THE ALMANAC OF AMERICAN POLITICS 2008

Author
Michael Barone

Co-Author
Richard E. Cohen

Editor
Charles Mahtesian

Contributing Writers
Charles Mahtesian, Mark Wegner

Research Associates
Emily Langer, Tricia Miller, Kyle Trygstad

Editorial Interns
Caleb Hannan, Jessica Taylor, Dean Treftz, Cory Vaughn

Photo Editor
Liz Lynch

Presidential Election Results
Polidata

State Maps
Polidata

Congressional Election Results
Election Data Services Inc.

The Almanac of American Politics
★ 2008 ★

THE **Senators,** THE **Representatives**
AND THE **Governors:**
THEIR **Records** AND **Election Results,**
THEIR **States** AND **Districts**

Michael Barone
Richard E. Cohen

National
Journal
GROUP
Washington, D.C.

Printed in the United States of America by United Book Press. Composition by Fry Communications Inc. Distributed to the trade by the University of Chicago Press.

Original cover concept by Adrian O. Constantyn. Photographs by Richard A. Bloom, Liz Lynch and Bruce Reedy. For information regarding photographs, contact: National Journal, 600 New Hampshire Ave., N.W., Washington, D.C. 20037; 202-739-8400. All rights reserved.

The Almanac of American politics. — 1972- —

v. : ill. ; 24 cm.

Biennial
Published by Gambit 1972– ; by National Journal 1988–

ISSN: 0362-076X
ISBN: 978-0-89234-116-0 (2008)
ISBN: 978-0-89234-117-7 (pbk. : 2008)

1. United States. Congress—Biography. 2. United States. Congress—Committees. 3. Election districts—United States—Handbooks, manuals, etc. I. Barone, Michael. II. Ujifusa, Grant. III. Matthews, Douglas.

JK1012 .A44
328.73/005   70-160417

TABLE OF CONTENTS

Guide to Usage 13
Key Votes. 18
Introduction 21
  by Michael Barone
President's Page 39
By the Numbers 1818
Congressional Leadership 1819
Closest 2006 Elections 1820
Class of 2006 1821
2008 Filing Deadlines and Primary
  Dates 1822
2008 Presidential Nominating Events . 1823
Senate Election Cycle 1824
Gubernatorial Election Cycle. 1825
Campaign Finance 1826
Senate Committee Leadership. 1829
Senate Committees 1830
House Committee Leadership 1836
House Committees 1837
Joint Committees 1846
Index 1848

ALABAMA. 41
Gov. Rilcy (R) 45
SENATORS
Shelby (R) 48
Sessions (R) 51
REPRESENTATIVES, (5R, 2D)
  1. Bonner (R) 53
  2. Everett (R) 55
  3. Rogers (R) 57
  4. Aderholt (R) 60
  5. Cramer (D) 62
  6. Bachus (R) 64
  7. Davis (D) 66

ALASKA. 68
Gov. Palin (R) 74
SENATORS
Stevens (R) 76
Murkowski (R) 80
REPRESENTATIVE-AT-LARGE, (1R)
  1. Young (R) 84

ARIZONA 87
Gov. Napolitano (D) 92

SENATORS
McCain (R) 94
Kyl (R) 100
REPRESENTATIVES, (4D, 4R)
  1. Renzi (R) 103
  2. Franks (R) 106
  3. Shadegg (R) 108
  4. Pastor (D) 111
  5. Mitchell (D) 113
  6. Flake (R) 115
  7. Grijalva (D) 117
  8. Giffords (D) 119

ARKANSAS 121
Gov. Beebe (D) 125
SENATORS
Lincoln (D) 127
Pryor (D) 129
REPRESENTATIVES, (3D, 1R)
  1. Berry (D) 132
  2. Snyder (D) 134
  3. Boozman (R) 137
  4. Ross (D) 139

CALIFORNIA. 141
Gov. Schwarzenegger (R). 153
SENATORS
Feinstein (D) 157
Boxer (D) 161
REPRESENTATIVES, (34D, 19R)
  1. Thompson (D) 165
  2. Herger (R) 167
  3. Lungren (R) 169
  4. Doolittle (R) 171
  5. Matsui (D) 174
  6. Woolsey (D) 177
  7. Miller (D) 179
  8. Pelosi (D) 182
  9. Lee (D) 189
  10. Tauscher (D) 191
  11. McNerney (D) 193
  12. Lantos (D) 196
  13. Stark (D) 199
  14. Eshoo (D) 201
  15. Honda (D). 204
  16. Lofgren (D) 206
  17. Farr (D) 208
  18. Cardoza (D) 211
  19. Radanovich (R) 213
  20. Costa (D) 215
  21. Nunes (R) 217

6   **Contents**

22. McCarthy (R) 220
23. Capps (D) 222
24. Gallegly (R) 224
25. McKeon (R) 226
26. Dreier (R) 228
27. Sherman (D) 231
28. Berman (D) 233
29. Schiff (D) 238
30. Waxman (D) 240
31. Becerra (D) 244
32. Solis (D) 247
33. Watson (D) 249
34. Roybal-Allard (D) 251
35. Waters (D) 253
36. Harman (D) 257
37. Richardson (D) 259
38. Napolitano (D) 261
39. Sanchez (D) 263
40. Royce (R) 265
41. Lewis (R) 268
42. Miller (R) 271
43. Baca (D) 273
44. Calvert (R) 275
45. Bono (R) 277
46. Rohrabacher (R) 279
47. Sanchez (D) 282
48. Campbell (R) 284
49. Issa (R) 287
50. Bilbray (R) 289
51. Filner (D) 292
52. Hunter (R) 295
53. Davis (D) 298

COLORADO **300**
Gov. Ritter (D) 305
SENATORS
Allard (R) 307
Salazar (D) 309
REPRESENTATIVES, (4D, 3R)
1. DeGette (D) 312
2. Udall (D) 315
3. Salazar (D) 317
4. Musgrave (R) 320
5. Lamborn (R) 322
6. Tancredo (R) 325
7. Perlmutter (D) 327

CONNECTICUT **329**
Gov. Rell (R) 334
SENATORS
Dodd (D) 336
Lieberman (ID) 340
REPRESENTATIVES, (4D, 1R)
1. Larson (D) 346
2. Courtney (D) 348

3. DeLauro (D) 350
4. Shays (R) 353
5. Murphy (D) 356

DELAWARE **358**
Gov. Minner (D) 361
SENATORS
Biden (D) 363
Carper (D) 367
REPRESENTATIVE-AT-LARGE, (1R)
1. Castle (R) 369

D.C. **372**
DELEGATE, (1D)
1. Norton (D) 375

FLORIDA **377**
Gov. Crist (R) 384
SENATORS
Nelson (D) 386
Martinez (R) 389
REPRESENTATIVES, (16R, 9D)
1. Miller (R) 392
2. Boyd (D) 395
3. Brown (D) 397
4. Crenshaw (R) 399
5. Brown-Waite (R) 401
6. Stearns (R) 403
7. Mica (R) 405
8. Keller (R) 408
9. Bilirakis (R) 410
10. Young (R) 412
11. Castor (D) 416
12. Putnam (R) 418
13. Buchanan (R) 420
14. Mack (R) 423
15. Weldon (R) 425
16. Mahoney (D) 427
17. Meek (D) 430
18. Ros-Lehtinen (R) 432
19. Wexler (D) 435
20. Wasserman Schultz (D) 437
21. Diaz-Balart (R) 439
22. Klein (D) 441
23. Hastings (D) 444
24. Feeney (R) 446
25. Diaz-Balart (R) 448

GEORGIA **451**
Gov. Perdue (R) 457
SENATORS
Chambliss (R) 459
Isakson (R) 462
REPRESENTATIVES, (7R, 6D)
1. Kingston (R) 464
2. Bishop (D) 466

3. Westmoreland (R) 469
4. Johnson (D) 471
5. Lewis (D) 473
6. Price (R) 475
7. Linder (R) 478
8. Marshall (D) 480
9. Deal (R) 483
10. Broun (R) 485
11. Gingrey (R) 487
12. Barrow (D) 490
13. Scott (D) 492

HAWAII **494**
Gov. Lingle (R) 499
SENATORS
Inouye (D) 502
Akaka (D) 505
REPRESENTATIVES, (2D)
1. Abercrombie (D) 507
2. Hirono (D) 510

IDAHO **512**
Gov. Otter (R) 516
SENATORS
Craig (R) 517
Crapo (R) 520
REPRESENTATIVES, (2R)
1. Sali (R) 523
2. Simpson (R) 525

ILLINOIS **527**
Gov. Blagojevich (D) 532
SENATORS
Durbin (D) 535
Obama (D) 538
REPRESENTATIVES, (10D, 9R)
1. Rush (D) 543
2. Jackson (D) 545
3. Lipinski (D) 548
4. Gutierrez (D) 550
5. Emanuel (D) 553
6. Roskam (R) 555
7. Davis (D) 557
8. Bean (D) 560
9. Schakowsky (D) 562
10. Kirk (R) 564
11. Weller (R) 567
12. Costello (D) 569
13. Biggert (R) 571
14. Hastert (R) 574
15. Johnson (R) 580
16. Manzullo (R) 582
17. Hare (D) 585
18. LaHood (R) 587
19. Shimkus (R) 589

INDIANA **591**
Gov. Daniels (R) 596
SENATORS
Lugar (R) 598
Bayh (D) 601
REPRESENTATIVES, (5D, 4R)
1. Visclosky (D) 604
2. Donnelly (D) 606
3. Souder (R) 608
4. Buyer (R) 610
5. Burton (R) 613
6. Pence (R) 616
7. Carson (D) 618
8. Ellsworth (D) 621
9. Hill (D) 623

IOWA **625**
Gov. Culver (D) 631
SENATORS
Grassley (R) 632
Harkin (D) 635
REPRESENTATIVES, (3D, 2R)
1. Braley (D) 639
2. Loebsack (D) 641
3. Boswell (D) 643
4. Latham (R) 646
5. King (R) 648

KANSAS **650**
Gov. Sebelius (D) 654
SENATORS
Brownback (R) 656
Roberts (R) 659
REPRESENTATIVES, (2D, 2R)
1. Moran (R) 663
2. Boyda (D) 665
3. Moore (D) 667
4. Tiahrt (R) 670

KENTUCKY **672**
Gov. Fletcher (R) 676
SENATORS
McConnell (R) 679
Bunning (R) 682
REPRESENTATIVES, (4R, 2D)
1. Whitfield (R) 685
2. Lewis (R) 687
3. Yarmuth (D) 690
4. Davis (R) 692
5. Rogers (R) 694
6. Chandler (D) 698

LOUISIANA **700**
Gov. Blanco (D) 706
SENATORS
Landrieu (D) 709
Vitter (R) 712

8   **Contents**

REPRESENTATIVES, (5R, 2D)
1. Jindal (R) 715
2. Jefferson (D) 718
3. Melancon (D) 722
4. McCrery (R) 725
5. Alexander (R) 728
6. Baker (R) 730
7. Boustany (R) 734

MAINE **736**
Gov. Baldacci (D) 740
SENATORS
Snowe (R) 743
Collins (R) 745
REPRESENTATIVES, (2D)
1. Allen (D) 748
2. Michaud (D) 751

MARYLAND **753**
Gov. O'Malley (D) 757
SENATORS
Mikulski (D) 759
Cardin (D) 761
REPRESENTATIVES, (6D, 2R)
1. Gilchrest (R) 763
2. Ruppersberger (D) 766
3. Sarbanes (D) 768
4. Wynn (D) 770
5. Hoyer (D) 772
6. Bartlett (R) 776
7. Cummings (D) 778
8. Van Hollen (D) 780

MASSACHUSETTS **783**
Gov. Patrick (D) 789
SENATORS
Kennedy (D) 790
Kerry (D) 794
REPRESENTATIVES, (9D, 1V)
1. Olver (D) 798
2. Neal (D) 800
3. McGovern (D) 802
4. Frank (D) 804
5. Vacant 809
6. Tierney (D) 810
7. Markey (D) 812
8. Capuano (D) 816
9. Lynch (D) 819
10. Delahunt (D) 821

MICHIGAN **823**
Gov. Granholm (D) 830
SENATORS
Levin (D) 833
Stabenow (D) 836

REPRESENTATIVES, (9R, 6D)
1. Stupak (D) 838
2. Hoekstra (R) 841
3. Ehlers (R) 844
4. Camp (R) 847
5. Kildee (D) 849
6. Upton (R) 851
7. Walberg (R) 853
8. Rogers (R) 855
9. Knollenberg (R) 857
10. Miller (R) 860
11. McCotter (R) 863
12. Levin (D) 865
13. Kilpatrick (D) 867
14. Conyers (D) 869
15. Dingell (D) 873

MINNESOTA **877**
Gov. Pawlenty (R) 882
SENATORS
Coleman (R) 885
Klobuchar (DFL) 888
REPRESENTATIVES, (5DFL, 3R)
1. Walz (DFL) 890
2. Kline (R) 892
3. Ramstad (R) 894
4. McCollum (DFL) 897
5. Ellison (DFL) 899
6. Bachmann (R) 902
7. Peterson (DFL) 904
8. Oberstar (DFL) 907

MISSISSIPPI **911**
Gov. Barbour (R) 916
SENATORS
Cochran (R) 919
Lott (R) 923
REPRESENTATIVES, (2D, 2R)
1. Wicker (R) 928
2. Thompson (D) 930
3. Pickering (R) 933
4. Taylor (D) 936

MISSOURI **938**
Gov. Blunt (R) 943
SENATORS
Bond (R) 945
McCaskill (D) 948
REPRESENTATIVES, (5R, 4D)
1. Clay (D) 950
2. Akin (R) 952
3. Carnahan (D) 954
4. Skelton (D) 956
5. Cleaver (D) 959
6. Graves (R) 961
7. Blunt (R) 963

8. Emerson (R) 967
9. Hulshof (R) 969

MONTANA 971
Gov. Schweitzer (D) 975
SENATORS
Baucus (D) 977
Tester (D) 980
REPRESENTATIVE-AT-LARGE, (1R)
1. Rehberg (R) 982

NEBRASKA 984
Gov. Heineman (R) 988
SENATORS
Hagel (R) 990
Nelson (D) 994
REPRESENTATIVES, (3R)
1. Fortenberry (R) 996
2. Terry (R) 998
3. Smith (R) 1001

NEVADA 1003
Gov. Gibbons (R) 1008
SENATORS
Reid (D) 1010
Ensign (R) 1014
REPRESENTATIVES, (2R, 1D)
1. Berkley (D) 1017
2. Heller (R) 1020
3. Porter (R) 1022

NEW HAMPSHIRE 1025
Gov. Lynch (D) 1030
SENATORS
Gregg (R) 1032
Sununu (R) 1035
REPRESENTATIVES, (2D)
1. Shea-Porter (D) 1038
2. Hodes (D) 1040

NEW JERSEY 1042
Gov. Corzine (D) 1047
SENATORS
Lautenberg (D) 1051
Menendez (D) 1055
REPRESENTATIVES, (7D, 6R)
1. Andrews (D) 1058
2. LoBiondo (R) 1061
3. Saxton (R) 1063
4. Smith (R) 1065
5. Garrett (R) 1068
6. Pallone (D) 1070
7. Ferguson (R) 1073
8. Pascrell (D) 1075
9. Rothman (D) 1077
10. Payne (D) 1079
11. Frelinghuysen (R) 1081

12. Holt (D) 1083
13. Sires (D) 1086

NEW MEXICO 1088
Gov. Richardson (D) 1092
SENATORS
Domenici (R) 1096
Bingaman (D) 1099
REPRESENTATIVES, (2R, 1D)
1. Wilson (R) 1101
2. Pearce (R) 1104
3. Udall (D) 1107

NEW YORK 1109
Gov. Spitzer (D) 1118
SENATORS
Schumer (D) 1122
Clinton (D) 1126
REPRESENTATIVES, (23D, 6R)
1. Bishop (D) 1133
2. Israel (D) 1135
3. King (R) 1137
4. McCarthy (D) 1140
5. Ackerman (D) 1142
6. Meeks (D) 1144
7. Crowley (D) 1147
8. Nadler (D) 1149
9. Weiner (D) 1152
10. Towns (D) 1155
11. Clarke (D) 1157
12. Velazquez (D) 1160
13. Fossella (R) 1163
14. Maloney (D) 1165
15. Rangel (D) 1168
16. Serrano (D) 1173
17. Engel (D) 1176
18. Lowey (D) 1178
19. Hall (D) 1180
20. Gillibrand (D) 1182
21. McNulty (D) 1185
22. Hinchey (D) 1187
23. McHugh (R) 1189
24. Arcuri (D) 1192
25. Walsh (R) 1194
26. Reynolds (R) 1197
27. Higgins (D) 1200
28. Slaughter (D) 1202
29. Kuhl (R) 1205

NORTH CAROLINA 1208
Gov. Easley (D) 1212
SENATORS
Dole (R) 1215
Burr (R) 1218

10   **Contents**

REPRESENTATIVES, (7D, 6R)
1. Butterfield (D) 1221
2. Etheridge (D) 1223
3. Jones (R) 1225
4. Price (D) 1228
5. Foxx (R) 1231
6. Coble (R) 1233
7. McIntyre (D). 1235
8. Hayes (R) 1237
9. Myrick (R) 1240
10. McHenry (R) 1242
11. Shuler (D). . . . . : . 1244
12. Watt (D) 1247
13. Miller (D) 1249

NORTH DAKOTA 1251
Gov. Hoeven (R) 1256
SENATORS
Conrad (D) 1258
Dorgan (D) 1261
REPRESENTATIVE-AT-LARGE, (1D)
1. Pomeroy (D) 1263

OHIO 1265
Gov. Strickland (D) 1272
SENATORS
Voinovich (R) 1273
Brown (D) 1276
REPRESENTATIVES, (10R, 7D, 1V)
1. Chabot (R) 1278
2. Schmidt (R) 1281
3. Turner (R) 1284
4. Jordan (R) 1286
5. Vacant 1288
6. Wilson (D) 1289
7. Hobson (R) 1291
8. Boehner (R) 1294
9. Kaptur (D) 1298
10. Kucinich (D) 1300
11. Tubbs Jones (D) 1303
12. Tiberi (R) 1305
13. Sutton (D) 1308
14. LaTourette (R) 1310
15. Pryce (R) 1312
16. Regula (R) 1315
17. Ryan (D). 1318
18. Space (D) 1321

OKLAHOMA 1323
Gov. Henry (D) 1327
SENATORS
Inhofe (R) 1329
Coburn (R) 1332
REPRESENTATIVES, (4R, 1D)
1. Sullivan (R) 1335
2. Boren (D) 1337

3. Lucas (R) 1339
4. Cole (R) 1341
5. Fallin (R) 1344

OREGON 1345
Gov. Kulongoski (D) 1350
SENATORS
Wyden (D) 1353
Smith (R) 1357
REPRESENTATIVES, (4D, 1R)
1. Wu (D) 1359
2. Walden (R) 1362
3. Blumenauer (D) 1364
4. DeFazio (D) 1366
5. Hooley (D) 1369

PENNSYLVANIA 1371
Gov. Rendell (D) 1377
SENATORS
Specter (R) 1380
Casey (D) 1385
REPRESENTATIVES, (11D, 8R)
1. Brady (D) 1387
2. Fattah (D) 1390
3. English (R) 1392
4. Altmire (D) 1394
5. Peterson (R) 1396
6. Gerlach (R) 1399
7. Sestak (D) 1401
8. Murphy (D) 1403
9. Shuster (R) 1405
10. Carney (D) 1408
11. Kanjorski (D) 1410
12. Murtha (D) 1412
13. Schwartz (D). 1417
14. Doyle (D) 1419
15. Dent (R) 1421
16. Pitts (R) 1424
17. Holden (D) 1426
18. Murphy (R). 1428
19. Platts (R) 1431

RHODE ISLAND 1433
Gov. Carcieri (R). 1437
SENATORS
Reed (D) 1439
Whitehouse (D) 1441
REPRESENTATIVES, (2D)
1. Kennedy (D) 1443
2. Langevin (D) 1446

SOUTH CAROLINA 1449
Gov. Sanford (R) 1454
SENATORS
Graham (R) 1457
DeMint (R) 1461

REPRESENTATIVES, (4R, 2D)
1. Brown (R) 1463
2. Wilson (R) 1466
3. Barrett (R) 1468
4. Inglis (R) 1470
5. Spratt (D) 1472
6. Clyburn (D) 1476

SOUTH DAKOTA **1478**
Gov. Rounds (R) 1483
SENATORS
Johnson (D) 1485
Thune (R) 1488
REPRESENTATIVE-AT-LARGE, (1D)
1. Herseth Sandlin (D) 1492

TENNESSEE **1494**
Gov. Bredesen (D) 1499
SENATORS
Alexander (R) 1502
Corker (R) 1506
REPRESENTATIVES, (5D, 4R)
1. Davis (R) 1508
2. Duncan (R) 1510
3. Wamp (R) 1512
4. Davis (D) 1514
5. Cooper (D) 1516
6. Gordon (D) 1519
7. Blackburn (R) 1521
8. Tanner (D) 1523
9. Cohen (D) 1525

TEXAS **1527**
Gov. Perry (R) 1535
SENATORS
Hutchison (R) 1539
Cornyn (R) 1541
REPRESENTATIVES, (19R, 13D)
1. Gohmert (R) 1545
2. Poe (R) 1547
3. Johnson (R) 1549
4. Hall (R) 1552
5. Hensarling (R) 1554
6. Barton (R) 1556
7. Culberson (R) 1559
8. Brady (R) 1561
9. Green (D) 1563
10. McCaul (R) 1566
11. Conaway (R) 1568
12. Granger (R) 1570
13. Thornberry (R) 1573
14. Paul (R) 1575
15. Hinojosa (D) 1577
16. Reyes (D) 1580
17. Edwards (D) 1582
18. Jackson Lee (D) 1586

19. Neugebauer (R) 1588
20. Gonzalez (D) 1591
21. Smith (R) 1593
22. Lampson (D) 1596
23. Rodriguez (D) 1599
24. Marchant (R) 1601
25. Doggett (D) 1603
26. Burgess (R) 1606
27. Ortiz (D) 1609
28. Cuellar (D) 1611
29. Green (D) 1614
30. Johnson (D) 1616
31. Carter (R) 1618
32. Sessions (R) 1620

UTAH **1623**
Gov. Huntsman (R) 1628
SENATORS
Hatch (R) 1630
Bennett (R) 1633
REPRESENTATIVES, (2R, 1D)
1. Bishop (R) 1635
2. Matheson (D) 1637
3. Cannon (R) 1640

VERMONT **1642**
Gov. Douglas (R) 1647
SENATORS
Leahy (D) 1649
Sanders (I) 1651
REPRESENTATIVE-AT-LARGE, (1D)
1. Welch (D) 1654

VIRGINIA **1655**
Gov. Kaine (D) 1659
SENATORS
Warner (R) 1661
Webb (D) 1664
REPRESENTATIVES, (7R, 3D, 1V)
1. Vacant 1667
2. Drake (R) 1670
3. Scott (D) 1672
4. Forbes (R) 1675
5. Goode (R) 1677
6. Goodlatte (R) 1679
7. Cantor (R) 1681
8. Moran (D) 1684
9. Boucher (D) 1686
10. Wolf (R) 1688
11. Davis (R) 1692

WASHINGTON **1695**
Gov. Gregoire (D) 1701
SENATORS
Murray (D) 1704
Cantwell (D) 1707

12   Contents

REPRESENTATIVES, (6D, 3R)
1. Inslee (D) 1710
2. Larsen (D) 1712
3. Baird (D) 1715
4. Hastings (R) 1717
5. McMorris Rodgers (R) 1720
6. Dicks (D) 1722
7. McDermott (D) 1726
8. Reichert (R) 1729
9. Smith (D) 1732

WEST VIRGINIA 1734
Gov. Manchin (D) 1738
SENATORS
Byrd (D) 1740
Rockefeller (D) 1744
REPRESENTATIVES, (2D, 1R)
1. Mollohan (D) 1747
2. Capito (R) 1750
3. Rahall (D) 1753

WISCONSIN 1755
Gov. Doyle (D) 1760
SENATORS
Kohl (D) 1763
Feingold (D) 1765

REPRESENTATIVES, (5D, 3R)
1. Ryan (R) 1769
2. Baldwin (D) 1771
3. Kind (D) 1773
4. Moore (D) 1776
5. Sensenbrenner (R) 1778
6. Petri (R) 1781
7. Obey (D) 1783
8. Kagen (D) 1788

WYOMING 1790
Gov. Freudenthal (D) 1794
SENATORS
Enzi (R) 1796
Barrasso (R) 1798
REPRESENTATIVE-AT-LARGE, (1R)
1. Cubin (R) 1800

TERRITORIES 1803
PUERTO RICO 1803
Fortuno 1807
VIRGIN ISLANDS 1808
Christensen 1809
GUAM 1810
Bordallo 1813
AMERICAN SAMOA 1814
Faleomavaega 1815

GUIDE TO USAGE

The following guide provides a brief description of each section and a list of sources from which information was derived, both of which serve as a road map to understanding the meaning behind the figures. Data in each category below is generated for *The Almanac of American Politics* by Polidata from data compiled by the United States Census Bureau, unless otherwise noted. Figures released by the Census may vary slightly from those used by the Almanac due to different methods of data aggregation or tabulation.

The People

Population. All population figures are from the 2000 Census, unless otherwise noted. Census estimates as of July 1, 2006 are used for cities and states. Official April 1, 2000 figures are used for district population; the 2005 district population estimates are compiled by Polidata and reflect a modification of the Census Bureau's American Community Survey estimates to include the number of persons who were counted in group quarters in the 2000 Census. These persons are added to the ACS estimate to derive a comparable estimate of the district for 2005.

Area Size. Area size is in square miles, including water.

State Native. Refers to persons born in their state of residence as a % of all persons.

Non-Citizen. Refers to persons foreign born and not a citizen as a % of all persons.

Language. Refers to the % of households speaking that language. The abbreviation *Other Eur.* refers to Other Indo-European languages.

Race and Ethnic Origin. For the 2000 Census, the Census Bureau asked people what their race or ethnic origin was. Race, as defined by the Census, reflects the individual respondent's perception of his or her racial identity and does not reflect any biological or anthropological definition. The basic racial categories are: American Indian or Alaska Native (designated in the box as *Native Am.*); Asian; Native Hawaiian or other Pacific Islander (*Hawaiian*); Black or African American; White; Two or more races (*Two + races*); Other non-Hispanic persons (*Other*). The race statistics used in the Almanac are drawn from respondents reporting only one race category, but the book also includes a total for those who responded to more than one race category. Hispanic origin is defined as an ethnicity, and includes those who classified themselves in one of three specific Hispanic categories (Cuban, Mexican, Puerto Rican) or as of "other Spanish/Hispanic origin." Persons of Latino or Hispanic origin may be of any race for Census purposes, but the Almanac includes only non-Hispanic Blacks in the Black population category and only non-Hispanic Whites in the White population category, so that the percentages add to 100%. The figures in the box are as a % of all persons in a state or congressional district.

Ancestry. Ancestry refers to ethnic origin or descent; categories are drawn from Census-designated possible groups. The question was intended by the Census to provide data for groups that were not included in the Hispanic origin and race questions; thus it does not reflect diversity within Hispanic and Asian subgroups. The % figure is calculated by using the average number of responses to estimate the % of the population that shares this ancestry characteristic. NOTE: The USA designation refers to "American" as a unique ethnicity, if it was provided alone as a response without any other ethnicity. *Subsaharan* refers to the Census category of Subsaharan African. *West Indian* excludes Hispanic groups.

Military Veterans. Refers to persons who were in the Armed Forces previously as a % of voting age persons. *Gulf War* % includes all veterans with service after 1990, but does not include those who also served in Vietnam.

Urban/Rural Population. Refers to the % of total population that lives in areas defined as urban or rural by the Census Bureau.

Education. *H.S. Grad* refers to persons with a high school diploma or higher, as a % of persons 25 years and older. *College Grad* refers to persons with a bachelor's degree or higher, as a % of persons 25 years and older.

Industry.   Refers to industry of occupation. The figure is of persons employed by that particular industry as a % of employed persons 16 years or older. Abbreviations: *Agri* (agriculture, forestry, fishing and mining); *Con* (construction); *Fin* (finance, insurance and real estate); *Info* (information); *Mfg* (manufacturing, durable and non-durable); *Prof* (professional and related services, including health and education); *Public* (public administration); *Trade* (trade, wholesale and retail); *Other* (primarily entertainment, recreation, hotel and food services).

Occupation.   Refers to type of job within industry. The figure is the % of employed persons 16 years and older in these occupations. *White collar* refers to management, professional, sales and administrative occupations. *Blue collar* refers to construction, production and transportation occupations. *Gray collar* refers to the balance of employed persons not classified as white or blue collar, such as farming, fishing and forestry or health care, protective service, food prep and personal care occupations.

Work Sector.   Refers to a classification of worker by economic sector. The figure is the % of employed persons 16 years and older. Abbreviations: *Private* (private for profit/not for profit wage/salary employers); *Govt* (federal, state and local government); *Self* (self-employed); *Family* (unpaid family workers).

Unemployment.   Unemployed civilians as a % of persons 16 years and older and as a % of the labor force.

Household Income/Poverty Status.   *Household Income* refers to household income in 1999, as a % of all households. *Poverty status* refers to % of persons below the poverty line.

Home Value.   Refers to self-estimated market value of owner-occupied units as % of owner-occupied housing units for which value was specified.

State Information.   Each legislature is referred to according to the proper name of its legislative body, followed by a breakdown by party membership. Partisan composition figures are as of May 25, 2007.

Legislative Term Limits.   Refers to whether a state has term limits for state legislators.

Registered Voters.   Refers to the number of registered voters by party, as close as possible to the November 2006 election. The individual states' election bureaus or political parties provide these figures. Some states have no voter registration. *D* refers to Democrat; *R* refers to Republican; *O* refers to independent, unaffiliated and minor parties.

Cook Partisan Voting Index.   Refers to the Partisan Voting Index (PVI) as used by Charlie Cook, Washington's foremost political handicapper. The PVI is designed to provide a quick overall assessment of generic partisan strength. For this volume, the PVI includes an average of the 2000 and 2004 presidential elections in the district as the partisan indicator. The PVI value is calculated by a comparison of the district average for the party nominee, compared to the 2004 national value for the party nominee. *The calculations are based upon the two-party vote.* The national values for 2004 are George W. Bush 51.2% and John Kerry 48.8%. The PVI value indicates a district with a partisan base above the national value for that party's 2004 presidential nominee. Thus a district with an R+15 is a district that voted 15 percentage points (as an average of its 2000 and 2004 presidential vote) higher for Bush than the national value of 51.2%. Similarly, a district with a D+15 is a district that voted 15 percentage points (as an average of its 2000 and 2004 presidential vote) higher for Kerry than the national value of 48.8%. An X +00 indicates an evenly balanced district.

Biography.   This section lists when each governor, senator and representative was elected or appointed, date and place of birth, home, college education and degrees obtained (if any), religion, marital status and, if applicable, spouse's name. The number of terms listed reflects full, elected terms. Also listed is a brief outline of the politician's past elected offices, professional career and military service and his or her office addresses and telephone numbers. Committee and subcommittee assignments, as of September 12, 2007, are provided as well. (Note: On many committees, the chairman and ranking minority member are ex officio members of each subcommittee on which they do not hold a regular assignment.)

Ratings

Group Ratings. The congressional rating statistics of 10 interest groups provide an idea of a legislator's general ideology and the degree to which the legislator represents different groups' interests. Not just a record of liberal/conservative voting behavior, these ratings come from a range of groups concerned with everything from single issues (environmental concerns) to the political interests of a particular sector (e.g., business). The order of the groups is such that the more "liberal" groups are on the left and the more "conservative" are on the right. Some groups only provide one rating for the two-year congressional session. Following is a general description of each organization.

ADA   Americans for Democratic Action

Liberal: Since its founding in 1947, ADA members have pushed for legislation designed to curtail rising defense spending, prevent encroachments on civil liberties and promote international human rights. The ADA uses 20 votes from the 109th Congress based on a broad spectrum of issues for its vote analysis.

ACLU   American Civil Liberties Union

Pro-individual liberties: ACLU seeks to protect individuals from legal, executive and congressional infringement on basic rights guaranteed by the Bill of Rights. The ACLU ratings are published for every Congress; the 2006 ratings include the years 2005 and 2006.

AFS   American Federation of State, County and Municipal Employees (AFSCME)

Liberal labor: As the nation's largest public service employees union, representing more than 1.4 million members, AFSCME is committed to improving working conditions through collective bargaining. The AFSCME voting records are based on a representative sample of roll call votes from the 109th Congress.

LCV   League of Conservation Voters

Environmental: Formed in 1970, LCV is the national, non-partisan arm of the environmental movement. LCV works to elect pro-environmental candidates to Congress. LCV ratings are based on key votes concerning energy, environment and natural resource issues.

ITIC   Information Technology Industry Council

High-tech industry: ITIC represents the leading U.S. providers of information technology products and services. ITIC's mission is to help shape policies that advance electronic commerce, open new markets, rely on market-based solutions, and foster innovation. The 2006 ratings include the years 2005 and 2006.

NTU   National Taxpayers Union

Pro-taxpayer rights: NTU is the nation's largest and oldest taxpayers' rights group, representing 362,000 members in all 50 states. NTU analyzes every roll call vote taken during both sessions of Congress that significantly affects federal taxes, spending, debt, or regulatory impact.

COC   Chamber of Commerce of the United States

Pro-business: Founded in 1912 as a voice for organized business, COC represents local, regional and state chambers of commerce in addition to trade and professional organizations.

ACU   American Conservative Union

Conservative: Since 1971, ACU ratings have provided a means of gauging the conservatism of members of Congress. Foreign policy, social and budget issues are their primary concerns.

CFG   Club for Growth

Pro-tax limitation: CFG supports limited government, lower taxes and policies that support economic growth. CFG ratings are based on key votes that deal with taxes, trade, and other economic proposals.

FRC   Family Research Council

Conservative: Founded in 1980, the FRC promotes marriage and family as the bedrocks of society and advocates policies that uphold Judeo-Christian values. FRC ratings are based on legislation dealing with abortion and family issues.

National Journal Ratings. *National Journal's* rating system establishes an objective method of analyzing congressional voting. A panel of *National Journal* editors and staff initially compiled a list of congressional roll call votes and classified them as either economic, social or foreign policy-related. The interrelationship of these votes was shown by a statistical procedure called "principal components analysis," which revealed which "yea" votes and which "nay" votes fit a liberal or a conservative pattern. The votes in each of the three subject areas were computer-weighted to reflect the degree they fit the common pattern. All members of Congress who participated in at least half of the votes in each area received ratings; those who missed more that half the votes were not scored (shown as *). Absences and abstentions were not counted.

Members of Congress were then ranked according to relative liberalism and conservatism. Finally, they were assigned percentiles showing their rank relative to others in their chamber. Percentile scores range from a minimum of 0 to a maximum of 99. Because some members voted liberal or conservative on every roll call, however, there are ties at the liberal and conservative ends of each scale. For that reason, the maximum percentiles often turn out to be less than 99.

Election Results

Listed for each member of the House are results of the 2006 general, runoff and primary elections, as well as the 2004 general elections (results of any intervening special elections are also listed). Gubernatorial and senatorial results are presented in a like manner. Votes and percentages are included, indicating the margin of victory (due to the process of rounding up and rounding down, some totals may equal more or less than 100%). Candidates receiving less than 4% of the total vote are grouped together and listed as "Other." Election returns were collected from the individual states. Where a state abbreviation and district number appear in parenthesis next to an election year, this indicates that the member ran in a differently numbered congressional district that year.

Prior Winning Percentage.   This feature provides winning percentage of the vote in past elections; in Senate profiles, the word "House" indicates the election that year was for the U.S. House. If no percentage is provided for an election year, it indicates that the member lost or did not run for reelection that year; generally this will occur where there has been a gap in service. An odd election year (e.g. 2001) indicates a special election; two elections in the same year indicate a special and a general election.

Presidential Vote.   The 2000 and 2004 presidential votes are included for each state. Results of the 2004 presidential primaries were provided by the Federal Election Commission; caucus results are not provided. The 2000 and 2004 presidential votes are included here for each congressional district. The 2000 presidential vote reflects the vote within the new district lines in effect for the 2002 election, except in Georgia and in Texas districts 15, 21, 23, 25, and 28, where the presidential vote reflects district lines in effect since the 2006 elections. The 2004 presidential vote reflects the vote within the district lines in effect for the 2004 election, except in Georgia and in Texas districts 15, 21, 23, 25, and 28, where the presidential vote reflects district lines in effect since the 2006 elections. The presidential vote by congressional district is estimated by Polidata, from information collected from state and local election offices. Only seven states provide district-level presidential vote data; by necessity, other results are aggregated from precinct-level returns. Voting data from districts with split precincts and centrally counted absentee votes thus should be considered estimates; the allocation of these unassigned votes is determined by Polidata. While estimates of votes are included in each district, the percentage values generally provide the more reliable information. The votes for minor party candidates are included where available but are not consistent across all 50 states. The total of the congressional district votes may not add up to the total state vote, because some votes (overseas, military and some absentee and early votes) are not assigned to a congressional district and because county election office reports sometimes conflict with reports from state election authorities.

Campaign Finance

All data are derived from candidates' campaign finance reports and party reports available from the Federal Election Commission (FEC). The dollar figure, in parentheses to the right of the election results, represents the candidates' net disbursements (expenditures) for the period beginning January 1, 2005, and ending December 31, 2006. *These figures may not include candidate loans that have been repaid, nor does it include any corrections or amendments filed with the FEC after June 2007.*

Abbreviations

ACLU	American Civil Liberties Union	H	Capitol Building Room-House side
ACU	American Conservative Union	HSOB	Hart Senate Office Building
ADA	Americans for Democratic Action, Americans with Disabilities Act	I	Independent
		IC	Independent Conservative
		ID	Independent Democrat
AFDC	Aid to Families with Dependent Children	IG	Independent Green
		IMC	Independent Maine Course
AFL-CIO	American Federation of Labor and Congress of Industrial Organizations	Ind	Independence Party
		IAP	Independent American Party (NV)
		ISTEA	Intermodal Surface Transportation Efficiency Act
AFS	American Federation of State, County & Municipal Employees (AFSCME)	IVP	Independent Voters Party
		L	Liberal Party
		LCV	League of Conservation Voters
AID	Agency for International Development	LDS	The Church of Jesus Christ of Latter-day Saints
AMI	American Independent (CA)	LHOB	Longworth House Office Building
ANWR	Arctic National Wildlife Refuge	Lib	Libertarian Party
BGH	Bovine Growth Hormone	Mod	Moderate Party
BL	Better Life Party	NAFTA	North American Free Trade Agreement
C	Conservative Party (NY)		
CAFE	Corporate Average Fuel Economy	NARAL	NARAL Pro-Choice America
CAFTA	Central America Free Trade Agreement	NEA	National Endowment for the Arts
		NFIB	National Federation of Independent Business
CFL	Connecticut for Lieberman		
CHOB	Cannon House Office Building	NL	Natural Law Party
CIA	Central Intelligence Agency	NP	Non-Partisan
CNP	Constitution Party	NPA	No Party Affiliation
CPF	Constitution Party of Florida	NRCC	National Republican Congressional Committee
COC	Chamber of Commerce of the United States	NRSC	National Republican Senatorial Committee
COLA	Cost of Living Adjustment	NSA	National Security Agency
DCCC	Democratic Congressional Campaign Committee	NTU	National Taxpayers Union
		PDP	Popular Democratic Party (PR)
DFL	Democratic-Farmer-Labor Party (MN)	PF	Peace and Freedom Party
		PJ	Peace and Justice Party (NY)
DLC	Democratic Leadership Council	PNTR	Permanent Normal Trade Relations
DNC	Democratic National Committee	POP	Populist Party
DSCC	Democratic Senatorial Campaign Committee	PRG	Progressive Party
		Ref	Reform Party
DSOB	Dirksen Senate Office Building	RHOB	Rayburn House Office Building
EMILY	EMILY's List (Early Money is Like Yeast)	RMM	Ranking Minority Member
		RNC	Republican National Committee
		RSOB	Russell Senate Office Building
ERISA	Employee Retirement Income Security Act	RTL	Right-to-Life Party
		S	Capitol Building Room, Senate side
FEC	Federal Election Commission	SDI	Strategic Defense Initiative
FERC	Federal Energy Regulatory Commission	SOC	Socialist Party
		SW	Socialist Workers Party
FTA	Free Trade Agreement	UAW	United Auto Workers
GATT	General Agreement on Tariffs & Trade	VNS	Voter News Service
		WF	Working Families
Green	Green Party	WI	Write In

Key Votes of the 109th Congress

Key Votes.   The Key Votes section attempts to illustrate a legislator's stance on important votes where he or she must vote for or against a national issue. The process grossly oversimplifies the legislative system where months of debate, amendment, pressure, persuasion, and compromise go into a final floor vote. However, the voting record remains the best indication of a member's general ideologies and position on specific issues. Following is a list of key votes used. A member who was absent, voted present, or who was not in office at the time of a particular vote receives an "*". Roll-call data were drawn from Congressional Observer Publications at www.proaxis.com/cop, a private legislative tracking company.

House Votes, 109th Congress:

1) **Estate Tax Repeal** (House Vote 102/HR 8) Permanently repeal federal estate and gift taxes. April 13, 2005. (272-162) (D: 42-160; R: 230-1; I: 0-1)

2) **Limit CAFE Standards** (House Vote 119/HR 6) Approve less stringent automobile fuel-efficiency standards. April 20, 2005. (259-172) (D: 70-130; R: 189-41; I: 0-1)

3) **FY06 Spending Curb** (House Vote 670/S 1932) Approve the conference report on fiscal 2006 budget reconciliation legislation to curb federal entitlement spending. December 19, 2005. (212-206) (D:0-196; R: 212-9; I: 0-1)

4) **Drilling in ANWR** (House Vote 209/HR 5429) Authorize oil and gas leases for Alaska's Arctic National Wildlife Refuge. May 25, 2006. (225-201) (D: 27-170; R: 198-30; I: 0-1)

5) **Limit Interstate Abortion** (House Vote 144/HR 748) Bar transportation of a minor girl across state lines to obtain an abortion without parental notification. April 27, 2005. (270-157) (D: 54-145; R: 216-11; I: 0-1)

6) **Extend Patriot Act** (House Vote 414/HR 3199) Reauthorize the USA PATRIOT Act, and make permanent most of its provisions for expanded law-enforcement authority to investigate potential terrorists. July 21, 2005. (257-171) (D: 43-156; R: 214-14; I: 0-1)

7) **Bar Same Sex Marriage** (House Vote 378/HJRes 88) Amend the Constitution to define marriage as the union of a man and a woman. July 18, 2006. (236-187; 282 votes required in this case to approve a constitutional amendment) (D: 34-159; R: 202-27; I: 0-1)

8) **Stem Cell Research $** (House Vote 388/HR 810) Override the president's veto of legislation permitting federal funds for embryonic stem cell research. July 19, 2006. (235-193; 286 votes required in this case to override the veto) (D: 183-14; R: 51-179; I: 1-0)

9) **Build Border Fence** (House Vote 446/HR 6061) Authorize 700 miles of fencing along the U.S.-Mexico border. September 14, 2006. (283-138) (D: 64-131; R: 219-6; I: 0-1)

10) **CAFTA** (House Vote 443/HR 3045) Approve the Central American Free Trade Agreement. July 28, 2005. (217-215) (D: 15-187; R: 202-27; I: 0-1)

11) **Oppose Iraq Withdrawal** (House Vote 288/HRes 861) Oppose setting a date to withdraw U.S. forces from Iraq. June 16, 2006. (256-153) (D: 42-149; R: 214-3; I: 0-1)

12) **Detainee Tribunals** (House Vote 491/HR 6166) Create military tribunals to try detainees described as unlawful enemy combatants. September 27, 2006. (253-168) (D: 34-160; R: 219-7; I: 0-1)

Senate Votes, 109th Congress:

1) **Bar ANWR Drilling** (Senate Vote 288/S 1932) Strike a provision to permit oil and gas leasing in Alaska's Arctic National Wildlife Refuge. November 3, 2005. (48-51) (D: 40-3; R: 7-48; I: 1-0)

2) **FY06 Spending Curb** (Senate Vote 363/S 1932) Approve, with revisions, the conference report on the fiscal 2006 budget reconciliation legislation to curb federal entitlement spending. December 21, 2005. (50-50; Vice President Cheney broke the tie) (D: 0-44; R: 50-5; I: 0-1)

3) **Estate Tax Repeal** (Senate Vote 164/HR 8) Limit debate on a proposal to permanently repeal the estate tax. June 8, 2006. (57-41; 60 votes required to invoke cloture) (D: 4-38; R: 53-2; I: 0-1)

4) **Raise Minimum Wage** (Senate Vote 179/S 2766) Increase the minimum wage to $7.25 per hour in two years. June 21, 2006. (52-46; 60 votes required because of a unanimous consent agreement) (D: 43-0; R: 8-46; I: 1-0)

5) **Confirm Samuel Alito** (Senate Vote 2) Confirm Samuel Alito as an associate justice on the Supreme Court. January 31, 2006. (58-42) (D: 4-40; R: 54-1; I: 0-1)

6) **Path to Citizenship** (Senate Vote 157/S 2611) Approve comprehensive immigration reform legislation providing a path to citizenship for most illegal immigrants but requiring those living in the United States for less than two years to return to their native country. May 25, 2006. (62-36) (D: 38-4; R: 23-32; I: 1-0)

7) **Bar Same Sex Marriage** (Senate Vote 163/SJRes 1) Limit debate on a constitutional amendment to define marriage as the union of a man and a woman. June 7, 2006. (49-48; 60 votes required to invoke cloture) (D: 2-40; R: 47-7; I; 0-1)

8) **Stem Cell Research $** (Senate Vote 206/HR 810) Permit federal funds for embryonic-stem-cell research. July 18, 2006. (63-37) (D: 43-1; R: 19-36; I: 1-0)

9) **Limit Interstate Abortion** (Senate Vote 216/S 403) Make it a federal crime to take a minor across state lines to obtain an abortion without parental notification or consent. July 25, 2006 (65-34) (D: 14-29; R: 51-4; I: 0-1)

10) **CAFTA** (Senate Vote 170/S 1307) Approve the Central American Free Trade Agreement. June 30, 2005. (54-45) (D: 10-33; R: 43-12; I: 1-0)

11) **Urge Iraq Withdrawal** (Senate Vote 182/S 2766) Express the sense of Congress that the president should start to withdraw U.S. troops from Iraq in 2006. June 22, 2006. (39-60) (D: 37-6; R: 1-54; I: 1-0)

12) **Provide Detainee Rights** (Senate Vote 255/S 3930) Remove provisions that limit habeas corpus rights for military detainees. September 28, 2006. (48-51) (D: 43-1; R: 4-50; I: 1-0)

Open-Field Politics

By Michael Barone

W e seem to be entering a new period in American politics. We have come through a period of trench warfare, in which two armies of approximately equal size faced each other across the battlefield and tried to rally their sides to achieve the incremental gains that would make the difference between victory or defeat. There were few defections from either army in this culture war, and almost no one crossing the lines. Like the trench warfare of World War I, our politics in this period, which stretched from 1995 to 2005, was a conflict of many bitter battles and no final victories.

Now we seem to be entering a new period, a period of open-field politics. It seems to be a time when there are no permanent alliances, when new leaders arise with new strategies and tactics, when the voters, instead of forming themselves into two coherent and cohesive armies, wander about the field, attaching themselves to one band and then another, with no clear lines of battle and no landmarks to rally beside.

Americans are facing the first presidential election since 1928—80 years ago!—that doesn't feature the incumbent president or the incumbent vice president as a candidate. We have gone through periods of open-field politics before, most recently between 1990 and 1995. In those years, a little-known governor of Arkansas challenged an incumbent president whose job approval rose to 89%; a Texas billionaire announced his candidacy on cable news and soon led the putative Republican and Democratic nominees in the polls; and the Republican Party, after 40 years in the minority in the House, won thumping majorities in the House and Senate. Few professional observers of politics predicted any of those three surprising developments.

Similar surprises, or quite different ones, may be in store for us. In the first months of 2007, the presidential candidates leading in the polls included the wife of a former president, a man who had never been a governor or a senator and who was far out of line with his party on issues important to its base, and a man who during the immediately preceding presidential contest was a state senator in Illinois. More surprises may be coming.

The 2006 Elections: One period is over, another begins   The results of the 2006 election were significantly different from those of the five biennial elections between 1996 and 2004. For a decade, we seemed to be an almost evenly divided and deeply politically polarized country. From the 1995-96 budget showdown between President Clinton and House Speaker Newt Gingrich until after Hurricane Katrina in 2005, the political balance across the country remained very much the same. We were a 49% nation, as was written in this space six years ago.

In the five House elections between 1996 and 2004, Republican candidates won between 49% and 51% of the vote, and Democratic candidates won between 46% and 48.5%—an unusually narrow range in American history. Clinton was re-elected with 49% of the vote in 1996; George W. Bush and Al Gore both won a rounded-off 48% in 2000; Bush beat John Kerry in 2004 by 51% to 48%, the narrowest percentage margin for a re-elected president since Woodrow Wilson beat Charles Evans Hughes 49% to 46% in 1916.

The electorate was divided primarily by cultural, even moral, issues: two armies in a culture war facing each other across the trenches. The bitterness of these divisions was exacerbated because the two men who occupied the White House—Clinton and Bush, both born in 1946, the first year of the Baby Boom, and both graduating in the high school class of 1964, which had the highest SAT scores since the test was first administered—happen to have personal characteristics that those on the other side of the cultural divide absolutely loathed. Elections became less a matter of persuading movable voters in the center and more a matter of turning out the party faithful on Election Day—or even before, thanks to the increasing trend toward absentee and early voting.

The 2006 election was at least somewhat different. Most glaringly different in a partisan sense: Democrats won a clear-cut victory, gaining majorities in both the Senate and the House, for the first time since 1992. (The Democrats' 2001-02 Senate majority was attained by a party switch rather than an election.) The Democratic capture of the Senate last year owed something to luck, as is often the case; Democrats won six of the seven closest races, and their candidates won in Montana and Virginia—both long shots at the start of the year—by a total of 12,891 votes. But parties have captured (or put themselves in position to capture) Senate majorities by winning most of the close races before—Republicans in 1980; Democrats in 1986 and 2000.

In House races, Democrats won 52% of the popular vote, compared with Republicans' 46%—a contrast to the Republicans' 50% to 47% advantage in 2004 and their 51% to 46% advantage in 2002. This shift was similar in magnitude to many others in American electoral history when one party or the other seemed to have a dominant majority. But coming as it did in a time of near-parity, it resulted in a decisive change in party control. House Democrats' popular vote ratio in 2006 was very similar to the House Republicans' 52% to 45% popular vote edge in 1994—the last year that either party got as much as 52% of the House vote.

Meanwhile, no presidential candidate has won as much as 52% of the popular vote since George H.W. Bush won 53% in 1988. The Democrats' 233-202 House majority after the 2006 election was nearly identical to the Republicans' 230-205 majority after the 1994 contest. (The majority grew to 235-200 after party switches and special-election victories later in that Congress; all numbers here count independent members as belonging to the party for which they voted to organize the House.) The Democrats' majority in the 110th Congress is also almost identical to the Republicans' 232-203 majority during most of the preceding Congress.

The contours of partisan support have not shifted greatly. Exit polls suggest that the Republicans' backing fell by similar percentages among just about every demographic group except those that have been mostly solidly moored to their party. The GOP's percentages fell more sharply among independents than among Democrats and Republicans, as one might expect, given the stronger partisan ties of the latter.

From 2002 to 2006, there was little difference in the parties' support among the elderly, many of whom have developed fixed preferences over the years, or among blacks, who have been voting overwhelmingly Democratic since 1964. Similarly, there was little change among demographic groups with large percentages of blacks—including voters with incomes under $15,000 and those who have not graduated from high school. In 2006 the Democrats held 92% of 2004 Kerry voters; the Republicans held a lower percentage, 83%, of 2004 Bush voters.

One of the triumphs of the 2004 Bush campaign was the registration and voter-turnout effort that increased the president's popular vote tally 23% from 2000 (Kerry's popular vote was 16% higher than Gore's in 2000). But looking at the 2006 figures, one gets the feeling that many of the new voters who came out for Bush in 2004 voted for Democratic members of Congress in 2006. Unfortunately, the exit poll did not identify those who voted for the first time in 2004.

Looking at the 2006 results in specific districts, one finds Democrats beating Republicans in districts that Bush carried by large ratios, as much as 62%, in 2004. Some Republican incumbents had specific problems, but these results also suggest that when Democrats seriously contested such districts, many voters were much more willing to cross party lines than they had been in the five elections between 1996 and 2004.

A couple of other demographic points are useful. The AFL-CIO and other unions again conducted a major voter-turnout drive in 2006, and that effort seems to have paid off. Fully 23% of 2006 voters said they were either union members or part of a household in which someone was a union member, and 63% of them voted Democratic. This is a startlingly high number, because only 8% of private-sector workers (and 36% of the many fewer public-sector workers) are union members. The unions seem to have leveraged a rather small movement into a much stronger political force, one to whom Democratic politicians owe very much indeed.

The GOP continues to owe a debt to white evangelical and born-again Protestants, who despite some grousing by leaders turned out strongly enough to form 24% of the electorate, and who voted 70% Republican. In contrast, people who said they never attend church services (15% of voters) voted 67% Democratic.

The 2006 election may turn out to be the beginning of a long period of Democratic dominance. Or it may not. The election was more a verdict on competence than on ideology, and it gave the Democrats an opportunity but, on most issues at least, not a mandate.

As the liberal columnist E.J. Dionne wrote, Democrats got their votes on loan. It was a negative verdict on the conduct of the military struggle in Iraq and on the government's response to Hurricane Katrina. It was a negative verdict on a Republican Congress that seemed casual about corruption and complacent about wasteful spending. It was a victory won after a campaign that was conducted largely in an idea-free zone. Republicans campaigned on pretty much the platform that Bush ran on in 2000 and 2004, though many of his promises had already been fulfilled, and others—such as Social Security reform—had been set aside as unachievable. Democrats campaigned pretty much as opponents of Bush, with a platform made up of planks that were minimalist (raise the minimum wage) or lacking in specifics in voters' minds (enact all the recommendations of the 9/11 commission, whatever they were).

The talented chairmen of the Democrats' House and Senate campaign committees, Rep. Rahm Emanuel of Illinois and Sen. Charles Schumer of New York, came out with books just before and after the election (Emanuel's was co-authored by Clinton White House domestic chief Bruce Reed) that advocated innovative and attractive ideas for changes in public policy. But Emanuel and Schumer did not press these ideas on their candidates. Instead, they shrewdly recruited and financed candidates who were out of line with the majority of the Democratic caucuses but in line with their districts and states, and the campaign chiefs had the satisfaction of seeing many of them win on Election Night.

This was quite a different victory from the Republicans' win in 1994. Then, the GOP largely defeated those Democrats who had supported liberal policies (the 1993 tax increase; the Clinton health care plan) in districts where majorities were considerably more conservative than their representative's voting records. In 2006, in contrast, as political scientist David Brady has pointed out, Democrats tended to defeat Republicans generally, especially those with relatively moderate records in relatively liberal districts and those who had scandal problems.

The 1994 election was a clear indication that voters would not have re-elected Bill Clinton had he been on the ballot that year; and he won his reelection in 1996 by changing his course on issues (most notably by signing the 1996 welfare reform act) and by campaigning as a champion of consensus against the kind of "angry white men" who bombed the federal building in Oklahoma City. The 2006 election was a clear indication that voters would not have re-elected George W. Bush had he been on the ballot that year. But he wasn't, and he won't be in 2008. Republicans have the chance to nominate a presidential candidate who will perhaps be in a different place on issues and will be able to argue, persuasively or not, that he has the competence that last year's voters believed that Bush lacked.

Voters in 1994 knew they could elect a Republican Congress without getting an entirely Republican government; they would just get a check on, or a goad to force a change of course on, Clinton. Voters in 2006 knew they could elect a Democratic Congress without getting an entirely Democratic government; they would just get a check on, or a goad to force a change of course on, Bush.

In 1996, as it turned out, voters decided they didn't want an entirely Republican government (though the margin in House races was exceedingly close). In 2008, voters may or not decide they want an entirely Democratic government. And it seems that they will be faced with that question, given that most political experts, looking at the lineup of Senate and House seats likely to be seriously contested, expect the Democrats to hold their congressional majorities in 2008. So the presidential election of 2008 will probably raise the question, more so than the 2000 presidential election did (because Democrats then had high hopes, which they nearly achieved, of winning a majority in the House), of whether voters want to turn the whole government over to one party.

The Democratic majorities in the 110th Congress emerged with a mandate, arguably, to end U.S. military involvement in Iraq. But they did not, given Bush's decision to "surge" additional troops into the conflict, have the means to put that mandate into effect, at least not immediately. They had the additional problem that a larger percentage of the public—59% versus 51% in the 2006 exit poll—believe that Republicans would make America safe from terrorism than would Democrats. The lingering reputation of the Democratic Party as weaker on protecting the nation and asserting U.S. interests—a reputation that dates from 1972 and was quite a reversal from the Democrats' reputation for being stronger on defense and more assertive in foreign policy that prevailed from 1940 to the 1960s-is a potential handicap for 2008, no matter how strong the party's position on Iraq was in the last half of 2006 and the first half of 2007.

As for domestic policy, here indeed is an open field. The issue is no longer, as it was from the 1920s to the 1980s, macroeconomic management. Voters in that era who remembered the Depression of the 1930s were ready, at the slightest sign of recession, to vote once again against Herbert Hoover's fecklessness and for Franklin Roosevelt's penchant for improvisational intervention. Voters who remembered the stagflation of the 1970s were ready, at the slightest sign of inflation and torpor, to vote against Jimmy Carter's dolorous insistence on sacrifice and for Ronald Reagan's optimistic faith that once the shackles were off, America's best economic times were ahead.

But almost none of today's voters remember the 1930s and fewer than half of them remember the 1970s. In the quarter-century since 1983, Americans have lived in a country that has enjoyed non-inflationary economic growth 95% of the time. They have come to think of this as the norm. They give politicians, particularly Bush, no credit when the economy performs this way, and they complain querulously about the slightest irritations, such as gasoline prices that in real dollar terms are far lower than they were in the early 1980s.

Polls show that public opinion on the state of the economy is so highly correlated with party identification that one must conclude it is less an assessment of objective conditions and more a matter of supporting the home team. Republicans complained about the vibrant economy in Clinton's second term; Democrats complained about the vibrant economy in Bush's second term. Macroeconomic numbers no longer move political numbers.

What does divide the parties is the way they frame economic issues. The Democrats want to redress economic inequality. The Republicans want to stimulate economic activity. But the Democrats haven't advanced policies that would reduce inequality substantially, nor have they answered the objection that policies that do—such as those adopted in Western Europe—also tend to produce economic stagnation.

The Republicans, meanwhile, went into the 2006 elections with a record of not holding down spending as much as taxes. House Speaker Dennis Hastert, faced with the need to hold together a small Republican majority, used money as his glue. Appropriators and Transportation Committee Republicans poured money into their districts (and let committee Democrats do the same) with increasing liberality. The ultimate earmark was Transportation Committee Chairman Don Young's $230 million "bridge to nowhere," an earmark in the 2005 transportation bill for a bridge to connect Ketchikan, Alaska (pop. 7,410) with its airport on the island of Gravina (pop. 50).

At the same time, neither party has come to terms with the looming long-range problem of entitlements. The Social Security, Medicaid, and Medicare programs are on a trajectory to eat up an ever-larger share of gross domestic product, to the point that in the lifetimes of many current members of Congress they will require far higher levels of taxation or borrowing to sustain them. Bush addressed Social Security in his 2000 and 2004 campaigns and tried to put it on Congress's agenda in 2005. He failed.

Young voters, the presumed beneficiaries of any change, seemed totally unmoved: Reagan and Clinton strengthened their parties among young voters, but Bush signally failed to do so. In response to his initiative, congressional Democrats were, almost to a member, prepared to entertain no changes. House Republicans were visibly reluctant to advance any proposal and gladly used the excuse of Hurricane Katrina to duck the issue in September 2005. Bush and members of Congress have come forward with arguably constructive approaches to changing health care finance. But in early 2007 none of those seemed ripe for passage.

In any event, the 2006 election was not a mandate for major domestic policy changes. It was an opportunity for congressional Democrats to demonstrate competence. The election may prove to be the harbinger of a long Democratic era. But it is scarcely a guarantee of one. And as the months go on, the struggle between Bush and the Democratic Congress—or the agreement they may reach on some serious issues, such as education and immigration—seem likely to be increasingly overshadowed by the competition between presidential candidates and, by some point in 2008, by the positions taken by the two parties' nominees.

The Open-Field Presidential Race   There was plenty of evidence by early 2007 that the 2008 presidential race was going to be starkly different from the races in 2004 or 2000. Partly, of course, because neither the president nor vice president was running. Voters were faced not with a choice between an incumbent and an alternative, but with a wide variety of alternatives. And initial polling suggested that voters were not as tightly moored to party labels as they were in recent years.

In 2004, poll results matching Bush and Kerry, taken before Kerry clinched the Democratic nomination, changed little from week to week and month to month. The vast majority of voters were clearly on one side or the other, and both the Bush and Kerry campaigns concentrated on motivating and mobilizing their supporters to get to the polls on Election Day, or, better yet, to vote early.

Early polls on the 2008 contest were different. They showed the best-known potential candidates for both parties—Hillary Rodham Clinton, Al Gore, Rudy Giuliani, John McCain—running well above 50% against little-known candidates of the other party. Voters who had never considered crossing party lines in the 2000 and 2004 cycles were apparently ready to do so. No more trench warfare: We were now in an open field.

Within the parties, the rules seemed to change as well. Early 2007 polling showed remarkable symmetry on the two parties' nominations. Leading in most polls were two candidates who were in opposition to or in tension with their parties' bases on issues that were or have been of great importance to the base—Giuliani (abortion and other cultural issues) and Clinton (the war in Iraq).

In second place in most polls were two candidates whose seeming lack of partisan edge was in contrast to the strong visceral feelings of both parties' bases—McCain (who worked with Democrats on campaign finance regulation and other issues) and Barack Obama (whose keynote speech at the 2004 Democratic National Convention stressed what Democrats and Republicans have in common rather than what divides them).

In third place were two candidates whose views and partisan edge seemed very much in line with their parties' bases, but who had arrived at those positions only recently—Mitt Romney (who changed his views on abortion and other issues) and John Edwards (who came out as a strong opponent of the Iraq war he had voted for).

Democratic voters seemed pretty pleased with their field of candidates and fairly confident that their party was headed to victory. Republican voters seemed less pleased with their field and less confident of victory—and two possible candidates with potentially wide followings, Gingrich and Fred Thompson, hovered over their field tantalizingly. But voters in both parties seemed willing to consider candidates who did not meet all of their litmus tests. And in spring 2007 many voters in both parties—in national polls and in polls in such potentially pivotal states as Iowa and New Hampshire—seemed to be moving from one candidate to another, with no firm commitment to any.

No candidate in either party seemed to be running as a clone of either of the two previous presidents, Clinton and Bush. Not even Hillary Rodham Clinton. She left behind the centrist tone of her husband's 1992 campaign and instead campaigned in line with the tone and substance of a party that has moved perceptibly to the left since he left the White House in January 2001.

Partly, this shift is simply because the issues are different: Reducing welfare and crime were the great public policy successes of the 1990s, for which the Clinton administration could take some credit. But Hillary Clinton, like most of her Democratic congressional colleagues, had moved away from the Clinton administration's staunch support of free-trade agreements and had not called for the kind of military interventions that Bill Clinton ordered in Bosnia and (without United Nations approval) in Kosovo.

The other Democratic contenders—Edwards, Obama, Sen. Joseph Biden of Delaware, Sen. Christopher Dodd of Connecticut, former Sen. Mike Gravel of Alaska, Rep. Dennis Kucinich of Ohio, New Mexico Gov. Bill Richardson—all called for more or less immediate withdrawal from Iraq. In the 2004 cycle, all of the Democratic candidates except Joe Lieberman and Dick Gephardt denounced the Bush administration in vitriolic terms, and those two quickly fell by the wayside. No Democratic candidate in the 2008 cycle seemed to be taking such an approach. Former Virginia Gov. Mark Warner and Sen. Evan Bayh of Indiana, who might have been expected to, decided not to run.

Among the Republicans, none was running as a clone of Bush. Senators Bill Frist and George Allen had been expected to do so and had taken issue positions similar to Bush's (except, in Allen's case, on immigration). But Allen lost reelection to the Senate and Frist, shortly after returning to Nashville, announced that he would not run. All of the candidates actively running took positions at odds with Bush's on some issues, and some criticized his performance on Iraq and other matters. Giuliani, McCain, and Romney all disagreed with Bush on important issues. Tommy Thompson, though he served four years in the Bush Cabinet, talked more about his 14 years as governor of Wisconsin. Sen. Sam Brownback of Kansas, former Virginia Gov. Jim Gilmore, former Arkansas Gov. Mike Huckabee, Rep. Duncan Hunter of California, and Rep. Tom Tancredo of Colorado campaigned as believers in various forms of conservatism, with different emphases. Rep. Ron Paul of Texas campaigned as a libertarian, against government intervention at home and abroad.

All of this has made the 2008 presidential race different from any other recent presidential race. So does the fact that, although voters expressed a generic preference for a Democratic president over a Republican president, at the same time in many polls respondents preferred Giuliani and, less often, McCain over Hillary Clinton and Gore, the best-known Democrats—and the ones most closely associated with the generally positively regarded Clinton administration. It does look like an open field.

One way to suggest how open is to advance three possible scenarios for the 2008 results, scenarios that are based on previous election results but are plausible extensions of trends apparent in early 2007. In each case, however, some differences exist between the historical example and the factors in the 2008 race.

The Blair Scenario   In the early 1990s, Britain's Conservative Party was regarded as nasty but competent. Then in September 1992 Britain was forced to exit from the European Rate Mechanism; interest rates and mortgage payments shot up, and the Conservatives' reputation for economic competence vanished. The Labor Party went ahead in the polls, to remain there until 2006, an impressive 14 years. Under the leadership of Tony Blair, New Labor, as he called it, won a sweeping victory in 1997. The House of Commons shifted from 343-273 Conservative to 419-165 Labor. Prime Minister Blair's party won a similarly sweeping victory in 2001 and won by a slightly reduced margin in 2005.

Today's Republicans, like the British Conservatives in the 1990s, have lost their reputation for competence. If things unfold here now as they did in Britain then, the result would be a 40-state presidential victory for the Democrats, a magnitude they have not achieved since 1964. It would also result in a considerably more Democratic Congress than at present, with Democrats winning seats previously regarded as utterly safe for Republicans—results that seemed as inconceivable in America in 2006 as they did in Britain in 1992.

But the two situations are not exactly parallel. Labor won in Britain only after Tony Blair rebranded the party as New Labor, with a renunciation of socialism and an embrace of market economics. If the old Labor Party's leader, John Smith, had not died suddenly in 1994, to be succeeded by the 41-year-old Blair, Labor might well have won in 1997 but probably by a much smaller and less durable margin.

America's Democrats in early 2007 didn't seem to be rebranding themselves as New Democrats, as Bill Clinton did in 1992. Moreover, it's not clear that the Republican nominee in 2008 will have the reputation for incompetence that Bush did in 2006. Giuliani's strength came not only from his response to the September 11 attacks but also from his well-known success in cutting crime and welfare dependency by more than half in New York City. Other possible Republican nominees had records that supported their claims of competence, and they will have the opportunity in the 2008 campaign to demonstrate that quality.

The Ike Scenario   In 1952 the United States was mired in a deadly conflict in Korea—a conflict that took 10 times as many lives as Iraq has and that President Truman could not end. There emerged a candidate with a record of making life-and-death decisions in war: Dwight D. Eisenhower. Ike captured the Republican nomination from "Mr. Republican," Robert Taft, and then defeated a refreshing new face from Illinois, Adlai Stevenson, who had little military experience. At a time when Democrats had a big advantage in party identification, Eisenhower won the election solidly, and Republicans captured small majorities in both houses of Congress.

This scenario does not fit perfectly with the situation in 2008. None of the Republican candidates can claim experience anything like Eisenhower's. But Giuliani did command a uniformed force of 40,000 that reduced crime in New York City by 64%. McCain served in combat and has had a record of close attention to military affairs ever since. None of the leading Democrats has comparable experience. Clinton has been a conscientious member of the Armed Services Committee. Obama is, like Stevenson, a fresh face from Illinois. Edwards was a senator for six years and has been a candidate for president for more than five. Perhaps the closest to Ike is Richardson, who has conducted serious negotiations with the North Koreans and served as ambassador to the United Nations.

There is another difference. Eisenhower was the nominee of the opposition party and was critical of the policy of the president. Today's Republicans have mostly supported Bush on Iraq. Yet a straight-line extrapolation from some of the early 2007 polls produces a result that looks something like the Ike scenario—that is, the election of a Republican president by a decisive margin, with Democrats holding narrow congressional majorities (or, as in 1952, narrowly losing them).

The Perot Scenario   In February 1992 a short billionaire from Texas told CNN's Larry King that he might run for president. Perot had enough money (he ultimately spent more than $60 million of his own money) and enough celebrity to make an independent candidacy plausible. What made Perot appealing to voters tired of stale, bitter division were his calls for reform and an end to partisan wrangling.

The short billionaire who is in a position to do something similar in 2008 is Michael Bloomberg, who spent $160 million getting elected mayor of New York City in 2001 and 2005. Bloomberg ranks 142nd on Forbes's list of the world's billionaires with a personal fortune of $5.5 billion, and he has demonstrated a willingness to spend unprecedented sums on campaigns. He can also argue, in a time of bitter partisanship, that he has a record of nonpartisan achievement. His job ratings from New Yorkers have been higher than Giuliani's were, and the Manhattan media elite, which appreciated Giuliani's success in cutting crime but was uncomfortable with his sharp challenges to conventional liberalism, find Bloomberg's less-confrontational style more congenial.

Of course, the two situations are somewhat different. For one thing, Bloomberg has no military experience or credibility. Perot's Texas twang enabled him to straddle cultural issues and to appeal to voters on both sides of the cultural divide. Bloomberg's Boston accent (he grew up outside the city) and self-assurance are perhaps not as broadly appealing. Bloomberg's chances as an independent would probably be highest if the Republicans nominated an unapologetic cultural conservative and the Democrats put forward a radical-sounding war opponent. But it's not clear that either party will do so.

In fact, in early 2007 it wasn't clear what either party, or any candidate or potential candidate, would do. What did seem fairly clear was that they were all running in an open field, with voters more liable than they had been to consider candidates different from those they supported in the past, and more ready to change their minds. Any of the above scenarios, or something like them, could conceivably happen—or at least one could see how they could happen by making straight-line extrapolations from the political facts in early 2007. But not all of them can happen. We have moved from trench warfare to open-field politics, and we don't know what's ahead.

THE HOUSE OF REPRESENTATIVES

"Tonight I have a high privilege and distinct honor of my own—as the first President to begin the State of the Union message with these words: Madam Speaker." With these words George W. Bush saluted Nancy Pelosi, the 60th Speaker of the House of Representatives. Bush went on to note that Pelosi's father, Congressman Thomas D'Alesandro, had watched Presidents Roosevelt and Truman speak at the podium. These two grace notes were a recognition of the fact that Pelosi at one and the same time represented innovation and tradition: she was the first woman Speaker and also one schooled and steeped in traditional politics. Growing up, she had helped her father, mayor of Baltimore after he served in the House, tend to ethnic precinct politics; as an adult (and the mother of five children) she advanced in the very different politics of ultraliberal San Francisco. To become speaker she also had to work with and for Democrats from many diverse districts—from inner city black neighborhoods to Midwestern farm country, country districts in the South and affluent precincts of liberal big cities where so much of her party's money is raised.

Her elevation to the speakership was a distinct break for the House from the 12 years of Republican control, just as Newt Gingrich's elevation was a distinct break from 40 years of Democratic majorities. It probably cannot be said of her, as it could of Gingrich, that her party would not have won a majority if she had not been there. She has been not so much a transformational as simply an effective political leader. Democrats in the 12 years before 2006 had never entirely given up on the hope of regaining a majority; Republican margins were simply too small to make their overturning unimaginable. But there had been trying times, and Pelosi did much to get Democrats through them. In contrast, from 1974 until the early 1990s few Republicans believed they could ever be in the majority again. Gingrich convinced them they could, and did much to make it happen.

There are two other former House members who were not present to see Pelosi at the Speaker's podium at the 2007 State of the Union, and who would have beamed as much as her father if they had: her predecessors in her district in San Francisco, Phillip Burton and Sala Burton. Phil Burton died suddenly in 1983 and Sala Burton, dying of cancer in 1987, wanted Pelosi to succeed her. The Burtons were an extraordinary couple who had an impact on the House as great in their time as Gingrich had in his, and through Pelosi they may be said to have an impact once again. Phil Burton was a spiritual heir of the longshoremen who led one of the nation's largest general strikes in San Francisco in 1934; as a young assemblyman he won a special election to the House in 1964. Soon he was the guiding force in the liberal Democratic Study Group, at a time when the Democratic leadership didn't whip votes for liberal causes. Under Burton and his hand-picked successors, the DSG stepped in in its place. Burton was a backer of Robert Kennedy and George McGovern in 1968 and 1972 and helped lead the California delegations in demanding reform of party rules. He demanded reform of party rules too. At the same time, he could play tough partisan politics with redistricting and became an expert on drawing lines not just in California but across the country. He helped to elect the young liberal Democrats of the Watergate class of 1974 and led them in demanding votes on committee chairmen. When the leadership said that there would be votes on those chairmanships in which a certain number of Democrats signed petitions, Burton got enough Democrats to sign petitions challenging every chairman. The leadership capitulated, and ordered automatic elections henceforth. Four committee chairmen were replaced—a warning that Democrats wouldn't elevate members who weren't sufficiently liberal or sufficiently capable. In 1960 Burton took part in a demonstration in San Francisco against the House Un-American Activities Committee. In 1974 he abolished it, by the typically backhanded ploy of seeing that no Democrats applied to be members.

The House as it was run by the liberal Democratic leadership from 1974 to 1994 was Burton's handiwork as much as anyone else's. But Burton did not lead it. After the 1976 election, in which Speaker Carl Albert retired and Majority Leader Tip O'Neill ascended to his post without opposition, Burton ran for Majority Leader. He had some unusual allies. He cultivated Wayne Hays, the autocratic Chairman of the House Administration Committee who expressed nothing but contempt for young liberal members. With Hays's help he accumulated some unlikely votes in his race for Majority Leader. But in the final round he lost to Jim Wright by one vote, 148-147. It's a secret ballot, and Burton spent years figuring out just who had cast the decisive votes against him.

Nancy Pelosi at this time was involved in California Democratic politics in various capacities: fundraising, working for candidates. She went back to her home state of Maryland in 1976 for Jerry Brown in the presidential primary and he won on unlikely turf, with help from some old D'Alesandro allies. She became chairman of the California Democratic Party in 1981, when she had to walk a fine line between Speaker Leo McCarthy and Majority Leader Howard Berman who was challenging him; both were running candidates in Democratic primaries in a fight which neither won and which resulted in the elevation, with Republican votes, of Speaker Willie Brown. She was an organizer for the 1984 Democratic National Convention in San Francisco. And, as the columnist Harold Meyerson wrote movingly, Sala Burton asked her to succeed her and her husband in Congress.

Pelosi did not start off seeking a leadership position. She got a seat on the Appropriations Committee and had to deal with a problem Phil Burton had left her: he put in an amendment saying that when the military left San Francisco's Presidio the installation would be turned over to the National Park Service. But the Presidio was expensive to maintain and renovate and threatened to eat up half the Park Service's budget. Pelosi had to find the money, and after several years she did. Starting in the late 1980s, she took a more open stand as the leader of a bipartisan group of members decrying China's human rights record, a stand directly opposite of that of her San Francisco neighbor, Senator Dianne Feinstein. In 1999, she began campaigning for a leadership post and made her move rapidly in 2001 when Minority Whip David Bonior, confronted with a partisan Republican redistricting, decided to run for governor. In a Democratic Caucus with many fewer Democrats than the Caucus that rejected Phil Burton by one vote—212 rather than 292—she assembled a coalition of Californians, liberals and, following the Burton example, some unlikely allies. Chief among them was John Murtha, from the coal country of western Pennsylvania, not far from Wayne Hays's coal country in eastern Ohio. She and her allies got Bonior to resign before his term in the House was up and when the Caucus met in October 2001 Murtha gave the nominating speech. Her opponent was Steny Hoyer of Maryland, whom she had known when they were interns in the office of Senator Daniel Brewster in 1963. Pelosi won 118-95. Whether she could have won in the more ideologically diverse caucus that rejected Burton was unclear, but like Burton she might have shaped her candidacy to suit her constituency.

Given the Republican leadership's determination to run the House despite their narrow majorities, a determination when Speaker Dennis Hastert held a 15-minute roll call open for three hours in order to get enough votes to pass the Medicare prescription drug bill in December 2003, it was not a hard choice for Pelosi to set a course of root-and-branch opposition to the Republican majority. In this she was as obdurate as Gingrich had wanted his Republicans before 1994. When Dick Gephardt, preparing to run for president, decided to resign as Minority Leader in November 2002, Pelosi was challenged by Harold Ford and won 177-29. After the 2004 election, she had no opposition.

For the 2006 cycle Pelosi chose Rahm Emanuel as head of the House Democrats' campaign committee. It was an inspired choice. From his days as a Clinton operative and his contacts in Chicago, he had developed great contacts for fundraising. And he chose a strategy that made eminent good sense. He extended his target list well beyond the Republican seats that seemed vulnerable on the basis of 2000, 2002 and 2004 election results. With partisan districting installed in many large states, with the Republican leadership aiding its weak members in many ways, there were not enough targets there to produce a Democratic takeover. Emanuel recruited candidates in unlikely districts and he searched especially for Iraq war veterans. He backed candidates where Republicans seemed susceptible to charges of encouraging a "climate of corruption," charges which were given strength by the (arguably unjust) indictment of Majority Leader Tom DeLay, and by the clear disgrace of Randy Cunningham and Bob Ney—all of this being underlined by the resignation of Mark Foley on the last day of the session in September and obscuring the Democrats' own corruption problem (the $90,000 of cash in Bill Jefferson's freezer). Not all of his long shot candidates came through. The Republicans' turnout efforts, stepped up from their success in 2004, helped save perhaps a dozen seats, and Republicans won more of the very closest races than did Democrats. Pelosi campaigned indefatigably around the country. Republicans tried to portray her as a dangerous San Francisco liberal, but that availed them little. The 232-203 Republican majority was transformed to a 233-202 Democratic majority.

As Speaker-elect and Speaker, Pelosi performed with smiling dignity but also with the sharp elbows she had shown in leadership races. She backed John Murtha for majority leader over Steny Hoyer. In an interview with *Fox News's* Brit Hume she said that Iraq was "a problem to be solved," not a war to be won, and she opposed George W. Bush's surge in January 2007. The rules changes the incoming Democrats made did not make as much institutional difference as those Burton had pushed through in 1974—election of committee chairmen, especially—or those that Newt Gingrich pushed through in 1994—six-year term limits on chairmen, which she kept in place. The House Democrats' reforms on transparency of earmarks did not go quite as far as promised. But they did pass the "Six for '06" agenda in the 100 hours promised—actually, 100 *legislative* hours. Committee chairmanships went in almost every case to members with seniority. But Pelosi effectively chose Bennie Thompson at Homeland Security when she made him the ranking minority member there in 2005, and she was obdurate in her insistence on ousting Jane Harman at the Intelligence Committee; she stumbled only when she first insisted on Alcee Hastings, an intelligent and active member of the committee but also a man who was impeached and removed from a federal judgeship by a Democratic Congress, then pushed him aside for Silvestre Reyes. To a greater extent than Gingrich in 1995, but to a lesser extent than earlier speakers, she deferred to committee chairmen. But not always. She set up a special committee to work on policies to combat climate change and reduce carbon dioxide emissions—an attempt to bypass Energy and Commerce Chairman John Dingell (to whose opponent, fellow incumbent Lynn Rivers, she contributed $10,000 in the 2002 primary).

She had the advantage here that the incoming chairmen, most of them older and more senior than their Republican counterparts, who had soldiered on during 12 years in the minority, were all members of proven ability and integrity: David Obey of Appropriations, Ike Skelton of Armed Services, John Spratt of Budget, George Miller (her fellow San Francisco Bay area resident and Burton acolyte) of Education, Dingell of Energy and Commerce, Barney Frank of Financial Services, Henry Waxman of Government Reform, Tom Lantos of International Relations, John Conyers of Judiciary, Louise Slaughter of Rules, Jim Oberstar of Transportation and Infrastructure, Charles Rangel of Ways and Means. Republicans may have treated them as bogeymen in campaigns, but they have to respect them in committee rooms and on the floor. Some of them embarked quickly on bipartisan initiatives—Miller on reauthorizing No Child Left Behind, Frank on regulating government-sponsored enterprises, Rangel on trade agreements. Others (and some of these chairmen) embarked on partisan agendas and partisan investigations.

What are the prospects for Democrats to continue their control of the House and for Pelosi to continue as Speaker? In early 2007 they looked pretty good. On the negative side, it was hard to see how they could easily expand their majority. Only 8 House Republicans represented districts that were carried by John Kerry in 2004; 6 of them were hard-pressed in 2006 and might figure that, having survived a bad year for their party, they are in fair shape to face 2008. But there are no guarantees in an era of open-field politics that 2006 was the worst possible year for Republicans, and surely some of these seats will be contested again. Moreover, DCCC Chairman Rahm Emanuel's decision to seriously contest districts which on the basis of 2004 figures were not winnable paid off: the prime example is the 8th District of Indiana, 62% for George W. Bush in 2004, 61% for Democrat Brad Ellsworth in 2006. Of the 30 seats Democrats picked up, 20 voted for Bush in 2004. Might there also be other Bush 2004 seats which were not seriously contested in 2006 but which might prove vulnerable in 2008? Quite possibly, and the new DCCC Chairman Chris Van Hollen seems very much alert to that prospect. But Republicans also have targets: 62 House Democrats hold seats that were carried by Bush in 2004. By no means are all of these vulnerable, and probably most aren't. But in a period of open field politics, some which would not appear on conventional targeting lists may turn out to be up for grabs.

One thing that is likely to be different in 2008 is that the two parties will be defined to a great extent by their presidential nominees. In the 2006 election the dominant figure was George W. Bush. Democrats campaigned almost exclusively against him and made only minimal references to their own party's platform. Republicans were seen as his followers, though many tried to campaign on their own personas or issues. In 2008 Bush will still be president, and the Republican party's image will still bear his imprint. But a Republican nominee with a perceptibly different approach to issues and a different persona will tend to define the party also. Bush, as compared to at least some possible 2008 nominees, had over his presidency greater appeal in the South and rural areas and less appeal in the Northeast and in the suburbs of our largest metropolitan areas outside the South. A Republican nominee with greater appeal in the latter and less in the former will be well positioned to compete for electoral votes in some states which Bush lost narrowly in 2004 and some which were not seriously contested at all; he could afford to lose some percentage points in the South and Great Plains and still win just about all the electoral votes Bush won there. The political map with which we are so familiar may be altered, if not beyond recognition, at least substantially in 2008.

Moreover, Democrats will probably not be able to campaign simply as the anti-Bush party. One of the advantages the out party usually has is that its candidates are free to adapt to local terrain. Democrats in 2006 ran successfully as moderates or even conservatives in Indiana and North Carolina, Texas and Arizona. They were also able to run as full-throated Bush and Iraq war opponents in Connecticut and suburban Pennsylvania, New Hampshire and Upstate New York. They may not have as much leeway to do that in 2008. The party's image will be set to a considerable extent by the character and issue positions of its nominee.

The presidential nominating process has been pushed back, so that both parties' nominees may be known after the contests held February 5, 2008. But that comes fairly late in the cycle of candidate recruitment and fundraising. Filing deadlines will already have passed in some states, notably Illinois and Texas, and will be coming soon in many others. Party strategists will thus be doing much of their recruiting and targeting in the dark. But the light is not always clear in open field politics.

THE SENATE

For six of the eight years of George W. Bush's presidency the Senate has been almost evenly divided. From January 2001 to June 2001, it was evenly divided, with Dick Cheney casting the 51st vote to give Republicans the majority. From June 2001 to January 2003, Democrats had a 51-49 majority. From January 2003 to January 2005 Republicans had a 51-49 majority. From January 2005 to January 2007, Republicans had a 55-45 majority—not enough to prevail on many issues. Starting in January 2007, Democrats have had a 51-49 majority but of course that could be reversed at any time if a seat becomes vacant and is filled by a nominee of the other party. In early 2007 that possibility was raised by the sudden disability of South Dakota Democrat Tim Johnson. But Johnson has been recovering, and he may very well serve out the term just as Strom Thurmond did his up through his 100th birthday in December 2002.

Why is the Senate so evenly divided, when George W. Bush carried 31 states in 2004 that elect 62 senators? The answer is that Democrats have done a much better job of electing Democratic senators in Republican-leaning states than Republicans have done electing Republican senators in Democratic-leaning states. Republican gains in 2002 and 2004 came primarily from Republican-leaning states: Georgia and Missouri in 2002, and Florida, Georgia, Louisiana, North Carolina, South Carolina and South Dakota in 2004. The exceptions in those cycles were Minnesota which turned Republican in 2002 and Colorado which turned Democratic in 2004. After the 2004 election Republicans held 18 of the 22 seats in the former Confederate states; they had few more to gain, and in fact lost Virginia in 2006. Republicans have lost seats because incumbents with political disabilities have insisted on running for reelection when non-incumbents could probably have won: Arkansas in 2002, Montana in 2006. And Republicans haven't been able to seriously dent the popularity of incumbent Democrats from Republican-leaning states like Arkansas, Florida, Indiana, Montana, Nebraska, Nevada, New Mexico, North Dakota and West Virginia. In 2006 DSCC Chairman Charles Schumer did a brilliant job of recruiting, getting Bob Casey, Jr., the one Democrat way ahead of Rick Santorum, to run in Pennsylvania; getting first-rate challengers to incumbents in narrowly Bush 2004 states like Missouri and Ohio; backing Jim Webb and capitalizing on George Allen's mistakes in Virginia; backing Jon Tester in Montana against a wounded Conrad Burns and Sheldon Whitehouse against Lincoln Chafee in heavily Democratic Rhode Island. It was an "inside straight," as Schumer acknowledged; but an inside straight, however unlikely, still wins the hand.

Schumer was tapped to run the DSCC for the 2007-08 cycle and started off with a better hand than two years before. Fully 21 of the 34 seats up are held by Republicans, including four in Kerry 2004 states: Maine, Minnesota, New Hampshire and Oregon. Democrats did very well in those states in 2006 and could field serious challengers in any or all of them. In addition, Wayne Allard's retirement left Democratic Congressman Mark Udall the favorite in Colorado, which went heavily Democratic in 2006, and subsequent retirements—of Pete Domenici in New Mexico and John Warner in Virginia—left attractive situations for Democrats. Of the 12 Democratic seats that are up, six are in Bush 2004 states: Arkansas, Iowa, Louisiana, Montana, South Dakota and West Virginia.

But at the beginning of the cycle only two looked vulnerable, Louisiana, where Mary Landrieu lost many black constituents after Hurricane Katrina, and South Dakota, where Tim Johnson's health made the outlook imponderable.

So who will control the Senate? The answer is that no one controls the Senate, no matter how big a majority one party or the other has. Majority Leader Bill Frist did not control the Senate, even in the two years his party had a 55-45 majority, and Majority Leader Harry Reid does not control the Senate, as shown by the fact that it took the Senate four months to pass just one item (the minimum wage) on the House Democrats' "Six for '06" agenda that they passed in 100 legislative hours in January.

It is a body of 100 men and women, most of whom think or thought that he or she should be president. It is a legislative chamber which conducts much of its business under rules that require unanimous consent for many matters and in which a supermajority of 60 votes is required for much that used to be routine business. The Framers created the Senate as a balance wheel, a cooling saucer for hot coffee, a place where superior experience and wisdom could prevent unwise and rash mistakes. With only one-third of its members elected every two years, with a fair number of its members free from political pressures because of their personal relationship with young voters in small or one-party states, with its rules allowing even the weakest and personally least regarded of its members to stop the forward motion of legislation for some precious period of time, with its allowance of unlimited discussion and non-germane amendments and its rules that require a 60% supermajority for passage of strongly-opposed legislation, the Senate supplies some caution to the enthusiasm of the House.

Before the ratification in 1913 of the Seventeenth Amendment providing for popular election of senators, the members of the Senate were elected by state legislatures and were something in the nature of ambassadors from the state governments to the federal government—in some cases, very high-ranking ambassadors. In the early republic they were great landowners and lawyers who were also political philosophers—Henry Clay, Daniel Webster and John C. Calhoun. In the late 19th and early 20th century, they were often wealthy industrialists of considerable intellect—Marcus Hanna, Boies Penrose, Leland Stanford, George Hearst, William A. Clark. After 1913 they were increasingly professional politicians—Republicans and Democrats who alternated in the Northern states with two-party politics and Democrats of great political skill and legislative acumen from the South. This is the Senate described by Robert Caro in *Master of the Senate*, his account of Lyndon Johnson as Senate Majority Leader from 1955 to 1961.

Before Johnson became Majority Leader, the post was of little importance. There was no majority leader at all until 1911. You will search through many histories of the Republican 80th Congress of 1947-49, a Congress which produced major partisan domestic legislation and supported a bipartisan Cold War policy before you find the name of the majority leader, Wallace White of Maine; the focus was all on committee chairmen like Robert Taft and Arthur Vandenberg. Johnson, operating in his first four years in a Senate closely divided between the parties, exercised extraordinary skills to produce an extraordinary flow of legislation, including the first civil rights act passed since the 1870s. But after Democrats gained 13 seats in the 1958 election, Johnson's power was diminished because liberal Democrats insisted on pressing for measures that, under Senate rules, could not be passed. Johnson's achievements between 1955 and 1959 created the idea, still lively, that the majority leader runs the Senate. A better understanding of the position's power came from the man who held it longest, Mike Mansfield, in a speech intended to be delivered on the day John F. Kennedy was murdered and which he only delivered in 1997 at the first Leader's Lecture, in which he argued that the majority leader was the servant, not the master, of the senators. Many people assume that the majority leader runs the Senate; what he does in fact is schedule business, and his schedule is usually subject to unanimous consent: He can stop things from happening, but he can't get things going if some significant body of opinion wants them stopped.

The Senate in which Mansfield worked and the Senate in which Robert Byrd, Howard Baker and Bob Dole were majority leaders was a Senate which was an incubator for presidential ambitions and an arena for legislative entrepreneurship, far less partisan than the House. The Senate in which Trent Lott, Tom Daschle, Bill Frist and Harry Reid have been majority leaders has been different. It is still an incubator for presidential ambitions. But it is less open to political entrepreneurship and more given to partisan battle. The filibuster was a rare procedure when it required 67 votes to defeat. Senators used it only on issues of the largest importance to them. But now that filibusters can be defeated by only 60 votes, they have become common—so common that it is constantly said that it requires 60 votes to pass major legislation. Points of order can also require 60 votes to overcome, and the Senate's parliamentary rules offer many more opportunities for obstruction. The impeachment of Bill Clinton in 1998 and the narrow and disputed victory of George W. Bush in 2000 heightened the partisan atmosphere: senators on both sides came to believe that the other side was acting illegitimately and to feel entitled to go full out to stop them. This seems likely to continue in a Senate whose majority leader, Harry Reid, is one of the most pugnacious men ever to have held the job, and whose minority leader, Mitch McConnell, is a strong partisan who is used to conducting political warfare over the long haul. The world's greatest deliberative body? Perhaps. But that may say more about the world's other representative assemblies than it does about the Senate.

House Reapportionment
After the 2010 Census

By Michael Barone

Reapportioning the seats in the U.S. House of Representatives at the start of every decade to account for population shifts inevitably boosts the political clout of some states and diminishes that of others. And, just as inevitably, the redistricting triggered by the redistribution of House seats influences the fortunes of both major political parties.

Since World War II, the shifting has cumulatively helped the Democratic Party more than the GOP. In the redistricting that followed the 1950 census, the Republicans netted about 10 seats. In each of the next three cycles—after the 1960, 1970, and 1980 censuses—Democrats picked up 10 to 15 seats. The 1990 census results did little to shift the partisan balance of power in the House. Then the 2000 census resulted in changes that enabled Republicans to pick up an initial five to 10 seats. Their party gained four more seats in 2004 after taking control of the Texas Legislature and redrawing congressional district lines for the second time in less than a decade.

Looking ahead to the round of musical chairs that will follow the 2010 census, we can safely predict that the Sun Belt will once again gain House seats at the expense of the manufacturing states of the Midwest and Northeast. And redistricting done in anticipation of the 2012 elections will very likely help the Republican Party somewhat—with the degree hinging on which party controls Ohio's state government.

Let's look at what redistricting will likely produce, given the current partisan lineup, the Census Bureau's latest population estimates and the people who will probably control the remapping process in each state. The greatest changes, of course, tend to come in states that gain or lose seats because of reapportionment. Using the nonpartisan data-gathering firm Polidata's estimates of winners and losers—based on straight-line extrapolations from population growth since 2000—we find that eight states' U.S. House delegations will expand in 2012.

States on Track to Gain Seats

Texas (+4) Not much chance of a change in control here by 2011. Gov. Rick Perry, who won a four-candidate race with a plurality last year, will presumably retire in 2010 and will probably be succeeded by a fellow Republican. The Texas GOP has proven its willingness to gerrymander, and can do it again. Most of the fast-growing sections of the state, except for some Hispanic areas along the border, are heavily Republican. Last November, Democrats flipped two seats into their column. Republicans might regain both, and they have an especially good chance of nabbing Tom DeLay's old seat, a district that gave President Bush 64% of its vote in 2004. The Voting Rights Act, which requires that minority voting strength be maximized, will compel creation of an additional Hispanic seat, which will probably go Democratic; but that may enable the legislators to add more Republicans to the district that Democrat Ciro Rodriguez took from Henry Bonilla.
Projection from current lineup: +4 Republican seats.

Arizona (+2) Arizona has a nonpartisan redistricting commission. After the 2000 census, the state gained two seats; the commission created a Democratic Hispanic district and an evenly balanced rural district—not what the Republican-controlled legislature would have done. Democrats picked up a pair of seats here in 2006, one based in Scottsdale, the other in Tucson. Population growth is likely to force creation of another Phoenix-area Republican seat. The Voting Rights Act probably won't require creation of a third Hispanic seat.
Projection from current lineup: +2 Republican seats.

Florida (+2) As in Texas, control of the state government isn't likely to change before redistricting. Popular Republican Gov. Charlie Crist can run for re-election in 2010. Republican legislative margins are wide. After Republican Mark Foley resigned from the House during last year's page scandal, Democrat Tim Mahoney picked up his Palm Beach-area district, where Bush won 54% of the vote in 2004. Mahoney may not be able to hold that seat. Last year, Democrats nearly picked up Katherine Harris's old district, which includes Sarasota. Look for the GOP to make those districts

more Republican. It's unlikely that the legislature will have to create another predominantly Hispanic district; there are three in Miami-Dade County.
   Projection from current lineup: +3 Republican seats, -1 Democratic seat.

Georgia (+1)   Here, Republicans drew up a relatively nonpartisan plan in 2005. A more partisan map, such as Florida's or Texas's, would almost certainly have resulted in the defeat of two South Georgia Democrats, who nearly lost anyway in the Democratic year of 2006. The state has five districts that are majority-black or almost majority-black. That number is unlikely to change.
   Projection from current lineup: +2 Republican seats, -1 Democratic seat.

Nevada (+1)   Hard to figure the odds. The new district will be in metro Las Vegas. The state most recently added a district in 2002, in suburban Las Vegas, that didn't tilt strongly toward either party; Republican Jon Porter won it and still holds it. If Democrats control the next round of redistricting, they will probably try to create a second safely Democratic seat. But control is likely to be in Republican hands, so Porter's position could be strengthened and a new balanced district created.
   Projection from current lineup: +1 toss-up seat.

Oregon (+1)   Democratic Gov. Ted Kulongoski can't run again. There's an outside chance that a Republican will win the Governor's Mansion, although that hasn't happened since 1982. But even with Democrats in control, they will have a hard time expanding their current 4-1 lead. They might want to protect Democrat Darlene Hooley, who holds a potentially competitive seat.
   Projection from current lineup: +1 toss-up seat.

Utah (+1)   In this very Republican state, it's impossible to imagine a new Democratic seat. The legislature has already tried once to shove Democrat Jim Matheson, who was first elected in 2000, into a district that he couldn't win. A second try isn't likely. But if Matheson retires, Republicans will capture the seat.
   Projection from current lineup: +1 Republican seat.

Washington (+1)   Washington uses a bipartisan commission; the lines can be changed by a two-thirds vote of the legislature. If the commission is deadlocked, the issue goes to the state Supreme Court. The Washington plan has been lauded by many for taking partisanship out of redistricting and for creating more districts that both parties can win. But in Washington, where the commission is not bound by the mathematical requirements that in Iowa have resulted in districts not tailored to incumbents, incumbent protection has been the result.
   Projection from current lineup: +1 Democratic seat.

   Altogether, the addition of 13 House seats to these eight states should translate into a 12-seat gain for the Republicans, a one-seat loss for the Democrats, and two toss-ups. Now let's look at the 11 states on track to lose House seats.

States on Track to Lose Seats

New York (-2)   Democratic Gov. Eliot Spitzer will likely win reelection in 2010. And Republicans could well lose their majority in the state Senate by redistricting time, putting Democrats in control. But there are limits to what they can gain: Republicans hold only six of 29 seats in the state's congressional delegation. The Census's 2005 estimates don't show New York City gaining as many people as it did in the 1990s. Democrats will thus find it hard to avoid eliminating a Democratic seat, because there are only two Republican districts left south of Albany—one on very Republican Staten Island, the other on Long Island (and New York pols may not want to lose Rep. Peter King's seniority in the U.S. House). At least one Republican upstate district will be eliminated.
   Projection from current lineup: -1 Republican seat, -1 Democratic seat

Ohio (-2)   Elected last November, Democratic Gov. Ted Strickland is quite popular. If his job-approval rating remains high, he'll easily win re-election in 2010. Republicans could lose their majorities in the Legislature, although they held them in 2006, a difficult year. The outcome depends on whether Democrats take control of both chambers. If they do, expect partisan redistricting with a vengeance.

Projection from current lineup: -4 Republican seats, +2 Democratic seats. (If Republicans retain one chamber, redistricting will focus on incumbent protection. *Projection from current lineup*: -1 Republican seat, -1 Democratic seat.)

Illinois (-1)   In the last round of redistricting, Illinois adopted a go-along-to-get-along plan, with one hapless downstate Democrat sacrificed because Chicago pols owed him nothing and Mayor Richard Daley didn't mind having Chicagoland's Dennis Hastert as Speaker of the House. Now the Chicago pols' Washington power broker is Democrat Rahm Emanuel. Democratic Gov. Rod Blagojevich can run again in 2010, but regardless of what he decides to do, the Republican nominee in this now very Democratic state is unlikely to win. Much of downstate Illinois has been losing population, so a downstate Republican may well get squeezed out. The demographics of metro Chicago suggest that city Democrats will have to extend their districts farther into the fast-growing suburbs, which will benefit currently embattled suburban Republicans.

Projection from current lineup: -1 Republican seat.

Iowa (-1)   This state has a nonpartisan redistricting commission, which presents a plan to the Legislature; lawmakers can veto any commission proposal. In 2001, the Legislature approved the commission's second plan. The commission's criteria emphasized following county lines and did not make protecting incumbents a priority. The question for 2011 is what the commission will do with Des Moines. The city is not in the same district as its main suburban counties. The commission could make the city the heart of a more compact district and divide it fairly evenly between the parties. Des Moines is represented by Democrat Leonard Boswell, who would be 78 in 2012.

Projection from current lineup: -1 Republican seat, -1 Democrat seat, +1 toss-up seat.

Louisiana (-1)   The Voting Rights Act compels the Legislature to create at least one majority-black district. Given the exodus of black residents from New Orleans, that district will probably have to connect African-American areas of New Orleans and Baton Rouge via a corridor along the Mississippi River. That would leave one very safe Republican district in suburban New Orleans and the state's four other districts divided among the five incumbents—a quartet of Republicans and one Democrat. Democrats almost certainly will not be in control, because Gov. Kathleen Blanco is retiring this year and Republican Bobby Jindal seems likely to succeed her and thus to be in charge when the census data are unveiled in 2011. Cajun country Democrat Charlie Melancon will probably find a way to hold on, so the casualty will likely be a Republican.

Projection from current lineup: -1 Republican seat.

Massachusetts (-1)   There's no question here. The congressional delegation is all Democratic. If the state loses a seat, a Democrat must go.

Projection from current lineup: -1 Democratic seat.

Michigan (-1)   Democratic Gov. Jennifer Granholm cannot run for a third term in 2010. And it's not clear which party will control either chamber of the Legislature in 2009, much less in 2011. Party control may well be divided, and that would enable Democrats to demand a plan more favorable than the very partisan Republican map now in effect.

Projection from current lineup: -2 Republican seats, +1 Democratic seat.

Minnesota (-1)   GOP Gov. Tim Pawlenty has not announced whether he will seek a third term in 2010, but the Democratic-Farmer-Labor Party could have control of the governorship during redistricting. The DFL's natural instinct would be to extend the population-losing 4th and 5th Districts farther out into the Minneapolis-St. Paul suburbs. That would make the fast-growing 2d, 3d, and 6th Districts more Republican. It's hard to see how any of those districts would be eliminated. The outcome may depend on whether Democrat Tim Walz can hold on in the 1st District. If he loses to a Republican, the DFL would be only too happy to carve up this narrow district, which runs across the south end of the state. House Agriculture Committee Chairman Collin Peterson's 7th District leans Republican; the DFL might redraw it if he retires.

Projection from current lineup: -1 Democratic seat.

Missouri (-1)   Republicans now have a shaky grip on the state. GOP Gov. Matt Blunt has had low job-approval ratings and is up for reelection in 2008. Democrats would have to gain a lot of seats, however, to take over either chamber of the Legislature. So let's assume that control is divided. Redistricting gets easier if Democrat Ike Skelton, chairman of the Armed Services Committee, decides to retire in 2012, when he would be 81. His 4th District seat is safe for him, but it is expected to go Republican once he leaves.
    Projection from current lineup: -1 Democrat seat.

New Jersey (-1)   New Jersey has a Congressional Redistricting Commission, made up of 12 members appointed by the legislative and party leaders of both parties; they pick a 13th as arbiter. The arbiter can break a tie, produce a compromise plan of his own and see if a majority will accept it or forward two plans to the state Supreme Court.
    Any new plan will surely maintain the heavily black 10th and the heavily Hispanic 13th Districts in their current form, and the lines are unlikely to be disturbed much in South Jersey, which has grown more than the rest of the state. Eliminating the seat of a retiring incumbent is one possibility but barring that scenario, it's likely a North Jersey seat gets squeezed out, perhaps setting up a fair fight between a Democratic and a Republican incumbent.
    Projection from current lineup: -1 Republican seat.

Pennsylvania (-1)   A very partisan Republican redistricting plan has collapsed: Democrats picked up four seats here in 2006. The party could pick up another, in the 6th District, very easily if the Democratic trend in the Philadelphia suburbs continues. But it's not clear who will control redistricting. Democratic Gov. Ed Rendell can't run for reelection in 2010, and the parties have been alternating the governorship every eight years since the 1950s. Democrats control the state House by a very narrow margin; the Republican majority in the state Senate is stronger. It is possible that the GOP will be in control again, as it was in 2001. But if Republicans have only veto power—by controlling the state Senate—incumbent protection would seem to be the order of the day. Western Pennsylvania will probably lose one seat.
    Projection from current lineup: -1 Republican seat.

    Let's add up these projections in the states losing seats. Assuming that Democrats don't control redistricting in Ohio, it's minus nine Republicans, minus five Democrats, plus one toss-up. If Democrats do get control in Ohio, it's minus 12 Republicans, minus two Democrats, plus one toss-up.
    Now let's add the states gaining seats and the states losing seats together. If Democrats don't get control in Ohio, we can expect Republicans to gain three seats, Democrats to lose six, and three toss-up districts to be created. If Democrats control the process in Ohio, Republicans will stay even, Democrats will lose three seats, and three toss-ups will be created.
    Although much seems to depend on Ohio at this point, redistricting after the 2010 census looks unlikely to help either party very much.
    Another way to look at it is this: If Democrats don't control Ohio, redrawing congressional boundaries will create a dozen new Republican districts, two new Democratic districts, and three new toss-ups. Eliminated would be nine Republican districts and eight Democratic districts. If Democrats control Ohio, redistricting will likely produce a dozen new Republican districts, four new Democratic districts, and three toss-ups. A dozen old Republican districts and seven Democratic districts would be eliminated.

States to Watch   Redistricting may well shift the political balance of the congressional delegations of seven other states even though they aren't projected to gain or lose House seats.

California   Having 53 seats in the U.S. House gives the Golden State plenty of room for redistricting maneuvers. Democrats hold a 34-19 majority within the congressional delegation. Republican Gov. Arnold Schwarzenegger and Democrats in the state Legislature would like to put a redistricting commission on the 2008 ballot, together with a proposal to relax term limits (and thus allow Assembly Speaker Fabian Nunez and Senate President Pro Tem Don Perata to remain in office). They would like to have the commission draw the lines for congressional as well as state legislative districts, but Speaker Nancy Pelosi and the Democratic House delegation are reportedly ready to spend $10 million to defeat such an initiative. The very Republican interior of the state has been growing more rapidly than the heavily Democratic coast. So a nonpartisan process might shift one seat to the Republicans. That would be unlikely if the Democratic-controlled legislature and Schwarzenegger's successor (probably a Democrat) control the process.

Projection from current lineup: unclear.

Colorado Democrats currently hold four of the state's seven U.S. House seats, having gained one in 2004 and another in 2006. They also control the governorship and the state legislature. But one Republican district will surely survive in the Denver suburbs and one will remain centered on Colorado Springs. In the 4th District, Marilyn Musgrave has been lagging other Republicans in her part of the state. If she survives through 2010, she could be hurt by redistricting.

Projection from current lineup: no change.

Connecticut Democrats hold four of the state's five U.S. House seats, having picked up two in 2006. Assuming that they keep all of those seats and that they retain control of the state legislature, Democrats can do no more than gain one seat—that of Christopher Shays. But Shays's district occupies the southwest corner of the state, and making it substantially more Democratic would be difficult. Republican Gov. M. Jodi Rell has sky-high job approval ratings and is eligible to run for reelection in 2010.

Projection from current lineup: no change.

Indiana Democrats gained three House seats in 2006 and now have a 5-4 majority in the delegation. Historically, Indiana's House seats have gone back and forth between the parties, and it is not clear whether Democrats will have an edge after the 2010 election. Nor is it clear that Republican Gov. Mitch Daniels will be reelected in 2008.

Projection from current lineup: unclear.

Kansas The delegation is now split 2-2, with Democrats Dennis Moore and Nancy Boyda holding districts that lean Republican in presidential elections. The legislature is Republican, and Democratic Gov. Kathleen Sebelius is ineligible to run in 2010. If Republicans are in control, they could try to weaken Moore or Boyda—but not both. Boyda, however, could be in danger long before redistricting.

Projection from current lineup: no change.

New Mexico Republicans currently hold two of the state's three House seats. Democratic Gov. Bill Richardson can't run for reelection in 2010, but his party is likely to keep control of the governorship and the legislature. That puts Republican Heather Wilson, who represents a competitive Albuquerque-based district, in jeopardy. She made plans to run for the Senate when Pete Domenici announced he would retire in 2008.

Projection from current lineup: -1 Republican seat, +1 Democratic seat.

Wisconsin Democrats hold a 5-3 advantage in the state's House delegation after picking up a seat in 2006. But in the past, that seat, based in Green Bay, has been hard for Democrats to hold. Democratic Gov. Jim Doyle is eligible to run in 2010, but even if he wins, Republicans might retain their small majority in the state House and might overcome the Democrats' small majority in the state Senate. All of this suggests that redistricting will produce an incumbent-protection plan.

Projection from current lineup: no change.

Taken together, these seven states are likely to lose one Republican seat and to add one Democratic one. That could vary in either direction by a few seats, but it's unlikely that a substantial enough shift will occur to offset the trends in the states whose congressional delegations will be growing or shrinking.

Finally, there is another group of states worth mentioning—the 14 states where redistricting is unlikely to make any significant political difference. In half of those, it literally can't: Alaska, Delaware, Montana, North Dakota, South Dakota, Vermont, and Wyoming have, and are projected to have, only one House seat. As for the others, Maine, New Hampshire, and Rhode Island are likely to keep their district boundaries much as they have for many years; Oklahoma also isn't expected to significantly change its congressional district lines; and Idaho and Nebraska are so Republican and Hawaii is so Democratic that any rearrangement of their congressional district lines is unlikely to produce a seat for the minority party.

President

Vice President

George W. Bush (R)

Elected 2000, seat up Jan. 2009, 2d term; b. July 6, 1946, New Haven, CT; home, Austin; Yale U., B.A. 1968, Harvard U., M.B.A. 1975; Methodist; married (Laura).

Military Career: TX Air Natl. Guard, 1968-73.

Elected Office: TX Gov., 1994-2000.

Professional Career: Founder & CEO, Bush Exploration Oil & Gas Co., 1975-87; Sr. Advisor, Bush Presidential Camp., 1988; Managing Gen. Partner, Texas Rangers baseball org., 1989-98.

Richard (Dick) B. Cheney (R)

Elected 2000, seat up Jan. 2009, 2d term; b. Jan. 30, 1941, Lincoln, NE; home, Casper, WY; U. of WY, B.A. 1965, M.A. 1966; United Methodist; married (Lynne).

Elected Office: U.S. House of Reps., 1978-89.

Professional Career: Spec. Asst. to the Dir. of OEO, 1969-70; White House Staff Asst., 1971; Asst. Dir., Cost of Living Cncl., 1971-73; V.P., Bradley, Woods & Co., 1973-74; Dep. Asst. to Pres. Gerald Ford, 1974-75; White House Chief of Staff, 1975-77; U.S. Secy. of Defense, 1989-93; Sr. Fellow, American Enterprise Inst., 1993-95; Chmn. & CEO, Halliburton Co., 1993-2000.

The People

Pop. 2006 (est):	299,398,484
Pop. 2000:	281,421,906
Pop. 1990:	248,709,873
Change 1990-2000:	Up 13.2%
% of U.S. total:	100.0%
Area size:	3,794,083 sq. mi.
State Native:	60.0%
Non-citizen:	6.6%

Language

English: 81.1%	Spanish: 10.2%
Other Eur.: 5.2%	

Race/Ethnic Origin

194,552,774	69.1%	White
33,947,837	12.1%	Black
10,123,169	3.6%	Asian
2,068,883	0.7%	Native Am.
353,509	0.1%	Hawaiian
4,602,146	1.6%	Two+ races
467,770	0.2%	Other
35,305,818	12.5%	Hisp. Origin

Ancestry

German: 12.0%	Irish: 8.5%
English: 6.8%	USA: 5.7%
Italian: 4.4%	

Military veterans: 26,403,703 (12.6%)

WWII: 20.5%	Korea: 13.6%
Vietnam: 31.7%	Gulf War: 10.2%

Most populous cities (2006):

1. New York	8,214,426
2. Los Angeles	3,849,378
3. Chicago	2,833,321
4. Houston	2,144,491
5. Phoenix	1,512,986

Urban population: 79.0%
Rural population: 21.0%

Education

H.S. Grad:	80.4%
College Grad:	24.4%

Industry

Agri: 1.9%	Con: 6.8%
Fin: 6.9%	Info: 3.1%
Mfg: 19.3%	Prof: 29.2%
Public: 4.8%	Trade: 15.3%
Other: 12.7%	

Occupation

Blue collar: 24.1%   White collar: 60.3%
Gray collar: 15.6%

Work Sector

Private: 78.5%	Govt: 14.6%
Self: 6.6%	Family: 0.3%
Unemployment: 5.7%	

Household Income

<15k: 15.8%	15-35k: 25.6%
35-50k: 16.5%	50-100k: 29.7%
100-150k: 7.7%	>150k: 4.6%
Median: $41,994	

Poverty status: 12.4%

Home Value

<50k: 14.9%	50-100k: 29.6%
100-200k: 35.2%	200-300k: 11.2%
300-500k: 6.1%	>500k: 2.9%

Median: $111,800

2004 Presidential Vote

George W. Bush (R)	62,040,606	(50.7%)
John Kerry (D)	59,028,109	(48.3%)
Other	1,217,895	(1.0%)

2000 Presidential Vote

George W Bush (R)	50,456,169	(47.8%)
Al Gore (D)	50,996,116	(48.4%)
Ralph Nader (Green)	2,831,066	(2.7%)

★ ALABAMA ★

Beginnings matter, and Alabama had its beginnings in two surges of settlement. One was from the north, when Jacksonian farmers from Tennessee surged into the red clay hills from which their hero, Andrew Jackson, expelled the Creek and other Indians. You can see their early Greek Revival buildings in historic Huntsville, surrounded by the boom town that has grown up around the Marshall Space Center, but Jacksonian Alabama is anything but cool and classical: the settlers brought the fighting faith of the Scots-Irish, a hot-spirited willingness to fight to the death against any perceived insult or threat. The other surge of settlement into Alabama came a few years later, as entrepreneurial Southern planters brought slaves in to pick cotton in the fertile Black Belt (so named for its soil) east and west of Montgomery in the middle of the state. The interplay between the offspring of these two streams of settlers has been the stuff of Alabama politics ever since. The Jacksonians' fighting spirit led them to join the planters and support secession; the first Confederate Congress convened and Jefferson Davis took the oath of office as president of the Confederacy in the Greek Revival Alabama Capitol in February 1861.

After the Civil War, Alabama, like other southern states, became solidly Democratic, but with an angry populist accent. Birmingham, with its solid-iron Red Mountain, became the South's first steel producer in the 1880s. Alabama politics in the first half of the 20th century was a struggle between angry populists who favored New Deal government spending to help the little guy— Senator and Supreme Court Justice Hugo Black, Senators Lister Hill and John Sparkman, Governor "Kissin' Jim" Folsom and the local economic potentates they called the "Big Mules"—and the plantation owners of the Black Belt.

Then Alabama became one of the birthplaces of the civil rights movement. Down the hill from the Capitol is the Dexter Avenue Baptist Church, where in December 1956 the 27-year-old Martin Luther King Jr. led the boycott that began when Montgomery seamstress Rosa Parks refused to move to the back of the bus. A hundred miles north in Birmingham, while King was held in jail, Birmingham Police Commissioner Bull Connor (then Alabama's Democratic National Committeeman) ordered police dogs and fire hoses to be turned on peaceful demonstrators in May 1963. Four months later four girls were killed when a bomb exploded in Birmingham's 16th Street Baptist Church (bombers were convicted in 1977, 2001 and 2002). In March 1965 a civil rights marcher was murdered in Montgomery two weeks after police beat dozens at Selma's Pettus Bridge; another activist was shot and killed in Lowndes County that August. These events had reverberations far beyond Alabama: in June 1963 John Kennedy endorsed what would become the Civil Rights Act of 1964, and in March 1965 Congress passed the Voting Rights Act.

While Alabamians like Parks were leading the nation toward civil rights, Alabama's leading politician of the time, George Wallace, was leading the other way. Elected governor in 1962, he made national news in June 1963 by standing in a schoolhouse door and pretending to defy a federal court desegregation order. In 1964 Wallace ran in northern Democratic presidential primaries against Lyndon Johnson; in 1968 he ran for president as a third-party candidate and won 13.5% of the vote. He ran in the Democratic primaries again in 1972 and was partially paralyzed by a gunshot wound while campaigning in May; he took delegates to the national convention, and did not lose his force as a national politician until he lost to Jimmy Carter in the March 1976 Florida primary. But he remained the key figure in Alabama for three decades, running his first wife to succeed him in 1966 (she died in mid-term), regaining the governorship again in 1970 and (when second terms were allowed) in 1974, then running and winning one last time in 1982. He spent his last sad years apologizing for his acts, meeting with the student he tried to block in the schoolhouse door, and proclaiming, "The South has changed, and for the better," until his death in September 1998.

It was during Wallace's last term as governor, in 1983, that state government started publishing a black heritage guide. Today heritage tourism commemorating the civil rights movement is one of the fastest-growing segments of the tourism business, and Alabama is leading the way. Montgomery boasts Maya Lin's circular Civil Rights Memorial, Troy University's Rosa Parks Museum, the Dexter Parsonage and the endpoint of the Selma-to-Montgomery trail. The Edmund Pettis Bridge in Selma, the Selma-to-Montgomery interpretive center in Lowndes County, the Tuskegee Airmen National Historic Site—all are on the Alabama Civil Rights Museum Trail.

Economically Alabama lost important ground in the Wallace years. While Atlanta was peacefully desegregating and beginning decades of vibrant white-collar growth, Birmingham was violently resisting the civil rights movement, only to see the shrinkage of its once substantial blue-collar base—the steel industry—and an outflow of talented people of all races. But Alabama's

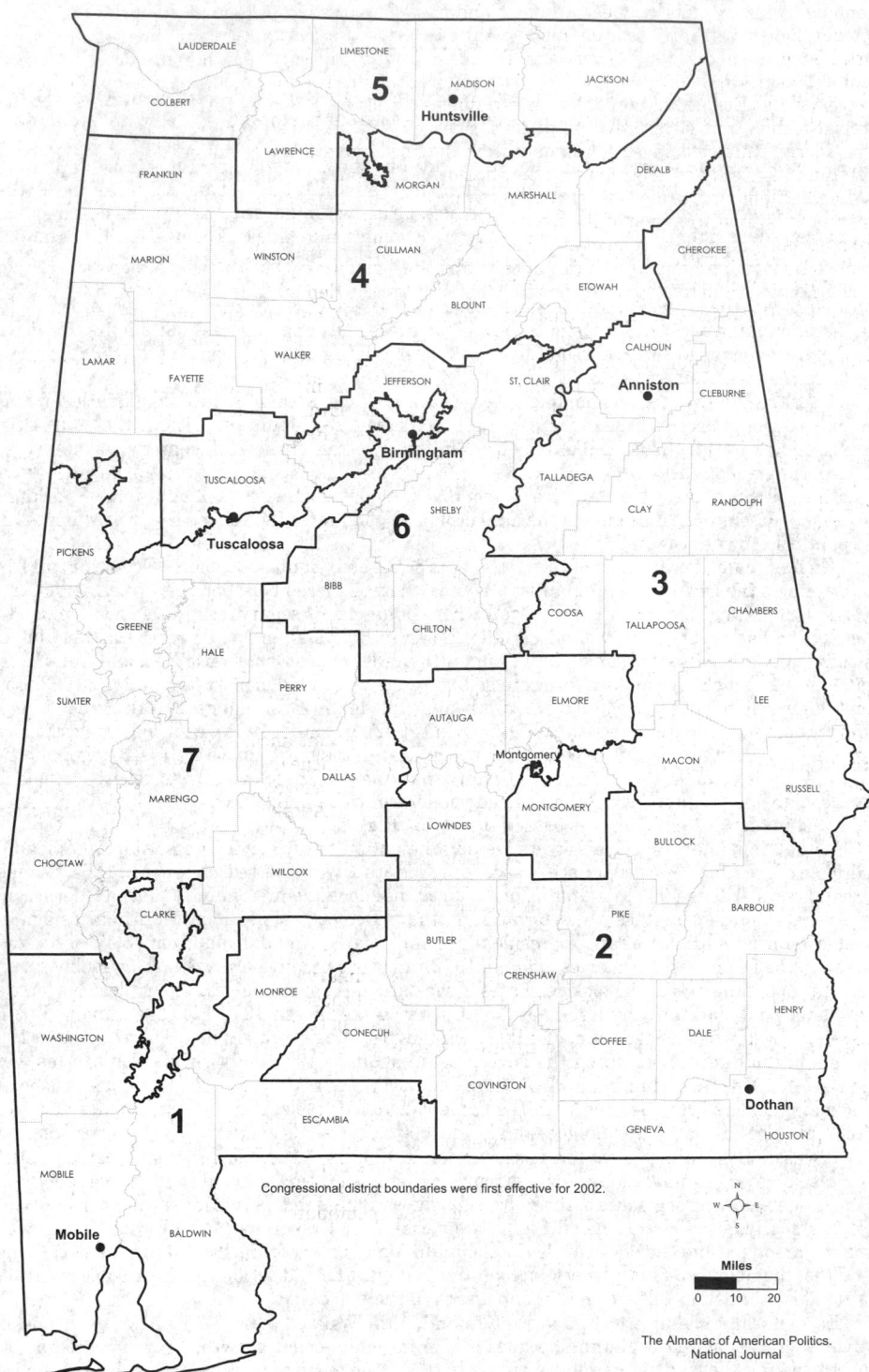

Congressional district boundaries were first effective for 2002.

Miles
0   10   20

The Almanac of American Politics.
National Journal

economy has been moving ahead recently and has been growing in tandem with the nation's; in October 2006 it had its lowest unemployment ever, 3.2%. Big new auto plants have played a role, with Mercedes in Tuscaloosa, Honda in Talladega County and Hyundai in Montgomery. Alabama produced nearly 500,000 vehicles in 2005 and Hyundai plans to add 200,000 more in production in a few years. Two European companies are building facilities near Mobile: EADS is expanding its new aircraft factory and ThyssenKrupp plans to open its $3.7 billion steel-processing facility in 2010.

George Wallace delayed for a generation the move toward the Republican party in Alabama and in much of the non-metropolitan South. But in the quarter-century since he last appeared on the ballot, Alabama has developed a two-party politics and, in presidential elections, has completed its transformation from one of the nation's most Democratic states to one of its most Republican. But state politics remains competitive. On one side of this political conflict are the Democrats: Their voting base is Alabama's large black minority and the institutional base is the state's well organized teachers' unions and trial lawyers. On the other side are the Republicans: Their voting base is white evangelical Protestants and their institutional base is small businessmen and the affluent young families filling the fast-growing suburban areas outside Birmingham, Montgomery, Mobile and Huntsville. The Republicans have tended to prevail, by large margins in presidential and Senate and state Supreme Court elections and by narrow margins in races for governor and statewide downballot offices. But the Democrats have fought back hard, holding onto the legislature and, since Wallace left office, bringing ethics charges against one Republican governor which led to his conviction and removal from office (Guy Hunt in 1993), defeating another (Fob James in 1998) and twice contesting election results with legal arguments (the Democratic runoff in 1986 and the general election in 2002).

The 2002 race for governor between Democrat Don Siegelman and Republican Congressman Bob Riley showed the close division between two Alabamas. Siegelman carried the central cities, the Black Belt and many of the poor-white rural counties in the north. This was the coalition of blacks and poor whites the political scientist V.O. Key, Jr., longed for in his mid-century classic *Southern Politics*. But it was not enough to win. Riley carried by big margins the suburban counties around Birmingham, Mobile, Montgomery and Huntsville and the smaller, robustly-growing counties along the Interstate highways.

Alabama politics has continued to run into turbulence since. One controversy raged over Chief Justice Roy Moore's installation in July 2001 of a huge monument with the Ten Commandments in the Supreme Court building. In 2002 a federal judge ruled that unconstitutional, and an appeals court affirmed the judgment and ordered him to remove the statue in 2003. Moore refused; the other eight justices complied; the Alabama Court of the Judiciary removed Moore in November 2003 and the U.S. Supreme Court declined to hear his appeal in 2004. Another controversy came when Bob Riley put on the ballot a referendum on a $1.2 billion tax increase. Riley argued that his changes would reduce taxes on low-income people and that such a move was in line with Christian morality. Alabama's Jacksonians did not buy it: the proposition was defeated 67%-33%, and won by unimpressive margins even in black-majority counties and the state capital. It won only 14% in Winston County, an independent-minded hill county which seceded from secessionist Alabama during the Civil War.

Sparks threatened to flare in the 2006 Republican primary when Moore ran against Riley, but Riley won 67%-33%. Moore evidently struck even many of those who had voted against Riley's tax increase as too extreme. Almost as many Alabamians voted in this Republican primary (460,000) as in the Democratic primary (467,000) the same day, a stark contrast with 20 years before, when George Wallace was the retiring incumbent and turnout in the Democratic primary (830,000) dwarfed that in the Republican primary (25,000). Riley won the general election by a solid 57%-42% margin. Democrat Jim Folsom Jr., was narrowly elected lieutenant governor, and Democrat Sue Bell Cobb beat Chief Justice Ryan Nabers, who had beaten a Moore ally in the Republican primary; Republicans won most other statewide offices. Alabama's hard-fought judicial races, pitting trial lawyer-backed Democrats versus business- and cultural conservative-backed Republicans, are costly: At least $52 million has been spent by high court candidates there since 1993.

The People		Race/Ethnic Origin			Military veterans: 447,397 (13.5%)	
Pop. 2006 (est):	4,599,030	3,125,819	70.3%	White	WWII: 17.5%	Korea: 14.0%
Pop. 2000:	4,447,100	1,150,076	25.9%	Black	Vietnam: 32.9%	Gulf War: 11.6%
Pop. 1990:	4,040,587	30,989	0.7%	Asian	**Most populous cities (2006):**	
Change 1990-2000:	Up 10.1%	21,618	0.5%	Native Am.	1. Birmingham	229,424
% of U.S. total:	1.6%	1,059	0.0%	Hawaiian	2. Montgomery	201,998
Pop. rank:	23rd of 50	39,086	0.9%	Two+ races	3. Mobile	192,830
Area size:	52,419 sq. mi.	2,623	0.1%	Other	4. Huntsville	168,132
State Native:	73.4%	75,830	1.7%	Hisp. Origin	5. Tuscaloosa	83,052
Non-citizen:	1.2%	**Ancestry**				
Language		USA: 14.8%		English: 6.8%	Urban population: 55.4%	
English: 94.2%	Spanish: 3.1%	Irish: 6.7%		German: 5.0%	Rural population: 44.6%	
Other Eur.: 1.8%		Scotch-Irish: 1.7%				

Education		Work Sector		Legislature		
H.S. Grad:	75.3%	Private: 77.9%	Govt: 15.5%	Senate	23 D 12 R	
College Grad:	19.0%	Self: 6.2%	Family: 0.3%	House	62 D 43 R	
Industry		Unemployment: 6.2%		Legislative Term Limits: No		
Agri: 1.9%	Con: 7.6%	**Household Income**		**Registered Voters**		
Fin: 5.8%	Info: 2.2%	<15k: 22.5%	15-35k: 28.4%	No party registration		
Mfg: 23.7%	Prof: 26.4%	35-50k: 16.5%	50-100k: 24.9%			
Public: 5.2%	Trade: 15.8%	100-150k: 4.9%	>150k: 2.7%			
Other: 11.4%		Median: $34,135				
Occupation		Poverty status: 16.1%				
Blue collar: 30.3%	White collar: 55.4%	**Home Value**				
Gray collar: 14.3%		<50k: 28.4%	50-100k: 38.3%	100-200k: 24.7%	200-300k: 5.2%	
		300-500k: 2.3%	>500k: 1.1%	Median: $76,700		

Presidential politics   George W. Bush carried Alabama by 56%-42% in 2000 and 62%-37% in 2004. Bush lost all but one of the black-majority counties in the Black Belt and, narrowly, two

nearby counties; in the exurban counties outside Birmingham, Montgomery and Mobile, he won 76% to 81% of the vote. Alabama whites voted 80%-19% for George W. Bush and Alabama blacks voted 91%-6% for John Kerry. So foreordained was the Alabama result that neither candidate set foot in the state except for Bush's visit to see Hurricane Ivan damage; the Bush campaign dispatched volunteers to Florida for the last week. And Alabama was one state which did not trend Democratic in 2006. Noting that Alabama rarely received visits from high-ranking Democrats, the Republican state chairwoman sent Democratic National Committee Chairman Howard Dean a gift certificate for airfare to Alabama and asked him to "outline, precisely, where the Democrats stand on issues like abortion, taxes, Second Amendment rights and gay marriage."

2004 Presidential Vote		
Bush (R)	1,176,394	(62%)
Kerry (D)	693,933	(37%)
Nader (I)	6,701	(0%)
Other	6,387	(0%)

2004 Democratic Presidential Primary		
Kerry (D)	164,021	(75%)
Uncommitted (D)	38,223	(17%)
Kucinich (D)	9,076	(4%)
Other	7,254	(3%)

2000 Presidential Vote		
Bush (R)	941,173	(56%)
Gore (D)	692,611	(42%)
Nader (Green)	18,323	(1%)
Other	14,165	(1%)

Alabama's presidential primary for years was held in June—too late to count for much. In April 2006 the legislature voted to hold the state's presidential primary on February 5, 2008, two weeks after the New Hampshire primary; Governor Bob Riley happily signed the bill. But in early 2007 much larger states like California and Florida moved their primaries to the same day, overshadowing Alabama. In any case, in late 2006 and early 2007 Alabama was seeing more campaign appearances and contributions from potential presidential candidates than ever before.

Congressional districting

110th Congress Lineup	
5 R	2 D
109th Congress Lineup	
5 R	2 D

The Democrats in control of redistricting in Alabama in 2002 did a pretty good job of helping their party in drawing the boundaries of the state's seven congressional districts—but not good enough to add to the two seats they have held since 1994. They marginally strengthened Democrat Bud Cramer in the 5th District and reduced the black percentage in the majority-black 7th District. The biggest change was to the 3d District, where incumbent Republican Bob Riley was leaving to run for governor. The 3d was made significantly more Democratic by the subtraction of fast-growing St. Clair County east of Birmingham and the addition of part of Montgomery County, including the area around the Capitol. The black percentage was raised from 25% to 32%, the second highest in the state. But Republican Mike Rogers still won narrowly in the 2002 open seat contest and easily held the seat in 2004 and 2006.

Governor

Bob Riley (R)

Elected 2002, term expires Jan. 2011, 2d term; b. Oct. 3, 1944, Ashland; home, Ashland; U. of AL, B.A. 1965; Baptist; married (Patsy).

Elected Office: Ashland City Cncl., 1972-76; U.S. House of Reps., 1996-2002.

Professional Career: Owner, egg & poultry co.; Rancher; Owner, Midway Transit, 1965-present.

Office: Alabama State Capitol, 600 Dexter Ave., Montgomery, 36130, 334-242-7100; Fax: 334-353-0004; Web site: www.governor.state.al.us.

Election Results

2006 general	Bob Riley (R)	718,327	(57%)
	Lucy Baxley (D)	519,827	(42%)
	Other	12,247	(1%)
2006 primary	Bob Riley (R)	306,665	(67%)
	Roy Moore (R)	153,354	(33%)
2002 general	Bob Riley (R)	672,225	(49%)
	Don Siegelman (D)	669,105	(49%)
	Other	25,273	(2%)

Bob Riley, elected governor of Alabama by a 3,120-vote margin in 2002, grew up in Clay County, off the beaten track east of Birmingham, where his family had lived for seven generations. Riley attended the University of Alabama during its desegregation in 1963 and after graduation returned home with a business degree; he and his brother started selling eggs door-to-door. Eventually, that became a large egg and poultry company; he also ran a grocery store, owned an airport, a pharmacy and sold real estate. He ended up with a car dealership (Midway Ford and Chrysler), a trucking company (Midway Transit), half a shopping center and a cattle farm, and served on the Ashland city council. In 1996, when the 3d District's Democratic congressman ran unsuccessfully for the Senate, Riley ran for the House. He started off little known outside Clay County, but he was a strong and energetic campaigner, a supporter of school prayer, term limits, tax cuts and a balanced budget amendment and an opponent of abortion, gun control and racial quotas. Riley won 50%-47%—a key victory in keeping the House Republican that year.

In the House, Riley had a solidly conservative voting record; he said he came to Washington intending to be bipartisan, but his first three months made him "become the most partisan person on Capitol Hill." Riley had serious competition in 1998 from former Democratic state Chairman Joe Turnham, but he spent $845,000 of his own money and won 58%-42%. Unopposed in 2000, he ran for governor in 2002.

The incumbent was Don Siegelman, a Democrat elected by 58%-42% in 1998 over embattled incumbent Republican Fob James. Siegelman's main policy was a lottery to fund education, but voters later rejected the lottery 54%-46% in an October 1999 referendum. Siegelman had success in attracting automakers Honda and Hyundai to the state and convinced voters to approve a ballot proposition for $425 million in bonds to fund road and bridge building. But he continued to have trouble on education funding. A special session in mid-2001 rejected his entire proposal; another in December 2001 passed $140 million in business and telephone taxes. Siegelman was also troubled by scandal. In September 1999, he was embarrassed when two young aides were revealed to have been getting tickets fixed. In 2002, it was revealed that Siegelman's personal finances were under investigation by a joint state-federal task force, and in June 2003 a former Siegelman aide and a lobbyist pleaded guilty to bribery for buying a utility trailer and a motorcycle at about the time Siegelman obtained such items.

Riley beat Lieutenant Governor Steve Windom 74%-18% in the June 2002 primary. George W. Bush came to Alabama the next month for a $4 million fundraiser; overall, Riley outspent the incumbent. The issues were pretty squarely posed. Siegelman said in May that he still favored a lottery, but his Plan B appeared to be raising taxes on business; in October 2002, anticipating victory, he called for a special session for that purpose. Riley charged that state government was "sinking into a quicksand of corruption and fraud." He called the lottery "the return of a bad idea." He opposed tax increases and called for limiting spending to the prior year's revenues. He called for a commission to recommend changes in the 1901 Constitution to give local governments more power to pass local laws that do not require approval by the legislature. In late summer, Riley was running ahead in polls, but in September he made several blunders and his standing fell. He stumped one day with National Rifle Association president Charlton Heston; the next day it was revealed that the NRA endorsed Siegelman (as it does all incumbents who oppose gun control). Then Riley aides hinted that Heston might have been affected by Alzheimer's disease.

This turned out to be the closest gubernatorial race in the nation in 2002. Siegelman won overwhelmingly among black voters and his denunciations of corporations who opposed his business tax increase probably helped him carry heavily white rural counties in northwestern Alabama. He carried Birmingham's Jefferson County and Montgomery County, but by narrower margins than in 1998. Riley won by big margins in fast-growing suburban counties. He ran far ahead of the 1998 Republican showing in his old congressional district, and around three widely separated cities— Huntsville in the north, Dothan in the southeast and Mobile, Siegelman's hometown, in the south. On election night, a clerical error in rapidly-growing and heavily Republican Baldwin County on the Gulf coast credited Siegelman with 7,000 more votes than he actually received, which put him ahead in the statewide count. Both Riley and Siegelman proclaimed themselves winners. Siegelman refused to recognize the 7,000-vote error in Baldwin County and called for a statewide recount which could take months and indicated he would not relinquish the governor's office. Only after two weeks, on November 18, did he concede.

Facing a $675 million budget shortfall and a Democratic legislature, Riley cut spending and came up with a broad-based proposal to transform state finances. It would eliminate many of the earmarkings in Alabama's 1901 constitution (now, with 772 amendments, the longest in the world) and raise state and local taxes by $1.2 billion by 2008. In return for support from the Alabama Education Association's head Paul Hubbert—a candidate for governor in 1990 and a key player in Alabama politics before and since—Riley agreed to maintain spending on teacher pay and to put the increased revenue into a non-earmarked Alabama Excellence Initiative. Why did a politician who was elected on a no-tax-increase program back such a plan? Riley said he was influenced by North Carolina Democratic Congressman Bobby Etheridge, who described how his state increased education spending in the 1960s and now had much higher test scores than Alabama. And he considered it a matter of Christian obligation. "When I read the New Testament, there are three things we're asked to do: That's love God, love each other and take care of the least among us."

Supporting Riley were the state Democratic party, Hubbert and the AEA and some leaders of the insurance, banking, utility and consumer products industry. In opposition were the state Republican party, timber companies, the state Christian Coalition and national organizations like Americans for Tax Reform and the American Conservative Union. As state Republican Chairman Marty Connors described the situation, "We've got a conservative, evangelical Christian Republican governor, trying to get a massive turnout of black voters to pass a tax increase so he can raise taxes on Republican constituents." Turnout in the September 2003 referendum was high—only 6% below the November 2002 general election. The result was unambiguous. Riley's proposal was rejected 67%-33%. It was approved in only 12 Black Belt counties and lost by more than 3–1 in most small counties in north Alabama.

For 2004 Riley proposed more cuts and foreswore broad-based tax increases; the cigarette tax, some fees and oil and gas severance taxes were increased. As revenues suddenly increased, the state ended the fiscal year with a $150 million surplus. Riley called a special session to cut the increases in health insurance for state employees and, with Hubbert's support, got a bill he signed into law. In the meantime, other controversies raged. Chief Justice Roy Moore was removed from the state Supreme Court after refusing to obey a federal court order to remove his Ten Commandments monument from the court's building.

Riley responded to Hurricane Katrina in 2005 by launching "Operation Golden Rule." The administration scoured the state's public resources—state parks, closed mental hospitals and dormitories at closed military bases—to find accommodations for 10,000 Katrina evacuees. Riley defended a decision to run criminal background checks on hurricane evacuees to block criminals with records of sexual and drug crimes from admission to evacuation housing. He told Congress it should postpone plans to cut federal Medicaid spending and said the federal government should pay for all of the state's Medicaid spending in areas hit by Katrina.

After the unpopularity of his tax increase plan in 2003, Riley focused on economic development, education and ethics; improved state revenues also helped by allowing him to propose tax cuts and more spending. He unveiled "Plan 2010," a legislative program that included reducing lower and middle class taxes, banning transfers of contributions between political action committees and improving education. In April 2006, Riley signed into law a $10.9 billion budget that gave non-education state employees a 5% pay raise, increased pensions for retired state employees and boosted spending for many state services. Riley signed a bill that increased the income thresholds at which families began paying state income taxes. He also gave his signature to the Rosa Parks Act, which allows individuals convicted under Jim Crow laws to apply for a pardon.

Riley stood for reelection in 2006 and faced Republican primary opposition from former Alabama Chief Justice Roy Moore, who won national attention by defying courts and keeping a monument of the Ten Commandments in the state judicial building; he was removed from office in 2003. In his October 2005 campaign announcement, Riley invoked his own religious faith. "Some say they can no longer acknowledge God in government. I think that's sad because I acknowledge him every day – in speeches, in the office, in meetings, schools and churches. We can all do that every day in the way we live our lives," Riley said. Religious conviction alone proved insufficient for Moore, especially against an incumbent who held Bible studies in the governor's office. In the June primary, Riley defeated Moore by a 2–1 margin and won 53 of 67 counties. "Tonight's victory means we go forward and that we will never again go back to a time when Alabama was 48th, 49th or 50th in everything," Riley said.

In the general election, Riley faced Lieutenant Governor Lucy Baxley, who had defeated Siegelman in the primary 60%-36%. Baxley and Sicgelman began the race tied in the polls but Siegelman lost support as his corruption trial got underway. Three weeks after the primary, a jury found Siegelman guilty of seven of 32 corruption charges. HealthSouth Corp. founder Richard Scrushy was also found guilty in a case related to $500,000 in donations made to Siegelman's failed 1999 lottery campaign. Riley ran an ad calling Baxley "just too liberal"; he picked up a string of 18 newspaper endorsements around the state that praised his effectiveness and clean administration. He outspent Baxley $13 million to $4 million, and won a second term by 57%-42%.

In early 2007, Riley worked to get his Plan 2010 program through the Democratic-controlled legislature. He convened a special legislative session in late February to approve a $400 million incentive package to lure German steelmaker ThyssenKrupp to build its new plant near Mobile; Alabama was locked in a bidding war with Louisiana for the $3.7 billion steel-processing facility, which could employ 2,700 workers and create as many as 29,000 construction jobs. Kicking off the regular session in March, Riley proposed $850 million for school construction and technology spending, a 7% teacher pay raise, a middle class tax cut, reducing income taxes on retirement income, and tax credits for worker training. His tax relief proposals faced opposition from the Alabama Education Association, which feared a loss in revenues dedicated to education spending. Riley's legislative program also faced discord in the 35-member Senate, where 18 Democrats adopted new operating rules and the remaining five Democrats and all 12 Republicans responded by slowing action in the chamber. Riley, the subject of local speculation about being picked as a 2008 vice presidential candidate, is prohibited by term limits from running again in 2010. Former Phoenix Suns basketball player Charles Barkley, who had considered running for governor in 1998 as a Republican, said in 2006 he is considering a 2010 gubernatorial bid as a Democrat. A more conventional choice might be Democratic Representative Artur Davis, who said he might also consider a run for Senate in 2010.

Senior Senator

Richard Shelby (R)

Elected 1986, seat up 2010, 4th term; b. May 6, 1934, Birmingham; home, Tuscaloosa; U. of AL, B.A. 1957, LL.B. 1963; Presbyterian; married (Annette).

Elected Office: AL Senate, 1970-78; U.S. House of Reps., 1978-86.

Professional Career: Practicing atty., 1963-78; City Prosecutor, Tuscaloosa, 1963-71; U.S. Magistrate 1966-70; Spec. Asst. to U.S. Atty. Gen., 1969-71.

DC Office: 110 HSOB, 20510, 202-224-5744; Fax: 202-224-3416; Web site: shelby.senate.gov.

State Offices: Birmingham, 256-731-1384; Huntsville, 256-772-0460; Mobile, 251-694-4164; Montgomery, 334-223-7303; Tuscaloosa, 205-759-5047.

Committees: *Aging (Special)* (2d of 10 R). *Appropriations* (7th of 14 R): Commerce, Justice, Science & Related Agencies (RMM); Transportation, Housing and Urban Development & Related Agencies; Financial Services & General Government; Homeland Security; Defense; Labor, Health and Human Services, Education & Related Agencies. *Banking, Housing & Urban Affairs* (RMM of 10 R).

Group Ratings

	ADA	ACLU	AFS	LCV	ITIC	NTU	COC	ACU	CFG	FRC
2006	10	17	0	0	75	67	83	74	55	100
2005	10	—	0	5	—	69	89	88	73	—

National Journal Ratings

	2005 LIB	—	2005 CONS		2006 LIB	—	2006 CONS
Economic	10%	—	89%		39%	—	60%
Social	0%	—	77%		26%	—	73%
Foreign	36%	—	61%		40%	—	58%

Key Votes of the 109th Congress

1. Bar ANWR Drilling	N	5. Confirm Samuel Alito	Y	9. Limit Interstate Abortion	Y
2. FY06 Spending Curb	Y	6. Path to Citizenship	N	10. CAFTA	N
3. Estate Tax Repeal	Y	7. Bar Same Sex Marriage	Y	11. Urge Iraq Withdrawal	N
4. Raise Minimum Wage	*	8. Stem Cell Research $	N	12. Provide Detainee Rights	N

Election Results

2004 general	Richard Shelby (R)	1,242,200	(68%)	($1,922,646)
	Wayne Sowell (D)	595,018	(32%)	($4,869)
2004 primary	Richard Shelby (R)	unopposed		
1998 general	Richard Shelby (R)	817,973	(63%)	($1,890,484)
	Clayton Suddith (D)	474,568	(37%)	($15,723)

Prior Winning Percentages: 1992 (65%); 1986 (50%); 1984 House (97%); 1982 House (97%); 1980 House (73%); 1978 House (94%)

Richard Shelby, Alabama's senior senator, has had a political career going back more than 30 years. Shelby grew up in Birmingham, the son of a steelworker. After earning two degrees from the University of Alabama, he stayed in Tuscaloosa and went into law practice with Walter Flowers, who was later a conservative Democratic congressman; Shelby was well enough politically connected to be elected state senator in 1970, at 36. When Flowers ran, unsuccessfully, for the Senate in 1978, Shelby ran for his House seat. The critical contest was the Democratic runoff against Chris McNair, a black legislator whose daughter had been killed in the 1963 Birmingham church bombing. The district had the highest black percentage in Alabama at the time; Shelby won 59%-41%. In the House Shelby had a conservative voting record, opposing the Voting Rights Act extension and the Martin Luther King Holiday. He ran for the Senate in 1986 and won the primary with 51% after getting then-Secretary of State (later Governor) Don Siegelman to withdraw. In the general, he ran ads against incumbent Republican Jeremiah Denton, a retired admiral who had been a prisoner of war in Vietnam, for voting to cut Social Security and owning two Mercedes (not a likely negative now, with the Mercedes plant in Tuscaloosa). Shelby won by 7,000 votes.

As one of half a dozen or so conservative southern Democrats in the Senate, Shelby at first attracted little notice. He voted for the confirmation of Clarence Thomas and for the Gulf War resolution. He voted against the campaign finance bill supported by almost all Democrats and he voted for the Strategic Defense Initiative. In 1992, he was re-elected 65%-33%; this broke the jinx on a seat which, before Shelby's election in 1986, had four occupants in 10 years.

Shelby broke with the Democratic Party soon after Bill Clinton took office. At a meeting with Vice President Al Gore, he turned to 19 Alabama TV cameras and opposed the Clinton program as "high on taxes, low on spending cuts." In response, it was announced that a multi-million dollar space facility would be built not in Alabama but in Texas (it eventually was built in Alabama). But, as Clinton's ratings slid downward, this only raised Shelby's popularity ratings to the highest level in the state, making a politician previously known more for his suppleness of maneuver now appear an embattled defender of principle. Relentlessly, Shelby voted against the administration again and again and lined up with Republicans on almost every partisan issue. The day after Republicans regained control of the Senate in 1994, Shelby announced he was switching parties and increased the Republican majority to 53-47. Republicans happily allowed him to keep his seniority on the Banking Committee and gave him seats on Appropriations and its Defense Subcommittee and on Intelligence as well.

This is the path that led Shelby to the chairmanship of the Intelligence Committee in 1997 and which made him, as ranking minority member on the committee, an important policymaker after September 11. Shelby took an adversarial posture toward the intelligence agencies during the Clinton years and in the Bush years as well. Soon after September 11, Shelby stopped just short of calling for the resignation of CIA Director George Tenet, who was appointed by Clinton and retained by Bush. He had evidently found Tenet excessively defensive in 1997 of his predecessor John Deutch for downloading classified material onto his personal laptop and was negatively impressed when, after India conducted three underground nuclear tests, Tenet told him. "We didn't have a clue." He was also concerned about the lack of information on the February 1993 World Trade Center bombing, the 1996 bombing of Khobar Towers, the 1998 attacks on the embassies in Kenya and Tanzania and the 2000 attack on the *U.S.S. Cole*. In June 2004, when Tenet announced his resignation, Shelby said, "This is not a surprise to me at all. What was a surprise was that he held onto the job as long as he did."

Shelby has been mostly supportive of the Bush administration's conduct of the war on terrorism. In December 2001, he was one of ten senators signing a letter saying, "it is imperative that we plan to eliminate the threat from Iraq." But he clashed with the two Intelligence Committee chairmen, Bob Graham and Porter Goss, in the joint investigations of the intelligence community. He helped push aside their choice as staff director and install his own choice. At first he opposed the appointment of an independent 9/11 commission as unnecessary, but in September 2002, nearing the end of the 107th Congress (and his tenure on the Intelligence Committee), he changed his mind. The organization of the families of September 11 victims insisted that Shelby and John McCain be given veto power over Republican Leader Trent Lott's two nominations to the independent commission. In September 2002, he complained, "We've made some adjustments, but the cultures have not changed between all the intelligence agencies. . . . I don't believe they're sharing information. There's no fusion, no central place yet to do it." He called for a separate Director of National Intelligence, a position later taken by the 9/11 Commission and in the intelligence reorganization approved by Congress in December 2004. That bill included a Shelby proposal to give the DNI ombudsman access to all intelligence for analytical reviews, and he supported the National Counterterrorism Center and immigration provisions, but he was displeased that the new DNI would not be a Cabinet member.

One other controversy remains from Shelby's service on the Intelligence Committee. Shortly after a June 2002 closed committee hearing, CNN reported the contents of two NSA intercepts received before September 11 but not analyzed until after. The administration argued these were harmful leaks, and an FBI investigation began. In August 2004 Fox News's Carl Cameron told FBI investigators that Shelby told him the contents of the classified intercepts in June 2002, and earlier the *Washington Post* reported that Shelby was a target of the probe. But no prosecution was brought, and the Justice Department referred the matter to the Senate Ethics Committee. In 2004 Shelby said, "I have never knowingly—and that is a very important word, and I've been told to use that by Senate counsel, by other counsel—that I have never knowingly, intentionally, willfully disclosed classified information. I think most people know that, believe that." In November 2005 the Ethics Committee informed Shelby that it had insufficient evidence to show that he had leaked national security information and would not pursue the matter further.

On domestic issues, Shelby has compiled a mostly conservative record. But he is not a free market purist. Despite his party switch he has remained friendly with trial lawyers, who usually support Democrats in Alabama. He opposed his colleague Jeff Sessions' amendment to cap lawyers' fees in tobacco cases, and insists tort reform should be only a state issue. He voted against a 2004 bill to protect gun manufacturers from liability for actions of users of their products. He was the only Senate Republican to vote against financial services deregulation in November 1999 and opposed allowing federally-insured banks to sell real estate or insurance. He opposes federal preemption of stricter state privacy laws. He has worked for repeal of the Public Utility Holding Company Act and opposes the current Community Reinvestment Act.

Shelby became chairman of the Banking Committee in January 2003, and on a hotly-lobbied issue supported defining stock options as expenses, a measure opposed by the high-tech industry. When the Financial Accounting Standards Board voted to require expensing and the House voted by a wide margin to overturn its ruling, Shelby together with ranking Democrat Paul Sarbanes blocked action in the Banking Committee, and the FASB rule became effective in June 2005. After Hurricane Katrina threatened to exhaust FEMA's National Flood Insurance program, he supported an increase in borrowing authority from $18.5 billion to $20.1 billion; that passed the Senate in February 2006 and, after negotiations with the House, the final bill passed in March with $20.8 billion. Shelby also pushed for higher premiums and wider coverage. He did not support Congressman Richard Baker's plan to spend $30 billion to buy up Katrina-damaged properties at 60% of pre-hurricane prices. In 2006 Shelby pushed through a bill to direct the SEC to designate ratings agencies as Nationally Recognized Statistical Ratings Organizations if they meet certain standards over three years; the SEC was enforcing a 1975 rule which prevented many ratings agencies from qualifying and left 80% of the business in the hands of Moody's and Standard & Poor's. "The dominant rating agencies failed millions of investors by neglecting to lower their ratings on Enron, WorldCom and other companies headed for bankruptcy. The absence of timely downgrades in these cases was the product of an industry that was beset by conflicts of interest and a lack of competition." His bill was unanimously approved in committee in March 2006 and passed on the floor in August; it was signed into law in September. With Shelby in the lead, the Fair Credit Act was reauthorized with a provision allowing consumers one free annual credit report a year. In July 2005 the committee voted on party lines for legislation that would impose tighter limits on Fannie Mae's and Freddie Mac's portfolios and which contained no affordable housing fund. A bill with less stringent limits passed in the House, but Senate Democrats strongly opposed Shelby's bill, and it was not brought to the floor.

Shelby also serves on the Appropriations Committee, where he looks out for Alabama interests. He authored a law allowing airliners to fly from Alabama to Dallas's in-town Love Field and, with Washington's Patty Murray, fashioned a compromise on Mexican trucks. The House wanted to keep them inside a zone within 20 miles of the border; the Bush administration wanted to let them in, subject to inspections, as required under NAFTA. Shelby and Murray won agreement that they can come in only at entry points where inspectors are on duty, that their drivers' licenses must be subject to electronic verification and that they must be insured by a company licensed in the U.S. When the sock industry in Ft. Payne's DeKalb County—the "sock capital of the world," with 150 sock mills— was hurt by the Trade Act of 2002, he held up a trade bill to get protection from socks mended in the Caribbean and in November 2004 got country-of-origin labeling for imported and domestic socks. He has obtained some $70 million for buildings at the University of Alabama at Birmingham medical campus, one of which is named for him, and funds for refurbishing the Vulcan statue on Birmingham's Red Mountain—a favorite target of John McCain. He called for more oversight when the FBI in March 2005 abandoned its Virtual Case System software after spending $170 million on it. His Commerce, Justice & Science Subcommittee appropriations in 2005 and 2006 prohibited changes in the Universal Services Fund, a favorite of full committee Chairman Ted Stevens; they also denied administration requests for some Justice programs and added more money for local law enforcement grants. In September 2005, after Katrina, Shelby called for freezing one-third of the federal budget and offered to give up his own earmarks. That course was not taken, and he worked to get $5 million for a computer security task force in Birmingham and $1 million for videoconferencing to enable prisoners at the Jefferson County Criminal Center talk to their attorneys.

Shelby's party switch caused him no trouble in increasingly Republican Alabama. He was reelected 63%-37% in 1998 over a retired ironworker who mortgaged his pickup truck to pay the $2,672 filing fee. For the 2004 election, he accumulated some $11 million, more than any other incumbent than New York's Charles Schumer. His opponent, Alabama's first black Senate nominee, was a telephone claims representative for the Social Security Administration in Birmingham. Shelby spent only $2.3 million of his money, and won 68%-32%, running behind in only nine black-majority counties in the Black Belt. In February 2006 he had $11.4 million in his campaign treasury, second in the Senate to Hillary Rodham Clinton; Public Citizen said that he got more contributions from lobbyists than any other senator.

Junior Senator

Jeff Sessions (R)

Elected 1996, seat up 2008, 2d term; b. Dec. 24, 1946, Hybart; home, Mobile; Huntingdon Col., B.A. 1969, U. of AL, J.D. 1973; Methodist; married (Mary).

Military Career: Army Reserves, 1973-86.

Elected Office: AL Atty. Gen., 1994-96.

Professional Career: Practicing atty., 1973-75, 1977-81, 1993-94; Asst. U.S. Atty., 1975-77; U.S. Atty., 1981-93.

DC Office: 335 RSOB, 20510, 202-224-4124; Fax: 202-224-3149; Web site: sessions.senate.gov.

State Offices: Birmingham, 205-731-1500; Huntsville, 256-533-0979; Mobile, 251-414-3083; Montgomery, 334-244-7017.

Committees: *Armed Services* (4th of 12 R): Strategic Forces (RMM); Seapower; Airland. *Budget* (6th of 11 R). *Energy & Natural Resources* (7th of 11 R): National Parks; Energy; Public Lands & Forests. *Judiciary* (5th of 9 R): Administrative Oversight & the Courts (RMM); Terrorism, Technology & Homeland Security; Immigration, Refugees & Border Security; Crime & Drugs.

Group Ratings

	ADA	ACLU	AFS	LCV	ITIC	NTU	COC	ACU	CFG	FRC
2006	0	8	0	0	75	83	92	92	79	100
2005	0	—	0	5	—	82	78	100	92	—

National Journal Ratings

	2005 LIB	—	2005 CONS		2006 LIB	—	2006 CONS
Economic	0%	—	94%		13%	—	82%
Social	0%	—	77%		0%	—	82%
Foreign	0%	—	74%		0%	—	92%

Key Votes of the 109th Congress

1. Bar ANWR Drilling	N	5. Confirm Samuel Alito	Y	9. Limit Interstate Abortion	Y
2. FY06 Spending Curb	Y	6. Path to Citizenship	N	10. CAFTA	Y
3. Estate Tax Repeal	Y	7. Bar Same Sex Marriage	Y	11. Urge Iraq Withdrawal	N
4. Raise Minimum Wage	N	8. Stem Cell Research $	N	12. Provide Detainee Rights	N

Election Results

2002 general	Jeff Sessions (R)	792,561	(59%)	($5,115,730)
	Susan Parker (D)	538,878	(40%)	($1,185,718)
	Other	21,584	(2%)	
2002 primary	Jeff Sessions (R)	unopposed		
1996 general	Jeff Sessions (R)	786,436	(52%)	($3,862,359)
	Roger Bedford (D)	681,651	(45%)	($2,284,801)
	Other	31,306	(2%)	

Jeff Sessions, Alabama's junior senator, grew up in the state's Black Belt, walked to school barefoot and is the son of a country store owner. He graduated from Huntingdon College and the University of Alabama Law School, practiced law in a small town near the Tennessee Valley, became a federal prosecutor and then practiced law in Mobile. He was appointed U.S. Attorney in 1981, at 35, where he became known as a tough, aggressive prosecutor, and served for 12 years. In 1985, he was nominated for federal judge, but was attacked by liberals for "gross insensitivity" in racial matters for prosecuting vote fraud cases. With Alabama's Senator Howell Heflin voting against him in the Judiciary Committee, his nomination never went to the floor. In 1994, Sessions challenged state Attorney General Jimmy Evans, who had successfully prosecuted Governor Guy Hunt the year before, and won 57%-43%. In March 1995, when Heflin announced his retirement, Sessions started running for his seat; he became the favorite among the seven Republicans and four Democrats.

Sessions relied on his base in southern Alabama, territory that not long ago cast almost no Republican primary votes. Long-distance carrier executive Sid McDonald spent more than $1 million and attacked Sessions. From Birmingham north, the primary was a close race: McDonald led by 30%-29%. But in the rest of the state, Sessions led 48%-12%, for a 38%-22% statewide margin. In the runoff, McDonald extended his lead north from Birmingham, 54%-46%, but almost half the votes were cast farther south, and there Sessions led 73%-27%, for a 59%-41% win. The Democratic nominee, trial lawyer and state Senator Roger Bedford, was financed by trial lawyers and endorsed by key public employee unions and black organizations—the heart of today's Alabama Democratic Party. In the past, Democratic primaries had turnouts of nearly 1 million, with the advantage going to moderate or conservative candidates, like Glen Browder, the 3d District congressman. But only 315,000 voted in the Democratic primary, about half of them black; Bedford led Browder 45%-29%. In the runoff, Bedford had more money and won 62%-38%. In the general Bedford was competitive in fundraising and seemed the better campaigner. He opposed abortion, gun control, and gays in the military. Sessions avoided debates and attacked the Democrat as a Ted Kennedy backer and for leading the battle against tort reform in the Alabama Senate in 1996. Sessions won 52%-45%, running best in the suburban counties around Alabama's cities; Bedford carried the Black Belt and other rural counties.

In the Senate, Sessions has a very conservative voting record. He serves on the Judiciary Committee which once rejected his own nomination, and in 2003 complained, "I'm angry and passionate about the way the Democrats refused to let the Senate vote on these judgeships." One was for Alabama Attorney General Bill Pryor; he received a recess appointment in February 2004, and the Senate finally confirmed him in June 2005. Sessions was an early booster of a reinforced fence along the border with Mexico. But Sessions also has taken on some causes that are not labeled conservative. With Edward Kennedy he co-sponsored a bill to combat sexual assault in prisons. And he cosponsored a bill to reduce the ratio between the amount of powder cocaine and the amount of crack cocaine required to justify a five-year sentence and to reduce mandatory minimum sentences for minor players in drug offenses. In 2005, based on his experience as U.S. attorney, he helped to enact a bill providing grants for prescription-drug monitoring programs in each state. In December 2006, he called for bipartisan action to create personal savings accounts outside the Social Security system, including an individual account for each American that the federal government would fund with $1,000 at their birth.

Although Sessions has sponsored few major bills, he has had considerable success in inserting provisions that set new federal policy into legislation likely to pass. Into the 2003 Medicare/prescription drug bill, Sessions inserted a provision for higher Medicare reimbursement for rural hospitals; he threatened to vote against the measure unless this was retained in conference committee. It was, providing $738 million to Alabama—more than any other state except Texas and Florida. On the Armed Services Committee, he has been a big advocate for missile defense, and focused on the needs of defense installations in Alabama. The 2004 special education bill included a Sessions provision giving school districts the authority to establish uniform discipline policies for all schools—and to be relieved of the Education Department's complex requirements for special ed discipline. In the 2004 defense authorization, Sessions and Charles Schumer included a provision giving the Justice Department authority to prosecute employees of civilian contractors for the U.S. military overseas; this was prompted by the Abu Ghraib abuses. He also got a provision increasing military life insurance payoffs to $325,000 (later raised to $350,000) and providing two years' salaries and benefits for the families of military personnel killed in hostile action.

Despite the devastation that Hurricane Katrina inflicted on Alabama along the Gulf of Mexico, Sessions voiced concern about the cost of the federal clean-up and criticized government waste. "It will be added straight to our debt, and our children and grandchildren will pay it plus the interest that accumulates," he said. He wanted to offset some of the federal costs and with Pete Domenici called on President Bush to name an independent manager to oversee rebuilding costs.

In 2002 Sessions was opposed by Democrat Susan Parker, the state auditor and a fundraiser for colleges. Parker had the support of teachers' unions, but Sessions outspent her 4–1. In October, she took note of the travails of New Jersey's Democratic Senator Bob Torricelli and attacked Sessions for seeking a provision, not passed, which would allow a group of investors to escape a $15 million debt owed to Lloyds of London. "Just like the Torch [Toricelli's nickname], Sessions tried to sneak in a bailout for millionaires who gave him money," she said, and then proceeded to dump thousands of dollars onto the floor at a press conference. A clever tactic, but it availed her little.

Sessions won 59%-40%, even as Republican Bob Riley was being elected governor by just a narrow margin. Parker carried two Tennessee River counties in the north and 12 Black Belt counties in the center of the state but Sessions carried everything else. In January 2007, he got a break when Congressman Artur Davis decided early not to challenge him in 2008; in August, state Senator Vivian Davis Figures of Mobile announced she would run against Sessions.

FIRST DISTRICT

Rep. Jo Bonner (R)

Elected 2002, 3d term; b. Nov. 19, 1959, Selma; home, Mobile; U. of AL, B.A. 1982, U. of AL Law Schl. 1988; Episcopalian; married (Janee).

Professional Career: Sr. Aide, U.S. Rep. Sonny Callahan, 1984-2002.

DC Office: 422 CHOB, 20515, 202-225-4931; Fax: 202-225-0562; Web site: www.bonner.house.gov.

District Offices: Foley, 251-943-2073; Mobile, 251-690-2811.

Committees: *Agriculture* (8th of 21 R): Department Operations, Oversight, Nutrition & Forestry (RMM); Conservation, Credit, Energy & Research. *Budget* (3d of 17 R). *Science & Technology* (10th of 20 R): Technology & Innovation; Space & Aeronautics. *Standards of Official Conduct* (2d of 5 R).

Group Ratings

	ADA	ACLU	AFS	LCV	ITIC	NTU	COC	ACU	CFG	FRC
2006	0	0	0	25	100	55	100	88	51	85
2005	0	—	0	11	—	61	89	100	67	92

National Journal Ratings

	2005 LIB	—	2005 CONS		2006 LIB	—	2006 CONS
Economic	17%	—	82%		27%	—	71%
Social	0%	—	89%		17%	—	83%
Foreign	17%	—	79%		6%	—	86%

Key Votes of the 109th Congress

1. Estate Tax Repeal	Y	5. Limit Interstate Abortion	Y	9. Build Border Fence	Y
2. Limit CAFE Standards	Y	6. Extend Patriot Act	Y	10. CAFTA	Y
3. FY06 Spending Curb	Y	7. Bar Same Sex Marriage	Y	11. Oppose Iraq Withdrawal	Y
4. Drilling in ANWR	Y	8. Stem Cell Research $	N	12. Detainee Tribunals	Y

Election Results

2006 general	Jo Bonner (R)	112,944	(68%)	($875,364)
	Vivian Beckerle (D)	52,770	(32%)	($13,211)
2006 primary	Jo Bonner (R)	unopposed		
2004 general	Jo Bonner (R)	161,067	(63%)	($1,015,702)
	Judy McCain Belk (D)	93,938	(37%)	($442,141)

Prior Winning Percentages: 2002 (60%)

The People		Race/Ethnic Origin	Ancestry		
Area size:	7,182 sq. mi.	67.8% White	USA: 12.4%		Irish: 6.7%
Urban population:	64.4%	28.0% Black	English: 6.6%		
Rural population:	35.6%	1.0% Asian	**2004 Presidential Vote**		
Pop. 2000:	635,300	1.0% Native Am.	Bush (R) 168,817		(64%)
Pop. 2005 (est):	657,380	0.0% Hawaiian	Kerry (D) 91,832		(35%)
Median income:	$34,739	0.9% Two+ races	Other 1,922		(1%)
Poverty status:	16.9%	0.1% Other	**2000 Presidential Vote**		
Military veterans:	14.3%	1.3% Hispanic Origin	Bush (R) 138,938		(60%)
			Gore (D) 86,142		(37%)
			Other 4,798		(2%)
			Cook Partisan Voting Index: R +12		

Occupation   Blue collar: 29.7%   White collar: 54.7%   Gray collar: 15.6%

Mobile, the port where the Tombigbee and Alabama rivers flow into the Gulf of Mexico, was long a key point on the American frontier. Spanish after the Revolutionary War, it was wrested away by threats of war from Secretary of State John Quincy Adams. During the Civil War, it was one of the major Confederate ports; here in 1864 Admiral David Farragut, while steaming into the harbor lashed to his mast, cried, "Damn the torpedoes! Full speed ahead." Today, Mobile is full of graceful signs of its slightly exotic past. Behind the docks and rail lines are downtown buildings and old houses with Spanish motifs, French accents, or tropical Art Deco lines. Further inland are neighborhoods with spacious houses, often with double porches, overhung by huge live oaks, graced with Spanish moss. Mobile is a Gulf Coast version of Charleston or a smaller, more comfortable New Orleans, with a taste for shellfish and spicy food and an even older Mardi Gras, which the locals have been celebrating since 1703. As befits a frontier city with a martial past, Mobile is bristling with arms: One of the city's proudest possessions is the battleship *U.S.S. Alabama*, moored at the head of Mobile Bay, with its guns aimed out toward the Gulf. Mobile's economy was based originally on docks and shipyards, factories and terminals, but with a determination to impose touches of beauty on its hot, flat landscape. Its economy has been thriving at the shipyards, chemical plants, and a new cruise terminal. The capital improvements include Mobile's State Docks, which serves Alabama's booming Mercedes, Honda, and Hyundai auto-production factories. In August 2005, Hurricane Katrina struck Mobile and its beaches with Category Four intensity. On Dauphin Island, the 15-mile spit of land south of Mobile Bay, 300 homes were swept away. Elsewhere in Mobile and Baldwin Counties, Katrina caused major damage to pecans, peanuts and cotton crops. Although the damage received far less national attention than in Louisiana and Mississippi, within a year FEMA had provided $970 million of post-Katrina assistance to Alabama.

Mobile is the focus of Alabama's 1st Congressional District, which extends north along the usually lazily flowing Tombigbee and Alabama Rivers, near the old forts and mansions. Monroeville was the home of great writers—Truman Capote and his childhood playmate, Harper Lee, whose *To Kill a Mockingbird* is set here; and Winston Groom, author of *Forrest Gump*. Also here are surviving backcountry settlements of blacks and Cajans (who may or may not be descended from Louisiana Cajuns) and Creek Indians. Once cotton fields, this is now timber land, a major contributor to Alabama's economy, though many stands were devastated by Hurricane Ivan in September 2004. East of Mobile Bay, along the shores of the Gulf of Mexico, are the condominium communities in Baldwin County, one of the two fastest-growing counties in Alabama. The area hosts the annual National Shrimp Festival, and its glorious Gulf beaches are one of the South's best-kept secrets. For years, this southern seaboard of the Confederacy and the Union has been one of the most hawkish parts of America, and today it is solidly Republican in national elections. But in elections held just before and after Katrina, Mobile had record voter turnout and elected its first African–American mayor: Sam Jones, a liberal Democrat who served with John McCain in Vietnam.

The congressman from the 1st District is Jo Bonner, a Republican first elected in 2002. Bonner was born in Selma and is just a little too young to remember the days when it was the focus of the civil rights movement; he grew up in Camden, where his father, who died when Jo was 13, was a probate judge appointed by the relatively moderate Governor Albert Brewer. Bonner majored in journalism and graduated from the University of Alabama in 1982; two years later, he started working as a campaign press secretary for Sonny Callahan, a gregarious nine-term Republican who rose to become an Appropriations subcommittee chairman. In 1989, Bonner was promoted to chief of staff and later moved his family back to Mobile, where he became the rare top aide permanently stationed in the district. That background left Bonner well positioned when Callahan announced his retirement just three months before the June 2002 primary.

Bonner's strongest opponent in the seven-candidate Republican primary had a similar background: Tom Young had been the chief of staff to Senator Richard Shelby for 12 years. Like Bonner, Young had his former boss's endorsement and showed a knack for campaign fundraising: the two raised more than $2 million between them, including lots of money from Washington lobbyists; some complained about the pressure to choose sides. Young contrasted his experience on intelligence and defense policy with Bonner's focus on more mundane constituent-service work. Bonner argued that Young had more connections in Washington than in southern Alabama; he jibed that Young should have been welcomed at a luncheon for "new Mobilians." Young outspent Bonner by $300,000 and was helped by ads from the pro-tax cut Club for Growth, but Bonner led the primary 40%-20%. In the runoff, Bonner was endorsed by the Republicans who ran third, fourth and fifth; he won 62%-38%. In a district held by Republicans since 1964, when Barry Goldwater swept Alabama, Bonner beat Democratic businesswoman Judy McCain Belk, who contributed more than $300,000 to her campaign, by a 60%-38% margin—almost the same as George W. Bush's margin here in 2000.

In the House, Bonner has a solidly conservative voting record. After Hurricane Katrina, he was so worried about the federal budget impact that he was willing to reassess his support for estate and gift-tax repeal. "I can't in good conscience say that everything shouldn't be on the table," he said. He secured $7.5 million for improved shelter space at the fairgrounds in Baldwin County. In 2006, he voted against renewal of the Voting Rights Act, saying that it was time to give the South "an opportunity to come out from under the burden of crawling to the U.S. Justice Department, on bended knee, and asking for its blessing to continue on the march for equality." He has been an assistant whip and pushed to get Callahan's seat on Appropriations, without success so far. Back home, Bonner has succeeded Callahan as host of the weekly "Gulf Coast Congressional Report," which has aired since 1972 and bills itself as the longest-running televised public service program hosted by a member of Congress. In a rematch against Belk, Bonner won by a 63%-37% margin, a margin very close to Bush's 2004 margin in the district. In 2006, he defeated former Mobile County treasurer Vivian Beckerle 68%-32%; he got 63% in Mobile County. Bonner seems likely to have a lengthy tenure in this safely Republican seat.

SECOND DISTRICT

Rep. Terry Everett (R)

Elected 1992, 8th term; b. Feb. 15, 1937, Dothan; homo, Enterprise; Dale County H.S.; Baptist; married (Barbara).

Military Career: Air Force, 1955-59.

Professional Career: Newspaper reporter, 1959-61, 1966-68; Businessman, 1961-64; Editor & Publisher, 1968-88; Real estate developer, 1988-92; Owner & Pres., *Union Springs Herald*, 1988-2003.

DC Office: 2312 RHOB, 20515, 202-225-2901; Fax: 202-225-8913; Web site: www.house.gov/everett.

District Offices: Dothan, 334-794-9680; Montgomery, 334-277-9113; Opp, 334-493-9253.

Committees: *Agriculture* (2d of 21 R): Specialty Crops, Rural Development & Foreign Agriculture; Conservation, Credit, Energy & Research. *Armed Services* (4th of 29 R): Strategic Forces (RMM); Seapower & Expeditionary Forces. *Permanent Select Committee on Intelligence* (2d of 8 R): Oversight & Investigations (RMM); Terrorism, Human Intelligence, Analysis & Counterintelligence; Technical & Tactical Intelligence.

Group Ratings

	ADA	ACLU	AFS	LCV	ITIC	NTU	COC	ACU	CFG	FRC
2006	5	0	0	8	86	60	93	88	51	100
2005	0	—	0	0	—	58	85	96	60	92

National Journal Ratings

	2005 LIB	—	2005 CONS	2006 LIB	—	2006 CONS
Economic	12%	—	87%	7%	—	93%
Social	17%	—	83%	21%	—	79%
Foreign	29%	—	70%	33%	—	63%

Key Votes of the 109th Congress

1. Estate Tax Repeal	Y	5. Limit Interstate Abortion	Y	9. Build Border Fence	Y
2. Limit CAFE Standards	Y	6. Extend Patriot Act	Y	10. CAFTA	Y
3. FY06 Spending Curb	Y	7. Bar Same Sex Marriage	Y	11. Oppose Iraq Withdrawal	Y
4. Drilling in ANWR	Y	8. Stem Cell Research $	N	12. Detainee Tribunals	Y

Election Results

2006 general	Terry Everett (R)	124,302	(69%)	($330,375)
	Charles James (D)	54,450	(30%)	($5,292)
2006 primary	Terry Everett (R)	unopposed		
2004 general	Terry Everett (R)	177,086	(71%)	($1,937,038)
	Charles James (D)	70,562	(28%)	($1,320)

Prior Winning Percentages: 2002 (69%); 2000 (68%); 1998 (69%); 1996 (63%); 1994 (74%); 1992 (49%)

The People		Race/Ethnic Origin	Ancestry	
Area size:	10,608 sq. mi.	67.0% White	USA: 15.7%	English: 6.2%
Urban population:	50.1%	29.4% Black	Irish: 5.9%	
Rural population:	49.9%	0.6% Asian	**2004 Presidential Vote**	
Pop. 2000:	635,300	0.4% Native Am.	Bush (R) 170,427	(67%)
Pop. 2005 (est):	652,515	0.0% Hawaiian	Kerry (D) 84,043	(33%)
Median income:	$32,460	0.9% Two+ races	Other 1,091	(0%)
Poverty status:	17.2%	0.1% Other	**2000 Presidential Vote**	
Military veterans:	15.1%	1.5% Hispanic Origin	Bush (R) 137,168	(61%)
			Gore (D) 84,435	(38%)
			Other 3,061	(1%)
			Cook Partisan Voting Index: R +13	
Occupation	Blue collar: 29.5%	White collar: 55.1%	Gray collar: 15.4%	

The thick green countryside is everywhere in southern Alabama. Even in Montgomery the stone and brick buildings that rise in the irregular downtown grid do not mask the contours of the hills or hide the lush foliage. You can look downhill from the restored Greek Revival Capitol toward Dexter Avenue Baptist Church where the young Martin Luther King Jr. was pastor in the 1950s, or out past the impressive Carolyn Blount Theater, host of the Alabama Shakespeare Festival, toward new subdivisions and shopping malls, and you can easily imagine when this land was covered with cotton fields and pine trees. The atmosphere is even more rural in southeast Alabama's Wiregrass region, named for the stiff native grass, in the fishing town of Eufaula along the Chattahoochee River, around the town of Dothan, past Daleville and the Army's Fort Rucker (the home of Army aviation flight training) to Enterprise, site of the Boll Weevil Monument that commemorates the insect that destroyed two-thirds of the cotton crop here in 1915 and then spread throughout the South. Timber is an important resource here, and peanuts are now the main crop in the area surrounding Dothan; the district ranks second in the nation in acres harvested for peanuts. But the area is diversifying: Hyundai built its first U.S. assembly plant in southwest Montgomery County, with about 3,000 local jobs.

The 2d Congressional District of Alabama covers the southeast corner of the state. It includes most of the city of Montgomery, but only a small part of Montgomery County; Democratic redistricters put the rest (which includes the Capitol and many black precincts) into the 3d District in an attempt to make that seat more Democratic. The result left the 2d heavily Republican. The Montgomery County precincts plus suburban Elmore and Autauga Counties vote heavily Republican, as does the area around Dothan and Houston County in the Wiregrass region. These places heavily outvote the district's Black Belt counties—Lowndes, Bullock, with a large black majority, and Barbour on the Georgia border, which was George Wallace's home base. It would be a mistake to see these preferences as purely racial, however. The civil rights laws of the 1960s have long since been accepted. Blacks here tend to support a larger and more generous government, and hence vote

Democratic. Alabama whites tend to take a hard line on defense and crime, want government to promote traditional cultural values and hence vote Republican.

The congressman from the 2d District is Terry Everett, a businessman first elected in 1992. He grew up in the Wiregrass region and served in Air Force Intelligence in Germany in the 1950s, where he learned Russian, then worked as a sports and police beat reporter and circulation manager for southern Alabama newspapers. He bought some newspapers himself and sold them for far more, and ended up heading an S&L and owning a large farm and real estate development firm. When he ran for the seat being vacated by 28-year incumbent Republican Bill Dickinson, Everett was far from the favorite. But he beat two career politicians, a Montgomery legislator in the Republican primary and, in the general, state Treasurer George C. Wallace, son of the former governor (Wallace, now a Republican, later was elected Public Service Commissioner, but he lost a primary runoff for lieutenant governor in 2006.). Everett spent $600,000 of his own money and, echoing an old George Wallace slogan, called on voters to, "Send them a message, not a politician." Everett carried the Montgomery area and the Wiregrass but lost the Black Belt and rural areas.

Everett's voting record is mostly conservative; he shows a practical-minded concern about local issues and demonstrates a real impact on some issues. A prime example is peanuts: In 1995, he formed a Peanut Caucus and on the Agriculture Committee held out against the Freedom to Farm Act until he got the peanut program continued, though with a 10% cut in the support price and a lower national quota. On the 2002 farm bill, as chairman of the Specialty Crops and Foreign Agriculture Programs Subcommittee, he concluded that Congress would no longer support the 30 cents per pound peanut subsidy. So, Everett worked with Saxby Chambliss and Sanford Bishop of Georgia on a compromise that reduced imports and guaranteed quota farmers 10 cents per pound, with new farmers receiving a fallback option of government purchase at 18 cents. That Everett was able to get the House to accept a $3.5 billion (over 10 years) program showed his skill in protecting the interests of local farmers. Everett, himself a holder of a peanut quota, estimated that he would get $30,000 over five years from the new program. The new program developed record yields for the district's peanut crop, though the number of farmers fell a bit. Another agricultural interest is the conversion of poultry waste to energy. If Republicans regain House control, he may be in line to chair the Agriculture Committee.

Later, as chairman of the Armed Services Strategic Forces Subcommittee, he sought to shift funding priorities "from longer-term efforts to those that will provide more immediate benefit to the war fighter" in Iraq, including space-based military capabilities that use global positioning satellites to guide aircraft and munitions. On another issue, he echoed the district's populist tradition when he filed a bill to require two months public notice before corporations could give big pay raises to their top executives. He called for reform of the Voting Rights Act "to ensure that it reflects our current society." Everett has been reelected easily against poorly-funded challengers. In September 2007, Everett announced he would not run for a ninth term in 2008.

THIRD DISTRICT

Rep. Mike Rogers (R)

Elected 2002, 3d term; b. July 16, 1958, Hammond, IN; home, Anniston; Jacksonville St. U., B.A. 1981, M.P.A. 1984, Birmingham Schl. of Law, J.D. 1991; Baptist; married (Beth).

Elected Office: Calhoun Cnty. Commission, 1986-90; AL House of Reps., 1994-2002, Min. Ldr., 1998-2000.

Professional Career: Practicing atty., 1991-2002; Owner, auto lot.

DC Office: 324 CHOB, 20515, 202-225-3261; Fax: 202-226-8485; Web site: www.house.gov/mike-rogers/.

District Offices: Anniston, 256-236-5655; Montgomery, 334-277-4210; Opelika, 334-745-6221.

Committees: *Agriculture* (9th of 21 R): Conservation, Credit, Energy & Research; Livestock, Dairy & Poultry. *Armed Services* (22d of 29 R): Readiness; Strategic Forces. *Homeland Security* (7th of 15 R): Management, Investigations & Oversight (RMM); Emergency Communications, Preparedness & Response.

Group Ratings

	ADA	ACLU	AFS	LCV	ITIC	NTU	COC	ACU	CFG	FRC
2006	10	9	14	17	86	53	87	84	43	100
2005	10	—	13	6	—	54	85	88	56	85

National Journal Ratings

	2005 LIB	—	2005 CONS		2006 LIB	—	2006 CONS
Economic	41%	—	59%		32%	—	67%
Social	22%	—	77%		15%	—	84%
Foreign	29%	—	70%		38%	—	59%

Key Votes of the 109th Congress

1. Estate Tax Repeal	Y	5. Limit Interstate Abortion	Y	9. Build Border Fence		Y
2. Limit CAFE Standards	Y	6. Extend Patriot Act	Y	10. CAFTA		Y
3. FY06 Spending Curb	Y	7. Bar Same Sex Marriage	Y	11. Oppose Iraq Withdrawal		Y
4. Drilling in ANWR	Y	8. Stem Cell Research $	N	12. Detainee Tribunals		Y

Election Results

2006 general	Mike Rogers (R)	98,257	(59%)	($1,046,764)
	Greg Pierce (D)	63,559	(38%)	($7,674)
	Other	3,485	(2%)	
2006 primary	Mike Rogers (R)	unopposed		
2004 general	Mike Rogers (R)	150,411	(61%)	($1,893,588)
	Bill Fuller (D)	95,240	(39%)	($240,774)

Prior Winning Percentages: 2002 (50%)

The People		Race/Ethnic Origin	Ancestry	
Area size:	7,988 sq. mi.	64.9% White	USA: 15.9%	Irish: 6.0%
Urban population:	53.3%	32.2% Black	English: 5.8%	
Rural population:	46.7%	0.6% Asian	**2004 Presidential Vote**	
Pop. 2000:	635,300	0.3% Native Am.	Bush (R) 146,380	(58%)
Pop. 2005 (est):	637,852	0.0% Hawaiian	Kerry (D) 103,456	(41%)
Median income:	$30,806	0.7% Two+ races	Other 1,501	(1%)
Poverty status:	18.8%	0.1% Other	**2000 Presidential Vote**	
Military veterans:	13.4%	1.2% Hispanic Origin	Bush (R) 112,320	(52%)
			Gore (D) 101,431	(47%)
			Other 3,769	(2%)
			Cook Partisan Voting Index: R + 4	

Occupation	Blue collar: 33.1%	White collar: 51.7%	Gray collar: 15.2%

Forty years ago, Lineville, Alabama, in the red hills of Clay County, was Ku Klux Klan country, with whites determined to resist race-mixing and blacks intimidated by threats of violence. More recently in Lineville, integrated crowds regularly cheer integrated high school teams, and people of all races work amicably together, though they tend to pray separately on Sundays. Lineville's progress perhaps echoes that of America's most integrated institution, the military, for the small town produced more men and women per capita for Operation Desert Storm than any other community in the nation. In 2003 Alabama was the nation's top contributor of National Guard personnel and in 2005, there were about 1,300 Alabama National Guard troops deployed in Iraq; Clay County has one of the highest concentrations of Guard enlistments and reservists in the state.

The 3d Congressional District of Alabama is centered geographically and perhaps spiritually in Lineville. The military presence is unmistakable throughout: Calhoun County is home to the Anniston Army Depot and formerly home to Fort McClellan, which survived several rounds of base closings until it was finally closed in 1999. Horseshoe Bend is where Andrew Jackson won a climactic battle against the Upper Creek Indians. Fort Mitchell, a 19th century frontier military outpost, is the site of a national military cemetery sometimes referred to as the "Arlington of the South." Phenix City, across the Chattahoochie River from Georgia's Fort Benning, served as a "sin city" in the 1940s and 1950s with virtually every imaginable vice for pleasure-seeking soldiers, a place so sleazy that General George Patton threatened to level it with his tanks; today, the huge military installation plays a more constructive role in the local economy. There are other places of distinction in the 3d: Tuskegee, home of Booker T. Washington's Tuskegee Institute, training ground for the Tuskegee Airmen, the first black pilots trained to fly for the U.S. military, and now the nation's only veterinary school at a historically black university; Auburn, home of Auburn University and its renowned sports teams and veterinary school; Talladega, home of the Alabama Institute for the Deaf and Blind, which is perhaps America's most user-friendly city for the disabled. NASCAR fans know it as the home of a famed speedway and for the International Motorsports Hall of Fame—the Cooperstown of auto racing. This looks and feels like rural country, though few people here make a living off their farms. Instead, they drive to work at Tyson Foods or Wal-Mart or in dozens of small- or medium-sized factories.

Politically, this was long one of the heartlands of the Democratic Party, the home of populist white Democrats—patriotic supporters of the military, cautious supporters of some domestic programs—who won power so often in the House and Senate. But the cotton mills have closed, and interstates have brought in new businesses, including a huge Honda assembly plant in Talladega County, where solid wages boosted local personal income by 22% in the three years after it opened. In Montgomery, state government is the largest employer. Except for Tuskegee's Macon County and the portions of Montgomery County added by the 2002 redistricting in an attempt by Democrats to make this district competitive, the area has become Republican, though Democrats have remained competitive in some state elections. George Bush won 52% here in 2000, and 58% in 2004.

The congressman from the 3d is Mike Rogers, a Republican first elected in 2002—the second Republican Mike Rogers in the House (the other is from the 8th District of Michigan). The Alabama Mike Rogers is a fifth generation resident of Calhoun County who, at the age of 28 in 1986, was the first Republican elected to the county commission. In 1994, he won a seat in the Alabama House and in his second term, he became Minority Leader. In 2002, the 3d District's congressman, Bob Riley, ran successfully for governor; Rogers easily won the Republican nomination to succeed him. But he had stiff competition from Democrat Joe Turnham, Jr., who served three years as state party chairman and challenged Riley unsuccessfully in 1998. Turnham and Rogers tried to "out-Bubba" each other. Turnham called for a congressional auto racing caucus and demanded that Rogers prove he had hunting and fishing licenses. Rogers touted his working class values and support from the National Rifle Association; he is an abortion opponent who supports a constitutional amendment for prayer in public school. Though both national parties targeted the district, Turnham did not risk bringing in national Democrats to campaign for him in this socially conservative district, while Rogers got frequent visits from national Republican leaders. Speaker Dennis Hastert promised him a seat on the Armed Services Committee. The contrast in national party support was evident in Rogers's big fundraising advantage. Still, Rogers won by only 50%-48%. Rogers did well in his base, Calhoun County, where he got 60% of the vote. In contrast, Turnham lost Lee County, his home, by a 52%-46% margin, and carried the district's portion of Montgomery County by only 57%-42%.

In the House Rogers has a voting record that leans conservative, though he is more centrist on economic issues. He bucked the Bush administration and won local praise by opposing the free trade agreement with Morocco on the grounds that it would reduce local textile and apparel jobs. On the Armed Services Committee he opposed a new round of base closings and won House passage of a bill to assure that universities would provide fair access to their facilities for military recruiters and ROTC personnel. As chairman of the Homeland Security Subcommittee on Management, Integration and Oversight, Rogers spotlighted in 2005 the defective equipment in a $239 million camera system installed on the borders with Mexico and Canada. He secured $47 million for an Anniston-based consortium that develops anti-terrorism training for emergency responders.

In this ancestrally Democratic district, Rogers worked hard to entrench himself and raise money to discourage strong Democratic opposition in 2004. He drew a credible challenger in Democrat Bill Fuller, the former state human resources commissioner and an 18-year veteran of the state House. Fuller called for limits on outsourcing of jobs and criticized Rogers for supporting the 2003 Medicare/prescription drug law; Rogers boasted of the law's increased payments for Alabama's rural hospitals. Though national and state Democrats hyped Fuller's prospects, he was inadequately funded and his campaign never posed a serious threat. Rogers won 61%-39%, carrying 11 of the 13 counties; he won 73% in Calhoun County. In 2006, he won 59% in a three-way contest; running as an independent, white supremacist Mark Layfield got 2%. Rogers seems to have made this a safe Republican district.

FOURTH DISTRICT

Rep. Robert Aderholt (R)

Elected 1996, 6th term; b. July 22, 1965, Haleyville; home, Haleyville; Birmingham-Southern Col., B.A. 1987, Samford U., J.D. 1990; Congregationalist; married (Caroline).

Professional Career: Haleyville Municipal Judge, 1992-96; Asst. Legal Advisor, Gov. Fob James, 1995-96.

DC Office: 1433 LHOB, 20515, 202-225-4876; Fax: 202-225-5587; Web site: www.aderholt.house.gov.

District Offices: Cullman, 256-734-6043; Decatur, 256-350-4093; Gadsden, 256-546-0201; Jasper, 205-221-2310.

Committees: *Appropriations* (15th of 29 R): Homeland Security; Transportation, HUD & Related Agencies; Commerce, Justice, Science & Related Agencies.

Group Ratings

	ADA	ACLU	AFS	LCV	ITIC	NTU	COC	ACU	CFG	FRC
2006	10	5	14	0	86	52	87	84	42	100
2005	0	—	0	0	—	57	85	92	57	92

National Journal Ratings

	2005 LIB	—	2005 CONS		2006 LIB	—	2006 CONS
Economic	9%	—	88%		25%	—	74%
Social	12%	—	86%		11%	—	85%
Foreign	23%	—	73%		30%	—	67%

Key Votes of the 109th Congress

1. Estate Tax Repeal	Y	5. Limit Interstate Abortion	Y	9. Build Border Fence	Y
2. Limit CAFE Standards	Y	6. Extend Patriot Act	Y	10. CAFTA	Y
3. FY06 Spending Curb	Y	7. Bar Same Sex Marriage	Y	11. Oppose Iraq Withdrawal	Y
4. Drilling in ANWR	Y	8. Stem Cell Research $	N	12. Detainee Tribunals	Y

Election Results

2006 general	Robert Aderholt (R)	128,484	(70%)	($622,248)
	Barbara Bobo (D)	54,382	(30%)	
2006 primary	Robert Aderholt (R)	unopposed		
2004 general	Robert Aderholt (R)	191,110	(75%)	($735,352)
	Carl Cole (D)	64,278	(25%)	($25,496)

Prior Winning Percentages: 2002 (87%); 2000 (61%); 1998 (56%); 1996 (50%)

The People		Race/Ethnic Origin	Ancestry	
Area size:	8,524 sq. mi.	90.4% White	USA: 21.3%	Irish: 8.2%
Urban population:	26.5%	5.1% Black	English: 6.8%	
Rural population:	73.5%	0.2% Asian	**2004 Presidential Vote**	
Pop. 2000:	635,300	0.4% Native Am.	Bush (R) 186,509	(71%)
Pop. 2005 (est):	643,409	0.0% Hawaiian	Kerry (D) 73,504	(28%)
Median income:	$31,344	0.8% Two+ races	Other 1,741	(1%)
Poverty status:	14.7%	0.0% Other	**2000 Presidential Vote**	
Military veterans:	12.9%	3.0% Hispanic Origin	Bush (R) 141,285	(61%)
			Gore (D) 87,062	(37%)
			Other 4,240	(2%)
			Cook Partisan Voting Index: R +16	
Occupation	Blue collar: 40.8%	White collar: 46.0%	Gray collar: 13.2%	

The Appalachians' corduroy ridges, dividing the Atlantic coast from the interior, are America's coal-and-steel industrial spine, from the black coal country of western Pennsylvania to the red hill country of northern Alabama. Here rose America's two premier steel cities, Pittsburgh and Birmingham. Around both, and for many miles in between them, is the country settled by feisty Scots-Irish farmers in the years between the Revolution and the Civil War. In valley land accessible to railroads are the great steel factories built in the 80 years after the Civil War and smaller factories that produce underwear and tires, glass and chemicals, socks and chickens. Politically, the two regions were separated by the Civil War: Western Pennsylvania was overwhelmingly Republican until the 1930s, while northern Alabama was solidly Democratic through the 1950s. But they shared the same political impulses—populist on economics, conservative on culture—which made them both Democratic heartlands during the New Deal and in congressional politics for years afterwards. Now they seem to have traded partisan allegiances: Western Pennsylvania is Democratic, though less solidly so when the Democrats emphasize cultural liberalism; northern Alabama has moved toward the Republicans, even though it has benefited from massive federal public works programs, and the movement is most pronounced in counties close to Birmingham and along the interstates.

Alabama's 4th Congressional District is a collection of small towns—Cullman, Jasper, Russellville, Fort Payne, and Albertville, the home of a new plant that equips military helicopters; gritty Gadsden, population 37,000, is the biggest city, with a large Goodyear tire plant. Sandwiched between Huntsville to the north and Birmingham to the south, the 4th crosses the state and the Appalachian ridges, from the Georgia line to the Mississippi line in rural counties. Decades of coal-mining scarred 150 square miles of landscape, about one-fourth of which has been reclaimed. This is Alabama's premier Scots-Irish district, with the lowest black percentage of the state's seven congressional districts. There are few vestiges of its Democratic heritage; George Bush won here with 71% in 2004.

The congressman from the 4th District is Robert Aderholt (pronounced *ADD-er-holt*), a Republican first elected in 1996 to replace 30-year Democrat Tom Bevill, a senior Appropriations member and benefactor of great federal projects, including the Tennessee-Tombigbee Waterway project. Aderholt is from Winston County, the one ancestrally Republican county in north Alabama, which opposed secession in the Civil War and declared itself the Free State of Winston. His father was a circuit judge for more than 30 years; his wife's father was a state senator and state commissioner of Agriculture and Industry. In 1992, Aderholt was appointed Haleyville municipal judge; in 1995, he became a top aide to Governor Fob James. With that pedigree, he decided to run for Congress when Bevill retired. As Republican nominee, he faced state Senator Bob Wilson Jr., who called himself a Democrat "in the Tom Bevill tradition." In this culturally conservative district, Aderholt didn't hedge on cultural issues. Against abortion, gun control and same-sex marriage, and for school prayer, he said, "We want to go to Washington to deliver a message, and that is, don't mess with our traditional family values." He attacked Wilson for his support from unions and trial lawyers. This was a nationally targeted race, seriously contested, and Aderholt won 50%-48%—one reason Republicans held their House majority in 1996.

Recognizing Aderholt's electoral vulnerability, Republican leaders put him on Appropriations; he has brought home more highway and sewer money than most Republicans. And he hasn't forgotten the social issues. After Alabama's ousted Chief Justice Judge Roy Moore called for a new law to prevent federal judges from interfering with public displays of the Ten Commandments, Aderholt sponsored legislation to work toward that goal. "The acknowledgment of God is not a legitimate subject of review by the federal courts," Aderholt said.

Aderholt's voting record is generally conservative. But he supported quotas on steel imports and sponsored a bill assessing additional antidumping duties on foreign steel, and he reached out to industrial unions with his vote against PNTR with China. After George W. Bush was elected—and after Aderholt got protection for the local sock industry (Fort Payne, with 150 plants, proclaims itself the Sock Capital of the World)—he voted for trade promotion authority. He opposed free trade agreements with Chile, Morocco and Singapore but voted in favor of the U.S.-Australia Free Trade Agreement. In 2005, he was a crucial vote for the Central American Free Trade Agreement, after he got a last-minute letter from the Bush administration delaying the phase-out on tariffs on socks. The House passed his bill to make it easier for the actions of notary publics to be recognized across state lines.

Aderholt faced serious challenges in his first two reelections, but has won easily ever since. In 2006, former Millport mayor Barbara Bobo, the Democratic challenger, said "We need checks and balances, not this bobblehead Congress." Aderholt won 70%-30%. He appears to have entrenched himself in what used to be a swing seat.

FIFTH DISTRICT

Rep. Bud Cramer (D)

Elected 1990, 9th term; b. Aug. 22, 1947, Huntsville; home, Huntsville; U. of AL, B.A. 1969, J.D. 1972; Methodist; widowed.

Military Career: Army, 1972; Army Reserves, 1976-78.

Professional Career: Instructor, U. of AL Law Schl., Dir., Clinical Studies Program, 1972-73; Madison Cnty. Asst. Dist. Atty., 1973-75; Practicing atty., 1975-80; Madison Cnty. Dist. Atty., 1981-90; Founder, Natl. Children's Advocacy Ctr., 1985.

DC Office: 2184 RHOB, 20515, 202-225-4801; Fax: 202-225-4392; Web site: www.cramer.house.gov.

District Offices: Decatur, 256-355-9400; Huntsville, 256-551-0190; Tuscumbia, 256-381-3450.

Committees: *Appropriations* (15th of 37 D): Defense; Transportation, HUD & Related Agencies; Financial Services & General Government. *Permanent Select Committee on Intelligence* (4th of 12 D): Oversight & Investigations (Chmn.); Technical & Tactical Intelligence (Vice Chmn.).

Group Ratings

	ADA	ACLU	AFS	LCV	ITIC	NTU	COC	ACU	CFG	FRC
2006	50	45	57	33	86	36	93	68	47	57
2005	75	—	63	28	—	32	81	54	31	46

National Journal Ratings

	2005 LIB	—	2005 CONS		2006 LIB	—	2006 CONS
Economic	50%	—	50%		53%	—	47%
Social	50%	—	50%		51%	—	48%
Foreign	51%	—	49%		50%	—	49%

Key Votes of the 109th Congress

1. Estate Tax Repeal	Y	5. Limit Interstate Abortion	Y	9. Build Border Fence	Y
2. Limit CAFE Standards	Y	6. Extend Patriot Act	Y	10. CAFTA	N
3. FY06 Spending Curb	N	7. Bar Same Sex Marriage	Y	11. Oppose Iraq Withdrawal	Y
4. Drilling in ANWR	Y	8. Stem Cell Research $	Y	12. Detainee Tribunals	Y

Election Results

2006 general	Bud Cramer (D)	...... unopposed		($589,469)
2006 primary	Bud Cramer (D)	...... unopposed		
2004 general	Bud Cramer (D)	 200,999	(73%)	($588,838)
	Gerald Wallace (R)	 74,145	(27%)	($12,610)

Prior Winning Percentages: 2002 (73%); 2000 (89%); 1998 (70%); 1996 (56%); 1994 (50%); 1992 (66%); 1990 (67%)

The People		Race/Ethnic Origin	Ancestry	
Area size:	4,689 sq. mi.	77.7% White	USA: 16.1%	Irish: 8.0%
Urban population:	59.4%	16.9% Black	English: 7.6%	
Rural population:	40.6%	1.0% Asian	**2004 Presidential Vote**	
Pop. 2000:	635,300	0.9% Native Am.	Bush (R) 167,552	(60%)
Pop. 2005 (est):	663,863	0.0% Hawaiian	Kerry (D) 110,633	(39%)
Median income:	$38,054	1.4% Two+ races	Other 2,225	(1%)
Poverty status:	12.5%	0.1% Other	**2000 Presidential Vote**	
Military veterans:	14.0%	2.0% Hispanic Origin	Bush (R) 131,608	(54%)
			Gore (D) 106,685	(44%)
			Other 5,241	(2%)
			Cook Partisan Voting Index: R + 6	

Occupation	Blue collar: 29.6%	White collar: 57.1%	Gray collar: 13.3%

Twice this century, the federal government has transformed the northern Alabama counties along the Tennessee River. The first time was when it created the Tennessee Valley Authority in 1933. Proposed by Nebraska Senator George Norris, a favorite of President Franklin Roosevelt, TVA took the World War I federal munitions plant at Muscle Shoals on the unnavigable Tennessee River, and built a series of dams to control flooding and produce cheap hydroelectric power. This was backward country then: Poor white farmers scratched an existence out of hardscrabble land, were housed in shacks without electricity or running water, and lived off a diet that produced pellagra and rickets. The TVA was intended to showcase what an enlightened, generous federal government could do. The second major federal project here was the space program. After the Soviets put up Sputnik in 1957, the Redstone Arsenal in Huntsville became the nation's major missile development center— the first of the large U.S. ballistic missiles were developed here. On the grounds of Redstone, NASA built its Marshall Space Flight Center in the 1960s and the Huntsville-Decatur area soon achieved high-tech critical mass. With leadership from Werner von Braun and other German engineers, Redstone and Marshall built Explorer 1, the first American orbiting satellite, the Mercury-Redstone vehicle that boosted astronaut Alan Shepard into suborbital flight and the Saturn V rocket that sent man to the moon. In the 1970s, Marshall produced Skylab and developed the Space Shuttle's main engines and solid rocket boosters, and the Boeing research center here has been a prime contractor for the space station. In 1990, it helped launch the Hubble Space Telescope. Boeing produces the Delta IV booster at its factory in Decatur. With the approaching retirement of the space shuttle, NASA expects that Marshall will help to prepare the next generation of space vehicles. Recently, space-related jobs have evolved with a broader defense focus. In 2005, the Pentagon base-closing commission moved 1,800 jobs in the Missile Defense Agency from northern Virginia to Redstone. Huntsville also was the beneficiary of 1,600 jobs with the Army's Materiel Command. Fifty years ago Huntsville was a sleepy town huddled around a well-preserved early 19th century residential district. Today it is the center of Alabama's third-largest and fast-growing metro area.

The 5th Congressional District of Alabama takes in most of the state's TVA and space counties. TVA and the space program were primarily Democratic projects, and for years most voters here were staunch New Deal Democrats, liberal on economics and not much interested in race, like the longtime Senator John Sparkman, the party's vice presidential nominee in 1952. But professional and technical people in the space business tend to combine high-tech and traditional values, and this made much of northern Alabama marginal-to-Republican country in the 1990s. This district has never elected a Republican to Congress, but it has voted Republican for president since the defeat of Jimmy Carter, and in the mid-1990s, it had seriously contested congressional elections.

The congressman from the 5th District is Bud Cramer, a Democrat first elected in 1990. He is a political survivor who has managed to become an active player for his district and now finds himself strategically positioned within the House. He grew up in Huntsville, served as an Army tank officer after law school, and beat the incumbent district attorney in 1980, at 33. In 1985, he set up the Child Advocacy Center, a child-friendly environment for abused children. When Congressman Ronnie Flippo ran unsuccessfully for governor in 1990, Cramer ran for Congress. He won the general election by a 2–1 margin.

In the House, Cramer has been a tireless booster of the Space Station and a leading advocate for missile defense spending. In the TVA tradition, he initially supported the Democratic leadership on key issues. But his votes for the Clinton budget and tax package in 1993 and for the Clinton crime bill with its gun control provisions were unpopular locally; in 1994, he was reelected by only a 50%-49% margin. Since then, Cramer's overall voting record frequently places him at the center of the House. But he has voted conservative on key issues, ranging from the Republicans' impeachment inquiry of Bill Clinton to the ban on partial-birth abortions and repeal of the estate and gift taxes. He is a founder of the Blue Dogs. With his seat on Appropriations, including its Defense Subcommittee, he has successfully pursued a nonpartisan approach toward federal dollars and contracts. On the Intelligence Committee, he was an early supporter of the proposal to create a national intelligence director to oversee the complex bureaucracy; in 2007, he became chairman of its oversight subcommittee. Drawing on his pre-congressional experience, he set up the National Child Advocacy Center, which assists abused children and has trained thousands of caregivers and case workers. "We are the Mayo Clinic there in Huntsville of child abuse," he boasted. The pork-busting Citizens Against Government Waste has listed many of Cramer's local projects in its "Pork Alert" listing, with a salute, "This Bud's for you!"

After the 2000 election, Cramer was said to be under consideration for a job in the Bush administration and later was touted as a possible challenger to Jeff Sessions in the 2002 Senate campaign. But neither option panned out. Before and after the 2002 election, Cramer was strikingly coy about persistent rumors that he might switch parties. "I don't plan on switching parties right now," or, "at this time," he would say. Amid this speculation, Democratic leadership tapped him for the Intelligence Committee. Since then, he has sounded more like a loyal Democrat. Despite being an early Republican target in 2006, Cramer ran unopposed and is unlikely to have much trouble holding this seat.

SIXTH DISTRICT

Rep. Spencer Bachus (R)

Elected 1992, 8th term; b. Dec. 28, 1947, Birmingham; home, Birmingham; Auburn U., B.A. 1969, U. of AL, J.D. 1972; Baptist; married (Linda).

Military Career: Natl. Guard, 1969-71.

Elected Office: AL Senate, 1983-84; AL House of Reps., 1984-87.

Professional Career: Owner, Lumber Co.; Practicing atty., 1972-92; AL Repub. Party Chmn., 1991-92.

DC Office: 2246 RHOB, 20515, 202-225-4921; Fax: 202-225-2082; Web site: www.house.gov/bachus.

District Offices: Birmingham, 205-969-2296; Clanton, 205-280-0704.

Committees: *Financial Services* (RMM of 33 R).

Group Ratings

	ADA	ACLU	AFS	LCV	ITIC	NTU	COC	ACU	CFG	FRC
2006	0	14	0	8	100	62	93	88	64	100
2005	5	—	0	0	—	58	93	92	60	92

National Journal Ratings

	2005 LIB	—	2005 CONS		2006 LIB	—	2006 CONS
Economic	17%	—	83%		19%	—	80%
Social	0%	—	89%		6%	—	92%
Foreign	34%	—	66%		15%	—	84%

Key Votes of the 109th Congress

1. Estate Tax Repeal	Y	5. Limit Interstate Abortion	Y	9. Build Border Fence	Y
2. Limit CAFE Standards	Y	6. Extend Patriot Act	Y	10. CAFTA	Y
3. FY06 Spending Curb	Y	7. Bar Same Sex Marriage	Y	11. Oppose Iraq Withdrawal	*
4. Drilling in ANWR	Y	8. Stem Cell Research $	N	12. Detainee Tribunals	Y

Election Results

2006 general	Spencer Bachus (R)........................... unopposed	($1,893,917)
2006 primary	Spencer Bachus (R)........................... unopposed	
2004 general	Spencer Bachus (R)........................... unopposed	($1,376,103)

Prior Winning Percentages: 2002 (90%); 2000 (88%); 1998 (72%); 1996 (71%); 1994 (79%); 1992 (52%)

The People		Race/Ethnic Origin	Ancestry	
Area size:	4,649 sq. mi.	88.8% White	USA: 14.5%	English: 10.1%
Urban population:	62.1%	7.7% Black	Irish: 8.1%	
Rural population:	37.9%	0.9% Asian	**2004 Presidential Vote**	
Pop. 2000:	635,300	0.3% Native Am.	Bush (R) 248,095	(78%)
Pop. 2005 (est):	691,309	0.0% Hawaiian	Kerry (D) 69,449	(22%)
Median income:	$46,946	0.7% Two+ races	Other 722	(0%)
Poverty status:	8.1%	0.0% Other	**2000 Presidential Vote**	
Military veterans:	12.9%	1.6% Hispanic Origin	Bush (R) 200,818	(74%)
			Gore (D) 67,975	(25%)
			Other 3,997	(1%)
			Cook Partisan Voting Index: R +25	

Occupation	Blue collar: 22.1%	White collar: 67.7%	Gray collar: 10.2%

Birmingham, once one of America's booming industrial cities, then the site of violence in the civil rights revolution, now has future prospects far more hopeful than seemed possible not long ago. This is a new city by southern standards: Before the Civil War there was nothing here but a few creeks running below Red Mountain. But Red Mountain is almost pure iron ore, and by 1890, Birmingham had the South's largest steel mills. In the early 20th century, as the statue of Vulcan, Roman god of fire and metalworking, looked out over the smokestack-rich valley, Birmingham seemed the most up-to-date and progressive city in the South. But the worldwide overcapacity in steel and technological obsolescence at home sent the American steel industry into long-term decline starting in the 1950s. Meanwhile, industrial Birmingham's political leaders plotted to avoid desegregation, and the city's violent reaction to civil rights—Police Commissioner (and Democratic National Committeeman at the time) Bull Connor set dogs and fire hoses against peaceful demonstrators, and Ku Klux Klansmen bombed the 16th Street Baptist Church, killing four young girls in 1963—made a vivid impression over the new medium of television news, spurring the Civil Rights Act of 1964, and created a reputation from which Birmingham still suffered a generation later.

But in recent years Birmingham has worked to improve race relations and has developed a new economic base to generate growth. Health care is one major industry: Birmingham has some of the largest and most advanced medical care centers in the South, and is especially renowned for its sports medicine facilities and specialists. Banking is the other: While Atlanta's banks foundered and were acquired by outsiders, Birmingham became the largest southern banking center after Charlotte, North Carolina. But city leaders worry that downtown may become "irrelevant," and white movement to newer suburbs has arguably increased racial polarization. The city's population has declined by 100,000 since 1960 and was 74% black in 2000. Whites have been moving out of Birmingham's Jefferson County southeast to Shelby County, which grew 44% in the 1990s—the fastest growth in the state. As a result, Jefferson County, once more Republican than most of Alabama, votes Democratic in close statewide elections, while Shelby County is one of the most Republican counties in the state.

The 6th Congressional District of Alabama, which once included all of Birmingham and most of Jefferson County, is now the suburban Birmingham-area district and strongly Republican. It includes parts of Jefferson County (such as prosperous Mountain Brook), and stretches southwest to Tuscaloosa and south along Interstate 65 halfway to Montgomery. In 2002, the Democratic line-drawers made it even more Republican, removing the last part of Birmingham and some black precincts in Tuscaloosa, and adding most of fast-growing St. Clair County north of Shelby County. Today, this is one of the most Republican districts in the nation: it voted 74% for George W. Bush in 2000—his second-best district outside of Texas. In 2004, it broke even harder for Bush, giving him 78% and ranking as his second-best district in the nation.

The congressman from the 6th District is Republican Spencer Bachus (pronounced *BACK-us*). A Birmingham native, he owned a sawmill company and practiced law. Elected to the state legislature in 1982, he was an activist—though one of very few Republicans. He was campaign manager when Guy Hunt was elected governor in 1986 and was the first Republican elected to the state school board in more than 100 years. After running unsuccessfully for attorney general in 1990, he became Republican state chairman. When the 6th District was radically redrawn in 1992, he won a Republican runoff and defeated incumbent Ben Erdreich, a moderate Democrat.

Bachus has a mostly conservative voting record and has been an aggressive lawmaker and investigator. As chairman of Banking's oversight subcommittee, he discovered that the Community Development Financial Institute, which Bill Clinton established in 1994, directed $11 million in loans to four banks with ties to Hillary Rodham Clinton without proper documentation; the two top CDFI officials resigned as a consequence. With George W. Bush in the White House, Bachus had a less adversarial role as chairman of the Financial Institutions and Consumer Credit Subcommittee, although he was an early critic of then-Securities and Exchange Commission chairman Harvey Pitt. He helped to enact changes in the Fair Credit Reporting Act, which provided consumers additional access to their credit reports and helped to cut back on identity theft, but also stripped away some state law privacy protections. In 2006, he helped to enact reforms of the federal deposit insurance system. Later that year, he pushed enactment of the controversial ban on Internet gambling, much of which is based overseas. He became something of a maverick on foreign policy, as an unlikely crusader for international debt relief for poor Third World nations. He criticized the Bush administration's dealings with the genocidal regime in Sudan and was a prime backer of the Sudan Peace Act, which threatens diplomatic reprisals and supports rebel groups. Locally, he helped to expand the Cahaba River National Wildlife Refuge.

For nearly two years, he competed with Richard Baker of Louisiana for what each hoped would be the chairmanship of the Financial Services Committee after the 2006 election. It turned out that the prize was only the ranking minority position, but the competition remained fierce. Bachus contended that he worked better with colleagues, and interest groups, than the sometimes independent

Baker. He benefited from his more generous campaign contributions to other Republicans (more than $800,000), and undoubtedly was helped by his early support for John Boehner for Majority Leader in early 2006; Baker had backed Roy Blunt. Bachus won on a 22–7 vote of the leadership-dominated Republican Steering Committee. "Barney Frank and I represent very different political philosophies, but when we disagree, we do so amicably," Bachus said, referring to the new Democratic chairman. "I look forward to working with him." Although the committee has had a recent history of bipartisanship, his willingness to cooperate likely will be tested frequently.

Bachus has not had a Democratic challenger since 1998. In 2004, he faced a primary challenge: Phillip Jauregui, the lawyer for ousted Alabama Chief Justice Roy Moore. This looked like a conflict between religious and business conservatives but Bachus emphasized his conservative credentials and proudly noted that he had the lowest ACLU rating in the Alabama delegation; he won 87%–13%. Although he has voiced interest in a statewide race, his new position on Financial Services might keep him in the House.

SEVENTH DISTRICT

Rep. Artur Davis (D)

Elected 2002, 3d term; b. Oct. 9, 1967, Montgomery; home, Birmingham; Harvard U., B.A. 1990, J.D. 1993; Lutheran; single.

Professional Career: Asst. U.S. atty., 1994-1998, Practicing atty., 1998-2002

DC Office: 208 CHOB, 20515, 202-225-2665; Fax: 202-226-9567; Web site: www.house.gov/arturdavis/.

District Offices: Birmingham, 205-254-1960; Demopolis, 334-287-0860; Livingston, 205-652-5834; Selma, 334-877-4414; Tuscaloosa, 205-752-5380.

Committees: *House Administration* (6th of 6 D). *Judiciary* (20th of 23 D): The Constitution, Civil Rights & Civil Liberties; Crime, Terrorism & Homeland Security; Immigration, Citizenship, Refugees, Border Security & International Law. *Ways & Means* (24th of 24 D): Income Security & Family Support; Social Security.

Group Ratings

	ADA	ACLU	AFS	LCV	ITIC	NTU	COC	ACU	CFG	FRC
2006	75	68	100	50	71	16	73	44	25	28
2005	80	—	100	56	—	18	70	28	11	8

National Journal Ratings

	2005 LIB	—	2005 CONS		2006 LIB	—	2006 CONS
Economic	62%	—	38%		61%	—	39%
Social	64%	—	36%		62%	—	37%
Foreign	56%	—	43%		56%	—	43%

Key Votes of the 109th Congress

1. Estate Tax Repeal	N	5. Limit Interstate Abortion	Y	9. Build Border Fence	Y
2. Limit CAFE Standards	Y	6. Extend Patriot Act	Y	10. CAFTA	N
3. FY06 Spending Curb	N	7. Bar Same Sex Marriage	Y	11. Oppose Iraq Withdrawal	N
4. Drilling in ANWR	Y	8. Stem Cell Research $	Y	12. Detainee Tribunals	Y

Election Results

2006 general	Artur Davis (D) .... unopposed		($579,160)
2006 primary	Artur Davis (D) 93,586	(91%)	
	Eddison Walters (D) 9,358	(9%)	
2004 general	Artur Davis (D) 183,408	(75%)	($1,068,606)
	Steve Cameron (R) 61,019	(25%)	

Prior Winning Percentages: 2002 (92%)

The People		Race/Ethnic Origin	Ancestry	
Area size:	8,780 sq. mi.	35.5% White	USA: 7.1%	English: 3.7%
Urban population:	72.2%	61.7% Black	Irish: 3.5%	
Rural population:	27.8%	0.6% Asian	**2004 Presidential Vote**	
Pop. 2000:	635,300	0.2% Native Am.	Kerry (D) 160,875	(64%)
Pop. 2005 (est):	610,950	0.0% Hawaiian	Bush (R) 88,433	(35%)
Median income:	$26,672	0.6% Two+ races	Other 233	(0%)
Poverty status:	24.7%	0.1% Other	**2000 Presidential Vote**	
Military veterans:	11.6%	1.3% Hispanic Origin	Gore (D) 158,580	(66%)
			Bush (R) 78,670	(33%)
			Other 1,827	(1%)
			Cook Partisan Voting Index: D +17	

Occupation   Blue collar: 28.6%   White collar: 53.4%   Gray collar: 18.0%

Alabama celebrates its black heritage more than any other state, building striking memorials to the civil rights movement in Montgomery and Birmingham, commemorating with dignified restraint a history that was full of raucous hatred and moving sacrifice. Blacks first came here as slaves; the last slave ship to the United States, the *Clotilde*, docked in Mobile in 1859, where its cargo was then set free. Blacks were part of the great migration into the cottonlands after the Jacksonians swept the Indians out of the Southeast and sent them on their Trail of Tears to what is now Oklahoma. Today, Alabama's rural blacks are still clustered in the Black Belt of fertile dark soil across the center of the state. In Selma, the site of one of the final battles of the Civil War and founded by Alabama's one vice president, William Rufus King, Sheriff Jim Clark's troops beat up peaceful marchers on the Edmund Pettus Bridge in demonstrations that led to the march on Montgomery and the 1965 Voting Rights Act. All 10 of Alabama's majority-black counties are in the rich farm country of the Black Belt but most Alabama blacks now live in urban areas—one-quarter in metropolitan Birmingham.

The 7th Congressional District of Alabama was created in 1992 as a black-majority district. It includes Black Belt counties where the Alabama and Tombigbee Rivers flow past old plantations and the catfish industry has thrived, plus part of Tuscaloosa, home of the University of Alabama, and nearby Vance, site of a Mercedes factory. Most of its people are in Birmingham and surrounding Jefferson County and it is solidly Democratic. John Kerry won 64%-35% here in 2004, one of his best showings in the Deep South.

The congressman from the 7th District is Artur Davis, first elected at age 35 in 2002. Davis grew up in Montgomery and was raised by his mother and grandmother. He graduated from Harvard and Harvard Law School (where he was impressed by a fellow student named Barack Obama), before returning to Alabama. After working as an intern in the Southern Poverty Law Center and as a clerk to federal Judge Myron Thompson, he served four years as an assistant U.S. attorney. Later, he practiced law in Birmingham. In 2000, he challenged 7th District incumbent Earl Hilliard in the Democratic primary. He criticized the incumbent's controversial trip to Libya, taken despite the State Department ban on travel in what was then a terrorist state, and argued that Hilliard failed to aid his financially pressed district. Davis ran a vigorous campaign, but lost 58%-34%. In 2002 Davis ran again; the district had been slightly altered by redistricting. Much of the dialogue focused on race and Middle East politics. Campaign surrogates for Hilliard questioned whether Davis was "black enough" to represent the district. Referring to Davis' background as a federal prosecutor, Hilliard claimed that, "the only thing has done for black people is put them in jail." Davis framed the debate as a generational battle between old-style black machine politics and a fresher, more effective approach. One key to Davis's victory appeared to be strong financial backing from supporters of Israel: Hilliard was one of only 21 House members to vote against a resolution supporting Israel's fight against terrorism, just weeks after Palestinian suicide bombers killed hundreds of Israelis. In the primary, Hilliard led Davis by only 46%-43% and was forced into a runoff. Several Congressional Black Caucus members, plus Al Sharpton, came in to campaign for Hilliard; Davis accused Hilliard of being divisive and called for "healing." Outspending Hilliard by nearly $180,000, Davis won the runoff 56%-44%. He had no trouble winning in November, or since then.

In the House Davis quickly reached out to other Black Caucus members, though some tensions remained with Hilliard's allies. Davis has a moderate voting record for House Democrats, with a less liberal ranking than Hilliard, and has become a far more active player in internal party politics. He focused on rural issues and led successful fights to reverse funding cuts for minority land-grant colleges and the HOPE program to revitalize public housing. He helped to win approval of a new interstate highway through Black Belt counties. With Christopher Smith of New Jersey, he filed a bill to increase the availability of umbilical cord blood and bone marrow for patients who need a transplant; President Bush signed the bill in December 2006. Working with a bipartisan coalition, he called for trade protection to level the playing field with China; his particular concerns were the steel and catfish industries.

Davis represents a new generation of African-American political leadership and has told local audiences that blacks must move beyond a preoccupation with race. But he also criticized national Democrats—including John Kerry's presidential campaign—for calling on black lawmakers only to rally black voters. Rahm Emanuel selected Davis as a vice-chairman of the DCCC for 2006, where Davis mentored prominent Democratic candidates, including Tim Mahoney of Florida. Davis has been a vice-chairman of the centrist New Democrats, and he warns Democrats about catering to special interests. Following the 2006 election, he was rewarded with a Ways and Means Committee seat. Amidst the legal problems of Louisiana's Bill Jefferson, which resulted in his removal from Ways and Means, some senior Democrats viewed Davis as the heir to that committee seat; Davis was cautious not to take sides in the dicey internal party politics. In May 2007, Davis was appointed to fill the vacancy on the House Administration Committee caused by Juanita Millender-McDonald's death.

In the 2004 primary, Davis was challenged by Albert Turner, a son of a leader of Selma's "Bloody Sunday" march. Turner criticized Davis for not giving sufficient priority to Black Belt needs and called him a self-promoter. With endorsements from most leading local Democrats, Davis won 88%-12%, a bigger margin than even he expected. He chaired a health subcommittee of Republican Governor Bob Riley's Black Belt Action Commission to improve the delivery of local services. Davis is interested in running for statewide office in the future, but he ruled out a bid for Senate in 2008. He said that his polling showed that whites in Alabama are ready to vote for a black candidate who shares their social values and that he could have won against Jeff Sessions, but that a contest would have diverted him from his opportunities in the House. "Alabama today is looking more like Tennessee or North Carolina," he said. Davis could have enticing opportunities in 2010, when Riley is term-limited, and Senator Richard Shelby will be 76 and might decide not to run for reelection. In a statewide race, he would be bolstered by his moderate voting record and style, not to mention Alabama's 26% black population. The near-win of Harold Ford in Tennessee "leads me to think, as I always believed, that if you have the right message and you are sustained and focused, you'll be in the game," Davis told a local publication after the 2006 election. As he prepares for a likely statewide bid, Davis appears to fit those descriptions.

★ ALASKA ★

With 16% of the nation's land area and 0.22% of the nation's population, Alaska is America in the Arctic, a state created by a federal government which it now often resents and an individualistic society that has responded to its unique situation in creative ways that commend themselves to the attention of what Alaskans call the Lower 48 or, more simply, Outside. Alaska would not be American at all but for the expansive dream of Secretary of State William Seward, who took advantage of a fleeting opportunity to create an American Pacific empire by purchasing it from Russia in 1867 for $7.2 million (the Russian Orthodox Church still claims 30,000 members in Alaska, many of them Alaska Natives). The Alaska Territory owed most of its early growth to decisions made by the federal government. It started growing feverishly with the Klondike gold rush in 1897, just as William McKinley reaffirmed the gold standard. Anchorage, the major city here, had its beginnings in 1913 as the chief worksite of the federal government's Alaska Railroad, completed in 1923. The Alcan Highway, connecting Alaska to the Lower 48, was built by the Army in the grim war days of 1942, when the Aleutian island of Attu was held by the Japanese, the only part of the United States occupied by a foreign enemy since the War of 1812. Alaska is the only state abutting Russia, across the Bering Strait and over the North Pole, and even today Alaska remains militarily strategic. The military remains a major presence at Fort Richardson and Elmendorf Air Force Base near Anchorage and Fort Wainwright and Eielson Air Force Base near Fairbanks; the Pentagon in 2004 installed interceptors for the national missile defense system at Fort Greely 100 miles southeast.

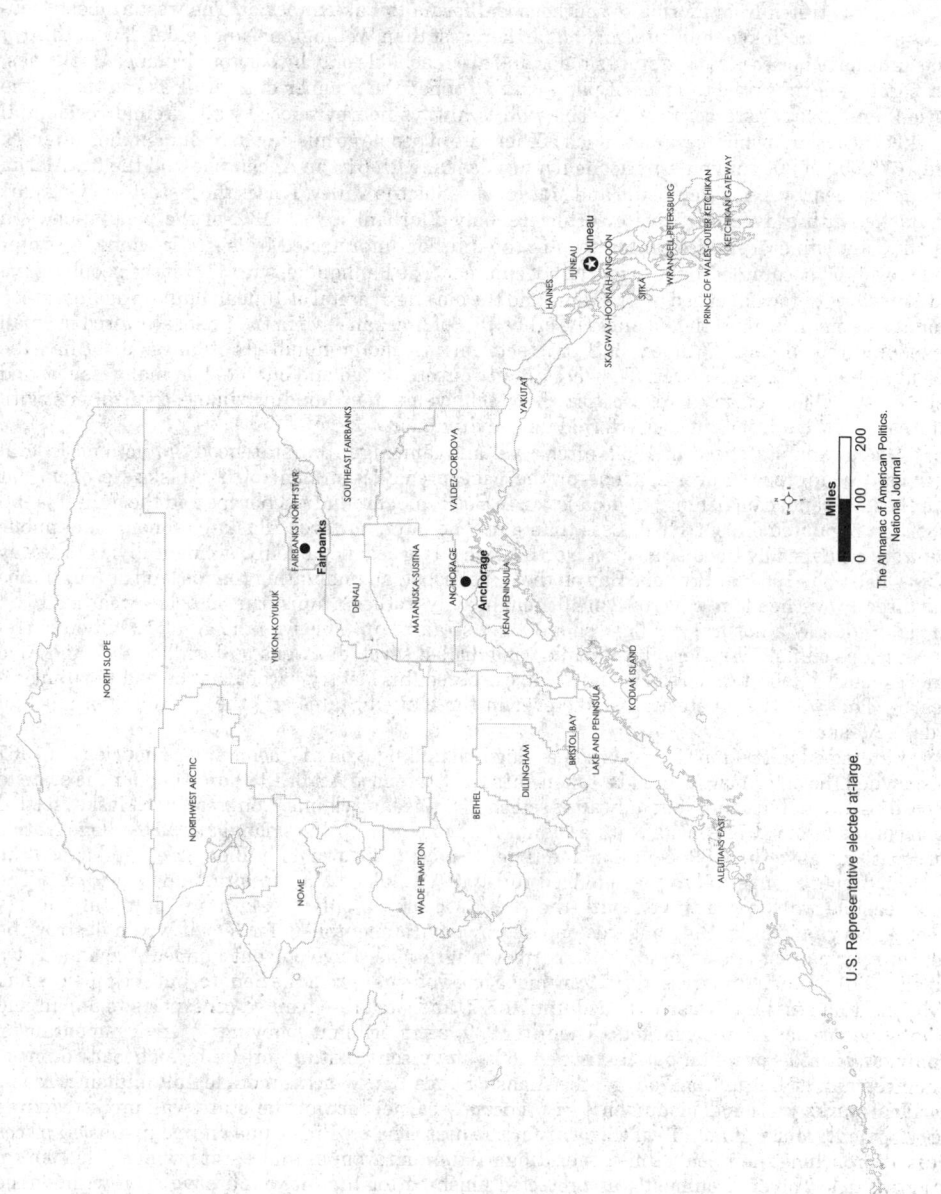

U.S. Representative elected at-large.

The Almanac of American Politics.
National Journal

Alaska's giant size remains hard for Americans to comprehend: If superimposed on the Lower 48, it would stretch from Florida to southern California to Lake Superior. The westernmost Aleutians are closer to Tokyo than Juneau and farther west than Wellington, New Zealand. One-third of Alaskans have no access to the state's roads and are reachable only by boat or airplane; Alaska has, per capita, six times the number of pilots and 16 times the number of aircraft as the rest of the nation, and 722 registered airports. The wild is always nearby; moose walk around residential neighborhoods in Anchorage, and a much higher rate of people go missing here than in the Lower 48. Only 670,000 of 300 million Americans live in Alaska, with 61% in Anchorage and the (by Alaska standards) nearby Kenai Peninsula and Matanuska-Susitna Valley. This is the fastest-growing part of Alaska, with a dynamic private sector economy. Fairbanks, with 13% of the population, is a pipeline and mineral service center deep in the interior, unprotected from Arctic winds in winter and crowds of mosquitoes in the brief but hot summer. The Panhandle, with 11% of the people, is the old Alaska, with towns settled by Russians and the old state capital of Juneau built up against steep mountains on inlets from the Pacific. The other 15% of Alaskans live in the Bush, scattered in small towns and the oil port of Valdez, in Native settlements and on hundreds of lakes; about half the people here are Alaska Natives. They are greatly outnumbered and outvoted on many issues, and yet are the object of awed respect for their achievement in building viable civilizations with impressive art traditions in such a forbidding environment.

Alaska won statehood in 1959, after a valiant campaign. But statehood did not end federal decision-making power over Alaska—or the widespread resentment of it. Alaska's economy at statehood depended on fishing, oil production in Cook Inlet around Anchorage and the military—all federally regulated or controlled. Less than a decade later, however, Alaska's economy and public life were reshaped by the discovery of North Slope oil. It began suddenly, accidentally: On the day after Christmas 1967, at Prudhoe Bay on the Arctic coast, an undulating roar as loud as four jumbo jets directly overhead drew a crowd of 40 men, heavily clothed against the 30-below weather, to an oil rig. Suddenly a natural gas flare shot 30 feet straight up: This was the great 12 billion barrel North Slope oil field. Earlier oil companies had drilled seven dry wells on Prudhoe Bay, and Arco chief executive Robert Anderson wouldn't have ordered this last try, except that he had a drilling rig nearby. This was the greatest oil strike ever in the United States and the beginning of much of today's Alaska.

Finding oil in Prudhoe Bay was something like finding it on the moon. It was not clear in 1967 who owned the oil or how it could be taken out. The Statehood Act of 1959 provided for the state to choose its own public lands, but only after settling Native land claims. Congress, not Alaska, settled such claims in the 1971 Alaska Native Claims Act which set up 12 regional and 220 village Native corporations, gave them $962 million and time to select their own 44 million acres, and ended the Interior Department's freeze that enabled the state to stake claims to mineral-rich acreage. The only feasible way to get the oil out—the Arctic Ocean ice only breaks up in late July for six weeks—was a pipeline. But that was opposed by environmentalists for fear it would destroy the delicate permafrost and interfere with caribou migrations. Development-minded Alaskans got a pipeline bill through Congress in 1973, by just a one-vote margin in the Senate, but the pipeline had to be built on stilts and wasn't opened until 1977, and Congress banned oil exports to Japan and other obvious East Asian markets. Then in 1980, after brilliant lobbying by environmentalists, Congress passed—over the objections of Alaska's two senators and in the face of tears from its Congressman-at-Large Don Young—the Alaska Lands Act, which set aside 159 million acres as national parks, national monuments or wilderness: One-third of the state was protected from development. Much, if not all, of this was for the best. The pipeline came on line just as oil prices were approaching their peak, thus generating maximum revenues to the state, which gets 100% of the royalties. The environment was protected much better than it would have been without the environmentalists' safeguards—though there was a major oil spill in March 2006 from a corroded transmission line. The caribou herd has risen from 3,000 animals to 32,000 and the Natives got more autonomy than the non-Native majority of Alaskans would have given them. With oil providing more than 80% of its revenue, the state abolished its income tax in 1980 and created a low-tax regime that has helped Alaska to grow even as oil revenues and military spending declined.

Wisely, Alaska did not squander its windfall. In 1976, Governor Jay Hammond persuaded the legislature to establish a Permanent Fund for most of the oil revenues. Each year it presents every one-year resident with a dividend of 20% of the average of profits for the preceding five years—$1,107 in 2006. More important, even though $14.3 billion has been paid in dividends, most of the money has been invested. The North Slope is producing less than half as much oil as in the late 1980s, but the Permanent Fund was worth $32.9 billion in 2006, and most of its income now comes from investments rather than oil. Some speculated that Alaska voters would pressure legislators for bigger payouts. But Alaskans have acted like investors: They want their dividend checks not just now, but in the future. In spring 2004, then-Governor Frank Murkowski urged the legislature to use earnings from the Permanent Fund to balance the budget. But the state Senate balked, and it turned out that sharply rising oil prices pushed the state's budget into surplus.

Similarly, the 12 regional Native Corporations created by the Alaska Native Claims Act have proved to be successful, not just in providing income for Natives, but in helping them preserve Native traditions and adapt to Alaska's market economy at their own pace. On Indian reservations in the Lower 48, all land is held by the tribe and supervised by the government; elections held on the political model have produced a winner-take-all politics that is too often corrupt and incapable of pursuing long-range strategies. The corporate model, on the other hand, allows the Alaska Native corporations' management more continuity in office—though some have made bad decisions and been thrown out. But the cumulative voting method, by which a minority can get a seat on the board, has produced management that is sensitive to all opinions. Huge windfalls are avoided because 70% of profits from mineral sales are shared by all corporations. But the corporation itself, not a distant federal bureaucracy, is left with the choice of how much ancestral land to retain and how much to exploit economically. Individual Natives can make the transition from their traditional communal economy, living on subsistence fishing and hunting, or make their way in the market economy; 43% of Natives now live in Anchorage, Fairbanks, Juneau, Matanuska-Susitna or the Kenai Peninsula. In 2004, the 42 regional and village Native corporations had revenues of $4.5 billion, and employed 13,000 Alaskans. Under federal law Native corporations are eligible for sole-source Pentagon contracts with no upper limit, and their federal contracts rose from $265 million in 2000 to $1.1 billion in 2004; but in 2006 there were charges of abuses in some contracts.

Not all is rosy here. Native villages in the Bush have little in the way of a private sector economy, and rates of alcoholism and suicide remain high. In the solemn mien so typical of Natives, one may be seeing the memory of great kill-offs by disease, which struck Native villages as recently as the 1920s. Native subsistence hunting was threatened by a 1989 state Supreme Court decision that struck down the subsistence preference for fishing and hunting by rural residents. The legislature refused to pass a constitutional amendment allowing it, and in 1999 the Interior Department took over regulation of fishing (it had regulated hunting since 1990) and shut down commercial and sports fishing for a time to protect Natives' subsistence. But in the long run, Natives have made great progress.

The federal government continues to make decisions that shape Alaska's economy—and not always Alaska's way, despite the clout of Ted Stevens, senator since 1968, and Don Young, Congressman-at-Large since 1973. They have failed to get approval of oil drilling in a small sliver of the Arctic National Wildlife Refuge—an area the size of Washington-area Dulles International Airport in an area the size of Delaware—although it was on the verge of being approved in 1989 when the Exxon *Valdez* ran aground in Prince William Sound in March 1989. Environmental groups have made ANWR oil drilling one of their main issues in their direct-mail fundraising even though ANWR is estimated to have between 9 and 16 billion barrels of oil, the most by far in any untapped U.S. oil field. In 2005 and 2006 the Senate approved ANWR drilling as part of its budget resolution, but that was stricken by the House when liberal Republicans threatened to withhold their votes; the House approved ANWR drilling as part of a defense appropriation, but Stevens fell three votes short of a filibuster-proof majority in the Senate to approve that. Prospects in early 2007 looked dim with Democrats in the majority in both houses. In the meantime oil production on the Slope, which peaked back in the 1980s, falls steadily—or even sharply. In March 2006 the Slope had its biggest oil spill ever, from a corroded BP transmission line, and in August 2006 BP shut down its largest field in Prudhoe Bay, eliminating half the oil production on the Slope.

The North Slope's oil has been pumped out through the pipeline since 1977, but there has been no way to get its vast quantities of natural gas out. So it's been burned off at the wellhead or pumped back into the ground; there is an estimated 30 trillion cubic feet in Prudhoe Bay and another 70 trillion cubic feet elsewhere on the Slope. Stevens worked for years to get an 80% federal loan guarantee for a gas pipeline into an energy bill, and in October 2004 inserted the proposal into the military construction appropriation. He omitted a provision guaranteeing producers a minimum price for the gas but did provide for rapid permit approval and avoidance of judicial review. Murkowski accepted two proposals—one from the three North Slope oil companies, another from a piepline company with Native corporations involved—to build the pipeline, and he urged that the state take an equity interest in the project as well. These plans faded after Murkowski's defeat in the 2006 primary; in the closing days of his administration, eight state legislators successfully sued to prevent him from signing a proposed contract with producers to develop North Slope gas reserves. In March 2007, Governor Sarah Palin, who had defeated Murkowski in the August 2006 primary, introduced the Alaska Gasline Inducement   Act, which would offer up to $500 million in seed money to help build the natural gas pipeline as well as freeze production taxes for 10 years.

Alaska remains heavily dependent on oil and on the federal government, but that is not all there is to its economy. Fishing, long its largest private employer, has stabilized as fishermen have come to accept state Fish and Game limits on boats and size of catches; the salmon fisheries here, unlike so many in the world, have not been dangerously depleted. Tourism, the number two private employer, is on the rise, with some 1.4 million tourists spending $2 billion a year; many arrive on cruise ships from which they view glaciers in the southeast, troop into Russian-settled Sitka and Juneau and, in some cases, make side trips as far inland as Denali National Park and Mount McKinley. In August 2006 voters by just 52%-48% approved a $50 per passenger cruise ship tax; the ballot proposition also taxed gambling revenues in Alaskan waters and required environmental observers to monitor the ships. Another spur is the air freight business. The Anchorage airport, near the top of the world, is seven hours from New York, Tokyo and London, and is a major cargo transfer point for UPS, FedEx, Northwest Airlines and the U.S. Postal Service. More all-cargo, wide-bodied aircraft move through Anchorage International than any other U.S. airport.

Alaska has also benefited from federal spending, including millions of dollars every year in "Stevens money"— construction, highway, sewer and harbor projects shepherded by Senator Stevens, chairman of the Appropriations Committee in 1997-2001 and 2003-05 and the most senior Republican in the Senate. Don Young, chairman of the House Transportation and Infrastructure Committee from 2001-07, has sponsored many projects as well. But in 2005 opponents of earmarking funds made a cause celebre of Young's provisions authorizing two huge proposed bridges, one from tiny Ketchikan to Gravina Island (population 50, plus the local airport) and the other from Anchorage to the largely uninhabited land two miles across Knik Arm. The former became known as "the bridge to nowhere," and attempts were made to delete it. Stevens's and Young's ability to channel funds into Alaska projects may be reduced by the fact that their party is now in the minority in both houses (though Stevens has long worked amicably with Democratic appropriators) and by new rules requiring identification of earmarks.

Politically, Alaska is heavily Republican, with a libertarian streak. In national politics, it has been solidly Republican since the 1970s because national Democrats have favored locking up natural resources. No Democrat has been elected to Congress since 1974, and if one came close in 2004, it was in unusual circumstances: Senator Frank Murkowski, elected governor in 2002, promptly appointed his daughter, state Representative Lisa Murkowski, to his U.S. Senate seat. That prompted a proposed state constitutional amendment revoking the appointive power from the governor. It passed, and the issue almost enabled former Governor Knowles, the Democrats' strongest Senate candidate in years, to beat Lisa Murkowski. But she won 49%-46%.

In state races, persona and specific issues matter more than party. Frank Murkowski was the first Republican nominee elected governor since 1978, and he was only the second governor in state history to be denied renomination in 2006. The biggest issue in the latter election was the natural gas pipeline, and the terms and conditions under which it could be built. Murkowski was criticized not only by Democrats but by many Republicans for proposing terms too favorable to the oil companies. He was opposed by former Wasilla Mayor Sarah Palin and former state Senator John Binkley. Palin, who opposed Murkowski's proposals on the gas pipeline, won 51% in the August primary; Binkley, by far the biggest spender, won 30%; Murkowski won only 19%, the most embarrassing primary performance for an incumbent governor since Democrat Preston Smith won 9% in the Texas primary in 1972. Murkowski ran ahead only in his home town of Ketchikan, at the very southern end of the Panhandle, and in the rest of the Panhandle he ran second or third. Palin's greatest strength was in her home area, the Matanuska Valley, and in greater Anchorage.

The Democratic nominee was Tony Knowles, governor from 1994 to 2002 and nearly successful Senate candidate in 2004. Knowles ran chiefly on his experience, which he claimed would allow him to negotiate the best pipeline deal for the state, while Palin cast herself as a fresh face and a maverick Republican who was unconnected to the Murkowski administration. Palin won by a 48%-41% margin, with 9% for Independent Andrew Halcro, a businessman and former Republican state representative. Palin carried greater Anchorage and her home area 54%-37%, and also carried the Fairbanks area 53%-37%. Knowles carried the Panhandle 56%-27%, where Palin had run a weak third in the Republican primary. But in the Bush, Knowles's big margins in the Native areas in the north were balanced off by Palin margins in the Valdez area and the hinterlands of Fairbanks. The Panhandle, as noted, was the odd man out, and one reason is the particular politics of Juneau.

The state's capital is remote from most Alaskans, reachable only by harrowing and often-cancelled plane rides through the fjords, and since statehood there have been efforts to move the capital to a site near Anchorage. Alaskans voted to do so in 1974, but rejected proposals to pay for it in 1978 and 1982. In 1994, Juneau, threatened with the loss of 40% of its economy, raised $1 million and defeated a proposal to move all state government by 55%-45%; in 2002 it helped defeat a proposal to move the legislature by 67%-33%.

The People		Race/Ethnic Origin			Military veterans: 71,552 (16.4%)	
Pop. 2006 (est):	670,053	423,788	67.6%	White	WWII: 7.9%	Korea: 6.9%
Pop. 2000:	626,932	21,073	3.4%	Black	Vietnam: 41.2%	Gulf War: 18.4%
Pop. 1990:	550,043	24,741	3.9%	Asian	**Most populous cities (2006):**	
Change 1990-2000:	Up 14.0%	96,505	15.4%	Native Am.	1. Anchorage	278,700
% of U.S. total:	0.2%	3,181	0.5%	Hawaiian	2. Fairbanks	31,142
Pop. rank:	48th of 50	30,454	4.9%	Two+ races	3. Juneau	30,737
Area size:	663,267 sq. mi.	1,338	0.2%	Other	4. Wasilla	9,236
State Native:	38.1%	25,852	4.1%	Hisp. Origin	5. Sitka	8,920
Non-citizen:	2.7%	**Ancestry**				
Language		German: 12.5%		Irish: 8.1%	Urban population: 65.7%	
English: 82.6%	Asian: 3.9%	English: 7.2%		USA: 4.3%	Rural population: 34.3%	
Spanish: 3.9%		Norwegian: 3.2%				

Education		Work Sector			Legislature	
H.S. Grad:	88.3%	Private: 64.9%		Govt: 26.8%	Senate	11 R 9 D
College Grad:	24.7%	Self: 8.0%		Family: 0.3%	House	23 R 17 D
Industry		Unemployment: 8.6%			Legislative Term Limits: No	
Agri: 4.9%	Con: 7.3%	**Household Income**			**Registered Voters**	
Fin: 4.6%	Info: 2.7%	<15k: 10.6%		15-35k: 21.6%	D: 66,636	(14.3%)
Mfg: 12.2%	Prof: 29.3%	35-50k: 16.0%		50-100k: 35.7%	R: 115,397	(24.7%)
Public: 10.7%	Trade: 14.2%	100-150k: 11.4%		>150k: 4.6%	O: 284,854	(61.0%)
Other: 14.2%		Median: $51,571				
Occupation		Poverty status: 9.4%				
Blue collar: 22.4%	White collar: 60.5%	**Home Value**				
Gray collar: 17.1%		<50k: 12.1%	50-100k: 17.7%	100-200k: 51.4%	200-300k: 13.7%	
		300-500k: 4.0%	>500k: 1.2%	Median: $137,400		

Presidential politics   When Alaska and Hawaii were admitted to the Union in 1959, it was expected that Alaska would vote Democratic and Hawaii Republican; it has turned out to be pretty much the other way around. Alaska voted eerily near the national average in the close elections of 1960 and 1968. Since then it has voted primarily on Alaska issues, which means against the national Democrats. In 1980, the year of the Alaska Lands Act, it gave only 26% of its votes to Jimmy Carter, who in some places ran behind Libertarian Ed Clark. In 1992, Ross Perot won 28% here, his second-best showing in the country. In 2000, George W. Bush won 59%-28%, but Ralph Nader got 10% of the vote—his best showing in the country. In 2004 Bush got

2004 Presidential Vote
Bush (R)	190,889	(61%)
Kerry (D)	111,025	(36%)
Nader (POP)	5,069	(2%)
Other	5,615	(2%)

2000 Presidential Vote
Bush (R)	167,398	(59%)
Gore (D)	79,004	(28%)
Nader (Green)	28,747	(10%)
Other	10,411	(4%)

61% and John Kerry improved on Al Gore's showing with 36%. Few expect Alaska to vote Democratic in 2008, but Democratic National Committee Chairman Howard Dean, as part of his 50-state strategy, did visit Alaska in May 2006 and urged the state party to hire more than one staffer. And in 2006 an Alaskan announced for president—former Democratic Senator (1969-81) Mike Gravel, who has lived mostly in the Washington area since his defeat in the 1980 Senate primary.

Alaska has no presidential primary. Party true believers tend to dominate the caucuses. In the January 1996 straw poll or "beauty contest," Alaska Republicans voted 33% for Pat Buchanan, 31% for Steve Forbes, and 17% for Bob Dole. But Buchanan got only 2% here in November 2000. In November 1999, the Republican Party committee voted 39-36 to hold precinct caucuses and a straw poll on January 24, 2000. About 4,000 Alaskans voted, and George W. Bush led Forbes by 5 votes. Alaska, unlike Florida, didn't have a recount. In 2004, Democrats here, like Democrats Outside, rallied early to John Kerry.

Governor

Sarah Palin (R)

Elected 2006, term expires Dec. 2010, 1st term; b. Feb. 11, 1964, Sandpoint, ID; home, Wasilla; U. of ID, B.S. 1987; Christian; married (Todd).

Elected Office: Wasilla City Cncl., 1992-96; Wasilla Mayor, 1996-2002.

Professional Career: Television sports reporter, 1987-89; Co-owner, commercial fishing operation, 1988-2007; Owner, snow machine, watercraft, and all-terrain vehicle business, 1994-97; Chairwoman, Alaska Oil and Gas Conservation Commission, 2003-2004.

Office: P.O. Box 110001, Juneau, 99811-0001, 907-465-3500; Fax: 907-465-3532; Web site: www.gov.state.ak.us.

Election Results

2006 general	Sarah Palin (R)	114,697	(48%)
	Tony Knowles (D)	97,238	(41%)
	Andrew Halcro (I)	22,443	(9%)
	Other	2,944	(1%)
2006 primary	Sarah Palin (R)	51,443	(51%)
	John Binkley (R)	30,349	(30%)
	Frank Murkowski (R)	19,412	(19%)
2002 general	Frank Murkowski (R)	129,279	(56%)
	Fran Ulmer (D)	94,216	(41%)

Sarah Palin, a Republican, was elected Alaska's youngest and first woman governor in 2006. When she began her political career she was viewed as a rising Republican star but she won election to the governorship as a maverick reformer at arm's length from her party. Born in Idaho, Palin moved to Alaska when she was three months old with her parents, a teacher and a school secretary. She grew up in Wasilla, just outside of Anchorage, played on Wasilla's state championship girls basketball team in 1982, wore the crown of Miss Wasilla in 1984 and competed in the Miss Alaska contest. She studied journalism and political science at the University of Idaho and graduated in 1987. After returning home, Palin eloped with her high school boyfriend in 1988 to save money on an expensive wedding. She helped out in her husband's family commercial fishing business and appeared occasionally as a television sportscaster.

Sounding themes that would resurface throughout her political career, Palin won a seat on the Wasilla City Council in 1992 as a "new face, new voice" and by opposing tax increases. Four years later she was elected mayor at 32 by knocking off a three-term incumbent. Palin conflicted with the city's staff and fired department heads who had stood by her predecessor, leading opponents to call her "Sarah barracuda", reviving a nickname she earned on the basketball court for her fierce and adversarial style. Palin relied on the tax revenue she once derided to help fuel the city's rapid growth by funding infrastructure improvements that attracted big-box stores; during her tenure as mayor, the city's operating budget grew from $3.9 million to $5.8 million. Wasilla's growth and booming sales tax revenues allowed her to cut property taxes; Republican Party leaders took notice and began grooming her for higher office. At the end of her second term, party leaders encouraged her to enter the 2002 race for the Republican nomination for lieutenant governor. Against veteran legislators with far more experience, Palin finished second by fewer than 2,000 votes, making a name for herself in statewide politics.

Palin campaigned actively for the Republican ticket, led by Frank Murkowski, who had served 22 years in the Senate before running for governor. After the election, Murkowski rewarded her with several job offers before she accepted an appointment in 2003 to the Alaska Oil and Gas Conservation Commission, which gave her a chance to learn about the state's energy industry. She was joined on the panel by state Republican Party Chairman Randy Ruedrich; months later, Palin emerged as the driving force behind an ethics probe of his activities. Ruedrich faced questions about conflicts of interest with oil companies; the most serious surrounded a sensitive document that was leaked to an energy lobbyist. Commission staff also complained that he had used the state office to do work for the party. As the commission's chairwoman and designated ethics officer, Palin spearheaded the investigation that ultimately prompted Ruedrich to resign from the commission. She was asked to personally search his desk and computer files for evidence relating to the allegations. Hamstrung by confidentiality rules, Palin was unable to talk about the case; she grew frustrated and resigned from the commission just 11 months after accepting the post. Her efforts were later vindicated when Ruedrich admitted ethics violations and paid a record $12,000 civil fine.

Ruedrich, however, had already been reconfirmed as Republican chairman and Palin grew estranged from the party. She contemplated a primary challenge in 2004 against Senator Lisa Murkowski, who had been appointed by her father to succeed him in the Senate; she instead endorsed conservative Mike Miller in the primary. Palin also joined with Democratic state Representative Eric Croft to file an ethics complaint against Alaska Attorney General Gregg Renkes, who had close political ties to Governor Frank Murkowski. The complaint alleged that Renkes' ownership in a coal company represented a conflict of interest when he negotiated an international trade deal with Taiwan; her stand was again vindicated when Renkes resigned his position.

While she firmly established herself as a party outsider, Palin still harbored statewide ambitions. She kept her name before the voters by appearing in a television ad in early 2005 to support a proposed pipeline that would carry natural gas from the North Slope to Valdez, where it could be liquefied and transported in tankers. The plan differed from the approach backed by Governor Murkowski and the state's major oil producers that would construct a pipeline from Alaska through Canada to the lower 48 states. In October 2005, before Murkowski decided whether he would seek another term, Palin entered the Republican gubernatorial primary.

Murkowski suffered politically from his decision to appoint his daughter as his Senate successor and for purchasing a state jet for his travel. He also faced criticism that the natural gas pipeline deal that he had negotiated was a sweetheart deal with oil producers. Against this backdrop, Palin's outsider status and engaging campaign style connected with voters even as opponents criticized her light resume and claimed her answers to policy questions lacked substance. In a profile just before the August 22 primary, the weekly newspaper *Anchorage Press* described Palin as "a small-town, angel-faced mother of four, an avid hunter and a fisher with a killer smile who wears designer glasses and heels, and hair like modern sculpture, who's taking it to the boys every so softly." Palin won the three-way gubernatorial primary with 51%, followed by former state Senator John Binkley with 30% and Murkowski with 19%.

In the general election, Palin faced former Democratic Governor Tony Knowles. He left office in 2002, barred from serving more than two consecutive terms, and lost a 2004 Senate race against Lisa Murkowski. Knowles, who had entered the race late, ran on experience and said he was the best candidate to negotiate a pipeline deal that could deliver Alaska's great natural gas reserves to the market. Palin entered the general election with a double digit advantage in the polls, but she also had the challenge of rallying the party and the leadership; this included Ruedrich, who rebuffed her calls to resign. But in an election year when the national mood seemed to be running against incumbent Republicans, Palin's outsider status was a blessing to the party. On Election Day, Palin defeated Knowles 48%-41% with independent Andrew Halcro, a businessman and former Republican state representative, winning 9%.

Dominating the state agenda in 2007 was the construction of a natural gas pipeline. Alaska legislators had filed a lawsuit in November that had prevented Murkowski from sealing the pipeline deal he had negotiated with the oil companies. Palin favored a market-driven plan aimed at getting large producers to compete against each other. In March she proposed the Alaska Gasline Inducement Act, which would provide up to $500 million in seed money to begin the process of constructing a natural gas pipeline. It would also freeze production taxes for 10 years for producers that agree to transport their gas through the pipeline. BP, Exxon Mobil and ConocoPhillips said that, under Palin's plan, they would neither bid on the project license nor commit their gas to the pipeline if another company was selected to build it. Palin also introduced ethics reform legislation and a budget that reduces state spending by $124 million, which was short of her goal of $150 million in cuts. Palin had exceptionally high approval ratings through mid-2007 and received high marks for her accessibility, a change from the Murkowski administration. But as she moved beyond the first 100 days, Palin faced the challenge of marshalling those positives into accomplishments, not the least of which is the multi-billion dollar construction of a project critical to the state's economy.

Senior Senator

Ted Stevens (R)

Appointed Dec. 1968, seat up 2008, 6th full term; b. Nov. 18, 1923, Indianapolis, IN; home, Girdwood; U.C.L.A., B.A. 1947, Harvard, LL.B. 1950; Episcopalian; married (Catherine).

Military Career: Army Air Corps, 1943-46 (WWII).

Elected Office: AK House of Reps., 1964-68.

Professional Career: Practicing atty., 1950-53, 1961-68; U.S. Atty., 1953-56; U.S. Dept. of Interior, Legis. Cnsl., 1956-58, Asst. to Secy., 1958-60, Solicitor, 1960-61.

DC Office: 522 HSOB, 20510, 202-224-3004; Fax: 202-224-2354; Web site: stevens.senate.gov.

State Offices: Anchorage, 907-271-5915; Bethel, 907-543-1638; Fairbanks, 907-456-0261; Juneau, 907-586-7400; Kenai, 907-283-5808; Ketchikan, 907-225-6880; Wasilla, 907-376-7665.

Committees: *Appropriations* (2d of 14 R): Defense (RMM); Interior, Environment & Related Agencies; Commerce, Justice, Science & Related Agencies; Homeland Security; Labor, Health and Human Services, Education & Related Agencies; Transportation, Housing and Urban Development & Related Agencies. *Commerce, Science & Transportation* (Vice Chmn. of 11 R). *Homeland Security & Governmental Affairs* (2d of 8 R): Disaster Recovery (RMM); Federal Financial Management, Government Information, Federal Services & International Security; Oversight of Government Management, the Federal Workforce & the District of Columbia. *Rules & Administration* (2d of 9 R).

Group Ratings

	ADA	ACLU	AFS	LCV	ITIC	NTU	COC	ACU	CFG	FRC
2006	5	17	13	14	100	63	100	64	47	87
2005	5	—	0	5	—	68	100	80	76	—

National Journal Ratings

	2005 LIB	—	2005 CONS	2006 LIB	—	2006 CONS
Economic	25%	—	72%	41%	—	58%
Social	47%	—	52%	41%	—	58%
Foreign	0%	—	74%	24%	—	74%

Key Votes of the 109th Congress

1. Bar ANWR Drilling	N	5. Confirm Samuel Alito	Y	9. Limit Interstate Abortion	Y
2. FY06 Spending Curb	Y	6. Path to Citizenship	Y	10. CAFTA	Y
3. Estate Tax Repeal	Y	7. Bar Same Sex Marriage	Y	11. Urge Iraq Withdrawal	N
4. Raise Minimum Wage	N	8. Stem Cell Research $	Y	12. Provide Detainee Rights	N

Election Results

2002 general	Ted Stevens (R)	179,438	(78%)	($2,295,429)
	Frank Vondersaar (D)	24,133	(11%)	($1,049)
	Jim Sykes (Green)	16,608	(7%)	
	Other	9,369	(4%)	
2002 primary	Ted Stevens (R)	64,315	(89%)	
	Mike Aubrey (R)	7,997	(11%)	
1996 general	Ted Stevens (R)	177,893	(77%)	($2,711,710)
	Jed Whittaker (Green)	29,037	(13%)	
	Theresa Obermeyer (D)	23,977	(10%)	

Prior Winning Percentages: 1990 (66%); 1984 (71%); 1978 (76%); 1972 (77%); 1970 (60%)

No other senator fills so central a place in his state's public and economic life as Ted Stevens of Alaska; quite possibly no other senator ever has. "They sent me here," Stevens said in one impassioned debate, "to stand up for the state of Alaska." He is the longest-serving Republican senator in the United States. He was President Pro Tempore of the Senate, and thus third in line for the presidency, from 2003-07. He was chairman of the Appropriations Committee for 6½ years (1997-2001, 2003-05), and chairman of the Commerce Committee for two years (2005-07); he has chaired or been ranking member on the Defense Appropriations Subcommittee for more than 20 years. He has also been for a quarter century the leading public policymaker for and about Alaska. "We ask for special consideration," Stevens is not too shy to say, "because no one else is that far away, no one else has the problems that we have or the potential that we have, and no one else deals with the federal government day in and day out the way we do." Probably more than any other senator, Stevens has shaped the public institutions and private economy of his state—and he doesn't seem finished yet.

Stevens grew up in Indiana and California in very modest surroundings, served in World War II flying C-46s and C-47s, graduated from UCLA and Harvard Law, then moved to Alaska in 1950, driving up the Alaska Highway with his new bride. He was U.S. attorney in Fairbanks and worked in the Interior Department in Washington. In 1962, he ran for the Senate and lost to Democrat Ernest Gruening by a 58%-42% margin. He then served in the legislature in Juneau and was appointed to the U.S. Senate by Governor Walter Hickel in December 1968, at 45. He quickly gained a seat on Appropriations and worked on Alaska issues of all description. He has not been entirely successful. He could not stop the Alaska Lands Act in 1980 and has failed repeatedly to win approval of oil drilling in the Arctic National Wildlife Refuge, often by agonizingly close margins. But he played a major role on the Native Claims Act in 1971 and got the oil pipeline through by one vote in 1973. In 1995, he and Frank Murkowski finally secured the repeal of the 1977 law forbidding exports of Alaskan oil, thus opening up the obvious East Asian markets.

On non-Alaska issues, Stevens has a moderate voting record. On the Defense Appropriations Subcommittee, he has worked for years with Democrat Daniel Inouye—another decorated World War II veteran who has represented an offshore state since the 1960s—to support robust defense spending and has been a staunch advocate of missile defense. On taking over the chairmanship of the Commerce Committee in 2005 (replacing John McCain, who has often attacked Stevens's Alaska projects as pork barrel spending), Stevens reshuffled the subcommittees to give him control over telecommunications. In June 2006 he got the committee to approve 15–7 a revision of the 1996 telecommunications law removing barriers to phone companies providing video services, in competition with cable companies; rejected by an 11-11 tie vote was a "net neutrality" provision which would have barred price discrimination by telephone and cable companies. His bill also stabilized the $7 billion Universal Service Fund which provides money for underserved communities, of which Alaska has many. Public radio has a larger audience in Alaska than in any other state—commercial radio is unprofitable in the Bush—and Stevens has been a strong supporter of public radio and television. For most of 2006 he struggled to get the 60 votes required to pass the bill on the floor over a filibuster, but was not able to do so. In 2007, as he turned over the chair to Inouye, it appeared that the telephone companies were less eager for a new bill because they feared Democrats would attach a net neutrality provision.

Stevens also led the Commerce Committee in revising the 1976 Magnuson-Stevens fisheries act, last updated in 1996. Changes were needed because most fish stocks have been depleted; Alaska, with strict state regulation, has done a better job of preserving its salmon stocks. His bill passed the Senate in June 2006, with provisions penalizing fisheries which exceed catch limits by lowering limits for the next year. The House Resources Committee produced a weaker bill; in December Stevens made concessions, dropping the penalties and instead required the eight regional fishery councils to develop and implement plans to end overfishing within two years. It had a 10-year time limit for permits and guidelines for cap-and-trade quotas. It passed in the closing days of the 109th Congress. Stevens responded to the March 2006 North Slope oil spill caused by a corroded pipeline with a bill, passed in December, to subject low-stress pipelines to the same standards and regulations as other hazardous-liquid pipelines. Stevens does not back all proposals for development in Alaska. In 2006 he opposed the proposed Pebble gold, copper and molybdenum mine in southwest Alaska because of its effect on commercial, sport and subsistence salmon fishing; on this he agreed with former Governor Tony Knowles and the *Anchorage Daily News*.

For years Stevens has been known for—and seems to want to be known for—his terrible temper. When he succeeded Mark Hatfield as Appropriations Committee chairman in 1997, he told his colleagues, "Senator Hatfield had the patience of Job and the disposition of a saint. I don't. The watch has changed. I'm a mean, miserable SOB." Some of this, at least, is an act: Stevens gets along with appropriators of all parties, at least if they do their homework and respect his prerogatives. He does not take kindly to those who vote against what he considers Alaska's interests for what he considers frivolous or bogus reasons. In the debate over oil drilling in the Arctic National Wildlife Refuge in March 2003, he said, "I have never broken a commitment in my life. I make this commitment: People who vote against this today are voting against me, and I will not forget it." But that may not mean direct retaliation; as Stevens put it on another occasion, "There are those people I am not going to go out of my way to help."

He showed his temper as he tried to open up the Arctic National Wildlife Refuge to oil drilling. Stevens has argued that he had a commitment when the Alaska Lands Act was passed in 1980 that Congress would allow drilling after a study. But the senators who made the commitment, Henry Jackson and Paul Tsongas, are long gone. Congress seemed on the point of allowing drilling in 1989, but support evaporated when the Exxon Valdez went aground and produced a giant oil spill. In 2005 Stevens got ANWR drilling into the budget resolution, so that it could pass the Senate with less than 60 votes. But the House wouldn't go along; liberal Republicans refused to support the budget resolution with ANWR drilling, and pro-drilling Democrats would not support the Republicans' budget resolution. In December 2005 Stevens put ANWR drilling into the defense appropriation. But his longtime Appropriations colleague Robert Byrd raised the point of order barring unrelated provisions from final bills. Stevens, noting that that point of order is seldom enforced, was furious. "This has been the saddest day of my life," he said. "It's a day I don't want to remember." With Democrats in control, Stevens has conceded that ANWR drilling is going nowhere soon.

At some point, probably in the 1990s, Alaskans began referring matter-of-factly to funding for federal projects as "Stevens money." He argues that Alaska has special needs and special handicaps and therefore deserves special treatment. "Congress has not awakened to the fact that we've got a state with one-fifth the land in this country. My mission is to try to make Congress understand that the promise of statehood is that we should have the ability to establish a workable private-enterprise economy in the areas of Alaska that want it. And that's basically 90% of the state." His prowess is legendary. In 1998, Stevens sought a land trade for a seven-mile road through the Izembeck National Wildlife Refuge—which the Clinton Interior Department wanted to declare off-limits—so that the tiny Aleutian village of King Cove would have access to medical facilities. The administration offered three alternatives; Stevens took all three: $37.7 million for an airport road, medical clinic and doctor and nurse. In 1998, he set up the Denali Commission (Denali is the Native name of Mount McKinley), which funds infrastructure projects—water and sewer, electricity—in central Alaska, to the tune of $38 million in 2001, $45 million in 2002 and $48 million in 2003. When a Stevens aide showed Stevens an *Anchorage Daily News* article about a volunteer group that had raised $6,000 to promote a string of public-use huts linked by hiking trails, he thought it was a good idea and, without consulting the group, put in $500,000 for a backcountry hut network at Snow River near Seward. "That's crazy!" exulted the group's vice president. "There's, like, tears in my eyes." It could be argued that Stevens is less a legislator than he is a philanthropist in the mode of John D. Rockefeller or Andrew Carnegie, although of course he is not spending his own money.

It might be said that Stevens is a philanthropist operating in the Senate Appropriations Committee. The list of Alaska projects Stevens has funded is long: $17 million for anti-alcohol funding, $5.5 million to the National Energy Technology Laboratory at the University of Alaska in Fairbanks, $35 million for Denali Commission rural health clinics, $10 million for the Alaska Fisheries Marketing Board (created in a 2002 appropriation), $16.8 million for sea lion research at the Alaska SeaLife Center (a pollock fishery was closed because of a decline in number of sea lions), $150,000 for a botanical garden in Anchorage, $900,000 for an aquarium in Ketchikan and $525,000 to upgrade a quarry in Nome, $400,000 for an Anchorage homeless shelter, $750,000 for quarry upgrades for the Bering Straits Native corporation, $7.5 million for Army housing in Alaska, $450,000 for research on salmon as baby food. He has inserted into appropriations provisions limiting judicial review of timber sales in the Tongass National Forest, 200 seasonal visas for Japanese technicians to evaluate salmon eggs (the Japanese will only buy them if they are Japanese-inspected and without those sales some fisheries would be unprofitable). Even Stevens's critics concede that he does not shovel money into projects willy-nilly. He shifts money around if he thinks it is not well spent and, past the age of 80, he is still prepared to defend every single project on the merits. Proposals to require identification of the proposers of earmarks seem unlikely to phase Stevens; he is happy to take credit for his work. And he can get angry when Alaska projects are challenged. In October 2005, when Senator Tom Coburn moved to defund the Ketchikan-Gravina bridge—a "bridge to nowhere" to its critics—and use the money to rebuild the I-10 bridge in New Orleans destroyed by Hurricane Katrina, Stevens responded stormily. "I will put the Senate on notice—and I don't kid people—if the Senate decides to discriminate against our state, to take money from our state, I'll resign from this body. This is not the Senate I came to. This is not the Senate I've devoted 37 years to, if one senator can decide he'll take all the money from one state to solve a problem of another." It was effective: Coburn's amendment was rejected 82-15.

Since the framing of the Native Claims Act—perhaps the most creative and successful legislation concerning American aboriginal peoples—Stevens has continued to work tirelessly to help Alaska Natives, who vote heavily Democratic in most elections. They have voted overwhelmingly for Stevens in recent elections, but he could win without their support easily. He skillfully elicits consensus with Native leaders when opinion is divided, getting more health and sanitation aid to Bush villages and funding for health research on fetal alcohol syndrome and cancers common among Natives, and to gain preference in federal contracting for Native corporations. At the same time, Stevens is not uncritical of Native leaders. In October 2002, he urged the Alaska Federation of Natives not to funnel their requests for federal money through the 229 individual village-based tribes granted official status by the Clinton administration, but to consolidate federal requests so that "the very, very poor communities that don't have that ability to hire consultants, to hire grantsmen, people to write applications," get assistance. In a January 2004 appropriation, he set up a commission to draw up a new legal and governmental system for rural Alaska and an economic development commission funded through the Denali Commission to "promote private sector investment to reduce poverty in economically distressed rural villages." He evidently wants to prevent the emergence of a separate Native legal system. As he said on the Alaska Public Radio Network, "The road they're on now is the road to the destruction of statehood, because the Native population is increasing at a much greater rate than the non-Native population. I don't know if you realize that. And they want to have total jurisdiction over anything that happens in a village without regard to state law and without regard to federal law."

Stevens played a crucial role in the 1970s in getting the oil pipeline approved. More recently he has tried to advance proposals for a natural gas pipeline. For years oil drillers in Prudhoe Bay have been pumping natural gas back into the ground; there are an estimated 30 trillion cubic feet there and another 70 trillion cubic feet elsewhere on the North Slope—all undeliverable to customers without a pipeline. Pipeline provisions had been included in the 2001 and 2003 energy bills—a loan guarantee of 80% of construction costs, a price floor for the producers, accelerated depreciation, limited judicial review—but the energy bill remained stalled for other reasons. In October 2004 Stevens decided to insert the pipeline provisions, except for the price floor, into the must-pass military construction appropriation; he also got accelerated depreciation into the corporate tax bill. The rider specified a route through central Alaska, not directly east into Canada, and provided for in-state use of gas. Governor Frank Murkowski quickly solicited contracts from two consortiums, one being the three North Slope oil companies, the other a pipeline company with Native corporation participation; Stevens endorsed Murkowski's proposal that the state have an equity share. There are still other barriers to overcome—federal and Canadian regulatory approval, private financing—but the gas pipeline, for the first time, seems likely to be built. And in 2004 he secured approval of loan guarantees for a natural gas pipeline.

Stevens's work has not gone unappreciated. In January 2000, he was named Alaskan of the Century. In July 2000, Anchorage Airport was named the Ted Stevens International Airport and the Challenger Center in Kenai became the Ted and Catherine Stevens Center for Space Science Technology. Stevens was criticized in a December 2003 *Los Angeles Times* story for investing in local Alaskan properties with his brother-in-law and for providing help to co-investors and a tenant (one of the Native corporations) in buildings he co-owned. Stevens insisted he was a "passive investor" and since sold the interests and placed the proceeds in a blind trust. In 2006 his son, state Senator Ben Stevens, was criticized for some of his business dealings and his office was searched by the FBI.

Stevens has been reelected easily. In the August 1996 Republican primary a banker and former legislator spent $1.3 million of his own money and charged that Stevens was insufficiently conservative. Stevens won 59%-27%. His Democratic opponent that year blamed Stevens for her husband's failure to pass the Alaska bar on 22 separate tries; Stevens won 77%-13%. In November 2002 his Democratic opponent, a denizen of the hip town of Homer, charged that Stevens was part of a government conspiracy to keep him under constant surveillance. Stevens was reelected 78%-11% margin, carrying all but three precincts. He campaigned actively for his 22-year colleague Frank Murkowski in the 2002 governor race and for his new colleague, Murkowski's daughter Lisa Murkowski, in the 2004 Senate race. Eight days after the 2006 election he announced that he would run for reelection in 2008, when he will be 85. "While the recent election did not go my party's way, I come out of the campaign more determined than ever to fight for Alaska's interests in Washington, D.C."

Stevens has shown no sign of slowing down and enters any contest with formidable strength. But Democrats nevertheless believed he might be vulnerable after news of an FBI corruption investigation in Alaska that produced guilty pleas from two close associates of Stevens, a July 2007 raid on the senator's home in Girdwood and 2006 raids on the offices of six Alaska state legislators, including his son, Ben. In May 2007, VECO Corp. executives Bill Allen and Rick Smith pleaded guilty to bribing four government officials, including an unnamed "State Senator B" who received hundreds of thousands of dollars from VECO, an Alaska-based oil-support contracting firm, for unspecified consulting work. Allen had donated over $50,000 to Ted Stevens' reelection campaigns since 2000 and had overseen the remodeling of the senator's Girdwood home. According to newspaper reports, bills for the construction were sent to Allen and VECO.

Days after Allen's guilty plea, Ted Stevens withdrew his support for an oft-maligned marketing program that had funneled over $100 million to select Alaska companies. In the subsequent month, the DSCC stepped up its candidate recruitment efforts, hoping to convince Anchorage Mayor Mark Begich or former state House Minority Leader Ethan Berkowitz to run. A host of other Democrats and Republicans also were said to be considering running. In June, Stevens candidly acknowledged his worries that the FBI probe would hurt him in 2008. "If this is still hanging around a year from November, it could cause me some trouble," he told the *Associated Press*.

Junior Senator

Lisa Murkowski (R)

Appointed Dec. 2002, seat up 2010, 1st full term; b. May 22, 1957, Ketchikan; home, Anchorage; Willamette U., 1975-77, Georgetown U., B.A. 1980, Willamette U., J.D. 1985; Catholic; married (Verne Martell).

Elected Office: AK House of Reps., 1998-02.

Professional Career: Anchorage Dist. Court Clerk's Office, atty., 1987-89; Practicing atty., 1989-98.

DC Office: 709 HSOB, 20510, 202-224-6665; Fax: 202-224-5301; Web site: murkowski.senate.gov.

State Offices: Anchorage, 907-271-3735; Bethel, 907-543-1639; Fairbanks, 907-456-0233; Juneau, 907-586-7400; Kenai, 907-283-5808; Ketchikan, 907-225-6880; Wasilla, 907-376-7665.

Committees: *Energy & Natural Resources* (3d of 11 R): Energy (RMM); National Parks; Public Lands & Forests. *Foreign Relations* (7th of 10 R): East Asian & Pacific Affairs (RMM); International Development & Foreign Assistance, Economic Affairs & International Environmental Protection; European Affairs. *Health, Education, Labor & Pensions* (6th of 10 R): Employment & Workplace Safety; Children & Families. *Indian Affairs* (Vice Chmn. of 7 R).

Group Ratings

	ADA	ACLU	AFS	LCV	ITIC	NTU	COC	ACU	CFG	FRC
2006	5	25	13	14	100	68	100	71	43	75
2005	20	—	0	10	—	70	100	83	81	—

National Journal Ratings

	2005 LIB	—	2005 CONS	2006 LIB	—	2006 CONS
Economic	25%	—	72%	42%	—	56%
Social	49%	—	50%	43%	—	55%
Foreign	0%	—	74%	26%	—	67%

Key Votes of the 109th Congress

1. Bar ANWR Drilling	N	5. Confirm Samuel Alito	Y	9. Limit Interstate Abortion	Y
2. FY06 Spending Curb	Y	6. Path to Citizenship	Y	10. CAFTA	Y
3. Estate Tax Repeal	Y	7. Bar Same Sex Marriage	Y	11. Urge Iraq Withdrawal	N
4. Raise Minimum Wage	N	8. Stem Cell Research $	Y	12. Provide Detainee Rights	N

Election Results

2004 general	Lisa Murkowski (R)	149,773	(49%)	($5,465,098)
	Tony Knowles (D)	140,424	(46%)	($5,768,963)
	Other	18,118	(6%)	
2004 primary	Lisa Murkowski (R)	45,710	(58%)	
	Mike Miller (R)	29,313	(37%)	
	Wev Shea (R)	2,857	(4%)	
	Other	748	(1%)	
1998 general	Frank Murkowski (R)	165,227	(74%)	($911,926)
	Joseph Sonneman (D)	43,743	(20%)	($26,091)
	Other	12,837	(6%)	

Lisa Murkowski became Alaska's sixth U.S. senator when Governor Frank Murkowski, her father, appointed her in December 2002 to fill the vacancy caused by his own resignation. She grew up in Ketchikan in Alaska's Panhandle and in Fairbanks, the second of six children. In her senior year of high school she worked five weeks as an intern in Senator Ted Stevens's Washington office. She attended Willamette University in Salem, Oregon, and graduated from Georgetown in 1980, the year her father was first elected to the Senate, and graduated from Willamette law school in 1985. She served as an Anchorage District Court attorney and worked for an Anchorage law firm for eight years, then established her own law practice. In 1998 she was elected to the state House from a north Anchorage district including her neighborhood of Government Hill.

Alaska's state government depends heavily on revenues from North Slope oil, and in early 2002 was facing a budget shortfall of $1.1 billion. Murkowski was one of the leaders of a bipartisan Fiscal Policy Caucus that sought tax increases—a position opposite to that of her father, who was running for governor on a platform of no new taxes. In March 2002 the House Finance Committee passed a package that included spending $900 million from the Permanent Fund, the first such spending since the Fund was created in 1977; that was eventually defeated. But Murkowski pushed hard for increasing the alcohol tax from 3 cents a drink to 10 cents. She fought fiercely—when another legislator proposed an amendment with a much smaller increase, she said, "I'm gonna kill some-body!"—and the tax was passed in May, giving Alaska the nation's highest alcohol tax. Some conservatives referred to her and her allies as RIMs, "Republican invertebrate moderates." She also angered conservatives when she was one of five Republicans to vote against a bill restricting publicly funded abortions. At the time she said, "I may have a very short-lived political future here. But you know, I've got great kids and a great husband, and I'm going to have a good heart, and I'm going to stand up for the women of the state of Alaska, and I'm going to vote no." But she has also said that abortion should be legal only when a mother's life is in danger or in cases of rape and incest, and in March 2003 said she was against partial-birth abortion. Nonetheless, Alaska Right to Life opposed her in 1998, claiming, "She is not pro-life."

Conservatives opposed her reelection in 2002, and against conservative Nancy Dahlstrom, who attacked her for favoring tax increases and tapping the Permanent Fund, she won by only 486-429—a margin of 57 votes. During this period she evidently stayed at arm's length from her father, who easily won the nomination for governor. "We have always maintained very separate identities at least for the time I have been in the legislature," Lisa Murkowski said. "I haven't called him for counseling and typically he doesn't offer." During and after the primary, she ran for House speaker. In November 2002, Republican House members chose the more conservative Pete Kott of Eagle River for that post and Murkowski for House majority leader.

That was just two days after Frank Murkowski had been elected governor. There were two years left in the Senate term to which he had been elected, and Republican legislators had seen to it that he, and not outgoing Democratic Governor Tony Knowles, would appoint his successor. Earlier in the year, they passed over Knowles's veto a law barring a governor from appointing a successor until five days after the vacancy occurred. Murkowski said he wanted to appoint someone who had legislative experience, was young enough and reelectable enough to serve for many years, who knew and shared his views on Alaska issues. On November 15 he unveiled a short list of 26 potential nominees, not all of whom met all his criteria. Many were experienced politicians, but some had different backgrounds—General Joseph Ralston, NATO Supreme Commander who had served in Alaska and was registered to vote there, as an Independent; retired General Mark Hamilton, President of the University of Alaska; Jerry Hood, secretary-treasurer of Teamsters Local 959 and a former Democrat who had become a Republican (and supported Murkowski for governor in 2002);

Francis Hurley, the retired Catholic Archbishop of Anchorage; John Troxel, an Anchorage plastic surgeon; incoming state Senate Majority Leader Ben Stevens, son of Ted Stevens. Also on the list was House Majority Leader Lisa Murkowski.

On December 20, Governor Murkowski appointed state Representative Murkowski as senator. This was the first time a governor had appointed his daughter, or for that matter his child, to the Senate. Most Republicans and many Democrats said nice things about the new senator. But there was some disapproval, even from the Republican side. Jim Whitaker, an ally of Murkowski in the Alaska House, said her appointment "is nepotism and therefore contrary to the democratic principles of representative government. An action of this type undermines the public trust and is therefore of great concern." All of which cast a shadow on her prospects for winning a full term in November 2004.

In the Senate, Lisa Murkowski has a moderate voting record, considerably closer to the middle of the road than her father. She got seats on the Energy, Environment, Veterans and Indian Affairs Committees. In March 2003 she was disappointed when the Senate voted down oil drilling in the Arctic National Wildlife Refuge. She was more upbeat in November 2003, when the Senate unanimously passed the Healthy Forests Act, authorizing fuel reduction treatment—cutting down disease- or insect-infested trees—in national forests; she worked to make sure that it included the Kenai peninsula forests infested by the spruce bark beetle. Her biggest success came in October 2004, when she sponsored the inclusion in the must-pass military construction appropriation of provisions from the stalled energy bill authorizing an Alaska gas pipeline; but the real mover was Ted Stevens, in his last months as Appropriations Chairman. Like many Alaskans, she was critical of the Patriot Act and called for greater judicial discretion in deciding whether federal officers could obtain "any tangible thing." She worked, with Stevens's help, to get 200 seasonal visas for Japanese experts to evaluate Alaska salmon eggs, needed to keep one salmon fishery economically viable.

No Alaska Republican senator had ever been defeated, but Murkowski entered the 2004 campaign in weak condition. She had primary opposition from conservative former legislator Mike Miller, who attacked her stands on abortion, the Second Amendment and the income tax; Miller was even supported by her father's lieutenant governor, Loren Leman. Murkowski was much better financed and had the support of Stevens and Congressman-at-Large Don Young, but she won the primary by only a 58%-37% margin—not a strong performance for an incumbent senator.

Her opponent in the general election was former Governor Tony Knowles, the most successful Alaska Democrat in recent times. A Vietnam veteran and Yale classmate and friend of George W. Bush, Knowles ran a restaurant in Anchorage and was twice elected the city's mayor in the 1980s. In 1994 he was elected governor in a multi-candidate field with 41% of the vote; in 1998 he won a second term, again against divided opposition, with 51%. Knowles strongly supported oil drilling in ANWR and the gas pipeline; he criticized Murkowski for not including the price floor and said that, as a Democrat, he would have a better chance of attracting votes on ANWR. National Republicans responded with an ad featuring John Kerry and saying he "wouldn't know a caribou if it dropped in for a bowl of Boston clam chowder," and Murkowski offered him space in her office to lobby for ANWR oil drilling. Knowles criticized Murkowski for not supporting full funding—that is, appropriating as much as was authorized—for veterans' health care and spotlighted a 49-48 vote (actually, on that occasion a 60-vote supermajority was needed). Stevens responded by saying that Murkowski supported $1.2 billion for veterans' health in committee. In October 2004 he said that, knowing what he did now, he would not have voted for war in Iraq; Murkowski said she would have.

Looming over the campaign was the issue of nepotism. Knowles's pollster said that 54% found it a convincing reason to vote against Murkowski, and she trailed, usually by narrow margins, during most polls conducted during the campaign. Frank Murkowski's job rating as governor suffered after his 2003 budget cuts. Organizers obtained 50,000 signatures for Ballot Measure No. 4, to ban governors from appointing new senators; it passed in November with 56% of the vote. Against this Republicans raised the issue of party and seniority. Stevens said Alaska would be hurt if Democrats gained a majority in the Senate, and Young said, "I do believe there's a lot of merit to Lisa being elected for the benefit of the state. Everybody says, 'Ted can work with the minority,' and, yes, he can. But there's a difference between working with the minority as a minority member and working in the majority and being chairman." They also made the point that Murkowski, at 47, would have a chance of amassing much more seniority than Knowles, at 61, would.

This was one of the national Democrats' best chances of picking up a Republican seat, but this Republican state ended up giving its Republican junior senator a full term, by a 49%-46% margin. Like her father in the 2002 governor's race, Murkowski ran behind by a wide margin in the Bush and a lesser margin in the Panhandle. In historically Republican Anchorage and Fairbanks,

Murkowski ran only narrowly ahead. Her winning margins came in south central Alaska, in the fast-growing arc around Anchorage. With her victory, she became the first woman elected to Congress from Alaska.

In her first full term, Murkowski pursued the Alaska delegation's longstanding goal of opening up ANWR to drilling. When the Senate in late December 2005 fell three shy of the 60 votes needed to cut off debate on ANWR legislation, Murkowski expressed deep disappointment. "It is the shortest day of the year, and it feels like it has gone on and on and on," she said. Murkowski opposed the idea of a temporary suspension of the federal gasoline tax to ease the consumer impact of high gas prices; she said the country instead needed a longterm energy solution that included ANWR. Her commitment to ANWR was shaken badly in September 2006 when BP announced it had not properly maintained its North Slope pipelines. Murkowski at a committee hearing said she felt betrayed because she worked hard to promote ANWR drilling in the belief that it was safe. "We have said the operations on Alaska's North Slope are the gold standard. That's what we believed; that's what we want to continue to believe. But that faith has been shattered by what we're seeing up north now."

Her independence and centrist positions have put her in the center of high-profile national debates. She came under pressure from conservatives in 2005 to support the "nuclear option," a proposed change in Senate rules that would have blocked Democrats from using a filibuster to block judicial nominations. Murkowski said she supported up-or-down votes on judicial nominations but did not reveal her position on the controversial rules change. Suspicious of her abortion stance, the conservative Christian group Focus on the Family called her a "squishy Republican" and ran radio and newspaper ads in the state that said she was likely to support Democratic obstruction of nominees. The nuclear option was averted when the so-called "gang of 14" senators–seven Democrats and seven Republicans–agreed not to filibuster Bush's judicial nominations except under "extraordinary circumstances." Murkowski had participated in some of the talks, but was not among the 14 senators: she had chosen to return to Alaska when the final deal was struck. When Bush asked Congress to reauthorize the Patriot Act, Murkowski was one of four Republican senators to insist the bill include more civil liberties protection. Their decision to join a Democratic filibuster forced the White House to accept a short-term extension in December 2005 and return the next year to negotiate a longer reauthorization.

Murkowski has fought for Alaska interests in the Senate and at home. (In 2006, she bested eight other senators during a Kenai River conservation fundraiser when she caught a 63-pound king salmon.) Murkowski fought along with Stevens against Pentagon plans to downgrade Eielson Air Force Base during the 2005 Base Realignment and Closure process. The senators backed a bill that would halt the BRAC process until the Pentagon met a number of requirements, including the return of most U.S. troops from Iraq. She criticized the Defense Department when it delayed declassification of information that would help the state make its case for keeping the base. The BRAC commission voted 7–0 to keep Eielson open by allowing 18 F-16 fighter jets to remain there, but it approved the transfer of another 18 other A-10 aircraft. The commission also voted to end the military's support of a former Air Force station in Galena, but signaled its closure might come toward the end of the latest round of realignments. Showing attention to native Alaskan issues, Murkowski authored a bill that would change existing law to make it easier for current stockholders of Alaska Native Corporations to issue new stock to descendants of the original holders. She also sponsored bills that would grant federal recognition and land to five landless native Alaskan communities. Conservationists opposed the recognition out of fear it could lead to logging of environmentally sensitive lands.

With the end of Stevens's tenure as Appropriations Committee chairman, Murkowski has worried publicly about Alaska's continuing ability to win federal earmarks and has invited constituents to make earmark suggestions on her website. Murkowski understands the importance of Senate seniority and Alaska's reliance on federal resources. She told reporters after the 2006 midterm elections that her party's transition to the minority would not prevent her from advocating the state's interests. "While I'm relatively junior in seniority, it's fair to say I've developed a rapport in a short time here of working with my Democratic colleagues. I'm not looking at this as a dark day for Republicans."

Representative-At-Large

Don Young (R)

Elected Mar. 1973, 17th full term; b. June 9, 1933, Meridian, CA; home, Fort Yukon; Yuba Jr. Col., A.A. 1952, Chico St. Col., B.A. 1958; Episcopalian; married (Lu).

Military Career: Army, 1955-57.

Elected Office: Fort Yukon City Cncl., 1960-64; Fort Yukon Mayor, 1964-68; AK House of Reps., 1966-70; AK Senate, 1970-73.

Professional Career: School teacher, Fort Yukon, 1960-68; Riverboat captain, 1960-68.

DC Office: 2111 RHOB, 20515, 202-225-5765; Fax: 202-225-0425; Web site: donyoung.house.gov.

District Offices: Anchorage, 907-271-5978; Bethel, 907-543-1639; Fairbanks, 907-456-0210; Juneau, 907-586-7400; Kenai, 907-283-5808; Ketchikan, 907-225-6880; Wasilla, 907-376-7665.

Committees: *Natural Resources* (RMM of 22 R). *Transportation & Infrastructure* (2d of 34 R): Coast Guard & Maritime Transportation; Highways & Transit.

Group Ratings

	ADA	ACLU	AFS	LCV	ITIC	NTU	COC	ACU	CFG	FRC
2006	25	29	29	0	100	58	100	72	52	71
2005	5	—	0	0	—	59	96	83	59	92

National Journal Ratings

	2005 LIB	—	2005 CONS		2006 LIB	—	2006 CONS
Economic	36%	—	63%		12%	—	86%
Social	51%	—	49%		51%	—	48%
Foreign	0%	—	89%		14%	—	85%

Key Votes of the 109th Congress

1. Estate Tax Repeal	Y	5. Limit Interstate Abortion	Y	9. Build Border Fence	N
2. Limit CAFE Standards	Y	6. Extend Patriot Act	Y	10. CAFTA	Y
3. FY06 Spending Curb	Y	7. Bar Same Sex Marriage	Y	11. Oppose Iraq Withdrawal	Y
4. Drilling in ANWR	Y	8. Stem Cell Research $	Y	12. Detainee Tribunals	Y

Election Results

2006 general	Don Young (R)	132,743	(57%)	($1,959,806)
	Diane Benson (D)	93,879	(40%)	($197,339)
	Other	8,023	(3%)	
2006 primary	Don Young (R)	unopposed		
2004 general	Don Young (R)	213,216	(71%)	($1,747,897)
	Thomas Higgins (D)	67,074	(22%)	
	Timothy Feller (Green)	11,434	(4%)	
	Other	8,272	(3%)	

Prior Winning Percentages: 2002 (75%); 2000 (70%); 1998 (63%); 1996 (59%); 1994 (57%); 1992 (47%); 1990 (52%); 1988 (63%); 1986 (57%); 1984 (55%); 1982 (71%); 1980 (74%); 1978 (55%); 1976 (71%); 1974 (54%); 1973 (51%)

Don Young has been Alaska's congressman-at-large since 1973. He was once a tugboat captain on the Yukon and is the only licensed mariner in Congress—in his words, "not one of these smooth, namby-pamby politicians." He is a hot-tempered, salty-tongued true believer, given to malapropisms ("Pribilof's dog") and tough talk (to critics who proposed channeling money earmarked for Alaska bridges to Katrina recovery efforts, he said, "They can kiss my ear"). Young grew up in rural California, served in the Army and graduated from college, then moved to Alaska, captained his tugboat and was elected mayor of Fort Yukon. He was elected to the legislature in 1966 and ran for Congress in 1972. His opponent, incumbent Democrat Nick Begich, was killed in a plane crash in October and was reelected posthumously; Young won the March 1973 special election to succeed him. Young is not a free-market conservative and has recently voted with liberals on some cultural issues. What he has been is an unceasing advocate of what he considers Alaska's interests.

For his first 22 years in the House, Young was in the minority, outvoted on what was then the Interior Committee and often on the floor by environmentalists—whom he once called a "self-centered bunch, the waffle-stomping, Harvard-graduating, intellectual idiots." Then in all 12 years of the Republican majority he was a committee chairman—of the Resources Committee in 1995-2001 and the Transportation and Infrastructure Committee in 2001-07. He steered to passage in the House bills allowing oil drilling in the Arctic National Wildlife Refuge in 1995, 2001 and 2006, only to see them defeated or bottled up in the Senate. His attempts to roll back some environmental rulings, like allowing logging in the Tongass National Forest, were frustrated in the 1990s by vetoes by Bill Clinton, or by adverse votes cast by Republicans from the Northeast, Florida and Arizona; in May 2006 the House voted 237-181 to prohibit roadbuilding in the forest, pretty much wiping out the logging business there. Young admonished his colleagues, "Each one of you, think about this, in this room: This should be a representative form government, and what you're doing is dead wrong, and I shall not forget it."

But on both committees he also forged bipartisan consensus. In May 2000 he got the House to pass, by a 315-102 vote, the Conservation and Reinvestment Act, to dedicate royalties from offshore oil and gas wells to provide federal dollars for state purchases of land. His original version would require that $3 billion be spent every year, independent of the appropriations process, for 15 years; Alaska would be guaranteed $163 million a year in compensation for the environmental costs of oil drilling, more than all but two other states. But many conservative Republicans opposed this, and only a scaled-down version, subject to appropriators, passed the Senate.

After the 2000 election, Young took over the rigorously bipartisan Transportation Committee. His predecessor Bud Shuster had turned it into the largest and arguably the most bipartisan committee in the House, because Shuster made sure every cooperating committee member received plenty of highway (or mass transit) projects and fought ruthlessly to keep transportation money flowing directly from the gasoline and airplane fuel taxes without any review by the Appropriations Committee. His biggest task was to reauthorize Shuster's masterpiece, the 1998 $218 billion TEA-21 surface transportation act, which expired in 2003. In November 2003 Young presented his TEA-LU (the LU stands for Legacy for Users; it was named after Young's wife Lu) version, with $375 billion in spending. It was financed with an increase in the gas tax—retroactive indexing, he said, to the last time the gas tax was increased in 1993, and indexed to rise in the future. But the Bush administration and the House Republican leadership were stoutly opposed to any gas tax increase. The administration set a limit of $256 billion; the Senate in early 2004 approved a $318 billion bill. In March 2004 the Transportation Committee approved Young's $375 billion package by voice vote, but Young promised the House leadership not to bring it to the floor; and in early April the House approved a $275 billion bill, without Young's gas tax increase. The Senate bill readjusted the funding formula, to give some states more money per dollar of gas tax revenue; the House bill didn't. The conference committee split the difference at $284 billion, a number the administration threatened to veto. The expiration date of TEA-21 was extended, and extended again, as conferees and the administration failed to agree. John McCain argued against the many earmarked highway projects and called for formula changes (Arizona got 90 cents for each dollar of revenue under the old formula, and 92 cents under the Senate formula; Alaska got $6.60), while Richard Shelby of Alabama wanted $319 billion in spending and wanted to shift mass transit money to highways; with Senate Democrats all voting against agreement, the conference was stymied and no bill passed when Congress adjourned in 2004. Young's proposal for a gas tax increase was clearly dead.

In 2005 Young tried again, and got the House to pass a $284 million bill in March. But there was mounting criticism of earmarked projects in the bill, particularly of two bridges in Alaska—one from Anchorage to the largely uninhabited land across the Knik Arm, the other from the town of Ketchikan (pop. 14,000) to the island of Gravina (pop. 50) with its airport, which could already be reached by local ferry. The "bridges to nowhere" they came to be called; Young's argument was that they were bridges to land which was the natural area of expansion for Alaska's largest city and the Panhandle town. Negotiations with the Senate and the Bush administration continued, and in July, just before the August recess, both houses passed by near-unanimous votes a $286 billion bill entitled SAFETEA-LU with some 6,376 earmarks (critics took a while to count them up). They included $230 million for the Knik Arm bridge (which Senator Ted Stevens insisted on naming Don Young's Way) and $220 million for the Ketchikan-Gravina bridge, plus $20 million to the Denali Commission for docks and waterfront projects, $15 million for a highway from Juneau to Skagway (or almost to Skagway), $10 million to relieve traffic congestion in Anchorage, and $3 million for a television documentary on Alaska infrastructure. Alaska got some 119 earmarks worth $941 million, more than any other state except California, New York and Illinois. Young's reaction was serene. "It is much-needed legislation that will move our country toward a stronger economy." As for the earmarks, "This is the time to take advantage of the position I'm in." And, "If I hadn't done fairly well for our state, I'd be ashamed of myself."

When the bill was passed, no one expected that it would become controversial when Congress reassembled. But after Hurricane Katrina hit the Gulf Coast and New Orleans in August, there were demands that funds be taken from Alaska's "bridges to nowhere" and sent to rebuild the damaged area. "That is the dumbest thing I ever heard," Young said. But for the next year criticism of earmarks and the bridges continued. Conservative Republicans as well as Democrats chimed in, and profligate spending emerged as an issue that damaged Republicans in the 2006 election.

Young has dealt with other contentious issues. After September 11 there was sharp conflict over the details of emergency aid for Amtrak, over provisions for federal aid to the airlines and over whether airport security personnel should be federal workers. Young, House Republican leaders and the Bush administration held out for federal supervision of private contractors—the system used in Israel and Europe—but had to retreat. Young was more successful on arming airline pilots, despite opposition from the administration. In summer 2004 Young and committee Democrats moved to require national biometric identification standards for personnel at U.S. airports; in October they pressed legislation to implement recommendations of the 9/11 Commission. In the midst of this, Young was stopped, mistaken for a suspected terrorist, another Don Young, in September 2004. "Apparently the guy is not a nice person. They had a reason for doing that and that is their job...It was sort of a shock, though. I'm the chair of the Transportation Committee. "I actually behaved myself." In summer 2005 he sought the chairmanship of the new Homeland Security Committee; it went instead to Peter King of New York. In 2006 he surprised many by opposing wind farms that come within 1.5 nautical miles of shipping lanes; this put him on the same side of the controversy over a proposed wind farm in waters off Cape Cod as Senator Edward Kennedy.

Young has had his ups and downs with Alaska voters over the years, with significant opposition in 1978, 1984, 1986, 1990 and 1992. In 2000, 2002 and 2004 he was reelected with 70% to 75% of the vote. In 2006 he had more trouble. His Democratic opponent Diane Benson did not seem formidable; as the Green party candidate for governor in 2002, she received only a handful of votes. But she attracted attention as the mother of a soldier who lost both his legs in an explosion in Iraq and she called for a graceful exit strategy from that conflict. The *Anchorage Daily News* (the "Daily Screw", Young calls it) described how Young received $20,000 in campaign contributions from Indian tribes that were clients of disgraced lobbyist Jack Abramoff, had used Abramoff's skybox at the MCI Center to hold two fundraisers and had urged the GSA to give preferential treatment to tribes on proposals to redevelop Washington's Old Post Office. Young had also blocked efforts in 2000 to apply U.S. labor laws to the Commonwealth of the Northern Mariana Islands, another Abramoff client. It was also noted that Young took 31 flights on corporate jets. It is not surprising that tribes contributed to Young, a former chairman and still high-ranking member of the committee with jurisdiction over Indian issues, and Young has done much work on Alaska Native issues; but the stories may have hurt. Young spent some $1.96 million on heavy advertising while avoiding joint appearances with Benson except for one public television broadcast; his campaign manager said he had no campaign events and he didn't even have a campaign website. Benson spent only $197,000 and did not tape her first television ad until late October. Young appeared upbeat and predicted in October that Republicans would lose no seats in the House. But on Election Day, Young won by the considerably reduced margin of 57%-40%. He ran even with Benson in the traditionally Democratic Panhandle (beating her 2–1 in the Ketchikan area) and, thanks to his long work for Alaska Native causes, including pushing for more federal jobs and contracts for Natives, carried the Bush 58%-39%, even though Benson is Tlingit. He won almost identical margins in greater Anchorage (58%-39%) and Fairbanks (57%-39%).

Young professed to be undaunted about being in the minority again. "I served 22 years in the minority and was very successful." He pointed out that he had increased Democrats' share of transportation funding to 45% and reported that incoming Transportation Chairman James Oberstar told him, "I'll treat you as good as you treated me." He is eighth in House seniority, and third among Republicans, and remains unashamed of his support of Alaska projects.

Young's 2008 reelection prospects became clouded by a far-reaching FBI corruption probe in Alaska. In May 2007, Rick Smith, an associate of Young's and the former CEO of the politically-connected oil-production services firm VECO Corp., whose PAC was the single largest contributor to Young since 1989, and several others plead guilty to bribery and conspiracy charges. *The Wall Street Journal* reported in July 2007 that the investigation had expanded to include Young.

Democrats, already encouraged by Young's relatively weak reelection performance in 2006, actively courted several candidates, including Anchorage Mayor Mark Begich and former state House Minority Leader Ethan Berkowitz; both were also considering running against Senator Ted Stevens, whose home was raided by the FBI in August 2007. Citing Young's ethics problems, former state Democratic party chairman Jake Metcalfe announced he would challenge Young in 2008; 2006 challenger Diane Benson also filed to run.

★ ARIZONA ★

Youth and age, new and old: Arizona is home to America's oldest continuous community and is America's fastest-growing and one of its most rapidly changing states. The Hopi Indians, living as shepherds on plateaus east of the Grand Canyon, have not changed much in perhaps 500 years. They have spurned Christianity since 1680, when they killed the local Franciscan priests and burned their churches; more recently they have been involved in land disputes with the far more numerous Navajo. The Hopi are the oldest Arizonans; the newest are moving in every day, into subdivisions rising up out of the empty desert east, north, and west of Phoenix, hemmed in only by dry river beds, upcroppings of mountains, and Indian reservation boundaries.

For Arizona is one of America's boom states. Its population grew 40% between 1990 to 2000, and another 20% between 2000 and 2006—nearly 1.5 million in 10 years, another 1 million in six. And growth is accelerating. Arizona's population grew between 2.5% and 2.9% annually from 2000 to 2004, then accelerated to 3.6% in 2004-06; in 2005-06 Arizona's growth rate topped Nevada's and was the highest in the nation. Arizona is now the 16th most populous state; if growth continues at 2005-06 rates, it will pass Indiana to rank 15th in 2007 and will pass Massachusetts and Washington to rank 13th in 2008. Maricopa County, which has 61% of the state's people, is the fourth most populous county in the nation (and, spreading far out from Phoenix, the 14th largest in area). It is a state with an economy now sophisticated and decentralized enough that there is no easy explanation, as there once was, of how and why Arizona grows. The original explanation was the five Cs, memorialized in the state seal. The first C was copper: The dome of the state Capitol dome is encased in copper; one of Arizona's leading public figures was Lewis Douglas, copper heir and congressman, Franklin D. Roosevelt's first budget director and Harry Truman's ambassador to Britain. The second C was cattle: as late as the mid-1960s a dozen or so cattlemen ran the state legislature. The third C was cotton: Carl Hayden, Democratic congressman from statehood in 1912 and senator from 1927-69, concentrated on bringing public works to Arizona; his signal achievement was the Central Arizona Project, so that big farmers could grow cotton in the flatlands around Phoenix. The water also helped with the fourth C, citrus. The fifth C was climate, which kept people out of Arizona for many years and then, after air conditioning came in during the early post-World War II years, started bringing them in.

In those years Arizona became less dependent on federal largesse except for military bases and defense contracts, as businessmen, lawyers, developers and water companies, notably the Salt River Project, built an Arizona based on something like the opposite of New Deal principles: With minimal government and precious little regulation of business, a welcoming of new technological ideas and shunning of new cultural liberalism; like Disneyland, a more gleaming and spotless embodiment of old values than America had ever been. Their political champion was Barry Goldwater, Phoenixcity council member and senator and the nation's Mr. Conservative for much of the 1950s and 1960s. He helped to make Arizona Republican, the only state to vote Republican for president in every election from 1952 to 1992.

This Arizona has grown phenomenally, from 700,000 people at the end of World War II to 3.6 million in 1990 and then to 6.2 million in 2006. It is growth based on high-tech and low taxes. It is not growth based on an influx of elderly retirees—Arizona may have Sun City, but just 13% of its residents are over 65, compared to 12% nationally. Nor is it based on subsidized farming, since thirsty cotton farms are being phased out for urban users who outbid them; the Valley around Phoenix lost nearly half its farmland between 1975 and 2000. It also is not based on (though it is helped by) immigration: Arizona has attracted immigrants from Mexico and Latin America eager for entry-level jobs, so eager that many cross the lightly guarded border in the desert even at the risk of death. More than anything else, the engine of Arizona's growth has been technology: Phoenix has been attracting high-tech industries since Motorola built a research center for military electronics there in 1948. Big employers include Honeywell, Raytheon, Motorola, Intel, Avnet and Northrop

District 2 is highlighted for visibility.

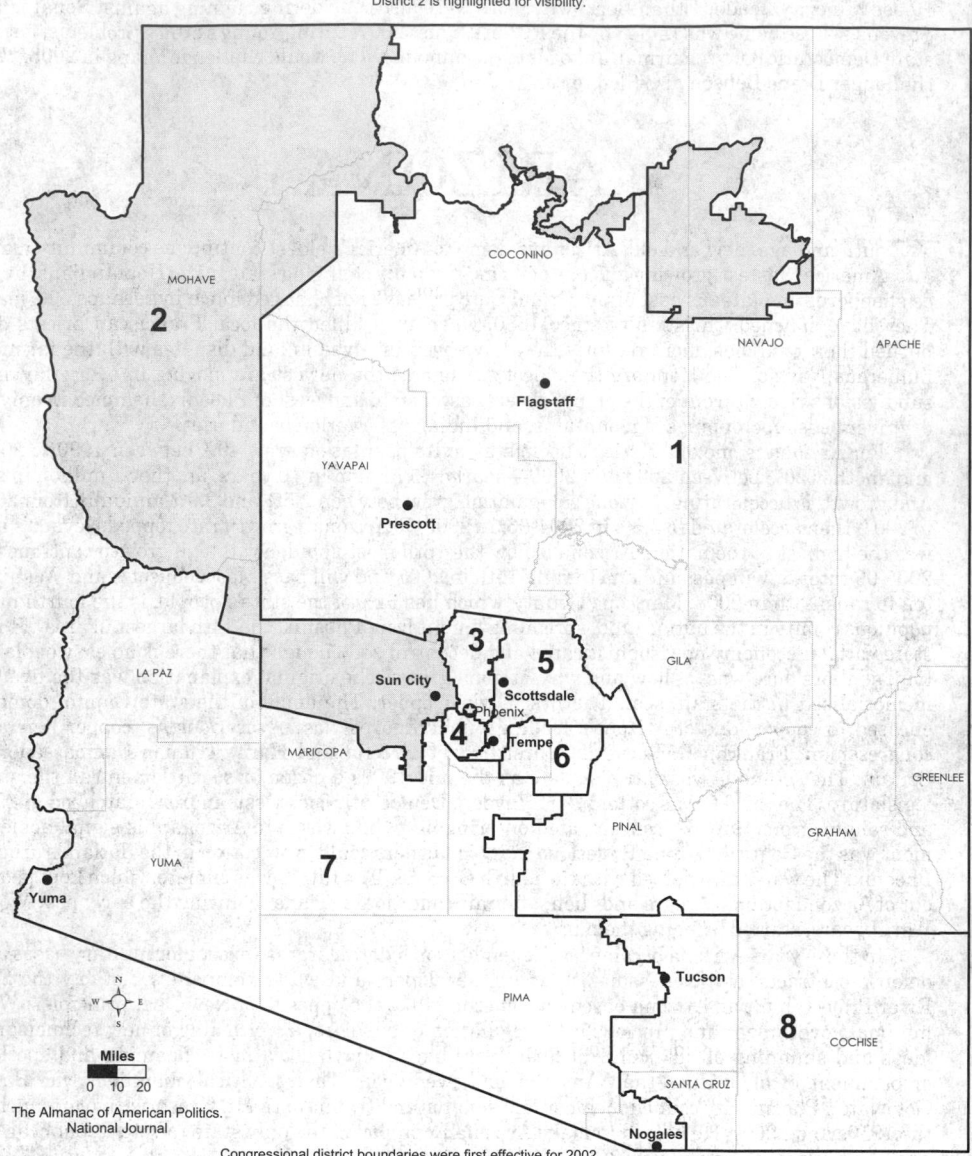

The Almanac of American Politics.
National Journal

Congressional district boundaries were first effective for 2002.

Grumman. Defense industries are important here: Arizona ranked number six in Defense Department contracts in 2006. The state counts two Air Force bases and a Marine Air Station plus the huge Barry M. Goldwater Range over which many of America's pilots have been trained. And for all its growth, Arizona still produces two-thirds of the nation's copper. The state's economy has kept humming while much of the nation was in recession and newcomers kept streaming in, nearly three-quarters of them from the rest of the United States, especially from California, but one-quarter of them immigrants.

In the past few years, Arizona has become the central focus of illegal immigration. With stronger border enforcement in Texas and a fence going up near San Diego, the hilly Arizona desert in Cochise and Santa Cruz Counties became a major entry point for illegals. Thousands streamed in over ranchlands; most who got through went on north to Phoenix or west to California, but the flow continued. Locals formed a Minuteman organization, reporting illegal aliens to authorities and demanding stronger enforcement by the federal government. Anger at the flood of illegals contributed to the passage of ballot propositions—Proposition 200 in 2004, denying certain welfare benefits and requiring government employees to report illegals, and in 2006, Proposition 102, denying punitive damages to illegals, Proposition 103, declaring English Arizona's official language, and Proposition 300, denying illegals in-state tuition at state colleges, state child care aid and adult literacy classes. These were characterized by some as signs of bigotry, but they were supported by at least 40% of Hispanics as well as majorities of Anglo whites. Arizona's congressional delegation was split on immigration: with Congressman J. D. Hayworth and Senator Jon Kyl for a border security measure and Congressmen Jim Kolbe and Jeff Flake and Senator John McCain, as well as the two House Democrats, favoring measures with guest worker and legalization provisions. But if anger at illegal immigration contributed to the success of some ballot propositions, it proved a losing issue for candidates for Congress. Hayworth was beaten in his affluent Phoenix-area district and Randy Graf, who made illegal immigration his chief issue while running against Kolbe in the 2004 primary and winning the nomination in 2006 to succeed him, was beaten and failed to carry even Cochise County.

Arizona is a place where the private sector is expanding and the public sector, if not shriveling away, is yielding ground. State taxes were cut sharply in the 1990s and there's been little increase since. Arizona pioneered in providing choice in education (at one point it had America's largest proportion of charter schools, some 20% of the total) and the for-profit University of Phoenix, based here but with branches in many states, which leases space and hires working-age adults to teach job-related skills to working-age adults. Local choice prevails: The inaptly named Youngtown, near Phoenix, bars children from living there; so does Superstition Heights. Where government once used to allocate precious water, now "shadow governments" (Joel Garreau's term) like the Salt River District do so, heeding the market signals that say urban users will pay more than farmers. It is a place wide open for entrepreneurs, some of them perhaps a bit shady, others at times wildly overoptimistic, many crossing traditional barriers. Phoenix is the number three metro area for women business owners per capita, and there is a burgeoning number of Latino-owned businesses. But there is a downside. Arizona also has one of the highest percentages of those without health insurance, and there is a wide income and education gap between affluent American newcomers and poor immigrants.

This wide-openness can be reflected in politics. In 1998 it became the first state to elect women to all its top five statewide downballot offices and in 2002 and 2006 it elected Democrat Janet Napolitano as governor. It is one of the relatively few states with more registered Republicans than Democrats. Although Bill Clinton carried Arizona in 1996 and came close in 1992, the state has generally tilted heavily Republican, except that Democrats have won the governorship in four of the last eight elections. Also, Democrats picked up two House seats in 2006, leaving the delegation evenly split, and they also reduced the Republican edge in the state House to 33-26 as Napolitano was reelected by a 63%-35% margin. Two recent governors left office under unusual circumstances: Republican Governor Fife Symington resigned in September 1997 when he was convicted of fraudulent dealings as a developer (the conviction was reversed on appeal and he was pardoned by Clinton in January 2001). Republican Governor Evan Mecham was impeached and removed from office by the state Senate in April 1987. If Napolitano serves out her second term she will be the first governor to serve eight consecutive years since Democrat Bruce Babbitt from 1978 to 1986. In other ways, Arizona has had political continuity. It has only had 10 U.S. senators, the lowest number of any state except Alaska (6) and Hawaii (5).

In the exuberance of growth, causes for anxiety remain. Congress passed a law in 2004 settling disputes over water between the state and the Gila River Indian Community and the Tohono

O'odham Nation but Arizona's congressional delegation was worried that one of its Air Force bases would fall victim to the 2005 base closing round and tried to discourage construction close to their boundaries. That approach may have worked: the state was largely unscathed when the Pentagon's recommendations were released in May 2005. Yet Arizona has been spared some of the worst effects of growth. The expansion of subdivisions has not led to abandonment of old downtowns or deterioration of central city neighborhoods as it has in eastern cities; the imperatives of growth in parched desert areas mean that lot sizes are smaller and land use more parsimonious than in a heavily-watered boom area like Atlanta. Arizona today is a mostly urban state, but it still has some of the look and feel of the Wild West.

The People		Race/Ethnic Origin			Military veterans: 562,916 (14.9%)	
Pop. 2006 (est):	6,166,318	3,274,258	63.8%	White	WWII: 21.3%	Korea: 14.7%
Pop. 2000:	5,130,632	149,941	2.9%	Black	Vietnam: 30.7%	Gulf War: 10.4%
Pop. 1990:	3,665,228	89,315	1.7%	Asian	**Most populous cities (2006):**	
Change 1990-2000:	Up 40.0%	233,370	4.5%	Native Am.	1. Phoenix	1,512,986
% of U.S. total:	1.8%	5,639	0.1%	Hawaiian	2. Tucson	518,956
Pop. rank:	20th of 50	76,372	1.5%	Two+ races	3. Mesa	447,541
Area size:	113,998 sq. mi.	6,120	0.1%	Other	4. Glendale	246,531
State Native:	34.7%	1,295,617	25.3%	Hisp. Origin	5. Chandler	240,595
Non-citizen:	9.0%	**Ancestry**				
Language		German: 12.2%		English: 8.1%	Urban population: 88.2%	
English: 73.6%	Spanish: 18.5%	Irish: 8.0%		USA: 3.7%	Rural population: 11.8%	
Other Eur.: 3.4%		Italian: 3.4%				

Education		Work Sector		Legislature	
H.S. Grad:	81.0%	Private: 78.1%	Govt: 15.2%	Senate	17 R 13 D
College Grad:	23.5%	Self: 6.4%	Family: 0.3%	House	33 R 27 D
Industry		Unemployment: 5.6%		Legislative Term Limits: Yes	
Agri: 1.5%	Con: 8.7%	**Household Income**		**Registered Voters**	
Fin: 7.9%	Info: 2.8%	<15k: 14.9%	15-35k: 27.9%	D: 1,010,451	(33.0%)
Mfg: 15.2%	Prof: 28.3%	35-50k: 17.5%	50-100k: 28.9%	R: 1,176,584	(38.4%)
Public: 5.4%	Trade: 15.6%	100-150k: 6.9%	>150k: 3.9%	O: 874,505	(28.6%)
Other: 14.7%		Median: $40,558			
Occupation		Poverty status: 13.9%			
Blue collar: 21.9%	White collar: 61.2%	**Home Value**			
Gray collar: 16.9%		<50k: 13.0%	50-100k: 31.4%	100-200k: 39.7%	200-300k: 9.5%
		300-500k: 4.5%	>500k: 1.9%	Median: $109,400	

Presidential politics   Far from the media centers of the East Coast, Arizona has tried every so often to make itself another Iowa or New Hampshire in presidential politics, with little success. In 1972 it had an early Democratic primary, the improbable winner of which was Republican-turned-Democrat New York Mayor John Lindsay. But he went nowhere any place else. In 1996 Arizona tried to set its primary for the same date as New Hampshire; when that failed the state set it one week later. The intended beneficiary was Republican Phil Gramm, running with the support of Arizona's John McCain. But Gramm pulled out of the race a week before New Hampshire, and Arizona became a battleground between Bob Dole, who now had McCain's support; Pat Buchanan, who urged his followers to "mount up and ride" after his narrow victory in New Hampshire; and Steve Forbes, who peppered the state with ads boosting his flat tax and attacking Washington politicians. Buchanan's campaigning in gunslinger costume wearing a black hat was a bit

2004 Presidential Vote
Bush (R) 1,104,294   (55%)
Kerry (D)....................... 893,524   (44%)
Badnarik (Lib)................. 11,856   (1%)
Other 2,911   (0%)

2004 Democratic Presidential Primary
Kerry (D)....................... 101,809   (43%)
Clark (D)........................ 63,256   (26%)
Dean (D) 33,555   (14%)
Edwards (D) 16,596   (7%)
Lieberman (D) 15,906   (7%)
Other............................. 3,896   (2%)

2000 Presidential Vote
Bush (R) 781,652   (51%)
Gore (D)........................ 685,341   (45%)
Nader (Green) 45,645   (3%)
Other............................. 19,268   (1%)

too much, and he finished third, with 27%; it was clear he had no chance to win the nomination. Dole finished second with 30%; Forbes won 33% and all the delegates, after which his campaign, like that of his fellow Easterner Lindsay a quarter-century before, went nowhere.

In 2000, Arizona tried again. McCain had irritated local Republicans enough that Governor Jane Hull and other party leaders endorsed George W. Bush. McCain, however, won a solid victory in his home state in the February primary, but it was overshadowed by his victory the same day in Michigan. Arizona Democrats ran and paid for their own primary in March, because the state's February date was outside the "window" permitted by national Democratic Party rules. They allowed voting by Internet, and about 35,000 Arizonans mouse-clicked their choices; another 20,000 voted by mail; still others voted by computer or paper ballot at the polls. But the Internet voting was not flawless and the primary didn't matter because Al Gore had already clinched the nomination. In 2004 a regular primary was held one week after New Hampshire, on February 3, the same day as Delaware, Missouri, New Mexico, North Dakota, Oklahoma and South Carolina. John Kerry and Wesley Clark were the only candidates who targeted the state, and Kerry got 43% of the vote to Clark's 26%. Only 603,000 voted in a state of 5.6 million people. In 2006 Arizona Democrats made a bid to have their state designated as the site for a caucus election soon after Iowa. But in August 2006 the Democratic National Committee picked Nevada instead.

In the 1990s, Arizona suddenly became competitive in presidential general elections. The national trend toward Clinton-Gore Democrats in the very largest metropolitan areas was operative in Phoenix and Maricopa County; once very heavily Republican, it was closely divided in 1996 and 2000. In 1996 Bill Clinton carried the state by a 47%-44% margin—the first Democrat to carry the state since Harry Truman in 1948. The winning issue was not Medicare—Arizona does not have an especially large elderly population, and the air seemed to go out of the Medicare issue in mid-October. Rather, it was the environment: Arizona's mostly metropolitan voters want to preserve the environment, not make a living off it as most voters in sparsely populated Western states do. Clinton's staging of the announcement of a Utah land preserve at the Grand Canyon may have carried Arizona single-handedly (it may also have defeated the only Democratic congressman in Utah at the time). Clinton went on to create new National Monuments in Arizona—four in 2000 alone—perhaps in the hope of aiding Al Gore. But George W. Bush won 51%-45%. He carried not only Phoenix and Maricopa County, as Republican nominees had in 1992 and 1996, but also the smaller counties outside the Phoenix and Tucson metro areas, which they had not.

Polls in spring and summer 2004 showed Arizonans closely divided, and John Kerry's campaign targeted the state. But Bush pulled ahead here after the Republican National Convention. In September, on a visit to Arizona, Teresa Heinz Kerry was asked about her husband's poor showing in local polls. "Oh, who cares?" she said. "You know, one state is not a whole [country]." Bush won 55%-44% in a record turnout. Once again Bush carried Maricopa County and the part of the state beyond the Phoenix and Tucson metro areas.

Congressional districting   Arizona gained two House seats in the 2000 Census, after gaining one each in the Censuses of 1960, 1970, 1980 and 1990: In 40 years it has moved from two districts to eight. This time redistricting was done not by the legislature but by a five-member Arizona Independent Redistricting Commission, a body created by the passage of Proposition 106 in November 2000. Two Republican and two Democratic legislators appoint four members, and the fifth, to be neither a Democrat nor a Republican, is picked by the other four. The commission held 66 hearings and meetings and in October 2001 approved a plan closely resembling a suggestion made in *The Almanac of American Politics 2002*. Democrats were disappointed because it didn't create a competitive seat in the Phoenix area; commissioners said such a district could be created only by drawing grotesque lines that, in their view, would be gerrymandering; as it turned out the Phoenix-area 5th District, assumed to be comfortably Republican, went Democratic in 2006, as did the Tucson-area 8th District. Arizona is expected to gain two more seats after the 2010 Census. At least one new district and perhaps part of another will have to be in Maricopa County, with its red hot population growth, but the county is no longer monolithically Republican and the political consequences at this point seem unclear.

An explanation may be due for the odd shape of the 2d District. The demographically and politically similar areas of Mohave County and western Maricopa County are connected by a thin

110th Congress Lineup	
4 D	4 R

109th Congress Lineup	
6 R	2 D

band of La Paz County (9 voters showed up there in both 2002 and 2004, 13 in 2006), and then Mohave County is connected by a strip that runs along the bottom of the Grand Canyon to the Hopi Reservation. The Hopi have had disputes for many years with the far more numerous Navajo, whose reservation surrounds theirs, and the commission evidently decided that the Hopi should have a congressman who doesn't also represent the Navajo. The Navajo sued to get the lines redrawn but did not succeed. Confusingly, most of the Hopi Reservation is in Navajo County and most of the Navajo Reservation is in Apache County.

Governor

Janet Napolitano (D)

Elected 2002, term expires Jan. 2011, 2d term; b. Nov. 29, 1957, New York City; home, Phoenix; Santa Clara U., B.A. 1979, U. of VA, J.D. 1983; Methodist; single.

Elected Office: AZ Atty. Gen., 1998-2002.

Professional Career: Clerk, U.S. Appeals Ct. Judge Mary Schroder, 1983-84; Practicing atty., 1984-93; AZ U.S. atty., 1994-98.

Office: State Capitol, 1700 W. Washington, Phoenix, 85007, 602-542-4331; Fax: 602-542-7601; Web site: www.governor.state.az.us.

Election Results

2006 general	Janet Napolitano (D)	959,830	(63%)
	Len Munsil (R)	543,528	(35%)
	Other	30,287	(2%)
2006 primary	Janet Napolitano (D)	unopposed	
2002 general	Janet Napolitano (D)	566,284	(46%)
	Matt Salmon (R)	554,465	(45%)
	Richard Mahoney (I)	84,947	(7%)
	Other	20,415	(2%)

Janet Napolitano, a Democrat, in 2002 became the second woman in a row to be elected governor of Arizona. Napolitano was born in New York City and grew up in Pittsburgh and Albuquerque, where her father helped establish the University of New Mexico Medical School. She graduated from Santa Clara University and the University of Virginia Law School, and moved to Phoenix in 1983 to clerk for Judge Mary Schroeder, currently the chief judge on the 9th Circuit Court of Appeals. She practiced corporate law, volunteered as an attorney for the state Democratic party and later joined the team of lawyers representing Anita Hill at the Clarence Thomas confirmation hearings in October 1991. In 1993 she was appointed U.S. Attorney for Arizona where she served until she ran for attorney general in 1998; she was elected by a 50%-47% margin in a year in which the top five statewide offices were all won by women, with Napolitano the only Democrat among them.

As attorney general, she got plenty of good publicity. By October 2001 Napolitano's work had earned her a 55% positive job rating, and she was obviously running for governor (incumbent Jane Hull was term limited). She was motivated, she said, after she was diagnosed with breast cancer in 2000 and after having a successful mastectomy; she wanted to work on health care. She announced in January 2002 and then in April 2002 presented the 6,000 nominating petitions and 6,000 $5 contributions that qualified her for financing under the Clean Elections Act passed by voters in 1998. She received public financing of $409,000 for the September primary and $615,000 for the general election. She campaigned as a "conservative Democrat" and was criticized as "too Republican" by one primary opponent. But she was able to enlist the help of the fire fighters' union and the United Food and Commercial Workers to amass her nominating petitions and $5 contributions.

The leading Republican candidate was former Congressman Matt Salmon, who was first elected in 1994 and kept his promise to serve just three terms by retiring in 2000. His high point in the House came in November 1998 when he announced he would not vote for Newt Gingrich for Speaker—a move that helped to prompt Gingrich's resignation three days after the election. Both candidates won their primaries by wide margins. Napolitano led former state Senator Alfredo

Gutierrez 57%-22% and Salmon led Secretary of State Betsey Bayless 56%-30%. In the race as an Independent was Richard Mahoney, a Democrat elected secretary of state in 1990, who also qualified for the Clean Elections Act money. He attacked both nominees. "Are Matt and Janet going to take on the oil companies or the special interests? Tweedledum and Tweedledee, Salmon and Napolitano." He portrayed himself as more conservative on fiscal issues than Salmon and more liberal on cultural issues than Napolitano.

In the general election, Napolitano relied on her record as attorney general and called for closing loopholes and cutting spending to make up the budget shortfalls; she supported the death penalty. Salmon opposed tax increases—"I will not raise taxes, go after shared revenues or make cuts in the classroom"—and announced a Workforce 2010 plan to create 500,000 jobs paying more than $40,000. The tone of their campaigns was different. Napolitano was businesslike and stressed her experience. Salmon said he wanted to bring God back into government and his ads showed him with his wife and four children (Napolitano is unmarried). The Clean Elections Act played a role: Salmon declined the Clean Elections money, and raised his own, more slowly than he had hoped. But the proceeds he got from a George W. Bush fundraiser were a mixed blessing: The law requires the state to pay candidates who have accepted the Clean Elections funding (and the concomitant limitations on spending) an amount equal to what candidates who decline the Clean Elections Act money raise above its limits. So every dollar Bush raised for Salmon above that amount put a dollar in Napolitano's campaign treasury.

This proved to be a very close election. Napolitano led on election night and Wednesday by 25,000 votes, but it took time to count 200,000 early ballots, mostly from the Phoenix and Tucson areas. On Sunday Napolitano led by 11,000 votes with just 11,000 more to count, and Salmon conceded. Salmon carried Phoenix's Maricopa County, but by only 48%-44%. Napolitano won Tucson's Pima County 52%-39%. In the smaller counties, the "conservative Democrat" led 46%-44%. Overall, Napolitano won 46%-45%, with 7% for Mahoney.

Napolitano faced a Republican legislature, but was able to pass most of her budget in 2003 with help from moderate Republicans; she negotiated with Senate President Ken Bennett, while she worked with rank-and-file House Republicans who refused to follow the lead of Speaker Jake Flake. In June 2003 she launched CopperRx, a program of discounts on prescription drugs for seniors and the disabled; only 15,000 enrolled that year, and in January 2004 she dropped the $9.95 enrollment fee and enrollments went up to 30,000 by June, when estimated savings for individuals totaled $3.2 million. In January 2004 she had to deal with a long standoff in a hostage-taking in a state prison; her actions were criticized by some Republicans. In 2004 she presented a $7.3 billion budget with no tax increases and $500 million of borrowing. Once again, working in different ways with Senate and House Republicans, she got it passed. It included $25 million for all-day kindergarten in 150 schools serving low-income pupils, which she pressed for hard. She also agreed on tax breaks for landowners who clear forests (Arizona was in its seventh year of drought) and doubled spending on forest crews and child abuse prevention. She signed a law requiring plaintiffs to get an expert opinion before their lawyers could file a medical malpractice suit. In 2003 she had vetoed an increase in unemployment benefits when unions complained about restrictions; in 2004 the legislature passed the increase without restrictions, and she signed it. She did not succeed in getting a statewide rating system for preschools or tax law changes. She vetoed a bill requiring a 24-hour waiting period for abortions.

"People are rejecting the notion that you can say no to everything and still grow a state," Napolitano said after passage of the 2004 budget. "This is a new day in Arizona." But not all were pleased by the new day. Several Republican legislators who supported Napolitano on the budget and other issues were defeated by conservatives in the September 2004 primary. In November Republicans increased their margin in the Senate to 18-12, and though their margin in the House was reduced to 38-22, there were fewer moderates there for Napolitano to work with. In April 2004 the general manager of the Central Arizona Project attacked her for not meeting with his organization and for not pushing for the reopening of a desalination plant near Yuma to produce some of the water the United States is obliged by treaty to transfer to Mexico. That would mean less diversion of Colorado River Water and less chance of the federal Interior Department declaring an emergency and shutting off delivery of Colorado River water to CAP. In November 2004 Napolitano ordered state agencies to reduce water usage by 5% and called for new water conservation efforts and new authority and more money for the Department of Water Resources.

In 2006, Arizona enjoyed a $1.5 billion revenue surplus leaving both parties with enough money to promote their agendas. The 2007 fiscal year budget included $545 million in income and property tax relief sought by the Republican legislature. Napolitano won expanded all-day kindergarten, with an extra $80 million in spending in each of the next two years, and pay raises for teachers and state employees. But nearing the end of her first term, Napolitano had tied the state record of 114 gubernatorial vetoes, which former Democratic Governor Bruce Babbitt set after nine years in office. She was up to 127 by the end of the 2006 legislative session. Many vetoes included budget measures, while other involved restrictions on abortion. Napolitano also vetoed GOP bills that would charge illegal immigrants with trespassing, establish a border radar system and penalize employers who hire undocumented workers. Republicans criticized her position on immigration, but Napolitano had endorsed tougher border security measures and succeeded in getting President George W. Bush to deploy more National Guard troops along the Mexican border.

Despite a nearly 150,000 state voter registration advantage, Republicans failed to recruit a top candidate against Napolitano in 2006 and instead nominated Len Munsil, a conservative activist. Munsil relied on strong organization to win a four-way primary, which included Don Goldwater, the nephew of the late Barry Goldwater. Munsil attacked Napolitano on immigration; Napolitano ran on passing full-day kindergarten, and on turning the state deficit into a budget surplus. Both candidates opted for public financing, which reduced the race's profile in comparison to competitive federal contests. With strong crossover support from Republicans, she won a second term by a 63%-35% margin. She became the state's first woman governor to be reelected, and the nation's first female governor to succeed another female.

Democrats also picked up seven seats in the state legislature, leaving Republicans with a 33-27 House majority and a 17-13 Senate margin. On the first day of her second term, Napolitano signed executive orders that created initiatives to curb sprawling development, reduce pollution on state lands and improve nursing homes and long-term care facilities. After three years of strong revenue growth, the state faced a tighter fiscal picture in 2007. Napolitano proposed an $11.4 billion budget for the 2008 fiscal year that included expanded children's health care, a 3.5% pay increase for state employees and protected the state's $650 million rainy-day fund. It also included $1 billion in state borrowing for road and school construction, which was received coolly by Republicans, as was a separate proposal for a commuter rail line between Phoenix and Tucson by 2012.

Term limits prevent Napolitano from seeking a third term in 2010. She could decide instead to run for Senate or seek a position in the next administration if Democrats win the presidency in 2008. Phoenix Mayor Phil Gordon, a moderate Democrat, has expressed interest in running for governor in 2010, while state attorney general Terry Goddard, a former Phoenix mayor and gubernatorial candidate, and Jim Pederson, who unsuccessfully challenged Senator Jon Kyl in 2006, are other Democratic possibilities. Republican candidates could include former Congressman J.D. Hayworth, current Congressman Jeff Flake, Transportation Secretary Mary Peters and former Maricopa County attorney Rick Romley.

Senior Senator

John McCain (R)

Elected 1986, seat up 2010, 4th term; b. Aug. 29, 1936, Panama Canal Zone; home, Phoenix; U.S. Naval Acad., B.S. 1958, Natl. War Col., 1973-74; Episcopalian; married (Cindy).

Military Career: Navy, 1958-80 (Vietnam).

Elected Office: U.S. House of Reps., 1982-86.

Professional Career: Dir., Navy Senate Liaison Ofc., 1977-81.

DC Office: 241 RSOB, 20510, 202-224-2235; Fax: 202-228-2862; Web site: mccain.senate.gov.

State Offices: Phoenix, 602-952-2410; Tempe, 480-897-6289; Tucson, 520-670-6334.

Committees: *Armed Services* (RMM of 12 R). *Commerce, Science & Transportation* (2d of 11 R): Aviation Operations, Safety & Security; Surface Transportation & Merchant Marine Infrastructure, Safety & Security; Interstate Commerce, Trade & Tourism; Science, Technology & Innovation; Consumer Affairs, Insurance & Automotive Safety. *Indian Affairs* (2d of 7 R).

Group Ratings

	ADA	ACLU	AFS	LCV	ITIC	NTU	COC	ACU	CFG	FRC
2006	15	33	0	29	100	88	100	65	76	62
2005	10	—	0	45	—	78	72	80	76	—

National Journal Ratings

	2005 LIB	—	2005 CONS		2006 LIB	—	2006 CONS
Economic	47%	—	52%		35%	—	64%
Social	23%	—	64%		53%	—	46%
Foreign	45%	—	54%		40%	—	58%

Key Votes of the 109th Congress

1. Bar ANWR Drilling	Y	5. Confirm Samuel Alito	Y	9. Limit Interstate Abortion	Y
2. FY06 Spending Curb	Y	6. Path to Citizenship	Y	10. CAFTA	Y
3. Estate Tax Repeal	Y	7. Bar Same Sex Marriage	N	11. Urge Iraq Withdrawal	N
4. Raise Minimum Wage	N	8. Stem Cell Research $	Y	12. Provide Detainee Rights	N

Election Results

2004 general	John McCain (R)	1,505,372	(77%)	($2,140,807)
	Stuart Starky (D)	404,507	(21%)	($12,716)
	Other	51,798	(3%)	
2004 primary	John McCain (R)	unopposed		
1998 general	John McCain (R)	696,577	(69%)	($2,461,900)
	Ed Ranger (D)	275,224	(27%)	($371,439)
	Other	41,479	(4%)	

Prior Winning Percentages: 1992 (56%); 1986 (60%); 1984 House (78%); 1982 House (66%)

For many Americans John McCain is the closest thing our politics has to a national hero, a presidential candidate widely admired in 2000 and an independent leader of great force in the years after. His personal story is a dramatic one, told beautifully by Robert Timberg in *The Nightingale's Song* and by McCain himself and Mark Salter in the 1999 bestseller *Faith of My Fathers*. McCain is the son and grandson of Navy admirals, a decorated Navy pilot himself. He volunteered for service in Vietnam and in July 1967 was injured in a flight deck explosion on the carrier Forrestal. He could have returned home but refused, and in October 1967 was shot down over Vietnam. He spent five and a half years, most of it in pain and torture, in Communist prisoner of war camps. He refused to be let out ahead of those who had been in longer when he was offered release because of his father's rank. McCain returned to the United States in March 1973. His final assignment in the Navy was as Senate liaison. In 1980 he retired and moved to Arizona, his wife's home state; in 1982 he ran for an open House seat. Attacked as an outsider, he responded, "The longest place I ever lived in was Hanoi." He led 32%-26% in a four-way primary, and won the 1982 and 1984 general elections and then the 1986 Senate contest easily.

In his first years in the Senate he had a low profile. His first major issue was one on which he had considerable expertise: Vietnam. In the early 1990s McCain worked hard with John Kerry, also a decorated Vietnam veteran, on the special committee investigating charges that American POWs or MIAs remained in Vietnam; they found no evidence of any. With Kerry he supported ending the trade embargo on, and pressed for, establishing diplomatic relations with Vietnam. But his support for reconciliation with our former enemies has not dimmed his memories of how his captors treated his fellow prisoners of war. On the Armed Services Committee, McCain has called for more defense spending and insisted military interventions be designed to achieve victory; he criticized the Clinton administration for using air power alone and ruling out ground troops in Bosnia and for not using "all necessary force" in Kosovo.

McCain's other major committee assignment is Commerce, which handles heavily lobbied regulatory issues. McCain's impulse on these is toward deregulation, but he took little part in shaping the 1996 telecommunications act and voted against it, arguing that it did not effectively ensure competition. In 2006 he called for relaxing franchise regulations for cable TV companies that offered programming on a per channel a la carte basis. Even when he served as chairman of the committee in 2003-05 he showed a distaste for the political deal-making and log-rolling that is so common. It appears to be his view that members of Congress, like members of the military, should serve the national interest honorably and without reference to political considerations. Linked to that is his opposition to what he considers pork barrel spending, which provides him plenty of material for his self-deprecating jokes about how unpopular he is with many colleagues. That has put him at odds with senators like Alaska's Ted Stevens, who after being term-limited as Appropriations chairman became chairman of Commerce in 2005.

The issue McCain has been most closely identified with over the years is campaign finance regulation. His interest came from his experience as one of the "Keating Five" senators investigated for meeting in 1987 with regulators on behalf of Charles Keating's Arizona savings and loan. Democrats kept McCain in the case, though he had done nothing for Keating; as the one Republican involved, he thus made the scandal bipartisan. Ultimately he was cited for nothing more than bad judgment. Vindicated by reelection in 1992, in the majority after the election of 1994, he sought out Democrat Russ Feingold, whose campaign finance bill had gotten nowhere that year. The McCain-Feingold bills went through several transformations. The 1998 bill purported to ban soft money contributions to political parties and to limit "issue ads" run by independent organizations within 60 days of an election. It was fiercely opposed as an infringement of free speech and as a threat to the Republican Party by Mitch McConnell of Kentucky. Majority Leader Trent Lott yanked the bill from the Senate floor in February 1998; it returned in September, after the House passed a similar bill, but could summon up no more than 52 votes and died. In September 1999, after the House passed a similar bill again, McCain and Feingold introduced a new version that attacked soft money but did not address issue ads. The intent was to get a bill to conference and generate enough public support that McConnell and other Republican opponents would have to back down. But in October McConnell, noting that McCain had charged that the current campaign finance system produces corruption, challenged McCain to name senators who had been corrupted. McCain refused to name names and said the system was corrupt in general. Against McConnell's filibuster a few days later, McCain and Feingold were able to summon up only 55 votes for cloture, five short of the 60 needed, and the bill was taken off the floor.

His work on campaign finance and his record of service in Vietnam provided solid credentials for the presidential campaign he embarked on in 1999. He decided to avoid the Iowa caucuses (McCain had long campaigned against ethanol subsidies as pork) and concentrated on New Hampshire, where he traveled around the state in his "Straight Talk Express" bus. At first only a few reporters traveled with him and crowds were sparse. But it soon became clear McCain was striking a chord. To increasingly large and fervent crowds he told his personal story in self-deprecating terms, and pledged, "I will never tell you a lie." He was asked to autograph hundreds of copies of *Faith of My Fathers*. He talked about defense and foreign policy issues—the only candidate to spend much time doing so—and invariably called for campaign finance reform. On the campaign bus, McCain was always available to answer reporters' questions and banter with the press, while making fun of his aides and consultant Mike Murphy (who later called the press "our constituency"). McCain did not have much support from politicians. Only four fellow senators endorsed him (Jon Kyl, Chuck Hagel, Fred Thompson and Mike DeWine). Back home, Arizona Governor Jane Hull, apparently because of abrasive treatment by McCain, endorsed George W. Bush; *The Arizona Republic* wrote editorials warning of McCain's "volcanic" temper. But the strength of feeling among his ever-larger crowds was palpable. Bush predicted victory in New Hampshire, but on February 1 McCain beat him by an impressive 49%-31% margin. Suddenly he became, if not the frontrunner, at least the most admired of either party's presidential candidates.

From there the "Straight Talk Express" had mixed success. It went down to South Carolina, where both the Republican establishment and Christian conservatives lined up with Bush in 2000. The campaigning got negative but what hurt even more was his failure to win over self-identified Republicans. His emphasis on campaign finance reform and his criticisms of Bush's tax plan for giving too much to the rich helped with independents, but sounded like enemy talk to Republicans. On February 18 Bush won 53%-42% in South Carolina, in what turned out to be as decisive a victory as his father's there had been 12 years before. The New Hampshire and South Carolina results were templates for what happened elsewhere; in New Hampshire and other Northeastern states, McCain ran about even with Bush among self-identified Republicans and way ahead among self-identified Independents and self-identified Democrats; in South Carolina and other states outside the Northeast, Bush ran way ahead among Republicans and behind among independents and Democrats. On February 22 McCain won in Arizona and, in a big 50%-43% upset, in Michigan, where 17% of Republican primary voters were self-identified Democrats and 35% Independents.

McCain might have done better if he had emphasized other issues on which he had consistently taken stands in line with most Republicans' thinking—defense, tax cuts (he had an interesting tax cut plan himself, but he spent less time on it than on attacking Bush's), abortion, Social Security individual investment accounts. Instead, after South Carolina, he gave a speech in Virginia Beach attacking the religious right and in an offhand comment on the bus called Pat Robertson and Jerry

Falwell "forces of evil." As he explained the next day, this was sarcastic "Luke Skywalker talk," which reporters often heard on the bus but which rarely appeared in their writings or broadcasts. But to many Christian conservatives, a large segment of the Republican primary vote, it sounded like angry hostility; McCain lost in Virginia and Washington on February 29. On Super Tuesday, March 7, McCain won in Massachusetts, Connecticut, Rhode Island and Vermont. But he lost decisively in New York, Ohio and California and "suspended" his campaign on March 9. Much attention was focused on the fact that he did not "endorse" Bush; when they finally met in Pittsburgh in May reporters practically had to extract the word from his mouth. He made it clear he did not want to be nominated for vice president and said he wanted no cabinet post, making the plausible argument that he operated better as his own man than as someone else's appointee. He insisted on having his wife Cindy McCain, not Jane Hull, head the Arizona delegation to the convention, and he gave a moving, elegiac speech that ended as if in a minor key.

Some defeated presidential candidates sulk in their tents; McCain became more legislatively active than ever—and on many issues allying himself with Democrats and against most Republicans. His first priority was the campaign finance bill; he had campaigned for Republican House candidates and tried, with some success, to get them to support it. In January 2001 he threatened to tie up the Senate unless Majority Leader Trent Lott set aside two weeks of debate on the issue. In March 2001, after two weeks of civilized but spirited debate, during which McCain and Feingold fended off several poison-pill amendments, the legislation passed April 2 by a 59-41 vote. An amendment by Fred Thompson and Dianne Feinstein was passed to raise limits on individual contributions from $1,000 to $2,000, but the bill retained the soft-money ban and limit on issue ads prior to the election, which some senators felt would be struck down by the courts as an unconstitutional ban of free speech. The House, which twice had passed similar bills, took up the issue in June 2001. But after the Republican leadership's rule was defeated—a very rare event indeed—Speaker Dennis Hastert pulled the bill from the floor. Supporters tried to get the 218 signatures needed for a discharge petition. For months the number hovered just under 218, but in January 2002 the signatures were obtained. The House passed its version of the bill in February 2002 by a 240-189 vote, and the bill became law in March 2002; initially, most of it was upheld by the Supreme Court. But McCain didn't rest on his victory. He was furious that the Bush administration didn't appoint a Democrat designated by Tom Daschle to a seat on the Federal Election Commission; the holdover Democrat was voting with the Republicans and passing regulations which McCain argued undercut the bill. In June he threatened to block all nominations until Bush made the appointment, and in October 2002 he invoked the Congressional Review Act to try to overturn the new regulations and also filed a lawsuit against the FEC.

McCain voted with the Democrats in July 2001 on HMO regulation. He was the only Republican to vote against the water projects bill in October, charging that it contained $1.2 billion of special projects earmarked for districts. He appeared in ads in Colorado and Oregon for ballot propositions requiring background checks for sales at gun shows. In 2002, after campaign finance regulation passed the Senate, he worked with many Democrats again. He, John Edwards and Edward Kennedy sponsored an HMO regulation bill. He supported funding of embryonic stem-cell research. With John Kerry he proposed CAFE standards for all cars and light trucks of 36 miles per gallon by 2015. He was one of two Republicans to vote against the conference report on the tax cut in May and, after Jim Jeffords switched parties, he invited Tom Daschle to a friendly visit to his vacation home near Sedona; speculation abounded that McCain would switch parties too, and liberals writing in *The Washington Monthly* and *The New Republic* argued that he would be the strongest Democratic nominee for president. But he turned that talk aside, and later accounts by participants differed on how serious McCain was about switching. He took strong stands with George W. Bush and most Republicans on some issues—the nomination of his tobacco bill adversary John Ashcroft for attorney general, repeal of ergonomics regulations, the May 2001 budget resolution, and allowing Mexican trucks into the United States.

McCain strongly supported Bush in the war on terrorism after September 11. In October 2001 he urged more ground troops in Afghanistan, and in December 2001 he was one of 10 members of Congress to sign a letter urging that Iraq be the next target. He called for the government to run airline security and he co-sponsored a bill with Ernest Hollings that effectively decided the issue; it passed 97–0 in October 2001. But he also proposed that screeners be fireable without regard to civil service rules—the position Bush insisted on and Democrats, to their political detriment, opposed on the homeland security bill in 2002. He called for a special commission to investigate intelligence failures before September 11, a proposal opposed for months by the Bush administration, and said that former Senators Gary Hart and Warren Rudman should serve on it. The final version of the law provided, at the insistence of relatives of September 11 casualties, that McCain and Richard Shelby get a veto over Trent Lott's appointees to the commission; McCain's attempts to get Lott to appoint Rudman failed. In 2002 he did much less campaigning for Republicans than in 2000, making appearances in tandem with promotion of his latest book *Worth the Fighting For* and only on behalf of Republicans who had supported his brand of campaign finance regulation; in September, he appeared with Richard Gephardt in support of the generic drug bill and said it was "very, very likely" that Republicans would lose their majority in the House.

They didn't and in fact regained their majority in the Senate, making McCain chairman of the Commerce committee again. There he promoted the bill he co-sponsored with Joseph Lieberman to reduce carbon dioxide emissions; it got 43 votes on the floor of the Senate in 2003. On Armed Services he persisted in his campaign against the proposed purchase of Boeing 767s as aerial refueling tankers and in his attacks on Pentagon improprieties. He questioned the fallback from Fallujah in April 2004. He also continued to call for a larger army and more troops in Iraq. "I have strenuously argued for larger troop numbers in Iraq, including the right kind of troops—linguists, special forces, civil affairs, etc. There are very strong differences of opinion between myself and Secretary Rumsfeld on that issue." In December 2004 he said he had "no confidence" in Rumsfeld but did not call on him to resign—an ominous note in that McCain was in line to become chairman of the committee in January 2007 (he became ranking minority member instead). He pushed for adoption of the 9/11 Commission's recommendations for changes in the intelligence community, but failed in October to get appropriations power for the Intelligence Committee. He opposed the constitutional amendment to ban same-sex marriage as "antithetical in every way to the core philosophy of Republicans. It usurps from the states a fundamental authority they have always possessed and imposes a federal remedy for a problem that most states believe does not confront them." On all these issues he was at odds with the Bush administration.

Two issues with an Arizona dimension on which McCain has worked are water and Indians. With Jon Kyl and the state's House delegation, he worked to pass the Arizona Water Settlements Act, resolving disputes between the state and Indian tribes and between the federal government over water rights; this was the most far-reaching Indian water settlement in history. The Senate passed it in October 2004, as the presidential campaign was raging, and the House passed it in November, after it was over. McCain served as chairman of the Indian Affairs Committee in 1995-97 and became chairman again in January 2005. In February 2004, after the *Washington Post* reported that lobbyist Jack Abramoff and publicist Michael Scanlon, both with strong Republican connections, had received $45 million in fees from Indian tribes, McCain demanded a hearing. It was held in September and McCain was fierce in his denunciation: "What sets this tale apart, what makes it truly extraordinary, is the extent and degree of the apparent exploitation and deceit." Abramoff later went to jail on unrelated charges.

Heading into the 2004 presidential campaign McCain was a major national figure, with high positives and very low negatives among Democrats as well as Republicans, a leading Republican who was nonetheless at odds with the Bush White House on many issues. The press, always enchanted with him, gave him plenteous coverage. As John Kerry, his fellow Vietnam veteran, clinched the Democratic nomination in March 2004, there was speculation that he would ask McCain to be his vice presidential nominee. Polls showed Kerry-McCain running far ahead of Bush-Cheney. After some days of speculation and some talks with Kerry, he firmly rejected the idea. "I am a pro-life, deficit hawk, free trade Republican," he said. Bush chief strategist Karl Rove sat down for a talk with McCain's 2000 strategist John Weaver, an old adversary from Texas politics, and made peace. In June 2004 McCain appeared with Bush at Fort Lewis, Washington, and at a campaign stop in Nevada and McCain endorsed him strongly. After press stories that suggested Bush would drop Dick Cheney from the ticket, McCain made a campaign appearance with Cheney. When the Swift Boat Veterans for Truth ads appeared against John Kerry, McCain called them "dishonorable" and said they should be dropped from the air. When Bush declined to join that demand, he didn't press the issue further, and conceded that, "Everybody is accountable for what they do, and certainly John Kerry is accountable for what he did after the war, and people can make a judgment." He said that he had advised Kerry to avoid mentioning the war, as he had done in his 2000 campaign, and to let others do it. In August he asked Kerry to stop running an ad showing him criticizing Bush in 2000; Kerry did so. On Monday night at the Republican National Convention McCain delivered another eloquent speech unequivocally endorsing Bush. "He has been tested and has risen to the most important challenge of our time, and I salute him." And he took a swipe at the "disingenuous filmmaker" Michael Moore, who was then sitting in the press section, to the delight of the delegates.

McCain made common cause with Bush not only on the campaign trail but on some important issues. McCain complained that heavy spending by mostly anti-Bush 527 organizations of millions of dollars of soft money violated McCain-Feingold. The Bush campaign took the same position, filing a complaint with the FEC in March 2004 and joining McCain in a lawsuit in August to force the FEC to act. In September McCain and Feingold filed a bill to limit the use of soft money by 527s and promised to push it forward in 2005. On immigration—a raging issue in Arizona—McCain said, "The truth is, border enforcement alone does not work." With Congressmen Jim Kolbe and Jeff Flake he sponsored a guest worker law, which would provide six-year temporary worker visas and three-year visas for those who are here illegally now. He also co-sponsored with Jon Kyl a bill to fund border security measures. He recognized Arizona voters' anger. "The nation has lost control of its southern border, and Arizona is paying the price through transient traffic, violence in our streets and deaths in our deserts." But he opposed Proposition 200, cutting off public benefits to illegal immigrants, arguing that it would"delay, possibly derail, the search for a solution." It passed, but with a less than overwhelming 56% of the vote.

In Washington, McCain continued to support Bush. He voted for extension of the Bush tax cuts, including some he had initially opposed. In May 2005 he and Edward Kennedy sponsored an immigration bill with legalization provisions; illegal immigrants could get two three-year visas and then "get in the back of the line" of legal immigrants. "Some Americans believe we must find all these millions, round them up and send them back to the countries they came from. I don't know how you do that. And I don't know why you would want to." That bill was similar to the Martinez-Hagel immigration bill that passed 62-36 in May 2006. On ethics issues, he began working quietly with his sometime adversary Trent Lott in January 2006 on a lobbyist gift ban and started working on a bipartisan basis with Barack Obama on the issue.   When in February 2006 Obama sent a letter favoring going through committee rather than a task force, McCain wrote back angrily. He "apologized" for taking Obama seriously. "I understand how important the opportunity to lead your party's effort to exploit this issue must seem to a freshman senator, and I hold no hard feelings over your earlier disingenuousness." Obama replied, "The fact that you have now questioned my sincerity and my desire to put aside politics for the public interest is regrettable, but does not in any way diminish my deep respect for you, nor my willingness to find a bipartisan solution to this problem," and they both quickly made up. But the Senate remained reluctant to embrace some McCain proposals: an independent Office of Public Integrity to monitor both houses of Congress, private jet travel to be billed at charter-flight rather than first-class rates. In 2005 and 2007 McCain and Lieberman introduced bills to reduce carbon dioxide emissions; the 2007 version would cap them at 2004 levels by 2012 and then mandate 2% annual reductions through 2020; it also had incentives for nuclear power development. After Hurricane Katrina showed the inadequacy of the Army Corps of Engineers' work, McCain worked with Russ Feingold to come up with language on an independent peer review of Corps projects.

On Iraq, McCain continually praised George W. Bush's resolve but called for more troops, to no avail while Donald Rumsfeld remained as Defense secretary. He said the administration's handling of the war "will go down as one of the worst" mistakes in U.S. military history. He dismissed the recommendations of the Iraq Study Group in December 2006 and called for the surge of troops that Bush ordered in January 2007. To those who said the troops were already overextended, he said, "There's only one thing worse than an overstressed Army and Marine Corps and that's a defeated Army and Marine Corps." He strongly opposed those who called for withdrawal of troops and pointed to what he said would be the consequences. "Failure means catastrophic consequences and then we are back. Maybe not in Iraq, but back in the Middle East." To those who said that his support of the surge would hurt his chances in the presidential race, he responded many times, "I would much rather lose an election than lose a war."

By mid-2006 it was clear that McCain was running for president again. In the 2006 election cycle he traveled around the country to support many Republicans, and raised $10.5 million for them. In May 2006 he delivered identical commencement speeches at Liberty University, where he was welcomed by Jerry Falwell, and The New School, a university where he was welcomed by his former colleague Bob Kerrey, though not by all the graduates. His long derision of pork barrel spending became a national issue, symbolized by the "bridge to nowhere" in Alaska authorized by the 2005 transportation bill. He voiced more frequently and fervently than in the past his longstanding opposition to abortion. Soon after the November 2006 elections, he set up an exploratory committee and announced in April 2007. In late 2006 he was running about even with Rudolph Giuliani in Republican primary polls and was generally considered the frontrunner. But in January 2007 Giuliani, despite his liberal stands on some cultural issues, started running ahead;

and in general election polling McCain was running not much better than even with, and sometimes behind, Hillary Rodham Clinton and Barack Obama. In April 2007 he encountered a setback when it turned out that his campaign had raised only $12.5 million in the first quarter of the year, far behind Mitt Romney's $23 million and Giuliani's $15 million, and that it had far less cash on hand than either; McCain announced he was reorganizing his fundraising and campaign apparatus. In April 2007 he delivered a fervent speech on Iraq and, a week later, another on taxes, opposing tax increases and promising to veto all pork barrel spending. As McCain continued his longstanding support of a surge in Iraq, his press coverage became less favorable. It was pointed out that he will turn 72 in August 2008, a year younger than Ronald Reagan was when he was reelected in 1984. But he continued to maintain a very active, indeed hyperkinetic, schedule, and he might be entitled to argue that voters shouldn't count the five and a half years he spent in Hanoi.

McCain's campaign struggled through the summer, waylaid by the June debate over illegal immigration. His sponsorship with Edward Kennedy of a bill to establish a temporary guest worker program met with fierce resistance from conservatives who labeled it amnesty. His polling numbers and fundraising sagged and the campaign faced high-profile departures of staffers. Yet he was adamant that his campaign would continue, saying nothing less than "contracting a fatal disease" would lead him to drop out of the race.

McCain's appeal in general elections has long been apparent in Arizona. He won his Senate seat in 1986 by 60%-40% and in 1992, after the Keating Five investigation, he was re-elected 56%-32%. In 1998 he won by an impressive 69%-27%, carrying heavily Democratic Apache County 54%-42% and winning the Hispanic vote 52%-42%. In late 2002 and early 2003 the Club for Growth encouraged Congressman Jeff Flake to challenge him in the Republican primary; Flake decided not to. In November 2004 McCain was reelected 77%-21%, while Bush was carrying the state 55%-44%.

Junior Senator

Jon Kyl (R)

Elected 1994, seat up 2012, 3d term; b. Apr. 25, 1942, Oakland, NE; home, Phoenix; U. of AZ, B.A. 1964, L.L.B. 1966; Presbyterian; married (Caryll).

Elected Office: U.S. House of Reps., 1986-94.

Professional Career: Practicing atty., 1966-86; Chmn., Phoenix Chamber of Commerce, 1984-85.

DC Office: 730 HSOB, 20510, 202-224-4521; Fax: 202-224-2207; Web site: kyl.senate.gov.

State Offices: Phoenix, 602-840-1891; Tucson, 520-575-8633.

Committees: *Republican Conference Chairman. Finance* (5th of 10 R): Taxation & IRS Oversight & Long-Term Growth (RMM); Social Security, Pensions & Family Policy; Health Care. *Judiciary* (4th of 9 R): Terrorism, Technology & Homeland Security (RMM); Human Rights & the Law; Immigration, Refugees & Border Security.

Group Ratings

	ADA	ACLU	AFS	LCV	ITIC	NTU	COC	ACU	CFG	FRC
2006	0	17	0	29	100	87	92	92	94	100
2005	5	—	0	5	—	87	83	100	100	—

National Journal Ratings

	2005 LIB	—	2005 CONS		2006 LIB	—	2006 CONS
Economic	16%	—	80%		0%	—	97%
Social	0%	—	77%		18%	—	74%
Foreign	26%	—	65%		0%	—	92%

Key Votes of the 109th Congress

1. Bar ANWR Drilling	N	5. Confirm Samuel Alito	Y	9. Limit Interstate Abortion	Y
2. FY06 Spending Curb	Y	6. Path to Citizenship	N	10. CAFTA	Y
3. Estate Tax Repeal	Y	7. Bar Same Sex Marriage	Y	11. Urge Iraq Withdrawal	N
4. Raise Minimum Wage	N	8. Stem Cell Research $	N	12. Provide Detainee Rights	N

Election Results

2006 general	Jon Kyl (R)	814,398	(53%)	($15,571,727)
	Jim Pederson (D)	664,141	(43%)	($14,709,241)
	Other	48,243	(3%)	
2006 primary	Jon Kyl (R)	unopposed		
2000 general	Jon Kyl (R)	1,108,196	(79%)	($2,503,674)
	William Toel (I)	109,230	(8%)	($21,491)
	Vance Hansen (Green)	108,926	(8%)	
	Barry J. Hess, II (Lib)	70,724	(5%)	

Prior Winning Percentages: 1994 (54%); 1992 House (59%); 1990 House (61%); 1988 House (87%); 1986 House (65%)

Jon Kyl, Arizona's junior senator, was first elected to the House in 1986 and to the Senate in 1994. His father John Kyl was a Republican congressman from Iowa (1959-65, 1967-73), who eventually lost his seat in reapportionment; Jon Kyl moved to a state that, in effect, was gaining the Republican seats that Great Plains states like Iowa were losing. Kyl went to college and law school in Arizona, practiced law in Phoenix, worked on Republican campaigns and headed the Phoenix Chamber of Commerce; he won the heavily Republican 4th District seat in 1986 by beating former (1973-77) Congressman John Conlan, who had support from the religious right, 60%-28%.

In the House, Kyl was a leader among Republicans on missile defense, the balanced budget amendment, and for disclosing the names of House members with overdrafts on the House bank—one of the causes that destabilized Democrats' control of the House in the years running up to 1994. By that time, Kyl was running for the Senate seat held for three terms by Democrat Dennis DeConcini, whose reputation was stained by his involvement in the Keating Five scandal. Kyl had no primary opposition and the further good fortune that one-term Congressman Sam Coppersmith won the September 13 Democratic primary by only 59 votes of 255,000 cast after a two-week recount. Kyl, with far more money, ran ads with home movie texture showing him traveling through the desert countryside, dressed in jeans and working on ranches, while talking about how he and his wife first fell in love with the state (he has climbed Camelback Mountain "more than 1,000 times"). Coppersmith stressed his support for abortion rights and said he would welcome a campaign visit from Bill Clinton. Kyl won easily, 54%-40%.

Kyl has a solidly conservative voting record. Quietly, he has become a major force on defense policy. He is perhaps the Senate's biggest champion of a missile defense system. In 1997 he led, with Jesse Helms, the losing fight against the Chemical Weapons Convention. Learning from that experience, he organized the winning fight to reject the Comprehensive Test Ban Treaty, submitted by Bill Clinton to the Senate in September 1997. Starting in 1998, Kyl studied the details and worked to persuade Republican colleagues to oppose the treaty. In May 1999 he told Majority Leader Trent Lott that he had 34 solid votes against, enough to prevent ratification, but Helms, the Foreign Relations chairman, insisted that Kyl get more before he would let the treaty come to the floor. All 45 Democrats, unaware in the increasingly partisan Senate of Kyl's efforts, wrote Helms in July demanding the treaty be brought forward by September. Helms replied dismissively that he would not do so until he got action on the Kyoto treaty and amendments to the ABM treaty. In September North Dakota Democrat Byron Dorgan promised to "plant myself on the floor like a potted plant" until the CTBT was considered. The ranking Foreign Relations Democrat still thought that 25 Republicans could be persuaded to vote for the treaty, and concurred when Lott promised to bring it up in October. Only then did Senate Democrats and the Clinton White House begin to discover that they had conspired to defeat their own treaty. Kyl had done his work well: The CTBT did not even get a majority, much less the required two-thirds, as it was defeated 48-51. Kyl continues to press forward on missile defense. He urged George W. Bush to abrogate the treaty, and when Senate Democrats on the Armed Services Committee tried to cut missile defense funds in May 2002 he was quick to respond, pointing out that Iran had just successfully tested an 800-mile-range missile. Kyl strongly supported the Bush administration on Afghanistan and Iraq. When Edward Kennedy attacked Bush in March 2004 for misusing intelligence on Iraq, Kyl replied, "The reality is, no one was duped. We were all working off the same data. Reasonable people reached different conclusions about what to do based on a commonly understood set of facts. There was nothing devious about that. One need not veer off into conspiracy theories to explain honest differences of opinion about policies."

On the Judiciary Committee, Kyl is the ranking Republican of the Terrorism, Technology and Homeland Security Subcommittee. Before September 11 he and ranking Democrat Dianne

Feinstein co-sponsored a bill to prepare defenses for attacks by terrorists with chemical and biological weapons, and in November 2001 they introduced a bill to establish a comprehensive lookout database, which would combine information from the CIA, the FBI and the State Department and make it available to border and consular personnel. In 2004 Kyl's bill passed the Senate to include terrorists not known to be affiliated with a group in the Patriot Act, and he held hearings on other potential changes in the law. He has pointed out how lax State Department visa policies— notably the Visa Express program in Saudi Arabia, which delegated visa issuance to travel agents— enabled most of the September 11 hijackers to enter the country and how the State Department resisted any tightening of procedures.

On other Judiciary issues, Kyl has worked to beef up the Border Patrol and to track legal immigrants who overstay their visas. He also has worked for more federal reimbursement of states and localities for the costs of hospitalizing and incarcerating illegal aliens. He took a central role in the illegal immigration debate, which put him at odds with McCain. In 2005, Kyl opposed a comprehensive immigration bill that McCain authored with Edward Kennedy, which included a controversial provision for an immigrant guest worker program. With John Cornyn, Kyl sponsored an immigration bill that focused heavily on border security and included a guestworker program that required immigrants to return home and apply for work permits before seeking a job in the U.S. Kyl's opposition to the Senate bill also put him at odds with the stance taken by fellow Arizona Reps. Jim Kolbe and Jeff Flake, both Republicans. The Senate passed the McCain-Kennedy bill, which was more in line with the White House's wishes, but the bill went nowhere because of stiff resistance in the House, which approved a border enforcement bill. Kyl and Cornyn failed in attempts to secure $3.9 billion worth of border security funding for new border agents and detention facilities. Kyl did succeed in attaching an amendment to a defense spending bill in the Senate that provided $1.8 billion for 370 miles of fencing along the U.S.-Mexican border. Bush in October 2006 signed into law a bill that allowed construction to begin on a 700-mile border fence, but provided no new money for the project. Congress had earlier approved $1.2 billion for the fence, but the bulk of the project depends now on whether the new Democratic Congress decides to fund it.

Water is one of the most sensitive issues in Arizona. For years Kyl worked, mostly behind the scenes, on settling Indian claims to Colorado and Gila River water and the dispute between the federal government and the state of Arizona of how much the state must pay the feds for the Central Arizona Project, completed in 1993 at a cost of $3.6 billion. The stakeholders were many and the stakes were huge; some of the litigation had been ongoing for 20 years. With John McCain as co-sponsor and with the support of the entire Arizona House delegation, Kyl succeeded in passing the Arizona Water Settlement Act in 2004. It settled Indian lawsuits against Arizona and New Mexico and set Arizona's reimbursement to the federal government at $1.65 billion; this was the most far-reaching Indian water settlement in history.

On other bills, Kyl had mixed results. He was the lead Senate sponsor for repealing the estate tax and had negotiated throughout 2005 and 2006 with Democrats on a compromise that would garner a filibuster-proof 60 votes. Hurricane Katrina in 2005 derailed plans for a scheduled vote. Kyl also became the lead Senate sponsor of an Internet gambling ban with a bill prohibiting credit card companies from processing online wagers. The House in July 2006 overwhelmingly passed a similar bill; in October 2006 President Bush signed port security legislation that included a ban on interstate and international online gambling transactions. (The ban prompted a group of poker players to start an online fundraising drive to support Kyl's 2006 opponent.)

Kyl is not an active seeker of publicity, and is far less well known in Arizona and Washington than his colleague McCain. He is pleasant and unassuming, but can surprise: He is a big fan of race cars and has been seen driving the lead car around the track in a warm-up lap at the Phoenix International Raceway. In June 2000 Kyl was interviewed as a possible vice presidential nominee by Dick Cheney, whom he had chosen as a kind of model when he came to the House, but he ultimately recommended against his own selection. He became the chairman of the Republican Steering Committee in 2001 and, moving up in the leadership, chairman of the Republican Policy Committee in 2003.

Kyl had no difficulty winning reelection in 2000: No Democrat filed to run against him and he won 79% of the vote against an Independent, a Green Party candidate and a Libertarian. When he first ran for the Senate in 1994, he said he would probably serve only two terms, but Kyl signaled early in the 2006 election cycle that he would run for a third term. His 2006 opponent was former state Democratic party chairman Jim Pederson, a wealthy real estate developer who had revitalized the state party by pouring millions of his personal wealth into it. Kyl portrayed Pederson as inexperienced and ran ads that accused him of attempting to buy the Senate seat and of supporting amnesty for illegal immigrants because of his support for an immigrant guestworker program. On the Iraq war, Kyl said it is better to fight terrorists in Iraq than at home. Pederson painted Kyl as a Washington insider and part of its "special interest" culture, while he also tied Kyl to the unpopular George W. Bush. Pederson called for the resignation of Defense Secretary Donald Rumsfeld and a stabilization plan for Iraq that included establishing conditions to bring U.S. troops home. The race remained on the margins for most of the election cycle, but Kyl took the challenge seriously, not least because Pederson spent more than $10.9 million of his own money in the race. Polls showed Kyl leading Pederson throughout the campaign but polling less than 50%. In October the Democratic Senatorial Campaign Committee reduced its spending in the state, but then Charles Schumer, citing positive early voting numbers, announced five days before the election that the party was pouring in $1 million to boost Pederson. In the end, Kyl spent $15.6 million in the race compared to Pederson's $14.7 million. Kyl won 53%-43%. He won all but four counties, carrying the Phoenix metro area but losing Flagstaff's Coconino County and Tucson's Pima County. Pederson won the Latino vote, but by only 54%-41%, and the African-American vote by only 53%-40%.

After the election, Kyl was poised to continue his more visible and assertive role in the Senate. His Republican colleagues promoted him to Republican Conference chairman, the third-ranking position in GOP leadership, which is responsible for developing and communicating the party's message. His role in drafting a compromise immigration reform measure in 2007 made him a lightning rod for criticism; his staff fielded thousands of emails and phone calls, almost all negative. "I have learned some new words from my constituents," he joked in May 2007. Speaking of the considerable political blowback, he told the *Associated Press*: "Obviously, I wasn't thinking of my political career when I took the leadership role I did in the immigration debate; sometimes you do what you have to do."

FIRST DISTRICT

Rep. Rick Renzi (R)

Elected 2002, 3d term; b. June 11, 1958, Ft. Monmouth, NJ; home, Flagstaff; N. AZ. U., B.S. 1980, Catholic U., J.D. 2002; Catholic; married (Roberta).

Professional Career: Admin., Defense Dept, 1984-89; Owner, Patriot Insurance Co., 1989-2002; Owner, Renzi & Campbell Dev. Inc., 1994-2002; Owner, Renzi Vino vineyard, 1998-present.

DC Office: 418 CHOB, 20515, 202-225-2315; Fax: 202-226-9739; Web site: www.house.gov/renzi/.

District Offices: Casa Grande, 520-705-2181; Flagstaff, 928-213-3434; Prescott, 928-708-9120; Show Low, 928-537-2800.

Group Ratings

	ADA	ACLU	AFS	LCV	ITIC	NTU	COC	ACU	CFG	FRC
2006	15	14	14	8	86	52	93	84	51	100
2005	15	—	13	0	—	56	93	92	56	92

National Journal Ratings

	2005 LIB	—	2005 CONS	2006 LIB	—	2006 CONS
Economic	42%	—	57%	36%	—	63%
Social	0%	—	89%	35%	—	63%
Foreign	0%	—	89%	42%	—	57%

Key Votes of the 109th Congress

1. Estate Tax Repeal	Y	5. Limit Interstate Abortion	Y	9. Build Border Fence	Y
2. Limit CAFE Standards	Y	6. Extend Patriot Act	Y	10. CAFTA	Y
3. FY06 Spending Curb	Y	7. Bar Same Sex Marriage	Y	11. Oppose Iraq Withdrawal	Y
4. Drilling in ANWR	Y	8. Stem Cell Research $	N	12. Detainee Tribunals	Y

Election Results

2006 general	Rick Renzi (R) 105,646	(52%)	($2,246,790)
	Ellen Simon (D) 88,691	(43%)	($1,514,638)
	David Schlosser (Lib) 9,802	(5%)	($30,628)
2006 primary	Rick Renzi (R) .... unopposed		
2004 general	Rick Renzi (R) 148,315	(59%)	($2,207,249)
	Paul Babbitt (D) 91,776	(36%)	($1,274,852)
	John Crockett (Lib) 13,260	(5%)	

Prior Winning Percentages: 2002 (49%)

The People		Race/Ethnic Origin	Ancestry	
Area size:	58,714 sq. mi.	58.4% White	German: 10.3%	English: 8.7%
Urban population:	55.5%	1.2% Black	Irish: 7.1%	
Rural population:	44.5%	0.5% Asian	**2004 Presidential Vote**	
Pop. 2000:	641,329	22.1% Native Am.	Bush (R) 139,221	(54%)
Pop. 2005 (est):	703,453	0.1% Hawaiian	Kerry (D) 117,673	(46%)
Median income:	$32,979	1.2% Two+ races	Other 1,726	(1%)
Poverty status:	20.3%	0.1% Other	**2000 Presidential Vote**	
Military veterans:	15.7%	16.4% Hispanic Origin	Bush (R) 102,068	(51%)
			Gore (D) 91,920	(46%)
			Other 7,931	(4%)
			Cook Partisan Voting Index: R + 2	

Occupation   Blue collar: 25.6%   White collar: 53.5%   Gray collar: 20.9%

Beyond Phoenix and the Valley of the Sun, Arizona is a vast state of stunning beauty: The awe-inspiring Grand Canyon, the subtle pastel hues of the Painted Desert, the sheer cliff walls of Canyon de Chelly, the still waters of Lake Powell, the mountainous pine forests around Flagstaff, the rust-and-rosy red rocks of Sedona. It is also the home of man-made landmarks: The celebrated U.S. 66, now mostly superseded by Interstate 40 (though you can still take the exit ramp and ride on the old unmarked 66 in Holbrook and Winslow and Williams); the old gold mining camp of Prescott, home since 1888 of America's oldest annual rodeo; Jerome, a mining town built improbably on hillside stilts, now reborn as an artist colony; plus old copper mining towns like Globe.

All of these places are in the 1st Congressional District of Arizona, which includes over half the state and is larger than Pennsylvania. It covers most of northern Arizona, except for Mohave County and the Hopi Indian Reservation and a narrow band of land connecting them. It reaches south to the northern edges of the Phoenix and Tucson metro areas. The 1st is the home of the nation's largest and fastest-growing Indian population: 22% of its residents identify themselves as American Indians. There are many reservations here—Fort Apache, San Carlos, Zuni—but by far the largest is the Navajo Nation. The Hopi are excluded because they have a long and angry boundary dispute with the Navajo and agreed to be part of the 2d District. Most of the Navajo are (oddly) in Apache County, with the rest in Navajo and Coconino Counties. They have a history of fiercely contested tribal elections and, alas, considerable corruption; their winner-take-all political governance does not seem to have served the community well. Unemployment has run close to 50%, nearly 60% are without phone service and 30% live without running water or electricity. Alcoholism and drug abuse remain rampant. Complex regulations have stifled economic development.

The 1st District was designed to be closely divided between the two parties. But there are sharp divisions. The copper mining counties (Greenlee, Graham, Gila) are historically Democratic and still register that way, but tend to vote Republican. Apache County, with its Navajo majority, has been heavily Democratic. Coconino County includes the college town and growing retirement mecca of Flagstaff, part of the Navajo Reservation, and New Age haven Sedona, where the Army drove the Apaches off the land in the 1870s after gold was discovered; it is increasingly Democratic. Yavapai County is heavily Republican. It includes Prescott, where Barry Goldwater always began his Arizona campaigns.

The congressman from the 1st District is Rick Renzi, a Republican elected in 2002 in his first bid for elective office. Renzi grew up in Sierra Vista, Arizona, near Fort Huachuca and the Mexican border, and was captain of the football team of Northern Arizona University in Flagstaff. His father, a retired Army general, is a senior executive for a Virginia-based defense contractor. During his first campaign for Congress, Renzi billed himself as a "hometown, Flagstaff boy," but he has spent most of his life outside the district. In 1986 he moved to Virginia to work for the Defense Department and in 1989 he started an insurance business in Virginia. In 2002, he received a law degree from Catholic

University in Washington. Since 1991, he and his family (Renzi is the father of 12 children, each of whose names begin with "R") have lived in Burke, Virginia, where he was a registered voter. In 1999 he declared himself an Arizona resident; he registered to vote as an independent in Santa Cruz County, near the Mexican border, where he owned some animals and a vineyard that has produced small quantities of wine. Soon after the Arizona Independent Redistricting Commission announced the new congressional map, Renzi bought a $216,000 house in Flagstaff, where he owned a real estate investment firm, and registered there, as a Republican.

This new seat attracted plenty of candidates—six Republicans, seven Democrats and two Libertarians—some, like Renzi, with only weak links to the district. Renzi quickly established himself as the frontrunner among Republicans by spending more than $500,000 of his own money for an early advertising blitz. He claimed to have worked on legislation for Congressman Jim Kolbe and Senator Jon Kyl; he was an unpaid intern in his office for two months in 1999, an annoyed Kyl said. Renzi opposed abortion and supported gun rights and a flat tax. He won the Republican primary with 24% of the vote, carrying Yavapai and Coconino Counties—Prescott, Sedona, Flagstaff—plus Pinal County in the south. The Democratic nominee was George Cordova, a venture capitalist and political neophyte who did grass roots campaigning on the Indian reservations. He won the primary in an upset with 22% of the vote. In the general, Cordova supported abortion rights, a prescription drug benefit, and environmental protection, but the key to the outcome was skillful opposition research. After the primary, the NRCC launched an intense attack on Cordova for four failed ventures in the 1980s that left behind a trail of lawsuits, tax liens and court-adjudicated debts. More than $2 million of Republican ads and a total of $4 million spent on Renzi's behalf weakened Cordova, on whose behalf national Democrats spent about $1 million. Renzi won 49%-46%. Cordova carried the three counties with large Navajo populations, but Renzi led 61%-33% in Yavapai, which cast one-third of the votes, and took the southern part of the district.

In the House, Renzi made few waves and usually voted with conservatives, especially on cultural issues. He focused his attention on topics with a local impact. One of his bills proposed an exchange of more than 56,000 acres of Forest Service and private lands to expand the Flagstaff airport. But it bogged down in disputes about other federal lands proposals. Renzi worked hard on Indian issues. He urged officials to locate a Veterans' Affairs hospital in the Navajo Nation, which would be the first ever on an Indian reservation, and he won enactment of his provision to study the inclusion of tribal governments in the high-intensity drug trafficking program. He also enacted a bill to reduce the risk to lenders for housing of Native Americans. Barney Frank gave him credit for focusing attention on Indian housing problems. Renzi sought federal funds for the state border guard to fight illegal immigration. He showed independence by opposing the Republican budget resolution in May 2006 and voting with Democrats on a minimum-wage increase.

Renzi has ranked high on the Democrats' target list, but they have nominated flawed candidates and made little progress. In 2004, Democratic challenger Paul Babbitt, former mayor of Flagstaff and the brother of former Interior Secretary and Arizona Governor Bruce Babbitt, criticized Renzi as a Republican loyalist. But there was some local resentment over Bruce Babbitt's actions as Interior Secretary. In contrast, there was great local appreciation for Renzi's work on Indian issues; he won important endorsements, including that of the Navajo Nation. In Indian country, he ran impressively. He carried Apache County with 56% of the vote; Bush got only 35% there. He carried Navajo County with 67%; Bush got only 53% there. And he lost Coconino County, Babbitt's home turf, by only 112 votes out of 51,000 cast; Bush got only 43% there. The result was a stunning 59%-36% victory for Renzi. In 2006, Democrats nominated Ellen Simon, a former Cleveland trial attorney who had settled in Sedona and ran into problems because of an ex-wife's child-support claims against her husband. Simon loaned her campaign more than $700,000. Democrats raised ethical questions about Renzi's involvement in an Arizona land deal that made a sizable profit for a business partner, but no charges were filed. Even in a difficult political climate, Renzi won 52%-43%. He lost Coconino 55%-40%, but took Yavapai County 55-39% and Navajo County by 57%-40%.

Renzi's business dealings remained in the headlines in 2007. He got entangled in the controversy surrounding the Bush administration firings of United States attorneys after his spokesman acknowledged calling one of the fired prosecutors to inquire about press accounts of a pending indictment. In April, Renzi's wife's insurance business was raided by the FBI. The congressman continued to deny any wrongdoing but took a leave of absence from his three committees. He also removed himself from an NRCC fundraising program for vulnerable incumbents, prompting speculation that he might resign or decline to seek reelection in 2008—rumors which Renzi denied. "For several weeks, I have been the subject of leaked stories, conjecture and false attacks about a land exchange," he said in late April. "None of them bear any resemblance to the truth, including the rumor that I am planning on resigning."

In August 2007, Renzi announced he would not seek reelection to a fourth term. Even before his announcement, a large field of potential challengers was taking shape. Among Democrats, state Representative Ann Kirkpatrick, attorney Howard Shanker, and former Phoenix television news reporter Mary Kim Titla by August had announced their intentions to run. Possible Republican candidates included businessman Lewis Tenney, former Sedona Mayor Alan Everett and political consultant Sydney Hay, all of whom challenged Renzi for the Republican nomination in 2002; former state Senators Tom O'Halleran and Jake Flake; and state Representative Bill Konopnicki.

SECOND DISTRICT

Rep. Trent Franks (R)

Elected 2002, 3d term; b. June 19, 1957, Uravan, CO; home, Glendale; Ottawa University, 1989-90; Baptist; married (Josie).

Elected Office: AZ House of Reps., 1984-86.

Professional Career: Director, AZ Governor's Office for Children, 1987-88; Exec. Director, AZ Family Research Institute, 1989-93; Writer-commentator, AZ radio station KTKP; Co-owner, Franks Brothers Independent Drilling; Pres.-CEO, Liberty Petroleum Corp.

DC Office: 1237 LHOB, 20515, 202-225-4576; Fax: 202-225-6328; Web site: www.house.gov/franks.

District Offices: Glendale, 623-776-7911.

Committees: *Armed Services* (23d of 29 R): Strategic Forces; Readiness. *Judiciary* (15th of 17 R): The Constitution, Civil Rights & Civil Liberties (RMM); Commercial & Administrative Law.

Group Ratings

	ADA	ACLU	AFS	LCV	ITIC	NTU	COC	ACU	CFG	FRC
2006	10	5	0	0	86	83	93	100	98	100
2005	5	—	0	6	—	80	81	100	100	100

National Journal Ratings

	2005 LIB	—	2005 CONS		2006 LIB	—	2006 CONS
Economic	0%	—	97%		16%	—	84%
Social	0%	—	89%		0%	—	94%
Foreign	0%	—	89%		17%	—	73%

Key Votes of the 109th Congress

1. Estate Tax Repeal	Y	5. Limit Interstate Abortion	Y	9. Build Border Fence	Y
2. Limit CAFE Standards	Y	6. Extend Patriot Act	Y	10. CAFTA	Y
3. FY06 Spending Curb	Y	7. Bar Same Sex Marriage	Y	11. Oppose Iraq Withdrawal	Y
4. Drilling in ANWR	Y	8. Stem Cell Research $	N	12. Detainee Tribunals	Y

Election Results

2006 general	Trent Franks (R)	135,150	(59%)	($474,707)
	John Thrasher (D)	89,671	(39%)	($37,231)
	Other	5,739	(2%)	
2006 primary	Trent Franks (R)	unopposed		
2004 general	Trent Franks (R)	165,260	(59%)	($738,525)
	Randy Camacho (D)	107,406	(39%)	($101,998)
	Other	6,637	(2%)	

Prior Winning Percentages: 2002 (60%)

The People		Race/Ethnic Origin	Ancestry	
Area size:	20,391 sq. mi.	78.4% White	German: 14.6%	English: 9.4%
Urban population:	89.0%	2.1% Black	Irish: 9.3%	
Rural population:	11.0%	1.7% Asian	**2004 Presidential Vote**	
Pop. 2000:	641,329	2.0% Native Am.	Bush (R) 182,326	(61%)
Pop. 2005 (est):	859,625	0.1% Hawaiian	Kerry (D) 112,620	(38%)
Median income:	$42,432	1.4% Two+ races	Other 1,634	(1%)
Poverty status:	8.9%	0.1% Other	**2000 Presidential Vote**	
Military veterans:	19.6%	14.2% Hispanic Origin	Bush (R) 119,386	(56%)
			Gore (D) 86,251	(41%)
			Other 5,760	(3%)
			Cook Partisan Voting Index: R + 9	

Occupation	Blue collar: 22.2%	White collar: 60.3%	Gray collar: 17.5%

Beyond the reach of metropolitan Phoenix and Tucson, much of Arizona looks as it did a century ago. Some is intentionally preserved in its natural state, such as the sere uplands of the Hopi Indian Reservation; other places maintain a timeless western look, like Wickenburg, the oldest Arizona town north of Tucson. Still others preserve antiquated ways of life, such as the polygamist community of Colorado City, just south of Utah, which prosecutes open polygamists. In some cases, nature and settlement juxtapose jarringly: the real London Bridge has been transplanted to Lake Havasu City, a retirement community on the Colorado River.

All these areas are part of the 2d Congressional District of Arizona, which stretches from the Hoover Dam and Lake Mead in the northwest corner of the state to the western suburbs of Phoenix, where 80% of its voters live. Astride Grand Avenue, the only diagonal street in the rigorous grid of metro Phoenix, is the mushrooming suburb of Glendale, not so long ago just a crossroads but with 239,000 people in 2005, big enough to be the scheduled host of the 2008 Super Bowl at its new stadium, and the planned spring-training home for the Los Angeles Dodgers and Chicago White Sox. Just west in the former desert are Peoria, as Middle American as its namesake in Illinois, and the huge retirement community of Sun City, where locals obsessively prune their Seussian hedges. The 2d also includes the fast-growing corridor along the I-10 Papago Freeway, past Luke Air Force Base—the largest fighter training wing in the Air Force and the only active duty F-16 training base in the U.S.—to the once open spaces of Goodyear and Buckeye. The 2d also includes Mohave County, with its growing Las Vegas suburbs, and the Hopi Indian Reservation, connected to the rest of the district by a narrow, oddly shaped corridor that runs along the bottom of the Grand Canyon.

This is Republican territory. The retirees here remember—and upwardly-striving, family-oriented young migrants who have populated these new towns in the desert still try to live—the culturally conservative, Ozzie-and-Harriet lifestyle of the 1950s. Culture, more than affluence, which by national standards is not all that striking here, accounts for their political conservatism. Republicans also control the new cities along the Colorado River.

The congressman from the 2d District is Trent Franks, a Republican first elected in 2002. He grew up in Colorado, attended college only briefly and started his own oil and gas exploration business. His political career began when he won a single term in the Arizona House in 1984; he was known for wearing a tie tack in the shape of the feet of a fetus. In 1987 he was the director of the Governor's Office for Children under Evan Mecham, a conservative Republican who was impeached and removed from office in April 1988. He was a consultant to Pat Buchanan's presidential campaign and in 1989 became executive director of the Arizona Family Research Institute, an organization associated with James Dobson's Focus on the Family. Franks sought unsuccessfully a 1992 ballot initiative to limit abortion rights and designed the state's 1997 scholarship tax credit legislation, a much-litigated measure that ultimately was upheld by the U.S. Supreme Court. The plan provides tax credits for donations to non-profits to help families pay for private education. In 1994, he ran for an open House seat but lost to John Shadegg in the Republican primary, 43%-30%.

In April 2002, Republican Bob Stump announced he was retiring and endorsed Lisa Atkins, his chief of staff throughout his 26-year congressional career. When the campaign started, Franks was not considered in the top tier of candidates. But his base of Christian conservatives and abortion opponents (plus more than $300,000 of his own money) made him a contender. Franks spent heavily on radio ads; he benefited from the distribution of a voter guide by the religious conservative Center for Arizona Policy, which describes itself as "the only organization in Arizona actively fighting in the legislature and media for conservative, traditional views on gambling, homosexuality and pornography." Franks called for overturning *Roe v. Wade* and for constitutional protection to fetuses. He endorsed a flat tax as a step toward eliminating the federal income tax, individual investment accounts under Social Security, tougher enforcement of immigration laws and minimal federal involvement in health care. His base of activists made the difference. He finished first with 28% of the vote, only 797 votes ahead of Atkins, who got 26%. In November he won 60%-37%.

In the House, Franks has a solidly conservative record. He sought co-sponsors for his Children's Hope Act, which was based on his 1997 state scholarship tax credit. He showed his outsider stripes by proposing that service on the Appropriations Committee be limited to a maximum of three terms in 10 years; redundantly, he commented that he had no interest in serving on Appropriations. He said he voted against the highway bill because it was bloated and also short-changed Arizona. But he succumbed to pressure from Republican leaders, and earned their gratitude, by switching his vote to support the Medicare/prescription drug bill while the roll call was held open for nearly three hours. On the Armed Services Committee, he worked to secure $27 million for Arizona to buy land adjacent to Luke Air Force Base in order to curtail housing development, and he worked to locate the new F-35 joint strike fighter planes at Luke. In the Republican Conference, he chairs the Voter Values Public Affairs Team. In 2007, he became ranking Republican on the Constitution subcommittee at Judiciary, where he has worked on border fence issues. Franks, who has had multiple surgeries on his cleft palate, has encouraged public awareness of the facial deformity.

Franks faced a competitive primary in September 2004 against Rick Murphy, a free-spending radio station owner, who criticized Franks for abandoning his conservative principles by supporting the Medicare/prescription drug bill. Murphy was endorsed by several local Republican officials who complained about their lack of contact from Franks; he attacked Franks for abandoning his promise not to take money from political action committees. Franks won 64%-36%—a wide margin, but less than incumbents usually get over primary challengers. He narrowly lost Mohave County, but he took 68% in Maricopa, which cast 76% of the total vote. In November Franks won 59%-39%, a downtick from 2002. With those warnings, he avoided a primary in 2006, and again won the general 59%-39%. In the early maneuvering for the 2008 GOP presidential nomination, Franks backed Duncan Hunter, the top Republican on his Armed Services Committee, as "an unequivocal social conservative and fiscal conservative," instead of John McCain, Arizona's senior senator.

THIRD DISTRICT

Rep. John Shadegg (R)

Elected 1994, 7th term; b. Oct. 22, 1949, Phoenix; home, Phoenix; U. of AZ, B.A. 1972, J.D. 1975; Episcopalian; married (Shirley).

Military Career: Air Natl. Guard, 1969-75.

Professional Career: Practicing atty., 1975-94; US Spec. Asst. Atty. Gen., 1983-90; Spec. Cnsl., AZ House Republican Caucus, 1991-92; Cnsl., AZ Wildlife Conservation, 1992.

DC Office: 306 CHOB, 20515, 202-225-3361; Fax: 202-225-3462; Web site: johnshadegg.house.gov.

District Offices: Phoenix, 602-263-5300.

Committees: *Energy & Commerce* (11th of 26 R): Health; Environment & Hazardous Materials; Energy & Air Quality. *Select Committee on Energy Independence and Global Warming* (2d of 6 R).

Group Ratings

	ADA	ACLU	AFS	LCV	ITIC	NTU	COC	ACU	CFG	FRC
2006	10	18	0	0	100	83	100	100	100	100
2005	0	—	0	6	—	79	81	100	100	92

National Journal Ratings

	2005 LIB	—	2005 CONS		2006 LIB	—	2006 CONS
Economic	21%	—	77%		26%	—	73%
Social	24%	—	74%		31%	—	68%
Foreign	0%	—	89%		30%	—	67%

Key Votes of the 109th Congress

1. Estate Tax Repeal	Y	5. Limit Interstate Abortion	Y	9. Build Border Fence	Y
2. Limit CAFE Standards	Y	6. Extend Patriot Act	Y	10. CAFTA	Y
3. FY06 Spending Curb	Y	7. Bar Same Sex Marriage	Y	11. Oppose Iraq Withdrawal	Y
4. Drilling in ANWR	Y	8. Stem Cell Research $	N	12. Detainee Tribunals	Y

Election Results

2006 general	John Shadegg (R)	112,519	(59%)	($1,167,473)
	Herb Paine (D)	72,586	(38%)	($96,976)
	Other	4,744	(2%)	
2006 primary	John Shadegg (R)	unopposed		
2004 general	John Shadegg (R)	181,012	(80%)	($794,256)
	Mark Yannone (Lib)	44,962	(20%)	

Prior Winning Percentages: 2002 (67%); 2000 (64%); 1998 (65%); 1996 (67%); 1994 (60%)

The People		Race/Ethnic Origin	Ancestry	
Area size:	599 sq. mi.	78.5% White	German: 14.5%	Irish: 10.0%
Urban population:	96.5%	2.3% Black	English: 8.6%	
Rural population:	3.5%	2.1% Asian	**2004 Presidential Vote**	
Pop. 2000:	641,329	1.2% Native Am.	Bush (R) 150,511	(58%)
Pop. 2005 (est):	659,949	0.1% Hawaiian	Kerry (D) 107,881	(41%)
Median income:	$48,108	1.6% Two+ races	Other 1,612	(1%)
Poverty status:	8.7%	0.1% Other	**2000 Presidential Vote**	
Military veterans:	13.4%	14.1% Hispanic Origin	Bush (R) 114,259	(54%)
			Gore (D) 89,308	(43%)
			Other 6,140	(3%)
			Cook Partisan Voting Index: R + 6	
Occupation	Blue collar: 17.7%	White collar: 68.2%	Gray collar: 14.1%	

In May 1998 Barry Goldwater died at his home in the Phoenix suburb of Paradise Valley. His life had spanned almost the whole history of Arizona. He was born on New Year's Day 1909, when Arizona was still a territory, and he could remember when it was the "baby state," with fewer people than every other state but Delaware, Wyoming and Nevada. When he returned from World War II, Paradise Valley was still empty land and Phoenix—founded after the Civil War as a hay market for cavalry horses at Fort McDowell 40 miles away—was not much more than a tiny outpost of American civilization in a sizzling desert. Today Arizona has 6.2 million people, with 4 million in metropolitan Phoenix; the city has been transformed from a frontier outpost to a diversified high-tech center, an example of how creativity and ingenuity can build a sophisticated city with relatively minimalist government and low taxes.

Like Los Angeles and San Francisco, Phoenix is dotted with mountains that rise grandly from the plains and are kept as undeveloped parkland. Some, such as Shaw Butte in the shadow of I-17, contain archeological evidence that Indians used them as a base for sophisticated astronomical observations. From Camelback Mountain, 1,800 feet above Phoenix and Paradise Valley, you can with equal awe get a sense of what this land was originally like and an understanding of how impressively Phoenix has grown. East of Camelback, subdivisions were often built with grass and greenery; in the affluent areas north of Camelback and spreading out Scottsdale Road and the Black Canyon Freeway, the natural desert look is more common. The master-planned community of Anthem 35 miles north of downtown, initially organized in 1999, already has about 40,000 residents. Grass is discouraged, and often banned by subdivision covenant; planting anything but desert flora is frowned upon. The architecture of the houses tends toward unadorned stucco with picture windows facing away from the sun; the idea is to suggest that there is a horse corral over in the next lot and sometimes, especially in the northern edges of Phoenix, there is.

The 3d Congressional District of Arizona includes the northern part of Phoenix plus Paradise Valley, bounded on the south by a zigzag line that approximates the Arizona Canal. The 3d also includes, 20 miles north of downtown Phoenix, the communities of New River, Cave Creek and Carefree (so named in 1955 by developers who hoped to lure retirees). Here the stores are more likely to feature horse feed than designer clothes—but that is changing fast, as metro Phoenix moves inexorably north, bringing with it more upscale malls in the adobe vernacular. This is an affluent, and comfortably Republican, district.

The congressman from the 3d District is John Shadegg, first elected in 1994, with a fine Arizona Republican pedigree. His father, Stephen Shadegg, managed Barry Goldwater's first campaign for the Senate in 1952, when Goldwater upset Senate Majority Leader Ernest McFarland; in those pre-fax, pre-email days, the older Shadegg helped deliver campaign press releases. The younger Shadegg is a lawyer who served as special assistant to the state attorney general and a special counsel to the Arizona House Republican Caucus. When Jon Kyl ran for the Senate in 1994, Shadegg ran for his House seat and won 43% in the Republican primary, to 30% for Trent Franks (now the 2d District congressman), and 21% for a county supervisor. He won the general election easily, 60%-36%.

In the House, Shadegg has mostly been a consistent conservative who has stuck to principle. As one of the firebrand 1994 Republican freshmen, he held firm against Democratic policies and often rebelled against his own party's leadership. He refused to back the balanced budget amendment without a three-fifths supermajority for tax increases, in defiance of Speaker Newt Gingrich. When he chaired the House's Republican Study Committee, Shadegg and his group agreed to support the annual budget resolution but they insisted—with occasional success—that appropriators strictly comply with budget limits. His anti-leadership stands cost him a seat on Ways and Means in 1997; it went to J.D. Hayworth instead. But he got a seat on Energy and Commerce Committee where, at the direction of Speaker Dennis Hastert, he often worked on health care policy. On HMO legislation, he battled with Charlie Norwood's bipartisan approach. In November 2003, Shadegg and Norwood were the only Republicans serving on Energy and Commerce, or Ways and Means, who voted against the Medicare/prescription drug bill. Still, he worked behind the scenes with GOP leaders to help them find the votes to pass the bill. On the Homeland Security Committee, he helped to enact in 2004 "Project Bioshield" legislation to address bio-terrorism. The energy bill enacted in August 2005 reflected his efforts to promote hydroelectric power; over the objections of environmentalists, Shadegg has promoted the use of hydro power to preserve Lake Powell. In July 2006, the House passed his bill to encourage joint ventures with Israel to develop alternative sources of energy.

Even with his independence, Shadegg has gained influence and respect among his colleagues. In January 2005, Shadegg ran unopposed to replace Christopher Cox as chairman of the Republican Policy Committee. All wings of the party praised him as open to ideas; he organized a series of "unity dinners" to try to find common ground on immigration legislation. In January 2006, he voluntarily gave up that post to run for majority leader after Tom DeLay stepped down and indirectly criticized Roy Blunt for not stepping down as majority whip. He finished a distant third with 40 votes to Blunt and John Boehner, and withdrew after the first ballot; his candidacy may have prevented a first-ballot win by Blunt, and most of his supporters went to Boehner. In November 2006, he ran against Blunt for minority whip in what was widely expected to a close contest. But it wasn't. Shadegg lost, 137-57. In contrast to other contenders, he did not have a leadership PAC to support GOP candidates.

No longer in leadership, Shadegg said he had no regrets about losing his seat at the table and was eager to return to his role as a reformer. During the 2006 campaign, he warned that the party was no longer aggressive enough and risked losing its majority. He cited the failure to strip pension rights from convicted members and to overhaul the rules for Indian gambling facilities to prevent further lobbying abuses.

Shadegg has shown his independence at home: In 2004, he opposed the tax increase for Phoenix-area transportation (which passed anyway), but he supported higher taxes on business to pay for full-day kindergarten for all Arizona children. Shadegg had won re-election each time with at least 64% of the vote against weak opponents; in 2006, a dismal year for local Republicans, he had his lowest margin, 59%-38% against Democrat Herb Paine, a former United Way executive. He has made known his interest in running for the Senate if either John McCain or Jon Kyl retires. His influence in the House, and Arizona's increasingly competitive political landscape, may give him second thoughts.

FOURTH DISTRICT

Rep. Ed Pastor (D)

Elected Sept. 1991, 8th full term; b. June 28, 1943, Claypool; home, Phoenix; AZ St. U., B.A. 1966, J.D. 1974; Catholic; married (Verma).

Elected Office: Maricopa Cnty. Bd. of Supervisors, 1976-91.

Professional Career: High schl. teacher, 1966-69; Asst., AZ Gov. Castro, 1975.

DC Office: 2465 RHOB, 20515, 202-225-4065; Fax: 202-225-1655; Web site: www.house.gov/pastor.

District Offices: Phoenix, 602-256-0551.

Committees: *Chief Deputy Majority Whip. Appropriations* (12th of 37 D): Transportation, HUD & Related Agencies; Energy & Water Development; Interior, Environment & Related Agencies.

Group Ratings

	ADA	ACLU	AFS	LCV	ITIC	NTU	COC	ACU	CFG	FRC
2006	100	100	100	92	14	11	33	8	9	0
2005	100	—	100	94	—	16	37	8	3	0

National Journal Ratings

	2005 LIB	—	2005 CONS		2006 LIB	—	2006 CONS
Economic	72%	—	26%		73%	—	27%
Social	90%	—	9%		96%	—	3%
Foreign	94%	—	4%		75%	—	23%

Key Votes of the 109th Congress

1. Estate Tax Repeal	N	5. Limit Interstate Abortion	N	9. Build Border Fence	N
2. Limit CAFE Standards	Y	6. Extend Patriot Act	N	10. CAFTA	N
3. FY06 Spending Curb	N	7. Bar Same Sex Marriage	N	11. Oppose Iraq Withdrawal	N
4. Drilling in ANWR	N	8. Stem Cell Research $	Y	12. Detainee Tribunals	N

Election Results

2006 general	Ed Pastor (D)	56,464	(73%)	($763,931)
	Don Karg (R)	18,627	(24%)	
	Ronald Harders (Lib)	2,770	(4%)	
2006 primary	Ed Pastor (D)	unopposed		
2004 general	Ed Pastor (D)	77,150	(70%)	($624,271)
	Don Karg (R)	28,238	(26%)	
	Gary Fallon (Lib)	4,639	(4%)	

Prior Winning Percentages: 2002 (67%); 2000 (69%); 1998 (68%); 1996 (65%); 1994 (62%); 1992 (66%); 1991 (56%)

The People		Race/Ethnic Origin	Ancestry		
Area size:	199 sq. mi.	29.3% White	German: 5.8%	Irish: 4.0%	
Urban population:	99.5%	7.5% Black	English: 3.4%		
Rural population:	0.5%	1.3% Asian	**2004 Presidential Vote**		
Pop. 2000:	641,329	2.4% Native Am.	Kerry (D)	71,805	(62%)
Pop. 2005 (est):	693,585	0.1% Hawaiian	Bush (R)	43,967	(38%)
Median income:	$30,624	1.5% Two+ races	Other	930	(1%)
Poverty status:	25.6%	0.1% Other	**2000 Presidential Vote**		
Military veterans:	9.6%	58.0% Hispanic Origin	Gore (D)	57,198	(63%)
			Bush (R)	31,542	(35%)
			Other	2,598	(3%)
			Cook Partisan Voting Index: D +14		

Occupation	Blue collar: 35.7%	White collar: 43.8%	Gray collar: 20.5%

Phoenix is a new American metropolis, grown to huge metropolitan size within most Americans' lifetimes. Yet it is also an ancient city, or built on top of one. The Arizona Canal, several miles north of downtown Phoenix, runs along the route of a canal built about 600 years ago by the Hohokam people. They distributed irrigated water diverted from the Salt River in its wet moments to farmers in what Phoenicians today call the Valley of the Sun and made sophisticated astronomical observations from the mountains that jut up from the plains. This society disappeared, for reasons that are not known, less than half a century before the Spaniards arrived in North America. So today's Phoenix is the second civilization to grow in this desert. Its growth is recent. Phoenix and Maricopa County had 331,000 people in 1950 and 3.8 million in 2006. Half a century ago, Phoenix spread half a dozen miles north, west and east of the downtown and only a few miles south. Downtown was its single office and main shopping district, and people blew fans over boxes of ice to keep cool. Today from downtown Phoenix's office towers the city seems to spread as far as the eye can see, including other clumps of office towers to the north and northwest.

The 4th Congressional District of Arizona is centered on downtown Phoenix and is based entirely in Maricopa County. It covers the Capitol in a rundown neighborhood a couple of miles to the west, and busy Sky Harbor International Airport in an industrial corridor several miles east. It includes most of southern Phoenix and its boundaries follow approximately the southern and western city limits; it extends as far north as Bethany Home Road and Northern Avenue. It stretches south into Guadalupe and northwest into Glendale. Geographically it covers most of the land between South Mountain and Camelback Mountain. The district is one of Arizona's two Hispanic districts; its population in 2000 was 58% Hispanic; most are Mexican, but there has been an influx of Guatemalans. The typical Latino neighborhood here is a collection of 1940s and 1950s bungalows, spaced out by empty lots. Here Habitat for Humanity built South Ranch, the organization's largest low-income subdivision in the U.S.; the idea was to cluster poor homeowners together and encourage them to stave off neighborhood decline collectively. Politically this is a solidly Democratic district, the most Democratic in Arizona.

The congressman from the 4th District is Ed Pastor, a Democrat who won a 1991 special election to replace Morris Udall at a time when the district's boundaries were quite different. He grew up in Claypool, a mining town in Gila County. Pastor is a career politician who does not seek much public attention. After teaching high school, he got a law degree at Arizona State, worked as an assistant to Governor Raul Castro in 1975, then was elected in 1976 to the Maricopa County Board of Supervisors, where he served until his election to Congress. In 1991, he defeated Republican Pat Connor 56%-44%. He has not faced stiff competition since then.

Pastor has been a faithful follower of the Democratic leadership and has a mostly liberal voting record. He supported NAFTA, despite strong labor opposition, but he opposed normal trade relations with China and CAFTA. He vigorously opposed Arizona's English Only law and supports bilingual ballots, but says, "everyone acknowledges that English is the common language of our country." In 2002 he sponsored legislation to provide amnesty to immigrants who were in the U.S. prior to January 2000. After a trip in 2002 to Cuba where he met with Fidel Castro for three hours, he urged the immediate end of the trade embargo. In July 2004, he narrowly lost in the Appropriations Committee on his proposal to remove a provision that prohibited banks from allowing the use of Mexican *matricula consular* identity cards. He serves in the leadership as a chief deputy whip.

Much of Pastor's work has been on the Appropriations Committee, where he often delivers projects of the kind that John McCain labels "pork." Home state demands on him have increased because he has become the only House or Senate appropriator from Arizona. On the Energy and Water Development and the Transportation subcommittees, he brings home the bacon. When money is needed, said a Maricopa County supervisor, "you go to Ed." But his prowess drew unfavorable publicity in June 2007 when the *Arizona Republic* reported that Pastor significantly increased the amount of federal grant money he delivered to a local community college scholarship program after his daughter Laura was hired in 2005 to help run it. In 2007, she ran for a seat on the Phoenix city council; in August, the newspaper reported that her campaign raked in "thousands of dollars in contributions from people and companies who also donate to her father."

Now in his eighth full term, Pastor may soon be in line to chair an Appropriations subcommittee. In the 2004 presidential campaign, he was an early supporter of Dick Gephardt. For the 2008 campaign, Pastor endorsed New Mexico Governor Bill Richardson and chaired his Arizona steering committee.

FIFTH DISTRICT

Rep. Harry Mitchell (D)

Elected 2006, 1st term; b. July 18, 1940, Phoenix; home, Tempe; AZ St. U., B.A. 1962, M.P.A. 1980; Catholic; married (Marianne).

Elected Office: Tempe City Cncl., 1970-78; Mayor, 1978-94; AZ Senate, 1998-2006.

Professional Career: High school teacher, 1964-1992.

DC Office: 2434 RHOB, 20515, 202-225-2190; Fax: 202-225-0096; Web site: mitchell.house.gov.

District Offices: Scottsdale, 480-946-2411.

Committees: *Science & Technology* (23d of 24 D): Technology & Innovation. *Transportation & Infrastructure* (35th of 41 D): Aviation; Water Resources & Environment; Highways & Transit. *Veterans' Affairs* (6th of 16 D): Oversight & Investigations (Chmn.).

Group Ratings and Key Votes: Newly Elected

Election Results

2006 general	Harry Mitchell (D)	101,838	(50%)	($1,933,184)
	J.D. Hayworth (R)	93,815	(46%)	($3,000,381)
	Other	6,357	(3%)	
2006 primary	Harry Mitchell (D)	unopposed		
2004 general	J.D. Hayworth (R)	159,455	(59%)	($1,356,723)
	Elizabeth Rogers (D)	102,363	(38%)	($4,898)
	Other	6,189	(2%)	

The People		Race/Ethnic Origin	Ancestry	
Area size:	1,423 sq. mi.	76.8% White	German: 14.3%	Irish: 9.5%
Urban population:	97.2%	2.7% Black	English: 9.0%	
Rural population:	2.8%	3.3% Asian	**2004 Presidential Vote**	
Pop. 2000:	641,329	1.8% Native Am.	Bush (R) 152,576	(54%)
Pop. 2005 (est):	684,531	0.2% Hawaiian	Kerry (D) 127,811	(45%)
Median income:	$51,780	1.7% Two+ races	Other 1,620	(1%)
Poverty status:	8.4%	0.2% Other	**2000 Presidential Vote**	
Military veterans:	12.4%	13.3% Hispanic Origin	Bush (R) 121,462	(54%)
			Gore (D) 97,604	(43%)
			Other 7,635	(3%)
			Cook Partisan Voting Index: R + 4	

Occupation	Blue collar: 14.2%	White collar: 73.1%	Gray collar: 12.7%

As metropolitan Phoenix grows over the expanse of the Valley of the Sun, around and beyond the mountains that block the passage of the grid streets from the plains below, it has encompassed and absorbed the crossroads towns that were separate and distinct—and much smaller—communities 50 years ago. Two such are Tempe and Scottsdale. Tempe is east of downtown Phoenix, south of the Arizona Canal. It was founded in 1871 as Hayden's Ferry, by the father of the future Senator (1927-69) Carl Hayden and was renamed in 1879 for an ancient Greek vale. The old town nucleus centered on Arizona State University; both the town and university have expanded greatly. The University sits astride a rise with a fine view of much of metropolitan Phoenix; the town is relatively affluent, with 161,000 people in 2005, an increase from 7,600 in 1950. Tempe has eight stations in Phoenix's new 20-mile light-rail project. Then there is Scottsdale, east of the affluent part of Phoenix and north of Tempe and the Salt River Indian Reservation; it now juts far north and encompasses Frank Lloyd Wright's Taliesin West, which was beyond the reach of electricity and telephone lines when it was built in the 1940s. Scottsdale features luxury shopping malls and resorts, lots of night life, the new Buffalo Bill Historical Center, plus the WestWorld equestrian center. Scottsdale has 226,000 people, as compared to, well, zero in 1940; it shows up first in the 1950 Census, with 2,000.

The 5th Congressional District of Arizona includes Tempe, Scottsdale and the northeast corner of Maricopa County—Fountain Hills, the Salt River and Fort McDowell Indian Reservations and part of the Tonto National Forest. Politically, this has been a Republican district, though less so than it was a dozen years ago. Some affluent people here, like so many in coastal metropolises, have been attracted to the Democrats by their stands on cultural issues; the 5th has the highest percentage of high school graduates of any district in Arizona. George W. Bush got 54% here in each of his presidential wins.

The new congressman from the 5th District is Harry Mitchell, a Democrat who rode the national anti-incumbent wave and became, at 66, the oldest member of the 2006 freshman class. A native Arizonan, he got his bachelor and master's degree from Arizona State University and for 28 years taught American government and economics at Tempe High School, from which he graduated. He also was an adjunct professor at ASU. He was elected at age 30 to the Tempe City Council and served 8 years before becoming mayor in 1978. In his 16 years as mayor, he led efforts to revitalize the downtown area and expand mass transit. After he stepped down, the city erected a 35-foot steel statue of Mitchell and renamed its government center in his name. Mitchell then served eight years in the state Senate, where he focused on education and job creation and was assistant minority leader. Mitchell was a reluctant candidate at first. He turned down the initial entreaties of DCCC Chairman Rahm Emanuel that he challenge six-term Representative J. D. Hayworth. He says he ultimately decided that Hayworth, a conservative Republican who grew up in North Carolina and moved up the hierarchy of local TV stations as a sportscaster, did not represent local values.

It's hard to imagine a starker difference in tone than between Mitchell and Hayworth. The incumbent was a bombastic and combative partisan who seemed to relish the opportunity to irritate Democrats with his fiery rhetoric. Mitchell was considered one of Arizona's elder statesmen. Hayworth asserted his outspoken positions on immigration and the Iraq war in loud and clear terms. By contrast, Mitchell earned a reputation in Arizona as a conciliator who worked both sides of a debate to build consensus. The endorsement of the Democrat by *The Arizona Republic*, the state's largest newspaper, bore the headline: "Mitchell Over the Bully." That favorable editorial prompted the DCCC to dump even more money into the race. During the campaign, immigration proved to be a contentious issue. Hayworth tried to cast his challenger as a supporter of "amnesty"— and Social Security benefits—for illegal immigrants. Mitchell supported the Senate-passed comprehensive immigration reform bill, which would have provided immigrants with a path to U.S. citizenship through a guest-worker program and criticized Hayworth for doing little other than writing a book on the topic, titled *Whatever It Takes*. But Mitchell stipulated that only legalized immigrants would get Social Security benefits. Mitchell focused heavily on Hayworth's ties to Tom DeLay and disgraced lobbyist Jack Abramoff, whose Indian tribal clients contributed about $100,000 to Hayworth; the 2002 redistricting removed the Indian counties from his district. The new constituents who tended to side with Republicans on economic issues were more inclined to embrace good-government positions and to back Democratic social policies. Hayworth also may have suffered because the Republican-controlled Congress failed to enact much legislation on immigration.

Mitchell faced the challenge of introducing himself to voters outside of Tempe, who were roughly three-fourths of the district. In an e-mail debate sponsored by *The Arizona Republic*, Mitchell said that he agreed with neighboring Representative John Shadegg that "divisive and emotional rhetoric is not helpful to [the immigration] debate." Hayworth said that "enforcement is a proven strategy" and that Mitchell had failed to offer alternatives to secure the border. Mitchell won 50.4%-46.4%—a margin of 8,000 votes. Post-election analysis suggested that Hayworth had been too negative in his campaign, and failed to focus enough on his local accomplishments. Hayworth returned to broadcasting in April 2007, hosting a Phoenix afternoon radio talk show.

SIXTH DISTRICT

Rep. Jeff Flake (R)

Elected 2000, 4th term; b. Dec. 31, 1962, Snowflake; home, Mesa; Brigham Young U., B.A. 1986, M.A. 1987; Mormon; married (Cheryl).

Professional Career: Pub. Plcy. Exec., Shipley, Smoak & Henry, 1987-89; Exec. Dir., Fndt. for Democracy (Namibia), 1989-90; Owner, Interface Pub. Affairs, 1990-92; Exec. Dir., The Goldwater Inst., 1992-99.

DC Office: 240 CHOB, 20515, 202-225-2635; Fax: 202-226-4386; Web site: flake.house.gov.

District Offices: Mesa, 480-833-0092.

Committees: *Foreign Affairs* (11th of 23 R): International Organizations, Human Rights & Oversight; Asia, the Pacific & the Global Environment. *Natural Resources* (8th of 22 R): Insular Affairs; National Parks, Forests & Public Lands.

Group Ratings

	ADA	ACLU	AFS	LCV	ITIC	NTU	COC	ACU	CFG	FRC
2006	20	41	0	8	57	92	79	100	100	85
2005	0	—	14	17	—	91	70	96	100	92

National Journal Ratings

	2005 LIB	—	2005 CONS		2006 LIB	—	2006 CONS
Economic	47%	—	53%		41%	—	58%
Social	48%	—	52%		52%	—	47%
Foreign	54%	—	46%		52%	—	47%

Key Votes of the 109th Congress

1. Estate Tax Repeal	Y	5. Limit Interstate Abortion	Y	9. Build Border Fence	Y
2. Limit CAFE Standards	Y	6. Extend Patriot Act	Y	10. CAFTA	Y
3. FY06 Spending Curb	Y	7. Bar Same Sex Marriage	Y	11. Oppose Iraq Withdrawal	Y
4. Drilling in ANWR	*	8. Stem Cell Research $	N	12. Detainee Tribunals	Y

Election Results

2006 general	Jeff Flake (R)	152,201	(75%)	($272,420)
	Jason Blair (Lib)	51,285	(25%)	
2006 primary	Jeff Flake (R)	unopposed		
2004 general	Jeff Flake (R)	202,882	(79%)	($675,055)
	Craig Stritar (Lib)	52,695	(21%)	

Prior Winning Percentages: 2002 (66%); 2000 (54%)

The People		Race/Ethnic Origin	Ancestry	
Area size:	724 sq. mi.	76.6% White	German: 14.1%	English: 10.2%
Urban population:	96.8%	1.9% Black	Irish: 8.6%	
Rural population:	3.2%	1.8% Asian	**2004 Presidential Vote**	
Pop. 2000:	641,329	0.8% Native Am.	Bush (R) 188,372	(64%)
Pop. 2005 (est):	874,033	0.2% Hawaiian	Kerry (D) 102,902	(35%)
Median income:	$47,976	1.4% Two+ races	Other 1,352	(0%)
Poverty status:	7.7%	0.1% Other	**2000 Presidential Vote**	
Military veterans:	15.8%	17.2% Hispanic Origin	Bush (R) 118,278	(61%)
			Gore (D) 72,093	(37%)
			Other 3,942	(2%)
			Cook Partisan Voting Index: R +12	

Occupation	Blue collar: 22.6%	White collar: 63.3%	Gray collar: 14.2%

The metropolis of Phoenix is exceedingly young. Barry Goldwater, born in 1909, grew up knowing people who remembered when the Valley of the Sun—or the Valley, as most people say—was virtually empty, with a few parched settlements set above the dry riverbed. As late as 1950, only 106,000 people lived in Phoenix and 331,000 in all of Maricopa County. But the air conditioner and military technology transformed Phoenix from a sleepy whistlestop to today's high-rise-studded metropolis, with 1.5 million people in Phoenix and 3.8 million in Maricopa—since 2000, it has posted the largest numerical gain of any county in the nation. This is not, as some people think, a giant retirement village, nor is it overrun by crooked land salesmen and fast-buck artists, though Phoenix has attracted its share of each.

The second largest city in Maricopa County is Mesa, south of the Salt River and east of Phoenix. It was founded by Mormons in 1878 on a square mile; it was laid out Salt Lake City-style on broad streets with huge blocks holding just four home sites, using canals built by Indians 1,100 years earlier. A gleaming white Mormon Temple was built in 1927, one of the few in the United States then. In 1950, Mesa had 17,000 people, enough to make it Arizona's third largest city. In 2000, it had 396,000 people, more than Minneapolis or Pittsburgh, though few people back east have ever heard of it. Five years later, it grew to 443,000; only 13 per cent were over age 65 in 2000.

The 6th Congressional District of Arizona is made up of Mesa and Chandler, Gilbert and Queen Creek to the south; it crosses the Pinal County line and includes fast-growing bedroom communities such as Apache Junction, Gold Camp and Sun Lakes. Growth has been constant here: In the 1990s Gilbert zoomed from a rail siding and a dot on the map to 110,000 people. The 6th includes some high-income precincts (interestingly, Asians lead whites in income in Chandler and Gilbert), but the district's cultural tone is resolutely middle class, hard-working and churchgoing. By most measures it is the most Republican district in Arizona. It continues to grow rapidly: a 36% increase since 2000, making it the third-fastest growing congressional district in the nation.

The congressman from the 6th District is Jeff Flake, a Republican elected in 2000, and something of a maverick—or, to some in House leadership, a "flake." A fifth-generation Arizonan, he is a practicing Mormon who was born and raised on a ranch in Snowflake; the town was named after his great-great grandfather. The fifth of 11 children, Flake served as a Mormon missionary in South Africa and Zimbabwe and graduated from Brigham Young University. In 1987 he moved to Washington, D.C., and worked in a lobbying firm. He returned to southern Africa to serve as executive director of the Foundation for Democracy, which monitored democratic progress in Namibia. Following Namibian independence in 1990 and two more years in Washington representing Namibian companies, he returned to Arizona and became executive director of the Goldwater Institute, where he led the fight for Arizona's charter school law. In 2000, when Matt Salmon kept his pledge to serve only three terms (he lost narrowly for governor in 2002), he handpicked Flake to succeed him. Flake faced four opponents in a hard-fought September primary, in which he was the most conservative candidate. He had the support of several prominent Republican state leaders and was bolstered by more than $200,000 from the Club for Growth. Flake won with 32% to 24% for Phoenix Councilman Sal DiCiccio. In the general, Flake won 54%-42% over Democrat David Mendoza, a longtime lobbyist for public employees.

Flake promised to serve no more than three terms and to "continue to rock the boat," much as Salmon had for six years. Less than a month after he took office, Flake—who favors replacing the income tax with a national sales tax—said that it would be a mistake for George W. Bush to limit his proposed tax cut to the "easy things," such as repeal of the marriage penalty, and estate and gift taxes. Flake organized the bipartisan Cuba Working Group to review the U.S. embargo of Cuba and he has pushed repeatedly to lift restrictions on travel by U.S. citizens to Cuba, with occasional victories on the House floor. House Republican leaders and the Bush administration have strongly opposed him and typically have removed his provisions in conference committee. Flake has a habit of taking lonely stands. He was one of two members who voted against a bill to punish Sudan for its human right abuses; Flake said he had seen in Africa the adverse impact of economic sanctions on poor nations. He was one of 33 Republicans who voted against final approval of the Bush education bill and one of 25 who opposed the Medicare/prescription drug bill.

As he gained experience, Flake's independence has solidified. His maverick views have placed his voting pattern toward the center of the House. He vowed never to ask appropriators for a dollar for any item or local project while he served in the House. When appropriators responded with his list of requests for the military, he responded that requests solely for defense were legitimate; he left the door open to making requests of other committees. He advocated reforms in spending "earmarks" and became a prolific sponsor of amendments on the House floor to spotlight many of the projects; he has become accustomed to losing, though he believes that he is making useful points. He reinforces his point with awards for the most egregious earmark of the week; although he does not name his colleague who sponsored it, he does list the locality that receives it. Limited-government groups have applauded his efforts. On immigration, he co-sponsored a guest worker bill with John McCain, to provide six-year temporary worker visas and three-year visas for those who are here

illegally now; he became an outspoken supporter and presciently warned of the political consequences if Republicans failed to act on the measure. On the Judiciary Committee, he also raised
questions about the Bush administration's domestic surveillance program. Flake paid a price for all
this at the start of 2007 when the leadership-controlled Republican Steering Committee ousted him
from the Judiciary Committee, where he was planning to join bipartisan initiatives. Minority
Leader John Boehner rejected Flake's claim that he had been punished for "bad behavior" but not
everyone believed him. Conservative pundit Bruce Fein noted, "The House Steering Committee's
rebuke of Mr. Flake demonstrates that, like the French Bourbons, it has learned nothing and
forgotten nothing."

Flake gave some thought to challenging McCain in the 2004 Senate primary, but decided not
to. Instead he faced a serious primary challenge himself. Former state Senator Stan Barnes called
Flake "fringe, libertarian and just a bit kooky," and attacked him on immigration issues. Flake won
59%-41%, an unimpressive margin for an incumbent. He had no Democratic opponent in November.
Days after the election he announced that he would abandon his term-limit pledge. "As much as I
hate to admit making a mistake, I made a big one here." He did not face a serious reelection
challenge in 2006. He has been mentioned as a possible Senate candidate if there is an opening.

SEVENTH DISTRICT

Rep. Raul Grijalva (D)

Elected 2002, 3d term; b. Feb. 19, 1948, Tucson; home, Tucson; U. of AZ,
B.A. 1985; Catholic; married (Ramona).

Elected Office: Tucson Unified Schl. Dist. Governing Bd., 1974-86;
Pima Cnty. Bd. of Supervisors, 1988-2002.

Professional Career: Asst. Dean of Hisp. Affairs, U. of AZ., 1987.

DC Office: 1440 LHOB, 20515, 202-225-2435; Fax: 202-225-1541; Web
site: www.house.gov/grijalva.

District Offices: Tucson, 520-622-6788; Yuma, 928-343-7933.

Committees: *Education & Labor* (15th of 27 D): Healthy Families & Communities; Early Childhood,
Elementary & Secondary Education. *Natural Resources* (10th of 27 D): National Parks, Forests & Public
Lands (Chmn.); Insular Affairs. *Small Business* (5th of 18 D): Finance & Tax; Investigations & Oversight.

Group Ratings

	ADA	ACLU	AFS	LCV	ITIC	NTU	COC	ACU	CFG	FRC
2006	100	100	100	100	14	12	27	4	4	0
2005	100	—	100	94	—	17	30	0	3	0

National Journal Ratings

	2005 LIB	—	2005 CONS		2006 LIB	—	2006 CONS
Economic	94%	—	0%		91%	—	6%
Social	84%	—	15%		97%	—	0%
Foreign	96%	—	0%		95%	—	0%

Key Votes of the 109th Congress

1. Estate Tax Repeal	N	5. Limit Interstate Abortion	N	9. Build Border Fence	N
2. Limit CAFE Standards	N	6. Extend Patriot Act	N	10. CAFTA	N
3. FY06 Spending Curb	N	7. Bar Same Sex Marriage	N	11. Oppose Iraq Withdrawal	N
4. Drilling in ANWR	N	8. Stem Cell Research $	Y	12. Detainee Tribunals	N

Election Results

2006 general	Raul Grijalva (D)	80,354	(61%)	($662,758)
	Ron Drake (R)	46,498	(35%)	($180,158)
	Joe Cobb (Lib)	4,673	(4%)	
2006 primary	Raul Grijalva (D)	unopposed		
2004 general	Raul Grijalva (D)	108,868	(62%)	($618,854)
	Joseph Sweeney (R)	59,066	(34%)	
	Dave Kaplan (Lib)	7,503	(4%)	

Prior Winning Percentages: 2002 (59%)

The People		Race/Ethnic Origin	Ancestry	
Area size:	22,891 sq. mi.	38.6% White	German: 7.8%	Irish: 5.4%
Urban population:	83.6%	2.8% Black	English: 4.8%	
Rural population:	16.4%	1.3% Asian	**2004 Presidential Vote**	
Pop. 2000:	641,329	5.3% Native Am.	Kerry (D) 105,532	(57%)
Pop. 2005 (est):	748,502	0.1% Hawaiian	Bush (R) 79,674	(43%)
Median income:	$30,828	1.3% Two+ races	Other 1,155	(1%)
Poverty status:	21.8%	0.1% Other	**2000 Presidential Vote**	
Military veterans:	13.3%	50.6% Hispanic Origin	Gore (D) 74,176	(58%)
			Bush (R) 49,343	(38%)
			Other 5,271	(4%)
			Cook Partisan Voting Index: D +10	

Occupation	Blue collar: 26.8%	White collar: 51.4%	Gray collar: 21.8%

Southern Arizona, though technically part of Mexico for hundreds of years, was never a home to Hispanic civilization like northern New Mexico. Here the hot desert land was inhabited mainly by Indians who kept their native ways and language until English-speaking whites came in on cavalry horses, miners' wagons and railroad cars in the late 19th century. This was after the 1854 Gadsden Purchase—$10 million to Mexico for 30,000 square miles of desert—cleared the way for a southern transcontinental railroad. Today's Hispanic Arizonans are mostly descendants of later immigrants from Mexico, some who came over the border in the sleepier days before World War II, when *la frontera* was scarcely patrolled, and many more who have come since the 1980s to partake in the dazzling economic growth that has served as both an attraction and an example to so many *norteno* Mexicans.

The 7th Congressional District of Arizona was newly created in 2002 and is the state's second Hispanic district; its population in 2000 was 51% Hispanic. It shares 300 miles of border with Mexico and is a collection of four distant communities connected by many square miles of uninhabited Sonoran desert. One is the suburb of Tolleson just west of downtown Phoenix. The second is the heavily Latino west side of Tucson. The third is Yuma, located at a Colorado River crossing in an irrigated agricultural valley, often the hottest place in the country. The fourth is the Mexican border town of Nogales, 94% Hispanic and near many maquiladora plants, long an entry point for illegal drugs and the scene of many illegal border crossings in recent years. The twin smuggling tides—drugs and people—have inflicted damage on the fragile desert ecosystem. In an interesting example of international cooperation the sister cities of Nogales, Arizona, and Nogales, Sonora, have signed an agreement to respond jointly to fire and hazardous material emergencies. Out in the desert there is the Organ Pipe Cactus National Monument, the Tohono O'odham Indian Reservation and the Barry M. Goldwater Air Force Range (the largest aerial gunnery range after Nevada's Nellis Air Force Range), which is twice the size of Delaware; 95% of it is not used for target practice as it is the habitat of the endangered Sonoran pronghorn antelope. Near Nogales, wilderness and wildlife—including endangered species such as the jaguar, peregrine falcon, Chiricahua leopard frog, and Mexican spotted owl—have been protected in the Tumacacori Highlands. With its brutal desert heat, the Baboquivari trail that runs north to the Tohono O'odham nation has been the deadliest immigrant crossing in the nation. Trash left behind by illegal crossers has caused growing environmental problems.

The 7th District, home to seven Indian tribes, is one of two solidly Democratic districts in Arizona.

The congressman from the 7th District is Raul Grijalva, a Democrat first elected in 2002. He grew up in Tucson and graduated from the University of Arizona; he has lived in the city all his life and has deep roots in the immigrant community on the city's southwest side. He was director of El Pueblo Neighborhood Center, and assistant dean for Hispanic student affairs at the University of

Arizona. In 1974 he was elected to the Tucson school board and served 12 years. In 1988 he was elected a Pima County Supervisor and served 14 years. As supervisor he backed an effort to extend medical and dental benefits to same-sex domestic partners of county employees and focused on affordable healthcare, family and children services, and growth. Developers and builders helped elect him to office, but his support for planned growth and impact fees later alienated them.

In 2002, the Democratic primary would obviously determine who would be the new congressman, and Grijalva entered with a home court advantage: 64% of the primary votes were cast in Pima County. His chief opponent was state Senator Elaine Richardson, who was endorsed by EMILY's List and spent more than $500,000 on ads. She criticized him for wasting taxpayer money on a $3.8 million contract to survey all the manholes in Pima County. Although outspent nearly 3–1, Grijalva had a well-organized grassroots effort and endorsements from labor unions, teachers' unions and the Sierra Club. Mocking his opponent's national funding, Grijalva created "Adelita's List"; the name alludes to the independent women who fought in the Mexican Revolution. He opposed any "privatization" of Social Security or increase in the retirement age. His proposals for immigration reform included an amnesty provision plus a comprehensive border policy with legalization, economic development, cost recovery, infrastructure enhancement and environmental protection. He won the primary with 41% to Richardson's 21%. In Pima County, Grijalva got 54% of the vote. He won easily in November and his daughter Adelita won a seat on the school board.

In the House, Grijalva's voting record is strongly liberal. On the Education and Workforce Committee, he promoted the "much improved" bipartisan agreement on the Individuals with Disabilities Education Act, and urged full funding. As an alternative to George W. Bush's immigration plan, he co-sponsored with Senator Edward Kennedy the SOLVE (Safe, Orderly, Legal Visas and Enforcement) Act, which would legalize millions of workers who have been in the United States for five years and who can prove that they have worked and paid taxes for at least two of those years. Grijalva joined Tucson activists in calling for an investigation of alleged Border Patrol abuse and mistreatment of illegal immigrants, including excessive force and racial profiling. He sought to educate other members about environmental problems in economically depressed communities, and pushed for wilderness designation for the Tumacacori highlands. In August 2006, he dismissed Republican immigration hearings held throughout the Southwest as "a political road show." He worked with other members of the Arizona delegation to resolve disputes over water rights with Indian reservations. In the majority, he became chairman of the influential Natural Resources Subcommittee on National Parks, Forests and Public Lands, and he hoped to restrict mining in the Santa Rita Mountains because of environmental hazards.

Grijalva has been reelected easily; in 2004, his Republican challenger called for the military to shoot illegal aliens seeking to cross the border.

EIGHTH DISTRICT

Rep. Gabrielle Giffords (D)

Elected 2006, 1st term; b. June 8, 1970, Tucson; home, Tucson; Scripps Col., B.A. 1993, Cornell U., M.S. 1996; Jewish; engaged.

Elected Office: AZ House of Reps., 2000-02; AZ Senate, 2002-05.

Professional Career: Price Waterhouse Coopers, 1996-97; CEO and Pres., El Campo Tire, 1997-2000.

DC Office: 502 CHOB, 20515, 202-225-2542; Fax: 202-225-0378; Web site: giffords.house.gov.

District Offices: Sierra Vista, 520-459-3115; Tucson, 520-881-3588.

Committees: *Armed Services* (30th of 34 D): Air & Land Forces; Readiness. *Foreign Affairs* (26th of 27 D): Western Hemisphere. *Science & Technology* (11th of 24 D): Energy & Environment.

Group Ratings and Key Votes: Newly Elected

Election Results

2006 general	Gabrielle Giffords (D)	137,655	(54%)	($2,442,119)
	Randy Graf (R)	106,790	(42%)	($1,341,943)
	Other..	9,275	(4%)	
2006 primary	Gabrielle Giffords (D)	33,375	(54%)	
	Patty Weiss (D)	19,148	(31%)	
	Jeffrey Latas (D)	3,687	(6%)	
	Alex Rodriguez (D)	2,855	(5%)	
	Other..	2,344	(4%)	
2004 general	Jim Kolbe (R)	183,363	(60%)	($1,146,714)
	Eva Bacal (D)	109,963	(36%)	($99,691)
	Other..	10,443	(3%)	

The People		Race/Ethnic Origin	Ancestry	
Area size:	9,057 sq. mi.	73.9% White	German: 14.4%	English: 9.7%
Urban population:	87.3%	3.0% Black	Irish: 9.1%	
Rural population:	12.7%	2.1% Asian	**2004 Presidential Vote**	
Pop. 2000:	641,329	0.8% Native Am.	Bush (R) 167,647	(53%)
Pop. 2005 (est):	716,011	0.1% Hawaiian	Kerry (D) 147,300	(46%)
Median income:	$40,656	1.8% Two+ races	Other 1,886	(1%)
Poverty status:	10.5%	0.1% Other	**2000 Presidential Vote**	
Military veterans:	19.1%	18.2% Hispanic Origin	Bush (R) 123,585	(50%)
			Gore (D) 114,055	(46%)
			Other 10,814	(4%)
			Cook Partisan Voting Index: R + 1	

Occupation	Blue collar: 16.5%	White collar: 66.7%	Gray collar: 16.8%

Arizona's first frontier was just south of today's Tucson, where Franciscan friars built San Xavier del Bac mission in the 18th century. To the east the late 19th century mining towns of Tombstone and Bisbee sprang up on desert mountainsides, where miners dug up gold and silver and much of America's copper; Cochise County, which includes those two towns, was the most populous county when Arizona became the 48th state in 1912. Here the white man last subdued the Indians, when the Apache leader Geronimo faced the U.S. Army in 1900. In the last decade Cochise County has been an active frontier again. After the Border Patrol reduced illegal crossings in California and Texas, Mexicans wishing to enter the United States came to Agua Prieta, just across the border from the town of Douglas. There they fan out, cross the border and use the area's numerous roads, mountain trails and ranch lands to get to Tucson and Phoenix. The Border Patrol's Tucson sector has become the most active on the border, with more than 490,000 illegal aliens apprehended in the 2004 fiscal year, almost four times the population of Cochise County. Numerous border-crossers are found dead in the mountains and the desert; in winter Border Patrol officers carry blankets and heat packs to treat cases of hypothermia. By the 2006 fiscal year, stepped-up federal efforts had brought the number of arrests down to under 390,000.

One immigrant destination is Tucson, Arizona's second metropolis, much smaller, more rough-hewn and politically less conservative than Phoenix. Tucson is a high-tech city and home of the University of Arizona. It is also a tourist destination, with famed resorts. For nearly 40 years, Tucson was the political base of the brothers Udall: Stewart, congressman in the 1950s, Interior secretary in the 1960s; Morris, congressman for 30 years and Interior Committee chairman, who retired in 1991 because of Parkinson's disease and died in 1998. Now their sons, Tom and Mark Udall, represent New Mexico and Colorado districts; a cousin, Stephen Udall, finished second in the 2002 primary in Arizona's 1st District.

The 8th Congressional District of Arizona includes all of Tucson except the Latino west side that is in the 7th District. The 8th also includes the eastern half of surrounding Pima County and much southeastern Arizona desert real estate: All of Cochise County (including Tombstone and Bisbee), Douglas and Sierra Vista near Fort Huachuca, site of the Army Military Intelligence Center, the training site for military interrogators; and very small portions of Santa Cruz and Pinal Counties. Politically it is closely divided, voting narrowly for George W. Bush in 2000 and 2004.

The congresswoman from the 8th District is Gabrielle Giffords, a Democrat first elected in 2006. Giffords grew up in Tucson, a third generation Southern Arizonan. She attended Scripps College in California, won a William Fulbright scholarship to study in Mexico and graduated from

Cornell University in 1996 with a master's degree in regional planning. After working briefly in New York, Giffords returned home to Tucson to take over for her father at the family tire business. Giffords was elected to the state House in 2000, and at 32 became the youngest woman elected to the state Senate in 2002. While in the legislature she was a managing partner for a commercial property management business.

When 11-term Republican Rep. Jim Kolbe announced his retirement in November 2005, her legislative experience and business background immediately made Giffords a contender for the swing district. Kolbe, the House's only openly gay Republican, had been a leader on free trade, Social Security reform and immigration issues. Except for a close race in 1998, the moderate Kolbe had little trouble winning re-election, but he faced tougher competition in the 2004 Republican primary. Then-state Representative Randy Graf criticized Kolbe for his support of an immigrant guest worker program and held the incumbent to a 57%-43% victory. The Congressman Mark Foley page scandal in 2006 took some of the shine off Kolbe's career when it was revealed that a former congressional page had come to him in 2001 to report an e-mail from Foley that made the page uncomfortable. An Ethics Committee report concluded Kolbe had not violated any rules but it raised questions about how much Kolbe knew of Foley's contact with pages.

Giffords resigned her seat in the state Senate in December 2005 to enter the race, which soon drew competitive primaries in both parties. Giffords faced Patty Weiss, a well-known Tucson news anchor. Backed by organized labor, EMILY's List and the Sierra Club, Giffords had a nearly 3-to-1 fundraising advantage and comfortably won the six-way September 12 primary, 54%-31%. Graf returned to run again in the Republican primary and his hard line on illegal immigration attracted support from the Minuteman Project border patrol group. Calculating that a single-issue candidate like Graf could not win the competitive seat, the National Republican Congressional Committee backed state Representative Steve Huffman and took the unusual step of running ads on his behalf; Huffman was joined in the race by former state Republican Chairman Mike Hellon. The Democratic Congressional Campaign Committee also weighed in on the Republican primary with ads attacking Huffman in an attempt to push Graf into the general election. Hellon and Huffman ended up splitting the moderate vote, allowing Graf to win the nomination with 42%. Huffman finished second with 38% and Hellon third with 13%.

After the primary, the NRCC ran ads against Giffords, but by October had canceled the airtime it reserved and effectively conceded the race to Democrats. Kolbe, with memories of the 2004 primary still fresh in his mind, refused to back Graf in the general. In contrast to Graf's polarizing campaign, Giffords portrayed herself as a pro-business moderate who could work across party lines and publicized her experience running the family tire store. Giffords carried Pima County by nearly 30,000 votes and she won Cochise County, where the Minuteman Project was active, by more than 1,000 votes (52%-48%). She carried the district overall 54%-42%.

Giffords has shown a flair for attracting attention: her campaign featured photos of her with her motorcycle and with her fiance, a NASA astronaut on the space shuttle *Discovery*. Her ambition has also drawn notice. "I wouldn't be surprised if she's the first or second female president of the United States," former Labor Secretary Robert Reich, a Giffords mentor, told *Congress Daily* in 2007. In Congress, Giffords won a seat on the Armed Services Committee, from which she can look after the district's two military bases. Graf said after the election he was unlikely to run again. By summer 2007, Republicans seemed to be coalescing behind state Senate President Tim Bee, who had not yet committed to a bid.

★ ARKANSAS ★

Two weeks after the 2004 election, four American presidents journeyed to Little Rock, Arkansas, to open the $165 million William J. Clinton Presidential Center. George H.W. Bush and George W. Bush gave gracious tribute to the president who defeated the former and was succeeded by the latter, and Jimmy Carter added words of praise. The Clinton Center is the largest of our presidential libraries, and the first with electronic records as well as paper documents; in its alcoves are exhibits and electronic connections to what the 42d president considers his great achievements along with a treatment of "the politics of persecution," Bill Clinton's take on the impeachment controversy. But not all is serious here: Clinton the hearty eater decreed that there be space on the grounds for picnics and cookouts. Bill Clinton may not have returned to live in Arkansas (nor did eight other presidents return to their home states), but he clearly is Arkansas's most distinguished

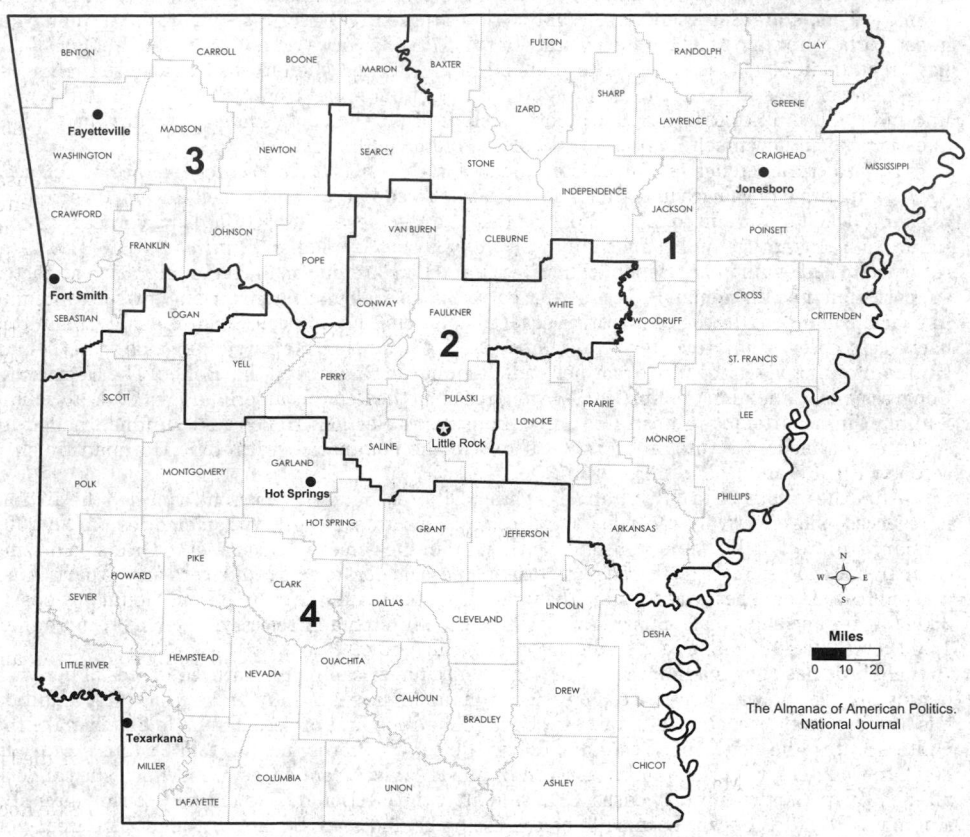

Congressional district boundaries were first effective for 2002.

politician and a man whose articulateness and earthiness, outsized ambitions and overly visible faults are redolent of the state from which he began his unlikely ascent to national and international prominence. Clinton still has his detractors in Arkansas, but as his presidential center opened most Arkansans and Americans considered him an outstanding or above average president. As one said when he left Little Rock for Washington in January 1993, "I distinctly remember thinking that this was finally going to wipe away the stain left by Faubus"—the governor whose disobedience of an order desegregating Little Rock's Central High School prompted President Dwight D. Eisenhower to dispatch federal troops to enforce it in 1957. Clinton certainly did that—no small accomplishment, but the scandals associated with him, if they did not bring him down, tarnished the reputations of many other Arkansans.

Arkansas, like Clinton, began life without many advantages. In area, it's the smallest state between the Mississippi River and the Pacific; in population, it's the smallest state in the South; it has not been blessed with any great natural resource—unless you count flame-retarding bromine, of which it produces half the world supply—or any growing major industry. Arkansas is the land left over when Louisiana and Missouri were carved out of the Louisiana Purchase and what is now Oklahoma was fenced off as Indian Territory. Settled by poor farmers with large families, few slaves and little cash, it has had no Atlanta or Dallas or even Memphis to be a focus of growth. Arkansas has the second lowest income levels of any state, the third lowest percentage of college graduates and the second lowest percentage of Internet use. Its economy—food processing, aerospace, auto parts, medical and construction equipment—recovered from the 2001 recession, despite some loss of manufacturing jobs, and the Clinton Center has been bringing in a steady stream of tourists. Growth is concentrated in the booming northwest corner of the state, in Little Rock and in counties along the Interstate highways. From 2000 to 2006, the Little Rock metro area grew 7%, the Fayetteville-Bentonville area in the northwest a whopping 21% (think Wal-Mart and Tyson Foods) and the Fort Smith metro area just to the south 6%; the rest of the state, with a little more than half the population, grew only 1%. It's the only southern state without a big auto plant; in February 2007 Toyota rejected for the second time a site in Marion, in favor of Tupelo, Mississippi. Arkansas prides itself on being a traditional values state—58% of adults are married, higher than any other state except Idaho and Utah. But the divorce rate has also been higher than average, prompting Governor Mike Huckabee to declare "a state of marital emergency" and, in February 2005, to convert his marriage into a covenant marriage. In 2004 voters passed an amendment prohibiting same-sex marriage and civil unions by 74%-26%.

As the late Arkansas political scientist Diane Blair noted, Arkansas never had a power elite of great plantation owners or economic robber barons. That has left it a heritage without honored traditions or tight standards, but has also made Arkansas a land of great opportunities, where talented people can move up fast, amassing huge fortunes by taking break-through ideas and making them work. Sam Walton believed that rural and small town America would support a chain of giant discount stores which, through tough bargaining with vendors and ultra-quick distribution, could undersell competitors, but through demanding management and employee profit-sharing could embody small town friendliness and service. Walton was the richest American when he died in April 1992, and Wal-Mart today is the largest private employer in the world, with a payroll of 1.8 million. Jack Stephens and his late brother Witt started an investment banking house in Little Rock specializing in underwriting municipal bonds and investing in businesses that are a mix of private enterprise, government subsidies and public regulation; their success—and political connections in Arkansas and elsewhere—amassed a billion dollar fortune. Don Tyson took his father's chicken business and made it one of the biggest food producers in America. Another big Arkansas operation is J.B. Hunt's trucking empire. These business giants have cultivated a down-home, laid-back style, but they have also skillfully united their interests with those of the state's politicians, including Bill Clinton.

Politically, Arkansas was long solidly Democratic, with Republican pockets in the mountains in the northwest. For years it produced politicians who accumulated great seniority and power in Washington—longtime House Ways and Means Chairman Wilbur Mills, Senators John McClellan and William Fulbright, who represented the state for a total of 65 years from the 1940s to the 1970s, and Senators Dale Bumpers and David Pryor, who served a total of 42 years from the 1970s to the 1990s. But in the 108th Congress, Arkansas was represented by two freshman senators and four House members with an average of four years of seniority—the delegation with the least clout of any state according to *Roll Call*. Republicans have won top of the line races occasionally—Winthrop Rockefeller, Sr., was elected governor in 1966 and 1968, following Orval Faubus, and Frank White beat Bill Clinton in 1980. Mike Huckabee took over as governor when Jim Guy Tucker was convicted and forced from office in 1996, and was reelected in 1998 and 2002; born in the same town as Bill Clinton, Hope, he launched a campaign for president in 2007. But he was succeeded by Democrat Mike Beebe, who won 56%-41%, and Arkansas's two Senate seats are held by Democrats: Blanche Lincoln was elected to succeed David Pryor in 1996, and Mark Pryor, David Pryor's son, beat one-term Republican Tim Hutchinson in 2002. Democrats now hold three of Arkansas's four House seats (although George W. Bush carried all four of them in 2004), and the legislature remains, as it has been since Reconstruction, overwhelmingly Democratic. One reason Republicans have not been able to convert their predominance in post-Clinton presidential politics into statewide victories is that Republican primaries tend to be dominated by voters from the atypically booming northwest corner of the state, and they have chosen nominees who had a hard time appealing to voters in Little Rock and the economically more quiescent counties in the east and south.

The People		Race/Ethnic Origin			Military veterans: 281,714 (14.1%)	
Pop. 2006 (est):	2,810,872	2,100,135	78.6%	White	WWII: 20.1%	Korea: 13.3%
Pop. 2000:	2,673,400	416,615	15.6%	Black	Vietnam: 32.0%	Gulf War: 10.5%
Pop. 1990:	2,350,725	19,892	0.7%	Asian	**Most populous cities (2006):**	
Change 1990-2000:	Up 13.7%	16,702	0.6%	Native Am.	1. Little Rock	184,422
% of U.S. total:	1.0%	1,494	0.1%	Hawaiian	2. Fort Smith	83,461
Pop. rank:	33rd of 50	30,364	1.1%	Two+ races	3. Fayetteville	68,726
Area size:	53,179 sq. mi.	1,332	0.0%	Other	4. Springdale	63,082
State Native:	63.9%	86,866	3.2%	Hisp. Origin	5. Jonesboro	60,489
Non-citizen:	1.9%	**Ancestry**				
Language		USA: 13.2%		Irish: 7.9%	Urban population: 52.4%	
English: 93.5%	Spanish: 4.0%	German: 7.7%		English: 6.5%	Rural population: 47.6%	
Other Eur.: 1.6%		French: 1.6%				

Education		Work Sector		General Assembly	
H.S. Grad:	75.3%	Private: 76.8%	Govt: 14.9%	Senate	27 D 8 R
College Grad:	16.7%	Self: 7.8%	Family: 0.4%	House	75 D 25 R
Industry		Unemployment: 6.1%		Legislative Term Limits: Yes	
Agri: 3.7%	Con: 7.0%	**Household Income**		**Registered Voters**	
Fin: 4.8%	Info: 2.2%	<15k: 22.0%	15-35k: 31.7%	No party registration	
Mfg: 25.3%	Prof: 25.0%	35-50k: 17.5%	50-100k: 22.8%		
Public: 4.3%	Trade: 16.3%	100-150k: 3.8%	>150k: 2.2%		
Other: 11.3%		Median: $32,182			
Occupation		Poverty status: 15.8%			
Blue collar: 31.6%	White collar: 52.8%	**Home Value**			
Gray collar: 15.6%		<50k: 34.1%	50-100k: 40.2%	100-200k: 19.8%	200-300k: 3.6%
		300-500k: 1.6%	>500k: 0.7%	Median: $67,400	

Presidential politics   Arkansas has voted for the winners of the last nine presidential elections. It voted 53% for Bill Clinton in 1992 and 54% in 1996, his best and eighth-best percentages those years. In 2000, it voted only 46% for Al Gore, his 29th-best state, and in 2004, only 44% for John Kerry, his 33d best. George W. Bush won 51% here in 2000, his lowest percentage in the South except of course for Florida; he won 54% in 2004. For a brief moment in mid-October, polls showed a tight race here. Bush already had headquarters across the state and ran radio ads, while Kerry and the Democrats went on TV and Bill Clinton returned to the state on Halloween. But Bush, who narrowly lost two of Arkansas's congressional districts in 2000, carried all four in 2004. Looking ahead to 2008, Arkansas seems like the southern state most likely to fall into the Democratic column. SurveyUSA's 50-state polling in 2006 showed that Hillary Rodham Clinton, even

2004 Presidential Vote
Bush (R)	572,898	(54%)
Kerry (D)	469,953	(45%)
Nader (POP)	6,171	(1%)
Other	5,923	(1%)

2004 Democratic Presidential Primary
Kerry (D)	177,754	(67%)
Uncommitted (D)	61,800	(23%)
Kucinich (D)	13,766	(5%)
LaRouche (D)	13,528	(5%)

2000 Presidential Vote
Bush (R)	472,940	(51%)
Gore (D)	422,768	(46%)
Nader (Green)	13,421	(1%)
Other	12,652	(1%)

though she left Arkansas behind and ran for the Senate instead in New York, leading Rudy Giuliani, John McCain, Mitt Romney and Arkansas's own Mike Huckabee in the state.

The Arkansas presidential primary, usually held in May, attracts little attention. So the legislature voted in 2005 to move it to the first Tuesday in February in an effort to give the state a more significant voice in the nominating process. In 2006 Arkansas sought the national Democratic party's sanction to hold an early primary, right after New Hampshire. But the Democratic National Committee awarded that plum to South Carolina, which has a much higher percentage of African-Americans, instead. Arkansas Republicans were not averse to holding an early primary, although with native son Huckabee in the race it might not have attracted many competitors.

Congressional districting

In April 2001, the boundaries of Arkansas's four congressional districts were adjusted slightly by the Democratic legislature to meet the equal-population standard. Because it didn't split counties, the legislature's plan had the highest population difference in the nation between the districts—6,698 people—but it also contained a backup provision that if a court found the plan invalid, it would be repealed and 4,400 voters would be shifted between districts; a court challenge did not materialize. Governor Mike Huckabee, lacking the votes to prevent an override of his veto, let the plan become law without his signature.

110th Congress Lineup	
3 D	1 R
109th Congress Lineup	
3 D	1 R

Governor

Mike Beebe (D)

Elected 2006, term expires Jan. 2011, 1st term; b. Dec. 28, 1946, Amagon; home, Searcy; AR St. U., B.A. 1968, U. of AR, J.D. 1972; Episcopal; married (Ginger).

Military Career: Army Reserve, 1968-74.

Elected Office: AR Senate, 1982-2002; AR Atty. Gen., 2002-06.

Professional Career: Practicing atty., 1972-2002.

Office: State Capitol, Rm. 250, Little Rock, 72201, 501-682-2345; Fax: 501-682-1382; Web site: www.arkansas.governor.gov.

Election Results

2006 general	Mike Beebe (D)	430,765	(56%)
	Asa Hutchinson (R)	315,040	(41%)
	Other	28,875	(3%)
2006 primary	Mike Beebe (D)	unopposed	
2002 general	Mike Huckabee (R)	427,082	(53%)
	Jimmie Lou Fisher (D)	378,250	(47%)

Mike Beebe, a Democrat, was elected governor in 2006. He was born to a single mother in his great-grandmother's country shack outside of tiny Amagon. As a child he moved frequently–St. Louis, Detroit, Houston and Alamogordo, New Mexico–as his mother worked through a succession of waitressing jobs and marriages. He never met his father and recalls going to five different schools in the fifth grade alone. "It taught me to adapt, to be resilient, and it taught me to make friends fast," he told the *Arkansas Democrat-Gazette*. His mother returned to Arkansas in time for him to enroll in high school and put down roots in the state. Beebe studied political science at Arkansas State University, earned a law degree at the University of Arkansas at Fayetteville and served in the U.S. Army Reserves. He excelled as a trial lawyer and he continued to practice during his years in the state legislature.

Beebe won election to the state Senate in 1982, where he served for two decades developing a reputation as a consensus-builder. He helped write Amendment 74, which set a uniform property tax rate for school funding, and Amendment 79, a $300 homestead property tax exemption. In 2002 Beebe, who had had run unopposed in every election, considered running for governor against Republican Governor Mike Huckabee, but he lacked statewide name recognition so he ran instead for attorney general. Unopposed again, Beebe became attorney general and over the next four years he oversaw the state's unsuccessful argument in a school funding case and pursued an investigation into whether Ford Motor Co. had engaged in false advertising on the sale of police cruisers to the state.

Term limits prevented Huckabee from running again in 2006, leaving no incumbent governor on the ballot for the first time since a young Bill Clinton won the office in 1978. The governor's office was the next logical move for Beebe, who told the *Democrat-Gazette* that he was unlikely to run for another office if he lost the race. "I'm not running for governor because I want to run for something else. I'm running for governor because that's what I want to be, nothing else, and for a very good reason: You can do a whole lot to lead your state," he said. Beebe had no opposition in the Democratic primary. At first it appeared Republicans would have a contested primary between former Congressman Asa Hutchinson and Lieutenant Governor Win Rockefeller, the billionaire heir to the Standard Oil fortune. But Rockefeller suffered from a rare blood ailment and dropped out of race in July 2005. He died a year later. Hutchinson, who had run unsuccessfully for Senate and for attorney general, had won three terms in Congress before resigning the seat to head the Drug Enforcement Agency. He later became a Homeland Security undersecretary. He was also the brother of former Senator Tim Hutchinson, who lost reelection in 2002.

Beebe reminded voters of his humble upbringing and campaigned on expanded pre-kindergarten programs, comprehensive health care, a $50 million discretionary fund to help attract business investment, and phasing out the state's 6-cent grocery tax. Hutchinson questioned Beebe's commitment to tax relief; Beebe suggested Hutchinson chose to run for governor because President Bush had not promoted him to secretary of the Homeland Security Department. The two candidates argued over how best to combat illegal immigration, and debated Hutchinson's record at Homeland Security; they sparred over past gun control votes and the No Child Left Behind act. Hutchinson attacked Beebe because the attorney general's office had not participated in a legal fight over the state Supreme Court's decision to strike down a state rule that prevented gay foster parenting. He also tried to link Beebe to a Democratic state senator convicted in 1999 of tax evasion and conspiracy charges. In the last two weeks of the campaign, one Hutchinson television spot featured children describing a politician as a "backslapper" and a "flip–flopper," and that politicians, "Tell voters what they want to hear." A girl concludes, "Just like Mike Beebe." Beebe called the ad shameful; Hutchinson called it lighthearted. Beebe's big financial advantage allowed him to start running ads before Labor Day: through Oct. 31, Beebe had raised $6.3 million to Hutchinson's $3.3 million. Bill Clinton campaigned for Beebe while Bush stumped for Hutchinson. On Election Day, Beebe won 56%-41% and helped sweep six other Democrats into statewide office.

With the help of a Democratic legislature, Beebe moved quickly in the first months to make good on campaign promises and had the good fortune of inheriting an estimated $919 million budget surplus. Beebe's years in the legislature and his hands-on approach to governing helped him avoid public battles with the lawmakers, and allowed him to advance much of his legislative agenda, including a bill that halved the state grocery sales tax from 6% to 3%. The grocery tax cut accounted for about $122 million of $197.5 million in total tax relief passed by the legislature, including an increase in the homestead property tax credit to $350, the elimination of state income tax for those earning below the poverty level and a reduction in the sales tax rate that manufacturers pay for natural gas and electricity. Rather than dedicate surpluses to a rainy day fund, legislators approved $456 million to build and improve public school buildings and gave the governor discretion to spend nearly $188 million on other projects. Beebe kept a low profile on a Republican proposal banning gays from serving as foster parents; the proposal died in committee. The legislature also fell short of passing campaign finance and ethics changes, animal cruelty legislation and limits on payday lending practices. Lawmakers wrapped up work in 86 days, making for the legislature's shortest session since Bill Clinton was governor.

Senior Senator

Blanche Lincoln (D)

Elected 1998, seat up 2010, 2d term; b. Sept. 30, 1960, Helena; home, Horseshoe Lake; U. of AR, 1979-80, Randolph Macon Col., B.S. 1982; Episcopalian; married (Steve).

Elected Office: US House of Reps., 1992-96.

Professional Career: Staff Asst., U.S. Rep. Bill Alexander, 1982-84; Lobbyist & govt. affairs rep., 1985-91.

DC Office: 355 DSOB, 20510, 202-224-4843; Fax: 202-228-1371; Web site: lincoln.senate.gov.

State Office: Little Rock, 501-375-2993.

Committees: *Aging (Special)* (3d of 11 D). *Agriculture, Nutrition & Forestry* (5th of 11 D): Production, Income Protection & Price Support (Chmn.); Nutrition and Food Assistance, Sustainable and Organic Agriculture & General Legislation; Rural Revitalization, Conservation, Forestry & Credit. *Energy & Natural Resources* (10th of 12 D): National Parks; Water & Power; Public Lands & Forests. *Finance* (6th of 11 D): International Trade & Global Competitiveness (Chmn.); Energy, Natural Resources & Infrastructure; Health Care.

Group Ratings

	ADA	*ACLU*	*AFS*	*LCV*	*ITIC*	*NTU*	*COC*	*ACU*	*CFG*	*FRC*
2006	90	75	75	43	100	18	67	8	12	12
2005	95	—	88	65	—	17	89	16	11	—

National Journal Ratings

	2005 LIB	—	*2005 CONS*	*2006 LIB*	—	*2006 CONS*
Economic	58%	—	41%	58%	—	41%
Social	65%	—	29%	64%	—	34%
Foreign	76%	—	15%	62%	—	35%

Key Votes of the 109th Congress

1. Bar ANWR Drilling	Y	5. Confirm Samuel Alito	N	9. Limit Interstate Abortion	N
2. FY06 Spending Curb	N	6. Path to Citizenship	Y	10. CAFTA	Y
3. Estate Tax Repeal	Y	7. Bar Same Sex Marriage	N	11. Urge Iraq Withdrawal	Y
4. Raise Minimum Wage	Y	8. Stem Cell Research $	Y	12. Provide Detainee Rights	Y

Election Results

2004 general	Blanche Lincoln (D)	580,973	(56%)	($5,816,913)
	Jim Holt (R)	458,036	(44%)	($148,682)
2004 primary	Blanche Lincoln (D)	231,037	(83%)	
	Lisa Burks (D)	47,010	(17%)	
1998 general	Blanche Lincoln (D)	385,878	(55%)	($3,122,776)
	Fay Boozman (R)	292,906	(42%)	($1,093,007)
	Other	21,860	(3%)	

Prior Winning Percentages: 1994 House (53%); 1992 House (70%)

Blanche Lambert Lincoln was elected to the Senate in 1998 after showing something close to perfect political pitch in her 1990s electoral career. She grew up in Helena, on the flat rice lands of eastern Arkansas, where her father and brother are the sixth and seventh generations running a farm raising rice, wheat, soybeans, and cotton, and where she stayed in public schools after they were integrated. Cheerful, active, endowed with good political sense, she lists her hobbies as duck hunting, fishing and yard sales. After college, in 1982, she worked as a staffer for 1st District Congressman Bill Alexander, then after two years worked as a lobbyist for, among others, Billy Broadhurst—Gary Hart's host on the 1987 *Monkey Business* cruise. In 1992, she moved back to Arkansas and, as Blanche Lambert (she was married in 1993) ran against Alexander, sensing he was in trouble. He had lost a leadership race in 1986, was named in a lawsuit for a $308,000 debt and had 487 overdrafts totaling $208,000 on the House bank. "I'll promise you one thing," the 31-year-old challenger said, "I can sure enough balance my checkbook." She won the primary 61%-39%, carrying 23 of 25 counties.

In the House, Lincoln compiled a moderate voting record and got a seat on the Commerce Committee. She supported much of the Contract with America in 1995. But when the moratorium on regulations threatened duck hunting season and national wildlife refuges were closed, she got laws changed to ensure it wouldn't happen again. Her re-election margin in 1994 was only 53%-47%, but she seemed well positioned to hold the seat when, in January 1996, she announced that she was pregnant with twin boys and would not run for reelection because of the strain of campaigning in an Arkansas summer during a difficult pregnancy.

When Senator Dale Bumpers announced he would not run for reelection in 1998, Lincoln got into the race. She flashed snapshots of her twins and ran ads showing her overseeing mealtime, balancing one twin on her lap, bouncing the other on her knee, laying her head on her husband's shoulder. "Daughter, wife, mother, congresswoman . . . Living our rock-solid Arkansas values." In the primary, she faced Attorney General Winston Bryant, the Democratic nominee in the 1996 Senate race. She led by an impressive 45%-27% in the May primary, with 64% in her old 1st District, which cast nearly one-third of the votes. She won the June runoff 62%-38%.

In the general election, Lincoln stanched the Republican tide that had been rising since Bill Clinton left the state. The Republican nominee was Fay Boozman, an ophthalmologist from Rogers in northwest Arkansas who attended the same church as Republican Senator Tim Hutchinson. Boozman had a profound religious experience in 1992, sold his medical practice, and ran for the state Senate; there he was the champion of the partial-birth abortion ban. Boozman called on Bill Clinton to resign and ran tough comparative ads on Lincoln. He said the Bible dictated his anti-tax philosophy and made a serious gaffe when he said it is rare for women to get pregnant by rape because fear triggers a hormonal change that blocks conception. Lincoln won 55%-42%; Boozman carried the northwest corner of the state and little else. She was the youngest woman ever elected to the Senate.

Lincoln's voting record has been a bit to the left of the midpoint of the Senate; she was one of nine Democrats to form a moderate caucus, similar to the House's Blue Dogs, in February 2000. Working with her 1st District successor, Marion Berry, she promoted farm exports; in May 2000 she visited Cuba, which, before Fidel Castro, purchased much of Arkansas's rice. She strongly supported ending the embargo on trade in Cuba. She voted for the partial-birth abortion ban, saying it was "always a difficult vote." In February 2001, Lincoln got a seat on the Finance Committee and played an important role in some key votes in the closely divided Senate. On the Finance Committee, she and other moderates negotiated with then-Chairman Charles Grassley and then-ranking member Max Baucus to get two provisions into the committee bill: to make the child care tax refundable to those who pay no income tax and to create a new 10% income bracket. She was one of 12 Democrats to vote for the tax cut in May 2001, but she voted against the Bush budget also in May 2001.

In 2003 and 2004 Lincoln continued to work to make the child tax credit totally refundable, and succeeded in conference in September 2004. She was also successful in extending the 10% bracket and relief from the marriage penalty. She worked for a $20 million cap on small businesses that qualify for industrial development bonds, tax breaks for production of electricity from municipal solid and agricultural wastes and tax credits for producers of biodiesel. In 2005, she opposed Republican attempts in the Finance Committee to reduce the growth of Medicare and Medicaid spending, and in 2006 she successfully fought for funding in the budget to combat methamphetamine. From her seat on the Finance Committee, Lincoln has also proposed numerous changes in tax law: legislation making it easier for disabled veterans to claim tax refunds, a bill permitting individuals to contribute $5,000 annually to tax-free accounts for long-term care, expanding the use of the "rehab tax credit" for the revitalization of older neighborhoods and low-income areas, and providing tax incentives for landowners that protect endangered species on their properties.

Lincoln supported the Iraq war but later criticized the administration for miscalculations and mismanagement. In 2004 she proposed a soldiers' bill of rights, including full disability and retirement benefits and retirement at 55 for reservists. She was the only Arkansas Democrat to vote for the Medicare/prescription drug bill supported by Bush in 2003. "I thought the good outweighed the bad. We really focused on the neediest and sickest." But in 2004 she co-sponsored a bill to eliminate health savings accounts and to authorize the government to negotiate with pharmaceutical companies. While she joined other Democrats in filibustering the nomination of Miguel Estrada and other appeals court nominees, Lincoln supported the nomination of Arkansan Leon Holmes after he was criticized for years-ago comments on abortion; he was confirmed 51-46. In 2006 Lincoln voted against a bill that would criminalize helping a minor avoid parental notification laws by taking her to another state for an abortion. (Her home-state colleague, Democrat Mark Pryor, voted for it.) Lincoln voted for John Roberts as chief justice but she opposed the nomination of Samuel Alito to the Supreme Court.

Never far from her mind are the rice farmers of Arkansas's Delta. She was one of two Democrats to vote against the farm bill in February 2002, because she said it was not generous enough to cotton and rice farmers; she also worked with Olympia Snowe of Maine to change the softwood lumber agreement with Canada. She fought unsuccessfully against limits on farm subsidies. Three rice farms in Stuttgart and Helena were among the top five recipients of farm subsidies in the country, with $106 million from 1996-2001, the largest concentration of subsidies in the United States. She has supported the $16 million Grand Prairie irrigation project, to replace water that rice farmers get from the nearly depleted alluvial aquifer. Lincoln in 2006 supported disaster relief assistance for farmers hurt by drought and fuel costs, and also sponsored a bill with Senator Jim Talent that would extend 2002 farm bill for a crop year while WTO negotiations continued on the crop payment and tariff issues. After Democrats won control of Congress, Lincoln earned a seat on the Energy and Natural Resources Committee, a position that will allow her to promote incentives for biofuels and biodiesel producers. Along with her seats on the Finance and Agriculture committees, Lincoln's new committee post positions her to be influential during the 2007 farm bill reauthorization, particularly on energy issues.

National Republicans, anticipating a Bush victory in Arkansas in 2004, hoped to target Lincoln. But Governor Mike Huckabee in August 2003 said he wouldn't run against her, and former Congressman Asa Hutchinson made no move to leave his number two post in the Department of Homeland Security. That left the Republican nomination to state Senator Jim Holt, who raised only $106,000. But Lincoln took nothing for granted. She raised $6.4 million, an Arkansas record. Holt emphasized his opposition to same-sex marriage, which Arkansans voted 74%-26% to prohibit in November, and Lincoln's vote against the federal Family Marriage Amendment. "It's been his one, only consistent message. I haven't heard him talking about anything else," she complained. Lincoln ran 11% ahead of John Kerry and won 56%-44%, losing 20 of Arkansas's 75 counties, mostly in the northwest. "If we had just had $500,000 or $1 million more we would have won this race," Holt said afterward.

Junior Senator

Mark Pryor (D)

Elected 2002, seat up 2008, 1st term; b. Jan. 10, 1963, Fayetteville; home, Little Rock; U. of AR, B.A. 1985, J.D. 1988; Christian; married (Jill).

Elected Office: AR House of Reps., 1990-94; AR Atty. Gen., 1998-02.

Professional Career: Practicing atty., 1988-96.

DC Office: 255 DSOB, 20510, 202-224-2353; Fax: 202-228-0908; Web site: pryor.senate.gov.

State Office: Little Rock, 501-324-6336.

Committees: *Armed Services* (11th of 13 D): Strategic Forces; Airland; Readiness & Management Support. *Commerce, Science & Transportation* (9th of 12 D): Consumer Affairs, Insurance & Automotive Safety (Chmn.); Space, Aeronautics & Related Sciences; Surface Transportation & Merchant Marine Infrastructure, Safety & Security; Interstate Commerce, Trade & Tourism; Science, Technology & Innovation; Aviation Operations, Safety & Security. *Ethics (Select)* (2d of 3 D). *Homeland Security & Governmental Affairs* (5th of 9 D): State, Local & Private Sector Preparedness & Integration (Chmn.); Investigations (Permanent); Disaster Recovery; Oversight of Government Management, the Federal Workforce & the District of Columbia. *Rules & Administration* (10th of 10 D). *Small Business & Entrepreneurship* (8th of 10 D).

Group Ratings

	ADA	ACLU	AFS	LCV	ITIC	NTU	COC	ACU	CFG	FRC
2006	75	67	88	43	75	20	75	20	18	25
2005	90	—	88	60	—	15	78	24	6	—

National Journal Ratings

	2005 LIB	—	2005 CONS		2006 LIB	—	2006 CONS
Economic	59%	—	40%		61%	—	38%
Social	58%	—	40%		59%	—	40%
Foreign	60%	—	38%		57%	—	42%

Key Votes of the 109th Congress

1. Bar ANWR Drilling	Y	5. Confirm Samuel Alito	N	9. Limit Interstate Abortion	Y
2. FY06 Spending Curb	N	6. Path to Citizenship	Y	10. CAFTA	Y
3. Estate Tax Repeal	N	7. Bar Same Sex Marriage	N	11. Urge Iraq Withdrawal	N
4. Raise Minimum Wage	Y	8. Stem Cell Research $	Y	12. Provide Detainee Rights	Y

Election Results

2002 general	Mark Pryor (D)	434,890	(54%)	($4,414,148)
	Tim Hutchinson (R)	369,069	(46%)	($5,063,923)
2002 primary	Mark Pryor (D)	unopposed		
1996 general	Tim Hutchinson (R)	445,942	(53%)	($1,604,014)
	Winston Bryant (D)	400,241	(47%)	($1,577,838)

Mark Pryor, the junior senator from Arkansas elected in 2002, is one of five children of former senators now serving in the Senate; the others are Christopher Dodd of Connecticut, Robert Bennett of Utah, Evan Bayh of Indiana, and Lisa Murkowski of Alaska (Jon Kyl of Arizona is the son of a congressman; Edward Kennedy's two brothers and Elizabeth Dole's husband were senators). His grandmother, Susie Newton Pryor, was the first woman in Arkansas to run for office when women got the vote. Mark Pryor grew up in southern Arkansas, the Washington area and Little Rock: His father, David Pryor, was elected to the House in 1966, lost a Senate race in 1972 and was elected governor in 1974 and 1976 and then senator in 1978. Mark Pryor graduated from the University of Arkansas and its law school in the 1980s. He practiced law in Little Rock and was elected to the Arkansas House in 1990 and 1992; in 1998, he was elected state attorney general, at 35 the youngest attorney general in the nation (but not in Arkansas history: Bill Clinton won the office at 30). In 1995 he was diagnosed with clear-cell sarcoma, a rare form of cancer. He underwent tendon transplant surgery in his left heel in 1996; the cancer has not returned.

As attorney general, he claimed to save the state $243 million in attorneys' fees in the tobacco settlement. He pushed for legislation to increase penalties for single-incident nursing home accidents (regulating nursing homes also was a big issue for young Congressman David Pryor in the 1960s) and to strengthen background checks for long-term care employees. He worked to reduce utility rates and to remove unsafe baby products from licensed day care centers.

In July 2001, Pryor announced that he would run against Senator Tim Hutchinson, the first Republican to win an Arkansas Senate seat since 1879, who was elected in 1996 to replace the retiring David Pryor. A Baptist minister, radio station owner and founder of a Christian school in Rogers, Hutchinson represented that conservative area in the legislature from 1984 and then for two terms as 3d District congressman. Hutchinson's conservative voting record would ordinarily have made him a favorite for reelection. But in June 1999, Hutchinson filed for divorce from his wife of 29 years, and in August 2000, he married Randi Fredholm, a former member of his House staff. For some senators, this would not have hurt politically. But for a Christian conservative, who criticized Bill Clinton strongly during the impeachment crisis, it was a severe handicap.

Pryor never mentioned Hutchinson's divorce and remarriage and instructed his pollster not to ask questions about them. When asked about Hutchinson's marital problems, he said, "They are what they are. Let the voters decide." But one recurrent theme in his campaign was "Tim Hutchinson has changed"—even though Hutchinson's positions on issues had not changed much, if at all. Pryor campaigned on his support for Second Amendment rights, repeal of the estate tax, increased military spending and, in October, of the Iraq war resolution. In 1998, he had run as a "pro-choice" candidate, but in 2002 he emphasized his belief that abortion was wrong except in cases of rape, incest or saving the life of the mother. But he avoided saying whether or not *Roe v. Wade* should be overturned. He attacked Hutchinson for working for special interests, especially the pharmaceutical companies, and for supporting plans that would risk Social Security benefits; he said he was "way too conservative" for Arkansas. But he carefully avoided identification with the national Democratic party, and made a point of being unavailable and elsewhere when Clinton paid visits to the state.

Pryor's ads were some of the most artful of the 2002 cycle. One showed him, his wife and their two children saying grace before a meal. Then Pryor, holding a Bible, said, "The most important lessons in life are in this book right here." The Pryors belonged to an evangelical church in Little Rock and sent their children to a private Christian school. He turned down an invitation to appear with Hutchinson on *Meet the Press*, explaining that voters wouldn't be able to watch "because they're in church Sunday morning." In another ad, Jill Pryor says laughingly, "I love my husband, but he's cheap." "You know me as Arkansas Attorney General, but I'm also my father's son," said Pryor, in one ad showing him with his father. He explained that not every Democratic idea is good and not every Republican idea is bad. He asked a meeting of municipal leaders in June to pray for George W. Bush. "I think he has done a pretty good job on the war on terrorism. He has a tremendous burden, an inhuman burden."

Against these ads, the Hutchinson ads showing his walking the halls on Capitol Hill or even those showing him playing with his three-year-old grandson were no match. Bush's visits to Arkansas to campaign for Hutchinson did not succeed, as they did in other southern states, in nationalizing the race. Pryor pulled ahead in polls in mid-year and never really fell behind. He won 54%-46%, a solid victory in a year when Democrats lost their majority in the Senate. A survey by pollster John Zogby showed that 12% said Hutchinson's divorce affected their vote—enough by itself to explain his drop from 53% in 1996 to 46% in 2002. Hutchinson's losses were particularly great in his home area. In 1996, he had won 65%-35% in the current 3d Congressional District; in 2002, he carried the 3d District by only 56%-44%.

Pryor entered the Senate ranked 100th in seniority. He got a seat on the Homeland Security and Governmental Affairs Committee, on which his father had served. With his senior colleague Blanche Lincoln, he was one of five Democrats voting to uphold George W. Bush's repeal of the Clinton New Source Review EPA regulations. But he voted against oil drilling in the Arctic National Wildlife Refuge. In March 2003 he voted for the partial-birth abortion ban and supported an amendment, which failed, granting an exception if the mother's physical health is at risk. He opposed an amendment by Dianne Feinstein that would allow an exception for a mother's mental health. He also voted against a resolution supporting *Roe v. Wade*. He voted against the Federal Marriage Amendment in July 2004, explaining that it's an issue that should be left to the states, but supported the amendment on the ballot in November 2004 banning same-sex marriage in Arkansas. In 2006 Pryor voted with Republicans for a bill that would make it a crime to help a minor avoid parental notification laws by traveling to another state for an abortion.

In 2003 Pryor voted against the omnibus appropriations bill which contained $300 million for Arkansas projects and against the $350 billion Bush tax cut. "I just can't support these budgets that send our deficits and national debt soaring out of control." He opposed the Bush Medicare/ prescription drug bill. He had success sponsoring a bill to allow combat pay to be considered as taxable income in calculating the earned income tax and child tax credits; this had the effect of lowering soldiers' taxes. He took care to get Charles Grassley and Max Baucus of the Finance Committee as co-sponsors; the bill passed. He also passed in the Senate a bill to help families get thorough information quickly about family members wounded in combat. In the Democratic majority, Pryor serves on six committees, having regained the Armed Services seat he lost after the 2004 elections: he had called it "an involuntary departure."

The breadth of his committee assignments is reflected in the range of bills he has introduced. He has sought more home heating assistance funding for Southern states, promoted stronger regulation of ammonium nitrate (it can be used in making explosives) while still allowing its use in fertilizer, sponsored with Trent Lott a bill that requires the Transportation secretary to establish new vehicle fuel economy standards and authored a bill with Bill Nelson that would prohibit Internet sales of illegally or deceptively collected private phone records. In 2006, he joined a bipartisan group of senators on a bill to bring narrow the disparities in federal sentencing guidelines for those convicted of possession of crack cocaine with those for possession of powder cocaine. Pryor has also advocated stronger parental controls for the Internet, including the creation of the ".xxx" domain for pornography websites. He has encouraged movie rental chains and retailers to put up signs warning parents about the content of video games.

Pryor's centrist voting record has put him in the center of the several high-profile debates. While Pryor opposed President Bush's "surge" plan to send more combat troops to Iraq, he also opposed a Democratic resolution in March 2007 setting a public timetable for withdrawing U.S. troops from Iraq. (He said he favors a deadline but that the timetable should remain classified to prevent terrorists from using it as a planning tool.) In 2005 he was one of the "Gang of 14" senators that brokered the compromise that allowed President Bush's judicial nominees to advance through the process while preventing GOP leaders from invoking the so-called nuclear option. In 2006, he voted for cloture allowing for the consideration of Supreme Court Justice Samuel Alito, but voted against his nomination. The Free Enterprise Fund, which advocates a repeal of the estate tax, hit Pryor with ads in 2006 for voting against cloture on a bill that would permanently repeal the estate tax. Pryor said he supports easing the burden of the estate tax for farms and small businesses. "Pryor is a liar," the ad declared.

Pryor is one of five Democratic senators from the South and seems acutely aware of the party's weakness in his region. On the issue of guns, he told the Democratic Leadership Conference, "Silence is an admission of guilt. If you don't talk about what your position is on guns, guess what? You're for gun control." He endorsed John Kerry in June 2004, months after he clinched the Democratic nomination, and suggested he go hunting in Arkansas. He admitted that the two "have a little different approach on some issues. But I'm comfortable with him as a person and a leader." Pryor enters the 2008 election cycle well positioned for reelection: he had more than $2 million cash-on-hand through the first quarter of 2007. But as the only Senate Democrat to vote against a public timetable for withdrawal from Iraq, he could get a primary challenge: Arkansas Lieutenant Governor Bill Halter, who won a four-way Democratic primary in 2006, has been mentioned as a possible candidate. Republicans said they plan to target Pryor; their strongest challenger would be Mike Huckabee, the former 10-year Republican governor. Huckabee, who lost a 1992 Senate race to Democrat Dale Bumpers and passed on the chance to run against Blanche Lincoln in 2004, had been encouraged by some Republicans to drop his 2008 presidential bid and run against Pryor. If Republicans cannot lure Huckabee into the race, they might turn to banker J. French Hill or former U.S. attorney Chuck Banks. Former state Senator Jim Holt, who challenged Lincoln unsuccessfully in 2004, and Congressman John Boozman both have said they are unlikely to run.

FIRST DISTRICT

Rep. Marion Berry (D)

Elected 1996, 6th term; b. Aug. 27, 1942, Bayou Meto; home, Gillett; U. of AR, B.S. 1965; Methodist; married (Carolyn).

Professional Career: Pharmacist, 1965-67; farmer, 1968-present; AR Soil & Water Conservation Comm., 1986-94, Chmn. 1992; Special Asst. to the Pres., Domestic Policy Cncl., White House, 1993-96.

DC Office: 2305 RHOB, 20515, 202-225-4076; Fax: 202-225-5602; Web site: www.house.gov/berry.

District Offices: Cabot, 501-843-3043; Jonesboro, 870-972-4600; Mountain Home, 870-425-3510.

Committees: *Appropriations* (26th of 37 D): Energy & Water Development; Military Construction, Veterans Affairs & Related Agencies; Transportation, HUD & Related Agencies. *Budget* (11th of 22 D).

Group Ratings

	ADA	ACLU	AFS	LCV	ITIC	NTU	COC	ACU	CFG	FRC
2006	50	50	86	25	57	24	73	56	26	71
2005	65	—	100	44	—	25	63	52	28	69

National Journal Ratings

	2005 LIB	—	2005 CONS		2006 LIB	—	2006 CONS
Economic	57%	—	43%		57%	—	43%
Social	54%	—	45%		54%	—	45%
Foreign	58%	—	41%		69%	—	30%

Key Votes of the 109th Congress

1. Estate Tax Repeal	Y	5. Limit Interstate Abortion	Y	9. Build Border Fence	Y
2. Limit CAFE Standards	Y	6. Extend Patriot Act	N	10. CAFTA	N
3. FY06 Spending Curb	N	7. Bar Same Sex Marriage	Y	11. Oppose Iraq Withdrawal	Y
4. Drilling in ANWR	Y	8. Stem Cell Research $	Y	12. Detainee Tribunals	N

Election Results

2006 general	Marion Berry (D) 127,577	(69%)	($1,320,295)
	Mickey Stumbaugh (R) 56,611	(31%)	($93,107)
2006 primary	Marion Berry (D) .... unopposed		
2004 general	Marion Berry (D) 162,388	(67%)	($947,839)
	Vernon Humphrey (R) 81,556	(33%)	($23,836)

Prior Winning Percentages: 2002 (67%); 2000 (60%); 1998 (100%); 1996 (53%)

The People		Race/Ethnic Origin	Ancestry	
Area size:	17,521 sq. mi.	80.2% White	USA: 15.3%	Irish: 7.5%
Urban population:	44.5%	16.6% Black	German: 6.8%	
Rural population:	55.5%	0.3% Asian	**2004 Presidential Vote**	
Pop. 2000:	668,360	0.4% Native Am.	Bush (R) 127,179	(52%)
Pop. 2005 (est):	676,359	0.0% Hawaiian	Kerry (D) 115,994	(47%)
Median income:	$28,940	0.9% Two+ races	Other 3,020	(1%)
Poverty status:	18.5%	0.0% Other	**2000 Presidential Vote**	
Military veterans:	13.8%	1.6% Hispanic Origin	Gore (D) 109,160	(50%)
			Bush (R) 105,547	(48%)
			Other 5,482	(2%)
			Cook Partisan Voting Index: D + 1	

Occupation   Blue collar: 35.0%   White collar: 48.8%   Gray collar: 16.2%

The Mississippi Delta, the flat, mushy, river-crossed lowland on both sides of the great river, was some of the country's first industrial farmland. This land was uncultivated in most of the 19th century, when plows were still pulled by mules and muddy flatlands were impassable. Then, about a century ago, big landowners used machines to drain the marshlands and persuaded poor blacks to move here to tend fields of cotton, rice, and later, soybeans. The results were bountiful agriculture and impoverished people. Around 1940, the Delta began to change slowly: the first minimum wage and war industry jobs up North drew young people out of the Delta and the mechanical cotton picker forced many off the farms. But this land—stretching flat as far as the eye can see, past rows of telephone poles and ribbons of asphalt that shimmer in the heat—remains poor by national standards, the people are undereducated, and the area has large pockets of unemployment. Local rice farmers are among the largest recipients of federal farm subsidies; this congressional district ranked fifth in the nation with $4.9 billion in farm subsidies from 1995-2005. In Stuttgart, Riceland Foods is the world's largest rice miller and marketer. The local rice fields also attract enough ducks to make Arkansas the nation's most productive for mallard hunters. There have been signs of change in the region. Several big auto parts plants have been built in Marion, across the Mississippi River from Memphis. But in February 2007, when Toyota chose a site for its seventh North American plant, Marion lost to Tupelo, Mississippi, in part because of local air-quality problems.

The 1st Congressional District of Arkansas includes most of the state's Delta lands and stretches west to the cool green Ozarks. The largest city in the district is Jonesboro, whose cheap labor and flat land has made it an industrial hub for food-processing companies like Nestle and Frito-Lay. The Delta with its large black population is the most Democratic part of Arkansas; some of the hill counties are ancestrally Republican, and there is a Republican trend in Jonesboro and in Lonoke County, which is part of the Little Rock metro area. The result is that the 1st District is closely divided in national politics: it voted 50%-48% for Al Gore in 2000 but 52%-47% for George W. Bush in 2004.

The congressman from the 1st District is Marion Berry, a Democrat who was first elected in 1996. He is the type of folksy small-town southern Democrat that has been prominent in Congress: "a pharmacist and a farmer, the owner of a loud laugh," profiled the *Arkansas Democrat-Gazette*. Berry grew up in Bayou Meto in Arkansas County in the Delta. When his rice-farming father suggested that he study something else, he earned a pharmacy degree in Little Rock, where he made some political connections and then ran a pharmacy for two years. He has been a family farmer since 1968, with a net worth of more than $1 million; for many years, he and his family received close to $100,000 annually in federal farm subsidies, but in 2005 they shifted to tenant farming. Governor Bill Clinton, when advocating changes in the state's water policy, appointed him to the Arkansas Soil & Water Conservation Commission in 1986; in 1993, as president, Clinton appointed him White House liaison to the Agriculture Department. Berry returned to Arkansas in 1996, after Blanche Lincoln did not run for reelection because she was pregnant with twins. Berry had tough opposition for the seat. Against Tom Donaldson, a 28-year-old deputy prosecutor in

Crittenden County who spent little money but ran rural radio ads criticizing Berry for accepting farm subsidies, Berry won the primary runoff by only 52%-48%. In the general, Berry faced Republican Warren Dupwe, a former Jonesboro city attorney. They sparred over Medicare; both candidates opposed abortion rights and gun control, and favored a balanced budget. Berry outspent Dupwe nearly 2–1 and, in a district that has never elected a Republican, won 53%-44%.

Berry's cooperation with Democratic leaders earned him a seat on leadership teams and a slot on the Appropriations Committee. His voting record is mostly moderate but a bit more liberal on foreign policy; a Blue Dog Democrat, he supported the balanced budget amendment and said he wanted to pay off the national debt and save Social Security and Medicare. He voted against Republican tax cuts because they are "just borrowing money from our children and grandchildren." He visited Cuba with Lincoln to promote an end to the trade embargo, so that Arkansas farmers could sell rice and feed products there. With his background, Berry was a natural as co-founder of Democrats' prescription drug task force and he co-chaired the House Democratic health care task force. He has filed the Fair and Speedy Treatment (FAST) of Medicare Prescription Drug Claims Act to get quicker reimbursement to pharmacists . He complained that Republicans added loopholes to his proposal for the re-importation of prescription drugs from other nations. Berry eagerly criticized George W. Bush's Medicare/prescription drug bill. In October 2003, he was one of three House Democrats appointed to the House-Senate conference committee, all of whom complained of being shut out of negotiations in which they said that they could be helpful. The enacted bill was "the sorriest piece of legislation" that Congress ever enacted, Berry said. "It is nothing but an expedited way to make it legal to cheat and steal from old people." His partisan instincts flared again on the House floor in November 2005, when he described Republican Adam Putnam as "a Howdy Doody-looking nimrod." In the majority, he got a seat on the Budget Committee. During their opening-days agenda, Speaker Nancy Pelosi sidestepped Berry's more sweeping approach to overhaul the prescription-drug program.

Berry has declined opportunities to run statewide, citing health and family responsibilities. He has been reelected easily; in 2006, Berry was endorsed by the National Rifle Association for the first time.

SECOND DISTRICT

Rep. Vic Snyder (D)

Elected 1996, 6th term; b. Sept. 27, 1947, Medford, OR; home, Little Rock; Willamette U., B.A. 1975, U. of OR, M.D. 1979, U. of AR, J.D. 1988; Methodist; married (Betsy Singleton).

Military Career: Marine Corps, 1967-69 (Vietnam).

Elected Office: AR Senate, 1990-96.

Professional Career: Practicing physician, 1982-present.

DC Office: 1330 LHOB, 20515, 202-225-2506; Fax: 202-225-5903; Web site: www.house.gov/snyder.

District Offices: Little Rock, 501-324-5941.

Committees: *Armed Services* (7th of 34 D): Oversight & Investigations (Chmn.); Military Personnel. *Veterans' Affairs* (3d of 16 D): Health.

Group Ratings

	ADA	ACLU	AFS	LCV	ITIC	NTU	COC	ACU	CFG	FRC
2006	75	91	100	92	86	14	43	17	14	14
2005	80	—	100	78	—	18	59	8	16	15

National Journal Ratings

	2005 LIB	—	2005 CONS		2006 LIB	—	2006 CONS
Economic	66%	—	33%		77%	—	22%
Social	66%	—	34%		64%	—	36%
Foreign	66%	—	33%		61%	—	39%

Key Votes of the 109th Congress

1. Estate Tax Repeal	N	5. Limit Interstate Abortion	Y	9. Build Border Fence	N
2. Limit CAFE Standards	N	6. Extend Patriot Act	N	10. CAFTA	Y
3. FY06 Spending Curb	N	7. Bar Same Sex Marriage	N	11. Oppose Iraq Withdrawal	Y
4. Drilling in ANWR	*	8. Stem Cell Research $	Y	12. Detainee Tribunals	N

Election Results

2006 general	Vic Snyder (D) 124,871	(61%)	($643,531)
	Andy Mayberry (R) 81,432	(39%)	($98,845)
2006 primary	Vic Snyder (D) .... unopposed		
2004 general	Vic Snyder (D) 160,834	(58%)	($880,496)
	Marvin Parks (R) 115,655	(42%)	($574,023)

Prior Winning Percentages: 2002 (93%); 2000 (58%); 1998 (58%); 1996 (52%)

The People		Race/Ethnic Origin	Ancestry	
Area size:	6,045 sq. mi.	75.6% White	USA: 11.7%	German: 8.4%
Urban population:	66.2%	19.4% Black	Irish: 7.9%	
Rural population:	33.8%	0.9% Asian	**2004 Presidential Vote**	
Pop. 2000:	666,058	0.4% Native Am.	Bush (R) 145,392	(51%)
Pop. 2005 (est):	697,168	0.0% Hawaiian	Kerry (D) 134,478	(48%)
Median income:	$37,221	1.1% Two+ races	Other 2,785	(1%)
Poverty status:	12.7%	0.1% Other	**2000 Presidential Vote**	
Military veterans:	14.5%	2.4% Hispanic Origin	Bush (R) 116,075	(49%)
			Gore (D) 112,720	(48%)
			Other 6,817	(3%)
			Cook Partisan Voting Index: R + 0	

Occupation   Blue collar: 25.0%   White collar: 60.5%   Gray collar: 14.5%

Little Rock has been the capital, largest city and central focus of Arkansas for more than a century, and now is the home of the nation's largest presidential library. It is one of those capitals located at its state's geographical center and, in a state that has no other metropolis, it stands out. For a long moment, Little Rock became internationally famous. That was in September 1957, when Governor Orval Faubus sent in the National Guard to block a desegregation order at Central High School. President Dwight D. Eisenhower sent in U.S. troops and federalized the National Guard to enforce the order, and Little Rock became a synonym for bigotry around the world. Forty years later, the Little Rock Nine who had integrated the high school returned for an anniversary commemoration with President Bill Clinton. "It was Little Rock that made racial equality a driving obsession in my life," he said, and added that American life still was in too many ways segregated. Also speaking was Republican Governor Mike Huckabee, who said, "Today we come to say once and for all that what happened here 40 years ago was simply wrong." For the 50th anniversary, the city planned to open a visitor center to highlight the Central High School experience.

Little Rock is the political center of Arkansas. It may not be upscale by national standards, but it is in Arkansas. Little Rock sets the tone of the public life of its state as do only a few other state capitals—Boston, Providence, Atlanta, Denver, Honolulu. It is home to the *Arkansas Democrat-Gazette*, the feisty, conservative paper whose editor Paul Greenberg christened Clinton "Slick Willie." On the bank of the Arkansas River is the Clinton Presidential Center and Park, designed to promote local economic revitalization and with architecture evocative of a "bridge to the 21st century." It opened in a November 2004 ceremony attended by the current and three former presidents.

The 2d Congressional District of Arkansas includes Little Rock, with its large black and affluent white neighborhoods, and North Little Rock, a kind of industrial suburb across the Arkansas River known informally for years as Dog Town. It is surrounded by Saline (named for its early salt works) and Faulkner (named for fiddle player Sanford C. Faulkner, the original Arkansas Traveler) Counties, which have grown rapidly as people move farther out on the freeways, and a couple of hill counties. In 2004, with turnout up sharply, George W. Bush got 63% of the vote in Saline County and 59% in Faulkner, but John Kerry won 55% in Little Rock's Pulaski County. Overall, the district gave Bush a 51%-48% margin—the same as in the national popular vote. This is the seat once held by legendary Ways and Means chairman Wilbur Mills, who retired in 1976.

The congressman from the 2d District is Vic Snyder, a Democrat first elected in 1996. Snyder is an unusual politician, "an inveterately private man in a public profession, quite content to be all alone," wrote the *Arkansas Democrat-Gazette*. He grew up fatherless in Medford, Oregon, dropped out of Willamette University, and at 20 signed up in the Marine Corps and served in Vietnam. Then he returned to Oregon for college and medical school, became a practicing physician, and went on medical missions in Thailand, Honduras, Sierra Leone and Sudan. While practicing medicine, he got a law degree, but never practiced law. In 1990, he was elected to the state Senate and made news when he called for repeal of Arkansas's anti-sodomy law and when he refused to accept a pension. When the seat opened in 1996, Snyder, consulting no one, decided to run for Congress. He campaigned as a reformer, promising not to accept a congressional pension until an equitable system was established for federal employees. His main Democratic opponents had more political backgrounds. But in a 51%-49% upset, Snyder won the runoff over Pulaski County prosecutor Mark Stodola, who was a strong Clinton supporter. Against Republican lawyer Bud Cummins, Snyder sounded reform themes while outspending him. Snyder won narrowly, 52%-48%.

Snyder's voting record is close to the center of House Democrats, but he is the most liberal in the Arkansas delegation and an occasional maverick. He voted for needle exchanges and against the partial-birth abortion ban. In 2004 he opposed a state constitutional amendment to ban same-sex marriage; the ballot measure passed 75%-25%. Snyder also has supported more moderate measures—the balanced budget, tax cuts, a strong education system—and has stressed his military record and service on the Armed Services Committee. He helped to organize the bipartisan Cuba working group to push the House to end the trade embargo of Cuba and the ban on travel there; he was the only Democrat from Arkansas to vote for trade promotion authority in 2001. He criticized the Bush administration for failure to provide increased security for embassies overseas and was the only Arkansas member to vote against the use of military force against Iraq. After the war began, he visited Iraq and called for more support of U.S. troops, but he criticized the Pentagon for failing to inform Congress of prison abuses. In March 2004, he sponsored legislation establishing separate medals for service in Afghanistan and Iraq; it was later signed into law by George W. Bush. Snyder has been active on internal House issues: He unsuccessfully sought changes in Democratic rules to spread committee assignments more equitably among members. He challenged as a possible violation of the House's anti-bribery rule the practice of interest groups that notify members that they will include an upcoming vote in their legislative scorecard. And he spoke out against members—mostly Democrats—who wanted to give governors the power to appoint new House members in the event of a catastrophic attack on the Capitol. In the majority, at first he chaired the Armed Services Subcommittee on Military Personnel, which deals with troop levels and benefits. The House unanimously passed his bill to improve health care for soldiers wounded in Iraq and Afghanistan, and he sought to provide members of the National Guard and Reserves the same G.I. benefits that are available to active duty personnel. In June 2007, after Martin Meehan resigned from Congress, Snyder was named to replace him as chairman of the Oversight and Investigations Subcommittee, which had been dissolved in 1995 by the new Republican majority and was reinstated when Democrats returned to power.

Since his initial tight election, he has been reelected with at least 58% of the vote. In 2004, Republican challenger Marvin Parks aligned himself with George W. Bush and criticized Snyder for being out of touch with local views, especially on issues such as abortion and gay marriage. Although he raised more than $500,000, Parks had little national Republican support. Parks carried Saline and Faulkner Counties, but Snyder won 58%-42%. In endorsing Snyder, the *Democrat-Gazette* wrote, "While we may abhor some of his political stances, there is no doubting the sincerity with which he takes them. Or his patriotism . . . We're endorsing an honorable opponent today, not his politics."

THIRD DISTRICT

Rep. John Boozman (R)

Elected Nov. 2001, 3d full term; b. Dec. 10, 1950, Shreveport, LA; home, Rogers; U. of AR, 1969-72, Southern Col. of Optometry, O.D. 1977; Baptist; married (Cathy).

Elected Office: Rogers School Bd., 1994-2001.

Professional Career: Optometrist, 1977-2001.

DC Office: 1519 LHOB, 20515, 202-225-4301; Fax: 202-225-5713; Web site: www.boozman.house.gov.

District Offices: Ft. Smith, 479-782-7787; Harrison, 870-741-6900; Lowell, 479-782-7787.

Committees: *Foreign Affairs* (15th of 23 R): Terrorism, Nonproliferation & Trade; Africa & Global Health. *Transportation & Infrastructure* (19th of 34 R): Aviation; Water Resources & Environment; Highways & Transit. *Veterans' Affairs* (7th of 13 R): Economic Opportunity (RMM).

Group Ratings

	ADA	ACLU	AFS	LCV	ITIC	NTU	COC	ACU	CFG	FRC
2006	5	18	14	8	100	57	100	92	61	100
2005	0	—	0	0	—	59	93	96	63	92

National Journal Ratings

	2005 LIB	—	2005 CONS		2006 LIB	—	2006 CONS
Economic	8%	—	92%		16%	—	81%
Social	24%	—	74%		23%	—	74%
Foreign	47%	—	52%		33%	—	67%

Key Votes of the 109th Congress

1. Estate Tax Repeal	Y	5. Limit Interstate Abortion	Y	9. Build Border Fence	Y
2. Limit CAFE Standards	Y	6. Extend Patriot Act	Y	10. CAFTA	Y
3. FY06 Spending Curb	Y	7. Bar Same Sex Marriage	Y	11. Oppose Iraq Withdrawal	Y
4. Drilling in ANWR	Y	8. Stem Cell Research $	N	12. Detainee Tribunals	Y

Election Results

2006 general	John Boozman (R)	125,039	(62%)	($651,611)
	Woodrow Anderson (D)	75,885	(38%)	($361,155)
2006 primary	John Boozman (R)	unopposed		
2004 general	John Boozman (R)	160,629	(59%)	($543,281)
	Janice Judy (D)	103,158	(38%)	($353,822)
	Other	7,016	(3%)	

Prior Winning Percentages: 2002 (99%); 2001 (56%)

The People		Race/Ethnic Origin	Ancestry	
Area size:	8,661 sq. mi.	87.3% White	USA: 11.8%	German: 10.0%
Urban population:	54.4%	2.0% Black	Irish: 8.8%	
Rural population:	45.6%	1.4% Asian	**2004 Presidential Vote**	
Pop. 2000:	672,756	1.2% Native Am.	Bush (R) 171,853	(62%)
Pop. 2005 (est):	737,861	0.2% Hawaiian	Kerry (D) 100,656	(36%)
Median income:	$33,915	1.6% Two+ races	Other 3,449	(1%)
Poverty status:	13.7%	0.1% Other	**2000 Presidential Vote**	
Military veterans:	14.3%	6.3% Hispanic Origin	Bush (R) 138,977	(60%)
			Gore (D) 86,739	(37%)
			Other 7,691	(3%)
			Cook Partisan Voting Index: R +11	

Occupation   Blue collar: 32.0%   White collar: 53.0%   Gray collar: 14.9%

The northwest corner of Arkansas has become one of America's boom areas—the nation's number one growth area in 2003, according to the Milken Institute—with major corporate headquarters and dozens of small factories, tourist attractions and retirement developments in the Ozarks, some of

America's richest families and growing numbers of hard-working Hispanic immigrants—about 20% of the population of Springdale and Rogers in 2000. This is home to the handsome University of Arkansas in Fayetteville (where young lawyers Bill Clinton and Hillary Rodham married in the living room of a brick bungalow) and the mountain-bound resort town of Eureka Springs. All this would have seemed unlikely during most of the 20th century, when these rounded green mountains and pleasant wide valleys, farmhouses and small towns seemed left behind. But the friendly atmosphere and strong religious faith of these communities have proved to be assets, not liabilities, conducive to economic creativity and personal serenity. There have also been touches of genius. Sam Walton, who opened his first Wal-Mart on the town square of Bentonville (it's now a small museum), had the inspiration to build a retail chain in tradition-minded small towns and rural areas using sophisticated computerized management; it made him the richest man in America, though he still drove a pickup truck and kept the corporate headquarters in a deliberately unsnazzy building in Bentonville. Don Tyson took his family chicken business and made Tyson Foods, in its sparkling headquarters outside Springdale, the world's leading chicken producer and processor. Other firms have flocked in, especially to do business with Wal-Mart, which is now also the world's largest food retailer. The area is attracting a diverse group of new residents, from upscale executives buying lavish homes in gated communities to immigrants seeking work in booming local industries.

The 3d Congressional District covers Northwest Arkansas, including Bentonville, Fayetteville and Springdale, plus Fort Smith on the Oklahoma line. It extends as far east as Marion County, home to Ranger Boats, the renowned manufacturer of tournament-quality fishing boats. Its population rose 30% in the 1990s and another 8% from 2000 to 2005—more than Arkansas's other three districts. Politically, this area has been the most Republican part of Arkansas since the Civil War, for there were few slaves here and much suspicion of planters. The area became more Republican in the 1950s, and John Paul Hammerschmidt was elected here in 1966 as one of the first Republican congressmen from the South. He was strong enough even in Democratic 1974 to beat Bill Clinton, then 28, in his first election, though Clinton did get an impressive 48% of the vote. Lately this area has become even more Republican, as Christian conservatives have entered politics and new migrants and millionaires have voted heavily Republican. After voting narrowly for Clinton in 1992 and narrowly against him in 1996, the 3d twice voted strongly for George W. Bush.

The congressman from the 3d District is John Boozman (it's pronounced like Bozeman, Montana), a Republican who won a special election in November 2001. He replaced Asa Hutchinson, who had resigned to head the Drug Enforcement Administration. A graduate of the University of Arkansas, where he was an offensive guard for the football team, Boozman became an optometrist in Rogers, part of rapidly growing Benton County. He served two terms on the local school board, and he worked for his brother Fay's unsuccessful campaign for the Senate in 1998.

To win the House seat, Boozman prevailed in three close contests in two months, even though he was outspent in each. In the wide-open primary, Boozman had the endorsement of Governor Mike Huckabee and was the only Republican to support George W. Bush's decision to permit limited federal funding of stem-cell research. His chief opponent initially, former state Representative Jim Hendren, was damaged by revelations that he had an extramarital affair. Boozman faced a runoff against state Senator Gunner DeLay, who raised few funds and had little support from local politicians (but was a cousin of Tom DeLay, who stayed neutral). In the three-week runoff, neither candidate spent heavily. With a stronger grass-roots organization, Boozman won 57%-43%. His opponent in the general was state Representative Mike Hathorn, a 28-year-old lawyer who, local Democrats hoped, could prevail with his Clinton-like personality. But House Democrats did little to help his campaign and only in the closing days ran ads that criticized Boozman's support for Social Security "privatization." Boozman won 56%-42%, with help from a sophisticated Republican voter-turnout operation.

Arriving in Washington for the first time in his life, Boozman was appointed to the Republican task force that prepared a bill for prescription drugs for seniors. His voting record has been reliably conservative, but not hard-edged. He showed his independence from the White House by voting to remove the embargo on trade with Cuba and to import prescription drugs from Canada; he opposed Bush's immigration proposal as amnesty for illegal aliens. Boozman sponsored bills to abolish the tax code and to display the Ten Commandments in the House and Senate chambers, and he voted against renewal of the Voting Rights Act because of the racial progress made in the South. An evangelical Christian, he wants to weaken restrictions on churches' political activities. With Democrat Tammy Baldwin, he filed the Veteran Vision Equity Act to improve benefits for veterans with impaired vision. On the Transportation Committee, he filed a proposal to give more flexibility to federal regulators setting maximum hours of service for truckers. He is an enthusiastic member of the I-49 caucus, whose members want to designate US-71 as an interstate and connect I-540 from Fort Smith to Bentonville with interstates running north to Kansas City and south to Texarkana and New Orleans. On Veterans Affairs, he is ranking Republican on the Economic Opportunity Subcommittee.

In the 2004 campaign, he was opposed by surprisingly well-funded Democratic state Representative Janice Judy, the owner of a Fayetteville pizza restaurant. Boozman criticized her opposition to a constitutional amendment to ban same-sex marriage and civil unions in Arkansas. He won 59%-38%, running 3% behind George W. Bush. He faced modest opposition in the tougher climate of 2006 and won 62%-38%. After the election, in which Democrats swept every statewide office, Boozman was left as the highest ranking Republican in Arkansas and the only one in the congressional delegation.

FOURTH DISTRICT

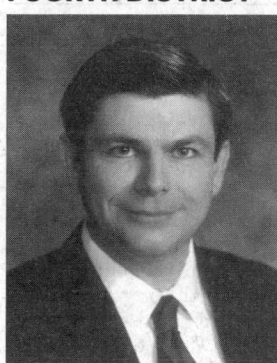

Rep. Mike Ross (D)

Elected 2000, 4th term; b. Aug. 2, 1961, Texarkana; home, Prescott; U. of AR, B.A. 1987; Methodist; married (Holly).

Elected Office: Nevada County Quorum Court, 1983-85; AR Senate, 1990-2000.

Professional Career: Chief of Staff, AR Lt. Gov. Winston Bryant, 1984-89; Owner, Holly's Health Mart, 1993-present.

DC Office: 314 CHOB, 20515, 202-225-3772; Fax: 202-225-1314; Web site: www.house.gov/ross.

District Offices: El Dorado, 870-881-0681; Hot Springs, 501-520-5892; Pine Bluff, 870-536-3376; Prescott, 870-887-6787.

Committees: *Energy & Commerce* (24th of 31 D): Commerce, Trade & Consumer Protection; Energy & Air Quality; Health. *Science & Technology* (18th of 24 D): Space & Aeronautics; Technology & Innovation.

Group Ratings

	ADA	ACLU	AFS	LCV	ITIC	NTU	COC	ACU	CFG	FRC
2006	50	50	71	25	29	22	67	60	27	71
2005	60	—	100	50	—	21	65	52	16	54

National Journal Ratings

	2005 LIB	—	2005 CONS		2006 LIB	—	2006 CONS
Economic	60%	—	40%		57%	—	43%
Social	56%	—	44%		54%	—	45%
Foreign	60%	—	40%		62%	—	38%

Key Votes of the 109th Congress

1. Estate Tax Repeal	Y	5. Limit Interstate Abortion	Y	9. Build Border Fence	Y
2. Limit CAFE Standards	Y	6. Extend Patriot Act	Y	10. CAFTA	N
3. FY06 Spending Curb	N	7. Bar Same Sex Marriage	Y	11. Oppose Iraq Withdrawal	Y
4. Drilling in ANWR	Y	8. Stem Cell Research $	Y	12. Detainee Tribunals	Y

Election Results

2006 general	Mike Ross (D)	128,236	(75%)	($1,254,480)
	Joe Ross (R)	43,360	(25%)	
2006 primary	Mike Ross (D)	unopposed		
2004 general	Mike Ross (D)	unopposed		($756,922)

Prior Winning Percentages: 2002 (61%); 2000 (51%)

The People		Race/Ethnic Origin	Ancestry	
Area size:	20,951 sq. mi.	71.0% White	USA: 14.0%	Irish: 7.3%
Urban population:	44.7%	24.4% Black	English: 5.7%	
Rural population:	55.3%	0.4% Asian	**2004 Presidential Vote**	
Pop. 2000:	666,226	0.5% Native Am.	Bush (R) 128,474	(51%)
Pop. 2005 (est):	663,951	0.0% Hawaiian	Kerry (D) 118,825	(48%)
Median income:	$29,675	0.9% Two+ races	Other 2,840	(1%)
Poverty status:	18.5%	0.0% Other	**2000 Presidential Vote**	
Military veterans:	13.9%	2.7% Hispanic Origin	Gore (D) 114,149	(49%)
			Bush (R) 112,341	(48%)
			Other 6,083	(3%)
			Cook Partisan Voting Index: D + 0	

Occupation   Blue collar: 34.9%   White collar: 47.8%   Gray collar: 17.2%

West from the Delta flatlands along the Mississippi River, where the water-soaked fields produce America's largest rice crop, across small cities with antique pasts like Pine Bluff and El Dorado, southern Arkansas runs to the Ouachita Mountains and the border town of Texarkana, where the main street divides two states and Texan Ross Perot grew up five blocks west of Arkansas. This is the northwestern corner of the Deep South. It includes the state's largest black population, a reminder that parts of southern Arkansas were once plantation country; there is also oil production, a reminder that this is the beginning of the Southwest. It includes the Crater of Diamonds State Park, the source of the 4.24 carat Kahn canary diamond that Hillary Rodham Clinton wore to her husband's second inauguration as president. The broiler chicken industry looms large in these parts, and the accent is clearly Arkansan: El Dorado, Nevada and Lafayette are all pronounced with long As and accents on the penultimate syllable, and Ouachita is, with a bow to the original French rendition of the Indian name, *waSHEEta*. The district includes the little railroad-crossing county-seat town of Hope, where President Bill Clinton and his first White House Chief of Staff Mack McLarty were classmates at Miss Mary's kindergarten, and where Governor Mike Huckabee grew up a decade later; and Hot Springs, the spa resort and gambling haven where Clinton's stepfather sold Buicks, his mother bet on the horses, and he excelled in high school as he began his climb from southern Arkansas obscurity to world prominence.

The 4th Congressional District occupies almost all of the southern half of Arkansas, from the Mississippi River to the Ouachita Mountains, the Delta to Texarkana. It is historically a Democratic district, and one that for most of the 20th century elected young men to the House and kept them there for years, to cut deals with the Democratic leadership and bring home the bacon. During the 1990s, it had a very different congressional politics: Bipartisan, with rancorous debates on national issues followed by narrow election victories. But this may be one part of the South returning to its heritage.

The congressman from the 4th District is Mike Ross, a Democrat who in 2000 defeated Republican Jay Dickey, the only House Republican outside California who was defeated that year. A fifth-generation Arkansan, Ross was born in Texarkana. He graduated from Hope High School and from the University of Arkansas at Little Rock. He got his start in local politics in 1982 as a travel aide for Bill Clinton's successful bid to recover from his 1980 loss and recapture the governorship. While in college, he served on the staff of Lieutenant Governor Winston Bryant and was executive director of the Arkansas Youth Suicide Prevention Commission. Ross sold insurance and worked as a sales manager for a pharmaceutical company. He owns Holly's Health Mart in rural Prescott, where he lives with his wife Holly, who is the store's pharmacist. He was elected to the state Senate in 1990 until term limits forced him out a decade later; then he ran for Congress. This was perhaps the only district in the nation where impeachment played a pivotal role in 2000. Dickey, representing Bill Clinton's boyhood homes, had voted for impeachment, and Clinton vowed to get back at him. Although Dickey often was a thorn to Republican leaders, Ross tied him to them and argued that "the real Jay Dickey" voted to cut Medicare and Social Security to fund tax cuts for the rich. Dickey responded that Ross was getting his script from "his liberal masters in Washington." Clinton had an impact: He helped raise $300,000 for Ross at fundraisers, orchestrated endorsements from administration officials with Arkansas roots, and campaigned for Ross in Pine Bluff on the Sunday before the election. There were plenty of independent expenditures as well, by pharmaceutical groups against Ross and by labor unions against Dickey. Ross won, 51%-49%.

In the House, Ross joined the Blue Dogs and he became a vocal proponent of prescription drug legislation, often citing his experiences as a small-town pharmacist. He cultivates his "country boy" image, including regular skeet shooting from the back of his pick-up truck. He got approval in 2002 of his proposal to remove Arkansas's constitutional limit on interest rates, which local bankers and consumer groups agreed had made financing difficult. His action won wide support from political leaders in Arkansas, which was the only remaining state to mandate such terms. But national banking interests voiced concerns about separate aspects of his measure, and it died when Congress adjourned. Although Ross voted for the use of force in Iraq, he later questioned whether the U.S. should finance reconstruction after the ouster of Saddam Hussein. Back home, Ross feuded with Huckabee. He accused the governor of running the Delta Regional Authority as a "slush fund," but refrained from criticizing specific local projects. Ross is an enthusiastic member of the I-49 caucus, and has sought funds for building it north across the Ouachita Mountains to Fort Smith. Following Hurricane Katrina, he criticized FEMA for failing to use more than 10,000 mobile homes parked at the airport in Hope. In 2006 he was a lieutenant to Rahm Emanuel at the DCCC and, in the majority, he has been a leader of the Blue Dogs and an outspoken defender of the Democrats' budget plan. He warned against the party moving to the left. "We didn't defeat the Republicans with liberal Democrats." On the Energy and Commerce Committee, he said that he hoped to fix the "flawed Medicare prescription drug bill."

Dickey decided to run again in 2002 and Ross seemed to face a serious challenge. Both candidates again raised substantial sums, but the Republican's campaign stumbled from the start. Dickey refused, as he had in the past, to accept funds from political action committees, but the Republicans' campaign committee got him to back down. Dickey constantly reminded voters that he had delivered federal money from his Appropriations Committee seat and carried a pledge from Speaker Dennis Hastert that he would get his seat back. Ross criticized Republican leaders for reversing after the 2000 election the appropriators' tentative decision to send $4 million to the district. Hastert defended the action, in an interview with the *Arkansas Democrat-Gazette*: "If we had a Republican in there, we could deliver the money. Jay is the one who worked for it. Ross wasn't even on the committee." Ross won by a convincing 61%-39% margin. That seems to have made the 4th a safe Democratic district again after more than a decade of fierce partisan contests. Ross had no Republican opposition in 2004, and Dickey became a Washington lobbyist.

★ CALIFORNIA ★

KAL-ee-for-nee-ah, as its current governor pronounces the name, more faithful to the original Spanish than any of his predecessors except perhaps Romualdo Pacheco, who served 10 months in 1875, is America's largest state, a nation-state really, with an economy larger than all but five nations. It is the site of the world's most advanced cutting-edge technology, yet it is a place with plenty of Third World neighborhoods and it greeted the 21st century with Third World-like rolling blackouts of electricity. Its growth has been awesome: The Census Bureau estimated that there were 36.5 million Californians in 2006, far ahead of second-place Texas's 23.5 million; metro Los Angeles had 17.8 million people, second only to metro New York's 22 million, and the San Francisco Bay area had 7.2 million, not so far behind Chicagoland's 9.7 million. The Central Valley and mountain counties had 6.8 million people; if this were a separate state it would rank 13th in population, yet it has only 19% of the population of California. San Diego County, with 2.9 million people the sixth largest county in the United States, contains only 8% of Californians. California owes this preeminence not to natural advantage but to human ingenuity. Los Angeles, with little in the way of natural resources and no natural harbor, is the nation's leading port and second-biggest manufacturer, as well as the world's entertainment center. The Bay area, which once lived by exporting food, is now the world's leader in computers and high tech. California has grown not because it had to but because people wanted it to. It has not grown without contradictions. California loves its physical environment, but also has the largest urban sprawl in the United States; it likes to think of itself as the America of the future, even as it watched the electricity flicker out earlier this decade; it likes to see itself as the political leader of the nation, but lives now with a president who did not come close to winning here and has a public sector that in important ways—in its public schools, fiscal condition, electricity regulation—has been deeply dysfunctional. California today is generally Democratic, well off to the left on cultural issues, secular more than religious. If it could imagine itself leading the nation when Bill Clinton was president, it was aware that the nation is not following its lead with George W. Bush in office. In installing Arnold Schwarzenegger

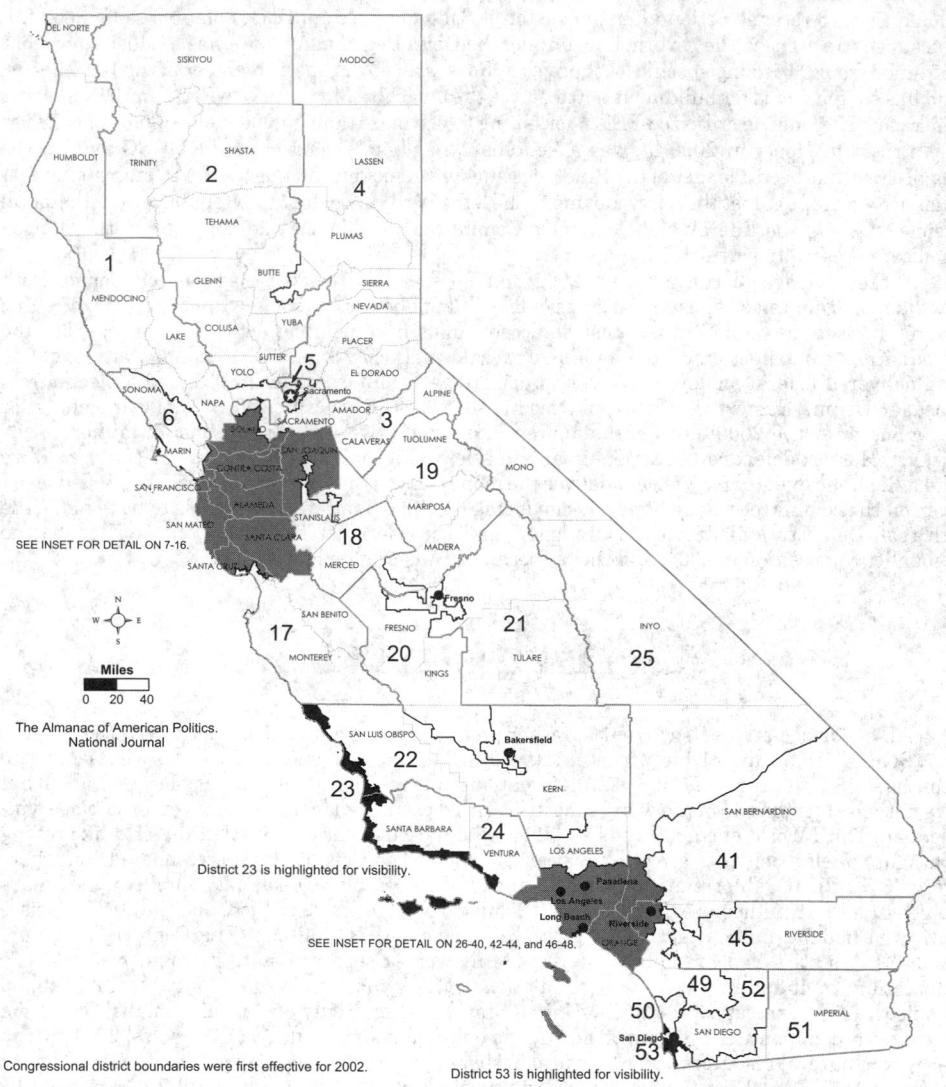

The Almanac of American Politics.
National Journal

SEE INSET FOR DETAIL ON 7-16.

District 23 is highlighted for visibility.

SEE INSET FOR DETAIL ON 26-40, 42-44, and 46-48.

District 53 is highlighted for visibility.

Congressional district boundaries were first effective for 2002.

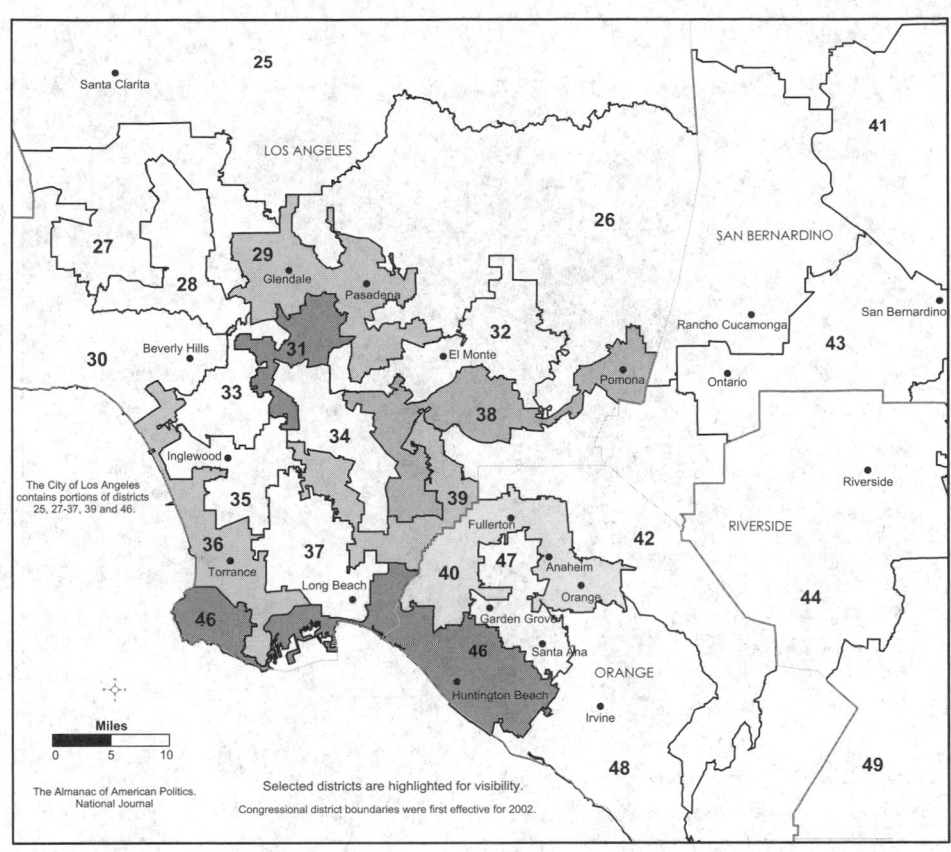

The City of Los Angeles contains portions of districts 25, 27-37, 39 and 46.

Miles
0   5   10

The Almanac of American Politics.
National Journal

Selected districts are highlighted for visibility.

Congressional district boundaries were first effective for 2002.

as governor (while recalling Gray Davis) and reelecting Schwarzenegger three years later, California set an interesting example, one that might be followed depending on who wins the Republican presidential nomination in 2008. But it won't be Schwarzenegger who as an immigrant is ineligible to run.

Most of all California has been a state that is always transforming itself, whose economy has been transformed several times over, whose population has been transformed by one group of newcomers after another and whose politics is periodically transformed with the suddenness of an earthquake. If other states have changed gradually on an analog scale over the years, California has changed sharply on a digital scale: this is quantum theory physics, not wave theory. So it has been from its American beginning. In 1848, when California passed from Mexico to the United States by the Treaty of Guadalupe Hidalgo, this was an almost entirely empty land, inhabited by a few thousand Indians and Mexicans and by a few hundred American soldiers and men on the make. Then in 1849 gold was found in Sutter's Mill and thousands arrived in the Gold Rush; within months San Francisco became one of America's 25 largest cities. The big money was made not by the miners but by the grocers and dry goods merchants who provisioned them, like the Big Four— Crocker, Hopkins, Huntington, Stanford—who built the Central and Southern Pacific Railroads. The railroads sold off vast chunks of the Central Valley to large farming operations and enticed settlers with low fares to newly-platted suburbs in the Los Angeles Basin. Engineers built great aqueducts that stretched hundreds of miles, from the Hetch Hetchy Valley in Yosemite to San Francisco and from the Owens River to Los Angeles, without which these metropolises could not exist. Early 20th century California was affluent and cultured, with great universities already, Berkeley and Stanford, and fine museums and libraries; it was America's window on the Pacific, alert to developments in China and Japan, Hawaii and the Philippines, eager to extend America's economic reach and military strength, but still, as Carey McWilliams wrote, an "island" separated

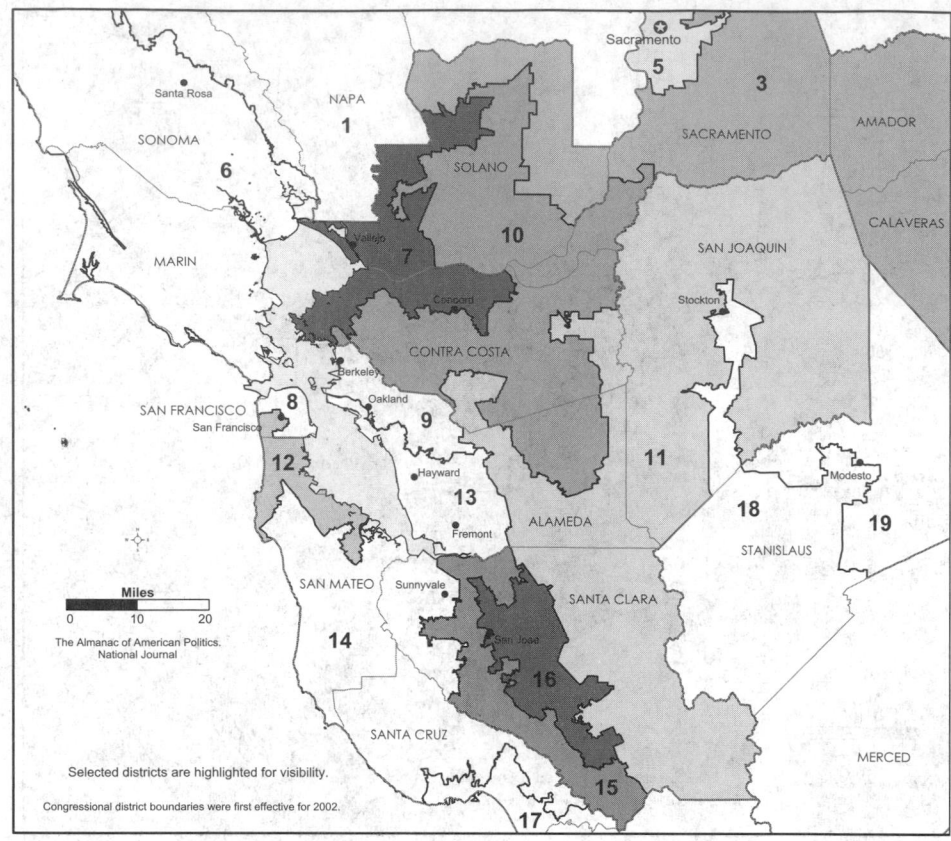

from the rest of the country. Then in World War II California became one of the great defense industry states, building ships and airplanes by the thousands. Millions of Americans came here and millions stayed: The population rose from 7 million in 1940 to 17 million in 1963, when California passed New York and became the nation's most populous state.

California's future was planned by the heads of the big units of government and business—Franklin D. Roosevelt and Henry J. Kaiser, who built vast shipyards and steel and aluminum factories; Governor Earl Warren, who husbanded tax monies to build schools and freeways in the years after the war; Robert Sproul and Clark Kerr, who built the University of California into what Kerr called "the multiversity;" Governor Pat Brown, who completed the vast system of canals and aqueducts that brought water from the wet north to the thirsty south. But the real engine of growth was the little people who took advantage of this infrastructure and built a humming economy on it. When California's defense plants closed down after World War II, leaders imagined that hundreds of thousands would have to head back east. Instead, as urbanologist Jane Jacobs pointed out, one-eighth of all the new jobs in the nation in the late 1940s were created in metro Los Angeles. This small-scale growth, multiplied thousands of times over, made California the nation's largest state. And this infusion of new people transformed California politically. Before World War II this was a Republican state, with progressive leanings; political struggles took place inside the Republican Party. The in-rush of the G.I. generation, with its allegiance to the New Deal, the building for the first time here of auto and steel factories with unionized work forces, made California a two-party state. These new migrants were middle class and working class, family men and women enjoying a life in suburbs in the lovely California climate and in the days—or remembering the days—when smog didn't make the sky of the Los Angeles Basin an angry gray-green most days of the year. Warren's progressive Republicans still were dominant through the mid-1950s, but with the election of Democratic Governor Pat Brown in 1958, a group of talented liberal Democrats took over. Things turned sour in the mid-1960s, when student rebellions starting in Berkeley in 1964 and the Watts riot of 1965 upset the New Deal order. Californians responded by calling in a disillusioned New Dealer espousing the conformist cultural conservatism of the G.I. generation, Ronald Reagan, who presaged the course the nation would follow in the 1980s. California was a harbinger: it showed the nation where the G.I. generation would go next.

California has turned out to be less of a harbinger, as the character of its migrants changed. California veered off on a different path in the 1970s, electing Jerry Brown as governor, entranced for a time by his original version of Baby Boomer liberalism (though he was too old to be a Boomer himself), as the World War II generation started to die out and California received a new infusion of migrants, well-educated whites attracted to the state's groovy lifestyle and, little noticed at first, Mexicans and other Latin Americans looking for work. Voters in time soured on Brown's liberalism: They passed Proposition 13 in 1978, banning property tax increases in a state where rapidly rising housing values were the chief source of people's wealth; they decried his spraying of Medfly-infested crops with an overly-effective insecticide that peeled paint on houses; they ousted, after he left office, three of his Supreme Court nominees who had overturned death penalty verdicts and struck down tough-on-crime laws. Brown, with Californian creativity, has since reinvented himself as a presidential candidate (in 1976, 1980 and 1992), as the law-and-order mayor of Oakland and since 2006 as attorney general, a post his father won in 1950 and 1954.

When Brown left Sacramento, politics and government more or less disappeared from TV stations' newscasts and voters' minds. In the 1980s, with Reagan as president and quiet Republican George Deukmejian as governor, California's defense industry boomed and Silicon Valley flowered off I-280 south of San Francisco. Migration continued, in vast numbers, in two streams: highly educated lawyers and show biz types, scientists and techies, enjoying the affluence of the Golden State; and Mexicans, other Latinos and East Asians, grappling to make a living in sweatshops and on construction sites and living in the dirty stucco bungalows and garden apartments the white blue collar class left behind. Neither influx had much effect on public policy, which was mostly set by Willie Brown, speaker of the California Assembly from 1980 to 1995 and later mayor of San Francisco, and the Democratic legislature furthered the causes of their clients—teachers' unions, trial lawyers and the criminal defense bar. The response of middle class voters was government by referendum, usually a clumsy matter but sometimes effective, on criminal justice, aid to immigrants, racial quotas and preferences. This continued under Republican Pete Wilson, elected governor in 1990 and 1994. In these years California went through another transformation, as a series of natural disasters and a massive economic downturn drained the state of confidence and set it off in a new political direction. Defense industry cutbacks hit metropolitan Los Angeles hard, costing hundreds of thousands of jobs and sending housing values that had skyrocketed in the 1980s plummeting downward in the early 1990s. Television screens were absorbed by disasters both natural and manmade—from floods and earthquakes to riots and the O. J. Simpson trial. Long proud of its efficient and incorruptible government, California saw it grow larger and increasingly dysfunctional, as documented by California's greatest reporter, Lou Cannon, in his book *Official Negligence*, the definitive story of the Rodney King beating, the Los Angeles riot and the trials that followed. In the 1990s California lost its trademark big businesses to mergers, so that today downtown Los Angeles has only one Fortune 500 company headquarters and San Francisco is no longer headquarters of the Bank of America. In the first half of the 1990s, about 2 million Californians, mostly white and affluent, abandoned California for other western states or went even farther back east.

In the meantime, and in increasing numbers, immigrants keep arriving. The Census Bureau reported that California's Hispanic percentage rose from 26% in 1990 to 32% in 2000 and to an estimated 35% in 2003; the Asian percentage was 10% in 1990, 11% in 2000 and 12% in 2003. Since 1990, California has had a net outflow of people to the rest of the United States offset by an even larger inflow of people from other countries. The pace accelerated from 2000 to 2004, with a net out-migration domestically of 415,000 and a net in-migration of 1.2 million from other countries. Los Angeles County has become what New York City was 100 years ago, the greatest immigrant entry point in the United States. The 2000 Census recorded Los Angeles County's population of 9.5 million as 45% Hispanic, 10% Black and 12% Asian. Here you can find the world's largest numbers of Mexicans, Iranians, Samoans, Filipinos, Salvadorans, Armenians, Guatemalans, Koreans and Thais outside their native countries. And immigrants are not just concentrated in Los Angeles County; they have spread through almost all parts of California. Orange County was 31% Hispanic in 2000, San Bernardino County 39%, Fresno County in the Central Valley 44%. Santa Clara County, home of Silicon Valley, was 26% Asian in 2000, San Francisco 31%, Alameda and San Mateo Counties 20%, Orange County 14%.

This new demographics—an outflow of Americans and an inflow of immigrants—helped make Proposition 187, denying non-emergency state government spending on illegal immigrants and their children became a central issue in 1994. Wilson, trailing state Treasurer Kathleen Brown in polls and concerned about fast-rising state spending on illegals, supported 187 and, though he was careful to differentiate between illegal and legal immigrant, also ran ads showing Mexicans sprinting across the border and stating in ominous tones, "They keep coming." Voters made that distinction too; 59% of all voters and about one-third of Hispanics voted for the proposition. Wilson won a decisive victory, 55%-41%, but one that came with considerable collateral damage for his party. In later elections Latino turnout increased and Latinos increasingly turned to the Democratic Party. The Latino vote increased from 10% of the vote in 1994 to 14% in 1998, and Gray Davis beat Republican Dan Lungren among Hispanics by 78%-16%—a huge drop for Republicans, since Wilson got almost 40% of the Latino vote in 1990. In 2000 Hispanics again cast 14% of California's votes, and voted 68%-29% for Al Gore. Those margins have since diminished; the NEP exit poll showed John Kerry leading George W. Bush 63%-34% in 2004. Asian immigrants seem also to have moved away from the Republicans. In the early 1990s Asians cast Republican margins, perhaps out of recoil from the 1992 riot, after the establishment showed great solicitude for the needs of the rioters but little sympathy for the Korean shopkeepers who were their victims. Later in the decade, Asians seemed to move toward Democrats, as Bill Clinton and Al Gore (remember his visit to the Buddhist temple in Hacienda Heights) courted them assiduously. The 2000 exit polls were in conflict: VNS showed Asians for Gore by only 48%-47% while the *Los Angeles Times* exit poll showed them giving Gore a 63%-33% margin. The 2004 NEP poll, showing Kerry carrying Asians 66%-34%, tends to confirm the *Times*'s numbers.

This Democratic trend among Latinos was one of two trends that moved California toward the Democrats in the 1990s; the other was the increasing prominence of cultural issues like abortion and gun control on which most affluent Californians in the big metropolitan areas have liberal views. Between 1980 and 1990 Republicans won seven of nine contests for president, senator and governor and nearly won another. From 1992 to 2002 Democrats won nine of ten such contests, the one exception being Wilson's reelection in 1994. Another key factor was Bill Clinton. After winning California in 1992 with 46% of the vote, Clinton understood that if he could lock up California's 54 electoral votes (it now has 55) he would be a long way toward being assured of re-election. He courted the state with dozens of appearances, with special attention to California issues and projects, with assiduous cultivation of Hollywood celebrities and Silicon Valley cybermillionaires. He carried the state 51%-38% in 1996. Clinton's combination of moderation on economic issues and liberalism on cultural issues was a perfect fit for a critical block of California voters, the affluent professionals and techies who support abortion rights and gun control and who are increasingly fearful of the prominence of Christian conservatives in the national and to some extent the state Republican party. Affluent Americans increasingly are not moored to any one locality, but can choose where they live, from an array of places with widely different cultural atmospheres. Those with traditional values and traditional religious views tend to pick metropolises like Atlanta, Dallas and Houston; those with liberation-minded values and secular or non-Christian religious attitudes tend to pick Los Angeles and the San Francisco Bay area. The quantum of all these personal decisions over the last decade and a half have made Georgia and Texas more Republican and made California more Democratic.

The Democratic trend in California reached its peak in 1998 when Gray Davis was elected governor by a 58%-38% margin and in 2000 when Al Gore carried the state 53%-42% over George W. Bush, even though Bush spent $20 million on California media and Gore not a penny. In the same years, Democratic Senators Barbara Boxer and Dianne Feinstein were both reelected by far wider margins than six years before. In 2002, with Clinton far less prominent, the Democrats' fortunes ebbed a bit in California. Gray Davis, with low job ratings after the 2001 electricity crisis, was reelected by only a 47%-42% margin. Democrats won every statewide downballot office for the first time since 1882, but not by overwhelming margins: their candidates' percentages varied from 45% to 51%, while Republicans' percentages varied from 40% to 45%, and conservative firebrand Tom McClintock came within 17,000 votes of being elected controller.

Then came the recall of Gray Davis and the election of Arnold Schwarzenegger. Recall was the project of conservative Republicans, who stumbled onto the idea. Davis represented an apotheosis of a political governing class which, thanks to its political competence and to California voters' faithfulness to a party which stood for liberal cultural values, had insulated itself largely from public control. The California legislature was the first in the nation to develop a large staff and to use the advantages of incumbency to protect against opposition; redistricting plans were adopted which reduced toward zero the chance of change in party control of seats. Davis capitalized on an apathetic electorate and an uninterested press to win elections by delivering the simple message that the opposition was unacceptable. But politicians who insulate themselves from public retaliation risk widespread revolt when things go sour. Things went sour on Davis with the electricity crisis and his handling of an electricity deregulation bill he had nothing to do with and when revenues fell by huge proportions after the dot.com bust of 2000; his 47% in 2002 was a harbinger of the problem he would have in 2003. The recount movement started and fizzled out in February 2003. Then Congressman Darrell Issa revived it with personal money, and Davis stimulated it by signing a bill (after vetoing others) authorizing driver's licenses for illegal aliens and unilaterally increased the license plate fee by 2% of vehicle value. By July it was apparent that enough petition signatures would be obtained to force a recall election. California law provides that in a recall election voters also get to choose who will succeed to the office if the incumbent is recalled; a relatively low number of signatures is required, and only a plurality is needed to win. The election was scheduled for October. Conservatives Tom McClintock and Issa put their names on the ballot; prominent Democrats, pledged to support Davis, did not. Schwarzenegger, who had spent fall 2002 campaigning for his own ballot proposition for after school programs, was busy publicizing Terminator 3. Then in early August Schwarzenegger went on *The Tonight Show* and surprised his political advisers by announcing he was running. Issa got off the ballot; Lieutenant Governor Cruz Bustamante got on, while saying he wanted Davis to stay in office.

In October 2003, recall won 55%-45% and on the replacement ballot Schwarzenegger won 49% of the vote to 32% for Bustamante and 13% for McClintock; a solid majority in this Democratic state had voted for Republicans. Turnout was way up from 2002—from 7.5 million to 9.0 million—and Schwarzenegger received more votes in 2003, 4.2 million, than Davis had in 2002, 3.5 million. Schwarzenegger's election seemed to mean the end of insider politics in California and the beginning of plebiscitary politics. Television stations rushed to set up news bureaus in Sacramento and newspapers headlined state government news: Schwarzenegger was the first governor since Jerry Brown to get such news coverage. Taking advantage of it, he ordered an audit of state government and forced the legislature to repeal driver's licenses for illegal immigrants. He forced changes in workmen's comp laws. He put two bond issues on the March 2004 ballot, campaigned for them vigorously and saw them passed with 63% and 71% of the vote. At the same time, 66% of voters rejected Democratic legislators' amendment to make it easier to raise taxes. In March 2004 he forced the legislature to accept his budget by using his star power and threatening to take the issue to the people. Schwarzenegger had his successes in November 2004 referenda as well: measures he favored passed (financing stem-cell research, limiting tort actions), while measures he opposed failed (expanding Indian casinos, relaxing the "three strikes and you're out" law). California voters seemed to be in line with their new Republican governor.

It was a different story in 2005. Schwarzenegger planned a frontal attack on the power structure in Sacramento. He called for defined contribution plans for state employees, which would sap the power of CalPERS, which invests the state defined benefit pension plan monies, and for merit pay for teachers, an anathema to teacher union. These he abandoned when they predictably went nowhere in the legislature. But he did put on the November 2005 ballot measures that would give the governor new powers to cut spending, increase the number of years teachers needed to get tenure and create a commission to redistrict the legislature and the House delegation. This time he got strong opposition. Public employees spent more than $100 million on anti-Schwarzenegger TV ads. Nurse union members told the cameras they were not, as he had said, "special interests." His poll ratings fell far under 50% and the three ballot propositions failed. Ironically, each got a smaller percentage than one Schwarzenegger supported only belatedly, a requirement that public employees get members' permission before using their dues money for political purposes. That, if passed, would prevent the unions from mauling anyone again as they did Schwarzenegger in 2005.

Schwarzenegger promptly changed course. He hired one of Gray Davis's top aides as his chief of staff and swapped Republican advisers for Democrats. He worked closely with Speaker Fabian Nunez and Senate President Don Perata, and in the spring they agreed to put $37 billion of bonds on the November ballot, for highways, housing, school construction and flood control: shades of Pat Brown. They reached agreement on a budget earlier than in the past 5 years. Schwarzenegger signed many measures which were opposed by most Republican legislators and supported by most Democrats. All of which put the Democratic candidate for governor, Treasurer Phil Angelides, in a tight corner. He seemed to campaign as much against the Iraq war as against Schwarzenegger's California record, and argued that the Republican would turn conservative again in 2007. Meanwhile Schwarzenegger was making appearances with Nunez in support of the bond issues. They all passed, and Schwarzenegger won 56%-39%. Only one other statewide Republican candidate, Steve Poizner for insurance commissioner, won. California appeared to be a solidly Democratic state, except that it was solid for the Terminator too.

Or is it two states, or perhaps three? Once upon a time people used to analyze California politics by distinguishing between Northern California and Southern California. Northern California—the Central Valley and the North Coast as well as the San Francisco Bay area—tended to vote for John Kennedy, Hubert Humphrey and Jimmy Carter. Southern California—Los Angeles County as well as the smaller suburban and desert counties—tended to vote for Richard Nixon and Gerald Ford. Today the divisions run the other way. The two states are Coastal California and Interior California. You can argue about the dividing lines and about whether there can really be said to be a difference between Los Angeles and Orange Counties on the one hand and the Inland Empire of Riverside and San Bernardino Counties on the other: you can't tell much difference between them when you cross the line on the I-10 Freeway. But the difference is demographic. Between 2000 and 2006 Coastal California, defined as all the counties that touch the Coast or San Francisco Bay, plus Napa—had an immigrant inflow of 6% and a domestic outflow of 7%. That's a lot of people: 1.4 million immigrants moving in, 1.8 million native-born Americans, net, moving out. Out to places with lower housing prices, fewer visible immigrants, more middle class accommodations, to the Inland Empire and the Central Valley, Arizona and Nevada, Texas and the Rocky Mountain states. Interior California from 2000 to 2006 saw quite different movements, an immigrant inflow of 3% overshadowed by a domestic inflow of 9%. The result is that Coastal California grew 4% in those years, less than the national average of 6%, while Interior California grew by 17%, more than any state except Nevada and Arizona. Coastal California by itself would still be the largest state, but would have only a bit more than 1 million people more than faster-growing Texas and would be soon overtaken by it. Interior California by itself would be slightly smaller than the seventh largest state, Ohio, and would seem likely to overtake it soon—and Pennsylvania and Illinois not much later.

The huge immigrant inflow and domestic outflow from Coastal California is making it a two-tiered society economically, with a very affluent elite in the professions, show biz, science, high tech, living in houses costing multiple millions, and with a very large body of immigrants, Central Americans living in the modest stucco houses built for Middle Americans in the 1950s and 1960s, working double shifts on and off the books in the hopes of making it to a more comfortable suburb. Democratic politicians complain about a widening gap between the rich and the poor, but it is widest in Coastal California, where secular affluent elites and religious low-income immigrants both vote very heavily Democratic—59%-40% for president in 2004, more Democratic than any other states except John Kerry's Massachusetts and Rhode Island. This is accentuated if you break off from Coastal California the South Coast—Orange and San Diego Counties. Demographically these two counties look like Coastal California, with immigrant inflow and domestic outflow, but politically they behave pretty much like Interior California. That's partly because for many years they've been very heavily Republican and partly because it appears that immigrants here, at least in Orange County, vote much less heavily Democratic than in Los Angeles County. Coastal California without the South Coast voted 64%-34% for John Kerry, a bigger Democratic margin than in any state or in any million-plus metro area.

Interior California is a very different kind of place, with twice as many native-born Americans moving in than immigrants. Growth is vibrant, even chaotic; the income gap is not so wide as in Coastal California, with not nearly so many high-income people and with low-income immigrants facing at least a somewhat lower cost of living. No Neiman Marcuses here and not so many swap-meets; more Wal-Marts and Target. In 2004 Interior California voted 57%-42% for George W. Bush, a result close to that in the demographically similar and somewhat smaller Georgia and North Carolina. If you put Interior California together with the demographically different but politically similar South Coast, you'd have a state of 17 million, just 1 million behind Florida, growing 12.8% since 2000, just under Florida's 13.2%. Politically, it voted 56%-42% for George W. Bush in 2004, versus Florida's 52%-47%. As a separate state, this Interior/South Coast California would cast 25 or 26 pretty sure Republican electoral votes. But it's part of California, which casts 55 pretty sure Democratic ones.

Coastal California and Interior California live uneasily together and uneasily within themselves. Coastal California has been utterly dominant since 1992 in presidential elections and in elections for senator: its sentiments on national issues, on cultural issues like abortion from 1992 to

2000, on foreign issues like the war in Iraq since 2003, all have resulted in strong Democratic majorities in the combined California. In 2006, for example, Senator Dianne Feinstein carried Coastal California from Los Angeles, which cast 54% of the state's votes, by 68%-26%, a margin so large it hardly mattered what she got in the rest of the state (she lost the rest of the state by 49%-46%). Down the ballot the effect has been similar: in races for congressman, state senator and Assembly you find scarcely any districts within Coastal California (except for the South Coast) which have elected Republicans starting with the 2002 redistricting. Rich, poor, the few left in the middle: they're all heavily Democratic. It is in races for governor that Coastal California has been less than totally dominant. Only once since 1992 has a Democrat won by a wide margin, Gray Davis in 1998, in the pattern seen in the senate and presidential races—overwhelming support in Coastal California except the South Coast, running about even in Interior California. In 1994 Pete Wilson was reelected by a wide margin; in 2002 and 2003 Davis got only 47% for reelection for 45% opposing recall. Interior California voted 67% and the South Coast 70% to recall Davis; Coastal California from Los Angeles north went 56%-44% for Davis, but was outvoted. Similarly, Schwarzenegger in 2006 won 65% in Interior California and 67% in the South Coast, while winning Coastal California from Los Angeles north by only several hundred votes. Schwarzenegger's stands on cultural issues are mostly acceptable in Coastal California, while his stands against the excesses of Coastal liberalism give him big majorities in the Interior and South Coast. Contests for governor have become the most embattled and hard to predict because the holder of the office is visible and can be held accountable for any negative consequences of Coastal liberalism.

Even so, Coastal liberalism depends not just on voters but on institutional strength, particularly the institutional strength of the public employee unions, which can mobilize thousands of volunteers and spend literally hundreds of millions of dollars. When Arnold Schwarzenegger took them on in 2005, he failed—and promptly changed course. He turned agilely to other issues, emphasizing carbon emission curbs, a cause sure to elicit great approval in Coastal California, probably including the South Coast, and not inspiring much in the way of negative feelings in Interior California, at least until negative practical effects become apparent; and to building and rebuilding infrastructure. These policy thrusts come as close to a shared vision of California, a vision that was put into action and subjected to tests as the Greatest Generation migrants, middle class and working class and sharing a common culture, streamed into the California of Earl Warren, Pat Brown and Ronald Reagan. Today there are different streams of migrants, and some are leaving the state rather than coming in: high-skill migrants from America and from Asia and other foreign lands as well, interested in enriching themselves in a socially tolerant paradise; low-skill migrants primarily from Latin America seeking to raise themselves up from hard work in the hope that their children can rise higher; and middle-skill migrants, most of the native-born Americans but some Hispanic immigrants as well, skilled workers and middle managers, frustrated with California's high housing prices and clogged traffic jams, tempted to move out of Los Angeles and into the Inland Empire, out of California and into Arizona, Nevada and Texas. Is the vision of the state's governing classes enough to hold them together?

The People		Race/Ethnic Origin			Military veterans: 2,569,340 (10.4%)	
Pop. 2006 (est):	36,457,549	15,816,790	46.7%	White	WWII: 20.5%	Korea: 13.7%
Pop. 2000:	33,871,648	2,181,926	6.4%	Black	Vietnam: 32.4%	Gulf War: 9.8%
Pop. 1990:	29,760,021	3,648,860	10.8%	Asian	**Most populous cities (2006):**	
Change 1990-2000:	Up 13.6%	178,984	0.5%	Native Am.	1. Los Angeles	3,849,378
% of U.S. total:	12.0%	103,736	0.3%	Hawaiian	2. San Diego	1,256,951
Pop. rank:	1st of 50	903,115	2.7%	Two+ races	3. San Jose	929,936
Area size:	163,696 sq. mi.	71,681	0.2%	Other	4. San Francisco	744,041
State Native:	50.2%	10,966,556	32.4%	Hisp. Origin	5. Long Beach	472,494
Non-citizen:	15.9%	**Ancestry**				
Language		German: 8.0%		Irish: 6.3%	Urban population: 94.5%	
English: 62.2%	Spanish: 22.4%	English: 6.1%		Italian: 3.5%	Rural population: 5.5%	
Asian: 8.6%		USA: 2.7%				

Education		Work Sector		Legislature	
H.S. Grad:	76.8%	Private: 76.5%	Govt: 14.7%	Senate	25 D 15 R
College Grad:	26.6%	Self: 8.5%	Family: 0.4%	Assembly	48 D 32 R
Industry		Unemployment: 6.9%		Legislative Term Limits: Yes	
Agri: 1.9%	Con: 6.2%	**Household Income**		**Registered Voters**	
Fin: 6.9%	Info: 3.9%	<15k: 14.0%	15-35k: 22.9%	D: 6,727,908　(42.5%)	
Mfg: 17.8%	Prof: 30.1%	35-50k: 15.2%	50-100k: 30.7%	R: 5,436,314　(34.3%)	
Public: 4.5%	Trade: 15.2%	100-150k: 10.4%	>150k: 6.9%	O: 3,672,886　(23.2%)	
Other: 13.4%		Median: $47,493			
Occupation		Poverty status: 14.2%			
Blue collar: 21.2%	White collar: 62.7%	**Home Value**			
Gray collar: 16.1%		<50k: 5.1%　　50-100k: 11.3%　　100-200k: 34.0%　　200-300k: 20.8%			
		300-500k: 17.8%　　>500k: 11.0%　　Median: $198,900			

Presidential politics　George W. Bush's chief strategist Karl Rove itched to make California a target state in 2000 and 2004. It just seems too large to ignore: 54 electoral votes in 2000, 55 in 2004, one-fifth of those needed to win the presidency. In 2000 Rove poured $20 million of California-raised money into ads on California TV stations. Al Gore's campaign, coolly assessing the polls, put in nothing at all, and won 53%-42%. Gore's California victory owed something to its increasing number of Latino voters and their distaste, rooted in California politics, for Republicans; it owed much to Californians' affection for and assiduous cultivation by Bill Clinton; it owed much as well to the liberal attitude on cultural issues here—abortion and gun control and the environment—which has trumped any desire for lower taxes. In 2004 Rove and Bush campaign manager Ken Mehlman kept a close eye on California, with a view toward putting money in and forcing Democrats to compete in this huge state if the race grew close here. After all, the memory of the 1994

2004 Presidential Vote		
Kerry (D)	6,745,485	(54%)
Bush (R)	5,509,826	(44%)
Badnarik (Lib)	50,165	(0%)
Other	145,328	(1%)

2004 Democratic Presidential Primary		
Kerry (D)	2,002,539	(64%)
Edwards (D)	614,441	(20%)
Kucinich (D)	144,954	(5%)
Dean (D)	130,892	(4%)
Sharpton (D)	59,326	(2%)
Other	155,457	(5%)

2000 Presidential Vote		
Gore (D)	5,861,203	(53%)
Bush (R)	4,567,429	(42%)
Nader (Green)	418,707	(4%)
Other	118,517	(1%)

campaign and Proposition 187 had faded among Latinos, Clinton was no longer head of the Democratic party, Bush's Israel policies had brought him new admirers among Jewish voters and Arnold Schwarzenegger's election as governor had projected a new image of the Republican party in the Golden State. But none of these things changed enough minds to make California close. Bush improved on his 2000 majorities in Interior California and the South Coast. But in coastal California from Los Angeles north Kerry ran better than Gore had four years before, and carried the state 54%-44%.

Some oldtimers can still recall when California's June primary was the national tiebreaker. This state was the center of national attention when Nelson Rockefeller lost here to Barry Goldwater in 1964, when Robert Kennedy and Eugene McCarthy slugged it out in 1968—Kennedy won and was murdered by a Palestinian terrorist on primary night—and when George McGovern edged Hubert Humphrey in 1972. California was all the more important because it was still winner-take-all in both parties. Democrats switched from winner-take-all after 1972, but few noticed because every four years California voted long after the nominations were clinched.

For 1996 California moved its presidential primary from the first week in June to March 26; that was still too late to make any difference. So in 2000 it moved it to March 7. In 2004 California voted on March 2, for John Kerry; this was the day Kerry clinched the Democratic nomination. In September 2004 Governor Arnold Schwarzenegger signed a bill rescheduling the presidential primary in June. But California was not ready to give up on getting in on the early action. In early 2007 it joined other major states, including New York and New Jersey, deciding to hold their primaries on February 5, not long after New Hampshire. Democratic legislative leaders supported the change and Schwarzenegger was happy to sign the bill in March 2007. Democrats said they would continue to pick all but 11 at-large delegates by proportional representation within districts, with 3 to 7 delegates per district. Republicans said they would assign the same number of delegates to each congressional district and that they would go to whoever finished number one in that district. That raised the specter of Republican presidential campaigns trolling for the handful of Republican votes cast in several Bay Area and Central Los Angeles districts. But this seems farfetched; there hardly seems time in the hurried national schedule for such pinpoint attention to so few people in such a large state.

More important was the possible June 2008 ballot proposal pushed by Republican strategists that would apportion California's electoral votes by congressional district, ending the state's winner-take-all system. Democrats began organizing in 2007 to oppose the initiative; had it been in place in 2004, George W. Bush would have taken 22 electoral votes out of California despite losing the state by more than 1.2 million votes.

Congressional districting

California has gained House seats in every Census going back to 1850, when it became a state; over that century and a half it has grown from 2 seats to 53, the most of any state in history. But California grew less rapidly in the early 1990s, and so it gained only 1 seat from the 2000 Census, the first time in a century it has not gained 2 or more. But this tradition may be coming to an end. Polidata's straight-line extrapolation to 2010 of the Census Bureau's estimates of 2000-06 population growth suggest that California, for the first time in history, will gain zero House seats after the 2010 Census. That's a projection with a margin of error, but the days are gone when California gained 7 seats in the 1950 Census, 8 in the 1960 Census and 7 in the 1990 Census.

110th Congress Lineup
34 D   19 R

109th Congress Lineup
33 D   20 R

The tradition of partisan redistricting here goes way back: Republicans drew the lines to their advantage in the 1940s and 1950s, Democrats in the 1960s, 1970s and 1980s, as the California House delegation grew from 23 in the 1940s to 30, 38, 43, 45 and 52. The great genius of redistricting here was Democratic Congressman Phillip Burton, who dominated the line-drawing for House seats and for the state Senate and Assembly as well (and intervened behind the scenes in other states too); his 1982 plan, slightly revised for 1984-90, left Democrats in secure control of the delegation even though he died in 1983. In the 1990s neither party had full control. Governor Pete Wilson, after hard-nosed bargaining with the Democratic legislature, persuaded the state Supreme Court to adopt a plan drawn up by his appointed commission in 1992. This was a relatively evenhanded plan, with generally regular boundaries; the fact that Democrats had a 32-20 margin in the delegation after the 2000 election reflected the party's strength in most parts of the state, not any acuity in drawing district lines.

The assumption after the 2000 election was that California would produce a Democratic redistricting plan. Democrats held the governorship and controlled the state Senate 26-14 and the Assembly 50-30. But that is not what happened; for the second decade in a row California ended up with a plan that gave neither party any great advantage. Democrats protected all incumbents and took the new seat created by reapportionment; Republicans got 20 seats for 19 of their incumbents in which the Bush 2000 percentage was at least 50%. Long Beach Republican Steve Horn, nearly beaten in 2000 and surrounded by mostly Democratic territory, was sacrificed to create a new Hispanic Democratic seat, and that Republicans would get a new seat in the Central Valley.

The plan, signed by Governor Gray Davis in 2001, has the elegance one would expect of today's foremost redistricter. Where the district shapes are contorted, there is often a demographic as well as political rationale: the 23d District, which connects a thin band of Pacific Coast in Ventura, Santa Barbara and San Luis Obispo Counties, collects a constituency with common interests and proclivities, quite different from those of the voters in the interior of those counties who were placed in the 22d and 24th Districts. Naturally there were some complaints. Moderate Democrat Ellen Tauscher complained that she was given a too Democratic district; she wanted one that matched her moderate record. Latino groups complained that only one additional Hispanic district was created. The Mexican American Legal Defense and Educational Fund filed a lawsuit against the plan, honing in on the fact that it reduced the Hispanic percentages in the districts held by Howard Berman and Bob Filner. The suit was dismissed in June 2002.

The plan was condemned by many journalists and political scientists for protecting incumbents and reducing competition. In 2002 in these 53 seats—12% of the nation's total—only one was seriously contested. In 2004, only one was arguably seriously contested, the open 20th in the Central Valley. In 2006, the 11th District seat, partly in the Central Valley but also partly in the San Francisco Bay Area, was seriously contested and Democrat Jerry McNerney beat incumbent Richard Pombo, the embattled chairman of the House Resources Committee. This was designed to be a Republican district, but trends in opinion had made it less so, as happens typically over larger areas during the 10-year period between censuses: the politically neutral 1990s plan had produced a solidly Democratic delegation by 2000.

Still, Governor Arnold Schwarzenegger kept taking aim at the redistricting process and after the 2006 election could point out that under current plans only 4 congressional and legislative seats had changed partisan hands in 459 contests. In November 2005 his ballot proposition setting up an independent commission of retired judges to draw redistricting plans was defeated by voters, as such proposals had been in 1930, 1948, 1960, 1962, 1982 and 1990. In December 2006 Schwarzenegger came up with a new way to create a commission: local election officials would produce lists of possible members, the political parties would be given the opportunity to veto a limited number of the names, then actual members would be chosen at random. In March 2007 Speaker Fabian Nunez said he would support putting such a commission on the February 2008 ballot for the Assembly and Senate, but hesitated at covering congressional districts; in return Schwarzenegger was ready to include an extension of term limits so that Assembly members could serve 12 years instead of only six. But Speaker Nancy Pelosi was said to be opposed and Zoe Lofgren, the state Democrats' delegation point person on the issue, came out for a federal law requiring each state to set up an independent redistricting commission, and opposed what she might have considered unilateral disarming by California Democrats. Nunez, however, in April came out for including House members as well as state legislators. "What we're looking for here is balance. What we're looking for here is fairness...Why? Because if it's good enough for the state legislature, it ought to be good enough for Congress."

Why are California Democrats considering giving up a partisan advantage in redistricting? Perhaps because they are not giving up very much at all, at least so long as the state's current political balance continues. Coastal California from Los Angeles north is now so heavily Democratic that it is very hard to create Republican districts. A few forlorn Republican enclaves don't add up to even an Assembly district, the smallest of those covered, which is about 456,000; House districts are about 688,000, state Senate districts 911,000. Political redistricters might be able to create a few such districts, with very careful drawing; politically neutral redistricters are very unlikely to do so. But in Interior California and in the South Coast counties of Orange and San Diego, it is possible to create Democratic districts, if you take the trouble to maximize the number of districts which are 50% or so Hispanic or more so—and that is exactly what the prevailing interpretation of the Voting Rights Act requires you to do. So a politically neutral commission would likely do what a partisan Democratic districter would do: create virtually no Republican districts in Coastal California and maximize the number of Democratic districts in Interior California and the South Coast. The only thing an independent commission could not be counted on to do was incumbent protection, which was the focus of the bipartisan 2001 redistricting. But there's an intellectually serious argument that it's rational for a state to want to keep in office powerful and experienced members. That's what an independent commission might put at risk.

Finally, demographics will make some difference. Interior California has been growing more rapidly than Coastal California, and if the state retains the 53 House seats it now has, this uneven growth will probably mean the movement of one or two districts from the Coast to the Interior—and perhaps one from the Democratic to the Republican party. The 2005 Census estimates show the 34 districts won by Democrats in 2006 with an average population of 646,000, a 1% gain since 2000, and the 19 districts won by Republicans in 2006 with an average population of 701,000, a 9% gain since 2000.

Governor

Arnold Schwarzenegger (R)

Elected Oct. 2003, term expires Jan. 2011, 1st full term; b. July 30, 1947, Thal, Austria; home, Pacific Palisades; U. of WI-Superior, B.A. 1979; Catholic; married (Maria Shriver).

Military Career: Austrian Army, 1965-66.

Professional Career: Bodybuilder, 1965-80; Chairman, President's Council on Physical Fitness and Sports, 1990-93; Actor, 1970-2003.

Office: State Capitol Bldg., Sacramento, 95814, 916-445-2841; Fax: 916-445-4633; Web site: gov.ca.gov.

Election Results

2006 general	Arnold Schwarzenegger (R)	4,850,157	(56%)
	Phil Angelides (D)	3,376,732	(39%)
	Other	452,527	(5%)
2006 primary	Arnold Schwarzenegger (R)	1,724,281	(90%)
	Robert Newman (R)	68,660	(4%)
	Other	123,139	(6%)
2003 special	Arnold Schwarzenegger (R)	4,206,284	(49%)
	Cruz Bustamante (D)	2,724,874	(32%)
	Tom McClintock (R)	1,161,287	(13%)
	Other	565,470	(7%)

Arnold Schwarzenegger, movie actor and entrepreneur, was elected governor of California in October 2003 and reelected in November 2006. He grew up in Graz, Austria, where his father was a police officer. At 13 he told his parents, "I want to be the best built man in the world." At 14, he started training; at 15, he studied psychology; at 17, he started competing in bodybuilding contests. Drafted into the Austrian army, he went off base to win the Mr. Europe Junior contest in Stuttgart, Germany; his superiors put him in the brig, then decided to let him spend the rest of his military career building his body. In 1966, at 19, he won the Mr. Europe competition in London. He lost a Mr. Universe contest that year but won in 1967. There were three organizations holding Mr. Universe contests; by 1970 he had won them all. In 1970 he won the Mr. Olympia contest for the first of seven times and was generally hailed as the strongest man in the world.

In the course of these competitions, Schwarzenegger came to California in September 1968 with $20 in his pocket. This was around the time that anyone's first impression of Los Angeles was smog: the gray-green area frowning over the city, leaving the mountains and ocean a mystery even in places where they were easily visible on a clear day. After listening to presidential candidates Richard Nixon and Hubert Humphrey, he decided he preferred the Republican. In between his training, he started buying commercial properties in Santa Monica. In 1970 he got a bit part in a movie called *Hercules in New York* and in 1977 was the chief subject of the documentary *Pumping Iron*. In 1978 he published an autobiography, *Arnold: The Education of a Bodybuilder*. He got a business degree from the University of Wisconsin at Superior in 1979. In 1982 he starred in *Conan the Barbarian*, the first in a string of box office hits that included *The Terminator*, *Predator*, *Total Recall*, and *True Lies*. In 1986 this Republican movie star married television journalist Maria Shriver, daughter of Sargent Shriver, first head of the Peace Corps and the Great Society's antipoverty program, and Eunice Kennedy Shriver, founder of Special Olympics. Schwarzenegger was active in promoting physical fitness among underprivileged children; from 1990 to 1993 he was chairman of George H. W. Bush's Council on Physical Fitness and Sports, and in 1995 he established the National Inner City Games Foundation. He became involved with the successful L.A.'s BEST after-school program and in 2002 sponsored a ballot proposition to establish a state after-school program; it provided that no money be spent until available in the budget. Proposition 49 passed 57%-43%, with roughly even support in all regions of the state—a departure from the usual partisan patterns of response to most ballot propositions.

Not many noticed, but Proposition 49 got 491,000 more votes than Governor Gray Davis did as he won reelection by a 47%-42% margin the same day. There was speculation that Schwarzenegger might run for governor in 2006, but many thought his liberal positions on cultural issues—pro-choice on abortion, pro-gun control, pro-civil unions for gays and lesbians—would make it hard for him to win a Republican primary. But there turned out to be another path to the governorship. In February 2003, after the state deficit was projected to be between $26 and $35 billion, and Davis mulled tax increases, conservative activist Ted Costa started a movement to recall Davis. California law provides that a recall election must be called if petitions are filed with signatures amounting to 12% of the votes most recently cast for the office; with turnout low in 2002, that meant 897,000 signatures. In March and April, it seemed to falter as polls showed most voters critical of Davis but opposed to recall. Then in May 2003 Congressman Darrell Issa, who made millions from a car alarm business, started pumping $1.7 million into the recall effort. After the July 4 weekend, organizers said they had 1.2 million signatures; on July 23 the secretary of state said the petitions qualified. Lieutenant Governor Cruz Bustamante set the election for October 7; voters would decide whether to recall Davis and could choose from a list of candidates who would replace him if he were recalled. Anyone could file by paying a $3,500 fee and filing 65 signatures by August 9. Would Schwarzenegger run? He said he had to promote *Terminator 3* and would only decide after that. On August 3 and 4 Davis filed lawsuits trying to get the recall called off or delayed; on August 5 the state AFL-CIO urged Democrats not to put their names on the replacement ballot; state Democratic leaders threatened that anyone who went on the replacement ballot would kill his chances for the nomination to succeed Davis in 2006. On the morning of August 6 Senator Dianne Feinstein, whom some Democrats wanted as a backup to hold the governorship if Davis was recalled, announced she would not run. That afternoon Schwarzenegger went to Burbank to tape *The Tonight Show*. His political consultants believed he would announce he was not running; he shocked them when he said he was. A few hours later Bustamante broke ranks with other Democratic leaders and announced he was running on the replacement ballot. Within 24 hours Issa withdrew from the race. In all, 135 candidates qualified for the replacement ballot. But the ranks of serious candidates soon dwindled. By mid-September it was clear that there were three serious candidates on the replacement ballot, Schwarzenegger, Bustamante and state Senator Tom McClintock, a fiscal and cultural conservative who had lost the 2002 race for state controller by only a 45.4%-45.1% margin. On September 15, a three-judge panel of the Ninth Circuit federal appeals court postponed the election to March 2004 at the urging of the ACLU; but on September 23 a full 11-judge panel ordered the recall to go ahead on October 7.

Throughout the campaign, in campaign rallies and in televised debates, Schwarzenegger made few specific proposals, but said that Davis must be removed, taxes must not be increased and spending needed to be cut. His campaign organized monster rallies which attracted thousands and where he spoke only briefly and did not mingle with the crowd. Davis rallies were sparsely attended, mainly by Democratic party and union officials. Bustamante, who announced his candidacy by fax, scarcely campaigned at all, though he did back driver's licenses for illegal immigrants. On October 2 the *Los Angeles Times* ran a story alleging that Schwarzenegger had groped various women some years ago. Recall advocates had considered the *Times's* coverage biased against their cause—its poll showed much more anti-recall sentiment than other public polls—and saw this as another attempt to keep Gray Davis in office. Schwarzenegger admitted that he had "behaved badly sometimes" and apologized. But the stories failed to stop the tide. Davis, elected 58%-38% in 1998 and reelected 47%-42% in 2002, was recalled 55%-45%. On the replacement ballot Schwarzenegger won 49% of the vote, Bustamante 32% and McClintock 13%. Turnout was actually up from 2002—from 7.5 million to 9.0 million—and Schwarzenegger received more votes in 2003, 4.2 million, than Davis had in 2002, 3.5 million. The San Francisco Bay Area voted 64%-36% against recall, but Los Angeles County rejected it by only 51%-49%. Southern California voted 69% and the rest of the state voted 64% for recall. Schwarzenegger trailed Bustamante 46%-33% in the Bay Area, but in Coastal California from Los Angeles north equaled him 40%-40%, and led 61%-20% in the South Coast and 56%-23% in Interior California.

Democrats were bitter over losing control of state government in this generally Democratic state after holding it for only five years of the preceding 21; some even threatened to recall Schwarzenegger in 2004. But Davis conceded graciously and ordered his appointees to cooperate with the new administration. On November 17 Schwarzenegger became governor and made state government suddenly visible; Los Angeles and San Francisco TV stations scrambled to open Sacramento bureaus. Schwarzenegger ordered a performance review of state government and plunged into the business of budget making. He pressed the legislature for repeal of the law Davis signed providing driver's licenses for illegal immigrants; he said he would sign a measure with sufficient security guarantees. He also repealed Davis's car tax increase and used deficiency appropriations to help local governments; they agreed to give up $1.3 billion in each of the next two years in return for a constitutional amendment making it harder for the state to take over local revenues. He got two constitutional amendments put on the March 2004 primary ballot: one to authorize $15 billion of debt to cover the current budget deficit, another to require a balanced budget in out-years. Both trailed in the polls, but after Schwarzenegger started campaigning for them, the first passed with 63% of the vote and the second with 71%; at the same time, voters rejected 66%-34% Democratic legislators' attempt to make it easier to raise taxes. In April 2004, by threatening to take the issue to the voters, he got the legislature to make changes in workmen's comp law without the rate regulation Democrats were seeking. In May 2004 he released a $99 billion budget with deficits that seemed likely to be $8 billion over two years. It called for higher payments from Indian casinos and cuts in pay and benefits for state employees. Unlike his Republican predecessors Ronald Reagan and Pete Wilson, he refused to support a tax increase in a budget crisis. California requires budgets to be approved by two-thirds votes in the legislature, so they always represent something of a consensus; after negotiations broke down, Schwarzenegger signed a $105 billion budget July 31.

Schwarzenegger campaigned for some Republican legislative candidates in fall 2004, but none won. But he had his successes in November 2004 referenda. A measure he backed promising $3 billion for stem-cell research passed 59%-41%. His measure to protect local government revenues from state takeover was approved 84%-16%. A measure to relax the "three strikes and you're out" law, which had been leading in the polls, lost 53%-47% after Schwarzenegger campaigned against it. A measure to limit tort actions passed 59%-41%. Indian tribes' attempts to augment their casino businesses were rejected by 77% and 84% of the voters. A telephone tax for emergency medical funding was rejected by 72%. And a measure to mandate health insurance coverage for small businesses was rejected, though by only 51%-49%. California voters seemed to be in line with their new Republican governor.

In January 2005 Schwarzenegger proposed a $111 billion budget, with cuts in scheduled increases in health care, transportation and school aid. Perhaps even more important, he went on the offensive, attacking the heart of the political system, by demanding action on four issues and, again, threatening to take them to the people in November 2005. They included a nonpartisan board of retired judges to redistrict California's congressional and legislative districts, automatic across-the-board spending cuts if spending grew faster than revenues, merit pay for teachers and defined contribution 401(k)-like pensions for state employees. All four threaten the roots of Democratic institutional power. Schwarzenegger said, "We're going right where all the evil is, and we're going to fix it." Redistricting would presumably put more Democrats (and Republicans) at risk of losing their seats, and Democrats might not be guaranteed the permanent majorities they have had under the current plan. Across-the-board spending cuts would give the governor huge leverage in budget negotiations and would repeal the provision the teacher unions got voters to pass guaranteeing a certain level of spending for education. Merit pay for teachers, furiously opposed by teacher unions, would further reduce the power of one of the Democrats' key supporting institutions. Defined contribution pension plans would reduce, over time, the power of CalPERS, which invests California's pension money and is one of the biggest institutional investors in the country; Democrats have dominated CalPERS and have used its leverage to influence the acts of major corporations. In early 2005 the Democratic legislature seemed certain to reject those measures; in June, Schwarzenegger called a November 2005 special election to get voters to approve them. Three of his favored measures qualified for the ballot: one would give the governor new authority to cut spending, another called for an increase in the service required before teachers could receive tenure and a third would create a non-partisan board of retired judges the authority to redistrict state legislative boundaries. Schwarzenegger dropped his initiative to overhaul the state employee pension system and got rid of the merit pay proposal. Democratic legislators and public employees vigorously opposed his plans, criticizing their cost; Schwarzenegger said the election was a "fantastic bargain" for taxpayers.

Schwarzenegger's attempt at plebiscitary government failed. He made a move to deprive the public employee unions of the roots of their power, the fact that they had the use of taxpayer dollars, in the form of public employees' union dues, to spend on politics. They spent heavily to keep that power to tap the private sector. Democrats and unions spent over $100 million on TV ads against Schwarzenegger, starting in early spring. In 2004 Schwarzenegger had referred to the nurses union as a "special interest" and said its leaders disliked him "because I am always kicking butts." Now television viewers saw a pleasant looking woman in a nurse's uniform quote these words back at him. Unaccountably, Schwarzenegger's political advisers did not respond with a campaign of their own, until the last two months before the November election. Evidently the Governator believed he could still get direct access to voters through the TV cameras stalking him walking through the Capitol grounds to his suite in the Sacramento Hyatt. But he couldn't: maybe local TV was tired of the Arnold story. Schwarzenegger's job rating dropped and support for his propositions went down. On Election Day they all lost. Ironically, the highest percentage, 47%, went to a proposition put together by others and only lukewarmly supported by Schwarzenegger, a ban on public employee unions spending dues money on politics without members'permission. This struck even more directly at the unions' power than Schwarzenegger's measures, and perhaps a more enthusiastic push for it could have put it over.

Schwarzenegger's response to this shattering defeat was almost immediate: a U-turn. As he later put it, "The people sent a very clear message. They said, 'Hey, don't come to us. We sent you to Sacramento. Work with them up there. That's what we expect you to do.' So I got that message last year." He hired a new chief of staff, Susan Kennedy, a top aide to Gray Davis. He cultivated Assembly Speaker Fabian Nunez and Senate President Don Perata and in spring 2006 agreed with them on a Let's Rebuild California program, four giant bond measures on the November 2006 ballot: $19.9 billion for transportation, $2.85 billion for housing, $10.4 billion for school construction and $4.1 billion for flood control. This looked like a return to the days of Earl Warren, Goodwin Knight and Pat Brown, as they responded to the huge domestic inflow into California during World War II and the postwar years. Schwarzenegger reached agreement with Nunez and Perata on a $131 billion budget earlier than in the preceding 6 years; most Republican legislators voted against it. This was made easier by the appearance of an $8 billion tax windfall, but of course there is no guarantee that such monies will keep coming in. Schwarzenegger also signed bills increasing the minimum wage and purporting to cut drug prices which most Republican legislators opposed. He signed many bills supported by gay rights groups but vetoed same-sex marriage. He signed a compact with Indian tribes allowing 22,000 more slot machines, but it was stopped by Democratic legislators. He signed a bill making drug treatment programs mandatory for convicts released after serving sentences for drug offenses.

His signature issue was reducing carbon emissions. For more than 50 years California has had an exemption from federal clean air legislation; it is authorized to pass more stringent legislation, for the very good reason that the Los Angeles Basin and other mountain-surrounded valleys in California are subject to inversion which holds pollutants in. California started regulating its air in the 1940s; smog peaked around 1970, when Schwarzenegger had just come to California. As governor, he converted his Hummers to run on hydrogen and biodiesel fuels; he popped in and said a few friendly words as Al Gore was signing books in Beverly Hills. He said the U.S. position on reducing emissions was "embarrassing" and urged California to fill "the vacuum" on carbon emissions policy. In March 2007 he signed a cap-and-trade system for reducing carbon emissions with four Western state governors. In July 2006 he signed an agreement with British Prime Minister Tony Blair to trade scientific and economic research. He met with the leaders of British Columbia and Baja California Norte on the issue. He journeyed to Detroit and told automakers that a low carbon fuel standard would not hurt domestic manufacturers. In September 2006 he was in California, signing a Global Warming Solutions Act, requiring a 25% cut in carbon dioxide emissions by 2020 and a 40% cut by 2050 (only one Republican legislator voted for it). He proclaimed his Hydrogen Highway and Million Solar Roofs plans. He contrasted his views on the issue with George W. Bush's. "What we're basically saying to the federal government is, 'Look, we don't need Washington.' And so let us create the partnerships and let the world know that America is actually fighting global warming." Leaders of some environmental groups still charged that his programs relied too much on markets. But on this issue, as on many others, voters were faced in 2006 with a very different Arnold Schwarzenegger than the one they repudiated in 2005.

And they responded very differently. Democrats had two serious choices in the Democratic primary: Controller Steve Westly, a Silicon Valley multimillionaire who campaigned as a "new Democrat," and state Treasurer Phil Angelides, a Sacramento area real estate developer and former state party chairman, who campaigned as a hard-charging partisan and vitriolic critic of George W. Bush. Angelides won the June primary 48%-43%. But he was not able to raise the large sums he had hoped for, and his angry criticisms went largely unheard as Schwarzenegger traveled the state with Fabian Nunez and Don Perata asking for bipartisan support of the bond ballot propositions and traded compliments with Senator Dianne Feinstein, who was running far ahead of a hapless conservative Republican legislator. In November Schwarzenegger won 56%-39% and Feinstein won 59%-35%. Schwarzenegger had little in the way of coattails for Republicans. Democrat John Garamendi beat Tom McClintock for lieutenant governor 49%-45%, and Secretary of State Bruce

McPherson, a Schwarzenegger appointee, was beaten by Democrat Debra Bowen 48%-45%. Leading the Democratic ticket was former Governor Jerry Brown, elected attorney general 56%-38%. One Republican, Silicon Valley millionaire Steve Poizner, beat Cruz Bustamante for insurance commissioner, 51%-39%. Schwarzenegger did better on the ballot propositions. His four bond issues won majorities ranging from 57% to 64%. Voters rejected a waiting period for abortion and an oil production tax by relatively narrow margins.   Schwarzenegger approached his second term optimistically and with a sense of command in Sacramento.

Schwarzenegger is a national figure of considerable prominence. Most voters outside California probably missed his drop in job approval in 2005 and his recovery in 2006, and perhaps have missed his change of course on policy as well. They may remember that he lauded George W. Bush at the 2004 Republican National Convention and they may note that in advancing his environmental initiatives he has been sharply critical of Bush. Term limits prevent Schwarzenegger from running for governor again in 2010, and the Constitution prevents him from running for president in 2008 or any future year unless an amendment passes allowing some or all those born in other countries to run. As for other offices, in February 2007 he said he would not rule out running for U.S. senator or mayor; that might mean taking on Senator Barbara Boxer in 2010 or running in an open race for mayor of Los Angeles in 2013. He said his wife Maria Shriver would "absolutely not" run for office. When asked whether he resented not being able to run for president, he said, "You will never hear me complain that I can't run for president. I look at the things that I was able to do rather than the things I am not able to do. I am very, very happy about how America has received me and the kind of things I was able to accomplish here."

Senior Senator

Dianne Feinstein (D)

Elected 1992, seat up 2012, 3d full term; b. June 22, 1933, San Francisco; home, San Francisco; Stanford U., B.A. 1955; Jewish; married (Richard C. Blum).

Elected Office: San Francisco Bd. of Supervisors, 1970-78, Pres., 1970-71, 1974-75, 1978; San Francisco Mayor, 1978-88.

Professional Career: CA Women's Parole Bd., 1960-66.

DC Office: 331 HSOB, 20510, 202-224-3841; Fax: 202-228-3954; Web site: feinstein.senate.gov.

State Offices: Fresno, 559-485-7430; Los Angeles, 310-914-7300; San Diego, 619-231-9712; San Francisco, 415-393-0707.

Committees: *Appropriations* (9th of 15 D): Interior, Environment & Related Agencies (Chmn.); Agriculture, Rural Development, Food and Drug Administration & Related Agencies; Energy & Water Development; Commerce, Justice, Science & Related Agencies; Defense; Transportation, Housing and Urban Development & Related Agencies. *Intelligence (Select)* (2d of 8 D). *Judiciary* (5th of 10 D): Terrorism, Technology & Homeland Security (Chmn.); Administrative Oversight & the Courts; Constitution; Immigration, Refugees & Border Security; Crime & Drugs. *Rules & Administration* (Chmn. of 10 D).

Group Ratings

	ADA	ACLU	AFS	LCV	ITIC	NTU	COC	ACU	CFG	FRC
2006	90	73	100	100	100	10	50	0	0	0
2005	95	—	75	90	—	13	50	12	14	—

National Journal Ratings

	2005 LIB	—	2005 CONS	2006 LIB	—	2006 CONS
Economic	75%	—	24%	67%	—	29%
Social	75%	—	24%	70%	—	29%
Foreign	76%	—	15%	88%	—	8%

Key Votes of the 109th Congress

1. Bar ANWR Drilling	Y	5. Confirm Samuel Alito	N	9. Limit Interstate Abortion	*
2. FY06 Spending Curb	N	6. Path to Citizenship	Y	10. CAFTA	Y
3. Estate Tax Repeal	N	7. Bar Same Sex Marriage	N	11. Urge Iraq Withdrawal	Y
4. Raise Minimum Wage	Y	8. Stem Cell Research $	Y	12. Provide Detainee Rights	Y

Election Results

2006 general	Dianne Feinstein (D)	5,076,289	(59%)	($8,030,489)
	Dick Mountjoy (R)	2,990,822	(35%)	($195,265)
	Other	474,365	(6%)	
2006 primary	Dianne Feinstein (D)	2,176,829	(87%)	
	Colleen Fernald (D)	199,170	(8%)	
	Martin Luther Church (D)	127,291	(5%)	
2000 general	Dianne Feinstein (D)	5,932,522	(56%)	($10,346,170)
	Tom Campbell (R)	3,886,853	(37%)	($4,378,283)
	Other	804,233	(8%)	

Prior Winning Percentages: 1994 (47%); 1992 (54%)

Dianne Feinstein, California's senior senator, is a Democrat first elected in 1992. Feinstein grew up in San Francisco, in lush Presidio Heights, graduated from Stanford and later studied criminology. She was appointed by Governor Pat Brown to the women's parole board in 1960, at 27. In 1969 she was elected to the San Francisco County Board of Supervisors—the city's council—and twice ran for mayor and lost. As president of the board, she became mayor in 1978 when Mayor George Moscone and Supervisor Harvey Milk were murdered by former Supervisor Dan White; she discovered Moscone's body and showed steadiness and a sense of command that calmed the city. She was elected to full terms in 1979 and 1983. In 1984, Walter Mondale seriously considered her for vice president, but passed over her for Geraldine Ferraro because of qualms about the business dealings of her husband, Richard Blum. Feinstein presided gracefully that year over the Democratic National Convention in San Francisco—while Ferraro juggled questions about *her* family's business. In fact, Feinstein and Blum's investments have thrived; *Roll Call* estimated their net worth in 2006 at more than $40 million.

Feinstein left the mayor's office in 1987, ineligible for a third full term, and ran for governor in 1990. She won the Democratic primary impressively, then lost 49%-46% to Pete Wilson. When Wilson appointed Orange County state Senator John Seymour—an unknown and bland choice—to replace him in the Senate, Feinstein quickly announced for the seat, even though the 1992 race was for only the last two years of Wilson's term, and she could have run for the seat being vacated by Alan Cranston the same year. She had primary competition from Gray Davis, then state controller, who ran an ad against her campaign finance practices comparing her to Leona Helmsley. Feinstein won 58%-33% and her relations with Davis, elected governor in 1998 and 2002 and recalled in 2003, were not always warm; she appeared in two spots for him in the 2003 recall campaign that did not mention his name. In the 1992 general election, nothing worked for the hapless Seymour—not his switches to pro-choice on abortion and anti-offshore oil drilling, not his attacks on Feinstein's arguably tricky financing of her 1990 gubernatorial campaign (which resulted in a $190,000 fine), not fears of immigration, not Seymour's tending to agricultural interests. Feinstein won 54%-38%, coming close even in Seymour's Southern California base.

In the Senate, Feinstein kept a certain distance from the Clinton administration, negotiating for changes before voting for the 1993 budget, voting against NAFTA, withdrawing her support of the Clinton health care plan in May 1994, condemning Bill Clinton's "I did not have sexual relations with that woman, Miss Lewinsky" comment which she had heard in person. She had two significant legislative achievements in her first two years. One was the attachment of the assault weapons ban to the 1994 crime bill. When Idaho's Larry Craig argued that her definition of assault weapons was not rigorous enough and challenged her knowledge of firearms, she responded by saying: "I know something about what firearms can do; I came to be mayor of San Francisco as a product of assassination." Her other major achievement was a California Desert Protection Act. Similar measures had been stymied by the state's Republican senators as too restrictive, but now that there was no Republican senator, Feinstein managed it through enactment.

Feinstein has a moderate to liberal voting record, and has differed on some issues from her colleague and Bay area neighbor Barbara Boxer. Feinstein sponsored the Y2K liability act opposed by trial lawyers, for example, and voted to repeal the marriage penalty and the estate tax. She supported the 2001 Bush tax cut and voted for the Iraq war resolution in October 2002 and the $87 billion supplemental in November 2003. She supported the Medicare/prescription drug bill in November 2003. When she ran for governor in 1990 she emphasized her support of the death penalty and of abortion rights, and on the Judiciary Committee she has taken tough stands. After September 11, Feinstein and Jon Kyl came forward with a bill to establish a central database of visa holders and other aliens in the country, to bar entry for people from nations that sponsor terrorism, to require the INS and the State Department to create biometric visa cards and passports, to require foreign nations to supply airlines with passenger manifest lists and to lift the 45-minute deadline for INS inspection of incoming foreigners. This was more stringent than a similar measure sponsored by Edward Kennedy and Sam Brownback. In December the two versions were melded and it was signed into law by Bush in May 2002. In February 2007 she criticized the US-VISIT program for lack of procedures to track the departures of visa holders.

Feinstein sought to crack down on Internet piracy of movies in 2003 and blocked for a time reauthorization of the moratorium on Internet taxation. She has sought to limit the sale of pseudophedrine to 9 grams to choke off the illegal meth trade; the amendment she sponsored with Jim Talent passed the Senate unanimously in September 2005. She opposed the Bush immigration plan in January 2004, arguing that it "could be a magnet for more illegal immigrants." She pressed in 2005 for reauthorization of the federal program reimbursing state and local governments for the cost of detaining illegal immigrants, under which California governments received $112 million in 2004. She got approval by voice vote of her measure establishing a process to handle unaccompanied child immigrants. In the debate on immigration in 2006, she opposed all outstanding guest worker proposals in March and in May called the Hagel-Martinez plan "100% calculated to fail." Her proposal, a system based on a bar-coded orange card, was rejected by a 61-37 vote. In July she and Barbara Boxer proposed a 20-year sentence for building or financing underground cross-border tunnels; sponsored by David Dreier in the House, it became part of the border fence bill that passed both houses in September. In February 2007 she was the first Democrat to write letters questioning the imprisonment of two Border Patrol agents for shooting an alleged Mexican drug smuggler on the Texas border.

In 2000 she introduced a bill to require licensing of all guns and in 2004 pressed fervently for reauthorization of the 1994 assault weapons ban. George W. Bush had said in 2000 that he would sign such a bill, but despite Feinstein's frequent pleas did nothing to bring it forward; the act expired in September 2004. With Patty Murray she co-sponsored an unsuccessful amendment in March 2004 which would have imposed multiple penalties for homicides causing the death of a fetus, but would not have defined the latter as a separate crime. With Orrin Hatch, she got 54 senators to sign a letter calling for more embryonic stem-cell research. She supported Arlen Specter's asbestos compensation bill and passed an amendment requiring that the sickest claimants be paid first; the measure came two votes short of the needed 60 in February 2006. In 2005 she stated that the Patriot Act had not led to violations of civil liberties, a statement cited by the Bush administration. She co-sponsored Specter's modification of FISA requirements for surveillance of those in contact with al Qaeda suspects abroad. She was the only Democrat on Judiciary to vote in June 2006 for the amendment authorizing prosecutions for flag desecration.

She has joined other Judiciary Committee Democrats in opposing and filibustering several Bush nominees to federal appeals court. With Boxer, she made an arrangement with the Bush administration to set up six-member panels to decide on the potential merits of federal trial judges in California; three members were appointed by each side, and four votes is required for approval of a nominee. This bypassed the senior Republicans in the House delegation. In May 2005, amid the Gang of 14 stand on judicial filibusters, she voted against the nomination of Priscilla Owen, but voted against a filibuster. After an interview with John Roberts in July 2005 she called him "very impressive," but opposed him in committee and on the floor out of concern that he might overturn *Roe v. Wade*. After Harriet Miers's nomination was withdrawn in October 2005, she said, "I don't believe they would have attacked a man the way she was attacked." After interviewing Samuel Alito in November 2005, she said he seemed sincere in saying he was no longer an advocate, but she voted against his nomination. In September 2006 she threatened a filibuster of a Ninth Circuit nominee from Idaho on the ground that the seat had been held by a Californian. She and Jim Inhofe sponsored a bill in September 2006 to penalize violent acts by animal rights activists against businesses that sell or use animals or animal products.

Feinstein voted for the Iraq war resolution in October 2002—an act unpopular with many California Democrats. In January 2003 she said U.S. troop deployments in the area were "deeply disturbing" in what she said was the absence of proof that Iraq had weapons of mass destruction. Hours after Colin Powell spoke at the United Nations in February 2003 she took a different view: "I no longer think inspections are going to work." In April 2004 she said she was misled into voting for the war by an exaggeration of the threat, and regretted her vote. In December 2004 she called on Bush to "tell the American people the truth" that troops would be required in Iraq for many years. But in January 2005 she introduced Condoleezza Rice to the Foreign Relations Committee and warmly supported her nomination to be secretary of state. In March 2006 she said, "It's time to change course, to bring in another team. We should not be putting American soldiers in the middle of a civil war with targets on their backs." On nuclear weapons, Feinstein has sought to deny funding to studies of the Robust Nuclear Earth Penetrator (the bunker buster bomb) and the Advanced Concepts Initiative (a low-yield nuclear bomb). Feinstein has supported trade ties with China since she established a sister city relationship between San Francisco and Shanghai with its then leader, Jiang Zemin, in 1980. She opposed Nancy Pelosi's efforts to impose penalties on China because of its human rights violations. In June 2005 she said China must crack down on piracy of intellectual property and revalue its currency, but she opposed the bill sponsored by Lindsey Graham and Charles Schumer to impose 27.5% tariffs on Chinese goods if it does not revalue. In April 2006 she urged China and Taiwan to negotiate a framework for closer business ties and a "mutually agreed upon status quo." On the Intelligence Committee, she called for a single national intelligence director in 2002, long before the 9/11 Commission recommended one.

Feinstein has a seat on Appropriations, where she can funnel money to California, and on Energy and Natural Resources, where she works on water issues. She has worked for several years to revive the CALFED water projects program. She was blocked in 2001 and 2002 by Republicans from other western states who thought California was drawing too much water from the Colorado River water until a January 2003 change. In 2003 and 2004 she worked with House Resources Chairman Richard Pombo to reauthorize CALFED and to protect water quality in San Francisco Bay and the Sacramento Delta. And in 2006, when the Delta levees were threatened by severe flood, she and Pombo called for coordinated evacuation plans, and she and Barbara Boxer backed $22 million to repair 29 sites on the levees. She has worked to protect California's strict emissions standards on small engines from federal preemption, in opposition to Christopher Bond, who has been concerned about the effect on lawn mower manufacturers in Missouri. She voted against the ethanol mandate in the energy bill in June 2005, and sought to have it not apply to California in the summer, and then voted against the energy bill in July. She opposed the bill seeking more deepwater oil and gas exploration in August 2006 and sought to extend the renewable moratorium on oil drilling in federal waters. In 2007 she sponsored a bill for a cap-and-trade market in carbon emissions and said, "Getting a moderate bill passed that can be strengthened . . . can become the most significant thing we can do." As ranking Democrat and then chairman of the Senate Rules Committee, she cosponsored with Trent Lott a requirement that conference committee earmarks be posted on the Internet for at least 24 hours, and she has sponsored a bill to require a paper trail on all state ballot systems. On Social Security, she has sought to repeal the offset in benefits for those with public pensions. In January 2007 she joined Pete Domenici in urging a bipartisan Social Security commission, with a timeline for Congress to act on its recommendations. That same month an article in the *Metro,* a free Bay Area weekly, charged that she had used her position as ranking minority member on the Military Construction Subcommittee to steer contracts to firms owned by her husband. URS Corp.had received $1.8 billion in defense contracts and Perini Corp. $200 million, but Feinstein said she had sought advice from the Ethics Committee on the matter and followed it. A subsequent *Metro* article said she had been forced off the Milcon subcommittee; her spokesman said she had rotated, as many members do, to chair the Interior Subcommittee, which was more important for California.

Feinstein has had only one serious challenge since she was first elected in the Senate, in the Republican year of 1994 from one-term Congressman Michael Huffington. In 1992 Huffington spent $3 million of his own money to unseat an 18-year incumbent in the Republican primary in the Santa Barbara area House seat. In 1994 he spent nearly $30 million of his own money against Feinstein. He pulled even in polls in September, and Feinstein was clearly flustered and angry that she could not count on heavily outspending him. Huffington slipped when it was revealed that he and his wife Arianna Huffington, now an outspoken liberal, employed an illegal alien as a nanny. On the Thursday before the election, it was revealed that Feinstein, despite her earlier denials, had employed a woman whose work permit had expired; the news media ran stories saying that federal officials cast doubt on whether the woman was an illegal. That probably made the difference. Feinstein won 47%–45%. She carried Los Angeles County 52%-40% and the San Francisco Bay area 63%-30%, offsetting Huffington's margins in Southern California and the rest of the state.

Since 1994 Feinstein has gotten positive ratings in the polls. In late 1997 she gave some thought to running for governor; in 2003 some Democrats tried to persuade her to put herself on the replacement ballot in the recall election. But both times she declined to seek the office she lost in 1990. In 2000 she was opposed by Republican Congressman Tom Campbell, a libertarian Stanford Law professor who had nearly won the 1992 nomination to run against Barbara Boxer and who, in a more Republican California than it is now, might have won. Campbell was outspent by $10.3 million to $4.4 million; Feinstein won 56%-37%, carrying all major regions of the state. She won 5,932,000 votes, the most popular votes cast for a senator in American history, a record eclipsed by Barbara Boxer in 2004. Feinstein made it plain early on that she would run for reelection in 2006. Republicans had to cast around to find a candidate. West Hollywood businessman Bill Mundell weighed a candidacy in 2005, but withdrew in November. In January 2006 conservative state Senator Richard Mountjoy started running. Some left-wing Democrats urged anti-war protester Cindy Sheehan to challenge Feinstein in the primary, but in February she declined to do so. Feinstein spent $8 million on her campaign, though she didn't purchase heavy ad buys until late October. Mountjoy spent $195,000 to reach an electorate of 8.5 million. Feinstein won 59%-35%. In Coastal California from Los Angeles north she won by the overwhelming margin of 69%-25%. She carried 35 of 58 counties, including nine of the 10 most populous.

Junior Senator

Barbara Boxer (D)

Elected 1992, seat up 2010, 3d full term; b. Nov. 11, 1940, Brooklyn, NY; home, Rancho Mirage; Brooklyn Col., B.A. 1962; Jewish; married (Stewart).

Elected Office: Marin Cnty. Bd. of Supervisors, 1976-82; U.S. House of Reps., 1982-92.

Professional Career: Stockbroker & researcher, 1962-65; Journalist, *Pacific Sun*, 1972-74; Dist. aide, U.S. Rep. John Burton, 1974-76.

DC Office: 112 HSOB, 20510, 202-224-3553; Fax: 415-956-6700; Web site: boxer.senate.gov.

State Offices: Fresno, 559-497-5109; Los Angeles, 213-894-5000; Sacramento, 916-448-2787; San Bernardino, 909-888-8525; San Diego, 619-239-3884; San Francisco, 415-403-0100.

Committees: *Commerce, Science & Transportation* (5th of 12 D): Oceans, Atmosphere, Fisheries & Coast Guard; Aviation Operations, Safety & Security; Interstate Commerce, Trade & Tourism; Science, Technology & Innovation. *Environment & Public Works* (Chmn. of 10 D): Public Sector Solutions to Global Warming, Oversight & Children's Health Protection (Chmn.). *Ethics (Select)* (Chmn. of 3 D). *Foreign Relations* (5th of 11 D): East Asian & Pacific Affairs (Chmn.); International Development & Foreign Assistance, Economic Affairs & International Environmental Protection; Near Eastern & South & Central Asian Affairs.

Group Ratings

	ADA	ACLU	AFS	LCV	ITIC	NTU	COC	ACU	CFG	FRC
2006	95	83	100	100	50	11	25	8	0	0
2005	100	—	100	90	—	11	24	12	0	—

National Journal Ratings

	2005 LIB	—	2005 CONS		2006 LIB	—	2006 CONS
Economic	90%	—	9%		87%	—	0%
Social	90%	—	0%		92%	—	7%
Foreign	95%	—	0%		98%	—	0%

Key Votes of the 109th Congress

1. Bar ANWR Drilling	Y	5. Confirm Samuel Alito	N	9. Limit Interstate Abortion	N
2. FY06 Spending Curb	N	6. Path to Citizenship	Y	10. CAFTA	N
3. Estate Tax Repeal	N	7. Bar Same Sex Marriage	N	11. Urge Iraq Withdrawal	Y
4. Raise Minimum Wage	Y	8. Stem Cell Research $	Y	12. Provide Detainee Rights	Y

Election Results

2004 general	Barbara Boxer (D)	6,955,728	(58%)	($14,886,426)
	Bill Jones (R)	4,555,922	(38%)	($7,802,657)
	Other	541,643	(4%)	
2004 primary	Barbara Boxer (D)	unopposed		
1998 general	Barbara Boxer (D)	4,410,056	(53%)	($13,737,548)
	Matt Fong (R)	3,575,078	(43%)	($10,764,892)
	Other	326,771	(4%)	

Prior Winning Percentages: 1992 (48%); 1990 House (68%); 1988 House (73%); 1986 House (74%); 1984 House (68%); 1982 House (52%)

Barbara Boxer, California's junior senator, was first elected to the House in 1982 and the Senate in 1992, and is now chairman of the Environment and Public Works Committee. She also serves as acting chairman of the Ethics Committee, pending the recovery of Senator Tim Johnson. She grew up in Brooklyn, where she was a victim of sexual harassment by a college professor and was refused work as a stockbroker. She and her husband moved to San Francisco in 1965 and then, in search of affordable housing, to Marin County in 1968. In 1968 she volunteered for Eugene McCarthy's presidential campaign; in 1970 she and some neighbors formed the Marin Alternative, to oppose the Vietnam War and a subdivision planned for a wetland near Sir Francis Drake Boulevard. Marin County was only on its way to being trendy then; the overall political tone was liberal Republican, but heading left: it was one of the few parts of the country where George McGovern won a higher percentage in 1972 than Hubert Humphrey had in 1968 and where abortion rights supporter Gerald Ford got a larger percentage margin over abortion critic Jimmy Carter in 1976 than Richard Nixon had over McGovern; in contrast, Marin voted 73%-25% for John Kerry in 2004. In 1972 Boxer ran for the Board of Supervisors and lost to an incumbent Republican. She then worked for Democratic Congressman John Burton. In 1976, when women candidates were more accepted, she ran again for the board and won. When Burton retired unexpectedly in 1982, she ran for the House and was easily elected. She made many splashes in the House, unearthing the Air Force's $7,622 coffee pot in 1984, denouncing the Gulf War with more ardor than just about anyone and leading a march of women on the Senate when Anita Hill was testifying against Clarence Thomas.

In the 1980s it seemed improbable that anyone as liberal as Boxer could be elected senator from California, which had after all voted Republican for president in all but one election from 1952 to 1988. But now Boxer has been elected three times, by decisive and rising margins. In 1992 she started off as neither the best-known nor the best-financed candidate, but this turned out to be the year of the woman, in which the enthusiasm of the feminist left produced important victories for Democratic women. Boxer won the June 1992 Democratic primary with 44% of the vote, to 31% for Lieutenant Governor Leo McCarthy and 22% for Congressman Mel Levine. Her general election opponent was Bruce Herschensohn, a Los Angeles TV and radio commentator, backer of a flat tax and offshore oil drilling and opponent of abortion. The Boxer-Herschensohn race was a battle of opposites, the far left versus the far right of the American electoral spectrum. Boxer was helped by the collapse of the Bush candidacy in California, by hearty support from Dianne Feinstein and by the revelation by state Democratic political director Bob Mulholland during the last week of the campaign that Herschensohn attended nightclubs that featured nude dancers.

Boxer's voting record has been strongly liberal, among the most liberal in the Senate in *National Journal's* ratings. She is perhaps the personification of the feminist left, and is one of the strongest proponents of abortion rights in the Senate; she has vehemently opposed the partial-birth abortion ban. But she was also a staunch defender of Bill Clinton. In 1998, the senator who had marched across the Capitol to protest the cross-examination of Anita Hill found little to believe in the charges against Clinton until he admitted their truth, and even then limited her condemnation to a perfunctory statement combined with a total commitment to defeat impeachment. And in 1999 the crusader against the Gulf War resolution solidly backed the bombing campaign against Serbia. In September 2001 she supported the use of force in Afghanistan. But in October 2002 she voted against the use of force in Iraq, and she voted against the $87 billion supplemental appropriation in October 2003. She has often charged that the Bush administration diverted its attention from Al Qaeda to Iraq.

Boxer has supported gun control and has sponsored amendments to require childproof safety locks on all handguns and to ban sales of guns to people who are intoxicated. But in summer 2002 she and Kentucky Republican Jim Bunning emerged as the Senate's leading advocates of allowing airline pilots to carry guns. Boxer argued that pilots could be trusted with that responsibility and that they could protect passengers against terrorists. The measure was initially opposed by the Bush administration but, after the House passed it, it passed the Senate by a wide margin. In April 2004 Boxer and Bunning charged that the TSA was stalling on implementation and urged it be speeded up. Also in 2003 Boxer warned of the danger to airliners from shoulder-fired missiles and called for installation of anti-missile devices on all airliners and beefed up Coast Guard and National Guard patrolling in airport perimeters. She called for air marshals to be stationed on high-risk flights after 9/11. In August 2006, after an FAA briefing on how a faulty circuit board outage in Palmdale caused the delay of 348 flights into LAX, she called for an investigation of the Los Angeles area air traffic control system. She hailed the FAA's decision to build a new air control tower in Palm Springs airport by 2010—she has moved her residence from Marin County to Rancho Mirage in the desert—but called for completing it earlier.

Boxer was frustrated when Republicans during the Clinton years held up nominations to the Ninth Circuit Court of Appeals, currently the most liberal in the country. In spring 2001 she opposed the nomination of Orange County Congressman Christopher Cox to the Ninth Circuit; when Dianne Feinstein said she might oppose him too, Cox withdrew. She and Feinstein worked to set up a procedure to give them approval of all federal district judges in California. In August 2005, after Feinstein said she was impressed by Supreme Court nominee John Roberts, Boxer said she would "use all the parliamentary tools I've been given as a U.S. senator" to delay a vote on his confirmation. She voted against him and against Samuel Alito. It was perhaps a case of life imitating art, or perhaps the other way around: October 2005 saw the publication of Boxer's novel *A Time to Run*, about a liberal woman senator from California opposing a conservative Supreme Court nominee. But on abortion issues, Boxer has pulled back when she has sensed she doesn't have the votes. In April 2005 she declined to bring forward a bill blocking a law that allowed health care providers to refuse to perform abortion, and in July 2006 she declined to filibuster a bill penalizing those who transport minors across state lines to get abortions.

As ranking minority member on the Environment and Public Works Committee, Boxer concentrated on blocking Bush nominations. She held up the nomination of EPA Administrator Stephen Johnson, a career professional, in April 2005 because of her opposition to a suspended program to pay parents to monitor the effects of pesticides on children. In November 2006, after Democrats won a Senate majority, she worked to block the nominations of acting EPA air chief William Wehrum and EPA inspector general nominee Alex Beehler. But she also moved to set her own agenda. "I really have two major goals. They are to protect the health of the American people. And the second is to make the environment a bipartisan issue again on Capitol Hill." She assigned herself the chairmanship on the subcommittee on Public Sector Solutions to Global Warming, Oversight, Children's Health Protection and Nuclear Safety—a pretty clear indication of her priorities. She sought to have the federal government limit perchlorates (from rocket fuels and dry cleaning solvents) in drinking water. She questioned the Nuclear Regulatory Commission's 5–0 ruling that nuclear power plants don't have to build shields made of steel I-beams and cabling to protect against air attacks. Most of all, she sought legislation to reduce carbon emissions which in her view contribute materially to global warming—"the greatest challenge of our generation." She called California's law, reducing carbon emissions by 25% by 2020 a "gold standard" and asked Governor Arnold Schwarzenegger and Assembly Speaker Fabian Nunez to testify in Washington. She championed legislation to cap carbon emissions from power plants, vehicles and other fossil fuel burners to reduce carbon emissions nationally to 1990 levels by 2020 and to 80% below 1990 levels by 2050. The latter standard was criticized by John Kerry as unrealistic, and others seemed by no means committed to her agenda—and not just outgoing chairman and now ranking minority member James Inhofe, who has called man-made climate change a "hoax." Energy Chairman Jeff Bingaman defended tax breaks for oil and gas producers and Louisiana Democrat Mary Landrieu has worked for more oil and gas exploration offshore in the Gulf of Mexico. Subcommittee Chairman Tom Carper seemed to take a less stringent approach on air pollution. Boxer called Al Gore to testify in a highly publicized hearing in March 2007, showering him with praise and telling Inhofe not to cut him off in mid-answer. But she has acknowledged that she must work with her colleagues and that most may not be prepared to go as far as she is. And in a bipartisan move, she endorsed a Bush administration initiative to boost the energy efficiency of federal buildings.

Boxer has weighed in on all manner of California issues. She has joined Oregon Democrat Ron Wyden in his attacks on FTC members who have not taken action against West Coast gasoline price increases which they said were the result of oil company mergers. When San Francisco Mayor Gavin Newsom was performing same-sex marriages in February 2004, she avoided endorsing his acts and said, "I have always been very strongly for domestic partnerships. I think the California law is a very good, workable law." In response to a killing in San Bernardino in 2005, she sponsored a gang prevention bill. She has noted the high levels of air pollution in the Central Valley and in December 2006, looking ahead to her committee duties, said, "It is not just the Central Valley alone which has a problem, which in a way is a good thing." She has sought $26 million to study how the Salton Sea might be restored.

During her first three years in the Senate, Boxer's job ratings were among the Senate's lowest. But California with its large metro areas trended sharply toward the Democrats in the mid-1990s, and in early 1997 Boxer's job rating was up to 50%. Prominent Republicans decided not to run against her in 1998. In the all-party primary, state Treasurer Matt Fong edged businessman (and now Congressman) Darrell Issa. On paper Fong was a strong candidate, with an Asian heritage and a moderate record on issues; his mother March Fong Eu, a Democrat, was California's secretary of state from 1974 to 1994. But Boxer raised $15 million and campaigned long and hard. She launched an ad campaign attacking Fong for his ambiguous stances on issues like abortion. She guarded herself from contact with reporters so she would not have to answer questions about Bill Clinton; the president's brother-in-law Tony Rodham was then married to her daughter Nicole. Fong attacked her for the hypocrisy of her stand on the Clinton scandals. But he spoke hesitantly and unconvincingly in the sound bytes that are the staple of California politics and never succeeded in raising much money. Boxer won 53%-43%. She won 61% of the vote in Los Angeles County and 63% in the San Francisco Bay area, and trailed not far behind in Southern California and the rest of the state—an impressive performance for a Democrat dismissed a few years before as too left-wing for much of the state.

Boxer says that before September 11 she had decided not to seek a third term in 2004. But when House Majority Leader Tom DeLay six months after the attacks criticized Democrats for criticizing the Bush administration, she changed her mind. "Then I got really fearful for my country. The greatest thing about our country is that we're free and that we debate and we talk." She began raising impressive amounts of money, and once again many well-known Republicans declined to make the race. The best-known candidate against her, Bill Jones, had been elected secretary of state by narrow margins in 1994 and 1998; but he was not well known outside his home base in Fresno County. He had the endorsement but not the active support of Governor Arnold Schwarzenegger. Nonetheless he won the March 2004 primary with 45% of the vote, to 20% for former U.S. Treasurer Rosario Marin and 11% for former Assemblyman Howard Kaloogian; Marin made a close race of it in Los Angeles County and Southern California, but Jones won by wide margins in the rest of the state. This turned out not to be a seriously contested race. George W. Bush's political advisers may still have been miffed that Jones in 2000 retracted his primary endorsement of Bush and endorsed John McCain; in any case, national Republicans made no effort to pump in the huge amounts of money needed to make a California Republican competitive. Boxer spent $16 million to Jones's $7 million; Boxer ran no attack ads, as she had done in 1998, while Jones ran no TV ads at all in September and October. Boxer, elected with 48% of the vote in 1992 and 53% in 1998, won 58% in 2004—almost a perfect arithmetical progression upward. Jones won only 38%. In Coastal California from Los Angeles north Boxer won 67%-29%. She ran essentially even in the rest of the state, carrying the South Coast 48%-47% and losing the rest of the state 47%-45%. Running in a presidential year, she won 6,956,000 votes—more popular votes than any other senator had ever won in American history, far ahead of Dianne Feinstein's previous records set in 1992 and 2000.

Boxer seems to have taken this huge victory in the nation's largest state as a mandate to speak out. In January 2005, as the electoral vote count was read out to a joint session of Congress, she was the one senator to protest the award of Ohio's electoral votes to George W. Bush. She remembered that four years before no senator had protested the Florida vote even though several members of the House had, and she said she regretted not having protested then. Her protest triggered the dissolution of the joint session and a debate in each of the two Houses—for one hour in the Senate, rather longer in the House. The Senate voted 74–1 to accept the Ohio count, with Boxer as the one dissenter; the House voted 267-31 on the same question. "I hate inconveniencing my friends, but I think it's worth a couple of hours to shine some light on these issues," Boxer said. Later in January, after her California colleague Dianne Feinstein escorted Condoleezza Rice to the Foreign Relations Committee hearing on her nomination to be secretary of state, Boxer attacked Rice stingingly. Her "loyalty to the mission," Boxer said, "overwhelmed your respect for the truth." Speaking of the troops, she said, "You sent them in there because of weapons of mass destruction. Later the mission changed when there were none." Rice responded, "I really hope you will refrain from impugning my integrity. I really hope that you will not imply that I take the truth lightly." She sought to delay the nomination of John Bolton to be ambassador to the United Nations by requesting internal documents. But she went to Connecticut in July 2006 to campaign for her colleague Joseph Lieberman in his primary. To her critics she explained, "Senator Lieberman has been one of my staunchest allies on the environment and choice, two issues very important to me."

There has been speculation that Governor Arnold Schwarzenegger might run for Boxer's seat in 2010, or that she might run for governor then, when term limits will force him to step down.

FIRST DISTRICT

Rep. Mike Thompson (D)

Elected 1998, 5th term; b. Jan. 24, 1951, St. Helena; home, St. Helena; CA St. U., B. A. 1982, M. A. 1996.; Catholic; married (Janet).

Military Career: Army, 1969-73 (Vietnam).

Elected Office: CA Senate, 1990-98.

Professional Career: Supervisor, Beringer Winery; CA Assembly fellow, 1982-83; Chief of Staff, CA Assemblyman Lou Papan, 1984-87; Chief of Staff, CA Assemblywoman Jacqueline Speier, 1987-90.

DC Office: 231 CHOB, 20515, 202-225-3311; Fax: 202-225-4335; Web site: mikethompson.house.gov.

District Offices: Eureka, 707-269-9595; Fort Bragg, 707-962-0933; Napa, 707-226-9898; Woodland, 530-662-5272.

Committees: *Permanent Select Committee on Intelligence* (9th of 12 D): Terrorism, Human Intelligence, Analysis & Counterintelligence (Chmn.); Intelligence Community Management. *Ways & Means* (13th of 24 D): Health; Select Revenue Measures.

Group Ratings

	ADA	ACLU	AFS	LCV	ITIC	NTU	COC	ACU	CFG	FRC
2006	90	95	86	92	57	19	47	20	12	0
2005	90	—	100	94	—	18	48	16	3	0

National Journal Ratings

	2005 LIB — 2005 CONS	2006 LIB — 2006 CONS
Economic	72% — 26%	69% — 30%
Social	76% — 23%	68% — 31%
Foreign	78% — 21%	88% — 10%

Key Votes of the 109th Congress

1. Estate Tax Repeal	N	5. Limit Interstate Abortion	N
2. Limit CAFE Standards	N	6. Extend Patriot Act	N
3. FY06 Spending Curb	N	7. Bar Same Sex Marriage	N
4. Drilling in ANWR	N	8. Stem Cell Research $	Y

9. Build Border Fence	N
10. CAFTA	N
11. Oppose Iraq Withdrawal	N
12. Detainee Tribunals	N

Election Results

2006 general	Mike Thompson (D)	144,409	(66%)	($1,382,639)
	John Jones (R)	63,194	(29%)	($64,164)
	Other	10,441	(5%)	
2006 primary	Mike Thompson (D)	unopposed		
2004 general	Mike Thompson (D)	189,366	(67%)	($1,272,329)
	Lawrence Wiesner (R)	79,970	(28%)	($28,993)
	Pamela Elizondo (Green)	13,635	(5%)	

Prior Winning Percentages: 2002 (64%); 2000 (65%); 1998 (62%)

The People		Race/Ethnic Origin	Ancestry	
Area size:	12,195 sq. mi.	71.2% White	German: 11.3%	Irish: 9.0%
Urban population:	76.0%	1.3% Black	English: 8.9%	
Rural population:	24.0%	3.9% Asian	**2004 Presidential Vote**	
Pop. 2000:	639,087	2.4% Native Am.	Kerry (D) 173,926	(60%)
Pop. 2005 (est):	677,636	0.2% Hawaiian	Bush (R) 111,754	(38%)
Median income:	$38,918	2.9% Two+ races	Other 5,508	(2%)
Poverty status:	15.3%	0.2% Other	**2000 Presidential Vote**	
Military veterans:	13.4%	17.9% Hispanic Origin	Gore (D) 131,376	(52%)
			Bush (R) 98,506	(39%)
			Other 24,220	(10%)
			Cook Partisan Voting Index: D +10	

Occupation	Blue collar: 20.9%	White collar: 58.3%	Gray collar: 20.8%

The North Coast of California is unlike any other place in America. It is the only part of the Lower 48 states first settled by Russians, who built Fort Ross in 1812; they sold it in 1841 to a Swiss named

John Augustus Sutter, whose discovery of gold near Sacramento started the Gold Rush eight years later. It is the only part of the world with large numbers of redwood trees, shooting up hundreds of feet in the moist and drizzly air. It is wet country, and for years it has been one of America's prime lumbering areas: Eureka and smaller lumber towns are filled with filigreed Victorian houses and old mills, art galleries, hiking trails, saloons and waterfront hotels. It has moved on to other crops: in sunny valleys sealed off from the Coast Range, some of the nation's premium wine grapes grow on ridges, and the Emerald Triangle area (Humboldt, Mendocino and Trinity Counties) is known for its premier marijuana fields. Thirty years ago, there were only 20 wineries in Napa Valley. Today, there are several hundred, with more just west of the ridges in Sonoma County; wineries were a favorite investment for Silicon Valley millionaires. Some of the land here has been planted in olive trees, and local olive production has sometimes topped $100 million annually. These valleys were some of California's earliest literary haunts: Robert Louis Stevenson took his honeymoon near Calistoga in Napa, and Jack London owned a giant house in Sonoma that mysteriously burned down in 1913. Along the coast, a 2006 law designated 273,000 acres of wilderness and restored the rights of commercial fishermen to drive trucks on the beaches of the Redwood National Park.

The 1st Congressional District of California consists of the North Coast from Mendocino County to the Oregon border. To the south, it includes Napa County and the eastern edge of Sonoma County—Healdsburg and the Alexander Valley and part of Sonoma Valley—plus part of the Yolo County flatlands to the east, including the University of California at Davis and industrial West Sacramento. The North Coast lumbering area from Mendocino on north, once filled with rough-hewn working men, was historically Democratic; but the timber business became hostage to concern about the northern spotted owl, and the area backlashed toward Republicans on environmental issues. The Pacific Lumber Company—long-time landlord of the town of Scotia, one of the last company-owned towns in the U.S.—announced in 2006 it would sell all of its 275 houses. Veterans of the counterculture settled in Mendocino County and along the coast, especially in Humboldt County, and the area became Democratic again; now, the focus is on sustainable forestry. Inland, the wine-growing country around Healdsburg and in Napa County was Republican in the 1970s, but now partakes of the San Francisco Bay area's liberal consensus. This district changed partisan hands four times during the 1990s, thanks largely to splits among Democrats, but the 2001 redistricting made it heavily Democratic.

The congressman from the 1st District is Mike Thompson, a Democrat first elected in 1998. Thompson grew up in the Napa Valley town of St. Helena, dropped out of high school, served in the Army in Vietnam and earned a Purple Heart. Later, he got a bachelor and master's degree from what has become California State University-Chico, owned a vineyard and worked as a maintenance supervisor for Beringer, a big winery in the valley. In 1982 he was chosen an Assembly Fellow, and from 1984-90 was chief of staff to two Bay Area Assembly members. In 1990, he was elected to the state Senate, where he chaired the Budget Committee. In 1998, he ran for the House seat held, precariously, by Republican Frank Riggs, who had been elected in 1990, 1994 and 1996. In January 1998 Riggs announced he was running for Barbara Boxer's Senate seat; with no name identification beyond the district and little money, he withdrew in April. Thompson faced weak opposition and won support from almost every interest group that matters in the 1st: unions, medical providers, vintners, oil and timber interests, environmental advocates, law enforcement groups, fishermen. His issue stands—opposition to oil drilling off the California coast, support of abortion rights and the death penalty—were broadly popular. He won the June primary easily, 78%-22%, and won the general by 62%-33%. He has won easily since then.

In the House, Thompson has styled himself as a moderate Democrat and his voting record is among the least liberal for coastal Californians. He joined both the New Democrats and the Blue Dogs, and pledged bipartisanship. With Republican George Radanovich, he started the Congressional Wine Caucus, but lost a battle with conservative senators and beer and alcohol wholesalers on a bill giving states new power to restrict sales over the Internet. He joined Jerry Lewis on a proposal to create a $1 billion pool to help pay for making buildings more resistant to earthquakes. Mindful of local businesses, he voted to override Bill Clinton's veto of the estate tax repeal; but he voted against the same proposal when it came from George W. Bush. He voted against trade promotion authority. After the massive fish kill caused by flooding of the Klamath River in 2002, he won emergency aid for local fishermen and businesses, and his provision for a salmon recovery plan passed the House in December 2006.

Thompson has been a close ally of Speaker Nancy Pelosi, which has bolstered his rising star among House Democrats. But his ambition to head the Democratic Congressional Campaign Committee after the 2002 election was frustrated after he joined at the last minute a trip, with

David Bonior and Jim McDermott, to Baghdad in September 2002, during which Bonior criticized George W. Bush and opposed the use of force in Iraq and McDermott suggested that Saddam Hussein was more credible than Bush. Thompson, who did not appear on television, said that he went to get first-hand information on the consequences of war and to urge Iraq to comply with demands for inspections. But it was obvious that making Thompson chairman of the campaign committee would give Republican candidates in every close race in the country a talking point, and no more was heard about his candidacy for that position. Years later, he conceded that it was a bad idea to criticize Bush from Iraq, and he eventually got some consolation prizes: With help from his well-placed California friend, he led the DCCC's incumbent protection program, won a seat on the Ways and Means Committee, and now chairs the Intelligence Subcommittee on Terrorism, Human Analysis and Counterintelligence. He enacted a tax break for landowners who place their land under conservation easements, and worked on other steps to preserve farm lands. In 2006, he helped to enact California's largest new wilderness bill since 1994. In March 2007, responding to several egregious incidents involving stranded passengers, he proposed an "airline passenger bill of rights" to assure a minimum level of service.

SECOND DISTRICT

Rep. Wally Herger (R)

Elected 1986, 11th term; b. May 20, 1945, Yuba City; home, Marysville; American River Comm. Col., A.A. 1967, CA St. U., 1968-69; Mormon; married (Pamela).

Elected Office: CA Assembly, 1980-86.

Professional Career: Rancher; Owner, Herger Gas Inc., 1969-80.

DC Office: 2268 RHOB, 20515, 202-225-3076; Fax: 202-226-0852; Web site: www.house.gov/herger.

District Offices: Chico, 530-893-8363; Redding, 530-223-5898.

Committees: *Joint Committee on Taxation* (5th of 5 R). *Ways & Means* (2d of 17 R): Trade (RMM); Income Security & Family Support.

Group Ratings

	ADA	ACLU	AFS	LCV	ITIC	NTU	COC	ACU	CFG	FRC
2006	0	5	0	0	100	67	93	92	75	100
2005	0	—	0	0	—	67	93	96	88	92

National Journal Ratings

	2005 LIB	—	2005 CONS		2006 LIB	—	2006 CONS
Economic	3%	—	94%		0%	—	98%
Social	0%	—	89%		8%	—	91%
Foreign	42%	—	55%		6%	—	86%

Key Votes of the 109th Congress

1. Estate Tax Repeal	Y	5. Limit Interstate Abortion	Y	9. Build Border Fence	Y
2. Limit CAFE Standards	Y	6. Extend Patriot Act	Y	10. CAFTA	Y
3. FY06 Spending Curb	Y	7. Bar Same Sex Marriage	Y	11. Oppose Iraq Withdrawal	Y
4. Drilling in ANWR	Y	8. Stem Cell Research $	N	12. Detainee Tribunals	Y

Election Results

2006 general	Wally Herger (R)	134,911	(64%)	($711,849)
	A.J. Sekhon (D)	68,234	(32%)	($157,449)
	Other	7,057	(3%)	
2006 primary	Wally Herger (R)	unopposed		
2004 general	Wally Herger (R)	182,119	(67%)	($580,670)
	Mike Johnson (D)	90,310	(33%)	($6,297)

Prior Winning Percentages: 2002 (66%); 2000 (66%); 1998 (63%); 1996 (61%); 1994 (64%); 1992 (65%); 1990 (64%); 1988 (59%); 1986 (58%)

The People		Race/Ethnic Origin	Ancestry		
Area size:	21,977 sq. mi.	76.2% White	German: 11.8%	English: 9.0%	
Urban population:	67.7%	1.2% Black	Irish: 8.9%		
Rural population:	32.3%	3.6% Asian	**2004 Presidential Vote**		
Pop. 2000:	639,087	1.9% Native Am.	Bush (R) 173,528	(62%)	
Pop. 2005 (est):	702,101	0.1% Hawaiian	Kerry (D) 102,254	(37%)	
Median income:	$33,559	2.8% Two+ races	Other 3,980	(1%)	
Poverty status:	17.0%	0.2% Other	**2000 Presidential Vote**		
Military veterans:	15.7%	14.0% Hispanic Origin	Bush (R) 150,196	(61%)	
			Gore (D) 81,861	(33%)	
			Other 13,609	(6%)	
			Cook Partisan Voting Index: R +13		

Occupation	Blue collar: 23.2%	White collar: 54.9%	Gray collar: 21.9%

Rising 14,000 feet over low foothills and the Central Valley, visible for 100 miles, is the snow-capped volcanic cone of Mount Shasta, one of a string of (supposedly) burnt-out volcanoes that march up and down the Pacific Coast states. This is the far northern end of California, where truck traffic on Interstate 5 is the only reminder of the choked metropolitan areas where most of the state's people live. This is lumber country mostly, where the mountains that rise on all sides—the Coast Range to the west, the Sierra Nevada to the east, the scattered mountains sealing off the Central Valley north of Redding—are carpeted with trees: rough flannel-shirt, two-lane-road country that was left behind economically when Los Angeles and San Francisco boomed after World War II. North of Shasta, the tiny town of Weed became a logging center and a noted locale for racial integration a half-century ago, but the loss of jobs has led younger blacks as well as whites to move out. Further south are the flat farm fields of the Sacramento Valley, spread across the 50 miles between the Sierra Nevada and the Coast Range. Since the 1980s, this northern end of California has been attracting people, mostly young families who come here to raise their children in a small town environment, but also retirees looking for a calm atmosphere and low cost of living. This is one part of California that remains overwhelmingly Anglo.

The 2d Congressional District of California covers most of this area. The district has three major population areas. One is around Redding, south of Mount Shasta, where increased high-altitude snowfall has allowed the Whitney Glacier to defy global warming trends by growing in the past century, the only glacier to do so. The second is further south, at the edge of the Sierra foothills, around the Butte County communities of Paradise and Chico, home to a state university campus and Sierra Nevada Pale Ale. Still further south are the farm counties of Colusa, Yuba and Sutter, not far north of Sacramento. The locally-cultivated rice hybrids from Colusa County, the leading rice-producing county in the nation, are a lucrative export. The region has a Democratic heritage, but is culturally conservative, angry at the diktats of urban environmentalists. Until 1980, it elected rough-and-ready Democrats who pulled strings in Sacramento and Washington to build roads and dams. Since then it has elected abstemious Republicans who have solidly conservative voting records and tend to local needs. George W. Bush won 62% of the vote here in 2004, his best showing in a northern California district.

The congressman from the 2d District is Republican Wally Herger, a Republican first elected in 1986. He grew up in the farm country north of Sacramento, where he remains a local farmer, worked as a rancher and propane gas company owner, and was elected in 1980 to the California Assembly. In 1986 he was elected to the House after winning solid margins over the mayor of Redding in the primary and a Shasta County supervisor in the general. He has a solidly conservative voting record and has served quietly on the Ways and Means Committee, favoring balanced budgets and lower taxes. When federal budget deficits disappeared in the late 1990s, Herger was a leader of the battle to create lock boxes for the surpluses in the Social Security and Medicare trust funds; that discussion became moot with the return of big deficits. As chairman of the Human Resources Subcommittee, he had responsibility for reauthorizing the 1996 welfare act. The House repeatedly passed the bill that he and other Ways and Means Republicans wrote to increase work requirements for recipients and incentives for states to reduce caseloads; it included provisions to encourage marriage and other Bush administration proposals. But few House Democrats supported his version, and it faced resistance in the Senate until 2006, when a deal was reached for additional benefits for children on welfare. With encouragement from Tom DeLay, he proposed an overhaul of foster care to give states more flexibility to prevent abuse of children who become lost in the system. He is the most senior among committee Republicans, but did not contest the move of Jim McCrery to jump over him and become the panel's ranking Republican. As senior Republican on the Trade Subcommittee, he worked across the aisle to seek consensus.

On local issues, Herger has tended to water projects and called for exemption of flood control programs from the Endangered Species Act. With Greg Walden of Oregon, he proposed full compensation of farmers and related businesses that suffered damages from the Klamath River flooding, but he rejected environmentalists' calls for management controls of the fisheries, which he called part of "an anti-agriculture agenda." He helped to enact a program to aid about 750 counties that have suffered from a loss of revenue from timber sales. Herger advocated increased basing of Global Hawk unmanned spy planes at Beale Air Force Base, which already housed the older U-2 and SR-71 reconnaissance aircraft. The huge base, whose rocky pastures were used before June 1944 to practice the Normandy invasion and to simulate combat in a fake European town, is about 40 miles north of Sacramento.

In this district, Herger has nothing to fear politically other than nuisance candidates. Since 1990, he has been consistently reelected with more than 60% of the vote against weak Democratic opponents, in what has become one of the safest Republican districts in the nation.

THIRD DISTRICT

Rep. Dan Lungren (R)

Elected 2004, 7th term; b. Sept. 22, 1946, Long Beach; home, Folsom; Notre Dame U., A.B. 1968, Georgetown U., J.D. 1971; Catholic; married (Bobbi).

Elected Office: U.S. House of Reps.1978-88; CA Atty. Gen. 1990-98.

Professional Career: Staff, U.S. Sen. George Murphy, 1969-70; Staff, U.S. Sen. Bill Brock, 1971; Spec. asst. RNC, 1971-72; Practicing atty., 1973-78.

DC Office: 2448 RHOB, 20515, 202-225-5716; Fax: 202-226-1298; Web site: lungren.house.gov.

District Offices: Gold River, 916-859-9906.

Committees: *Budget* (7th of 17 R). *Homeland Security* (6th of 15 R): Transportation Security & Infrastructure Protection (RMM); Emerging Threats, Cybersecurity & Science and Technology. *House Administration* (2d of 3 R). *Judiciary* (7th of 17 R): Immigration, Citizenship, Refugees, Border Security & International Law; Crime, Terrorism & Homeland Security.

Group Ratings

	ADA	ACLU	AFS	LCV	ITIC	NTU	COC	ACU	CFG	FRC
2006	10	14	14	8	86	67	80	84	78	100
2005	0	—	0	0	—	63	93	92	77	92

National Journal Ratings

	2005 LIB	—	2005 CONS		2006 LIB	—	2006 CONS
Economic	9%	—	88%		16%	—	81%
Social	24%	—	74%		35%	—	63%
Foreign	11%	—	86%		33%	—	63%

Key Votes of the 109th Congress

1. Estate Tax Repeal	Y	5. Limit Interstate Abortion	Y	9. Build Border Fence		Y
2. Limit CAFE Standards	Y	6. Extend Patriot Act	Y	10. CAFTA		Y
3. FY06 Spending Curb	Y	7. Bar Same Sex Marriage	Y	11. Oppose Iraq Withdrawal		Y
4. Drilling in ANWR	Y	8. Stem Cell Research $	N	12. Detainee Tribunals		Y

Election Results

2006 general	Dan Lungren (R)	135,709	(59%)	($633,991)
	Bill Durston (D)	86,318	(38%)	($313,766)
	Other	6,142	(3%)	
2006 primary	Dan Lungren (R)	unopposed		
2004 general	Dan Lungren (R)	177,738	(62%)	($1,407,970)
	Gabe Castillo (D)	100,025	(35%)	($98,284)
	Other	9,310	(3%)	

Prior Winning Percentages: 1986 (73%); 1984 (73%); 1982 (69%); 1980 (72%); 1978 (54%)

The People		Race/Ethnic Origin	Ancestry	
Area size:	3,422 sq. mi.	74.4% White	German: 12.4%	Irish: 9.0%
Urban population:	86.4%	4.3% Black	English: 8.9%	
Rural population:	13.6%	5.9% Asian	**2004 Presidential Vote**	
Pop. 2000:	639,088	0.8% Native Am.	Bush (R) 176,512	(58%)
Pop. 2005 (est):	752,101	0.3% Hawaiian	Kerry (D) 123,671	(41%)
Median income:	$51,313	3.5% Two+ races	Other 2,936	(1%)
Poverty status:	8.5%	0.2% Other	**2000 Presidential Vote**	
Military veterans:	15.7%	10.7% Hispanic Origin	Bush (R) 142,946	(55%)
			Gore (D) 107,690	(41%)
			Other 9,820	(4%)
			Cook Partisan Voting Index: R + 7	

Occupation	Blue collar: 18.4%	White collar: 67.8%	Gray collar: 13.8%

Until recently, Sacramento was chiefly the metropolis of a fertile valley that produced a marvelous variety of crops: rice, plums, almonds, olives, asparagus, pears, hops, beans, celery, onions, potatoes, plus caviar-yielding sturgeon in pools of filtered water. The farmlands remain, and the capital city flourishes as a center of government; greater Sacramento is one of the fastest-growing metro areas in the country. Almost all the growth has been away from the flood plain of the Sacramento River, in the higher land east of the city that eventually turns into hills rising toward the Sierra Nevadas. Here is the Mother Lode country in Amador and Calaveras Counties, which filled up with people in the Gold Rush days, when Mark Twain was inspired to write his story about the famous jumping frog of Calaveras County. Only in recent decades has Calaveras County had more than the 16,000 people who lived there in Twain's time. In rapidly growing Rancho Cordova, local leaders created a "new urbanist" development plan with a new downtown in place of aging strip malls. But some things have not changed. When an animal-rights group tried to cancel the annual Jumping Frog Jubilee, a local official said that the frogs are not tortured and that the jubilee would continue.

The 3d Congressional District of California includes much of suburban Sacramento, some territory in Solano County to the west and some of the Mother Lode country to the east, where it reaches over the Sierras to Alpine County, the smallest county in California (1,180 people in 2006) with the state's highest mountain ridge line, and the Nevada line. More than 80% of the people in the district live in Sacramento County, in suburbs like Carmichael, Citrus Heights, Arden-Arcade and the old town of Folsom, where an Intel campus has grown to 6,500 employees and created a prosperous company town. Historically Sacramento was Democratic. But Sacramento County, with its rapid private-sector growth and 32% population increase from 1990 to 2006, has become more Republican. The district voted 58% for George W. Bush in 2004 and is safely Republican.

The congressman from the 3d District is Dan Lungren, first elected here in 2004 but with an earlier decade in the House. Lungren grew up in Long Beach, and his father was Richard Nixon's personal physician; young Dan worked on the staffs of Senators George Murphy and Bill Brock. After a few years of law practice in Long Beach, he unsuccessfully challenged a "Watergate baby" in 1976, then came back and won rather easily in 1978 with a boost from the anti-tax Proposition 13. He entered a freshman class that included Dick Cheney, Newt Gingrich, and Jerry Lewis and Bill Thomas from California; one unsuccessful Republican that year was George W. Bush. During his initial years in Congress, Lungren focused on criminal code reform at the House Judiciary Committee; he was a member of the Conservative Opportunity Society, the influential young House conservatives organized by Gingrich. He played a key role on major immigration legislation in 1986, which was enacted despite reservations from Mexican-American groups, Democratic leaders and the Reagan administration. In 1989 he was nominated as state treasurer but was not confirmed by the state Senate, despite court challenges; in 1990, he was elected to the first of two terms as

California attorney general. After losing 58%-38% to Democrat Gray Davis in the 1998 race for governor, Lungren worked in the Sacramento area as a visiting professor and radio talk show host and joined a Washington-based law firm.

In 2004 3d District incumbent Republican Doug Ose honored his pledge to retire after serving three terms, and Lungren ran for the seat. His toughest competition was in the Republican primary, in which he faced Mary Ose, the incumbent's sister, and state Senator Rico Oller. The contest split the California delegation, with John Doolittle backing Oller and Ways and Means Chairman Bill Thomas supporting Lungren. Ose, a real estate developer, raised more than $2 million, much of it from her own pocket, but despite an almost 2-to-1 fundraising advantage over the others, she won only 23% of the votes. Oller, with a geographic base in Amador and Calaveras Counties, attacked Lungren as soft on immigration; Lungren ran an ad with praise from Gingrich for his work on the 1986 immigration bill. Lungren beat Oller 39%-36%, winning 42%-32% in Sacramento County, which cast 82% of the total vote. In the general election, Lungren criticized his successor as attorney general, Bill Lockyer, for not immediately stopping San Francisco Mayor Gavin Newsom from issuing marriage licenses to same-sex couples. He won 62%-35%. He returned to a Congress that had become a very different place with its Republican majority, and representing a district nearly 400 miles north of his old one.

On his return, Lungren quickly resumed his status as an influential player and usually voted with conservatives, though he moved a bit to the center on social issues. He claimed credit for his previous service and gained senior positions on the Judiciary Committee and Homeland Security, where he chaired the Economic Security, Infrastructure Protection, and Cybersecurity Subcommittee. Although he lost a bid in September 2005 to chair Homeland Security, he worked with Jane Harman to enact a bill enhancing port security, including requirements to scan cargo containers for radioactive materials—but not the firm deadline that Democrats sought. On Judiciary, he opposed restrictions on the Patriot Act as "compromising our ability to investigate terrorist cases," and helped to write the House-passed bill for warrantless surveillance. He sided with most House Republicans in opposing the Senate-passed immigration reform bill and emphasizing the need to "get control of our border." In May 2006, he was part of a bipartisan group that wrote new House rules for travel paid by interest groups. Lungren filed a constitutional amendment to ban gay marriage, and was an outspoken opponent of embryonic stem-cell research. He opposed some aspects of the Republican-run Congress: the huge growth of earmarks, and the increased influence of staff. In November 2006, he ran fourth of four candidates to chair the Republican Conference.

He was reelected 59%-38% against Bill Durston, a physician who served with the Marines in Vietnam and was endorsed by a national group that funded candidates who backed impeachment of President Bush.

FOURTH DISTRICT

Rep. John Doolittle (R)

Elected 1990, 9th term; b. Oct. 30, 1950, Glendale; home, Rocklin; U. of CA at Santa Cruz, B.A. 1972, U. of the Pacific, J.D. 1978; Mormon; married (Julia).

Elected Office: CA Senate, 1980-90, Repub. Caucus Chmn., 1987-90.

Professional Career: Practicing atty., 1978-80.

DC Office: 2410 RHOB, 20515, 202-225-2511; Fax: 202-225-5444; Web site: doolittle.house.gov.

District Offices: Granite Bay, 916-786-5560.

Group Ratings

	ADA	ACLU	AFS	LCV	ITIC	NTU	COC	ACU	CFG	FRC
2006	5	0	14	0	86	53	93	84	46	100
2005	0	—	0	0	—	55	85	92	58	100

National Journal Ratings

	2005 LIB	—	2005 CONS		2006 LIB	—	2006 CONS
Economic	40%	—	59%		16%	—	81%
Social	0%	—	89%		0%	—	94%
Foreign	16%	—	84%		6%	—	86%

Key Votes of the 109th Congress

1. Estate Tax Repeal	Y	5. Limit Interstate Abortion	Y	9. Build Border Fence	Y
2. Limit CAFE Standards	Y	6. Extend Patriot Act	Y	10. CAFTA	Y
3. FY06 Spending Curb	Y	7. Bar Same Sex Marriage	Y	11. Oppose Iraq Withdrawal	Y
4. Drilling in ANWR	Y	8. Stem Cell Research $	N	12. Detainee Tribunals	Y

Election Results

2006 general	John Doolittle (R)	135,818	(49%)	($2,449,428)
	Charlie Brown (D)	126,999	(46%)	($1,650,458)
	Dan Warren (Lib)	14,076	(5%)	
2006 primary	John Doolittle (R)	63,731	(67%)	
	Mike Holmes (R)	31,162	(33%)	
2004 general	John Doolittle (R)	221,926	(65%)	($912,648)
	David Winters (D)	117,443	(35%)	($2,061)

Prior Winning Percentages: 2002 (65%); 2000 (63%); 1998 (63%); 1996 (60%); 1994 (61%); 1992 (50%); 1990 (50%)

The People		**Race/Ethnic Origin**	**Ancestry**	
Area size:	17,159 sq. mi.	83.8% White	German: 13.1%	English: 11.2%
Urban population:	67.4%	1.2% Black	Irish: 10.1%	
Rural population:	32.6%	2.3% Asian	**2004 Presidential Vote**	
Pop. 2000:	639,088	1.1% Native Am.	Bush (R) 216,838	(61%)
Pop. 2005 (est):	727,601	0.1% Hawaiian	Kerry (D) 132,267	(37%)
Median income:	$49,387	2.4% Two+ races	Other 4,119	(1%)
Poverty status:	8.7%	0.2% Other	**2000 Presidential Vote**	
Military veterans:	16.6%	8.9% Hispanic Origin	Bush (R) 172,169	(59%)
			Gore (D) 104,437	(36%)
			Other 15,633	(5%)
			Cook Partisan Voting Index: R +11	

Occupation	Blue collar: 19.6%	White collar: 63.1%	Gray collar: 17.3%

California sprang suddenly into existence: The Gold Rush of 1849 was followed by statehood and the creation of the first 27 counties in 1850. The new state's first boom area was the Mother Lode country in the foothills of the Sierras above Sacramento. Mining camps the size of eastern cities grew up in vacant valleys locked amid steep hills, with thousands of would-be millionaires gathered to find gold—though most of those who actually got rich did so by catering to miners' needs. In Placerville, John Studebaker had a buggy shop, Phillip Armour ran a butcher shop and Mark Hopkins had a dry goods store. The biggest mine in California was sunk in Grass Valley in 1857 and worked for half a century. But long before that, most of the Mother Lode country emptied out, leaving ghost towns and villages with hundreds of deserted houses: an antique vacation country left behind in time.

When local residents celebrated the sesquicentennial, the area had been resurrected as a booming exurban and tourist mecca. "The American River near Coloma becomes a virtual freeway of whooping rafters on summer weekends," reported *USA Today*. "The Mother Lode also offers modern-day prospectors an intriguing pastiche of bed-and-breakfast inns, musty antique stores and such blink-and-you'll-miss-'em outposts as Volcano, Fiddletown, Rough and Ready"—named after President Zachary Taylor. Thousands of Californians—many of them families from smog-filled, middle-class suburbs of the Los Angeles Basin and the San Francisco Bay area—looking for a more pleasant, small-town, orderly environment, have found it along fast-flowing creeks where the '49ers camped. The population of these counties has risen sharply in recent decades. Placer County, which includes Sacramento suburbs and part of the Mother Lode country, grew 78% from 1990 to 2006, more than any other county in California. It also has the highest percentage of registered Republicans in the state and ranks high among its most wealthy counties. On Lake Tahoe, Truckee has grown with the development of ski resorts. Politically, this growth has changed the Mother Lode country from Democratic to Republican. In 1976, nine Mother Lode counties from Sierra to

Mariposa cast 118,000 votes and voted 50%-47% for Jimmy Carter over Gerald Ford: close to the California average. In 2004 they cast 370,000 votes and voted 61% for George W. Bush—a percentage closer to Idaho's than California's. The culture here could not be more different than what prevails less than 50 miles away in the Bay Area.

The 4th Congressional District of California consists of the northern half of the Mother Lode country and the Placer County suburbs of Sacramento, plus a small slice of Sacramento County. It extends northward through thinly populated mountain counties like Modoc County, site of a World War II detention facility for Japanese-Americans, which shares a border with Oregon and Nevada. Most residents here live within the I-80 corridor, clustered near Sacramento County in suburban places like Roseville (the district's most populous city, and the fifth fastest-growing in the nation from 2000 to 2004) and Rocklin, or in the Mother Lode country from Placerville to Nevada City. Some 33% live in areas classified as rural, the largest percentage of the state's 53 districts.

The congressman from the 4th District is John Doolittle, a Republican first elected in 1990. Doolittle grew up in the Los Angeles area and went to high school in Cupertino, in what now is Silicon Valley. His conservatism was annealed in the fires of adversity: He graduated from the University of California at Santa Cruz in 1972, when the campus was 97% for George McGovern. After law school he moved to the edge of the Sacramento metro area where the foothills begin, and in 1980 was elected to the state Senate at 30. When the Republican incumbent retired in 1990, Doolittle ran for the seat. He had tougher competition than expected from Democrat Patricia Malberg, who was pro-choice on abortion, against nuclear power and for defense spending cuts; he won 50%-46%.

In the House, Doolittle has been a solid conservative. As a freshman, he was one of the Republicans' Gang of Seven, who were the advance guard for Newt Gingrich's 1994 revolution. He supported the Auburn Dam, which he and other Sacramento area congressmen for decades wanted to build on the American River, 35 miles east of Sacramento. But for years he deadlocked with a combination of environmentalists and spending opponents led by the 5th District's Robert Matsui. Doolittle contended that alternative plans by the Army Corps of Engineers to repair and strengthen the Folsom Dam, which was completed in 1955, would be a waste of money. In 2003, Doolittle and Matsui reached an agreement to raise the Folsom Dam by seven feet and to spend $135 million on upstream water projects that will take more than a decade to complete. The once fiscally tight-fisted Doolittle had loosened up, and Sacramento got its long-sought flood protection. By mid-2005, Doolittle again was raising the possibility that the Auburn Dam might be needed and the House approved his proposal for a new study. But the Democratic takeover of Congress became another setback.

The iPod-toting Doolittle has taken a consumer interest in copyright policy. He introduced with Rick Boucher a bill to permit fair use copying of certain communications software; it would weaken the anti-circumvention rules of a 1998 copyright law and brought criticism from the motion picture industry. With Zoe Lofgren, he filed a bill on behalf of film preservationists and archivists to make it easier to restore old movies without having to pay copyright fees. For many years, Doolittle worked closely with Tom DeLay, notably in opposition to the Shays-Meehan campaign finance bill. (Critics said that the duo preferred a "do little and delay" Congress.) As a leader of House conservatives, Doolittle was a co-founder of the renamed Republican Study Committee, which has become a force in attempting to limit domestic spending. After the 2002 election, he gained a seat at leadership meetings as secretary of the House Republican Conference. On the Appropriations Committee, he directed many millions of dollars to his district, for land acquisition, wastewater treatment facilities and restoration projects in the Lake Tahoe basin.

He gained unwanted attention with news reports that he had been a beneficiary of the fundraising largess of convicted lobbyist Jack Abramoff and that Doolittle's wife Julie, who runs a fund-raising firm, was among those under investigation; as Doolittle's campaign fundraiser, his wife was paid 15% of what she raised. In January 2006, he conceded that the reports "were hanging over our heads" and that he had been a friend of Abramoff, but added that investigators had not contacted him. Doolittle had won reelection regularly with more than 60% of the vote but the shadow of the Abramoff scandal, combined with the difficult environment for Republicans, made the 2006 campaign unexpectedly competitive. After winning the primary 67%-33% over Auburn vice mayor Mike Holmes, he faced Democrat Charlie Brown, a retired Air Force lieutenant colonel who charged that Doolittle was part of "congressional bribery scandals." Doolittle denied any ethical violations and emphasized his conservative record plus his work for the district. In a debate, Doolittle called Brown "a flim-flam man" who campaigns as a conservative but raised money from liberals in San Francisco. Doolittle survived, but barely, 49%-46%; he had the identical margin in Placer County, which cast 44% of the vote. He won all of the counties except for Nevada.

After the election, he took several steps to stabilize his precarious situation. He relinquished his leadership post. He promised to spend more time on district issues. And he said that he would hire an outside fundraiser to replace his wife, but he also agreed to pay her $137,000 that she claimed she was owed. Then, in April 2007, the FBI raided Doolittle's suburban Virginia home in search of documents related to his wife's fundraising business. In response, after a private meeting with Minority Leader John Boehner, Doolittle temporarily stepped down from his Appropriations seat. "I understand how the most recent circumstances may lead some to question my tenure on the Appropriations Committee," he wrote in a letter to Boehner. But Doolittle was not repentant: he claimed in an opinion article for a local newspaper that the FBI raid was politically motivated, part of an attempt to bolster the image of Attorney General Alberto Gonzales before he was due to appear before the Senate Judiciary Committee, which was investigating the firings of federal prosecutors.

In May 2007, Doolittle said he would not resign and that his intention was to run for reelection. Three Republicans, including 2006 primary challenger Mike Holmes, Assemblyman Ted Gaines, and Air Force Reservist Eric Egland, all made moves to run against Doolittle in the 2008 primary. Brown was also gearing up for another run.

FIFTH DISTRICT

Rep. Doris Matsui (D)

Elected March 2005, 1st full term; b. Sept. 25, 1944, Poston, AZ; home, Sacramento; U. of CA, B.A. 1966; United Methodist; widowed.

Professional Career: Transition team, President-elect Bill Clinton, 1992-93; Dep. Asst. to the Pres., Dep. Dir. of Public Liaison, White House, 1993-98; Lobbyist, 1998-2005.

DC Office: 222 CHOB, 20515, 202-225-7163; Fax: 202-225-0566; Web site: www.house.gov/matsui.

District Offices: Sacramento, 916-498-5600.

Committees: *Rules* (4th of 9 D): Rules & Organization of the House (Vice Chmn.). *Transportation & Infrastructure* (26th of 41 D): Water Resources & Environment; Aviation; Highways & Transit.

Group Ratings

	ADA	ACLU	AFS	LCV	ITIC	NTU	COC	ACU	CFG	FRC
2006	95	100	100	100	50	12	33	4	7	0
2005	100	—	100	94	—	11	46	0	3	0

National Journal Ratings

	2005 LIB	—	2005 CONS	2006 LIB	—	2006 CONS
Economic	87%	—	13%	79%	—	18%
Social	91%	—	9%	86%	—	13%
Foreign	84%	—	15%	88%	—	10%

Key Votes of the 109th Congress

1. Estate Tax Repeal	N	5. Limit Interstate Abortion	N	9. Build Border Fence	N
2. Limit CAFE Standards	N	6. Extend Patriot Act	N	10. CAFTA	N
3. FY06 Spending Curb	N	7. Bar Same Sex Marriage	N	11. Oppose Iraq Withdrawal	N
4. Drilling in ANWR	N	8. Stem Cell Research $	Y	12. Detainee Tribunals	N

Election Results

2006 general	Doris Matsui (D)	105,676	(71%)	($2,463,336)
	Claire Yan (R)	35,106	(24%)	
	Jeff Kravitz (Green)	6,466	(4%)	($12,632)
	Other	2,018	(1%)	
2006 primary	Doris Matsui (D)	unopposed		
2005 special	Doris Matsui (D)	56,175	(68%)	($941,224)
	Julie Padilla (D)	7,158	(9%)	
	John Thomas Flynn (R)	6,559	(8%)	
	Serge Chernay (R)	3,742	(5%)	
	Other	8,841	(11%)	

The People		Race/Ethnic Origin	Ancestry	
Area size:	150 sq. mi.	43.4% White	German: 7.5%	Irish: 5.9%
Urban population:	99.7%	14.4% Black	English: 5.3%	
Rural population:	0.3%	14.9% Asian	**2004 Presidential Vote**	
Pop. 2000:	639,088	0.8% Native Am.	Kerry (D) 125,378	(61%)
Pop. 2005 (est):	675,773	0.8% Hawaiian	Bush (R) 77,788	(38%)
Median income:	$36,719	4.7% Two+ races	Other 2,172	(1%)
Poverty status:	19.7%	0.3% Other	**2000 Presidential Vote**	
Military veterans:	12.2%	20.8% Hispanic Origin	Gore (D) 113,987	(60%)
			Bush (R) 66,011	(35%)
			Other 9,239	(5%)
			Cook Partisan Voting Index: D +14	

Occupation   Blue collar: 20.1%   White collar: 62.9%   Gray collar: 17.0%

Sacramento, capital of the nation's largest state, focus of California's third-largest media market (19th in the nation), home of a national sports franchise (the NBA's Sacramento Kings) and an 18-mile light rail system, is no longer just a small city with a lot of civil servants and a vegetable-packing economy. It is a vibrant American metropolis, with some of the nation's highest job growth. Sacramento started as a river port on the sluggish waters of the Sacramento and American rivers. It was the destination of many overland migrants, the site of Sutter's Fort, where John Augustus Sutter found the gold that set off the Gold Rush of 1849, and the western terminus of the Pony Express in 1860. This was the natural choice at the time to be California's capital, halfway between the San Francisco Bay and the Mother Lode country in the foothills of the Sierras, and in the middle of California's vast valley. Agriculture continues to be important today in Sacra-tomato (as some call it): it has the world's largest almond processing plant. A growing local concern is the city's location in a flood plain, inadequately protected by levees, which has occasionally resulted in heavy flooding.

In the old days, government was not a big business. Just a few lobbyists hung out in saloons on K or J streets, the governor's mansion was a musty antique, and the 100-plus degree summers emptied out what there was of the city. But air conditioning has replaced awnings, freeways and shopping malls have followed the city's growth east and north toward the Sierra foothills and affluence has made this one of America's higher income metropolitan areas. In the 1980s metropolitan Sacramento grew 35% and in the 1990s by 22%, so that it now has two million people, about the same as metro Cincinnati or Orlando. Some high-tech firms have moved east from Silicon Valley, with Intel and Hewlett-Packard housing large campuses, and Bay Area refugees have welcomed less expensive and more comfortable living standards; the increase has continued in recent years, but at a slower pace due to housing shortages. Government expanded, too, and platoons of lobbyists, lawyers and consultants have set up permanent shop here, and new hotels have been built to serve them. Today, 1,000 registered lobbyists prowl the halls of the Capitol. The closing of Mather and McClellan Air Force Bases appeared to have little economic impact. As Sacramento has grown, this once Democratic, pro-government, working-class bastion has become closer to an upscale Sun Belt boomtown. In 1966, Sacramento was just about the only part of California beyond the Bay Area that stuck with Pat Brown over challenger Ronald Reagan. But when John Kerry carried California 54%-44% in 2004, he carried Sacramento County by only 49.6%-49.3%. In the 2003 recall election, 60% of county voters voted to remove Gray Davis, and Schwarzenegger won 52% of the vote on the replacement ballot.

The 5th Congressional District of California consists of the center of metropolitan Sacramento, all of the city of Sacramento and some of its close-in suburbs. The 5th contains affluent neighborhoods on older grid streets and scattered low-income black and Mexican-American neighborhoods, plus new condominiums north of the American River and middle-class subdivisions south of downtown. According to the Public Policy Institute of California, Sacramento's neighborhoods are more ethnically diverse than those of any other big city in California. They are home to, among others, recent Hmong refugees from Laos, Vietnamese and, since the late 1980s, evangelical Russians and Ukrainians. This is the solidly Democratic part of metro Sacramento, and the 5th is the most Democratic district in the great valley from Bakersfield north to Oregon.

The congresswoman from the 5th District is Doris Matsui, who won a special election in March 2005 to replace her late husband Robert Matsui. She was born in an Arizona internment camp and was a well-known figure during her husband's career in Congress. She grew up in Dinuba in Fresno County and graduated from UC-Berkeley; in Sacramento she chaired the board of the local public television station and participated in many civic organizations. After working on Bill Clinton's presidential campaign, she joined his transition team and then served as deputy director of public liaison, where she coordinated with both the public and private sectors on economic and budget priorities. When she left the White House in 1998, she became a senior adviser at a Washington law firm. Robert Matsui died of complications from a rare blood disorder in January 2005, after serving 13 terms as a senior member of the House Ways and Means Committee and was a confidant to Nancy Pelosi as chairman of the Democratic Congressional Campaign Committee. As an infant, he and his family were among the Japanese Americans forced into internment camps in 1942; he was one of the lead sponsors of the 1988 Japanese American redress law that apologized for the internment policy and provided monetary compensation for every survivor of the camps and for so-called "voluntary evacuees."

A few days after the Washington and Sacramento memorial services for her husband, Doris Matsui announced that she would run in the special election. "People lose their spouses every day and make decisions about what they'll do next. I'm no different than anyone else," she said. With her strong support from Pelosi, other prominent Sacramento Democrats decided not to run. None of Matsui's 10 opponents in the nonpartisan contest had significant political experience or name recognition. Matsui emphasized her support for local water projects and said that she opposed George W. Bush's proposal for personal retirement accounts in Social Security; she opposed the war in Iraq but supported maintaining U.S. troops there to avoid a political vacuum. Her investment in a partnership with a long-time friend who was a Sacramento land developer sparked a brief flurry of criticism, but she emphasized that her husband had nothing to do with the deal and that there was no conflict of interest. Some called the contest a "coronation," but the lack of competition surely reflected the respect the Matsuis had won over the years. She won the all-party primary with 68% of the vote to 9% for the runner up. Pelosi rewarded her with a seat on the Rules Committee.

She had a reliably liberal voting record and quickly showed that she knew how to get things done. In addition to her seat on Rules, she joined the Transportation and Infrastructure Committee to tend to the many highway and water resource needs of her district. Working with John Doolittle, she expedited funding for flood control in flood-prone Sacramento, an issue with increased urgency following the devastation that Hurricane Katrina caused in New Orleans. She also worked to improve safety of the Folsom Dam and to strengthen levees. She opposed a renewed push for the Auburn Dam as "not a politically viable option."

Matsui has taken on leadership assignments and fought for party priorities such as federal funding for stem-cell research, reduced prescription-drug prices, and opposition to the Central American Free Trade deal. She cited her family's experience in internment camps to warn of potential civil liberties abuses in the Patriot Act and with detainees at Guantanamo. She was reelected easily.

SIXTH DISTRICT

Rep. Lynn Woolsey (D)

Elected 1992, 8th term; b. Nov. 3, 1937, Seattle, WA; home, Petaluma; U. of San Francisco, B.S. 1981; Presbyterian; divorced.

Elected Office: Petaluma City Cncl., 1985-92, Vice Mayor, 1986, 1991.

Professional Career: Human Resources Mgr., Harris Digital Telephone, 1969-80; Owner, Woolsey Personnel Svc., 1980-92.

DC Office: 2263 RHOB, 20515, 202-225-5161; Fax: 202-225-5163; Web site: woolsey.house.gov.

District Offices: San Rafael, 415-507-9554; Santa Rosa, 707-542-7182.

Committees: *Education & Labor* (6th of 27 D): Workforce Protections (Chmn.); Early Childhood, Elementary & Secondary Education. *Foreign Affairs* (16th of 27 D): Africa & Global Health. *Science & Technology* (4th of 24 D): Energy & Environment.

Group Ratings

	ADA	ACLU	AFS	LCV	ITIC	NTU	COC	ACU	CFG	FRC
2006	100	100	100	100	14	16	20	4	5	0
2005	100	—	100	100	—	19	33	8	8	8

National Journal Ratings

	2005 LIB	—	2005 CONS	2006 LIB	—	2006 CONS
Economic	88%	—	9%	90%	—	9%
Social	96%	—	4%	97%	—	0%
Foreign	96%	—	0%	95%	—	0%

Key Votes of the 109th Congress

1. Estate Tax Repeal	N	5. Limit Interstate Abortion	N
2. Limit CAFE Standards	N	6. Extend Patriot Act	N
3. FY06 Spending Curb	N	7. Bar Same Sex Marriage	N
4. Drilling in ANWR	N	8. Stem Cell Research $	Y

9. Build Border Fence	N
10. CAFTA	N
11. Oppose Iraq Withdrawal	N
12. Detainee Tribunals	N

Election Results

2006 general	Lynn Woolsey (D)	173,190	(70%)	($1,443,910)
	Todd Hooper (R)	64,405	(26%)	($12,156)
	Richard Friesen (Lib)	9,028	(4%)	
2006 primary	Lynn Woolsey (D)	72,058	(66%)	
	Joe Nation (D)	36,845	(34%)	
2004 general	Lynn Woolsey (D)	226,423	(73%)	($562,533)
	Paul Erickson (R)	85,244	(27%)	($6,309)

Prior Winning Percentages: 2002 (67%); 2000 (64%); 1998 (68%); 1996 (62%); 1994 (58%); 1992 (65%)

The People		Race/Ethnic Origin	Ancestry	
Area size:	2,119 sq. mi.	76.1% White	German: 11.1%	Irish: 10.6%
Urban population:	89.8%	2.0% Black	English: 9.8%	
Rural population:	10.2%	3.7% Asian	**2004 Presidential Vote**	
Pop. 2000:	639,087	0.6% Native Am.	Kerry (D) 226,051	(70%)
Pop. 2005 (est):	637,563	0.2% Hawaiian	Bush (R) 90,432	(28%)
Median income:	$59,115	2.7% Two+ races	Other 4,574	(1%)
Poverty status:	7.7%	0.2% Other	**2000 Presidential Vote**	
Military veterans:	12.2%	14.5% Hispanic Origin	Gore (D) 178,746	(62%)
			Bush (R) 87,082	(30%)
			Other 21,514	(7%)
			Cook Partisan Voting Index: D +21	

Occupation	Blue collar: 17.2%	White collar: 68.0%	Gray collar: 14.8%

When the Golden Gate Bridge was opened in 1937, San Francisco was one of the nation's best-known cities, but few knew much about the land beyond the bridge's north pier head. There were fewer than 50,000 people in Marin County then and another 65,000 just to the north in Sonoma County. For San Franciscans, Marin was known for the ferry terminus in Sausalito, a fishing village and art colony, and as the beginning of the Redwood Empire, with its giant trees in Muir Woods (the largest is 253 feet tall and 13 feet in diameter), with a dense concentration of spotted owls that demand quiet during the mating season. Near the Bay and adjacent to the I-580 bridge is the state prison at San Quentin, one of the oldest in the nation, with its famous gas chamber and crowded Death Row; plans for a $233 million overhaul of the facility led to local calls to demolish it and use the valuable land for more commercial enterprises. Farther north is the Point Reyes peninsula with its organic farming and recreational activities, and the wine country of Sonoma County, sunny valleys protected from the fog by the Coast Range. In one such valley was Santa Rosa, destroyed by the 1906 earthquake and later the site of agronomist Luther Burbank's laboratory, a town that looked Middle American enough to be the set for dozens of movies. Politically, the area was then typical of the nation: traditionally Republican, but favoring Franklin D. Roosevelt in the 1930s.

Today this part of California is far more populous, with 249,000 people in Marin County and 467,000 in Sonoma, affluent beyond the dreams of post-World War II Americans, extreme in its cultural attitudes, and with relatively few racial minorities compared to other counties in the Bay Area. Until it was surpassed by the Silicon Valley in the late 1990s, it was the nation's most expensive housing market. Santa Rosa is thriving, thanks to the wine and telecommunications industries. Trendy Marin, with its hot tubs and its fashionable people getting in touch with themselves, became a national caricature: economically affluent, culturally liberationist; this was the home of "American Taliban" John Walker Lindh. When the war in Iraq began, "many of the same people who marched against the Vietnam War have held nightly peace vigils," *The Washington Post* reported. They included a group of feminists who "bared witness" by using their nude bodies to spell out "PEACE." After a while such an image feeds on itself; a place like Marin attracts affluent people who share its values, while those who don't, go elsewhere—in the Bay Area to the more conservative San Ramon Valley, beyond the mountains east of Oakland. Indeed the Bay Area as a whole seems to attract liberals and repel conservatives, just as the Dallas-Fort Worth Metroplex does the opposite. Marin and Sonoma attract the most liberal of the liberal—averse to traditional religion, derisive of traditional sexual and marriage mores, viscerally anti-military.

The 6th Congressional District of California includes all of Marin County and all of Sonoma County except for its rural eastern border. These counties have been transformed politically over the past generation. In 1980 they voted for Ronald Reagan over Jimmy Carter by a 47%-36% margin. Then they moved left and voted in 1988 for Michael Dukakis over George H. W. Bush by 57%-41%. Now Republicans seem almost an endangered species here: in 2004 the two counties voted for John Kerry over George W. Bush by 69%-29%.

The congresswoman from the 6th District is Lynn Woolsey, a Democrat first elected in 1992. Woolsey grew up in the Pacific Northwest, moved to Marin and was a housewife with three children under 6 when her marriage ended in 1968. She went on welfare, got a low-paying job and left her children with 13 different babysitters in a year. Deliverance appeared in the form of a job with a high-tech startup firm where she rose to become a top executive. She remarried and moved to a house in Petaluma where her mother could live and look after the kids. She put herself through business school at night, earned a degree in human resources and started her own personnel service. In 1984 Woolsey won a seat on the Petaluma Council. In 1992 she won the House seat in a nine-candidate primary with 26%, well ahead of 19% for the runner-up. In the general she faced liberal Republican Assemblyman Bill Filante. But he had surgery for a brain tumor and stopped campaigning; she won 65%-34%.

An apt representative of her district, Woolsey has one of the most liberal voting records in the House. As the first former welfare recipient in Congress, she opposed the 1996 welfare law and supports easing work requirements and providing more child care; she wants mothers to be able to stay at home until their children are 11. She lobbied against banning gays in the military, accompanied by her son who is gay. Republicans sought to embarrass Democrats by calling for a vote on Woolsey's bill to revoke the federal charter for the Boy Scouts because the group excludes gays; her bill was defeated 362-12. On the Science Committee, Woolsey worked to promote energy efficiency and increase support for alternative energy sources. She wants to repeal portions of the Patriot Act on civil liberties grounds, and sponsored a resolution in January 2005 for the immediate withdrawal of U.S. troops from Iraq as part of a "complete reevaluation" of national security policy; it lost, 128-300. For President Bush's State of the Union message in 2006, she gave a gallery ticket to antiwar protestor Cindy Sheehan, who was arrested during the speech. As co-chair of the Progressive Caucus in January 2007, Woolsey called for withdrawal in six months, when Speaker Nancy

Pelosi was pushing for a 2008 deadline. She has failed to win Appropriations seats that have gone to more junior members. In the majority, she chaired the Education and Labor Subcommittee on Workforce Protections.

For her district, she got the House to authorize $15 million to renovate the immigration complex on Angel Island—now a state park in the Bay not far from Golden Gate Bridge, but a place where countless Chinese arrivals were detained in deplorable conditions—and turn it into an Ellis Island of the West. In 2004, she apologized for intervening on behalf of the son of an office aide who was convicted as a rapist; the victim rejected the gesture. Woolsey has been easily reelected. She was challenged in the 2002 primary by Santa Rosa Mayor Mike Martini, the founder of a winery in Sebastopol, who criticized her for lack of leadership, excessively liberal votes and failure to bring sufficient funds to the district. Woolsey responded that she had delivered $430 million since 1997, and defended her record on civil-liberties grounds; she won 80%-20%. Term-limited Assemblyman Joe Nation, who lost to Woolsey in the 1992 open seat primary, challenged her in 2006, calling her ineffective. Woolsey ran negative ads in the closing days before the vote, and won 66%-34%.

SEVENTH DISTRICT

Rep. George Miller (D)

Elected 1974, 17th term; b. May 17, 1945, Richmond; home, Martinez; San Francisco St. U., B.A. 1968, U. of CA at Davis, J.D. 1972; Catholic; married (Cynthia).

Professional Career: Legis. aide, CA Senate Majority Ldr., 1969-74; Practicing atty., 1972-74.

DC Office: 2205 RHOB, 20515, 202-225-2095; Fax: 202-225-5609; Web site: www.house.gov/georgemiller.

District Offices: Concord, 925-602-1880; Richmond, 510-262-6500; Vallejo, 707-645-1888.

Committees: *Democratic Steering Committee Co-Chair. Education & Labor* (Chmn. of 27 D): Higher Education, Lifelong Learning & Competitiveness; Health, Employment, Labor & Pensions. *Natural Resources* (15th of 27 D): Water & Power.

Group Ratings

	ADA	ACLU	AFS	LCV	ITIC	NTU	COC	ACU	CFG	FRC
2006	90	100	100	100	57	18	29	4	7	0
2005	100	—	100	100	—	17	35	0	7	0

National Journal Ratings

	2005 LIB	—	2005 CONS	2006 LIB	—	2006 CONS
Economic	92%	—	6%	94%	—	0%
Social	93%	—	6%	95%	—	5%
Foreign	91%	—	7%	95%	—	0%

Key Votes of the 109th Congress

1. Estate Tax Repeal	N	5. Limit Interstate Abortion	N	9. Build Border Fence	N
2. Limit CAFE Standards	N	6. Extend Patriot Act	N	10. CAFTA	N
3. FY06 Spending Curb	N	7. Bar Same Sex Marriage	N	11. Oppose Iraq Withdrawal	N
4. Drilling in ANWR	N	8. Stem Cell Research $	Y	12. Detainee Tribunals	N

Election Results

2006 general	George Miller (D)	118,000	(84%)	($719,639)
	Camden McConnell (Lib)	22,486	(16%)	
2006 primary	George Miller (D)	unopposed		
2004 general	George Miller (D)	166,831	(76%)	($571,957)
	Charles Hargrave (R)	52,446	(24%)	

Prior Winning Percentages: 2002 (71%); 2000 (76%); 1998 (77%); 1996 (72%); 1994 (70%); 1992 (70%); 1990 (61%); 1988 (68%); 1986 (67%); 1984 (66%); 1982 (67%); 1980 (63%); 1978 (63%); 1976 (75%); 1974 (56%)

The People		Race/Ethnic Origin	Ancestry	
Area size:	443 sq. mi.	43.2% White	German: 7.5% Irish: 6.7%	
Urban population:	98.7%	16.8% Black	English: 5.6%	
Rural population:	1.3%	13.3% Asian	**2004 Presidential Vote**	
Pop. 2000:	639,088	0.5% Native Am.	Kerry (D) 153,988	(67%)
Pop. 2005 (est):	649,003	0.6% Hawaiian	Bush (R) 72,994	(32%)
Median income:	$52,778	3.9% Two+ races	Other 2,300	(1%)
Poverty status:	10.0%	0.3% Other	**2000 Presidential Vote**	
Military veterans:	12.5%	21.4% Hispanic Origin	Gore (D) 139,421	(66%)
			Bush (R) 64,477	(31%)
			Other 6,824	(3%)
			Cook Partisan Voting Index: D +19	

Occupation   Blue collar: 22.7%   White collar: 60.1%   Gray collar: 17.1%

The journey inward from the Pacific Ocean to the vast flatness of California's Central Valley passes through a wondrous variety of terrain. The traveler starts at the Golden Gate, with the lush green Presidio on one side and the bluff of the Marin mountains on the other; through the waters of San Francisco Bay, looked down upon by ridges above the East Bay on one side and the cone of Mount Tamalpais on the other; through the narrow Carquinez Strait to Suisun Bay, with its sloughs and marshes and ships ready for scrap, fed by the sluggish waters of the Sacramento and San Joaquin Delta; and finally past the mountains and waters, to the flat, fertile expanse of California's great interior. This is not a journey most tourists make, but it was a familiar route to the first Americans in California and it passes by much of the industrial base of the Bay Area. On the east side of the bay is Richmond, developed almost instantaneously during World War II when Henry J. Kaiser built a shipyard in its deep-water port and 91,000 people from all over the country were put to work building ships for the Pacific theater; what became known as Rosie the Riveter Memorial Park is now a national park, and the city now has a 36% black population and is attracting high-tech spinoffs, despite a downtown that has seen better days. Across Carquinez Strait is Vallejo, named for a Mexican general and member of the first California Senate, the site from 1853 to 1996 of the giant Mare Island Naval Shipyard, where 41,000 worked during World War II. Farther up the bay, on the south, is Concord, the largest city in Contra Costa County, whose city officials were unique in that they lobbied the Pentagon to close the mostly unused Concord Naval Weapons Station; they wanted to use the land for business and residential development, which is banned beyond the urban limit that county voters imposed in 1990. The Defense Department complied and included about half of the site on the 2005 base closure list, with plans now underway for mixed-use development; the Army retains the remaining parcel for ammunition and cargo shipping. These shores are the industrial part of the Bay area, with tank farms and refineries. The towns are among the most ethnically diverse in the country, with large percentages of blacks, Hispanics and Asians and large numbers of Filipinos in Vallejo and other towns.

The 7th Congressional District of California includes most of this passage, from Richmond to Vallejo (the 7th's largest city), Hercules, Martinez and Pittsburg. It also proceeds inland through the intermountain interstices of Contra Costa County to include part of Concord and northeast from Vallejo over the sloughs and up I-80 to include Vacaville, on flat land beneath Vaca Mountain. Politically, this industrial area was blue-collar, labor union Democratic back in the days when San Francisco, with its larger white-collar population, often voted Republican. Today housing values have risen, as they have just about everywhere in the Bay Area, but it remains heavily Democratic, liberal on most issues. But not as leftish as other San Francisco Democrats: John Kerry's 67%-32% win over George W. Bush in 2004 was closer than in six other Bay Area districts.

The congressman from the 7th District is George Miller, one of three remaining Democrats of the Watergate class of 1974 (the others are James Oberstar and Henry Waxman), the first baby-boom liberal to chair a House committeeand now chairman of the Education and Labor Committee. He is heir to a tradition of Bay Area working class politics. His father was chairman of the state Senate Finance Committee; when he died in 1969, Miller lost the race to succeed him, but became a staffer for Senate Leader (and later San Francisco Mayor) George Moscone. Miller was a protege of San Francisco Congressman Phillip Burton, who did so much to establish liberal hegemony in the House in the 1970s. His work is marked by one of the most liberal voting records in the House, and hebrings an aggressiveness and zest for political combat reminiscent of Burton. Miller is a strong backer of protecting the environment against what he sees as greedy private sector operators and of furthering the causes of labor unions. Like Burton, Miller has grasped for top party leadership posts but hasn't made it. But he has learned a legislator's virtues of patience, timing and creativity. Now, his close alliance with Burton's successor—Speaker Nancy Pelosi—places him in a position of great influence.

Miller began the 1990s in a position of power, able to advance his causes forward. In 1991 he became chairman of the Interior Committee (he renamed it Natural Resources in 1993, Republicans renamed it Resources in 1995, and Democrats have returned it to Natural Resources) and proceeded, in his words, "to kick ass and take names." He had long crusaded against water reclamation projects that provided cheap water to farmers. In 1992, amid a California drought, he passed a Central Valley Project law that raised farmers' prices closer to those of urban users and imposed environmental restrictions, over the fierce opposition of Central Valley politicians and Governor Pete Wilson. He passed the California desert bill, with Senator Dianne Feinstein, in October 1994; it was the last major legislation of the Democratic Congress.

For several years in the minority he worked more to prevent change than to make change. He helped to stymie John Doolittle's attempt to revise the Central Valley Project. He harshly criticized Republicans for trying to change the Endangered Species Act, EPA regulations, the bans on Arctic National Wildlife Refuge oil drilling and Tongass National Forest logging and for commercial sponsorship of national parks; for the most part, he was successful, with help from the Clinton administration.

The election of George W. Bush unexpectedly returned Miller to the center ring. He replaced the retired Bill Clay as ranking Democrat on the Education and the Workforce Committee. The incoming chairman, John Boehner, recommended that Bush include Miller and other Democrats in a pre-inauguration meeting in Austin. They struck up a cordial relationship; Bush started calling Miller "Big George." Miller is a Democrat who doesn't always follow the dictates of the teacher's unions; he seems genuinely concerned that too many American children are getting a rotten education. He came to believe that Bush shared that concern. Miller wanted more spending on education, but he also wanted more rigorous standards, with consequences. Boehner and Miller worked on a bipartisan basis on a committee that usually had bitter partisan divisions from the 1960s through the 1990s. This effort became the No Child Left Behind Act; at the bill signing in January 2002, Bush took care to praise Miller for his contributions. Miller has not been entirely happy with the way the administration implemented the law, however. He has continually complained that the administration and Congress have not appropriated the full amounts authorized (though that is standard practice on many programs). But he has also said that there has been progress by minority and poor students—his goal in the first place.

Miller has fought the Bush administration and committee Republicans on many issues. He worked to defeat the Department of Labor overtime regulations and lost on the floor. In 2004 he proposed, as an alternative to Ways and Means Chairman Bill Thomas's corporate tax bill, an American Jobs Plan that read like a Democratic wish list: rollbacks of incentives for outsourcing jobs, $40 billion of research and development spending, doubling of Pell grants, a federal broadband program, extension of unemployment benefits. He has sponsored a bill to allow unions to be recognized as bargaining representatives by securing signatures on cards and requiring arbitration of initial contracts. That was a cause going nowhere in a Republican House, but Miller made passage of this "card-check" bill an early accomplishment of the Democratic-controlled House; it passed 241-185 in March 2007, with 13 Republican votes.

On the 2001 education bill Boehner worked closely with Miller, and in 2004 and early 2005 he seemed prepared to do that again on the issue of pensions. Miller praised Boehner for raising the subject in 2004, and in September 2004 the House placed on an appropriation Miller's amendment to require the Pension Benefit Guaranty Corporation to disclose corporate pension funding levels to participants. In October 2004 he sponsored a bill, "as a public marker," to freeze for five years the pensions of corporate executive who terminate employee pension plans or vastly reduce benefits. In early 2005, Boehner said he would work on pension law in terms that suggested a bipartisan approach might be possible. But when pension reform legislation was enacted in 2006, it was with considerable Democratic support but steadfast opposition from Miller.

His ascension to committee chairman in January 2007 was all the more significant because Pelosi relies heavily on his advice, judgment and protection from potential adversaries within the Democratic Caucus. "She is the leader that I've been waiting for for 30 years," Miller said in a 2005 interview with *National Journal*. "She is the complete package. She understands policy, politics, and has a core of values that is clear and solid. She is a rare breed." Their working relationship clearly works both ways. He has described his role as "Hamburger Helper," adding, "I'll do whatever she wants." Pelosi named Miller as chairman of the Democratic Policy Committee, where he was instrumental in preparing the "New Direction" agenda for the 2006 campaign. He often spends time in Pelosi's office and even gave up his long-time staff director and close adviser to become Pelosi's chief of staff in 2005. Some have said that Miller serves as Pelosi's enforcer, as evidenced by Miller's strong support for John Murtha's November 2006 campaign against Steny Hoyer for Majority Leader, which became an embarrassment for Pelosi. But the Democrats' return to the House majority shifted some of his focus back to the Education and Labor Committee where he has ambitious plans. As chairman, his priorities included renewal of the No Child Left Behind Act, with increased funding and incentives for improved teacher quality; increased support for college student loans; and pursuit of his long-time interests in services to poor children and nutrition programs. In May 2007, he won enactment of an increase in the minimum wage to $7.25 per hour.

In local matters, Miller worked to reduce the number of slot machines in the Lytton Band of Pomo Indians casino in San Pablo from 5,000 to 2,500, though he had passed in 2000 an amendment freeing the casino from federal and state restrictions; Senator Dianne Feinstein in January 2005 moved to rescind the 2000 measure. Later in 2005, Miller reversed his earlier view, and joined in calling for repeal of the compact because the proposed casino was too large.

Miller has been reelected by wide margins in this very Democratic district. In 2006, he won without major-party opposition.

EIGHTH DISTRICT

Rep. Nancy Pelosi (D)

Elected June 1987, 10th full term; b. Mar. 26, 1940, Baltimore, MD; home, San Francisco; Trinity Col., B.A. 1962; Catholic; married (Paul).

Professional Career: CA Dem. Party, Northern Chmn., 1977-81, St. Chmn., 1981-83; DSCC Finance Chmn., 1985-87; PR exec., Ogilvy & Mather, 1986-87.

DC Office: 235 CHOB, 20515, 202-225-4965; Fax: 202-225-8259; Web site: www.house.gov/pelosi.

District Offices: San Francisco, 415-556-4862.

Committees: *Speaker of the House.*

Group Ratings

	ADA	ACLU	AFS	LCV	ITIC	NTU	COC	ACU	CFG	FRC
2006	95	100	100	100	57	11	40	8	7	0
2005	95	—	100	94	—	11	36	0	3	0

National Journal Ratings

	2005 LIB	—	2005 CONS	2006 LIB	—	2006 CONS
Economic	91%	—	8%	94%	—	0%
Social	96%	—	3%	86%	—	13%
Foreign	82%	—	17%	92%	—	5%

Key Votes of the 109th Congress

1. Estate Tax Repeal	N	5. Limit Interstate Abortion	N	9. Build Border Fence	N
2. Limit CAFE Standards	N	6. Extend Patriot Act	N	10. CAFTA	N
3. FY06 Spending Curb	N	7. Bar Same Sex Marriage	N	11. Oppose Iraq Withdrawal	N
4. Drilling in ANWR	N	8. Stem Cell Research $	Y	12. Detainee Tribunals	N

Election Results

2006 general	Nancy Pelosi (D)	148,435	(80%)	($1,853,040)
	Mike DeNunzio (R)	19,800	(11%)	($149,248)
	Krissy Keefer (Green)	13,653	(7%)	($32,091)
	Other	2,751	(1%)	
2006 primary	Nancy Pelosi (D)	unopposed		
2004 general	Nancy Pelosi (D)	224,017	(83%)	($1,240,543)
	Jennifer Depalma (R)	31,074	(12%)	($5,704)
	Leilani Dowell (PF)	9,527	(4%)	
	Other	5,446	(2%)	

Prior Winning Percentages: 2002 (80%); 2000 (85%); 1998 (86%); 1996 (84%); 1994 (82%); 1992 (82%); 1990 (77%); 1988 (76%); 1987 (63%)

The People		Race/Ethnic Origin	Ancestry	
Area size:	114 sq. mi.	42.9% White	Irish: 6.9%	German: 6.4%
Urban population:	100.0%	8.6% Black	English: 5.1%	
Rural population:	0.0%	28.7% Asian	**2004 Presidential Vote**	
Pop. 2000:	639,088	0.3% Native Am.	Kerry (D) 244,009	(85%)
Pop. 2005 (est):	606,714	0.5% Hawaiian	Bush (R) 40,558	(14%)
Median income:	$52,322	2.9% Two+ races	Other 4,024	(1%)
Poverty status:	12.2%	0.3% Other	**2000 Presidential Vote**	
Military veterans:	6.8%	15.7% Hispanic Origin	Gore (D) 196,878	(77%)
			Bush (R) 37,737	(15%)
			Other 20,869	(8%)
			Cook Partisan Voting Index: D +36	

Occupation   Blue collar: 11.9%   White collar: 72.9%   Gray collar: 15.1%

On February 20, 1915, Governor Hiram Johnson and Mayor James Rolph led 150,000 people onto the grounds of the Panama-Pacific International Exposition to see the Spanish-Italian baroque style building built on reclaimed land in what became San Francisco's Marina district. The Exposition ostensibly celebrated the completion of the Panama Canal, but it was clearly intended to show off San Francisco's recovery from the 1906 earthquake. It also spotlighted San Francisco as the central focus of an America that was becoming, with its acquisition of Hawaii and the Philippines and its interest in an open-door policy with China and trade with Japan, a power in the Pacific. The Exposition set the physical style of San Francisco: It encouraged the use of Mediterranean color, accent and detail that characterizes most post-Victorian houses and commercial structures in The City (as the *San Francisco Examiner* called it for years). It created the picturesque Marina district, whose old buildings were among those damaged in the 1989 earthquake, and today's tourist waterfront around Fisherman's Wharf and Ghirardelli Square. This San Francisco has many facets: On a sunny day it looks almost tropical, with brown mountains baking in the sun and light shining off the pastel stucco buildings; when the clouds scud in from the Pacific, it can look sinister, full of dark corners where a private detective's partner might be ambushed by a pretty girl. The buildings can be majestic, like the monumental Beaux Arts City Hall, or tawdry, like the hotels of the Tenderloin; it is a city that looks exotic at first but, when you look closely, can only be American.

San Francisco has been a dynamic city, capable of great growth, carrying the American tradition of tolerance of diversity to new lengths; it grew from nothing to a major city in the single year of 1850; its American origins are obvious from the regular grids of streets named after politicians and local developers. The San Francisco of 1915 was proud of the writers who had flourished there—Jack London, Ambrose Bierce, Frank Norris—and of the hometown traditions of the arts and crafts movement, just as San Francisco later would have a Herb Caen-ish pride in the beats of the 1950s North Beach, the hippies who thronged Haight-Ashbury in 1967, and the gays of Castro in the 1970s and since (although lately straights have been moving in). Over the years, the city's booming economy, based initially on food processing, but now on finance, high-tech and clothing (Levi Strauss, The Gap) attracted talented newcomers, weighted increasingly toward those who find its liberation-minded cultural attitudes congenial. Today its population is increasingly high-income and low-income, with new condominiums rising on the waterfront (construction workers found the remains of an 1849 sailing ship under one) and a splendid new Transbay Terminal planned for the booming yet funky South of Market area. It has the lowest percentage of children (15%) of any major city; half of parents of preschool children in a 2005 survey said they were planning to move out.

Politically, San Francisco was a progressive Republican town, like the two men who led the way into the Exposition. The sour-tempered Hiram Johnson made his name as a reformer throwing out crooked city politicians; his administration gave California primary elections, referenda and recall, and strong civil service laws. "Sunny Jim" Rolph, mayor from 1911-30 and then governor, built the civic center, parks, schools, streetcars and the Hetch Hetchy aqueduct—the antique infrastructure of San Francisco today. Sympathetic to the conservation movement, willing to deal with organized labor in a union town that had America's only general strike in 1934, tolerant of the diversity of California, these progressive Republicans were the recognizable ancestors of, though certainly not identical to, the latter-day San Franciscans who became increasingly liberal and even radical.

But San Francisco's hipness can be overstated. For if its distinctive style attracted liberal singles and gays in increasing numbers, its economic dynamism on the Pacific Rim has attracted Asians—as indeed San Francisco did from 1850 until immigration was shut off by the Chinese Exclusion Act in 1882. The city has elected strong liberal politicians—notably, Mayor George Moscone and openly gay Supervisor Harvey Milk, who were shot to death in 1978 by a political opponent who was acquitted of murder by a jury on the bizarre theory that he had been crazed by junk food. Over the next decade, the city's cultural liberalism was tempered by Mayor Dianne Feinstein, who vetoed a domestic partnership ordinance and opposed commercial rent control. In 1995, Willie Brown, ousted after 15 years as Speaker of the Assembly, returned home and was elected mayor. After reaping admiring publicity following his takeover of the office, Brown's record turned dismal. While the affluent neighborhoods were enriched with new Silicon Valley million-aires, the Chinese, Filipino and other Asian immigrants in the southern and western parts of the city were beleaguered by high taxes that supported the pampered public employee unions. After sparking protests for his crackdown on the homeless, the term-limited Brown stepped down in 2003. As his successor, San Francisco passed over the radical Matt Gonzalez and installed Gavin Newsom, who in February 2004 started issuing marriage licenses to same-sex couples, more than 4,000 in all, although California voters outlawed same-sex marriage and the courts declined to overturn that law. The state Supreme Court ordered him to stop after a month, and later declared that Newsom had exceeded his authority and that the marriages were "void and of no legal effect from their inception." Some talked of Newsom as a future governor; after an affair with his chief fundraiser's wife was revealed in 2007 that seemed unlikely.

The 8th Congressional District of California takes in four-fifths of San Francisco, all but the southwest corner. It includes all of San Francisco's high-rise downtown, the crowded and bustling Chinatown, Telegraph, Nob and Russian Hills, North Beach (which was once really a beach), Pacific Heights (which is still on heights) and the Marina District (which does not have a very big marina). In the valleys are the mostly black Fillmore and Western Addition areas; the 8th is 9% black, 16% Hispanic and 29% Asian—the second highest Asian percentage of any district outside Hawaii. The 8th also has the gay Castro district and Noe Valley, Haight-Ashbury, once the bedraggled center of hippiedom and now another yup-and-coming San Francisco neighborhood, and Portrero Hill with its restored houses overlooking downtown. Farther south are the old residential areas overlooking I-280, with pastel houses strewn along grid streets that hug the steep hills. San Francisco's population has been declining since the dot com bust, and the 8th District's population dropped 5% between 2000 and 2006; Census estimates for 2005 show it to rank 413th in population among the 435 districts, ahead only of 10 central city districts in Illinois, Massachusetts, Minnesota, Ohio, Pennsylvania and Rhode Island, 10 districts in Iowa, Nebraska and West Virginia and the at-large districts of Delaware and Wyoming. The district is overwhelmingly Democratic and voted 85%-14% for John Kerry in 2004. In 2006, 60% of San Franciscans voted for Measure J, calling for the impeachment of George W. Bush and Dick Cheney.

The 8th District is represented by Nancy Pelosi, the Speaker of the House, who was first elected in June 1987. She has the energy and shrewdness of one who has handled the most delicate political chores, and the charm and unflappability of one who is the mother of five and grandmother of six. Pelosi grew up on Albemarle Street in Baltimore's Little Italy, just east of downtown and north of the harbor. Her father, Thomas D'Alesandro Jr., served in the House from 1939-47 and was mayor of Baltimore for 12 years after that; her mother Annunciata, was an indefatigable political organizer and her brother, Thomas D'Alesandro III, was mayor from 1967 to 1971. She says of her parents, "What I got from them was about economic fairness. That was the difference between Democrats and Republicans all those years ago." She graduated from Trinity College in Washing-ton, where she met her husband; they married and moved to his hometown, San Francisco. There he became a successful real estate investor. She raised her family and got into local Democratic politics. At first she impressed rough-hewn Congressman John Burton as just another stylish hostess in a city that has many of them.

But she soon impressed Burton and his older brother, Congressman Phillip Burton, the de facto liberal leader of the House in the 1970s, who lost his race for majority leader to Jim Wright by a 148-147 margin in December 1976. In 1976 she returned to Maryland to run the presidential primary campaign of Governor Jerry Brown. She was able to relate both to "Governor Moonbeam" and to the practical-minded politicians she had met around her father and mother. Brown was never president (he is now California's attorney general), but Pelosi was, unknowingly, on her way to becoming Speaker. In 1979 she became chairman of the Northern California Democratic party; in 1981 she became chairman of the California Democratic party. These positions required a consider-able amount of diplomacy: Assembly Majority Leader Howard Berman of Los Angeles was attempt-ing to oust Assembly Speaker Leo McCarthy of San Francisco, and in 1980 they both ran candidates in the primary to get more votes. That led to a protracted struggle in 1981, out of which Willie Brown of San Francisco emerged with the speakership, which he held for 15 years. Pelosi managed to remain on good terms with all of them and to help Democrats hold majorities in the legislature and nearly elect Los Angeles Mayor Tom Bradley governor in 1982.

That was the year that Phillip Burton's crowning gerrymander went into effect, but to the surprise of all, John Burton declined to run in his new Marin-and-San-Francisco district. Some Democrats sounded out Pelosi, whose Presidio Heights home was in the district, but she declined to run; the seat went instead to Marin-based Barbara Boxer. In the next few years Pelosi worked with Mayor Dianne Feinstein to land the 1984 Democratic National Convention for San Francisco. In 1985 she ran for Democratic National Chairman, but lost to longtime Kennedy aide Paul Kirk. The people Pelosi was dealing with, while still technically a housewife, were all politicians of the first order of magnitude at the time or soon became so. Jerry Brown was governor and a presidential candidate in 1976 and 1992, Phil Burton was a major power in the House and John Burton was later president of the California Senate and negotiator with Governor Arnold Schwarzenegger, Berman was elected to Congress and is a behind-the-scenes power there still, McCarthy became lieutenant governor and a Senate candidate, Willie Brown was Speaker for 15 years and mayor of San Francisco for eight years after that, Bradley was mayor of Los Angeles for 20 years, Feinstein was a candidate for governor in 1990 and was elected to the Senate in 1992, the same year in which Boxer won the state's other Senate seat. This was a fast political track. In April 1983 Phil Burton, who chain-smoked Pall Malls and drank vodka from tumbler glasses, dropped dead at 57. Elected to succeed him was his widow, Sala Burton, who idolized his record and whose political instincts were as shrewd as his. But her health failed too. In 1987, as she was dying of cancer, she told her intimate friends who she wanted to succeed her: Nancy Pelosi.

Only two years before Pelosi had told the press, "I won't be running for office." Her children were not yet grown, her husband's business interests kept him mostly in California and their net worth was not yet such that she could afford to self-finance a campaign. (In 2006 *Roll Call* reported her net worth at more than $14 million, with houses in San Francisco, a vineyard in the Napa Valley, a townhome in the Sierras and a condominium in Washington: pretty good for a kid from Little Italy.) But in 1987 she ran, moving her residence from Presidio Heights to a Pacific Heights rental apartment (Presidio Heights is back in her district now). Her chief opponent in the Democratic primary was San Francisco Supervisor Harry Britt, the gay successor of Harvey Milk who had been murdered by Supervisor Dan White along with Mayor George Moscone in 1978. San Francisco's gay community at that time was not as mainstream as it became, but Britt had a good record in office and Pelosi had to work hard to beat him 35%-31%. As has been the case on other occasions, this politician who is positioned on the left side of the national Democratic party is on the political right in San Francisco.

There seemed to be no clue in Pelosi's early work in the House that she would seek a leadership position as Phil Burton did. Instead she took the lead on important issues of local sensitivity. One was the Presidio: Burton inserted in some must-pass bill a provision that when the military left the Presidio, it would go to the Interior Department. The problem was that it was so expensive to maintain that it threatened to swallow up the National Park Services budget. Through several Congresses, Pelosi worked to get bipartisan support for a funding source, and in 1997 created the Presidio Trust, with a declining appropriation scheduled to be phased out in 2012. Another sensitive issue was human rights, especially in China. After the Tiananmen Square massacre, she sponsored an amendment to give Chinese students the right to remain in the United States; George H.W. Bush vetoed it. In 1991 she became the lead sponsor of the bill to condition China's Most Favored Nation status on human rights reforms; the House overrode Bush's veto but it was upheld in the Senate. After that, Pelosi led the annual fight against normal trade relations and sharply criticized China. When Bill Clinton in 1999 agreed to terms for China's entry into the World Trade Organization, Pelosi led even more furious opposition to normal trade relations with China. Although bitter about the setbacks, she vowed to maintain her human rights vigil. She did all this at some political risk: Pelosi's position is by no means universally popular with Asian Americans in her district; many think the U.S. should trade and negotiate quietly with China. One of her chief adversaries on the issue was her San Francisco neighbor, Senator Dianne Feinstein; for many years they lived in houses just a few blocks apart in Presidio Heights. In addition to working with some Republicans like religious conservatives Christopher Smith and Frank Wolf on China, she usually cooperated with chairman Porter Goss as the senior Democrat on the Intelligence Committee, especially after the September 11 attacks. She joined in the committee's report that, while the intelligence community did not have specific evidence in advance, it did have information that was clearly relevant to the attacks. On other issues Pelosi had an almost perfectly liberal voting record. She has been a leader in encouraging family planning and environmental protection overseas.

Her move into the leadership was persistent, shrewd and well-organized. In 1997, as a member of the House ethics committee, she doggedly pursued charges against Speaker Newt Gingrich and worked with Minority Whip David Bonior's scorched earth tactics against him. In 1999, she launched a campaign for Majority Whip, anticipating that Democrats would win a majority in 2000 (which they nearly did: it was their best year between 1992 and 2006), against Steny Hoyer of Maryland. They were old acquaintances, having served as interns in the office of one-term Senator Daniel Brewster in the 1960s, but not confreres: there were considerable stylistic and ideological differences. Rosa DeLauro had just been defeated for Conference Chairman by Martin Frost, and many Democrats felt there should be a woman in the leadership. Pelosi, who raised $3 million for Democratic candidates that cycle, said she was not running as a woman, but "the fact that I am a woman is an enhancement because we absolutely must have diversity in the leadership." But Republicans barely held onto their majority, and the race for majority whip was moot. But not for long. Michigan's Republican legislature put Bonior in a district it was plain he could not win, and he decided to run for governor. Pelosi and her allies pushed him to resign as minority whip, and Pelosi was off and running against Hoyer. Pelosi said that Democrats needed to refocus on grassroots organization, money and message. Some supporters played up her potential to become a celebrity— "a glamorous grandmother who knocks people off their feet," as Hawaii's Neil Abercrombie put it. With nearly unanimous support from the 32 California Democrats and from most women members, Pelosi started off with a strong base. But her support crossed ideological lines. She was nominated by John Murtha, a mostly hawkish and cultural conservative Vietnam veteran from the coal country of western Pennsylvania, with a following among old-line Democrats—an alliance similar to that between Phil Burton and the hard-bitten conservative Wayne Hays from the coal country of eastern Ohio a quarter-century before. Pelosi won by a convincing 118-95 margin in October 2001, in a much smaller and more liberal Democratic Caucus than the one that rejected Phil Burton 148-147 in 1976. She had 29 fewer votes than Burton; Hoyer won 53 fewer votes than Jim Wright, a measure of the reduction of moderate and conservative ranks in the Democratic Caucus.

As whip, Pelosi moved quickly to assert herself, sometimes independently from Minority Leader Dick Gephardt. She sparked controversy when she contributed $10,000 to Representative Lynn Rivers in a redistricting-forced Michigan primary against John Dingell—the ranking Democrat on Energy and Commerce, who had been a strong supporter of Hoyer for whip. Normally, party leaders do not take sides in such elections. Dingell handily won the primary. Her biggest conflict came in fall 2002 when she actively encouraged opponents of the resolution authorizing the use of force in Iraq, which Gephardt had enthusiastically endorsed with George W. Bush at the White House. Pelosi contended that supporters had not made the case for using force, and that she had seen no evidence that Iraq "poses an imminent threat to our nation." To the surprise of many, her efforts helped win 126 Democratic votes against the resolution, while only 81 backed the position of Gephardt, which also was backed by Democratic Caucus chairman Martin Frost. In retrospect, that split signaled the transition in the caucus—and showed that Pelosi, who had brushed aside former friends and allies like Bonior and Hoyer on her way to power, was willing to brush aside Gephardt too. Once the disappointing 2002 election results were in and Gephardt said that he was stepping down, Pelosi had all but locked up the support of a majority of the caucus. Martin Frost announced his candidacy with warnings that the selection of Pelosi might create a "permanent minority party";

he withdrew from the contest a day later, conceding that he could not win. Harold Ford made a belated, quixotic bid designed to appeal to a combination of blacks and New Democrats, but Pelosi won 177-29.

As Democratic leader in the House, she brought a burst of energy—and favorable press coverage—to a party that badly needed it. She showed hands-on management in selecting members for House committee vacancies and developing a Democratic message designed to highlight the shortcomings of the Bush agenda. There were bruised feelings over some committee assignments, particularly of Max Sandlin to Ways and Means (he was dating one of Pelosi's daughters), but even allies of Hoyer and Frost credited her with bringing a breath of fresh air and enthusiasm to party deliberations and a critical conservative reporter called her "charming, gracious and constructively energetic." As Republicans pressed their agenda, Pelosi declared that Democrats would take "a party position" in opposition to the Republican Medicare/prescription drug bill. But 16 Democrats voted for the final deal in November 2003, providing the critical margin for passage; she was largely silent about the renegades, many of whom were responding to local pressures. This was a painful lesson for Pelosi in the limited power of the minority leader in the House. She called President Bush an "incompetent" leader for his handling of the war in Iraq. Working with Robert Matsui as chairman of the DCCC, she tirelessly traveled the country raising money and boosting local candidates. If she became Speaker, Pelosi pledged, she would reform the House to give a greater voice to all members and assure fairness. She cited Democratic gains of open seats in Kentucky and South Dakota in special elections in early 2004 as proof that the political tide was turning their way. But the three-seat loss in the November election turned out to be yet another crushing disappointment for House Democrats, though Pelosi noted correctly that they won a net gain apart from the effects of the 2003 Texas redistricting. She also cast some of the blame on the presidential campaign of John Kerry.

In early 2005, she firmly insisted that House Democrats would not sit down with Republicans on Social Security until they removed personal retirement accounts from discussion. The declining job approval of George W. Bush and the rising prospects of Democrats in the 2006 election helped her establish and maintain party discipline. She saluted her longtime supporter John Murtha's November 2005 speech calling for a redeployment of troops out of Iraq and suggested without saying so that it would be the party's position. "A vote on the war is an individual vote. It may be viewed as the position of the party, it is not. But I do know that a majority of House Democrats will support Mr. Murtha." Hoyer, in contrast, said withdrawing from Iraq would be a "disaster." Pelosi paid careful attention to critics who said she was trying to impose San Francisco liberalism on the party. Hoyer, whatever his private feelings, declared in June 2006 that he had no intention of challenging Pelosi if once again Democrats failed to win a majority. "If we lose, it will not be Nancy Pelosi's fault. She's done everything she possibly can. Win, lose or draw, she's going to be our leader." Just days later Murtha announced he was running for majority leader, presumably against Hoyer, and said that Pelosi neither encouraged nor discouraged him from saying so. Pelosi faced some criticism from the Congressional Black Caucus when she removed William Jefferson from the Ways and Means Committee after federal authorities found $90,000 cash in his home freezer, and she faced opposition from the left in San Francisco for her refusal to vote against military appropriations. "The money is for the troops. I'm not prepared to go against the troops having the equipment they need." In the Democratic Caucus in May 2006 she came out firmly against impeachment and censure of George W. Bush and reined in John Conyers, ranking Democrat on Judiciary, who was fond of talking of such things. For months House Democrats struggled to come up with something in the nature of a platform for 2006, and after many postponements emerged with a "six for '06" program of increasing the minimum wage and enacting the remaining recommendations of the 9/11 Commission. Pelosi campaigned tirelessly across the country and was rewarded with a Democratic majority on November 7.

"I understand my role as leader of the Democrats. And I very, very much respect that I will be the Speaker of the House, not of the Democrats," she said when it was clear Democrats had won—not an accurate forecast, perhaps, and a bit of boilerplate, yet representing some sincere hope in her as it had in her Republican and Democratic predecessors. She said the resignation of Donald Rumsfeld was "a fresh start toward a new policy in Iraq, signaling a willingness on the part of the president to work with the Congress to devise a better way forward" and told Fox News's Brit Hume that Iraq was "a problem to be solved, not a war to be won." She made some missteps along the way, as new leaders often do. She vigorously supported John Murtha for majority leader, as Murtha said, "There's Nancy Pelosi, Dave Obey and myself, and then Hoyer is listed after me in the power plays." Hoyer was supported by most of the Blue Dogs and most freshmen and by senior incoming chairmen like John Dingell, Henry Waxman, Ike Skelton, Jim Oberstar and Barney Frank, and won 149-86. She finessed DCCC Chairman Rahm Emanuel, who wanted to serve as majority whip as a reward for his role in capturing the House, by persuading him to take the caucus chairmanship with newly-broadened responsibilities, and gave the majority whip position to the very well-liked James Clyburn. She did see her candidate John Larson beat Hoyer's, Joseph Crowley, for vice chairman 116-87. Pelosi had long been at odds with Jane Harman, the ranking Democrat on Intelligence, who had voted for the Iraq war resolution and was determined not to allow her to chair the committee. But the next Democrat in seniority, Alcee Hastings, although bright and charming, had been impeached and removed from his office as federal judge by a Democratic Congress (John Conyers was one of the impeachment prosecutors). After an embarrassing interval, the position went to Silvestre Reyes.

Pelosi staged four days of celebration of her elevation as speaker—an excessive display, said some Republicans, though Newt Gingrich had arranged celebrations of similar magnitude though different style with his elevation to the job. First, Little Italy in Baltimore, then the Trinity College chapel, the Italian embassy (with Tony Bennett recounting which part of his anatomy he left in San Francisco), brunch at the Capitol, dinner at the Building Museum, a reception at the Cannon House Office Building. As she assumed the office which put her third in line for the presidency, she said, "This is an historic moment, for Congress, and for the women of this country. It is a moment for which we have waited more than 200 years. For our daughters and granddaughters, today we have broken the marble ceiling. To our daughters and granddaughters, the sky is the limit." Minority Leader John Boehner echoed the sentiment as he handed her the gavel that Dick Gephardt handed Newt Gingrich 12 years before, "In a few moments, I'll have the high privilege of handing the gavel of the House of Representatives to a woman for the first time in history. Whether you're a Republican, a Democrat or an Independent, this is a cause for celebration."

There was some awkwardness in her first months as Speaker. The 100 hours to pass the "six for '06" program turned out to be 100 legislative hours, stretched over a couple of weeks. A request for a military plane to fly her to her district seemed to be a request for a huge plane with room for relatives, staffers and campaign contributors; but Speaker Dennis Hastert had had use of military planes to go back to his Illinois district, and Pelosi not unreasonably wanted aircraft that could fly nonstop to San Francisco. She was criticized when the Democrats' minimum wage law exempted American Samoa, where the big employer is the tuna plant owned by San Francisco-based Del Monte. But it seems unlikely that there was some local connection there. Beneath the velvet glove, Pelosi continued to operate with something like an iron fist. One of her key issues is reducing carbon dioxide emissions, because many scientists believe that they have increased and will increase global warming. So she announced the creation of a Select Committee on Energy Independence and Global Warming, to be headed by Energy and Commerce member Edward Markey. Energy and Commerce Chairman John Dingell protested; Pelosi said the special committee would have no legislative power. But clearly this was a dust-off pitch directed at one of Congress's all-time heavy hitters. And, one must add, by one of Congress's all-time heavy hitters. Nancy Pelosi, gracious in manner, always ready with a chocolate and a compliment, has proved herself to be a hardball politician of whom her predecessors Phil and Sala Burton would have been proud.

Pelosi represents one of the most Democratic districts in the nation and regularly wins with percentages in excess of 80%. Anti-war activist Cindy Sheehan has said she will run as an independent against Pelosi in 2008 because the Speaker failed to move to impeach President George W. Bush.

NINTH DISTRICT

Rep. Barbara Lee (D)

Elected April 1998, 5th full term; b. July 16, 1946, El Paso, TX; home, Oakland; Mills Col., B.A. 1973, U. of CA, M.A. 1975; no religious affiliation; divorced.

Elected Office: CA Assembly, 1990-96; CA Senate, 1996-98.

Professional Career: Chief of Staff, U.S. Rep. Ron Dellums, 1975-87.

DC Office: 2444 RHOB, 20515, 202-225-2661; Fax: 202-225-9817; Web site: lee.house.gov.

District Offices: Oakland, 510-763-0370.

Committees: *Appropriations* (27th of 37 D): Legislative Branch; State, Foreign Operations & Related Programs; Labor, HHS, Education & Related Agencies.

Group Ratings

	ADA	ACLU	AFS	LCV	ITIC	NTU	COC	ACU	CFG	FRC
2006	100	100	100	100	14	20	20	4	8	0
2005	95	—	100	89	—	21	31	4	7	0

National Journal Ratings

	2005 LIB	—	2005 CONS		2006 LIB	—	2006 CONS
Economic	94%	—	0%		90%	—	9%
Social	97%	—	2%		97%	—	0%
Foreign	96%	—	0%		95%	—	0%

Key Votes of the 109th Congress

1. Estate Tax Repeal	N	5. Limit Interstate Abortion	N	9. Build Border Fence	N
2. Limit CAFE Standards	N	6. Extend Patriot Act	N	10. CAFTA	N
3. FY06 Spending Curb	N	7. Bar Same Sex Marriage	N	11. Oppose Iraq Withdrawal	N
4. Drilling in ANWR	N	8. Stem Cell Research $	Y	12. Detainee Tribunals	N

Election Results

2006 general	Barbara Lee (D)	167,245	(86%)	($1,054,307)
	John Den Dulk (R)	20,786	(11%)	($38,769)
	Other	5,655	(3%)	
2006 primary	Barbara Lee (D)	unopposed		
2004 general	Barbara Lee (D)	215,630	(85%)	($783,143)
	Claudia Bermudez (R)	31,278	(12%)	($482,942)
	Other	8,131	(3%)	

Prior Winning Percentages: 2002 (81%); 2000 (85%); 1998 (83%); 1998 (67%)

The People		Race/Ethnic Origin	Ancestry	
Area size:	152 sq. mi.	35.2% White	German: 5.9%	English: 5.1%
Urban population:	99.9%	26.0% Black	Irish: 5.0%	
Rural population:	0.1%	15.4% Asian	**2004 Presidential Vote**	
Pop. 2000:	639,088	0.4% Native Am.	Kerry (D) 228,642	(86%)
Pop. 2005 (est):	615,585	0.4% Hawaiian	Bush (R) 33,450	(13%)
Median income:	$44,314	3.6% Two+ races	Other 4,082	(2%)
Poverty status:	16.9%	0.4% Other	**2000 Presidential Vote**	
Military veterans:	8.4%	18.7% Hispanic Origin	Gore (D) 184,030	(79%)
			Bush (R) 31,464	(13%)
			Other 18,868	(8%)
			Cook Partisan Voting Index: D +38	

Occupation	Blue collar: 17.3%	White collar: 69.0%	Gray collar: 13.7%

Oakland and Berkeley, on the East Bay opposite San Francisco, stand today on one of the lushest sites in America, overlooking the Bay Bridge and the Golden Gate, basking in the sunshine that is more common here than across the Bay. Both cities are the homes of great institutions, but in different ways they are also museum pieces, antiques from a moment in the 1960s when both, especially Berkeley, gained identities that became hard to shake. Berkeley was founded as a university town, named after the 18th century Irish philosopher Bishop George Berkeley, for his proclamation, "Westward the course of empire takes its way." Famous for years as the home of first-rate scholarship at the University of California, Berkeley became famous politically in 1964 as the home of student rebellion when the Free Speech Movement, protesting an administrator's refusal to let students set up a card table to sign up volunteers for Lyndon Johnson's campaign, led to months of riots, student strikes and classroom confrontation. In 1969, students led protests at "People's Park," a lot owned by the university, and Governor Ronald Reagan sent in the National Guard to protect state property from conversion to a playground: an episode in which both sides relished the confrontation. Berkeley in the 1960s gave birth to a street culture that still exists. Its denizens made common cause with the quasi-political Black Panthers from nearby Oakland, and smoked marijuana with the Hell's Angels motorcycle gang. Berkeley's city council features bizarre political wars in which Democrats who are very liberal by national standards are the right wing. The campus, with its view of the Bay, remains beautiful, and old buildings like the shingled Claremont Hotel are grand. But Berkeley has had little commercial development, and its public facilities have an almost Third World look.

Oakland has a different history, centered around commerce and building its own civic institutions (Gertrude Stein was wrong: there is a there there). It became the western terminus of the transcontinental railroad in 1870 and was connected by ferry to San Francisco; it has always had heavy industry, and its port today is the busiest on the bay. The docks attracted young roustabouts like the writer Jack London, after whom a downtown square is named; civic affairs were run by the local elite, like the Knowland family who owned the *Oakland Tribune*. With the Bay Area's largest black community, Oakland spawned the Black Panthers; African-Americans took control of city government in the 1970s and the *Tribune* in the 1980s. Onto the scene came Jerry Brown, governor of California 20 years earlier, unsuccessful presidential candidate in 1976, 1980 and 1992; in 1998, he ran an unorthodox campaign for mayor, and won. Brown irritated local factions by firing department heads and ignoring longstanding alliances, but he seemed to take seriously his mission of propelling Oakland to prominence. He sounded like a conservative, with his tough talk on crime and advocacy of big commercial development projects that drove up rents; he set up a military high school. Crime rates dropped and the local economy thrived, partly with the growth of middle-income refugees from the exorbitant housing costs of San Francisco. But many long-time residents, especially African-Americans, complained about rising costs and they, in turn, moved to the outskirts; the black population has fallen from 47% in 1980 to about 30% in 2005. After two terms, Brown was elected state attorney general; his successor as mayor was former Congressman Ron Dellums—a revival of the 1970s liberals.

The 9th Congressional District of California consists of Oakland and Berkeley, plus Castro Valley. It has the largest black percentage of any northern California district (26% in 2000, down from 32% in 1990); almost as high were its percentages of Hispanics (19%) and Asians (15%). Politically, it may be the most activist left-wing district in the nation. It voted 86%-13% for John Kerry.

The congresswoman from the 9th District is Barbara Lee, a Democrat first chosen in an April 1998 special election. Lee grew up in Texas and the San Fernando Valley, where she was the first black cheerleader at her high school. She graduated from Mills College in Oakland, got a degree in social work at Berkeley, and has brought that training to her work since then. She started a community mental health center in Berkeley and then worked as a staffer for 12 years for Congressman Ron Dellums, a liberal Democrat who became chairman of the Armed Services Committee. Lee was elected to the California Assembly in 1990 and to the Senate in 1996. After Dellums announced he was resigning, he endorsed Lee as his successor; she won the special election with 67% of the vote.

In the House, Lee stands at the far left of the ideological spectrum. She wants to reduce the nation's weapons stockpiles and cut Pentagon spending sharply. She won enactment of her bill to require that federal cancer data collection include information on benign brain tumors in order to assist health research. In negotiations with Henry Hyde, she increased support for international AIDS programs, but later criticized administration emphasis on abstinence programs. After a visit to Cuba, she called for steps to end the 40-year embargo of Castro's island; the House accepted her amendment to lift restrictions on education travel to Cuba. As co-chair of the Progressive Caucus, she laid out an agenda with three priorities: economic justice and security, protection of civil rights and liberties, and promotion of global peace. She was a founder of the Out of Iraq Caucus. In mid-2006, she abandoned a plan to challenge Carolyn Cheeks Kilpatrick as head of the Congressional Black Caucus, and instead became vice-chair. In 2007, Speaker Pelosi gave Lee a seat on the Appropriations Committee, where she opposed party leaders on their timetable to withdraw from Iraq.

Lee has consistently opposed military action to the point of being a lonely but principled voice. She criticized Bill Clinton's bombing of Iraq in 1998. As most Democrats voted to authorize bombing of Serbia in 1999, Lee was the only House member to oppose a resolution supporting U.S. troops. In September 2001 she was the only member of Congress to vote against the resolution authorizing the use of force in response to the terrorist attacks. Her vote brought a torrent of national attention and protest, but there were supportive rallies in her district. She received threats of violence and the Capitol police provided her with 24-hour protection. During debate in October 2002 on whether to authorize the use of force in Iraq, Lee offered an alternative calling for diplomatic rather than military action; it was defeated 355-72.

With Democrats in the majority, Lee became outspoken in seeking a quick end to the Iraq war. In March 2007, she was among the seven liberal members who initially voted against the House Democrats' war funding bill, because she believed that it made too many concessions to the Bush administration. "My conscience is that we can't put up more money to fund this war," said Lee, who supported what she called "a fully funded withdrawal." As a new member on the Appropriations Committee, she was the only Democrat in committee who voted against the withdrawal timetable assembled by party leaders; then, she was 1 of 14 Democrats to vote against the funding bill on the House floor. But, despite some occasionally confrontational rhetoric, Lee backed away from efforts to seek the votes of additional Democrats to defeat that alternative, and has praised Speaker Nancy Pelosi's handling of the Iraq war issue. "She did what she could to get the maximum number of votes to begin the end of the war."

Lee has been reelected easily. She won the 2002 primary 85%-15% over an opponent who criticized her vote against military force. In the 2006 general, John Den Dulk ran against Lee and said that she "speaks for bin Laden, not for me." Lee won 86%-11%.

TENTH DISTRICT

Rep. Ellen Tauscher (D)

Elected 1996, 6th term; b. Nov. 15, 1951, Newark, NJ; home, Alamo; Seton Hall U., B.A. 1973; Catholic; divorced.

Professional Career: Wall Street Invest. Banker, 1974-88, NYSE member, 1977-79; Founder & CEO, Registry Cos., 1992-96.

DC Office: 2459 RHOB, 20515, 202-225-1880; Fax: 202-225-5914; Web site: www.house.gov/tauscher.

District Offices: Antioch, 925-757-7187; Fairfield, 707-428-7792; Walnut Creek, 925-932-8899.

Committees: *Armed Services* (11th of 34 D): Strategic Forces (Chmn.); Oversight & Investigations; Air & Land Forces. *Transportation & Infrastructure* (12th of 41 D): Highways & Transit; Water Resources & Environment; Aviation.

Group Ratings

	ADA	ACLU	AFS	LCV	ITIC	NTU	COC	ACU	CFG	FRC
2006	95	95	100	100	86	13	40	12	16	0
2005	90	—	100	94	—	17	52	8	13	8

National Journal Ratings

	2005 LIB — 2005 CONS		2006 LIB — 2006 CONS	
Economic	68%	— 32%	79%	— 18%
Social	79%	— 21%	76%	— 23%
Foreign	76%	— 24%	73%	— 26%

Key Votes of the 109th Congress

1. Estate Tax Repeal	N	5. Limit Interstate Abortion	N	9. Build Border Fence	N
2. Limit CAFE Standards	N	6. Extend Patriot Act	N	10. CAFTA	N
3. FY06 Spending Curb	N	7. Bar Same Sex Marriage	N	11. Oppose Iraq Withdrawal	N
4. Drilling in ANWR	N	8. Stem Cell Research	$	12. Detainee Tribunals	N

Election Results

2006 general	Ellen Tauscher (D) 130,859	(66%)	($830,579)
	Darcy Linn (R) 66,069	(34%)	($7,366)
2006 primary	Ellen Tauscher (D) .... unopposed		
2004 general	Ellen Tauscher (D) 182,750	(66%)	($780,196)
	Jeff Ketelson (R) 95,349	(34%)	($159,219)

Prior Winning Percentages: 2002 (76%); 2000 (53%); 1998 (53%); 1996 (49%)

The People		Race/Ethnic Origin	Ancestry	
Area size:	1,085 sq. mi.	65.4% White	German: 10.7%	Irish: 9.1%
Urban population:	96.5%	5.7% Black	English: 8.2%	
Rural population:	3.5%	9.1% Asian	**2004 Presidential Vote**	
Pop. 2000:	639,088	0.4% Native Am.	Kerry (D) 169,373	(59%)
Pop. 2005 (est):	698,326	0.4% Hawaiian	Bush (R) 117,037	(40%)
Median income:	$65,245	3.7% Two+ races	Other 3,098	(1%)
Poverty status:	6.3%	0.2% Other	**2000 Presidential Vote**	
Military veterans:	13.4%	15.0% Hispanic Origin	Gore (D) 145,996	(55%)
			Bush (R) 109,149	(41%)
			Other 9,273	(4%)
			Cook Partisan Voting Index: D + 9	

Occupation   Blue collar: 17.8%   White collar: 69.0%   Gray collar: 13.2%

In the 1950s, when the streets of San Francisco and Oakland were already crowded, the rolling grasslands on the east of the mountain ridges, over the hill and through the tunnel from Oakland, were still mostly empty. In the years since, they have filled up. Freeways took the first commuters through the Caldecott Tunnel to the woodsy trail-like roads of Orinda and Lafayette; I-580 brought people east from the southern East Bay towns to the Amador Valley and Livermore, site of one of the nation's nuclear laboratories, with nuclear warhead research and the world's fastest computer; I-680 running north-south provided a spine for businesses and shopping centers up and down the San Ramon Valley, from burgeoning Concord through Walnut Creek in Contra Costa County and points south; BART stations in Walnut Creek and Orinda took commuters to downtown San Francisco. Not all of the inhabitable areas are filled in yet, and local voters have passed measures to keep growth inside an urban limit. But what has evolved in this sunny land, shielded by the mountains from the ocean fogs and rains, is an advanced civilization of highly skilled and educated people. Affluent and generally tolerant of—if a little put off by—what happens in San Francisco, they are respectful of economic markets and wary of government, but concerned about preserving a physical environment that is one of America's most pleasant.

This remains the heart of the 10th Congressional District of California. The 2001 redistricting removed the San Ramon Valley south of Walnut Creek, and added part of the Sacramento River Delta and parts of booming Solano County to the north—Fairfield (now the largest city in the 10th), nearby Travis Air Force Base with its C-17 cargo haulers, and Suisun City. This made the district more working-class and Democratic. In 2004 John Kerry carried the district 59%-40%—a solid margin, but nothing like his one-sided margins in the San Francisco and Oakland-Berkeley districts.

The congresswoman from the 10th District is Ellen Tauscher, a Democrat first elected in 1996. Tauscher grew up in New Jersey, where her father ran a grocery store; at 25, she became the youngest woman with a seat on the New York Stock Exchange, where she was a stock trader and investment banker. In 1989, she and her then-husband, owner of Vanstar (formerly ComputerLand), moved to California. After a difficult childbirth followed by trouble finding quality childcare for her daughter, Tauscher started the ChildCare Registry, the first company to offer (for $140) background information on child-care providers. In 1996 she challenged Republican Congressman Bill Baker, a fiscal conservative who was also a tart-tongued conservative on cultural issues. She ran as a moderate Democrat and spent liberally of her own money, some $1.7 million in all. Baker ran ads comparing her to a lottery winner buying a congressional seat. Tauscher's ads called Baker an "extremist" on gun control, abortion and the environment. This proved a winning combination, though only barely. Tauscher won 49%-47%.

In the House, Tauscher has a more moderate and activist bipartisan voting record than other Bay Area Democrats—"Tauscherism," as *Time* once called it. She voted for the Republicans' impeachment inquiry resolution and called on Bill Clinton to stop "legal hairsplitting and speak plain English to the American people." On transportation issues, she has taken the lead for the region on behalf of highway projects and Bay Area transit plans. She has shown the ability to make bipartisan deals: "I feel like I'm back on Wall Street. If you have a sensory touch that can tell there's a deal in the room—and I have a great one—you can get things done." Alone among Bay Area Democrats, she favored normal trade relations with China; after initially opposing trade promotion authority, which disappointed the high-tech industry, she voted for the final version. But she grew critical of the Bush administration's trade policies, and opposed CAFTA. Despite her Wall Street background, she called Republican proposals for personal retirement accounts in Social Security "ill-advised." In 2005, she became chair of the New Democrats, with a pledge to find new areas of collaboration, including a greater emphasis on national security, but lamented that Republicans were not amenable. Once her party took control, she moved the New Democrats into a key role in building consensus in their party.

On the Armed Services Committee, the activist Tauscher was an early advocate of improving America's homeland security and the nation's ability to deal with the threat of terrorism, which led her to join a bipartisan group urging creation of the Homeland Security Department. She supported use of force in Iraq. She criticized the failure of the Pentagon to provide information to Congress, including intelligence on Iraq and nonproliferation programs. She has worked to stop the spread of nuclear, chemical and biological weapons, including the "bunker buster," and to shift research from nuclear to conventional weapons. She led Democratic calls to increase military forces, including 40,000 in increased Army troop levels. Worried about the future of Travis, which is home to 13,000 jobs and is a center of the Air Mobility Command, Tauscher called the "precipitous rush to close bases . . . just irresponsible"; Travis survived the review. In the majority, she chairs the Strategic Forces Subcommittee—a good fit for the representative of Livermore Lab.

Among Democrats, Tauscher showed her centrism and independence with early support for Steny Hoyer against San Francisco's Nancy Pelosi in the 2001 contest for minority whip. That displeased many local colleagues and may have been a reason the redistricters removed San Ramon Valley from her district. She complained and accused other Democrats of giving her a district where her moderate voting record would be a liability. In the old 10th District, Tauscher had competitive re-election contests. In 2002, she was the only California Democrat without Republican opposition. In 2004 and 2006, she easily defeated token opponents. Although still a centrist, she has become more aggressive in showing her partisan colors, perhaps in part because of intra-party pressures; she has been a target of Internet-based progressive activists who fault her as being insufficiently liberal and too compliant with business interests. Tauscher does not discourage speculation that she might run if either of California's Democratic senators steps down, but neither has shown any inclination to do so and the crowd of aspirants is growing. When liberal activists promised to challenge her in the 2008 Democratic primary, she moved quickly to defend herself; the opposition faded, and no serious local challenger stepped forward through the summer of 2007.

ELEVENTH DISTRICT

Rep. Jerry McNerney (D)

Elected 2006, 1st term; b. June 18, 1951, Albuquerque, NM; home, Pleasanton; Attended U.S. Military Academy, 1969-71, U. of NM, B.S. 1973, M.S. 1975, Ph.D. 1981; Catholic; married (Mary).

Professional Career: National security contractor, Sandia National Laboratories, 1979-85; Engineer, U.S. Windpower, Kenetech, 1985-94; Energy consultant, 1994-99; CEO, start-up wind turbine manufacturer, 2000-06.

DC Office: 312 CHOB, 20515, 202-225-1947; Fax: 202-225-4060; Web site: mcnerney.house.gov.

District Offices: Pleasanton, 925-737-0727; Stockton, 209-476-8552.

Committees: *Science & Technology* (12th of 24 D): Research & Science Education; Energy & Environment. *Select Committee on Energy Independence and Global Warming* (9th of 9 D). *Transportation & Infrastructure* (40th of 41 D): Water Resources & Environment; Highways & Transit. *Veterans' Affairs* (14th of 16 D): Economic Opportunity.

Group Ratings and Key Votes: Newly Elected

Election Results

2006 general	Jerry McNerney (D)	109,868	(53%)	($2,422,962)
	Richard Pombo (R)	96,396	(47%)	($4,629,983)
2006 primary	Jerry McNerney (D)	23,598	(53%)	
	Steve Filson (D)	12,744	(28%)	
	Steve Thomas (D)	8,390	(19%)	
2004 general	Richard Pombo (R)	163,582	(61%)	($1,017,709)
	Jerry McNerney (D)	103,587	(39%)	($154,701)

The People		Race/Ethnic Origin	Ancestry	
Area size:	2,316 sq. mi.	64.1% White	German: 11.4%	Irish: 8.3%
Urban population:	90.1%	3.4% Black	English: 7.5%	
Rural population:	9.9%	8.7% Asian	**2004 Presidential Vote**	
Pop. 2000:	639,088	0.5% Native Am.	Bush (R) 151,397	(54%)
Pop. 2005 (est):	766,101	0.2% Hawaiian	Kerry (D) 127,102	(45%)
Median income:	$61,996	3.2% Two+ races	Other 2,306	(1%)
Poverty status:	8.8%	0.2% Other	**2000 Presidential Vote**	
Military veterans:	12.0%	19.7% Hispanic Origin	Bush (R) 125,876	(53%)
			Gore (D) 106,354	(45%)
			Other 5,882	(2%)
			Cook Partisan Voting Index: R + 3	

Occupation	Blue collar: 19.1%	White collar: 67.6%	Gray collar: 13.3%

People from back East looking for clues about California might consider avoiding Beverly Hills and Nob Hill and taking a look at the Central Valley directly east of San Francisco. This is an old part of California with much recent growth. Stockton on the San Joaquin River was a Gold Rush trading town founded in 1847, named after Robert Stockton, the second U.S. military governor of California, who captured Santa Barbara and Los Angeles from Mexico and proclaimed California U.S. territory. The Central Valley around Stockton, criss-crossed with railroads and canals, became one of the world's greatest agriculture areas; the San Joaquin River channel was deepened to 37 feet and Stockton today is the Central Valley's ocean port. The rich farming attracted immigrants from all over: Mexicans coming up Route 99 joined North Dakotans flocking to the town of Lodi; Italian and Yugoslav immigrants bringing their Old World crops; Yankees and Okies bringing their distinct churches and systems of belief; and Southeast Asian refugees crowd into the older streets of Stockton. More recently, Stockton has positioned itself to take advantage of the region's economic strength by turning into a warehouse and distribution center for northern California. This growth came even though the farm economy was threatened by moves toward reducing water subsidies, the difficulty of attracting migrant workers for harvests, and declines in crop prices. But it may benefit because many of its crops (especially, fruits and vegetables) are not subject to the vagaries of federal controls, though the area is still a big cotton producer. And the Central Valley has also become a suburb: with the high cost of living in San Francisco, Bay Area workers with modest incomes are increasingly buying cheaper houses around Tracy and Stockton and commuting to work on I-580 past the windmills of Altamont, where some of the blades are shut down in winter to protect migrating birds. While the Bay area's population rose only 1%, Stockton's San Joaquin County had a population increase of 19% from 2000 to 2006; in that period, the Hispanic share grew from 30% to 35%. What was not long ago a rundown farm town has become a growing urban center, with a $125 million waterfront renovation project.

The 11th Congressional District of California includes much of this area plus the Bay Area suburbia of San Ramon Valley in Contra Costa County. The central part of Stockton is not in the district; rather, it is connected by a thin corridor to the 18th District further south in the valley. But the 11th does include northwest Stockton and most of the rest of San Joaquin County—Tracy, Lodi, and the almond center of Manteca. Connected to this is the adjacent town of Brentwood in Contra Costa County, the fastest-growing city in the Bay Area in the 1990s. The farm town of Morgan Hill anchors the far southern edge of the 11th in Santa Clara County. The San Ramon Valley towns— Danville and San Ramon in Contra Costa County and Dublin and Pleasanton in Alameda County, are much more affluent than the Central Valley parts of the district. Politically, both parts are Republican. It has been moving cautiously toward Republicans on cultural issues and on farm interests' hostility to environmental restrictions. The San Ramon Valley is the most Republican part of the Bay Area, but not very Republican by national standards, fairly liberal on cultural issues but conservative on economics. This district, whose lines were drawn by Republicans in 2001 to safeguard their interests, voted 54% for George W. Bush in 2004.

The new congressman from the 11th District is Jerry McNerney, a Democrat who won in one of the nastiest and most hard-fought contests of 2006. He defeated Richard Pombo, a local rancher in an area that many had called Pombo Country, leader of the property rights movement in Congress and the chairman of the House Resources Committee. McNerney's father was a union organizer in the 1930s and later worked for the U.S. Geological Survey in Albuquerque, where Jerry McNerney was born. Along with his twin brother, McNerney was sent to a military boarding school in Hays, Kansas, and he later won an appointment to the United States Military Academy at West Point; he left after two years because he opposed the war in Vietnam, and then went to the University of New Mexico for his bachelor's, master's and a doctorate degree in differential geometry. He spent several years as a contractor to Sandia National Laboratories, working on national security programs. In 1985, he moved to the private sector with U.S. Windpower; later, he consulted for several firms, including Pacific Gas & Electric, the Electric Power Research Institute, and other utility companies that built windmills in the Altamont Pass. He became chief executive of a firm that planned to manufacture wind turbines. McNerney, who named his daughter Windy, claimed that his work contributed to saving the equivalent of 8.3 million tons of carbon dioxide. Prior to running for Congress, he had never held elected office.

McNerney was an unlikely winner. Pombo crushed him 61%-39% in 2004, after McNerney secured the nomination as a write-in candidate. That led Democratic Congressional Campaign Committee officials to take the unusual step of endorsing another challenger in the 2006 primary because they didn't think much of McNerney's repeat bid. And in the general election, Pombo outspent McNerney by nearly 2-to-1. Despite all of those factors, McNerney managed to turn the election into a referendum on the controversial seven-term incumbent. Pombo, in fact, had come under a withering assault long before Democrats chose their nominee. Environmental groups—including the Defenders of Wildlife, the Sierra Club, and the League of Conservation Voters—teamed up for a well-funded grassroots campaign against the Republican chairman they labeled an "eco-thug" and "Wildlife Enemy No. 1." Their first shot at Pombo came in the Republican primary, where he faced 78-year-old former Republican Congressman Pete McCloskey, a carpetbagger in this district, who was best known for running against the renomination of President Richard Nixon in 1972 and calling for his impeachment. Pombo was attacked over his ethics and spending practices. The campaign contributions he received from disgraced lobbyist Jack Abramoff also came under close scrutiny because Abramoff's Native American and overseas clients fell under the jurisdiction of Pombo's committee. With campaign help from Vice President Cheney, Pombo won his primary by an unimpressive margin, 62%-32%. In the Democratic primary, the DCCC unsuccessfully urged local legislators to run and then endorsed Steve Filson, an airline pilot and political neophyte who turned out to be a disappointment. McNerney, endorsed by the state party and by local organized labor, soundly defeated Filson, 53%-28%.

Even after McNerney's impressive primary upset, and with the endorsement of McCloskey, the DCCC was not sold on his viability. But over the summer, he began picking up extensive "netroots" support and captured the imagination of liberal Internet activists. He also won the "Grassroots All-Star" online voting contest run by Democracy for America, a political action committee inspired by Howard Dean. The group's endorsement triggered campaign contributions for McNerney from around the country. As McNerney inched closer in the polls, the DCCC began to air ads against Pombo. McNerney, emphasizing his background as an energy consultant, focused his attacks on Pombo's environmental voting record. Campaigning for Pombo, President Bush said that each of them was a straight-shooter with a background in ranching. The two candidates disagreed on virtually every issue: Iraq, Social Security personal accounts, oil exploration in Alaska, and permanent repeal of the estate tax. Each candidate had plenty of money. But Pombo was running against a strong anti-Republican wind. McNerney won 53%-47%. In San Joaquin County, which cast a bit more than half of the vote, Pombo led 51%-49%. But McNerney won comfortably in the parts of the district closer to the Bay, with 54% in Contra Costa, 63% in Alameda, and 61% in Santa Clara.

He got seats on the Transportation and Infrastructure, Science and Technology, and Veterans Affairs Committees. Democratic leaders gave him an early opportunity to sponsor a bill that won House passage, 368-59: a pilot program to develop alternative water-source projects. Widely viewed as one of the most vulnerable Democratic freshmen, McNerney worked the district aggressively with gatherings called "Congress at Your Corner" and citizen advisory panels for issues such as agriculture, health care and small business. Pombo announced in May 2007 that he would not seek to win his seat back; former Assemblyman Dean Andal became the frontrunner for the Republican nomination after Assemblyman Guy Houston declined to run in the interests of avoiding a bruising primary.

TWELFTH DISTRICT

Rep. Tom Lantos (D)

Elected 1980, 14th term; b. Feb. 1, 1928, Budapest, Hungary; home, San Mateo; U. of WA, B.A. 1949, M.A. 1950, U. of CA, Ph.D. 1953; Jewish; married (Annette).

Professional Career: Economist, Bank of America, 1952-53; TV Commentator, San Francisco, 1955-63; Dir. of Intl. Programs, CA St. U., 1962-71; Advisor, U.S. Sen. Joseph R. Biden Jr., 1978-79; Mbr., Pres. Task Force on Defense & Foreign Policy, 1976; Prof., San Francisco St. U., 1950-80.

DC Office: 2413 RHOB, 20515, 202-225-3531; Fax: ; Web site: lantos.house.gov.

District Offices: San Mateo, 650-342-0300.

Committees: *Foreign Affairs* (Chmn. of 27 D). *Oversight & Government Reform* (2d of 23 D): Domestic Policy; National Security & Foreign Affairs.

Group Ratings

	ADA	ACLU	AFS	LCV	ITIC	NTU	COC	ACU	CFG	FRC
2006	100	91	100	92	43	10	33	9	5	0
2005	95	—	100	94	—	11	38	0	3	8

National Journal Ratings

	2005 LIB	—	2005 CONS		2006 LIB	—	2006 CONS
Economic	88%	—	12%		94%	—	0%
Social	76%	—	24%		83%	—	17%
Foreign	68%	—	32%		77%	—	20%

Key Votes of the 109th Congress

1. Estate Tax Repeal	N	5. Limit Interstate Abortion	N	9. Build Border Fence	N
2. Limit CAFE Standards	N	6. Extend Patriot Act	N	10. CAFTA	N
3. FY06 Spending Curb	N	7. Bar Same Sex Marriage	N	11. Oppose Iraq Withdrawal	N
4. Drilling in ANWR	N	8. Stem Cell Research $	Y	12. Detainee Tribunals	N

Election Results

2006 general	Tom Lantos (D)	138,650	(76%)	($695,534)
	Mike Moloney (R)	43,674	(24%)	
2006 primary	Tom Lantos (D)	61,510	(83%)	
	Kevin Hearle (D)	6,973	(9%)	
	Robert Barrows (D)	5,401	(7%)	
2004 general	Tom Lantos (D)	171,852	(68%)	($1,190,646)
	Mike Garza (R)	52,593	(21%)	
	Pat Gray (Green)	23,038	(9%)	($44,685)
	Other	5,116	(2%)	

Prior Winning Percentages: 2002 (68%); 2000 (75%); 1998 (74%); 1996 (72%); 1994 (67%); 1992 (69%); 1990 (66%); 1988 (71%); 1986 (74%); 1984 (70%); 1982 (57%); 1980 (46%)

The People		Race/Ethnic Origin	Ancestry	
Area size:	363 sq. mi.	48.2% White	Irish: 8.2%	German: 7.4%
Urban population:	99.9%	2.5% Black	Italian: 6.4%	
Rural population:	0.1%	28.5% Asian	**2004 Presidential Vote**	
Pop. 2000:	639,088	0.2% Native Am.	Kerry (D) 193,689	(72%)
Pop. 2005 (est):	626,324	0.9% Hawaiian	Bush (R) 73,740	(27%)
Median income:	$70,307	3.6% Two+ races	Other 2,646	(1%)
Poverty status:	5.4%	0.3% Other	**2000 Presidential Vote**	
Military veterans:	8.9%	15.7% Hispanic Origin	Gore (D) 164,490	(67%)
			Bush (R) 70,468	(29%)
			Other 11,103	(5%)
			Cook Partisan Voting Index: D +22	

Occupation	Blue collar: 14.6%	White collar: 72.8%	Gray collar: 12.6%

Running south from San Francisco is the Peninsula, which connects the city with the mainland of the United States. This is geologically interesting, and active, country: The San Andreas Fault runs just east of the Coast Range, underneath the reservoirs that store San Francisco's water supply. To the west are green mountains running down into the foggy ocean. To the east is a zone of flat land between mountain and bay, an unbroken chain of suburbs and urban settlement, with light industry and salt flats along the bay front, and residential neighborhoods and some commercial strips from the Bayshore Freeway up through the Junipero Serra Freeway atop the mountain ridge. Historically, the Peninsula has seemed separate from San Francisco. But Daly City and Pacifica on the ocean are a kind of extension of San Francisco's old working class districts, with boxy houses on streets looking out on the ocean or the freeway; now they are the home of many of the Bay Area's Asian immigrants and Asian supermarkets. Pacific Islanders, too: the mainland's biggest concentration of Samoans is in Daly City and the biggest concentration of Tongans in San Bruno; King Taufa'ahau Tupou IV of Tonga, who died in September 2006, had a house in the high-income suburb of Hillsborough, though most of the local Tongans live in poverty. On the Bay side is South San Francisco which, a sign on the side of San Bruno Mountain proclaims, is "the Industrial City." Actually, these days it is post-industrial, for it is here that Herb Boyer and Bob Swanson sketched on a napkin their plans for the first biotechnology company, Genentech; they bought space in an old warehouse on the waterfront near a Bethlehem Steel plant; today, Genentech has a market capitalization approaching $100 billion, and the area is one large biotech campus overlooking the Bay, with lawns, parkways and earth-tone office complexes, the center of the biotech industry. Further south, between the Bayshore Freeway and I-280, there are middle-class suburbs that are now also cities with office complexes—Millbrae, Burlingame, San Mateo, San Carlos.

The 12th Congressional District of California consists of these northern Peninsula suburbs plus the southwest quadrant of San Francisco—the city's middle-income Sunset district, with older houses amid unburied telephone and electric wires, lying on curving hills that were once sand dunes, and affluent St. Francis Wood and West Portal. It is an ethnically and racially diverse, economically productive part of America; 29% of its residents are Asian—the third highest of any district outside Hawaii—and another 16% are Hispanic. The economic orientation here was historically toward San Francisco, then south toward the Silicon Valley, now to its own burgeoning biotech industries. Income levels are among the highest in the state, very far above average. Politically, the Peninsula historically was a bastion of progressive Republicanism, a lively force in California from the election of Governor Hiram Johnson in 1910 until the liberal Democratic breakthrough in 1958. But that tradition is only a memory now. In national and California elections the 12th District is now overwhelmingly Democratic.

The congressman from the 12th District, Tom Lantos, has several distinctions, but none more important than the fact that he is the only Holocaust survivor ever to serve in Congress. Lantos was born in Hungary and grew up in Budapest. In 1944, as a teenager, he was sent to a labor camp, escaped, was captured and beaten, escaped again, then lived with his aunt in a building whose occupants were protected by Swedish diplomat Raoul Wallenberg. His wife Annette, his childhood sweetheart (and a first cousin of actress Zsa Zsa Gabor), also survived by going into hiding and escaping to Switzerland with fake documents; these two Holocaust survivors have two daughters and 17 grandchildren, one of whom performed a concert as a soprano soloist at the Kennedy Center in Washington, accompanied by Secretary of State Condoleezza Rice. Lantos immigrated to the United States in 1947, and graduated from the University of Washington and got a Ph.D. in economics at Berkeley. He taught economics at San Francisco State, made money as an investor and appeared on television as a foreign policy expert. He had the political insight to challenge a Republican incumbent in the Peninsula in 1980, a Republican year nationally though not so much here; he has shown great capacity for publicizing his crusades in congressional hearings and on television.

Lantos has spent much of his time in the House on foreign policy and is now chairman of the House Foreign Affairs Committee. The first major bill that he passed gave Wallenberg an honorary American citizenship. Unlike other Bay Area Democrats, he has not brought to his work an instinctive mistrust of American policy or doubts of American good intentions. He founded the Congressional Human Rights Caucus, focusing on Communist regimes as well as the right-wing dictatorships other liberal Democrats denounced. During the collapse of Communism, Lantos stayed in close touch with Eastern Europe, especially Hungary, as new democracies rose up. He sponsored the first U.S. aid to the newly free countries of Eastern Europe and strongly backed NATO expansion. He has attacked human rights violations in China, opposes normalizing of Chinese trade status and in September 2000 sponsored a resolution urging that Beijing not be selected as the site of the 2008 Olympics; in February 2006, he criticized Google, Yahoo, Microsoft and Cisco Systems for agreeing to comply with Internet censorship demands of China. He is among the most enthusiastic supporters of Israel and called for economic sanctions against Iraq back in 1988 for its gassing of the Kurds; he continued to support sanctions against Iraq in 2000 when other Bay area members tried to end them. He helped lead the debate in favor of the Iraq war resolution in October 2002, although he had urged that it be debated after the election. Later, he grew increasingly critical of the war effort and the pace and cost of reconstruction. In February 2007, he helped draft a House resolution to oppose George W. Bush's troop surge.

In 2004 Lantos sponsored a bill to keep off the UN Human Rights Commission nations that violate human rights themselves. In April 2002 he introduced a resolution expressing "solidarity with Israel in its fight against terrorism," co-sponsored by Majority Whip Tom DeLay. They delayed it at the request of the White House, but it passed 352-21 in May 2002. He worked with then-committee Chairman Henry Hyde to get $1.3 billion to fight AIDS around the world in December 2001 and $3 billion as down payment on the $15 billion pledged by Bush in May 2003. In 2005, he opposed Republican proposals to withhold U.S. dues if the UN failed to reorganize its operations. With Hyde, he won congressional approval in December 2006 of the agreement for export of U.S. nuclear technology to India in exchange for cooperation with international inspectors. He has been a leading advocate of trade sanctions against the regime in Myanmar.

Lantos was among the first members of Congress to visit Libya since the 1960s in January 2004 and hailed Muammar el-Qaddafi's renunciation of weapons of mass destruction; he said Libya had "turned the corner" but called for a measured response in line with Libyan actions. He proposed converting 25% of military aid to Egypt to economic assistance and got the House to pass in October 2004 a bill suspending aid to Ethiopia and Eritrea until they settled their border dispute. Lantos was among five members of Congress arrested during a protest at the Embassy of Sudan in April 2006. "If you're looking for lack of international morality, Darfur encompasses all aspects," he said. "I'm appalled by the relative lack of interest in most civilized countries. This is murder on a grand scale." Five months later, he helped to enact the Darfur Peace and Accountability Act, imposing sanctions on Sudan for its failure to end the genocide. When George W. Bush called for doubling aid to Palestinians in February 2005, Lantos said he would delay the aid until Arab countries made promised contributions; a year later, after Hamas won control of the Palestinian government, he called for strict limits on U.S. aid. In February 2006, he cosponsored a House-passed resolution that condemned Iran for violating nuclear non-proliferation agreements and calling for economic sanctions.

In the majority, Lantos moved away from his previous bipartisan approach and held numerous oversight hearings that were critical of Bush administration foreign policy. As an outspoken ally of Speaker Nancy Pelosi, he encouraged and was part of her controversial visit to Syria in April 2007, where they advocated what Lantos termed "the bipartisan foreign policy" of the United States. He said that Republican criticisms that the visit was inappropriate were "outrageous."

Lantos spent $1.7 million on his 1980 and 1982 campaigns and has won easily ever since. He helped his son-in-law Dick Swett get elected from the 2d District of New Hampshire in 1990 and 1992; Swett lost in 1994 and in the 1996 Senate race, as did Lantos's daughter Katrina Swett in the 2d District House race in 2002. She has indicated she will challenge Senator John Sununu in 2008. In 2004 Lantos had his first primary opposition in the 12th District since 1992, from two candidates who criticized his support of the war in Iraq. To that he said, "Had I been older and had I been in power, clearly I would have preferred in the mid-30s preempting Hitler because the Second

World War cost slightly over 50 million innocent lives." He won with 74% of the vote. In 2006, against token opposition from a poet who said that he didn't want to serve in Congress and a public relations executive who composed a rap song titled, "Run for Office," Lantos won 83% of the primary vote.

THIRTEENTH DISTRICT

Rep. Pete Stark (D)

Elected 1972, 18th term; b. Nov. 11, 1931, Milwaukee, WI; home, Fremont; MIT, B.S. 1953, U. of CA, M.B.A. 1960; Unitarian; married (Deborah).

Military Career: Air Force, 1955-57.

Professional Career: Founder, Beacon Savings & Loan Assn., 1961; Founder & Pres., Security Natl. Bank, Walnut Creek, 1963-72.

DC Office: 239 CHOB, 20515, 202-225-5065; Fax: 202-226-3805; Web site: www.house.gov/stark.

District Offices: Fremont, 510-494-1388.

Committees: *Joint Committee on Taxation* (2d of 5 D). *Ways & Means* (2d of 24 D): Health (Chmn.); Income Security & Family Support.

Group Ratings

	ADA	ACLU	AFS	LCV	ITIC	NTU	COC	ACU	CFG	FRC
2006	95	100	100	100	14	23	8	4	8	0
2005	90	—	100	100	—	24	32	0	7	0

National Journal Ratings

	2005 LIB	—	2005 CONS	2006 LIB	—	2006 CONS
Economic	94%	—	0%	78%	—	21%
Social	98%	—	0%	97%	—	0%
Foreign	96%	—	0%	95%	—	0%

Key Votes of the 109th Congress

1. Estate Tax Repeal	N	5. Limit Interstate Abortion	N	9. Build Border Fence	N
2. Limit CAFE Standards	N	6. Extend Patriot Act	N	10. CAFTA	N
3. FY06 Spending Curb	N	7. Bar Same Sex Marriage	N	11. Oppose Iraq Withdrawal	N
4. Drilling in ANWR	N	8. Stem Cell Research $	Y	12. Detainee Tribunals	N

Election Results

2006 general	Pete Stark (D)	110,756	(75%)	($645,573)
	George Bruno (R)	37,141	(25%)	($24,061)
2006 primary	Pete Stark (D)	unopposed		
2004 general	Pete Stark (D)	144,605	(72%)	($455,735)
	George Bruno (R)	48,439	(24%)	($31,883)
	Mark Stroberg (Lib)	8,877	(4%)	

Prior Winning Percentages: 2002 (71%); 2000 (70%); 1998 (71%); 1996 (65%); 1994 (65%); 1992 (60%); 1990 (58%); 1988 (73%); 1986 (70%); 1984 (70%); 1982 (61%); 1980 (55%); 1978 (65%); 1976 (71%); 1974 (71%); 1972 (53%)

The People		Race/Ethnic Origin	Ancestry	
Area size:	281 sq. mi.	38.4% White	German: 6.9%	Irish: 5.7%
Urban population:	99.3%	6.3% Black	English: 4.8%	
Rural population:	0.7%	28.2% Asian	**2004 Presidential Vote**	
Pop. 2000:	639,088	0.4% Native Am.	Kerry (D) 153,598	(71%)
Pop. 2005 (est):	642,543	0.8% Hawaiian	Bush (R) 60,559	(28%)
Median income:	$62,415	4.5% Two+ races	Other 2,378	(1%)
Poverty status:	7.1%	0.3% Other	**2000 Presidential Vote**	
Military veterans:	9.6%	21.1% Hispanic Origin	Gore (D) 126,477	(67%)
			Bush (R) 55,803	(30%)
			Other 6,472	(3%)
			Cook Partisan Voting Index: D +22	

Occupation   Blue collar: 22.3%   White collar: 66.8%   Gray collar: 10.9%

The East Bay is the workaday, unglamorous side of the San Francisco Bay area—a narrow strip of land between San Francisco Bay and the surprisingly high mountains that rise just to the east. The shoreline is not picturesque, with its closed-down Navy bases, docks, airports and salt evaporators. The Bay Bridge, bisected by Yerba Buena Island, cuts an inspiring figure, though it requires constant patching and is getting a new span; the San Mateo Bridge to the south is at best utilitarian. In World War Two, when the shipyards of Richmond and the Navy yard in Oakland were buzzing, the East Bay south of Oakland was still largely uninhabited farm fields. After the war, it filled up, south along the old Route 17: San Leandro, originally settled by Portuguese; Hayward with its Cal State University campus and seafood industry; Union City with its rail yards; Fremont, home of the NUMMI joint venture auto plant where Pontiac Vibes and Toyota Corollas are produced together; and Newark, with dozens of manufacturing plants that range from salt processing to computer network servers. Hit hard by the dot-com bust, the East Bay revived with biotech, construction and health care. Underneath is the Hayward Fault, not as famous as the San Andreas, but just as dangerous.

The 13th Congressional District of California is made up of this string of East Bay towns in Alameda County, with lower income than the Peninsula towns across the Bay. The district is racially and ethnically mixed in the California manner. Fremont is home to the Little Kabul neighborhood of Afghans; Koreans and other Asians have moved in large numbers not only to Fremont, but to Hayward and other East Bay towns. The district is 28% Asian—the fourth highest Asian percentage in any district outside Hawaii—21% Hispanic and 6% black. This has long been a Democratic area, and it has become more Democratic than ever: in 2004, John Kerry got 71% of the vote here.

The congressman from the 13th District is Pete Stark, a liberal Democrat and product of the peace movement of the 1960s, first elected in 1972. Stark grew up in Wisconsin, served in the Air Force, got an engineering degree at MIT and an M.B.A. at Berkeley, and in 1963 started a bank in Walnut Creek, which he later sold. He attracted attention, and accounts, all over the Bay Area when he put a giant peace symbol atop the bank headquarters and peace symbols on all checks. In 1972 he ran for Congress, spending his own money freely; he beat an 81-year-old incumbent in the primary 56%-22% and held on in the McGovern undertow to win the general with 53%. By his third term he had a safe seat back home and was on Ways and Means, on which he now is the number-two Democrat; he has regained the chairmanship of its Health Subcommittee.

Stark brought to that post a desire to use government powers to make health care more available, but his record of legislative success is mixed. He has expanded Medicare benefits and provided COBRA benefit continuation to younger workers. His major achievement was the Catastrophic Health Care Act of 1988, which created a new benefit for Medicare recipients, but then was repealed by an overwhelming vote in 1989 after an outpouring of public protest: the problem was that its tax on the high-income elderly was very unpopular while benefits seemed puny. He has supported universal health insurance in various forms. During his dozen years in the minority, Stark mostly criticized and found few areas of agreement with Republicans, and had testy personal dealings. He was one of two votes against the 1996 Kennedy-Kassebaum bill, on the grounds it did not include mental health coverage and extended patent protection for a drug. When George W. Bush presented his proposal for prescription drug coverage for seniors, Stark countered with a plan that would guarantee affordable and comprehensive coverage for all seniors under Medicare. But other than criticism from the sidelines, he played little role in the debate on the Medicare/ prescription drug bill in 2003. He led the second-guessers when new cost projections revealed that the 10-year cost had ballooned to $720 billion. "I told you so. We can't trust numbers provided by administration officials," he said. Stark continued to push to permit reimportation of prescription drugs and opposed trade agreements that barred that. When the AARP offered its own prescription-drug plan, he attacked the group for seeking to "leverage a trusting membership of America's seniors to pass legislation that you know will do little more than line your own pocket." In the majority, he moved to improve the children's health insurance program.

As the senior Democrat on the Joint Economic Committee, Stark produced reports that criticized Republican policies. He was one of two House members to vote against repeal of the 3% telephone excise tax. His willingness to go his own way extended to cultural issues when he was one of three who opposed the resolution denouncing the Ninth Circuit Court of Appeals decision that declared the Pledge of Allegiance unconstitutional. In March 2003 he called the bombing of Iraq "an act of extreme terrorism." He co-sponsored a plan to reinstate the military draft, and was on the losing side of a 402–2 vote on the proposal in October 2004.

Stark has a habit of making provocative comments about other members; he later conceded that some were "unnecessary." After he incorrectly stated at a committee hearing in May 2001 that all children of Republican Conference chairman J.C. Watts had been born out of wedlock, Watts confronted him in the House chamber and Stark reportedly gave a flippant response that further angered Watts. At a hearing on prescription drug coverage in February 2003, he said that George W. Bush did not have to pay a penny when he went to Alcoholics Anonymous to quit drinking (Bush has never said that he attended AA or that he was an alcoholic). In July 2003, when committee Democrats gathered in a room adjacent to the Ways and Means room and Chairman Bill Thomas called the Capitol Police to evict them, Stark called Thomas a "fascist." The *San Francisco Chronicle* reported "rumblings that it might be time for the veteran Congressman to retire," but Stark said, "I've got to keep running. I've got 2-year-old twins and I've got to get them through college. Our retirement plan is good, but it ain't that good." After reports in 2005 that Representative Duke Cunningham was being investigated for bribery with a defense industry lobbyist, Stark paid for an ad in *Congress Daily* that headlined, "Attention Powerful Lobbyists. House for sale by influential member of Congress."

Stark is next in line on Ways and Means behind chairman Charles Rangel. There has been talk that, should Rangel retire, another committee Democrat might challenge Stark for Rangel's post. It seems likely that Speaker Nancy Pelosi would protect her Bay Area colleague, but keep a tight leash on him. Despite occasional talk in his district of a serious primary challenge, well-known local politicians have shown no interest in running, and Stark seems even at his most flamboyant to be expressing the views of many Democrats in the district. In March 2007, he gained attention by saying in response to a survey that his religious affiliation is "a Unitarian who does not believe in a supreme being." Atheist groups rejoiced, claiming that Stark was the first member of Congress and the highest-ranking American politician to say he did not believe in God. There was no immediate impact on Capitol Hill or in his district.

FOURTEENTH DISTRICT

Rep. Anna Eshoo (D)

Elected 1992, 8th term; b. Dec. 13, 1942, New Britain, CT; home, Atherton; Canada Col., A.A. 1975; Catholic; divorced.

Elected Office: San Mateo Cnty. Bd. of Supervisors, 1982-92, Pres., 1986.

Professional Career: Chmn., San Mateo Cnty. Dem. Party, 1980; Chief of Staff, CA Assembly Speaker, 1981.

DC Office: 205 CHOB, 20515, 202-225-8104; Fax: 202-225-8890; Web site: www.eshoo.house.gov.

District Offices: Palo Alto, 650-323-2984.

Committees: *Energy & Commerce* (9th of 31 D): Health; Telecommunications & the Internet. *Permanent Select Committee on Intelligence* (5th of 12 D): Intelligence Community Management (Chmn.).

Group Ratings

	ADA	ACLU	AFS	LCV	ITIC	NTU	COC	ACU	CFG	FRC
2006	95	95	100	100	67	15	40	4	13	0
2005	100	—	100	94	—	14	38	4	7	0

National Journal Ratings

	2005 LIB	—	2005 CONS	2006 LIB	—	2006 CONS
Economic	81%	—	18%	94%	—	0%
Social	98%	—	0%	88%	—	12%
Foreign	76%	—	23%	83%	—	14%

Key Votes of the 109th Congress

1. Estate Tax Repeal	N	5. Limit Interstate Abortion	N	9. Build Border Fence	N
2. Limit CAFE Standards	N	6. Extend Patriot Act	N	10. CAFTA	N
3. FY06 Spending Curb	N	7. Bar Same Sex Marriage	N	11. Oppose Iraq Withdrawal	N
4. Drilling in ANWR	N	8. Stem Cell Research $	Y	12. Detainee Tribunals	N

Election Results

2006 general	Anna Eshoo (D)	141,153	(71%)	($1,069,186)
	Rob Smith (R)	48,097	(24%)	
	Other	9,325	(5%)	
2006 primary	Anna Eshoo (D)	unopposed		
2004 general	Anna Eshoo (D)	182,712	(70%)	($939,389)
	Chris Haugen (R)	69,564	(27%)	($52,623)
	Brian Holtz (Lib)	9,588	(4%)	

Prior Winning Percentages: 2002 (68%); 2000 (70%); 1998 (69%); 1996 (65%); 1994 (61%); 1992 (57%)

The People		Race/Ethnic Origin	Ancestry	
Area size:	1,030 sq. mi.	59.6% White	German: 9.7%	English: 8.3%
Urban population:	93.6%	3.0% Black	Irish: 7.2%	
Rural population:	6.4%	16.0% Asian	**2004 Presidential Vote**	
Pop. 2000:	639,088	0.3% Native Am.	Kerry (D) 188,864	(68%)
Pop. 2005 (est):	651,108	0.7% Hawaiian	Bush (R) 83,326	(30%)
Median income:	$77,985	2.7% Two+ races	Other 3,981	(1%)
Poverty status:	6.4%	0.3% Other	**2000 Presidential Vote**	
Military veterans:	9.5%	17.5% Hispanic Origin	Gore (D) 155,165	(62%)
			Bush (R) 84,637	(34%)
			Other 12,451	(5%)
			Cook Partisan Voting Index: D +18	

Occupation	Blue collar: 12.1%	White collar: 77.1%	Gray collar: 10.8%

Silicon Valley is a place and a state of mind, an area that had no distinctive identity three decades ago but which people all over the world have recognized, admired and tried to imitate. In the 1980s and 1990s Silicon Valley emerged as the center of America's computer industry, a place where creative minds have developed products that large corporations never thought would sell. Its beginnings can be traced back to 1939, when William Hewlett and David Packard started their electronics firm in a Palo Alto garage, or perhaps to 1891, when Stanford University was founded on the estate of a California governor and senator. Not every aspect of the computer business is centered here. Microsoft, routinely disparaged in every Palo Alto espresso shop and bar, is up in Redmond, Washington, and IBM is off in Armonk, New York. But Silicon Valley is where most of the giants, and very much of the creativity, of the high-tech business—as well as the ghosts of many dot.coms—have been based.

How did Silicon Valley come to be where it is? One reason is Stanford, the students it attracts and produces, and the fact that it has always encouraged profit-making activity by faculty. Another is venture capital, widely available from innovation-minded old San Francisco money, dispensed mostly from nondescript office buildings on Sand Hill Road off I-280 on the reclaimed flatlands along San Francisco Bay. A third, perhaps the greatest, is that Silicon Valley is the kind of place where smart young innovators like to live. Elite law and medical school graduates head to the prestigious, high-salary jobs of central cities; but techies are free to live in this pleasant, healthy environment. Sheltered by hills from coastal fogs and rains, Silicon Valley boasts a sunny climate with perceptible but gentle seasons, perfect for year-round outdoor sports; there may well be more jogging trails and bicycle paths here than anywhere else in the country. There is a sort of pure

Americana here: these communities were rustic but never poor, rural but never bigoted, country-like but still easily accessible to the luxuries of civilization. People here were ahead of the rest of the nation in fighting for the environment, in favoring natural over processed foods and in indulging in regular exercise. And they have been quick to adapt to change. In the 1980s, in the face of threats from Japanese firms, Silicon Valley shifted to microprocessors and personal computers. In the 1990s, when PCs became a low-profit commodity business, Silicon Valley shifted to the Internet. Yahoo and Hotmail reportedly were conceived at Buck's restaurant, the networking nexus in Woodside. When the Internet bubble burst in 2000, Silicon Valley fell on hard times. By one estimate, it lost 220,000 jobs, nearly two-thirds of the 350,000 jobs created during the dot.com era. Stock prices plummeted and real estate prices have too, though they are still the highest in the nation; the Valley actually lost population from 2000 to 2003. Billions in paper wealth disappeared, and technology exports from California fell. The question became whether Silicon Valley still had the ability to adapt. Since then, the Valley has been on the upturn, with rising profits and a net gain of jobs in 2005 and 2006. Defenders said that traffic congestion and high cost of living do not signal the demise of a community. No one knows what the next big thing in high-tech will be, but there are still lots of people working in Silicon Valley's bland office parks or in someone's garage who think they're on the way to it, and perhaps some are.

The 14th Congressional District of California includes much of Silicon Valley, with Menlo Park, Palo Alto, home of Stanford, and most of Redwood City, where tech office parks went up on the old salt flats and large condominium projects followed. Further south along El Camino Real are Mountain View and the several thousand employees of Google, Los Altos and Sunnyvale (the district's largest city). There are some ultra-wealthy enclaves here: Woodside, with its 1850s country store and mansions dotting the hills; Portola Valley and Los Altos Hills, with stark contemporary homes overlooking the Bay. Atherton, with its stone-walled lots, ranked as the most expensive zip code (94027) in the nation in 2005, with a median home-sale price of $2.5 million; it fell to 17th in 2006. Over the mountains it includes the little town of Half Moon Bay, with its pumpkin farms rising over the ocean, and the mountains where imposing redwoods grow within five miles of spectacular beaches. The 14th's political heritage is progressive: a sort of environmentalist, dovish, healthy-lifestyle, but entrepreneurial Republicanism, typified by former Congressmen Pete McCloskey, Ed Zschau and Tom Campbell, each of whom quit the House to run unsuccessfully for the Senate between 1982 and 2000. But this kind of Republican is virtually extinct, and Silicon Valley has become heavily Democratic. It is liberal on cultural issues and was enchanted by the attention it received from Bill Clinton and Al Gore. In 2004 George W. Bush got only 30% of the vote here.

The congresswoman from the 14th District is Anna Eshoo, a Democrat first elected in 1992. Born back East, she is the only member of Congress of Assyrian descent. She was a full time homemaker, then chaired the San Mateo County Democratic Party and was elected to the San Mateo Board of Supervisors in 1982. In 1988, she ran for the House against Tom Campbell. The two spent a total of $2.5 million, and Eshoo was the first congressional candidate to distribute video-tapes to voters. Campbell won 52%-46%. But in 1992 he ran for the Senate and Eshoo ran for the House again. In the primary she beat an assemblyman redistricted out of his seat by 40%-36%. In the general, Eshoo outspent her opponent and won 57%-39%. She has not faced a serious challenge for reelection.

In the House, Eshoo's voting record has been mostly liberal and occasionally moderate on foreign policy. She was a bit nervous in 1993 about supporting the Clinton budget and tax package, which hit this high-income area hard, and hesitated before supporting NAFTA. She joined Republicans and high-tech interests on securities litigation, liability relief for Y2K computer problems, normal trade relations with China and electronic signatures. Despite local pressure, she voted against trade promotion authority and CAFTA on labor and environmental grounds. With Richard Baker, she passed a House bill to oppose the FASB accounting board proposal to charge stock options against earnings, which would hit hard in Silicon Valley. Eshoo fought telecom legislation that would allow Internet carriers to have a two-tier pricing system, contending that it would disadvantage start-up firms.

With Minority Leader Nancy Pelosi's help, Eshoo got a seat on the Intelligence Committee, where she now chairs the Subcommittee on Intelligence Community Management. They have been close friends and confidants since they first met at a Democratic event in the Bay Area in the early 1970s, and their families have spent time together. Now, she is in the Speaker's inner circle, and was instrumental in preparing the party's Innovation Agenda. Although she does not seek attention, she is a fierce advocate for Pelosi.

FIFTEENTH DISTRICT

Rep. Mike Honda (D)

Elected 2000, 4th term; b. June 27, 1941, Walnut Creek; home, San Jose; San Jose St. U., B.S. 1969, B.A. 1970, M.A. 1973; Protestant; widowed.

Elected Office: San Jose Unified Sch. Bd., 1981-90; Santa Clara Cnty. Bd. of Supervisors, 1990-96; CA Assembly, 1996-2000.

Professional Career: Peace Corps, 1965-67; Elem. schl. principal, 1978-90.

DC Office: 1713 LHOB, 20515, 202-225-2631; Fax: 202-225-2699; Web site: www.house.gov/honda.

District Offices: Campbell, 408-558-8085.

Committees: *Appropriations* (30th of 37 D): Legislative Branch; Commerce, Justice, Science & Related Agencies; Labor, HHS, Education & Related Agencies. *Science & Technology* (16th of 24 D): Technology & Innovation.

Group Ratings

	ADA	ACLU	AFS	LCV	ITIC	NTU	COC	ACU	CFG	FRC
2006	95	100	100	100	57	13	33	4	5	0
2005	100	—	100	94	—	16	37	4	3	0

National Journal Ratings

	2005 LIB	—	2005 CONS		2006 LIB	—	2006 CONS
Economic	94%	—	0%		94%	—	0%
Social	98%	—	0%		93%	—	6%
Foreign	91%	—	7%		92%	—	5%

Key Votes of the 109th Congress

1. Estate Tax Repeal	N	5. Limit Interstate Abortion	N	9. Build Border Fence	N
2. Limit CAFE Standards	N	6. Extend Patriot Act	N	10. CAFTA	N
3. FY06 Spending Curb	N	7. Bar Same Sex Marriage	N	11. Oppose Iraq Withdrawal	N
4. Drilling in ANWR	N	8. Stem Cell Research $	Y	12. Detainee Tribunals	N

Election Results

2006 general	Mike Honda (D)	115,532	(72%)	($763,242)
	Raymond Chukwu (R)	44,186	(28%)	($46,274)
2006 primary	Mike Honda (D)	unopposed		
2004 general	Mike Honda (D)	154,385	(72%)	($539,475)
	Raymond Chukwu (R)	59,953	(28%)	($84,998)

Prior Winning Percentages: 2002 (66%); 2000 (54%)

The People		Race/Ethnic Origin	Ancestry	
Area size:	289 sq. mi.	47.1% White	German: 8.0% Irish: 6.3%	
Urban population:	99.3%	2.4% Black	English: 6.1%	
Rural population:	0.7%	29.2% Asian	**2004 Presidential Vote**	
Pop. 2000:	639,088	0.3% Native Am.	Kerry (D) 145,007	(63%)
Pop. 2005 (est):	651,067	0.3% Hawaiian	Bush (R) 82,742	(36%)
Median income:	$74,947	3.2% Two+ races	Other 2,903	(1%)
Poverty status:	6.6%	0.2% Other	**2000 Presidential Vote**	
Military veterans:	8.4%	17.2% Hispanic Origin	Gore (D) 124,880	(60%)
			Bush (R) 74,974	(36%)
			Other 7,108	(3%)
			Cook Partisan Voting Index: D +14	

Occupation   Blue collar: 16.9%   White collar: 73.6%   Gray collar: 9.6%

The broad valley of Santa Clara County around San Jose a few decades ago was mostly orchards and vineyards. Sheltered by mountains from the chilly ocean fogs, with soil incredibly fertile once it was irrigated, this valley produced peaches, plums, prunes, apricots and grapes and made San Jose half a century ago the nation's biggest fruit-packing center. Today, subdivisions, shopping centers and office buildings have replaced almost all the orchards, and San Jose and Santa Clara County have a population of 1.73 million people. San Jose, with a growing downtown, an arena for its National Hockey League team, and a population of 912,000,has become a major American city. In 2005, it replaced Detroit on the list of the nation's 10 largest cities. But this has not been a family-friendly increase: a shortage of kids has led to the closure of several local schools. San Jose and some towns to the west are part of Silicon Valley, which has no official boundaries.

The 15th Congressional District consists of the central slice of Santa Clara County. It includes 295,000 people in San Jose, nearly half of the district's population; for the most part these are San Jose's affluent neighborhoods. West of San Jose, the district includes the cities of Santa Clara and Cupertino, where Steve Jobs started Apple in a garage in the 1970s and where the company is still headquartered, Los Gatos and Campbell. The district also includes the salt flats of San Jose, site of the Great America theme park not far from where a huge Lockheed plant was once the nation's largest defense contractor, the heavily Asian city of Milpitas and, far to the south, connected by a swath of mountains, Gilroy, the garlic capital of the world, where you can marinate a steak by hanging it outside your house. Outside of Hawaii, this district has the highest percentage of Asians in the nation (29.2%). In Cupertino, where nearly a majority are Asians, their influence has made them a political force. This area was once marginal political territory but is now heavily Democratic. John Kerry got 63% of the vote here in 2004.

The congressman from the 15th District is Mike Honda, a Democrat first elected in 2000. Honda's grandparents arrived in the U.S. at the turn of the century from Japan's Kumamoto Prefecture, which served as the primary battleground for the Seinan Civil War in the 1870s (it was memorialized in the film, *The Last Samurai*). Honda was born in Walnut Creek and spent 14 months during his childhood in a World War II internment camp in Colorado. His wife Jeanne, who died in 2004, was born in Hiroshima and survived the atomic bombing before immigrating to the United States several years later. Honda received his bachelor's and master's degrees from San Jose State University and served two years in the Peace Corps in El Salvador, where he gained a passion for teaching. In 1971, San Jose Mayor Norman Mineta appointed him to the city Planning Commission. From 1978 to 1986, Honda was a principal at two area elementary schools; during these years he was elected to the San Jose Unified School Board and later to the Santa Clara County Board of Supervisors. In 1996, he was elected to the California Assembly. He worked to reduce classroom sizes and increase teacher benefits, and to secure an apology from Japan for its wartime atrocities against other Asian nations. For relaxation, the once-shy Honda sings karaoke.

In 2000, Republican Congressman Tom Campbell decided to run against Senator Dianne Feinstein. At first Honda was reluctant to run for the House, even though California's term limits meant that a third term in the Assembly would be his last. Days before the filing deadline, he told supporters that he would not run for the open seat. But persuasive telephone calls from several leading House Democrats and, finally, from Bill Clinton changed his mind. One reason for his initial reluctance was the prospect of running against former Carter administration Pentagon official Bill Peacock, a venture capitalist who was ready to spend $1 million of his own money and had gotten significant endorsements. But the primary was no contest: Honda won 67% to 24% for Peacock. His Republican opponent was Republican Assemblyman Jim Cunneen. A Campbell protégé, Cunneen was strongly supported by national Republican leaders; the contest seemed likely to be one of the year's most competitive. Cunneen favored liberal positions on cultural issues; he had support from many Silicon Valley capitalists. He tried to depict the contest as a referendum on the old economy versus the new economy. Honda, despite his close ties to unions, supported normal trade relations with China, a position strongly backed by the high tech industry. Honda won 54%-42%.

Honda has been among the most liberal members of the House. He chairs the Congressional Asian Pacific American Caucus, which advocates for under-represented groups on issues such as immigration and health care. He helped to enact the Cyber Security Research and Development Act, which funds training and programs to protect computer data and networks. He also was a major architect of the Nanotechnology Research and Development Act of 2003 to improve planning and encourage the development of networked facilities, which involve the manipulation of molecules at the atomic level; this has become a booming technology in the Bay Area. He publicized the cause of American POWs from World War II who were taken on "hell ships" as slave laborers in Japan, and sought apologies from Japan and its companies that profited from them; the 1951 peace treaty with Japan waived the rights of Americans to file such suits. Later, he signed on to an amendment with Dana Rohrabacher to prevent the State Department from opposing the POWs in court, but the amendment disappeared in conference committee after it passed both the House and

Senate. In 2003, he demanded an apology from North Carolina's Howard Coble, who said the internment of Japanese Americans in World War II was necessary to protect them.

Honda also sought to pass a resolution calling for an apology from Japan for forcing as many as 200,000 women into sexual slavery during the 1930s and World War II and he was not swayed when the Japanese prime minister in March 2007 denied such a practice had taken place. His efforts to secure an apology have generated controversy in Japan; *The New York Times* referred to him as "one of the most famous American congressmen in his ancestral land." Honda cast one of the three votes against the resolution condemning the Ninth Circuit decision that found the words "under God" in the Pledge of Allegiance unconstitutional. He filed the Student Privacy Protection Act, stating that military recruiters must have parents' consent to contact their children. Honda took up the cause of Army Ranger Pat Tillman, a San Jose native and National Football League star, who died in a "friendly fire" incident in Afghanistan; he echoed the family's criticism of the Pentagon's "deeply flawed and possibly dishonest series of prior investigations." In 2007, with help from Speaker Nancy Pelosi, he got a seat on the Appropriations Committee.

Honda, who has breezed to reelection in his own district, calls the nation's low voter turnout a "serious illness," and has filed a bill to reschedule federal elections for the first full weekend in November.

SIXTEENTH DISTRICT

Rep. Zoe Lofgren (D)

Elected 1994, 7th term; b. Dec. 21, 1947, San Mateo; home, San Jose; Stanford U., B.A. 1970, U. of Santa Clara Law Schl., J.D. 1975; Protestant; married (John Collins).

Elected Office: Santa Clara Bd. of Supervisors, 1980-94.

Professional Career: Staff Asst., U.S. Rep. Don Edwards, 1970-78; Practicing atty., 1978-80; Prof., U. of Santa Clara Law Schl., 1981-94.

DC Office: 102 CHOB, 20515, 202-225-3072; Fax: 202-225-3336; Web site: lofgren.house.gov.

District Offices: San Jose, 408-271-8700.

Committees: *Homeland Security* (9th of 19 D): Emerging Threats, Cybersecurity & Science and Technology; Border, Maritime & Global Counterterrorism. *House Administration* (2d of 6 D). *Judiciary* (7th of 23 D): Immigration, Citizenship, Refugees, Border Security & International Law (Chmn.); Commercial & Administrative Law; Courts, the Internet & Intellectual Property.

Group Ratings

	ADA	ACLU	AFS	LCV	ITIC	NTU	COC	ACU	CFG	FRC
2006	100	95	100	92	57	12	33	4	6	0
2005	100	—	100	100	—	15	37	4	3	0

National Journal Ratings

	2005 LIB	—	2005 CONS		2006 LIB	—	2006 CONS
Economic	85%	—	13%		86%	—	14%
Social	92%	—	7%		89%	—	10%
Foreign	85%	—	15%		83%	—	14%

Key Votes of the 109th Congress

1. Estate Tax Repeal	N	5. Limit Interstate Abortion	N	9. Build Border Fence	N
2. Limit CAFE Standards	N	6. Extend Patriot Act	N	10. CAFTA	N
3. FY06 Spending Curb	N	7. Bar Same Sex Marriage	N	11. Oppose Iraq Withdrawal	N
4. Drilling in ANWR	N	8. Stem Cell Research $	Y	12. Detainee Tribunals	N

Election Results

2006 general	Zoe Lofgren (D) 98,929	(73%)	($622,369)
	Charel Winston (R) 37,130	(27%)	
2006 primary	Zoe Lofgren (D) .... unopposed		
2004 general	Zoe Lofgren (D) 129,222	(71%)	($598,739)
	Douglas McNea (R) 47,992	(26%)	($244)
	Other.. 5,067	(3%)	

Prior Winning Percentages: 2002 (67%); 2000 (72%); 1998 (73%); 1996 (66%); 1994 (65%)

The People		Race/Ethnic Origin	Ancestry		
Area size:	232 sq. mi.	31.9% White	German: 5.7%		Irish: 4.6%
Urban population:	98.7%	3.4% Black	English: 4.2%		
Rural population:	1.3%	23.4% Asian	**2004 Presidential Vote**		
Pop. 2000:	639,088	0.4% Native Am.	Kerry (D) 125,415	(63%)	
Pop. 2005 (est):	633,610	0.4% Hawaiian	Bush (R)............... 70,190	(36%)	
Median income:	$67,689	2.8% Two+ races	Other 2,089	(1%)	
Poverty status:	9.8%	0.2% Other	**2000 Presidential Vote**		
Military veterans:	7.6%	37.6% Hispanic Origin	Gore (D) 109,632	(64%)	
			Bush (R).............. 57,160	(33%)	
			Other 4,832	(3%)	
			Cook Partisan Voting Index: D +16		

Occupation	Blue collar: 24.7%	White collar: 60.9%	Gray collar: 14.4%

With more people than San Francisco, a tradition of high-tech innovation that rivals any on earth, and a major league sports team, San Jose finally has great claims on national attention and respect. Yet San Jose does not bulk as large in the national consciousness as it should. At the southern end of the Bay, it remains in the shadow of the city on the Golden Gate. San Francisco is every tourist's idea of a city: geographically compact, with picturesque public transportation, old-time and new immigrant groups, an economy historically based on heavy industry and sea trade, a large city bureaucracy and a monumental city hall. San Jose is quite different. It got its start as a farm-market town, with canneries and fruit-packing operations for the produce from the surrounding fertile plains. Farm-labor icon Cesar Chavez settled with his family in the East San Jose barrio. San Jose sits not on the Bay, but on the Southern Pacific line above the marshes and salt evaporators; its major transportation arteries are the freeways—U.S. 101, Interstates 280, 680 and 880, California 17—that encircle its revitalized downtown.

Starting in the 1950s, San Jose has grown out in every direction, developers hip-hopping across the farmland, putting up subdivisions faster sometimes than the few city employees could update the street map. Economically, San Jose has been sustained by everything from its traditional agriculture to manufacturing to the high-tech businesses that are centered in Silicon Valley towns just to the west but are omnipresent here: an American city, 21st century style. For many years San Jose had Northern California's largest Mexican-Americans community, many of whom were farm workers; now there is a diverse immigrant presence, with large numbers from Latin America and East and South Asia. Nearly half of all Santa Clara County residents speak a language other than English at home, mostly Spanish, Vietnamese or Chinese; one in three are foreign-born.

The 16th Congressional District of California consists of about two-thirds of San Jose, plus nearby unincorporated area to the south; 92% of its residents live inside the jagged city limits of San Jose. It includes the old and new downtowns and the heavily Mexican-American areas to the east. This has the largest Hispanic (38%) share of any district in the Bay Area; included is the largest concentration of Vietnamese in the U.S (the next highest district is the Orange County-based 47th). Politically, it is solidly Democratic; John Kerry won here 63%-36%.

The congresswoman from the 16th District is Zoe Lofgren, a Democrat first elected in 1994. Lofgren grew up in the Bay Area, where her father was a Teamster truck driver and her mother worked for the Machinists Union. She graduated from Stanford and Santa Clara law school and was a staffer for eight years to Congressman Don Edwards; as a law student, she worked for him while he was a leader on the Judiciary Committee that voted to impeach Richard Nixon. In 1980 she was elected to the Santa Clara County Board of Supervisors. When Edwards retired, Lofgren ran for the seat. Her chief Democratic opponent, former San Jose Mayor Tom McEnery, started off better known. But Lofgren raised almost twice as much money, with the support of the national women's organizations and women in the California delegation. She won the primary 45%-42%, and easily won the general.

Edwards, her predecessor, never spent a day in the minority during 32 years in the House. To Lofgren's surprise, that's where she found herself for 12 years. But she had some impact, and her voting record, while mostly liberal, includes some bipartisan free market positions responsive to local businesses. Working with David Dreier, she won expanded allotments in the H-1B visa program for high-tech workers. She pushed for looser controls on encryption exports, securities litigation limitation and relaxation of trade restraints on supercomputers: all big Silicon Valley causes. She has cosponsored bipartisan legislation to impose criminal penalties for "spyware" violations. When the House split 210-210 on a proposal to restrict government spying on library records, Lofgren was the only member to vote "present"; the amendment went too far in preventing legitimate law-enforcement searches, she said. In December 2005, she voted against extension of some provisions of the Patriot Act, including library searches. Finally in the majority in January 2007, she became chairwoman of the Immigration Subcommittee of Judiciary, where she made plans to move a comprehensive reform measure and voiced hope that it could draw bipartisan support. "I am encouraged," she told *National Journal* in March 2007. "Shortly, we will find out if my optimism is justified." Lofgren also chaired the Election Subcommittee at House Administration, where she investigated problems with electronic voting machines.

Her more partisan efforts have taken several directions. After backing normal trade relations with China, she opposed President's Bush request for trade promotion authority. Her earlier support for repealing the estate tax changed in April 2005, when she voted against repeal. In 2001, the Republicans' energy plan included her proposal to accelerate the development of fusion as an energy source, but she voted against the overall bill. When Republicans brought up a bill to make it a separate offense to injure or kill a fetus while committing a crime against a pregnant woman, she offered an alternative simply to make it a crime to attack a pregnant woman, without conferring rights to the fetus; that lost 229-196. In July 2006, she criticized Representative Rob Simmons for failing to hold more hearings in the Homeland Security Intelligence Subcommittee to investigate alleged government spying on civilians.

Lofgren has had no trouble winning reelection. After the 2002 election, she ran for vice chairman of the Democratic Caucus. But Nancy Pelosi, also from the Bay Area, had already been elected Minority Leader, and the Congressional Black Caucus was pressing to have one of its members in the leadership. Lofgren got 53 votes to 95 for James Clyburn and 56 for Gregory Meeks. As chair of the California Democratic delegation, she led efforts to oppose the recall in 2003 of Governor Gray Davis.

SEVENTEENTH DISTRICT

Rep. Sam Farr (D)

Elected June 1993, 7th full term; b. July 4, 1941, San Francisco; home, Carmel; Willamette U., B.S. 1963; Episcopalian; married (Shary).

Elected Office: Monterey Cnty. Bd. of Supervisors, 1975-80, Chmn., 1979; CA Assembly, 1980-93.

Professional Career: Peace Corps, Colombia, 1963-65; Staff, CA Assembly, 1965-75.

DC Office: 1221 LHOB, 20515, 202-225-2861; Fax: 202-225-6791; Web site: www.farr.house.gov.

District Offices: Salinas, 831-424-2229; Santa Cruz, 831-429-1976.

Committees: *Appropriations* (19th of 37 D): Military Construction, Veterans Affairs & Related Agencies; Agriculture, Rural Development, FDA & Related Agencies; Homeland Security.

Group Ratings

	ADA	ACLU	AFS	LCV	ITIC	NTU	COC	ACU	CFG	FRC
2006	95	95	100	100	50	13	27	4	7	0
2005	100	—	100	100	—	17	42	8	11	8

National Journal Ratings

	2005 LIB	—	2005 CONS	2006 LIB	—	2006 CONS
Economic	81%	—	18%	91%	—	6%
Social	97%	—	2%	96%	—	3%
Foreign	91%	—	7%	95%	—	0%

Key Votes of the 109th Congress

1. Estate Tax Repeal	Y	5. Limit Interstate Abortion	N	9. Build Border Fence	N
2. Limit CAFE Standards	N	6. Extend Patriot Act	N	10. CAFTA	N
3. FY06 Spending Curb	N	7. Bar Same Sex Marriage	N	11. Oppose Iraq Withdrawal	N
4. Drilling in ANWR	N	8. Stem Cell Research $	Y	12. Detainee Tribunals	N

Election Results

2006 general	Sam Farr (D)	120,750	(76%)	($678,902)
	Anthony DeMaio (R)	35,932	(23%)	
	Other	2,611	(2%)	
2006 primary	Sam Farr (D)	unopposed		
2004 general	Sam Farr (D)	148,958	(67%)	($616,323)
	Mark Risley (R)	65,117	(29%)	($144,619)
	Other	9,150	(4%)	

Prior Winning Percentages: 2002 (68%); 2000 (69%); 1998 (65%); 1996 (59%); 1994 (52%); 1993 (52%)

The People		Race/Ethnic Origin	Ancestry	
Area size:	5,386 sq. mi.	46.3% White	German: 7.6%	English: 6.3%
Urban population:	90.0%	2.6% Black	Irish: 6.3%	
Rural population:	10.0%	4.8% Asian	**2004 Presidential Vote**	
Pop. 2000:	639,088	0.4% Native Am.	Kerry (D) 149,029	(66%)
Pop. 2005 (est):	642,703	0.3% Hawaiian	Bush (R) 75,005	(33%)
Median income:	$49,234	2.5% Two+ races	Other 3,144	(1%)
Poverty status:	13.3%	0.3% Other	**2000 Presidential Vote**	
Military veterans:	10.4%	42.9% Hispanic Origin	Gore (D) 124,580	(60%)
			Bush (R) 68,717	(33%)
			Other 14,819	(7%)
			Cook Partisan Voting Index: D +17	

Occupation	Blue collar: 19.7%	White collar: 55.4%	Gray collar: 24.9%

The California coast around Monterey Bay is for many a working definition of paradise. This kernel of California, where Spanish and then Mexicans governed a virtually empty land and Californians set up their first state capital, still makes a fine living off the land and sea, as it has for 150 years. The locale for *The Grapes of Wrath* and many other John Steinbeck novels, the fields around Salinas supply much of the nation's lettuce and cauliflower (the area is often referred to as "the salad bowl of the world"). Nearby, the fields around Castroville supply almost all of its artichokes, and the vast greenhouses around Watsonville supply a goodly portion of its roses. The fishing fleet and the 18 now-closed canneries of Monterey (the last sardines were canned in 1964) have generated a new industry: Once described by Steinbeck as "a poem, a stink, a grating noise, a quality of light, a tone, a habit, nostalgia, a dream," Cannery Row now is refurbished with upscale shops and hotels. The magnificent Monterey Bay Aquarium is one of California's top tourist destinations; the National Marine Sanctuary here holds more than 400 shipwrecks and ditched aircraft. The Monterey Bay area calls itself the world's language learning capital, with the Defense Language Institute, Language Line Services and Cal State's Monterey Bay Center for Intensive Language and Culture on the site of Fort Ord, which was closed in 1994. There are other attractions on the Monterey peninsula: the lush 17-Mile Drive along the Pacific Coast Highway, Pebble Beach golf courses, Del Monte Lodge, and Carmel, whose restrictive laws—no house numbers, no door-to-door mail delivery, no live entertainment, no stop lights, no cutting trees without city council permission—reflect an effort to maintain the atmosphere of nearly a century ago, when it really was an artists' colony.

The 17th Congressional District of California includes all the coast of Monterey Bay and follows the stunning Big Sur coastline south along the steep slopes almost to William Randolph Hearst's castle, San Simeon, past some of the most beautiful scenery in America; to the north along Monterey Bay, it extends past Watsonville to Santa Cruz and the last boardwalk amusement park on the West Coast. The district extends inland, into sunny valleys sheltered from ocean mists, and covers some of the nation's richest farmland. In San Benito County is Hollister, where tens of thousands of motorcyclists assemble annually at an oval dirt racetrack for the Independence Rally. Most of the farm workers are Latino (mainly Mexican), and in the 1990s the district's Latino population rose from 31% to 43%—the largest increase in any Northern California district. The gap between rich and poor in Monterey County has widened: More than 2,000 homes were valued at more than $1 million, while the county ranked seventh statewide in the share of households below the poverty line; of course many of these people were living in much greater poverty in other countries a decade earlier. This area is a prime example of how the California coast has trended Democratic. Forty years ago this was a solidly Republican area, dominated politically by the landowners in Salinas and the townspeople who sympathize with them, plus retirees in Santa Cruz and the Monterey peninsula. But an influx of liberation-minded young people, attracted less by the economy than by the atmosphere, moved the coast to the left. As late as 1980, Monterey and Santa Cruz Counties were voting less Democratic than the nation. But since 1984 they have become steadily more Democratic than the nation, and each now exceeds the Democratic presidential vote by more than 10%. In 2004 John Kerry won by 66%-33% a district that was carried four times by Ronald Reagan.

The congressman from the 17th is Sam Farr, a Democrat first elected in June 1993. A fifth-generation Californian, he grew up in Monterey County, where his father was a state senator for many years. Farr signed up for the Peace Corps after college, learned Spanish at the Monterey Institute of International Studies and served two years in Colombia. He was a California Assembly staffer for a decade, became a Monterey County supervisor in 1975, and was elected to the Assembly in 1980. There, he wrote one of the nation's strictest oil spill liability laws. In 1993, Leon Panetta resigned from the House to become Office of Management and Budget director, and Farr ran for his seat. He entered the race as the overwhelming favorite, and in the all-party primary won 26% to beat two other Democrats who had 19% and 14%. But in the runoff, after the Clinton budget and tax increase had been introduced, he had trouble against Republican Bill McCampbell, whom Panetta had defeated 72%-24% seven months earlier. Farr won, but by just 52%-43%.

In the House, Farr has a solidly liberal voting record. In voting against trade promotion authority, Farr cited the Clinton administration's failure to restrict imports of cut flowers from Colombia, which compete with a major local industry. On the Appropriations Committee, Farr has focused on two major local concerns: farming and military bases. He helped to negotiate the final agreement that conveyed the former Fort Ord to civilian hands, and he took the lead in transferring the lands to local governments and in refusing to permit the Navy to establish a practice bombing range near Big Sur. Working with Senator Patrick Leahy, he led a successful effort in 2003 to repeal a little-noted provision of an appropriations bill that would have allowed poultry and beef to be raised on non-organic food but still be labeled organic. George W. Bush signed his bill to add 55,000 acres to Big Sur wilderness area, and Farr helped to pass in 2004 the California Missions Preservation Act; 5 of those 21 missions are in his district. After the local spinach crop in 2006 was damaged by an E-coli outbreak, Farr held a press conference to urge constituents to "go Popeye" and eat spinach. He pushed for $25 million to aid producers, a provision that generated controversy after it was added to the emergency war spending bill; House and Senate conferees stripped it from the bill in April 2007. "It's easy to make fun of spinach," Farr said in defense of the subsidy. "But if we had eaten more of it, we would be a stronger society."

An advocate of post-conflict reconstruction, Farr helped to set up the Center for Stabilization and Reconstruction at Monterey's Naval Postgraduate School. As co-chair of the Oceans Caucus, he has pushed a major proposal to overhaul ocean management, with national and regional governance; he helped to write the 2006 law revising rules for offshore fisheries. He also filed a bill to encourage research on sea otters.

Farr was elected to a full term in 1994 against McCampbell by only 52%-44%. Since then California has moved toward the Democrats and he has been reelected easily. His ability to work well with diverse interests has made Farr an influential member on statewide issues; he has been a close ally of Speaker Nancy Pelosi.

EIGHTEENTH DISTRICT

Rep. Dennis Cardoza (D)

Elected 2002, 3d term; b. Mar. 31, 1959, Merced; home, Atwater; U. of MD, B.A. 1982, CA St. U. Stanislaus; Catholic; married (Kathleen McLoughlin).

Elected Office: Atwater City Cncl., 1984-86; Merced City Cncl., 1994-95; CA Assembly, 1996-2002.

Professional Career: Agribusiness owner.

DC Office: 435 CHOB, 20515, 202-225-6131; Fax: 202-225-0819; Web site: www.house.gov/cardoza.

District Offices: Merced, 209-383-4455; Modesto, 209-527-1914; Stockton, 209-946-0361.

Committees: *Agriculture* (7th of 25 D): Horticulture & Organic Agriculture (Chmn.); Livestock, Dairy & Poultry; Conservation, Credit, Energy & Research. *Rules* (5th of 9 D): Legislative & Budget Process (Vice Chmn.).

Group Ratings

	ADA	ACLU	AFS	LCV	ITIC	NTU	COC	ACU	CFG	FRC
2006	60	73	67	58	43	21	79	46	28	28
2005	85	—	100	61	—	25	67	44	15	33

National Journal Ratings

	2005 LIB	—	2005 CONS		2006 LIB	—	2006 CONS
Economic	57%	—	43%		59%	—	41%
Social	59%	—	41%		63%	—	37%
Foreign	55%	—	45%		57%	—	43%

Key Votes of the 109th Congress

1. Estate Tax Repeal	Y	5. Limit Interstate Abortion	Y	9. Build Border Fence	Y
2. Limit CAFE Standards	Y	6. Extend Patriot Act	N	10. CAFTA	N
3. FY06 Spending Curb	N	7. Bar Same Sex Marriage	N	11. Oppose Iraq Withdrawal	Y
4. Drilling in ANWR	Y	8. Stem Cell Research $	Y	12. Detainee Tribunals	N

Election Results

2006 general	Dennis Cardoza (D)	71,182	(65%)	($952,158)
	John Kanno (R)	37,531	(35%)	($138,766)
2006 primary	Dennis Cardoza (D)	unopposed		
2004 general	Dennis Cardoza (D)	103,732	(68%)	($809,014)
	Charles Pringle (R)	49,973	(33%)	($11,095)

Prior Winning Percentages: 2002 (51%)

The People		Race/Ethnic Origin	Ancestry	
Area size:	3,101 sq. mi.	39.1% White	German: 6.2%	Irish: 4.8%
Urban population:	91.3%	5.6% Black	English: 4.0%	
Rural population:	8.7%	8.9% Asian	**2004 Presidential Vote**	
Pop. 2000:	639,088	0.7% Native Am.	Bush (R) 80,157	(50%)
Pop. 2005 (est):	706,335	0.3% Hawaiian	Kerry (D) 79,764	(49%)
Median income:	$34,211	3.2% Two+ races	Other 1,677	(1%)
Poverty status:	22.7%	0.2% Other	**2000 Presidential Vote**	
Military veterans:	10.1%	41.9% Hispanic Origin	Gore (D) 77,908	(53%)
			Bush (R) 65,105	(44%)
			Other 3,690	(3%)
			Cook Partisan Voting Index: D + 3	

Occupation   Blue collar: 31.0%   White collar: 46.0%   Gray collar: 23.1%

The Central Valley of California is a miraculous man-made landscape, an outdoor factory stretching as far as the eye can see. Nature created the vast flatlands, rimmed by mountains rising in the distant haze. But man in the last century has disciplined the land with a remorseless mile-square grid of roads, and the sluggish-flowing California Aqueduct and dozens of arrow-straight canals;

pipes fitted with valves and gauges to pump water and fertilizer and pesticides to the fields in measured quantities give an air of industrial precision. The crops grow in carefully spaced rows, filling the fields; the rich soil and the irrigated water are too precious to waste on decoration or flower gardens. Farming here has been a business, not a way of life. In the 19th century the land was not given to 160-acre homesteaders, but sold to thousands-of-acres capitalist enterprises. Among the most famous local capitalists were the Gallo brothers, Ernest and Julio, who started a winery in Modesto in 1933 with virtually no money, and grew it to more than 10,000 acres of vineyards and 80 million cases each year.

The Central Valley in recent years has become one of California's surprise boom areas, growing not just crops but people. Middle-income employees in the San Francisco Bay area drive east at the end of the day on I-580, past surreal windmills whirling on the bare hills of the Altamont pass, across the Westlands fields to modestly priced homes in Modesto, the town immortalized (when it was much smaller) in *American Graffiti* and made famous more recently as the home of Gary Condit and Scott Peterson. Warehouses and factories have sprung up on land that, for all its farming value, is cheaper than industrial land in the Bay Area, and some croplands have been given over to pasture, as subsidized water was cut off from cultivators of cotton, and water prices move slowly toward market levels far above those of government subsidy. The result is not stagnation but growth, and a more well-rounded economy; Inland California had a 46% increase in jobs from 1990 to 2005, while jobs in coastal California grew by 10% in the same period. But there are costs. Traffic is a problem, air pollution on bad days can be among the worst in the nation, and the pace of life has become more hectic.

The 18th Congressional District of California includes a large chunk of the Central Valley from Stockton, south to Modesto and through Merced County to the fringes of Fresno. The political tradition here had been Democratic: Democrats in Washington and Governor Pat Brown in California built the irrigation canals and authorized the water subsidies; Democrats owned the McClatchy newspapers, the predominant Valley chain; Democrats staffed the Bank of America, long the dominant financial force here; on the walls of insider law firms were signed pictures of Franklin D. Roosevelt and Pat Brown, not Ronald Reagan and Pete Wilson. The district produced two House Democratic whips, John McFall in the late 1970s and Tony Coelho in the late 1980s. But the Central Valley is the part of California with the highest proportion of families and children, and there is a natural cultural conservatism here, shared by successful local politicians. In the 1980s and 1990s the Central Valley trended Republican, and even Latinos here are less heavily Democratic than in Los Angeles. The 18th District is still modestly Democratic, because of very careful redistricting. The old Central Valley district had voted 53% for George W. Bush in 2000. By removing much of fast-growing Stanislaus County and adding a corridor along I-5 in San Joaquin County, including the central part of Stockton, the Bush 2000 vote dropped to 44%; in 2004 Bush carried the district 50%-49%.

The congressman from the 18th District is Dennis Cardoza, a Democrat first elected in a 2002 contest that drew international attention because of the notoriety of his predecessor, Gary Condit. Cardoza grew up in Merced and Stanislaus Counties and graduated from the University of Maryland; he is of Portuguese descent (like Jim Costa of the adjacent 20th District and Devin Nunes of the 21st, also in the Central Valley). In the mid-1980s Cardoza worked as an aide to Condit, then an assemblyman, assisted Condit's 1989 special election campaign and served on his Washington staff. In 1997 Cardoza was elected to the Assembly; he undoubtedly would have remained loyal to Condit had Chandra Levy, a Modesto resident who was working as an intern in the executive branch, not disappeared in Washington in April 2001.

Her disappearance generated saturation media coverage. It was revealed that Condit had a relationship with her, though he steadfastly denied it was sexual in nature. In those pre-September 11 days, the Levy case suddenly became top news; Condit was harried by reporters and cameramen as he left his Adams Morgan apartment or walked from the Capitol to the Rayburn Building. For constituents, the case was a revelation. Condit had always portrayed himself as a family man, the son of a preacher; his wife was well known and beloved in the Modesto area. Now it appeared that Condit had been living another life in Washington, acting decidedly unlike a family man. After September 11 Condit disappeared from the cable news networks, but the question remained whether he would seek reelection. Cardoza was careful not to criticize or question Condit's actions at a time when his conduct with Levy generated worldwide speculation. National and local Democrats urged him to enter the contest because they feared that Condit could not survive a general election. Cardoza entered the race in October; Senators Dianne Feinstein and Barbara Boxer endorsed him, as did many members of the House delegation. In the primary, Cardoza won

53%-39%. The embittered Condit all but disappeared from the airwaves. For Cardoza, the election was not over. Republicans nominated state Senator Dick Monteith, whose seat included 73% of the congressional district; he claimed Cardoza was too liberal for an agriculture-oriented constituency. Cardoza allies responded by citing his business-oriented reputation in the Legislature. Cardoza tried to mollify Condit supporters, but Condit would not speak to him and predicted that Monteith would win in November. In October, Condit's children released a letter that harshly criticized Cardoza and urged a vote against him; Cardoza won, 51%-43%. Stockton made the difference. Cardoza led 67%-27% in San Joaquin County, a 10,000-vote margin that wiped out Monteith's 2,000-vote lead elsewhere.

In the House, Cardoza cast a Condit-like independent and centrist voting record, and gravitated to the obvious issues of agriculture and resources. The father of two adopted children, he backed steps to encourage placement of more children in foster care, an interest that he shared with Tom DeLay. He bucked environmentalists and worked with Resources Committee chairman Richard Pombo (from the adjacent district) and other Republicans on farmer-friendly revisions to the Endangered Species Act, including changes in designating critical habitat. He advocated solar power and other sources of renewable energy. He is a member of the Blue Dog Democrats, and emphasizes the need for fiscal discipline. In the majority, he became chairman of the Agriculture Subcommittee on Horticulture and Organic Agriculture, a title that sounds more coastal than Valley; but the position gave Cardoza a seat at the table on the farm bill, where he sought more supports for "specialty crops," notably the fruits and vegetables that are grown in his district. Despite occasional differences with Speaker Nancy Pelosi, including his public support for Steny Hoyer against Jack Murtha for Majority Leader, she gave him a seat on the leadership-friendly Rules Committee.

Cardoza has won reelection handily and with far less attention than in his first race.

NINETEENTH DISTRICT

Rep. George Radanovich (R)

Elected 1994, 7th term; b. June 20, 1955, Mariposa; home, Mariposa; CA Polytechnic U., B.S. 1978; Catholic; married (Ethie).

Elected Office: Mariposa Cnty. Planning Comm., 1982-86, Chmn., 1985-86; Mariposa Cnty. Bd. of Supervisors, 1989-92.

Professional Career: Farmer; Founder & Owner, Radanovich Winery, 1986-2003.

DC Office: 438 CHOB, 20515, 202-225-4540; Fax: 202-225-3402; Web site: www.radanovich.house.gov.

District Offices: Fresno, 559-449-2490; Modesto, 209-579-5458.

Committees: *Energy & Commerce* (15th of 26 R): Commerce, Trade & Consumer Protection; Environment & Hazardous Materials; Telecommunications & the Internet.

Group Ratings

	ADA	ACLU	AFS	LCV	ITIC	NTU	COC	ACU	CFG	FRC
2006	5	10	0	0	100	65	100	88	66	100
2005	0	—	0	6	—	64	96	92	74	100

National Journal Ratings

	2005 LIB	—	2005 CONS	2006 LIB	—	2006 CONS
Economic	13%	—	87%	3%	—	97%
Social	32%	—	68%	0%	—	94%
Foreign	23%	—	73%	41%	—	58%

Key Votes of the 109th Congress

1. Estate Tax Repeal	Y	5. Limit Interstate Abortion	Y	9. Build Border Fence	Y
2. Limit CAFE Standards	Y	6. Extend Patriot Act	Y	10. CAFTA	Y
3. FY06 Spending Curb	*	7. Bar Same Sex Marriage	Y	11. Oppose Iraq Withdrawal	Y
4. Drilling in ANWR	Y	8. Stem Cell Research $	N	12. Detainee Tribunals	*

Election Results

2006 general	George Radanovich (R)	110,246	(61%)	($1,197,702)
	T.J. Cox (D)	71,748	(39%)	($886,086)
2006 primary	George Radanovich (R)	unopposed		
2004 general	George Radanovich (R)	155,354	(66%)	($919,414)
	James Bufford (D)	64,047	(27%)	
	Larry Mullen (Green)	15,863	(7%)	

Prior Winning Percentages: 2002 (67%); 2000 (65%); 1998 (79%); 1996 (67%); 1994 (57%)

The People		Race/Ethnic Origin	Ancestry	
Area size:	6,781 sq. mi.	59.9% White	German: 10.0%	English: 7.3%
Urban population:	80.6%	3.4% Black	Irish: 6.9%	
Rural population:	19.4%	4.4% Asian	**2004 Presidential Vote**	
Pop. 2000:	639,088	1.0% Native Am.	Bush (R) 151,603	(61%)
Pop. 2005 (est):	729,300	0.1% Hawaiian	Kerry (D) 93,918	(38%)
Median income:	$41,225	2.8% Two+ races	Other 2,308	(1%)
Poverty status:	14.8%	0.2% Other	**2000 Presidential Vote**	
Military veterans:	12.4%	28.2% Hispanic Origin	Bush (R) 125,465	(58%)
			Gore (D) 84,559	(39%)
			Other 6,823	(3%)
			Cook Partisan Voting Index: R +10	

Occupation   Blue collar: 22.0%   White collar: 59.3%   Gray collar: 18.8%

The city of Fresno started as a farm-marketing center—one high-income neighborhood is called Fig Garden because that's what it used to be—and as a tourist stop-off point on the way to Yosemite National Park. But it has long since grown out north, east and west from its old downtown, and its economy has diversified. Like all the Central Valley, Fresno has always been ethnically diverse, with a telephone book that reads like the United Nations; it has America's second largest Armenian community, after Los Angeles. Its already large Latino population has more than doubled in the past 20 years, and Fresno County was 44% Hispanic in 2000; Asians, including Chinese, Filipinos, Vietnamese and Hmong, were 8% of the county's population. The city grew a lusty 29% from 1990 to 2004, despite some serious problems: high unemployment rates, violent teenage gangs and air pollution that made the Sierra Nevada invisible on many days. The growth was accompanied by some success in addressing those problems, though Fresno remained number-one in poverty levels among the nation's 50 largest cities. Tighter border patrolling has encouraged illegal Mexican immigrants to remain in Fresno County year round, even during the off season for farm work; migrants have been crowding into trailers and makeshift homes on formerly vacant farmland. Historically, Fresno was a Democratic town, the prime Democratic bastion in the Central Valley south of Sacramento. Since the 1990s, it has moved toward the Republicans. It voted for Bob Dole and twice for George W. Bush, for Republican governor candidates Dan Lungren in 1998 and Bill Simon in 2002, none of whom came close statewide.

The 19th Congressional District of California includes nearly half of Fresno, the relatively affluent north side of the city, and the farm towns of Madera County to the north. This is one of the two heavily populated parts of the district. The other nearly 100 miles away is the northern and eastern half of Stanislaus County, including the northern edge of Modesto and towns like Turlock, Riverbank and Oakdale. These two areas are linked and surrounded by mountainous Mariposa and Tuolumne Counties, including Sierra foothills, the peaks of the Sierra Nevada and Yosemite National Park. Gold was once prospected in these butterfly-filled hills and a chain of mining camps ran along what is now Highway 49.

The congressman from the 19th District is George Radanovich, a Republican first elected in 1994. Radanovich is the son of Croatian immigrants, with relatives all over the Valley. He worked on the family farm, served on the Mariposa County Planning Commission in the 1980s and won a seat on the Board of Supervisors in 1989. In 1986, after studying local microclimates, he opened the first winery in Mariposa County and made it work; the Radanovich Winery shipped 4,000 cases annually of sauvignon blanc, merlot, zinfandel and cabernet sauvignon. In 1992 he ran for Congress, losing the primary 33%-30% to 28-year-old Tal Cloud, who lost to incumbent Democrat Richard Lehman 47%-46%. In 1994, Radanovich, an easy winner in this primary, attacked Lehman for supporting the Clinton administration and California Democrat George Miller's efforts to raise the price of Valley water. Radanovich won 57%-40% in the widest defeat of a non-freshman incumbent that year.

In the House, where Radanovich was elected president of his 74-member freshmen Republican class, he has a mostly conservative voting record that briefly turned a bit moderate as he contemplated statewide office. In 1996 he passed with David Bonior an amendment to require Turkey to acknowledge the Armenian genocide of 1915; Turkey spurned aid under such conditions. In 2000, Radanovich secured $90 million in aid for Armenia—one of the largest recipients of U.S. aid; but Speaker Dennis Hastert acceded to Bill Clinton's personal appeal to abandon another resolution that recognized the Armenian genocide. In 2004, the House initially approved a similar resolution by Democrat Adam Schiff, but Hastert and other Republican leaders insisted on dropping it as an amendment from a foreign aid bill. With Democrats in the majority, Radanovich refiled the resolution and had better prospects for success. Radanovich was more enthusiastic about supporting trade promotion authority after George W. Bush became president.

At the Resources Committee, he chaired the National Parks, Recreation and Public Lands Subcommittee; he pledged a greater local voice in planning for the parks but his proposed changes in the master plan for Yosemite encountered widespread opposition, and he made changes before the House passed the bill. He enacted proposals to improve the remote schools serving families that work at the park. He faced opposition from conservatives on his proposal designating the 318-mile Highway 49 as a national heritage corridor; property rights advocates worried that private landowners would lose their rights and Radanovich modified the plan. As chairman of the Water and Power Subcommittee, his ambitious plans to restore the San Joaquin River caused clashes with Devin Nunes and farmers in the adjacent district.

After his initial pledge to serve only 10 years in the House, he said that he needed "some flexibility" to accomplish his priorities and he suffered no apparent retribution. He explored a race against Barbara Boxer in 2004, but decided to hold onto his safe seat in the House. He suffered a black eye when the *Fresno Bee* in July 2004 published a lengthy report about the collapse of his winery, which left several investors short hundreds of thousands of dollars while Radanovich continued to own the land and other assets; the story raised the question of whether the investors' losses amounted to a gift to Radanovich contrary to House rules. He said that the newspaper was representing the views of "unhappy investors." The controversy has not caused reelection problems. Against chemical engineer T.J. Cox in 2006, Radanovich sent a mailer late in the campaign that included praise from Dianne Feinstein, who objected to the unauthorized use of her photo.

TWENTIETH DISTRICT

Rep. Jim Costa (D)

Elected 2004, 2d term; b. Apr. 13, 1952, Fresno; home, Fresno; CA State U. Fresno, B.A. 1974; Catholic; single.

Elected Office: CA Assembly, 1978-94; CA Senate, 1994-2002.

Professional Career: Consultant, 2002-04.

DC Office: 1314 LHOB, 20515, 202-225-3341; Fax: 202-225-9308; Web site: www.costa.house.gov.

District Offices: Bakersfield, 661-869-1620; Fresno, 559-495-1620.

Committees: *Agriculture* (12th of 25 D): Conservation, Credit, Energy & Research; Livestock, Dairy & Poultry. *Foreign Affairs* (24th of 27 D): Middle East & South Asia; Europe. *Natural Resources* (12th of 27 D): Energy & Mineral Resources (Chmn.); Water & Power.

Group Ratings

	ADA	ACLU	AFS	LCV	ITIC	NTU	COC	ACU	CFG	FRC
2006	70	67	71	42	86	23	93	56	34	42
2005	80	—	100	61	—	23	70	32	22	25

National Journal Ratings

	2005 LIB	—	2005 CONS	2006 LIB	—	2006 CONS
Economic	59%	—	41%	57%	—	43%
Social	59%	—	41%	62%	—	38%
Foreign	60%	—	39%	58%	—	41%

Key Votes of the 109th Congress

1. Estate Tax Repeal	Y	5. Limit Interstate Abortion	Y	9. Build Border Fence	Y
2. Limit CAFE Standards	N	6. Extend Patriot Act	N	10. CAFTA	N
3. FY06 Spending Curb	N	7. Bar Same Sex Marriage	N	11. Oppose Iraq Withdrawal	Y
4. Drilling in ANWR	Y	8. Stem Cell Research $	Y	12. Detainee Tribunals	N

Election Results

2006 general	Jim Costa (D) .... unopposed			($722,335)
2006 primary	Jim Costa (D) .... unopposed			
2004 general	Jim Costa (D) 61,005	(53%)		($1,937,317)
	Roy Ashburn (R) 53,231	(47%)		($1,093,429)

The People		Race/Ethnic Origin	Ancestry	
Area size:	4,989 sq. mi.	21.4% White	German: 3.2%	Irish: 2.7%
Urban population:	91.2%	7.2% Black	USA: 2.3%	
Rural population:	8.8%	5.6% Asian	**2004 Presidential Vote**	
Pop. 2000:	639,088	0.7% Native Am.	Kerry (D) 58,534	(51%)
Pop. 2005 (est):	683,528	0.1% Hawaiian	Bush (R) 56,045	(48%)
Median income:	$26,800	1.7% Two+ races	Other 1,023	(1%)
Poverty status:	32.2%	0.2% Other	**2000 Presidential Vote**	
Military veterans:	8.1%	63.1% Hispanic Origin	Gore (D) 57,790	(55%)
			Bush (R) 46,058	(44%)
			Other 1,844	(2%)
			Cook Partisan Voting Index: D + 5	

Occupation	Blue collar: 27.2%	White collar: 37.8%	Gray collar: 35.0%

California's Central Valley by car seems a monotonous landscape: mile after mile of farmland with mile-square grid roads, cut across by diagonal railroads and canals, with an occasional cluster town. The land is hilly and gets more water near the Sierra Nevada, and this is where you find the larger cities. On the other side are the Westlands, where the land is flatter and the water scarcer. Its 600,000 acres are the nation's largest irrigation district. Here the land was always developed and sold in large plots; it has some of the world's largest farming operations today. And it produces plenty: alfalfa, cantaloupes, cotton, grapes, lima beans, olives, peaches, plums, raisins, sugar beets, tomatoes, walnuts, wheat. The owners are a hardy lot, but like most entrepreneurs they have been happy to have government help over the years: crop price supports (in the case of cotton), agricultural research, exceptions to the immigration laws, irrigation systems and (most important) subsidized water. They have fought hard against liberals' efforts at change, from Governor Jerry Brown's attempts to encourage Cesar Chavez's United Farm Workers in the 1970s to former House Natural Resources Committee Chairman George Miller's 1992 law to draw off more water to the Sacramento delta and charge higher prices for it in the Valley. But the greatest threats could come from conservatives: Congress has deadlocked on guest worker programs pushed by Valley members. Farmers also worry that Los Angeles users might outbid them for water. But the Bush administration has signed contracts that deliver water to them for $31 an acre foot, while southern California cities pay more than $200 for water from the state.

The 20th Congressional District of California includes most of the Westlands of the Central Valley, from Bakersfield to a point northwest of Fresno. Its irregular boundaries were drawn to maximize the Hispanic population and Democratic percentage, so the 20th includes the old downtown neighborhoods of both Bakersfield and Fresno, but not their more affluent neighborhoods; it includes heavily Latino towns like Delano, long Chavez's headquarters and the site of a potentially large natural gas discovery, but not more Anglo places like Tulare. Just 36% of Fresno's population is included within the 20th and just 18% of Bakersfield's; the district's Hispanic population is 63%, about double that in other Central Valley districts. This is the most Democratic Valley seat between Sacramento and Los Angeles, though in 2004 George W. Bush won 48% here and in 2006 Arnold Schwarzenegger won 54% in the governor's race.

The congressman from the 20th District is Jim Costa, a Democrat elected in 2004. Costa was born in Fresno and worked on the family farm. In 1978 he was elected to the Assembly where he was known as a moderate Democrat. In 2002 he was forced to retire because of term limits. He turned down an opportunity that year to run in the less familiar 18th District against the politically vulnerable Gary Condit; he founded a consulting firm instead. In 2004, when Cal Dooley retired after 14 years, Costa entered the race and started off with wide name recognition—his former state Senate district covered the entire congressional district. But in the March primary, he faced a bruising challenge from Lisa Quigley, chief of staff to Dooley. Quigley grew up in the Central Valley, but she hadn't lived in the district in nearly two decades, not since she left for the University of California at Berkeley and a career on Capitol Hill. Costa, a third-generation farmer and a Fresno native, questioned her residency and her agricultural credentials. Quigley, who was endorsed by Dooley and national abortion-rights groups, bashed Costa's legislative record and painted him as a special interest lobbyist. In the final days Quigley ran ads mentioning Costa's 1986 arrest for soliciting a prostitute and a 1994 incident in which police found drug paraphernalia in his home. Costa shrugged off the attacks and won the primary by an unexpectedly large 73%-27%.

In the general, Costa began as a clear favorite in this Democratic-leaning district. But state Senator Roy Ashburn, the Republican nominee, ran a formidable campaign. He focused on cultural issues, including same-sex marriage, hoping to win Latino votes. He criticized Costa for supporting tax policies that he said hurt low-income families. He brought in Vice President Dick Cheney, Speaker Dennis Hastert and Governor Arnold Schwarzenegger and benefited from $1.5 million in ads from the National Republican Congressional Committee that claimed, "Jim Costa—he's gonna cost ya." But Costa's lengthy legislative record didn't readily lend itself to the "liberal" label. He criticized Ashburn as an "extreme partisan" who would be a tool of the Republican leadership. In a relatively low turnout, Costa won 53%-47%. In Fresno County, which cast 42% of the vote, he won 61%-39%. Costa also carried Bakersfield-centered Kern County, 55%-45%. Ashburn won in the geographically central Kings County 61%-39%, but its vote was too little to make a difference. After the election, Ashburn attacked the 22d District's Bill Thomas and other Republican moderates for "sabotaging" his efforts.

In the House, Costa got seats on Agriculture and Resources, both important committees to the Valley. His voting record placed him toward the center of the House. He cosponsored a bill that would require states to establish independent commissions to perform redistricting. In the majority, he became chairman of the Energy and Mineral Resources Subcommittee, a panel of interest to many Democrats who criticized recent sweetheart deals for offshore oil and gas leasing. He also was named as vice-chair of the Transatlantic Legislators' Dialogue, a biannual meeting between members of Congress and European parliaments to discuss global issues. In 2006, he had no opposition in the primary or general election.

TWENTY-FIRST DISTRICT

Rep. Devin Nunes (R)

Elected 2002, 3d term; b. Oct. 1, 1973, Tulare; home, Visalia; Col. of the Sequoias, A.D. 1993, CA Poly. U., B.S. 1995, M.A. 1996; Catholic; married (Elizabeth).

Elected Office: Col. of the Sequoias Governing Bd., 1996-2002.

Professional Career: State Dir., USDA Rural Dev., 2001

DC Office: 1013 LHOB, 20515, 202-225-2523; Fax: 202-225-3404; Web site: www.nunes.house.gov/.

District Offices: Clovis, 559-323-5235; Visalia, 559-733-3861.

Committees: *Ways & Means* (15th of 17 R): Oversight; Social Security.

Group Ratings

	ADA	ACLU	AFS	LCV	ITIC	NTU	COC	ACU	CFG	FRC
2006	0	10	0	0	100	56	100	84	52	85
2005	5	—	13	0	—	59	96	84	59	92

National Journal Ratings

	2005 LIB	—	2005 CONS		2006 LIB	—	2006 CONS
Economic	26%	—	73%		4%	—	94%
Social	39%	—	60%		30%	—	70%
Foreign	11%	—	86%		14%	—	85%

Key Votes of the 109th Congress

1. Estate Tax Repeal	Y	5. Limit Interstate Abortion	Y	9. Build Border Fence	Y
2. Limit CAFE Standards	Y	6. Extend Patriot Act	Y	10. CAFTA	Y
3. FY06 Spending Curb	Y	7. Bar Same Sex Marriage	Y	11. Oppose Iraq Withdrawal	Y
4. Drilling in ANWR	Y	8. Stem Cell Research $	N	12. Detainee Tribunals	Y

Election Results

2006 general	Devin Nunes (R)	95,214	(67%)	($991,874)
	Steven Haze (D)	42,718	(30%)	($154,339)
	Other	4,729	(3%)	
2006 primary	Devin Nunes (R) .... unopposed			
2004 general	Devin Nunes (R)	140,721	(73%)	($667,520)
	Fred Davis (D)	51,594	(27%)	

Prior Winning Percentages: 2002 (70%)

The People		**Race/Ethnic Origin**	**Ancestry**	
Area size:	8,090 sq. mi.	46.4% White	German: 7.7%	English: 5.6%
Urban population:	79.9%	2.1% Black	Irish: 5.5%	
Rural population:	20.1%	4.9% Asian	**2004 Presidential Vote**	
Pop. 2000:	639,088	0.9% Native Am.	Bush (R) 133,004	(65%)
Pop. 2005 (est):	726,294	0.1% Hawaiian	Kerry (D) 68,501	(34%)
Median income:	$36,047	2.2% Two+ races	Other 1,646	(1%)
Poverty status:	20.7%	0.2% Other	**2000 Presidential Vote**	
Military veterans:	10.6%	43.4% Hispanic Origin	Bush (R) 107,645	(60%)
			Gore (D) 65,268	(37%)
			Other 5,120	(3%)
			Cook Partisan Voting Index: R +13	

Occupation	Blue collar: 22.0%	White collar: 52.8%	Gray collar: 25.2%

Fresno, in California's Central Valley, between the flat Westlands and the Sierras, is a city agricultural and industrial, middle American and ethnically diverse. It is a creation of the industrial age, founded by the Central Pacific Railroad; its city fathers bred the local wine grape, developed the raisin industry and introduced the Smyrna fig. These are among Fresno's 300-plus crops, which include cotton, lima beans, nectarines, almonds, tomatoes, cantaloupes, plums, peaches and alfalfa. Dairy products, however, are now the biggest commodity here. Fresno County produces more farm products in dollar value than any other county in the United States and neighboring Tulare County is close behind. Central Valley agriculture is industrial in its precision, its thoroughness and its ownership by large corporations. The vineyards outside Fresno radiate in mechanical precision, with vines just 10 feet apart and exposed to the relentless summer sun: nothing romantic or quaint about it. Times have been good here: The weak dollar of recent years has boosted farm exports, as did the temporary break in the longstanding local drought; large citrus groves benefited from hurricanes in Florida, and nuts have found new export markets. While the city of Fresno started as a farm-marketing center and as a tourist stop-off point on the way to Yosemite National Park, it has long since grown out north, east and west from its old downtown, and its economy has diversified. New home builders can barely keep up with the demand by farm workers.

The 21st Congressional District of California, the most productive farm district in the nation, covers most of Fresno County east of Fresno and all of Tulare County to the south; 42% of the population is in Fresno County and 58% in Tulare. Here and there amid the farm fields are small cities— Visalia (fast-growing, and the largest in the district), Tulare, Clovis, Reedley, Porterville. Connecting many of these places is State Route 99, the old Farm-to-Market Corridor and a future Interstate. Past Kings Canyon and Sequoia National Parks loom the giant peaks of the Sierra Nevada, including Mount Whitney, at 14,494 feet, the highest point in California and in the lower 48 states. This part of the Central Valley has had vigorous growth between 1990 and 2005; the district is 43% Hispanic. In 2004, George W. Bush got 65% of the vote, his second highest percentage in a California district.

The congressman from the 21st District is Devin Nunes, a Republican of Portuguese ancestry, first elected in 2002. He grew up in Tulare County on a dairy farm that has been in his family for three generations. He graduated from Cal Poly in San Luis Obispo with degrees in agriculture and worked on the dairy farm. He is politically well connected. In 1998, at 25, he ran for the House in the 20th District and finished second in the primary, losing by just 52%-48%. In 2000 he was Tulare County campaign chairman for former Congressman and Ways and Mean Chairman Bill Thomas. In 2001, with help from Thomas, he was appointed California director of rural development for the Agriculture Department.

When California's redistricting plan was unveiled in September 2001, there was no incumbent in the 21st District, and Nunes moved quickly to run. He was supported by Thomas and in time by nine other California Republican incumbents—half the state Republican delegation. His $5,000 contribution from Thomas opened doors in Washington, and many in the pharmaceutical and insurance industries supported him. At home he won the endorsement of the California Farm Bureau, the state's largest farm organization and a powerful voice in Central Valley politics. But Nunes had serious primary competition. The best known candidate was Jim Patterson, the conservative former mayor of Fresno, who was well-financed by the Club for Growth. Another serious candidate was Assemblyman Mike Briggs, who worked on agriculture issues in Sacramento, but he was criticized for being one of only four Republicans to cross the aisle and vote for the state budget in 2001; he defended his vote by saying he got large tax breaks for farmers. There were few differences on policy. All three said that agriculture was their top priority and promised to seek new water sources. All called for cuts in taxes and regulations and endorsed expanded guest worker programs. Nunes won the endorsement of *The Fresno Bee*. He won with 37% of the vote, to 33% for Patterson and 26% for Briggs. In his base of Tulare County, which cast 49% of the Republican votes, Nunes led with 46% of the vote. In Fresno County he finished third with 27%, but his two opponents divided the vote: Patterson got 37% and Briggs 30%. Nunes won easily in November 70%-26%.

Nunes began what could be a lengthy House career with a very good friend as chairman of Ways and Means. He had a mostly conservative voting record, though toward the center on social issues. Speaker Dennis Hastert tapped him for a group of about a dozen House members who met informally with him each week. He worked to prevent a trade dispute when South Korea banned the import of local oranges because of what Nunes said was an unwarranted report of a fungus. He got a feasibility study for a new water reservoir near Temperance Flat, but he clashed with George Radanovich in the adjacent district over his more senior colleague's push to increase water flow over Friant Dam so salmon could be returned to the parched San Joaquin River; Nunes believes it would drive local farmers out of business by weakening the area's water supply. In January 2005, his well-placed friends maneuvered to get Nunes a seat on Ways and Means, but he took an immediate leave of absence until there was an opening. Meanwhile, he became chairman of the National Parks, Recreation and Public Lands Subcommittee at Resources. He received a permanent seat on Ways and Means in May after Rob Portman of Ohio exited the House, and Ways and Means, to become special trade representative. Ohio Republicans objected and stated that the seat ought to be given to an Ohioan but they were outmaneuvered by Nunes and his patron Bill Thomas. The only downside was that Nunes was forced to relinquish his National Parks subcommittee gavel. Nunes was an early backer of Arnold Schwarzenegger's referendum for a new non-partisan redistricting plan, which was handily defeated.

Like most California members of both parties, Nunes has been easily reelected. After the 2006 election, Nunes said Republicans "would have kept the Senate, and maybe the House" if President Bush had not waited until the day after the election to announce the resignation of Defense Secretary Don Rumsfeld. As an early ally of John Boehner, Nunes won some leadership assignments, including at the NRCC.

TWENTY-SECOND DISTRICT

Rep. Kevin McCarthy (R)

Elected 2006, 1st term; b. Jan. 26, 1965, Bakersfield; home, Bakersfield; Attended Bakersfield Col., 1984-85, CA St. U., B.S. 1989, M.B.A. 1994; Baptist; married (Judy).

Elected Office: Kern Comm. Col. Board, 2000-02, CA Assembly, 2002-06, Min. Ldr., 2003-06.

Professional Career: Owner, Kevin O's Deli, 1986-87, Mesa Marin Batting Range, 1991-92; Dist. Dir., U.S. Rep. Bill Thomas, 1987-2002.

DC Office: 1523 LHOB, 20515, 202-225-2915; Fax: 202-225-2908; Web site: kevinmccarthy.house.gov.

District Offices: Atascadero, 805-461-1034; Bakersfield, 661-327-3611.

Committees: *Agriculture* (20th of 21 R): Horticulture & Organic Agriculture; General Farm Commodities & Risk Management. *House Administration* (3d of 3 R). *Natural Resources* (21st of 22 R): National Parks, Forests & Public Lands.

Group Ratings and Key Votes: Newly Elected

Election Results

2006 general	Kevin McCarthy (R)	133,278	(71%)	($682,340)
	Sharon Beery (D)	55,226	(29%)	($27,673)
2006 primary	Kevin McCarthy (R)	63,399	(86%)	
	Steve Nichols (R)	5,995	(8%)	
	David Evans (R)	4,637	(6%)	
2004 general	Bill Thomas (R)	unopposed		($1,493,678)

The People		Race/Ethnic Origin	Ancestry	
Area size:	10,454 sq. mi.	66.8% White	German: 10.7%	Irish: 8.1%
Urban population:	82.5%	5.6% Black	English: 7.8%	
Rural population:	17.5%	2.9% Asian	**2004 Presidential Vote**	
Pop. 2000:	639,088	0.9% Native Am.	Bush (R) 180,584	(68%)
Pop. 2005 (est):	731,581	0.1% Hawaiian	Kerry (D) 82,356	(31%)
Median income:	$41,801	2.5% Two+ races	Other 2,747	(1%)
Poverty status:	13.7%	0.2% Other	**2000 Presidential Vote**	
Military veterans:	14.8%	21.0% Hispanic Origin	Bush (R) 141,156	(64%)
			Gore (D) 73,338	(33%)
			Other 5,043	(2%)
			Cook Partisan Voting Index: R +16	

Occupation   Blue collar: 23.1%   White collar: 57.8%   Gray collar: 19.1%

Bakersfield, at the apex of the southern end of California's Central Valley, has been the focus of great migrations four times—in a gold rush in 1885, when oil was discovered here in 1899, during the 1930s when the Okies drove their jalopies from the Dust Bowl of Oklahoma and Kansas and Texas across the Southwest on U.S. 66, and again in the 1980s and 1990s, when Bakersfield and Kern County grew more rapidly than California's biggest metro areas, with their rigs pumping more oil than is produced annually in Oklahoma. The migration that made the deepest imprint was in the 1930s. The Okies drove over one thousand miles of brown landscape, then through the Tehachapi Pass, and found this vast green valley, with its irrigated fields and its eucalyptus-shaded towns, the richest farming country in the world. The story is told vividly in John Steinbeck's *The Grapes of Wrath*, though his vision of the Okies as workers eager to join together with their fellow proletarians and rise up against their bosses did not get the picture quite right. More accurate is Dan Morgan's *Rising in the West*, which shows the strong Pentecostal beliefs that drove many migrants and, unlike Steinbeck, explains how they prospered in California.

The area around Bakersfield has become the one Southern-accented part of California, the home of country singers Buck Owens and Merle Haggard and a thriving country music scene. People here are culturally conservative with a strong drive toward discipline and little empathy for the therapy that is so common in Los Angeles, 110 miles south. But Bakersfield's uniqueness may be diluted as southern California spreads north: city officials want to expand its boundaries and developers are planning Centennial, a town of 70,000 on land where I-5 plunges downhill from the Tejon Pass.

The 22d Congressional District of California, the southernmost district in the Central Valley, includes most of Bakersfield and Kern County, most of the land area of San Luis Obispo County, over the mountains to the west, and a slice of northern Los Angeles County including half the desert town of Lancaster and the tiny desert town of Gorman, which has tried unsuccessfully to secede from Los Angeles County to join Kern. At the eastern end in the desert is Edwards Air Force Base where Chuck Yeager flew the X-1 and where the Space Shuttle has frequently landed; not far away is Mojave, the end of the Twenty Mule Team Trail where borate from Death Valley was loaded onto trains. The district's boundaries are designed to maximize the Hispanic percentage of the next-door 20th District, but the population of the 22d is still 21% Hispanic. The 22d includes oil fields but also high-income subdivisions. The rich farmland produces most of the olives grown in the United States and more than 70% of the carrots. This is where the standardized baby carrot was born: local breeders figured out how to grow an 8-inch carrot; an automated cutter then snips uniformly-sized 2-inch pieces from it. Politically, Kern County was Democratic territory in the early 1960s—when, for that matter, so was Oklahoma. By the late 1960s, both had become solidly Republican in national politics. The inland portion of San Luis Obispo County has always been Republican. George W. Bush won 64% of the vote here in 2000 and 68% in 2004, in both cases his best showing in any California district; with 74% here, it was also Arnold Schwarzenegger's top performing district in the 2006 governor's race.

The new congressman from the 22d District is Kevin McCarthy, who won the seat in 2006 without serious competition in the primary or general. He comes from a fourth-generation Bakersfield family and has a political background that suggests he will be on the leadership track. In college, he was chairman of the California Young Republicans and later chairman of the national Young Republicans organization. A graduate of California State University in Bakersfield, with bachelor and MBA degrees, he started his own deli with $5,000 in winnings from the state lottery. He joined Thomas's district office as a volunteer and eventually became his district director and local protege. In 2002, McCarthy followed in his boss's footsteps by winning election to the state legislature. Part of a large freshman class in the state House, he built relationships with his colleagues by fraternizing, playing pickup basketball with them, and traveling to their home districts. A mainstream conservative, McCarthy quickly impressed his colleagues and was elected minority leader during his first term when the previous leader had to step down because of term limits. He served on the transition team for newly-elected GOP Gov. Arnold Schwarzenegger. McCarthy later worked closely with the governor on reducing the state's budget deficit, overhauling its workers' compensation system, and crafting a redistricting proposal that drew districts in which no political party had more than a 7% advantage among registered voters.

When Thomas, the chairman of the powerful House Ways and Means Committee, announced in March 2006 that he would not seek reelection to a 15th term, McCarthy was the logical successor. He faced only token opposition in the June primary—a testament both to the strength of his candidacy and to the fact that Thomas announced his retirement just four days before the filing deadline, leaving little time for other prospective challengers to organize for a campaign. In this solidly Republican district, winning the GOP nomination was tantamount to victory; in November, McCarthy won 71%-29%. Yet he didn't rest on his laurels. He raised more than $1 million and traveled the country campaigning for other Republican congressional candidates. He parceled out at least $80,000: $50,000 to the National Republican Congressional Committee and most of the rest to more than a dozen Republican candidates for open seats across the nation. Nine of his 12 other freshman Republican House colleagues got contributions from him. Those contributions put McCarthy in good stead with party leaders. In the House, he got seats on House Administration and Agriculture, where he got to work on the farm bill. He also helped other freshmen with committee assignments as their representative on the Republican Steering Committee.

TWENTY-THIRD DISTRICT

Rep. Lois Capps (D)

Elected March 1998, 5th full term; b. Jan. 10, 1938, Ladysmith, WI; home, Santa Barbara; Pacific Lutheran U., B.S. 1959, Yale U., M.A. 1964, U. of CA at Santa Barbara, M.A. 1990; Lutheran; widowed.

Professional Career: Staff nurse, Visiting Nurses Assn., 1963-64; Head nurse, Yale New Haven Hospital, 1960-63; Instructor, Santa Barbara City Col., 1983-95; Nurse, Santa Barbara Schl. Dist., 1979-96.

DC Office: 1110 LHOB, 20515, 202-225-3601; Fax: 202-225-5632; Web site: www.house.gov/capps.

District Offices: San Luis Obispo, 805-546-8348; Santa Barbara, 805-730-1710; Ventura County, 805-985-6807.

Committees: *Energy & Commerce* (15th of 31 D): Environment & Hazardous Materials; Health; Telecommunications & the Internet. *Natural Resources* (21st of 27 D): Fisheries, Wildlife & Oceans; National Parks, Forests & Public Lands.

Group Ratings

	ADA	ACLU	AFS	LCV	ITIC	NTU	COC	ACU	CFG	FRC
2006	95	91	100	100	43	16	27	4	11	0
2005	95	—	100	94	—	14	32	0	4	8

National Journal Ratings

	2005 LIB	—	2005 CONS		2006 LIB	—	2006 CONS
Economic	85%	—	13%		90%	—	9%
Social	85%	—	14%		91%	—	8%
Foreign	90%	—	9%		80%	—	18%

Key Votes of the 109th Congress

1. Estate Tax Repeal	N	5. Limit Interstate Abortion	N	9. Build Border Fence	N
2. Limit CAFE Standards	N	6. Extend Patriot Act	N	10. CAFTA	N
3. FY06 Spending Curb	N	7. Bar Same Sex Marriage	N	11. Oppose Iraq Withdrawal	N
4. Drilling in ANWR	N	8. Stem Cell Research $	Y	12. Detainee Tribunals	N

Election Results

2006 general	Lois Capps (D)	114,661	(65%)	($922,774)
	Victor Tognazzini (R)	61,272	(35%)	($79,530)
2006 primary	Lois Capps (D)	unopposed		
2004 general	Lois Capps (D)	153,980	(63%)	($1,009,290)
	Don Regan (R)	83,926	(34%)	($148,631)
	Other	6,391	(3%)	

Prior Winning Percentages: 2002 (59%); 2000 (53%); 1998 (55%); 1998 (53%)

The People		Race/Ethnic Origin	Ancestry	
Area size:	2,479 sq. mi.	48.7% White	German: 8.3%	English: 7.2%
Urban population:	98.0%	1.9% Black	Irish: 6.5%	
Rural population:	2.0%	4.9% Asian	**2004 Presidential Vote**	
Pop. 2000:	639,088	0.5% Native Am.	Kerry (D) 147,361	(58%)
Pop. 2005 (est):	656,110	0.2% Hawaiian	Bush (R) 101,817	(40%)
Median income:	$44,874	2.0% Two+ races	Other 3,464	(1%)
Poverty status:	15.7%	0.1% Other	**2000 Presidential Vote**	
Military veterans:	11.0%	41.7% Hispanic Origin	Gore (D) 119,795	(53%)
			Bush (R) 90,550	(40%)
			Other 13,574	(6%)
			Cook Partisan Voting Index: D + 9	

Occupation	Blue collar: 20.3%	White collar: 57.3%	Gray collar: 22.4%

Santa Barbara is one of California's most paradisiacal places, a collection of red tile roofs and leafy live oaks, sheltered by towering mountains just above the sea. The impression is a bit misleading, for Santa Barbara has its problems, and its Spanish style is a creation not of 18th century Mission culture, but of the 20th century. Most of its white stucco buildings were put up after a 1925 earthquake leveled much of the town and the most distinguished of the Spanish Revival buildings were designed by an architect with the marvelously un-Latin name of George Washington Smith. Santa Barbara, like Disneyland, does not reproduce the past but presents a bigger, more attractive, cleaner version of it, maintained not by a company but by an architectural review board. But Santa Barbara's affluence isn't ersatz. This has long been one of the nation's richest retirement communities, and one determined to preserve its environment and serenity. Both features came under threat spectacularly in 1969, when an underwater oil well ruptured, coating the beach with oil; pictures of the oil slick in the channel and of volunteers trying to wash oil off grounded birds, helped to launch the environmental movement. Almost all the wells are closed now (though some old 19th century wells still send globs of oil to the beach at nearby Summerland). But the oil spill did leave a residue in Santa Barbara's politics. This was once a mostly Republican community, uninterested in redistribution of wealth, but very concerned about the environment (it has built the nation's largest desalination plant) and moderate to liberal on cultural issues. Like most of coastal California, it moved decisively to the left in the past decade. But some of those changes have not gone smoothly, as pressures grew to split Santa Barbara into two counties of roughly equal population: a proposed Mission County to the west and north, which would be more conservative; and the rest in the more liberal Santa Barbara County. In June 2006, county voters overwhelmingly rejected the proposal.

The 23d Congressional District of California is a thin strip of Pacific coastline, from two to 12 miles deep, from the industrial ports of Oxnard and Port Hueneme southeast of Santa Barbara to the north end of San Luis Obispo County on the Big Sur coast, just north of William Randolph Hearst's San Simeon. There are nodes of populated territory. The largest city is Oxnard, in Ventura County, which is anything but upscale, with a large number of immigrants and booming development; overall the district is 42% Hispanic. Santa Barbara and nearby Montecito are far more upscale. Much of the Santa Barbara coastline is occupied by Vandenberg Air Force Base, which launches unmanned government and commercial satellites into polar orbit. The largest towns in northern Santa Barbara County, like San Luis Obispo to the north, are pleasant, comfortable places, as untrendy as you can find in coastal California. Environmentalists want to extend the Monterey Bay National Marine Sanctuary to cover the waters off San Luis Obispo. This was a marginal district, seriously contested several times in the 1990s. But in its current iteration, it has become safely Democratic.

The congresswoman from the 23d District is Lois Capps, a Democrat first chosen in a March 1998 special election to replace her late husband Walter Capps. Lois Capps grew up in Wyoming and Montana, the daughter of a Lutheran minister; she graduated from college with a nursing degree and was head nurse at Yale New Haven Hospital where she met Walter Capps, a student at Yale Divinity School. In 1964 he became a professor at the University of California at Santa Barbara. Lois Capps became the head elementary school nurse for the Santa Barbara school system, director of the county's teenage pregnancy and parenting project, and a part-time instructor at Santa Barbara City Community College. In 1994, Walter Capps ran for the House seat and lost 49.3%-48.5% to Andrea Seastrand, a conservative Republican assemblywoman from San Luis Obispo County. Capps ran again in 1996 and won 48%-44%, but died of a heart attack in October 1997. After a spirited primary, Republicans nominated Assemblyman Tom Bordonaro, the favorite of Christian conservatives. Bordonaro, a paraplegic since a car accident in college, emphasized his "blue-collar roots and common values," and was backed by Tom DeLay. Lois Capps had help from labor and environmental groups. In the January 1998 primary she finished first with 45% to 29% for Bordonaro. In the runoff Bordonaro suffered from continuing GOP divisions and voter backlash against outside groups' advertising. Capps won by a surprisingly large 53%-45% margin. The same two candidates were on the ballot in November. But national Republicans had few hopes of winning this time, and it was not a priority race. Capps won 55%-43%.

With her seat on Energy and Commerce and background as a health care professional (she is one of three nurses in the House, all Democrats), Capps has focused on HMO regulation and protecting the privacy of medical records, including genetic tests. She began as less of a down-the-line liberal than her husband, and she worked more successfully with Republicans than the typical California Democrat. Perhaps it is her disposition: A 2006 survey of congressional aides for *Washingtonian* magazine named Capps "the nicest member of Congress."

After she voted for normal trade relations with China, the Teamsters claimed that Capps betrayed them and withdrew their endorsement. When George W. Bush took over, she patched things up with labor by opposing trade promotion authority and her voting record has moved toward the liberal end of the Democratic Caucus. She stood by Bush's side during a White House signing ceremony of her bill to attract more students into the nursing profession. When the AARP endorsed Bush's Medicare/prescription drug bill, Capps said that she was "stunned and offended" and resigned from the group.

Capps represents a coastal district and it is reflected in her other legislative interests. In 2004, the House passed her amendment to stop a comprehensive inventory of oil and gas resources beneath the Outer Continental Shelf; she has also opposed the Bush administration plan for drilling in the Los Padres National Forest and has been outspoken against off-shore drilling. She organized the National Marine Sanctuaries Caucus. In December 2005, she successfully opposed an attempt by Armed Services Committee chairman Duncan Hunter to convert part of the Channel Islands into a private recreation area for the military.

In 2000, Capps had serious competition from moderate Republican Mike Stoker, a former Santa Barbara County Supervisor and California Agricultural Labor Relations Board chairman. Capps had a big fundraising edge and won 53%-44%. After promising in 1998 to serve only three terms, she abandoned that pledge; since 2002, she has not been seriously challenged. Her biggest problem in the 2004 campaign was that law enforcement officials discovered that a former finance director had embezzled $200,000 from her campaign.

TWENTY-FOURTH DISTRICT

Rep. Elton Gallegly (R)

Elected 1986, 11th term; b. Mar. 7, 1944, Huntington Park; home, Simi Valley; Los Angeles St. Col., 1962-63; Protestant; married (Janice).

Elected Office: Simi Valley City Cncl., 1979-80; Simi Valley Mayor, 1980-86.

Professional Career: Owner, real estate firm.

DC Office: 2309 RHOB, 20515, 202-225-5811; Fax: 202-225-1100; Web site: www.house.gov/gallegly.

District Offices: Solvang, 805-686-2525; Thousand Oaks, 805-497-2224.

Committees: *Foreign Affairs* (4th of 23 R): Europe (RMM); Western Hemisphere. *Judiciary* (4th of 17 R): Immigration, Citizenship, Refugees, Border Security & International Law; Courts, the Internet & Intellectual Property. *Natural Resources* (3d of 22 R): Insular Affairs.

Group Ratings

	ADA	ACLU	AFS	LCV	ITIC	NTU	COC	ACU	CFG	FRC
2006	0	9	0	8	100	53	100	84	49	85
2005	0	—	0	6	—	54	92	80	54	100

National Journal Ratings

	2005 LIB — 2005 CONS	2006 LIB — 2006 CONS
Economic	30% — 68%	11% — 89%
Social	0% — 89%	15% — 84%
Foreign	14% — 85%	30% — 67%

Key Votes of the 109th Congress

1. Estate Tax Repeal	Y	5. Limit Interstate Abortion	Y	9. Build Border Fence	Y
2. Limit CAFE Standards	Y	6. Extend Patriot Act	Y	10. CAFTA	Y
3. FY06 Spending Curb	Y	7. Bar Same Sex Marriage	Y	11. Oppose Iraq Withdrawal	Y
4. Drilling in ANWR	Y	8. Stem Cell Research $	N	12. Detainee Tribunals	Y

Election Results

2006 general	Elton Gallegly (R)	129,812	(62%)	($944,852)
	Jill Martinez (D)	79,461	(38%)	($131,905)
2006 primary	Elton Gallegly (R)	51,923	(80%)	
	Michael Tenenbaum (R)	12,903	(20%)	
2004 general	Elton Gallegly (R)	178,660	(63%)	($551,059)
	Brett Wagner (D)	96,397	(34%)	($207,432)
	Other	9,321	(3%)	

Prior Winning Percentages: 2002 (65%); 2000 (54%); 1998 (60%); 1996 (60%); 1994 (66%); 1992 (54%); 1990 (58%); 1988 (69%); 1986 (68%)

The People		Race/Ethnic Origin	Ancestry		
Area size:	4,157 sq. mi.	68.6% White	German: 11.7%		English: 9.0%
Urban population:	94.2%	1.6% Black	Irish: 8.8%		
Rural population:	5.8%	4.4% Asian	**2004 Presidential Vote**		
Pop. 2000:	639,088	0.5% Native Am.	Bush (R)	165,430	(56%)
Pop. 2005 (est):	668,099	0.1% Hawaiian	Kerry (D)	127,875	(43%)
Median income:	$61,453	2.2% Two+ races	Other	3,473	(1%)
Poverty status:	7.2%	0.2% Other	**2000 Presidential Vote**		
Military veterans:	13.1%	22.3% Hispanic Origin	Bush (R)	140,755	(54%)
			Gore (D)	112,436	(43%)
			Other	9,220	(4%)
			Cook Partisan Voting Index: R + 5		

Occupation   Blue collar: 17.1%   White collar: 67.8%   Gray collar: 15.1%

On a golden mountainside, looking westward over a valley hemmed in by mountains north and south, five United States presidents gathered in November 1991 to dedicate the Ronald Reagan Library. This was the first time in 202 years that five presidents stood together in one place—one which the Founding Fathers probably did not imagine would ever be American and yet today seems quintessentially so. Simi Valley, famous a few months later as the site of the trial of police officers accused of assaulting Rodney King, is a product of the 1960s, the expansive postwar years when the vast stream of migrants who had come from all over the United States to Los Angeles spread beyond city and county limits to fill up barren valleys between golden mountains. To an area that much earlier had attracted Spanish settlers, they brought a willingness to work hard, high competence and high tech, an appreciation of the local environment and a distaste for crime and rioting that seemed all too common in the Los Angeles basin they left behind. Simi Valley is just one of several communities in the valleys of Ventura County, west of Los Angeles, that have been filling up with people leaving Los Angeles and the San Fernando Valley and building new communities in what had been orange and lemon groves. Ventura County "is part of an attempt by lots of very desirable areas to control growth," said author Joel Kotkin. "It's an elitist strategy. The irony is that the elitists are so numerous that they prompt growth by themselves." To the south, in another valley, is upscale Thousand Oaks, one of the safest large cities in the nation. Farther west in Pleasant Valley is Camarillo; in inland valleys still farther west are Santa Paula and Ojai. Academy Award nominee *Sideways*, which dealt with the abundant consumption of local wines by two friends, was filmed in nearby Buellton. Looking out toward these valleys and to the Pacific beyond at the Reagan Library are 55 million pages of presidential documents and a large piece of the Berlin Wall, which Reagan urged Mikhail Gorbachev to tear down and which fell two years later.

The 24th Congressional District of California includes all of the interior of Ventura County and Santa Barbara County to the west, plus a stretch of the Ventura County coastline including the Santa Monica Mountains and Point Mugu Naval Weapons Test Center; more than 2,000 of the naval jobs were shifted to Kern County in the 2005 base realignment. The Santa Barbara County interior is lightly inhabited; it includes the small towns of Lompoc, the Danish town of Solvang with windmills and museums, and Santa Ynez, near Reagan's beloved cabin in the mountains. It shares Vandenberg Air Force Base and the five Channel Islands and their steep cliffs with the 23d District. Most of the population is in eastern Ventura County. Politically, these areas are solidly Republican. The district voted 56% for George W. Bush in 2004.

The congressman from the 24th District is Elton Gallegly, a Republican first elected in 1986. He grew up in the working class (and now entirely Latino) suburb of Huntington Park in Los Angeles County, dropped out of college and became a real estate broker. In 1979 he was elected to the Simi Valley city council, became mayor in 1980, then was elected to Congress in 1986. In 1992, when redistricting moved much of Republican Robert Lagomarsino's district into the new Ventura County-based seat, Gallegly moved fast to push Lagomarsino into running in the district to the north, where he lost the primary to Michael Huffington's $3 million campaign.

Gallegly has a moderate-to-conservative voting record and has played a role on major issues. On immigration, he called for a constitutional amendment to deny citizenship to babies of illegal immigrants, a tougher Border Patrol, an end to welfare for illegal immigrants and a tamperproof identification card for legal aliens. In 1996, he got the House to pass his amendment allowing states to deny education to children who are illegal immigrants. In 2007, he filed a bill to require the IRS to report people suspected of working illegally in the U.S. to the Homeland Security Department. On other issues, despite pressure from local citrus growers, he decided in the final hours to support normal trade relations with China. In 2004 he passed a resolution calling on the United Nations to take action to respond to the threat that Burma poses to Southeast Asia. Locally, he earlier helped to save the Point Mugu Navy base, threatened with closure in 1996, and Ventura County's largest employer; he worked to get a wing of 16 E-2 radar planes assigned there, plus two new C-130s to fight forest fires. When the facility lost jobs in the 2005 base realignment to neighboring Kern County, Gallegly and local leaders appeared to have been outmaneuvered by Congressman Bill Thomas.

Gallegly, a non-lawyer, passed up several opportunities to chair a Judiciary subcommittee and declined to serve as a House manager during the Senate impeachment trial of Bill Clinton. In 2003, he was one of several senior members of the Resources Committee who were passed over when Richard Pombo became chairman. At home, he has become entrenched. He spent a few days campaigning for governor in the 2003 recall, but withdrew because he lacked statewide name recognition. In March 2006, he had an unusual episode in which he unexpectedly announced he would not seek reelection because of unspecified health problems, only to change his mind five days later under pressure from party leaders. After handily winning reelection in November, he abandoned his earlier plan to serve only one more term—and said he would run in 2008.

TWENTY-FIFTH DISTRICT

Rep. Buck McKeon (R)

Elected 1992, 8th term; b. Sept. 9, 1938, Los Angeles; home, Santa Clarita; Brigham Young U., B.S. 1985; Mormon; married (Patricia).

Elected Office: William S. Hart Schl. District Bd., 1979-87; Santa Clarita Mayor, 1987-88; Santa Clarita City Cncl., 1988-92.

Professional Career: Small businessman; Owner, Howard & Phil's Western Wear, 1973-00; Chmn., Valencia Natl. Bank, 1987-88.

DC Office: 2351 RHOB, 20515, 202-225-1956; Fax: 202-226-0683; Web site: mckeon.house.gov.

District Offices: Palmdale, 661-274-9688; Santa Clarita, 661-254-2111.

Committees: *Armed Services* (6th of 29 R): Air & Land Forces; Readiness. *Education & Labor* (RMM of 22 R): Health, Employment, Labor & Pensions; Healthy Families & Communities.

Group Ratings

	ADA	ACLU	AFS	LCV	ITIC	NTU	COC	ACU	CFG	FRC
2006	5	5	0	8	100	57	100	80	53	85
2005	0	—	0	6	—	54	93	84	56	83

National Journal Ratings

	2005 LIB	—	2005 CONS		2006 LIB	—	2006 CONS
Economic	19%	—	79%		12%	—	86%
Social	14%	—	85%		17%	—	79%
Foreign	23%	—	73%		17%	—	83%

Key Votes of the 109th Congress

1. Estate Tax Repeal	Y	5. Limit Interstate Abortion	Y	9. Build Border Fence	Y
2. Limit CAFE Standards	Y	6. Extend Patriot Act	Y	10. CAFTA	Y
3. FY06 Spending Curb	Y	7. Bar Same Sex Marriage	Y	11. Oppose Iraq Withdrawal	Y
4. Drilling in ANWR	Y	8. Stem Cell Research $	Y	12. Detainee Tribunals	Y

Election Results

2006 general	Buck McKeon (R)	93,987	(60%)	($1,370,664)
	Robert Rodriguez (D)	55,913	(36%)	($230,516)
	David Erickson (Lib)	6,873	(4%)	
2006 primary	Buck McKeon (R)	unopposed		
2004 general	Buck McKeon (R)	145,575	(64%)	($954,938)
	Tim Willoughby (D)	80,395	(36%)	($47,171)

Prior Winning Percentages: 2002 (65%); 2000 (62%); 1998 (75%); 1996 (62%); 1994 (65%); 1992 (52%)

The People		Race/Ethnic Origin	Ancestry		
Area size:	21,622 sq. mi.	57.2% White	German: 10.3%	Irish: 7.6%	
Urban population:	88.2%	7.9% Black	English: 7.1%		
Rural population:	11.8%	3.7% Asian	**2004 Presidential Vote**		
Pop. 2000:	639,087	0.9% Native Am.	Bush (R)	142,052	(59%)
Pop. 2005 (est):	752,711	0.2% Hawaiian	Kerry (D)	96,355	(40%)
Median income:	$49,002	2.7% Two+ races	Other	3,057	(1%)
Poverty status:	12.6%	0.2% Other	**2000 Presidential Vote**		
Military veterans:	12.7%	27.1% Hispanic Origin	Bush (R)	108,627	(56%)
			Gore (D)	81,893	(42%)
			Other	5,055	(3%)
			Cook Partisan Voting Index: R + 7		

Occupation	Blue collar: 23.6%	White collar: 60.3%	Gray collar: 16.1%

One tragedy of the 1994 Northridge earthquake was at the intersection of the I-5 and Route 14 freeways at the north edge of the San Fernando Valley, where an overpass collapsed and a motorcycle patrolman hurtled to his death. Destruction of the interchange had a major economic and personal impact, for the settled area of Los Angeles County no longer ends at the mountains at the northern rim of the San Fernando Valley. It continues along Route 14 past the mountain-surrounded city of Santa Clarita, with 168,000 people in 2004 and home of the Six Flags Magic Mountain theme park, past the former gold mining center of Acton, to where the mountains stop at the San Andreas Fault and the desert stretches out low and flat. This is the Antelope Valley, with huge aerospace plants and military bases around the fast-growing towns of Palmdale and Lancaster (named after the founder's hometown in Pennsylvania), where more than 253,000 people live; not far from upscale shopping centers, there has been a resurgence of specialty farm crops such as baby carrots, organic onions and parsnips. Traffic congestion and incidents of gang crime have supplanted the once rural lifestyle; a new expressway is planned to link the Antelope and Victor valleys. The long runways of Palmdale airport remain a little-used alternative to crowded LAX but the adjacent Air Force Plant 42 is home to many defense contractors, with projects that include the B-2 Stealth Bomber, the F-117 Stealth Fighter and the Joint Strike Fighter. Beyond the Antelope Valley the desert stretches for miles, with clumps of human settlement—Edwards Air Force Base, where Chuck Yeager flew the X-1 and where the Space Shuttle has frequently landed, and the desert towns of Victorville and Barstow.

The 25th Congressional District of California covers all of these areas (though it shares Edwards AFB with the 22d). It is enormous, geographically the largest in the state, extending far to the north, across the almost uninhabited Mojave Desert and mountains, to include Death Valley and the Owens Valley, the starting point of the Los Angeles Aqueduct, one of the glories of early 20th century engineering. The military occupies hundreds of thousands of acres with its China Lake Naval Air Weapons Station, the Goldstone deep space communications complex, and the battlefield training center at Fort Irwin. It then swings north to include mountainous Inyo and Mono Counties. But less than 10% of the district's people live in this vast expanse. Politically, this is a solidly Republican district.

The congressman from the 25th District is Howard "Buck" McKeon, a Republican first elected in 1992. He grew up in Southern California, graduated from Brigham Young University and was a co-owner of Howard and Phil's Western Wear, a family business that expanded to 52 stores in California, Arizona, Nevada and Utah in the early 1990s, but closed in 2000. McKeon was the first mayor of Santa Clarita when it was incorporated in 1987. He ran for the new House seat in 1992 and won the crucial primary 40%-38% over Assemblyman Phil Wyman, who once proposed to ban the allegedly satanic practice of recording certain words into songs backwards. McKeon became Republican freshman class president and helped abolish four select committees in 1993. On the Armed Services Committee, he worked to save local defense jobs. He helped get new contracts for the X-33, the next generation Space Shuttle and the Joint Strike Fighter; at his urging, the Pentagon is building part of the fighter in the Antelope Valley. With Howard Berman, he filed a bill to grant full Social Security benefits to teachers and other public servants who receive local pensions and take a second job; in 13 states, these retirees must take cuts in Social Security.

With a voting record that has been reliably conservative, but not sharp-edged, McKeon has been a leader at the Education and the Workforce Committee (as Republicans called it). In 2001, after losing out to John Doolittle for an Appropriations seat, he became chairman of the 21st Century Competitiveness Subcommittee, which dealt mostly with higher education issues. In handling the renewal of the higher education bill, he advocated steps that would penalize hundreds of universities and colleges that have raised tuition much faster than inflation. Many schools and Democrats complained loudly that he was advocating price controls. McKeon disagreed, responding that he simply was calling for removal of federal aid from schools that push their rates too high; but in the face of opposition from the Bush administration he later abandoned the proposal, claiming that many colleges had moved to rein in tuition hikes. In 2004, he enacted the Assistive Technology Act to benefit individuals with disabilities. When John Boehner stepped down as Education Committee chairman to become Majority Leader in February 2006, McKeon succeeded him by leapfrogging senior Republicans—Tom Petri and Pete Hoekstra—more interested in other chairmanships. In the remaining months of the Republican majority, he completed the reform of employment training programs, plus the sweeping overhaul of pension laws with Boehner's continued active role. In 2007, he became ranking Republican, a challenging post with activist chairman George Miller.

McKeon has been reelected without serious opposition.

TWENTY-SIXTH DISTRICT

Rep. David Dreier (R)

Elected 1980, 14th term; b. July 5, 1952, Kansas City, MO; home, San Dimas; Claremont McKenna Col., B.A. 1975, Claremont Grad. Schl., M.A. 1976; Christian Scientist; single.

Professional Career: Corp. Relations Dir., Claremont McKenna Col., 1976-78; Mktg. Dir., Industrial Hydrocarbons, 1978-80; V.P., Dreier Development Co., 1985-present.

DC Office: 233 CHOB, 20515, 202-225-2305; Fax: 202-225-7018; Web site: dreier.house.gov.

District Offices: San Dimas, 909-575-6226.

Committees: *Rules* (RMM of 4 R): Legislative & Budget Process.

Group Ratings

	ADA	ACLU	AFS	LCV	ITIC	NTU	COC	ACU	CFG	FRC
2006	10	18	0	17	100	57	100	72	60	57
2005	0	—	0	6	—	55	93	84	56	77

National Journal Ratings

	2005 LIB	—	2005 CONS		2006 LIB	—	2006 CONS
Economic	19%	—	79%		16%	—	81%
Social	23%	—	76%		41%	—	58%
Foreign	34%	—	61%		17%	—	73%

Key Votes of the 109th Congress

1. Estate Tax Repeal	Y	5. Limit Interstate Abortion	Y	9. Build Border Fence	Y
2. Limit CAFE Standards	Y	6. Extend Patriot Act	Y	10. CAFTA	Y
3. FY06 Spending Curb	Y	7. Bar Same Sex Marriage	N	11. Oppose Iraq Withdrawal	Y
4. Drilling in ANWR	Y	8. Stem Cell Research $	Y	12. Detainee Tribunals	Y

Election Results

2006 general	David Dreier (R)	102,028	(57%)	($2,540,691)
	Cynthia Matthews (D)	67,878	(38%)	($17,182)
	Other	9,238	(5%)	
2006 primary	David Dreier (R)	29,569	(65%)	
	S. Sonny Sardo (R)	12,186	(27%)	
	Melvin Milton (R)	3,826	(8%)	
2004 general	David Dreier (R)	134,596	(54%)	($1,338,730)
	Cynthia Matthews (D)	107,522	(43%)	($25,535)
	Randall Weissbuch (Lib)	9,089	(4%)	

Prior Winning Percentages: 2002 (64%); 2000 (57%); 1998 (58%); 1996 (61%); 1994 (67%); 1992 (58%); 1990 (64%); 1988 (69%); 1986 (72%); 1984 (71%); 1982 (65%); 1980 (52%)

The People		Race/Ethnic Origin	Ancestry		
Area size:	755 sq. mi.	52.7% White	German: 9.6%	English: 7.5%	
Urban population:	98.8%	4.4% Black	Irish: 6.9%		
Rural population:	1.2%	15.2% Asian	**2004 Presidential Vote**		
Pop. 2000:	639,088	0.3% Native Am.	Bush (R)	148,352	(55%)
Pop. 2005 (est):	689,524	0.1% Hawaiian	Kerry (D)	117,532	(44%)
Median income:	$58,968	2.6% Two+ races	Other	3,202	(1%)
Poverty status:	8.4%	0.2% Other	**2000 Presidential Vote**		
Military veterans:	10.5%	24.4% Hispanic Origin	Bush (R)	127,468	(53%)
			Gore (D)	105,023	(44%)
			Other	7,044	(3%)
			Cook Partisan Voting Index: R + 4		

Occupation   Blue collar: 17.3%   White collar: 70.7%   Gray collar: 12.0%

It was the great route west to California in the first half of the 20th century: Passengers on the Santa Fe railroad's *Super Chief* or motorists on U.S. 66, after hours and days in barren desert, descended through the Cajon Pass into the Los Angeles Basin, then moved in a stately procession beneath the 10,000-foot snow-capped San Gabriel Mountains, marveling at orange groves and exotic plants. The railroad and highway ran through a line of towns built by Midwestern Protestants as independent communities and now mostly high-income suburbs with their own civic institutions: Claremont, home of the academically renowned Claremont Colleges; La Verne and Glendora and San Dimas with its rodeo and horse trails; Monrovia and Arcadia, site of the Santa Anita race track and the Los Angeles County Arboretum; and, a few miles from the tracks, luxurious San Marino, home of the Huntington Library, one of the world's great museums and scholarly institutions, with more than 150 acres of botanical gardens. Today, the traveler arriving in Los Angeles can see the same sights, if the air is clear, much more quickly as the jet glides down the flight path to LAX.

The 26th Congressional District of California covers these foothill communities in what once were citrus groves in the San Gabriel Valley. It includes, east of Claremont, the newer San Bernardino cities of Upland, Montclair and Rancho Cucamonga, the largest city in the district and home of the Quakes minor league baseball team who play at a stadium called the Epicenter. It includes the new suburb of Walnut to the south and, far to the west, the mountain-enclosed suburb of La Canada-Flintridge, home of NASA's Jet Propulsion Laboratory. Historically, the towns running east from Los Angeles have been heavily Republican. But the area now has large Hispanic and Asian populations—San Marino, Arcadia, San Dimas and Walnut have sizable Chinese populations—that have trended Democratic. The communities in the 26th District, however, have remained Republican, even San Marino, whose population was 49% Asian in 2000. George W. Bush won 55% of the vote here in 2004; Arnold Schwarzenegger won 65% in the governor's race in 2006.

The congressman from the 26th District is David Dreier, a Republican first elected in 1980 and an influential legislator. Dreier grew up in Kansas City, Missouri, where he remains active with his family's real-estate investment firm. He spent a decade mostly on the Claremont McKenna campus, as a student and administrator, before he was elected to Congress. Dreier first ran in 1978, at 25, and lost to Democratic incumbent Jim Lloyd. He beat Lloyd in 1980, and in 1982 beat fellow Republican Wayne Grisham after they were redistricted together. At that point, Dreier evidently decided never to be pressed for funds again; he raised plenty and spent little, which takes more self-discipline than one might think. After the 2002 campaign he had $2.5 million cash on hand, the highest in the House. In 2006, the balance was $2.2 million. Dreier personifies the intellectually rigorous conservatism and free market economics that have thrived at Claremont and maintains a California cheerfulness and good humor—while serving in both the minority and majority, chiefly on the Rules Committee, where partisanship is expected and the minority fights for crumbs. As chairman from 1999 to 2006, he was a top lieutenant of Speaker Dennis Hastert and he helped to keep the legislative trains running.

Rules chairmen, once upon a time independent operators, have become an operating part of the House leadership since Democrats instituted election of committee chairmen in 1974 and Republicans did so in 1994. Rules sets the terms for debate and limits the amendments that can be offered—an essential procedural function in a legislature with 435 members, and one which can be and often is used to shape substantive outcome. The 9–4 ratio and the careful selection of members guarantee the chairman and leadership control over committee votes, but over time it must be tempered by a dose of fairness: An outraged minority party can store up grievances and wait for a chance to overturn a rule on the floor, with help from dissidents in the majority party. As chairman for eight years, Dreier's Rules Committee produced hundreds of rules, and he lost only two on the House floor. He also led a bipartisan review that reduced the number of standing House rules from 51 to 28. After September 11, he opposed conducting congressional sessions electronically and helped establish the Homeland Security Committee. In 2003 he pushed through rules changes to allow the Speaker to adjust, in case of a catastrophic attack, the number of House members required for a quorum. In April 2004 he led the House in setting a 45-day limit for special elections to fill vacancies if more than 100 seats are declared vacant by the Speaker. In 2005 he won another rule change allowing the Speaker in case of catastrophe to hold extended quorum calls and then declare vacancies and set an emergency quorum; Democrats criticized the lack of minority party input, and scholars questioned its constitutionality.

Dreier also has a policy agenda: free trade, high-tech and San Gabriel Valley water. His voting record is mostly conservative, but towards the center on cultural issues. He was a chief advocate of normal trade relations with China, and led the fight for many months when it seemed short of votes. In 2001 and 2002 he worked to pass trade promotion authority. On high-tech, he was a leading sponsor, with the Silicon Valley's Zoe Lofgren, of increasing the number of H1-B visas. In response to France's opposition to the United States invasion of Iraq, Dreier suggested increasing the number of immigration slots to citizens of France, so that more of its most talented citizens can come to the United States. With David Price, he led the House's democracy assistance commission to work with legislatures of emerging democracies.

Dreier has played a role in Republican party politics. He serves on the Republican Steering Committee and has been parliamentarian at national conventions, in which capacity he produced the rationale for the three-day "rolling roll call." He supported George W. Bush early in the 2000 race for president; they have been acquainted since Dreier sat next to Bush at a training school for Republican congressional candidates in 1978. Both lost, but their friendship endured, and more than two decades later the Rules Committee chairman was positioned to assist the President. Dreier took the lead for California Republicans on redistricting in 2001, and reached an agreement with Democratic redistricter Michael Berman under which 19 of the 20 Republican incumbents got safe districts and the GOP got a newly created seat in return for Republican support in the legislature. That helped Dreier, whose district was becoming more Hispanic and more Democratic.

He supported Arnold Schwarzenegger for governor in the recall election in 2003, and appeared with him at almost every campaign rally. In the six weeks between Schwarzenegger's election and his inauguration, Dreier acted as head of his 65-member transition team in Sacramento. Dreier originally opposed Schwarzenegger's proposal to redistrict all the state's legislative districts, arguing that the congressional district boundary lines should stay in place until after the 2010 Census. But after a meeting with the governor, Dreier publicly backed the proposal in September 2005; voters rejected it two months later.

In January 2005, Hastert changed GOP Republican rules to permit Dreier to continue as Rules chairman. But before that, he had a reelection scare. He was opposed by a conservative in the March 2004 primary who attacked him on trade and illegal immigration; Dreier won 84%-16%. Then, in August Los Angeles radio talk show hosts John Kobylt and Ken Chiampou, who had been inveighing against illegal immigration, started a Fire Dreier campaign. In September they held a rally outside Dreier's office with his Democratic opponent Cynthia Matthews, who spent only $26,000. Dreier protested, "I take a back seat to no one on the issue of illegal immigration, yet I'm being painted as a coyote." Dreier spent $1.3 million and won by 54%-43%, the first time since 1980 he finished with under 57%.

In 2005, with Judiciary Committee chairman Jim Sensenbrenner, Dreier won enactment of the "Real ID" bill to increase penalties on employers and prevent states from issuing drivers' licenses to illegal immigrants; his related proposal to require a more secure plastic Social Security card with a digitized photo was supported by T.J. Bonner, president of the Border Patrol employees' union and co-sponsored by Democrat Silvestre Reyes, the former head of the Border Patrol in El Paso, Texas. The 2005 session gained added turbulence when a Texas state grand jury indictment forced Tom DeLay to step down as Majority Leader. Hastert tentatively agreed to designate Dreier as acting Majority Leader, and the Speaker's aides discussed the details with Dreier. But some conservatives objected, and Majority Whip Roy Blunt privately urged Hastert to give the position to him and the Speaker agreed; the disappointed Dreier gained additional duties in working with committee chairmen. When John Boehner in February 2006 was elected by Republicans to replace DeLay, Dreier was assigned to push a reform package of lobbying and ethics reforms. The House passed the package, some of which became part of House rules, but failed to reach agreement with the Senate.

His November 2006 rematch against Matthews got far less attention, and Dreier won 57%-38%. In the minority, he became ranking Republican on Rules and clashed with new chairman Louise Slaughter, but showed a new zest in challenging Democratic procedural moves and occasionally outmaneuvering them.

TWENTY-SEVENTH DISTRICT

Rep. Brad Sherman (D)

Elected 1996, 6th term; b. Oct. 24, 1954, Los Angeles; home, Sherman Oaks; U.C.L.A., B.A. 1974, Harvard U., J.D. 1979; Jewish; married (Lisa).

Elected Office: CA St. Board of Equalization, 1990-95, Chmn., 1991-95.

Professional Career: Accountant, 1980-90.

DC Office: 2242 RHOB, 20515, 202-225-5911; Fax: 202-225-5879; Web site: www.house.gov/sherman.

District Offices: Sherman Oaks, 818-501-9200.

Committees: *Financial Services* (10th of 37 D): Capital Markets, Insurance & Government Sponsored Enterprises; Financial Institutions & Consumer Credit; Domestic and International Monetary Policy, Trade & Technology. *Foreign Affairs* (6th of 27 D): Terrorism, Nonproliferation & Trade (Chmn.); Middle East & South Asia. *Judiciary* (17th of 23 D): Courts, the Internet & Intellectual Property.

Group Ratings

	ADA	ACLU	AFS	LCV	ITIC	NTU	COC	ACU	CFG	FRC
2006	95	95	100	100	43	11	33	4	5	0
2005	100	—	100	100	—	12	41	0	3	8

National Journal Ratings

	2005 LIB	—	2005 CONS		2006 LIB	—	2006 CONS
Economic	88%	—	9%		86%	—	11%
Social	76%	—	24%		81%	—	18%
Foreign	76%	—	23%		74%	—	25%

Key Votes of the 109th Congress

1. Estate Tax Repeal	N	5. Limit Interstate Abortion	N	9. Build Border Fence	N
2. Limit CAFE Standards	N	6. Extend Patriot Act	N	10. CAFTA	N
3. FY06 Spending Curb	N	7. Bar Same Sex Marriage	N	11. Oppose Iraq Withdrawal	P
4. Drilling in ANWR	N	8. Stem Cell Research $	Y	12. Detainee Tribunals	N

Election Results

2006 general	Brad Sherman (D)	92,650	(69%)	($851,404)
	Peter Hankwitz (R)	42,074	(31%)	($42,311)
2006 primary	Brad Sherman (D)	unopposed		
2004 general	Brad Sherman (D)	125,296	(62%)	($871,672)
	Robert Levy (R)	66,946	(33%)	
	Eric Carter (Green)	8,956	(4%)	

Prior Winning Percentages: 2002 (62%); 2000 (66%); 1998 (57%); 1996 (49%)

The People		Race/Ethnic Origin	Ancestry	
Area size:	152 sq. mi.	44.9% White	German: 6.3% Irish: 5.0%	
Urban population:	99.7%	4.5% Black	English: 4.6%	
Rural population:	0.3%	10.5% Asian	**2004 Presidential Vote**	
Pop. 2000:	639,088	0.3% Native Am.	Kerry (D)	130,567 (59%)
Pop. 2005 (est):	672,326	0.1% Hawaiian	Bush (R)	86,397 (39%)
Median income:	$46,781	3.1% Two+ races	Other	3,034 (1%)
Poverty status:	13.4%	0.2% Other	**2000 Presidential Vote**	
Military veterans:	8.4%	36.5% Hispanic Origin	Gore (D)	117,120 (60%)
			Bush (R)	70,557 (36%)
			Other	6,568 (3%)
			Cook Partisan Voting Index: D +13	

Occupation   Blue collar: 19.9%   White collar: 66.2%   Gray collar: 13.9%

The San Fernando Valley, in the early 20th century when the movie business was young, was a vast expanse of empty land, annexed to Los Angeles in 1915. Moviemakers, looking for filming sites for a western, drove past the vacant lots of Westwood, up narrow roads through the Santa Monica Mountains and over into the vast Valley, sheltered from ocean breezes and rain-bearing clouds by the mountains. Since then this vast bowl of land has been transformed, first into 1950s suburbia, then into a postmodern city of its own, economically vital and yeastily ethnic. Even in its suburban years, the San Fernando Valley was not entirely residential: big factories—the General Motors Van Nuys assembly plant, the Anheuser Busch brewery, Rockwell (now, Boeing) and Litton (now, Northrop Grumman) defense plants—provided jobs. In those years this was fast-growing, family-friendly territory; politically, it was turf fought over hard by Republicans and Democrats. By the 1970s young Anglo families were fleeing, as the Los Angeles Unified School District was hit by a busing order. There is plenty of upscale territory left in the uplands in the rims of the Valley, in Granada Hills and Tarzana; the office blocks and mini-malls show unmistakable signs of affluence. In what had been the culturally arid Valley, lounges and bars have become prevalent. Urban planners have revived the planned community of Panorama City, which was the busy center of the Valley during the 1950s. In the inner lowlands of the Valley, new immigrants have moved to the growing communities of Reseda and Van Nuys. Some old neighborhoods have become rough enclaves, with youth gangs and boarded-up houses and apartments; Iranians and Chinese, Mexicans and Koreans, Israelis and Filipinos are keeping other neighborhoods diverse and solidly middle-class. Even this multiethnic Valley has been unhappy to be linked with the city of Los Angeles, whose city council imposes high taxes and irksome regulations that have stopped in the Valley the kind of vibrant economic growth seen in independent municipalities like Burbank and Glendale. A Valley secession movement arose and the issue was put on the November 2002 ballot, and the Valley voted 51%-49% for it, with stronger support in the western part of the Valley. But it needed a majority in all of Los Angeles to pass, and failed. In 2005, its 1.74 million people—41% of them foreign-born—would have made the Valley the fifth-largest city in the nation; its separate geographic status with the Census Bureau allows its state and federal representatives to pursue funding geared specifically to the region.

The 27th Congressional District of California on the map looks like an inverted "U" over the San Fernando Valley, between the Santa Monica and San Gabriel mountains. On the east it includes part of Burbank, the home of NBC studios and Disney headquarters, and blue-collar and heavily Hispanic neighborhoods filled with renters. To the north are Sunland and Tujunga at the base of the San Gabriel Mountains. The larger and more settled parts of the district are west of the 405 Freeway (roughly the dividing line between the East and West valleys), including most of Granada Hills, Northridge, Van Nuys and Tarzana. This is a diverse district indeed, 37% Hispanic and 11% Asian, roughly half of whom are Filipino or Korean. The district is comfortably Democratic.

The congressman from the 27th District is Brad Sherman, a Democrat first elected in 1996. Sherman grew up in Monterey Park, in the San Gabriel Valley east of Los Angeles; he started working on Democratic campaigns at age 6, licking stamps and stuffing envelopes for Congressman George Brown, and he set up his own stamp-wholesaling firm at 14. He graduated with high honors from UCLA, worked as an accountant, then went to Harvard Law School and practiced tax law in L.A.; he represented the Philippines in its successful effort to seize the assets of deposed president Ferdinand Marcos. He always had the political bug, and in 1990 was elected from Los Angeles County to the state Board of Equalization, which is a sort of tax court. He was known as a stickler for detail, a "tax nerd," as one former staffer said, who used the office with a keen scent for political advantage. He irritated cartoonists with a ruling that exempted them from the state tax on artwork but not on illustrations; they set up a website, the Sherman Gallery, in which they vied in caricaturing the balding and bespectacled Sherman.

Sherman decided to run for Congress in 1996, and moved his residence from Santa Monica to Sherman Oaks, when the seat became open. Both he and his Republican opponent, businessman Rich Sybert, were self-financers (Sherman spent $578,000 of his own money) who stressed their moderation. Sherman ran against Newt Gingrich and the Republican Congress, but he also supported the death penalty, wanted racial quotas and preferences phased out and favored tough measures on illegal immigration. Sybert stressed his independence of Gingrich, favoring abortion rights and environmental protections. Sybert was intense; Sherman a bit humorous (he handed out combs to voters, saying "You'll be able to use it more than I can"). Sherman won 49%-44%.

In the House, Sherman's voting record has been more moderate than those of most other Los Angeles County Democrats. One of the few CPAs in Congress, he serves on the Financial Services Committee; there, he has worked on corporate accounting issues. In 2002 he voted for the use of force in Iraq, after initially backing language to urge more support from the United Nations. The House accepted his "Halliburton" amendment to require competitive bidding procedures for the procurement of oil from Iraq, but a conference committee later dropped it. He sought to limit the use of franked mailings by House committee chairmen. He proposed a revision of the Presidential Succession Act to permit both the presidential and vice-presidential nominees to designate "successors" and make it unlikely that a leader of the Legislative Branch could become president. On the Foreign Affairs Committee, he chairs the Terrorism, Nonproliferation and Trade Subcommittee, where his priority is preventing Iran from obtaining nuclear weapons; he has sought tighter economic sanctions on Iran and companies that do business there.

Sherman has won reelection easily, even after redistricting gave him a district that was two-thirds new to him and 37% Hispanic. He has not had serious opposition. Sherman opposed Arnold Schwarzenegger's 2005 redistricting referendum, which could have placed him at greater risk.

TWENTY-EIGHTH DISTRICT

Rep. Howard Berman (D)

Elected 1982, 13th term; b. Apr. 15, 1941, Los Angeles; home, N. Hollywood; U.C.L.A., B.A. 1962, LL.B. 1965; Jewish; married (Janis).

Elected Office: CA Assembly, 1973-82, Maj. Ldr., 1974-79.

Professional Career: Practicing atty., 1967-72.

DC Office: 2221 RHOB, 20515, 202-225-4695; Fax: 202-225-3196; Web site: www.house.gov/berman.

District Offices: Van Nuys, 818-994-7200.

Committees: *Foreign Affairs* (2d of 27 D): Middle East & South Asia. *Judiciary* (2d of 23 D): Courts, the Internet & Intellectual Property (Chmn.); Immigration, Citizenship, Refugees, Border Security & International Law.

Group Ratings

	ADA	ACLU	AFS	LCV	ITIC	NTU	COC	ACU	CFG	FRC
2006	90	100	100	100	57	11	43	8	9	0
2005	90	—	100	94	—	13	41	4	7	0

National Journal Ratings

	2005 LIB	—	2005 CONS		2006 LIB	—	2006 CONS
Economic	88%	—	9%		94%	—	0%
Social	85%	—	14%		91%	—	9%
Foreign	67%	—	32%		69%	—	30%

Key Votes of the 109th Congress

1. Estate Tax Repeal	N	5. Limit Interstate Abortion	N	9. Build Border Fence		N
2. Limit CAFE Standards	N	6. Extend Patriot Act	N	10. CAFTA		N
3. FY06 Spending Curb	N	7. Bar Same Sex Marriage	N	11. Oppose Iraq Withdrawal		Y
4. Drilling in ANWR	N	8. Stem Cell Research $	Y	12. Detainee Tribunals		N

Election Results

2006 general	Howard Berman (D)	79,866	(74%)	($954,004)
	Stanley Kesselman (R)	20,629	(19%)	
	Byron DeLear (Green)	3,868	(4%)	($68,714)
	Other	3,679	(3%)	
2006 primary	Howard Berman (D)	31,048	(80%)	
	Charles Coleman (D)	7,547	(20%)	
2004 general	Howard Berman (D)	115,303	(71%)	($902,390)
	David Hernandez (R)	37,868	(23%)	($32,611)
	Kelley Ross (Lib)	9,339	(6%)	

Prior Winning Percentages: 2002 (71%); 2000 (84%); 1998 (82%); 1996 (66%); 1994 (63%); 1992 (61%); 1990 (61%); 1988 (70%); 1986 (65%); 1984 (63%); 1982 (60%)

The People		Race/Ethnic Origin	Ancestry	
Area size:	78 sq. mi.	31.4% White	German: 3.7%	Irish: 3.2%
Urban population:	99.9%	4.1% Black	English: 2.9%	
Rural population:	0.1%	5.9% Asian	**2004 Presidential Vote**	
Pop. 2000:	639,087	0.2% Native Am.	Kerry (D) 125,351	(71%)
Pop. 2005 (est):	664,778	0.1% Hawaiian	Bush (R) 49,220	(28%)
Median income:	$40,439	2.4% Two+ races	Other 2,011	(1%)
Poverty status:	19.1%	0.2% Other	**2000 Presidential Vote**	
Military veterans:	5.9%	55.6% Hispanic Origin	Gore (D) 112,332	(73%)
			Bush (R) 36,762	(24%)
			Other 5,021	(3%)
			Cook Partisan Voting Index: D +25	

Occupation   Blue collar: 26.2%   White collar: 58.0%   Gray collar: 15.8%

A hiker looking north from the crest of the Santa Monica Mountains in 1910 would have seen spread out, almost totally empty and barren, 20 miles wide and 12 miles deep, the San Fernando Valley. Separated by the Cahuenga Pass from rapidly growing Los Angeles and Hollywood, the Valley was bought up in massive tracts by civic leaders even as they were urging city engineer William Mulholland to build a huge 250-mile aqueduct from the Owens Valley to give Los Angeles water and persuading the city in 1915 to annex 200 square miles of the Valley. In the years after World War II, this was modern suburbia, filled with *Leave It to Beaver* families. Today the San Fernando Valley is postmodern urban, with a look you can see in exaggerated form in Disney headquarters buildings in Burbank or Universal City's CityWalk shopping mall: The driver topping the crest today sees office towers looming out over slightly hazy air, shopping centers, occasional palm trees, lines of grid streets stretching out into the distance beyond stucco subdivisions and the squat factory and warehouse buildings that have made Los Angeles County a top manufacturing locale. The Valley has aged, sometimes gracefully; homeowners in Van Nuys, Sun Valley and Granada Hills are now forming preservation districts, maintaining the antic architecture of the Valley in the 1950s.

The people in the Valley have also changed. The white Anglo families with stay-at-home moms in the 1950s have been replaced by hard-working Latino families, with children waiting at the bus stops for schools and parents juggling two jobs. But there is continuity: These remain places where people work hard and try to raise children who will have better chances and make better livings than they have. Pacoima, at the northern end of the Valley, where Rodney King was pulled over and beaten and arrested, is mostly Latino. Farther south, in Canoga Park, Van Nuys and Burbank, was the industrial base—the aircraft and GM assembly plants—of the Valley in the 1950s and 1960s; the GM plants were shut down in the 1980s and only one of the defense plants, the old Rocketdyne plant now owned by Boeing, remains open, and a Neiman Marcus is going up across the street. Less visible are the hundreds of small factories and multimedia plants where thousands of jobs have been created. The lower income areas here are farther from the central city; the southern rim of the Valley, around Studio City and North Hollywood, is still heavily Jewish and is attracting new families who often send their kids to religious schools; there is a trendy and lively shopping strip along Ventura Boulevard. People with money cluster near the rims of the mountains around the Valley; those less well off settle on the flatlands beyond.

The 28th Congressional District of California consists of about half of the San Fernando Valley and some of the mountains in the south. It includes parts of Van Nuysand several miles of land on either side of the Hollywood Freeway from where it comes through the Cahuenga Pass from Hollywood up to the junction with the Golden State Freeway; much of the northern end of the Valley around the Golden State, including Pacoima and the small city of San Fernando, is in the district. Mulholland Drive, which runs along the crest of the Santa Monica Mountains and the Ventura Freeway, is the southern border until the district dips south to Hollywood Boulevard. Within these borders are affluent North Hollywood, Studio City, Sherman Oaks and Encino, with big houses on twisting streets overlooking the Valley and just above the shops of Ventura Boulevard. The population of the district in 2000 was 56% Hispanic; the central and northern parts are much more Hispanic, while the southern end has a large Jewish population. But Hispanics are still not the majority voting bloc here; many are not citizens, many are children or young people not yet in the voting stream; and the tradition among Hispanics today, as among Italians 100 years ago, is to trust family and hard work, not politics and government, to get ahead. The high Democratic percentages here are due as much to Jewish as to Latino voters, who both trended Democratic in the late 1990s, one group in response to the emergence of the Christian right, the other in response to the campaign for cutting off aid to illegal aliens which suggested, incorrectly, that Latinos are interested more in welfare than hard work. The trend now may be a little bit in the other direction: George W. Bush's percentage here rose from 24% in 2000 to 28% in 2004.

The congressman from the 28th District is Howard Berman, one of the most aggressive and creative members of the House—and one of the most clear-sighted operators in American politics. He grew up in Los Angeles in modest circumstances, got interested in politics in high school and went to UCLA where he became friends with Henry Waxman, his ally in politics ever since. At UCLA law schoolhe got an internship at the California Assembly. "I was assigned to the Assembly Agriculture Committee. It was dealing with farm labor issues and Cesar Chavez's movement. From then on, I was hooked." Just a few years later he and Waxman were elected to the Assembly, Waxman in 1968 by beating an incumbent in the heavily Jewish Fairfax district, Berman (after working as a Vista volunteer) in 1972 by beating the Assembly Republican leader in a Hollywood Hills district. This was the beginning of the so-called Berman-Waxman political machine—not so much a precinct organization as a group of consultants who raised money, redrew district lines and endorsed candidates through direct mail; a key player was Berman's brother Michael Berman, who became an expert on redistricting and who drew the new lines in 2001. "We don't have a machine any more, if we ever did," Howard Berman said in 2004. "We just helped some friends." Their core constituency was liberal Westside Jews. Berman became Assembly Majority Leader in his first term. In 1980 he tried to unseat Speaker Leo McCarthy; ultimately both lost to Willie Brown, who served 15 years. Berman's consolation prize was a Valley-based congressional seat in 1982. The machine fell on hard times in the 1990s, as Republicans wrested away control of redistricting and the feminist left became the Democratic Party's driving force. Since then, Berman has been a political force on his own, with a record that is mostly but not always liberal.

Berman has been an active legislator even more than a political operator, and on all manner of issues, but not one who gets much publicity. On foreign policy, he started off less as a Vietnam War dove than as a backer of Israel. For a decade he floor-managed foreign aid authorization bills, defending aid to many countries as well as Israel. With Henry Hyde he wrote the law authorizing embargoes on nations that condone terrorism; in April 1990 he called for sanctions on Iraq, four months before Saddam Hussein invaded Kuwait. Berman voted for the Gulf War resolution, but was understandably critical of the first Bush administration—if it had followed his advice there might well have been no need for war. He is supportive of organized labor and opposed trade promotion authority. Berman passed a law banning the double-issuing of U.S. passports to coddle

Arab countries that refuse to honor passports with Israeli marks. He offered an amendment to revoke normal trade relations with China if it attacks, invades or blockades Taiwan and, when that was rejected, voted against it. Berman played a critical role in winning passage by a wide margin of the Iraq war resolution in October 2002. He strongly supported military action against Iraq, and in September he came out from behind the scenes and organized a group of Democrats who shared his views. They broke off from the negotiations between Republicans and John Spratt, who ended up offering an alternative to the administration's resolution, and talked directly to the Bush administration. He didn't seek the permission of Minority Leader Richard Gephardt but Berman's discussions led to Gephardt's agreement with the administration on the terms of the resolution—talks that undercut the demands of Spratt, Minority Whip Nancy Pelosi and Senate Foreign Relations Chairman Joseph Biden. Iraq. In June 2006 he voted for the Republican resolution to reject a timetable for withdrawal from Iraq. "I voted for today's resolution on Iraq because I agree with what it calls for: success in the 'mission to create a sovereign, free and united Iraq.' I still have hope that we can accomplish that mission."He voted for the Democrats' nonbinding resolution disapproving Bush's surge policy in February 2007.

Immigration is another issue on which Berman has been a major legislator. In 1988 he sponsored the provision allowing 20,000 immigrant visas for migrants without close relatives here, to be selected randomly by computer—"Berman visa applications," they are called. He secured in 1990 more family reunification slots, expediting the immigration of Soviet Jews (a vivid presence in L.A.), and gaining amnesty provisions for more family members to remain in this country. In 2003 he worked out a farm workers bill with Chris Cannon and Senators Larry Craig and Edward Kennedy. Worked out laboriously with farm organizations and farm workers unions, it would legalize temporary agricultural workers, provide for good working conditions and allow them eventually to become legal residents; it was set aside as George W. Bush proposed a broader guest worker program with different terms, but it was reintroduced in January 2005.

In 1999 Berman took the ranking position on the Courts and Intellectual Property Subcommittee of Judiciary, one of vital importance to Hollywood interests. There he passed an anti-cybersquatting law to discourage pouncing on website names. In 2003 Berman cosponsored with John Conyers and Lamar Smith a bill to create new judgeships to determine copyright royalty rates and distribution of royalties and to remedy defects in Copyright Arbitration Royalty Panels. It passed the House unanimously in March 2004 and the Senate unanimously in October and was signed into law in November. In 2003 Berman, Conyers and Smith also sponsored a bill providing for criminal penalties of mass downloaders of music and requiring file-sharing software to contain warnings of security risk. In July 2004 Berman was unable to prevent an amendment to the bill allowing firms to sell software that could delete offensive passages from movie DVDs; Berman still supported the overall bill which was approved by the Judiciary Committee in September 2004. In 2005 he and Smith sponsored a bill to create a blanket licensing system that would make it easier for online services to get permission to sell music which passed the subcommittee unanimously but went no further. He also sponsored a bill with Rick Boucher to crack down on "patent trolls" who file spurious patents and collect royalties.

In January 2007 Berman became chairman of the subcommittee, now called Courts, the Internet and Intellectual Property, with jurisdiction over copyrights, trademark and patents, of great interest to the entertainment, biotech, broadcasting, pharmaceutical, telecom, consumer electronics and information technology industries. He continued to work closely with Lamar Smith, now ranking minority member. He indicated his basic orientation. "I want to protect fair use, but sometimes I hear some of these arguments about digital freedom meaning freedom to make permanent copies to spread around to everyone for free. Sometimes I look at that as stealing." Record industry lobbyist Mitch Bainwol said, "Everybody views him as a wonderfully honest broker with a deep substantive grasp of the issues and an unusual ability to legislate." Electronics industry lobbyist John Palafoutas saw him a little differently. "There are two problems with Howard Berman," he told *The Los Angeles Times.* "One, he's really smart. And two, he knows how to represent his constituents, which in this case is Hollywood." Berman said he wanted to crack down on piracy and update music licensing and royalty standards for the digital age. He also called for streamlining the patent system, and predicted that the pharmaceutical industry, a foe of his approach in 2006, would be more willing to work with the subcommittee. On patents, he noted that the Supreme Court ruled in 2006 that injunctions against alleged infringement can be granted only on a case-by-case basis. His goal was to discourage litigation and create a streamlined mediation process. He said "the call for legislative action is loud" on the need for a system to review already-granted patents, and said he would try to work out language on how long third parties could challenge decisions of the Patent and Trademark Office. Sometimes his work on intellectual property has a local angle; in June 2006, prompted by a complaint from a Malibu distributor of Russian films, he called for an investigation of Aeroflot crews smuggling pirated DVDs into LAX.

From 1997 to 2003 Berman was the ranking Democrat on the House ethics committee. During his tenure, few complaints were filed for partisan reasons. After he left the committee in 2003, that no longer was the case. Berman opposed the Republican changes in ethics rules including the elimination of admonishments for conduct unbecoming a member of Congress—the action taken by the ethics committee against Majority Leader Tom DeLay in 2004, even as it declared that he had violated no House rule. In April 2006, when ethics committee Democrat Alan Mollohan was pushed by Minority Leader Nancy Pelosi to resign the post because of ethics charges raised against him, she asked Berman to take the post. "This is an honor I could have done without," Berman said. "The ethics committee should be neither a member protection agency nor a forum for deciding partisan and ideological battles. If the committee chooses to pursue either option, then expect my tenure to be even briefer than it is intended to be." He worked amicably with Chairman Doc Hastings and the existing committee staff. After Mark Foley resigned on September 29, there was a demand for an ethics investigation. Hastings and Berman formed an investigative subcommittee consisting of themselves and Stephanie Tubbs Jones, a former county prosecutor in Cleveland and Judy Biggert. Berman promised that the investigation would take "weeks not months," and the subcommittee worked late hours throughout October, interviewing Speaker Dennis Hastert, his top aides and others who had knowledge of Foley's suggestive emails and explicit instant messages sent to former House pages. Norman Ornstein of the American Enterprise Institute wrote, "The House ethics committee's tattered reputation is on the line, and two words are keeping it from total collapse: Howard Berman." The committee issued an exhaustive report on December 8, finding fault with carefully calibrated judgments but declining to recommend any disciplinary action against House members or staffers.

Berman is not the most senior member of the California delegation, but he is the go-to guy on many state issues. One California Assembly lobbyist said of him, "He's the conscience and dad of the delegation. In this era of term limits and turnover, Howard Berman is the constant. He has a vast institutional knowledge of issues in both Congress and the legislature that is rare these days." One issue on which he was the dad of the delegation was redistricting. California gained one seat in the 2000 Census and Democrats controlled the process. Michael Berman, his brother, was hired as redistricting consultant by all U.S. House and state Senate Democrats at $20,000 per member. When the lines were unveiled in August 2001, the biggest controversy came over the San Fernando Valley. Brad Sherman, the Democrat from the 27th District, claimed that Howard Berman had been given too much of his territory south of Ventura Boulevard, while Sherman would be given too many Hispanics to have a secure seat over the decade. "Howard Berman stabbed me in the back," Sherman said. At first Berman was dismissive but agreed to negotiate. Adjustments were made in the lines, and Sherman's district ended up 37% Hispanic and Berman's 56%. The Mexican American Legal Defense Fund immediately took the plan to court, arguing that seats in the San Fernando Valley and San Diego tended to reduce Hispanic representation. The court approved the plan in June 2002.

In any case, Hispanics are not a majority of voters in this district and are not likely to be before 2010, and Berman has in fact worked on issues like farm labor and immigration long before he had any significant number of Hispanic constituents. Against Republican David Hernandez, a proponent of Valley secession, he won 71%-23% in both 2002 and 2004. In 2006, he won with 74%.

TWENTY-NINTH DISTRICT

Rep. Adam Schiff (D)

Elected 2000, 4th term; b. June 22, 1960, Framingham, MA; home, Burbank; Stanford U., B.A. 1982; Harvard U., J.D. 1985; Jewish; married (Eve).

Elected Office: CA Senate, 1996-00.

Professional Career: Prosecutor, U.S. Atty. Gen. Ofc., L.A., CA 1987-93; Practicing atty., 1986-87, 1995-96.

DC Office: 326 CHOB, 20515, 202-225-4176; Fax: 202-225-5828; Web site: www.house.gov/schiff.

District Offices: Pasadena, 626-304-2727.

Committees: *Appropriations* (29th of 37 D): State, Foreign Operations & Related Programs; Commerce, Justice, Science & Related Agencies; Financial Services & General Government. *Judiciary* (19th of 23 D): Courts, the Internet & Intellectual Property.

Group Ratings

	ADA	ACLU	AFS	LCV	ITIC	NTU	COC	ACU	CFG	FRC
2006	85	91	86	100	57	15	47	12	12	0
2005	85	—	100	94	—	12	42	0	8	0

National Journal Ratings

	2005 LIB	—	2005 CONS		2006 LIB	—	2006 CONS
Economic	82%	—	18%		74%	—	23%
Social	74%	—	25%		76%	—	23%
Foreign	61%	—	39%		77%	—	20%

Key Votes of the 109th Congress

1. Estate Tax Repeal	N	5. Limit Interstate Abortion	N	9. Build Border Fence	N
2. Limit CAFE Standards	N	6. Extend Patriot Act	N	10. CAFTA	N
3. FY06 Spending Curb	N	7. Bar Same Sex Marriage	N	11. Oppose Iraq Withdrawal	N
4. Drilling in ANWR	N	8. Stem Cell Research	$	Y	12. Detainee Tribunals	N

Election Results

2006 general	Adam Schiff (D)	91,014	(63%)	($900,377)
	William Bodell (R)	39,321	(27%)	
	William Paparian (Green)	8,197	(6%)	($45,741)
	Other	4,872	(4%)	
2006 primary	Adam Schiff (D)	33,750	(83%)	
	Bob McCloskey (D)	7,102	(17%)	
2004 general	Adam Schiff (D)	133,670	(65%)	($955,782)
	Harry Scolinos (R)	62,871	(30%)	($605,280)
	Other	10,291	(5%)	

Prior Winning Percentages: 2002 (63%); 2000 (53%)

The People		Race/Ethnic Origin	Ancestry
Area size:	102 sq. mi.	39.1% White	Armenian: 10.6% German: 6.2%
Urban population:	99.4%	5.9% Black	English: 5.5%
Rural population:	0.6%	23.7% Asian	**2004 Presidential Vote**
Pop. 2000:	639,088	0.2% Native Am.	Kerry (D) 136,796 (61%)
Pop. 2005 (est):	637,269	0.1% Hawaiian	Bush (R) 83,448 (37%)
Median income:	$43,895	4.7% Two+ races	Other 3,097 (1%)
Poverty status:	14.5%	0.2% Other	**2000 Presidential Vote**
Military veterans:	6.8%	26.1% Hispanic Origin	Gore (D) 119,396 (58%)
			Bush (R) 79,210 (38%)
			Other 7,671 (4%)
			Cook Partisan Voting Index: D +12

Occupation   Blue collar: 16.0%   White collar: 70.2%   Gray collar: 13.8%

In the early years of the 20th century, when Los Angeles was growing rapidly, on its way to one of America's major cities, its richest citizens settled not on the beach (too clammy and cold) or on the west side (too dusty and remote), but in communities they built at the base of the San Gabriel Mountains that rise 10,000 feet above the city, their snow-capped peaks visible most of the year. The premier such community was Pasadena, with its institutions of national stature—the Rose Bowl and Rose Parade, Cal Tech; its premier structure is its baroque-domed City Hall. Pasadena and South Pasadena have proudly preserved their bungalow neighborhoods, and Pasadena preserved and rebuilt the 80-year old curving Colorado Boulevard Bridge over Arroyo Seco. More middle class is Glendale, north of downtown Los Angeles, site of Forest Lawn Cemetery and DreamWorks Animation; just west, beneath the Verdugo Mountains, is Burbank (named not for botanist Luther Burbank but for a local dentist-developer), famous now for NBC Studios, ABC Studios, Warner Brothers, and Disney, plus many small entertainment multimedia companies. With their lower taxes and business-friendly attitude, and despite earlier loss of aerospace jobs, Glendale and Burbank are booming while inside the city limits of high-tax and high-regulation Los Angeles, Hollywood has become seedy and plagued by commercial buildings with huge vacancy rates. To reduce traffic congestion, planners are exploring a lengthy tunnel to link the freeways in South Pasadena and Pasadena.

The 29th Congressional District of California, which extends to the San Gabriel Mountains, includes Pasadena, South Pasadena, Glendale and the eastern half of Burbank. Historically, these were solidly Republican cities, but they have become more Democratic in recent years, for various reasons—Pasadena because of affluent voters' cultural liberalism and a growing black community; Glendale because of large communities of Armenians (the nation's largest), Iranians, Koreans and Filipinos; Burbank from the trendiness of show business. The district also includes, south of South Pasadena, cities with large Asian populations: Vietnamese in San Gabriel, Chinese in Alhambra, Temple City and the northern edge of Monterey Park (which calls itself the nation's first Chinese suburb). This is a polyglot district—26% Hispanic, 24% Asian, 11% Armenian and 6% black. It has become solidly Democratic, casting only 38% of its votes for George W. Bush in 2000 and 37% in 2004.

The congressman from the 29th District is Adam Schiff, a Democrat elected in 2000 over Republican James Rogan in what was then the most expensive House race ever. Schiff's father was a traveling salesman, and Schiff grew up throughout the country, graduating from high school in northern California, and went on to Stanford and Harvard Law School. From 1987 to 1993, he worked in the U.S. attorney's office in Los Angeles. He ran for the Assembly and lost three times, twice to Rogan. But in 1996 he was elected to the state Senate, where he became its youngest member. In his first two years, he authored dozens of measures that Governor Pete Wilson signed into law, including landmark school textbook legislation. Schiff also taught political science at Glendale Community College.

When Schiff ran for the House, this was one of the few races in which the impeachment of Bill Clinton was an important issue. Rogan was a leading player in the Judiciary Committee's deliberations, and a persuasive voice for the case against Clinton. He obviously knew that supporting impeachment carried political risks; he had won reelection in 1998 by just 51%-46%. Entertainment mogul—and then-Clinton pal—David Geffen promised to raise millions to oppose him. The Schiff-Rogan race became a fundraising marathon; the candidates, buoyed by responses to direct mail, raised more than $10 million combined, and more was spent independently by Clinton lovers and Clinton haters. Rogan had no apologies for his work on impeachment. The candidates disagreed on health care, abortion, gun control and taxes. Rogan branded his opponent as a traditional tax-and-spend liberal, who would "run naked through the Treasury, spending everything he can." Schiff attacked Rogan for calling abortion a "Holocaust" for the African-American community and saying that the Ku Klux Klan "couldn't do a better job on committing genocide on African Americans." They also battled for the support of more than 67,000 local Armenians. Rogan was a lead sponsor of a House resolution commemorating their genocide from 1915 to 1923 by the Ottoman Turks; he was promised a floor vote in October 2000, but Speaker Dennis Hastert reneged after phone calls from Clinton and his foreign policy appointees. Schiff cosponsored a state Senate resolution declaring "a day of remembrance of Armenian genocide," and got $400,000 from state taxpayers to produce a documentary about Armenian issues. Schiff said that Rogan's focus on Washington led him to ignore local problems. He won by a surprisingly large 53%-44% margin.

In the House, Schiff's voting record has been moderate, especially on foreign policy. He joined the Blue Dog Democrats and said that he was ready to work across party lines. He worked with freshman Republicans to help pass the McCain-Feingold campaign reform bill. He helped to enact the bill to make "identity theft" a crime. On the bill to implement recommendations of the 9/11 Commission, he was the only Democrat voting with Judiciary Committee Republicans on added immigration restrictions; the final bill included his provisions to establish new penalties for developing a "dirty bomb," and to give new tools to law enforcement to crack down on weapons of mass destruction. With Republican Jeff Flake, he filed a bill to revise domestic surveillance procedures. On International Relations, he took up the cause of Armenian genocide, and called it a "symbolic victory" when the House passed a foreign aid bill with his provision, even though Hastert later insisted on its removal; his support for the legislation became the focus in 2007 of a documentary film, "Screamers." He stirred complaints from liberal constituents when he supported the Patriot Act, and he voted for the use of force in Iraq, though he later criticized intelligence gathering. Schiff co-founded a Democratic study group on national security and made that a personal priority, and sought action to secure nuclear materials in the former Soviet Union so that terrorists don't gain access to them. In March 2006, his provisions on port and rail security were enacted as part of a terrorism prevention bill. In 2007, he got a seat on the Appropriations Committee, where he was assigned to the intelligence oversight panel.

Schiff has been easily reelected. In 2006, he chaired the mentoring program for the DCCC's prime candidates.

THIRTIETH DISTRICT

Rep. Henry Waxman (D)

Elected 1974, 17th term; b. Sept. 12, 1939, Los Angeles; home, Los Angeles; U.C.L.A., B.A. 1961, J.D. 1964; Jewish; married (Janet).

Elected Office: CA Assembly, 1968-74.

Professional Career: Practicing atty., 1965-68.

DC Office: 2204 RHOB, 20515, 202-225-3976; Fax: 202-225-4099; Web site: www.house.gov/waxman.

District Offices: Los Angeles, 323-651-1040.

Committees: *Energy & Commerce* (2d of 31 D): Health; Oversight & Investigations; Energy & Air Quality; Environment & Hazardous Materials. *Oversight & Government Reform* (Chmn. of 23 D).

Group Ratings

	ADA	ACLU	AFS	LCV	ITIC	NTU	COC	ACU	CFG	FRC
2006	95	100	100	100	43	15	33	4	8	0
2005	100	—	100	100	—	15	38	0	7	0

National Journal Ratings

	2005 LIB	—	2005 CONS		2006 LIB	—	2006 CONS
Economic	94%	—	0%		90%	—	9%
Social	83%	—	16%		89%	—	10%
Foreign	87%	—	13%		82%	—	17%

Key Votes of the 109th Congress

1. Estate Tax Repeal	N	5. Limit Interstate Abortion	N	9. Build Border Fence	N
2. Limit CAFE Standards	N	6. Extend Patriot Act	N	10. CAFTA	N
3. FY06 Spending Curb	N	7. Bar Same Sex Marriage	N	11. Oppose Iraq Withdrawal	*
4. Drilling in ANWR	N	8. Stem Cell Research $	Y	12. Detainee Tribunals	N

Election Results

2006 general	Henry Waxman (D)	151,284	(71%)	($553,049)
	David Jones (R)	55,904	(26%)	($21,825)
	Other	4,546	(2%)	
2006 primary	Henry Waxman (D)	unopposed		
2004 general	Henry Waxman (D)	216,682	(71%)	($453,715)
	Victor Elizalde (R)	87,465	(29%)	($262,130)

Prior Winning Percentages: 2002 (70%); 2000 (76%); 1998 (74%); 1996 (68%); 1994 (68%); 1992 (61%); 1990 (69%); 1988 (72%); 1986 (88%); 1984 (63%); 1982 (65%); 1980 (64%); 1978 (63%); 1976 (68%); 1974 (64%)

The People		Race/Ethnic Origin	Ancestry	
Area size:	388 sq. mi.	76.4% White	German: 8.4%	English: 6.8%
Urban population:	97.5%	2.6% Black	Irish: 6.8%	
Rural population:	2.5%	8.8% Asian	**2004 Presidential Vote**	
Pop. 2000:	639,088	0.2% Native Am.	Kerry (D) 220,181	(66%)
Pop. 2005 (est):	648,127	0.1% Hawaiian	Bush (R) 109,014	(33%)
Median income:	$60,713	3.3% Two+ races	Other 3,660	(1%)
Poverty status:	9.0%	0.3% Other	**2000 Presidential Vote**	
Military veterans:	8.3%	8.3% Hispanic Origin	Gore (D) 199,282	(68%)
			Bush (R) 81,336	(28%)
			Other 11,464	(4%)
			Cook Partisan Voting Index: D +20	

Occupation	Blue collar: 6.9%	White collar: 84.4%	Gray collar: 8.7%

The Westside: The term was not much used 20 years ago, but is now shorthand for what might be the biggest and flashiest concentration of affluence in the world. It is the heartland of one of America's most productive and creative industries and one of the nation's major exports, show business. The first moviemakers came here earlier in the century, looking for a place to shoot silent films where the sunlight was more dependable than in Astoria, Queens, or Englewood, New Jersey. They found it in Hollywood, a suburb just annexed by burgeoning Los Angeles when the first movie studio was built in 1911. In 1923 came the Hollywood sign, overlooking the soon-famous intersection of Hollywood and Vine. By the 1930s, big studio lots were scattered around town, over the mountains in Burbank or out toward the ocean in Westwood and Culver City. Miraculously, the studio bosses of that era—most of them Jewish immigrants with little ancestral experience of America—created a popular culture that was universally accessible and embodied the American spirit in a way that still captures the imagination.

Showbiz still sets the tone for the Westside. It remains tremendously profitable, and not just for the big studios which are owned by large conglomerates; there are thousands of entrepreneurs, actors, writers and craftsmen who are the best in the world at what they do and who tend to cluster on the Westside because so many of the others they do business with are here. Showbiz rejoiced in the election of Bill Clinton and in his frequent forays into California and obvious fascination with entertainers; it rejected with fury the notion that there was something wrong about his affair with a White House intern (from the Westside, it turns out) or with lying under oath in a sexual harassment case in a federal court. It responded with rage to George W. Bush and the war in Iraq, but its shrill endorsements of his opponent probably inspired more votes for Bush than against him.

Not everyone on the Westside is in show business, of course. The West Side has become metro Los Angeles's biggest office center, with horrifying traffic inbound in the morning and outbound in the evening: most office workers can't afford to live anywhere nearby. Also, Los Angeles ranks first in the nation in percentage of people who work at home and this is a place where thousands of small entrepreneurs, manufacturers, and inventors and marketers of everything imaginable helped spark the huge growth of the Los Angeles Basin, and there are even traces of pre-show business Los Angeles money, which is also plentiful. There are large numbers of singles and gays here. The Fairfax neighborhood remains solidly middle-class Jewish—though many of its Jews today are recent Russian immigrants. The Westside was the home of a former president who does not at all exemplify its politics, Ronald Reagan; before his Alzheimer's disease worsened, he kept his office on the former Fox lot that is now Century City. It is the center of the second-largest Jewish community in the United States, as well as the focus of the 1980s immigration of Iranians to the United States; Iranians accounted for 6% of the district's residents in 2000 and in 2006, 20% in Beverly Hills, which elected an Iranian-American mayor. There were complaints that the new residents have been building garish houses, but there have been such complaints about others before, whose houses are now seen as timeless classics. Beverly Hills and the Westside remain the locus of some of America's most expensive residential real estate, where people buy houses for multiples of $1 million, knock down the structure and build something new for more millions, and of one of the world's premier high-priced shopping areas—Rodeo Drive, once a quite ordinary shopping street.

The 30th Congressional District of California contains most of Westside Los Angeles plus territory to the west. It includes the Fairfax neighborhood east to La Brea Avenue, heavily gay West

Hollywood, Beverly Hills and the heavily Jewish Los Angeles neighborhoods to the south, Westwood and UCLA, Bel Air and Brentwood, Santa Monica and the whole 27 miles of Malibu on the ocean; most of the workload of the California Coastal Commission comes from Malibu. The district also includes the western end of the San Fernando Valley, the high-income neighborhoods of Woodland Hills and Chatsworth up against the mountains that rim the Valley. And it includes the high-income suburbs of Hidden Hills, Calabasas, Agoura Hills and Westlake Village, nestled amid mountains along the Ventura Freeway west of the San Fernando Valley. This is a mostly high-income district, with a large number of Jews and immigrants from Russia and Iran, but by today's definitions it is the least diverse district in metro Los Angeles. Only 3% of its residents in 2000 were black; no L.A. County district has a lower percentage. Only 8% of its residents are Hispanic, by a considerable margin the lowest percentage in southern California. Many Latinos work in the district, but few are interested in paying the prices for housing that has been bid up by rich people who can't imagine living anywhere else. Politically, the 30th District is heavily Democratic, but perhaps not quite as heavily as is generally believed. In 2000 it cast only 28% of its votes for George W. Bush, but in 2004 he got 33% here, even as his percentages declined in the San Francisco Bay area. One reason is the response of many Jewish voters to his support for Israel and policy of overthrowing or undermining tyranny in the Middle East. Bush's share of the vote rose from 20% to 42% in Beverly Hills; showbiz celebrities may regard Bush as a tyrant, but Iranian immigrants know what real tyranny is like.

The congressman from the 30th District is Henry Waxman, a Democrat first elected in 1974, one of the ablest members of the House, a shrewd political operator who is a skilled and idealistic policy entrepreneur, who is now chairman of the Oversight and Government Reform Committee. There is no Westside glitz about him: He grew up over his family's store in Watts, his personal demeanor is quiet, and he has never attended the Oscars ceremony. He graduated from UCLA and its law school, where he met Howard Berman, his longtime political ally and colleague. He moved up rapidly in politics by spying openings before others did and taking advantage of them. He ran against Assemblyman Lester McMillan in the mostly Jewish Fairfax area in 1968, at 28, and won 64% in the primary. From 1971-72 he chaired the redistricting committee, a good place to make friends, but he went to Congress in 1974 in a district designed, he points out, not by his committee but by a court. Waxman's biggest break in Congress came after the 1978 election, when he was elected chairman of the Commerce Committee's Health and Environment Subcommittee. This was one of the first times House Democrats decided to ignore seniority in handing out subcommittee chairs. Nevertheless, Waxman argued his case on the issues and—in a move quite unprecedented at the time, though common in Sacramento then and soon in Washington—made campaign contributions to other Democrats on the full committee, and won the post, 15-12, over the widely respected Richardson Preyer of North Carolina.

The campaign contributions were no accident. In the 1970s and 1980s Waxman and Berman built their own political machine in Los Angeles. Its power came not from patronage but from fundraising and savvy. They raised huge sums on the Westside for favored candidates. For them they put out carefully targeted direct mail, with hundreds of customized letters and endorsement slates sent out to different lists of people. In the apolitical commonwealth of California, where television advertising is exceedingly expensive and people seem to avoid politics, this made them critical though not always successful players. But in 1992 their machine foundered; since then, Waxman has rarely taken an active role in Los Angeles area politics, though he did endorse former Assembly Speaker Antonio Villaraigosa in his successful race against Los Angeles Mayor James Hahn in 2005.

As part of the Democratic majority and chairman of a key subcommittee from 1978 to 1994, Waxman was a major national policymaker, usually from behind the scenes. In 1981 and 1982 he prevented the Reagan administration and Commerce Committee Chairman John Dingell from revising the Clean Air Act; biding his time, he worked to strengthen the law in its 1990 revision. He also worked on the Safe Drinking Water Act, the Radon Abatement Act and the Lead Contamination Act. Another Waxman project was expanding Medicaid for the poor. Between 1984 and 1990, he got coverage for all poor children up to 18, all children under seven and pregnant women in families under 133% of poverty income. This helped raise Medicaid from 9% to 14% of state spending in the 1980s, and helps to explain why Waxman was so disliked by many governors because many of these mandates were unfunded. Waxman had less success on reforming national health care. He wanted to move to something like a single-payer program and supported the Clinton plan but to no avail. He has secured more funding for AIDS research, important in the 30th District with its large gay population. In early 1994, in widely publicized hearings, he lined up the chief executive officers of leading tobacco companies and accused them of adding nicotine and other substances to cigarettes and of lying in their testimony. All this had no immediate legislative result, and when Thomas Bliley of Virginia became Commerce Committee chair, the hearings stopped. But Waxman brought the tobacco issue into public view, and he helped to inspire the lawsuits against tobacco companies which have resulted in the biggest redistribution of corporate assets—from the tobacco companies to state governments and trial lawyers—in history.

Waxman reacted with dismay to the Republican takeover of Congress, but with no slackening of effort. Largely shut out of the legislative process by the Republican leadership, in 1996 he gave up the ranking position on the Health Subcommittee to become ranking Democrat on the Government Reform Committee and concentrated more on holding separate hearings and seeking and publicizing GAO reports than on crafting legislation. "When the Republicans excluded me and other Democrats from legislating, we had to figure out something else to do. So we did our own investigations." There he sharply attacked Chairman Dan Burton's investigation of Clinton campaign misdeeds, arguing that Burton had given himself unprecedented subpoena power and was misusing it, and he emerged as perhaps the House's most articulate defender of Bill Clinton against scandal charges. In 2001, Waxman switched from being a defender of the White House to being a critic, frequently writing letters to Burton calling for investigations. In May 2001 he and John Dingell asked the GAO for the names of company executives who had been consulted by Vice President Dick Cheney's energy task force. In June he asked Burton to seek the names. In July the GAO sent a letter to Cheney asking for the names, the first such demand letter the GAO had ever sent; Cheney declined. In February 2002 the GAO brought a lawsuit against Cheney. In December 2002 a federal judge ruled against the GAO, and the agency declined to appeal.

In January 2003 the House Republicans' term limits removed Burton as chairman and the Republican leadership installed Tom Davis, who promised a more constructive chairmanship and on occasion worked with Waxman on issues. Nevertheless Waxman indefatigably wrote multi-page letters with dozens of footnotes and questions, called for GAO investigations and invoked the 1920s seven-member rule, which entitles any seven members of the committee to seek information from the executive branch. He assembled a staff of dozens of investigators, squirreled in tiny offices around the Capitol Hill complex. He noted that the 2003 Medicare/prescription drug bill "will set up a dynamic in the future that requires us to add more revenue," and, when the cost proved to be higher than the $400 billion claimed when the bill was passed, sought internal administration estimates by March 2004. When those were denied he and 18 other committee Democrats filed suit in May. With Carolyn Maloney, he proposed an amendment to restore non-prescription sale of morning-after contraceptive drugs. In February 2004 he and Sherrod Brown asked 10 pharmaceutical companies to reveal how much they paid in consulting fees and stock options to NIH scientists; this and other inquiries resulted in a stricter NIH policy on ethics and disclosure in February 2005, of which Waxman said he approved.

Waxman has issued continual criticisms of Halliburton and other government contractors in Iraq, pointing out relentlessly that Vice President Dick Cheney was once Halliburton's CEO. In October 2004 he said an investigation of U.S. management of Iraqi oil revenue should come before any investigation of the UN Oil for Food program. In November 2004 he said State Department documents showed that Halliburton employees tried to extract bribes for fuel contracts. But he also targeted baseball steroid use and the TaekwondoUnion policy of allowing 12-year-olds to kick opponents in the head (they raised the age to 14). Air pollution of varying types continued to attract his attention. He and Adam Schiff sponsored a bill to reduce carbon emissions by 2% a year starting in 2010 and by 5% a year starting in 2021. He and Martin Meehan sponsored an amendment to the legislative appropriation banning smoking in all House buildings, which could be interpreted as a direct attack on Minority Leader John Boehner, who routinely smoked in the Speaker's lobby, John Murtha, who used to smoke in the "Murtha corner" on the House floor, and George Miller and Barney Frank, who have been known to enjoy cigars in the Speaker's lobby. He amended the Postal Service reorganization bill to bar the USPS from delivering cigarettes purchased online to underage customers. He acquiesced in a reversal of his 1985 ban on building the Los Angeles subway under Wilshire Boulevard when he was convinced there was no seismic danger.

"If I were chairman, it would be a lot different. The biggest things that we're not taking up are oversight issues, in a lot of areas where I think we should be very, very active," Waxman said in 2004. He mentioned the flawed intelligence about yellowcake uraniumin Niger, the Valerie Plame incident and Halliburton contracts. The committee did hold hearings on contracting in Iraq in March 2004, for which Waxman commended Davis. They worked together on investigations on mad cow disease and D.C. drinking water, and on the bipartisan project of changing the Postal Service. But Waxman blistered Davis in a seven-page letter for investigating former National Security Adviser

Sandy Berger in July 2004; Berger said then that he only inadvertently took classified documents out of the National Archives, but in 2005 he admitted that he took them on purpose. In January 2005 he called for a GAO investigation of how a flawed HHS report on obesity was allowed to be released. When Davis called for restoring the executive branch's reorganization powers and for reducing the number of appointments requiring congressional confirmation, Waxman strongly disagreed.

"There has been no cop on the beat," Waxman said on taking over as chairman—a slight exaggeration, since Davis did cooperate with him on some investigations of the administration, but there is arguably no cop like Henry Waxman. Thanks to a Republican rule change, he is the only committee chairman entitled to issue subpoenas without a committee vote, and the committee has a pretty much unlimited jurisdiction over the federal government. When asked whether he would issue a flurry of subpoenas, Waxman said, "I'd prefer not to. I am determined to restore some stability and bipartisanship." He pointed out that as chairman of the committee Dan Burton had issued over 1,000 unilateral subpoenas, while Waxman in his 16 years as chairman of the Health Subcommittee had never issued one. "We want to return to civility and bipartisanship. Legislation ought to be based on evidence, not ideology," said Waxman. Tom Davis, now ranking minority member, said, "There is no question that life is going to be different for the administration. Henry is going to be tough. . . . And he's been waiting a long time to do this." Waxman reduced the number of subcommittees from seven to five, barring Diane Watson and Stephen Lynch from subcommittee chairmanships. He did not, as he suggested before becoming chairman, launch investigations of the Abu Ghraib prison or the presentation of intelligence before the Iraq war. His first hearings were on whether the administration had interfered with the work of climate scientists and on fraud and waste in reconstruction projects in Iraq. Witnesses denied that, as Waxman suggested, there was $10 billion in fraud, but Davis noted that there was "an arcane, ill-suited management structure." He prepared to examine the reconstruction process after Hurricane Katrina and the 2001 Bush executive order restricting access not only to his but to previous presidents' papers, an order criticized by many historians and far more restrictive than Ronald Reagan's executive order of 1989. When Speaker Nancy Pelosi created a special committee headed by Edward Markey examining global warming, he co-wrote a letter with Energy and Commerce Committee Chairman John Dingell asserting their understanding that the Markey committee would have no legislative authority. There was some tension in this: Waxman ranks just behind Dingell on Energy and Commerce and just ahead of Markey; Dingell and Waxman both voted for Majority Leader Steny Hoyer against Pelosi's choice, John Murtha. This was an assertion of the power of experienced and competent committee chairmen against a new speaker, even though Dingell and Waxman had differed on clean air legislation many times over the years.

Waxman has always won reelection easily, and has contributed generously to other Democrats' campaigns. Redistricting added Malibu and the San Fernando Valley to his district but it is still very heavily Democratic; the lines were drawn by Howard Berman's brother, Michael Berman.

THIRTY-FIRST DISTRICT

Rep. Xavier Becerra (D)

Elected 1992, 8th term; b. Jan. 26, 1958, Sacramento; home, Eagle Rock; Stanford U., B.A. 1980, J.D. 1984; Catholic; married (Carolina Reyes).

Elected Office: CA Assembly, 1990-92.

Professional Career: Staff Atty., Legal Assistance Corp. of Central MA; Dist. Dir., CA Sen. Art Torres, 1986; CA Dep. Atty. Gen., 1987-90.

DC Office: 1119 LHOB, 20515, 202-225-6235; Fax: 202-225-2202; Web site: becerra.house.gov.

District Offices: Los Angeles, 213-483-1425.

Committees: *Budget* (8th of 22 D). *Ways & Means* (9th of 24 D): Oversight; Health; Social Security.

Group Ratings

	ADA	ACLU	AFS	LCV	ITIC	NTU	COC	ACU	CFG	FRC
2006	95	100	100	100	29	10	21	4	8	0
2005	95	—	100	94	—	14	37	0	3	0

National Journal Ratings

	2005 LIB	—	2005 CONS	2006 LIB	—	2006 CONS
Economic	91%	—	9%	94%	—	0%
Social	90%	—	9%	90%	—	9%
Foreign	91%	—	7%	95%	—	0%

Key Votes of the 109th Congress

1. Estate Tax Repeal	N	5. Limit Interstate Abortion	N	9. Build Border Fence	N
2. Limit CAFE Standards	N	6. Extend Patriot Act	N	10. CAFTA	N
3. FY06 Spending Curb	N	7. Bar Same Sex Marriage	N	11. Oppose Iraq Withdrawal	N
4. Drilling in ANWR	N	8. Stem Cell Research $	Y	12. Detainee Tribunals	N

Election Results

2006 general	Xavier Becerra (D)	.... unopposed		($767,138)
2006 primary	Xavier Becerra (D)	 26,904	(89%)	
	Sal Genovese (D)	 3,227	(11%)	
2004 general	Xavier Becerra (D)	 89,363	(80%)	($623,023)
	Luis Vega (R)	 22,048	(20%)	

Prior Winning Percentages: 2002 (81%); 2000 (83%); 1998 (81%); 1996 (72%); 1994 (66%); 1992 (58%)

The People		Race/Ethnic Origin	Ancestry	
Area size:	40 sq. mi.	9.8% White	USA: 1.6%	German: 1.5%
Urban population:	100.0%	4.2% Black	Irish: 1.3%	
Rural population:	0.0%	13.8% Asian	**2004 Presidential Vote**	
Pop. 2000:	639,088	0.3% Native Am.	Kerry (D) 92,894	(77%)
Pop. 2005 (est):	635,804	0.1% Hawaiian	Bush (R) 26,054	(22%)
Median income:	$26,093	1.5% Two+ races	Other 1,815	(2%)
Poverty status:	30.1%	0.2% Other	**2000 Presidential Vote**	
Military veterans:	3.7%	70.2% Hispanic Origin	Gore (D) 79,560	(77%)
			Bush (R) 19,400	(19%)
			Other 4,156	(4%)
			Cook Partisan Voting Index: D +30	

Occupation	Blue collar: 33.7%	White collar: 44.1%	Gray collar: 22.2%

Surrounding downtown Los Angeles are neighborhoods just now becoming antique, as mid-20th century buildings stop looking familiar and start taking on the patina of the historic. Downtown LA, with its 1980s marble slabs and pink cylinders jutting up to 70 stories from what was once a low-rise business district, has become surprisingly pedestrian-friendly, with attractive plazas like the one around the dazzlingly redesigned Los Angeles Library. But downtown is detached from the neighborhoods around, which change character with every new immigration flow. South of downtown is the garment district, with factories in nondescript buildings, an economically vibrant area with high rents and one of the reasons Los Angeles has become the largest manufacturing city in America today; the anti-sweatshop movement has struggled to maintain new facilities here, while attempting to compete with overseas manufacturers. To the north are Lincoln Heights, a heavily Hispanic area centering on the busy shopping street of North Broadway where residents have been fighting gangs and graffiti, and the neighborhoods of Highland Park and Eagle Rock, white middle-class 30 years ago, now mostly Latino but with Asians as well, and with middle-class housing prices. West of downtown are Pico Union, an entry point for new immigrants; lower Sunset Boulevard; University Park, which surrounds the University of Southern California campus; and Thai Town along Hollywood Boulevard between Normandie and Western. Lower Sunset Boulevard and Echo Park have become lively shopping strips filled with that rare L.A. commodity: pedestrians. Hollywood has long had a seedy look—it has not sprouted the office buildings you can see in Burbank or Glendale, because of Los Angeles's high taxes and daffy regulations—but has recently been spiffied up.

Almost all of these areas, centering geographically on Dodger Stadium, are part of California's 31st Congressional District. In Los Angeles's booming 1980s these neighborhoods were suddenly thronged with immigrants, more thickly populated than a quarter-century before, with small houses and garden apartments full of large families and many children. In the 1990s, the population surge stopped and this became the slowest-growing district in California, as the newcomers of the decade before moved out to middle class neighborhoods and as incoming immigrants spread more evenly around the Los Angeles Basin; the trend continued between 2000 and 2005, when this was one of only two L.A.-area districts to lose population. This remains a district of immigrants, though: In the 2000 Census, it ranked first in the nation with its non-citizens (41%) and last in the nation in homes where English is spoken (21%).

The congressman from the 31st District is Xavier Becerra, a Democrat first elected in 1992. He grew up in Sacramento, went to college and law school at Stanford, helped his parents to fight a real-estate scam and worked for legal services, then joined state Senator Art Torres and Attorney General John Van de Kamp, and married a Harvard Medical School graduate who became vice president of California's largest health-care foundation. In 1990 he was elected to the Assembly. In 1992, when Edward Roybal, California's first Latino congressman, announced that he was retiring, Becerra jumped into the race. His main Latino competitor, Leticia Quezada, was a member of the Los Angeles school board, a powerful engine for publicity. But Becerra had the endorsements of Roybal and County Supervisor Gloria Molina. In a primary in which only 33,000 voters turned out, Becerra won with 32% to 22% for Quezada. His 10,417 votes effectively made him the representative of more than 600,000 people. Since then, he has not faced a serious campaign challenge.

In the House, he has been a consistent liberal. His pleasant and businesslike manner, combined with his obvious ambition, have made him a force in the House now that Democrats have regained control. In March 2005, he took pride in his selection by House leaders to fill the seat on the board of regents of the Smithsonian Institution. In February 2007, he won House support for a commission to study creation of a new museum of the American Latino, which would be located on the National Mall and would be part of the Smithsonian.

On the Ways and Means Committee, where he is the only Hispanic member, Becerra advocated tax changes to prevent the overseas exodus of jobs in the entertainment industry, including a tax credit for labor costs of independent film producers. He supported normal trade relations with China and won House approval of his resolution supporting reunification efforts between North and South Korea. His support for free-trade deals with Chile and Singapore led to local protests by union activists, but he demanded changes in the labor standards in the Central American Free Trade Agreement. He sponsored a bill that would forgive student loans for graduates who work as librarians in poor neighborhoods and another to assist low-income taxpayers in preparing their tax returns while protecting them from predatory tax refund anticipation loan providers.

Becerra ran for mayor of Los Angeles in 2001, a campaign that dimmed his rising star. He did not raise enough money to establish name recognition outside his district and was overshadowed by former Assembly Speaker Antonio Villaraigosa. In the primary, Becerra finished fifth, with 6% of the vote, far behind Villaraigosa's 30% and James Hahn's 25%; Hahn won the runoff. Among the 21% of voters who were Hispanic, Villaraigosa led Becerra 62%-17%. Post-election analyses noted that Becerra damaged his standing among Latino leaders with negative campaign telephone calls. Villaraigosa ran again in 2005 and defeated Hahn; Becerra seemed content to build influence in the House and at Ways and Means. In December 2006, he got his reward when Nancy Pelosi gave him the vaguely defined position of Assistant to the Speaker, where he helps to set priorities and drive legislative decision-making: the most senior Latino in Democratic leadership. "A seat at the table has been priceless," he told *Congress Daily*.

THIRTY-SECOND DISTRICT

Rep. Hilda Solis (D)

Elected 2000, 4th term; b. Oct. 20, 1957, Los Angeles; home, El Monte; CA St. Polytechnic U., B.A. 1979; U. of S. CA, M.A. 1981; Catholic; married (Sam Sayyad).

Elected Office: CA Assembly, 1992-94; CA Senate 1994-00.

Professional Career: Editor, White House Ofc. of Hispanic Affairs, 1980-81; Management Analyst, Ofc. of Management & Budget, 1981.

DC Office: 1414 LHOB, 20515, 202-225-5464; Fax: 202-225-5467; Web site: solis.house.gov.

District Offices: East Los Angeles, 323-307-9904; El Monte, 626-448-1271.

Committees: *Energy & Commerce* (20th of 31 D): Environment & Hazardous Materials (Vice Chmn.); Health; Telecommunications & the Internet. *Natural Resources* (25th of 27 D): Energy & Mineral Resources. *Select Committee on Energy Independence and Global Warming* (5th of 9 D).

Group Ratings

	ADA	ACLU	AFS	LCV	ITIC	NTU	COC	ACU	CFG	FRC
2006	100	100	100	100	29	13	27	4	4	0
2005	100	—	100	94	—	15	35	0	7	0

National Journal Ratings

	2005 LIB	—	2005 CONS		2006 LIB	—	2006 CONS
Economic	94%	—	0%		94%	—	0%
Social	93%	—	6%		93%	—	6%
Foreign	94%	—	4%		95%	—	0%

Key Votes of the 109th Congress

1. Estate Tax Repeal	N	5. Limit Interstate Abortion	N	9. Build Border Fence	N
2. Limit CAFE Standards	N	6. Extend Patriot Act	N	10. CAFTA	N
3. FY06 Spending Curb	N	7. Bar Same Sex Marriage	N	11. Oppose Iraq Withdrawal	N
4. Drilling in ANWR	N	8. Stem Cell Research $	Y	12. Detainee Tribunals	N

Election Results

2006 general	Hilda Solis (D)	76,059	(83%)	($882,866)
	Leland Faegre (Lib)	15,627	(17%)	
2006 primary	Hilda Solis (D)	unopposed		
2004 general	Hilda Solis (D)	119,144	(85%)	($527,054)
	Leland Faegre (Lib)	21,002	(15%)	

Prior Winning Percentages: 2002 (69%); 2000 (79%)

The People		Race/Ethnic Origin	Ancestry	
Area size:	93 sq. mi.	14.8% White	German: 3.1% Irish: 2.5%	
Urban population:	100.0%	2.6% Black	English: 2.2%	
Rural population:	0.0%	18.4% Asian	**2004 Presidential Vote**	
Pop. 2000:	639,087	0.3% Native Am.	Kerry (D)	99,286 (62%)
Pop. 2005 (est):	663,846	0.1% Hawaiian	Bush (R)	58,341 (37%)
Median income:	$41,394	1.4% Two+ races	Other	1,756 (1%)
Poverty status:	18.0%	0.1% Other	**2000 Presidential Vote**	
Military veterans:	6.3%	62.3% Hispanic Origin	Gore (D)	96,217 (67%)
			Bush (R)	45,018 (31%)
			Other	3,057 (2%)
			Cook Partisan Voting Index: D +17	

Occupation	Blue collar: 32.7%	White collar: 51.3%	Gray collar: 16.0%

Anyone interested in the future of America and today's immigrants should drive straight east from downtown Los Angeles on I-10, the San Bernardino Freeway, through the string of suburbs that grew up in the 1940s and 1950s. These were once white middle-class communities, with grid streets of stucco houses above the dry riverbeds; they were filled with Midwest and East Coast migrants who discovered California during World War II and decided to stay, or who learned of its golden reputation from the new medium of television in the days before smog became part of the language. The atmosphere then was Midwestern, cheerful, busy, with children always underfoot. The next generation resulted in almost a complete population turnover here, but some things remained the same. Mexican-Americans spread out from their original East Los Angeles base to become majorities in blue-collar suburbs like El Monte, Baldwin Park, Azusa and West Covina, all with many more residents than in their Anglo days. Chinese and other Asians are the majority in Monterey Park and 49% of the population in Rosemead. The late *New York Times* food maven R.W. Apple Jr. described "a memorable week in the gastronomic trenches" of the local Asian restaurant scene, and reported that "it is easier to buy bok choy than iceberg" in Monterey Park. The same town hosts an annual Cherry Blossom Festival, sponsored by the local Japanese community. Almost every neighborhood here is mixed, with people whose origins are in different continents and cultures. The new people here have upgraded the neighborhoods, bringing in energy and money, the enthusiasm of the young and the community-spiritedness of the homeowner. There are busy shops with new signs, newly painted homes with carefully tended gardens, neighborhoods still filled with children whose parents believe in traditional values. When blacks and Latinos were rioting in South Central and Hollywood in 1992, East Los Angeles and the San Gabriel Valley were quiet and orderly. Now, some leaders of East Los Angeles want to incorporate to stake their claim as a city of 140,000. The progress and pride of these immigrant suburbs surely tell more about the human condition than stories about the clueless youth of Beverly Hills.

The 32d Congressional District of California covers much of this territory. It includes part of East Los Angeles and a small part of Los Angeles, most of Monterey Park and all of Rosemead, El Monte, Baldwin Park, Azusa, West Covina and Covina. It is 62% Hispanic and 18% Asian—the second-highest Asian percentage and one of the lowest percentages of non-Hispanic whites in southern California. Politically, the new Latinos and Asians have been up for grabs. In the early 1990s Asians, dismayed that the civic elite seemed more interested in ministering to the complaints of rioters than compensating the store owners whose property was ruined and lives threatened, moved toward the Republicans. In the middle 1990s Latinos, because of Republican immigration and welfare laws removing aid to legal immigrants—and because Republican campaign ads suggested Latinos were more interested in welfare than work—moved heavily toward the Democrats; Asians moved a bit in the same direction. This was assumed to be a heavily Democratic district. But Republicans Arnold Schwarzenegger and Tom McClintock together won nearly half of the Latino vote in the 2003 recall of Gray Davis as governor, according to exit polls. Then, 13 months later, the percentage here for George W. Bush rose from 31% to 37%, and Governor Schwarzenegger in 2006 lost by a respectable 54%-42%.

The congresswoman from the 32d District is Hilda Solis, a Democrat first elected in 2000. She is the daughter of a Teamsters Union shop steward from Mexico and an assembly line worker from Nicaragua who met while taking citizenship courses in Los Angeles. She graduated from California State Polytechnic University in 1979 and got a master's of public administration from the University of Southern California. She worked in the Carter White House's Office of Hispanic Affairs. Solis was first elected in 1984 to the Rio Hondo Community College Board of Trustees. She won an Assembly seat in 1992, and in 1994 became the first Latina elected to the state Senate. Her work for environmental justice led the John F. Kennedy Library Foundation to name her as the first woman to get a Profiles in Courage Award. In 2000, she ran against Congressman Matthew Martinez, who was originally elected in 1982 with the support of Congressman Howard Berman and Henry Waxman; he lost support among feminist and labor activists by voting for a ban on late-term abortions and fast-track trade authority and helping to stall gun control. Solis was endorsed by labor unions, EMILY's List, the Sierra Club, Senator Barbara Boxer and Congresswoman Loretta Sanchez. Martinez was supported by colleagues Lucille Roybal-Allard and Grace Napolitano; Berman and Waxman, no longer much involved in local politics, were neutral. Solis raised four times as much money as Martinez and had hundreds of volunteers from reinvigorated unions and local grass-roots organizations. The contest was caustic; she won 62%-29%, and had no Republican opposition. After the primary, a bitter Martinez switched parties, but his efforts to urge Latinos to vote Republican fell flat.

Solis has been among the most liberal members of the House and rarely casts a conservative vote. In the minority, she was a tenacious defender of her community. She fought proposals to weaken worker safety regulations and complained that the Nielsen television ratings undercounted Latinos. She showed her good standing with Nancy Pelosi by gaining a highly-sought seat on the Energy and Commerce Committee, and has been active on its Environment and Hazardous Materials Subcommittee—a good fit with her career work. Solis has scored some legislative successes. She was among the early sponsors of the bill to give citizenship eligibility to immigrants who have served a year in the military, which George W. Bush signed in November 2003; previous law required three years of service. She enacted a bill for the Interior Department to restore the water flow of the San Gabriel River and study ways to create more green space and urban recreation areas. She enacted another bill to name a post office in Duarte for Francisco Martinez Flores, a Marine who was among the first casualties in the Iraq war. As a Pelosi loyalist, she has been active in leadership circles and was named to the select committee on global warming; she has cosponsored legislation that sets greenhouse gas emission targets.

Solis has been easily reelected. She broke her earlier alliance and had bitter arguments with Loretta Sanchez by backing Hector De La Torre against her sister Linda Sanchez in the 2002 primary for the 39th District. In February 2007, amidst feuding within the Hispanic Caucus, it was reported that Caucus Chairman Joe Baca called her a "kiss-up" to Pelosi. Baca publicly apologized.

THIRTY-THIRD DISTRICT

Rep. Diane Watson (D)

Elected June 2001, 3d full term; b. Nov. 12, 1933, Los Angeles; home, Los Angeles; U.C.L.A., B.A. 1954, CA State L.A., M.A. 1968, Claremont U., Ph.D. 1987; Catholic; single.

Elected Office: L.A. Bd. of Education, 1975-78; CA Senate, 1978-98.

Professional Career: Teacher & school psychologist, 1954-75; lecturer, CA State L.A. & CA State Long Beach; U.S. Ambassador, Micronesia 1999-2001.

DC Office: 125 CHOB, 20515, 202-225-7084; Fax: 202-225-2422; Web site: www.house.gov/watson.

District Offices: Los Angeles, 323-965-1422.

Committees: *Foreign Affairs* (11th of 27 D): Africa & Global Health; Asia, the Pacific & the Global Environment. *Oversight & Government Reform* (11th of 23 D): Domestic Policy.

Group Ratings

	ADA	ACLU	AFS	LCV	ITIC	NTU	COC	ACU	CFG	FRC
2006	80	95	100	100	40	14	33	0	1	0
2005	95	—	100	100	—	13	37	4	4	0

National Journal Ratings

	2005 LIB	—	2005 CONS		2006 LIB	—	2006 CONS
Economic	94%	—	0%		94%	—	0%
Social	93%	—	6%		97%	—	0%
Foreign	88%	—	11%		95%	—	0%

Key Votes of the 109th Congress

1. Estate Tax Repeal	N	5. Limit Interstate Abortion	N	9. Build Border Fence	N
2. Limit CAFE Standards	N	6. Extend Patriot Act	N	10. CAFTA	N
3. FY06 Spending Curb	N	7. Bar Same Sex Marriage	N	11. Oppose Iraq Withdrawal	N
4. Drilling in ANWR	N	8. Stem Cell Research $	Y	12. Detainee Tribunals	N

Election Results

2006 general	Diane Watson (D) .... unopposed		
2006 primary	Diane Watson (D) 47,461	(91%)	
	Mervin Evans (D) 4,774	(9%)	
2004 general	Diane Watson (D) 166,801	(89%)	($259,663)
	Bob Weber (Lib) 21,513	(11%)	

Prior Winning Percentages: 2002 (83%); 2001 (75%)

The People		Race/Ethnic Origin	Ancestry		
Area size:	48 sq. mi.	19.9% White	German: 2.8%		Irish: 2.4%
Urban population:	100.0%	29.9% Black	English: 2.1%		
Rural population:	0.0%	12.1% Asian	**2004 Presidential Vote**		
Pop. 2000:	639,088	0.2% Native Am.	Kerry (D) 172,382		(83%)
Pop. 2005 (est):	643,566	0.1% Hawaiian	Bush (R) 33,132		(16%)
Median income:	$31,655	2.8% Two+ races	Other 2,631		(1%)
Poverty status:	23.5%	0.4% Other	**2000 Presidential Vote**		
Military veterans:	6.5%	34.6% Hispanic Origin	Gore (D) 148,978		(83%)
			Bush (R) 24,214		(14%)
			Other 6,067		(3%)
			Cook Partisan Voting Index: D +36		

Occupation	Blue collar: 17.8%	White collar: 63.9%	Gray collar: 18.4%

One of the myths of the Los Angeles riots of 1992 and 1965 is that black Angelenos live in conditions of isolation and poverty. Some do. But in levels of income and in degree of residential integration with non-blacks, Los Angeles blacks rank among the top in the United States. Its black-owned businesses have the highest revenues of any city in the nation. Californians have historically shown less prejudice toward blacks than most Americans, and job opportunities in Los Angeles—up to and including the office of mayor for 20 years—have been plenteous for blacks. This is apparent in the hills just west of Crenshaw, an Art Deco neighborhood built in the 1920s and 1930s in vacant flat land southwest of downtown LA and the birthplace of West Coast hip-hop music. Here, in Baldwin Hills, where on clear days you can see the towers of downtown and the snow-capped San Gabriel Mountains beyond, is a high-income black neighborhood, one of the strongest in the country. Near Windsor Hills along Slauson Avenue, other comfortable black-majority neighborhoods have been built. In the more rundown Crenshaw area, former L.A. Laker Magic Johnson built his successful multiplex theaters. With Olympic Boulevard as its main street, Koreatown has become a center for the city's cultural and business life and an investment opportunity for many South Koreans; Aroma, a large futuristic shopping center and spa along Wilshire Boulevard, caters to affluent Koreans. On the site of the old Ambassador Hotel, the Los Angeles Unified School District decided to build a school rather than approve retail shops. To the north at Hollywood Boulevard, near the tourist mecca of the famed Grauman's Chinese Theatre, a huge new complex includes the Kodak Theater, which hosts the Oscars and many television and award events, including the American Idol finals.

These parts of central Los Angeles are the heart of the 33d Congressional District, which is bisected by the Santa Monica Freeway, and runs from the Golden State Freeway southwest to the economically revived Culver City and almost to Venice on the Pacific Ocean. It includes most of Koreatown, centered on Western Avenue and Olympic Boulevard, plus the Wilshire Corridor, some of Hollywood and the affluent Los Feliz neighborhoods to the east. It is 35% Hispanic, 30% black and 12% Asian, with a sizable Korean population. But many Latinos are not citizens or registered voters, and a majority of Democratic primary voters here have been black, though that may no longer be true for the next redistricting. Here, affluent, well-educated blacks seem if anything to be culturally more liberal than low-income black voters who may have closer ties to church and tradition. Many have profited on the way up from some form of government intervention—a student loan, a public sector job, affirmative action—and many still hold public sector jobs. This is one of the most Democratic districts in the nation: John Kerry got 83% of the vote in 2004.

The congresswoman from the 33d District is Diane Watson, first elected in a June 2001 special election. She grew up in Los Angeles, graduated from UCLA, and later got her master's from California State and a doctorate in educational administration from Claremont. She worked as an elementary school teacher, school psychologist and lecturer at Cal State Los Angeles. Watson began her political career in 1975 as the first black woman elected to the Los Angeles Board of Education, where she worked on school desegregation issues. Three years later, she ran for the state Senate, again becoming the first black woman in that body. She served as chairman of the Health and Human Services Committee for 17 years before term limits forced her to retire in 1998. She stirred controversy in 1989 when she defended legislative perks that have since been outlawed; she argued that legislators deserved special treatment because they were not "ordinary people." In 1999, Watson was confirmed as U.S. Ambassador to Micronesia; she returned home to run in the special election to replace Julian Dixon, who died in December 2000. In that contest, which effectively was decided in the Democratic primary, her chief opponents were state Senator Kevin Murray and Councilman Nate Holden. Watson's theme was familiarity. Murray argued that, at 41 and 26 years younger than Watson and 30 years younger than Holden, he could build seniority; Watson countered by campaigning with her 91-year-old mother. Watson was funded by EMILY's List and was endorsed by Magic Johnson. Murray was endorsed by Dixon's widow Bettye, Maxine Waters, Henry Waxman and Howard Berman. Holden was endorsed by outgoing Mayor Richard Riordan. Watson won 33% of the vote, to 26% for Murray and 17% for Holden. On her victory night, she angrily attacked the party leaders who opposed her. In the June runoff, she won 75%-20% over a Republican who spent $709,000 of her own money on her campaign.

Watson has a solidly liberal voting record, and was the most liberal member of the House in 2006. She drew protests from California dentists by sponsoring a bill to prohibit the use of mercury amalgams in dental fillings; Watson responded that the California legislature had banned mercury thermometers and was reviewing the use of dental amalgams. Later, she demanded that Kellogg stop placing a Spiderman toy in its cereal boxes because it contained a mercury battery. She joined other Black Caucus members in calling for United Nations monitors of the 2004 U.S. presidential election. In November 2004, she gained attention when she claimed that she had tipped off federal agents to an alleged terror plot at an Albany, New York mosque; law enforcement authorities said that they had launched a sting operation months earlier. She showed an interest in media issues: In November 2005, the House passed a resolution that she cosponsored urging Russia to protect intellectual property rights. In October 2006, she told an FCC field hearing that further relaxation of media-ownership rules serves corporate interests, not consumer interests.

In future redistricting, small shifts of lines could have a considerable impact on Watson, altering the district's racial and ethnic balance of power and possibly generating serious primary competition from a Latino challenger.

THIRTY-FOURTH DISTRICT

Rep. Lucille Roybal-Allard (D)

Elected 1992, 8th term; b. June 12, 1941, Los Angeles; home, Los Angeles; CA State L.A., B.A. 1965; Catholic; married (Edward Allard).

Elected Office: CA Assembly, 1986-92.

DC Office: 2330 RHOB, 20515, 202-225-1766; Fax: 202-226-0350; Web site: www.house.gov/roybal-allard.

District Offices: Los Angeles, 213-628-9230.

Committees: *Appropriations* (18th of 37 D): Labor, HHS, Education & Related Agencies; Homeland Security; Transportation, HUD & Related Agencies. *Standards of Official Conduct* (3d of 5 D).

Group Ratings

	ADA	ACLU	AFS	LCV	ITIC	NTU	COC	ACU	CFG	FRC
2006	100	100	100	100	14	8	33	4	4	0
2005	90	—	100	89	—	10	43	0	3	0

National Journal Ratings

	2005 LIB	—	2005 CONS		2006 LIB	—	2006 CONS
Economic	94%	—	0%		74%	—	23%
Social	96%	—	4%		89%	—	10%
Foreign	80%	—	19%		75%	—	23%

Key Votes of the 109th Congress

1. Estate Tax Repeal	N	5. Limit Interstate Abortion	N	9. Build Border Fence	N
2. Limit CAFE Standards	N	6. Extend Patriot Act	N	10. CAFTA	N
3. FY06 Spending Curb	*	7. Bar Same Sex Marriage	N	11. Oppose Iraq Withdrawal	N
4. Drilling in ANWR	N	8. Stem Cell Research $	Y	12. Detainee Tribunals	N

Election Results

2006 general	Lucille Roybal-Allard (D)	57,459	(77%)	($658,270)
	Wayne Miller (R)	17,359	(23%)	
2006 primary	Lucille Roybal-Allard (D)	unopposed		
2004 general	Lucille Roybal-Allard (D)	82,282	(74%)	($572,055)
	Wayne Miller (R)	28,175	(26%)	

Prior Winning Percentages: 2002 (74%); 2000 (85%); 1998 (87%); 1996 (82%); 1994 (81%); 1992 (63%)

The People		Race/Ethnic Origin	Ancestry	
Area size:	59 sq. mi.	11.4% White	German: 2.0%	USA: 1.9%
Urban population:	100.0%	4.4% Black	Irish: 1.5%	
Rural population:	0.0%	5.5% Asian	**2004 Presidential Vote**	
Pop. 2000:	639,088	0.3% Native Am.	Kerry (D) 82,942	(69%)
Pop. 2005 (est):	669,403	0.1% Hawaiian	Bush (R) 35,926	(30%)
Median income:	$29,863	0.9% Two+ races	Other 1,654	(1%)
Poverty status:	26.0%	0.1% Other	**2000 Presidential Vote**	
Military veterans:	4.8%	77.2% Hispanic Origin	Gore (D) 76,876	(72%)
			Bush (R) 27,384	(26%)
			Other 1,901	(2%)
			Cook Partisan Voting Index: D +23	

Occupation   Blue collar: 40.0%   White collar: 43.7%   Gray collar: 16.4%

A block from the 452-foot white tower of Los Angeles's "modern architecture" City Hall—long the symbol of the city, but now less spectacular than the nearby Westin Bonaventure Hotel and dwarfed by 60- and 70-story postmodern marble slabs and pink cylinders a few blocks away—is the huge retail shopping street of Broadway. The sidewalks are thronged with Latinos, the signs are mostly in Spanish, the merchandise is often strewn on tables: this could be Mexico City or Lima. It is Latin America transplanted a block from a gleaming symbol of Yankee propriety and gaudy emblems of North American prosperity. Broadway is neither the geographical nor spiritual center of Los Angeles's Latino communities and it is just one of many shopping and dining areas. But it is an emblem of the entry-level Latino neighborhoods of the nation's second-largest city, the places where many immigrants, not only from Mexico but from Central and South America, come to find a cheap place to live—doubling and tripling up with other families and single newcomers, close enough to drive an old car to work in factories and warehouses that fill so much of the acreage south and east of downtown.

Broadway and many of these entry-level neighborhoods are part of the 34th Congressional District of California. It includes downtown and Boyle Heights, once an entry neighborhood for Irish and Jewish immigrants and for the last 40 years predominantly Mexican-American. Near the Hollywood Freeway is the Cathedral of Our Lady of the Angels, the $190 million center of the nation's largest and most ethnically diverse Roman Catholic archdiocese, which Cardinal Roger Mahony dedicated as an "anchor for the ages." Another new landmark is the Walt Disney Concert Hall, home of the Los Angeles Philharmonic. Even though prostitution and drug sales flourish not far from City Hall, the commercial revival has spurred residential development in the central business district, with both new housing and renovations. The 34th also includes the giant factories south of downtown along the Southern Pacific Railroad and Santa Ana Freeway and it takes in part of East Los Angeles. To the south it includes the garment factories of Vernon and the 1940s working-class suburbs: Huntington Park—with its vibrant shopping strip on the wide Pacific Boulevard and with a youthful population that has more than doubled since 1980—Bell and Bell Gardens, Commerce, Maywood and Cudahy, all of which are now heavily Latino; city officials have declared Maywood a "sanctuary city" for illegal immigrants. Beyond those areas are the more affluent suburbs of Downey, home of the Boeing (formerly Rockwell) plant that built the space shuttle, and Bellflower, which was a prime shopping area decades ago and recently has started a comeback. Bisecting much of the district is the concrete-lined Los Angeles River.

The 34th District is 77% Hispanic, the highest percentage in any California district. Politically, this area is heavily Democratic, but with just 4% black residents the 34th is less Democratic than some neighboring districts. It is not clear what the future political preferences of people here will be, for the large majority of adults here do not vote. In 2006, in a constituency of 669,000 people, only 75,000 voted in the general election, far less than the 211,000 who voted in the Westside 30th District.

The congresswoman from the 34th District is Lucille Roybal-Allard, first elected in 1992, the daughter of 30-year Congressman Edward Roybal. His roots were in New Mexico, not Mexico, and in 1949 he was the first Latino elected to the Los Angeles city council. Lucille Roybal-Allard dreamed of a show business career as a teenager and later worked as a department store clerk and for non-profit organizations. After raising a family— two of her children are lawyers—she entered politics at age 45, with the encouragement of local activists. She was elected to the Assembly in 1986. She entered the 1992 House race before her father announced his retirement in the adjacent district, and she easily won, with 75% in the primary and 63% in the general election.

The first Mexican-American woman elected to Congress, Roybal-Allard has compiled a solidly liberal voting record. On the Appropriations Committee, where her father had been a subcommittee chairman, she has worked on immigration issues. In June 2004, the House passed her amendment to prevent the privatizing of services for immigration information officers or investigators. With Republican Chris Cannon, she filed a bill to provide in-state college tuition rates for children of illegal immigrants. With Howard Berman and Lincoln Diaz-Balart, she sponsored the American Dream Act to provide a path to legal immigration for college-bound students. On other issues, she won House passage of an amendment to allow breastfeeding in national parks and museums. She has sought to focus on underage drinking, including a call for higher taxes on alcohol and restraints on advertising; her STOP bill (Sober Truth on Preventing) underage drinking was enacted in 2006. With George Miller, she filed a bill to require the Labor Department to issue a standard requiring employers to pay for needed protective equipment. She formed a bipartisan study group on public health with Kay Granger. In November 2006, Roybal-Allard showed her independence of Nancy Pelosi by seconding the nomination of Steny Hoyer in the contest against John Murtha for Majority Leader.

Back home, in her office at the Edward R. Roybal Federal Building, Roybal-Allard sponsors health fairs and workshops on home buying and U.S. citizenship. She has been reelected without difficulty.

THIRTY-FIFTH DISTRICT

Rep. Maxine Waters (D)

Elected 1990, 9th term; b. Aug. 15, 1938, St. Louis, MO; home, Los Angeles; CA State L.A., B.A. 1970; Christian; married (Sidney Williams).

Elected Office: CA Assembly, 1976-90.

Professional Career: Head Start teacher, 1966; Dpty., City Councilman David Cunningham, 1973-76.

DC Office: 2344 RHOB, 20515, 202-225-2201; Fax: 202-225-7854; Web site: www.house.gov/waters.

District Offices: Los Angeles, 323-757-8900; Los Angeles, 310-642-4610.

Committees: *Chief Deputy Majority Whip. Financial Services* (3d of 37 D): Housing & Community Opportunity (Chmn.); Domestic and International Monetary Policy, Trade & Technology; Oversight & Investigations; Financial Institutions & Consumer Credit. *Judiciary* (9th of 23 D): Crime, Terrorism & Homeland Security; Immigration, Citizenship, Refugees, Border Security & International Law.

Group Ratings

	ADA	ACLU	AFS	LCV	ITIC	NTU	COC	ACU	CFG	FRC
2006	90	100	100	100	14	14	31	4	13	0
2005	95	—	100	94	—	19	32	8	8	8

National Journal Ratings

	2005 LIB	—	2005 CONS		2006 LIB	—	2006 CONS
Economic	80%	—	20%		89%	—	11%
Social	98%	—	0%		95%	—	4%
Foreign	87%	—	12%		88%	—	10%

Key Votes of the 109th Congress

1. Estate Tax Repeal	N	5. Limit Interstate Abortion	N	9. Build Border Fence	N
2. Limit CAFE Standards	N	6. Extend Patriot Act	N	10. CAFTA	N
3. FY06 Spending Curb	N	7. Bar Same Sex Marriage	N	11. Oppose Iraq Withdrawal	N
4. Drilling in ANWR	N	8. Stem Cell Research $	Y	12. Detainee Tribunals	N

Election Results

2006 general	Maxine Waters (D)	82,498	(84%)	($759,619)
	Gordon Mego (AMI)	8,343	(8%)	
	Paul Ireland (Lib)	7,665	(8%)	
2006 primary	Maxine Waters (D)	34,338	(86%)	
	Carl McGill (D)	5,538	(14%)	
2004 general	Maxine Waters (D)	125,949	(81%)	($330,980)
	Ross Moen (R)	23,591	(15%)	($3,540)
	Other	6,867	(4%)	

Prior Winning Percentages: 2002 (78%); 2000 (87%); 1998 (89%); 1996 (86%); 1994 (78%); 1992 (83%); 1990 (79%)

The People		Race/Ethnic Origin	Ancestry		
Area size:	55 sq. mi.	10.4% White	German: 2.0%	Irish: 1.7%	
Urban population:	100.0%	34.1% Black	Subsaharan: 1.6%		
Rural population:	0.0%	5.6% Asian	**2004 Presidential Vote**		
Pop. 2000:	639,088	0.2% Native Am.	Kerry (D)	130,764	(79%)
Pop. 2005 (est):	701,097	0.3% Hawaiian	Bush (R)	33,110	(20%)
Median income:	$32,156	1.8% Two+ races	Other	1,726	(1%)
Poverty status:	26.4%	0.2% Other	**2000 Presidential Vote**		
Military veterans:	7.2%	47.4% Hispanic Origin	Gore (D)	118,450	(82%)
			Bush (R)	24,495	(17%)
			Other	2,262	(2%)
			Cook Partisan Voting Index: D +33		

Occupation   Blue collar: 28.3%   White collar: 53.0%   Gray collar: 18.7%

Los Angeles in the years just after World War II was the fastest growing metropolitan area in America. If a traveler deplaning today at LAX could suddenly put himself in the postwar Los Angeles of 50 years ago, he would see quite a different city. LAX, today the nation's third-busiest airport, with eight central terminals, was then a small airfield, standing amid open country. The mile-square grids east, north and south of the airport were just filling up with rapidly built subdivisions. North of the airport on open fields you would find the spanking new middle class Westchester subdivision; just beyond you would see the wetlands along Ballona Creek, where Howard Hughes took his Spruce Goose, the largest airplane ever built, up for its one and only flight. Inglewood, the rapidly growing suburb just east of the airport around the Hollywood Park Race Track, was filling up with the young families of people who had moved to Los Angeles during or after the war—workers in the giant aircraft factories or in the small factories built by entrepreneurs manufacturing products that Californians got from factories back East before the war. Inglewood would become a focus of sports fans when the Forum opened in 1967, the home of the Los Angeles Lakers for 32 years. In Hawthorne, just to the south, home of a big Northrop Grumman plant, future celebrities were growing up—Sonny Bono and the Beach Boys. Gardena, east of Hawthorne, was famous for its legal poker clubs and its Japanese American residents, back from the wartime internment camps. East of Gardena is the part of Los Angeles called South Central or, more recently, South Los Angeles, after the city council in 2003 officially renamed this community to rid it of the stigma as a place of gang wars and race riots. In the days of residential segregation, much of this area was the home of Los Angeles's black community, its numbers greatly expanded by migration from the South during and after the war. Here you could find the Central Avenue entertainment district, at whose clubs and theaters you could see the likes of Ella Fitzgerald, Sarah Vaughn, Billy Eckstine, Duke Ellington, Louis Armstrong, Count Basie, Dizzy Gillespie and Charlie Parker. Later, it was the epicenter of L.A.'s two postwar riots, in the Watts district of Los Angeles in 1965 and at the corner of Florence and Normandie in 1992. In the last 20 years, Latinos have been buying houses here, which are among the cheapest in the metro area—only five L.A. zip codes have median prices below $200,000—and new businesses have been cropping up in garages and small factories.

The 35th Congressional District of California today is made up of all these areas, with a landscape and populations very different from what you would have found 50 years ago. At its west and east ends are two of the Los Angeles area's great transportation facilities. One is LAX and the cluster of hotels and office buildings all around; the swooping arches of LAX's theme building, intended in 1961 to symbolize the jet era, are now an historic landmark, like Disneyland's Tomorrowland or the *Jetsons*, an antique version of a surpassed future. In December 2004 the Los Angeles Council approved Mayor James Hahn's $11 billion expansion plan, which includes $500 million for soundproofing and other measures to placate nearby communities. The other is the Alameda Corridor, the 20-mile rail express line connecting the ports of Los Angeles and Long Beach with rail distribution points near downtown Los Angeles in a trench 33 feet below ground, built between 1997 and 2002 at a cost of $2.4 billion. Westchester, once all white, now is home to many blacks and Latinos. Inglewood, once all white, later mostly black, is now 46% Hispanic; it also has a school system that is producing some of the state's highest test scores. Hawthorne, with more Hispanics than whites or blacks, is home of the Western Museum of Flight. Gardena still has its poker clubs and a large Asian population. South Los Angeles, an almost entirely black neighborhood at the time of the Watts riot, now is home to more Hispanics than blacks. As Los Angeles expanded in the post-World War II era, this was mostly white working-class and middle-class country; from 1954 to 1970 much of the area was part of the assembly district that elected Jesse Unruh, legendary Speaker of the Assembly from 1960 to 1968. The area has since changed: the 35th District's population in 2000 was 34% black and 47% Hispanic. Since the 1992 riot, local businesses have revived though it still has high crime rates and plenty of mistrust of local police, exacerbated in February 2005 when a policeman shot a 13-year-old boy who was stopped after a freeway chase and backed his stolen car toward police officers and into their cruiser. Politically, this is an overwhelmingly Democratic district.

The congresswoman from the 35th District is Maxine Waters, a Democrat first elected in 1990. She grew up in St. Louis, one of 13 children; she has said, "I know all about welfare. I remember the social workers peeking in the refrigerator and under the beds." She moved to California in 1961; she worked in a garment factory and raised two children, got a sociology degree at California State University in Los Angeles and became an assistant Head Start teacher after the Watts riot of 1965. She likes to call herself "The Organizer", and has shown the capacity to draw big supportive crowds to her protests over the years. From 1973 to 1976 she worked on the staff of a Los Angeles councilman. In 1976 she won a seat in the California Assembly. She helped pass legislation divesting state pension funds from South Africa, setting up a child abuse prevention training program and prohibiting police strip searches for nonviolent offenses. She became a Democratic national committeewoman in 1980 and Phil Burton consulted her on the 1982 redistricting. When Augustus Hawkins retired in 1990 after 28 years in the House and 28 years in the California Assembly, Waters was the obvious choice for the seat and won it easily.

Waters comes from a background of poverty and believes with fervor in federal aid for the poor and for racial preferences to help blacks overcome years of slavery, segregation and discrimination; she has favored drastic reductions in defense spending. She was one of six members who voted against supporting the Gulf War once it started, asking how urban gang members could be expected to stop fighting when America's own leaders were waging battles. In March 2003 she was one of 11 members who voted against the resolution to support the troops in Iraq after battle began. She brings to her work a fury that is almost palpable, and an insistence that she will assert herself regardless of protocol, partly perhaps a result of anger but also a weapon she uses shrewdly to get both publicity and results. "I don't have time to be polite," she says, beginning her House career by getting herself included in a post-riot White House meeting with George H. W. Bush. The Los Angeles riot was occasion for both Waters' best and worst moments. She flew home immediately and roused the Department of Water and Power to restore water to the riot area, and was effective in gaining provisions to the post-riot emergency act that eventually made it through Congress and was signed into law. But she also suggested rioters were morally justified and claimed ominously, "Los Angeles is under siege," she said. "The violence could spill over to many other cities in this country."

Waters isn't afraid to step on toes in pursuit of her legislative agenda. She has produced specific legislation and pushed Section 108 loan guarantees to cities for economic and infrastructure development. In a rare legislative success in the Republican House, Waters sponsored an amendment to triple spending for the erasure of the debts of poor nations, mostly in Africa; many Republicans agreed, and it passed 216-211. She has sponsored bills to repeal mandatory minimum sentences for drug crimes, and charges that the war on drugs has created "apartheid." In 2006 she sponsored a bill to provide routine HIV/AIDS testing of federal prison inmates, with an opt-out provision for those who objected.

Her husband, a former professional football player and Mercedes Benz salesman, became Bill Clinton's ambassador to the Bahamas. But she voted against the crime bill rule in August 1994 when the administration desperately needed votes. In 1996 and 1997, she attracted attention for pushing the theory, supported in a story in the *San Jose Mercury News* (later repudiated by the paper), that the CIA had worked with Nicaraguan Contras to import crack cocaine into South Central Los Angeles. During the Judiciary Committee's Clinton impeachment inquiry, she assailed "trumped-up charges" and said Kenneth Starr was "guilty" of "raw, unmasked, unbridled hatred and meanness that drives this impeachment coup d'etat." She has been a staunch opponent of the Iraq war. In the summer of 2006 she campaigned in Connecticut for Ned Lamont in his successful primary challenge of Senator Joseph Lieberman. "I believe this is the most significant election of all the Democrats that are running." In March 2007, though a chief deputy majority whip, she whipped against the Iraq supplemental with a timetable for withdrawal supported by the Democratic leadership

Waters is a force to be reckoned with in L.A. politics as well. Other politicians are eager to be included on her Progressive Connections slates that are mailed out to many thousand black voters. Politicians pay to be included—a common California practice. In the April 2001 primary for city attorney Councilman Mike Feuer paid $10,000 to be on the slate and ran even in black areas with Deputy Mayor Rocky Delgadillo. But Feuer wouldn't pay $25,000 to be on the slate for the June runoff; Delgadillo paid $35,000 and got 65% in black areas. For mayor in 2001 she strongly supported City Attorney James Hahn over former Assembly Speaker Antonio Villaraigosa. After Hahn won, Waters approached banker and *LA Focus* owner Jheryl Busby and insisted he fire columnist Najee Ali, who had backed Villaraigosa. Busby fired Ali in July 2001. Ali sued Busby, and Busby's attorney said Busby "told me he needs a positive relationship with Waters because of her ability to help him with his bank and other business interests." (Waters is on the Financial Services Committee). In the March 2005 rematch between Hahn and Villaraigosa, she supported Villaraigosa against Hahn. As a footnote, she and Najee Ali had a confrontation in a church parking lot in October 2006, after which each sought temporary restraining orders against the other; they abandoned those requests in November. She was one of the most visible opponents of an Inglewood referendum to permit a Wal-Mart superstore; in April 2004, it was defeated 61%-39% amid turnout of 11,000 in a city of 115,000. Waters was one of the few officials to oppose November 2004's Measure A, a .5% sales tax increase to pay for more police officers; it failed to get the needed two-thirds majority and got less than 50% in South Los Angeles. In September 2005 she was listed as one of the "13 most corrupt members of Congress" by the liberal-leaning Citizens for Responsibility and Ethics in Washington, on the grounds that members of her family made more than $1 million in eight years doing business with companies, candidates and causes that she had helped. Her reply: "They do their business and I do mine." No charges of any kind have been brought against her.

Waters has been reelected without difficulty. The 2001 redistricting removed some black areas from the district and added Westchester, LAX and Lawndale, which do not have large black percentages. The one potential threat to her tenure is the rising Hispanic percentage in the district; blacks were still a majority of Democratic primary voters in 2000, but that may no longer be true in 2010. Her strong support of Hahn over Villaraigosa in the 2001 mayor's race risked angering Latino voters; the late labor leader Miguel Contreras said that many Latinos in her district felt that she "played the race card against the Latino candidate." But her support of Villaraigosa in 2005 may have soothed any angry feelings on this.

THIRTY-SIXTH DISTRICT

Rep. Jane Harman (D)

Elected 2000, 7th term; b. June 28, 1945, New York, NY; home, Venice; Smith Col., B.A. 1966, Harvard U., J.D. 1969; Jewish; married (Sidney).

Elected Office: U.S. House of Reps., 1992-98.

Professional Career: Legis. Dir., U.S. Sen. John Tunney, 1972-73; Chief Cnsl. & Staff Dir., Senate Judiciary Subcmtee., 1973-77; Dep. Cabinet Secy., White House, 1977; Defense Dept. Special Cnsl., 1979; Harman Intl. Industries, Corp. Secy., 1985-92, Dir., 1990-92; Practicing atty., 1970-72, 1982-92; Regents Prof., U.C.L.A., 1999.

DC Office: 2400 RHOB, 20515, 202-225-8220; Fax: 202-226-7290; Web site: www.house.gov/harman.

District Offices: El Segundo, 310-643-3636; Wilmington, 310-549-8282.

Committees: *Energy & Commerce* (17th of 31 D): Telecommunications & the Internet; Energy & Air Quality. *Homeland Security* (5th of 19 D): Intelligence, Information Sharing & Terrorism Risk Assessment (Chmn.); Border, Maritime & Global Counterterrorism.

Group Ratings

	ADA	ACLU	AFS	LCV	ITIC	NTU	COC	ACU	CFG	FRC
2006	90	85	100	100	71	11	40	12	13	0
2005	70	—	100	78	—	20	58	5	9	8

National Journal Ratings

	2005 LIB	—	2005 CONS		2006 LIB	—	2006 CONS
Economic	64%	—	36%		83%	—	17%
Social	71%	—	29%		73%	—	26%
Foreign	70%	—	30%		73%	—	26%

Key Votes of the 109th Congress

1. Estate Tax Repeal	N	5. Limit Interstate Abortion	N	9. Build Border Fence	N
2. Limit CAFE Standards	Y	6. Extend Patriot Act	Y	10. CAFTA	N
3. FY06 Spending Curb	*	7. Bar Same Sex Marriage	N	11. Oppose Iraq Withdrawal	N
4. Drilling in ANWR	N	8. Stem Cell Research $	Y	12. Detainee Tribunals	N

Election Results

2006 general	Jane Harman (D)	105,323	(63%)	($1,173,313)
	Brian Gibson (R)	53,068	(32%)	($11,513)
	Other	7,762	(5%)	
2006 primary	Jane Harman (D)	30,333	(62%)	
	Marcy Winograd (D)	18,227	(38%)	
2004 general	Jane Harman (D)	151,208	(62%)	($763,781)
	Paul Whitehead (R)	81,666	(33%)	($68,635)
	Other	11,170	(5%)	

Prior Winning Percentages: 2002 (61%); 2000 (48%); 1996 (52%); 1994 (48%); 1992 (48%)

The People		Race/Ethnic Origin	Ancestry	
Area size:	122 sq. mi.	48.4% White	German: 8.0%	Irish: 6.6%
Urban population:	100.0%	4.1% Black	English: 6.2%	
Rural population:	0.0%	13.4% Asian	**2004 Presidential Vote**	
Pop. 2000:	639,087	0.3% Native Am.	Kerry (D) 154,010	(59%)
Pop. 2005 (est):	650,393	0.4% Hawaiian	Bush (R) 103,425	(40%)
Median income:	$51,633	2.9% Two+ races	Other 3,558	(1%)
Poverty status:	12.7%	0.3% Other	**2000 Presidential Vote**	
Military veterans:	8.8%	30.3% Hispanic Origin	Gore (D) 130,752	(57%)
			Bush (R) 88,619	(39%)
			Other 9,423	(4%)
			Cook Partisan Voting Index: D +11	

Occupation	Blue collar: 16.1%	White collar: 71.1%	Gray collar: 12.8%

For many southern Californians, there is no better place to be than the beach. It is not a perfect environment: In the morning there may be mists, the winter air is damp and clammy, even in summer the weather can be chilly, the water is never very warm and is sometimes polluted. But for many this is echt-California, and in this democratic polity, there is a beach to suit the taste of just about everyone, many of them with their unique piers and athletes, especially volleyball. The funkiest of all is Venice: "Muscle Beach," with its beach houses and some expensive new mansions jammed together, its long-stagnant canals dug by a developer in 1904 and paved over in the late 1920s to make way for cars, and the chaotic boardwalk where skateboarding got its start and roller blade sports are *de rigueur*. The 2005 movie "Lords of Dogtown" was about the group of Venice surfers who revolutionized the skateboarding culture in the 1970s. To the south is Marina Del Rey, with sleek modern apartment complexes and expensive yacht moorings, and, south of LAX, El Segundo, named for Chevron's second oil refinery; now it has big office buildings. Next is South Bay with Manhattan Beach, a favorite of the Beach Boys who grew up a couple of miles inland in Hawthorne and where the first surf shop opened in 1949, and tiny Hermosa Beach, with tightly packed frame houses, originally the homes of elderly retirees, now filled with the young and would-be young. Many of the beaches enforce no-smoking rules. Farther south are the flower-planted rises of Redondo Beach and the larger city of Torrance, whose vast inland expanse is the home of the North American headquarters of both Toyota and Honda, plus a new design center for Honda (and to large Korean and Japanese communities). Just to the east, overlooking L.A.'s eerily modern container port, are Wilmington and San Pedro, once working-class, but moving up as well.

The 36th Congressional District of California includes most of this beach territory, from Venice south to San Pedro (both of which are within the Los Angeles city limits, though the area in between is not). California today is mostly multiethnic, but the beach communities are still, as if in the 1950s, filled mostly with white Anglos. This area is still leery of taxes, but culturally it is libertarian—against restrictions or even aspersions on its various lifestyles. This has been one of America's leading defense and aerospace areas, where Howard Hughes built planes half a century ago and where much of the 1980s defense buildup took place. With its many military and space operations, Boeing is the largest private employer in the area, including its assembly operation in El Segundo. The Los Angeles Air Force Base, which has no runways but works closely with nearby aerospace companies, survived the 2005 base closure review.

The congresswoman from the 36th District is Democrat Jane Harman, who regained the seat in 2000 that she held for six years before running for governor in 1998. Born in New York City, she grew up in Los Angeles as the daughter of a Westside physician and was in the gallery as a volunteer usher when John F. Kennedy was nominated at the 1960 Democratic convention in Los Angeles. She graduated from Smith College and Harvard Law School, when women were still rare there. In the 1970s, she worked for California Senator John Tunney and the Senate Judiciary Committee. She served in the Carter White House and as a special counsel in the Defense Department. Later, Harman practiced law and worked as a lobbyist in Washington. She is one of the most wealthy members of Congress; her husband Sidney Harman is founder of audio-equipment maker Harman International Industries, and she has spent large amounts of her own money on her campaigns.

In 1992, she campaigned as "pro-choice and pro-change," defeating a pro-life Republican woman 48%-42% in a new district; she was narrowly reelected in 1994 and 1996. She ran for governor in 1998 and spent more than $20 million, including $15 million of her own money, but finished a disappointing third among Democrats, far behind Gray Davis. Congressional and state Democrats lobbied her hard to reclaim her former House seat, which Republican Steven Kuykendall narrowly won in 1998. Kuykendall supported abortion rights and took liberal stands on environmental issues; many Democrats believed that only Harman could defeat him. She decided to run again in 2000, attacking Kuykendall for failing to support the Democrats' proposal for a prescription drug benefit in Medicare and for voting to repeal the estate tax, and tried to tie him to House Republican leaders. She stressed her earlier House record, economically somewhat conservative and culturally liberal. Kuykendall was hurt by the lack of appeal of George W. Bush in coastal California. This was a race targeted by both parties, with each candidate spending nearly $2 million. After more than a week of absentee ballot counting, Harman won 48%-47%.

On her return to the House, Harman joined Energy and Commerce. Her voting record has been the most conservative of Democrats from Los Angeles. She disappointed many Democrats by voting for the final version of trade promotion authority after initially opposing it; she cited improved worker training provisions. After September 11, her focus turned to national security. On the Intelligence Committee, she became ranking Democrat of the new Terrorism and Homeland Security Subcommittee. Working closely with chairman Saxby Chambliss, she criticized the CIA, FBI and National Security Agency for moving too slowly to share information and respond to terrorism threats. She was an early supporter of a Department of Homeland Security and she voted for the use of force in Iraq. Minority Leader Nancy Pelosi, who was ranking Democrat on Intelligence, chose Harman to replace her after the 2002 election, despite a vigorous campaign by Sanford Bishop. "I live and breathe security 24–7," she said. Harman agreed with the thrust of the 9/11 Commission's recommendations to give more authority to a national intelligence director and to unify intelligence resources. She worked closely with chairman Pete Hoekstra and Senate Governmental Affairs Chairman Susan Collins in getting Congress to complete the intelligence reorganization bill in December 2004. In February 2005, she called for a ban on torture by U.S. interrogators and a prohibition on transfer of detainees to countries that engage in torture; later, she said that President Bush lacked authority for his domestic surveillance program. She fought for increased security at the ports, and worked with Dan Lungren in 2006 to enact standards for cargo-container screening.

Her bipartisanship and pragmatism occasionally rankled other Democrats on the committee and in the House. In 2006, she had reason to believe that she would chair the Intelligence Committee if Democrats regained the majority. But Pelosi had other ideas. Having earlier promised other members that Harman would be the top Democrat for only four years, Pelosi made clear that the position was up for grabs. But Harman did not get the message; the more she defended her qualifications, stated her intention to remain and had allies lobby for her, the more Pelosi was angered by the pressure. Silvestre Reyes won the position, and Harman got the consolation prize as chairman of the Homeland Security Subcommittee on Intelligence, Information Sharing and Terrorism Risk Assessment: a big title, but less authority.

In 2006, Harman survived a primary with Marcy Winograd, president of Progressive Democrats of Los Angeles, who harshly attacked Harman for supporting the Iraq war and for backing President Bush on intelligence issues. Harman defended her record as independent, and won 62%-38%. She might be interested in another statewide bid.

THIRTY-SEVENTH DISTRICT

Rep. Laura Richardson (D)

Elected August 2007, 1st term; b. Apr. 14, 1962, Los Angeles; home, Long Beach; U.C.L.A., B.A. 1984, U. of S. CA, M.B.A. 1996; Christian; divorced.

Elected Office: Long Beach City Cncl., 2000-06; CA Assembly, 2006-07.

Professional Career: Teacher, 1984-87; Mktg. rep., Xerox Corp., 1987-2001; Field Dpty., Rep. Juanita Millender-McDonald, 1996-98; Southern CA dir., Lt. Gov. Cruz Bustamante, 2001-05.

DC Office: 2233 RHOB, 20515, 202-225-7924; Fax: 202-225-7926; Web site: richardson.house.gov.

Group Ratings and Key Votes: Newly Elected

Election Results

2007 spec. general	Laura Richardson (D)	15,559	(67%)	
	John Kanaley (R)	5,837	(25%)	
	Daniel Brezenoff (Green)	1,274	(5%)	
	Other	551	(2%)	
2007 spec. primary	Laura Richardson (D)	11,956	(37%)	
	Jenny Oropeza (D)	9,960	(31%)	
	Valerie McDonald (D)	3,027	(9%)	
	John Kanaley (R)	2,425	(8%)	
	Other	4,820	(15%)	
2006 general	Juanita Millender-McDonald (D)	80,716	(82%)	($355,784)
	Herb Peters (Lib)	17,246	(18%)	

The People		Race/Ethnic Origin	Ancestry		
Area size:	75 sq. mi.	16.6% White	German: 3.2%		Irish: 2.7%
Urban population:	100.0%	24.8% Black	English: 2.4%		
Rural population:	0.0%	11.1% Asian	**2004 Presidential Vote**		
Pop. 2000:	639,088	0.3% Native Am.	Kerry (D) 126,068	(74%)	
Pop. 2005 (est):	682,348	1.4% Hawaiian	Bush (R) 43,160	(25%)	
Median income:	$34,006	2.4% Two+ races	Other 2,281	(1%)	
Poverty status:	25.2%	0.2% Other	**2000 Presidential Vote**		
Military veterans:	8.1%	43.2% Hispanic Origin	Gore (D) 112,235	(76%)	
			Bush (R) 31,832	(22%)	
			Other 3,712	(3%)	
			Cook Partisan Voting Index: D +27		

Occupation	Blue collar: 29.0%	White collar: 53.5%	Gray collar: 17.5%

Long Beach, founded in 1888, with 473,000 people in 2006, would be a major metropolis almost anywhere but in Los Angeles County, where it seems just the largest of many suburbs. But it has an identity of its own. Started as a beach resort, it soon became a port when Los Angeles civic leaders decided that if their town were to be a world-class city it must have a world-class harbor; nature not having provided one, they built it where the Los Angeles River flows into the ocean at the western edge of Long Beach. By 1909, Los Angeles had annexed the harbor towns of San Pedro and Wilmington on the other side of the river; over the next decades the two cities persuaded the federal government to dredge channels and build a breakwater and turning basins. Long Beach was developing other businesses as well. It sprouted oil derricks in the 1920s and briefly became one of the nation's big oil producers; it was the site of major aircraft plants in the 1940s and beyond. Since then, the Los Angeles-Long Beach port has become the nation's largest, the fastest-growing major cargo center in the world, with huge steel-gray container ships pulling quietly up to enormous automated loading facilities—a 21st century contrast to the rotting docks of New York and San Francisco. The length of three football fields, these ships unload a daily average of 18,400 containers, which accounts for 13% of goods passing through U.S. ports; from there, about half of the cargo leaves by rail in 50 daily trains along the new $2.4 billion, high-speed 20-mile Alameda Corridor to the large rail yards near downtown Los Angeles. The cargo has faced a huge increase in inspections since September 11, with scanning at the port of all high-risk containers and frequent directives from Washington; but with three major highways threading through the port, cargo security remains a major concern. Long Beach's naval station was closed in the 1990s and there were job losses at the huge McDonnell Douglas aircraft plant. Boeing, the new owner, announced in January 2005 that it would stop producing commercial jets here; it continues to build military planes here, although there have been fewer orders for the giant C-17 transport. Small businesses have grown, and Long Beach's beachfront has thrived; the *Queen Mary,* converted into a floating hotel, is a big tourist attraction, and there is a glittering array of high-rises along the beach.

The 37th Congressional District of California includes 80% of the city of Long Beach (but not the harbor), and Signal Hill, surrounded by Long Beach, where the oil rigs are still pumping. It includes two industrial suburbs of Compton and Carson. Compton switched from all-white to all-black in the 1960s and in the 1980s became heavily Latino and economically depressed; lately it has been mentioned as a possible site for an Indian casino. Carson, with recent subdivisions amid freeway interchanges and tank farms, has a multiethnic population. The district includes the south end of South Central Los Angeles, including the Watts tower near which the riot of 1965 broke out. In 2000 the district's population was 25% black and 43% Hispanic, but many of the Latinos are not U.S. citizens and were only an estimated 22% of registered voters in 2007. It is a heavily Democratic district.

The new congresswoman from the 37th District is Laura Richardson, a Democrat who won the seat in an August 2007 special election. The seat was temporarily vacant following the April 22, 2007, death of Juanita Millender-McDonald, a Democrat who served 11 years and was chairman of the House Administration Committee.

A former field deputy for Millender-McDonald, Richardson majored in political science at UCLA, worked as a marketing representative for Xerox and got an MBA from the University of Southern California. In 2000, she began her career in elected office by winning a seat on the Long Beach City Council and simultaneously served as Southern California director for Lieutenant Governor Cruz Bustamante. In 2006, Richardson ran for an open Assembly seat and won the primary 54% to 46%; she won the general with 68% of the vote.

The June 26 special primary election was viewed as a critical test of black and Hispanic voting clout in a district where power is transitioning from African-Americans to Hispanics. Richardson's victory all but assured that the seat would remain under African-American representation.

Seventeen candidates filed for the special but the frontrunners were Richardson and state Senator Jenny Oropeza, both of Long Beach. Oropeza, who is Latina, had served six years in the Assembly, where she chaired the Budget and Transportation Committees, before she was elected to the state senate in 2006. Each candidate sought to downplay the racial component of the contest, but Richardson's endorsements came chiefly from African-American leaders, including Congresswoman Maxine Waters of the adjacent 35th District, and Oropeza got her support mostly from Hispanics, including some Los Angeles-area members of Congress and state legislators. Assembly Speaker Fabian Nunez, however, supported Richardson. Oropeza and Richardson both called for an end to the war in Iraq and said that they would focus on the needs of the local port, such as additional security. Oropeza got significant financial support for voter turnout efforts from an Indian tribe in Riverside County; organized labor's opposition to the tribe's proposed casino led national and county labor federations to back Richardson.

In the low-turnout June voting, Richardson won 37% to win the Democratic nomination, while Oropeza got 31%. Valerie McDonald, daughter of the late congresswoman, finished third with 9%. John Kanaley, a Long Beach policeman and Iraq war veteran, finished first among Republicans with 8%. Since none of the candidates received more than 50% of the vote, each party's leading candidate faced an August 21 runoff. But this was a pro forma contest in this solidly Democratic district, with Richardson winning 67% to Kanaley's 25%.

THIRTY-EIGHTH DISTRICT

Rep. Grace Napolitano (D)

Elected 1998, 5th term; b. Dec. 4, 1936, Brownsville, TX; home, Norwalk; Brownsville H.S.; Catholic; married (Frank).

Elected Office: Norwalk City Cncl., 1986-92; Norwalk Mayor, 1989-92; CA Assembly, 1992-98.

Professional Career: Employee, Ford Motor Co., 1970-1992.

DC Office: 1610 LHOB, 20515, 202-225-5256; Fax: 202-225-0027; Web site: www.napolitano.house.gov.

District Offices: Santa Fe Springs, 562-801-2134.

Committees: *Natural Resources* (8th of 27 D): Water & Power (Chmn.). *Transportation & Infrastructure* (24th of 41 D): Railroads, Pipelines & Hazardous Materials; Highways & Transit; Water Resources & Environment.

Group Ratings

	ADA	ACLU	AFS	LCV	ITIC	NTU	COC	ACU	CFG	FRC
2006	100	100	100	100	14	10	33	8	4	0
2005	100	—	100	89	—	12	35	0	3	0

National Journal Ratings

	2005 LIB	—	2005 CONS		2006 LIB	—	2006 CONS
Economic	85%	—	15%		91%	—	6%
Social	83%	—	17%		83%	—	16%
Foreign	87%	—	12%		91%	—	9%

Key Votes of the 109th Congress

1. Estate Tax Repeal	N	5. Limit Interstate Abortion	N	9. Build Border Fence	N
2. Limit CAFE Standards	N	6. Extend Patriot Act	N	10. CAFTA	N
3. FY06 Spending Curb	N	7. Bar Same Sex Marriage	N	11. Oppose Iraq Withdrawal	N
4. Drilling in ANWR	N	8. Stem Cell Research $	Y	12. Detainee Tribunals	N

Election Results

2006 general	Grace Napolitano (D)	75,181	(75%)	($317,822)
	Sidney Street (R)	24,620	(25%)	($8,704)
2006 primary	Grace Napolitano (D) .... unopposed			
2004 general	Grace Napolitano (D) .... unopposed			($273,757)

Prior Winning Percentages: 2002 (71%); 2000 (71%); 1998 (68%)

The People		Race/Ethnic Origin	Ancestry	
Area size:	105 sq. mi.	13.6% White	German: 2.7% Irish: 1.8%	
Urban population:	100.0%	3.6% Black	English: 1.8%	
Rural population:	0.0%	10.2% Asian	**2004 Presidential Vote**	
Pop. 2000:	639,088	0.3% Native Am.	Kerry (D) 106,652	(65%)
Pop. 2005 (est):	643,261	0.1% Hawaiian	Bush (R) 54,869	(34%)
Median income:	$42,488	1.4% Two+ races	Other 1,846	(1%)
Poverty status:	16.3%	0.1% Other	**2000 Presidential Vote**	
Military veterans:	6.8%	70.6% Hispanic Origin	Gore (D) 104,612	(70%)
			Bush (R) 41,706	(28%)
			Other 2,929	(2%)
			Cook Partisan Voting Index: D +20	

Occupation   Blue collar: 34.1%   White collar: 50.7%   Gray collar: 15.2%

One of the great population surges in the United States is the upward social movement of the hundreds of thousands of immigrants in the Los Angeles Basin, from crowded entry-level neighborhoods out on freeways to the suburbs. It is visible east and southeast of Los Angeles, in suburbs that over a generation have changed from solidly white Anglo to largely Latino. Many people here have made their way up working in small smokeless factories along railroad tracks and near river beds, beneath roaring freeways and on grid streets near stucco garden apartment blocks and in small business offices and stores; these have made Los Angeles the nation's top manufacturing metro area, surpassing Chicago. Their values resemble those of working-class Americans of the 1960s: pro-family and respectful of traditional personal morals (L.A.-area Latinos have lower than average divorce rates), patriotic and hard-working (Latino males have the highest work force participation of any measured group and the incomes of U.S.-born Los Angeles County Latinos are at the county average).

Vast numbers of these new residents live in the 38th Congressional District of California, where the percentage of Hispanics in 2000 was 71%, the second highest of any California district. This is a swath of Los Angeles County anchored by four primarily Hispanic suburbs. To the northwest is Montebello (Italian for "beautiful hill"), a working-class suburb just beyond East Los Angeles, where there is a cultural divide between Americanized residents and the "TJ" crowd that acts as though they are still in Tijuana; heavy traffic on the Union Pacific tracks from the Long Beach port has produced calls to place the rail line underground to minimize dangers and routine traffic interference. To the east is La Puente, a center of the light manufacturing economy that created hundreds of thousands of jobs in the Los Angeles Basin, and in which increasing numbers of small businesses are owned by Asians, Latinos and blacks. Farther east is the old town of Pomona, the district's largest city, now much expanded and site of the Los Angeles County Fair, but troubled for decades by gang wars. To the south are Norwalk, a rail crossroad astride the Santa Ana Freeway, 63% Hispanic, and Santa Fe Springs.

The congresswoman from the 38th District is Grace Napolitano, a Democrat first elected in 1998. Napolitano grew up in the Lower Rio Grande Valley of Texas, married at 18, and had five children and moved to California by the time she was 23. She worked as a secretary at Ford Motor Company for 22 years. After her first husband died, she married Frank Napolitano and in 1980 they started a pizzeria business. She served on the city council in Norwalk from 1986 to 1992 and served one term as mayor, becoming the first Latino to hold each position. In 1992 she was elected to the California Assembly from a seat that covered much of this congressional district. Term-limited in 1998, she got the opportunity to run for Congress when 16-year incumbent Esteban Torres announced three days before the filing deadline that he was retiring. Torres' surprise move seemed designed to promote the election of Jamie Casso, his son-in-law and chief of staff, who immediately announced his candidacy. But Napolitano was not deterred. She convinced the state AFL-CIO to vote an "open endorsement," although the executive board had backed Casso, and Torres had been a senior United Auto Workers official in the 1960s. Napolitano and Casso waged a fierce campaign. She criticized him for not living in the district; he criticized her $180,000 loan to her campaign at an unusual 18% interest rate. Napolitano had the financial backing of national women's organizations, including EMILY's List, plus the benefit of higher name identification. The two candidates had few differences on major issues; Napolitano signed a pledge to serve only three terms. Napolitano won the primary by 618 votes. Her victory in November was routine.

In the House, she has a mostly liberal voting record. As chairman of the Congressional Hispanic Caucus in 2005, she urged efforts to reshape the way that the Democratic Party reaches out to Hispanic voters, and was more consensus-oriented than some members on immigration reform. On the Resources Committee, Napolitano was active in the reauthorization in 2004 of the California Bay-Delta water allocation program, which featured unusual bipartisanship among Californians. In committee, Napolitano removed the 25% limit on how much of the federal total for new water conservation projects can go to CALFED; she later sponsored her own version of the bill that removed approval of additional projects outside California. In the majority, she became chairwoman of the Water and Power Subcommittee, with a focus on southern California's acute need for water supply and quality.

With Pennsylvania's Tim Murphy, she co-founded the congressional Mental Health Caucus, on which Napolitano focused on the needs of veterans. She initially became interested in mental health issues after reading a report that showed one in three Hispanic girls contemplated suicide. "Mental health is treatable. But we [the Latino community] have a stigma attached to it. We don't want to see it, we don't want to hear it, we don't want to feel it. We hide it."

Napolitano's work has played well at home. She has not been seriously challenged for reelection. In February 2003, she abandoned her earlier pledge and announced she planned to run for reelection two more times and then retire after serving five terms. But through August 2007, she had not announced her intentions for 2008; a spokesman explained that she planned to stay in office until a successor could be found who shared her value for constituent service. Democrats ought to have no trouble retaining the district.

THIRTY-NINTH DISTRICT

Rep. Linda Sanchez (D)

Elected 2002, 3d term; b. Jan. 28, 1969, Orange; home, Lakewood; U. of CA, B.A. 1991, U.C.L.A., J.D. 1995; Catholic; divorced.

Professional Career: Practicing atty., 1995-98; Exec. Secy. Treas. of Orange Cnty. AFL-CIO, 2000-02.

DC Office: 1222 LHOB, 20515, 202-225-6676; Fax: 202-226-1012; Web site: www.house.gov/lindasanchez.

District Offices: Cerritos, 562-860-5050.

Committees: *Education & Labor* (17th of 27 D): Health, Employment, Labor & Pensions; Early Childhood, Elementary & Secondary Education. *Foreign Affairs* (22d of 27 D): Western Hemisphere; Europe. *Judiciary* (12th of 23 D): Commercial & Administrative Law (Chmn.); Immigration, Citizenship, Refugees, Border Security & International Law.

Group Ratings

	ADA	ACLU	AFS	LCV	ITIC	NTU	COC	ACU	CFG	FRC
2006	100	100	100	100	14	9	33	4	5	0
2005	100	—	100	94	—	13	30	0	3	0

National Journal Ratings

	2005 LIB	—	2005 CONS		2006 LIB	—	2006 CONS
Economic	94%	—	0%		91%	—	9%
Social	98%	—	0%		97%	—	0%
Foreign	94%	—	4%		83%	—	14%

Key Votes of the 109th Congress

1. Estate Tax Repeal	N	5. Limit Interstate Abortion	N	9. Build Border Fence	N
2. Limit CAFE Standards	N	6. Extend Patriot Act	N	10. CAFTA	N
3. FY06 Spending Curb	N	7. Bar Same Sex Marriage	N	11. Oppose Iraq Withdrawal	N
4. Drilling in ANWR	N	8. Stem Cell Research $	Y	12. Detainee Tribunals	N

Election Results

2006 general	Linda Sanchez (D)	72,149	(66%)	($639,354)
	James Andion (R)	37,384	(34%)	($19,095)
2006 primary	Linda Sanchez (D)	23,893	(78%)	
	Kenneth Graham (D)	5,083	(17%)	
	Frank Amador (D)	1,738	(6%)	
2004 general	Linda Sanchez (D)	100,132	(61%)	($782,521)
	Tim Escobar (R)	64,832	(39%)	($772,577)

Prior Winning Percentages: 2002 (55%)

The People		Race/Ethnic Origin	Ancestry	
Area size:	65 sq. mi.	21.0% White	German: 4.3%	Irish: 3.3%
Urban population:	100.0%	6.1% Black	English: 3.0%	
Rural population:	0.0%	9.5% Asian	**2004 Presidential Vote**	
Pop. 2000:	639,088	0.3% Native Am.	Kerry (D) 102,660	(59%)
Pop. 2005 (est):	683,943	0.3% Hawaiian	Bush (R) 70,635	(40%)
Median income:	$45,307	1.5% Two+ races	Other 2,110	(1%)
Poverty status:	15.7%	0.1% Other	**2000 Presidential Vote**	
Military veterans:	7.1%	61.2% Hispanic Origin	Gore (D) 98,478	(62%)
			Bush (R) 56,067	(36%)
			Other 3,390	(2%)
			Cook Partisan Voting Index: D +13	

Occupation	Blue collar: 31.2%	White collar: 55.0%	Gray collar: 13.9%

In the years just after World War II much of southeast Los Angeles County was farmland—citrus groves, dairy farms. Then in the next two decades subdivisions were built and new cities incorporated so that what had been a few separate towns separated by farmland became one continuous swatch of suburbia. The separate towns were different in character. Whittier, founded by Midwestern Quakers, was the hometown of Richard Nixon, a young lawyer thinking about running for Congress in early 1946 who was inaugurated as vice president of the United States seven years later. South Gate and Lynwood, with new auto and other factories, filled up with newcomers from the South. Lakewood, just north of Long Beach, was built up so rapidly in the 1950s from former lima bean fields that it was featured in *Life* magazine as one of the first mass-produced suburbs; in recent years, real estate prices soared again. Other towns grew later; there were still dairy farms in Cerritos in the 1970s, though few remain now.

The 39th Congressional District of California is made up of a heterogeneous and oddly shaped collection of these suburbs. It is shaped like a U. On the east end are two-thirds of Whittier, all of South and West Whittier and La Mirada. The bottom end of the U includes Lakewood, the classic fast-growing post-war suburb, and in former dairy country, Cerritos, Artesia and Hawaiian Gardens. The west end includes South Gate, Lynwood, Paramount and the eastern fringe of South Central Los Angeles: these were once working class white, then mostly black, then heavily Latino. The district's population is 61% Hispanic and 10% Asian. More evidence of the 39th's diversity can be found at a local motor vehicle office, where the written exam can be taken in 33 languages. As this area grew in the postwar years it was pretty closely divided between the parties. But in the 1990s it trended Democratic. This district was created in 2001 to be a safe seat for California Democrats; it voted 62%-36% for Al Gore in 2000 but only 59%-40% for John Kerry in 2004.

The congresswoman from the 39th District is Linda Sanchez, a Democrat first elected in 2002, and the junior member of the first pair of sisters ever elected to Congress. They are the oldest and youngest of seven children of Mexican immigrant parents Ignacio Sanchez, a machinist, and Maria Macias, a bilingual education aide in an elementary school. Loretta Sanchez, who is nine years older, was elected to the House in 1996 from Orange County. Linda Sanchez graduated from Berkeley and UCLA law school. She became a civil rights lawyer and was executive secretary-treasurer of the Orange County Federation of Labor. "She's definitely the more liberal one," Loretta has said. Their five siblings include two business owners, a mortgage broker, a securities broker, and a civil engineer.

When the district lines were unveiled for this newly-created seat, Linda Sanchez was one of six Democrats who ran. Her most important asset was her sister's support. Linda Sanchez tapped Loretta's extensive fundraising network, walked precincts with her, and appeared in a television commercial with her. In the Spanish language ad, their mother urged voters to send both of her daughters to Capitol Hill. All this gave Linda Sanchez an advantage over her two chief opponents, who started off better known—two-term Assemblywoman Sally Havice and South Gate Councilman Hector De La Torre, who had worked several years in Washington as a legislative aide and Labor Department official. There were few differences between them on major issues, and the campaign turned negative in the closing weeks. Sanchez's labor ties helped her build a strong voter turnout operation; the L.A. County AFL-CIO endorsed both Sanchez and Havice. With help from her sister, Sanchez was endorsed by then-Minority Whip Nancy Pelosi. Her opponents replied that Sanchez had received no endorsements from other Latino members of Congress; Hilda Solis, whom Loretta Sanchez backed in her first House race in 1998, endorsed De La Torre. They charged that Linda Sanchez was a political opportunist who changed her name and residence to run in the newly-created district; like her sister, Sanchez had used her non-Latino married name until she started to run for the House. Sanchez won with 33% of the vote, to 29% for De La Torre and 19% for Havice. Afterwards the Long Beach *Press-Telegram* attacked Sanchez's tactics: "It may have been the only way for Sanchez to win, as an unemployed labor activist with little political experience, but the tactics were deceptive, dishonest and mean." This district is not as Democratic as the four other LA-based Hispanic-majority districts, and Sanchez's negative primary campaign may have hurt her. Republican Tim Escobar, a financial adviser and former Army helicopter pilot, said Sanchez was an inexperienced liberal extremist; he quoted the bitter remarks of her primary opponents. But Sanchez won 55%-41%.

In the House, the election of the two sisters generated largely flattering national press coverage. But their service in the minority party in the House limited their influence and activity. Linda Sanchez has a strongly liberal voting record, more so than Loretta. She filed the "Bullying Prevention for School Safety and Crime Reduction Act," with federal funds to help stop bullying; she got the proposal included in the Justice Department authorization bill, but it died in the Senate. Other legislative priorities included an increase in small-business loan limits from $35,000 to $50,000. She attacked the House Republican proposal to deny drivers' licenses to undocumented immigrants, for "using national security as a facade to alienate law-abiding and taxpaying immigrants." She was co-founder of the Labor and Working Families Caucus. In the majority, she gained attention as chairwoman of the Judiciary Subcommittee on Commercial and Administrative Law, where she worked with senior Democrats on hearings to oversee the Bush administration firings of U.S. Attorneys.

In 2004, Escobar ran again and spent $773,000, more than three times as much money as in his first race and more than the total spent by Sanchez. But she had a bigger win this time, 61%-39%, and attributed the improvement to her efforts as an incumbent. She had an easy win in 2006. In Washington, she gained attention for her comedy routines at the D.C. Improv. One that has been oft-cited: "Republicans make love like they make war. They lie to get in, and they don't know what to do when they get there."

FORTIETH DISTRICT

Rep. Ed Royce (R)

Elected 1992, 8th term; b. Oct. 12, 1951, Los Angeles; home, Fullerton; CA State Fullerton, B.A. 1977; Catholic; married (Marie).

Elected Office: CA Senate, 1982-92.

Professional Career: Tax Mgr., 1979-82.

DC Office: 2185 RHOB, 20515, 202-225-4111; Fax: 202-226-0335; Web site: www.royce.house.gov.

District Offices: Fullerton, 714-992-8081.

Committees: *Financial Services* (6th of 33 R): Oversight & Investigations; Financial Institutions & Consumer Credit; Capital Markets, Insurance & Government Sponsored Enterprises. *Foreign Affairs* (7th of 23 R): Terrorism, Nonproliferation & Trade (RMM); Asia, the Pacific & the Global Environment.

Group Ratings

	ADA	ACLU	AFS	LCV	ITIC	NTU	COC	ACU	CFG	FRC
2006	5	5	0	17	100	72	100	96	84	85
2005	0	—	0	22	—	79	77	96	100	92

National Journal Ratings

	2005 LIB	—	2005 CONS		2006 LIB	—	2006 CONS
Economic	32%	—	67%		27%	—	71%
Social	30%	—	69%		11%	—	85%
Foreign	0%	—	89%		38%	—	59%

Key Votes of the 109th Congress

1. Estate Tax Repeal	Y	5. Limit Interstate Abortion	Y	9. Build Border Fence	Y
2. Limit CAFE Standards	Y	6. Extend Patriot Act	Y	10. CAFTA	Y
3. FY06 Spending Curb	Y	7. Bar Same Sex Marriage	Y	11. Oppose Iraq Withdrawal	Y
4. Drilling in ANWR	Y	8. Stem Cell Research $	N	12. Detainee Tribunals	Y

Election Results

2006 general	Ed Royce (R)	100,995	(67%)	($1,317,274)
	Florice Hoffman (D)	46,418	(31%)	($140,406)
	Other	3,876	(3%)	
2006 primary	Ed Royce (R)	unopposed		
2004 general	Ed Royce (R)	147,617	(68%)	($736,717)
	Tilman Williams (D)	69,684	(32%)	

Prior Winning Percentages: 2002 (68%); 2000 (63%); 1998 (63%); 1996 (63%); 1994 (66%); 1992 (57%)

The People		Race/Ethnic Origin	Ancestry	
Area size:	102 sq. mi.	49.3% White	German: 9.3%	English: 6.8%
Urban population:	100.0%	2.2% Black	Irish: 6.8%	
Rural population:	0.0%	15.6% Asian	**2004 Presidential Vote**	
Pop. 2000:	639,088	0.3% Native Am.	Bush (R) 138,766	(60%)
Pop. 2005 (est):	679,886	0.4% Hawaiian	Kerry (D) 88,631	(39%)
Median income:	$54,356	2.4% Two+ races	Other 2,740	(1%)
Poverty status:	10.2%	0.2% Other	**2000 Presidential Vote**	
Military veterans:	10.1%	29.6% Hispanic Origin	Bush (R) 119,443	(56%)
			Gore (D) 86,460	(41%)
			Other 5,886	(3%)
			Cook Partisan Voting Index: R + 8	

Occupation	Blue collar: 22.1%	White collar: 64.5%	Gray collar: 13.4%

Orange County is the fifth most populous county in the United States, having grown steadily from 130,000 in 1940 to 703,000 in 1960, 1.9 million in 1980, 2.8 million in 2000 and 3,002,000 in 2006. It is now a community with the patina of maturity—in some places an aging community, fraying around the edges. The county can no longer double its population, as it did for several decades, when Disneyland sprung up on empty land and mile-square grids of orange groves and bean fields were transformed into one suburban subdivision, shopping center or office tower after another. Although developers have plans for a few more huge projects in the next decade, "We're outta land. We don't have any dirt left," a real estate analyst told the *Los Angeles Times* in 2003. A distinctive civilization was implanted here by ranchers and farmers, who settled the place and then gave way to Cold War aerospace engineers: mostly white and middle-class, confident of its traditional values and its market capitalism, proud of American principles and American military might. Orange County has been transformed in the years since by its openness to economic and ethnic change. Its economy was constantly reshaped by the inevitable upheavals of capitalism and it continues to be. In 2006, Boeing announced it would close its plant in Anaheim and shift the 3,700 workers to Huntington Beach. Tourism remains key to the local economy, but there is no single industry here that is responsible for the prosperity of Orange County. It was hit hard by the defense cutbacks and recession of the early 1990s but it bounced back, pitched forward by new startups and small entrepreneurial successes not anticipated by government or corporate planners.

Always Republican, Orange County became a symbol of conservatism first in California and then nationally. This was a solid base for Ronald Reagan in his campaigns for governor and president. In 1988 its 317,000-vote plurality for George H. W. Bush was his largest in any county in the nation. Orange County's conservatism reflected a belief in technological progress and traditional values as unyielding as the mile-square grid the county's founders imposed on most of its land, a belief in market economies that produced such wonders as Disneyland and the area's advanced military technologies. But problems developed. In 1994, the county government declared bankruptcy because of the county treasurer's sloppy investment and bookkeeping practices; shortly afterwards, the Disney company shelved plans for a $2 billion resort development that would have doubled the size of Disneyland. Orange County has rebounded, and so has Disney, with its California Adventure amusement park on Disneyland property. Over the years Orange County has become racially and ethnically more diverse; contrary to the images presented in the since-cancelled TV series *The OC*, the all-white Orange County stereotype is now thoroughly out of date, especially with the election in 2007 of the county's first Vietnamese supervisor. In 2005, Orange County's population was 33% Hispanic and 16% Asian, percentages that seem likely to rise; the median age of non-Hispanic whites was 40 while for Hispanics it was 25. In 2000 the county gave George W. Bush only a 149,000-vote margin; four years later, his lead was 222,000 votes, still well below his father's margin 16 years before.

The 40th Congressional District of California, located entirely in Orange County, consists of acreage that was mostly farmland when Disneyland was being laid out. At the geographic center is Fullerton, with 36,000 students at its own branch of Cal State University, named after rail executive George Fullerton, who extended the railroad there; to the southwest are Buena Park, home of Knott's Berry Farm, the earliest theme park (1940), plus Cypress, Los Alamitos, La Palma, Stanton, and parts of Garden Grove and Westminster. Southeast of Fullerton the district includes most of Placentia, part of eastern Anaheim and all of Villa Park and Orange, the district's largest city. Overall the 40th District is 30% Hispanic, 16% Asian (primarily Korean, Vietnamese and Filipino) and 2% black.

The congressman from the 40th District is Ed Royce, a Republican first elected in 1992. His life almost precisely covers the area's growth. He grew up in Fullerton; he was in the Young Americans for Freedom at Cal State Fullerton and was the head of Youth for Reagan in California during his 1976 challenge to Gerald Ford. He worked several years as a tax and capital projects manager for a cement company. In 1982, a bunch of conservative legislators known as "the Cave Men" took him to a Black Angus restaurant—no avocado and sprout sandwiches for them—and persuaded him to run for the state Senate. He won at age 31. When the legislature refused to pass his bill allowing crime victims to object to trial delays, giving grand juries more power and ending shopping for juries, he put it on the ballot as an initiative and it passed by a wide margin. In 1992 Royce ran for the House. With the blessing of Orange County Republican leaders, he was unopposed in the Republican primary and easily won the general.

In the House, Royce has a conservative voting record, though a bit less so on economic issues. He co-chaired the House "porkbusters," risking others' wrath by opposing appropriations bills with dubious projects; in July 2005, he was among eight Republicans, and the only Californian, to vote against the highway bill. His proposal to ensure that nonprofit religious organizations have access to all necessary financial resources was a forerunner of George W. Bush's faith-based initiative. On the Financial Services Committee, he has worked with Paul Kanjorski to expand lending authority for credit unions and to put them on an equivalent status with banks.

As chairman of the International Relations Subcommittee on Africa and an ardent free-trader, Royce backed an Africa free trade bill with Ways and Means senior Democrat Charles Rangel; displaying legislative creativity, he helped steer the bill to enactment. When Congress passed trade promotion authority, he revised the bill to raise the cap on duty-free apparel imports from Africa. Although Royce had never set foot in Africa before he became chairman, he was widely praised for learning about the continent. His other initiatives on Africa included steps to encourage oil production while also promoting human rights, and encouragement of the Bush administration to stop the genocide in Sudan. Royce is the former co-chair of the Congressional Caucus on India and Indian Americans and urges stronger strategic and trade relationships between the United States and India. George W. Bush signed his bill establishing Radio Free Afghanistan as a tool in the fight against terrorism; with Zoe Lofgren, he filed a bill to open communication in Vietnam. In 2006, he enacted a bill to promote nuclear nonproliferation in North Korea. He joined other Republicans in demanding tighter controls on immigration at the border. Royce is ranking Republican on the Subcommittee on Terrorism, Nonproliferation and Trade, where he has focused on the spread of radical Islam.

Royce has been reelected by wide margins. After redistricting in 2001, half of the district was new to him, but he has continued to win easily.

FORTY-FIRST DISTRICT

Rep. Jerry Lewis (R)

Elected 1978, 15th term; b. Oct. 21, 1934, Seattle, WA; home, Redlands; U.C.L.A., B.A. 1956; Presbyterian; married (Arlene).

Elected Office: CA Assembly, 1968-78.

Professional Career: Insurance exec., 1959-78; Field rep., U.S. Rep. Jerry Pettis, 1968.

DC Office: 2112 RHOB, 20515, 202-225-5861; Fax: 202-225-6498; Web site: www.house.gov/jerrylewis.

District Offices: Redlands, 909-862-6030.

Committees: *Appropriations* (RMM of 29 R).

Group Ratings

	ADA	ACLU	AFS	LCV	ITIC	NTU	COC	ACU	CFG	FRC
2006	15	14	14	0	100	54	93	67	49	71
2005	0	—	0	6	—	53	93	76	55	69

National Journal Ratings

	2005 LIB	—	2005 CONS		2006 LIB	—	2006 CONS
Economic	28%	—	71%		12%	—	86%
Social	38%	—	61%		47%	—	52%
Foreign	31%	—	67%		28%	—	71%

Key Votes of the 109th Congress

1. Estate Tax Repeal	Y	5. Limit Interstate Abortion	Y	9. Build Border Fence	Y
2. Limit CAFE Standards	Y	6. Extend Patriot Act	Y	10. CAFTA	Y
3. FY06 Spending Curb	Y	7. Bar Same Sex Marriage	Y	11. Oppose Iraq Withdrawal	*
4. Drilling in ANWR	Y	8. Stem Cell Research $	Y	12. Detainee Tribunals	Y

Election Results

2006 general	Jerry Lewis (R)	109,761	(67%)	($1,806,532)
	Louie Contreras (D)	54,235	(33%)	
2006 primary	Jerry Lewis (R) .... unopposed			
2004 general	Jerry Lewis (R)	181,605	(83%)	($1,450,053)
	Peymon Mottahedek (Lib)	37,332	(17%)	

Prior Winning Percentages: 2002 (67%); 2000 (80%); 1998 (65%); 1996 (65%); 1994 (71%); 1992 (63%); 1990 (61%); 1988 (70%); 1986 (77%); 1984 (85%); 1982 (68%); 1980 (72%); 1978 (61%)

The People		Race/Ethnic Origin	Ancestry	
Area size:	13,350 sq. mi.	63.5% White	German: 11.7%	English: 8.4%
Urban population:	89.4%	5.3% Black	Irish: 8.3%	
Rural population:	10.6%	3.7% Asian	**2004 Presidential Vote**	
Pop. 2000:	639,087	1.0% Native Am.	Bush (R) 149,673	(62%)
Pop. 2005 (est):	758,647	0.2% Hawaiian	Kerry (D) 89,424	(37%)
Median income:	$38,721	2.7% Two+ races	Other 2,729	(1%)
Poverty status:	15.2%	0.2% Other	**2000 Presidential Vote**	
Military veterans:	16.1%	23.4% Hispanic Origin	Bush (R) 114,498	(56%)
			Gore (D) 83,584	(41%)
			Other 5,116	(3%)
			Cook Partisan Voting Index: R + 9	

Occupation	Blue collar: 25.0%	White collar: 57.3%	Gray collar: 17.8%

Over the last quarter-century the great American movement west has turned back east, at least in California. As settlement reached the Pacific Coast, young families looking for affordable houses, neighborhoods and schools, where traditional values are respected, moved away from the liberation-minded and high-crime coast and toward the sunny, often hot, valleys inland. This impulse has resulted in rapid growth in the Central Valley, the repopulation of the Mother Lode country in the foothills of the Sierras and the startling growth in the Inland Empire at the eastern end of the Los Angeles Basin, around San Bernardino and Riverside, and east and north past the mountain rims into the High Desert. This Inland Empire, generally defined as San Bernardino and Riverside Counties, though other definitions abound—grew from 1.6 million people in 1980 to 2.6 million in 1990, 3.2 million in 2000 and 3.8 million in 2005. "The L.A. dream still exists, it just moved east," says author and California expert Joel Kotkin.

The 41st Congressional District covers some of the Inland Empire and the desert beyond the mountains. It includes most of the land area of San Bernardino County, which with 20,052 square miles is the largest county in the United States and is more than twice the size of New Jersey. Nearly half its population is concentrated in its southwest corner, in the Inland Empire, including the northern and eastern edges of San Bernardino and all of Loma Linda, Redlands, Highland, Yucaipa—small towns founded by pious Midwesterners at the base of 10,000-foot mountains. It also includes towns in Riverside County just to the south—Calimesa, Beaumont, Banning, San Jacinto. East of the mountains is the vast Mojave Desert, mostly uninhabited, but with growing clusters of population. In the Victor Valley are Hesperia and Apple Valley, new towns in the desert with 129,000 people between them, and Victorville, another high-growth high desert community that was once home to Roy Rogers and Dale Evans. The district includes the mountain country around Lake Arrowhead and Big Bear Lake, Desert Hot Springs, the rustic town north of posh Palm Springs, and Twentynine Palms and the huge Twentynine Palms Marine Corps Base, the largest Marine base in the world and the Marines' leading live-fire training facility. This fast-growing area is Republican country—62%-37% for George W. Bush in 2004 and 69%-27% for Arnold Schwarzenegger in the 2006 governor's race.

The congressman from the 41st District is Jerry Lewis, a Republican first elected in 1978 and former chairman of the Appropriations Committee. Lewis grew up in San Bernardino, worked as a lifeguard and graduated from UCLA. (He maintains his swimming skills, and once saved former Speaker Jim Wright off the shore of Hawaii.) He was an insurance agent in Redlands, a joiner in civic causes, and was elected to the local school board in the early 1960s. He was elected to the California Assembly in 1968, at 34. In 1978, the incumbent congressman retired and Lewis was elected to the House. In 1980, he got a seat on the Appropriations Committee, where bipartisan cooperation was the norm, enabling even minority members to confer favors on their districts. With a small city background and an accommodationist attitude toward Democrats, he steadily won leadership positions—chairman of the Republican Research Committee in 1984, chairman of the Republican Policy Committee in 1986, Republican Conference chairman in 1988, and seemed headed towards the minority leader post. But a small group of young conservatives around Newt Gingrich resented Lewis's cooperation with Democrats and believed that Republicans could break out of the minority if they confronted Democrats more. In March 1989 the minority whip position came open when Dick Cheney was appointed Secretary of Defense. Lewis considered running, but declined; Gingrich won by an 87-85 vote. In December 1992 Dick Armey, with support from Gingrich, challenged Lewis for the Conference chairmanship and won 88-84. Those two votes put in place the two top leaders of the Republican majority that emerged after November 1994.

Lewis recovered from that setback, and when Republicans won their majority in 1994, he became chairman of the VA-HUD Appropriations Subcommittee—a member of the "college of cardinals," as Appropriations subcommittee chairmen are known. Here he got his agencies' attention by reporting a bill making deep cuts in NASA. In 1999 Lewis became chairman of the Defense Subcommittee, with the largest share of federal spending of any of the 13 subcommittees. He attracted attention when the subcommittee voted unanimously to cut $1.8 billion for building the first six of the Air Force's F-22s. Funds were restored by the Senate, but the program was cut by $500 million and the Pentagon's attention was gained. Lewis continued to promote the Predator unmanned air vehicle, which had been tested on the Mojave Desert; this proved to be of prime importance in Afghanistan and Iraq.

In August 2001 Lewis said that he would press for the $18.4 billion George W. Bush had requested over the original $310.5 billion. On the morning of September 11, the subcommittee was debating an increase in funding for counterterrorism when news of the attacks came; in November a $317 billion defense appropriation was passed. In June 2002 Lewis steered a $354.7 billion defense appropriation to passage in the House. In October the final $355.4 billion appropriation was passed. In 2003 and 2004 the defense appropriations bill were approved in a smooth process. The House accepted a $368 billion conference report in September 2003, with Iraq left to be dealt with in a supplemental. Bowing to the Senate and civil liberties groups, Lewis eliminated the Pentagon's Total Information Awareness program in the U.S. early in the year, and the House acceded in having five rather than six Virginia class submarines built over five years. In early 2004 Lewis warned Defense Secretary Donald Rumsfeld that "people will be targeting our budget in a serious way." But the House passed a $417 billion appropriation in June, including $25 billion for Iraq; Lewis insisted that only $1 billion of that, rather than all, as the administration had sought, be available for flexible use. The conference report was approved a month later.

As an appropriator, Lewis has been unapologetic about channeling funds into his district. One special beneficiary has been Loma Linda University, where he has promoted cancer treatment and NASA research. He played a role in converting the former George and Norton Air Force bases into successful airports. Some are sentimental projects. Lewis got $1 million to rebuild the Perris Hill Plunge, a WPA-built pool where he was a lifeguard and taught dozens of children to swim; he helped to get another $1 million for the Jerry Lewis Community Center in his hometown of Highland. In December 2003 he got $40 million for district projects, which included national forest protection and emergency watershed protection in the Inland Empire. Drought and bark beetles have threatened the San Bernardino National Forest, and Lewis responded in 2004 by raising aid from $1 million to $24 million a year. "I don't know exactly if it will be $20 million a year or $50 million a year, but I know Congress will be there for the forest," he said. It was $30 million in 2005. Also in 2005, he took credit for $10 million for flood control and debris clearance along San Timoteo Creek, and $62 million for the Santa Ana River Mainstem project.

In the 1990s Lewis, noticing the rising Hispanic population, took Spanish lessons and spent time with a family in Mexico City to learn the language. But Latinos were not the only constituency to which he paid heed. Appropriations Chairman Bill Young reached the end of House Republicans' six-year term limit in 2004, and Lewis, third in seniority among committee Republicans, sought the chairmanship. So did the more senior Ralph Regula, who voted less often with the House leadership, and the less senior Hal Rogers. The House Republican leadership urged aspirants to chairmanships to raise money for fellow Republicans; Regula, who refused to accept PAC contributions, contributed little before 2004; Rogers, at a meeting in July 2004, came forward with a check for $300,000, at which point Lewis proffered his own check for $600,000. In all, he contributed $1.35 million to Republicans in the 2004 cycle. The Republican Steering Committee interviewed all three in January 2005 and, after Speaker Dennis Hastert said it was a marginal difference, chose Lewis. In February Lewis, following a suggestion by Majority Leader Tom DeLay, reduced the number of subcommittees from 13 to 10.

He had a rocky two years as chairman. Lewis said that he wanted to streamline funding and avoid omnibus spending bills. But he failed to achieve either goal, and spending increased significantly: The combination of Iraq war funding and Katrina relief and reconstruction added more than $200 billion to the original budget in 2005. In 2006, Lewis's committee finished most of its work, but breakdowns in the Republican-controlled Senate meant that most spending decisions were deferred to the Democrats when they took over in January 2007. Even worse for Lewis, in spring 2006, the Justice Department began an investigation of his dealings with a lobbying shop led by former Representative Bill Lowery of California, a long-time Lewis friend, who obtained abundant appropriations earmarks for the defense industry and California communities. News reports linked Lewis to the continuing investigation of corruption charges involving convicted former Congressman Randy (Duke) Cunningham and defense contractors. Lewis denied wrongdoing, but he piled up hundreds of thousands of dollars in lawyers' bills. Although some Republicans urged him to resign, Lewis managed to continue as the ranking Republican on Appropriations. In the minority in March 2007, he criticized Democrats for their bill that "ties the hands of our commander in chief during a time of war, places military decisions in the hands of politicians and attempts to buy votes for its passage—on the left and on the right—by literally promising something for everyone."

Despite these problems, Lewis remained popular at home in his solidly Republican and fast-growing district. In 2006, Democratic challenger Louie Contreras, an insurance agent in Hesperia, was little-known and did not mount a serious bid. Lewis won 67%-33%, similar to his past margins. But in 2007, House Democrats eyed his seat as potentially vulnerable because of his legal troubles. In June, syndicated columnist Robert Novak wrote that Lewis would not seek reelection; his office denied the report and in August Lewis announced he would seek reelection in 2008.

FORTY-SECOND DISTRICT

Rep. Gary Miller (R)

Elected 1998, 5th term; b. Oct. 16, 1948, Huntsville, AR; home, Diamond Bar; Mt. San Antonio Col. 1971, 1988-89; Christian; married (Cathy). Military Career: Army, 1967-1968.

Elected Office: Diamond Bar City Cncl., 1989-95; Diamond Bar Mayor, 1992; CA Assembly, 1995-98.

Professional Career: Businessman, real estate developer, G. Miller Development Co., 1971-98.

DC Office: 2438 RHOB, 20515, 202-225-3201; Fax: 202-226-6962; Web site: www.house.gov/garymiller.

District Offices: Brea, 714-257-1142; Mission Viejo, 949-470-8484.

Committees: *Financial Services* (14th of 33 R): Oversight & Investigations (RMM); Housing & Community Opportunity. *Transportation & Infrastructure* (12th of 34 R): Railroads, Pipelines & Hazardous Materials; Water Resources & Environment; Highways & Transit.

Group Ratings

	ADA	ACLU	AFS	LCV	ITIC	NTU	COC	ACU	CFG	FRC
2006	0	0	0	0	100	62	100	88	62	100
2005	0	—	0	0	—	65	92	96	74	100

National Journal Ratings

	2005 LIB	—	2005 CONS		2006 LIB	—	2006 CONS
Economic	27%	—	73%		7%	—	93%
Social	0%	—	89%		0%	—	94%
Foreign	0%	—	89%		17%	—	73%

Key Votes of the 109th Congress

1. Estate Tax Repeal	Y	5. Limit Interstate Abortion	Y	9. Build Border Fence	Y
2. Limit CAFE Standards	Y	6. Extend Patriot Act	Y	10. CAFTA	Y
3. FY06 Spending Curb	*	7. Bar Same Sex Marriage	Y	11. Oppose Iraq Withdrawal	Y
4. Drilling in ANWR	Y	8. Stem Cell Research $	N	12. Detainee Tribunals	Y

Election Results

2006 general	Gary Miller (R)	.... unopposed		($365,812)
2006 primary	Gary Miller (R)	.... unopposed		
2004 general	Gary Miller (R)	 167,632	(68%)	($421,841)
	Lewis Myers (D)	 78,393	(32%)	

Prior Winning Percentages: 2002 (68%); 2000 (59%); 1998 (53%)

The People		Race/Ethnic Origin	Ancestry	
Area size:	317 sq. mi.	54.4% White	German: 10.2%	Irish: 7.4%
Urban population:	98.7%	2.9% Black	English: 7.4%	
Rural population:	1.3%	15.9% Asian	**2004 Presidential Vote**	
Pop. 2000:	639,088	0.3% Native Am.	Bush (R) 164,998	(62%)
Pop. 2005 (est):	673,932	0.2% Hawaiian	Kerry (D) 98,108	(37%)
Median income:	$70,463	2.4% Two+ races	Other 2,578	(1%)
Poverty status:	6.0%	0.2% Other	**2000 Presidential Vote**	
Military veterans:	9.6%	23.8% Hispanic Origin	Bush (R) 139,655	(59%)
			Gore (D) 92,169	(39%)
			Other 5,157	(2%)
			Cook Partisan Voting Index: R +10	

Occupation	Blue collar: 15.2%	White collar: 74.1%	Gray collar: 10.7%

The fastest growth in the Los Angeles metropolitan area over the last 25 years has been in the Inland Empire at eastern end of the Los Angeles Basin. Mostly orange groves and dairy farms a few decades ago, this territory now is the site of a booming economy, personal upward mobility, and ethnic and cultural harmony. The main ingredient of this economic growth has been small entrepreneurial businesses, usually started by people with no particular connections or advantages—often, of Asian or Latino immigrant background. California has never been a land of leisure, as stereotype would have it, but rather a place for hard work, where the fertility of the soil and the productivity of the people have prospered with considerable effort and tolerance toward newcomers. California hasn't always welcomed people from distant places: anti-Asian sentiment expressed itself in the Chinese Exclusion Act of 1882 and the Japanese American internment camps of 1942-44. But since World War II this has been one of the least prejudiced and most welcoming places on earth, which helps to explain why it has received more immigrants than any other state.

The 42d Congressional District of California is one place where such trends are visible. It is centered in the Inland Empire on the point where Los Angeles, San Bernardino and Orange Counties come together. In San Bernardino County it includes Chino, site of a large low-security prison, and Chino Hills, incorporated in 1991 and full of subdivisions for commuters who battle the heavy traffic on Interstate 5 to Orange and L.A. Counties. In Los Angeles County it includes Diamond Bar, where the local high school had the best College Board scores in the world on the calculus exam, and La Habra Heights and the eastern part of Whittier. Nearly two-thirds of the district's population is in Orange County. Here it includes Yorba Linda, birthplace of Richard Nixon in 1913 (when only 40,000 people lived in Orange County, short of the 3,002,000 in 2006) and the site now of his nine-acre presidential library; Brea and La Habra to the west; the eastern part of Anaheim; and, connected only by the uninhabited Santa Ana Mountains, the newer condominium communities of Mission Viejo and Rancho Santa Margarita. Ethnically diverse, its residents in 2000 were 24% Hispanic and 16% Asian, believers still in traditional values (the 42d has the highest percentage of married people in the state), working their way up through the private sector—and leaning Republican. In 2004, George W. Bush won 62% here; in 2006, Governor Arnold Schwarzenegger won 71%-25%.

The congressman from the 42d District is Gary Miller, a Republican first elected in 1998. He was born in Arkansas but grew up in Whittier. In his early 20s, he became a homebuilder and later developed planned communities; he is one of the most wealthy members of the House. He began his public service in 1988 when he was appointed to the Diamond Bar Municipal Advisory Council. A year later, after Diamond Bar was incorporated, Miller was elected to the city council and served as mayor. In 1995 he was elected to the Assembly in a special election. After chairing the Assembly's Budget Committee, he decided in 1997 to run for the House against scandal-tarred incumbent Jay Kim. Kim and his wife had pleaded guilty to accepting and concealing $230,000 in illegal campaign contributions. In March 1998 Kim was sentenced to house arrest, confined to the House and his apartment in suburban Virginia, and was required to wear an electronic bracelet around his ankle for two months. As a result, he could not campaign back home. Miller was endorsed by Governor Pete Wilson; the National Republican Congressional Committee, which normally endorses incumbents, remained neutral. Miller emphasized standard Republican themes—lower taxes, tougher penalties for crime, improved local education—and largely financed his campaign. Miller won the all-party primary 48% to 26% for Kim. Democrats did not pose a serious challenge in November.

Miller has a very conservative voting record in the House and has advanced some original proposals. He sponsored anti-spam legislation in the California Assembly well before it became a notorious problem; in Congress, he sponsored a bill to allow Internet Service Providers to decide whether they want to allow spamming and, if not, to give them a cause of action against spammers, with $500 per message in damages. On Financial Services, he used his familiarity with housing development to focus on affordable housing programs. He won House passage of amendments for additional funding of brownfield redevelopment. A Civil War buff who discovered that nearly 20% of the major battle sites have been lost, he successfully sponsored a bill to preserve Civil War battlefields by authorizing matching grants to local governments and nonprofits for unprotected sites. As the only California Republican on the Transportation and Infrastructure Committee, Miller had the daunting task of representing the state's diverse interests on the highway bill in 2005; Ways and Means chairman Bill Thomas won a disproportionate share of the state's funds for his Bakersfield district. In 2006, the IRS implemented Miller's proposal to stop collecting the excise tax on long-distance phone calls.

Miller has been easily reelected against token opposition. But that pattern might not continue. News outlets have reported on and raised questions about a variety of lucrative property transactions to which Miller, as a House member, has been a party. In one case, the *Los Angeles Times* reported in December 2006, he urged the Monrovia city council in 2000 to secure federal funds to purchase 165 acres that he owned. In another case, he got a $1.28 million earmark in funds to improve streets in front of development property he co-owned in Diamond Bar. News media reported in 2007 that the FBI was investigating several land deals where Miller avoided paying capital gains taxes by claiming that the land was about to be acquired through the use of eminent domain powers. Miller replied that he did nothing wrong and that he was the victim of a smear campaign. Democrats promised an active challenge in 2008.

FORTY-THIRD DISTRICT

Rep. Joe Baca (D)

Elected Nov. 1999, 4th full term; b. Jan. 23, 1947, Belen, NM; home, Rialto; CA State L.A., B.A., 1971; Catholic; married (Barbara).

Military Career: Army, 1966-68.

Elected Office: CA Assembly, 1992-98; CA Senate, 1998-99.

Professional Career: Community affairs rep., General Telephone and Electric, 1974-89; Co-owner, Interstate World Travel, 1989-present.

DC Office: 1527 LHOB, 20515, 202-225-6161; Fax: 202-225-8671; Web site: www.house.gov/baca.

District Offices: San Bernardino, 909-885-2222.

Committees: *Agriculture* (6th of 25 D): Department Operations, Oversight, Nutrition & Forestry (Chmn.); Livestock, Dairy & Poultry. *Financial Services* (17th of 37 D): Capital Markets, Insurance & Government Sponsored Enterprises; Financial Institutions & Consumer Credit. *Natural Resources* (24th of 27 D): Water & Power.

Group Ratings

	ADA	ACLU	AFS	LCV	ITIC	NTU	COC	ACU	CFG	FRC
2006	95	77	100	75	29	13	47	20	13	0
2005	90	—	100	56	—	16	58	32	9	23

National Journal Ratings

	2005 LIB	—	2005 CONS	2006 LIB	—	2006 CONS
Economic	63%	—	36%	67%	—	32%
Social	65%	—	34%	68%	—	32%
Foreign	77%	—	22%	72%	—	27%

Key Votes of the 109th Congress

1. Estate Tax Repeal	N	5. Limit Interstate Abortion	Y
2. Limit CAFE Standards	Y	6. Extend Patriot Act	Y
3. FY06 Spending Curb	*	7. Bar Same Sex Marriage	N
4. Drilling in ANWR	N	8. Stem Cell Research $	Y

9. Build Border Fence	N
10. CAFTA	N
11. Oppose Iraq Withdrawal	N
12. Detainee Tribunals	N

Election Results

2006 general	Joe Baca (D)	52,791	(64%)	($744,228)
	Scott Folkens (R)	29,069	(36%)	($16,597)
2006 primary	Joe Baca (D)	unopposed		
2004 general	Joe Baca (D)	86,830	(66%)	($450,287)
	Ed Laning (R)	44,004	(34%)	($40,391)

Prior Winning Percentages: 2002 (66%); 2000 (60%); 1999 (51%)

The People		Race/Ethnic Origin	Ancestry		
Area size:	193 sq. mi.	23.4% White	German: 4.6%	Irish: 3.4%	
Urban population:	99.3%	12.4% Black	English: 3.0%		
Rural population:	0.7%	3.1% Asian	**2004 Presidential Vote**		
Pop. 2000:	639,087	0.4% Native Am.	Kerry (D) 79,946		(58%)
Pop. 2005 (est):	719,698	0.3% Hawaiian	Bush (R) 55,952		(41%)
Median income:	$37,390	1.9% Two+ races	Other 1,497		(1%)
Poverty status:	20.7%	0.2% Other	**2000 Presidential Vote**		
Military veterans:	8.9%	58.3% Hispanic Origin	Gore (D) 76,710		(64%)
			Bush (R) 41,272		(34%)
			Other 2,293		(2%)
			Cook Partisan Voting Index: D +13		

Occupation　　Blue collar: 36.2%　　White collar: 46.4%　　Gray collar: 17.4%

The gateway to the Los Angeles Basin for decades was San Bernardino, situated on flat land where the route through the twisting, windy Cajon Pass took passengers on the Santa Fe Railroad and motorists on U.S. 66 from the hot and dusty desert to the greener, tree-lined Los Angeles basin. There were orange groves around the little railroad towns and vineyards to the west; this was an agricultural zone until World War II, when Henry J. Kaiser built the West Coast's first major steel mill between the Santa Fe and Southern Pacific lines in Fontana, just west of San Bernardino. Today, these lands have largely filled up. This Inland Empire, as it is called, may be where the smog piles up against the mountains, but it also has some of the lowest real estate prices in the Los Angeles Basin and an energetic small business economy. Business growth has been spurred by huge distribution and warehouse centers that service overseas cargo from the Long Beach port. Within 26 miles of San Bernardino, there are 17 Wal-Marts—and counting. The area's farmlands and dairy pastures have been reduced substantially, and the land sold to developers. From 1990 to 2005, jobs in the county grew from 408,000 to 643,000.

The 43d Congressional District of California includes most of San Bernardino and Colton and the towns running west—Rialto; Fontana, where many new businesses supplanted the steel mill closed in 1994 (and reassembled in China) and property values have increased sharply; and Ontario, with its expanded airport and international service. Every year Ontario celebrates the 4th of July at the longest picnic table in the world. San Bernardino's economy turned downward after the closure of Norton Air Force Base and the Santa Fe rail repair yard. But the base is now San Bernardino's new airport, the city has built a new baseball stadium and Northrop Grumman has opened a new Missile Engineering Center here. Politically this area—and San Bernardino County, in general—trended Republican in the 1980s, due to the cultural liberalism of California Democrats. But as the economy slowed in the early 1990s, and California's growing Latino population (the district was 58% Hispanic in 2000) and its continuing aversion to Republicans shifted it farther to the left, the district trended to the Democrats. It remains Democratic, but with some apparent second thoughts: George W. Bush's percentage here increased from 34% in 2000 to 41% in 2004, his second biggest increase in California's 53 districts.

The congressman from the 43d District is Joe Baca, a Democrat first elected in November 1999. He was born in Belen, New Mexico, the youngest of 15 children. His family moved to Barstow, California, in the desert, when he was four years old. His father worked as a laborer for the Santa Fe Railroad; Baca shined shoes at age 10 and later sold newspapers and worked as a janitor. He served in the Army as a paratrooper during the Vietnam War, but did not see combat. After graduating from California State University at Los Angeles, Baca moved to the San Bernardino area, where he spent 15 years as a community affairs representative for General Telephone and Electric and was elected four times to the San Bernardino Community College board. After two unsuccessful campaigns, the persistent Baca was elected to the Assembly in 1992. He became speaker pro tempore of the Assembly, the first Latino to hold the position in California. He earned a reputation as a hard worker, introducing more bills than any other member in his first year, but his aggressiveness rubbed some colleagues the wrong way. A moderate to conservative Democrat, he worked to reduce welfare rolls, lower taxes on middle-income earners and increase penalties for drug dealers. Facing term limits in 1998, he threatened to run in the primary against veteran Congressman George Brown. Instead he ran for the state Senate, spending $2 million to raise his local profile.

His opportunity came in July 1999, when Brown died in his 18th term. His widow Marta Macias Brown ran for the seat. Widows of members had won in 35 of the last 36 such races, but Minority Leader Richard Gephardt refused her request to clear the field, and Baca ran. He won the endorsement of organized labor and had a base among Latino voters. Brown attacked Baca for his endorsement by the National Rifle Association. Baca won the all-party primary with 32% of the vote; Brown got 30%, losing by 518 votes. The Republican nominee was real estate developer Elia Pirozzi, who in 1998 lost to Brown 55%-40%. Baca emphasized his centrist voting record and his support for targeted tax cuts, a minimum wage increase and abortion rights. Brown did not endorse Baca. In a light turnout, Baca won 51%-45%.

In the House, Baca has one of the more conservative voting records of California Democrats. He lobbied for a seat on the Rules Committee, and complained that he had been "bypassed" after Gephardt filled openings there with an African-American from Florida and a white from Massachusetts; Nancy Pelosi, too, did not accommodate his request for a higher-profile assignment. He opposed the resolution authorizing the use of force in Iraq and later called for a timeline for withdrawal. In 2007, he became chairman on the Agriculture Subcommittee on Department Operations, Oversight, Nutrition and Forestry and was the most senior Californian working on the farm bill; dairy production is the chief agricultural business in his district. He also became chairman of the Congressional Hispanic Caucus, and hoped to become a national spokesman on Hispanic issues. He co-sponsored the Flake-Gutierrez immigration bill. But Baca ran into trouble at the CHC. In March 2006, some members protested when the PAC's funds were used to support bids for office by members' relatives, including two of Baca's sons. In 2007, several women members complained about his handling of the caucus and about allegedly sexist remarks; all but one woman abstained from the vote naming Baca as chairman.

With redistricting changes, the district became significantly more Democratic and less competitive. And there have been shades of Dynasty, San Bernardino style: Joe Baca Jr. was elected to the state Assembly in 2004, becoming the first such parent-child team in California history. But two years later, he was defeated in a state Senate primary, and Jeremy Baca, another son, lost a primary to replace his brother in the Assembly.

FORTY-FOURTH DISTRICT
Rep. Ken Calvert (R)

Elected 1992, 8th term; b. June 8, 1953, Corona; home, Corona; Chaffey Col., 1972-73; San Diego St. U., B.A. 1975; Protestant; divorced.

Professional Career: Restaurant owner, 1975-80; Real estate broker, 1980-92; Chmn., Riverside Cnty. Repub. Party, 1984-88.

DC Office: 2201 RHOB, 20515, 202-225-1986; Fax: 202-225-2004; Web site: www.house.gov.calvert.

District Offices: Las Flores, 949-888-8498; Riverside, 909-784-4300.

Committees: *Appropriations* (29th of 29 R): Financial Services & General Government; Interior, Environment & Related Agencies.

Group Ratings

	ADA	ACLU	AFS	LCV	ITIC	NTU	COC	ACU	CFG	FRC
2006	5	9	0	8	100	54	100	80	54	85
2005	0	—	0	11	—	55	93	84	56	85

National Journal Ratings

	2005 LIB	—	2005 CONS	2006 LIB	—	2006 CONS
Economic	19%	—	79%	12%	—	86%
Social	12%	—	86%	35%	—	63%
Foreign	0%	—	89%	33%	—	63%

Key Votes of the 109th Congress

1. Estate Tax Repeal	Y	5. Limit Interstate Abortion	Y	9. Build Border Fence	Y
2. Limit CAFE Standards	Y	6. Extend Patriot Act	Y	10. CAFTA	Y
3. FY06 Spending Curb	Y	7. Bar Same Sex Marriage	Y	11. Oppose Iraq Withdrawal	Y
4. Drilling in ANWR	Y	8. Stem Cell Research $	Y	12. Detainee Tribunals	Y

Election Results

2006 general	Ken Calvert (R)	89,555	(60%)	($857,529)
	Louis Vandenberg (D)	55,275	(37%)	($3,154)
	Other	4,486	(3%)	
2006 primary	Ken Calvert (R)	unopposed		
2004 general	Ken Calvert (R)	138,768	(62%)	($687,467)
	Louis Vandenberg (D)	78,796	(35%)	($6,196)
	Other	7,559	(3%)	

Prior Winning Percentages: 2002 (64%); 2000 (74%); 1998 (56%); 1996 (55%); 1994 (55%); 1992 (47%)

The People		Race/Ethnic Origin	Ancestry	
Area size:	549 sq. mi.	51.3% White	German: 9.5%	Irish: 7.0%
Urban population:	97.7%	5.5% Black	English: 6.8%	
Rural population:	2.3%	4.8% Asian	**2004 Presidential Vote**	
Pop. 2000:	639,088	0.5% Native Am.	Bush (R) 139,476	(59%)
Pop. 2005 (est):	790,991	0.3% Hawaiian	Kerry (D) 94,374	(40%)
Median income:	$51,578	2.4% Two+ races	Other 2,562	(1%)
Poverty status:	12.1%	0.2% Other	**2000 Presidential Vote**	
Military veterans:	11.2%	35.0% Hispanic Origin	Bush (R) 101,897	(53%)
			Gore (D) 84,048	(44%)
			Other 5,143	(3%)
			Cook Partisan Voting Index: R + 6	
Occupation	Blue collar: 26.0%	White collar: 59.3%	Gray collar: 14.6%	

Riverside was a sleepy town of 34,000, a couple hours' drive from Los Angeles, when Richard and Pat Nixon were married there in 1940 in the gaudy Mission Inn, originally built in 1876 and with several wings that included bell towers, altars, fountains, rotunda, stained-glass windows and wrought-iron grilles. Riverside was not much larger, with 46,000 people, when Ronald and Nancy Reagan spent their honeymoon at the Mission Inn a dozen years later, in 1952. Riverside then was a citrus center, a market town amid orange groves, where the local agricultural college developed among other things, the navel orange. Today the Mission Inn is again doing business, after being closed from 1985 to 1992, but Riverside has changed completely. The city has expanded to some 281,000 people, and Riverside County, which had 105,000 people in 1940, had 2 million in 2006, more than doubling since 1980 and a 31% increase since 2000. Much of that growth came in the Inland Empire around Riverside, where the flat Los Angeles Basin plains are interrupted by oddly shaped hills and ridges, and the vegetation has an other-worldly air. This has been a boom part of California, where modest-income families found new houses in inexpensive developments and small businesses expanded mightily. After being hit hard by the recession of the early 1990s, it rebounded strongly. Near Moreno Valley, the former March Air Force Base has become a business park and regional hub for shipping giant DHL.

The 44th Congressional District of California, which covers much of this area, has been one of the fastest-growing congressional districts in the nation in the past two decades; from 2000 to 2005, it grew another 24%, making this currently the fastest-growing district in the state. Some 40% of its residents live in the city of Riverside and most others in nearby towns like Corona and Norco, the self-proclaimed Horsetown USA and the home of a Naval Surface Warfare Center, which evaluates weapons systems. In May 2005, the Pentagon recommended closing the base, which would have resulted in a loss of 3,300 local jobs; the base closure commission unexpectedly decided to save the base and to build a new lab. The district includes the eastern edge of Orange County all the way to the ocean, much of it uninhabited mountainsides but also including San Clemente, where Richard Nixon lived after he resigned the presidency, and half of San Juan Capistrano, to which the swallows famously return every March. This is a solidly Republican district.

The congressman from the 44th District is Ken Calvert, a Republican first elected in 1992. Calvert grew up in Corona; during college, he was a congressional intern at the Senate Watergate hearings of 1973. Later, he ran the family restaurant back home and in 1980 entered the commercial real estate business. In 1982, at 29, he ran for Congress in a district that included almost all the geographic expanse of Riverside County and lost a nine-candidate primary to Al McCandless by 868 votes. In 1992 he ran in a new district and won the primary with 28% of the vote. His Democratic opponent was Mark Takano, an eighth grade teacher with support from teachers' unions and Japanese Americans. In a district where George H.W. Bush beat Bill Clinton by 797 votes, Calvert beat Takano by 519 votes. He ran into trouble back home soon after he was elected, when the

Riverside *Press-Enterprise* reported that he had been stopped by police with a convicted prostitute in his car; Calvert apologized, and said that he was upset because his wife had divorced him the month before and his father had recently committed suicide. It was, as he said, "an extremely embarrassing situation," of which his opponents rushed to take advantage. Calvert won the 1994 primary 51%-49%, with only an 884-vote margin, against business professor Joseph Khoury. Takano, running again in the general, ran an ad with the song "The Liar" and accused him of "flagrant womanizing." But with the Republican tide that year, Calvert won 55%-38%.

In the House, Calvert has compiled a moderate-to-conservative voting record. He worked quietly as a subcommittee chairman, and usually has been a Republican team player. He also has co-chaired the Caucus to Fight and Control Methamphetamine. In 2001, Calvert took over as chairman of the Water and Power Subcommittee at Resources, which distributes public works projects. He focused intensively on building support for reauthorization of the vital water supply program (CALFED) for California's Central Valley. During the middle of the water fight, Calvert was one of several contenders seeking to chair the Resources Committee in 2003, but he lost to fellow Californian Richard Pombo, who was backed by Tom DeLay; he kept the Water and Power chairmanship. With help from Pombo, Calvert negotiated with Senator Dianne Feinstein, and they reached a compromise among the competing users, including new levees and recycling projects. After the bill was enacted in October 2004, southern California was deluged with rain for months. With the water issues largely resolved, Calvert became chairman in 2005 of Science's Space and Aeronautics Subcommittee; he enacted that year a reauthorization of NASA programs, which included a goal to return man to the moon by 2020 and incentives for private entrepreneurs to develop space technologies. Calvert also served on the Armed Services Committee, where he advocated the interests of local defense contractors and the area's shrinking military facilities. He defended the National Security Agency's data-mining techniques to identify possible terrorists.

Calvert steadily increased his margins in Republican primaries; he has not had serious Democratic opposition. In early 2003 he said he would not keep his 1992 pledge to serve only 12 years; he has been reelected easily anyway. Calvert reportedly became the focus of federal investigators after the *Los Angeles Times* in May 2006 wrote that he made a significant profit from a four-acre tract after steering earmarks to a nearby area. Calvert described the newspaper story as "scurrilous" and denied any wrongdoing. "They still haven't passed a law that you can't make personal investments," he said. But a year later, when Calvert was tapped to replace the ethically-tainted John Doolittle on the Appropriations Committee, the story came back to haunt him. Conservative bloggers reacted angrily to his selection in the wake of recent Republican ethics scandals; the popular www.redstate.com blog wrote, "We must scalp one member. That member's name is Ken Calvert."

FORTY-FIFTH DISTRICT

Rep. Mary Bono (R)

Elected April 1998, 5th full term; b. Oct. 24, 1961, Cleveland, OH; home, Palm Springs; U. of S. CA, B.F.A. 1984; Protestant; engaged.

Professional Career: Gen. Mgr., Bono restaurant, 1986-90.

DC Office: 104 CHOB, 20515, 202-225-5330; Fax: 202-225-2961; Web site: www.house.gov/bono.

District Offices: Hemet, 909-658-2312; Palm Springs, 760-320-1076.

Committees: *Energy & Commerce* (17th of 26 R): Commerce, Trade & Consumer Protection; Energy & Air Quality; Telecommunications & the Internet.

Group Ratings

	ADA	ACLU	AFS	LCV	ITIC	NTU	COC	ACU	CFG	FRC
2006	25	29	0	25	100	50	86	68	44	42
2005	15	—	0	11	—	55	93	71	51	42

National Journal Ratings

	2005 LIB	—	2005 CONS	2006 LIB	—	2006 CONS
Economic	30%	—	68%	38%	—	62%
Social	42%	—	57%	51%	—	49%
Foreign	45%	—	55%	29%	—	70%

Key Votes of the 109th Congress

1. Estate Tax Repeal	Y	5. Limit Interstate Abortion	Y	9. Build Border Fence	Y
2. Limit CAFE Standards	Y	6. Extend Patriot Act	Y	10. CAFTA	Y
3. FY06 Spending Curb	Y	7. Bar Same Sex Marriage	N	11. Oppose Iraq Withdrawal	Y
4. Drilling in ANWR	Y	8. Stem Cell Research $	Y	12. Detainee Tribunals	Y

Election Results

2006 general	Mary Bono (R)	99,638	(61%)	($1,528,130)
	David Roth (D)	64,613	(39%)	($722,765)
2006 primary	Mary Bono (R)	unopposed		
2004 general	Mary Bono (R)	153,523	(67%)	($501,088)
	Richard Meyer (D)	76,967	(33%)	($262,288)

Prior Winning Percentages: 2002 (65%); 2000 (59%); 1998 (60%); 1998 (64%)

The People		Race/Ethnic Origin	Ancestry	
Area size:	6,062 sq. mi.	50.1% White	German: 8.9%	English: 7.1%
Urban population:	89.9%	6.3% Black	Irish: 6.6%	
Rural population:	10.1%	2.8% Asian	**2004 Presidential Vote**	
Pop. 2000:	639,088	0.6% Native Am.	Bush (R) 132,288	(56%)
Pop. 2005 (est):	777,101	0.2% Hawaiian	Kerry (D) 101,679	(43%)
Median income:	$40,468	1.9% Two+ races	Other 2,102	(1%)
Poverty status:	15.0%	0.1% Other	**2000 Presidential Vote**	
Military veterans:	14.5%	38.0% Hispanic Origin	Bush (R) 93,802	(51%)
			Gore (D) 85,427	(47%)
			Other 4,029	(2%)
			Cook Partisan Voting Index: R + 3	

Occupation   Blue collar: 23.1%   White collar: 53.2%   Gray collar: 23.7%

From the air two decades ago, a night flight east from Los Angeles showed the lights of 10 million persons' streets and houses and then almost perfect darkness: a vast metropolis surrounded by almost uninhabited territory. Today the sprinkled pattern of white lights has spread into the Inland Empire around Riverside and San Bernardino and is multiplying outward into the desert. The Inland Empire has filled up with instant towns like family-oriented Moreno Valley, which did not exist in 1980 and had 178,000 people in 2005. Over the 10,000-foot San Jacinto Mountains, desert communities have boomed: Palm Springs, once the lone winter resort for the stars and now popular for its retro architecture such as flying-saucer roofs and steel-and-glass buildings, is one of a string of communities along Highway 111 and Frank Sinatra and Bob Hope Drives. Among rich retirees, the vogue for the coast lessened as beach cities filled up with roller bladers and rent control crusaders; the clean, dry, roomy desert, where the days are almost always crystal clear and the sky usually blue and cloudless, became more attractive, and, with everything air-conditioned, a comfortable year-round home. Two presidents retired to the desert here: Dwight Eisenhower in Palm Desert for the winters, and Gerald Ford who resided for 30 years after his presidency in nearby Rancho Mirage. Rancho Mirage is called the "playground of presidents" not for its connection to Ford, but rather for the corporate CEOs who retire and keep second homes there. The population is nearly 300,000 for the entire desert corridor if you count Indio and Coachella, the heavily Latino and fast-growing cities in the agricultural Coachella Valley, which has 75% of the country's date palms and features camel races at its annual date festival; *Rolling Stone* magazine called the launch of the annual music festival in Coachella one of the 50 greatest moments in rock history.

The 45th Congressional District of California covers almost all the desert in Riverside County from Blythe on the Nevada border to Palm Springs. The Joshua Tree National Park, with its high desert sands, is a popular tourist spot (it's shared with the 41st District, though most of it is in the 45th) and real estate values are growing in nearby towns. About half its population lives west of the 10,000-foot peak that looms above Palm Springs, in fast-growing Moreno Valley, socially conservative Murrieta and in the old town of Hemet surrounded by surreal landscape. This area tends to vote Republican; it voted 51% for George W. Bush in 2000 and 56% in 2004.

The congresswoman from the 45th District is Mary Bono, who won the seat in April 1998 after the death of her husband Sonny Bono, onetime showbiz celebrity and mayor of Palm Springs. Mary Bono grew up as Mary Whitaker in South Pasadena, where she was an accomplished gymnast; she remains a fitness buff, a certified personal fitness instructor who has studied karate and Tae Kwan Do. She met Sonny Bono when she was celebrating her college graduation at his Los Angeles restaurant in 1984; they were married two years later. He was on a family vacation when he died in a skiing accident in South Lake Tahoe, California. Before her campaign, she had no political experience and was little known in Washington. She was strongly encouraged to run for the seat by House Republican leaders who believed that only she could avert a divisive Republican primary and that she had the best chance to hold the seat. In the special election, Democrats backed actor Ralph Waite, best known as Pa Walton in *The Waltons*. Waite was hurt during the brief campaign because he kept a commitment to play Willy Loman in *Death of a Salesman* six times a week in a New Jersey theater. The campaign's biggest controversy came when Sonny's 83-year-old mother said that her son would have opposed Mary's candidacy, preferring that she care for their children. But it was no contest. Bono won 64%-29%, a bigger margin than Sonny's two victories.

Bono has a moderate voting record, especially on social issues; the least conservative voting record of California Republicans. She helped pass the reauthorization of the Ryan White AIDS research law in 2006, and supported embryonic stem-cell research.

Her initial legislative priority was passage of Sonny's bill to restore the Salton Sea, an artificial body of water in the desert created when a canal burst in 1905; it has been shrinking in recent decades, increasing the salinity of the water and the pollution from agricultural runoff. Although some Democrats objected to taking funds from other California projects, Mary Bono initially secured $13.4 million for what became the Sonny Bono Salton Sea National Wildlife Refuge. She later pushed for engineering projects to reduce the heavy salinity of the lake and to assure continuing sources of fresh water, but progress was slow and millions of fish were dying. Final costs likely would be billions of dollars. Later, she enacted a bill to establish the Santa Rosa and San Jacinto National Monument in the Palm Springs area. With a seat on the Energy and Commerce Committee, she worked on her legislation to crack down on invasive computer "spyware"; the House passed her bill in May 2005, but it died in the Senate. Bono, who collects about $100,000 annually from her late husband's royalties, has opposed legislation to relax controls on digital piracy. On immigration, she supported tougher enforcement at the border plus an expanded guest-worker program but opposed amnesty for illegal aliens.

Mary Bono has been easily reelected. In 2006, educational consultant David Roth raised more than $720,000 and ran an active campaign, but Bono won 61%-39%. She thought about running for Barbara Boxer's Senate seat in 2004: Sonny Bono had run for the seat in 1992, and finished third in the Republican primary. She also was mentioned as the possible new head of the Recording Industry Association of America, but she decided to remain in the House. She was an early supporter of Rudy Giuliani for president.

FORTY-SIXTH DISTRICT

Rep. Dana Rohrabacher (R)

Elected 1988, 10th term; b. June 21, 1947, Coronado; home, Huntington Beach; Long Beach St. Col. B.A. 1969, U. of S. CA, M.A. 1975; Baptist; married (Rhonda).

Professional Career: Radio & print journalist, 1970-80; Sr. Speechwriter, Special Asst. to Pres. Reagan, 1981-88.

DC Office: 2300 RHOB, 20515, 202-225-2415; Fax: 202-225-0145; Web site: www.house.gov/rohrabacher.

District Offices: Huntington Beach, 714-960-6483.

Committees: *Foreign Affairs* (5th of 23 R): International Organizations, Human Rights & Oversight (RMM); Asia, the Pacific & the Global Environment. *Science & Technology* (4th of 20 R): Investigations & Oversight; Space & Aeronautics.

Group Ratings

	ADA	ACLU	AFS	LCV	ITIC	NTU	COC	ACU	CFG	FRC
2006	15	9	0	17	71	75	93	88	86	71
2005	5	—	0	17	—	76	81	96	95	92

National Journal Ratings

	2005 LIB	—	2005 CONS		2006 LIB	—	2006 CONS
Economic	9%	—	88%		16%	—	81%
Social	42%	—	58%		39%	—	60%
Foreign	23%	—	73%		17%	—	73%

Key Votes of the 109th Congress

1. Estate Tax Repeal	Y	5. Limit Interstate Abortion	Y	9. Build Border Fence	Y
2. Limit CAFE Standards	Y	6. Extend Patriot Act	N	10. CAFTA	Y
3. FY06 Spending Curb	Y	7. Bar Same Sex Marriage	Y	11. Oppose Iraq Withdrawal	Y
4. Drilling in ANWR	Y	8. Stem Cell Research $	Y	12. Detainee Tribunals	Y

Election Results

2006 general	Dana Rohrabacher (R)	116,176	(60%)	($354,651)
	Jim Brandt (D)	71,573	(37%)	($80,078)
	Dennis Chang (Lib)	7,303	(4%)	
2006 primary	Dana Rohrabacher (R)	unopposed		
2004 general	Dana Rohrabacher (R)	171,318	(62%)	($517,315)
	Jim Brandt (D)	90,129	(33%)	($85,456)
	Tom Lash (Green)	10,238	(4%)	
	Other	5,005	(2%)	

Prior Winning Percentages: 2002 (62%); 2000 (62%); 1998 (59%); 1996 (61%); 1994 (69%); 1992 (55%); 1990 (59%); 1988 (64%)

The People		Race/Ethnic Origin	Ancestry	
Area size:	825 sq. mi.	62.8% White	German: 10.7%	English: 8.5%
Urban population:	99.9%	1.4% Black	Irish: 8.4%	
Rural population:	0.1%	15.4% Asian	**2004 Presidential Vote**	
Pop. 2000:	639,088	0.3% Native Am.	Bush (R)	168,158 (57%)
Pop. 2005 (est):	662,649	0.3% Hawaiian	Kerry (D)	122,991 (42%)
Median income:	$61,567	2.6% Two+ races	Other	3,734 (1%)
Poverty status:	7.8%	0.2% Other	**2000 Presidential Vote**	
Military veterans:	11.3%	16.9% Hispanic Origin	Bush (R)	145,729 (55%)
			Gore (D)	110,984 (42%)
			Other	9,413 (4%)
			Cook Partisan Voting Index: R + 6	

Occupation	Blue collar: 15.4%	White collar: 72.7%	Gray collar: 11.9%

In the 1950s, when the Beach Boys were at blue-collar Hawthorne High School, surfers would drive far down the coast to the vast expanse of Huntington Beach in Orange County to catch a wave. This was empty country then, vegetable fields and orange groves, with nary a freeway or shopping center in sight. Today a long stretch of the beach itself is eerily empty, with swampland across the highway where surfers' pickups are parked, but the rest of the 42-mile shoreline of Orange County is pretty much filled in. Pricey coastal resorts have become a popular destination. Huntington Beach is a city of 194,000, a mixture of family subdivisions and garden apartments and home of the International Surfing Museum. To the north is Westminster, the center of the nation's most prominent Vietnamese-American community, with miles of malls where all the shops have Vietnamese names and the area has its own Vietnamese-language daily newspaper. Southeast along San Diego Freeway is Fountain Valley, the central focus of many Asian-owned high-tech businesses, an engine of Southern California growth. Near the coast is Costa Mesa, site of South Coast Plaza's luxury stores and a grand performing arts center. Out on the beach in Huntington Beach you can see the curving coastline to the west, past the port of Los Angeles and Long Beach to where the mountains of the seismically active and economically upscale Palos Verdes Peninsula rise above the water.

The 46th Congressional District of California includes all of this beachfront plus the Long Beach Harbor area and the Palos Verdes Peninsula. It also includes territory inland: the eastern end of Long Beach and next-door Seal Beach, areas settled by many retirees, most of Westminster, all of Fountain Valley, Costa Mesa, the southwest corner of Santa Ana and a tiny slice of Los

Angeles. The eastern part of the district is connected to the Palos Verdes Peninsula by a thin strip of beach or the port area. Politically, the two ends of the district are solidly Republican, from high-income Palos Verdes to Westminster. This is no longer the monoracial Orange County of the 1960s: the district's population is 17% Hispanic and 15% Asian.

The congressman from the 46th District is Dana Rohrabacher, a Republican first elected in 1988. He calls himself a surfer Republican and sports an American flag surfboard. He grew up in southern California, went to college and experimented with drugs, and once had a folk band called the Goldwaters. He was a press aide in the 1976 and 1980 Reagan presidential campaigns, wrote editorials for the *Orange County Register* and was a speechwriter in the Reagan White House. He returned to Southern California in 1988 when Long Beach-based Congressman Dan Lungren decided not to run again. Rohrabacher, with fundraising help from Oliver North, won the primary with 35% of the vote, to 22% for an Orange County supervisor and 20% for Steve Horn, who later represented a Long Beach-based district. After redistricting in 1992, Rohrabacher tussled with Robert Dornan and won, running in this heavily Republican district while Dornan ran in the inland seat which, after a quixotic presidential campaign, he lost in 1996.

A self-styled free spirit, Rohrabacher likes to make waves in the House. His website once featured the motto: "Fighting for freedom and having fun." His voting record can be unpredictable, especially on cultural issues; he supported medical marijuana and embryonic stem-cell research, and has been skeptical of the Patriot Act. That helps to explain why this maverick has found himself on second-level committees, but he has made the most of his opportunities. As chairman of the Science Subcommittee on Space and Aeronautics, he worked for the single-stage-to-orbit vehicle. He said that a manned space flight to repair the Hubble space telescope was not worth the risk. In December 2004, George W. Bush signed his bill to promote the development of the commercial human space flight industry. He has encouraged an obscure NASA program to search for and knock off course asteroids and comets that could slam into Earth. In 2007, he lost to Ralph Hall for the ranking minority position on the Science committee.

In 2005, he became chairman of the Oversight and Investigations Subcommittee on International Relations, an area where he already had stirred the waters. As a White House aide, he traveled in November 1988 with a mujahedeen militia unit for one week. Soon after the September 11 attacks, he visited the exiled King of Afghanistan in Rome, encouraged him to return to Kabul and promised that the United States would oust the Taliban and help rebuild Afghanistan. Rohrabacher has been a long-time critic of China's rulers and strongly opposed normal trade relations with China and Vietnam. He organized a Victims of Communism memorial near Union Station in Washington.

Despite the Bush administration's criticism that it would violate the peace treaty, he won House passage of his amendment to allow World War II prisoners of war to sue Japanese companies for enslaving them. In July 2002, after a lengthy delay while he paced the House floor, he cast one of the final votes that secured the passage by one vote of trade promotion authority for President Bush. He went through a similar routine in November 2003 before voting for the Medicare/prescription drug bill; in exchange, Republican leaders gave him a vote on his bill to require hospitals to report potential illegal immigrants to the Homeland Security Department. He has led voter initiatives to remove illegal aliens from California welfare and school rolls. In 2004, with in-vitro fertilization and at age 56, he and wife Rhonda became the parents of triplets.

Rohrabacher has been routinely reelected by wide margins. In the 2004 primary, he was challenged by his former colleague Robert Dornan, who had become a radio talk-show host. Rohrabacher won 84%-16%. His hold on the district is secure enough that he could maintain his friendship with convicted lobbyist Jack Abramoff, whom Rohrabacher first met in the 1980s when he worked for Reagan and Abramoff led the College Republicans, and defend his character in the press. "I see him more as a good person who's done bad things and has to be punished for doing bad things."

FORTY-SEVENTH DISTRICT

Rep. Loretta Sanchez (D)

Elected 1996, 6th term; b. Jan. 7, 1960, Lynwood; home, Santa Ana; Chapman U., B.A. 1982, American U., M.B.A. 1984; Catholic; divorced.

Professional Career: Mgr. & Financial Analyst, Orange Cnty. Transp. Auth., 1984-87; Asst. Vice Pres., Fieldman, Rolapp & Assoc., 1987-90; Assoc., Booz, Allen & Hamilton, 1990-93; Principal, Amiga Advisors.

DC Office: 1230 LHOB, 20515, 202-225-2965; Fax: 202-225-5859; Web site: www.house.gov/sanchez.

District Offices: Garden Grove, 714-621-0102.

Committees: *Armed Services* (9th of 34 D): Military Personnel; Oversight & Investigations; Readiness. *Homeland Security* (2d of 19 D): Border, Maritime & Global Counterterrorism (Chmn.); Emergency Communications, Preparedness & Response. *Joint Economic Committee* (4th of 10 D).

Group Ratings

	ADA	ACLU	AFS	LCV	ITIC	NTU	COC	ACU	CFG	FRC
2006	100	91	100	100	57	14	47	12	13	0
2005	90	—	100	94	—	22	52	16	15	25

National Journal Ratings

	2005 LIB	—	2005 CONS		2006 LIB	—	2006 CONS
Economic	69%	—	29%		71%	—	28%
Social	75%	—	24%		80%	—	19%
Foreign	76%	—	23%		70%	—	28%

Key Votes of the 109th Congress

1. Estate Tax Repeal	Y	5. Limit Interstate Abortion	N	9. Build Border Fence	N
2. Limit CAFE Standards	N	6. Extend Patriot Act	N	10. CAFTA	N
3. FY06 Spending Curb	N	7. Bar Same Sex Marriage	N	11. Oppose Iraq Withdrawal	N
4. Drilling in ANWR	N	8. Stem Cell Research $	Y	12. Detainee Tribunals	N

Election Results

2006 general	Loretta Sanchez (D)	47,134	(62%)	($1,829,971)
	Tan Nguyen (R)	28,485	(38%)	($547,646)
2006 primary	Loretta Sanchez (D)	unopposed		
2004 general	Loretta Sanchez (D)	65,684	(60%)	($1,837,079)
	Alex Coronado (R)	43,099	(40%)	($356,372)

Prior Winning Percentages: 2002 (61%); 2000 (60%); 1998 (56%); 1996 (47%)

The People		Race/Ethnic Origin	Ancestry	
Area size:	55 sq. mi.	17.3% White	German: 3.5%	Irish: 2.5%
Urban population:	100.0%	1.5% Black	English: 2.3%	
Rural population:	0.0%	13.9% Asian	**2004 Presidential Vote**	
Pop. 2000:	639,087	0.3% Native Am.	Bush (R) 56,226	(50%)
Pop. 2005 (est):	642,692	0.4% Hawaiian	Kerry (D) 54,623	(49%)
Median income:	$41,618	1.3% Two+ races	Other 1,393	(1%)
Poverty status:	19.1%	0.1% Other	**2000 Presidential Vote**	
Military veterans:	5.2%	65.3% Hispanic Origin	Gore (D) 59,515	(56%)
			Bush (R) 43,752	(41%)
			Other 2,257	(2%)
			Cook Partisan Voting Index: D + 5	
Occupation	Blue collar: 37.9%	White collar: 40.9%	Gray collar: 21.2%	

When Walt Disney began planning Disneyland in the late 1940s, he did not have to drive far from downtown Los Angeles before finding agricultural land. Dairy farms and orange groves covered most of southeast Los Angeles County and adjacent Orange County, which had only 216,000 people in 1950. As Disneyland opened there in 1955 and became a vast success for families and fun, the area around it—a mass of flat land surrounded by mountains and sea—found itself directly in the path of the most explosively growing metropolitan area in the United States. With 3,002,000 people, it is the nation's fifth-largest county, just a bit ahead of San Diego County.

Just as Orange County was once transformed by newcomers from Los Angeles County and the Midwest, so it is again being transformed by immigrants, from Mexico and other parts of Latin America, and from Vietnam, Taiwan, Korea and other parts of East Asia. By 1990 the county's population was 23% Hispanic and 10% Asian; in 2005, the figures were 33% Hispanic and 16% Asian. Some of these new Orange County residents are direct migrants: Santa Ana, the county seat, is a major arrival point for immigrants from Mexico, and its increasingly settled population is 76% Hispanic. Others have moved farther out, like so many southern Californians before them, working hard at jobs, commuting on freeways and living in stucco subdivisions. There are concentrations in various places—Latinos in Santa Ana and much of Anaheim; Vietnamese in Westminster and Garden Grove, who comprise the largest expatriate Vietnamese community in the nation—but many of these new Californians are just speckled through the county. These changes have made for some political wobble. But until the mid-1990s, Asians were split between the parties and few Latinos were registered to vote. After the 1994 approval of Proposition 187, which sought to deny most social services to illegal immigrants, many more Latinos began voting, and mostly Democratic; Asian voters were less predictable.

The 47th Congressional District of California is the geographic heart of Orange County. About half its people live in Santa Ana, in neighborhoods full of large families and many workers. The district includes most of Garden Grove and Anaheim. It includes many Orange County landmarks—Angel Stadium of Anaheim, Disneyland and Disney's California Adventure. The district's population in 2000 was 65% Hispanic and 14% Asian (primarily Vietnamese). This core area has always been the most Democratic part of Orange County. But it is not overwhelmingly Democratic like most majority-Hispanic districts in Los Angeles County. In 2003 the district voted 62% to recall Democratic Governor Gray Davis. George W. Bush, who lost the district 56%-41% to Al Gore in 2000, won it 50%-49% over John Kerry in 2004. This was the biggest increase for Bush in California's 53 districts. In 2006, Governor Arnold Schwarzenegger won 54%-40% here.

The congresswoman from the 47th District is Loretta Sanchez, a Democrat first elected in 1996. Sanchez was raised in Anaheim by Mexican immigrant parents, graduated from Chapman University in Orange, and got an MBA from American University in Washington. She worked as a financial analyst, providing advice on municipal finances to public agencies and private businesses; she created her own firm in the early 1990s. For a time she and her husband lived in affluent Palos Verdes Estates, far from Orange County. In 1994 she ran for the city council in Anaheim under her married name, Loretta Sanchez-Brixcy, and lost. In 1996, she ran for the House, this time as Loretta Sanchez, against one of the loudest voices of American conservatism, Robert Dornan. In the primary against three Anglo male Democrats, she won with 35%. That victory attracted little attention, not even from Dornan. But she shrewdly counted on increasing Latino turnout, plus attracting contributions from the many enemies that Dornan had made over a political career that went back to 1976 and included a quixotic presidential campaign that took him far from Orange County during 1995 and 1996. Bill Clinton came to Santa Ana late in the campaign to stump for Sanchez, and may have made the difference. She won by 984 votes, 47%-46%. Dornan charged vote fraud, and, using the privileges afforded to former members, he regularly appeared on the House floor trying to convince his former colleagues to call for a special election; Democrats charged that he was abusing his privileges and the House voted to bar him from the floor after a heated discussion between Dornan and Bob Menendez. In February 1998, the House Administration Committee upheld Sanchez's victory.

After the election Sanchez was named general co-chairwoman of the Democratic National Committee to lead a Hispanic voter registration drive, and Al Gore tapped her as honorary chair of his political action committee. But that proved a mixed blessing for both Sanchez and her party. She scheduled a fundraiser during the 2000 Democratic National Convention in Los Angeles at Hugh Hefner's Playboy Mansion. Gore and many House Democrats—including other Latinos, from whom she had kept her distance—said that she was undermining the party's image. At first quietly, then more bluntly, she was urged to choose a new site and was warned that she was jeopardizing her political future. Belatedly she relented and moved the event to Universal Studio's City Walk.

In the House, Sanchez's voting record leaned to the Democratic middle. Vietnam has been a focus: Accompanying Clinton on his November 2000 visit there, she met with dissidents to discuss human rights. Her plans to return in 2004 were blocked when she was denied an entry visa because her visit "would not serve Vietnam-U.S. relations." On the Armed Services Committee, she has worked to bring jobs to local high tech firms; in 2004, the House passed her provision for the Pentagon to study the loss of civilian income by reservists on active duty. As the senior woman on the committee, she wants to update the sexual assault crimes in the Uniform Code of Military Justice to comply with federal sexual assault crimes. She is the number two Democrat on the Homeland Security Committee, where she has focused on port security, including her proposal for a secure, long-range automated vessel tracking system; she chairs the Border, Maritime and Global Counterterrorism Subcommittee.

Sanchez has been reelected comfortably and voters appear to have grown accustomed to her unconventional style. She is renowned for her quirky Christmas cards, which feature her aging white cat Gretzky, and she hosts a monthly cable access show titled, "Loretta Live" (though it's actually taped). In October 2006, Republican leaders urged her GOP challenger—a Vietnamese immigrant—to withdraw after he mailed a campaign letter that threatened Latino voters with potential prosecution; he denied wrongdoing, but lost 62%-38%. Her focus has extended beyond the 47th District. In 2002 she angered some Latino Democrats when she worked hard to elect her sister Linda Sanchez in the new 39th District. Ever ambitious, Sanchez has said that she might like to be a senator some day; for a few days in August 2003, she floated her name as a Democratic candidate in the governor recall election. In January 2007, she quit the Congressional Hispanic Caucus after she said that its chairman Joe Baca had called her a "whore."

FORTY-EIGHTH DISTRICT

Rep. John Campbell (R)

Elected Dec. 2005, 1st full term; b. July 19, 1955, Los Angeles; home, Irvine; U.C.L.A., B.A. 1976, U. of S. CA, M.B.T., 1977; Presbyterian; married (Catherine).

Elected Office: CA Assembly, 2000-04; CA Senate, 2004-05.

Professional Career: Tax accountant, 1977-78; Auto dealership executive, 1978-2003.

DC Office: 1728 LHOB, 20515, 202-225-5611; Fax: 202-225-9177; Web site: campbell.house.gov.

District Offices: Newport Beach, 949-756-2244.

Committees: *Budget* (12th of 17 R). *Financial Services* (27th of 33 R): Housing & Community Opportunity; Capital Markets, Insurance & Government Sponsored Enterprises; Financial Institutions & Consumer Credit.

Group Ratings (Only Served Partial Term)

	ADA	ACLU	AFS	LCV	ITIC	NTU	COC	ACU	CFG	FRC
2006	0	8	0	25	100	74	87	88	84	85
2005	—	—	—	—	—	—	—	—	—	—

National Journal Ratings (Only Served Partial Term)

	2005 LIB	—	2005 CONS	2006 LIB	—	2006 CONS
Economic	*	—	*	32%	—	67%
Social	*	—	*	16%	—	84%
Foreign	*	—	*	6%	—	86%

Key Votes of the 109th Congress (Only Served Partial Term)

1. Estate Tax Repeal	*	5. Limit Interstate Abortion	*	9. Build Border Fence	Y
2. Limit CAFE Standards	*	6. Extend Patriot Act	*	10. CAFTA	*
3. FY06 Spending Curb	Y	7. Bar Same Sex Marriage	Y	11. Oppose Iraq Withdrawal	Y
4. Drilling in ANWR	Y	8. Stem Cell Research $	N	12. Detainee Tribunals	Y

Election Results

2006 general	John Campbell (R) 120,130	(60%)	($2,254,028)
	Steve Young (D) 74,647	(37%)	($434,792)
	Other 5,750	(3%)	
2006 primary	John Campbell (R) .... unopposed		
2005 special	John Campbell (R) 46,184	(44%)	
	Steve Young (D) 28,853	(28%)	
	Jim Gilchrist (AI) 26,507	(25%)	
	Other 2,404	(2%)	
2005 spec. primary	John Campbell (R) 41,420	(45%)	
	Marilyn Brewer (R) 15,595	(17%)	
	Jim Gilchrist (AI) 13,423	(15%)	
	Steve Young (D) 7,941	(9%)	
	John Graham (D) 3,667	(4%)	
	Other 9,116	(10%)	

The People		Race/Ethnic Origin	Ancestry	
Area size:	301 sq. mi.	68.0% White	German: 11.3%	English: 9.3%
Urban population:	99.9%	1.4% Black	Irish: 8.3%	
Rural population:	0.1%	12.7% Asian	**2004 Presidential Vote**	
Pop. 2000:	639,087	0.2% Native Am.	Bush (R) 178,739	(58%)
Pop. 2005 (est):	685,473	0.2% Hawaiian	Kerry (D) 123,664	(40%)
Median income:	$69,663	2.7% Two+ races	Other 3,364	(1%)
Poverty status:	6.3%	0.2% Other	**2000 Presidential Vote**	
Military veterans:	10.3%	14.7% Hispanic Origin	Bush (R) 156,340	(58%)
			Gore (D) 106,809	(39%)
			Other 7,421	(3%)
			Cook Partisan Voting Index: R + 8	

Occupation   Blue collar: 10.1%   White collar: 79.8%   Gray collar: 10.1%

If you drove south on the Santa Ana and San Diego Freeways in Orange County 35 years ago, once you got past Santa Ana and John Wayne Airport you would have found yourself in open land for the next 25 miles, a vacant landscape of flat plains and low mountains, all beneath the 4,600-foot Trabuco Peak in the distance. This was the land of the Irvine Ranch, purchased by Gold Rush merchant James Irvine from the Sepulveda and Yorba families and maintained as a ranch until the early 1970s, the last large plot of vacant land in metro Los Angeles. Irvine sold some of it to create the cities of Santa Ana and Tustin, but in the 1970s there was still this great swath of land, 10 miles along the Pacific Coast and 22 miles inland to the mountains, where the freeway traveler could see what the California the first American settlers saw looked like. As Orange County grew up to the limits of the Irvine Ranch, the Irvine family realized that they owned immensely valuable land. In 1959 they donated a site for the University of California at Irvine, which has grown to more than 25,000 students; in the 1970s they sold the rest of the property to developers. The resulting city of Irvine was a planned community, with eight-lane parkways, huge office parks and shopping malls, and attractive subdivisions and condominiums. Irvine has attracted high-tech and high-growth businesses, highly educated and affluent people, including Asian immigrants; its population is 37% Asian, with enough Chinese to support a Chinese supermarket and a Chinese-language library. Irvine is one planned city that respects free market economics; the expressways on the Irvine Ranch land were built by private companies and paid for by tolls. Now the El Toro Marine Corps Air Station that closed in 1999 is being developed as the Great Park, with 1,300 acres parkland ringed by 2,400 acres of development, 3,600 homes and 3 million square feet of commercial and industrial space. Efforts by Los Angeles Mayor James Hahn to have the land developed as an airport were rebuffed by the Navy, which auctioned off the property for $649 million in 2005.

Irvine is set amid a raft of affluent communities, except for low-income and 76% Hispanic Santa Ana. To the north is Tustin, an older town built on Irvine land. To the south is Newport Beach, one of California's richest cities; Newport Harbor is chock full of expensive boats, and nearby Balboa Island is filled with multi-million dollar homes. To the east is Lake Forest; the name used to be El Toro, and some residents now complain that it has few lakes or forests. To the southeast, on the ocean is Laguna Beach with its art galleries and cute shops, and more conventionally affluent Dana Point. Inland are Laguna Niguel, Laguna Hills, and the Laguna Woods retirement community.

The 48th Congressional District of California, entirely contained within Orange County, is centered geographically on the Irvine Ranch lands and includes all of these communities. Politically, this is a conservative area, and for a long time it was one of the most Republican districts in the United States. In the 1990s, like most of metro Los Angeles, it trended to the Democrats. It is still Republican, but far from the most Republican district in the state; it voted 58% for George W. Bush in 2000 and 2004.

The congressman from the 48th District is John Campbell, a Republican who won a special election in December 2005. He has deep roots in southern California, with a great-grandfather who was elected to the Republican state Assembly in 1860, and a grandfather who was managing editor of the now-defunct *Herald-Examiner*, W.R. Hearst's rival to the *Los Angeles Times*. Campbell's father was an oil field geologist and investor who later edited the *Herald-Examiner*'s financial pages; he ran unsuccessfully for state Senate in 1966 against Anthony Beilenson, who later won election to Congress. John Campbell graduated from UCLA and got a master's degree in business taxation from USC. A certified public accountant, he joined an Orange County automobile dealership group as controller in 1978 after a stint with Ernst & Young; upon reviewing the books, Campbell discovered that the company's management had diverted $500,000 towards personal expenses. He alerted shareholders, including his father. The CEO was fired, and Campbell was given the job. He later declared a no-haggling policy at each of Campbell Automotive's car dealerships. "We want to be the Nordstrom of auto retailing," he told the *Orange County Register* in 1989. In the 1990s, Campbell's plan for a nationwide Saturn dealership group came close to an initial public offering, but the deal fell through and he sold off Campbell Automotive's Mazda, Ford and Nissan dealerships to focus on its remaining Saab franchises—and on politics.

In 2000, term limits opened up an Irvine-based California Assembly seat; he won the general election with 60% of the vote and became a prolific legislator, introducing three dozen bills in his first session. In 2003, when Democratic Governor Gray Davis tripled the state's vehicle licensing fee to 2% of a vehicle's value, Campbell called on citizens to flood the department of motor vehicles with refund claims. He was elected to the state senate in 2004.

Campbell got his opportunity to run for Congress when Christopher Cox, the chairman of the Homeland Security Committee, was nominated in June 2005 by George W. Bush to chair the Securities and Exchange Commission. At first, state Senate Minority Leader Dick Ackerman announced his candidacy for the seat, and Campbell voiced support for him. But Campbell changed his mind and decided to run, taking Ackerman's political consultant with him. Ackerman withdrew and Campbell was instantly frontrunner in this solidly Republican district. Also entering the race was Marilyn Brewer, whom Campbell had succeeded in the Assembly. Brewer supported abortion rights and embryonic stem cell research, and drew support from the moderate Republican Main Street Partnership. Campbell was endorsed by Governor Arnold Schwarzenegger, whom he had worked closely with in Sacramento, and by the state and Orange County Republican parties.

With 19 candidates running for the seat in the all-party October 4 special primary, none was able to meet the 50% threshold required to win the seat outright and avoid a special general election. Campbell finished first with 45%, well above Brewer's 17%, to win the Republican nomination; Steve Young was the Democratic nominee after winning 9%. Jim Gilchrist, founder of the anti-illegal-immigrant Minuteman Project, finished third with 15% and was the nominee of the American Independent Party. When Congressman Tom Tancredo endorsed Gilchrist, neighboring 49th District Congressman Darrell Issa urged Colorado Republicans to expel him from the party. In the December 4 campaign, Gilchrist criticized Campbell for his votes in the Assembly; Campbell admitted that he made a mistake in 2001 when he voted to allow illegal immigrants to receive in-state college tuition. Gilchrist's single-issue campaign caught Campbell off guard and turned the contest into a referendum on immigration. Campbell won, though with a surprisingly modest 44% to 28% for Democrat Steve Young and 25% for Gilchrist. Nearly 13,000 more votes were cast in December than October, but Campbell picked up just 4,800 votes over his October performance; the bulk of the other votes went to Young and Gilchrist.

In the House, Campbell's voting record was mostly conservative but toward the center on economic issues. He has seats on the Budget and Financial Services committees. He moved quickly into a leadership role among conservatives as chairman of the budget and spending task force of the Republican Study Committee. He said that the Democrats' fiscal policies would lead to "the largest tax increase in American history." At home, Campbell won his first full term 60%-37%. In this district, he should be secure.

FORTY-NINTH DISTRICT

Rep. Darrell Issa (R)

Elected 2000, 4th term; b. Nov. 1, 1953, Cleveland, OH; home, Vista; Sienna Heights U., B.A. 1976; Antioch Orthodox Christian; married (Kathy).

Military Career: Army, 1970-72; 1976-80.

Professional Career: Founder & Pres., Directed Electronics, 1982-99.

DC Office: 211 CHOB, 20515, 202-225-3906; Fax: 202-225-3303; Web site: www.issa.house.gov.

District Offices: Temecula, 909-693-2447; Vista, 760-599-5000.

Committees: *Judiciary* (10th of 17 R): The Constitution, Civil Rights & Civil Liberties; Courts, the Internet & Intellectual Property. *Oversight & Government Reform* (11th of 18 R): Domestic Policy (RMM); Federal Workforce, Postal Service & the District of Columbia. *Permanent Select Committee on Intelligence* (8th of 8 R): Intelligence Community Management (RMM).

Group Ratings

	ADA	ACLU	AFS	LCV	ITIC	NTU	COC	ACU	CFG	FRC
2006	5	14	0	0	100	62	100	80	67	71
2005	0	—	0	6	—	59	93	84	66	83

National Journal Ratings

	2005 LIB	—	2005 CONS		2006 LIB	—	2006 CONS
Economic	19%	—	79%		23%	—	76%
Social	28%	—	70%		21%	—	79%
Foreign	29%	—	70%		15%	—	84%

Key Votes of the 109th Congress

1. Estate Tax Repeal	Y	5. Limit Interstate Abortion	Y	9. Build Border Fence	Y
2. Limit CAFE Standards	Y	6. Extend Patriot Act	Y	10. CAFTA	Y
3. FY06 Spending Curb	Y	7. Bar Same Sex Marriage	Y	11. Oppose Iraq Withdrawal	Y
4. Drilling in ANWR	Y	8. Stem Cell Research $	Y	12. Detainee Tribunals	Y

Election Results

2006 general	Darrell Issa (R)	98,831	(63%)	($1,102,601)
	Jeeni Criscenzo (D)	52,227	(33%)	($88,834)
	Other	5,079	(3%)	
2006 primary	Darrell Issa (R)	unopposed		
2004 general	Darrell Issa (R)	141,658	(63%)	($882,952)
	Mike Byron (D)	79,057	(35%)	($69,035)
	Other	5,751	(3%)	

Prior Winning Percentages: 2002 (77%); 2000 (61%)

The People		Race/Ethnic Origin	Ancestry		
Area size:	1,778 sq. mi.	57.9% White	German: 10.7%	Irish: 7.9%	
Urban population:	90.3%	5.0% Black	English: 7.8%		
Rural population:	9.7%	3.5% Asian	**2004 Presidential Vote**		
Pop. 2000:	639,087	0.9% Native Am.	Bush (R)	149,283	(63%)
Pop. 2005 (est):	729,089	0.5% Hawaiian	Kerry (D)	86,998	(36%)
Median income:	$46,445	2.5% Two+ races	Other	2,389	(1%)
Poverty status:	11.9%	0.2% Other	**2000 Presidential Vote**		
Military veterans:	15.3%	29.5% Hispanic Origin	Bush (R)	114,193	(59%)
			Gore (D)	75,561	(39%)
			Other	5,217	(3%)
			Cook Partisan Voting Index: R +10		

Occupation   Blue collar: 24.4%   White collar: 58.1%   Gray collar: 17.5%

The California coast between Los Angeles and San Diego has never entirely filled up with development—and never will as long as the Marine Corps retains custody of Camp Pendleton, the giant training base just south of the Orange-San Diego County line and the Corps' largest expeditionary training facility on the West Coast. The land along the coast and inland in northern San Diego County, usually referred to as North County, was largely empty territory a quarter century ago—never fertile enough to produce a large farm community, never endowed with much manufacturing, never actively promoted as a retirement community. But North County has been growing rapidly since then. Today about one million people live here, and who can blame them? For this is one of America's most beautiful and comfortable environments, with ocean and mountain scenery, sunny and warm weather, no rural poverty and low crime. Here, amid dry but not desert landscape, you can see miles of rolling hills, with occasional surrealistic trees and sagebrush-like bushes; mountains clump up not in ridges, but here and there, seemingly at random. This land has attracted thousands of new migrants—many, but by no means all, retirees.

The 49th Congressional District of California occupies the northern part of San Diego County and the southwestern corner of Riverside County. It was the fastest-growing California district in the 1990s, with a population increase of 35%; it grew another 14% between 2000 and 2005. On the coast next to Camp Pendleton is Oceanside, a lower-middle-income town heavily dependent on the base; local business declined in early 2003 when thousands of residents went off to war. Inland is Vista, a higher-income community that calls itself the "climatic wonderland of the United States," with day after day of blue skies, sunshine and average high temperatures that range from 68 degrees in January to 82 degrees in July. About 40% of the district's population is in these two areas. About 30% are in small communities in North County, including a small portion of San Diego. Another 30% are in Riverside County. Here is the instant city of Temecula: a corner-grocery town serving a vineyard district in the mid-1980s, it is now the center of an increasingly congested area with more than 100,000 people, mostly commuters attracted by low-priced homes and traditional values. To the north are the older communities of Lake Elsinore, Canyon Lake and Perris. Politically, this is a heavily Republican area, which rarely elects Democrats to any office; it voted 63% for George W. Bush in 2004.

The congressman from the 49th District is Darrell Issa (pronounced *EYE-sah*), a Republican first elected in 2000. He grew up in a Lebanese-Christian family in a heavily Jewish neighborhood of Cleveland, and graduated from Sienna Heights University in Adrian, Michigan. To compensate for dyslexia, he studies hard and attempts to memorize prepared statements. After his Army service, Issa started the Viper car alarm company in Cleveland, moved the business to North County and renamed it Directed Electronics, where it became the world's largest manufacturer of vehicle security systems, with the industry's largest R&D budget. The firm, the first with a programmable personal computer system, made him a fortune estimated at $200 million as he found a way to capitalize legally on America's high property crime rates. He became active in the high-tech industry, serving as chairman of the Consumer Electronics Association. In the early 1990s he turned to politics, contributing to Republicans and chairing the 1996 campaign to pass Proposition 209, which banned state use of racial quotas and preferences. In 1998 he ran for the Senate seat of Barbara Boxer and spent $9.8 million of his own money. But he lost the Republican primary 45%-40% to Matt Fong.

In November 1999, when North County incumbent Ron Packard announced his retirement, it was obvious that his successor would be chosen in the Republican primary. Although there were 10 candidates, the race turned into a bruising two-man contest between Issa and state Senator Bill Morrow; former Congressman Robert Dornan expressed interest in a comeback attempt, but he deferred to his son, Mark Dornan, who trailed well behind. Morrow questioned Issa's business practices. Issa raised questions about his opponent's honesty. On most issues, the candidates took similar positions; they supported streamlining government, opposed abortion and favored rebuilding the military. Issa spent $1.5 million of his own money on the primary, and beat Morrow 46%-30%. In the fall the Democratic nominee disconnected his phone and abandoned his campaign because his party, predictably, gave him little support. Issa won 61%-28%.

In the House, Issa's voting record has been relatively moderate, especially on foreign issues where he is unusually active. On the eve of George W. Bush's decision to start military action in Afghanistan, Issa joined Democrat Robert Wexler, who is Jewish, in a visit to several Middle East nations to build support for the United States. During that trip, he suggested that he was the victim of racial profiling when he was kept off an Air France flight to Paris; the airline claimed that he was late. After he hesitatingly voted for a House resolution expressing solidarity with Israel, he voiced reservations about its lack of evenhandedness. In December 2001, the issue of terrorism hit close to home: two members of the militant Jewish Defense League were charged with plotting to blow up Issa's office in San Clemente and a Culver City mosque; one died in 2002 and the other pled guilty to civil rights and weapons violations in September 2005.

In 2005, he took a leave of absence from Energy and Commerce, and reclaimed his seniority at the International Relations and Judiciary Committees. Issa has sought to cut back on illegal immigrants in the United States and to prevent them from getting driver's licenses, and he demanded more vigorous prosecution of smuggling across the border. Drawing on his experience as a patent holder (he holds 37 of them), Issa has been a key player on patent reform issues. He co-sponsored Howard Berman's legislation to create a post-grant review of already-issued patents and to establish an "apportionment rule" for calculating damages in a patent lawsuit; he worked to broker a deal that would satisfy both the drugmakers who oppose the bill and the high-tech firms that support it. On the Government Reform Committee, he chaired the Energy and Resources Subcommittee, and sought to use his private sector technology experience to oversee federal programs. Twice, he ran and lost for chairman of the Republican Policy Committee.

Issa decided against another challenge to Boxer in 2004. In 2003, he spent $1.7 million of his own money on the campaign to get the signatures needed for a special election to recall Governor Gray Davis; without his money, the drive would have failed. He hinted that he would run for governor on the replacement ballot. But when Arnold Schwarzenegger entered the field just before the deadline, Issa tearfully announced that he would not run. He had been weakened by Democratic charges against him that were linked to decades-old news reports of possible criminal activity in Ohio; a judge had dismissed the prosecutor's charges. After Schwarzenegger won, Issa was an early supporter of his non-partisan redistricting proposal and made known his interest in running for lieutenant governor in 2006. But Republicans chose conservative Tom McClintock. In 2005, Issa castigated Tom Tancredo for supporting the anti-illegal immigrant Minuteman Party candidate for the open House seat in the adjacent 48th District. He has continuing ambition to run statewide.

FIFTIETH DISTRICT

Rep. Brian Bilbray (R)

Elected June 2006, 4th full term; b. Jan. 28, 1951, Coronado; home, Carlsbad; Attended SW Commun. Col., 1970-72, 1974; Catholic; married (Karen).

Elected Office: Imperial Beach City Cncl., 1976-78; Imperial Beach Mayor, 1978-84; San Diego Cnty. Bd. of Supervisors, 1984-94; U.S. House of Reps., 1994-2000.

Professional Career: Tax consultant, 1972-present; Lobbyist, 2001-05.

DC Office: 227 CHOB, 20515, 202-225-0508; Fax: 202-225-2558; Web site: www.house.gov/bilbray.

District Offices: Solana Beach, 858-350-1150.

Committees: *Oversight & Government Reform* (16th of 18 R): Government Management, Organization & Procurement (RMM); Domestic Policy. *Science & Technology* (18th of 20 R): Research & Science Education. *Veterans' Affairs* (10th of 13 R): Oversight & Investigations.

Group Ratings (Only Served Partial Term)

	ADA	ACLU	AFS	LCV	ITIC	NTU	COC	ACU	CFG	FRC
2006	5	25	0	0	100	—	100	94	—	83
2005	—	—	—	—	—	—	—	—	—	—

National Journal Ratings (Only Served Partial Term)

	2005 LIB	—	2005 CONS		2006 LIB	—	2006 CONS
Economic	*	—	*		*	—	*
Social	*	—	*		27%	—	73%
Foreign	*	—	*		*	—	*

Key Votes of the 109th Congress (Only Served Partial Term)

1. Estate Tax Repeal	*	5. Limit Interstate Abortion	*	9. Build Border Fence	Y
2. Limit CAFE Standards	*	6. Extend Patriot Act	*	10. CAFTA	*
3. FY06 Spending Curb	*	7. Bar Same Sex Marriage	Y	11. Oppose Iraq Withdrawal	Y
4. Drilling in ANWR	*	8. Stem Cell Research $	Y	12. Detainee Tribunals	Y

Election Results

2006 general	Brian Bilbray (R)	118,018	(53%)	($2,619,848)
	Francine Busby (D)	96,612	(43%)	($3,596,185)
	Other	7,472	(3%)	
2006 primary	Brian Bilbray (R)	41,545	(54%)	
	Eric Roach (R)	10,617	(14%)	
	Bill Hauf (R)	9,952	(13%)	
	Bill Morrow (R)	4,788	(6%)	
	Howard Kaloogian (R)	3,689	(5%)	
	Other	6,305	(8%)	
2006 special	Brian Bilbray (R)	78,341	(50%)	
	Francine Busby (D)	71,146	(45%)	
	William Griffith (I)	6,027	(4%)	
	Other	2,519	(1%)	
2006 spec. primary	Francine Busby (D)	60,010	(44%)	
	Brian Bilbray (R)	20,952	(15%)	
	Eric Roach (R)	19,891	(14%)	
	Howard Kaloogian (R)	10,207	(7%)	
	Bill Morrow (R)	7,369	(5%)	
	Alan Uke (R)	5,477	(4%)	
	Other	13,297	(10%)	
2004 general	Randy (Duke) Cunningham (R)	169,025	(58%)	($939,542)
	Francine Busby (D)	105,590	(36%)	($212,406)
	Other	14,713	(5%)	

Prior Winning Percentages: 1998 (49%); 1996 (53%); 1994 (49%)

The People		Race/Ethnic Origin	Ancestry		
Area size:	365 sq. mi.	65.8% White	German: 11.5%	English: 8.8%	
Urban population:	97.8%	1.8% Black	Irish: 8.6%		
Rural population:	2.2%	10.3% Asian	**2004 Presidential Vote**		
Pop. 2000:	639,087	0.3% Native Am.	Bush (R)	169,935	(55%)
Pop. 2005 (est):	697,741	0.2% Hawaiian	Kerry (D)	135,007	(44%)
Median income:	$59,813	2.6% Two+ races	Other	2,891	(1%)
Poverty status:	8.1%	0.2% Other	**2000 Presidential Vote**		
Military veterans:	13.4%	18.8% Hispanic Origin	Bush (R)	136,311	(54%)
			Gore (D)	107,436	(43%)
			Other	8,996	(4%)
			Cook Partisan Voting Index: R + 5		

Occupation   Blue collar: 15.7%   White collar: 70.8%   Gray collar: 13.5%

Soledad Mountain looms over La Jolla, the affluent San Diego neighborhood, overlooking the Pacific Ocean to the west, the hills of San Diego and, past them, the flat expanse of Miramar Marine Corps Air Station. Here a visitor to San Diego can stand in the sunshine and see the Blue Angels perform aerial stunts. It is a sight no one could have seen half a century before: Miramar then was a small airfield, military planes could do nothing like those stunts and San Diego, even after heavy activity in its Navy bases in World War II, was still a small urban center well to the south. Most of the land you would see looking east and north from Soledad Mountain was empty landscape. Since then San Diego has become the nation's eighth-largest city, barely behind San Antonio. Development has jumped over Miramar, where plans are underway to locate a national veterans' cemetery, to the inland communities of Escondido and San Marcos and beyond the old Del Mar race track. These are pleasant and affluent communities, attractively planned, many with red tile roofs that contrast with the tan hillsides. Local officials have explored sites to replace the San Diego airport, which is on a small piece of downtown land with one runway and little room for expansion. In November 2006, voters rejected a referendum to use part of Miramar as a civilian airport.

The 50th Congressional District of California covers much of this part of San Diego County. About 40% of its population is in the city of San Diego, including most of scenic La Jolla with its pricey boutiques, hillside Clairemont, Carmel Valley and University City to the west and, north of Miramar, Mira Mesa, Rancho Penasquitos and part of Rancho Bernardo. About 25% are on or near the coast, from Del Mar, where a 1,000 foot pier was opened in 1917 but washed away in 1926, to Encinitas and Carlsbad, home of the La Costa resort. Just inland is Rancho Santa Fe, one of the wealthiest communities in the nation, with multi-million dollar mansions set amid rolling hills and lush greenery. About 30% of the people are in Escondido and fast-growing San Marcos. Politically, this has been Republican territory, more so as one gets away from the coast, but liberal Democratic Senator Barbara Boxer nearly carried it in 2004. In 2006, though, the 50th delivered 70% to Arnold Schwarzenegger in the governor's race.

The congressman from the 50th District is Brian Bilbray, a Republican who served in Congress from 1995-2001 and then returned to win a June 2006 special election. Bilbray was born in Coronado and grew up on naval bases and in Imperial Beach. He owned a tax preparation business and was elected to the Imperial Beach Council in 1976, at 25, then mayor two years later, and to the San Diego County Board of Supervisors in 1984, where he worked for environmental protections and economic development. He made his first big splash in 1980, when he mounted a skiploader and built a berm to keep the sewage-polluted Tijuana River from seeping into the San Diego County beaches. An experienced surfer, he made news again in 1984 when as Imperial Beach mayor he paddled out on his surfboard to battle a fire raging on the city pier. In 1994, he defeated first-term Democrat Lynn Schenck, who had a moderate voting record but voted for the 1993 Clinton budget and tax increases. In a politically marginal district, Bilbray worked on many immigration issues; he voted for the impeachment of Bill Clinton, though he conceded at the time that it may be the issue that "drives a nail through my political coffin." That comment proved prescient as Bilbray lost 50%-46% in 2000 to Susan Davis, who said that Bilbray "talks moderate in San Diego but votes conservative in Washington."

After spending the intervening years as a lobbyist, Bilbray returned to Congress in a more Republican district than the one he previously represented for three terms. The seat opened when Republican Randy (Duke) Cunningham, a former decorated Navy pilot, pleaded guilty in November 2005 to evading taxes and taking more than $2 million in bribes for using his influence to help a defense contractor and was sentenced to eight years in federal prison. Bilbray was an early frontrunner in the contest, but he faced competitive contests in the special primary and special general election. His chief Republican opponents were more conservative: state senator Bill Morrow, former Assemblyman Howard Kaloogian and wealthy businessman Eric Roach. They criticized Bilbray for serving as a lobbyist and claimed his voting record in Congress had been too liberal. Bilbray highlighted his work with a non-profit group that opposed illegal immigration. Bilbray won the Republican nomination in the April special primary with 15% of the total vote cast to 14% for Roach, 7% for Kaloogian and 5% for Morrow. Francine Busby, a professor of women's studies and local school board member, who got 36% against Cunningham in 2004, cruised to the Democratic nomination with 44% of the total vote.

Spotting an opportunity to take a long-time Republican seat and gain momentum for the 2006 national campaign, Democrats invested heavily in Busby, even as they conceded that she was a flawed candidate. EMILY's List, which had ignored Busby in 2004, became an active supporter with hundreds of thousands of dollars in contributions; by mid-May, Busby had collected more than $2 million, roughly 10 times the amount she raised against Cunningham. Exploiting local disgust with Cunningham and other recent San Diego politicians who suffered from legal problems, Busby embraced the national Democratic theme that Washington was mired in a "culture of corruption," and she criticized Bilbray for taking campaign money from oil companies. Bilbray said that Busby had been "disingenuous" about her negative campaigning and had no positions of her own on immigration and pollution at the border with Mexico. The two national parties spent millions of dollars on the contest. Busby made a crucial mistake at a campaign event five days before the June 6 special general election when she told a questioner at a group of campaign supporters that "you don't need papers for voting, you don't need to be a registered voter to help." Busby later explained that she misspoke but Republicans seized on the comment as an invitation for illegal aliens to vote and blitzed the air waves with a final round of ads highlighting the gaffe. Bilbray won 50%-45% in what had once been thought of as a solidly Republican district. Bilbray said that anti-immigration sentiment drove his victory.

Upon his return to the House, Bilbray joined the Armed Services Committee and his voting record became more conservative on social issues. On the Veterans Affairs Committee, he won approval of a provision to give free credit monitoring and insurance against costs to veterans affected by computer security breaches. He was reelected 53%-43% against Busby in a November

2006 rematch that received far less national attention than their contest five months earlier. In 2007, he replaced Tom Tancredo as chairman of the Immigration Reform Caucus. But he lost his seat on Armed Services because of the Democratic takeover.

FIFTY-FIRST DISTRICT

Rep. Bob Filner (D)

Elected 1992, 8th term; b. Sept. 4, 1942, Pittsburgh, PA; home, San Diego; Cornell U., B.A. 1963, Ph.D. 1973, U. of DE, M.A. 1969; Jewish; married (Jane Merrill).

Elected Office: San Diego Schl. Bd., 1979-83, Pres., 1982-83; San Diego City Cncl., 1987-92, Dpty. Mayor, 1991.

Professional Career: Prof., San Diego St. U., 1970-92; Legis. Asst., U.S. Sen. Hubert Humphrey, 1974; Legis. Asst., U.S. Rep. Don Fraser, 1975.

DC Office: 2428 RHOB, 20515, 202-225-8045; Fax: 202-225-9073; Web site: www.house.gov/filner.

District Offices: Chula Vista, 619-422-5963; Imperial, 760-355-8800.

Committees: *Transportation & Infrastructure* (8th of 41 D): Aviation; Water Resources & Environment; Highways & Transit. *Veterans' Affairs* (Chmn. of 16 D).

Group Ratings

	ADA	ACLU	AFS	LCV	ITIC	NTU	COC	ACU	CFG	FRC
2006	95	100	86	92	14	15	33	12	13	0
2005	95	—	100	89	—	20	37	4	10	8

National Journal Ratings

	2005 LIB	—	2005 CONS		2006 LIB	—	2006 CONS
Economic	81%	—	18%		72%	—	27%
Social	87%	—	12%		97%	—	0%
Foreign	96%	—	0%		92%	—	5%

Key Votes of the 109th Congress

1. Estate Tax Repeal	Y	5. Limit Interstate Abortion	N	9. Build Border Fence		N
2. Limit CAFE Standards	N	6. Extend Patriot Act	N	10. CAFTA		N
3. FY06 Spending Curb	N	7. Bar Same Sex Marriage	N	11. Oppose Iraq Withdrawal		N
4. Drilling in ANWR	N	8. Stem Cell Research $	Y	12. Detainee Tribunals		N

Election Results

2006 general	Bob Filner (D)	78,114	(67%)	($2,001,750)
	Blake Miles (R)	34,931	(30%)	($66,656)
	Other	2,794	(2%)	
2006 primary	Bob Filner (D)	23,312	(51%)	
	Juan Vargas (D)	19,364	(43%)	
	Daniel Ramirez (D)	2,862	(6%)	
2004 general	Bob Filner (D)	111,441	(62%)	($657,867)
	Michael Giorgino (R)	63,526	(35%)	($111,778)
	Other	5,912	(3%)	

Prior Winning Percentages: 2002 (58%); 2000 (68%); 1998 (99%); 1996 (62%); 1994 (57%); 1992 (57%)

The People		Race/Ethnic Origin	Ancestry	
Area size:	4,896 sq. mi.	21.3% White	German: 4.2%	Irish: 3.3%
Urban population:	95.6%	9.4% Black	English: 2.9%	
Rural population:	4.4%	12.4% Asian	**2004 Presidential Vote**	
Pop. 2000:	639,087	0.5% Native Am.	Kerry (D) 100,062	(53%)
Pop. 2005 (est):	688,278	0.6% Hawaiian	Bush (R) 85,762	(46%)
Median income:	$39,243	2.4% Two+ races	Other 1,731	(1%)
Poverty status:	16.3%	0.2% Other	**2000 Presidential Vote**	
Military veterans:	12.2%	53.3% Hispanic Origin	Gore (D) 85,561	(57%)
			Bush (R) 61,008	(41%)
			Other 3,819	(3%)
			Cook Partisan Voting Index: D + 7	

Occupation   Blue collar: 23.5%   White collar: 54.7%   Gray collar: 21.8%

San Diego, at one corner of the continental United States, not so long ago a small Navy town known for its good harbor and splendid weather, is now a major metropolis, a city of 1.26 million people and the center of a county of 2.9 million. It is also, to its sometime discomfort, one of the largest cities anywhere directly on an international border and between countries with strikingly different economic conditions, political systems and cultural traditions. On a daily basis, agents for the Border Patrol play a cat-and-mouse and sometimes violent game with illegal immigrants trying to make the crossing. About 127,000 were apprehended in 2005, but many more crossed the border in this area without being captured. In 2006, authorities found a sophisticated tunnel dug under the border for drug-running.

This is the busiest border crossing in the world, but most of San Diego seems to look away, toward the ocean. Tijuana looks to the United States, to the lower-income part of San Diego—the industrial zone on brown hills in Otay Mesa and San Ysidro, the industrial suburbs of Chula Vista and National City and the grid streets south of downtown and behind the harbor in San Diego itself. Many children from Mexico cross the border daily to attend public and private schools. Latinos pour billions into the San Diego economy and are scattered in various parts of the city, in the southern corridor and in Encanto and Chollas Park in the east. Thousands of workers legally cross the border every day; without them, this would be a much quieter place. Outside of the Sacramento area, this is the fastest growing region in California. Oddly, there is not much evidence of Mexican style in San Diego—less even than in Los Angeles, as if the border city was insisting on its Yanqui origins, just as San Diego's civic leaders bridled at the idea of a bi-national airport on the border, even though their single-runway airport is unable to meet demand. Even the city's favorite symbol, the red Tijuana Trolley that takes tourists from downtown to the San Ysidro-Tijuana border station, is as resolutely Yanqui as Main Street in Disneyland.

The 51st Congressional District of California covers all of California's border with Mexico, including the southeast corner of San Diego, National City and Chula Vista on San Diego Bay, and San Ysidro and Otay Mesa, which are part of the city of San Diego, connected to the rest by lines running down the harbor. The 51st also extends east to the Arizona border to include all of Imperial County, with its string of farms and towns running south from the Salton Sea to Mexicali, Mexico. The water comes from the Colorado River through the All-American Canal; the Salton Sea was created when the canal burst in 1905 and water flowed into the lowest part of the desert. With farm land being turned into moderately priced subdivisions, rapidly growing Imperial County in 2005 had 144,000 people, 77% Hispanic. With its abundant open land, some planners in San Diego see Imperial as a promising site for their new airport—connected, perhaps, by a magnetic levitation train at 270 miles per hour. Districtwide in 2000, 73% of the people lived in San Diego, National City and Chula Vista, 19% in Imperial County and only 8% elsewhere. Minorities now make up 80% of the population; Hispanics are a majority here and there are large numbers of Filipinos. This was created to be a solidly Democratic district, but may be becoming less so: Al Gore won 57% of the vote here, and John Kerry won only 53%. In 2006, Republican Governor Arnold Schwarzenegger carried the district 52%-43%, with most of that margin coming from the San Diego County portion.

The congressman from the 51st District is Bob Filner, a Democrat first elected in 1992. Filner grew up in New York City and was a Freedom Rider in 1961, imprisoned for two months in Mississippi. He earned a Ph.D. at Cornell, taught history at San Diego State and directed the Lipinsky Institute for Judaic Studies; he took time off to work on Senator Hubert Humphrey's staff in the 1970s, was elected to the San Diego school board in 1979 and to the city council in 1987. The 1992 redistricting created a new Democratic seat in San Diego County, and Filner decided to run.

He was strongly backed by local activists although he had two better-known rivals. Filner won with 26%, to 23% for Waddie Deddeh, state senator and assemblyman since 1966; 20% for Jim Bates, four-term congressman defeated in 1990 after being disciplined for sexual harassment; and 19% for Juan Carlos Vargas.

Filner is politically savvy, with some original ideas about policy, aggressive in articulating his views, and has one of the most liberal voting records in the House. His style can be confrontational. He engaged in a heated argument with Joe Wilson of South Carolina on C-SPAN in 2002, and in August 2007 made headlines when he was charged with assault and battery after an altercation with an airline employee at Dulles International Airport. His office released a statement calling the charges "ridiculous." It was later revealed that in 2003 Filner had been involved in a dispute at an immigration detention facility surrounding a visit to a detainee; according to a Justice Department incident report, Filner told officials, "I am a Congressman and I can do whatever I want, I want to see my constituent and I am not moving from here until I do so." The report also noted that Filner later apologized and "admitted handling the situation incorrectly."

In 1998, Filner was one of only five House members to vote against both parties' impeachment inquiries. He voted against the use of force in Iraq. In 2004, he was the only member of the California delegation not to sign a letter seeking a waiver from a Clean Air Act provision requiring the state to add oxygenates to fuel; Filner saw an opportunity for ethanol made from sugar cane grown in Imperial County. He supported truckers blockading the border because of long waits they were facing, but he opposed an expansion of the border station at San Ysidro because he feared that I-5 construction would split the community geographically.

The new chairman of the Veterans' Affairs Committee, Filner has long been a vocal advocate of veterans' rights, a popular cause in a district of many military retirees. He sought to pay benefits to merchant mariners who served during World War II and often encountered hazardous conditions. Outraged by the treatment of Filipino veterans to whom promises were made but not delivered, he got Congress to hold hearings and approve some benefits. Filner took interim duties as ranking Democrat at the Veterans committee in May 2006, due to the lengthy illness of Lane Evans, who retired at the end of the year. Later that year, he won bipartisan action in the House to improve data security at the Veterans Affairs Department, following reports of a major computer security lapse. He became chairman following a heated contest with Mike Michaud of Maine, who criticized Filner's problems in working with Republicans and some of the veterans' groups. Filner cited praise from major veterans' organizations; bolstered by Nancy Pelosi, with whom he sometimes had a testy relationship, he won the Caucus vote over Michaud, 112-69. In January 2007, Filner announced plans for a major overhaul of the GI Bill, first enacted in 1944. He said that revelations of disrepair at the Walter Reed Army Medical Center were "the tip of the iceberg."

In the 1996 primary, Filner was again opposed by Juan Carlos Vargas, by then on the San Diego Council. Filner won, but by just 55%-45%. After redistricting replaced heavily Latino parts of San Diego with Imperial County, in 2002 he faced Danny Ramirez, an Imperial County businessman. Filner won 70%-30%, despite losing 60%-40% in Imperial County. In 2006, Vargas challenged Filner for a third time. The bitter primary contest featured ethics charges from each side. Vargas, by then a term-limited assemblyman, said that Filner had paid his wife more than $500,000 in campaign funds for her consulting services, which she operated from their condominium in Washington. Filner spotlighted questionable campaign payments by Vargas to his brother-in-law, who was a lobbyist for realtors. Each cited potential parallels to recently imprisoned former Congressman Duke Cunningham from the neighboring 50th District. Filner benefited from his constituent work in Imperial County, where Vargas was not well known despite his Hispanics ties, and won 51%-43%. In San Diego County, which cast 78% of the total vote, Filner led 50%-45%. He took Imperial County 55%-34%. "People vote for the person who's going to be the most effective for them, not by their last name," Filner said. He had his usual easy win in November.

FIFTY-SECOND DISTRICT

Rep. Duncan Hunter (R)

Elected 1980, 14th term; b. May 31, 1948, Riverside; home, Alpine; U. of MT, U. of CA, Western St. U., B.S.L & J.D. 1976; Baptist; married (Lynne).

Military Career: Army, 1969-71 (Vietnam).

Professional Career: Practicing atty., 1976-80.

DC Office: 2265 RHOB, 20515, 202-225-5672; Fax: 202-225-0235; Web site: www.house.gov/hunter.

District Offices: El Cajon, 619-448-5201.

Committees: *Armed Services* (RMM of 29 R).

Group Ratings

	ADA	ACLU	AFS	LCV	ITIC	NTU	COC	ACU	CFG	FRC
2006	5	5	0	0	71	62	93	88	63	100
2005	5	—	0	6	—	56	88	92	49	100

National Journal Ratings

	2005 LIB	—	2005 CONS		2006 LIB	—	2006 CONS
Economic	9%	—	88%		21%	—	77%
Social	0%	—	89%		10%	—	90%
Foreign	17%	—	79%		16%	—	84%

Key Votes of the 109th Congress

1. Estate Tax Repeal	Y	5. Limit Interstate Abortion	Y	9. Build Border Fence	Y
2. Limit CAFE Standards	Y	6. Extend Patriot Act	Y	10. CAFTA	N
3. FY06 Spending Curb	Y	7. Bar Same Sex Marriage	Y	11. Oppose Iraq Withdrawal	Y
4. Drilling in ANWR	Y	8. Stem Cell Research $	N	12. Detainee Tribunals	Y

Election Results

2006 general	Duncan Hunter (R)	123,696	(65%)	($1,042,928)
	John Rinaldi (D)	61,208	(32%)	($80,423)
	Other	6,465	(3%)	
2006 primary	Duncan Hunter (R)	unopposed		
2004 general	Duncan Hunter (R)	187,799	(69%)	($1,058,126)
	Brian Keliher (D)	74,857	(28%)	($14,828)
	Other	8,782	(3%)	

Prior Winning Percentages: 2002 (70%); 2000 (65%); 1998 (76%); 1996 (65%); 1994 (64%); 1992 (53%); 1990 (73%); 1988 (74%); 1986 (77%); 1984 (75%); 1982 (69%); 1980 (53%)

The People		Race/Ethnic Origin	Ancestry	
Area size:	2,129 sq. mi.	72.9% White	German: 12.5% Irish: 9.1%	
Urban population:	93.6%	3.7% Black	English: 8.5%	
Rural population:	6.4%	5.4% Asian	**2004 Presidential Vote**	
Pop. 2000:	639,087	0.7% Native Am.	Bush (R)	177,055 (61%)
Pop. 2005 (est):	683,859	0.3% Hawaiian	Kerry (D)	108,806 (38%)
Median income:	$52,940	3.2% Two+ races	Other	2,509 (1%)
Poverty status:	8.1%	0.2% Other	**2000 Presidential Vote**	
Military veterans:	16.0%	13.7% Hispanic Origin	Bush (R)	143,081 (57%)
			Gore (D)	98,633 (40%)
			Other	7,833 (3%)
			Cook Partisan Voting Index: R + 9	

Occupation	Blue collar: 18.2%	White collar: 67.7%	Gray collar: 14.1%

San Diego began as a port, but today most metropolitan area residents live out of sight of the sea, in hilltop neighborhoods inland that look out over distant ridges and freeways or in warm, sunny valleys amid the mountains which become denser and higher as one travels east from the Pacific.

There is a discernible difference in attitudes and values between those who have settled inland and those nearer the ocean, part of the split between Coastal California and Interior California that has been crucial in the state's political struggles and culture wars. In San Diego, both groups tend to identify as Republicans, and coastal people may be more affluent. But those who settle inland are more likely to be conventionally religious and to have traditional moral values; they tend to be more supportive of the military and assertive foreign policy; they are more dubious about the ability of government to shape poor citizens' lives. They are more conservative on most of the cultural and foreign issues of recent times, and therefore more reliably Republican: When oceanfront voters in San Diego shifted sharply toward Democrats in the 1990s, the movement was much less among voters inland. Inland San Diego County produced higher percentages for George W. Bush in 2004 than in 2000, while coastal San Diego County did not.

The 52d Congressional District of California takes in many of the inland San Diego suburbs and most of the mountain and desert interior of San Diego County. It includes the part of San Diego north of I-8 and east of I-15; Santee, an East County city of 53,000; and El Cajon, which has the nation's second largest (after the Detroit area) community of Chaldeans, Catholic Arabs from Iraq, who own perhaps half of San Diego County's independent retail convenience storesand are known for their toughness—it was not easy being a Christian in Saddam Hussein's Iraq. The district also includes high-income Poway, north of San Diego, and more modest La Mesa, east of San Diego. The mountains and the desert to the east are lightly inhabited. In the mountains is tiny Alpine with one Indian casino and another sought by a tribe with a membership of seven adults and one child. In the desert is the town of Borrego Springs amid the giant Anza-Borrego Desert State Park. This East County area was swept by horrific fires in October and November 2003, which killed 17 people and destroyed more than 2,400 homes; in 2006 wildflowers were growing in the burnt-out El Capitan trail. Politically, this is a solidly Republican district.

The congressman from the 52d District is Duncan Hunter, a Republican first elected in 1980, an upset winner in the Reagan landslide who served four years as chairman of the House Armed Services Committee. He grew up on a ranch outside Riverside, where his father was a real estate developer. He dropped out of college to serve in the Army, and was awarded a Bronze Star for his service in 24 helicopter combat assaults in Vietnam. He farmed briefly in the Snake River Valley in Idaho, then attended Western State University law school and graduated in 1976. After that he practiced law in San Diego's Barrio Logan. In 1980 his father urged him to run against Democratic Congressman Lionel Van Deerlin in what had been a safe Democratic district. But it was a Republican year in southern California and Hunter won 53%-47%. "Your real campaign is just starting," his father told him. "You've got to get on Armed Services." He did, and redistricting gave him a safe Republican seat. In the 1980s he was part of the group of young conservative Republicans around Newt Gingrich, but he concentrated on military issues.

On the committee, Hunter supported the Reagan defense buildup and was an ardent backer of the Strategic Defense Initiative, which had few backers in the services or among senior committee members, and of the 600-ship Navy. After the 1994 election he failed in his attempt to get into the Republican leadership when he lost the Conference chairmanship to John Boehner. But he became chairman of the Military Procurement Subcommittee. He worked to accelerate development of the F-22, arguing that the Navy needed a stealth-equipped carrier plane. He argued for building more B-2s and against reducing the number of B-1s. He tried to push the Pentagon to build more nuclear submarines and match apparent Russian gains in quiet technology.

Hunter argued for many years that the Clinton administration cut defense spending far too much, and he was willing to buck the Republican leadership and the incoming Bush administration to get more spending. He was disappointed with the increase in the first Bush budget, and in November 2001 called for a $32 billion increase in current spending, and said the administration was trying to "conduct an aggressive Ronald Reagan foreign policy with a Jimmy Carter defense budget." By January 2002 he was asking the Bush administration for a $50 billion increase in the next fiscal year; later, when the administration called for a $45 billion increase, he said he wanted $30 billion more than that.

As chairman of the Armed Services Committee, in January 2003 he revised the subcommittee structure, establishing a new subcommittee on emerging threats and giving the other subcommittees jurisdiction based on service activities rather than Pentagon procedures. On some issues Hunter was at odds with the Bush administration. He said that the campaign in Afghanistan, fought with no area air bases, showed the need for more B-2s and B-1s. He called for more F-22s than the Pentagon wanted and was an enthusiastic supporter of the Joint Strike Fighter. He said there was a danger that the military was no longer capable of fighting two wars at the same time and he argued that Defense Secretary Donald Rumsfeld's plans for transforming the military should be accompanied by a buildup in troops. In November 2002 he argued that the administration's budget request still left the military $30 billion behind on modernization projects; he got the administration to back down on the issue of full retirement and disability benefits for veterans with Purple Hearts or injured during training or hazardous duty. Hunter has also frustrated the Senate: Senator Richard Lugar charged that he and Curt Weldon took money away from the Nunn-Lugar program to dismantle Russian weapons of mass destruction to pay for weapons programs.

In 2003 Hunter supported the administration budget request but disagreed with the cancellation of the Crusader armed vehicle and tried to postpone the 2005 base closing round. He added more B-1s and B-2s and authorization for a new bomber. Hunter has long favored restrictions on trade—he opposed NAFTA, GATT, normal trade relations with China and trade promotion authority and endorsed Patrick Buchanan in the 1996 presidential primaries—and in 2001 he barred the Army from buying berets made in China. In the 2003 defense authorization he increased the percentage of purchases that must be bought in America; this was opposed by the administration and led to a long deadlock with the Senate. In September 2003 Hunter and ranking Democrat Ike Skelton backed a permanent increase in the Army from 485,000 to 525,000. In early 2004 Hunter lined up House Republicans to back George W. Bush's $421 billion defense spending request against other claims on the money and called for a new international agency to keep weapons from terrorists. He supported Defense Secretary Donald Rumsfeld during the clamor about the Abu Ghraib abuses in May 2004 and pointedly refused to hold hearings on the subject as the Senate Armed Services Committee was doing; despite the media prominence of the charges, he argued that the abuse didn't warrant a congressional investigation. He worked to give combat commanders "an available checkbook" to buy needed equipment like protective armor without going through the Pentagon procurement process.

Hunter played a major role on the intelligence reorganization bill in late 2004. In October Joint Chiefs Chairman Richard Myers told him that the new director of national intelligence could use his budgetary power to interrupt the flow of intelligence to the battlefield; Hunter urged him to put that in writing, which he did. At a closed-door meeting of House Republican leaders November 20 Hunter demanded changes in the intelligence bill that had come out of the conference committee, because the Senate had removed White House language assuring the secretary of defense power over military intelligence. He said that troops in the field would be imperiled and noted that his son Duncan Duane Hunter, who enlisted in the Marine Corps after September 11, was serving in Iraq. Speaker Dennis Hastert pulled the bill from the floor and negotiations commenced. On December 6 Hunter accepted language proposed by Senator Susan Collins that the bill "respects and does not abrogate the statutory responsibilities of the heads of departments," and the administration agreed to issue regulations maintaining the flow of intelligence from aircraft and satellites to troops in the field. In June 2005 he held up the nomination of John Negroponte until he agreed to meet with him before transferring anyone from DOD intelligence work to other duties.

In 2005 Hunter again supported administration requests but sought more. He and Skelton questioned whether the Navy would have enough ships. He insisted the refueling tankers be built by an American firm. He abandoned an effort to regulate women in combat and removed an amendment extending the Tricare medical insurance program to all National Guard units regardless of activation status. The $441.6 billion bill included an across-the-board 3.1% pay raise for members of the military. Hunter pushed a $512.9 billion authorization, approved by committee in May 2006. He amended it with substitute language on military tribunals; the conference committee dropped a provision requiring reporting of CIA secret prisons. This bill eventually went to $532.8 billion, with a 2.2% pay increase and provisions limiting the retirement of B-2s and U-2s, and continued purchases of C-17s.

Hunter was angered by the large number of illegal immigrants in the early 1990s, and at one point he called for using military aircraft for "deep deportation" of illegal immigrants. He wrote the 1997 law requiring the 14-mile, 15-foot-high steel mesh fence along the Mexican border from the Pacific Ocean to Otay Mountain. When the California Coastal Commission rejected the plan to build the remaining four miles to the ocean because it would fill in gulleys and interrupt the flow of a stream, Hunter denounced the decision as "nutty." In February 2005 he managed to include an override of this state decision in James Sensenbrenner's driver's license and asylum bill. In May 2006 he included language in the defense authorization finishing the San Diego fence and building another on the border on either side of Laredo. In September 2006, the House passed Hunter's law authorizing 700 miles of border fence; it passed the Senate 80-19 on the last day of the session. Hunter was one of the leading opponents of the Dubai Ports deal in March 2006. He and Orrin

Hatch have worked on bills to compensate World War II veterans captured by the Japanese and used as slave laborers. For years he has been fighting to get around a 1999 federal court decision ordering the city of San Diego to take down the memorial cross atop Soledad Mountain, east of La Jolla. In July 2006 he got a provision in the defense authorization to transfer the land to the federal government; it was signed into law in August. He also got a provision prohibiting civilian use of Miramar Field and two other military airbases near San Diego and another extending, for military veterans and their families, private hunting operations on Santa Rosa Island in the Channel Islands National Park past a court-ordered 2011 deadline. In 2007, California's two senators teamed up with Lois Capps to try to repeal the provision.

When Hunter's San Diego colleague Duke Cunningham was convicted of bribery, Hunter insisted that he was still his friend and at his sentencing said his much decorated service in Vietnam should be taken into account as well as his crimes. He wrote a $39,650 check to the Injured Marine Semper Fi Fund—the amount of the contributions he had received from those connected with the companies implicated in the Cunningham scandal.

On October 30, as he was once again cruising to easy reelection, Hunter announced that he would not run for reelection again in 2008, but instead would be a candidate for president. He summed up his platform: "I believe in a strong national defense, a strong and enforceable border, a two-way street on trade." In January 2007 he won a straw poll of 458 precinct committeemen in Phoenix's Maricopa County, Arizona, with 21% of the votes to 18% for Mitt Romney. In March 2007 Hunter's son Duncan Duane Hunter announced he would run for the seat; several weeks later he was called back to active duty for another tour in Iraq. It appeared he would return in time to campaign before the June 2008 Republican primary; his wife and brother were expected to stand in for him while he was overseas. Mentioned as possible GOP opponents were businessman Ken King, radio talk show host Mark Larson, former Assembly members Charlene Zettel and Jan Goldsmith.

FIFTY-THIRD DISTRICT

Rep. Susan Davis (D)

Elected 2000, 4th term; b. Apr. 13, 1944, Cambridge, MA; home, San Diego; U.of CA, B.A. 1964, U. of NC, M.A. 1968; Jewish; married (Steven).

Elected Office: San Diego School Bd., 1983-92; CA Assembly, 1994-2000.

Professional Career: Devel. Assoc., KPBS Radio, 1980-82.; Exec. Dir., Aaron Price Fellows, 1990-94.

DC Office: 1526 LHOB, 20515, 202-225-2040; Fax: 202-225-2948; Web site: www.house.gov/susandavis.

District Offices: San Diego, 619-280-5353.

Committees: *Armed Services* (14th of 34 D): Military Personnel (Chmn.); Oversight & Investigations. *Education & Labor* (13th of 27 D): Early Childhood, Elementary & Secondary Education; Higher Education, Lifelong Learning & Competitiveness. *House Administration* (5th of 6 D).

Group Ratings

	ADA	ACLU	AFS	LCV	ITIC	NTU	COC	ACU	CFG	FRC
2006	90	95	100	92	57	14	33	8	14	0
2005	90	—	100	100	—	14	41	0	7	0

National Journal Ratings

	2005 LIB	—	2005 CONS		2006 LIB	—	2006 CONS
Economic	82%	—	16%		85%	—	15%
Social	80%	—	19%		78%	—	21%
Foreign	66%	—	33%		70%	—	28%

Key Votes of the 109th Congress

1. Estate Tax Repeal	N	5. Limit Interstate Abortion	N	9. Build Border Fence	N
2. Limit CAFE Standards	N	6. Extend Patriot Act	N	10. CAFTA	N
3. FY06 Spending Curb	N	7. Bar Same Sex Marriage	N	11. Oppose Iraq Withdrawal	N
4. Drilling in ANWR	N	8. Stem Cell Research $	Y	12. Detainee Tribunals	N

Election Results

2006 general	Susan Davis (D)	97,541	(68%)	($430,945)
	John Woodrum (R)	43,312	(30%)	($90,750)
	Other	3,534	(2%)	
2006 primary	Susan Davis (D)	unopposed		
2004 general	Susan Davis (D)	146,449	(66%)	($387,177)
	Darin Hunzeker (R)	63,897	(29%)	($68,081)
	Other	11,090	(5%)	

Prior Winning Percentages: 2002 (62%); 2000 (50%)

The People		Race/Ethnic Origin	Ancestry	
Area size:	251 sq. mi.	51.0% White	German: 8.8%	Irish: 7.4%
Urban population:	99.9%	7.2% Black	English: 6.3%	
Rural population:	0.1%	8.3% Asian	**2004 Presidential Vote**	
Pop. 2000:	639,087	0.5% Native Am.	Kerry (D) 146,160	(61%)
Pop. 2005 (est):	612,984	0.4% Hawaiian	Bush (R) 89,890	(38%)
Median income:	$36,637	3.1% Two+ races	Other 2,953	(1%)
Poverty status:	20.2%	0.3% Other	**2000 Presidential Vote**	
Military veterans:	12.1%	29.4% Hispanic Origin	Gore (D) 114,435	(58%)
			Bush (R) 74,526	(37%)
			Other 9,944	(5%)
			Cook Partisan Voting Index: D +12	

Occupation   Blue collar: 16.3%   White collar: 64.6%   Gray collar: 19.1%

When the United States was dictating the terms of the Treaty of Guadalupe Hidalgo in 1848, after its successful war with Mexico, it made sure the southern boundary of its new California territory was just south of the port of San Diego. This is one of three splendid natural harbors on the Pacific Coast and in 1914 the Marine Corps established a base on North Island. This was just the first of many military bases in San Diego, with its mild climate, deep harbor and plentiful land for aircraft maneuvers. This has been the major West Coast U.S. Navy base for more than 50 years, and home to about 30,000 active duty Navy and Marine personnel on shore, the second-largest Navy port behind Norfolk. Also based here are the retired aircraft carriers *Midway* and *Constellation*, plus the *Ronald Reagan*, which is the Navy's newest carrier, with a flight deck that covers 4.5 acres.

The port and Navy base in the sheltered harbor remain the central focus of a rapidly growing metropolis that now stretches far inland and to the north. On one side is downtown, booming with postmodern buildings like the Horton Plaza amid a few well-preserved early 20th century relics like the Spreckels Theatre. Across the harbor, on the sand spit that guards it against the ocean, is the white frame castle of the Hotel Del Coronado, with its surprisingly dark wooden interior—the U.S.'s largest wooden structure, opened in 1888 and a favored resort of past American presidents; the town of Coronado has long been a favorite retirement mecca for Navy admirals and captains. But San Diego is not all harbor and Navy. To the north, the Pacific waves pound against the beach beneath erose cliffs of unique rock formations that stride up and down the coast. Here stand some of San Diego's great cultural institutions: the Scripps Institute of Oceanography, the University of California San Diego campus, the Salk Institute and the Torrey Pines reserve, home of the unique, wide-spreading pine tree. To the south are raffish Mission Beach, Ocean Beach, with its strong rip currents, and Point Loma, overlooking the entrance to the harbor. The weather—a sunny 70 degrees most of the time—lures tourists and new residents. But this also is a working town, a sophisticated high-tech center with around 200,000 full and part-time students at its colleges and universities and growing biotech, electronics, software and telecommunications industries. It is a manufacturing center as well, with maquiladora factories clustering near the Mexican border. Despite earlier fears that it might lose its Naval Surface Warfare Center, the San Diego areawas unscathed in the 2005 base closure review. The city has had a long-running battle over proposals to expand or move Lindbergh Field, its land-locked airport, with options ranging from a floating airport in the ocean to a site nearly 100 miles away in Imperial County.

The 53d Congressional District of California—the only 53d Congressional District in American history—consists of the center of San Diego, the San Diego beaches from Blacks Beach to Ocean Beach, the port that has become the home of several cruise lines, La Jolla beach (but not its interior) and Balboa Park. It includes the heavily Latino neighborhoods south and east of downtown; the Gaslamp District, with its glitzy night-life scene that has driven out most of the porn shops; and the older neighborhoods of University Heights and East San Diego. Altogether, 85% of the district population is inside the San Diego city limits. It also includes Coronado and Imperial Beach, just north of the Mexican border, and the inland suburbs of La Presa and Lemon Grove, site of a celebrated school-desegregation case in the 1930s. Historically, this was a Republican district, but after Coastal California's trend toward cultural liberalism and redistricting, it is now solidly Democratic. The Hispanic percentage is 29%, and John Kerry carried the district 61%-38%.

The congresswoman from the 53d District is Susan Davis, a Democrat first elected in 2000. She grew up in Richmond, California, graduated from the University of California at Berkeley and got a degree in social work at the University of North Carolina. She lived for a time in Japan while her husband served as an Air Force doctor during the Vietnam War. She moved to San Diego in 1972 and became president of the local League of Women Voters and a community producer for the local public television station. In 1983 she was elected to the San Diego school board. In 1990, she became the executive director of the Aaron Price Fellows Program, which helps teach leadership and citizen skills to high school students. In 1994, she won the first of three terms in the California Assembly, where she chaired the Consumer Protection Committee. Facing term limits, Davis in 2000 challenged Republican Brian Bilbray, who had won three close elections. She portrayed him as a conservative, even though he took liberal positions on abortion and the environment and made a point of not attending the Republican National Convention. He supported John McCain's campaign finance bill and said that he was comfortable with votes to impeach a president he called "a perpetual liar." She attacked Bilbray for supporting bills that would deny citizenship to U.S.-born children of illegal immigrants and that would allow private insurers to provide prescription drug benefits to seniors; she called for coverage under Medicare. The AFL-CIO ran so much advertising on her behalf that Davis requested it stop. Bilbray criticized Davis for her handling of utility deregulation, but Davis won 50%-46%. Bilbray returned to Congress in June 2006 when he won a special election in the neighboring 50th District.

In the House, she has a less liberal voting record than most coastal Californians, leaning to the center on foreign policy. Assigned to the Armed Services and Education and Labor committees, her priorities included higher military pay, increased aid for school districts with a large military presence, increased student loans and incentives for better teachers. She angered organized labor and some Democratic activists by voting for trade promotion authority, one of only 21 House Democrats to do so. She called the vote "agonizing," but in the interests of a city that has been built on trade; organized labor rescinded its endorsement. In 2005, Davis went in a different direction by voting against CAFTA. She crusaded against dietary supplements that contain the herbal stimulant ephedra, and introduced legislation removing them from the marketplace. With Republican Ginny Brown-Waite, she won House passage of a bill to increase the maximum loan amount that the Veterans Administration approves for home mortgages. In 2005, Davis criticized Armed Services Committee Republicans for seeking to limit women from service in combat units. She voted against the use of force in Iraq in 2002 and against President Bush's troop "surge" proposal in 2007 but voted to continue war funding in May 2007. Davis has been reelected easily.

★ COLORADO ★

At the Front Range of the Rocky Mountains, Colorado has also been at the front edge of economic, cultural and political change. Colorado is an island of nearly 5 million people surrounded by the sea of the Great Plains and the ramparts of the Rockies. With vistas of vast emptiness, it is mostly an urban state: More than half its people live in metropolitan Denver and four-fifths in the urban strip paralleling the Front Range, where the Rockies rise suddenly from the mile-high plateau. And its very ruggedness is inviting more settlement. While the eastern plains continue to lose population, the valley-crevices between the mountains are being filled with second-home condominiums and ranchettes and the rolling land on three sides of metro Denver is being platted into subdivisions.

Colorado started off with a boom, and its recent history has been punctuated by booms—and then by pauses of moderate growth. The first boom came with the discovery of gold and silver in the Rockies. Evidence of this mining boom still can be seen in the opera houses and storefronts of Cripple Creek and Central City, Aspen and Telluride, built when Denver was just a village on the creek that is the South Platte River. Then Denver grew, as a meatpacking, banking and manufacturing center, and also as the state capital and regional headquarters of the federal government. After that came the boom of the high-energy-price 1970s, when the Denver skyline sprouted new

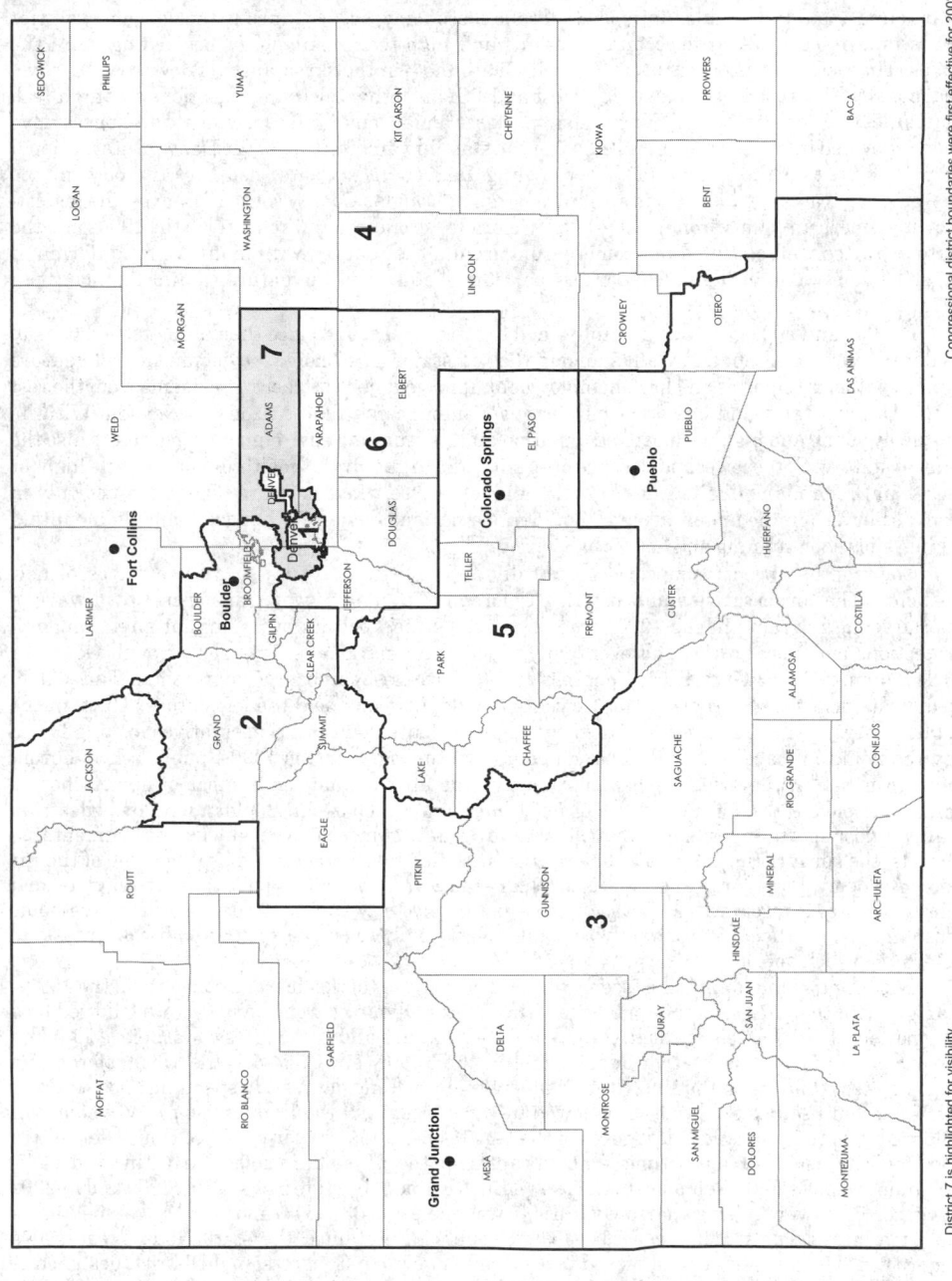

Congressional district boundaries were first effective for 2002.

District 7 is highlighted for visibility.

buildings overlooking the Capitol's golden dome and entrepreneurs built ever more ski resorts and year-round mountain condominiums. Colorado's economy sagged during the low-energy-price 1980s but, based more on telecommunications and high-tech than energy, boomed again in the 1990s. The visible signs of this boom are still all around—in the skyscrapers of downtown Denver, bearing at various times, the names of Qwest and TCI and other telecommunications and high-tech companies; in the retro Coors Field baseball park set amid Denver's LoDo, where warehouses have been renovated into restaurants and clubs; in the startling architecture of the Denver International Airport far out in the plains; in the sprawling Denver Tech Center south of the city; in the fast-growing tracts of subdivisions and office parks in Douglas County south of Denver, the fastest-growing American county from 1990 to 2003. Colorado's economy grew robustly in the 1990s and the state attracted well-educated newcomers from around the country, with many from California; it ranked number one in high-tech workers per capita and third in venture capital financing per capita.

In 2001 and 2002 Colorado painfully shed high-tech jobs, and since then it has settled back to moderate growth. Although it ranks among the top states in economic development and venture capital, with high salaries and low unemployment, it has not been attracting residents from the rest of the United States and has attracted far fewer immigrants than Arizona or Nevada. With its relatively young and highly educated population and its stunning environment, Colorado is also the leanest state, with the lowest percentage of obesity, and arguably the healthiest. In the mile high (or more) air, Coloradans like to ride, jog, bike and, of course, ski. There are bike paths not only in Denver but also in the mountains and Boulder is a national center for bungee jumping, mountain biking, snowshoe running and hot air ballooning.

Colorado has been reshaped, economically and politically, by its successive waves of new residents. The conservative and boosterish Colorado of the 1960s was transformed by a wave of liberal young migrants in the 1970s who swept the state's politics by calling for environmental protections and slow growth and eventually reached the national stage—slow-growth Governor Dick Lamm, Senator Gary Hart, Congresswoman Patricia Schroeder, Congressman Tim Wirth. Democrats held the governorship for 24 years but Republicans held the legislature. Then, in the 1990s, a new wave of migrants—tech-savvy, family-oriented cultural conservatives looking for an environment to prosper—moved Colorado politics to the right. In the 1990s, public school enrollment rose 14%, while private school enrollment was up 33% and the number of home-schooled children tripled. If the spirit of the 1970s newcomers was embodied in Boulder, with its pedestrian mall, outdoor sports shops and vegetarian restaurants, dominated politically by environmentalist liberals, the spirit of the 1990s newcomers was embodied in Colorado Springs, the home of the Air Force Academy, Fort Carson and Focus on the Family, and dominated politically by religious and family-oriented conservatives. Both of these politically very different communities have some reason to believe that they exemplify the state; elections here can be seen as political contests to determine which one does.

But the newcomers' influence seems to ebb. The victories of the liberal Democrats in the 1970s, starting with the 1972 referendum blocking the Winter Olympics from Denver, were followed by a long period where Republicans held control of the legislature and the congressional delegation. And the victories of the conservative Republicans in the 1990s, starting with the 1990 referendum imposing term limits and the 1992 "Tabor" amendment holding down state spending and requiring referenda to raise taxes, have been followed by a resurgence of the Democratic party, which now holds the governorship and both houses of the legislature, a majority in the U.S. House delegation and one Senate seat—and is optimistic about capturing the other one in 2008. Earlier in the decade, Colorado seemed solidly Republican. George W. Bush carried the state 51%-42% in 2000 and in 2002 Governor Bill Owens, elected narrowly in 1998, was reelected 63%-34% and Senator Wayne Allard, after trailing in many polls, won 51%-46%. Republicans retained the state House, regained a majority in the state Senate and picked up Colorado's new 7th Congressional District, designed to be competitive for both parties, by 121 votes. Then Colorado Democrats went on the offensive. Heiress Patricia Stryker and tech millionaire Tim Gill spent large sums on the 2004 elections, backing Democratic candidates in carefully chosen districts; this gave Democrats control of the state Senate 18-17. A budget crisis was forced by Amendment 23, put on the 2000 ballot by teachers' unions and approved 53%-47%, which required that the state education budget increase by the rate of inflation, and by big transportation spending programs backed by Owens. This led Owens to join the Democrats in fall 2005 in support of Referendum C, which suspended the Tabor rules, denying taxpayers the refunds it would have required and pumping the money into state government. Many conservative Republicans opposed this, but with the support of most media outlets and business leaders it passed 52%-48%, running ahead in many normally Republican affluent suburbs and trailing in some low-income Democratic areas.

At the same time, demographic trends seemed to be favoring Democrats. John Kerry's campaign made Colorado a target state for most of the 2004 campaign and so did the Bush campaign. Democrats registered and turned out the anti-Bush vote in Denver, Boulder and the ski resorts—Telluride, Aspen, Vail, Crested Butte, Steamboat Springs, all full of liberal-minded trustfunders—and ran just about even in the close-in Denver suburbs. This was not enough to put Kerry over the top: Bush carried the state by the reduced margin of 52%-47%, but Kerry's increase over the Gore percentage was his highest in all but three other mountainous states (Alaska, Montana, Vermont). Democrats were even more successful at the state level. Senator Ben Nighthorse Campbell (who switched to the Republican party in 1995) announced he would not seek reelection in March 2004, and Democrats united around moderate Attorney General Ken Salazar while Republicans had a divisive primary between former Congressman Bob Schaffer and beer scion Pete Coors. In November Salazar beat Coors 51%-47%. In addition, Salazar's brother John won the 3d District House seat vacated by Republican Scott McInnis—one of only two open Republican seats nationally captured by Democrats in 2004. And Democrats won control of both houses of the legislature, with help from a Democratic redistricting plan; Republicans actually won more popular votes in state House races.

In 2006 Democrats swept the board. Denver District Attorney Bill Ritter, a moderate who opposed abortion, beat Congressman Bob Beauprez for governor by a whopping 57%-40% margin. Ritter carried metro Denver 62%-35% and won in most of the state except Colorado Springs, the eastern plains and the mining area around Grand Junction. Beauprez's suburban Denver House seat, designed to be evenly divided between the parties, was swept by Democrat Ed Perlmutter, and Republican Marilyn Musgrave came within 3% of losing her hitherto safe House seat. Democratic margins in the legislature were dramatically increased. Beauprez warned that Democratic control would mean that unions and trial lawyers would be in charge, and raised the familiar conservative issues of same-sex marriage, gun control and immigration. Ritter campaigned as a moderate and said, "The people of this state want problem-solvers who are pragmatic and who won't allow government to be polarized." In celebration of these victories and in anticipation of more—Republican Senator Wayne Allard announced he would retire as promised in 2008 and Democratic Congressman Mark Udall was an early frontrunner for the seat—the Democratic National Committee chose to hold its 2008 national convention in Denver. National Chairman Howard Dean said the decision was a sign that Democrats could make critical breakthroughs in the West. The omens were good, but precedent was unnerving. Democrats held their national convention in Denver once before, 100 years ago in 1908, and there nominated William Jennings Bryan for the third time. In November he carried Colorado and Nevada (New Mexico and Arizona weren't states yet) plus the then Solid South, but lost nationally 52%-43% to William Howard Taft.

The People		Race/Ethnic Origin			Military veterans: 446,385 (13.9%)	
Pop. 2006 (est):	4,753,377	3,202,880	74.5%	White	WWII: 15.0%	Korea: 11.3%
Pop. 2000:	4,301,261	158,443	3.7%	Black	Vietnam: 36.3%	Gulf War: 13.1%
Pop. 1990:	3,294,394	93,277	2.2%	Asian	**Most populous cities (2006):**	
Change 1990-2000:	Up 30.6%	28,982	0.7%	Native Am.	1. Denver	566,974
% of U.S. total:	1.5%	3,845	0.1%	Hawaiian	2. Colorado Springs	372,437
Pop. rank:	24th of 50	72,721	1.7%	Two+ races	3. Aurora	303,582
Area size:	104,094 sq. mi.	5,512	0.1%	Other	4. Lakewood	140,024
State Native:	41.1%	735,601	17.1%	Hisp. Origin	5. Fort Collins	129,467
Non-citizen:	5.9%	**Ancestry**				
Language		German: 16.3%		Irish: 9.0%	Urban population: 84.5%	
English: 82.5%	Spanish: 11.3%	English: 8.8%		USA: 3.8%	Rural population: 15.5%	
Other Eur.: 3.9%		Italian: 3.5%				

Education		Work Sector		General Assembly	
H.S. Grad:	86.9%	Private: 78.1%	Govt: 13.9%	Senate	20 D 15 R
College Grad:	32.7%	Self: 7.7%	Family: 0.3%	House	39 D 26 R
Industry		Unemployment: 4.3%		Legislative Term Limits: Yes	
Agri: 2.0%	Con: 9.1%	**Household Income**		**Registered Voters**	
Fin: 7.7%	Info: 4.9%	<15k: 11.9%	15-35k: 23.8%	D: 904,767	(30.2%)
Mfg: 14.0%	Prof: 28.7%	35-50k: 17.0%	50-100k: 33.1%	R: 1,070,190	(35.7%)
Public: 4.6%	Trade: 15.2%	100-150k: 9.1%	>150k: 5.2%	O: 1,025,812	(34.2%)
Other: 13.8%		Median: $47,203			
Occupation		Poverty status: 9.3%			
Blue collar: 21.0%	White collar: 64.5%	**Home Value**			
Gray collar: 14.5%		<50k: 6.0% 50-100k: 13.4% 100-200k: 48.1% 200-300k: 19.3%			
		300-500k: 9.4% >500k: 3.8% Median: $160,100			

Presidential politics

Colorado was a battleground state in 2004, as it was in the three-way race in 1992 (it was one of Ross Perot's best states) and was not in 2000. George W. Bush and John Kerry both paid several visits to the state; both campaigns ran TV ads here, and both parties launched major organizational efforts. The Democrats seem to have been more successful: they increased their margins by 34,000 votes in Denver and 33,000 in Boulder County, while Bush margins went up only 17,000 in El Paso County and 12,000 in Douglas County.

One additional fillip in Colorado was Amendment 36, financed by Jorge Klor de Alva, a California multimillionaire who runs a for-profit university in Brazil, which would have split Colorado's 9 electoral votes in proportion to its popular

2004 Presidential Vote		
Bush (R)	1,101,255	(52%)
Kerry (D)	1,001,732	(47%)
Nader (Ref)	12,718	(1%)
Other	13,925	(1%)

2000 Presidential Vote		
Bush (R)	883,748	(51%)
Gore (D)	738,227	(42%)
Nader (Green)	91,434	(5%)
Other	27,959	(2%)

vote. In addition, it stated it would take effect immediately, i.e., when the electoral votes were cast in December 2004. Proponents said it would more accurately reflect voters' views and would serve as an example to the rest of the nation (Maine and Nebraska already give the winner in each congressional district an electoral vote, but this has never resulted in a split in those states' electoral votes.) Amendment 36 was vociferously opposed by Governor Bill Owens and other Republicans as an attempt to steal four electoral votes from George W. Bush, and others raised the specter of litigation over the immediate applicability clause determining the outcome of the 2004 presidential race. But as it became clear that John Kerry was contesting the state, and as polls showed him running even (most Colorado public polls in 2002 and 2004 seemed to lean Democratic), some Democrats decided that they would rather go for the full nine electoral votes rather than settle for the additional one they would get under Amendment 36 for carrying the state. Democratic Senate nominee Ken Salazar opposed the amendment, and support in polls slipped from 51% in mid-September to 36% in late October. The amendment was defeated 65%-35%; it lost in both Republican and Democratic counties. That likely dooms similar efforts in other states: partisans on both sides will oppose it in a closely divided state, while partisans of the minority party in a safe state will find it hard to muster enough votes to pass.

Colorado has had an early March presidential primary since 1992, when Jerry Brown won it. It has not attracted much attention since; in 2003, to save money, the legislature voted to eliminate its presidential primary in 2004. In 2007, the legislature passed a law leaving it to the major parties to decide when to hold 2008 caucuses and both selected February 5.

Congressional districting

110th Congress Lineup
4 D   3 R

109th Congress Lineup
4 R   3 D

Colorado gained a House seat from the 2000 Census, just as it did from the Censuses of 1970 and 1980. Republicans would have controlled the redistricting process, except that they lost control of the state Senate in 2000. When the legislature proved unable to reach a compromise, a state court judge selected a Democrat-designed plan. The judge did not make major changes in the existing districts, but Republicans still responded angrily—they wanted the new district drawn in the fast-growing Republican counties on the south side of Denver. Instead, the newly created 7th District was anchored in the inner Denver suburbs to the north of the city—making it highly competitive for both parties.

The Republicans' one-seat takeover of the Senate in 2002 gave them another opportunity to take a crack at the congressional map. They prepared a new map, then introduced and passed it in late May 2003, in the final days of the legislative session. The new Republican map significantly strengthened 7th District Republican Bob Beauprez, who won in 2002 by 121 votes, the closest margin in the nation. They also increased the Republican base of the 3d District. Attorney General (now Senator) Ken Salazar sued in the Colorado courts, and in December 2003 the state Supreme Court threw out the new plan on the grounds that the state constitution prohibited more than one plan every 10 years; it rejected the argument that the court that drew the plan left it open for the legislature to act. A Republican challenge of that decision was rejected by a federal court in July 2005; in 2006, when Beauprez left the 7th to run for governor, Democrat Ed Perlmutter captured it with 55%.

Governor

Bill Ritter (D)

Elected 2006, term expires Jan. 2011, 1st term; b. Sept. 6, 1956, Denver; home, Denver; CO St. U., B.A. 1978; U. of CO, J.D. 1981; Catholic; married (Jeannie).

Elected Office: Denver dist. atty., 1993-2004.

Professional Career: Denver chief deputy dist. atty., 1981-87, 1992-93; Catholic missionary to Zambia, 1987-90; Asst. U.S. atty., 1990-92; practicing atty., 2005-06.

Office: 136 State Capitol, Denver, 80203, 303-866-2471; Fax: 303-866-2003; Web site: www.colorado.gov/governor.

Election Results

2006 general	Bill Ritter (D)	888,095	(57%)
	Bob Beauprez (R)	618,342	(40%)
	Other	44,424	(3%)
2006 primary	Bill Ritter (D)	unopposed	
2002 general	Bill Owens (R)	884,583	(63%)
	Rollie Heath (D)	475,373	(34%)
	Other	52,646	(4%)

Bill Ritter, a Democrat, was elected governor in 2006. He grew up on a five-acre wheat farm in eastern Arapahoe County, the sixth of 12 children. His father worked the farm and earned extra money as a heavy equipment operator; an alcoholic, he left the family when Ritter was 13. (The family reconciled in the father's later years.) Ritter's mother applied for welfare and worked as a bookkeeper, while he and his siblings got jobs to support the household. Ritter found work in construction at age 14; he then won a scholarship to a Catholic prep school in San Antonio, but after two years decided to return home. He joined the local pipelayers union at 18 and worked his way through Colorado State University and later law school at the University of Colorado.

After earning his law degree in 1981, he joined the Denver district attorney's office. He rose to chief deputy prosecutor, but in 1987 Ritter shocked his colleagues by quitting and moving with his wife Jeannie and young son to Zambia, where the couple volunteered for three years as Catholic missionaries to expand a food distribution and nutrition center. While driving slowly through a crowd, Ritter killed a man who had abruptly stepped in front of the vehicle; accidents were common there and Ritter was cleared of wrongdoing. Ritter, who rarely talks of the incident, later told the *Denver Post* he was devastated: "It is a very big tragedy."

Ritter returned home in 1990 to work as a prosecutor in the U.S attorney's office and in 1992 rejoined the Denver district attorney's office. When Ritter's boss left for private practice, Democratic Governor Roy Romer appointed Ritter as his successor in 1993. Ritter was elected to the position three times and served until 2004, when he was term limited.

In 2006, term limits also prevented Republican Gov. Bill Owens from seeking a third term. Ritter jumped into the race to succeed him in May 2005, which gave him an early start in establishing his candidacy. Party leaders worried about his abortion stance—he said he personally opposed abortion but would enforce Roe v. Wade, though if it were overturned, he would sign a law banning abortions except in cases of rape, incest or to save the life of the mother—and some went so far as to urge him to change his position or drop out of the race. Ritter recounted an emotional meeting with more than 50 women in September 2005, who aggressively questioned about him about his abortion position. "It was the most intense moment of this campaign by far," he said. Ritter held to his stance, but he did not embrace the term "pro-life" or the anti-abortion agenda. In January 2006, Ritter picked Barbara O'Brien, the head of a children's advocacy group, as his running mate. O'Brien supported abortion rights and her choice helped Ritter in his efforts to alleviate party fears about his candidacy. None of the state's other prominent Democrats—state President Joan Fitz-Gerald, House Speaker Andrew Romanoff, House Majority Leader Alice Madden or Denver Mayor John Hickenlooper—made the race, and Ritter won the state party endorsement in May 2006.

Ritter's Republican opponent, two-term Congressman Bob Beauprez, had a much harder time winning the party nomination, and his primary fight required him to court anti-tax and social conservatives. Beauprez faced former University of Denver President Marc Holtzman, who criticized him for his opposition to Referendum C. The measure, which passed in 2005, amended parts of the 1992 Taxpayer Bill of Rights and allowed legislators to tap budget surpluses for health care, transportation and education, rather than refund them to taxpayers. Beauprez won the state GOP convention 72%-28%. Holtzman failed to submit enough valid signatures to get on the primary ballot but his criticism of "Both Ways Bob" stuck with Beauprez to the general election. By the end of the summer, a series of gaffes was beginning to take a toll on Beauprez's general election campaign: in one interview he incorrectly suggested that 70% of African-American pregnancies end in abortion. In August, he picked first-term Mesa County Commissioner Janet Rowland to be his running mate. The choice ignited controversy because she had once compared gay marriage to bestiality: "Do we allow a man to marry a sheep?"

By July Ritter had nearly matched Beauprez in fundraising by collecting $2 million, and he had run a solid campaign throughout the race. Ritter found support within the business community because he had supported Referendum C. Beauprez accused Ritter of supporting amnesty for illegal immigrants; Ritter countered that a Republican Congress had failed to address the issue. Then, in October, the FBI began a criminal investigation into whether a federal agent had illegally supplied Beauprez's campaign with information that was used in an ad attacking Ritter's prosecution of an illegal immigrant. Ritter's campaign quickly cut its own spot against Beauprez, asking "How can we trust him to be governor?" Beauprez continued to sink in the polls; frustration with President Bush and the Iraq war exacerbated his situation. Ritter won a lopsided 57%-40% victory, winning 38 of 64 counties, and for the first time in 40 years, Democrats won control of governor and both chambers of the legislature. Ritter lost only Colorado Springs, Douglas County, Grand Junction and the lightly-populated eastern plains.

Ritter, the first governor in three decades not to come out of the legislature, had a ready-made agenda. He had campaigned on the "Colorado Promise," a series of policy objectives laid out in a 51-page booklet: renewable energy, education reforms, affordable healthcare and highway funding. After his election, Ritter named veteran former legislator Norma Anderson, a moderate Republican, to his transition team. He also convened expert panels to develop long-term plans for transportation and health care coverage. In February 2007, he angered labor by vetoing a bill that would have made it easier for unions to organize non-union shops.

Senior Senator

Wayne Allard (R)

Elected 1996, seat up 2008, 2d term; b. Dec. 2, 1943, Fort Collins; home, Loveland; CO St. U., D.V.M. 1968; Protestant; married (Joan).

Elected Office: CO Senate, 1982-90; US House of Reps., 1990-96.

Professional Career: Veterinarian, 1968-present; Loveland City Health Officer, 1970-78; Owner, Allard Animal Hosp., 1970-90.

DC Office: 521 DSOB, 20510, 202-224-5941; Fax: 202-224-6471; Web site: allard.senate.gov.

State Offices: Colorado Springs, 719-634-6071; Durango, 970-375-6311; Englewood, 303-220-7414; Grand Junction, 970-245-9553; Loveland, 970-461-3530; Pueblo, 719-545-9751.

Committees: *Appropriations* (13th of 14 R): Legislative Branch (RMM); Military Construction, Veterans Affairs & Related Agencies; Financial Services & General Government; Interior, Environment & Related Agencies; Energy & Water Development; Transportation, Housing and Urban Development & Related Agencies. *Banking, Housing & Urban Affairs* (3d of 10 R): Securities, Insurance & Investment (RMM); Financial Institutions; Housing, Transportation & Community Development. *Budget* (4th of 11 R). *Health, Education, Labor & Pensions* (9th of 10 R): Employment & Workplace Safety; Children & Families.

Group Ratings

	ADA	ACLU	AFS	LCV	ITIC	NTU	COC	ACU	CFG	FRC
2006	0	8	0	29	100	84	92	88	90	100
2005	0	—	0	5	—	80	89	96	98	—

National Journal Ratings

	2005 LIB	—	2005 CONS	2006 LIB	—	2006 CONS
Economic	0%	—	94%	13%	—	82%
Social	0%	—	77%	18%	—	74%
Foreign	0%	—	74%	0%	—	92%

Key Votes of the 109th Congress

1. Bar ANWR Drilling	N	5. Confirm Samuel Alito	Y	9. Limit Interstate Abortion	Y
2. FY06 Spending Curb	Y	6. Path to Citizenship	N	10. CAFTA	Y
3. Estate Tax Repeal	Y	7. Bar Same Sex Marriage	Y	11. Urge Iraq Withdrawal	N
4. Raise Minimum Wage	N	8. Stem Cell Research $	N	12. Provide Detainee Rights	N

Election Results

2002 general	Wayne Allard (R)	717,893	(51%)	($5,223,592)
	Tom Strickland (D)	648,130	(46%)	($5,160,517)
	Other	50,059	(3%)	
2002 primary	Wayne Allard (R)	unopposed		
1996 general	Wayne Allard (R)	750,325	(51%)	($2,233,429)
	Tom Strickland (D)	677,600	(46%)	($2,894,916)
	Other	41,686	(3%)	

Prior Winning Percentages: 1994 House (72%); 1992 House (58%); 1990 House (54%)

Wayne Allard, Colorado's Republican senator, was first elected to the House in 1990 and to the Senate in 1996. Allard grew up in the northern end of the Front Range, the son of a cattle rancher and developer, attended veterinary school, then in 1970 started a veterinary practice in Loveland—a lively business in an area with vast feedlots. His father was a Democrat—Allard's colleague Edward Kennedy remembers him from the 1960 campaign—and a friend of conservative Democratic Congressman Wayne Aspinall, but both father and son switched parties after Aspinall was defeated by a liberal in the 1972 primary. In 1982, Allard was elected to the state Senate, where he succeeded in limiting the length of legislative sessions to 120 days, so legislators would be more in touch with their constituents. In 1990, when Congressman Hank Brown ran for the Senate, Allard ran for the House in the 4th District, which covered much of the High Plains and the northern end of the Front Range. Against a former local university president and legislator, Allard won a 54% victory. He was easily re-elected in 1992 and 1994 and, when Brown retired from the Senate after just one term, Allard ran for the seat.

Allard's voting record was one of the most conservative in the House. He was scarcely the most prominent candidate going into 1996, but others better known declined to run—former Senator Gary Hart, Governor Roy Romer, former Governor Dick Lamm. In the August 13 primary, Allard won 57%-43% over Attorney General Gale Norton, who later became George W. Bush's Interior Secretary.

The Democratic nominee was Tom Strickland, who had more money and sophistication, but Allard ended up with more votes. Strickland held fundraisers with Robert Redford and Gloria Steinem and attacked Allard's "Neanderthal" positions on the environment; Allard said he was interested in "sound science" rather than emotional appeals, more local decision-making and less bureaucracy. Allard won 51%-46%.

Allard has a very conservative voting record in the Senate and is not much of a headline-maker. "I try not to be on the front burner of every issue that comes through." As ranking member and former chairman of the Armed Services Strategic Forces Subcommittee, he strongly supported missile defense and pushed to develop space-based radar and defenses for space-based assets. He gets low ratings from national environmental groups, but has done much work on his own environmental causes. With 2d District Democrat Mark Udall, he has worked successfully to create a wildlife refuge at Rocky Flats, a much-polluted nuclear plant near Denver that closed in 1989; this was modeled on his action as a House member, when he joined with Democrat Patricia Schroeder to make the Rocky Mountain Arsenal site a wildlife refuge. In 2006, Allard pressed Health and Human Services Secretary Michael Leavitt to consider a petition that sought compensation for employees who fell ill after working at Rocky Flats.

One of Allard's few moments in the national spotlight came in 2004, when he was the lead Senate sponsor of the Family Marriage Amendment sponsored in the House by Colorado's Marilyn Musgrave. The amendment fell far short of the 67 votes needed; Allard was defeated 48-50 on a procedural vote. Allard's amendment fared little better in 2006, when it picked up just one more vote and also failed on a 49-48 procedural vote. In 2004 he was mentioned as a possible chairman of the Budget Committee; he ended up with a seat on the Appropriations Committee and is now ranking member of the Legislative Branch Subcommittee, which oversees construction of the Capitol Visitors Center. As an appropriator, Allard secured $70 million in additional funding to renovate Fort Carson to accommodate the arrival of at least 7,000 new troops at the base near Colorado Springs.

On the Banking Committee, Allard sponsored legislation to restrict banks from offering real estate services. After Hurricane Katrina hit the Gulf Coast, Allard authored a bill that would clear damaged or abandoned properties on federal land and turn it over to local governments for rebuilding. As chairman of Banking Committee's Housing and Transportation Subcommittee, Allard in 2005 was named as a conferee to the House-Senate negotiations over a long-stalled transportation bill. To help keep up with the state's growing population, Allard fought to recapture 92 cents, up from 90.5 cents, of every dollar that Colorado pays into the highway trust fund. When the final $286.4 billion was approved, Colorado received nearly $2.5 billion, a 47% increase in federal highway spending.

In his 2002 reelection race, Allard faced the same opponent as in 1996, Tom Strickland. Polls showed he remained relatively little known, perhaps because he has kept his promise to visit all 63 of Colorado's counties—64 since the creation of Broomfield County in November 2001—every year, even though 10 of those counties have 80% of the state's population. Allard was not troubled by his low name identification. "At the end of the day, there are work horses, and there are show horses. As a veterinarian, I know the difference." There was a vast contrast in style between the rural and stolid Allard and the urban and urbane Strickland: The candidate of the simple rural areas versus the candidate of the sophisticated urban core in a mostly suburban state. Strickland said his favorite food (in landlocked Colorado) was sushi; Allard said his was his wife's Crisco cherry pie. Allard constantly called Strickland a lawyer-lobbyist; Strickland called Allard a far right-winger and ran ads saying he lived in a right-wing "Wayne's World." Strickland described himself as a conservative Democrat, ready and able to work with senators in both parties; he called for broader access to health care and a $12,000 per year deduction for college tuition.

Much of the campaign dialogue focused on corporate wrongdoing and the candidates' involvement in it. Some of the accusations came in the candidates' 13 debates, but voters saw it more in the independent expenditure ads. Over the summer, the bulk was run by liberal groups against Allard; the Club for Growth and the NRA chimed in with ads against Strickland later. Strickland accused Allard of promoting the 1999 acquisition by Qwest of USWest, which had turned out badly, and criticized him for buying 50 shares of Qwest one day after the acquisition was announced. Allard responded that in 1998 Strickland made a profit of $25,000 in one day because he was let in to the IPO of Global Crossing (which later failed). Allard called Strickland a liberal "elitist" who had worked for a company that wanted to build a medical waste incinerator in north Denver in the late 1980s.

In the end, even though many public polls showed Strickland leading, the result was exactly the same as in 1996: Allard won 51%-46%. The percentage and the contours of support were strikingly similar to George W. Bush's 2004 Colorado victory. Allard was shellacked in Denver and Boulder and carried the old-line suburban Jefferson and Arapahoe Counties with only 51% and 52% of the vote. But he won 65% in fast-growing Douglas County, where the turnout was up 40% from the last off-year election, and 66% in Colorado Springs's El Paso County. Strickland carried some fashionable resort areas in the Western Slope and a few Hispanic counties in the south; Allard won large margins in most of the Western Slope and most of the Eastern Plains counties. Strickland carried metro Denver 51%-45%, but Allard carried the rest of the state 57%-39%.

In January 2007, Allard announced he would not seek reelection in order to fulfill a campaign promise not to serve more than two Senate terms. "In an age when promises are cast away as quickly as yesterday's newspaper, I believe a promise made should be a promise kept," he said. Allard's decision made him the first senator to announce he would not seek reelection in 2008 and handed GOP leaders their first major Senate contest of the election cycle. Democratic Rep. Mark Udall had positioned himself as the 2008 Democratic frontrunner long before Allard's announcement: Udall had entered the 2004 Senate race only to drop out 24 hours later in deference to then-Attorney General Ken Salazar. Denver Mayor John Hickenlooper said he would not run for the Democratic nomination if Udall was in the race. Republicans, whose failures in the 2004 Senate and 2006 gubernatorial races began with divisive primaries, at first faced the prospect of another contested statewide primary. But Attorney General John Suthers bowed out and former Congressman Scott McInnis, who retired from the House in 2004 with nearly $1 million still in his campaign account, announced in March 2007 that he would not run, clearing the field for former Congressman Bob Schaffer, who lost to beer magnate Pete Coors in the 2004 Senate primary.

Junior Senator

Ken Salazar (D)

Elected 2004, seat up 2010, 1st term; b. Mar. 2, 1955, Alamosa; home, Denver; CO College, B.A. 1977; U. of MI, J.D. 1981; Catholic; married (Hope).

Elected Office: CO Atty. Gen., 1998-2004.

Professional Career: Practicing atty., Exec. Dir., CO Nat. Resources Dept., 1990-94; Chairman, Rio Grande Compact Comm., 1995-98.

DC Office: 702 HSOB, 20510, 202-224-5852; Fax: 202-228-5036; Web site: salazar.senate.gov.

State Offices: Alamosa, 719-587-0096; Colorado Springs, 719-328-1100; Denver, 303-455-7600; Durango, 970-259-1710; Fort Collins, 970-224-2200; Fort Morgan, 970-542-9446; Grand Junction, 970-241-6631; Pueblo, 719-542-7550.

Committees: *Aging (Special)* (8th of 11 D). *Agriculture, Nutrition & Forestry* (8th of 11 D): Energy, Science & Technology; Domestic & Foreign Marketing, Inspection, & Plant & Animal Health; Rural Revitalization, Conservation, Forestry & Credit. *Energy & Natural Resources* (8th of 12 D): National Parks; Water & Power; Public Lands & Forests. *Ethics (Select)* (3d of 3 D). *Finance* (11th of 11 D): Taxation & IRS Oversight & Long-Term Growth; Energy, Natural Resources & Infrastructure; Health Care.

Group Ratings

	ADA	ACLU	AFS	LCV	ITIC	NTU	COC	ACU	CFG	FRC
2006	85	58	100	71	75	20	64	17	4	12
2005	100	—	88	80	—	14	72	32	3	—

National Journal Ratings

	2005 LIB	—	2005 CONS		2006 LIB	—	2006 CONS
Economic	61%	—	38%		72%	—	27%
Social	56%	—	43%		69%	—	30%
Foreign	62%	—	37%		61%	—	38%

Key Votes of the 109th Congress

1. Bar ANWR Drilling	Y	5. Confirm Samuel Alito	N	9. Limit Interstate Abortion	Y
2. FY06 Spending Curb	N	6. Path to Citizenship	*	10. CAFTA	N
3. Estate Tax Repeal	N	7. Bar Same Sex Marriage	N	11. Urge Iraq Withdrawal	Y
4. Raise Minimum Wage	Y	8. Stem Cell Research $	Y	12. Provide Detainee Rights	Y

Election Results

2004 general	Ken Salazar (D)	1,081,188	(51%)	($9,886,551)
	Pete Coors (R)	980,668	(47%)	($7,858,598)
	Other..	45,616	(2%)	
2004 primary	Ken Salazar (D)	173,167	(73%)	
	Mike Miles (D)	63,973	(27%)	
1998 general	Ben Nighthorse Campbell (R)	829,370	(62%)	($3,045,982)
	Dottie Lamm (D)	464,754	(35%)	($1,818,801)
	Other...	33,111	(3%)	

Ken Salazar was elected to the Senate in 2004, the first Democratic senator elected in Colorado since 1992. Salazar grew up in Conejos County, in the San Luis Valley in south central Colorado, on a 217-acre ranch and farm owned by his family since 1850. He was one of eight children; the family spoke Spanish at home, though Ken was fluent in English thanks to his three older brothers—one of whom, John Salazar, was elected to the House in 2004. (The brothers share an apartment in Washington.) The San Luis Valley is one of the oldest parts of Colorado, settled by Spanish-speaking people who came north from New Mexico; it has also been one of the poorest, and the Salazars did not have electricity when Ken was growing up. He spent two of his teen years in a Catholic seminary, but decided not to become a priest. Instead, he graduated from Colorado College and the University of Michigan Law School. Then he moved to Denver and practiced law. But when he was married in 1985, the wedding was at Our Lady of Guadalupe Church in Conejos, the oldest church in Colorado.

In 1987, as he was on the brink of making partner in his Denver law firm, Salazar was asked by incoming Governor Roy Romer to be his chief legal counsel, and accepted. In 1990 Romer appointed him head of the state Department of Natural Resources; in 1994 he resigned and joined a Denver law firm. Senator Ben Nighthorse Campbell, then still a Democrat, recommended him for a post in the Bureau of Land Management, but he evidently wasn't interested. In 1998, when Attorney General Gale Norton—later the U.S. Interior Secretary—was barred from running because of term limits, Salazar ran for attorney general. It was a Republican year and he was expected to lose to Colorado Springs District Attorney John Suthers. But he won by a 50%-47% margin, making him the first Hispanic elected to statewide office in Colorado.

In 2002 Salazar was reelected 58%-38%, even as Republican Governor Bill Owens was winning by a wider margin. In late 2003 and early 2004 it was widely assumed that Salazar would run for governor in 2006; with his moderate record and his talents as a conciliator he seemed a strong candidate.

No one at that time expected him to run against Campbell, whose Senate seat was up in 2004 and who seemed determined to run for a third term. Indeed Democrats struggled to come up with a candidate against Campbell; former Senator Gary Hart and Congressman Mark Udall decided they weren't interested. But in March 2004 Campbell suddenly announced he was retiring for health reasons.

Campbell's retirement set off a scramble for his seat. The strongest candidate seemed to be Governor Bill Owens but on March 9 he announced he would not run. The next day Democratic Congressman Mark Udall and former Republican Congressman Bob Schaffer announced they were running. Also in was Democrat Rutt Bridges, a software millionaire and geophysicist who originated Colorado's popular do-not-call registry in 2001. Then on March 10, Salazar announced that he was running. He was accompanied by former Governor Dick Lamm and Denver Mayor John Hickenlooper—and by Udall and Bridges, who announced that they were no longer running and were supporting Salazar. On the Republican side, Schaffer thought he had the support of high-ranking party officials, including Owens. But many Republicans believed that with his strong conservative record on cultural issues and his base far from metro Denver, Schaffer would be hard to sell statewide. They encouraged Pete Coors, chairman of the Coors brewing company and a long-time backer of Republican and conservative causes, to run; when Coors became a candidate, Schaffer's campaign reacted angrily. What had looked like a race with a strong Republican nominee and a fractious Democratic primary became, within a few days, a race with a strong Democratic nominee and a fractious Republican primary. Actually, Salazar did have a primary opponent, former Army Ranger and State Department officer Mike Miles, who backed universal health care and said he would "de-Halliburton" Iraq. Miles's leftish views won him a majority at the activist-filled Democratic state convention but Salazar won the August primary 73%-27%.

Coors had a more difficult time. A familiar figure from his appearances in Coors beer ads, he was less than adept in debates; Schaffer flustered him by recalling his proposals to lower the drinking age and pointing out that he couldn't name the Prime Minister of Canada. Schaffer supporters pointed to Coors ads showing scantily clad women and the company's sponsorship of Denver's gay PrideFest and provision of benefits for same-sex couples. In July Coors announced that he was changing the company's health insurance which was paying for abortions. Just before the August primary Coors lent $400,000 of his own money to his campaign; he won the primary 61%-39%.

Up to the August primary, Salazar raised more money and Coors spent more; in the fall, the Democrats' Senate campaign committee put more money into this race than its Republican counterpart. Salazar kept distant from the Kerry campaign, avoiding joint appearances in Colorado; he proclaimed himself "an independent voice for the people of Colorado" and asked the Sierra Club and other independent expenditure groups to stay out of the state. But Salazar also engaged in edgy attacks: Coors was "fronting for his drug company backers," his company was "one of Colorado's biggest polluters" and cut 900 jobs. He attacked Coors for supporting Referendum A in 2003; he favored the death penalty while Coors was opposed. Coors hit Salazar for his various stances on vouchers; Salazar hit Coors for conflicting statements on the 2002 Bush education act. Other differences were more predictable: Coors was for the Family Marriage Amendment, Salazar against; Coors backed Bush on the Iraq war (though in October he suggested he might not vote for it if he had known what we did then), while Salazar called him a "rubber stamp" for Bush in the war on terrorism. Salazar, like Kerry, would rescind the Bush tax cut on top earners; Coors ran an ad on taxes showing Salazar and Kerry together. Salazar was attacked by independent groups for acting as a lawyer for polluters and for taking money from casino interests. Their frequent debates could be fractious. Coors: "I'm a businessman; my opponent is a bureaucrat. I'm a job creator, and my opponent is a litigator." Salazar: "You know, he says we have too many lawyers in the United States Senate. Many of them—in fact, more than half—are Republicans. My point of view, Pete, is that we have too many multimillionaires in the United States Senate."

Republicans won almost all the close Senate races in 2004—but not this one. Salazar came out ahead 51%-47%—almost the same margin by which George W. Bush beat John Kerry in the state. Coors lost all of the suburban Denver counties except Douglas County; Salazar ran about even on the Western Slope, even as his brother John was winning the 3d Congressional District there. Coors ran far behind Bush in areas with large Hispanic populations. Salazar, along with Florida's Mel Martinez, became the first Hispanic in the Senate since Joseph Montoya of New Mexico lost in 1976, but he rejected the role of group tribune: "I sometimes bristle when people say I'm the first Hispanic elected statewide or I would be the first Hispanic senator in 30 years. I'm an American, and I represent all the people in the state."

Salazar's actions in his first months in office were hard to predict. During the campaign he indicated he would not oppose Bush on judicial nominations but in December 2004, he suggested he would join other Democrats in filibustering appeals court nominees. He introduced Alberto Gonzales at his confirmation hearings for Attorney General and was one of only six Democrats to vote for him. In March, he called for Bush to withdraw controversial judicial nominees, including William Myers, whom he had endorsed for the 9th Circuit Court of Appeals in 2004 while sitting as Colorado's attorney general. In a conference call with reporters that same month, he refused to rule out a bid for governor in 2006.

Salazar quickly found himself at the center of many of the Senate's leading debates. He sided with Democratic colleagues in opposing President Bush's proposed Social Security overhaul, passage of the Central America Free Trade Agreement and drilling in the Arctic National Wildlife Refuge. He joined with a bipartisan group of senators in 2005 to force the White House to negotiate on the reauthorization of USA Patriot Act. Salazar voted with Republicans for a constitutional flag burning amendment, bankruptcy legislation and curbs on class action lawsuits. He supported the confirmation of Condoleezza Rice as Secretary of State. "I'm a moderate Democrat with an independent streak," he said. "That's why I won three statewide offices in six years. I'm not a puppet for either party."

Salazar's first real controversy came in April 2005 when he fought back against ads the political arm of the Colorado Springs-based Focus on the Family ran to pressure Salazar to give Bush's judicial nominations an up or down vote. Salazar called the tactics "un-Christian" and in another interview referred to the group as "the anti-Christ." Salazar apologized for his latter comment, but not the former. "I didn't choose to fight with them. They attacked me first." Salazar joined the "Gang of 14" senators who agreed not to filibuster Bush's judicial nominees except in "extraordinary circumstances." He disappointed abortion rights groups when he announced his support for John Roberts as Chief Justice, but he voted against the nomination of Samuel Alito.

When Salazar came to the Senate, he chose Senator John McCain as his mentor, and it was McCain in 2006 who turned to Salazar to help win Senate passage of key elements of his immigration bill, including an immigrant guestworker program and a legalization process for undocumented workers. Harry Reid named Salazar to the House-Senate conference committee on immigration, although sharp differences with the House-passed bill stood in the way of a negotiated compromise.

Energy, the environment and agriculture are critical issues for Colorado, and Salazar inserted himself in debates on each. He was the cosponsor of an amendment to the 2005 energy bill that requires that refiners use 8 billion gallons of renewable fuels by 2012. Salazar identified the 2007 farm bill as a vehicle to promote biofuels and wind farms; he opposed plans to auction off oil and gas leases in the Colorado's national forests until the state could finish a study. In January 2007 he sought up to $5 billion to aid farmers and ranchers on the state's eastern plains in their recovery from drought and blizzards. Salazar helped negotiate language on a bill that would give liability protections to "good samaritans" that clean up abandoned hard-rock mines. He supported a bill that would guarantee the Veterans Affairs health system annual funding increases based on cost of living adjustments.

By the end of his first year, Salazar had impressed Democratic leaders, who had looked for opportunities to give him a larger national profile. Salazar resisted efforts to be recruited into the governor's race in 2006, and after the 2006 election won a coveted seat on the Finance Committee, a post that will allow him to seek tax incentives for renewable energy. By January 2007 Salazar was being mentioned as a potential 2008 vice-presidential candidate, speculation he did not discourage.

FIRST DISTRICT

Rep. Diana DeGette (D)

Elected 1996, 6th term; b. July 29, 1957, Tachikawa, Japan; home, Denver; CO Col., B.A. 1979, N.Y.U., J.D. 1982; Presbyterian; married (Lino Lipinsky).

Elected Office: CO House of Reps., 1992-96, Asst. Min. Ldr., 1994-95.

Professional Career: Practicing atty., 1982-96.

DC Office: 2421 RHOB, 20515, 202-225-4431; Fax: 202-225-5657; Web site: www.house.gov/degette.

District Offices: Denver, 303-844-4988.

Committees: *Chief Deputy Majority Whip. Energy & Commerce* (Vice Chmn. of 31 D): Oversight & Investigations; Health; Commerce, Trade & Consumer Protection; Environment & Hazardous Materials.

Group Ratings

	ADA	ACLU	AFS	LCV	ITIC	NTU	COC	ACU	CFG	FRC
2006	95	100	100	100	43	14	33	4	11	0
2005	90	—	100	100	—	15	37	0	8	0

National Journal Ratings

	2005 LIB	—	2005 CONS	2006 LIB	—	2006 CONS
Economic	87%	—	12%	85%	—	14%
Social	95%	—	4%	84%	—	15%
Foreign	81%	—	18%	92%	—	5%

Key Votes of the 109th Congress

1. Estate Tax Repeal	N	5. Limit Interstate Abortion	N	9. Build Border Fence	N
2. Limit CAFE Standards	N	6. Extend Patriot Act	N	10. CAFTA	N
3. FY06 Spending Curb	N	7. Bar Same Sex Marriage	N	11. Oppose Iraq Withdrawal	N
4. Drilling in ANWR	N	8. Stem Cell Research $	Y	12. Detainee Tribunals	N

Election Results

2006 general	Diana DeGette (D) 129,446	(80%)	($642,405)
	Thomas Kelly (Green) 32,825	(20%)	
2006 primary	Diana DeGette (D) .... unopposed		
2004 general	Diana DeGette (D) 177,077	(73%)	($620,599)
	Roland Chicas (R) 58,659	(24%)	($16,968)
	Other.. 5,193	(2%)	

Prior Winning Percentages: 2002 (66%); 2000 (69%); 1998 (67%); 1996 (57%)

The People		Race/Ethnic Origin	Ancestry	
Area size:	173 sq. mi.	54.3% White	German: 11.6% Irish: 7.8%	
Urban population:	100.0%	10.1% Black	English: 6.9%	
Rural population:	0.0%	2.7% Asian	**2004 Presidential Vote**	
Pop. 2000:	614,465	0.7% Native Am.	Kerry (D) 180,064	(68%)
Pop. 2005 (est):	616,265	0.1% Hawaiian	Bush (R) 81,265	(31%)
Median income:	$39,658	1.9% Two+ races	Other 2,817	(1%)
Poverty status:	13.7%	0.2% Other	**2000 Presidential Vote**	
Military veterans:	11.3%	30.0% Hispanic Origin	Gore (D) 134,187	(61%)
			Bush (R) 72,455	(33%)
			Other 14,430	(7%)
			Cook Partisan Voting Index: D +18	
Occupation Blue collar: 20.4% White collar: 64.3% Gray collar: 15.3%				

Denver is serious about being the mile high city: there are three markers on the granite steps of the gold-domed Capitol that proclaim the elevation of 5,280 feet. Denver is situated a few miles from where the High Plains yield to the sharp peaks of the Front Range of the Rockies, on no historic trade route and with a fresh water supply adequate for a town one-tenth of its size. With 557,000 people, the city has been the economic and cultural capital for 100 years of the whole Rocky Mountain region. On top of its Old West heritage and early 20th century elegance, Denver has developed an exuberant postmodern style. The National Western Stock Show held here every year and the LoDo entertainment district redeveloped near the railyards along the South Platte evoke the Old West; the Capitol, the spacious parks, the aspens which line so many streets, give the city a lush, burnished air, in contrast to the dry high plains and the stark Rocky peaks. Amid its downtown grid, slanted on a 45-degree angle to align with the South Platte and the railroads, are the skyscrapers of the 1970s energy and 1990s high-tech booms, plus the new-old Coors Stadium, Elitch Gardens amusement park and the expanded Museum of Nature and Science. Rather than losing population as many central cities have, it has gained people since 1990; most of its neighborhoods have vitality, including the black neighborhoods of northeastern Denver, filled with well-maintained 1950s bungalows, and the Hispanic quarter northwest of downtown. But more than three-quarters of the metro area's people now live in the suburbs, and Denver has disproportionate numbers of singles and cultural liberals who value an urban and physically active lifestyle in the gentrified areas south of the Capitol, and the rich neighborhood that is home to the posh Cherry Creek Shopping Center.

Denver has become the liberal heart of Colorado, heavily Democratic while the state mostly voted Republican, strongly liberation-minded on cultural issues, cautiously liberal on economic issues. Though it remains majority Anglo, it has elected Hispanic and black mayors. In the early 1970s, Denver liberals were hostile to growth and boosterism; today's Denver, from Cherry Creek to the night life of LoDo, has shown that growth can produce more of the distinctiveness that people here appreciate. As has been evident in the selection and planning for the city to host the 2008

Democratic convention, civic pride is rampant. There is good reason: Denver has been ranked among the nation's top 10 cities in its business climate, livability, libraries, and bikeways. In the lower downtown near Coors Field, dilapidated bars have been replaced by art galleries over the past decade. In 2004, voters easily approved a sales tax increase to pay for the "FasTracks" expansion of commuter rail and bus service across the metro area.

The 1st Congressional District of Colorado includes all of Denver and extends northeast to take in Denver International Airport, encompassing places with warehouses and trucking terminals on main streets and curved-street subdivisions behind. The district extends to affluent suburbs, long-settled Englewood and newly settled Cherry Hills Village, in Arapahoe County. It counts most of metro Denver's blacks and Hispanics, singles and gays: The percentage of households with married couples and children has been among the lowest in America, and was lower in 2000 than in 1990. In an era when cultural attitudes are a better clue to voting behavior than economic status, this district, which last elected a Republican in 1970, is solidly Democratic.

The congresswoman from the 1st District is Diana DeGette, a Democrat elected in 1996. She is a fourth-generation Denverite (though she was born on a military base in Japan) who went away to law school, returned to practice employment law and became involved in politics. In 1992, at 35, she was elected to the Colorado House. In 1995, when Patricia Schroeder, a pioneer of the feminist left, announced she was retiring after 24 years in the House, DeGette decided to run for the seat. DeGette—feminist, organizationally adept and legislatively creative—has become a worthy successor.

Until 2007, DeGette had never served in the majority party—either in Denver or Washington. Yet even with a liberal voting record, she managed to achieve some legislative successes, both in the leadership and on the Energy and Commerce Committee. She has focused especially on health care issues. She supported trade relations with China but returned to organized labor's graces by opposing trade promotion authority. Teaming with Republican Mike Castle of Delaware, who pressured GOP leaders for a vote, she formed a broad bipartisan coalition to expand federal funds for stem cell research and remove President George W. Bush's restrictions; in May 2005, they won majority support and the Senate passed the bill a year later. "It took four years, hundreds of one-on-one meetings, and a heck of a lot of shoe leather to win," she said. But Bush vetoed the measure—the first veto in his first six years as president—and the House fell 51 votes short of an override. Speaker Nancy Pelosi responded by including the measure in the House's "100-hour" agenda as the third bill passed by the new majority; the vote was 253-174, still 32 votes short of the two-thirds necessary to override. She opposed the war in Iraq, and said that Bush's handling had created a "credibility gap." In 2005, she secured $50 million for redevelopment of the downtown Union Station, the hub of Denver's transit expansion.

DeGette backed Steny Hoyer in his unsuccessful leadership race against Pelosi; when Hoyer became Minority Whip he named DeGette a chief deputy whip. She deliberately moved into a role as a party strategist. In the majority, DeGette seriously considered a run for Majority Whip against James Clyburn. She said that she could have won, but decided that it would have been disruptive to have another intra-party brawl at the same time that John Murtha was challenging Hoyer for Majority Leader; Clyburn retained her as a chief deputy whip. DeGette emerged with additional responsibilities: She is one of two Democrats on the Page Board (her daughter served as a page). John Dingell named her as vice-chairman of the Energy and Commerce Committee, which positioned her to broker the often intricate clashes among the panel's combative Democrats. She has played a leadership role for the 2008 Democratic National Convention in Denver.

In 2002, DeGette fared impressively against credible primary and general election opponents. Ramona Martinez, a 15-year term-limited member of the Denver City Council and a Democratic National Committeewoman, criticized DeGette for having lost touch with the district. DeGette returned her family to Denver from the Maryland suburbs in 2001 and won by an unexpectedly large 73%-27% margin. In November, she faced Republican Ken Chlouber, a rural state senator known for folksy humor and a flame-painted pickup truck, who won the Teamsters' endorsement; DeGette won 66%-30%. She won 80%-20% in 2006 against the Green Party's Thomas Kelly; Republicans had no candidate.

SECOND DISTRICT

Rep. Mark Udall (D)

Elected 1998, 5th term; b. July 18, 1950, Tucson, AZ; home, Boulder; Williams Col., B.A. 1972; no religious affiliation; married (Maggie L. Fox).

Elected Office: CO House of Reps., 1996-98.

Professional Career: CO Outward Bound Course Dir., 1975-85, Exec. Dir., 1985-95.

DC Office: 100 CHOB, 20515, 202-225-2161; Fax: 202-226-7840; Web site: www.house.gov/markudall.

District Offices: Minturn, 970-827-4154; Westminster, 303-650-7820.

Committees: *Armed Services* (19th of 34 D): Terrorism, Unconventional Threats & Capabilities; Readiness. *Natural Resources* (23d of 27 D): Water & Power; National Parks, Forests & Public Lands. *Science & Technology* (5th of 24 D): Space & Aeronautics (Chmn.); Energy & Environment.

Group Ratings

	ADA	ACLU	AFS	LCV	ITIC	NTU	COC	ACU	CFG	FRC
2006	85	91	86	100	57	16	53	16	10	0
2005	90	—	100	100	—	16	37	8	4	0

National Journal Ratings

	2005 LIB	—	2005 CONS		2006 LIB	—	2006 CONS
Economic	71%	—	28%		74%	—	23%
Social	67%	—	33%		68%	—	32%
Foreign	67%	—	32%		77%	—	20%

Key Votes of the 109th Congress

1. Estate Tax Repeal	N	5. Limit Interstate Abortion	N	9. Build Border Fence	N
2. Limit CAFE Standards	N	6. Extend Patriot Act	N	10. CAFTA	N
3. FY06 Spending Curb	N	7. Bar Same Sex Marriage	N	11. Oppose Iraq Withdrawal	N
4. Drilling in ANWR	N	8. Stem Cell Research $	Y	12. Detainee Tribunals	N

Election Results

2006 general	Mark Udall (D)	157,949	(68%)	($932,188)
	Rich Mancuso (R)	65,481	(28%)	($14,748)
	Other	7,976	(3%)	
2006 primary	Mark Udall (D)	unopposed		
2004 general	Mark Udall (D)	207,900	(67%)	($885,440)
	Stephen Hackman (R)	94,160	(30%)	($10,262)
	Other	7,304	(2%)	

Prior Winning Percentages: 2002 (60%); 2000 (55%); 1998 (50%)

The People		Race/Ethnic Origin	Ancestry	
Area size:	5,664 sq. mi.	78.9% White	German: 16.9% Irish: 9.8%	
Urban population:	87.3%	1.0% Black	English: 9.1%	
Rural population:	12.7%	3.2% Asian	**2004 Presidential Vote**	
Pop. 2000:	614,465	0.5% Native Am.	Kerry (D)	188,538 (58%)
Pop. 2005 (est):	669,194	0.1% Hawaiian	Bush (R)	132,642 (41%)
Median income:	$55,204	1.5% Two+ races	Other	1,975 (1%)
Poverty status:	7.4%	0.1% Other	**2000 Presidential Vote**	
Military veterans:	11.2%	14.7% Hispanic Origin	Gore (D)	126,607 (52%)
			Bush (R)	103,518 (43%)
			Other	13,107 (5%)
			Cook Partisan Voting Index: D + 8	

Occupation	Blue collar: 20.2%	White collar: 66.3%	Gray collar: 13.5%

Nestled right up against the Front Range of the Rockies is Boulder, the home of the 29,000-student University of Colorado, once billed by its convention bureau as "a combination of lycra-clad athletes,

New Age artists, and thoughtful intellectuals sipping cappuccinos." Dubbed the "adventure capital of the U.S.", Boulder is one of the nation's leading centers for bungee jumping, mountain biking, snowshoe running, rock and ice climbing, downhill skiing, land surfing and hot-air ballooning. It has been called the nation's number one town for outdoor sports by *Outdoor* magazine. Marathoners from around the world train in several camps here. It is also the home of the Buddhist Naropa Institute and the Boulder School of Massage Therapy. All of which is suggested by the terrain: The grid streets of Boulder literally look up at craggy peaks rising to 14,000 feet from a mile-high plain stretching farther east than the eye can see. Five of the top 10 counties in the nation with the highest life expectancy rates are in this district.

The 2d Congressional District of Colorado is centered on Boulder. It includes most of Boulder County and extends west along Interstate 70 on its awesome course through the mountains as it takes in some once-remote and lightly-populated but picturesque Rocky Mountains acreage, including the old mining town of Central City, the nearby casino mecca of Black Hawk, and the lodges and resorts of Vail; some local officials want to widen the often congested I-70. Once dependent on mining and agriculture, Vail evolved into an international resort after the 10th Mountain Division ski troops were introduced to the Eagle River Valley in the 1940s; following World War II, a group of Army buddies returned and developed a ski resort. The district also contains some of the northwest suburbs of Denver—Northglenn, Federal Heights, Lafayette and most of Westminster and Thornton—and the old Rocky Flats nuclear weapons plant, so toxic it required a $7 billion clean-up before being turned into a national wildlife refuge. The plant, where plutonium triggers were once manufactured, was home to the notorious Building 771—once known as the "most dangerous building in America" because of its immeasurably high levels of radioactive contamination.   More than $2 billion has been paid to workers who were exposed to radiation and toxic chemicals at the site. Politically, the Metro North area is marginal while Boulder is heavily Democratic and the mountain counties have been trending Democratic. Overall, this remains one of a half dozen safe Democratic districts in the Rocky Mountain states.

The congressman from the 2d District is Mark Udall, a Democrat elected in a close race in 1998. Udall is the son of longtime (1961-91) Arizona Congressman Morris Udall, who ran for president in 1976 and later chaired the Natural Resources Committee, and the nephew of Stewart Udall, who served in the House before his brother and was Interior secretary from 1961-68. "I can remember the excitement I felt sitting in a corner of Stewart's kitchen listening to my father, Stewart, Bob McNamara, Bobby Kennedy and Justice Douglas talk about the issues of the day, and there was a sense of optimism and sense of involvement and sense of meaning," Mark recalls. He is also a cousin of Oregon Senator Gordon Smith, a Republican, and of New Mexico Congressman Tom Udall, a Democrat also elected in 1998. Another Udall ran in the Arizona 1st District in 2002, but lost the Democratic nomination. "Vote for the Udall nearest you," as Mark put it. As a family, he says, they share "a belief that the 11th Commandment is that thou shalt protect the environment."

Soon after college, Udall moved to Boulder to work for the Colorado Outward Bound School and headed it for 10 years. He is an accomplished mountaineer (though he didn't quite make it to the top of Mount Everest), rock climber, kayaker and he captained his golf team as an undergraduate at Williams College. In 1996, he ran for the state House, and with his family and ideological connections raised 40% of his money out of state and won. In 1998 Udall ran when Democratic Congressman David Skaggs retired. Republicans nominated Boulder Mayor Bob Greenlee, who put more than $1 million of his own money into his campaign; Udall stressed environmental protection, growth management and education. Greenlee ran well in the Metro North suburbs, but even with all his involvement in its local government and charities, he still lost Boulder County, where nearly half the votes were cast, 56%-41%. That gave Udall a 50%-47% victory.

With seats on the Natural Resources, Science and Armed Services committees and his co-chairmanship of the Renewable Energy and Energy Efficiency Caucus, Udall has been a relatively centrist Democrat. His focus has been on the West and environmental issues. He opposed the Interior Department's decision to permit western states to designate roads across thousands of acres of federal land that might otherwise be designated as wilderness areas. With Zach Wamp, he got several provisions in the 2005 energy law to promote energy efficiency, including tax breaks and federal standards. In an unusual twist, local environmentalists opposed his efforts to cut forests in order to combat bug infestations by bark beetles and reduce wildfire threats; Udall responded that the risk to mountain communities was high. Also in 2006, he enacted a bill to establish a national drought information system, including timely forecasts plus assessments of current droughts. Explaining his 2002 opposition to the resolution authorizing force against Iraq, he cited his father's regret over supporting the Tonkin Gulf resolution in 1964. A year later, he opposed as a "blank check" the $87 billion bill to finance the war. In 2005, he led House efforts to seek a redeployment of U.S. troops from Iraq and in December 2006, he called for implementation of the Iraq Study Group's recommendations. He also worked with a bipartisan group of lawmakers to add 10,000 troops to the Army. After Democrats regained House control, he said that their challenge was "to govern well and broaden the Democratic tent."

Udall has had relatively easy reelections and has often been mentioned as a contender for statewide office. He declined to run against Senator Ben Nighthorse Campbell in 2003, but when Campbell suddenly announced his retirement in March 2004, he quickly said that he was running even if it meant a contested primary. Within 24 hours he changed his mind and endorsed Attorney General Ken Salazar as he announced his candidacy. Salazar, unencumbered with serious primary opposition, won in November. Udall soon made clear his planned candidacy in 2008, even before Senator Wayne Allard announced in January 2007 that he would not seek another term. With Allard's announcement, he became the Democratic frontrunner for the open seat and a reasonable prospect to win the general in this increasingly competitive state. With Democrats likely to hold Udall's House seat, contenders included state Senate President Joan Fitz-Gerald, philanthropist Jared Polis and Will Shafroth, head of the Colorado Conservation Trust. Former Eagle County commissioner Tom Stone, a Republican, said that he would be the best candidate and could win.

THIRD DISTRICT

Rep. John Salazar (D)

Elected 2004, 2d term; b. July 21, 1953, Alamosa; home, Manassa; Adams St. Col., B.A. 1981; Catholic; married (Mary Lou).

Military Career: Army Criminal Investigations Unit, 1973-76.

Elected Office: CO House, 2002-04.

Professional Career: Farmer.

DC Office: 1531 LHOB, 20515, 202-225-4761; Fax: 202-226-9669; Web site: www.house.gov/salazar.

District Offices: Alamosa, 719-587-5105; Durango, 970-259-1012; Grand Junction, 970-245-7107; Pueblo, 719-543-8200.

Committees: *Agriculture* (13th of 25 D): General Farm Commodities & Risk Management; Specialty Crops, Rural Development & Foreign Agriculture; Conservation, Credit, Energy & Research. *Transportation & Infrastructure* (23d of 11 D): Aviation; Water Resources & Environment. *Veterans' Affairs* (11th of 16 D): Health.

Group Ratings

	ADA	ACLU	AFS	LCV	ITIC	NTU	COC	ACU	CFG	FRC
2006	60	59	67	58	43	24	64	44	23	57
2005	75	—	100	72	—	26	67	44	15	58

National Journal Ratings

	2005 LIB	—	2005 CONS		2006 LIB	—	2006 CONS
Economic	60%	—	40%		58%	—	42%
Social	62%	—	38%		59%	—	40%
Foreign	56%	—	43%		59%	—	40%

Key Votes of the 109th Congress

1. Estate Tax Repeal	Y	5. Limit Interstate Abortion	Y	9. Build Border Fence	N
2. Limit CAFE Standards	Y	6. Extend Patriot Act	N	10. CAFTA	N
3. FY06 Spending Curb	N	7. Bar Same Sex Marriage	N	11. Oppose Iraq Withdrawal	Y
4. Drilling in ANWR	N	8. Stem Cell Research $	Y	12. Detainee Tribunals	Y

Election Results

2006 general	John Salazar (D)................................	146,488	(62%)	($2,033,671)
	Scott Tipton (R)	86,930	(37%)	($819,314)
	Other..	4,444	(2%)	
2006 primary	John Salazar (D).............................	unopposed		
2004 general	John Salazar (D)................................	153,500	(51%)	($1,625,022)
	Greg Walcher (R)	141,376	(47%)	($1,562,081)
	Other..	8,770	(3%)	

The People		Race/Ethnic Origin	Ancestry	
Area size:	54,100 sq. mi.	74.6% White	German: 13.6%	English: 9.0%
Urban population:	61.0%	0.7% Black	Irish: 8.1%	
Rural population:	39.0%	0.5% Asian	**2004 Presidential Vote**	
Pop. 2000:	614,467	1.4% Native Am.	Bush (R) 171,115	(55%)
Pop. 2005 (est):	661,014	0.1% Hawaiian	Kerry (D) 135,755	(44%)
Median income:	$35,970	1.2% Two+ races	Other 3,787	(1%)
Poverty status:	12.8%	0.1% Other	**2000 Presidential Vote**	
Military veterans:	15.3%	21.5% Hispanic Origin	Bush (R) 140,191	(54%)
			Gore (D) 102,100	(39%)
			Other 19,585	(7%)
			Cook Partisan Voting Index: R + 6	

Occupation   Blue collar: 25.0%   White collar: 56.1%   Gray collar: 18.9%

On a clear night from the air, they look like tiny mottled veins with small clots here and there, thicker near Denver but never very bright: These are the lights of the civilization Americans have built on the Western Slope of the Rockies in Colorado. The lights follow the trails of valley roads and mountainside switchbacks. The nodes mark the dozens of little towns built during mining boom years: The gold rush of the 1870s, the uranium boom of the 1950s, and the oil shale boomlet of the 1970s. The Western Slope—everything west of the Front Range, with dozens of peaks over 14,000 feet—has always blocked east-west movement; except for mining and now skiing, few would have followed the Ute Indians and settled here. The miners who tracked gold and silver and lead ores also built Victorian towns with opera houses and gingerbread storefronts in Aspen and Telluride in valleys and defiles scarcely accessible to the outside world. Now, many of these towns have been restored by ski resort operators and joined by dozens of new condominiums and shopping malls. Cries of overdevelopment have followed. Amid the tourism, some resource development continues with gas deposits trapped beneath the Roan Plateau.

The political map of the Western Slope is as diverse as its history. Aspen and Telluride, with Victorian houses and counter-cultural substrata, are liberal and Democratic; the former coal-mining center of Crested Butte and Steamboat Springs, with contemporary condominiums, for-merly Republican, are now Democratic as well. Durango, an old frontier town, has moved in the same direction; Republicans still have a voter registration edge in surrounding La Plata County. The rough-handed mining area around Grand Junction, where piles of tailings still crackle with radioactivity, Glenwood Springs, with its old hot springs hotel once visited by President Taft, and the northwest corner of the state, where people remember the oil shale boom with nostalgia, are hostile to environmentalists and heavily Republican. Thus high-income areas, with lots of liberal-minded trustfunders, are the lead Democratic areas, while modest-income, working-class towns are the lead Republican areas on the Western Slope.

The 3d Congressional District of Colorado is the state's largest—roughly the size of Arkansas—and includes most of the Western Slope. It extends east of the Front Range to include the small industrial city of Pueblo. There, on the banks of the Arkansas River, the Rockefellers built large steel factories before World War I to make barbed wire and rails; now, this blue-collar town has attracted large medical centers and some industrial plants. Pueblo is heavily Democratic and so are the counties on the plains and in the San Luis Valley to the south. These inhabitants are Hispanic, not Mexican-American: Spanish-speaking people have been living here, as in northern New Mexico, for 350 years. Politically, the 3d District has moved to the right, voting for Bill Clinton in 1992 but for Bob Dole in 1996 and George W. Bush in 2000 and 2004. On balance, it is a Republican district, but it can be unpredictable.

The congressman from the 3d District is John Salazar, a Democrat and the older brother of Senator Ken Salazar; both were first elected in 2004. They are the third pair of brothers in Congress. The Salazar brothers grew up on a family ranch without running water or electricity in the San Luis Valley, east of the Front Range just north of the New Mexico border. After high school, John Salazar served in the Army, including a tour of duty in a criminal investigations unit overseas. After his service he returned to Colorado and got a business degree from Adams State College. He settled on the ranch, which has been in his family since 1850, and developed a seed potato farming operation that grows millions of potatoes in huge fields; he was active in the Colorado Certified Seed Growers and on state farming boards. When a private developer in the mid-1990s tried to buy up water rights in the San Luis Valley to ship it to the Denver area, Salazar organized a citizens' revolt. Younger brother Ken Salazar had held high state office from the 1980s and was elected attorney general in 1998; John Salazar did not run for office until 2002, when he was elected to the state House.

When Republican Scott McInnis announced his retirement in September 2003, Salazar moved quickly to run. Rather than emphasizing his Hispanic heritage, he called himself a farmer. And wisely in this district, he cast himself as a pragmatic centrist and a friendly guy, not a partisan Democrat. But he proved to be a good fundraiser and won labor endorsements which helped him win 69% of the delegate votes in the May 2004 state party convention and avoid a primary. Meanwhile, five candidates battled for the Republican nomination. Former state Department of Natural Resources Director Greg Walcher narrowly beat McInnis's brother-in-law, state Representative Matt Smith, 32%-31%. Walcher, considered the most socially conservative of the candidates, was the only one who in 2003 supported Governor Bill Owens's Referendum A to authorize $2 billion in bonds for water storage projects, which was defeated 67%-33% statewide and 85%-15% on the Western Slope. John Salazar, who was state co-chairman of the anti-Referendum A campaign, hammered the issue relentlessly. Walcher accused Salazar of being a pro-tax liberal and attempted to tie him to Democratic presidential nominee John Kerry. But Salazar proved to be an elusive target. Though he supported abortion rights and opposed a constitutional amendment banning same-sex marriage, the folksy, cowboy-hat wearing Democrat crafted a moderate image by keeping Kerry at a safe distance, embracing tax cuts for farmers and ranchers and supporting estate tax repeal. He also sported an "A" rating from the National Rifle Association. Salazar won 51%-47%, taking 16 of the 29 counties and running far ahead of Kerry in Pueblo and in the Hispanic counties on the plains.

In the House, Salazar had a centrist voting record and he joined the Hispanic Caucus. At the urging of a local college student, he enacted a bill to enhance protections against improper uses of the congressional Medal of Honor and other military decorations. Following an August 2006 trip to Iraq, he opposed a timetable for withdrawal, which brother Ken supported. On the Transportation and Infrastructure Committee, he got $32 million for his district in the 2005 highway bill, which was among the highest totals for a freshman. On the Agriculture Committee, he won approval of his proposal to require forest managers to consider using some dead logs as an alternative fuel. He worked with Republicans on tougher immigration enforcement. In the majority, he planned to focus on energy independence; he has opposed big subsidies to oil companies.

His legislative accomplishments discouraged serious opposition in 2006. Republican Scott Tipton, who ran a pottery business, crisscrossed the rural district in a Ford F-350 pickup but Salazar noted that Tipton's other car was a Jaguar. This was a bad year for Republican challengers, even in districts like this one, and especially against a Democrat like Salazar who had deemphasized partisanship. Salazar won 62%-37%. He won 24 of the 29 counties, including 73%-26% in Pueblo. Tipton took five counties along the western border.

FOURTH DISTRICT

Rep. Marilyn Musgrave (R)

Elected 2002, 3d term; b. Jan. 27, 1949, Greeley; home, Ft. Morgan; CO St. U., B.A. 1972; First Assembly of God; married (Steve).

Elected Office: Ft. Morgan Schl. Bd., 1990-94; CO House of Reps., 1994-98; CO Senate, 1998-2002.

DC Office: 1507 LHOB, 20515, 202-225-4676; Fax: 202-225-5870; Web site: www.house.gov/musgrave.

District Offices: Fort Morgan, 970-867-4414; Greeley, 970-352-4037; Las Animas, 719-456-0925; Longmont, 720-494-4336; Loveland, 970-663-3536; Sterling, 970-522-1788.

Committees: *Agriculture* (11th of 21 R): Specialty Crops, Rural Development & Foreign Agriculture (RMM); Conservation, Credit, Energy & Research. *Small Business* (6th of 15 R): Rural & Urban Entrepreneurship; Regulations, Healthcare & Trade.

Group Ratings

	ADA	ACLU	AFS	LCV	ITIC	NTU	COC	ACU	CFG	FRC
2006	0	10	0	8	100	75	100	96	85	100
2005	0	—	0	0	—	70	92	100	88	100

National Journal Ratings

	2005 LIB	—	2005 CONS		2006 LIB	—	2006 CONS
Economic	3%	—	94%		11%	—	89%
Social	17%	—	82%		6%	—	92%
Foreign	0%	—	89%		17%	—	73%

Key Votes of the 109th Congress

1. Estate Tax Repeal	Y	5. Limit Interstate Abortion	Y	9. Build Border Fence	Y
2. Limit CAFE Standards	Y	6. Extend Patriot Act	Y	10. CAFTA	Y
3. FY06 Spending Curb	Y	7. Bar Same Sex Marriage	Y	11. Oppose Iraq Withdrawal	Y
4. Drilling in ANWR	Y	8. Stem Cell Research $	N	12. Detainee Tribunals	Y

Election Results

2006 general	Marilyn Musgrave (R)	109,732	(46%)	($3,212,143)
	Angie Paccione (D)	103,748	(43%)	($1,951,180)
	Eric Eidsness (Ref)	27,133	(11%)	($31,808)
2006 primary	Marilyn Musgrave (R)	unopposed		
2004 general	Marilyn Musgrave (R)	155,958	(51%)	($3,314,507)
	Stan Matsunaka (D)	136,812	(45%)	($868,439)
	Bob Kinsey (Green)	12,739	(4%)	($6,946)

Prior Winning Percentages: 2002 (55%)

The People		Race/Ethnic Origin	Ancestry	
Area size:	31,048 sq. mi.	79.4% White	German: 20.3%	English: 8.7%
Urban population:	75.1%	0.7% Black	Irish: 8.4%	
Rural population:	24.9%	1.1% Asian	**2004 Presidential Vote**	
Pop. 2000:	614,466	0.5% Native Am.	Bush (R) 180,017	(58%)
Pop. 2005 (est):	679,200	0.1% Hawaiian	Kerry (D) 128,002	(41%)
Median income:	$43,389	1.2% Two+ races	Other 2,637	(1%)
Poverty status:	10.9%	0.1% Other	**2000 Presidential Vote**	
Military veterans:	12.3%	17.0% Hispanic Origin	Bush (R) 145,056	(57%)
			Gore (D) 92,602	(36%)
			Other 16,271	(6%)
			Cook Partisan Voting Index: R + 9	

Occupation	Blue collar: 24.0%	White collar: 59.8%	Gray collar: 16.2%

The High Plains of eastern Colorado are dusty brown, gently rolling grasslands that seem flat but actually slope imperceptibly up toward the Rocky Mountains. The land is fertile, but dry; rainfall is rare, the rivers are just a trickle most of the year, and in many places groundwater is equally scarce. It is fine wheat country when irrigated and one of the foremost beef cattle regions. But it has been squeezed in recent decades between declining prices for wheat plus declining demand for beef and increased prices for water because of high demand in Denver and along the Front Range. Bitter confrontations have erupted over who gets access to the South Platte River, leading to limitations on pumping from the basin. Local farmers are now finding that the value of their water rights to metro Denver far exceeds what they hope to gain by farming; their neighbors condemn them for selling out and betraying a way of life that seems destined to decline. The prairie lands and small towns of the High Plains have small reminders of their past: The Pawnee National Grasslands, where antelope, coyotes and prairie dogs still roam, and Burlington's 1905 carousel, one of the few with the original paint. But the free market that once peopled the High Plains with farmers and ranchers and made it the scene of farm protests and revolts is now causing it to empty out and revert to untamed land, ready again for now increasingly numerous buffalo, elk, deer and bighorn sheep.

The 4th Congressional District of Colorado contains almost all of the High Plains plus the medium-sized and fast-growing area around Greeley, Fort Collins and Loveland—the northern end of the densely populated Front Range, off I-25 toward Cheyenne, Wyoming. It includes all of fast-growing Larimer County just east of the mountains and reaches into Boulder County to pick up the city of Longmont. Fort Collins became a center for California transplants seeking a different lifestyle at start-up telecommunications firms, and appeared to survive the dot.com bust by spending its money on infrastructure instead of corporate incentives. Fort Collins also is home to a Centers for Disease Control and Prevention lab that conducts cutting-edge research in the war against bio-terrorism. To the east is Weld County, still mostly rural and more conservative in its politics. By heritage and usually by inclination, this is Republican territory: It was evenly split in 1992, but later gave solid margins to Bob Dole and George W. Bush.

The congresswoman from the 4th District is Marilyn Musgrave, first elected in 2002; she replaced Bob Schaffer, a Republican who reluctantly abided by his pledge to limit himself to three terms and who lost the Republican Senate nomination in 2004 to Pete Coors. Musgrave grew up in rural Weld County, where she worked as a waitress, cleaned houses and cared for children. She first became interested in politics when a liberal teacher in her high school government class inspired her with his interest in issues. She pursued her interest in social studies at Colorado State, where she found herself increasingly disturbed by socialist ideas. She and her husband Steve, whom she married at college, started a hay-stacking business. Musgrave was first elected to public office in 1990 as a member of the Fort Morgan school board and in 1994, she was elected to the state House. In 1998, she successfully challenged a popular Democratic state senator. In the statehouse, she earned a reputation as an honest, uncompromising social conservative. She was one of the legislature's strongest Second Amendment supporters, an advocate of tax cuts and a sponsor of bills opposing abortion, same-sex marriage and adoptions by same-sex parents.

When Schaffer announced he would retire, Musgrave became the front-runner to replace him. In the primary, she was opposed by a Greeley lawyer who criticized her focus on cultural issues. Musgrave got Schaffer's backing, and easily won the primary 65%-35%. In the general, she faced state Senate president Stan Matsunaka of Loveland who, after the Democrats won a one-seat majority in the Senate in 2000, thwarted many of her legislative initiatives. Matsunaka emphasized his fiscal conservatism and his support for gun ownership rights and at every opportunity depicted Musgrave as an ineffective extremist and as a zealot on cultural issues. But Musgrave raised more money and criticized Matsunaka's record on tax issues. At the end of the campaign, voters could be excused for thinking that Matsunaka's name was "Stan Taxsunaka" or "Stan the Tax Man." Musgrave won 55%-42% and carried all 18 counties. In Larimer County, which cast about 45% of the vote, Musgrave won 50%-47%. In the eastern plains, she won overwhelmingly.

In the House, Musgrave quickly made a name for herself with her independent style and outspoken conservatism. After only three months in office, she drew attention when she wrote a letter to Speaker Dennis Hastert that criticized the pork-barrel habits of Transportation and Infrastructure Committee Chairman Don Young and called his proposal to raise the gas tax "ill-timed." That caught Young's attention: On the House floor, he walked toward her and, as she recounted, "he proceeded to browbeat me." Later, he rejected her requests for highway projects in her district. She opposed the Bush Medicare/prescription drug bill as too expensive. During the extended three-hour roll call, Hastert urged her to switch, but she waved off his entreaties. Later that night she told George W. Bush too that she was a firm "no" vote. Musgrave moved into the national spotlight as the lead sponsor of the Federal Marriage Amendment banning same-sex marriage, to reverse what she called "the modern assault on marriage." Musgrave dismissed gay rights advocates who called her an extremist, and she added that her views were well known to her constituents. When the House in September 2004 fell 49 votes short of the required two-thirds support to pass the constitutional amendment, Musgrave called it "a victory to me that we had a vote." In 2006, the proposed amendment fell 46 votes short and its immediate future was dim. Also that year, the House passed her amendment to prevent enforcement of a law passed in 2005 that gun dealers sell trigger locks with the weapons that they sell.

In this firmly Republican district, Musgrave has struggled with reelection. In 2004, Matsunaka decided at the last minute to run again. He was even more heavily outspent than in 2002; Musgrave called him "the same old Stan." But he benefited from independent advertising that harshly criticized Musgrave for voting to cut veterans' benefits, including a TV spot that depicted her taking money from a dead soldier's pocket. The NRCC spent about $1 million to bail out Musgrave. Musgrave won this time by only 51%-45%. She lost Larimer County by 49%-46%. Most of her margin came from the sparsely populated eastern plains, which she carried 64%-33%. Democrats targeted her again in 2006, though with an unconventional candidate for this rural district: state Representative Angie Paccione, a part-Italian, part African-American former professional basketball player and an avowed liberal. Paccione criticized Musgrave's focus on social issues as a distractions from more immediate needs of the district, including the need for federal drought relief and farm subsidies; she was aided by more than $3 million in spending by outside groups. Musgrave defended her record and conservative views. Republican worries about the contest led Bush to make a campaign stop for Musgrave the final weekend of the campaign. "Marilyn Musgrave understands the importance of defending traditional values," he said. Her victory margin grew still tighter, 46%-43%, with 11% for Reform Party candidate Eric Eidsness; she had the lowest winning percentage of anyone elected to the House in 2006. Paccione took Larimer County, 49%-40% but Musgrave won by 2-to-1 and 3-to-1 margins in some of the rural counties. After not making a campaign appearance on Election Night or the next day, she issued a statement three weeks later emphasizing her bipartisan approach. But in early 2007 she voted against the key pieces of the Democrats' agenda and criticized their "raw power" in barring GOP amendments.

Paccione dropped her bid to run again in 2008; Eidsness planned to run as a Democrat. Betsy Markey, a former aide to Senator Ken Salazar, also declared her candidacy.

FIFTH DISTRICT

Rep. Doug Lamborn (R)

Elected 2006, 1st term; b. May 24, 1954, Leavenworth, KS; home, Colorado Springs; U. of KS, B.S. 1978, J.D. 1986; Christian; married (Jeanie).

Elected Office: CO House of Reps., 1994-98; CO Senate, 1998-2006.

Professional Career: Practicing atty., 1987-2007.

DC Office: 437 CHOB, 20515, 202-225-4422; Fax: 202-226-2638; Web site: lamborn.house.gov.

District Offices: Colorado Springs, 719-520-0055.

Committees: *Natural Resources* (20th of 22 R): Water & Power; National Parks, Forests & Public Lands. *Veterans' Affairs* (11th of 13 R): Disability Assistance & Memorial Affairs (RMM).

Group Ratings and Key Votes: Newly Elected

Election Results

2006 general	Doug Lamborn (R)	123,264	(60%)	($997,973)
	Jay Fawcett (D)	83,431	(40%)	($669,121)
2006 primary	Doug Lamborn (R)	15,126	(27%)	
	Jeff Crank (R)	14,234	(25%)	
	Bentley Rayburn (R)	9,735	(17%)	
	Lionel Rivera (R)	7,213	(13%)	
	John Anderson (R)	6,474	(12%)	
	Duncan Bremer (R)	3,310	(6%)	
2004 general	Joel Hefley (R)	193,333	(71%)	($93,332)
	Fred Hardee (D)	74,098	(27%)	($8,949)
	Other	6,627	(2%)	

The People		Race/Ethnic Origin	Ancestry	
Area size:	7,732 sq. mi.	77.4% White	German: 16.1%	Irish: 9.1%
Urban population:	85.7%	5.7% Black	English: 8.9%	
Rural population:	14.3%	2.2% Asian	**2004 Presidential Vote**	
Pop. 2000:	614,467	0.7% Native Am.	Bush (R) 190,190	(66%)
Pop. 2005 (est):	667,666	0.2% Hawaiian	Kerry (D) 93,684	(33%)
Median income:	$45,454	2.5% Two+ races	Other 3,248	(1%)
Poverty status:	8.3%	0.2% Other	**2000 Presidential Vote**	
Military veterans:	19.9%	11.1% Hispanic Origin	Bush (R) 151,751	(63%)
			Gore (D) 74,940	(31%)
			Other 13,116	(5%)
			Cook Partisan Voting Index: R +16	

Occupation	Blue collar: 21.3%	White collar: 63.2%	Gray collar: 15.5%

In 1893, Katherine Lee Bates took the cog railway up from Colorado Springs to the top of 14,110-foot Pikes Peak and, looking out at the purple mountain's majesty above amber waves of grain, wrote the lines of "America the Beautiful." Pike's Peak, espied by Zebulon Pike in 1806, and Colorado Springs, with the Garden of the Gods and the Broadmoor Hotel, have been tourist attractions for more than 100 years. In the second half of the 20th century, Colorado Springs, safe in the vastness of North America, has also become a great American military fortress. During the height of the Cold War in the 1960s, the Pentagon constructed the North American Aerospace Defense Command more than 1,000 feet below Cheyenne Mountain, a fortified bunker able to survive a nuclear strike from a Soviet missile. The Pentagon decided in 2006, in part because of local traffic congestion, to move NORAD's surveillance operations to nearby Peterson Air Force Base, site of space-based defense research. The 5th is also the home of Fort Carson, the site of the Air Force Academy, and Schriever Air Force Base, formerly Falcon AFB but renamed in 1998 for General Bernard A. Schriever, a pioneer in the development of ballistic missile programs.

Around them, Colorado Springs has built a high-tech, innovative economy. And with the arrival of Dr. James Dobson's Focus on the Family in 1994 and other Christian organizations, it has been a center of conservative Christianity, the home of Colorado's young conservatism, the counterpoint to Denver's aging liberalism. This was the birthplace of Colorado's anti-tax initiatives and of Amendment 2, which in 1992 repealed city gay rights ordinances but was overturned by the U.S. Supreme Court. It is one of America's most Republican metropolitan areas: Colorado Springs's El Paso County in 2004 cast more votes than Denver County, and its 83,000-vote margin for George W. Bush almost counterbalanced Denver's 96,000-vote margin for John Kerry.

The 5th Congressional District consists of Colorado Springs and El Paso County, plus all or most of four mountain counties to the west. One of them, Lake County, includes the old mining town of Leadville and usually votes Democratic. But 87% of the district's population is in El Paso County and in effect this is the Colorado Springs congressional district. The 5th District is the most Republican district in Colorado and one of the most Republican in the nation.

The new congressman from the 5th District is Doug Lamborn, a Republican elected in 2006 to succeed Republican Joel Hefley, who retired after 10 terms. Lamborn, the son of a prison guard, was born in Leavenworth, Kansas, and studied journalism at the University of Kansas. He said he voted in 1976 for Jimmy Carter, which he calls a mistake, but was then drawn to Republican politics by Ronald Reagan. Lamborn ran unsuccessfully in 1982 as the Republican candidate for a heavily Democratic seat in the Kansas legislature, then returned to his alma mater to earn a law degree. In

1987, Lamborn moved his family to Colorado Springs, where he practiced business and real estate law and became an avid mountain climber. In 1994, he won the first of two terms in the Colorado House and in 1998 was appointed to a vacant state Senate seat. Lamborn ran unopposed in the next election, and later served as state Senate president pro tem. During 12 years in the legislature, Lamborn compiled a reliably conservative record on social and fiscal issues. He opposed abortion, sponsoring bills to limit late-term abortions, and he advocated tax cuts, including a reduction in state income taxes. He backed legislation that would have ended some benefits to illegal immigrants, and increased penalties for illegal immigrant smugglers.

During two decades in Congress, Hefley had never won with less than 66 percent, and the chance to represent a safe Republican seat drew six GOP candidates, including Lamborn, Jeff Crank, a former aide for Hefley, retired Air Force Major General Bentley Rayburn, Colorado Springs Mayor Lionel Rivera, former El Paso County Sheriff John Anderson and former El Paso County Commissioner Duncan Bremer, brother of Paul Bremer, the administrator of the Coalition Provisional Authority in Iraq. Crank had endorsements from Hefley and the president of Focus on the Family; Lamborn had the backing of the anti-tax Club for Growth and the Colorado Christian Coalition. At the May party convention, Crank won the delegate vote 46%-40%, but Lamborn had more than the minimum 30% needed to secure a place on the primary ballot. Lamborn emphasized his conservative voting record and vowed never to raise taxes. The state Christian Coalition sent a mailer suggesting Crank backed the "radical homosexual lobby."

In the August primary, Crank won five of the district's six counties and appeared headed to victory. With absentee ballots still to be counted, Lamborn decided to go for a walk. On his return, he was greeted on the sidewalk by staffers and reporters who told him he had won the nomination. Asked why he went for a walk, Lamborn replied, "I had to say a prayer and ask that God's will be done." He won the nomination by 892 votes, winning only El Paso County with 27% to Crank's 23%. Overall, he defeated Crank 27%-25%, while Rayburn placed third with 17%.

In the general election, Lamborn faced Democrat Jay Fawcett, an Air Force Academy graduate who won a Bronze star during the Gulf War. In most years, the Democratic nominee would not have drawn a second look. But the bruising Republican primary and a tough national election environment made for an unusually competitive general election campaign. Hefley, displaying his usual candor, refused to endorse Lamborn for the general election. "I made this clear at the start of this campaign that I would never again support a Republican who ran a sleazy campaign against another Republican, and that's what Doug Lamborn did," Hefley said. He rejected attempts to recruit him back into the race as a write-in candidate. Fawcett sought to take advantage of the Republican discord, going so far as to purchase a newspaper ad featuring the names and photos of three dozen prominent local Republicans who also declined to endorse Lamborn. He tried to appeal to Republicans and unaffiliated voters by emphasizing his military experience, a strong selling point in a military-oriented district that is also home to many retired veterans.

During two debates, the candidates disagreed on Iraq and abortion, and in October, polls reflected a dead heat, an alarming result for a district that national Republicans were unaccustomed to worrying about—no Democrat had won the seat since it was created in 1972. But on Election Day, voters overcame any lingering animosity toward Lamborn and gave him a 60%-40% victory. Asked after the election about Republican defectors, Lamborn said, "Those people represented some whiners and some of the most liberal Republicans."

In Congress, Lamborn won a seat on the Armed Services Committee, a critical committee for a member from this district, but there were no Republican vacancies at the time and he was forced to take "on leave" status to await the committee's next opening. Back home, lingering resentment over Lamborn's 2006 primary election victory may lead to a tough challenge in 2008. In August 2007, Crank announced he would run again in the 2008 primary while Rayburn was considering it.

SIXTH DISTRICT

Rep. Tom Tancredo (R)

Elected 1998, 5th term; b. Dec. 20, 1945, Denver; home, Littleton; U. of N. CO, B.A. 1968; Presbyterian; married (Jackie).

Elected Office: CO House of Reps., 1976-81.

Professional Career: Jr. high teacher, 1968-81; Regional rep., U.S. Dept. of Education, 1981-93; Pres., Independence Inst., 1993-98.

DC Office: 1130 LHOB, 20515, 202-225-7882; Fax: 202-226-4623; Web site: www.house.gov/tancredo.

District Offices: Castle Rock, 303-688-3430; Centennial, 720-283-9772; Littleton, 720-283-7575.

Committees: *Foreign Affairs* (9th of 23 R): Africa & Global Health; Terrorism, Nonproliferation & Trade. *Natural Resources* (7th of 22 R): National Parks, Forests & Public Lands.

Group Ratings

	ADA	ACLU	AFS	LCV	ITIC	NTU	COC	ACU	CFG	FRC
2006	10	9	0	8	67	76	100	92	80	100
2005	5	—	13	11	—	80	77	100	88	92

National Journal Ratings

	2005 LIB	—	2005 CONS	2006 LIB	—	2006 CONS
Economic	44%	—	56%	19%	—	81%
Social	21%	—	78%	11%	—	85%
Foreign	42%	—	55%	47%	—	51%

Key Votes of the 109th Congress

1. Estate Tax Repeal	Y	5. Limit Interstate Abortion	Y	9. Build Border Fence	Y
2. Limit CAFE Standards	Y	6. Extend Patriot Act	Y	10. CAFTA	N
3. FY06 Spending Curb	Y	7. Bar Same Sex Marriage	Y	11. Oppose Iraq Withdrawal	Y
4. Drilling in ANWR	Y	8. Stem Cell Research $	N	12. Detainee Tribunals	Y

Election Results

2006 general	Tom Tancredo (R)	158,806	(59%)	($1,754,235)
	Bill Winter (D)	108,007	(40%)	($806,518)
	Other	4,118	(2%)	
2006 primary	Tom Tancredo (R)	unopposed		
2004 general	Tom Tancredo (R)	212,778	(59%)	($1,178,724)
	Joanna Conti (D)	139,870	(39%)	($827,526)
	Other	5,093	(1%)	

Prior Winning Percentages: 2002 (67%); 2000 (54%); 1998 (56%)

The People		Race/Ethnic Origin	Ancestry	
Area size:	4,111 sq. mi.	87.7% White	German: 18.9%	Irish: 10.9%
Urban population:	84.7%	1.9% Black	English: 10.5%	
Rural population:	15.3%	2.6% Asian	**2004 Presidential Vote**	
Pop. 2000:	614,466	0.4% Native Am.	Bush (R) 223,156	(60%)
Pop. 2005 (est):	725,209	0.1% Hawaiian	Kerry (D) 144,683	(39%)
Median income:	$73,393	1.5% Two+ races	Other 2,553	(1%)
Poverty status:	2.7%	0.1% Other	**2000 Presidential Vote**	
Military veterans:	13.6%	5.8% Hispanic Origin	Bush (R) 169,205	(60%)
			Gore (D) 104,126	(37%)
			Other 7,580	(3%)
			Cook Partisan Voting Index: R +10	

Occupation	Blue collar: 13.2%	White collar: 77.4%	Gray collar: 9.4%

Two generations ago, most people in metro Denver lived in the city itself; at the city limits, the tree-shaded sidewalks gave way to the empty High Plains. Today, more than three-quarters of metro Denver residents live outside the city, some in long-settled suburbs, some in huge new subdivisions raised up in the 1990s and 2000s on bare rolling land with magnificent views of the Rockies. You can see the boundaries to these areas in Littleton, originally a small, long-settled suburb just south of Denver, but now extending to vast new tracts; this is the site of the massacre at Columbine High School in April 1999. Just south of Littleton is Douglas County, which until the 1970s was a sparsely populated patch of the High Plains just east of the Front Range. From 1990 to 2003 it was the fastest-growing county in the United States, as young families moved into 35-acre "ranchettes," or huge subdivisions around Castle Rock and Parker just south of the Denver Tech Center, and took high-paying telecommunications jobs at local employers Echo Star and AT&T Broadband, now a part of Comcast. Lockheed is attracting scientists to build the Orion space exploration vehicle in Jefferson County. In 2000, Douglas was the nation's most affluent county in median household income ($84,645) and had the smallest percentage of people living in poverty (1.8%). The rapid growth has continued: From 2000 to 2004, it grew by 35%, making it the third-fastest growing county in the nation over that period. This is Patio Land, as David Brooks has described, with a high-tech economy, a highly educated population with relatively conservative cultural values, family men and women who want to create a safe, comfortable environment for their children with the serenity if not the close personal ties of the traditional small town and the economic vibrancy and creativity of the great metropolis. "The fastest-growing regions of the country tend to have the highest concentrations of children. Young families move away from what they perceive as disorder, vulgarity and danger and move to places like Douglas County," Brooks wrote in *The New York Times*.

The 6th Congressional District of Colorado is centered on Littleton and Douglas County. To the west, it includes much of Jefferson County, including part of affluent Evergreen in the mountains. To the east, it includes much of Arapahoe County and, southeast, Elbert County, long empty land but now sprouting new subdivisions on the high plains. After the Colorado Springs-based 5th, this is the state's second most Republican district.

The congressman from the 6th District is Tom Tancredo (pronounced *tan-CRAY-doe*), a self-described religious right Republican, who was first elected in a turbulent 1998 campaign. Tancredo grew up on the north side of Denver, taught junior high school civics, and in 1976, at 30, was elected to the state House. He got his political start, he says, when as an eighth-grader he imitated Fidel Castro. In the state legislature, he was part of a group called "the Crazies," who zeroed out the sales tax on food and utilities, the inheritance tax and the auto safety inspection tax. In 1981, he became head of the regional office of the Education Department, and cut its staff by two-thirds. A lapsed Catholic who began attending an evangelical Presbyterian church in 1990, he became in 1993 head of the Independence Institute, a libertarian think tank in Golden.

When the congressional seat opened in 1998, Tancredo, an energetic and voluble speaker, jumped into the race. He had four opponents in the Republican primary, spanning the ideological spectrum. Tancredo campaigned by walking the district and running radio ads the last 10 days; his big break was an endorsement by former Senator (1979-91) Bill Armstrong, a religious conservative who has stayed politically active. Armstrong's endorsement was worth 5% of the vote, Tancredo said, and he needed it: He defeated moderate Bill Schroeder 25%-22%. In the general election, Tancredo was smeared by a self-financing 70-year-old Democrat, who ran a TV ad linking Tancredo with a white supremacist militia. But Tancredo won 56%-42%.

Tancredo drew attention from the start. He declined to attend a Clinton White House reception for new members. Then came the shootings at Columbine High School, six blocks from Tancredo's house. An outcry arose for new gun controls. Tancredo, a Second Amendment supporter, pointed out that Colorado has stronger gun-control laws than the federal government. Gun control measures failed to pass; Tancredo was the only Colorado House member to vote for the National Rifle Association's bill. In November 2003, he was one of 25 House Republicans to vote against the final version of the Medicare/prescription drug bill, which he said would trigger a "catastrophic fiscal crisis." His voting record sometimes veers toward the center, especially because of his protectionist views on trade.

Immigration is the chief cause that animates Tancredo, who is himself the grandson of an Italian immigrant. He is the leading voice in Congress for tougher border enforcement and increased immigration regulation, and he founded the Immigration Reform Caucus. In April 2002, in an editorial meeting with *The Washington Times,* Tancredo earned the enmity of the White House by charging that George W. Bush's "open door" border policy was a threat to national security and an invitation to terrorism. Tancredo said that Bush strategist Karl Rove called him disloyal and told him, "Don't ever darken the doorstep of the White House." But six months later, Tancredo was invited to the White House for the signing of the Sudan Peace Act, which he co-sponsored. While

Bush was calling for a legalized guest worker program, Tancredo remained relentless. He opposed proposals to grant regularized status to illegal immigrants who entered the country illegally or overstayed visas and proposed an amendment to the Colorado constitution to deny state services to illegal immigrants. He called for taxes on the checks that immigrants send to their families that have remained south of the border. At the 2004 Republican convention he criticized the platform's "open-border policy" for pandering to corporate desires for cheap labor. When Bush suggested in March 2005 that the Minuteman Project activists who patrolled the Arizona-Mexico border were "vigilantes," Tancredo told them, "You are not vigilantes, you are heroes." He has endorsed primary challengers to GOP incumbents who don't share his views, and is not likely to win a popularity contest among fellow Republicans; some contend that House leaders' embrace of his hard line was a factor in their 2006 election setback. He has called Miami "a Third World country," and said that the Congressional Black Caucus and other race-based groups condone segregation and should be abolished. His book, *In Mortal Danger*, denounced "the cult of multiculturalism." Democrats have welcomed the opportunity to make him a face of the Republican party. "I'm all for more and more nuts in their party speaking up," said Rahm Emanuel, referring to Tancredo. Critics maintain a "Tancredo Watch" blog.

With his controversial views, Tancredo in 2000 was reelected by the slimmer margin of 54%-42%. Redistricting made reelection much easier; he won 67%-30% in 2002. But in 2004 he ran behind George W. Bush. Against Bill Winter, a modestly funded ex-Marine, lawyer and high school football coach, Tancredo won 59%-40% in 2006, a much tougher year for Republicans. After talking about running for president for two years, spending time in Iowa and New Hampshire and logging many appearances on cable TV—during which he urged more serious candidates in the presidential race to take on the immigration issue—Tancredo declared his presidential candidacy in April 2007. He has worked closely with Bay Buchanan, who has presidential campaign experience. Tancredo was critical of Bush, telling the *Politico* that the president has been a "disaster in so many ways." He added, "To be at odds with the president of the United States who's in my party or the leadership in my party wasn't my intention, but it certainly developed that way."

Tancredo has said he is not interested in running for Colorado's open Senate seat in 2008 and through mid-2007 did not indicate whether he would seek reelection to his House seat.

SEVENTH DISTRICT

Rep. Ed Perlmutter (D)

Elected 2006, 1st term; b. May 1, 1953, Denver; home, Golden; U. of CO, B.A. 1975, J.D. 1978; Protestant; married (Deana).

Elected Office: CO Senate, 1994-2002.

Professional Career: Practicing atty., 1979-2006.

DC Office: 415 CHOB, 20515, 202-225-2645; Fax: 202-225-5278; Web site. perlmutter.house.gov.

District Offices: Lakewood, 303-274-7944.

Committees: *Financial Services* (32d of 37 D): Capital Markets, Insurance & Government Sponsored Enterprises; Financial Institutions & Consumer Credit. *Homeland Security* (18th of 19 D): Management, Investigations & Oversight; Intelligence, Information Sharing & Terrorism Risk Assessment; Transportation Security & Infrastructure Protection.

Group Ratings and Key Votes: Newly Elected

Election Results

2006 general	Ed Perlmutter (D) 103,918	(55%)	($2,945,170)
	Rick O'Donnell (R) 79,571	(42%)	($2,771,913)
	Other 5,683	(3%)	
2006 primary	Ed Perlmutter (D) 15,598	(53%)	
	Peggy Lamm (D) 11,047	(38%)	
	Herb Rubenstein (D) 2,625	(9%)	
2004 general	Bob Beauprez (R) 135,571	(55%)	($2,970,799)
	Dave Thomas (D) 106,026	(43%)	($1,125,677)
	Other 6,167	(2%)	

The People		Race/Ethnic Origin	Ancestry	
Area size:	1,265 sq. mi.	68.9% White	German: 16.0%	Irish: 8.9%
Urban population:	97.7%	5.8% Black	English: 8.4%	
Rural population:	2.3%	2.9% Asian	**2004 Presidential Vote**	
Pop. 2000:	614,465	0.6% Native Am.	Kerry (D) 130,984	(51%)
Pop. 2005 (est):	646,651	0.1% Hawaiian	Bush (R) 122,772	(48%)
Median income:	$46,149	1.9% Two+ races	Other 1,150	(0%)
Poverty status:	8.9%	0.1% Other	**2000 Presidential Vote**	
Military veterans:	14.1%	19.6% Hispanic Origin	Gore (D) 103,592	(50%)
			Bush (R) 101,632	(49%)
			Other 2,783	(1%)
			Cook Partisan Voting Index: D + 2	

Occupation	Blue collar: 23.8%	White collar: 62.6%	Gray collar: 13.6%

The inner circle of suburbs around Denver was developed in the 1950s, 1960s and 1970s. West of Denver, on broad avenues running toward the mountains, is Lakewood, where growth was sparked by the Denver Federal Center; affluent in the south, more marginal near the Denver city limits, a place not of uniformity but of suburban diversity. Out to the west is the town of Golden, with the old Colorado School of Mines and the Coors brewery. To the north are Arvada (which is shared with the 2d District) and Wheat Ridge, middle-income suburbs with an increasing number of Latinos. On the other side of Denver, to the east of the now-closed Stapleton Airport, is Aurora, as vast as Lakewood, and somewhat newer, with its huge regional mall and an increasing number of middle class blacks. East of Aurora are rolling, empty plains that stretch to the Kansas line.

The 7th Congressional District of Colorado, newly created for the 2002 election, covers parts of three counties and most of the inner Denver suburbs. The bulk of its land area, but only 15% of its voters, are in Adams County, which includes the industrial zone along the South Platte River and the Rocky Mountain Arsenal National Wildlife Refuge. Adams County has long been the most Democratic of the suburban Denver counties, but its political future cannot be predicted safely: This empty area is likely to fill up with new subdivisions in the next decade. Aurora, partly in Adams County with a larger part in Arapahoe County, has long been Republican. But with more black and Latino residents, it has been trending Democratic. Lakewood and the other towns in Jefferson County (or Jeffco, as people call it) is perhaps Colorado's premier political battleground. Long solidly Republican, it is now more marginal. And it is crucial here: Jeffco has 62% of the 7th District's voters. The judge who handed down the redistricting plan deliberately chose to make the 7th evenly divided between the parties, and so it has been. The areas within its boundaries voted 50%-49% for Al Gore in 2000 and 51%-48% for John Kerry in 2004, and in the 2002 House election this was the most closely divided district in the nation.

The new congressman from the 7th District is Ed Perlmutter, a Democrat elected in 2006. He grew up in Jefferson County, walking precincts with his father on Democratic campaigns at an early age. He attended the University of Colorado and earned a law degree in 1978, and then went into private practice. In 1994, a bad political year for Democrats, Perlmutter won election to the state Senate from a northern Jefferson County district that had not elected a Democrat in nearly 30 years. In the legislature, where he gained a reputation as a mediator, he chaired the renewable energy caucus and worked on legislation protecting consumer rights and promoting responsible growth. He won a second term in 1998 and served two years as Senate president pro tem and then retired from the chamber in 2002, when term limits forced him from office.

Perlmutter was considered the early frontrunner for the newly-created 7th District, but he opted not to run in 2002, citing the time it would take him away from his three daughters. The new district elected Republican Bob Beauprez by just 121 votes; when Beauprez entered the governor's race in 2006, Democrats immediately touted it as one of their top pick-up opportunities. Perlmutter polled his family and this time entered the race. His most significant primary opposition came from Peggy Lamm, a former state representative who used to be the sister-in-law of former Governor Richard Lamm. Perlmutter criticized Lamm's relationship with the gun lobby and for backing Republican Bill Owens for governor in 2002. At a time when gas prices were flirting with $3 a gallon, Lamm pointed to Perlmutter's sponsorship of an oil and gas bill to portray him as beholden to those interests. Perlmutter campaigned in favor of stem cell research, and in his first commercial, his oldest daughter talked about how stem-cell research might find a cure for her epilepsy. EMILY's List had endorsed Lamm, but she trailed Perlmutter in fundraising. Perlmutter won the primary by a solid 53%-38%.

In the general election, he faced Republican Rick O'Donnell, a rising Republican star who left his post as executive director of the Colorado Higher Education Department to run. O'Donnell had finished second to Beauprez in the 2002 Republican primary, and he was unopposed for the nomination this time. At a time when the public was focused on lobbying-related ethics scandals in Congress, O'Donnell argued that Perlmutter's marriage to a Denver lobbyist for a D.C.-based lobbying firm would lead to conflicts of interest, an argument Lamm had also made in the primary. Perlmutter seized on an article that O'Donnell wrote 11 years earlier, which called for abolishing Social Security. In an effort to bolster Perlmutter, Democrats selected him to deliver the Democratic response to President Bush's weekly radio address in August, and he used the opportunity to lambaste Republicans for threatening to "privatize" the program. O'Donnell countered that he had tempered his position since then and had even enrolled his mother in Social Security, but Perlmutter and independent groups nevertheless ran numerous attack ads on Social Security.

The two candidates also debated illegal immigration: Perlmutter supported a guest worker program for immigrants while O'Donnell opposed it. Both called for Defense Secretary Donald Rumsfeld's resignation, a position that enabled O'Donnell to distance himself from the Bush administration. By October the two were closely matched in fundraising, each with well over $2 million. However the strength of Perlmutter's candidacy, Beauprez's poor showing in the governor's race and Bush's unpopularity all worked against O'Donnell. A week before the election, the NRCC redirected funding it had reserved for him to shore up the reelection of nearby Republican Congresswoman Marilyn Musgrave. The DCCC kept spending, investing nearly $2 million on the race. Perlmutter won by 55%-42%. He carried Jefferson County by nearly 15,000 votes, 55%-43%.

★ CONNECTICUT ★

Connecticut is by many measures the nation's highest-income state and quite likely the wealthiest, not through any natural advantage but largely by virtue of its own pluck. Through most of its history this small chunk of rocky terrain has been isolated and insular, and politically Connecticut has been an odd duck, one of the last to renounce an established church (in 1818) and one of the last to impose an income tax (in 1991), one of the last to back the Federalist Party (1816) and one of the few to vote to reelect Herbert Hoover (1932). Connecticut was founded by Puritans who found Massachusetts too lenient and backsliding; Connecticut Yankees for years were flintier and more unyielding, more tight-fisted and set in their ways. Yet they were also open to reform: the state's schools now tell pupils that Connecticut once had slavery, but neglect to mention how remarkable it was that in 1784 it voted for gradual emancipation—one of the first societies to do so. Life here still bears the imprint of the original 17th century settlers, even though most Connecticut residents today are descendants of Catholic immigrants who arrived here between 1840 and 1924.

A tenacity to principle and an openness to innovation: these Yankee characteristics pervade the state's history. Connecticut's affluence came not from any windfall but from a knack for tinkering and making good productive use of savings. In 1831 Alexis de Tocqueville was struck by how this spot on the map gave America "the clock-peddler, the schoolmaster, and the senator. The first gives you time, the second tells you what to do with it, and the third makes your law and civilization." Connecticut made clocks of wood and metal and hats of felt; it produced combs, cigars, clocks, silk

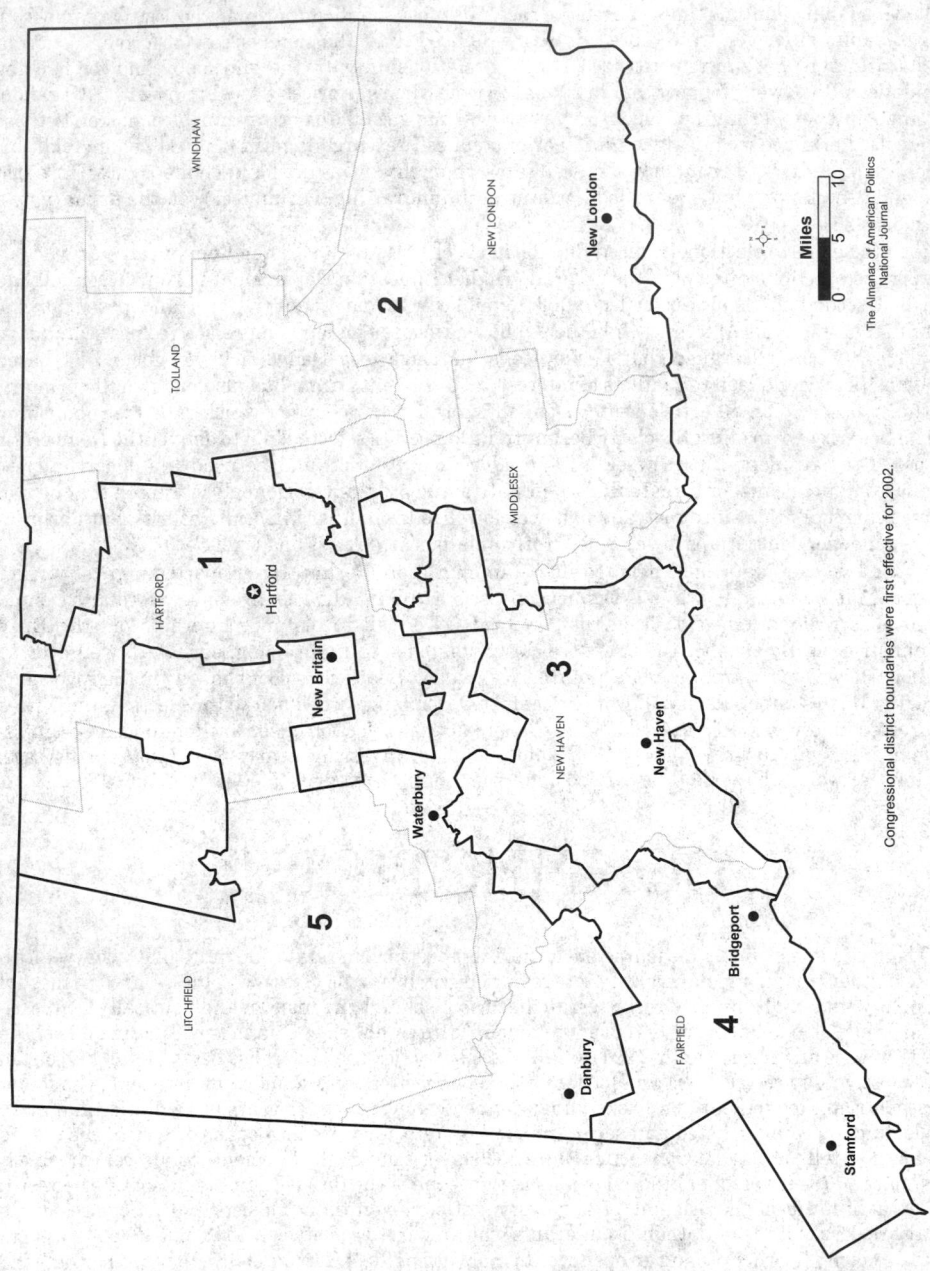

The Almanac of American Politics
National Journal

Congressional district boundaries were first effective for 2002.

thread, pins, matches, furniture; it invented and still manufactures Pez candy in Orange, Pepperidge Farm bread and Nivea cream in Norwalk, the Stanley Powerlock tape measure in New Britain and the Wiffle Ball in Shelton. Connecticut, one of the least violent parts of America, has always specialized in arms. The quintessential Connecticut Yankee, Eli Whitney, was the inventor not only of the cotton gin but also of rifles with interchangeable parts. Connecticut has been an arms maker ever since Samuel Colt won a War Department contract to manufacture guns for the Mexican-American War; during the Reagan defense buildup of the 1980s it produced Air Force jets and Army helicopters and, in the Electric Boat Shipyard in New London, most of the Navy's nuclear submarines. These arms industries, like Connecticut's civilian manufacturers, depend heavily on meticulous work. For years, the state was the center of the brass industry, the nation's main producer of precision instruments. Through decades of immigration Connecticut workers never lost the Yankee knack: Connecticut ranks second in new patents per capita, and a Milken Institute study ranked Connecticut number three among states in its ability to excel in the information economy. Over the years Connecticut has accumulated capital and invested shrewdly, with great skill at assessing risk; it is the home of several of the nation's great insurance companies, and its laws are uniquely friendly to creditors and harsh on bankrupts.

But Connecticut may be finding its success hard to sustain. Connecticut has never entirely recovered from the recession of the early 1990s and has had the slowest rate of job growth of any state since. Its insurance companies were hit by huge casualty losses, and cuts in defense spending cost Connecticut nearly 150,000 manufacturing jobs. Its small central cities—New Haven, Hartford, Bridgeport—have been plagued by crime and have lost manufacturing jobs and people; in 1950 those three cities had 500,000 people in a state of 2.0 million, while in 2005 they had 388,000 in a state of 3.5 million. Connecticut's post-1990 economic growth has been concentrated in two corners of the state, on opposite sides of the invisible divide that separates Yankee fans and Red Sox fans. In the southeast is the state's biggest employer and taxpayer, the Foxwoods Resort Casino, opened in 1992, run by a battery of lawyers and lobbyists and developers working for the 650-member Mashantucket Pequot tribe; its big competitor is Mohegan Sun, owned by the 1,600-member Mohegans. In 2006 both casinos were embarking on $700 million expansions. In the southwest, Stamford and Greenwich have become major financial services centers and the headquarters of the burgeoning hedge fund industry. But population growth is limited in Stamford and lower Fairfield County by sky-high housing prices and constraints on growth. Otherwise growth has been most vigorous along Interstate 84 and Route 2; new subdivisions are cutting into open land, though there is enough of it for Connecticut to have 47,000 horses, one for every 72 people, the highest ratio in the country. Connecticut's work force is aging, as over the last decade its 18-to-34-year-old population has declined by about 200,000, at the third fastest rate of any state. There has been an influx of immigrants from Mexico, Peru, the Dominican Republic and other parts of Latin America, who fill jobs others let go begging; Hispanics are now the state's largest minority group. Small business growth is inhibited by high taxes, heavy regulation and requirements that health insurance policies cover every imaginable contingency: a comfortable enough situation for those who are already well off, but a "get out" sign to those who want to move up the ladder. Corruption has been widespread; mayors of Waterbury and Bridgeport were sent to jail and Governor John Rowland was forced out of office in July 2004. As former legislator Kevin Rennie wrote, "Affluence, high scholastic scores and verdant hills have masked an increasingly corrupt political system that thrives on a complacent public and political elite." Demographically, Connecticut resembles Western Europe more than just about any other American state, and the question arises whether the achievements of the tinkerers and investors who built this state can be sustained in what now is a center for gambling and hedge funds.

For most of the 20th century, Connecticut politics was an ethnic struggle between Yankee Republicans and Catholic Democrats. Slowly, as Catholic birthrates exceeded Protestant, Democrats gained ground; their great leader was John Bailey, state Democratic chairman from 1946-75, a master legislative strategist and ticket-balancer, who was one of the first to endorse John Kennedy for president. Some traces of the old Protestant-Catholic divide are apparent today in geographic voting patterns, but not much in political rhetoric; splitting tickets is now common in a state where the straight-party lever dominated politics a generation ago. Then the central cities and Catholic suburbs voted Democratic, the WASPy suburbs and rural towns Republican. Today that pattern has almost disappeared, although it reappeared in the 2006 Senate primary, when challenger Ned Lamont carried most of the old Republican areas and incumbent Joe Lieberman carried most of the historic Democratic strongholds. As in other major metropolitan areas, high-income voters have trended toward the Democrats on cultural issues. The state whose ban on contraceptives produced the Supreme Court's *Griswold* decision in 1965, the precursor of *Roe v. Wade*, is now solidly for abortion rights, and its legislature passed a law in 2005 legalizing civil unions for same-sex couples. Perhaps in reaction, there has been a smaller countervailing move by some blue-collar workers and Catholics toward the Republicans. The 2004 NEP exit poll has Connecticut Protestants voting 52%-47% for John Kerry and Connecticut Catholics voting 53%-47% for George W. Bush. Kerry carried affluent Fairfield, Guilford and Farmington and lost Greenwich, where Prescott Bush was first selectman before he was U.S. senator, by only 52%-47%. Bush carried working class Naugatuck and Beacon Falls and came within 161 votes of carrying Waterbury, where a crowd of 100,000 waited until 2:00 a.m. to cheer John F. Kennedy in 1960.

On balance Connecticut these days is mostly a Democratic state. It has two Democratic senators, though Lieberman, triumphant over Lamont in November, calls himself an Independent Democrat. Four of its five congressmen are Democrats and Christopher Shays, the last remaining Republican House member from New England, barely held onto his seat in 2006. Democrats have 2–1 margins in the legislature. It has not elected a Democratic governor since 1986, but Lowell Weicker, a former Republican elected as an Independent in 1990, pushed through a state income tax and Jodi Rell, the popular incumbent who succeeded the disgraced Rowland, has proposed a major tax increase.

The People		Race/Ethnic Origin			Military veterans: 310,069 (12.1%)	
Pop. 2006 (est):	3,504,809	2,638,845	77.5%	White	WWII: 25.4%	Korea: 15.3%
Pop. 2000:	3,405,565	295,571	8.7%	Black	Vietnam: 29.6%	Gulf War: 6.3%
Pop. 1990:	3,287,116	81,564	2.4%	Asian	Most populous cities (2006):	
Change 1990-2000:	Up 3.6%	7,267	0.2%	Native Am.	1. Bridgeport	137,912
% of U.S. total:	1.2%	958	0.0%	Hawaiian	2. Hartford	124,512
Pop. rank:	29th of 50	52,896	1.6%	Two+ races	3. New Haven	124,001
Area size:	5,543 sq. mi.	8,141	0.2%	Other	4. Stamford	119,261
State Native:	57.0%	320,323	9.4%	Hisp. Origin	5. Waterbury	107,251
Non-citizen:	5.6%	**Ancestry**				
Language		Italian: 13.7%		Irish: 12.2%	Urban population: 87.7%	
English: 78.8%	Other Eur.:10.6%	English: 7.6%		German: 7.3%	Rural population: 12.3%	
Spanish: 8.4%		Polish: 6.2%				

Education		Work Sector		General Assembly	
H.S. Grad:	84.0%	Private: 79.9%	Govt: 13.3%	Senate	24 D 12 R
College Grad:	31.4%	Self: 6.5%	Family: 0.2%	House	107 D 44 R
Industry		Unemployment: 5.2%		Legislative Term Limits: No	
Agri: 0.4%	Con: 6.0%	**Household Income**			
Fin: 9.8%	Info: 3.3%	<15k: 12.0%	15-35k: 19.7%	**Registered Voters**	
Mfg: 18.7%	Prof: 32.1%	35-50k: 14.4%	50-100k: 33.6%	D: 704,811	(34.4%)
Public: 4.0%	Trade: 14.4%	100-150k: 11.7%	>150k: 8.5%	R: 433,029	(21.2%)
Other: 11.2%		Median: $53,935		O: 908,647	(44.4%)
Occupation		Poverty status: 7.9%			
Blue collar: 19.9%	White collar: 65.6%	**Home Value**			
Gray collar: 14.5%		<50k: 2.5% 50-100k: 14.2%	100-200k: 48.6% 200-300k: 17.7%		
		300-500k: 10.2% >500k: 6.7%	Median: $160,600		

Presidential politics   Why does the nation's highest income state vote Democratic for president? Because liberal stands on cultural issues have trumped the hunger for tax cuts among most of these often cynical voters; because most people here regard themselves as members of ethnic groups with a historic Democratic heritage. The Gore-Lieberman ticket carried Connecticut 56%-38%, better than Kerry-Edwards's 54%-44% in 2004. Over the years Connecticut oscillated between the parties, moving toward Republicans in the 1970s and 1980s as cultural conflicts split the old Democratic majority, moving toward Democrats in the 1990s in response to the 1990-91 recession and also out of increasing distaste for Southern-accented Republican conservatism.

2004 Presidential Vote		
Kerry (D)	857,488	(54%)
Bush (R)	693,826	(44%)
Nader (I)	12,969	(1%)
Other	14,486	(1%)

2004 Democratic Presidential Primary		
Kerry (D)	75,860	(58%)
Edwards (D)	30,844	(24%)
Lieberman (D)	6,705	(5%)
Dean (D)	5,166	(4%)
Kucinich (D)	4,133	(3%)
Other	7,315	(6%)

2000 Presidential Vote		
Gore (D)	816,015	(56%)
Bush (R)	561,094	(38%)
Nader (Green)	64,452	(4%)
Other	17,920	(1%)

Connecticut's presidential primary, though held fairly early in the process, has not been quite early enough and has made little difference. Edward Kennedy won here in 1980, Gary Hart in 1984, Jerry Brown in 1992, John McCain in 2000; but they fared no better than the Federalists Connecticut favored in 1816. Connecticut's Democratic primary has never produced a president: Al Gore and John Kerry won in 2000 and 2004 but were not elected. Joe Lieberman never made it to Connecticut's March primary in 2004; Christopher Dodd, off and running in 2006, must make an impact in Iowa and New Hampshire if he hopes to get to Connecticut in 2008.

Congressional districting   Connecticut has devised a bipartisan process for redistricting. Two Republicans and two Democrats from each house of the legislature meet and try to draw lines; if they are approved by a two-thirds vote in both chambers, they become law. Otherwise, a ninth member is chosen by the other eight, and they try to reach consensus. It worked in 1991, when a plan that made minimal changes in the congressional district lines was approved. And it worked in 2001, with a nudge from the state Supreme Court, when the task was much harder: Connecticut lost one of its six seats in the 2000 Census, and two incumbents had to be put together in one district. Legislators of both parties said they wanted a "fair fight" between a Republican and a Democrat. Some Democrats called for dividing the 2d District in eastern Connecticut, which Republican Rob Simmons won from veteran incumbent Democrat Sam Gejdenson in 2000. But Simmons argued that eastern Connecticut had been a single district since 1843, and the commission moved in another direction.

110th Congress Lineup	
4 D	1 R

109th Congress Lineup	
3 R	2 D

The commission decided to create a new seat out of the 5th District represented by Democrat Jim Maloney and the 6th District represented by Republican Nancy Johnson. The narrow and elongated 5th, the only district to have boundaries with all the others, seemed to many the obvious district to eliminate. But the commissioners haggled over precisely what boundaries would set up a fair fight. Maloney wanted to keep the three biggest cities in the 5th in the new district: Danbury, his hometown, and Waterbury and Meriden had a community of interest, because they were linked by I-84, had a common labor market and had been in the same district for 37 years. But some Republicans tried to put Danbury into the heavily Republican 4th District. Johnson insisted on keeping her hometown of New Britain, even though it is heavily Democratic and she had not always carried it. The four-member commission failed to come up with a plan by the September 2001 deadline, and it appointed as its tie-breaker 79-year-old former Speaker Nelson Brown, a Republican, who had served in the same capacity 10 years before. The commission tried out various plans, but couldn't reach agreement by a November 30 deadline. Then the issue went to the state Supreme Court, but the commissioners asked for an extension and the court granted one to December 21. Ninety minutes before the deadline the commission reached unanimous agreement. Some 27,000 of

Waterbury's residents were put into the 3d District, but otherwise Maloney kept his three cities. Johnson kept New Britain. Both incumbents said they were happy. Johnson ended up winning 54%-43%. But in 2006 she and Rob Simmons were swept to defeat.

Connecticut is not expected to lose a seat after the 2010 Census, but if it does the fight may well be among Democrats, who now hold four of the five seats.

Governor

M. Jodi Rell (R)

Assumed office July 2004, term expires Jan. 2011, 1st full term; b. June 16, 1946, Norfolk, VA; home, Brookfield; Attended Old Dominion U., Western CT St. U.; Protestant; married (Louis).

Elected Office: CT House of Reps., 1989-1994; Lt. Gov., 1994-2004.

Office: 210 Capitol Ave., Hartford, 06106, 860-566-4840; Fax: 860-566-4677; Web site: www.state.ct.us/governor.

Election Results

2006 general	M. Jodi Rell (R)	710,048	(63%)
	John DeStefano (D)	398,220	(35%)
	Other	15,198	(1%)
2006 primary	M. Jodi Rell (R)	unopposed	
2002 general	John Rowland (R)	573,958	(56%)
	Bill Curry (D)	448,984	(44%)

M. Jodi Rell, a Republican, became the 87th governor of Connecticut in July 2004 after the resignation of her predecessor John Rowland. Rell was born Mary Carolyn Reavis and grew up in Norfolk, Virginia. Her mother died when she was 7, and her father remarried; she spent summers with relatives in North Carolina, picking tobacco and driving a truck. A teenage boyfriend nicknamed her Jodi, after actress Joey Heatherton. She attended Old Dominion University and dropped out to marry her husband, Louis Rell, a Navy pilot. After military service, he became a pilot with TWA, and the Rells moved to Parsippany, New Jersey, and then to an 1843 house with views of wild turkeys, deer and foxes in Brookfield, Connecticut. (Airline pilots can live where they want, and neither New Jersey nor Connecticut had a state income tax when the Rells moved there.) Before her children were born, Rell worked as an office clerk for an investment firm in Danbury. Then she became a stay-at-home mom, active in the PTA and a volunteer for the local Republican party. She took classes at Western Connecticut State University but did not graduate. In 1984 Brookfield state Representative David Smith, an Eastern pilot, told Rell he was not running for reelection and that he wanted her to run for the seat. After twice rejecting the idea, she agreed. Connecticut has small legislative districts, and this one was heavily Republican; she was elected with 64%. At a campaign event, she met John Rowland, then a 27-year-old state representative, who was running for Congress and beat a Democratic incumbent that Reagan landslide year.

In the state House Rell supported tax cuts and fiscal responsibility. Her maternal manner helped weld the minority Republicans together as a solid block. House Minority Leader Robert Ward describes how: "When it appeared that most of us were supporting something that was good for the state, a good Republican issue, and say 90% of us were behind it, she knew if she could get us to 100% we'd be a more effective voice. That became known as 'Rell's Rule.'" Rell's rule helped her move up on the leadership ladder, to become Assistant Minority Leader and Deputy Minority Leader. In 1994 Rowland, running for governor, asked Rell to be his lieutenant governor candidate. The Rowland-Rell ticket won a narrow victory in a three-way race in 1994, then was reelected with 63% of the vote in 1998 and 56% in 2002. As lieutenant governor, Rell presided over the state Senate, where she was regarded as businesslike and fair. Rowland named her his chief liaison to municipalities, and she traveled to all 169 Connecticut cities and towns. By all accounts she was not part of Rowland's inner circle. She continued to live in Brookfield, where she rose each morning at 5:30 a.m.

and started the day with a two-hour walk, listening to tapes; she was known for writing personal notes, baking brownies for her staff, delivering rye bread to a sick friend.

Scandals dominated the headlines during the Rowland administration, beginning in September 1999 with former state Treasurer Paul Silvester, a Republican appointed by Rowland who pleaded guilty to federal charges arising out of a scheme to steer state pension funds to conspiring investment firms in return for campaign contributions. Rowland was forced to fire his two co-chiefs of staff in connection to the troubled Connecticut Resources Recovery Authority (the state trash agency) and in March 2003 Rowland's former deputy chief of staff pleaded guilty to accepting bribes. Then, in December 2003, charges surfaced that Rowland had accepted gifts from contractors who had received $100 million-plus no-bid contracts and from appointees for his family's cottage on Bantam Lake in Litchfield. Rowland said he hadn't received gifts and that the cabinets had been purchased off the shelf at Home Depot. On December 12, 2003, Rowland admitted that he had lied about the cottage renovations.

Rowland's poll numbers plummeted to a record low. Three newspapers called for his resignation. After his December 12 announcement, Rell said, "I feel sick at heart. I'm disappointed and I'm angry." The state House set up a Select Committee of Inquiry to consider Rowland's impeachment and set a deadline of June 30. On June 18 the state Supreme Court ruled that Rowland had to testify before the committee. On June 21 Rowland announced he would resign on July 1. In December he pleaded guilty to income tax evasion. He served 10 months in a federal prison before his February 2006 release.

At noon on July 1 Rell walked up the steps of the Capitol and was sworn in as governor. She was still little known to the public. "Today, we begin to restore faith, integrity and honor to our government," she said. "It is our solemn obligation. It will be our lasting legacy." Rell announced that she would accept no gifts of any kind; she donated T-shirts and caps to the state or charities. She demanded that all appointees submit resignations, and proceeded to fire four commissioners and accept another's resignation. She installed an ethics lawyer in the governor's office, ordered a review of contracting provisions, announced a zero tolerance policy on ethics violations and banned lobbyists from her office. In October she suspended four transportation managers after irregular contracting procedures were discovered. She worked to change procedures at the State Ethics Commission. In January 2004, polls showed that 70% of voters had no opinion of Rell; in June her favorable job rating was just 34%. But it rose rapidly, to 73% in August, 77% in September, 80% in November.

In December Rell was diagnosed with breast cancer and days after Christmas underwent a mastectomy. Against doctors' advice she went to the Capitol to deliver a State of the State address on January 5 as legislators of both parties applauded and wept. Her job rating fell from 83% in January 2005 to 74% in February—still stellar, but a reflection of her recently unveiled budget which proposed raising cigarette, alcohol, and gasoline taxes to close a projected $1.2 billion deficit. Democratic leaders insisted on a "millionaire's tax" on those who earn more than $1 million per year; Rell said it was possible if Democrats considered spending cuts. In June, when the budget deal was hammered out, neither side got exactly what they wanted. The sin and gasoline taxes were not increased and no millionaire's tax was enacted; instead, the state restored its estate tax on the transfer of estates valued at $2 million or more. Rell also signed legislation establishing a 10-year, $100 million plan to fund embryonic and adult stem cell research, an increase in the minimum wage and a measure creating civil unions for same-sex couples. She vetoed a heavily lobbied bill that would have restricted the sale of junk food in schools and mandated at least 20 minutes of recess every day for elementary school; Rell said it was an infringement of local control of schools (and some school officials were reluctant to give up vending machine revenues). She also vetoed a major ethics bill, prompted by the Rowland scandal, designed to stop corrupt contracting practices; instead she issued an executive order with many of the same provisions that gave the governor the power to appoint all 5 members to a state contracting standards board.

After refusing for a time to say whether she would seek a full term in 2006, Rell finally announced in October 2005 that she was running. "I want you to believe in me," she said. "I want you to know I'm a different kind of governor." That same month, she called a special session on campaign finance reform, which the legislature failed to pass in the regular session that ended in June. She proposed public financing for campaigns for the General Assembly, governor and other statewide constitutional offices; in December she signed into law a wide-ranging measure that created a voluntary system of public financing and banned contributions from lobbyists and state contractors.

As with many of her other accomplishments, Rell worked with Democrats, who hold large margins in both the state House and Senate, to get the law passed; Republican leaders criticized it as loophole-ridden and largely voted against it.

In 2006, Rell called for a second phase of ethics reform. A budget surplus led her to seek elimination of the property tax on non-commercial motor vehicles, partially paid for by eliminating the property tax credit on the state income tax—a credit created by Democrats. All in all, her tax relief proposals totaled about $295 million, pleasing even Republicans who had voted against her budget the year before. Her earnest and pragmatic style kept her riding high in the polls through all this, and in April 2006, when she became a grandmother, it sparked speculation she might actually become even more popular. "She's already at 80 percent," Douglas Schwartz, director of the Quinnipiac University Polling Institute, told the *Connecticut Post* in April 2006. "I don't know if she can get any higher."

On the Democratic side, New Haven Mayor John DeStefano and Stamford Mayor Dannel Malloy battled for the nomination through the summer. With support from labor, DeStefano won 51%-49%, but ended up paired with Molloy's designated running mate for lieutenant governor, former Simsbury First Selectman Mary Glassman, who defeated his preferred candidate, West Hartford Mayor Scott Slifka.

Sprawl and job creation were key issues in the general election; Rell campaigned on her record and created an Office of Responsible Growth by executive order in October. DeStefano sought to link Rell to Rowland, running an ad with video from the 2002 Republican state convention where she says "I'm proud of Governor John G. Rowland" and refers to him as "the greatest governor Connecticut has ever had." But with 3 closely contested House races and a contentious Senate race involving Senator Joe Lieberman, the governor's race took a back seat. Rell ran a low-key campaign, eschewed negative ads and raised nearly $4 million without accepting contributions from lobbyists or PACs. The closely fought August primary, where both Democrats raised about $3.5 million, had drained DeStefano's resources and left him struggling for funds in the final weeks. Rell won 63%-35%, carrying Stamford, Waterbury and nearly everywhere else outside the bigger cities. DeStefano won Bridgeport 56%-42% and carried New Haven and Hartford with 65% or more, but turnout in those places was too low to overcome suburban margins across the state.

Senior Senator

Christopher Dodd (D)

Elected 1980, seat up 2010, 5th term; b. May 27, 1944, Willimantic; home, East Haddam; Providence Col., B.A. 1966, U. of Louisville, J.D. 1972; Catholic; married (Jackie Clegg).

Military Career: Army Reserves, 1969-75.

Elected Office: U.S. House of Reps., 1974-80.

Professional Career: Peace Corps, Dominican Republic, 1966-68; Practicing atty., 1972-74.

DC Office: 448 RSOB, 20510, 202-224-2823; Fax: 202-224-1083; Web site: dodd.senate.gov.

State Office: Hartford, 860-258-6940.

Committees: *Banking, Housing & Urban Affairs* (Chmn. of 11 D): Security & International Trade & Finance. *Foreign Relations* (2d of 11 D): Western Hemisphere, Peace Corps & Narcotics Affairs (Chmn.); Near Eastern & South & Central Asian Affairs; European Affairs. *Health, Education, Labor & Pensions* (2d of 11 D): Children & Families (Chmn.); Employment & Workplace Safety. *Rules & Administration* (4th of 10 D).

Group Ratings

	ADA	ACLU	AFS	LCV	ITIC	NTU	COC	ACU	CFG	FRC
2006	95	80	100	100	33	10	42	8	0	0
2005	100	—	88	90	—	11	39	8	2	—

National Journal Ratings

	2005 LIB	—	2005 CONS	2006 LIB	—	2006 CONS
Economic	81%	—	17%	83%	—	13%
Social	76%	—	23%	93%	—	5%
Foreign	76%	—	15%	72%	—	26%

Key Votes of the 109th Congress

1. Bar ANWR Drilling	Y	5. Confirm Samuel Alito	N	9. Limit Interstate Abortion	N
2. FY06 Spending Curb	N	6. Path to Citizenship	Y	10. CAFTA	N
3. Estate Tax Repeal	N	7. Bar Same Sex Marriage	*	11. Urge Iraq Withdrawal	Y
4. Raise Minimum Wage	Y	8. Stem Cell Research $	Y	12. Provide Detainee Rights	Y

Election Results

2004 general	Christopher Dodd (D)	945,347	(66%)	($3,938,132)
	Jack Orchulli (R)	457,749	(32%)	($1,462,401)
	Other	21,630	(2%)	
2004 primary	Christopher Dodd (D)	unopposed		
1998 general	Christopher Dodd (D)	628,306	(65%)	($4,442,567)
	Gary A. Franks (R)	312,177	(32%)	($1,478,307)
	Other	23,974	(2%)	

Prior Winning Percentages: 1992 (59%); 1986 (65%); 1980 (56%); 1978 House (70%); 1976 House (65%); 1974 House (59%)

Christopher Dodd, the senior senator from Connecticut, was almost born into politics, one of five senators who are children of former senators (Lisa Murkowski, Mark Pryor, Evan Bayh and Bob Bennett are the others). His father Thomas Dodd, a lead prosecutor at the Nuremberg trials, was elected to the House in 1952, when Chris was eight; he lost a Senate race to Prescott Bush, George W. Bush's grandfather, in 1956, then won in 1958. Chris Dodd served in the Peace Corps in the Dominican Republic from 1966-68. In 1967 the older Dodd was censured by the Senate for misuse of funds; he ran as an independent in 1970 and Chris Dodd managed his campaign, in which he finished behind Republican Lowell Weicker and Democrat Joseph Duffey, for whom Yale Law School student Bill Clinton was working as a volunteer. Almost immediately after law school, Chris Dodd ran for the House in the open-seat eastern Connecticut 2d District and, in the Watergate year of 1974, won comfortably. He was reelected easily and in 1980 outmaneuvered fellow Watergate Democrat Toby Moffett to get the Democratic nomination to succeed Senator Abraham Ribicoff; he won that race by a wide margin and became the youngest senator from Connecticut in history.

Dodd, who speaks fluent Spanish, has often played a role on Latin American issues. On the Western Hemisphere Subcommittee in the 1980s he took the lead in opposing U.S. military aid to El Salvador's government and aid to the Nicaraguan contras. He has long backed freer travel to Fidel Castro's Cuba and an end to the embargo on trade with Cuba. In contrast to his wariness of U.S. military aid in Central America in the 1980s, he supported the Clinton administration's Plan Colombia, to provide equipment and military training to Colombians fighting the FARC guerrillas. In September 2002 he called for international cooperation to disarm Saddam Hussein but said that lacking that, "I don't think we have any choice but to act alone." He voted for the Iraq war resolution in October 2002 but later had second thoughts. In November 2003, when the turnover to Iraqis in June 2004 was announced, Dodd said, "The good news is that they're doing it. The bad news is that it took so long to do it. Iraqi people have to choose their own leaders." In September 2004, he said of the Iraqi war resolution, "There wouldn't have been a vote if we knew then what we know now. Only the threat of weapons of mass destruction caused us to vote as we did." In late 2006 he said, "I'd love to see a democratic Middle East. But you've got to have a coherent society before you can be a democracy." In January 2007, he sponsored a bill to prohibit increases in forces in Iraq without a vote by Congress. "If we're going to stop this, we have to stop it before the new troops get to Iraq. You're not going to cut off funds once they're there. The window is closing." But that bill was not taken up by the Senate. On a related issue, Dodd was the Senate's most outspoken opponent of the military commissions bill and in September 2006 considered filibustering against it. Citing his father's experience at Nuremberg, he argued that the United States had to uphold the rule of law against its enemies, and he sponsored a bill to give habeas corpus protection to anyone, including unlawful combatants, in U.S. custody; it also would have given Congress and the judiciary oversight of the Executive Branch's interpretations of the Geneva Conventions. He was an outspoken opponent of the nomination of John Bolton to be ambassador to the United Nations, which in his view would "send a dreadful, dreadful signal about our credibility to the world." On his general approach to foreign policy, he has said, "I'm in the Brent Scowcroft school, the world as it is."

In 2007 Dodd became chairman of the Banking Committee. He has not always taken liberal stands on economic and regulatory issues; Connecticut, with its big insurance companies, has long been a creditor state, and one that is leery of trial lawyers. In 1995 he was the chief Democratic sponsor of the securities litigation bill sought by high-tech companies and fought by trial lawyers. When Bill Clinton vetoed it, Dodd immediately started lobbying Senate and House Democrats, and both houses in December 1995 voted to override. He was a lead sponsor of the product liability bill vetoed by Clinton in May 1996. Dodd supported the bill to limit class action lawsuits, requiring many to be transferred to federal court, but cast a critical vote against cloture in October 2003 when he said Republican leaders were not addressing his concerns. He voted for the measure when it passed in February 2005. He supported the bankruptcy bill passed in March 2005, but sought an amendment banning the issuance of credit cards to people under 21. But he has criticized card issuers for "turning credit cards into nothing less than wallet-sized predatory loans," and has called for more disclosure, a ban on finance charges for on-time payments and a study of fees banks charge merchants. He has opposed federal regulations of hedge funds, many of which are headquartered in Greenwich, Connecticut; he suggested he may hold hearings on them, but said, "I'm not hostile to them at all." He helped write the Sarbanes-Oxley Act of 2002, and after the 2006 election stated, "I'm not quite as convinced as others are that there is as big a problem with Sarbanes-Oxley as some have suggested. At some point we're going to look at it. I don't know exactly when but obviously it's an issue that needs to be examined." Elevated to the chairmanship by the Republican defeat and the retirement of senior Democrat Paul Sarbanes, Dodd said he would work on a bipartisan basis for a bill creating a new regulator for the Government Sponsored Enterprises Fannie Mae and Freddie Mac and setting new limits on their portfolios. Other items on his priority list: combating terrorist financing, a transit security bill like the one the committee passed unanimously in 2005, an overhaul of flood insurance and a rewriting of the CFIUS restrictions of foreign direct investment in the U.S.—an issue raised by the Dubai Ports deal in early 2006. He said he was inclined to support more federal housing programs, a priority of new House Financial Services Chairman Barney Frank. He seemed less interested in federal insurance chartering and reining in executive pay. Dodd appeared aware that financial regulation can have enormous negative consequences, as in the savings and loan industry in the 1980s. As he said, "At the end of my tenure on this committee, I want it to be said that the safety and soundness of our financial institutions was not weakened on my watch."

Dodd was the lead Democratic sponsor of the terrorism insurance bill, which passed the Senate in June 2002. His original version would have had the government pay for the first $10 billion of terrorism claims each year and then 90% of the rest. The House version, passed in December 2001, required insurers to repay the government and provided full coverage of only the first $1 billion of damage. In lengthy negotiations, Dodd managed to get a bill limiting claims to a sliding scale of percentages of premiums and placing a surcharge on all commercial insurance if companies' claims exceeded a sliding scale of limits. But there was intense argument over the House's provision shielding property owners from pain and suffering damages in lawsuits. Finally Dodd's compromise was accepted by the Republicans, consolidating lawsuits in a single federal court and setting up rigid tests for holding property owners liable. In 2004 and 2005 he pressed for a two-year extension of the act, and it was extended to December 2007. He has said that as chairman he will press for a further extension.

As ranking member on and then as chairman of the Senate Rules Committee, Dodd worked with Mitch McConnell on the elections procedure bill that just about everyone thought was necessary after the Florida controversy. There were significant differences between the House bill passed in December 2001 and the Senate bill passed in April 2002. Most matters were agreed on: provisional voting, computerized voter lists, improved access to the polls for the disabled, $3.9 billion to help states upgrade their equipment. But approval was delayed over disagreement over whether first-time voters who register by mail should have to show driver's licenses. Finally it was agreed that they could use utility bills, bank statements, paychecks, government documents with their names and addresses instead, and the bill was signed in October 2002. In 2005 Dodd and Christopher Bond proposed changes in the act. In 2006 Dodd worked on proposed Senate rule changes; he persuaded the Senate to reject Russ Feingold's amendment that would have defined as a lobbyist any employee of an organization that hired lobbyists. In September 2006, at the direction of Senate party leaders, he worked with Trent Lott on a version that would eliminate anonymous holds on bills.

Dodd was one of the chief sponsors of the Family and Medical Leave Act, vetoed by George H. W. Bush but signed in 1993 by Bill Clinton. In 2007 he called for expanding the law to allow six weeks of paid leave for family emergencies. In fall 2005, after oil prices rose sharply, he and Byron Dorgan proposed a 50% tax on oil companies' windfall profits not invested in domestic oil and gas exploration, new refineries or renewable energy sources. In 2005 he and Charles Grassley sponsored a bill to increase public access to FDA data on prescription drug clinical trials and another to establish an independent office of drug safety in the FDA. In November 2006 Dodd opposed what he called "sweeping immunity" for vaccine makers. He and Richard Lugar have been the Senate sponsors of a press shield bill which would allow reporters to conceal the identity of confidential sources in federal courts. In 2007 he and House Republican Vern Ehlers called for $4 million in grants to states that agree to administer the national standard NAEP science and mathematics tests. In April 2005 he brought the Senate to a halt with an amendment to cancel the Navy's decision to award the contract to build a new presidential helicopter to AgustaWestland; he wanted Connecticut's Sikorsky to get the contract, but was opposed by Charles Schumer, presumably because of a big subcontractor in New York.

Dodd has a cheerful manner, seems unfazed by opposition and approaches debates with an affable air, deflating opponents' indignation and suggesting that they are all in this game together. In November 1994 he made an attempt to get a position in the national spotlight after Jim Sasser, who had expected to run for Senate majority leader, was defeated for reelection by Bill Frist. Dodd spent a month campaigning among colleagues for the minority leadership and lost to Tom Daschle by just 24-23. Dodd was promptly asked by Bill Clinton to be Democratic National Committee chairman. Dodd performed ably in public debates and set-tos with Republican Chairman Haley Barbour, but was embarrassed in October 1996 when he followed White House orders to stonewall on charges that DNC top-level fundraiser John Huang raised millions in illegal foreign contributions. Dodd left the chairmanship in January 1997. In 2000 he lobbied hard to get his junior colleague Joe Lieberman nominated for vice president, assuring Jesse Jackson, NEA head Bob Chase and AFL-CIO President John Sweeney that Lieberman was a good Democrat. In 2003 Dodd gave some consideration to running for president in 2004, but in March 2003 announced he would not and endorsed Lieberman. After the defeat of Tom Daschle in November 2004, he made soundings to run for majority leader but did not when it became quickly apparent that Harry Reid had the votes.

Dodd has never faced a tough election in Connecticut and for years he had a cordial relationship with his colleague Joe Lieberman. He supported Lieberman in his August 2006 primary against Ned Lamont, but the morning after Lamont won, Dodd endorsed him and later appeared in an ad for him, saying, "People want different leadership in Washington." When asked why he didn't support Lieberman's third-party candidacy, he said, "What do I tell a 20-year-old, what do I tell someone who wants to be a Democrat and join the process. I'm sorry, the primary doesn't count, it doesn't make a difference'? It was painful. I didn't like it. But I wasn't going to turn around and tell people this doesn't mean anything." After Lieberman won the general election, the two shook hands perfunctorily in the Democratic caucus room, but their relationship seemed frosty at best. But Dodd's support for Lamont will probably be an asset in his own quest for the Democratic presidential nomination. He made visits to neighboring New Hampshire in 2006, noting, "I used to have a head of black hair when I came to New Hampshire." He announced his candidacy in January 2007, noting that he was a "dark horse" and "an unknown quantity with experience"—indeed if elected he will have had 34 years of experience in Congress, more than any president in history. He approached the race with characteristic optimism. "It's a long way away, and there are plenty of chances to break through."

If he does not win the presidency, his political strength in Connecticut will not be in doubt. He was reelected by 65%-32% in 1998 over former Congressman Gary Franks. In 2004 he faced fashion entrepreneur Jack Orchulli who spent $1.38 million of his own money on the campaign. Dodd won 66%-32%, carrying all but five of Connecticut's 169 cities and towns. In February 2007 he passed the mark of Republican Orville Platt and became the longest-serving Connecticut senator in history.

Junior Senator

Joe Lieberman (ID)

Elected 1988, seat up 2012, 4th term; b. Feb. 24, 1942, Stamford; home, New Haven; Yale U., B.A. 1964, LL.B. 1967; Jewish; married (Hadassah).

Elected Office: CT Senate, 1970-80, Maj. Ldr., 1974-80; CT Atty. Gen., 1982-88.

Professional Career: Practicing atty., 1967-70, 1980-82.

DC Office: 706 HSOB, 20510, 202-224-4041; Fax: 202-224-9750; Web site: lieberman.senate.gov.

State Office: Hartford, 860-549-8463.

Committees: *Armed Services* (4th of 13 D): Airland (Chmn.); Seapower; Personnel. *Environment & Public Works* (3d of 10 D): Private Sector & Consumer Solutions to Global Warming & Wildlife Protection (Chmn.); Clean Air & Nuclear Safety; Public Sector Solutions to Global Warming, Oversight & Children's Health Protection. *Homeland Security & Governmental Affairs* (Chmn. of 9 D). *Small Business & Entrepreneurship* (4th of 10 D).

Group Ratings

	ADA	ACLU	AFS	LCV	ITIC	NTU	COC	ACU	CFG	FRC
2006	75	75	100	71	100	15	44	17	1	12
2005	80	—	100	70	—	9	61	8	3	—

National Journal Ratings

	2005 LIB	—	2005 CONS		2006 LIB	—	2006 CONS
Economic	74%	—	25%		73%	—	26%
Social	65%	—	29%		74%	—	25%
Foreign	54%	—	45%		54%	—	45%

Key Votes of the 109th Congress

1. Bar ANWR Drilling	Y	5. Confirm Samuel Alito	N	9. Limit Interstate Abortion	N
2. FY06 Spending Curb	N	6. Path to Citizenship	Y	10. CAFTA	*
3. Estate Tax Repeal	N	7. Bar Same Sex Marriage	N	11. Urge Iraq Withdrawal	N
4. Raise Minimum Wage	Y	8. Stem Cell Research	$	12. Provide Detainee Rights	Y

Election Results

2006 general	Joe Lieberman (CFL)	564,095	(50%)	($17,210,710)
	Ned Lamont (D)	450,844	(40%)	($20,557,217)
	Alan Schlesinger (R)	109,198	(10%)	($204,113)
	Other	10,643	(1%)	
2006 primary	Ned Lamont (D)	146,404	(52%)	
	Joe Lieberman (D)	136,490	(48%)	
2000 general	Joe Lieberman (D)	828,902	(63%)	($3,786,665)
	Phil Giordano (R)	448,077	(34%)	($1,080,020)
	Other	34,282	(3%)	

Prior Winning Percentages: 1994 (67%); 1988 (50%)

Joseph Lieberman, Connecticut's junior senator, was the Democratic nominee for vice president in 2000 and now classifies himself an Independent Democrat. He grew up in Stamford, the son of a liquor store owner, and was interested in politics early on; he remembers coming home from school at age nine eager to watch the televised Kefauver hearings. He graduated from Yale College and Yale Law School, became chairman of the *Yale Daily News* and worked summers for Senator Abraham Ribicoff and the Democratic National Committee. His political ambitions were no secret— other students called him "the Senator." In college he wrote an admiring yet revealing biography of that quintessential political boss John Bailey, Connecticut Democratic chairman from 1946-1975. Writing a book that was intellectually honest enough to pass academic scrutiny but tactful enough not to displease a man who could make or break his political career was a challenge, and Lieberman met it. At the same time, he was not afraid to challenge the political establishment. He helped found a reform and anti-war Caucus of Connecticut Democrats; in 1970 he ran for state Senate in New Haven against state Senate Majority Leader Edward Marcus, and won with help from, among others, a Yale Law student volunteer named Bill Clinton. In 1980 he ran for an open House seat and lost 52%-46% in a Republican year. In 1982 he was elected Connecticut attorney general.

In 1988 Lieberman challenged Senator Lowell Weicker, another maverick, but of a different sort. Weicker was well to the left of most Republicans on economic and cultural issues; Lieberman was to the right of most Democrats on cultural issues and foreign policy. Lieberman is an Orthodox Jew—he didn't attend the convention that nominated him for senator because it was held on Saturday, and sent in videotape instead—and a believer that "we in government should look to religion as a partner, as I think the Founders of our country did." He ran witty ads, one showing a bear sleeping through work—a nice take-off on the growling but erratic Weicker. Lieberman won 50%-49%.

From his first years in the Senate Lieberman has made a distinctive mark in foreign policy. He was one of the leaders in the fight for the Gulf War resolution in January 1991, and without his earnest but vehement support it might not have passed. Presciently, he called for "final victory" over Saddam Hussein. He is a strong supporter of Israel but favored F-15 sales to Saudi Arabia in 1992. He has strongly opposed Fidel Castro's regime in Cuba—a difference between him and his colleague Christopher Dodd—and in May 2001 sponsored with Jesse Helms a bill to give $100 million to Cuban opposition groups. After September 11 he strongly supported the war against terrorism in Afghanistan and in December 2001 was one of 10 members who signed a letter urging George W. Bush to target Iraq next. And his vision is broader: in January 2002 he urged the administration to move its putative allies in the Arab world toward political freedom to prevent a "theological iron curtain" behind which terrorism can build. In May 2002, when Tom DeLay introduced a resolution supporting Israel in the House, Lieberman introduced one in the Senate, but with fewer condemnations of Palestinian leaders. While running for president in July 2003, he criticized Democrats for attacking Bush and continued to steadfastly support him on Iraq. With Chuck Hagel, he introduced a bill to provide $1 billion yearly to promote democratic institutions, development aid for infrastructure and help for small enterprises in the Middle East and Central Asia. He and John McCain called for more troops in Iraq, decried the April retreat from Fallujah and insisted the handover of power to Iraqis must be genuine. Like McCain, he continued to call for more troops in 2005 and 2006, even when he attracted primary opposition from the antiwar candidate Ned Lamont. Lieberman's strong convictions on foreign policy may have been the key factor in his decision to run as an "Independent Democrat" after losing the August 2006 primary by 52%-48%, and after his 50%-40% victory in November, as almost all other Democrats and some Republicans called for accepting the recommendations of the Iraq Study Group, Lieberman supported George W. Bush when he took another course. He strongly supported the surge and in the debate on supplemental funds in April 2007 rose to argue that the strategy behind the Democratic resolution would be disastrous.

On economic issues, Lieberman has backed capital gains tax cuts for small business ("you can't be pro-jobs and anti-business") and urged Bill Clinton to sign the 1996 welfare bill—both stands opposed by many Democrats. In November 2001 he threatened to filibuster against oil drilling in the Arctic National Wildlife Refuge. He subpoenaed documents from the Bush Interior and Agriculture departments and EPA on scalebacks of Clinton environmental regulations. He called Bush's leadership on emissions "feeble" and said his energy policy was "mired in crude oil." With McCain, increasingly a legislative partner, he has sponsored bills to reduce carbon dioxide and other emissions with an economy-wide cap and to sanction emissions trading; one version was rejected 55-43 in October 2003 and another was voted down 60-38 in June 2005. As ranking Democrat on Governmental Affairs, Lieberman worked closely with Chairman Susan Collins. In June 2005 they threatened to launch an investigation of the base closing process unless the Pentagon released certain documents; this was part of Lieberman's successful campaign to prevent the recommended closing of the submarine base at Groton. They investigated the government's response to Hurricane Katrina and recommended the appointment of an inspector general to monitor recovery efforts. In 2006 they called for an independent Office of Public Integrity, in which non-members would conduct investigations requiring final approval by the Senate ethics committee, but the plan was rejected. Lieberman was part of the "Gang of 14" that promised to prevent the filibuster of judicial nominees except in extreme cases.

Lieberman played a key—and frustrating—role on the issue of homeland security. He became convinced well before George W. Bush that there should be a cabinet department combining the government agencies involved in homeland security, and in October 2001 he sponsored a bill to create one. Then, in June 2002, Bush came out with his proposal for such a department. Lieberman said, with good reason, that Bush's plan resembled his own, and drafted a bill in July 2002. But in late August Bush said that the personnel provisions of Lieberman's bill would not give him sufficient flexibility to manage the department. The main issue was whether the president could get rid of unions in divisions of the department. Lieberman argued that his version allowed removal on a case-by-case basis if there was a showing that union rights were a threat to national security. Bush administration spokesmen said that such civil service procedures were too cumbersome and that Lieberman's version actually reduced the president's ability to move employees. In October, the bill was pulled for a while for consideration of the Iraq war resolution and other issues. Lieberman evidently had a 51-vote majority for his version, but Republicans were able to keep it from coming to the floor. Democrats, in refusing to give in to Bush's demands, were being faithful to their longtime supporters, the government employee unions. But the issue played a major role in the defeats of Senators Max Cleland in Georgia and Jean Carnahan in Missouri. After the election, Democrats meekly conceded most of the issue.

Lieberman has spoken out eloquently on moral issues. In 1995 he joined with *Book of Virtues* author William Bennett and criticized gangsta rap records, and shamed Time Warner into selling their Interscope label. In highly publicized Commerce Committee hearings in September 2000 he denounced the marketing of violent movies, music and video games to children. But during that fall campaign, after he attended a Hollywood fundraiser and spoke of being a "noodge" to the industry, Bennett criticized him for abandoning their fight against obscenity and violence. One thing that made Lieberman an attractive running mate for Al Gore was the fact that he was one of the few Democrats who was not a lockstep defender of Bill Clinton. He was dismayed by Clinton's August 17, 1998, speech in which he grudgingly admitted lying about the Lewinsky affair for seven months. When the Senate resumed in September, Lieberman took the floor and said, "Such behavior is . . . wrong and unacceptable and should be followed by some measure of public rebuke and accountability." But he was persuaded by Senate Minority Leader Tom Daschle not to call for censure, and he stopped well short of backing impeachment or resignation. Lieberman has long believed, as he said in 2002, that "faith-based groups can help government solve pressing social problems." But he opposed the faith-based charities bill the House passed in July 2001, and with Rick Santorum developed a different approach, based on tax incentives for corporate giving, for matching by banks of poor people's "development accounts," plus charitable deductions of up to $400 a year for taxpayers who take the standard deduction. He has supported gun control measures, but worked to get a gun produced by Connecticut-based Colt removed from the 1994 assault weapon ban and voted against making lawsuits against gunmakers non-dischargeable in bankruptcy.

After his presidential candidacy ended in February 2004, Lieberman returned to work vigorously in the Senate. He reacted positively to the recommendations of the 9/11 Commission on intelligence restructuring. He and committee Chairman Susan Collins introduced a bill that adopted many of them, including a national intelligence director with control over 2/3 of the intelligence budget and the power to move personnel and assets among intelligence agencies, and the creation of a National Counterterrorism Center. It passed the Senate 96–2 in October 2004. The House took a different view. Speaker Dennis Hastert pulled the bill off the floor in November because of opposition by committee chairmen. In December the House and Senate agreed on a version that included a provision recognizing the existing military chain of command. Other Lieberman legislation: a bill with Orrin Hatch to give incentives to companies developing antidotes and vaccines against bioterrorism, a bill with John McCain to impose the hard money requirements of McCain-Feingold on the 527 organizations which spent so freely in the 2004 campaign and a proposal that the United States maintain a global system of warning against tsunamis.

Lieberman's distinctive positions on issues and his differences with Democrats on many issues, his independence of mind and civility of spirit helped him to win the nomination for vice president in 2000 and to fall far short of winning the nomination for president in 2004. Al Gore's decision to make him his vice presidential nominee in 2000 was history-making: He was the first Jew on a major party ticket in American history. Gore knew Lieberman from the Senate, where they were friends. But two things probably pushed Gore toward his choice: Lieberman's reputation for probity and denunciation of Clinton, which gave the ticket some insulation from the Clinton scandals, and Lieberman's moderate record on many issues and undoubted ability. Another asset proved to be Lieberman's fervent avowals of religious faith and that it has a rightful place in politics; what might have been resented from a Christian conservative seemed attractive coming from an Orthodox Jew.

Overall, Lieberman was clearly an asset to the ticket. His poll ratings were high, and if there was general agreement that Dick Cheney excelled at the October 6 vice presidential debate,

Lieberman also performed well; some observers wondered whether the order of the tickets should be reversed. Lieberman's Judaism seems not to have hurt the ticket anywhere, and it probably helped in crucial Florida; he made memorable campaign appearances in heavily Jewish Broward and Palm Beach Counties, which together voted 65%-32% for Gore-Lieberman. But there was some tension between positions Lieberman had taken before August 2000 and what he said during the campaign. He had questioned racial quotas and preferences, and refused to oppose Proposition 209 in California in 1996, which banned racial quotas and preferences by paraphrasing the Civil Rights Act of 1964. Lieberman had supported vouchers for students in the failing District of Columbia schools; he told teachers' union leaders that he was for demonstration vouchers, but overall wanted to put money into public schools. In the Florida controversy, Lieberman took what to some was a surprisingly partisan role—though of course this was a quintessentially partisan issue. On Sunday interview shows he said that he and Gore would never challenge legitimately cast military absentee ballots. But on the preceding Friday night, lawyers working for the Gore-Lieberman ticket did precisely that.

Lieberman's nomination for vice president was greeted warmly by most Democrats. But his unswerving support of the Iraq war has won him many detractors in his party and led to defeats in Democratic primaries in 2004 and 2006. There was some tension apparent when he got into a post-mortem argument with Gore over campaign strategy. In August 2002 he said, "Al said some things in the campaign that were not the logical continuation of things—his voting record in the Senate and his career in public service. The people versus the powerful unfortunately left that track and gave a different message, which may have been caused by the pressure that the Nader campaign was giving us. But I think it was not the New Democratic approach." Gore responded in a *New York Times* opinion article that people versus the powerful was "the right choice." Lieberman kept to his pledge not to run if Gore did, and he began active fundraising and campaigning only after Gore announced in December 2002 he would not run. Lieberman started off ahead in the polls. But that just reflected his name identification, and there remained his chief problem, that he was out of step with most active Democrats on the war on terrorism and was unable to create a mass Democratic constituency which took his view. Lieberman supported Bush on going into Afghanistan and going into Iraq, and he supported him not just perfunctorily or after the fact, but was in fact urging these actions, fervently and cogently, before Bush acted. He was one of the most prominent voices calling for the remaking of the Middle East and the encouragement of democracy and human rights in the region.

He stuck to those positions in spring and summer 2003 even as Howard Dean attracted a mass constituency over the Internet and rose in the polls, and as other candidates echoed his stringent criticism of Bush on Iraq. In August 2003 Lieberman said, "I share the anger of my fellow Democrats with George Bush and the wrong direction he has taken our nation. But the answer to his outdated, extremist ideology is not to be found in outdated extremes of our own. That path will not solve the challenges of our time and it could well send us Democrats back to the political wilderness for a long time." He told unions that foreign trade is good for the American economy and criticized John Kerry for "ambivalence" on Iraq. He cautioned Democrats not to abandon the policies of Bill Clinton, who "made our party once again fiscally responsible, pro-growth, strong on values, for middle-class tax cuts, and Howard Dean is against all of these."

Like other hawkish candidates—Gore in 1988, McCain in 2000—Lieberman decided to avoid dovish Iowa. He was stung in December 2003 when Gore endorsed Dean, with no notice to Lieberman. "I don't have anything to say today about Al Gore's sense of loyalty, I really don't, and I have no regrets about the loyalty that I had to him when I waited until he decided whether he would run to make my decision because that was the right thing to do," he said. While Dean, Kerry, John Edwards and Dick Gephardt were attracting attention in Iowa, Lieberman spent the month before the January 27 primary living in a basement apartment in New Hampshire, chatting with voters over coffee, speaking to groups wherever he could. But Dean was attracting far more volunteers and far larger crowds and Kerry, after his come-from-behind victory in Iowa, was also far better organized. "We have JOE-mentum," the always cheerful Lieberman proclaimed, but it wasn't enough. He finished fifth in New Hampshire, with 9% of the vote. For another week he persisted in campaigning for the February 3 primaries in Delaware, Oklahoma, Arizona, Missouri, New Mexico and South Carolina. But the best he could do was a second-place finish in Delaware, with 11% of the vote. He announced the end of his campaign election night in an Arlington, Virginia, hotel. Lieberman did not formally endorse Kerry, whom he had known at Yale, until May, and at the Democratic National Convention he was perhaps the only speaker to refer to "the liberation of Iraq."

In 2005, after he delivered his State of the Union address, George W. Bush embraced Lieberman as he was leaving the floor; many thought Bush kissed him—and "the kiss" became one of the war cries of Lieberman's critics in the blogosphere. The Democratic leadership was not pleased when he continued to support the Iraq war, voted to confirm Alberto Gonzales and supported faith-based initiatives. In Connecticut, John Orman, a professor at Fairfield University, spent the summer of 2005 traveling around the state exploring the possibility of running against Lieberman in the Democratic primary. He concluded the race was unwinnable: "After five months, I looked around. Joe had $4 million and I had $1,000." But money was not a problem for Ned Lamont. The great-grandson of J. P. Morgan partner Thomas Lamont, owner of a big house in Greenwich, owner of a business that installs cable TV systems on college campuses and the husband of a successful venture capitalist, Lamont had enough money to finance a campaign. He had served as a selectman in Greenwich in 1987-89 and lost a race for the state Senate in 1990, and had contributed to many Democratic candidates, including Lieberman in 2000. He was repelled by Lieberman's vote on the Terri Schiavo bill and was angered by his continued support of the war. Lamont called Orman, who suggested that he contact Tom Swan, head of the Connecticut Citizen Action Group. Lamont and Swan got together in December 2005, and a month later Lamont was running and Swan was managing his campaign.

At first Lamont's campaign seemed a long shot. To get on the primary ballot, he had to get 15% of the votes at the state party convention in May (or signatures from 2% of registered Democrats, an avenue he didn't pursue). That was not an overwhelming obstacle, given the antiwar views of most Connecticut Democrats, but Lieberman had been deeply involved in Connecticut Democratic politics for 40 years and had built up many close personal relationships during that time; he was also, given his easy reelections in 1994 and 2000, certain to keep the seat out of the hands of the Republicans. Lieberman's work on saving the Groton base was sure to pay dividends in eastern Connecticut, and Lieberman had support from key Democratic groups from the state AFL-CIO to the Human Rights Campaign. Also, Lamont was an inexperienced candidate not given to easy repartee and he made some mistakes along the way: he said that job losses from free trade agreements were a necessary "transition cost" and said that the No Child Left Behind Act was now "irrelevant." But he had enthusiastic support, and not just in Connecticut. Lowell Weicker, the man whom Lieberman beat in 1988 and who was elected governor as an Independent, came out for Lamont; so did Jim Dean, brother of Democratic National Chairman Howard Dean. National blogs like Daily Kos and MyDD heaped vitriol on Lieberman and film clips championing Lamont's candidacy got wide airing on You Tube. Lieberman was booed at the state Jefferson Jackson Bailey dinner. At the May 19 state convention, Lamont won one-third of the delegates. Lieberman emphasized his Democratic credentials and his support from Hillary Clinton and Harry Reid. "I'm probably the only person in America to run against George W. Bush twice," he said. He said that he had criticized Bush for being too unilateral, for not sending enough troops, for not following the State Department's reconstruction plan. On August 1 he said that he hoped troops could be pulled out by the end of the year. Polls showed the race closing. Lieberman had some $4 million, and used some of it on an ad showing Lamont as a bear cub, a suggestion that he was a pawn of Weicker which may have been lost on those who had not seen his bear ad 18 years before, and another on saving the submarine base. "I've always been a Democrat, and I'll remain a Democrat," Lieberman said. At a July 6 debate, while Lamont attacked him on Iraq, Lieberman said, "The people of Connecticut and I have known each other for a long time. We have laughed and cried together. We prayed and dreamed together. And, most of all, we have worked together." But by July 10 he had staffers taking steps to register an independent party on whose line he could run; the papers would have to be filed two days after the August 8 primary; he was endorsed by Republican Congressman Christopher Shays. But Lamont was also spending liberally, both his own money—he ultimately put in $17 million—and funds raised over the Internet.

It turned out to be a close election. Lamont won 52%-48%. Lieberman won over 60% in working class New Haven suburbs, Waterbury and the industrial Naugatuck Valley. Lieberman won the votes of 61% of Jews and 55% of Catholics, but still lost; John Bailey would have been amazed to learn that you could carry Catholics and Jews in a Democratic primary and still not win.

Lamont carried the upscale suburbs, with 68% in Greenwich, and his network of campaigners helped him carry almost all of the small towns, with percentages ranging up to 91% in tony Cornwall. On election night Lamont rehearsed his primary themes; right behind him on the podium, in the shot that went in every newscast, stood Jesse Jackson and Al Sharpton. Lieberman declared that he would run in the general on the Connecticut for Lieberman party line. "The old politics of partisan polarization won today," he said, offering "a new politics of unity and purpose."

The next morning Christopher Dodd (whose father ran as an Independent in 1970 when he was not renominated by the Democrats) endorsed Lamont, went to a unity rally and later appeared in a TV spot for him. Asked later whether Dodd was still his best friend in the Senate, Lieberman said, "I have so many good friends in the Senate. John McCain is a very good friend." Most Democrats shunned him when he returned to Washington in September. "Some of the Democrats said, 'I'm sorry it didn't turn out better, but we hope you come back.' I won't disclose which one said that." It could have been more than one. Five Senate Democrats did endorse Lieberman: Mary Landrieu, Tom Carper, Ben Nelson, Mark Pryor and Ken Salazar. He got better treatment from Republicans. In April, former state Representative and Derby Mayor Alan Schlesinger emerged as a Republican; he was little known and had little money. Quickly leading Republicans sent out unmistakable signals that the White House was for Lieberman. On August 13, Republican National Chairman Ken Mehlman said that his practice was to consult "our leadership in the states and they say, 'You ought to stay out of this one.'" On August 15, presidential press secretary Tony Snow said, "The Republican party of Connecticut has suggested that we not make an endorsement in that race, so we're not." Lieberman called himself a "noncombatant" in the three Connecticut House races where Democrats were seriously challenging Republicans (two of them won); he appeared with Christopher Shays, the one who ended up winning, in a motorcycle rally. Lieberman started running ads referencing the 7/7 London bombings and his work on Connecticut projects, and ignored the calls by Howard Dean and John Kerry that he drop out of the race. He hired a new campaign team, including a Republican pollster. He said he was still a "proud Democrat," but added, "People treat parties as if they are the only thing that matters." Republicans like former vice presidential nominee Jack Kemp, Senator Susan Collins and New York Mayor Michael Bloomberg voiced support of Lieberman; so did Democrats like former New York Mayor Edward Koch and former Senator Bob Kerrey.

Most polls from primary day through November showed Lieberman leading Lamont. Bloggers on Daily Kos and MyDD speculated hopefully that Schlesinger would surge and take votes from Lieberman, but that never happened. Lamont seemed unprepared for this second struggle. Tom Swan admitted that 98 percent of his planning was for the primary, and Lamont took several more tranches from his checkbook to finance his campaign. Most of the national Democrats who had endorsed him turned out to have scheduling problems that prevented them from coming to Connecticut. Lieberman researchers revealed that Lamont had missed a vote on increasing property taxes on the Greenwich Board of Selectmen, even as they found that he had recently spent $1 million to buy a painting. He resigned from the Round Hill Club in Greenwich, having discovered after many years that it didn't have many black members. Lieberman charged that Lamont was "surrounded by people who are either naïve or are isolationists or, frankly, some more explicitly against Israel." Then Swan was quoted as saying that the industrial town of Waterbury was "where the forces of slime meet the forces of evil." This was a reference to crooked local politicians, but it looked like a slur against a working class city that was famous in Democratic lore as the place where 100,000 people waited until three o'clock in the morning to cheer John Kennedy on the Monday before the 1960 election.

The polls proved to be on point. Lieberman won 50%-40%, with only 10% for the hapless Schlesinger. "We never wavered in our beliefs or in our purpose, did we? And we never gave up, did we?" asked Lieberman on election night. "I would like to see this election day as a declaration of independence from the politics of partisanship." This time it was Lieberman who carried most of the small towns and cities in the state; Lamont's patches of support in such areas came only from the towns around the University of Connecticut in the east and the tony residences of New York expatriates in the far northwest of Litchfield County. Lamont carried Hartford, New Haven and Bridgeport, where Democratic party loyalty prevailed. But Lieberman carried most of the suburbs, many by wide margins. Exit polls showed Lieberman winning 70% of Republicans, 54% of Independents and 33% of Democrats. He won whites by 52%-36% and lost blacks by only 61%-38%: Lamont had the lowest percentage among blacks of any Democratic candidate in a seriously contested race in 2006. Lieberman carried 52% of Protestants, 55% of Catholics and 65% of Jews; Lamont carried 68% of those with other religions and 66% of those with none.

In the lame duck session in December, Lieberman was welcomed to the Democratic Caucus by Majority Leader-elect Harry Reid, who said, "We're all family." But family with edgy relationships. Senate Democrats—and Republicans—were very much aware that it was Lieberman's vote alone that gave them a Senate majority and that, for all his professions of loyalty to the Democratic party, the quick withdrawal of that vote would lead them back into the minority. George W. Bush, aware of that, cited Lieberman when he came out in November 2005 against a timetable for withdrawal from Iraq, and in his January 2007 nationally televised speech cited Lieberman's "good advice" for the establishment of a bipartisan working group including congressional leaders. Democratic leaders disagreed, arguing that there were already venues for bipartisan discussions. Lieberman for his part enlisted as a co-sponsor with John McCain and Lindsey Graham of a resolution opposing the Democrats' calls for withdrawal from Iraq. And his impassioned and meticulously detailed critiques of Democrats' proposals led blogger Hugh Hewitt in April 2007 to call for Lieberman to leave the Democratic party and transfer the majority to the Republicans. Lieberman did not heed or note this advice, but observers were left with the impression that if Democrats were to use their majority to cut off funds for the military effort in Iraq he might.

FIRST DISTRICT

Rep. John Larson (D)

Elected 1998, 5th term; b. July 22, 1948, Hartford; home, E. Hartford; Central CT St. U., B.S. 1971; Catholic; married (Leslie).

Elected Office: E. Hartford Bd. of Ed., 1977-79; E. Hartford Town Cncl., 1979-83; CT Senate, 1983-95, Pres. Pro-Tem 1986-95.

Professional Career: H.S. teacher, 1972-77; Insurance broker, 1977-98; Sr. Fellow, Yale Bush Ctr., 1995-1998.

DC Office: 1005 LHOB, 20515, 202-225-2265; Fax: 202-225-1031; Web site: www.house.gov/larson.

District Offices: Hartford, 860-278-8888.

Committees: *Democratic Caucus Vice Chairman. Select Committee on Energy Independence and Global Warming* (4th of 9 D). *Ways & Means* (14th of 24 D): Trade; Select Revenue Measures.

Group Ratings

	ADA	ACLU	AFS	LCV	ITIC	NTU	COC	ACU	CFG	FRC
2006	95	90	100	33	57	14	43	8	9	0
2005	100	—	100	89	—	10	44	0	6	8

National Journal Ratings

	2005 LIB	—	2005 CONS		2006 LIB	—	2006 CONS
Economic	76%	—	24%		94%	—	0%
Social	77%	—	23%		83%	—	16%
Foreign	83%	—	16%		83%	—	14%

Key Votes of the 109th Congress

1. Estate Tax Repeal	N	5. Limit Interstate Abortion	N	9. Build Border Fence	N
2. Limit CAFE Standards	N	6. Extend Patriot Act	N	10. CAFTA	N
3. FY06 Spending Curb	N	7. Bar Same Sex Marriage	N	11. Oppose Iraq Withdrawal	N
4. Drilling in ANWR	N	8. Stem Cell Research $	Y	12. Detainee Tribunals	N

Election Results

2006 general	John Larson (D)	154,539	(74%)	($953,971)
	Scott MacLean (R)	53,010	(26%)	
2006 primary	John Larson (D)	unopposed		
2004 general	John Larson (D)	198,802	(73%)	($604,516)
	John Halstead (R)	73,601	(27%)	

Prior Winning Percentages: 2002 (67%); 2000 (72%); 1998 (58%)

The People		Race/Ethnic Origin	Ancestry		
Area size:	673 sq. mi.	71.6% White	Italian: 12.1%	Irish: 11.1%	
Urban population:	93.4%	12.6% Black	English: 6.9%		
Rural population:	6.6%	2.4% Asian	**2004 Presidential Vote**		
Pop. 2000:	681,113	0.2% Native Am.	Kerry (D) 187,089	(60%)	
Pop. 2005 (est):	695,979	0.0% Hawaiian	Bush (R) 121,263	(39%)	
Median income:	$50,227	1.7% Two+ races	Other 5,809	(2%)	
Poverty status:	9.6%	0.2% Other	**2000 Presidential Vote**		
Military veterans:	12.0%	11.4% Hispanic Origin	Gore (D) 178,977	(62%)	
			Bush (R) 96,411	(33%)	
			Other 13,731	(5%)	
			Cook Partisan Voting Index: D +14		

Occupation   Blue collar: 19.7%   White collar: 65.8%   Gray collar: 14.5%

In 1871, Mark Twain moved to Hartford to become director of an insurance company, and in time became the Connecticut capital's most famous citizen. Hartford, already more than two centuries old, home of the nation's longest circulating newspaper (since 1764), *The Hartford Courant,* boyhood home of the financier J. P. Morgan, was becoming the nation's best-known insurance center. This was not what the harsh Puritans who founded Hartford had in mind, but Connecticut's Yankees turned out to be shrewd businessmen. Thanks to the broad Connecticut River, Hartford also became a seaport; its merchants, prevented from trading and writing marine insurance by Thomas Jefferson's Embargo Act of 1807, turned to writing fire insurance and using the capital they had accumulated in the Napoleonic Wars to finance their ventures. One was Samuel Colt's gun factory just south of downtown Hartford, which became one of the nation's great arms plants.

Insurance and arms are still economic mainstays of Hartford, Connecticut's capital and the center of its largest metropolitan area. Insurance carriers account for 4% of local jobs, leaving Connecticut with the largest concentration of insurance jobs in the nation. The Phoenix Companies and the Hartford Financial Services Group are the two largest employers; several other insurance companies have been sold or moved. Across the river is the Pratt & Whitney jet engine plant in East Hartford, cornerstone of Connecticut-based United Technologies; even though its local work force is less than one-fourth its size in 1980, it still builds engines for more than 600 customers around the world. The small central city of Hartford otherwise has been in bad shape, its high-crime neighborhoods abandoned and bedraggled, its school system deeply troubled. Many words have been written about the sad decline of this once rich city: where 177,000 people lived in 1950, there were 124,000 in 2000. Today, its population is 41% Hispanic (the largest share for a city in the Northeast, and heavily Puerto Rican) and 38% black. Beyond Hartford, the metropolitan area is mostly affluent and growing slowly, spread out over pleasant hills.

The 1st Congressional District of Connecticut is centered on Hartford and upscale West Hartford. On the map it looks like a lobster claw. The claw extends west, excluding some affluent suburbs from the district while including small towns and part of Torrington in the north. Southwest of Hartford, the district includes the industrial town of Bristol, where along a two-lane country road is the sprawling headquarters of ESPN, the multi-media network that revolutionized sports broadcasting and employs about 3,000 locally. East of the Connecticut River are East Hartford, home of the Pratt & Whitney plant, and more affluent suburbs. Politically, the Hartford area has long been more Democratic than the rest of Connecticut: Hartford is something like Boston, a commercial metropolis more statist than its surroundings. It owes some of its Democratic character to longtime state (1946-75) and national (1961-68) Democratic chairman John Bailey, an old-fashioned political boss with a scandal-free career who promoted a raft of first-class candidates.

The congressman from the 1st District is John Larson, a Democrat first elected in 1998 to replace Barbara Kennelly (John Bailey's daughter), who ran unsuccessfully for governor. Larson grew up in the Mayberry Village public housing project in East Hartford, one of eight children; his father was a fireman at Pratt & Whitney, and his mother worked at the state Capitol. He graduated from Central Connecticut State, taught high school and coached athletics; he then became an insurance agent. He comes from a political family—his brother Timothy was mayor of East Hartford—and in 1982, at 34, John Larson was elected to the state Senate. Four years later he was Senate president. There Larson sponsored one of the nation's first family medical leave laws, a prototype for the law sponsored by Senator Christopher Dodd and signed by Bill Clinton in 1993. He seemed headed for the governorship, and in 1994 he won the party designation at the state convention. But Comptroller Bill Curry built an organization of unionists and liberal activists, and beat him 55%-45% in the primary. When Kennelly announced her retirement, Larson ran against Secretary of State Miles Rapoport. Rapoport led in polls and fundraising. But Larson raised impressive sums as well, built a local organization, did lots of door-to-door campaigning, and benefited from the support of Hartford Mayor Mike Peters. Larson won 46%-43%. The general election was vigorously contested by Kevin O'Connor, a 31-year-old former law clerk and SEC lawyer who was endorsed by the *Hartford Courant*, but Larson won 58%-41%.

In the House Larson's voting record places him near the center of his party. He voted against normal trade relations with China, he said, because of a promise he had made to labor unions. Larson actively opposed authorizing the use of force in Iraq; he worried that unilateral action would unite the Arab world against the United States. In 2004, he added a provision to the defense bill to reimburse soldiers and their families who have purchased body armor before deploying to Iraq. As ranking Democrat on the House Administration Committee, he responded to colleagues' concerns and questions about how to run their offices, and worked with Capitol officials on security. When the House approved a bipartisan package of steps to reconstitute Congress in the event of a catastrophic attack on its members, it defeated proposals by Larson to give states additional time to fill vacancies. He gave up that post in 2005, when Minority Leader Nancy Pelosi tapped him for a seat on the Ways and Means Committee. That year's energy bill included his efforts to expand tax incentives for fuel-cell technologies.

In February 2006, Larson was the unexpected winner of the contest for vice-chairman of the Democratic Caucus. After Jan Schakowsky finished third on the first ballot, he consolidated support among allies of Nancy Pelosi and defeated Joe Crowley, an ally of Steny Hoyer, by 116-87. Bolstered by John Murtha, his campaign manager, Larson ran a low-key, back-room campaign that emphasized his services to members. In the majority, he planned to run for Caucus chairman after James Clyburn relinquished that post, but he stepped aside when Rahm Emanuel had broad support for the job. At home, he wants to make the Colt site a national historic landmark.

Larson has not been seriously challenged for reelection.

SECOND DISTRICT

Rep. Joe Courtney (D)

Elected 2006, 1st term; b. Apr. 6, 1953, Hartford; home, Vernon; Tufts U., B.A. 1975, U. of CT, J.D. 1978; Catholic; married (Audrey).

Elected Office: CT House of Reps., 1986-94.

Professional Career: Practicing atty., 1978-2006; CT coordinator, John Edwards pres. campaign, 2004.

DC Office: 215 CHOB, 20515, 202-225-2076; Fax: 202-225-4977; Web site: courtney.house.gov.

District Offices: Enfield, 860-741-6011; Norwich, 860-886-0139 .

Committees: *Armed Services* (26th of 34 D): Seapower & Expeditionary Forces; Readiness. *Education & Labor* (26th of 27 D): Higher Education, Lifelong Learning & Competitiveness; Health, Employment, Labor & Pensions.

Group Ratings and Key Votes: Newly Elected

Election Results

2006 general	Joe Courtney (D)	 121,248	(50%)	($2,410,306)
	Rob Simmons (R)	 121,165	(50%)	($3,177,694)
2006 primary	Joe Courtney (D)	.... unopposed		
2004 general	Rob Simmons (R)	 166,412	(54%)	($2,516,937)
	Jim Sullivan (D)	 140,536	(46%)	($1,056,756)

The People		Race/Ethnic Origin	Ancestry	
Area size:	2,143 sq. mi.	88.6% White	Irish: 13.3%	Italian: 10.2%
Urban population:	66.7%	3.3% Black	English: 10.2%	
Rural population:	33.3%	1.7% Asian	**2004 Presidential Vote**	
Pop. 2000:	681,113	0.5% Native Am.	Kerry (D) 180,235	(54%)
Pop. 2005 (est):	710,458	0.0% Hawaiian	Bush (R) 147,819	(44%)
Median income:	$54,498	1.5% Two+ races	Other 6,208	(2%)
Poverty status:	5.8%	0.1% Other	**2000 Presidential Vote**	
Military veterans:	14.6%	4.3% Hispanic Origin	Gore (D) 162,762	(54%)
			Bush (R) 119,184	(40%)
			Other 19,587	(6%)
			Cook Partisan Voting Index: D + 8	

Occupation   Blue collar: 20.9%   White collar: 62.9%   Gray collar: 16.2%

Eastern Connecticut, one of the longest-settled parts of the United States, had great, and sometimes painful, change in recent years—a change comparable to those of the 1640s or 1810s or 1950s. When the Puritan settlers from Massachusetts and England arrived, these flinty hills were the home of small Indian tribes, whose numbers were decimated by warfare and even more by disease. This was never fertile farming country, but New London and Norwich were among the 13 colonies' leading workshops and ports. Not long after, factories developed around mills in little villages on the fast-flowing Quinebaug and Shetucket Rivers. Sandbars kept oceangoing ships out of the rivers, but they docked at New London. Norwich was the home of Samuel Huntington, signer of the Declaration of Independence, and the president of the Continental Congress in 1781 when the nation officially was named the United States of America. In the mid-20th century new technology shaped the area. Four nuclear power plants were built here, more than in any similarly populated part of the United States. In Groton, the "Submarine Capital of the World" across the Thames River from New London and downriver from the Coast Guard Academy, is General Dynamics' Electric Boat Company, which built the nuclear submarines that may very well have deterred nuclear war. New London is also the site of the Coast Guard Museum; the local congressional delegation passed a measure in 2004 barring its relocation.

In the 1990s, this local economy was in trouble. Nuclear plants were wearing out and being shut down across the country. After the end of the Cold War much of the Electric Boat work force was laid off, though some remained to work on the next-generation Virginia-class submarine; the base is home port to more than 20 subs, still the nation's most active submarine port, and about 10,000 employees. The area's economic base then shifted to entertainment. Some of that was tourism—Mystic Seaport and the Coast Guard Academy. Much more important was the Foxwoods Casino, built by the 650-member Mashantucket Pequot tribe and opened in 1992. Foxwoods is now the largest casino in the world, and with hotels, golf courses and a convention center. It is the largest employer in Connecticut and is pushing ahead with plans for a $700 million expansion. With the Mohegan Sun casino (the second largest casino in the world), opened near Norwich in 1996, gambling establishments now provide more tax dollars to the state than any insurance or defense company.

The 2d Congressional District of Connecticut includes most of the eastern part of the state, centering on the small cities of New London and Norwich, including mill towns and the University of Connecticut town of Storrs nestled in the rocky hills to the north. The northeastern edge of Windham County, long known as Quiet Corner for its small towns and dairy farms, is now drawing the attention of Rhode Island and Massachusetts residents looking to escape high taxes and housing prices. The 2d also stretches west to the outskirts of Hartford, and to antique-filled small towns like Essex and Old Lyme on Long Island Sound. For many years this was a politically marginal district, with close battles between Yankee Republicans and Catholic Democrats. More recently it has trended Democratic and has become volatile, with substantial votes for Ross Perot and Ralph Nader.

The new congressman from the 2d District is Joe Courtney, a Democrat elected in 2006. Courtney studied at Tufts University, graduated from University of Connecticut's law school and went into private practice. In 1986, he won the first of four terms in the state House, where he served as chairman of the public health and human services committees. He ran unsuccessfully for lieutenant governor in 1998, and then unsuccessfully against Republican Congressman Rob Simmons in 2002. Simmons, who earned two Bronze Stars in Vietnam and later served as a CIA operations officer, had defeated 20-year Democratic Congressman Sam Gejdenson two years earlier.

Courtney ran on the standard Democratic themes of Social Security, prescription drug coverage for seniors and against the Bush tax cut. Friends of the Earth endorsed Simmons, saying that he had the most pro-environment record of the freshmen Republicans. Courtney gained ground late in the 2002 campaign, but Simmons won 54%-46%. Courtney stepped aside for Democrat Jim Sullivan in 2004, but Sullivan lost by the same 54%-46% score.

Courtney announced his second bid against Simmons in March 2005, which was early enough to discourage other Democrats from running in 2006. Economic uncertainty abounded when the Pentagon in May 2005 named the New London submarine base for closure. From his seat on the Armed Services Committee, Simmons lobbied the Pentagon, held hearings on the need for more submarines, met with Base Realignment and Closure Commission members and touted the synergy with nearby submarine builder Electric Boat. In August 2005, the base closing commission recommended the New London base remain open, which boded well for Simmons's reelection chances.

But Democrats worked diligently to nationalize the race by exploiting voter anger over the Iraq war and GOP scandals. Simmons was attacked for donating $1,000 to Tom DeLay's legal defense fund; after DeLay left Congress, Democrats sought to tether Simmons to President Bush. Courtney called Simmons the President's "Number 1 supporter in Connecticut" and said the incumbent voted with Bush "more than any congressman from Connecticut." At the May 2006 Democratic district convention, Courtney said Simmons had entrusted his vote to George Bush. "If we want change in this country, we need to take George Bush's vote in the 2d Congressional District back," he said. Simmons touted his independence from the administration by pointing to votes on partial-birth abortion and same-sex marriage, and he criticized Courtney for supporting higher gasoline taxes as a state legislator. There was concern that Joe Lieberman's independent Senate candidacy and support for the Iraq war would distract voter attention from Connecticut's House races, while others like DCCC chairman Rahm Emanuel predicted the Lieberman race would keep the spotlight on the war and energize Democratic voters. To demonstrate the value of a bipartisanship delegation, Simmons appeared with Lieberman on the anniversary of saving the submarine base. Courtney called for the resignation of Defense Secretary Donald Rumsfeld, and used television ads to portray Simmons as aligned with Bush on energy policy, Medicare prescription drug coverage and Iraq.

More than 242,000 voters turned out on Election Day, which was 25,000 more voters than in 2002. Courtney won towns like Old Lyme that he had lost four years earlier, and he posted larger margins in Mansfield, Norwich, New London and Vernon. Simmons did well in smaller towns in Windham County. The outcome was uncertain on election night, and Courtney held a slim 167-vote lead the next day, a margin which was small enough to trigger an automatic recount. A week later, Courtney's lead was cut in half but official results gave Courtney an 83-vote victory. There was some precedent for this in the 2d: Sam Gejdenson won reelection in 1994 by just 21 votes. Democrats appointed Courtney to the Armed Services Committee on which his predecessor had served. For 2008, Republicans have lined up behind Sean Sullivan, former commander of the Groton submarine base, in what is expected to be a competitive contest.

THIRD DISTRICT

Rep. Rosa DeLauro (D)

Elected 1990, 9th term; b. Mar. 2, 1943, New Haven; home, New Haven; Marymount Col., B.A. 1964, London Sch. of Econ., 1962-63, Columbia U., M.A. 1966; Catholic; married (Stanley Greenberg).

Professional Career: Exec. Asst., New Haven Mayor Frank Logue, 1976-77; Exec. Asst. & Develop. Admin., City of New Haven, 1977-79; Chief of Staff, U.S. Sen. Christopher Dodd, 1980-87; Exec. Dir., Countdown '87, 1987-88; Exec. Dir., EMILY's List, 1989.

DC Office: 2262 RHOB, 20515, 202-225-3661; Fax: 202-225-4890; Web site: www.house.gov/delauro.

District Offices: New Haven, 203-562-3718; Stratford, 203-378-9005.

Committees: *Democratic Steering Committee Co-Chair. Appropriations* (9th of 37 D): Agriculture, Rural Development, FDA & Related Agencies (Chmn.); Labor, HHS, Education & Related Agencies; Commerce, Justice, Science & Related Agencies. *Budget* (2d of 22 D).

Group Ratings

	ADA	ACLU	AFS	LCV	ITIC	NTU	COC	ACU	CFG	FRC
2006	100	95	100	100	29	12	27	8	4	0
2005	95	—	100	100	—	11	37	0	0	0

National Journal Ratings

	2005 LIB	—	2005 CONS		2006 LIB	—	2006 CONS
Economic	88%	—	9%		94%	—	0%
Social	85%	—	14%		89%	—	10%
Foreign	79%	—	21%		95%	—	0%

Key Votes of the 109th Congress

1. Estate Tax Repeal	N	5. Limit Interstate Abortion	N	9. Build Border Fence	N
2. Limit CAFE Standards	N	6. Extend Patriot Act	N	10. CAFTA	N
3. FY06 Spending Curb	N	7. Bar Same Sex Marriage	N	11. Oppose Iraq Withdrawal	N
4. Drilling in ANWR	N	8. Stem Cell Research $	Y	12. Detainee Tribunals	N

Election Results

2006 general	Rosa DeLauro (D)	150,436	(76%)	($860,821)
	Joseph Vollano (R)	44,386	(22%)	
	Other	3,089	(2%)	
2006 primary	Rosa DeLauro (D)	unopposed		
2004 general	Rosa DeLauro (D)	200,638	(72%)	($714,890)
	Richter Elser (R)	69,160	(25%)	($21,416)
	Other	7,182	(3%)	

Prior Winning Percentages: 2002 (66%); 2000 (72%); 1998 (71%); 1996 (71%); 1994 (63%); 1992 (66%); 1990 (52%)

The People		Race/Ethnic Origin	Ancestry	
Area size:	485 sq. mi.	76.1% White	Italian: 18.7%	Irish: 12.5%
Urban population:	96.6%	11.5% Black	German: 6.7%	
Rural population:	3.4%	2.5% Asian	**2004 Presidential Vote**	
Pop. 2000:	681,113	0.2% Native Am.	Kerry (D) 174,382	(56%)
Pop. 2005 (est):	690,372	0.0% Hawaiian	Bush (R) 128,960	(42%)
Median income:	$49,752	1.5% Two+ races	Other 5,980	(2%)
Poverty status:	8.8%	0.2% Other	**2000 Presidential Vote**	
Military veterans:	11.8%	8.0% Hispanic Origin	Gore (D) 168,196	(60%)
			Bush (R) 96,446	(34%)
			Other 15,455	(6%)
			Cook Partisan Voting Index: D +12	

Occupation	Blue collar: 21.1%	White collar: 64.7%	Gray collar: 14.2%

The beginnings of Connecticut's defense industry came more than two centuries ago, in 1798, when Eli Whitney, a young Yale graduate, won an order from the federal government to produce 10,000 muskets at $13.40 each. Six years before, Whitney had invented the cotton gin, which revolutionized the South but for years only embroiled him in a patent suit. On the musket contract, he was determined to make a profit right off, so he set up a system of interchangeable parts and invented a milling machine and gauges: The beginning of standardized American manufacturing. It was also the beginning of New Haven as a manufacturing center, for Whitney set up his factory along a small, rapidly flowing river just north of this town, established more than 150 years earlier as a religious haven for strict Puritans. For the next 150 years or so, the town mass-produced rifles, clocks, locks, hardware and toys—anything its tinkerers and entrepreneurs could fashion. Today few factories remain in New Haven, and the state's defense contracts are cut way back. The factory that produced Winchester rifles and guns for 140 years closed in 2006; the Sikorsky plant in Stratford failed to get the contract to produce a new Marine One helicopter. Southern Connecticut around New Haven is mostly prosperous, with scores of small technology and biomedical firms. In Orange, Pez Candy Inc. produces several million of its distinctive candy tablets each day. But the city, with significant crime rates and many neighborhoods scarred by abandoned homes, has shrunk: 164,000 people in 1950 and 125,000 in 2005. Yale, with its Gothic spires and redbrick halls, has always been the visual focus of New Haven, and now is its largest employer. Some local revival has been sparked by a state development program that has turned old retail and office buildings into residences, and by $1 billion in investments by biotech firms. Lately, New Haven has a new historic claim. It was the birthplace of George W. Bush in 1946, and he lived his first two years on Hillhouse Avenue in a building that now houses the economics department.

The 3d Congressional District of Connecticut covers the New Haven metropolitan area, which has long since spread beyond the narrow city limits over the hills of what were once Yankee villages and countryside; New Haven cast only 12% of its votes in 2004. For many years the 3d was a marginal district, changing partisan hands in the 1980s as well as the 1940s and 1950s. But it is now a strongly Democratic district.

The congresswoman from the 3d District is Rosa DeLauro, first elected in 1990. She is well connected in New Haven and Washington. She grew up in New Haven's Wooster Square. Both her parents were elected as New Haven aldermen; her mother, Luisa DeLauro, retired in 1999 after 35 years as New Haven's longest-serving alderman. Rosa DeLauro's husband, Stanley Greenberg, was Bill Clinton's chief pollster from 1991-94 and worked for Al Gore in 2000 and John Kerry in 2004. Rahm Emanuel lives in the basement apartment of their Capitol Hill home. DeLauro has been in politics nearly all of her life. She was a development administrator in New Haven in the 1970s, chief of staff to Senator Christopher Dodd from 1980-87, then spent a year working to stop U.S. military aid to Nicaraguan contras before going on to become director of EMILY's List, the feminist campaign fundraising group. When 3d District incumbent Bruce Morrison ran for governor in 1990, DeLauro ran for Congress and won 52%-48% over anti-tax and anti-abortion legislator Tom Scott.

DeLauro has had a consistently liberal voting record and is one of the Democratic leadership's loudest champions on the floor. She has been an active and enthusiastic supporter of feminist issues. A cancer survivor, she sponsored the law to require 48-hour hospital stays for mastectomies, argued for insurance coverage of early-detection tests of cervical cancer, and helped to enact "Johanna's Law" to increase awareness of gynecological cancers. She voted against NAFTA and normal trade relations with China. As a member of the committee that drafted in 2002 the bill creating the Homeland Security Department, she embarrassed House Republican leaders by winning a vote to prevent the department from contracting with corporations that move overseas for tax purposes; the House-Senate conference committee later watered down that provision. DeLauro organized the House's food safety caucus, and she has demanded additional steps to prevent bioterrorism.

She remains an active and intense political strategist, "a live wire whose words rush out like sparks," wrote the *New York Times*. She has run twice for chairman of the Democratic Caucus and suffered two painfully close losses. In 1998, she lost 108-97 to Martin Frost, but Dick Gephardt then named her an assistant to the leader to work on the party message. In 2002 she lost by 104-103 to Bob Menendez after an intense yearlong contest. The deciding vote was cast for Menendez by Mike Feeley of Colorado, whose election was in question at the time; it later turned out that he lost his race and so was never actually a member of Congress. DeLauro was an active supporter of Nancy Pelosi in her races for minority whip and minority leader, and she was probably hurt in her own race by the reluctance of some Democrats to put so many liberal women in the party leadership. But she has found other opportunities for leadership. Pelosi named her to co-chair the Democratic Steering Committee, which assigns members to House committees. In 2004, working in close coordination with the Kerry campaign, DeLauro led the drafting panel of the Democratic Platform Committee. In 2006, she co-chaired the successful campaign by John Larson for Caucus vice-chairman. In the majority, she chairs the Appropriations Subcommittee on Agriculture, Rural Development, and Food and Drug Administration. She listed consolidation of food-safety programs as a top priority and has worked with farm groups for mandatory country-of-origin labels. She wants retailers to increase the availability of emergency contraceptives.

DeLauro's last serious competition in the 3d District came in 1992, when she won a rematch against Scott 66%-34%. She has expressed interest in running for the Senate if Joe Lieberman's or Christopher Dodd's seat becomes open.

FOURTH DISTRICT

Rep. Christopher Shays (R)

Elected Aug. 1987, 10th full term; b. Oct. 18, 1945, Darien; home, Bridgeport; Principia Col., B.A. 1968, NYU, M.B.A. 1974, M.P.A. 1978; Christian Scientist; married (Betsi).

Elected Office: CT House of Reps., 1974-87.

Professional Career: Peace Corps, Fiji, 1968-70; Aide, Trumbull Mayor, 1971-72.

DC Office: 1126 LHOB, 20515, 202-225-5541; Fax: 202-225-9629; Web site: www.house.gov/shays.

District Offices: Bridgeport, 203-579-5870; Norwalk, 203-866-6469; Ridgefield, 203-438-5953; Shelton, 203-402-0426; Stamford, 203-357-8277.

Committees: *Financial Services* (13th of 33 R): Capital Markets, Insurance & Government Sponsored Enterprises; Housing & Community Opportunity. *Homeland Security* (3d of 15 R): Intelligence, Information Sharing & Terrorism Risk Assessment. *Oversight & Government Reform* (3d of 18 R): National Security & Foreign Affairs (RMM); Domestic Policy.

Group Ratings

	ADA	ACLU	AFS	LCV	ITIC	NTU	COC	ACU	CFG	FRC
2006	65	59	20	92	86	38	62	36	31	0
2005	55	—	50	78	—	44	70	20	33	8

National Journal Ratings

	2005 LIB	—	2005 CONS		2006 LIB	—	2006 CONS
Economic	53%	—	47%		54%	—	45%
Social	55%	—	44%		60%	—	40%
Foreign	53%	—	46%		52%	—	47%

Key Votes of the 109th Congress

1. Estate Tax Repeal	Y	5. Limit Interstate Abortion	N	9. Build Border Fence	Y
2. Limit CAFE Standards	N	6. Extend Patriot Act	Y	10. CAFTA	Y
3. FY06 Spending Curb	Y	7. Bar Same Sex Marriage	N	11. Oppose Iraq Withdrawal	Y
4. Drilling in ANWR	N	8. Stem Cell Research $	Y	12. Detainee Tribunals	Y

Election Results

2006 general	Christopher Shays (R)	106,510	(51%)	($3,804,187)
	Diane Farrell (D)	99,450	(48%)	($2,961,500)
	Other	3,059	(1%)	
2006 primary	Christopher Shays (R)	unopposed		
2004 general	Christopher Shays (R)	152,493	(52%)	($2,255,210)
	Diane Farrell (D)	138,333	(48%)	($1,542,410)

Prior Winning Percentages: 2002 (64%); 2000 (58%); 1998 (69%); 1996 (60%); 1994 (74%); 1992 (67%); 1990 (77%); 1988 (72%); 1987 (57%)

The People		Race/Ethnic Origin	Ancestry	
Area size:	539 sq. mi.	70.9% White	Italian: 13.5%	Irish: 11.6%
Urban population:	95.9%	10.9% Black	German: 7.1%	
Rural population:	4.1%	3.2% Asian	**2004 Presidential Vote**	
Pop. 2000:	681,113	0.1% Native Am.	Kerry (D) 162,166	(52%)
Pop. 2005 (est):	690,098	0.0% Hawaiian	Bush (R) 143,280	(46%)
Median income:	$66,598	1.7% Two+ races	Other 4,121	(1%)
Poverty status:	7.4%	0.3% Other	**2000 Presidential Vote**	
Military veterans:	10.0%	12.8% Hispanic Origin	Gore (D) 148,022	(53%)
			Bush (R) 120,140	(43%)
			Other 10,219	(4%)
			Cook Partisan Voting Index: D + 5	

Occupation	Blue collar: 15.5%	White collar: 71.8%	Gray collar: 12.7%

No one in colonial America imagined that the rocky shore of southern Connecticut on Long Island Sound would some day lodge one of the largest concentrations of wealth in the world. The soil was stony, the terrain unaccommodating, the harbors not as convenient as those in New York and Rhode Island and Massachusetts. Yet that is what has happened. For 200 years this was the home of unnoticed Yankee farmers, sailors and tinkerers; then, factories were built on its fast-running stream. In the 19th century, Bridgeport became famous as the home of P.T. Barnum (the city's mayor before he started his circus), and around that same time rich New Yorkers began taking the train north to country houses in Connecticut. In the 20th century, Greenwich and other Yankee villages clustered around commuter railroad stations became the home of some of New York's elite. Greenwich has beautifully manicured hills, elaborately simple boat docks, carefully casual roads, good manners and dull haircuts, over a dozen private clubs and nearly a dozen private schools—and houses that routinely sell for more than $3 million and are then torn down to make way for grander mansions. Many towns report nearly as many demolitions as new homes. Starting in the 1950s, New York-based CEOs, eager to minimize their commutes and avoid New York income taxes, moved their headquarters to Greenwich and farther, including General Electric in Fairfield and several firms in Stamford. Greenwich, sometimes referred to as "Wall Street by the Sea" for its proliferation of hedge fund offices and financial firms, is closest to New York and commands the highest commercial rents of all these places; these firms manage more than $300 billion in assets. Not all of the businesses are gigantic: In Shelton, Wiffle Ball Inc. sells millions of wiffle balls and bats each year.

The 4th Congressional District covers Connecticut along Long Island Sound, from industrial Bridgeport to affluent Greenwich, and goes inland to Ridgefield, Redding, Monroe and Oxford. This is the wealthiest district in the nation's wealthiest state. It includes bustling and pricey Stamford, woodsy Darien, modest Norwalk, artsy-craftsy Westport, Fairfield and then Bridgeport, an odd duck, an industrial and low-income town, though spruced up when the state-financed Harbor Yard sports complex opened for minor league baseball, and a major downtown rehabilitation resulted. The basic political balance has been the same since the 1940s, when the heavily affluent suburbs out-voted Bridgeport and elected Republican Clare Boothe Luce to the House. More than the rest of Connecticut, the 4th is oriented to New York rather than Hartford or Boston. People here watch New York TV stations: They are Yankee, not Red Sox, fans; their political attitudes are shaped by what is happening in the City as much as in Hartford. Opposition to high taxes has helped Republicans to win here; in tax year 2004, the 4th District had the third-highest federal individual income tax burden of all congressional districts. But the influence of Christian conservatives in the GOP has repelled Episcopalians and other mainline Protestants, and they have been increasingly voting Democratic. This is the district where George H. W. Bush grew up and one which he carried in 1988 and 1992. But George W. Bush lost it in 2000 and 2004.

The 4th District's congressman, Christopher Shays, is a product of the upscale towns and he has been a pivotal Republican in the House. Shays grew up in Darien. After college he and his wife volunteered for the Peace Corps and served in Fiji; after graduate school he was elected to the Connecticut House in 1974, at 29, and served for 12 years. He was elected to Congress in a 1987 special election by beating a culturally conservative Democrat from Bridgeport. Shays is a pleasant man with a stubborn streak and considerable legislative savvy; his voting record is near the middle of the House, a bit left on cultural issues. When he feels strongly, he will risk everything: He registered for conscientious objector status during the Vietnam War, and says he would not have served if drafted; as a legislator, he went to jail for seven days in 1986 to protest judicial system corruption; he is one of two congressmen (the other is Frank Wolf) who have made trips to Iraq on their own, without guides from the Defense Department, and he has made 18 trips altogether—more than any other member of Congress.

Despite his dissent from many Republicans' views—on campaign finance reform, abortion, gun control, arts subsidies, gay rights, the minimum wage, defense spending, Census sampling—he was a partisan Republican from the time he was ignored by the House's Democratic leaders and impressed by a speech in Connecticut by a backbencher named Newt Gingrich. The first major bill of the Republican Congress was managed by Shays: the Congressional Accountability Act, imposing on Congress the laws it imposes on others, passed unanimously on the first day. Shays supported Gingrich on ethics charges and warned him of the other leaders' attempted coup in 1997. But he soured on Republican leaders after they went to great lengths to sink his Shays-Meehan campaign finance bill. On some big issues he was solidly with George W. Bush: He voted for trade promotion authority and to authorize the use of force in Iraq. After the ouster of Saddam Hussein, Shays made several visits to Iraq to meet with local groups, and he typically returned with suggestions for the

Bush administration. In 2002, he became a leading supporter of Bush's proposal for a Homeland Security Department and he helped to defeat an amendment to permit its employees to join unions. In 2004, he pressed harder than most House Republicans wished to enact the intelligence-reform recommendations of the 9/11 Commission. He harshly criticized the response to Hurricane Katrina. At a hearing one month after the disaster, he told former FEMA head Michael Brown, "I'm happy you left." Shays has been a leader on initiatives to encourage national service.

Shays's great cause has been campaign finance regulation. As enacted in March 2002, his Shays-Meehan bill—or McCain-Feingold, as it was known in the Senate and more widely—banned in federal elections soft money from corporations, labor unions and wealthy individuals and barred issue advocacy ads within 60 days of an election unless hard money has paid for them. Although the House passed the bill 240-189, all but 41 House Republicans voted against it, with many contending it was harmful to their party. The conflict caused bitter divisions and anger by Republicans toward Shays. Shays defended the new law in federal court; after lengthy review, the Supreme Court in December 2003 upheld most of the provisions. Then, he turned his attention to abolishing the Federal Election Commission and creating a more assertive agency to enforce the nation's campaign finance laws. On other domestic issues, he chaired a bipartisan group that filed the Climate Stewardship Act, to focus attention on global warming and set a schedule to reduce harmful emissions. After the 2004 election, he spoke out against proposed Republican rules changes to remove the requirement that a party leader step down after being indicted. "The power has gotten to our heads," he said. His call for Majority Leader Tom DeLay's resignation in April 2005 compounded his isolation, though success by Shays in scuttling the Republican rules change assured that DeLay soon was forced out. Shays also called Nancy Pelosi a "fraud" on ethics issues, because of her own actions and attacks on him.

The chairmanship of the Government Reform Committee was open following the 2002 election, and Shays was next in line in seniority. He actively sought the post; he argued that it was best suited for him and that his work on campaign finance ought not to be held against him. But he clearly was not popular with Republican leaders, and the Steering Committee chose Tom Davis of Virginia, who had maintained the Republican majority for four years at the National Republican Congressional Committee. Shays retained the chairmanship of the Government Reform subcommittee with the most far-reaching investigative authority, on national security issues. He chaired nearly 100 hearings on terrorism, including 22 prior to September 11.

Back home, Shays faced opposition from Democrats who have attacked him for supporting Gingrich and, in 2000, from a Republican primary opponent who said he was too independent and too liberal. Until 2004, none caused him serious difficulty. But Shays faced a big challenge that year from Democrat Diane Farrell, the First Selectman of Westport. Farrell got extensive financial support from House Democrats and argued that Shays was a "rubber stamp" for Bush and House GOP leaders. National Republicans found themselves in the curious position of citing and defending Shays's independence based on roll-call vote analysis; to the NRCC's dismay, he ordered the campaign committee not to run ads attacking Farrell. Both candidates were well-funded but Shays won 52%-48%. He carried 13 of the 17 cities and towns, losing narrowly in Norwalk, Stamford and Westport and by a big margin in Bridgeport. In affluent Greenwich, Darien, New Canaan and Wilton he ran 8% or 9% ahead of George W. Bush.

In 2006, Farrell ran again. This time, she criticized him more harshly on Iraq—both for his frequent travels and continued support of Bush's policy. "I don't think he's being honest with himself about what's happening over there," she told a reporter in July. Shays said that Farrell "doesn't know the first thing about what is going on in Iraq," but he increasingly attacked the administration's actions there and conceded that at least two-thirds of his constituents opposed the war. He showed bipartisanship with an early endorsement of Joe Lieberman's reelection, but the Senator did not return the favor. As his election neared, it seemed increasingly unlikely that Shays's independent views would prevail. But he persevered in defending his credibility and his commitment to fighting terrorism. "My hero is Churchill," he told the *Hartford Courant* in June 2006. "If I lost over Iraq, I would be unhappy. But I would live with the knowledge that I've taken what I believe to be the right stand." Shays survived again, even as Connecticut's two other House Republicans were defeated. The margin this time was 51%-48% and the local patterns were similar to 2004; Farrell was hurt by a much smaller turnout in Bridgeport, where her lead fell by about 8,000 votes.

Back in Washington, where Shays survives as the only House Republican from New England, some party colleagues continued to view him as a sanctimonious troublemaker. But once again, he laid plans to become top Republican on the Government Reform Committee, after the 2008 election.

That would require concurrence by both House GOP leaders and Connecticut voters—and in 2007 there already were signs that Shays would get a tough challenge from Greenwich Democrat Jim Himes, a former investment banker.

FIFTH DISTRICT

Rep. Chris Murphy (D)

Elected 2006, 1st term; b. Aug. 3, 1973, White Plains, NY; home, Cheshire; Attended Exeter College (England), 1994-95; Williams Col., B.A. 1996; U. of CT, J.D. 2002; Protestant; married (Cathy Holahan).

Elected Office: CT House of Reps., 1998-2002; CT Senate, 2002-06.

Professional Career: Southington zoning commission, 1997-99; Practicing atty., 2002-06.

DC Office: 501 CHOB, 20515, 202-225-4476; Fax: 202-225-5933; Web site: chrismurphy.house.gov.

District Offices: New Britain, 860-223-8412.

Committees: *Financial Services* (33d of 37 D): Housing & Community Opportunity; Capital Markets, Insurance & Government Sponsored Enterprises. *Oversight & Government Reform* (21st of 23 D): Government Management, Organization & Procurement; Domestic Policy.

Group Ratings and Key Votes: Newly Elected

Election Results

2006 general	Chris Murphy (D)	117,186	(54%)	($2,486,251)
	Nancy Johnson (R)	94,824	(44%)	($5,095,844)
	Other	5,794	(3%)	
2006 primary	Chris Murphy (D)	unopposed		
2004 general	Nancy Johnson (R)	168,268	(60%)	($1,241,036)
	Theresa Gerratana (D)	107,438	(38%)	($128,229)
	Other	5,741	(2%)	

The People		Race/Ethnic Origin	Ancestry	
Area size:	1,282 sq. mi.	80.2% White	Italian: 14.5%	Irish: 12.7%
Urban population:	85.9%	5.2% Black	German: 8.2%	
Rural population:	14.1%	2.1% Asian	**2004 Presidential Vote**	
Pop. 2000:	681,113	0.2% Native Am.	Kerry (D) 153,616	(49%)
Pop. 2005 (est):	715,783	0.0% Hawaiian	Bush (R) 152,504	(49%)
Median income:	$53,118	1.5% Two+ races	Other 5,325	(2%)
Poverty status:	7.7%	0.3% Other	**2000 Presidential Vote**	
Military veterans:	11.9%	10.5% Hispanic Origin	Gore (D) 146,599	(52%)
			Bush (R) 121,424	(43%)
			Other 13,887	(5%)
			Cook Partisan Voting Index: D + 4	
Occupation	Blue collar: 22.4%	White collar: 62.9% Gray collar: 14.6%		

Over the years, Connecticut's stony soil has become the home of some of the most affluent people in the nation and the world. This is true even in the hills of northwest Connecticut, off the interstates and far from Connecticut's small urban capital of Hartford and its sometime booming edge city of Stamford. Here are exquisite Yankee towns like Washington and Kent, once prosperous in the post-Revolutionary era when Connecticut's ship owners accumulated capital and invested it in factories and mills, and now the "anti-Hamptons," a country-home mecca for ultra-rich New Yorkers seeking to avoid the glitz of Southampton and East Hampton. Not far away are small industrial cities like New Britain, America's ball bearing capital for years; Meriden, which turned from ivory combs, clocks, cutlery, and silver, to producing electrical signaling equipment, jewelry, biotech filters, and nuclear instruments; Waterbury, once the nation's largest producer of brass, where political corruption and economic malaise resulted in the state taking over its finances in 2001; and Danbury, once the nation's leading producer of hats, but now a growing corporate headquarters with an eclectic mix of recent immigrants from South America, the Caribbean and Southeast Asia. Over the hills from Hartford are Avon and Simsbury, booming towns that have become comfortable bedroom communities and the home of champion international ice-skaters.

The 5th Congressional District of Connecticut covers much of the western side of the state, dipping down to include the northern towns of Fairfield County. It has two arms that reach into the hills of central Connecticut—one to Democratic Meriden, and the other to the affluent and Republican-leaning Farmington Valley suburbs of Hartford. This district was carefully drawn by a bipartisan redistricting commission to provide a "fair fight" between two incumbents forced into the same district because Connecticut lost a House seat in the 2000 Census. Small towns like Kent and Salisbury in Litchfield County were, until recently, dominated by Republicans, but the influx has altered voting patterns. In 2006 the district recorded 17,000 new registered voters, including 48% who were unaffiliated, 34% Democrats and 17% Republican.

The new congressman from the 5th District is Chris Murphy, a Democrat elected in 2006 by ousting Republican Nancy Johnson, Connecticut's senior House member. Murphy grew up in Wethersfield, and his father is a prominent lawyer at a Hartford law firm. He graduated from Williams College in 1996 and that same year, at age 22, became the campaign manager for Democrat Charlotte Koskoff, whose campaign came 1,587 votes short of ousting Nancy Johnson. The lessons that Murphy learned during that campaign served him well in the political career that followed, and in his own campaign against Johnson a decade later. Murphy won a seat in the state House in 1998, graduated from the UConn law school in 2002, and later that year won election to the state Senate. He served as co-chairman of the public health committee where he worked to curb hospital collection practices, ban smoking in the workplace, and to increase investment in stem cell research.

Democrats took a pass on Johnson in 2004 and she began the 2006 cycle as the favorite in the seat she had occupied for 24 years. Murphy in early 2005 moved into Johnson's 5th District and announced his campaign in April. He was backed by the Democratic establishment and faced no primary opposition. Unlike Connecticut's two other competitive congressional races in 2006, this one did not revolve around the Iraq war and President Bush. Much of the debate instead focused on the Medicare prescription drug benefit that the moderate Johnson helped design in 2003 as chairwoman of the House Ways and Means Health Subcommittee.

The liberal group MoveOn.org ran ads in April 2006 tying Johnson to disgraced former lobbyist Jack Abramoff and to the oil and pharmaceutical industries, spots designed to elevate the competitiveness of what was then viewed as a second tier race. For his part, Murphy contended that the Medicare prescription drug program's enrollment deadlines penalized seniors; he spotlighted drug industry contributions to Johnson to portray her as a shill for the industry. "My opponent Nancy Johnson deserves part of the blame. She wrote the confusing Medicare law in 2003," Murphy said in September, when he was tapped by Democratic leaders to give the party's weekly radio address. "She refuses to make Medicare better, and works tirelessly to stop reform."

National security issues did not play a major role in the race until the day after the fifth anniversary of the September 11, 2001 terrorist attacks. In a television ad resembling a movie trailer for an espionage thriller, Johnson attacked Murphy for opposing the Bush administration's warrantless wiretapping program. The 30-second spot, which featured a series of rapid images, suggested that seeking a court warrant for surveillance takes too long and could jeopardize national security. "A call is placed from New York to a known terrorist in Pakistan. A terrorist plot may be unfolding," the announcer warned. The security focus briefly put Murphy on the defensive and some Democrats feared Murphy was too slow to respond. But Murphy then struck back with an ad that implied Johnson was slow to help a mother obtain health coverage to pay for a surgery to fix her infant's cleft palate. In October Johnson used an ad to accuse Murphy of voting to raise taxes 27 times and for being weak on terrorism and soft on drug dealers; the negative campaign may have undermined Johnson's image as an experienced legislator and a grandmotherly figure. Johnson, who collected over $1.2 million from the health care industry alone, outspent Murphy $5 million to $2.5 million. But Murphy won 54%-44%. Republican State Senator David Cappiello announced he would challenge Murphy in 2008.

★ DELAWARE ★

Delaware, the first state to ratify the Constitution, the second smallest state in area, sixth smallest in population, is a small corner of America, with some considerable claims on the national attention. The mouth of the Delaware River was explored by Henry Hudson, and the Dutch and Swedes built settlements on the west bank in the 1630s. But the three counties of Delaware owe their separate existence to the politics of the proprietors of William Penn's colony of Pennsylvania, and to Delawareans' own speed in ratifying the Constitution which made it literally the "First State."

Through most of its history, Delaware has been unusually affluent. It had the nation's highest income levels during the early 20th century and still has high income levels today. It houses, in beautiful cobblestone mansions in its chateau country, many members of the most numerous wealthy family in America, the du Ponts. Delaware's racial and ethnic mix is much like that of the rest of the East Coast and not that much different from the nation's, though with more blacks and fewer Hispanics; there is a mixture here of suburbs, old immigrant neighborhoods, urban black neighborhoods, attractive beach towns and farmlands. Sussex County in southern Delaware is a world of its own. It produces more chickens that any other county in the country (chickens outnumber people by 300–1 in Delaware) and also thousands of tons of processed chicken dung (or "broiler litter"). Its beach communities are bustling with growth and there is a move toward historic preservation in the old towns inland.

For much of the last two centuries the central focus of Delaware's economy was the business started when Eleuthere Irenee du Pont, the practical-minded son of a dreamy, idealistic French immigrant, built a gunpowder mill on the banks of Brandywine Creek in 1802. This was the first enterprise of the family du Pont, and it expanded to become one of America's great munitions and chemical companies. It switched from gunpowder to dynamite in the 1880s and grew especially rapidly during World War I, generating so much capital that the company bought a large share of General Motors stock in the 1920s and controlled GM for 30 years when it was America's largest corporation. DuPont capital also financed what was arguably the world's finest research and development program. In the years on either side of World War II, DuPont prospered by bringing to the consumer and industrial markets new synthetics and plastics like rayon, nylon, synthetic dyes, cellophane, lucite, teflon, dacron, orlon, kevlar: "Better Living Through Chemistry."

Delaware has used its status as a state to pass laws that set national policy. In the late 19th century, it passed pioneering laws of incorporation, giving more flexibility and power to managers and owners. About half of the nation's publicly traded companies are incorporated in Delaware—their legal births take place in a federal-style building near the Capitol in Dover—which means that much of the nation's corporate law, especially on mergers and acquisitions, is made in Delaware's Chancery Court. Delaware takes care in choosing judges and writing corporate law to produce a reliable legal environment. In the last quarter century, Delaware has fostered a new industry: credit cards. In 1981 Governor Pete du Pont pushed through a law abolishing Delaware's usury laws and lowering its bank franchise tax. Inflation was high, and banks were looking for a state with no limit on interest rates to locate their credit card operation. South Dakota abolished its usury law in 1980, but didn't have a labor force large enough to support many banks; Delaware did. MBNA moved in from Maryland in 1982 and invented the affinity card in 1983; it became the nation's largest credit card issuer and its CEO Charles Cawley replaced the du Ponts as Delaware's most visible philanthropist and community leader. Cawley retired in 2003 and MBNA was acquired by Bank of America in 2005. But Delaware still issues most of the nation's credit cards, DuPont is developing alternative fuels, life sciences businesses are growing (AstraZeneca has its U.S. headquarters here) and the state's economy may surge again from the rise of an industry as little anticipated now as the credit card business was in 1980.

One way Delaware thrives is by "exporting taxes." As Jonathan Chait, irritated at the $2 tolls and the traffic jams in the toll booths on the Delaware Turnpike, wrote in the *New Republic*, "The organizing principle of Delaware government is to subsidize its people at the rest of the country's expense." State government gets 3% of its operating budget from the Turnpike tolls, 22% from corporate and franchise taxes and 9% from slot machines, mostly patronized by out-of-staters. A 1993 U.S. Supreme Court decision has allowed Delaware to tax unclaimed property from other states. Exporting taxes has allowed Delaware to be one of the five states with no sales tax and, first under du Pont and then under Republican Mike Castle and Democrat Tom Carper, to lower its income tax several times. The Census Bureau reports that Delaware's state government has the

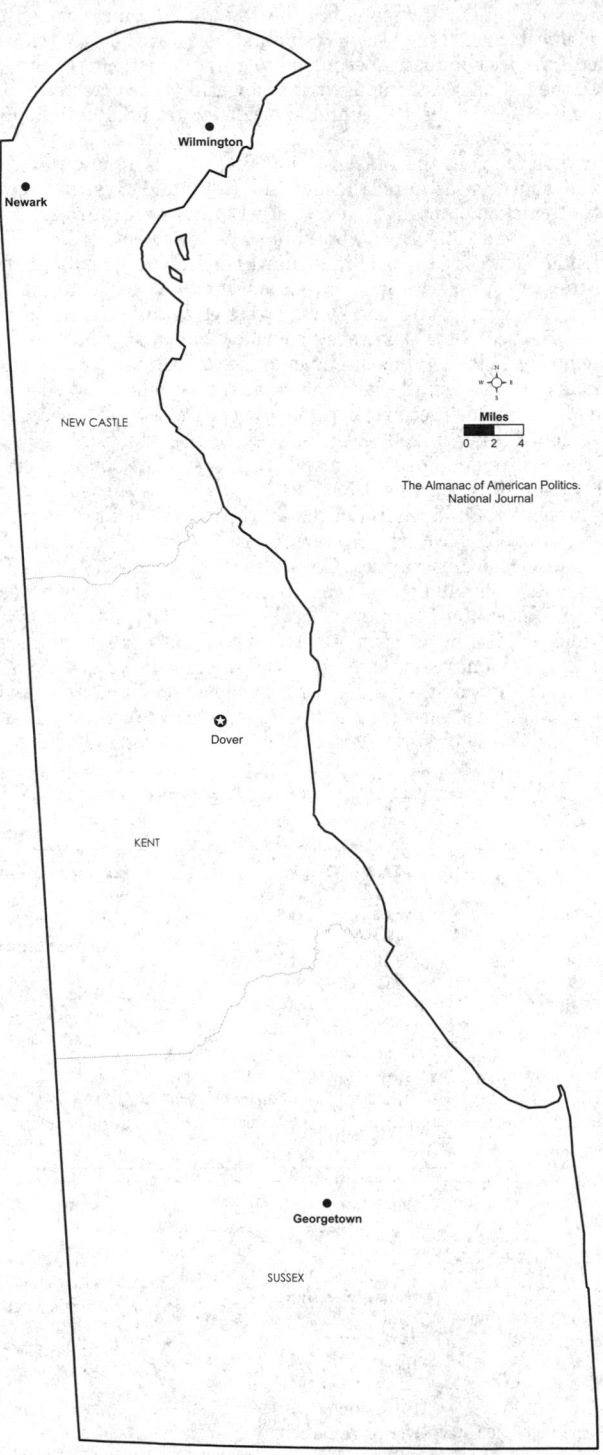

The Almanac of American Politics.
National Journal

U.S. Representative elected at-large.

fifth highest revenue per capita of any state, but the Tax Foundation reports that it has the third lowest per capita revenue derived from its own residents. Delaware boosters can argue that its state policies have enabled America's industrial economy to grow robustly, have provided easy credit to millions and have led the nation in a virtuous cycle of lowering taxes. Certainly Delaware has done well. Its population grew 18% in the 1990s and another 9% from 2000 to 2006—faster than any other state in the East or Midwest.

Delaware is on both sides of the Mason-Dixon line; it has immigrant communities in the Wilmington area and southern-accented farmers in Kent and Sussex Counties (plus Latino migrants working in its chicken plants); its New Castle County suburbs range from very affluent to not-so-affluent. Well-preserved 18th century buildings line the streets of New Castle, the capital in 1776-77, while mansions gaze out over rolling countryside in Centreville, north of Wilmington. Newark has grown from a country crossroads to a small city as the University of Delaware has expanded; new housing has sprung up along U.S. 40 west of Wilmington while some country towns have changed little since the 1950s. Delaware's considerable variety has produced a robust two-party politics in which tiny Delaware has often voted like the nation as a whole. But in the 1990s Delaware, like so many of America's largest metro areas, trended toward the Democrats. Now Democrat Ruth Ann Minner holds the governorship and both U.S. Senate seats—Joseph Biden was first elected in 1972, Tom Carper in 2000—are held by Democrats. Former Republican Governor Mike Castle holds the state's single seat in the U.S. House. In 2000 Al Gore carried the state 55%-42% and in 2004 John Kerry carried it 53%-46%; it was not a target state, but it got plenty of ads because most of it is in the Philadelphia media market. New Castle County, which casts nearly two-thirds of its votes, went 60% for Kerry, Sussex County 60% and Kent County 56% for George W. Bush. In 2006 there was a Democratic uptick. Carper's majority surged to 70%, Castle's fell to 57%; Democrats picked up seats in, but did not win control of, the state House. In a closer contest, Joseph Biden's son Beau Biden was elected attorney general by a 53%-47% margin.

Delaware elections are not bitter contests. Thanks to the state's small size there is still an intimacy to politics here. Personal campaigning is still important; voters are not surprised to run into their senators in the supermarket. Successful Delaware politicians are almost always nice people; they couldn't get elected otherwise. Then there is Delaware's unique custom, dating back to 1792, of "Return Day." On the Thursday after the election, winning and losing candidates come to the Sussex County seat of Georgetown and ride together in carriages to receive the bipartisan cheers of the voters and, literally, bury a hatchet in a box of Lewes beach sand. Not a bad example for the nation.

The People		Race/Ethnic Origin			Military veterans: 84,289 (14.3%)	
Pop. 2006 (est):	853,476	567,973	72.5%	White	WWII: 19.2%	Korea: 13.7%
Pop. 2000:	783,600	148,435	18.9%	Black	Vietnam: 31.7%	Gulf War: 10.1%
Pop. 1990:	666,168	16,110	2.1%	Asian	**Most populous cities (2006):**	
Change 1990-2000:	Up 17.6%	2,324	0.3%	Native Am.	1. Wilmington	72,826
% of U.S. total:	0.3%	234	0.0%	Hawaiian	2. Dover	34,735
Pop. rank:	45th of 50	10,222	1.3%	Two+ races	3. Newark	30,014
Area size:	2,489 sq. mi.	1,025	0.1%	Other	4. Middletown	10,272
State Native:	48.3%	37,277	4.8%	Hisp. Origin	5. Milford	7,852
Non-citizen:	3.3%	**Ancestry**				
Language		Irish: 12.6%		German: 10.9%	Urban population: 80.0%	
English: 88.1%	Spanish: 5.4%	English: 9.2%		Italian: 7.1%	Rural population: 20.0%	
Other Eur.: 4.6%		USA: 4.6%				

Education		Work Sector		General Assembly	
H.S. Grad:	82.6%	Private: 81.1%	Govt: 13.8%	Senate	13 D 8 R
College Grad:	25.0%	Self: 5.0%	Family: 0.2%	House	22 R 19 D
Industry		Unemployment: 5.1%		Legislative Term Limits: No	
Agri: 1.1%	Con: 7.4%	**Household Income**		**Registered Voters**	
Fin: 11.6%	Info: 1.9%	<15k: 12.2%	15-35k: 23.5%	D: 246,141	(44.1%)
Mfg: 18.0%	Prof: 28.6%	35-50k: 16.9%	50-100k: 33.3%	R: 178,635	(32.0%)
Public: 5.2%	Trade: 14.3%	100-150k: 9.4%	>150k: 4.6%	O: 132,927	(23.8%)
Other: 11.9%		Median: $47,381			
Occupation		Poverty status: 9.2%			
Blue collar: 22.0%	White collar: 62.9%	**Home Value**			
Gray collar: 15.1%		<50k: 9.7%	50-100k: 26.0%	100-200k: 47.9%	200-300k: 11.3%
		300-500k: 3.7%	>500k: 1.4%	Median: $122,000	

Presidential politics   Delaware has been competitive in most presidential elections since the Federalists were battling the Jeffersonians. Until 2000, it could claim to be a presidential bellwether: It had voted for every winner from 1952 to 1996, the longest winning streak of any state. But in 2000 and, to a lesser extent, 2004, Delaware voted distinctly more Democratic than the rest of the nation. The New Castle County suburbs, like other affluent parts of major metropolitan areas, tilted toward the Democrats and away from the Republicans on cultural issues. This leaves Delaware, more affluent than the nation, also more Democratic. The 2004 Bush campaign, advertising in the Philadelphia market in pursuit of Pennsylvania's 21 electoral votes, also covered most of Delaware and, to add the rest, bought time in the tiny Salisbury, Maryland, market that reaches Kent and Sussex Counties; but otherwise Delaware didn't see much of the candidates.

2004 Presidential Vote		
Kerry (D)	200,152	(53%)
Bush (R)	171,660	(46%)
Nader (I)	2,153	(1%)
Other	1,225	(0%)

2004 Democratic Presidential Primary		
Kerry (D)	16,787	(50%)
Lieberman (D)	3,706	(11%)
Edwards (D)	3,674	(11%)
Dean (D)	3,462	(10%)
Clark (D)	3,165	(10%)
Other	2,497	(8%)

2000 Presidential Vote		
Gore (D)	180,638	(55%)
Bush (R)	137,081	(42%)
Nader (Green)	8,288	(3%)
Other	1,863	(1%)

In 1996 Delaware vied for attention by holding its presidential primary February 24, just four days after New Hampshire. But New Hampshire Republicans put pressure on candidates to ignore Delaware, and only Steve Forbes and Alan Keyes showed up here. For 2000 Republicans decided to hold a primary on February 9, nine days after New Hampshire. George W. Bush, who spent two full days in Delaware, led with 51%, well ahead of John McCain (25%) and the still-remembered Forbes (20%). The Democratic primary, held February 5, was outside the Democrats' rules and neither candidate campaigned, and only 11,000 voters turned out; Al Gore led Bill Bradley 57%-40%. In 2004, Delaware scheduled its primary one week after New Hampshire, on February 3, but it was only one of several states voting that day. Joseph Lieberman, endorsed by Senator Tom Carper, Lieutenant Governor John Carney and Treasurer Jack Markell, paid several trips to Delaware. Other candidates were scarcer. John Kerry won the primary with 50% of the vote; Lieberman ran second with 11%, in what amounted to a tie with John Edwards, Howard Dean and Wesley Clark.

Governor

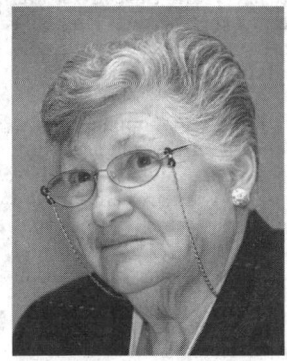

Ruth Ann Minner (D)

Elected 2000, term expires Jan. 2009, 2d term; b. Jan. 17, 1935, Slaughter Neck; home, Milford; G.E.D. 1968; Methodist; widowed.

Elected Office: DE House of Reps., 1974-82; DE Senate, 1982-92; Lt. Gov. 1992-2000.

Professional Career: Owner, Roger Minner Towing, 1969-present; Receptionist, Gov. Sherman Tribbitt, 1973.

Office: Tatnall Bldg., Dover, 19901, 302-744-4101; Fax: 302-739-2775; Web site: www.state.de.us/governor.

Election Results

2004 general	Ruth Ann Minner (D)............................ 185,687	(51%)
	Bill Lee (R)...................................... 167,115	(46%)
	Other.. 12,206	(3%)
2004 primary	Ruth Ann Minner (D)......................... unopposed	
2000 general	Ruth Ann Minner (D)............................ 191,484	(59%)
	John M. Burris (R) 128,436	(40%)
	Other.. 3,263	(1%)

Ruth Ann Minner, a Democrat, was elected governor in 2000. She was born in Slaughter Neck in southern Delaware, the daughter of a sharecropper; one grandfather was an oysterman and a grandmother a midwife. She dropped out of high school to work on the farm, and got married at 17. In 1967, her husband died; at 32, she was left with three sons and no high school diploma. She worked as an agricultural worker and a librarian, got her GED, and in 1972 landed a job as a receptionist in the office of Governor Sherman Tribbitt. In 1974 she ran for the state House ("Tribbitt Greeter Will Seek Office" read the headline in *The Evening Journal*) and, in one of Delaware's small districts (they average 20,000 residents today), won. In 1982 she was elected to the state Senate. She also married again, and she and her husband started a car-towing business; he died in 1991, but her sons still run the business. In 1992 she ran for lieutenant governor as Democratic Congressman-at-Large Tom Carper's running mate, but the offices are elected separately. She won 61% of the vote in 1992 and 70% in 1996.

Minner was the favorite in the 2000 election and was unopposed in the Democratic primary. The Republicans had a close primary between former state Senate Majority Leader John Burris and former Judge Bill Lee; Burris won by exactly 46 votes. Both nominees were from southern Delaware, and both were generally regarded as moderates. Minner ran as a successor to Carper, who had continued former Governor Pete du Pont's policy of cutting income taxes even as, helped by the state's surging economy, he increased state spending by 40%.

Minner was ahead in polls all along; she won 59%-40% and became the state's first female governor. At first, the state's fiscal situation looked good enough that she backed a 2% pay increase in May 2001. But by December she was cutting back. She imposed a hiring freeze in March 2002, lifted it in June, and then reimposed it in November. She failed to get the legislature to increase the cigarette tax, but did get it to pass a law banning smoking in public buildings, including restaurants and bars; she failed to get a ban on discrimination on the basis of sexual orientation. She opposed expansion of gambling. She put in place a Liveable Delaware program, to steer development to places where public services exist or are planned and to encourage historic preservation.

During her first term Minner faced controversies about the state police and corrections system. In 2001 the state NAACP demanded the firing of the state police chief. In 2002 white troopers brought a lawsuit claiming they were the victims of racial quotas. In July 2004 an inmate was injured in a fight and, according to a lawsuit he filed, denied proper medical treatment. Two days later a prison counselor was abducted and raped by a rapist sentenced to 699 years; the convict was shot dead by a sharpshooter. Minner responded, "There are problems at every prison. This isn't something that is unique to Delaware. In prisons, you almost expect this to happen. The people who work in our prisons are doing an outstanding job." She said she was talking about the training of prison personnel, but many thought her words were brusque.

The incident played a major part in the 2004 campaign. Minner's Republican opponent was retired Judge Bill Lee, the narrow loser of the 2000 primary, and well known for his role presiding over the trial of Thomas Capano, an adviser to Governor Tom Carper, for killing Anne Marie Fahey in 1996. Lee called for doing away with the three-tier high school diploma program, revamping the state's educational tests, better enforcement of environmental laws and new revenue sources that wouldn't inhibit growth. But he also criticized Minner's handling of the state police and prisons and was endorsed by police and prison guard groups. In October the Republican Governors Association ran an ad recounting the July abduction and rape, accusing Minner of resisting an independent investigation and dismissing the incident. Observers had expected Minner to win easily. But the result was close. She won by just 51%-46%, carrying New Castle County and losing Kent and Sussex Counties.

Prison scandals continued to challenge Minner's administration in her second term. The Wilmington *News Journal* ran a series beginning in September 2005 about the state's poor prison facilities. A bill to reform the prisons died in 2006 after lawmakers balked at its $30 million annual cost. In December 2006 the Justice Department concluded an investigation that found inadequate health treatment for prisoners throughout the system and civil rights violations at four prisons. The state agreed to an 87-point plan with Justice to improve the prison system, and soon after two top prison officials announced their retirements. Minner also faced the challenge of keeping the charter for Wilmington-based MBNA Corp. in Delaware after its January 2006 acquisition by Bank of America. In 2007, Minner proposed a $3.2 billion budget that included a 5-cent per gallon gas tax increase to help make up a projected $1.5 billion shortfall in the state's transportation fund. It also included a 45-cent per pack increase in cigarette taxes to pay for increased health care costs.

Minner is limited to two terms as governor and has said she will not seek another office after 2008. Rumors began circulating as early as 2006 suggesting that Minner might resign her seat early to give Democratic Lieutenant Governor John Carney, her preferred successor, a head start in the 2008 campaign. It seems likely Carney will face opposition in the Democratic primary from state Treasurer Jack Markell, who announced in June 2007 despite efforts by state party leaders to convince him to run for lieutenant governor instead. Former Happy Harry's drugstore chain CEO Alan Levin, a former aide to Senator William Roth, is considering a run for the Republican nomination. Beyond him, the Republican bench is thin.

Senior Senator

Joseph Biden (D)

Elected 1972, seat up 2008, 6th term; b. Nov. 20, 1942, Scranton, PA; home, Wilmington; U. of DE, B.A. 1965, Syracuse U., J.D. 1968; Catholic; married (Jill).

Elected Office: New Castle Cnty. Cncl., 1970-72.

Professional Career: Practicing atty., 1968-72.

DC Office: 201 RSOB, 20510, 202-224-5042; Fax: 202-224-0139; Web site: biden.senate.gov.

State Offices: Milford, 302-424-8090; Wilmington, 302-573-6345.

Committees: *Foreign Relations* (Chmn. of 11 D). *Judiciary* (3d of 10 D): Crime & Drugs (Chmn.); Immigration, Refugees & Border Security; Antitrust, Competition Policy & Consumer Rights; Terrorism, Technology & Homeland Security; Human Rights & the Law.

Group Ratings

	ADA	ACLU	AFS	LCV	ITIC	NTU	COC	ACU	CFG	FRC
2006	100	92	100	100	33	11	45	4	1	0
2005	100	—	100	90	—	10	44	8	0	—

National Journal Ratings

	2005 LIB — 2005 CONS		2006 LIB — 2006 CONS	
Economic	73%	— 26%	87%	— 0%
Social	83%	— 10%	73%	— 26%
Foreign	76%	— 15%	65%	— 34%

Key Votes of the 109th Congress

1. Bar ANWR Drilling	Y	5. Confirm Samuel Alito	N	9. Limit Interstate Abortion	N
2. FY06 Spending Curb	N	6. Path to Citizenship	Y	10. CAFTA	N
3. Estate Tax Repeal	N	7. Bar Same Sex Marriage	N	11. Urge Iraq Withdrawal	Y
4. Raise Minimum Wage	Y	8. Stem Cell Research $	Y	12. Provide Detainee Rights	Y

Election Results

2002 general	Joseph Biden (D)	135,253	(58%)	($3,152,762)
	Raymond Clatworthy (R)	94,793	(41%)	($1,983,141)
2002 primary	Joseph Biden (D)	unopposed		
1996 general	Joseph Biden (D)	165,465	(60%)	($2,466,499)
	Raymond Clatworthy (R)	105,088	(38%)	($1,126,427)
	Other	5,038	(2%)	

Prior Winning Percentages: 1990 (63%); 1984 (60%); 1978 (58%); 1972 (51%)

Joseph Biden, Delaware's longest-serving senator, was first elected in 1972, at age 29 (he reached the constitutional age of 30 by the time he took office); he has spent most of his life as a senator. Biden grew up in the suburbs of Wilmington in a middle class home; his father was a car salesman and one grandfather was a state senator in Pennsylvania. As a teenager he had a stutter, but taught himself to deliver a speech to his whole school. He graduated from the University of Delaware and Syracuse Law School; he married and started a family while still in law school. After school he moved back to the Wilmington suburbs, practiced law, and in 1970, at 27, was elected to the New Castle County Council. In 1972 he ran for the Senate against a popular incumbent who seemed ready to retire, while this young challenger had energy, an attractive extended family and an ability to connect with voters' emotions. He won 51%-49%. A month later his wife and daughter were killed in an auto accident; his two young sons were injured. He thought about resigning, but was persuaded to serve, and began his practice, kept to this day, of commuting from his home near Wilmington on Amtrak, 80 minutes to and from Washington every day. He remains a familiar figure in, and one familiar with, his constituency (and to Amtrak employees).

In the Senate, Biden has a moderate-to-liberal voting record. For many years he did much of his most visible work on the Judiciary Committee, which he chaired from 1987-95 and served as ranking Democrat on from 1981-87 and 1995-97. The issues that arise here—abortion, flag-burning, capital punishment, crime control—cut deeply, and for years the cultural liberals in the Democratic Party differed sharply on most of them from the constituents Biden saw in Delaware every day. As chairman, Biden presided over the most contentious Supreme Court confirmation hearings in history. In his 1987 hearings, nominee Robert Bork set a high standard for intellectual seriousness, but some of his opponents used his candor to vote against him, from which Biden's attempts to construct an honestly based, anti-Bork rationale proved politically indistinguishable; no other nominee since has testified so candidly. The 1991 hearings on Clarence Thomas exploded when someone leaked charges of sexual harassment by Anita Hill against the nominee. Biden was bitterly criticized for covering up this information, but he had shared it with committee members, who agreed that Hill's initial unwillingness to testify publicly meant that any reference to it would be unfair to Thomas. Once the story was out though, Hill and then Thomas testified to fascinated television audiences; Thomas was confirmed, over Biden's opposition.

In the middle of the Bork hearings came a climactic moment for Biden, who in 1987 started running for president. He hoped to inspire a new generation as John Kennedy had inspired his. But Biden decided to leave the race when a Michael Dukakis staffer leaked an "attack video" showing similarities between Biden's stump speech about his background and a speech by British Labour Party leader Neil Kinnock. Paraphrasing someone else's words is not a political crime—most political discourse is conducted in familiar shorthand terms—but Biden in dramatizing his back-ground actually distorted it, for unlike Kinnock he did not rise from working class roots, and unlike in Britain, upward social mobility is a common experience in the United States. In 1988, Biden was stricken by an aneurysm on the night of the New Hampshire primary; he was rushed to the hospital and nearly died, but recovered fully.

After the Thomas hearings, Biden seemed defensive about attacks from the feminist left, then the greatest source of activism in the Democratic Party. He sought out women to serve on Judiciary and worked hard on the 1994 Violence Against Women Act; he helped renew it in 2000, although the Supreme Court declared part of it unconstitutional, and again in 2005. He opposed the nominations of Chief Justice John Roberts and Justice Samuel Alito, and after the hearings on their nominations said, "I have reached a conclusion that we should not even have these hearings, that we should just go right to the floor like they used to do in the old days."

Biden has been the sponsor in Judiciary of the bankruptcy bill, backed strongly by Delaware's MBNA and other credit card issuers, which was vetoed by Bill Clinton in 2000. It was brought up again in 2001 with a president ready to sign it, and versions passed both the Senate and the House. But there were two contentious issues blocking final passage. One was the homestead exemption; the Senate voted to limit it to $125,000, but the House version allowed unlimited exemptions once a home had been owned for two years (Florida and Texas have unlimited exemptions, and some bankrupts hold onto $5 million houses). Biden agreed to accept the House version. The other issue was Charles Schumer's amendment making fines incurred by anti-abortion protesters undischargeable in bankruptcy. On this, Biden would not yield. In November 2002 the bill, with a version of the Schumer provision was defeated in the House when 87 anti-abortion Republicans spurned the leadership's pleas and defeated the bill. In 2005, Biden again voted for the Schumer amendment, which failed, but also voted for the final bankruptcy bill.

Biden has also used his seat on Judiciary to combat what he considers harmful drugs. In April 2003 he amended an Amber Alert bill with a version of the RAVE Act, with prison terms up to nine years for club owners sponsoring raves at which Ecstasy and other illegal drugs are used. In October 2004 he persuaded the Senate to pass a bill criminalizing steroid precursors like androstenedione, the supplement used by baseball slugger Mark McGwire; it was reconciled with the House version and became law. In December 2004 Biden threatened to sponsor legislation addressing drug use in baseball if Major League Baseball failed to clamp down; he hailed the agreement on the issue between the baseball commissioner and the players' union in November 2005.

Biden became ranking Democrat on the Foreign Relations Committee in 1997 and chairman in June 2001 and again in January 2007. To the surprise of many, he entered into a constructive working relationship with Jesse Helms, chairman from 1995 to 2001. When democracy in the former Yugoslavia was thwarted by state-led terrorism and when multilateral instrumentalities proved ineffective, Biden was among the strongest voices to call for lifting the arms embargo on Bosnia and training Bosnian Muslims, demanding that the United States and NATO investigate war crimes there, and arguing for NATO air strikes. To the incoming Bush administration he was friendly but sometimes critical. Then Biden became chairman of Foreign Relations in June 2001 and America was attacked on September 11. In the weeks following the attack Biden praised Bush for being "patient, resolute and cautious." In July and August 2002 he held two days of hearings on Iraq, with administration witnesses. In August he said the United States has "no choice but to eliminate" Saddam Hussein and that "probably" it means war with Iraq. He conferred frequently with Secretary of State Colin Powell and pushed for the U.S. to bring the issue to the United Nations; he said a unilateral attack would be the "single worst option." In late September 2002, he and ranking Republican Richard Lugar were working to bring forward a resolution that would authorize the president to take action to remove weapons of mass destruction, but not Saddam Hussein himself, only after exhausting diplomatic options. Bush opposed this, and forestalled Biden and Lugar by getting agreement on terms of a resolution from Trent Lott, Dennis Hastert and Richard Gephardt. Biden voted for it in October 2002.

As fighting and casualties continued and rose after major military operations were completed, Biden became more critical of the administration. In June 2003 he said Bush should "level with the American people" about the cost and length of the Iraq commitment; he was angry when administration officials refused to put a price tag on the effort. In August 2003 he said he did not regret his vote for the war, but added, "There's nothing international about this until we get NATO in there and we get Islamic forces in there." He said the administration was filled with "control freaks who are allowing their ideology to get in the way of common sense," and mentioned Dick Cheney. In April 2004, looking ahead to the June 30 turnover of power, he said, "Our goal should be to take the 'American face' off the occupation so that we are not blamed for everything that doesn't go right in Iraq." He said that Bush should call a summit conference of allies and broaden the coalition. In September 2005 he called for a postponement of the constitutional referendum until after the elections for the national assembly, so that Sunnis could participate. In May 2006 he and former Council on Foreign Relations head Leslie Gelb announced a plan for Iraq. The country should be divided into three semi-autonomous regions, they argued, for Kurds, Shiites and Sunnis—much as Bosnia had been. Oil revenues should be shared among the regions; American aid should be conditioned on respect shown for women's rights; the U.S. military should withdraw by 2008; there should be a United Nations or internationally sanctioned regional conference in which Iraq's neighbors should agree to work for stability. He continued to call for this approach through the year and in December criticized the Iraq Study Group proposal for not saying more about a political settlement. In December 2006 he came out against George W. Bush's surge strategy. "We've tried the military surge option before and it failed. If we try it again, it will fail again." He co-sponsored with Carl Levin a nonbinding resolution declaring that "it is not in the national interest of the United States to deepen its military involvement in Iraq." It passed in committee by only a 12–9 vote though, as Biden noted, most Republicans at committee hearings expressed reservations about or even (in the case of Chuck Hagel) downright opposition to the surge.

Biden continued to campaign against missile defense and opposed abrogation of the ABM Treaty. But Bush's withdrawal from the treaty did not prevent the May 2002 nuclear disarmament treaty, which Biden hailed as "an important step forward." Biden traveled widely as chairman and for a time at least seemed to have been taken into the confidence of the administration: Condoleezza Rice encouraged him to sound out Iranian diplomats at the United Nations when they requested a meeting. As ranking minority member again in 2003, he did not have as much power, but he worked closely with the new chairman, Richard Lugar, and said that he and Lugar are in agreement on a great many issues. Biden has urged caution on Iran and has called for the U.S. to engage in unilateral negotiations with North Korea and in 2005 suggested that we extend economic incentives for an agreement. He co-sponsored a resolution with Mitch McConnell calling for restriction on aid to the Palestinian Authority until the Hamas government renounces violence, recognizes Israel and moves against terrorist groups. He supported the nuclear agreement with India in 2006 and defended it against those who argued that it undermined nonproliferation efforts.

Biden remains an everyday figure in Delaware and has tended to its most local needs. Sussex County is America's number one chicken-producing county, and he held up a bill for favorable trade status for Russia when that country blocked the import of U.S. chickens. He has gotten more than 1,000 acres of federal land in the beach areas turned over to the state. Naturally, he has supported Amtrak funding and has sought, unsuccessfully to get $1.1 billion spent on rail security. On his daily commutes, he has come to know the Amtrak crew members personally and hosts an annual Christmas dinner for the crews.

Being elected a senator at age 29 makes you think about running for president some day, and Biden has done that twice, once in his 40s and now in his 60s. He passed up the 1992 campaign, fresh after his vote against the Gulf war; in 1996 Bill Clinton was renominated without opposition and in 2000 Clinton tried to clear the field for Al Gore. In early 2003 he said he might run, but in August 2003 he announced he would not. In 2004 Biden campaigned for John Kerry, whom he has known since 1972, when they both hired the same political consultant. Biden was frequently mentioned as a possible secretary of state if Kerry had been elected, but said he liked serving in the Senate. After Kerry's defeat he made little secret that he was interested in running again. "My intention is to seek the nomination," he said on *Face the Nation* in June 2005. "I know I'm supposed to tell you, you know, that I'm not sure. But if, in fact, I think that I have a clear shot at winning the nomination by this November or December, then I'm going to seek the nomination." He made his first trip of the cycle to New Hampshire in May 2006 and to Iowa in August 2006. Some of his off-the-cuff statements caused him some embarrassment. "You cannot go to a 7-Eleven or a Dunkin' Donuts franchise unless you have a slight Indian accent," he remarked, presumably based on everyday observation; but some in the press suggested this was off bounds. When Fox News's Chris Wallace suggested he couldn't draw votes in the South, he said, "You don't know my state. My state was a slave state. My state is a border state. My state has the eighth-largest black population in the country." Again, some tut-tutted, but this was a valid historical point. On January 31, 2007, he officially announced his candidacy. Unfortunately, that day the *New York Observer* released a story in which he called Barack Obama "the first mainstream African-American who is articulate and bright and clean and a nice-looking guy." Critics pointed out that this overlooked or insulted Shirley Chisholm, Jesse Jackson, Carol Moseley Braun and Al Sharpton; by six o'clock, in time for the evening news, Biden said, "I deeply regret any offense my remark in the *New York Observer* might have caused anyone." Washington insiders wrote off his candidacy, and he raised only $4 million in the first quarter of 2007. But as he pointed out, he has had more experience in office than any other candidate and has served more than 30 years on the Foreign Relations Committee. Indeed, no president has ever had nearly as many years experience in Congress. "If the national Democratic primary and caucus voters conclude this is a really big-ticket election in the sense that what's at stake is literally our place in the world and the restoration of the middle class, then I'm in the game. If it's about who has the most money, who has the most early endorsements, then I'm not going to be in that game." And he got credit for the wittiest response in the first Democratic candidates' debate. When MSNBC's Brian Williams asked him if he had the self-discipline to refrain from overlong statements, he answered, "Yes."

Biden's seat comes up in 2008. Delaware law allows him to run for reelection to the Senate and for president (or vice president) at the same time; the filing deadline is in late July. His electoral record has been strong. He was reelected by wide margins in 1978, 1984, 1990 and 1996. His 1996 opponent Raymond Clatworthy was a Naval Academy graduate, Marine aviator and businessman who walked, rode a bicycle and rollerbladed through the state, raised $1 million and questioned the sale of Biden's house to an executive of MBNA, the big credit card company whose top executives gave generously to Biden's campaign. Biden won 60%-38%. In 2002 Clatworthy ran again and raised $1.8 million: Evidently Biden has raised the hackles of many Republicans across the country, and you can raise money by direct mail against him. Clatworthy argued that he would support George W. Bush more fully on defense and foreign policy. This time the result was a little closer: Biden won 58%-41%, the same margin he had in 1978. He actually lost Kent County, which includes Dover, and only narrowly carried Sussex County; together the two counties cast 37% of the state's votes, up from 33% in 1996. On Return Day, two days after the November 2006 election, he told

Delaware reporters, "I've told the staff to prepare for a regular reelection campaign." Biden is one of 12 current incumbents who has spent more than half his life as a member of Congress; he can probably go on for many years more. One possible successor: his oldest son Beau Biden, who was elected attorney general of Delaware in 2006.

Junior Senator

Thomas Carper (D)

Elected 2000, seat up 2012, 2d term; b. Jan. 23, 1947, Beckley, WV; home, Wilmington; OH St. U., B.A. 1968, U. of DE, M.B.A. 1975; Presbyterian; married (Martha).

Military Career: Navy, 1968-73 (Vietnam); Naval Reserves, 1973-91.

Elected Office: DE Treas., 1976-82; U.S. House of Reps., 1982-92; DE Gov. 1992-2000.

Professional Career: Industrial Devel. Specialist, DE Div. of Econ. Devel., 1975-76.

DC Office: 513 HSOB, 20510, 202-224-2441; Fax: 202-228-2190; Web site: carper.senate.gov.

State Offices: Dover, 302-674-3308; Georgetown, 302-856-7690; Wilmington, 302-573-6291.

Committees: *Aging (Special)* (5th of 11 D). *Banking, Housing & Urban Affairs* (6th of 11 D): Economic Policy (Chmn.); Housing, Transportation & Community Development; Financial Institutions. *Commerce, Science & Transportation* (10th of 12 D): Oceans, Atmosphere, Fisheries & Coast Guard; Consumer Affairs, Insurance & Automotive Safety; Surface Transportation & Merchant Marine Infrastructure, Safety & Security; Aviation Operations, Safety & Security. *Environment & Public Works* (4th of 10 D): Clean Air & Nuclear Safety (Chmn.); Transportation & Infrastructure; Public Sector Solutions to Global Warming, Oversight & Children's Health Protection. *Homeland Security & Governmental Affairs* (4th of 9 D): Federal Financial Management, Government Information, Federal Services & International Security (Chmn.); Investigations (Permanent); Disaster Recovery; Oversight of Government Management, the Federal Workforce & the District of Columbia.

Group Ratings

	ADA	ACLU	AFS	LCV	ITIC	NTU	COC	ACU	CFG	FRC
2006	90	67	100	71	100	21	58	20	6	25
2005	90	—	75	80	—	22	72	8	15	—

National Journal Ratings

	2005 LIB	—	2005 CONS		2006 LIB	—	2006 CONS
Economic	63%	—	36%		67%	—	29%
Social	65%	—	29%		63%	—	36%
Foreign	76%	—	15%		67%	—	29%

Key Votes of the 109th Congress

1. Bar ANWR Drilling	Y	5. Confirm Samuel Alito	N	9. Limit Interstate Abortion	Y
2. FY06 Spending Curb	N	6. Path to Citizenship	Y	10. CAFTA	Y
3. Estate Tax Repeal	N	7. Bar Same Sex Marriage	N	11. Urge Iraq Withdrawal	Y
4. Raise Minimum Wage	Y	8. Stem Cell Research $	Y	12. Provide Detainee Rights	Y

Election Results

2006 general	Thomas Carper (D)	170,567	(70%)	($2,632,603)
	Jan Ting (R)	69,734	(29%)	($212,765)
	Other	2,671	(1%)	
2006 primary	Thomas Carper (D)	unopposed		
2000 general	Thomas Carper (D)	181,387	(56%)	($2,608,942)
	William V. Roth Jr. (R)	142,683	(44%)	($4,366,884)
	Other	2,144	(1%)	

Prior Winning Percentages: 1990 House (66%); 1988 House (68%); 1986 House (66%); 1984 House (59%); 1982 House (52%)

Democrat Thomas Carper was elected Delaware's junior senator in 2000, after already serving 24 years in statewide elective office. Carper grew up in Southside Virginia and Ohio and went to college in Ohio. He first came to Delaware as an ensign in the Navy, then returned to get his M.B.A. after service in Southeast Asia, where he served as a mission commander piloting submarine-hunting planes. In 1976, he was elected state treasurer, at 29; he ran for Congress in 1982 and beat a scandal-tarred incumbent. In the House, Carper had a moderate voting record and worked to let banks into the securities business and to prevent ocean sludge dumping, both causes supported by Delaware constituencies. In 1992, when Republican Governor Mike Castle had served his two allotted terms and ran for Congress, Carper ran for governor and won the general election with 65% of the vote.

As governor, Carper pursued an agenda in many ways more conservative than liberal. He continued his Republican predecessor Pete du Pont's policy of cutting taxes, reducing income tax rates about 10% and also cutting small business and utility taxes. Revenues kept gushing in from Delaware's strong economy, and he boosted the state's credit rating to an historic high even as state spending rose 40% in eight years. He was re-elected by 70%-30% over then-Treasurer Janet Rzewnicki. Barred from a third term, he was an obvious candidate for the Senate seat held by Republican William Roth since 1970.

This was a battle of positives. Both candidates had very high approval ratings, and both were familiar figures to many voters; they brought a combined total of 58 years in statewide office to the race. Roth had a record of achievements that paid direct benefits to people in this generally affluent state: The Kemp-Roth tax cut of 1981, the Roth IRAs enacted in 1997, the reform of the Internal Revenue Service passed in 1998, $2.3 billion for Amtrak capital improvements in 1998 and $10 billion in bonds in 2000. Roth's main problem was that he was 79 in 2000. When Carper announced his candidacy in September 1999, a poll showed him ahead 48%-38%. He was careful not to campaign negatively against Roth or to attack him for his age, but his slogan "A Senator for Our Future" spotlighted the contrast between their ages. Carper's 16-hour days of campaigning at factories, bowling alleys and parades was a contrast with Roth, who stayed in Washington legislating much of the time and made a dwindling number of campaign appearances with his trademark St. Bernards. As Roth unveiled initiatives—Amtrak funding, a program to aid states to pay for prescription drugs for low-income seniors—Carper suggested that Roth's tax cuts were too large and his prescription drug plan too stingy. Roth, able to raise large sums as Finance chairman, outspent Carper by $4.3 million to $2.5 million, but the Democratic Party spent some $4 million of soft money in Delaware, more than evening the score. In October, Roth fainted twice on the campaign trail, once in full view of cameras. Polls showed the race close to even in September and October, but in November Carper won by a solid 56%-44% margin.

In the Senate, Carper has a moderate voting record and supports centrist proposals. With five Republicans and five other Democrats he moved unsuccessfully to condition the Bush tax cut on deficit reduction. In June 2001 he and Judd Gregg got $125 million for public school choice programs and $400 million for charter schools. He voted with Jim Jeffords to impose on old power plants the standards of the Clean Air Act. But he also put forward, with Lincoln Chafee, John Breaux and Max Baucus, a milder bill that would not impose those standards on old plants when remodeled and require 2001 levels of carbon dioxide by 2012. He has worked for reauthorization of the 1996 welfare act, with higher work requirements, funding for transitional jobs, funding for abstinence programs and more funding for child care. Since September 11 he has pressed for more spending on rail security, and he has sought $30 billion in bond financing for railroad projects. With Robert Bennett, Carper sponsored a bill in 2006 that would establish a uniform system of notifying customers when the security of their personal data is breached. Carper's own personal information was put at risk when a Veterans Affairs laptop computer that contained files on 26.5 million veterans was stolen.

Carper has taken the lead on several issues. One is Postal Service reform, where he and Governmental Affairs Chairman Susan Collins collaborated on a bill to allow more flexibility on rates and worksharing with private firms, but only on a profitable basis; it did not pass in 2004 but set up the framework for the next Congress. It nearly died again in 2006, until sponsors worked out a compromise in the December lame duck session that resulted in the first comprehensive change in postal policy since 1970. The bill capped rate increases to inflation and resolved several labor and retirement issues. He worked with Lamar Alexander, another former governor, on the extension of the moratorium on Internet taxation, to preserve existing state taxes on DSL and Voice Over Internet Protocol. He also collaborated with Alexander on a bill to limit emissions not only of sulphur dioxide, nitrous oxide and mercury (as in the Bush Clear Skies bill), but also carbon dioxide, with a cap and emissions trading. With Alexander he also authored a bill that would allow farmers who cut their carbon dioxide emissions to take part in a cap-and-trade program to reduce industrial emissions. After the 2006 elections, Carper became chairman of the Clean Air, Nuclear Plant Security and Community Development Subcommittee. He worked with Mary Landrieu to add amendments to the D.C. school voucher bill, to ban schools from charging additional tuition and limiting eligibility to students in failing schools. He strongly supported the bill limiting class actions and was angry when Majority Leader Bill Frist refused to allow non-germane amendments in July 2004; that killed the bill for the year, but it was passed in February 2005. He declined to vote on the tobacco buyout because he owns tobacco-growing land in North Carolina. Delaware is the only state without a National Park Service facility, and in August 2004 Carper proposed a Coastal Heritage Park, to consist of four interpretive centers in Wilmington, Port Penn, Little Creek and Lewes. The Senate in 2005 approved a bill authorizing a study of the proposed park, and the House considered it in committee.

Carper, who is vice chairman of centrist Democratic Leadership Council, has been "bitterly disappointed" by the reduction of the number of centrist Democratic senators after the 2002 and 2004 elections. On Social Security, in December 2004 he said, "I don't think it's sufficient for Democrats just to say no." But in January 2005 he added, "The better part of valor [would be] for the administration to present their proposal. Let us read it and understand it. . . . I don't rule out at some point having private accounts." Carper supported Bush's nomination of John Roberts as Chief Justice, but opposed the president's later choice of Samuel Alito to the Supreme Court.

In 2006 Carper faced Republican opposition from law professor Jan Ting, a first-time candidate who worked in George H.W. Bush's administration. Ting falsely accused Carper of taking contributions from disgraced former lobbyist Jack Abramoff, although Carper did take over $7,000 from his Indian tribal clients, which he gave to charity. Carper won a second term 70%-29%. After the election, Carper won a seat on the Commerce, Science and Transportation Committee and a second term as a deputy whip in Democratic leadership.

Representative-At-Large

Michael Castle (R)

Elected 1992, 8th term; b. July 2, 1939, Wilmington; home, Wilmington; Hamilton Col., B.A. 1961, Georgetown U., LL.B. 1964; Catholic; married (Jane).

Elected Office: DE House of Reps., 1966-68; DE Senate, 1968-76, Minority Ldr., 1975-76; DE Lt. Gov., 1980-84; DE Gov., 1984-92.

Professional Career: Practicing atty., 1964-80; DE Dep. Atty. Gen., 1965-66.

DC Office: 1233 LHOB, 20515, 202-225-4165; Fax: 202-225-2291; Web site: www.house.gov/castle.

District Offices: Dover, 302-736-1666; Georgetown, 302-856-3334; Wilmington, 302-428-1902.

Committees: *Education & Labor* (4th of 22 R): Early Childhood, Elementary & Secondary Education (RMM); Higher Education, Lifelong Learning & Competitiveness. *Financial Services* (4th of 33 R): Domestic and International Monetary Policy, Trade & Technology; Capital Markets, Insurance & Government Sponsored Enterprises; Financial Institutions & Consumer Credit.

Group Ratings

	ADA	ACLU	AFS	LCV	ITIC	NTU	COC	ACU	CFG	FRC
2006	40	47	14	83	100	52	83	52	48	14
2005	40	—	25	67	—	51	78	28	43	23

National Journal Ratings

	2005 LIB	—	2005 CONS		2006 LIB	—	2006 CONS
Economic	51%	—	49%		50%	—	50%
Social	58%	—	42%		54%	—	46%
Foreign	49%	—	51%		43%	—	57%

Key Votes of the 109th Congress

1. Estate Tax Repeal	Y	5. Limit Interstate Abortion	N	9. Build Border Fence	Y
2. Limit CAFE Standards	N	6. Extend Patriot Act	Y	10. CAFTA	Y
3. FY06 Spending Curb	Y	7. Bar Same Sex Marriage	N	11. Oppose Iraq Withdrawal	Y
4. Drilling in ANWR	N	8. Stem Cell Research $	Y	12. Detainee Tribunals	*

Election Results

2006 general	Michael Castle (R)	143,897	(57%)	($1,112,716)
	Dennis Spivack (D)	97,565	(39%)	($386,890)
	Other	10,232	(4%)	
2006 primary	Michael Castle (R)	unopposed		
2004 general	Michael Castle (R)	245,978	(69%)	($902,706)
	Paul Donnelly (D)	105,716	(30%)	($4,429)
	Other	4,351	(1%)	

Prior Winning Percentages: 2002 (72%); 2000 (68%); 1998 (66%); 1996 (70%); 1994 (71%); 1992 (55%)

Michael Castle, a Republican first elected in 1992, is Delaware's congressman-at-large. A direct descendant of Benjamin Franklin, he grew up in Delaware, the son of a DuPont patent lawyer. He graduated from Hamilton College and Georgetown Law School, and returned to Delaware and worked as a deputy attorney general. In 1966, at 27, local Republicans urged him to run for the state House in a Democratic seat; the competitive Castle was elected. Two years later he was elected to the state Senate, and in time became minority leader. He left the legislature in 1976 to practice law in Wilmington; he still lives there, in the same house, and commutes to Washington. In 1980 Governor Pete du Pont asked him to run for lieutenant governor; he did and won. He was elected governor in 1984 and 1988. In 1992, barred from running for re-election by term limits, he traded jobs with Democratic Congressman-at-Large Thomas Carper. Castle won the Republican primary for Congress by 56%-30% over state Treasurer Janet Rzewnicki, and won the general election 55%-43% over former Senate candidate and Lieutenant Governor S. B. Woo.

At that point it seemed unlikely that Castle, as a moderate member of a conservative minority party, could be influential; yet he was. He was a leader of the bipartisan freshmen who offered their own budget cuts. In August 1994 he withdrew his support from the crime bill when he thought Democrats overreached; then, at Newt Gingrich's suggestion, he led a group of moderate Republicans to negotiate with the Clinton administration. This delivered a stinging rebuke to Democrats—it broke their majority apart, in fact—and yet ultimately produced a crime bill with less spending on prevention but with the gun control provisions that Castle, unlike most Republicans, supported.

Castle has had a voting record at the middle of the House; he was one of the 10 Republicans to support Clinton administration positions on most issues, has been a leader of the informal Tuesday Group which meets for lunch on Wednesdays (don't ask), is a co-founder and former president of the Republican Main Street Partnership and is one of three Republicans who voted for all six of the Democrats' 100 hours agenda items in early 2007. He voted for the 2001 Bush tax cut with some ambivalence; he had voted against repeal of the estate tax and wanted the tax cuts made contingent. He initially opposed the 2003 tax cut, but voted for it when it was reduced to $350 billion, with $20 billion in aid to the states. He voted against the budget resolution in March 2004 because it "does not address real reform, shared restraint and elimination of waste." Castle is cautious about tax cuts, because he wants to reduce deficits and is pessimistic about holding down spending. In November 2005, when the leadership pressed for a budget measure with spending cuts, Castle and the RMSP resisted, and demanded the removal of oil drilling in the Arctic National Wildlife Refuge; the leadership complied, and Castle provided a key vote as it passed 217-215. The next month labor unions ran TV ads attacking Castle for the cuts. In March 2006 he held out against the budget resolution and called for an additional $7 billion for education and health, which the Senate had already voted. He also wanted specific allocations for all 11 appropriations in the budget resolution. In April he continued to resist. "Right now, it appears they do not have the votes to do this. They're nervous. They really can't solve it. If they give us anything, in any way, they'll lose conservative votes." When the leadership offered in May to move $4 billion to those programs but maintain the overall caps, he said, "It's a very generous offer. I'd like to see if more could be done." After midnight on May 18, moderates gave their support after leadership promised to find another $3 billion for health, education and jobs programs and it passed 218-210.

Castle noted in late 2005 that the fact that Democrats were increasingly voting as a solid bloc gave Republican moderates more leverage. But that seemed to be sharply reduced when Republicans lost their majority in November 2006, with several of Castle's allies defeated or otherwise gone—Nancy Johnson, Mike Fitzpatrick, Charlie Bass, Rob Simmons, Joe Schwarz (who lost his primary) and Sherwood Boehlert (who retired). But sometimes Castle made a difference. He voted in February 2007 for the nonbinding resolution against the surge in Iraq. But he did not vote for the supplemental with deadlines for withdrawal, and the Democrats had to scramble to get a majority.

For six years Castle chaired the Education Reform Subcommittee, and while he may support higher spending than some other Republicans, he also questions the worth of programs originally fashioned by Democrats. That was evident in his work on the No Child Left Behind Act in 2001 and on Head Start in 2003. Castle's bill, passed in subcommittee and full committee in June 2003, maintained the core program. But he cited studies showing that the progress Head Start children make tends to disappear by third or fourth grade, and he inserted provisions requiring more teaching of literacy and academics. He also had a provision allowing eight states to get waivers to fashion their own programs. This brought down a storm of criticism from Democrats and from Head Start employees, who said these measures would gut a program that was a proven success. Castle persevered. The bill was pulled off the floor once, then passed in July 2003 by only a 217-216 vote; one Republican was brought in fresh from an auto accident. The Senate HELP committee passed a version cutting out the pilot projects but the bill did not receive a floor vote in 2003. In May 2007, in the minority, Castle worked with subcommittee Chairman Dale Kildee to pass a bill reauthorizing the program for the first time since 1998. The measure increased spending from $6.9 billion to $7.4 billion and increased teacher qualification requirements but eliminated the testing program designed to emphasize literacy education.

Castle's approach on reauthorization of the Carl Perkins vocational education act required states to impose new academic standards and accountability measures and merged the funding of Perkins grants and Tech-Prep but it also failed to get a floor vote. But in May 2005 the House voted 416–9 to reauthorize the Perkins act, despite the Bush administration proposal to zero it out. In 2005, when most assumed Republicans would retain their majority, he considered running for the chairmanship. But he noted that he had not been a leadership loyalist and had not raised much money for other Republicans. In February 2006, when Chairman John Boehner was elected Majority Leader and the chairmanship came open, he announced he wouldn't seek it. "The bottom line is, I wouldn't make it. Let's face it, once you become the head of a committee, you have to totally support the leadership on everything. And that's never been one of my interests. . . . I'd give up my independence if I were a committee chairman. I'd have to worry about committee business instead of what I consider the important issues." But he maintained good relations with the new chairman, Buck McKeon, now ranking Republican; the two cosponsored a bill in January 2007 to provide a clearinghouse for information on college tuition and financial aid.

Castle serves on the Financial Services Committee, which is of great importance to Delaware. He has supported measures to prevent identity theft and to promote low-income housing programs. His special project there has been coins. He sponsored the 1997 law establishing commemorative quarters, with different designs for each state. He sponsored the Sacagawea dollar coin, and in 2004 sponsored a bill for new dollar coins, with likenesses of each president replacing Sacagawea and the Statue of Liberty replacing the eagle. The bill did not come to the floor in 2004, but in December 2005 it passed 291-113 in the House on suspension calendar. It was at risk of not getting the required two-thirds when Mike Pence's Republican Study Committee attacked as an unfunded mandate a provision requiring vending machines on federal property or on property receiving federal money to accept $1 coins. The coins have done more than just encouraging numismatics. The government makes a profit off seignorage, the difference between the value of the metal and the face value of the coin; the state quarters have become collector's items and have brought in a cool $6 billion.

Contact with constituents in Delaware led Castle to support federal financing of embryonic stem-cell research. He initially supported George W. Bush's August 2001 decision to fund research only on existing lines, but then decided that there were too few; he argued that embryos which are created for fertility treatments, but then are discarded, should be available if there was donor consent. "There is more potential here than anything that has ever happened in the history of medicine," he has said. In 2004 he and Democrat Diana DeGette co-sponsored a bill to permit and fund such research, and in 2005 he threatened to vote against the budget resolution unless it was given a vote on the floor. The leadership acceded and it passed in May 2005 by 238-194. That was not enough for an override of Bush's veto, the first of his presidency. In January 2007 Democrats brought it forward in January as part of their 100 hours program. It passed 253-174, still less than the two-thirds required to override a veto, but a stronger showing than two years before.

Castle is a strong supporter of Amtrak and opposed the Bush administration proposals to divide it into three units and to spin off control of rails, stations and infrastructure to the states. He negotiated a $1.225 billion compromise funding level in 2003 and in 2004, and has opposed the lower funding or defunding in Bush's budgets. He is co-chairman of the Passenger Rail Caucus and laments that, "The problem is getting any money for rails is so difficult in Washington, D.C., because the rails only serve certain places in the country." He opposed the firing of Amtrak CEO David Gunn in November 2005 and called for an expansion of the board of directors. He hailed an October 2005 GAO report on rail security and sponsored a bill to provide grants for security training programs, to fund security personnel and technology, and to require DHS to develop timelines and cost and feasibility estimates for stronger security programs and a strategy for increasing public awareness

For years Castle was reelected by wide margins in Delaware, 68%-31% in 2000, 72%-27% in 2002, 69%-30% in 2004. He has often been mentioned as a candidate for the Senate in this small state, and said that he would have run if Republican Senator William Roth had retired in 1994. But Roth chose to run then and again in 2000 when he lost to Democrat Tom Carper. In September 2006 Castle suffered a minor stroke and was off the campaign trail for four weeks; he made a public appearances walking with reporters around the Rockford Tower on October 13 and appeared at a debate on October 25 with Democrat Dennis Spivack and Green party candidate Michael Berg, father of the contractor Nick Berg who was beheaded in Iraq in 2004. Castle won by the sharply reduced margin of 57%-39%, after outspending Spivack by $1.1 million to $387,000. This race was not on the DCCC target list, but Democratic strategists quickly said they would target the Delaware seat in 2008; it is one of eight Republican-held seats that was carried by John Kerry in 2004. In mid-2007 they didn't have a well-known challenger. State Treasurer Jack Markell and Lieutenant Governor John Carney were running for governor in 2008 and Beau Biden, elected attorney general in 2006, had pledged to serve out his four-year term. Mentioned as a possible candidate was New Castle County Executive Chris Coons. Meanwhile, incoming NRCC Chairman Tom Cole appointed Castle as one of his top lieutenants, with a mandate to recruit moderate candidates.

★ DISTRICT OF COLUMBIA ★

The District of Columbia, the seat of government of the most powerful and affluent nation in the history of the world, is a beautiful city of great achievements and astonishing contrasts—and one which finally seems to have a competent local government. For most of a century it was governed directly by Congress, not an ideal state of affairs. In 1974 the District got self-government. But for 16 out of the 20 years from 1978-98 the District government was run by Mayor Marion Barry, a talented politician but disastrous mayor. Under him the District was a dysfunctional polity, a city with above-average incomes and a vibrant commercial property base, but with a local government so bloated with employees yet so indifferent to its responsibilities that it destroyed one marginal neighborhood after another. Now things are different. The District's population has been increasing since 2000, according to revised Census estimates; affluent professionals and eager immigrants are flowing in, gentrifying and giving vitality to neighborhoods long given up to decline—Columbia Heights, Logan Circle, Shaw; new apartment buildings are springing up on land left empty for years. There are still problems: The outflow of middle class blacks from the District to the suburbs continues, and some neighborhoods, especially east of the Anacostia River, continue to be plagued by crime and flight. But overall Washington is safer and more prosperous than it was a decade ago.

The problem of how to govern the nation's capital is not new. In 1787 the framers of the Constitution, familiar with contemporary London and Paris mobs and remembering how crowds had threatened Congress in Philadelphia, purposely gave the new federal government control of the 10-mile-square enclave that came to be called the District of Columbia (the portion across the Potomac River was retroceded to Virginia in 1846). Over the years Congress kept control, for its own advantage and, later, out of distrust of the city's large black population. Blacks have consistently made up one-quarter of the population of Washington and surrounding counties since the 1790s, and the city was a center for free blacks even before the Civil War and Emancipation. Radical Republicans gave the District self-government in the era of Reconstruction in 1871, but Governor Alexander "Boss" Shepherd in building great public works spent the District into bankruptcy, and the experiment ended in 1874. Later, Washington's vast growth, starting with the New Deal and World War II, resulted in the growth of large, mostly white suburbs, and blacks became a larger percentage of the city's population—a majority in the 1960 Census. Amid the 1960s civil rights revolution, it began to seem absurd to deny the vote to Washington. So in 1964, after the Constitution was amended, District residents began to cast three electoral votes for president, in 1968 they were allowed to vote for school board, in 1971 they got to elect a non-voting delegate to Congress and in 1974, they got home rule and could vote for a mayor and city council.

The results were tragic. Marion Barry, a man of great ability and charm, inherited a government that was already overlarge and undermanaged, and over the years made it more so. He raised money from public employee unions and real estate developers and increasingly won votes from poor blacks by attacking any critic as racist. In January 1990, he was arrested in a D.C. hotel using crack cocaine, and was prosecuted and sent to jail. Later that year voters chose a reform-minded mayor, Sharon Pratt Kelly, but she flinched when it came time to cut the payroll. Barry, out of prison and elected to the council in 1992, ran for mayor in 1994 and won the Democratic primary with 47% to 37% for Councilman John Ray and only 13% for Kelly. Against Republican Carol Schwartz, a longtime council member, Barry won 56%-42% in November.

In the meantime, the District had changed. Even as the District payroll was peaking—at 51,300 in 1992—the District's population was falling, and becoming more white. Washington's population fell from 802,000 in 1950 to 572,000 in 2000. In the 1950s and 1960s, the District saw white flight; in the Barry years, it saw black flight. The District lost 6% of its population in the 1990s, as blacks headed to majority-black Prince George's County and other suburbs, where three-quarters of Washington-area blacks live. At the same time, Ward 3 and gentrifying neighborhoods near downtown grew in population, so that the black percentage of the population has declined from a peak of 71% in 1970 to 60% in 2000 and 57% in 2005. With higher turnout in affluent areas, whites may now cast half or almost half of the District's votes. But the electorate remains overwhelmingly Democratic: In 2004, John Kerry carried the District over George W. Bush by an 89%-9% margin. Whites voted for Kerry 80%-19%—a higher percentage than in any state and almost every county. Bush got over 20% of the vote in only 14 of 142 precincts, and over 30% in only two.

The District's fiscal crisis after Barry's return in 1995 led Congress to take most of the government out from under his control. This was not a hostile takeover: House Speaker Newt Gingrich appointed as chairman of the D.C. subcommittee Tom Davis, a Republican congressman from Northern Virginia long sympathetic to the District, and Davis worked closely with the District's elected delegate, Eleanor Holmes Norton. They got Congress to establish a five-member financial control board in April 1995, and the control board's CFO, Anthony Williams, hacked away at the payroll, reformed management practices and literally cleaned up messes in District government offices. When Barry announced in May 1998 that he wouldn't run again, there was a move, encouraged by *The Washington Post*, to draft Anthony Williams. He was an unlikely candidate. He grew up in Los Angeles, a speechless foster child adopted when he was 3. He was once an alderman in New Haven, Connecticut; when he took the CFO job in 1995, he moved first to Virginia and only later to Washington's Foggy Bottom. Williams graduated from Yale, Harvard Law and the Kennedy School and worked in Connecticut, Boston and St. Louis. Always dressed in a bow tie, diffident in crowds, he did not seem to have a political touch. But that may have been an asset. In the Democratic primary Williams beat Councilman Kevin Chavous 50%-35%, and in the general he beat Carol Schwartz 66%-30%. The control board immediately delegated power to the new mayor, and in fall 2000, judges returned control of most District departments to the city.

Williams proved to be an impolitic but successful mayor. There was sharp criticism when he closed down D.C. General Hospital. He sought control of the school system in July 2004 but the city council blocked his plan. He won reelection in 2002 by defeating Schwartz again, 61%-34%. Quietly, city services began to improve; departments were removed from court control; the city's finances were in excellent shape, as gentrification and rising real estate values swelled revenues. Williams was pleased when in September 2004 Major League Baseball decided to move the Montreal Expos to Washington, provided the city built a new stadium to replace Robert F. Kennedy stadium, where the 2005 season would be played. Williams proposed a $440 million stadium next to the Washington Navy Yard, on the Anacostia River, in a neighborhood of empty lots and little-used industrial sites. But many council members bridled at the cost, and there were continuing adverse votes and negotiations in public and behind the scenes, placing the city in jeopardy of losing the team. But with help from City Council Chair Linda Cropp and Councilman Marion Barry, the council after missing a December 2005 deadline approved a plan in March 2006 that capped the District's share of the cost to $611 million. The stadium is scheduled to be ready by Opening Day 2008.

By that time the 2006 race for mayor was well under way. Williams announced that he would not seek another term in September 2005. The frontrunner to succeed him was Cropp, who had years of experience in city government, going back to the time when her husband was a top aide to Barry. But the winner was 35-year-old Councilman Adrian Fenty. The son of a black father and white mother who grew up over their shoe store in the diverse Adams-Morgan area, Fenty had an undistinguished record as a practicing lawyer and a strong ambition for political office. In 2000 he ran for the council seat in Ward 4, an affluent mostly black area just east of Rock Creek Park. Campaigning relentlessly, he beat longtime incumbent Charlene Drew Jarvis (who had beaten Cropp 12 years before). In the council he cast dissenting votes on issues like D.C. General, the baseball stadium and, in summer 2006, an anti-crime bill. He specialized in constituent services, and won a reputation for getting almost instant action from the D.C. bureaucracy. He had little time for the intricacies of legislation; in council meetings he constantly worked his BlackBerry. He did initiate two major pieces of legislation that passed—an indoor smoking ban and a flow of funding for a major school repair program. But the details on the latter were worked out by Council members Kathy Patterson and Jack Evans, with assistance from Cropp.

Fenty announced an exploratory committee for running for mayor in January 2005, much earlier in the cycle than usual in D.C., and began to campaign door-to-door. Accompanied often by some of his many volunteers, he knocked on about half the doors in the District of Columbia, clicking his BlackBerry on the way to the door. He ran on his strengths, his energy and his ability to get government working as it should. "Government, like business, is about follow-through, responsiveness, attention to detail. That's what I do. Some people say I am too eager. I am very hungry. I want this job more than anybody else." Political reporters interviewing voters heard dozens of stories about how he had solved people's problems, and fast; every neighborhood in the District was sprouting green Fenty signs. By August 2006 Fenty's energetic campaigning had put him ahead in the polls. Cropp responded with ads criticizing Fenty sharply for his lack of experience, for his thin legislative record and for his mishandling of legal cases. Fenty's response: "It's right out of the political playbook. 'He's young, he's inexperienced,' they say, and they have to say that because they're defending the politics of patronage, and I represent the politics of accountability." She had the support of most of the local business community. But Fenty got most of the voters. In the September 12 primary he led Cropp by 57%-31%. He carried all eight wards, with his highest percentage in Ward 4, his home and Cropp's; he carried all 142 precincts in the city. Electoral politics in Washington has often divided voters on lines of race. Fenty, with his biracial background, did not do so. "There's no question that gives me a tolerance and an appreciation for the views of everyone. I always heard politicians talk about race, but not the people. They were just talking about making sure every neighborhood gets the same attention."

Fenty spent much of the fall traveling around the country, seeking the advice of the mayors of Baltimore, New York, Chicago, Los Angeles and San Francisco. The general election was an anticlimax: Fenty won 89% of the vote. Soon afterwards, on the advice of New York's Michael Bloomberg, he proposed that the public schools should be run by the mayor. Williams's proposal to do that had been rejected in 2004, but within days Fenty got most of the incoming council members to say that they agreed with him in principle. In April 2007, the city council approved Fenty's plan by a 9–2 vote. The official takeover still required congressional approval. The District's school system, despite some of the highest spending levels in the nation, has been considered abysmal, with enrollments declining every year; by 2006, 25% of the students were enrolled in charter schools, one of the highest rates in the country. As mayor, Fenty signaled his new style by literally knocking down walls: his office is in the middle of a large room resembling a Wall Street trading floor, with desks for 33 staffers and two conference areas separated by glass partitions.

2004 Presidential Vote			**2000 Presidential Vote**		
Kerry (D)	202,970	(89%)	Gore (D)	171,923	(85%)
Bush (R)	21,256	(9%)	Bush (R)	18,073	(9%)
Nader (I)	1,485	(1%)	Nader (Green)	10,576	(5%)
Other	1,875	(1%)	Other	1,322	(1%)

The People		Race/Ethnic Origin			Military veterans: 44,484 (9.7%)	
Pop. 2006 (est):	581,530	159,178	27.8%	White	WWII: 22.1%	Korea: 14.4%
Pop. 2000:	572,059	340,088	59.4%	Black	Vietnam: 29.5%	Gulf War: 10.4%
Pop. 1990:	606,900	15,039	2.6%	Asian	**Most populous cities (2006):**	
Change 1990-2000:	Down 5.7%	1,274	0.2%	Native Am.	1. Washington	581,530
% of U.S. total:	0.2%	273	0.0%	Hawaiian		
Area size:	68 sq. mi.	9,584	1.7%	Two+ races	Urban population: 100.0%	
State Native:	39.2%	1,670	0.3%	Other	Rural population: 0.0%	
Non-citizen:	9.0%	44,953	7.9%	Hisp. Origin		
		Ancestry				
Language		Irish: 4.3%		German: 4.2%		
English: 81.0%	Spanish: 9.1%	English: 3.9%		Subsaharan: 2.5%		
Other Eur.: 6.2%		Italian: 1.9%				

Education		Work Sector		Registered Voters	
H.S. Grad:	77.8%	Private: 68.7%	Govt: 25.9%	D: 285,486	(73.6%)
College Grad:	39.1%	Self: 5.2%	Family: 0.1%	R: 30,560	(7.9%)
Industry		Unemployment: 10.7%		O: 71,894	(18.5%)
Agri: 0.1%	Con: 3.9%	**Household Income**			
Fin: 7.4%	Info: 6.4%	<15k: 20.7%	15-35k: 23.7%		
Mfg: 5.1%	Prof: 36.8%	35-50k: 14.2%	50-100k: 24.9%		
Public: 15.0%	Trade: 6.9%	100-150k: 8.4%	>150k: 8.0%		
Other: 18.4%		Median: $40,127			
Occupation		Poverty status: 20.2%			
Blue collar: 10.0%	White collar: 73.9%	**Home Value**			
Gray collar: 16.1%		<50k: 1.9% 50-100k: 19.4%	100-200k: 42.4% 200-300k: 12.0%		
		300-500k: 14.5% >500k: 9.7%	Median: $153,500		

Delegate

Eleanor Holmes Norton (D)

Elected 1990, 9th term; b. June 13, 1937, Washington, D.C.; home, Washington, D.C.; Antioch Col., B.A. 1960, Yale, M.A. 1963, LL.B. 1964; Episcopalian; divorced.

Professional Career: Asst. Legal Dir., ACLU, 1965-70; New York City Human Rights Comm., 1970-77; Equal Empl. Oppor. Comm., 1977-81; Sr. Fellow, The Urban Inst., 1981-82; Prof., Georgetown U. Law Ctr., 1982-present.

DC Office: 2136 RHOB, 20515, 202-225-8050; Fax: 202-225-3002; Web site: www.norton.house.gov.

District Offices: Washington, D.C., 202-678-8900; Washington, D.C., 202-783-5065.

Committees: *Homeland Security* (8th of 19 D): Transportation Security & Infrastructure Protection; Emergency Communications, Preparedness & Response. *Oversight & Government Reform* (16th of 23 D): Federal Workforce, Postal Service & the District of Columbia. *Transportation & Infrastructure* (5th of 41 D): Economic Development, Public Buildings & Emergency Management (Chmn.); Water Resources & Environment; Aviation.

Election Results

2006 general	Eleanor Holmes Norton (D) .... unopposed			
2006 primary	Eleanor Holmes Norton (D) 95,419	(93%)		
	Andy Miscuk (D)..................................... 6,681	(7%)		
2004 general	Eleanor Holmes Norton (D) 202,027	(91%)	($213,604)
	Michael Andrew Monroe (R) 18,296	(8%)	
	Other... 890	(0%)	

Prior Winning Percentages: 2002 (93%); 2000 (90%); 1998 (90%); 1996 (90%); 1994 (89%); 1992 (85%); 1990 (62%)

Eleanor Holmes Norton, who was first elected Delegate from the District of Columbia in 1990, grew up in Washington. She graduated from Antioch and Yale Law School, worked for the ACLU and the

New York City Commission on Human Rights, and was head of the Equal Employment Opportunity Commission in the Carter administration. Afterward, she taught law at Georgetown. When the delegate seat came open in 1990, she ran and drew criticism because her husband hadn't filed their income taxes for several years. But in the primary she edged past city Councilwoman Betty Anne Kane, 39%-33%. Norton has been re-elected easily since.

In the House, she had the difficult and sometimes vexing task of responding to the fiscal collapse of the District government just as Republicans took over Congress. She has been hard-working, competent, intellectually honest, able to get along with opponents as well as fellow partisans and willing to take personal and political risks. She established good relations with Republicans active on District matters before 1994, even though she led the drive, much resented by Republicans in 1993 and repealed by them in 1995, to give her and the four territorial delegates to the House—all of whom were then Democrats—votes on most legislation in the House. In April 2007, the House passed the D.C. House Voting Rights Act introduced by Norton and northern Virginia's Tom Davis, making the city a congressional district with full voting rights in the House. In 1995, she worked with Davis and Newt Gingrich to create the fiscal control board to superintend District finances; in 1997, she and Davis came up with the package that rescued District finances and removed control over most of the District government from Marion Barry. It also included tax breaks for downtown and some other areas. In return, the District gave up the $660 million federal payment for a $198 million "contribution," which, Norton argues, should in the long run remove the District from the superintendency of Congress. That came one step closer when in September 2006 Congress passed a bill with an amendment allowing the District to spend money in midyear without getting approval from Congress in a supplemental appropriation. "It takes us close to budget autonomy," she said.

Norton understands that statehood for the District is improbable—it was defeated 277-153 by a Democratic Congress in 1993—and has sought voting representation in Congress. But she has opposed proposals by Republicans Ralph Regula and Dana Rohrabacher to count the District as part of Maryland for purposes of House representation. Norton originally declined to support the 2004 proposal by Tom Davis, with whom she has worked closely on District affairs, to increase the House temporarily by two new members — one from the District and one from the state entitled under the statutory formula to the 436th seat (which under the 2000 Census happens to be heavily Republican Utah). But in 2006 she decided to back a bill adding two permanent House seats and in November 2006 she and Mayor-elect Adrian Fenty urged Congress to pass it in the lame duck session.

In December, Utah legislators did their part by passing a four-district redistricting plan, which included a relatively safe seat for Utah's one House Democrat, Jim Matheson. But the outgoing House Republican leaders declined to let it go to the floor; some Republicans argued that the Constitution provides that only states shall be represented in the House, and that representation for the District can only come from a constitutional amendment, like the one that gave District residents the right to vote for president. The measure had the support of incoming Speaker Nancy Pelosi and in April 2007 the House passed it by a 241-177 vote. It still faced a steep climb since Senate Democrats did not have enough votes to avoid a filibuster and there was the threat of a presidential veto.

Despite her lack of a floor vote, Norton has effectively moved District legislation in the House. She successfully pushed the Southeast Federal Center Public-Private Development Act which provided a coordinated approach to the area around the Washington Navy Yard; this has resulted in new federal and private sector buildings near the Navy Yard. She supported the transfer of 200 acres of federal land to the District that passed in November 2006 and the decision to place the Coast Guard headquarters on the grounds of St. Elizabeth's Hospital. She protested vigorously when Congress has made decisions for the District, as in September 2004 when the House voted to repeal the District's ban on handguns; the bill didn't pass. She also objected in November 2004 to an amendment that would require the city to offer surplus school property to public charter schools for at least 25% less than the appraised value before selling it to anyone else.

After the terrorism threat level was raised in August 2004, streets around the Capitol were closed and 14 vehicle checkpoints established. Norton exploded, "We concede this makes it easier for security. You want to make it really easier? Close down all the streets! Close down the city! You can make it real safe." When the terrorism threat level was lowered in November and the checkpoints dismantled, she said, "While I am pleased that change is on the way, we will not be satisfied until the nation's capital no longer looks like an armed camp." But she concedes there is a need to balance interests here.

Norton has been regularly reelected with 90% or more of the vote.

★ FLORIDA ★

For a moment in history, a moment that lasted 36 days, Florida was the center of the political world, the state whose vote count would determine who would become president of the United States, the most evenly balanced political state in the nation. To students of political history this seemed astonishing. Sixty years before, Florida was the smallest Southern state, with just 5 congressional districts and 7 electoral votes, overwhelmingly Democratic. In 2000 it was the fourth-largest state in the nation, with 23 congressional districts and 25 electoral votes—and about to get 2 more from the 2000 Census. Only 12 years earlier, Florida had voted 61% for then-Vice President George Bush, who carried 66 of its 67 counties. Military-minded Southerners in the northern part of the state, affluent retirees on the Gulf Coast, middle-class conservatives in Tampa Bay and Orlando and around Disney World, Cubans in Miami and Dade County—all voted Republican, easily outnumbering the state's scattered black communities and its Jewish voters concentrated in Broward and Palm Beach Counties on the Gold Coast. But by 2000 Florida had become a state with political divisions as deep and political preferences as starkly different as any in the nation. Broward and Palm Beach on the Gold Coast voted 65%-33% for Al Gore; Escambia, Santa Rosa and Okaloosa Counties, on the western end of the Panhandle around what is called, perhaps unkindly, the Redneck Riviera, voted 68%-30% for George W. Bush. During the 2004 presidential campaign the focus again was on Florida more than any other state, as Republicans and Democrats brought in their nominees and organized to register new voters and get them to vote by absentee ballot or on Election Day. This time Florida turned out not to be close: John Kerry got 23% more votes there than Al Gore, but George W. Bush got 36% more than he had four years before, and he carried the state 52%-47%. Florida was only 1% less Republican than New Jersey was Democratic, though New Jersey was on no one's list of battleground states. Yet Florida was still closely enough divided—much more closely than the three larger states, that it remains crucial, for both parties. The story of how Florida became the pivot of American politics is a story of growth and change, and over the past 60 years Florida has grown more rapidly and changed more vividly than just about any other part of the United States.

Florida has an exotic past. It is the only Atlantic Coast state that was not part of the colonial United States; through the exertions of John Quincy Adams and Andrew Jackson, then political allies but later bitter political enemies, it was acquired from Spain in 1819. Starting off as a forgotten swamp and semitropical resort, Florida has emerged as almost an empire of its own, a prototype in many ways of America's future, with an international flavor and sometimes almost with its own foreign policy. Pivotal has been the rise of air conditioning: in 1950 only 20% of Florida houses had it, in 2000, 95% did. For many years, Florida was the place which millions of retirees looked forward to: the sunny, year-round warmth after eternal gray skies over winter factories and dark offices. But in the 1980s and 1990s Florida's population of children grew rapidly as young couples, from the South, from various points north and from Latin America, chose to raise their families and make their livings in a booming economy, with jobs and opportunities in communities that did not exist a generation ago. Some 17% of Florida's population today is over 65, more than the national average of 12%, but not enormously so; and the state's percentage of those under 18, is 22%, not much below the national average of 25%. For refugees from Cuba and Haiti and immigrants from all over the Caribbean and Latin America, Florida has been a land of freedom and security from authoritarian regimes and totalitarian police states. For Americans and foreigners of all kinds—some 80 million of them—Florida is the place to visit, with lively attractions, year-round swimming, restaurants and rooms to suit every taste and pocketbook. Yet all is not sunny: crime is down, but still a threat; the economic future is, as always, uncertain; the melting pot seems to work slowly and Florida's Hispanic population seems often to live in a world apart.

Florida is a creation not of America's elite—though a few millionaires like Henry Flagler and Marcus Plant pioneered tourism here—but a place for which ordinary people have voted with their feet. Before World War II it was the least populous state in the South, with 1.4 million people, isolated, disease-ridden, bigoted, with phosphate mines but no mineral resources, not much agriculture outside its citrus groves, and hardly any manufacturing at all. In 2006 Florida had 18 million people, within reach of New York's 19 million. It is a state one-fifth of whose economy is based on tourism in a country where tourism is one of the great growth industries; a state with an economy based on services in a country increasingly service-oriented; the state with the largest proportion of elderly and retired citizens in a country where an increasing percentage will live many years in retirement; a state also with a growing number of school children in a country which, replenished by

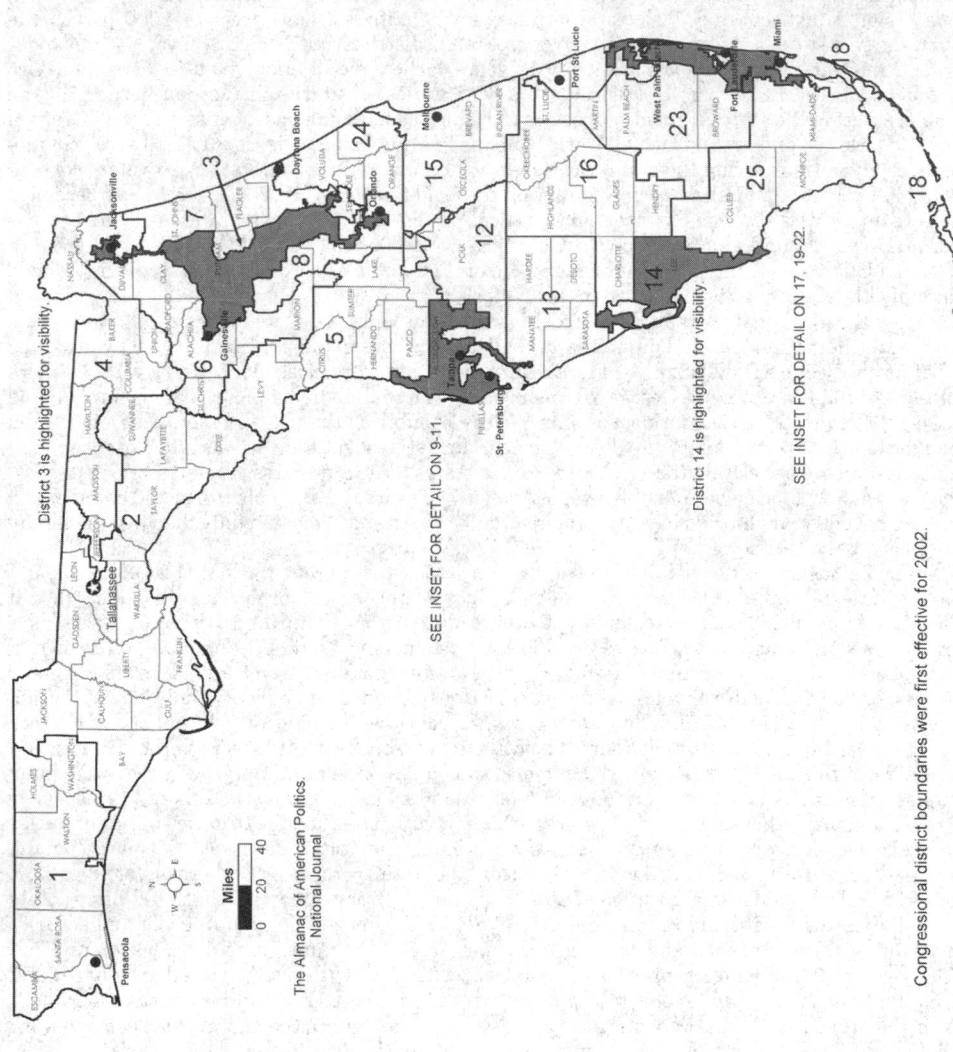

District 3 is highlighted for visibility.

SEE INSET FOR DETAIL ON 9-11.

District 14 is highlighted for visibility.

SEE INSET FOR DETAIL ON 17, 19-22.

The Almanac of American Politics.
National Journal

Miles
0   20   40

Congressional district boundaries were first effective for 2002.

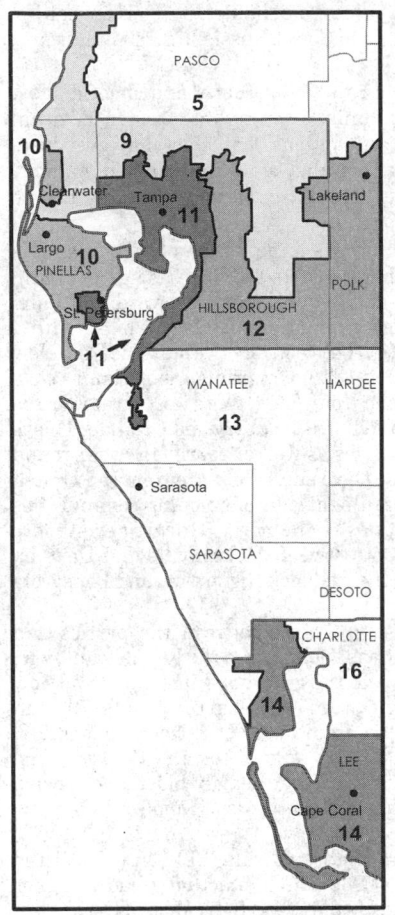
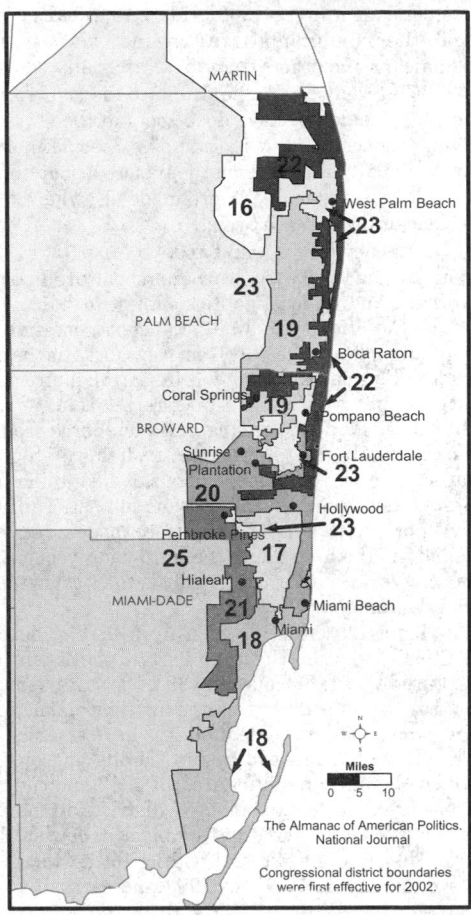

immigration, is growing faster and more robustly than any other advanced nation. It is a state continually replenished with people from out of state, two-thirds of them from the United States, one-third from foreign countries: in just the six years from 2000 to 2006, Florida had a domestic inflow of 8% and an immigrant inflow of 4% of its 2000 population.

Florida in recent years has had one of America's most buoyant economies—it has gained jobs consistently over the last 10 years except during the three months after September 11—though its economic base often seems a mystery to outsiders. This is an economy based heavily on small business—98% of businesses have fewer than 100 employees and in the 1990s Florida ranked number one in small business starts—with a significant high-tech sector (fifth in the country) and retirees, who account for 52% of Florida's consumer spending and pay 47% of its property taxes (though some of this may be in jeopardy, as retirees head to other states). Florida's economy is also based on international merchandise trade, which increased from $24 billion in 1987 to $81 billion in 2004; while foreign investment increased from $9.5 billion to $34.3 billion in 2002. Miami for three decades has been the economic and commercial capital of Latin America, as well as its mecca for political exiles. You can fly nonstop from Miami to just about any place in Latin America, both English and Spanish are commonly understood, and it has been the one place where many Latins could be sure their money and their persons were safe from government takeover. Recent ructions in their countries have brought thousands of Argentinians, Venezuelans, Bolivians and Ecuadorans, some very affluent and some struggling, to south Florida; Puerto Ricans and other Latinos have also been moving into central Florida, and Cubans now account for less than half of Florida's Hispanics. And other immigrants have come in as well, especially to the Gold Coast: Russians, Arabs, Haitians, Jamaicans and others from the Caribbean.

What may be fragile in Florida is civil society; Florida can be disorderly and chaotic. Most people here do not have deep roots in the state, most communities sprang into existence within living memory and, if Florida gives people more freedom and options than they may ever have imagined, it has also given them more disruption and crime than they surely anticipated. Many of Florida's great fortunes were made elsewhere, and brought here partly because the state has no income or inheritance taxes.

This new Florida, like today's America, has no real center. Its largest urban focus, Miami, is geographically off to one corner and culturally uniquely Cuban, with its eyes increasingly on Latin America and its local politics subject to ridicule. The rest of the Gold Coast, Broward and Palm Beach Counties, with 3 million people (one-sixth of Florida's population), is also atypical, with a population drawn heavily from New York (the largest migration between any two states is from New York to Florida) and other Northeastern metro areas, plus non-Latino migrants from Miami-Dade, large numbers of Jews and huge retiree condos lining the ocean front. Then there is Central Florida, the I-4 corridor from Tampa-St. Petersburg through citrus and tourist country and Orlando. This is mostly family, not retiree, country, living off high-tech industries as well as tourism: A year-round rather than seasonal megalopolis of 4.8 million people. Most newcomers here are from the United States, not from abroad. There is also the Gulf Coast, the affluent and burgeoning communities south of Tampa Bay and the more modest retirement counties to the north. Growing even more rapidly is the area along the hard-sand-beach Atlantic Coast between Jacksonville and Daytona Beach. Very Southern culturally is the western Panhandle, the Redneck Riviera around Pensacola and Panama City.

Politically, this all adds up to a Florida that is closely divided between the parties and politically volatile. The trend in state politics since the 1990s has been toward the Republicans, who captured the state House in 1994, the state Senate in 1996, and the governorship in 1998 and now hold most statewide offices and have big majorities in the legislature—26-14 in the Senate, 79-41 in the House. Similarly, Republicans have established an 16–9 margin in the U.S. House delegation. They have been helped by term limits and by shrewdly adapting to local terrain. Redistricting, which Republicans influenced in 1992 and controlled in 2002, helped: heavily black and Jewish areas are concentrated in a few districts, to the point that nearly two-thirds of Democrats holding legislative and House seats are black or Jewish.

The trend in national politics in the 1990s was toward the Democrats. Bill Clinton lost the state by only 41%-39% in 1992 and carried it 48%-42% in 1996. Al Gore actually had a higher percentage when he lost the state by the excruciating margin of 48.85%-48.84%. Most of the change was due to movement toward Democrats on the Gold Coast and in the I-4 corridor from Tampa-St. Petersburg to Orlando. Drops in crime and welfare rolls deprived Republicans of issues in these metro areas as they did in the big metro areas of the Northeast, industrial Midwest and West Coast, and after 1995 the tax issue was taken off the table; cultural issues like abortion and gun control favored Democrats. Also, the increasing Jewish population in Broward and Palm Beach Counties moved the Gold Coast toward Democrats; Joe Lieberman campaigned there and drew enthusiastic crowds in 2000. In the I-4 corridor, what had been a big Republican margin for Bush in 1988 was transformed to a Clinton margin in 1996 and a standoff in 2000. The biggest drop in the Republican percentage in any county in Florida between 1988 and 2000 was in Osceola County, which contains part of Disney World and the Disney-sponsored "new town" of Celebration. In the 1980s, Disney World was still an epitome of traditional conservative values; by 2000, Disney was hosting Gay Day.

The closeness of Florida's political divisions was shown not only in the 2000 presidential race but in the two races for open Senate seats. In 2000, when Republican Connie Mack retired, Insurance Commissioner and former Democratic Congressman Bill Nelson beat Republican Congressman Bill McCollum 51%-46%. In 2004, when Democrat Bob Graham retired, Republican former HUD Secretary and Orange County Commission Chairman Mel Martinez beat former state Education Commissioner Betty Castor 49%-48%. Both winners made inroads in the other party's strongholds. Nelson, with his Florida roots and accent, lost the part of the state outside the Gold Coast and the I-4 corridor by only 52%-46%. Martinez, who was born in Cuba, ran ahead of George W. Bush among Miami-Dade's Cubans and lost the Gold Coast by only 57%-41%. The open race for governor in 2006 was also reasonably close. Republican Attorney General Charlie Crist beat Democratic Congressman Jim Davis 52%-45%. Crist lost the Gold Coast 59%-40% but won the I-4 corridor 54%-43% and won 59%-38% in the rest of the state.

A pivotal role in Florida politics—and government—has been played by Jeb Bush. In 1994 he challenged incumbent Governor Lawton Chiles and, after Democrats targeted elderly voters with a last minute claim that Bush would (somehow) cut Social Security, he lost 51%-49%. If he had won it might have been the Florida rather than the Texas Bush as the Republican nominee in 2000, with who knows what consequences for history. In 1998 Jeb Bush won 55%-45% and, with the help of a heavily Republican legislature, proceeded to make a record that made him arguably the best governor of his time. Over the opposition of the teachers' unions, he improved the rigor and accountability of the schools and provided alternatives for those in schools that kept failing; he resolutely and continuously cut taxes; he overturned, to great protest, racial quotas and preferences; he involved local governments and the private sector in accommodating growth with enhanced infrastructure and limits on the exploitation of groundwater and swampy land; he prepared meticulously for the natural disasters which are part of Florida's natural heritage. He achieved overwhelming approval for his response to hurricanes and, if his brother's FEMA was unprepared for Hurricane Katrina, it may have been because it was used to dealing with hurricanes in which the response was handled by Jeb Bush and competent state and local Florida public servants. After the controversy over Florida's electoral votes in 2000, Democrats targeted Jeb Bush for defeat, although he had no role in counting the votes; in fall 2002, DNC Chairman Terry McAuliffe said that the Florida governor's race was the national party's number one priority. But Bush was reelected by a 56%-43% margin, and at the same time, Republican Charlie Crist was elected attorney general, replacing the last Democrat holding a non-federal statewide office, and Republican margins in the U.S. House delegation and the state Senate and House were increased. Then came the 2004 presidential election, in which Florida was supposed to be close, yet was carried by George W. Bush by a 52%-47% margin—380,000 votes in this large state.

In 2006 Jeb Bush was obliged by term limits to retire as governor and Florida politics, in a year that turned out to be good for Democrats, was up for grabs. The Republican nominee for governor was Attorney General Charlie Crist, known as tough on law enforcement but as less conservative on other issues than Jeb Bush. The Democratic nominee, the winner by only 47%-41% in the primary, was Tampa Congressman Jim Davis, also from the I-4 corridor. The Senate race was a contest between incumbent Democrat Bill Nelson and Republican Katherine Harris, the secretary of state who did play a pivotal role in the Florida 2000 controversy, and who won the Republican primary with 49% of the vote; if Republicans had not, for political reasons of their own, abolished the state's runoff law, she might have been replaced by a stronger candidate. Nelson won as expected, by a 60%-38% margin, and Democrats had downballot successes, picking up 6 seats in the state House and having their nominee Alex Sink, wife of the 2002 gubernatorial nominee, win the statewide office of chief financial officer. But Crist was elected governor by a 52%-45% margin over Davis, carrying 59 of the 67 counties—losing only the three Gold Coast counties, four counties in and around the state capital of Tallahassee and the county containing the University of Florida. Democrats gained two congressional seats—one where the Republican incumbent, Mark Foley, had been disgraced and resigned; the other a Gold Coast oceanfront seat which John Kerry had carried in 2004. Crist in his first months as governor charted a somewhat different course from the rigorously conservative Jeb Bush. But Florida's basic affinity for the Republican party seemed, on balance, intact—in what is on course to be in just a couple of years the nation's third largest state.

Two more things are worth noting about Florida politics. The first is that politics here is not driven by an elderly population terrified of losing government benefits. To be sure, the elderly are a larger percentage of the electorate here than in any other state, 19% in 2004, but the difference is not overwhelming; most new residents come here to work, not to retire. Florida has the five congressional districts with the most Social Security recipients in the nation; Republican congressmen with elderly districts who have supported changes in the Social Security system have been reelected in all but one case by wide margins. In 2000 and 2004 George W. Bush called for personal retirement accounts in Social Security and according to exit polls carried the over 65 vote in Florida by a 52%-46% and 51%-48%. The elderly tend to vote in line with long-established partisan preferences, not in panicky response to the latest campaign ad on Social Security.

The second point is that the environment is an increasingly important issue in Florida, but one that may not cut in a partisan way. People come to Florida partly because of the kind of place it is; migrants from New York or Illinois may not have cared much about environmental issues when they lived there, but they came to Florida in large part because of the climate and setting, and don't want to see oil drilled on the Gulf Coast or the Everglades paved over. This is a change from history. The Everglades were seen as a nuisance for years. In 1845, when Florida was admitted to the Union, the legislature called for "reclaiming" the Everglades, and in 1850 Congress passed the Swamp and

Overflowed Lands Act. The Army Corps of Engineers started building a dike across Lake Okeechobee in 1930 and for nearly 50 years worked to straighten the Kissimmee River and build dikes and channels to reclaim land for farming. But with the 1947 publication of *The Everglades: River of Grass* by Marjory Stoneman Douglas, who died in 1998 at 108, Floridians began to appreciate the Everglades, which is essentially a flow of water south, from the Kissimmee River near Disney World, through Lake Okeechobee down to Florida Bay and the Gulf of Mexico. Governor Jeb Bush worked with national politicians of both parties on a gigantic, multiyear project to reverse the projects of the past and restore the Everglades.

The People		Race/Ethnic Origin			Military veterans: 1,875,597 (15.2%)	
Pop. 2006 (est):	18,089,888	10,458,509	65.4%	White	WWII: 25.6%	Korea: 15.0%
Pop. 2000:	15,982,378	2,264,268	14.2%	Black	Vietnam: 28.0%	Gulf War: 9.2%
Pop. 1990:	12,937,926	261,693	1.6%	Asian	**Most populous cities (2006):**	
Change 1990-2000:	Up 23.5%	42,358	0.3%	Native Am.	1. Jacksonville	794,555
% of U.S. total:	5.7%	6,887	0.0%	Hawaiian	2. Miami	404,048
Pop. rank:	4th of 50	236,954	1.5%	Two+ races	3. Tampa	332,888
Area size:	65,755 sq. mi.	28,994	0.2%	Other	4. St. Petersburg	248,098
State Native:	32.7%	2,682,715	16.8%	Hisp. Origin	5. Orlando	220,186
Non-citizen:	9.2%	**Ancestry**				
Language		German: 9.5%		Irish: 8.3%	Urban population: 89.3%	
English: 76.2%	Spanish: 15.7%	English: 7.4%		USA: 6.4%	Rural population: 10.7%	
Other Eur.: 6.3%		Italian: 5.0%				

Education		Work Sector		Legislature	
H.S. Grad:	79.9%	Private: 79.8%	Govt: 13.7%	Senate	26 R 14 D
College Grad:	22.3%	Self: 6.2%	Family: 0.3%	House	79 R 41 D
Industry		Unemployment: 5.5%		Legislative Term Limits: Yes	
Agri: 1.3%	Con: 8.0%	**Household Income**		**Registered Voters**	
Fin: 8.1%	Info: 3.1%	<15k: 16.3%	15-35k: 28.7%	D: 4,219,531 (40.4%)	
Mfg: 12.6%	Prof: 28.7%	35-50k: 17.4%	50-100k: 27.2%	R: 3,935,675 (37.7%)	
Public: 5.2%	Trade: 17.5%	100-150k: 6.3%	>150k: 4.1%	O: 2,278,643 (21.8%)	
Other: 15.6%		Median: $38,819			
Occupation		Poverty status: 12.5%			
Blue collar: 21.1%	White collar: 61.1%	**Home Value**			
Gray collar: 17.8%		<50k: 16.5%	50-100k: 38.7%	100-200k: 32.1%	200-300k: 7.1%
		300-500k: 3.6%	>500k: 2.1%	Median: $93,200	

Presidential politics   Going into the 2004 campaign, just about every strategist and pundit thought that Florida would be crucial once again, and very narrowly decided. Crucial it certainly was: George W. Bush would not have won without Florida's 27 electoral votes. But narrowly decided it turned out not to be. Bush's .01% percentage margin in 2000 ballooned into a 5.01% margin—larger than the percentage margins in 10 other states. Bush was declared the winner in Florida at 11:39 p.m. by ABC, at 11:43 by CBS, at 11:51 by Fox, at 12:10 by CNN and at 12:24 by NBC and MSNBC.

Bush's biggest gains were among minorities. According to the NEP exit poll, whites voted 57% for Bush, the same as in 2000; blacks voted 13% for Bush, up 6% from 2000; Latinos voted 56% for Bush, up 7% from 2000. The Latino numbers are all the more remarkable, since he seems to have lost ground among still heavily Republican Cuban-Americans; he seems to have done particularly well among Nicaraguans and surprisingly well among Puerto Ricans. Osceola County, which includes part of Disney World, has a rapidly expanding Latino population; it voted for Al Gore in 2000 and for Bush in 2004. Jews voted

2004 Presidential Vote
Bush (R) 3,964,522   (52%)
Kerry (D).................... 3,583,544   (47%)
Nader (Ref) 32,971   (0%)
Other.......................... 28,773   (0%)

2004 Democratic Presidential Primary
Kerry (D)...................... 581,672   (77%)
Edwards (D) 75,703   (10%)
Sharpton (D)................... 21,031   (3%)
Dean (D) 20,834   (3%)
Kucinich (D) 17,198   (2%)
Other.......................... 37,324   (5%)

2000 Presidential Vote
Bush (R) 2,912,790   (49%)
Gore (D)..................... 2,912,253   (49%)
Nader (Green) 97,488   (2%)
Other.......................... 40,579   (1%)

80%-20% for John Kerry, but Bush's share was up from 2000; despite increased voter turnout, Broward and Palm Beach Counties produced lower Democratic popular vote margins. In the heavily Jewish 19th and 20th Congressional Districts, Bush's percentage rose from 27% to 34% and from 31% to 36%.

That difference was made because the Republicans built an effective statewide organization manned by some 109,000 volunteers, who made 3 million voter contacts on Election Day and increased Republican turnout just about everywhere. The Bush campaign may have been helped by the fact that Florida was badly hit by four hurricanes in August and September; Governor Jeb Bush and also his brother the president got great credit for their response. And Florida's economy, unlike those of other battleground states like Ohio, Michigan and Pennsylvania, was humming along. But the organization may have made the difference. Bush won 2.9 million votes in Florida in 2000 and 3.9 million in 2004. He did not increase his percentage much in the Gold Coast—which he lost 60%-38% in 2000 and 59%-40% in 2004—but he prevented Democrats from increasing their popular vote margin there. In the I-4 corridor, Bush led 51%-49% in 2000 and 54%-46% in 2004, increasing a 50,000-vote margin to 230,000 votes. And in the rest of the state, Bush increased his 2000 popular vote margin from 316,000 votes to 524,000. In counties with small populations, with more trailer parks than gated communities, with more swampland than sandy beaches, the Bush percentage rose by 4% to 12%.

Florida has had a presidential primary in March for many years; since 1988 it has been part of Southern Super Tuesday. In recent years, as one of many states voting on a single day, it has attracted less attention. In 2004 it came too late to matter: the primary was held March 9, but John Kerry clinched the Democratic nomination on March 2. For 2008 the Florida legislature decided to move even earlier. It initially considered joining the several other states holding their primaries on February 5, two weeks after New Hampshire. But in 2007 the House passed a bill setting the primary one week earlier, on January 29. In May, after some hesitation, the Senate agreed, and Governor Charlie Crist signed the bill. One motive: to pressure presidential candidates to back a national catastrophic insurance fund. Since the January 29 date did not conform to the national party's nominating calendar, the Democratic National Committee voted in August to strip Florida of all of its delegates if the state party did not act within 30 days to comply with party rules.

Congressional districting

Florida has gained congressional districts from every Census since 1930, when it was still the smallest state in the South: in 1930 it elected four House members; in the 2000 Census it gained two seats, for a total of 25. In 2002, the redistricting process was controlled by Republicans; they agreed on a plan and passed it in March 2002. Disagreement between the state House and Senate was resolved when senators agreed to create a district tailor-made for House Speaker Tom Feeney; the other new district was tailor-made for Mario Diaz-Balart, chairman of the House Congressional Districting Committee. When Democratic Attorney General Bob Butterworth failed to pass it along to the Department of Justice for Voting Rights Act review, Governor Jeb Bush sent it there in May 2002. Democrats filed lawsuits against the plan in state and federal courts. The Justice Department approved the plan on June 7. A state court on June 17 dismissed the suit and said the federal court had jurisdiction. On July 9, in time for the filing deadline, a three-judge federal court approved the plan.

110th Congress Lineup	
16 R	9 D

109th Congress Lineup	
18 R	7 D

This was one of the most successful partisan redistrictings of the 2002 cycle. Feeney and Diaz-Balart were both elected to the House by wide margins. Karen Thurman was defeated by Republican state Senator Ginny Brown-Waite. Two senior Republicans, Bill Young of St. Petersburg and Clay Shaw of Fort Lauderdale, were strengthened; both represented areas which were among the first in Florida to elect Republican congressmen, but which had become more Democratic in the 1980s and 1990s. Democrat Allen Boyd of the 2d District was weakened. The seats of the three black Democrats and two Latino Republicans were protected, although the black percentage in Alcee Hastings's 23d District was reduced. The 2002 plan produced a delegation of 18 Republicans and 7 Democrats, a lopsided Republican majority in a state that was evenly divided in the 2000 presidential election. But the Democratic trend in 2006, though it produced only modest gains in Florida state politics, was evident in the results for U.S. House elections. Clay Shaw, possibly in line to be chairman of Ways and Means, was defeated. Democrats picked up the 16th District represented by disgraced Republican incumbent Mark Foley. And other Republicans incumbents' percentages were sharply down, leading to the possibility that Democrats might target them in 2008.

In early 2007 it seemed likely, though by no means assured, that Republicans would control redistricting in Florida after the 2010 Census. Governor Charlie Crist had high job approval in his first year, and Republican margins in the legislature are large enough that they seemed unlikely to be reversed in 2008 or 2010. Democrats had tried to put on the ballot a referendum to take the redistricting process away from the legislature, but in March 2006 the Florida Supreme Court ruled that it didn't meet state requirements and kept it off the ballot.

Governor

Charlie Crist (R)

Elected 2006, term expires Jan. 2011, 1st term; b. July 24, 1956, Altoona, PA; home, St. Petersburg; Attended Wake Forest U., FL St. U., B.A. 1978, Samford U. Cumberland Schl. of Law, J.D. 1981; Methodist; divorced.

Elected Office: FL Senate, 1992-98; FL Commissioner of Educ., 2000-02; FL Atty. Gen., 2002-06.

Professional Career: Gen. counsel, Minor League Baseball, 1982-88; practicing atty., 1988-89; state dir., U.S. Sen. Connie Mack, 1989-91; dep. sec., FL Dept. of Bus. and Prof. Regulation, 1998-2000.

Office: The Capitol, Tallahassee, 32399, 850-488-4441; Fax: 850-487-0801; Web site: www.flgov.com.

Election Results

2006 general	Charlie Crist (R)	2,519,845	(52%)
	Jim Davis (D)	2,178,289	(45%)
	Other	131,136	(3%)
2006 primary	Charlie Crist (R)	630,816	(64%)
	Tom Gallagher (R)	330,165	(33%)
	Other	25,005	(3%)
2002 general	Jeb Bush (R)	2,856,845	(56%)
	Bill McBride (D)	2,201,427	(43%)

Charlie Crist, a Republican, was elected governor of Florida in 2006. He was born in Altoona, Pennsylvania, where his grandfather, a Greek immigrant from Cyprus who arrived in America in 1912, ran a shoe-shine parlor. He moved to Atlanta before his first birthday when his father, who shortened the family name from Christodoulos to Crist, was accepted to medical school at Emory University. In 1960 the Crist family settled in sleepy St. Petersburg; a nearby Greek community and a rising population of retirees made it a nice fit for a young doctor looking to build a practice. By the time he was 10, Charlie Crist was campaigning for his father, who won a seat on the Pinellas County School Board. In high school, he was the starting football quarterback and class president. He was a walk-on player at Wake Forest University but transferred after his sophomore year to Florida State, where he was student body vice-president and homecoming king before graduating in 1978. In 1982 he got his law degree from Cumberland School of Law in Alabama, then worked as general counsel for the minor league division of Major League Baseball.

His first run for the state Senate in 1986 was unsuccessful. After that he served a stint as Senator Connie Mack's state director, then ran again for the state Senate and twice won election. There, he was nicknamed "Chain Gang Charlie" for his tough stances on crime. Over the years, he gained a reputation as an ambitious, media-savvy pol, always sporting a healthy tan and blessed with terrific retail campaigning skills. He has been on the statewide ballot in 4 of the last 5 elections—in 1998, as the Republican nominee against Senator Bob Graham, he lost 62%-38%; in 2000, he won election as state education commissioner; in 2002, he won election as attorney general; in 2006, he won the governorship.

As attorney general, Crist surprised some with attention to civil rights issues. He pushed a landmark civil rights bill through the legislature, named for Tampa civil rights leader Marvin Davies, that enabled the attorney general's office to go after businesses that engage in a pattern or practice of discrimination based on race, sex or disability; it was signed into law by Governor Jeb Bush in 2003. He also reopened in December 2004 the murder probe into the deaths of Harry and Harriette Moore, two Florida civil rights pioneers killed by a bomb planted at their home in 1951. At an August 2006 press conference, Crist declared that four dead Ku Klux Klansmen were responsible; some scholars raised questions about the findings and critics claimed political motives were behind Crist's actions.

Crist's office was up for election in 2006; so too was the governor's office, where term limits prevented Republican Governor Jeb Bush from running for a third term. On the Republican side, the three most prominent possible candidates were Crist, Lieutenant Governor Toni Jennings and Chief Financial Officer Tom Gallagher. By mid-2005, Crist and Gallagher had raised nearly $7 million between them; Jennings eventually decided not to run, leaving the other two veteran statewide candidates to battle for the nomination.

Gallagher, a former legislator from Miami, was making his third try for governor: he had dropped out of the 1982 race, and lost in the 1986 and 1994 primaries. He had been considered a moderate for much his career but he positioned himself as a social conservative this time and referred to Crist as a liberal. Gallagher opposed adoptions by gay parents and supported efforts to add a gay marriage ban to the state constitution; Crist said the marriage ban was unnecessary because state law already forbids it. Crist highlighted his school reform work as education commissioner and his accomplishments as attorney general; he said he was "fine" with civil unions between gays and that gay adoption "is not a major focus in my campaign." Crist also took another position that did not endear him to religious conservatives, saying he disagreed with President Bush's veto of a stem cell research bill.

Below the surface of the campaign, and perhaps driving its themes, were persistent rumors that Crist is gay. A bachelor, Crist was divorced in the early 1980s after a seven-month marriage. At several public events, Crist was asked if he was gay and denied it; the issue did not get much attention in the newspapers, despite determined public efforts by the Reform Party candidate. Gallagher also found his own personal life closely scrutinized: in June, court documents pertaining to his bitter 1979 divorce (he had since remarried) were leaked to a Tampa newspaper, forcing him to admit he had used drugs and committed adultery in the 1970s. The sleazy disclosures didn't stop there. Shortly before the September primary, Crist had to confront an 18-year-old paternity claim after sealed records were anonymously faxed and emailed to various reporters; Crist had denied the claim at the time and had relinquished any parental rights to the child, who was put up for adoption. Thus the 2006 Republican primary election will go down in the annals of dirty politics: here a candidate was attacked both for being gay *and* for fathering a child out of wedlock.

The final result was not close. Crist won 64%-33%, carrying all but a handful of small counties, mainly in the Panhandle. On the Democratic side, Tampa Congressman Jim Davis won the nomination by defeating state Senator Rod Smith 47%-41%. There were ominous signs for November. Crist raised some $14 million for his primary; Davis, accustomed to soft reelections in his solidly Democratic district, had raised about $9 million less. In victory, Crist won 631,000 votes—225,000 more than Davis. In the Republican primary, 986,000 votes were cast, Democrats cast 858,000 votes—a difference of 128,000. Davis still had a ways to go in introducing himself to voters—while he won across central Florida and the I-4 corridor, he lost nearly every county north and west of Ocala and failed to carry Palm Beach and Miami-Dade Counties.

Crist ran as a fiscal conservative and portrayed Davis as a liberal, "do-nothing congressman" who raised taxes. He pointed out that Davis attended private schools, contrasting that with his own background as a "proud product of Florida's public school system," with two sisters who became teachers and a father who sat on the local school board. He called for doubling homestead exemptions and talked about the environment and civil rights; when asked, he said he had opposed congressional intervention in the Terry Schiavo case. Davis promised $1 billion in property tax relief and raising teachers' salaries; he criticized Crist's record as attorney general by highlighting Florida's rising murder rate. Davis also sought to tie Crist to the national Republican party and claimed Crist was ducking President Bush when Bush made an election eve appearance in Pensacola and Crist campaigned elsewhere.

Crist outspent Davis $20 million to $7 million and won 52%-45%, the fourth time in the last six elections that Republicans have won the Florida governorship. Voters saw some 21,000 Crist ads from August through October, the most of any candidate nationwide. Crist carried 59 of 67 counties, winning by large margins in the western Panhandle and in the Jacksonville area and carrying central Florida and the I-4 corridor. He lost the Gold Coast (Miami-Dade, Broward and Palm Beach Counties) 59%-40%, the University of Florida's Alachua County, and four counties around Tallahassee. He won 59%-38% among white voters, ran evenly with Latino voters (70%-29% among Cubans; 33%-66% among other Hispanic groups) but lost badly with African-Americans, 81%-18%, despite his outreach efforts.

His first step as governor-elect was a shaky one: After considerable negative publicity, he was forced to backtrack and cancel plans for an expensive inaugural ball where donations as high as $500,000 were solicited to pay for the event. He was immediately confronted with the state's property insurance crisis, with skyrocketing rates and private insurers leaving the market, and a weeklong January special legislative session was called. Crist ended up winning several property insurance revisions, including a rate freeze for the state-backed insurer. By March, his 73% approval rating made him one of the most popular governors in the nation.

Senior Senator

Bill Nelson (D)

Elected 2000, seat up 2012, 2d term; b. Sept. 29, 1942, Miami; home, Melbourne; Yale U., B.A. 1965; U. of VA, J.D. 1968; Protestant; married (Grace Cavert).

Military Career: U.S. Army, 1968-70; U.S. Army Reserves, 1965-71.

Elected Office: FL House of Reps., 1972-78; U.S. House of Reps., 1978-90; FL Treasurer, Insurance Comm. & Fire Marshal, 1994-2000.

Professional Career: Practicing atty., 1970-79, 1991-94; Legis. asst., FL Gov. Reubin Askew, 1971; Crew member, Space Shuttle Columbia, 1986.

DC Office: 716 HSOB, 20510, 202-224-5274; Fax: 202-228-2183; Web site: billnelson.senate.gov.

State Offices: Coral Gables, 305-536-5999; Davie, 954-693-4851; Fort Myers, 239-334-7760; Jacksonville, 904-346-4500; Orlando, 407-872-7161; Tallahassee, 850-942-8415; Tampa, 813-225-7040; West Palm Beach, 561-514-0189.

Committees: *Aging (Special)* (6th of 11 D). *Armed Services* (7th of 13 D): Strategic Forces (Chmn.); Emerging Threats & Capabilities; Seapower. *Budget* (6th of 12 D). *Commerce, Science & Transportation* (6th of 12 D): Space, Aeronautics & Related Sciences (Chmn.); Consumer Affairs, Insurance & Automotive Safety; Oceans, Atmosphere, Fisheries & Coast Guard; Aviation Operations, Safety & Security. *Foreign Relations* (6th of 11 D): International Operations & Organizations, Democracy & Human Rights (Chmn.); African Affairs; Western Hemisphere, Peace Corps & Narcotics Affairs. *Intelligence (Select)* (7th of 8 D).

Group Ratings

	ADA	ACLU	AFS	LCV	ITIC	NTU	COC	ACU	CFG	FRC
2006	60	58	63	57	75	29	83	40	25	12
2005	80	—	88	90	—	16	50	20	8	—

National Journal Ratings

	2005 LIB	—	2005 CONS		2006 LIB	—	2006 CONS
Economic	78%	—	19%		57%	—	42%
Social	62%	—	37%		64%	—	34%
Foreign	56%	—	43%		58%	—	41%

Key Votes of the 109th Congress

1. Bar ANWR Drilling	Y	5. Confirm Samuel Alito	N	9. Limit Interstate Abortion	Y
2. FY06 Spending Curb	N	6. Path to Citizenship	Y	10. CAFTA	Y
3. Estate Tax Repeal	Y	7. Bar Same Sex Marriage	N	11. Urge Iraq Withdrawal	N
4. Raise Minimum Wage	Y	8. Stem Cell Research $	Y	12. Provide Detainee Rights	Y

Election Results

2006 general	Bill Nelson (D)	2,890,548	(60%)	($16,116,224)
	Katherine Harris (R)	1,826,127	(38%)	($9,334,232)
	Other	76,859	(2%)	
2006 primary	Bill Nelson (D)	unopposed		
2000 general	Bill Nelson (D)	2,989,487	(51%)	($6,535,832)
	Bill McCollum (R)	2,705,348	(46%)	($8,664,112)
	Other	161,896	(3%)	

Prior Winning Percentages: 1988 House (61%); 1986 House (73%); 1984 House (61%); 1982 House (71%); 1980 House (70%); 1978 House (61%)

Bill Nelson was elected Florida's junior senator in 2000, after nearly 30 years in politics. He grew up in Melbourne, on what is now the Space Coast, the son of a developer and real estate investor who died when he was 14; Nelson likes to recall that his great-grandfather arrived in Florida from Denmark on a boat as a stowaway. From his family home, Rock Point, he could see rockets blast off from what is now the Kennedy Space Center in the 1950s and 1960s. Nelson was active in student government and has always been something of a straight arrow; he doesn't drink, smoke or swear. He went to the University of Florida for two years, then graduated from Yale and the University of Virginia law school. He served two years in the Army, then returned to Melbourne and briefly practiced law and worked on the staff of Governor Reubin Askew. In 1972, at 30, he was elected to the state House of Representatives.

In 1978, when Republican Congressmen Louis Frey retired, Nelson ran for Congress, from a seat that then included the Space Coast's Brevard County and most of Orlando's Orange County. His religious faith and traditional values, his indefatigable campaigning and folksy manner helped make him popular in an area that was trending Republican. He won the seat 61%-39% and in five succeeding elections won between 61% and 73% of the vote, in a district that voted 29% for Michael Dukakis in 1988. On the Science Committee, he got his fellow Democrats to vote him rather than the more liberal George Brown chairman of the Space Subcommittee—obviously of prime importance to the district. Nelson not only boosted the space program in every possible way, he also rode the space shuttle *Columbia* himself, spending 6 days orbiting the earth, in early January 1986. Less than two weeks later the *Challenger* exploded. After the *Columbia* was lost in February 2003, he called for continued manned space flight despite the risks.

In 1989, with the support of leading Florida Democrats, Nelson set out to run against Republican Governor Bob Martinez, who was not faring well in polls. But in early 1990, some Democrats became antsy about Nelson's prospects and persuaded Lawton Chiles, who had retired from the Senate in 1988 after three terms, to run. Chiles was always far ahead, and won the September primary 69%-31%. Nelson returned to his 77-acre oceanfront home in Melbourne, his political career seemingly over. But in 1994 he found an opening when state Insurance Commissioner Tom Gallagher, a Republican, ran for governor. Nelson was elected in November to an office whose full title was Treasurer, Insurance Commissioner and State Fire Marshal, and proceeded to compile a highly publicized activist record.

Nelson was obviously setting himself up to run for higher statewide office, and his opening came in March 1999, when Republican Senator Connie Mack said he would not run for reelection in 2000. Mack's retirement left a seat up for grabs in a state that, as election night viewers learned in November 2000, was very closely divided between the parties. Republicans nominated 20-year, Orlando-based Congressman Bill McCollum, one of the House's impeachment managers. A possible problem for Nelson was the independent candidacy of Willie Logan, a veteran African-American legislator whom Democrats had ousted as Speaker-designate in January 1998 on the grounds that he wasn't raising enough money. But Logan, who was getting 5% in many polls, ended up winning just 1.4% in November.

Washington observers considered the race a contest over the wisdom of impeachment but mostly it was a battle of competing styles. Nelson, running his fourth statewide race in 10 years, always led in polls. His easygoing, folksy manner contrasted favorably with McCollum's stiff, often aggressive manner. McCollum, with a long conservative record on abortion and gun control, attempted to modulate his positions, but only succeeded in antagonizing his base; his charge that Nelson was a "liberal" and a proponent of "class warfare" proved unconvincing. This was the most expensive Senate race in Florida history, with the two candidates spending over $15 million between them; Nelson won 51%-46%. Nelson won 60%-37% in the Gold Coast, almost exactly the same margin as in the presidential race. In the I-4 corridor, which included McCollum's district and most of the district Nelson had represented in the House, Nelson won 51%-46%; superior name identification was not Nelson's only advantage. In the rest of the state Nelson lost by only 52%-46%, compared to the 55%-42% margin by which Al Gore lost there. Folksiness and Florida roots counted.

In the Senate, Nelson focused on insurance issues and voted on the Budget Committee to limit the Bush tax cut, then voted against it on the floor in May 2001. In March 2004 he agreed with John Kerry's call for a delay in military base closings and an increase of 40,000 troops. On the Foreign Relations and Armed Services committees, Nelson kept pushing with Pat Roberts to get Iraq to provide information about Scott Speicher, the Navy pilot shot down in 1991 who was classified as Missing In Action; Speicher's family lives in Orange Park, near Jacksonville. In February 2004 he recommended a multilateral peacekeeping force for Haiti, and in April 2004 became the first member of Congress to meet with heads of its provisional government since the resignation in

February of Jean-Bertrand Aristide. In January 2005, with two Senate colleagues, he met with Venezuela's President Hugo Chavez, who told him he would cooperate in keeping Colombian FARC guerrillas from reaching sanctuary in Venezuela. Nelson voted for the Iraq war resolution in October 2002, but in May 2004 said he regretted the vote. Defying the White House, Nelson in December 2006 traveled to Damascus to meet with Syrian President Bashar Assad to gauge the Syrians level of interest in aiding efforts to stabilize Iraq.

Nelson serves on the Commerce subcommittee with jurisdiction over the space program, where he has strongly supported the space shuttle. After the loss of *Columbia*, he called for accelerated development of a reusable space vehicle to ferry astronauts to the Space Station. When George W. Bush proposed sending spacecraft to the Moon by 2020 and Mars by 2030, Nelson praised the idea but said funding was insufficient. When the committee was considering reauthorization of the space program in September 2004, Nelson passed an amendment calling on NASA to report to Congress on the costs of extending the space shuttle past 2010, but did not get approval of another amendment requiring NASA to find laid-off shuttle workers similar jobs in the agency. In the majority, Nelson became chairman of the Commerce Committee's space subcommittee.

After weeks of study, he voted against the Medicare/prescription drug bill in November 2003 and said in August 2004, "When seniors see how miniscule the coverage is and the costs escalate, there will be a lot of moaning and groaning. People will demand change." In 2007, Nelson introduced a bill with Harry Reid that would increase the number of physician training positions supported by Medicare. He voted against the constitutional amendment banning same-sex marriage on the grounds it "could limit civil rights—including inheritance and hospital visitation—for a whole class of people." Nelson voted for John Roberts as chief justice, but against the nomination of Samuel Alito to the Supreme Court. He voted for an amendment to an immigration bill that would establish English as the national language.

In July 2004 he called for an independent audit of Florida's new touch-screen voting machines. After the disputed 2006 election in Florida's 13th District raised questions about the dependability of electronic voting machines, Nelson introduced a bill requiring that voting equipment produce a paper record. In the atmosphere of increased ethics disclosure, Nelson began posting his daily schedule on the Internet, allowing the public to see with whom he met each day, including lobbyists. After hurricanes hit Florida in August and September 2004, he pushed successfully to get $1 billion of agricultural assistance in the homeland security appropriation. Nelson worked with Senator Mel Martinez on efforts to block oil and gas exploration in the eastern part of the Gulf of Mexico. He also supported a Senate bill lifting a moratorium on offshore oil and gas exploration after receiving assurances from Senate Majority Leader Frist that bill conferees would not abandon protections for Florida's coast that had been negotiated by Martinez.

In 2004 he was mentioned several times as a possible running mate for John Kerry, but tended to defer to his senior colleague Bob Graham. In January 2005 he made it clear that he wanted to run for reelection and not for governor in 2006. Elected with 51% of the vote, Nelson was an obvious Republican target and he positioned himself accordingly. In January 2005 he opposed George W. Bush's Social Security plan. After the Pentagon limited access to military bases for the Boy Scouts, apparently in response to criticism of their policy of excluding gays and requiring belief in God, Nelson introduced a resolution supporting the Scouts and embarked on a tour of Florida in their support.

In June 2005, two-term Congresswoman Katherine Harris, who decided not to run for the Senate in 2004 after consultations with White House strategist Karl Rove, announced she would challenge Nelson in 2006. But many Republican leaders believed that Harris' prominent role as secretary of state during the disputed 2000 presidential election made her too polarizing for the general election. Still, Harris enjoyed celebrity status among many rank-and-file Republican voters.

Contrary to Nelson's image as a centrist Democrat, Harris portrayed him as "ultra-liberal" on taxes, abortion, gay marriage and immigration. But the contest was defined almost entirely by the erratic behavior of Harris and her hapless campaign. Governor Jeb Bush had repeatedly indicated he was not interested in running, and Republicans unsuccessfully appealed to former Florida House Speaker Allen Bense and former Representative Joe Scarborough to run for the seat. In February 2006, former defense contractor Mitchell Wade, who had illegally contributed $32,000 to Harris' 2004 campaign and had asked Harris for legislative favors, pleaded guilty to bribing former Congressman Randy (Duke) Cunningham. Harris, who had given the money to charity, responded to Wade's guilty plea by avoiding the media and canceling campaign events. Harris badly needed a jump start to her campaign. Amid speculation she would resign her House seat or withdraw from the Senate race, she announced in March she would spend $10 million of her personal wealth on her Senate campaign. (She ended up spending a third of that amount.) By June, the Harris campaign had hemorrhaged nearly two dozen staffers, including veteran strategists like Ed Rollins. Many were frustrated by her unwillingness to heed their advice or had been driven away by the candidate's campaign style. Harris was notably absent from the party's "unity tour" after the September primary, and by then the national party had already written off the race. Nelson won in a 60%-38% landslide; he lost in the Panhandle but carried 57 of 67 counties and even Harris's home county of Sarasota.

Junior Senator

Mel Martinez (R)

Elected 2004, seat up 2010, 1st term; b. Oct. 23, 1946, Sagua La Grande, Cuba; home, Orlando; FL St. U., B.A. 1969, J.D. 1973; Catholic; married (Kitty).

Elected Office: Orange County chairman, 1998-2001.

Professional Career: Practicing atty., 1973-98; Secy., U.S. Dept. of Housing and Urban Dev., 2001-03.

DC Office: 356 RSOB, 20510, 202-224-3041; Fax: 202-228-5171; Web site: martinez.senate.gov.

State Offices: Coral Gables, 305-444-8332; Jacksonville, 904-398-8586; Naples, 239-774-3367; Orlando, 407-254-2573; Pensacola, 850-433-2603; Tampa, 813-207-0509.

Committees: *Aging (Special)* (4th of 10 R). *Armed Services* (11th of 12 R): Seapower (RMM); Emerging Threats & Capabilities. *Banking, Housing & Urban Affairs* (10th of 10 R): Security & International Trade & Finance (RMM); Housing, Transportation & Community Development. *Energy & Natural Resources* (10th of 11 R): National Parks; Energy.

Group Ratings

	ADA	ACLU	AFS	LCV	ITIC	NTU	COC	ACU	CFG	FRC
2006	0	25	0	0	100	76	100	84	75	100
2005	5	—	0	10	—	70	83	100	82	—

National Journal Ratings

	2005 LIB	—	2005 CONS		2006 LIB	—	2006 CONS
Economic	36%	—	61%		25%	—	72%
Social	0%	—	77%		42%	—	57%
Foreign	0%	—	74%		8%	—	85%

Key Votes of the 109th Congress

1. Bar ANWR Drilling	N	5. Confirm Samuel Alito	Y	9. Limit Interstate Abortion	Y
2. FY06 Spending Curb	Y	6. Path to Citizenship	Y	10. CAFTA	Y
3. Estate Tax Repeal	Y	7. Bar Same Sex Marriage	Y	11. Urge Iraq Withdrawal	N
4. Raise Minimum Wage	N	8. Stem Cell Research $	N	12. Provide Detainee Rights	N

Election Results

2004 general	Mel Martinez (R)	3,672,864	(49%)	($12,836,836)
	Betty Castor (D)	3,590,201	(48%)	($11,472,071)
	Other	166,829	(2%)	
2004 primary	Mel Martinez (R)	522,994	(45%)	
	Bill McCollum (R)	360,474	(31%)	
	Doug Gallagher (R)	158,360	(14%)	
	Johnnie Byrd (R)	68,982	(6%)	
	Other	55,121	(5%)	
1998 general	Bob Graham (D)	2,436,402	(62%)	($5,094,581)
	Charlie Crist (R)	1,463,749	(38%)	($1,487,498)

Melquiades "Mel" Martinez, a Republican, was elected Florida's junior senator in 2004. He grew up in the Cuban countryside, near Sagua La Grande, where his father made his living as a veterinarian inseminating cows. After a neighboring 16-year-old was shot by a firing squad for dealing with the underground, Martinez's parents sent him to the United States in February 1962, as part of Operation Pedro Pan, a Catholic Church program that brought 14,000 unaccompanied children to the United States. He stayed in a camp along the St. John's River west of St. Augustine, then was taken in as a foster child by Eileen and Walt Young of Orlando, still unable to speak much English; later he was taken in by June and Jim Berkmeyer. Martinez attended Orlando Junior College and worked at a Publix supermarket; his parents arrived in 1966, and he bought them a used Chevy. He transferred to Florida State, graduated from its college and law school and practiced law in Orlando with Orlando Mayor Bill Frederick's firm. A Democrat in college and law school, he became a Republican in 1979. As one of the few bilingual lawyers in town, he got many Spanish-speaking clients. As a personal injury plaintiff's lawyer, Martinez made lots of money and became head of the Florida Academy of Trial Lawyers. He and his college roommate, Ken Connor, started a law practice; Connor ran for governor in 1994 as a pro-life Republican and asked Martinez to be his running mate. Jeb Bush won the primary with 46% of the vote and Connor finished fifth with 9%, but Martinez was noticed. In 1998 Martinez ran for chairman of the Orange County government and in a nonpartisan three-way race won by a wide margin. In 2000 Martinez, a Cuban-American not involved in Cuban-American politics in Miami, was named co-chairman of George W. Bush's Florida campaign, and after the election he was appointed Secretary of Housing and Urban Development.

There he set up a $1.7 billion tax credit program for investors building affordable housing and a $1 billion program to help 650,000 low-income families make down payments over five years; spending on Section 8 housing vouchers increased from $12 billion to $18 billion. But his attempt to streamline the closing process on housing purchases was unsuccessful. Martinez traveled extensively and was constantly available to Spanish language television and radio media; he commented not only on HUD programs but in defense of administration domestic and foreign policy generally.

Up through 2003 he was a distant observer of politics in Florida, where Senator Bob Graham's seat came up for reelection in 2004. Graham was widely popular, a long-term fixture in Florida politics, first elected governor in 1978 and then to the Senate in 1986. In May 2003 he announced he was running for president. When asked whether he would run for reelection to the Senate, he would say he did not anticipate doing so. Suddenly a Senate seat that had seemed to be safe seemed to be open. Graham's apparent withdrawal from the Senate race led many Republicans and Democrats to run, the latter all insisting that they would withdraw if he decided to run for reelection. In early October Graham withdrew from the presidential race but left his intentions in the Senate race unclear.

This left both parties with candidates and potential candidates whose ability to win many party leaders doubted. On the Democratic side Broward County Congressman Peter Deutsch was running hard: he was well financed but had a liberal voting record and a strong partisan edge that seemed unlikely to go over well statewide; former Miami-Dade County Mayor Alex Penelas had strong support from Cuban-Americans but uncertain appeal statewide. On the Republican side, former Congressman Bill McCollum was an active and earnest campaigner but had already demonstrated in a 51%-46% loss to Bill Nelson in 2000 that he was capable of running 3% behind George W. Bush; businessman Doug Gallagher was ready to spend his own money, but was unknown; Congresswoman Katherine Harris, who was expressing interest in the race, was well known for her role as secretary of state in the 2000 Florida recount controversy, but was a target who would clearly attract a huge response from Democratic moneygivers and activists. So both parties found other candidates who ended up winning their nominations. Democrats found Betty Castor, a former legislator from Tampa, elected state education commissioner in 1986 and 1990 and later president of the University of South Florida. White House strategist Karl Rove met with Harris, who decided not to run after serving only one House term, while Senators George Allen and Rick Santorum met with Mel Martinez and urged him to run. Martinez had earlier expressed interest in running for governor in 2006—a better natural fit for his executive experience than a run for the Senate. But in December 2003 Martinez resigned as HUD Secretary and announced he was running for the Senate. He quickly raised sufficient money to make himself competitive.

Both parties' primaries proved fractious. McCollum attacked Martinez as a trial lawyer and as a "failed" HUD secretary. To the first charge Martinez replied, "I'm proud of what I did as a lawyer helping people, fighting big insurance companies. There is nothing in my life I would run away from." Martinez ran a nine-minute spot showing him as a teenager in a refugee camp, old home movie footage and a statement by George W. Bush: "The American dream is alive and well, and Mel Martinez represents it all." Doug Gallagher spent $6.3 million on ads calling his opponents "the

M&M boys" and citing his accomplishments in business and diabetes research. In the week before the August 31 primary, Martinez ads attacked McCollum as "anti-family" because of his support of embryonic stem cell research and said he was appeasing "the radical homosexual lobby" because of his support of a hate crimes bill. In a debate McCollum called the ads "despicable" and said Martinez was "unfit" to serve; Governor Jeb Bush phoned Martinez on the subject, and Martinez pulled the ads over the weekend. Polls had consistently showed Martinez ahead, with many undecided. But Martinez won big, with 45% of the vote, to 31% for McCollum and 14% for Gallagher. McCollum declined to endorse Martinez until 13 days after the primary. But two days after the primary, Martinez went to New York and spoke in prime time to the Republican National Convention. "Only in America can a 15-year-old boy arrive on our shores alone, not speaking the language—with a suitcase and the hope of a brighter future—and rise to serve in the Cabinet of the president of the United States. And only in America can that same young boy today stand one step away from making history as the first Cuban-American to serve in the United States Senate."

The Democratic primary was just as fractious. Deutsch, an aggressive spokesman for Al Gore during the 2000 Florida controversy, attacked Penelas for not supporting Gore vigorously enough. In ads he attacked Castor for not taking enough action against Sami al-Arian, a professor at the University of South Florida, who was indicted on terrorism charges in 2003. Castor avoided attacks on her primary opponents and, on her specialty issue, attacked the 2002 education act as fundamentally flawed; she said little about abortion. Statewide Castor won with 58% of the vote to 28% for Deutsch and 10% for Penelas.

Throughout September and October public polls showed the race a dead heat. There was plenty of contrast between the candidates on issues—the Iraq war, abortion, stem-cell research, Cuba, tax cuts, Social Security, education. Both sides spent plenty of money—Martinez $12.8 million, Castor $11.4 million. But it was a hard environment in which to get messages through: Florida airwaves were filled with ads by the presidential candidates and 527 organizations and by backers and opponents of a medical malpractice ballot measure, and local newscasts in late August and most of September were dominated by the four hurricanes that swept through the state. The Senate candidates differed on hurricane relief: Martinez called for tax-exempt development bonds for the areas worst hit and for zero interest loans to help damaged businesses; Castor called for incentives for insurance companies to open their disaster relief funds and for FEMA to pay insurance deductibles for afflicted homeowners. Martinez accused Castor of going soft on the "terrorist cell" in the University of South Florida and ran an ad featuring a retired INS agent criticizing Castor. Castor said Martinez's ads were "despicable" and said she was the only one who had taken any action against al-Arian. She ignored John Kerry and featured Bob Graham; she depicted herself as independent and Martinez as a rubber stamp for George W. Bush. The Human Rights Campaign ran an ad, aimed at Martinez's opposition to hate crimes legislation, featuring pictures recalling the murders of James Byrd in Texas and Matthew Shepard in Wyoming. In the final days Castor ran ads charging Martinez with ethical improprieties at HUD. Both also ran positive ads—Martinez more bio spots on his rise from Cuba and the refugee camp, Castor on her work on education.

On election night, the returns showed a very close race, and Castor claimed a recount would be needed. But when more complete returns came in the next morning, she conceded. Martinez won by less than 100,000 votes, 49%-48%; Castor led 57%-41% in the Gold Coast, and the I-4 corridor produced a 49%-49% tie; Martinez won 56%-42% in the rest of the state. Martinez ran ahead of Bush among Cuban-Americans. Some were unhappy with the Bush administration's limits on trips that could be made and remittances that could be sent to Cuba, measures supported by Martinez; but the prospect of a Cuban-American senator proved attractive even to some Cubans who voted for John Kerry. Martinez carried Latino voters 60%-39%, better than Bush's 56%-43%; he carried Miami-Dade County 49.2%-49.0% while Bush lost it 53%-47%. Martinez ran 1% behind Bush in the rest of the Gold Coast, 4% behind in the I-4 corridor and 3% behind in the rest of the state—but it was enough to win.

So Martinez joined Democrat Bill Nelson in the Senate. Nelson was no stranger to him: as far back as 1978, Martinez had campaigned for Nelson in his first race for the House. He got seats on the Foreign Relations, Banking and Energy committees. On the Banking Committee, Martinez has advocated legislation that would overhaul the mortgage process for consumers and implement policies he had backed at HUD. Martinez promised to work on local issues—getting a veterans hospital for Orlando, the nation's largest metropolitan area without one; alleviating traffic in central Florida—and he said that, as a former trial lawyer and a Republican, he would try to be an "honest broker" on medical malpractice. He flew to the Middle East to monitor the Palestinian elections in January 2005 and in his maiden speech in February 2005 he defended Attorney General

Alberto Gonzalez. Martinez expressed disappointment that Bush did not use his 2006 State of the Union speech to challenge Cuba for its undemocratic practices. He introduced a bill that would deny a visa to foreign entities that help Cuba to develop its oil exploration program. With Senator Ken Salazar, he introduced a bill allowing Puerto Rico to determine whether to keep is territorial status. He took a lead role in March 2005 on the bill seeking federal judicial review in the case of Terri Schiavo but was embarrassed after he unknowingly handed to Democrat Tom Harkin a memo, drafted by one of his staffers, that made mention of the political advantages presented by the case.

Martinez became the Senate's dealmaker on offshore drilling and immigration legislation. He worked with Pete Domenici, then-chairman of the Senate Energy committee, to reach a compromise on a bill that would open up a large section of the Gulf of Mexico to offshore oil and gas drilling. Concerned about Florida's beaches and tourism industry, Martinez negotiated a ban on drilling within 125 miles of the Florida Panhandle and 235 miles of Tampa and Naples. The job fell to Martinez because Nelson had irritated Domenici the year before by threatening to filibuster the legislation. Environmentalists, who opposed the deal, said he caved to pressure from his leadership, and they ran ads in Florida media urging him to rethink the compromise. When the Senate appeared headed for deadlock on a major overhaul of the nation's immigration policy, Martinez worked out a compromise with Senator Chuck Hagel in April 2006 that allowed the Senate debate to proceed by establishing different requirements for illegal immigrants to legalize their status depending on their length of time in the country. Martinez advised members of his party that anti-immigrant rhetoric and policies could alienate Hispanic voters that the party had worked hard to court. While party leaders wanted Martinez to represent the party on immigration, Martinez told the *Washington Post* he was careful to advance the issue for what he considered the right reasons. "I think it's important that just because I happen to be Hispanic that I don't allow those who might have a point of view that I wouldn't necessarily agree with to utilize who I am, my heritage, to cover for bad policy." The Senate passed the bill but clashed with the House's border enforcement approach. The Democratic takeover in 2006 gave immigration legislation new life and Martinez played a prominent role as one of 12 senators pushing for a new compromise around a guest worker program. He helped temporarily revive the bill in June 2007 after waves of amendments stalled progress. His emergence as a key player in favor of the Senate bill came at some cost back home; his approval rating in summer 2007 dropped to a three-year low.

After the 2006 election, Bush backed Martinez as his choice to become general chairman of the Republican party, which was seen as an effort to shore up support among Hispanic and Catholic voters. The choice drew criticism from some Republican National Committee members, who viewed Martinez's immigration position as "amnesty." The party approved Martinez as general chairman in January 2007, giving him a voice in the 2008 presidential election.

FIRST DISTRICT

Rep. Jeff Miller (R)

Elected Oct. 2001, 3d full term; b. June 27, 1959, St. Petersburg; home, Chumuckla; U. of FL, B.A. 1984; Methodist; married (Vicki).

Elected Office: FL House of Reps., 1998-2001.

Professional Career: Real estate broker, Henry Co. homes; Owner, Jeff Miller Real Estate; deputy sheriff.

DC Office: 1535 LHOB, 20515, 202-225-4136; Fax: 202-225-3414; Web site: jeffmiller.house.gov.

District Offices: Ft. Walton Beach, 850-664-1266; Pensacola, 850-479-1183.

Committees: *Armed Services* (13th of 29 R): Air & Land Forces; Oversight & Investigations. *Veterans' Affairs* (6th of 13 R): Health (RMM).

Group Ratings

	ADA	ACLU	AFS	LCV	ITIC	NTU	COC	ACU	CFG	FRC
2006	5	14	0	8	86	72	93	92	76	100
2005	0	—	0	17	—	72	80	92	96	100

National Journal Ratings

	2005 LIB	—	2005 CONS		2006 LIB	—	2006 CONS
Economic	29%	—	71%		9%	—	90%
Social	17%	—	83%		8%	—	92%
Foreign	0%	—	89%		0%	—	94%

Key Votes of the 109th Congress

1. Estate Tax Repeal	Y	5. Limit Interstate Abortion	Y	9. Build Border Fence	Y
2. Limit CAFE Standards	Y	6. Extend Patriot Act	Y	10. CAFTA	Y
3. FY06 Spending Curb	Y	7. Bar Same Sex Marriage	Y	11. Oppose Iraq Withdrawal	Y
4. Drilling in ANWR	Y	8. Stem Cell Research $	N	12. Detainee Tribunals	Y

Election Results

2006 general	Jeff Miller (R)	135,786	(69%)	($322,726)
	Joe Roberts (D)	62,340	(31%)	($48,383)
2006 primary	Jeff Miller (R)	unopposed		
2004 general	Jeff Miller (R)	236,604	(77%)	($279,318)
	Mark Coutu (D)	72,506	(23%)	($33,000)

Prior Winning Percentages: 2002 (75%); 2001 (66%)

The People		Race/Ethnic Origin		Ancestry	
Area size:	5,241 sq. mi.	78.0% White		USA: 10.7% German: 8.8%	
Urban population:	77.5%	14.0% Black		Irish: 8.5%	
Rural population:	22.5%	1.9% Asian		**2004 Presidential Vote**	
Pop. 2000:	639,295	0.9% Native Am.		Bush (R) 231,199	(72%)
Pop. 2005 (est):	675,685	0.1% Hawaiian		Kerry (D) 88,686	(28%)
Median income:	$36,738	2.0% Two+ races		Other 2,135	(1%)
Poverty status:	13.1%	0.2% Other		**2000 Presidential Vote**	
Military veterans:	21.7%	3.0% Hispanic Origin		Bush (R) 173,896	(69%)
				Gore (D) 78,469	(31%)
				Cook Partisan Voting Index: R +19	

Occupation   Blue collar: 24.4%   White collar: 57.1%   Gray collar: 18.6%

The "Redneck Riviera" is the affectionate local name for the Gulf Coast beaches of Florida's Panhandle, stretching from Pensacola east to Destin. This has been military country ever since John Quincy Adams persuaded Spain to sell Florida to the U.S. in 1819 to get the port of Pensacola. In October 1861, the Union defeated the Confederates in a battle to control Santa Rosa Island, the outermost spit of land protecting Pensacola Bay. A quarter century later, the site of that clash, Fort Pickens, became Apache warrior Geronimo's prison. In the 20th century, the Pensacola Naval Air Station was turned into the nation's first naval aviation training base, giving birth to carrier aviation. Today, about 20,000 people are employed at Eglin Air Force Base, which spreads over three counties and, with approximately 100,000 square miles of airspace stretching over the Gulf of Mexico to the Florida Keys, is considered the largest air base in the free world. Eglin developed the BLU-82 "Daisy Cutter" bomb that was used in Afghanistan, and this was the test site for the largest conventional bomb in the U.S. arsenal, the 21,000-pound ordnance referred to as the "Mother of All Bombs."

The western panhandle of Florida, closer to Houston than to Miami, is culturally part of Dixie. Until recently, it was economically backward and heavily dependent on the military. As the South has become more prosperous, however, the shore has attracted vacationing and retiring Southerners to its vast, fine-grained white sand beaches, perhaps the finest in the Lower 48, and its pleasant inlet-filled bays; it also has become a leading spring break destination for college students. The region has long been culturally and economically conservative, with a strong pro-military bent.

The 1st Congressional District of Florida is so far west that it's in the Central time zone. Pensacola's Escambia County, where about half the district's people live, is the state's westernmost county. The time zone issue became a sore point in 2000, when TV networks announced that Florida's polls had closed at 7 p.m. Eastern time, though they were still open in the Panhandle, and then declared Al Gore the winner of Florida's electoral votes 10 minutes before the Panhandle's polls had closed; without that misinformation, a few thousand votes might have been cast for George W. Bush here and made the whole Florida controversy unnecessary. The district's shoreline runs from Pensacola, adjoining the Alabama border, through Fort Walton Beach to the west side of Destin. Inland, the 1st stretches further east, taking in rural Walton, Holmes and Washington Counties.

The population here has grown steadily, with young civilians, not just military retirees, moving in and shifting attention towards education and quality-of-life issues. In 2004, four massive hurricanes roared through the region, with devastating effect: in Pensacola alone, 45,000 homes were deemed unlivable. In 2005, Hurricane Katrina also left its mark here. With the most military veterans of any district in the nation, the 1st District is strongly Republican. It voted 69%-31% for George W. Bush in 2000 and 72%-28% in 2004, his best numbers in the state. In 2004, a columnist for the *Pensacola News Journal* wrote that it was time to consider creation of a separate state, or independent commonwealth, of West Florida. "We don't have much in common with the people inhabiting what I call peninsular Florida," wrote Jerry Maygarden. "I'm convinced that the further south you drive, the further north you get."

The congressman from the 1st District is Jeff Miller, a Republican who won a special election in October 2001. The son of a pioneering farm family that settled in central Florida in the mid-1800s, Miller grew up in Levy County, where his parents raised cattle. He graduated from the University of Florida and became an aide to the state's long-time agriculture commissioner, Democrat Doyle Conner. In 1998 he moved to Santa Rosa County, his wife's family's home, and began to sell real estate. Also in 1998, a year after he switched to the Republican Party, he ran his first campaign, challenging a Republican state representative who had received some negative press after an altercation with a state trooper. Miller won 53%-47% out of only 6,000 votes cast. Not long afterwards, the 1st District seat came open with the resignation of Joe Scarborough, one of the most outspoken members of the Republican Class of 1994 and now a talk show host on MSNBC; Miller quickly became the favorite of national party leaders. Sensitive to coastal interests, the major candidates claimed to be ardent environmentalists, an unusual twist in a Republican primary. Miller's best-known opponent was state Representative Randy Knepper, chief of staff to the district's former Democratic Congressman Earl Hutto, who retired in 1994. Scarborough endorsed Miller as "a strong voice for northwest Florida." In the six-candidate contest, Miller got 54% to only 15% for Knepper, just behind the 16% for businessman Michael Francisco, a decorated combat pilot. National Democrats made no perceptible effort to win this seat that they held less than seven years earlier, and Miller won the general election by 66%-28% over a former Republican.

In the House, Miller has compiled a mostly conservative record, though a bit to the center on economic issues. In contrast to the vocal Scarborough, he gained a reputation for being soft-spoken and a good listener. He won seats on the Armed Services and Veterans' Affairs committees, obvious assignments for this district. He made multiple visits to U.S. troops in Afghanistan and Iraq and praised the conduct of the war. He worked to protect local military facilities in the base-closing review. When Jacksonville subsequently cooled to its proposed acquisition of the 250 F-18 fighter jets and support staff from Oceana naval air station in Virginia Beach, he proposed Pensacola Bay as an alternative for the jets. In 2004, when Democrats were seeking to force a House vote on Miller's bill to provide a 100% annuity to surviving military spouses, he convinced Republican leaders to call up the bill and avoid a partisan conflict; the measure was passed into law. He joined Senator Bill Nelson in seeking a review by the Environmental Protection Agency of a 1994 decision that allowed toxic chemicals to collect in the aquifer that supplies drinking water to Pensacola. A long-standing foe of oil and gas drilling in the eastern Gulf of Mexico, he relented to a deal in 2006 that opened up some drilling off shore but included a bar on drilling rigs in a military training range that extends at least 200 miles south of Fort Walton Beach. He sponsored a bill to place the face of Ronald Reagan on the half-dollar coin. With a group of former federal officials, Miller called for denying pensions to members of Congress who have been expelled from office. To the dismay of some Republicans, the House did not pass the bill until the Democratic takeover in 2007. In the minority, he became the ranking Republican on the Health Subcommittee at Veterans' Affairs.

In the 2002 primary, Miller faced a rematch with special election primary runner-up Francisco, who criticized his lack of military experience. Miller won 64%-36%. Since then, Democrats have run token challengers against him.

SECOND DISTRICT

Rep. Allen Boyd (D)

Elected 1996, 6th term; b. June 6, 1945, Valdosta, GA; home, Monticello; N. FL Jr. Col., A.A. 1966, FL St. U., B.S. 1969; Methodist; married (Cissy).

Military Career: Army 1969-71 (Vietnam).

Elected Office: FL House of Reps., 1989-96.

Professional Career: Farmer.

DC Office: 1227 LHOB, 20515, 202-225-5235; Fax: 202-225-5615; Web site: www.house.gov/boyd.

District Offices: Panama City, 850-785-0812; Tallahassee, 850-561-3979.

Committees: *Appropriations* (22d of 37 D): Agriculture, Rural Development, FDA & Related Agencies; Military Construction, Veterans Affairs & Related Agencies; Defense. *Budget* (12th of 22 D).

Group Ratings

	ADA	ACLU	AFS	LCV	ITIC	NTU	COC	ACU	CFG	FRC
2006	50	62	71	33	71	27	93	63	38	57
2005	80	—	100	78	—	21	70	42	25	25

National Journal Ratings

	2005 LIB	—	2005 CONS		2006 LIB	—	2006 CONS
Economic	56%	—	44%		56%	—	44%
Social	58%	—	41%		58%	—	42%
Foreign	58%	—	41%		55%	—	45%

Key Votes of the 109th Congress

1. Estate Tax Repeal	N	5. Limit Interstate Abortion	Y	9. Build Border Fence	Y
2. Limit CAFE Standards	Y	6. Extend Patriot Act	N	10. CAFTA	N
3. FY06 Spending Curb	N	7. Bar Same Sex Marriage	Y	11. Oppose Iraq Withdrawal	P
4. Drilling in ANWR	Y	8. Stem Cell Research $	Y	12. Detainee Tribunals	Y

Election Results

2006 general	Allen Boyd (D)	unopposed		($615,784)
2006 primary	Allen Boyd (D)	unopposed		
2004 general	Allen Boyd (D)	201,577	(62%)	($2,064,646)
	Bev Kilmer (R)	125,399	(38%)	($1,132,998)

Prior Winning Percentages: 2002 (67%); 2000 (72%); 1998 (100%); 1996 (59%)

The People		Race/Ethnic Origin	Ancestry	
Area size:	11,141 sq. mi.	71.5% White	USA: 10.3%	English: 8.0%
Urban population:	62.1%	22.1% Black	Irish: 7.9%	
Rural population:	37.9%	1.2% Asian	**2004 Presidential Vote**	
Pop. 2000:	639,295	0.5% Native Am.	Bush (R) 181,300	(54%)
Pop. 2005 (est):	685,407	0.0% Hawaiian	Kerry (D) 153,164	(46%)
Median income:	$34,718	1.3% Two+ races	Other 1,346	(0%)
Poverty status:	16.5%	0.1% Other	**2000 Presidential Vote**	
Military veterans:	15.3%	3.3% Hispanic Origin	Bush (R) 132,275	(53%)
			Gore (D) 118,758	(47%)
			Cook Partisan Voting Index: R + 2	
Occupation	Blue collar: 19.3%	White collar: 61.7%	Gray collar: 19.1%	

For most of the 36 days from November 7 to December 12, 2000, Tallahassee was the center of the political universe. Many wondered why this small city, in the middle of swampy lowlands and far from Florida's booming cities and beachfronts, should be the capital of the nation's fourth-largest state. The answer is that it was chosen back when Florida's modest population lived mostly along the state's northern tier, placing Tallahassee, more or less, at the state's center of gravity. Ralph Waldo Emerson, visiting Tallahassee in the 19th century, called it a "grotesque place, rapidly settled by public officers, land speculators and desperadoes." Today the countryside around Tallahassee is distinctly Dixie: Cotton fields, soft pine stands, catfish farms, large families, small towns with big churches. Until recently, Tallahassee was little more than a Spanish-mossed county seat with a handsome Creole capitol, built in 1845 and preserved opposite its 1977 skyscraper replacement, and a pair of state universities. Since the 1980s, it has spread out and become a middling-sized city, with a tight-knit and sometimes fractious political and legal elite, bringing a taste of newly urbanized Florida to the state's north. Tallahassee has not yet attained the critical mass of Sacramento, Austin, or Albany, but perhaps it is on its way as the state legislature inches closer to professional status.

The 2d Congressional District of Florida is centered on Tallahassee, and extends along the Gulf coast west to Destin and east to the Suwanee River, which empties into the Gulf in the only part of Florida where the beach is still undeveloped. Inland, the 2d runs north to the Alabama and Georgia borders, and far enough east to be within an hour's drive of Jacksonville. Historically, this was Democratic country, Jeffersonian and segregationist. Today, it is still mostly Democratic, though for different reasons: More than one in three Tallahassee area jobs are in city and state government, three times the statewide level. The district, 22% black, includes Gadsden County, the state's only black-majority county. Growth is spreading south into Wakulla County, which grew 91% from 1990 to 2004, more than all but three others in Florida. There is similar growth along the beach areas near Destin which have attracted affluent families to "new urbanist" communities like Seaside and Rosemary Beach. In Tallahassee, the recent growth rate has surpassed that of Miami and Tampa. But for all this recent growth, this remains the part of Florida with the highest percentage of native Floridians.

With state government, two universities and many public employee union members, Tallahassee and Leon County have voted solidly for Democratic presidential nominees; the Florida law that establishes Leon County as the venue for election cases clearly favors Democrats. Beyond Leon County, which casts nearly 40% of the district's votes, partisan performance is less predictable. Gadsden County is heavily Democratic; the Gulf beach areas tend to be Republican. The 2d District voted twice for George W. Bush, but in 2002 it gave a hefty margin to Democrat Bill McBride over Governor Jeb Bush, who was disliked by most public employee unions. The antipathy was mutual: In his second inaugural speech in 2003, Bush said a goal should be to "make these buildings around us empty of workers." In 2006, Charlie Crist also struggled here. He lost only 8 of 67 counties, but 3 of them—Gadsden, Leon and Jefferson—were here.

The congressman from the 2d District is Allen Boyd, a Democrat first elected in 1996. A lifelong farmer, Boyd grew up in Monticello in Jefferson County just east of Tallahassee. He graduated from Florida State and served in Vietnam. His political career began when he won a special election to the state House in 1989. Boyd decided to run for the House in 1996 when Pete Peterson, a moderate Democrat and Vietnam prisoner-of-war, retired after three terms, saying he believed in term limits. In the Democratic primary, Boyd took 48% of the vote to 26% for Leon County Commissioner Anita Davis. Boyd easily won the runoff 64%-36%. In the general, Boyd campaigned with Blue Dog conservative Democrats and outspent the Republican by 2–1 to win a solid 59%-40% victory.

In the House, Boyd has worked as a behind the scenes consensus builder. With one of the House's most centrist voting records, he called himself a "moderate Democrat with a social conscience." He was unperturbed when animal rights advocates picketed the Annual Boyd Family Dove Hunt, and was the only Florida Democrat to vote for an amendment that helped kill the 1999 gun control bill. He opposed George W. Bush's 2001 tax cut but voted to repeal the Clinton administration's ergonomics regulation. Later, he opposed trade promotion authority, but he voted to authorize the use of force in Iraq, though he said that he wanted Bush to get a United Nations resolution before launching the invasion. In 2003 he was one of 16 House Democrats who voted for the Medicare/prescription drug bill; Minority Leader Nancy Pelosi voiced her unhappiness to Boyd. With Republican John Peterson of Pennsylvania, Boyd chairs the Rural Caucus. As a member of the Appropriations Committee, he has delivered largess to local universities, farmers and military facilities. He joined the Defense Subcommittee in 2007.

In December 2004, Boyd created some heartburn among Democrats when he co-sponsored with Republican Jim Kolbe a bipartisan Social Security package including personal retirement accounts and lower benefits. He said that he would seek additional Democratic supporters, but he ultimately found none in the House. His goal, he said, was "a fair balance between preserving the basic benefit of Social Security while also encouraging individual responsibility"; he blamed Bush for failing to reach across the aisle, and for having "invoked fear among our nation's retirees." In February 2005, Moveon.org ran television ads in Boyd's district criticizing Bush's proposals. Soon after the 2006 election, he and other Blue Dog leaders met with Bush to explore possible areas of agreement, without preconditions. "The Blue Dogs believe in partnership, not partisanship," he said.

Boyd has been easily reelected, despite unfavorable redistricting changes. In early 2003, after Senator Bob Graham launched a presidential campaign, Boyd made moves to run for the Senate. By July, he had raised significant money and had a team of consultants in place. But in October, Boyd announced he would not run. In 2004, he was challenged by state Representative Bev Kilmer. She raised substantial funds and said she would support George W. Bush's agenda on defense, terrorism, health care and the economy. Boyd countered that he sometimes supported Bush, but said that voters wanted somebody who would be independent and represent their interests. He won handily, 62%-38%, despite losing big in the two western counties along the beach; he won 71% of the vote in Leon County. He endorsed a 2006 proposal by Florida Democrats to take redistricting from the Legislature by creating a commission.

THIRD DISTRICT

Rep. Corrine Brown (D)

Elected 1992, 8th term; b. Nov. 11, 1946, Jacksonville; home, Jacksonville; FL A&M, B.S. 1969, M.S., 1971; Baptist; single.

Elected Office: FL House of Reps., 1982-92.

Professional Career: Prof., FL Commun. Col., 1977-82, Guidance Counselor, 1982-92.

DC Office: 2336 RHOB, 20515, 202-225-0123; Fax: 202-225-2256; Web site: www.house.gov/corrinebrown.

District Offices: Jacksonville, 904-354-1652; Orlando, 407-872-0656.

Committees: *Transportation & Infrastructure* (7th of 41 D): Railroads, Pipelines & Hazardous Materials (Chmn.); Coast Guard & Maritime Transportation; Aviation. *Veterans' Affairs* (2d of 16 D): Health.

Group Ratings

	ADA	ACLU	AFS	LCV	ITIC	NTU	COC	ACU	CFG	FRC
2006	100	95	100	92	29	10	40	20	10	0
2005	95	—	100	94	—	11	42	0	0	8

National Journal Ratings

	2005 LIB	—	2005 CONS	2006 LIB	—	2006 CONS
Economic	80%	—	19%	74%	—	23%
Social	74%	—	26%	75%	—	25%
Foreign	69%	—	31%	73%	—	26%

Key Votes of the 109th Congress

1. Estate Tax Repeal	N	5. Limit Interstate Abortion	*	9. Build Border Fence	Y
2. Limit CAFE Standards	N	6. Extend Patriot Act	N	10. CAFTA	N
3. FY06 Spending Curb	N	7. Bar Same Sex Marriage	N	11. Oppose Iraq Withdrawal	N
4. Drilling in ANWR	N	8. Stem Cell Research $	Y	12. Detainee Tribunals	N

Election Results

2006 general	Corrine Brown (D)	unopposed	($476,775)
2006 primary	Corrine Brown (D)	unopposed	
2004 general	Corrine Brown (D)	unopposed	($450,589)

Prior Winning Percentages: 2002 (59%); 2000 (58%); 1998 (55%); 1996 (61%); 1994 (58%); 1992 (59%)

The People		Race/Ethnic Origin	Ancestry	
Area size:	2,097 sq. mi.	38.4% White	USA: 6.4%	German: 5.2%
Urban population:	89.7%	49.3% Black	Irish: 4.9%	
Rural population:	10.3%	1.6% Asian	**2004 Presidential Vote**	
Pop. 2000:	639,295	0.3% Native Am.	Kerry (D) 151,466	(65%)
Pop. 2005 (est):	634,503	0.0% Hawaiian	Bush (R) 81,778	(35%)
Median income:	$29,785	2.1% Two+ races	Other 42	(0%)
Poverty status:	21.5%	0.2% Other	**2000 Presidential Vote**	
Military veterans:	14.2%	8.0% Hispanic Origin	Gore (D) 110,501	(65%)
			Bush (R) 59,144	(35%)
			Cook Partisan Voting Index: D +16	

Occupation   Blue collar: 26.6%   White collar: 51.8%   Gray collar: 21.6%

Before the Civil War, most of Florida was still an uncharted watery wilderness, festooned with exotic greenery, inhabited by unusual animals: a part of the United States so far out of the experience of most Americans as to seem foreign. As late as 1940, Florida had the smallest population of any southern state, and most of the people here lived in classic Dixie rural counties with small courthouse towns, where civic affairs were run by the richest white men; blacks lived in poorly constructed, unpainted shotgun shacks propped up on blocks, with little money and no vote. This was a land of swamps, lakes and orange groves, of Marjorie Kinnan Rawlings's Cross Creek, where she wrote the great children's classic *The Yearling*, and the Florida of the broad St. Johns River, one of the few North American rivers that flows (if only sluggishly) north, through orange grove country to the port of Jacksonville, which was for many years Florida's largest city.

The 3d Congressional District of Florida occupies much of this swampy terrain. The district was created in 1992 to be north Florida's black majority seat, and has had three sets of boundaries. The district borders five Republican-held districts, each of which was designed to shift as many Democrats as possible to the 3d to strengthen Republicans elsewhere. In its current form it follows the St. Johns River upstream from center city Jacksonville to downtown Orlando, reaching out to pluck additional minority and Democratic voters from Sanford, where Amtrak's Auto Train unloads its Florida-bound travelers, and Gainesville, home of the University of Florida. Along the way, the district takes in smaller black settlements, such as lettuce-producing Zellwood, and Eatonville, home of author Zora Neale Hurston. In time, this relatively unpopulated, lake-filled region may see itself become Florida's next development frontier. But between 2000 and 2005, despite the sizable growth in the more prosperous neighboring districts, the 3d District was one of only 2 districts in the state to lose population. The district is 49% black—the third-highest of any Florida district—and 8% Hispanic. It is solidly Democratic.

The congresswoman from the 3d District is Corrine Brown, a Democrat first elected in 1992. She grew up in Jacksonville, taught at the community college, was a guidance counselor and in 1982 was elected to the Florida House. With her Jacksonville base, she was the clear favorite in this new district. In the Democratic primary, she faced white talk radio host Andy Johnson, who called himself "the blackest candidate in the race." Brown led 43%-31% in the primary and won 64%-36% in the runoff; she won the general 59%-41%. Brown has compiled a liberal record on most issues. In this district where many voters work at military bases she tends to support high defense spending; she argues that the military can be a source of opportunity. On the Veterans Committee she sought additional veterans cemeteries for Florida, which is the home to more veterans than any other state except California; new cemeteries were approved for Jacksonville and Sarasota in 2003. On the Transportation and Infrastructure Subcommittee, she worked on legislation to strengthen security at the ports. In the majority, she chairs the Railroads, Pipelines and Hazardous Materials Subcommittee; she listed rail safety and security as top priorities and planned to deal with long-term Amtrak funding issues.

Brown has had spirited campaign opposition, resulting largely from personal issues of her own making. Her most difficult contest came in 1998. That April the *St. Petersburg Times* reported that she received $10,000 from Baptist minister Henry Lyons, who had since been indicted on theft charges. In June the same paper reported that her daughter was given a $50,000 Lexus by agents of African millionaire Foutanga Sissoko; he had been imprisoned in Miami on federal charges of paying an illegal gratuity to a Customs Service officer, and Brown worked furiously to get him released, lobbying Attorney General Janet Reno to have him deported to Africa to continue his humanitarian work. A third charge was that she kept a jazz singer on her payroll as a "congressional outreach specialist," who occasionally visited the district from her New York City home. Brown reacted with fury: she filed a criminal contempt charge against the *Times* reporters with the Capitol Police, claiming they "accosted" her and their questions made her cry. A federal prosecutor said there was not enough to indict them for impeding a member of Congress. These charges attracted national Republican attention and a presentable candidate: Bill Randall, also black, a former General Motors manager who had become a minister. He opposed abortion, favored local control of schools and school vouchers. The charges hurt Brown: she won by only 55%-45%.

The Congressional Accountability Project subsequently requested that the House ethics committee investigate the $10,000 contribution and the Lexus gift; her daughter later sold the car and gave the proceeds to charity. In September 2000 the committee concluded that Brown "demonstrated, at the least, poor judgment and created substantial concerns regarding both the appearance of impropriety and the reputation of the House," but dropped the case because it was unable to question key witnesses, including Sissoko. She faced a vigorous reelection challenge from Republican Jennifer Carroll, a retired Navy officer with 20 years of service, who criticized Brown for lack of vision and an inability to work with people. Brown, who called Carroll "a zero" and "a Republican puppet," was outspent by Carroll, who is also black. With help from an October campaign rally with Bill Clinton and a strong grass-roots organization, Brown won 58%-42%. In 2002 Carroll again challenged Brown. But local Republicans were not enthusiastic about Carroll's candidacy in this heavily Democratic district. Brown won 59%-41%, again with huge leads in Jacksonville and Orlando. She has been unopposed since then. Barring unexpected problems, she appears secure until the next redistricting.

Her outspoken partisan views caused her problems when Republicans ran the House. In February 2004, she criticized a briefing on the Haiti crisis by saying that administration representatives were "a bunch of white men," and reportedly said, "you all look alike to me." After Republican Henry Bonilla said that she should resign, Brown apologized, but she continued to call the Haiti policy racist. In July, under parliamentary pressure, she rescinded her comment to the House that Republicans "stole the election" in 2000.

FOURTH DISTRICT

Rep. Ander Crenshaw (R)

Elected 2000, 4th term; b. Sept. 1, 1944, Jacksonville; home, Jacksonville; U. of GA, B.A. 1966, U. of FL, J.D. 1969; Episcopalian; married (Kitty).

Elected Office: FL House of Reps., 1972-78; FL Senate 1986-93.

Professional Career: Investment banker, 1980-2000.

DC Office: 127 CHOB, 20515, 202-225-2501; Fax: 202-225-2504; Web site: crenshaw.house.gov.

District Offices: Jacksonville, 904-598-0481; Lake City, 386-365-3316.

Committees: *Appropriations* (25th of 29 R): Military Construction, Veterans Affairs & Related Agencies; State, Foreign Operations & Related Programs.

Group Ratings

	ADA	ACLU	AFS	LCV	ITIC	NTU	COC	ACU	CFG	FRC
2006	0	5	0	8	100	53	100	84	56	100
2005	5	—	0	11	—	55	89	92	60	92

National Journal Ratings

	2005 LIB	—	2005 CONS		2006 LIB	—	2006 CONS
Economic	24%	—	74%		12%	—	86%
Social	15%	—	84%		11%	—	85%
Foreign	15%	—	84%		17%	—	73%

Key Votes of the 109th Congress

1. Estate Tax Repeal	Y	5. Limit Interstate Abortion	Y	9. Build Border Fence	Y
2. Limit CAFE Standards	Y	6. Extend Patriot Act	Y	10. CAFTA	Y
3. FY06 Spending Curb	Y	7. Bar Same Sex Marriage	Y	11. Oppose Iraq Withdrawal	Y
4. Drilling in ANWR	Y	8. Stem Cell Research $	N	12. Detainee Tribunals	Y

Election Results

2006 general	Ander Crenshaw (R) 141,759	(70%)	($1,202,193)
	Robert Harms (D) 61,704	(30%)	($42,727)
2006 primary	Ander Crenshaw (R) .... unopposed		
2004 general	Ander Crenshaw (R) .... unopposed		($279,540)

Prior Winning Percentages: 2002 (100%); 2000 (67%)

The People		Race/Ethnic Origin	Ancestry	
Area size:	4,368 sq. mi.	77.8% White	USA: 9.7%	German: 9.0%
Urban population:	78.2%	13.5% Black	Irish: 8.7%	
Rural population:	21.8%	2.4% Asian	**2004 Presidential Vote**	
Pop. 2000:	639,295	0.3% Native Am.	Bush (R) 227,431	(69%)
Pop. 2005 (est):	690,981	0.1% Hawaiian	Kerry (D) 100,414	(31%)
Median income:	$43,947	1.5% Two+ races	Other 744	(0%)
Poverty status:	9.1%	0.1% Other	**2000 Presidential Vote**	
Military veterans:	17.1%	4.2% Hispanic Origin	Bush (R) 154,615	(66%)
			Gore (D) 80,227	(34%)
			Cook Partisan Voting Index: R +16	

Occupation	Blue collar: 20.6%	White collar: 64.8%	Gray collar: 14.7%

With a metropolitan area of 1.2 million people, Jacksonville is beginning to overcome its reputation as Florida's overlooked city. Not long ago, Jacksonville was considered a backwater, dominated by insurance and smelly paper mills. It now boasts a National Football League franchise, the Jaguars; bold new skyscrapers looming above a wide river; a shopping mall that overshadows gridded streets and tiny shotgun houses; the wide freeways sidestep primeval wetlands on their way to huge beachfront subdivisions. The city received favorable reviews when it hosted the 2005 Super Bowl, even though it has far fewer hotel rooms than the usual sites; to meet the demands for lodging, cruise ships docked in the harbor, which has grown as a destination for cargo and passenger operations. With the Mayport Naval Station and the Naval Air Station, Jacksonville has a significant military employment base (they are the two largest metro area employers). Shrewd marketing has lured big-name private sector companies; Jacksonville is the headquarters of railway giant CSX and has big operations of Publix supermarkets, UPS and Bank of America. Business leaders have talked of making the area into the "Silicon Valley of Logistics," to build on its land, air and sea transportation facilities. The metro area grew 33% from 1990 to 2004.

The 4th Congressional District of Florida includes much of Jacksonville (minus the mostly black neighborhoods, which are in the 3d District) as well as a northern tier of counties along the Georgia border that runs all the way west to Tallahassee. This northern tier is sleepy territory punctuated by small towns like White Springs, Lake City, and Raiford (home to a big state prison); it is criss-crossed by Interstates 10 and 75. Some 70% of the population is in Jacksonville and rapidly growing Nassau County, just to the north. The boosterish Jacksonville civic culture and significant military presence make the 4th a pro-business, pro-military and pro-Republican district. George W. Bush won 66% of the district's vote in 2000 and 69% in 2004, both his second highest percentage in Florida.

The congressman from the 4th District is Ander Crenshaw, a Republican first elected in 2000. He grew up in Jacksonville and attended the University of Georgia on a basketball scholarship, then graduated from the University of Florida law school. His wife's father, Claude Kirk, was elected governor, the first Republican since Reconstruction, in 1966, then defeated in 1970. Crenshaw was elected to the state House in 1972 and served for six years until he ran unsuccessfully for secretary of state; he then became an investment banker. In 1980 he ran for the Senate and finished third of six in the 1980 Republican primary won by Paula Hawkins. From 1986 until 1993 he served in the state Senate, and in 1992 became the first Republican state Senate president in 118 years. He ran for governor in 1994 but finished fourth in the primary, far behind Jeb Bush, who narrowly lost to Lawton Chiles in November. Crenshaw's opportunity to run for the House came in 2000 when Republican Tillie Fowler announced that she would honor her promise to serve only four terms. Crenshaw was promptly endorsed by local Republican leaders, which discouraged several potential candidates. He won the primary 70%-30% and the general election 67%-31%.

In the House, Crenshaw is a reliable conservative. Although his tall frame makes him hard to miss in a crowd, he has not sought attention. He has cited approvingly the comment by Ronald Reagan: "There's no limit to what you can do as long as you don't care who gets the credit." He displayed his political savvy by becoming freshman class liaison to the Republican leadership, which admitted him to weekly leadership meetings, and he became friends with Majority Leader Tom DeLay and Majority Whip Roy Blunt. Blunt later named him to chair a House GOP budget task force. In his second term, he won a seat on Appropriations, where his top priorities were the district's large military and veterans' facilities. He pushed hard to pass a bill for new veterans' cemeteries in Jacksonville and Sarasota, which George W. Bush signed in November 2003, and he fought for expanded disability coverage for Gulf War veterans. In January 2005, Crenshaw described as "short-sighted, short-term thinking" reports that the *USS John F. Kennedy*, which was scheduled for an overhaul in Mayport, might instead be decommissioned. "Our national security demands at least 12 carriers, if not more." The carrier was one of only two that is oil-powered and its fate became clear once the Pentagon announced it planned to reduce its carriers to 11. When the Navy announced in April 2005 it was canceling a $378 million overhaul of the ship, Crenshaw attached a provision to the 2005 emergency supplemental that would delay plans to decommission the *Kennedy*. But the military barons on Capitol—led by Senate Armed Services Committee chairman John Warner, who was focused on other spending priorities—ultimately went along with the Pentagon. Still, Crenshaw claimed some credit for local success in the base-review process, which is expected to bring several thousand jobs to Jacksonville. He raised nearly $1 million for other House Republican candidates as part of his campaign against Paul Ryan of Wisconsin for the chairmanship of the House Budget Committee after the 2006 election; the post turned out to be ranking minority member, and Ryan won.

Crenshaw obviously has a safe seat, and has turned down opportunities for other statewide bids. He was reelected twice without general election opposition. In 2006, after downplaying his past ties to DeLay, he defeated lightly-funded Democratic challenger Robert Harms, 70%-30%.

FIFTH DISTRICT

Rep. Ginny Brown-Waite (R)

Elected 2002, 3d term; b. Oct. 5, 1943, Albany, NY; home, Brooksville; S.U.N.Y. Albany, B.S. 1976, Russell Sage Col., M.S. 1984; Catholic; married (Harvey).

Elected Office: Hernando Cnty. Commissioner, 1990-92; FL Senate, 1992-2002.

Professional Career: Small business owner; Legis. Dir., NY Senate, 1972-90.

DC Office: 414 CHOB, 20515, 202-225-1002; Fax: 202-226-6559; Web site: www.house.gov/brown-waite/.

District Offices: Brooksville, 352-799-8354; Dade City, 352-567-6707.

Committees: *Financial Services* (19th of 33 R): Capital Markets, Insurance & Government Sponsored Enterprises; Financial Institutions & Consumer Credit. *Homeland Security* (12th of 15 R): Transportation Security & Infrastructure Protection; Emerging Threats, Cybersecurity & Science and Technology. *Veterans' Affairs* (8th of 13 R): Oversight & Investigations (RMM).

Group Ratings

	ADA	ACLU	AFS	LCV	ITIC	NTU	COC	ACU	CFG	FRC
2006	15	10	14	17	86	63	87	88	71	71
2005	10	—	0	11	—	58	88	87	57	85

National Journal Ratings

	2005 LIB	—	2005 CONS		2006 LIB	—	2006 CONS
Economic	40%	—	60%		37%	—	63%
Social	36%	—	63%		15%	—	84%
Foreign	21%	—	78%		17%	—	73%

Key Votes of the 109th Congress

1. Estate Tax Repeal	Y	5. Limit Interstate Abortion	Y	9. Build Border Fence	Y
2. Limit CAFE Standards	Y	6. Extend Patriot Act	Y	10. CAFTA	Y
3. FY06 Spending Curb	Y	7. Bar Same Sex Marriage	Y	11. Oppose Iraq Withdrawal	Y
4. Drilling in ANWR	Y	8. Stem Cell Research $	Y	12. Detainee Tribunals	Y

Election Results

2006 general	Ginny Brown-Waite (R)	162,421	(60%)	($784,889)
	John Russell (D)	108,959	(40%)	($88,703)
2006 primary	Ginny Brown-Waite (R)	unopposed		
2004 general	Ginny Brown-Waite (R)	240,315	(66%)	($787,436)
	Robert Whittel (D)	124,140	(34%)	($140,742)

Prior Winning Percentages: 2002 (48%)

The People		Race/Ethnic Origin	Ancestry	
Area size:	4,801 sq. mi.	87.7% White	German: 13.0%	Irish: 10.5%
Urban population:	64.5%	4.5% Black	English: 10.1%	
Rural population:	35.5%	0.8% Asian	**2004 Presidential Vote**	
Pop. 2000:	639,295	0.3% Native Am.	Bush (R) 221,259	(58%)
Pop. 2005 (est):	811,341	0.0% Hawaiian	Kerry (D) 156,632	(41%)
Median income:	$34,815	0.9% Two+ races	Other 1,948	(1%)
Poverty status:	10.6%	0.1% Other	**2000 Presidential Vote**	
Military veterans:	21.5%	5.6% Hispanic Origin	Bush (R) 147,231	(54%)
			Gore (D) 124,982	(46%)
			Cook Partisan Voting Index: R + 5	

Occupation   Blue collar: 26.1%   White collar: 55.2%   Gray collar: 18.7%

Over the past quarter century, Florida's urban areas have grown in almost every direction, occupying the high ground between the swamps that still take up much of the state's peninsula. The pattern of development is evident in counties to the north and east of St. Petersburg and Tampa, where subdivisions, trailer parks and shopping centers with Eckerd drug stores and Publix and Winn-Dixie supermarkets sprang up in what previously were sleepy little towns and farm areas with low brick buildings baking in the Florida sun. This area—a haven for manatees, the unusual and beloved sea mammal—has seen suburban development run up the spines of U.S. 19, just off the Gulf Coast, and U.S. 41 and I-75 inland alongside orange groves. Though there are plenty of working people here, this is mainly retirement country; residents are comfortable though not usually affluent. One of every four residents is over 65, and Citrus and Hernando County have a higher percentage of military veterans than any other Florida county but one; Citrus County has the second-highest percentage of retirees (33%) in the state. Drawn by plenteous lakes, green scenery and a pleasant climate, retirees from Michigan, Indiana and Ohio flocked here by taking Interstate 75 south—a pattern distinct from the retirees who drove Interstate 95 from the Boston-Washington corridor to such destinations as Palm Beach, Fort Lauderdale and Miami.

The 5th Congressional District of Florida occupies much of this rapidly-growing area. Between 2000 and 2005 it added 172,000 new residents, more than any other congressional district in the state. The beach areas in Levy, Citrus and Hernando Counties are largely undeveloped; the bulk of the population lives inland, in such places as Citrus Springs in Citrus County, Brooksville in Hernando County, Zephyrhills and Land o' Lakes in Pasco County, and Clermont in Lake County. More than two-thirds of the population is in Pasco, Hernando and Citrus; Sumter County is growing rapidly in part due to a massive retirement community of 65,000 persons known as the "Villages," which is split between the 5th and 6th Districts. The district has 251,000 Social Security recipients, 39% of the population, more than any other district in the country and 65,000 more than any other district in Florida. Politically, this is marginal territory. The district lines were drawn by Republicans in 2002 to make the district more Republican; they raised the Bush 2000 percentage from 46% to 54%. That percentage went up to 58% in 2004, as volunteers in the Bush campaign registered new Republicans and made sure they voted absentee or on election day. In Pasco County turnout was up 31% from 2000 to 2004, and the Bush percentage rose from a losing 48% to a winning 54%.

The congresswoman from the 5th District is Ginny Brown-Waite, a Republican first elected in 2002. She grew up in Albany, New York, and graduated from State University of New York at Albany and from Russell Sage College. She worked for two decades as a Republican staffer in the New York state Senate. She moved to Spring Hill in 1987, worked as a health care consultant and became active in politics. In 1990 she was elected to the Hernando County Commission. In 1992 she was elected to the state Senate, after drawing attention for her successful efforts to block a local mining company's controversial plan to burn hazardous waste. As a member of the Senate congressional redistricting committee, Brown-Waite was well positioned to shape the 5th District boundaries. Republican leaders had asked her to run for the House in 1996, but she didn't think the district was winnable; in 2002, she helped to draw a district that was, and she gave it a try. In the primary, health care consultant Don Gessner said he was the only "true conservative" and he criticized Brown-Waite's willingness to vote across party lines. His attacks had some resonance, but she won 58%-42%. In the general, she faced Democratic incumbent Karen Thurman, who won the district in 1992 after chairing the state Senate congressional redistricting committee. This was one of the most competitive contests in the country. Abortion was a key area of disagreement. Both said they supported abortion rights, but Brown-Waite highlighted Thurman's vote against the partial-birth abortion ban as evidence of Thurman's fealty to the Democratic party line. Thurman outspent Brown-Waite 2-to-1 but Brown-Waite benefited from a late visit by George W. Bush and the strong showing of Governor Jeb Bush, who carried every county in the district. Brown-Waite won 48%-46%. This was an election decided by redistricting: Thurman carried the parts of the district she had previously represented, which cast 49% of the votes, by a 52%-43% margin. But Brown-Waite carried the new parts of the district 53%-41%.

In the House, Brown-Waite was one of five Republicans to vote against the bill to get federal courts to review the case of Terri Schiavo in March 2005. But she has a mostly conservative voting record, toward the center on some economic issues. On budget issues, she styled herself as a fiscal hawk with demands for spending restraint. But she took a different approach at the Veterans' Affairs Committee, where she stressed her independence and worked hard to expand benefits. The House passed her proposal to reduce long waits for veterans to get medical treatment, and she cosponsored another bill for faster filling of prescriptions. She helped to broker the deal to permit disabled retirees to receive both their pensions and their full veterans disability benefits. When France opposed military action in Iraq, Brown-Waite proposed removal of the remains of World War II veterans buried in France. As the Social Security debate opened in 2005, she was cautious as she told Bush that she "won't drink the Kool Aid." On Financial Services, she filed a bill seeking to limit rising insurance costs, following recent hurricanes. After House leaders objected to the FBI raid on the office of Rep. William Jefferson, she countered that lawmakers should not be immune from office searches in a criminal case. An adoptive parent, she co-chairs the Congressional Coalition on Adoption Institute, which seeks to facilitate adoption. In 2007, she became ranking Republican at the Veterans Affairs' Subcommittee on Oversight and Investigations.

Her narrow win in 2002 placed Brown-Waite high on the worry list for House Republicans in 2004. But several prime candidates, including Thurman, decided not to run. Democrats nominated a former Republican who had never voted before and who demanded that the congresswoman return $14,000 in contributions from Majority Leader Tom DeLay. Brown-Waite won 66%-34%. In 2006, while Republicans elsewhere struggled, she easily took each county and defeated nurse practitioner John Russell 60%-40%; he accused her of covering up for disgraced Congressman Mark Foley, and she called him a "cockroach."

SIXTH DISTRICT

Rep. Cliff Stearns (R)

Elected 1988, 10th term; b. Apr. 16, 1941, Washington, DC; home, Ocala; George Washington U., B.S. 1963; Presbyterian; married (Joan).

Military Career: Air Force, 1963-67.

Professional Career: Data Control Systems Inc., 1967-68; Negotiator, CBS, 1969-70; Pres., Stearns House Inc., 1972-present.

DC Office: 2370 RHOB, 20515, 202-225-5744; Fax: 202-225-3973; Web site: www.house.gov/stearns.

District Offices: Gainesville, 352-337-0003; Ocala, 352-351-8777; Orange Park, 904-269-3203.

Committees: *Energy & Commerce* (5th of 26 R): Commerce, Trade & Consumer Protection (RMM); Environment & Hazardous Materials; Telecommunications & the Internet. *Veterans' Affairs* (2d of 13 R): Health; Oversight & Investigations.

Group Ratings

	ADA	ACLU	AFS	LCV	ITIC	NTU	COC	ACU	CFG	FRC
2006	10	5	14	8	86	75	93	96	85	100
2005	10	—	13	11	—	71	89	88	87	92

National Journal Ratings

	2005 LIB	—	2005 CONS		2006 LIB	—	2006 CONS
Economic	43%	—	56%		36%	—	63%
Social	12%	—	88%		0%	—	94%
Foreign	0%	—	89%		41%	—	59%

Key Votes of the 109th Congress

1. Estate Tax Repeal	Y	5. Limit Interstate Abortion	Y	9. Build Border Fence		Y
2. Limit CAFE Standards	Y	6. Extend Patriot Act	Y	10. CAFTA		Y
3. FY06 Spending Curb	Y	7. Bar Same Sex Marriage	Y	11. Oppose Iraq Withdrawal		Y
4. Drilling in ANWR	Y	8. Stem Cell Research $	N	12. Detainee Tribunals		Y

Election Results

2006 general	Cliff Stearns (R)	136,601	(60%)	($455,531)
	David Bruderly (D)	91,528	(40%)	($150,508)
2006 primary	Cliff Stearns (R)	unopposed		
2004 general	Cliff Stearns (R)	211,137	(64%)	($283,334)
	David Bruderly (D)	116,680	(36%)	($118,904)

Prior Winning Percentages: 2002 (65%); 2000 (100%); 1998 (100%); 1996 (67%); 1994 (100%); 1992 (65%); 1990 (59%); 1988 (54%)

The People		Race/Ethnic Origin	Ancestry	
Area size:	3,026 sq. mi.	78.9% White	German: 10.7% Irish: 9.1%	
Urban population:	69.4%	11.9% Black	English: 8.9%	
Rural population:	30.6%	2.2% Asian	**2004 Presidential Vote**	
Pop. 2000:	639,295	0.3% Native Am.	Bush (R)	210,101 (61%)
Pop. 2005 (est):	741,103	0.0% Hawaiian	Kerry (D)	136,622 (39%)
Median income:	$36,846	1.4% Two+ races	Other	838 (0%)
Poverty status:	13.4%	0.1% Other	**2000 Presidential Vote**	
Military veterans:	18.3%	5.2% Hispanic Origin	Bush (R)	142,489 (58%)
			Gore (D)	102,179 (42%)
			Cook Partisan Voting Index: R + 8	

Occupation   Blue collar: 21.7%   White collar: 61.4%   Gray collar: 16.9%

The flat grasslands of central Florida, once bypassed by southbound tourists heading for the coast, has over the past two decades become a prime growth area in this high-growth state. Central Florida's economy once depended on farming, on tourists getting off the interstate, and on state institutions, most notably the University of Florida in Gainesville. Then retirees began settling in places like the bluegrass country around Ocala, one of America's prime horse-breeding grounds, and Leesburg, perched on a narrow spit of land between Lake Griffin and Lake Harris. Initially, these areas were studded with trailer parks and mobile home developments, but the 1990s brought more upscale development, albeit nothing approaching the high-rise apartments and gated communities that line the coasts further south. At the same time, the large citrus groves have been cut back— victims of booming property values, plus environmental changes that have resulted in more diseases. Some of this development is at the intersection of Lake, Marion and Sumter Counties in the rapidly expanding "Villages" retirement community. This part of central Florida grew by 62% from 1990 to 2004.

The 6th Congressional District of Florida includes much of central Florida and also part of the Jacksonville metropolitan area, connected by a strip of lightly populated counties. In the south it includes parts of Marion and Sumter Counties, around Ocala, and a corner of Lake County. In the north it includes the western part of Jacksonville's Duval County and most of Clay County just to the south. In between it includes most of Alachua County except for Gainesville. On balance, this is a Republican district. Alachua is one of the few Florida counties to regularly vote Democratic, but its most heavily Democratic precincts are located in the strongly Democratic 3d District. The country around Ocala and the Villages in the south is pretty heavily Republican; western Jacksonville and

Clay County, with many military retirees, are even more Republican. In the 2006 governor's race, Republican Charlie Crist won 73% of the vote in Clay County, his second-highest percentage in any of Florida's 67 counties.

The congressman from the 6th District is Cliff Stearns, a Republican first elected in 1988. Stearns grew up and attended public schools in Washington, D.C., and served in the Air Force. In 1972 he went into Florida real estate and ended up owning five motels, three restaurants and other property. He was "someone who works in the community, goes to church with his neighbors, and doesn't live in Tallahassee," as he put it in his 1988 campaign, when he beat the favorite, state House Speaker Jon Mills, 54%-46%. "I was elected to put the federal government on a diet," Stearns said, and went on to compile a conservative voting record, though less so on foreign policy. Since losing a low-level leadership contest in 1994, he has been an occasional maverick. He bucked party leaders on NAFTA, IMF funding and normal trade relations with China. He complains about the growth in the federal deficit since George W. Bush took office. "We used to be the party of account-ability and fiscal responsibility," he said. He wants to end the automatic cost-of-living increases for members of Congress.

Stearns has become an active and productive legislator. On the Veterans Committee, he sponsored a research center on Gulf War syndrome and won new medical facilities and benefits for disabled vets. On Energy and Commerce, he has worked on health care and Internet policy. He enacted a bill that encourages states to permit asthmatic children to carry and self-administer medication at school. After failing to win the chairmanship of the Telecommunications Subcommit-tee, Stearns became chairman of the revamped Commerce, Trade and Consumer Protection Sub-committee, where he took on many Internet issues. In 2004, he won House passage of the bill to restrict abuses of computer spyware; he got committee approval of database protection legislation, but ran into jurisdictional squabbles with the Judiciary and Financial Services Committees. His Do-Not-Call Implementation Act became law, authorizing the Federal Trade Commission to estab-lish a national registry of consumers who opt out of telemarketing calls. He helped to enact the anti-spam law that requires most commercial e-mail to be labeled and have a valid return address. In October 2005, he enacted a bill limiting lawsuits against the firearms industry. The House also passed a bill with his provision to protect consumers from price-gouging during fuel emergencies. He backed a measure that opened parts of the Outer Continental Shelf to oil and gas leasing but he opposed new drilling in Florida waters. He held hearings on the U.S. Olympic Committee and on problems in college athletics, including gambling and recruitment. But Stearns suffered some setbacks, even while Republicans held the majority. The House defeated his proposal for a Federal Boxing Commission, with enforcement of uniform standards, and he lost on an amendment in the House to prohibit funds for ballot and language assistance under the Voting Rights Act. Although some critics contend that he could have done more on oversight of product-safety issues, committee Democrats were surprised by his relatively nonpartisan and productive course. His role appeared likely to diminish with the changing dynamics of Democratic control.

At home, he has faced no problems. In 2006, his reelection with 60% in his third contest with retired Navy officer David Bruderly was his lowest since 1990.

SEVENTH DISTRICT

Rep. John Mica (R)

Elected 1992, 8th term; b. Jan. 27, 1943, Binghamton, NY; home, Winter Park; Miami-Dade Commun. Col., A.A. 1965, U. of FL, B.A. 1967; Episcopa-lian; married (Patricia).

Elected Office: FL House of Reps., 1976-80.

Professional Career: Exec. Dir., Palm Beach & Orange Cnty. Govt. Charter Study Commissions, 1970-74; Pres., MK Development, 1975-92; A.A., U.S. Sen. Paula Hawkins, 1981-85; Partner, Mica, Dudinsky & Assoc., 1985-92.

DC Office: 2313 RHOB, 20515, 202-225-4035; Fax: 202-226-0821; Web site: www.house.gov/mica.

District Offices: Deltona, 386-860-1499; Maitland, 407-657-8080; Ormond Beach, 386-676-7750; Palatka, 386-328-1622; Palm Coast, 386-246-6042; St. Augustine, 904-810-5048.

Committees: *Oversight & Government Reform* (5th of 18 R): Federal Workforce, Postal Service & the District of Columbia; Domestic Policy. *Transportation & Infrastructure* (RMM of 34 R).

Group Ratings

	ADA	ACLU	AFS	LCV	ITIC	NTU	COC	ACU	CFG	FRC
2006	0	10	0	0	100	61	100	92	64	85
2005	0	—	0	0	—	63	92	100	78	92

National Journal Ratings

	2005 LIB	—	2005 CONS		2006 LIB	—	2006 CONS
Economic	28%	—	71%		0%	—	98%
Social	22%	—	78%		11%	—	85%
Foreign	0%	—	89%		17%	—	73%

Key Votes of the 109th Congress

1. Estate Tax Repeal	Y	5. Limit Interstate Abortion	Y	9. Build Border Fence	Y
2. Limit CAFE Standards	N	6. Extend Patriot Act	Y	10. CAFTA	Y
3. FY06 Spending Curb	Y	7. Bar Same Sex Marriage	Y	11. Oppose Iraq Withdrawal	Y
4. Drilling in ANWR	Y	8. Stem Cell Research $	N	12. Detainee Tribunals	Y

Election Results

2006 general	John Mica (R) 149,656	(63%)	($665,785)
	John Chagnon (D) 87,584	(37%)	($11,282)
2006 primary	John Mica (R) .... unopposed		
2004 general	John Mica (R) .... unopposed		($256,103)

Prior Winning Percentages: 2002 (60%); 2000 (63%); 1998 (100%); 1996 (62%); 1994 (73%); 1992 (56%)

The People		Race/Ethnic Origin	Ancestry	
Area size:	2,221 sq. mi.	81.3% White	German: 11.7%	Irish: 10.6%
Urban population:	86.7%	8.8% Black	English: 9.9%	
Rural population:	13.3%	1.4% Asian	**2004 Presidential Vote**	
Pop. 2000:	639,295	0.3% Native Am.	Bush (R) 204,454	(57%)
Pop. 2005 (est):	762,287	0.0% Hawaiian	Kerry (D) 155,302	(43%)
Median income:	$40,525	1.1% Two+ races	Other 964	(0%)
Poverty status:	10.1%	0.1% Other	**2000 Presidential Vote**	
Military veterans:	17.6%	6.9% Hispanic Origin	Bush (R) 143,672	(54%)
			Gore (D) 122,818	(46%)
			Cook Partisan Voting Index: R + 4	

Occupation   Blue collar: 20.3%   White collar: 63.2%   Gray collar: 16.4%

In 1513, Spanish explorer Ponce de Leon headed to Florida, hoping to discover the Fountain of Youth; instead, he found Ponte Vedra Beach, located just south of modern-day Jacksonville. A few decades later and a little farther south, Spanish colonists founded St. Augustine, the oldest permanent European settlement in North America—42 years older than Jamestown, Virginia, and 55 years older than the Plymouth colony in Massachusetts. Some communities here are old: John D. Rockefeller used to winter in Ormond Beach, and cars have been zooming on Daytona's rock-hard beach for decades. Near long-settled St. Augustine are a Northrop Grumman aircraft plant and some of the newest communities in America. St. Johns and Flagler Counties, the two coastal counties between Jacksonville and Daytona Beach, grew 31% and 53% between 2000 and 2005; Flagler County was the fastest growing county in the nation between 2003 and 2004 and then again between 2004 and 2005. Nearby DeLand is a mecca for skydivers, while Heathrow, just off Interstate 4, serves as the home base of the American Automobile Association. Other places are much newer, instant cities: the Palm Coast development on the beach in Flagler County, and Deltona, which was built inland on a drained swamp in Volusia County. Although disappearing, some farming and ranching continues to fill lands between these growing areas.

The 7th Congressional District of Florida covers the Atlantic coast for nearly 100 miles, from Ponte Vedra Beach to Daytona Beach. Inland it includes affluent Seminole County suburbs of Orlando as well as the timber center of Palatka. Nearly two-thirds of the population is in the south, around Orlando, Deltona and Daytona Beach. The political tendencies in this area are mixed. Seminole County and St. Augustine's St. Johns County are affluent and heavily Republican. Palm Coast's Flagler County is marginal; Daytona Beach's Volusia County leans Democratic, but about 40% of it is in the 24th District.On balance, this is a Republican district, but not overwhelmingly so.

The congressman from the 7th District is John Mica, a Republican first elected in 1992. He grew up in south Florida, in a bipartisan political family: His younger brother Dan Mica was a Democratic congressman from Palm Beach County from 1978 to 1988, when he lost a primary for U.S. Senate, and then became a credit union lobbyist; another brother, David Mica, worked for Democratic Governor Lawton Chiles and became executive director for the Florida Petroleum Council. John Mica made a small fortune by turning 360 feet of New Smyrna beachfront into a real estate business. He was elected to the state House in 1976 and served four years, worked on Senator Paula Hawkins's staff from 1981 to 1985, and then became a lobbyist. He ran for the House when this district was created after the 1990 Census. After he was attacked in the Republican primary as an insider representing special interests, he said, "Some of the finest folks I've met are lobbyists." He still managed to win the primary 53%-34%. In the general election, against an opponent he attacked as a liberal backed by trial lawyers and labor unions, he won 56%-44%. He has since been reelected easily.

Mica has been a consistent conservative but also a brash reformer, leading the charge to abolish House select committees and to make public the names of those signing petitions to discharge legislation. When Republicans took control of the House, Mica became chairman of Government Reform's Civil Service Subcommittee. There he helped pass the White House Accountability Act of 1996, imposing on the White House the laws that are imposed on the private sector. His image is that of a congressional tightwad, though with one exception: he was an early backer of the Congressional Visitors Center, whose cost estimates have risen and completion date is routinely extended; he called CVC critics a "chorus of prima donnas." Mica has focused on fighting drugs by promoting eradication and interdiction programs.

His chief legislative front has been at the Transportation and Infrastructure Committee. When he took over in 2001 as chairman of the Aviation Subcommittee, he pledged faster building of runways across the nation. But after the September 11 attacks, he focused on security. After congressional leaders moved within days to pass a bill to aid the airlines, Mica played a major role in designing the next legislation: improved screening at all airports. The Senate, by 100–0, approved a bill that federalized the screeners; Mica and House Republicans objected to a complete federal takeover and sought to preserve some role for the private sector. They reached a deal to allow airports to opt out of the federal system after three years if they met certain standards. A few months later, Mica introduced a bill to permit commercial airline pilots to carry guns in the cockpit. The bill was initially opposed by the Bush administration and the Senate; airlines worried about the risks of having firearms aboard planes. Mica brought to the floor a bill permitting a few pilots to carry the weapons during a two-year demonstration period. But the House, to his surprise, voted 310-113 to allow all pilots to carry guns. The Senate agreed by an 87–6 margin, and President Bush bowed to popular will. Since then, Mica has raised alarms about gaps in security. When Congress passed intelligence reform in the 2004 lame-duck session, it included some demands from Mica for quicker action by the Homeland Security Department on aviation security. On local transportation issues, he has fought for mass transit in the traffic-clogged Orlando area; he has secured a pledge from federal officials of $250 million for a commuter rail system in Central Florida. He was the only House member from Florida who voted to lift the moratorium on oil drilling off the coasts of his state.

In 2006, he was one of several Republicans seeking the chairmanship of the Transportation Committee in the new Congress. Although he was less senior than adversaries Tom Petri and John Duncan, Mica was more of a party regular; he won the backroom contest of the leadership-controlled Steering Committee, reportedly by one vote. The prize was less valuable after the GOP lost House control in November, but Mica retained some clout because the panel has a history of bipartisanship and, of course, he would be in line for the chairmanship in the majority.

In 2002, Mica faced a serious challenge at home from Democrat Wayne Hogan, a Jacksonville trial lawyer who spent $2.7 million of his own money on his campaign. Hogan, part of the legal team that won Florida's settlement with the tobacco industry, from which he netted $54 million, said that he would fight for "ordinary families against powerful interests." Mica responded that Hogan was trying to buy the seat, and that his pledge not to take contributions from political action committees was like "Rockefeller saying he won't take food stamps." Mica won comfortably, 60%-40%, carrying all six counties. Since then, he has not been seriously challenged.

EIGHTH DISTRICT

Rep. Ric Keller (R)

Elected 2000, 4th term; b. Sept. 5, 1964, Johnson City, TN; home, Orlando; E. TN St. U., B.S. 1986, Vanderbilt U., J.D. 1992; Methodist; divorced.

Professional Career: Practicing atty., 1992-2000.

DC Office: 419 CHOB, 20515, 202-225-2176; Fax: 202-225-0999; Web site: www.keller.house.gov.

District Offices: Eustis, 888-642-1211; Ocala, 888-642-1211; Orlando, 407-872-1962.

Committees: *Education & Labor* (9th of 22 R): Higher Education, Lifelong Learning & Competitiveness (RMM); Early Childhood, Elementary & Secondary Education. *Judiciary* (9th of 17 R): Commercial & Administrative Law; Courts, the Internet & Intellectual Property.

Group Ratings

	ADA	ACLU	AFS	LCV	ITIC	NTU	COC	ACU	CFG	FRC
2006	0	10	0	17	100	62	100	88	68	85
2005	5	—	0	17	—	64	88	96	87	92

National Journal Ratings

	2005 LIB	—	2005 CONS		2006 LIB	—	2006 CONS
Economic	23%	—	77%		34%	—	65%
Social	0%	—	89%		0%	—	94%
Foreign	17%	—	79%		28%	—	71%

Key Votes of the 109th Congress

1. Estate Tax Repeal	Y	5. Limit Interstate Abortion	Y	9. Build Border Fence	*
2. Limit CAFE Standards	Y	6. Extend Patriot Act	Y	10. CAFTA	Y
3. FY06 Spending Curb	Y	7. Bar Same Sex Marriage	Y	11. Oppose Iraq Withdrawal	Y
4. Drilling in ANWR	Y	8. Stem Cell Research $	N	12. Detainee Tribunals	*

Election Results

2006 general	Ric Keller (R)	95,258	(53%)	($1,691,408)
	Charlie Stuart (D)	82,526	(46%)	($998,271)
	Other	2,660	(1%)	
2006 primary	Ric Keller (R)	30,707	(72%)	
	Elizabeth Doran (R)	11,661	(28%)	
2004 general	Ric Keller (R)	172,232	(61%)	($292,257)
	Stephen Murray (D)	112,343	(39%)	($62,420)

Prior Winning Percentages: 2002 (65%); 2000 (51%)

The People		Race/Ethnic Origin	Ancestry	
Area size:	1,158 sq. mi.	69.9% White	German: 10.7% Irish: 9.0%	
Urban population:	91.7%	7.2% Black	English: 8.6%	
Rural population:	8.3%	3.0% Asian	**2004 Presidential Vote**	
Pop. 2000:	639,295	0.3% Native Am.	Bush (R)	160,722 (55%)
Pop. 2005 (est):	733,281	0.1% Hawaiian	Kerry (D)	133,328 (45%)
Median income:	$41,568	1.6% Two+ races	Other	261 (0%)
Poverty status:	9.4%	0.3% Other	**2000 Presidential Vote**	
Military veterans:	14.9%	17.6% Hispanic Origin	Bush (R)	119,139 (54%)
			Gore (D)	102,538 (46%)
			Cook Partisan Voting Index: R + 3	

Occupation	Blue collar: 19.3%	White collar: 63.6%	Gray collar: 17.2%

Who would have supposed 40 years ago that the most popular tourist destination in the world would rise amid the swamps and orange groves of central Florida? The answer: Walt Disney, and just about no one else. In the mid-1960s, Disney looked at the map and decided that the intersection of

I-4 and Florida's Turnpike, the "crossroads of Florida," just a few miles southwest of Orlando, was the perfect place for the vast theme park he was planning. The spirit of this place was set by a man who never lived here but created something now taken for granted. Disney conceived the first theme park in the flatlands of Orange County, California, in 1955, but he perfected it in the 17,000 acres of swamp and lakes in Florida's Orange County that his associates had stealthily snapped up and where Disney World opened in 1971. With the invention of the theme park, Disney also pioneered sophisticated communications, utility, and waste-disposal methods—all out of sight and under-ground. Disney World is not just an engineering marvel; it requires some 56,000 people with know-how and earnest cheerfulness to entertain its 40 million-plus visitors. But it is hardly the only site that has made Orlando one of the world's great tourist destinations: other popular theme parks here include Sea World and Universal Studios and Cape Canaveral is less than 40 miles away. The high-tech economy also has moved into Greater Orlando; defense contractor Lockheed Martin has a big missile facility southwest of Orlando, which has been growing since 1956, now with more than 6,000 employees. Continuing growth—of the downtown skyline and in the expanding metropolitan region—has spurred what may be uphill efforts to control the sprawl and congestion in one of the nation's booming areas.

The 8th Congressional District of Florida includes parts of Orlando and surrounding Orange County and most of the enormous Walt Disney World complex, including the Disney new urbanist town of Celebration. It includes most of the southeast and southwest parts of Orlando and adjoining suburbs; the heavily black areas of central Orlando are in the 3d District. More than three-quarters of the district's residents live in Orange County. The rest live in a ribbon of territory to the northwest, past Lake Apopka to little market towns like Mount Dora and Umatilla in Lake County that seem insulated from the booming metro area; around here, turtles, alligators and river otters go about their lives underneath cypress trees draped with Spanish moss. Nearby is Silver Springs, where tourists can view the world's largest formation of clear artesian springs from glass-bottomed boats—a theme park from an earlier era. Beyond that is the horse farm country of Marion County, around Ocala. In the 1980s the Orlando area was heavily Republican, but in the 1990s it moved perceptibly toward national Democrats. The 8th District was designed to be a Republican district, though it's not comfortably so. Some 18% of its residents are Hispanic, most of them not Cuban Republicans, but Puerto Ricans and people with roots in other parts of Latin America; many work in the tourism industry. They favored Governor Jeb Bush in 2002 and Charlie Crist in 2006, and trended toward George W. Bush in 2004, when he got 55% of the total vote.

The congressman from the 8th District is Ric Keller, a Republican first elected in 2000 in one of the closest races in the country. He was born in Tennessee but grew up mostly in Orlando, in a one-bedroom house with his brother, sister, mother and grandmother. With financial help from Pell grants, he graduated first in his class at East Tennessee State University, then graduated from Vanderbilt law school. In 1992 he moved to Orlando and practiced law and quickly earned conserva-tive credentials. His firm served as general counsel to a business coalition that won passage of changes in tort law in the Florida legislature.

When Congressman Bill McCollum decided to run for the Senate in 2000, Keller ran for the House. He had tough primary competition from state Representative Bill Sublette, who boasted of delivering state funds to the area and was supported by most Republican leaders. With greater name recognition, Sublette led in most polls. Keller focused on issues like abortion and gun owners' rights. Sublette led Keller in the September primary 43%-31%. In the October 3 runoff, helped by $400,000 in contributions and issue ads by the conservative Club for Growth, Keller won 52%-48%. In the five-week general election, Keller again was the underdog against Linda Chapin, former Orange County Commission chairman, who argued that her moderate views plus her experience as a county official put her more in line with district voters. Keller played up his anti-tax views and outsider status, while Republican ads lampooned Chapin for providing frills for the county jail and other local facilities, including $150,000 for palm trees and an $18,500 statue of a frog. Keller's 50.8%-49.2% win was a great disappointment to House Democratic leaders. It may have been decided by the personal touch: Keller's folksy, self-deprecating style made him "an easy man to like," wrote the *Orlando Sentinel*.

In the House, Keller has mostly been a reliable conservative. His strong support for tax cuts plus his advocacy of increased education funding for the disadvantaged made him "a bootstrap conservative," in the *Sentinel's* words. On oil drilling in the Gulf of Mexico and the Clinton adminis-tration's proposed regulations on arsenic in drinking water, he surprised many by voting against the Republican leadership. On the Judiciary Committee, he carved a niche in the tort-reform wars by authoring the House-passed "Cheeseburger bill," which prohibits most obesity-related lawsuits against the food industry. "The gist of this legislation is there should be common sense in the food court, not blaming other people in the legal court," he explained. On Education and Labor, where he is ranking Republican on the Higher Education subcommittee and the only Floridian on the full panel, he helped to win increases in Pell grants, especially for low-income students, and he joined Democrats in opposing a Bush administration proposal to change the funding formula; the House in March 2006 passed a five-year extension of the higher-ed law, but the bill stalled in the Senate. He helped to enact bipartisan changes in the special education program, including paperwork reduction and sanctions against students who bring a gun to school. In 2005, the House passed his bill to make it a crime to aim a laser beam at the cockpit of a flying airplane. He showed independence in February 2007 as one of 17 House Republicans to vote for the resolution opposing President Bush's troop-increase initiative in Iraq.

In 2002 and 2004, Keller won with more than 60% of the vote. But as with many other House Republicans, the 2006 election was considerably more difficult. Democratic challenger Charlie Stuart, a marketing consultant from a politically experienced Orlando family, said that he represented mainstream values and criticized Republican "rhetoric that divides us rather than brings us together." The National Restaurant Association ran $100,000 in ads on behalf of Keller. He won 53%-46%, and led in each county, though only 51%-48% in Orange. "I knew it was going to be a close race but not this close," he said on election night.

In 2000, Keller had pledged to serve only four terms. But two weeks after the 2006 election, he said that he made a mistake. "As a rookie candidate, I underestimated the value of experience and seniority." He planned to seek a fifth term, but not spend "my entire career in Congress." Keller seemed certain to have tough opposition again in 2008 as conservative radio host Todd Long declared his candidacy and 2000 Republican primary challenger Bob Hering also voiced interest in running. On the Democratic side, Stuart said he would run again; several other Democrats also made plans to run.

NINTH DISTRICT

Rep. Gus Bilirakis (R)

Elected 2006, 1st term; b. Feb. 8, 1963, Gainsville; home, Palm Harbor; Attended St. Petersburg Jr. Col., U. of FL, B.A. 1986, Stetson U., J.D. 1989; Greek Orthodox; married (Eva Lialios).

Elected Office: FL House of Reps., 1998-2006.

Professional Career: Intern, U.S. Pres. Ronald Reagan, 1983; Intern, NRCC, 1984; Aide, U.S. Rep. Don Sundquist, 1985; Teacher, St. Petersburg Col., 1997-2001; Practicing atty., 1989-2006.

DC Office: 1630 LHOB, 20515, 202-225-5755; Fax: 202-225-4085; Web site: bilirakis.house.gov.

District Offices: Palm Harbor, 727-773-2871; Temple Terrace, 813-985-8541.

Committees: *Foreign Affairs* (23d of 23 R): Europe; Middle East & South Asia. *Homeland Security* (13th of 15 R): Transportation Security & Infrastructure Protection; Border, Maritime & Global Counterterrorism. *Veterans' Affairs* (12th of 13 R): Disability Assistance & Memorial Affairs.

Group Ratings and Key Votes: Newly Elected

Election Results

2006 general	Gus Bilirakis (R)	123,016	(56%)	($2,574,356)
	Phyllis Busansky (D)	96,978	(44%)	($1,419,414)
2006 primary	Gus Bilirakis (R)	40,603	(82%)	
	David Langheier (R)	8,915	(18%)	
2004 general	Michael Bilirakis (R)	unopposed		($596,389)

The People		Race/Ethnic Origin	Ancestry	
Area size:	800 sq. mi.	85.2% White	German: 13.3% Irish: 11.2%	
Urban population:	93.8%	3.5% Black	English: 9.2%	
Rural population:	6.2%	1.8% Asian	**2004 Presidential Vote**	
Pop. 2000:	639,296	0.2% Native Am.	Bush (R) 196,837	(57%)
Pop. 2005 (est):	726,088	0.0% Hawaiian	Kerry (D) 148,694	(43%)
Median income:	$40,742	1.1% Two+ races	Other 953	(0%)
Poverty status:	8.6%	0.1% Other	**2000 Presidential Vote**	
Military veterans:	17.2%	7.9% Hispanic Origin	Bush (R) 146,735	(54%)
			Gore (D) 124,242	(46%)
			Cook Partisan Voting Index: R + 4	

Occupation	Blue collar: 17.6%	White collar: 68.0%	Gray collar: 14.4%

Half a century ago, the land north of St. Petersburg and Tampa was scarcely inhabited. Behind the barrier island of beaches, the land along the Gulf shore was swampy; further inland was dense, semitropical forest spotted with lakes. Over the years, development has moved up the coast and inland via the major highways, first to Clearwater and Tarpon Springs in Pinellas County and then up the once-empty coast of Pasco County. Much of this area originally was designed for retirees, offering everything from condominiums to garden apartments to trailer parks to what is probably the largest array of Medicare HMO plans in the nation. But it has attracted others. Clearwater, in Pinellas County north of St. Petersburg, in 2000 had a higher percentage of senior citizens than any other city over 100,000 but it also features the spiritual headquarters for the Church of Scientology, which has transformed its downtown by buying 200 businesses and building a yet-unfinished $50 million, 384,000-square-foot Mediterranean Revival-style Scientology religious center. Businesses have sprouted in northern Pinellas County and inland off the I-75 corridor; nearly half of Pasco County's workers commute to jobs in other counties. The people who settled here in recent decades brought their ancestral political beliefs with them: In the 1950s and 1960s, only white-collar retirees could afford to buy new places in Florida, and they were heavily Republican. As Florida retirements became more feasible for people with modest incomes in the 1970s and 1980s, the partisan balance shifted toward Democrats. In the 1990s, young immigrants with professional and technical backgrounds flooded the area; their political independence has turned this into one of Florida's most politically marginal areas. In 2004 Republican organizers brought out a lot of new voters, many of them Christian conservatives.

The 9th Congressional District of Florida covers part of the area north of St. Petersburg and north and east of Tampa. It includes the string of towns on the coast of Pasco County—Holiday, New Port Richey, Bayonet Point, Hudson. In Pinellas County to the south, the 9th includes Tarpon Springs, an old resort first settled by Greek sponge divers a century ago, the affluent neighborhoods of mid- and upper-level managers in East Lake, the young commuter families of Oldsmar, the bayside community of Safety Harbor and Clearwater. The district also includes the northern Tampa suburbs in Hillsborough County and much of the eastern part of the county, including part of strawberry-growing Plant City (named not for plants but for Tampa pioneer Henry B. Plant). The borders were drawn by Republican redistricters to produce a district that would elect a Republican. The district gave Jeb Bush a big margin in 2002 and voted 54% for George W. Bush in 2000 and 57% in 2004.

The new congressman from the 9th District is Gus Bilirakis, a Republican elected in 2006 to succeed his father, 12-term Republican Michael Bilirakis. Perhaps no state is better suited than Florida for a legacy candidate like Bilirakis, who joined Connie Mack and Kendrick Meek in the delegation as members who followed a parent into Congress. At seven, the younger Bilirakis stuffed envelopes for Republican Louis "Skip" Bafalis, who lost his 1970 bid for Florida governor but was elected to five terms in Congress. Bilirakis interned in the Reagan White House and worked for former Congressman Don Sundquist before he became Tennessee governor. Bilirakis earned a law degree from Stetson University and worked as a probate lawyer and estate planner. In 1998 he was elected to the first of four terms in the Florida state House. Bilirakis' career has always been closely tied to his father's. On Election Day 2002, the two were campaigning together on a street corner when a driver lost control of his car and struck the younger Bilirakis, leaving him with bruises and just missing his father.

The elder Bilirakis announced before the 2006 cycle began that he would not seek a 13th term and his son was already presumed to be a candidate for the seat. He drew only nominal opposition for the Republican nomination. Bilirakis was not shy about running on the family name. He appeared on the ballot as Gus Michael Bilirakis and raised money from many political action committees that were familiar with his father's work on the House Energy and Commerce Committee. Bilirakis's campaign website praised the father's patriotism, integrity and work ethic during 12 terms in office, and declared, "There is no one better suited to carry on the mission than Gus, who has been instilled with these vital attributes." Rahm Emanuel recruited Democrat Phyllis Busansky, a former 8-year member of the Hillsborough County Commission and the first executive director of the state's welfare-to-work program. Busansky played up her background in health care and on senior citizens issues. Bilirakis, whose law practice focused on elder law, pointed to his own health care credentials. In the Florida House, he spearheaded legislation supporting community health care centers that treat the uninsured. He called for expanding tax incentives for health savings accounts and for low-to-middle-income families who purchase private health care coverage.

The soft-spoken Bilirakis contrasted in style with Busansky's assertive personality. Busansky ran television ads portraying Bilirakis as a follower, and she accused Bilirakis of ducking public debate and relying heavily on his father's reputation. She ambushed Bilirakis as he arrived at one event by filling the parking lot with supporters. "I was hoping he'd come here and stand up with me," she said. "Gus has hidden always from these kinds of encounters." In October, the Bilirakis campaign distributed mailers that dredged up a 1991 debate over an ordinance on swimsuits to charge that Busansky "advocates nudity on public streets." The flyer showed the Democrat's photo next to the censored image of a naked woman, charging that "Phyllis Busansky will bankrupt our values."

Busansky trailed in the polls for much of the campaign, but she gained some short-lived momentum in October after criticizing Bilirakis for his "deep and lucrative ties to the 'Foley Five,'" a reference to contributions he accepted from House Republicans who had early knowledge of the e-mails sent by disgraced Congressman Mark Foley to congressional pages. The national party did not leave this race to chance: President Bush, Vice President Dick Cheney and Speaker Dennis Hastert all stumped for Bilirakis, enabling him to outspend Busansky $2.6 million to $1.4 million. Bilirakis won 56%-44%. After the election, Bilirakis introduced a bill that would extend veterans disability benefits to former prisoners of war who suffered from diabetes and osteoporosis. With his family name and the district's Republican edge, Bilirakis is well-positioned for reelection. Attorney Bill Mitchell, who withdrew from the Democratic primary in 2006, said he plans to run in 2008.

TENTH DISTRICT

Rep. Bill Young (R)

Elected 1970, 19th term; b. Dec. 16, 1930, Harmarville, PA; home, Largo; St. Petersburg H.S.; Baptist; married (Beverly).

Military Career: Army Natl. Guard, 1948-57.

Elected Office: FL Senate, 1960-70, Min. Ldr., 1966-70.

Professional Career: Aide, U.S. Rep. William Cramer, 1957-60.

DC Office: 2407 RHOB, 20515, 202-225-5961; Fax: 202-225-9764; Web site: www.house.gov/young.

District Offices: Seminole, 727-391-6030; St. Petersburg, 727-893-3191.

Committees: *Appropriations* (2d of 29 R): Defense (RMM); Military Construction, Veterans Affairs & Related Agencies.

Group Ratings

	ADA	ACLU	AFS	LCV	ITIC	NTU	COC	ACU	CFG	FRC
2006	10	10	14	50	86	57	87	84	57	85
2005	5	—	0	22	—	56	92	87	64	83

National Journal Ratings

	2005 LIB	—	2005 CONS		2006 LIB	—	2006 CONS
Economic	41%	—	58%		39%	—	61%
Social	35%	—	64%		31%	—	68%
Foreign	27%	—	71%		6%	—	86%

Key Votes of the 109th Congress

1. Estate Tax Repeal	Y	5. Limit Interstate Abortion	Y	9. Build Border Fence	Y
2. Limit CAFE Standards	Y	6. Extend Patriot Act	Y	10. CAFTA	Y
3. FY06 Spending Curb	Y	7. Bar Same Sex Marriage	Y	11. Oppose Iraq Withdrawal	Y
4. Drilling in ANWR	Y	8. Stem Cell Research $	N	12. Detainee Tribunals	Y

Election Results

2006 general	Bill Young (R)	131,488	(66%)	($506,473)
	Samm Simpson (D)	67,950	(34%)	($39,744)
2006 primary	Bill Young (R)	unopposed		
2004 general	Bill Young (R)	207,175	(69%)	($681,749)
	Bob Derry (D)	91,658	(31%)	($85,865)

Prior Winning Percentages: 2002 (100%); 2000 (76%); 1998 (100%); 1996 (67%); 1994 (100%); 1992 (57%); 1990 (100%); 1988 (73%); 1986 (100%); 1984 (80%); 1982 (100%); 1980 (100%); 1978 (79%); 1976 (65%); 1974 (76%); 1972 (76%); 1970 (67%)

The People		Race/Ethnic Origin	Ancestry	
Area size:	448 sq. mi.	88.0% White	German: 14.0%	Irish: 11.6%
Urban population:	100.0%	3.6% Black	English: 10.2%	
Rural population:	0.0%	2.3% Asian	**2004 Presidential Vote**	
Pop. 2000:	639,295	0.3% Native Am.	Bush (R) 158,082	(51%)
Pop. 2005 (est):	646,138	0.0% Hawaiian	Kerry (D) 150,761	(49%)
Median income:	$37,168	1.3% Two+ races	**2000 Presidential Vote**	
Poverty status:	8.9%	0.1% Other	Gore (D) 137,286	(51%)
Military veterans:	18.3%	4.4% Hispanic Origin	Bush (R) 133,004	(49%)
			Cook Partisan Voting Index: D + 1	

Occupation   Blue collar: 19.9%   White collar: 64.9%   Gray collar: 15.2%

St. Petersburg was first settled in the 1870s, reached by railroad in 1888 and in 1892 named, after a coin toss, by one of the rail partners, Pyotr Dementyev, for his native city in Russia; if his partner had won the toss, it would have been named Detroit. For decades, it was known as the American city with the largest percentage of elderly residents, sitting on its green park benches and playing shuffleboard. In the early 1900s, *St. Petersburg Times* editor W. L. Straub sought to reverse the industrialization of the waterfront, establishing the parks that continue to define the city's character. Starting out on the grid streets facing Tampa Bay, St. Petersburg later spread toward the Gulf Coast as the migration of retirees accelerated. Mostly from the North and modestly affluent, the newcomers adapted easily to a city whose civic tone was set by the *St. Petersburg Times* and its longtime owners Nelson and Henrietta Poynter: Sober, good-humored, supportive of clean government, and civil rights. More recently, retirees have come to prefer homes in less urbanized settings, and St. Petersburg has become a more conventional central city, with a larger working population, more families and minorities, and more office buildings and civic attractions—the Salvador Dali Museum, the Florida International Museum, the Museum of Fine Arts. The new balance has brought new politics. White-collar Yankee retirees in the 1940s and 1950s made St. Petersburg and surrounding Pinellas County the first Republican county in ancestrally Democratic Florida. Then, in the early 1970s, Social Security was vastly increased and indexed to inflation and St. Petersburg basked in prosperity. More workers came to afford a Florida retirement, the affluent moved farther down the Gulf Coast, and St. Petersburg trended Democratic in the 1970s and 1980s. The whole of St. Petersburg and Pinellas County are now pretty well built up, with new projects replacing old buildings in downtown St. Pete and elsewhere; except for the county containing the Florida Keys, this was the slowest growing large county in the state, with virtually no growth between 2000 and 2006.

The 10th Congressional District is the only Florida district entirely within one county. It includes all of Pinellas County south of Clearwater except for heavily black precincts in south St. Petersburg, which are part of the Tampa-based 11th District. It includes all the Pinellas County beach communities on the barrier islands facing the Gulf from Belleair Beach to Mullet Key and, north of Clearwater, includes middle-class Dunedin and pricey Palm Harbor in the north to the new subdivisions of Largo in the center of the peninsula. In 2004 it voted 51% for George W. Bush.

The congressman from the 10th District is Bill Young, a Republican first elected in 1970, the most senior Republican in the House. Young grew up in a dirt-poor Pennsylvania coal town. His first home was a shotgun shack that was swept down a river when he was 6; at 16 he was shot in a hunting accident. The family moved to Florida, and Young dropped out of high school to support his ill mother by hauling concrete blocks and mixing mortar; at 25 he applied for a job as an insurance salesman, and ultimately ran a successful insurance agency. In the 1950s he worked for St. Petersburg's first Republican congressman, William Cramer. Young was elected to the state Senate in 1960, at 29, and was the lone Republican there. When Cramer ran for the U.S. Senate in 1970, Young ran for his House seat and won.

Young has a moderate to conservative voting record. Early on, he got a seat on Appropriations, where he, like many Republicans, worked closely with the Democratic chairmen. One of Young's special projects has been the bone marrow donor program, originated by Dr. Robert Good of All Children's Hospital in St. Petersburg. Working from his seat on the Defense Subcommittee, he originally placed the program in the Pentagon; in 1987 it started off with $2.1 million; by 2006 it had matched nearly 25,000 patients with one of 6 million volunteers.

Despite his seniority, Young did not become full committee chairman after Republicans won their majority in 1994. Speaker-designate Newt Gingrich passed over him and two more senior Republicans for being too accommodating to Democrats. With some reason: after 34 years as a minority party legislator Young's instincts were bipartisan. "I came into the majority party with this strong conviction that every member of Congress has been elected by their constituents and should be given respect. I've tried to deal with anybody on that basis, whether it is a first-term freshman or a 20-year veteran." Young says that Gingrich offered him the job, but that he preferred to chair the Defense Subcommittee, on which he had done much of his work. In that post he worked to produce bipartisan appropriations out of the spotlight; he has said he knew every dime that goes into secret "black" military and intelligence operations. In 1998 Young considered retiring, but at the end of the year he was suddenly catapulted into the Appropriations chairmanship. It happened three days after the November election, when Gingrich decided to resign; Appropriations Chairman Bob Livingston quickly became the Speaker-designate, and Young became chairman.

In 2001 and 2002 Young was caught between demands by OMB Director Mitch Daniels that spending be held down to Bush administration limits and demands by appropriators for more spending. For the most part he came down on Bush's side. When the administration proposed an end to earmarking money for members' projects (there were 7,803 earmarks in 2001, totaling $15 billion), Young demurred. In early May 2002 he proposed to add $2.5 billion to the $27.3 billion emergency spending bill, but after a meeting where George W. Bush expressed his "disappointment" and stormier sessions with Daniels and Speaker Dennis Hastert, Young held to the $27.3 billion level, partly through accounting legerdemain. In September he tried to get Hastert to move the $130 billion Labor-HHS appropriation to the floor under an open rule, to see if the Bush limits would be accepted by the House; Hastert declined, and work on appropriations was not completed until early 2003. After the November election, House Republicans adopted a new rule requiring Appropriations subcommittee chairmen—the college of cardinals—to be approved by the Republican Steering Committee. This was seen as a move to rein in appropriators; when it passed by a close voice vote, Young did not call for a roll call vote. "I could not let that meeting conclude with the Speaker having lost."

Young resolved to make the appropriations process go more smoothly in 2003 and managed to pass all 13 bills through the House by early September. But delays in the Senate and in resolving differences between the chambers resulted in the postponement of final action until January 2004 on an omnibus package with seven of the bills. In 2004, appropriators got a late start because the House and Senate could not agree on a budget resolution. In June 2004, leading a coalition of appropriators and Democrats, Young beat a proposal to impose budget caps on spending. The House passed more appropriations bills than the Senate in the summer and fall, but Young agreed to a continuing resolution and an omnibus appropriation bill after the election. The House also was able to pass disaster relief after Florida was hit by four hurricanes in August and September. In early September Congress approved $2 billion; in early October another $11.6 billion was included in the military construction appropriation. Finally the House approved the omnibus appropriation in November, but not until after Tom DeLay pressured Young into including an extra $300 million for NASA.

Like other appropriators, Young has worked on projects in his district. "I don't appropriate for my state or my district for junk. I don't think anybody can really complain about the value of what we do," he has said. And he adds, "I try to make sure things that are needed in the whole state of Florida are taken care of." He refused repeated leadership demands that he reduce the amount of projects for Democratic appropriators. But anti-pork lobbyists like Keith Ashdown of Taxpayers for

Common Sense agree that he has not put too much money into his area. "I'd probably put him at the top of the list of people in Congress I most admire. If you could clone him 434 times, the Congress would be a better place."

As chairman of the Defense Appropriations Subcommittee before and after his six years as full committee chairman, Young has taken an interest in local defense facilities. The 2004 omnibus included $72 million in local defense projects, and a replacement for the Belleair Causeway Bridge. MacDill Air Force Base in Tampa, just across the bay from St. Petersburg, is the headquarters of Central Command and Special Operations Command. Young has pushed through a $25 million intelligence and operations center and $78 million for a conference center for SOCOM and $31 million for more family housing and a new headquarters for CentCom. MacDill has been thought to be in jeopardy because few planes are based there; Young was pleased when the Air Force announced it would station 32 of the 100 KC-767 aerial refueling tankers built by Boeing at MacDill in June 2003 and dismayed when the Boeing project was held up by the Senate in December 2003.

After the 2004 election, House Republicans' term limits ended Young's tenure as Appropriations chairman. He said that he was confident he could still work on district projects. "I appointed most of the subcommittee chairmen to their positions. We have a very strong mutual respect, and we have worked together for so long. They know I'm not going to bring anything to the markup that can't be justified." He chaired the Defense Subcommittee instead. Appropriations bills were mostly passed on time in 2005, and Young got $240 million for district and $80 million for other Florida projects. Some projects: $500,000 for an Eckerd College science center, $100,000 for a waterfront park at St. Petersburg Airport, $344,000 for research on the interaction of medications and grapefruit juice, $20 million for Florida National Guard responses to emergencies, $750,000 for state police athletic leagues and $2.1 million to help colleges and universities prepare for hurricanes. In 2006 only two of the 11 appropriations were completed in the 109th Congress, one of which was defense. As a result, Young got only $90 million for district and Florida projects.

Young has always paid close attention to veterans issues. In the 1970s Young persuaded Congress and Gerald Ford to build the Bay Pines Veterans Medical Center in St. Petersburg, now the second largest VA hospital; it will be named after him, as will be the Center for Biodefense and Emerging Infectious Diseases at NIH in Bethesda, Maryland, but, at his insistence, only when he is no longer in Congress. In February 2004 he called for an investigation of poor care there and held hearings the next month; the hospital's chief of staff was promptly transferred elsewhere. In October 2003 he persuaded the House to vote 399–0 to end the practice of charging military personnel in military hospitals $8.10 a day for meals. In October 2004 the Veterans Affairs Department gave speedy approval to a Fisher House for families of wounded military personnel at the Haley Veterans Medical Center in Tampa. Since 2003 Young and his wife have been visiting wounded soldiers almost every week at military hospitals including Walter Reed Army and Bethesda Naval Hospitals. Sometimes they found care lacking—a soldier sitting in a pool of urine, a sergeant's brain surgery was delayed because of malfunctioning equipment at Walter Reed and denial of transfer to Bethesda, a corporal with a head injury fell out of bed because he had not been properly secured—and they regularly complained to General Kevin Kiley at Walter Reed and others in charge. "We got in General Kiley's face on a regular basis." They brought Mother's Day gifts for soldiers to give their mothers and skipped family gatherings to be with the wounded. In February 2007 the Washington Post wrote a series of stories about wretched conditions—moldy, rat-infested rooms in outpatient dormitories. Young, whose visits were to inpatient facilities which were not in such bad shape, was asked why he hadn't made his complaints public or brought them before his committee. He said he "did not go public with these concerns because we did not want to undermine the confidence of the patients and their families and give the Army a black eye while fighting a war." And his wife wrote in a *St. Petersburg Times* blog, "I have given most of my time and all of my energy to making a better life for the wounded returning home...We never once turned our backs on a soldier in need."

The trend toward Democrats in Pinellas County had not previously posed any threat to Young. But Republican redistricters in 2002 made the district more Republican, so that the party could hold it if and when he retired. He was reelected unopposed in 2002 and won 69%-31% in 2004 and 66%-34% in 2006. But after the 2006 election, Democrats began talking about targeting the district, which had voted 51%-49% for Al Gore in 2000 and which George W. Bush carried by only 51%-49% in 2004. When the Walter Reed story broke in 2007, he was attacked by Democratic campaign staffers and by Florida Democratic Chairwoman and former Congresswoman Karen Thurman for not having reported the abuses he saw there. He wrote Thurman, "You have changed the personal smear campaign that my family and I have endured for several weeks into a political smear campaign based on what has become the big lie."

Young had considered retiring in April 2006, but in March 2007, after the Walter Reed criticism, he said, "I can guarantee I would not consider retiring in view of a major smear campaign because it's based on a big lie," he told *The St. Petersburg Times*. "It would look like I was running away." Democrats floated the names of many possible candidates, though some quickly said they had no intention of running: former Speaker Peter Wallace, former state Representative Lars Hafner, state Representatives Bill Heller and Rick Kriseman, state Senator Charlie Justice, his campaign manager Mitch Kates (a former professional wrestler known as Jason the Terrible), Bayfront Medical CEO Sue Brody, County Commissioner Ken Welch (who lives just outside the district). Among the Republicans mentioned as candidates if Young retired was County Commissioner Karen Seel and St. Petersburg Mayor Rick Baker, though he said in late 2006 that he was unlikely to run. Some speculated that Young would like to be succeeded by his son Bill Young, who will not reach the constitutional age to take office until 2010, or by his wife, Beverly. But Young said his wife is unlikely to run.

ELEVENTH DISTRICT

Rep. Kathy Castor (D)

Elected 2006, 1st term; b. Aug. 20, 1966, Miami; home, Tampa; Emory U., B.A. 1988, FL St. U., J.D. 1991; Presbyterian; married (William Lewis).

Elected Office: Hillsborough Cnty. Comm., 2002-06.

Professional Career: Asst. Gen. Counsel, FL Dept. of Community Affairs, 1991-94; Practicing atty., 1994-2000.

DC Office: 317 CHOB, 20515, 202-225-3376; Fax: 202-225-5652; Web site: castor.house.gov.

District Offices: Tampa, 813-871-2817.

Committees: *Armed Services* (33d of 34 D): Terrorism, Unconventional Threats & Capabilities; Air & Land Forces. *Rules* (7th of 9 D): Rules & Organization of the House.

Group Ratings and Key Votes: Newly Elected

Election Results

2006 general	Kathy Castor (D)	97,470	(70%)	($1,221,825)
	Eddie Adams (R)	42,454	(30%)	($27,990)
2006 primary	Kathy Castor (D)	21,310	(54%)	
	Les Miller (D)	13,474	(34%)	
	Scott Farrell (D)	1,721	(4%)	
	Al Fox (D)	1,653	(4%)	
	Other	1,336	(3%)	
2004 general	Jim Davis (D)	191,780	(86%)	($630,804)
	Robert Johnson (Lib)	31,579	(14%)	($21,141)

The People		Race/Ethnic Origin	Ancestry	
Area size:	460 sq. mi.	48.3% White	German: 7.6%	Irish: 6.6%
Urban population:	99.6%	27.4% Black	English: 5.8%	
Rural population:	0.4%	2.0% Asian	**2004 Presidential Vote**	
Pop. 2000:	639,295	0.3% Native Am.	Kerry (D) 145,831	(58%)
Pop. 2005 (est):	660,997	0.1% Hawaiian	Bush (R) 103,748	(41%)
Median income:	$33,559	1.7% Two+ races	Other 1,764	(1%)
Poverty status:	17.5%	0.2% Other	**2000 Presidential Vote**	
Military veterans:	13.1%	20.0% Hispanic Origin	Gore (D) 120,926	(61%)
			Bush (R) 77,367	(39%)
			Cook Partisan Voting Index: D +11	

Occupation	Blue collar: 21.2%	White collar: 61.4%	Gray collar: 17.4%

Tampa, one of America's boomtowns, has a history that goes back not much more than a century. Its industrial past can be traced to 1886, when Cuban cigarmakers left Key West for what became the Ybor City neighborhood. Then Tampa became the major embarkation port for U.S. troops in the Spanish-American War of 1898. It also became a major citrus distribution center. The old industrial city developed along the waterfront, where today you can find what is billed as the world's longest sidewalk (6.5 miles along Bayshore Boulevard); you can also see the 13 minarets on the Arabian-style Tampa Bay Hotel built by railroad and real-estate tycoon Henry B. Plant in the 1890s (now part of the University of Tampa). For a time, Tampa was Florida's one industrial city. Now, it has a diversified economy: A healthy service sector, the University of Tampa and the University of South Florida, and tourist attractions led by Busch Gardens. Tampa's subdivisions and condominiums, office towers and low-rise commercial buildings have spread inland across swamps and lowlands.

Through all of this, and in contrast to St. Petersburg with its many retirees, Tampa has remained a city of families and young people; seniors account for only about one in eight residents here, an unusually low percentage for Florida. As Tampa expands, its blue-collar character is quickly moving upscale. In January 2005, Donald Trump announced a 52-story luxury condominium project on the Hillsborough River in the city, although financing issues led to construction delays and a lawsuit by condo buyers. Tampa is also an important military center. MacDill Air Force Base, on the south side of Tampa jutting into Tampa Bay, is the headquarters of Central Command, which ran the Persian Gulf War and the campaigns in Afghanistan and Iraq, and of Special Operations Command. Generals Norman Schwarzkopf and Tommy Franks, retired after their successful commands in the same gated community in Tampa.

The 11th Congressional District of Florida is centered on Tampa, but has irregular boundaries. It includes most of the city of Tampa and close-in suburbs, the east shore of Tampa Bay, plus two areas across Tampa Bay. One is the heavily black and lower-income neighborhoods south of Central Avenue in St. Petersburg. The other is a strip of Manatee County bordering Tampa Bay that includes working-class neighborhoods in Memphis, Palmetto and Bradenton. Tropicana moved its headquarters to Chicago in 2004, but the distinctive – some say nauseating – smell of oranges from its citrus plant in Bradenton still occasionally fills the air. Connecting them is the distinctive Sunshine Skyway Bridge, a four-mile span completed in 1987 that has come to symbolize the Tampa Bay area. The district has a population that is 27% black and 20% Hispanic, making it the most heavily minority district in Florida outside the Gold Coast and the Jacksonville-to-Orlando 3d District. While Hillsborough County as a whole voted for George W. Bush in 2000 and 2004, the 11th District cast solid majorities for Al Gore and John Kerry.

The new congresswoman from the 11th District is Kathy Castor, a Democrat elected in 2006. Castor studied political science at Emory University, earned her law degree from Florida State University and worked as a land use attorney. Her parents were heavily involved in public service. Her father, Don Castor, sat on the Hillsborough County court for two decades; her mother, Betty Castor, served in the state Senate, as state education commissioner and president of the University of South Florida. In 2004 Betty Castor ran as the Democratic Senate nominee and lost 49%-48% to Republican Mel Martinez. Kathy Castor herself appeared on the ballot twice, first in 2000, when she ran unsuccessfully for the state Senate, and again in 2002, when she won a 4-year term on the Hillsborough County Commission. Castor was 1 of 2 Democrats on the 7-member commission and frequently cast lone votes, including opposition to a proposed beltway project. The commission's Republicans stripped her of assignments on several local boards and panels.

Castor family political fortunes began to change when five-term Democrat Jim Davis decided to run for governor in 2006, opening up a safe Democratic district. Kathy Castor announced her candidacy for Congress in April 2005 and benefited from the high name recognition from her mother's close Senate election just months earlier. In a district where Democrats enjoy a nearly 2–1 advantage over Republicans, Castor faced four opponents in the September 5 Democratic primary. The most formidable was state Senate Minority Leader Les Miller, a veteran African-American legislator. Although Miller was familiar to voters from his service in the state House and Senate, he proved unable to keep pace with Castor's prolific fundraising. With the support of EMILY's List, Castor raised nearly $1 million before the primary and outspent Miller by 3-to-1. Whites make up slightly less than half the district's population, and Miller contended the seat was drawn to elect a minority candidate after the 2000 census; the Tampa-St. Petersburg area has never elected a black representative to Congress. Castor trailed Miller in the heavily African-American portion of the Pinellas County, but she defeated him by more than 8,600 votes in Tampa's Hillsborough County, to win a 54%-34% victory.

The outcome of the general election in this comfortably Democratic district was never in doubt as Republican Eddie Adams, an architect, struggled to raise money and was absent from the campaign trail for three weeks in October while recovering from a ruptured appendix. Castor campaigned for expanded health care for low-income families and for stronger ethics and lobbying rules. Both were issues she advocated as a county commissioner and would later champion in Congress. She advocated a rapid withdrawal of U.S. troops from Iraq. She won the general election 70%-30%.

Well before Election Day, Castor began positioning herself as a congressional insider. She participated in leadership-sponsored fundraisers with the goal of getting good committee assignments. She told Nancy Pelosi in October that she wanted to serve as freshman representative on the Democratic Steering and Policy Committee, which determines committee assignments. Pelosi said no one had asked her for the position; Castor won the post after the election. Castor also claimed choice seats on the Rules and the Armed Services committees. As a member of the Rules panel, she was the first freshman to speak on the House floor when Congress took up its first legislative business in the new Democratic majority by changing House ethics rules. In early 2007, she introduced a bill to increase the number of Medicare-funded physician training slots in states facing a shortage. Castor appears well-positioned to hold onto this safe Democratic seat.

TWELFTH DISTRICT

Rep. Adam Putnam (R)

Elected 2000, 4th term; b. July 31, 1974, Bartow; home, Bartow; U. of FL, B.S. 1995; Episcopalian; married (Melissa).

Elected Office: FL House of Reps., 1996-2000.

Professional Career: Rancher, Putnam Groves, Inc.

DC Office: 1725 LHOB, 20515, 202-225-1252; Fax: 202-226-0585; Web site: www.adamputnam.house.gov.

District Offices: Bartow, 863-534-3530.

Committees: *Republican Conference Chairman. Financial Services* (28th of 33 R): Capital Markets, Insurance & Government Sponsored Enterprises.

Group Ratings

	ADA	ACLU	AFS	LCV	ITIC	NTU	COC	ACU	CFG	FRC
2006	0	5	0	8	100	55	100	84	53	100
2005	5	—	0	11	—	57	85	92	57	100

National Journal Ratings

	2005 LIB	—	2005 CONS		2006 LIB	—	2006 CONS
Economic	24%	—	74%		15%	—	85%
Social	0%	—	89%		28%	—	70%
Foreign	31%	—	67%		6%	—	86%

Key Votes of the 109th Congress

1. Estate Tax Repeal	Y	5. Limit Interstate Abortion	Y	9. Build Border Fence	Y
2. Limit CAFE Standards	Y	6. Extend Patriot Act	Y	10. CAFTA	Y
3. FY06 Spending Curb	Y	7. Bar Same Sex Marriage	Y	11. Oppose Iraq Withdrawal	Y
4. Drilling in ANWR	Y	8. Stem Cell Research $	N	12. Detainee Tribunals	Y

Election Results

2006 general	Adam Putnam (R)	124,452	(70%)	($991,101)
	Joe Viscusi (NPA)	34,976	(20%)	($36,935)
	Ed Bowlin (NPA)	12,590	(11%)	($14,833)
2006 primary	Adam Putnam (R)	unopposed		
2004 general	Adam Putnam (R)	179,204	(65%)	($700,625)
	Bob Hagenmaier (D)	96,965	(35%)	($54,002)

Prior Winning Percentages: 2002 (100%); 2000 (57%)

The People		Race/Ethnic Origin	Ancestry	
Area size:	2,096 sq. mi.	72.1% White	German: 9.9%	USA: 9.8%
Urban population:	84.3%	13.0% Black	Irish: 8.4%	
Rural population:	15.7%	1.1% Asian	**2004 Presidential Vote**	
Pop. 2000:	639,296	0.3% Native Am.	Bush (R) 167,216	(58%)
Pop. 2005 (est):	739,405	0.0% Hawaiian	Kerry (D) 119,825	(42%)
Median income:	$37,769	1.3% Two+ races	Other 798	(0%)
Poverty status:	12.4%	0.1% Other	**2000 Presidential Vote**	
Military veterans:	17.0%	12.0% Hispanic Origin	Bush (R) 121,083	(55%)
			Gore (D) 99,826	(45%)
			Cook Partisan Voting Index: R + 5	

Occupation   Blue collar: 26.1%   White collar: 55.9%   Gray collar: 18.0%

With their skyscrapers rising over bays and rivers, the great gleaming cities of Florida are found near the Atlantic or Gulf coasts. But the most expansive inland county in the state, billed as the heart of central Florida, is Polk County. It is filled with modest lakes and small and medium-sized cities: Lakeland, Bartow, Lake Wales, Winter Haven, Frostproof and Haines City. It is the part of Florida most dependent on agriculture: strawberries, cattle and citrus remain economic mainstays, though periodic freezes have convinced some orange growers to move south or produce tomatoes instead. Turpentine distilleries, dependent on the big stands of pine, and phosphate mining businesses can be found as well. There are more manufacturing jobs here proportionately than almost anywhere else in Florida (though still not very many). Retired *Ladies Home Journal* editor Edward Bok in 1929 built the most prominent landmarks here: the 205-foot gothic Bok Tower with carillon, and the surrounding Mountain Lake Sanctuary and gardens. A remnant of the old Florida, this area has not become a major retiree haven; it grew 23% between 1990 and 2004—rapid growth in most of the country, but not by Florida standards. About half the growth has been a large influx of Latinos. Devastating hurricanes in recent years have caused the loss of thousands of jobs for migrants and seasonal laborers.

The 12th Congressional District of Florida includes almost all of Polk County, which is about 60% of the population. This was the home of Spessard Holland and Lawton Chiles, two legendary Democrats who each served as governor and senator. Even today, there are more registered Democrats than Republicans, but Polk County, like most of the Deep South, increasingly votes Republican; in the 2006 governor's race, Republican Charlie Crist won the county with 56% of the vote. The 12th District includes a sliver of Osceola County and the rapidly growing suburbs just east of Tampa in Republican-leaning Hillsborough County—places like Brandon, home to strip malls and younger, pro-business families. Overall this district is becoming reliably Republican. It voted 55% for George W. Bush in 2000 and 58% in 2004.

The congressman from the 12th District is Adam Putnam, a Republican first elected in 2000 and, at one time, the youngest member of the House. He grew up in Polk County, a fifth-generation member of a Bartow family, graduated from the University of Florida and worked in his family's citrus and cattle business. In 1996, at 22, he was elected to the state House ("I was 22 and looked about 12," he said later); as Agriculture Committee chairman he supported a "sovereign lands" bill that would have given shoreline property on inland waters to adjacent property owners and that was strongly opposed by environmental groups. In 2000, when Congressman Charles Canady kept his term-limits pledge, Putnam ran and was unopposed in the Republican primary. He supported most parts of the Republican agenda; opposed abortion and gun control; wanted to lower the capital gains tax; and favored missile defense and personal retirement accounts in Social Security. In his first election, Putnam had a tougher than expected challenge from auto-dealer and first-time candidate Michael Stedem, who said Putnam did not have enough life experience for the job. Stedem's message gained some traction; Putnam was ridiculed in the press. "Putnam is 26 and looks as if he's going on 13," the *Tampa Tribune* wrote in October 2000, in a story headlined, "Opie runs for Congress." But he won the seat 57%-43%. Though he has been reelected easily since then, his youthful looks continue to draw mention. President Bush calls him "Red" (for his hair). A less-admiring Congressman Marion Berry referred to him as "a Howdy-Doody looking Nimrod" during a House debate in November 2005.

With one notable exception, Putnam has been a reliably conservative vote. That one case was the December 2001 vote on trade promotion authority, where he sided with the citrus industry, despite considerable pressure from party leaders and from Bush on Air Force One a week before the vote. When the bill returned to the House a few months later to resolve final details, Putnam got what he viewed as a stronger commitment to protect citrus interests and he voted in favor. Putnam had another memorable ride with Bush three months earlier. On September 11, he was with Bush during a visit to an elementary school in Sarasota when word came of the attacks on the World Trade Center towers. After their rapid and steeply-banking exit and before they landed at Barksdale Air Force Base in Louisiana, Bush called in Putnam and the 13th District's Dan Miller for a briefing of his options that morning. The two congressmen returned to Washington on another plane. On immigration, an important local issue, Putnam supported Bush's guest worker proposal, based partly on his own family's hiring experiences. After the 2004 hurricanes, he helped to get $500 million in disaster relief for his state's agricultural industry.

In 2003 he became chairman of the Technology, Information Policy, Intergovernmental Relations and Census Subcommittee on Government Reform, making him the youngest subcommittee chair in the post-World War II era. As chairman, he passed an amendment to the 2004 intelligence bill that required federal agencies to emphasize information security in planning new systems. Speaker Dennis Hastert rewarded his party faithfulness with a seat on the House Rules Committee. That enhanced his status as a rising star, and led to quick moves up the leadership ladder. In February 2006, he defeated three other candidates to become chairman of the Republican Policy Committee; Hastert tasked him to develop the party's partisan approach on immigration policy. He helped to broker the deal to permit limited oil drilling off the coast of Florida; he said that the measure enhanced protection in environmentally sensitive areas.

In November 2006, he continued his leadership climb, defeating three opponents to become chairman of the Republican Conference, the third-ranking leadership position in the minority. In the latter post, he moved aggressively to coordinate the party's message in opposition to the Democratic majority. He formed a rapid-response team and assembled a new communications strategy that focused on small media markets. He said his party's challenge was to get noticed against the backdrop of a new congressional majority, a presidential election cycle and "the historical nature of a woman Speaker." With his impressive rise in the House, he continues to be mentioned as a possible statewide candidate.

THIRTEENTH DISTRICT

Rep. Vern Buchanan (R)

Elected 2006, 1st term; b. May 8, 1951, Detroit, MI; home, Longboat Key; Cleary U., B.B.A. 1975, U. of Detroit, M.B.A. 1986; Baptist; married (Sandy).

Military Career: MI Air Natl. Guard, 1970-76.

Professional Career: Tae kwon do instructor, 1971-74; Marketing representative, Burroughs Corp., 1975-76; Founder, Vern Buchanan and Associates, 1976-78; Founder and CEO, American Speedy Printing Centers, 1976-92; Founder and chmn., Buchanan Automotive Group, 1992-2007; Founder and chmn., Buchanan Enterprises, 1992-2007.

DC Office: 1516 LHOB, 20515, 202-225-5015; Fax: 202-226-0828; Web site: buchanan.house.gov.

District Offices: Bradenton, 941-747-9081; Sarasota, 941-951-6643.

Committees: *Small Business* (14th of 15 R): Finance & Tax; Regulations, Healthcare & Trade. *Transportation & Infrastructure* (34th of 34 R): Aviation; Highways & Transit. *Veterans' Affairs* (13th of 13 R).

Group Ratings and Key Votes: Newly Elected

Election Results

2006 general	Vern Buchanan (R)	119,309	(50%)	($8,112,752)
	Christine Jennings (D)	118,940	(50%)	($3,002,798)
2006 primary	Vern Buchanan (R)	20,918	(32%)	
	Nancy Detert (R)	15,804	(24%)	
	Tramm Hudson (R)	15,535	(24%)	
	Mark Flanagan (R)	6,465	(10%)	
	Donna Clarke (R)	5,972	(9%)	
2004 general	Katherine Harris (R)	190,477	(55%)	($3,556,976)
	Jan Schneider (D)	153,961	(45%)	($655,790)

The People		Race/Ethnic Origin	Ancestry	
Area size:	2,948 sq. mi.	86.0% White	German: 14.1%	English: 10.8%
Urban population:	89.4%	4.4% Black	Irish: 10.2%	
Rural population:	10.6%	0.8% Asian	**2004 Presidential Vote**	
Pop. 2000:	639,295	0.2% Native Am.	Bush (R) 200,932	(56%)
Pop. 2005 (est):	728,736	0.0% Hawaiian	Kerry (D) 156,727	(43%)
Median income:	$40,187	0.8% Two+ races	Other 2,642	(1%)
Poverty status:	9.4%	0.1% Other	**2000 Presidential Vote**	
Military veterans:	19.2%	7.7% Hispanic Origin	Bush (R) 152,725	(54%)
			Gore (D) 127,751	(46%)
			Cook Partisan Voting Index: R + 4	

Occupation   Blue collar: 21.0%   White collar: 58.5%   Gray collar: 20.5%

When the Ringling Brothers made a success of the circus they founded in the 1880s, they needed a place for performers and animals to rest during the winter months. They settled on the bayfront village of Sarasota, located behind a barrier island on the Gulf of Mexico. It was just far enough north to be reachable by railroad, just far enough south to be semitropical so the elephants would not get sick and die. Here, on the calm Sarasota Bay, John Ringling established the Ringling Museum of Art, a huge sculpture garden and his own Venetian palace, the Ca'd'Zan; next door, his brother Charles built a pair of neoclassical revival mansions made of pink Georgia marble, now part of New College of Florida. After World War II, the balmy Gulf Coast attracted new settlers— affluent, well-educated Republicans from WASPy, upper-crust suburbs in the north. The population exploded, with Manatee and Sarasota Counties leaping from 63,000 in 1950 to 683,000 in 2006. This part of Florida is no longer a winter community for snow birds from the North; it has generated its own economy, one with considerably more vitality than and just as much diversity as the places from which its residents have come.

The 13th Congressional District of Florida runs from just below Tampa Bay to Charlotte Harbor, north of Fort Myers. It includes all of Sarasota County, which accounts for just over half the district's population, and all of lightly populated, rural DeSoto and Hardee Counties, most of Manatee County to the north and an adjoining sliver of Charlotte County to the south. The barrier islands include much idyllic beachfront, from sleepy Anna Maria down through pricey Longboat Key and Lido Key to more casual Siesta Key. The bayfront area, along the Intracoastal Waterway, is lined with high rises and often clogged with traffic, running from Bradenton south to Sarasota. Below that, Venice—established in 1920 as a speculative land venture by the Brotherhood of Locomotive Engineers and, since 1960, the winter quarters for the circus sits directly on the Gulf. Though some high-tech firms diversify the economy, this remains a place of tourists and well-off retirees: 29% of the population is over 65, and it has 182,000 Social Security recipients, third highest of all U.S. congressional districts. The large number of retirees that take prescription drugs has made Manatee County a major battleground in the competition between the Walgreens and CVS pharmacy chains. For many years, the 13th District was heavily Republican, and it remains that way in party registration, but like the affluent northern suburbs from which so many of its voters came, it trended toward the Democrats in the 1990s. George W. Bush has carried this district, but with just 54% of the vote in 2000 and 56% in 2004. Democratic successes at the local level in 2006 have challenged Republican domination in the Sarasota area.

The new congressman from the 13th District is Vern Buchanan, a Republican elected in 2006. Buchanan grew up outside of Detroit the eldest of six children and the son of a factory foreman. He joined the Michigan Air National Guard and worked his way through college as a tae kwon do instructor, while earning a business degree from Cleary University and later an MBA from the University of Detroit. Buchanan founded American Speedy Printing Centers and made his fortune by selling 700 quick-printing franchises before his 40th birthday. In 1990 Buchanan moved his family to Florida, where he found new success as an automobile dealer with franchises throughout the Southeast. Buchanan became active in Republican Party politics, serving as a top fundraiser for Republicans such as Florida Governor Jeb Bush and Senator Mel Martinez. He had considered a 2002 bid for this seat when Republican Dan Miller retired but stepped aside when then-Secretary of State Katherine Harris, a national Republican figure after her role in the 2000 presidential race, entered the race.

Buchanan got his chance to run for Congress in 2006, when Harris announced she would challenge Democratic Senator Democrat Bill Nelson. His party connections and personal finances made him the frontrunner. In the primary, Buchanan worked to appeal to conservatives, and challenged his chief rival, former Sarasota Republican party Chairman Tramm Hudson for his positions on abortion and immigration. Other Republican candidates included state Representatives Nancy Detert and Donna Clarke and former state Representative Mark Flanagan. Buchanan said he opposed abortion without any exceptions and claimed in a fundraising letter he was the only anti-abortion Republican in the race. Hudson stumbled when he retold a story about his days in the Army and said that black soldiers were poor swimmers. Buchanan faced withering assaults on his business dealings: Hudson leveled the fiercest attacks, reminding voters that Buchanan resigned from his printing company just days before it declared bankruptcy. This recasting of Buchanan's success story took a toll: After spending more than $2 million of his own money, Buchanan limped to a 32% victory in the five-way primary. Detert and Hudson finished next with 24% each.

The bruising primary took place September 5 and left Buchanan little time to recover before the general election. The Democratic nominee was Christine Jennings, who like Buchanan, was a transplanted Midwesterner who became a self-made business success. Jennings, who unsuccessfully sought the Democratic nomination in 2004, was an Ohio native whose rise from bank teller to bank owner made a compelling story. The Democratic Congressional Campaign Committee backed Jennings, who won the primary with 62%, over Jan Schneider, who had twice lost to Katherine Harris. Democrats continued pummeling Buchanan through the fall, hammering him over the American Speedy Printing Centers bankruptcy and over a messy real estate deal involving the Sarasota Ritz-Carlton that ended up in litigation. Buchanan responded by characterizing Jennings as a pro-tax liberal, a charge that was tough to stick on the former Republican with a business background. Despite the Republican advantage in the district, Buchanan was hurt by the attacks on his business dealings, the poor political environment for Republicans and late-breaking revelations about Mark Foley's contact with congressional pages. Buchanan's free-spending ways kept him in contention and made this the most expensive House race in 2006. He spent $8.1 million, including $5.5 million of his own money, compared to Jennings, who spent $3 million, $2.1 million out of her own pocket.

Buchanan prevailed on Election Day, but Democrats disputed the results for months. After a recount, Republican election officials certified Buchanan the winner by 369 votes out of nearly 240,000 votes cast. Democrats decried the more than 18,000 "undervotes" on ballots that registered a vote for other offices but did not indicate a choice in the congressional race. The Jennings campaign suggested that a software glitch on touch-screen voting machines in Sarasota County was to blame for the unusually high number of undervotes, while a poor ballot design or intentional voter choice were also suggested as possibilities. Tests run after the election did not provide a conclusive answer and Jennings filed a lawsuit in state courts and contested the election with the House Administration Committee, which in March 2007 named a three-member task force to look into the dispute. Democrats seated Buchanan in the House but reserved the option of removing him if Jennings succeeded in one of her challenges. Jennings also filed a motion to stay her appeal of the results in the First District Court of Appeals, saying that "issues of practicality and timing weight heavily in favor of deferring to the House investigation."

The three member task force, which included two Democrats and one Republican, instructed the Government Accountability Office to test the reliability of the voting machines and determine whether they were responsible for the lower number of votes cast and report back to the committee by July 27. That report was finally delivered on August 4; the investigator testified that no "smoking gun" was found and that a deeper inquiry was needed to find the problem in Sarasota County's election system. Jennings' legal team continued to allege that codes could have malfunctioned within the system; the GAO report said they were permitted to review the source code only a week before the report was issued, but more testing on those codes was needed.

In contrast to the primary campaign he waged as a Reagan conservative, Buchanan appeared to soften his ideological positions in Congress. He voted for five of the Democrats' "Six for '06" legislative priorities, opposing only the stem cell research bill. "I ran as a conservative, but I also ran as someone who is going to be independent," he told the *Sarasota Herald-Tribune* . "Obviously, some of the industry groups are, initially maybe, not happy about it. But the other side of it is I've gotten a lot of positive feedback in our community." Buchanan's difficult elections and the ongoing legal challenges have marked him as a Democratic target in 2008. Jennings announced in July 2007 that she would again challenge Buchanan. "I didn't lose," she said. "I just don't have the seat." Buchanan was taking his reelection seriously: he reported raising $826,000 by July 2007.

FOURTEENTH DISTRICT

Rep. Connie Mack (R)

Elected 2004, 2d term; b. Aug. 12, 1967, Fort Myers; home, Fort Myers; U. of FL, B.S. 1993; Catholic; engaged.

Elected Office: FL House, 2000-03.

Professional Career: Marketing consultant, 1994-2004.

DC Office: 115 CHOB, 20515, 202-225-2536; Fax: 202-226-0439; Web site: mack.house.gov.

District Offices: Cape Coral, 239-573-5837; Naples, 239-774-8035.

Committees: *Budget* (10th of 17 R). *Foreign Affairs* (17th of 23 R): Western Hemisphere; Middle East & South Asia. *Transportation & Infrastructure* (26th of 34 R): Water Resources & Environment; Aviation.

Group Ratings

	ADA	ACLU	AFS	LCV	ITIC	NTU	COC	ACU	CFG	FRC
2006	25	23	0	17	86	68	93	84	75	71
2005	5	—	0	22	—	67	81	92	84	92

National Journal Ratings

	2005 LIB	—	2005 CONS	2006 LIB	—	2006 CONS
Economic	21%	—	77%	40%	—	60%
Social	42%	—	58%	43%	—	56%
Foreign	33%	—	66%	17%	—	73%

Key Votes of the 109th Congress

1. Estate Tax Repeal	Y	5. Limit Interstate Abortion	Y	9. Build Border Fence	Y
2. Limit CAFE Standards	Y	6. Extend Patriot Act	N	10. CAFTA	N
3. FY06 Spending Curb	Y	7. Bar Same Sex Marriage	Y	11. Oppose Iraq Withdrawal	Y
4. Drilling in ANWR	Y	8. Stem Cell Research $	Y	12. Detainee Tribunals	Y

Election Results

2006 general	Connie Mack (R)	151,615	(64%)	($973,082)
	Robert Neeld (D)	83,920	(36%)	($41,314)
2006 primary	Connie Mack (R)	unopposed		
2004 general	Connie Mack (R)	226,662	(68%)	($1,854,028)
	Robert Neeld (D)	108,672	(32%)	($25,275)

The People		Race/Ethnic Origin	Ancestry	
Area size:	1,718 sq. mi.	83.8% White	German: 14.5% Irish: 11.0%	
Urban population:	90.7%	5.1% Black	English: 10.2%	
Rural population:	9.3%	0.7% Asian	**2004 Presidential Vote**	
Pop. 2000:	639,295	0.2% Native Am.	Bush (R)	222,234 (62%)
Pop. 2005 (est):	777,621	0.0% Hawaiian	Kerry (D)	136,049 (38%)
Median income:	$42,541	1.0% Two+ races	Other	2,631 (1%)
Poverty status:	8.8%	0.1% Other	**2000 Presidential Vote**	
Military veterans:	19.8%	9.0% Hispanic Origin	Bush (R)	163,750 (61%)
			Gore (D)	103,118 (39%)
			Cook Partisan Voting Index: R +10	

Occupation   Blue collar: 21.1%   White collar: 59.6%   Gray collar: 19.3%

On the edge of the tropics, in a physical environment once teeming with diseases and inhospitable to advanced civilization three generations ago, Florida's Gulf Coast has sprung up as a model for retirement living. Early on, there were only a few white settlements here; one was Fort Myers, built in 1850 as an Army base to help get rid of the Seminole Indians. The fort achieved its goal: In 1858, the last Seminoles were sent west on boats. For another century after that, this corner of Florida was mostly deserted. But in time, it became resort country, thanks to its wide, white-sand beaches with gentle breakers; the inlets and broad estuaries that are perfect for boating; and the wetlands graced with exotic birds. Thomas Edison had his winter home in Fort Myers, Henry Ford used to visit here and tourists came to a beach thick with sea shells on nearby Sanibel and Captiva islands. But the local economy could not support many permanent residents, and at the beginning of World War II, there were only 68,000 people living on the Gulf Coast from Bradenton south to Naples.

By 2004, there were 1.6 million. The climate and environment, and the fact that Florida has no state income or inheritance tax, attracted waves of affluent suburbanites from the Midwest and Northeast. Developers like Barron Collier, who built the Tamiami Trail across the soggy Everglades and designed Naples with the wealthy in mind (and gave his name to Collier County, the richest and from 1990 to 2003 the third fastest-growing in Florida), were determined to avoid the high-rise canyons that line the Atlantic from Palm Beach to Miami. Their alternative was to construct low-rise, city-style developments, such as rapidly growing Cape Coral, with 409 miles of canals running through most backyards; thinly-paved roads run along the sand spits next to the sultry, lapping waves of the Gulf, and luxurious boutique towns like Naples, set amidst preserved coastal islands, St. Augustine grass and banyan trees. This is very much retirement country, for those who can afford it. Although much of this area has been damaged by multiple hurricanes the past few years, there has been no appreciable slowdown in new residential or commercial development; the Cape Coral-Fort Myers metro area was the third fastest-growing in the nation between 2000 and 2006.

The 14th Congressional District of Florida occupies the southern half of the habitable Gulf Coast below Tampa Bay; much of its growth is driven by retirees, who account for more than one of every four residents. The 14th includes a small part of Port Charlotte and Charlotte County, all of Lee County and the coastal strip of Collier County including Naples and Marco Island. Two-thirds of the district's residents live in Lee County, in places like Fort Myers, Bonita Springs and Sanibel and Captiva Islands. In a state where Republican registration rates often understate Republican voting strength, the 14th District counts 49% of its electorate as registered Republicans. Just 27% are registered Democrats, the lowest percentage of any Florida district.

The congressman from the 14th District is Connie Mack IV, a Republican elected in 2004, whose father Connie Mack III held the same seat for three terms in the 1980s and then served two terms in the Senate. His great-grandfather and best-known forebear was Philadelphia Athletics baseball owner and manager for 50 years Cornelius McGillicuddy, who shortened his name to Connie Mack. Connie Mack IV graduated from the University of Florida after seven years and worked as a marketing consultant. In 2000 he was elected to the state House from a district across the state in Broward and Palm Beach Counties. In Tallahassee, he formed the anti-tax Freedom Caucus, which fought against increased state spending and in favor of lower taxes and limits on attorneys' fees in personal injury and malpractice cases.

To political observers, Mack seemed a more logical candidate to one day succeed 22d District Republican Clay Shaw (as it turns out, Shaw lost his 2006 reelection bid). But in 2004 Porter Goss, chairman of the House Intelligence Committee since 1997, was not running for reelection in the 14th District; Goss was nominated to be Director of the CIA and, after his confirmation by the Senate, resigned from the House in September 2004. Mack resigned from the state House in October 2003 and moved across the state to Lee County and ran for the seat. He faced three opponents in the Republican primary: state Representative Carole Green from Lee County, Lee County Commissioner Andy Coy and Naples physician Frank Schwerin. Mack raised $1.4 million for the primary, outpacing his nearest Republican rival by more than 2–1, and blanketed southwestern Florida with TV ads. His opponents attacked him as a carpetbagger who hadn't lived in the 14th District since he was a teenager and had moved there simply to run for Congress. Mack, who refused interviews with reporters and responded only to written questions, countered that he was the only candidate who had been born and raised in the district. Green was endorsed by the *Fort Myers News-Press* and by Mariel Goss, wife of Porter Goss. Editorialists were dismissive of Mack's qualifications, as well as his carpetbagging. "What a hoot," wrote the *Palm Beach Post,* which noted that his marketing consulting included sending Hooters girls to charity events. Mack's opponents claimed that he was an inexperienced lightweight who spoke in platitudes. The four Republicans differed little on the issues. All campaigned as conservatives and all backed George W. Bush's war on terrorism and tax cuts. Mack campaigned as a budget hawk and said that national security would top his agenda. While he opposed abortion, he broke with the Bush administration on federal funding of embryonic stem-cell research. He supported reimportation of prescription drugs from Canada; the 14th District has the fourth highest number of Social Security recipients in the nation.

Mack won the primary with 36% of the vote; Green narrowly carried Lee County, which cast 73% of the total vote, but fell short district-wide with 32%; Coy won 22% and Schwerin 10%. In November Mack won 68%-32%.

In the House, his votes fell toward the center, especially on social issues. He made few waves during his first term, except to show his independence from other Florida Republicans by opposing a compromise to permit oil drilling off the state's coast. He broke with national environmentalists with his support for drilling in the Arctic National Wildlife Refuge. He listed his top local priority as more scientific research on the causes of algae and red tide, which have been killing local dolphins and manatees. He claimed credit for $81 million to widen I-75. He was reelected easily. In September 2007, he announced his engagement to California Congresswoman Mary Bono.

FIFTEENTH DISTRICT

Rep. Dave Weldon (R)

Elected 1994, 7th term; b. Aug. 31, 1953, Amityville, NY; home, Palm Bay; S.U.N.Y. Stony Brook, B.A. 1978, S.U.N.Y. Buffalo, M.D. 1981; Christian; married (Nancy).

Military Career: Army Medical Corps, 1981-87, Army Reserves, 1987-92.

Professional Career: Practicing physician, 1987-94.

DC Office: 2347 RHOB, 20515, 202-225-3671; Fax: 202-225-3516; Web site: weldon.house.gov.

District Offices: Melbourne, 321-632-1776.

Committees: *Appropriations* (21st of 29 R): Labor, HHS, Education & Related Agencies; State, Foreign Operations & Related Programs.

Group Ratings

	ADA	ACLU	AFS	LCV	ITIC	NTU	COC	ACU	CFG	FRC
2006	5	5	0	0	86	55	93	88	54	100
2005	0	—	0	11	—	59	81	88	59	92

National Journal Ratings

	2005 LIB	—	2005 CONS		2006 LIB	—	2006 CONS
Economic	36%	—	64%		25%	—	74%
Social	12%	—	88%		11%	—	85%
Foreign	11%	—	86%		6%	—	86%

Key Votes of the 109th Congress

1. Estate Tax Repeal	Y	5. Limit Interstate Abortion	Y	9. Build Border Fence	Y
2. Limit CAFE Standards	Y	6. Extend Patriot Act	Y	10. CAFTA	Y
3. FY06 Spending Curb	Y	7. Bar Same Sex Marriage	Y	11. Oppose Iraq Withdrawal	Y
4. Drilling in ANWR	Y	8. Stem Cell Research $	N	12. Detainee Tribunals	Y

Election Results

2006 general	Dave Weldon (R)	125,965	(56%)	($925,951)
	Bob Bowman (D)	97,834	(44%)	($115,380)
2006 primary	Dave Weldon (R)	unopposed		
2004 general	Dave Weldon (R)	210,388	(65%)	($733,711)
	Simon Pristoop (D)	111,538	(35%)	($54,355)

Prior Winning Percentages: 2002 (63%); 2000 (59%); 1998 (63%); 1996 (51%); 1994 (54%)

The People		Race/Ethnic Origin	Ancestry	
Area size:	3,253 sq. mi.	77.8% White	German: 12.2%	Irish: 10.6%
Urban population:	89.6%	7.3% Black	English: 9.7%	
Rural population:	10.4%	1.6% Asian	**2004 Presidential Vote**	
Pop. 2000:	639,295	0.3% Native Am.	Bush (R) 195,076	(57%)
Pop. 2005 (est):	743,985	0.0% Hawaiian	Kerry (D) 146,914	(43%)
Median income:	$39,397	1.4% Two+ races	Other 2,128	(1%)
Poverty status:	9.8%	0.2% Other	**2000 Presidential Vote**	
Military veterans:	19.4%	11.3% Hispanic Origin	Bush (R) 141,242	(54%)
			Gore (D) 121,611	(46%)
			Cook Partisan Voting Index: R + 4	

Occupation	Blue collar: 21.5%	White collar: 58.4%	Gray collar: 20.1%

When Cape Canaveral was chosen as the nation's rocket testing site in the 1940s, there were only 20,000 people in all of Brevard County, which stretches along 63 miles of the coast north and south of the Cape. It was a backward place reliant on fishing and citrus-growing, chosen because it was on the sunny Atlantic coast: rockets here have to be launched eastward so that spent parts fall into the ocean. In 1948, the Brooklyn Dodgers established their spring-training home in Vero Beach, located 60 miles south of Canaveral in Indian River County; it remained segregated through the mid-1950s, until Dodger executives used an ingenious method to flex their economic muscle in the service of integration: They stamped the team's name on 20,000 dollar bills and told players and reporters to spend them freely at local establishments. Local officials got the message, easing off on Jim Crow, at least when Jackie Robinson and his teammates were in town. Today, the region has come a long way. Brevard County has 519,000 people, and the Kennedy Space Center attracts 2 million visitors annually. Brevard County is a prototype of America's future, with no city center but plenty of shopping centers along strip highways, with a white-collar, service economy, knitted together by interest in the space program, which constitutes 16% of local jobs. Even with cutbacks in commercial satellite launches, development continued strong. Proximity to Disney World has spawned growth in the cruise line business, Port Canaveral is the second-largest passenger port in the world. But the Dodgers planned to move their spring training facilities to Arizona in 2009, breaking one of the last connections to the franchise's Brooklyn era.

The 15th Congressional District of Florida includes much, but not all, of the 72-mile Space Coast; the area code here is 321. Its northern end is at Cape Canaveral itself, but most of the Space Center facilities, including the visitors' center, are in the 24th District. It runs south along the Atlantic Coast and includes 75% of Brevard, and all of Indian River County; among the bigger towns are Cocoa Beach, Melbourne, Palm Bay and Vero Beach. To the west the district includes all but a small piece of Osceola County; the population here is just south of Disney World and concentrated around Kissimmee and St. Cloud. This is the fastest-growing part of the district, with a rapidly increasing Puerto Rican and Latino population. The district also includes the northern tip of Polk County. The population here is a mixture of young workers and retirees, plus military families stationed at Patrick Air Force Base, home of the 45th Space Wing. Politically, the district leans Republican. In 2004, George W. Bush won more easily here than in 2000. The Bush campaign worked intensively on the new Latino voters in Osceola County; Bush lost the county 52%-48% in 2000 but carried it 52%-47% in 2004. Brevard—the home of Senator Bill Nelson—remains Republican, but it is becoming less so; Republican Charlie Crist got 54% there in his successful 2006 governor's race.

The congressman from the 15th District is Dave Weldon, a Republican first elected in 1994. Weldon grew up on Long Island, went to medical school in Buffalo, and served in the Army as a major at Fort Stewart, Georgia. In 1987, he joined Melbourne Internal Medicine Associates in Florida; two years later, he founded the Space Coast Family Forum "to promote family-friendly issues and positions." In 1994 Weldon ran for the House when moderate Democrat Jim Bacchus retired after two terms; he was considered a weak candidate because of his strong conservative views on cultural issues. But Weldon led the seven-candidate Republican primary with 24% of the vote, and in the runoff won 54%-46% over moderate Carole Jordan. Democrats ran Sue Munsey, a former Republican and Space Coast Chamber of Commerce head who supported abortion rights. Weldon called for phasing out welfare and banning abortion; he won 54%-46%. Speaker Newt Gingrich, whom Weldon called an "idol," gave him a seat on the Science Committee and made him vice chairman of the Space and Aeronautics Subcommittee.

Weldon has a mostly conservative voting record. He is the co-founder and chairman of the Congressional Aerospace Caucus and represents one of the few districts where a seat on the Science committee would be considered a plum assignment. He started off defending the Kennedy Space Center and promoting the space shuttle, protecting their funding even when NASA funding was going down. With Senator Bob Graham, he passed a bill in 1998 to move toward commercialization of space. But commercial competition and the response to the loss of the space shuttle Columbiain February 2003, may bring long-term challenges to the Cape Canaveral area. Even before the shuttle blew up over Texas, Weldon complained that budget cuts were "slowly killing space explora- tion" and that NASA requirements are "fluid" and its designs "overly complex"; he cited reduced spending as a factor in the failure of two Mars missions. In 2003, he gained a seat on the Appropria- tions Committee, giving him more direct impact on NASA's budget. Weldon's interest in space and technology is not limited to his day job: in 2002, he co-authored with writer William Proctor *Moongate,* a sci-fi novel about a Brevard County congressman who chairs the House Space Commit- tee and gains the power to cure many ills through genetic engineering. Another off-hours pursuit: Weldon plays bass guitar in the Second Amendments, a bipartisan group of musical congressmen.

Weldon favors increased defense spending, a 17% flat tax, school vouchers and education IRAs. Citing labor and human rights abuses plus undercutting of the U.S. space launch industry, he voted against normal trade relations with China; but he voted for trade promotion authority. Weldon has been a leader in the campaign to ban cloning, including embryonic stem cell research, which he views as immoral. Although he does not oppose research on adult stem cells, he resisted efforts to find middle ground and avoid a veto by President Bush. Over strong objections from abortion advocates, he has helped to enact a provision to block states and localities from requiring health care providers and insurers to provide abortion services. He worked with Christian conservatives as the lead sponsor in March 2005 of the bill for the federal government to intervene on behalf of Terri Schiavo in the "right to die" case. "As a doctor, I would never pull her tube out," he said. On a more practical matter, he won a change in House rules to drop restrictions on members who are physi- cians from earning income from their medical practice. He worked to protect Patrick Air Force Base in the base-closing review.

Weldon's outspoken conservatism has inspired vigorous electoral opposition, but he has sur- vived with mostly comfortable margins. In 2002, Weldon beat a primary opponent who criticized him for violating his term-limit pledge by 83%-17%. In 2004, he was reelected with 65%. He had a closer race in 2006 against retired Air Force rocket scientist Robert Bowman, who criticized the Bush administration for committing "many young Americans to a battle that has absolutely nothing to do with the security of Americans." Bowman raised little money, but he held Weldon to a 56%-44% win in a year when Florida Republicans lost two House seats in districts to the south. That career-low reelection percentage has national Democrats looking closely at this district for 2008.

SIXTEENTH DISTRICT

Rep. Tim Mahoney (D)

Elected 2006, 1st term; b. Aug. 16, 1956, Aurora, IL; home, Venus; WV U., B.A. 1978, George Washington U., M.B.A. 1983; Methodist; married (Terry).

Professional Career: Sales exec., Computer Sciences Corp., 1978-79; Sales manager, Automatic Data Processing, 1979-81; Dir. of Government Sales, General Electric Information Systems, 1981-84; VP of marketing and sales, Tecmar, 1984-86; President, Rodime Systems, 1986-91; Pres., SyDOS Division, SyQuest Technology, 1991-94; Founder and COO, vFinance, 1994-06; Founder and Pres., Center for Innovative Entrepre- neurship, 2004-06.

DC Office: 1541 LHOB, 20515, 202-225-5792; Fax: 202-225-3132; Web site: www.mahoney.house.gov.

District Offices: Highlands, 863-471-1813; Martin, 772-878-3181; Port Charlotte, 941-627-9100.

Committees: *Agriculture* (25th of 25 D): Horticulture & Organic Agriculture; Livestock, Dairy & Poultry. *Financial Services* (30th of 37 D): Oversight & Investigations; Capital Markets, Insurance & Government Sponsored Enterprises; Financial Institutions & Consumer Credit.

Group Ratings and Key Votes: Newly Elected

Election Results

2006 general	Tim Mahoney (D)	115,832	(50%)	($2,783,045)
	Joe Negron (R)	111,415	(48%)	($814,562)
	Other	6,526	(3%)	
2006 primary	Tim Mahoney (D)	unopposed		
2004 general	Mark Foley (R)	215,563	(68%)	($1,839,746)
	Jeff Fisher (D)	101,247	(32%)	

The People		Race/Ethnic Origin		Ancestry		
Area size:	5,249 sq. mi.	81.8% White		German: 12.3% Irish: 11.3%		
Urban population:	84.5%	5.8% Black		English: 9.7%		
Rural population:	15.5%	1.0% Asian		**2004 Presidential Vote**		
Pop. 2000:	639,295	0.3% Native Am.		Bush (R)	183,339	(54%)
Pop. 2005 (est):	739,847	0.0% Hawaiian		Kerry (D)	154,632	(46%)
Median income:	$39,408	1.0% Two+ races		Other	1,312	(0%)
Poverty status:	10.0%	0.1% Other		**2000 Presidential Vote**		
Military veterans:	18.9%	10.1% Hispanic Origin		Bush (R)	141,029	(53%)
				Gore (D)	124,752	(47%)
				Cook Partisan Voting Index: R + 2		

Occupation	Blue collar: 21.8%	White collar: 57.5%	Gray collar: 20.6%

Urban Florida has fanned far across the swamplands from its original nuclei in beachfront resort communities. Once, metro Palm Beach was a narrow stretch along Lake Worth; now it runs inland almost halfway to Lake Okeechobee. Thus Palm Beach has spread out from its original locus around the posh Breakers Hotel and the Addison Mizner villas, across Lake Worth and well beyond West Palm Beach: These are now just neighborhoods within a vast metropolitan area. Old beach towns, such as Hobe Sound, located northward along the ocean, have become the hub of very affluent developments that stretch all the way to Stuart in Martin County. Farther north, near the old town of Fort Pierce, are larger but more modest developments like Port St. Lucie, which in 2006 began to shake its image as a sleepy bedroom community by winning the $40 million relocation of the Torrey Pines Institute of Molecular Studies. This is a stretch of Florida where spring training sites compete for baseball franchises that direct millions of dollars to local economies.

The 16th Congressional District of Florida stretches from the Atlantic almost to the Gulf of Mexico; it is one of the most oddly designed districts in the nation. In 2000, before redistricting, 44% of the 16th District's vote was cast in Palm Beach County; after redistricting, just 15% was cast there. On the Atlantic Coast it includes most of Martin County, with its very affluent towns of Stuart and Hobe Sound; much of St. Lucie County, where it includes the new developments of Port St. Lucie and Hutchinson Island and the white neighborhoods of Fort Pierce; and just a bit of Palm Beach County—Tequesta, its northernmost beach town, inland Royal Palm Beach and Wellington, a town for rich horse fanciers. By a thin corridor of land this Atlantic Coast area is connected to rural territory north and west of Lake Okeechobee: here huge farms produce citrus, tomatoes and other vegetables or support large dairy herds; the only population cluster is around Sebring, with its car racing track. In recent years, encroaching development, hurricanes and citrus diseases have threatened the viability of the citrus industry, and rising land prices have tempted farmers to get out of the business. This area is connected by the swamps of eastern Charlotte County with the Gulf Coast towns of Port Charlotte and Punta Gorda, on the wide Peace River where it empties into Port Charlotte and the Gulf of Mexico.

The new congressman from the 16th District is Tim Mahoney, a Democrat elected in 2006 to replace a Republican who resigned in disgrace. Mahoney was born in Illinois and grew up in New Jersey in a large Irish Catholic family of Kennedy Democrats. He studied computer science at West Virginia University, got his MBA from George Washington University and went to work selling computer equipment. Mahoney, by this time a Reagan Republican, moved to Florida in 1986 and founded Rodime Systems, which packaged disk drives for retail sale. He sold the business when its parent company moved to Singapore, and he helped found vFinance Inc., a financial services company based in Boca Raton. Recruited by state and national Democrats, Mahoney switched his party affiliation to Democrat in July 2005 and launched in October what appeared to be a long-shot campaign against six-term Republican Mark Foley.

Mahoney, a first-time candidate, ran a respectable campaign and proved an able fundraiser. He collected money from finance and technology interests and ended up spending over $500,000 out of pocket. Still, Foley was again favored to win reelection in this Republican-leaning district. The race tightened in the fall as Mahoney attacked Republicans for their growing appetite for earmarks and tried to link Foley to disgraced former lobbyist Jack Abramoff. In August, Mahoney filed a defamation lawsuit against Foley for television ads that claimed Mahoney had once fired workers and outsourced their jobs to Singapore. Another Foley ad noted Mahoney's company had been fined by the Securities and Exchange Commission.

Then, less than six weeks before the election, the race took a major turn when ABC News began reporting about inappropriate electronic instant messages sent by Foley to male congressional pages. Foley abruptly resigned his seat in Congress on September 29; the scandal grew quickly when it was revealed that Foley had a history of sending sexually explicit instant messages to underage pages. Foley went into seclusion, checked himself into an alcohol rehabilitation clinic and accused a Catholic priest of molesting him in his youth.

Coming so close to the election, the Foley scandal reverberated across the national political landscape. Republicans had just begun to gain traction in their efforts to talk about national security issues, but the Foley scandal halted the modest recovery. The House Ethics Committee launched an investigation that raised questions about how much House Speaker Dennis Hastert and National Republican Congressional Committee Chairman Tom Reynolds knew of Foley's contact with pages. Republicans scrambled to find a replacement nominee for Foley and on October 2 selected state Representative Joe Negron, a conservative who had abandoned a run earlier that year for state attorney general. The change came too close to the election to remove Foley's name from the ballot but all votes cast for Foley would be counted for Negron. State and local election officials announced that they would post signs in polling places explaining that a vote for Foley counted for Negron; Democrats challenged the legality of such signs, but an appeals court eventually permitted their posting as long as they also named the other candidates in the race.

Under the circumstances, a Mahoney victory seemed inevitable. But Negron gained on Mahoney in the five-week sprint to Election Day, using the snappy slogan, "Punch Foley for Joe." Negron, who at one time had been considered Foley's likely successor in this seat, had the support of the Republican establishment. The NRCC poured $1.6 million into the race; three weeks out from the election, one poll showed Mahoney ahead by only 7 points. But Mahoney provided a palatable alternative for Republicans who could not bring themselves to cast a vote in Foley's name. A wealthy businessman, he had described himself as a fundamentalist Christian. His 100-acre cattle ranch in Highlands County also helped to broaden his appeal in the rural parts of the district, where cattle and citrus dominate. With strong margins in Palm Beach and St. Lucie Counties, Mahoney won 50%-48%.

After the election, Mahoney won a seat on the Agriculture Committee, which oversees the 2007 farm bill reauthorization and positioned him to aid the district's citrus, sugar, and cattle interests. He pledged to work for lower homeowners insurance premiums, and introduced a bill with Alcee Hastings to fund the Indian River Lagoon and a cleanup of the St. Lucie River. Negron said he would not run in 2008, but Mahoney is still likely to face credible Republican opposition. State Representative Gayle Harrell, attorney Tom Rooney, the grandson of Pittsburgh Steelers founder Art Rooney, and Palm Beach Gardens Councilman Hal Valeche announced they would run for the Republican nomination. *The Hill* newspaper reported in May 2007 that Democratic party leaders were concerned about Mahoney's vulnerability and his frustration with the congressional pace; Mahoney told the paper, "Very candidly, this isn't the greatest job I've had."

SEVENTEENTH DISTRICT

Rep. Kendrick Meek (D)

Elected 2002, 3d term; b. Sept. 6, 1966, Miami; home, Miami; FL A&M U., B.S. 1989; Baptist; married (Leslie).

Elected Office: FL House of Reps., 1994-98; FL Senate, 1998-2002.

DC Office: 1039 LHOB, 20515, 202-225-4506; Fax: 202-226-0777; Web site: http://kendrickmeek.house.gov.

District Offices: Miami Gardens, 305-690-5905; Pembroke Pines, 954-450-6767.

Committees: *Armed Services* (32d of 34 D): Air & Land Forces. *Ways & Means* (22d of 24 D): Income Security & Family Support; Trade.

Group Ratings

	ADA	ACLU	AFS	LCV	ITIC	NTU	COC	ACU	CFG	FRC
2006	95	86	100	92	43	14	57	8	13	0
2005	95	—	100	89	—	15	52	9	3	8

National Journal Ratings

	2005 LIB	—	2005 CONS		2006 LIB	—	2006 CONS
Economic	71%	—	28%		69%	—	31%
Social	72%	—	28%		71%	—	29%
Foreign	66%	—	34%		62%	—	37%

Key Votes of the 109th Congress

1. Estate Tax Repeal	N	5. Limit Interstate Abortion	N	9. Build Border Fence	N
2. Limit CAFE Standards	Y	6. Extend Patriot Act	N	10. CAFTA	N
3. FY06 Spending Curb	N	7. Bar Same Sex Marriage	N	11. Oppose Iraq Withdrawal	N
4. Drilling in ANWR	N	8. Stem Cell Research $	Y	12. Detainee Tribunals	N

Election Results

2006 general	Kendrick Meek (D) .... unopposed		($976,658)
2006 primary	Kendrick Meek (D) 32,426	(89%)	
	Dufirstson Neree (D) 3,850	(11%)	
2004 general	Kendrick Meek (D) .... unopposed		($488,407)

Prior Winning Percentages: 2002 (100%)

The People		Race/Ethnic Origin	Ancestry
Area size:	99 sq. mi.	18.4% White	West Indian: 20.3% USA: 4.7%
Urban population:	100.0%	55.2% Black	Italian: 2.4%
Rural population:	0.0%	1.5% Asian	**2004 Presidential Vote**
Pop. 2000:	639,296	0.2% Native Am.	Kerry (D) 178,605 (83%)
Pop. 2005 (est):	671,344	0.0% Hawaiian	Bush (R) 35,642 (17%)
Median income:	$30,426	3.1% Two+ races	**2000 Presidential Vote**
Poverty status:	23.3%	0.3% Other	Gore (D) 145,341 (85%)
Military veterans:	7.2%	21.2% Hispanic Origin	Bush (R) 26,081 (15%)
			Cook Partisan Voting Index: D +35

Occupation   Blue collar: 24.0%   White collar: 52.5%   Gray collar: 23.5%

North from downtown Miami, alongside the railroad tracks that Henry Flagler built shortly after Miami was founded in 1896, and alongside Interstate 95, Miami's main north-south artery, is the city's largest black community, stretching from the Miami Arena in downtown Miami north through Allapattah and Liberty City, to the brightly painted minarets and Moorish arches of Opa-Locka. This has been a kind of frontierland in Miami, the scene where hostilities between Miami's blacks and its Cuban-American majority have played out. Many Miami blacks have resented the economic upward mobility and political strength of the Cubans, the first generation of which rose while still speaking mostly Spanish, and of other Latinos—including the Haitians in Little Haiti, the Creole-speaking community whose heart is in N.E. 54th Street, north of downtown—who have been moving upward as well, though they have been less unified politically. The Elian Gonzalez affair reminded many local blacks of the refugee status granted to Cubans even as many black Haitians were deported without notice or turned away at the shore. This animosity is reflected in partisan politics: The increasingly politically assertive Haitian-American community is solidly Democratic and blacks in Miami-Dade County vote more than 90% Democratic, while Cuban Americans have voted 70% to 80% Republican..

The 17th Congressional District of Florida covers much of northeast Miami-Dade County, including Opa-Locka and Miami Gardens, right up to Biscayne Boulevard; it does not include the affluent enclaves facing Biscayne Bay or the beach towns north of Miami Beach nor does it include heavily Latino Hialeah to the west. Within its borders is the historic, socially active Greater Bethel AME Church in Overtown; the district also includes part of Hollywood and other communities in southern Broward County, with fewer blacks, but still very heavily Democratic. Some 55% of the 17th District's residents are black, the highest percentage of any Florida district, which helps explain why this district has the lowest number of registered Republicans—just 38,000—of any Florida district.

The congressman from the 17th District is Kendrick Meek, a Democrat first elected in 2002. He is the son of his predecessor, Carrie Meek, who was first elected when the district was created in something like its present form in 1992. She is the granddaughter of a slave and was elected to the state legislature in 1978, when Kendrick Meek was 12. In July 2002, just two weeks before the filing deadline, Carrie Meek announced that she would not run again and promised to work "24 hours a day, seven days a week" to elect her son. The election did not require that much effort: the timing of her announcement left little time for a candidate to emerge against her son and no Democrat or Republican filed to run against him. The Meeks are not the first mother-son combination in the House. In 1952 Oliver Bolton, an Ohio Republican, was elected to the House from a district adjoining the one which had been represented by his mother Frances Bolton since 1940 and by his father Chester Bolton before that.

Kendrick Meek would have been a formidable candidate even without the succession scheme. He was a page in the Florida legislature when his mother was elected. At Florida A&M in Tallahassee he was president of state College Young Democrats. After receiving his degree in criminology, he worked as a captain in the Highway Patrol and became security aide to Lieutenant Governor Buddy MacKay. He was elected to the Florida House in 1994, at 28, and to the Senate in 1998; in each case he took on longtime, respected incumbents and waged contentious campaigns to oust them. In January 2000, he staged a 25-hour sit-in at the lieutenant governor's office to protest Governor Jeb Bush's "One Florida" executive orders, which called for ending the use of racial preferences in state contracting and university admissions. Meek failed to change Bush's mind, but his act of political theater helped spark the largest-ever protest march on the state Capitol two months later. In 2002 he was well known as the chief proponent of the class size initiative which qualified for the November ballot and which, despite the opposition of Bush, was approved 52%-48%.

In Washington, Democratic leaders were impressed by Meek's political and fundraising skills and predicted a bright future for him. He was comfortable in front of the camera, especially in his appeals to young voters; he scored points with Nancy Pelosi as co-chairman of her 30-Something Working Group (though he is now actually 40-something). At the Congressional Black Caucus, he chaired the fundraising arm. Meek's voting record is toward the center of House Democrats, especially on foreign policy issues. Much of his legislative energy is directed toward Haiti; he visited the island in April 2007. He filed a bill to make it easier for Haitians to become permanent residents, urged the Bush administration not to take sides in conflicts on the island, and sought a constructive role for himself in internal disputes. After failing to win his mother's seat on Appropriations in 2005, he got on the Ways and Means Committee two years later, where he is the only Floridian on the panel. He promised to focus on low-income programs that benefit his constituents.

In 2006, Meek faced the first primary or general election opponent in his congressional career: Haitian-born Democratic challenger Durfirstson Neree, who founded Little Haiti's first credit union. Neree ran against the Meek dynasty and said that voters deserved a greater chance to participate. Meek had little reason to worry: He won 89%-11%.

EIGHTEENTH DISTRICT

Rep. Ileana Ros-Lehtinen (R)

Elected Aug. 1989, 9th full term; b. July 12, 1952, Havana, Cuba; home, Miami; Miami-Dade Comm. Col., A.A. 1972, FL Intl. U., B.A. 1975, M.S. 1986, U. of Miami, Ph.D. 2004; Catholic; married (Dexter).

Elected Office: FL House of Reps., 1982-86; FL Senate, 1986-89.

Professional Career: Teacher, Principal & Owner, Eastern Academy Elem. Schl., 1978-85.

DC Office: 2160 RHOB, 20515, 202-225-3931; Fax: 202-225-5620; Web site: www.house.gov/ros-lehtinen.

District Offices: Miami, 305-220-3281.

Committees: *Foreign Affairs* (RMM of 23 R).

Group Ratings

	ADA	ACLU	AFS	LCV	ITIC	NTU	COC	ACU	CFG	FRC
2006	15	37	0	33	67	49	87	63	43	71
2005	10	—	0	11	—	56	93	88	51	85

National Journal Ratings

	2005 LIB	—	2005 CONS		2006 LIB	—	2006 CONS
Economic	27%	—	73%		29%	—	70%
Social	53%	—	46%		53%	—	47%
Foreign	27%	—	73%		37%	—	62%

Key Votes of the 109th Congress

1. Estate Tax Repeal	Y	5. Limit Interstate Abortion	Y	9. Build Border Fence	N
2. Limit CAFE Standards	Y	6. Extend Patriot Act	Y	10. CAFTA	Y
3. FY06 Spending Curb	Y	7. Bar Same Sex Marriage	N	11. Oppose Iraq Withdrawal	Y
4. Drilling in ANWR	Y	8. Stem Cell Research $	N	12. Detainee Tribunals	Y

Election Results

2006 general	Ileana Ros-Lehtinen (R)	79,631	(62%)	($1,439,442)
	David Patlak (D)	48,499	(38%)	($75,698)
2006 primary	Ileana Ros-Lehtinen (R)	unopposed		
2004 general	Ileana Ros-Lehtinen (R)	143,647	(65%)	($859,083)
	Sam Sheldon (D)	78,281	(35%)	($11,882)

Prior Winning Percentages: 2002 (69%); 2000 (100%); 1998 (100%); 1996 (100%); 1994 (100%); 1992 (67%); 1990 (60%); 1989 (53%)

The People		Race/Ethnic Origin	Ancestry	
Area size:	3,196 sq. mi.	29.7% White	German: 4.0%	English: 3.5%
Urban population:	99.1%	5.7% Black	Irish: 3.3%	
Rural population:	0.9%	0.9% Asian	**2004 Presidential Vote**	
Pop. 2000:	639,295	0.1% Native Am.	Bush (R) 127,746	(54%)
Pop. 2005 (est):	635,514	0.0% Hawaiian	Kerry (D) 107,073	(46%)
Median income:	$32,298	0.7% Two+ races	**2000 Presidential Vote**	
Poverty status:	19.3%	0.1% Other	Bush (R) 109,596	(57%)
Military veterans:	6.6%	62.7% Hispanic Origin	Gore (D) 83,524	(43%)
			Cook Partisan Voting Index: R + 4	

Occupation   Blue collar: 20.6%   White collar: 60.1%   Gray collar: 19.3%

A century ago it was a tiny tropical village where the Miami River empties into Biscayne Bay. Today it is a world city, not just America's "Gateway to Latin America" but the "Capital of the Americas," as welcoming signs proclaim. The surrealistic high-rises of Brickell Boulevard, the reminders of the 1920s in the pseudo-Spanish Villa Vizcaya and the winding lanes of Coral Gables, the shimmer of orange and pink neon signs in the hot night air: the lights of the grid streets stretching for miles and then abruptly turning to darkness at the bayfront or the Everglades: This is Miami today. It lives on the cusp of two civilizations, North American and Latin American, with different traditions, styles and sensibilities converging in this one place, despite some friction, toward an amalgam with the strengths of both. Miami has become commercially and economically the capital of Latin America, the one place from which it is easiest to fly directly to any other part of Latin America, where top business and banking services are available to a sophisticated Spanish-speaking (and usually also English-speaking) clientele.

The 1980s TV program *Miami Vice* showed the underside of Miami, the air of menace in streets where many were armed and vast quantities of drugs and cash regularly changed hands and killings were not at all unusual. The news columns focused on violence: The riots in 1980 and 1989; the late 1990s shenanigans of local politicians, when corruption charges were lodged at several officeholders; and on the controversy over six-year-old Elian Gonzalez in 2000. But the negatives were often exaggerated. What is striking about Miami is less its vices than its virtues—the vitality and creativity of entrepreneurs and artists, the cosmopolitan sophistication of people living and prospering in two (or more) cultures, the successful Americanization of Cubans and other Latinos, with the retention of a cultural flavor that is linked to the past but headed fast into the future. In 2006, a movie version of *Miami Vice* depicted a more modern and glitzy portrayal of the city.

John Quincy Adams believed that Cuba would inevitably become a part of the United States. That never happened, but many of Cuba's people have become Americans, and the focus of Cuban America has been Miami, ever since the first refugees fled Fidel Castro in 1959. That caused some resentment among the previous majority. In the 1960s, as the Cuban population grew, the tone of Miami civic life was set by the large Jewish community and the liberal voice of the *Miami Herald*: But the Cubans, implacably opposed to the totalitarian Castro and estranged by John F. Kennedy's betrayal of their cause at the Bay of Pigs, entered the voting stream heavily Republican. In the early 1960s Cubans were a noisy minority in the Miami area; now they are dominant in a Latino majority in Miami-Dade County (as Dade County was renamed in 1997). In 2005, the population of Miami-Dade was 61% Hispanic and 19% black, leaving Anglo whites a fading minority; the city has the highest percentage of immigrants of any large city in the world. South Florida's Jewish community has mostly moved north to Broward and Palm Beach Counties. Little Havana around Calle Ocho (Southwest 8th Street in English) is now home to many Nicaraguans, Hondurans and Peruvians; its annual spring carnival has featured the world's largest paella (serving 300,000 people) and the longest conga line (four miles). Latinos in Miami-Dade tend to go to school at Miami-Dade Community College (one of the nation's largest) and Florida International University, and start businesses or join the professions in Miami's vibrant economy.

Politically, Miami-Dade has been volatile. It voted 57%-38% for Bill Clinton in 1996, after he signed the Helms-Burton Act and responded angrily to the shooting down of two Brothers to the Rescue planes. But it soured on him after he suspended Helms-Burton and clashed with the Cuban community during the Elian Gonzalez affair. Al Gore, despite overwhelming support from Miami-Dade's blacks and Jews, carried the county by only 53%-46%. In 2004, Bush's share of the Cuban-American vote declined, partly because younger Cubans are not so focused on Fidel Castro, partly through resentment of the limits placed on visits and remittances sent to Cuba. At the same time, Democrats improved at turning out more African-American votes in the county. The result was that John Kerry carried Miami-Dade 53%-47%; Bush's percentage rose 2% in Florida as a whole but only 0.3% in Miami-Dade County.

The 18th Congressional District of Florida is one of Miami-Dade's three Hispanic-majority districts. It is 63% Hispanic and only 6% black. The district includes most of the city of Miami. It follows Calle Ocho west to heavily Hispanic West Miami and Westchester. It includes most of metro Miami's high-income residential areas—Coral Gables, with luxurious streets laid out in the 1920s with Spanish, French country and even Chinese style houses; Cocoplum, the gated community with huge houses of rich Cuban-Americans with docks for their boats; the postmodern apartment buildings and upscale hotels along Brickell Boulevard; and Key Biscayne, with its high-rise apartments mostly owned by Latin Americans in need of a safe harbor if their countries are threatened with revolution or asset confiscation. The district includes parts of Miami Beach: South Beach, where old art deco hotels used to house elderly retirees and have become the crowded home to the glitziest celebrities of North America, Latin America and Europe; the high-rises along Collins Avenue facing the ocean; and the Latino neighborhoods around 63d Street to the north. South of Miami, the district is connected to the Florida Keys by U.S. 1, the sturdier successor to Henry Flagler's "folly" of a railway that was built on an archipelago of calcified outcroppings and destroyed, two decades after its construction, by a hurricane in 1935. The highway ends in bustling, tropical Key West, the southernmost city in the continental United States. Key West was long accessible only by sea, and treasures from shipwrecks along the miles of coral reefs once provided its residents the highest per capita income in the nation. Key West has attracted famous residents—Ernest Hemingway, Tennessee Williams, Jimmy Buffett—and a large gay population, many living in quaint clapboard bungalows called "conch houses." The gay communities in Key West and Miami Beach are solidly Democratic, and they wield some clout: Gay leaders in Miami-Dade spearheaded a successful effort to reject a countywide gay-rights repeal ordinance in 2002. Overall the 18th is Republican, but George W. Bush's percentage fell here in 2004.

The congresswoman from the 18th District is Ileana Ros-Lehtinen, the first Cuban-American and the first Hispanic woman elected to Congress, in 1989. She was born in Havana, came to Miami at the age of 8 not knowing English, graduated from Miami-Dade Community College and Florida International University. She became a teacher, then was the owner of a private school. In 2004, she got her doctorate in education from the University of Miami; her dissertation was on the views of House members regarding national testing for high school students. She was elected to the Florida House in 1982, at 30, and to the state Senate in 1986; while there, she met her husband Dexter Lehtinen, who also served in both houses of the legislature, and as U.S. attorney in Miami during the first Bush administration. Ros-Lehtinen ran for the House in the special election after the death of Claude Pepper, one of the most enduring liberals in American politics and a staunch opponent of Castro. It was an acrimonious contest, with voting almost entirely on ethnic lines: exit polls showed that 96% of blacks and 88% of non-Hispanic whites voted for Democrat Gerald Richman, while 90% of Hispanics voted for Ros-Lehtinen. Overall, she won 53% of the vote. With a much more heavily Latino district since 1992, she has not faced serious opposition.

Ros-Lehtinen has a mixed voting record: moderate on cultural policy, more conservative on economic and foreign issues. She refused to sign the Contract with America, and was a harsh critic of Republican attempts to pass English-only legislation, to cut off welfare for legal immigrants and to reduce the immigration quota for relatives of U.S. citizens. During the 2007 debate over immigration, she pleaded with Republican colleagues not to rebuff the growing Hispanic voting bloc. She has been the chief sponsor of the Child Custody Protection Act, to bar the transport of minors across state lines for abortions; the House passed it, but it died in the Senate because, she said, the chamber is "controlled by the abortion lobby." She has urged the Pentagon to allow gay men and lesbians in the military.

Ros-Lehtinen has focused her committee work on the now-renamed Foreign Affairs panel, where much of her energy has been devoted to Cuban and Latin issues and the protection of human rights. She strongly backed the Cuban Democracy Act and the 1996 Helms-Burton law that tightened sanctions against Fidel Castro. She has opposed farm state Republicans who have sought to relax the trade embargo on Cuba that has been in effect since 1961; when these were passed by the Republican-controlled House, party leaders ensured that they were deleted in conference. With the Democratic takeover, she and her Cuban-American allies lost ground on this. Even though George W. Bush firmly supports the embargo, its opponents—a coalition of liberal Democrats, farm state Republicans and foreign policy left-wingers—have gained strength. As chairwoman of the Middle East and Central Asia Subcommittee, she was a booster of Israel and won enactment of bills to impose additional economic sanctions on Libya and Iran. She got the Bush administration to extend permits for Salvadorans, Nicaraguans and Hondurans to remain in the United States. Ros-Lehtinen ran an intensive campaign to succeed Henry Hyde as the top Republican on the committee; she succeeded, but the 2006 election results made her the ranking minority member instead. Still, with her affable personality, she has positioned herself among the most influential congressional players on foreign policy. On Iraq, she remained an outspoken supporter of the war; she repeatedly espoused the view that if the U.S. were to leave, terrorists would use the country to strike American targets. For her, the war hit close to home: her stepson served as a Marine in Iraq. Dexter Lehtinen, who was severely wounded as an Army Ranger during the Vietnam War, was an outspoken critic of John Kerry during the 2004 presidential campaign for his 1971 testimony against the war.

In 2006, Ros-Lehtinen won 62%-38% against David Patlak, a retired Coast Guard officer.

NINETEENTH DISTRICT

Rep. Robert Wexler (D)

Elected 1996, 6th term; b. Jan. 2, 1961, Queens, NY; home, Boca Raton; U. of FL, B.A. 1982, George Washington U., J.D. 1985; Jewish; married (Laurie).

Elected Office: FL Senate, 1990-96.

Professional Career: Practicing atty., 1985-96.

DC Office: 2241 RHOB, 20515, 202-225-3001; Fax: 202-225-5974; Web site: www.wexler.house.gov.

District Offices: Boca Raton, 561-988-6302; Margate, 954-972-6454.

Committees: *Financial Services* (35th of 37 D): Oversight & Investigations; Domestic and International Monetary Policy, Trade & Technology; Capital Markets, Insurance & Government Sponsored Enterprises. *Foreign Affairs* (7th of 27 D): Europe (Chmn.); Middle East & South Asia. *Judiciary* (11th of 23 D): Courts, the Internet & Intellectual Property.

Group Ratings

	ADA	ACLU	AFS	LCV	ITIC	NTU	COC	ACU	CFG	FRC
2006	90	95	100	100	50	12	33	8	7	0
2005	100	—	100	100	—	15	26	0	3	0

National Journal Ratings

	2005 LIB	—	2005 CONS	2006 LIB	—	2006 CONS
Economic	94%	—	0%	91%	—	6%
Social	88%	—	12%	83%	—	17%
Foreign	78%	—	22%	64%	—	36%

Key Votes of the 109th Congress

1. Estate Tax Repeal	N	5. Limit Interstate Abortion	N
2. Limit CAFE Standards	N	6. Extend Patriot Act	N
3. FY06 Spending Curb	N	7. Bar Same Sex Marriage	N
4. Drilling in ANWR	N	8. Stem Cell Research $	Y

9. Build Border Fence	Y
10. CAFTA	N
11. Oppose Iraq Withdrawal	N
12. Detainee Tribunals	N

Election Results

2006 general	Robert Wexler (D) .... unopposed	($793,904)
2006 primary	Robert Wexler (D) .... unopposed	
2004 general	Robert Wexler (D) .... unopposed	($939,363)

Prior Winning Percentages: 2002 (72%); 2000 (72%); 1998 (100%); 1996 (66%)

The People

Area size:	234 sq. mi.
Urban population:	99.6%
Rural population:	0.4%
Pop. 2000:	639,295
Pop. 2005 (est):	714,878
Median income:	$42,237
Poverty status:	7.7%
Military veterans:	16.6%

Race/Ethnic Origin

77.5% White	
6.1% Black	
2.0% Asian	
0.1% Native Am.	
0.0% Hawaiian	
1.4% Two+ races	
0.3% Other	
12.7% Hispanic Origin	

Ancestry

Italian: 9.0%	German: 8.4%
Irish: 7.6%	

2004 Presidential Vote

Kerry (D)	210,695	(66%)
Bush (R)	107,348	(34%)

2000 Presidential Vote

Gore (D)	191,382	(73%)
Bush (R)	71,544	(27%)

Cook Partisan Voting Index: D +21

Occupation   Blue collar: 17.1%   White collar: 67.1%   Gray collar: 15.7%

When the first millionaires came to Palm Beach in the 1920s to winter in their new Addison Mizner pseudo-Mediterranean mansions, and as the first real estate speculators arrived in Miami, there was virtually nothing man-made between these two cites. In 1920, Dade, Broward and Palm Beach Counties boasted a mere 66,000 residents. In 1990, 4 million people lived in the 5- to 15-mile strip between the Atlantic Ocean and the protected Everglades, a number that grew to 5.4 million in 2004. The contrast between the 1920s and today is especially striking in Boca Raton, where Mizner built in 1926 what is now the Boca Raton Resort and Club. Its azure fountains and red-tiled roofs, its pseudo-Moorish columns and pink stucco walls bespeak a vision of a holiday Florida, a bit mannered and antique to today's eye, but still exuberant and benefiting from tasteful refurbishing. Boca Raton has grown inland and is still solidly affluent, but it has become more functional and workaday. Affluent retirees from the Northeast and Canada ("snow birds") live in unadorned high-rise towers, enjoying the weather and the lack of a state income tax.

The 19th Congressional District of Florida includes former swampland and citrus groves in Palm Beach and Broward Counties. It does not touch the ocean at all, kept inland by the majority-black 23d District, which collects poorer black neighborhoods just behind the Intracoastal Waterway, and the 22d District, which ties together more affluent oceanside precincts. The boundaries of the 19th District are erose and irregular, obviously drawn with an eye to political advantage; the Republicans who controlled the redistricting process were happy to pack heavily Democratic precincts into the 19th. It extends north from Fort Lauderdale to Okeechobee Boulevard in unglamorous but booming West Palm Beach; the district also takes in Margate, Mission Bay, Boca Raton and parts of Boynton Beach. What ties these communities together is that they have large Jewish populations and have voted heavily Democratic; more than 20% of Palm Beach County is Jewish. Senior citizens are an especially important voting bloc here: the 19th ranks second among all 435 congressional districts in the number of Social Security recipients. Democrats traditionally have maximized turnout in the big condominiums with confidence that they would produce huge Democratic majorities. But George W. Bush's Israel and Middle East policies seemed to win over many Jewish voters here. His percentage in the district rose from 27% in 2000 to 34% in 2004, the biggest rise in any Florida district and one of the biggest in the nation.

The congressman from the 19th is Robert Wexler, a Democrat first elected in 1996. Wexler is one of South Florida's two Queens-born members (the other is Debbie Wasserman Schultz); he grew up in Florida from age 10, and after law school went into practice in Boca Raton. In 1990, at 29, he was elected to the state Senate. When the seat opened, Wexler was one of three Democratic legislators who jumped into the race. In the primary he led with 47% to 29% for state Senator Peter Weinstein. The runoff was bitter. Wexler won 65%-35%; afterwards Weinstein filed a $10 million defamation suit against him, citing an unflattering picture of himself in a Wexler TV ad (the suit soon was dropped). In this heavily Democratic district, Wexler has not faced serious Republican opposition.

Wexler has a fairly liberal voting record in the House and a flair for gaining attention. Wexler made his greatest mark as an ardent defender of Bill Clinton during impeachment. Producers of cable TV shows are always looking for someone who can be relied on to take one side of an issue and to bring energy to the broadcast: Wexler filled the bill, and he seemed to turn down few invitations. Wexler also appeared often on cable TV news during the Florida vote controversy in 2000 and in 2004 he relentlessly demanded that Florida election officials provide paper printouts from touch-screen voting machines to assure a credible paper trail and avoid what he continued to argue was the theft of the 2000 election. After losing several court proceedings, he prepared a legislative alternative. In 2005, Wexler again became a frequent face on national news shows, this time with a less welcome voice for his party as he introduced his own Social Security bill, to impose a 6% tax on income above the existing $90,000 cap. Democratic leaders were unhappy with his defection and sought to isolate him, but Wexler said, "My allegiance to seniors is greater than my allegiance to the Democratic party." He said he wanted to show that the financial problems of Social Security could be solved without a cut in benefits or privatization.

An orthodox Jew, Wexler said in December 2002 that Israel was engaged in full-scale war, and that it was time for the United States to force the ouster of terrorist leaders in the Mideast, including Yassir Arafat and Saddam Hussein; he voted for the Iraq war resolution. In November 2005, he called for an immediate withdrawal of U.S. troops from Iraq. On the now-renamed Foreign Affairs Committee, he chairs the Europe Subcommittee. On the Judiciary Committee he was the only Democrat to favor a three-year pilot program giving temporary visas to an unlimited number of foreign workers for seasonal farm work. In 2006, he sought unsuccessfully to force the Justice Department to turn over documents related to the National Security Agency's collection of millions of telephone records.

Despite frequent speculation, Wexler has not run for statewide office. In 2006, he and his staff were the subjects of a Sundance Channel documentary, "The Hill," which was described as a congressional version of "The West Wing" television show; they welcomed the attention. Wexler also made a July 2006 appearance on "The Colbert Report" that ended up drawing criticism back home. Responding to prodding from the show's comedic host, Stephen Colbert, Wexler jokingly said, among other things, "I enjoy cocaine because it's a fun thing to do." Former Broward County

Commissioner and 1996 primary opponent Ben Graber, who is challenging Wexler in the 2008 primary, seized on the remark and said it sent the wrong message to teenagers.

TWENTIETH DISTRICT

Rep. Debbie Wasserman Schultz (D)

Elected 2004, 2d term; b. Sept. 27, 1966, Queens, NY; home, Weston; U. of FL, B.A. 1988, M.A. 1990; Jewish; married (Steve).

Elected Office: FL House, 1992-2000; Min. leader pro tem., 1999-2000; FL Sen., 2000-04.

Professional Career: State legislative aide, 1989-1992.

DC Office: 118 CHOB, 20515, 202-225-7931; Fax: 202-226-2052; Web site: www.house.gov/schultz.

District Offices: Aventura, 305-936-5724; Pembroke Pines, 954-437-3936.

Committees: *Chief Deputy Majority Whip. Appropriations* (36th of 37 D): Legislative Branch (Chmn.); Financial Services & General Government. *Judiciary* (21st of 23 D): The Constitution, Civil Rights & Civil Liberties.

Group Ratings

	ADA	ACLU	AFS	LCV	ITIC	NTU	COC	ACU	CFG	FRC
2006	95	95	100	100	33	11	40	4	7	0
2005	100	—	100	94	—	14	44	0	0	0

National Journal Ratings

	2005 LIB	—	2005 CONS		2006 LIB	—	2006 CONS
Economic	85%	—	13%		83%	—	16%
Social	83%	—	16%		84%	—	16%
Foreign	72%	—	28%		67%	—	31%

Key Votes of the 109th Congress

1. Estate Tax Repeal	N	5. Limit Interstate Abortion	N	9. Build Border Fence	N
2. Limit CAFE Standards	N	6. Extend Patriot Act	N	10. CAFTA	N
3. FY06 Spending Curb	N	7. Bar Same Sex Marriage	N	11. Oppose Iraq Withdrawal	N
4. Drilling in ANWR	N	8. Stem Cell Research $	Y	12. Detainee Tribunals	N

Election Results

2006 general	Debbie Wasserman Schultz (D) .... unopposed		($828,658)
2006 primary	Debbie Wasserman Schultz (D) .... unopposed		
2004 general	Debbie Wasserman Schultz (D) 191,195	(70%)	($1,468,898)
	Margaret Hostetter (R) 81,213	(30%)	($35,045)

The People		Race/Ethnic Origin	Ancestry	
Area size:	218 sq. mi.	66.9% White	Italian: 7.9%	German: 7.7%
Urban population:	99.7%	7.9% Black	Irish: 7.5%	
Rural population:	0.3%	2.3% Asian	**2004 Presidential Vote**	
Pop. 2000:	639,295	0.2% Native Am.	Kerry (D) 183,510	(64%)
Pop. 2005 (est):	692,885	0.0% Hawaiian	Bush (R) 104,039	(36%)
Median income:	$44,034	1.6% Two+ races	**2000 Presidential Vote**	
Poverty status:	9.6%	0.3% Other	Gore (D) 161,154	(69%)
Military veterans:	11.3%	20.6% Hispanic Origin	Bush (R) 72,553	(31%)
			Cook Partisan Voting Index: D +18	
Occupation	Blue collar: 16.0%	White collar: 69.4%	Gray collar: 14.6%	

Fort Lauderdale, back when Connie Francis made it famous in the 1960 spring break movie *Where the Boys Are*, was just a small town with a strip of motels along the beach and some nice houses fronting canals. Now it is a more stylish beach resort and the center of a sprawling metropolitan area that bills itself as a place where well-heeled Europeans, sophisticated Northerners and laid-back Midwesterners come to relax and vacation. In 1950, Fort Lauderdale and Broward County had 183,000 people; in 2004 they had 1.8 million. The land from the strip of beach along the Atlantic Ocean west to the Sawgrass Expressway and the Everglades Wildlife Management Area has filled up with subdivisions, shopping centers, office complexes, warehouses and trucking terminals. Broward County is no longer just vacation country; it is also a major port and business center with high-tech companies and startups that have become national giants, including Blockbuster Video.

As it has grown, the ethnic composition of Broward County has changed. In the 1950s, it was understood that Jews couldn't buy houses or rent hotel rooms this far north of Miami. Today, after four decades of Cubans moving into the Miami area and many Jews moving out, Broward County is one of the most heavily Jewish parts of the United States. Nearer the coast, especially in the huge high-rises of Hollywood and Hallandale, most of Broward's Jews are retirees from New York and other Northeastern metro areas. But inland, in towns like booming Davie, Plantation and Sunrise that didn't exist a few decades ago, there are many young Jewish parents raising families in communities that pride themselves on fine schools and high property values. Places like Weston, a 15,000-home development built on 16 square miles on the edge of the Everglades, drew affluent transplants to its gated communities, including many from Venezuela who have fled the rule of President Hugo Chavez. This is one reason that in the 1990s the number of children in Florida rose more rapidly than the number of seniors, with school enrollment growing more than 35% in Broward alone.

The 20th Congressional District of Florida includes much of southeastern Broward County and the northern Biscayne Bay shoreline in Miami-Dade. Precinct by precinct, its computer-generated borders are drawn to include heavily Democratic and Jewish areas; with its large gay and lesbian community, Wilton Manors trails only Provincetown, Massachusetts, and Guerneville, California, in its proportion of same-sex households. It includes much of Fort Lauderdale, Hollywood and Dania Beach on the coast, but its biggest blocks of territory are inland. In Miami-Dade County, it includes the shores of Biscayne Bay both on the Miami and Miami Beach side, with expensive homes and huge high-rises. This is a strongly Democratic district, though a considerable number of Jewish voters did swing toward George W. Bush over his first term; his percentage in the district rose from 31% in 2000 to 36% in 2004.

The congresswoman from the 20th District is Debbie Wasserman Schultz, a Democrat elected in 2004. She accomplished the unusual feat of winning her seat in Congress without a primary opponent or a significant general election foe. Like many of her constituents she was born in Queens; she grew up on Long Island, where she ran for student council every year and always lost. After getting her bachelor's and master's degrees in political science from the University of Florida, in 1992, at age 26, she became the state's youngest woman ever elected to the state House. Many of her constituents treat her like a granddaughter. She served eight years in the state House, including two years as minority leader, followed by four years in the state Senate. She calls herself "a pragmatic liberal" but sponsored a controversial law to require an equal number of men and women on state boards and a bill that failed to pass requiring that dry cleaners and some other businesses charge the same prices for women as for men.

When 20th District incumbent Peter Deutsch ran for the Democratic nomination for Bob Graham's open Senate seat, Wasserman Schultz moved to replace him in Congress, as she had earlier replaced him in Tallahassee; earlier still, Deutsch hired her as an aide. She began laying the groundwork early. In July 2003, more than a year before the primary, she had raised $115,000. By February 2004 she had lined up endorsements from Minority Leader Nancy Pelosi and six of Florida's seven House Democrats. Wasserman Schultz ultimately collected more than $1 million for what turned out to be an uncompetitive race; in June 2004, she pledged $100,000 to the Democratic Congressional Campaign Committee, a staggering contribution from a non-incumbent. Wasserman Schultz called for repeal of the Bush tax cuts, a reduction in the budget deficit, greater use of diplomacy, improved prescription drug coverage, and gay and abortion rights. Against a Republican who attacked the "homosexual agenda" in the public schools, she won 70%-30%.

In the House, she was a reliably liberal vote, though more to the center on foreign policy. She wanted a seat on Energy and Commerce, but that was a long shot for a freshman, even with her ambition, insider savvy, and fundraising skills. Instead, she was placed on Financial Services. Within days, she was making an impact, and she hasn't looked back. *The Miami Herald* reported that her first year made "a Cinderella-worthy impression." In the debate over whether to intervene to retain the feeding tube for Terri Schiavo, she argued that Congress would set a dangerous precedent if it attempted to circumvent the courts. She won approval of a resolution designating American Jewish History Month. On Financial Services, she called for a commission to examine the state of natural disaster insurance. After an insurance company denied her additional life-insurance coverage because she might travel to Israel at some time, she filed a bill making such a practice illegal; the bill never made it out of the House. She testified before the Senate Judiciary Committee against the nomination of Samuel Alito to the Supreme Court, warning that his support of government intrusion could lead to more Schiavo cases. Wasserman Schultz also moved quickly into national campaign work. To the dismay of Florida Republicans, including Clay Shaw in the neighboring 22d District, she joined House Democratic efforts to target their seats in the 2006 campaign, as co-chairman of the party's "Red to Blue" campaign. Working closely with DCCC chairman Rahm Emanuel, she became a party spokesman and a mentor for Democratic recruits. "We have much more member involvement than in the past," Wasserman Schultz said in 2006. "It's important to have members run this program. We can do better in motivating others."

When Democrats won House control, she was a prime beneficiary. Majority Whip James Clyburn tapped her as a chief deputy whip. Although her initial preference was the Ways and Means Committee, she won a seat on Appropriations—not a bad trade-off. She immediately and unexpectedly became a "cardinal" as chairman of the Legislative Branch Subcommittee; she used that post to demand more accountability in the construction of the long-delayed and budget-busting Capitol Visitors Center. She continued in a leadership role at the DCCC, as head of the Frontline program to protect vulnerable incumbents—mostly freshmen. She also was an early supporter of Hillary Rodham Clinton for president.

TWENTY-FIRST DISTRICT

Rep. Lincoln Diaz-Balart (R)

Elected 1992, 8th term; b. Aug. 13, 1954, Havana, Cuba; home, Miami; U. of S. FL, B.S. 1977, Case Western Reserve U., J.D. 1979; Catholic; married (Cristina).

Elected Office: FL House of Reps., 1986-89; FL Senate 1989-92.

Professional Career: Practicing atty., 1979-92; Asst. FL Atty., 1983-84.

DC Office: 2244 RHOB, 20515, 202-225-4211; Fax: 202-225-8576; Web site: diaz-balart.house.gov.

District Offices: Miami, 305-470-8555.

Committees: *Rules* (2d of 4 R): Legislative & Budget Process (RMM).

Group Ratings

	ADA	ACLU	AFS	LCV	ITIC	NTU	COC	ACU	CFG	FRC
2006	15	33	0	17	86	48	93	60	47	71
2005	5	—	0	11	—	59	89	87	55	85

National Journal Ratings

	2005 LIB	—	2005 CONS	2006 LIB	—	2006 CONS
Economic	38%	—	62%	14%	—	85%
Social	53%	—	46%	53%	—	46%
Foreign	30%	—	70%	17%	—	73%

Key Votes of the 109th Congress

1. Estate Tax Repeal	Y	5. Limit Interstate Abortion	Y	9. Build Border Fence	N
2. Limit CAFE Standards	Y	6. Extend Patriot Act	Y	10. CAFTA	Y
3. FY06 Spending Curb	Y	7. Bar Same Sex Marriage	N	11. Oppose Iraq Withdrawal	Y
4. Drilling in ANWR	Y	8. Stem Cell Research $	Y	12. Detainee Tribunals	Y

Election Results

2006 general	Lincoln Diaz-Balart (R)	66,784	(59%)	($926,106)
	Frank Gonzalez (D)	45,522	(41%)	($16,598)
2006 primary	Lincoln Diaz-Balart (R)	unopposed		
2004 general	Lincoln Diaz-Balart (R)	146,507	(73%)	($451,555)
	Frank Gonzalez (Lib)	54,736	(27%)	

Prior Winning Percentages: 2002 (100%); 2000 (100%); 1998 (75%); 1996 (100%); 1994 (100%); 1992 (100%)

The People		Race/Ethnic Origin	Ancestry	
Area size:	140 sq. mi.	21.0% White	USA: 3.2%	German: 2.6%
Urban population:	99.9%	6.5% Black	West Indian: 2.6%	
Rural population:	0.1%	1.8% Asian	**2004 Presidential Vote**	
Pop. 2000:	639,295	0.1% Native Am.	Bush (R) 127,326	(57%)
Pop. 2005 (est):	681,288	0.0% Hawaiian	Kerry (D) 96,232	(43%)
Median income:	$41,426	0.8% Two+ races	**2000 Presidential Vote**	
Poverty status:	13.0%	0.2% Other	Bush (R) 104,888	(58%)
Military veterans:	4.8%	69.7% Hispanic Origin	Gore (D) 76,322	(42%)
			Cook Partisan Voting Index: R + 6	

Occupation	Blue collar: 22.6%	White collar: 63.6%	Gray collar: 13.9%

Miami's Cuban-American community has been one of America's most dynamic over the last 40 years, growing from 50,000 in 1960, the year after Fidel Castro took over Cuba, to well over 1 million today. Over those years, the Cuban-American neighborhoods centered along 8th Street—Calle Ocho—expanded to the southwest, west and northwest. In the 1980s, development reached outward to the Homestead extension of Florida's Turnpike. In the 1990s, Cuban-Americans moved out and beyond Hialeah, whose 90% Hispanic population is the highest in the Miami area; Hialeah's famed racetrack was built in the 1920s beyond the edge of urban development, but the stables were demolished in 2006 after years of neglect and the area could become another development. The suburbs of Miami have spread through former swampland, with planned communities and subdivisions leading to streets that fan out around lakes and golf courses.

The 21st Congressional District of Florida is an irregular rectangle about 20 miles long and two to six miles wide on the western side of settled territory in Miami-Dade County and southern Broward County. In Miami-Dade it includes Kendall and Cutler, southwest of Miami, and Westwood Lakes and Sweetwater, directly to the west. It includes low-income Hialeah and nearby Miami Lakes, developed in the 1960s by future Senator Bob Graham and his brothers. In Broward County the 21st District includes much of Miramar and Pembroke Pines. It includes Florida International University and Miami International Airport, which ranks third in the nation for international travel and first for overseas freight. The population of the district is 70% Hispanic, the highest of any Florida district, but only 58% of these are of Cuban origin. Cuban voters continue to be heavily Republican; other Latino voters are less so, but by no means overwhelmingly Democratic. Many here do not vote at all: The 21st has the lowest number of registered voters of any Florida district. With relatively few Hispanics, the Broward County portion of the district tends to vote Democratic. Overall, this is a Republican district, but one that sometimes votes for Democrats who support the Cuban community. Some Cuban-Americans—typically, the more recent arrivals—have been unhappy with the Bush administration's tightened restrictions on travel and remittances to Cuba, but others supported any steps that kept dollars from Castro. Bush's vote in the district was 58% in 2000 and 57% in 2004.

The congressman from the 21st District is Lincoln Diaz-Balart, a Republican first elected when the district was created in 1992. Diaz-Balart was born in Cuba where his grandfather, father and uncle served in the Cuban Congress; the family left Cuba in 1959, shortly after Castro took over and after their house was looted and burned while they were vacationing in Paris. His aunt was briefly the wife of Fidel Castro and the mother of Castro's only recognized child. His education included stops in Spain and England. Diaz-Balart started off as a poverty lawyer and a Democrat, but switched parties. He was elected to the state House in 1986, two years before his younger brother Mario was elected to the same chamber. (Unlike Mario, who is now the congressman from the 25th District, Lincoln Diaz-Balart was not born in the United States and is ineligible to be President.) The Diaz-Balarts are sometimes called the "Cuban Kennedys": one other brother is a TV anchorman on Telemundo and another is an investment banker. In 1989 Jorge Mas Canosa's Cuban American National Foundation convinced Diaz-Balart not to run against Ileana Ros-Lehtinen in the special election to replace Claude Pepper, and he instead took her state Senate seat. In 1992 the organization endorsed him in the 21st. State Senator Javier Souto, also Cuban-born, opposed him in the primary, charging that he was backed by wealthy contributors and was not a lifelong Republican. Diaz-Balart won 69%-31%.

Diaz-Balart has a voting record that is centrist on social issues and occasionally liberal on economics, veering from market principles on issues from the minimum wage to NAFTA, though he has said that a hemispheric common market is inevitable. He was one of three Republican incumbents who refused to sign the Contract with America, and he voted against the Republican welfare bills because of their provisions denying benefits to legal immigrants. Many older Cubans who have not taken U.S. citizenship because they hope some day to return to Cuba are dependent on Supplemental Security Income and other aid. He persevered, and his bill to restore SSI benefits to legal immigrants passed. In 2006, he objected to the deal opening the areas off the Florida coast to oil drilling, citing the need to protect "environmental treasures." In 2007, he spoke in favor of Democrats' efforts to expand collective bargaining rights but said he could not support a bill that undermined secret ballot elections.

Diaz-Balart, who shares a birthday with Castro, hopes that he will return some day to his freed homeland (Castro has referred to the Diaz-Balarts as "his most repulsive enemies" and "miserable Judases"). Naturally he has favored sanctions against Cuba, and when the Clinton administration announced in 1995 that it would no longer give automatic safe haven to Cuban refugees and instead would return them to Cuba, Diaz-Balart was arrested while protesting this switch. The next year, he wrote the section of the Helms-Burton Act codifying the embargo against Cuba. During the Elian Gonzalez controversy, Diaz-Balart closely advised the Miami family—he gave the six-year-old a black Labrador puppy—and he was a prominent spokesman for the local community. When farm state Republicans, working with Democrats, got the House to pass bills relaxing the trade embargo on Cuba, Diaz-Balart sought to assure the Bush administration's unyielding opposition to significant trade openings to Cuba; when Congress finally agreed to some trade, he made sure that payments for the goods were received in advance. He created the House's Cuba Democracy Group, as a counterpoint to the trade-opening Cuba Working Group. In 2006, he strongly objected when the Cuban team was permitted to play in the World Baseball Classic, some of which was played in Florida, and he unsuccessfully urged its players to "escape totalitarianism."

Although he is the second-most senior Republican at the Rules Committee, the chairman is selected by the Speaker and some Republicans contend that Diaz-Balart is too independent for the post. At home, Diaz-Balart has had no problem winning reelection. In 2006, he faced his first Democratic opponent since 1998: Frank Gonzalez, who challenged Diaz-Balart two years earlier as a Libertarian. Gonzalez called the Cuban embargo an "act of war" and supported the legalization of drugs. Diaz-Balart won 59%-41%; Gonzalez got 57% in Broward County, but it cast only 19% of the total vote.

TWENTY-SECOND DISTRICT

Rep. Ron Klein (D)

Elected 2006, 1st term; b. July 10, 1957, Cleveland, OH; home, Boca Raton; OH St. U., B.A. 1979, Case Western Reserve U., J.D. 1982; Jewish; married (Dori Dragin).

Elected Office: FL House of Reps., 1992-96; FL Senate, 1996-2006; FL Senate Min. Ldr., 2002-04.

Professional Career: Practicing atty., lobbyist, 1982-2006.

DC Office: 313 CHOB, 20515, 202-225-3026; Fax: 202-225-8398; Web site: klein.house.gov.

District Offices: Ft. Lauderdale, 954-522-4579; West Palm Beach, 561-651-7594.

Committees: *Financial Services* (29th of 37 D): Oversight & Investigations; Capital Markets, Insurance & Government Sponsored Enterprises; Financial Institutions & Consumer Credit. *Foreign Affairs* (27th of 27 D): Terrorism, Nonproliferation & Trade; Middle East & South Asia; Western Hemisphere.

Group Ratings and Key Votes: Newly Elected

Election Results

2006 general	Ron Klein (D)	108,688	(51%)	($4,185,922)
	Clay Shaw (R)	100,663	(47%)	($5,226,161)
	Other	4,254	(2%)	
2006 primary	Ron Klein (D)	unopposed		
2004 general	Clay Shaw (R)	192,581	(63%)	($1,237,966)
	Robin Rorapaugh (D)	108,258	(35%)	($9,800)
	Other	5,887	(2%)	

The People		Race/Ethnic Origin	Ancestry	
Area size:	500 sq. mi.	82.3% White	German: 11.7%	Irish: 11.0%
Urban population:	99.2%	3.8% Black	Italian: 9.5%	
Rural population:	0.8%	1.7% Asian	**2004 Presidential Vote**	
Pop. 2000:	639,295	0.1% Native Am.	Kerry (D) 169,161	(52%)
Pop. 2005 (est):	669,368	0.0% Hawaiian	Bush (R) 153,265	(48%)
Median income:	$51,200	1.2% Two+ races	**2000 Presidential Vote**	
Poverty status:	7.1%	0.2% Other	Gore (D) 135,868	(52%)
Military veterans:	14.9%	10.7% Hispanic Origin	Bush (R) 123,302	(48%)
			Cook Partisan Voting Index: D + 4	

Occupation   Blue collar: 16.0%   White collar: 69.4%   Gray collar: 14.7%

The barrier islands of Florida's Gold Coast have been developed in spasms of speculative frenzy, not just as vacation places and retirement homes but as embodiments of dreams and fantasies. Consider Palm Beach, the great beach resort of the 1920s, where rich WASPs would leave their snow-covered Tudor or Georgian mansions and live in Addison Mizner's pseudo-Mediterranean confections. Or Boca Raton, where Mizner built the Boca Raton Hotel in 1926. Or Fort Lauderdale, a tiny town when Clyde Beatty brought his circus there for the winter in the 1930s (locals complained about the roaring lions) and then, from the 1950s to the 1980s, the favored winter break beach resort of college students. Starting in the 1970s, high-rise condominiums sprouted up and down the Atlantic coast of Broward and Palm Beach Counties. In recent years the old town centers have been revived. Palm Beach remains, as it has been since the 1920s, the precinct of the very rich, including Rush Limbaugh, who broadcasts from there. Boca Raton now sports the stylish Mizner Park, a collection of upscale stores on a walking street. Downtown Fort Lauderdale is the home of new condominiums and museums, the Museum of Art Fort Lauderdale, the Museum of Discovery and Space, the Broward Center for the Performing Arts and the International Swimming Hall of Fame.

The 22d Congressional District of Florida covers most of the Atlantic oceanfront in Palm Beach and Broward Counties, from Jupiter in Palm Beach County to Fort Lauderdale in Broward County. It is rarely more than a few miles wide and in some places it is not much wider than the barrier islands separated from the mainland by the Indian River and Lake Worth. But it also has jagged salients that extend several miles inland. The district, a testament to the advances made in redistricting software, was drawn by Republican redistricters in an attempt to provide a safe seat for Republican Congressman Clay Shaw after he barely won reelection in 2000. The Miami-Dade County portion of the district was removed, as was heavily Democratic Hollywood in Broward County. Inland salients in Broward County brought in Republican precincts in Plantation and Coral Springs. Much new territory was added in Palm Beach County—an inland finger in wealthy Boca Raton, a long strand parallel to the oceanfront of affluent areas from Delray Beach to Glen Ridge (here the 22d surrounds the heavily black 23d district on three sides) and an inland slice in north Palm Beach County including parts of Palm Beach Gardens and Jupiter. The resulting district is affluent and elderly, with a large Jewish population politically very active in condominium groups.

The new congressman for the 22d District is Ron Klein, a Democrat elected in 2006 after defeating 26-year Republican incumbent Clay Shaw. Klein was born in Cleveland, where his father owned a five-and-dime store and his mother was a school teacher. He interned in the Ohio House and for Ohio Congressman Tom Luken, a Democrat. Klein studied at Ohio State University, got his law degree from Case Western Reserve and entered private practice. In 1985, Klein moved to Boca Raton where he became a name partner at a law firm that also did lobbying. He was elected to the state House in 1992, seven years after arriving in Florida, and to the state Senate in 1996, where he served as minority leader. While in the legislature, Klein worked to pass bills requiring mandatory education of the Holocaust in public schools, trade initiatives that benefited Florida and the Jimmy Ryce Act, which extended jail time for sexual predators. Klein was a Democratic partisan, but also became a dealmaker in the Republican-controlled state Senate. Term limits barred Klein from seeking another term in 2006 so he entered the race against Clay Shaw in March 2005, early enough to discourage primary opposition and to raise the large sums needed to challenge a well-funded incumbent.

Shaw had won reelection in 2000 by just 599 votes, but Republican-led redistricting shored up his seat since then and helped him win easy re-elections despite vigorous Democratic challenges. Shaw, who was recovering from lung cancer surgery in January 2006, claimed his seniority positioned him to become the next Ways and Means chairman, even though most insiders considered Congressman Jim McCrery of Louisiana as the frontrunner. Klein campaigned as a "moderate pro-business Democrat," but he had liberal stances on social issues, supporting abortion rights and stem cell research and opposing a ban on same-sex marriage. Each courted Jewish voters and pledged their support for Israel. Each offered fixes to bring down hurricane insurance premiums for homeowners and businesses: Shaw proposed a federal fund to back up insurance companies while Klein proposed a federal income tax deduction for homeowners who weather-proof their properties.

Shaw slammed Klein as a well-heeled lobbyist with deep connections to special interests; Klein insisted he had never lobbied state colleagues and had only advocated on behalf of a few clients before local governments. Klein's prodigious fundraising allowed him to counter with ads that charged Shaw had let down the district's large senior population by supporting a Medicare/ prescription drug bill that prevents the government from negotiating lower drug prices. Shaw touted his plan to fund private investment accounts as an add-on to the Social Security program. Klein called the proposal fiscally irresponsible, although his own alternative came late in the campaign and relied on establishing a commission to review the issue. Tapping into the national current of discontent with Republicans, Klein attacked Shaw for supporting the Iraq war and accused the incumbent of voting with President Bush "90% of the time." (Shaw corrected him in one debate, noting that it was 83%.) Klein supported calls for Defense Secretary Donald Rumsfeld to resign, but fell short of calling for a timetable to withdraw U.S. troops.

The race attracted national attention and drew top party leaders. President Bush helped Shaw raise $800,000 during a single trip in May, in addition to appearances by Dick Cheney, Laura Bush and Rudolph Giuliani. In September, Shaw appeared with Interior Secretary Dirk Kempthorne to underscore his work on Everglades restoration. In October, debates about Iraq and Social Security were overshadowed by the scandal enveloping Congressman Mark Foley, who represented an adjoining district. During one debate, Shaw called Foley's behavior a "tragedy" but declined to call on Speaker Dennis Hastert to resign as speaker over questions that he had handled the matter poorly. The scandal helped Klein reinforce his contention that Shaw was too closely tied to national Republicans. "The concern that many Americans have right now is that Congress has lost its integrity, has lost its leadership and lost its accountability on many issues," Klein said. The race was one of the most expensive House contests in 2006: Shaw spent $5.2 million to Klein's $4.2 million. Klein won 51%-47%.

After the election, Klein won a seat on the Financial Services Committee, and Chairman Barney Frank appointed Klein to lead the panel's efforts on property insurance reform. Klein represents a marginally Democratic district that voted against Bush in 2000 and 2004. He will likely be well-funded in 2008. One possible Republican challenger in 2008 is attorney Alan Schlesinger, the 2006 Republican Senate nominee against Joe Lieberman in Connecticut, who has ties to the district and was contemplating a move to the Florida to run for the seat. Two other Republicans made moves to run: Marc Flagg, a former Navy pilot whose parents were aboard the plane that crashed into the Pentagon on September 11, and former Army Lt. Col. Allen West, who retired after a 2003 incident in which he fired a gun near the head of an Iraqi detainee in an effort to make him reveal information about plans to attack U.S. troops.

TWENTY-THIRD DISTRICT

Rep. Alcee Hastings (D)

Elected 1992, 8th term; b. Sept. 5, 1936, Altamonte Springs; home, Miramar; Fisk U., B.A. 1958, Howard U., 1958-60, FL A&M, J.D. 1963; Methodist; single.

Elected Office: Broward Cnty. Circuit Court Judge, 1977-79.

Professional Career: Practicing atty., 1964-77; Federal Judge, U.S. District Court, 1979-89.

DC Office: 2353 RHOB, 20515, 202-225-1313; Fax: 202-225-1171; Web site: www.alceehastings.house.gov.

District Offices: Ft. Lauderdale, 954-733-2800; West Palm Beach, 561-684-0565.

Committees: *Permanent Select Committee on Intelligence* (Vice Chmn. of 12 D): Oversight & Investigations (Vice Chmn.); Terrorism, Human Intelligence, Analysis & Counterintelligence. *Rules* (3d of 9 D): Legislative & Budget Process (Chmn.).

Group Ratings

	ADA	ACLU	AFS	LCV	ITIC	NTU	COC	ACU	CFG	FRC
2006	95	95	100	92	29	13	33	8	13	0
2005	90	—	100	89	—	13	31	4	0	8

National Journal Ratings

	2005 LIB	—	2005 CONS		2006 LIB	—	2006 CONS
Economic	87%	—	12%		82%	—	18%
Social	83%	—	17%		93%	—	7%
Foreign	73%	—	27%		61%	—	39%

Key Votes of the 109th Congress

1. Estate Tax Repeal	N	5. Limit Interstate Abortion	Y	9. Build Border Fence	N
2. Limit CAFE Standards	Y	6. Extend Patriot Act	*	10. CAFTA	N
3. FY06 Spending Curb	N	7. Bar Same Sex Marriage	N	11. Oppose Iraq Withdrawal	N
4. Drilling in ANWR	N	8. Stem Cell Research $	Y	12. Detainee Tribunals	N

Election Results

2006 general	Alcee Hastings (D) .... unopposed	($427,924)
2006 primary	Alcee Hastings (D) .... unopposed	
2004 general	Alcee Hastings (D) .... unopposed	($947,430)

Prior Winning Percentages: 2002 (77%); 2000 (76%); 1998 (100%); 1996 (73%); 1994 (100%); 1992 (59%)

The People		Race/Ethnic Origin	Ancestry	
Area size:	3,703 sq. mi.	29.4% White	West Indian: 16.2% USA: 5.0%	
Urban population:	97.9%	51.2% Black	German: 4.1%	
Rural population:	2.1%	1.2% Asian	**2004 Presidential Vote**	
Pop. 2000:	639,295	0.2% Native Am.	Kerry (D) 155,915	(76%)
Pop. 2005 (est):	692,701	0.1% Hawaiian	Bush (R) 50,138	(24%)
Median income:	$31,309	3.9% Two+ races	Other 28	(0%)
Poverty status:	21.9%	0.4% Other	**2000 Presidential Vote**	
Military veterans:	9.1%	13.7% Hispanic Origin	Gore (D) 130,518	(80%)
			Bush (R) 33,034	(20%)
			Cook Partisan Voting Index: D +29	

Occupation   Blue collar: 25.8%   White collar: 48.0%   Gray collar: 26.2%

In the morning shadow of the high-rise condominiums that line the Atlantic Ocean, behind the quiet waters that separate the barrier islands from the mainland, usually a few blocks off of old U.S. 1 and behind the railroad lines, are the black neighborhoods of South Florida's Gold Coast. They are gatherings of older stucco homes and commercial storefronts, ranging from enclaves of upper-middle-class residents to rundown slums. These neighborhoods, populated by the working poor and with relatively few seniors, are bypassed by most tourists.

The 23d Congressional District of Florida gathers together many of South Florida's black neighborhoods in a geographically contrived, but demographically coherent, constituency. Geographically most of the district is in the Everglades, east and south of Lake Okeechobee. This is a land of swamps and drainage canals, with some farms and citrus groves—and very few people, some in migrant worker camps, some on the Miccosukee Indian Reservation, some in places like Southwest Ranches, a new community where residents have opposed roads and street lights. Almost all of the people in the district live within four narrow tentacles that extend east from the Everglades and get close to but never reach the Atlantic Ocean. The northernmost reaches into St. Lucie County and takes in black neighborhoods in Fort Pierce. In northern Palm Beach County a tentacle reaches past high-income Wellington into West Palm Beach and then continues south along the railroad tracks and U.S. 1 to Delray Beach, which was the site of a civil rights showdown in 1956 and now has a big Haitian community. The most populated tentacle reaches east into Broward County to take in heavily black areas in Lauderhill, Fort Lauderdale, Pompano Beach and Deerfield Beach. Farther south in Broward County there is a much smaller tentacle that reaches into parts of fast-growing Miramar and Pembroke Pines, home to upwardly mobile Haitians and also to one of the Century Village communities, the retirement development known for its politically powerful, liberal associations led by "condo commandos." Overall, the population is 51% black and 14% Hispanic. In 2004 to 2005, Broward had the largest increase of black residents of any county in the nation. This is a heavily Democratic district, where registered Democrats outnumber Republicans 64%-16%, though turnout has been low and voting power in the state has been shifting elsewhere.

The congressman from the 23d District is Alcee Hastings, a Democrat first elected in 1992, the only member of Congress ever to have been impeached and removed from office as a federal judge. Hastings is charming but with a partisan edge, the only child of a hotel maid from Orlando, who later worked as a domestic for wealthy families across the nation. He practiced law, finished fourth in the five-candidate Democratic primary when he ran for the U.S. Senate in 1970, and was confirmed as a federal judge in 1979. Hastings was charged with conspiring with a friend to take a $150,000 bribe and give two convicted swindlers light sentences. A Miami jury acquitted Hastings in 1983, but the friend was convicted. Under a new judicial disciplinary code, the 11th Circuit Court of Appeals called for impeachment in 1987 and referred the case to Congress. Hastings was impeached by the House by a vote of 413–3 and convicted by the Senate, 69-26. In the House, John Conyers, senior member of the Congressional Black Caucus, made the case for impeachment; an investigative panel of 12 senators was badly divided, and the full Senate acted in 1989 without hearing all of the arguments. As a footnote, during a 1997 investigation into the FBI crime lab, the Department of Justice found that an agent falsely testified against Hastings; he and Conyers moved to reopen the case but nothing came of it.

After his removal Hastings was unapologetic. In 1990 he ran an abortive campaign for governor, then lost in a primary for secretary of state. When the 23d District was created, he entered that race and led in the primary 28%-27%. In the October runoff he faced Palm Beach County legislator Lois Frankel, who blasted Hastings for his record; he responded, "The bitch is a racist." Hastings was helped by a ruling by federal Judge Stanley Sporkin that his removal from office was invalid since the full Senate did not hear the charges; the Supreme Court later ruled to the contrary in a case of another convicted federal judge in 1993, but by that time Hastings was in Congress. He won the runoff 58%-42%, with voting closely following racial lines. He won the general election 59%-31%. Since then, he has not had a serious primary or general election challenge.

In the House, his voting record has been mostly liberal, but toward the center on foreign policy. He strongly supported the U.S. intervention in Kosovo but opposed the use of force in Iraq. Naturally, Hastings's opinion was sought when the subject of impeachment arose, and it was exuberantly given. He saw Bill Clinton's impeachment as being driven by prosecutors, like the judges in his own case, abusing their powers: "In my case, they nullified a jury. In this case, they are nullifying an election." He moved to impeach Independent Counsel Kenneth Starr; his motion was voted down 340-71. In 2004, with the support of Speaker Dennis Hastert, he was elected president of the Organization for Security and Cooperation in the pan-European Parliamentary Assembly and served two one-year terms; in 2007, he became chairman of the counterpart U.S. commission. His extensive travels—more foreign trips since 1994 than any other current member of Congress, according to PoliticalMoneyLine—caused him to miss some House votes, but he told the *Palm Beach Post*, "It's hard to apologize for working." In December 2006, the House passed his resolution condemning Iran for hosting a conference on Holocaust denial. He serves on the House Rules Committee, a more influential post with Democrats in the majority. Following the 2006 election, he was seriously considered for chairman of the House Intelligence Committee. He had support from the Congressional Black Caucus but was opposed by the Blue Dogs and others who maintained that his controversial past disqualified him from such an assignment. Hastings attacked his critics as "misinformed fools" but Nancy Pelosi nevertheless selected Texas Democrat Silvestre Reyes. "I am not angry," he told *National Journal* afterwards. "At some point along the way, it became too much to explain. That is legitimate politics. But it's unfortunate for me." He remained a member of the panel.

TWENTY-FOURTH DISTRICT

Rep. Tom Feeney (R)

Elected 2002, 3d term; b. May 21, 1958, Abington, PA; home, Oviedo; PA St. U., B.A. 1980, U. of Pittsburgh, J.D. 1983; Presbyterian; married (Ellen).

Elected Office: FL House of Reps., 1990-94, 1996-2002, Speaker, 2000-02.

Professional Career: Practicing atty., 1983-2002.

DC Office: 323 CHOB, 20515, 202-225-2706; Fax: 202-226-6299; Web site: www.house.gov/feeney.

District Offices: Orlando, 407-208-1106; Port Orange, 386-756-9798; Titusville, 321-264-6113.

Committees: *Financial Services* (16th of 33 R): Financial Institutions & Consumer Credit; Capital Markets, Insurance & Government Sponsored Enterprises. *Judiciary* (14th of 17 R): Courts, the Internet & Intellectual Property; Commercial & Administrative Law. *Science & Technology* (11th of 20 R): Space & Aeronautics (RMM); Investigations & Oversight.

Group Ratings

	ADA	ACLU	AFS	LCV	ITIC	NTU	COC	ACU	CFG	FRC
2006	10	10	0	8	86	72	93	96	84	100
2005	0	—	0	17	—	74	81	96	97	100

National Journal Ratings

	2005 LIB	—	2005 CONS	2006 LIB	—	2006 CONS
Economic	30%	—	70%	27%	—	71%
Social	18%	—	82%	23%	—	74%
Foreign	23%	—	73%	38%	—	59%

Key Votes of the 109th Congress

1. Estate Tax Repeal	Y	5. Limit Interstate Abortion	Y	9. Build Border Fence	Y
2. Limit CAFE Standards	Y	6. Extend Patriot Act	Y	10. CAFTA	Y
3. FY06 Spending Curb	Y	7. Bar Same Sex Marriage	Y	11. Oppose Iraq Withdrawal	Y
4. Drilling in ANWR	Y	8. Stem Cell Research $	N	12. Detainee Tribunals	Y

Election Results

2006 general	Tom Feeney (R)	123,795	(58%)	($1,571,417)
	Clint Curtis (D)	89,863	(42%)	($84,804)
2006 primary	Tom Feeney (R)	unopposed		
2004 general	Tom Feeney (R)	unopposed		($705,578)

Prior Winning Percentages: 2002 (62%)

The People		Race/Ethnic Origin	Ancestry	
Area size:	1,915 sq. mi.	80.0% White	German: 12.4% Irish: 10.5%	
Urban population:	91.2%	6.3% Black	English: 9.3%	
Rural population:	8.8%	2.0% Asian	**2004 Presidential Vote**	
Pop. 2000:	639,295	0.3% Native Am.	Bush (R) 188,973	(55%)
Pop. 2005 (est):	742,225	0.0% Hawaiian	Kerry (D) 153,130	(45%)
Median income:	$43,954	1.4% Two+ races	Other 476	(0%)
Poverty status:	8.7%	0.2% Other	**2000 Presidential Vote**	
Military veterans:	17.1%	9.8% Hispanic Origin	Bush (R) 133,531	(53%)
			Gore (D) 116,502	(47%)
			Cook Partisan Voting Index: R + 3	

Occupation	Blue collar: 19.4%	White collar: 65.3%	Gray collar: 15.3%

In 1960, central Florida was a sleepy place: Orlando was a small city surrounded by citrus groves; the Atlantic Coast from Cape Canaveral north was a quiet winter vacation spot, with small motels lining U.S. 1 or along the beach on Highway A1A. Then two outsiders transformed this part of America, and made it in two different ways a leader in the world: John F. Kennedy and Walt Disney. Kennedy promised in 1961 to put a man on the moon before the end of the decade, and the Kennedy Space Center was built on an island near Cape Canaveral. This part of Florida suddenly became the Space Coast, from which Americans traveled directly to the moon. Disney in 1971 opened Disney World southwest of Orlando, near the intersection of I-4 and Florida's Turnpike. Other theme parks followed, and metro Orlando became the number one tourist destination in the world. In the process, the populations of metro Orlando and the Space Coast have more than tripled since the 1960s. People from all over the United States and, more recently, immigrants from Latin America and elsewhere, have come here in large numbers and, with the aid of ubiquitous air conditioning, have transformed sleepy backwaters into vibrant metropolitan areas. This is a part of Florida that has attracted many more young families and people in their working years than retirees: people who have built all-American communities where there used to be orange groves and swamps.

The 24th Congressional District of Florida has about half its population in the Orlando area, much of it in affluent Orange and Seminole County suburbs north and northeast of Orlando— all of Oviedo and parts of Maitland and Altamonte Springs.The other half is on the coast. The 24th covers nearly 80 miles of coastline and includes the northern half of Brevard County, including the main grounds of the Space Center itself, the Canaveral National Seashore and the county seat of Titusville; with cutbacks in the space shuttle program, whose last flight is expected by 2010, the economy here has diversified to include commercial and military satellites. It contains the southern half of Volusia County, including part of Daytona Beach, where NASCAR is a big employer and Bike Week and Speed Week are held every year but Spring Break has shrunk for the kids; also here is New Smyrna Beach, founded as a colony by Andrew Turnbull, a Scotch doctor, where you can see the ruins of an 1820s sugar mill. This is as close as Florida gets to a typical suburban district: There are higher than average numbers of homeowners, families with children, working women and white-collar employees. This is on balance a Republican district; it voted 53% for George W. Bush in 2000 and 55% in 2004.

The congressman from the 24th District is Tom Feeney, a Republican first elected in 2002 who was a prominent political player in the Bush versus Gore machinations in Florida. His political career has been marked by ambition, impulsiveness and a quick rise through the ranks but with some bumps along the way. He grew up in Pennsylvania, the son of schoolteachers, and was an unsuccessful candidate to be a delegate for Ronald Reagan in 1980. After graduating from Penn State and University of Pittsburgh law school, he moved to Florida and practiced real estate law. In 1990 he was elected to the state House, where his early focus was on education. In 1994 Jeb Bush picked him as his running mate. The statewide race was a sobering experience. Democrats zeroed in on Feeney's conservative voting record—he opposed abortion rights and favored school prayer and vouchers—and attacked him as an extremist bent on injecting religion into the public schools. Bush and Feeney lost to Lawton Chiles and Buddy MacKay 51%-49%. In 1996, Feeney was returned to the state House. In November 2000, he became Speaker and suddenly found himself in the national spotlight. During the 36-day presidential recount he aggressively challenged the rulings of the Florida Supreme Court and supported Secretary of State Katherine Harris. When it was unclear whether the U.S. Supreme Court would review the Florida court's second decision, he called a special session of the House to appoint presidential electors for Bush; that became moot after the U.S. Supreme Court decision on December 12.

As Speaker, Feeney took a lead role on congressional redistricting. Central Florida's population had increased robustly in the 1990s, and that part of the state gained one of Florida's two additional seats in 2002. He ran in the new 24th District and was unopposed in the Republican primary. The Democratic nominee was Harry Jacobs, a wealthy trial lawyer who in November 2000 filed a lawsuit challenging some 16,000 absentee ballots in Seminole County; a trial judge dismissed the suit. Jacobs spent $3.2 million of his own money, boasted about his work as a schoolteacher and attacked Feeney's "questionable ethics." Feeney said that Jacobs tried to disenfranchise military voters with his lawsuit. He won 62%-38%.

In the House, Feeney usually sides with conservatives and has chaired the House Conservatives Fund, the campaign arm of the Republican Study Committee. On the Judiciary Committee, he enacted a controversial proposal to restrict judges from imposing sentences in sexual assault cases that are more lenient than federal guidelines. Chief Justice William Rehnquist criticized the proposal as an "unwarranted and ill-considered effort to intimidate individual judges." Liberal lawmakers criticized the proposal, but many voted for it as part of the bill to create a nationwide "Amber Alert" system to recover abducted children. Feeney also sponsored a bill to prohibit federal judges from citing foreign laws in their rulings. On the Financial Services Committee, he pushed to weaken accounting requirements on business from the Sarbanes-Oxley law. After the death of Ronald Reagan, he called the former president "our Moses." Although he made an exception for NASA, where he wants to extend the retirement date for the shuttle, he joined other conservatives who said that the federal government was spending too much money. Feeney ignored the pleas of Republican leaders, including George W. Bush, to vote for the Medicare/prescription drug bill in November 2003; while asking for his vote, Bush reportedly hung up when Feeney told him that he came to Washington to cut entitlements, not increase them. He got a change in House rules to remove the prohibition on referring to the Senate or individual Senators. "The rule was antiquated," he said. When the ethics committee admonished Tom DeLay in October 2004, Feeney said that the majority leader "stands strong as our leader." Some called him Tom DeLay Lite. In 2006, he called lobbying reform "a joke," and far less important than budget overhaul; he denied that he did favors for convicted lobbyist Jack Abramoff in exchange for a golf trip to Scotland, but he later reimbursed the Treasury $5,643 for that trip. In April 2007, Feeney released a statement saying he was cooperating with a Justice Department investigation into activity surrounding Abramoff. In June, he established a legal defense fund; Feeney has said he is not a target of the investigation.

In 2006, Feeney faced Democratic challenger Clint Curtis, who had worked for a computer firm that once had Feeney as a client. Curtis accused Feeney of asking him to write a computer program designed to fix elections. Feeney dismissed the charges ("I didn't lead the purple Martian invasion of Earth either," he replied), and won 58%-42%. Democrats were looking closely at this district for 2008, but a top-tier challenger had not yet emerged as of August 2007. Curtis said he would run again in 2008.

TWENTY-FIFTH DISTRICT

Rep. Mario Diaz-Balart (R)

Elected 2002, 3d term; b. Sept. 25, 1961, Ft. Lauderdale; home, Miami; U. of S. FL; Catholic; married (Tia).

Elected Office: FL House of Reps., 1988-92, 2000-02; FL Senate, 1992-00.

Professional Career: A.A., Miami Mayor Xavier Suarez, 1985-88; Public relations executive.

DC Office: 328 CHOB, 20515, 202-225-2778; Fax: 202-226-0346; Web site: mariodiaz-balart.house.gov.

District Offices: Miami, 305-225-6866; Naples, 239-348-1620.

Committees: *Budget* (5th of 17 R). *Science & Technology* (16th of 20 R): Energy & Environment. *Transportation & Infrastructure* (22d of 34 R): Railroads, Pipelines & Hazardous Materials; Aviation; Highways & Transit.

Group Ratings

	ADA	ACLU	AFS	LCV	ITIC	NTU	COC	ACU	CFG	FRC
2006	15	28	0	17	86	55	93	64	49	71
2005	5	—	0	11	—	68	96	92	84	85

National Journal Ratings

	2005 LIB	—	2005 CONS	2006 LIB	—	2006 CONS
Economic	18%	—	81%	21%	—	77%
Social	51%	—	49%	53%	—	47%
Foreign	0%	—	89%	29%	—	71%

Key Votes of the 109th Congress

1. Estate Tax Repeal	Y	5. Limit Interstate Abortion	Y	9. Build Border Fence	N
2. Limit CAFE Standards	Y	6. Extend Patriot Act	Y	10. CAFTA	Y
3. FY06 Spending Curb	Y	7. Bar Same Sex Marriage	N	11. Oppose Iraq Withdrawal	Y
4. Drilling in ANWR	Y	8. Stem Cell Research $	N	12. Detainee Tribunals	Y

Election Results

2006 general	Mario Diaz-Balart (R) 60,765	(58%)	($697,936)
	Michael Calderin (D) 43,168	(42%)	($35,161)
2006 primary	Mario Diaz-Balart (R) .... unopposed		
2004 general	Mario Diaz-Balart (R) .... unopposed		($322,024)

Prior Winning Percentages: 2002 (65%)

The People		Race/Ethnic Origin	Ancestry	
Area size:	4,724 sq. mi.	24.3% White	USA: 3.8%	West Indian: 3.7%
Urban population:	94.4%	10.0% Black	German: 3.2%	
Rural population:	5.6%	1.6% Asian	**2004 Presidential Vote**	
Pop. 2000:	639,295	0.1% Native Am.	Bush (R) 122,342	(56%)
Pop. 2005 (est):	773,848	0.0% Hawaiian	Kerry (D) 95,001	(44%)
Median income:	$44,489	1.4% Two+ races	**2000 Presidential Vote**	
Poverty status:	13.7%	0.2% Other	Bush (R) 88,308	(55%)
Military veterans:	6.0%	62.4% Hispanic Origin	Gore (D) 72,050	(45%)
			Cook Partisan Voting Index: R + 4	

Occupation	Blue collar: 20.8%	White collar: 61.7%	Gray collar: 17.5%

An interconnected sea of wetlands once covered 8.9 million acres of southern Florida, stretching from present-day Orlando down to the peninsula's southern tip. It was once a coherent ecosystem, a "river of grass" in which water moved slowly down a gentle slope to the ocean, buffering plants and animals from meteorological extremes, and providing different micro-environments for flora and fauna based on an inch or two gained or lost in elevation. It was long a dream of Florida's white settlers to control this land and make it more useful, but for decades this goal proved elusive. It took three attempts between 1915 and the late 1920s to build the Tamiami Trail from Miami to Tampa; to this day, it is one of only two roads that cross the South Florida interior from coast to coast. Over time, man managed to reshape the Everglades. In 1948, Congress approved the Central and South Florida Project, which authorized the construction of 1,000 miles of canals and 720 miles of levees to channel and drain the Everglades. Since then, about half of the original ecosystem has been turned over to agriculture and housing, and the amount of water discharged into the ocean has fallen by 70%. Floridians later had second thoughts and called for restoration of the Everglades. Politicians of both parties took notice, and called for change. In 2000, Congress passed a law to restore the Everglades in 16 counties, authorizing $7.8 billion over 30 years. In 2002 President George W. Bush and his brother Jeb, the governor of Florida, signed an agreement to proceed. After a slow start, initial steps have included a huge storage reservoir and a safety valve to protect Lake Okeechobee and its dikes.

A century of meddling has produced an often-surreal landscape. Farmers came to the Fakahatchee Strand in the early 20th century, but they found that crops would not grow reliably, and livestock often escaped, leaving a legacy of feral, mean-spirited swamp pigs. Timbering came next, until there were no more trees to chop down. Then the timber barons sold their land to real estate speculators who made hundreds of millions of dollars duping customers into buying wretched plots for $10 a month, using patently false promises, spying on their customers' private conversations in their hotel rooms and driving potential buyers to remote areas of the site and threatening to let them walk home if they did not sign a contract. Much of the landholdings became an untamed state park.

The 25th Congressional District of Florida sprawls almost all the way across this uninhabitable portion of South Florida, connecting population centers near (but not on) each of Florida's two coasts. About 13% of its residents live in Collier County, in new housing wedged between decidedly upscale and artsy Naples and the wild Everglades and in the farm town of Immokalee, where an estimated 80% of workers are illegal aliens. The large majority live in western and southern edges of metropolitan Miami, mostly close to the swamps. Here you can drive out on roads past the subdivisions and find strawberry, tomato and citrus farms; the trees thin out and then the road just ends, and the Everglades begin. The towns in the northern part of Miami-Dade are heavily Cuban and Latino—Hialeah Gardens, Tamiami, Kendale Lakes, South Miami Heights, Cutler Ridge. Farther south the 25th takes in low-income agricultural areas along South Dixie Highway (U.S. 1), like Princeton and Naranja, as well as a few older tourist attractions, like the Metrozoo, the innovative Monkey Jungle and Coral Castle. Even further south is what was the country town of Homestead. The Air Force Base once was a major employer here. But in August 1992 Hurricane Andrew ravaged Homestead, with massive property destruction; Homestead was leveled and the base closed, though limited facilities remained for some reserve units. In one of his last acts as president, Bill Clinton rejected a plan to convert the base to a commercial airport, citing environmental concerns. Instead, 700 acres were transferred to the county for use by developers, resulting in a new boomtown, with residential developments, shops, hospitals, parks and schools, plus a Coast Guard base; NASCAR has an annual race at the speedway. The district as a whole is one of Florida's fastest-growing, with 21% population growth between 2000 and 2005. Politically, this area leans Republican, thanks to the allegiance of its many Cuban Americans, though this is the least Cuban of the three South Florida Hispanic majority districts.

The congressman from the 25th District is Mario Diaz-Balart, a Republican first elected in 2002. His father, Rafael Lincoln Diaz-Balart, served as majority leader in pre-revolution Cuba's House of Representatives. His uncle and grandfather also served in the Cuban House. His aunt was once married to Fidel Castro. He comes from a prominent family sometimes called "the Cuban Kennedys," which seems to have politics in its blood. One of his three older brothers is Lincoln Diaz-Balart, congressman from the 21st District just to the east. Mario Diaz-Balart, unlike Lincoln, was born in the United States after his family fled Cuba.

Even for a scion of one of Miami's most prominent political families, his ascent has been impressive. He dropped out of the University of South Florida at 24 to work for former Miami Mayor Xavier Suarez and was elected in 1988 to the Florida House. In 1992, at 31, he became the youngest person ever elected to the Florida Senate. Soon after that, Diaz-Balart was named chairman of the Senate Ways and Means Committee, where he was a budget hawk. His 1995 order calling for state agencies to cut spending by 25% earned him the nickname "The Slasher"—a moniker he wore with pride. The eight-year term limit forced him from the state Senate in 2000, so he again ran for the Florida House and was elected. No ordinary freshman, Diaz-Balart requested and received the chairmanship of the congressional redistricting committee. The resulting plan included a central Florida district tailored to Speaker Tom Feeney and this western Miami-Dade district tailored for Diaz-Balart. The election proved anticlimactic. Diaz-Balart went to court and eliminated all his would-be Republican opponents. In the general, he coasted to victory over state Representative Annie Betancourt, a former social worker and the widow of a Bay of Pigs veteran. Her campaign was underfinanced and she remained largely unknown; Diaz-Balart had support from teachers and other unions. Betancourt called to end the "failed" embargo of Cuba in a way "that doesn't pander to the Cuban regime but likewise doesn't punish the Cuban people." This was a bold move in a strongly anti-Castro constituency. Diaz-Balart did not pursue the issue vigorously, perhaps because he sensed that the increasing non-Cuban Latinos in south Florida are less concerned about Castro. He won 65%-35%.

In the House, his voting record has generally been more conservative than brother Lincoln on economic and foreign policy, and he has been a moderate on cultural issues. With Tom Feeney and Jeb Hensarling, he founded Washington Waste Watchers, to combat government waste, fraud and abuse. At home, he worked to include parts of his district in the clean-up program following Hurricane Katrina, but he criticized FEMA for supporting puppet shows and gumbo cook-offs elsewhere. He organized the Congressional Hispanic Conference, a Republican alternative to the Democrats' Congressional Hispanic Caucus. He has been a hard-line foe of Fidel Castro and predicted that the regime would not last long under brother Raul Castro. Also like brother Lincoln, his reelection margin shrunk in 2006—to 58%-42% against 26-year-old Michael Calderin, a computer software specialist at the University of Miami medical school who criticized him for "blindly supporting the president." Calderin planned to run again in 2008.

★ GEORGIA ★

Georgia and Atlanta—the megacity whose metropolitan area spreads out over the red clay hills of 20 of Georgia's 159 counties—have been one of the great boom areas of America over the last dozen years and have been the site as well of one of the great political transformations of the first decade of the 21st century. From 1990 to 2006, Georgia's population grew by 45%, the fifth highest rate of population growth among states, after Nevada, Arizona, Utah and Idaho, ahead of Florida and Texas and far ahead of California. The 2000 Census recorded it as the tenth-largest state—the first time it has been in the top 10 since the Census of 1850—and in 2002 it passed New Jersey to become number nine. Metro Atlanta, now spreading over 28 North Georgia counties, has grown by 67% in that period. This is the highest rate of growth for Georgia since the 1870s, when Atlanta rose literally from the ashes of the Civil War and Henry Grady's New South sprang into being. Atlanta and Georgia have been in many ways, for many years, the center of the South, at least since General William Tecumseh Sherman marched here in 1864. This is where John Stith Pemberton invented Coca-Cola, where Margaret Mitchell wrote *Gone With the Wind*, where Martin Luther King Jr. grew up, and where most of the civil rights organizations that changed America were headquartered. But in growth and flamboyance, Georgia for decades was outdazzled by other parts of the South—by Texas with its oil wells and high-tech industries, by Florida with Miami Beach and Disney World, even by North Carolina with its Research Triangle and college basketball champions.

Neither Atlanta's rise to world eminence nor its role as the capital of the South was inevitable. Georgia was the last of the seaboard colonies, founded by James Oglethorpe in 1733 as an "Asilum of the Unfortunate"; Oglethorpe forbade slavery, but the settlers rebelled and repealed his ban in 1750. This was only a small, though well located, railroad crossroads when it was burned by Sherman's troops on their "march to the sea." Richmond, Charleston and New Orleans all had stronger claims to being the central focus of the South a century ago. But in the 20th century two figures imprinted Atlanta on the national imagination. One was Margaret Mitchell, whose 1936 novel *Gone with the Wind* inspired the 1939 movie. The other was Martin Luther King Jr., reared in Atlanta and based there during most of his career, as a leader and ultimately the national symbol of the civil rights revolution that changed the South and the nation. Linking the two was Atlanta's business community, notably Robert Woodruff, who headed Coca-Cola from 1932-60 and made Coke a worldwide enterprise. Perhaps aware that a world company could not indefinitely be associated with racial segregation, Woodruff and William Hartsfield, mayor from 1937-61, cooperated with blacks and promoted Atlanta as "the city too busy to hate." Hartsfield's successor, Ivan Allen, elected in 1961 and 1965, supported the Civil Rights Act of 1964, as Peachtree Center and the first atriumed Hyatt Regency were going up in downtown Atlanta.

This new Atlanta was growing up amid a mostly rural, deeply segregationist Georgia that as late as 1960 cast the second-highest Democratic percentage of any state for president: Hatred of Sherman was still strong 96 years after he marched through Georgia. Political contests typically matched Atlanta-supported moderates against rural-supported segregationists, and the latter invariably won: Georgia's electoral votes were cast for Barry Goldwater in 1964 and George Wallace in 1968. Then came change in the person of Jimmy Carter, a one-term state senator who was elected governor in 1970 with a rural base as well as conspicuous black support. On taking office he proclaimed a reconciliation of the races and installed a portrait of Martin Luther King Jr. in the Capitol. Carter thus became one of the first politicians from the rural South to celebrate and honor the civil rights revolution and in the process set himself on the road to being elected president in 1976.

Since then, Georgia and Atlanta have seen an in-migration of black Americans. The state's population was 29% black in 2000, the highest figure since 1950; the state has more blacks than any other state except New York and Texas, and will surpass them soon if present trends continue. The presence of nine historically black colleges, of large numbers of prominent black public officials and businessmen, the growth of middle- and upper-income predominantly black suburban neighborhoods in DeKalb County and, more recently, Cobb County—all have made metro Atlanta in some sense the capital of black America. Arguably, Georgia has developed what Charles Moskos and John

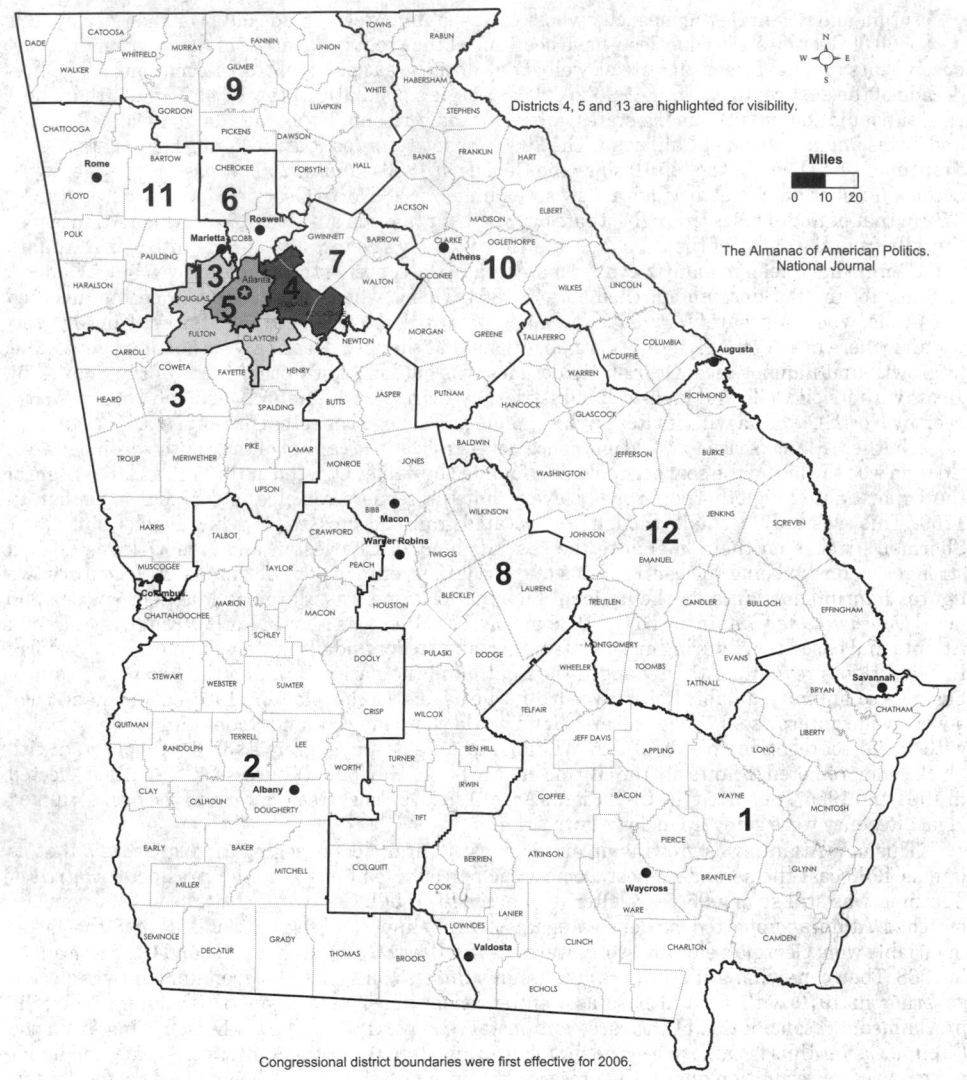

Districts 4, 5 and 13 are highlighted for visibility.

Miles
0   10   20

The Almanac of American Politics.
National Journal

Congressional district boundaries were first effective for 2006.

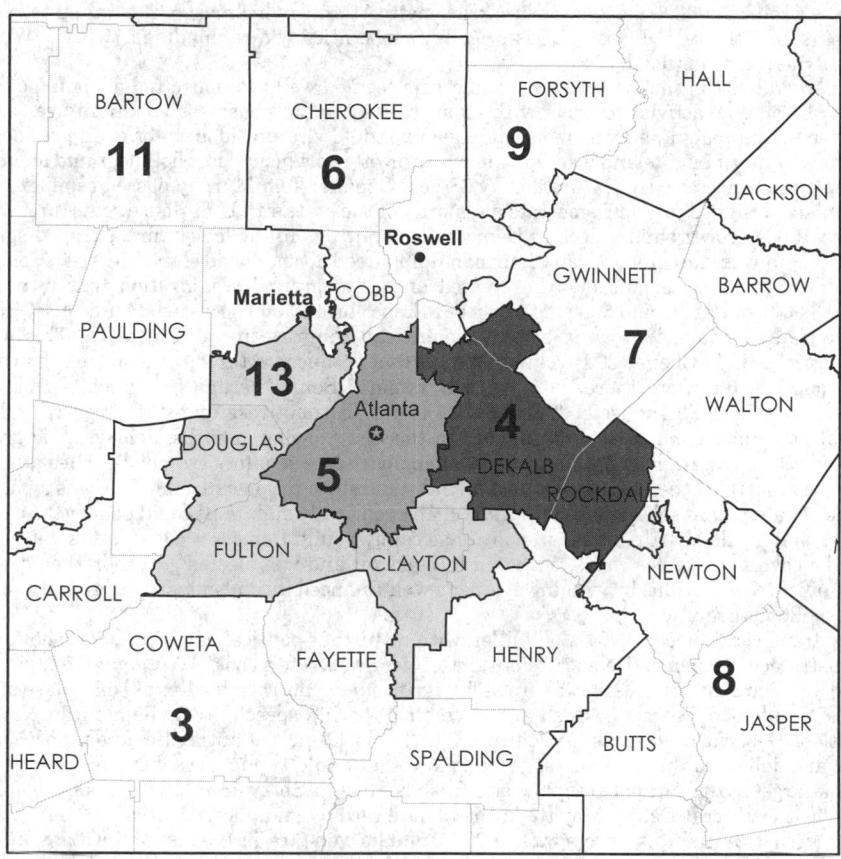

Sibley Butler described in their book on race in the Army, *All We Can Be*, an Anglo-African culture, a merger of traditions that were long associated intimately in private life but rigidly and even violently separated in public.Georgia has four black Democratic congressmen, two from non-black majority districts, and Andrew Young won in a white-majority district as long ago as 1972; black Democrats Thurbert Baker and Michael Thurmond have been elected attorney general and labor commissioner statewide, and reelected despite a strong Republican trend; in 2004 Georgia elected its first black Republican state representative since Reconstruction, and blacks came in second in the contests for the Republican nomination for the Senate and the 8th District House seat. Georgia also has been attracting immigrants, and 7% of its residents in 2005 were Hispanic and 3% Asian—quite a change over the past quarter-century. And it has been attracting even more internal migrants from the United States: domestic inflow in 2000-06 was 5% of 2000 population. These newcomers were attracted by, and in turn stimulated, Georgia's booming and vibrant private sector economy, which has generated more population growth than in any state east of Arizona.

Demographic change and economic change in Georgia have been followed by political change, to the point that this once heavily Democratic state now seems to be solidly Republican. In retrospect, this change seems to have been a long time coming. It was delayed by the presence of politically skillful Southern and Georgia Democrats with rural bases—George Wallace, who carried the state in 1968; Jimmy Carter, who sent it in a different direction in 1970, and carried it solidly in 1976 and 1980; Carter's successors as governor, each of whom served for eight years, George Busbee, Joe Frank Harris and Zell Miller; by Bill Clinton, who carried the state 43.5%-42.9% in 1992 and lost it by only 47%-46% in 1996. Then, in 2000, a sign of change: George W. Bush carried

Georgia by a solid 55%-43% margin. Bush carried metro Atlanta (which cast 53% of the state's votes) by 52%-45% and the rest of Georgia, historically Democratic, by a resounding 57%-41%. William Tecumseh Sherman was dead.

The trend has continued ever since. Democrats seemed well positioned to hold onto power in 2002. Roy Barnes, an activist governor with strong ties to Atlanta's business community, raised $19 million for his campaign and was mentioned as a possible vice presidential or even presidential candidate. Senator Max Cleland was well known as a veteran who had lost both legs and an arm in Vietnam. The Democratic legislature, led by 28-year Speaker Tom Murphy passed complex redistricting plans designed to give Democrats a majority of the state's 13 U.S. House seats (up from 11 thanks to 1990s growth) and to lock in Democratic majorities in the legislature. Arrayed against this juggernaut was state Republican Chairman Ralph Reed, former head of the Christian Coalition and later a campaign consultant, who created an on-the-ground organization that ultimately deployed 3,000 volunteers and 500 paid workers to knock on 150,000 doors in 600 precincts. He ran registration drives in fast-growing heavily Republican counties in metro Atlanta. This was a prototype of the Bush-Cheney 2004 volunteer effort that produced votes in rural and exurban areas that no one thought were there. Former state Senator Sonny Perdue beat Barnes 51%-46%; Congressman Saxby Chambliss beat Cleland 53%-46%. Turnout rose robustly in central Atlanta and in black counties, but it rose even more in the fast-growing suburbs: demographic growth translated into votes. In the week after the election, four state senators switched parties and gave Republicans control of the state Senate for the first time since Reconstruction. This was a political revolution of a sort that seldom occurs in a state. The politically ambitious could ponder the careers of Barnes and Perdue. Both started in politics as canny young Democratic legislators with ambitions to be governor. Barnes chose to remain a Democrat and was elected governor, then couldn't hold the office. Now Perdue, by winning against a well-financed incumbent, showed that it is easier to win as a Republican.

The trend continued in 2004. Zell Miller, with no further political ambitions, also showed the way. Frustrated with Senate Democrats' obstructionism, he wrote a book, *A National Party No More* ("the modern South and rural America are as foreign to our Democratic leaders as some place in Asia or Africa"), endorsed George W. Bush and gave a rip-roaring speech at the Republican National Convention. Georgia Democrats reviled him, but he spoke in the authentic accents of Andrew Jackson and delivered the same message Georgia voters would two months later. Though Georgia was not a target state, turnout rose 28% and Bush beat John Kerry 58%-41%. Republican Johnny Isakson beat Democrat Denise Majette in the Senate race by an almost identical 58%-40%. Bush won 56% in metro Atlanta, up from 52% in 2000, and he won 60% in the rest of the state, up from 57% in 2000. Kerry won among blacks, who cast 25% of the votes, by 88%-12%; most Kerry voters were black. But Bush won among whites, who cast 70% of the votes, by 76%-23%. Turnout was up sharply from 2000 in fast-growing counties in metro Atlanta—up 67% in Paulding, 65% in Henry, 59% in Forsyth and Newton, 45% in Walton, 41% in Cherokee, 38% in Carroll and Spalding, 37% in Douglas and 25% in Fayette. Bush carried these counties by 200,000 votes, 72%-27%. Republicans increased their majority in the state Senate to 34-22 and transformed the state House from a 102-77 Democratic majority to a 99-80-1 Republican majority.

The Republican trend continued in 2006, as most other states trended Democratic. The new Republican majorities passed the nation's toughest law on illegal immigrants, requiring employers to consult a federal database when hiring, welfare recipients to prove their legal status and jailers to inform federal authorities of illegal inmates. They cut income, corporate and property taxes. Democrats had a spirited primary for governor in 2006, but it no longer seemed to matter much: Perdue was reelected in November by a 58%-38% margin. Georgia became one of just 10 states with a Republican governor and legislature (the others are Alaska, Florida, Idaho, Missouri, North Dakota, South Carolina, South Dakota, Texas and Utah). Republican Casey Cagle, who beat Ralph Reed in the primary, was elected lieutenant governor; Democrats Baker and Thurmond were reelected attorney general and labor commissioner. Leah Ward Sears became Chief Justice of the state supreme court in 2005, the first black woman in that position in Georgia. Two Democratic congressmen, Jim Marshall and John Barrow, came very close to losing central Georgia House seats—the Republicans' strongest challenges in the nation in 2006. Georgia Democrats will surely figure out how to compete in this economically surging environment some day, but they haven't found the formula yet.

The People		Race/Ethnic Origin			Military veterans: 768,675 (12.8%)	
Pop. 2006 (est):	9,363,941	5,128,661	62.6%	White	WWII: 13.5%	Korea: 10.8%
Pop. 2000:	8,186,453	2,331,465	28.5%	Black	Vietnam: 34.4%	Gulf War: 15.4%
Pop. 1990:	6,478,216	171,513	2.1%	Asian	**Most populous cities (2006):**	
Change 1990-2000:	Up 26.4%	17,670	0.2%	Native Am.	1. Atlanta	486,411
% of U.S. total:	2.9%	3,278	0.0%	Hawaiian	2. Augusta	194,398
Pop. rank:	10th of 50	87,364	1.1%	Two+ races	3. Columbus	188,660
Area size:	59,425 sq. mi.	11,275	0.1%	Other	4. Savannah	127,889
State Native:	57.8%	435,227	5.3%	Hisp. Origin	5. Athens	112,787
Non-citizen:	5.0%	**Ancestry**				
Language		USA: 11.6%		English: 7.0%	Urban population: 71.7%	
English: 88.6%	Spanish: 6.0%	Irish: 6.7%		German: 6.0%	Rural population: 28.3%	
Other Eur.: 3.2%		Italian: 1.7%				

Education		Work Sector			General Assembly	
H.S. Grad:	78.6%	Private: 78.9%		Govt: 15.0%	Senate	34 R 22 D
College Grad:	24.3%	Self: 5.9%		Family: 0.3%	House	106 R 74 D
Industry		Unemployment: 5.4%			Legislative Term Limits: No	
Agri: 1.4%	Con: 7.9%	**Household Income**			**Registered Voters**	
Fin: 6.5%	Info: 3.5%	<15k: 16.0%		15-35k: 24.9%	No party registration	
Mfg: 20.8%	Prof: 27.0%	35-50k: 16.7%		50-100k: 30.1%		
Public: 5.0%	Trade: 15.8%	100-150k: 7.8%		>150k: 4.6%		
Other: 11.9%		Median: $42,433				
Occupation		Poverty status: 13.0%				
Blue collar: 26.5%	White collar: 59.5%	**Home Value**				
Gray collar: 14.0%		<50k: 16.9%	50-100k: 32.8%	100-200k: 34.4%	200-300k: 9.3%	
		300-500k: 4.7%	>500k: 1.9%	Median: $100,600		

Presidential politics   For many years Georgia seemed to vote against General Sherman, shunning Republican presidential candidates even when states less ravaged by Sherman's troops, like next-door South Carolina and Ala-
bama, embraced them. It was the second most Democratic state for John Kennedy in 1960, voted for opponents of the Civil Rights Act of 1964 (Barry Goldwater in 1964 and George Wallace in 1968), delivered big margins for Jimmy Carter in both 1976 and 1980 and voted heavily Republican only in 1972, 1984 and 1988. A residual anti-Sherman vote in rural Georgia can perhaps explain why Bill Clinton carried the state outside metro Atlanta in 1992 and lost it by only 2% in 1996. But no more. George W. Bush carried Georgia by wide margins and the half of the state outside metro Atlanta by even wider margins in 2000 and 2004. It will take a major shift of opinion to make Democrats competitive for Georgia's electoral votes again.

2004 Presidential Vote		
Bush (R)	1,914,254	(58%)
Kerry (D)	1,366,149	(41%)
Badnarik (Lib)	18,387	(1%)

2004 Democratic Presidential Primary		
Kerry (D)	293,225	(47%)
Edwards (D)	259,361	(41%)
Sharpton (D)	39,123	(6%)
Dean (D)	11,320	(2%)
Kucinich (D)	7,699	(1%)
Other	16,110	(3%)

2000 Presidential Vote		
Bush (R)	1,419,720	(55%)
Gore (D)	1,116,230	(43%)
Other	47,258	(2%)

Georgia's presidential primary comes early in the cycle and has been of some importance. In 1992 Governor Zell Miller had it scheduled one week before Super Tuesday in order to help Clinton, and it did: Clinton won solidly to balance losses in Maryland and Colorado the same day. In 1996 and 2000, Georgia was of little importance except as a measure of turnout: Democratic turnout fell from 622,000 in 1988 to 284,000 in 2000, while Republican turnout rose from 400,000 in 1988 to 643,000. In the March 2, 2004, primary Democratic turnout zoomed to 627,000, as there was no Republican contest. John Edwards visited Georgia five times after the Iowa caucuses and John Kerry only once, but Kerry beat Edwards 47%-41%. Edwards carried white voters and won 101 of the 159 counties, but Kerry carried black voters and carried Atlanta's Fulton County and the two other majority-black counties in the Atlanta metro area by 47,000 votes—more than his 33,000-vote statewide plurality. Edwards's loss here made it plain that he had no chance to win the nomination and would be hard pressed to win other Southern states, and he withdrew from the race. For 2008, Georgia has moved up its primary to February 5. But even though it's now the ninth largest state, it's not clear it will get much attention. In early 2007, well-known Republican politicians were lining up behind Rudy Giuliani, Mitt Romney and John McCain; there appeared to be less activity on the Democratic side.

Congressional districting

110th Congress Lineup
7 R   6 D
109th Congress Lineup
7 R   6 D

After the 1990 and 2000 Censuses, Georgia Democrats pushed through convoluted redistricting plans—arguably the most convoluted in the nation each time—to guarantee majorities for their party in the state's House delegation. Both times they failed. In the 1990s, Speaker Thomas Murphy tried to end the career of Newt Gingrich and strengthen incumbent Democrats. Instead, what was a 9–1 Democratic delegation in October 1992 was 8–3 Republican in April 1995, and Gingrich was Speaker of the House. A court-ordered redistricting in 1995 left virtually all incumbents with safe seats, and the balance remained 8–3. In 2001 the Democrats tried again, drawing several plans and negotiating among themselves. This time the boundaries were even more convoluted, and Democrats had a bit more success. But only a bit—with some unintended consequences. Congressman Saxby Chambliss, placed in the new 1st District with fellow Republican Jack Kingston, ran for the Senate and beat incumbent Max Cleland. The new 11th and 12th Districts, created to elect Democrats, elected Republicans instead, and Democrats only narrowly won the new 3d District. The new 13th District did elect a black Democrat, Georgia's fourth, but the delegation remained Republican by an 8–5 margin. And Georgia's plan prompted the House Republicans' campaign committee head Tom Davis to push successfully for a similarly convoluted Republican gerrymander in Pennsylvania, one which netted the Republicans more gains than the Democrats achieved in Georgia.

But now the Democrats' convoluted handiwork has been undone. In March 2004, a court redrew the district lines for the state House and state Senate, which helped the Republicans increase their Senate margin and gain control of the state House in November. In February 2005, Republicans by then in control of the governorship and the legislature worked with congressional Republicans in Washington to make redistricting of the U.S. House districts one of their top priorities; freshman Congressmen Lynn Westmoreland and Tom Price had previously served as legislative leaders in Atlanta. Moving more deliberately and facing far less Democratic resistance than Republicans encountered in Texas in 2003, they passed the plan in March with a few Republican defections and with limited Democratic support; federal review was mandatory under the Voting Rights Act, and Democratic leaders said that they would file court challenges. Another difference between Texas and Georgia: Georgia Republicans could argue they had popular support for redrawing the congressional map since they campaigned on the issue in 2002 and 2004.

The 2005 Republican plan had much more regularly shaped districts than the 2001 Democratic and splits many fewer counties (19 rather than 34). It strengthened Republican Phil Gingrey in the 11th District and weakened Democrats Jim Marshall and John Barrow of the 3d and 12th Districts. Republicans quietly worked with some of the African-American congressional Democrats to accommodate their personal concerns with the new districts; two Atlanta-area districts are 56% and 53% black while three others have black percentages of 48%, 45% and 41%. In the 2006 election Republicans came very close to defeating Marshall and Barrow; if the Republican redistricters had drawn the kind of convoluted lines Democratic redistricters used, they could have insured that the two Democrats would lose. In March 2006 Governor Sonny Perdue appointed an independent redistricting task force. It recommended a constitutional amendment establishing an independent commission which would submit recommendations for redistricting plans that would be voted up or down by the legislature. Perdue's initiative was evidence of Republicans' confidence that relatively regularly-shaped and neutrally-drawn districts would leave them with majorities in the economically surging Georgia of the 21st century.

Governor

Sonny Perdue (R)

Elected 2002, term expires Jan. 2011, 2d term; b. Dec. 20, 1946, Perry; home, Bonaire; U. of GA, D.V.M 1971; Baptist; married (Mary).

Military Career: Air Force, 1971-74 (Vietnam).

Elected Office: GA Senate, 1990-2001; Maj. Ldr. 1994-97.

Professional Career: Veterinarian; owner, Houston Fertilizer and Grain; owner, Perdue Inc.; owner, AgroStar.

Office: 203 State Capitol, Atlanta, 30334, 404-656-1776; Fax: 404-657-7332; Web site: www.gov.state.ga.us.

Election Results

2006 general	Sonny Perdue (R)	1,229,724	(58%)
	Mark Taylor (D)	811,049	(38%)
	Garrett Hayes (Lib)	81,412	(4%)
2006 primary	Sonny Perdue (R)	370,756	(88%)
	Ray McBerry (R)	48,498	(12%)
2002 general	Sonny Perdue (R)	1,041,677	(51%)
	Roy Barnes (D)	937,062	(46%)
	Other	47,122	(2%)

Sonny Perdue, the first Republican governor of Georgia since Reconstruction, grew up on his family's farm in Bonaire, near Warner Robins in central Georgia. He was a high school football quarterback and earned a veterinarian degree at the University of Georgia, where he was a walk-on football player. He served in the Air Force from 1971 to 1974, practiced as a veterinarian for two years in North Carolina, then returned to Georgia and started a fertilizer and grain business and a trucking firm near Warner Robins. In 1990 he was elected to the state Senate as a Democrat; he was easily reelected and was elected Senate majority leader in 1994 and Senate president pro tem in 1997. In 1998 he announced that he was switching parties and running for reelection as a Republican. He was stripped of his leadership posts and staff, but was reelected as a Republican with 70% of the vote. In December 2001, after his Senate seat had been hacked up in redistricting, he resigned his seat and announced he was running for governor.

He had taken on the daunting task of running against Governor Roy Barnes, elected in 1998 by a 52%-44% margin over businessman Guy Millner. Barnes had pushed through an ambitious program. In 1999 he persuaded the legislature to create the Georgia Regional Transportation Authority that gave him control over transportation and development in the 20-county metro Atlanta area. In 2000 he produced an education reform plan that required annual testing and held teachers accountable for results, with bonuses for some and adverse consequences for others; it also ended tenure for newly-hired teachers. In January 2001 Barnes persuaded the legislature to replace the Confederate battle flag, which had been chosen the state flag in 1956, and replace it with a design in which the state seal occupied most of the flag and which included at the bottom small depictions of five flags that have flown over the state, including the battle flag. One by one he antagonized many groups—Confederate battle flag lovers, the Georgia Association of Education, opponents of the Northern Arc highway he wanted to build north of Atlanta.

On all this Perdue capitalized. He called for dismantling the Office of Education Accountability, and relying less on yearly tests and state standards and more on local teachers and parents to enforce standards. He attacked Barnes for the Democrats' highly partisan redistricting of state legislative and U.S. House seats. Coming from south (or at least central) Georgia, he employed a rural strategy. "We're trying to capture the basic voting instincts of the non-metro voter," he said. He also promised a referendum on the state flag. This worked in tandem with state Republican Chairman Ralph Reed's program of building Republican organizations and volunteer corps not just in heavily Republican metro Atlanta counties, but also in 70 target counties outside the metro area. With a big turnout and solid majorities outside metro Atlanta, Perdue won the August primary with 51% of the vote, just enough to avoid a runoff.

Barnes still had a positive job approval and outspent Perdue $19 million to $3 million. But he was put on the defensive when the Georgia Association of Educators refused to endorse anyone for governor and endorsed Republican Kathy Cox, another opponent of the Barnes education reform, for school superintendent. Barnes put a hold on the Northern Arc. Still, it was a shock on election night when Perdue beat Barnes 51%-46%. Barnes led very narrowly in metro Atlanta, 49%-48%, but Perdue won the rest of the state 55%-43%—just 2% below George W. Bush's 2000 showing there. There were two electoral keys to Perdue's victory. One was the rural strategy. Barnes carried only 41 of the 159 counties, most of them either central city or very small rural counties, down from 118 in 1998. The other factor was increased turnout in the fast-growing suburbs. Turnout was up 13% statewide and 15% in metro Atlanta. It was up far more in the heavily Republican fast-growing counties. These counties gave Perdue a 116,000-vote margin, more than his statewide margin of 104,000 votes.

It turned out to be a Republican victory up and down the line. Within a week of the election four Democratic state senators switched parties and gave Republicans a 30-26 margin in the Senate.

All was not easy for Perdue once in office. He was forced to cut some $1.7 billion of projected spending and still got the legislature to raise the cigarette tax; he vetoed local projects sponsored by Democratic legislators. With help from Jimmy Carter, he proposed a new design for the state flag, with a red, white and blue background similar to the first Confederate flag (but wholly unlike the familiar battle flag); this and Barnes's 2001 flag, but not the Confederate battle flag, were put on the March 2004 ballot, and voters approved the Carter-Barnes flag 73%-27%. In 2004 Perdue proposed no tax increases and again started off cutting projected spending. For teachers he proposed a 2% pay increase and tax deductions for purchases of school supplies.

Perdue gave ordinary Georgians a chance to meet briefly with the governor through his "Saturdays with Sonny" initiative and he has periodically conducted barnstorming tours of the state; on one such trip, in April 2004, he announced that two more Democratic legislators had switched to the Republican party. He had even more success in the 2004 election. As George W. Bush was carrying the state with 58% of the vote, Republicans raised the majority in the state Senate to 34-22 and transformed a 77-102 deficit in the state House to a 99-80–1 majority. In his 2005 State of the State address, Perdue explained the new governing philosophy. "We don't want a busybody government—a boss—that butts into our lives every chance it gets to tell us how to work, how to play, where to live and on and on."

The new majorities helped Perdue get his legislation passed: in February, he signed a medical malpractice bill that capped pain-and-suffering awards and punished frivolous lawsuits. A month later, he signed a bill requiring a 24-hour waiting period for women seeking an abortion and parental notification for minors, measures long blocked by majority Democrats. In May he signed two bills strengthening ethics rules. He also signed a modest tax deduction for teachers. But he angered some black legislators when he signed a bill requiring voters to show government-issued photo identification at the polls. In September 2005 he signed an executive order suspending the gas tax after fuel supply disruptions caused by Hurricane Katrina led to a spike in gas prices and runs on Atlanta gas stations.

As Perdue came up for reelection in 2006, he was careful to attend to the needs of those who put him into office. Public school teachers had been disappointed by the postponement of school class size reductions and a 2% pay raise in 2004; Perdue made plans to dedicate 72% of the state's new revenues to education, to further increase teacher salaries by 4% and to provide teachers with a $100 gift card to purchase school supplies. He called for funding broadband Internet access in rural areas and for distributing $234 million in road and highway improvements in all of Georgia's 159 counties. In March 2006, he was able to announce that South Korean automaker Kia planned to build an automobile manufacturing plant in West Point; this helped cushion the blow of impending Ford and GM auto plant closings in Atlanta. Perdue also signed into law one of the nation's toughest immigration laws, a wide-ranging measure so restrictive that it drew criticism from President Vicente Fox of Mexico.

Perdue kicked off his reelection campaign in May with a 20-stop tour across the state and an endorsement from Zell Miller. He was attacked from the right by a little-known "Southern nationalist" challenger, still angry over the Confederate flag compromise; Perdue ignored him and won the primary with 88%. Democrats had a far more contentious and high-profile primary that featured Lieutenant Governor Mark Taylor and Secretary of State Cathy Cox, both from south Georgia. Taylor won 52%-44% but spent more than $4 million, depleting his resources for the general election against Perdue, who had raised more than $10 million by July.

Taylor focused on Perdue's cuts to school and health care funding; Perdue responded that he had spent $1 billion in additional education spending. Ethics issues played a noticeable role. Taylor was criticized for his family's business dealings with the state; Perdue was dogged by questions surrounding a land purchase next to his home and a Florida land purchase from a developer whom he appointed to the state economic development board. Taylor claimed Perdue had used the governor's office to enrich himself. "He made more money in four years as Gov. Perdue than he made in 54 years as Sonny Perdue," he said in one debate. Perdue dismissed Taylor's attacks as "wild allegations". In one television ad, Perdue reminded voters of Taylor's role in the bitter Democratic primary by turning to his wife Mary and observing that it would be nice "if we could go the whole campaign without those negative ads like they had in the Democratic primary." She responds, "Yeah, that'd be great. But just in case Mark tries to do to you what he did to Cathy Cox, tell everybody about [the new Perdue campaign] website where they can go to find out the facts."

Perdue won 58%-38%. He won 2–1 margins across much of north Georgia and again won big majorities in heavily Republican, fast-growing counties in the Atlanta metro area; he carried Forsyth County 82%-13% and Cherokee County 77%-17%. Taylor won the University of Georgia's Clarke County and mainly in majority-black counties and those with high percentages of African-Americans. Perdue's victory celebration was short-lived. In April 2007, he vetoed the state's mid-session budget, which included a $142 million property tax rebate and was passed unanimously by the legislature, amid fights over spending priorities. The Republican-controlled House overrode the veto by an overwhelming margin; Perdue later "rescinded" his veto without restoring the tax rebate.

Senior Senator

Saxby Chambliss (R)

Elected 2002, seat up 2008, 1st term; b. Nov. 10, 1943, Warrenton, NC; home, Moultrie; U. of GA, B.A. 1966, U. of TN, J.D. 1968; Episcopalian; married (Julianne).

Elected Office: U.S. House of Reps., 1994-2002.

Professional Career: Practicing atty., 1968-94.

DC Office: 416 RSOB, 20510, 202-224-3521; Fax: 202-224-0103; Web site: chambliss.senate.gov.

State Offices: Atlanta, 404-763-9090; Augusta, 706-738-0302; Macon, 478-741-1417; Moultrie, 229-985-2112; Savannah, 912-232-3657.

Committees: *Agriculture, Nutrition & Forestry* (RMM of 10 R). *Armed Services* (6th of 12 R): Personnel; Readiness & Management Support; Airland. *Intelligence (Select)* (4th of 7 R). *Rules & Administration* (6th of 9 R).

Group Ratings

	ADA	ACLU	AFS	LCV	ITIC	NTU	COC	ACU	CFG	FRC
2006	0	17	0	0	100	83	92	96	93	100
2005	5	—	0	0	—	73	94	96	85	—

National Journal Ratings

	2005 LIB	—	2005 CONS	2006 LIB	—	2006 CONS
Economic	15%	—	84%	8%	—	89%
Social	0%	—	77%	0%	—	82%
Foreign	0%	—	74%	16%	—	82%

Key Votes of the 109th Congress

1. Bar ANWR Drilling	N	5. Confirm Samuel Alito	Y	9. Limit Interstate Abortion	Y
2. FY06 Spending Curb	Y	6. Path to Citizenship	N	10. CAFTA	Y
3. Estate Tax Repeal	Y	7. Bar Same Sex Marriage	Y	11. Urge Iraq Withdrawal	N
4. Raise Minimum Wage	N	8. Stem Cell Research $	N	12. Provide Detainee Rights	N

Election Results

2002 general	Saxby Chambliss (R)	1,071,153	(53%)	($7,743,004)
	Max Cleland (D)	931,857	(46%)	($9,116,775)
	Other	26,981	(1%)	
2002 primary	Saxby Chambliss (R)	300,371	(61%)	
	Bob Irvin (R)	132,132	(27%)	
	Robert Brown (R)	59,109	(12%)	
1996 general	Max Cleland (D)	1,103,993	(49%)	($2,926,391)
	Guy Millner (R)	1,073,969	(48%)	($9,858,955)
	Other	81,270	(4%)	

Prior Winning Percentages: 2000 House (59%); 1998 House (62%); 1996 House (53%); 1994 House (63%)

Saxby Chambliss, the senior senator from Georgia, was elected in 2002 after serving four terms in the House. Chambliss grew up in Shreveport, Louisiana, the son of an Episcopalian minister, went to college in Georgia, and practiced business and agriculture law in Moultrie starting in 1968. In 1992 he ran for the House and lost the Republican primary; in 1994 he was the sole Republican candidate, while Democrats, as in days of yore, had a multi-candidate contest. The winner was Craig Mathis, the 32-year-old son of Congressman (1971-81) Dawson Mathis. Chambliss won 63%-37%. Speaker Newt Gingrich saw that Chambliss got the committee assignments he needed most—Armed Services, to look after Warner Robins Air Force Base, and Agriculture, to protect subsidies for peanut farmers.

When Budget Chairman John Kasich announced his retirement in July 1999, Chambliss started a campaign for the post. In July 2000, after Senator Paul Coverdell died suddenly, Chambliss considered running in the November election to replace him. Speaker Dennis Hastert persuaded him to stay in the House, and Chambliss came away feeling he would get the Budget chair. But he had competition from Jim Nussle of Iowa; the Republican Steering Committee interviewed both candidates and in December 2000 picked Nussle. Chambliss got an Agriculture subcommittee chairmanship and Hastert made him head of a working group on terrorism. After September 11, Hastert made that into an Intelligence Subcommittee on Terrorism and Homeland Security.

These were obviously good political credentials for a Senate candidacy, and Chambliss had two other reasons to consider challenging Democratic Senator Max Cleland in 2002. One was Cleland's narrow 49%-48% margin of victory in 1996 and Georgia's Republican trend, evident in George W. Bush's 55%-43% margin there in 2000. The other was the uncertainty of his House seat. Democratic redistricters passed a plan in September 2001 that left him with two unpleasant options: run in a primary against Savannah-based Republican incumbent Jack Kingston or in the new Democratic-leaning 3d District. The Bush White House and Senate campaign committee chairman Bill Frist urged Chambliss to run for the Senate, and in October 2001 he announced he would. Chambliss was not an initial favorite to win. Cleland had a compelling biography. After college he volunteered for the Army and went to Vietnam in 1967; he lost both legs and his right arm when a loose grenade exploded. After Senator Sam Nunn announced his retirement after four terms, he ran for the Senate in 1996 and beat Republican businessman Guy Millner 49%-48%. He served on the Armed Services Committee and had a moderate voting record. But in 2001 and 2002 he tended to stick with the close-knit Democratic Caucus while his new colleague, Zell Miller, dissented vociferously on issues from the tax cut to the Department of Homeland Security personnel rules. On the Republican side, Chambliss won the August 2002 primary 61%-27%. "From Rabun Gap to Tybee Light, voters continue to tell me that Max Cleland is too liberal for Georgia," he said on primary election night.

Cleland's two major strengths—his sacrifice in Vietnam and his support from the highly popular Miller—seemed formidable. Cleland supporters noted that Chambliss had received four student deferments in the 1960s and then was found ineligible for service because of a bad knee. Miller, in ads, told voters of Cleland's "rock solid Georgia values." But that did not deter Chambliss from launching sharp attacks. He ran a series of 10-second spots, mentioning Cleland's opposition to an amendment banning aid for schools that barred the Boy Scouts, his votes against the partial-birth abortion ban, his support of school clinics passing out morning-after pills without parental permission, his vote against confirming Attorney General John Ashcroft, his vote against speeding elimination of the marriage penalty—all ending with an apparently astounded announcer asking, "Why would he do that?"

But probably the most important issue was homeland security. Cleland stood with other Senate Democrats in opposing the degree of flexibility over work rules in the new department. The dispute occupied the Senate for much of October and prevented passage of the bill to create the department. On the other side, standing loudly in his support of Bush and his opposition to other Senate Democrats was Zell Miller. Chambliss ran an ad, much attacked in the press, showing pictures of Osama Bin Laden, Saddam Hussein and Max Cleland, and saying that Cleland "voted against the President's vital homeland security efforts 11 times."Against this, Cleland's ads attacking Chambliss for opposing an increase in the minimum wage and financing children's health insurance, for cutting student loans and school aid for the disabled, were weak stuff. In a late October debate, Cleland, echoing John Randolph of Roanoke on Henry Clay, said that the Osama Bin Laden ad was "like a mackerel in the moonlight—it both shines and stinks at the same time." But Cleland's record in Vietnam did not inoculate him against charges that he had given short shrift to homeland security. The tide of opinion, as measured by very late polls, was moving toward Chambliss. George W. Bush visited the state three times in his behalf, with visits to Atlanta and Savannah the Saturday before the election. On Election Day Chambliss won 53%-46%, a much bigger margin than just about anyone expected for either candidate. Chambliss carried metro Atlanta 52%-47%, running ahead of Republican governor candidate Sonny Perdue, and he carried the rest of Georgia 54%-45%. It was a slightly stronger showing than Coverdell made four years before, primarily because of increasing Republican percentages in the outer counties of metro Atlanta. In the three black-majority counties of 20-county metro Atlanta (Fulton, DeKalb and Clayton), turnout was up 26,000 from 1998 and the Democratic margin was up 34,000. But in the other 17 counties, turnout was up 123,000 and the Republican margin was up 40,000.

In the Senate Chambliss has had a conservative voting record and has taken a lead role on several issues. He was chairman of the Immigration Subcommittee of Judiciary, and in 2003 succeeded in passing a law modifying L-1 visas, so that international companies who bring in foreign employees cannot shop them out to other employers. He continued to be favorable to firms seeking more H-1B visas for high-tech foreign employees. He also pressed to change the law so that immigrants seeking to stay in the U.S. through the lottery procedure are not disqualified if the immigration authorities fail to process their applications on time. He called for "total overhaul" of immigration, but conceded that wasn't practicable. Initially, he was favorable to George W. Bush's proposal for a guest worker program, at least for farm workers, but unlike some Democrats who back similar proposals he argued that putting such workers on the road to citizenship unfairly rewards those who broke the law. He opposed a proposal by Republicans in Atlanta to cut off state financing of services to illegal immigrants. In May 2006, he was 1 of 36 Senators who voted against the bipartisan immigration reform bill and in June 2007 he joined Johnny Isakson to oppose the immigration bill they had helped draft because they felt it wouldn't do enough to secure the borders.

On the Armed Services Committee, Chambliss was alert to the needs of Georgia military bases and defense contractors. He objected in April 2005 when the Pentagon announced plans to discontinue the building of the C-130 cargo plane by Lockheed Martin in Marietta. In 2006, he moved successfully to reverse plans to cut back on procurement of the F-22 Raptor, also produced by Lockheed Martin. Chambliss supported the Bush administration on Iraq, but in November 2003 voted to have the $20 billion in reconstruction aid classified as a loan rather than a grant. He showed his frustration with "a lot of bad decisions" in the war in Iraq when he was 1 of 14 Senators who voted in February 2007 against the nomination of George Casey as Army chief of staff.

In 2005, Chambliss became chairman of the Agriculture Committee—the first Senator since 1947 to chair a standing committee after serving only two years, according to the Congressional Research Service. He resisted demands to impose income caps on wealthy farmers and other budget cuts in cotton and other commodity programs important to Georgia, and advocated domestic production of sugar ethanol. In the minority, he remained senior Republican on the committee during handling of the farm bill, and argued to keep programs at existing levels. He has been a backer of Representative John Linder's Fair Tax, a 23% retail sales tax to replace all income taxes. He also sought to bar states from requiring catalytic converters on lawn mowers under 50 horsepower (Briggs & Stratton produces them in Statesboro). Chambliss has been rated the second-best golfer in the Senate behind John Ensign.

In the early skirmishing for reelection in 2008, Cleland turned down a rematch; in July 2007, DeKalb County Chief Executive Officer Vernon Jones formally announced his candidacy, with hopes for a large black voter turnout. Atlanta TV reporter Dale Cardwell also announced his candidacy. Given the political direction in Georgia, Democrats faced an uphill challenge.

Junior Senator

Johnny Isakson (R)

Elected 2004, seat up 2010, 1st term; b. Dec. 28, 1944, Atlanta; home, Marietta; U. of GA, B.B.A. 1966; Methodist; married (Dianne).

Military Career: GA Air Natl. Guard, 1966-72.

Elected Office: GA House of Reps., 1976-90, Repub. Ldr., 1983-90; GA Senate, 1993-96; U.S. House of Reps., 1999-2004.

Professional Career: Northside Realty, 1967-99, Pres., 1979-99; Co-chair, Dole GA presidential campaign, 1988, 1996; Chmn., GA Board of Ed., 1997.

DC Office: 120 RSOB, 20510, 202-224-3643; Fax: 202-228-0724; Web site: isakson.senate.gov.

State Office: Atlanta, 770-661-0999.

Committees: *Environment & Public Works* (4th of 9 R): Transportation & Infrastructure (RMM); Clean Air & Nuclear Safety; Private Sector & Consumer Solutions to Global Warming & Wildlife Protection. *Ethics (Select)* (3d of 3 R). *Foreign Relations* (9th of 10 R): Western Hemisphere, Peace Corps & Narcotics Affairs; East Asian & Pacific Affairs; International Operations & Organizations, Democracy & Human Rights. *Health, Education, Labor & Pensions* (5th of 10 R): Employment & Workplace Safety (RMM); Retirement & Aging. *Small Business & Entrepreneurship* (9th of 9 R). *Veterans' Affairs* (7th of 7 R).

Group Ratings

	ADA	ACLU	AFS	LCV	ITIC	NTU	COC	ACU	CFG	FRC
2006	0	17	0	0	100	83	92	96	79	100
2005	5	—	0	5	—	77	94	100	86	—

National Journal Ratings

	2005 LIB	—	2005 CONS		2006 LIB	—	2006 CONS
Economic	14%	—	85%		4%	—	93%
Social	0%	—	77%		0%	—	82%
Foreign	0%	—	74%		16%	—	82%

Key Votes of the 109th Congress

1. Bar ANWR Drilling	N	5. Confirm Samuel Alito	Y	9. Limit Interstate Abortion	Y
2. FY06 Spending Curb	Y	6. Path to Citizenship	N	10. CAFTA	Y
3. Estate Tax Repeal	Y	7. Bar Same Sex Marriage	Y	11. Urge Iraq Withdrawal	N
4. Raise Minimum Wage	N	8. Stem Cell Research $	N	12. Provide Detainee Rights	N

Election Results

2004 general	Johnny Isakson (R)	1,864,202	(58%)	($8,038,200)
	Denise Majette (D)	1,287,690	(40%)	($2,391,248)
	Other	69,089	(2%)	
2004 primary	Johnny Isakson (R)	346,670	(53%)	
	Herman Cain (R)	170,370	(26%)	
	Mac Collins (R)	133,952	(21%)	
2000 special	Zell Miller (D)	1,413,224	(58%)	($2,533,746)
	Mack Mattingly (R)	920,478	(38%)	($1,093,408)
	Other	94,540	(4%)	

Prior Winning Percentages: 2002 House (80%); 2000 House (75%); 1999 House (65%)

Johnny Isakson, a Republican, was elected Georgia's junior senator in 2004. Isakson grew up outside Atlanta, in south Fulton County; his father drove a Greyhound bus and his parents bought old houses, renovated them and sold them for a profit. Isakson graduated from the University of Georgia and served in the Air National Guard. He went to work for Northside Realty in 1967 and eventually became president of the firm. He volunteered for Barry Goldwater in 1964 and Richard Nixon in 1972, and in 1974 he ran for the state House as a Republican and lost. In 1976 he ran again and won, and in 1983 became Minority Leader. He ran for governor in 1990 and lost 53%-45% to Zell Miller. Two years later he was elected to the state Senate. In 1996 he ran statewide again, and lost the Republican runoff for senator to self-financing businessman Guy Millner, who lost in November to Max Cleland 49%-48%. In December 1996 Miller appointed Isakson head of the state Board of Education. His partisan political career seemed over, but it would be revived by two timely retirements.

In November 1998 Newt Gingrich announced that he was stepping down as Speaker and would resign from the House. That opened up a vacancy in the heavily Republican 6th District which included much of Atlanta's northern suburbs plus the affluent Buckhead neighborhood. Isakson was by far the best known of the six candidates in the February 1999 nonpartisan election. He raised $1 million and spent $500,000 of his own money and won the seat with 65% of the vote. In the House Isakson served on the Transportation Committee, where he pushed for a rapid transit line for the overburdened Georgia 400 corridor on the north side. On the Education Committee he took a leading role in negotiations of the No Child Left Behind Act, working to give schools more discretion in using funds. Committee Chairman John Boehner credited Isakson for the provision requiring that 25% of technology funds be used for teacher classroom training.

Isakson passed up a chance to run against Cleland in 2002, but when Zell Miller announced his retirement in January 2003, Isakson announced for the seat a week later. For months he had no well-known opponent but eventually he had two serious competitors in the Republican primary. One was Herman Cain, who grew up in a black neighborhood in Atlanta, worked for Pillsbury and Burger King, then became CEO and owner of Omaha-based Godfather's Pizza. In 1994, as president of the National Restaurant Association, Cain attended one of Bill Clinton's meetings on health care and denounced the Clinton plan. Afterwards he left the company, became a motivational speaker and returned to Atlanta. The other was Congressman Mac Collins, whose district included the southern edge of metro Atlanta. Cain and Collins were both solid conservatives and abortion rights opponents, and they made abortion a major issue. During the primary, Isakson said he opposed abortion rights except in cases of incest, rape or to save the mother's life; he received an 82% rating from the National Right to Life Committee in the 108th Congress. But he had voted against the Mexico City policy preventing foreign aid money from funding abortions, in favor of importation of RU-486 pills, and to allow servicewomen to have abortions at their own expense in military hospitals. In the 1996 Senate primary, he irked religious conservatives when he appeared in a TV ad opposing a constitutional amendment banning abortion, saying, "I will not vote to amend the Constitution to make criminals of women and their doctors. I trust my wife, my daughter and the women of Georgia to make the right choices."

That may have made him unacceptable in a Republican primary then; it was not so disqualifying in 2004. Collins called him "a certified moderate," and Cain, in a TV spot, said, "There's a big difference between me and Johnny Isakson. And it's not just the color of our eyes." Cain also backed a consumption tax and individual investment accounts in Social Security; Collins criticized Isakson for favoring an extension of the date for the turnover of sovereignty in Iraq. Isakson called for staying the course in Iraq, tax reform and support of Bush judicial nominees. One of the big differences between the candidates was money. With his business contacts, Isakson raised $5.5 million for the primary; Cain spent $3 million, much of it his own money and Collins only $1.9 million. For two months before July 20 primary, Isakson was on the air, mostly with biographical spots. Early on, most observers thought this race would end with a runoff. But Isakson got 53% of the vote to 26% for Cain and 21% for Collins. Isakson won 55% in metro Atlanta and 52% in the rest of the state. This was the first state primary in which more Georgians chose the Republican ballot (650,000) over the Democratic (625,000). Democrats had a hard time finding a candidate for a seat held by a Democrat—albeit, one who usually voted with Republicans in the Senate and supported George W. Bush for reelection. The Democratic race came down to two late entering candidates, 4th District Congresswoman Denise Majette and businessman Cliff Oxford. Majette had served just one term after her upset victory over Cynthia McKinney in the 2002 primary, and she had a solidly liberal voting record. Oxford was accused of spousal abuse by a former wife. Oxford spent $1 million of his own money, but in a primary in which a majority of votes appear to have been cast by blacks, Majette led 41%-21%. In the August runoff Majette won 59%-41%. In both contests Majette had big leads in metro Atlanta but ran behind in the rest of the state—not a good harbinger for November.

In the general, Zell Miller backed neither candidate; he had appointed Majette to a judgeship and Isakson as head of the Board of Education. Through most of the fall Isakson continued to run positive ads; in the last two weeks he attacked Majette's liberal voting record, including her vote against the $87 billion supplemental appropriation for Iraq. Majette criticized Isakson for not voting funding for the full amounts authorized by No Child Left Behind. Isakson won 58%-40%, almost the same margin by which George W. Bush beat John Kerry in the state. Majette carried only

19 of 159 counties—Atlanta's Fulton County and the two black-majority counties in metro Atlanta, the counties including the central cities of Athens, Columbus and Augusta and 12 Black Belt rural counties.

Isakson had one of the most conservative voting records in the Senate, and he moved quickly to take on major issues. On the Health, Education, Labor and Pensions Committee, he worked actively on pension reform, with the chief goal of advocating the interests of Delta Airlines, which was bankrupt and had huge pension obligations to its workers. Isakson sponsored a proposal to give the airlines additional time beyond the limits set in the bill to make payments to cover the liabilities of their defined-benefit plans. It was crucial, he said, for the airlines to get pension relief. "The aviation industry doesn't have the luxury of time." In November 2005, the Senate passed a pension-reform measure that included Isakson's amendment to give the airlines 20 additional years to meet their obligations. House Education Committee chairman Boehner, who had been Isakson's ally, countered that he opposed "any industry-specific relief." Negotiations between the House and Senate dragged on until August 2006. The final version gave Delta and Northwest 17 years to amortize their pension payments, while American and Continental got only 10 years. "The winners are tens of thousands of employees in the airline industry," Isakson said, and he received much of the credit for the final deal.

He was an outspoken opponent of the bipartisan McCain-Kennedy immigration reform bill. He joined other Georgia Republicans who strongly opposed illegal immigration, which was "tearing the country apart right now," and he took a hard-line approach on tougher enforcement at the border. On his amendment to delay the guest worker program until the Homeland Security Department certified that the borders were secure, Isakson lost, 55-40.He also wanted an enhanced identification system to verify the legality of workers. In June 2007, he joined Saxby Chambliss to oppose the immigration bill they had originally helped draft because they felt it wouldn't do enough to secure the borders. When the Senate took up a proposal to expand funding for embryonic stem-cell research, Isakson at first advocated the limited alternative offered by President Bush. When that failed, he said that researchers should use the thousands of malformed but fertilized eggs that are not viable embryos and are routinely disposed as medical waste. In April 2007, the Senate approved his proposal, 70-28, in tandem with the main proposal that was vetoed in June.

FIRST DISTRICT

Rep. Jack Kingston (R)

Elected 1992, 8th term; b. Apr. 24, 1955, Bryan, TX; home, Savannah; U. of GA, B.S. 1977; Episcopalian; married (Libby).

Elected Office: GA House of Reps., 1984-92.

Professional Career: Insurance agent, 1979-92.

DC Office: 2368 RHOB, 20515, 202-225-5831; Fax: 202-226-2269; Web site: www.house.gov/kingston.

District Offices: Baxley, 912-367-7403; Brunswick, 912-265-9010; Savannah, 912-352-0101; Valdosta, 229-247-9188.

Committees: *Appropriations* (9th of 29 R): Agriculture, Rural Development, FDA & Related Agencies (RMM); Defense.

Group Ratings

	ADA	ACLU	AFS	LCV	ITIC	NTU	COC	ACU	CFG	FRC
2006	5	9	0	17	100	61	100	92	67	100
2005	0	—	0	6	—	61	92	88	69	77

National Journal Ratings

	2005 LIB	—	2005 CONS		2006 LIB	—	2006 CONS
Economic	13%	—	86%		19%	—	81%
Social	35%	—	65%		9%	—	90%
Foreign	0%	—	89%		0%	—	94%

Key Votes of the 109th Congress

1. Estate Tax Repeal	Y	5. Limit Interstate Abortion	Y	9. Build Border Fence	Y
2. Limit CAFE Standards	Y	6. Extend Patriot Act	Y	10. CAFTA	Y
3. FY06 Spending Curb	Y	7. Bar Same Sex Marriage	Y	11. Oppose Iraq Withdrawal	Y
4. Drilling in ANWR	Y	8. Stem Cell Research $	N	12. Detainee Tribunals	Y

Election Results

2006 general	Jack Kingston (R)	94,961	(69%)	($1,237,548)
	Jim Nelson (D)	43,668	(31%)	($117,749)
2006 primary	Jack Kingston (R)	unopposed		
2004 general	Jack Kingston (R)	unopposed		($783,347)

Prior Winning Percentages: 2002 (72%); 2000 (69%); 1998 (100%); 1996 (68%); 1994 (77%); 1992 (58%)

The People		Race/Ethnic Origin	Ancestry	
Area size:	12,243 sq. mi.	68.8% White	USA: 14.4%	English: 6.9%
Urban population:	57.3%	24.9% Black	Irish: 6.8%	
Rural population:	42.7%	0.9% Asian	**2004 Presidential Vote**	
Pop. 2000:	629,727	0.3% Native Am.	Bush (R) 148,806	(66%)
Median income:	$34,912	0.1% Hawaiian	Kerry (D) 75,399	(34%)
Poverty status:	15.9%	1.1% Two+ races	Other 878	(0%)
Military veterans:	15.5%	0.1% Other	**2000 Presidential Vote**	
		3.8% Hispanic Origin	Bush (R) 111,883	(62%)
			Gore (D) 67,477	(38%)
			Cook Partisan Voting Index: R +13	

Occupation	Blue collar: 29.9%	White collar: 52.8%	Gray collar: 17.3%

Georgia's South Atlantic coast, long one of the poorest parts of the country, was settled in the 1730s by James Oglethorpe as Britain's 13th coastal colony as a refuge and reformatory for convicts. It did not take long for the sea islands and lowlands along the wide rivers and inlets to become plantation country. It is here where General William Tecumseh Sherman and his troops famously set their sights when they marched from Atlanta in 1864. Without supplies or lines of communication, they burned plantation houses, destroyed crops and captured the Confederacy's leader. When their march was complete, they left behind memories of property destroyed and slaves freed, which were handed down as family lore for more than a century.

The 1st Congressional District of Georgia includes much of the southeast and south part of the state. It includes the state's whole Atlantic coast, and runs west approximately to Interstate 75 at Valdosta, the largest city in the district. It heads toward the center of the state just short of Vidalia, and runs from the Ocmulgee and Altamaha Rivers in the north to the Florida border. It takes in almost one-third of Chatham County's population but only a sliver of Savannah, most of which is now in the 12th District, and all of the Sea Islands, which house a vibrant resort economy with efforts to preserve the African-American Gullah culture and its eponymous West African-originated creole language. One of those coastal communities is the historic black settlement of Pin Point, 11 miles southeast of Savannah. Its 300 citizens are mostly descendants of the first slaves here and its most famous son is Supreme Court Justice Clarence Thomas. The 2005 redistricting shifted Warner Robins Air Force Base to the new 8th District; added in its place were Telfair and Wheeler Counties. There are a few modest-sized cities like Brunswick, a World War II shipbuilding center and increasingly the gateway to the Sea Islands, and isolated Waycross, a railroad junction town and gateway to the Okefenokee Swamp, the largest swamp in North America. Prior to the abolitionist movement, this swamp-filled area was a site of the Underground Railroad, with trails to north Florida. Much of the district is rural, with cotton and tobacco fields and softwood forests inhabited by wild hogs and bears. Appling County and Berrien County are known for their turpentine and bell peppers. Many popular films have been produced in the region, including *Glory* and *Forrest Gump*. This was Democratic country for a century after General Sherman's troops marched through Georgia, but voters here are solidly conservative on most issues. For two decades this part of south Georgia voted for national Republicans but Georgia Democrats; since 2000, it has voted solidly Republican for governor and senator, as well. The redistricting changes increased the black population from 23% to 25% and reduced President Bush's vote in 2004 from 68% to 66%.

The congressman from the 1st District is Jack Kingston, a Republican first elected in 1992. Kingston grew up in Texas, Ethiopia, and Athens, Georgia, the son of a professor. After college he moved to Savannah and became a commercial insurance agent. In 1984 he was elected to the

Georgia House, at 29, and served eight years. In 1992, when Democrat Lindsay Thomas retired to work on the Atlanta Summer Olympics, Kingston ran for Congress. Against Democrat Barbara Christmas, a school principal, he won decisively—58%-42%—with a 2–1 margin in his home base of Savannah and Chatham County. He has not been seriously challenged since then.

In the House, Kingston has a mostly conservative voting record and has tended to district interests. During the Clinton presidency, he parted company with Republicans on trade issues, notably NAFTA, GATT and normal trade relations for China, and he decried the World Trade Organization; but he voted to give trade promotion authority to George W. Bush and was a late vote for the Central American Free Trade Agreement. In 2007, he became ranking Republican on the Agriculture Subcommittee of Appropriations, where he has been an advocate of the peanut warehousing program. He retained his seat on the Defense Subcommittee, another locally useful position. For two years, Kingston chaired the Appropriations Legislative Branch Subcommittee, which placed him on the firing line for the huge cost overruns of the underground Capitol Visitors Center, whose initial cost estimate (in 1991) of $71 million has ballooned to more than $600 million, and counting. But he lost his chairmanship in 2005 when the subcommittee was eliminated in an Appropriations Committee restructuring.

Kingston has been an active member of leadership. As head of the Republicans' "theme team," which coordinates the party's national message on the House floor and at home, he became a spokesman on late-night television shows. In 2002 he was elected vice-chairman of the Republican Conference—the party's fifth-highest leadership post—and stepped up his role in setting the party's message, including encouraging regular appearances on Comedy Central and more use of blogs. But he may have been the victim of a desire for change when he fell short after the 2006 election in a bid for chairman of the conference, losing to Adam Putnam on the third ballot. In 2004 he played a key role in convincing House Republican leadership to back the $10 billion tobacco buyout, which ended the quota system in place since 1938. In 2005, he joined Eliot Engel in a bipartisan initiative to reduce oil use by increasing auto fuel efficiency. "The age of cheap oil and gas is over."

On local issues, Kingston has fought for historic preservation and looked after local military facilities. During the base-closing process, he criticized former President Carter for "going against the home team in the 11th hour" by supporting the continuation of the submarine base in Connecticut; a shutdown there would have been a big boost for the Kings Bay base near St. Marys. As an appropriator and co-chairman of the Congressional Waterways Caucus, he has brought millions of dollars to improve the water flow of the Savannah River and complete the Sidney Lanier drawbridge in Brunswick.

Kingston considered but turned down opportunities to run for the Senate in 2002 and 2004. With two first-term Republican senators now representing Georgia, he may not have that opportunity again.

SECOND DISTRICT

Rep. Sanford Bishop (D)

Elected 1992, 8th term; b. Feb. 4, 1947, Mobile, AL; home, Albany; Morehouse Col., B.A. 1968, Emory U., J.D. 1971; Baptist; divorced.

Military Career: Army, 1970-71.

Elected Office: GA House of Reps., 1976-90; GA Senate, 1990-92.

Professional Career: Practicing atty., 1971-92.

DC Office: 2429 RHOB, 20515, 202-225-3631; Fax: 202-225-2203; Web site: www.house.gov/bishop.

District Offices: Albany, 229-439-8067; Columbus, 706-320-9477.

Committees: *Appropriations* (25th of 37 D): Agriculture, Rural Development, FDA & Related Agencies; Military Construction, Veterans Affairs & Related Agencies; Defense.

Group Ratings

	ADA	ACLU	AFS	LCV	ITIC	NTU	COC	ACU	CFG	FRC
2006	65	71	86	25	71	22	87	64	29	57
2005	85	—	100	44	—	23	74	45	18	38

National Journal Ratings

	2005 LIB	—	2005 CONS		2006 LIB	—	2006 CONS
Economic	56%	—	43%		58%	—	42%
Social	62%	—	38%		58%	—	41%
Foreign	57%	—	43%		47%	—	51%

Key Votes of the 109th Congress

1. Estate Tax Repeal	Y	5. Limit Interstate Abortion	Y	9. Build Border Fence	Y
2. Limit CAFE Standards	Y	6. Extend Patriot Act	Y	10. CAFTA	N
3. FY06 Spending Curb	N	7. Bar Same Sex Marriage	Y	11. Oppose Iraq Withdrawal	Y
4. Drilling in ANWR	Y	8. Stem Cell Research $	Y	12. Detainee Tribunals	Y

Election Results

2006 general	Sanford Bishop (D)	88,662	(68%)	($745,257)
	Bradley Hughes (R)	41,967	(32%)	($27,142)
2006 primary	Sanford Bishop (D)	unopposed		
2004 general	Sanford Bishop (D)	129,984	(67%)	($761,275)
	Dave Eversman (R)	64,645	(33%)	($25,277)

Prior Winning Percentages: 2002 (100%); 2000 (54%); 1998 (57%); 1996 (54%); 1994 (66%); 1992 (64%)

The People		Race/Ethnic Origin	Ancestry	
Area size:	11,001 sq. mi.	47.7% White	USA: 11.3%	English: 4.8%
Urban population:	58.1%	47.5% Black	Irish: 4.5%	
Rural population:	41.9%	0.5% Asian	**2004 Presidential Vote**	
Pop. 2000:	629,727	0.3% Native Am.	Bush (R) 104,014	(50%)
Median income:	$29,843	0.1% Hawaiian	Kerry (D) 103,163	(50%)
Poverty status:	21.9%	0.8% Two+ races	Other 756	(0%)
Military veterans:	13.4%	0.1% Other	**2000 Presidential Vote**	
		3.0% Hispanic Origin	Gore (D) 90,010	(52%)
			Bush (R) 81,657	(48%)
			Cook Partisan Voting Index: D + 2	

Occupation	Blue collar: 32.0%	White collar: 49.7%	Gray collar: 18.3%

Before the Civil War, the southwest corner of Georgia was plantation country. It was in this part of Georgia that Confederates ran the Andersonville military prison, which within 14 months killed about 13,000 of the 45,000 Union soldiers confined there, through disease, poor sanitation, malnutrition, overcrowding and exposure; they are remembered at the National Prisoner of War Museum at Andersonville, dedicated to all Americans who have endured wartime captivity. The military has been unscathed by base closings and remains a major presence here, most notably at Fort Benning—the Army's third largest installation, home of the Army Infantry School and soon to be the home of the relocated Army Armor Center and School; Benning can train as many as 16,000 soldiers at a time, with the annual total expected to reach 105,000 trainees. But the region is mostly farmland: Cotton fields, peanut acreage (this has been the nation's top peanut producing district), pecan groves, pine lands. In the south, near the Florida border, is the Cairo birthplace of baseball's black pioneer Jackie Robinson, plus the Plantation Trace area around Thomasville, where rich Northerners have come to shoot quail and ducks in winters since the 1880s—a part of Georgia memorialized in Tom Wolfe's *A Man in Full*. A bit to the north is Albany, with several factories, a civil rights museum and the site of Martin Luther King Jr.'s least successful civil rights protests in the 1960s. Not far from Albany, between upland pine stands and bottomland habitats, lies the Chickasawatchee Swamp, one of the Southeast's largest freshwater swamps and home to rare plant species such as the needle palm and the green fly orchid. Two counties north is the village of Plains, the home since childhood of Jimmy Carter and the site of a huge new biofuels factory; Carter has said that he will be buried in his front yard, rather than at his library in Atlanta. This has been hardscrabble country: As recently as World War II most rural residents lived in clapboard cabins without power or running water, eking a living out of over-tilled soil.

This is the land of Georgia's 2d Congressional District. In the 2005 redistricting, the district lost virtually all of Valdosta, but increased to two-thirds its share of Columbus and Muscogee

County. That round of redistricting removed Turner, Tift, Colquitt and part of Worth County, and added eight rural counties between Columbus and Macon. The resulting effect was to raise the black percentage of the district from 45% to 48%, reduce the vote for George W. Bush in 2004 from 54% to 50.02% and create a new minority-majority district.

The congressman from the 2d District is Sanford Bishop, a Democrat first elected in 1992. Bishop grew up in Mobile, Alabama, where his father was a state college president. He went to Morehouse College in Atlanta, where he was student body president in 1968 and sang at Martin Luther King Jr.'s funeral. He was an award-winning student at Emory Law School, then served in the Army. After a year in New York he settled in Columbus, practiced law, and was elected to the state legislature in 1976, at 29. He served there until 1990, when he was elected to the Georgia Senate. In 1992 he ran for the House against Democratic incumbent Charles Hatcher, who revealed he had 819 overdrafts on the House bank. Bishop defeated Hatcher in the runoff 53%-47%, and won the general election 64%-36%.

Bishop describes himself as "a moderate conservative on fiscal issues and a 'traditionalist' on so-called family issues." His style is not confrontational, and his voting record has been the most conservative in the Congressional Black Caucus. After first voting for the assault weapons ban, he switched, joined the NRA and started hunting doves. He joined the conservative Blue Dog Democrats, and supported the balanced budget, school prayer, anti-flag burning and gay-marriage ban amendments, plus the partial-birth abortion ban. He was one of 10 House Democrats to vote for George W. Bush's tax cuts in 2001. But he opposed a federal court-stripping bill on gay-rights issues.

In 2003, after Nancy Pelosi turned down his bid to become ranking Democrat on the Intelligence Committee, Bishop won a long-sought seat on Appropriations. For several years, he pushed unsuccessfully for a requirement that FEMA study ways to improve how it warns and rescues people in a disaster; following Katrina, he said that the catastrophic failures showed that "someone in the Administration didn't do what they should have done." He has worked to safeguard local military facilities and claimed credit for more than $200 million in local military projects. They include the School of the Americas that trains Latin American soldiers at Fort Benning, which was renamed the Western Hemisphere Institute for Security Cooperation. Bishop also has been active on farm programs, working with Republicans on the 1996 Freedom to Farm Act to fashion a "market-oriented, no-net cost" program for peanuts. In 2002, he helped to craft the scaled-back program for peanut support, which was based on a combination of phasing out quotas and price guarantees. In 2005, he decided at virtually the last minute to oppose the Central American Free Trade Agreement; there had been speculation that he was seeking special protections for the peanut industry. After the 2006 election, he was considered for the chairmanship of the Intelligence Committee, which ultimately went to Silvestre Reyes. Instead, Bishop gained seats on the Agriculture, Defense and Military Construction subcommittees at Appropriations. In March 2007, he got committee approval of $74 million for peanut storage in the supplemental spending bill. When Bush objected, Bishop responded that the money would help farmers compete internationally. "What the president does not like is he is being asked to be accountable" on spending in Iraq, Bishop added.

In 2000, Bishop faced serious reelection competition from Dylan Glenn, a former aide to George H.W. Bush and RNC staffer. The unprecedented contest between two African-Americans in a rural, then-majority-white district was strikingly lacking in racial overtones. Bishop largely ignored the challenger and ran on his record, while Glenn offered the perspective of a new generation focusing on economic growth. Bishop won 54%-46%. Redistricting changes have made a serious challenge less likely.

THIRD DISTRICT

Rep. Lynn Westmoreland (R)

Elected 2004, 2d term; b. Apr. 2, 1950, Atlanta; home, Grantville; Attended GA State U., 1969-71; Baptist; married (Joan).

Elected Office: GA House of Reps., 1992-2004; Min. Ldr. 2000-03.

Professional Career: Real estate developer; Owner, L.A.W. Builders, 1982-present.

DC Office: 1213 LHOB, 20515, 202-225-5901; Fax: 202-225-2515; Web site: http://www.house.gov/westmoreland/.

District Offices: Newnan, 770-683-2033.

Committees: *Oversight & Government Reform* (13th of 18 R): National Security & Foreign Affairs. *Small Business* (9th of 15 R): Regulations, Healthcare & Trade (RMM); Investigations & Oversight. *Transportation & Infrastructure* (28th of 34 R): Railroads, Pipelines & Hazardous Materials; Aviation.

Group Ratings

	ADA	ACLU	AFS	LCV	ITIC	NTU	COC	ACU	CFG	FRC
2006	5	5	0	0	100	80	100	92	92	100
2005	5	—	0	0	—	70	85	96	90	77

National Journal Ratings

	2005 LIB	—	2005 CONS		2006 LIB	—	2006 CONS
Economic	6%	—	93%		12%	—	86%
Social	0%	—	89%		6%	—	92%
Foreign	0%	—	89%		0%	—	94%

Key Votes of the 109th Congress

1. Estate Tax Repeal	Y	5. Limit Interstate Abortion	*	9. Build Border Fence	Y
2. Limit CAFE Standards	Y	6. Extend Patriot Act	Y	10. CAFTA	Y
3. FY06 Spending Curb	Y	7. Bar Same Sex Marriage	Y	11. Oppose Iraq Withdrawal	Y
4. Drilling in ANWR	Y	8. Stem Cell Research $	N	12. Detainee Tribunals	Y

Election Results

2006 general	Lynn Westmoreland (R)	130,428	(68%)	($936,111)
	Mike McGraw (D)	62,371	(32%)	($55,060)
2006 primary	Lynn Westmoreland (R)	unopposed		
2004 general (GA 8)	Lynn Westmoreland (R)	227,524	(76%)	($1,943,512)
	Silvia Delamar (D)	73,632	(24%)	($28,846)

The People		Race/Ethnic Origin	Ancestry	
Area size:	4,180 sq. mi.	76.4% White	USA: 15.0%	Irish: 8.0%
Urban population:	56.4%	19.1% Black	English: 8.0%	
Rural population:	43.6%	1.1% Asian	**2004 Presidential Vote**	
Pop. 2000:	629,727	0.2% Native Am.	Bush (R) 207,252	(70%)
Median income:	$47,553	0.0% Hawaiian	Kerry (D) 86,361	(29%)
Poverty status:	9.0%	0.8% Two+ races	Other 1,401	(0%)
Military veterans:	14.8%	0.1% Other	**2000 Presidential Vote**	
		2.2% Hispanic Origin	Bush (R) 143,802	(67%)
			Gore (D) 70,834	(33%)
			Cook Partisan Voting Index: R +18	

Occupation   Blue collar: 29.6%   White collar: 57.7%   Gray collar: 12.6%

Running south from Atlanta, within an hour or so by car, you leave behind the newest parts of Georgia—like Henry County, the eighth-fastest growing county in America with a 49% increase from 2000-06—and come upon some of the most traditional. Henry County's flourishing residential, commercial and industrial development has risen near its seven I-75 interchanges and has benefited from its proximity to Hartsfield-Jackson Atlanta International Airport. To the west is the old courthouse town of Fayetteville, now surrounded by new suburbs, whose Holliday-Dorsey-Fife

House is thought to have inspired the columned architecture of Tara in Margaret Mitchell's *Gone With the Wind*. Peachtree City is the headquarters of struggling Delta Airlines, which emerged from bankruptcy in April 2007. Further west, metro Atlanta is spreading through the countryside to Newnan and Carrollton, and further south past tourist-appealing Barnesville to Thomaston. In the old textile town of West Point in Troup County, along the Alabama border, South Korean automaker Kia is building a $1.2 billion plant that is expected to create 2,500 direct jobs and another 2,000 jobs for suppliers. Even farther to the southwest is yet another Georgia, the small industrial city of Columbus and next-door Fort Benning, long the home of the Army's Infantry School; it is the place where General George Marshall's talents were first noted and where he kept his little black book with a list of gifted officers whom he would make generals in World War II.

Much of this territory is within the redrawn and renumbered 3d Congressional District of Georgia. It has replaced the old 8th District, which had been an unsightly splatter in metro Atlanta. The 3d includes roughly one-third of the city of Columbus (the rest is in the 2d District, which also contains most of Fort Benning), but Fayette County is the largest population center, and the ring of five counties that are closest to Atlanta include roughly half of the district population. This remains conservative country, with young tradition-minded families with busy breadwinners and with a heavy military background. People here are upwardly mobile, but not necessarily at the upper end of the income scale. The ancestral politics of most of this area was Democratic, but that is as much a part of history now as Tara; this is one of the most heavily Republican congressional districts in Georgia. George W. Bush won 70% here in 2004.

The congressman from the 3d District is Lynn Westmoreland, a Republican elected in 2004. Westmoreland grew up in the Atlanta area, left Georgia State University after two years and became a real estate broker and homebuilder in Fayette County. After losing two races for the state Senate, Westmoreland was elected in 1992 to the Georgia House, where he founded the Conservative Policy Caucus, a group of fiscally conservative, anti-tax lawmakers; longtime Democratic House Speaker Tom Murphy once called him "a braying jackass." In 2000 he was elected House Minority Leader and in that position refused to agree to tax increases, even when it meant defying newly elected Republican Governor Sonny Perdue.

In 2004, Congressman Mac Collins ran for the Senate seat vacated by Zell Miller. Westmoreland faced a choice between staying in Georgia, where he stood to become Speaker if Republicans won a majority in the state House (as they did), or taking advantage of a rare opportunity to run for a safe Republican open seat in the U.S. House. He chose the latter and ran on an anti-spending platform. The primary race became a contest between him and Dylan Glenn, a former staffer for George H.W. Bush and Perdue. Glenn, who is black and from Columbus, had run twice in the 2d District; he lost the Republican nomination 53%-47% in 1998 and lost to Democratic incumbent Sanford Bishop by the same margin in 2000. Against Westmoreland, Glenn was endorsed by former Speaker Newt Gingrich, who argued in what he later said was a personal letter to Westmoreland's wife that a Glenn victory would "strengthen us in our area of greatest weakness" and that Republicans needed "representation from every aspect of America." Senator Saxby Chambliss and four current Georgia congressional members endorsed Westmoreland. In the primary, he led Glenn 46%-38%. He won 60% of the vote in his base in Fayette and Coweta Counties; Glenn led in the three counties nearest his home base in Columbus. During the three weeks between the primary and the August runoff, Glenn accused Westmoreland of taking excessive gifts from lobbyists (with an ad that depicted his opponent as a hog), while Westmoreland labeled Glenn a "Washington insider" with an inflated resume. Westmoreland won 55%-45%, carrying 12 of the 18 counties.

In the House, Westmoreland had one of the most conservative voting records. On the Transportation and Infrastructure Committee, he opposed cuts in the number of security screeners at Hartsfield-Jackson International Airport. He got $250,000 for a study of the feasibility of moving the rail yard from downtown Columbus to a more rural setting. Following Hurricane Katrina, he worked with other conservatives to propose "Operation Offset," in an attempt to limit the cost to the budget. When he visited New Orleans six months later, he said that the devastation was "unbelievable," worse than what he had seen on television. Westmoreland was outspoken in his opposition to extension of the Voting Rights Act, and said that the preclearance procedure that covered mostly southern states should either be eliminated or applied nationwide. He cited the "great progress" made by Georgia since the enactment of the law in 1965, and noted that many local communities that had problems at the time now "are controlled by minorities." He criticized GOP leaders for having "purposefully ignored" the objections by many southern Republicans. When the House debated the bill in July 2006, he offered an amendment to make it easier for states to opt out of the law's requirements; he lost, 302-118, and then was 1 of 33 Republicans voting against the bill.

In the weeks after taking office, Westmoreland worked intensively with the newly Republican-controlled legislature in Atlanta to redraw congressional district lines to create more compact districts, with the not unintended benefit of entrenching another Republican seat and jeopardizing two incumbent Democrats; in March 2005, the legislature passed a new congressional map designed by a 23-year-old legislative aide to Westmoreland. In 2006, Westmoreland was reelected with token opposition in the general. He has floated his name as a possible candidate for governor in 2010.

FOURTH DISTRICT

Rep. Hank Johnson (D)

Elected 2006, 1st term; b. Oct. 2, 1954, Washington, D.C.; home, Lithonia; Clark Atlanta U., B.A. 1976, Texas S. U., J.D. 1979; Buddhist; married (Mereda Davis).

Elected Office: DeKalb Cnty. Comm., 2001-06.

Professional Career: Practicing atty., 1980-2006; Associate Judge, DeKalb Cnty. Magistrate Court, 1989-2006.

DC Office: 1133 LHOB, 20515, 202-225-1605; Fax: 202-226-0691; Web site: hankjohnson.house.gov.

District Offices: Lithonia, 770-987-2291; Tucker, 770-939-2016.

Committees: *Armed Services* (24th of 34 D): Oversight & Investigations; Air & Land Forces. *Judiciary* (14th of 23 D): Commercial & Administrative Law; Crime, Terrorism & Homeland Security; Courts, the Internet & Intellectual Property. *Small Business* (15th of 18 D): Finance & Tax; Rural & Urban Entrepreneurship.

Group Ratings and Key Votes: Newly Elected

Election Results

2006 general	Hank Johnson (D)	106,352	(75%)	($786,158)
	Catherine Davis (R)	34,778	(25%)	($230,444)
2006 runoff	Hank Johnson (D)	41,281	(59%)	
	Cynthia McKinney (D)	28,915	(41%)	
2006 primary	Cynthia McKinney (D)	29,216	(47%)	
	Hank Johnson (D)	27,529	(44%)	
	John Coyne (D)	5,253	(8%)	
2004 general	Cynthia McKinney (D)	157,461	(64%)	($569,680)
	Catherine Davis (R)	89,509	(36%)	($39,874)

The People		Race/Ethnic Origin	Ancestry	
Area size:	333 sq. mi.	29.6% White	English: 4.6%	USA: 4.4%
Urban population:	98.5%	52.6% Black	German: 4.0%	
Rural population:	1.5%	4.9% Asian	**2004 Presidential Vote**	
Pop. 2000:	629,726	0.2% Native Am.	Kerry (D) 167,666	(71%)
Median income:	$47,943	0.0% Hawaiian	Bush (R) 67,040	(28%)
Poverty status:	10.3%	1.7% Two+ races	Other 587	(0%)
Military veterans:	11.1%	0.2% Other	**2000 Presidential Vote**	
		10.7% Hispanic Origin	Gore (D) 129,189	(70%)
			Bush (R) 55,200	(30%)
			Cook Partisan Voting Index: D + 22	
Occupation	Blue collar: 23.7%	White collar: 62.4%	Gray collar: 13.9%	

In 1920, when Gutzom Borglum began sculpting Jefferson Davis, Robert E. Lee and Stonewall Jackson into the side of Stone Mountain, the huge outcropping of granite was a day's drive into the country from central Atlanta and was soon to become a rallying point for the Ku Klux Klan. Even when the memorial (the largest single piece of sculpture in the world) was completed in 1972, suburban development barely reached this far. But today, after three decades of some of the most explosive metropolitan growth in the country, DeKalb County, which Stone Mountain overlooks, is part of the core of the Atlanta metropolitan area, and this monument to the Confederacy sits in one of the most cosmopolitan and liberal constituencies in the South.

All around in north DeKalb County are affluent suburbs, including much of Atlanta's Jewish community, with voting habits much more liberal than in other suburbs. South DeKalb has been transformed from mostly rural territory 30 years ago to one of the nation's largest collections of affluent black neighborhoods, rivaled only by Prince George's County, Maryland. DeKalb's population grew by 22% in the 1990s, and 8% from 2000 to 2006. These demographic changes have moved DeKalb County's politics well to the left: It was a Republican county when rural Georgia was almost all Democratic in the 1960s; now it is the most heavily Democratic major county in Georgia, even more than next-door Fulton County which includes central Atlanta; in 2004 DeKalb voted 73%-27% for John Kerry, his best percentage except for one tiny rural county in all the 159 counties of Georgia. DeKalb County was a prime destination for evacuees from New Orleans following Hurricane Katrina, a migration that started long before August 2005.

The 4th Congressional District of Georgia consists of more than two-thirds of DeKalb County, a corner of the more Republican Gwinnett County and much of Rockdale County, including Conyers, to the southeast. About 75% of the population of the district now is in DeKalb, compared to more than 95% prior to 2005 redistricting. In the new boundaries, John Kerry received 71% in 2004 and Al Gore got 70% in 2000—virtually the same as with the old lines. The 4th and next-door 5th Districts, both with African-American majorities, are the most Democratic in Georgia.

The new congressman from the 4th District is Hank Johnson, a Democrat who was an unexpected winner in 2006. He is the third person to hold this seat in as many election cycles, all Democrats, and the second primary challenger to oust controversial Democratic Congresswoman Cynthia McKinney. Johnson was born in Washington D.C., where his father was director of classifications and paroles for the Bureau of Prisons and his mother was a school teacher. He practiced law as a civil and criminal litigator, served 12 years as a magistrate judge in DeKalb County and then 5 years on the DeKalb County Commission before he resigned his seat to run for Congress. Although his immediate family members are Presbyterians, he has been a Buddhist since the 1970s; he and fellow freshman Congresswoman Mazie Hirono of Hawaii are the first practicing Buddhists elected to Congress.

McKinney, who served five terms in the House before losing her seat to Denise Majette in a 2002 primary, won an unexpectedly easy return two years later when Majette decided to run for the Senate. She got 51% in the 2004 primary against three state senators and a former Atlanta city council president and won convincingly in the general election. With that strong performance, she was thought to have rehabilitated herself following a bitter campaign loss in 2002, when her bombastic reaction to the events of September 11 proved to be her undoing. Among other things, McKinney had charged that George W. Bush "may" have had prior knowledge of the September 11 attacks and did not act on it because the war on terrorism would boost the defense stocks of associates of his father. Senator Zell Miller called her comments "loony." During her second act, however, McKinney appeared to pick up where she left off. In March 2006, she drew national attention after an altercation with a Capitol Police officer who stopped her at a security checkpoint. Nancy Pelosi, who had a chilly relationship with her, had this reaction: "I find it hard to see any set of facts that would justify striking a police officer." McKinney apologized on the House floor a week later, but the damage had been done.

Until that scuffle, McKinney was cruising past Johnson to the Democratic nomination. The incident, however, galvanized opposition to McKinney and energized Johnson's flagging campaign. In the July 18 primary, the incumbent led Johnson, 47%-44%, but her failure to break the 50% threshold in the three-candidate field forced a runoff three weeks later between the top two vote-getters. Johnson gained additional momentum after the primary. His fundraising, which had been anemic, suddenly picked up as donors from both parties—including former Democratic Gov. Roy Barnes and his 1998 opponent, Republican Guy Millner—took notice of the close contest and weighed in against McKinney. She responded by criticizing Johnson's past financial troubles, which included declaring bankruptcy in the late 1980s. But in the runoff, turnout rose and Johnson easily outdistanced McKinney, 59%-41%. He carried all three counties, including 57%-43% in McKinney's stronghold of DeKalb; he led by margins of 3-to-1 and more in Gwinnett and Rockdale. McKinney was a victim not only of her only mishaps, but also of the changing political and cultural demographics in DeKalb. Johnson breezed in the general against minor opposition.

In the House, Johnson got seats on the Armed Services, Judiciary and Small Business Committees. With his low-key style, he was intent on becoming the first incumbent in the 4th District to win reelection since 2000. But amid suspicion that he was an "accidental" congressman who was in the right place at the right time, he could face a serious Democratic primary—perhaps from McKinney, who in spring 2007 was also mentioned as a possible Green party candidate for president, or from Majette. There was also speculation that term-limited DeKalb County Chief Executive Officer Vernon Jones might drop his Senate candidacy to challenge Johnson.

FIFTH DISTRICT

Rep. John Lewis (D)

Elected 1986, 11th term; b. Feb. 21, 1940, Troy, AL; home, Atlanta; Amer. Baptist Theol. Seminary, B.A. 1961, Fisk U., B.A. 1963; Baptist; married (Lillian).

Elected Office: Atlanta City Cncl., 1981-86.

Professional Career: Chmn., Student Nonviolent Coord. Cmte., 1963-66; Field Foundation, 1966-67; Community Organization Dir., Southern Regional Cncl., 1967-70; Exec. Dir., Voter Educ. Project, 1970-76; Assoc. Dir., ACTION, 1977-80; Community Affairs Dir., Natl. Coop. Bank, 1980-82.

DC Office: 343 CHOB, 20515, 202-225-3801; Fax: 202-225-0351; Web site: www.house.gov/johnlewis.

District Offices: Atlanta, 404-659-0116.

Committees: *Senior Chief Deputy Majority Whip. Ways & Means* (5th of 24 D): Oversight (Chmn.); Income Security & Family Support.

Group Ratings

	ADA	ACLU	AFS	LCV	ITIC	NTU	COC	ACU	CFG	FRC
2006	80	100	100	100	33	14	10	4	5	0
2005	85	—	100	94	—	17	33	0	4	0

National Journal Ratings

	2005 LIB	—	2005 CONS		2006 LIB	—	2006 CONS
Economic	94%	—	0%		84%	—	15%
Social	95%	—	5%		92%	—	8%
Foreign	93%	—	6%		95%	—	0%

Key Votes of the 109th Congress

1. Estate Tax Repeal	N	5. Limit Interstate Abortion	N	9. Build Border Fence	N
2. Limit CAFE Standards	N	6. Extend Patriot Act	N	10. CAFTA	N
3. FY06 Spending Curb	N	7. Bar Same Sex Marriage	N	11. Oppose Iraq Withdrawal	N
4. Drilling in ANWR	N	8. Stem Cell Research $	*	12. Detainee Tribunals	*

Election Results

2006 general	John Lewis (D)	.... unopposed	($702,246)
2006 primary	John Lewis (D)	.... unopposed	
2004 general	John Lewis (D)	.... unopposed	($547,098)

Prior Winning Percentages: 2002 (100%); 2000 (77%); 1998 (79%); 1996 (100%); 1994 (69%); 1992 (72%); 1990 (76%); 1988 (78%); 1986 (75%)

The People		Race/Ethnic Origin	Ancestry	
Area size:	247 sq. mi.	34.4% White	English: 5.6%	German: 4.4%
Urban population:	99.7%	55.7% Black	Irish: 4.3%	
Rural population:	0.3%	2.2% Asian	**2004 Presidential Vote**	
Pop. 2000:	629,728	0.1% Native Am.	Kerry (D) 179,576	(74%)
Median income:	$37,802	0.0% Hawaiian	Bush (R) 62,351	(26%)
Poverty status:	21.2%	1.1% Two+ races	Other 1,803	(1%)
Military veterans:	9.3%	0.2% Other	**2000 Presidential Vote**	
		6.2% Hispanic Origin	Gore (D) 137,497	(73%)
			Bush (R) 51,417	(27%)
			Cook Partisan Voting Index: D +25	

Occupation	Blue collar: 17.5%	White collar: 66.8%	Gray collar: 15.7%

Venture out of the quiet of the Ebenezer Baptist Church or the shade of Martin Luther King Jr.'s boyhood home two blocks away and into the steamy heat of the sun on Auburn Avenue—Sweet Auburn—and you can see, a mile away, downtown Atlanta's atrium-skyscrapers towering in their glory. They are evidence of the wealth and vibrant growth of the commercial capital of the South, the metropolis that has grown up where there was little more than a railroad junction at the time of the War Between the States. But the awesome achievement that is downtown Atlanta is overshadowed by the revolution made in very large part by a man who grew up on Auburn Avenue, where people who never felt air-conditioning moved slowly in the sweltering heat, and around Morehouse and Spelman colleges, where proud professionals struggled and worked hard to raise their families. Atlanta's white establishment, led by Mayors William Hartsfield and Ivan Allen and Coca-Cola's Robert Woodruff, deserve credit for abandoning segregation, but it was King and other civil rights leaders who took the risks that led them to do so. Atlanta's city fathers acted out of good will, but also with an eye for the economic growth of their city, which they knew would be hurt by violent resistance.

Today Atlanta is the center of the nation's ninth largest metropolitan area that spreads far out from Sweet Auburn into 28 counties of North Georgia. Its Hartsfield-Jackson Airport is the busiest in the world, with 86 million passengers in 2005 and nearly 1 million takeoffs and landings. All is not well in the city of Atlanta: some neighborhoods are emptying out, and middle-income blacks have moved in large numbers to the suburbs in DeKalb, Cobb and Douglas Counties. But Atlanta also has vibrant office centers, in downtown, midtown and Buckhead to the north. Coca-Cola's skyscraper headquarters looms up, the symbol of Atlanta's most successful worldwide business, near the stadiums and sports facilities built for the 1996 Summer Olympics. November 2005 was a month of openings, with the new Georgia Aquarium and the expanded High Museum of Art. The World of Coca-Cola museum opened in May 2007. In October 2006 Coca-Cola donated a $10 million parcel of land near Centennial Park for a $100 million civil rights museum to house the Martin Luther King papers; Mayor Shirley Franklin had organized a $32 million loan to rescue them from a Sotheby's auction.

The 5th Congressional District of Georgia includes all of the city of Atlanta, down to the suburb of East Point to the south. As redistricted by Republicans in 2005, it occupies most of the land inside the I-285 ring road—the city of Atlanta, including posh and Republican Buckhead; the westernmost part of DeKalb County; the northern edge of Clayton County, including the airport. The 5th District is overwhelmingly Democratic.

The congressman from the 5th District is John Lewis, who made history a long generation ago as a hero of the civil rights movement, as he recounted in his 1998 autobiography, *Walking With the Wind*. A sharecropper's son from Troy, Alabama, he was seized by religious fervor as a child, preaching in the barnyard, determined to be a minister. Lewis was the first in his family to finish high school; he wrote to Ralph Abernathy for help in suing for the right to enter Troy State College; he met Martin Luther King Jr. when he was 18. In 1959, at 19, he helped organize the first lunch-counter sit-in, which was received with open hostility hard to imagine today. In 1960, the day after John Kennedy was elected, Lewis sat in the Krystal Diner in Nashville while a waitress poured cleansing powder down his back and water over his food; he went to talk to the manager, who turned a fumigating machine on him. In May 1961, he was on the first of the Freedom Rides, riding buses as they were attacked and burned; he was viciously beaten in Rock Hill, South Carolina, and Montgomery, Alabama. He spoke at the 1963 March on Washington, criticizing Kennedy liberals for inaction on civil rights and calling for massive help for the poor. In 1964, he helped coordinate the Mississippi Freedom Project. In March 1965, he led the Selma-to-Montgomery march to petition for voting rights and was beaten by policemen who fractured his skull. Modestly, quietly, maintaining his poise and good judgment under harsh circumstances, Lewis was one of the people who risked their lives many times to make the civil rights revolution happen. He worked for Robert Kennedy for president in 1968, and was with him in Indianapolis when they heard King was killed, and in Los Angeles just before Kennedy himself was shot.

Lewis's first foray into electoral politics was unsuccessful: He ran in 1977 to replace Andrew Young in the House and was soundly beaten by Wyche Fowler (but ran ahead of Republican Paul Coverdell, who beat Fowler in the 1992 Senate election). After winning a seat on the Atlanta Council in 1981, Lewis ran for Congress in 1986, and trailed Julian Bond 47%-35% in the primary. But even though Bond won more than 60% of the black vote, Lewis won the runoff by assembling a coalition of poor blacks and affluent whites: "Vote for the tugboat, not the showboat" was his slogan, stressing his hard work on local issues. He has been re-elected easily since.

Lewis has been a strong partisan, with one of the most liberal voting records in the House. Usually quiet, he can speak in the cadences of black preachers, as he did on the Gulf War resolution in January 1991 and the impeachment of Bill Clinton in December 1998. He is the Democrats' Senior Chief Deputy Whip, a member of the leadership, and has a seat on Ways and Means. Only occasionally does he defect from his party, as when he opposed the 1994 crime bill because of his disapproval of capital punishment and when he voted against the Iraq supplemental in March 2007 because it contained funds for continuing military action. He furiously voiced his disappointment when Republicans captured the House in 1994 and argued passionately against the Republican welfare bills.

Lewis has worked to commemorate the civil rights revolution in which he played such a large part. He got a federal building in Atlanta named for Martin Luther King Jr. and got the route from Selma to Montgomery designated a National Historic Trail. He has said affirmative action should move from race to class as a criterion, but he has stoutly defended racial quotas and preferences. Since 1998 he has led pilgrimages of members of Congress to civil rights sites. In June 2005 Georgia colleagues Saxby Chambliss and David Scott sponsored a bill to rename a building at the Martin Luther King Jr. National Historic Site the John Lewis Civil Rights Institute.

In August 1999, Lewis declared that he was running for majority whip should Democrats win a House majority; Nancy Pelosi and Steny Hoyer had already started lining up support. But not all Congressional Black Caucus members supported him, and Lewis left the race (which turned out to be academic) in July 2000. He strongly championed the reauthorization of the Voting Rights Act, including preclearance and redistricting provisions attacked by critics as outdated, and his support helped ensure it carried by a large majority. Appointed Senior Chief Deputy Majority Whip, with a remit to work with the Progressive Caucus, the Congressional Black Caucus, the Blue Dogs and the New Democrats, he said, "The Democratic Caucus is a very diverse group. We have to hold everyone together under the big tent." Political reporters in early 2007 looked for hints that Lewis would endorse Hillary Clinton or Barack Obama. He said he was endorsing neither, but "I'm going to be involved in someone's campaign along the way."

Lewis was reelected without opposition in 2002, 2004 and 2006.

SIXTH DISTRICT

Rep. Tom Price (R)

Elected 2004, 2d term; b. Oct. 8, 1954, Lansing, MI; home, Roswell; U. of MI, B.A. 1976, M.D. 1979; Presbyterian; married (Betty).

Elected Office: GA Senate, 1996-2004; Maj. Ldr., 2002-03.

Professional Career: Practicing orthopedic surgeon, 1979-2002; Asst. prof., Emory U., 2002-present.

DC Office: 424 CHOB, 20515, 202-225-4501; Fax: 202-225-4656; Web site: www.house.gov/tomprice.

District Offices: Marietta, 770-565-4990.

Committees: *Education & Labor* (14th of 22 R): Workforce Protections; Health, Employment, Labor & Pensions. *Financial Services* (24th of 33 R): Financial Institutions & Consumer Credit; Oversight & Investigations; Domestic and International Monetary Policy, Trade & Technology.

Group Ratings

	ADA	ACLU	AFS	LCV	ITIC	NTU	COC	ACU	CFG	FRC
2006	0	5	0	8	100	77	100	92	88	100
2005	0	—	0	0	—	68	93	96	93	92

National Journal Ratings

	2005 LIB	—	2005 CONS		2006 LIB	—	2006 CONS
Economic	9%	—	88%		7%	—	91%
Social	32%	—	66%		23%	—	74%
Foreign	0%	—	89%		17%	—	73%

Key Votes of the 109th Congress

1. Estate Tax Repeal	Y	5. Limit Interstate Abortion	Y	9. Build Border Fence	Y
2. Limit CAFE Standards	Y	6. Extend Patriot Act	N	10. CAFTA	Y
3. FY06 Spending Curb	Y	7. Bar Same Sex Marriage	Y	11. Oppose Iraq Withdrawal	Y
4. Drilling in ANWR	Y	8. Stem Cell Research $	N	12. Detainee Tribunals	Y

Election Results

2006 general	Tom Price (R)	144,958	(72%)	($2,281,556)
	Steve Sinton (D)	55,294	(28%)	($104,821)
2006 primary	Tom Price (R)	47,925	(82%)	
	John Konop (R)	10,322	(18%)	
2004 general	Tom Price (R)	unopposed		($2,283,545)

The People		Race/Ethnic Origin	Ancestry	
Area size:	695 sq. mi.	81.0% White	English: 10.7%	German: 10.7%
Urban population:	93.5%	6.7% Black	Irish: 9.7%	
Rural population:	6.5%	4.4% Asian	**2004 Presidential Vote**	
Pop. 2000:	629,726	0.2% Native Am.	Bush (R) 215,437	(70%)
Median income:	$71,699	0.0% Hawaiian	Kerry (D) 90,348	(29%)
Poverty status:	4.5%	1.2% Two+ races	Other 2,394	(1%)
Military veterans:	11.3%	0.2% Other	**2000 Presidential Vote**	
		6.2% Hispanic Origin	Bush (R) 163,855	(68%)
			Gore (D) 76,501	(32%)
			Cook Partisan Voting Index: R +18	

Occupation   Blue collar: 12.4%   White collar: 78.2%   Gray collar: 9.3%

In the red clay hills north of Atlanta, over the past four decades an almost wholly new metropolitan quarter has grown up as affluent Atlanta has spread out past the I-285 Perimeter into territory that was once just farms, small towns and little factory cities. Where there were perhaps 100,000 people in the 1950s, there are more than 1 million today. No longer is downtown Atlanta the only focus: The edge cities of Perimeter Center and the area near Cumberland Mall are not just for shopping; they are major office centers, rivaling downtown Atlanta in square footage. Along the usually jammed Georgia 400 highway, in the fast-growing northern part of Fulton County, are the affluent suburbs of Sandy Springs, Roswell and Alpharetta; at the tip of the county, near the Chattahoochee River, the new cities of Johns Creek and Milton were incorporated in 2006 to free residents of county government. Cobb County is the headquarters of The Weather Channel. Farther out in Cherokee County, the big issue has been the proposed Northern Arc highway; commuters have ached for relief, but approval has been a political football. For all this economic and demographic change, this Golden Crescent north of the Perimeter and between I-75 in Cobb County and I-85 in Gwinnett County outwardly does not seem to have changed greatly: The buildings are tree-shaded, and lush foliage and large-lot requirements have given most of the communities a woodsy look.

The 6th Congressional District of Georgia occupies a large portion of this Golden Crescent north of Atlanta, including the eastern slice of Cobb County, much of northern Fulton, the northwest tip of DeKalb, and all of Cherokee County. It contains affluent Alpharetta, fast-growing Canton and historic Roswell. This seat was in effect created after the 1990 Census, and its boundaries have twice been reshaped by redistricting. The changes in 2005 cut back more than half of the previous parts of Cobb and added the remainder of Cherokee; the result left about 40% of the population in Fulton County, roughly 25% each in Cobb and Cherokee, and the remainder in DeKalb. It would surely surprise Georgians a generation or two ago to learn that one of their congressional districts would rank among the nation's richest and most educated: Now the 6th and the 7th, to the east, both do. It is one of several heavily Republican Georgia districts, and the political tension here tends to be between economic and cultural conservatives. In 2004, George W. Bush defeated John Kerry 70%-29% under both the old and new boundaries.

The congressman from the 6th District is Tom Price, a Republican elected in 2004. Price grew up in Michigan and graduated from the University of Michigan and its medical school; his father and grandfather were physicians. He did his residency in orthopedic surgery at Emory Medical School and moved to Roswell, where he was involved in civic affairs and was president of the Rotary Club. Working closely with the Medical Association of Georgia, he campaigned locally against the Clinton health care plan. When a seat opened in the state Senate in 1996, he was elected and quickly moved up the leadership ranks to become Majority Leader when Republicans captured the Senate in 2002 for the first time since Reconstruction.

In January 2003, Congressman Johnny Isakson announced he was running for the Senate seat being vacated by Zell Miller. The contest for this heavily Republican open seat was hard-fought and big-spending. Three state senators ran—Price from Fulton County, and Robert Lamutt and Chuck Clay from Cobb County. Price spent $499,000 of his own money and contrasted his work in medicine with the legal and business careers of his two main opponents. He highlighted his fiscal conservatism and strong support for limiting jury awards in malpractice suits, a position that won him considerable support from the medical community. Calling the federal income tax "broken," he advocated 7th District Republican John Linder's national retail sales tax. He said that he had "a surgeon's mentality . . . . I get things done." Price led the first round of the primary with 35%; Lamutt made it into the runoff with 28% to 21% for Chuck Clay. Lamutt, who cited his success in creating an assets management firm and gave $1.5 million to his campaign, criticized Price as a "special interest" candidate because he raised large sums from fellow doctors. He attacked Price's 2003 support for a 25-cent state tax increase on a pack of cigarettes. Price defended his vote as a tool to reduce local property taxes. "Bob Lamutt helped cigarette makers but voted against tax relief for you," a Price ad said. In the runoff the Cobb vote was nearly twice as large as in Fulton. But Price got 79% in Fulton County and held Lamutt to 59% in Cobb; with the small vote in Cherokee County split nearly evenly, Price won 54%-46%. Lamutt was one of two candidates in Georgia runoffs endorsed by former Speaker Newt Gingrich, who once represented this district; both lost. With obstetrician Phil Gingrey and dentist Linder, Price is the third medical professional in the Georgia Republican delegation.

In the House, Price has a conservative voting record, though it is less conservative on cultural issues than most of his Georgia Republican colleagues. On the Terri Schiavo case, he thought that Congress went too far in a private conflict. On the pension reform bill, he worked with Isakson to protect the interests of Delta Airlines and its employees, and got the initially reluctant chairman John Boehner to agree to separate treatment for the airline industry. As a member of the Financial Services Committee, he sponsored a bill to limit identity theft. On health care, he opposed government intervention to negotiate Medicare drug prices, which he said were being reduced by market forces. He joined Tammy Baldwin on a proposal to increase health-insurance coverage by giving the states more authority with a "state health innovation commission." At the Capitol, he helped to create the Medical and Dental Doctors Caucus to work with Capitol Physician John Eisold to create an emergency response team. Price became active in party leadership by helping to create the "Official Truth Squad" to "shed light" on statements made by House Democrats.

The redistricting in 2005 served the Fulton County-based Price's interest by reducing the opportunity for a primary challenge from Cobb County Republicans; the county is now divided between the 6th, 11th and 13th Districts. He was reelected in 2006 with minor opposition in the primary and general.

SEVENTH DISTRICT

Rep. John Linder (R)

Elected 1992, 8th term; b. Sept. 9, 1942, Deer River, MN; home, Duluth; U. of MN, B.S. 1964, D.D.S., 1967; Presbyterian; married (Lynne).

Military Career: Air Force, 1967-69.

Elected Office: GA House of Reps., 1974-80, 1982-90.

Professional Career: Practicing dentist, 1969-82; Founder & Pres., Linder Financial Corp., 1977-92.

DC Office: 1026 LHOB, 20515, 202-225-4272; Fax: 202-225-4696; Web site: linder.house.gov.

District Offices: Lawrenceville, 770-232-3005.

Committees: *Ways & Means* (14th of 17 R): Oversight; Select Revenue Measures.

Group Ratings

	ADA	ACLU	AFS	LCV	ITIC	NTU	COC	ACU	CFG	FRC
2006	0	0	0	0	100	75	100	96	85	100
2005	0	—	0	11	—	69	93	96	92	100

National Journal Ratings

	2005 LIB	—	2005 CONS		2006 LIB	—	2006 CONS
Economic	3%	—	94%		3%	—	97%
Social	21%	—	78%		23%	—	74%
Foreign	0%	—	89%		0%	—	94%

Key Votes of the 109th Congress

1. Estate Tax Repeal	Y	5. Limit Interstate Abortion	Y	9. Build Border Fence	Y
2. Limit CAFE Standards	Y	6. Extend Patriot Act	Y	10. CAFTA	Y
3. FY06 Spending Curb	Y	7. Bar Same Sex Marriage	Y	11. Oppose Iraq Withdrawal	Y
4. Drilling in ANWR	Y	8. Stem Cell Research $	N	12. Detainee Tribunals	Y

Election Results

2006 general	John Linder (R)	130,561	(71%)	($398,794)
	Allan Burns (D)	53,553	(29%)	($33,213)
2006 primary	John Linder (R)	unopposed		
2004 general	John Linder (R)	unopposed		($746,763)

Prior Winning Percentages: 2002 (79%); 2000 (100%); 1998 (69%); 1996 (64%); 1994 (58%); 1992 (51%)

The People		Race/Ethnic Origin	Ancestry	
Area size:	978 sq. mi.	75.6% White	USA: 10.6%	English: 9.1%
Urban population:	86.8%	11.5% Black	German: 8.8%	
Rural population:	13.2%	5.1% Asian	**2004 Presidential Vote**	
Pop. 2000:	629,727	0.2% Native Am.	Bush (R) 199,492	(70%)
Median income:	$60,450	0.0% Hawaiian	Kerry (D) 85,472	(30%)
Poverty status:	5.4%	1.3% Two+ races	Other 1,895	(1%)
Military veterans:	11.6%	0.2% Other	**2000 Presidential Vote**	
		6.1% Hispanic Origin	Bush (R) 141,986	(69%)
			Gore (D) 63,336	(31%)
			Cook Partisan Voting Index: R +18	

Occupation   Blue collar: 20.5%   White collar: 69.5%   Gray collar: 10.1%

In the last two decades, greater Atlanta has grown out in every direction, south past the airport, west over the Chattahoochee, north past far Buckhead and the Perimeter Mall, and east and northeast past Stone Mountain. The outer suburbs north of Atlanta have grown fastest of all: Gwinnett County to the east features more mature neighborhoods of affluent professionals and entrepreneurs. The closer-in portions of Gwinnett, near I-85, with their older shopping districts, have been attracting Georgia's largest concentration of Hispanics and also middle class blacks; the county's rapidly growing school system boasts that its students speak more than 100 languages. Further out in Lawrenceville, Duluth and Buford, downtown Atlanta seems very far away, both physically—it is 30 to 50 miles, and more than an hour of clogged rush-hour driving, to Peachtree Street—and in state of mind. For many, Atlanta is something that whizzes by on the way to Hartsfield-Jackson Atlanta International Airport.

The growth here and its diversity are hard to overstate. Gwinnett County cast 21,000 votes in 1972 and 243,000 in 2004, not so far behind Fulton County (336,000), which includes central Atlanta, or DeKalb County (276,000) just to the east. And the trend has continued in Gwinnett, with a 22% increase from 2000 to 2006 to a population of 757,000. Like other metro Atlanta counties, the non-Hispanic white population has been dropping in the schools, while the overall numbers soar. There is some international flavor here: Mexicans in Norcross, Koreans in Duluth and Bosnians in Lawrenceville. Beyond Gwinnett, recent increases have been even more robust, with spurts from 24% to 32% in Barrow, Walton and Newton Counties. These were once rural, low-income and heavily Democratic areas; now they are full of strivers and achievers, with many religious conservatives and many economic conservatives, and relatively few liberals and Democrats.

The 7th Congressional District of Georgia owes its existence to the rapid growth here in the 1990s. Prior to the 2005 redistricting, this was a new crescent-shaped district created by Democrats with a few odd twists to cordon off Republican votes from districts they hoped to win. The newest iteration gave it a more compact shape and recentered the district in Gwinnett, which has 78% of the population, compared to 58% with the previous lines. In addition to all of Barrow and Walton Counties, the 7th includes thin slices of Forsyth and Newton Counties. The changes increased the black population from 7% to 12% and had the effect of reducing the 2004 vote here for George W. Bush from 76% to 70%.

The congressman from the 7th District is John Linder, a Republican first elected in 1992 in the old 4th District (which combined north DeKalb County and half of Gwinnett). After a court-ordered redistricting, he moved in 1996 to the 11th District (which stretched from Gwinnett to Athens and the South Carolina border). Like many in the Georgia delegation, Linder grew up elsewhere, in his case Minnesota, where he went to college and dental school. After two years in the Air Force he moved to greater Atlanta and practiced dentistry for 13 years. In 1977 he started Linder Financial Corporation, a lending institution for entrepreneurial ventures in the South. In 1974, at 32, he was elected to the Georgia House, where he served all but two of the next 16 years. In 1990 he challenged Congressman Ben Jones and lost 52%-48%. After the 1992 redistricting, Linder ran first in a six-candidate primary and won the runoff with 62% of the vote. In the general, he faced Democratic state Senator Cathey Steinberg and, in a race that broke along national party lines, won 51%-49%.

From this tenuous beginning Linder quickly became an important congressman. For a time he was a close ally to Newt Gingrich. They went back a ways: In 1975 Linder, Gingrich and Paul Coverdell began meeting to try to build a strong Georgia Republican Party, surely not imagining that within 20 years they would be Congressman, Speaker and Senator. But Gingrich resigned in 1998 and Coverdell died in 2000; now, only Linder survives in office.

Linder has a calm, sometimes humorous demeanor; his views are solidly conservative—though a bit more Wall Street than Main Street. After Republicans won control, Gingrich gave Linder a seat on the House Rules Committee and called on him often to preside over contentious debates. After the 1996 election, Gingrich chose Linder as chairman of the National Republican Congressional Committee. He excelled at fundraising, and relentlessly prevailed on incumbents to contribute to Republican challengers. He did a good job at recruiting candidates and shared the assumption of most observers that Republicans would gain seats as the out party in an off-year election. But one of his ads misfired: At the behest of Gingrich, it raised the trust and impeachment issues against Bill Clinton. While run in only a few districts, the ad was publicized nationally; it yielded a minimum of gain and a maximum of pain. When Republicans lost five seats, Linder was in deep trouble. He said the problem was the lack of a "strong message," which "was not my responsibility"—an obvious reference to Gingrich. Tom Davis of Virginia started running for the job, with the support of Whip Tom DeLay. Linder reacted bitterly: "I remember when Newt Gingrich's wife left a press conference in tears when he blamed her. So I don't think he has any compunction about blaming me." That was Thursday, two days after the election. Gingrich announced his resignation late on Friday; 12 days later, Linder lost to Davis 130-77.

Taking a far lower profile, Linder resumed his legislative work and got on well with the new Republican leadership. He turned his attention toward the fight for fundamental tax reform. With more than 50 co-sponsors, including DeLay, his FairTax plan would abolish all federal income taxes, including payroll taxes, and replace them with a single 23% national retail sales tax, with no exceptions for food or medical expenses but a monthly rebate for low-income citizens. As Linder explains, "the FairTax gives the American people control over their own lives again by allowing them to keep 100% of their pay checks and shielding their personal information from bureaucrats." Late in the 2004 campaign, many Democratic candidates sought to turn the issue in their favor with alarming descriptions of increased costs for consumers. By Election Day, the furor had died down, and George W. Bush listed tax reform as one of his second-term priorities. Linder had longed to serve as chairman of Rules, but Speaker Hastert in January 2005 decided that the six-year limit on committee chairmen did not apply at the Rules Committee and gave David Dreier of California another term as chairman. Linder was disappointed, but he did not cause a fuss; he left the committee and got a seat on Ways and Means. With Republicans consumed by Social Security reform, he made no legislative headway on tax reform. But he continued to generate grass-roots interest and in 2005 his *FairTaxBook*, written with radio host Neal Boortz, debuted at number one on the *New York Times* nonfiction bestseller list. Linder also joined the Homeland Security Committee, where he chaired the Prevention of Nuclear and Biological Attack Subcommittee. In fighting terrorism, he warned, "We should be looking for nuclear devices, and I think we should not spend all of our money on the airline industry."

In 2002, Linder was unexpectedly inconvenienced by the redistricting plan drawn by Georgia Democrats. Although the new 7th appeared tailor-made for him, he found himself in a primary contest with Representative Bob Barr. The new 7th had only 18% of Barr's old district, and most Republicans expected that he would run in the new 11th, which contained more of his old seat and which in fact elected a Republican, albeit narrowly. The race was a contrast of styles, not of voting records. Linder campaigned as a political insider who quietly got things done. Barr, an early advocate of the impeachment of Bill Clinton, campaigned as a champion of conservative principle. Linder had more local financial support; Barr had contributors across the nation. The campaign grew bitter, but the final result was unambiguous. Linder won 64%-36%. He got 74% in Gwinnett County, which cast 57% of the votes. He appears secure in the redrawn district.

EIGHTH DISTRICT

Rep. Jim Marshall (D)

Elected 2002, 3d term; b. Mar. 31, 1948, Ithaca, NY; home, Macon; Princeton U., B.A. 1972, Boston U., J.D. 1977; Catholic; married (Camille).

Military Career: Army, 1968-70 (Vietnam).

Elected Office: Macon Mayor, 1995-99.

Professional Career: Mercer U. Law Professor, 1979-95, 1999-2002.

DC Office: 504 CHOB, 20515, 202-225-6531; Fax: 202-225-3013; Web site: www.house.gov/marshall.

District Offices: Macon, 478-464-0255; Tifton, 229-556-7418.

Committees: *Agriculture* (9th of 25 D): Specialty Crops, Rural Development & Foreign Agriculture; General Farm Commodities & Risk Management. *Armed Services* (17th of 34 D): Terrorism, Unconventional Threats & Capabilities; Readiness; Air & Land Forces. *Financial Services* (36th of 37 D): Domestic and International Monetary Policy, Trade & Technology; Capital Markets, Insurance & Government Sponsored Enterprises.

Group Ratings

	ADA	ACLU	AFS	LCV	ITIC	NTU	COC	ACU	CFG	FRC
2006	35	32	43	42	71	29	73	72	27	100
2005	70	—	63	61	—	24	63	46	22	77

National Journal Ratings

	2005 LIB	—	2005 CONS		2006 LIB	—	2006 CONS
Economic	56%	—	44%		53%	—	46%
Social	45%	—	55%		51%	—	49%
Foreign	52%	—	48%		45%	—	54%

Key Votes of the 109th Congress

1. Estate Tax Repeal	N	5. Limit Interstate Abortion	Y	9. Build Border Fence	Y
2. Limit CAFE Standards	N	6. Extend Patriot Act	Y	10. CAFTA	N
3. FY06 Spending Curb	N	7. Bar Same Sex Marriage	Y	11. Oppose Iraq Withdrawal	Y
4. Drilling in ANWR	N	8. Stem Cell Research $	N	12. Detainee Tribunals	Y

Election Results

2006 general	Jim Marshall (D) 80,660	(51%)	($1,849,155)
	Mac Collins (R) 78,908	(49%)	($1,981,928)
2006 primary	Jim Marshall (D) .... unopposed		
2004 general (GA 3)	Jim Marshall (D) 136,273	(63%)	($1,307,926)
	Calder Clay (R) 80,435	(37%)	($1,054,493)

Prior Winning Percentages: 2002 (51%)

The People		Race/Ethnic Origin	Ancestry	
Area size:	7,239 sq. mi.	62.9% White	USA: 15.4%	English: 6.6%
Urban population:	56.6%	32.4% Black	Irish: 5.9%	
Rural population:	43.4%	0.8% Asian	**2004 Presidential Vote**	
Pop. 2000:	629,728	0.2% Native Am.	Bush (R) 147,729	(61%)
Median income:	$36,294	0.0% Hawaiian	Kerry (D) 93,875	(39%)
Poverty status:	15.8%	0.8% Two+ races	Other 1,114	(0%)
Military veterans:	14.0%	0.1% Other	**2000 Presidential Vote**	
		2.8% Hispanic Origin	Bush (R) 111,240	(58%)
			Gore (D) 80,383	(42%)
			Cook Partisan Voting Index: R + 8	
Occupation	Blue collar: 31.2%	White collar: 52.8%	Gray collar: 16.0%	

Macon, the hub of central Georgia, is a city proud of its restored houses and its Japanese cherry trees, of which it shows off 20 times as many as Washington, D.C., during its annual International Cherry Blossom Festival. It is the home of music legends Otis Redding, James Brown, Little Richard and the Allman Brothers, and of the Harriet Tubman Historical and Cultural Museum. Surrounding it are the farm and forest lands of central Georgia. Much of this land was the site of General William Tecumseh Sherman's 1864 march from Atlanta to the sea. To the east, Twiggs and Wilkinson Counties have been among the world's major sources of kaolin, a clay used for china and ceramics. A short drive north on Interstate 75 is Juliette, an old mill town that's too small for most maps; it is the place where many scenes in the movie *Fried Green Tomatoes* were filmed.

The 8th Congressional District of Georgia includes all of Macon and Bibb County and stretches about 200 miles north and south, from fast-growing Newton County in metro Atlanta to Colquitt County nearly at the Florida border. About one-half of its votes are cast in the five-county Macon metro area. With its Air Logistics Center and repair site for the F-22 Raptor, the Warner Robins Air Force Base and the surrounding city of Warner Robins have grown significantly in recent years. This was Democratic country from the time of Sherman's march until the civil rights revolution of the 1960s. Today the political balance is different. More than 70% of whites usually vote Republican; about 90% of blacks usually vote Democratic. So the political leanings of any district in this part of Georgia depend on the racial percentages.

Redistricters in 2005 significantly changed this district with the goal of increasing the prospect of electing a Republican. The seat was renumbered from the 3d to the 8th District, and its shape was elongated to add unfamiliar territory, much of it Republican. Slightly more than half of the population is new to the district and the new lines reduced the black population from 40% to 33%. The result was to increase President Bush's 2004 performance in this district from 55% to 61%.

The congressman from the 8th District is Jim Marshall, first elected in 2002. The son and grandson of Army generals, he grew up at several Army posts. He graduated from high school in Mobile, Alabama, and went on to Princeton but interrupted his education to enlist in the Army and volunteer for infantry combat in Vietnam. He served there in the elite Airborne Ranger reconnaissance platoon, was wounded in combat and awarded two Bronze Stars and a Purple Heart. After military service, he graduated from Princeton and Boston University Law School. He joined the faculty of Mercer University law school in Macon, practiced business law and became active in Democratic politics. His wife Camille is a federal bankruptcy trustee. In his first political contest, Marshall was elected mayor of Macon in 1995. He made his first run for Congress in 2000 against Saxby Chambliss in the old 8th District (that was 3 maps ago in Georgia). He campaigned almost exclusively on prescription drugs for seniors, and lost 59%-41%.

When Democrats redrew the district, Marshall quickly entered the contest and made his military experience the centerpiece of his 2002 campaign. Against three opponents in the Democratic primary, his toughest competitor was politically-connected attorney Chuck Byrd, whose father Garland Byrd was lieutenant governor from 1959-63. Byrd ran as a conservative in the Sam Nunn tradition and as an opponent of abortion, but Marshall carried Bibb County solidly and won 54% of the total vote, enough to avoid a runoff. In the general election, Marshall faced Bibb County Commissioner Calder Clay, an energetic fundraiser who claimed Marshall was too liberal for the district. Marshall kept emphasizing his military record; Clay had not served in the military. Both supported George W. Bush on Iraq, but they differed on abortion and Social Security. Each candidate got a pledge of a seat on the House Armed Services Committee. In one of 2002's closest contests, Clay carried most of the eastern counties and the Warner Robins area. But Marshall won 61%-39% in Bibb County and 50.5%-49.5% overall.

In the House, Marshall has cast a moderate voting record that placed him virtually at the center of the chamber. It didn't take long for him to get noticed in the Democratic Caucus. In March 2003, on the day after hostilities began in Iraq, Marshall showed up, uninvited, to a press conference convened by a group of anti-war House Democrats. "The time for debate is past," he announced. He then invoked an obscure House rule to cancel a Democratic Caucus meeting organized to debate war alternatives. After a September 2003 visit to Iraq, he criticized news coverage of the war for focusing disproportionately on the coalition's "death, mistakes and setbacks." He said the "Pentagon's version is far closer to reality" than the media's portrayal. In an *Atlanta Journal-Constitution* opinion article, he urged Democrats to "carefully avoid using the language of failure" which he said could be "unforgivably self-fulfilling." The following Christmas, he secretly returned to Iraq to visit some of the most dangerous areas, observe the conditions, and thank U.S. soldiers. Three times, he has spent Christmas with the Army Chief of Staff and troops in Iraq. An increasingly lonely voice among Democrats, he continued to support the war. In November 2005, he was the only Democrat to vote against Nancy Pelosi's resolution for a "thorough investigation of . . . abuses relating to the Iraq war." In January 2007, he said that U.S. and Iraqi forces were having success in reducing insurgent activity. A month later, he was one of two Democrats voting against a resolution condemning the military surge in Iraq. He called the proposal "akin to sitting on the sidelines and booing in the middle of our own team's play, because we don't like the coach's call."

Marshall avidly backed "concurrent receipt" legislation to permit veterans to receive full retirement pay plus disability compensation at the same time; within months, Republicans took up and passed a modified version. In 2005, he turned his attention to another inequity for veterans: an 1891 law that required a dollar-for-dollar offset for those receiving both retirement pay and disability compensation. He voted against the Central American Free Trade Agreement. Unusual in the House, he sits on three major committees: Agriculture, Armed Services and Financial Services.

In 2004, Marshall turned down pleas from national and state Democrats to run for the Senate seat left open by Zell Miller's retirement. Instead, he faced a rematch with Calder Clay. Marshall was the only Democratic candidate endorsed by Miller, who called him "the kind of Democrat we need to keep in Washington." In an unexpectedly strong showing, Marshall won 63%-37%; he won 74%-26% in Bibb County, which cast 20% of the vote. But the March 2005 redistricting gave Marshall new headaches and cause to think about running statewide. In 2006, Republicans nominated former Congressman Mac Collins, who served six terms before running unsuccessfully in 2004 for the Republican Senate nomination. Marshall, with the advantage of greater name recognition in the Macon area, ran against "extremists on both sides." Collins ran ads criticizing him for support of food stamps to illegal immigrants. The result was one of the closest in the nation and took a week before it became official: Marshall won by 1,752 votes. His margin of victory came in Bibb, which he took 63%-37%. Collins won 11 of the 21 counties, including Houston and most of the counties to the north. Some Republicans criticized the national party for failing to spend more money on the contest.

In 2007, Senate Democrats encouraged Marshall to challenge Saxby Chambliss for reelection in 2008. In the district, Republican Rick Goddard, the former commander of the Warner Robins Air Logistics Center at Robins Air Force Base who was heavily recruited by the National Republican Congressional Committee, announced he will run against Marshall in 2008. But Goddard might face a primary challenge from Mac Collins, who has said he is considering a rematch.

NINTH DISTRICT

Rep. Nathan Deal (R)

Elected 1992, 8th term; b. Aug. 25, 1942, Millen; home, Clermont; Mercer U., B.A. 1964, J.D. 1966; Baptist; married (Sandra).

Military Career: Army, 1966-68.

Elected Office: Hall Cnty. Juvenile Court Judge, 1971-72; GA Senate, 1980-92, Pres. Pro-Tem, 1989-90, 1991-92.

Professional Career: Hall Cnty. Atty., 1966-70; Asst. Dist. Atty., NE Judicial Circuit, 1970-71; Practicing atty., 1971-92.

DC Office: 2133 RHOB, 20515, 202-225-5211; Fax: 202-225-8272; Web site: www.house.gov/deal.

District Offices: Dalton, 706-226-5320; Gainesville, 770-535-2592; Lafayette, 706-638-7042.

Committees: *Energy & Commerce* (6th of 26 R): Health (RMM); Environment & Hazardous Materials; Telecommunications & the Internet.

Group Ratings

	ADA	ACLU	AFS	LCV	ITIC	NTU	COC	ACU	CFG	FRC
2006	5	5	0	0	83	78	92	92	79	100
2005	5	—	0	0	—	67	89	96	89	100

National Journal Ratings

	2005 LIB	—	2005 CONS	2006 LIB	—	2006 CONS
Economic	6%	—	93%	2%	—	97%
Social	0%	—	89%	8%	—	91%
Foreign	0%	—	89%	27%	—	73%

Key Votes of the 109th Congress

1. Estate Tax Repeal	Y	5. Limit Interstate Abortion	Y	9. Build Border Fence	Y
2. Limit CAFE Standards	Y	6. Extend Patriot Act	Y	10. CAFTA	Y
3. FY06 Spending Curb	Y	7. Bar Same Sex Marriage	Y	11. Oppose Iraq Withdrawal	Y
4. Drilling in ANWR	Y	8. Stem Cell Research $	N	12. Detainee Tribunals	Y

Election Results

2006 general	Nathan Deal (R)	128,685	(77%)	($959,845)
	John Bradbury (D)	39,240	(23%)	($15,737)
2006 primary	Nathan Deal (R)	unopposed		
2004 general (GA 10)	Nathan Deal (R)	unopposed		($372,286)

Prior Winning Percentages: 2002 (100%); 2000 (75%); 1998 (100%); 1996 (66%); 1994 (58%); 1992 (59%)

The People		Race/Ethnic Origin	Ancestry	
Area size:	4,418 sq. mi.	86.1% White	USA: 17.5%	Irish: 8.4%
Urban population:	47.3%	2.9% Black	English: 7.9%	
Rural population:	52.7%	0.6% Asian	**2004 Presidential Vote**	
Pop. 2000:	629,728	0.3% Native Am.	Bush (R) 196,023	(77%)
Median income:	$41,116	0.0% Hawaiian	Kerry (D) 58,530	(23%)
Poverty status:	10.8%	0.8% Two+ races	Other 1,471	(1%)
Military veterans:	12.4%	0.1% Other	**2000 Presidential Vote**	
		9.3% Hispanic Origin	Bush (R) 135,583	(71%)
			Gore (D) 55,416	(29%)
			Cook Partisan Voting Index: R +23	

Occupation   Blue collar: 36.7%   White collar: 51.0%   Gray collar: 12.3%

In the last years of the 20th century, the hills and mountains of north Georgia suddenly became one of the boom areas of the South. This was a sharp turn in their history: Since the Cherokee were driven out early in the 19th century this was poor country, where small farmers scratched a living off rocky land. It was devastated by the Civil War, by General Sherman's troops and because so many young men who left to fight for the Confederacy (and a few who left from mountain counties to fight for the Union) never returned. After the war, not much changed for a while. Most communities lived in isolation; roads with hairpin curves led to remote hills where until very recently moonshine stills were more common than summer cabins (the novel *Deliverance* was a thinly-disguised portrait of life along the Coosawatee River in Gilmer and Murray Counties, though the movie was filmed on the Chattooga River in Rabun County). In time, textile mills began springing up along the railroads, poultry production became a big business around Gainesville, and in Dalton the craft tradition of tufted bedspread handiwork was transformed into the world's largest carpet industry, producing 60% of the world's tufted carpet. But these were low-wage industries and all white; there had never been many slaves here and there are few blacks here today.

Since the 1980s, there has been a rush of change. Interstate highways have brought north Georgia in easy range of the world-city of Atlanta; the carpet industry has become more high-tech; small manufacturing is booming, with higher-skill work replacing low-tech mills; vacation and retirement communities have been built in mountains and around lakes. Agribusiness remains important, with huge poultry processors in Hall County around Gainesville. The carpet industry still plays a key economic role, too: The area economy is vulnerable to fluctuations in new construction activity. Once rural counties are now part of the booming ring around Atlanta, and Lake Sidney Lanier, named for the 19th century poet who wrote *Song of the Chattahoochee*, is filled with vacation and second homes and is the most visited lake served by the Army Corps of Engineers. So tight are the labor markets that tens of thousands of Latinos from Mexico and other Latin countries have come to Dalton, Gainesville, and the area around to snap up the jobs the boom is creating. This area 1,200 miles from the border now has three times as many Hispanics as blacks, and the apparent surge of illegal immigrants that has rescued the carpet industry also has strained local services. Debate continued over a highway, similar to the controversial Northern Arc road, to link I-75 and I-85, which would cross Forsyth County plus three other north Georgia counties.

The 9th Congressional District covers most of northwest Georgia. Its northern tier of counties borders North Carolina, Tennessee and Alabama, much of it in the Chattanooga—not the Atlanta—media market. Here are some of the few mountainous parts of Georgia, where within living memory the major product was moonshine whiskey and which in the days of the Democratic Solid South had a robust two-party politics. The district reaches south to the outer reaches of metro Atlanta to include most of Forsyth County, which grew by 53% between 2000 and 2006—the fifth fastest-growing county in the nation. The 2005 redistricting renumbered this seat from the 10th to the 9th and gave it a more compact and logical shape. It retains Gainesville and Hall County but lost a thin strip of counties on the east edge of metro Atlanta—Gwinnett, Walton, Rockdale—and added rural Lumpkin, Union and White Counties toward the northeast corner of Georgia. Today the Democratic history of most of this region is forgotten and this is a solidly Republican area in national and state elections. Under both the old and new boundaries, Bush got 77% here in 2004, his biggest margin in Georgia and one of his largest in the nation.

The congressman from the 9th District is Nathan Deal, first elected in 1992 as a Democrat, who switched parties and became a Republican in April 1995. Deal grew up in Gainesville, went to Mercer University, then served in the Army from 1966-68; he returned home to practice "street level law," with offices always on the ground floor, and public offices a young lawyer takes as civic duty: Assistant district attorney, juvenile court judge, county attorney. In 1980, at 38, he was elected to the state Senate as a Democrat. Jimmy Carter was still president, the legislature was overwhelmingly Democratic; it would have been quixotic to run as a Republican. A capable legislator, he twice was elected Senate president pro tem. In 1992, when boll weevil Democrat Ed Jenkins retired from Congress, Deal ran and defeated a Republican abortion opponent with 59% of the vote.

In the House, Deal opposed the new Clinton administration's economic policies, voting against the 1993 budget, for the line-item veto and balanced budget amendment. Many saw Deal as a potential party-switcher, but while campaigning in 1994 he said, "If I choose to switch during the term, I think the honest thing to do is resign and have a special election." He beat an underfunded Republican, but with a slightly lower percentage than two years before. In early 1995, he worked with other Democrats to offer an alternative to the Republicans' welfare reform package. On April 3, Deal said how pleased he was by Democrats' support for that plan. Two days later, he was unhappy with Democrats' opposition to tax cuts and with senior Democrats' criticisms of Clean Water Act revisions he had won on a bipartisan committee vote. On April 10, back home in Gainesville, Deal announced he was a Republican—but he did not resign and run in a special election. He said the national Democratic Party was unwilling to admit it was "out of touch with mainstream America," and "I think that it is important that at some point you get away from the schizophrenia I have had to deal with." Democrats were stunned, and Newt Gingrich was clearly delighted; Deal was rewarded with a seat on the Energy and Commerce Committee.

Deal's voting record is mostly conservative, with an occasional split on foreign issues. Although he has not been a reflexive Republican, he has not made dramatic breaks from the party line either. He repeatedly filed a bill to cut up to 10% of congressional salaries if the budget is not balanced. Working with the Federation for American Immigration Reform, he sponsored higher penalties for illegal aliens plus citizenship restrictions on their U.S.-born children, and he opposed the Bush administration's study of legalization of immigrants from Mexico. On the Immigration Reform Caucus, he led efforts to define birthright citizenship. But Deal made some accommodation to a district with a rapidly growing Hispanic population by backing increased spending for bilingual education; a majority of school children in Dalton are Hispanic. On the Telecommunications and the Internet Subcommittee, he was the leading proponent of "a la carte" proposals to give cable television subscribers greater choice. He called his plan "a step toward protecting the American family from indecency;" opponents said that the proposal could lead to higher prices and fewer programming choices. As chairman of the Health Subcommittee in 2005, he assembled $11 billion in Medicaid cuts over five years, including elimination of prescription coverage for Viagra. "Taxpayers are willing to pay for somebody's heart medication, but they are not going to buy their beer or their Viagra."

Deal has not faced serious primary or general election opposition since he switched parties in 1995.

TENTH DISTRICT

Rep. Paul Broun (R)

Elected July 2007, 1st term; b. May 14, 1946, Atlanta; home, Athens; U. of GA, B.S.1967; Medical Col. of GA, M.D. 1971; Baptist; married (Niki Bronson).

Military Career: Marine Corps Reserves, 1964-1967; Naval Reserves, 1967-1973; GA Air Natl. Guard, 1972-1973; Air Force Reserves, 1973-1988.

Professional Career: Practicing physician, 1971-present; owner, Travel and Adventure, 1985-92.

DC Office: 2104 RHOB, 20515, 202-225-4101; Fax: 202-226-0776; Web site: broun.house.gov.

District Offices: Toccoa, 706-886-1008.

Committees: *Homeland Security* (15th of 15 R): Emerging Threats, Cybersecurity & Science and Technology; Transportation Security & Infrastructure Protection. *Science & Technology* (20th of 20 R).

Group Ratings and Key Votes: Newly Elected

Election Results

2007 spec. runoff	Paul Broun (R)	23,529	(50%)
	Jim Whitehead (R)	23,135	(50%)
2007 special	Jim Whitehead (R)	23,555	(44%)
	Paul Broun (R)	11,208	(21%)
	James Marlow (D)	11,010	(20%)
	Other	5,790	(11%)
	Denise Freeman (D)	2,574	(5%)
2006 general	Charlie Norwood (R)	117,721	(67%)
	Terry Holley (D)	57,032	(33%)
2006 primary	Charlie Norwood (R)	unopposed	($1,158,294)
2004 general (GA 9)	Charlie Norwood (R)	197,869	(74%) ($905,590)
	Bob Ellis (D)	68,462	(26%) ($113,330)

The People		Race/Ethnic Origin	Ancestry	
Area size:	6,061 sq. mi.	74.0% White	USA: 14.3%	English: 8.0%
Urban population:	50.4%	19.8% Black	Irish: 7.3%	
Rural population:	49.6%	1.6% Asian	**2004 Presidential Vote**	
Pop. 2000:	629,728	0.2% Native Am.	Bush (R) 168,831	(65%)
Median income:	$36,615	0.1% Hawaiian	Kerry (D) 90,304	(35%)
Poverty status:	14.8%	1.0% Two+ races	Other 1,547	(1%)
Military veterans:	13.1%	0.1% Other	**2000 Presidential Vote**	
		3.3% Hispanic Origin	Bush (R) 126,960	(63%)
			Gore (D) 75,238	(37%)
			Cook Partisan Voting Index: R +13	

Occupation	Blue collar: 29.5%	White collar: 55.7%	Gray collar: 14.8%

Northeastern Georgia is a land where the coastal plains and cotton fields yield first to gently rolling hills, then finally near the North Carolina border to the Appalachian Mountains. For most of its history, this has been quiet rural country, with courthouse towns and a few small cities, mostly forgotten by national elites, bypassed even by General Sherman on his march to the sea. But in the last two decades, economic growth has radiated outward from Atlanta and has spread across much of the region. The effects can be seen as far away as the old city of Augusta, on the Savannah River across from South Carolina. Founded in 1735, with an old Cotton Exchange and mansions untouched by Sherman, it is rich in history. It is also a center for newer industries, which are replacing the paper industry and the nuclear industry that has abandoned the Savannah River weapons site over the border in South Carolina. Augusta is best known as the home of the Augusta National Golf Club, the site of the Masters tournament every year, its entrance barely visible off four-lane Washington Road. The city also houses the Army base at Fort Gordon and it has become a site for Hollywood film production.

The 10th Congressional District of Georgia includes much of the northeast corner of the state. It includes about 40% of Augusta in Richmond County, but not heavily black precincts in Augusta itself. The 2005 redistricting renumbered this seat from the 9th to the 10th and added Clarke County and the liberal enclave of Athens, site of the gracious campus of the University of Georgia since 1801 and home to the rock bands R.E.M. and the B-52s, graceful Greek Revival mansions, boxwood gardens and magnolias. This was a key alteration for the addition of Athens to the 10th District undermined Democratic prospects in the neighboring 12th District. Clarke and Richmond Counties are now the two largest population centers here. Columbia County, next to Augusta, and Oconee County, next to Athens, are particularly affluent and rapidly growing; the Lake Oconee area has close to 100 subdivisions and developments, marked by gated communities and golf courses that beckon to 2nd home buyers and retirees. Voters here prefer traditional values: several counties recently rejected ballot propositions to end prohibition of alcohol. The redistricting changes increased the black population from 14% to 20%, but this remains a solidly Republican district in national politics. The vote for President Bush in 2004 dropped from 72% to 65%.

The new congressman from the 10th District is Paul Broun Jr., a Republican who was the surprise winner of a special election to fill this seat following the February 2007 death of Republican incumbent Charlie Norwood. Born in Atlanta, Broun is a lifelong Georgia resident who got his bachelor's degree from the University of Georgia and his medical degree from the Medical College of Georgia in Augusta. His father, Paul Broun Sr., was a state senator for 38 years, serving as a moderate Democrat from Athens.

The younger Paul Broun was also active in politics, though he has said that he was "far, far apart on the issues" from his father. He served as president of the Georgia Sport Shooting Association (an affiliate of the National Rifle Association) and as vice president of political action for Safari Club International, a national advocacy group for hunters. But his record as a candidate suggests he lacks his father's politicking skills. He first ran for the House in 1990 against Democratic incumbent Richard Ray in the old 3d District, which was then based in west-central Georgia; Ray won 63%-37%. After redistricting two years later, Broun ran in the revamped and more Republican 3d District south of Atlanta; he lost the primary 55%-45% to Mac Collins, who held the seat for 12 years. In 1996, Broun closed his medical practice to campaign full-time for a year for Georgia's open Senate seat. He was vastly outspent, and finished a distant fourth in the primary with an anemic 3%, well behind Guy Millner, who led with 42%, and now-Senator Johnny Isakson, who won 35%. Millner went on to defeat Isakson in the runoff but lost 49%-48% to Democrat Max Cleland; Isakson would later win election to Georgia's other Senate seat in 2004.

There was little doubt that a Republican would succeed Norwood in this conservative district, but few would have predicted that Broun would be that Republican. State Senator Jim Whitehead entered the special election contest early and became the frontrunner after state Senator Ralph Hudgens of Athens reversed his plans to run in mid-March. Whitehead had attended the University of Georgia, where he was a star offensive lineman for the football team. He returned home to the Augusta area, where he opened a tire and auto shop, served seven years on the Columbia County Commission—the final two as chairman—and won a state Senate seat in 2004. Norwood had encouraged him to run for that seat and the two had held fundraisers together. Whitehead often mentioned their friendship while campaigning to succeed him and got the endorsement of Norwood's widow Gloria in June.

The seat seemed to be his to lose, which is exactly what he did. He avoided debates and committed several gaffes, including the remark that, "Iraq has not been a big thing in our district." He also was forced to explain a 2004 comment that dismissed the University of Georgia as a "bunch of liberals" that, except for the football team, ought to be bombed. Whitehead said illegal immigration was the number one issue in the campaign but his approach led critics to complain he was insufficiently vigorous in his opposition. In the June 19 special election, he won 44%, ahead of Broun who won 21%, but not enough to avoid a runoff. Broun barely squeezed into the runoff against Whitehead: he finished 198 votes ahead of Democrat James Marlow, a former Yahoo executive, who came in third with 20%.

Whitehead got 69% in Columbia County, the district's second–largest county, but he won barely 10% in the largest, Democratic-leaning Clarke County. This was a sign of trouble for Whitehead in the July 17 runoff as the race turned into contest between candidates representing the district's two population centers, Augusta and Athens, with Whitehead serving as the Augusta-area candidate and Broun serving as the Athens designee. Broun touted his medical background, claiming he was perhaps the only physician in Georgia who regularly made house calls. "I've got an old-fashioned medical bag," he said. "My office is my GMC Yukon." Broun said he opposed any steps to permit illegal immigrants to gain legal status, highlighted his connections to Christian conservatives on social issues, and also reached out to African-Americans and other Democrats, especially in Athens. Whitehead talked up his Augusta-area roots and complained about his Athens-based opposition. Whitehead had a considerable advantage in campaign dollars, but Broun skillfully exploited Whitehead's assertion that it was an Athens-versus-Augusta contest to win with 50.4%, just 394 votes ahead of Whitehead, who had 49.6%. Broun carried Athens's Clarke County with a remarkable 90%, while holding Whitehead to 73% in Columbia County, and won 12 other counties; Whitehead's strength was confined mostly to the Augusta area. The race was close enough that there was a one-week delay in certifying the vote; Whitehead decided not to press for a recount.

Hours after he was sworn into the House, Broun expressed his libertarian instincts by voting for an amendment to bar the Justice Department from prosecuting the use of marijuana for medicinal purposes. He called the vote "a constitutional issue pertaining to 'restraining' the federal government from interfering with the rights of the states," and joined 14 other Republicans backing the proposal, which was defeated, 165-262. Back home, Republicans expected that he would receive a competitive primary challenge in 2008; state House Majority Whip Barry Fleming of Augusta seemed a likely opponent.

ELEVENTH DISTRICT

Rep. Phil Gingrey (R)

Elected 2002, 3d term; b. July 10, 1942, Augusta; home, Marietta; GA Inst. of Tech., B.S. 1965, Med. Col. of GA, M.D. 1969; Catholic; married (Billie).

Elected Office: Marietta Schl. Bd., 1993-97; GA Senate, 1998-2002.

Professional Career: Practicing obstetrician, 1976-present.

DC Office: 119 CHOB, 20515, 202-225-2931; Fax: 202-225-2944; Web site: www.house.gov/gingrey/.

District Offices: Cartersville, 678-721-2509; Marietta, 770-429-1776; Rome, 706-290-1776.

Committees: *Armed Services* (21st of 29 R): Oversight & Investigations; Air & Land Forces. *Science & Technology* (17th of 20 R): Technology & Innovation (RMM).

Group Ratings

	ADA	ACLU	AFS	LCV	ITIC	NTU	COC	ACU	CFG	FRC
2006	5	0	0	0	71	68	87	92	78	100
2005	0	—	0	6	—	59	89	100	62	92

National Journal Ratings

	2005 LIB	—	2005 CONS		2006 LIB	—	2006 CONS
Economic	14%	—	83%		0%	—	98%
Social	0%	—	89%		17%	—	79%
Foreign	16%	—	83%		30%	—	67%

Key Votes of the 109th Congress

1. Estate Tax Repeal	Y	5. Limit Interstate Abortion	Y	9. Build Border Fence	Y
2. Limit CAFE Standards	Y	6. Extend Patriot Act	Y	10. CAFTA	Y
3. FY06 Spending Curb	Y	7. Bar Same Sex Marriage	Y	11. Oppose Iraq Withdrawal	Y
4. Drilling in ANWR	Y	8. Stem Cell Research $	N	12. Detainee Tribunals	Y

Election Results

2006 general	Phil Gingrey (R)	118,524	(71%)	($1,011,322)
	Patrick Pillion (D)	48,261	(29%)	($3,318)
2006 primary	Phil Gingrey (R) .... unopposed			
2004 general	Phil Gingrey (R)	120,696	(57%)	($2,254,633)
	Rick Crawford (D)	89,591	(43%)	($280,307)

Prior Winning Percentages: 2002 (52%)

The People		Race/Ethnic Origin	Ancestry	
Area size:	2,718 sq. mi.	80.4% White	USA: 15.8%	Irish: 8.1%
Urban population:	70.4%	11.7% Black	English: 7.6%	
Rural population:	29.6%	1.3% Asian	**2004 Presidential Vote**	
Pop. 2000:	629,727	0.2% Native Am.	Bush (R) 183,750	(71%)
Median income:	$45,710	0.0% Hawaiian	Kerry (D) 74,268	(29%)
Poverty status:	9.8%	1.0% Two+ races	Other 1,569	(1%)
Military veterans:	12.5%	0.1% Other	**2000 Presidential Vote**	
		5.1% Hispanic Origin	Bush (R) 128,971	(65%)
			Gore (D) 68,073	(35%)
			Cook Partisan Voting Index: R + 17	

Occupation	Blue collar: 29.2%	White collar: 58.2%	Gray collar: 12.6%

Northwest Georgia, home of the Cherokee Nation before they were sent west in the 1830s on the Trail of Tears, has been manufacturing country for the last century. There were once hundreds of textile mills and dozens of carpet mills located near the supply of natural cotton and along the railroad lines heading southwest at the base of the southern Appalachian chain. The late 19th century propagandists of the New South hailed factories as the vanguard of technological progress, and in fact the factories produced a higher standard of living than farms on this stubborn land. But mill work put scant premium on education or the cultivation of civic virtues and did little to bring in higher-skill white-collar work. All-white hiring practices maintained racial segregation in mostly white north Georgia. Today, this area is developing a different kind of economy, as metro Atlanta spreads out highways north and west into sprawling subdivisions in what once were mill towns. Floyd County is home to an auto-parts manufacturing cluster, in addition to the carpet mills of Rome, where Latino immigrants have become a major part of the workforce.

The 11th Congressional District of Georgia includes much of this part of the state, taking in small industrial towns and rural cotton, poultry and cattle-producing areas and a cluster of older suburbs around Atlanta. It stretches from Rome in the north to suburban Marietta, which is about 15 miles up I-75 from Atlanta and where Lockheed Martin builds the F-22 Raptor and the C-130 cargo plane. West of Atlanta is Carrollton, once the home of an untenured West Georgia College professor who in his third try became a Republican congressman: Newt Gingrich. The district includes all of Rome and Kennesaw, most of Marietta and part of Carrollton. In 2002, Democrats drew the absurdly shaped 11th District to target controversial Republican Congressman Bob Barr. But he decided to run instead in the new 7th District, very little of which he had represented, and lost in the Republican primary to fellow incumbent John Linder. The 2005 redistricting made the 11th significantly more compact (it's more than 1,000 square miles smaller than the previous version) and more Republican, by drawing lines to include the northern part of Cobb County, all of exurban Bartow County and all of Paulding County, which was the ninth fastest-growing county in the nation between 2000 and 2006. The changes shifted many African-American precincts of Cobb County to the 13th District and reduced the black share in the new 11th from 28% to 12%; the result considerably altered the partisan composition, changing this from a somewhat competitive seat to one that is probably out of reach for Democrats.

The congressman from the 11th is Republican Phil Gingrey, an obstetrician first elected in his party's sweep of Georgia in 2002. Gingrey grew up in Augusta, graduated from Georgia Tech, and returned home to attend the Medical College of Georgia. After his medical training in Georgia hospitals, he settled in Marietta, where he set up an obstetrics and gynecology practice and delivered more than 5,200 babies. During his spare time, he served on the local school board, and was chosen as chairman. In 1998, he was elected to the state Senate, where he had a reputation as a staunch social conservative but one who could work with Democrats on other issues. When Bob Barr decided not to run in the 11th, Gingrey got into the race, and faced tough competition in both the primary and general election. The issue differences were small among the three candidates in the Republican primary. Gingrey, who is Catholic, styled himself as the only native Georgian. Cecil Staton, an ordained Baptist minister, vowed to view all legislation from the perspective of the traditional family. In the primary, Gingrey won 40% of the vote to 32% for Staton and 28% for Bob Herriott, a pilot for Delta Airlines. The bitter September runoff revolved around their respective religions and allegations by Staton that Gingrey supported homosexual causes. Voters who knew Gingrey from his state Senate tenure didn't buy it; he won 64%-36%, carrying every county. The Democrats, meanwhile, had their own brawl featuring former Congressman (1983-1995) Buddy Darden, and Roger Kahn, a millionaire beer distributor who in 2000 lost to Barr 55%-45%. Kahn won, 52%-48%. In the general, Kahn accused Gingrey of seeking special favors for cocaine-dealing felons and violent criminals who had assaulted police officers. He spent $2.8 million from his own pocket, and complained that national Democrats did not give him more help. Spending $600,000 of his own money, Gingrey portrayed Kahn as a wealthy liquor distributor posing as a modest farmer. With a boost from the Georgia Republican tide and the National Republican Congressional Committee, Gingrey won 52%-48%.

In the House, Gingrey became an active member of the majority and had a mostly conservative voting record. In May 2003, the House passed his bill authorizing funding to agencies that aid runaway and homeless youths; it also funded George W. Bush's initiative to create maternal group homes. After Bush signed it into law in October, Gingrey claimed he was the first freshman that year to get substantive legislation passed. In dozens of local town hall meetings, he enthusiastically supported the new prescription drug benefit for seniors, which he said should end "the days of forgoing, rationing and splitting pills." He sought and failed to get a seat on the Ways and Means Committee in 2005, but got a seat instead on the Rules Committee. Insisting that there are "no throwaway lives," he opposed embryonic stem cell research. He helped to organize the Medical and Dental Doctors Caucus, which would offer its services during a catastrophe on Capitol Hill. After receiving assurances on protection for the textile industry, he voted for the Central American Free Trade Agreement. In February 2006, Gingrey lost a bid for the chairmanship of the Republican Policy Committee. In the minority, he lost his seat on Rules and shifted back to the Armed Services Committee, where he has been an avid booster of Lockheed's Marietta plant.

Democrats claimed they would seriously contest Gingrey in 2004 but he had an easier than expected reelection. He raised $2.3 million, much of it from the medical community. The campaign of his opponent, conservative Democrat Rick Crawford, failed to impress national Democrats. Gingrey won 57%-43%, but he lost Cobb County 52%-48%, evidently because of the increased number of black voters there. The Republican-controlled redistricting in early 2005 took care of that problem and shored up Gingrey by giving him all of Bartow County. With the removal of much of south Cobb County from his district, he won 71%-29% in 2006 and now may be immune from another serious Democratic challenge.

TWELFTH DISTRICT

Rep. John Barrow (D)

Elected 2004, 2d term; b. Oct. 31, 1955, Athens; home, Savannah; U. of GA, B.A. 1976, Harvard U., J.D. 1979; Baptist; married (Victoria).

Elected Office: Athens-Clarke City-Co. comm., 1990-2004.

Professional Career: Practicing atty, 1981-2004.

DC Office: 213 CHOB, 20515, 202-225-2823; Fax: 202-225-3377; Web site: www.house.gov/barrow.

District Offices: Augusta, 706-722-4494; Sandersville, 478-553-1923; Savannah, 912-354-7282; Vidalia, 912-537-9301.

Committees: *Agriculture* (22d of 25 D): Horticulture & Organic Agriculture; Specialty Crops, Rural Development & Foreign Agriculture. *Energy & Commerce* (30th of 31 D): Energy & Air Quality; Commerce, Trade & Consumer Protection; Environment & Hazardous Materials.

Group Ratings

	ADA	ACLU	AFS	LCV	ITIC	NTU	COC	ACU	CFG	FRC
2006	45	36	43	50	43	30	87	76	38	71
2005	75	—	75	78	—	21	56	40	20	62

National Journal Ratings

	2005 LIB	—	2005 CONS		2006 LIB	—	2006 CONS
Economic	62%	—	38%		54%	—	46%
Social	52%	—	48%		49%	—	51%
Foreign	53%	—	47%		52%	—	47%

Key Votes of the 109th Congress

1. Estate Tax Repeal	Y	5. Limit Interstate Abortion	Y	9. Build Border Fence	Y
2. Limit CAFE Standards	N	6. Extend Patriot Act	Y	10. CAFTA	N
3. FY06 Spending Curb	N	7. Bar Same Sex Marriage	Y	11. Oppose Iraq Withdrawal	Y
4. Drilling in ANWR	N	8. Stem Cell Research $	Y	12. Detainee Tribunals	Y

Election Results

2006 general	John Barrow (D)	71,651	(50%)	($2,265,762)
	Max Burns (R)	70,787	(50%)	($2,173,231)
2006 primary	John Barrow (D)	unopposed		
2004 general	John Barrow (D)	113,036	(52%)	($1,866,177)
	Max Burns (R)	105,132	(48%)	($2,798,725)

The People		Race/Ethnic Origin	Ancestry	
Area size:	8,734 sq. mi.	50.8% White	USA: 12.1%	Irish: 5.0%
Urban population:	59.9%	44.5% Black	English: 4.8%	
Rural population:	40.1%	0.8% Asian	**2004 Presidential Vote**	
Pop. 2000:	629,727	0.2% Native Am.	Bush (R) 112,735	(50%)
Median income:	$30,383	0.0% Hawaiian	Kerry (D) 110,192	(49%)
Poverty status:	21.9%	0.9% Two+ races	Other 871	(0%)
Military veterans:	13.6%	0.1% Other	**2000 Presidential Vote**	
		2.7% Hispanic Origin	Gore (D) 92,527	(52%)
			Bush (R) 84,605	(48%)
			Cook Partisan Voting Index: D + 2	

Occupation	Blue collar: 31.5%	White collar: 48.9%	Gray collar: 19.6%

In Georgia, the focus is usually on Atlanta. But Georgia also has some gracious smaller cities, with roots deep in the past. One is Savannah, the state's first capital, which by the 1830s was one of America's booming cotton ports; it languished after the Civil War, living off paper mills and chemical plants in the 20th century, while impoverished blacks on the islands a few miles away still spoke Gullah dialects. Then, a few decades ago, preservationists started restoring houses and churches on the grid punctuated by 24 squares that James Oglethorpe had laid out more than 200 years before. Today Savannah is one of the most graciously preserved cities in the country, home to a rollicking annual St. Patrick's Day parade, and a major tourism destination thanks to the popularity of John Berendt's *Midnight in the Garden of Good and Evil*, a somewhat-based-on-facts story of eccentricity and murder on the bestseller lists for four years in the 1990s. The city actively competes with neighboring—and equally well-preserved—Charleston, South Carolina, not only for tourists but for shipping. Another such city is Augusta, upriver on the Savannah River, founded in 1735 as a fur-trading post, home of the Medical College of Georgia since 1835 and boyhood home of President Woodrow Wilson, with its own Cotton Exchange and Riverwalk.

The 12th Congressional District of Georgia, newly created by the Democratic redistricting of 2001, runs along the Savannah River and combines almost all of Savannah (but only some of its suburbs) and about 60% of Augusta (but not much of its suburbs). It contains the Depression-wracked farm country near Augusta that Erskine Caldwell chronicled in his scandalous bestseller, *Tobacco Road*; the titular dirt thoroughfare, which led to a small port on the Savannah River, is now paved and passes a nondescript mix of residential and commercial areas. The 2005 redistricting removed from the 12th a narrow but politically meaningful finger that extended to Clarke County and the relatively liberal enclave of the University of Georgia campus at Athens and added 11 rural counties that extend toward central Georgia. The district was originally designed in 2001 to elect a Democrat from rural Georgia but the current iteration makes the 12th a good bit more competitive, even though the Democratic-voting black population actually increased from 42% to 45%. These new changes shifted the 2004 vote from 54%-46% for John Kerry to 50.4%-49.2% for George W. Bush.

The congressman from the 12th District is Democrat John Barrow, who was one of only two successful challengers to House Republican incumbents in 2004. Barrow claims seven generations of Georgians in his family; his father handled school desegregation cases as a lawyer and as a Superior Court judge in the Athens area. A graduate of the University of Georgia and Harvard Law School, Barrow became a trial lawyer who made his name in local politics by winning four terms as an Athens-Clarke city-county commissioner. In 2004 he decided to run against Republican Max Burns, who had won an upset victory in 2002. In that win, Burns ran a vigorous campaign but he had help from the flawed Democratic candidate Charles "Champ" Walker Jr., whose credibility eroded after local newspapers reported a past littered with failed business ventures and run-ins with the law. Burns won 55%-45%, but was an obvious Democratic target in 2004 and House Republican leaders gave him all the help they could.

Barrow worked hard to win. Although most Democratic voters here are black, all four candidates in the Democratic primary were white. Barrow raised more than $700,000 and, with the endorsements of former Senator Max Cleland, the Sierra Club and the Georgia AFL-CIO, extended his appeal beyond his home base. He won 51% of the vote and all 14 counties, enough to avoid a runoff. In the general election, Barrow focused on Burns's support of a national retail sales tax to replace the income tax; he attacked the proposal as a tax increase that "just doesn't add up for Georgia families," and labeled it "the Max Tax." Burns replied that Barrow distorted the proposal; he called Barrow a "liberal trial attorney" controlled by "Atlanta party bosses," who "would let France determine our national defense policy." Barrow criticized Burns for supporting the Medicare prescription drug bill and ran an ad that claimed Burns had cut funding for Georgia's rural hospitals. Barrow distanced himself from John Kerry and the national Democratic party. Burns sought to turn the focus to same-sex marriage, an issue on which Barrow struggled to find a consistent position; this debate occurred against the backdrop of a proposed state constitutional amendment banning same-sex marriage that was approved overwhelmingly on the November ballot. But this was not enough to save Burns. He ran well in rural areas but Barrow won big margins among the heavily black electorates in the three counties which cast two-thirds of the district's votes—62% in Richmond, 58% in Chatham, and 58% in Clarke. Overall, Barrow won 52%-48%.

In the House, Barrow had a moderate voting record. He filed a bill to give tax credits equal to 50% of an employer's health insurance costs. He frequently broke with Democratic leaders. In May 2006 he voted for the Republican lobbying reform measure; he took a hard line against illegal immigrants and cast votes in early 2007 against proposals to limit war funding in Iraq. Democratic leaders gave him an upfront role in pushing for an increase in the minimum wage and farm disaster aid. In 2007, he gained a seat on the powerful Energy and Commerce Committee.

Barrow's political life was made more difficult by the 2005 redistricting, which moved his Clarke County base into the heavily Republican 10th District. He said that he would run in the new district that included the largest part of his former district, which turned out to be the 12th. Burns announced in May 2005 that he would run for his redesigned seat, declaring that the new district had no incumbent and preempting the Republican field. Barrow moved his residence to Savannah and emphasized his independence. "No boss, no leader, no caucus can tell me how to vote. And none of them has." Burns, who got fundraising help and two campaign visits from George W. Bush, criticized national Democratic themes and said that Barrow was ineffective. Barrow responded with ads that he agreed with Bush—and against Burns—in opposing a national sales tax. They disagreed over global warming, abortion policy, and photo identification requirements for voters. The outcome was even closer this time, and Burns took nine days before conceding. In his 50.3%-49.7% win, Barrow won only 8 of 22 counties but he rolled up 62% in Chatham and 65% in Richmond, the two largest counties. In a warning for Barrow, the 11 new counties in the district cast almost 30% of the vote and went to Burns 55%-45%.

THIRTEENTH DISTRICT

Rep. David Scott (D)

Elected 2002, 3d term; b. June 27, 1946, Aynor, SC; home, Atlanta; FLA&M U., B.A. 1967, U. of PA, M.B.A. 1969; Baptist; married (Alfredia).

Elected Office: GA House of Reps., 1974-82; GA Senate, 1982-2002.

Professional Career: Founder and Pres., Dayn-Mark Advertising, 1979-present.

DC Office: 417 CHOB, 20515, 202-225-2939; Fax: 202-225-4628; Web site: house.gov/davidscott.

District Offices: Jonesboro, 770-210-5073; Smyrna, 770-432-5405.

Committees: *Agriculture* (8th of 25 D): General Farm Commodities & Risk Management; Conservation, Credit, Energy & Research. *Financial Services* (20th of 37 D): Capital Markets, Insurance & Government Sponsored Enterprises; Financial Institutions & Consumer Credit. *Foreign Affairs* (23d of 27 D): Terrorism, Nonproliferation & Trade; Middle East & South Asia.

Group Ratings

	ADA	ACLU	AFS	LCV	ITIC	NTU	COC	ACU	CFG	FRC
2006	85	68	86	75	43	17	60	32	17	42
2005	80	—	100	56	—	19	74	38	13	31

National Journal Ratings

	2005 LIB	—	2005 CONS		2006 LIB	—	2006 CONS
Economic	58%	—	41%		62%	—	38%
Social	58%	—	42%		63%	—	37%
Foreign	64%	—	36%		64%	—	35%

Key Votes of the 109th Congress

1. Estate Tax Repeal	Y	5. Limit Interstate Abortion	N	9. Build Border Fence	N
2. Limit CAFE Standards	Y	6. Extend Patriot Act	Y	10. CAFTA	N
3. FY06 Spending Curb	N	7. Bar Same Sex Marriage	Y	11. Oppose Iraq Withdrawal	N
4. Drilling in ANWR	N	8. Stem Cell Research $	Y	12. Detainee Tribunals	Y

Election Results

2006 general	David Scott (D)	103,019	(69%)	($1,364,825)
	Deborah Honeycutt (R)	45,770	(31%)	($1,319,909)
2006 primary	David Scott (D)	29,179	(67%)	
	Donzella James (D)	14,157	(33%)	
2004 general	David Scott (D)	unopposed		($980,333)

Prior Winning Percentages: 2002 (60%)

The People		Race/Ethnic Origin	Ancestry	
Area size:	577 sq. mi.	46.7% White	USA: 8.7%	Irish: 5.8%
Urban population:	96.6%	41.0% Black	English: 5.1%	
Rural population:	3.4%	2.8% Asian	**2004 Presidential Vote**	
Pop. 2000:	629,727	0.2% Native Am.	Kerry (D) 144,870 (60%)	
Median income:	$46,477	0.0% Hawaiian	Bush (R) 96,393 (40%)	
Poverty status:	8.8%	1.4% Two+ races	Other 1,200 (0%)	
Military veterans:	13.7%	0.2% Other	**2000 Presidential Vote**	
		7.6% Hispanic Origin	Gore (D) 105,521 (57%)	
			Bush (R) 80,699 (43%)	
			Cook Partisan Voting Index: D +10	

Occupation	Blue collar: 26.0%	White collar: 60.7%	Gray collar: 13.4%

Many great landmarks of the civil rights movements, the headquarters of major civil rights organizations and the campuses of six historically black colleges are all in the central city of Atlanta. The city's cohesive and talented black community, more than any other, provided the leadership and inspiration for the civil rights movement that changed America so much for the better. In the 1960s, Atlanta's blacks were clustered in ghetto neighborhoods on the south and west side of the city; the north side of Atlanta and the suburbs in every direction were heavily or entirely white. Today, a long generation after the great days of the civil rights movement, blacks have moved outward from Atlanta in almost all directions in one of the nation's fastest-growing metro areas. The central city of Atlanta has an increasing white percentage, as whites move into affluent Buckhead and the thriving communities of Midtown Atlanta, while the crime-ridden ghettoes in south and west Atlanta lose population. But this is a story not of failure but of success: members of metro Atlanta's thriving black middle class have been moving elsewhere in the metro area—to south DeKalb County to the east, to Clayton County directly south of the city and Hartsfield-Jackson Atlanta International Airport, to southwest Fulton County outside Atlanta, to eastern and southern Cobb and Douglas Counties to the west.

The 13th Congressional District of Georgia, newly created in the 2001 redistricting, is a collection of areas into which Atlanta-area African-Americans have been moving or are likely to be moving in the next 10 years—Sweet Auburn marching south and west to the suburbs. Its nucleus is Clayton County, heavily dependent on the airport and almost all of which is in the district: a county that voted for George Wallace in 1968 but now has the highest black percentage of any metro Atlanta county. Its small slice of Fulton County includes the headquarters of Home Depot. Prior to the 2005 redistricting, the original boundaries could rightfully be depicted as the most geographically grotesque district in the country. The new shape is much more coherent. The biggest change was the addition of Cobb County; now Cobb and Clayton Counties each contain about one-third of the district population and the rest are parceled out across DeKalb, Douglas, Fulton and Henry Counties. Even with all of the changes, the 13th remained 41% black and heavily Democratic.

The congressman from the 13th District is David Scott, a Democrat first elected in 2002. Born in rural South Carolina, he grew up around the country—in Scranton, Pennsylvania, Scarsdale, New York, and Daytona Beach, Florida. He graduated from Florida A&M and the Wharton School of Finance. He was elected to the Georgia House in 1974 and to the Georgia Senate in 1982; there he chaired the Rules Committee. Since 1979 he has owned the Dayn-Mark Advertising Company, which creates and places radio, television and print advertising; the firm is now operated by his wife and two daughters.

In 2002 Scott ran for the newly-created 13th District seat, though he lived near Midtown Atlanta. It was obvious that the primary would be decisive in this heavily Democratic district. Four other Democrats ran; the best known was former state party chairman David Worley, who nearly defeated Newt Gingrich in 1990. Scott, however, was far more familiar to most voters, after more than a quarter-century in the legislature. His brother-in-law Hank Aaron, baseball's true home run king and an Atlanta icon, co-chaired his campaign. Scott brought his advertising expertise to the campaign, plastering the Interstates with eye-catching billboards—a clever idea in a district that closely tracked Atlanta's Perimeter. His chief competitors, Worley and state Senator Greg Hecht of Clayton County, were both white, and ran ads against each other; racial appeals seem to have played little part in the campaign. Scott won the primary without a runoff, with 54% of the vote and at least 50% in every county but one. The son of a minister and grandson of a deacon, Scott credited God and said that "a divine hand worked with us." He won the general election 60%-40%—not a huge margin, but a decisive one.

In the House, Scott's voting record was far more centrist than that of an Atlanta liberal. His business background and nearly three decades' experience in representing multiracial, multiethnic constituencies were unique credentials to bring to the Congressional Black Caucus and the House. Scott joined the Blue Dogs group of moderate Democrats, and showed no reluctance about going his own way. In May 2003, he was one of seven House Democrats to vote for final passage of the Bush tax cut. In June 2004, he was one of 11 Democrats who angered their party leaders by joining Republicans on a procedural vote in support of the buyout of tobacco farmers, which Scott helped to write before it reached the House floor. He split with most of his party by voting for the constitutional amendment to ban same-sex marriages. On the Financial Services Committee, Scott criticized predatory lenders that exploit would-be homeowners in poor communities but he was reluctant to pass new laws to eliminate favorable interest deals. He spoke out strongly for extension of the Voting Rights Act and against claims by Georgia Republicans that it had achieved its goals. At home, he hosted annual job and health fairs for constituents.

In 2006, Scott faced a primary challenge from Donzella James, who served 10 years in the state senate and criticized Scott for living outside the district. Scott won 67%-33% and took every county, including 74%-26% in Clayton, which cast the largest vote. In the general, he was opposed by first-time candidate Deborah Honeycutt, a family physician who surprisingly raised $1.3 million, but had little name recognition and unsurprisingly lost 69%-31%.

★ HAWAII ★

Hawaii, geographically the most isolated archipelago in the world, geologically some of the youngest land on earth, is continuing to undergo transformations. These islands were settled by human beings only about 1,000 years ago, when Polynesians paddled across vast Pacific expanses in small outrigger canoes; when Captain Cook came here in 1776, he found his Maori interpreter from New Zealand could understand Hawaiian. On this subtropical land, teeming with food and seldom inconvenienced by bad weather, Hawaiians built a fierce civilization, with harsh taboos and cannibalism as well as alluring music and dance. The islands were united politically in 1779 by King Kamehameha I, who ate one of his rivals and maintained the old culture. In 1819, within a year of his death, his consort Kaahumanu outlawed the Hawaiian religious taboos and welcomed the American missionary Hiram Bingham. New England missionaries and their trader cousins came—while British and Russian ships occasionally put into port—and established the predominant culture. By the 1850s, laborers from China, Japan, Portugal and the Philippines streamed in to work the sugar and pineapple plantations. American planters and businessmen bridled at the caprices of the royal family and, in January 1893, with the help of U.S. Marines, ousted Queen Liliuokalani from the Iolani Palace and called on the United States to annex Hawaii. President Grover Cleveland demurred, and Hawaii for five years was a republic; President William McKinley annexed it in July 1898. This history is a source of regret for some; an *Onipa'a* ceremony remembering Liliuokalani's overthrow was staged by John Waihee, the first governor of Native Hawaiian descent, in January 1993, with the American flag conspicuously absent. Later that year Congress passed and Bill Clinton signed an apology for the overthrow of Liliuokalani 100 years before.

Yet Hawaii is an American civilization in the Pacific, which has created a better life for its citizens than almost any other island or native commonwealth. Its people have not been walled off in ethnic blocs, but have been mixing for the last century, when the native Hawaiian population was down to 45,000, sharing the islands with 3,000 Americans, 20,000 Chinese and 25,000 Japanese. To that Americana, each group has made positive contributions. The Asian migrant laborers brought traditions of hard work, family loyalty and group solidarity that found expression most vividly in the performance of the 442d "Go for Broke" Regimental Combat Team, made up mostly of sons of Japanese immigrants, which became the most decorated unit in U.S. military history. The Yankee spirit has been evident in Hawaii's commercial success and in its attachment to the rule of Anglo-American law. The Hawaiian spirit is apparent in the vitality of the *aloha* ambience, the welcoming of others despite their differences, and a willingness to absorb the teachings of others while maintaining a certain Polynesian attitude toward life. When the Japanese attacked Pearl Harbor in December 1941, no one in Hawaii or on the mainland doubted that this was part of America. It was Hawaii's super-American tolerance that inspired segregationist Southern Democrats to block its admission to the Union for years. Today's Hawaiians can take pride in their ethnic

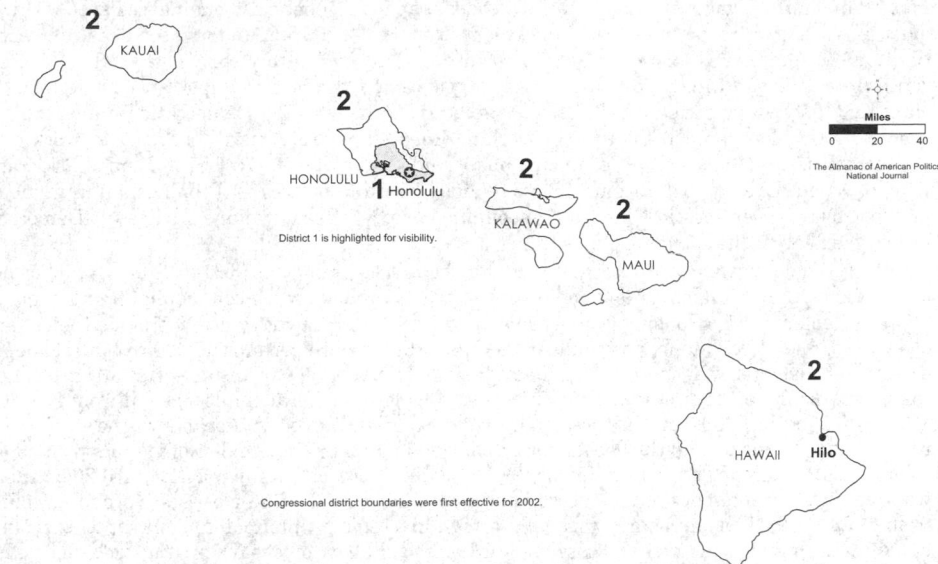

District 1 is highlighted for visibility.

Congressional district boundaries were first effective for 2002.

heritage—or, more likely, heritages: about half of marriages are across ethnic or racial lines. In the 2000 Census, 18% of Hawaiians identified themselves as being of two races and 7% said three or more. Some 23% described themselves as at least partly Native Hawaiian—nearly 225,000 descendants of the 45,000 Native Hawaiians of the late 19th century. By census category, Hawaii in 2000 was 41% Asian, 23% white, 2% black, 9% Native Hawaiian or Pacific Islander and 7% Hispanic. But those categories seem artificial when looking at Hawaii. Local experts identify Hawaiians by ethnicity and give estimates of the size of each group: Hawaiian 22%, Caucasian 21%, Japanese 18%, Filipino 12%, Chinese 5%. The 2004 NEP exit poll classified the electorate as 42% white, 26% Asian, 10% Latino, 1% black and 22% "other."

Politically, the Hawaii Territory was Republican; after all, southern Democrats were blocking statehood and championing racial segregation. John Kennedy carried it in 1960 by just 115 votes. But from 1962 to 2002, its politics was dominated by a Democratic machine which had its beginning in the 1950s, when returning World War II veterans like Daniel Inouye, Spark Matsunaga and George Ariyoshi joined forces with former mainlander John Burns, who as a policeman during the war helped prevent persecution of Japanese Americans. They allied themselves with the then-powerful International Longshoremen's and Warehousemen's Union, and cemented the allegiance of Japanese-American voters. The Burns-Inouye machine built on the grievances against the *haole* (the Hawaiian word for white) owners of the big companies and triumphed. Inouye was elected as a Democrat to the House in 1959 and to the Senate in 1962; Burns was elected governor in 1962, and for 40 years the office was passed down in lineal succession to George Ariyoshi, John Waihee and Benjamin Cayetano—balanced tickets, of Japanese, Native Hawaiian and Filipino descent. Over the years this machine has built a large government. Despite some 1990s tax cuts, Hawaii had the third highest per capita tax burden in the nation in 2000 and by far the highest number of state and local employees per capita. This is centralized government: Hawaii has five counties (and one, Honolulu, has 71% of the population), one school district and one statewide health care plan. Landholdings are centralized too. Eight public and private entities own 69% of Hawaii's land: The federal government 16%, the state 29%, and six private landowners 24%. The Bishop Estate (Mrs. Bishop was the last surviving descendant of Kamehameha I), now called the Kamehameha Schools Estate, owns 8%.

During the 40 years of Democratic dominance, Hawaii's economy was transformed. By the 1960s tourism edged out agriculture—mainly pineapples and sugar—as Hawaii's number one industry. Pineapple acreage declined from 77,000 to 10,000, and Del Monte closed its last pineapple operations in 2006. Sugar production declined 67% in the 1990s, and most of the sugar produced is now processed into biofuel. Hawaii's agriculture is now dedicated to specialty crops whose high cost of production can be recovered in local, national or international markets: flowers, wasabi, macadamia nuts, Kona coffee, bananas, avocados, papayas, genetically engineered seeds. Hawaii even sells sea water: a Japanese company scoops it up from 2,000 feet underwater, desalinates it on the Kona cost and sells it in Japan for $5.50 a bottle. As big agriculture shriveled, the ILWU, which represented agricultural workers as well as longshoremen, dimmed in importance as its membership inevitably slumped; politically it was replaced by the strongly Democratic public employee unions. Voting long tended to run along ethnic lines. Japanese Americans, used to working in organizations in unions and government, have tended to be the heart of the Democratic Party; whites, with relatively high incomes, have tended toward Republicans; Filipinos, often in menial jobs, are heavily Democratic; Chinese, somewhat less so; Native Hawaiians are heavily Democratic but not as likely to be active in politics.

But as it changed, Hawaii found it had vulnerabilities. It imports 90% of its food, and has only one week's supply available at any one time; this was a problem when commercial flights were cut off after September 11. Housing is expensive, bid up by luxury buyers who have made their money elsewhere. The state's number two industry is the military, with perhaps 50,000 troops and dependents on the islands, with more than 100 military installations of varying size. But after the end of the Cold War the number of military personnel and civilian federal employees fell from 97,800 in 1988 to 67,750 in 2000. And in those same years tourism proved vulnerable to the early 1990s recession in California and the decade-long deflation in Japan. The number of visitors peaked at 7 million in 1990, dropped to 6.1 million in 1993, and did not reach 7 million again until 2000; then it was cut back by September 11 and recession to 6.4 million in 2003. The gross state product declined from 1992 to 1998, the number of jobs fell, foreign investment plummeted, bankruptcies zoomed, home sales dropped and welfare caseloads increased. Labor force participation declined as the number of young adults fell and the number of elderly rose: the combination of high housing costs and comparatively low wages led many young Hawaiians to seek work on the Mainland. The tourism industry finally bounced back, to 7 million in 2004, 7.5 million in 2005, 7.4 million in 2006. But the number of Japanese tourists, who tend to spend more per day than any others, went down, despite the revival of the Japanese economy; some worry that the state's strict smoking ban, enacted in 2006, will further dissuade them from vacationing in Hawaii. Unemployment in late 2006 was 2.1%, the lowest in the nation. But Hawaii's economy was still not generating as many high-paying jobs as its young people were seeking. Senator Barack Obama, who has chronicled his anxiety growing up black in the seemingly tolerant Hawaii of the 1970s (and in one of its most elite private schools, Punahou Academy), has become the first presidential candidate born and raised in the state. But he chose to be educated in California, New York and Massachusetts and to make his living in Illinois.

By 2004, Hawaii's economy otherwise had come back. Tourism revived, housing prices zoomed upward—the median sale price was over $500,000 on Maui and just under that on Oahu—and the construction industry boomed. Military cutbacks ended after September 11 and deployments overseas followed. Hawaii's small high-tech sector grew while Silicon Valley contracted. This economic turnaround coincided with a political turnaround, the election of Republican Linda Lingle as governor in 2002 after Democrats had held the office and controlled state government for 40 years. The question now is whether Hawaii can sustain its economic boom and at the same time preserve the defining characteristics that have made Hawaii strong and tolerant in the six decades since Pearl Harbor. The sluggish economy, high taxes and insider control all worked to undermine the hold of the Democratic machine on voters. The opposition to the machine, often carried on in primaries or in the form of third party candidacies by longtime Honolulu Mayor Frank Fasi, coalesced in 1998 in the person of Republican Linda Lingle. She lost to incumbent Ben Cayetano by only 50%-49% and in 2000 Republicans made gains in state legislative races. In 2002 Lingle won 52%-47%. She proved highly popular as governor and was reelected 63%-35% in 2006. But union-backed Democrats increased their already large margins in the legislature, and in 2005 implemented a law putting price controls on gasoline (it was predictably counterproductive and repealed in April 2006). In 2006 Congressman Ed Case challenged three-term Senator Daniel Akaka in the Democratic primary. Akaka won 55%-45%. "The machine won," said Case. "This was a clear and convincing victory for the Democratic machine that has been increasingly hanging on to power in Hawaii by their fingernails."

Hawaiians like to see their state as an archipelago of tolerance and good feeling. But that reputation has been marred by controversy over the status of Native Hawaiians and by occasional violence, including attacks on military personnel by Native Hawaiians. A Native Hawaiian protest movement grew in the 1990s, with demonstrations on the anniversaries of the overthrow of Queen Liliuokalani and the U.S. annexation of the islands. A state sovereignty commission sponsored a referendum on electing delegates to create a Native Hawaiian government; this raised the question of just who is a Native Hawaiian, since almost no one is of pure Native ancestry. Advocates of special treatment for Natives argued that they ranked below all other Hawaii ethnic groups (except perhaps Filipinos) in income and education and some called for independence from the United States. Native activist Haunani-Kay Trask disagreed: "As a nationalist, I hate the United States of America. But [independence] doesn't live in the political-military world we live in, with 26 military bases in Hawaii and 7 million tourists a year." She has also said that, "Our native people have been essentially confined to a servant class," but of course they have higher living standards than Polynesians in other islands which lack Hawaii's military installation and tourism infrastructure. In February 2000 the U.S. Supreme Court declared unconstitutional the 1978 Hawaii state constitutional amendment setting up Native-Hawaiian-only elections for the Office of Hawaiian Affairs, which administers a $400 million trust fund. That decision casts doubt on other provisions of the 1978 amendment, including the Hawaiian Homes Commission and the recognition of native gathering rights on private property. Senator Daniel Akaka responded with a bill granting Native Hawaiians sovereignty; a version was passed by the House in September 2000, but it was not brought up in the Senate. Meanwhile, Congress passed laws with benefits for those of Native Hawaiian ancestry: the Hawaiian Homelands Homeownership Act in 2000, the Native Hawaiian Education Act in 2001. Legal challenges were brought, and in August 2005 a Ninth Circuit panel ruled 2–1 that the Kamehameha Schools's policy of admitting only Native Hawaiians violated federal civil rights laws; the decision was reversed by an en banc panel by an 8–7 vote in December 2006. Meanwhile, Akaka worked to get his Native sovereignty bill onto the floor. It would allow a separate sovereign Native Hawaiian government, with apparently no territorial jurisdiction, but with potential custody of the Office of Hawaiian Affairs's $400 million trust monies; Akaka argues that this would be similar to Indian tribal governments. A vote was scheduled for September 2005, but put aside because of Hurricane Katrina. Akaka finally got it to the floor in June 2006, with an amendment prohibiting gambling (Hawaii is one of two states with no legal gambling whatsoever). Lingle and a delegation of Hawaiian leaders flew to Washington to lobby for the bill. But opponents rallied 41 Republicans to vote against cloture. Its chances in the Democratic Congress appear to be better, but the Bush administration has opposed it and if passed it presumably would be vetoed.

This is not the only Hawaii issue Bush has weighed in on. In June 2006 he issued an order dedicating the Northwestern Hawaiian Islands Marine National Monument, covering an expanse of ocean with a few uninhabited islands 1,400 miles long and 100 miles wide, which contain 70% of the nation's tropical, shallow-water coral reefs, some 7,000 marine species (one-quarter found nowhere else), the endangered Hawaiian monk seal population and threatened species of predatory fish (sharks, groupers, jacks); it is the largest marine sanctuary in the world. This followed up on more limited protection ordered by Bill Clinton in 2000 and 2001 and was supported strongly by Governor Lingle, Congressman Case and former Speaker Newt Gingrich. Senators Daniel Inouye and Daniel Akaka, apprehensive about the effect on a tiny fishing fleet employing fewer than 20 fishermen and the precedental effect it might have on others, were dubious if not hostile to the designation. Nature, which after all has been here long before the Hawaiian Natives, has its claims, and forces its own transformations: the Kilauea volcano on the Big Island began erupting in 1983 and is still sending lava down the slopes.

The People		Race/Ethnic Origin			Military veterans: 120,587 (13.1%)	
Pop. 2006 (est):	1,285,498	277,091	22.9%	White	WWII: 17.6%	Korea: 12.0%
Pop. 2000:	1,211,537	20,829	1.7%	Black	Vietnam: 34.5%	Gulf War: 13.2%
Pop. 1990:	1,108,229	494,149	40.8%	Asian	**Most populous cities (2000):**	
Change 1990-2000:	Up 9.3%	2,539	0.2%	Native Am.	1. Honolulu CDP	371,657
% of U.S. total:	0.4%	108,441	9.0%	Hawaiian	2. Hilo CDP	40,759
Pop. rank:	42nd of 50	218,700	18.1%	Two+ races	3. Kailua CDP	36,513
Area size:	10,931 sq. mi.	2,089	0.2%	Other	4. Kaneohe CDP	34,970
State Native:	56.9%	87,699	7.2%	Hisp. Origin	5. Waipahu CDP	33,108
Non-citizen:	7.0%	**Ancestry**				
Language		German: 4.6%		Irish: 3.5%	Urban population: 91.6%	
English: 65.7%	Asian: 29.1%	English: 3.4%		Portuguese: 3.2%	Rural population: 8.4%	
Spanish: 2.7%		Italian: 1.4%				

Education		Work Sector		Legislature	
H.S. Grad:	84.6%	Private: 70.9%	Govt: 21.0%	Senate	20 D 5 R
College Grad:	26.2%	Self: 7.6%	Family: 0.4%	House	43 D 8 R
Industry		Unemployment: 5.9%		Legislative Term Limits: No	
Agri: 2.3%	Con: 6.0%	**Household Income**		**Registered Voters**	
Fin: 7.0%	Info: 2.5%	<15k: 12.5%	15-35k: 21.9%	No party registration	
Mfg: 9.8%	Prof: 28.5%	35-50k: 15.7%	50-100k: 33.3%		
Public: 8.1%	Trade: 15.4%	100-150k: 11.1%	>150k: 5.4%		
Other: 20.5%		Median: $49,820			
Occupation		Poverty status: 10.7%			
Blue collar: 17.5%	White collar: 60.3%	**Home Value**			
Gray collar: 22.2%		<50k: 2.3% 50-100k: 7.4% 100-200k: 26.8% 200-300k: 27.6%			
		300-500k: 26.3% >500k: 9.6% Median: $249,300			

Presidential politics   Hawaii's presidential voting over the years has been the product of two, sometimes countervailing, forces. One is the Islands' historic preference for the Democratic party. Thus Hawaii voted Democratic when few other states did in 1980 and 1988. The other is an inclination to support incumbents in a state that takes patriotism very seriously, in part because the patriotism of so many of its citizens was once unjustly questioned and in part because of the large presence of the military, greater than almost any other state. This helps explain why Hawaii supported Ronald Reagan solidly in 1984 and came close to voting for Gerald Ford in 1976, though it wasn't nearly enough to help George H. W. Bush in 1992: Ross

2004 Presidential Vote		
Kerry (D)	231,708	(54%)
Bush (R)	194,191	(45%)
Cobb (Green)	1,737	(0%)
Other	1,377	(0%)

2000 Presidential Vote		
Gore (D)	205,286	(56%)
Bush (R)	137,845	(37%)
Nader (Green)	21,623	(6%)
Other	3,197	(1%)

Perot's military background, and the presence of Hawaiian Orson Swindle among his top leaders, gave him 14% and helped Bill Clinton carry Hawaii 48%-37%. In 1996 and 2000, as in 1968 and 1980, both those forces were moving in the same direction, and Hawaii voted 57%-32% for Clinton and 56%-37% for Al Gore.

In 2004, Hawaii's two countervailing forces were in tension and suddenly, in late October, this state which had given the Democrat a 19% majority four years before, was a battleground state. The *Honolulu Star-Bulletin* and the *Honolulu Advertiser* both ran polls showing the state a dead heat. The polls and attendant reporting suggested that Filipino and Japanese Americans, usually heavily Democratic, were leaning toward the Commander-in-Chief. On October 29 Al Gore appeared at a Filipino concert in Kalihi and, well briefed, noted that John Kerry favored higher benefits for Filipino World War II veterans and supported a Native Hawaiian federal recognition bill that would create a process for sovereignty. Kerry gave satellite TV interviews, Bill Clinton was interviewed by four Hawaii TV reporters and Democratic National Chairman Terry McAuliffe held a conference call with Hawaii reporters. Governor Linda Lingle stepped up her campaigning for Bush. On October 31 Dick Cheney flew into Honolulu at 10 p.m. "I was in the neighborhood and I thought I'd stop by and say, 'Aloha,'" he said (actually, he flew 8,270 miles to make the appearance). "Some candidates may take Hawaii for granted—President Bush and I take it seriously." He left two hours after he arrived. No presidential or vice presidential nominee had campaigned in Hawaii since Richard Nixon did in 1960 to keep his pledge to campaign in all 50 states. Now there was a battle for Hawaii's four electoral votes.

It was a battle Kerry won. The race was closest on Oahu, which Kerry carried by only a 51%-48% margin. He led 60%-39% on Kauai and 61%-38% on Maui and the Big Island for a statewide margin of 54%-45%. This is contrary to the usual pattern (Maui usually votes more Republican than Oahu), and the NEP exit poll showed unusual patterns of support: whites 58%-42% for Kerry, Latinos 54%-46% for Kerry, Asians only 52%-48% for Kerry. Kerry carried all but five precincts on the Big Island, all but one on Kauai and all but two on Maui. On Oahu, Bush carried the affluent Kahala and Koko Head areas, but ran behind on the Windward Coast where Republicans usually do best in legislative races. Instead he carried most of Oahu west of Honolulu, places like Aiea, Waipahu, Wahiawa, Ewa and Kapolei, around the big military bases of Pearl Harbor and Schofield Barracks, areas that voted mostly for Democrats in the legislative races.

Hawaii chooses presidential delegates by caucus. Sometimes insurgent candidates have been able to swamp thinly-attended meetings and win, as Jesse Jackson and Pat Robertson did in 1988. Between 1992 and 2000, frontrunners won. In 2004 Dennis Kucinich campaigned twice in the state and two days before the caucus attracted a crowd of 200 in a Honolulu theater. Fewer than 4,000 appeared at the caucus, and the preference poll gave John Kerry 46% and Kucinich 30%; Kerry got 12 delegates and Kucinich 8.

Congressional districting

110th Congress Lineup
2 D
109th Congress Lineup
2 D

Hawaii has two congressional districts: The 1st includes urban Honolulu (city elections now cover all of Oahu) and extends westward to Pearl Harbor and the rural area beyond; the 2d includes the rest of Oahu and the Neighbor Islands. The 1st District elected a Republican in 1986 and 1988; the 2d District has elected only Democrats since it was created in 1970; before that Hawaii elected one Democrat at large in 1959 and 1960 and two Democrats at-large from 1962 to 1968. The Democratic legislature made minor and politically insignificant changes in the district lines in 2002.

Governor

Linda Lingle (R)

Elected 2002, term expires Dec. 2010, 2d term; b. June 4, 1953, St. Louis, MO; home, Honolulu; CA St. U. at Northridge, B.A. 1975; Jewish; divorced.

Elected Office: Maui Cnty. Cncl., 1980-90; Mayor, Maui Cnty., 1990-98.

Professional Career: Founder and editor, *Moloka'i Free Press*, 1977-80.

Office: State Capitol, Executive Chambers, Honolulu, 96813, 808-586-0034; Fax: 808-586-0006; Web site: www.hawaii.gov/gov.

Election Results

2006 general	Linda Lingle (R)	215,313	(63%)
	Randy Iwase (D)	121,717	(35%)
	Other	7,285	(2%)
2006 primary	Linda Lingle (R)	unopposed	
2002 general	Linda Lingle (R)	197,009	(52%)
	Mazie Hirono (D)	179,647	(47%)

Linda Lingle is the first woman elected governor of Hawaii and the first Republican elected since 1959. She grew up in the St. Louis area and Los Angeles's San Fernando Valley; after graduating from California State University at Northridge in 1975, she moved to Hawaii, where her father owned a Ford dealership. She worked for the Teamsters and Hotel Workers unions in Honolulu and then founded the *Moloka'i Free Press* on that island, which is part of Maui County. In 1980 she was elected to the Maui Council and for six years represented Molokai and for four more held an at-large seat. She was elected mayor of Maui in 1990 over former Mayor and House Speaker Elmer Carvalho and reelected in 1994 over a 40-year member of the council.

In 1998 she ran for governor. She hailed what she called "the Maui miracle"—job growth in at least one part of Hawaii—and said, "It's time for a change, and change is about joining the other 49 states with economic revitalization that is taking place across the country." Lingle led in polls throughout the campaign, but incumbent Ben Cayetano appealed to Hawaii's ethnic groups and Democratic tradition. In August, Lingle accused the Cayetano campaign of spreading the false rumor that she is gay (she has been divorced twice). The outcome may have been determined by Lingle's decision to take state matching funds and abide by a $2.7 million spending limit; she was heavily outspent by Cayetano in the last two weeks. Cayetano won 50%-49%.

Lingle immediately set out to run again. She became Republican state chairman, traveled around the state and built an organization much stronger than what she had in 1998; in 2000, Republicans made notable gains in state House seats. She raised plenty of money, much of it from the mainland and changed the mindset in Hawaii that Democratic victories were inevitable. In the meantime, Cayetano struggled with budget problems. In April 2001 teachers in the state's single public school district went out on strike seeking a 22% raise. Prominent Democrats were caught up in scandals. Against this backdrop, Lingle led in the polls from the start. She was by no means conservative on all issues; she called for 20% of energy to come from renewable sources by 2020 and backed Native Hawaiian groups' claims for some form of sovereignty. She favored parental consent for abortions and a partial-birth abortion ban, but did not oppose abortion rights altogether. But the chief theme of her campaign was change.

Meanwhile Democrats were in disarray. The initial party insider favorite, Honolulu Mayor Jeremy Harris, was accused of violating fundraising laws and was ruled by a court to be ineligible to run until he resigned as mayor in March 2002. He suspended his campaign for two months, and then withdrew from the race in May. Lieutenant Governor Mazie Hirono, who had been running for mayor, entered the race for governor. She was part of the ruling Democratic machine, and there were two candidates who were running as outsiders, both regarded as archenemies by the Democratic machine and the powerful public employees union, which campaigned furiously for Hirono. It was just barely enough. She won the September 21 primary with 41% of the vote.

Hirono had an appealing life story. She was born in Japan and raised by a single mother who came to Hawaii to escape an abusive husband. She was a legislator from 1980 to 1994, then lieutenant governor from 1994 to 2002 where she worked to set up a state-owned workmen's comp insurer. When Lingle ran an ad highlighting Hawaii's poor test scores, low rate of job creation and growing poverty, Hirono said that Lingle was "always putting our people down." But Democrats remained on the defensive on corruption and Hirono was far behind Lingle in fundraising. With the Democrats no longer seen as inevitable winners, and after the Harris fundraising charges, many business interests were no longer ponying up for the party that had held the governorship for 40 years. Ethnic balance for once helped Republicans; they had a ticket with a white Caucasian and a Native Hawaiian, Lingle and retired Judge James "Duke" Aiona, while the Democrats had a ticket with two Japanese Americans, Hirono and former state Senator Matt Matsunaga.

Hirono did manage to narrow the gap by appealing to the party loyalties and by now ancient memories that had rallied late victories for Cayetano in 1998 and Waihee in 1986. But it all wasn't quite enough. Lingle won 52%-47%.

Lingle proclaimed her governorship a "New Beginning" and held a series of talk-story town meetings around the state, eating stew and rice and listening to citizens' complaints. With Democrats controlling the state Senate 20–5 and the state House 36-15, she had little leverage. The legislature overrode Lingle's veto of a raise for 23,000 white-collar state employees and did not act on her calls for changes in workmen's comp and reducing business fees, but she set up a www.eHawaii.gov website to make applying for permits easier. Lingle called for two privately funded 500-bed substance abuse correctional facilities but later dropped those efforts, explaining that no community appeared to want them. Hawaii has the nation's highest gas prices, and the legislature passed a law capping wholesale prices; Lingle criticized it and claimed it would lead to higher prices, and its effective date was postponed until September 2005. After that radical approach took effect, Lingle urged legislators to repeal the policy. "While the gas cap law was well-intentioned, it has become the de facto energy policy of the state," she said. "It has focused attention and government resources away from the state's actual energy problem, which is an overdependence on the use of oil."

Lingle came to office determined to change education in Hawaii. She called for the creation of seven local school boards, instead of a statewide board, which would require a constitutional amendment, and she called for giving school principals control over 90% of operational money. She also called for allocating money for schools not according to the number of pupils but according to a new formula taking into account special education spending and students' incomes. The legislature rejected the constitutional amendment, but in April 2004 passed a bill with a new spending formula and giving principals power to oversee 70% of operational money. Lingle vetoed it, and asked for five changes; the legislature overrode the veto in May. Lingle also signed a bill creating a new junior kindergarten program for children turning five after August 1.

In November 2004 Republicans lost five seats in the state House and after that Lingle took a different approach to governing. She found common ground with Democrats on alternative energy, education and affordable housing. In 2005, Lingle approved a 9.6% pay raise for public school teachers and a bill appropriating more money to charter schools while removing the cap on public schools that convert to charter schools. In July 2004 she had called for building 17,000 units of affordable housing in five years; she identified state land as sites for some of the housing, and the legislature gave her $100 million in bonding authority. In her December 2005 supplemental budget request she called for $20 million to repair homeless shelters and to provide additional services for the homeless, including temporary housing. In January 2006, with a projected $574 million budget surplus, she proposed $300 million in tax relief; she was pleased enough when the legislature approved $50 million and directed much of the rest to education. Addressing the gas price cap, Lingle said the state should require internal price, product and profit data from oil companies. She also called for a law to deter price-gouging during market disruptions. After gas prices rose in 9 of 10 weeks beginning in February 2006, the legislature suspended the gas cap in May 2006. In June 2006 Lingle signed into law part of her Energy for Tomorrow initiative that provided financing, funds and tax credits for renewable energy projects.

Not all of Lingle's stands pleased her (few) fellow Republicans. She said Oahu should raise taxes to finance its $2.64 billion light-rail system. She lobbied the White House and Republican senators for the Native Hawaiian recognition legislation supported by the Hawaii delegation; the measure failed but the Bush administration established the Northwestern Hawaiian Islands (NWHI) Coral Reef Ecosystem Reserve as a Marine National Monument in June 2006. She angered conservatives by not vetoing a tax increase for mass transit or increases to the cigarette and real estate conveyance taxes.

Still, Lingle's standing in the polls remained strong and no top-tier challenger emerged. Democrats sought to handicap her fundraising by passing in 2005 a campaign finance law that placed limits on mainland donations—an attempt to hinder Lingle's national fundraising efforts after her record-breaking campaign spending in 2002, when she spent $5.4 million. The ploy did not work as planned: Lingle ramped up her mainland fundraising before the law took effect in 2006, holding events in Houston, Los Angeles, New York and Philadelphia, putting her on a pace to meet her ambitious goal of $6 million. In January 2006, former state Senator Randall Iwase announced he would seek the Democratic nomination but he was little known; the party continued to solicit candidates right up until the July filing deadline. By then, Lingle already had $3.3 million cash-on-hand; with a strong economy and low unemployment, she was well-positioned for reelection.

Through the summer, the governor's race was overshadowed by the contentious September 23 Democratic Senate primary where 2d District Congressman Ed Case unsuccessfully challenged Senator Daniel Akaka. Iwase won the Democratic nomination over two political newcomers but his performance was uninspiring: a quarter of primary voters cast blank votes for governor. In the fall campaign he was underfunded and claimed Lingle exaggerated her accomplishments and took too much credit for the state economy and budget surplus. He criticized her for sending Hawaii inmates to mainland prisons; she touted her crime-fighting efforts against sexual predators. Iwase also seized on the Iraq war issue, calling for a timetable for withdrawal, and sought to tie Lingle to President Bush. "Are you ready to admit that you and President Bush were wrong about Iraq, and will you pick up the phone and call your friend George Bush on behalf of Hawaii's people and demand an exit strategy for our troops?" he said in their only televised debate. Lingle responded that she had visited Iraq to support the troops but "we should never telegraph a timetable to the terrorists." The result wasn't close: Lingle won 63%-35%, impressive enough for a Hawaii Republican, but especially so in the face of a strong Democratic wind. In the Senate general election, Akaka had won 61%-37%; in the two House races, Abercrombie won 69%-31% and Mazie Hirono, Lingle's 2002 opponent, won the open 2d District by 61%-39%. This was a victory built on Lingle's appeal to independent voters—exit polls revealed Lingle won 66%-29% among independents. She grew her vote from 31,000 votes in the Republican primary to more than 215,000 in the general. By contrast, Iwase won 119,000 votes in the Democratic primary but just 122,000 in the general.

Senior Senator

Daniel Inouye (D)

Elected 1962, seat up 2010, 8th term; b. Sept. 7, 1924, Honolulu; home, Honolulu; U. of HI, B.A. 1950, George Washington U., J.D. 1952; United Methodist; widowed.

Military Career: Army, 1943-47 (WWII).

Elected Office: HI House of Reps., 1954-58; HI Senate, 1958-59; U.S. House of Reps., 1959-62.

Professional Career: Honolulu Dpty. Public Prosecutor, 1953-54.

DC Office: 722 HSOB, 20510, 202-224-3934; Fax: 202-224-6747; Web site: inouye.senate.gov.

State Offices: Hilo, 808-935-0844; Honolulu, 808-541-2542; Kauai, 808-245-4611; Kona, 808-935-0844; Maui, 808-242-9702; Molokai, 808-642-0203; West Oahu, 808-623-8334.

Committees: *Appropriations* (2d of 15 D): Defense (Chmn.); Commerce, Justice, Science & Related Agencies; Homeland Security; Labor, Health and Human Services, Education & Related Agencies; Military Construction, Veterans Affairs & Related Agencies; State, Foreign Operations & Related Programs; Energy & Water Development. *Commerce, Science & Transportation* (Chmn. of 12 D). *Indian Affairs* (2d of 8 D). *Rules & Administration* (3d of 10 D).

Group Ratings

	ADA	ACLU	AFS	LCV	ITIC	NTU	COC	ACU	CFG	FRC
2006	95	82	100	71	50	12	50	8	2	12
2005	90	—	100	65	—	7	44	5	1	—

National Journal Ratings

	2005 LIB	—	2005 CONS		2006 LIB	—	2006 CONS
Economic	64%	—	35%		65%	—	34%
Social	72%	—	27%		75%	—	24%
Foreign	71%	—	28%		74%	—	25%

Key Votes of the 109th Congress

1. Bar ANWR Drilling	N	5. Confirm Samuel Alito	N	9. Limit Interstate Abortion	Y
2. FY06 Spending Curb	N	6. Path to Citizenship	Y	10. CAFTA	N
3. Estate Tax Repeal	N	7. Bar Same Sex Marriage	N	11. Urge Iraq Withdrawal	Y
4. Raise Minimum Wage	Y	8. Stem Cell Research $	Y	12. Provide Detainee Rights	Y

Election Results

2004 general	Daniel Inouye (D)	313,629	(76%)	($1,768,886)
	Cam Cavasso (R)	87,172	(21%)	($57,123)
	Other	14,546	(4%)	
2004 primary	Daniel Inouye (D)	157,367	(94%)	
	Brian Evans (D)	8,051	(5%)	
	Other	2,437	(1%)	
1998 general	Daniel Inouye (D)	315,252	(79%)	($1,375,601)
	Crystal Young (R)	70,964	(18%)	
	Other	11,908	(3%)	

Prior Winning Percentages: 1992 (57%); 1986 (74%); 1980 (78%); 1974 (83%); 1968 (83%); 1962 (69%); 1960 House (74%); 1959 House (68%)

The largest figure in Hawaii's public life remains Senator Daniel K. Inouye, who has held elective office here since before Hawaii attained statehood in 1959. Inouye (pronounced *in-NO-ay*) grew up in Honolulu, the son of Japanese immigrants; his ambition was to become a surgeon. He was 17 and teaching a first aid course when Pearl Harbor was attacked; he tended the wounded for a week. He served in the 442d Regimental Combat Team in World War II in France and Italy, and earned 15 medals and citations; 17 days before the end of the war in Europe, he lost his right arm. Unsure of what to do, recovering in a Michigan veterans' hospital, he asked a Kansas veteran whose right arm had been shattered what his plans were; the man said he was going to law school, would run for the legislature and "when the opportunity presents itself, I am going to Congress": It was Bob Dole, who was also wounded in Italy, exactly one week before Inouye. They served together two years in the House and 28 in the Senate. Inouye graduated from the University of Hawaii and George Washington University Law School, then became a leader of a group of young veterans who took over Hawaii's creaking Democratic party. He was elected to the territorial legislature in 1954, the House in 1959, and the Senate in 1962. He was keynoter at the turbulent 1968 Democratic National Convention, a tenacious member of the Senate Watergate Committee in 1973-74 and the first chairman of the Senate Intelligence Committee, in 1976. Inouye believes in the Senate, the Democratic Party, Hawaii, the armed services, and Native Americans—among other things. He is the third most senior member of the Senate, after Robert Byrd and Edward Kennedy. In June 2000 he was awarded the Congressional Medal of Honor for his heroism in World War II.

Inouye is chairman of the Senate Commerce Committee and of the Defense Appropriations Subcommittee; in each post his Republican counterpart is Ted Stevens of Alaska, and on the latter they have rotated as chairman and ranking minority member since 1989. These two senators who have been in office since the 1960s representing the two states most recently admitted to the Union and geographically the most distant from other states refer to each other as brother; Republican Stevens has contributed money to Democrat Inouye's campaign. Inouye and Hawaii colleague Daniel Akaka were two of the four Democrats who joined all Republicans in 1998 in seeking to deploy a ballistic missile defense system; the Clinton administration's opposition to deployment was based in part on an intelligence estimate that there will be no missile threat within the next 10 years to the continental 48 states—which seems to exclude Hawaii and Alaska from the "common defense" the Constitution promises. In March 2005 Inouye and Akaka were two of the three Democrats (Louisiana's Mary Landrieu was the other) who voted for authorizing oil drilling in the Arctic National Wildlife Refuge into the Senate budget resolution; it passed 51-49. Three months later, Inouye journeyed to Alaska and told the base closing commission that it should not shut down Eielson Air Force Base there.

Inouye has long used his seat on Appropriations to fund projects he finds worthy, from his alma mater of George Washington University to Native Hawaiian education. Like Stevens, Inouye takes a kind of proprietary interest in the public policy of his home state, with a sense of responsibility for its long-term development and character. From 1998 to 2003 he steered $1.4 billion to military projects in Hawaii. There are sound military reasons for much of this: Hawaii occupies a forward geographical position, and the U.S. has shut down other facilities in the Pacific since the end of the Cold War. The 2005 defense appropriation contained $496.7 million for Hawaii projects, many of them high-tech: an Army high-tech intelligence center, telemedicine research at Tripler Army Medical Center, the Maui Space Surveillance System, the Pacific Missile Range Facility on Kauai. One can see Inouye is thinking ahead in small legislation, such as the 2004 authorization of a study of establishing a Pacific Region of the Department of Homeland Security, an appropriation amendment passed by voice vote of $20 million to integrate federal coastal and ocean mapping activities. In 2005 he got funding for an upgrade of harbors in Maui, sought home-porting of an additional aircraft carrier in Hawaii, got $20 million for a new long-term care facility for veterans in Hilo and obtained $125 million for health, education and social services in Hawaii, including $63 million for Native Hawaiians, and $44 million for Hawaii transportation, anti-drug and housing projects. In 2006 he got $372 million for Hawaii-based programs, including $25 million for the Maui satellite tracking facility. Altogether in 2006 Hawaii got $904 million in earmarks, including $22 million for the Hawaiian Federal Health Care Network in the defense appropriation. After the November 2006 election he explained to *The Honolulu Advertiser,* "I had a chat with Senator Stevens before the election and we pledged to each other that no matter what happens, we will continue with our tested system of bipartisanship, and we've been doing this for the past 25 years, and it's worked." To those who called for changes in earmarks, he told *The New York Times,* "I don't see any monumental changes...If something is wrong we should clean house, but if they can explain it and justify it, I will look at it." But his concerns are not limited to Hawaii. He has sought increased funding for railroad security, although Hawaii has not much in the way of rail lines. And he and Stevens co-sponsored a bill that passed the Senate in July 2005 to reduce dumping of trash and debris in the ocean from ships.

Inouye chaired the Indian Affairs Committee from 1989-94 and again in 2001-03, and was moved by the tragic history. Inouye evidently sees many analogies between the condition of mainland Indians and Native Hawaiians. In February 2006 he removed from a lobbying regulation bill a provision that would require Indian tribes to report contributions to the FEC. The next month in committee he sponsored an amendment, defeated 6–6, to give tribes the right to appeal a rejection by the states of their bids for casinos. He was a co-sponsor of the 1993 law in which the United States apologized for overthrowing the Hawaiian monarchy. He supported the Hawaiian Homes Commission Act and in 2000 finally secured funding for Native Hawaiians purchasing property in the Home Lands, the 200,000 acres set aside in 1920 for a permanent homeland for Native Hawaiians. On the heated issue of Native Hawaiian sovereignty, some Native Hawaiian activists considered him lukewarm. Since 2000 he has worked with his colleague Daniel Akaka on Native Hawaiian recognition legislation, which has been approved by committee but was filibustered successfully in June 2006; Akaka has said it "holds the promise for all of us in Hawaii to come to terms with Hawaii's unique and often painful history."

On the Commerce Committee, Inouye has long been involved in communications issues and tends to favor government regulation over markets. He and Stevens were successful in October 2004 in preventing the transfer of jurisdiction over TSA and the Coast Guard from Commerce to the Governmental Affairs Committee. He and Stevens co-sponsored a bill in 2005 that passed the Senate, setting April 7, 2009, as the "hard date" for the end to analog broadcasting to free up spectrum for other users. In May 2006 he formally co-sponsored, but didn't necessarily support, Stevens's far-ranging rewrite of the 1996 telecommunications act. He supported the net neutrality amendment, which was defeated in committee 11-11, but then voted for Stevens's bill in June, which passed 15–7. It was not enacted, however, and when taking over the chairmanship in 2007 he indicated that he was not interested in such sweeping legislation. Instead he pushed more modest measures, like one setting criteria for Commerce Department grants to strengthen emergency communications.

Over the years Inouye has taken more moderate positions on some issues than many Democrats. He was one of the Gang of 14 senators who in May 2005 pledged not to filibuster judicial nominees except in extraordinary circumstances. But he and Akaka voted against the Iraq war resolution in October 2002, and they were two of the 12 Democrats who voted for Russ Feingold's resolution in June 2006 to withdraw all combat troops from Iraq by July 2007. And he spoke out against the confirmation of Alberto Gonzales in 2005, saying, "I am appalled that he has professed only a 'vague knowledge' of the racial and ethnic disparities in the imposition of the death penalty in federal cases." He sponsored a law passed in December 2006 with $38 million in grants to restore and research sites where Japanese-Americans were interned in World War II, and in January 2007 he sponsored a bill to investigate the cases of people of Japanese origin in Latin America who were deported from countries there (there are more people of Japanese descent in Brazil than in this country) and sent to the United States, evidently as possible hostages for exchanges of prisoners of war.

Honolulu is a long two flights from Washington, and Inouye's local influence has varied, but is generally great. He is part of the faction of Hawaii's Democratic party that held the governorship from 1962 to 2002. In 2002 he vigorously supported Lieutenant Governor Mazie Hirono in her nearly successful attempt to extend this 40-year string; but he has worked with Republican Governor Linda Lingle on Hawaii issues. Inouye has always been re-elected by wide margins. His greatest trouble came in 1992, when Republican Rick Reed ran an ad with tapes of Inouye's longtime barber, a woman who made charges about events many years before. On Election Day, Inouye won with a much reduced percentage, 57%, to 27% for Reed and 14% for the Green Party's Linda Martin. He was reelected by huge margins in 1998 (79%-18%) and 2004 (76%-21%). Inouye and Akaka were both born in September 1924, and both have said they intend to continue in the Senate. Akaka beat Congressman Ed Case 55%-45% in a seriously contested primary in September 2006; Inouye seems certain not to face such competition when his seat comes up in 2010. Congressman Neil Abercrombie, when asked whether Inouye would retire, said, "May that day not come for many years. Someone will take his position, but not his place."

Hawaii law requires that, in filling legislative vacancies, the governor must appoint someone of the same party as the person leaving office. In 2006 and 2007, Lingle vetoed bills requiring the governor to choose from a list of candidates submitted by the chairman of the incumbent's party. But in May 2007, the legislature overrode her veto, enacting a law that requires the governor to select from three nominees named by the political party. Unless she wants to challenge the constitutionality of the state law, it appears she would have to choose a Democrat to fill any Senate vacancy.

Junior Senator

Daniel Akaka (D)

Appointed May 1990, seat up 2012, 3d full term; b. Sept. 11, 1924, Honolulu; home, Honolulu; U. of HI, B.Ed. 1952, M.A. 1966; Congregationalist; married (Mary Mildred).

Military Career: Army Corps of Engineers, 1945-47 (WWII).

Elected Office: U.S. House of Reps., 1976-90.

Professional Career: Public schl. teacher, principal & admin., 1953-71; Dir., HI Office of Econ. Oppor., 1971-74; Asst., HI Gov. Ariyoshi, 1975-76; Dir., Progressive Neighborhoods Program, 1975-76.

DC Office: 141 HSOB, 20510, 202-224-6361; Fax: 202-224-2126; Web site: akaka.senate.gov.

State Offices: Hilo, 808-935-1114; Honolulu, 808-522-8970.

Committees: *Armed Services* (6th of 13 D): Readiness & Management Support (Chmn.); Airland; Seapower. *Banking, Housing & Urban Affairs* (8th of 11 D): Housing, Transportation & Community Development; Financial Institutions; Securities, Insurance & Investment. *Energy & Natural Resources* (2d of 12 D): National Parks (Chmn.); Energy; Public Lands & Forests. *Homeland Security & Governmental Affairs* (3d of 9 D): Oversight of Government Management, the Federal Workforce & the District of Columbia (Chmn.); State, Local & Private Sector Preparedness & Integration; Federal Financial Management, Government Information, Federal Services & International Security. *Indian Affairs* (4th of 8 D). *Veterans' Affairs* (Chmn. of 8 D).

Group Ratings

	ADA	ACLU	AFS	LCV	ITIC	NTU	COC	ACU	CFG	FRC
2006	95	92	100	100	25	12	30	0	0	12
2005	95	—	100	75	—	7	39	8	1	—

National Journal Ratings

	2005 LIB	—	2005 CONS	2006 LIB	—	2006 CONS
Economic	69%	—	30%	74%	—	25%
Social	83%	—	10%	79%	—	20%
Foreign	76%	—	15%	95%	—	2%

Key Votes of the 109th Congress

1. Bar ANWR Drilling	N	5. Confirm Samuel Alito	N	9. Limit Interstate Abortion	N
2. FY06 Spending Curb	N	6. Path to Citizenship	Y	10. CAFTA	N
3. Estate Tax Repeal	N	7. Bar Same Sex Marriage	N	11. Urge Iraq Withdrawal	Y
4. Raise Minimum Wage	Y	8. Stem Cell Research $	Y	12. Provide Detainee Rights	Y

Election Results

2006 general	Daniel Akaka (D)	210,330	(61%)	($2,651,026)
	Cynthia Thielen (R)	126,097	(37%)	($356,413)
	Other	6,415	(2%)	
2006 primary	Daniel Akaka (D)	129,158	(55%)	
	Ed Case (D)	107,163	(45%)	
2000 general	Daniel Akaka (D)	251,215	(73%)	($428,516)
	John Carroll (R)	84,701	(25%)	($97,407)
	Other	9,707	(3%)	

Prior Winning Percentages: 1994 (72%); 1990 (54%); 1988 House (89%); 1986 House (76%); 1984 House (82%); 1982 House (89%); 1980 House (90%); 1978 House (86%); 1976 House (80%)

Daniel Kahikina Akaka is the first senator of Native Hawaiian descent and Hawaii's second senator of Chinese descent. Born four days after Daniel Inouye, he served in the Army Corps of Engineers in the 1940s, went to college, taught school and became a principal. In 1971, at 47, he became director of the Hawaii antipoverty program; in 1975, he became an assistant to Governor George Ariyoshi. The next year, when both of Hawaii's congressmen ran for the Senate, he was elected to the House, where he served quietly on the Appropriations Committee. In May 1990, after the death of Senator Spark Matsunaga, Governor John Waihee appointed Akaka to the Senate. He has thus been an integral part of the dominant Democratic organization and a quiet but diligent worker on Hawaii issues for nearly 30 years.

Akaka, though a member of Congress since 1976, is not well known in Washington. "I was taught not to be a showhorse but a workhorse," he told *The Honolulu Advertiser* in 2006. "So, in a way, it's been a part of me not to brag." He has a mostly liberal voting record, somewhat less so on foreign and defense issues; he and Inouye were two of the four Democrats supporting deployment of a ballistic missile defense system in 1998. Hawaii, out in the Pacific, is much more vulnerable to North Korean missiles than the U.S. mainland.

Much of Akaka's time has been spent on the issue of Native Hawaiian sovereignty. He was the sponsor of the 1993 Apology Resolution, signed by Bill Clinton, in which the United States acknowledged as illegal the overthrow of the Kingdom of Hawaii in 1893 and the denial of Native Hawaiians' right to self-determination. In 1998 and 1999 he pushed the Clinton administration to recognize Native Hawaiians as an aboriginal people with whom the U.S. has a special relationship, as it does with Indian tribes. But in February 2000 the U.S. Supreme Court ruled that the Hawaii Constitution provision limiting voting for the Office of Hawaiian Affairs to those of Native Hawaiian descent was unconstitutional racial discrimination; the Clinton administration assertion of a special relationship was rejected. Other lawsuits were brought against OHA activities. In response, in July 2000 Akaka introduced a native recognition bill, which would recognize Native Hawaiians as an indigenous people with a right to self-determination and set up a process for formation of a Native Hawaiian governing body to have, as many Indian tribes do, a government-to-government relationship with the United States. This passed the House in September 2000 but died in the Senate in December. Akaka brought the bill up again in 2001 and it was passed by Inouye's Indian Affairs Committee in July. It had passed the House committee in May 2001, but House Republican leaders refused to bring it to the floor. In the Senate, Akaka had lobbying help from Alaska Native and American Indian groups, but a hold was placed on the bill by a Republican perhaps influenced by the opposition of some Native Hawaiians, who argue that it would make them wards of the government.

In April 2004 the bill, with some changes, was approved by the Indian Affairs Committee, but again faced a hold, apparently by Jon Kyl of Arizona. The House Resources Committee voted unanimously for the bill in September. Akaka's colleague Daniel Inouye put it on an appropriation as an amendment. But Kyl was vigorous in his opposition. "Persons of different races, who live together in the same society, would be subject to different legal codes. This would not produce racial reconciliation in Hawaii. Instead, it is a recipe of permanent racial conflict." In October Akaka and Inouye agreed to drop the bill in return for a promise, made by Frist and Kyl as well, that the bill would come to the floor before August 7, 2005. In July, just before a vote was expected, the Justice Department raised "serious policy concerns" about the bill in a letter to Indian Affairs Chairman John McCain and questioned whether a Native Hawaiian government would conflict with the Supreme Court's 2000 ruling. The Bush administration had not yet taken an official position; Republican Governor Linda Lingle traveled to Washington to lobby for the bill with the White House and Republican senators. But Nevada Senator John Ensign placed a hold, claiming the assertion of native rights could lead to legalized gambling in Hawaii, one of only two states without it, and an expansion of gambling on the mainland. Then Hurricane Katrina struck and a vote was delayed indefinitely. In June 2006, the bill finally got a vote; in a 56-41 vote, the Senate fell 4 votes short of the 60 needed to bring it to the floor for consideration, effectively killing it for the 109th Congress. Republicans cast all 41 votes.

Other Akaka causes include the 1995 law for a review of World War II service records with a view to awarding higher medals to deserving Asian Americans (under this, Senator Daniel Inouye was awarded the Congressional Medal of Honor in 2000), and a law making permanent the waiver of visa requirements from certain countries including Japan (2 million Japanese visit Hawaii every year). He has called for a commission to determine the facts involving the relocation, internment, and deportation of Latin Americans of Japanese descent during World War II and the late 1940s and for the creation of a National Foreign Language Director to oversee efforts to increase the number of multi-lingual workers. On the bankruptcy bill in 2005, the Senate rejected his amendment barring credit card companies from collecting accruing interest and fees from consumers in credit counseling and another Akaka amendment requiring them to provide detailed information about the long-term costs of paying only the minimum balance every month and to inform consumers how much they would have to pay every month in order to eliminate their balances within 3 years. He has taken a lead role on the 1989 and 1994 laws to protect whistleblowers in government and with Susan Collins he has sought to expand whistleblower protections and allow federal workers to make classified disclosures to congressmen and aides with security clearances. Akaka was one of the nine senators (Inouye was another) voting against the homeland security bill in November 2002, arguing that it gave the government too much power to compile information about citizens and failed to protect the rights of whistleblowers. In 2006, he was one of 9 Senate Democrats who voted against renewing the Patriot Act. He supported oil drilling in the Arctic National Wildlife Refuge, perhaps in part out of solidarity with colleagues from Alaska, who like Hawaiians often feel resentment that policy is made for their states by mainlanders who have little knowledge and understanding of their needs. But Akaka also believes his position represents the will of the majority of local native peoples, which include the Inupiat Eskimos and the Gwich'in. "To some of my colleagues, the debate about the Arctic National Wildlife Refuge is about energy. To others, it is about the environment. To me, the [refuge] is really about whether or not the indigenous people who are directly impacted have a voice about the use of their lands."

Since his initial 54%-45% victory in 1990 against Republican Congresswoman Pat Saiki, Akaka has won reelection by large margins—72%-24% in 1994 and 73%-25% in 2000. But in 2006, at the age of 82, he faced a competitive primary challenge from 2d District Congressman Ed Case. This was a remarkable election for Hawaii, where the creaky Democratic party establishment retains a tight grip on elections and no incumbent member of Congress has ever been defeated for reelection. Akaka was the establishment candidate, strongly supported by labor, Daniel Inouye and Hawaii's other Democratic congressman, Neil Abercrombie. Case was an archenemy of the establishment after challenging the machine-backed candidate in the 2002 primary for governor. The 54-year-old Case argued that Hawaii, with its two octogenarian senators, needed to begin preparing for the inevitable transition by electing a more youthful Democrat who could begin accumulating seniority. In most other states, Case would have had ample ammunition between Akaka's low profile, the failure of the Native Hawaiian federal recognition bill and a recent *Time* magazine article ranking Akaka as one of the five worst senators. But in Hawaii, Akaka is revered for his gentleness and modesty—there were limits to how far Case could go. Case highlighted his outsider status and noted that Akaka was a "product" of a "culture that perceives any innovation, any advance, any progress and even any disagreement as a threat to their power"; Akaka played up his vote against authorizing the use of force in Iraq, his close relationship with Inouye and suggested Case was not a real Democrat. He won 55%-45%. "The machine won," said Case, "this was a clear and convincing victory for the Democratic machine that has been increasingly hanging on to power in Hawaii by their fingernails." Akaka carried Oahu, where 69% of the votes were cast, 53%-47%; he won larger margins elsewhere, including 64% in Maui. The general election was an easier endeavor. The Republican nominee was forced to withdraw for health reasons; state Representative Cynthia Thielen, a moderate who supported abortion rights, was selected as a replacement in September. For a Hawaii Republican who had just six weeks to assemble a Senate campaign, she didn't do half bad. Akaka won easily, but Thielen held him to a 61%-37% victory—his lowest Senate reelection percentage.

FIRST DISTRICT

Rep. Neil Abercrombie (D)

Elected 1990, 9th full term; b. June 26, 1938, Buffalo, NY; home, Honolulu; Union Col., B.A. 1959, U. of HI, M.A.1964, Ph.D. 1974; no religious affiliation; married (Nancie Caraway).

Elected Office: HI House of Reps., 1974-78; HI Senate, 1978-86; U.S. House of Reps., 1986-87; Honolulu City Cncl., 1988-90.

Professional Career: College prof., 1959-63; Probation Officer, Marin Cnty., CA, 1964-67; Sociologist, 1967-74; Asst. prof., HI Loa Col., 1979-80; Consultant, 1983-87, 1989-90; Asst., HI Superintendent of Educ., 1987-88.

DC Office: 1502 LHOB, 20515, 202-225-2726; Fax: 202-225-4580; Web site: www.house.gov/abercrombie.

District Offices: Honolulu, 808-541-2570.

Committees: *Armed Services* (5th of 34 D): Air & Land Forces (Chmn.); Seapower & Expeditionary Forces. *Natural Resources* (4th of 27 D): National Parks, Forests & Public Lands; Fisheries, Wildlife & Oceans.

Group Ratings

	ADA	ACLU	AFS	LCV	ITIC	NTU	COC	ACU	CFG	FRC
2006	90	100	71	75	29	19	40	12	15	0
2005	100	—	100	67	—	14	42	12	5	8

National Journal Ratings

	2005 LIB	—	2005 CONS		2006 LIB	—	2006 CONS
Economic	64%	—	35%		66%	—	34%
Social	97%	—	0%		82%	—	18%
Foreign	92%	—	5%		79%	—	20%

Key Votes of the 109th Congress

1. Estate Tax Repeal	N	5. Limit Interstate Abortion	N	9. Build Border Fence	N
2. Limit CAFE Standards	N	6. Extend Patriot Act	N	10. CAFTA	N
3. FY06 Spending Curb	N	7. Bar Same Sex Marriage	N	11. Oppose Iraq Withdrawal	N
4. Drilling in ANWR	N	8. Stem Cell Research $	Y	12. Detainee Tribunals	N

Election Results

2006 general	Neil Abercrombie (D)	112,904	(69%)	($823,229)
	Richard Hough (R)	49,890	(31%)	($16,551)
2006 primary	Neil Abercrombie (D)	82,169	(79%)	
	Alexandra Kaan (D)	21,667	(21%)	
2004 general	Neil Abercrombie (D)	128,567	(63%)	($1,055,643)
	Dalton Tanonaka (R)	69,371	(34%)	($213,639)
	Other	6,243	(3%)	

Prior Winning Percentages: 2002 (73%); 2000 (69%); 1998 (62%); 1996 (50%); 1994 (54%); 1992 (73%); 1990 (60%); 1986 (30%)

The People		Race/Ethnic Origin	Ancestry	
Area size:	326 sq. mi.	17.7% White	German: 3.8%	English: 2.9%
Urban population:	99.3%	1.9% Black	Irish: 2.8%	
Rural population:	0.7%	53.6% Asian	**2004 Presidential Vote**	
Pop. 2000:	606,718	0.1% Native Am.	Kerry (D) 110,702	(53%)
Pop. 2005 (est):	627,635	6.6% Hawaiian	Bush (R) 99,256	(47%)
Median income:	$50,798	14.4% Two+ races	**2000 Presidential Vote**	
Poverty status:	9.7%	0.2% Other	Gore (D) 100,403	(55%)
Military veterans:	13.0%	5.4% Hispanic Origin	Bush (R) 70,674	(39%)
			Other 10,211	(6%)
			Cook Partisan Voting Index: D + 7	

Occupation   Blue collar: 15.7%   White collar: 63.8%   Gray collar: 20.5%

Tourists in Honolulu see the airport and adjacent Hickam Air Force Base, the *Arizona* monument in Pearl Harbor, perhaps the downtown with its wondrously Victorian Iolani Palace, and of course Waikiki, with its 40-story hotels rising within a few feet of one another. This is tight-packed Hawaii, between the 3,000-foot Koolau Range and the beaches and harbor, where tropical bungalows and garden apartments house Hawaiians of all incomes. Here are Hawaii's largest shopping centers and its state university; here are neighborhoods where the rich overlook the ocean and neighborhoods where the relatively poor are packed into people-clogged streets. Hawaii's topography also jams cars into just a few freeways and avenues, where traffic slows during rush hour and the *aloha* spirit is sorely tested. For much of the last decade Hawaii's high taxes and high land and utility costs have limited growth, but by 2005 the tourism business was reaching record levels, and the local economy has once again been growing. The military remains an important presence on Oahu. Hickam is home to eight new C-17 Air Force cargo carriers that can transport 20-ton armored Stryker vehicles. The Pentagon left the Pearl Harbor Naval Shipyard, which generates $1.3 billion in economic activity each year, off the base-closing list in 2005.

All of these areas are in the 1st District of Hawaii. It is mostly built up now, with well-established neighborhoods, and is growing less rapidly than the rest of the state. Politically, the neighborhoods around Honolulu's downtown and the university campus are middle and lower income and usually Democratic. To the west, around the harbor, are many military families in modest neighborhoods who may vote for Democrats but can be attracted to Republicans, including

George W. Bush in 2004. To the east, past Waikiki, around Diamond Head and out to the Kahala and Koko Head beach areas, is higher-income territory, often voting for Hawaii Republicans as well as for Bush.

The congressman from the 1st District is Neil Abercrombie, a Democrat with a graying beard who used to sport a ponytail. He has been called an aging hippie but he has bench-pressed 260 pounds in the House gym; he debates with an aggressiveness and bombast tempered by enthusiasm and good humor. After college in upstate New York, he taught school, moved to Hawaii, earned a Ph.D. in American studies, and at various times worked as a waiter, custodian and probation officer. In those years he got to know Illinois Senator Barack Obama's parents before Obama was born. Abercrombie was elected to the Hawaii legislature in 1974 and served 12 years. He first came to the House in 1986, when he won a special election, and served only three months; he lost a primary for the full term to Democrat Mufi Hanneman (now mayor of Honolulu) who then lost to Republican Pat Saiki. When she ran for the Senate in 1990, Abercrombie won a three-way primary for the House seat and won the general election easily.

Abercrombie is one of the distinctive and often delightful figures in the House. His voting record is mostly, but not entirely, liberal. He serves on the Armed Services Committee and sees no contradiction between his protests of war, and votes for military spending in Hawaii and elsewhere. But he still gets things done on Armed Services. "I see my work on Armed Services as a fulfillment of my principles and the motivating force of my life. I never opposed the military. . . . It's not about pro-war or anti-war, but how do you keep the peace." He and Dennis Kucinich were the lead sponsors of a resolution calling for a date certain withdrawal of U.S. troops from Iraq. Abercrombie was a vocal opponent of the Bush administration's "surge" proposal for adding more combat troops. "This is the craziest, dumbest plan I've ever seen or heard of in my life," he told Joint Chiefs of Staff chairman Peter Pace during a hearing in January 2007. Abercrombie has urged the Bush administration to fund U.S. operations in Iraq and Afghanistan out of the regular defense budget rather than through supplemental spending bills.

In the Democratic majority, the administration must contend with Abercrombie as chairman of the Air and Land Forces Subcommittee. When he was the panel's ranking member, Abercrombie helped to get $3 billion in military construction for Hawaii, which became strategically more important with the closing of facilities elsewhere in the Pacific. He has worked to assure adequate funding for Micronesia and the Marshall Islands 2,500 miles to the southwest in the Pacific. He has also pressed the Army to explain the dumping of 8,000 tons of chemical munitions off Oahu after World War II. Though his district had no bases at risk during the 2005 base closing round, Abercrombie has been a critic of reducing the domestic military infrastructure through the Base Realignment and Closure process saying that projected savings of $15 billion over 20 years does not justify the economic "grief and suffering."

Abercrombie is protective of Hawaii interests but is not always predictable. He voted for a Republican energy bill in 2005 because it included a study for turning sugar cane into ethanol—Hawaii is a sugar producer. He co-sponsored repeal of the estate tax—there are a lot of small businesses in Hawaii, he said. He filed a bill to allow businesses to write off the travel costs of spouses on business trips—Hawaii has lots of hotels. He opposed a Department of Agriculture proposal that would subject Hawaii's specialty fruit industry to competition from Thailand. He angered environmentalists when he joined with Republican John Peterson of Pennsylvania to sponsor legislation that would allow for offshore natural gas drilling and share revenues with states, such as Hawaii, that open their coasts to new natural gas leasing. But despite Hawaii's trade interests, he voted against normal trade relations with China and opposed trade promotion authority.

In September 2000, he won a surprising victory as House sponsor of a bill to recognize Native Hawaiians as an indigenous people with a right to self-determination. The Senate Indian Affairs Committee, chaired by Daniel Inouye, approved the bill, but some Republicans objected when it was brought to the floor the next month, and the bill died. After that, the House Republican leadership did not allow the bill to come to the floor, though the Resources Committee unanimously approved it in September 2004. After Democrats took control of Congress, he reintroduced the bill in the House with Hawaii colleague Mazie Hirono.

Abercrombie considered running for governor against Republican Linda Lingle but withdrew his name from consideration in late 2005. He was critical of then-2d District Congressman Ed Case's decision to challenge Senator Daniel Akaka in the 2006 Democratic primary. "Some people have forgotten what it is to be a Democrat," he said at the state party convention.

The 1st District is usually solidly Democratic, but in 1994 Abercrombie had serious competition from Orson Swindle, Marine Corps pilot and Vietnam POW, a national leader of Ross Perot's United We Stand America, and later member of the Federal Communications Commission. Swindle charged that Abercrombie was too dovish, but Abercrombie raised more money and won 54%-43%. Swindle ran again in 1996, labeled Abercrombie a far left hippie and called for big spending cuts. Abercrombie narrowly outspent him, and won by only 50%-46%. Since then, he has been reelected by overwhelming margins.

SECOND DISTRICT

Rep. Mazie Hirono (D)

Elected 2006, 1st term; b. Nov. 3, 1947, Fukushima, Japan; home, Honolulu; U. of HI, B.A. 1970, Georgetown U., J.D. 1978; Buddhist; married (Leighton Kim Oshima).

Elected Office: HI House of Reps., 1980-94, HI Lt. Gov. 1994-2002.

Professional Career: Dep. Atty. Gen., 1978-80; Practicing atty., 1984-88.

DC Office: 1229 LHOB, 20515, 202-225-4906; Fax: 202-225-4987; Web site: hirono.house.gov.

District Offices: Honolulu, 808-541-1986.

Committees: *Education & Labor* (21st of 27 D): Early Childhood, Elementary & Secondary Education; Higher Education, Lifelong Learning & Competitiveness. *Transportation & Infrastructure* (29th of 41 D): Water Resources & Environment; Highways & Transit; Aviation.

Group Ratings and Key Votes: Newly Elected

Election Results

2006 general	Mazie Hirono (D)	106,906	(61%)	($1,374,988)
	Bob Hogue (R)	68,244	(39%)	($230,411)
2006 primary	Mazie Hirono (D)	24,487	(22%)	
	Colleen Hanabusa (D)	23,643	(21%)	
	Matt Matsunaga (D)	16,001	(14%)	
	Clayton Hee (D)	12,649	(11%)	
	Gary Hooser (D)	10,730	(10%)	
	Brian Schatz (D)	8,254	(7%)	
	Ron Menor (D)	8,030	(7%)	
	Nestor Garcia (D)	4,479	(4%)	
	Other	3,862	(3%)	
2004 general	Ed Case (D)	133,317	(63%)	($784,823)
	Mike Gabbard (R)	79,072	(37%)	($484,160)

The People		Race/Ethnic Origin	Ancestry	
Area size:	10,605 sq. mi.	28.0% White	German: 5.4%	Portuguese: 4.2%
Urban population:	83.8%	1.5% Black	Irish: 4.0%	
Rural population:	16.2%	28.0% Asian	**2004 Presidential Vote**	
Pop. 2000:	604,819	0.3% Native Am.	Kerry (D) 120,633	(56%)
Pop. 2005 (est):	646,305	11.3% Hawaiian	Bush (R) 94,860	(44%)
Median income:	$48,686	21.7% Two+ races	Other 1,214	(1%)
Poverty status:	11.7%	0.2% Other	**2000 Presidential Vote**	
Military veterans:	13.3%	9.0% Hispanic Origin	Gore (D) 104,830	(56%)
			Bush (R) 67,118	(36%)
			Other 14,577	(8%)
			Cook Partisan Voting Index: D +10	

Occupation	Blue collar: 19.3%	White collar: 56.7%	Gray collar: 24.0%

The 2d District of Hawaii includes not only the Neighbor Islands but most of Oahu's acreage beyond the old limits of Honolulu. It has Wheeler Army Airfield and the farmlands north of Pearl Harbor, between two jagged chains of mountains that lift the island out of the sea. Over the mountains to the

west on Oahu is the Leeward Coast—calm, sultry and lightly populated; over the mountains to the northeast is the Windward Coast with many prosperous and Republican subdivisions in and around Kaneohe and Kailua. The 137 islands have distinct personalities. Hawaii, the Big Island, is the size of Connecticut and boasts huge cattle ranches, the active volcano of Kilauea, which started erupting in 1983 and has not stopped since, and Mauna Kea, the highest mountain in the world if you count from its base far under the ocean to the peak; tourists are told that it is bad luck to take pieces of lava home, and many send them back. Notwithstanding an October 2006 earthquake that caused $200 million in damage, the Big Island enjoyed increased retail activity and development in the second half of 2006 and into 2007. On the north shore, with heavy rainfall and tropical foliage, is the old port of Hilo and Hawaii's macadamia nut industry; this is a blue-collar Democratic area in a natural wonderland. On the Kona Coast, where there is little rainfall and the landscape is dominated by lava flows, there are retirement condominiums and a higher-income, more Republican population. Maui, favored more by North American than Asian tourists, has dozens of luxury condominiums and vast upscale resorts. Workers are employed chiefly in tourism, the military, social services and agriculture. Kauai, much of which was devastated by Hurricane Iniki in 1992, is the least developed and most agricultural of the main islands; parts of it have the nation's highest rainfall, while others seldom get wet. Its large farm work force—a reminder of what most of Hawaii was like a century ago—makes it the most Democratic of the islands.

The new congresswoman from the 2d District is Mazie Hirono, a Democrat elected in 2006. Hirono was born in Fukushima, Japan, and immigrated to Hawaii in 1955 just before her eighth birthday with her mother, who fled an abusive husband with an alcohol and a gambling problem. As a child, she shared a single bed in a boarding-house room with her mother and older brother, and at age 10 was forced to work to help support the family. These childhood struggles with poverty and the adjustment to a new country shaped her later feminist and liberal politics. "I know what it feels like to be discriminated against, to feel powerless, to have landlords who threaten to kick you out, and not having a place to go," she told *The Honolulu Advertiser*. Hirono mastered English in the public schools and became a naturalized citizen in 1959, the same year Hawaii became a state.

After graduating from the University of Hawaii, she ran for a seat in the state House and lost, then earned a law degree from Georgetown University and worked in the Hawaii attorney general's office. She ran again for the state House in 1980 and won a seat that she held for 14 years; in 1994 she was elected to the first of two terms as lieutenant governor. Hirono set out to run for Honolulu mayor in 2002 as then-mayor Jeremy Harris was the leading candidate for governor. After Harris got caught up in a fundraising scandal and dropped out, Hirono reversed course and ran instead for governor. She defeated Democrat Ed Case, who was then a state representative, in the primary, but her poorly organized campaign struggled to gain momentum in the general election and she was undermined by Democratic corruption scandals, budget woes and an acrimonious teachers strike. She lost the general election by 52%-47% to Linda Lingle, the first Republican to win the office since 1959.

Hirono's defeat proved to be a painful setback but not a career-ender. She formed the Patsy Mink political action committee (named for the late Hawaii congresswoman), to assist state-level Democratic female candidates who support abortion rights. When then-Congressman Ed Case, who won the seat after Mink died in 2002, announced in January 2006 he would challenge Daniel Akaka in the Democratic Senate primary, Hirono was one of 10 Democrats and 2 Republicans—including one-fifth of the state Senate—who sought to succeed him. The field included experienced campaigners such as state Senators Colleen Hanabusa and Clayton Hee, and former state Senator Matt Matsunaga, the son of the late U.S. Senator Spark Matsunaga. Hirono entered the race in April 2006 and was endorsed by EMILY's List; she had more money and name recognition than the other candidates and was considered a frontrunner. She ran radio ads that highlighted her efforts on early childhood education, land reform, workers compensation, and a television ad that featured an endorsement from Eugene Takemoto, Patsy Mink's brother. Hirono was forced to confront criticism about her record of accomplishment in state government and lingering doubts about the strength of her candidacy in the wake of her 2002 gubernatorial defeat. But with support on the Big Island and Maui, Hirono narrowly won the splintered September 23 primary with 22% of the vote and finished 844 votes ahead of Hanabusa, who garnered 21%. Matsunaga was third with 14%.

After clinching the Democratic nomination, Hirono had a much easier time winning the general election in a district that had never elected a Republican. Republican state Senator Bob Hogue, a former sportscaster, struggled to stay competitive with Hirono. Republicans portrayed Hirono as too liberal even for Hawaii: they mocked her as a "big-government peacenik" for her support for Dennis Kucinich's proposal to create a federal Department of Peace. Hirono emphasized her experience and raised more money, winning the general election 61%-39%. Hirono's 86-year-old mother attended her swearing in after making what was her first trip to the mainland. Hirono entered office as one of only two Buddhists ever to serve in Congress. (The other is Hank Johnson of Georgia, also elected in 2006). One of her first official acts in the new Democratic majority was to reintroduce, along with Neil Abercrombie, the Native Hawaiian recognition bill.

★ IDAHO ★

Idaho, tucked off near the northwest edge of the country, has been one of America's unnoticed success stories in recent years. Since 1990 its population has grown by 42%, from 1.0 million to nearly 1.5 million, thanks to technological progress and economic creativity. From 2000 to 2004 it had a higher rate of positive internal migration than all but three other states (Nevada, Arizona and Florida, all considerably sunnier). It has spawned some awesomely large businesses. Mining is less important here than potatoes, of which Idaho produces one-third of the nation's total. And it processes them: back in 1953, J. R. Simplot perfected the process of freezing French fries; his company soon got a contract with McDonald's and has become one of the biggest potato processors in the world, selling 3 billion pounds a year. Idahoans complain about the Atkins diet, and bellyached when Governor Dirk Kempthorne put the peregrine falcon and not the potato on the Idaho quarter; but the potato business continues to thrive. In the 1980s Simplot put up $1 million to finance Micron Technology, which is now the state's largest employer. In 1939 Joe Albertson opened a grocery store in Boise; in 2006 Albertsons had become the second largest grocery chain and was sold off to Supervalu, CVS and Cerberus for $17.4 billion; the headquarters has stayed in Boise. Idaho is home also to Morrison-Knudsen, the huge contractor, and dozens of smaller high-tech and service businesses that have recently sprung up. A few highly publicized liberal entertainment personalities and investment bankers have moved to Sun Valley or over the line from Jackson Hole, Wyoming, and some liberal professionals are appearing in Boise. But a much larger number of conservative engineers and entrepreneurs have come, from California and all over, to Idaho for a fresh environment and fresh start, clean air and few crowds, and no cumbersome or expensive regulations, where family lifestyles are still prevalent, traditional values respected and traditional rules enforced. As Governor Jim Risch said in 2006, "People are coming not because they want to change Idaho, but because they like what they see." Outsiders may not notice, but national football fans did when Boise State University beat Oklahoma in the 2007 Tostitos Fiesta Bowl 43-42, with a dramatic two-point conversion in overtime.

Idaho is big—Montpelier, in the southeast, is closer to Farmington, New Mexico, than to Bonner Springs in the northern panhandle—and the wilderness is never far away. Towering over the state Capitol in Boise is the vast peak of Shafer Butte, and not far away are impassable mountains of the Frank Church River of No Return Wilderness, the largest wilderness area outside Alaska, and the Salmon River, at 425 miles the longest undammed river in the Lower 48. Idaho was the last North American area European pioneers—fur traders—set eyes on. In the 1840s, New England Yankees led by ministers made their way west on the Oregon Trail through southern Idaho. Idaho's northern panhandle, an extension of Washington's Columbia Valley, was first settled by miners seeking gold and silver, then by loggers seeking timber. Mormons moved north from Utah and settled eastern Idaho. But federal water reclamation projects first authorized in 1894 brought the most settlers, and they transformed the barren Snake River Valley into some of the nation's best volcanic soil-enriched farmland, which with its warm days and cool nights proved ideal for the Burbank russet potato. Idaho potatoes are ideal for baked potatoes and frozen French fries. Fresh in family lore are the people who pioneered this state, built the first towns and farms, established the first churches and schools and became its community leaders. Yet Idaho is also cosmopolitan. It exports potatoes—mostly frozen French fries—across the Pacific Rim, and its high-tech companies have competitors all over the world. If Idaho politicians used to concentrate on water and maintaining irrigation, now they also work to curb Canadian potato imports and South Korean semiconductor subsidies.

Not so long ago Idaho was a state of farms and small towns; Boise, the pleasant state capital, was just the largest of the small towns. Today Idaho is increasingly urbanized. Nearly 60% of its people live in just five counties, in and around Boise, Idaho Falls, Coeur d'Alene and Pocatello, and all but the last are growing rapidly. Some 38% live in Boise's Treasure Valley, which has been growing rapidly, with big increases in the towns west of Boise—Eagle, Meridian, Middleton,

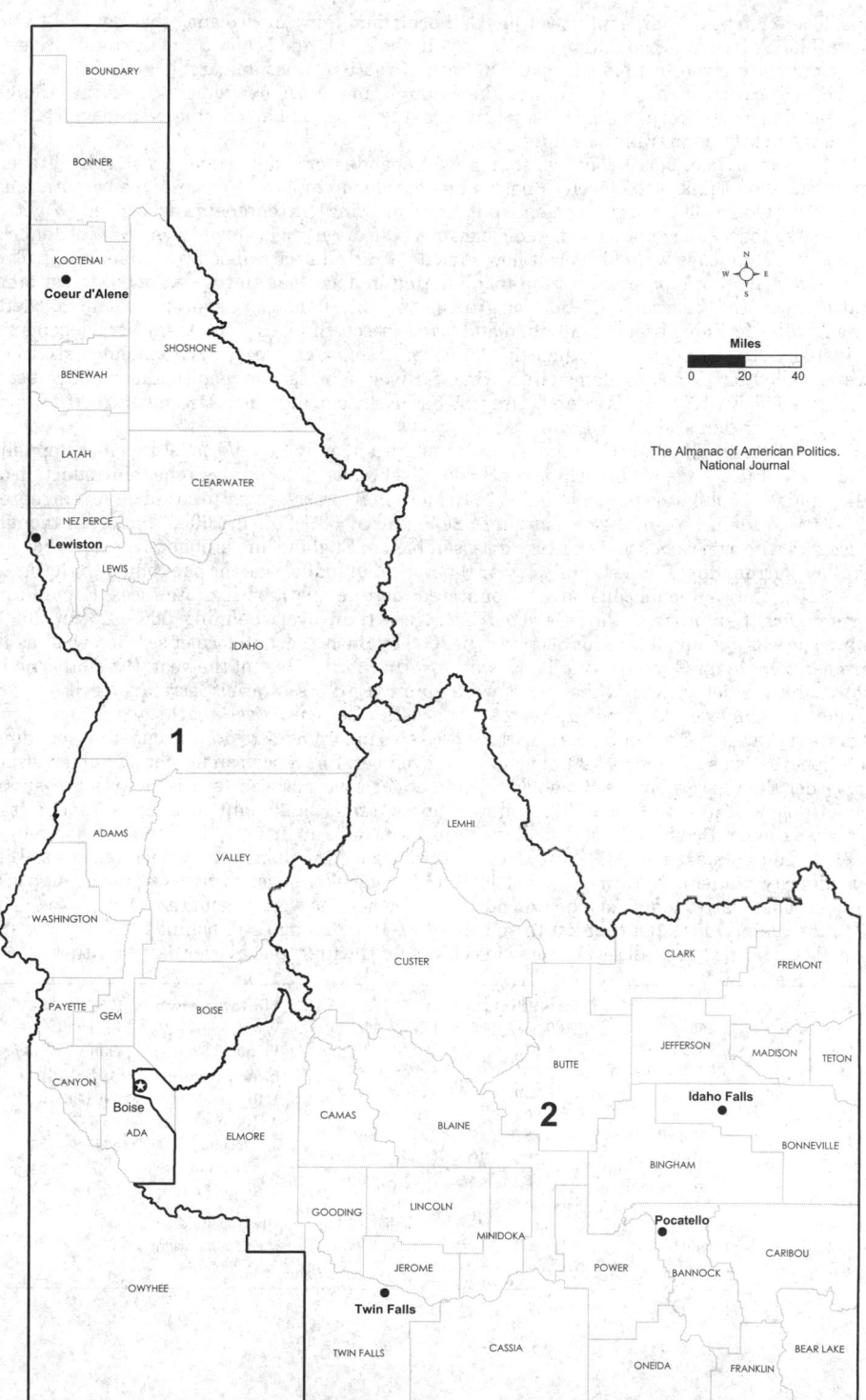

Congressional district boundaries were first effective for 2002.

Nampa. There have been large influxes from California and from Mexico and other parts of Latin America. Idaho's Hispanic population grew by 92% in the 1990s and is now 8% of the total; driver's license exams are given in English, Spanish, Serbo-Croatian, Russian, Arabic and Vietnamese. Here the political trend has been toward the Republicans: Most newcomers are from Orange County, not San Francisco, and they seek not cultural liberation, but an environment in which they can raise their children in traditional lifestyles.

At the same time, small counties that have depended on mining and grazing have been hurting. But they think of themselves not as downtrodden employees of absentee corporations needing a protective federal government, but as pioneering entrepreneurs who need to get a bloated, bossy federal government off their backs. The federal government owns 62% of Idaho's land, and most Idahoans were furious at how President Bill Clinton's appointees managed it. The Clinton administration's proposal to stop roadbuilding in about one-third of national forest land was bitterly opposed. Federal limitations on grazing on public lands have squeezed cattle ranchers already hurt by declining beef consumption and lower prices. Similarly, potato farmers dependent on irrigated water were enraged when the *Idaho Statesman* and local environment restriction advocates called for breaching dams on the Snake River to protect salmon. Idahoans have been furious as a federal judge in Portland, Oregon, has been moving since December 2000 toward requiring that the dams be taken down.

The political result of all these things was to make a heavily Republican state more Republican. George W. Bush—against breaching the Snake River dams, dubious about the reintroduction of grizzlies and the prohibition of roadbuilding in the national forests, eager to cut taxes on entrepreneurs—carried Idaho by a 67%-28% margin in 2000 and by 68%-30% in 2004. That, even though John Kerry's wife owns a house—a cottage disassembled in England and brought over to Idaho—in Sun Valley; surrounding Blaine County, by far the richest in Idaho, was the one county in the state that voted for Kerry. Republicans have encountered more competition in state races. Republican Governor Dirk Kempthorne was reelected by a less than overwhelming 56%-42% in 2002. Kempthorne was appointed Interior Secretary in 2006 by Bush and, as a former senator, was easily confirmed; Lieutenant Governor Jim Risch was governor for the rest of the year. (Kempthorne is Idaho's third Cabinet secretary; the others were Jimmy Carter's Interior Secretary Cecil Andrus and Dwight Eisenhower's Agriculture Secretary Ezra Taft Benson.) Risch got the legislature to cut local property taxes by $260 million, raise the state sales tax from 5% to 6% and cut state spending $50 million; that was ratified by 72% of voters in November. But Risch ran for lieutenant governor again rather than governor; the Republican nominee for governor was 1st District Congressman Butch Otter, once the son-in-law of J. R. Simplot and a former lieutenant governor himself. Otter had spirited competition from Democrat Jerry Brady, who had run in 2002; the Republican won by a somewhat reduced margin of 53%-44%. Democrats also gave 1st District Republican nominee Bill Sali, a minority winner in the primary, a battle. But his outspoken conservatism was not enough of a liability in conservative Idaho, and he won 50%-45%. Democrats were gleeful that they picked up 6 seats in the Idaho House, but that left them behind 51-19 there, and still behind 28–7 in the state Senate; Republicans swept all seven statewide offices for the first time in over half a century.

The People		Race/Ethnic Origin			Military veterans: 136,584 (14.8%)	
Pop. 2006 (est):	1,466,465	1,139,291	88.0%	White	WWII: 18.6%	Korea: 12.6%
Pop. 2000:	1,293,953	4,889	0.4%	Black	Vietnam: 32.3%	Gulf War: 13.5%
Pop. 1990:	1,006,749	11,641	0.9%	Asian	**Most populous cities (2006):**	
Change 1990-2000:	Up 28.5%	15,789	1.2%	Native Am.	1. Boise	198,638
% of U.S. total:	0.5%	1,200	0.1%	Hawaiian	2. Nampa	76,587
Pop. rank:	39th of 50	18,261	1.4%	Two+ races	3. Meridian	59,832
Area size:	83,570 sq. mi.	1,192	0.1%	Other	4. Pocatello	53,932
State Native:	47.2%	101,690	7.9%	Hisp. Origin	5. Idaho Falls	52,786
Non-citizen:	3.3%	**Ancestry**				
Language		German: 13.8%		English: 13.3%	Urban population: 66.4%	
English: 88.4%	Spanish: 7.4%	Irish: 7.3%		USA: 6.1%	Rural population: 33.6%	
Other Eur.: 2.7%		Norwegian: 2.6%				

Education		Work Sector		Legislature	
H.S. Grad:	84.7%	Private: 73.8%	Govt: 16.4%	Senate	28 R 7 D
College Grad:	21.7%	Self: 9.3%	Family: 0.5%	House	51 R 19 D
Industry		Unemployment: 5.7%		Legislative Term Limits: No	
Agri: 5.8%	Con: 8.1%	**Household Income**		**Registered Voters**	
Fin: 5.1%	Info: 2.3%	<15k: 15.8%	15-35k: 30.3%	No party registration	
Mfg: 17.8%	Prof: 27.2%	35-50k: 19.1%	50-100k: 27.6%		
Public: 5.1%	Trade: 16.2%	100-150k: 4.8%	>150k: 2.5%		
Other: 12.5%		Median: $37,572			
Occupation		Poverty status: 11.8%			
Blue collar: 25.0%	White collar: 56.7%	**Home Value**			
Gray collar: 18.3%		<50k: 12.3%	50-100k: 36.3%	100-200k: 39.5%	200-300k: 7.5%
		300-500k: 2.8%	>500k: 1.6%	Median: $102,100	

Presidential politics

Idaho is one of the most Republican states in national politics. George W. Bush and Bob Dole carried it easily; in 1992 Bill Clinton only narrowly beat out Ross Perot for second place, 28%-27%. It was Bush's third best state in both 2000 and 2004. Idaho saw John Kerry, on his visit to Sun Valley, and Dick Cheney, at a Boise fundraiser, in 2004, but not the president. British Prime Minister Tony Blair, in his July 2003 speech to Congress, said that he would like to visit people in Idaho, and Senator Larry Craig complained to Bush that Blair would get there before he did; Bush finally got there in August 2005, for a vacation in the resort of Tamarack. Since 1988, Idaho's presidential primary has been held in late May and has been little noticed elsewhere.

2004 Presidential Vote

Bush (R)	409,235	(68%)
Kerry (D)	181,098	(30%)
Badnarik (Lib)	3,844	(1%)
Other	4,199	(1%)

2004 Democratic Presidential Primary

Kerry (D)	25,921	(82%)
None (D)	2,479	(8%)
Kucinich (D)	1,568	(5%)
Sharpton (D)	927	(3%)
LaRouche (D)	590	(2%)

2000 Presidential Vote

Bush (R)	336,937	(67%)
Gore (D)	138,637	(28%)
Nader (Green)	12,292	(2%)
Other	13,749	(3%)

Congressional districting

Idaho has two congressional districts, which split Boise

110th Congress Lineup
2 R

109th Congress Lineup
2 R

between them. After the 2000 Census, a bipartisan commission drew new boundaries. It moved the boundary of the districts in Boise about a mile to the west, along Cole Road—a minor and uncontroversial change. If Idaho ever gets a third district, redistricting should be a cinch: most of the Boise area would get one district, eastern Idaho and northern Idaho one each.

Governor

Butch Otter (R)

Elected 2006, term expires Jan. 2011, 1st term; b. May 3, 1942, Caldwell; home, Star; Col. of ID, B.A. 1967; Catholic; married (Lori Easley).

Military Career: ID Natl. Guard, 1967-73.

Elected Office: ID House of Reps., 1972-76; ID Lt. Gov., 1986-2000; U.S. House of Reps., 2000-06.

Professional Career: Rancher; Dir., Food Products Div., Pres., Simplot Livestock, Pres., Simplot Intl., 1963-1993.

Office: P.O. Box 83720, Boise, 83720, 208-334-2100; Fax: 208-334-3454; Web site: http://gov.idaho.gov.

Election Results

2006 general	Butch Otter (R)	237,437	(53%)
	Jerry Brady (D)	198,845	(44%)
	Other	14,550	(3%)
2006 primary	Butch Otter (R)	96,045	(70%)
	Dan Adamson (R)	29,093	(21%)
	Jack Johnson (R)	7,652	(6%)
	Other	4,385	(3%)
2002 general	Dirk Kempthorne (R)	231,566	(56%)
	Jerry Brady (D)	171,711	(42%)
	Other	8,200	(2%)

Clement Leroy "Butch" Otter, something of a free-spirited Republican, was elected governor in 2006. He is the sixth of nine children and the first in his family to get a college degree; his father was a journeyman electrician and carpenter and a lifelong Democrat. Butch Otter entered an abbey to pursue the priesthood but quickly decided that was not his calling; in 1967, at the age of 25, he graduated from the College of Idaho, now known as Albertson College of Idaho. He went to work for his then father-in-law, billionaire J.R. Simplot, at the J.R. Simplot Company, one of the largest potato processors in the world, owner of the largest feedlot in the nation, and an early investor in Micron Technology. In 1972, Otter won the first of two terms in the state House. He ran for governor in 1978, finishing third in the Republican primary and, in 1986, he was elected lieutenant governor. Otter, a wealthy ranch owner after his 1993 divorce, held that post longer than anyone else in Idaho history; he served under three governors until he was elected to Congress in 2000.

Otter espouses a libertarian philosophy and believes strongly in gun ownership and property rights. But he is not the social conservative that other Idaho Republicans have been (in 1992, he won the "Mr. Tight Jeans" contest at the Rockin' Rodeo bar in Boise). In Congress, where he served three terms, he sought to check the power of the federal government; as a ranch owner, he was well-acquainted with its reach after having been charged three times by the EPA for violating the Clean Water Act. In 2001, after fighting the agency for two years, he paid a fine of $50,000 for dredging and filling wetlands without a permit. That same year, Otter was one of three House Republicans to vote against the USA Patriot Act. In July 2004 he sponsored an amendment with independent Bernie Sanders to prevent authorities from using the Patriot Act to demand information on book buyers and library users; he lost on a tie vote after Republican leaders held the roll call open for 23 extra minutes to turn the outcome their way.

In December 2004, Otter announced his intention to run for governor, giving him an organizational and fundraising head start over then-Lieutenant Governor Jim Risch, a Republican who was also considering running. In November 2005, Risch decided to run for reelection as lieutenant governor; he became governor in May 2006 when Republican Gov. Dirk Kempthorne left office to serve as President George W. Bush's Interior Secretary, but remained in the lieutenant governor's race. (He won 58%-39% over former Democratic Congressman Larry LaRocco).

Without competition from Risch, Otter won 70% in the May 2006 primary to easily outdistance his three opponents. He then faced Democrat Jerry Brady, a former publisher of the Idaho Falls *Post Register* making his second consecutive bid for governor. In heavily Republican Idaho, which hasn't elected a Democratic governor since 1990, Otter began as the frontrunner. But Brady, who highlighted environmental issues and compared himself to former Democratic Gov. Cecil Andrus, gained momentum by criticizing Otter's co-sponsorship of a bill that would have sold millions of acres of federal land in Idaho and the western United States to raise money for Hurricane Katrina relief; Otter eventually rescinded his support for the bill in January 2006. Brady also attacked Otter for accepting $6,000 from a company attempting to build a coal-fired power plant in Idaho. Otter countered by highlighting controversial editorials written by Brady's newspaper, the second largest in Idaho, including one that called for breaching Snake River dams to protect endangered salmon.

Otter ran a Rose Garden campaign, avoiding the traditional Idaho public television debate and initially refusing to take a position on Proposition 2, a controversial property rights initiative that he later opposed. In August, he found time to get married to a former Miss Idaho whom he had first met at a Fourth of July parade in 1991. Brady, the great-grandson of former Idaho Republican Governor James Brady, proved to be the more energetic candidate and remained competitive through Election Day; polls taken a week before the election showed him within striking distance. Despite national discontent with the Republican party and his own lackluster campaign, Otter managed to hold on, 53%-44%. He lost 8 of the state's 44 counties, including Boise's Ada County, the state's most populous, and the counties including Sun Valley and the University of Idaho. In heavily Mormon eastern Idaho, where Otter's libertarian stands and lifestyle hurt him in prior statewide elections, he lost just two counties: Bannock (home to Pocatello and Idaho State University) and Teton County, which shares a border with Wyoming's wealthy Teton County (Jackson Hole).

Senior Senator

Larry Craig (R)

Elected 1990, seat up 2008, 3d term; b. July 20, 1945, Midvale; home, Payette; U. of ID, B.A. 1969; United Methodist; married (Suzanne).

Military Career: Army Natl. Guard, 1970-74.

Elected Office: ID Senate, 1974-80; U.S. House of Reps., 1980-90.

Professional Career: Rancher, farmer.

DC Office: 520 HSOB, 20510, 202-224-2752; Fax: 202-228-1067; Web site: craig.senate.gov.

State Offices: Boise, 208-342-7985; Coeur d'Alene, 208-667-6130; Idaho Falls, 208-523-5541; Lewiston, 208-743-0792; Pocatello, 208-236-6817; Twin Falls, 208-734-6780.

Committees: *Aging (Special)* (5th of 10 R). *Appropriations* (10th of 14 R): Interior, Environment & Related Agencies; Military Construction, Veterans Affairs & Related Agencies; Labor, Health and Human Services, Education & Related Agencies; Energy & Water Development; Agriculture, Rural Development, Food and Drug Administration & Related Agencies; Homeland Security. *Energy & Natural Resources* (2d of 11 R): Public Lands & Forests; Energy; Water & Power. *Environment & Public Works* (7th of 9 R): Public Sector Solutions to Global Warming, Oversight & Children's Health Protection; Superfund & Environmental Health. *Veterans' Affairs* (1st of 7 R).

Group Ratings

	ADA	ACLU	AFS	LCV	ITIC	NTU	COC	ACU	CFG	FRC
2006	0	25	0	0	75	82	100	88	87	100
2005	15	—	13	5	—	69	89	96	72	—

National Journal Ratings

	2005 LIB	—	2005 CONS		2006 LIB	—	2006 CONS
Economic	22%	—	76%		4%	—	93%
Social	38%	—	61%		37%	—	61%
Foreign	40%	—	58%		8%	—	85%

Key Votes of the 109th Congress

1. Bar ANWR Drilling	N	5. Confirm Samuel Alito	Y	9. Limit Interstate Abortion	Y
2. FY06 Spending Curb	Y	6. Path to Citizenship	Y	10. CAFTA	N
3. Estate Tax Repeal	Y	7. Bar Same Sex Marriage	Y	11. Urge Iraq Withdrawal	N
4. Raise Minimum Wage	N	8. Stem Cell Research $	N	12. Provide Detainee Rights	N

Election Results

2002 general	Larry Craig (R)	266,215	(65%)	($3,045,521)
	Alan Blinken (D)	132,975	(33%)	($2,170,928)
	Other	9,354	(2%)	
2002 primary	Larry Craig (R)	unopposed		
1996 general	Larry Craig (R)	283,532	(57%)	($2,992,451)
	Walt Minnick (D)	198,422	(40%)	($2,140,878)
	Other	15,279	(3%)	

Prior Winning Percentages: 1990 (61%); 1988 House (66%); 1986 House (65%); 1984 House (69%); 1982 House (54%); 1980 House (54%)

Larry Craig, Idaho's senior senator, was first elected to the House in 1980 and to the Senate in 1990. Born on a ranch 70 miles north of Boise homesteaded by his grandfather in 1899, he was first elected to the state Senate in 1974, at 29, and served six years before running for the U.S. House. In 1990, when Senator James McClure retired, he was elected to the Senate; he won the Republican primary with 59% of the vote and the general election with 61%. Craig has been a well-informed and persistent critic of Western lands policies favored by environmentalists or, as he once put it, "environmental extremism." As he has said, "All of us who spend any time outdoors recognize that man and woman, properly assisted and directed, are a much better steward of Mother Nature than Mother Nature herself." He opposed Bill Clinton's efforts to revise the Mining Act of 1872 and increase grazing fees and the Clinton proposal to introduce grizzly bears into Idaho's Bitterroot Range. He opposed expansion of the Craters of the Moon National Monument, and sponsored a bill to create certain requirements for presidents to declare national monuments, as Clinton frequently did. He has steadfastly opposed breaching the Snake River dams to allow salmon to swim more easily upstream and sponsored a bill to require the Fish and Wildlife Service to consider many factors, including the effect on farming, when it makes decisions on salmon protection programs. In 2003 a federal judge in Portland, Oregon, after years of litigation demanded a "major overhaul" of the Snake River dams in order to protect endangered salmon and ordered spills over the dams; Craig has supported trucking salmon around the dams. In 2005 Craig passed an amendment zeroing out funding of the Fish Passage Center in Portland, which he said was providing biased data; in January 2007, the Ninth Circuit Court of Appeals, the most reversed federal appeals court, ruled that that was illegal. Craig has called for the governors of Washington, Oregon, Idaho and Montana (three of the four are Democrats) to meet with federal officials to produce a consensus plan to manage the Columbia and Snake River systems to meet the needs of all concerned—including the salmon, electricity ratepayers and shippers—and for a suspension of lawsuits.

As chairman of the Public Lands and Forests Subcommittee in the 1990s, Craig worked to change the policies and institutional culture of the Forest Service. The agency during the Clinton years reduced by nearly 80% the timber harvest on public lands, and in the process eliminated the livelihoods of many in small towns in Idaho and the West. While attacking Clinton policies publicly, he also worked behind the scenes with Oregon Democrat Ron Wyden; they came up with a bill, passed in 2000, to compensate local governments which had used timber revenues for roads and schools. In 2006, when it came up for renewal, the two took different approaches: Craig stressed that the program was temporary and called for more timber harvesting, while Wyden sought a more permanent system. Hearings were held on the bill, but it was never voted on in the Senate; it was reintroduced in March 2007. He opposed the Clinton regulation to ban construction of roads in national forests and supported the Bush administration's attempts to repeal it. He also backed the Bush administration's 2002 proposal to give regional managers power to approve commercial or recreational use without environmental impact statements and the Bush Healthy Forest Initiative streamlining approval of forest thinning. He has worked to waive penalties on local governments with less than 10,000 people for exceeding EPA's raised levels of arsenic in drinking water and to bar the classification of manure as a hazardous waste under Superfund or EPA hazardous waste laws.

Another Craig cause is nuclear waste. He has pushed relentlessly for the government to meet its commitment to establish a permanent nuclear waste repository at Yucca Mountain in Nevada. Opposition has come from Nevada's two senators and came from Bill Clinton, who carried Nevada twice by narrow margins after promising to veto bills to establish a temporary waste facility there. In July 2002, Craig's efforts came to fruition: George W. Bush signed a resolution establishing the repository. In March 2002 Craig inserted into the energy bill a Nuclear Power 2010 program for the Energy Department, and in March 2003 he got Energy Committee Chairman Pete Domenici to insert into the energy bill a $1.2 billion nuclear reactor for the Idaho National Laboratory in Butte

County. In 2005 he got $40 million to begin an experimental nuclear reactor to produce electricity and hydrogen at the Idaho National Laboratory and he inserted into an appropriation a report on whether there should be compensation for downwinders, residents of four Idaho counties subjected to radiation from above-ground nuclear weapons tests in Nevada in the 1950s.

Craig has taken on a variety of national issues. He was a lead sponsor of the constitutional amendment to require a balanced budget in the House in 1982 and in the Senate in 1995. He has supported free trade measures but opposed what he considers dumping of Korean microchips (Micron is Idaho's biggest employer) and Canadian softwood lumber. He opposed the Central American Free Trade Agreement because it would allow more sugar imports and insisted that sugar should be considered only in the Doha Round, not in regional trade agreements. In 2004 he sponsored with Minnesota Senator Mark Dayton a bill imposing tariffs on milk protein concentrates. Craig has supported opening up trade with Cuba, once a big purchaser of Idaho lentils and peas, and oil exploration by U.S. firms in Cuban waters. He opposed the Bush administration proposal to require payment in advance for Cuban purchases. In 2004 he sponsored a bill, backed by some liberals and conservatives, to repeal or limit portions of the Patriot Act.

Craig was chairman of the Special Committee on Aging in 2003 and 2004, and sponsored a bill with Evan Bayh of Indiana to enable seniors to purchase state-approved long-term care policies. In 2005 and 2006 he was chairman of the Veterans Affairs Committee. He joined with Robert Byrd in June 2005 in backing a $1.5 billion Veterans supplemental against the House's $975 million. In December 2006 he pushed to passage a comprehensive bipartisan veterans bill, authorizing major construction projects, more access to mental health services, more tele-health outreach and making non-VA facilities eligible for home per diem payments. In July 2002 he, John McCain, Edward Kennedy and Charles Schumer were an "odd duck" coalition sponsoring a bill to improve the National Instant Check background check system; they want to make sure that it includes all those convicted of crimes or otherwise ineligible to buy guns. In March 2004 he sponsored the bill to protect gun manufacturers from lawsuits seeking money for injuries committed by gun users. It seemed to have a majority, but when liberals attached to it a reauthorization of the assault weapons ban, he successfully killed the whole measure; he was pleased when the assault weapons ban expired in September 2004. In October 2005 his measure to protect gun dealers from prosecution for unknowing illegal sales became law.

Craig agreed in November 2004 to support the Boulder-White Clouds wilderness area sponsored by 2d District Congressman Mike Simpson and the Owyhee Canyonlands wilderness proposal, worked out after lengthy negotiations with his Senate colleague Mike Crapo, the Owyhee County commissioners, local landowners, in-state environmentalists and the Shoshone-Paiute Tribe. The bills did not pass, and Craig's subcommittee held hearings on them in September 2006. Craig sought to have landowners receive compensation before any wilderness is designated; environmental groups opposed that, and Oklahoma Senator Tom Coburn came out against any bill with a payout. In December 2006 Craig and Simpson had side-by-side articles in the *Idaho Statesman*—a rare public disagreement in the monopartisan Idaho delegation—and neither wilderness provision made it into the December 2006 tax bill.

Craig has used his seat on the Appropriations Committee to advance Idaho projects. In November 2004 he attached to the omnibus bill the agreement worked out by the Interior Department, Governor Dirk Kempthorne and the Nez Perce tribe settling water claims on the Snake River. He obtained funding for a new tower at Boise's airport and for a new VA clinic that opened in Caldwell in 2007. The year before he inserted into an appropriation a provision barring the FAA from shifting a Terminal Radar Approach Control System from Boise to Salt Lake City.

In the 1990s Craig was chairman of an informal committee whose members seemed to win most leadership positions. After Senator Bob Dole's resignation in June 1996, Craig was elected chairman of the Republican Policy Committee, the number four leadership position. In December 2000 Craig was challenged for this position by the more senior and more conciliation-minded Pete Domenici, and Craig just barely hung on, 26-24. Term limits prevented him from running again in 2002. He considered running for whip in the fall, but evidently became convinced that Mitch McConnell had the votes and did not run.

Winning reelection is ordinarily not difficult for an Idaho Republican, but Craig has had to run twice against Democrats who largely self-financed their campaigns. In 1996 building materials tycoon Walt Minnick spent $945,000 of his own money and attacked Craig sharply for backing Governor Phil Batt's nuclear waste compact. Craig responded by rafting down the river with his family and running ads predicting toxic desolation if the nuclear waste compact was not carried out. Craig won 57%-40%. In 2002 retired investment banker Alan Blinken, owner of a Sun Valley house who registered to vote there in 2001, spent $1.5 million of his own money on the campaign. Blinken had points against him: he had been Clinton's ambassador to Belgium and had lived for many years in New York City. But he boasted that he owned eight pistols, eight rifles and eight shotguns, "and I use them all. I'm a gun-totin' Idaho Democrat." Craig spent more than $3 million and Idaho did not drift far from its usual voting habits. Craig won 65%-33%; he carried 43 counties and Blinken carried the county that includes Sun Valley. He drew mention as a possible Cabinet appointee in November 2004, but he wasn't asked. In March 2006 he was embarrassed when Congressman Duke Cunningham—a friend since they became Washington neighbors at the Capitol Yacht Club—was convicted on bribery charges. "Duke and I have been friends over the years. I will be the first to tell you I was phenomenally disappointed in what I found out he was doing, and could never understand quite why all of that happened." He donated to charity some $43,000 from lobbyists implicated in the Cunningham case and their clients; he defended an amendment that he had introduced at their urging in 2002 as filling legitimate defense needs.

Craig's seat comes up for reelection in 2008. Through late August 2007, he had not announced whether he would run again. Then *Roll Call* reported that Craig had been arrested June 11 at the Minneapolis-St. Paul International Airport by a plainclothes police officer investigating lewd conduct in a public restroom. On August 8, he pleaded guilty to misdemeanor disorderly conduct charges. After the *Roll Call* story appeared, the *Idaho Statesman* reported on its own five-month-long inquiry into previous allegations that Craig was gay; the newspaper had ended its inquiry in May after Craig denied the allegations.

The *Statesman* story included an account from an anonymous source who claimed to have engaged in a sexual act with Craig three years earlier in a men's bathroom in Washington's Union Station. In an August 28 press conference, Craig strongly denied any wrongdoing in Minneapolis and said the *Statesman* had "relentlessly and viciously harassed" him while tracking down its story, which involved interviewing classmates from college. "I was not involved in any inappropriate conduct at the Minneapolis airport or anywhere else. I chose to plead guilty to a lesser charge hoping it would go away," he said. "I am not gay. I never have been gay." Senate Republican leaders called for an ethics committee review of the June arrest.

Craig refused to say at the press conference whether he would seek a fourth term. But one day later, Senate Republican leadership stripped him of his committee leadership assignments; on September 1, Craig announced his intention to resign by September 30.

Governor Butch Otter, who would appoint Craig's successor, said potential candidates included Lieutenant Governor Jim Risch, Attorney General Lawrence Wasden, 2d District Congressman Mike Simpson, former Attorney General and Lieutenant Governor David Leroy, state Senator John McGee and former state Senator Dane Watkins. Simpson later withdrew from consideration. Prior to the incident, Craig was a heavy favorite to win reelection, if he chose to run. On the Democratic side, former Congressman Larry LaRocco was already running for the seat. LaRocco won the 1st District House seat with 53% of the vote in 1990 and 58% in 1992, but was defeated in 1994 and lost the 2006 lieutenant governor's race to Risch by a 58%-39% margin.

Junior Senator

Mike Crapo (R)

Elected 1998, seat up 2010, 2d term; b. May 20, 1951, Idaho Falls; home, Idaho Falls; Brigham Young U., B.A. 1973, Harvard U., J.D. 1977; Mormon; married (Susan).

Elected Office: ID Senate, 1984-92, Senate Ldr., 1988-92; U.S. House of Reps., 1992-98.

Professional Career: Practicing atty., 1977-92.

DC Office: 239 DSOB, 20510, 202-224-6142; Fax: 202-228-1375; Web site: crapo.senate.gov.

State Offices: Boise, 208-334-1776; Caldwell, 208-455-0360; Coeur D'Alene, 208-664-5490; Idaho Falls, 208-522-9779; Lewiston, 208-743-1492; Pocatello, 208-236-6775; Twin Falls, 208-734-2515.

Committees: *Agriculture, Nutrition & Forestry* (8th of 10 R): Rural Revitalization, Conservation, Forestry & Credit (RMM); Domestic & Foreign Marketing, Inspection, & Plant & Animal Health; Nutrition and Food Assistance, Sustainable and Organic Agriculture & General Legislation. *Banking, Housing & Urban Affairs*

(7th of 10 R): Housing, Transportation & Community Development (RMM); Financial Institutions; Securities, Insurance & Investment. *Budget* (8th of 11 R). *Finance* (8th of 10 R): International Trade & Global Competitiveness; Taxation & IRS Oversight & Long-Term Growth; Energy, Natural Resources & Infrastructure.

Group Ratings

	ADA	ACLU	AFS	LCV	ITIC	NTU	COC	ACU	CFG	FRC
2006	0	9	0	0	75	82	83	88	78	100
2005	10	—	0	5	—	69	94	100	69	—

National Journal Ratings

	2005 LIB	—	2005 CONS		2006 LIB	—	2006 CONS
Economic	16%	—	80%		13%	—	82%
Social	0%	—	77%		18%	—	74%
Foreign	43%	—	55%		8%	—	85%

Key Votes of the 109th Congress

1. Bar ANWR Drilling	N	5. Confirm Samuel Alito	Y	9. Limit Interstate Abortion	Y
2. FY06 Spending Curb	Y	6. Path to Citizenship	N	10. CAFTA	N
3. Estate Tax Repeal	Y	7. Bar Same Sex Marriage	Y	11. Urge Iraq Withdrawal	N
4. Raise Minimum Wage	N	8. Stem Cell Research $	N	12. Provide Detainee Rights	N

Election Results

2004 general	Mike Crapo (R)	499,796	(99%)	($1,031,912)
	Other	4,136	(1%)	
2004 primary	Mike Crapo (R)	unopposed		
1998 general	Mike Crapo (R)	262,966	(70%)	($1,563,811)
	Bill Mauk (D)	107,375	(28%)	($241,443)
	Other	7,833	(2%)	

Prior Winning Percentages: 1996 House (69%); 1994 House (75%); 1992 House (61%)

Mike Crapo (pronounced *CRAY-poe*) is a Republican elected to the House in 1992 and the Senate in 1998. He grew up in Idaho Falls, graduated from Brigham Young University and Harvard Law School, and is a faithful Mormon who was named a bishop in the church at 31. A former congressional intern, he was elected to the state Senate at 33 in 1984, two years after leukemia took his older brother Terry's life. Terry Crapo had been state House majority leader and a rising star in state politics; the two were close and Mike Crapo decided to follow in his brother's path to the legislature. He became state Senate leader in 1988 and ran for the House in 1992, campaigning against all tax increases, for spending cuts, a balanced budget amendment and the line-item veto—the Contract with America two years early. He won the primary 68%-32%. "Cowboy Democrat" J. D. Williams, the state controller, ran on a "put America first" stand on industrial policy and trade. Crapo won 61%-35%.

With a self-professed "passion for reform," Crapo became Republican freshman class leader and championed institutional reforms—on discharge petitions, select committees, closed rules, closed committee meetings, open voting—many of which were adopted after Republicans won control in 1994. Like many Republicans then, he favored simple, hard-and-fast rules—a balanced budget, term limits, across-the-board discretionary spending cuts (excluding Social Security)—to force tough decisions. He sponsored the deficit reduction lockbox bill that passed the House in 1995; he served on Agriculture as it passed the Freedom To Farm Act. His overall voting record has been very conservative, with some exceptions on economics. He opposed NAFTA in 1993 but supported PNTR with China in 2000. In 2002, he voted in favor of trade promotion authority. He has criticized many recent trade agreements for accepting limits on U.S. agricultural exports as leverage for opening up access for other products, but has said that negotiators did less of that at the WTO meetings in Seattle and Cancun.

In 1997 Crapo, who prides himself on returning to Idaho Falls to be with his family every weekend, faced a career choice that many House members would like to face. In September Governor Phil Batt announced his retirement and in October Senator Dirk Kempthorne said he would run for governor. Within days Crapo announced he would run for the Senate. His opponent was former Democratic chairman and Boise trial lawyer Bill Mauk. Idaho, one-quarter Mormon, had never elected a Mormon senator; this time it did. Crapo led in polls by a wide margin and won 70%-28%, carrying every county.

In his first years in the Senate, Crapo became chairman of the subcommittee with jurisdiction over the troubled Superfund program and many EPA programs. He worked on the farm bill in 2001 and 2002, and helped write the conservation provisions; he sought to free farmers taking part from complying with federal water standards. He was troubled with the bill's dairy provisions, which he said would take money away from Western producers and give it to Eastern dairies; Idaho has a growing dairy industry. He passed a bill providing $1 million for small Idaho communities to comply with federal water quality standards, and seeks to extend it to the whole nation. He sponsored the Senate version of the Healthy Forests Restoration Act. He worked on changing the Endangered Species Act, and in November 2004 he produced a draft bill directing the Interior Secretary to set deadlines based on specific criteria. With Senator Blanche Lincoln, Crapo in 2006 sponsored legislation that would provide states with a greater role in species conservation and provide tax breaks and incentives for landowners to help the recovery of species on their land.

In his second term, Crapo won a seat on the Finance Committee, where he worked quietly and productively. Crapo succeeded in making permanent a tax break for state 529 college plans by getting it attached to a pension bill, while separately he headed off a cut in food stamps. Crapo also urged the IRS to implement a tax break that would help the country's short-line railroads, one of the largest of which is used by Idaho farmers to move crops and equipment. During the debate over Social Security, Crapo offered a bill with Jim DeMint that would use the program's surplus money to create personal "lockbox" retirement accounts. Crapo came under fire from Democrats in 2006 for traveling to the Virgin Islands and raising $41,000 in donations from businesses that sought to expand a tax break that Crapo supported. From his seat on the Banking Committee, Crapo won passage in 2006 of a bill that would ease outdated regulation of the banking industry. In a bid to protect Boise-based chipmaker Micron Technology, Crapo also sponsored a bill that would limit the type of companies that could receive loans from the Export-Import Bank.

In the Senate and in working on issues in Idaho, Crapo has met with groups with very different views and has tried to forge consensus. Of Crapo, Oregon Democrat Ron Wyden said, "He is not a showboat. He is somebody who day in and day out is always a constructive force for sensible public policy." With Harry Reid of Nevada he got the Senate in June 2002 to pass unanimously a bill providing for continuous production of the American Eagle Silver Bullion Coin by having the Treasury replenish its silver supply on the open market. Blanks for coins are manufactured at Sunshine Minting Inc.in Coeur d'Alene and Idaho's Silver Valley mines produce $70 million of silver per year. Crapo opposed reintroduction of grizzly bears to the Bitterroot Mountains and breaching the Snake River dams and opposed spring drawdowns on lower Snake River dams; he wrote a bill to compensate businesses around the Dworshak Reservoir for summer drawdowns to help migrating salmon. He has worked to get compensation for downwinders, residents of four Idaho counties subjected to radiation from above-ground nuclear weapons tests in Nevada in the 1950s, and worked on the Snake River Water Rights Act, which was passed as part of the omnibus appropriation in November 2004.

From 2001 to 2004 he worked to forge a consensus on the Owyhee Canyonlands wilderness proposal with the Owyhee County Commissioners, landowners and cattlemen, environmental groups and the Shoshone-Paiute Tribe. In November 2004, consensus resulted—199,000 acres formerly off limits would be opened to fence-building and pipelines, with independent review of BLM decisions; 517,000 acres would be set aside as wilderness and 384 miles of rivers would be protected, and open to hikers and boaters; the habitat of the California bighorn sheep and sage grouse would be protected. His Idaho colleague Larry Craig promised to steer it through his Public Lands and Forests Subcommittee in 2005. But getting the compromise enacted into law continues to require Crapo's efforts: In 2006, he won the support of then-Governor Jim Risch while a working group negotiated individual cash and land deals with 15 ranchers.

On other issues, Crapo and colleague Larry Craig supported the DREAM Act, allowing young illegal aliens to earn temporary resident status by graduating from high school and enrolling in college. They both opposed a provision blocking disposal of radioactive sludge in cement containers at Idaho National Laboratory and the Savannah River Site; they said INL would not do any of this. Crapo arranged to get the Senate to donate used surplus computer equipment to five Idaho schools in July 2005.

Crapo had expressed interest in a federal district judgeship but sought reelection in 2004; he had no Democratic opponent and won with 99% of the vote. In 2005, Harry Reid named Crapo to a list of four GOP senators he thought would make good Supreme Court justices.

FIRST DISTRICT

Rep. Bill Sali (R)

Elected 2006, 1st term; b. Feb. 17, 1954, Portsmouth, OH; home, Kuna; Boise St. U., B.A. 1981; U. of ID, J.D. 1984; Christian; married (Terry).

Elected Office: ID House, 1990-2006.

Professional Career: Musician; Practicing atty., 1984-2006.

DC Office: 508 CHOB, 20515, 202-225-6611; Fax: 202-225-3029; Web site: sali.house.gov.

District Offices: Boise, 208-336-9831; Caldwell, 208-454-5602; Caldwell, 208-667-0127; Lewiston, 208-743-1388.

Committees: *Natural Resources* (19th of 22 R): Energy & Mineral Resources; Fisheries, Wildlife & Oceans; National Parks, Forests & Public Lands. *Oversight & Government Reform* (17th of 18 R): Information Policy, Census & National Archives.

Group Ratings and Key Votes: Newly Elected

Election Results

2006 general	Bill Sali (R)	115,843	(50%)	($1,061,340)
	Larry Grant (D)	103,935	(45%)	($768,324)
	Other	12,196	(5%)	
2006 primary	Bill Sali (R)	18,985	(26%)	
	Robert Vasquez (R)	13,624	(19%)	
	Sheila Sorensen (R)	13,472	(18%)	
	Keith Johnson (R)	13,186	(18%)	
	Norman Semanko (R)	7,976	(11%)	
	Rocky Brandt (R)	6,289	(9%)	
2004 general	Butch Otter (R)	207,662	(70%)	($512,498)
	Naomi Preston (D)	90,927	(31%)	($15,152)

The People		Race/Ethnic Origin	Ancestry	
Area size:	39,972 sq. mi.	89.0% White	German: 15.4%	English: 10.6%
Urban population:	65.8%	0.3% Black	Irish: 8.2%	
Rural population:	34.2%	0.9% Asian	**2004 Presidential Vote**	
Pop. 2000:	648,774	1.2% Native Am.	Bush (R) 215,069	(69%)
Pop. 2005 (est):	750,148	0.1% Hawaiian	Kerry (D) 94,915	(30%)
Median income:	$38,364	1.5% Two+ races	Other 3,540	(1%)
Poverty status:	11.0%	0.1% Other	**2000 Presidential Vote**	
Military veterans:	15.5%	6.8% Hispanic Origin	Bush (R) 171,364	(68%)
			Gore (D) 70,523	(28%)
			Other 11,983	(5%)
			Cook Partisan Voting Index: R +19	

Occupation	Blue collar: 26.2%	White collar: 56.1%	Gray collar: 17.7%

The 1st District of Idaho stretches from the Nevada border to Canada, including some of usually Republican Boise and all of the panhandle, historically Democratic but more recently leaning Republican. It includes two of Idaho's big growth areas, the western suburbs of Boise and the Coeur d'Alene area to the north in Kootenai County; high-tech and tourism have fueled the economy. In Nampa, whose population nearly doubled in the 1990s and replaced Pocatello as Idaho's second-largest city, commercial developers have taken over land outside Boise that not long ago grew wheat and alfalfa. Subdivisions with as many as 1,000 homes are being constructed in nearby Meridian, the fastest-growing city in Idaho, as city planners struggle to upgrade their infrastructure. The growth is turning these once-rural areas to urban centers, but that has reinforced rather than altered the political landscape: newcomers routinely say they moved to conservative Idaho to "escape" from places like California. Some old-timers worry that their areas may become a new version of San Jose or Orange County, but support for property rights remain strong here. Politically, the 1st District is overwhelmingly Republican. Kootenai County, once a Democratic stronghold, is now as likely to cast as many Republican votes as communities in conservative Canyon County west of Boise. Northern mining counties were once the district's Democratic base; now it is the university town of Moscow in Latah County, one of only two in Idaho to vote against a 2006 constitutional amendment outlawing same-sex marriage. But every county here voted for George W. Bush in 2000 and 2004.

The congressman from the 1st District is Bill Sali, a Republican first elected in 2006. Sali was born in Ohio, moved with his family to Connecticut and then to Idaho, where his father worked in the mining industry. Sali started playing the drums while in high school and later performed as a professional musician in a number of bands, while also working jobs as farmer and a Caterpillar machinery salesman. He studied economics at Boise State University, earned a law degree at the University of Idaho and had a solo law practice until he ran for the state House in 1990.

In his 16 years in the state House, Sali was often viewed by his colleagues as an uncompromising grandstander. He frequently antagonized his party leaders, making him perhaps the most unpopular man elected to Congress in 2006. When the legislature took up an abortion bill in 2006, Sali insisted on forcing a debate over purported links between abortions and breast cancer. The debate pushed the Democratic leader, who was a breast cancer survivor, to tears. Republican state House Speaker Bruce Newcomb, who had feuded with Sali during his entire eight years as speaker and stripped him of a committee chairmanship in 2004, lashed out at Sali. "That idiot is just an absolute idiot," Newcomb said. "He doesn't have one ounce of empathy in his whole fricking body. And you can put that in the paper." After the abortion debate, Sali was unapologetic: "If people want go-along, get-along politics, I am not their guy." Newcomb's predecessor as speaker also found Sali difficult to work with; he once threatened to throw Sali out the third floor of the state Capitol. That would-be defenestrator, Mike Simpson, now represents eastern Idaho's 2d District.

Sali entered the race for Congress after Republican Rep. Butch Otter decided to run for governor, and faced five other Republicans in the primary. The opposition included Canyon County Commissioner Robert Vasquez, a conservative best known for his anti-immigration stance, and former state Sen. Sheila Sorensen, a moderate who was backed by Simpson. The obstinacy that made Sali a pariah to the Idaho Republican establishment earned him praise from social conservatives, who admired his maverick, no-nonsense style. His abortion opposition won him the backing of the National Right to Life organization and other conservative groups, but it was the anti-tax Club for Growth that gave him a decided advantage in the crowded primary. Sali boasted that he never voted for a tax increase during his 16 years in the legislature, and the Club ran television ads praising Sali's anti-tax stance and attacking Vasquez and Sorenson. In the primary, Sali won with just 19,000 votes and an unimpressive 26%; he carried just eight of the 19 counties that make up the 1st District. Vasquez placed second with 19%, followed by Sorensen and then state controller Keith Johnson, both of whom finished with 18%.

This was a tough year for Republican candidates even in Idaho and many Republicans worried Sali had burned so many bridges in the legislature that he might actually lose a district that President Bush won in 2004 with 69%. His Democratic opponent was former Micron Technology executive Larry Grant, who raised enough money to run competitively but got little help from Democrats in Washington. Vice President Dick Cheney and House Speaker Dennis Hastert campaigned for Sali, and a strong Republican organization elevated Sali to a 50%-45% victory. Grant carried five counties and ran competitively in Coeur d'Alene and around Boise but not well enough to overcome Sali.

In a curious twist, once in Washington his fellow Republican freshmen put him in the unlikely position of bridgebuilder with the Democratic freshmen by electing Sali as Republican class president. He immediately displayed his irreverence in his opposition to a minimum wage raise: Sali proposed a bill to bring down obesity rates by reducing Earth's gravity, explaining that his bill was just as foolish as trying to overturn the "natural laws" of the economy with a wage hike. Sali explained his style to *Congress Daily:* "I'm a real, honest-to-God conservative who has a vision of where I want to take this country and a lot of people have said that I have a unique way of articulating that."

Sali should be able to hold onto this solidly Republican seat, although any serious misstep in his first term might give Democrats reason to give the seat more of a look than they did in 2006. Grant has said he will run again, though in a presidential election year it is likely to be a more uphill battle than in 2006.

SECOND DISTRICT

Rep. Mike Simpson (R)

Elected 1998, 5th term; b. Sept. 8, 1950, Burley; home, Blackfoot; UT St. U., 1968-72; Washington U., D.D.S. 1977; Mormon; married (Kathy).

Elected Office: Blackfoot City Cncl., 1980-84; ID House of Reps., 1984-98, Speaker, 1993-98.

Professional Career: Practicing dentist, 1977-98.

DC Office: 1339 LHOB, 20515, 202-225-5531; Fax: 202-225-8216; Web site: www.house.gov/simpson.

District Offices: Boise, 208-334-1953; Idaho Falls, 208-523-6701; Pocatello, 208-233-2222; Twin Falls, 208-734-7219.

Committees: *Appropriations* (22d of 29 R): Energy & Water Development; Labor, HHS, Education & Related Agencies. *Budget* (8th of 17 R).

Group Ratings

	ADA	ACLU	AFS	LCV	ITIC	NTU	COC	ACU	CFG	FRC
2006	5	9	14	0	71	51	93	80	49	85
2005	10	—	0	6	—	53	89	92	38	85

National Journal Ratings

	2005 LIB	—	2005 CONS		2006 LIB	—	2006 CONS
Economic	34%	—	65%		21%	—	77%
Social	32%	—	66%		23%	—	74%
Foreign	23%	—	73%		33%	—	63%

Key Votes of the 109th Congress

1. Estate Tax Repeal	Y	5. Limit Interstate Abortion	Y	9. Build Border Fence	Y
2. Limit CAFE Standards	Y	6. Extend Patriot Act	Y	10. CAFTA	N
3. FY06 Spending Curb	Y	7. Bar Same Sex Marriage	Y	11. Oppose Iraq Withdrawal	Y
4. Drilling in ANWR	Y	8. Stem Cell Research $	N	12. Detainee Tribunals	Y

Election Results

2006 general	Mike Simpson (R)	132,262	(62%)	($571,630)
	Jim Hansen (D)	73,441	(34%)	($162,639)
	Other	7,629	(4%)	
2006 primary	Mike Simpson (R)	unopposed		
2004 general	Mike Simpson (R)	193,704	(71%)	($498,082)
	Lin Whitworth (D)	80,133	(29%)	($68,209)

Prior Winning Percentages: 2002 (68%); 2000 (71%); 1998 (53%)

The People		Race/Ethnic Origin	Ancestry	
Area size:	43,598 sq. mi.	87.1% White	English: 16.0%	German: 12.2%
Urban population:	67.0%	0.5% Black	Irish: 6.4%	
Rural population:	33.0%	0.9% Asian	**2004 Presidential Vote**	
Pop. 2000:	645,179	1.2% Native Am.	Bush (R) 194,166	(69%)
Pop. 2005 (est):	676,982	0.1% Hawaiian	Kerry (D) 86,183	(30%)
Median income:	$36,934	1.3% Two+ races	Other 2,665	(1%)
Poverty status:	12.6%	0.1% Other	**2000 Presidential Vote**	
Military veterans:	14.0%	8.9% Hispanic Origin	Bush (R) 165,559	(67%)
			Gore (D) 68,055	(28%)
			Other 12,319	(5%)
			Cook Partisan Voting Index: R +19	

Occupation   Blue collar: 23.8%   White collar: 57.3%   Gray collar: 18.9%

The 2d District of Idaho, from central Boise east to the Utah and Wyoming borders, is one of America's most Republican districts. It's also one of the most picturesque. The thick forests, mountain ranges and river valleys close by the Montana border are strongly Republican and suspicious of government. Southeast Idaho is part of the Mormon heartland, and the LDS presence runs deep; eastern Idaho's first Mormon settlements were in Franklin, Bear Lake and Caribou Counties. The old frontier and railroad town of Pocatello was once a Democratic outpost, home to unionized rail workers, a liberal college campus and a far more diverse population than the surrounding parts (Idaho State University used to be known as the place where Mormon kids went to lose their religion). But Pocatello has moved in a Republican direction as union strength declined and the conservative Mormon influence increased. Fifty miles north on I-15, Idaho Falls serves as the metropolis for a vast region stretching from West Yellowstone, Wyoming to the Salmon River Mountains. The nearby Idaho National Laboratory (so renamed in 2005 when it was combined with Argonne National Laboratory-West), a massive facility that occupies 890 square miles and employs more than 8,000 workers, is located on a windswept, desolate range—exactly why the federal government selected the site in the 1940s to test nuclear reactors. West of INL, in the year-round resort community of Sun Valley (Blaine County) where celebrities from Bill Gates and Arnold Schwarzenegger to John Kerry and Teresa Heinz keep homes, rapid development has led to calls for restrictions on growth. Blaine is the one Idaho county that voted for Kerry, 59%-40%. In 2006, it was one of only two counties to vote against a constitutional amendment outlawing same-sex marriage; Butch Otter lost here 70%-28% in his successful run for governor. The other counties in the 2d District voted for George W. Bush by percentages that range between 61% (Teton County) and 92% (Madison County). The district also includes the east side of Boise.

The congressman from the 2d District is Mike Simpson, a Republican first elected in 1998 when incumbent Mike Crapo ran successfully for the Senate. Simpson grew up in Blackfoot, became a dentist and joined his father's practice there. He was elected to the city council in 1980 and to the state House in 1984; he didn't declare himself as a Republican until then and was opposed by the local Republican organization. In 1993 he became Speaker, but kept up his dental practice as well. In the legislature he was known as a moderate in a conservative House, affable and able to get differing sides together. When Governor Phil Batt announced he would retire in 1998, Simpson wanted to run for his office; Senator Dirk Kempthorne's decision to seek the office closed that option. Crapo's decision to run for Kempthorne's Senate seat opened up the House seat for Simpson.

There was a serious contest for the district. In the Republican primary, state Representative Mark Stubbs called for lower payroll taxes; he had opposed nuclear programs at INL, while Simpson wanted more work at the facility. But the big issue was term limits. Simpson refused to take a pledge to serve only three terms; the other candidates did. Term limits advocates spent large sums against Simpson. Angry at these ads, Batt endorsed Simpson five days before the election. Simpson ran ads against "outsiders" and "out-of-state folk." Simpson beat Stubbs, 47%-41%. The Democratic nominee was Richard Stallings, a former history professor elected to the House in 1984 and re-elected three times; in 1992 he ran against Kempthorne for the Senate and lost 57%-43%. Stallings talked about his conservative voting record in the House, called for more education spending and pointed with anxiety at falling farm commodity prices. Simpson wanted a smaller federal role in education; he favored tax cuts and individual investment accounts in Social Security. Simpson won 53%-45%, losing the most visible parts of the district—Pocatello, Sun Valley, Boise—but carrying just about everything else.

In the House, Simpson has been relatively moderate for a western Republican. In his first two years, he set out to build relationships with each of his 434 colleagues—preferably, he said, in one-on-one informal conversations. But he only got up to about 350 members—the House is a big place—and that reinforced his opposition to term limits. More than most western Republicans, he has reached out to Democrats on economic and social issues. The *Idaho Statesman* called him "a savvy and solutions-oriented lawmaker." He helped to establish a bipartisan caucus to talk about the trade-related needs of farmers and ranchers. Simpson voted against the White House in 2005 by opposing the Central America Free Trade Agreement because of its potential impact on Idaho's sugar industry. "When I came to Congress, I was a free trader. But we don't live in an ideal world and I've come to understand that more and more. I'm starting to become one of those people I disagreed with a few years ago," he said in 2007. But George W. Bush has signed two of his bills; one, to protect hunting rights in the expanded portions of the Craters of the Moon monument, and the other to overhaul a job-training program for veterans.

In 2003, Simpson showed his skills as a party insider when he got a seat on the Appropriations Committee, a post he has used to win funding for the Idaho National Laboratory, including $40 million to develop an experimental nuclear reactor and $20 million to build four new buildings at the lab. Simpson became a leading defender of appropriations earmarks; he opposed restricting earmarks but did support greater transparency in the process. After Democrats took control of the House, Simpson called incoming Appropriations Chairman David Obey one of Congress's most honest members and noted that he once toured Obey's northern Wisconsin district. "He's the kind of guy I can work with," he said. In 2007 Simpson kept his full committee seat, but nearly lost his slot on the Energy-Water Appropriations Subcommittee, which oversees nuclear energy spending. To keep the seat, he gave up his slot on the Interior Appropriations Subcommittee.

Simpson has said he would "die trying" to create the Boulder-White Cloud Management Area and has spent five years negotiating the plan with opposing constituencies. The plan would preserve 312,000 acres in the central Idaho mountains, but would also transfer 68 acres in the Sawtooth National Recreation Area, a winter range for elk, to the city of Stanley, which could be sold to developers. It would also transfer 3,600 acres of BLM rangeland to Custer County. Motorized recreation groups have opposed the plan even though Simpson has proposed a new 960 acre motorized park south of the Boise airport. To entice environmental groups, which are divided over the plan, Simpson has added 630 acres of state land along the Salmon River, and proposed a land exchange that would turn over federal land in eastern Idaho for a new state park. Simpson got the bill passed in the House in 2006, but reservations from Larry Craig slowed Senate progress. In the lame-duck session, Simpson nearly succeeded in attaching it to a tax-extenders bill, but it got dropped from the package at the last minute by outgoing Ways and Means Chairman Bill Thomas to make room for an Illinois tax break sought by Dennis Hastert. In the new Democratic Congress, Simpson faces the challenge of satisfying incoming House Natural Resources Chairman Nick Rahall, a supporter of wilderness preservation who has criticized Simpson's bill for creating too many loopholes.

Simpson won three straight reelections with a better than 2–1 margin, but his lead slipped to 62%-34% in 2006, when he faced former Democratic state Rep. Jim Hansen, the son of former Republican Congressman Orval Hansen, who represented the district for six years (1969-75). After Senator Larry Craig announced that he would resign in September 2007, Simpson was mentioned by Governor Butch Otter as a possible successor, but he withdrew his name from consideration. He is a solid bet for reelection to the House.

★ ILLINOIS ★

At the beginning of the 20th century Chicago seemed destined to be the center of America. This brash new city on the lake had grown from 112,000 residents in 1860, when it was host to the Republican Convention that nominated Illinois's Abraham Lincoln, to 1.4 million when it hosted the Columbian Exposition in 1893 and 1.7 million in 1900. "Make no little plans," Chicago architect Daniel Burnham exhorted. And Chicago was making vast plans: building grand parks on the lakefront, erecting America's first downtown of skyscrapers, building expansive retail palaces, becoming the headquarters of the new American Medical and American Bar Associations, creating a great university from scratch on the Exposition's Midway Plaisance, housing union agitators and their liberal advocate Clarence Darrow as well as corporate leaders and attorneys who bested them, hosting the Democratic Convention of 1896 that nominated 36-year-old William Jennings Bryan after his "cross of gold" speech, and becoming the headquarters of the brilliant campaign Mark Hanna waged for William McKinley that beat Bryan in the fall. Chicago started with the advantage of a great location, where the Great Lakes meet the prairies of the vast Mississippi Valley, and Chicago's entrepreneurs made it the hub of the nation's railroad network and the center of the nation's trade in lumber, grain and meat, as William Cronon describes in *Nature's Metropolis*.

A century later, Chicago is the nation's third-largest metropolis, sometimes overshadowed by and often ignored by the media of coastal New York and Los Angeles, but still a productive and creative world-class city. Illinois, after near-zero population growth in the 1970s and 1980s, saw its population rise 12% from 1990 to 2006, more than other big states like New York, Pennsylvania, Ohio or Michigan. In commerce, Chicago remains a prime producer and processor of food products, the nation's number one manufacturing center with the strongest white-collar and service economy between the coasts, the home of the world's greatest commodities exchanges and futures markets. O'Hare Airport, promoted and nurtured by longtime (1955-76) Mayor Richard J. Daley and long one of the world's busiest airports, is one of its great hubs of commerce. But for the most part Chicago was established not by government but by markets; it has always been a free enterprise city, settled by pioneers from New England and Kentucky, by immigrant Irishmen who dug the first canal connecting Lake Michigan and the Illinois River, and by railroad promoters who saw its potential as the great connecting point between East and West, the Great Lakes and the Mississippi Valley. Its

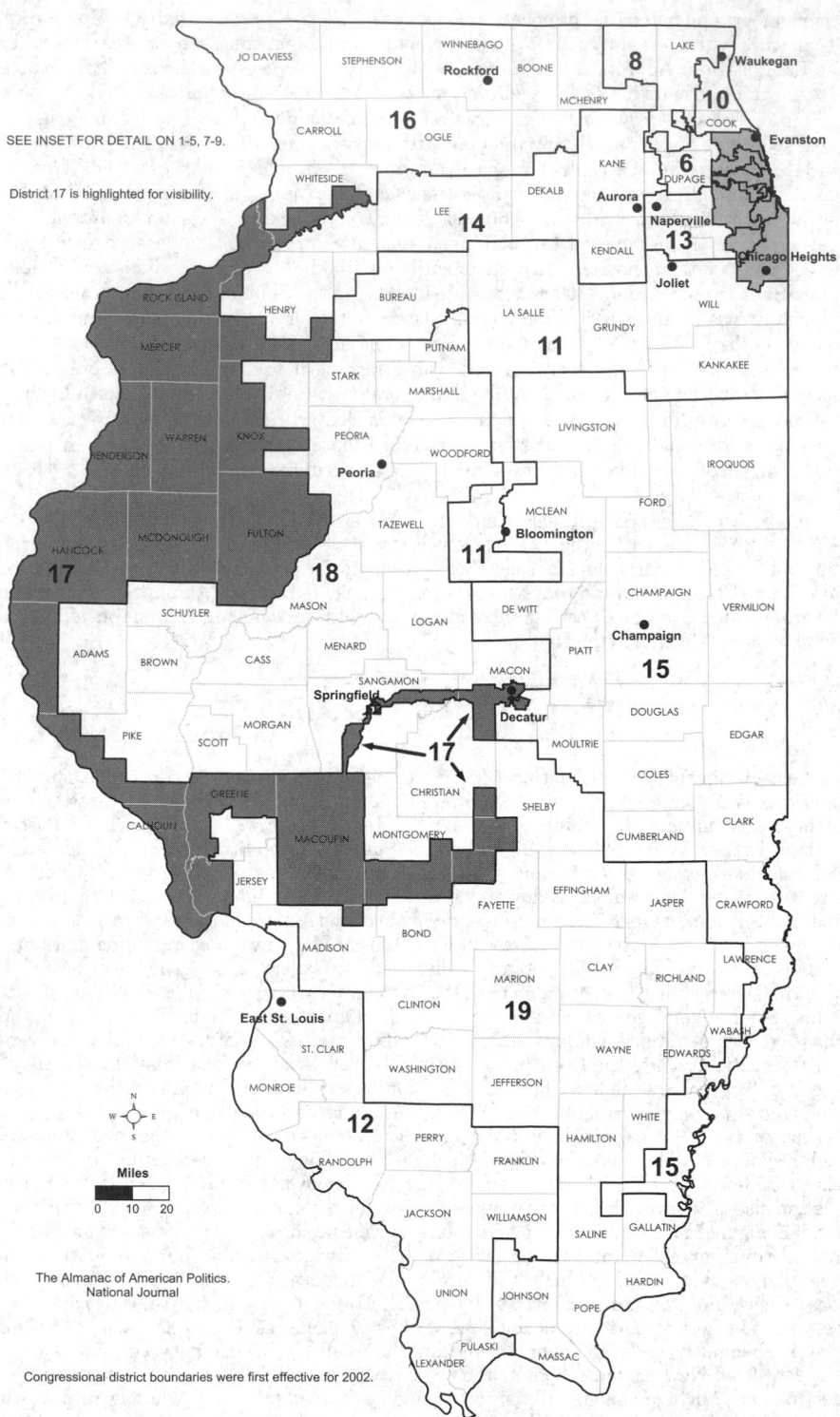

SEE INSET FOR DETAIL ON 1-5, 7-9.

District 17 is highlighted for visibility.

Miles
0   10   20

The Almanac of American Politics.
National Journal

Congressional district boundaries were first effective for 2002.

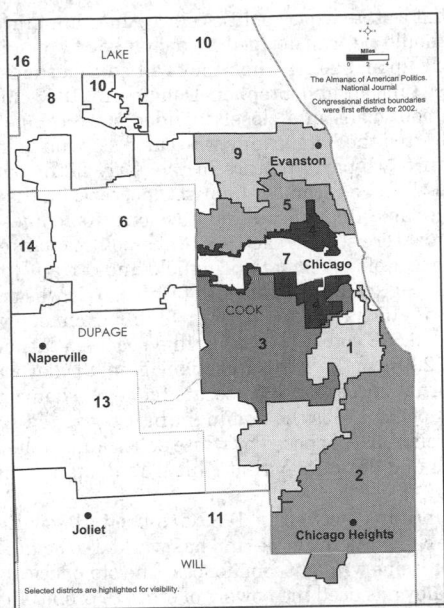

factories, built where iron ore from Great Lakes freighters and coal from inland hills came together, attracted migrants from near and far. Today many of the old factories have been closed or demolished, and some of the Chicago area's biggest corporations have had problems. But Chicago's economy, based on finance and commodities, manufacturing and food, and undergirded by thousands of small firms, continues to thrive. The O'Hare area rivals downtown Chicago in number of jobs; central city neighborhoods north and south of the Loop are attracting new affluent residents, many to houses worth over $1 million; Latinos are thronging to the Chicago area and adding vitality to tired old neighborhoods; in April 2007, Chicago was selected to be the host city for the U.S. bid for the 2016 Olympics.

Chicago and Illinois produced no presidents in the 20th century, but they have produced crucial votes and pivotal politicians. The list starts with Charles Dawes, a 30-year-old lawyer sent to Chicago by Hanna to manage McKinley's campaign—later he was a World War I general, the first director of Budget Bureau (now Office of Management and Budget) and vice president under Calvin Coolidge. Next comes Chicago lawyer Harold Ickes, who was Franklin Roosevelt's great Interior secretary. Prominent Illinois Republicans have included House Speaker Joseph Cannon, Senate Republican Leader Everett Dirksen, Senator Charles Percy and House Republican Leader Robert Michel; prominent Democrats have included Governor Adlai Stevenson, Mayor Richard J. Daley and Ways and Means Chairman Dan Rostenkowski. But it has not produced a serious presidential candidate in the half-century separating Stevenson and Senator Barack Obama.

For most of the 20th century, Illinois was a key political battleground, closely divided between (usually) Democratic Chicago and (mostly) Republican Downstate, with the growing ring of suburbs around Chicago becoming increasingly pivotal. Its mixture of blacks and whites and Hispanics, immigrants and pioneers, city-dwellers and suburbanites and farmers, the affluent and the impoverished, heavy industry and high-tech, make it a rough proxy for the nation. For a century Illinois was a political bellwether, voting only twice for losing presidential candidates between 1896 and 1996—in 1916 and 1976. But in the 1990s Illinois became steadily more Democratic than the nation. In 2000 Illinois was one of Al Gore's best states. He won 55%-43%, running even ahead of Clinton in winning metro Chicago by 61%-37%; he did slightly worse Downstate, which George W. Bush won 51%-46%. This was in line with the national trend toward Clinton and Gore in the suburbs and slightly away from Democrats in rural areas; if Democrats' stands on abortion and gun control hurt them in rural areas, they clearly helped in the suburbs of Chicago. Illinois was not a target state in 2004, and it voted pretty much as it did in 2000—55%-44% for John Kerry, with Kerry leading in metro Chicago 60%-39% and Bush leading Downstate 55%-45%. Bush ran 3% ahead of his father's 1988 showing in Downstate Illinois, but Kerry ran 11% ahead of Michael Dukakis in metro Chicago.

It may seem strange that a state whose politics since Abraham Lincoln's time has mostly been run by political machines should be transformed by a change of opinion in the suburbs. Illinois's party machines were already up and going when they rallied thousands of partisans to cheer and boo at the debates between Lincoln and Stephen Douglas in 1858. Machine politics continued through the Gilded Age as politicians in a closely divided state competed for public jobs and as politicians of both parties courted the immigrants who came streaming into Chicago. Both Chicago and Downstate had a thriving two-party politics in the early 20th century; it was not until the Depression of the 1930s that Chicago became reliably Democratic. In the decades that followed, the suburbs, wary of Chicago, became Republican and developed machines of their own. Starting in 1950, Illinois's political trends were set by reactions to the political officeholder most visible to the voters, who was not the governor off in remote Springfield and certainly not the senators who have to work "out of town" in Washington, but the mayor of Chicago. It was only through the herculean efforts of mayor and party boss Richard J. Daley that John F. Kennedy was able to win Illinois by exactly (or so it was certified) 8,858 votes out of 4.7 million cast—a turnout that has been exceeded since only in 1984, 1992 and 2004. In the 1970s, reaction against Daley was key to the rise of James Thompson, who as U.S. Attorney successfully prosecuted machine denizens and served as governor from 1976 to 1990. For most of the 1980s the dominant figure was Mayor Harold Washington, the able black mayor who was vociferously opposed by white politicians in the "council wars." Suburban-ites, repelled by the hubbub and out of fear that Chicago's demands might increase their taxes, voted heavily Republican.

The dominant figure since his election in 1989 has been Mayor Richard M. Daley. Like his father, he seems to know the city block by block, and has worked to beautify it—planting thousands of trees and encouraging handsome wrought-iron fences. The old political machine which his father so ably led is no more, but Daley has used the powers of office to propitiate the black politicians who at first seemed to be obdurate opponents; he has been reelected by overwhelming majorities. He has kept on good terms with presidents of both parties. Daley's luster has extended to his party. His example as the state's leading Democrat undoubtedly helped ease the way for suburbanites to move toward Democrats over the last 15 years.

The last dozen years have seen a turnover of state government from Republicans to Democrats. In 1994 Republican Governor Jim Edgar was reelected and Republicans won majorities in both houses of the legislature. They lost their House majority in 1996 and their Senate majority in 2002. Democrat Richard Durbin was elected to the Senate in 1996 and easily reelected in 2002. In 1998 Republican Secretary of State George Ryan was elected governor and Republican Peter Fitzgerald beat ethics-challenged Senator Carol Moseley Braun but both had political problems. Ryan's top aides in the Secretary of State office were implicated in a bribery scandal; Ryan prudently decided not to run for reelection in 2002 and was convicted on racketeering and fraud charges in April 2006. The Republican nominee to succeed him, Attorney General Jim Ryan, was no relation, but having the same last name did not help him; he lost to Chicago Congressman Rod Blagojevich, who had the advantage of a name that no one could confuse with Ryan, 52%-45%. Blagojevich carried metro Chicago 57%-40% while losing Downstate 52%-46%: the key was the suburbs. In 2003 Fitzgerald, who had criticized George Ryan and many other Republican leaders, decided not to seek reelection; Democratic state senator and University of Chicago Law Professor Barack Obama won the seat by 70%-27%, the most one-sided Senate victory in Illinois history. In 2006 Blagojevich was reelected by a 50%-39% vote over state Treasurer Judy Baar Topinka; he carried metro Chicago 56%-34%, while losing Downstate 48%-40%. Democrats increased their margins in the state Senate to 37-22 and the state House to 66-52.

The People		Race/Ethnic Origin			Military veterans: 1,003,572 (10.9%)	
Pop. 2006 (est):	12,831,970	8,424,140	67.8%	White	WWII: 22.7%	Korea: 14.4%
Pop. 2000:	12,419,293	1,856,152	14.9%	Black	Vietnam: 30.1%	Gulf War: 9.0%
Pop. 1990:	11,430,602	419,916	3.4%	Asian	**Most populous cities (2006):**	
Change 1990-2000:	Up 8.6%	18,232	0.1%	Native Am.	1. Chicago	2,833,321
% of U.S. total:	4.4%	3,116	0.0%	Hawaiian	2. Aurora	170,617
Pop. rank:	5th of 50	153,996	1.2%	Two+ races	3. Rockford	155,138
Area size:	57,914 sq. mi.	13,479	0.1%	Other	4. Naperville	142,901
State Native:	67.1%	1,530,262	12.3%	Hisp. Origin	5. Joliet	142,702
Non-citizen:	7.5%	**Ancestry**				
Language		German: 15.1%		Irish: 9.3%	Urban population: 87.8%	
English: 80.3%	Spanish: 9.6%	Polish: 5.8%		English: 5.1%	Rural population: 12.2%	
Other Eur.: 7.1%		Italian: 4.6%				

Education		Work Sector		General Assembly	
H.S. Grad:	81.4%	Private: 81.8%	Govt: 12.7%	Senate	37 D 22 R
College Grad:	26.1%	Self: 5.3%	Family: 0.3%	House	66 D 52 R
Industry		Unemployment: 6.0%		Legislative Term Limits: No	
Agri: 1.1%	Con: 5.7%	**Household Income**		**Registered Voters**	
Fin: 7.9%	Info: 3.0%	<15k: 13.8%	15-35k: 23.2%	No party registration	
Mfg: 22.0%	Prof: 29.5%	35-50k: 16.2%	50-100k: 32.3%		
Public: 4.0%	Trade: 14.9%	100-150k: 9.0%	>150k: 5.4%		
Other: 11.9%		Median: $46,590			
Occupation		Poverty status: 10.7%			
Blue collar: 24.0%	White collar: 61.8%	**Home Value**			
Gray collar: 14.3%		<50k: 11.2% 50-100k: 26.1% 100-200k: 39.7% 200-300k: 13.6%			
		300-500k: 6.6% >500k: 2.8% Median: $127,800			

Presidential politics   Illinois's presidential primary, for years held fittingly on or around St. Patrick's Day, clinched the nominations for Republican victors Gerald Ford in 1976, Ronald Reagan in 1980 and George Bush in 1988, and Democratic victors Jimmy Carter in 1980, Walter Mondale in 1984 and Bill Clinton in 1992. In 1988 the Democratic nomination would probably have been clinched here for Michael Dukakis, except for the dominance of two Illinois candidates, Paul Simon and Jesse Jackson. But as more states voted earlier, Illinois has voted too late to decide any nomination. In January 2007 Speaker Michael Madigan proposed moving the primary to February 5, to help Illinois's Barack Obama; the bill was signed into law in June. Other candidates may well ignore Illinois—and avoid the expense of running ads in the nation's third largest media market.

In the 1990s, as Republican margins in the suburban Collar Counties dwindled and in suburban Cook County disappeared, Illinois became a solidly Democratic state in presidential politics. Bush strategists in 2004 kept an eye out for favorable developments in California, with its 55 electoral votes, but they didn't pay attention to Illinois, with its 21.

2004 Presidential Vote
Kerry (D).................... 2,891,550   (55%)
Bush (R) 2,345,946   (44%)
Badnarik (Lib)................. 32,442   (1%)
Other........................... 4,384   (0%)

2004 Democratic Presidential Primary
Kerry (D)..................... 873,230   (72%)
Edwards (D) 131,966   (11%)
Braun (D) 53,249   (4%)
Dean (D) 47,343   (4%)
Sharpton (D).................... 36,123   (3%)
Other........................... 75,604   (6%)

2000 Presidential Vote
Gore (D)..................... 2,589,026   (55%)
Bush (R) 2,019,421   (43%)
Nader (Green) 103,759   (2%)
Other........................... 29,902   (1%)

Congressional districting   Illinois lost one of its 20 House seats in the 2000 Census, and control of redistricting was split between the Democratic state House and the then-Republican state Senate and governor. In similar circumstances, the 1980s and 1990s redistricting plans had been drawn by courts, with results that were politically unpredictable and unpalatable to incumbents: in 1992, four incumbents lost their primaries. Things worked differently in

110th Congress Lineup
10 D   9 R

109th Congress Lineup
10 D   9 R

2001. Speaker Dennis Hastert and 3d District Democrat William Lipinski started negotiating early, to produce an incumbent-protection plan that would pass both houses of the legislature. Before the Census data came in, it was assumed that the 5th District would be eliminated, since Democratic incumbent Rod Blagojevich had announced that he was running for governor. But the Census figures showed that the 5th District and adjacent districts in Chicago, swelled with new immigrants, had gained population, while rural southern Illinois had lost population. Mayor Richard M. Daley let it be known that he would not like to see Chicago lose a seat.

So Hastert and Lipinski concocted a new plan taking a district away from southern Illinois. The victim was 19th District Democratic Congressman David Phelps, a former professional gospel singer with little seniority and a somewhat conservative voting record. His hometown was connected by a narrow band of land on the eastern edge of the state with the central Illinois 15th District held by Republican Tim Johnson. Phelps had no clout in the legislature, and the Hastert-Lipinski plan became law in May 2001. Phelps sued unsuccessfully and then ran, also unsuccessfully, against Republican incumbent John Shimkus in the new 19th District. Why were Lipinski, Daley and Speaker Michael Madigan willing to sacrifice a fellow Democrat and lose their party's 10-10 parity in the House delegation? Because the low-seniority Phelps could do little for them in the House, while Hastert had been generous in using his powers as Speaker to aid Daley, Lipinski and other Chicago Democrats on Chicago issues and projects. Maintaining a Republican majority that would keep Hastert in the speakership was in the interests of Chicago Democrats.

The resulting map is a nightmare for those who believe redistricting plans should have compact and competitive districts. Aside from Phelps and perhaps Shimkus, every other incumbent was strengthened. And the resulting district lines are grotesque. The 17th District, long confined to west central Illinois, now has a narrow finger extending to downtown Springfield and Decatur. The 15th District in central Illinois has a long narrow tentacle along the eastern border of the state, then snakes south to the Kentucky border. Hastert's 14th District extends from the Chicago suburbs to a point six miles from the Iowa border. Incumbents were accommodated in the most minute fashion. A small portion of Livingston County was added to Jerry Weller's 11th District so his parents could vote for him. Complicated boundaries were drawn to Philip Crane's 8th District so that his Palatine office would still be in his district (he lost anyway in 2004). Jesse Jackson Jr.'s 2d District was extended southward to be nearer to Peotone, the site for the proposed third Chicago airport that he has been tirelessly promoting. Lipinski lost a heavily black ward in Chicago and majority-Hispanic Cicero and in return got the white Bridgeport neighborhood that is the homeland of the Daleys and some heavily white suburbs (he engineered the nomination of his son to succeed him in 2004).

In 2005, Congressman Rahm Emanuel, the newly-installed chairman of the Democratic Congressional Campaign Committee, sought to revisit the issue of the state's congressional map; the idea was to draw a new map to retaliate for post-2002 Republican redistricting efforts in Colorado, Georgia and Texas. But the legislature didn't seem to have much interest in drawing new lines and neither did a majority of the Democratic congressional delegation, and the idea was shelved.

Governor

Rod Blagojevich (D)

Elected 2002, term expires Jan. 2011, 2d term; b. Dec. 10, 1956, Chicago; home, Chicago; Northwestern U., B.A. 1979, Pepperdine U., J.D. 1983; Eastern Orthodox; married (Patti).

Elected Office: IL House of Reps., 1992-96; U.S. House of Reps., 1996-2002.

Professional Career: Practicing atty., 1984-96; Asst. Cook County Atty., 1986-88.

Office: Office of the Governor, 207 State House, Springfield, 62706, 217-782-0244 ; Fax: 217-524-4049; Web site: http://www.illinois.gov/gov/.

Election Results

2006 general	Rod Blagojevich (D)	1,736,731	(50%)
	Judy Baar Topinka (R)	1,369,315	(39%)
	Rich Whitney (Green)	361,336	(10%)
	Other	14,574	(1%)
2006 primary	Rod Blagojevich (D)	669,006	(71%)
	Edwin Eisendrath (D)	275,375	(29%)
2002 general	Rod Blagojevich (D)	1,847,040	(52%)
	Jim Ryan (R)	1,594,960	(45%)
	Other	96,883	(3%)

Rod Blagojevich was elected governor of Illinois in 2002, the first Democrat elected to the office since 1972, when Blagojevich was in high school. He grew up in Chicago, the son of a Serbian immigrant who worked at the A. Finkl & Sons steel works on the North Side; his mother worked as a ticket-taker for the Chicago Transit Authority. He lived in a five-room walkup near Cicero and Armitage and worked as a shoeshine boy and a dishwasher on the Alaskan pipeline. Blagojevich (pronounced *blah-GOY-eh-vich*) graduated from Northwestern and Pepperdine Law School and was a Golden Gloves boxer. A fine athlete, he runs marathons and climbs perilous mountains. He practiced law and worked two years in State's Attorney Richard M. Daley's office. But he got his start in politics through his father-in-law, 33d Ward Alderman and Democratic Ward Committeeman Richard Mell. In 1988 Blagojevich met Mell's daughter Patti at a Mell fundraiser, and in 1990 they were married. In 1988 he got a job on Mell's staff; in 1992 he was elected to the Illinois House. His opportunity to run for the U.S. House came after Republican Michael Flanagan upset Ways and Means Chairman Dan Rostenkowski in 1994. Flanagan, who had little backing, was obviously a one-termer. In 1996 Blagojevich outspent Flanagan and won 64%-36%.

The initial impulse for Blagojevich's gubernatorial candidacy may have come from uncertainty about redistricting. It was fairly clear early on that Illinois would lose a seat in the 2000 Census, and most politicians assumed one of the Chicago districts would have to go—and Blagojevich's 5th District was vulnerable because it could easily be sliced up by its neighbors and was not represented by a black or Hispanic. Moreover, it was apparent that unpopular incumbent Republican Governor George Ryan, embroiled in scandal, would be hard put to win a second term. In July 2001, Blagojevich announced that he was running for governor. He plunged ahead, although the redistricting plan passed two months earlier had preserved his 5th District in almost identical form.

There were crowded races in both parties' March 2002 primaries. In the Democratic primary, Blagojevich faced former Chicago schools CEO Paul Vallas and former Attorney General Roland Burris. Burris was relying on his appeal to black voters, Vallas on his record in improving Chicago's public schools, although he had left office at odds with his original patron, Mayor Richard M. Daley. In metro Chicago Vallas led with 38% of the vote to 32% for Burris and 29% for Blagojevich. But Blagojevich won 56% of the vote Downstate, for a 37%-34%-29% victory over Vallas and Burris. There was more acrimony on the Republican side. All three candidates vied to distance themselves from George Ryan. Jim Ryan, no relation to the incumbent, well known from his years as DuPage County state's attorney and state attorney general, was pummeled from both sides. But he won convincingly, with 45% of the vote.

Ordinarily in Illinois politics it is an advantage to have an Irish name shared by other successful politicians. Candidates named Ryan, Hynes or Hines, or Cullerton are often elected to downballot state and Cook County offices without much difficulty and can easily become serious contenders for the top positions. But in 2002 it was not an advantage to be a Ryan. Jim Ryan was at pains to distinguish himself from George Ryan; his campaign signs said simply "Jim." Jim Ryan lamented that Blagojevich was not being hurt by his ties to machine politicians. But Richard Mell was not a political liability in 2002 and Mayor Daley, the chairman of Blagojevich's campaign, was a decided political asset.

Blagojevich campaigned for "changing the old way of doing business"—an obvious attack on George Ryan. Always ahead in the polls, he got support from big lobby groups which usually back Republicans—the Illinois State Medical Society, the Illinois Retail Merchants Association—and raised $25 million, far more than Jim Ryan. The only surprise about the outcome was that it was a bit closer than expected. Blagojevich won 52%-45%; he carried metro Chicago by a solid 57%-40% and lost Downstate by only 52%-46%—a good return on the time and money he spent there. On election night, at a gathering held at the A. Finkl & Sons steel works, Blagojevich, a big Elvis Presley fan, said he was "all shook up" and full of "a whole bunch of hunk o', hunk o' burnin' love for each one of you." Democrats captured a majority in the state Senate, and Chicagoan Emil Jones succeeded longtime Republican leader Pate Philip as Senate Majority Leader; Democratic State Chairman and Speaker Michael Madigan remained in charge of the Illinois House. Federal investigators, led by U.S. Attorney Patrick Fitzgerald—an out-of-stater nominated by Republican Senator (and George Ryan critic) Peter Fitzgerald—zeroed in on George Ryan, and in December 2003 he was indicted on bribery charges; he was convicted in April 2006.

Democrats were in control of state government for the first time since 1976, and Democrats with friendly ties to Chicago politicians for the first time since 1968. But all was not harmony. "Illinois has voted for change," Blagojevich proclaimed, and proceeded to oppose the kind of pork spending which George Ryan had lavished on legislators of both parties. As co-chairman of his transition team he named former Governor Jim Thompson, a Republican who had built his career on opposition to the Chicago machine. He announced that he would govern from Chicago, and traveled to the gritty state capital of Springfield only rarely (a not unheard of procedure: current or recent governors of California, New York and Illinois have spent more time in Los Angeles, New York City and Chicago, rather than their state capitals, than most voters would guess). He hired his law school roommate from California and a former top aide to Senator Charles Schumer and Mayor Michael Bloomberg of New York as top aides in a state where politics is an intensely parochial matter. Senate Majority Leader Emil Jones said, "Well, he does a pretty good job of communicating—if I read the papers in time." Blagojevich's response: "The system has to change. I know it, I presume you know it and I know the people know it. We are going to keep fighting to change this system, a system that has way too much cynicism, a system that has too many misplaced priorities and a system that spends the people's money with reckless disregard."

On many issues the new governor prevailed. In 2003 he vetoed one ethics package passed by the legislature and got it to pass a much stronger version. He succeeded in keeping his promise not to allow increases in the sales or income taxes. He got steep cuts in some programs and an increase in education spending; borrowing $10 billion to shore up pension systems freed $2 billion for operating expenses. He got changes in the death penalty law, and got the legislature to strike a provision on police perjury which was supported by Emil Jones but opposed by police unions. Richard M. Daley's plan for vastly expanding O'Hare Airport—the mayor's absolute number one priority—was approved. The minimum wage was increased. But there were clashes along the way, with Secretary of State Jesse White over spending for his office, with Michael Madigan over the 2004 budget. In 2004 Blagojevich and Jones were allies on the budget, with Madigan and Senate Republican leaders as their adversaries seeking cuts in education and Medicaid: scrambled political alignments reminiscent of the city-states of Renaissance Italy.

Riverboat gambling has become a big business in Illinois, and state government faces current gambling issues. In May 2004, one day after Mayor Daley called for a city-run casino in Chicago, Blagojevich abruptly rejected the proposal; he said that gambling should be confined to depressed riverfront areas. In the Chicago area most interstates are named after local politicians and road builders; Blagojevich named I-88 after Ronald Reagan. During most of 2003 and 2004 Blagojevich's job approval remained at or above 50%, far better than his predecessor's. But his poll ratings dropped as one appointee pleaded guilty to criminal charges and a Blagojevich fundraiser was indicted. A family feud with his powerful father-in-law, Alderman Richard Mell, also drew considerable attention. Daley blamed Blagojevich for failing to push gun control laws and for not funding the Chicago transit authority. Blagojevich got the legislature to give him the power to appoint most members of the State Board of Education, then complained when the new Board did not produce its independent recommendation for school spending. Some Blagojevich proposals never went anywhere: a federal court struck down his ban on violent video games for minors, his plan to sell the state lottery to raise $10 billion remained on the back burner. But others did. The AllKids children's health insurance program was expanded to include families with incomes up to $80,000; a medical malpractice bill limiting punitive damages was passed; preschool was expanded to kids at age three; tuition grants of $500 were offered to students attending Illinois colleges and maintaining B grades with family incomes up to $200,000.

The campaign season begins early in Illinois; the filing deadline is in December. Blagojevich was opposed in the 2006 Democratic primary by former Chicago Alderman Edwin Eisendrath, who charged that the governor had not ended "business as usual", but Blagojevich won the March contest 71%-29%. As in 2002, the Republicans had a fractious primary. Dairy magnate Jim Oberweis, an unsuccessful Senate candidate in 2002 and 2004, ran as a conservative; so did Bloomington state Sen. Bill Brady and Chicago businessman Ron Gidwitz. In the summer of 2005 many Republicans tried to persuade former Governor Jim Edgar to enter the race, but in September he said he wouldn't run. He supported Treasurer Judy Baar Topinka, the only Republican left in statewide office, a supporter of abortion rights, opponent of gun control and a fiscal moderate. She won the primary with 38% of the vote, to 32% for Oberweis, 18% (mostly from Downstate) for Brady and 11% for Gidwitz. She lambasted Blagojevich for overspending and for increasing the state debt, by her count, from $7.6 billion to $21.4 billion. Blagojevich, who outspent her by $17 million to $6 million, ran a barrage of negative ads, depicting her as "George Ryan's Treasurer" and showing her dancing the polka with him. Topinka, the granddaughter of Czech immigrants, said she was willing to "polka with anyone, any time." By October her negatives were approaching 50%. Blagojevich, whose job approval numbers were in similar territory, won with 50% of the vote (actually slightly less than an absolute majority), while Topinka got only 39%; the Green party candidate, with 10%, got his party a place on the ballot for the next four years. Turnout was down from 2002—in contrast to most other states and a sign that many voters were displeased with both major party candidates.

Blagojevich carried metro Chicago by 56%-34% while Topinka led Downstate by 48%-40%; she won the usually Republican suburban Collar Counties by only 46%-42%.

Blagojevich entered his second term as a champion of "an activist government offering bold solutions that make a difference for people." He called for universal health care for Illinois, even as Speaker Michael Madigan grumbled about the possible cost. In March 2007, Blagojevich proposed funding his health care plan with the largest tax increase in Illinois history—an idea not well received by legislators. After failing to compromise and pass a budget by the July 31 deadline, on August 10 legislators finally passed a budget that included more funding for education, local earmarks, and a legislative pay raise—but no increase in health care spending. Blagojevich threatened to veto the proposed budget, though an override was certain; he called legislators into special sessions which they refused to attend. In late August, Blagojevich sued Madigan and requested that a judge order the Speaker to hold special sessions at the governor's behest.

Blagojevich had talked with Democratic allies about running for president as early as November 2002, but he made no moves to enter the 2008 race, and his 50% reelection percentage in what is now a solidly Democratic state was not stellar enough to propel him into national prominence.

Senior Senator

Richard Durbin (D)

Elected 1996, seat up 2008, 2d term; b. Nov. 21, 1944, E. St. Louis; home, Springfield; Georgetown U., B.S. 1966, J.D. 1969; Catholic; married (Loretta).

Elected Office: U.S. House of Reps., 1982-96.

Professional Career: Staff, Lt. Gov. Paul Simon, 1969-72; Legal Cnsl., IL Sen. Judiciary Cmte., 1972-82; Prof., S. IL Schl. of Medicine, 1978-82.

DC Office: 309 HSOB, 20510, 202-224-2152; Fax: 202-228-0400; Web site: durbin.senate.gov.

State Offices: Chicago, 312-353-4952; Marion, 618-998-8812; Springfield, 217-492-4062.

Committees: *Majority Whip. Appropriations* (10th of 15 D): Financial Services & General Government (Chmn.); Legislative Branch; Agriculture, Rural Development, Food and Drug Administration & Related Agencies; State, Foreign Operations & Related Programs; Transportation, Housing and Urban Development & Related Agencies; Defense; Labor, Health and Human Services, Education & Related Agencies. *Judiciary* (8th of 10 D): Human Rights & the Law (Chmn.); Constitution; Immigration, Refugees & Border Security; Terrorism, Technology & Homeland Security; Crime & Drugs. *Rules & Administration* (6th of 10 D).

Group Ratings

	ADA	ACLU	AFS	LCV	ITIC	NTU	COC	ACU	CFG	FRC
2006	100	92	100	100	25	12	45	4	0	0
2005	100	—	100	95	—	4	28	0	0	—

National Journal Ratings

	2005 LIB	—	2005 CONS		2006 LIB	—	2006 CONS
Economic	94%	—	5%		87%	—	0%
Social	77%	—	18%		95%	—	4%
Foreign	86%	—	13%		95%	—	2%

Key Votes of the 109th Congress

1. Bar ANWR Drilling	Y	5. Confirm Samuel Alito	N	9. Limit Interstate Abortion	N
2. FY06 Spending Curb	N	6. Path to Citizenship	Y	10. CAFTA	N
3. Estate Tax Repeal	N	7. Bar Same Sex Marriage	N	11. Urge Iraq Withdrawal	Y
4. Raise Minimum Wage	Y	8. Stem Cell Research $	Y	12. Provide Detainee Rights	Y

Election Results

2002 general	Richard Durbin (D)	2,103,766	(60%)	($4,979,865)
	Jim Durkin (R)	1,325,703	(38%)	($794,634)
	Other	57,382	(2%)	
2002 primary	Richard Durbin (D)	unopposed		
1996 general	Richard Durbin (D)	2,384,028	(56%)	($4,966,804)
	Al Salvi (R)	1,728,824	(41%)	($4,696,065)
	Other	137,870	(3%)	

Prior Winning Percentages: 1994 House (55%); 1992 House (57%); 1990 House (66%); 1988 House (69%); 1986 House (68%); 1984 House (61%); 1982 House (50%)

Richard Durbin, Illinois's senior senator, is a Democrat first elected to the House in 1982 and the Senate in 1996. Durbin grew up in East St. Louis, and graduated from Georgetown and its law school. For almost all his adult life he has been in politics: he was an intern in the office of Senator Paul Douglas and after law school joined Paul Simon's staff when he was lieutenant governor (1969-73), then was a state Senate staffer in the 1970s. He lost races for the state Senate in 1976 and lieutenant governor in 1978, but in 1982 won the nomination to oppose Republican Congressman Paul Findley, who had characterized himself as Yasir Arafat's best friend in Congress; that helped Durbin raise large sums from Israel supporters. Durbin won that race, got a seat on the Agriculture Committee and then moved to Appropriations, where in 1993 he became chairman of the Agriculture Subcommittee. Durbin's father died of lung cancer when he was 14, and Durbin's most prominent achievement in the House was the 1988 ban on smoking on domestic airline flights; he followed that up by trying to limit tobacco subsidies and in 1994 moved unsuccessfully to direct the FDA to regulate tobacco as a health hazard. "I didn't realize it would trigger a change in America," he later said of the airline smoking ban, but indeed it has led to smoking bans in many settings.

Durbin won his Senate seat in 1996 after his onetime boss Senator Paul Simon announced his retirement; the race may have looked more attractive because Democrats had lost control of the House in 1994 and because Durbin's own margins in the 1992 and 1994 House races were fairly close. Raising more than $1 million, he outspent former state Treasurer (and current Lieutenant Governor) Pat Quinn in the March 1996 primary and won 65%-30%. In the general he faced trial lawyer and abortion opponent Al Salvi and won 56%-41%.

In the Senate, Durbin has compiled a liberal voting record—in 2006, he was the most liberal senator, according to *National Journal*—though he has supported welfare reform and the death penalty. He has been an active and dependable Democratic partisan on the floor and on cable news networks. After the defeat of Tom Daschle in 2004 and the elevation of Harry Reid as minority leader, Durbin became minority whip—a natural promotion since he has held the floor for Democrats on many seriously contested issues. He serves on the Judiciary Committee and has been a strong opponent of many Bush judicial nominees, including John Roberts and Samuel Alito. In his early years in the Senate he attempted to move his goal of gun control incrementally forward. But many Democrats have concluded that gun control helped defeat Al Gore in 2000 and these moves have not been successful. While serving in the House, Durbin favored restrictions on abortion, including the Hyde Amendment and the Human Life amendment. But in the Senate he has opposed restrictions on abortion, including the partial-birth abortion ban; he said it should include an exception for health of the mother. This has caused some controversy among his fellow Catholics. In April 2004 the priest at his home church in Springfield said that he wouldn't give Holy Communion to Durbin; he said that earlier leafletters had subjected him to a "rather uncomfortable atmosphere" there. In June 2004 he presented a report showing how senators voted on positions taken by the U.S. Conference of Catholic Bishops, including international and domestic issues beyond abortion; it showed Democratic senators, including John Kerry, Edward Kennedy and Durbin himself with records above 60%.

On other domestic issues, Durbin has had a very strong pro-union voting record, but split with labor on trade, supporting NAFTA in the House and normal trade relations with China in the Senate: Illinois is a big exporter. But in 2006 he said he felt "betrayed" by the results of NAFTA and he has opposed more recent trade agreements, though he hailed the agreement by which Mexico removed its tax on beverages with high-fructose corn syrup and the U.S. provided duty-free access to the same amount of Mexican sugar.

Durbin took a lead role on asbestos legislation in 2003. Called on by Illinois-based businesses to support a bill establishing quick recovery for injured plaintiffs and reducing the burden on businesses only tangentially connected with asbestos, he negotiated with Judiciary Committee

Chairman Orrin Hatch. But Durbin insisted on a "collateral source" amendment which would grandfather in existing asbestos cases and settlements—a poison pill, in the view of the National Association of Manufacturers. His amendment was not approved and an asbestos bill was not passed. In 2006 he helped to defeat the asbestos trust fund sponsored by Arlen Specter but admitted the need for "significant changes in the existing tort system." In July 2003 Minority Leader Tom Daschle asked Durbin to be the Democrats' point man on medical malpractice, and he successfully blocked action on the legislation. He has opposed a $250,000 cap on pain and suffering awards but has favored medical panels to review the merit of malpractice claims. He has sought funding to treat childhood asthma, promoted organ and tissue donation and moved to ban ephedra.

Durbin voted against the Gulf War resolution in January 1991 and the Iraq war resolution in October 2002, though he voted to authorize the use of force in Iraq when Bill Clinton was president in February 1998. In July 2003 he took to the Senate floor to charge that the Bush White House was trying to push him off the Intelligence Committee; some Republican senators said that Durbin may have disclosed classified information. In June 2005, Durbin was at the center of a storm over remarks he made from the Senate floor concerning detainees at Guantanamo Bay. Citing an FBI report that described the mistreatment of some prisoners, Durbin likened the American interrogators to "Nazis, Soviets in their gulags, or some mad regime—Pol Pot or others—that had no concern for human beings." His over-the-top comments dominated the news cycle for days; Durbin said he regretted any misunderstanding over his remarks. After Mayor Richard M. Daley criticized them, Durbin issued an emotional apology from the Senate floor. In 2006 he co-sponsored the successful bipartisan bill to prohibit demonstrations at federal and private cemeteries; this was aimed at war opponents who had distressed the families of fallen service members.

After the 2006 election Durbin became the majority whip; as he remarked, his job in the minority was to get 41 of 45 Democrats to go along but now he needed to get 60 votes with only 51 Democrats. He noted that his position enabled him to promote local issues. "So if I'm in the huddle, so is Illinois." These include ethanol, for which he worked for tax incentives and pushed for an ethanol research pilot plant at SIU-Edwardsville. He and Barack Obama opposed increased ethanol imports. In January 2007 he rearranged jurisdictions to get the Commodity Futures Trading Commission under his Appropriations subcommittee. This has jurisdiction over Chicago's commodities exchanges; Durbin has opposed new fees for the exchanges and has supported the planned merger of the Chicago Mercantile Exchange and the Board of Trade. He has supported farm disaster aid, deductibility of health insurance for the self-employed, reductions in interest rates on student loans and full funding of Pell grants. He has sought Medicaid waivers for Illinois and funding for the FutureGen clean coal project.

Durbin was mentioned briefly in 2000 as a possible vice presidential nominee; he said that he had been contacted by the Gore campaign in June and asked for information, but had called back four days later to say they he did not want to be considered. He was reelected 60%-38% in 2002 against an opponent who raised very little money; the parties' Senate campaign committees are unwilling to put money into a long shot race in a large state like Illinois when they can target races in much smaller states with much less money. In 2004, he was not much mentioned as a vice presidential nominee and played only a small role—introducing his soon-to-be colleague Obama—at the Democratic National Convention. He had known Obama for more than a decade and appeared not to be jealous of his junior colleague's increasing national prominence. "I think it would be great for Illinois if he's president." He continues to live in an "animal house" communal house on Capitol Hill with Charles Schumer, George Miller and Bill Delahunt; there was coverage in the *New York Times* when Durbin killed a rat but failed to dispose of the carcass.

Durbin comes up for reelection in 2008. Prominent Republicans including Congressmen Mark Kirk, Ray LaHood and John Shimkus have said they're not interested in running; one possible opponent is Downstate state Senator Bill Brady, who ran third in the Democratic gubernatorial primary in 2006, though he said in May 2007 he was focusing on another run for governor in 2010. It is unlikely that national Republicans will fund a candidate in a state where advertising is very expensive and which seems almost sure to vote Democratic for president.

Junior Senator

Barack Obama (D)

Elected 2004, seat up 2010, 1st term; b. Aug. 4, 1961, Honolulu, HI; home, Chicago; Attended Occidental College, 1979-81, Columbia U., B.A. 1983, Harvard U., J.D. 1991; United Church of Christ; married (Michelle).

Elected Office: IL Senate, 1996-2004.

Professional Career: Dir., Illinois Project Vote!, 1992; Practicing atty.; Lecturer, U. of Chicago, 1993-2004.

DC Office: 713 HSOB, 20510, 202-224-2854; Fax: 202-228-4260; Web site: obama.senate.gov.

State Offices: Chicago, 312-886-3506; Marion, 618-997-2402; Moline, 309-736-1217; Springfield, 217-492-5089.

Committees: *Foreign Relations* (7th of 11 D): European Affairs (Chmn.); African Affairs; East Asian & Pacific Affairs; International Development & Foreign Assistance, Economic Affairs & International Environmental Protection. *Health, Education, Labor & Pensions* (9th of 11 D): Employment & Workplace Safety; Children & Families. *Homeland Security & Governmental Affairs* (7th of 9 D): Federal Financial Management, Government Information, Federal Services & International Security; Investigations (Permanent); State, Local & Private Sector Preparedness & Integration. *Veterans' Affairs* (4th of 8 D).

Group Ratings

	ADA	ACLU	AFS	LCV	ITIC	NTU	COC	ACU	CFG	FRC
2006	95	83	100	100	75	16	55	8	7	0
2005	100	—	100	95	—	6	39	8	0	—

National Journal Ratings

	2005 LIB	—	2005 CONS		2006 LIB	—	2006 CONS
Economic	87%	—	12%		87%	—	0%
Social	77%	—	18%		77%	—	21%
Foreign	76%	—	15%		85%	—	12%

Key Votes of the 109th Congress

1. Bar ANWR Drilling	Y	5. Confirm Samuel Alito	N	9. Limit Interstate Abortion	N
2. FY06 Spending Curb	N	6. Path to Citizenship	Y	10. CAFTA	N
3. Estate Tax Repeal	N	7. Bar Same Sex Marriage	N	11. Urge Iraq Withdrawal	Y
4. Raise Minimum Wage	Y	8. Stem Cell Research $	Y	12. Provide Detainee Rights	Y

Election Results

2004 general	Barack Obama (D)	3,595,299	(70%)	($14,532,493)
	Alan Keyes (R)	1,389,850	(27%)	($2,545,325)
	Other	153,158	(3%)	
2004 primary	Barack Obama (D)	655,923	(53%)	
	Daniel Hynes (D)	294,717	(24%)	
	Blair Hull (D)	134,453	(11%)	
	Maria Pappas (D)	74,987	(6%)	
	Gery Chico (D)	53,433	(4%)	
	Other	29,483	(2%)	
1998 general	Peter Fitzgerald (R)	1,709,041	(50%)	($17,678,198)
	Carol Moseley-Braun (D)	1,610,496	(47%)	($7,200,895)
	Other	74,984	(2%)	

Barack Obama, Illinois's junior senator, was a national political celebrity even before he was elected to the Senate in November 2004. His background is unusual, quite different from that of most black politicians, yet as quintessentially American as that of Tiger Woods. Obama's father was from Kenya, his mother from Kansas; they met in Hawaii, where her parents had gone to live and where Barack Jr. was born in 1961. When he was 2, Obama's father left to get a degree at Harvard, then returned to Kenya where he was a prominent politician and then, after a downward spiral, died in an auto accident in 1982; Obama recalls meeting him only once, when he was 10. Obama's mother married an Indonesian, and the family moved there, where he attended both Muslim and Catholic schools; he lived there from age 6 to 10, during the years 1967-71 that were so turbulent in U.S.

politics. He returned to Hawaii and, when his mother moved back to Indonesia, stayed and lived with his maternal grandparents and attended the elite Punahou Academy. Classmates remember him as a bright and cheerful young man who played basketball and helped the team win a state championship in 1979. His memories, as recounted in his 1995 autobiography *Dreams from My Father: A Story of Race and Inheritance,* are that he was preoccupied and almost tormented by his racial background, even in multiracial and tolerant Hawaii, and that he got into drugs (marijuana and cocaine but not heroin). "Junkie. Pothead. That's where I'd been headed: the final, fatal role of the young would-be black man." He went to the Mainland to college, first to Occidental College in Los Angeles, then to Columbia University in New York. After graduation he worked as a community organizer in Chicago from 1985 to 1988. He then attended Harvard Law School, where he graduated *magna cum laude* and was the first black president of the *Harvard Law Review* (and was also a classmate of former Republican National Chairman Ken Mehlman). He and his wife, also a Harvard Law graduate, then moved to Chicago, her hometown, where in 1993 he became a lecturer at the University of Chicago law school.

Politics always seems to have been on his mind. In 1992 he worked on voter registration for the Democratic ticket. In 1996 he ran for the state Senate and was unopposed in the decisive Democratic primary. Next came a political misstep: in 2000 he ran in the primary against 1st District Democratic Congressman Bobby Rush, who the year before had lost the February 1999 race for mayor to incumbent Richard M. Daley by 72%-28%. Obama was attacked for missing a vote on a gun control measure sought by Daley and Governor George Ryan because he was in Hawaii, visiting family, and one of his daughters was ill. Rush was endorsed by Bill Clinton and won 61%-30%. Obama compiled an impressive record in the state Senate. He played important roles in welfare legislation, on the state earned income tax credit and on the 2003 ethics legislation. In 2003 he pushed successfully for a law requiring electronic recording of interrogations and confessions in homicide cases; prosecutors resisted it, but he argued persuasively that it would ensure convictions in the large majority of cases. He voted against requiring medical care for fetuses who survived abortions, for allowing retired police to carry concealed weapons and against allowing people who used banned handguns to defend against intruders in their houses to be exempt from prosecution for possessing the guns. He sponsored a bill against job and housing discrimination against gays and got a study of racial profiling in traffic stops. He provided the key vote in 2004 to pass Governor Rod Blagojevich's bill to raise $300 million in taxes after first voting against it. In October 2002 he made a public statement opposing the Iraq war resolution. "I know that even a successful war against Iraq will require a U.S. occupation of undetermined length, at undetermined cost, with undetermined consequences," he said at an anti-war rally. "I know that an invasion of Iraq without a clear rationale and without strong international support will only fan the flames of the Middle East, and encourage the worst, rather than best, impulses of the Arab world, and strengthen the recruitment arm of Al Qaeda. I am not opposed to all wars. I'm opposed to dumb wars."

Looming not too far ahead was the 2004 Senate race. Illinois has one of the earliest filing deadlines and state primaries in the nation, in December 2003 and in March 2004 in this case, and the incumbent senator, Republican Peter Fitzgerald, was obviously in trouble. Elected in 1998 in large part because of the ethical shortcomings of incumbent Democrat Carol Moseley Braun, he had compiled an attractive record on ethics himself. But Fitzgerald would have to run in an increasingly Democratic state, and without the support of leading Illinois Republicans; the Republican state committee declined to support Fitzgerald for reelection. In 1998 Fitzgerald had largely self-financed his campaign, but his wealth would have been seriously diminished by another such race, and in April 2003 he announced he would not seek reelection.

With Democratic Senator Richard Durbin comfortably reelected in 2002 and still in the prime of life, it seemed that another Illinois Senate seat would not come open for many years, perhaps a generation, so a host of candidates—eight Democrats and eight Republicans, many of them capable of self-financing a campaign—entered the 2004 race. Initially Obama did not stand out. As an African-American he had an edge with black voters, who would probably make up 25% of the primary electorate. But some prominent black politicians, notably Bobby Rush, endorsed other candidates, though Obama was backed by state Senate Majority Leader Emil Jones, 2d District Congressman Jesse Jackson Jr. and 1984 and 1988 presidential candidate Jesse Jackson Sr. His positions on issues were not particularly distinctive among Illinois Democrats—he favored abortion rights, background checks on all gun sales and was willing to filibuster Bush judicial nominees. He was for civil unions but against same-sex marriage; he backed only the middle-class Bush tax cuts and favored pay-as-you-go budgeting, which is consistent with tax increases on the wealthy.

Other candidates seemed better positioned. State Comptroller Dan Hynes, elected to that office in 1998 at age 30, from a prominent Cook County Democratic family, was backed by Cook County Board President John Stroger and Cook County Commissioner John Daley, brother of Mayor Richard M. Daley. Blair Hull, who sold his trading firm to Goldman-Sachs in 1999 for $531 million, had contributed $260,000 to Governor Rod Blagojevich in 2002 and announced that he was willing to spend $40 million of his own money on his campaign. He imitated Blagojevich's 2002 tactic by buying Downstate TV starting in June 2003 and spent $29 million by the March primary, including $75 a day for anyone who would put up a lawn sign. Also running were Cook County Treasurer Maria Pappas and former Chicago School Board President Gery Chico, each with plausible claims on the nomination. Hull turned out to have serious problems. It was revealed that he had struck his first wife in the shin in 1998 and that she had sought a protection order, calling him "a violent man with an ungovernable temper." His lead in the polls collapsed. Hynes was unable to translate his support from prominent officeholders in the face of Obama's poised performances in endorsement meetings. Obama's opposition to the Iraq war resolution and his dismissive criticism of some Bush policies helped establish a bond with the Bush-hating Dean supporters of his party. And he had some other endorsements—a $10,000 contribution from Michael Jordan and an ad featuring Sheila Simon, daughter of former (1984-96) Senator Paul Simon, a fondly remembered and thoughtful politician who had died in December 2003. Obama was endorsed by the *Chicago Tribune*, no reflexive backer of Democrats, as "one of the strongest Democratic candidates Illinois has seen in some time"—something of a slap in the face to Senator Durbin and Governor Blagojevich. The March primary was a blowout victory for Obama. He won 53% of the vote in an eight-candidate race, to 24% for Hynes, 11% for Hull, 6% for Pappas and 4% for Chico. In metro Chicago, where 74% of the votes were cast, and where the race received the most coverage in the free media, Obama led Hynes 63%-17%. Hull, benefiting from his early ads, won a plurality of 24% Downstate, but that didn't matter. As Obama said on election night, "I think it is fair to say the conventional wisdom was we could not win. We didn't have enough money. We didn't have enough organization. There was no way that a skinny guy from the South Side with a funny name like Barack Obama could ever win a statewide race. Sixteen months later we are there." Moreover, the primary turnout showed huge Democratic strength. Some 1,242,000 voted in the Democratic primary, while only 661,000 voted in the Republican primary—just a tad bit over the 656,000 votes Obama won.

The Senate race was over except for the shouting—but there turned out to be quite a lot of that. The Republican nominee was Jack Ryan, who led the eight-candidate field with 35% of the vote and, like Obama, had an attractive life story. He had graduated from Harvard Law and Harvard Business schools, made a fortune working for Goldman Sachs and had then gone to teach in an inner city school. He and Obama might have had a series of civil exchanges on the issues. But Ryan, like Hull, had a divorce problem. Before the primary he released the records of his California divorce from television actress Jeri Ryan, except for some passages which he said would be harmful to his nine-year-old son. After the primary the *Chicago Tribune* pressed for full disclosure. In June a California judge agreed. It turned out that Ryan had pressed his former wife, against her wish, to go to sex clubs in Paris. Republican party leaders were furious that Ryan had not told them of this vulnerability, and pressed him to get out of the race. After an agonizing interval he did—and then the Republicans had to figure out who to put in his place. The candidates who lost the primary proved either unwilling or unacceptable. Former Chicago Bears coach Mike Ditka thought about it, and said no.

While this was going on, Obama delivered the keynote speech at the Democratic National Convention. In quietly elegant prose, with echoes of the rhythms of black preachers, Obama proclaimed to delegates of a party that tends to divide its ranks into discrete constituencies, "There's not a liberal America and a conservative America, there is the United States of America. There's not a black America and white America and Latino America and Asian America, there is the United States of America." Drawing on his own experiences campaigning in Illinois, he said, "We worship an awesome God in the Blue States, and we don't like federal agents poking around in our libraries in the Red States. We coach Little League in the Blue States, and yes, we've got some gay friends in the Red States." And, echoing Bill Cosby, he spoke about the black community. "Go into any inner city neighborhood, and folks will tell you that government alone can't teach our kids to learn—they know that parents have to teach, that children can't achieve unless we raise their expectation and turn off the television sets and eradicate the slander that says a black youth with a book is acting white. They know these things." Immediately, and not without justification, commentators were hailing this state senator from Hyde Park as a national leader and possible future president.

Republicans still did not have a candidate against him, and it was clear none could do very well. As Peter Fitzgerald said, "Taking the Republican nomination in Illinois for the U.S. Senate would be akin to accepting a cancer transplant." Cultural conservatives, including 16th District Congressman Don Manzullo, put forward the name of Alan Keyes, the fiery conservative who had run for president in 1996 and 2000. Keyes is a Harvard Ph.D. who believes that the purpose of America is defined by the Declaration of Independence and that abortion is a violation of the Declaration's principle of respect for life, liberty and the pursuit of happiness. He had run for the Senate twice before, in Maryland, losing 62%-38% to Paul Sarbanes in 1988 and 71%-29% to Barbara Mikulski in 1992. Inconveniently, he still lived in Maryland and in 2000 had sharply criticized Hillary Rodham Clinton's move into New York to run for the Senate. But this was different, Keyes said; he was being invited to run by the Illinois Republican party. On August 4 he became its nominee.

In a state where liberal cultural views had moved critical suburban votes to the Democrats, Keyes chose to campaign primarily on abortion and same-sex marriage. Polls showed Obama with huge majorities, and the state Republican party sent out mailers omitting Keyes's name. Former Governor Jim Thompson said he wouldn't vote for him; former Governor Jim Edgar and Speaker Dennis Hastert said they'd vote for the Republican ticket; Manzullo said he was still for Keyes, but "I don't like the way he says some things"; state Republican Chairman Judy Baar Topinka said one of his comments was "idiotic." In mid-October the FEC fined Keyes $23,000 for receiving $180,000 in illegal donations to his 2000 presidential campaign. Obama meanwhile was confident enough to contribute $283,000 to other campaigns and send volunteers into Wisconsin to campaign for the Kerry-Edwards ticket.

Obama won 70%-27%, the widest victory margin in Illinois history. Keyes carried 9 heavily Republican counties in southern Illinois; Obama carried the other 93. Obama carried blacks 92%-8% and whites 66%-31%; he won 70% or more from all income groups; Keyes carried Republicans by only 56%-40% and, in a state where there are almost as many liberals as conservatives, carried conservatives by only 61%-33%. Obama appeared on *Meet the Press* and *This Week* and was featured on the cover of *Newsweek*. *Dreams from My Father* was brought out in paperback and sold more than half a million copies, and he got a $1.9 million book contract for *The Audacity of Hope*, which appeared in 2006 and also sold well.

In the Senate he proceeded cautiously. He compiled a mostly liberal voting record, but was one of 18 Democrats to support the class action bill that passed in 2005. He voted against the nominations of John Roberts and Samuel Alito and against CAFTA. His first bill, introduced in April 2005, was to increase the maximum Pell grant to $5,100; he noted that he hadn't paid off his school loans till he received the advance for *The Audacity of Hope*. In March, he pushed successfully in the Foreign Relations Committee to get $25 million for research and responses to avian flu and got the support of Chairman Richard Lugar. He worked with Lugar on the Cooperative Threat Reduction Program Lugar had started in 1991 with Sam Nunn; in August they went together to Russia, Azerbaijan and Ukraine to investigate weapons facilities, and in November they sponsored a bill to add shoulder-fired missiles, abandoned land mines and other conventional weapons to the program originally aimed at nuclear, chemical and biological weapons. He delivered his first major foreign policy speech in November 2005 in Chicago, calling for a phased withdrawal from Iraq starting in 2006. He worked with Republican Sam Brownback on response to the slaughter in Darfur. He co-sponsored a comprehensive immigration package with Republican Mel Martinez. He worked on investigating no-bid contracts to recover from Hurricane Katrina with Republican Tom Coburn. With Hillary Rodham Clinton he sponsored a bill to encourage health professionals to disclose errors early on and analyze them. He worked on changing Senate ethics rules with John McCain, but when in February 2006 he sent a letter favoring going through committee rather than a task force, McCain wrote back angrily. He "apologized" for taking Obama seriously. "I understand how important the opportunity to lead your party's effort to exploit this issue must seem to a freshman senator, and I hold no hard feelings over your earlier disingenuousness." Obama replied, "The fact that you have now questioned my sincerity and my desire to put aside politics for the public interest is regrettable, but does not in any way diminish my deep respect for you, nor my willingness to find a bipartisan solution to this problem," and they quickly made up. While the Senate voted to ban meals and gifts from lobbyists and full disclosure of privately funded travel in March, it did not include Obama's proposal for a special outside panel to police members' ethics. He and McCain were among the eight senators who voted against the final bill.

Despite his national prominence, Obama took care to hold nearly 50 town meetings in Illinois, mostly Downstate, in his first 16 months as a senator. He sponsored a bill for a 50% tax credit for gas stations that installed E-85 pumps with ethanol fuel, co-sponsored another with funding for Mississippi and other river locks and dams and got more VA claims specialists in Chicago. He tried to get agreement between Will County officials and Jesse Jackson, Jr., on the governing body for the airport in Peotone that Jackson had long been promoting and which he supported in the 2004 campaign. He and Dick Durbin challenged the Defense Department's shutdown (out of concern they would interfere with radar) of new wind farms in Illinois, and he sponsored a successful amendment to get the Air Force to report on the future missions of the 183rd Fighter Wing after it was transferred from Springfield to Fort Wayne, Indiana. With Durbin, he opposed ethanol imports from Brazil and other countries. He and Kentucky's Jim Bunning sponsored a coal liquefication bill, noting that "Illinois basin coal has more untapped energy potential than the oil reserves of Saudi Arabia and Kuwait combined." With his book advance and royalties, and his wife's promotion to vice president of the University of Chicago Hospitals, they bought a large house in Kenwood and also, from neighbor and lobbyist Tony Rezko, part of a lot next door. After Rezko was indicted in October, Obama said he had used bad judgment in making the purchase. "There's no doubt I should have seen some red flags in terms of me purchasing a piece of property from him."

In early 2005 Obama downplayed his presidential prospects. He was urged to run by the *New Republic* and by Oprah Winfrey, who said, "He's really more than a politician. He is the real deal." He started a PAC, Hopefund, in January 2005, to encourage young people, especially blacks and Latinos, to work on political campaigns, and maintained a small staff. By mid-2005 he had visited 25 states and was receiving 300 requests a week to make speeches. He stumped for governor candidates Tim Kaine in Virginia and Jon Corzine in New Jersey in October and November 2005 and, despite his stated dislike of fundraising, raised $1 million for Robert Byrd and $6.5 million for other Democrats. He spoke to 10,000 in Detroit upon receiving an NAACP lifetime achievement award in May 2005, went to Omaha to visit with billionaire Warren Buffett in November 2005, spoke (with Sam Brownback) at Rick Warren's Saddleback Church in December 2006, gave the Democratic response at the Gridiron Dinner in Washington in March 2006. He took the time to tape a reading of *Dreams From My Father* and won a Grammy for it. His first eight podcasts averaged 10,000 downloads each by fall 2005. He posted on the liberal website Daily Kos and urged Democrats to tone down their rhetoric and not to "exaggerate or demonize" their opponents. *Time* put him on the cover in October 2006, with a very positive cover story by Joe Klein. There was some less favorable coverage. The liberal writer Ezra Klein called him "a leader who's never led" in the *Los Angeles Times*. Some partisan Democrats criticized him for not taking up major issues; some Republicans complained that he had little experience. Some blacks complained that he was not "really black," and he is not, like most American blacks, the descendant of American slaves and he grew up not in a black ghetto but in the nation's most multiracial state.

Nonetheless in January 2006 Obama told Tim Russert on *Meet the Press* that, "I will serve out my full six-year term" and "I will not" run for president or vice president in 2008. But in 2005 he hired Anita Dunn, one of Bill Bradley's top staffers in his 2000 presidential campaign, and he spoke at Iowa Senator Tom Harkin's annual steak fry in September 2006. That same month, as he was campaigning for Democrats around the country, his 2004 primary opponent Dan Hynes wrote him an open letter urging him to run. On October 22, Obama appeared again on *Meet the Press* and told Russert that he had "thought about the possibility" of running for president. In December 2006 he went, for the first time in his life, to New Hampshire, where he spoke to crowds of thousands. In January 2007 he announced he was setting up an exploratory committee, and in February he went to Springfield and announced he was indeed running. The choice of Springfield naturally evoked the memory of Abraham Lincoln, whom Obama often cites, who ran for president with less experience in public office and only a tad more experience in military affairs than Obama. At the beginning of his campaign he, like almost all the other candidates of both parties, had little in the way of a specific issues platform, and didn't have much to say on complex issues like health care. In his stump speeches he had been attacking the Bush tax cuts for favoring the rich, calling for energy independence and criticizing the administration's handling of Iraq—and sounding the themes of his 2004 convention speech. "We've come to be consumed by a 24-hour, slash-and-burn, negative ad, bickering, small-minded politics that doesn't move us forward. Sometimes one side is up and the other side is down. But there's no sense that they are coming together in a common sense, practical, non-ideological way to solve the problems we face." With black audiences, as he has explained, he takes a slightly different approach. "I know if I'm in an all-black audience that there's going to be a certain rhythm coming back at me from the audience. They're not just going to be sitting there. That creates a different rhythm in your speaking." He is not the first black candidate for president: Shirley Chisholm ran in 1972, Jesse Jackson in 1984 and 1988, Alan Keyes in 1996 and 2000, Carol

Moseley Braun and Al Sharpton in 2004. But he is the first black candidate whose showing in the polls suggests he has a chance to win. Polls after the November 2006 election and up through August 2007 showed him running second to Hillary Rodham Clinton nationally and in most states; his support from black voters increased as the months went on, with no diminishment in support from others; he polled well against the leading Republicans in general election pairings. Many who watched his 2004 convention speech thought they were looking at a future President of the United States; there is some considerable chance that they may turn out to be right.

FIRST DISTRICT

Rep. Bobby Rush (D)

Elected 1992, 8th term; b. Nov. 23, 1946, Albany, GA; home, Chicago; Roosevelt U., B.A. 1973, U. of IL, M.A. 1994, McCormick Seminary, M.A. 1998; Baptist; married (Carolyn).

Military Career: Army, 1963-68.

Elected Office: Chicago City Alderman, 1983-92; 2d Ward Committeeman, 1984-present.

Professional Career: Member, Student Non–Violent Coord. Cmte., 1966-68; Co–founder, IL Black Panther Party, 1968; Med. Clinic Dir., 1970-1973; insurance agent, 1978-83.

DC Office: 2416 RHOB, 20515, 202-225-4372; Fax: 202-226-0333; Web site: www.house.gov/rush.

District Offices: Chicago, 773-224-6500; Midlothian, 708-385-9550.

Committees: *Energy & Commerce* (8th of 31 D): Commerce, Trade & Consumer Protection (Chmn.); Telecommunications & the Internet.

Group Ratings

	ADA	ACLU	AFS	LCV	ITIC	NTU	COC	ACU	CFG	FRC
2006	80	100	100	58	33	17	46	9	19	0
2005	100	—	100	72	—	13	44	4	3	0

National Journal Ratings

	2005 LIB	—	2005 CONS		2006 LIB	—	2006 CONS
Economic	72%	—	26%		64%	—	36%
Social	96%	—	3%		81%	—	18%
Foreign	90%	—	10%		88%	—	10%

Key Votes of the 109th Congress

1. Estate Tax Repeal	N	5. Limit Interstate Abortion	N	9. Build Border Fence	N
2. Limit CAFE Standards	Y	6. Extend Patriot Act	N	10. CAFTA	N
3. FY06 Spending Curb	N	7. Bar Same Sex Marriage	N	11. Oppose Iraq Withdrawal	N
4. Drilling in ANWR	N	8. Stem Cell Research $	Y	12. Detainee Tribunals	N

Election Results

2006 general	Bobby Rush (D)	146,623	(84%)	($684,692)
	Jason Tabour (R)	27,804	(16%)	
2006 primary	Bobby Rush (D)	81,593	(82%)	
	Phillip Jackson (D)	18,427	(18%)	
2004 general	Bobby Rush (D)	212,109	(85%)	($361,032)
	Raymond Wardingley (R)	37,840	(15%)	

Prior Winning Percentages: 2002 (81%); 2000 (88%); 1998 (87%); 1996 (86%); 1994 (76%); 1992 (83%)

The People		Race/Ethnic Origin	Ancestry	
Area size:	99 sq. mi.	27.3% White	Irish: 7.1%	German: 6.2%
Urban population:	100.0%	65.2% Black	Polish: 4.5%	
Rural population:	0.0%	1.4% Asian	**2004 Presidential Vote**	
Pop. 2000:	653,647	0.1% Native Am.	Kerry (D) 234,086	(83%)
Pop. 2005 (est):	644,450	0.0% Hawaiian	Bush (R) 47,533	(17%)
Median income:	$37,222	1.0% Two+ races	Other 565	(0%)
Poverty status:	19.7%	0.1% Other	**2000 Presidential Vote**	
Military veterans:	10.8%	4.8% Hispanic Origin	Gore (D) 213,244	(84%)
			Bush (R) 39,400	(15%)
			Other 2,097	(1%)
			Cook Partisan Voting Index: D +35	

Occupation   Blue collar: 21.6%   White collar: 61.3%   Gray collar: 17.1%

The South Side of Chicago has been the nation's largest urban black community for nearly a century now. A hundred years ago there were just a few blocks where black families from the South could settle; this ghetto grew rapidly with the first influx of blacks from the Mississippi Delta in the 1910s. By the 1920s the South Side was well established, a center of music in America from blues to Jazz and of black-owned businesses. Politically, the South Side was a heavily Republican constituency throughout those years; the comfortable white Protestants who settled in solid brick houses here believed in the party of Yankee propriety, and the blacks had faith in the party of Lincoln. This was one of the heartlands of the Republican Party, represented in the House in the 1920s by Appropriations Chairman Martin Madden. After Madden died in the Appropriations Committee room in 1928, the 1st District elected Oscar DePriest, the first black elected to the House in the 20th century. Blacks remained faithful to the party of Lincoln even during the Depression, voting for Herbert Hoover and DePriest in 1932.

The New Deal and the racial liberalism of New Dealers like Eleanor Roosevelt and Interior Secretary Harold Ickes (both former Republicans themselves) attracted blacks to the Democratic Party, and black Democrat Arthur Mitchell beat DePriest in 1934. The South Side has been Democratic ever since. For 40 years it was a cooperative part of Chicago's Democratic machine; then, after the death of longtime Congressman William Dawson, it rebelled against Mayor Richard J. Daley. The South Side seemed to take over the city when Congressman Harold Washington was elected mayor in 1983 and 1987. After he died in November 1987, other black South Side politicians flailed at each other, even though Chicago's electorate peaked at about 40% black (because so many blacks have been moving to the suburbs) and black candidates need non-black voters to win.

The 1st Congressional District of Illinois includes about half of Chicago's black South Side community plus many suburbs beyond. The 1st has a northern salient that includes some of Chicago's first black neighborhoods plus the Gothic spires of the University of Chicago and the mansions of Kenwood, once the home of Chicago's Jewish aristocracy and more recently the headquarters of the Nation of Islam and home to its leader, Louis Farrakhan. Bronzeville, once a destination point for million of black families, lately has become popular with upscale professionals. It includes most of the South Side from Stony Island west almost to the city limit and from 60th Street to 95th—miles and miles of bungalow neighborhoods, with single-family houses lining arrow-straight streets. In neighborhoods such as Englewood, which lost more than half of its population after 1970, thousands of private residential homes have been built with federal support in recent years in hopes of creating a new black middle-class community; some have been placed on vacant lands or in abandoned buildings that housed gangs. From there a narrow neck connects the 1st with a still mostly white collection of suburbs, starting with Blue Island and fanning southwest to Palos Heights, Orland Park and Oak Forest. The 1st remains overwhelmingly Democratic: Only 15% for George W. Bush in 2000, his weakest district in Illinois that year, and just 17% for him in 2004.

The congressman from the 1st District is Bobby Rush, a man who has gone through several transformations. He grew up on the North Side, a Boy Scout whose mother was a Republican precinct captain. In the Army he became involved in the Student Non-Violent Coordinating Committee in the South, then went AWOL. He has received masters' degrees in political science and theological studies. He founded the Illinois Black Panthers, with its "Power to the People" slogan; there he recruited Fred Hampton, who became chairman but was later killed by police in a 1969 raid; the next day, police raided Rush's family's apartment, but he wasn't there. Rush served six months in prison for illegal possession of firearms, but also during his time with the Black Panthers he ran a free breakfast for children program and a medical clinic that developed the nation's first mass sickle cell anemia testing program. "I don't repudiate any of my involvement in the Panther party—it was part of my maturing," Rush later said. Lately, he has commemorated the anniversary of the raid by holding a job fair to promote the future. In 1983 he was elected 2d Ward alderman and became a strong Harold Washington supporter. In 1992, he challenged Congressman Charles Hayes, an older generation politician with a union background. Just before the primary it was revealed that Hayes had 716 overdrafts on the House bank. Rush won 42%-39%.

In the House, Rush has a liberal voting record and serves on the Energy and Commerce Committee. Rush's rhetoric has toned down over the years, and his more deliberate style contrasts sharply with his days as a Panther. Gun violence caused great pain to Rush in 1999, when his son Huey Rich—who was born three weeks before the 1969 police raid, and, although raised by an aunt, had recently grown close to his father—was murdered by a man wielding a handgun as he returned to his South Side home with his fiancée. The experience moved him spiritually to the point that he was ordained as a Baptist minister; he founded in 2002 a church in the depressed Englewood community, but it struggled financially. In 2003, he ran for chairman of the Congressional Black Caucus, but Elijah Cummings of Maryland defeated him. Legislatively, he has focused on children's health and the nursing shortage. In 2006, the House passed his telecom bill with Energy and Commerce chairman Joe Barton to exempt Bell companies and cable operators from the need to obtain local franchises. News reports accused him of a conflict because a community center founded by him received a $1 million grant from AT&T. Rush denied the charge, and cited a verbal approval from the House ethics committee. In the majority in 2007, he took over the chairmanship of the Commerce, Trade and Consumer Protection Subcommittee.

Rush waged a quixotic mayoral campaign in 1999 against Richard M. Daley, of whom he has sometimes been a harsh critic. During the campaign, he attacked the mayor for tolerating police brutality, inadequate mass-transit service and "cronyism." House colleagues Jesse Jackson Jr. and Danny Davis were at his side, but only three of the 50 aldermen endorsed him. Rush insisted that he wanted to build a multiracial coalition, but for practical purposes his only chance was with black voters. Daley's record was too popular and his financial advantage overwhelming. Daley won the primary by 72%-28%, with nearly 45% of the black vote and the support of many prominent black ministers. After that pounding, Rush found himself challenged in the primary in 2000 by two state senators—Donne Trotter and the then little-known Barack Obama. Obama waged an active campaign, but was attacked for being absent from the legislature for two months and missing a vote on a gun control bill. He was on a family trip to Hawaii that was extended after his daughter got sick, he said—South Side voters may not have known that Obama grew up in Hawaii and may have had little sympathy for a candidate who escaped a Chicago January for Hawaii's sunny climate. Rush was also helped by an endorsement from Bill Clinton and beat Obama 61%-30%. Surely not by coincidence, redistricting shifted Obama's Hyde Park home two blocks outside the new lines and removed the 19th Ward that he had carried. Rush has been routinely reelected since then. In the 2004 Senate primary, he was campaign chairman for free spending ($29 million) self-financer Blair Hull, who finished third; after the primary, he warmly supported Obama. In January 2007, calling it "one of the most difficult decisions I've had to make in politics," Rush endorsed Obama for president. "Barack is a favorite son, and I'm going to be with Barack," he said.

SECOND DISTRICT

Rep. Jesse Jackson Jr. (D)

Elected Dec. 1995, 6th full term; b. Mar. 11, 1965, Greenville, SC; home, Chicago; NC A&T, B.S. 1987, Chicago Theological Seminary, M.A. 1990, U. of IL, J.D. 1993; Baptist; married (Sandra).

Professional Career: Civil rights activist; Pres., Keep Hope Alive PAC, 1989-90; V.P., Operation PUSH, 1991-95; Field Dir., Natl. Rainbow Coalition, 1993-95.

DC Office: 2419 RHOB, 20515, 202-225-0773; Fax: 202-225-0899; Web site: www.house.gov/jackson.

District Offices: Chicago, 773-241-6500; Homewood, 708-798-6000.

Committees: *Appropriations* (20th of 37 D): State, Foreign Operations & Related Programs; Labor, HHS, Education & Related Agencies; Agriculture, Rural Development, FDA & Related Agencies.

Group Ratings

	ADA	ACLU	AFS	LCV	ITIC	NTU	COC	ACU	CFG	FRC
2006	100	100	100	92	14	13	27	4	7	0
2005	100	—	100	94	—	12	30	0	7	8

National Journal Ratings

	2005 LIB	—	2005 CONS		2006 LIB	—	2006 CONS
Economic	92%	—	6%		83%	—	16%
Social	86%	—	14%		93%	—	6%
Foreign	94%	—	4%		92%	—	5%

Key Votes of the 109th Congress

1. Estate Tax Repeal	N	5. Limit Interstate Abortion	N	9. Build Border Fence	N
2. Limit CAFE Standards	N	6. Extend Patriot Act	N	10. CAFTA	N
3. FY06 Spending Curb	N	7. Bar Same Sex Marriage	N	11. Oppose Iraq Withdrawal	N
4. Drilling in ANWR	N	8. Stem Cell Research $	Y	12. Detainee Tribunals	N

Election Results

2006 general	Jesse Jackson Jr. (D)	146,347	(85%)	($946,866)
	Robert Belin (R)	20,395	(12%)	
	Other	5,748	(3%)	
2006 primary	Jesse Jackson Jr. (D)	unopposed		
2004 general	Jesse Jackson Jr. (D)	207,535	(88%)	($527,367)
	Stephanie Sailor (Lib)	26,990	(12%)	

Prior Winning Percentages: 2002 (82%); 2000 (90%); 1998 (89%); 1996 (94%); 1995 (76%)

The People		Race/Ethnic Origin	Ancestry	
Area size:	192 sq. mi.	25.6% White	German: 5.8%	Polish: 4.4%
Urban population:	99.9%	62.0% Black	Irish: 4.4%	
Rural population:	0.1%	0.6% Asian	**2004 Presidential Vote**	
Pop. 2000:	653,647	0.1% Native Am.	Kerry (D) 230,613	(84%)
Pop. 2005 (est):	677,669	0.0% Hawaiian	Bush (R) 43,822	(16%)
Median income:	$41,330	1.2% Two+ races	Other 353	(0%)
Poverty status:	15.2%	0.1% Other	**2000 Presidential Vote**	
Military veterans:	11.7%	10.4% Hispanic Origin	Gore (D) 204,372	(82%)
			Bush (R) 41,005	(17%)
			Other 2,455	(1%)
			Cook Partisan Voting Index: D +35	

Occupation	Blue collar: 23.8%	White collar: 60.1%	Gray collar: 16.1%

Chicago is a great center of both commerce and industry, and if its white-collar offices are heavily concentrated in the Loop, its blue-collar heavy industries are most visible on the far South Side. This Chicago, diminished in importance economically today, is historically significant and, with the remnants of its great hulking factories around Lake Calumet and the nearby rail yards, has a certain undeniable majesty. Thomas Geoghegan has told in his book, *Which Side Are You On?*, of the fights to wrest severance benefits and pension rights for the workers whose steel mills shut down, of the decline in the labor movement in a place where it got much of its inspiration. This is where the Pullman strike of 1894 was broken by federal troops and where policemen killed 10 union supporters in the Little Steel strike of 1937. Over the years, Chicago grew around the tight ethnic neighborhoods where workers went home at shift break each afternoon or midnight; today they are mostly empty buildings that suburbanites speed past on the Calumet and Dan Ryan Expressways. A local historic preservation group has listed the Hulett Iron Ore Unloaders, built in 1912 and resembling a giant preying mantis, as endangered structures.

The 2d Congressional District of Illinois includes much of Chicago's old South Side industrial area, the old Comiskey Park which was replaced by U.S. Cellular Field across the street (and turned into a parking area), and many Cook County suburbs to the south. The district reaches north to include Jackson Park, where the Columbian Exposition of 1893 was held, and the South Shore neighborhood to the south, once heavily Jewish and now home to middle-class blacks. The district includes all of Chicago south of 95th Street and east of I-57, including the old industrial area around Lake Calumet. The Chicago portion of the 2d is overwhelmingly black, though many blacks, especially young parents fleeing Chicago public schools, are moving into suburbs directly to the south—Harvey, Dolton, Markham, and down to Hazel Crest and Lynwood. Farther south are economically revitalized Homewood and Flossmoor, with significant Jewish populations, high-income Olympia Fields, the planned town of Park Forest, and Chicago Heights, home town of America's premier political reporter for a half-century, David Broder. In the south is Ford Heights; once a steel-industry hub known as East Chicago Heights, it is now the nation's leader in single mothers per capita, the vast majority of whom live in public housing. The 2d District now has more people in the suburbs than in Chicago; the district spills slightly into Will County, to include Governors State University in University Park. These extensions reduced the black share from 76% to 62%, but the district remains middle class and still one of the most Democratic in the nation.

The congressman from the 2d District is Jesse Jackson Jr., a Democrat first elected at age 30 in December 1995, son of civil rights activist and 1984 and 1988 presidential candidate Jesse Jackson. Jesse Jackson Jr. was born in Greenville, South Carolina, while his father was marching to Selma; he went to the St. Albans School in Washington, then to North Carolina A&T (as did his father), and got a masters degree at Chicago Theological Seminary and a law degree at the University of Illinois. He worked for his father's Rainbow Coalition and did not run for office until the spectacular rise and fall of Congressman Mel Reynolds, who was hailed nationally when he defeated the anti-Semitic Gus Savage in the 1992 primary and then disgraced when he was convicted and sentenced to five years in prison for having sexual relations with a teenage campaign worker. Jackson had serious competition in the 1995 special election from Emil Jones, then a legislator for 23 years and now the state Senate President, who had the support of Mayor Richard M. Daley. Jones emphasized his clout and political experience; Jackson said being his father's son was a lifetime of political experience. He talked of bringing dollars to the South Side and, echoing the argument Dan Rostenkowski made to Mayor Richard J. Daley in 1957, said, "The only way one grows into leadership in Congress is to get elected young enough that you become speaker of the House or chairman of the Ways and Means Committee." Jackson won the primary 46%-37% and easily won the special general election.

In the House, Jackson has combined liberal advocacy with careful attention to the interests of his district and a steady advancement of his own influence. In recent years, he has sponsored few legislative bills, but nine constitutional amendments with proposed 21st century rights such as "health care of equal high quality," "decent, safe, sanitary and affordable housing," and "full employment and balanced economic growth." He plans to keep introducing his amendments "as long as I am alive and in Congress." All are unlikely to pass, even in a Democratic Congress. In 2005, President Bush signed his bill to erect a statue in the Capitol for civil-rights icon Rosa Parks.

Jackson has worked on local projects, notably the long-time proposal for a third Chicago area airport in Peotone, 45 miles south of the Loop and just south of the 2d District along Interstate 57. The fight pitted him against fellow Democrats, including Daley, whose number one priority is expansion of O'Hare. Jackson's allies have included Republicans from the northern suburbs who are worried about O'Hare noise.

He seems content to remain in the House after years of flirting with the mayoral race. "I'm not interested in the job of mayor of Chicago," Jackson told the *Chicago Tribune* in 2002. "I'm not interested in it today, I'm not interested in it tomorrow. I'm not ever going to be interested in being the mayor of the city of Chicago." But indeed he still was. In 2005, his increasingly sharp criticism of Mayor Richard M. Daley led to speculation that he would mount a challenge in the February 2007 Democratic primary. In September 2006, Jackson announced "it's more likely than not" that he would run against Daley; he added that there was a 75% chance he would be a candidate for mayor. Soon after Democrats won back the House in 2006, he reversed himself again and decided to stay in Congress, though he said he could have won. With a new Democratic majority and a seat on the Appropriations Committee, "It means I'm Dan Rostenkowski," he told the *Chicago Sun Times*, with some overstatement. After nearly a decade on the committee, he is gaining seniority: Except for Patrick Kennedy, every Democrat with more seniority than Jackson is at least 13 years older.

Jackson has been careful not to exploit his huge name recognition or to be seen as exclusively the "black issues" congressman. The movement of middle-class blacks to the suburbs reduces his core constituency, but Jackson's advocacy of the Peotone airport suggests he has anticipated this and is set on representing a mostly suburban, mostly black district for some time. His connection to city politics is still strong though: In 2006, his wife Sandi, a deputy political director of the DNC, was elected alderman in Chicago's 7th Ward.

Jackson seems to be succeeding with his plan to build clout and connections for the long term, an often successful approach in Illinois.

THIRD DISTRICT

Rep. Daniel Lipinski (D)

Elected 2004, 2d term; b. July 15, 1966, Chicago; home, Western Springs; Northwestern U., B.S. 1988, Stanford U., M.A. 1989, Duke U., Ph.D. 1998; Catholic; married (Judy).

Professional Career: Asst. professor, U. of TN, 2001-04.

DC Office: 1217 LHOB, 20515, 202-225-5701; Fax: 202-225-1012; Web site: www.house.gov/lipinski.

District Offices: Chicago, 312-886-0481; LaGrange, 708-352-0524; Oak Lawn, 708-424-0853.

Committees: *Science & Technology* (Vice Chmn. of 24 D): Research & Science Education; Energy & Environment. *Small Business* (9th of 18 D): Regulations, Healthcare & Trade. *Transportation & Infrastructure* (25th of 41 D): Aviation; Railroads, Pipelines & Hazardous Materials; Highways & Transit.

Group Ratings

	ADA	ACLU	AFS	LCV	ITIC	NTU	COC	ACU	CFG	FRC
2006	70	52	100	92	71	13	47	33	7	71
2005	85	—	88	83	—	15	46	16	12	62

National Journal Ratings

	2005 LIB	—	2005 CONS		2006 LIB	—	2006 CONS
Economic	65%	—	34%		71%	—	28%
Social	57%	—	42%		58%	—	42%
Foreign	65%	—	34%		62%	—	37%

Key Votes of the 109th Congress

1. Estate Tax Repeal	N	5. Limit Interstate Abortion	Y	9. Build Border Fence	Y
2. Limit CAFE Standards	N	6. Extend Patriot Act	Y	10. CAFTA	N
3. FY06 Spending Curb	N	7. Bar Same Sex Marriage	P	11. Oppose Iraq Withdrawal	Y
4. Drilling in ANWR	N	8. Stem Cell Research $	N	12. Detainee Tribunals	N

Election Results

2006 general	Daniel Lipinski (D)	127,768	(77%)	($414,167)
	Raymond Wardingley (R)	37,954	(23%)	
2006 primary	Daniel Lipinski (D)	44,401	(54%)	
	John Kelly (D)	20,918	(26%)	
	John Sullivan (D)	16,231	(20%)	
2004 general	Daniel Lipinski (D)	167,034	(73%)	($49,004)
	Ryan Chlada (R)	57,845	(25%)	
	Other	5,077	(2%)	

The People		Race/Ethnic Origin	Ancestry	
Area size:	126 sq. mi.	68.2% White	Irish: 14.2%	Polish: 13.5%
Urban population:	100.0%	5.8% Black	German: 11.0%	
Rural population:	0.0%	2.8% Asian	**2004 Presidential Vote**	
Pop. 2000:	653,647	0.1% Native Am.	Kerry (D)	144,657 (59%)
Pop. 2005 (est):	652,310	0.0% Hawaiian	Bush (R)	100,257 (41%)
Median income:	$48,048	1.7% Two+ races	Other	533 (0%)
Poverty status:	8.3%	0.1% Other	**2000 Presidential Vote**	
Military veterans:	10.9%	21.3% Hispanic Origin	Gore (D)	131,650 (58%)
			Bush (R)	91,471 (40%)
			Other	4,913 (2%)
			Cook Partisan Voting Index: D +10	

Occupation	Blue collar: 27.6%	White collar: 58.1%	Gray collar: 14.3%

A century ago, Finley Peter Dunne's fictional Mr. Dooley pontificated on matters political in a saloon on Archery Road. This was, and is, Archer Avenue on the South Side of Chicago, one of the radial streets that cut across what was once open prairie near the Loop and out the Chicago River and the Chicago and Sanitary Ship Canal. Archer Avenue was one of the paths of outward migration and upward mobility for the children and grandchildren of Chicago's ethnic and cultural groups, and still is. (Even today, in Archer Heights, you can scarcely go a block without hearing someone speaking Polish). Italians from the river wards along the Canal moved west; the South Side Irish moved west and south along Cicero Avenue toward Oak Lawn; the Bohemians (as they were called then; now Czechs) were heavily concentrated in the neat bungalows of industrial suburbs like Berwyn. Today, Latinos are driving these same avenues, up before dawn to arrive at large factories and small, or heading to the Loop on the CTA or to "edge city" jobs out the expressways or the Tollway, then home past storefronts with Spanish signs to carefully refurbished old bungalows. The growing Hispanic community has required construction of new schools. Midway Airport, Chicago's main airport before O'Hare opened in 1955 and now a low-cost facility, has been expanding its congested terminals and parking lots squeezed into the heart of a busy commercial area on the southwest side.

The 3d Congressional District of Illinois consists of much of this territory, crisscrossed by the Canal, the radial streets and the railroad lines and switching yards so common in this, the center of the nation's rail network. It includes much of the Bungalow Belt; in his book, *The Lost City,* Alan Ehrenhalt describes the houses as "so close together that one had to make a special effort even to notice the side of the building. Driving down the street, what you saw was one front after another, and the fronts, clean and well-laid in dark-brown brick by Swedish and Italian immigrant masons, always looked good." The 3d also includes the far southwest edge of Chicago and most of Berwyn; Riverside, with its early 20th century prairie-style houses; a few older affluent suburbs like Western Springs and the more recent and middle-income expanses of Oak Lawn and Palos Hills. In the Archer Avenue neighborhoods, Poles defiantly cling to their heritage with more than 20 weekend schools teaching Polish to local kids and adults. A narrow corridor extends to the famed Bridgeport neighborhood, the lifetime home of the late Mayor Richard J. Daley and the storied Irish stronghold that produced four other Chicago mayors. Politically, this is marginal territory: ancestrally Democratic, culturally conservative, multiethnic and viscerally patriotic. Of the seven districts that include parts of Chicago, this has cast the highest percentages, though well short of majorities, for George W. Bush.

The congressman from the 3d District is Dan Lipinski, elected in 2004, son of Congressman Bill Lipinski, who represented the district for 22 years. Dan Lipinski grew up in Chicago, in the 23d Ward, and first served as a campaign volunteer for his father in 1979. He got engineering degrees from Northwestern and Stanford, before switching to political science to get his doctorate at Duke. He worked on the staffs of four House Democrats from Illinois, though not on his father's, and was an American Political Science Association congressional fellow for the House Democratic Policy Committee. He wrote his doctoral thesis on the topic of congressional newsletters (*Congressional Communication,* published by the University of Michigan Press); at the beginning of 2004, he was an assistant professor of political science at the University of Tennessee in Knoxville. His skimpy campaign resume did not list his scholarly or teaching experiences, nor his out-of-state connections; they might not have been great selling points in the 3d District.

Bill Lipinski filed for reelection in December 2003 and was nominated without opposition in the March 2004 primary. Although he had denied widespread rumors that he was going to give up his seat, he announced on August 13 he would not seek reelection. "I want to come back to Chicago and spend more time with my wife," he explained; he later became a lobbyist on transportation issues. The deadline to replace a withdrawing candidate was August 26; a meeting was scheduled for August 17 for the 19 ward and township Democratic committeemen in the 3d District, who would choose the new nominee by weighted vote. Among them were 11th Ward Committeeman John Daley, Cook County Commissioner, son of the late Mayor Richard J. Daley and brother of Mayor Richard M. Daley; 13th Ward Committeeman Michael Madigan, Speaker of the Illinois House and father of Illinois Attorney General Lisa Madigan; 14th Ward Committeeman Edward Burke, who succeeded his father as 14th Ward Alderman and whose wife is a judge on the Illinois Appeals Court; 19th Ward committeeman Tom Hynes, former Cook County Assessor and father of Illinois Comptroller Dan Hynes; and 23d Ward Committeeman Bill Lipinski: Politics is a family business in Chicago. Bill Lipinski advanced his son's name and said, "I'm optimistic, but one never knows in politics until the votes are counted." It did not take long to count them and resolve any doubts: Dan Lipinski was nominated without opposition. To charges that the nomination was rigged, one participant dryly noted that anyone could have run.

Dan Lipinski, who had not lived in Illinois for 15 years, quickly reestablished his residency. But at his first press conference, he stumbled: He admitted that he rooted for North Side Chicago's baseball Cubs since he was three years old, rather than the South Side White Sox—this in a city that has two separate St. Patrick's Day parades, one downtown and one on the South Side. A local legislator signaled Lipinski from the back of the room to cut off his politically embarrassing remarks. It did not matter much. In the solidly Democratic 3d District, the Democratic nomination is tantamount to election. But local critics charged that Bill Lipinski had further predetermined the outcome by putting up a stooge as the Republican nominee. Ryan Chlada, the 26-year-old college dropout and bar owner who won the Republican nomination unopposed, was a political ally of former Cicero Mayor Betty Loren-Maltese, who was serving prison time for racketeering. Chlada avoided publicity, had no website, filed no reports with the FEC (legal, if you don't raise or spend much money) and was unknown to local Republicans; the Cook County Republican chairman said he was a sham candidate. Unsurprisingly, Dan Lipinski won, 73%-25%.

In the House, Dan Lipinski kept his pledge that he would be "not really that different from my father," who was the most conservative Democrat in the Illinois delegation and focused on local transportation projects, especially Midway Airport, which generates more jobs than any other 3d District employer. In his second term, he won a seat on the Transportation and Infrastructure Committee. His priorities include improvement of Chicago's rail infrastructure. His Hospital Price Disclosure Act would require hospitals to post the costs of common procedures online so patients could compare prices. Lipinski filed another bill to make it a federal crime to sell private phone records. He opposed same-sex marriage and opposed abortion except when the mother's life is at stake.

At home, the family influence held firm and Lipinski was reelected without serious competition. In the primary, he faced two challengers: John Sullivan, an assistant Cook County state's attorney, said that Lipinski got his seat in "a backroom deal" and often had voted in Chicago while living out of state; financial planner John Kelly used "no tricks, no fix" as his campaign slogan. Despite the fact that he initially listed an incorrect home address on his campaign petition, Lipinski won easily, with 54% to 26% for Kelly and 20% for Sullivan. The general election was a foregone conclusion; Lipinski won with 77%. Lyons Township High School Board President Mark Pera, an abortion rights supporter, has announced he will challenge Lipinski in the 2008 Democratic primary.

FOURTH DISTRICT

Rep. Luis Gutierrez (D)

Elected 1992, 8th term; b. Dec. 10, 1953, Chicago; home, Chicago; NE IL U., B.A. 1975; Catholic; married (Soraida).

Elected Office: Chicago City Alderman, 1986-92, Pres. Pro Tem, 1989-92.

Professional Career: Teacher, Puerto Rico, 1977-78; Social Wkr., Chicago Dept. of Children & Family Svcs., 1979-83; Advisor, Chicago Mayor Harold Washington, 1984-86.

DC Office: 2266 RHOB, 20515, 202-225-8203; Fax: 202-225-7810; Web site: luisgutierrez.house.gov.

District Offices: Northside Chicago, 773-384-1655; Southside Chicago, 312-666-3882.

Committees: *Financial Services* (5th of 37 D): Domestic and International Monetary Policy, Trade & Technology (Chmn.); Oversight & Investigations; Financial Institutions & Consumer Credit. *Judiciary* (16th of 23 D): Immigration, Citizenship, Refugees, Border Security & International Law.

Group Ratings

	ADA	ACLU	AFS	LCV	ITIC	NTU	COC	ACU	CFG	FRC
2006	80	100	100	100	17	14	31	4	8	0
2005	90	—	100	78	—	18	38	0	3	0

National Journal Ratings

	2005 LIB	—	2005 CONS		2006 LIB	—	2006 CONS
Economic	87%	—	13%		91%	—	6%
Social	86%	—	13%		94%	—	6%
Foreign	91%	—	7%		90%	—	9%

Key Votes of the 109th Congress

1. Estate Tax Repeal	N	5. Limit Interstate Abortion	N	9. Build Border Fence	N
2. Limit CAFE Standards	N	6. Extend Patriot Act	N	10. CAFTA	N
3. FY06 Spending Curb	*	7. Bar Same Sex Marriage	N	11. Oppose Iraq Withdrawal	*
4. Drilling in ANWR	N	8. Stem Cell Research $	*	12. Detainee Tribunals	N

Election Results

2006 general	Luis Gutierrez (D)	69,910	(86%)	($315,779)
	Ann Melichar (R)	11,532	(14%)	
2006 primary	Luis Gutierrez (D)	unopposed		
2004 general	Luis Gutierrez (D)	104,761	(84%)	($233,086)
	Tony Cisneros (R)	15,536	(12%)	
	Jacob Witmer (Lib)	4,845	(4%)	

Prior Winning Percentages: 2002 (80%); 2000 (89%); 1998 (82%); 1996 (94%); 1994 (75%); 1992 (78%)

The People		Race/Ethnic Origin	Ancestry	
Area size:	39 sq. mi.	18.4% White	Polish: 5.0%	German: 3.4%
Urban population:	100.0%	3.7% Black	Irish: 3.1%	
Rural population:	0.0%	1.7% Asian	**2004 Presidential Vote**	
Pop. 2000:	653,647	0.1% Native Am.	Kerry (D) 105,419	(79%)
Pop. 2005 (est):	650,767	0.0% Hawaiian	Bush (R) 27,684	(21%)
Median income:	$35,935	1.4% Two+ races	Other 809	(1%)
Poverty status:	20.2%	0.1% Other	**2000 Presidential Vote**	
Military veterans:	4.3%	74.5% Hispanic Origin	Gore (D) 93,266	(79%)
			Bush (R) 23,809	(20%)
			Other 317	(0%)
			Cook Partisan Voting Index: D +31	
Occupation	Blue collar: 39.2%	White collar: 43.5%	Gray collar: 17.3%	

Just west of the Loop, the Chicago River splits into North and South Branches, both penetrating the heart of old neighborhoods where immigrants fresh off the boat first got their start in Chicago. The South Branch is the guts of Chicago, the site of one of Western civilization's astonishing engineering feats: in 1900 the course of the river was reversed so that sewage flowed Downstate through a canal rather than out into Lake Michigan. Just blocks away was Maxwell Street, then thronged with market stalls, long the arrival neighborhood for Chicago's Jews; not far away, in an Italian-American neighborhood on Halsted Street, was Jane Addams's Hull House, the original settlement house, where social workers told new immigrants not how to rebel against middle-class American mores but how to live up to them. To the south were Pilsen, arrival neighborhood for the Bohemians (Czechs), and the Irish neighborhoods along Archer Avenue. To the north was Milwaukee Avenue, the main street of Polish-Americans and Ukrainian-Americans for a century now.

Today, many of these places are arrival neighborhoods again, mostly for Chicago's wide variety of Hispanic immigrants. On the South Side, in the old river wards, is Chicago's Mexican-American community, extending west into the once Bohemian suburb of Cicero (famous as a haven for Al Capone's mobsters in the 1920s) and to Pilsen, where residential development has increased; this is the largest community of Mexican-Americans in the nation outside California. In the gentrifying North Side are many Puerto Ricans and other Hispanics. In the 1990s, Chicago's Hispanic population increased from 545,000 to 754,000, by far the largest Latino concentration north of Texas and Florida and between the two coasts, and not all that much less than the 1.1 million blacks in Chicago. By 2005, the city population was almost 30% Hispanic. Spanish-language radio stations have become a local force.

The 4th Congressional District of Illinois is the Hispanic-majority district created in 1992. With the South Side Mexican-American and the smaller North Side Puerto Rican communities separated by the West Side black ghetto, the solution was the creation of one of the most bizarrely-shaped congressional districts in the country. Essentially these two Latino communities, defined by careful boundaries to maximize the Hispanic percentage, are connected by a thin line of territory stretching around the West Side black-majority 7th District to meet at the Cook-DuPage County line. The district is sandwiched between the 5th District to the north and the 3d District to the south; it is shaped something like a pair of earmuffs. More than 95% of the votes are in Chicago or Cicero. The 2001 redistricting raised the Hispanic share of the district population to 75% (75% of these Hispanics are Mexican; 10% are Puerto Rican). Even so, because many have not become citizens and some who have do not vote, Latinos may be only a bare majority of the electorate; the community has sought to increase turnout, which is about half of that in nearby suburban districts.

The congressman from the 4th District is Luis Gutierrez, a Democrat who has held the seat since its creation in 1992. He is of Puerto Rican descent, grew up in Chicago and returned for two years to Puerto Rico as a teacher after college. Back in Chicago, he worked as a cab driver and social worker. In 1983 he ran for 32d Ward committeeman against Dan Rostenkowski, and lost decisively. Then he became a staffer for Mayor Harold Washington, ran for alderman in 1984 and lost; in 1986 he ran again and won in one of two new Hispanic-majority aldermanic seats. After Washington died, Gutierrez backed Richard M. Daley in the 1989 election to succeed him. In the 1992 primary for the new seat, rival alderman Juan Solis called Gutierrez a machine candidate; Gutierrez won anyway, 60%-40%. After easily winning a rematch in 1994, Gutierrez has not had serious competition.

In the House, Gutierrez has staked out liberal positions and his in-your-face style has produced mixed results. As a freshman, his outspoken opposition to congressional pay raises and his appearance on a *60 Minutes* broadcast—in which he called the House "the belly of the beast" and charged that Democratic leaders stifled reform and that some freshmen Democrats "sold out"—was not well received. "I've gotten my rear end kicked around here," Gutierrez told *The Washington Post*; a leadership staffer said Gutierrez "will never get a choice committee" and "will always end up on the Banking Committee." True enough, though he's moved into the senior ranks of what is now the Financial Services Committee, and now chairs the Domestic and International Monetary Policy, Trade and Technology Subcommittee. In the Hispanic Caucus, he chaired the immigration task force, where he pushed efforts to restore food stamp eligibility and other benefits to legal immigrants. He filed other bills to grant automatic citizenship to immigrants in military combat, and legal status to immigrants without documentation who are making major contributions in the United States. "I want to be a spokesperson for people that are new to this country," he said. He attacked CNN's secure-borders advocate Lou Dobbs for encouraging "anti-immigration extremists." In 2005, he became the lead Democratic sponsor of the House version of comprehensive immigration reform, which passed the Senate in 2006 but was throttled by House Republicans. In the 110th Congress, it was revived with a provision to allow illegal immigrants who have been in the U.S. for six years to apply for "conditional nonimmigrant status." "We're tired of going to church on Sunday and seeing that the person who sat next to us during Mass the week before has disappeared," he told a rally. To pursue his interest in immigration reform, he joined the Judiciary Committee in 2007.

Gutierrez often takes the posture of the political rebel, but he has been capable of making accommodations with the locally powerful. He consolidated Chicago's previously fractious Democratic politicians so as to maximize Latino influence and has made plans to build a Latino political empowerment organization in Chicago.

In December 2005, Gutierrez said he would retire after seeking one final term in November 2006 and would explore a mayoral bid in February 2007. But after Democrats regained the House majority in 2006, Gutierrez decided against challenging Democratic Mayor Richard M. Daley. He wavered nearly all year on whether or not he would run again for Congress in 2008. Then, in early August, came a fortuitous sign: 10 elected officials from the 4th District sent Gutierrez a letter "imploring" him not to retire; it was also signed by one of his likely successors, Alderman Ricardo Munoz. On August 16, Gutierrez announced he would heed their wishes and indeed run for a 9th term. "I want to be there to make sure that now that we have a Democratic Congress, we'll have a Democratic president, we can get the issue that I'm so passionate about—that I've committed my life's work doing the last 15 years—comprehensive immigration reform," Gutierrez told WBBM-AM radio.

FIFTH DISTRICT

Rep. Rahm Emanuel (D)

Elected 2002, 3d term; b. Nov. 29, 1959, Chicago; home, Chicago; Sarah Lawrence Col., B.A. 1981; Northwestern U., M.A. 1985; Jewish; married (Amy).

Professional Career: Pol. Dir., DCCC, 1985-86; Natl. Campaign Dir., DCCC, 1988; Sr. White House adviser, 1993-99; Investment bank dir., 1999-2002.

DC Office: 1319 LHOB, 20515, 202-225-4061; Fax: 202-225-5603; Web site: www.house.gov/emanuel.

District Offices: Chicago, 773-267-5926.

Committees: *Democratic Caucus Chairman. Ways & Means* (15th of 24 D): Health; Select Revenue Measures.

Group Ratings

	ADA	ACLU	AFS	LCV	ITIC	NTU	COC	ACU	CFG	FRC
2006	90	81	100	92	71	11	47	4	10	0
2005	100	—	100	72	—	12	48	0	13	0

National Journal Ratings

	2005 LIB	—	2005 CONS	2006 LIB	—	2006 CONS
Economic	74%	—	26%	74%	—	23%
Social	73%	—	27%	76%	—	23%
Foreign	72%	—	27%	67%	—	31%

Key Votes of the 109th Congress

1. Estate Tax Repeal	N	5. Limit Interstate Abortion	N	9. Build Border Fence	N
2. Limit CAFE Standards	*	6. Extend Patriot Act	Y	10. CAFTA	N
3. FY06 Spending Curb	*	7. Bar Same Sex Marriage	N	11. Oppose Iraq Withdrawal	N
4. Drilling in ANWR	N	8. Stem Cell Research $	Y	12. Detainee Tribunals	N

Election Results

2006 general	Rahm Emanuel (D)	114,319	(78%)	($1,380,457)
	Kevin White (R)	32,250	(22%)	($31,038)
2006 primary	Rahm Emanuel (D)	53,727	(83%)	
	Mark Fredrickson (D)	6,050	(9%)	
	John Haptonstall (D)	4,876	(8%)	
2004 general	Rahm Emanuel (D)	158,400	(76%)	($689,463)
	Bruce Best (R)	49,530	(24%)	

Prior Winning Percentages: 2002 (67%)

The People		Race/Ethnic Origin	Ancestry	
Area size:	58 sq. mi.	65.9% White	Polish: 13.5%	German: 11.5%
Urban population:	100.0%	2.2% Black	Irish: 9.9%	
Rural population:	0.0%	6.5% Asian	**2004 Presidential Vote**	
Pop. 2000:	653,647	0.2% Native Am.	Kerry (D) 161,348	(67%)
Pop. 2005 (est):	620,387	0.0% Hawaiian	Bush (R) 79,349	(33%)
Median income:	$48,531	2.2% Two+ races	Other 1,539	(1%)
Poverty status:	8.5%	0.2% Other	**2000 Presidential Vote**	
Military veterans:	6.7%	23.0% Hispanic Origin	Gore (D) 143,106	(66%)
			Bush (R) 73,793	(34%)
			Other 885	(0%)
			Cook Partisan Voting Index: D +18	

Occupation   Blue collar: 21.5%   White collar: 64.9%   Gray collar: 13.6%

Few places in America today have more variety—ethnic and cultural—than the North Side of Chicago. This has been the homeland of one immigrant group after another and the chosen neighborhoods of all manner of successful middle-class people. Wooden workingman's cottages from the late 19th century give way to sturdy huge brick houses of the early 1900s and then to the prairie bungalows of the 1920s and white-shuttered, orange-brick colonials of the 1950s. Chicago was America's number one immigrant destination for Poles, Lithuanians, Czechs, Slovaks, Ukrainians and Romanians; something about the heavy dull clouds of the long winters, the short hot summers, a climate suited to potatoes and cabbage and other hardy vegetables, may have reminded them of central and eastern Europe. By the late 1980s, upwardly mobile immigrants from Mexico and Guatemala, Korea and the Philippines moved in; the 1990s witnessed new rounds of immigrants from Poland and Ukraine, plus Pakistan, India and Bosnia. Family ties, webs of acquaintance that reach back to ancestral villages, have made the North Side of Chicago a natural port of entry for Eastern bloc migrants, even as other newcomers arrive with webs of relationships extending to Latin America and Southeast Asia.

The 5th Congressional District of Illinois covers an oddly shaped swath across Chicago's North Side, running from the lakefront to the suburbs directly south of O'Hare Airport. The 5th includes Chicago's most glamorous lakefront apartments facing the Oak Street beach and the gentrified neighborhoods of Old Town, where old houses and factories are being converted into upscale condominiums, often over the objections of preservationists to the loss of neighborhood architecture. Nearby Lincoln Park has the highest median household income of Chicago's 77 community areas. The district takes in baseball's famed Wrigley Field, the Polish-American and Ukrainian-American neighborhoods with their own museums around Milwaukee Avenue, and the old Italian neighborhoods running west on Grand Avenue. It includes, a couple of blocks from the Chicago River, the grand old church of St. Stanislaus Kostka—a traditional center of the Polish community since the 19th century but now with Masses in Spanish—and the residence across from Pulaski Park of Dan Rostenkowski, chairman of the House Ways and Means Committee from 1981 to 1994, for whom the district was designed in 1992. It reaches the Cook County suburbs, beyond River Grove and Franklin Park into Schiller Park and Northlake. This is a solidly Democratic district.

The congressman from the 5th District is Rahm Emanuel, a Democrat elected in 2002 and a major force in the House. Emanuel was born in Chicago and grew up in Wilmette, the son of an Israeli immigrant. He graduated from Sarah Lawrence, got a master's degree in communications from Northwestern and began his career with Illinois Public Action, a consumer rights group. California Representative Tony Coelho recruited him to join the staff of the Democratic Congressional Campaign Committee in 1985. He worked for Mayor Richard M. Daley, before joining Bill Clinton's presidential campaign in 1991. He was rewarded with a high-level staff post in the Clinton White House, where he gained wide respect for his political savvy but drew criticism, even from allies, for an arrogant and abrasive style. In 1999 he left the White House and returned to Chicago where he made millions as an investment banker. His decision to run for Congress was greeted with disdain by those who had toiled for years in the vineyards of Chicago politics. His strongest opponent was former state Representative Nancy Kaszak, who lost the 1996 primary to Rod Blagojevich; she portrayed Emanuel as an interloper with few ties to the district. But Emanuel had his own local connections. He was endorsed by Daley and by labor unions (despite his support of NAFTA), and he raised large sums—nearly $2 million for the primary—from his extensive Chicago and national Democratic fundraising networks. Emanuel benefited from controversy two weeks before the primary, when a local Polish-American leader supporting Kaszak charged that Emanuel served in the Israeli army in 1991 during the Gulf War and suggested he had dual loyalties. The charge was false—Emanuel is a U.S. citizen who volunteered as a civilian at an Israeli supply base—and Kaszak's campaign was thrown off-stride. Emanuel won 50%-39%, with large majorities on the Lakefront and in Lincoln Park. He carried all of the 13 wards in the district, except for the heavily Polish 30th. In the general election, Emanuel faced a feisty challenger who attacked him as overly ambitious, but the result was never in doubt; he won 67%-29%. That made him the district's fourth congressman in a decade; before he was indicted and eventually served prison time, Rostenkowski served this area for 36 years.

Moving quickly up the ranks in the House, Emanuel cut an unusually high-profile figure. Even before winning election in 2002, he strategized for the national party, met with the national media and sought a prime committee assignment: Rosty's old haunt at Ways and Means. Although he was delayed for two more years—freshmen seldom get on Ways and Means—his aggressiveness, political skills and fundraising prowess quickly made him a congressman to watch. "He's very strategic, very good at message, smart on the legislative process, and disciplined," said Democrat Jan Schakowsky, who represents the neighboring 9th District. He also showed skill in working across the aisle. He cosponsored with Representative Gil Gutknecht the House-passed bill allowing Americans to import prescription drugs from other nations. "Few members here have Rahm's energy, or know what reporter to talk to at *The New York Times,*" Gutknecht marveled. NRCC chairman Tom Reynolds became Emanuel's chief co-sponsor of a proposal to spend billions of dollars to clean up the Great Lakes. "He came to me, and I liked his concept," Reynolds said. "I think that Hillary [Rodham Clinton] told him he should get to know me."

In January 2005, Minority Leader Nancy Pelosi appointed him as the DCCC chairman to succeed Robert Matsui, who had died. Emanuel thus chaired the committee on which he had once been a staffer. He quickly imposed his take-no-prisoners approach on the committee, allowing nothing to stand in his way of gaining the House majority. With the popularity of President Bush and Republicans in decline because of the war in Iraq and the federal government's weak response to Hurricane Katrina, he recruited actively to expand the playing field of competitive House contests. With his promises of party support came demands that candidates meet benchmark requirements for fundraising, local news clips and a campaign field operation. His demand for more financial support from the national party led to a bitter confrontation in which Emanuel complained that Howard Dean was spending too much money on his "50 state" strategy and not enough to win the House in 2006; the DCCC chairman seemed to be prepared to blame the DNC chairman if Democrats failed to capture the House. This was another element of Emanuel's hard-edged tactical skills, which combined with his total commitment and seemingly inexhaustible energy to give the DCCC the aura of a presidential campaign. "He's brilliant, he's articulate, he's politically astute, and he's as cold-blooded as I need him to be to make the decisions," Pelosi told *National Journal* in May 2006. The *Chicago Tribune* profiled him as "a portrait in power of a brutally effective taskmaster."

Meanwhile, Emanuel did not ignore the policy debate. With friend and former White House colleague Bruce Reed, he coauthored *The Plan*, a book filled with mostly centrist Democratic proposals on how to fix the nation's problems and published three months before the 2006 election. He has called for sweeping tax reform to reduce the complexity of the tax code and lower rates for the middle class; ironically, it was Rostenkowski in 1986 who was instrumental in enacting the most recent major tax reform law. In the usually back-slapping Illinois delegation, Emanuel had a testy relationship with then-Speaker Dennis Hastert, which began in 1986 when he waged an aggressive fight as a DCCC aide against Hastert's election to an open House district and continued with his confrontational rhetoric after he was elected to his own seat.

Emanuel's stock skyrocketed after Election Night, and he faced pressure to decide quickly what leadership post he wanted in the new majority. Allies had urged that he run for majority whip, a job for which he was well-suited because of its emphasis on both policy and arm-twisting. But Democratic Caucus chairman James Clyburn already had moved to claim the whip position, and Emanuel was reluctant to challenge the respected Clyburn, a past chairman of the Congressional Black Caucus. So, with strong encouragement from Pelosi and her agreement to strengthen the post, he ran without opposition to replace Clyburn as chairman of the Democratic Caucus. He quickly became a top strategist, spokesman and enforcer for the new majority. With each of the top three Democratic leaders about 20 years older than him, Emanuel is well-positioned to become Speaker within the next decade if he is willing to be patient.

SIXTH DISTRICT

Rep. Peter Roskam (R)

Elected 2006, 1st term; b. Sept. 13, 1961, Hinsdale; home, Wheaton; U. of IL, B.A. 1983, Chicago-Kent Col. of Law, J.D. 1989; Anglican; married (Elizabeth).

Elected Office: IL House, 1992-98; IL Senate, 2000-06, Min. Whip, 2003-06.

Professional Career: Aide, U.S. Rep. Tom DeLay, 1985-86, U.S. Rep. Henry Hyde, 1986-87; High school teacher, 1983-85; Exec. Dir., Educational Assistance Ltd., 1987-1993; Practicing atty., 1994-2006.

DC Office: 507 CHOB, 20515, 202-225-4561; Fax: 202-225-1166; Web site: roskam.house.gov.

District Offices: Bloomingdale, 630-893-9670.

Committees: *Financial Services* (30th of 33 R): Oversight & Investigations; Domestic and International Monetary Policy, Trade & Technology; Capital Markets, Insurance & Government Sponsored Enterprises.

Group Ratings and Key Votes: Newly Elected

Election Results

2006 general	Peter Roskam (R) 91,382	(51%)	($3,302,702)
	Tammy Duckworth (D) 86,572	(49%)	($4,556,495)
2006 primary	Peter Roskam (R) .... unopposed		
2004 general	Henry Hyde (R) 139,627	(56%)	($804,197)
	Christine Cegelis (D) 110,470	(44%)	($193,947)

The People		Race/Ethnic Origin	Ancestry	
Area size:	215 sq. mi.	75.3% White	German: 16.7% Irish: 11.0%	
Urban population:	100.0%	2.7% Black	Polish: 9.4%	
Rural population:	0.0%	8.1% Asian	**2004 Presidential Vote**	
Pop. 2000:	653,647	0.1% Native Am.	Bush (R) 139,028	(53%)
Pop. 2005 (est):	661,493	0.0% Hawaiian	Kerry (D) 121,344	(47%)
Median income:	$62,640	1.3% Two+ races	**2000 Presidential Vote**	
Poverty status:	4.3%	0.1% Other	Bush (R) 126,254	(53%)
Military veterans:	9.6%	12.5% Hispanic Origin	Gore (D) 103,616	(44%)
			Other 6,945	(3%)
			Cook Partisan Voting Index: R + 3	

Occupation	Blue collar: 20.2%	White collar: 69.5%	Gray collar: 10.3%

In World War II, what is now the nation's second-busiest airport was an apple orchard on which a defense plant was built (hence its current three-letter code: ORD). To the east was the Forest Preserve along the Des Plaines River, to the west little suburban villages strung along rail lines, separated by cornfields. But later in the 1940s, Chicago politicians, in search of a new airport site, annexed the orchard and named it after a World War II airman awarded the Medal of Honor, who got a military appointment from the feds after his father turned state's evidence against Al Capone and was gunned down. Mayor Richard J. Daley opened O'Hare in 1955 and promoted its development, correctly concluding that a great airport could maintain in the 20th century the economic strength Chicago gained from railroad stations and rail yards in the 19th century. For years O'Hare has vied with Atlanta's Hartsfield-Jackson as America's number one or two airport in passenger traffic, and number one in combined passenger and cargo traffic; it has done much to maintain Chicago as the most vibrant center of commerce in the Midwest. With O'Hare operating close to capacity, Mayor Richard M. Daley's plans to reconfigure the runways and expand the airport are aimed at maintaining that preeminence. They are not popular, however, with the suburbs that surround O'Hare on all sides and are almost as densely settled as the bungalow wards of the city. Politically, these suburbs were for many years solidly Republican, convinced that civic virtues could best be realized by opposing the party of City Hall in Chicago and that economic growth could best be assured by opposing the party that backed stifling government regulation. But in the 1990s they became less Republican, as voters here recoiled from the national party's cultural conservatism.

The 6th Congressional District of Illinois includes O'Hare and much of the suburban area to its west. Most of the district is in DuPage County, the second largest county in Illinois. It includes the string of long-settled suburbs due west of the Loop: Elmhurst, Villa Park, Lombard, Glen Ellyn, Wheaton, plus the newer suburbs along I-290: Bensenville, Addison, Wood Dale, Bloomingdale. Economically, this remains high-income territory; culturally, it is now cautiously moderate or even liberal. In 1988 George Bush carried DuPage by 124,000 votes, with 68% of the vote, but in 2004 George W. Bush carried the county by only 39,000, with 54% of the vote—which tells you in a nutshell why the elder Bush carried Illinois in 1988 and the younger Bush twice wrote it off.

The new congressman from the 6th District is Peter Roskam, a Republican who replaced the iconic Henry Hyde, one of the most intellectually honest members of the House. Hyde retired after 32 years and as chairman of the House International Relations Committee. A native of DuPage County, Roskam graduated from the University of Illinois and got his law degree while directing a charitable organization that used corporate resources to fund college scholarships. During law school, he was part of a team that won a national mock trial competition. Prior to law school, he worked in Washington for Hyde and for Tom DeLay. Roskam served six years in the state House, and six years in the Senate. Between those legislative stints, he ran unsuccessfully in 1998 for the open congressional seat in the neighboring 13th District, but lost 45% to 40% against state House colleague Judy Biggert in the primary; he attacked her for support of abortion rights and was backed by DeLay, but she raised far more money and had the endorsement of Governor Jim Edgar and the incumbent, Harris Fawell. After Hyde in April 2005 announced his retirement, Roskam raised nearly $400,000 in the next two months, and managed to scare off potentially competitive Republican challengers. He ran unopposed for the GOP nomination and was able to conserve his funds for the general election.

His Democratic opponent was Tammy Duckworth, a former manager for Rotary International and an Iraq war veteran. The daughter of a retired Marine and an ethnic Chinese, she was born in Bangkok and spent much of her early life in southeast Asia. She was famous as a Black Hawk helicopter pilot who served with the Illinois National Guard and lost both legs in Iraq in a crash after her helicopter was hit by a rocket-propelled grenade. As part of an effort to nominate military veterans for Congress, the Democratic Congressional Campaign Committee (chaired by Rahm Emanuel, from the neighboring 5th District) hand-picked Duckworth; her high profile made this one of the nation's most closely watched House races — and one of the most expensive. First, she faced a competitive primary from technology consultant Christine Cegelis, who ran against Hyde in 2004 and held him to a 56%-44% win, his smallest margin since he was first elected. Contrasting herself to Duckworth, who lived three miles outside the district, Cegelis said that she had been a local resident for 20 years and assembled her own campaign organization. A political novice, Duckworth was slow to learn campaign skills, but she was bolstered by Emanuel and other party leaders. She also benefited from a wave of favorable news coverage for her compelling personal story. Duckworth won the primary 44% to 40% and 16% for Lindy Scott, a Wheaton College professor of Latin American studies.

The two nominees sparred over tax cuts, spending earmarks, the Iraq war, and immigration policy. They also clashed over abortion rights, federal funding for stem-cell research, and expansion at O'Hare; Roskam opposed each. The campaign debate often degenerated into personal attacks. Duckworth criticized Roskam as "a rubber stamp" for the Bush administration, and referred to DeLay as Roskam's "mentor." A Duckworth spokesman said, "While Peter Roskam was climbing up the political ladder, using connections to disgraced leaders like Tom DeLay, Tammy Duckworth was climbing into helicopters and serving her country." Bill Clinton and actor Michael J. Fox made late campaign appearances for her. Roskam disparaged Duckworth as the "candidate from the Chicago Democratic machine" because of her ties to Emanuel. He also sought to portray her as a carpetbagger with little connection to the district. In one of the few Republican successes in a competitive House contest, Roskam won with 51.4% of the vote. Duckworth took 53% in Cook County, but it cast only 20% of the total vote; Roskam won 52% to 48% in DuPage—sufficient, though not overwhelming. Senator Dick Durbin promised that Democrats would give Roskam a strong challenge in 2008, but in July 2007 Duckworth, the party's top prospect, said she would not seek a rematch.

SEVENTH DISTRICT

Rep. Danny Davis (D)

Elected 1996, 6th term; b. Sept. 6, 1941, Parkdale, AR; home, Chicago; AR AM&N Col., B.A. 1961, Chicago St. U., M.S. 1968, Union Inst., Ph.D. 1977; Baptist; married (Vera).

Elected Office: Chicago City Alderman, 1979-90; Cook Cnty. Commissioner, 1990-96.

Professional Career: Teacher, Chicago Public Schls., 1962-69; Health Care Planner, 1969-79.

DC Office: 2159 RHOB, 20515, 202-225-5006; Fax: 202-225-5641; Web site: www.house.gov/davis.

District Offices: Broadview, 708-345-6857; Chicago, 773-533-7520.

Committees: *Education & Labor* (14th of 27 D): Early Childhood, Elementary & Secondary Education; Higher Education, Lifelong Learning & Competitiveness. *Oversight & Government Reform* (8th of 23 D): Federal Workforce, Postal Service & the District of Columbia (Chmn.); Domestic Policy.

Group Ratings

	ADA	ACLU	AFS	LCV	ITIC	NTU	COC	ACU	CFG	FRC
2006	90	100	100	83	43	15	40	8	13	0
2005	100	—	100	83	—	17	41	4	12	0

National Journal Ratings

	2005 LIB	—	2005 CONS		2006 LIB	—	2006 CONS
Economic	69%	—	29%		77%	—	22%
Social	93%	—	6%		92%	—	7%
Foreign	94%	—	4%		91%	—	9%

Key Votes of the 109th Congress

1. Estate Tax Repeal	N	5. Limit Interstate Abortion	N	9. Build Border Fence	N
2. Limit CAFE Standards	Y	6. Extend Patriot Act	N	10. CAFTA	N
3. FY06 Spending Curb	N	7. Bar Same Sex Marriage	*	11. Oppose Iraq Withdrawal	N
4. Drilling in ANWR	N	8. Stem Cell Research $	Y	12. Detainee Tribunals	N

Election Results

2006 general	Danny Davis (D)	143,071	(87%)	($414,881)
	Charles Hutchinson (R)	21,939	(13%)	
2006 primary	Danny Davis (D)	77,287	(89%)	
	Jim Ascot (D)	6,646	(8%)	
	Other	2,921	(3%)	
2004 general	Danny Davis (D)	221,133	(86%)	($438,680)
	Antonio Davis-Fairman (R)	35,603	(14%)	($43,718)

Prior Winning Percentages: 2002 (83%); 2000 (86%); 1998 (93%); 1996 (83%)

The People		Race/Ethnic Origin	Ancestry	
Area size:	59 sq. mi.	27.3% White	German: 5.6%	Irish: 5.2%
Urban population:	100.0%	61.6% Black	Italian: 2.9%	
Rural population:	0.0%	3.8% Asian	**2004 Presidential Vote**	
Pop. 2000:	653,647	0.1% Native Am.	Kerry (D) 227,018	(83%)
Pop. 2005 (est):	627,239	0.0% Hawaiian	Bush (R) 45,071	(17%)
Median income:	$40,361	1.2% Two+ races	Other 887	(0%)
Poverty status:	24.0%	0.1% Other	**2000 Presidential Vote**	
Military veterans:	8.0%	5.8% Hispanic Origin	Gore (D) 199,064	(83%)
			Bush (R) 38,196	(16%)
			Other 1,985	(1%)
			Cook Partisan Voting Index: D +35	

Occupation	Blue collar: 15.5%	White collar: 70.6%	Gray collar: 13.9%

The cross-country flyer on a lucky day can get a clear view of the biggest man-made cityscape between the Atlantic and Pacific Oceans: Chicago's Loop. High-rise buildings and the parks along Lake Michigan were pioneered a century ago in the Loop—named in 1897 for the quadrilateral the elevated train forms around the city's center—by architects like Louis Sullivan and Daniel Burnham. International School modernists built their most impressive collection of buildings here and along Lake Shore Drive in the years after World War II; in recent years, postmodernists have decorated the Chicago River and reinvented the skyscraper. The Loop now spreads beyond the El, up the wondrous shopping street of North Michigan Avenue with a peak at the John Hancock Tower plus the new Millennium Park and band shell along the lakefront, and west beyond the financial exchanges to the Sears Tower on the Chicago River. This is the face Chicago likes to present to the world: giant structures rising where the prairies meet the inland sea, a vast concentration of brains and muscle, the nerve center of the markets of the nation and the world.

Behind the lakefront, where the air traveler sees the grid spread out below with occasional radials, are the muscle and sinew, gristle and fat of the city. There are parts that do not work so well: houses and apartment buildings are abandoned; commercial space stands empty and vandalized; giant, crime-racked housing projects, like the Robert Taylor Homes off the Dan Ryan Expressway, built by Mayor Richard J. Daley in the 1960s (he preferred low-rise projects, but the feds wouldn't finance them) and torn down by Mayor Richard M. Daley. The West Side of Chicago, the vast acres directly west of the Loop, for years was a dreadful slum, with some areas almost emptied out; the decay spread west to the Austin neighborhood, just before the border of upper-income—and for decades racially integrated—Oak Park. Many factories that made Chicago the chocolate and candy center of the nation were shuttered, and production went mostly overseas. In the 1990s, there was some revival. The United Center, the erstwhile home court of Michael Jordan, sparked commercial development of the West Side, and lower crime rates raised land values once again. Former meatpacking buildings have been turned into art galleries. A massive new downtown dormitory houses students from nearby DePaul University, Roosevelt University and Columbia College.

The 7th Congressional District of Illinois contains the Loop and most of the North Michigan corridor and the Near North Side, where the infamous Cabrini-Green housing project has been replaced by new, mixed-market housing. It goes south, past landmark museums, Soldier Field stadium and 19th century Prairie Avenue mansions to take in a few of the heavily black South Side neighborhoods chronicled in the groundbreaking 1945 book *Black Metropolis*. Its heart, demographically and spiritually, is the black ghetto of the West Side, more depopulated and socially disorganized than the South Side. To the west, just outside city limits, are Oak Park, the boyhood home of Ernest Hemingway and location of the Frank Lloyd Wright home and museum and many of his prairie-style houses; River Forest; and the much more modest Maywood, which is black-majority; plus Broadview and Hillside, site of a one-lane Chicago expressway bottleneck known as the Hillside Strangler. As with the South Side districts, redistricting in 2001 added nearly 100,000 people to the 7th and reduced slightly the share of black population but left George W. Bush with only 16% and 17% in his two campaigns. Just under two-thirds of the people here are black; there are relatively few Hispanics, since Latino neighborhoods were carefully placed in the 4th District.

The congressman from the 7th District is Danny Davis, a Democrat first elected in 1996 after two unsuccessful tries in the 1980s. Davis grew up on a cotton farm in Arkansas, graduated from college there, then moved to Chicago and worked as a teacher, assistant principal and guidance counselor in Chicago public schools. For 10 years, he ran a community health project on the West Side. He was elected alderman in the 29th Ward on the boundary of Oak Park in 1979 and supported Mayor Harold Washington in the council wars of the 1980s. In 1990 he was elected a Cook County commissioner; in 1991 he made a quixotic run for mayor against Richard M. Daley; he lost his 29th Ward committeeman post to a Daley-backed challenger in 2000.

In 1996, when Cardiss Collins retired after nearly 24 years in the House, Davis decided to run for the House again. His major opponents were 3d Ward Alderman Dorothy Tillman, a Daley ally, and 37th Ward Alderman Ed Smith. Davis campaigned as a big-government liberal, calling for a $7.60 minimum wage, affirmative action, and a national health care plan. Davis won with 33%. He won the general with ease and has not faced a serious challenge since then.

In the House, Davis has a mostly liberal voting record, though he's moved closer to the center on economic issues. He has opposed income tax cuts, even when advocated by Bill Clinton. He opposed the sugar program as corporate welfare (Chicago remains the nation's leading candy manufacturer). On the Government Reform Committee, he was a champion of organized labor as he worked with a bipartisan coalition that in 2006 enacted major changes in the Postal Service. With his wife Vera, who was then president of the West Side NAACP, Davis advocated a local program to increase the low share of black home ownership in his district by offering credit counseling and innovative forms of mortgage financing. He has created dozens of advisory task forces to get views from constituents.

Davis speaks in an impressive sepulchral tone, and his self-evident sincerity and concern for the poor helped him to some success in the Republican-controlled House. With the view that everybody deserves a second chance, Davis has taken a deep interest in the problems of former convicts seeking to transition back to the mainstream. He and conservative Republican Mark Souder proposed the Public Safety ex-Offender Self-Sufficiency Act, to use tax credits to encourage transitional housing and job training for former prisoners.

In 2006, he sought to become Cook County Board president when incumbent John Stroger suffered a serious stroke. But Democratic committeemen overwhelmingly supported Stroger's son Todd for the nomination and Davis was a distant second; with Davis's endorsement, Stroger went on to win easily in November. When Democrats regained the House majority, Davis became chairman of the Federal Workforce Subcommittee at the Oversight and Government Reform panel.

EIGHTH DISTRICT

Rep. Melissa Bean (D)

Elected 2004, 2d term; b. Jan. 22, 1962, Chicago; home, Barrington; Oakton Comm. Col., A.A. 1982, Roosevelt U., B.A. 2002; Serbian Orthodox; married (Alan).

Professional Career: Technology and sales consultant, 1982-2004.

DC Office: 318 CHOB, 20515, 202-225-3711; Fax: 202-225-7830; Web site: www.house.gov/bean.

District Offices: Schaumburg, 847-925-0265.

Committees: *Financial Services* (23d of 37 D): Capital Markets, Insurance & Government Sponsored Enterprises; Financial Institutions & Consumer Credit. *Small Business* (7th of 18 D): Finance & Tax (Chmn.); Regulations, Healthcare & Trade.

Group Ratings

	ADA	ACLU	AFS	LCV	ITIC	NTU	COC	ACU	CFG	FRC
2006	60	64	43	83	100	46	80	48	47	0
2005	80	—	88	78	—	34	73	12	44	23

National Journal Ratings

	2005 LIB	—	2005 CONS		2006 LIB	—	2006 CONS
Economic	59%	—	40%		55%	—	44%
Social	60%	—	39%		61%	—	38%
Foreign	58%	—	42%		56%	—	43%

Key Votes of the 109th Congress

1. Estate Tax Repeal	Y	5. Limit Interstate Abortion	N	9. Build Border Fence	Y
2. Limit CAFE Standards	N	6. Extend Patriot Act	Y	10. CAFTA	Y
3. FY06 Spending Curb	N	7. Bar Same Sex Marriage	N	11. Oppose Iraq Withdrawal	Y
4. Drilling in ANWR	N	8. Stem Cell Research $	Y	12. Detainee Tribunals	Y

Election Results

2006 general	Melissa Bean (D)	93,355	(51%)	($4,299,589)
	David McSweeney (R)	80,720	(44%)	($5,140,109)
	Bill Scheurer (Mod)	9,312	(5%)	($46,299)
2006 primary	Melissa Bean (D)	unopposed		
2004 general	Melissa Bean (D)	139,792	(52%)	($1,586,829)
	Phil Crane (R)	130,601	(48%)	($1,618,074)

The People		Race/Ethnic Origin	Ancestry	
Area size:	646 sq. mi.	78.8% White	German: 19.5%	Irish: 11.0%
Urban population:	96.1%	3.2% Black	Polish: 8.3%	
Rural population:	3.9%	5.6% Asian	**2004 Presidential Vote**	
Pop. 2000:	653,647	0.1% Native Am.	Bush (R) 153,245	(56%)
Pop. 2005 (est):	720,063	0.0% Hawaiian	Kerry (D) 121,710	(44%)
Median income:	$62,762	1.2% Two+ races	**2000 Presidential Vote**	
Poverty status:	4.4%	0.1% Other	Bush (R) 131,967	(56%)
Military veterans:	10.6%	10.8% Hispanic Origin	Gore (D) 98,664	(42%)
			Other 6,954	(3%)
			Cook Partisan Voting Index: R + 5	

Occupation	Blue collar: 21.8%	White collar: 67.3%	Gray collar: 10.9%

Schaumburg may not be nationally known, but it is one of America's major corporate headquarters cities and one of several edge cities northwest of Chicago. Sixty years ago this was farmland, half a dozen miles beyond the orchard that is now O'Hare Airport. Today, Schaumburg—near the intersection of the Northwest Tollway and I-290, with lots of office space and Woodfield Mall and miles of subdivisions—is the site of the headquarters of Motorola and Zurich American Insurance; nearby are the headquarters of Sears and Kemper Insurance. Yet Schaumburg yearns for traditions. It has built a performing arts center, formed an orchestra for young people, and has built from scratch a traditional downtown.

The 8th Congressional District of Illinois is made up of Schaumburg and dozens of similar communities to the north, on the hilly lakelands north and northwest of Chicago. Just to the north are Palatine and country-manor Barrington Hills (in-between Inverness is connected by a narrow corridor to the 10th District). The district includes the rapidly-growing western half of Lake County, with little lake communities being surrounded by new suburbs like Deer Park and Volo, and also includes the Lake Michigan town of Zion at the Wisconsin border. To the west, the 8th includes about half of fast-growing McHenry County, where Democrats have begun to show some life. The tone of life is not elite, but people here are affluent. Culturally, this is part of the great rural Midwest perhaps more than it is of yeasty, lusty Chicago, though it lacks much regional identity other than the "northwest suburbs." Economically, its suspicion of government and trade restrictions has declined, as Motorola has become the victim of overseas competition, which has caused job upheaval in Schaumburg. Historically, this area was one of the most Republican places in the nation. In the past decade, like other suburban Chicago areas, it moved toward the Democrats, and if the 8th is still one of Illinois's most Republican districts, as measured by its support of George W. Bush in 2000 and 2004, it is far less Republican than districts with similar demographics in Texas or Georgia.

The congresswoman from the 8th District is Melissa Bean, who on her second attempt defeated Phil Crane, the senior Republican in the House and one of only two Republican incumbents defeated in 2004. Bean was born in Chicago and grew up in Park Ridge, where her father owned a company that manufactured conveyor belts. She attended a local community college, then worked from home as a business consultant in technology sales, training executives at Motorola and other companies how to develop marketing and sales campaigns; at 40, she got a bachelor's degree in political science from Roosevelt University. She served on the local PTA and volunteered for Crane's Democratic challenger in 2000; two years later, she ran for the seat herself. When Bean challenged Crane in 2002, she got little assistance from national Democrats. But she held him to 57%, the second-lowest performance of his long career, and never stopped campaigning.

In 2004, her energetic campaign offered a vivid contrast to Crane's sluggish and late-starting effort. Downplaying her party identification and keeping her distance from Democratic leaders, she handed voters jelly beans to help them remember her name, framed her candidacy as "a fresh start" and consistently talked about the need for a vigorous new voice. In this Republican district, she sharply attacked Crane for having lost touch back home and showing little influence in Washington; her attacks were directed at Crane rather than the Republican majority. Bean supported the war in Iraq, opposed the Bush tax cuts and favored abortion rights. Crane tried to depict her as an inexperienced newcomer who would be unable to deliver federal dollars for the district: but this is not a district with visible infusions of federal money. In October, the *Chicago Tribune*, historically Republican and still less liberal than most other big metro area newspapers, endorsed Bean. Crane "has used his seat in Congress as a cozy sinecure." Bean "will, unlike Crane, pay close attention to the folks back home." Crane complained, "I have been busting my hump for about five straight weeks" in the campaign. Bean won 52%-48%. She won 56%-44% on her home turf of Cook County, won 50.3%-49.7% in Lake County and trailed 49%-51% in McHenry County, running in each case well ahead of usual Democratic percentages in this historically Republican territory.

In the House, Bean has a centrist voting record and focused her work on the Financial Services Committee. She worked on the issue of identity theft and on tax credits for adoptive families; Bean was adopted as a baby. She backed a bill to permit small businesses to join together and offer health coverage to employees. She won business support—and angered unions—as 1 of 15 House Democrats to vote for the Central American Free Trade Agreement; she said it would benefit local companies. In 2007, she again drew fire from labor and progressive adocacy groups when she was the only Democrat to vote against the $607 billion FY08 Labor-HHS appropriations bill; a spokesman said she had concerns about the overall level of spending in the measure.

Bean immediately became a top Republican target for 2006. But she made skillful use of incumbency and constituency service, and moved quickly to build a campaign warchest. Bean also benefited from a divisive six-candidate Republican primary. The frontrunners were former investment banker David McSweeney, who got 35% when he challenged Crane in the 1998 primary, and Kathy Salvi, a personal-injury attorney with connections to local conservatives; the national party did not take sides. McSweeney, who won the primary with 43% to 33% for Salvi, mostly self-financed his campaign and said that he was independent of the Republican party; he criticized Speaker Dennis Hastert for large budget deficits. In the general, attorney Bill Scheurer ran as an independent with support from some national labor unions who felt "betrayed" by Bean; Scheurer called Bean "a corporate candidate." National Republicans spent more than $2 million here, some of it to encourage Scheurer, though he failed to get much traction. Bean won with 51% to 44% for McSweeney and 5% for Scheurer. She carried each county, though she won by only 43 votes in McHenry. In Lake County, which cast 55% of the total vote, she led 50% to 45%. Bean cannot take this seat for granted, but Republicans will need unity and a top-flight challenger to oust her.

NINTH DISTRICT

Rep. Jan Schakowsky (D)

Elected 1998, 5th term; b. May 26, 1944, Chicago; home, Evanston; U. of IL, B.S. 1965; Jewish; married (Robert Creamer).

Elected Office: IL House of Reps., 1990-98.

Professional Career: Founder, Natl. Consumers Unite, 1969-73; Prog. Dir., IL Public Action, 1976-85; Exec. Dir., IL State Cncl. of Sr. Citizens, 1985-90.

DC Office: 1027 LHOB, 20515, 202-225-2111; Fax: 202-226-6890; Web site: www.house.gov/schakowsky.

District Offices: Chicago, 773-506-7100; Evanston, 847-328-3409; Park Ridge, 847-298-2128.

Committees: *Chief Deputy Majority Whip. Energy & Commerce* (19th of 31 D): Commerce, Trade & Consumer Protection (Vice Chmn.); Oversight & Investigations; Health; Environment & Hazardous Materials. *Permanent Select Committee on Intelligence* (10th of 12 D): Oversight & Investigations.

Group Ratings

	ADA	ACLU	AFS	LCV	ITIC	NTU	COC	ACU	CFG	FRC
2006	95	100	100	100	14	14	20	0	0	0
2005	100	—	100	89	—	15	29	0	0	0

National Journal Ratings

	2005 LIB	—	2005 CONS		2006 LIB	—	2006 CONS
Economic	94%	—	0%		90%	—	9%
Social	97%	—	2%		95%	—	5%
Foreign	96%	—	0%		92%	—	5%

Key Votes of the 109th Congress

1. Estate Tax Repeal	N	5. Limit Interstate Abortion	N	9. Build Border Fence	N
2. Limit CAFE Standards	N	6. Extend Patriot Act	N	10. CAFTA	N
3. FY06 Spending Curb	N	7. Bar Same Sex Marriage	N	11. Oppose Iraq Withdrawal	N
4. Drilling in ANWR	N	8. Stem Cell Research $	Y	12. Detainee Tribunals	N

Election Results

2006 general	Jan Schakowsky (D)	122,852	(75%)	($1,134,762)
	Michael Shannon (R)	41,858	(25%)	
2006 primary	Jan Schakowsky (D)	unopposed		
2004 general	Jan Schakowsky (D)	175,282	(76%)	($1,068,961)
	Kurt Eckhardt (R)	56,135	(24%)	($2,624)

Prior Winning Percentages: 2002 (70%); 2000 (76%); 1998 (75%)

The People		Race/Ethnic Origin	Ancestry	
Area size:	78 sq. mi.	62.5% White	German: 10.5%	Polish: 8.4%
Urban population:	100.0%	10.7% Black	Irish: 8.2%	
Rural population:	0.0%	12.3% Asian	**2004 Presidential Vote**	
Pop. 2000:	653,647	0.2% Native Am.	Kerry (D) 175,288	(68%)
Pop. 2005 (est):	601,741	0.1% Hawaiian	Bush (R) 81,138	(32%)
Median income:	$46,531	2.6% Two+ races	Other 677	(0%)
Poverty status:	11.0%	0.3% Other	**2000 Presidential Vote**	
Military veterans:	8.0%	11.5% Hispanic Origin	Gore (D) 155,529	(67%)
			Bush (R) 71,064	(31%)
			Other 4,331	(2%)
			Cook Partisan Voting Index: D +20	

Occupation   Blue collar: 16.1%   White collar: 69.8%   Gray collar: 14.0%

"Make no little plans," commanded architect Daniel Burnham, who made no little plans for the Chicago lakefront. The glorious parks he designed are among America's urban jewels, and the row of high-rise apartment buildings—some austere works of masters of the International style, some in traditional styles evocative of some other place and time, some sleek Art Deco works of the 1920s and 1930s—are a splendid accompaniment. Behind the lakefront is all the diversity of Chicago. In sturdy brick houses, with scarcely a shoehorn's space between them, or in stubby apartment buildings, are ethnic and racial groups of all sorts, from Argentineans to Slavs, Plains Indians to Indian plainsmen. In the 1970s the neighborhoods behind the lakefront seemed to be getting grimier and heading downhill. But since the late 1980s, they have been busy gentrifying, as young couples and gays, professionals and entrepreneurs renovate old houses and open new businesses. Today this part of Chicago has as much urban energy and lively diversity as any place in America.

The lakefront has long been the most heavily Jewish part of Chicago. The local Jewish community, prominent for more than a century, has never been as much a force for big government as in New York, nor is it connected as much to a glamorous industry as in Los Angeles. Yet these Jewish voters' liberal impulses have been strong: the 19th century impulse to resist state authority and imposition of cultural uniformity and the 20th century impulse to increase state responsibility for individuals' lives. Chicago's North Side Jews, on the lakefront or in neighborhoods like Rogers Park and nearby suburbs like Skokie and Niles, have been a solidly Democratic voting bloc, involved with—but skeptical of—the old Democratic machine. In city politics since the 1980s Jewish voters and lakefront liberals of all backgrounds have been a key swing group.

The 9th Congressional District of Illinois covers most of Chicago's lakefront, from just north of Diversey Harbor past the thriving Asian and orthodox Jewish communities in West Rogers Park and on to Evanston, founded by Methodists to promote temperance (a cause that never prospered in Chicago). The home of Northwestern University, Evanston has moved gracefully from historic Yankee Republican-ness to trendy post-graduate Democratic-ness. From Evanston and nearby Wilmette (which is shared with the 10th), the 9th presses inland through heavily Jewish Skokie to Morton Grove and Niles and includes most of Des Plaines. These bustling inner-ring suburbs near O'Hare Airport have become the center of Chicagoland's job base; with its financial markets and the professionals that support them, the city once known as the hog butcher of the world has evolved into the hog belly trader. The district extends west to once rock-solid Republican territory—Park Ridge, with its characteristic Chicago brick houses in orderly rows, where Hillary Rodham Clinton grew up at 235 Wisner, and the cluster of office buildings and interchanges in Rosemont, next to O'Hare. Though much less Republican than it was before the 1990s, that territory lowered the district's Democratic percentage. But this remains an overwhelmingly Democratic district.

The congresswoman from the 9th District is Jan Schakowsky, a Democrat elected in 1998 and an outspoken progressive. She grew up in Rogers Park and worked two years as a teacher; in 1969 she formed National Consumers Unite and worked for date-of-freshness labels on dairy products and other food. Later she joined Illinois Public Action, a consumer group; in 1985 she became executive director of the Illinois State Council of Senior Citizens, where she organized the 1989 protest to Dan Rostenkowski's Medicare catastrophic health care law for seniors, which resulted in televised pictures of him fleeing from elderly protestors and led Congress to repeal the benefit. In 1990 she was elected to the state House from Evanston and Skokie, and served as Democratic floor leader.

In 1998 Schakowsky was selected in the Democratic primary to replace Sidney Yates, who had represented the lakefront in Congress for 48 of the preceding 50 years. Her strategy was to run from the left—"I don't think I can be defined as too far left in a district like this"—and to build a volunteer organization. With ads in college papers, she got 400 young people to apply for 20 field organizer jobs; they set about identifying Schakowsky voters. She raised $1.4 million, with help from EMILY's List. Against state Senator Howard Carroll, who had the support of most Democratic ward committeemen and attacked her opposition to the death penalty, Schakowsky's 1,500 workers, 250 from unions, helped to give her a 45%-34% win. She easily won the general election then, and subsequently.

Schakowsky has one of the most liberal voting records in the House and regularly scores perfect ratings from liberal interest groups. She harshly criticized the 2003 enactment of prescription-drug coverage for seniors, joining Democrats seeking to overhaul the law. Drawing on her experience as a consumer advocate, she urged the Consumer Product Safety Commission to recall yo-yo balls, a water-filled toy with a long cord that has resulted in hundreds of reports of injuries. To encourage food safety, she filed a bill to create a national database of school food suppliers. In 2006, after Republicans filed changes that made the measure "toothless," she abandoned support of a bill to require automakers to share technical information with repair shops. In the majority, she called for aggressive oversight of the Bush administration.

Schakowsky has worked with party leaders on electoral strategy, gaining their support to expand her training program for political organizers. An early supporter of Nancy Pelosi for party whip, Schakowsky was rewarded with a chief deputy whip slot, which she retained as Steny Hoyer and then James Clyburn took the Whip job. She has used her post to convey an often tough partisan message and to underscore her loyalty to Pelosi. Her contacts with national liberal groups have helped her to become a major party fundraiser. When the McCain-Feingold law ended big soft-money contributions after the 2002 election, Schakowsky helped to assemble the House Democrats' program to expand contributions from small donors.

Schakowsky briefly considered a run for the Senate in 2004 but decided to remain in the House. When Bob Menendez was appointed to a vacant Senate seat in early 2006, she campaigned actively for the opening that resulted for vice-chairman of the Democratic Caucus; with support from Pelosi, she seemed to be the early frontrunner against Joe Crowley and John Larson. But she unexpectedly was eliminated on the first ballot, and it became apparent that Larson had picked up much of her support. John Murtha, a close ally of Pelosi, managed Larson's campaign. Some Democrats speculated that she was the victim of bad timing: The Caucus was skittish of selecting her so soon after her husband Robert Creamer, longtime head of Illinois Public Action Fund, pleaded guilty in August 2005 on bank fraud charges for a check-kiting scheme; he later was sentenced to a five-month prison term. Schakowsky said that her husband had "made mistakes," but that she was unaware of his financial problems and was "proud of who Bob is . . . .He has been a constant crusader." After Democrats won House control, Schakowsky seconded the nomination of Pelosi for Speaker, calling her "my treasured friend," and she was part of the inner circle.

TENTH DISTRICT

Rep. Mark Kirk (R)

Elected 2000, 4th term; b. Sept. 15, 1959, Champaign; home, Kenilworth; Universidad Nacional Autonoma de Mexico, 1977-78, Cornell U., B.A. 1981, London Sch. of Econ., M.Sc. 1982; Georgetown U., J.D. 1992; Congregationalist; married (Kimberly Vertolli-Kirk).

Military Career: U.S. Naval Reserve, 1989-present.

Professional Career: Parliamentary aide, British House of Commons, 1981-83; A.A., U.S. Rep. John E. Porter, 1984-89; Staffer, World Bank, 1990-91; Spec. Asst., U.S. Dept. of State, 1991-93; Practicing atty., 1993-95; Counsel, U.S. House Cmte. on Intl. Relations, 1995-2000.

DC Office: 1030 LHOB, 20515, 202-225-4835; Fax: 202-225-0837; Web site: www.house.gov/kirk.

District Offices: Northbrook, 847-940-0202.

Committees: *Appropriations* (24th of 29 R): Financial Services & General Government; State, Foreign Operations & Related Programs.

Group Ratings

	ADA	ACLU	AFS	LCV	ITIC	NTU	COC	ACU	CFG	FRC
2006	45	55	14	75	86	47	80	54	37	14
2005	30	—	25	39	—	51	81	36	49	31

National Journal Ratings

	2005 LIB	—	2005 CONS		2006 LIB	—	2006 CONS
Economic	49%	—	50%		47%	—	53%
Social	57%	—	42%		55%	—	45%
Foreign	48%	—	51%		43%	—	55%

Key Votes of the 109th Congress

1. Estate Tax Repeal	Y	5. Limit Interstate Abortion	N	9. Build Border Fence	Y
2. Limit CAFE Standards	N	6. Extend Patriot Act	Y	10. CAFTA	Y
3. FY06 Spending Curb	Y	7. Bar Same Sex Marriage	N	11. Oppose Iraq Withdrawal	Y
4. Drilling in ANWR	N	8. Stem Cell Research $	Y	12. Detainee Tribunals	Y

Election Results

2006 general	Mark Kirk (R)	107,929	(53%)	($3,512,971)
	Dan Seals (D)	94,278	(47%)	($1,882,795)
2006 primary	Mark Kirk (R)	unopposed		
2004 general	Mark Kirk (R)	177,493	(64%)	($1,653,529)
	Lee Goodman (D)	99,218	(36%)	($88,520)

Prior Winning Percentages: 2002 (69%); 2000 (51%)

The People		Race/Ethnic Origin	Ancestry	
Area size:	252 sq. mi.	75.2% White	German: 14.4%	Irish: 9.9%
Urban population:	99.6%	5.3% Black	Polish: 7.3%	
Rural population:	0.4%	5.9% Asian	**2004 Presidential Vote**	
Pop. 2000:	653,647	0.1% Native Am.	Kerry (D) 150,267	(53%)
Pop. 2005 (est):	669,028	0.0% Hawaiian	Bush (R) 134,536	(47%)
Median income:	$71,663	1.1% Two+ races	**2000 Presidential Vote**	
Poverty status:	4.8%	0.2% Other	Gore (D) 134,149	(51%)
Military veterans:	10.5%	12.3% Hispanic Origin	Bush (R) 123,982	(47%)
			Other 6,097	(2%)
			Cook Partisan Voting Index: D + 4	

Occupation	Blue collar: 14.4%	White collar: 75.9%	Gray collar: 9.7%

Since 1855, when the Chicago & Northwestern opened the railroad line from downtown Chicago north along the lakeshore, the North Shore suburbs along Lake Michigan have been the favorite residence for Chicago's elite. The North Shore starts in Evanston, and goes on to Wilmette and Winnetka and Glencoe, then crosses into the eastern Lake County towns of Highland Park and Lake Forest—each with a slightly different personality, each long established, mightily prosperous and with a patina of age. Not far from the gritty, monosyllabic city, these are communities of pleasant, affluent, well-educated people living in an environment whose natural beauty—the long water vista and blue light off the lake, the gentle hills and fine trees—is carefully disciplined. Corporate headquarters fit comfortably here, including Baxter Healthcare, Abbott Laboratories, Allstate Insurance. This is the home of the Great Lakes Naval Training Center and also of Highland Park, which provided the setting for the 1980s films *Risky Business*, *Sixteen Candles* and *Ferris Bueller's Day Off.*

The 10th Congressional District of Illinois is the North Shore district, starting on the Wilmette lakefront, running north to the city of Waukegan (once famous as the home of comedian Jack Benny) and almost to the Wisconsin border. The district goes inland to Northbrook and Deerfield through what for many years were cornfields. Farther inland are suburbs like Arlington Heights, developed in the 1950s and 1960s on the Northwestern railroad line, and Wheeling, developed in the 1970s near I-294. To the north is Libertyville, near where the Adlai Stevensons, the late presidential candidate and his son the former senator, owned what is now one of the last farms only a few miles from Lake Michigan. With the big movement toward Democrats in the Chicago suburbs in the 1990s, this establishment Republican district voted narrowly for Al Gore in 2000 and by a slightly larger margin for John Kerry in 2004.

The congressman from the 10th District is Mark Kirk, a Republican first elected in 2000. Kirk was born in downstate Illinois but grew up mostly in Kenilworth, on the Lake between Wilmette and Winnetka. He graduated from Cornell and the London School of Economics, worked in Congressman John Porter's Washington office and became the chief of staff in just three years. Kirk left Capitol Hill in 1990 and moved on to a number of Washington jobs, first at the World Bank, then as a State Department aide working on the Central American peace process, during which time he got his law degree at Georgetown. After two years of international law practice, he served four years as counsel to the House International Relations Committee. He is also a commander in the Naval Reserves, serving as an aviator with tours of duty in Turkey, Serbia, Bosnia, Haiti, and Panama. In flights during the Gulf War, he was a frequent target of Iraqi guns; he continues to work one weekend each month at the Pentagon's "war room," monitoring intelligence reports.

In 1999, when Porter announced his retirement, Kirk returned home to the 10th District, where he was one of 11 competitors in the Republican primary. This contest included six millionaires who spent nearly $4 million of their own money. Kirk did not spend nearly as much, but he had great advantages: the endorsement of the highly popular Porter, the fact that he was the only candidate with moderate views on cultural issues and his greater experience in government. His 31% put him well ahead of the 15% for R.R. Donnelley & Sons printing company heiress Shawn Margaret Donnelley, and the 14% for Northbrook Mayor Mark Damisch. Democrats nominated state Representative Lauren Beth Gash. Kirk and Gash campaigned as candidates in the Porter mold, promising to carry on his fiscally conservative, culturally moderate record. Gash tried to downplay Kirk's years in Washington, touting her own legislative experience while talking about Social Security and prescription drugs. But Kirk won 51%-49%.

In the House, Kirk has compiled a centrist voting record, though a bit more liberal on social issues and conservative on foreign policy. He said that he wanted to strengthen moderate Republicans with a libertarian approach. His familiarity with the workings of the House and a helpful connection enabled him to get a seat on the Appropriations Committee. His explanation for the assignment: "Three words—J. Dennis Hastert."

Kirk joined forces between Republican moderates and deficit hawks in 2004 on steps to limit federal spending; the House passed his amendment that requires the Congressional Budget Office to publish an annual report that compares projected annual spending for entitlements to the actual spending in the preceding year. He fought to eliminate funding for Alaska's "bridge to nowhere." Citing intelligence failures in Iraq, the well-informed Kirk pushed for reform of the intelligence community. "For the president, it's incumbent on him to say mistakes were made and it's incumbent on him to fix it," he said. In October 2006, he demanded that the Pentagon do more about the opium crisis in Afghanistan and terrorism fueled by the sale of illegal narcotics. He filed the "American Heroes Act" proposal for a statue in the new Capitol Visitors Center to commemorate the victims of the United Airlines flight that crashed in Pennsylvania after passengers struggled with terrorists to prevent them from reaching their target, which was probably the Capitol. With Democrat Jesse Jackson Jr. and backed by the Everglades Foundation, he fought unsuccessfully in the Appropriations Committee to end subsidized loans for storage by sugar processing companies; Chicago-area candy producers have complained that high sugar prices forced them to cut thousands of jobs. He pushed for O'Hare expansion and opposed a proposal for suburban rail commuters to subsidize the beleaguered Chicago Transit Authority. He worked with the 5th District's Rahm Emanuel on a sweeping package to clean up Lake Michigan.

In the 109th Congress, Kirk co-chaired the mainstream Republicans' Tuesday Group, and said that Congress should reflect the nation's preponderant moderates. He unveiled a suburban agenda that he termed "pro-defense, pro-personal responsibility, pro-environment, and pro-science." He also established the 55-member Suburban Agenda Caucus. In May 2005, with other GOP moderates, he successfully demanded a House vote on legislation to promote embryonic stem-cell research as a condition for his support of that year's budget resolution. He spoke out against House Republicans' "DeLay rule", which sought to abandon the requirement that an indicted party leader must step down from the post; the proposal was dropped.

In 2006, he faced his most competitive reelection challenge. Democrats nominated Dan Seals, a marketing specialist who built a well-financed grass-roots campaign and espoused Democratic talking points. While largely maintaining his support for the war in Iraq, Kirk emphasized centrist positions on domestic policy that distanced himself from President Bush. Rahm Emanuel's DCCC, which did not target this race, did some last-minute spending for Seals, including a mailing in which Bush had his arm around Kirk. But it wasn't enough. Kirk won 53%-47%. He took 51% in Lake and 55% in Cook, which cast 57% of the total vote. Seals announced he would run again in 2008 but faced the prospect of primary opposition from former Clinton administration aide Jay Footlik. Some

Republicans wanted Kirk to run against Senator Richard Durbin in 2008; Kirk dismissed the possibility. For now, at least, he has become the "go to" Republican in the northern suburbs.

ELEVENTH DISTRICT

Rep. Jerry Weller (R)

Elected 1994, 7th term; b. July 7, 1957, Streator; home, Morris; U. of IL, B.S. 1979; Christian; married (Zury Rios Sosa).

Elected Office: IL House of Reps., 1988-94.

Professional Career: Farmer; Aide, U.S. Rep. Tom Corcoran, 1980-81; Aide, U.S. Agriculture Secy. John Block, 1981-85.

DC Office: 108 CHOB, 20515, 202-225-3635; Fax: 202-225-3521; Web site: weller.house.gov.

District Offices: Joliet, 815-740-2028.

Committees: *Ways & Means* (7th of 17 R): Income Security & Family Support (RMM); Trade.

Group Ratings

	ADA	ACLU	AFS	LCV	ITIC	NTU	COC	ACU	CFG	FRC
2006	5	14	14	25	100	51	100	80	52	85
2005	5	—	0	0	—	57	93	92	63	92

National Journal Ratings

	2005 LIB	—	2005 CONS		2006 LIB	—	2006 CONS
Economic	26%	—	73%		34%	—	65%
Social	41%	—	59%		26%	—	74%
Foreign	34%	—	61%		33%	—	63%

Key Votes of the 109th Congress

1. Estate Tax Repeal	Y	5. Limit Interstate Abortion	Y	9. Build Border Fence		Y
2. Limit CAFE Standards	Y	6. Extend Patriot Act	Y	10. CAFTA		Y
3. FY06 Spending Curb	Y	7. Bar Same Sex Marriage	Y	11. Oppose Iraq Withdrawal		Y
4. Drilling in ANWR	Y	8. Stem Cell Research $	N	12. Detainee Tribunals		Y

Election Results

2006 general	Jerry Weller (R)	109,009	(55%)	($1,906,882)
	John Pavich (D)	88,846	(45%)	($593,324)
2006 primary	Jerry Weller (R)	unopposed		
2004 general	Jerry Weller (R)	173,057	(59%)	($1,792,779)
	Tari Renner (D)	121,903	(41%)	($315,600)

Prior Winning Percentages: 2002 (64%); 2000 (56%); 1998 (59%); 1996 (52%); 1994 (61%)

The People		Race/Ethnic Origin	Ancestry	
Area size:	4,284 sq. mi.	83.7% White	German: 18.4% Irish: 11.8%	
Urban population:	78.2%	7.8% Black	Italian: 6.0%	
Rural population:	21.8%	0.8% Asian	**2004 Presidential Vote**	
Pop. 2000:	653,647	0.1% Native Am.	Bush (R) 162,779	(53%)
Pop. 2005 (est):	720,349	0.0% Hawaiian	Kerry (D) 140,619	(46%)
Median income:	$47,800	0.9% Two+ races	Other 1,018	(0%)
Poverty status:	8.4%	0.1% Other	**2000 Presidential Vote**	
Military veterans:	12.5%	6.7% Hispanic Origin	Bush (R) 128,280	(50%)
			Gore (D) 122,979	(48%)
			Other 7,269	(3%)
			Cook Partisan Voting Index: R + 1	
Occupation	Blue collar: 29.4%	White collar: 55.3% Gray collar: 15.3%		

The low-lying land west and south of Chicago, where sluggishly flowing rivers run circles around industrial sites, is a great divide over which French explorers portaged the easiest path from the inland oceans of the Great Lakes to the Mississippi River valley. Today there is still a kind of borderland here, as the factories and shopping centers and subdivisions stop somewhere past the Cook County line and downstate prairies begin, cornfields bisected by highways and railroads radiating out from the Loop and the rail yards of the nation's transportation hub. Politically, this is a borderland as well, between the traditionally Democratic Chicago metropolitan area, with its hard-bitten machine politics, and heavily Republican Downstate Illinois, with its tradition of governance by local civic leaders that stretches back to the days of Abraham Lincoln.

The 11th Congressional District of Illinois covers much of this borderland. It includes most of Will County, the fastest-growing of the large suburban Chicago counties, and its county seat of Joliet—politically marginal territory. Once a canal boat town, and later the producer of one-third of America's wallpaper, Joliet was home to the famed Joliet Correctional Center (the prison of *Blues Brothers* fame) until it closed in 2002. It is the location of a 75,000-seat NASCAR racetrack; it owes its current prosperity and growing tourist locales in part to riverboat gambling. Nearby Plainfield doubled its population between 2000 and 2005 on what had been mostly farmland, and at the same time the number of Hispanic residents nearly doubled in Will County. Farther west, on bluffs above the Illinois River heading down to the Mississippi, are the factory towns of Ottawa and LaSalle and, to the south, Streator; this is LaSalle County, also politically marginal. South of Joliet is Kankakee, a county seat amid rich prairie earth on the Illinois Central main line and the home of convicted former Governor George Ryan; this is Republican territory. The 11th no longer includes the south-ernmost townships of Cook County, which were increasingly Democratic, but it has added two ungainly-looking appendages. One goes west to rural Bureau County; the other heads south at the intersection of I-80 and I-39 and includes most of Bloomington in McLean County, one of the faster-growing Downstate counties. Another addition was a small corner of Livingston County, which includes the home of the parents of the 11th District's congressman. The 2001 redistricting made this district more Republican than its 1990s incarnation; George W. Bush won here with 53% in 2004.

The congressman from the 11th District is Jerry Weller, a hard-working, politically savvy Republican who won the seat in 1994. Weller grew up on a farm, where his family raised hogs. Out of college, he was a staffer to Congressman Tom Corcoran and Agriculture Secretary John Block; in the mid-1980s he returned to Illinois and was elected to the state House in 1988. In 1994, when Democratic Congressman George Sangmeister retired, Weller was one of six Republicans and seven Democrats to run for the seat. He called for reforming health care via market-based principles; he was proud of replacing the "granny tax" on nursing home residents with a cigarette tax as a way to pay for health care. Against Democrat Frank Giglio, a 20-year state legislator, who said of Congress, "Wouldn't this be a nice way to finish my career?" Weller won 61%-39%.

In the House, Weller has leaned toward conservatives on economic policy and is slightly more moderate on cultural issues. He showed impressive insider skills when he won in 1996 a seat on the Ways and Means Committee, arguing that no one there represented Chicago. He became a prime sponsor of ending the marriage penalty. He backed several other tax cuts, including the end of the Social Security earnings limit on seniors, which Bill Clinton signed, and elimination of the estate tax, which Clinton opposed and George W. Bush signed, though on a phased schedule and with a sunset date. The energy bill enacted in 2005 included his provision for a $300 tax credit to encourage homeowners to make energy-efficient repairs. Weller did not neglect local concerns. With Democrat Jesse Jackson Jr., he promoted the third Chicago-area airport for Peotone, 45 miles south of Chicago and a few miles north of Kankakee. In December 2005, Congress passed Weller's amendment giving Will County control of the airport; Jackson, who envisioned substantial control by Cook County officials, said the measure would sabotage the project with legal and regulatory delays. Weller opposed Jackson's proposal for a new casino in Lynwood in southern Cook County.

Weller has been active in internal House Republican politics, with mixed success. He lost a race for Republican Conference secretary in 1997 and withdrew from a race for chairman of the Policy Committee in 1998. When Speaker-designate Bob Livingston stunned everyone by announcing his retirement, Weller worked the phones for Hastert, along with Tom DeLay and Tom Davis, and helped Hastert win the speakership within hours. In early 2001, he was named finance chairman of the NRCC but suffered another setback to his leadership ambitions in 2002, when Tom Reynolds defeated him for the NRCC chairmanship 119-90.

Weller gained unusual attention in 2004 when he announced his engagement to Zury Rios Sosa, a Guatemalan congresswoman and the daughter of Jose Efrain Rios Montt, who seized power in that country in 1982 in a military coup that was followed by a bloody revolt and thousands of deaths. Congressional historians said that he is the first U.S. lawmaker to marry a member of the legislature from another nation. Weller said that his personal life was a private matter, and criticized as "disgraceful" Democrats who criticized the background of his fiancée, whom he met at a reception hosted by the U.S. Ambassador in Guatemala. That didn't stop Tari Renner, Weller's Democratic opponent that year, a McLean County Board member and political science professor at Illinois Wesleyan University. Weller got Ethics Committee advice that his marriage did not pose a conflict unless he had a direct interest in the outcome of legislation, plus a unanimous Federal Election Commission ruling that Sosa could take part in his campaign, even though she is a foreign national. Renner criticized Weller for lockstep support of George W. Bush; Weller referred to his opponent simply as "the college professor." He won 59%-41%, and carried seven of the eight counties; Renner carried his home county, McLean, 53%-47%. Weller and Sosa were married later that month at a Guatemalan mansion guarded by tight security.

In 2006, Weller faced a competitive challenge from John Pavich, a former CIA officer—and political neophyte—who criticized his handling of the Peotone airport. In the closing days, Weller sent a mailing that depicted Jackson as a puppeteer "pulling the strings" on Pavich; the ad was "race baiting," Pavich said. Despite Weller's big fundraising advantage, his victory was reduced to 55%-45%; he carried all eight counties. In September 2007, Weller announced he would not seek reelection to an eighth term.

TWELFTH DISTRICT

Rep. Jerry Costello (D)

Elected Aug. 1988, 10th full term; b. Sept. 25, 1949, E. St. Louis; home, Belleville; Belleville Area Col., A.A. 1971, Maryville Col., B.A. 1973; Catholic; married (Georgia).

Elected Office: Chmn., St. Clair Cnty. Bd. of Supervisors, 1980-88.

Professional Career: Dir., IL Court Svcs. & Probation, 1973-80; Chmn., Region's Cncl. of Govts., 1980-84.

DC Office: 2408 RHOB, 20515, 202-225-5661; Fax: 202-225-0285; Web site: www.house.gov/costello.

District Offices: Belleville, 618-233-8026; Carbondale, 618-529-3791; Chester, 618-826-3043; E. St. Louis, 618-397-8833; Granite City, 618-451-7065; West Frankfort, 618-937-6402.

Committees: *Science & Technology* (2d of 24 D): Energy & Environment; Investigations & Oversight. *Transportation & Infrastructure* (4th of 41 D): Aviation (Chmn.); Water Resources & Environment; Railroads, Pipelines & Hazardous Materials.

Group Ratings

	ADA	ACLU	AFS	LCV	ITIC	NTU	COC	ACU	CFG	FRC
2006	70	64	86	75	43	21	40	48	10	71
2005	80	—	100	72	—	22	52	40	23	77

National Journal Ratings

	2005 LIB	—	2005 CONS		2006 LIB	—	2006 CONS
Economic	62%	—	38%		62%	—	38%
Social	57%	—	43%		60%	—	39%
Foreign	67%	—	32%		80%	—	18%

Key Votes of the 109th Congress

1. Estate Tax Repeal	Y	5. Limit Interstate Abortion	Y	9. Build Border Fence		Y
2. Limit CAFE Standards	Y	6. Extend Patriot Act	N	10. CAFTA		N
3. FY06 Spending Curb	N	7. Bar Same Sex Marriage	Y	11. Oppose Iraq Withdrawal		Y
4. Drilling in ANWR	N	8. Stem Cell Research $	N	12. Detainee Tribunals		N

Election Results

2006 general	Jerry Costello (D) .... unopposed		($757,056)
2006 primary	Jerry Costello (D) 45,600	(90%)	
	Kenneth Wiezer (D) 4,991	(10%)	
2004 general	Jerry Costello (D) 198,962	(69%)	($637,567)
	Erin Zweigart (R) 82,677	(29%)	($15,983)
	Other 4,796	(2%)	

Prior Winning Percentages: 2002 (69%); 2000 (100%); 1998 (60%); 1996 (72%); 1994 (66%); 1992 (71%); 1990 (66%); 1988 (53%); 1988 (51%)

The People		Race/Ethnic Origin	Ancestry	
Area size:	4,556 sq. mi.	79.7% White	German: 18.6% Irish: 8.7%	
Urban population:	76.7%	16.3% Black	English: 6.6%	
Rural population:	23.3%	0.8% Asian	**2004 Presidential Vote**	
Pop. 2000:	653,647	0.2% Native Am.	Kerry (D) 152,055	(52%)
Pop. 2005 (est):	652,484	0.0% Hawaiian	Bush (R) 139,710	(48%)
Median income:	$35,198	1.0% Two+ races	Other 1,600	(1%)
Poverty status:	15.0%	0.1% Other	**2000 Presidential Vote**	
Military veterans:	15.3%	1.8% Hispanic Origin	Gore (D) 144,548	(54%)
			Bush (R) 116,724	(43%)
			Other 7,634	(3%)
			Cook Partisan Voting Index: D + 5	

Occupation	Blue collar: 26.2%	White collar: 55.1%	Gray collar: 18.7%

The nation's two mightiest rivers, the Mississippi and Missouri, their waters roiling together, join just a few miles above St. Louis and just a few miles below Alton, Illinois. Most views of this center of the Mississippi Valley focus on the Gateway Arch and the buildings of downtown St. Louis. But the Mississippi shoreline of Illinois is worthy of attention as well. Alton's 19th century buildings recall its turbulent history, when it was the home of the anti-slavery agitator Elijah Lovejoy, who was murdered by a mob. More recently it was the longtime home of conservative crusader and columnist Phyllis Schlafly. Nearby in Hartford, Lewis and Clark spent five months preparing their team and collecting supplies for their journey westward. Just across from the Gateway Arch is East St. Louis, where dozens of rail lines and highways funnel into bridges over the river. Once a rail and stockyards center second only to Chicago, East St. Louis is now almost entirely black and one of America's poorest and most troubled cities, a half-abandoned slum with one of the nation's highest crime rates and a rapidly declining tax base; it is almost entirely dependent on a riverboat casino and an adjacent waterfront hotel for local revenue, but casino taxes have increased and revenues have dipped, leaving the future of gambling in Illinois in question. After peaking at 82,000 in 1960, its population is now less than 30,000. East St. Louis is in St. Clair County, long heavily Democratic; Alton is in Madison County, politically more marginal and famous as a prime locale for trial lawyers to file tort suits. George W. Bush campaigned here in 2005 to change tort law.

South of East St. Louis and the industrial area around Belleville, the river counties are lightly inhabited, but they were not always unimportant. This was the site of the French Kaskaskia settlement that became Illinois's first capital in 1818, but repeated flooding turned it into an island and reduced its population to 9 people and many more egrets. Farther south, the river abuts coal country and is not far from Carbondale, once a coal center but now, as the home of Southern Illinois University, bustling with students from Downstate Illinois and Chicago; in 2006, Maytag shut its plant and eliminated 1,000 jobs in nearby Herrin. The land here is sometimes known as Egypt, the southern end of Illinois where the Ohio River meets the Mississippi: flat, fertile farmland, protected by giant man-made levees because it is susceptible to yearly floods. The marshy landscape has created the Sinkhole Plain, with more than 10,000 sinkholes. There is more than a touch of Dixie here: The unofficial capital of Egypt, Cairo (pronounced *KAY-roh*), is a declining town closer to Mississippi and Atlanta than to Chicago. In his 1842 work, *American Notes*, Charles Dickens described the town in these unflattering terms: "The hateful Mississippi circling and eddying before it, and turning off upon its southern course a slimy monster hideous to behold; a hotbed of disease, an ugly sepulchre, a grave uncheered by any gleam of promise: a place without one single quality, in earth or air or water, to commend it: such is this dismal Cairo." A more enticing locale not far from Cairo is the Shawnee National Forest, which has preserved Native American sites that are 10,000 years old; the Cherokee Nation left here in the 1830s on its devastating forced march to Oklahoma, which became known as the Trail of Tears.

The 12th District of Illinois covers all of this riverfront from Alton south to Cairo, with some inland territory as well. Most of its population is in the Metro East area in St. Clair and Madison Counties. The largest employer in southern Illinois is Scott Air Force Base near Belleville, where local officials hoped that a relocation of planes for the 932d Airlift Wing would protect the facility in the 2005 base-closing review. When the Pentagon's recommendations were released, there was joy in Belleville: Scott ended up gaining 797 jobs, upgraded medical transport planes, and 12 refueling tankers.

The congressman from the 12th District is Jerry Costello, a Democrat first elected in 1988. He grew up in a St. Clair County political family, worked for the courts after college, then became chairman of the St. Clair County Board of Supervisors. He waited with some impatience for the retirement of Congressman Mel Price, first elected in 1944; Price died in office in April 1988. Experienced, well connected, supported by organized labor, Costello was the obvious successor. Yet he received only 51% of the votes in the special election and 53% for a full term.

Costello is a practical-minded politician with a centrist voting record that is a bit more liberal on economics than on cultural issues. Seniority has moved him toward top posts on both the Science and the Transportation and Infrastructure committees, where he is chairman of the Aviation Subcommittee. In 2006, he pushed a bill to require contract talks between the Federal Aviation Administration and the air traffic controllers union, but it fell nine votes short of the two-thirds required to pass on the "suspension" calendar. He has opposed changes in fees for airlines in the air traffic control system. Concern over their local economic impact led him to oppose the Clean Air Act and NAFTA. He voted against authorizing to use force against Iraq in January 1991 and October 2002; his son was a paratrooper during the 1991 war. Attempting to revive his district's largely dormant high-sulfur coal mines, he authored several provisions for expanded clean-coal research and development that the House has included in energy legislation; he also got $18 million from the House Appropriations Committee for a projected FutureGen clean coal power plant, which is designed to burn coal without releasing pollutants. Despite setbacks, Costello has continued to urge a new Mississippi River bridge slightly north of the current congested bridge on Interstate 70, plus extensive highway relocation; the existing Poplar Street bridge serves three interstates in the St. Louis area.

Costello was opposed in 1998 by Bill Price, an orthopedic surgeon and son of Mel Price, who switched parties and ran as a Republican. Costello won by a solid 60%-40%. Since then, he has been reelected without significant opposition. In 2006, he easily defeated a four-time challenger in the primary; he was unopposed in November.

THIRTEENTH DISTRICT

Rep. Judy Biggert (R)

Elected 1998, 5th term; b. Aug. 15, 1937, Chicago; home, Hinsdale; Stanford U., B.A. 1959, Northwestern U., J.D. 1963; Episcopalian; married (Rody).

Elected Office: Hinsdale Bd. of Ed., 1982-85; IL House of Reps., 1992-98.

Professional Career: Clerk, U.S. Ct. of Appeals, 1963-64; Practicing atty., 1975-98.

DC Office: 1034 LHOB, 20515, 202-225-3515; Fax: 202-225-9420; Web site: judybiggert.house.gov.

District Offices: Willowbrook, 630-655-2052.

Committees: *Education & Labor* (7th of 22 R): Early Childhood, Elementary & Secondary Education; Higher Education, Lifelong Learning & Competitiveness. *Financial Services* (12th of 33 R): Housing & Community Opportunity; Financial Institutions & Consumer Credit (RMM). *Science & Technology* (8th of 20 R): Technology & Innovation; Energy & Environment.

Group Ratings

	ADA	ACLU	AFS	LCV	ITIC	NTU	COC	ACU	CFG	FRC
2006	30	41	0	33	100	59	93	64	54	0
2005	20	—	0	22	—	53	89	60	61	54

National Journal Ratings

	2005 LIB	—	2005 CONS		2006 LIB	—	2006 CONS
Economic	42%	—	57%		36%	—	63%
Social	52%	—	48%		52%	—	48%
Foreign	51%	—	48%		43%	—	55%

Key Votes of the 109th Congress

1. Estate Tax Repeal	Y	5. Limit Interstate Abortion	N	9. Build Border Fence	Y
2. Limit CAFE Standards	N	6. Extend Patriot Act	Y	10. CAFTA	Y
3. FY06 Spending Curb	Y	7. Bar Same Sex Marriage	N	11. Oppose Iraq Withdrawal	Y
4. Drilling in ANWR	Y	8. Stem Cell Research $	Y	12. Detainee Tribunals	Y

Election Results

2006 general	Judy Biggert (R)	119,720	(58%)	($1,014,819)
	Joseph Shannon (D)	85,507	(42%)	($225,842)
2006 primary	Judy Biggert (R)	52,900	(80%)	
	Bob Hart (R)	13,564	(20%)	
2004 general	Judy Biggert (R)	198,823	(65%)	($542,733)
	Gloria Schor Andersen (D)	106,525	(35%)	($42,129)

Prior Winning Percentages: 2002 (70%); 2000 (66%); 1998 (61%)

The People		Race/Ethnic Origin	Ancestry	
Area size:	362 sq. mi.	81.6% White	German: 16.5%	Irish: 13.1%
Urban population:	98.8%	4.9% Black	Polish: 10.0%	
Rural population:	1.2%	6.6% Asian	**2004 Presidential Vote**	
Pop. 2000:	653,647	0.1% Native Am.	Bush (R) 175,705	(55%)
Pop. 2005 (est):	759,047	0.0% Hawaiian	Kerry (D) 142,397	(45%)
Median income:	$71,686	1.2% Two+ races	**2000 Presidential Vote**	
Poverty status:	2.9%	0.1% Other	Bush (R) 148,621	(55%)
Military veterans:	9.9%	5.5% Hispanic Origin	Gore (D) 113,450	(42%)
			Other 7,166	(3%)
			Cook Partisan Voting Index: R + 5	

Occupation	Blue collar: 15.8%	White collar: 74.9%	Gray collar: 9.4%

Most residents of Chicagoland now live not in the city but in the suburbs, and increasingly not even in Cook County but in the Collar Counties all around. DuPage County, straight west of Chicago, had 103,000 residents in 1940; in 2006, there were 933,000, with new subdivisions still springing up at the western edges. There are not just bedroom communities. Since 1970 DuPage County has generated nearly half the new jobs in metro Chicago. Here in Oak Brook are the headquarters of Ace Hardware, Federal Signal, and, most famously, McDonald's and its Hamburger University, an 80-acre campus where more than 80,000 trainees have received Bachelor of Hamburgerology degrees since it was founded in 1961. Nearby are gracefully older railroad commuter towns like Hinsdale and Downers Grove, but also Naperville, once a country village, now an edge city, with a school district ranked number one in the world in science in an international exam and a top-rated public library. The Argonne National Laboratory, which conducts basic and applied research in disciplines that range from high-energy physics to biotechnology, has sparked numerous private research firms along the Sanitary and Ship Canal, the Des Plaines River and the Illinois and Michigan Canal, built way back in 1848.

The 13th Congressional District of Illinois includes the southern part of DuPage County (including Oak Brook, Downers Grove and Naperville), a small section of the southwest corner of Cook County and the northern slice of Will County (including Bolingbrook, Romeoville and Lockport). *Money* magazine rated Naperville number-two among the best places to live in the United States in 2006. Politically, this has been a heavily Republican area, suspicious of the motives and operations of Chicago Democrats, devoted to free enterprise and hostile to higher taxes. Republican margins shrunk in DuPage County as the Chicago suburbs have became more Democratic, but the 13th District has not been in danger of going Democratic.

The congresswoman from the 13th District is Judy Biggert, a Republican first elected in 1998. She grew up in Kenilworth on the affluent North Shore, graduated from New Trier Township High School, Stanford and Northwestern Law School and clerked for a federal appeals judge. She raised four children in Hinsdale, practicing estate and real estate law out of her home, served on the Hinsdale Township Board of Education, was chairman of the Visiting Nurses Association of Chicago—a "former car pool mom and assistant soccer coach," as her campaign put it. In 1992 she was elected to the state House, and was soon part of the leadership. Biggert started running for the U.S. House in 1997 when incumbent Republican Harris Fawell announced his retirement; he endorsed her. She said she supported abortion rights and opposed most gun control measures for constitutional reasons, though she had campaigned for gun control in 1992. She had primary opposition from state Representative Peter Roskam, now her 6th District colleague, who moved into the district to run. Biggert put in $402,000 of her own money and got support from Planned Parenthood and the Human Rights Campaign. She won the primary 45%-40% and the general election 61%-39%.

In the House, Biggert has a moderate voting record, especially on cultural issues. On the Education and the Workforce Committee, she was the prime sponsor of a bill to allow employees to take compensatory time rather than overtime, a measure she said would allow flexibility, especially for working mothers. The AFL-CIO lobbied heavily against it, and Republican leaders cancelled a roll call after it was apparent they didn't have the votes. A year later Biggert and other committee members sought to amend the transportation bill to remove Davis-Bacon and other labor provisions inconsistent with committee policy. After Hurricane Katrina, she strongly opposed the proposed school voucher program for evacuees, and advocated existing mechanisms to address education problems. Less controversially, she and Harold Ford passed a bill to allow church pension plans to pool their funds in collective trusts.

Biggert has been a strong supporter of the Argonne Lab. On the Science Committee, she sponsored a bill authorizing $180 million for university nuclear science and engineering programs, and later she inserted a 65% funding increase for the Office of Science into the energy bill. She sponsored a bill to fund the Energy Department with $165 million over three years to build a supercomputer with a sustained performance of 100 trillion teraflops (floating-point operations per second). It passed the House and became law in November 2004. Biggert has also sponsored bills to make sure homeless children get schooling, to help children with eating disorders and to finance school construction. She has paid heed to local issues, getting Lake Michigan water for Downers Grove when wells were contaminated there and seeking funds for two electric fish barriers on the Chicago ship canal to keep the huge Asian carp from invading the Great Lakes.

Biggert's attempts to move into the Republican leadership have been less successful. In November 2000 she ran for secretary of the Republican Conference and lost to Barbara Cubin of Wyoming, 122-73. In July 2002, when Cubin was moving up to another position, she ran for one day for the same post, but withdrew when it became clear that John Doolittle of California had the votes. Placed on the House ethics committee by Speaker Dennis Hastert, who hails from a neighboring district, she was willing to investigate in 2005 Majority Leader Tom DeLay, but the committee could not agree to investigate. Biggert also served on the four-member panel that investigated former Representative Mark Foley and the House page program, which issued a report following the 2006 election detailing the failures of Republican leaders and their top aides, but did not call for sanctions.

Biggert has not been seriously challenged for reelection, even after she abandoned her pledge to serve only three terms in October 1999. In July 2004 Republican leaders asked if she wanted the vacant nomination to oppose Barack Obama for the U.S. Senate; she passed. In 2006, trial lawyer and political neophyte Joseph Shannon challenged her as a "career politician." But, for a Democrat, his prospects were limited by his opposition to abortion rights and embryonic stem-cell research. Biggert won 58%-42%, and carried all three counties.

FOURTEENTH DISTRICT

Rep. Dennis Hastert (R)

Elected 1986, 11th term; b. Jan. 2, 1942, Aurora; home, Yorkville; Wheaton Col., B.A. 1964, N. IL U., M.A. 1967; Protestant; married (Jean).

Elected Office: IL House of Reps., 1980-86.

Professional Career: H.S. teacher & coach, 1965-80.

DC Office: 2304 RHOB, 20515, 202-225-2976; Fax: 202-225-0697; Web site: www.house.gov/hastert.

District Offices: Batavia, 630-406-1114; Dixon, 815-288-0680; Geneseo, 309-944-3558.

Committees: *Energy & Commerce* (3d of 26 R): Energy & Air Quality (RMM); Telecommunications & the Internet; Commerce, Trade & Consumer Protection.

Group Ratings and Key Votes: *As Speaker, did not usually vote.*

Election Results

2006 general	Dennis Hastert (R)	117,870	(60%)	($5,206,105)
	Jonathan Laesch (D)	79,274	(40%)	($306,020)
2006 primary	Dennis Hastert (R)	unopposed		
2004 general	Dennis Hastert (R)	191,616	(69%)	($5,013,947)
	Ruben Zamora (D)	87,590	(31%)	($18,028)

Prior Winning Percentages: 2002 (74%); 2000 (74%); 1998 (70%); 1996 (64%); 1994 (76%); 1992 (67%); 1990 (67%); 1988 (74%); 1986 (52%)

The People		Race/Ethnic Origin	Ancestry	
Area size:	2,866 sq. mi.	74.0% White	German: 18.9%	Irish: 9.9%
Urban population:	86.2%	4.6% Black	English: 6.0%	
Rural population:	13.8%	1.8% Asian	**2004 Presidential Vote**	
Pop. 2000:	653,647	0.1% Native Am.	Bush (R) 158,428	(55%)
Pop. 2005 (est):	770,672	0.0% Hawaiian	Kerry (D) 125,269	(44%)
Median income:	$56,314	1.0% Two+ races	Other 1,828	(1%)
Poverty status:	7.0%	0.1% Other	**2000 Presidential Vote**	
Military veterans:	10.3%	18.5% Hispanic Origin	Bush (R) 129,745	(54%)
			Gore (D) 101,369	(42%)
			Other 7,428	(3%)
			Cook Partisan Voting Index: R + 5	
Occupation	Blue collar: 26.8%	White collar: 59.9%	Gray collar: 13.3%	

A few dozen miles beyond the Loop there is an invisible line marking two different Chicagos. One is the Chicago dominated by blacks and descendants of the vast immigrations of 1840-1924 and 1970-2000, a Chicago where certain loyalties are taken for granted: loyalty to ethnic group, to church (usually the Catholic Church, often with an ethnic prefix), and to party (almost always the

Democrats). This Chicago is a gritty city, where personal cheerfulness and courtesy lighten up days otherwise as cold and impersonal as the gray winter sky. The other Chicago is the beginning of the Great Plains, originally a white Anglo-Saxon Protestant Chicago, a place whose residents are products of the first great wave of immigration to America. The tone of this Chicago is lighter, its streets and highways cleaner and neater, its daily life generally free from evidence of unpleasantness and deprivation. Ronald Reagan grew up in Downstate Illinois within the orbit of this Chicago (though he did live in the city briefly), and its spirit helped to characterize his presidency. His migration to southern California, incidentally, is not atypical: You can see in the geometric grids and Republican voting patterns of Orange County or Phoenix almost exact replicas of the grids and patterns in Chicago's suburban Collar Counties, transported to the once-empty Southwest on the Atchison, Topeka & Santa Fe or out the old U.S. 66 from their beginnings in Chicago's Loop.

The 14th Congressional District of Illinois straddles this line between metropolitan Chicago and Downstate Illinois. It gets as close as 30 miles to Chicago's Loop, in western DuPage County, with two great Chicagoland landmarks—Cantigny, the estate of Colonel Robert McCormick, longtime publisher of the *Chicago Tribune*, and FermiLab, the world's fastest energy particle accelerator and employer of some 2,500 people—icons of political conservatism and high technology within two miles of each other. The 14th also contains the Fox River Valley and its industrial cities of Elgin and Aurora, now the third-largest city in Illinois and home to a sizable Hispanic population, plus antique St. Charles with its annual Scarecrow Festival; local debates rage over whether to tear down the dams on the Fox River.

To the south is Kendall County, the fastest-growing county in Illinois, where new subdivisions are growing up outside the old town of Yorkville; Kendall's surge helps make this the fastest-growing congressional district in Illinois. Farther west, amid what may be the world's richest cornfields, the 14th passes through DeKalb, long the world's leading manufacturer of barbed wire, and goes on to Lee County, including Reagan's boyhood home in Dixon. Since the 2001 redistricting, the 14th moves farther west, almost to the Mississippi River, to include farmlands in parts of Whiteside, Bureau and Henry Counties. This was traditionally some of the most heavily Republican territory in the country. Northern Illinois was settled when Chicago was just a frontier village by Yankees from Ohio, Indiana, Upstate New York and New England, and by Germans emigrating after the failed revolutions of 1848: people who formed the heart of the Republican Party from its founding in 1854 and who would form the core of the Grand Army of the Republic a few years later. Their descendants, in this extension of Chicagoland, remain mostly Republican today.

The congressman from the 14th District is Dennis Hastert, a Republican first elected in 1986, and from 1999 to 2007 the 51st Speaker of the House of Representatives. He comes from the Fox River Valley, outside the Chicago metro orbit when he was growing up, but now part of its booming outer edge. His great-grandfather emigrated from Luxembourg to Aurora, on the Fox River, in the 19th century, to work on the railroads. His father, originally an embalmer, opened a feed supply business in Oswego. Denny and his two younger brothers hoisted 100-pound bags and delivered milk in the early morning; his parents also had a restaurant where he worked as a fry cook. At high school in Oswego—then a rural town, now exploding with subdivisions—he wrestled and played football. He graduated from Wheaton College, a religious school in nearby DuPage County, and then he became a high school teacher at Yorkville High School, a few miles south of Oswego. There he taught history and coached wrestling for 16 years and met his wife, a physical education teacher. But his experience was not entirely local. In summers he traveled as a teacher for the YMCA or other groups to Japan, Colombia, Venezuela, Europe and the Soviet Union. And as a wrestling coach he excelled. His team won the state championship and he was named the national coach of the year in 1976; he tries to attend the NCAA wrestling tournament every year. He continues to live on a 127-acre farm near the Fox River, where he owns nine antique vehicles, including two fire engines and a pickup truck; he likes to carve duck decoys and fish nearby for walleye.

After a trip to Washington in 1978, when Democrats had a 2–1 majority in the House, Hastert got involved in politics, interning with state Senator John Grotberg. In 1980 he finished third in a primary race for two seats in the Illinois House; then the incumbent became fatally ill and Hastert was chosen to take his place on the November ballot and was elected. After the March 1986 primary, Grotberg, at that point a member of Congress, was fatally stricken with cancer and Hastert again was chosen by the party as a replacement. The election was unusually close, but Hastert won 52%-48%.

In his early years in the House, Hastert had a conservative voting record and made few waves. But he gained valuable experience. He got a seat on the Commerce committee and on the subcommittees handling health, energy and telecommunications issues. He built a relationship with

Minority Leader Robert Michel, from the 18th District of Illinois. He worked together with Tom DeLay of Texas for Illinois's Ed Madigan in the race for minority whip in March 1989; Madigan lost by just two votes to an upstart from Georgia named Newt Gingrich. In 1994 he was chief organizer for DeLay's campaign for whip, the one leadership post won by a non-Gingrichite after the big Republican gains that fall. Afterwards Hastert was named chief deputy whip and shared an office and staff with DeLay. If he had not stopped in the hall to answer a reporter's question, he would have been in the line of fire when a crazed killer stormed into DeLay's office in July 1998.

To his work Hastert brought the habits of a coach, listening long to colleagues' goals and complaints, sizing up their character and capacity, then insisting firmly on a course of action when he reached a judgment. He operated with minimal ego and a bear-like friendliness, putting his arm around a colleague when asking advice or seeking intelligence; increasingly he was looked to by other leaders to help Republicans reach consensus and to negotiate difficult issues with Democrats, particularly health care. Over the years, Hastert has continued his trips abroad, including to Japan, and has been supportive of free trade; central Illinois, where the largest company is Caterpillar, produces more exports than just about anywhere else in the country.

Then suddenly one day in December 1998 he was chosen Speaker of the House. Speaker Newt Gingrich announced his retirement three days after the November election. Members scrambled for leadership positions, and Hastert was urged to run against Majority Leader Dick Armey. But Hastert had pledged to support him and, when he asked to be released from the pledge, Armey said no; so he kept his word and didn't run for a position he probably could have won. Then on December 19, just before the House voted on impeachment, Speaker-designate Bob Livingston announced his retirement too. Gingrich told Hastert, "You are the only one in this conference who could pull this body together. You are going to have to be the next speaker of the House." At 1 p.m. he announced; by the end of the day he had more than 100 votes, and the speakership.

He may have been "the accidental Speaker," but he ended up serving as Speaker longer than any other Republican and longer than all but three Democrats (Sam Rayburn, Tip O'Neill, John McCormack) and one Whig (Henry Clay). In many ways he resembles O'Neill, who likely would never have been Speaker but for the death of Hale Boggs in a plane crash in 1972. Like O'Neill, Hastert is tall and heavy, is from a modest background, speaks in a rough and tumble manner but has a sophisticated understanding of politics and a command of policy; and like O'Neill, he is a tough partisan and a man of his word. Unlike O'Neill, he never had large majorities. In his five terms as Speaker, O'Neill had an average of 267 Democrats—49 more than the 218 needed for a majority in the House. In his four terms Hastert had an average of 226 Republicans—8 more than 218. That's a smaller average than any other speaker since John Nance Garner, in his single term. Hastert never had more than 231 Republicans; in all time since the House reached its present size of 435 members until 1999, speakers have had fewer members of their own party only during seven Congresses (and the Speaker in two of those Congresses was Newt Gingrich). The job of the Speaker in a partisan age is to hold his party together and muster 218 votes on the floor; by that measure Hastert did a much better job than almost anyone expected when he was chosen.

Some of this was the legacy of decisions taken by Gingrich. After the Republicans' big victory in 1994, he personally installed committee chairmen and passed two institutional changes which tended to maintain the leadership's—and particularly the Speaker's—power over them. One was a rule limiting chairmen (of Appropriations subcommittees as well as full committees) to six years in that position; the other was selection of these chairmen by the Republican Steering Committee, on which the Speaker had five of up to 33 votes. That meant that when Hastert became Speaker, many chairmen were serving their last terms, and others were jockeying to succeed them. Hastert and Majority Whip Tom DeLay made it clear that they were expected to make substantial campaign contributions to endangered Republicans. Gingrich's second change was, even as he temporarily reined in appropriators on overall spending, to encourage them to distribute pet projects—pork—to incumbents facing hard reelection battles. At the same time, Gingrich did not prevent Transportation and Infrastructure Chairman Bud Shuster from passing generous highway and transportation bills with pet projects for every cooperating member of both parties. In this system that Hastert inherited, the glue holding the Republican Conference together was money. Appropriators' overall spending was restrained only by the limits set by the Clinton and then the Bush administrations.

It was a system that mostly worked—until it stopped working. In eight years as Speaker, the leadership brought to the floor hundreds of rules, terms and conditions under which legislature can be considered, and was only beaten on two. Only five times did the Democrats pass a motion to recommit a bill to committee. Maintaining control of the floor to this extent with such small majorities was a considerable achievement. During 1999 and 2000 Hastert also cooperated with the

Clinton administration on some foreign policy issues. In March 1999 he supported and even took the unusual step, for a Speaker, of voting on the floor for a resolution backing the military intervention in Kosovo—and had the embarrassment of seeing it nearly defeated by the opposition of Tom DeLay. After the election of George W. Bush, Hastert's position changed. In general he supported administration priorities and produced majorities for them. But he refused to deal with the White House staff on the transportation bill in 2003 and 2004, when House members wanted to spend much more than the administration, and he bluntly told Bush in early 2003 that a Medicare/prescription drug bill could not pass if it blocked seniors from fee-for-service health care. In 2001 and 2003 the House quickly passed versions of the Bush tax cuts and Medicare/prescription drug bill, and then waited to hammer out a conference committee report with a slower-acting Senate (it came only in 2003 on the latter). Hastert led the fight for trade promotion authority, which passed, with little Democratic help, by 215-214 in December 2001 and then again by 215-212 in July 2002. When the Enron and WorldCom accounting scandals hit the headlines, Hastert got Financial Services Chairman Michael Oxley to abandon his own bill, which had been passed by the House in April 2002, and accept Senator Paul Sarbanes's version, which had passed the Senate unanimously; it became law before the August recess.

Probably Hastert's chief—and most controversial—achievement was passage of the Medicare/prescription drug bill in November 2003. The Bush White House wanted to have all benefits provided entirely by private insurers, outside the Medicare structure; Hastert waved that off as a nonstarter. The Senate first passed a bill to the liking of Democrats like Edward Kennedy. House Ways and Means Chairman Bill Thomas drafted a different measure, with health savings accounts and nationwide competition between Medicare and private insurers. The conference committee worked for many days, with clashes between Thomas and Senate Finance Chairman Charles Grassley. Hastert stepped in at many points and finally pressed Thomas to drop the nationwide competition. Thomas walked out and said he was going to fly home to California; Hastert insisted he come back. Competition was limited to a few geographic areas, and the AARP promptly endorsed the bill. When it came to the floor, Hastert hoped that many Democrats would support it, but only a few did; with many conservatives opposed to the creation of a new entitlement, Hastert decided to hold the 15-minute roll call (a Republican innovation in 1995) open until he could switch enough votes. It was held open for nearly three hours—an unprecedented amount, and one much criticized by Democrats and by conservatives who opposed the bill. "Our job was to get people on board. It took some time," Hastert said. "It took 30 years for seniors to get their drug benefit. Three hours is not too long to wait." Many Democrats predicted that leaving the prescription drug benefit to competition between private insurers would prove unworkable and that the health savings accounts embedded in the bill would be of little import. But overwhelming majorities of seniors signed up for the benefit when it became effective in 2006 and expressed great satisfaction with it, while health savings accounts proliferated.

Grinding out continued majorities proved difficult. The House and Senate were unable to agree on a budget resolution in 2004 and 2006, though they did so in 2005. Tax cuts were extended in 2004 and 2005. In November 2004, adhering to his policy not to bring up bills that did not have the support of "a majority of the majority," Hastert refused to bring to the floor an intelligence reorganization measure without Judiciary Chairman James Sensenbrenner's requirement that states not issue driver's licenses to illegal aliens and provisions to make it easier to deport immigrants involved in terrorism and without a provision insisted on by Armed Services Chairman Duncan Hunter that preserved military control of military intelligence. He prodded the White House to resolve the differences and got Dick Cheney to come to the Capitol to mediate. In December Hunter agreed on a provision that stated that the military chain of command would not be altered by the new National Intelligence Director, and Sensenbrenner's provisions were put aside, with a promise that they could be attached to the first must-pass legislation of 2005. The bill passed 336-75. Confidence in Hastert among Republicans remained high. In January 2003 House Republicans repealed the eight-year limit on Speakers' terms and in December 2004 Bush urged him to remain in office until the end of his own second term. "I hope you're going to run again. We need you."

In 2005 and 2006 a couple of logjams were broken. The energy bill, long delayed, was finally passed in July 2005, without a provision allowing oil drilling in the Arctic National Wildlife Refuge. That same month, after years of dispute on the overall funding level between the White House and the Transportation and Infrastructure Committee, the highway bill was finally passed. But one provision—the $200 million-plus "bridge to nowhere" in Alaska, a priority of Chairman Don Young—attracted much adverse attention, from Republicans even more than Democrats. After Hurricane Katrina, critics like Senator Tom Coburn called for transferring the "bridge to nowhere" money to help hurricane evacuees and people in New Orleans and the Gulf Coast; that focused attention on pork barrel spending. The money Hastert had used to cement House Republicans together started becoming a political liability. Ethics problems became highlighted as well. In 1997 the two parties agreed not to use ethics complaints as a political weapon. The truce was broken in June 2004, when Texas Democrat Chris Bell, defeated in his primary after redistricting, filed a complaint against Tom DeLay for, among other things, allegedly offering to support Nick Smith's son in the race to succeed him if Smith voted for the Medicare prescription drug bill. Smith didn't vote for the bill, his son lost in the Republican primary and Smith's story changed during the investigation. The ethics committee did vote in late September 2004 to admonish DeLay—the lightest sanction possible—for conduct putting the House in a bad light. Democrats crowed, and many Republicans believed the offense was too loosely defined. Hastert moved to change the rule after the election, but backed down when many Republicans complained. He also moved to change the Republican Conference rule requiring a member to resign a leadership position if indicted; some DeLay aides had been indicted by the Travis County, Texas, district attorney, a liberal Democrat who had brought what turned out to be a baseless indictment against Senator Kay Bailey Hutchison in 1993; many Republicans feared he would do the same thing to DeLay. But in the face of bad publicity he had to back down on the rules change. But in January and February 2005 Hastert removed ethics committee Chairman Joel Hefley—it's normal for ethics chairmen to serve just two terms, he said—and the Steering Committee removed Veterans Committee Chairman Christopher Smith, who was seen as unresponsive to the leadership and supportive of too much spending. In contrast, Hastert decreed that the usual six-year term limit on chairmanships did not apply to Rules Committee Chairman David Dreier. The ouster of Hefley and the installation of Washington's Doc Hastings, regarded as a leadership loyalist, led ranking Democrat Alan Mollohan to boycott the committee. Then DeLay was indicted in Texas on campaign finance charges; he resigned as Majority Leader and in June 2006 resigned from the House.

In what turned out to be his last term as Speaker, Hastert blocked action on two important issues. In early 2005, as George W. Bush pushed for action on Social Security and sought dialogue with Democrats, Hastert behind the scenes let it be known he was not eager to address the issue. Bush found only one House Democrat willing to consider the issue, backbencher Allen Boyd of Florida, and no reliable Democratic interlocutors in the Senate. In July Ways and Means Chairman Bill Thomas said he would present a plan to address retirement issues in September, but then after Hurricane Katrina came along in late August, other issues were swept aside and changes in Social Security forgotten. On immigration, the House did take action. In February 2005 it passed the Real-ID bill sought by Sensenbrenner setting requirements for more tamper-proof driver's licenses. And in December 2005 it passed Sensenbrenner's border security bill. The Senate, after an extended debate, passed a bill in May 2006 with border security, guest worker and legalization provisions, and Bush and Republicans like John McCain pressed the House to take action. Instead, Hastert asked members to hold hearings on the issue in their districts in the August recess. When they came back in September, it was clear that there was no "majority of the majority" for anything like the Senate measure, and the House passed another border security bill instead.

On September 29, 2006, on the last day in session prior to the election, ABC News reported that Florida Republican Mark Foley had sent sexually explicit electronic instant messages to former House pages. This was a thunderclap: Foley resigned from the House the same day and flew off to rehab, and Hastert had tough questions to answer. It turned out that Hastert aides had been told a number of times over the years that Foley had been unusually friendly to male pages and that they had been told that he had sent "overfriendly" emails to a former page; they did not see or request to see the emails. This information, as it turned out, was also in the hands of DCCC staffers. Hastert aides, the Clerk of the House and Republican John Shimkus, head of the three-member page board, had told Foley on a number of occasions to steer clear of the pages; but Shimkus had not notified the other two members of the page board, Democrat Dale Kildee and Republican Shelley Moore Capito. NRCC Chairman Tom Reynolds and John Boehner, who had been elected majority leader to replace DeLay, both said they had talked to Hastert about Foley's conduct; Hastert said he had no recollection of such conversations. On October 2, Hastert said that the "overfriendly" emails should have raised a "red flag;" four days later he apologized. The House ethics committee was ordered to conduct an investigation, although Foley by his resignation had removed himself from its jurisdiction. Amid calls from some conservatives, including the *Washington Times*, that Hastert should step down as Speaker, he said in a news conference in his district that he would stay on. Minority Leader Nancy Pelosi said any action should be postponed until the ethics committee reported, and no incumbent Democrat called on Hastert to resign, although at least 20 non-incumbent Democratic

House candidates did so. On October 12, Bush appeared at a Chicago fundraiser for Hastert and spoke in his behalf; Hastert, who had been campaigning across the nation most of the year, remained mostly at home in his district and took the unusual step of running ads on Chicago radio. The four-member ethics subcommittee worked long hours taking testimony, including Hastert's on October 24, and issued its report in December 2006. It found no evidence that House members and staffers had knowledge of the sexually explicit emails and ruled that no House rules had been broken, but said that a number of members and staffers had shown bad judgment; it tended to give credence to Reynolds's and Boehner's testimony that they had told Hastert about the "overfriendly" emails.

By this time, the question of Hastert's tenure as Speaker was moot. The Foley case took up most of the political oxygen for the first two or three weeks of October, and any chance the Republicans had of holding their House majority vanished. Pork barrel spending and overspending in general demoralized many Republican-inclined voters; the troubles of Tom DeLay and of two other Republican members—Randy "Duke" Cunningham, convicted of taking bribes, and Bob Ney, accused at that time of taking bribes and later convicted—gave the Democrats a basis for saying the House Republicans were corrupt. On election day Hastert was reelected by a 60%-40% margin over an underfunded Democrat; it was his lowest margin since he was first elected in 1986. Republicans ended up losing 30 seats and control of the House. "As a former wrestling coach, I know what it is like when your team takes second place in the state tournament," Hastert said. "It hurts. And so it is with politics." In Washington the Republican defeat was seen as a repudiation of Hastert and his leadership, and indeed the spending practices of the House Republicans contributed to their loss. But it is not unusual in history for a Speaker to lose his majority: of the 26 House Speakers since the Civil War up through 2006, 12 have lost their majorities, two of them (Sam Rayburn and Joseph Martin) twice. On the day after the election, Hastert announced that he wouldn't be a candidate for a leadership position. Energy and Commerce ranking Republican Joe Barton offered to relinquish that position for Hastert; he declined, but became ranking minority member on the Energy and Air Quality Subcommittee. The new (and past) full committee chairman, John Dingell, said he and Hastert had been friends and worked well together. Incoming Speaker Nancy Pelosi assigned him a large office on the ground floor of the Capitol.

Hastert remains the longest-serving Republican Speaker in history, and one with significant legislative and political accomplishments. Not least with respect to Illinois. He has worked closely with Mayor Richard M. Daley on any number of projects, notably including the expansion of O'Hare Airport (and extracted a promise that it would have expressway access on its western edge), and Daley obviously appreciated having a Chicago-area Speaker of the House; in 2001 he blessed a redistricting agreement that protected all incumbents except for one sacrificed Downstate Democrat. In his last term as Speaker Hastert got an E-85 tax credit in the energy bill, a Metra railroad extension to LaFox and Elburn and $250,000 for a Mental Health Court in Kane County. When he lost the Speakership, Democratic Governor Rod Blagojevich said, "It's clearly a loss for Illinois." Another longstanding Hastert project, promotion of the Prairie Parkway in Kane and Kendall Counties, led to some criticism in June 2006, when it was announced that Hastert had made a profit of more than $1.5 million on land bought in 2002 and 2004 in Kendall County, some 5.5 miles from a planned Prairie Parkway interchange. But Hastert had backed the project since he was a freshman in the Illinois House, and land values have been rising sharply in Kendall County, the second fastest-growing county in the United States in 2000-06.

In August 2007, Hastert confirmed what many had suspected since the midterm election—that he would not seek a 12th term. Announced Republicans included dairy company owner Jim Oberweis, who ran unsuccessfully for the Republican nominations for senator in 2002 and 2004 and for governor in 2006, state Senator Chris Lauzen and Geneva Mayor Kevin Burns. Democrats included wealthy physicist Bill Foster, attorney Jotham Stein and 2006 challenger John Laesch. This is a tough district for a Democratic candidate to win, but it is not entirely out of reach.

FIFTEENTH DISTRICT

Rep. Tim Johnson (R)

Elected 2000, 4th term; b. July 23, 1946, Champaign; home, Sidney; U. of IL, B.A. 1969, U. of IL, J.D. 1972; Assembly of God; divorced.

Elected Office: Urbana City Council, 1971-76; IL House of Reps., 1976-2000.

Professional Career: Practicing atty., Johnson, Frank, Frederick & Walsh.

DC Office: 1207 LHOB, 20515, 202-225-2371; Fax: 202-226-0791; Web site: www.house.gov/timjohnson.

District Offices: Bloomington, 309-663-7049; Champaign, 217-403-4690; Charleston, 217-348-6759; Mt. Carmel, 618-262-8719.

Committees: *Agriculture* (6th of 21 R): General Farm Commodities & Risk Management. *Transportation & Infrastructure* (15th of 34 R): Railroads, Pipelines & Hazardous Materials; Highways & Transit.

Group Ratings

	ADA	ACLU	AFS	LCV	ITIC	NTU	COC	ACU	CFG	FRC
2006	20	36	29	83	100	43	86	76	40	85
2005	40	—	50	72	—	40	70	52	34	92

National Journal Ratings

	2005 LIB	—	2005 CONS		2006 LIB	—	2006 CONS
Economic	52%	—	48%		49%	—	50%
Social	51%	—	48%		48%	—	51%
Foreign	49%	—	50%		38%	—	59%

Key Votes of the 109th Congress

1. Estate Tax Repeal	Y	5. Limit Interstate Abortion	Y	9. Build Border Fence		Y
2. Limit CAFE Standards	N	6. Extend Patriot Act	N	10. CAFTA		Y
3. FY06 Spending Curb	N	7. Bar Same Sex Marriage	Y	11. Oppose Iraq Withdrawal		Y
4. Drilling in ANWR	N	8. Stem Cell Research $	N	12. Detainee Tribunals		Y

Election Results

2006 general	Tim Johnson (R)	116,810	(58%)	($493,982)
	David Gill (D)	86,025	(42%)	($234,168)
2006 primary	Tim Johnson (R)	unopposed		
2004 general	Tim Johnson (R)	178,114	(61%)	($428,750)
	David Gill (D)	113,625	(39%)	($100,106)

Prior Winning Percentages: 2002 (65%); 2000 (53%)

The People		Race/Ethnic Origin	Ancestry		
Area size:	10,122 sq. mi.	88.5% White	German: 18.8%	Irish: 9.2%	
Urban population:	64.2%	5.7% Black	English: 8.4%		
Rural population:	35.8%	2.3% Asian	**2004 Presidential Vote**		
Pop. 2000:	653,647	0.2% Native Am.	Bush (R)	174,928	(59%)
Pop. 2005 (est):	667,336	0.0% Hawaiian	Kerry (D)	121,814	(41%)
Median income:	$38,583	1.0% Two+ races	Other	2,227	(1%)
Poverty status:	11.7%	0.1% Other	**2000 Presidential Vote**		
Military veterans:	12.4%	2.2% Hispanic Origin	Bush (R)	148,176	(54%)
			Gore (D)	116,436	(42%)
			Other	9,616	(4%)
			Cook Partisan Voting Index: R + 6		

Occupation	Blue collar: 26.3%	White collar: 57.7%	Gray collar: 16.0%

South from Chicago, the Illinois Central Railroad heads to the city of New Orleans on a railbed elevated a few feet above the rich black soil of the Illinois prairie, topsoil reaching down not just inches but feet. This land dazzled its first settlers, who were accustomed to land that had to be cleared of trees and stumps before it could be plowed; this treeless prairie could be cultivated almost immediately, and with bounteous results. Today this remains farming country, made up not of small family farms but of large commercial operations, typically of 1,000 acres or more. Cultivating this soil is a business, requiring informed decisions about crop selection, maximizing yields, proper pesticides, marketing decisions, watching farm export prospects and taking advantage of government programs. The prairie landscape of eastern Illinois is marked by only a few towns, the largest of which are the sites of universities (the University of Illinois in Champaign-Urbana and Illinois Wesleyan, and Illinois State in Bloomington-Normal). Politically, these prairie lands incline much more to the party of former House Speaker Joseph Cannon, a Republican from the manufacturing city of Danville east of Urbana, than to that of Vice President Adlai Stevenson, a Democrat from Bloomington, who served under *laissez-faire* Democrat Grover Cleveland and was the grandfather of the Adlai Stevenson nominated by Democrats for president in 1952 and 1956.

The 15th Congressional District of Illinois occupies much of this prairie, beginning 60 miles from Chicago, where the Illinois Central heads south into Iroquois County, and covering some 130 miles south to the old National Road and U.S. 40, traditionally the line between northern Republican and southern Democratic Downstate Illinois. The biggest city here is Champaign-Urbana and the district includes parts of Normal and next-door Bloomington. The twin cities of Normal and Bloomington are split mostly along U.S. 51. Downtown Normal and Illinois State University are in the 11th District, while southern Normal and eastern Bloomington are in the 15th. The district also features a narrow corridor of land extending more than 100 miles along the Wabash River border with Indiana as far south as the Ohio River, with an extension to the town of Eldorado. The university towns are somewhat liberal but the prairie counties have long been Republican, and this on balance is a Republican-oriented district. There are many farms here, with corn and soybeans as the chief crops.

The congressman from the 15th District is Tim Johnson, a Republican first elected in 2000. Johnson was born in Champaign, grew up in Urbana, and graduated from the University of Illinois and its law school. He was elected to the Urbana City Council while still in law school and served there four years before winning election to the state House in 1976. In the legislature, Johnson worked his way up to deputy majority leader. He is a trial lawyer and managed a small local farm operation until he sold it in April 2005. He is often mistaken for the Democratic senator from South Dakota of the same name, who suffered a stroke in December 2006.

Johnson ran for Congress after Republican Tom Ewing announced his retirement in October 1999. Ewing and Speaker Dennis Hastert had been close friends in Congress and previously in the state House, and Ewing was part of the team that backed him for speaker. But Hastert was unhappy that Ewing delayed his retirement announcement until his 29-year-old son Sam could move back to the district from Texas to launch his own candidacy. The Speaker endorsed state Representative Bill Brady, the scion of a prominent real estate family from Bloomington. Johnson had more political experience than either and was a ferocious campaigner. The primary results broke along regional lines. Brady won his base of McLean County, 62%-20% over Johnson. In Champaign, Johnson led Brady, 61%-28%. Johnson carried seven of the 11 counties; he won 44% of the vote, to 36% for Brady and 17% for Ewing. Against Illinois State University instructor Mike Kelleher in the general, the voting pattern was similar: Kelleher narrowly won his home of McLean County, while Johnson again took Champaign and nine of the 11 counties, winning 53%-47% overall.

In the House, Johnson compiled a moderate voting record, with maverick tendencies, a low profile and notable independence from Hastert, which helps to explain his modest committee assignments compared to other Illinois Republicans. He has taken issue with the Bush administration's environmental record and voted against opening the Alaska National Wildlife Refuge to oil drilling, winning him a reelection endorsement from the League of Conservation Voters. In November 2005, he was 1 of 14 House Republicans who voted against $50 billion in domestic spending cuts. On the Agriculture Committee, he advocated the expansion of bio-fuels and opposed reduction of Farm Service Agency offices.

Johnson makes a point of keeping in touch with the grass roots, making what he says are 200-250 calls to constituents most weeks (but not on Sundays or holidays). "That's 90% of the job," he said. He figures he has called more than 200,000 of his constituents. In May 2006, after the NCAA had taken steps to limit the ability of the University of Illinois to host tournaments as a reprimand for its "demeaning" Chief Illiniwek mascot, Johnson filed a bill to limit the NCAA's ability to sanction colleges because of their athletic team's name, symbol or mascot. At a field hearing in Champaign, Johnson told an NCAA official, "You do a good job of running basketball tournaments . . . but you don't do a good job of social engineering." Yet the mascot made his last appearance in February 2007.

Since redistricting Johnson has won easily against weak opposition. In October 2002 he announced that he had changed his mind and renounced the term-limit pledge he had made during his first campaign. In both 2004 and 2006, emergency-room physician David Gill ran as the Democratic nominee, promoting a universal health care system. Johnson won with 61% and 58% of the vote, respectively.

SIXTEENTH DISTRICT

Rep. Don Manzullo (R)

Elected 1992, 8th term; b. Mar. 24, 1944, Rockford; home, Egan; American U., B.A. 1967, Marquette U., J.D. 1970; Baptist; married (Freda).

Professional Career: Practicing atty., 1970-92; author.

DC Office: 2228 RHOB, 20515, 202-225-5676; Fax: 202-225-5284; Web site: www.house.gov/manzullo.

District Offices: Crystal Lake, 815-356-9800; Rockford, 815-394-1231.

Committees: *Financial Services* (10th of 33 R): Domestic and International Monetary Policy, Trade & Technology; Capital Markets, Insurance & Government Sponsored Enterprises. *Foreign Affairs* (6th of 23 R): Asia, the Pacific & the Global Environment (RMM); Terrorism, Nonproliferation & Trade.

Group Ratings

	ADA	ACLU	AFS	LCV	ITIC	NTU	COC	ACU	CFG	FRC
2006	10	23	0	0	100	66	100	91	67	100
2005	0	—	0	0	—	66	93	100	86	100

National Journal Ratings

	2005 LIB	—	2005 CONS		2006 LIB	—	2006 CONS
Economic	37%	—	62%		11%	—	89%
Social	37%	—	62%		32%	—	68%
Foreign	40%	—	58%		0%	—	94%

Key Votes of the 109th Congress

1. Estate Tax Repeal	Y	5. Limit Interstate Abortion	Y	9. Build Border Fence	Y
2. Limit CAFE Standards	Y	6. Extend Patriot Act	N	10. CAFTA	Y
3. FY06 Spending Curb	Y	7. Bar Same Sex Marriage	Y	11. Oppose Iraq Withdrawal	Y
4. Drilling in ANWR	Y	8. Stem Cell Research $	N	12. Detainee Tribunals	Y

Election Results

2006 general	Don Manzullo (R)	125,951	(64%)	($1,334,337)
	Richard Auman (D)	63,627	(32%)	($105,581)
	John Borling (WI)	8,523	(4%)	($89,832)
2006 primary	Don Manzullo (R)	unopposed		
2004 general	Don Manzullo (R)	204,350	(69%)	($1,078,353)
	John Kutsch (D)	91,452	(31%)	($2,911)

Prior Winning Percentages: 2002 (71%); 2000 (67%); 1998 (100%); 1996 (60%); 1994 (71%); 1992 (56%)

The People		Race/Ethnic Origin	Ancestry	
Area size:	4,158 sq. mi.	85.7% White	German: 21.8%	Irish: 10.0%
Urban population:	78.4%	5.3% Black	English: 6.7%	
Rural population:	21.6%	1.3% Asian	**2004 Presidential Vote**	
Pop. 2000:	653,647	0.2% Native Am.	Bush (R) 168,303	(55%)
Pop. 2005 (est):	710,658	0.0% Hawaiian	Kerry (D) 133,701	(44%)
Median income:	$48,960	1.0% Two+ races	Other 1,539	(1%)
Poverty status:	7.3%	0.1% Other	**2000 Presidential Vote**	
Military veterans:	12.8%	6.5% Hispanic Origin	Bush (R) 141,878	(54%)
			Gore (D) 113,020	(43%)
			Other 8,163	(3%)
			Cook Partisan Voting Index: R + 4	

Occupation   Blue collar: 29.7%   White collar: 57.2%   Gray collar: 13.0%

The far northwest corner of Illinois is one of the heartlands of the Republican Party. Here in the town square of Freeport, some 15,000 people came to hear Abraham Lincoln and Stephen Douglas in one of their seven debates in 1858, the one on the terrain most partial to Lincoln. Settled by New England Yankees, northern Illinois was one of the strongest Republican constituencies in 1860 and for years after. Not far away, on a little river once navigable by Mississippi River steamboats, is Galena, one of the earliest settlements in northern Illinois, the home of Ulysses S. Grant before he became general and then president. Once larger than Chicago, Galena is now a tourist attraction. The largest city here is Rockford, on the Rock River, settled by Swedes as well as Yankees, one of America's leading furniture manufacturers at one time, then a major center for machine tools, today the nation's leading manufacturer of fasteners, with a big Chrysler plant a few miles east in Belvidere. Rockford, 90 miles from the Loop, has been promoting its airport as an alternative to O'Hare, though for a time it was served only by Hooters Air and TransMeridian.

Politically, northern Illinois, perhaps repelled by Democratic Chicago, remained steadfastly Republican for many years; it backed Herbert Hoover in 1932, Barry Goldwater in 1964 and George H.W. Bush in 1992 when most of America and Illinois were going the other way. But in recent years the trend here has been the other way. In 2004 George W. Bush ran ahead of his father's 1988 percentages in almost every Illinois county south of Champaign. But he ran far behind in metro Chicago and behind in every one of the state's three northern tiers of counties, carrying all but two of them but not by margins large enough to carry the state.

The 16th Congressional District of Illinois consists of much of the northwest part of the state. It includes the hilly, almost mountainous country around Galena and the Mississippi River, and the flatter plains in the farming counties to the east and south. Rockford remains the biggest city, but the fastest-growing part of the district is in the east, where it contains part of McHenry County and all of Boone and Winnebago Counties, three of the fastest-growing counties in Illinois in recent years.

The congressman from the 16th District is Donald Manzullo, a Republican first elected in 1992. He grew up in Rockford, where his father ran a grocery store, and his father and brother owned Manzullo's Famous Italian Restaurant from 1953 until it closed in December 2004. While in college in Washington in the mid-1960s Manzullo worked for Republican candidates and he started practicing law in Illinois in 1970. He lives on a cattle-breeding farm, writes poetry and books on constitutional law, and ran a radio talk show; he and his wife home-schooled their three children until high school and started the Northern Illinois Crisis Pregnancy Center. Manzullo ran for Congress in 1990 and lost the primary 54%-46% to a moderate, who after revelations of personal problems then lost the general to Democrat John Cox. Cox favored increased taxes, opposed capital punishment and was hurt when heavily Republican McHenry County was added in redistricting. Manzullo ran again and, with support from conservative Christians, beat a moderate 56%-44% in the primary. In the general election, Cox campaigned for higher taxes; Manzullo for a 10% across-the-board income tax cut. Manzullo won with 56% of the vote.

Manzullo has a generally conservative voting record, though he voted against reauthorizing the Patriot Act. He passed an amendment to the Clean Air Act in 1995 which had the effect on ending mandatory car pooling in McHenry County, a law in 1998 requiring federally funded family planning clinics to report evidence of child abuse and molestation and a law in 2002 eliminating the requirement that colleges and universities determine whether parents paid tuition for Hope scholarship students. He has said that his proudest legislative achievement was helping to pass the 2001 law ordering the VA to recognize Gulf war syndrome.

In 2001 Manzullo became the chairman of the Small Business Committee. He used the committee to hold hearings on all manner of issues, in Washington and around the country. He journeyed to West Yellowstone, Montana, in January 2002, to hold a hearing in which he encouraged allowing snowmobiles in Yellowstone National Park; several Rockford-area factories produce snowmobile parts. Manzullo came to Congress as a market conservative and a strong supporter of free trade, and he supported NAFTA, GATT, the WTO and normal trade relations with China. He criticized the Bush administration's imposition of steel tariffs in March 2002 and cited Rockford manufacturers' increased costs; he worked to exclude products like tool-grade steel from the tariffs. But he has been dismayed by local job losses in manufacturing—some 13,000 in the Rockford area since 2000—which he attributes to Chinese competition. In November 2004 he said the Bush administration should do more to shore up the defense industrial base. He has worked to encourage a revival of manufacturing in America, and has listed 17 priorities, including tax cuts for businesses that create jobs in the United States, an end to Chinese currency manipulation and enforcement of Buy American laws.

Manzullo was exercised when funding for the Small Business Administration's 7(a) program lapsed in January 2004; the SBA had previously guaranteed lenders 75% if the borrower defaulted on loans up to $750,000. Stories appeared about hapless entrepreneurs in Chicago and Rockford newspapers, and Manzullo demanded reinstatement of the program. But the Bush administration insisted on abolishing the SBA subsidy and funding the program with higher fees to borrowers and lenders. In June 2004 Manzullo got the House, 281-137, to add $79 million to the SBA budget but the funds would not go straight to 7(a). The SBA reauthorization foundered on this issue, but in November 2004 Manzullo and Senate Chairman Olympia Snowe got the administration to agree on increased fees, with increases in the amounts of loans; Manzullo was agreeable since 7(a) lending remained strong after the authorization expired on October 1. In 2005, when the SBA was criticized for not processing loans to Katrina victims rapidly enough, Manzullo defended the agency, noting that it had processed the same level of claims in almost the same time frame as it had after the Northridge earthquake in 1994. In 2006 he sponsored bills to allow small business owners to deduct health care costs from their FICA and Medicare taxes and to create national Association Health Plans. He worked on reauthorization of the SBA in 2006 and supported an amendment which would let franchises of large corporations qualify as small businesses. Manzullo reached the end of the Republicans' six-year term limit on chairmen in January 2007 and is no longer on the committee.

Manzullo has worked on local projects, often in cooperation with Senators Dick Durbin and Barack Obama. He helped obtain $12 million for Rockford's EIGER*lab*, a city-state-university center for the study of advanced manufacturing technologies like micromachining, with startup assistance available, which opened in May 2004 in an old Ingersoll Machine Tool building in Rockford. In the 2005 transportation bill, he got $51.6 million for district projects. With Durbin he has secured $7 million for design and $34 million for construction of a new federal courthouse in Rockford.

In June 2004, after Republican Senate nominee Jack Ryan left the race, Manzullo was among those who urged that Republicans nominate former presidential candidate (and Maryland resident) Alan Keyes. Keyes was nominated, and turned out to be a disastrous candidate who was repudiated by many Republican pols. In October Manzullo said he still supported him but admitted, "I don't like the way he says some things." Manzullo was reelected 69%-31% in 2004 and 64%-32% in 2006.

SEVENTEENTH DISTRICT

Rep. Phil Hare (D)

Elected 2006, 1st term; b. Feb. 21, 1949, Galesburg; home, Rock Island; Attended Black Hawk Community College, 1967-69; Catholic; married (Becky).

Military Career: Army Reserves, 1969-75.

Professional Career: Factory worker, Seaford Clothing Factory, 1969-82, Dist. Dir., U.S. Rep. Lane Evans, 1982-2006.

DC Office: 1118 LHOB, 20515, 202-225-5905; Fax: 202-225-5396; Web site: hare.house.gov.

District Offices: Carlinville, 217-854-2290; Decatur, 217-422-9150; Galesburg, 309-342-4411; Moline, 309-793-5760.

Committees: *Education & Labor* (24th of 27 D): Workforce Protections; Health, Employment, Labor & Pensions; Early Childhood, Elementary & Secondary Education. *Veterans' Affairs* (8th of 16 D): Disability Assistance & Memorial Affairs; Health.

Group Ratings and Key Votes: Newly Elected

Election Results

2006 general	Phil Hare (D)	115,025	(57%)	($808,792)
	Andrea Lane Zinga (R)	86,161	(43%)	($405,650)
2006 primary	Lane Evans (D)	unopposed		
2004 general	Lane Evans (D)	172,320	(61%)	($752,444)
	Andrea Lane Zinga (R)	111,680	(39%)	($270,256)

The People		Race/Ethnic Origin	Ancestry	
Area size:	8,289 sq. mi.	87.3% White	German: 18.2%	Irish: 9.0%
Urban population:	71.1%	7.2% Black	English: 7.7%	
Rural population:	28.9%	0.6% Asian	**2004 Presidential Vote**	
Pop. 2000:	653,647	0.2% Native Am.	Kerry (D) 148,562	(51%)
Pop. 2005 (est):	634,013	0.0% Hawaiian	Bush (R) 139,251	(48%)
Median income:	$35,066	1.0% Two+ races	Others 1,333	(0%)
Poverty status:	12.5%	0.1% Other	**2000 Presidential Vote**	
Military veterans:	14.4%	3.7% Hispanic Origin	Gore (D) 146,548	(54%)
			Bush (R) 119,563	(44%)
			Other 7,807	(3%)
			Cook Partisan Voting Index: D + 5	
Occupation	Blue collar: 29.9%	White collar: 51.7%	Gray collar: 18.4%	

Illinois's western prairies are some of America's richest agricultural land. They were first settled by Yankees coming overland from northern Indiana and Ohio and Upstate New York. After 1848, Germans left their homeland in search of better opportunities and settled this land that in so many ways resembles the flat, orderly plains of northern Germany. All these migrants farmed quarter-sections and built small towns, with banks and stores, community churches and libraries. As farming expanded, so did the need for agricultural equipment. Entrepreneurs and investors built farm machinery factories, and the Quad Cities of the Mississippi—Davenport and Bettendorf, Iowa, and Rock Island and Moline, Illinois—became one of the nation's biggest agricultural equipment manufacturing centers. These plants were unionized in the 1930s and 1940s, and in post-World War II America their wages went up as the demand for ever more sophisticated machines rose among the Midwest's government-subsidized farmers. But eventually the cost of subsidies rose too high and the market had its revenge. In the early 1980s farm profits vanished, land values declined and orders for new machinery and equipment dried up. The result was a depression in western Illinois and neighboring Iowa, and a political swing toward the Democrats and away from the Republicans who had been the ancestral party in most of this area. The Democratic tide has receded a bit, but this was still one of the few parts of rural America carried by Al Gore and John Kerry. Recent job losses and wildly oscillating farm prices have helped Democrats maintain majorities here.

The 17th Congressional District of Illinois includes the state's portion of the Quad Cities plus several rural counties to the south: All of the Mississippi River border with Iowa and south almost to

St. Louis. From there, the geography gets more imaginative. A thin strip of land along the Mississippi River and the lower Illinois River connects the district to an extension that includes rural Macoupin County and some parts east of there. Then another thin reed sprouts north from Macoupin to include central Springfield (but not the state Capitol building) and then reaches some 40 miles further east to take in a portion of Decatur. Decatur is home to politically influential Archer Daniels Midland, the largest agricultural processor in the world and a key promoter of ethanol. It would be fairly easy to drive directly from any part of the 17th District to another, but only if you crossed over into the 18th or 19th Districts. To drive from one end of the 17th to the other while remaining entirely inside the district would take many more miles and many, many more hours than to drive from Chicago to the southern tip of Illinois in Cairo. There is, of course, a good political explanation for this weird configuration. By removing the Republican counties east and north of the Quad Cities during redistricting, the 17th was made more safely Democratic and neighboring districts were reinforced for Republicans. Macoupin County is historically Democratic; central Springfield and Decatur are solidly Democratic. The old 17th district gave George W. Bush a 6% margin in 2000; the new gerrymandered 17th gave Al Gore a 10% margin.

The new congressman from the 17th District is Phil Hare, a Democrat elected to succeed his long-time boss Lane Evans. Hare was born in Galesburg and is the son of a machinist. He attended Black Hawk Community College in Moline and was a union leader at the Seaford Clothing Factory in Rock Island, where he was a lining cutter for 13 years. He worked on the presidential campaigns of Fred Harris and Ted Kennedy. For 23 years, he was an aide to Evans, chiefly as his district director.

Evans had served in Congress since 1982, became the ranking minority member on the Veterans Affairs Committee, and was a leading prairie populist before suffering the debilitating effects of a long-running battle with Parkinson's disease. He was diagnosed in 1995 but did not make his condition public until 1998; for several years, little was heard of his illness. But in 2004 his Republican opponent, onetime Quad Cities TV anchor Andrea Zinga, raised it loudly. By this time Evans had trouble getting up from a chair and pouring a soft drink, and he had speech therapy once a week to prevent "lazy tongue," though he said he still went out running some mornings and regularly traveled throughout the district. Zinga said he was not physically fit to serve. "People who are on the medications he is on may have trouble with judgment, which can be worsened by excitement or stress." Evans assured friendly audiences, "I may be slow, but I know which way to go." In November 2004, he was reelected 61%-39%, carrying every county except heavily Republican Adams. But one week after winning the March 2006 Democratic primary, Evans announced that he would not run for a 13th term, citing his long-running battle with Parkinson's.

After Evans announced his retirement, Hare quickly received his endorsement as well as the backing of organized labor and the Rock Island Democratic Party establishment. Hare said that his top priorities were fixing the health care system, fighting for working families, and expanding renewable fuels. On social issues, he expressed his support for abortion rights but said he favored parental notification for minors who seek abortions. He opposed a constitutional amendment to ban same-sex marriage. State Senator John Sullivan, state Representative Mike Boland and Rock Island Mayor Mark Schweibert were his chief Democratic opponents. Under Illinois law, precinct committeemen from the 17th District were authorized to choose the party's replacement nominee in a weighted selection process; party leaders jousted over who was an eligible voter and how the votes should be weighted. Voting was by mail, and the results were counted on June 6. Hare spoke personally with nearly 350 of the roughly 400 eligible voters. He won 64% of the weighted vote, to 28% for Sullivan and 5% for Schweibert. Boland criticized the "insiders game" and pressure from party and union leaders to support Hare.

Zinga ran again in the general, but her campaign never really threatened Hare. She struggled to raise money, and the national GOP took no interest in the race. After a controversial September 11 speech in which she supported racial profiling at airports, her campaign backpedaled, explaining that she had meant that airport screeners shouldn't face anti-discrimination lawsuits for focusing on travelers from certain ethnic groups. In another blow to her campaign, the Illinois Farm Bureau chose not to endorse either candidate, despite having endorsed Zinga in 2004. Hare won 57%-43%. Zinga carried Adams County and three adjoining rural counties, all located well to the south of Rock Island. Evans spoke softly at Hare's victory celebration and "looked fragile, but he walked briskly to the podium with some assistance," the *Quad-City Times* reported.

EIGHTEENTH DISTRICT

Rep. Ray LaHood (R)

Elected 1994, 7th term; b. Dec. 6, 1945, Peoria; home, Peoria; Canton Jr. Col., 1963-65, Bradley U., B.S. 1971; Catholic; married (Kathy).

Elected Office: IL House of Reps., 1982.

Professional Career: Jr. High Schl. Teacher, 1971-77; Dir., Rock Island Youth Svcs., 1972-74; Chief Planner, Bi–state Planning Comm., 1974-76; Dist. A.A., U.S. Rep. Tom Railsback, 1977-82; Dist. A.A., U.S. Rep. Bob Michel, 1983-90, Chief of Staff, 1990-94.

DC Office: 1424 LHOB, 20515, 202-225-6201; Fax: 202-225-9249; Web site: www.house.gov/lahood.

District Offices: Jacksonville, 217-245-1431; Peoria, 309-671-7027; Springfield, 217-793-0808.

Committees: *Appropriations* (20th of 29 R): Legislative Branch; Agriculture, Rural Development, FDA & Related Agencies.

Group Ratings

	ADA	ACLU	AFS	LCV	ITIC	NTU	COC	ACU	CFG	FRC
2006	5	19	14	25	100	49	87	80	39	85
2005	5	—	0	22	—	49	92	65	47	85

National Journal Ratings

	2005 LIB	—	2005 CONS		2006 LIB	—	2006 CONS
Economic	46%	—	54%		38%	—	61%
Social	44%	—	55%		35%	—	63%
Foreign	48%	—	52%		47%	—	51%

Key Votes of the 109th Congress

1. Estate Tax Repeal	Y	5. Limit Interstate Abortion	Y	9. Build Border Fence	Y
2. Limit CAFE Standards	N	6. Extend Patriot Act	N	10. CAFTA	Y
3. FY06 Spending Curb	Y	7. Bar Same Sex Marriage	Y	11. Oppose Iraq Withdrawal	Y
4. Drilling in ANWR	Y	8. Stem Cell Research $	N	12. Detainee Tribunals	Y

Election Results

2006 general	Ray LaHood (R)	150,194	(67%)	($1,262,225)
	Steve Waterworth (D)	73,052	(33%)	
2006 primary	Ray LaHood (R)	unopposed		
2004 general	Ray LaHood (R)	216,047	(70%)	($955,764)
	Steve Waterworth (D)	91,548	(30%)	($4,519)

Prior Winning Percentages: 2002 (100%); 2000 (67%); 1998 (100%); 1996 (59%); 1994 (60%)

The People		Race/Ethnic Origin	Ancestry	
Area size:	8,302 sq. mi.	90.0% White	German: 21.2%	Irish: 9.7%
Urban population:	68.0%	6.4% Black	English: 8.8%	
Rural population:	32.0%	0.9% Asian	**2004 Presidential Vote**	
Pop. 2000:	653,647	0.2% Native Am.	Bush (R) 181,058	(58%)
Pop. 2005 (est):	660,990	0.0% Hawaiian	Kerry (D) 130,669	(42%)
Median income:	$41,934	0.9% Two+ races	Other 1,954	(1%)
Poverty status:	8.9%	0.1% Other	**2000 Presidential Vote**	
Military veterans:	14.2%	1.5% Hispanic Origin	Bush (R) 159,475	(54%)
			Gore (D) 128,411	(43%)
			Other 7,464	(3%)
			Cook Partisan Voting Index: R + 5	

Occupation	Blue collar: 24.7%	White collar: 59.1%	Gray collar: 16.2%

Old vaudeville bookers, presented with a new act, used to ask, "Will it play in Peoria?" The implication was that if an act went over in this small city on the bluffs above the Illinois River, 154 miles from Chicago and 171 miles from St. Louis, it would go over just about anywhere. In the first half of the 20th century, Peoria did seem pretty typical of America. If its citizens were mostly of British or German descent, with a small percentage of blacks, that was the image of ordinary

America that prevailed through the 1960s, despite the great immigrations of 1880-1924 and the northward urban migrations of southern rural blacks of 1940-1965. But Peoria's economy today has changed, much as America's has changed. This is still a heavy manufacturing town, dominated by big plants that produce farm machinery and earth-moving equipment. Its biggest employer is Caterpillar, the world's leading producer of earth-moving and construction equipment, and one of America's major exporters. There are more than just memories here of the sharp divide between blue collar and white collar, union and management, Democrat and Republican—the basis of the class warfare politics that was the norm in heavy industrial metropolises of the Great Lakes region starting with the sit-down strikes of the late 1930s. But the blue-collar workers now are not as numerous and the unions not as strong. The Peoria area went through terrible times in the 1980s, as big farm machinery plants laid off workers and even closed down. Then Caterpillar, struck by the United Auto Workers in 1992, hired replacement workers and continued to operate—not without some friction and inefficiency, but profitably—something unheard of a decade or more earlier. Not until 1998 did union members approve a settlement, pretty much on the company's terms. There was no population growth here in the 1990s, and Peoria slipped from 3d to 7th among the largest cities in Illinois.

The 18th Congressional District of Illinois, variously configured, has been the Peoria district since the 1940s. It has been represented by two national Republican leaders: from 1933-49 by Everett McKinley Dirksen, who was elected senator in 1950 and was Senate Republican leader from 1959-69, and Robert Michel, congressman from 1957-95 and House Republican leader from 1981-95. The 18th's boundaries currently extend through rich farm land south along the Illinois River and east to include half of Springfield (including the state Capitol) and west within a few miles of Iowa, away from historically Republican Peoria toward the historically marginal counties of central Illinois. It is the home of Eureka College, which dedicated the Ronald Reagan Peace Garden in honor of its 1932 graduate and the end of the Cold War that he helped to achieve.

The congressman from the 18th District is Ray LaHood, a Republican elected in 1994. LaHood grew up in Peoria, the grandson of an immigrant from Lebanon and son of a restaurant manager. He worked his way through school, spent six years teaching in Catholic schools, then moved to Rock Island, where he worked with delinquent teens and became a staffer for Congressman Tom Railsback. He served in the Illinois House in 1982, then worked for Congressman Michel in Peoria and, from 1990-94, was his chief of staff in Washington. When Newt Gingrich pointedly declined to rule out running against Michel for Republican leader after the 1994 election, Michel decided to retire. LaHood ran to replace his boss, and in the Republican primary beat state Representative Judy Koehler, 50%-40%. LaHood's Democratic opponent was Douglas Stephens, a labor lawyer and small businessman, who held Michel to 52% in 1982. In a Republican year, LaHood carried all but one county and won 60%-39%.

LaHood's voting record has made him a centrist in the House, both in substance and style. He's an institutional maverick: He has a keen appreciation and respect for the House, and insists on asserting his prerogatives. An odd man out under Speaker Gingrich, LaHood became more visible during and after Gingrich's final days as Speaker. He was one of only three Republicans who did not sign the Contract with America; he had reservations about voting for tax cuts until the budget was balanced. He filled a niche by frequently presiding over the House. With his experience in monitoring the floor for Michel, LaHood's evenhanded rulings, his surefooted mastery of parliamentary procedure and his determination to maintain decorum were widely appreciated. Most famously, he presided over the impeachment of Bill Clinton.

When Dennis Hastert replaced Gingrich as Speaker, LaHood suddenly was well placed with House leaders and he got seats on the Appropriations and Intelligence committees. But he continued to go his own way. As a self-styled deficit hawk, he supported a freeze in federal spending. He seized on the disputed 2000 count in Florida as an opportunity to advance his cause of abolishing the Electoral College and replacing it with a national popular vote count. But the moment passed without action. He was the only House member to speak out against the creation of the commission to investigate the causes of the September 11 attacks. When the House debated the commission's proposed reforms of intelligence operations, LaHood opposed them for "creating another bureaucracy." He has been active in internal House politics. In 2002, he considered running for majority whip, but he backed off when it became clear that Roy Blunt had locked up the votes; in January 2006, he was an early backer of John Boehner over Blunt for majority leader. After he lost a bid for the Intelligence Committee chairmanship, LaHood said that he would not agree to Hastert's requirement that he give up his Appropriations seat. After the base-review commission in 2005 decided to move 15 F-16 jets from the Air National Guard unit in Springfield, LaHood filed a House resolution to reject its entire list; the House overwhelmingly defeated his proposal. In June 2006, he was among seven Republicans on the House Appropriations Committee who supported a Democratic amendment to raise the minimum wage to $7.25 an hour. As a result, GOP leaders kept the bill off the House floor. Following revelations of improper conduct by Representative Mark Foley with House pages, LaHood called for suspending what he called the "antiquated" page program so that it could be reevaluated.

LaHood has been re-elected by wide margins throughout his district, and he has been outspoken about problems among Illinois Republicans. When Senator Peter Fitzgerald attacked Hastert for not imposing federal bidding requirements on the Abraham Lincoln Library project, LaHood told the *Chicago Sun-Times*, "I'm thinking about trying to make sure that Peter has an opponent" in the Republican primary. "I think we can do better than him." Fitzgerald retired. When court records opened by court order revealed that 2004 Senate nominee Jack Ryan took his former wife to sex clubs, LaHood said that he should leave the race; Ryan did. In early 2005, LaHood toured the state to explore a run for governor, but he decided in August that former Governor Jim Edgar, who was considering the race then but later decided not to run, would be a better candidate.

LaHood won in November 2006 with 67% of the vote and appeared to have a lock on the seat, but in June 2007 he announced he had suspended his political fundraising and was considering applying for the presidency of Bradley University, his alma mater. In July, LaHood said he had decided not to apply for the job, and later that month announced he would not seek reelection in 2008. Among the Republicans talking about running were state Representative Aaron Schock, who at 26 is the youngest member of the state legislature, former Peoria City Council member John Morris and Peoria businessman Jim McConoughey. Among the Democrats mentioned were former state Representative Bill Edley, former Indiana Pacers basketball head coach Dick Versace, and civil rights attorney Patricia Benassi.

NINETEENTH DISTRICT

Rep. John Shimkus (R)

Elected 1996, 6th term; b. Feb. 21, 1958, Collinsville; home, Collinsville; West Point Military Acad., B.S. 1980, Christ Col., Teaching Cert., 1990, S. IL U., M.B.A. 1997; Lutheran; married (Karen).

Military Career: Army 1980-85; Army Reserves, 1985-present.

Elected Office: Collinsville Township Trustee, 1989-93; Madison Cnty. Tres., 1990-96.

Professional Career: High schl. teacher, 1986-90.

DC Office: 2452 RHOB, 20515, 202-225-5271; Fax: 202-225-5880; Web site: www.house.gov/shimkus.

District Offices: Centralia, 618-532-9676; Collinsville, 618-344-3065; Harrisburg, 618-252-8271; Olney, 618-392-7737; Springfield, 217-492-5090.

Committees: *Energy & Commerce* (9th of 26 R): Environment & Hazardous Materials (RMM); Energy & Air Quality; Telecommunications & the Internet.

Group Ratings

	ADA	ACLU	AFS	LCV	ITIC	NTU	COC	ACU	CFG	FRC
2006	0	14	0	0	100	60	93	83	55	85
2005	10	—	0	0	—	60	89	92	70	83

National Journal Ratings

	2005 LIB	—	2005 CONS	2006 LIB	—	2006 CONS
Economic	30%	—	68%	9%	—	90%
Social	32%	—	68%	11%	—	85%
Foreign	42%	—	55%	17%	—	73%

Key Votes of the 109th Congress

1. Estate Tax Repeal	Y	5. Limit Interstate Abortion	Y	9. Build Border Fence	Y
2. Limit CAFE Standards	Y	6. Extend Patriot Act	Y	10. CAFTA	Y
3. FY06 Spending Curb	Y	7. Bar Same Sex Marriage	Y	11. Oppose Iraq Withdrawal	Y
4. Drilling in ANWR	Y	8. Stem Cell Research $	N	12. Detainee Tribunals	Y

Election Results

2006 general	John Shimkus (R)	143,491	(61%)	($826,242)
	Danny Stover (D)	92,861	(39%)	($166,732)
2006 primary	John Shimkus (R)	unopposed		
2004 general	John Shimkus (R)	213,451	(69%)	($544,784)
	Tim Bagwell (D)	94,303	(31%)	($38,229)

Prior Winning Percentages: 2002 (55%); 2000 (63%); 1998 (61%); 1996 (50%)

The People		Race/Ethnic Origin	Ancestry	
Area size:	11,646 sq. mi.	94.0% White	German: 21.6%	USA: 8.8%
Urban population:	52.2%	3.5% Black	Irish: 8.6%	
Rural population:	47.8%	0.5% Asian	**2004 Presidential Vote**	
Pop. 2000:	653,647	0.2% Native Am.	Bush (R) 192,678	(61%)
Pop. 2005 (est):	661,436	0.0% Hawaiian	Kerry (D) 123,172	(39%)
Median income:	$38,955	0.7% Two+ races	Other 1,287	(0%)
Poverty status:	9.1%	0.1% Other	**2000 Presidential Vote**	
Military veterans:	14.4%	1.1% Hispanic Origin	Bush (R) 164,541	(56%)
			Gore (D) 121,210	(41%)
			Other 7,621	(3%)
			Cook Partisan Voting Index: R + 8	

Occupation   Blue collar: 28.2%   White collar: 55.4%   Gray collar: 16.4%

Southern Illinois is a land of prairies, of flat, treeless land sloping imperceptibly down to the Ohio and Mississippi Rivers. It was settled almost entirely from the south by farmers coming overland from Kentucky, such as Abraham Lincoln's family. Just beyond the Ohio River, they found hilly terrain, some of which turned out to have coal deposits. To the north they must have been astonished, after miles of thick forest, to see the great American prairie stretch before them, a vast sea of empty land extending past the horizon. The prairie lands proved wondrously rich, and were soon crisscrossed by rail lines taking their produce away and bringing in industrial products from St. Louis, Chicago and points east. About the same time, vast coal deposits were found in southern Illinois, producing one mining town after another: This was the home turf of John L. Lewis, the imperious leader of the United Mine Workers for half a century and, in the late 1930s and early 1940s, one of the most powerful and eloquent figures in American public life.

The 19th Congressional District of Illinois, the largest in the state, extends more than 200 miles up, down and across. It covers all or part of 30 counties in the rich heartland of southern Illinois—most of the land area south of Springfield, from the Ohio River to the Mississippi.Much of it is south of the old National Road, which became U.S. 40 and is paralleled by Interstate 70, the traditional boundary between the part of Downstate settled by Southerners and that settled by Yankees. Effingham, which straddles that line, is where the flat prairie with corn and soybeans soon gives way to hills and valleys with orchards and woodlands. The boundaries of the 19th are jagged, but there is a rational political explanation for them. The biggest voting blocs are in Madison, Clinton and Washington Counties, part of the St. Louis metropolitan area, and the Sangamon County suburbs of Springfield, the state capital. The district includes the coal mining area around Mount Vernon, sparsely settled areas along the Ohio River and prairie counties along U.S. 40. Traditional Democrats have become harder to find here. George W. Bush won 61% here in 2004, his best performance in the state.

The congressman from the 19th District is John Shimkus, a Republican first elected in 1996. Shimkus grew up in Collinsville, in Madison County. His father was an installer for Illinois Bell, and his mother a township trustee; he is of Lithuanian descent, as is his predecessor in the House, Democratic Senator Richard Durbin. Shimkus graduated from West Point, trained in the Army as a ranger and paratrooper, studied in California, then came back to Collinsville to teach high school. Almost immediately he began running for local office. In 1988 he ran for the Madison County Board, and lost; in 1989 he was elected Collinsville Township trustee. In 1990, at 32, he beat a 12-year incumbent and was elected Madison County treasurer. He ran for the House against Durbin in 1992, and lost 57%-43%, a closer margin for Durbin than in his previous campaigns. In 1996, when Durbin ran for the Senate, Shimkus easily won the Republican primary with 51% against seven other candidates. In the general election he faced state Representative Jay Hoffman. Both were anti-abortion, anti-gun control, and pro-balanced budget amendment. Hoffman raised more money and had the benefit of AFL-CIO ads but Shimkus won by 50.3%-49.7%. The following August, after taking classes part-time for six years, he received an MBA from Southern Illinois University.

In the House, Shimkus's voting record has been a bit right of center. He got a seat on the Energy and Commerce Committee and used it to sponsor a locally important piece of legislation: his amendment that qualified the soybean-diesel fuel blend B-20 for the alternative fuels program. The Clinton administration opposed it, arguing that any standard diesel fuel engine would qualify. But Shimkus got it enacted. On the committee, he worked with Anna Eshoo to educate the public about "911" emergency response systems; the plan was enacted with the port security law in October 2006.

Shimkus has made several visits to Iraq and occasionally criticized the news media for not fully reporting the conditions there. By not reporting good news, he said the press was hurting the morale of the U.S. military. Shimkus remains a lieutenant colonel on active duty in the Army Reserves, and occasionally teaches at West Point. As a former high school teacher, he took what seemed to be a routine assignment as chairman of the House page board and imposed stricter review procedures for applicants. But five weeks before the 2006 election, the revelations of inappropriate instant messages and e-mails between Representative Mark Foley and past and current pages became a political bombshell for which Republicans—including Shimkus and Speaker Dennis Hastert, who gave him the position—had no satisfactory explanation. Shimkus, who had in 2005 confronted Foley with reports of e-mail traffic and alerted House officials to the problems, defended his own actions: "I don't know of a single thing I would have done differently." He called Foley a "slimeball" and emphasized "I love these kids." The House Ethics Committee found that Shimkus should have alerted other House members on the page board to the private reports and should have demanded copies of all of Foley's e-mails, but it called for no sanctions against him. After the election, Shimkus said he wished that he had done more to investigate allegations about Foley and he stepped down from the page board.

When the state's redistricting plan in 2001 eliminated the seat held by David Phelps, a conservative Democrat and former professional gospel singer from far south Illinois, he decided to run against Shimkus in the new 19th, of which Shimkus had been representing 63% of the voters and Phelps 34%. Chicago-based Democrats, interested in colleagues who could help them with Chicago priorities, did not care much about Phelps. The result was a spirited contest. The AFL-CIO spent more than $1.5 million attacking Shimkus; he was helped by campaign ads paid by the pharmaceutical industry. But the numbers were all for Shimkus. In the portions of the district he had represented he won 59%-41%, with a popular vote margin of 29,000. Phelps, in the portions he had represented, won by only 53%-47%, with a popular vote margin of 5,000. Overall, Shimkus won 55%-45%. Since then, he has been reelected easily. When he first ran for the seat in 1996, he said he would limit himself to 12 years in the House. At Hastert's urging, Shimkus reconsidered the pledge and announced in September 2005 that his earlier plan was "a mistake at the time . . . .Unless everyone plays by the same rules, term limits don't make sense." The term limit repudiation and the page scandal do not appear to have damaged him with local voters; he won with 61% in 2006.

★ INDIANA ★

On Memorial Day every year the nation's eyes turn to Indianapolis, the center of a state with the nation's most distinctive nickname—Hoosier—and some of its least distinctive borders, for a sports spectacle celebrating the knack for tinkering and the taste for powerful machines that make the Midwest the nation's manufacturing center: the Indianapolis 500. This combination of sports and manufacturing is symbolic of Indiana's historic strengths and successes. The image of its manufacturing base and sports heritage seems as antique as the bricks with which the Indianapolis Speedway was originally paved, though all but one yard at the start/ finish line has long since been asphalted. The Speedway is literally at the center of American manufacturing: Almost precisely half the country's manufacturing jobs are east of Indiana and the other half west, almost half are north and half south. Indiana itself has the nation's highest percentage of workers in manufacturing (20% in 2005) and the highest percentage of gross product attributable to manufacturing. It is the number two steel producer with its giant, heavily automated steel mills on the south shore of Lake Michigan and mini-mills scattered across the state. Indiana leads the nation in making elevators, refrigerators, engines, engine-electrical equipment, recreational vehicles, mobile homes, and truck and bus bodies. It gave the world canned pork and beans, tomato juice, the Coca-Cola bottle and Alka-Seltzer. Nor are Indiana's days of innovation over. Just as it has attracted new teams and events to Indianapolis's sports facilities, the small factories set amidst farm landscape or at the edge

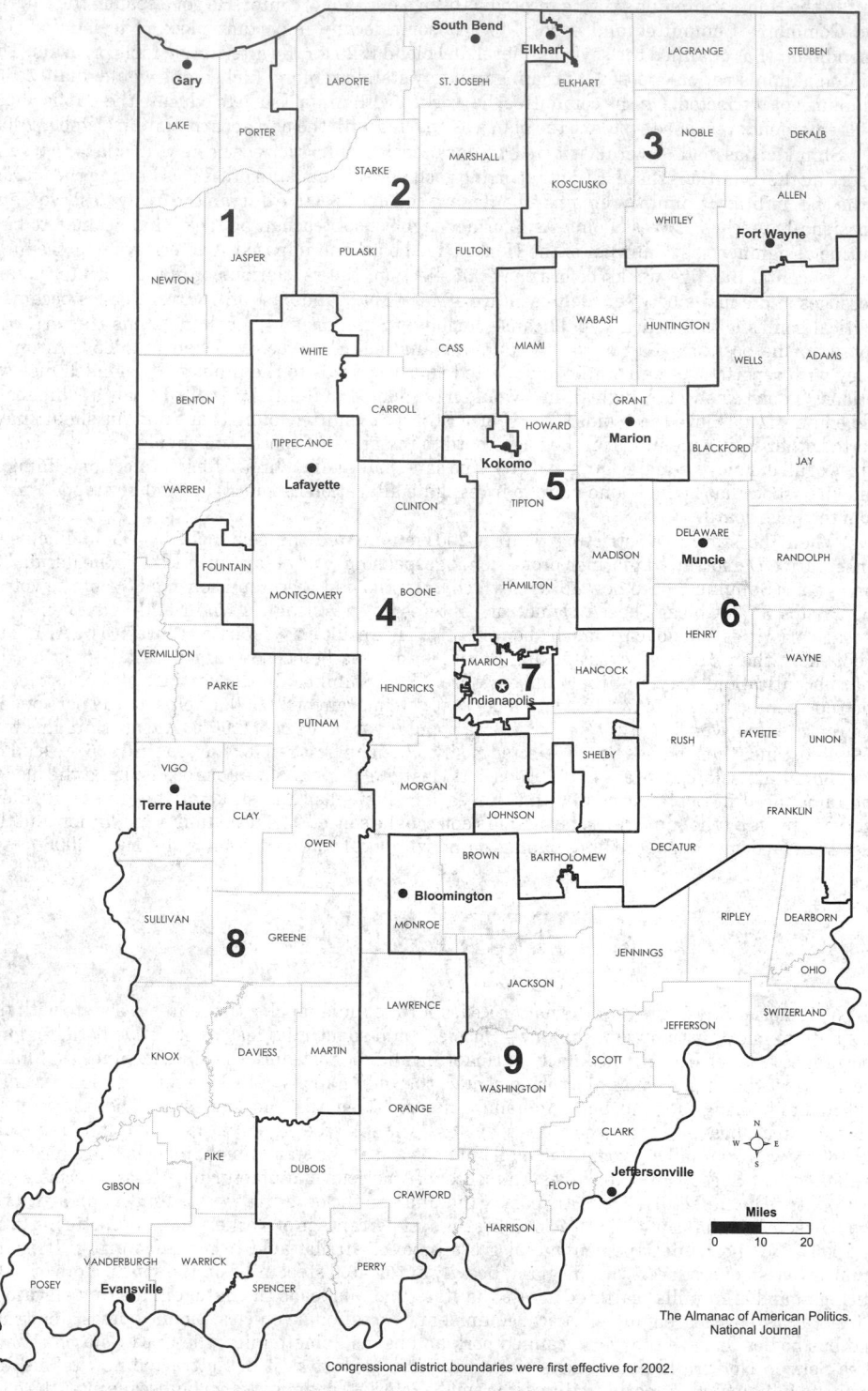

The Almanac of American Politics.
National Journal

Congressional district boundaries were first effective for 2002.

of small cities have become centers of advanced manufacturing innovation. And in 2006 a team of Purdue University undergraduates won the Rube Goldberg Machine Contest for the fourth year in a row, for a 215-step paper shredder.

But there is one downside to a manufacturing economy: It is subject to sharp contraction in times of recession. The economic slowdown of 2000-02 was not by historic standards a major one, but jobs peaked in Indiana in May 2000 and, after bottoming out in July 2003, were still below the peak in 2006. More seem on the way: Toyota is going to build Camrys in a Suburu plant in Lafayette in addition to its plant in Gibson County, and Honda picked Greensburg, Indiana, over an Ohio site, for a new plant; Governor Mitch Daniels hopes to attract Honda suppliers and the planned HondaJet plant too. Cummins and American Commercial Lines opened new factories in 2007. But manufacturing is increasingly capital-intensive; Indiana continues to churn out huge tonnages of steel to meet Chinese demands, but with only 19,000 workers. And so Indiana is turning to other things—especially life sciences, with biopharmaceuticals by Indianapolis-based Eli Lilly, university research at Purdue and IU, prosthetics and orthopedics, biofuels—to the point that Indiana was rated one of the nation's top three life sciences centers by the Battelle Institute. Growth has been strong in metro Indianapolis, which with about one-quarter of the state's population accounted for 60% of its population growth in 2000-06; it grew 9%, versus 2% in the rest of the state and population loss in the belt of counties east and north of Indianapolis which have long depended heavily on the Big Three auto companies.

Culturally, Indiana is like an earlier America; it retains some of the old norms that in the 1920s and 1930s brought sociologists Robert and Helen Lynd in their search for the typical American place to "Middletown" (actually Muncie). Ethnically, Indiana seems like an earlier America too: Except for the steel area around Gary—really an extension of the Chicago metropolitan area—Indiana has relatively few descendants from the 1840-1924 wave of immigration and only a small flow of recent Hispanic or Asian immigrants. But it does have religious diversity, with 109 denominations according to the Glenmary Center; only six states have more. The major metropolitan area, Indianapolis, now has 1.6 million people but still doesn't have the big singles and gay neighborhoods of larger cities. What it does have is one of the nation's largest foundations, the Lilly Endowment (which gives much of its money locally) and a willingness to create and innovate. In the 1980s, the Lilly Endowment urged Indianapolis to make itself a sports center. The city attracted the Colts professional football team to the Hoosier Dome (now the RCA Dome). In the late 1990s, Indianapolis's downtown filled with new construction projects: the pro basketball Pacers' Conseco Fieldhouse, the new NCAA headquarters (the lease has been extended to 2039), a conservatory and the Indiana State Museum. In the 1990s Indianapolis Mayor Stephen Goldsmith, a Republican, pioneered the privatization of city services and cut taxes, while in the state Capitol four blocks away, Governors Evan Bayh and Frank O'Bannon, both Democrats, also cut taxes. But after 2000 job losses led to a revenue crunch, and there has been movement in the other direction.

The partisan patterns in Indiana state politics sometimes seem typical of an older America, with preferences anchored in the Civil War era and a small overlay of change from the union-organizing days of the 1930s. Indiana's cultural conservatism has kept it Republican in presidential elections for the last generation, but it was a crucial state from the Civil War to the New Deal in the struggles between Republicans and Democrats. Party identification was handed down like religious affiliation—the Lynds noted that Presbyterians had little to do with Methodists, but that was nothing next to divisions between Republicans and Democrats—in a state still peopled largely by descendants of its original settlers, Yankees from Ohio and New England and "Butternuts" (as they were called in the Civil War years) from Kentucky and the South.

Most Yankees became Republicans and most Butternuts Democrats, and that split has persisted over generations and can still be seen in election returns today. Of the 26 Indiana counties carried by Bill Clinton in 1996, 18 were south of Indianapolis, most near the Ohio River. The others are clustered around industrial towns that were organized by the CIO unions, the United Steelworkers and the United Auto Workers, in the 1930s. In the 1920s the Lynds, liberal academics influenced by Marx's idea that political beliefs were determined by economic interests, were puzzled why the factory workers in "Middletown" didn't vote against the bosses; in the 1930s and since in some parts of industrial Indiana they have. But not so in other cities, including metro Indianapolis.

Why not? One answer is that cultural identity and personal values tend to be permanent and so have usually been the critical determinants of political allegiance in an America where economic status can often be changeable. Another is that the economic interests of Indiana's high-skill workers and its small and large factory owners are not necessarily as adversarial as academics suppose.

Indiana's partisan allegiances have remained remarkably steady. There is an historic base here large enough to allow Democrats to win: Evan Bayh broke a 20-year Republican hold on the governorship in 1988, with his strongest support from southern Indiana and the far northwest industrial zone. His successor, Democrat O'Bannon—from a Butternut town near the Ohio River—with similar moderate policies beat Indianapolis's Goldsmith 52%-47% in 1996 and Congressman David McIntosh by 57%-42% in 2000, with voting patterns much the same as in 1988. In 2004 Republican Mitch Daniels beat Democrat Joe Kernan, who had succeeded O'Bannon after his death in September 2003, by 53%-45%. Daniels carried 75 of 92 counties, losing in the three Lake Michigan counties and Kernan's home town of South Bend, in a few industrial counties (Muncie, Terre Haute, Evansville) and one university county (Bloomington), in Indianapolis's Marion County (but he carried the suburban counties by much wider margins) and nine smaller counties, all but two of them south of Interstate 70 which bisects the state. But two policies that Daniels pushed through the Republican legislature provoked an uproar—the leasing for 75 years of the North Indiana Toll Road to Spanish and Australian companies and the adoption of Daylight Saving Time. Indiana has always straddled the Eastern and Central time zones, with most counties in Eastern time not observing Daylight Savings. Few issues impinge so closely on personal lives, and several counties ended up outside the time zone they wanted. Democrats put up an outcry and gained three seats in the state House, enough for a 51-49 majority, the sixth time control of the state House has changed in 20 years; the state Senate remains solidly Republican. Republicans won the offices of secretary of state, auditor and treasurer. But the biggest impact may have been in U.S. House races. Democrats picked up three seats here, one anchored in industrial South Bend and two in Butternut territory, adjoining the Ohio River. The Democrats' county percentages there look very much like those of Bayh and O'Bannon—or of Butternut Democrats in the late nineteenth century.

The People		**Race/Ethnic Origin**			**Military veterans:** 590,476 (13.1%)	
Pop. 2006 (est):	6,313,520	5,219,373	85.8%	White	WWII: 19.7%	Korea: 13.7%
Pop. 2000:	6,080,485	505,462	8.3%	Black	Vietnam: 31.3%	Gulf War: 9.3%
Pop. 1990:	5,544,159	58,424	1.0%	Asian	**Most populous cities (2006):**	
Change 1990-2000:	Up 9.7%	13,654	0.2%	Native Am.	1. Indianapolis	795,484
% of U.S. total:	2.2%	1,573	0.0%	Hawaiian	2. Fort Wayne	248,637
Pop. rank:	14th of 50	61,115	1.0%	Two+ races	3. Evansville	115,738
Area size:	36,418 sq. mi.	6,348	0.1%	Other	4. South Bend	104,905
State Native:	69.3%	214,536	3.5%	Hisp. Origin	5. Gary	97,715
Non-citizen:	1.9%	**Ancestry**				
Language		German: 17.6%		USA: 9.3%	Urban population: 70.8%	
English: 91.7%	Spanish: 4.1%	Irish: 8.4%		English: 6.9%	Rural population: 29.2%	
Other Eur.: 3.1%		Polish: 2.3%				

Education		**Work Sector**		**General Assembly**	
H.S. Grad:	82.1%	Private: 83.4%	Govt: 10.9%	Senate	33 R 17 D
College Grad:	19.4%	Self: 5.4%	Family: 0.3%	House	51 D 49 R
Industry		Unemployment: 4.9%		Legislative Term Limits: No	
Agri: 1.4%	Con: 6.6%	**Household Income**		**Registered Voters**	
Fin: 5.7%	Info: 2.1%	<15k: 14.3%	15-35k: 27.2%	No party registration	
Mfg: 28.0%	Prof: 25.6%	35-50k: 17.9%	50-100k: 31.5%		
Public: 3.3%	Trade: 15.2%	100-150k: 6.3%	>150k: 2.8%		
Other: 12.0%		Median: $41,567			
Occupation		Poverty status: 9.5%			
Blue collar: 31.4%	White collar: 54.0%	**Home Value**			
Gray collar: 14.6%		<50k: 15.7%	50-100k: 40.6%	100-200k: 34.5%	200-300k: 6.1%
		300-500k: 2.2%	>500k: 0.9%	Median: $92,500	

Presidential politics   Democrats are not, however, competitive in Indiana's presidential politics; the one time they have carried the state since 1936 was in 1964. Since then it has been close only in 1976, when Gerald Ford beat Jimmy Carter here by 53%-46%, and in 1996, when Bob Dole beat Bill Clinton 47%-42%. George W. Bush won here 57%-41% in 2000 and, with big percentage increases in small counties, 60%-39% in 2004. So Indiana sees little of presidential candidates in election year autumns, nor does it see much of them in spring or summer: Indiana's May presidential primary has not been influential since 1968. That might have been different if Senator Evan Bayh had run for president. He made frequent trips to Iowa and New Hampshire in 2005 and 2006 and on December 3, 2006, announced he was setting up a presidential exploratory committee. He went to Iowa on December 4 and New Hampshire December 9. But his crowds were far smaller than Barack Obama's, and he evidently concluded that, with his moderate record, he wouldn't be able to break through. He announced he was not running on December 16.

2004 Presidential Vote

Bush (R)	1,479,438	(60%)
Kerry (D)	969,011	(39%)
Badnarik (Lib)	18,058	(1%)
Other	1,495	(0%)

2004 Democratic Presidential Primary

Kerry (D)	231,047	(73%)
Edwards (D)	35,651	(11%)
Dean (D)	21,482	(7%)
Clark (D)	17,437	(5%)
Kucinich (D)	7,003	(2%)
Other	4,591	(1%)

2000 Presidential Vote

Bush (R)	1,245,836	(57%)
Gore (D)	901,980	(41%)
Other	51,489	(2%)

Congressional districting   Indiana lost one congressional district in the 2000 Census, and that required significant changes in district lines that had stayed pretty much the same for 20 years. In charge were Democrats, who then had the governorship and a majority in the state House, though Republicans had a majority in the state Senate; Indiana law provides that if the House and Senate cannot agree, the decision goes to a five-member commission, with the tie-breaking member appointed by the governor. In May 2001, the commission adopted a plan largely identical to that passed by the state House. Democrats hoped to retain the four seats they held and improve their chances in at least one more. But as happens often with redistricting, the initial results were disappointing. In the marginal 2d District Tim Roemer retired in 2002, and Republican Chris Chocola picked up the seat. In 2004 Republican Mike Sodrel beat incumbent Democrat Baron Hill in the 9th District. But the plan paid off when Republican numbers plunged in 2006. The 2nd and 9th districts went 54% and 50% to Democrats Joe Donnelly and Baron Hill, who reclaimed his former seat, and Democrat Brad Ellsworth walloped six-term incumbent John Hostettler 61%-39% in the 8th, which in the 1970s and 1980s was one of the nation's most frequently seriously contested districts. Indiana is not expected to lose another district in the 2010 Census, and redistricting will depend on whether Republican Governor Mitch Daniels is reelected in 2008. If he is and Republicans hold their big margin in the state Senate, they will likely control the process, whichever party holds onto the closely divided and often changing state House. If Daniels is defeated, Democrats will be assured of control only if they elect a majority in the state House in 2010.

110th Congress Lineup
5 D   4 R

109th Congress Lineup
7 R   2 D

Governor

Mitch Daniels (R)

Elected 2004, term expires Jan. 2009, 1st term; b. Apr. 7, 1949, Monongahela, PA; home, Indianapolis; Princeton U., B.A. 1971, Georgetown U., J.D. 1979; Presbyterian; married (Cheri).

Professional Career: Advisor, Mayor of Indianapolis Richard Lugar, 1971-76; Chief of Staff, U.S. Sen. Lugar, 1976-82; Exec. Dir., NRSC, 1983-84; senior adv., White House, 1985-87; CEO, Hudson Institute, 1987-90; executive, Eli Lilly, 1990-2001; Dir., OMB, 2001-02.

Office: 206 State House, Indianapolis, 46204, 317-232-4567; Fax: 317-232-3443; Web site: www.in.gov/gov.

Election Results

2004 general	Mitch Daniels (R)	1,302,907	(53%)
	Joe Kernan (D)	1,113,879	(45%)
	Other	31,717	(1%)
2004 primary	Mitch Daniels (R)	335,228	(66%)
	Eric Miller (R)	169,930	(34%)
2000 general	Frank O'Bannon (D)	1,232,525	(57%)
	David McIntosh (R)	908,285	(42%)
	Other	38,458	(1%)

Mitch Daniels, elected governor of Indiana in 2004, grew up in Indianapolis and graduated from Princeton and Georgetown law school. He worked as a staffer for Richard Lugar when he was mayor of Indianapolis in the early 1970s, as chief of staff for Lugar from 1976 to 1983 when he was in the Senate, and then as political director in the Reagan White House. In 1987, he returned to Indianapolis to work at the Hudson Institute and then went to work for the Eli Lilly company in 1990 where he climbed high in its ranks to president of Lilly's North American pharmaceutical operations; when he resigned to reenter government in 2001, he made $27 million from liquidating his stock holdings. He reentered government at the top level, as George W. Bush's director of the Office of Management and the Budget. There he developed a reputation for cutting spending and for having disdain for members of Congress, whose motto he said should be, " 'Don't just stand there. Spend something.' This is the only way they feel relevant." Bush insiders referred to him as "the Blade"; Senator Robert Byrd called him "Little Caesar." Senator Ted Stevens said the only way he could fix his relationship with Congress was to "go home to Indiana."

Which is what he did, in May 2003. Daniels's family had remained in Indianapolis, he was tired of commuting on weekends and he saw an opportunity to run for governor. Democrats had held the office in mostly Republican Indiana since 1988—first Evan Bayh, elected in 1988 and 1992, then Frank O'Bannon, elected in 1996 and 2000. For most of that time Bayh and O'Bannon cut taxes, cut the welfare rolls and instituted education testing. But after the 2001 recession cost the state jobs and revenues plummeted, O'Bannon was forced to take a different course. In 2002, the sales tax was raised. Out-year deficits loomed. Small scandals were exposed—DMV employees selling black market IDs, a state contracting official accepting favors, child protective workers filing false reports. Lieutenant Governor Joseph Kernan, a Vietnam veteran and POW for 11 months and a popular three-term mayor of South Bend, was widely assumed to be the strongest Democrat to succeed the term-limited O'Bannon. But in December 2002 Kernan shocked just about everyone by announcing that he would not run. "I just want to have a beer in my back yard on a Tuesday night. I've got a great job. I've enjoyed it, but I want to go back to South Bend." That left the Democratic field to former Democratic state and national Chairman Joe Andrew and state Senator Vi Simpson.

Soon after he returned home, Daniels announced he was running for governor. All but one of the Republicans then running, including 2000 nominee David McIntosh, left the race and endorsed him. Bush, on a visit to the state, referred to "my man Mitch," and in time Dick Cheney, Laura Bush and Andy Card made appearances for him. He campaigned around the state in checked shirts and sweaters, traveling in an RV with supporters' signatures all over it; he touched down in every one of Indiana's 92 counties and eventually visited each of them three times.

Then in September 2003 O'Bannon was found in his hotel room in Chicago paralyzed by a stroke. Two days later, Kernan was sworn in as acting governor. Three days after that, on September 13, O'Bannon died and Kernan became governor in his own right. He handled the tragic transition gracefully and, perhaps inevitably, reconsidered his decision not to run in 2004. In November he announced he was running; quickly Andrew and Simpson ended their campaigns and supported him, as did Indianapolis Mayor Bart Peterson, often mentioned as a potential candidate himself.

From there on in it was a two-man race, although Daniels did have primary opposition. While his former boss George W. Bush was put on the defensive about losses of manufacturing jobs nationally, Daniels was attacking Kernan and local Democrats for losses of manufacturing jobs in Indiana and said it was time for a "new crew." He called for tax breaks for new business property investments, new hires and research and development. He said he would put more emphasis on winning federal grants. He said he would create a state agriculture department and would provide tougher enforcement of child support obligations. Daniels opposed drug reimportation and favored an online referral service to match patients with drug discount programs. He called for health savings accounts for state employees and credits for employees who stop smoking and stay fit.

Kernan called for lower property taxes and for tax abatements for new business on a case-by-case basis. He endorsed full-day kindergarten. He criticized Daniels for his budget cuts as OMB Director, and for signing off on foreign contracts and job outsourcing; he blamed Indiana job losses on federal trade policy. He dropped a state contract with a company based in India to process unemployment claims. He charged that I-69 from Indianapolis to Evansville would have been built if Daniels had put in the money; Daniels said it had to be financed as a toll road.

Daniels had modest leads in polls during most of the campaign and won 53%-45%. He carried metro Indianapolis 57%-42% but ran behind in northern Indiana and Kernan's home town of South Bend. In southern rural counties, places where people are used to voting Democratic in state races, he ran farther behind Bush than in the north. Republicans increased their margin in the state Senate to 33-17 and converted a 51-49 deficit in the state House to a 52-48 majority: it was the first time Republicans had won control of state government since 1986. Fiscal problems loomed: state government faced a $645 million deficit and owed $710 million in back payments to schools, universities and local governments.

In his first year as governor, Daniels showed that his talent for infuriating legislators had not diminished. He said Democrats "car-bombed" his agenda after they killed close to 130 bills by boycotting the House floor at the deadline for legislation to be passed and transferred to the Senate. And toward the end of the legislative session, Daniels caused a Senate floor walk-out by Democrats after he said they had "zero interest" in the budget process and that the minority leader was a "throwback politician."

But Daniels achieved some notable successes in his first two years. With the help of business interests, he convinced lawmakers to enact daylight saving time to stop Indiana from being one of three states that does not go on daylight-savings time, and he persuaded the Department of Transportation to allow eight counties to switch to the Central time zone. He created a state economic development corporation to replace the Department of Commerce and a new inspector general post for ethics; he also got a small funding increase for schools, a voter identification bill, a methamphetamine crackdown, and signed a bill requiring state vehicles to run on agricultural-based fuels when possible. Daniels led trade delegations to Japan, South Korean and Taiwan to promote agricultural exports and to court foreign investment. He reduced the state's property tax relief payments, and in turn sought to give local governments more control over how they raise revenue.

Daniels launched his most controversial plan in 2005 when he unveiled "Major Moves" a 10-year transportation plan that aimed to cover shortfalls in the state's transportation budget by privatizing transportation assets rather than raising gasoline taxes or state borrowing. The center-piece was a 75-year deal to lease the Indiana Toll Road, a 157-mile-long span across northern Indiana that connects Ohio and Illinois, to an Australian-Spanish consortium in exchange for a $3.8 billion lump sum payment. Daniels sold the plan as a way to raise cash to improve state's road system and create jobs, while leaving toll collection and highway maintenance to someone else. Democrats protested the state would lose control of toll increases and decades of future revenue. (This was despite the fact the highway was losing money because tolls had not been raised in 20 years.) Daniels and the state Republican party dipped into their campaign funds to run ads to promote the plan. After the Republican legislature approved the deal in 2006, Daniels proposed a spend $12 billion on the state's infrastructure over the next decade, including the construction of an

Illiana Expressway to ease traffic congestion between Illinois and Indiana, and building a privately funded extension of I-69 around metropolitan Indianapolis.

The unpopularity of the Toll Road lease and the switch to daylight-saving time kept Daniels largely off the campaign trail in 2006 and in part contributed to Republican losses, including the ouster of three members of Congress. Democrats also won a narrow 51-49 seat majority in the state House and a check on Daniels' legislative agenda, particularly new efforts to privatize state transportation, lottery, welfare administration and other state services. The governor indicated a willingness to support a "reasonable" minimum wage increase, and had laid out an agenda that includes all-day kindergarten, low-income health insurance, a cigarette tax increase, increased veterans benefits, a public infrastructure plan and a ceiling on state spending. In spite of the Republicans' poor showing in 2006, Daniels will be formidable if he runs for reelection in 2008. The governor took on and won unpopular initiatives and his opponent faces the challenge of proposing alternatives or advocating a return to the status quo; perhaps as important, he entered January 2007 with more than $2.5 million cash on hand. Among the announced Democratic candidates were Jim Schillinger, an architect and South Bend native, Democratic state Senate Minority Leader Richard Young and former Congresswoman Jill Long Thompson.

Senior Senator

Richard Lugar (R)

Elected 1976, seat up 2012, 6th term; b. Apr. 4, 1932, Indianapolis; home, Indianapolis; Denison U., B.A. 1954, Rhodes Scholar, Oxford U., M.A. 1956; Methodist; married (Charlene).

Military Career: Navy, 1957-60.

Elected Office: Indianapolis Bd. of Schl. Commissioners, 1964-67; Indianapolis Mayor, 1968-75.

Professional Career: Mgr., family farm; V.P. & Treas., Thomas L. Green & Co., 1960-67; Prof., U. of Indianapolis, 1976.

DC Office: 306 HSOB, 20510, 202-224-4814; Fax: 202-228-0360; Web site: lugar.senate.gov.

State Offices: Evansville, 812-465-6313; Ft. Wayne, 260-422-1505; Indianapolis, 317-226-5555; Jeffersonville, 812-288-3377; Valparaiso, 219-548-8035.

Committees: *Agriculture, Nutrition & Forestry* (2d of 10 R): Nutrition and Food Assistance, Sustainable and Organic Agriculture & General Legislation; Rural Revitalization, Conservation, Forestry & Credit; Energy, Science & Technology. *Foreign Relations* (RMM of 10 R).

Group Ratings

	ADA	ACLU	AFS	LCV	ITIC	NTU	COC	ACU	CFG	FRC
2006	15	25	25	14	100	67	100	64	52	75
2005	10	—	0	20	—	61	100	88	69	—

National Journal Ratings

	2005 LIB	—	2005 CONS		2006 LIB	—	2006 CONS
Economic	45%	—	54%		44%	—	55%
Social	45%	—	54%		48%	—	51%
Foreign	50%	—	49%		42%	—	54%

Key Votes of the 109th Congress

1. Bar ANWR Drilling	N	5. Confirm Samuel Alito	Y	9. Limit Interstate Abortion	Y
2. FY06 Spending Curb	Y	6. Path to Citizenship	Y	10. CAFTA	Y
3. Estate Tax Repeal	Y	7. Bar Same Sex Marriage	Y	11. Urge Iraq Withdrawal	N
4. Raise Minimum Wage	Y	8. Stem Cell Research $	Y	12. Provide Detainee Rights	N

Election Results

2006 general	Richard Lugar (R)	1,171,553	(87%)	($3,133,830)
	Steve Osborn (Lib)	168,820	(13%)	
2006 primary	Richard Lugar (R)	unopposed		
2000 general	Richard Lugar (R)	1,427,944	(67%)	($4,251,603)
	David L. Johnson (D)	683,273	(32%)	($1,179,029)
	Other	33,992	(1%)	

Prior Winning Percentages: 1994 (67%); 1988 (68%); 1982 (54%); 1976 (59%)

Richard Lugar, still running 5K races at the annual Dick Lugar Run and Walk in Indianapolis, has a career in public life going back to the late 1950s, when as a young Navy officer he prepared intelligence briefings for Chief of Naval Operations Arleigh Burke and briefed President Eisenhower over closed-circuit television. Now he is the first Indiana senator ever elected to fourth, fifth and sixth terms and a powerful voice on foreign policy. Lugar grew up in Indianapolis, near his family's farm and food machinery firm, which was founded in 1893. He was an Eagle Scout, a straight-A student at Denison College and a Rhodes scholar. After military service Lugar returned to the family business, was elected to the school board in 1964, then was elected mayor of Indianapolis in 1967, at 35. As mayor, he consolidated the city and Marion County into Unigov, which brought in tax resources and suburban voters, keeping the city both solvent and Republican (until 1999, when a Democrat was finally elected mayor). In the late 1960s, Lugar bucked fashion and called for fewer rather than more federal programs and became known as Richard Nixon's favorite mayor. This was not a political asset in the Watergate year of 1974, when Lugar ran against Senator Birch Bayh, father of his current junior colleague, and lost 51%-46%. But in the more favorable climate of 1976 and against a weaker Democratic incumbent, Vance Hartke, Lugar won 59%-40%.

Throughout his public life, Lugar's strength has been that he has followed where his stubborn convictions and his considerable intellect led, regardless of political risk or reward: He has plenty of accomplishments but also some disappointments. His lone course has served him well in Indiana, but has had mixed results in the Senate and in the national arena. He has a mostly conservative voting record, but not entirely; he has voted to raise auto mileage standards, fund embryonic stem-cell research, and for the low income heating program and increasing the minimum wage. Lugar started off in the Senate leading the 1978 filibuster to defeat the AFL-CIO's labor law reform bill, although unions were then a major power in Indiana. He strongly supported NAFTA in 1993, in a Midwest manufacturing state where many thought foreigners were taking their jobs. He ran for president in 1996 on his own platform and without any concessions to the political shorthand or the TV sensibility of the day, but his candidacy made little impact. Lugar based his campaign on "nuclear security and fiscal sanity"—deterring nuclear terrorism and backing a 17% national sales tax. But he got little coverage, and finished 7th in Iowa and 5th in New Hampshire and soon left the race.

Lugar's great interest is foreign policy. He has been chairman of the Foreign Relations Committee, first in 1985-87 and then again in 2003-07. In 1985 he quickly took command over a committee sharply divided between Jesse Helms and liberal Democrats. Lugar was in the middle, backing Contra aid and favoring sanctions on South Africa. Helms had allowed him to become chairman in 1985, despite his lower seniority, because of a campaign promise in 1984 to take the chairmanship of the Agriculture Committee. But after Republicans lost their Senate majority in 1986, Helms said he was no longer bound by his promise and invoked seniority; Lugar took the issue to the Republican Conference, but lost a vote there. So Helms was the ranking minority member and chairman for 16 years, while Lugar waited. Helms left Lugar off conference committees and seldom communicated with him; Lugar led the fight to ratify the Chemical Weapons Agreement over Helms' opposition in April 1997, and won. Lugar favored other arms control treaties about which some conservatives have been skeptical—INF in 1988, START I in 1992, START II in 1996. He supported NATO expansion and U.S. payment of U.N. dues. But in October 1999, he joined other Republicans in voting against the Comprehensive Test Ban Treaty, arguing that the U.S. must keep testing to maintain its nuclear arsenal.

His greatest achievement has been the Nunn-Lugar Cooperative Threats Reduction program to pay Russia, Ukraine, Belarus and Kazakhstan to dismantle and destroy their nuclear weapons and some chemical and biological weapons as well, to prevent them from falling into the hands of hostile powers or terrorists. This was passed by Congress in 1991, and Lugar has been active in seeing that it is effective ever since. Lugar has gained considerable notice for this work—he and Nunn have been nominated for the Nobel Peace Prize and an Indianapolis TV station filmed a documentary of him inspecting weapons in Russia—but perhaps not enough. As of August 2005, the Nunn-Lugar program had deactivated 13,300 nuclear warheads, 1,473 ICBMs, 831 ICBM silos, 442 ICBM mobile missile launchers, 233 bombers, 906 nuclear ASMs, 728 SLBM launchers, 936 SLBMs, 48 SSBMs and all 194 nuclear test tunnels and holes; all nuclear weapons have been removed from Ukraine, Belarus and Kazakhstan. A nerve gas destruction facility has been built at Shchuchye, Russia and a pathogen storage facility in Tblisi, Georgia. After September 11 Lugar called for a Nunn-Lugar approach to prevent chemical and biological weapons throughout the world from falling into the hands of terrorists. In October 2004, legislation was signed extending Nunn-Lugar to Albania. Amid charges by John Kerry that the Bush administration slighted Nunn-Lugar, Lugar credited the administration with getting $10 billion for the program from the other members of the Group of Eight, with establishing the Global Threat Reduction Initiative to secure radioactive materials globally, with the ending of weapons of mass destruction programs in Libya, and with the IAEA Additional Protocol and UN Resolution 1540 requiring states to criminalize proliferation. Lugar continues to monitor this work closely; in August 2005 he and Barack Obama made a trip to Russia, Ukraine and Azerbaijan to monitor progress; there was a minor incident when Russian officials insisted on inspecting their military plane and relented only after several hours' delay.

Lugar kept a vigilant eye on Iraq throughout the 1990s. Starting in August 1990, he called for an end to Saddam Hussein's regime and said that Saddam might have to be killed and U.S. ground troops needed to accomplish that. But he has not necessarily been a team player for the Bush administration. In summer 2002, he and then-Chairman Joseph Biden conducted hearings on Iraq to which the administration declined to send witnesses. In September 2002 he and Biden drafted their own resolution, which limited the authorization geographically and required the administration either to obtain a U.N. resolution or to certify to Congress that its efforts at the U.N. had failed; this was bypassed when House Democratic Leader Dick Gephardt and Senators Joe Lieberman and Evan Bayh agreed with the administration on a resolution. In late 2002 Lugar complained that he had not been briefed on postwar plans for Iraq. In April 2004 he said the administration "failed to communicate" its plans to Congress and argued that the June 30 turnover to Iraqis was too soon and said the Army needed to be increased by 80,000 soldiers. In September 2004 he said the failure to spend more than $1 billion of $18 billion appropriated for Iraqi reconstruction was the result of a "lack of planning." While Democrats have accused Republicans of failing to perform oversight while in the majority, Lugar in four years as chairman held 40 hearings on Iraq. In June 2007, he dealt an unexpected blow to the Bush administration when he sharply criticized the President's Iraq policy and called for a change in course in a speech on the Senate floor. "In my judgment, the costs and risks of continuing down the current path outweigh the potential benefits that might be achieved."

As chairman and now as ranking Republican, Lugar kept at arm's length from the administration and has worked cooperatively with his Democratic counterpart Joseph Biden. When the nomination of John Bolton to be Ambassador to the United Nations came under attack, he pressed the administration to supply emails, memos and documents. He does not always go along with established authorities. In May and July 2004 he held hearings on Third World nations' corrupt use of World Bank funds. In 2005 he and Norm Coleman sponsored a bill to withhold half of U.S. dues to the United Nations if the UN failed to make specific changes in its operations.

Lugar was chairman of the Agriculture Committee from 1995 to 2001. He liked to point out that he was the only working farmer on the committee—his 604 acres, thanks to Unigov, is inside the city of Indianapolis—and he played a key role in the 1996 passage of the Freedom to Farm Act, which purported to phase out over seven years the farm subsidies of which he had long been a critic. But low crop prices starting in 1998 resulted in disaster relief payments that kept in place something very much like the old subsidy system. In October 2001 he opposed the House farm bill with its big increases for historically subsidized crops, and proposed his own bill, guaranteeing up to 80% of income of qualified farmers, but at far less cost. But with key Senate races in states with historically subsidized farmers, the Senate passed a farm bill similar to the House's and George W. Bush signed it. Lugar has called for addressing "the fundamentals" on energy; he switched in 2002 and voted for oil drilling in the Arctic National Wildlife Refuge and, despite the importance of auto manufacturing in Indiana, he has voted to raise the CAFE auto gas mileage standards. Lugar was one of the 23 Republicans who in May 2006 supported the Senate immigration bill with its guest worker and legalization provisions; he sponsored a bill to give conditional legal status to young illegal immigrants who graduate from U.S. high schools. With Christopher Dodd, he sponsored a bill to give journalists a privilege not to testify about information they received confidentially.

In Indiana, Lugar has remained vastly popular. He was reelected 68%-32% in 1988, 67%-31% in 1994 and 67%-32% in 2000—pretty monotonous. In 2005 former Congressman and 9/11 Commission member Tim Roemer declined to run against him. In 2006 he had no Democratic opponent; Democratic state Chairman Dan Parker said, "Let's be honest. Richard Lugar is beloved not only by Republicans, but by Independents and Democrats." Lugar took the trouble to run some ads in October and in November was reelected over a Libertarian by an 87%-13% margin. If he serves out this term, he will have served twice as long as any Indiana senator before him.

Junior Senator

Evan Bayh (D)

Elected 1998, seat up 2010, 2d term; b. Dec. 26, 1955, Shirkieville; home, Indianapolis; IN U., B.S. 1978, U. of VA, J.D. 1981; Episcopalian; married (Susan).

Elected Office: IN Secy. of State, 1986-88; IN Gov., 1988-96.

Professional Career: Practicing atty., 1981-86, 1997-98; Visiting Prof., Indiana U., 1997-98.

DC Office: 131 RSOB, 20510, 202-224-5623; Fax: 202-228-1377; Web site: bayh.senate.gov.

State Offices: Evansville, 812-465-6500; Fort Wayne, 260-426-3151; Hammond, 219-852-2763; Indianapolis, 317-554-0750; Jeffersonville, 812-218-2317; South Bend, 574-236-8302.

Committees: *Aging (Special)* (4th of 11 D). *Armed Services* (9th of 13 D): Airland; Readiness & Management Support; Emerging Threats & Capabilities. *Banking, Housing & Urban Affairs* (5th of 11 D): Security & International Trade & Finance (Chmn.); Securities, Insurance & Investment; Financial Institutions. *Intelligence (Select)* (4th of 8 D). *Small Business & Entrepreneurship* (7th of 10 D).

Group Ratings

	ADA	ACLU	AFS	LCV	ITIC	NTU	COC	ACU	CFG	FRC
2006	85	67	100	100	75	12	45	16	1	0
2005	95	—	100	85	—	12	56	20	2	—

National Journal Ratings

	2005 LIB	—	2005 CONS	2006 LIB	—	2006 CONS
Economic	66%	—	33%	83%	—	13%
Social	83%	—	10%	71%	—	28%
Foreign	58%	—	40%	62%	—	35%

Key Votes of the 109th Congress

1. Bar ANWR Drilling	Y	5. Confirm Samuel Alito	N	9. Limit Interstate Abortion	Y
2. FY06 Spending Curb	N	6. Path to Citizenship	Y	10. CAFTA	N
3. Estate Tax Repeal	N	7. Bar Same Sex Marriage	N	11. Urge Iraq Withdrawal	Y
4. Raise Minimum Wage	Y	8. Stem Cell Research $	Y	12. Provide Detainee Rights	Y

Election Results

2004 general	Evan Bayh (D)	1,496,976	(62%)	($2,250,428)
	Marvin Scott (R)	903,913	(37%)	($2,242,526)
	Other	27,344	(1%)	
2004 primary	Evan Bayh (D)	unopposed		
1998 general	Evan Bayh (D)	1,012,244	(64%)	($3,914,375)
	Paul Helmke (R)	552,732	(35%)	($642,784)
	Other	23,641	(1%)	

Evan Bayh was elected in 1998 to the Senate seat his father Birch Bayh first won in 1962 when Evan was just 6. He grew up mostly in Washington, graduated from Indiana University and the University of Virginia Law School, then returned to Indiana to practice law—and politics. His father, a charismatic candidate, beat three serious opponents: Incumbent Senator Homer Capehart in 1962, later-Deputy Attorney General William Ruckelshaus in 1968, and future Senator Richard Lugar in 1974. But in 1980, with Evan helping run the campaign, he lost to Dan Quayle. In 1986, at 30, Evan Bayh was elected secretary of state, often a steppingstone office. In 1988, at 32, he ran for governor. Republicans had held the office and controlled most of Indiana state government for 20 years. However, their smoothly run machine had grown sluggish: The Republican nominee promised innovation, but Bayh was a young and fresh face. As governor, he balanced the budget, cut taxes and piled up a $1.6 billion budget surplus. He trimmed a deficit in state pension plans and sliced Medicaid spending. He claimed credit for the creation of 350,000 jobs, as Indiana's manufacturing economy revived. He did less to reform education and other government services, but he was immensely popular when he left office.

It was widely expected that Bayh would run for the Senate in 1998, and in December 1996, incumbent Republican Dan Coats announced he would not run for reelection. Bayh's 1998 opponent was Fort Wayne Mayor Paul Helmke, who had backed tax increases in Fort Wayne and who even had kind words for Bill and Hillary Rodham Clinton, whom he had known since law school; he narrowly won the Republican primary with 35% against two more conservative candidates. Helmke argued that Bayh "still comes across a little the empty suit." But Bayh's platform—a balanced budget, saving Social Security, raising education standards and a "fairer, flatter" tax—preempted the Hoosier political center. He ran ads showing his wife extolling his accomplishments, saying he "cracked down on deadbeat dads, sponsored Indiana's fatherhood initiative . . . worked to make our schools safer and drug-free and to move people from welfare to work." Bayh won 64%-35%, carrying 88 of 92 counties, although it is a victory that probably never would have happened if Birch Bayh had not beaten Homer Capehart by 10,000 votes 36 years before—one election can make a big difference.

In the Senate, Bayh has pursued the issues he campaigned on. If his father had a mostly liberal voting record, Evan Bayh has often been one of the more moderate Democratic senators. He has irritated important Democratic constituency groups. He voted for normal trade relations with China in 2000. In 2004 he took a somewhat different approach, sponsoring a trade bill that would allow countervailing duties on China and other non-market countries and revive Super 301 actions. In April 2005 he placed a hold on the nomination of Rob Portman to be special trade representative in order to get a vote on his bill to allow the Commerce Department to impose countervailing duties on subsidized imports from non-market countries, i.e., China, and he co-sponsored a bill to create a special trade prosecutor. In February 2006 he called for tariffs on Chinese imports "until they get right the currency issue." After voting for Free Trade Agreements with Singapore and Chile, he voted against CAFTA in June 2005. He voted in 1999 and 2003 to ban partial-birth abortions; he says he opposes abortion personally, but in most instances doesn't want to impose his religious beliefs on others; as governor, he vetoed an 18-hour waiting period. He was one of two Democrats and one of only 21 senators to vote against allowing the importing of foreign price-controlled prescription drugs in July 2000. This was portrayed as truckling to Eli Lilly, one of Indiana's biggest employers and on whose board Bayh served in 1997-98, but his stand was vindicated when HHS Secretary Donna Shalala declined to enforce the law later in the year. He has since voted against the Medicare/prescription drug bill and voted to give the federal government authority to negotiate lower drug prices. In 2004 and 2005 he sponsored a bill to have the government buy back excess vaccines and provide tax credits to encourage vaccine production.

In May 2000, Bayh and Connecticut Senator Joe Lieberman sponsored a revision of the basic federal aid to education act, which would increase spending by $35 billion over five years, target poor-performing school districts, foster English proficiency among immigrants, promote public school choice and demand accountability of teachers and students. Many of these measures became part of the Bush education bill, for which Bush gave Bayh some of the credit. But Bayh voted against the Bush tax cut, voted against the confirmation of Attorney General John Ashcroft and criticized the Bush energy package. In January 2004 he and Larry Craig introduced a bill to require the CDC to estimate need for vaccines and to buy back unused doses; later in the year there was a flu vaccine shortfall but the bill was not passed. In May 2004 he got the Armed Services Committee to vote $610 million for more humvees that could be armored (the vehicles are produced in South Bend but armored in Fairfield, Ohio); this became a hot issue in December 2004 when Defense Secretary Donald Rumsfeld was asked about the armor by a reservist in Iraq. In April 2005 an amendment he sponsored with Edward Kennedy to add $213 million for armored humvees passed 60-40. In May he sponsored an amendment to get the Defense Department to make sure military personnel were informed of a 2003 law protecting them from eviction or foreclosure. In February 2006 he called for expanding the Army by 100,000 soldiers.

Bayh serves on the Intelligence and Armed Services committees. He was one of the Democrats who early on indicated he would support a resolution authorizing military force in Iraq and continued to support the administration in 2003 and 2004. But when Rumsfeld came before Armed Services after publication of the Abu Ghraib abuse photos, he asked him if he might step down to "demonstrate how seriously we take the situation and therefore help to undo some of the damage to our reputation." Rumsfeld replied, "That's possible." He supported the intelligence overhaul bill recommended by the 9/11 Commission and sponsored an amendment to allow the Intelligence Committee to set its own priorities. He called for Rumsfeld's resignation in December 2004, and he was one of 13 Democrats voting against the confirmation of Condoleezza Rice in February 2005; he said that as an architect of the Iraq war she "did not deserve a promotion." But the same month he said, "To cut and run at this juncture would be a terrible mistake." In early 2006 he called for sanctions on Iran and said, "If action had been taken four or five years ago, we perhaps wouldn't be at this juncture. The president was right to label Iran part of the axis of evil, but then did nothing about it." In June 2006 he voted against withdrawing troops by July 2007 but for the non-binding resolution calling for troops to begin returning by the end of 2006, to "put pressure on the Iraqis to make the hard choices and necessary compromises to stabilize the country."

After then-Lieutenant Governor Joe Kernan said in December 2002 he wouldn't run for governor in 2004, some Democrats wanted Bayh to run, but he said no a month later. His reelection was never in doubt. He won 62%-37%, with a slightly lower percentage than in 1998, carrying 86 of 92 counties, but with the highest number of popular votes ever for an Indiana senator—a considerable achievement as George W. Bush was carrying the state 60%-39%.

Birch Bayh ran for president in 1976 and Evan Bayh has often been mentioned as a candidate for national office. In July 2000, he was on Al Gore's short list of vice presidential possibilities. But leaders of feminist organizations opposed him because of his vote for a partial-birth abortion ban. In June 2001, he announced he wouldn't run for president in 2004; it would keep him away for too long from his young children. But he held the door open for a vice presidential nomination. From February 2001 to June 2005 he was chairman of the moderate Democratic Leadership Council, which helped foster the national career of Bill Clinton. After the November 2004 election Bayh seemed open to running for president in 2008. "I do think that whatever's right for the Democratic party and right for the American people will be found in the center, both geographically and ideologically. National security, economic growth, making government accountable and fiscal discipline, and then showing we're in tune with middle American values—I think that's the right approach." His voting record in 2005 was more in line with other Senate Democrats than it had been before; he joined filibusters to stop the constitutional amendment to ban same-sex marriage, the bill to limit medical malpractice lawsuits and several judicial nominations; he joined almost all other Democrats in rejecting individual investment accounts in Social Security; he took a harder line stance on trade; he voted not only against Samuel Alito but also against John Roberts. In 2005 and 2006 he made frequent trips to Iowa and New Hampshire and many other states and raised enough money that he had $10.6 million by September 2006. "I'm doing some of the practical things that you think would be necessary to make that decision when the time comes, if it's the appropriate thing to do." Bayh was clearly contemplating running as a relatively centrist Democrat. On December 3, 2006, Bayh announced the creation of an exploratory committee and said he wouldn't make the final decision about running until after the first of the year. Then on December 16, he announced he was out. "I concluded that due to circumstances beyond our control the odds were longer than I felt I could responsibly pursue. This path—and these long odds—would have required me to be essentially absent from the Senate for the next year instead of working to help the people of my state and the nation." The Democrats' victory in 2006 seems to have made many Democratic voters and activists confident that they could win without nominating a candidate who had taken moderate stands on issues. Bayh, just 50 at the time, may have a chance to run at some time in the future and in the meantime seems to have a safe seat in Indiana.

FIRST DISTRICT

Rep. Peter Visclosky (D)

Elected 1984, 12th term; b. Aug. 13, 1949, Gary; home, Merrillville; IN U. Northwest, B.S. 1970, U. of Notre Dame, J.D. 1973, Georgetown U., LL.M. 1982; Catholic; divorced.

Professional Career: Practicing atty., 1973-76, 1983-84; Aide, U.S. Rep. Adam Benjamin, 1976-82.

DC Office: 2256 RHOB, 20515, 202-225-2461; Fax: 202-225-2493; Web site: www.house.gov/visclosky.

District Offices: Merrillville, 219-795-1844.

Committees: *Appropriations* (6th of 37 D): Energy & Water Development (Chmn.); Defense; Financial Services & General Government.

Group Ratings

	ADA	ACLU	AFS	LCV	ITIC	NTU	COC	ACU	CFG	FRC
2006	100	82	100	92	14	11	27	12	5	0
2005	85	—	100	72	—	12	37	8	3	0

National Journal Ratings

	2005 LIB	—	2005 CONS		2006 LIB	—	2006 CONS
Economic	71%	—	29%		70%	—	29%
Social	69%	—	31%		71%	—	29%
Foreign	74%	—	25%		83%	—	14%

Key Votes of the 109th Congress

1. Estate Tax Repeal	N	5. Limit Interstate Abortion	N
2. Limit CAFE Standards	Y	6. Extend Patriot Act	N
3. FY06 Spending Curb	N	7. Bar Same Sex Marriage	N
4. Drilling in ANWR	N	8. Stem Cell Research $	Y

9. Build Border Fence	N
10. CAFTA	N
11. Oppose Iraq Withdrawal	N
12. Detainee Tribunals	N

Election Results

2006 general	Peter Visclosky (D)	104,195	(70%)	($1,208,010)
	Mark Leyva (R)	40,146	(27%)	($10,899)
	Charles Barman (I)	5,266	(4%)	
2006 primary	Peter Visclosky (D)	unopposed		
2004 general	Peter Visclosky (D)	178,406	(68%)	($1,076,753)
	Mark Leyva (R)	82,858	(32%)	($20,755)

Prior Winning Percentages: 2002 (67%); 2000 (72%); 1998 (73%); 1996 (69%); 1994 (56%); 1992 (69%); 1990 (66%); 1988 (77%); 1986 (73%); 1984 (71%)

The People		Race/Ethnic Origin	Ancestry	
Area size:	2,443 sq. mi.	69.8% White	German: 13.8%	Irish: 8.9%
Urban population:	87.0%	18.2% Black	Polish: 7.3%	
Rural population:	13.0%	0.8% Asian	**2004 Presidential Vote**	
Pop. 2000:	675,562	0.2% Native Am.	Kerry (D) 148,698	(55%)
Pop. 2005 (est):	694,785	0.0% Hawaiian	Bush (R) 118,417	(44%)
Median income:	$44,087	1.0% Two+ races	Other 2,214	(1%)
Poverty status:	10.5%	0.1% Other	**2000 Presidential Vote**	
Military veterans:	13.4%	10.0% Hispanic Origin	Gore (D) 141,163	(56%)
			Bush (R) 104,917	(42%)
			Other 4,759	(2%)
			Cook Partisan Voting Index: D + 8	

Occupation	Blue collar: 31.2%	White collar: 53.1%	Gray collar: 15.7%

At the southernmost shore of Lake Michigan is a part of America made by steel. Here, in the northwest corner of Indiana, where the water highway of the Great Lakes comes closest to the rail highway of the transcontinental railroads, America's leading capitalists a century ago identified an ideal site for manufacturing steel. On empty sand dunes United States Steel, then the nation's largest corporation, founded Gary in 1906 and named it for the company's chairman, Chicago Judge Elbert Gary. For nearly 70 years the steel mills attracted a diverse work force, like Chicago and quite unlike the rest of Indiana: Irish, Poles, Czechs, Ukrainians and blacks from the American South. Politics here has always been turbulent, from the Communist-led long and unsuccessful steel strike of 1919 to the racially polarized politics of the 1960s and 1970s. The city has been the setting for other historical events: the birthplace of rock star Michael Jackson and the name of a famous tune from the Broadway musical "The Music Man." But the tone of public life—the clash between union stewards and management foremen, between blacks and eastern European ethnics, between the stalwarts of different factions vying for control of Gary's massive City Hall—was always abrasive, like the clash of steel on steel.

Steel brought sudden growth and sudden depression to northwest Indiana. The massive storefronts built on Gary's aptly named Broadway bear witness to the confidence and exuberance of the 1920s. But today they stand vacant—vandalized, whole blocks burned down—witness to steel layoffs, crime waves and an acute sense of loss. The steel mills went cold during the Depression of the 1930s, but were thronged with workers during World War II, and in the years afterward their massiveness helped create the illusion that life in the steel towns of Gary, Hammond and East Chicago would go on forever just like it was in the 1950s. But technological advances replaced increasingly expensive workers with increasingly efficient machines. And the efforts to seal off the U.S. steel market from the world inevitably failed. The oil crunch of 1979 was the catalyst for change, reducing the demand for large-sized autos, the biggest customer for steel. Steel employed 70,000 workers in northwest Indiana in 1979, 35,000 a few years later, 19,000 in 2004. Obsolete mills were closed, old mills modernized and new ones built that cut the number of man-hours needed by two-thirds. Just-in-time methods were introduced, management and high-skill workers cooperated to engineer higher-quality, less expensive steel to meet customers' needs. For the last decade, Indiana has been the number one or two steel-producing state; in 2005, US Steel announced a $260 million project to modernize its largest blast furnace in Gary.

But as the steel industry was changing, Gary was falling almost into ruins—with "the same problems facing less-developed countries," said Nobel Prize-winning economist Joseph Stiglitz in 2006. As long ago as 1967, Gary elected a black mayor, Richard Hatcher, who was determined to use city government to cure poverty. But high crime rates gave Gary the national distinction as the "Murder Capital" for nine consecutive years with the most homicides per capita, and led to white flight to the suburbs. The city's population fell 12% in the 1990s to 102,000 and in 2005 to 97,000 (of whom 83% were black), far below its peak of 178,000 in 1960; in nearby majority-white Hammond, with many Hispanic immigrants, the population loss was much less. Local officials tried to promote the city's airport as a third Chicago-area airport, but with only limited success. After Hooters Air suspended operations in January 2006, the airport had no regularly scheduled passenger service; Chicago-based Boeing has parked its private jet fleet at the airport.

Indiana's 1st Congressional District stretches from Gary and Hammond along the Lake Michigan shore, east almost to Michigan City. It includes Lake County, 25% black and 12% Hispanic in 2000, and Porter County to the east, which includes Valparaiso, known locally as Valpo, notable for its annual Popcorn Festivals, honoring longtime resident and developer of 300 popcorn hybrids, Orville Redenbacher. The district includes three small Republican-leaning counties south of Gary, but nearly three-quarters of the population is in Lake County. This remains the most Democratic district in Republican-leaning Indiana, as it has been since the United Steelworkers' organizing drives of the late 1930s.

The congressman from the 1st District is Pete Visclosky, a Democrat first elected in 1984. Visclosky grew up in Lake County (his father was mayor of Gary in the early 1960s), went to college there and law school at Notre Dame. He practiced law, and then worked for six years for 1st District Congressman Adam Benjamin. Benjamin died suddenly in 1982 and Visclosky returned to Indiana. In 1984 he ran against Katie Hall, a black state senator who had been given the 1982 nomination— and thus the election, in this Democratic district—by Mayor Hatcher, then district party chairman. But Hall was able to win only 33% of the 1984 primary vote; Visclosky had 34% and another white candidate got 31%. In two later primaries Visclosky twice beat Hall by more than 20%.

Visclosky's voting record has trended moderate and he concentrates much of his effort on projects to help the local economy, especially the steel industry. He has a solid pro-union voting record. He is a leader of the Congressional Steel Caucus and has been vigilant in monitoring surges in steel imports. When George W. Bush was elected with critical help from steel-producing areas, Visclosky had greater leverage, and Bush did impose steel import quotas. But when the quotas were removed, Visclosky protested that Bush "stabbed the American steelworkers in the back." Visclosky, meanwhile, sought health benefits for unemployed and retired workers whose steel companies were unable to pay them, and he again called for closer monitoring of imports. In 2005, he joined a bipartisan group of House members calling for repeal of permanent trade relations with China, which he termed "a one-way street." He criticized Bush for rejecting a recommendation for relief to American pipe steel producers suffering from Chinese imports.

As senior Democrat—and now, chairman—of the Appropriations Subcommittee on Energy and Water Development, Visclosky has been well-positioned and adept in securing federal funding for projects in his district. He pushed through an exception to the Johnson Act, making Lake Michigan waters eligible for gambling and thus allowing riverboat casinos for Gary. In 2005, he took credit for $20 million for the "Marquette Plan" for projects on the shoreline plus another $15 million for local flood control projects. His longevity on Appropriations and the advanced age of the five Democrats more senior than him increases the prospect that he might one day chair the full committee.

At home, he appears secure. In heavily Republican 1994, with an opponent who spent more than $100,000, Visclosky lost some conservative suburbs and won by just 56%-44%. Since then he has won without difficulty.

SECOND DISTRICT

Rep. Joe Donnelly (D)

Elected 2006, 1st term; b. Sept. 29, 1955, Queens, NY; home, Granger; U. of Notre Dame, B.A. 1977, J.D. 1981; Catholic; married (Jill).

Elected Office: Mishawaka Marian High School Board, 1997-2001.

Professional Career: Practicing atty., 1981-96; Owner, Marking Solutions, 1996-2006.

DC Office: 1218 LHOB, 20515, 202-225-3915; Fax: 202-225-6798; Web site: donnelly.house.gov.

District Offices: La Porte, 219-326-6808 ext. 414; Logansport, 574-753-2671; Michigan City, 219-873-1403 ext. 308; South Bend, 574-288-2780.

Committees: *Agriculture* (24th of 25 D): Livestock, Dairy & Poultry; Conservation, Credit, Energy & Research. *Financial Services* (34th of 37 D): Housing & Community Opportunity; Capital Markets, Insurance & Government Sponsored Enterprises. *Veterans' Affairs* (13th of 16 D): Economic Opportunity.

Group Ratings and Key Votes: Newly Elected

Election Results

2006 general	Joe Donnelly (D)	103,561	(54%)	($1,561,420)
	Chris Chocola (R)	88,300	(46%)	($3,415,742)
2006 primary	Joe Donnelly (D)	30,589	(83%)	
	Steve Francis (D)	6,280	(17%)	
2004 general	Chris Chocola (R)	140,496	(54%)	($1,480,546)
	Joe Donnelly (D)	115,513	(45%)	($700,728)
	Other	3,346	(1%)	

The People		Race/Ethnic Origin	Ancestry	
Area size:	3,719 sq. mi.	84.4% White	German: 18.3% Irish: 8.8%	
Urban population:	72.8%	8.1% Black	USA: 6.4%	
Rural population:	27.2%	0.8% Asian	**2004 Presidential Vote**	
Pop. 2000:	675,766	0.3% Native Am.	Bush (R)	146,000	(56%)
Pop. 2005 (est):	685,371	0.0% Hawaiian	Kerry (D)	112,671	(43%)
Median income:	$40,381	1.3% Two+ races	Other	1,964	(1%)
Poverty status:	9.5%	0.1% Other	**2000 Presidential Vote**	
Military veterans:	13.5%	5.0% Hispanic Origin	Bush (R)	128,803	(53%)
			Gore (D)	107,344	(44%)
			Other	5,276	(2%)
			Cook Partisan Voting Index: R + 4	
Occupation	Blue collar: 34.7%	White collar: 50.7%	Gray collar: 14.6%	

When Notre Dame University was founded in 1842, Catholics were still a rarity in most of America and certainly rare on the limestone-bottomed plains of northern Indiana. This was still farm country and South Bend no more than a crossroads on the St. Joseph River. But by the 1920s, both had grown. Notre Dame, thanks to its football team, "the Fighting Irish," was the most famous Catholic university in the land, and South Bend was a significant industrial city, home of Studebaker and Bendix and dozens of other factories. In the past 50 years, Notre Dame has grown in size and reputation, but South Bend has had the experience of many Midwestern industrial cities: In the 1960s, Studebaker went out of business, in the early 1980s there were big layoffs at big factories, and in the early 1990s there were well-publicized layoffs in nearby Elkhart. But these high-visibility job losses were accompanied by the much less visible creation of jobs in small factories throughout the region. The work here requires more skill than did the old assembly lines, and the products must be more responsive to just-in-time prime contractors or computer-inventory retailers. In the late 1990s, many employers had trouble filling job openings, and the economic base was more secure than when it depended on the fate of two or three big companies. There have been painful layoffs since then as part of the nation's continuing industrial shrinkage, but nothing like the agony of 20 years before. In recent years, foreign automotive investment has flowed into the state economy with DaimlerChrysler now considering the construction of a new $550 million transmission plant in Kokomo.

The 2d Congressional District of Indiana is centered on South Bend, which for three decades has seen plenty of close congressional contests. This is an industrial and ethnic city—with one of the nation's largest percentage of Hungarian-Americans, plus a growing community of Mexicans—that has long been Democratic; so is LaPorte County around Michigan City. Elkhart County to the east is heavily Republican and conservative—there used to be a six-foot Ten Commandments monument in front of Elkhart City Hall until an ACLU lawsuit led to its removal. The 2d District also includes several counties on the limestone plains to the south down past the Wabash River. This is an area rural in appearance but with much small manufacturing; politically, it has been part of the Republican heartland since the party was created in the 1850s. Moderate Democrat Tim Roemer represented this area for 12 years before he retired in 2002; he later gained renown as a member of 9/11 Commission. Indiana Democrats drew the lines of the 2d to maximize their chance to hold it by including Democratic Michigan City, excluding much of heavily Republican Elkhart County and adding the industrial town of Kokomo at its southern edge. But Roemer did not run for reelection in 2002, and the partisan lines were not enough to elect a Democrat that year.

The new congressman from the 2d District is Joe Donnelly, a Democrat first elected in 2006. Donnelly was born in Massapequa, New York, and grew up on Long Island's South Shore. He attended the University of Notre Dame, earning an undergraduate degree in government and then a law degree in 1981. He practiced law in the area until 1996 when he opened Marking Solutions, a printing and rubber stamp company. Donnelly served on the state election board from 1988-1989. He ran unsuccessfully for the Democratic nomination in 1988 for state attorney general and in 1990 lost a bid for the state Senate. From 1997-2001, he served on the board, including a year as president, of a local Catholic high school.

Donnelly failed in his first attempt to run for Congress in 2004, his third consecutive election loss, when Republican incumbent Chris Chocola defeated him 54%-45%. Chocola, a businessman who was one of the wealthiest members of Congress, had won the open seat in 2002 even after Democrats had drawn the district to maximize their chances of holding it. In the 2004 race, Donnelly compared himself to former Congressman Tim Roemer and said he would be more independent of his party than Chocola. But he raised less than half as much money as Jill Long Thompson, the 2002 Democratic nominee, and the DCCC made the race a low priority.

The 2006 election cycle was a much more difficult political environment for Republicans like Chocola. At home, Republican Gov. Mitch Daniels' move to daylight saving time and privatization of the Indiana Toll Road, which runs through the district, proved unpopular. The liberal group MoveOn.org identified Chocola as an early target and ran negative television ads. This time, the DCCC took a much greater interest in the race by installing its choice for Donnelly's campaign manager and by elevating the race to its "Red to Blue" program. Republicans recognized the seriousness of his predicament: President Bush's first 2006 campaign visit for a House candidate was for Chocola, who collected about $650,000 from the February appearance. But the wealthy Chocola had not done enough to connect with the district's middle class workforce. Donnelly also made Bush's handling of the Iraq war an issue, but he declined to call for Defense Secretary Donald Rumsfeld's resignation out of fear it would give Republicans ammunition that could be used to paint him as a liberal. Chocola again outspent him by more than 2-to-1, spending over $3.4 million to

Donnelly's $1.5 million, a financial advantage that might have led the NRCC to pull its money out of the race in October; the DCCC, meanwhile, continued to fund it. Donnelly won the election 54%-46% and carried five of the district's 12 counties. Donnelly increased his margin in South Bend's St. Joseph County from 621 votes in 2004 to over 12,700 in 2006.

An opponent of abortion rights and federal stem cell research, Donnelly urged his party leadership to advance a moderate agenda in Congress. He secured a seat on the Financial Services Committee, which will prove beneficial to his future fundraising. Bush won this swing district twice; Republicans are likely to target Donnelly in 2008.

THIRD DISTRICT

Rep. Mark Souder (R)

Elected 1994, 7th term; b. July 18, 1950, Ft. Wayne; home, Ft. Wayne; IN U., B.S. 1972, Notre Dame U., M.B.A. 1974; Protestant; married (Diane).

Professional Career: Furniture salesman, 1976-83; Staff Dir., U.S. House Select Cmte. on Children, Youth & Families, 1984-89; Legis. Dir., U.S. Sen. Dan Coats, 1989-91, Dep. Chief of Staff, 1991-93.

DC Office: 2231 RHOB, 20515, 202-225-4436; Fax: 202-225-3479; Web site: www.house.gov/souder.

District Offices: Ft. Wayne, 260-424-3041; Goshen, 574-533-5802; Winona Lake, 574-269-1940.

Committees: *Education & Labor* (5th of 22 R): Early Childhood, Elementary & Secondary Education; Higher Education, Lifelong Learning & Competitiveness. *Homeland Security* (4th of 15 R): Border, Maritime & Global Counterterrorism (RMM); Emergency Communications, Preparedness & Response. *Oversight & Government Reform* (6th of 18 R): Domestic Policy.

Group Ratings

	ADA	ACLU	AFS	LCV	ITIC	NTU	COC	ACU	CFG	FRC
2006	0	14	0	0	100	55	100	88	54	100
2005	5	—	0	0	—	57	100	96	60	92

National Journal Ratings

	2005 LIB	—	2005 CONS	2006 LIB	—	2006 CONS
Economic	3%	—	94%	12%	—	86%
Social	21%	—	78%	17%	—	79%
Foreign	27%	—	71%	30%	—	67%

Key Votes of the 109th Congress

1. Estate Tax Repeal	Y	5. Limit Interstate Abortion	Y	9. Build Border Fence	Y
2. Limit CAFE Standards	Y	6. Extend Patriot Act	Y	10. CAFTA	Y
3. FY06 Spending Curb	Y	7. Bar Same Sex Marriage	Y	11. Oppose Iraq Withdrawal	Y
4. Drilling in ANWR	Y	8. Stem Cell Research $	N	12. Detainee Tribunals	Y

Election Results

2006 general	Mark Souder (R)	95,421	(54%)	($642,282)
	Thomas Hayhurst (D)	80,357	(46%)	($708,181)
2006 primary	Mark Souder (R)	39,449	(71%)	
	William Larsen (R)	15,845	(29%)	
2004 general	Mark Souder (R)	171,389	(69%)	($238,176)
	Maria Parra (D)	76,232	(31%)	($18,761)

Prior Winning Percentages: 2002 (63%); 2000 (62%); 1998 (63%); 1996 (58%); 1994 (55%)

The People		Race/Ethnic Origin	Ancestry		
Area size:	3,292 sq. mi.	87.6% White	German: 22.8%		USA: 8.4%
Urban population:	65.1%	5.6% Black	Irish: 7.1%		
Rural population:	34.9%	0.9% Asian	**2004 Presidential Vote**		
Pop. 2000:	675,457	0.2% Native Am.	Bush (R) 172,919		(68%)
Pop. 2005 (est):	701,925	0.0% Hawaiian	Kerry (D) 79,674		(31%)
Median income:	$44,013	1.1% Two+ races	Other 737		(0%)
Poverty status:	7.8%	0.1% Other	**2000 Presidential Vote**		
Military veterans:	11.9%	4.5% Hispanic Origin	Bush (R) 147,106		(66%)
			Gore (D) 73,775		(33%)
			Other 3,682		(2%)
			Cook Partisan Voting Index: R +16		

Occupation   Blue collar: 35.9%   White collar: 51.7%   Gray collar: 12.4%

The northeast corner of Indiana, in the center of a flat agricultural and manufacturing area, can claim to be the center of Middle America. Its first settlers were of New England Yankee stock, establishing orderly communities with public schools and even colleges. They were joined by German immigrants, who built tidy farms and their own civic institutions. In the northern part of the state there are hills and lakes, and the strange swamp that is the central focus of Gene Stratton Porter's children's classic, *A Girl of the Limberlost*. The one large city here, Fort Wayne, was built on the flat terrain along the Maumee River that flows to Toledo, Ohio. It grew as a factory town, surging ahead and then falling back as large factories, often tied to the auto industry, opened and closed over the years. As much as anything else, this part of Indiana is a place where people make things. Northwest of Fort Wayne on U.S. Route 33, Elkhart County is a manufacturing hub where local companies make everything from pharmaceuticals to musical instruments—oboes, bassoons, piccolos. The county is best known as the nation's manufacturing center for recreational vehicles ("I represent the biggest gas guzzling district in the U.S.," says the congressman), a business that flourished after the September 11 attacks as travelers stayed closer to home. Neighboring Kosciusko County is renowned for medical supplies; in Warsaw, the orthopedics manufacturing capital of the world, residents have been making orthopedic devices in for more than a century. But reflecting national trends, manufacturing jobs in the Fort Wayne area dropped by 22 per cent from 1998 to 2005. In April 2006, local officials announced construction in Claypool of a $135 million biodiesel complex, including a soybean processing plant, capable of producing 80 million gallons of fuel annually. This is a surprisingly diverse area. Its eclectic population mix includes a concentration of Amish that ranks with those in central Ohio and Lancaster, Pennsylvania, plus Central Americans, Bosnians, Somalis and the nation's largest population of dissident Burmese.

The 3d Congressional District of Indiana consists of most of eight counties in the northeast part of the state. This part of Indiana has been heavily Republican since the Civil War, though it has sometimes veered Democratic in times of economic distress. The seat recently has had members who have gone on to other high positions: Dan Quayle, elected here in 1976, later was elected senator and vice president, and Dan Coats, a Quayle aide elected here in 1980, succeeded to Quayle's Senate seat and served as ambassador to Germany for George W. Bush.

The congressman from the 3d District is Mark Souder (pronounced *SOW-dur*), a Republican first elected in 1994. Souder grew up in Grabill, 10 miles from Fort Wayne, where his Amish great-great-grandfather's family settled. There the family started Souders of Grabill in 1907, originally a harness shop and now a furniture store and manufacturer of store fixtures. As an undergraduate at Indiana University, where he was student body president, he wore a button, "I'm proud to be a square." Souder worked in the furniture business, returned to Grabill, then went to work in 1984 for Coats, as staff director of the House Select Committee on Children, Youth and Families. He moved with Coats to the Senate in 1989, where he served as his legislative director. In 1993, he returned to Fort Wayne and started running against Democrat Jill Long, who had won a special election to succeed Coats when he was appointed to the Senate. With a moderate record and a farm background, she was not an easy target. But Souder, after winning a six-candidate primary with 40%, raised more money. When the state Republican ticket ran far ahead of the Democrats, Souder won a 55%-45% victory.

Souder says that he is "most defined by the fact that I'm an evangelical Christian." He told an interviewer with the Fort Wayne *Journal-Gazette* that it "isn't like it takes away all problems. It's just that you get a peace about the problems." In Washington, despite his solidly conservative views, he initially was a rebel in the House, especially against his own party's leaders. His independence frequently left senior Republicans muttering. As a leader of the Conservative Action Team, Souder challenged House appropriators for excessive spending, including the close-to-home House members' office allowances. He voted against the balanced budget amendment because it did not require a supermajority to raise taxes. In the 2004 omnibus appropriation, he inserted a requirement for the Veterans' Administration to reexamine its plan to eliminate in-patient services at its Fort Wayne facility. He successfully fought the closing of the hospital in the 2005 base review. In February 2006, when he nominated John Shadegg in the contest to replace Tom DeLay as majority leader, he warned that the selection of Roy Blunt would tell the public "that we have not changed"; as a fallback, he said that John Boehner was a better alternative than Blunt.

Souder has been active on drug issues and blamed Bill Clinton's "half-hearted" anti-drug message for increased drug use by teens. As chairman of the Government Reform subcommittee dealing with criminal justice and drug policy, Souder held hearings on growing addiction to methamphetamines, and he blamed weak enforcement in the 1990s for reviving drug abuse problems. In 2004, the House passed his bill to rescind the District of Columbia's ban on gun ownership, but it died in the Senate. Before Republicans lost control of the House, Souder made considerable legislative progress. In March 2006, Bush signed his "Combat Methamphetamine Epidemic Act," as a rider on the extension of the Patriot Act. Souder called his measure the most comprehensive attack on meth trafficking; it included restrictions on consumer purchases, monitoring of sales at the wholesale level, and increased criminal enforcement. He also enacted a reauthorization of the Office of Drug Control Policy Act. To clarify a controversial Clinton-era law he helped enact that denied those with past drug convictions access to federal student loans, Souder inserted the "Drug-Free Student Loans" amendment in the deficit-reduction law that specifies only students enrolled in college at the time of their drug conviction can lose access to loans. He has worked for years to ensure that faith-based programs are eligible for federal funds, a cause that Bush has pursued. With Democrat Brian Baird, he formed a National Parks Caucus to assure adequate funding; he chaired hearings to document the shortfalls in the park system.

Souder has been comfortably reelected since 1994 against poorly funded opponents. In 2002, former Fort Wayne Mayor Paul Helmke challenged him in the primary. Helmke ran as a moderate and criticized Souder's use of congressional perks. Souder said that Helmke had been a liberal mayor and called him "a Clinton clone." He carried all eight counties to win by 60%-37%. He abandoned his original pledge to serve no more than 12 years. After a string of weak Democratic challengers, he faced credible opposition in 2006 from Tom Hayhurst, a retired pulmonary physician and Fort Wayne city council member for a decade. Hayhurst opposed repeal of the estate tax, called for affordable health care, and opposed making abortion illegal. Souder purchased sizable TV and radio advertising explaining his record; he objected when the NRCC orchestrated phone calls that attacked Hayhurst on immigration and taxes. In a dismal year for Indiana Republicans, Souder was outspent by Hayhurst and held to a 54%-46% win. Souder won all eight counties, though by fewer than 1,000 votes in Allen County, where he lost Fort Wayne. After the election, he returned as ranking Republican on Border, Maritime and Global Counterterrorism Subcommittee at Homeland Security.

FOURTH DISTRICT

Rep. Steve Buyer (R)

Elected 1992, 8th term; b. Nov. 26, 1958, Rensselaer; home, Monticello; The Citadel, B.S. 1980, Valparaiso U., J.D. 1984; Methodist; married (Joni).

Military Career: Army, 1984-87, 1990-91 (Persian Gulf); Army Reserves, 1980-84, 1987-present.

Professional Career: IN Dep. Atty. Gen., 1987-88; Vice Chmn., White Cnty. Repub. Party, 1988-90; Practicing atty., 1988-92.

DC Office: 2230 RHOB, 20515, 202-225-5037; Fax: 202-225-2267; Web site: stevebuyer.house.gov.

District Offices: Bedford, 812-277-9590; Monticello, 574-583-9819; Plainfield, 317-838-0404.

Committees: *Energy & Commerce* (14th of 26 R): Health; Energy & Air Quality. *Veterans' Affairs* (RMM of 13 R).

Group Ratings

	ADA	ACLU	AFS	LCV	ITIC	NTU	COC	ACU	CFG	FRC
2006	10	10	17	0	86	60	87	83	67	100
2005	0	—	13	0	—	61	93	96	72	92

National Journal Ratings

	2005 LIB	—	2005 CONS	2006 LIB	—	2006 CONS
Economic	21%	—	77%	11%	—	88%
Social	22%	—	77%	11%	—	85%
Foreign	23%	—	73%	15%	—	84%

Key Votes of the 109th Congress

1. Estate Tax Repeal	Y	5. Limit Interstate Abortion	Y	9. Build Border Fence	Y
2. Limit CAFE Standards	Y	6. Extend Patriot Act	Y	10. CAFTA	Y
3. FY06 Spending Curb	N	7. Bar Same Sex Marriage	Y	11. Oppose Iraq Withdrawal	Y
4. Drilling in ANWR	Y	8. Stem Cell Research $	N	12. Detainee Tribunals	Y

Election Results

2006 general	Steve Buyer (R)	111,057	(62%)	($536,985)
	David Sanders (D)	66,986	(38%)	($133,260)
2006 primary	Steve Buyer (R)	50,695	(73%)	
	Mike Campbell (R)	18,799	(27%)	
2004 general	Steve Buyer (R)	190,445	(69%)	($509,517)
	David Sanders (D)	77,574	(28%)	($15,480)
	Other	6,117	(2%)	

Prior Winning Percentages: 2002 (71%); 2000 (61%); 1998 (63%); 1996 (65%); 1994 (70%); 1992 (51%)

The People		Race/Ethnic Origin	Ancestry	
Area size:	4,033 sq. mi.	93.6% White	German: 17.0%	USA: 11.7%
Urban population:	68.2%	1.3% Black	Irish: 8.9%	
Rural population:	31.8%	1.5% Asian	**2004 Presidential Vote**	
Pop. 2000:	675,617	0.2% Native Am.	Bush (R) 196,010	(69%)
Pop. 2005 (est):	729,145	0.0% Hawaiian	Kerry (D) 85,179	(30%)
Median income:	$45,947	0.8% Two+ races	Other 1,700	(1%)
Poverty status:	8.0%	0.1% Other	**2000 Presidential Vote**	
Military veterans:	13.0%	2.6% Hispanic Origin	Bush (R) 156,747	(66%)
			Gore (D) 74,660	(31%)
			Other 5,739	(2%)
			Cook Partisan Voting Index: R +17	

Occupation   Blue collar: 29.6%   White collar: 56.5%   Gray collar: 13.9%

The landscape of central Indiana is some of the most prosaic in the United States, mostly flat, with neat farms and frame-bungalowed towns, looking mostly unchanged from many years ago. Across this landscape run some of the nation's chief transportation arteries. The earliest was the old National Road, from Baltimore to St. Louis, which was paralleled by U.S. 40 in the 1930s. Also here are the great east-west rail lines, on which famed railroad passenger trains like the old *Wabash Cannonball* rumbled along Indiana's Wabash River. Today the *Cannonball* no longer runs: People bounce around the Midwest on commuter airlines from small city to hub, and U.S. 40 has been replaced for through traffic by Interstate 70. The landscape still looks rural, and there are some large farms. But the economy here is more industrial, with small factories at crossroads and in courthouse towns. This is a part of America with little heritage from the early waves of immigration, relatively few blacks, and only a handful of Latin and Asian immigrants. Traditional cultural values have not been shaken so much here as in other parts of the nation.

The 4th Congressional District of Indiana covers much of this territory, running from Indiana's northern plains to its southern hills. It includes all or part of 12 counties in western Indiana, including the far western edge of Indianapolis and Marion County, and extends south past (but not including) Bloomington to Lawrence County, which was the source of the limestone used to rebuild the Pentagon after the September 11 attacks. The largest city is Lafayette, where the main business is Purdue University, Indiana's land-grant college and the alma mater of C-SPAN founder Brian Lamb. Growing and prosperous, the city expects to benefit from a 2006 partnership between Toyota and long-time local manufacturer Subaru to annually produce 100,000 Camry sedans. Lafayette tends to vote Republican. Even more Republican are the small counties and the suburban territory outside Indianapolis—places like fast-growing Hendricks County, which delivered 73% for George W. Bush in 2004.

The 4th District's congressman is Steve Buyer (pronounced *BOO-yer*), a Republican elected in 1992. Buyer grew up in White County, graduated from The Citadel, served in the Army, worked in Indianapolis and started a family law practice in Monticello, where he joined all the civic organizations. As a captain in the Army reserve, he was called to active duty in fall 1990, serving as legal adviser at a prisoner-of-war camp in the Persian Gulf. Buyer was enraged that most House Democrats, including then-Congressman Jim Jontz, voted against the war. After Buyer returned to Indiana, where he was White County Republican vice chairman, he began making speeches around the Hoosier heartland attacking Jontz on his Gulf War stand. Jontz was a skilled politician, but Buyer won 51%-49%.

As a mainstream conservative, Buyer has made a legislative mark in the House. On the Veterans' Affairs Committee, he spent much time on the lingering effects of Gulf War illness—which Buyer says is incorrectly referred to as "Gulf War syndrome." Still in the Army Reserves, Buyer was called to duty again in March 2003 during the war with Iraq. He returned home, collected his gear and had received a leave of absence from Speaker Dennis Hastert. But the Army later notified Buyer that his high-profile status jeopardized both him and his Army colleagues; he was not deployed. In 2004, he led an investigation that uncovered lapses in the hiring process for medical practitioners at VA hospitals. When he chaired the Military Personnel Subcommittee on Armed Services, he won enactment of what military officials call the greatest expansion of health care benefits for military retirees in at least three decades. But Buyer later took issue with Veterans Committee chairman Chris Smith over the implementation of that law, contending that some wealthy veterans had taken advantage of the new benefits, causing costs to soar. In January 2005, the Republican Steering Committee voted Smith out of the Veterans' Affairs Committee chairmanship, evidently because of his opposition to the leadership on budget and labor issues, and installed Buyer. During two years as chairman, his top priorities centered around creating a seamless transition between the Defense Department and the VA, including the development of an interoperable system to share electronic medical records. Following a major data theft in May 2006, the House approved his proposal for raising the oversight and protection levels of the VA's cybersecurity by creating an undersecretary of information services. To stop protestors from interfering with funerals for soldiers killed in Iraq, he filed a bill to restrict demonstrations at federal cemeteries.

Buyer can be blunt. In 2004, when he learned that House Democrats had requested that the United Nations send "monitors" for the presidential election, he furiously forced a vote stating the House's opposition. On the Energy and Commerce Committee, he focused on telecom and health care issues, including the creation of health savings accounts to pay for medical expenses. He defended the Indianapolis-based Eli Lilly Company, a major local employer, from industry critics—notably, fellow Republican Dan Burton from an adjacent district—who want to permit states to create preferred lists for mental health drugs for Medicaid patients.

Probably his most self-assured—and politically successful—strategy was his handling of redistricting in 2002. Democratic redistricters sliced up Buyer's old 5th District so that its remains were grafted onto seven of Indiana's nine surviving districts. Buyer chose to run in the district with his hometown of Monticello (population 5,723) in which he resided, and that happened to be the most heavily Republican, and that happened to include the least senior member of the delegation—first-term Republican Brian Kerns. This district, the new 4th, was 97% new to Buyer. He charged Democrats with trying to end his career because of his work as a manager of the impeachment of Bill Clinton and in the Florida recount. He emphasized that Kerns's home in Vigo County was 70 miles outside the new 4th, and argued that he should run against the 8th District's John Hostettler. Kerns said Buyer should run elsewhere, and when he didn't, Kerns seemed dumbfounded. Kerns's reelection effort moved in fits and starts. With Buyer outraising Kerns by more than 3–1, the result wasn't close. Buyer bested Kerns 55%-30%, and carried every county. Buyer has won easily since then.

FIFTH DISTRICT

Rep. Dan Burton (R)

Elected 1982, 13th term; b. June 21, 1938, Indianapolis; home, Indianapolis; IN U., 1958-59, Cincinnati Bible Seminary, 1959-60; Protestant; married (Samia).

Military Career: Army, 1956-57, Army Reserves, 1957-62.

Elected Office: IN House of Reps., 1966-68, 1976-80; IN Senate, 1968-70, 1980-82.

Professional Career: Real estate broker; Founder, Dan Burton Insurance Agency, 1968.

DC Office: 2308 RHOB, 20515, 202-225-2276; Fax: 202-225-0016; Web site: www.house.gov/burton.

District Offices: Indianapolis, 317-848-0201; Marion, 765-662-6770.

Committees: *Foreign Affairs* (3d of 23 R): Western Hemisphere (RMM); Asia, the Pacific & the Global Environment. *Oversight & Government Reform* (2d of 18 R): National Security & Foreign Affairs; Domestic Policy.

Group Ratings

	ADA	ACLU	AFS	LCV	ITIC	NTU	COC	ACU	CFG	FRC
2006	0	5	0	0	100	63	92	88	67	100
2005	0	—	0	0	—	63	92	96	80	100

National Journal Ratings

	2005 LIB	—	2005 CONS	2006 LIB	—	2006 CONS
Economic	13%	—	87%	20%	—	79%
Social	0%	—	89%	15%	—	85%
Foreign	0%	—	89%	0%	—	94%

Key Votes of the 109th Congress

1. Estate Tax Repeal	Y	5. Limit Interstate Abortion	Y	9. Build Border Fence	Y
2. Limit CAFE Standards	Y	6. Extend Patriot Act	Y	10. CAFTA	Y
3. FY06 Spending Curb	Y	7. Bar Same Sex Marriage	Y	11. Oppose Iraq Withdrawal	*
4. Drilling in ANWR	Y	8. Stem Cell Research $	N	12. Detainee Tribunals	Y

Election Results

2006 general	Dan Burton (R)	133,118	(65%)	($781,677)
	Katherine Carr (D)	64,362	(31%)	($12,956)
	Sheri Sharlow (Lib)	7,431	(4%)	
2006 primary	Dan Burton (R)	61,150	(84%)	
	Clayton Alfred (R)	6,869	(9%)	
	Victor Wakley (R)	4,822	(7%)	
2004 general	Dan Burton (R)	228,718	(72%)	($777,535)
	Katherine Carr (D)	82,637	(26%)	($10,229)
	Other	7,008	(2%)	

Prior Winning Percentages: 2002 (72%); 2000 (70%); 1998 (72%); 1996 (75%); 1994 (77%); 1992 (72%); 1990 (63%); 1988 (73%); 1986 (68%); 1984 (73%); 1982 (65%)

The People		Race/Ethnic Origin	Ancestry	
Area size:	3,291 sq. mi.	93.2% White	German: 18.7%	USA: 9.6%
Urban population:	74.5%	2.6% Black	Irish: 9.1%	
Rural population:	25.5%	1.3% Asian	**2004 Presidential Vote**	
Pop. 2000:	675,577	0.3% Native Am.	Bush (R) 233,215	(71%)
Pop. 2005 (est):	770,357	0.0% Hawaiian	Kerry (D) 91,955	(28%)
Median income:	$52,800	0.9% Two+ races	Other 1,506	(0%)
Poverty status:	5.2%	0.1% Other	**2000 Presidential Vote**	
Military veterans:	12.9%	1.6% Hispanic Origin	Bush (R) 187,489	(69%)
			Gore (D) 80,945	(30%)
			Other 5,110	(2%)
			Cook Partisan Voting Index: R +20	

Occupation   Blue collar: 24.4%   White collar: 63.2%   Gray collar: 12.4%

Indiana's most rapid growth these days is in the suburban ring of counties around Indianapolis, and especially in Hamilton County, directly north of the city. This is affluent suburbia, with subdivisions full of spacious houses on cul de sacs, shopping centers, office developments and life science complexes in what were not too long ago farm fields. Hamilton County's population increased from 82,000 in 1980 to 108,000 in 1990, 182,000 in 2000 and 250,000 in 2006—tripling in a quarter-century. It's now the fifth largest county in the state, soon to become the fourth, and it is certainly the most affluent: Rich people in the Indianapolis area used to be concentrated on the north side of the city; now they're more likely to be in Carmel, Fishers or Noblesville. These are not wealthy suburbs with a penchant for Democrats: Hamilton County is the most Republican county in Indiana and one of the most Republican in the nation. It voted 74%-24% for George W. Bush in 2004.

Almost half the people of the 5th Congressional District of Indiana live in Hamilton County. The district also includes the somewhat suburban but less affluent and Republican Hancock County (where the U.S. Lawn Mower Racing Association's championship is held every September) and parts of Shelby and Johnson Counties to the south. To the north the district also includes quite different parts of Indiana, with small industrial cities like Marion heavily dependent on the auto industry and now suffering from auto parts companies' bankruptcies and layoffs. Here the population is declining and new subdivisions just about nonexistent. In the far north are Miami County, the birthplace of Cole Porter, and Wabash and Huntington Counties, a cradle of vice presidents: Thomas Marshall, Woodrow Wilson's vice president, was from North Manchester in Wabash County, and Dan Quayle, the first George Bush's vice president, spent his high school years and later practiced law in Huntington (which was in the Fort Wayne-based district when Quayle represented it in the House).

The congressman from the 5th District is Dan Burton, an active and enthusiastic Republican first elected to the House in 1982. He has been running for office since he was in his 20s. He had a horrific childhood: His father was abusive and left the family, his mother worked as a waitress and bought the kids' clothes at Goodwill, his father ultimately kidnapped his mother and went to jail, and the kids were sent to the county home. "I think part of my aggressive nature is because of my childhood," Burton told author Studs Terkel in an interview for *Hope Dies Last*. "The highest moment of hope in my childhood was when we finally got away from my father. When I was five, six years old, my mother used to stand between me and him when he'd start to beat me and take the blows. I was black and blue from my neck to my ankles." As a teenager, Burton earned money shining shoes and at 18 enlisted in the Army. He never finished college but made his way up as a real estate broker and insurance salesman. He also ran for public office, often unsuccessfully. He was elected to the Indiana House in 1966, 1976 and 1978 and to the Indiana Senate in 1968 and 1980; he lost races for Congress in 1970 and 1972 and finally won in 1982 when a Republican legislature created a heavily Republican suburban seat.

For years, Burton was regarded by many Democrats as a nut, excitably pursuing lost causes. He opposed sanctions on South Africa, backed UNITA in Angola and Renamo in Mozambique, offered dozens of spending cuts that were overwhelmingly defeated, and pushed for universal mandatory AIDS testing. He has spent much time investigating the alleged link between thimerosal, a mercury-based vaccine preservative, and autism. He contends his grandson's autism was caused by thimerosal, and in December 2002, he bitterly criticized the Department of Homeland Security bill provision ending lawsuits against vaccine makers. He held hearings on vaccine safety and pressed for the removal of thimerosal; in May 2004, he criticized the Institutes of Medicine ("pawns for the pharmaceutical industry") when they found no link between thimerosal and autism. In December 2005 he voted present on the defense appropriation because it included an amendment that limited the liability of avian flu vaccine makers. His position on the issue puts him at odds with one of his district's major employers, Indianapolis-based Eli Lilly and Co., the company that developed thimerosal; some 5,000 Lilly employees live in the district, and he has received no contributions from Lilly's PAC since 2002. Burton is at odds with many Republicans on some other health issues. He is an enthusiastic supporter of alternative medicine and he favors importation of prescription drugs from Canada. He was one of the 25 Republican House members who voted against the Medicare/prescription drug bill; he argued that the drug benefit would cost too much. Some of his opinions he developed as his wife was battling cancer; she died in 2002 and in August 2006 he married her cancer doctor.

Burton has had some significant legislative successes but his biggest achievement was the Helms-Burton Act. It was a response to the Cuban Air Force's downing of the "Brothers to the Rescue" planes and it stated that foreign companies could be sued in American courts if, as part of business deals with Fidel Castro's regime, they took over property expropriated from American owners. Helms-Burton passed both houses in fall 1995 and was signed by Bill Clinton, who carried Florida in 1996 after losing it in 1992.

As chairman of the Government Reform Committee, he conducted tumultuous hearings on the Clinton-Gore campaign finance scandals from 1997 to 2000. Many Republicans were queasy about having Burton conduct the hearing; they felt he was too excitable and vulnerable to attack by Democrats and remembered with dismay his 1994 speech questioning whether White House counsel Vincent Foster had been murdered and his body moved. Burton promised a bipartisan approach but encountered early and fierce opposition; ranking Democrat Henry Waxman, one of the brainiest Democrats in the House, set the tone, calling it "a partisan witch hunt." Burton helped that impression along when, in reference to Clinton, he told The Indianapolis Star editorial board in April 1998, "This guy's a scumbag. That's why I'm after him." Burton faced great resistance –some 90 witnesses took the Fifth Amendment or left the country—and perhaps official retaliation: In July 1997, the FBI subpoenaed Burton's finance records of his House campaigns. Burton worked doggedly to get hold of memos to Attorney General Janet Reno with recommendations on dealing with Clinton-Gore campaign fundraising irregularities, or worse; he was still seeking them in 2002, when the Bush administration claimed executive privilege. In May 2000, when it was revealed that White House e-mails from 1996-98 sought in the investigation had been erased, Burton angrily sought an investigation, an independent counsel and he sent a criminal referral to the Justice Department; the e-mail stonewall continued until the end of the Clinton presidency. Burton has also tried to get internal Justice documents about an FBI scandal in which agents covered up evidence of crime by mobster informants in Boston from the 1960s to the 1980s and allowed an innocent man to go to jail for 30 years; citing that case, he has called for taking J. Edgar Hoover's name off the FBI headquarters. His efforts to get those documents were opposed by the Bush administration, and he harshly criticized the November 2001 Bush administration executive order which limited accessibility to current and previous White House documents and records; that prompted erstwhile critic Barney Frank to say, "I see now a genuine intellectual integrity in his approach."

Burton had to relinquish the Government Operations chairmanship in January 2003 because of House Republicans' six-year limit on committee chairmen; he was seeking the chairmanship of what was then the Middle East and South Asia Subcommittee of International Relations. But he has been a backer of Pakistan and critic of India's treatment of Sikhs and Kashmiris so instead he got the chairmanship of the Western Hemisphere Subcommittee, which he had held in 1995-96. In 2007 he became ranking minority member on the subcommittee; he sought that post on the full committee, but it went to the less senior Ileana Ros-Lehtinen. He was the only member of the House who opposed the 2007 restrictions on gifts and travel from lobbyists, as he had opposed earlier changes in 1995; he argued that full disclosure is sufficient.

For all the pasting Burton has taken from the national press, he has never been in trouble for reelection—not even when it was revealed in 1998 that he had fathered an illegitimate son some 15 years before. The woman had not notified Burton until her companion, long presumed to be the father, left her five years later. Burton took a blood test and afterward paid child support. Any district that contains Hamilton County will be heavily Republican, so the only real threat to Burton would be in a Republican primary. He already has one serious primary challenger for 2008: John McGoff, a former twice-elected Marion County Coroner, who has taken advantage of negative publicity surrounding Burton's decision to skip 19 House votes to play in a California golf tournament in January 2007.

SIXTH DISTRICT

Rep. Mike Pence (R)

Elected 2000, 4th term; b. June 7, 1959, Columbus; home, Elwood; Hanover Col., B.A. 1981, IN U., J.D. 1986; Protestant; married (Karen).

Professional Career: Practicing atty., 1986-91; Pres., IN Policy Review Fndt., 1991-93; Radio broadcaster, Network Indiana, 1992-99; Host, Pub. Affairs TV, UPN-23, 1995-99.

DC Office: 1317 LHOB, 20515, 202-225-3021; Fax: 202-225-3382; Web site: mikepence.house.gov.

District Offices: Anderson, 765-640-2919; Muncie, 765-747-5566; Richmond, 765-962-2883.

Committees: *Foreign Affairs* (13th of 23 R): Middle East & South Asia (RMM). *Judiciary* (11th of 17 R): The Constitution, Civil Rights & Civil Liberties; Courts, the Internet & Intellectual Property.

Group Ratings

	ADA	ACLU	AFS	LCV	ITIC	NTU	COC	ACU	CFG	FRC
2006	15	14	0	0	100	83	100	100	97	100
2005	0	—	0	6	—	75	92	100	100	100

National Journal Ratings

	2005 LIB	—	2005 CONS		2006 LIB	—	2006 CONS
Economic	0%	—	97%		21%	—	77%
Social	14%	—	85%		30%	—	70%
Foreign	16%	—	84%		0%	—	94%

Key Votes of the 109th Congress

1. Estate Tax Repeal	Y	5. Limit Interstate Abortion	Y	9. Build Border Fence	Y
2. Limit CAFE Standards	Y	6. Extend Patriot Act	Y	10. CAFTA	Y
3. FY06 Spending Curb	Y	7. Bar Same Sex Marriage	Y	11. Oppose Iraq Withdrawal	Y
4. Drilling in ANWR	Y	8. Stem Cell Research $	N	12. Detainee Tribunals	Y

Election Results

2006 general	Mike Pence (R)	115,266	(60%)	($1,319,503)
	Barry Welsh (D)	76,812	(40%)	($45,424)
2006 primary	Mike Pence (R)	52,188	(86%)	
	George Holland (R)	8,406	(14%)	
2004 general	Mike Pence (R)	182,529	(67%)	($1,010,228)
	Melina Fox (D)	85,123	(31%)	
	Other	4,397	(2%)	

Prior Winning Percentages: 2002 (64%); 2000 (51%)

The People		Race/Ethnic Origin	Ancestry	
Area size:	5,572 sq. mi.	93.4% White	German: 16.8% USA: 12.7%	
Urban population:	59.3%	3.8% Black	English: 7.7%	
Rural population:	40.7%	0.5% Asian	**2004 Presidential Vote**	
Pop. 2000:	675,669	0.2% Native Am.	Bush (R) 177,214	(64%)
Pop. 2005 (est):	670,889	0.0% Hawaiian	Kerry (D) 97,781	(35%)
Median income:	$39,002	0.8% Two+ races	Other 2,096	(1%)
Poverty status:	9.7%	0.1% Other	**2000 Presidential Vote**	
Military veterans:	13.6%	1.3% Hispanic Origin	Bush (R) 148,415	(58%)
			Gore (D) 100,231	(40%)
			Other 5,090	(2%)
			Cook Partisan Voting Index: R +11	

Occupation	Blue collar: 35.0%	White collar: 49.7%	Gray collar: 15.3%

Muncie, Indiana, became famous as the "Middletown" that sociologists Robert and Helen Lynd lived in and reported on in 1924-25 and again in 1935, and where a team of sociologists investigated again in 1976-78. The Lynds were attracted to Muncie by its typicalness—"every small city from Maine to

California," said *Life* magazine. But it wasn't exactly: It was a factory town in a country still almost half rural, it was almost entirely Protestant and Northern in a country one-quarter Catholic and one-third Southern. Muncie was more typical in being culturally homogeneous but economically riven. In the 1920s, when General Motors opened its first Chevrolet plant in Muncie, the city celebrated its common values and was loath to admit its economic disparities; in the 1930s they came out into the open when Muncie, like much of the industrial Midwest, was unionized in what were sometimes violent uprisings. Workers who were joining CIO unions and voting for Democrats fiercely opposed the business elite—local bankers, merchants, GM executives and the Ball family's glass company. Partisan politics took on the sharp, bitter tone of a struggle for wealth between two rival classes whose claims seemed irreconcilable. Echoes of this class-warfare politics reverberate only faintly today. They grow louder with local economic distress, when the Ball headquarters moved to Colorado in 1998 and as Muncie continues to suffer with layoffs. In March 2006, GM closed its local manual transmission plant, which had opened in 1935 and once had 3,000 workers. The loss was tempered by the announcement three months later that Honda would build a car assembly plant on farmland in Greensburg, about 60 miles south of Muncie and on I-74.

There are higher Democratic percentages in towns with union traditions, like Muncie and Anderson, than in others such as Richmond. But Indiana's more recent prosperity, based on high-skill manufacturing, has brought something like a political consensus here for tax cuts, trimmed budgets and quiet support of traditional values, with strong support for candidates of either party who agree. Basketball is the civic religion here. Indiana has nine of the nation's 10 largest high school gyms; The Fieldhouse, in New Castle near the Indiana Basketball Hall of Fame, is number one. Also at hand is Tom Raper Inc. in Richmond, the nation's largest RV dealer.

The 6th Congressional District of Indiana covers most of the east-central part of the state. It includes Muncie and Anderson in the north; and Richmond, founded by a major branch of American Quakers and the home of their Earlham College. In the north and south are suburban fringes of Fort Wayne and Cincinnati. The district is solidly Republican in presidential politics, but has been a swing district in some state races.

The congressman from the 6th District is Mike Pence, a Republican first elected in 2000. He grew up in Columbus as a John F. Kennedy-admiring Catholic but graduated from Hanover College as a Republican evangelical Christian. He got his law degree from Indiana University, then practiced law. Starting before he was 30, he ran as the Republican nominee for this seat in 1988 and 1990 against longtime Democratic Congressman Philip Sharp, then wrote an article after the second contest called "Confessions of a Negative Campaigner," in which he apologized for running negative advertisements. He was president of the conservative Indiana Policy Review Foundation, a think tank based in Fort Wayne, and began broadcasting "The Mike Pence Show," a conservative talk radio program that was syndicated statewide starting in 1994 and lasted until he launched his 2000 campaign.

The seat opened up when Republican Congressman David McIntosh left to challenge Governor Frank O'Bannon. In the six-candidate Republican primary, Pence beat state Representative Jeff Linder, 44%-24%. Robert Rock, Anderson lawyer and son of former Lieutenant Governor Robert Rock, won the Democratic primary. The general election became complicated when Bill Frazier, a former Republican state senator and four-time loser against Sharp, entered the race as an independent after the primary. All three candidates opposed abortion rights and gun control, and supported increased military spending; Frazier tried to tap into populist sentiment. Rock, a former Marine, attacked Pence for not serving in the military (Pence was 13 when the draft was abolished and U.S. troops left Vietnam) and supported tax cuts for middle-income families. Pence called for across-the-board tax cuts, and reform of Medicare financing. Pence won 51% to 39% for Rock and 9% for Frazier. He has won reelection easily.

Pence quickly made his mark as one of the House's more outspoken conservative members. He antagonized the business community by abandoning the bankruptcy bill because he objected to a provision on abortion. As the only House member to become a plaintiff in the lawsuit challenging the constitutionality of the McCain-Feingold campaign finance law, Pence said that Senator John McCain was "so deep in bed with the Democrats that his feet are coming out of the bottom of the sheets." He was one of 33 House Republicans to vote against final action on George W. Bush's education bill, and one of 25 to oppose the Medicare/prescription drug bill as too costly; he claimed vindication when budget estimates showed rising costs, though the costs eventually dropped. He did vote for the big-spending farm bill in 2002, conceding, "I don't have clean hands"; later, he voiced regret about his vote. With Richard Lugar, he filed in 2005 a federal shield bill to protect journalists. He was the first House member to install a radio studio in his office.

In 2005, Pence took over as chairman of the Republican Study Committee, and promoted greater attention to the party's conservative message. "We win as conservatives when we communicate," Pence said. "If you can't communicate, you can't govern." Cable TV talk shows producers often issue invites because they find him smart and charming. He likes to call himself, "Rush Limbaugh on decaf." He placed a strong emphasis on the need to control federal spending, advocating changes in how Congress handles the budget. Pence's group worked with Majority Whip Roy Blunt and Budget Committee Chairman Jim Nussle to impose procedural roadblocks on appropriations bills that exceed annual spending limits. Although some House insiders dismissed the outcome as a "fig leaf," Pence contended that the change would increase budget discipline. He has shown skill and good timing in making political moves. When Majority Leader Tom DeLay in September 2005 said that it would be difficult to offset the budget costs of cleaning up for Katrina because Republicans already had cut most waste in government, Pence quickly called a press conference to document for reporters and TV cameras $24 billion of proposed spending cuts. "Katrina broke my heart," he said. "But we must not let Katrina break the bank." GOP leaders were miffed with his stunt and appropriators spotlighted the earmarks he had secured for his own district. Pence changed the terms of debate, though not the eventual outcome. The conservative publication *Human Events* named him Man of the Year in 2005.

In 2006, his career took some unexpected twists. On immigration, he teamed with Senator Kay Bailey Hutchison to file what they hoped would become a compromise proposal to break the deadlock between the hard-line approach of House Republicans and the bipartisan deal in the Senate. Their plan would strengthen security along the border with Mexico and send home illegal immigrants, but permit most of them to return quickly. He won an audience with President Bush but conservative activist Phyllis Schlafly called the proposal "a sick joke." Republican leaders abandoned hope that the lame-duck session could yield a deal on immigration reform, and Pence's plan went nowhere. Pence, meanwhile, hoped that his RSC activism could lead to a bid for a GOP leadership post. When Tom DeLay gave up his post in January 2006, he decided not to run and said that he would seek to increase conservative influence. After the November election, he decided to run for minority leader. He told Republicans that the results showed, "We didn't just lose our majority. I believe we lost our way." But John Boehner, who had spent less than a year as majority leader, distanced himself from the leadership failures and embraced most conservative principles, including a leaner budget and entitlement reforms. Pence fared poorly in the showdown, with just 27 votes to 168 for Boehner. He recovered with the post of ranking Republican on the Middle East and South Asia Subcommittee at International Relations, and became a favorite conservative spokesman on the talk shows.

Back home, some speculate that he might run for a Senate seat in the next few years, in the event one opens up.

SEVENTH DISTRICT

Rep. Julia Carson (D)

Elected 1996, 6th term; b. July 8, 1938, Louisville, KY; home, Indianapolis; attended Martin U., IN U.-Purdue U. Indianapolis; Baptist; divorced.

Elected Office: IN House of Reps., 1972-76; IN Senate, 1976-90; Marion Cty. Center Township Trustee, 1991-96.

Professional Career: Secy., UAW, 1962-63; Legis. Aide, U.S. Rep. Andy Jacobs, 1965-72.

DC Office: 2455 RHOB, 20515, 202-225-4011; Fax: 202-225-5633; Web site: www.juliacarson.house.gov.

District Offices: Indianapolis, 317-283-6516.

Committees: *Financial Services* (9th of 37 D): Housing & Community Opportunity; Financial Institutions & Consumer Credit. *Transportation & Infrastructure* (18th of 41 D): Railroads, Pipelines & Hazardous Materials; Highways & Transit.

Group Ratings

	ADA	ACLU	AFS	LCV	ITIC	NTU	COC	ACU	CFG	FRC
2006	90	100	100	100	67	9	43	4	4	0
2005	100	—	100	89	—	14	40	0	7	0

National Journal Ratings

	2005 LIB	—	2005 CONS		2006 LIB	—	2006 CONS
Economic	79%	—	21%		94%	—	0%
Social	89%	—	11%		92%	—	7%
Foreign	83%	—	17%		83%	—	14%

Key Votes of the 109th Congress

1. Estate Tax Repeal	N	5. Limit Interstate Abortion	N	9. Build Border Fence	N
2. Limit CAFE Standards	Y	6. Extend Patriot Act	N	10. CAFTA	N
3. FY06 Spending Curb	N	7. Bar Same Sex Marriage	N	11. Oppose Iraq Withdrawal	N
4. Drilling in ANWR	N	8. Stem Cell Research $	Y	12. Detainee Tribunals	N

Election Results

2006 general	Julia Carson (D)	74,750	(54%)	($604,962)
	Eric Dickerson (R)	64,304	(46%)	($74,288)
2006 primary	Julia Carson (D)	29,503	(81%)	
	Kris Kiser (D)	4,052	(11%)	
	Bob Hidalgo (D)	1,690	(5%)	
	Other	1,036	(3%)	
2004 general	Julia Carson (D)	121,303	(54%)	($419,603)
	Andy Horning (R)	97,491	(44%)	($25,303)
	Other	4,381	(2%)	

Prior Winning Percentages: 2002 (53%); 2000 (59%); 1998 (58%); 1996 (53%)

The People		Race/Ethnic Origin	Ancestry	
Area size:	265 sq. mi.	63.0% White	German: 12.3% Irish: 7.8%	
Urban population:	99.7%	29.4% Black	USA: 7.8%	
Rural population:	0.3%	1.3% Asian	**2004 Presidential Vote**	
Pop. 2000:	675,674	0.2% Native Am.	Kerry (D)	130,779 (58%)
Pop. 2005 (est):	641,626	0.0% Hawaiian	Bush (R)	93,347 (42%)
Median income:	$36,522	1.5% Two+ races	**2000 Presidential Vote**	
Poverty status:	13.5%	0.2% Other	Gore (D)	109,800 (55%)
Military veterans:	12.6%	4.4% Hispanic Origin	Bush (R)	84,362 (43%)
			Other	3,795 (2%)
			Cook Partisan Voting Index: D + 9	

Occupation	Blue collar: 26.2%	White collar: 57.7%	Gray collar: 16.1%

Indianapolis, radiating outward from the Soldiers and Sailors statue in Monument Circle, is precisely at the center of Indiana, dominating it as few other cities do a state. What the locals once disparaged as Nap Town has become a thriving metropolis, including downtown. It is the political and governmental capital, industrial and financial center, and the intellectual center of Indiana as well. It is symmetrically laid out: Just to the west of the circle is the state Capitol, to the north is the American Legion headquarters, to the east is the City-County building, and to the south is the Circle Center mall, and the RCA Dome (formerly Hoosier Dome). Farther out are some classic and some new Indianapolis institutions: the Indiana University Medical Center, the Convention Center, the Eiteljorg Museum of Native American and Western Art and the new Indiana State Museum, Conseco Fieldhouse and the NCAA headquarters. Indianapolis has become the nation's amateur sports capital, especially for basketball, and it is a popular place for religious conventions. The city also has the world's biggest children's museum. In 2006, a Brookings Institution study found that Indianapolis had the highest job growth of the 25 large Rust Belt cities.

Politically, Indianapolis has long had robust competition in national as well as local races. Republicans held the mayor's office from 1967, when Richard Lugar won it, until 1999, when Stephen Goldsmith retired and became an adviser to George W. Bush. Lugar expanded Indianapolis's city limits to include all of Marion County in UniGov, which made it a solidly Republican constituency then. But more recently affluent young people have been moving to counties farther out, and Marion County has been trending Democratic. In 2004, Marion County voted for John Kerry by 51%-49%, even as seven surrounding suburban counties gave Bush 70% to 75% of their votes.

Indiana's 7th Congressional District includes all of Indianapolis and most of Marion County. It includes all of Center Township, a Democratic stronghold with a large black population and gentrified middle class, but does not include all of the affluent, Republican northern edge of the county. It extends west to include Speedway, where the Indianapolis 500 has been held on a 2.5 mile track since 1911, southward and east to modest neighborhoods, and includes Amtrak's largest repair yard in Beech Grove. The Mexican population, which nearly tripled in size during the 1990s, is the newest immigrant community; the 60% increase in Hispanic-owned businesses from 1997 to 2002 was twice the national average. Within these boundaries, the 7th District leans Democratic, and it gave Bill Clinton, Al Gore and John Kerry solid margins.

The congresswoman from the 7th District is Julia Carson, a Democrat first elected in 1996. Carson was born to an unmarried teenage mother and grew up in poverty, working as a waitress, newspaper deliverer and summer farm laborer; she can remember going to the welfare office for a ration of cornmeal and lard. As a divorced mother, she raised two children and then two grandchildren. In 1965 she was hired away from her job as a secretary at UAW Local 550 by newly-elected Congressman Andy Jacobs to do casework in his Indianapolis office. When his election prospects looked dim in 1972 (he did lose, but won the seat back two years later), he encouraged Carson to run for the state House; she won, then was elected to the state Senate in 1976. In 1990 she was elected as Center Township trustee, the position responsible for running welfare in central Indianapolis. In 1996, when Jacobs retired, Carson decided to run. She won his endorsement and that of the local Democratic organization. She was outspent by former prosecutor and party chairman Ann DeLaney, but won the primary 49%-31%. The Republican nominee was Virginia Blankenbaker, a stockbroker and state senator. In this race between two grandmothers, both were pro-choice on abortion and against the death penalty. Many commentators wondered whether a black Democrat could beat a white Republican in this district, but Carson raised almost as much money as Blankenbaker; she won 53%-45%.

Carson has compiled a liberal voting record, but chronic health problems have limited her activity and impact. She was sworn into office from her hospital bed after heart surgery in January 1997, and was hospitalized in 1999 with a serious case of pneumonia. In 2004, she missed close to 200 House votes, complaining of a lack of energy; her doctor imposed a diet and exercise regimen, and halted her weekly commute to Washington. Carson can be unpredictable. One of the last House members to decide how to vote on normal trade relations with China, she spent the final hours before the vote chatting with President Clinton for 45 minutes at the White House, listening to union officials, and then talking to CNN. Her vote for the measure left organized labor steaming, but its state officials supported her reelection because they liked her overall record. In November 2001, human-rights concerns caused her to agonize over the anti-terrorism bill, which she finally supported. She voted against the war in Iraq, plus supplemental spending bills to pay for it. In April 2005, when the city-county council opposed a bill to prohibit mistreatment of gays and transgendered persons, she lamented, "I see the erosion of the Democratic Party, which makes me nervous."

Carson has faced serious competition at home. In 2002, public affairs specialist and former Senate Republican aide Brose McVey ran, saying that Indianapolis needs "a congressman with energy and creativity" and that Carson was "out of step with her own constituency." Carson cited the federal funds that she delivered for local development and anti-violence programs; she said that Congress should put "the skids on the tax cuts" until the economy strengthened. McVey raised large amounts from the local business community and received national Republican backing in an ad that accused Carson of not paying her property taxes on time from 1997 to 2001. During their final pre-election debate, Carson walked off the stage to protest "the lowest common denominator" and "racial polarization" campaign run by McVey. Using that message to motivate her strong grass-roots network, Carson won 53%-44%. In 2004 her Republican opponent raised little money and was unable to arrange joint appearances; when the *Indianapolis Star* endorsed Carson, he protested outside its offices and burned a copy of the newspaper. Still, Carson won by only 54%-44%, suggesting that there is an entrenched anti-Carson (as well as a pro-Carson) vote. Carson, who said during the campaign that her work was not limited to votes in the House, returned to the hospital an hour after her victory speech but claimed that she was visiting a friend. She accused political rivals of fueling speculation about her health. In 2006, Republicans nominated Eric Dickerson—a Buick dealer, not the former running back with the Indianapolis Colts football team. He had problems with modest fundraising and unpaid bank loans, which forced him to sell his dealership. Dickerson's campaign slogan: "A seat in Congress is a terrible thing to waste." In an excellent year for Democrats, Carson struggled to rally her base. But she prevailed, 54% to 46%.

Carson's weak 2006 performance and questions about her health have sparked speculation that she may soon retire. One possible successor is her grandson Andre Carson, who has been active in local Democratic politics and who filed in August 2007 to run for a vacant seat on the city-county council.

EIGHTH DISTRICT

Rep. Brad Ellsworth (D)

Elected 2006, 1st term; b. Sept. 11, 1958, Huntingburg; home, Evansville; U. of S. IN, B.S. 1981, IN St. U., M.A. 1993; Catholic; married (Beth).

Elected Office: Vanderburgh Cnty. Sheriff, 1998-2006.

Professional Career: Chief Deputy, Vanderburgh Cnty. Sheriff's Office, 1982-98.

DC Office: 513 CHOB, 20515, 202-225-4636; Fax: 202-225-3284; Web site: www.ellsworth.house.gov.

District Offices: Evansville, 812-465-6484; Terre Haute, 812-232-0523.

Committees: *Agriculture* (14th of 25 D): Conservation, Credit, Energy & Research; General Farm Commodities & Risk Management. *Armed Services* (21st of 34 D): Seapower & Expeditionary Forces; Terrorism, Unconventional Threats & Capabilities. *Small Business* (14th of 18 D): Rural & Urban Entrepreneurship; Finance & Tax.

Group Ratings and Key Votes: Newly Elected

Election Results

2006 general	Brad Ellsworth (D) 131,019	(61%)	($1,742,341)
	John Hostettler (R) 83,704	(39%)	($580,161)
2006 primary	Brad Ellsworth (D) .... unopposed		
2004 general	John Hostettler (R) 145,576	(53%)	($494,781)
	Jon Jennings (D) 121,522	(45%)	($1,504,920)
	Other 5,680	(2%)	

The People		Race/Ethnic Origin	Ancestry	
Area size:	7,132 sq. mi.	93.7% White	German: 18.1%	USA: 11.9%
Urban population:	58.1%	3.7% Black	Irish: 8.1%	
Rural population:	41.9%	0.6% Asian	**2004 Presidential Vote**	
Pop. 2000:	675,564	0.2% Native Am.	Bush (R) 170,390	(62%)
Pop. 2005 (est):	680,251	0.0% Hawaiian	Kerry (D) 104,625	(38%)
Median income:	$36,732	0.8% Two+ races	Other 2,006	(1%)
Poverty status:	10.7%	0.1% Other	**2000 Presidential Vote**	
Military veterans:	13.9%	0.9% Hispanic Origin	Bush (R) 144,848	(56%)
			Gore (D) 106,850	(42%)
			Other 4,808	(2%)
			Cook Partisan Voting Index: R + 9	
Occupation	Blue collar: 31.9%	White collar: 51.9%	Gray collar: 16.2%	

"Evansville," wrote John Bartlow Martin in 1947, "is the capital of a tri-state area comprising the neglected tag ends of Indiana, Kentucky and Illinois." It was a factory town then, building car parts and refrigerators, drawing workers from Kentucky, Tennessee and the picturesque but not very fertile hills of southern Indiana. Today Evansville has become the headquarters for many mid-size companies, bringing with them many high-paying and skilled jobs. Car parts still get made here, though it's auto assembly that helps anchor the local manufacturing economy. Toyota in 2000 opened a plant in nearby Princeton that builds SUVs and minivans and employs 5,200 workers, some making $28 an hour. It has seen hard times, such as the terrible flood of March 1997 and a

November 2005 tornado that killed 24, but it also has Indiana's first riverboat casino and claims to have the nation's second largest street festival, second only to New Orleans's Mardi Gras celebration.

Evansville is one of two major focuses of the 8th Congressional District, which covers most of southwest and west central Indiana. The other, in Vigo County, is Terre Haute, an old manufacturing town and the boyhood home of Socialist Eugene Debs. It hosts a maximum-security penitentiary, which includes the only federal death chamber, where Oklahoma City bomber Timothy McVeigh was executed in June 2001. This southwest corner of Indiana was the first part of the state settled by whites. Vincennes, now a small town on the banks of the Wabash River, was once the metropolis of Indiana, and Scottish philanthropist and visionary Robert Owen established the town of New Harmony downstream. Owen's son was the first congressman from the area, elected in 1842 and 1844. Southern Indiana is ancestrally Democratic, just as northern Indiana is ancestrally Republican; these southern counties were hostile to the Civil War. In New Deal times, workers in Evansville moved again toward the Democrats.

The result has been a very close political balance, and this district has become known as the "Bloody Eighth" for its tight congressional races. At one point in the 1970s it elected four different congressmen in four successive elections. In 1984, the state certified the Republican as the winner by exactly 34 votes, but the Democratic U.S. House, in a fight that left many Republican members bitterly aggrieved, overturned the result. Since then, it has been as fiercely contested as ever. The trend in presidential politics, however, is away from national Democrats: Bill Clinton twice carried it by 2%, but in 2000 George W. Bush won 56% followed by 62% in 2004.

The new congressman from the 8th District is Brad Ellsworth, a Democrat elected in 2006. He was born in Jasper, not far outside the current district, and his family moved to Evansville when he was 10 so his father could take a job as crane operator at a nearby Alcoa plant. He graduated in 1981 from what was then called Indiana State University at Evansville, where he worked in the Sears paint and hardware departments to pay for college, and joined the Vanderburgh County sheriff's department as a deputy a year later. Ellsworth steadily rose through the ranks while also earning a master's degree in criminology during weekend courses at Indiana State University. He easily won his first election as county sheriff in 1998 and ran unopposed in 2002. During his eight years as sheriff, Ellsworth became a familiar name in Vanderburgh County, which is part of the district's largest media market.

Ellsworth entered the race early against John Hostettler, a conservative Republican iconoclast who had held the seat for six terms. Hostettler had never won with more than 53% of the vote, and his policy of never accepting PAC donations made him a poor fundraiser and a perennial Democratic target. He frequently bucked party leadership and took unconventional positions, such as votes against the 1995 balanced budget amendment, the Violence Against Women Act and the use of force against Iraq. Republican strategists each election cycle worried about Hostettler's re-election, but also took comfort in his uncanny ability to eke out victories by mobilizing support among anti-abortion and Christian conservative groups.

After a string of disappointing challengers, Democrats thought they'd found the ideal candidate for this culturally conservative district. Ellsworth supports gun ownership rights, and he opposes abortion, gay marriage and a hasty withdrawal of troops from Iraq. He could run on a quarter century of local law enforcement experience. When a tornado devastated parts of Southern Indiana in November 2005, Ellsworth was the face of the disaster recovery; Hostettler was nearly invisible. Hostettler was also in the uncomfortable position of asking for federal disaster aid just two months after he had voted against Hurricane Katrina relief.

Hostettler made relatively few appearances during the campaign and did not run a campaign ad until October, leading to rumors that he had given up the race. In October he did run a radio spot, in which an announcer impersonated Clint Eastwood's *Dirty Harry* character and warned that a vote for Ellsworth would be a vote for Nancy Pelosi as House speaker. "Pelosi will then put in motion her radical plan to advance the homosexual agenda," the announcer warned. The attacks alienated many women, while most voters did not know who Pelosi was and were baffled by the attacks against her. Ellsworth shone as a top-tier candidate for Democrats. Weeks before the election, *The Washington Post* featured a photo of the "swaggering Indiana sheriff" on the front page with a story about the unusually good looks of Democratic candidates running in 2006. Hostettler's lackluster campaign was not enough to overcome the unpopularity of President Bush and Governor Mitch Daniels. Nor could it trump Ellsworth's strong candidacy and financial advantage: Ellsworth had spent more than $1.7 million, more than three times Hostettler's $580,000 campaign. On Election Day, Ellsworth crushed Hostettler 61%-39%—a stunningly weak election performance for a non-scandal-ridden incumbent. Ellsworth carried 14 of the district's 18 counties, beat Hostettler by 11,500 votes in Vigo County and by nearly 15,000 more votes in Vanderburgh County (63%-37%).

NINTH DISTRICT

Rep. Baron Hill (D)

Elected 2006, 4th term; b. June 23, 1953, Seymour; home, Seymour; Furman U., B.A. 1975; Methodist; married (Betty).

Elected Office: IN House of Reps., 1982-90; U.S. House of Reps., 1998-2004.

Professional Career: The Hill Agency (insurance), 1975-90; Exec. Dir., IN Student Assistance Comm., 1990-94; Financial analyst, Merrill Lynch, 1994-98; Sr. Advisor, mCapitol Management, 2005-06.

DC Office: 223 CHOB, 20515, 202-225-5315; Fax: 202-226-6866; Web site: baronhill.house.gov.

District Offices: Bloomington, 812-336-3000; Jeffersonville, 812-288-3999.

Committees: *Energy & Commerce* (31st of 31 D): Commerce, Trade & Consumer Protection; Telecommunications & the Internet; Environment & Hazardous Materials. *Joint Economic Committee* (3d of 10 D). *Science & Technology* (22d of 24 D): Research & Science Education.

Group Ratings and Key Votes: Newly Elected

Election Results

2006 general	Baron Hill (D)	110,454	(50%)	($1,888,695)
	Mike Sodrel (R)	100,469	(45%)	($2,724,285)
	Eric Schansberg (Lib)	9,893	(4%)	($22,120)
2006 primary	Baron Hill (D)	53,883	(79%)	
	Gretchen Clearwater (D)	9,415	(14%)	
	Lendall Terry (D)	2,501	(4%)	
	Other	2,267	(3%)	
2004 general	Mike Sodrel (R)	142,197	(49%)	($1,546,877)
	Baron Hill (D)	140,772	(49%)	($1,634,699)
	Other	4,541	(2%)	

Prior Winning Percentages: 2002 (51%); 2000 (54%); 1998 (51%)

The People		Race/Ethnic Origin	Ancestry	
Area size:	6,670 sq. mi.	94.0% White	German: 19.9%	USA: 12.2%
Urban population:	52.3%	2.3% Black	Irish: 8.7%	
Rural population:	47.7%	0.9% Asian	**2004 Presidential Vote**	
Pop. 2000:	675,599	0.2% Native Am.	Bush (R)	171,926 (59%)
Pop. 2005 (est):	697,177	0.0% Hawaiian	Kerry (D)	117,647 (40%)
Median income:	$39,011	0.9% Two+ races	Other	1,568 (1%)
Poverty status:	10.5%	0.1% Other	**2000 Presidential Vote**	
Military veterans:	13.0%	1.5% Hispanic Origin	Bush (R)	142,694 (56%)
			Gore (D)	106,417 (42%)
			Other	4,288 (2%)
			Cook Partisan Voting Index: R + 7	
Occupation	Blue collar: 34.4%	White collar: 50.6%	Gray collar: 15.0%	

The southeastern corner of Indiana was a busy place when settlers rafted down the Ohio River in the early 19th century. They were mostly Southerners, "Butternuts," from across the river in Kentucky or over the mountains in Virginia, and they built the first large Indiana settlements. Today, you can see their work in the marvelous old buildings of Madison, now quiet but once one of the busiest ports on the Ohio River. Its Broadway Fountain was originally cast in iron and was displayed at the Centennial Exposition in Philadelphia in 1876. Farther down the river is Corydon, from 1816-25 the state capital. The early 19th century buildings here have been well preserved because these towns were bypassed first by the railroads, then by U.S. routes and interstate highways, and they certainly are remote from major airports. The river remains an artery of commerce, but utilitarian barges have replaced steamers, except for riverboat casinos.

Butternut Indiana retained its affection for things Southern into the Civil War and beyond. Local politician Jesse Bright was expelled from the U.S. Senate in 1862 for "supporting the rebellion." The hills along the Ohio River typically have voted Democratic, but the growing Clark County suburbs of Louisville have trended Republican. To the east, Indiana is now filling up with migrants from Cincinnati—a Yankee and German abolitionist bastion in Jesse Bright's time, an overwhelmingly Republican stronghold in ours—who are moving the southeast corner of Indiana away from its ancestral party.

The 9th Congressional District of Indiana is made up of most of the state's Ohio River counties. It includes tiny Milan, home to the championship high school of *Hoosiers* movie fame, and the Indiana University campus in the rolling hills of Democratic-leaning Bloomington. To the east is Batesville, home of the Batesville Casket Company, which makes the caskets used for U.S. military personnel who die in the line of duty. To the west is French Lick—a former rural resort town famous to basketball fans as the hometown of Boston Celtics basketball star Larry Bird and the site of a new casino. Most of the district is culturally conservative; much of it has been trending Republican, particularly in the suburbs of Cincinnati.

The congressman from the 9th District is Baron Hill, a Democrat first elected in 1998 and then again in 2006. He served three terms in Congress before losing in 2004, when he was the only Democratic incumbent to lose a seat for reasons other than redistricting. Hill grew up in Seymour, the small town of John Mellencamp's song "Small Town." A former high school and college basketball standout at Furman University—he was inducted into the Indiana Basketball Hall of Fame alongside Larry Bird in 2000–Hill returned home after graduation to a family insurance business and eventually served four terms in the state House. In 1990, he ran against Senator Dan Coats and, despite a huge money disadvantage, held him to a 54%-46% win. Governor Evan Bayh appointed Hill to head the state student assistance agency; then he worked for Merrill Lynch. In 1998, he won a competitive contest to replace Democratic Congressman Lee Hamilton, who served 34 years and became chairman of the Foreign Affairs Committee.

During his three prior terms in the House, Hill was a member of the moderate Blue Dog Coalition, served as a chief deputy whip, and had a seat on the Agriculture Committee. In 2002, Hill was challenged by bus-company owner Mike Sodrel, who spent more than $1 million from his own pocket, but won 51% to 46%. Two years later, Sodrel returned to defeat Hill by 1,425 votes in a campaign that centered on social issues such as gay marriage, abortion, and flag-burning. The National Republican Congressional Committee spent more than $1 million on ads against Hill, and top GOP leaders made numerous visits to the district on his behalf. Sodrel got coattail support that year from President Bush, who carried the district with 59%. In 2006, Sodrel's party affiliation wasn't so helpful. Bush, the Republican-controlled Congress, and Republican Governor Mitch Daniels were far less popular than in 2004, and Democrats portrayed Sodrel as a drone for the Bush administration. Sodrel tried to counter by attacking Hill as a career politician who had become a Washington lobbyist. Hill insisted that he did consulting for local businesses and wasn't a lobbyist, even though the Washington consulting firm he worked for, mCapitol Management, did have a lobbying arm. Illegal immigration loomed large during the campaign, as did social issues such as same-sex marriage, but Hill left little daylight between his and Sodrel's positions on those issues. In early October, Hill put Sodrel on the defensive by turning the focus to the congressional page scandal involving Mark Foley. Hill was the first candidate in the nation to air a commercial featuring Foley's picture, and he slammed Sodrel for refusing to return contributions from House GOP leaders "who did nothing to stop sexual predator Congressman Foley." The same day, Speaker Dennis Hastert canceled a campaign appearance with Sodrel. Hill called himself "a family man with deep religious convictions," and he ran an ad opposing gay marriage. Visits by the President and Laura Bush, Vice President Cheney and several Cabinet officials were less helpful for Sodrel in their third match, Hill won 50%-45%—a 9,985 vote margin. His big advantage was in Bloomington-based Monroe County, where he won 63%-32%, with a lead of nearly 8,000 votes.

Returning to Capitol Hill, Hill got a seat on Energy and Commerce and served in the majority for the first time. He said that he would work on energy independence and promote increased use of ethanol plus biodiesel fuels and hybrid vehicles. Sodrel was considering a rematch with Hill in 2008—which would mark the fourth contest between the two pols.

★ IOWA ★

As Americans were surging westward in the 1840s, Iowa was filling up with Yankee farmers and German immigrants, watching as wagon trains headed to the Oregon Trail and the Mormon thousands mustered by Brigham Young headed from the Mississippi across the rolling hills to Council Bluffs on the Missouri and then west. Iowa was a young state then, proud of its hundreds of schools and dozens of colleges, sending more than its share of young men back east to fight for the cause of the Union. After that war Iowans built a solid civilization based on farming, farm-machine manufacturing and meat processing that resisted the blandishments of William Jennings Bryan's populism and cheap money, and Iowa became one of the most solidly Republican states in the nation.

But starting around 1900, Iowa grew old. "If you build it, they will come" was the theme from the movie *Field of Dreams*, set in Iowa, and in the 19th century, Iowans built a model society. Yet for most of the 20th century very few people came. Iowa's commercial and financial center remained in the railroad hub of Chicago, its economy failed to diversify and develop the dense manufacturing base of the Great Lakes states, and its young people started to move east or west to make their fortunes. Iowa's population, up from 674,000 in 1860 to 2.2 million in 1900, increased only slowly, and has not reached 3 million to this day: In 1900, Iowa had 11 congressional districts and California 7; now Iowa has 5 and California 53, and Iowa is expected to lose 1 and California gain 1 after the 2010 Census. Iowa's solid Capitol—a memorial to its Civil War dead—and its courthouses, its sturdy but mostly old housing stock, give testimony to Iowa's strengths but also suggest a lack of dynamism. Even its great economic achievement—the development of high-tech, ever more productive, but also less labor-intensive agriculture—has made this a state that did not grow much. Iowa is number one in pork, number one in corn, and number one in soybeans, but it has been down near the bottom in population growth.

Iowa suffered especially in the 1980s. The number of Iowans whose principal occupation was farming dropped from 86,000 in 1982 to 56,000 in 1997, and the state's population dropped by 4.7% between 1980 and 1990—down to the 1960 level. In the 1990s its high level of literacy and good work habits have produced white-collar and high-tech growth in and around its pleasant small cities, especially in Des Moines and Cedar Rapids, even as many old factories closed, and it grew by 5.4% in the 1990s—the biggest population increase since the 1910s. But the recession of 2001 hit hard, and Iowa lost 10,000 jobs, and growth slowed. Young Iowans with good educations left the state; Governor Tom Vilsack took to hosting parties for Iowa natives in New York City and Chicago where he urged them to come back home. The outflow was offset a bit by Mexican and other immigrants, who moved to small towns like Denison as well as to Des Moines and the old industrial cities of Sioux City and Waterloo. But over-65 population is expected to increase 47% over the next 20 years, while the number of children is projected to fall. Ethanol has boosted the Iowa economy, since Senator Charles Grassley in 1998 got the ethanol tax credit extended to 2007, and by then Iowa was producing 30% of the nation's ethanol. That has pushed corn prices above $3 a bushel and increased the value of farmland, and soybean prices have been helped by Iowa's biofuel plants; cattle producers are using the distiller fuel produced by ethanol production as a nutritious feed. But ethanol plants are capital-intensive and produce relatively few jobs, while some factory jobs are disappearing; Iowa's Maytag was purchased by Whirlpool, which announced it was moving its Newton headquarters and factory to Ohio.

For much of the 20th century Iowa was been a culturally and politically countercyclical state, headed in just the opposite direction of the rest of the nation—determinedly, with confidence in its own chipper rectitude, unembarrassedly out of step. In the industrial New Deal era, it stayed mostly agricultural and Republican, even as Davenport and Des Moines radio announcer Ronald Reagan became an enthusiastic Roosevelt Democrat and headed to Hollywood. Iowa partook little of postwar economic growth. It was dovish during the Vietnam War and after. In the 1980s, as Reagan, by then a conservative Republican, became president, Iowa's economy was hit hard and self-pity became the dominant note of Iowa's politics, as voters sought protection from the vagaries of the market even as commercial real estate and stock prices boomed elsewhere. In the 1988 caucuses Iowa Republicans voted against Reagan's vice president, George Bush, and Iowa Democrats voted for the populist Dick Gephardt. In the fall it gave Michael Dukakis his second highest percentage of any state.

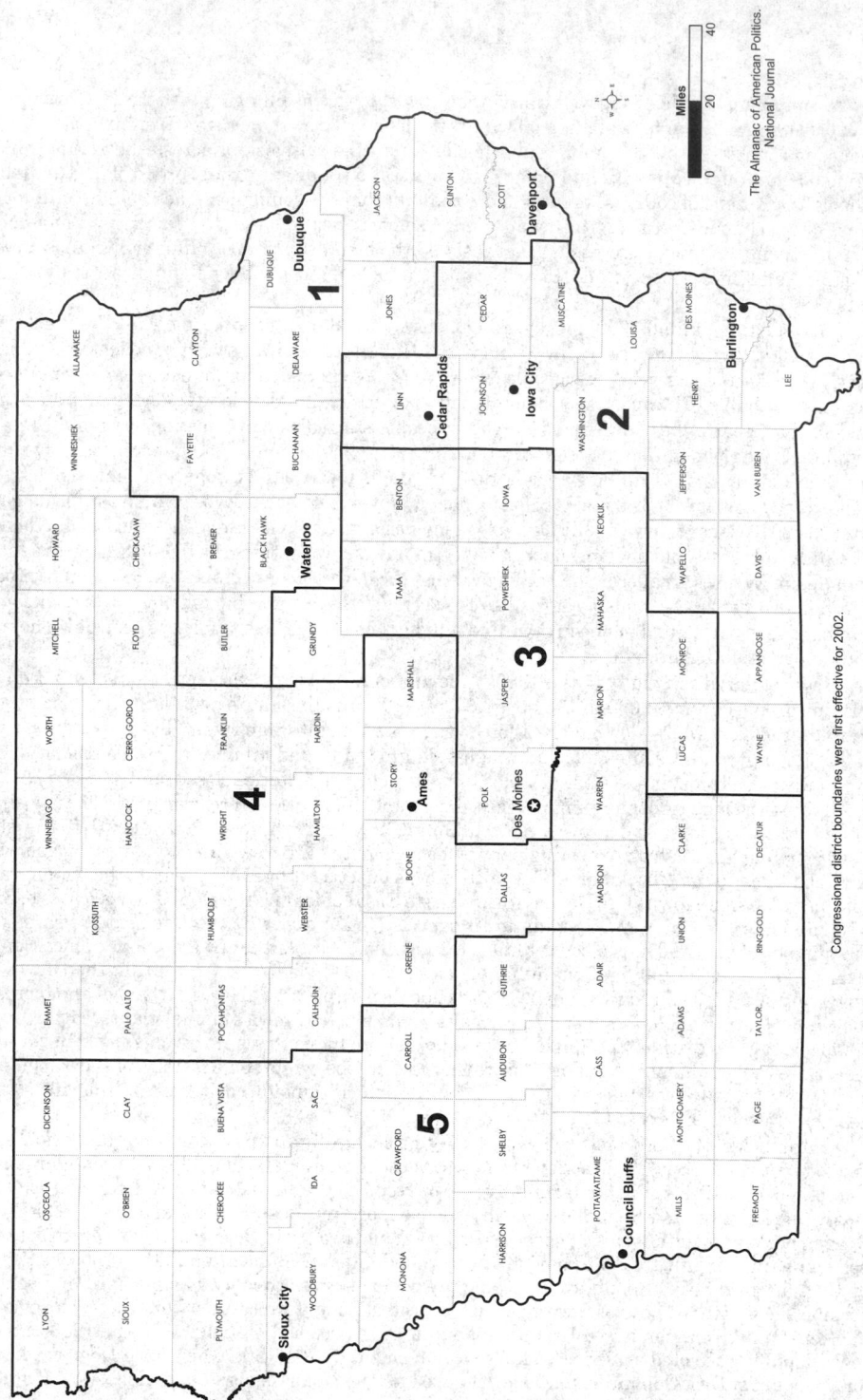

Congressional district boundaries were first effective for 2002.

The Almanac of American Politics.
National Journal

Since then, Iowa and the nation have converged politically. If its economic rebellion against America's move toward free markets failed in the 1980s, its cultural qualms about America's move away from traditional values may have set an example for the rest of the country in the 1990s. It voted twice for Bill Clinton and went for Al Gore by 4,144 votes in 2000 and for George W. Bush by 10,059 in 2004. It has reelected both its Republican and its Democratic senator. After 30 years of Republican governors, it elected Democrats three times starting in 1998. Republicans held majorities in the legislature, until 2004 in the state Senate and 2006 in the state House. Collectively these results indicate a sort of steady moderation, a desire to accept the verdict of the markets and to honor traditional values with some hedging on both counts. Iowa remains quirky in some respects. It is still probably one of the most dovish, isolationist-prone states, though very much aware of its role as an international exporter: Its delegation voted for NAFTA in 1993 and normal trade relations with China in 1999 (Mexicans eat lots of corn and Chinese lots of pork). It is thrift-minded, seeing a balanced budget more as a badge of moral rectitude than as a prudent economic policy. It pioneered legal riverboat gambling in 1989, but also has a large anti-abortion movement. And it has its own traditional gatherings, which are often of political significance. One is the Iowa State Fair held every August on the east side of Des Moines, complete with the traditional 600-pound butter cow. Another is RAGBRAI, the *Des Moines Register*'s Annual Great Bike Ride Across Iowa, held every year in late summer since 1973. And then there are the Iowa precinct caucuses held on a cold night in January in presidential years, the first occasion in which ordinary Americans decide who will be their president.

The People		Race/Ethnic Origin		Military veterans: 292,020 (13.3%)	
Pop. 2006 (est):	2,982,085	2,710,344 92.6%	White	WWII: 22.6%	Korea: 15.6%
Pop. 2000:	2,926,324	60,744 2.1%	Black	Vietnam: 31.4%	Gulf War: 8.3%
Pop. 1990:	2,776,755	36,345 1.2%	Asian	**Most populous cities (2006):**	
Change 1990-2000:	Up 5.4%	7,955 0.3%	Native Am.	1. Des Moines	193,886
% of U.S. total:	1.0%	888 0.0%	Hawaiian	2. Cedar Rapids	124,417
Pop. rank:	30th of 50	25,472 0.9%	Two+ races	3. Davenport	99,514
Area size:	56,272 sq. mi.	2,103 0.1%	Other	4. Sioux City	83,262
State Native:	74.8%	82,473 2.8%	Hisp. Origin	5. Waterloo	65,998
Non-citizen:	2.1%	**Ancestry**			
Language		German: 26.0%	Irish: 9.8%	Urban population: 61.1%	
English: 92.5%	Spanish: 3.7%	English: 6.9%	USA: 4.9%	Rural population: 38.9%	
Other Eur.: 2.6%		Norwegian: 4.1%			

Education		Work Sector		General Assembly	
H.S. Grad:	86.1%	Private: 77.8%	Govt: 13.6%	Senate	30 D 20 R
College Grad:	21.2%	Self: 8.2%	Family: 0.4%	House	54 D 46 R
Industry		Unemployment: 4.2%		Legislative Term Limits: No	
Agri: 4.4%	Con: 6.2%	**Household Income**		**Registered Voters**	
Fin: 6.7%	Info: 2.8%	<15k: 14.9%	15-35k: 29.0%	D: 645,554	(31.1%)
Mfg: 21.9%	Prof: 27.8%	35-50k: 19.0%	50-100k: 29.8%	R: 623,863	(30.0%)
Public: 3.4%	Trade: 15.6%	100-150k: 4.9%	>150k: 2.4%	O: 807,822	(38.9%)
Other: 11.1%		Median: $39,469			
Occupation		Poverty status: 9.1%			
Blue collar: 27.0%	White collar: 57.2%	**Home Value**			
Gray collar: 15.8%		<50k: 22.9%	50-100k: 42.2%	100-200k: 27.5%	200-300k: 5.0%
		300-500k: 1.8%	>500k: 0.6%	Median: $82,100	

Presidential politics   On a frosty evening in January every four years, some 200,000 Iowans troop to caucuses in nearly 2,000 precincts and begin the formal process of choosing a president of the United States. The precinct caucuses were scheduled early in the cycle for 1972 by Democratic doves who wanted more leverage for their views, and that year they started George McGovern on his way to the Democratic nomination. But the caucuses have had other, unanticipated consequences. In 1976, Jimmy Carter's strategist Hamilton Jordan determined that intensive campaigning could produce a surprise victory that could make a little-known candidate a national contender: Without Iowa and the next-week New Hampshire primary, Carter would never have become president.

2004 Presidential Vote		
Bush (R)	751,957	(50%)
Kerry (D)	741,898	(49%)
Nader (I)	5,973	(0%)
Other	7,080	(0%)
2000 Presidential Vote		
Gore (D)	638,517	(49%)
Bush (R)	634,373	(48%)
Nader (Green)	29,374	(2%)
Other	13,299	(1%)

Then, for the next 20 years, the Iowa caucuses were less nomination determinative. In 1980, George H.W. Bush's intensive campaigning gave him a victory among Republicans, while Carter, still profiting from his 1976 contacts, trounced Senator Edward Kennedy. But Bush lost the nomination to Ronald Reagan, and Carter lost in November. In 1984 Democratic favorite Walter Mondale won 49% of the "delegate strength" (Democrats don't compute the actual number of votes), but the momentum went to the 17% second place finisher Gary Hart, though Mondale did win the nomination. In 1988, Iowa failed to pick the winners on either side: Dick Gephardt capitalized on Iowa's economic woes to win among Democrats, while George H.W. Bush finished in third place behind Kansas Senator Bob Dole and televangelist Pat Robertson among Republicans—a sign of the rising strength of Christian conservatives here. But Gephardt and Dole lost in New Hampshire, and neither was nominated. In 1992, Iowa went dark: No Democrat challenged Iowa's Tom Harkin here, and Pat Buchanan began his campaign against Bush in New Hampshire. In 1996, Dole had the support of leading Republicans, led by Governor Terry Branstad and Senator Charles Grassley, and farm state roots as well: Dole's very narrow victory was an omen of the weakness of his candidacy later.

In 2000, Iowa moved its caucus date back to Monday, January 24, after New Hampshire surprised everyone by scheduling its primary for Tuesday, February 1. And in 2000, Iowa turned out to be important again. George W. Bush won the August 1999 straw poll at Ames with 31% of the vote, to 21% for Steve Forbes and 14% for Elizabeth Dole; Dole soon dropped out, as did Dan Quayle and Lamar Alexander, while Pat Buchanan left the Republican party altogether and, as the Reform party candidate in November, won 0.4% of the popular vote. In January Bush won the caucuses with 41% of the vote while Forbes got 30%, not the upset victory he needed. Both got a share of religious conservatives, as did Alan Keyes, who was third with 14%. On the Democratic side the race was between Al Gore and Bill Bradley. In his 1988 campaign, Gore skipped what he called "madness" in "the small state of Iowa"; in June 1997 he was proclaiming, "I love Iowa," and in November 1998, he was on the phone congratulating Tom Vilsack before Vilsack himself realized he had been elected governor. Gore did not get Vilsack's support—he stayed carefully neutral—but Gore did get vigorous support from Vilsack's wife, from Senator Tom Harkin and, perhaps most important, from Iowa's labor unions. Gore won in "delegate strength" with 63% to Bradley's 35%. That gave Gore momentum in New Hampshire, which he won eight days later, by only 50%-46%. With five weeks to the next Democratic contest, Bradley dropped out and Gore was the nominee.

Iowa was dispositive in 2004 as well. George W. Bush had no opposition: this was the Democrats' show. The leader in Iowa polls from summer 2003 through the second week of January 2004 was Howard Dean. His opposition to the war in Iraq was popular among Iowa's overwhelmingly dovish caucusgoers; his thousands of out-of-state volunteers seemed to have built the best turnout organization. But as the new year opened, Democrats suddenly confronted the possibility that they could actually defeat George W. Bush, and the question for many became not who could most stridently criticize the president and his policies but who could defeat him. Al Gore's December 9 endorsement of Dean didn't help Dean with the party regulars and union operatives who had won the caucuses for Gore four years before; Dean's comment that the December 13 capture of Saddam Hussein "has not made America safer" raised doubts about his electability. Dean's irritated outshouting of a 68-year-old Republican questioner in Oelwein January 11 was a breach of Iowa manners; his poll numbers immediately started plummeting. The question was who would rise.

Dick Gephardt, supported by private sector unions and veterans of his campaign 16 years before, failed to gather new adherents. John Edwards, endorsed by the *Des Moines Register*, had only a few chipper out-of-staters organizing things. John Kerry, who mortgaged his Boston house for $6.4 million and put all his efforts into Iowa, had the best organization, led by 2002 congressional candidate John Norris, the endorsement of Christie Vilsack—the governor was again technically neutral—and a message. Just days before the caucuses he was joined by a Green Beret whom he had rescued in the waters of Vietnam. Kerry proclaimed that he could stand up to Bush on Iraq because he had volunteered and been decorated in Vietnam.

That was enough for victory on caucus night—and the nomination. Howard Dean's 3,500 orange-stocking-capped Perfect Stormers were swarming in the streets of Des Moines. But Kerry got the votes. Under Iowa Democrats' procedures, the supporters of candidates who fail to meet a 15% threshold of the votes in any precinct can choose to caucus for another candidate; this gives a premium to front-runners and penalizes also-rans. Entry polls at the caucuses showed Kerry well ahead, with Edwards, Dean and Gephardt trailing. But Edwards had shrewdly targeted supporters of Dennis Kucinich and their second-choice support for Edwards helped swell his numbers in the final standings, while Dean and Gephardt, failing to make the threshold in many precincts, saw their numbers dwindle below the entry poll. The final results, in "delegate strength": Kerry 38%, Edwards 32%, Dean 18%, Gephardt 11%. Gephardt soon left the race; Dean was effectively finished even before he emitted his famous scream on caucus night; Edwards was left to finish second or third to Kerry until Kerry clinched the nomination six weeks and one day later. But it was Iowa Democrats—some 122,000 of them—who did the deciding.

Iowa has been a closely contested state in three of the last four presidential elections and has cast percentages for the two parties close to their national averages in all four. One reason is that Iowa Democrats have used the competitive caucuses in 2000 and 2004 and the strong organization developed by Senator Tom Harkin in his 1996 and 2002 campaigns to develop a strong voter turnout organization. They have been especially effective in getting votes cast by mail in early voting (which started September 23 in 2004). This enabled Democrats to carry the state in 2000—Al Gore lost among those who cast their votes on Election Day but won because of absentees—and to come very close four years later. But in 2004, more quietly and without the hoopla of a presidential caucus fight, Iowa Republicans also developed a strong organization. In November 2004 this resulted in increased Republican popular vote margins (or decreased Democratic margins) in 72 of Iowa's 99 counties. Democrats produced hefty popular vote margins increases in the counties including Iowa City (the University of Iowa) and Cedar Rapids (Quaker Oats) and smaller increases in the counties including Ames (Iowa State University) and Newton (Maytag). But Republicans produced a hefty increase in Pottawatomie County (east of Omaha, Nebraska) and Dallas and Warren Counties (both Des Moines suburbs) and actually produced improved popular vote margins in the counties including Des Moines (the state capital) and Davenport (Oscar Mayer). Moreover, Republicans increased their popular vote margins in most of Iowa's unglamorous and non-growing rural counties, especially in western Iowa: a considerable political achievement, delivering Iowa's seven electoral votes to George W. Bush.

Iowa's first-in-the-nation status was preserved against challenges at the 2004 Republican National Convention and by the rules adopted by the Democratic National Committee in August 2006; its caucuses were set for January 14, 2008. Democrats, provoked by the complaint by Michigan's Senator Carl Levin and others that these two states lack racial diversity (Iowa is 2% black and 3% Hispanic), staged a second early caucus in Nevada January 19 and, after the New Hampshire primary, originally scheduled for January 22, a second early primary in South Carolina January 29. By 2006 presidential candidates were already making the rounds in Iowa; John Edwards, with no need to meet Senate roll calls, made more than a dozen trips there in 2005 and 2006. None of the best-known candidates seemed likely to skip Iowa, as Al Gore did in 1988, John McCain in 2000 and Joe Lieberman and Wesley Clark in 2004; they surely have noticed that none won his party's nomination. On the Republican side, John McCain seemed prepared to contest Iowa, despite his longstanding opposition to farm subsidies and ethanol tax credits; long shot candidates, including Chicago accountant John Cox, were accumulating pledges of support in all 99 counties. The state Republicans' August 2007 straw poll in Ames winnowed the field, as it did in 1999. On the Democratic side, Edwards's frequent trips helped put him in the lead or near it in Iowa polls in late 2006 and early 2007, although these may be discounted; getting an accurate sample of the relatively small number of Iowa voters who attend caucuses—about 15% of those who vote in November—is pretty tricky. But Barack Obama and Hillary Rodham Clinton attracted large crowds when they came calling. Outgoing Governor Tom Vilsack became the first Democrat to declare his candidacy, soon after the November 2006 election. But his poll numbers were not dazzling, and there was no sign that other Democrats were dropping out as most did when Senator Tom Harkin ran in 1992; and Vilsack left the race in February 2007, saying that he wasn't able to raise enough money. The scheduling of other early contests in Nevada and South Carolina and the decision of several big states to vote on February 5 led some pundits to opine that Iowa wouldn't be as important as in the past. But the *Des Moines Register's* David Yepsen, by common consent Iowa's leading political reporter, disagreed. "Packing so many events so closely after the Iowa events just makes Iowa more important. There is not enough time between these caucuses and primaries for a candidate to recover from a setback here—or to slow the winner's momentum." Iowa seems determined to have the first word—and quite possibly the last.

Congressional districting

110th Congress Lineup	
3 D	2 R

109th Congress Lineup	
4 R	1 D

Iowa's congressional district lines are drawn by the nonpartisan Legislative Services Bureau and then approved by the (Democratic in 2002) governor and (Republican in 2002) legislature—a process that is praised by many critics of partisan gerrymandering and bipartisan incumbent protection plans. But it is not entirely apolitical. The Legislative Service Bureau is not supposed to take past voting patterns or legislator's place of residence into account, and in good Iowa fashion, they don't. But the governor and legislators can and do. In May 2001, the Iowa Senate rejected the Legislative Service Bureau's first plan; Republicans said the population disparities were too large; Democrats contended that Republicans thought it was politically damaging to them. So a special session was called in June to consider the Bureau's second plan. That plan placed Republican congressmen Jim Nussle and Jim Leach in the same district and separated Des Moines from suburban Dallas and Warren Counties, with which it arguably has a community of interests. Indeed, with the exception of the 5th District in western Iowa, all the districts combine very disparate parts of Iowa. Nevertheless Democratic Governor Vilsack and the Republican legislature approved the plan. Two incumbents moved their residences, Leach into the 2d District, most of which he had been representing, and Democrat Leonard Boswell into Des Moines in the new 3d District, whose incumbent, Republican Greg Ganske, was running for the Senate.

The Iowa plan did produce more strenuous competition than was seen in most states, in 2002. Four of the five districts were contested seriously by both Democrats and Republicans that year, and the 5th had a spirited Republican primary. In 2004 only one district was seriously contested, and four of the five incumbents improved their percentages. In 2006 three districts were seriously contested, and Democrats picked up two Republican-held seats—the district Nussle abandoned to run, unsuccessfully, for governor, and the district held for 30 years by liberal Republican Jim Leach. Democrats could argue that this was simple justice: both districts voted for John Kerry in 2004 and until 2006 Democrats held only one of the five districts in a state closely divided between the parties. But Republicans could argue that the results were unfair in that they won a 50%-47% majority of the vote for the House but got only two of the five seats. Low population growth means that Iowa is likely to lose a seat in the reapportionment following the 2010 Census, and there is no telling who will be the victim—or victims—of the Legislative Services Bureau and the governor and legislature. The 2005 estimates show the current districts as having between 581,000 and 613,000 people; the average district in a four-district plan would have 745,000—close to the 2006 population of a district made up of Des Moines's Polk County and including the eight surrounding counties. If the Legislative Services Bureau created such a district it would be, based on 2004 presidential numbers, competitive between the parties, and the rest of the state would be divided between a heavily Republican western district and two eastern districts in which Democrats would have the edge.

Governor

Chet Culver (D)

Elected 2006, term expires Jan. 2011, 1st term; b. Jan. 25, 1966, Washington, D.C.; home, Des Moines; VA Tech, B.A. 1988; Drake U., M.A.T. 1994; Presbyterian; married (Mari Thinnes).

Elected Office: IA Sec. of State, 1998-2006.

Professional Career: Consumer & environmental advocate, IA Atty. Gen.'s Office, 1991-95; Teacher, Roosevelt High, 1995, Hoover High, 1996-1998.

Office: 1007 East Grand Avenue, Des Moines, 50319, 515-281-5211; Fax: 515-281-0217; Web site: www.governor.iowa.gov.

Election Results

2006 general	Chet Culver (D)	569,021	(54%)
	Jim Nussle (R)	467,425	(44%)
	Other	16,809	(2%)
2006 primary	Chet Culver (D)	58,131	(39%)
	Michael Blouin (D)	50,728	(34%)
	Ed Fallon (D)	38,253	(26%)
	Other	1,639	(1%)
2002 general	Tom Vilsack (D)	540,449	(53%)
	Doug Gross (R)	456,612	(45%)
	Other	28,741	(3%)

Chet Culver, a Democrat, was elected governor of Iowa in 2006. He is the son of former Representative (1965-75) and Senator (1975-81) John Culver, a Democrat who served a single Senate term before losing to Charles Grassley in 1980. Chet Culver was born in Washington, D.C., during his father's first term in the House, went to high school in Maryland and then to college in Virginia. He is from a family not just of politicians but of athletes: His father was a star football player at Harvard, good enough to be drafted by the NFL, and his mother was a champion diver and speedskater. His three sisters were college athletes; he won a football scholarship to Virginia Tech before a knee injury ended his career.

After college, Culver moved to Iowa, where his family name still could open some doors. He was a field staffer for the state Democratic party, which at the time was chaired by Bonnie Campbell, who had run his father's Senate office in Iowa. Then he worked for Campbell's husband, a statehouse lobbyist, before serving as Campbell's field director during her successful 1990 election as state attorney general. He spent several years working in the attorney general's office. Campbell ran for governor in 1994 and lost to Republican Terry Branstad; in 1995, President Clinton appointed her to a Justice Department position and Culver took a job coaching football and teaching government and history at a Des Moines high school.

In 1998, Culver decided to run for office himself and at 32 he was elected Iowa's secretary of state—the youngest in the nation at the time. A politician who wins statewide office at that age is immediately marked as future prospect for governor; Culver did nothing in his two terms that would take him off that track. His critics saw a partisan edge to his work. As the state's elections administrator, he frustrated Republican legislators who wanted changes to Iowa's voting system and was criticized by Republicans in 2004 for mailing to every household a voter guide that included an absentee-ballot request (traditionally this worked to the advantage of Iowa Democrats); Culver said he was "offended" by the insinuation and merely sought to increase voter participation. He further angered Republicans when he failed to declare President Bush as the winner in Iowa until days after the 2004 election—making Iowa the last state to declare a winner even though few thought the remaining uncounted ballots could change the outcome.

Iowa has had only 4 governor's elections in the last 40 years in which the incumbent was not running. The fourth election came in 2006 when Democratic Governor Tom Vilsack fulfilled a promise made in his 1998 and 2002 campaigns to serve only 2 terms. Vilsack was the only Democrat elected governor of Iowa since 1966; he was making plans to run for president in 2008. Culver had two main opponents in the primary, former Congressman Michael Blouin, who had succeeded Culver's father in the House, and state Representative Ed Fallon, who refused to take PAC money or contributions from paid lobbyists. Blouin resigned his position as Iowa's economic development director to run and assembled support from most of the state's Democratic legislators and from much of organized labor. Fallon ran as a progressive and an outsider; he had supported Ralph Nader over Al Gore in 2000. Culver announced his candidacy in November 2005, months after Fallon and Blouin, and highlighted economic development, education and energy issues. He proposed a $100 million Iowa Power Fund to create energy-oriented businesses and attract new investment in alternative fuels and technologies. "In the past, Iowa has fed the world," he said. "Now it's time for Iowa to fuel the world." Culver wasn't always articulate on the campaign trail but he was the better fundraiser and his solid support for abortion rights gave him an edge among party activists. He won 39% to 34% for Blouin. Fallon finished third with 26%. Culver carried 80 of 99 counties, but lost Dubuque County, the University of Iowa's Johnson County, and Cedar Rapids's Linn County to Blouin. Fallon's strength didn't extend far beyond his Des Moines home: he won Des Moines's Polk County and Iowa State University's Story County just to the north.

Congressman Jim Nussle, unopposed in the Republican primary, awaited Culver. An eight-term House veteran and the Budget Committee chairman, Nussle had more experience and polish, which Republicans sought to highlight; the Culver campaign responded to the perception that Culver was rough around the edges with a smart ad where his wife Mari Culver fondly refers to her husband as "a big lug." Culver tied Nussle to the unpopular Bush administration and the national Republican party, while pointing out growth in the size of the federal budget deficit under Nussle's watch. Both Culver and Nussle urged more education spending; they were at odds on immigration, taxes and economic development issues. The abortion debate was especially divisive. Culver said Nussle's opposition to abortion rights and embryonic stem cell research was an "extreme position"; Nussle appeared to backtrack on abortion in the fall, though he later clarified his stance and reiterated that he favored banning abortion except to save the life of the mother.

This was an awful year to run as a Republican in Iowa: Culver won 54%-44%. He won Des Moines's Polk County (56%-42%), Davenport's Scott County (56%-41%) and carried Cedar Rapids's Linn County and Waterloo's Black Hawk County by 59%-40%. In the University of Iowa's Johnson County, he won 68%-29%. As of early November, Democrats had cast 89,000 absentee ballots to 50,000 for Republicans—this accounted for more than one-third of Culver's 99,000 vote margin. Democrats also picked up Nussle's open 1st District seat, defeated Republican Congressman Jim Leach in the 2d District, and won majorities in the state House and Senate for the first time since 1992. Going into the election, the Senate was tied 25-25; Culver took office with a 30-20 Democratic advantage. Republicans had a 50-49 edge (with one vacancy) in the House; Democrats ended up with a 54-46 majority.

The 2007 legislative session marked the first time in 42 years that Democrats controlled the governor's office and both chambers. State spending increased by roughly 10 percent and the legislature raised the tax on cigarettes. Culver boasted some successes, among them: a pay raise for teachers, legislation extending anti-discrimination protections to gays and lesbians, and an increase in the minimum wage. He also signed a bill allowing same-day voter registration.

Senior Senator

Charles Grassley (R)

Elected 1980, seat up 2010, 5th term; b. Sept. 17, 1933, New Hartford; home, New Hartford; U. of N. IA, B.A. 1955, M.A. 1956, U. of IA, 1957-58; Baptist; married (Barbara).

Elected Office: IA House of Reps., 1958-74; U.S. House of Reps., 1974-80.

Professional Career: Farmer.

DC Office: 135 HSOB, 20510, 202-224-3744; Fax: 202-224-6020; Web site: grassley.senate.gov.

State Offices: Cedar Rapids, 319-363-6832; Council Bluffs, 712-322-7103; Davenport, 563-322-4331; Des Moines, 515-284-4890; Sioux City, 712-233-1860; Waterloo, 319-232-6657.

Committees: *Agriculture, Nutrition & Forestry* (10th of 10 R): Production, Income Protection & Price Support; Energy, Science & Technology. *Budget* (3d of 11 R). *Finance* (RMM of 10 R): Health Care. *Joint Committee on Taxation* (4th of 5 R). *Judiciary* (3d of 9 R): Administrative Oversight & the Courts; Immigration, Refugees & Border Security; Antitrust, Competition Policy & Consumer Rights; Crime & Drugs.

Group Ratings

	ADA	ACLU	AFS	LCV	ITIC	NTU	COC	ACU	CFG	FRC
2006	5	25	13	14	100	77	92	88	86	87
2005	5	—	0	10	—	71	100	96	84	—

National Journal Ratings

	2005 LIB	—	2005 CONS		2006 LIB	—	2006 CONS
Economic	31%	—	68%		28%	—	69%
Social	23%	—	64%		0%	—	82%
Foreign	0%	—	74%		26%	—	67%

Key Votes of the 109th Congress

1. Bar ANWR Drilling	N	5. Confirm Samuel Alito	Y	9. Limit Interstate Abortion	Y
2. FY06 Spending Curb	Y	6. Path to Citizenship	N	10. CAFTA	Y
3. Estate Tax Repeal	Y	7. Bar Same Sex Marriage	Y	11. Urge Iraq Withdrawal	N
4. Raise Minimum Wage	N	8. Stem Cell Research $	N	12. Provide Detainee Rights	N

Election Results

2004 general	Charles Grassley (R)	1,038,175	(70%)	($6,403,445)
	Arthur Small (D)	412,365	(28%)	($135,503)
	Other	28,688	(2%)	
2004 primary	Charles Grassley (R)	unopposed		
1998 general	Charles Grassley (R)	648,480	(68%)	($2,781,940)
	David Osterberg (D)	289,049	(30%)	($165,429)
	Other	10,378	(1%)	

Prior Winning Percentages: 1992 (70%); 1986 (66%); 1980 (54%); 1978 House (75%); 1976 House (57%); 1974 House (51%)

Charles Grassley, the senior senator from Iowa, was first elected to the House in 1974 and to the Senate in 1980. He grew up on a farm in Butler County near Waterloo; his parents switched to the Republican party when Franklin Roosevelt ran for a third term in 1940. He graduated from the University of Northern Iowa and, while in graduate school, ran for the state House in 1956 and lost by 70-some votes. Two years later he ran again and was elected, at 25, in a Democratic year; while in the legislature he worked as a sheet metal shearer and an assembly line worker. He won an open U.S. House seat in the Democratic year of 1974 and a Senate seat by beating incumbent Democrat John Culver, father of Governor Chet Culver, in 1980. Grassley inherited an 80-acre farm in 1960, and has added to it over the years—he got a big raise when elected to the House at a time the salary was $42,000—until he now owns 710 acres, which he helps his son run. He goes back to Iowa just about every weekend and has held meetings in each of the state's 99 counties every year he has served in the Senate. Starting in 1997, he led the Senate in consecutive roll call votes; the last one he missed came when he was inspecting flood damage in Iowa in 1993.

Grassley started off in Congress as a freshman in a party outnumbered by 51 seats in a House where the majority ran things untrammeled; he has been serving more recently as a senior member in a roughly evenly-divided Senate in which few issues can be settled without some kind of consensus. His first major legislation was the 1986 Federal False Claims Act, which authorizes suits for fraud on behalf of the government; he says it brought in more than $17 billion by 2006. He long sponsored the bill to apply to Congress the same laws it applies to others, and was the chief sponsor of the Congressional Accountability Act of 1995. He has conducted intensive and critical oversight over the FBI, the Department of Homeland Security, Centers for Medicare and Medicaid Services and the FDA; he has criticized specific corporations from pharmaceuticals to nursing home companies for cheating the government or evading appropriate regulation.

As a farmer, Grassley supported both the 1996 act which attempted to replace subsidies and also the subsequent disaster farm aid programs. He opposed the May 2002 farm bill, drafted by his Iowa Democratic colleague Tom Harkin, on the grounds that it had a higher limit on subsidies than the $275,000 he had persuaded the Senate to vote for. "A number of folks have been saying this is a good bill, and I'd say those folks are part right. It's a good bill if you're a cotton and rice producer. The problem is, we don't grow those commodities in my state of Iowa." He has consistently sought to limit subsidies, arguing that high payments to individual farmers put the whole program into political jeopardy, and has been joined by North Dakota Democrat Byron Dorgan. He also attacked the bill for lacking the ban on meatpacker ownership of livestock, which he has long supported. When state bans on meatpacker ownership, including Iowa's, were overturned to the courts, Grassley returned to the issue, with the co-sponsorship of Harkin, in 2007.

Grassley has served two stints as chairman of the Senate Finance Committee, in the first half of 2001 and from 2003 to 2007. Both as chairman and as ranking minority member, he has had close relations and weekly meetings with his Democratic counterpart Max Baucus; as chairman, he had far more difficult relations with the acrimonious and often sarcastic House Ways and Means Chairman Bill Thomas. He has used his committee seat to get advantageous tax treatment of ethanol, and in 1998 he got the ethanol tax credit extended to 2007—a key incentive to the creation of dozens of ethanol plants across Iowa and the increase in corn prices they've sparked. He has also sought tax incentives for biodiesel, made with soybean oil or recycled cooking oil. The United States is a major exporter of agricultural products, and Grassley has been a supporter of free trade, with one major exception. He supported NAFTA and strongly supported normal trade relations with China in the 1990s. He managed trade promotion authority to passage in May 2002. He helped push through the Australia Free Trade Agreement in 2004 and the Central American Free Trade Agreement in 2005. But he proposed an amendment to the Caribbean Basin Initiative to limit the import of duty-free ethanol only partly produced in the Caribbean, lest it give entry to Brazil's sugar-based ethanol. In 2006 he came to believe that the Doha round would not succeed and attempted to advance bilateral trade agreements; he asked the administration not to send the Vietnam free trade agreement up until it sent the one with Peru. After Charles Schumer and Lindsey Graham sponsored a bill to impose trade sanctions on China if it does not revalue its currency, Grassley and Baucus sponsored a bill that would seek sanctions through the IMF.

As chairman of Finance in May 2001 and again in May 2003, Grassley played a key role in rounding up bipartisan support for the Bush tax cuts. And he was one of the lead players on the Medicare/prescription drug act of 2003. He worked with Baucus to put together the Senate bill that got the approval even of Edward Kennedy. A different version passed the House, and after an abrasive conference committee Grassley successfully worked to sell the new version on the Senate floor. Throughout the process he was careful to look after the interests of rural health care providers and to seek changes in the Medicare reimbursement formula which had Iowa receiving the lowest reimbursement per beneficiary of any state. After the bill was passed, he defended it against continuing Democratic attacks. He complained, "The drug discount card has been the target of a deliberate campaign to discredit it and confuse seniors," and continued to closely monitor the workings of Medicare and Medicaid. He questioned CMS's oversight of fraud and abuse and sponsored a bill to insure that low-income seniors get $800 a year to pay for Medicare Part B premiums. In June 2006 he sought to eliminate the penalty for those who had not signed up for the Part D drug benefit by the May deadline; but that was held over, and in time a larger percentage of seniors enrolled than expected, with insurance premiums and total program costs both lower than projected. In January 2007 Grassley said he would filibuster Democratic bills requiring direct government negotiations with pharmaceuticals over drug prices, arguing that Part D had saved more than the Democrats' proposal would. "Eventually, we have to ask them to prove how they're going to save more money than we are."

Grassley argued in 2006 that major changes in Social Security could not happen even if Republicans had retained their majorities. "If you're going to change our entitlement programs or have a simplified tax system, it has to be an issue of national debate, and that can only happen in presidential election." Instead he worked for incremental changes. In May 2006 he blocked the extension of the 2003 capital gains and dividend taxes pending disagreements with Thomas; in September 2006 he wanted to act on the extensions rather than combine them with estate tax repeal and raising the minimum wage. He sought a charitable deduction for non-itemizers and tighter rules for foundations, with tougher penalties. He led the committee to tighten the rules on partial gifts of art, which allowed donors to retain possession while getting tax deductions. "Call it what it is, a subsidy for millionaires to buy art. Where I come from the word 'giving' doesn't mean keeping." He sent a letter to the Museum of Modern Art demanding to know the number of partial gifts and staff salaries. It was in the same spirit that he had once brought in the mounted head of a springbok to protest what he considered inflated values for donations of trophy heads. In January 2007 Grassley joined Baucus in backing a bill to repeal the Alternative Minimum Tax, which has been threatening to hit millions in high-income states, most of them heavily Democratic. But Grassley also said it would be unfair to raise other taxes to repeal the AMT. Grassley has also weighed in on other issues. In 2006 he asked administration officials whether there should be greater oversight of hedge funds. In January 2007 he questioned the tax exemption for college and university athletic activities, suggesting that donations going to coaches' salaries amounted to a taxpayer subsidy.

On the Judiciary Committee, Grassley was for years the chief sponsor of the bankruptcy bill which failed because of a provision on abortion; it finally passed in 2005 and Bush signed it in April.

He took special care to see that Chapter 12, applying to farmers, would allow them to reorganize their debt without creditors' consent. Large issues claim much of Grassley's attention, but he is willing to devote much time to smaller issues as well. He worked on the money-laundering bill after September 11 and said of bank lobbyists, "They are being very unpatriotic in their approach." In April 2006 he called on Bush to fire drug czar John Walters; he said the office wasn't doing enough to stop meth use. In December 2006 he accused the FDA of withholding key information about the antibiotic Ketek. He defended funding for a rain forest near Pella, Iowa. "[T]his wasn't snuck in in the middle of the night. I looked at this project as something that would be good for Iowa, and I was open about getting these funds for it."

For more than 20 years, Grassley has been the most popular politician in Iowa. As he said in the runup to the 2004 election, "I commune with Iowans on a regular basis and I think they know that, they appreciate it and they don't feel like Washington has gone to my head. I suppose if I don't get smug and overconfident, I'll be reelected." In 1986, he became the first Iowa senator to win reelection in 20 years, with a record 66% of the vote. In 1992, he broke the record when he won 70%-27%, carrying all 99 counties. In 1998, against a Democrat who campaigned by taking trips down Iowa rivers, he won 68%-30%, carrying all 99 counties again. Against a Democrat with whom he served in the legislature in the early 1970s, he was reelected in 2004 by 70%-28%. He carried all 99 counties again, from Johnson County and its college town Iowa City (53%-43%) to heavily Dutch-American Sioux County (92%-7%). In 2006, Grassley's 23-year-old grandson, Patrick, was elected as a Republican to represent his old district in the Iowa General Assembly. Charles Grassley has indicated he will run for reelection in 2010, and has now served Iowa longer in the Senate than anyone but William B. Allison, whose record he will beat if he serves until June 2016, three months before he turns 83.

Junior Senator

Tom Harkin (D)

Elected 1984, seat up 2008, 4th term; b. Nov. 19, 1939, Cumming; home, Cumming; IA St. U., B.S. 1962, Catholic U., J.D. 1972; Catholic; married (Ruth).

Military Career: Navy, 1962-67; Naval Reserves, 1969-72.

Elected Office: U.S. House of Reps., 1974-84.

Professional Career: Practicing atty., 1972-74; Staff Aide, House Select Cmte. on U.S. Involvement in SE Asia, 1973-74.

DC Office: 731 HSOB, 20510, 202-224-3254; Fax: 202-224-9369; Web site: harkin.senate.gov.

State Offices: Cedar Rapids, 319-365-4504; Davenport, 563-322-1338; Des Moines, 515-284-4574; Dubuque, 563-582-2130; Sioux City, 712-252-1550.

Committees: *Agriculture, Nutrition & Forestry* (Chmn. of 11 D). *Appropriations* (4th of 15 D): Labor, Health and Human Services, Education & Related Agencies (Chmn.); Agriculture, Rural Development, Food and Drug Administration & Related Agencies; State, Foreign Operations & Related Programs; Defense; Commerce, Justice, Science & Related Agencies; Transportation, Housing and Urban Development & Related Agencies. *Health, Education, Labor & Pensions* (3d of 11 D): Retirement & Aging; Employment & Workplace Safety. *Small Business & Entrepreneurship* (3d of 10 D).

Group Ratings

	ADA	ACLU	AFS	LCV	ITIC	NTU	COC	ACU	CFG	FRC
2006	100	100	100	71	50	9	36	8	0	0
2005	100	—	100	95	—	7	33	4	0	—

National Journal Ratings

	2005 LIB	—	2005 CONS		2006 LIB	—	2006 CONS
Economic	83%	—	16%		83%	—	13%
Social	83%	—	10%		96%	—	0%
Foreign	95%	—	0%		92%	—	6%

Key Votes of the 109th Congress

1. Bar ANWR Drilling	Y	5. Confirm Samuel Alito	N	9. Limit Interstate Abortion	N
2. FY06 Spending Curb	N	6. Path to Citizenship	Y	10. CAFTA	N
3. Estate Tax Repeal	N	7. Bar Same Sex Marriage	N	11. Urge Iraq Withdrawal	Y
4. Raise Minimum Wage	Y	8. Stem Cell Research $	Y	12. Provide Detainee Rights	Y

Election Results

2002 general	Tom Harkin (D)	554,278	(54%)	($6,897,168)
	Greg Ganske (R)	447,892	(44%)	($5,392,510)
	Other..	20,905	(2%)	
2002 primary	Tom Harkin (D)	unopposed		
1996 general	Tom Harkin (D)	634,166	(52%)	($6,070,137)
	Jim Ross Lightfoot (R)	571,807	(47%)	($2,439,679)

Prior Winning Percentages: 1990 (54%); 1984 (55%); 1982 House (59%); 1980 House (60%); 1978 House (59%); 1976 House (65%); 1974 House (51%)

Tom Harkin, a Democrat first elected to the House in 1974 and the Senate in 1984, is an accomplished veteran of Capitol Hill who brings the attitude of the aggrieved outsider to his work. Harkin grew up poor in a rural town, where his father was a coal miner and his mother, a Slovenian immigrant, died when he was 10. He worked his way through college and law school, and spent five years in the Navy during the 1960s, ferrying planes from Vietnam for repair. Returning there in 1970 as an aide to Congressman Neal Smith, he discovered the infamous "tiger cages" prison cells. He ran for the House in 1972 and lost narrowly, then ran again and won in 1974. In that campaign he invented "work days," a campaign technique widely imitated since: he spent a day working at each of a dozen or so local jobs. He won and then held the seat with solid percentages. Well before the 1984 election, he cornered the Democratic nomination to run against Senator Roger Jepsen. In the midst of Iowa's farm depression of the 1980s, Harkin was elected with 55% of the vote.

Harkin was chairman of the Agriculture Committee from June 2001 to January 2003 and has been chairman again since January 2007. He came into that position both times rather unexpectedly, and in both cases when the major farm legislation was coming up for reauthorization. The first time he steered to passage the 2002 farm bill, a considerable achievement and one somewhat out of line with his previous record. His earlier initiative was the 1987 Harkin-Gephardt supply management farm bill, which would have raised overall food costs in order to benefit small farmers. But it was a nonstarter even in the 1980s, when Iowa farmers were hurting. Harkin opposed the Republicans' 1996 farm act, which purported to phase out farm subsidies. But starting in 1998, Congress approved disaster relief every year for farmers, which had much the same economic effect. Harkin supported these efforts and worked to make conservation payments an entitlement and to promote the use of ethanol and alcohol fuels. Farm exports are important to Iowa, and Harkin, despite his warm feelings for labor unions, voted, apparently with some reluctance, for NAFTA in 1993 and normal trade relations with China in 2000. But he and Charles Grassley worked to stop the importation of Brazilian sugar-based ethanol tariff-free through El Salvador.

On taking the chairmanship in June 2001, Harkin worked to fashion a farm bill that would restore much of the subsidies (and end the need, some supporters said, for annual disaster relief) and that could win bipartisan support. His top goals were to increase conservation programs, come up with a formula for countercyclical aid and fight concentration in agribusiness. In November 2001, Harkin introduced his bill, with no limit on subsidies (though Harkin had proposed one) and more spending for conservation and food stamps (to secure votes from non-farm states). The bill was defeated in December 2001, but revived and passed in February 2002, with increased but limited subsidies for grain and cotton and a doubling of conservation money in an expanded Conservation Security Program. The total cost was estimated at $73.5 billion over 10 years. Harkin put in subsidies to discourage the use of irrigated water and added dairy and peanut provisions that won votes from New England and the Deep South; it passed 58-40. It included a ban on meatpackers owning livestock—a key issue for Grassley. The bill went to conference committee, in which the House Republicans, led by Larry Combest from cotton-farming west Texas, insisted on higher subsidy limits and deletion of the ban on meatpacker ownership of livestock. Harkin brought the bill back and got the Senate to pass it.

In the minority Harkin continued to follow farm issues closely. For much of 2003 and 2004 he criticized Agriculture Secretary Ann Veneman's Conservation Security Program regulations as tardy and narrow. In October 2004 he held up the corporate tax bill to protest an appropriation that paid for $2.8 billion in drought aid by deferring conservation spending and the dropping of FDA regulation of tobacco; he got a non-binding resolution to restore the conservation money. In the face of a Supreme Court decision leaving open meatpacking ownership of livestock, he sought to set up a special counsel at USDA to investigate meatpacker price-fixing; he joined Republicans Charles Grassley and Mike Enzi in sponsoring a bill to bar meatpacker ownership of livestock. The Democratic victory in 2006 made Harkin chairman once again, as the farm bill came up for reauthorization in 2007. One problem they faced was a 2005 WTO ruling outlawing the cotton subsidy program and threatening subsidy programs for other commodities. Harkin and incoming House Agriculture Chairman Collin Peterson quickly said that they could write a new bill that would not be affected by any limits on subsidies in an agreement in the Doha trade negotiations, which were stalled. The two said that stronger energy and conservation programs were their first priority; Peterson called for a permanent weather-related disaster relief program. Harkin said, "We're going to have to think about how we are moving our agricultural agenda toward energy independence."

Harkin has had a substantial impact on health policy. Two of his sisters died from breast cancer and one brother of thyroid cancer; another brother became deaf at age nine. He was a key player in shaping the Americans with Disabilities Act of 1990. This was a great achievement, one that required overcoming resistance based on cost and qualms about the real-world effect of regulations, to build a bipartisan coalition with the first Bush administration. As chairman and ranking Democrat on the Labor-HHS Appropriations Committee, Harkin worked creatively and determinedly with his Republican counterpart Arlen Specter to double the budget for the National Institutes of Health over five years—strengthening one of America's greatest research institutions in a way that may be remembered gratefully 50 or 100 years from now. He also sponsored a national institute on alternative medicine. "We need a new paradigm in American health care, a prevention paradigm," he said in 2004, and sponsored a multi-part bill to encourage better nutrition and fitness. Provisions passed include requiring schools to set nutritional standards for food available during the school day, making Harkin Fresh Fruit and Vegetable grants to schools permanent. In 2005 he called for food companies to do less marketing to children and sponsored a bill to give the FTC authority to regulate advertising directed at children. He is a crusader against childhood obesity, pushing for nutritional standards for food sold in schools by sponsoring bills in the beginning of the 110th Congress that would expand federal research seeking solutions, require labels on menus in chain restaurants and form a federal task force on childhood obesity. A bill he sponsored in 2006 would have removed French fries, ice cream bars, non-diet soft drinks and candy bars from schools. Opposition comes not only from food companies but from school districts eager for food revenues. Harkin sponsored the bill for federal funding of embryonic stem-cell research; it passed 63-37 in July 2006 and 63-34 in April 2007—not enough to override a presidential veto.

On foreign policy, Harkin's views seem to have been shaped by the Vietnam War. He was a vocal opponent of Contra aid in the 1980s and of the Gulf War resolution in 1991, bringing a lawsuit against President George H.W. Bush to prevent him the use of force without congressional approval. But he favored the threat of force in Haiti in 1994. He voted to authorize the use of force in Iraq in 1998, when Bill Clinton sought it, and in October 2002, when George W. Bush did. But as the violence continued in Iraq, he said in December 2003, it "may not be Vietnam, but, boy, it sure smells like it." In May 2004, he said the Abu Ghraib prison abuses reminded him of the tiger cages in Vietnam and said, "I believe it's time to fire the secretary of defense." On the campaign trail, he responded in August 2004 to Dick Cheney's attacks on John Kerry by saying, "When I hear this coming from Dick Cheney, who was a coward, who would not serve during the Vietnam War, it makes my blood boil. He'll be tough, but he'll be tough with someone else's kid's blood." And in September he said, "If, God forbid, another attack happens here, I see the president using that as a linchpin to reinstate the draft."

As an appropriator, Harkin has directed spending toward Iowa. As he said in November 2006, "I happen to be a supporter of earmarks, unabashedly. But I don't call them earmarks. It is 'congressional directed spending.'" He cited the millions he directed toward breast cancer research. "Now, was that bad? If you left it to the Defense Department, they never would have done it." From 2000 to 2006 he got more than $275 million in spending on Iowa projects, including $800,000 million for the National Mississippi River Museum in Dubuque, $250,000 for the National Cattle Congress in Waterloo, $1.8 million for University of Northern Iowa projects, $200,000 to redevelop an abandoned military base outside Waverly and $3 million for the National Advanced Driving Simulator in Coralville.

Harkin has been a major force in Iowa politics. His fervent stands on issues and his hard-edged campaigning give him a large base of strong supporters and a large base of strong detractors as well. He has never won by a large margin but in his career he has beaten no less than five members of

Congress—according to his office, more than anyone else in history—while never winning more than 55% of the vote in his Senate campaigns. He ran for president in 1992. In angry phrases, with a Trumanesque zest, Harkin preached that George H.W. Bush and the Republicans helped only the rich and that government must get involved to help the poor and middle class. But organized labor withheld an early endorsement despite his 90%-plus AFL-CIO voting record—a great tactical victory for Bill Clinton. Harkin's sweep of the Iowa caucuses February 10, actually an impressive testimonial to his home state popularity, was mostly discounted by the media. He finished with only 10% in New Hampshire; though he won the Minnesota and Idaho caucuses March 3, he got only 7% in South Carolina March 7 after campaigning there with Jesse Jackson, and quit the race. In Iowa Harkin has built a strong political organization that helped him win reelection in 1990—the first time Iowa has elected a Democratic senator to a second full term—1996 and 2002. In 2000 he endorsed Al Gore in the Iowa precinct caucuses and appeared with him all over the state—an important factor in Gore's smashing victory.

In 2002 Harkin's opponent was Congressman Greg Ganske, a Des Moines plastic surgeon who had upset 36-year incumbent Neal Smith in 1994 and had been one of the lead supporters of HMO regulation in the House. Ganske won the June 2002 primary, but by an unimpressive 59%-41% margin over a more conservative candidate. Against Harkin, Ganske argued that his work on HMO regulation showed that he could work on a bipartisan basis for solutions to problems. Harkin argued that with his seniority he could best serve Iowa's interests. Harkin attacked Ganske for supporting "privatization" of Social Security and touted passage of the farm bill; Ganske said it gave too much in subsidies to southern cotton and rice farmers and didn't include a ban on meatpacker ownership of livestock. Polls showed the race fairly close after the June primary. But Harkin had far more money and, for the first time, the endorsement of the Iowa Farm Bureau Federation.

Then, in September, scandal struck. A Des Moines Democrat and former Harkin staffer, who changed his registration to Republican and contributed $50 to Ganske, attended a meeting of Ganske fundraisers with a tape recorder in his pocket. After the meeting, he turned it over to a 21-year-old Harkin campaign staffer. A transcript was leaked to a political reporter by "Democratic sources." Harkin's campaign manager said his campaign had nothing to do with it. That lie was exposed and by the end of the week, the campaign manager resigned and Harkin apologized. At the candidates' next debate angry words flowed. Many observers speculated that in squeaky-clean Iowa this caper would cost Harkin votes. Perhaps it did, but not very many. Harkin's campaign and the Iowa Democratic party also ran an effective, high-tech voter registration and turnout operation; they appear to have maximized the Democratic vote not only in factory towns but in rural counties Democrats usually don't carry. Harkin won 54%-44%. Regional patterns of support evident in Harkin's 1990 and 1996 runs were not evident in 2002. He carried Des Moines, Cedar Rapids and all of Iowa's significant cities except Council Bluffs, but he won in most rural areas as well, carrying 79 of Iowa's 99 counties—far more than the 50 he carried in 1996 or the 63 he carried in 1990.

Harkin seemed likely to be a key figure in the 2004 Iowa presidential precinct caucuses. As he noted, "Every candidate I have supported in Iowa has gone on to be the nominee of our party." In May 2003 he organized the first of 10 Hear It From the Heartland meetings, each featuring a different presidential candidate. Most attended his September 2003 Harkin Steak Fry. For months he did not endorse. On January 9, just ten days before the caucuses, he endorsed Dean. It proved not a big help: Dean's standing in the polls started declining a few days later. He finished third and on election night Harkin awkwardly cheered on stage as he watched Dean deliver "the scream" speech. In November 2006, when outgoing Governor Tom Vilsack announced he was running for president, Harkin endorsed him; that left him with no candidate when Vilsack withdrew in February 2007. But after Barack Obama appeared at Harkin's fall 2006 steak fry, Harkin said that the only comparison to him as one who could draw an enthusiastic crowd was Robert Kennedy. Looking forward to his own 2008 campaign for reelection, he said, "The way things are looking now, Democrats will be in the majority for the next several years," and "Until I tell you differently, the Democratic presidential nominee will have Harkin on the ballot in Iowa." In early 2007 there was some speculation that one of Iowa's two remaining Republican congressmen, Tom Latham and Steve King, might run, but observers noted that Harkin has beaten an incumbent member of Congress each time he has won reelection. In March 2007 Linn County businessman Steve Rathje declared his candidacy and embarked on a bus tour.

FIRST DISTRICT

Rep. Bruce Braley (D)

Elected 2006, 1st term; b. Oct. 30, 1957, Grinnell; home, Waterloo; IA St. U., B.A. 1980, U. of IA, J.D. 1983; Presbyterian; married (Carolyn).

Professional Career: Practicing atty., 1983-2006.

DC Office: 1408 LHOB, 20515, 202-225-2911; Fax: 202-225-6666; Web site: braley.house.gov.

District Offices: Davenport, 563-323-5988; Dubuque, 563-557-7789; Waterloo, 319-287-3233.

Committees: *Oversight & Government Reform* (15th of 23 D): National Security & Foreign Affairs; Domestic Policy. *Small Business* (12th of 18 D): Contracting & Technology (Chmn.). *Transportation & Infrastructure* (30th of 41 D): Railroads, Pipelines & Hazardous Materials; Aviation; Highways & Transit.

Group Ratings and Key Votes: Newly Elected

Election Results

2006 general	Bruce Braley (D)	114,322	(55%)	($2,418,625)
	Mike Whalen (R)	89,729	(43%)	($2,385,532)
	Other	3,570	(2%)	
2006 primary	Bruce Braley (D)	10,489	(36%)	
	Rick Dickinson (D)	9,971	(34%)	
	Bill Gluba (D)	7,453	(26%)	
	Denny Heath (D)	1,161	(4%)	
2004 general	Jim Nussle (R)	159,993	(55%)	($1,622,743)
	Bill Gluba (D)	125,490	(43%)	($524,168)
	Other	4,571	(2%)	

The People		Race/Ethnic Origin	Ancestry	
Area size:	7,291 sq. mi.	92.1% White	German: 31.5% Irish: 11.1%	
Urban population:	66.3%	3.8% Black	English: 6.0%	
Rural population:	33.7%	0.8% Asian	**2004 Presidential Vote**	
Pop. 2000:	585,302	0.2% Native Am.	Kerry (D)	157,380 (53%)
Pop. 2005 (est):	585,693	0.0% Hawaiian	Bush (R)	138,073 (46%)
Median income:	$38,727	1.0% Two+ races	Other	2,381 (1%)
Poverty status:	10.1%	0.1% Other	**2000 Presidential Vote**	
Military veterans:	13.8%	2.0% Hispanic Origin	Gore (D)	135,856 (52%)
			Bush (R)	116,588 (45%)
			Other	7,737 (3%)
			Cook Partisan Voting Index: D + 5	

Occupation	Blue collar: 28.3%	White collar: 55.7%	Gray collar: 16.0%

Northeast Iowa, along the Mississippi River and westward, has some of the loveliest landscape in America. Here the Mississippi flows past green bluffs, then broadens out in great quiet pools and flows past picturesque towns. A century and a half ago settlers surged west of the Mississippi. Germans stopped at the river bluffs reminiscent of their native land and built neat farmhouses and substantial towns. Inland, on the rolling hills portrayed with surprisingly little exaggeration in the paintings of Iowa's Grant Wood, and in the more open territory to the west, New England and Midwestern Yankees built their characteristic farmhouses, barns, town halls, church spires and small colleges. Railroad builders, headquartered in Chicago, extended their networks of steel rails over the plains and rivers. You can see the stamp of these pioneers today, though the old ethnic folkways have faded and giant barges and riverboat casinos have replaced the old river steamboats; much of this is in the Silos and Smokestacks National Heritage Area. Davenport, on the hills over the Mississippi River, still has the look of the city where Ronald Reagan got his first radio job more than 70 years ago. German Catholics settled Dubuque, whose giant Victorian courthouse looks down on the Mississippi and up at the Fenelon Place Elevator that rides up the bluff. Dubuque, which houses a giant John Deere facility, has other large—and growing—factories. Farther west is Waterloo, which grew rapidly after 1900 as its John Deere tractor factory expanded and the eight-floor Rath factory became the largest meat-packing plant in the world; Rath closed in 1984 and Deere had thousands of layoffs, but Waterloo has rebounded somewhat with new businesses from telemarketing to a high-tech Iowa Beef Processing (IBP) factory, acquired by Tyson Foods in 2001.

The 1st Congressional District covers much of northeast Iowa, including the Mississippi riverfront from the antique town of McGregor south to Davenport, Iowa's part of the Quad Cities and heading west 100 miles as far as Butler County. There is considerable political variation here. Davenport and next-door Bettendorf were historically Republican, but in 2000 and 2004, like much of eastern Iowa, they voted narrowly for Al Gore and John Kerry. Dubuque, heavily German Catholic, was for years Iowa's most Democratic city, and still is sometimes unless abortion is the issue. But the rural counties along the river and farther west—more German Protestant, Scandinavian and Yankee—were traditionally Republican. Waterloo and Cedar Falls, originally Republican, trended sharply Democratic in the troubled 1980s. Overall this district is pretty evenly balanced and was a key battleground in the 2000 and 2004 presidential races. At one point George W. Bush and John Kerry were campaigning within blocks of each other in Davenport (thieves took advantage of the distraction and robbed three local banks). Bush lost the district by seven points each time.

The new congressman from the 1st District is Bruce Braley, a Democrat from Waterloo who replaced Jim Nussle, who ran unsuccessfully for governor. A native of Brooklyn (Iowa), his mother was a teacher and his father died a few years after a severe injury when he fell down a grain elevator. He graduated from Iowa State University and got his law degree from the University of Iowa. He was an active trial lawyer and is a former president of the Iowa Trial Lawyers Association. His candidacy drew considerable financial support from the Association of Trial Lawyers of America and many of its members and officers. Those connections also made him the target of lawyer-bashing: The NRCC disparaged Braley as "a trial lawyer's trial lawyer." In the June 6 primary, Braley overcame two competitive opponents: former state Rep. Rick Dickinson, an economic development official in Dubuque, and 2004 Democratic nominee Bill Gluba, a real estate agent in Davenport. Although Braley was making his first run for office, he had a distinct fundraising advantage and the support of the Iowa AFL-CIO. He won 36% to 34% for Dickinson and 26% for Gluba; each comfortably won his home county. Republicans nominated Mike Whalen, a graduate of Harvard Law School, wealthy entrepreneur and owner of the Machine Shed restaurant chain; he took the primary with 48% to 37% for state Representative Bill Dix.

From the start, Republicans knew that this would be a tough contest. In his eight terms, Nussle—who chaired the House Budget Committee from 2001 to 2006—never got more than 57% of the vote. This was one of only 18 Republican-held congressional districts that Kerry carried in 2004. The candidates disagreed on many issues, including Iraq, tort reform, international trade deals, abortion rights and stem cell research. Braley framed Whalen as an out-of-touch millionaire. He claimed that Whalen wanted to privatize Social Security, and he attacked Whalen's opposition to raising the minimum wage. When Whalen insisted that his employees all receive better than the federal minimum wage, Braley produced a Machine Shed waitress who claimed that, even with tips, she and many of her co-workers earned only minimum wage. Whalen charged that the litigious Braley contributed to higher health care costs and the medical liability crisis; Braley called for expanding health care for the uninsured. Although the NRCC spent heavily on direct-mail and television ads against Braley, it wasn't enough to keep the seat in GOP control.

Braley won surprisingly easily: 55%-43%. He took each of the 12 counties, except for two rural counties. As expected, he ran strongly in Waterloo's Black Hawk County, with 59%; but he also took Whalen's Quad Cities base in Scott County, with 53%. He got seats on the Transportation and Infrastructure Committee (to tend to local projects) and on the Oversight and Government Reform Committee (to utilize his trial-lawyer skills.) Some local Democrats have mentioned Braley as a possible contender when Iowa's two veteran senators retire.

SECOND DISTRICT

Rep. Dave Loebsack (D)

Elected 2006, 1st term; b. Dec. 23, 1952, Sioux City; home, Mt. Vernon; IA St. U., B.S. 1974, M.A. 1976, U. of CA, Ph.D., 1985; Methodist; married (Teresa).

Professional Career: Professor, Cornell Col., 1982-2006.

DC Office: 1513 LHOB, 20515, 202-225-6576; Fax: 202-226-0757; Web site: loebsack.house.gov.

District Offices: Cedar Rapids, 319-364-2288; Iowa City, 319-351-0789.

Committees: *Armed Services* (27th of 34 D): Strategic Forces; Readiness. *Education & Labor* (20th of 27 D): Health, Employment, Labor & Pensions; Early Childhood, Elementary & Secondary Education.

Group Ratings and Key Votes: Newly Elected

Election Results

2006 general	Dave Loebsack (D)	107,683	(51%)	($488,385)
	Jim Leach (R)	101,707	(49%)	($533,734)
2006 primary	Dave Loebsack (D)	unopposed		
2004 general	Jim Leach (R)	176,684	(59%)	($479,605)
	Dave Franker (D)	117,405	(39%)	($122,489)
	Other	5,792	(2%)	

The People		Race/Ethnic Origin	Ancestry	
Area size:	7,684 sq. mi.	92.4% White	German: 24.0% Irish: 10.4%	
Urban population:	66.0%	2.0% Black	English: 7.3%	
Rural population:	34.0%	1.5% Asian	**2004 Presidential Vote**	
Pop. 2000:	585,241	0.2% Native Am.	Kerry (D) 171,561	(55%)
Pop. 2005 (est):	596,954	0.0% Hawaiian	Bush (R) 135,991	(44%)
Median income:	$40,121	1.0% Two+ races	Other 3,090	(1%)
Poverty status:	9.9%	0.1% Other	**2000 Presidential Vote**	
Military veterans:	13.0%	2.7% Hispanic Origin	Gore (D) 141,487	(53%)
			Bush (R) 113,255	(43%)
			Other 11,581	(4%)
			Cook Partisan Voting Index: D + 7	

Occupation	Blue collar: 26.5%	White collar: 58.6%	Gray collar: 14.9%

Eastern Iowa is a land little known to outsiders. It is a land of rolling hills and deep river valleys, of undulant farm fields and big skies, of prosperous small towns and grain elevators and factories. Even political writers, who come to Iowa by the thousands for the quadrennial precinct caucuses tend to hang out in Des Moines and to do their reporting there or in small counties within an hour's drive; this is a lot bigger state than New Hampshire, and driving from Des Moines east to the second largest city, Cedar Rapids, takes more than two hours—only worth it for some major event. Eastern Iowa was not accessible even to candidate George W. Bush in 2000, since his campaign plane was too big to land in any of the airports here. So Al Gore ran well in eastern Iowa—it was one of the few parts of the country where he carried most rural counties—and carried the state by 4,000 votes. But by 2004 a local airport runway had been extended and George W. Bush improved his showing enough to carry Iowa by 10,000 votes.

Cedar Rapids, the metropolis in these parts, has high-tech employers and contemporary office buildings; it boomed in the past decade, and per capita income, adjusted for the local cost of living, is among the nation's highest. Yet traditional industries still make themselves known: Go down by the river and you can't miss the smell of burnt oats coming from the Quaker Oats factory. Iowa City, just to the south, is a university town complete with trendy bookstores and vegetarian eateries; the University of Iowa is known for its Writer's Workshop. Travel farther afield, and you will come on increasing oddities. Rural Cedar County, the birthplace of Herbert Hoover, reported a tie on election night 2000, the only county in the nation to do so; a recount gave Al Gore a 4,033–4,031 vote lead. In

2004 George W. Bush carried it 4,869–4,747—a 122-vote landslide. Bentonsport, in Van Buren County near the Missouri border, was mostly bought up by the county's conservation board in the 1970s, and restored; now it is an artists' and craftsmen's colony. Conesville, in Muscatine County near the Mississippi, has an Hispanic majority—the only city in Iowa that does—attracted at first by farm work in the fields and more recently by the IBP plant in nearby Columbus Junction. Anamosa, in Jones County just east of Cedar Rapids, features the house painted by Anamosa native Grant Wood in *American Gothic*—the models for the two figures were his dentist and his sister, who died only in 1990—and you can have your picture taken there too. The oddest of all is Iowa's newest city, incorporated in 2001, Vedic City. It's just outside the fading town of Fairfield, in Jefferson County, where followers of the Maharishi Mahesh Yogi built Maharishi University in 1973, where believers in transcendental meditation study and meditate and practice yogic flying (the first step is hopping around). Vedic City "believes in the creativity-enhancing, stress-reducing, intelligence-increasing, health-promoting and world-peace-increasing properties of TM, and it really, really wants you to believe in them too," wrote a visiting reporter from the *Los Angeles Times*. There's a political angle too: TM followers supported John Hagelin of the Natural Law party for president in 1996, and he won 21% of the vote in Jefferson County in 1996 and 15% in 2000. Hagelin didn't run in 2004 and his votes evidently went to John Kerry, who carried the county.

All these parts of eastern Iowa are in the state's 2d Congressional District. It is by most measures Iowa's most Democratic congressional district, thanks in large part to big Democratic majorities in Iowa City's Johnson County; Cedar Rapids's Linn County has also inclined toward the Democrats in recent years.

The new congressman from the 2d District is Dave Loebsack, a Democrat elected in a stunning 2006 upset. In a result that was a fluke in many ways, he defeated Jim Leach, a Republican who often was out of step with his party but with views that seemed well-connected to this district. A native of Sioux City, Loebsack lived as a child in poverty with his mother, grandmother and three siblings in a two-bedroom house, and worked as a high school janitor to pay for college. He got his bachelor and master degrees at Iowa State University and went to the University of California at Davis for his Ph.D. in political science. Since 1982, he had been a professor of international relations at Cornell College in Mount Vernon, a few miles from Cedar Rapids. For three years before his campaign, he was fundraising chairman for Linn County Democrats. His initial foray into the race—and, for that matter, into electoral politics—did not inspire confidence in his candidacy: He failed to gain the appropriate number of signatures required to get on the ballot. But under Iowa law, if no candidate files for a party's nomination, the party can designate a candidate; so, Democrats chose Loebsack anyway. He insisted that his campaign was not an attack on Leach's tenure in Congress but rather on GOP leadership and he called the moderate Republican an "enabler" for party leaders. In fact, the two candidates had a cordial relationship. Over the years, Loebsack had invited Leach, a member of the House International Relations Committee, to address his classes. During the spring 2006 semester, even as Loebsack geared up to unseat Leach, the often-idiosyncratic congressman spent a month guest-teaching a Cornell College class. "There's no doubt Jim Leach is more than qualified to teach all my courses at Cornell College, and there's no doubt that I can represent the residents of Iowa's 2d District," Loebsack said in January 2006.

The war in Iraq was a prominent issue from the start of this contest. In 2002, Leach was the only member of the Iowa delegation to oppose the war. Yet Loebsack sought to tie Leach to Secretary of Defense Donald Rumsfeld because Leach had been an aide to Rumsfeld for two years in the late 1960s while Rumsfeld served as an Illinois congressman, and he later served a stint under him at the Office of Economic Opportunity; both were Princeton alums. Despite their disagreement on the war, Leach refused to disparage his former boss, calling him a friend and insisting that his ouster would not change the administration's policy in Iraq. The candidates remained civil to each other with Leach discussing the need to promote ethanol and Loebsack calling for national health insurance. But Leach underestimated the hostility toward the war in the most populous counties in the district, which also happened to be home to university communities that welcomed Loebsack's candidacy and anti-Iraq war message. Loebsack raised $522,000, which ordinarily would have been not nearly enough to win a competitive House race; he had little support from the Democratic Congressional Campaign Committee. But Leach eschewed modern campaign practices and was a notoriously reticent fundraiser. When the Iowa Republican Party sent negative mailers on Loebsack, Leach told them to stop and he warned that he would refuse to caucus with House Republicans if the negative tactics continued. He refused to accept contributions from political action committees or from outside the district, and raised only $491,000. Three weeks before the election, he said that U.S. troops should be withdrawn from Iraq within a year, but that wasn't enough to return him to Washington from this Democratic-leaning district in a year when the Bush administration and the Iraq war dominated headlines.

Leach earned the endorsement of the district's major newspapers but Loebsack won 51% to 49%. Of the district's 15 counties, Leach carried 10. Loebsack won by 367 votes in Linn County (Cedar Rapids), the largest county in the district. The election swung on the second-largest: Johnson County (Iowa City), where Loebsack got 58%, a margin of 8,525 votes. He won in three other counties—Des Moines (Burlington), Lee (Fort Madison) and Wapello (Ottumwa)—by a total of nearly 5,000 votes. In a concession speech to teary supporters, Leach maintained his civil decorum. "For three decades, I've had . . . the goal from the beginning of running positive campaigns. I want to express my deep respect for the Loebsack campaign." He called the end of his career "the happiest day of my life. It's as if a burden has been lifted."

Loebsack gained seats on Armed Services, and Education and Labor and sponsored a measure to designate the federal building in Davenport as the James A. Leach United States Courthouse; it passed the House in May 2007. Given Loebsack's political inexperience and the predilections of this district, the biggest threat to his reelection could come in a Democratic primary.

THIRD DISTRICT

Rep. Leonard Boswell (D)

Elected 1996, 6th term; b. Jan. 10, 1934, Harrison Cnty., MO; home, Davis City; Graceland Col., B.A. 1969; Reorganized Latter Day Saints; married (Dody).

Military Career: Army, 1956-76 (Vietnam).

Elected Office: IA Senate, 1984-96, Pres., 1992-96.

Professional Career: Farmer.

DC Office: 1427 LHOB, 20515, 202-225-3806; Fax: 202-225-5608; Web site: boswell.house.gov.

District Offices: Des Moines, 515-282-1909.

Committees: *Agriculture* (5th of 25 D): Livestock, Dairy & Poultry (Chmn.). *Permanent Select Committee on Intelligence* (3d of 12 D): Terrorism, Human Intelligence, Analysis & Counterintelligence (Vice Chmn.). *Transportation & Infrastructure* (13th of 41 D): Railroads, Pipelines & Hazardous Materials; Aviation.

Group Ratings

	ADA	ACLU	AFS	LCV	ITIC	NTU	COC	ACU	CFG	FRC
2006	70	55	86	50	29	20	67	44	24	28
2005	60	—	100	50	—	20	55	32	11	33

National Journal Ratings

	2005 LIB	—	2005 CONS		2006 LIB	—	2006 CONS
Economic	62%	—	37%		58%	—	42%
Social	59%	—	41%		58%	—	41%
Foreign	68%	—	32%		63%	—	36%

Key Votes of the 109th Congress

1. Estate Tax Repeal	Y	5. Limit Interstate Abortion	Y	9. Build Border Fence	Y
2. Limit CAFE Standards	Y	6. Extend Patriot Act	Y	10. CAFTA	N
3. FY06 Spending Curb	N	7. Bar Same Sex Marriage	N	11. Oppose Iraq Withdrawal	Y
4. Drilling in ANWR	N	8. Stem Cell Research $	Y	12. Detainee Tribunals	Y

Election Results

2006 general	Leonard Boswell (D)	115,769	(52%)	($2,060,474)
	Jeff Lamberti (R)	103,722	(46%)	($1,994,605)
	Other	3,796	(2%)	
2006 primary	Leonard Boswell (D)	unopposed		
2004 general	Leonard Boswell (D)	168,007	(55%)	($1,545,133)
	Stan Thompson (R)	136,099	(45%)	($862,304)

Prior Winning Percentages: 2002 (53%); 2000 (63%); 1998 (57%); 1996 (49%)

The People		Race/Ethnic Origin	Ancestry	
Area size:	7,034 sq. mi.	90.1% White	German: 20.7% Irish: 9.6%	
Urban population:	73.1%	3.2% Black	English: 7.7%	
Rural population:	26.9%	1.9% Asian	**2004 Presidential Vote**	
Pop. 2000:	585,305	0.4% Native Am.	Bush (R) 154,919	(50%)
Pop. 2005 (est):	612,950	0.0% Hawaiian	Kerry (D) 154,652	(50%)
Median income:	$43,176	1.1% Two+ races	Other 2,443	(1%)
Poverty status:	8.0%	0.1% Other	**2000 Presidential Vote**	
Military veterans:	12.7%	3.2% Hispanic Origin	Gore (D) 132,890	(49%)
			Bush (R) 131,319	(48%)
			Other 7,226	(3%)
			Cook Partisan Voting Index: D + 1	

Occupation	Blue collar: 23.5%	White collar: 62.0%	Gray collar: 14.5%

Iowa, which today seems very much in the middle of the country, was once part of the West. It was not only the home of sober farmers and pious burghers, but also the eastern terminus of the first Transcontinental Railroad, a way stop for people in a hurry to get across the Great Plains to the Rockies and the Pacific Northwest. Those who stayed behind were determined to use the wealth accumulated by methodical husbandry of their fertile farmlands to implant firmly the glories of Western civilization. You can feel that impulse today in Des Moines when you look across the river from downtown at the Victorian Capitol, its gold dome above a Corinthian pediment, or Terrace Hill, the beautifully restored governor's mansion, atop a hill overlooking the Raccoon River. The nearby Living History Farms, which recreate Indian villages, frontier towns and turn-of-the-century farms, show the effort the new settlers made to put their imprint on the environment.

The 3d Congressional District covers 12 counties in central Iowa, including Des Moines's Polk County and extends mostly to the east. It is the most urbanized Iowa district and the only one that does not border another state or a mighty river on the east or west. Some 65% of its votes are cast in Polk County, but it does not include Dallas or Warren Counties which are in the Des Moines metropolitan area. Des Moines remains classically Middle America, even as it becomes more lively downtown and spreads into the countryside, and even as Iowa farm counties' population continues to decline. The area has become a sanctuary for people from around the nation who are seeking a family-friendly urban lifestyle. More than 12,000 Bosnians also have settled in Des Moines because the climate reminds them of home and they have been well received. Insurance, agricultural supply, and printing and service businesses are expanding in office centers downtown and at freeway interchanges; Iowans are driving 100 miles or more to fill the shopping malls at cities' edges.

The remainder of the district is largely rural, with no city larger than 30,000. But these small towns continue to house some giant manufacturing plants. Pella (9,800) is the home of the Pella window and door maker, which employs 3,000 workers. With considerable outside criticism of its federal funding, Pella also is the site of the planned Earthpark—a combination rain forest, aquarium and education center. The famed Amana colonies, with seven quaint villages, were founded in 1855 by the Community of True Inspiration, German pietists who have retained many of their old customs. This was the home of the Amana appliance business, acquired by Iowa-based Maytag in 2001, which in turn was purchased and then closed by Michigan-based Whirlpool in 2007. An ethanol plant being built in Tama is set to begin production in 2008. Polk County has historically voted Democratic, but has become more Republican as its white collar businesses grow and its blue collar businesses fade; the rural counties here have mostly been historically Republican. The result is a district split right down the middle, about as evenly divided as any in the nation: 49%-48% for Al Gore in 2000, 49.7%-49.6% for George W. Bush in 2004.

The congressman from the 3d District is Leonard Boswell, a Democrat first elected in 1996. Boswell grew up on farms in Ringgold and Decatur Counties, near the Missouri border. He was drafted in 1956, at 22, and was a private in the Army. He re-enlisted as an officer, graduated first in his class in both fixed wing and helicopter flying school, served two years in Vietnam, and retired as a lieutenant colonel in 1976; he was a teacher at the Army command college at Fort Leavenworth, Kansas. Boswell settled down on his Decatur County farm and became head of the local Farmers' Co-op. He managed to keep it out of bankruptcy during the farm depression of the 1980s and decided to go into politics. He was elected state senator from a six-county Republican district in 1984, served as chairman of Appropriations and, after 1992, Senate president; he was the Democratic nominee for lieutenant governor in 1994. In 1996, he ran for an open seat in the old 3d District, which was largely rural and extended across the southern tier of Iowa. Boswell flew his four-seater Piper

Comanche 250 across the district and called for balancing the budget, higher education aid and protections against Medicare reductions, all to be financed with Pentagon cuts and elimination of Medicare waste. Poweshiek County attorney Mike Mahaffey ran as a moderate Republican. Boswell was endorsed by the Farm Bureau, which usually backs Republicans. He raised more money than Mahaffey and, like other Democrats, ran ads attacking Newt Gingrich and the Republican Medicare plan. The result was a 49%-48% Boswell victory.

Boswell got a seat on Agriculture and supported the Freedom to Farm Act. Along with all of the delegation's Republicans, he voted for normal trade relations with China, the world's biggest market for pork. His voting record has consistently placed him in the most conservative quadrant of House Democrats. Focusing on health care, he has called for expanded tax breaks for insurance coverage. Assigned to the Intelligence Committee, his extensive military background and security clearance left him well positioned to investigate the nation's response to terrorism. He voted to authorize military action in Iraq, but later criticized the Bush administration for not spending enough money for counter-terrorism. In May 2006, when *The Washington Post* reported that he was absent from a closed committee meeting, he said that he was "appalled" that Republicans had leaked the information. His attendance was a sensitive issue because he was absent from the House for three months in 2005 following removal of a non-cancerous tumor from his abdomen and subsequent chemotherapy; he lost 70 pounds, but his doctors said that he could meet the House's schedule.

The non-partisan June 2001 redistricting plan left Boswell with a dilemma. Only seven of the 27 counties and 24% from the population in his former district were moved to the new 3d District. Decatur County, where he continued to operate his family farm, was one of eight counties moved to western Iowa's new, heavily Republican 5th District. The other option was to move to the new 2d District, which leans Democratic but where he would have faced a tough contest against incumbent Republican Jim Leach. Boswell decided to move to Des Moines and run in the 3d. But Democratic state Senator Matt McCoy had already said he would run in the Polk County district; local fundraising events for Boswell by Minority Leader Dick Gephardt eventually convinced him to defer. Republican challenger Stan Thompson was less accommodating. A Des Moines lawyer who worked for George W. Bush in the 2000 Iowa caucuses, Thompson argued that Boswell was out of step with the new district's geography and philosophy. Thompson ran a credible campaign and won several endorsements, including a joint designation with Boswell from the Farm Bureau. Boswell won by a 53%-45% margin. In a 2004 rematch, Thompson said, "It's time we elect a congressman who is on the way up and not one on the way out." Thompson won endorsements from the Iowa Farm Bureau and from the *Des Moines Register*, which praised his energy and job-creating proposals, and said that Boswell had become "almost so low-key he is no longer heard." This time, Boswell won 55%-45% and carried Polk County 57%-43%.

In 2006, he faced another tough challenge—this time, from state Senate co-president Jeff Lamberti, an active fundraiser; his family owned a chain of convenience stores and gas stations. The NRCC made Boswell one of its prime incumbent targets. Lamberti highlighted his differences with Boswell on taxes, excessive spending, and border control. Boswell cited Lamberti's support from Republican leaders to raise doubts about the "change" that he would bring and called him a "multi-millionaire." This was Boswell's closest win since he was first elected: 52%-46%. His 13,269-vote lead in Polk County accounted for more than his district-wide margin. Lamberti's showing was all the more impressive given the poor Republican performance elsewhere in Iowa.

After the election, Boswell initially took a seat on the Energy and Commerce Committee, but he changed his mind when the 110th Congress convened and kept his previous committee assignments. He said that he wanted to help write the new farm bill; he chairs the Agriculture Subcommittee on Livestock, Dairy and Poultry.

FOURTH DISTRICT

Rep. Tom Latham (R)

Elected 1994, 7th term; b. July 14, 1948, Hampton; home, Alexander; Wartburg Col., 1966-67, IA St. U., 1967-70; Lutheran; married (Kathy).

Professional Career: Farmer; Bank Teller/Bookkeeper, 1970-72; Independent Insurance Agent, 1972-74; Hartford Insurance Mktg. Rep., 1974-76; Co–Owner, Latham Seed Co., 1976-present.

DC Office: 2447 RHOB, 20515, 202-225-5476; Fax: 202-225-3301; Web site: www.tomlatham.house.gov.

District Offices: Ames, 515-232-2885; Clear Lake, 641-357-5225; Fort Dodge, 515-573-2738.

Committees: *Appropriations* (14th of 29 R): Agriculture, Rural Development, FDA & Related Agencies; Commerce, Justice, Science & Related Agencies.

Group Ratings

	ADA	ACLU	AFS	LCV	ITIC	NTU	COC	ACU	CFG	FRC
2006	5	14	14	0	100	56	100	84	53	85
2005	5	—	0	6	—	52	93	84	48	85

National Journal Ratings

	2005 LIB	—	2005 CONS		2006 LIB	—	2006 CONS
Economic	24%	—	74%		12%	—	86%
Social	23%	—	76%		23%	—	74%
Foreign	34%	—	61%		17%	—	73%

Key Votes of the 109th Congress

1. Estate Tax Repeal	Y	5. Limit Interstate Abortion	Y	9. Build Border Fence	Y
2. Limit CAFE Standards	Y	6. Extend Patriot Act	Y	10. CAFTA	Y
3. FY06 Spending Curb	Y	7. Bar Same Sex Marriage	Y	11. Oppose Iraq Withdrawal	Y
4. Drilling in ANWR	Y	8. Stem Cell Research $	N	12. Detainee Tribunals	Y

Election Results

2006 general	Tom Latham (R)	121,650	(57%)	($1,125,580)
	Selden Spencer (D)	90,982	(43%)	($478,932)
2006 primary	Tom Latham (R)	unopposed		
2004 general	Tom Latham (R)	181,294	(61%)	($988,369)
	Paul Johnson (D)	116,121	(39%)	($287,843)

Prior Winning Percentages: 2002 (55%); 2000 (69%); 1998 (100%); 1996 (65%); 1994 (61%)

The People		Race/Ethnic Origin	Ancestry	
Area size:	15,833 sq. mi.	94.7% White	German: 27.1%	Norwegian: 9.1%
Urban population:	50.5%	0.8% Black	Irish: 8.9%	
Rural population:	49.5%	1.1% Asian	**2004 Presidential Vote**	
Pop. 2000:	585,305	0.2% Native Am.	Bush (R) 155,587	(51%)
Pop. 2005 (est):	590,275	0.0% Hawaiian	Kerry (D) 148,331	(48%)
Median income:	$38,242	0.6% Two+ races	Other 2,711	(1%)
Poverty status:	8.9%	0.1% Other	**2000 Presidential Vote**	
Military veterans:	13.1%	2.5% Hispanic Origin	Bush (R) 131,391	(49%)
			Gore (D) 129,280	(48%)
			Other 8,506	(3%)
			Cook Partisan Voting Index: D + 0	

Occupation	Blue collar: 27.2%	White collar: 56.2%	Gray collar: 16.6%

Central Iowa is where the Great Plains begin—a land of farm fields marked off by straight roads every mile and rolling slightly upward to the west, punctuated by occasional crossroads towns and grain elevators, with a sky that seems to fill the eyes. Pioneers coming here in the 1840s and 1850s found prairie grass whose roots were two feet thick and girded trees with grubbing machines that cut off their roots below ground. Central Iowa has some of the world's most productive soil, and it has also had some of its most productive and creative agricultural scientists and farmers. A monument to one of them is the 12-foot statue of Norman Borlaug in his home town of Cresco, in Howard County near the Minnesota border. This is long-settled land now, and Iowans' productivity means that there are fewer people living here on farms than there were 50 and 100 years ago. But its towns and small cities remain centers of creativity. One is Ames, in Story County, home of Iowa State University, and home of Iowa Republicans' straw poll that has launched several Republican presidential contests. Ames is part of the growth zone around Des Moines, which is 30 miles to the south; so is Boone County to the west. Directly west of Des Moines and its most affluent suburbs is Dallas County, the fastest-growing county in Iowa in the 1990s. To the south is Madison County, famous for the wooden covered bridges that gave their name to a best-selling novel and movie; in 2002 one of the bridges caught fire and burned, so now there are only five left. Toward the north is Mason City, the boyhood home of *The Music Man* author Meredith Willson. Algona in rural Kossuth County opened a museum with a replica of the prisoner of war camp that housed more than 10,000 Germans during World War II. In nearby Winnebago County is Winnebago Industries, which manufactures motor homes and recreation vehicles on computer-controlled assembly lines with robotic equipment; the main factory in Forest City employs more than 3,000 workers. The first tractors were manufactured in Charles City, which calls itself "America's Hometown."

The 4th Congressional District includes all these parts of central and northern Iowa, and covers 28 counties. It does not include Des Moines, but counties around Des Moines cast more than one-third of its votes. Like Iowa, the 4th District is closely divided politically: George W. Bush carried the district 49%-48% in 2000 and 51%-48% in 2004.

The congressman from the 4th District is Tom Latham, a Republican first elected in 1994. Latham grew up on a farm in Franklin County, near Alexander (population 162) where his family has owned a seed company—a very Iowa business—since 1947. For years Latham was active in Republican politics, attending the national convention and serving as a farm adviser to Congressman Fred Grandy. In 1994 Grandy ran against Governor Terry Branstad and lost a close primary, and Latham ran for the House. His Democratic opponent Sheila McGuire had been one of 47 health care professionals to sit on an advisory panel for Hillary Rodham Clinton's health care plan; Latham opposed it. He won 61%-39%.

In the House, Latham has a moderately conservative record and has usually been a quiet but diligent member who avoids the national spotlight. He has pursued local interests on the Appropriations Committee and its Agriculture Subcommittee. In 2006, he passed an amendment to force the Agriculture Department to accept electronic certificates for horses shipped overseas instead of requiring the department's paper forms. He strongly opposed legislation to permit states to allow physician-assisted suicide. He criticized the Senate Appropriations Committee, where Tom Harkin is a senior Democrat, for reducing funds needed to complete the National Animal Disease Center in Ames, which he described as essential to "agro-terrorism" prevention. In 2006, he enacted a bill to award a congressional gold medal to Norman Borlaug, a scientist from Cresco who worked on increasing crop yield and ending hunger. On House Appropriations, Latham is the most senior Republican waiting for a top subcommittee post. He has been a close ally of Minority Leader John Boehner.

In 2002, after redistricting made the district more competitive, he faced the most vigorous campaign since he was elected. Latham had not been an active fundraiser and Democrats targeted the race. Their nominee was John Norris, former chief of staff to Governor Tom Vilsack and, in 2003 and 2004, John Kerry's Iowa manager in the precinct caucuses. Norris talked about jobs, education and Social Security and sounded the theme of working hard for "Iowa's working families"; he attacked Latham for supporting Republican positions on taxes and health care. He was an aggressive campaigner and raised more than $1 million. But Latham won by a relatively comfortable 55%-43%, winning all 28 counties—though, only by 9 votes in Ames's Story County, which cast the most votes. Angry at Latham's negative ads, Norris refused to make the customary election-night concession call to Latham. Latham responded that Norris attacked him from the start, and forced him to respond. In 2006, his opponent was Selden Spencer, a neurologist in Ames, who spent two weeks in Afghanistan treating patients and training doctors three months before the election; Spencer filed a blog and viewed the effort as good campaign publicity. Spencer called for withdrawal of U.S. forces from Iraq. Latham commended Spencer for his travel, but disagreed with his views on the war. Latham won, 57%-43%, and carried every county except for Story County, which gave 52% to Spencer. Latham said that "all options are open" for a possible challenge to Tom Harkin in 2008. If he does not seek reelection, the 4th District will likely be seriously contested. Spencer said that he might run again.

FIFTH DISTRICT

Rep. Steve King (R)

Elected 2002, 3d term; b. May 28, 1949, Storm Lake; home, Kiron; NW MO St. U., 1967-70; Catholic; married (Marilyn).

Elected Office: IA Senate, 1996-2002.

Professional Career: Construction co. owner, 1975-2002.

DC Office: 1609 LHOB, 20515, 202-225-4426; Fax: 202-225-3193; Web site: www.house.gov/steveking.

District Offices: Council Bluffs, 712-325-1404; Creston, 641-782-2495; Sioux City, 712-224-4692; Spencer, 712-580-7754; Storm Lake, 712-732-4197.

Committees: *Agriculture* (10th of 21 R): Conservation, Credit, Energy & Research; Department Operations, Oversight, Nutrition & Forestry; Livestock, Dairy & Poultry. *Judiciary* (13th of 17 R): Immigration, Citizenship, Refugees, Border Security & International Law (RMM); The Constitution, Civil Rights & Civil Liberties. *Small Business* (7th of 15 R): Regulations, Healthcare & Trade; Finance & Tax.

Group Ratings

	ADA	ACLU	AFS	LCV	ITIC	NTU	COC	ACU	CFG	FRC
2006	15	5	0	0	86	77	93	100	94	100
2005	0	—	0	0	—	70	93	100	93	100

National Journal Ratings

	2005 LIB	—	2005 CONS		2006 LIB	—	2006 CONS
Economic	0%	—	97%		42%	—	58%
Social	0%	—	89%		0%	—	94%
Foreign	0%	—	89%		17%	—	73%

Key Votes of the 109th Congress

1. Estate Tax Repeal	Y	5. Limit Interstate Abortion	Y	9. Build Border Fence	Y
2. Limit CAFE Standards	Y	6. Extend Patriot Act	Y	10. CAFTA	Y
3. FY06 Spending Curb	Y	7. Bar Same Sex Marriage	Y	11. Oppose Iraq Withdrawal	Y
4. Drilling in ANWR	Y	8. Stem Cell Research $	N	12. Detainee Tribunals	Y

Election Results

2006 general	Steve King (R)	105,580	(59%)	($620,071)
	Joyce Schulte (D)	64,181	(36%)	($73,262)
	Roy Nielsen (I)	8,159	(5%)	($149,777)
	Other	2,544	(1%)	
2006 primary	Steve King (R)	unopposed		
2004 general	Steve King (R)	168,583	(63%)	($553,171)
	Joyce Schulte (D)	97,597	(37%)	($59,976)

Prior Winning Percentages: 2002 (62%)

The People		Race/Ethnic Origin	Ancestry	
Area size:	18,429 sq. mi.	93.7% White	German: 26.8% Irish: 9.2%	
Urban population:	49.4%	0.6% Black	English: 6.7%	
Rural population:	50.6%	0.9% Asian	**2004 Presidential Vote**	
Pop. 2000:	585,171	0.4% Native Am.	Bush (R)	167,387 (60%)
Pop. 2005 (est):	580,838	0.0% Hawaiian	Kerry (D)	109,974 (39%)
Median income:	$36,773	0.7% Two+ races	Other	2,428 (1%)
Poverty status:	8.9%	0.0% Other	**2000 Presidential Vote**	
Military veterans:	14.0%	3.6% Hispanic Origin	Bush (R)	141,820 (57%)
			Gore (D)	99,004 (40%)
			Other	7,623 (3%)
			Cook Partisan Voting Index: R + 8	

Occupation   Blue collar: 29.5%   White collar: 53.3%   Gray collar: 17.2%

Sioux City, one of the oldest market towns on the Great Plains, is situated picturesquely, nestled below and running up the loess bluffs above the Missouri River. Although still the largest city on the Plains west of Des Moines and north of Omaha, Sioux City has not grown much in the past five decades. Its original economic base has become obsolete, and so has some of the city itself: The waterfront, once raucous with boatmen and stockyard workers, is now quiet; the downtown stores have been replaced by shopping malls at the edge of town where people still spend a day doing a season's shopping and then drive for hours back home. The stockyards, which employed thousands and slaughtered millions of hogs during their peak years in the 1920s, have closed. But there are still many hogs in western Iowa. Instead of meeting sellers in the markets of the Sioux City stockyard, packers now contract directly with large farms and build their modern slaughterhouses nearby; Tyson Foods has facilities in Buena Vista and Crawford Counties. Wind farming has grown; Iowa trails only California and Texas in generating electricity from wind.

Sioux City is the largest city in the 5th Congressional District of Iowa, which covers the western part of the state from Minnesota to Missouri and borders South Dakota and Nebraska to the west. This is the state's largest congressional district, the one with the most 4-H members and the nation's top hog-and-pig producing district. The 2001 redistricting removed 15 counties centered around Fort Dodge and added 17 counties centered around Council Bluffs. That city houses the mansion of General Grenville Dodge, who in 1859 lobbied Illinois lawyer Abraham Lincoln on the need for a transcontinental railroad; Lincoln got it through Congress in 1863, Dodge became its chief engineer, and Council Bluffs became its eastern terminus when it was completed in 1869. Surrounded by beef grazing territory, where federal intrusion has long been resented, Council Bluffs looks west across the Missouri River to Omaha, taking on the culturally more conservative tone of Nebraska and the conservative politics of the *Omaha World-Herald*. In Crawford County, Denison houses the Donna Reed Heritage Museum that commemorates the former Hollywood film-star and middle-America mom. This is by far the most Republican district in Iowa and George W. Bush twice carried it by wide margins.

The congressman from the 5th District is Steve King, a Republican who won the open seat in 2002. He was born in Storm Lake in western Iowa and attended Northwest Missouri State University. He founded the King Construction Company in 1975. He began his political career in 1996, at 47, when he was elected to the state Senate; he quickly gained a reputation as a conservative's conservative. He opposed abortion, racial quotas and preferences, and same-sex marriage. He sponsored Iowa's "God and Country" bill, which would require Iowa schools to recognize that the United States "has derived its strength from biblical values," and was a driving force behind the state's English-only law. In 2000, King filed suit to repeal Governor Tom Vilsack's executive order banning workplace discrimination based on sexual orientation. On economic matters, King supported repeal of the state's inheritance tax, backed a 15% state income tax reduction and a national right-to-work law.

In 2002 there were four main contenders in the Republican primary. King ran as a strong conservative and the only rural candidate, and called for limiting federal control over local schools. King led in the June primary with 30% of the vote. Because nobody received the required 35% of the primary vote, the nomination was determined by a special party convention three weeks later. The 533 voting delegates needed three ballots to select a winner. King led on each ballot and defeated House Speaker Brent Siegrist of Council Bluffs 272-253 in the final round, marking the first time in 38 years that Iowans used a convention to select a congressional nominee. The general election outcome was never in doubt. Democrat Paul Shomshor attempted to paint King as too conservative for the district, and won the endorsement of the *Omaha World-Herald*—perhaps because his home city of Council Bluffs had not elected a member to Congress since the 1920s—but he fell far short, 62%-38%. *National Review* called King the "Great Right Hope."

In the House, King has a firmly conservative record, though he voted for the 2003 Medicare/prescription drug bill, which contained higher Medicare reimbursement rates for Iowa. In 2005, the House passed his amendment to prohibit Medicare funds to reimburse for Viagra. The House defeated his amendment to limit the United States contribution to the United Nations to the largest assessment of any other Security Council member. He has been a proponent of tougher enforcement of immigration laws, including a border fence, and contends that illegal immigrants have been the source of many crimes. The House has twice passed his amendment to enforce a 1996 law that forbids localities from preventing police officers from reporting immigration information to the federal government. He advocates English as the official language of the United States, and said that Iowa officials violated the state law he wrote in 2002 by posting voter information on a Web site in other languages. In May 2006, the House Judiciary Committee defeated his amendment to ban bilingual ballots from polling places. A *Carroll Daily Times Herald* columnist who has assembled some of King's quotes into a book, "King Kong Krazy," calls him "maniacally nationalistic." In 2007, King became ranking Republican on the Immigration Subcommittee of Judiciary, which put him in the middle of the high-profile debate.

On local issues, he called for expansion of "value-added agriculture," including biotechnology and ethanol, to strengthen the local economy; he successfully promoted an expanded tax credit for small ethanol and biodiesel producers as part of the 2005 energy law. He joined Christian conservatives who demanded that the Iowa Supreme Court display a donated copy of the Ten Commandments.

In November 2004 he carried all but one small county and won 63%-37% over Democrat Joyce Schulte. She ran again in 2006, accused him of "racist remarks" on immigration, and lost 59%-36%. King refused to debate, and said that most voters know his views. He said that Senator Tom Harkin was vulnerable because of his liberal views, and that he was considering a challenge in 2008.

★ KANSAS ★

"The image of Kansas wasn't negative," the state director of travel and tourism told the *New York Times* in 2005, reporting on a national survey, "it was blank." Well, not entirely: Kansas made national news at the time as it arrested the BTK killer in Wichita, as Steve Fossett took off from Salina in his glider-like Global Flyer and flew nonstop around the world, as the state attorney general sought abortion clinic records to investigate illegal abortions and sex offenses against minors. Those stories suggested that Thomas Frank, author of the bestselling *What's the Matter with Kansas?*, had a better point when he says, "Kansas may be the land of averageness, but it is a freaky, militant, outraged averageness." For the history of seemingly placid Kansas—it actually is flatter than a pancake, geographers announced in 2004 after comparing its geography to an IHOP product—has been punctuated by uprisings, intellectual and violent, by moments of anger and rage sweeping through the tall sheaves like a tornado wind. Kansas literally began in a moment of violence, the Bleeding Kansas of the 1850s that led proximately to the terrible war that split the whole nation. The trigger was the Kansas-Nebraska Act of 1854, which left to local settlers the question of whether this new Kansas Territory would be a free or slave state. Pro-slavery "bushwhackers" rode over the line from Missouri, stealing elections and writing a pro-slavery constitution. But much larger numbers of free-soil "jayhawkers" from New England and the New England-Yankee-settled Great Lakes states put down roots and, despite the massacres of the mad John Brown, prevailed and established their own law and order. This was a civil war before the Civil War and, as Wichita State historian Charles Miner points out, one conducted by literate people who produced mountains of documents that have not been fully mined by historians.

Kansas's effect on national politics was tumultuous: The Democratic Party was split, the Republican Party was created, and the nation was plunged into Civil War. The ultimate effect on Kansas was calming: The anti-slavery majority bent the soil to the plow and built small towns thick with schools, churches and colleges, to the point that in the 1939 color movie, *The Wizard of Oz*, the Kansas scenes were shot in dreary black and white as the image of dull, prim, old-fashioned Middle America, while the scenes in imaginary Oz were shot in brilliant color. But the rebellious impulse did not totally die out. Kansans' livelihoods were always at risk: Hailstorms, grasshopper invasions, dry seasons or a drop in world farm prices could mean disaster for thousands. The high-rainfall 1880s attracted hundreds of thousands of new settlers to Kansas; the low-rainfall 1890s produced a bust and a populist rebellion. "What you farmers should do," said orator Mary Ellen Lease, "is to raise less corn and more hell." For a few years in the 1890s, and then in farm rebellions of the 1930s, 1950s and 1970s, Kansans did, but afterwards always returned to jayhawker Republicanism.

Kansas remains mostly Republican in the 21st century, but not in quite the same old way. Its most famous politician, Bob Dole, still returns occasionally to his small hometown of Russell, out on the plains. But Kansas' population is increasingly metropolitan. Some 52% of Kansans live in just five counties, which include Kansas City, Lawrence, Topeka and Wichita, and in 84 of the 100 other counties the population declined between 2000 and 2006. A majority of Kansans are in or within easy reach of metropolitan Kansas City, which has a diverse economy that is by no means dependent on farming. Small towns on the plains see their city halls and post offices padlocked and high schools closed because of low attendance; some towns have bought land to be distributed free to homesteaders, others have courted call centers. The state promotes agri-tourism at buffalo ranches

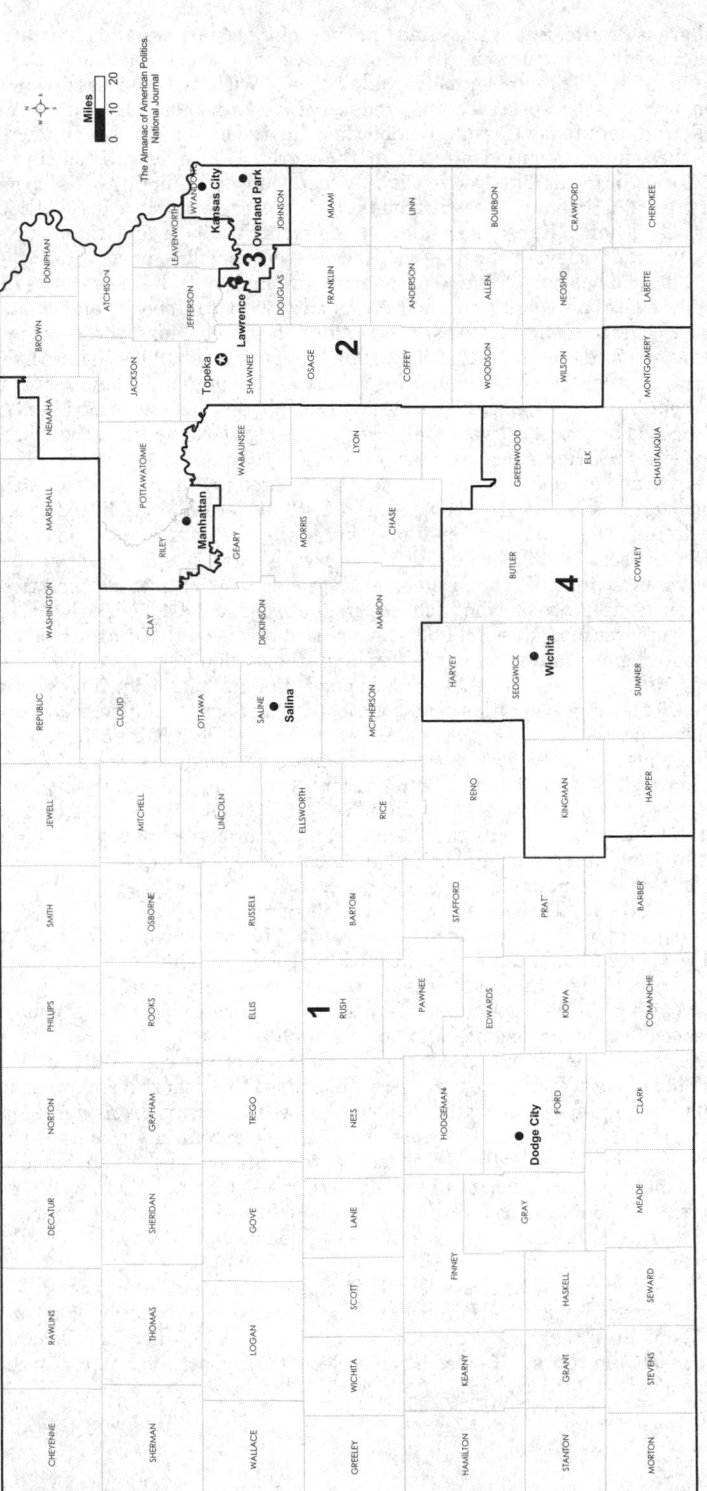

The Almanac of American Politics.
National Journal

Congressional district boundaries were first effective for 2002.

and the wild Tallgrass Prairie. But at the same time new office complexes and corporate headquarters are rising amidst the affluent suburbs of Johnson County, which has one of the highest job growth rates in the country. The smaller metropolitan area of Wichita, while less diversified, has an economy built on its role as the world's leading producer of small airplanes: Here many World War II planes were built and here today Cessna, Bombardier, Raytheon and other manufacturers make more than half the general aviation aircraft in the world. Hispanics are flocking to work in meatpacking factories in towns like Dodge City, Garden City and Liberal, whose populations in 2000 were more than 40% Hispanic and which had pro-immigration marches in April 2006. Hispanics accounted for nearly half of Kansas's population growth in the 1990s, and 8% of its population in 2005. There is no warrant today for shooting the Kansas scenes in black and white.

This transformation has had political consequences. Some 40% of Kansas's votes in 2004 were cast in the mostly suburban counties from Kansas City west to Topeka, and another 15% in Wichita's Sedgwick County. If rural Kansas once produced farm rebellions, these urban and suburban Kansans have produced their own kind of rebellion. Since the mid-1990s Kansas has had a kind of three-party politics—conservative Republicans versus moderate Republicans versus Democrats. Republican Governor Bill Graves, elected in 1994 and 1998, favored abortion rights and gun control; he was fiercely opposed by conservative Republicans in the legislature. Graves beat back a conservative challenge in the 1998 Republican primary by nearly 3–1, but conservatives won a majority on the state school board and in 1999 issued guidelines that treated evolution as a theory. That aroused a national uproar and was reversed in 2001, and in 2003 moderate Republicans took leadership posts in the legislature. The Republican split opened the way for Democrats, who captured the 3d Congressional District seat in 1998 by beating a conservative who was hated by suburban moderates and the governorship in 2002 when Democrat Kathleen Sebelius beat conservative Treasurer Tim Shallenburger. Conservatives won victories in the August 2004 legislative primaries and gained a 6–4 majority over moderate Republicans and Democrats on the state school board, which voted to teach non-religious alternatives to Darwinian theory, founded, its leader said, on "good science that's empirically based." But that aroused opposition in the 2006 primaries. So did a bill, vetoed by Sebelius, for stricter regulation of abortion clinics, an unsuccessful legislative move to ban state-funded embryonic stem cell research and Attorney General Phill Kline's move to see abortion clinic records. Sebelius recruited former Republican state chairman Mark Parkinson to be her running mate and won 58%-40%. Johnson County District Attorney Paul Morrison switched to the Democratic party, ran against Kline and beat him 59%-41%. Conservatives lost their majority on the State Board of Education in the August Republican primaries. Republican Congressman Jim Ryun was upset by Democrat Nancy Boyda in November. The conservatives had some successes; they got a ban on same-sex marriage on the ballot in April 2005, which passed easily. But the balance went against them. "These are people who felt banished," Sebelius told the *Washington Post.* " We have some remarkable conversions. My favorite kind of revival is going to a place where someone says, 'I've been a Republican all my life, and I've seen the light.'"

Frank's book argued that Kansas voters have been hornswoggled into voting against their economic interests by big business operatives. That's not an accurate picture. His hometown, which he cites as evidence of economic decline, is in booming Johnson County, and Kansas's unemployment rate has been well below the national average. And lots of other voters—liberal Frank fans on the Upper East Side of New York, for example—vote against their short-term economic interests because cultural issues are more important to them. The switch toward the moderate Republicans and the Democrats in 2006 came not in the drought-stricken farm counties in southern and western Kansas, which are sustained by subsidized crop insurance and federal disaster payments, but in the economically vital metropolitan areas of Kansas, where the key swing voters were motivated, as Kansas's conservative Republican voters have been, by cultural issues. And where the balance seems to have shifted, as it has several times in Kansas in the last decade, by the perceived excesses of the side in power.

Democrats now hold two of Kansas's four U.S. House seats, but otherwise the state seems solidly Republican in national politics. It voted 58%-37% for George W. Bush in 2000 and 62%-37% in 2004. Its two Republican senators were both first elected in 1996, when Bob Dole resigned and Nancy Landon Kassebaum retired. Kansas has not elected a Democratic senator since 1932—the only state that hasn't.

The People		Race/Ethnic Origin			Military veterans: 267,452 (13.5%)	
Pop. 2006 (est):	2,764,075	2,233,997	83.1%	White	WWII: 21.2%	Korea: 13.1%
Pop. 2000:	2,688,418	151,407	5.6%	Black	Vietnam: 32.6%	Gulf War: 10.9%
Pop. 1990:	2,477,574	46,301	1.7%	Asian	**Most populous cities (2006):**	
Change 1990-2000:	Up 8.5%	22,322	0.8%	Native Am.	1. Wichita	357,698
% of U.S. total:	1.0%	1,154	0.0%	Hawaiian	2. Overland Park	166,722
Pop. rank:	32nd of 50	42,508	1.6%	Two+ races	3. Kansas City	143,801
Area size:	82,277 sq. mi.	2,477	0.1%	Other	4. Topeka	122,113
State Native:	59.5%	188,252	7.0%	Hisp. Origin	5. Olathe	114,662
Non-citizen:	3.3%	**Ancestry**				
Language		German: 19.5%		Irish: 8.7%	Urban population: 71.4%	
English: 89.7%	Spanish: 6.0%	English: 8.1%		USA: 6.7%	Rural population: 28.6%	
Other Eur.: 2.6%		French: 2.3%				

Education		Work Sector		Legislature	
H.S. Grad:	86.0%	Private: 76.3%	Govt: 15.5%	Senate	30 R 10 D
College Grad:	25.8%	Self: 7.8%	Family: 0.4%	House	77 R 48 D
Industry		Unemployment: 4.2%		Legislative Term Limits: No	
Agri: 3.8%	Con: 6.5%	**Household Income**		**Registered Voters**	
Fin: 6.1%	Info: 3.3%	<15k: 14.9%	15-35k: 27.8%	D: 438,327	(26.6%)
Mfg: 20.3%	Prof: 29.1%	35-50k: 18.1%	50-100k: 29.9%	R: 760,745	(46.1%)
Public: 4.4%	Trade: 14.8%	100-150k: 6.1%	>150k: 3.2%	O: 450,866	(27.3%)
Other: 11.6%		Median: $40,624			
Occupation		Poverty status: 9.9%			
Blue collar: 24.9%	White collar: 59.7%	**Home Value**			
Gray collar: 15.5%		<50k: 27.3%	50-100k: 35.6%	100-200k: 28.6%	200-300k: 5.6%
		300-500k: 2.2%	>500k: 0.7%	Median: $81,000	

Presidential politics   Except for 1964, when it narrowly favored Lyndon Johnson over Barry Goldwater, Kansas has voted Republican for president throughout the last 60 years. In 2000 and 2004 George W. Bush carried 103 of its 105 counties, losing only those containing the old industrial city of Kansas City and the university town of Lawrence. Bush's percentage rose from 58% to 62%, and rose by more in most rural counties. But it rose only a little in suburban Johnson County and fell in Douglas County, home of the University of Kansas. Kansas is so one-sidedly Republican that it sees little of presidential candidates. But on May 17, 2004, both George W. Bush and John Kerry came to Topeka and, in separate appearances, commemorated the Brown v. Board of Education decision, which outlawed Topeka's segregated schools.

2004 Presidential Vote		
Bush (R)	736,456	(62%)
Kerry (D)	434,993	(37%)
Nader (I)	9,348	(1%)
Other	6,959	(1%)

2000 Presidential Vote		
Bush (R)	622,332	(58%)
Gore (D)	399,276	(37%)
Nader (Green)	36,086	(3%)
Other	14,522	(1%)

In 1996 the state legislature voted to cancel the April primary and none has been held since.

Congressional districting   In 2002 Republicans had full control of redistricting in Kansas for the first time since the 1960s, but did not use it to partisan advantage. Why? As one legislator put it, "What's ground zero with reapportionment? I'd say it's Lawrence." In the previous plan, Lawrence, midway between Kansas City and Topeka, and home of the University of Kansas, was in the 3d District captured by Democrat Dennis Moore in 1998 and held in 2000. The 3d District had to shed 61,000 people, and the obvious partisan move was to remove Lawrence, which Moore carried by wide margins, and place it in the heavily Republican 2d District, where incumbent Republican Jim Ryun was thought to be unbeatable anyway. But Lawrence civic

110th Congress Lineup	
2 D	2 R

109th Congress Lineup	
3 R	1 D

leaders insisted that Lawrence be kept together in the 3d District—they wanted the university to be in the same district as its hospital in Kansas City—and Republicans in the state House in March 2002 passed a plan splitting the city but keeping most of it, including the university, in the 3d. The state Senate in April 2002 passed a different plan, promoted by national Republicans, which extended the western 1st District all the way to the southeast corner of the state. But the House's plan prevailed and was adopted in June. As it turned out, in 2006 Democrat Nancy Boyda won the portion of Douglas County included in the 2d District 61%-38%; overall, she won by a much smaller margin in her 51%-47% upset win over Ryun.

Governor

Kathleen Sebelius (D)

Elected 2002, term expires Jan. 2011, 2d term; b. May 15, 1948, Cincinnati, OH; home, Topeka; Trinity Col., B.A. 1970, U. of KS, M.P.A. 1977; Catholic; married (Gary).

Elected Office: KS House of Reps., 1986-94; KS Insurance Commissioner, 1994-2002.

Professional Career: KS Dept. of Corrections, 1975-77; Dir., KS Trial Lawyers Assoc., 1977-87.

Office: State Capitol, 2d Fl., Topeka, 66612, 785-296-3232; Fax: 785-296-7973; Web site: www.ksgovernor.org.

Election Results

2006 general	Kathleen Sebelius (D)	491,993	(58%)
	Jim Barnett (R)	343,586	(40%)
	Other	14,117	(2%)
2006 primary	Kathleen Sebelius (D)	unopposed	
2002 general	Kathleen Sebelius (D)	441,858	(53%)
	Tim Shallenburger (R)	376,830	(45%)

Kathleen Sebelius was elected governor of Kansas in 2002 and reelected in 2006, the second Democratic woman to win the office. Sebelius grew up in Cincinnati, where her father John Gilligan was elected to the city council in 1953, when she was 5. Campaigns were very much a part of her life. Her father was elected to Congress in a usually Republican district in the very Democratic year of 1964; he was defeated in 1966 by Robert Taft Jr. In 1970, Gilligan was elected governor of Ohio and in 1971 pushed through the state's first income tax. A man of wry humor, he was given to self-deprecating statements; when asked at the Ohio State Fair in 1972 whether he would join the sheep-shearing, he said, "I shear taxpayers, not sheep." Comments like this helped defeat him in 1974 by a 49%-48% margin. Still active and a member of the Cincinnati school board in 2002, he had the satisfaction of being the first governor to see his daughter elected governor.

Kathleen Sebelius graduated from Trinity College in Washington, D.C., where she met her husband, the son of Kansas Republican Congressman (1969-81) Keith Sebelius. After graduation the Sebeliuses moved to Topeka, where they live just 12 blocks from the state Capitol. Kathleen Sebelius worked for the state trial lawyers association and in 1986 was elected to the state House as a Democrat. With a Topeka base and a name well known in western Kansas, she was elected state insurance commissioner in 1994. It was a position held since its creation by Republicans, and by just three men over the preceding 50 years.

Sebelius's moderate image and her political savvy made her the obvious Democrat to run for governor in 2002, and she had no primary opposition. Term-limited Governor Bill Graves was a moderate who engaged in fierce feuds with conservatives in the Republican party, and there was a rip-roaring battle for the Republican nomination. Attorney General Carla Stovall, the choice of the moderate wing, left the race just two months before the filing deadline. That left moderates with no candidate against conservative state Treasurer Tim Shallenburger, a strong opponent of abortion who pledged not to increase taxes and said he would cut state spending by 10%. State Senate President Dave Kerr and Wichita Mayor Bob Knight jumped in but the one conservative beat the two moderates. Shallenburger won the August primary with 41% of the vote.

The general election provided a clear contrast on issues. Sebelius promised a top-to-bottom review of state government and refused to pledge she would veto any tax increase. "No one is talking about a tax increase," she said in an October debate. "We need to do more with less." She favored abortion rights, opposed capital punishment and favored banning concealed weapons except for retired law enforcement officers. She picked a Republican, a retired Cessna executive, for her running mate. She called for a $1,000 increase in per pupil spending and said she would institute character education in schools. She proved to be an excellent fundraiser and spent $3.2 million to Shallenburger's $1.5 million. Graves waited until six weeks after the primary to grudgingly endorse Shallenburger, and the Kansas Farm Bureau in September decided to stay neutral. Sebelius made one slip when she said that Missouri's underfunded highways were "much more terrifying to me than the attacks on the World Trade Center," but she quickly apologized. She got some mileage attacking Shallenburger for calling her, in a fundraising letter, "a lying dangerous liberal who will ruin our schools and endanger our children." Polls showed her well ahead all along, and she won 53%-45%. She carried most counties in eastern Kansas and lost heavily Republican Johnson County by only 52%-46%.

In her first year as governor, Sebelius faced a budget deficit estimated at $1.1 billion. Her top-to-bottom review of state government resulted, she said, in $76 million in savings. In one efficiency initiative, she had the state automobile fleet surveyed (until then nobody could tell her how many vehicles were owned by any agency or where they were) and then sold several hundred excess cars. Still, there were no tax increases in 2003. Trouble came in December 2003 when a trial judge in Shawnee County ruled on a suit brought by Dodge City and Salina in 1999 that Kansas's school funding formula was unconstitutional; Sebelius and the legislature were given until July 2004 to come up with changes. In January 2004 Sebelius announced a balanced budget but then added that she favored a $300 million increase in education spending and proposed increases in the sales, income and property taxes to pay for it. This proposal was rejected; in January 2005, the state supreme court ruled that the legislature had inadequately funded education and ordered it to come up with a solution by April. The dispute dragged on for months and into a special session in June and July, the longest special session since 1966; the legislature finally agreed to a $148.4 million school funding bill.

On other issues, Sebelius worked for a new Indian gambling casino in Kansas City. Sebelius's program to provide more flexibility on pay raises for state employees was bitterly criticized by public employee unions. She traveled to Iraq, with stops in Pakistan and Afghanistan, to support the troops and to China on a trade mission to promote Kansas businesses. In 2006 she proposed a property tax break for some Kansas businesses and continued to support an expansion of gambling to help fund schools; she won the tax break but failed on gambling. In May, responding again to the state supreme court, Sebelius signed a 3-year, $466 million school finance plan, the largest increase in education aid in state history. In July, the court ruled the state had complied with its previous orders to increase spending and dismissed the underlying lawsuit.

Through mid-2006, Sebelius managed solid approval ratings in the polls even after taking some controversial positions. She signed a bill to allow young illegal immigrants who graduated from high school and were admitted to college in-state tuition rates—proof that neither side in Kansas politics is reflexively hostile to the state's growing Hispanic population. She vetoed a concealed weapons bill; the legislature overrode her. Sebelius has said she personally believes abortion is wrong, but she proved to be a vigilant defender of abortion rights. She vetoed funding in 2004 for a program designed to promote alternatives to abortion and vetoed a 2006 bill that would have required abortion providers to report information about why late-term abortions were performed and the conditions surrounding them.

In May 2006, Sebelius stunned the state political establishment by naming a new running mate for the 2006 election—Mark Parkinson, the former state Republican chairman. Parkinson, a moderate and an ambitious former state legislator from Johnson County, had switched his party registration to Democratic one day before Sebelius made the announcement that he was her choice to replace Lieutenant Governor John Moore, who planned to step down after his term ended. This was a brilliant political play, for all at once it exploited the deep divisions between Kansas Republicans, made Sebelius a more attractive candidate to disaffected moderate Republicans, and laid the groundwork for a Democratic successor to Sebelius in 2010, when term limits will prevent her from running again. The move occasioned harsh criticism from Republicans who noted that Parkinson had referred to Sebelius's 2002 selection of Moore, also a Republican before joining the ticket, as a "gimmick." He also had referred to Sebelius as "an extreme liberal" and said that "any Republican who supports Kathleen Sebelius for governor is either insincere or uninformed."

The general election campaign was not nearly as interesting as the Parkinson announcement. State Senator Jim Barnett, a conservative, won the Republican nomination over six other candidates. Barnett opposed an expansion of state-run gambling; he had voted against the school finance plan and called for tax cuts. Sebelius touted what she said was more than $1 billion in savings from increased government efficiency, and pointed to her job creation efforts and the accomplishment of a constitutional school finance plan. She proudly noted that in 2005 she was ranked by *Time* magazine as one of America's 5 best governors. The race never got close and failed to generate much attention; Sebelius won reelection 58%-40%. She carried Wichita's Sedgwick County 51%-46% and won populous suburban Johnson County and Topeka's Shawnee County by 62%-37% margins.

Her runaway win in a state where registered Republicans outnumber Democrats by more than 300,000, and her 2007 chairmanship of the Democratic Governors Association, attracted national notice, leading to talk that she would make an attractive vice-presidential candidate in 2008. "It's hard to imagine that her name's not going to appear on everybody's list," Democratic pollster Mark Mellman told the *Associated Press*. Others have speculated that Sebelius will be a Senate candidate in 2010, when Senator Sam Brownback has said he will not seek another term. But Kansas has not elected a Democratic senator since 1932—the only state that hasn't. Sebelius drew further attention in May 2007 when, after the town of Greensburg was devastated by a tornado, she suggested that the state National Guard was underequipped in its response because of the Iraq war; the White House responded forcefully, blaming Sebelius for not following proper procedures for requests.

Senior Senator

Sam Brownback (R)

Elected 1996, seat up 2010, 2d full term; b. Sept. 12, 1956, Garnett; home, Topeka; KS St. U., B.S. 1978, U. of KS, J.D. 1982; Catholic; married (Mary).

Elected Office: U.S. House of Reps., 1994-96.

Professional Career: Radio broadcaster, KKSU, 1978-79; Practicing atty., 1982-86, 1993; Prof., KS St. U. Law Schl., 1982-86; Ogden & Leonardville City Atty., 1983-86; KS Secy. of Agriculture, 1986-93; White House Fellow, Office of USTR, 1990-91.

DC Office: 303 HSOB, 20510, 202-224-6521; Fax: 202-228-1265; Web site: brownback.senate.gov.

State Offices: Garden City, 620-275-1124; Overland Park, 913-492-6378; Pittsburg, 620-231-6040; Topeka, 785-233-2503; Wichita, 316-264-8066.

Committees: *Appropriations* (12th of 14 R): Financial Services & General Government (RMM); Military Construction, Veterans Affairs & Related Agencies; State, Foreign Operations & Related Programs; Transportation, Housing and Urban Development & Related Agencies; Agriculture, Rural Development, Food and Drug Administration & Related Agencies; Commerce, Justice, Science & Related Agencies. *Joint Economic Committee* (8th of 10 R). *Judiciary* (8th of 9 R): Constitution (RMM); Antitrust, Competition Policy & Consumer Rights; Terrorism, Technology & Homeland Security; Human Rights & the Law.

Group Ratings

	ADA	ACLU	AFS	LCV	ITIC	NTU	COC	ACU	CFG	FRC
2006	5	25	0	29	100	84	100	87	98	100
2005	10	—	0	10	—	75	89	100	88	—

National Journal Ratings

	2005 LIB — 2005 CONS		2006 LIB — 2006 CONS	
Economic	16%	— 80%	7%	— 92%
Social	23%	— 64%	46%	— 53%
Foreign	0%	— 74%	34%	— 64%

Key Votes of the 109th Congress

1. Bar ANWR Drilling	N	5. Confirm Samuel Alito	Y	9. Limit Interstate Abortion	Y
2. FY06 Spending Curb	Y	6. Path to Citizenship	Y	10. CAFTA	Y
3. Estate Tax Repeal	Y	7. Bar Same Sex Marriage	Y	11. Urge Iraq Withdrawal	N
4. Raise Minimum Wage	N	8. Stem Cell Research $	N	12. Provide Detainee Rights	N

Election Results

2004 general	Sam Brownback (R)	780,863	(69%)	($2,476,585)
	Lee Jones (D)	310,337	(27%)	($102,931)
	Other..	37,822	(3%)	
2004 primary	Sam Brownback (R)	286,839	(87%)	
	Arch Naramore (R)	42,880	(13%)	
1998 general	Sam Brownback (R)	474,639	(65%)	($1,719,612)
	Paul Feleciano Jr. (D)	229,718	(32%)	($39,500)
	Other..	22,879	(3%)	

Prior Winning Percentages: 1996 (54%); 1994 House (66%)

Sam Brownback grew up on a farm in Anderson County, some 50 miles from Kansas City; he has family roots in Osawatomie, a center of evangelical abolitionism in the bleeding Kansas of the 1850s. He was state president of Future Farmers of America while in high school and student body president at Kansas State University. He worked briefly as a farm broadcaster and then graduated from the University of Kansas law school. He practiced law for four years in Manhattan, Kansas, then was appointed secretary of the state Board of Agriculture in 1986 and served until it was abolished in 1993. He was a White House Fellow, working from 1990-91 for Special Trade Representative Carla Hills. In March 1994, after 2d District Democrat Jim Slattery ran for governor, Brownback announced for Congress, condemning "a welfare system that discourages the work ethic and encourages the disintegration of families and a government that can't say no to spending or yes to reform." He won the primary by a 48%-35% margin over Bob Bennie, who campaigned as a strong opponent of abortion. In the general election he beat John Carlin, governor from 1978-86, by 66%-34%, carrying every county.

Brownback was one of the enthusiastic 1994 freshmen who tried to shake up the House. He headed a group of "New Federalists," which sought to abolish three cabinet departments. He backed the McCain-Feingold campaign finance bill and in 1995 spoke at Ross Perot's United We Stand convention denouncing "influence peddling" in Washington. On immigration, he played a key role in separating the legal and illegal immigration issues, which led to passage of a tough measure against illegal immigrants but no major reductions in the number of legal immigrants. In 1995 he had a melanoma removed, and this brush with a fatal disease led him toward a deeper evangelical faith. "I did a lot of internal examination. My conclusion was that if this were to be terminal, at that point in time I would not be satisfied with how I had lived life," he told *The Weekly Standard*. From the Prison Fellowship's Charles Colson, he learned of the British politician William Wilberforce, who led the move to abolish the slave trade in 1807 and slavery itself in 1833. In 2002 he converted to Catholicism, with Rick Santorum as his sponsor; on Sundays in Topeka he attends both Catholic mass and a service at the Topeka Bible Church. "You can find the Lord in a lot of places if you're willing to look for Him." He believes the nation has "re-engaged with its faith" in a spiritual revival. He chairs weekly meetings of the Values Action Team on Capitol Hill.

In May 1996 Bob Dole surprised just about everyone when he announced he was resigning from the Senate in June. Two days later Brownback said he would seek the seat. Governor Bill Graves' choice to fill the vacancy, Lieutenant Governor Sheila Frahm, delayed ten days before accepting. There were strong differences between the two on issues. She was pro-choice on abortion, he was pro-life. Brownback accused her of voting as a state legislator to raise taxes by $500 million; she criticized his "slash and burn" approach to federal spending. Brownback won the August primary 55%-42%. In the fall race for the remaining two years of Dole's term, Brownback faced Democrat Jill Docking, a Wichita stockbroker and wife of a former lieutenant governor whose father and grandfather both served as governor. Docking promised "Kansas common sense" and likened herself to Senator Nancy Landon Kassebaum. Brownback campaigned on the 3 R's: "Reduce, reform and return. Reduce the size and scope of the federal government. Reform the Congress. Return to the basic values that built the country: Work and family and the recognition of a higher moral authority." He promised to serve only two terms—presumably two full terms. Both candidates spent liberally, and some fall polls showed the race close. But Brownback won by the convincing though not overwhelming margin of 54%-43%.

Brownback has had a conservative voting record in the Senate and has taken on many issues because of his strong moral views. "I think every life is sacred and beautiful, whether it's the unborn or whether it's Ted Kennedy," he has said. "I really try to reach out and work with anybody and everybody I can." After September 11, Brownback and Kennedy co-sponsored a bill to strengthen the nation's borders. It provided for an automatic entry and exit system, the development of biometric identifiers and tracking of foreign students and called for greater sharing of information about potential terrorists by the INS, State Department and intelligence agencies. The bill became law in May 2002. On the Foreign Relations Committee he worked to ease sanctions against Pakistan and urged a tough approach on Iraq; he called the Iraqi National Congress, a group shunned by many in the State Department and the CIA, "invaluable in the fight to rid the world of Saddam's threat."

He worked with Paul Wellstone to gain passage of the Victims of Trafficking and Violence Protection Act of 2000. He led the fight for the Sudan Peace Act of 2002 and has worked to end slavery and the civil war there; he and Congressman Frank Wolf visited refugee camps in Darfur in June 2004. He co-sponsored the North Korea Refugee Act with Edward Kennedy and in December 2002 said, "If hell is the absence of God, I think you can see North Korea is the closest place to that on Earth." Using his seat on Appropriations, in 2005 he added $3 million to an appropriation to promote democracy in Iran; in 2006 he called for $100 million for that purpose, and applauded Secretary of State Condoleezza Rice when she called for $75 million for Farsi broadcasts and aid to unions and human rights activists focusing on Iran. He has pushed for action to combat AIDS and malaria in Africa. He supported the 2004 congressional declaration of genocide in Darfur and in 2005, with Jon Corzine, successfully pressed for passage of the Darfur Peace and Accountability Act and called for the dispatch of more African Union troops there and prosecution of human rights violators in an international court. In 2005 he and Barack Obama called for a larger African Union force and a NATO or UN force and for pressure on the rebels to unite in negotiations with the Sudan government.

Brownback has taken the initiative on many domestic issues. He hailed the Bush administration for bringing a WTO action against Airbus, and said that if European subsidies to Airbus were not removed, U.S. subsidies to Boeing (a big Kansas employer) should be considered. In 2004 he tried, ultimately unsuccessfully, to increase the fine on broadcasters for indecency to $500,000; in 2005, after the Janet Jackson "wardrobe malfunction" at the Super Bowl, his bill for raising the maximum fine from $32,500 to $325,000 passed. On taxes, he said in April 2004, "I think we need fundamental tax reform—flat, or a consumption-based tax system." With Congressman John Lewis, he worked to authorize the African-American Museum on Washington's Mall, and with Byron Dorgan he sponsored a resolution apologizing to Native Americans for past government misdeeds. He has sponsored bills to require doctors to tell women seeking abortion that fetuses can feel pain and to bar doctors from prescribing controlled drugs for use in assisted suicides. He held a hearing on capital punishment in February 2006 with relatives of murder victims and academics on both sides of the death penalty debate. "If use of the death penalty is contrary to promoting a culture of life, we need to have a national dialogue and hear both sides of the issue." Serving on the Judiciary Committee in 2005-06, he supported most Bush appointees, but said in October 2005 that he was undecided on the Supreme Court nomination of Harriet Miers and for some weeks in December 2006 held up the approval of a district court nominee who had attended a lesbian commitment ceremony. He was a leading co-sponsor of the immigration bill passed by the Senate in May 2006, which had guest worker and legalization as well as border security provisions.

As chairman of the D.C. Appropriations Subcommittee, he warned Mayor Anthony Williams in April 2005 that a legal ruling allowing same-sex couples to submit joint tax returns would generate a backlash and jeopardize D.C. domestic partner benefits; the District's chief fiscal official ruled in May that such couples couldn't file joint returns. Brownback briefly sponsored a bill to allow D.C. school vouchers to be used in private schools in Maryland and Virginia. He sponsored a bill to allow funds put into accounts by low earners for buying a first home, financing college educations and starting a business to be matched on a 3-to-1 basis by the federal government up to $9,000. Brownback has visited many prisons, even spent the night in them, and has worked with the Prison Fellowship's InnerChange Freedom Initiative; he sponsored a bill to provide $40 million for housing, drug treatment, counseling, job training and education for released prisoners.

In 2003 and 2004 Brownback used his chairmanship of the Science Subcommittee of Commerce to hold hearings on cloning and genetic testing. In 2002 he and Mary Landrieu had sponsored a bill to ban reproductive human cloning and the cloning of embryos for use in research; as a fallback, he called for a two-year moratorium on cloning. But the Senate remained stymied over several competing bills and took no legislative action. In 2005 Brownback again sponsored a cloning ban prohibiting therapeutic cloning or somatic cell nuclear transfer. He compared the destruction of human life in embryonic stem cell research to Nazi experimentation on Jews. "While researchers in the private sector are free to destroy young human lives through embryonic stem cell research, the government should not be in the business of funding this ethically troubling research with taxpayer dollars." That bill did not pass, but his amendment to outlaw fetus farming passed unanimously in July 2006.

Brownback supported the Bush administration on Iraq until he returned from a trip there in January 2007. "I do not believe that sending more troops to Iraq is the answer," he said. "Iraq requires a political rather than a military solution." After meeting with Iraqi officials and U.S. military leaders, he called for Iraq to be divided into three relatively autonomous zones.

Brownback was elected to a full six-year term in 1998 by a 65%-32% margin after well-known Democrats declined to run. In November 2002 Brownback announced he would run again, and Democrats had a hard time finding a candidate to run against him. Former Congressman and Agriculture Secretary Dan Glickman bowed out in September 2003; Governor Kathleen Sebelius wasn't interested. The winner of the August 2004 primary withdrew from the race. Brownback was reelected 69%-27%, carrying 104 of Kansas's 105 counties. After the 2004 elections, some conservatives were talking about Brownback running for president. In June 2006 he said he was giving it serious consideration. "I could be the right person with the right message at the right moment. And I could be completely wrong and I'll still be happy about it," he told *The Washington Post*. He made several trips to Iowa, where his background in agriculture and his strong religious convictions might resonate with Republican caucusgoers. After George Allen lost his Senate race and Bill Frist announced he was not running, Brownback seemed to be one of the few potential candidates whose stand on issues was in line with the cultural conservatives who have dominated the Republican selection process since 1980. In January 2007, he announced he was running.

Junior Senator

Pat Roberts (R)

Elected 1996, seat up 2008, 2d term; b. Apr. 20, 1936, Topeka; home, Dodge City; KS St. U., B.A. 1958; United Methodist; married (Franki).

Military Career: Marine Corps, 1958-62.

Elected Office: U.S. House of Reps., 1980-96.

Professional Career: Co–owner, editor, *The Westsider* (AZ newspaper) 1962-67; A.A., U.S. Sen. Frank Carlson, 1967-68; A.A., U.S. Rep. Keith Sebelius, 1968-80.

DC Office: 109 HSOB, 20510, 202-224-4774; Fax: 202-224-3514; Web site: roberts.senate.gov.

State Offices: Dodge City, 620 227 2241; Overland Park, 913-451-9343; Topeka, 785-295-2745; Wichita, 316-263-0416.

Committees: *Agriculture, Nutrition & Forestry* (5th of 10 R): Production, Income Protection & Price Support (RMM); Domestic & Foreign Marketing, Inspection, & Plant & Animal Health. *Ethics (Select)* (2d of 3 R). *Finance* (9th of 10 R): Taxation & IRS Oversight & Long-Term Growth; International Trade & Global Competitiveness; Health Care. *Health, Education, Labor & Pensions* (8th of 10 R): Employment & Workplace Safety; Children & Families.

Group Ratings

	ADA	ACLU	AFS	LCV	ITIC	NTU	COC	ACU	CFG	FRC
2006	5	8	13	0	100	68	92	84	57	100
2005	0	—	0	0	—	69	100	88	76	—

National Journal Ratings

	2005 LIB	—	2005 CONS		2006 LIB	—	2006 CONS
Economic	25%	—	72%		20%	—	77%
Social	37%	—	62%		0%	—	82%
Foreign	26%	—	65%		34%	—	64%

Key Votes of the 109th Congress

1. Bar ANWR Drilling	N	5. Confirm Samuel Alito	Y	9. Limit Interstate Abortion	Y
2. FY06 Spending Curb	Y	6. Path to Citizenship	N	10. CAFTA	Y
3. Estate Tax Repeal	Y	7. Bar Same Sex Marriage	Y	11. Urge Iraq Withdrawal	N
4. Raise Minimum Wage	N	8. Stem Cell Research $	N	12. Provide Detainee Rights	N

Election Results

2002 general	Pat Roberts (R)	641,075	(83%)	($1,038,984)
	Steven Rosile (Lib)	70,725	(9%)	
	George Cook (Ref)	65,050	(8%)	($3,473)
2002 primary	Pat Roberts (R)	233,642	(84%)	
	Tom Oyler (R)	45,491	(16%)	
1996 general	Pat Roberts (R)	652,677	(62%)	($2,305,898)
	Sally Thompson (D)	362,380	(34%)	($659,066)
	Other	37,243	(4%)	

Prior Winning Percentages: 1994 House (77%); 1992 House (68%); 1990 House (63%); 1988 House (100%); 1986 House (75%); 1984 House (76%); 1982 House (68%); 1980 House (62%)

Pat Roberts, the state's junior senator, is from a fine Kansas Republican background. His abolitionist great-grandfather "arrived in Kansas with a flat-bed press, a six-gun and a Bible" and founded Kansas' second-oldest newspaper, the *Oskaloosa Independent*, and his father, Wes Roberts, was briefly Republican National Committee chairman during the Eisenhower years. Pat Roberts graduated from Kansas State University, served four years in the Marine Corps, then spent five years running an Arizona newspaper. He worked for two years as an aide to Senator Frank Carlson and 12 years as chief aide to 1st District Congressman Keith Sebelius, Bob Dole's successor in the House and the father-in-law of Democratic Governor Kathleen Sebelius. When Sebelius retired in 1980, Roberts won the seat with 56% in a three-candidate Republican primary. For 14 years, in the minority in the House, he concentrated on farm issues, learning their intricacies and minutiae, traveling in a van to keep in touch with constituents in a district so large that it took two weeks to visit every county seat. His voting record was moderate and he looked after Kansas interests.

In January 1995, after Republicans won their majority, Roberts became chairman of the House Agriculture Committee. He had long believed that the huge subsidies of the early 1980s would never return. Faced with Republican budget parameters, Roberts fashioned a Freedom to Farm bill designed to phase out subsidies over seven years. In September 1995 his bill failed in committee when Southern Republicans eager to protect cotton, rice and peanut subsidies voted against it. But in November 1995, Roberts persuaded Agriculture conferees to include most of his bill in the 1996 budget reconciliation bill, which Bill Clinton vetoed. He agreed to maintain cotton and rice marketing loans and managed to preserve the popular Conservation Reserve Program. But overall this was the biggest change in agriculture policy since the New Deal act of 1933. Roberts' new bill passed the Agriculture Committee 29-17 in January 1996, the full House in February, and became law in April. But after the Asian financial collapse in 1997, world crop prices fell and Congress started voting disaster relief to farmers every year—the subsidies in another form.

Amid this furious legislative activity, one of Kansas' Senate seats came open when in November 1995 Nancy Landon Kassebaum announced her retirement. At first Roberts said he was too busy working on the farm bill and declined to run. When the bill's fortunes improved, he announced his candidacy in January 1996; the law seemed likely to remove much of the power of the committee, and under new Republican rules he was limited to three terms as chairman. He won the August primary with an overwhelming 78% in a four-way race. In the general election he faced state Treasurer Sally Thompson and won easily, 62%-34%. Thus Roberts became the first House member to give up a committee chairmanship to run for the Senate since Lister Hill in 1938 (and Hill got appointed to his Senate seat).

Roberts is on the Senate Agriculture Committee and has spent much time on farm issues. The Freedom to Farm Act worked well in 1997, and farmers seemed pleased to be able to decide what crops to plant without getting government approval. But in 1998 crop prices plunged—in line with the long-run trend of falling prices for basic commodities—and some demanded a return to the old system. Roberts resisted that, and bills were passed to give temporary aid and accelerate $4.5 billion in payments and give farmers an extra $4 billion in disaster assistance. In 2000 the pattern continued: Roberts argued that increased subsidies for crop insurance would mean less need for yearly assistance and argued that limiting production would not raise prices because the U.S. accounts for less than one-fifth of world production. The problem seems intractable. The number of family farmers continues to fall in places like western Kansas, where farm communities are tending to disappear, yet prices are not sufficient to maintain many operations.

The Freedom to Farm Act came up for reauthorization in 2002, and this time Roberts was not chairman of an Agriculture Committee but the fifth-ranking member of the minority. He admitted the Freedom to Farm Act "didn't work out as anybody would have hoped," and with Thad Cochran pushed for farm savings accounts. But in committee that was rejected in favor of Chairman Tom Harkin's approach: Revival of countercyclical subsidies when crop prices are low, plus a larger Conservation Reserve Program, which pays farmers not to farm their land in order to protect environmentally sensitive areas. Harkin prevailed on the Senate floor 58-40 in February 2002; Roberts wasn't even on the conference committee. "I've never seen such partisanship in a farm bill," Roberts said. "This policy fails farmers." He argued that it would provide no aid when production was low and crop prices rose, which is exactly what happened when drought struck the Great Plains in summer 2002. Roberts has tried to encourage farm exports in many ways, opposing cargo preferences, urging passage of trade promotion authority and replenishment of IMF funds. He was a lead sponsor of the 2000 law to end the embargo on food to Cuba, and he and Kansas colleague Sam Brownback sponsored the 1999 law allowing the president to lift the embargo on India and Pakistan and in 2000 sought to end food sanctions altogether. He supported normal trade relations with China and met with Fidel Castro in Cuba in 2000. In 2004 he said that Brazil's cotton complaint to the WTO was "the most serious, full-frontal assault on the U.S. farm program in our history"; Brazil won its case in the WTO in 2005, which threatens not only the cotton but other subsidy programs.

In January 2005 Roberts let the less senior Saxby Chambliss became chairman of Agriculture so he could keep the chairmanship of the Intelligence Committee; after Republicans lost their majority, he let Chambliss take the ranking minority position. As he said in 2005 of his service on the committee, "When you're from Kansas, you're not appointed to [the Agriculture committee]. You're sentenced to it." Roberts has continued to promote the food aid programs which use U.S. surplus commodities. In January 2005 he and Harkin urged food aid to victims of the Asian tsunami. In February 2005 he and Larry Craig sought to reverse a Treasury regulation that required Cuba to pay in advance for U.S. agricultural and medical shipments. In May 2005 he opposed an administration plan to allow purchase of foreign commodities for the food aid program. In October 2005 Roberts cast a deciding vote for $3 billion in Agriculture cuts over the next five years, and predicted disaster because of rising oil prices. "We are facing a Category 5 energy and fertilizer hurricane. The concern of farmers and lenders is at a level not seen since the 1980s." In May 2006 he co-sponsored a bill to have federal food labeling laws override state and local laws. In June 2006 he and Kent Conrad sponsored legislation to place trade sanctions on Japan unless it agreed to end its embargo on U.S. beef imports by the end of August; later in the month Japan announced it would do that. As the Agriculture Committee reauthorized the 2002 farm bill in 2007, Roberts was again a mid-ranking member on the minority side, with Harkin in the chair.

In 1999 Roberts was named chairman of the new Emerging Threats and Capabilities Subcommittee of Armed Services. In hearings that attracted little attention, he probed the nation's vulnerability to terrorists and predicted that targets would be "selected for their symbolic value, like the World Trade Center in the heart of Manhattan." He warned of the dangers of information and biological warfare. He gave strong support to the Bush administration on Iraq.

In January 2003 Roberts became chairman of the Intelligence Committee. There were signs of increasing partisanship there; in October 2002 ranking Democrat Jay Rockefeller had said that if Democrats were to retain their majority he would diminish the entire traditionally bipartisan staff and replace them with partisan appointees. Roberts started off favorably disposed toward CIA Director George Tenet and in summer 2003 resisted Democratic calls for investigation of how administration officials used intelligence on Iraq and for declassification of the 28 pages of the White House report which were classified. In November Fox News's Sean Hannity obtained a memo prepared by Democratic committee staffers saying that in the hearings on pre-March 2003 Iraq intelligence they should "pull the majority along" on getting information out and then in early 2004 should "pull the trigger" and use it to attack the Bush administration. Majority Leader Bill Frist demanded an apology on behalf of Roberts, and the committee's weekly meeting was cancelled. Rockefeller tried to mend relations, but refused to apologize; the next day he said he was "profoundly surprised" by a November 13 opinion article in *The Washington Post* written by Roberts. "The Democrats planned to undermine the integrity of the committee by conducting a partisan attack, which threatens to destroy the credibility of an institution that has served the U.S. Senate and the nation well for nearly 30 years. I oppose them, and for this I make no apologies."

In January 2004 the Senate and House Intelligence Committee reported that the CIA did not seriously consider the possibility that Saddam Hussein had no weapons of mass destruction. In April 2004 Roberts proposed that the Intelligence Committee take over from Armed Services oversight of Defense Department intelligence operations; the proposal was resisted. In July 2004 the committee unanimously approved a report criticizing pre-war intelligence on Iraq; Democrats demanded an additional Phase II investigation of how Bush administration officials used the intelligence. After the 9/11 Commission recommended changes in intelligence organizations, including a new national intelligence director, Roberts and committee Republicans came up with their own proposal, to abolish the CIA and arrange its functions in three component organizations under a new national intelligence director. The CIA opposed this; the White House had not been informed, and was frosty to the idea; John Kerry mentioned the proposal favorably; the 9/11 Commission was neutral. But soon thereafter there was bipartisan agreement in the Senate on the proposal made by the Governmental Affairs Committee's Susan Collins and Joseph Lieberman; it was not entirely accepted in conference committee with the House.

In February 2005 Roberts launched a "preemptive" investigation of intelligence on Iran. He criticized the CIA for not learning enough about the Iraq insurgency. In March 2005, when Rockefeller called for an investigation of CIA treatment of terrorism suspects and renditions, Roberts refused, arguing that the committee covered that in normal oversight. "Let me assure you the Senate Intelligence Committee is well aware of what the CIA is doing overseas in the defense of our nation and they are not torturing detainees." When Rockefeller filed an amendment to the emergency supplemental appropriations bill to require such an investigation, Roberts said that some members had an "almost a pathological obsession with calling into question the actions" of intelligence agencies. In May 2005 the committee debated a Roberts bill to allow the FBI to subpoena certain records without judicial oversight; it was approved 11–4 in June. Committee Democrats continued to resist Roberts's proposal that in the Phase II evaluation of statements by administration officials and others in the runup to the Iraq action of March 2003, no names be attached to the statements under consideration by the committee; Democrats may have feared that they would end up condemning statements made by themselves. On November 1, Democrats, protesting the failure to complete Phase II, forced a closed-door secret session of the Senate. Roberts was furious. "I understand the minority has held yet another press conference today," he said. "If they would work so hard on getting Phase II completed, we might be done by now. This senator has been and is ready to roll up his sleeves and get going." Roberts opposed the Democrats' proposal to have staff members make preliminary evaluation of statements in Phase II.

When the *New York Times* in December 2005 revealed that the NSA was surveilling contacts between al Qaeda suspects abroad and persons in the United States, Roberts noted that he and Rockefeller had been briefed on the program and that Rockefeller had often said he approved it. Rockefeller nonetheless sought a committee investigation; Roberts said that the program was within the president's constitutional powers, which could not be extinguished by Congress, and that the program was "legal, necessary and reasonable." In February 2006, however, the *Times* reported that he said he wanted the surveillance conducted under the authority of the FISA and wanted the committee to get regular briefings on it; a staffer said the story didn't reflect the ongoing negotiations between the administration and Congress. In March 2006 the committee voted on party lines not to conduct an investigation into the domestic surveillance program but instead to establish a seven-member panel, approved by the Bush administration, charged with that responsibility; Roberts said that some Democrats "believe the gravest threat we face is not Osama bin Laden and al Qaeda, but rather the president of the United States" and wrote, perhaps with reference to a 2003 Democratic staff memo, that they "seem less interested in fixing the intelligence community's problems than in the political benefit to be achieved by exploiting them." In June 2006 he asked the Director of National Intelligence for an assessment of the damage done to intelligence efforts by the *Times*'s disclosure of the NSA surveillance program and its later disclosure of data-mining in the Swift banking consortium in Belgium. In November 2006, after Democrats won their majority, Rockefeller said that he would lead investigations of the NSA surveillance, CIA detention practices and the use of prewar intelligence on Iraq; Phase II had yet to be completed.

On other issues, Roberts worked successfully in 2005 to get from an Agriculture Department program an additional $25 million for affordable housing for troops and civilians at Fort Riley; the base came out of the base closing process with additional forces, including the 1st Infantry Division which was to be moved from Germany to Kansas. In 2005 he and Hillary Rodham Clinton sponsored a bill to set up an electronic tracking system for vaccines. In 2006, for the fourth year in a row, Roberts was voted the funniest senator in *Washingtonian*'s biennial poll of congressional staffers. But he wasn't satisfied. "I was lobbying for the 'hottie of the year,' but I can't even get to lukewarm."

Roberts came up for reelection in 2002. No Democrat filed to run against Roberts and against Libertarian and Reform party candidates he won 83% of the vote. In November 2006, after Republican losses, he confirmed he would run again in 2008. In mid-2007 he seemed to be in a strong position to win reelection.

FIRST DISTRICT

Rep. Jerry Moran (R)

Elected 1996, 6th term; b. May 29, 1954, Great Bend; home, Hays; U. of KS, B.S. 1976, J.D. 1981; Methodist; married (Robba).

Elected Office: KS Senate, 1988-96, Majority Ldr., 1995-96.

Professional Career: Operations Officer, Consolidated State Bank, 1975-77; Mgr., Farmers State Bank & Trust Co., 1977-78; Practicing atty., 1981-96; Instructor, Ft. Hays St. U., 1986.

DC Office: 2202 RHOB, 20515, 202-225-2715; Fax: 202-225-5124; Web site: www.house.gov/moranks01.

District Offices: Hays, 785-628-6401; Hutchinson, 620-665-6138; Salina, 785-309-0572.

Committees: *Agriculture* (4th of 21 R): General Farm Commodities & Risk Management (RMM); Department Operations, Oversight, Nutrition & Forestry; Conservation, Credit, Energy & Research. *Transportation & Infrastructure* (11th of 34 R): Railroads, Pipelines & Hazardous Materials; Aviation. *Veterans' Affairs* (3d of 13 R): Economic Opportunity; Health.

Group Ratings

	ADA	ACLU	AFS	LCV	ITIC	NTU	COC	ACU	CFG	FRC
2006	5	27	0	8	100	60	93	84	58	85
2005	15	—	13	0	—	64	93	96	76	92

National Journal Ratings

	2005 LIB	—	2005 CONS		2006 LIB	—	2006 CONS
Economic	30%	—	68%		39%	—	60%
Social	22%	—	78%		41%	—	59%
Foreign	47%	—	53%		56%	—	43%

Key Votes of the 109th Congress

1. Estate Tax Repeal	Y	5. Limit Interstate Abortion	Y	9. Build Border Fence	Y
2. Limit CAFE Standards	Y	6. Extend Patriot Act	Y	10. CAFTA	Y
3. FY06 Spending Curb	Y	7. Bar Same Sex Marriage	Y	11. Oppose Iraq Withdrawal	Y
4. Drilling in ANWR	Y	8. Stem Cell Research $	N	12. Detainee Tribunals	N

Election Results

2006 general	Jerry Moran (R)	156,728	(79%)	($723,063)
	John Doll (D)	39,781	(20%)	($62,274)
	Other	2,869	(1%)	
2006 primary	Jerry Moran (R)	unopposed		
2004 general	Jerry Moran (R)	239,776	(91%)	($349,807)
	Jack Warner (Lib)	24,517	(9%)	

Prior Winning Percentages: 2002 (91%); 2000 (89%); 1998 (81%); 1996 (73%)

The People		Race/Ethnic Origin	Ancestry	
Area size:	57,576 sq. mi.	84.5% White	German: 23.2%	English: 7.3%
Urban population:	52.4%	2.1% Black	USA: 7.2%	
Rural population:	47.6%	0.9% Asian	**2004 Presidential Vote**	
Pop. 2000:	672,091	0.4% Native Am.	Bush (R) 199,554	(72%)
Pop. 2005 (est):	653,879	0.0% Hawaiian	Kerry (D) 73,309	(26%)
Median income:	$34,869	1.1% Two+ races	Other 3,962	(1%)
Poverty status:	11.0%	0.1% Other	**2000 Presidential Vote**	
Military veterans:	13.4%	10.9% Hispanic Origin	Bush (R) 177,857	(67%)
			Gore (D) 76,448	(29%)
			Other 12,514	(5%)
			Cook Partisan Voting Index: R +20	

Occupation	Blue collar: 28.5%	White collar: 52.8%	Gray collar: 18.8%

"A prairie is not any old piece of flatland in the Midwest," writes Kansas-born reporter Dennis Farney. "No, a prairie is wine-colored grass, dancing in the wind. A prairie is a sun-splashed hillside, bright with wild flowers. A prairie is a fleeting cloud shadow, the song of the meadowlark. It is the wild land that has never felt the slash of the plow." This prairie once covered almost all of Kansas. Now only a little virgin prairie can still be found, in the Flint Hills region west and south of Topeka, where you can see 30 miles on a clear day and the waist-deep sea of grass still waves in the wind as it did when the pioneers on the Santa Fe Trail went west through here some 150 years ago. The 11,000-acre Tallgrass Prairie National Preserve was created in 1996 to protect this unique landscape and it is the largest privately owned unit in the National Park system. "The Flint Hills do not take your breath away," wrote western folklorist Jim Hoy. "They give you a chance to catch it." Much of the area was grazing land, first for buffalo, then for the cattle driven to Kansas railheads like Abilene and Dodge City in the 1870s and 1880s. This brief moment in history has been recaptured with varying accuracy in movies over a much longer span, and commemorated in the Boot Hill Museum of kitschy Dodge City, where Wyatt Earp Boulevard is the main street.

After the harsh winter of 1886-87 wiped out the cattle herds, came the plow and barbed wire (commemorated in LaCrosse's Barbed Wire Museum), which enabled farmers to keep livestock out of their wheat fields and later became the foundation for a cheap telephone system. The farmers also brought to this vacant landscape Yankee civilization, with its schools and churches, and some foreign traditions as well, like the Cathedral of the Plains built by German Catholics. Now this civilization is threatened. "My great-grandparents and grandparents were part of the stream of settlers who migrated to western Kansas after the Civil War to become wheat farmers," writes James Dickenson in his elegiac *Home on the Range*. "They broke the virgin sod, erected houses, barns, schools, churches and towns, and made the area one of the most agriculturally productive in the world. A little more than a century later, the population has ebbed away from this area and many of the farms, schools, churches and towns lie vacant, dilapidated and boarded up like old boomtowns." The average age of Kansas farmers has approached 60. But there are also signs of new life, including growing agri-tourism to supplement the family farm. Some towns are attracting new residents by giving away lands as homesteads, and big meatpacking plants in Dodge City, Garden City and Liberal (the "Golden Triangle of meatpacking") have attracted large numbers of Hispanic immigrants, many living in trailer parks; nearly two-thirds of the school children in these counties are Hispanic and Spanish-language radio is prominent. Wind farms have grown on prairie land, though some worry that they may disturb the tallgrass and the delicate prairie ecosystem.

The 1st Congressional District consists of most of this expanse of Kansas, almost everything west of the Flint Hills and Abilene, the boyhood home of Dwight Eisenhower. Its 66 full counties (it also contains parts of three others; only the Nebraska 3d District has more counties) increased from 76,000 people in 1870 to 570,000 in 1890; but it has not grown much since then. With its aging population, it has the most hospitals of any district in the nation. Kansas now has more "frontier counties," with between two and six people per square mile, than it did in 1890. The "Big First," which stretches 350 miles east from the Colorado border, is roughly the size of Illinois. It is also a district of firsts: it has more farms and more acres in grain sorghum production than any other, and more cattle than any other. Politically, the 1st District is heavily Republican. It voted better than 2–1 for George W. Bush in 2000 and by nearly 3–1 in 2004, and his county percentages were as high as 85%. But it also voted narrowly for Democratic Governor Kathleen Sebelius, whose late father-in-law, Republican Keith Sebelius, represented the district in the House for 12 years.

The congressman from the 1st District is Jerry Moran, a Republican first elected in 1996. Moran grew up in Plainville in Rooks County and got his start in politics as an intern for Keith Sebelius; he got a seat at the hearings on the impeachment of Richard Nixon. Moran worked as a banker for four years before attending the University of Kansas Law School. He practiced law and was elected to the state Senate in 1988. In 1995 he became state Senate majority leader. When Congressman Pat Roberts ran for the Senate in 1996, Moran stepped into the 1st District race and, with the help of Republican leaders, avoided serious primary competition. He won 76% of the vote in the primary, which was tantamount to election.

Moran's voting record has been sporadically moderate on economic and foreign issues, and he has sometimes gone his own way in pursuing district causes. He praised the 2002 farm bill for improving the safety net to farmers. During international trade negotiations in Geneva, he defended U.S. farm subsidies and called for more market access for U.S. farmers. He called for sanctions if Japan did not open its borders to U.S. beef shipments. In the 2006 supplemental spending bill, he pushed for $75 million in energy aid to compensate farmers in his district, the most in the nation. To the dismay of Speaker Dennis Hastert, he "ran and hid" as one of the 25 House Republicans who opposed the Medicare/prescription drug bill in 2003 because it did not reduce drug prices. "I have never been under such pressure to vote contrary to what I thought was right as I was with this vote," Moran wrote. Later, he sought to give federal officials negotiating authority to lower prescription drug costs. He has bucked Republican leadership to lead bipartisan efforts to bar the Treasury Department from enforcing sanctions against the sale of food and medicine to Cuba; he called the embargo "a failed policy." In 2005, Cuba purchased 25,000 metric tons of Kansas wheat.

Each year, Moran has logged about 50,000 miles around the district visiting every county. He began his 2007 annual "listening tour" in late 2006 because of uncertainties surrounding the new Democratic majority's voting schedule; people here expect to see their congressman without driving to the next county over. He was reelected in 1998 with a record 81% of the vote and did not face another Democratic challenger until 2006, when he got 79% against first-time candidate John Doll, a former school teacher; that was the second-best result for any House Republican facing a Democratic foe. He resisted state party leaders' pressure to challenge popular Governor Kathleen Sebelius in 2006. But a statewide bid remains possible. If Senator Pat Roberts retires in 2008, Moran is viewed as his preferred successor.

SECOND DISTRICT

Rep. Nancy Boyda (D)

Elected 2006, 1st term; b. Aug. 2, 1955, Clayton, MO; home, Topeka; William Jewell Col., B.A. 1977; Methodist; married (Steve).

Professional Career: Teacher, 1977-79; EPA, 1979-81; Marion Laboratories/Marion Merrill Dow, 1981-93; IMTCI/PRA, 1993-95; CYDEX, Inc., 1995-2001; Independent Consultant, 2001-03.

DC Office: 1711 LHOB, 20515, 202-225-6601; Fax: 202-225-7986; Web site: boyda.house.gov.

District Offices: Pittsburg, 620-231-3011; Topeka, 785-234-8111.

Committees: *Agriculture* (15th of 25 D): General Farm Commodities & Risk Management; Department Operations, Oversight, Nutrition & Forestry; Conservation, Credit, Energy & Research. *Armed Services* (22d of 34 D): Military Personnel; Readiness.

Group Ratings and Key Votes: Newly Elected

Election Results

2006 general	Nancy Boyda (D)	114,139	(51%)	($726,738)
	Jim Ryun (R)	106,329	(47%)	($1,075,223)
	Other	5,094	(2%)	
2006 primary	Nancy Boyda (D)	unopposed		
2004 general	Jim Ryun (R)	165,325	(56%)	($1,136,464)
	Nancy Boyda (D)	121,532	(41%)	($1,105,838)
	Other	7,579	(3%)	

The People		Race/Ethnic Origin	Ancestry		
Area size:	14,318 sq. mi.	87.3% White	German: 19.3% Irish: 9.1%		
Urban population:	59.8%	4.9% Black	English: 8.2%		
Rural population:	40.2%	1.0% Asian	**2004 Presidential Vote**		
Pop. 2000:	672,102	1.2% Native Am.	Bush (R)	176,764	(59%)
Pop. 2005 (est):	678,278	0.1% Hawaiian	Kerry (D)	117,924	(39%)
Median income:	$37,855	1.7% Two+ races	Other	4,103	(1%)
Poverty status:	11.2%	0.1% Other	**2000 Presidential Vote**		
Military veterans:	14.6%	3.8% Hispanic Origin	Bush (R)	144,721	(54%)
			Gore (D)	109,133	(41%)
			Other	13,723	(5%)
			Cook Partisan Voting Index: R + 7		
Occupation	Blue collar: 26.1% White collar: 57.6% Gray collar: 16.3%				

The green plains of eastern Kansas have seen more than their share of American history. Here, on bluffs above the Missouri River, Fort Leavenworth was built in 1827, famous in later years for its war college and military prison and now the oldest U.S. fort west of the Mississippi. In the 1850s, newly founded towns along the Kansas River and along the Missouri line were the centers of Bleeding Kansas, where the pro-slavery bushwhackers set up a state capital in tiny Lecompton and anti-slavery New Englanders set up their stronghold down the river at Lawrence.

Farther up the river is Manhattan, home of Kansas State University, and Fort Riley, once an outpost against the Indians, then a major Army base often threatened with closure. In 2005, the Pentagon designated Fort Riley as the headquarters of the 1st Infantry Division—the "Big Red One"—which is expected to create several thousand local jobs. Topeka, the state capital, sits here on a low bluff above the river; it was this city whose system of legal segregation was overturned in the 1954 landmark case, *Brown v. Board of Education*. Farther south, on the Missouri border, are the hills called "the Balkans." Here coal miners, often of Eastern European origin, lived in and near towns like Pittsburg and Girard, once a center of American socialism, where Clarence Darrow and Upton Sinclair made pilgrimages; the local paper, *Appeal to Reason*, had circulation of 750,000 across the nation. Population loss is not as great here as in western Kansas. The area around Lawrence has been booming as, in effect, the perimeter of metropolitan Kansas City; coal-bed methane gas wells have been a growth industry in southeast Kansas.

These disparate areas, Topeka and Manhattan, Fort Riley and Fort Leavenworth, the wheat-growing counties and the Balkans—most of eastern Kansas except the Kansas City metropolitan area—make up the 2d Congressional District. The heritage of most of this area has been Republican ever since the jayhawks defeated the bushwhackers once the votes were counted honestly in the 1850s. Yet Democrats in recent decades have been competitive in state races, especially in Topeka. For 20 of the years from 1970-94, Democrats held the 2d District seat. In the following dozen years, it voted for strongly conservative Republicans, usually by comfortable margins.

The new congresswoman from the 2d District is Nancy Boyda, who defeated Republican Jim Ryun in 2006 on her second attempt. A native of Clayton, Missouri, she graduated from William Jewell College, where she majored in chemistry and education. She was a school teacher and a chemist with the Environmental Protection Agency. In 2003, Boyda quit her job as a pharmaceutical company executive and switched parties to challenge Ryun the following year. She had not previously held elected office, and she acknowledged participating in protests before the invasion of Iraq in March 2003. Ryun tried to link her to radical groups opposed to the hunt for Osama bin Laden. Although she had help from national Democrats, a hefty contribution from labor, almost $300,000 of her own money, and managed to out-fundraise the incumbent by $130,000, she still lost the election, 56%-41%.

Boyda returned two years later, saying, "My momma didn't raise a quitter. I don't give up." But this contest failed to appear on the national political radar until late in the cycle: The perception was that this had become a solidly Republican district and Ryun—whose initial fame came in 1965 when he was the first high-schooler to break the four-minute mile and he made the cover of *Sports Illustrated*—appeared to have become entrenched. Boyda also had been unimpressive in her earlier challenge. But the 2006 political tremors reached Kansas, too, and her candidacy suddenly became more appealing. This time, Boyda had the advantage of an environment in which voters were hostile to Republicans and disillusioned with the course of the Iraq war. Ryun's support for Bush and the war never wavered, even as Boyda reiterated her mantra, "Had enough? Nothing will change until we change Congress." While Ryun spent his money blanketing the eastern Kansas district with television spots, Boyda bicycled across much of the district and used a $99 software program to produce 12- and 16-page newspaper inserts to familiarize voters with her background and positions on Iraq, immigration, health care, the federal deficit, energy, education and other issues. After Ryun returned from Iraq in the summer of 2006 with the claim that the U.S. strategy was making progress, Boyda said that the Bush administration and its supporters had no answers on how to end the war. She also criticized the failure of Republicans to stem the tide of illegal immigration.

National Democrats—including EMILY's List, which backed her in 2004 but failed to endorse her this time—all but ignored Boyda until the final weeks of the 2006 campaign, and her fundraising lagged behind Ryun. "People in Washington still don't have a clue," she said in early October. "We are still beneath the radar in Washington, D.C., and I think the pundits are going to eat their words on November 8." When Boyda's strong grassroots campaign (her husband was her campaign manager) suddenly bolted into close contention, Republicans began to take notice. Vice President Cheney stumped for Ryun, and President Bush appeared at a rally in Topeka just two days before the election. By then, it was too late. Ryun, who appeared to have been caught off guard and was unaccustomed to such a competitive election, painted Boyda as a radical liberal who supported a "cut and run" approach to Iraq and amnesty for illegal immigrants, a harsh attack that may have seemed out of character for the five-term incumbent. The Democratic Congressional Campaign Committee's heavy investment in TV spots late in the campaign also took its toll as Ryun was forced to answer charges that he voted against a $1,500 combat bonus for troops while giving himself two pay raises.

After having won only in historically Democratic Crawford County in the Balkans two years earlier, Boyda won 12 of the district's 26 counties for an overall 51%-47% victory. She won Crawford County 57%-41% and carried Atchison and Douglas Counties by even larger margins.

In the House, Boyda said that she would pursue her interest in health care issues, such as policies that encourage consumers to purchase prescription drugs from local pharmacists rather than through the mail; she refused to accept congressional medical benefits until the nation's health care problems were solved. But as one of five freshman Democrats who won districts where President Bush captured at least 59% in 2004, Boyda ranks as a top Republican target. The Democratic leadership sought to guard against her vulnerabilities by placing her on the Agriculture and Armed Services committees—prime assignments for a Kansan—and by featuring her bill to revoke the pensions of members of Congress convicted of certain crimes. But she invited criticism in January 2007 when she told ABC News that people who are dissatisfied with the Iraq war "should have thought about that before they voted for President Bush, not once, but twice"—an ill-considered statement from a congresswoman in this particular district—she later apologized for "an unclear and poorly stated response" and cited "first-week jitters." She also weathered attacks from the left after she said she would support the Bush administration's troop "surge." At home, the state Republican Party placed volunteers at nearly every post office in the district on Tax Day to distribute literature linking Boyda to "liberal San Francisco Speaker" Nancy Pelosi.

In April, Ryun announced he would challenge Boyda in 2008, but many Republicans doubted his chances at winning back the seat; Republican state Treasurer Lynn Jenkins, a moderate, also filed in April. Promising to run an independent reelection bid, Boyda declined funding from a DCCC program for vulnerable incumbents.

THIRD DISTRICT

Rep. Dennis Moore (D)

Elected 1998, 5th term; b. Nov. 8, 1945, Anthony; home, Lenexa; U. of KS, B.A. 1967; Washburn U. Law Schl., J.D. 1970; Protestant; married (Stephene).

Military Career: Army, 1970; Army Reserves, 1971-73.

Elected Office: Johnson Cnty. Dist. Atty., 1976-88; Johnson Cnty. Comm. Coll. Bd. of Trustees, 1993-98.

Professional Career: Asst. KS Atty. Gen., 1971-73; Practicing atty., 1973-76, 1989-98.

DC Office: 1727 LHOB, 20515, 202-225-2865; Fax: 202-225-2807; Web site: moore.house.gov.

District Offices: Kansas City, 913-621-0832; Lawrence, 785-842-9313; Overland Park, 913-383-2013.

Committees: *Budget* (19th of 22 D). *Financial Services* (12th of 37 D): Capital Markets, Insurance & Government Sponsored Enterprises; Financial Institutions & Consumer Credit; Domestic and International Monetary Policy, Trade & Technology.

Group Ratings

	ADA	ACLU	AFS	LCV	ITIC	NTU	COC	ACU	CFG	FRC
2006	85	77	100	92	100	16	60	23	17	0
2005	80	—	100	78	—	21	59	16	19	8

National Journal Ratings

	2005 LIB	—	2005 CONS		2006 LIB	—	2006 CONS
Economic	63%	—	37%		64%	—	35%
Social	65%	—	35%		69%	—	30%
Foreign	58%	—	42%		60%	—	39%

Key Votes of the 109th Congress

1. Estate Tax Repeal	N	5. Limit Interstate Abortion	N	9. Build Border Fence	Y
2. Limit CAFE Standards	N	6. Extend Patriot Act	N	10. CAFTA	Y
3. FY06 Spending Curb	N	7. Bar Same Sex Marriage	N	11. Oppose Iraq Withdrawal	Y
4. Drilling in ANWR	N	8. Stem Cell Research $	Y	12. Detainee Tribunals	Y

Election Results

2006 general	Dennis Moore (D)	153,105	(65%)	($1,852,080)
	Chuck Ahner (R)	79,824	(34%)	($433,456)
	Other	4,051	(2%)	
2006 primary	Dennis Moore (D)	unopposed		
2004 general	Dennis Moore (D)	184,050	(55%)	($2,362,887)
	Kris Kobach (R)	145,542	(43%)	($1,191,231)
	Other	6,147	(2%)	

Prior Winning Percentages: 2002 (50%); 2000 (50%); 1998 (52%)

The People		Race/Ethnic Origin	Ancestry	
Area size:	787 sq. mi.	79.6% White	German: 18.0%	Irish: 10.5%
Urban population:	94.7%	8.8% Black	English: 9.0%	
Rural population:	5.3%	2.6% Asian	**2004 Presidential Vote**	
Pop. 2000:	672,124	0.6% Native Am.	Bush (R)	186,476 (55%)
Pop. 2005 (est):	726,527	0.0% Hawaiian	Kerry (D)	150,598 (44%)
Median income:	$51,118	1.5% Two+ races	Other	3,262 (1%)
Poverty status:	7.8%	0.1% Other	**2000 Presidential Vote**	
Military veterans:	12.1%	6.8% Hispanic Origin	Bush (R)	152,832 (53%)
			Gore (D)	122,463 (42%)
			Other	13,452 (5%)
			Cook Partisan Voting Index: R + 4	

Occupation	Blue collar: 17.3%	White collar: 70.4%	Gray collar: 12.3%

Though its central city is in Missouri, 40 percent of metropolitan Kansas City's residents now live west of the state line in Kansas. Some are in Kansas City, Kansas, (or KCK as it is sometimes called) where the low-lying land near the Missouri River used to house one of the nation's largest stockyards. This is still a working-class town with a few dilapidated looking streets and lots of modest frame houses, new Latino neighborhoods, the largest black neighborhood and the oldest Catholic ethnic neighborhoods in Kansas. Kansas City's Wyandotte County has lost 35,000 people since the 1970s and its population was 28% black and 16% Hispanic in 2000. South of Kansas City and Wyandotte is Johnson County, much more affluent and more than three times larger than Wyandotte, separated from the affluent Kansas City, Missouri, neighborhood around the old Country Club Plaza shopping center by just a single small street. The newer neighborhoods are arrayed along the interstates, as subdivisions have replaced croplands. They have grown to the point that Overland Park, Olathe, Shawnee and Lenexa are among the largest cities in the state. These suburbs are not just residential; Applebee's restaurant chain, a J.C. Penney catalog center, as well as lots of thriving small businesses, are in Johnson County. A huge theme park is planned for Olathe. But capitalism produces creative destruction: Sprint, headquartered here, merged with Nextel and moved its corporate headquarters to Northern Virginia. Politically, Wyandotte County has an old Democratic machine politics, though its influence has been tempered by the consolidation of city and county governments. Johnson County has long been heavily Republican, but with plenty of voters moderate or even liberal on cultural issues; this has been the scene of fierce fights between moderate and conservative Republicans, with Democrats as the beneficiaries.

The 3d Congressional District of Kansas consists of Johnson County, Wyandotte County and part of Douglas County to the west including the portion of Lawrence that is the home of the University of Kansas campus; Douglas County was the only one of Kansas's 105 counties to oppose a 2005 constitutional amendment banning same-sex marriage. More than two-thirds of the district lives in Johnson County, which grew by 27% in the 1990s and had a $62,000 median household income. This is an affluent metropolitan district in a rough-hewn, historically rural state.

The congressman from the 3d District is Dennis Moore, a Democrat first elected in 1998. Moore grew up in Wichita, where his father Warner Moore ran for Congress in the 4th District and lost the general by only 50.3%-49.7% in 1958. Moore went to college and law school in Kansas, served in the Army and practiced law in Johnson County. In 1976, at 31, he was elected Johnson County district attorney and was twice re-elected. He went into private law practice, and was elected to the local community college board in 1993. In 1998, when national Democrats were recruiting a candidate to run against conservative Republican incumbent Vince Snowbarger, Moore's electoral success made him a natural choice. The contest attracted independent expenditure campaigns, with the Sierra Club and the AFL-CIO spending heavily on TV ads, mailings and phone banks to elect Moore. Moore won 52%-48%, carrying Kansas City and Lawrence by wide margins, but his key wins came in the affluent, long-settled suburbs in northeast Johnson County.

In the House, Moore has become a prominent voice among Blue Dogs and moderate Democrats who have sought to straddle party lines and move their own party toward the center. He has styled himself as tight-fisted on spending, pro-business, and eager to address entitlements and long-term fiscal problems. To the dismay of organized labor, he voted for normal trade relations with China and trade promotion authority. In July 2005, his vote was up for grabs on the Central America Free Trade Agreement and he was one of 15 Democrats who bucked his party leaders to vote in favor. He led the effort in 2004 and 2005 to raise the death benefit for military personnel killed since September 11. After Democrats regained House control, he joined a Blue Dog and New Democrat delegation to meet President Bush. "I told the President that we are mortgaging the future of [our] children and grandchildren if we don't turn this around and start living like American families do, within a budget," Moore recounted, and he voiced hope for a bipartisan response to the nation's fiscal problems.

Republicans have tried hard to recapture this seat, but have been hampered by the bitter division between conservative and moderate Kansas Republicans. In 2000, the primary was between tax-cutting state Representative Phill Kline and Greg Musil, an Overland Park councilman with support from moderates and the backing of National Republican Congressional Committee Chairman Tom Davis. Kline won the primary 50%-37%. In the general, Moore appealed to moderates by portraying himself as a fiscal conservative and a crime-fighter. He won 50%-47%. In 2002, the NRCC supported reconstructive surgeon Jeff Colyer, the anti-abortion candidate, against United Airlines pilot and former Naval F-18 aviator Adam Taff, who supported abortion rights. Colyer outspent him 2-to-1, but Taff unexpectedly won the primary, 52%-48%. Taff emphasized his military experience and top-secret clearance, but he was outspent by Moore and did not run negative ads. He carried Johnson County by 53%-44% but lost overall, 50%-47%. His backers complained that NRCC support was too little and too late. In 2004, Taff ran again. But he lost the primary to Kris Kobach, a conservative former Overland Park councilman and a top aide to Attorney General John Ashcroft who helped to create the Justice Department program to collect information about foreign visitors following the September 11 attacks. In the general, Kobach sought to rally the party base, but Moore had his biggest win yet: 55%-43%. He even prevailed 50%-48% in Johnson County, which cast 74% of the total vote. With that discouraging history, national Republicans in 2006 took a pass on the district and Moore had his first easy win: 65%-34% against West Point graduate and Overland Park businessman Chuck Ahner.

"Maybe we have to wait for Dennis Moore to retire," said a Johnson County Republican activist after the 2004 election—and he may be right. But there are too many Republicans here for a Democrat to take this district for granted. Moore has appealed to enough of them to hold the seat but he is probably not secure enough to avoid another tough challenge, especially now that House Republicans are in the minority and eager to pursue any possible opportunity. One option for Moore would be a Senate run, particularly if there is a vacancy. But he faces the daunting reality that Kansas has not elected a Democrat to the Senate since the 1930s. In August 2007, state Senator Nick Jordan said he would run against Moore.

FOURTH DISTRICT

Rep. Todd Tiahrt (R)

Elected 1994, 7th term; b. June 15, 1951, Vermillion, SD; home, Goddard; SD Sch. of Mines, 1969-71; Evangel Col., B.A. 1975; SW MO St. U., M.B.A. 1989; Assembly of God; married (Vicki).

Elected Office: KS Senate, 1992-94.

Professional Career: Project Engineer, Zenith Corp., 1978-81; Proposal Mgr., Boeing Co., 1981-94.

DC Office: 2441 RHOB, 20515, 202-225-6216; Fax: 202-225-3489; Web site: www.house.gov/tiahrt.

District Offices: Wichita, 316-262-8992.

Committees: *Appropriations* (12th of 29 R): Interior, Environment & Related Agencies (RMM); Defense. *Permanent Select Committee on Intelligence* (6th of 8 R): Intelligence Community Management.

Group Ratings

	ADA	ACLU	AFS	LCV	ITIC	NTU	COC	ACU	CFG	FRC
2006	5	0	17	0	100	56	93	84	50	100
2005	0	—	0	0	—	61	93	96	67	92

National Journal Ratings

	2005 LIB — 2005 CONS		2006 LIB — 2006 CONS	
Economic	6%	94%	29%	71%
Social	0%	89%	16%	83%
Foreign	11%	86%	30%	67%

Key Votes of the 109th Congress

1. Estate Tax Repeal	Y	5. Limit Interstate Abortion	Y	9. Build Border Fence	Y
2. Limit CAFE Standards	Y	6. Extend Patriot Act	Y	10. CAFTA	Y
3. FY06 Spending Curb	Y	7. Bar Same Sex Marriage	Y	11. Oppose Iraq Withdrawal	Y
4. Drilling in ANWR	Y	8. Stem Cell Research $	N	12. Detainee Tribunals	Y

Election Results

2006 general	Todd Tiahrt (R)	116,386	(64%)	($1,085,348)
	Garth McGinn (D)	62,166	(34%)	($25,612)
	Other	4,655	(3%)	
2006 primary	Todd Tiahrt (R)	unopposed		
2004 general	Todd Tiahrt (R)	173,151	(66%)	($491,456)
	Michael Kinard (D)	81,388	(31%)	($15,083)
	Other	7,376	(3%)	

Prior Winning Percentages: 2002 (61%); 2000 (54%); 1998 (58%); 1996 (50%); 1994 (53%)

The People		Race/Ethnic Origin	Ancestry	
Area size:	9,596 sq. mi.	81.0% White	German: 17.7%	English: 8.0%
Urban population:	78.8%	6.8% Black	Irish: 7.9%	
Rural population:	21.2%	2.4% Asian	**2004 Presidential Vote**	
Pop. 2000:	672,101	1.1% Native Am.	Bush (R) 173,643	(64%)
Pop. 2005 (est):	685,882	0.0% Hawaiian	Kerry (D) 93,129	(34%)
Median income:	$40,917	2.0% Two+ races	Other 3,783	(1%)
Poverty status:	9.6%	0.1% Other	**2000 Presidential Vote**	
Military veterans:	14.0%	6.6% Hispanic Origin	Bush (R) 146,921	(59%)
			Gore (D) 91,232	(37%)
			Other 10,918	(4%)
			Cook Partisan Voting Index: R +12	

Occupation	Blue collar: 28.3%	White collar: 57.0%	Gray collar: 14.6%

Wichita is the largest Kansas-only metropolitan area, smaller than million-plus metro Kansas City, but a Great Plains metropolis of the magnitude of Omaha or Tulsa, and still growing. It began as a farm market town and grew with local oil and gas discoveries in the 1920s. But its real impetus came during World War II and the years just after, when aircraft factories sprouted up here on the Kansas plains and Wichita suddenly became the nation's major producer of small planes. Today the big four—Cessna, Raytheon, Boeing, Bombardier—are all located here. In the early 1990s, general aviation was hurt by the recession and by lawsuits that held manufacturers liable for planes they had produced years, even decades, before. A few years later, Wichita recovered: The demand for small planes was robust, and a federal limit on liability enlivened the industry. The September 11 attacks were a severe blow to the airline industry, with the loss of some 15,000 jobs in Wichita. But the Navy gave the area a boost in 2004 with a contract for 100 modified 737's to hunt submarines. And more good news came with the opening of Cessna's huge hangar center to service business jets and increased production of new Cessna planes. Boeing, the area's largest employer, sold its commercial airplane operations in Kansas but its military division remained strong. The aviation industry is just one facet of the local economy: Wichita also has become a regional health-care center in the Great Plains pattern, as people from miles around come to the metropolis for treatment.

Kansas' 4th Congressional District is centered around Wichita, covering wheat-growing areas to the east and west, but with most of its people in Wichita and Sedgwick County. Politically, it has voted Republican in federal elections but has voted Democratic occasionally in state contests.

The congressman from the 4th District is Todd Tiahrt (pronounced TEE-hart), a Republican first elected in 1994 and a party stalwart since then. He grew up on a farm in South Dakota, went to the same high school as South Dakota Senator Tim Johnson, played football for the South Dakota School of Mines and Technology and graduated from Evangel College. In 1976 he moved to the Wichita area to be closer to his wife's family and worked at Zenith as a project engineer and at Boeing as a proposal manager on the Space Station, Air Force One, KC-135, B-52, B-1, B-2, A-67, YF-22 and Comanche helicopter programs. In 1990 he went to the courthouse to file to run for the Kansas House and decided he was a Republican; he lost that race by eight votes. His grandfather raised him to be a Democrat, but he found his strong religious views were more in line with Republicans. In 1992 he was elected to the Kansas Senate, where his great cause was a concealed weapons law.

In 1994 Tiahrt decided to run against Democratic Congressman Dan Glickman, who had served for 18 years. Tiahrt ran ads showing Glickman's face morphing into Bill Clinton's, and attacked him for voting for gun control. With his base among Wichita's numerous religious conservatives, who had taken over the local Republican Party, he assembled a corps of 1,800 volunteers, many from church contacts. Glickman outspent him more than 3-to-1, but he suffered serious losses in middle-income areas in Sedgwick County. Tiahrt won a solid 53%-47% victory.

In the House, Tiahrt has a strongly conservative voting record and has wielded influence on the Appropriations Committee, particularly on its Defense Subcommittee. He has sponsored measures that help aircraft manufacturers and supported the Air Force's proposal to buy KC-767 aerial refueling tankers from Boeing. He sided with aerospace workers in opposing George W. Bush's proposal to change rules on overtime pay. He has been active on other issues as well. He tried to zero out—and later, to reduce—AmeriCorps, but with no success. He won approval of his proposal to bar enforcement of certain record-keeping requirements for gun dealers. He kept the pressure on Metro officials in the Capitol region to make sure that their signs included the correct name of Ronald Reagan Washington National Airport. He chairs the House Economic Competitiveness Caucus, which seeks to eliminate federal regulations with the goal of making U.S. businesses more competitive in global trade. Following the suicide of his teenage son Luke in 2004, Tiahrt created a foundation to help troubled teens.

Democrats targeted Tiahrt during his early years with well-financed opponents, but he appears to have locked up the district. In 2000, Wichita attorney and former Glickman aide Carlos Nolla ran a tougher-than-expected challenge against him. Tiahrt won 54%-42%. In a rematch two years later, Nolla doubled his fundraising with support from national Hispanics, and said that Tiahrt was beholden to pharmaceutical companies, but he lost 61%-37%. Since then, Tiahrt's opponents have been poorly funded and got little attention. This has enabled Tiahrt to pursue moves up the political ladder. He considered running for governor in 2002, but backed off. In the House, Tiahrt—a close ally of Tom DeLay—pushed for Roy Blunt to appoint him as chief deputy whip, but the job went to the more junior Eric Cantor of Virginia. In early 2006, Tiahrt was among several Republicans who prepared to run for party Whip when Blunt campaigned for Majority Leader; but Blunt lost and there was no opening. In December 2006, senior members of the Republican Study Committee backed him as the group's new chairman, but he lost to insurgent Jeb

Hensarling of Texas, whose backers said that Tiahrt was too close to Republican leaders. Despite his failed leadership bids, Tiahrt's experience and ideological convictions continue to stamp him as an influential backroom leader.

★ KENTUCKY ★

Kentucky is a state that in many ways remains close to its beginnings. This is, literally, a Jeffersonian commonwealth: It is one of four commonwealths (the others are Virginia, Pennsylvania and Massachusetts) and when the first settlers came here, in the years Thomas Jefferson was writing his *Notes on Virginia*, it was part of Virginia. Kentucky was admitted to the Union in 1792, when Jefferson was secretary of state; when Jefferson was aroused at the Federalists' anti-sedition acts, he ghostwrote the Kentucky Resolutions in 1798. Kentucky's largest county is named after Jefferson and what has long been its largest city after the monarch to whom he was credentialed as ambassador to France, Louis XVI. To this day, Kentucky still has a constitution informed by a Jeffersonian jealousy of power. Its one-term limit on governors was raised to two only in 1995; it limited its state legislature to one 60-day session every two years until 2001, so that much important business was done in special sessions; every governor must swear that he or she has not participated in a duel (remember what Jefferson thought of Aaron Burr). Kentucky for many long years favored the Democratic Party, which can trace its ancestry at least tenuously back to Jefferson. But here too there has been change recently. George W. Bush carried Kentucky twice, after it was carried twice, by diminishing margins, by William Jefferson Clinton. Both of Kentucky's senators and four of its six House members are Republicans; a Republican was elected governor in 2003, for the first time since 1967, and Republicans have had a majority in the state Senate since 1999.

The agrarian Jefferson would approve of Kentucky's demography, which is still quite rural, with well under half its population in the big metropolitan areas of Louisville, Lexington and the Northern Kentucky counties across the Ohio River from Cincinnati. And the tobacco planters who once presided over what one historian called "the alcoholic republic" might not entirely disapprove of a Kentucky economy that remained for years heavily dependent on century-old industries such as whiskey (Bourbon County, where the beverage was invented in the 18th century, is in Kentucky; its county seat is Paris), tobacco (Kentucky is the nation's number two producer after North Carolina, and it has the largest number of tobacco farms) and coal. But change is coming here too. Kentucky has ranked number one in percentage of smokers, but the city-county council voted a ban on smoking in public places in Lexington, the site of Kentucky's burley market, and the buyout of already dwindling tobacco quotas voted by Congress in 2004 will likely result in the end of tobacco farming in the Appalachian mountains and a shift of production to central and western Kentucky. Louisville's Brown & Williamson Tobacco was absorbed by R. J. Reynolds, based in North Carolina. Employment is sharply down in coal and tobacco, and Kentucky has big plants producing appliances, Toyotas, Ford trucks and Lexmark printers; it also has big companies that specialize in things not traditionally Kentuckian, such as Humana health services and Ashland Oil. Still, this is an economy that did not partake in much of the bounteous growth of the past two decades.

Many of the buildings here are old: The small-town 19th century courthouses, the cabins in the coal mining Appalachians, the unpainted houses in the soggy lowlands beneath the levees by the Mississippi River. Kentucky is the home of some of the nation's oldest traditions, from bourbon to bluegrass music to religious revivals (the Disciples of Christ got their start in the enormous revival at Cane Ridge in 1801); it was the home of the inventor of Mother's Day in 1887 and a Louisville restaurant that claims credit for inventing the cheeseburger. Some things have changed. Satellite dishes and four-lane highways have brought modern civilization into hollows and lowland farms that lacked indoor plumbing and electricity within living memory and farmers have begun to diversify their crops; Eastern Kentucky farmers raise goats for meat production and the state touts its grape vineyards and fruit orchards. But people in this state still have a strong attachment to place and family; the continuity is real. Kentucky's population has grown just 42% over the past 50 years, while the nation's almost doubled; few outsiders have moved in, though the number increased since 1990, so today's Kentuckians are mostly descendants of settlers who poured over the mountains in the 40 years after Daniel Boone made his way through the Cumberland Gap in 1775, when Kentucky's population rose from 73,000 in the Census of 1790 to 564,000 in 1820.

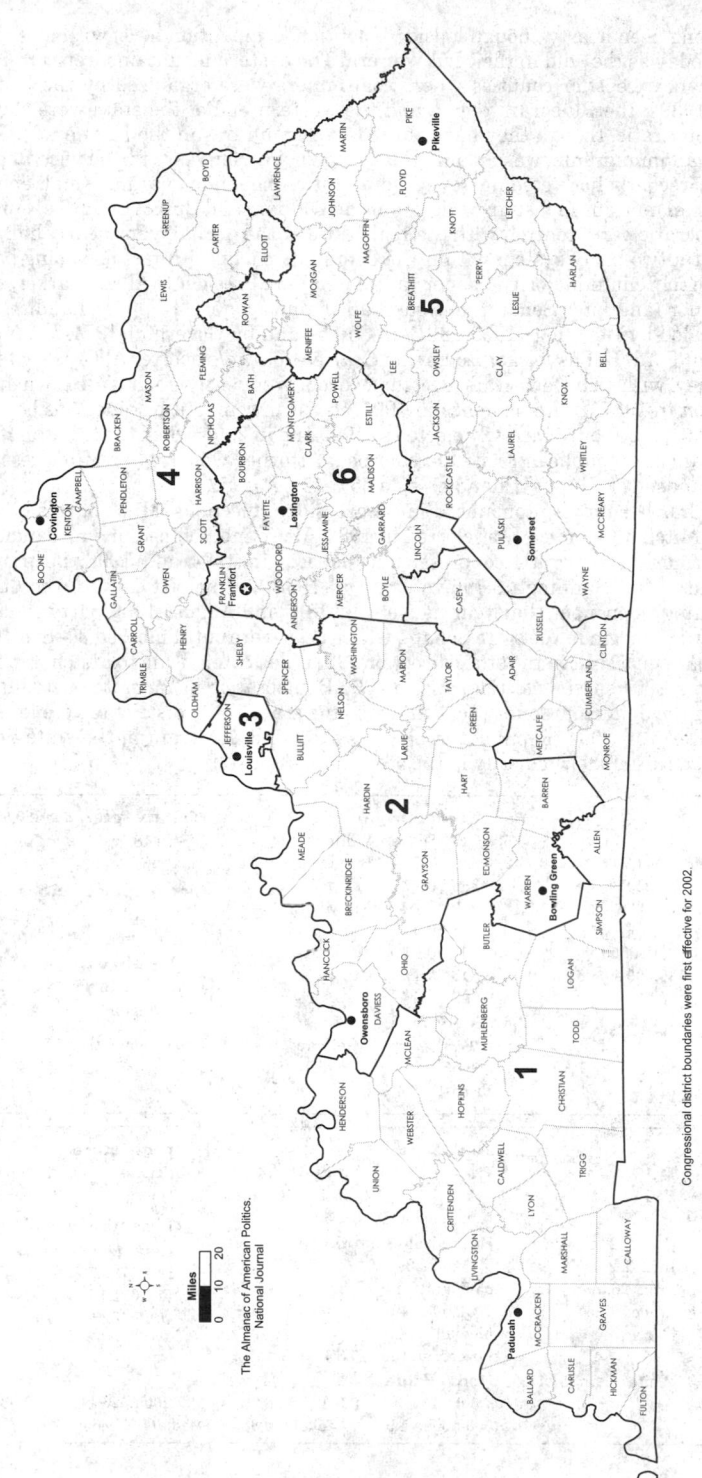

The Almanac of American Politics.
National Journal

Miles
0   10   20

Congressional district boundaries were first effective for 2002.

There has long been hearty, though lopsided, political competition here, with most of the 120 counties voting today as they did in the Civil War era. The eastern mountains were pro-Union and remain Republican, except for counties where coal miners were organized by the United Mine Workers in the 1930s; the Bluegrass region and the western end of the state were slaveholding territory and Democratic, though they have shifted to Republicans in the last decade. Louisville, with many German immigrants, was an anti-slavery town, and for years flirted with Republicans; Jefferson County recently has voted narrowly Democratic, though by margins small enough to be offset by Republican margins in fast-growing suburban Oldham and Bullitt Counties. For years, all this meant Democratic party control, with the real battle in the primary. For nearly half a century there was almost a two-party system within the dominant party, with factions going back to the 1938 primary when Senate Majority Leader (and later Vice President) Alben Barkley was challenged by Governor (and later Senator and baseball commissioner) "Happy" Chandler. Barkley's faction was later led by Governor (1959-63) Bert Combs and by Governor (1971-74) and Senator (1974-99) Wendell Ford. But as former Louisville *Courier-Journal* reporter Al Cross noted, faction gave way to money, with rich Democrats elected governor frequently—John Y. Brown Jr. in 1979, Wallace Wilkinson in 1987, Brereton Jones in 1991. Partisan competition since has been sharper. Democrat Paul Patton was only narrowly elected in 1995 and in 2003; when the term-limited Patton was tarred by scandal, Republican Ernie Fletcher beat Attorney General (now Congressman) Ben Chandler, the grandson of "Happy" Chandler, by a 55%-45% margin.

The change has been most pronounced in congressional elections. Much of this has been the work of Senator Mitch McConnell, first elected in 1984. McConnell helped line up candidates who carried three formerly Democratic congressional districts in 1994 and 1996; he provided key support for Senator Jim Bunning's 6,766-vote win in 1998 and helped capture the 6th District vacated by Bunning's opponent that year as well. In July and August 1999 party switches gave Republicans a 20-18 margin in the state Senate, where they were outnumbered 30–8 in 1990. More recently there has been a shift in the other direction. Chandler, after losing to Fletcher in 2003, won his House seat in a 2004 special election, and in 2006 Democrat John Yarmuth ousted Republican Anne Northup in the Jefferson County seat that was the state's only district to vote for Al Gore in 2000 and John Kerry in 2004. Republicans now have a 21-16–1 margin in the state Senate, but Democrats in 2006 raised their majority in the state House to 61-39.

The People

Pop. 2006 (est):	4,206,074		
Pop. 2000:	4,041,769		
Pop. 1990:	3,685,296		
Change 1990-2000:	Up 9.6%		
% of U.S. total:	1.4%		
Pop. rank:	25th of 50		
Area size:	40,409 sq. mi.		
State Native:	73.7%		
Non-citizen:	1.3%		

Language

English: 94.4%	Spanish: 2.7%
Other Eur.: 2.0%	

Race/Ethnic Origin

3,608,013	89.3%	White
293,639	7.3%	Black
29,368	0.7%	Asian
7,939	0.2%	Native Am.
1,275	0.0%	Hawaiian
37,750	0.9%	Two+ races
3,846	0.1%	Other
59,939	1.5%	Hisp. Origin

Ancestry

USA: 17.3%	German: 10.5%
Irish: 8.6%	English: 8.0%
Scotch-Irish: 1.4%	

Military veterans: 380,618 (12.5%)

WWII: 18.9%	Korea: 13.5%
Vietnam: 32.6%	Gulf War: 10.8%

Most populous cities (2006):

1. Louisville	701,500
2. Lexington	270,789
3. Owensboro	55,525
4. Bowling Green	53,176
5. Covington	42,797

Urban population: 55.7%
Rural population: 44.3%

Education

H.S. Grad:	74.1%
College Grad:	17.1%

Industry

Agri: 3.3%		Con: 7.2%
Fin: 5.4%		Info: 2.2%
Mfg: 23.6%		Prof: 26.6%
Public: 4.3%		Trade: 15.5%
Other: 12.0%		

Occupation

Blue collar: 30.7%	White collar: 54.1%
Gray collar: 15.2%	

Work Sector

Private: 78.5%		Govt: 14.4%
Self: 6.7%		Family: 0.4%
Unemployment: 5.7%		

Household Income

<15k: 22.3%	15-35k: 29.2%
35-50k: 16.4%	50-100k: 24.9%
100-150k: 4.6%	>150k: 2.6%
Median: $33,672	
Poverty status: 15.8%	

Home Value

<50k: 27.3%	50-100k: 38.9%	100-200k: 26.1%	200-300k: 5.1%
300-500k: 1.9%	>500k: 0.8%	Median: $79,600	

Legislature

Senate	21 R 16 D 1 I
House	61 D 39 R

Legislative Term Limits: No

Registered Voters

D: 1,578,273	(57.1%)
R: 1,011,186	(36.6%)
O: 176,829	(6.4%)

Presidential politics   For many years Kentucky was a competitive state when Democrats ran a Southerner or two on their ticket, as in such widely separated years as 1952, 1976, 1980, 1992 and 1996. In 2000 Al Gore initially targeted Kentucky, which is just north of his home state of Tennessee and which the Clinton-Gore ticket carried twice. But Kentucky was part of the rural trend away from Clinton Democrats and toward Republicans in the 1990s, and Gore had taken stands seen as hostile to the state's leading industries—tobacco, coal and automobiles. Early polls showed Bush far ahead, and Gore took his ads off Kentucky stations and took the state off his schedule. Bush swept the state, 57%-41%. In 2004 Kentucky was never on anyone's list of battleground states and Bush won 60%-40%. Bush lost Jefferson County 50%-49% but carried 108 of the 119 other counties; Kerry carried just 11 counties in the eastern mountains. Bush's percentage increased robustly in the southeastern mountains, in the Bluegrass region around Lexington and in the Jackson

2004 Presidential Vote		
Bush (R) 1,069,439	(60%)
Kerry (D) 712,733	(40%)
Nader (I) 8,856	(0%)
Other 4,832	(0%)

2004 Democratic Presidential Primary		
Kerry (D) 138,175	(60%)
Edwards (D) 33,403	(15%)
Uncommitted (D) 21,199	(9%)
Lieberman (D) 11,062	(5%)
Dean (D) 8,222	(4%)
Other 17,855	(8%)

2000 Presidential Vote		
Bush (R) 872,520	(57%)
Gore (D) 638,923	(41%)
Nader (Green) 23,118	(1%)
Other 9,465	(1%)

Purchase in far western Kentucky; he lost ground appreciably only in some northeastern mountain counties. Bush carried voters in all age and income groups; he won 71% among white evangelical or born again Protestants, who made up 45% of the electorate.

Kentucky was part of the Super Tuesday primary in March 1988, but switched back to a May date in 1992, so that state and presidential contests can be held on the same day. It has had no effect on the outcome of the presidential contest.

Congressional districting   Kentucky's 1991 redistricting plan, drawn by Democrats after the state lost one House seat in the 1990 Census, was intended to protect Democratic incumbents, but instead produced a delegation that was 5–1 Republican by 1996. Party control of the legislature in 2001 was split. House Democrats prepared a plan that would have chopped off the east end of the 1st District and added Owensboro to it, making it more difficult for Republican Ed Whitfield. Senate Republicans were prepared to pass the incumbent Republicans' plan that would have added heavily Republican Oldham County to the 3d District to strengthen Anne Northup. The impasse continued through January 2002, delaying the January 29 filing deadline for candidates. On February 1, the legislature finally adopted a compromise plan that changed the lines very little. With one important exception: It removed increasingly Republican suburban Shelby County from the 4th District and added three and one-half traditionally Democratic counties.

110th Congress Lineup	
4 R	2 D

109th Congress Lineup	
5 R	1 D

Governor

Ernie Fletcher (R)

Elected 2003, term expires Dec. 2007, 1st term; b. Nov. 12, 1952, Mt. Sterling; home, Lexington; U. of KY, B.S. 1974, M.D. 1984; Baptist; married (Glenna).

Military Career: Air Force, 1974-80.

Elected Office: KY House of Reps., 1994-96; U.S. House of Reps., 1998-2003.

Professional Career: Practicing physician, 1984-present; CEO, St. Joseph Medical Foundation, 1997-99.

Office: State Capitol, 700 Capitol Ave., Frankfort, 40601, 502-564-2611; Fax: 502-564-2517; Web site: gov.state.ky.us.

Election Results

2003 general	Ernie Fletcher (R)	596,284	(55%)
	Ben Chandler (D)	487,159	(45%)
2003 primary	Ernie Fletcher (R)	90,912	(57%)
	Rebecca Jackson (R)	44,084	(28%)
	Steve Nunn (R)	21,167	(13%)
	Other	2,365	(1%)
1999 general	Paul Patton (D)	352,099	(61%)
	Peppy Martin (R)	128,788	(22%)
	Gatewood Galbraith (Ref)	88,930	(15%)
	Other	6,934	(1%)

There is no question who ordinarily stands at the apex of Kentucky politics: The governor. The governor's appointment powers are wide; until the passage of a constitutional amendment in 2000, the legislature met in regular session for only 60 days in even-numbered years. Beginning in 2001, the legislature began meeting for 30 days in odd-numbered years also but the governor still can shift around line items in the state budget and call special sessions. Kentucky's governor, elected in 2003, is Ernie Fletcher, a Republican who grew up in Mount Sterling, about an hour's drive east of the state capitol. Fletcher got an engineering degree from the University of Kentucky, was an Air Force pilot for five years, intercepting Soviet aircraft; then he went to medical school, practiced medicine, and was CEO of a company that managed medical practices. He did volunteer medical work in India and was a lay minister. In 1994 he was elected to the Kentucky House. In 1996 he won the Republican primary—by exactly 4 votes—and ran against Democratic Congressman Scotty Baesler, a onetime University of Kentucky basketball star. With help from national Republicans, Fletcher raised and spent nearly as much as the incumbent and ran a spirited campaign. He lost 56%-44%, but kept his taste for campaigning.

When Baesler ran for the Senate in 1998, Fletcher decided to run for Congress again and won 53%-46%. In the House, Fletcher established a conservative record and became an activist legislator. Unlike other recent Republican doctors elected to the House who have taken on HMOs, he worked to craft the less sweeping Republican alternative on HMO regulation. He twice won reelection; in 2002, no Democrat filed to run.

Kentucky is one of five states that hold governor's elections in odd years, which enabled Fletcher to run in 2003 without the risk of giving up his House seat, a necessary consideration in a state where Republicans last won the governorship in 1967. He did not have a clear path to the nomination. He faced two serious candidates, former Jefferson County Judge-Executive Rebecca Jackson and state Representative Steve Nunn, the son of Louie Nunn, the state's last Republican governor. Jackson stressed her credentials as an executive and zeroed in on outgoing Governor Paul Patton; she called for his resignation during his scandal-plagued second-term.

The Patton administration scandals gave the Republican field a strong theme to run on but Fletcher and Nunn, both of whom campaigned as agents of change, became enmeshed in legal struggles. Fletcher's original choice for lieutenant governor, Hunter Bates, a former top aide to Senator Mitch McConnell, was disqualified after a lawsuit successfully challenged his eligibility. Steve Nunn's choice for lieutenant governor, Bob Heleringer, then sued to prevent Fletcher from choosing another running mate, a gambit which, if successful, would have made Fletcher himself ineligible for the nomination. The state supreme court ruled in Fletcher's favor and he then named U.S. Attorney Steve Pence as Bates's replacement.

Among Republican primary voters, the legal maneuvering appeared to hurt Nunn far worse than Fletcher. Fletcher won a solid 57% victory, with 28% for Jackson and just 13% for Nunn. State Senator Virgil Moore finished fourth with 1%. Fletcher showed his greatest strength in the counties he represented in Congress and racked up 84% in Lexington's Fayette County, his home. In the general, Fletcher faced Attorney General Ben Chandler, the grandson of former Governor and Senator (and pro baseball commissioner) A.B. "Happy" Chandler. Ben Chandler had narrowly won the nomination over House Speaker Jody Richards 50%-47% after weathering a tough primary season as the main target of health care entrepreneur Bruce Lunsford, who spent more than $8 million, much of it attacking Chandler as a career politician. Lunsford withdrew his candidacy four days before the May 20 primary and backed Richards after the Chandler campaign ran a tough ad stating Lunsford didn't care about the abuse of a patient in one of his nursing homes; he eventually endorsed Fletcher in the general.

Chandler, who was unpopular with some insiders but popular with voters for his prosecution of Patton's chief of staff, labor liaison and two union leaders for violating campaign finance laws, reminded voters that he had taken on Patton and had "convicted corrupt politicians." But Fletcher, as the nominee of the party that hadn't held the governor's office in over three decades, had the more persuasive argument. He promised to "clean up the mess in Frankfort." In the background loomed a $300 million budget deficit facing the next governor. Both Fletcher and Chandler promised to address the shortfall by cutting waste, abuse and fraud in state government. Fletcher also signed a pledge not to raise taxes. Chandler focused on job losses and national Republican economic policies, a questionable tack considering George W. Bush's popularity in Kentucky (he would win 60% in 2004). Chandler also hammered Fletcher for a 2003 congressional vote against reimportation of prescription drugs from Canada; he said Fletcher was too close to drug manufacturers, who were big contributors to Fletcher while he was in Congress.

Fletcher won 55% to 45%, carrying 86 of 120 counties. He carried Northern Kentucky, won Lexington's Fayette County 54%-46% and only narrowly lost Louisville's Jefferson County 51%-49%; Fletcher ran weakest in traditionally Democratic areas, the Pennyrile to the west and in the coal-mining eastern mountain counties. He outspent Chandler $5.7 million to $3.8 million and was assisted by close to $2 million in television ads bought by the Republican Governors Association. His win capped a decade-long Republican surge that, by the end of 2004, left Republicans in control of both Senate seats, 5 of 6 House seats, and a majority in the state Senate. Republicans also in 2003 won two state offices that had been in Democratic control since 1971—secretary of state and commissioner of agriculture —and picked up 7 state House seats to the narrow the Democratic margin to 57-43.

Kentucky governors begin their terms in December and by mid-January 2004 Fletcher could point to several accomplishments. He reduced the number of executive branch cabinets that operate state government, abolished the mismanaged Kentucky Racing Commission and replaced it with a Kentucky Horse Racing Authority, and balanced the 2004 budget with $302 million in spending cuts. But his first year as governor failed to achieve much beyond that. The legislature adjourned in April without having passed a budget, divided over Fletcher's proposal to overhaul the state's tax code. The state teachers association voted to strike in October in response to Fletcher's 2005 state health plan, which they claimed would increase out-of-pocket costs. Fletcher had to call the legislature back into special session in October; the final plan that emerged cost close to $200 million more than Fletcher's original and the strike was averted. In November, death penalty opponents sought an opinion from the Kentucky Board of Medical Licensure as to whether Fletcher, still a licensed doctor, violated medical guidelines by signing a death warrant for a convicted killer. The board unanimously dismissed the complaint, saying that the governor had acted as a governor, not a doctor, when he signed the order. Fletcher also attracted additional unwanted attention in June when the state police plane taking him to the funeral of Ronald Reagan was nearly shot down by two F-16 fighters in Washington airspace after air defense officials were unable to identify the aircraft; the incident caused the evacuation of thousands from the U.S. Capitol and the Supreme Court building.

Fletcher has focused on balanced budgets, tax relief and job creation. He passed tax reform that cut individual and corporate income tax rates, and eliminated the state's corporate license tax rate and the intangible property tax. In 2006 he vetoed $370 million worth of projects approved by the General Assembly and said the money could be used for small business tax relief. Notable in the nation's leading burley tobacco producing state, Fletcher signed an executive order that bans smoking in state buildings, and passed a cigarette tax increase from 3 cents to 30 cents per pack. Fletcher has cracked down on the transport of overloaded coal trucks, which had caused traffic fatalities, and signed emergency regulations that sped up new safety laws designed to protect coal miners. Fletcher has faced criticism that he did not back bigger tobacco tax increases and that his tax proposals have not done more to aid the state's growing service economy.

Fletcher endured a 15-month investigation over a political patronage scandal and he faced the prospect that he would run for reelection in 2007 while under indictment. In May 2005, a former Fletcher supporter and transportation cabinet official gave state Attorney General Greg Stumbo copies of e-mails and documents that included a list of civil service workers to be fired or transferred. It also revealed the existence of 12 officials called the Disciples, who were tasked with replacing Democrats in state government. The hiring practice involved all sectors of state government, but activity centered on transportation officials.   At the instruction of Stumbo, a Democrat, a special Franklin County grand jury began hearing the case in June 2005 and issued its first indictments of three transportation cabinet officials. But Fletcher in August 2005 issued a blanket pardon, which excluded himself, that protected anyone in his administration from being prosecuted in the case. One year after the investigation began, the grand jury on May 11, 2006 indicted Fletcher on misdemeanor charges of criminal conspiracy, official misconduct and political discrimination. By that time, the grand jury had indicted 29 administration officials, including Fletcher. Polls showed the governor's approval rating had plummeted to below 30 percent and a majority of voters supported Fletcher's resignation.

Fletcher aides accused Ben Chandler, Fletcher's 2003 opponent and Stumbo's predecessor as attorney general, of being the "driving force" behind the investigation that led to Fletcher's indictment, and they speculated that Chandler and Stumbo, both Democrats, were both considering a run for governor in 2007. Chandler called accusations about his involvement false. A judge in July 2006 did bar Stumbo from taking part in the case, even though he concluded Stumbo did not appear to be a "direct active participant" in the prosecution. Before the case went to trial, a judge ruled in August 2006 that Fletcher had immunity from prosecution for official acts and cannot be tried until he is impeached or out of office. Impeachment even in the Democrat-controlled House was unlikely and Fletcher's possible reelection could have delayed a trial until 2011. Stumbo and Fletcher settled the case in August 2006: Fletcher was cleared of the charges and admitted no personal wrongdoing, but was forced to accept concessions on hiring for the state Personnel Board. The grand jury's report, released in November 2006, concluded the Fletcher administration attempted to bypass the state's merit system through a "widespread political patronage" scheme. "People were wrongfully fired and demoted. Others were transferred to distant locations to pressure them to retire or resign. People less qualified were hired simply because they supported Governor Fletcher financially or politically," the report concluded.

Fletcher thus avoided running for reelection while under indictment. But the scandal tarnished Fletcher's reputation and left many Republicans wondering whether Fletcher could win reelection. Republican Lieutenant Governor Steve Pence announced he would not run on the ticket again with Fletcher and refused the governor's request to resign. Two Republicans and six Democrats lined up to run against Fletcher in 2007. In the May Republican primary, he faced Paducah businessman Billy Harper, his former finance chairman, and former Congresswoman Anne Northup, who represented Louisville until her 2006 defeat. On the Democratic side, Chandler said he would not seek a rematch with Fletcher. State Treasurer Jonathan Miller entered the race but dropped out two weeks before the primary and threw his support to former Lieutenant Governor Steve Beshear, a former attorney general and legislator who lost statewide races for governor in 1987 and Senate in 1996.   Also running were House Speaker Jody Richards, former Lieutenant Governor Steve Henry and Bruce Lunsford, who ran in 2003.

Despite Northup's contention that Fletcher would be unable to win in November, he won by a decisive 50%-37% margin. Harper finished third with 13%. "Well, I guess we answered the electability question," he said afterwards. The Democratic nominee was Beshear, who won 41% to Lunsford's 21% and narrowly avoided a runoff.   The general election campaign focused on the issue of legalizing limited casino gambling, which Beshear favored to generate tax revenues for education and health care; Fletcher strongly opposed expanded gambling.

Senior Senator

Mitch McConnell (R)

Elected 1984, seat up 2008, 4th term; b. Feb. 20, 1942, Sheffield, AL; home, Louisville; U. of Louisville, B.A. 1964, U. of KY, J.D. 1967; Baptist; married (Elaine Chao).

Elected Office: Jefferson Cnty. Judge Exec., 1977-84.

Professional Career: Chief Legis. Asst., U.S. Sen. Marlow Cook, 1968-70; Dpty. Asst. U.S. Atty. Gen., 1974-75.

DC Office: 361-A RSOB, 20510, 202-224-2541; Fax: 202-224-2499; Web site: mcconnell.senate.gov.

State Offices: Bowling Green, 270-781-1673; Ft. Wright, 859-578-0188; Lexington, 859-224-8286; London, 606-864-2026; Louisville, 502-582-6304; Paducah, 270-442-4554.

Committees: *Minority Leader. Agriculture, Nutrition & Forestry* (4th of 10 R): Domestic & Foreign Marketing, Inspection, & Plant & Animal Health; Nutrition and Food Assistance, Sustainable and Organic Agriculture & General Legislation; Rural Revitalization, Conservation, Forestry & Credit. *Appropriations* (6th of 14 R): State, Foreign Operations & Related Programs; Energy & Water Development; Agriculture, Rural Development, Food and Drug Administration & Related Agencies; Commerce, Justice, Science & Related Agencies; Military Construction, Veterans Affairs & Related Agencies; Defense. *Rules & Administration* (3d of 9 R).

Group Ratings

	ADA	ACLU	AFS	LCV	ITIC	NTU	COC	ACU	CFG	FRC
2006	5	25	0	0	100	81	100	84	87	100
2005	5	—	0	0	—	75	94	100	89	—

National Journal Ratings

	2005 LIB	—	2005 CONS	2006 LIB	—	2006 CONS
Economic	0%	—	94%	4%	—	93%
Social	23%	—	64%	29%	—	69%
Foreign	0%	—	74%	8%	—	85%

Key Votes of the 109th Congress

1. Bar ANWR Drilling	N	5. Confirm Samuel Alito	Y	9. Limit Interstate Abortion	Y
2. FY06 Spending Curb	Y	6. Path to Citizenship	Y	10. CAFTA	Y
3. Estate Tax Repeal	Y	7. Bar Same Sex Marriage	Y	11. Urge Iraq Withdrawal	N
4. Raise Minimum Wage	N	8. Stem Cell Research $	N	12. Provide Detainee Rights	N

Election Results

2002 general	Mitch McConnell (R)	731,679	(65%)	($5,336,099)
	Lois Combs Weinberg (D)	399,634	(35%)	($2,244,035)
2002 primary	Mitch McConnell (R)	unopposed		
1996 general	Mitch McConnell (R)	724,794	(55%)	($5,031,293)
	Steven L. Beshear (D)	560,012	(43%)	($2,073,794)
	Other	22,240	(2%)	

Prior Winning Percentages: 1990 (52%); 1984 (50%)

Mitch McConnell, Kentucky's senior senator, is the Senate Minority Leader; his wife Elaine Chao is Secretary of Labor, the only original member of the Bush cabinet still in office. McConnell grew up in Alabama, where he overcame polio, and at age 13 moved to Louisville. He has been in politics almost his whole career. He was an intern for Senator John Sherman Cooper in 1964 and, after finishing law school, became chief legislative assistant to Senator Marlow Cook. He served in the Ford administration Justice Department, then moved back to Louisville and in 1977, at 35, won by a narrow margin the office that had been Cook's political stepping stone, Jefferson County judge-executive. In 1981 he was re-elected, again narrowly. In 1984 he ran for the Senate, against incumbent Dee Huddleston. McConnell ran ads showing bloodhounds sniffing for Huddleston in vacation locales where he had collected fees for speeches while the Senate was in session. McConnell won by 5,169 votes of 1.2 million cast.

McConnell began his Senate career with a seat on Foreign Relations and switched to Appropriations in 1992, and there served as chairman or ranking member on the Foreign Operations Subcommittee. He has worked since the early 1990s in opposing the dictators in Myanmar (formerly Burma) who have imprisoned Nobel Prize and election winner Aung San Suu Ki, and with Dianne Feinstein has sponsored bills imposing trade sanctions on Myanmar and trying to isolate its regime. He has long been a strong supporter of Israel and passed a Palestinian Anti-Terrorism bill in the Senate, and has been an advocate for human rights in Cambodia, Egypt and other nations. He has often opposed trial lawyers, backing product liability and medical malpractice laws that would reduce their leverage and sponsoring the auto choice plan that would let car owners pay less for insurance by disclaiming pain and suffering damages. He ran for chairman of the NRSC and lost to Phil Gramm in 1990 and in 1992 by one vote; he won the post in November 1996. But he was unable to get Republican senators to contribute as much to campaigns as Democratic senators did in 1998 and the party gained no seats. In the 2000 cycle, he had tougher sledding; Republicans lost most of the close races, and the result was a 50-50 split that put Democrats in position to gain a majority when Jim Jeffords left the Republican party in May 2001.

McConnell might argue that what ties his record together is a concern for free speech and free political competition, perhaps because he came out of a state politically dominated by one party. He became interested in campaign finance regulation while teaching a night course at the University of Louisville, and in 1990 he drafted a bill that would have banned PACs, cut in half out-of-state donations and banned soft money. But in a few years he came to believe that these provisions and those in the various bills sponsored by John McCain and Russ Feingold are unconstitutional infringements of free speech; his critics have said that he changed about the time when Republicans gained majorities. Yet before that, earlier in 1994, he spoke all night to filibuster a campaign finance bill. In October 1999, with more than 40 senators on his side, he killed a version of the McCain-Feingold campaign finance bill. In March 2001, McCain insisted on bringing campaign finance forward again, and despite McConnell's efforts, managed to pass his measure. But it did not include many provisions in previous McCain-Feingold bills, including public subsidies for candidates and voluntary spending limits. McCain's bill was also amended by a doubling of the limit on individual contributions—something McConnell supported. McConnell insisted he was working to protect First Amendment freedoms; when challenged about his vote for amending the Constitution to allow the banning of flag burning, he switched his position and became one of the few Republicans to consistently vote against those measures.

In 2001 the House Republican leadership blocked consideration of the similar Shays-Meehan bill. But after the implosion of Enron, Shays and Meehan got enough signatures on a discharge petition to bring their bill to the floor, and it passed in February 2002. For more than a month, McConnell put forward 13 "technical corrections," and Majority Leader Tom Daschle refused to bring the issue to the floor until he and McCain settled their differences. The bill passed on March 27, and immediately McConnell filed a lawsuit charging it was unconstitutional. In May 2003 a deeply divided three-judge federal court issued 1,700 pages of opinions and upheld some provisions of the law but not others. In December 2003 the Supreme Court upheld almost all the provisions of the bill. "There won't be any less speech or money spent. Dramatically more will be spent, just in a different way," McConnell predicted, and warned that 527 organizations would raise and spend huge amounts of money, as indeed they did in the 2004 cycle. "You must have money in politics, because it's the only way the candidates can get their message across." More quietly, as ranking member of the Rules Committee, McConnell helped put together the bipartisan Help America Vote Act.

McConnell has frequently used his seat on Appropriations to insert riders that help Kentucky and channel aid to the state. He has also worked hard on tobacco issues. In 2003 he was working for a buyout of tobacco quotas from farmers, and said he would support FDA regulation of tobacco in order to get it. In July 2004 the Senate voted 78-15 to add the buyout and FDA regulation to the must-pass corporate tax bill. But the House refused to support FDA regulation, and in October 2004 the Senate backed the tobacco buyout without it and passed the corporate tax bill by 69-17. When residents of Richmond County protested the Pentagon's plan to burn chemical weapons at the Blue Grass Army Depot, he used the appropriations process to force the Army to use other means; in October 2006 ground was broken on a new neutralization plant there, where the caustic agents would be broken down by hydrolysis, breaking them down into basic elements which could be safely stored.

McConnell has done much to build up Kentucky's long ailing Republican Party. In 1994 he helped Ed Whitfield pick up the 1st District and Republican legislative candidates win in western Kentucky. He backed Anne Northup in her win in Louisville's 3d District in 1996. In 1998 McConnell strongly backed Jim Bunning's candidacy for the Senate and in 2004 helped rescue his reelection campaign. In 2000 McConnell helped the Bush campaign target and carry Kentucky; he backed the ballot proposition to merge the Jefferson County and Louisville city governments. He helped to persuade two Democratic state senators to switch parties in July and August 1999, which gave Republicans a 20-18 margin in the state Senate, and he has helped them hold that majority ever since. In 2003 he backed the gubernatorial candidacy of Congressman Ernie Fletcher, who beat Democrat Ben Chandler 55%-45%. But Chandler came back to win Fletcher's House seat in the general election, and in 2006 Northup, from the only Kentucky district carried by Al Gore and John Kerry, was defeated for reelection. In early 2007 he seemed uninterested in helping Fletcher, who had faced legal charges of making unlawful appointments, as he faced opposition not only from Democrats but from Northup and his former campaign treasurer in the Republican primary. But after Fletcher won the nomination, McConnell weighed in with his support.

McConnell has now won reelection three times. In 2002 McConnell's opponent was Lois Combs Weinberg, daughter of former (1959-63) Governor Bert Combs. She had the support of the state's Democratic establishment, but memories of her father, one of the state's most notable governors, had evidently dimmed. In the primary she squeaked past former 1st District Congressman Tom Barlow, who spent only $6,000; after that, national Democrats put little money into the race. McConnell refused to debate and ran ads showing how he had done things for Kentuckians—helping the widow of a police officer killed in the line of duty, getting compensation for the families of workers sickened by radiation poisoning at the Paducah uranium plant. McConnell spent $5.3 million to Weinberg's $2.2 million and won 65%-35%, carrying 112 of 120 counties, losing only in a few Democratic strongholds in the eastern mountains. It was the highest percentage won by any Kentucky senator.

Back in Washington, he won another election in November 2002, to become majority whip. He had been campaigning for months among colleagues and his only opponent, Larry Craig, dropped out several days before the contest. In December, when Trent Lott was criticized for his comments at Strom Thurmond's 100th birthday party, McConnell was at first his strongest public defender, suggesting on December 15 that Lott might resign from the Senate if ousted (which would have meant a Democrat would get his seat and the Republicans would no longer have a majority) and threatening that if Democrats moved to censure Lott, he would amend the motion to add censure of some Democrats' comments. But on December 20 he privately recommended to Lott that he "step down as soon as possible"; McConnell did not challenge Bill Frist for the majority leadership, and urged Rick Santorum not to either. McConnell advised Frist, who was relatively unversed in Senate procedures; in June 2003 he and House Whip Roy Blunt started attending each others' whip meetings.

After Republicans gained four Senate seats in the 2004 election, McConnell declined to join in the laments about partisan divisiveness in Washington. "I'm amazed at all the hand-wringing over the level of discourse and partisanship. It leads me to believe that nobody has read any history. The level of divisiveness now is really quite mild when it's compared with numerous periods in our history." He showed considerable mastery of Senate rules and, anticipating Frist's long announced plans to retire in 2006, ran for what he hoped would be majority leader. It was a behind the scenes campaign, as described by his ally Bob Bennett. "Brick by brick, he built a firewall. So whenever somebody decided they wanted to run, all we had to do was sit down and say to them, 'This is what you're going to have to deal with.' One by one potential opponents said, 'Wait a minute, I don't want to run and lose.'" The election results meant that he was running for minority leader instead, but he won without opposition, while Trent Lott narrowly beat Lamar Alexander for minority whip.

He continued to raise large sums—$1 million in the 2006 cycle—for the Senate Republican campaign committee. In mid-October 2006 the *Lexington Herald Leader* ran a four-part series on McConnell's fundraising over the years, which it said amounted to $220 million, and on legislative work he had done for bills supported by contributors. Before it ran, McConnell protested that the series was financed by a $37,500 grant from an investigative reporting center, which got the money from a foundation, both of which he characterized as left-leaning. The paper's owner, the McClatchy chain, said that the paper should have paid for the story out of its own funds and returned the money; two weeks later the *Herald Leader* ran a column by McConnell chiding the paper for its conduct.

As minority whip and minority leader, McConnell has supported the Bush administration on most issues. To charges that there is some conflict in his marriage to a cabinet member, he said, "I'm a Republican, and I generally support what the Bush administration is trying to do. She takes her orders from the White House." "There will be nothing here they can do without some degree of cooperation from a very robust 49-vote minority," he said soon after the election. "The question is,

Are you going to work together and try to do good things for the country or not? I would like to see us quit playing games with Social Security. They know and we know it is a huge problem. This is the kind of thing divided government might be able to conquer." He has supported the administration staunchly on Iraq, although when he returned from a trip to Baghdad in August 2006 he admitted the city was "not secure" and said, "Clearly in some ways it hasn't gone as well as we would like." But when Majority Leader Harry Reid in February 2007 advanced a resolution disapproving George W. Bush's troop surge, McConnell led 33 Republicans (plus Joseph Lieberman) to prevent it from coming to the floor unless another resolution, forswearing any cuts in spending on the troops, could be voted on also.

McConnell's Senate seat seems secure, but his support for the Bush administration on Iraq and on immigration in 2007 makes it possible he might face competitive opposition in 2008. Larry Forgy, the unsuccessful Republican nominee for governor in 1995, has been mentioned as a possible primary challenger. Potential Democratic candidates include businessman Charlie Owen, Attorney General Greg Stumbo and Andrew Horne, an Iraq War veteran.

Junior Senator

Jim Bunning (R)

Elected 1998, seat up 2010, 2d term; b. Oct. 23, 1931, Campbell Cnty.; home, Southgate; Xavier U., B.S. 1953; Catholic; married (Mary).

Elected Office: Ft. Thomas City Cncl., 1977-79; KY Senate, 1979-83; U.S. House of Reps., 1986-98.

Professional Career: Pro baseball player, 1950-71; Investment broker & agent, 1960-86.

DC Office: 316 HSOB, 20510, 202-224-4343; Fax: 202-228-1373; Web site: bunning.senate.gov.

State Offices: Ft. Wright, 859-341-2602; Hazard, 606-435-2390; Hopkinsville, 270-885-1212; Lexington, 859-219-2239; Louisville, 502-582-5341; Owensboro, 270-689-9085.

Committees: *Banking, Housing & Urban Affairs* (6th of 10 R): Economic Policy (RMM); Financial Institutions; Securities, Insurance & Investment. *Budget* (7th of 11 R). *Energy & Natural Resources* (8th of 11 R): Water & Power; Energy; Public Lands & Forests. *Finance* (7th of 10 R): Energy, Natural Resources & Infrastructure (RMM); International Trade & Global Competitiveness; Health Care.

Group Ratings

	ADA	ACLU	AFS	LCV	ITIC	NTU	COC	ACU	CFG	FRC
2006	0	17	0	0	75	88	91	96	94	87
2005	5	—	0	0	—	75	94	92	82	—

National Journal Ratings

	2005 LIB	—	2005 CONS		2006 LIB	—	2006 CONS
Economic	6%	—	90%		11%	—	88%
Social	0%	—	77%		0%	—	82%
Foreign	0%	—	74%		0%	—	92%

Key Votes of the 109th Congress

1. Bar ANWR Drilling	N	5. Confirm Samuel Alito	Y	9. Limit Interstate Abortion	Y
2. FY06 Spending Curb	Y	6. Path to Citizenship	N	10. CAFTA	Y
3. Estate Tax Repeal	Y	7. Bar Same Sex Marriage	Y	11. Urge Iraq Withdrawal	N
4. Raise Minimum Wage	N	8. Stem Cell Research $	N	12. Provide Detainee Rights	N

Election Results

2004 general	Jim Bunning (R)	873,507	(51%)	($6,075,399)
	Daniel Mongiardo (D)	850,855	(49%)	($3,104,981)
2004 primary	Jim Bunning (R)	96,545	(84%)	
	Barry Metcalf (R)	18,395	(16%)	
1998 general	Jim Bunning (R)	569,817	(50%)	($3,746,540)
	Scotty Baesler (D)	563,051	(49%)	($3,841,950)
	Other	12,546	(1%)	

Prior Winning Percentages: 1996 House (68%); 1994 House (74%); 1992 House (62%); 1990 House (69%); 1988 House (74%); 1986 House (55%)

Jim Bunning, a Republican elected to the Senate in 1998, is the first player elected to the Baseball Hall of Fame to serve in Congress. Bunning grew up in Northern Kentucky, just across the Ohio River from Cincinnati. He started in minor league baseball in 1950, but at his father's insistence finished high school and college. He made the majors in 1956 and the next year became the only pitcher to strike out Ted Williams three times in one game. Bunning threw a no-hitter for the Detroit Tigers in 1958 and pitched a perfect game for the Philadelphia Phillies on Father's Day 1964; he also played for the Pittsburgh Pirates and the Los Angeles Dodgers. He retired in 1971 with a 224-184 record, a 3.24 ERA and 2,855 strikeouts; he was the second pitcher (Cy Young was the first) to achieve 1,000 strikeouts and 100 wins in both the American and the National Leagues. He was inducted into the Baseball Hall of Fame in August 1996, and private autograph signings account for more than half of the money his Jim Bunning Foundation raises each year, according to *The Wall Street Journal*. He is a family man, with nine children (two sets of twins) and at last count 35 grandchildren and 2 great-grandchildren; his son David Bunning, after 10 years as a federal prosecutor, was unanimously confirmed as a federal judge in February 2002. Jim Bunning and fellow pitcher Robin Roberts set up the Major League Baseball Players Association and hired Marvin Miller in 1966, when the minimum player salary was $6,000; in 2002, however, he was criticizing the players for not accepting a salary cap, the big metro area teams for not accepting revenue sharing and the owners for not opening their books.

The skill, energy and aggressiveness he showed in baseball—Bunning registered one of the highest totals in baseball history for hitting batters—he brought to politics in his native northern Kentucky. He was elected to the Fort Thomas City Council in 1977, to the state Senate in 1979, and won a respectable 44% against Martha Layne Collins in the 1983 race for governor (the best showing for a Republican gubernatorial candidate between 1971 and 1995). When incumbent 4th District Congressman Gene Snyder retired in 1986, Bunning won the seat with 55% of the vote. He served six years on the ethics committee, starting off in March 1992 by leading the charge against the House bank overdraft scandal. In September 1993, he called Bill Clinton "the most corrupt, the most amoral, the most despicable person I've ever seen in the presidency."

In February 1997, Senator Wendell Ford announced he would retire in 1998, and Bunning, with typical aggressiveness, made plans to run for his seat. The Democratic nominee was Lexington Congressman Scotty Baesler, who was still known as a star on one of Adolph Rupp's University of Kentucky basketball teams in the early 1960s.

Baesler emerged from the primary ahead of Bunning in the polls but out of money; Bunning, with extensive help from Senator Mitch McConnell, had plenty of money. Bunning ran an ad showing actors thanking Baesler, in Spanish and (with subtitles) Chinese, for voting for NAFTA and for normal trade relations with China. This was perhaps the country's closest race for months. And, despite Kentucky's early poll closing times and rapid count, it was not until late in the evening that Bunning was declared the winner. His margin was 49.7%-49.2%, or 6,766 votes.

Citing interviews with his Senate colleagues, *Time* magazine in 2006 named Bunning the "Underperformer" for not demonstrating the same effort he put forth as a pitcher. "Bunning shows little interest in policy unless it involves baseball," the magazine reported. Bunning has made steroid use in baseball a leading issue, and has threatened legislation against professional baseball's anti-trust exemption if the Major League Baseball did not impose tougher penalties requiring abusers to sit out more games. Bunning testified as the lead witness in a high-profile House hearing on steroid use in March 2005. He said athletes accused of steroid use should be stripped of their records and barred from entry into the Baseball Hall of Fame.

Bunning has made headlines from his seat on the Banking Committee, which he has used to wage a campaign against the Federal Reserve. Bunning cast the Senate's lone dissenting vote against President Bush's nomination of Ben Bernanke as Federal Reserve chairman in 2006. He criticized Bernanke for not being more independent from outgoing chairman Alan Greenspan and for stating he would continue the Fed's policy of raising interest rates to keep inflation in check. He was also one of two Republican senators (the other was Senator Rick Santorum, who had just lost reelection) to oppose Robert Gates as successor to Defense Secretary Donald Rumsfeld because he said Gates lacked solutions for Iraq and Afghanistan. On other issues, Bunning unsuccessfully opposed efforts to increase Federal Deposit Insurance Corporation coverage limits from $100,000 to $250,000 because of the money taxpayers paid during the 1980s savings-and-loan crisis. Bunning succeeded in attaching to the Senate's 2006 budget resolution an amendment aimed at repealing

1993 taxes imposed on upper income Social Security recipients. He has sought to restrict certain "intergovernmental" transfers of Medicaid funding that allow states to increase their federal contributions. When Republicans elected McConnell their leader in 2006, Bunning inherited the Senate desk used by legendary Henry Clay. McConnell had moved to the desk traditionally used by the GOP leader, and he offered a Senate resolution that enabled someone other than Kentucky's senior senator to use Clay's desk.

Bunning has compiled one of the most conservative voting records in the Senate and he has worked on many Kentucky issues, including legislation promoting clean coal and other coal technologies. He has also criticized the Energy Department's cleanup of the USEC uranium enrichment plant in Paducah, ongoing since 1988, on which $823 million had been spent by 2003. He has been especially angry at DOE's failure to compensate workers stricken with radiation-related disease. He held several hearings on the issue and blocked the nomination of the agency's CFO to get attention. In December 2003 he supported the workers' union's efforts to get laid-off workers hired by the new contractor with continued pension and service credit. In June 2004 he got a unanimous vote to put in the defense authorization an amendment moving the compensation process to the Labor Department and to have the government rather than private contractors compensate workers. It was part of the final bill passed in October 2004. The first Kentucky claimant got $125,000 in December 2004; Bunning pointed out that there were 24,000 claims pending and only 30 had been acted on.

Bunning came up for reelection in 2004. For some time it seemed he would face Governor Paul Patton, ineligible to seek a third term in 2003. But in September 2002 Patton admitted that he had had an affair with a nursing home operator who sued him that month for sexual harassment. Patton, after denying the affair, admitted it after phone records showed 440 calls from his office to her home or business; a few days later he announced, unsurprisingly, that he would not run for the Senate. Other well known Democrats dropped out for one or another reason. That left Bunning the heavy favorite. But he ended up facing a serious challenge from state Senator Daniel Mongiardo. Mongiardo, a physician from the eastern mountains, had beaten a longtime incumbent for one state Senate seat, then won another that Republicans had redistricted three hours away from his home; he started off by putting $168,000 of his own money into his campaign. Bunning raised and spent $6.5 million in all, but the Democratic Senatorial Campaign Committee started spending money on Mongiardo in July. Mongiardo got ammunition from what some considered Bunning's strange behavior. He refused to give the press advance notice of his appearances—Kentucky Republicans believe the state's dominant paper, the Louisville *Courier-Journal*, is biased against them—and traveled with a security guard, because of "classified briefings that I have received in the U.S. Senate," Bunning said. At one campaign stop, Bunning said that Mongiardo looked like one of Saddam Hussein's sons. Bunning ran ads attacking Mongiardo on national security, taxes and as a "Medicaid millionaire." Mongiardo promised to reduce the cost of health care and called for reimportation of prescription drugs from Canada; his ads pointed out that Bunning accepted $75,000 from pharmaceutical PACs. Mongiardo said he was against abortion and same-sex marriage and in favor of gun rights.

The contest came to a head in the single debate October 11. Bunning participated on video from Washington, where he said he needed to be to vote in the Senate. Democrats complained loudly about this because Bunning read his opening and closing statements from a teleprompter, though that did not violate the agreed on rules. Bunning accused Mongiardo and his staff of passing on "horrible rumors" about his health (he was 73) and asked for an apology. "I hope that you are healthy," Mongiardo said, and accused Bunning of behavior "unbecoming of a U.S. senator. You have conduct that has been unbecoming of a Kentucky gentleman." Bunning apologized for "an inappropriate comment," presumably the Saddam Hussein comment. Both continued in that vein in post-debate comments. "When we went to Fancy Farm," Bunning said, referring to the traditional July political gathering in Graves County, "my wife was black and blue from their staff or someone connected with the Mongiardo campaign—absolutely running into her." He said that members of the media were hostile because they "don't believe the same way I believe." Mongiardo said, "Senator Bunning has the history and record of throwing high, hard fastballs and we were ready for a beanball. Senator Bunning's arrogance and his mean-spiritedness prevents him from seeing the impact of his policies on the people of Kentucky." The commentary continued from others. The *Courier-Journal* editorialized, "Is he, as he ages, just becoming a more concentrated version of himself: more arrogant, more prickly? Certainly that would be a normal occurrence. Or is his increased belligerence an indication of something worse? Has Senator Bunning drifted into territory that indicates a serious health concern?" Republicans were also throwing punches at

Mongiardo. State Senate President David Williams said he had a "limp wrist," and another state senator said Mongiardo "is not a gentleman. I'm not even sure the word 'man' applies to him." A constitutional amendment to ban same-sex marriage was on the ballot, and passed in November 75%-25%.

The DSCC shrewdly poured money into this race, $466,000 in five days in October alone, and the polls tightened; a Democratic poll showed Bunning leading by only 47%-39% and a Bunning poll showed him ahead by the not entirely reassuring margin of 50%-39%. Bunning provided his critics with more material on October 21 when asked about a unit of Army Reserve soldiers in Iraq who refused an order to deliver fuel because they said their trucks were lightly armored. Bunning said he was unaware of the incident. "Let me explain something. I don't watch the national news, and I don't read the paper. I haven't done that for the last six weeks. I watch Fox News to get my information."

On November 2 Bunning just barely squeaked to victory, 51%-49%, as George W. Bush was carrying the state 60%-40%. Mongiardo ran far ahead of John Kerry in his home area in the eastern mountains—30% ahead in his home of Perry County—and 12% to 22% ahead in the ring of counties around Lexington. But Bunning was rescued, as he had been in 1998, by his strong showing in his home area, the three counties of Northern Kentucky, where he won 66.5% of the vote (to Bush's 66.6%), and which he carried by 48,000 votes, more than double his statewide margin of 22,000. Bunning, asked whether he had made mistakes, said, "Sure we made mistakes. Everybody makes mistakes. The only time I've ever been perfect was for about two hours and 10 minutes on June 21, 1964."

In January 2007, Bunning said he plans to run for reelection in 2010, when he will be 79 years old. Democratic Congressman Ben Chandler is frequently mentioned as a potential opponent.

FIRST DISTRICT

Rep. Ed Whitfield (R)

Elected 1994, 7th term; b. May 25, 1943, Hopkinsville; home, Hopkinsville; U. of KY, B.S. 1965, J.D. 1969; Methodist; married (Connie).

Military Career: Army Reserves, 1967-73.

Elected Office: KY House of Reps., 1973-75.

Professional Career: Practicing atty., 1969-79; Owner, Rhodes Oil Co., 1975-79; Cnsl., Seaboard System Railroad, 1979-83; V.P., CSX, 1983-91; Cnsl., Interstate Commerce Comm., 1991-93.

DC Office: 2411 RHOB, 20515, 202-225-3115; Fax: 202-225-3547; Web site: www.house.gov/whitfield.

District Offices: Henderson, 270-826-4180; Hopkinsville, 270-885-8079; Paducah, 270-442-6901; Tompkinsville, 270-487-9509.

Committees: *Energy & Commerce* (7th of 26 R): Oversight & Investigations (RMM); Commerce, Trade & Consumer Protection; Energy & Air Quality.

Group Ratings

	ADA	ACLU	AFS	LCV	ITIC	NTU	COC	ACU	CFG	FRC
2006	0	14	0	25	86	50	93	76	41	100
2005	10	—	13	6	—	56	85	88	58	92

National Journal Ratings

	2005 LIB	—	2005 CONS	2006 LIB	—	2006 CONS
Economic	29%	—	70%	42%	—	57%
Social	19%	—	80%	6%	—	92%
Foreign	31%	—	67%	6%	—	86%

Key Votes of the 109th Congress

1. Estate Tax Repeal	Y	5. Limit Interstate Abortion	Y	9. Build Border Fence	Y
2. Limit CAFE Standards	Y	6. Extend Patriot Act	Y	10. CAFTA	Y
3. FY06 Spending Curb	Y	7. Bar Same Sex Marriage	Y	11. Oppose Iraq Withdrawal	Y
4. Drilling in ANWR	Y	8. Stem Cell Research $	N	12. Detainee Tribunals	Y

Election Results

2006 general	Ed Whitfield (R) 123,618	(60%)	($1,063,078)
	Tom Barlow (D) 83,865	(40%)	($120,956)
2006 primary	Ed Whitfield (R) .... unopposed		
2004 general	Ed Whitfield (R) 175,972	(67%)	($557,233)
	Billy Cartwright (D) 85,229	(33%)	

Prior Winning Percentages: 2002 (65%); 2000 (58%); 1998 (55%); 1996 (54%); 1994 (51%)

The People		Race/Ethnic Origin	Ancestry	
Area size:	12,058 sq. mi.	89.7% White	USA: 19.5%	English: 7.8%
Urban population:	36.5%	7.2% Black	Irish: 7.7%	
Rural population:	63.5%	0.3% Asian	**2004 Presidential Vote**	
Pop. 2000:	673,629	0.2% Native Am.	Bush (R) 180,446	(63%)
Pop. 2005 (est):	673,889	0.0% Hawaiian	Kerry (D) 102,346	(36%)
Median income:	$30,360	0.9% Two+ races	Other 1,866	(1%)
Poverty status:	16.5%	0.1% Other	**2000 Presidential Vote**	
Military veterans:	12.9%	1.5% Hispanic Origin	Bush (R) 147,486	(58%)
			Gore (D) 101,551	(40%)
			Other 3,961	(2%)
			Cook Partisan Voting Index: R +10	

Occupation   Blue collar: 37.3%   White collar: 46.6%   Gray collar: 16.0%

The point where the Ohio River flows into the Mississippi—the intersection Huckleberry Finn and Jim missed in the fog—must have struck early settlers as a site for a great city. But no Pittsburgh or St. Louis grew up on this fertile black soil. Instead, the Kentucky land west of the dammed-up Tennessee and Cumberland rivers, bought from the Chickasaw Indians by General Andrew Jackson and Governor Isaac Shelby in 1818—the Jackson Purchase, it is still called—was settled by farmers. Most people here today are the descendants of these farmers, with memories of earlier generations living in family lore. Just to the east of the Tennessee and the Cumberland rivers is the Pennyrile (after pennyroyal, a common variety of local wild mint), a land of low hills and small farms, where you find the west Kentucky coal fields. Here is Lyon County, founded by Matthew "Spitting" Lyon, who earned his epithet while a congressman from Vermont, and who later represented western Kentucky from 1803 to 1811. These areas are separated by the Land Between the Lakes, the boating and recreational haven created by the damming of the Tennessee and Cumberland Rivers just before the debouche into the Ohio; this is the fastest-growing area in these parts, as the Jackson Purchase and the Pennyrile struggle economically. The biggest problem is the USEC uranium enrichment plant, under federal cleanup since 1988 and slated to be closed; in the meantime the government has been slow to compensate workers stricken with radiation-related sickness. Nuclear power now has the potential to improve the district, as a bipartisan delegation drawn from Kentucky, Illinois and Missouri is helping Western Kentucky to vie for a new Department of Energy nuclear fuel recycling plant.

The 1st Congressional District of Kentucky is made up of the Jackson Purchase and much of the Pennyrile, plus a line of counties stretching some 200 miles east of the Mississippi in the mountains along the Tennessee border and then north toward the center of the state. There is a distinctive Southern atmosphere here—in the crops that are grown, in historically low wage levels, and in the fact that the big city that people look to is more often Nashville than Louisville. Paducah has its own big plans. Its artist relocation program has boosted development and made the small Ohio River town a U.S art destination. Turkey hunting has become a big business here. The Jackson Purchase and the Pennyrile are ancestrally Democratic; Paducah produced one of the most enduring Democratic politicians of this century, Alben Barkley, whose career from 1912 to 1956 included 14 years in the House, 24 in the Senate and four as vice president; he was Senate majority and minority leader, keynoted four Democratic National Conventions, and died while delivering the peroration at Washington and Lee University's mock political convention in 1956. But the hills far from the Mississippi are Republican country and this, combined with the Republican trend that reached north from Dixie to Paducah, has made the 1st District seriously contested territory in state elections—and one of the longtime Democratic rural areas that went solidly for George W. Bush in 2000 (58%) and 2004 (63%). In the close Senate election of 2004, Republican Jim Bunning won 48% in the Jackson Purchase and most state legislators elected in the region were Republicans.

The congressman from the 1st District is Ed Whitfield, a Republican first elected in 1994. Whitfield grew up in Hopkinsville and Madisonville, in a family with Pennyrile roots going back before 1800. He served in the Army Reserves, practiced law in Hopkinsville, and was elected to the legislature in 1973 as a Democrat where he was something of an insider; former Governor (1963-67) Edward Breathitt was best man at his wedding. After one term in Frankfort, Whitfield ran an oil distributorship in the west Kentucky coalfields, then in 1979 moved to Washington to become an executive for the Seaboard and CSX railroads. He was legal counsel to the chairman of the Interstate Commerce Commission from 1991-93, when he returned to west Kentucky and ran for Congress as a Republican. He was returning to a district that since Barkley's time had been represented by quiet, long-serving, conservative Democrats. But the one-term incumbent, Tom Barlow, was a free-spirited supporter of the Clinton administration. Encouraged to run by Senator Mitch McConnell, Whitfield turned aside criticism that he was carpetbagging and concentrated on attacking Barlow's vote for the Clinton budget and tax increase. With help from the mountain counties added by redistricting, and running strongly in the Pennyrile, Whitfield won a 51%-49% win in the big Republican sweep of 1994.

In the House, Whitfield has a moderate-to-conservative voting record and a seat on the Energy and Commerce Committee. One major concern has been aid to workers exposed to radiation at the USEC plant in Paducah. He also overcame objections from the Bush administration to cleaning up the site, which is projected to cost more than $3 billion and last more than another decade. He voted for normal trade relations with China after the Chinese agreed to lower tariffs on imported tobacco, and he voted for trade promotion authority. He supported the tobacco buyout bill, which hand-somely benefited local farmers. President Bush in 2005 signed into law a bill Whitfield sponsored to discourage "doctor shopping" by addicts of prescription drugs, through the use of an electronic data base in which each state would participate to monitor people who cross state lines to buy pharma-ceuticals. A thoroughbred owner, Whitfield co-sponsored legislation to ban the killing of horses for meat; the House overwhelmingly passed a horse slaughter ban in September 2006, but the ban did not make it out of the Senate.

In January 2005, he became chairman of the Oversight and Investigations Subcommittee at Energy and Commerce. Whitfield held hearings on Hewlett-Packard's "pretexting" to spy on poten-tial dissenters, on private data brokers who collect telephone records without customer permission, on the sexual exploitation of children on the Internet, on medical insurance for horse jockeys, and on the transfer of human tissue research samples. In the 110th Congress, Whitfield lost his subcom-mittee gavel and became ranking Republican as Democrats turned toward investigating the Bush administration.

Whitfield has entrenched himself to the point that he is no longer much of a Democratic target. In 1996, when lawyer Dennis Null opposed him, Whitfield carried 18 of the district's 31 counties, including Paducah, which he lost in 1994, and won 54%-46%. In 1998, Tom Barlow ran again, this time with a lightly funded "grass roots" campaign. Whitfield won 55%-45%. In 2000, Whitfield increased his margin to 58%-42%, carrying for the first time several counties in the far western corner. Since then, Whitfield has won easily. He defeated Barlow a third time in 2006, increasing his winning margin to 60%-40%. This longtime Democratic stronghold now seems to be a safe Republi-can seat.

SECOND DISTRICT

Rep. Ron Lewis (R)

Elected May 1994, 7th full term; b. Sept. 14, 1946, South Shore, KY; home, Cecilia; U. of KY, B.A. 1969, Morehead St. U., M.A. 1981; Southern Baptist; married (Kayi).

Military Career: Navy OCS, 1972.

Professional Career: Heavy Equip. Sales Rep., 1975-80; Baptist Minis-ter, 1980-present; Prof., Watterson Col., 1980-85; Owner, Alpha Christian Bookstore, 1985-94.

DC Office: 2418 RHOB, 20515, 202-225-3501; Fax: 202-226-2019; Web site: www.house.gov/ronlewis.

District Offices: Bowling Green, 270-842-9896; Elizabethtown, 270-765-4360; Owensboro, 270-688-8858.

Committees: *Ways & Means* (9th of 17 R): Social Security; Trade.

Group Ratings

	ADA	ACLU	AFS	LCV	ITIC	NTU	COC	ACU	CFG	FRC
2006	5	9	14	17	100	62	100	84	67	100
2005	10	—	13	0	—	60	85	88	70	100

National Journal Ratings

	2005 LIB	—	2005 CONS	2006 LIB	—	2006 CONS
Economic	14%	—	83%	21%	—	77%
Social	0%	—	89%	11%	—	85%
Foreign	0%	—	89%	0%	—	94%

Key Votes of the 109th Congress

1. Estate Tax Repeal	Y	5. Limit Interstate Abortion	Y	9. Build Border Fence	Y
2. Limit CAFE Standards	Y	6. Extend Patriot Act	Y	10. CAFTA	Y
3. FY06 Spending Curb	Y	7. Bar Same Sex Marriage	Y	11. Oppose Iraq Withdrawal	Y
4. Drilling in ANWR	Y	8. Stem Cell Research $	N	12. Detainee Tribunals	Y

Election Results

2006 general	Ron Lewis (R)	118,548	(55%)	($1,975,693)
	Mike Weaver (D)	95,415	(45%)	($883,819)
2006 primary	Ron Lewis (R)	unopposed		
2004 general	Ron Lewis (R)	185,394	(68%)	($688,898)
	Adam Smith (D)	87,585	(32%)	($4,172)

Prior Winning Percentages: 2002 (70%); 2000 (68%); 1998 (64%); 1996 (58%); 1994 (60%); 1994 (55%)

The People		Race/Ethnic Origin	Ancestry	
Area size:	7,669 sq. mi.	90.6% White	USA: 18.7%	German: 9.2%
Urban population:	47.2%	5.7% Black	Irish: 8.5%	
Rural population:	52.8%	0.7% Asian	**2004 Presidential Vote**	
Pop. 2000:	673,224	0.2% Native Am.	Bush (R) 190,612	(65%)
Pop. 2005 (est):	714,748	0.1% Hawaiian	Kerry (D) 100,580	(34%)
Median income:	$35,724	1.0% Two+ races	Other 2,065	(1%)
Poverty status:	13.3%	0.1% Other	**2000 Presidential Vote**	
Military veterans:	13.7%	1.7% Hispanic Origin	Bush (R) 152,236	(62%)
			Gore (D) 90,086	(37%)
			Other 4,288	(2%)
			Cook Partisan Voting Index: R +13	

Occupation	Blue collar: 35.2%	White collar: 49.6%	Gray collar: 15.1%

In the 1770s and 1780s, Americans began settling the limestone-soiled country of central Kentucky, staking out towns like Bardstown and Elizabethtown and starting academies and colleges; they were well-settled when Stephen Foster wrote "My Old Kentucky Home" just before the Civil War. That conflict tore deeply here: This part of Kentucky gave birth to Abraham Lincoln and in the Civil War it lost thousands of soldiers, Union and Confederate; it would suffer disproportionate casualties in the 20th century wars as well. This area is the home of several Kentucky landmarks—Fort Knox, the nation's gold depository; some of the nation's largest bourbon distilleries; and Mammoth Cave, the world's largest accessible cavern, near Bowling Green. And Kentucky culture is more broadly disseminated than one might think: Japanese executives at the five Japanese-owned plants in Bardstown feel at home there because Stephen Foster's songs, apparently well adapted to Japanese tones, are universally known in Japan. In 2004, a Japanese blue-grass band played at a bluegrass festival in Owensboro.

The 2d Congressional District of Kentucky consists of much of the territory south and southwest of Louisville, starting with fast-growing Spencer County southeast of Louisville and proceeding south to Bowling Green and west along the Ohio River to Owensboro, the home of the International Bluegrass Music Museum and a port with warehouses that receive aluminum alloys to make lightweight engine parts. Owensboro is the home of an annual international barbecue festival where mutton, a throwback to Welsh sheep herders who settled in Western Kentucky, remains a favorite. Much of this is rural and small-town country, where most people have family roots that go back generations and a connection with the past not often found in big metropolitan areas. Civil War loyalties are reflected in the election returns here; Kentucky was deeply split on secession, and a color-coded map of the current 2d District would show various splotches of counties pro-South and splotches pro-Union. For many years, the balance of opinion here favored the

Democrats. But in the 1990s, the Civil War gave way to the culture war, and opinion moved toward the Republicans. In 2000 and 2004 this was George W. Bush's best district in Kentucky.

The congressman from the 2d District is Ron Lewis, a Republican first elected in a May 1994 special election that had national implications. Lewis was born in a log cabin and raised in eastern Kentucky; he worked his way through Morehead State as a laborer at Armco Steel. He worked in the highway department, at a state hospital, then served in the Navy. In 1980, he became a Baptist minister; in 1985 he started a Christian bookstore in Elizabethtown, two counties south of Louisville; he was the opposite of a political insider. Then, in March 1994, Democratic Congressman William Natcher died. He was chairman of the Appropriations Committee and a politician of a very old school, so hard-working and conscientious that he never missed a roll call vote in 41 years. Though the district voted for George H.W. Bush in 1992, Democratic leaders assumed they would win: They handpicked former state Senate President Joe Prather. Before the election, Prather even flew to Washington to go apartment hunting. But they failed to account for the national and local conservative trend. The NRCC spent $200,000, while Prather raised campaign money belatedly and asserted that he was quite a different sort of Democrat than Bill Clinton. Lewis won a solid 55%-45% victory.

In the House, Lewis has a solidly conservative voting record and is attentive to local concerns. He backed tobacco buyout proposals, phasing out tobacco price supports and providing a mandatory buyout of tobacco farmers' entitlements. With a seat on the Ways and Means Committee, Lewis—who doesn't drink—took up the cause of local distillers and got more than 60 co-sponsors on his bill to reduce the excise tax on liquor by 26%. But by the time the lobbying campaign was in full gear, the budget surplus had disappeared. He cited his own experience as the father of an adopted child to oppose stem-cell research on embryos. Lewis helped Fort Knox survive the 2005 round of base closing by emphasizing its international renown as a former gold depository and by winning $200 million for the Army to spend on housing at what has become mostly a training facility. After the 9th Circuit appeals court ruled that the Pledge of Allegiance was unconstitutional, Lewis sponsored a bill that would allow two-thirds majorities in the House and Senate to override Supreme Court rulings that overturn federal statutes.

His growing seniority has increased his influence in the House and at Ways and Means, where he works on his promises to cut the capital gains tax to 15% and fix the long-term financing of Social Security. Lewis included a provision in a 2006 tax bill that allows songwriters to claim the lower capital gains rate when they sell song catalogs rather than the higher income tax rate. He also introduced legislation to exempt interest income from agricultural property and some housing loans in rural areas, and he sought to extend the New Markets Tax Credit designed to promote investment low income and rural communities. Lewis in 2005 challenged his colleagues to give up their earmarks for district projects and direct federal funds to the rebuilding effort after hurricanes Katrina and Rita. He won praise from conservative groups but found little support from within his own delegation.

In 1994, many Democrats assumed that Lewis's special election victory was aberrational and that Democratic Owensboro Mayor David Adkisson would win in November. But Lewis projected sincerity, and his strong religious views and opposition to the Clinton tax increase and health care plan were pluses. Lewis won by a resounding 60%-40% margin. In 1998, Lewis reversed his 1994 campaign pledge to serve no more than four full terms, announcing he had changed his mind. Breaking the pledge caused barely a ripple back home.

After largely giving Lewis a pass for a decade, Democrats in 2006 fielded conservative state Representative Mike Weaver, who fit the Democrats' model for challenging entrenched Republicans. Weaver, a Vietnam veteran and retired Army colonel, was able to talk with authority about national security issues as he advocated gradually handing over control of Iraq to the Iraqis. Weaver emphasized his humble farm roots and moral values, while Lewis countered that Weaver's election could make the liberal Nancy Pelosi Speaker of the House (Weaver said he would not vote for Pelosi). When the state Democratic party ran an ad criticizing him for abandoning term limits, Lewis responded by admitting he had made a mistake in 1998 when he said he would limit himself to three more terms. Lewis sounded national security themes as he campaigned on energy policy, immigration and border security. He outspent Weaver by more than 2-to-1 and won reelection 55%-45%.

THIRD DISTRICT

Rep. John Yarmuth (D)

Elected 2006, 1st term; b. Nov. 4, 1947, Louisville; home, Louisville; Yale, B.A. 1969, attended Georgetown, 1972-74, attended U. of Louisville, 1975; Jewish; married (Catherine).

Professional Career: Stockbroker, 1969-71; Sr. aide, U.S. Sen. Marlow Cook, 1971-74; Publisher, Louisville Today magazine, 1976-82; Asst. VP of university relations, U. of Louisville, 1983-86; VP, Caretenders, 1986-90; Owner, Columnist & Executive Editor, Louisville Eccentric Observer, 1990-2006; co-host, Yarmuth & Ziegler, 2003; commentator, Hot Button, 2004-05.

DC Office: 319 CHOB, 20515, 202-225-5401; Fax: 202-225-5776; Web site: yarmuth.house.gov.

District Offices: Louisville, 502-582-5129.

Committees: *Education & Labor* (23d of 27 D): Higher Education, Lifelong Learning & Competitiveness; Healthy Families & Communities. *Oversight & Government Reform* (14th of 23 D): National Security & Foreign Affairs; Information Policy, Census & National Archives.

Group Ratings and Key Votes: Newly Elected

Election Results

2006 general	John Yarmuth (D)	122,489	(51%)	($2,224,248)
	Anne Northup (R)	116,568	(48%)	($3,421,281)
	Other...	2,908	(1%)	
2006 primary	John Yarmuth (D)	30,962	(54%)	
	Andrew Horne (D)	18,662	(32%)	
	James Moore (D)	4,582	(8%)	
	Burrel Farnsley (D)	3,322	(6%)	
2004 general	Anne Northup (R)	197,736	(60%)	($3,339,760)
	Tony Miller (D)	124,040	(38%)	($1,221,092)
	Other...	6,363	(2%)	

The People		Race/Ethnic Origin	Ancestry	
Area size:	379 sq. mi.	76.0% White	German: 14.8%	Irish: 10.4%
Urban population:	98.3%	19.1% Black	USA: 8.8%	
Rural population:	1.7%	1.4% Asian	**2004 Presidential Vote**	
Pop. 2000:	674,032	0.2% Native Am.	Kerry (D) 167,440	(51%)
Pop. 2005 (est):	680,825	0.0% Hawaiian	Bush (R) 160,772	(49%)
Median income:	$39,468	1.3% Two+ races	**2000 Presidential Vote**	
Poverty status:	12.4%	0.2% Other	Gore (D) 141,337	(50%)
Military veterans:	13.7%	1.8% Hispanic Origin	Bush (R) 134,234	(48%)
			Other 5,628	(2%)
			Cook Partisan Voting Index: D + 2	

Occupation	Blue collar: 23.7%	White collar: 62.0%	Gray collar: 14.3%

At the falls of the Ohio River, Americans more than 200 years ago founded one of their first inland metropolises, the river port and industrial city of Louisville (pronounced *LOOuhv'l*). The city has always retained an air of the South; when Kentucky decided not to secede in 1861, the decision was not unanimous, and the culture of tidewater Virginia is still visible in the Louisville lawn party. Steamboats are tied up in front of Louisville's downtown, primed to follow the channel around the falls of the Ohio that prompted George Rogers Clark to found the town in 1778. Mint juleps are served on the verandas of mansions, especially (but not only) during Kentucky Derby week in May; horse racing is a preoccupation throughout the year. Although the Ohio River is crossed with many bridges and the accent across the river in Indiana may sound the same to outsiders, Louisville partakes of the cavalier culture that second sons of big landowners from England brought to Virginia in the 17th century and their heirs brought over the Appalachians to the valleys of Kentucky in the 18th century.

Louisville is Kentucky's largest city, though in the 2000 Census it was ranked number two, behind Lexington, which includes all of Fayette County. One of the arguments that persuaded voters in November 2000 by a 54%-46% margin to consolidate the city and surrounding Jefferson

County is that it would make Louisville number one again; the merger took effect in January 2003. Louisville has not been growing as rapidly as many other Southern and Midwestern cities. Its economy is in many ways pre-postindustrial: It produces cigarettes and whiskey, large appliances and automobiles. But it is also the headquarters of Humana health services and of Yum! Brands, which owns KFC, Pizza Hut, Taco Bell and Long John Silver's and is expanding most rapidly in China. It has a new medical services center downtown, as well as the Muhammad Ali Center and the Owsley Brown Frazier Historical Arms Museum. The Louisville Bats's Slugger Field, opened in April 2000 on the riverfront, has attracted $100 million in development nearby. But this growth is less than in the ring of Kentucky counties around Jefferson County, whose populations increased from 40% to 118% from 1990 to 2004, or in the counties across the river in Indiana. This regional growth has fueled plans to build two massive bridges over the Ohio River, at an estimated cost of $3.9 billion, to help Louisville untangle Spaghetti Junction, the knotted convergence of Interstates 64, 65 and 71. Louisville has not yet attracted large numbers of immigrants, but has an interesting variety—Vietnamese, Bosnians, Cubans, Chinese, Indians, Koreans, Mexicans.

The 3d Congressional District of Kentucky includes all but a dozen or so precincts of Louisville-Jefferson County. There is a large black population in the West End of Louisville and just south of the old city limits and a lower-income white population along the strip highway that leads to Fort Knox. The suburbs to the east tend to be affluent; little elite neighborhoods—Mockingbird Valley, Glenview, Ten Broeck—nestled in the hills above the Ohio River. Louisville has long been an odd duck in Kentucky politics. If its elite were Virginia cavaliers, many of its burghers were Germans and Pennsylvanians who made this river town a Republican and anti-slavery island in a secessionist and pro-slavery sea. That tradition helps explain why Republican Mitch McConnell was able to get elected Jefferson County judge-executive in 1977 and 1981 when the state was electing Democrats to most other offices. In the 1990s Louisville, like so many bigger metro areas, trended toward the Democrats, even as the rest of Kentucky trended Republican. The 3d District voted by narrow margins for Al Gore in 2000 and John Kerry in 2004, while the state's other five districts all voted twice for George W. Bush.

The congressman from the 3d District is John Yarmuth, who won the district in 2006 by defeating five-term Republican Anne Northup. Yarmuth never held elected office before Congress, but draws political experience from four years as a Senate aide and more than two decades as a newspaper editor, publisher and columnist. He comes from a wealthy family: His father Stanley Yarmuth founded National Industries, a conglomerate that started as a used car business; his maternal grandfather Samuel Klein ran the Bank of Louisville. John Yarmuth grew up in Louisville, and graduated from Atherton High School, where he was elected student government president. (He was also inducted to the school's hall of fame in 2002). After graduating from Yale University in 1969, he worked briefly as a stockbroker and then as an aide for Republican Sen. Marlow Cook, who was defeated for re-election in 1974. Yarmuth attended two years of law school at Georgetown University while working for Cook but returned home to attend the University of Louisville; he left without finishing his law degree. In 1976 he founded *Louisville Today* magazine, served as publisher through 1982, he ran unsuccessfully for Louisville alderman in 1975 and for county commissioner in 1981. He worked in public relations from 1983-1990 for the University of Louisville and a healthcare company. Unhappy with the policies of President Reagan and the Republican Party, Yarmuth switched his party affiliation in 1985. (He first registered as a Republican as a favor to his father, who was a major Nixon fundraiser.) In 1990 Yarmuth founded the *Louisville Eccentric Observer*, a free newsweekly popularly known as LEO, where for 15 years he penned a column called "Hot Coals" that he used to promote mostly liberal views. He sold the newspaper in 2003, but his columns continued to appear until he began his campaign for Congress. In 2003 he became a television commentator, offering the liberal viewpoint on a political talk show.

The incumbent he defeated was Anne Northup, a perennial Democratic target who consistently won close elections in this Democratic-leaning seat. Northup brought millions of dollars to the district with her seat on the Appropriations Committee; Democrats appeared to come up short for the 2006 cycle when Louisville attorney Jack Conway, who held Northup to 52% in 2002, announced he would not run. Without Conway in the race, the Democratic Congressional Campaign Committee touted attorney Andrew Horne, an Iraq war veteran and first-time candidate. But Yarmuth raised more money and proved a more formidable candidate than Horne, winning the four-way primary 54%-32%. He called for an immediate pullout of troops from Iraq and referred to Northup as a "rubber stamp" for President Bush.

Republicans, at the expense of the DCCC, took pleasure in noting Horne's defeat. But Yarmuth remained competitive throughout the summer and by late October he had earned a second look by the DCCC, which then began to spend money in the race. Northup campaigned on Republican economic policies, including tax cuts, and her work for the district. Yarmuth ran on universal health coverage, a minimum wage increase and revamping the No Child Left Behind Act. Northup, the mother of six children, suffered a personal tragedy when her son died of an undiagnosed heart condition in mid-July. She suspended her campaign for six weeks before returning to campaigning at the end of the summer. Northup in September unleashed a radio, television and Internet offensive that blasted Yarmuth for his past writings. She charged that Yarmuth supported abolishing Social Security, doubling payroll taxes, raising taxes on sport utility vehicles and trucks, removing "under God" from the Pledge of Allegiance, lowering the drinking age and legalizing marijuana use. Yarmuth's campaign responded the portrayals were inaccurate or outdated. Northup raised nearly $3.4 million compared to Yarmuth's $2.3 million, which included $708,000 of his own money. But Northup, who carried the district while Bush lost it in 2000 and 2004, could not overcome a national tide against Republicans, an environment made worse by a patronage scandal surrounding Republican Gov. Ernie Fletcher. Yarmuth defeated Northup 51%-48%.

Yarmuth has had the luxury to wander through most of his professional career and faces an adjustment to Congress. "He had a pretty decent life, a son he adores, a gorgeous wife, and the freedom to go and do. It is hard to give that all up," his mother, 79-year-old Edna Yarmuth, told the Louisville *Courier-Journal* just before Election Day. Yarmuth, a scratch golfer who said he plays as many as 100 rounds of golf a year, said he will scale back plans to spend four weeks a year at a home he recently built near a golf course in Ireland. He expected to continue Northup's work on vital district projects, including a new veterans hospital and funding for the Ohio River bridges. He won a seat on the Education and Workforce Committee, a good post for a candidate who ran on pocketbook issues. He said he plans to donate his congressional salary to charity. Given Yarmuth's freshman status and the district's only marginal Democratic leanings, he could face a competitive reelection challenge in 2008. Erwin Roberts, an African-American and the former director of the state's Office of Homeland Security, was thought to be a promising Republican candidate with some appeal to traditionally Democratic black voters; state Senator Dan Seum, who is white, was also considering running.

FOURTH DISTRICT

Rep. Geoff Davis (R)

Elected 2004, 2d term; b. Oct. 26, 1958, Montreal, Canada; home, Hebron; U.S.M.A., B.S. 1981; Christian; married (Pat).

Military Career: Army, 1976-87.

Professional Career: Technology consultant, 1989-2004; Owner, Republic Consulting, 1992-2004.

DC Office: 1108 LHOB, 20515, 202-225-3465; Fax: 202-225-0003; Web site: www.geoffdavis.house.gov.

District Offices: Ashland, 606-324-9898; Fort Mitchell, 859-426-0080; LaGrange, 502-222-2233; Maysville, 606-564-6004; Williamstown, 859-824-3320.

Committees: *Armed Services* (28th of 29 R): Oversight & Investigations; Air & Land Forces. *Financial Services* (25th of 33 R): Housing & Community Opportunity; Capital Markets, Insurance & Government Sponsored Enterprises; Financial Institutions & Consumer Credit.

Group Ratings

	ADA	ACLU	AFS	LCV	ITIC	NTU	COC	ACU	CFG	FRC
2006	5	14	14	8	100	59	93	84	55	100
2005	0	—	0	6	—	55	93	88	57	92

National Journal Ratings

	2005 LIB	—	2005 CONS		2006 LIB	—	2006 CONS
Economic	30%	—	68%		30%	—	68%
Social	0%	—	89%		28%	—	70%
Foreign	21%	—	78%		6%	—	86%

Key Votes of the 109th Congress

1. Estate Tax Repeal	Y	5. Limit Interstate Abortion	Y
2. Limit CAFE Standards	Y	6. Extend Patriot Act	Y
3. FY06 Spending Curb	Y	7. Bar Same Sex Marriage	Y
4. Drilling in ANWR	Y	8. Stem Cell Research $	N

9. Build Border Fence — Y
10. CAFTA — Y
11. Oppose Iraq Withdrawal — Y
12. Detainee Tribunals — Y

Election Results

2006 general	Geoff Davis (R)	105,845	(52%)	($4,255,379)
	Ken Lucas (D)	88,822	(43%)	($1,469,555)
	Brian Houillion (Lib)	10,100	(5%)	
2006 primary	Geoff Davis (R)	unopposed		
2004 general	Geoff Davis (R)	160,982	(54%)	($2,959,526)
	Nick Clooney (D)	129,876	(44%)	($1,448,282)
	Other	5,069	(2%)	

The People

Area size: 5,770 sq. mi.
Urban population: 59.7%
Rural population: 40.3%
Pop. 2000: 673,588
Pop. 2005 (est): 712,091
Median income: $40,150
Poverty status: 11.4%
Military veterans: 13.0%

Race/Ethnic Origin

95.1% White
2.2% Black
0.5% Asian
0.2% Native Am.
0.0% Hawaiian
0.8% Two+ races
0.1% Other
1.1% Hispanic Origin

Ancestry

German: 17.6% USA: 13.6%
Irish: 10.4%

2004 Presidential Vote
Bush (R) 195,055 (63%)
Kerry (D) 111,049 (36%)
Other 2,547 (1%)

2000 Presidential Vote
Bush (R) 152,856 (61%)
Gore (D) 92,768 (37%)
Other 6,060 (2%)

Cook Partisan Voting Index: R +12

Occupation Blue collar: 29.6% White collar: 56.0% Gray collar: 14.3%

The commonwealth of Kentucky has gone to court more than once to assert its claim to all of the Ohio River up to its northern bank: This is one of the northernmost extensions of the South. The Ohio sees many different parts of Kentucky. Ashland, near the West Virginia border, is industrial, the home of Ashland Oil; the river here is bound in by tight hills that hold smoke and soot close in the air. Farther down the river, the country is more bucolic: Here Eliza fled across the ice floes in Harriet Beecher Stowe's *Uncle Tom's Cabin*. Farther west, between Louisville and Cincinnati, are counties that still look like they're in the 19th century. But metropolitan growth obtrudes. Oldham County, just upriver from Louisville, has some of Kentucky's oldest homes, though the horse country is also sprouting affluent subdivisions; this is by far the most affluent county in the state. The three Northern Kentucky counties across the river from Cincinnati—Campbell, Kenton and fast-growing Boone—are urban and suburban. Overlooking the suspension bridge built by John Roebling 16 years before the Brooklyn Bridge are new buildings on the Covington waterfront while Newport is sprucing up, and office buildings and new subdivisions are rising on the hills in Boone County above the river and near the Cincinnati-Northern Kentucky International Airport. The airport opened a new runway in 2005 and is the second largest hub for Delta Air Lines. Newport, controlled for decades by an organized crime syndicate based in Cleveland, with its panoramic view of the Cincinnati skyline plus its entertainment and nightlife, has become a regional hot spot; local features include the aquarium, Labor Day fireworks on the river, and its hometown status for one-time Republican presidential candidate Gary Bauer.

The 4th Congressional District of Kentucky spans all these variations of Ohio River country; it also includes lightly populated counties just inland. Economically, it runs the gamut from coal mining towns to rich suburbs. Politically, it has some of the most Democratic counties in America, like mountain-bound Elliott County (70%-30% for John Kerry in 2004), and some of the most Republican territory in Kentucky, like Oldham County (69%-30% for George W. Bush). The three northern Kentucky counties across the river from Cincinnati cast nearly half the district's votes, and they too are heavily Republican; in 2004, Bush won the district, 63%-36%.

The congressman from the 4th District is Geoff Davis, a Republican elected in 2004. He grew up in Pittsburgh and graduated from West Point. He was an Army ranger and served as a helicopter flight commander, then directed Army air operations enforcing the peace between Israel and Egypt. After 11 years in the Army, he moved to Fort Worth, Texas, then to Northern Kentucky, where in 1992 he started a consulting firm that advised companies on how to streamline manufacturing technology. In 2002 he ran against Congressman Ken Lucas, a conservative Democrat first elected in 1998; Davis lost 51%-48% after receiving very little assistance from the national party. After some hesitation, Lucas decided to honor his pledge to serve only three terms and announced his retirement in November 2003.

That left Davis the frontrunner in this heavily Republican district in 2004, but he still faced a formidable challenge from Democrat Nick Clooney, a locally famous newspaper columnist and television commentator, and the father of actor George Clooney and the brother of the late singer Rosemary Clooney. Through his son's Hollywood connections, Nick Clooney got checks from Paul Newman, Kevin Costner and Catherine Zeta-Jones. Davis said his opponent had more in common with the people of Southern California than with those in northern Kentucky, and national Republicans called the Democrat, "Looney Clooney." Clooney said he was a moderate and supported the Bush tax cuts and opposed same-sex marriage and abortion except when the mother's life was in danger. The Davis campaign unearthed columns Clooney had written over a period of 15 years, including a 1998 column in which he had criticized gun ownership; Davis, by contrast, said he was a lifetime member of the National Rifle Association membership and supported gun ownership rights. Davis had a big fundraising advantage: he spent $2.6 million to Clooney's $1.5 million. Clooney won rural and mining areas in the eastern end of the district, but Davis carried the three Cincinnati-area suburban counties and won the race 54%-44%.

Davis got seats on the Armed Services and Financial Services Committees, which catered to his experience and provided him a platform for his first major achievement as a freshman. In 2006, President Bush signed into law Davis's bill to protect military personnel from being sold overpriced insurance and investment products. He initially opposed Senate language that would cap interest rates on "payday" loans, but reversed his position and supported the cap in a defense bill after stories about a donation he had taken from a payday loan chain owner generated criticism.

In January 2006, Democrats succeeded in recruiting former congressman Lucas for a rematch. Lucas, a conservative who opposed abortion, gay marriage and gun control, held the district for three terms and previously served as Boone County judge-executive. The race had the attention of the Democratic Congressional Campaign Committee, whose executive director, John Lapp, had previously served as Lucas's campaign manager. Republicans promptly criticized Lucas for not passing a single freestanding bill during his earlier tenure in Congress. Davis, usually a reliable vote for Bush administration policies, distanced himself from Bush by saying he strongly disagreed with the White House on Social Security private accounts, immigration and port security. But Lucas had difficulty tapping into national anti-Republican sentiment or disenchantment with the Iraq war. (Lucas had voted for the Iraq invasion, which he later said he regretted.) Davis attempted to make the race a referendum on who could be more effective in Congress. He also criticized Lucas for urging a judge to give a lighter sentence to John Finnan, a banker involved in a building scandal. Davis spent nearly three times as much as Lucas and got the endorsement of Democratic Covington Mayor Butch Callery, who appeared in a commercial for him. He also focused his voter turnout program on the populous suburban Cincinnati counties of Boone, Kenton and Campbell, as well as Oldham County, outside of Louisville. On Election Day, Davis carried all four–while losing 15 of the district's 24 counties–to win 52%-43%. Davis has now won two tough races in this Republican district; it will take a strong Democratic candidate to seriously challenge him again.

FIFTH DISTRICT

Rep. Harold Rogers (R)

Elected 1980, 14th term; b. Dec. 31, 1937, Barrier; home, Somerset; U. of KY, B.A. 1962, J.D. 1964; Baptist; married (Cynthia).

Military Career: Army Natl. Guard, 1957-64.

Professional Career: Practicing atty., 1964-69; Pulaski–Rockcastle Commonwealth's Atty., 1969-80.

DC Office: 2406 RHOB, 20515, 202-225-4601; Fax: 202-225-0940; Web site: www.house.gov/rogers.

District Offices: Hazard, 606-439-0794; Prestonburg, 606-886-0844; Somerset, 606-679-8346.

Committees: *Appropriations* (4th of 29 R): Homeland Security (RMM); Commerce, Justice, Science & Related Agencies.

Group Ratings

	ADA	ACLU	AFS	LCV	ITIC	NTU	COC	ACU	CFG	FRC
2006	10	9	29	17	100	54	87	80	50	100
2005	0	—	0	0	—	55	93	92	56	92

National Journal Ratings

	2005 LIB	—	2005 CONS	2006 LIB	—	2006 CONS
Economic	9%	—	88%	27%	—	71%
Social	24%	—	74%	23%	—	74%
Foreign	17%	—	79%	6%	—	86%

Key Votes of the 109th Congress

1. Estate Tax Repeal	Y	5. Limit Interstate Abortion	Y
2. Limit CAFE Standards	Y	6. Extend Patriot Act	Y
3. FY06 Spending Curb	Y	7. Bar Same Sex Marriage	Y
4. Drilling in ANWR	Y	8. Stem Cell Research $	N

9. Build Border Fence	Y
10. CAFTA	Y
11. Oppose Iraq Withdrawal	Y
12. Detainee Tribunals	Y

Election Results

2006 general	Harold Rogers (R)	147,201	(74%)	($916,202)
	Kenneth Stepp (D)	52,367	(26%)	($1,747)
2006 primary	Harold Rogers (R)	unopposed		
2004 general	Harold Rogers (R)	unopposed		($737,589)

Prior Winning Percentages: 2002 (78%); 2000 (74%); 1998 (78%); 1996 (100%); 1994 (79%); 1992 (55%); 1990 (100%); 1988 (100%); 1986 (100%); 1984 (76%); 1982 (65%); 1980 (67%)

The People		Race/Ethnic Origin	Ancestry	
Area size:	10,759 sq. mi.	97.1% White	USA: 29.5%	English: 6.8%
Urban population:	21.3%	1.1% Black	Irish: 5.7%	
Rural population:	78.7%	0.3% Asian	**2004 Presidential Vote**	
Pop. 2000:	673,670	0.2% Native Am.	Bush (R) 159,489	(61%)
Pop. 2005 (est):	687,351	0.0% Hawaiian	Kerry (D) 102,142	(39%)
Median income:	$21,915	0.6% Two+ races	Other 1,911	(1%)
Poverty status:	28.1%	0.0% Other	**2000 Presidential Vote**	
Military veterans:	10.0%	0.7% Hispanic Origin	Bush (R) 131,494	(57%)
			Gore (D) 97,104	(42%)
			Other 3,423	(1%)
			Cook Partisan Voting Index: R + 8	

Occupation	Blue collar: 35.3%	White collar: 48.4%	Gray collar: 16.3%

The mountains of eastern Kentucky have been a special place since Daniel Boone came through the Cumberland Gap in 1775. As Virginians poured through and created their version of a Tidewater civilization in the Bluegrass country, the people who settled the mountain counties and the Cumberland Plateau, most of them of Irish Protestant or Border Scot descent, brought different values—an assertive egalitarianism, loyalty to family and community, and passionate willingness to defend honor by feuds or violence. Most of the people in the mountains today are descendants of families who settled there in the two or three generations after Boone. Handed down are living memories of the old ways of doing things from the time not so far distant when there was little contact here with the outside world and the ties to the rest of American civilization were secured mainly by school primers and the King James Bible. Only when people's lives have been changed and uprooted by outside events and institutions have their basic political attitudes been changed— and with a lasting imprint. The first agent of such change here was the Civil War; the second was the great United Mine Workers organizing drives in the coalmines around the 1930s. The Civil War made the mountains and the Cumberland Plateau a stronghold of the Republican Party. This was never slave territory—hardly any blacks have ever lived here, yet communities and families were riven by the rebellion of the South. People have not forgotten: The counties around Somerset and Corbin in south central Kentucky cast some of the highest Republican percentages in the nation, election after election.

Then came coal. Early in the 20th century, vast seams of coal were discovered under the Kentucky mountains; representatives of eastern capitalists (including the young Franklin D. Roosevelt) began prowling through these hills, hiring town lawyers to buy up mineral rights from unsuspecting farmers, building industrial slum towns in hollows and creek beds beneath glowering, heavily forested mountainsides. Coal mining was harsh and deadly work: Mine accidents, black lung disease and simple exhaustion killed tens of thousands of miners, while low wages and company stores kept them poor. Then John L. Lewis's United Mine Workers came in and something like open warfare followed, with neither mine operators nor union organizers loath to use violence and threats. The union mostly won in eastern Kentucky and in the short run raised wages and built hospitals for miners and their families; in the longer run, the UMW phased out many jobs in the mines in return for job security and health benefits, as use of oil expanded. Today there are just over 400 mines in Kentucky, a drop from over 2,000 25 years ago. Politically, the UMW counties in the eastern part of the state became heavily Democratic. In the mid-1960s Lyndon B. Johnson came to eastern Kentucky and cited the poverty here in pushing for his Appalachian and anti-poverty bills. The high energy prices of the 1970s sparked strip mining, and eastern Kentucky's economy moved upward; the lower energy prices of the 1980s and 1990s were something of a setback; high coal prices in 2004 stepped up the pace at existing mines, but the big mining companies who increasingly control production were wary of opening new mines. Mountaintop mining has become common, requiring huge machines and few workers; some say it wrecks the scenery, others say it produces more useful level land. Most eastern coal counties have lost population since 1980, and counties off the interstate highways have a hard time attracting new businesses, but life here today is much closer to the ordinary American standard of living than it was in Johnson's time. There is less insularity and less defensiveness, and more celebration of heritage, as in the Hillbilly Days Festival that draws 100,000 people every June to Pikeville; the mine-scarred hills of Harlan County are now a mecca for all terrain vehicles. Income levels are low, but so is the cost of living.

The 5th Congressional District of Kentucky includes much of the Cumberland Plateau and most of the eastern mountains, a mixture of heavily Republican and heavily Democratic territory. There are huge political differences here between counties separated by just a mountain ridge or two, evidence of the depth of Civil War and United Mine Workers political loyalties, and only somewhat modulated by the trend toward George W. Bush in the coal country. Jackson County, which Bill Clinton visited on his "poverty tour" in 1999, voted 84%-15% for Bush in 2004; a few counties over, Knott County voted 63%-36% for John Kerry. On one matter there is widespread agreement: More people here identify their ancestry as "American" than any other congressional district in the nation. And this part of Kentucky has produced stars in that quintessentially American medium, country music—Loretta Lynn, Ricky Skaggs, Dwight Yoakum, Crystal Gayle. The 5th District, created in the 1991 redistricting and modified just slightly in 2001, spans these lines and combines most of two former districts, one heavily Democratic and the other heavily Republican. But overall this is a solidly Republican district—57% for Bush in 2000, 61% in 2004.

The congressman from the 5th District is Harold Rogers, a Republican first elected in 1980. Rogers grew up in Wayne County, went off to the University of Kentucky and served in the National Guard, then practiced law in Somerset; in 1969, at 34, he was elected Pulaski-Rockcastle Common-wealth's Attorney. In 1979 he was the Republican nominee for lieutenant governor. In between he with others bought the Citizens National Bank in Somerset. In 1980, when the 5th District congressman retired, Rogers was one of 11 Republicans in the primary; he won with 23% of the vote in the primary (Kentucky has no runoffs) and then easily in November. His toughest race came in 1992, with redistricting. At first his likely opponent was 7th District incumbent Chris Perkins, longtime Congressman Carl Perkins's son; but then Perkins retired at 37, before it was revealed he had 514 overdrafts on the House bank. Rogers ended up facing state Senator John Doug Hays of Pike County, whose grandfather Doug "Sawloggin" Hays was state senator before him. Rogers won with 55% of the vote. He won 71% in his old 5th District, which cast 52% of the new district's votes.

Rogers is now the fourth ranking Republican on the Appropriations Committee. From 2001 until 2003, he was chairman of its Transportation Subcommittee. In February 2003 he became the first chairman of the Homeland Security Appropriations Subcommittee; now he is its ranking minority member. His voting record is mostly, but not always, conservative. Representing a low-income district, he is sympathetic to some spending bills. Rogers represents a district that has long been hungry for federal aid, and does not have a uniformly conservative record on economic issues. He supported most of the Contract with America, but prevented the zeroing out of several pro-grams—the Appalachian Regional Commission, the Legal Services Corporation—by straightfor-wardly negotiating deals, then sticking to them. Over the years he has worked to provide $162 million to protect the solvency of the funds for the United Mine Workers Combined Benefit Fund. After he became chairman of the Transportation Subcommittee, Kentucky became the fourth highest state in transportation funding per capita. The Daniel Boone Parkway, from London to Hazard, has been renamed the Hal Rogers Parkway, and Rogers has been pushing for an expansion of I-66, which now connects Washington and the Shenandoah Valley, with a portion running across

Kentucky from Pikesville to Paducah. He has pushed for $100 million to rebuild the town of Martin above the floodplain, though the town's building are worth one-tenth that sum. He has gotten $7 million for a freight transfer facility in Pulaski County to be leased to the Norfolk Southern for $1 a year, $500,000 to pave a parking lot for Lee's Ford Marina Resort. One big Rogers project is the $15.5 million Center for Rural Development on U.S. 27 near Somerset, nicknamed the Taj Ma-Hal. It contains a 760-seat theater, a 23,000-square foot exhibition hall and houses the Southeast Kentucky Economic Development Corporation and the National Institute for Hometown Security, which with Kentucky schools has gotten $34 million in homeland security grants. In 2006 he was working with the Kentucky delegation and Governor Phil Bredesen of Tennessee to get a federal Bio-Agro Disease Facility built at a former airport 10 miles north of Somerset. The *Lexington Herald Leader* called him "the Prince of Pork." Rogers says, "I'm two people. I'm a national legislator, and I'm a local congressman."

Even before September 11, Rogers was lamenting that most airport screeners were not U.S. citizens. After Congress voted to federalize airport screeners, he kept close watch on the new TSA, insisting that it get rid of the Argenbright Security firm, objecting when it got around Congress's 45,000-employee cap by classifying 9,000 five-year workers as temporary. Rogers has superintended the Department of Homeland Security and its divisions closely. In August 2005 his subcommittee froze FEMA funds for digitizing maps, many of them old and arguably out of date, used to determine premiums for the National Flood Insurance Program, and ordered modernized maps made for Kentucky and other subcommittee members' home states. After Hurricane Katrina he berated FEMA for not changing policy so that it could reduce payments to contractors who fail to perform on time. In February 2006 he told Homeland Security Secretary Michael Chertoff that his budget request was insufficient and focused too much on border security, immigration enforcement and nuclear detection. "While these are homeland security priorities, the increases come at the expense of everything else, resulting in reduced funding for first responders, transit security, research and development and little new money for essential work of federal air marshals and the U.S. Secret Service." The subcommittee bill in May 2006 was $1.8 billion above administration requests, but withheld funds from some department priorities and rejected its proposed increase in airline passenger fees; it withheld $1.3 billion in spending until further information was provided. Noting that border security spending had increased from $5.1 billion in 1995 to $17.9 billion in 2006, but that the flow of illegal immigrants increased, Rogers said, "The policy of more money and no results is no longer in effect." He favored keeping FEMA in Homeland Security, siding with the leaders of the Homeland Security authorizing committee and against the chairmen of the Transportation and Government Oversight committees. The Homeland Security appropriation was finally passed in September, after nearly foundering over disagreements on chemical plant security and whether prescription drugs from Canada should be impounded. The final version exceeded the administration request by $2.7 billion.

Moves in the House to eliminate earmarks or to identify their sponsors obviously would impinge on Rogers's customary ways of doing business. He was criticized in May 2006 by a *New York Times* article detailing the problems of the Transportation Worker Identification Credential program. In 1998 the Clinton administration, perhaps to please Rogers, set up a $5.2 million plant to produce credential card production in Corbin, Kentucky (otherwise famous as the site of Colonel Sanders's first Kentucky Fried Chicken restaurant). When a tamperproof identity card for transportation workers was proposed in 2002, Rogers put in language requiring that green cards, with data recorded on reflective optical stripes, be produced at the Corbin plant, though department officials were pushing smart cards, with data recorded on embedded computer chips. In a 2002 report, Rogers said, "The committee does not want TSA to develop new technologies if existing ones, already developed by other federal agencies, are good enough." In 2003, a $4 million study found the smart card superior; production of 5,000 test cards was scheduled to be under way in Pennsylvania in 2004, but was then moved to Corbin. In 2005 Rogers inserted language into the appropriation requiring DHS to hire for work on background checks of transportation officials a Virginia trade association from which he had received 11 trips to trade association meetings since 2000; when DHS objected, Rogers argued, "Doing so [hiring another contractor] increases both the cost to the federal government and the time it takes to begin conducting background checks." But the no-bid contract was cancelled, and it took time to bid a contract out. When the *Lexington Herald Leader* criticized Rogers's actions keeping TWIC production in Corbin, Rogers replied in a column in the paper that Corbin was one of the three government facilities with high security able to produce the cards, and that it made no sense to have it done by private firms, which might not have such tight security.

Since 1992, Rogers has been re-elected by overwhelming margins, carrying even the most Democratic counties. Many Republicans urged him to run for governor in 2003, but in March 2002 he said he could do more for the state from his current position. He donated some $423,000 to 64 Republican candidates during the 2004 cycle, and sent $5,000 to the South Dakota Republican party and $1,000 to Missouri governor candidate Matt Blunt, son of House Republican Whip Roy Blunt. After the 2004 election he was one of three senior appropriators who sought the chairmanship of the Appropriations Committee. Rogers said he would impose a "sweeping attitudinal change of the entire committee," crack down on earmarks, negotiate aggressively with the Senate and impose fundraising quotas on members. All this may have pleased the Steering Committee, but not enough; the chair went to the more senior Jerry Lewis. His fundraising activity continued, with many contributions from those associated with firms that have won homeland security contracts, some of which have also located facilities in southeast Kentucky; a long *Washington Post* article in December 2005 detailed these relationships, but did not allege any violations of House ethics rules or the law. Rogers's response to the criticism: "I've had a lot of fundraisers. Campaign contributions mean nothing on my watch." In 2006, Rogers won the general election 74%-26%.

SIXTH DISTRICT

Rep. Ben Chandler (D)

Elected Feb. 2004, 2d full term; b. Sept. 12, 1959, Versailles; home, Versailles; U. of KY, B.A. 1983, J.D. 1986; Presbyterian; married (Jennifer).

Elected Office: KY Auditor, 1991-95; KY Atty. Gen. 1995-2004.

Professional Career: Practicing atty., 1986-91.

DC Office: 1504 LHOB, 20515, 202-225-4706; Fax: 202-225-2122; Web site: www.house.gov/chandler.

District Offices: Lexington, 859-219-1366.

Committees: *Appropriations* (35th of 37 D): State, Foreign Operations & Related Programs; Interior, Environment & Related Agencies. *Science & Technology* (19th of 24 D): Technology & Innovation; Space & Aeronautics.

Group Ratings

	ADA	ACLU	AFS	LCV	ITIC	NTU	COC	ACU	CFG	FRC
2006	60	50	71	92	50	16	57	50	15	42
2005	85	—	88	83	—	21	52	36	21	54

National Journal Ratings

	2005 LIB	—	2005 CONS		2006 LIB	—	2006 CONS
Economic	64%	—	36%		65%	—	34%
Social	52%	—	47%		58%	—	42%
Foreign	56%	—	43%		54%	—	45%

Key Votes of the 109th Congress

1. Estate Tax Repeal	Y	5. Limit Interstate Abortion	Y	9. Build Border Fence	Y
2. Limit CAFE Standards	Y	6. Extend Patriot Act	Y	10. CAFTA	N
3. FY06 Spending Curb	N	7. Bar Same Sex Marriage	Y	11. Oppose Iraq Withdrawal	Y
4. Drilling in ANWR	N	8. Stem Cell Research $	Y	12. Detainee Tribunals	Y

Election Results

2006 general	Ben Chandler (D)	158,765	(85%)	($723,278)
	Paul Ard (Lib)	27,015	(15%)	
2006 primary	Ben Chandler (D)	unopposed		
2004 general	Ben Chandler (D)	175,355	(59%)	($1,623,086)
	Tom Buford (R)	119,716	(40%)	($137,072)
	Other	4,146	(1%)	

Prior Winning Percentages: 2004 (55%)

The People		Race/Ethnic Origin	Ancestry	
Area size:	3,775 sq. mi.	87.1% White	USA: 15.3%	English: 9.5%
Urban population:	71.3%	8.2% Black	German: 9.3%	
Rural population:	28.7%	1.2% Asian	**2004 Presidential Vote**	
Pop. 2000:	673,626	0.2% Native Am.	Bush (R) 182,787	(58%)
Pop. 2005 (est):	704,533	0.0% Hawaiian	Kerry (D) 128,967	(41%)
Median income:	$37,544	1.1% Two+ races	Other 2,505	(1%)
Poverty status:	13.2%	0.1% Other	**2000 Presidential Vote**	
Military veterans:	11.7%	2.1% Hispanic Origin	Bush (R) 145,606	(55%)
			Gore (D) 109,602	(42%)
			Other 7,282	(3%)
			Cook Partisan Voting Index: R + 7	

Occupation   Blue collar: 25.8%   White collar: 58.8%   Gray collar: 15.4%

With its white picket fences, horse farms and Georgian brick house-filled small towns, the rolling plateau of the Bluegrass country almost plumb in the middle of Kentucky is the part of interior America longest settled by English speakers: Lexington was founded in 1775; the town of Hopewell was renamed Paris in 1789 out of gratitude for French help during our Revolution and in a salute to theirs (though the county name remained Bourbon even after Louis XVI was guillotined). Tobacco farming started here in the 1770s, horse racing in 1787, and the first whiskey distillery, in Bourbon County, was built in 1790. Tobacco, whiskey and racehorses remained the staples of the Bluegrass economy for six generations until 1956, when IBM built its typewriter plant in Lexington. IBM's arrival "really was the beginning of Lexington's industrial revolution," as University of Kentucky historian Carl Cone put it. But capitalism, as Joseph Schumpeter wrote, is a process of creative destruction. The PC eventually outclassed the typewriter, and the IBM plant was put on the block. The big employer here became Lexmark International, an independent IBM spinoff that makes inkjet and laser printers. Another mainstay of the local economy is the Toyota plant, built in the 1980s, in Georgetown, a town with early 19th century houses and lush countryside, just one county north of Lexington and west of Paris. Toyota's $5 billion worth of investment has attracted auto parts and suppliers to move nearby as an adjunct to the Georgetown plant, which can produce 500,000 cars annually. The engineering school at the University of Kentucky has created additional manufacturing job opportunities. Lexington, which includes all of Fayette County, grew by a sprightly 18% between 1990 and 2004, and the 2000 Census showed it the largest city in Kentucky, just ahead of Louisville. But Louisville voters decided to merge the city and Jefferson County, and in January 2003 Louisville became number one again.

The 6th Congressional District of Kentucky includes Lexington and the surrounding counties—a natural unit, unlike some other Kentucky districts. Lexington casts 40% of the votes. It was the home base of the Whig Party's great leader Henry Clay, but in the 150 years after his death, the Bluegrass country was mostly Democratic. In the 1990s the area became more Republican, and George W. Bush carried the district in 2000 and 2004.

The congressman from the 6th District is Ben Chandler, a Democrat who won a special election in February 2004. He grew up in Versailles, in the horse country just west of Lexington, the grandson of A.B. "Happy" Chandler, the former governor and senator who for five years was commissioner of baseball before eventually serving another term as governor. His father owned a local newspaper. Ben Chandler got his bachelor's and law degree from the University of Kentucky and practiced law for five years. In 1991 he was elected state auditor and in 1995 and 1999 attorney general. In that job he made a name for himself by prosecuting corrupt politicians. But he, like other Kentucky Democrats, was hurt in 2002 when Governor Paul Patton admitted an extramarital affair with a woman who owned a nursing home and who was given preferential treatment by the state. In 2003 Chandler ran for governor and beat Speaker Jody Richards in the Democratic primary by a 50%-47% margin. But he lost the general election to 6th District Congressman Ernie Fletcher 55%-45%. Fletcher resigned the 6th District House seat on December 9.

Chandler quickly decided that if he could not defeat Fletcher, he would try to succeed him. He won the Democratic nomination without opposition, and faced low-profile Republican state Senator Alice Forgy Kerr. Both candidates supported the Iraq war, a constitutional amendment to ban same-sex marriage and opposed amnesty for illegal aliens. National Democrats strongly backed Chandler, who carefully kept his distance from then-Minority Leader Nancy Pelosi. Chandler scored an unexpectedly easy victory, 55%-43%, marking the first time since 1991 that Democrats had captured a Republican seat in a special election. "It was a big, big deal," said Chandler. "I couldn't believe the enthusiasm I was greeted with on my arrival in Washington — my election was hailed at the time as a turning of the tide." It wasn't, but in the regular November general election, Chandler defeated state Senator Tom Buford, 59%-40%. His victories in 2004 kept alive Kentucky's record of electing at least one Democrat to Congress every year since Andrew Jackson founded the party in 1828.

In the House, Chandler has a moderate voting record, though a bit more liberal on economic issues. In 2006 he proposed spending up to $32 billion over five years for grants and loans to fix and construct the nation's schools, but the bill died without a hearing. From his seat on the Transportation and Infrastructure Aviation Subcommittee, Chandler hounded Federal Aviation Administration officials about the adequacy of air traffic control staffing at Lexington's Blue Grass Airport and nationally after the crash of Comair Flight 5191, which killed 49 people in August 2006.

After Chandler lost the governor's race in 2003, the expectation was that Chandler would serve several years in Congress while plotting a 2007 rematch against Fletcher. Wary of Chandler's potential candidacy, Fletcher aides, with little evidence, accused Chandler of being the driving force behind an investigation into a patronage scandal that engulfed Fletcher's administration. But once in Congress, Chandler learned about the importance of seniority and saw the power that junior Republicans enjoyed just by being in the majority. "If you can maintain yourself here, if you can keep your nose clean, you will increase in your seniority and power," he told the *Lexington Herald Leader*. "Just as important, you will learn how this institution works and how you can make it work." Chandler was his party's consensus favorite to run for governor in 2007, but after winning reelection with 85% in 2006 and after Democrats won control of the House, Chandler in late November 2006 turned down another chance to seek the seat held by his grandfather. He said he was enthusiastic about his job in the Democratic House majority, and soon secured a plum seat on the Appropriations Committee, which should put him in a strong position to defend this Republican-leaning seat. Chandler draws frequent mention as a possible challenger for Republican Senator Jim Bunning's seat in 2010.

★ LOUISIANA ★

"Louisiana," it was written in this space two years ago, "often seems to be America's banana republic, with its charm and inefficiency, its communities interlaced by family ties and its public sector sometimes laced with corruption, with its own indigenous culture and its tradition of fine distinctions of class and caste. It is a state with an economy uncomfortably like that of an underdeveloped country, based on pumping minerals out of soggy ground and shipping grain produced in the vast hinterland drained by its great river, an economy increasingly dependent on businesses typical of picturesque Third World countries—tourism (now the second largest industry, hard hit by September 11) and gambling. Its politics too has a Third World quality, with its own peculiar election laws and a heritage of no-holds-barred conflict and demagoguery no other state can match: what other state has produced a Huey Long or an Edwin Edwards? Louisiana has a hereditary rich class and a large low-wage working class. It has conservative cultural attitudes: Louisiana and Utah have the most restrictive abortion laws in the U.S.—its partial-birth abortion ban and optional "Choose Life" license plates have been ruled illegal by federal courts—and Louisiana in 1997 became the first state to offer covenant marriages, in which spouses would agree not to be covered by no-fault divorce laws. But Louisiana also has a lazy tolerance of rule-breaking, and feels more like the Caribbean or the Mediterranean than the North Atlantic or the Pacific Rim. This is not an entirely original observation. Five decades ago, A. J. Liebling described Louisiana as an outpost of the Levant along the Gulf of Mexico. Most of the United States faces east toward the vast Atlantic Ocean or west toward the vast Pacific; Louisiana faces south, to the Gulf of Mexico and the steamy heat and volatile societies of the Caribbean and Latin America."

Not much of this needs to be rewritten in the wake of Hurricane Katrina, which struck New Orleans on August 29, 2005, and resulted in flooding which devastated most of the city and sent hundreds of thousands of evacuees to shelter on higher ground. Katrina destroyed large parts of Louisiana, but it also highlighted its faults, exposed its weaknesses and shredded the fabric of a society that was already deep in decay. Katrina struck the Gulf Coast of Mississippi with Category 5 winds and New Orleans with only Category 4; in a few hours it destroyed far more structures in Mississippi than it did in Louisiana; New Orleans mostly survived the initial rains and winds. But then the levees broke and the destruction of New Orleans followed as water sought its level. The

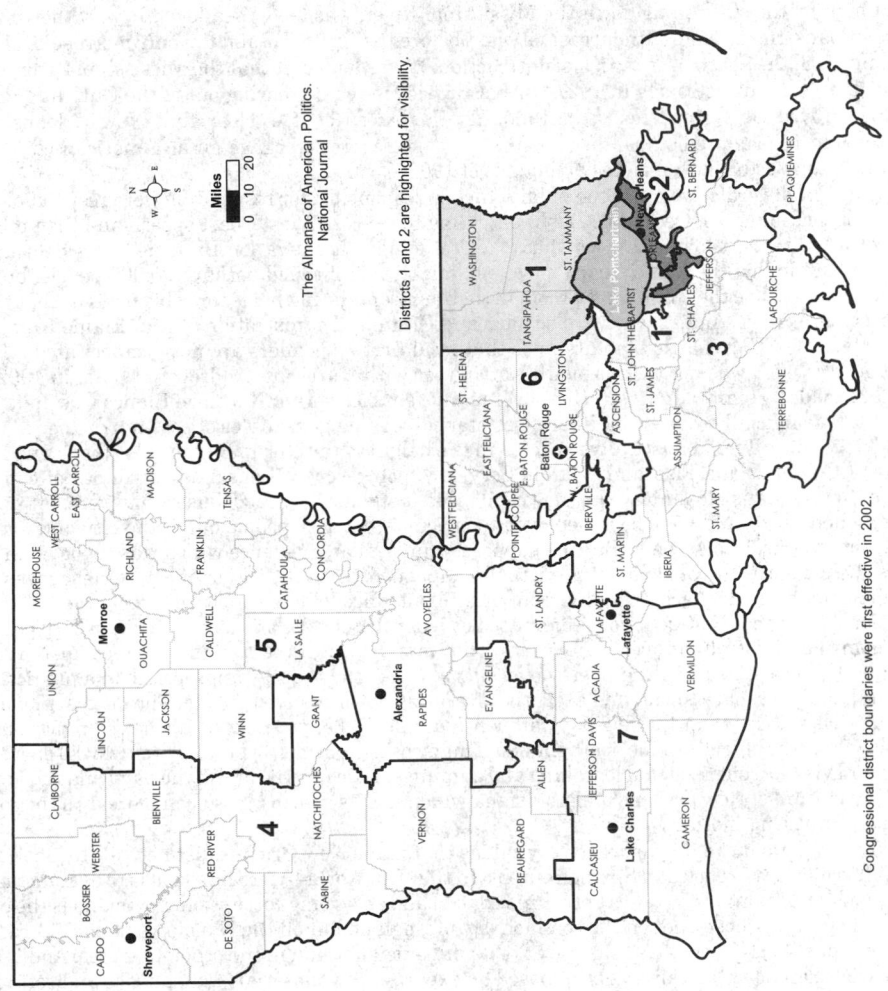

The Almanac of American Politics.
National Journal

Districts 1 and 2 are highlighted for visibility.

Congressional district boundaries were first effective in 2002.

17th Street Canal, constructed by one of several Louisiana levee boards, sprung a 200-foot hole through which much of the waters inundating 80% of New Orleans came. The Industrial Canal, along the picturesquely poverty-stricken Ninth Ward, had a similar break. The Mississippi River Gulf Outlet, built by the Army Corps of Engineers as a shipping channel though precious few ships ever chose to use it, funneled waters and winds into St. Bernard Parish east of the city and the lowlands of eastern New Orleans and devastated all in its wake. It had been known since New Orleans was founded by the French in 1718 that most of the land around here, beyond the two ridges piled high by the silt coming down the Mississippi River, was below sea level. It was known that New Orleans, the nation's fifth largest city just before the Civil War and the only metropolis of any magnitude in the South, was at risk of destruction. It was no secret that the Mississippi River often flooded, as it did disastrously in 1927, or that hurricanes came roaring out of the Gulf, as one did that destroyed Galveston, Texas, in 1900. Yet in retrospect it is clear that New Orleans was unprepared for the predictable disaster that wreaked more wreckage on an American city than anything since the San Francisco earthquake of 1906.

The initial verdict was that the public officials responsible for responding were responsible for the grim consequences. George W. Bush, unwilling to cancel a West Coast speech and then telling his FEMA Director Michael Brown that, "You're doing a heckuva job Brownie," was held up to ridicule. But in fact the Coast Guard moved in quickly and rescued perhaps 20,000 people; but no one knew it because they didn't have room in their helicopters and boats for cable news anchors and their camera crews. And, as Harvard scholar and Clinton administration official Elaine Kamarck has noted, the FEMA battle plan assumes that local first responders are not incapacitated by the emergency, which was not the case with Katrina (or with Hurricane Andrew in Miami in 1992): a mistake made by many administrations over many years. Governor Kathleen Blanco was undoubtedly tardy in officially requesting federal assistance, seeking guarantees of post-hurricane aid that could never have been realistically expected in the height of the storm. But she also dispatched the boats of the Louisiana Fish and Wildlife Service which rescued thousands, again out of camera range. New Orleans Mayor Ray Nagin was pilloried justly for the school buses that were left under water when they could have been deployed to evacuate helpless people out of the city and for not ordering an evacuation sooner. But the supposed murders and violence which was reported in the city's shelter in the Super Dome never actually happened. The inundation of New Orleans was the result not of the inadequacies of the current incumbent officeholders supposedly in charge but of the decisions made and the derelictions committed by federal and state and local officials of both parties and many administrations over many years. The New Orleans levee boards were incompetent and corrupt; the Army Corps of Engineers never had a long-term strategy appropriate to a predictable disaster, and its congressional and executive overlords never insisted on one. The destruction of so much of New Orleans in the few days after August 29, 2005, was the result not so much of the negligence of the officials in the spotlight but of many other officials, over many years, who operated out of full view, of congressional logrolling and administrative inertia, and of the particular civic and political culture of New Orleans and Louisiana which, for its charms, has been more dysfunctional than any other in America.

This is a product of history. The very things that made New Orleans distinctive—the look and feel it has had as a French and Spanish outpost in the New World—were linked also to dysfunctional traditions, traditions of *dirigiste* centralized control and easygoing corruption. Louisiana is the only state whose law is based not on the common law of England but on the Napoleonic Code of France; the concept of civil liberties has shallower roots in Louisiana than in the other 49 states. And it is a state whose economy has always been based on export of raw materials—sugar, rice and cotton in the 19th century, oil and gas in the 20th. Antebellum Louisiana's agricultural abundance generated the wealth which built grand plantation houses behind alleys of oaks running in from the Mississippi and made New Orleans the one significant city by the time of the Civil War. Then came oil, first discovered in 1901, at the dawn of the automobile age; the first offshore well, out of sight of land, came in 1947, at the start of the postwar boom. In 1921 Governor John Parker and a young Public Service Commission Chairman Huey Long got the idea of putting a severance tax on oil; in the 1970s Governor Edwin Edwards, a man similar in many ways to Long, changed it from a tax on amount of production to a tax on market value. Oil money came gushing into the Louisiana treasury and financed state government for six decades—and found its way into other pockets as well.

The most enduringly famous politician here, and by far the most talented, was Huey Long, who in less than a single term each as governor (1928-32) and senator (1932-35), left an imprint on the state's public life and imposed an organization to its politics that have faded into history only recently. Long's genius was not that he promised to tax the rich to help the poor—hundreds of idealists and demagogues in America have done that—but that, to an amazing extent, he actually delivered. He dominated the legislature so thoroughly that, as governor, he roamed the floors of both chambers at will, bringing to the podium bills he insisted be passed without changing a comma—and they were. He was ready to use bribery, intimidation and physical violence. He built a new skyscraper Capitol, a new Louisiana State University and more miles of roads than any state but rich New York and huge Texas. He also built a national following, and by 1935, he was planning to run for president on the platform of "Share the wealth, every man a king," when he was assassinated at age 42 in the hallway of the Capitol, where the bullet holes can still be seen in the marble walls.

For America, the Long threat may have moved Franklin D. Roosevelt to embrace the liberal programs—the Wagner Labor Act, social security, steeply graduated taxes—of the second New Deal. For Louisiana, Long delivered a political structure that revolved around him even after he was dead—and a class of political leaders who, lacking his talents, treated the state as Long's incompetent doctors had treated his fatal wound, leaving Louisiana without either a fully developed economy or a fully competent public sector. For 50 years, until Huey's son Senator Russell Long retired in 1986, Longs and Long proteges held high political office in Louisiana and elections were run along pro- and anti-Long lines. The Long experience has strengthened Louisiana's already strong predispositions—tolerance of corruption, disinterest in abstract reform and taste for colorful extremists regardless of their short-term means or long-term ends—in a way that helps explain the rise and fall of such unlikely politicians as the four-term Governor Edwin Edwards and the onetime Ku Klux Klan leader and state legislator David Duke, both of whom by 2003 were spending time in jail. It also helps to explain the state's lack of dynamism. It has been a state with low incomes and work force participation and low levels of education, with income disparities greater than almost anywhere else in the United States; New Orleans's rich, like many in Latin America, are notoriously unventuresome and tight-knit, determined to hold on to their wealth against the grasp of the impecunious and unlearned masses. This has made a huge difference over time. Metro New Orleans in 1940 had a population of 564,000; it was about the same size then as metro Houston (610,000) and metro Dallas (624,000). But in 2004, just before Katrina, metro Houston had 5.1 million people and metro Dallas 5.8 million, to New Orleans's 1.3 million.

The oil shocks of 1973 and 1979 did for Louisiana what they did for Saudi Arabia, Nigeria and Venezuela: they made it suddenly hugely richer. Louisiana incomes reached up to national levels and 500,000 new jobs were generated between 1972 and 1981. But oil prices plummeted in the 1980s, Louisiana's rig count dropped by two-thirds, the state lost 150,000 jobs and energy taxes fell from 41% of state revenues in 1982 to 9% in 1996. The state's economy has never regained much forward momentum. Gambling, legalized in 1991, produced less revenue than expected and nothing like the boom that some promised. People have been leaving the state: From 1980 until 2005 Louisiana's population increased only 7%, far less than any other Southern state, less than any state except two in the Great Plains and the industrial triangle of Ohio, Pennsylvania and West Virginia. Then, as evacuees left New Orleans, its population fell sharply, by 5% in mid-2006 according to Census Bureau estimates, by more according to others.

Louisiana has long had natural political divides. One is by religion: Catholic Cajun parishes (Louisiana has parishes rather than counties) cast about 30% of the state's vote, the New Orleans area casts around 25% or so, and about 45% are cast in Protestant parishes from Baton Rouge on north. White Protestants for years have wanted nothing to do with national Democrats, while Cajuns tend to mull it over. Another divide is by race: Blacks are overwhelmingly Democratic, whites split in seriously contested elections. A third divide is by income: Low- and high-income whites vote very differently and are much less influenced than voters in most other states by candidates' cultural values, marital status, lifestyles and the like. As a result, Louisiana politics since Huey P. Long's time has often been a struggle between reformist and conservative forces on one side and roguish populists on the other, a struggle waged in lavishly financed campaigns and with grandiloquent rhetoric.

For a quarter-century, the lead role was played by Edwin Edwards as the roguish populist, with a number of rivals as reformist conservatives. Edwards was elected governor in 1971 and 1975 and was not eligible to run in 1979. In 1983 he beat incumbent Republican David Treen; in 1987 he lost to Buddy Roemer, a Democratic congressman who later switched parties. For much of this third term, Edwards faced corruption charges, until he was acquitted by a jury in 1986. In 1991 he ran again, and this time an even odder character surfaced. David Duke was an active Nazi sympathizer up through 1989, but he also had a knack for speaking to mainstream political issues in attractive political language. In 1989 he was narrowly elected to the state legislature from a district in suburban Jefferson Parish as a nominal Republican—a victory that got enormous national publicity. Then in 1991, Duke ran for governor against Roemer and Edwards. Louisiana has a unique primary system, invented by Edwards, and now no longer applicable in races for senator and governor: candidates of all parties run in a single primary; any candidate who gets 50% is elected; otherwise, the top two finishers, regardless of party, have a runoff. Edwards received only 34% of the votes in that 1991 race, and Duke made the runoff by finishing second with 32%. All articulate opinion in Louisiana moved to Edwards's side, and Republicans from George H.W. Bush on down endorsed Edwards, who won 61%-39%.

In the years leading up to Katrina, Louisiana was not on a clear political course. In 2000 the state, after voting twice for Bill Clinton, voted 53%-45% for George W. Bush. In 2002 Democratic Senator Mary Landrieu, elected by 5,788 votes in 1996, failed to win a majority in the November primary and faced a runoff with Republican Suzanne Haik Terrell. Shrewdly Landrieu cast this as a choice between an independent who would fight for Louisiana interests and a Republican who would vote in lockstep with Bush; she won 52%-48%. In 2003, when Republican Governor Mike Foster was ineligible for a third term, Republican Bobby Jindal led in the October primary with 33% of the vote to 18% for Democratic Lieutenant Governor Kathleen Babineaux Blanco. In the November runoff Jindal's youth, Indian ancestry and policy wonkishness didn't set well with voters in northern parishes who vote heavily Republican for president, and Blanco, a Catholic Cajun, was elected 52%-48%. In the 2004 Senate race, left open by the retirement of Democrat John Breaux, the balance fell the other way. Democrats had two serious candidates running, Congressman Chris John and state Treasurer John Kennedy. There was just one serious Republican, suburban New Orleans Congressman David Vitter and, as George W. Bush was carrying the state 57%-42% over John Kerry, Vitter surprised the pundits by winning outright with 51% of the vote. Vitter, who jousted with almost every other legislator when he served in Baton Rouge, fits the mold of the Republican reformer; neither Landrieu nor Blanco fits the mold of rogue populist.

Katrina changed the political balance, but no one is sure by how much. Commentators speculated that the departure from New Orleans of perhaps 200,000 blacks would tilt the state to the Republicans and make it impossible for Democrats to win narrow victories like Landrieu's in 1996 and 2002 and Blanco's in 2003. Under-sea level black neighborhoods like New Orleans's Ninth Ward and East New Orleans were devastated, while the French Quarter and the Garden District, on higher land built up by the Mississippi over many years, were relatively unscathed. But the partisan effect may not be so one-sided. Comparison of turnout in the 2006 and 2002 U.S. House elections—the closest thing to commensurate races—shows the biggest percentage turnout decline, 72%, came in devastated St. Bernard Parish, which votes Republican. Turnout in suburban Jefferson Parish, also Republican, declined 18%. The combined turnout decline in the two parishes was (rounded off) 38,000 votes. Turnout declined 42% in Orleans Parish (coterminous with the city of New Orleans), or by 54,000 votes. And not all those were black Democrats. The 17th Street canal breach flooded adjacent Lakeview, relatively high-income and heavily white, the only part of the city that voted for George W. Bush. Evacuees may continue to vote in Louisiana in 2007 and 2008. Secretary of State Al Ater set up absentee polling stations around the state to increase voter turnout, while a state Senate bill that would have set up out-of-state voting locations never made it out of committee. Evacuees were reached by mail with absentee ballots, which accounted for 22% of the May 2006 New Orleans mayoral runoff. It is possible that white evacuees have been more assiduous about voting, but not certain; Ray Nagin, supported by most blacks and opposed by most whites, managed to get reelected over Lieutenant Governor Mitch Landrieu in May 2006.

These calculations may not make much difference when Louisiana elects a governor in 2007. Kathleen Blanco, widely criticized for her handling of Katrina, announced in March 2007 she wouldn't run for a second term. Bobby Jindal, elected congressmen to succeed Vitter in 2004 and 2006, announced early on that he was running. Polls showed him far ahead of Blanco and also ahead of former Senator John Breaux, his onetime boss. Breaux showed some interest in the race, but after leaving the Senate he had registered to vote in Maryland, and Jindal made it clear that he would challenge his eligibility under the Louisiana law requiring five years of residence in the state. Louisiana judges tend to be easy going about these things but Breaux, noting that a court challenge could take up most of the campaign, announced in April 2007 he would not run. New Orleans Mayor Ray Nagin flirted with a bid up until the September filing deadline but chose not to run either. Polls showed Republican frontrunner Bobby Jindal running much better in northern Louisiana than he had in 2003.

The People		Race/Ethnic Origin			Military veterans: 392,486 (12.1%)	
Pop. 2006 (est):	4,287,768	2,794,391	62.5%	White	WWII: 19.5%	Korea: 12.7%
Pop. 2000:	4,468,976	1,443,390	32.3%	Black	Vietnam: 32.2%	Gulf War: 12.4%
Pop. 1990:	4,219,973	54,256	1.2%	Asian	**Most populous cities (2006):**	
Change 1990-2000:	Up 5.9%	24,129	0.5%	Native Am.	1. Baton Rouge	229,553
% of U.S. total:	1.6%	1,076	0.0%	Hawaiian	2. New Orleans	223,388
Pop. rank:	22nd of 50	39,260	0.9%	Two+ races	3. Shreveport	200,199
Area size:	51,840 sq. mi.	4,736	0.1%	Other	4. Lafayette	114,214
State Native:	79.4%	107,738	2.4%	Hisp. Origin	5. Lake Charles	70,224
Non-citizen:	1.3%	**Ancestry**				
Language		French: 10.2%		USA: 8.4%	Urban population: 72.7%	
English: 85.9%	Other Eur.: 9.3%	German: 5.9%		Irish: 5.9%	Rural population: 27.3%	
Spanish: 3.5%		English: 4.4%				

Education		Work Sector		Legislature	
H.S. Grad:	74.8%	Private: 76.2%	Govt: 17.4%	Senate	24 D 15 R
College Grad:	18.7%	Self: 6.1%	Family: 0.3%	House	63 D 41 R 1 I
Industry		Unemployment: 7.3%		Legislative Term Limits: Yes	
Agri: 4.2%	Con: 7.9%	**Household Income**		**Registered Voters**	
Fin: 5.7%	Info: 2.0%	<15k: 24.1%	15-35k: 28.5%	D: 1,554,877	(53.8%)
Mfg: 15.5%	Prof: 29.3%	35-50k: 15.7%	50-100k: 24.2%	R: 708,752	(24.5%)
Public: 5.8%	Trade: 15.4%	100-150k: 4.8%	>150k: 2.6%	O: 627,262	(21.7%)
Other: 14.3%		Median: $32,566			
Occupation		Poverty status: 19.6%			
Blue collar: 25.8%	White collar: 56.6%	**Home Value**			
Gray collar: 17.5%		<50k: 28.3%	50-100k: 38.5%	100-200k: 25.4%	200-300k: 5.0%
		300-500k: 2.0%	>500k: 0.9%	Median: $77,500	

Presidential politics   Louisiana's presidential politics is racially polarized. In 2004 the state voted 57%-42% for Bush; whites voted 75%-24% for him and blacks voted 90%-9% for John Kerry. Louisiana's black percentage is the second highest in the country, after Mississippi's, and until Katrina was rising. Katrina obviously changed the racial balance, with blacks disproportionately leaving the state, at least temporarily, and political experts predicted that the political balance would be tilted toward Republicans. That's probably right, but the effect may be overstated. Bill Clinton carried Louisiana in 1992 and 1996, and George W. Bush's success here may have owed something to the contrast between him and his opponents on cultural issues like abortion—Louisiana is one state with a solid anti-abortion majority. A Republican nominee with a more nuanced position on that issue might not be able to count on the huge rural majorities Bush won (and which Bobby Jindal failed to win in the 2003 race for governor) and so it may be unwise to count Louisiana as indisputably Republican in 2008.

2004 Presidential Vote		
Bush (R)	1,102,169	(57%)
Kerry (D)	820,299	(42%)
Nader (BL)	7,032	(0%)
Other	13,606	(1%)

2004 Democratic Presidential Primary		
Kerry (D)	112,639	(70%)
Edwards (D)	26,074	(16%)
Dean (D)	7,948	(5%)
Clark (D)	7,091	(4%)
McGaughey (D)	3,161	(2%)
Other	4,740	(3%)

2000 Presidential Vote		
Bush (R)	927,871	(53%)
Gore (D)	792,344	(45%)
Nader (Green)	20,473	(1%)
Other	24,968	(1%)

Louisiana has never played a significant role in presidential primaries and caucuses, with one odd exception. That was in 1996, when Republican allies of Phil Gramm set up a pre-Iowa-and-New Hampshire February 6 caucus. The aim was to jump-start Gramm's campaign; instead the caucuses killed it. Only 20,000 Republicans showed up at 42 voting sites voted (as compared to 100,000 at 2,000 sites in Iowa), and Pat Buchanan won more votes than Gramm and took 13 of the 21 delegates. Gramm's campaign in Iowa faltered, and he left the race before the vote in New Hampshire.

In December 1999, Governor Mike Foster got the state central committee to cancel the caucus and hold a March primary. He cited the low turnout in 1996 and the fact that only Orrin Hatch, Gary

Bauer and Alan Keyes were competing in Louisiana. George W. Bush, Foster's candidate, won in March. In 2004 the primary was held March 9, when both party's nominations had already been clinched. In 2008 Louisiana is scheduled to vote on February 9. Early endorsements came on the Republican side: Congressmen Jim McCrery and Rodney Alexander endorsed Mitt Romney; Senator David Vitter and Congressman Charles Boustany endorsed Rudolph Giuliani.

Congressional districting   Louisiana redistricted its congressional districts three times in the 1990s. The first two plans created two black-majority districts, one of them in each case highly irregular in shape; they were declared unconstitutional in federal court in December 1993 and July 1994. The first plan was used in the 1992 elections, the second in 1994. In January 1996 a federal court came up with a plan, adopted by the legislature, that cut through few parish boundaries and had much more regular lines, and had only one black-majority district, centered in New Orleans. It was upheld by the Supreme Court in June 1996.

110th Congress Lineup
5 R   2 D
109th Congress Lineup
5 R   2 D

In August 2001 six of the seven House incumbents (all except John Cooksey, who was running for the Senate) submitted their own plan to the legislature. Governor Mike Foster called a special session for redistricting in October, and the legislators made minor tweaks in the House incumbents' plan. It was opposed by the Black Legislative Caucus, which drew up a plan with a second black-majority district stretching from Lafayette and Baton Rouge along the Mississippi River to the Arkansas border. But that was rejected by solid margins. Foster signed the new plan in October; it certainly seemed likely to be upheld by the courts, since the Supreme Court had already approved an almost identical plan. It was submitted to the Justice Department in January 2002 and approved in April. Unexpectedly, the plan turned out to have an effect on the results. In the December 2002 runoff, Democrat Rodney Alexander won an upset victory for Cooksey's old seat. His margin of victory came from heavily black areas added to the district. But he switched to the Republican party in August 2004. In 2005 some Democrats urged the Democratic legislature to redistrict again, as Republicans in Texas had in 2003, to help their party gain a seat or two; but Democratic Governor Kathleen Babineaux Blanco seemed uninterested.

Louisiana's big population loss after Hurricane Katrina made it clear that the state would lose one House seat after the 2010 Census; that might have happened anyway, given the state's sluggish pre-Katrina growth. Demographically, the 2d District centered in New Orleans suffered the greatest population loss by far. But Voting Rights Act jurisprudence forbids the elimination of the state's one black-majority district and practically commands the 2011-12 legislature to create a black majority seat, perhaps by connecting part of New Orleans with part of Baton Rouge through a corridor running up the Mississippi River. That would leave a heavily Republican suburban New Orleans seat and four more districts in territory currently represented by four Republicans and one Democrat.

Governor

Kathleen Babineaux Blanco (D)

Elected 2003, term expires Jan. 2008, 1st term; b. Dec. 15, 1942, Coteau; home, Lafayette; U. of LA at Lafayette, B.A. 1964; Catholic; married (Raymond).

Elected Office: LA House of Reps., 1984-88; Public Service Comm., 1988-1995; Lt. Gov., 1996-2003.

Professional Career: H.S. teacher, 1964-65; District Mgr., US Census Bureau, 1979-80. Political Consultant, 1981-84.

Office: Office of the Governor, P.O. Box 94004, Baton Rouge, 70804, 225-342-0991; Fax: 225-342-7099; Web site: gov.state.la.us.

Election Results

2003 runoff	Kathleen Babineaux Blanco (D)	731,358	(52%)
	Bobby Jindal (R)	676,484	(48%)
2003 primary	Bobby Jindal (R)	443,389	(33%)
	Kathleen Babineaux Blanco (D)	250,136	(18%)
	Richard Ieyoub (D)	223,513	(16%)
	Claude Leach (R)	187,872	(14%)
	Randy Ewing (D)	123,936	(9%)
	Hunt Downer (R)	84,718	(6%)
	Other	48,960	(4%)
1999 primary	Mike Foster (R)	805,203	(62%)
	William Jefferson (D)	382,445	(30%)
	Other	107,557	(8%)

Kathleen Babineaux Blanco, a Democrat, was elected governor of Louisiana in November 2003. She was born in the Cajun village of Coteau, in the sugar cane-producing region south of Lafayette. At her inauguration, she took the oath of office in English and French. Her father was an Electrolux vacuum salesman and ran a carpet-cleaning business. The family later moved south to New Iberia; they loaded their three-bedroom house onto a flatbed truck and took it with them. Blanco graduated from the University of Louisiana at Lafayette, taught high school in southwest Louisiana, got married and raised six children. With her husband, she ran a market research and political polling business. In 1971, together they managed then-state Senator J. Bennett Johnson's campaign for governor in the Acadiana region, no picnic in an election where Congressman Edwin Edwards was seeking to become the state's first Cajun governor. Edwards narrowly defeated Johnston in the December runoff.

Blanco began her own political career in 1984 with an upset victory in an open state House race; outspent by a wealthy opponent, this was the first in a series of low budget, winning campaigns. In 1988, she was elected to the Public Service Commission, where she became the first woman to serve as a commissioner; she chaired the commission, which regulates utilities and phone companies, in 1993 and 1994. In 1991, she entered the race for governor against incumbent Buddy Roemer, in a contest that also featured former Governor Edwards and former Ku Klux Klansman David Duke; she withdrew after failing to raise enough money to compete.

In 1995, Blanco won the first of two terms as lieutenant governor. The low-profile position has little responsibility but it offered one role that turned out to be consequential. As the chief of the state Department of Culture, Recreation and Tourism, Blanco had a platform that enabled her to travel to all 64 parishes to promote the state and, of course, herself.

Blanco joined in May 2003 what was already a very large field to succeed term-limited Republican Governor Mike Foster. In Louisiana, candidates of all parties compete in the October primary and then, if no one gets 50% of the vote, the top two finishers regardless of party compete in the November runoff. Blanco had two advantages that made her candidacy stand out in the primary—she was the only woman in the race and the only candidate from Acadiana. Her Democratic opponents included Attorney General Richard Ieyoub, former Congressman Buddy Leach, former state Senate President Randy Ewing; Republican candidates included state Senator Hunt Downer and Bobby Jindal, appointed by Foster at 24 as president of the Department of Health and Hospitals and later as head of the Louisiana state university system, and appointed by George W. Bush as HHS Assistant Secretary.

Blanco said she wanted to move beyond "the tired old politics of Louisiana" and stressed health care and education themes. She called for investing in pre-kindergarten programs for all 4-year-olds, laptops for 7th graders and increased teacher salaries. She opposed a processing tax on oil and gas and said her experience promoting Louisiana gave her greater economic development expertise than her opponents. For much of the primary campaign, Blanco remained atop the polls but insiders dismissed her candidacy, claiming she was too nice to win, lacked key interest group support or worse, that she was a lightweight. But in the October primary she finished second with 18% to Jindal's 33%, and ahead of Ieyoub, who had 16%, and Leach, who had 14%.

In the runoff against Jindal, Blanco focused on his youth, saying he was too immature to be governor. "The ship of state does not come with training wheels," she said. She promised to hold an emergency health care policy summit, chaired by Senator John Breaux and said she would not raise taxes unless education and health care spending was deeply threatened. Jindal signed a pledge not to raise taxes at all; he highlighted this as a key difference. Jindal often mentioned his connections to the Bush administration; Blanco ran radio ads that said the administration's negotiations in the

Central American Free Trade Agreement would lead to lower tariffs on imported sugar, a volatile issue in sugar-producing Louisiana. Both candidates opposed abortion. In the final debate with Jindal, she was asked to name the "defining moment" in her life; she gave an emotional response, recalling the death of her 19-year-old son in an industrial accident in 1997.

She won 52%-48% to become the state's first female governor. Jindal carried the New Orleans, Baton Rouge, Shreveport and Monroe metro areas and won by wide margins in the fastest-growing parts of the state: St. Tammany Parish outside New Orleans, Livingston and Ascension Parishes outside Baton Rouge, Bossier Parish outside Shreveport. But Blanco carried her home area, the Cajun country, by a wide margin, and Jindal carried only one of the northern parishes which most Republicans have been carrying in other statewide races.

Her first year in office was cautious and did not feature an ambitious legislative agenda. After that, she focused on health care, economic development and education. In 2005, the centerpiece of her legislative agenda, a plan to increase cigarette taxes, was rejected but she managed to win passage of a tax on private and community hospitals that was expected to generate $300 million for health care. Then, on August 29, 2005, Hurricane Katrina struck New Orleans and resulted in flooding which devastated most of the city and sent hundreds of thousands of evacuees to shelter on higher ground. The hurricane wreaked more wreckage on an American city than anything since the San Francisco earthquake of 1906; large swaths of Louisiana outside New Orleans were also destroyed. In the days and weeks afterwards, her performance was uneven. Blanco was described by *Time* magazine as "dazed and unsteady" and questions were raised about her preparation efforts as well as her timing in officially requesting federal assistance. Bickering between Blanco and the Bush administration reflected poorly on both; when the president visited the state for a second time in three days in early September, Blanco learned of his plans through a reporter. The Bush administration had requested federalizing Louisiana law enforcement officials to clarify the lines of authority and the command structure among the various responding local, state and federal agencies. Blanco refused to relinquish control, stating that she needed the flexibility to operate the Louisiana National Guard. The next day she named former Clinton administration FEMA Director James Lee Witt to oversee relief efforts. Some, including Blanco, saw sexism in the widespread criticism of her leadership and her displays of emotion. She was frustrated by frequent comparisons to former New York City Mayor Rudy Giuliani and his response to the events of 9/11. "I'm not a guy," Blanco told *The New York Times* in December. "I can't be Rudy, whatever that is."

On September 14, one day after President Bush accepted some blame for the ineffective governmental response, Blanco told legislators that "there were failures at every level of government" and that "as your governor, I take full responsibility." Yet her position did not improve. Another storm, Hurricane Rita, slammed into southwestern Louisiana on September 24. In November, *Time* named her one of the worst governors in the nation. That same month, in a special legislative session, she alienated her allies in the Legislative Black Caucus with deep budget cuts and tax breaks for businesses; they filed a lawsuit charging that the budget cuts were unconstitutional because she did not consult with the legislature. A November poll by Southern Media and Opinion Research revealed that just 19% of Louisiana voters would definitely vote to reelect Blanco.

Blanco's poll ratings improved slightly over the next year but she entered 2007 lagging in polls behind Bobby Jindal, who was elected to Congress a year after losing to Blanco in the 2003 governor's race. In January, in an email to supporters, Jindal confirmed that he would run for governor. Blanco said she would seek reelection and stepped up her criticism of the Bush administration. After former FEMA Director Michael Brown in January 2007 accused the White House of deliberately trying to undermine Blanco in the days after Katrina, she asked Congress to create a commission to investigate whether the Republican party played politics in the federal response to Hurricanes Katrina and Rita. She claimed Louisiana was being shortchanged in federal hurricane relief funding allocations. "For 18 months, the Washington Republicans have consistently punished and discriminated against our people, all for partisan political purposes," she said.

Despite this potent message and $3 million in campaign cash, Blanco continued to trail Jindal by a wide margin in polls. Some Democrats wanted her to step aside, having concluded she was too damaged to win a campaign that essentially would be a referendum on her performance. Certainly the state's new political landscape did not work in her favor. Blanco had won by 55,000 votes in 2003 with strong support in New Orleans, but after Katrina the most hurricane-impacted counties had hemorrhaged 220,000 people, according to census estimates, most of them from New Orleans and many of them African-Americans who helped form Blanco's base. In early March, there were signals that popular former Democratic Senator John Breaux was interested in running, though only if Blanco stepped aside. The state Republican party responded by running ads claiming Breaux, who was working as a lobbyist, was ineligible to run because he had lived outside the state for more than five years and was registered to vote in Maryland. On March 14, Blanco said she was running whether or not Breaux entered the race. But less than a week later, amid news of complications and delays in her Road Home hurricane recovery program, Blanco announced she had decided against running for a second term. By then she had already drawn one prominent Democratic challenger in the October 20th open primary, Public Service Commissioner Foster Campbell of north Louisiana.

On the Republican side, Jindal had the support of the state party establishment but state Senator Walter Boasso of St. Bernard Parish was also running, joined by free-spending business-man John Georges of Jefferson Parish. The dynamics of the race changed again in April when Breaux announced he would not run after the Democratic state attorney general declined to issue a legal opinion as to whether Breaux met the state's citizenship requirement; Breaux noted that a court challenge could take up most of the campaign. Not long afterwards, Boasso switched parties to run as a Democrat, with a plan to run to the right of Campbell; Georges also switched parties and ran as an independent. Democratic New Orleans Mayor Ray Nagin flirted with a bid and his intentions were not known until after the September filing deadline; he chose not to run. Boasso ran ads against Jindal, hoping to take advantage of George W. Bush's low approval ratings and keep Jindal below the 50%-plus-one threshold necessary to win the October primary outright and avoid a November 17 runoff. "Some things just go together," said Boasso in one ad. "Like red beans and rice. Gumbo and Tabasco. And, unfortunately for Louisiana, George W. Bush and Bobby Jindal."

Senior Senator

Mary Landrieu (D)

Elected 1996, seat up 2008, 2d term; b. Nov. 23, 1955, Arlington, VA; home, New Orleans; LA St. U., B.A. 1977; Catholic; married (Frank Snellings).

Elected Office: LA House of Reps., 1979-88; LA Treasurer, 1987-96.

DC Office: 724 HSOB, 20510, 202-224-5824; Fax: 202-224-9735; Web site: landrieu.senate.gov.

State Offices: Baton Rouge, 225-389-0395; Lake Charles, 337-436-6650; New Orleans, 504-589-2427; Shreveport, 318-676-3085.

Committees: *Appropriations* (12th of 15 D): Legislative Branch (Chmn.); Military Construction, Veterans Affairs & Related Agencies; Financial Services & General Government; Labor, Health and Human Services, Education & Related Agencies; Energy & Water Development; Homeland Security; State, Foreign Opera-tions & Related Programs. *Energy & Natural Resources* (6th of 12 D): National Parks; Public Lands & Forests; Energy. *Homeland Security & Governmental Affairs* (6th of 9 D): Disaster Recovery (Chmn.); State, Local & Private Sector Preparedness & Integration; Oversight of Government Management, the Federal Workforce & the District of Columbia. *Small Business & Entrepreneurship* (5th of 10 D).

Group Ratings

	ADA	ACLU	AFS	LCV	ITIC	NTU	COC	ACU	CFG	FRC
2006	65	58	75	43	50	19	75	24	11	37
2005	95	—	71	50	—	23	76	44	13	—

National Journal Ratings

	2005 LIB	—	2005 CONS		2006 LIB	—	2006 CONS
Economic	56%	—	43%		56%	—	43%
Social	57%	—	42%		60%	—	39%
Foreign	60%	—	38%		55%	—	44%

Key Votes of the 109th Congress

1. Bar ANWR Drilling	N	5. Confirm Samuel Alito	N	9. Limit Interstate Abortion	Y
2. FY06 Spending Curb	N	6. Path to Citizenship	Y	10. CAFTA	N
3. Estate Tax Repeal	N	7. Bar Same Sex Marriage	N	11. Urge Iraq Withdrawal	N
4. Raise Minimum Wage	Y	8. Stem Cell Research $	Y	12. Provide Detainee Rights	Y

Election Results

2002 runoff	Mary Landrieu (D)	638,654	(52%)	($7,384,554)
	Suzanne Haik Terrell (R)	596,642	(48%)	($2,760,276)
2002 primary	Mary Landrieu (D)	573,347	(46%)	
	Suzanne Haik Terrell (R)	339,506	(27%)	
	John Cooksey (R)	171,752	(14%)	
	Tony Perkins (R)	119,776	(10%)	
	Other	41,952	(3%)	
1996 runoff	Mary Landrieu (D)	852,945	(50%)	($2,504,815)
	Woody Jenkins (R)	847,157	(50%)	($1,878,242)

Mary Landrieu, a Democrat, was elected to the Senate in 1996 and reelected in 2002. Landrieu grew up in New Orleans, the oldest of nine children of Moon Landrieu (all with names starting with M), mayor of New Orleans in the 1970s. Her brother is Mitch Landrieu, Louisiana's lieutenant governor, who was defeated by incumbent Ray Nagin in the 2006 New Orleans mayor's race. She was educated at Ursuline Academy and LSU and in 1979, at 23, became the youngest woman ever elected to the Louisiana state legislature, where she was sometimes the object of undue ridicule. In 1987 she was elected state treasurer; she was a sharp critic of Governor Edwin Edwards. In 1995 she ran for governor, and in the September primary finished third, just 1% and 8,983 votes behind second-place finisher Congressman Cleo Fields. She immediately started running for the Senate seat held by Bennett Johnston, who was retiring 24 years after he was elected to the Senate.

With a well-known name and a moderate platform—for a balanced budget amendment and capital gains tax cut, promising to make education a top priority—Landrieu shared a lead in the polls with Attorney General Richard Ieyoub, also a Democrat. Woody Jenkins, a 25-year state legislator and strong abortion opponent, who had run twice unsuccessfully for the Senate as a Democrat, claimed the Republican endorsement; he surged in the polls, and led the September primary with 26%, to 22% for Landrieu and 20% for Ieyoub; David Duke got 12%.

At this point Jenkins looked like the favorite; Republican candidates had won 55% of the total votes and Democrats only 44%. But he had little money left, and Landrieu, who ultimately outspent him, ran ads attacking him as an extremist. The result was an exceedingly close election. The official results showed Landrieu ahead by 5,788 votes, 50.2%-49.8%. Jenkins filed a lawsuit claiming vote fraud, but withdrew it, and submitted his case to the Senate; in October 1997, the Senate Rules Committee voted unanimously to end the inquiry. While concluding that "isolated instances" of voter fraud did occur, Rules Chairman John Warner said there was no evidence to prove that there was a "widespread effort to illegally affect the outcome of this election," or that Landrieu had any involvement in the violation of election laws.

In the Senate, Landrieu's voting record has been among the more conservative Democrats. Her first bill was for a $5 million block grant for adoption services; her two children are adopted. She backs adoption tax credits and wants higher breaks for those who adopt special needs or foster children. She was the lead co-sponsor of the law providing for speedy citizenship for foreign-born children adopted by U.S. citizens; when it went into effect it created the largest number of new U.S. citizens ever on a single day. Landrieu was the only Democrat who co-sponsored Sam Brownback's bills to prohibit human cloning for reproduction or research. In 2001, she won a seat on the Appropriations Committee.

All the while she was running hard for reelection in 2002. She was an obvious Republican target, because of the closeness of her margin in 1996 and because George W. Bush carried Louisiana in 2000. In early 2001 the only active Republican candidate was 5th District Congressman John Cooksey, a north Louisiana ophthalmologist. But on September 18, 2001, a week after September 11, in a radio interview in Louisiana, he said, "If I see someone comes in that's got a diaper on his head and a fan belt wrapped around the diaper on his head, the guy needs to be pulled over." Cooksey spent $200,000 on radio ads defending his comments.

Cooksey's candidacy was undone by one word, "diaper." It was obvious that the Bush White House did not want to have the president portrayed as supporting a candidate whose remark would be an embarrassment to the United States in the Middle East. For such a candidate no flow of Republican money and no presidential visits would be forthcoming. The National Republican Senatorial Committee, headed by Bill Frist, started encouraging other Republicans to run. In May 2002 state Representative Tony Perkins, a sponsor of a school prayer bill, met with Frist and decided to run. Perkins telegraphed Frist's strategy. "Republicans' best shot is to get a multiple field of candidates in this race. If we can get Landrieu in a runoff, it will be like the Coverdell runoff [in

Georgia] in 1992. This is our seat." Perkins also encouraged Elections Commissioner Suzanne Haik Terrell to run. "I would like to see Suzie Terrell in the race because she would draw votes from Mary in New Orleans." Terrell announced on July 9.

In July the NRSC started running what would eventually be $2 million of TV ads against Landrieu. "There's just something about Mary and higher taxes," said one. "Landrieu voted in favor of higher taxes over 120 times." Playing defense, Landrieu ran ads saying she supported Bush 74% of the time and that only two Democrats, Georgia's Zell Miller and Louisiana's John Breaux, had voted more often with Bush. At the end of August Frist announced that the NRSC would support Terrell and spend the allowed $464,000 on her behalf. His strategy was obviously to hold Landrieu below 50% in November, and he evidently calculated, as Perkins had, that Terrell, a New Orleans Catholic, was better positioned than the two north Louisiana Protestants to take votes away from Landrieu in the New Orleans area. Other Republicans were angry. Governor Mike Foster endorsed Cooksey. In mid-October Landrieu started running anti-Terrell ads, charging that taxes and spending went up in New Orleans when she was on the council. Perkins ran ads attacking Landrieu for living in a "Washington mansion"; she said she wanted to be close to her small children. The NRSC ran ads saying that Landrieu's voting record was similar to Hillary Rodham Clinton's. On November 5, as Republicans were gaining a majority in the Senate, Landrieu failed to clinch a victory. She won 46% of the vote, to 27% for Terrell, 14% for Cooksey and 10% for Perkins. The three Republicans together led Landrieu 51%-46%.

In the runoff, there was discontent on the Democratic side among black leaders about Landrieu's ads proclaiming her 74% support of Bush. In debates the two candidates tangled about abortion. In one case, on leaving the TV studio, Landrieu said to Terrell, "This is your last campaign." Terrell, taken aback, said "She threatened me." The candidates continued to argue about tax cuts, personnel rules for the Department of Homeland Security and privatizing government jobs. Then a Democratic opposition researcher made a propitious find—an article in the Mexican center-left newspaper *Reforma* reporting that the Bush administration had agreed with the Mexican government to double the amount of sugar that could be imported from Mexico. The Office of Special Trade Representative and the State Department denied that any such agreement had been made. But Landrieu trumpeted the claim in ads and promised to do everything she could to stop any such agreement. Sugar is a heavily protected crop, with U.S. prices kept at levels far above the world price; Louisiana is the prime cane sugar producing state. So it was a fine issue for Landrieu to document her claim that Terrell would be a "rubber stamp" for Bush, even though Terrell said she opposed any such deal as well. It turned out the *Reforma* story was wrong; Landrieu met with trade and State Department officials in January 2003 and reported that there was no deal. But it may have changed enough votes to give Landrieu her 52%-48% victory.

In her second term Landrieu from time to time made waves. As ranking Democrat on the District of Columbia Appropriations Subcommittee, she insisted on restrictions on D.C. school vouchers. Voucher supporters ran an ad in the New Orleans newspaper saying, "My mom wants you to know that Sen. Mary Landrieu doesn't want me to go to the same school where her children go." She has supported oil drilling in the Arctic National Wildlife Refuge and, when it passed in March 2005, was one of three Democrats voting for it (the others were the two senators from Hawaii). In 2004 she passed an amendment eliminating the reduction in veterans' widows pensions when they became eligible for Social Security. She supported an amendment to the bill criminalizing the killing of unborn children which would have funded domestic violence programs; she had a meeting with backers of the bill which she described as "contentious." In May 2004 she stalled the flood insurance bill because she opposed higher premiums for those making repetitive claims. In October 2004 she filibustered the corporate tax bill for three days in support of an amendment to give tax credits to employers who make up lost pay for Reservists and Guards troops called to active duty; she accepted a compromise limiting the tax credit to companies with 50 or fewer workers. In 2004 and 2005 she and George Allen, both representing Confederate states, sponsored a resolution apologizing for the Senate's refusal, from the 1890s to the 1940s, to pass anti-lynching legislation.

Landrieu voted for the Iraq war resolution in October 2002. But in October 2003 she wanted the Iraq reconstruction money in the supplemental appropriation to be a loan, not a grant. She made her case to George W. Bush at the White House. "He looked at me and said, 'It's not negotiable, and I don't want to debate it.'" In the 2004 campaign she endorsed neither of the two well-known Democrats running for John Breaux's seat, but campaigned extensively around the state against Republican David Vitter. "Don't send me a puppet to work with, send me a partner," she said over and over. On election night she had an abrupt conversation with Vitter, who against expectations won the seat with 51% of the vote; she told him the second-place finisher, Democrat Chris John, was not conceding and he evidently hung up. They pledged later to work together on Louisiana issues, but already had 2 public disputes in the months after his election.

Hurricane Katrina, sadly, was an event that forced the two senators to work together and put the outspoken Landrieu in the national spotlight as advocate for her pained state. "If my heart is a little heavy today, it's because I've seen more in the last two weeks than I've seen in my entire life," she said on her return to the Senate. Three of her siblings lost their homes to Katrina; her tension was evident. In response to the post-Katrina comment by George W. Bush that nobody "anticipated the breach of the levees," she said, "Everybody anticipated the breach of the levees, Mr. President." In early September, Landrieu said on national television that if anyone, including Bush, criticized the state and local government response to Katrina, "I might likely have to punch him. Literally." Six weeks after the catastrophe, she objected that Louisiana was being treated less sympathetically on the forgiveness of debts to struggling communities than had other states during emergencies; on the Senate floor, Vitter disagreed with her protest. "She needs to learn a little statesmanship. She's been way too hotheaded," local political analyst Elliott Stonecipher told the Baton Rouge *Advocate*. In April 2006, she said that she would block every presidential nomination until Bush agreed to $6 billion for repair of Louisiana levees. When the Senate approved that money and more a few weeks later, Landrieu backed off her general threat but promised to block nominees at the Energy and Interior Departments until there was agreement on using royalties from offshore oil and gas production to pay for coastal restoration and additional hurricane protection. She played a major role when that bill finally was enacted in December 2006. "It is the cornerstone that has been laid down to protect and rebuild the Gulf Coast," she said.

In 2007, the Democratic takeover of the Senate positioned Landrieu for a more influential role. On the Homeland Security Committee, she became chairman of the new Disaster Recovery Subcommittee, with plans to find ways to avoid the mistakes that were made in response to Katrina. She became co-chair with Olympia Snowe of the new bipartisan Common Ground Coalition. At home, she was expected to face another tough reelection campaign in 2008, with the prospect of a considerably smaller Democratic voting base in New Orleans. The NRSC viewed her as perhaps its top target, though local Republicans suggested that they might not agree on a challenger until after the November 2007 election for governor. Congressman Richard Baker declined to run; Secretary of State Jay Dardenne and Treasurer John Kennedy were mentioned as possible challengers. In August 2007, Kennedy switched parties and became a Republican, a move widely seen as a sign he intended to run against Landrieu.

Junior Senator

David Vitter (R)

Elected 2004, seat up 2010, 1st term; b. May 3, 1961, New Orleans; home, Metairie; Harvard U., A.B. 1983, Rhodes Scholar, Oxford U., B.A. 1985, Tulane Law Schl., J.D. 1988; Catholic; married (Wendy).

Elected Office: LA House of Reps., 1991-99; U.S. House of Reps., 1999-2004.

Professional Career: Practicing atty., 1988-99; Adjunct Law Prof., Tulane U. & Loyola U., 1995-98.

DC Office: 516 HSOB, 20510, 202-224-4623; Fax: 202-228-5061; Web site: vitter.senate.gov.

State Offices: Alexandria, 318-448-0169; Baton Rouge, 225-383-0331; Lafayette, 337-262-6898; Lake Charles, 337-436-0453; Metairie, 504-589-2753; Monroe, 318-325-8120; Shreveport, 318-861-0437.

Committees: *Aging (Special)* (8th of 10 R). *Commerce, Science & Transportation* (10th of 11 R): Oceans, Atmosphere, Fisheries & Coast Guard; Consumer Affairs, Insurance & Automotive Safety; Surface Transportation & Merchant Marine Infrastructure, Safety & Security; Aviation Operations, Safety & Security. *Environment & Public Works* (5th of 9 R): Transportation Safety, Infrastructure Security & Water Quality (RMM); Superfund & Environmental Health; Transportation & Infrastructure. *Foreign Relations* (10th of 10 R): International Operations & Organizations, Democracy & Human Rights (RMM); African Affairs; East Asian & Pacific Affairs. *Small Business & Entrepreneurship* (4th of 9 R).

Group Ratings

	ADA	ACLU	AFS	LCV	ITIC	NTU	COC	ACU	CFG	FRC
2006	0	17	0	0	50	77	92	92	77	100
2005	15	—	0	10	—	70	83	96	76	—

National Journal Ratings

	2005 LIB	—	2005 CONS		2006 LIB	—	2006 CONS
Economic	24%	—	75%		25%	—	72%
Social	23%	—	64%		0%	—	82%
Foreign	36%	—	61%		8%	—	85%

Key Votes of the 109th Congress

1. Bar ANWR Drilling	N	5. Confirm Samuel Alito	Y	9. Limit Interstate Abortion Y
2. FY06 Spending Curb	Y	6. Path to Citizenship	N	10. CAFTA N
3. Estate Tax Repeal	Y	7. Bar Same Sex Marriage	Y	11. Urge Iraq Withdrawal N
4. Raise Minimum Wage	N	8. Stem Cell Research $	N	12. Provide Detainee Rights N

Election Results

2004 primary	David Vitter (R)	943,014	(51%)	($7,206,714)
	Chris John (D)	542,150	(29%)	($4,868,165)
	John Kennedy (D)	275,821	(15%)	($1,919,874)
	Other...	87,071	(5%)	
1998 primary	John Breaux (D)	620,502	(64%)	($3,858,472)
	Jim Donelon (R)	306,616	(32%)	($364,073)
	Other...	42,047	(4%)	

Prior Winning Percentages: 2002 House (81%); 2000 House (80%); 1999 House (51%)

Louisiana's junior senator is David Vitter, a Republican elected in 2004. He grew up in the New Orleans area, the son of a Chevron petroleum engineer, graduated from Harvard and Tulane law school and was a Rhodes Scholar. He was a business attorney and taught law at Tulane and Loyola. Vitter was elected in 1991 to the state House, the successor to former Ku Klux Klansman and state legislator David Duke's seat. There he passed a term-limits bill through a reluctant state legislature. Slim and boyish-looking, he was noted for his ability to irritate other politicians; many were enraged by his crusade for term limits, and a popular sheriff sued him three times after Vitter criticized his ethics.

He ran for Congress and won in a May 1999 special election after the abrupt retirement of 1st District Congressman Bob Livingston, the Speaker-designate who announced in December 1999 that he would resign after confessing that he had extramarital affairs. Many Republicans jumped into the race, but the chief fear of Louisiana and national Republicans was that David Duke would run and make it into the runoff. The establishment choice was David Treen, 70, who won four terms in the House starting in 1972 and was elected governor in 1979. In contrast, Vitter said, "We need a younger congressman like me, so we can start building up the seniority we lost when Bob Livingston resigned." Treen, with 25%, and Vitter, with 22%, advanced to the runoff. Duke, unnervingly close to making the runoff, finished third with 19%. Low turnout was probably a factor in deciding this contest, as Vitter rallied his troops and won 51%-49%.

In the House, Vitter had the most conservative voting record in the delegation and one of the most conservative in the House. He enacted easier access to prescription drug coverage for military retirees and advocated aggressive controls of HMOs. When the House debated the education bill in 2001, it passed his amendment to require secondary schools that take federal money to allow military recruiters to visit the schools. Vitter twice won reelection in the heavily Republican, suburban New Orleans district with at least 80% of the vote.

In December 2003, Senator John Breaux announced he would not seek a fourth term. Two days later Vitter said he was running. Wooden in manner, a self-described loner and highly conservative, the suburban Vitter was the stylistic opposite of Breaux, a gregarious dealmaker and noted centrist from Cajun country who was a major force for reform of entitlements and health care. But the state party and national Republicans worked hard to clear the field for Vitter, viewing him as the strongest possible candidate thanks to his suburban political base and his habit of traveling the state to announce projects secured from his perch on Appropriations. He was also familiar in Cajun country after his well-publicized opposition to an Indian casino in southwestern Louisiana.

On the Democratic side, three serious candidates joined the race: Congressman Chris John, a native of Crowley, the town which produced not only Breaux but Congressman and later Governor

Edwin Edwards; two-term state Treasurer John Kennedy; and state Representative Arthur Morrell, an African-American from New Orleans. There was little doubt that Vitter would win the state's unique Election Day primary against a divided Democratic field; the real issue for Democrats was holding him below the 50%-plus-one threshold necessary to avoid a December runoff. Vitter ran as a strong supporter of George W. Bush and called for making Bush's tax cuts permanent, new job creation and medical malpractice reform. He opposed abortion, gay marriage and gun ownership restrictions. He said he best represented "mainstream Louisiana values"; he painted John as an out-of-touch Washington liberal who was close to John Kerry. John, the Democratic frontrunner who had Breaux's endorsement, responded by referring to Vitter as a Republican party puppet and strove to distance himself from Kerry's presidential campaign—a wise move in a state that Bush carried with 57% in November.

Sugar was an important issue, as it was during Senator Mary Landrieu's 2002 reelection campaign. Louisiana is the prime cane sugar producing state and worries about being undercut by cheap imports. Vitter broke with the Bush administration over the Central American Free Trade Agreement, opposing it because it did not exempt sugar imports from the deal. Vitter ran some of the best and most creative television ads of the election cycle. He managed to make light of his public image as a stiff politician through the use of several humorous commercials, including one involving his daughter's home movies. John, meanwhile, failed to gain momentum and was caught in the crossfire between Vitter on the right and Kennedy and Morrell on the left.

With Vitter leading in the polls going into November, the Democratic candidates began scrambling to hold him below the 50% threshold. The Democratic Senatorial Campaign Committee assisted their efforts by spending more than $1.5 million in attack ads criticizing Vitter's positions on prescription drug reimportation and Social Security. It wasn't enough. Vitter won the race outright with 51%; he became the first Republican in 121 years to represent Louisiana in the Senate. John was the leading Democratic vote-getter with 29% to 15% for Kennedy and 3% for Morrell. George W. Bush's strong performance helped Vitter, but he ran well on his own, winning Mississippi River parishes that Bush lost, carrying nearly all of Louisiana north of Baton Rouge and posting large margins in the New Orleans suburbs. In populous St. Tammany Parish, which he represented in Congress, Vitter won by more than 5–1; his 60,000-vote margin there was more than enough to erase John's 25,000-vote advantage in New Orleans and Orleans Parish.

In the Senate, Vitter posted a relatively conservative voting record but with maverick touches. He continued his efforts to encourage the importation of prescription drugs, which included Senate passage in July 2006 of his amendment to prohibit federal customs agents from preventing Americans not engaged in business from importing small amounts of an FDA-approved drug for their personal use. In January 2007, during Senate debate of the lobbying reform bill, he won passage of his amendments to increase penalties, including criminal sanctions for willful violations. He also sought to prohibit lobbying by spouses of senators. He advocated what appeared to be a lost cause in the Senate: a constitutional amendment to limit members of the House and Senate to 12 years of service.

At a Senate hearing two months before Hurricane Katrina, Vitter predicted that a huge storm someday would smash the city and leave it under water. "It's not a question of if. It's a question of when." But he, like other Louisiana politicians over the years, had been slow to take steps to strengthen the levees and to restore the coastal swamps. In his reaction to the catastrophe, Vitter abandoned partisanship and collaborated with the Senate's Katrina Caucus on issues such as relief and recovery, additional oil and gas drilling in the Gulf of Mexico. With Mary Landrieu he filed a proposal that had been prepared by a Louisiana commission for $250 billion in post-Katrina funds. Most experts regarded the plan as utterly unrealistic. He also displayed some of his trademark independence. He criticized the Army Corps of Engineers for its slowness in providing flood protection.

Despite their post-Katrina cooperation, he occasionally criticized Landrieu for alleged grandstanding or lack of cooperation. In a Senate floor speech in October 2005, he said in reference to Landrieu, "When others have been filibustering . . . .I tried to do something constructive." He was not nearly as aggressive as Landrieu in demands for action. Vitter told local reporters that he was well aware of the widespread view among Republicans in Congress that Louisiana would waste federal reconstruction funds.

Vitter's image was tarnished in July 2007 when it was revealed that his phone number appeared on the call list of "D.C. Madam" Deborah Jeane Palfrey between 1999 and 2001. A week after the allegations were made public, Vitter appeared with his wife Wendy by his side and issued a public apology, but did not clarify whether he used the escort service for sex. He said he had told his wife about the incident years ago, and they had dealt with it in counseling. "I believe I received forgiveness from God," he said. It's not yet clear whether the episode will significantly weaken him when he comes up for reelection in 2010.

FIRST DISTRICT

Rep. Bobby Jindal (R)

Elected 2004, 2d term; b. June 10, 1971, Baton Rouge; home, Kenner; Brown U., B.A. 1991, Oxford U., M.Lit. 1994; Catholic; married (Supriya).

Professional Career: Secy., LA Dept. of Health and Hospitals, 1996-98; Exec. Dir., Natl. Bipartisan Comm. on the Future of Medicare, 1998-99; Pres., U. of LA System, 1999-2001; Asst. Sec., U.S. Dept. of HHS, 2001-03.

DC Office: 1205 LHOB, 20515, 202-225-3015; Fax: 202-226-0386; Web site: jindal.house.gov.

District Offices: Hammond, 985-340-2185; Mandeville, 985-893-9064; Metairie, 504-837-1259.

Committees: *Homeland Security* (8th of 15 R): Border, Maritime & Global Counterterrorism; Emergency Communications, Preparedness & Response. *Natural Resources* (13th of 22 R): Energy & Mineral Resources; Fisheries, Wildlife & Oceans.

Group Ratings

	ADA	ACLU	AFS	LCV	ITIC	NTU	COC	ACU	CFG	FRC
2006	0	5	0	8	86	58	100	92	55	100
2005	10	—	0	6	—	62	89	100	67	92

National Journal Ratings

	2005 LIB	—	2005 CONS	2006 LIB	—	2006 CONS
Economic	3%	—	94%	39%	—	61%
Social	19%	—	80%	6%	—	92%
Foreign	21%	—	78%	33%	—	63%

Key Votes of the 109th Congress

1. Estate Tax Repeal	Y	5. Limit Interstate Abortion	Y	9. Build Border Fence	Y
2. Limit CAFE Standards	Y	6. Extend Patriot Act	Y	10. CAFTA	N
3. FY06 Spending Curb	Y	7. Bar Same Sex Marriage	Y	11. Oppose Iraq Withdrawal	Y
4. Drilling in ANWR	Y	8. Stem Cell Research $	N	12. Detainee Tribunals	Y

Election Results

2006 primary	Bobby Jindal (R)	130,508	(88%)	($3,573,550)
	David Gereighty (D)	10,919	(7%)	($18,139)
	Other	6,701	(5%)	
2004 primary	Bobby Jindal (R)	225,708	(78%)	($1,656,964)
	Roy Armstrong (D)	19,266	(7%)	
	M. V. Mendoza (D)	12,779	(4%)	
	Dan Zimmerman (D)	12,135	(4%)	
	Other	18,009	(6%)	
2002 primary	David Vitter (R)	147,117	(81%)	($1,703,084)
	Monica Monica (R)	20,268	(11%)	
	Robert Namer (R)	7,229	(4%)	
	Other	5,956	(3%)	

The People		Race/Ethnic Origin	Ancestry	
Area size:	2,840 sq. mi.	79.6% White	French: 13.3%	German: 10.9%
Urban population:	79.6%	12.8% Black	Irish: 9.4%	
Rural population:	20.4%	1.5% Asian	**2004 Presidential Vote**	
Pop. 2000:	638,355	0.3% Native Am.	Bush (R) 215,538	(71%)
Pop. 2005 (est):	667,527	0.0% Hawaiian	Kerry (D) 87,009	(28%)
Median income:	$40,948	1.0% Two+ races	Other 3,076	(1%)
Poverty status:	12.1%	0.1% Other	**2000 Presidential Vote**	
Military veterans:	13.1%	4.7% Hispanic Origin	Bush (R) 179,196	(66%)
			Gore (D) 83,779	(31%)
			Other 6,650	(2%)
			Cook Partisan Voting Index: R +18	

Occupation   Blue collar: 20.2%   White collar: 65.3%   Gray collar: 14.5%

New Orleans, founded in 1718, the nation's fifth-largest city at the outbreak of the Civil War, is ancient for an American metropolis; yet it is still closely girded by the peculiar wilderness of the mushy Delta lands of the sluggish Mississippi River. For decades, you could climb a levee overlooking the Mississippi and see an expanse of water with untidy clumps of trees and disorganized-looking, seemingly abandoned docks—what Mark Twain had in his mind's eye while writing *Life on the Mississippi* in the 1870s. Or drive just past the last block of a suburban subdivision, and you were in unreclaimed swamp, vegetation and wetness, thick with herons and alligators, flat as far as the eye can see. For years the river has funneled the products of half a continent down to a single port with an international heritage and flair; the New Orleans metropolitan area has lived off that geography and history, with an inward-looking elite preoccupied with who is in which Mardi Gras krewe and interested more in old families' genealogy than in Oil Patch geology. The old buildings of New Orleans were finely proportioned and its old neighborhoods charming, like those in France; and its early 20th century improvements, like Olmstead's City Park, were grand. But its middle and late 20th century streetscapes and subdivisions, like those of France, were without ornament or charm, utilitarian works of man made to master the below-sea-level environment.

After Hurricane Katrina struck with Category Four force on August 29, 2005, many of those details changed dramatically: population plummeted, housing stock was devastated, some levees were breached and others were no longer reliable. The last act of nature to have wreaked so much damage on an American city was the San Francisco earthquake of 1906.

The 1st Congressional District of Louisiana includes some of the places hardest hit by Katrina. It includes much of the newer part of the New Orleans metropolitan area, spread over the soggy lands of the lower Mississippi and Lake Pontchartrain. A bit less than half of its people live south of the lake in affluent white neighborhoods in New Orleans, in the Uptown area and west of City Park, in mostly white neighborhoods on the West Bank of the Mississippi opposite New Orleans and in the vast suburb of Metairie in Jefferson Parish, divided by slanting grids and elevated only where bridges jut out over the many canals. It also includes part of suburbanizing St. Charles Parish to the west. The boundaries have been drawn so that the next-door 2d District has a black majority; the black percentage in the 1st (13%) is the lowest of any Louisiana district. The 1st extends across the 26-mile Lake Pontchartrain Causeway to include St. Tammany Parish, with old towns lush with trees and clusters of new growth around giant intersections. This has been the growth area of metropolitan New Orleans: the population of the city fell 7% between 1990 and 2004 and Jefferson Parish's increased only 1%, while St. Tammany Parish's population increased 40%. Those figures were in flux after Katrina, but previous trends seemed likely to continue. Nearly 75% of the homes in St. Tammany were damaged to some degree, but much of the parish, with the notable exception of Slidell, was spared from the worst effects. Because of this, the neighborhoods of St. Tammany recovered more quickly than elsewhere and many evacuees found their way to its higher ground in the ensuing months. The local real estate market surged; St. Tammany officials estimated that the parish population had grown by as much as 23% in the first year after Katrina. The 1st District also includes, to the north and west, Washington and Tangipahoa Parishes, still mostly rural country. More than half of the district's population is north of Lake Pontchartrain. This is the most upscale, affluent, highly educated district in Louisiana, and by far the most Republican, supportive of political reformers and against economic redistribution. George W. Bush got 71% of the vote here in 2004, by far his best performance in the state.

The congressman from the 1st District is Bobby Jindal, a talented and ambitious Republican first elected in 2004. He grew up in Baton Rouge, the son of immigrants from India; they came so his mother could do graduate work at LSU. He was born in the United States and named Piyush, but as a boy insisted on being called Bobby, after the youngest brother in "The Brady Bunch." As a teenager he converted from Hinduism to Catholicism. Jindal graduated from Brown University and was a Rhodes scholar; he worked briefly for the McKinsey consulting firm. His first political job was an internship with 4th District Congressman Jim McCrery and he quickly built a glittering resume. He was appointed to head Louisiana's state Health and Hospitals Department at 24 after McCrery recommended him to Governor Mike Foster, though he had little experience to suggest he could run a 13,000-employee agency that accounted for about 40% percent of the state budget. Foster, at first a skeptic, was impressed by Jindal and hired him. Jindal erased a $400 million deficit within two years, then returned to Washington and, at 27, was executive director of the National Bipartisan Commission on the Future of Medicare, co-chaired by Senator John Breaux and Representative Bill Thomas. Next he served as president of the 80,000-student Louisiana state university system and was appointed by George W. Bush as Assistant Secretary for Planning and Evaluation at the Health and Human Services Department. In 2003 he ran for governor as a Republican, his first race for elective office, and narrowly lost a bid to become the nation's first Indian-American governor. He campaigned as a policy expert with ideas for restructuring state government and attracted national and international attention (his candidacy was front-page news in India). In the October 2003 primary he ran first, with 33% of the vote, ahead of three Democrats, Lieutenant Governor Kathleen Blanco, with 18%, Attorney General Richard Ieyoub, with 16%, and former Congressman Buddy Leach, with 14%. In the November runoff he lost to Blanco 52%-48%. He carried the New Orleans, Baton Rouge, Shreveport and Monroe metro areas. But Blanco carried her home area, the Cajun country, by a wide margin, and Jindal carried only one of the northern parishes which most Republicans have won in other statewide races.

In 2004, Jindal considered running for the seat of retiring Senator John Breaux, but deferred to Congressman David Vitter. He then decided to run in Vitter's House district, where his wife's family lived and where he won 68% in his campaign for governor. Republican state Representative Steve Scalise abandoned his campaign in August while trailing badly in fundraising and the polls, and Jindal was endorsed by state Republican leaders. He won 78% of the vote in November and was elected without a runoff. He is the first Asian Indian American elected to Congress since Dalip Saund won in the 29th District of California in 1956, 1958 and 1960.

In the House, his voting record was moderate to conservative and his approach was earnest. With help from McCrery, Jindal lobbied Republican leaders for assignment to the Energy and Commerce Committee. But no freshman has been assigned there for years. Instead Jindal has retained seats on Homeland Security and Natural Resources. He had the promise of a bright future in the House, with influential mentors in Thomas and McCrery. He was elected president of the Republican freshman class and spoke out early for personal retirement accounts in Social Security. During President Bush's State of the Union address, he took the lead in dipping his finger in purple ink and raising it in solidarity with the Iraqis who had voted in their election three days before; he invited all members of the House to use the ink, but most who did were Republicans. Following the devastation of Katrina, his legislative work included reform of FEMA and the flood insurance program, the governance of levee boards, financial aid to state and local school boards, and waiver authority for campus-based aid programs. Perhaps his most significant work was with the enactment in December 2006 of a measure to direct offshore oil and gas revenues to Louisiana for the first time.

But Katrina also drew his focus back to Louisiana, and Jindal declared his candidacy for governor in January 2007, two months before Blanco announced that she would not seek reelection. For the state to recover, he said, "We need a plan that won't just rebuild things the way they were, where we were 50th in health care and 50th in the best places to do business. We need to move to the top of those lists and others."

SECOND DISTRICT

Rep. William Jefferson (D)

Elected 1990, 9th term; b. Mar. 14, 1947, Lake Providence; home, New Orleans; Southern U., B.A. 1969, Harvard U., J.D. 1972, Georgetown U., LL.M. 1996; Baptist; married (Andrea).

Military Career: Army Reserves, 1969-78, Army Judge Advocate Corps, 1975.

Elected Office: LA Senate, 1979-90.

Professional Career: Law clerk, U.S. Dist. Judge Alvin Rubin, 1972-73; Legis. aide, U.S. Sen. Bennett Johnston, 1973-75; Practicing atty., 1975-90.

DC Office: 2113 RHOB, 20515, 202-225-6636; Fax: 202-225-1988; Web site: www.house.gov/jefferson.

District Offices: New Orleans, 504-589-2274.

Group Ratings

	ADA	ACLU	AFS	LCV	ITIC	NTU	COC	ACU	CFG	FRC
2006	60	90	83	50	57	25	86	35	42	14
2005	85	—	100	50	—	19	59	29	22	17

National Journal Ratings

	2005 LIB	—	2005 CONS		2006 LIB	—	2006 CONS
Economic	62%	—	38%		56%	—	43%
Social	70%	—	30%		74%	—	26%
Foreign	71%	—	28%		77%	—	20%

Key Votes of the 109th Congress

1. Estate Tax Repeal	Y	5. Limit Interstate Abortion	N	9. Build Border Fence	N
2. Limit CAFE Standards	Y	6. Extend Patriot Act	N	10. CAFTA	Y
3. FY06 Spending Curb	N	7. Bar Same Sex Marriage	Y	11. Oppose Iraq Withdrawal	N
4. Drilling in ANWR	Y	8. Stem Cell Research $	Y	12. Detainee Tribunals	N

Election Results

2006 runoff	William Jefferson (D)	35,153	(57%)	($1,396,091)
	Karen Carter (D)	27,011	(43%)	($1,258,965)
2006 primary	William Jefferson (D)	28,283	(30%)	
	Karen Carter (D)	20,364	(22%)	
	Derrick Shepherd (D)	16,799	(18%)	($462,787)
	Joseph Lavigne (R)	12,511	(13%)	($291,129)
	Troy Carter (D)	11,304	(12%)	($171,850)
	Other	4,765	(5%)	
2004 primary	William Jefferson (D)	173,510	(79%)	($960,790)
	Art Schwertz (R)	46,097	(21%)	($15,139)
2002 primary	William Jefferson (D)	90,310	(64%)	($1,049,231)
	Irma Dixon (D)	28,480	(20%)	
	Silky Sullivan (D)	15,440	(11%)	
	Other	7,926	(6%)	

Prior Winning Percentages: 2000 (100%); 1998 (86%); 1996 (100%); 1994 (75%); 1992 (73%); 1990 (52%)

The People		Race/Ethnic Origin	Ancestry	
Area size:	444 sq. mi.	28.3% White	French: 6.3%	German: 4.3%
Urban population:	99.4%	63.7% Black	Irish: 3.6%	
Rural population:	0.6%	2.7% Asian	**2004 Presidential Vote**	
Pop. 2000:	638,562	0.3% Native Am.	Kerry (D) 183,928	(75%)
Pop. 2005 (est):	617,138	0.0% Hawaiian	Bush (R) 58,855	(24%)
Median income:	$27,514	1.0% Two+ races	Other 1,858	(1%)
Poverty status:	26.8%	0.2% Other	**2000 Presidential Vote**	
Military veterans:	10.9%	3.8% Hispanic Origin	Gore (D) 165,587	(76%)
			Bush (R) 48,726	(22%)
			Other 4,457	(2%)
			Cook Partisan Voting Index: D +28	

Occupation   Blue collar: 21.4%   White collar: 56.2%   Gray collar: 22.4%

Founded by the French in 1718, ruled by the Spanish from 1763 to just days before the French took over to sell it to the United States in 1803, New Orleans was a Creole city—part French, a bit Spanish, more than a touch Caribbean—when the American flag was raised over what is now Jackson Square. The statue of Andrew Jackson still seems an alien intrusion in a square set off by a French Market, the Cabildo, the Presbytere, the Pontalba apartments and Cathedral St. Louis. New Orleans was the fifth largest American city from 1840 until the Civil War and the only sizable city in the South; yet even as it was sending southern cotton out to the mills of Lancashire, it was an alien cultural force in both the nation and region. Urbanized, yet poor and in many ways primitive, New Orleans had yellow fever epidemics late in the 19th century, even as it was installing electric lights; it had a riot in which Italian immigrants were massacred, even as it was laying streetcar tracks and telephone lines. This was one of the most corrupt American cities during Reconstruction and the Gilded Age, when its votes were regularly bid for and bought; like other Southern cities, it became rigidly segregated after 1890.

For a time during the 1970s oil boom, New Orleans seemed to be a fast-growing Sun Belt city. But in the 1980s, it reverted to its rougher traditions and was beset by woes big and small. Its port lost business—oil to Houston, and Latin American trade to Miami—though it still ships large amounts of grain. In the 1990s, New Orleans took a turn for the better. Crime plummeted and no longer depressed tourism. Incomes went up and home ownership increased among blacks as well as whites. Mayor Ray Nagin campaigned to tackle corruption but he was criticized by fellow African-Americans for not paying enough attention to community needs. Harrah's Casino opened in 1999, and it got the state to lower its minimum tax payment. People came to New Orleans for things other than gambling. They wanted to see the gaudy bars of Bourbon Street, the restored houses there and in the Garden District, and Mardi Gras and the krewes that parade for weeks before. And they wanted to dine in New Orleans's storied restaurants, with a cuisine all New Orleans's own, spicy and rich and unaffected by today's taste for low-fat food.

But the city—and the nation and world—have since acquired other images of New Orleans for their memories. As Hurricane Katrina made landfall early on a Monday morning, more than 20,000 people huddled at the downtown Superdome in the shelter of last resort. Although they were told to bring food, water and medicine, many did not. The scene inside was nightmarish, with no power or provisions, and conditions worsened when the storm ripped two holes in the roof. A few days later, city officials began to load these people on buses for transport to cities that were better positioned to provide services. The breach of the 17th Street canal levee led to a surge that churned through the mostly low-income Ninth Ward. At the more advantageously situated French Quarter, largely untouched by the floodwaters, the debauchery never quite stopped even during the grimmest times. A month later, when parts of the city had started to dry out, Mayor Ray Nagin begged people to return, even though services obviously were limited. In April 2006, elections that had been postponed in February were held for mayor and city council; Nagin faced 21 challengers and ended up winning a May runoff against Lieutenant Governor Mitch Landrieu, brother to Senator Mary Landrieu and son of Moon Landrieu, the city's last white mayor. Thousands of people returned on buses from out of state to cast a ballot and then departed again to their not-so-temporary homes.

During these months, there were plenty of outsiders who moved into New Orleans for a spell: the news media, insurance and other financial-service agents, government officials, unemployed workers looking for a paycheck. But a year later, the numbers still told a troubling story for the city and Orleans Parish: the city's population cut from 462,000 to about 220,000; 18,700 FEMA trailers occupied; 60% of electricity and 41% of gas customers reconnected; 350,000 vehicles flooded or abandoned; 1.5 million appliances removed as debris. The recovery proceeded, but expectations repeatedly were downsized. In May 2007, the Kaiser Family Foundation issued a report on the people of New Orleans: "Hurricane Katrina and the failure of government at all levels to respond to it more effectively, was personally devastating for a large percentage of the Greater New Orleans population in ways that continue to reverberate today. Overall, a third of Greater New Orleans residents (32%) said their life remains 'very disrupted' or 'somewhat disrupted' by the storm. This rose to 59% among African Americans living in Orleans Parish."

The 2d Congressional District of Louisiana includes almost all of the city of New Orleans, everything except a few affluent white neighborhoods, plus nearly half of Jefferson Parish, black neighborhoods in Metairie and Kenner, the West Bank towns of Harvey, Marrero and Westwego, between the levee and the swamp. Here is the French Quarter—the *Vieux Carre*—its 19th century homes still intact because the Americans who moved here after 1803 wanted to stay away from the snobbish Creoles and then built a new downtown across Canal Street. Many neighborhoods remained where preservation of old buildings was not a priority; blacks and some working-class whites lived in rickety frame houses that were not always strong enough to keep the rain out and never tight enough to protect against the summer humidity or the damp winter chill, along the vividly named streets—Elysian Fields, Spain, Desire, Arts—that go north from the river wharves. South of the quarter is the downtown flecked with skyscrapers and the ominous Superdome, and to the east is the old slum known as the Irish Channel—a reminder that New Orleans had more foreign immigrants than any other part of the South. Up St. Charles Avenue is the Garden District. This was the home of rich early American settlers, and its antebellum homes are still covered with vines and Spanish moss. New Orleans, for many years a speckled black-and-white city, had a 67% black majority in the 2000 Census (a figure that is all but certain to decline in the next Census), and the 2d District was overwhelmingly Democratic. John Kerry won 75% of the vote here; it is the only Louisiana district where he got more than 41%.

The congressman from the 2d District is Bill Jefferson, a Democrat first elected in 1990. Jefferson grew up in the northeast corner of Louisiana in Lake Providence. He graduated from Southern University and Harvard Law School, clerked for a federal judge, worked for Senator Bennett Johnston and settled in New Orleans to set up what became the largest black law firm in the South; later, while serving in Congress, he received an LL.M. from Georgetown. Jefferson was elected to the state Senate in 1979; he twice ran for mayor and lost. In 1990, when Lindy Boggs retired, Jefferson won 25% in the primary to 22% for Marc Morial, whose father was New Orleans's first black mayor and who was later elected mayor himself. In the runoff, charges flew: Jefferson was dogged by reports of defaults on outstanding loans and mortgages, while Morial admitted he was the father of an eight-year-old girl living in the Ivory Coast. Jefferson won with 52% and became the first Louisiana black elected to Congress since Reconstruction.

In the House Jefferson has shown impressive political skills and has a moderate voting record among Democrats, especially on economic issues. From his seat on Ways and Means, Jefferson opposed Social Security personal accounts and questioned reliance on the payroll tax. He wants to expand the availability of Individual Retirement Accounts, and to repeal estate taxes. Jefferson co-sponsored the Africa free-trade law, and he bucked most Democrats on Ways and Means to support trade promotion authority, which he said was vital to Louisiana's economy. He also worked with chairman Bill Thomas to reduce corporate taxes (in exchange for a tax break for shipping companies) and was one of the few Democrats on Ways and Means to speak positively about free trade with Central America.

Jefferson has eyed other offices, seeking to become the first black elected statewide since Reconstruction. In 1991, he filed to run for governor, but withdrew; in 1995, he began running for governor again, but withdrew in favor of Cleo Fields, and said he would run for Senate; in May 1996 he bowed out of that race. In January 1999, after Republican Mike Foster and other statewide officials met at the Governor's Mansion and promised not to oppose each other regardless of party, Jefferson was evidently peeved and ran for governor. Voting ran pretty much along racial lines, and Foster won 62%-30%. After the 2002 election, with support from the Congressional Black Caucus, Jefferson sought the chairmanship of the Democratic Congressional Campaign Committee. He cited his active fundraising for the committee plus his success in helping to elect Democrats in Louisiana; some union officials who were unhappy about his free trade views opposed him. Some black members were upset when Nancy Pelosi instead selected fellow Californian Bob Matsui, with whom she had a closer relationship.

In 2005, his career took a downhill plunge from which it seemed unlikely that Jefferson could ever recover. On July 30, he met at a Ritz-Carlton Hotel outside Washington, D.C., with a Virginia woman, to whom he was providing assistance for her investment in a project in Nigeria. That conversation was taped by the FBI, including her agreement to provide him a briefcase with $100,000 in marked bills; Jefferson had said that he would need the money to bribe officials in Nigeria. FBI video cameras showed Jefferson driving away with the briefcase. Four days later, FBI agents raided his home and found $90,000 of "cold cash" in the kitchen freezer of his Capitol Hill home. Hurricane Katrina hit a few weeks later; five days after that, Jefferson drew notice when he was accompanied by National Guard troops to his home in New Orleans, where he retrieved personal items. In May 2006, the FBI obtained a search warrant to conduct a Saturday night raid of his congressional office in the Rayburn building, where agents removed records and computer drives. Speaker Dennis Hastert and Pelosi had received no advance notice; they objected to this as an infringement on congressional prerogatives. In an affidavit released after the raid, the FBI accused Jefferson of receiving more than $400,000 in bribes to assist a Kentucky-based company to invest in Africa. Jefferson denied wrongdoing and said that the government was viewing the facts in the worst possible light. "I certainly did not sell my office." A former aide to Jefferson and a business associate pleaded guilty to related crimes to which Jefferson evidently was the accomplice. In July, a federal judge upheld the constitutionality of the search. The raid had considerable political repercussions. In June 2006, Pelosi sought to remove Jefferson from his seat on the Ways and Means Committee. "Anybody with $90,000 in their freezer has a problem," she said understatedly. Jefferson objected and was supported by some members of the Congressional Black Caucus; a few were harsh in their condemnations of Pelosi. But she persisted, and the Democratic Caucus on a 99-58 vote sustained her plan to strip his assignment. Democratic Caucus chairman James Clyburn, a former CBC chairman, backed Pelosi. Republicans, meanwhile, spotlighted the Jefferson case as an example of corruption among Democrats at the very time that the GOP was experiencing a litany of its own ethics problems.

To the surprise of many, Jefferson sought reelection. He faced 12 opponents in the unusual November contest. The most prominent were state representative Karen Carter and state senator Derrick Shepherd. The state Democratic party endorsed Carter, while the city and parish committees stayed with Jefferson; the DCCC mostly kept its distance, though Pelosi's animosity toward Jefferson was obvious. He spent far less money than he had in past elections, but he campaigned actively among his diminished post-Katrina constituents, many of whom believed that he had been unfairly targeted by law enforcement officials. Carter raised substantial sums and ran as a good-government candidate. In the primary, Jefferson got 30% of the vote, with 22% to Carter and 18% to Shepherd. In the December 9 runoff, Shepherd endorsed Jefferson, saying Carter did not share his conservative views on social issues; viewed another way, the endorsement might have enhanced Shepherd's future chances of winning the seat if Jefferson was reelected. Carter emphasized that Jefferson was tainted and could not be effective in a district desperately in need of assistance. Jefferson cautioned against a rush to judgment and bragged about the federal assistance that he continued to deliver back home. Jefferson prevailed 57%-43%. Jefferson had won a battle, but his bigger war continued. Failing to regain his Ways and Means seat, he returned to the ignominy of a seat on the Small Business Committee. When Republicans objected to his assignment to Homeland Security, Democratic leaders backed off, all the more so after two Republican members under separate investigations gave up their committee seats in April 2007.

In June 2007, Jefferson was indicted on 16 counts related to his alleged bribery scheme. The next day, he temporarily gave up his sole remaining committee seat on Small Business. He pleaded innocent to the federal corruption charges and trial was set for January 2008.

THIRD DISTRICT

Rep. Charlie Melancon (D)

Elected 2004, 2d term; b. Oct. 3, 1947, Napoleonville; home, Napoleonville; U. of SW LA, B.S. 1971; Catholic; married (Peachy).

Elected Office: LA House, 1987-93.

Professional Career: Ex. Dir., South Central Planning and Dev. Comm., 1973-79; Owner, Melancon Insurance Agency, 1980-93; Baskin-Robbins franchise owner; Pres. & Gen. Mgr., American Sugar Cane League, 1993-2004.

DC Office: 404 CHOB, 20515, 202-225-4031; Fax: 202-226-3944; Web site: melancon.house.gov.

District Offices: Chalmette, 504-271-1707; Gonzales, 225-621-8490; Houma, 985-876-3033; New Iberia, 337-367-8231.

Committees: *Energy & Commerce* (29th of 31 D): Energy & Air Quality; Oversight & Investigations (Vice Chmn.); Commerce, Trade & Consumer Protection. *Science & Technology* (21st of 24 D): Space & Aeronautics.

Group Ratings

	ADA	ACLU	AFS	LCV	ITIC	NTU	COC	ACU	CFG	FRC
2006	40	50	57	8	57	32	93	76	42	71
2005	80	—	100	33	—	29	67	61	25	62

National Journal Ratings

	2005 LIB	—	2005 CONS		2006 LIB	—	2006 CONS
Economic	55%	—	45%		51%	—	48%
Social	55%	—	45%		51%	—	48%
Foreign	55%	—	45%		53%	—	46%

Key Votes of the 109th Congress

1. Estate Tax Repeal	Y	5. Limit Interstate Abortion	Y	9. Build Border Fence	Y
2. Limit CAFE Standards	Y	6. Extend Patriot Act	Y	10. CAFTA	N
3. FY06 Spending Curb	N	7. Bar Same Sex Marriage	Y	11. Oppose Iraq Withdrawal	Y
4. Drilling in ANWR	Y	8. Stem Cell Research $	Y	12. Detainee Tribunals	Y

Election Results

2006 primary	Charlie Melancon (D)	75,023	(55%)	($2,596,270)
	Craig Romero (R)	54,950	(40%)	($1,936,495)
	Other	6,358	(5%)	
2004 runoff	Charlie Melancon (D)	57,611	(50%)	($1,761,978)
	Billy Tauzin III (R)	57,042	(50%)	($1,924,780)
2004 primary	Billy Tauzin III (R)	84,680	(32%)	
	Charlie Melancon (D)	63,328	(24%)	
	Craig Romero (R)	61,132	(23%)	($1,033,107)
	Damon Baldone (D)	25,783	(10%)	($359,449)
	Charmaine Caccioppi (D)	19,347	(7%)	($247,253)
	Kevin Chiasson (R)	10,350	(4%)	($12,110)

The People

Area size:	12,675 sq. mi.
Urban population:	73.0%
Rural population:	27.0%
Pop. 2000:	638,322
Pop. 2005 (est):	651,411
Median income:	$34,463
Poverty status:	18.6%
Military veterans:	10.8%

Race/Ethnic Origin

69.7% White
24.6% Black
1.0% Asian
1.6% Native Am.
0.0% Hawaiian
1.0% Two+ races
0.1% Other
2.1% Hispanic Origin

Ancestry

French: 17.4%   USA: 8.7%
German: 5.9%

2004 Presidential Vote

Bush (R)	162,269	(58%)
Kerry (D)	115,011	(41%)
Other	3,826	(1%)

2000 Presidential Vote

Bush (R)	133,749	(52%)
Gore (D)	115,734	(45%)
Other	7,967	(3%)

Cook Partisan Voting Index: R + 5

Occupation   Blue collar: 33.6%   White collar: 50.3%   Gray collar: 16.2%

Below sea level, veined with bayous and creeks and wide streams of water, crossed by only an occasional road or railroad, the wetlands of southern Louisiana are one of America's unique landscapes. Technically, most of this waterlogged land rests on islands in a broad river mouth, through which the waters of the Mississippi and its tributaries drain into the Gulf of Mexico. It is rich with animal life, herons and egrets, shrimp and crawfish, muskrats and alligators. Until August 2005, it supported more people than one might have thought, in surprisingly sturdy small towns, with shopping malls on high ground, and in cabins along the bayous and crossroad towns where Cajun French remains the first language and roadside diners feature crawfish etoufee. The steep-roofed Cajun houses were not the only structures: Here and there, jutting out of the swampy land, are huge elaborate metal sculptures—petrochemical plants and refineries, processing the oil and natural gas trapped under these wetlands and the shallow continental shelf of the Gulf. In the 1960s and 1970s, the oil industry, by providing good jobs for young people here, helped preserve Cajun culture and built a Cajun pride that was seldom articulated a generation ago. Then oil payrolls plummeted and the wetlands were threatened by coastal erosion and battered by Hurricane Andrew in 1992. The erosion continued, as the wetlands get less water because the Mississippi is not permitted to flood, and the shrimp fishermen, who still sailed out in Blessing of the Fleet (La Benediction des Bateaux) ceremonies in April or May, found their catch declining and their profits threatened by competition from aquaculture-raised Asian and Latin American shrimp. But so long as the petrochemical plants, oil refineries, aluminum smelters and sugar refineries provided well-paying jobs in these parts, most Cajuns remained in this land of good hunting and good food.

The good life changed in many of these places on August 29, 2005. On that day, the eye of Hurricane Katrina made a direct hit on this district, and inflicted more immediate damage here than anywhere else along the Gulf. Plaquemines and St. Bernard Parishes were ravaged by high winds and floodwaters; a year after Katrina, St. Bernard's population was estimated at 15,000, down from 67,000. In August 2006, *National Journal's* Jonathan Rauch described the desolation. "Some houses are under repair; trailers are parked in their yards. A family is barbecuing at a gas grill outside a half-renovated garage. Next to another trailer, a few people chat in a pool of light. On most blocks, however, one encounters no people, hears no human sounds. There are no dogs or cats. The odd car prowls by, picking its way amid potholes. By day, people come and work on their houses. By night, the sense of desertion is overpowering. Even a graveyard feels less desolate, because it is not meant for living."

The 3d Congressional District of Louisiana includes about half the Cajun country. It includes most of Louisiana's swamplands, covering Houma, where seven bayous converge; St. Charles, St. John the Baptist, St. James and Ascension Parishes on both sides of the Mississippi, once the greatest sugar producers in America, now studded with refineries and petrochemical plants; roughneck Morgan City, which services many offshore oil rigs; Iberia Parish, the home of McIlhenny's Tabasco sauce; plus the remains of St. Bernard and Plaquemines Parishes, downriver from New Orleans. Behind the Mississippi's western levee, hunkered side by side in Vacherie, are twin reminders of the region's grandeur and pain: the stately Oak Alley plantation, whose stunning vista stood in for the home of a fictional, aristocratic governor in the 1998 movie *Primary Colors;* and the slave cabins of Laura Plantation, believed to be the original home of the famous Br'er Rabbit stories. The ancestral language here is French, mainly Cajun but also Creole; the ancestral religion is Roman Catholic and the ancestral politics Democratic, though very conservative. There has been an influx of Mexicans and other immigrants from Central America, many of whom work on the oil rigs or at the chemical plants. George W. Bush won 58% here in 2004 but it's anybody's guess as to how many voters will show up for the 2008 election and how they will respond. A comparison of voter turnout between the 2006 and 2002 House elections offers one small clue: the biggest percentage turnout decline in the state, 72%, came in white and working-class St. Bernard Parish, which votes Republican.

The congressman from the 3d District is Charlie Melancon (pronounced, *meh-LAW-sawn*), a Democrat elected in 2004 in a contest that was decided in the December runoff. He grew up in Napoleonville, on a dead-end street called Hog-Pen Alley; his father was mayor. After graduating with a bachelor's in agribusiness from the University of Southwestern Louisiana, he worked on the 1971 campaign of Edwin Edwards for governor, and then on his transition team. He returned to Napoleonville, where he worked on the South Central Planning and Development Commission; later, he ran an insurance agency and owned several Baskin-Robbins ice cream franchises. He ran for the state House in 1975 and lost; he ran again in 1987 and was elected to the first of three terms. He co-sponsored the bill that resulted in creation of the state-backed Louisiana Workers Compensation Corporation. He resigned in 1993 to become president of the American Sugar Cane League.

Melancon was one of six candidates to replace Billy Tauzin, who chaired the Energy and Commerce Committee from January 2001 to February 2004. In late 2003 rumors spread that Tauzin would resign to take a high-paying lobbying job but Tauzin vigorously denied them. Then in February he resigned the chairmanship and underwent surgery for cancer; in December 2004, he was named to head PhRMA, the giant pharmaceutical lobby. The early frontrunner for the seat was his son Billy Tauzin III, who left the Coast Guard Academy after less than three years and returned to Louisiana to work for BellSouth—at first, selling mobile phones and eventually becoming a lobbyist and regional manager. But Little Billy, as his detractors called him, did not clear the field. Craig Romero, an Iberia Parish cattle farmer and oil field supply salesman who had served in the state Senate as a Republican since 1996, criticized Tauzin's lack of experience in politics and in south Louisiana. He said that the senior Tauzin was seeking to "anoint" his successor, and criticized him for directing at least $200,000 to the state Republican party that was recycled to his son's campaign; Dad ran ads in October that thanked voters for their best wishes during his convalescence but did not make clear that he was retiring. In the nonpartisan November primary, some Democrats feared that Tauzin and Romero would be the two frontrunners and there would be no Democrat in the runoff. But in the final weeks before the initial vote, Melancon benefited from several hundred thousand dollars in advertising by the Democratic Congressional Campaign Committee. That spending proved to be a wise investment. In the November vote, Tauzin won 32% of the vote and led in eight parishes, mostly in the Bayous. Melancon edged out Romero, 24%-23%; each ran very strongly in his base.

In the runoff, Romero expressed anger over Tauzin's late advertising that painted him as a liberal who voted to repeal Louisiana's ban on sodomy; he did not endorse either candidate. The candidates split over tax cuts for the wealthy, school vouchers, tort reform and missile defense. Melancon voiced doubts about the war in Iraq, but said that he would not "second-guess" the decision. He said that he was pro-gun, anti-abortion and opposed to gay marriage (though he opposed amending the Constitution to ban same-sex marriage); he emphasized his experience, and said that he would protect sugar interests from the Central America Free Trade Agreement. Tauzin said that he was his own man, but he benefited from large contributions by interest groups that benefited from his father's blessings. Each national party spent close to $2 million in the runoff, mostly on negative ads. The final tally gave Melancon a win by 569 votes, 50.2%-49.8%. He carried six parishes in the northern and western parts of the district, including Romero's base of Iberia Parish. Tauzin won all of the parishes along the Gulf, but it wasn't enough.

In the House, Melancon's voting record was among the most conservative Democrats, and he joined the congressional Blue Dogs. Following Katrina, he was the only one of the seven House members from Louisiana to join Mary Landrieu and David Vitter in filing the proposed $250 billion relief package prepared by a home-state commission. Despite objections from Minority Leader Nancy Pelosi, he participated in a select committee chaired by Tom Davis that investigated the federal response to the disaster. He worked with Republicans to craft details of the landmark legislation for Louisiana to share royalties from offshore drilling.

Craig Romero returned to challenge him in 2006. Although Romero would have had a good chance to win in 2004, much had transpired since then and Melancon had proven himself to his constituents with his post-Katrina advocacy work. In a contest that became something of an afterthought, Melancon won 55%-40%; Romero led only in Iberia Parish, his home base. The vote turnout in St. Bernard was 4,741; in November 2004, there were 28,378 voters. In January 2007, Melancon got a seat on the Energy and Commerce Committee, which left him well-positioned for additional work on oil and gas issues. In February, he criticized House Democratic leaders for "not moving fast enough" to address Katrina issues. In response, Democrats created a working group on Gulf Coast recovery, led by James Clyburn.

FOURTH DISTRICT

Rep. Jim McCrery (R)

Elected Apr. 1988, 10th full term; b. Sept. 18, 1949, Shreveport; home, Shreveport; LA Tech. U., B.A. 1971, LA St. U., J.D. 1975; Methodist; married (Johnette).

Professional Career: Practicing atty. 1975-78; Asst. Shreveport City Atty., 1979-80; Legis. Dir., U.S. Rep. Buddy Roemer, 1981-84; Regional Mgr., Georgia–Pacific Corp., 1984-88.

DC Office: 242 CHOB, 20515, 202-225-2777; Fax: 202-225-8039; Web site: mccrery.house.gov.

District Offices: Leesville, 337-238-0778; Shreveport, 318-798-2254.

Committees: *Joint Committee on Taxation* (4th of 5 R). *Ways & Means* (RMM of 17 R).

Group Ratings

	ADA	ACLU	AFS	LCV	ITIC	NTU	COC	ACU	CFG	FRC
2006	0	14	0	0	100	58	100	88	55	85
2005	0	—	0	0	—	57	92	92	56	92

National Journal Ratings

	2005 LIB	—	2005 CONS		2006 LIB	—	2006 CONS
Economic	17%	—	82%		4%	—	94%
Social	20%	—	79%		31%	—	68%
Foreign	31%	—	67%		6%	—	86%

Key Votes of the 109th Congress

1. Estate Tax Repeal	Y	5. Limit Interstate Abortion	Y	9. Build Border Fence	Y
2. Limit CAFE Standards	Y	6. Extend Patriot Act	Y	10. CAFTA	Y
3. FY06 Spending Curb	Y	7. Bar Same Sex Marriage	Y	11. Oppose Iraq Withdrawal	Y
4. Drilling in ANWR	Y	8. Stem Cell Research $	N	12. Detainee Tribunals	Y

Election Results

2006 primary	Jim McCrery (R)	77,078	(57%)	($2,246,203)
	Artis Cash (D)	22,757	(17%)	($7,619)
	Patti Cox (D)	17,788	(13%)	
	Chester Kelley (R)	16,649	(12%)	($79,783)
2004 primary	Jim McCrery (R)	unopposed		($939,484)
2002 primary	Jim McCrery (R)	114,649	(72%)	($1,117,836)
	John Milkovich (D)	42,340	(26%)	
	Other	3,104	(2%)	

Prior Winning Percentages: 2000 (71%); 1998 (100%); 1996 (71%); 1994 (80%); 1992 (63%); 1990 (55%); 1988 (68%); 1988 (51%)

The People		Race/Ethnic Origin	Ancestry	
Area size:	11,151 sq. mi.	62.0% White	USA: 10.2%	Irish: 6.9%
Urban population:	59.3%	33.3% Black	English: 5.6%	
Rural population:	40.7%	0.7% Asian	**2004 Presidential Vote**	
Pop. 2000:	638,466	0.8% Native Am.	Bush (R) 156,298	(59%)
Pop. 2005 (est):	646,059	0.1% Hawaiian	Kerry (D) 105,962	(40%)
Median income:	$31,085	1.1% Two+ races	Other 2,771	(1%)
Poverty status:	20.0%	0.1% Other	**2000 Presidential Vote**	
Military veterans:	14.7%	2.0% Hispanic Origin	Bush (R) 129,908	(55%)
			Gore (D) 102,228	(43%)
			Other 5,466	(2%)
			Cook Partisan Voting Index: R + 7	
Occupation	Blue collar: 28.5%	White collar: 52.7%	Gray collar: 18.9%	

Northwestern Louisiana, south of Arkansas and just east of Texas, is part of the Deep South. The overwhelming majority of people here are Protestants, not Catholics, often very tradition-minded, with names that are English or Scottish, not French. The tone is set not by wide-open New Orleans—which was not easily accessible by interstate until 1996, when the last chunk of I-49 was completed—but by the much smaller Shreveport, which could be just another East Texas oil town, albeit one which has its own, comparatively sedate, Mardi Gras. The countryside is agricultural, though there are few vestiges of large riverfront plantations and backward farm country. Roots go back here a long way. Natchitoches is the oldest town, founded by Louis Antoine Juchereay de St. Denis in 1714; since 1927 it has been running a Christmas Festival of Lights on the riverfront, with plenty of food and entertainment. Shreveport was founded when Captain Henry Miller Shreve, with the Army Corps of Engineers, in the 1830s dispatched a young deputy named Robert E. Lee to break up a 100-mile blockade of logs in the Red River, moving the region's epicenter upriver to a new town, which was named after him. Oil provided the basis for much of the economic growth of the 20th century, but natural gas has taken off in the 21st. Gas was discovered here in 1870 and the nation's first gas pipeline built from Caddo Field to Shreveport in 1908, but it wasn't economical to drill until gas prices zoomed in 2000. There are defense installations nearby, notably Barksdale Air Force Base in Bossier City (pronounced BOHzhir), where George W. Bush landed on September 11, 2001 and spoke briefly to the nation. Politically, northern Louisiana voters, for more than 100 years, have been voting against cosmopolitan New Orleans and the Catholic Cajun south, sometimes for rip-roaring populists, and more often recently for market-oriented Republicans.

The 4th Congressional District of Louisiana consists of the northwest corner of the state. More than half the votes here are cast in Caddo and Bossier Parishes in the far corner around Shreveport, with the rest scattered around rural areas, like picturesque Natchitoches and strip-highway towns like Leesville near Fort Polk. This area seemed to be trending Republican in the 1980s, but in the middle 1990s it went the other way: Both Bill Clinton and Senator Mary Landrieu carried the district in 1996, a critical factor in her narrow 5,788-vote statewide margin. In 2000 George W. Bush carried the area by a comfortable 55% margin, but it voted for Landrieu again in the close 2002 Senate race and for Democratic Governor Kathleen Blanco in 2003 over Bobby Jindal. In 2004, the district gave Bush 59% of the vote.

The congressman from the 4th District is Jim McCrery, a Republican first elected in April 1988. McCrery grew up in Leesville, graduated from Louisiana Tech in Ruston (next door to Grambling, site of the football-famous historically black college) and LSU law school, and practiced law in Leesville and Shreveport. In 1981 he worked for Congressman Buddy Roemer, then a Democrat; in 1984 he went to work for Georgia Pacific. After Roemer was elected governor in 1987, McCrery ran as a Republican and won the special election 51%-49%. McCrery's toughest reelection race was in 1992, when the creation of the black-majority 4th District put him in the 5th District with 16-year incumbent Jerry Huckaby, a conservative Democrat. But the district, with few black voters, was heavily Republican and Huckaby had 88 overdrafts on the House bank. McCrery weathered some negative personal attacks, led in the October primary 44%-29% and won the November runoff 63%-37%.

McCrery has compiled a mostly conservative voting record and has worked on major legislation from his seat on the Ways and Means Committee, on which he is now ranking minority member. Armed with the intuition that made him one of only 72 House members to vote against the disastrous 1988 catastrophic health care bill, he advanced a Republican alternative to the Clinton health care plan in 1994. He worked on the Republicans' Medicare and prescription drug bills and on the party task force on HMO regulation. He sponsored a bill in 2004 to allow workers to transfer unused money from "use it or lose it" flexible savings accounts into health savings accounts; it passed in May. In energy bills he has sponsored tax credits for energy companies and green bond tax credits for projects that improve the environment; one intended beneficiary was a riverfront shopping center in Bossier City with a Hooters restaurant—the subject of some ridicule from Senator John McCain. He worked hard on mastering the intricacies of tax, trade and health care finance legislation and evidently impressed Bill Thomas, who became chairman in 2001. McCrery became chairman of the Select Revenue Measures Subcommittee in that year, and in that position helped shepherd to passage the Bush tax cuts of 2001 and 2003. He worked closely with Thomas, who retired in 2006, but his more diplomatic approach enabled him to be an intermediary between Thomas and colleagues with whom he was not on speaking terms. He has said that he favors a consumption-based tax, but has evidently thought the time not propitious for that.

In January 2005 McCrery was named chairman of the Social Security Subcommittee, over the more senior Wally Herger. He has long favored personal retirement accounts in Social Security, and on taking the chairmanship called them "an absolute necessity." He said Social Security was "one of the most successful programs ever" and that he was ready to listen to all ideas. He thought in similar terms to Thomas politically. "I just think we've got to go outside the Social Security box to get us a bill that some Democrats will feel comfortable with and Republicans will feel comfortable with and the president would sign." But in February 2005, after a meeting with White House economic counselor Al Hubbard, he said he favored Bush's approach of dealing more narrowly with Social Security. In July 2005 he came forward with a plan to use the surplus of Social Security revenues over obligations to finance personal accounts, but acknowledged that this would not address the solvency of the system and that money would cease flowing into the accounts as the surplus vanished on or about 2017. Thomas had promised to bring up Social Security in September 2005, but the issue was laid aside after Hurricane Katrina, and McCrery admitted that a comprehensive plan "has not yet taken hold in the minds of many Americans and their elected representatives." In December he said, "The president made a valiant effort to highlight that issue. But unfortunately we were not able to sell the president's plan to enough of the public to get that done." He expressed the hope that it might be addressed in 2007, with broader tax reform waiting until 2009; he said the idea of another bipartisan Social Security commission was "hogwash."

At the time McCrery made no secret that he hoped to succeed Thomas as chairman when the six-year term limit clicked in after the 2006 election. McCrery ranked behind Clay Shaw, Nancy Johnson and Wally Herger in seniority on the committee. But his mastery of complex issues had impressed the House leadership as it had Thomas; Johnson may have been too liberal for the leadership and Herger seems never to have been under serious consideration. "I think part of Bill Thomas's legacy will be that he got things done. I hope to continue that legacy, using maybe a little different style, but be as effective as he was at getting things passed," he said in December 2005. "If I'm fortunate enough to become chairman, I've got to figure out a way to make Ways and Means, if necessary, a place where there is more interaction between both sides of the aisle." He worked to raise enormous sums of money for House Republicans. His Committee for the Preservation of Capitalism PAC raised $4.3 million between 1997 and 2005; he chaired the June 2006 President's Dinner and raised $1.2 million of the $15 million total himself. He was a bit embarrassed when Democrats opposing Shaw highlighted McCrery's chances of being chairman and downplayed Shaw's; he took care to contribute the maximum $10,000 to Shaw's campaign. The chairmanship became unavailable when the Democrats won a majority in the November 2006 election, but the ranking minority position was easily his: Shaw and Johnson were defeated for reelection and Herger was not a contender.

McCrery set out to build an amiable relationship with the new chairman, Charles Rangel, whom Thomas had mostly ignored and excluded from conference committees on important issues; he was now seeking the bipartisanship which he had promised a year before. "I'll do my best to be productive. I think it's possible. I get along with Charlie Rangel." Not on every issue. In January 2007 he opposed the Democrats' energy taxes, an increased period of amortization of oil and gas investments and removal of the oil and gas industries from a program designed to aid manufacturing—measures that would hurt his district. He and Buck McKeon of the Education Committee put together a package of small business tax cuts as an amendment to the minimum wage bill; it did not reach the floor in January, but in February he worked with Rangel to draft a $1.8 billion package, financed largely by denying capital gains to persons under 24 with low incomes and rich parents, for negotiations with the Senate; it passed the committee unanimously. He derided Democratic arguments that vast sums could be gained by collecting unpaid taxes and argued that the IRS had been making great progress in reducing the amount of unpaid taxes in the past six years. On trade he said in December 2006, "I'm optimistic that we can find some language that satisfies the Democrats' desire to make labor a more evident part of our trade agreements, while not doing injury to Republicans' strongly held beliefs of protecting our own country's sovereignty." He reached agreement in May with Rangel on labor and environmental provisions in the Panama and Peru Free Trade Agreements and continued to negotiate with him on terms for renewing trade promotion authority.

Since 1994 McCrery has not faced serious competition at the polls. In early 2004 he talked about retiring, so he could be in Shreveport with his wife, who had a part-time job there, and his two young children. George W. Bush and Dick Cheney called him and failed to persuade him to run again. But then his wife called and said she had decided that the family should move to the Washington area and she should get a job there. They moved in early 2005, but McCrery continued to deal with district matters. On the 2005 highway bill he got $150 million to build I-49 north from Shreveport to the Arkansas border, and he helped pass business tax incentives for investors in New Orleans after Katrina and money for unemployment benefits for evacuees. In 2006 he was reelected with 57% of the vote against three little-known opponents; he won more than 50% in all but one small parish. Democrat Patti Cox, the third-place finisher, filed suit in state and federal court after the election claiming McCrery, whose family had been living in Virginia, was not a Louisiana resident when he won the election. The courts dismissed the case; in June 2007, the House Administration Committee also voted to dismiss her complaint.

Footnote: Just as McCrery once worked as a staffer for Congressman Buddy Roemer, 1st District Congressman and 2007 gubernatorial candidate Bobby Jindal once worked as an intern in McCrery's office.

FIFTH DISTRICT

Rep. Rodney Alexander (R)

Elected 2002, 3d term; b. Dec. 5, 1946, Quitman; home, Quitman; attended LA Tech. U., 1965; Baptist; married (Nancy).

Military Career: Air Force Reserves, 1965-71.

Elected Office: Jackson Parish Police Jury, 1972-87; President, 1980-87; LA House of Reps., 1988-2002.

Professional Career: Insurance agent, 1990-93; contractor, 1993-present.

DC Office: 316 CHOB, 20515, 202-225-8490; Fax: 202-225-5639; Web site: www.house.gov/alexander.

District Offices: Alexandria, 318-445-0818; Monroe, 318-322-3500.

Committees: *Appropriations* (28th of 29 R): Financial Services & General Government; Agriculture, Rural Development, FDA & Related Agencies. *Budget* (15th of 17 R).

Group Ratings

	ADA	ACLU	AFS	LCV	ITIC	NTU	COC	ACU	CFG	FRC
2006	5	9	14	0	100	56	100	80	48	100
2005	0	—	0	0	—	56	93	92	56	92

National Journal Ratings

	2005 LIB	—	2005 CONS		2006 LIB	—	2006 CONS
Economic	9%	—	88%		12%	—	86%
Social	12%	—	86%		17%	—	79%
Foreign	23%	—	73%		17%	—	73%

Key Votes of the 109th Congress

1. Estate Tax Repeal	Y	5. Limit Interstate Abortion	Y	9. Build Border Fence	Y
2. Limit CAFE Standards	Y	6. Extend Patriot Act	Y	10. CAFTA	Y
3. FY06 Spending Curb	Y	7. Bar Same Sex Marriage	Y	11. Oppose Iraq Withdrawal	Y
4. Drilling in ANWR	Y	8. Stem Cell Research $	N	12. Detainee Tribunals	Y

Election Results

2006 primary	Rodney Alexander (R)	78,211	(68%)	($1,199,376)
	Gloria Williams Hearn (D)	33,233	(29%)	($156,927)
	Other	3,138	(3%)	
2004 primary	Rodney Alexander (R)	141,495	(59%)	($1,344,520)
	Zelma Blakes (D)	58,591	(25%)	($20,303)
	Jock Scott (R)	37,971	(16%)	($149,557)
2002 runoff	Rodney Alexander (D)	86,718	(50%)	($831,088)
	Lee Fletcher (R)	85,744	(50%)	

The People		Race/Ethnic Origin	Ancestry	
Area size:	14,225 sq. mi.	63.4% White	USA: 13.2%	Irish: 6.4%
Urban population:	52.9%	33.7% Black	French: 5.6%	
Rural population:	47.1%	0.5% Asian	**2004 Presidential Vote**	
Pop. 2000:	638,517	0.4% Native Am.	Bush (R) 168,484	(62%)
Pop. 2005 (est):	633,854	0.0% Hawaiian	Kerry (D) 100,511	(37%)
Median income:	$27,453	0.6% Two+ races	Other 3,410	(1%)
Poverty status:	23.6%	0.0% Other	**2000 Presidential Vote**	
Military veterans:	12.0%	1.3% Hispanic Origin	Bush (R) 143,628	(57%)
			Gore (D) 100,287	(40%)
			Other 7,706	(3%)
			Cook Partisan Voting Index: R +10	

Occupation	Blue collar: 26.9%	White collar: 53.5%	Gray collar: 19.5%

Northeast Louisiana is perhaps the least known part of the state. Along the Mississippi River and the Red River and their dozens of tributaries, it was plantation country before the Civil War, with black majorities still in many parishes. Away from the larger rivers, it is hill country, places where small farmers scratched out a living on land connected to parish courthouses by dusty lanes. Such was Winn Parish, where Huey P. Long, the pivotal figure in modern Louisiana politics, was born in 1893, and from which he began his meteoric political career—elected governor in 1928, senator in 1930, a national figure threatening both parties when he was assassinated in 1935 in the new high-rise Capitol he built in Baton Rouge.

The 5th Congressional District of Louisiana contains much of this country, from the river parishes to the hills of Winn Parish. The biggest urban areas here, with about 50,000 people each, are Monroe in the north and Alexandria in the south. Alexandria in Rapides Parish sits at the northernmost extension of Cajun, Catholic Louisiana, and is majority black. Monroe in Ouachita Parish is heavily WASP and Baptist, and is home to one of the world's leading Bible collections, assembled by an heir to an early Coca-Cola bottler. Redistricting added some Cajun areas in Allen and Evangeline Parishes and heavily black precincts in Pointe Coupee and Iberville Parishes, all Democratic areas. Overall, population has been declining in this area. George W. Bush increased his vote here from 57% in 2000 to 62% in 2004, his second-best showing in the state.

The congressman from the 5th District is Rodney Alexander, who was elected as a Democrat in December 2002 and switched parties to become a Republican in August 2004. Alexander graduated from Louisiana Tech and won election to the Jackson Parish police jury in 1972 at the age of 25. In 1988 he was elected to the state House, where he chaired the Health and Welfare Committee. He characterized himself as pro-guns, pro-life and pro-prayer. The 5th District seat opened in 2002 when Republican John Cooksey ran unsuccessfully for the Senate after serving three terms in the House. The primary turned out to be a regional contest. Alexander led with 29% of the vote, carrying three hill counties in his legislative district and five heavily black parishes along the Mississippi River. Republican Lee Fletcher, Cooksey's chief of staff for five years, was second with 25%, carrying Monroe's Ouachita Parish and three nearby parishes. Close behind, with 23%, was Republican Clyde Holloway, elected congressman by narrow margins in 1986, 1988 and 1990 from the old 8th District. Holloway, a tree farmer from Rapides Parish, carried seven parishes in the southern end of his district. After the primary, he was angry because he thought the House Republicans' campaign committee was steering contributors to Fletcher's campaign despite Holloway's prior service in the House; he called a press conference to denounce Fletcher as someone who "will do anything to win and he scares me." Alexander attacked Fletcher as a Washington insider and contrasted his "blue jeans" supporters with Fletcher's "blue blood" contributors. Alexander squeaked by with a 50.3%-49.7% victory, a margin of 974 votes. He carried two hill parishes, all the Mississippi River parishes and all but one of the parishes in the southern end of the district.

In the House, Alexander got seats on Agriculture and Armed Services, and had a voting record virtually in the center of the House. In November 2003, he showed independence from Democratic leaders when he voted for the Medicare/prescription drug bill. He voted to extend the tax cuts that Republicans enacted in 2001, and cosponsored legislation to prohibit desecration of the flag and bar gay marriages. Despite his occasional independence, Democratic leaders worked to keep Alexander happy and helped him to raise money for reelection. So they and many others were stunned when in the last hour before the election filing deadline Alexander switched parties. One factor, he explained, was the candidacy of Democratic Zelma Blakes, an African American and political neophyte who he feared would draw votes from him and would leave him vulnerable to attacks from both the left and the right. Democrats were outraged and called him a liar. "I've seen some cowardly things in my career, but this is the worst," said Senator Mary Landrieu.

National Republicans, who were not enthusiastic when Fletcher expressed interest in running again and had failed to attract a strong challenger for the district, quickly embraced Alexander. He explained that he came close to switching parties earlier in 2004, but that he held off because "I didn't want anyone thinking I changed because I couldn't win as a Democrat." Louisiana Democrats filed suit to reopen the qualifying period, but the state appeals court rejected their case. After he switched, Alexander said he would return contributions from Democratic colleagues; in October, after they complained about the delay, Alexander repaid them. But this election turned out to be an afterthought for both parties in Louisiana, where there were two hotly contested open seat House races and a serious contest for the Senate seat Breaux was vacating. Alexander won 59% of the vote, to 25% for Blakes and 16% for former state representative Jock Scott, a Republican. He carried all parishes except for two on the riverfront near Baton Rouge, where Blakes led.

Although Alexander and House Republican leaders insisted that they had made no deal before his switch, he got a seat in January 2005 on the Appropriations Committee and its Agriculture Subcommittee, where he quickly got earmarks for a supplier of water packs to the Pentagon, several road projects, and a transportation and parking facility for the University of Louisiana at Monroe. He said that his views remained the same. But his voting record became markedly more conservative, as though he were liberated from past obligations. The Mark Foley scandal unexpectedly focused attention on Alexander when it was revealed that he sponsored a page who received inappropriate e-mails from Foley, and that Alexander and his chief of staff later conveyed this information to Republican leaders and other officials but they failed to act; Alexander said that his office "did everything we thought we should have," and he voiced frustration that others did not respond. In its December report, the House Ethics Committee commended Alexander for his actions. With his seat on Appropriations, he voiced confidence that he would retain influence while in the minority. Whether leaders of his former party would work with him was a separate issue.

House Democrats tried but failed to find a credible challenger here in 2006. Alexander won 68%-29% against Gloria Hearn, who generated little attention.

SIXTH DISTRICT

Rep. Richard Baker (R)

Elected 1986, 11th term; b. May 22, 1948, New Orleans; home, Baton Rouge; LA St. U., B.A. 1971; United Methodist; married (Kay).

Elected Office: LA House of Reps., 1972-86.

Professional Career: Real estate developer, 1972-86.

DC Office: 341 CHOB, 20515, 202-225-3901; Fax: 202-225-7313; Web site: baker.house.gov.

District Offices: Baton Rouge, 225-929-7711.

Committees: *Financial Services* (2d of 33 R): Capital Markets, Insurance & Government Sponsored Enterprises; Financial Institutions & Consumer Credit. *Transportation & Infrastructure* (9th of 34 R): Water Resources & Environment (RMM); Highways & Transit. *Veterans' Affairs* (4th of 13 R): Economic Opportunity; Health.

Group Ratings

	ADA	ACLU	AFS	LCV	ITIC	NTU	COC	ACU	CFG	FRC
2006	0	0	0	0	100	63	100	92	67	100
2005	0	—	0	0	—	61	92	92	65	92

National Journal Ratings

	2005 LIB	—	2005 CONS	2006 LIB	—	2006 CONS
Economic	14%	—	86%	10%	—	89%
Social	0%	—	89%	17%	—	79%
Foreign	0%	—	89%	0%	—	94%

Key Votes of the 109th Congress

1. Estate Tax Repeal	Y	5. Limit Interstate Abortion	Y	9. Build Border Fence	Y
2. Limit CAFE Standards	Y	6. Extend Patriot Act	Y	10. CAFTA	Y
3. FY06 Spending Curb	Y	7. Bar Same Sex Marriage	Y	11. Oppose Iraq Withdrawal	Y
4. Drilling in ANWR	Y	8. Stem Cell Research $	N	12. Detainee Tribunals	Y

Election Results

2006 primary	Richard Baker (R)	94,658	(83%)	($1,604,762)
	Richard Fontanesi (Lib)	19,648	(17%)	
2004 primary	Richard Baker (R)	189,106	(72%)	($1,090,347)
	Rufus Craig (D)	50,732	(19%)	($17,346)
	Edward Galmon (D)	22,031	(8%)	
2002 primary	Richard Baker (R)	146,932	(84%)	($790,953)
	Rick Moscatello (I)	27,898	(16%)	

Prior Winning Percentages: 2000 (68%); 1998 (51%); 1996 (69%); 1994 (81%); 1992 (51%); 1990 (100%); 1988 (100%); 1986 (51%)

The People		Race/Ethnic Origin	Ancestry	
Area size:	3,210 sq. mi.	62.7% White	French: 10.3%	USA: 7.4%
Urban population:	75.5%	33.2% Black	Irish: 6.3%	
Rural population:	24.5%	1.4% Asian	**2004 Presidential Vote**	
Pop. 2000:	638,324	0.2% Native Am.	Bush (R) 172,080	(59%)
Pop. 2005 (est):	662,252	0.0% Hawaiian	Kerry (D) 117,255	(40%)
Median income:	$37,931	0.7% Two+ races	Other 2,524	(1%)
Poverty status:	16.6%	0.1% Other	**2000 Presidential Vote**	
Military veterans:	11.2%	1.6% Hispanic Origin	Bush (R) 142,239	(55%)
			Gore (D) 111,602	(43%)
			Other 5,716	(2%)
			Cook Partisan Voting Index: R + 7	

Occupation   Blue collar: 23.6%   White collar: 61.5%   Gray collar: 15.0%

Baton Rouge is the central node of Louisiana, on the boundary between the French-speaking, Catholic Cajun country and the heavily Baptist Deep South, its skyscraper Capitol and Exxon refinery sitting just beyond the levees that line the Mississippi River. Historically, it was part of the Florida Parishes, the territory west of the Mississippi River and north of Lake Pontchartrain which was not included in the Louisiana Purchase in 1803; it still belonged to Spain, until the locals rebelled and declared their own Republic of West Florida in 1810. It quickly became part of Louisiana and the United States, but the Florida Parishes, like the states of Texas, California, Vermont and Hawaii, can claim to have been a separate republic (and kingdom in the case of Hawaii) before people here became Americans. But the remote history of the Florida Parishes presses more lightly on Baton Rouge than the impress of the man who dominated Louisiana politics for much of the 20th century, Huey P. Long. Here Long became governor at 36 in the old (and still-standing) Gothic Capitol, when Baton Rouge had only 30,000 people, and was assassinated in 1935 in the hallway of the 34-story Art Deco Capitol he built, next door to the Governor's Mansion, which he also built. To the south are the buildings of Louisiana State University, much of which he built, in an amazingly short time. Today Baton Rouge is the center of a metro area of 766,000, almost all on the east bank of the Mississippi, and reaching far inland to Livingston Parish. This is one of the faster-growing parts of Louisiana: Livingston and Ascension Parishes outside Baton Rouge grew 25% and 27% between 2000 and 2006, faster than any other parishes in the state. Baton Rouge grew more than that—no one knows how much more—in the weeks and months after Hurricane Katrina, when evacuees moved into motel rooms, spare rooms in people's houses, dorm rooms in LSU and Southern University and the city's population may have momentarily doubled; certainly the traffic jams suggested it had. Many have moved on since then, but Baton Rouge is still the largest city in Louisiana, and while much of the state lost jobs in 2006, Baton Rouge gained.

The 6th Congressional District of Louisiana includes just about all of metropolitan Baton Rouge, plus three small mostly rural parishes to the north. The city of Baton Rouge itself in 2000 had a 50% black majority; suburban East Baton Rouge Parish was 40% black and Livingston Parish 4% black. Overall the district is 33% black. Historically, all of this territory was Democratic. In the 1980s the Baton Rouge area moved toward the Republicans and in the 1990s it was fairly closely balanced. In 2004 East Baton Rouge Parish voted 54% for George W. Bush and Livingston Parish 77% for Bush; overall the 6th District voted 59% for Bush.

The congressman from the 6th District is Richard Baker, a Republican first elected in 1986. Baker has spent most of his adult life in public office. He came to Baton Rouge to attend LSU, then in 1972, at 23, was elected as a Democrat to the Louisiana House from a blue-collar district in Baton Rouge. In 1974 he successfully sponsored a highway priority program, allocating roadbuilding funds on the basis of need rather than patronage. He became a Republican in 1985 (the result of "Edwin Edwards pushing me and Ronald Reagan pulling me") and in 1986, when Baton Rouge Republican Congressman Henson Moore ran for the Senate, Baker ran for the House and beat a Democratic state senator 51%-46%. In 1992 he was redistricted in the same district with Republican Congressman Clyde Holloway. The new district lines put Baker at a disadvantage, and he trailed 37%-33% in the September primary. But he won the November runoff 51%-49%.

Baker has spent much of his House career working on regulation issues on the Financial Services Committee, where he chaired the Capital Markets, Insurance and Government Sponsored Enterprises Subcommittee from 2001 to 2007. But after Hurricane Katrina struck New Orleans in August 2005 he devoted much of his time and energy to responding to the disaster.

Baker worked on financial services deregulation, one of the most heavily lobbied issues in the 1990s; the issue was how, under what terms and conditions, to dismantle the wall separating banks and other institutions created by the Glass-Steagall Act of 1933. Baker generally favored deregulation, and served on the conference committee that finally reached agreement in November 1999. The issue of auditor independence was raised by the collapse of Enron in 2001. Financial Services Chairman Michael Oxley and Baker avoided flamboyant hearings; they cancelled a hearing after former Enron Chairman Kenneth Lay said he would take the Fifth Amendment. In February 2002 they rolled out a bill which would create an accounting oversight board inside the SEC, require far more disclosure and would bar external auditing firms from doing certain financial systems consulting and internal auditing. The committee approved the Oxley-Baker approach in April 2002 and the bill passed the House later that month. Meanwhile, in the Senate, Banking Committee Chairman Paul Sarbanes was preparing a bill with bipartisan support which went farther than Oxley and Baker. That bill was languishing when disclosure of the WorldCom accounting scandal in June propelled it forward. It passed the Senate by a wide margin and in conference, at the prodding of the Bush White House, Oxley and Baker yielded on most points of disagreement; the bill was passed and signed before the August recess. In the process, Baker proposed a Federal Account for Investor Restitution (FAIR) Fund, with money raised from monetary penalties levied against corporations and funds disgorged from executives guilty of fraud or malfeasance to be paid over to defrauded investors; this was included in what became the Sarbanes-Oxley Act.

In 2004 Baker opposed the trade-through rule imposed by SEC Chairman William Donaldson. He has taken an "incrementalist approach" to legislation imposing uniformity on regulation of insurance, which historically has been left to the states. In 2004 he got the House to pass a law delaying the FASB rule requiring expensing of stock options, but Senate Banking Chairman Richard Shelby opposed it and it did not become law.

For many years Baker worked almost alone to change the rules governing the government-sponsored enterprises (GSEs) Fannie Mae and Freddie Mac, which purchase and securitize home mortgages. These are for-profit enterprises, yet the fact that they each have $2.25 billion lines of credit with the U.S. Treasury creates an impression in the marketplace that the government will bail them out if they become insolvent. Baker started off conceding that they were well-managed and not at risk, and argued that that was the best time for reform. In February 2000 Baker introduced legislation to create a new regulatory agency for the GSEs and terminate their line of credit, increase disclosure requirements, toughen capital mandates and give regulators more say in approving new activities. Fannie Mae and Freddie Mac vigorously opposed the bill and predicted it would never pass. In October they reached agreement. Fannie Mae and Freddie Mac agreed to increase their equity capital and subordinated debt to 4% of assets and to disclose more information to investors. By February 2001 Fannie Mae CEO Franklin Raines was praising Baker, but they still disagreed: Baker still wanted an independent regulator instead of OFHEO, which is part of Treasury; Raines was opposed. In summer 2001 Baker introduced a bipartisan bill to require Fannie Mae and Freddie Mac to register their stock with the SEC; they agreed to do so voluntarily, but did not issue SEC prospectuses for the securitized instruments they sell to investors—who are, they say, sophisticated enough to evaluate them. The GSEs seemed to have fended off a new regulator. But new developments weakened their position. In June 2003, Freddie Mac's CEO suddenly resigned amid charges of accounting irregularities; in September 2004 OFHEO issued a report charging that Fannie Mae had manipulated earnings. After the OFHEO report was issued, Baker said, "The outrageous conduct outlined in OFHEO's report suggests that for too long Fannie

Mae has acted as if it were somehow above the law while arrogantly flouting all accountability to the Congress, and that must come to an end." Fannie Mae increased its capital level and in December 2004 its CEO was forced to resign. In January 2005 an incredulous Baker demanded that Fannie Mae executives return the huge bonuses they made which turned out to result from flawed accounting. In April 2005, Baker introduced legislation calling for a new regulator, renaming OFHEO and moving it within the Treasury Department rather than HUD.

Baker has twice sought the chairmanship of the Financial Services Committee and has come up short each time. The second time, Baker and the less senior Spencer Bachus both vied for the chair. Baker's support of Roy Blunt for majority leader in February 2006 may have hurt his bid; Bachus supported the winner, John Boehner. The Republican leadership reportedly felt that Baker had not raised enough money for Republican candidates. Baker argued that Bachus would not be a match for his Democratic counterpart, Barney Frank, generally considered one of the smartest members of the House, and that putting Bachus in would put two Alabamians in the lead position on corresponding committees, since Alabama's Richard Shelby was chairman of the Senate Banking Committee. After the election, when the post in question became ranking minority member, the Steering Committee chose Bachus over Baker.

Hurricane Katrina had an enormous impact on the 6th District; hundreds of thousands of evacuees from the New Orleans area streamed up Interstate 10 and U.S. 61 into Baton Rouge. Baker spent the next year concentrating on Katrina-related legislation. He sponsored amendments in October 2005 to allow use of the Agriculture Department's rural housing program to assist evacuees and to loosen HUD restrictions on Community Development Block Grants so they could be spent on public services in damaged areas. He inserted provisions in the Gulf Coast Recovery Act passed in December 2005: federal grants to pay state and local employees, an increase in the cap on community disaster loans from 25% to 50% of local government budgets, 100% federal payment for the cost of debris removal, an extension of unemployment insurance from 26 to 52 weeks. In December 2005 he proposed a Louisiana Recovery Act, using up to $30 billion in the proceeds of sale of federal bonds over 10 years to buy storm-damaged properties and pay off the mortgages; owners would get between 60% and 80% of how much they paid into their house; a Louisiana Recovery Commission would accumulate properties and repackage large tracts for developers, with evacuees getting right of first refusal. To meet objections, he deleted a provision giving the LRC the power of eminent domain. This passed the Financial Services Committee 50–9 and was backed by New Orleans Mayor Ray Nagin, Governor Kathleen Babineaux Blanco and 3d District Democrat Charles Melancon. Other members of the Louisiana delegation were noncommittal. But in January 2006 White House economic aide Al Hubbard rejected the plan, on the grounds that it would add a duplicative bureaucracy and that the problems could be handled by a $6.2 billion supplemental for CDBGs, with hazard mitigation and no replacement of structures on flood-vulnerable land. In March Baker asked federal Katrina coordinator Donald Powell whether he would object to a state agency doing something similar; Powell said, "That's a decision for the local people to make." Baker called on Blanco and the legislature to move in this direction.

At the same time, he worked to authorize the National Flood Insurance Program to borrow up to $25 million and commission a study of mandatory coverage in 100-year-floodplain land. Baker then worked on getting provisions in the homeland security appropriation that would allow the use of "Katrina cottages," modular housing, rather than the trailers FEMA had been providing; that was included in September 2006. He also got amendments to waive a restriction subtracting flood insurance and federal disaster payments from the state's Road Home program, a waiver of the requirement that Road Home recipients use proceeds to pay off SBA loans and $15 million to allow the New Orleans Redevelopment Authority to acquire contiguous properties in distressed neighborhoods and aggregate them to sell to developers. In December 2006, with Melancon and Mary Landrieu, he tried to get approval of an $886.7 million Morganza-to-the-Gulf flood protection system in Terrebonne and Lafourche Parishes, but the Senate did not act; in April 2007 it was approved by the House as part of a $13.2 billion water projects bill, which also provided for closure of the Mississippi River Gulf Outlet (which had funneled waters into St. Barnard Parish and eastern New Orleans) and for $105 million for damaged wetlands there, plus $178 million for flood control in East Baton Rouge Parish. Over the years Baker has worked to build local institutions, including the Pennington Biomedical Research Center in Baton Rouge and (he is an astronomy buff) the underground Laser Interferometer Gravitational-Wave Observatory in Livingston Parish.

With one exception, Baker has not had difficulty winning reelection since 1992. That exception was in 1998, when he was challenged then by Democrat Marjorie McKeithen, the granddaughter of former Governor (1964-72) John McKeithen and daughter of Secretary of State Fox McKeithen, and won by only 50.7%-49.3%. Since then Baker has been reelected by wide margins. In August 2007, he said he would not challenge Senator Mary Landrieu in 2008.

SEVENTH DISTRICT

Rep. Charles Boustany (R)

Elected 2004, 2d term; b. Feb. 21, 1956, New Orleans; home, Lafayette; U. of SW LA, B.S. 1978, LA St. U., M.D. 1982; Episcopalian; married (Bridget).

Professional Career: Practicing surgeon, 1982-2004.

DC Office: 1117 LHOB, 20515, 202-225-2031; Fax: 202-225-5724; Web site: boustany.house.gov.

District Offices: Lafayette, 337-235-6322; Lake Charles, 337-433-1747.

Committees: *Agriculture* (13th of 21 R): General Farm Commodities & Risk Management; Department Operations, Oversight, Nutrition & Forestry. *Education & Labor* (16th of 22 R): Health, Employment, Labor & Pensions; Early Childhood, Elementary & Secondary Education. *Transportation & Infrastructure* (29th of 34 R): Water Resources & Environment; Highways & Transit.

Group Ratings

	ADA	ACLU	AFS	LCV	ITIC	NTU	COC	ACU	CFG	FRC
2006	0	14	0	0	86	53	100	80	50	100
2005	15	—	0	6	—	56	89	96	49	92

National Journal Ratings

	2005 LIB	—	2005 CONS		2006 LIB	—	2006 CONS
Economic	6%	—	93%		32%	—	67%
Social	30%	—	70%		23%	—	74%
Foreign	34%	—	61%		17%	—	73%

Key Votes of the 109th Congress

1. Estate Tax Repeal	Y	5. Limit Interstate Abortion	Y	9. Build Border Fence	Y
2. Limit CAFE Standards	Y	6. Extend Patriot Act	Y	10. CAFTA	N
3. FY06 Spending Curb	Y	7. Bar Same Sex Marriage	Y	11. Oppose Iraq Withdrawal	Y
4. Drilling in ANWR	Y	8. Stem Cell Research $	N	12. Detainee Tribunals	Y

Election Results

2006 primary	Charles Boustany (R)	113,720	(71%)	($1,622,109)
	Mike Stagg (D)	47,133	(29%)	($57,011)
2004 runoff	Charles Boustany (R)	75,039	(55%)	($2,785,524)
	Willie Mount (D)	61,493	(45%)	($1,340,886)
2004 primary	Charles Boustany (R)	105,761	(39%)	
	Willie Mount (D)	69,079	(25%)	
	Don Cravins (D)	67,389	(25%)	($212,315)
	David Thibodaux (R)	26,526	(10%)	($118,238)
	Other	5,177	(2%)	

The People		Race/Ethnic Origin	Ancestry	
Area size:	7,294 sq. mi.	72.0% White	French: 14.1% USA: 11.6%	
Urban population:	68.9%	24.8% Black	Fr. Canadian: 6.6%	
Rural population:	31.1%	0.7% Asian	**2004 Presidential Vote**	
Pop. 2000:	638,430	0.2% Native Am.	Bush (R) 168,645	(60%)
Pop. 2005 (est):	647,471	0.0% Hawaiian	Kerry (D) 110,623	(39%)
Median income:	$31,453	0.7% Two+ races	Other 3,103	(1%)
Poverty status:	19.9%	0.1% Other	**2000 Presidential Vote**	
Military veterans:	11.8%	1.4% Hispanic Origin	Bush (R) 141,378	(55%)
			Gore (D) 107,190	(42%)
			Other 7,357	(3%)
			Cook Partisan Voting Index: R + 7	

Occupation   Blue collar: 27.9%   White collar: 54.9%   Gray collar: 17.2%

More than 200 years ago, French-speaking settlers were forced to leave their land of Acadie, which the British had taken over and renamed Nova Scotia, and make their way to the wetlands of southern Louisiana. Here, without much notice, they built steep-roofed houses to slough off nonexistent snow and adapted French cuisine to the crawfish and muskrat they found in abundance in the pelican-tended swamps. The heart of the Cajun country is around Lafayette, just west of the Atchafalaya Basin, where Mississippi waters pour through bayous and canals, with only occasional bits of solid land visible on the 30-mile section of Interstate 10 built on elevated stilts. For half a century the Cajun country thrived, thanks to the oil and gas plentiful here and just off shore in the Gulf of Mexico; oil rigs are common, and every once in a while the swampy foliage parts to reveal a giant refinery or petrochemical plant. Cajun pride has experienced a resurgence: Cajun French is surviving decades of efforts to eliminate it; Cajun music—and its black-influenced variant, zydeco— are popular here and nationally; spicy Cajun cooking has become a tourist attraction here and, in understated form, familiar all over the United States. About 45% of the people in Acadiana speak French as a second language. Lafayette, with its Acadian Village and plethora of oil exploration firms, features its annual *Festivals Acadiens* to celebrate music, food and crafts. Unlike New Orleans, its Mardi Gras reveries do not require anti-discrimination statements; the result has been an all-white parade and an all-black parade.

The oil price crash of the middle 1980s hit the Cajun country hard. Rising expectations, and the giddy sense that the oil industry promised lasting prosperity, suddenly collapsed, leaving borrowers overextended and ordinary homeowners unable to maintain the standard of living they expected. Politically, the Cajun country seemed to move then toward national Democrats, whom it had shunned because their cultural liberalism seemed alien to the Cajun tradition of respecting the authority of Church and state while tolerating a certain amount of *laissez les bons temps rouler* spirit. The Cajun country voted for Bill Clinton in 1992 and 1996, as it had voted for Louisiana's foremost Cajun politician, Edwin Edwards, who was elected governor four times. It has given solid majorities to George W. Bush, but also favored Lafayette-based Governor Kathleen Babineaux Blanco.

Hurricane Rita, not Katrina, was the natural disaster with the most devastating local impact in 2005. While most of the state and nation remained preoccupied by circumstances in New Orleans, this second hurricane left its own path of destruction 200 and 300 miles to the west. Rita struck with winds of 120 miles per hour and a storm surge of up to 15 feet that virtually erased some coastal communities, especially in Cameron Parish; local residents and officials complained that they were the victims of "Rita amnesia" in the lack of public attention. Plans were hatched to move some villages along the coast more than 10 miles inland to higher ground.

The 7th Congressional District of Louisiana covers much of the Cajun country, from Lafayette and the Atchafalaya west along I-10 to Lake Charles and the Texas border. Refineries and oil-field support industries provide many jobs, as do the rice and crawfish farming fields. Some 21% of the population claims either French or French Canadian ancestry.

The congressman from the 7th District is Charles Boustany, elected in 2004 and the first Republican elected from this area since 1884. Of Lebanese ancestry, he grew up in Lafayette, where his father was parish coroner; he graduated from the University of Southwestern Louisiana and LSU Medical School. He worked as a cardio-thoracic surgeon and was active in civic and political affairs.

In 2004, Democrat Chris John ran for the Senate, and Boustany was one of five candidates running to succeed him. The other Republican was David Thibodeaux of Lafayette, who had run unsuccessfully for this seat three times, most recently in 1996; but he raised little money, some party leaders viewed him as too conservative and Boustany quickly became the Republican favorite. The Democratic frontrunners were two state senators: Don Cravins of the Breaux Bridge area, who was seeking to become the first black to hold this seat, and state Senator Willie Mount of Lake Charles. Boustany raised plenty of money early and campaigned on his "prescription for prosperity"—expansion of health-savings accounts, high-speed Internet access for local small businesses, and opposition to the Central American Free Trade Agreement. The National Republican Congressional Committee ran ads attacking Mount's support for higher taxes in the Legislature, presumably because it saw Cravins as a weaker candidate in a runoff. Boustany led the November primary with 39% of the vote, to 25.2% for Mount, 24.6% for Cravins, and 10% for Thibodeaux. In the December runoff, Cravins refused to endorse Mount because of his anger over the state Democratic Party's "unity ballot" sent to black voters, which included Mount's name and not his. Cravins's neutrality hurt Mount in the Lafayette area. Mount pointed to her legislative experience, while Boustany emphasized his "values" agenda. Boustany won 55%-45%. Mount won 60% in Lake Charles's Calcasieu Parish, which cast 32% of the vote. But Boustany trumped that with 70% in Lafayette Parish, which cast 30% of the vote.

In the House, Boustany's voting record was relatively moderate for a southern Republican. He has seats on three prime committees: Agriculture, Education and the Workforce, and Transportation and Infrastructure. On the Education committee, he was an active proponent of legislation to permit small businesses to join together in associations to pay less for health insurance. On Transportation, his priorities included use of the Water Resource and Development Act to restore Louisiana's eroding coastline and funding to complete Interstate 49 from Shreveport to Lafayette. He enacted post-Hurricane Katrina and Rita initiatives to provide special rules for disaster-relief employment for individuals displaced by the storms, and to assist individuals with disabilities. In October 2005, he pledged to local groups that he would make sure "southwest Louisiana is not a stepchild" in hurricane recovery. He pushed for expedited assistance payments from FEMA and criticized the slow clean-up of debris in Cameron Parish. When Speaker Dennis Hastert and Minority Leader Nancy Pelosi led a delegation of House members in March 2006 to Katrina recovery sites, Boustany complained loudly that they overlooked his area. In July, Hastert returned to Boustany's district.

The Democratic Congressional Campaign Committee recruited Chris John to run for his old seat in 2006; he was not interested, but left the door open for another statewide bid. With John out of the running, Boustany had an easy win against Democrat Mike Stagg, 71%-29%. He ruled out a run for the Senate in 2008.

★ MAINE ★

Maine is a state with a distinctive personality—ornery, contrary-minded, almost bullheaded, rough-hewn. It is the state closest geographically to Europe, but it was not heavily settled until the mid-19th century, and then by people coming from the south and west—the opposite of America's usual pattern. In an urbanizing and rapidly changing country, Maine was famous for its pointed firs and steady habits, with a few dozen small factory and paper mill towns but nothing like a major metropolis. Maine grew in a rush and then mostly stopped: There were 600,000 people here in 1860 but its population did not top 1 million until the 1970s. Then the tremors of the New England high-tech booms of the 1980s and 1990s reverberated up I-95 and shook Maine. The simple, back-to-nature Yankee style came into vogue. The antique dockside buildings on Portland's waterfront were restored and an old-style Public Market was constructed; the Maine Mall expanded and saw office parks spring up nearby, a miniature edge city; real estate prices rose by hundreds of percents, not just in vacation coves, but in Portland and small towns that had never considered themselves picturesque. The L.L. Bean headquarters in Freeport, open 24 hours a day, 365 days a year, symbolized the boom: The two chaste initials and the Anglo-Saxon monosyllable suggesting the dry understatement of Down East Yankees; the 24-hour-a-day schedule recalling the hard work needed to eke out a living from the cold waters of the North Atlantic to the pine-covered North Woods; the commercial success of the enterprise a prime example of Maine's unexpected boom. Something like the Maine slogan: "The way life should be."

Over these years, Maine's economy was transformed. It lost jobs in shoes, chicken processing, papermaking and timber, but gained in tourism, call centers and high-tech. The Grand Banks have

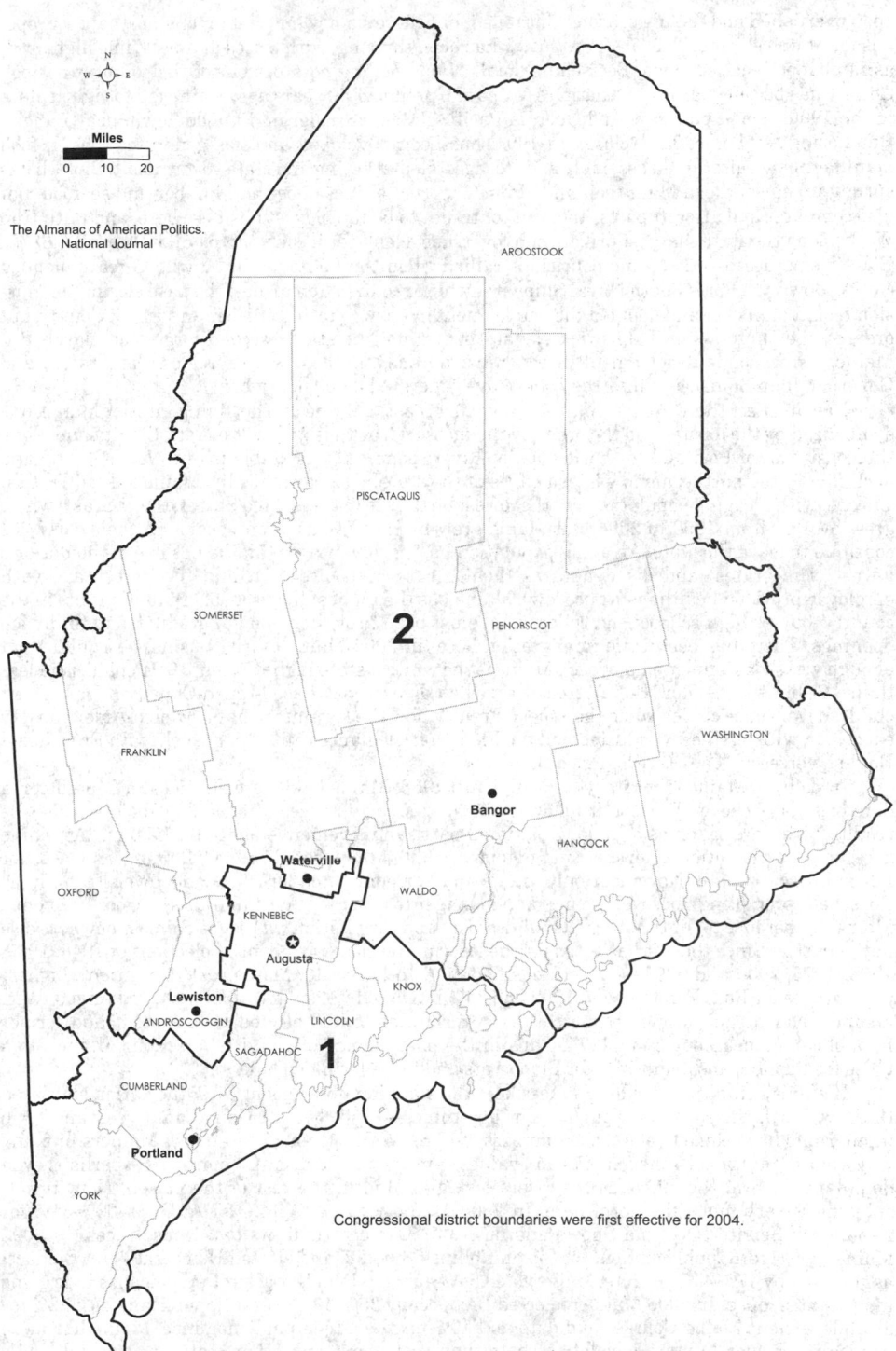

The Almanac of American Politics.
National Journal

Congressional district boundaries were first effective for 2004.

been overfished and fishing seasons shortened, but there's a new market among northern Europeans for Maine shrimp. The lobster industry has been thriving, with prices at an all-time high, even as lumber mills close down. Scratching small Maine boiling potatoes out of the soil of Aroostook County has become harder; the nation's top potato producer 50 years ago, Maine fell to eighth place in the 1990s: small potatoes. And Georgia-Pacific closed its paper mill in Old Town, near Bangor. But Loring Air Force Base, closed in 1994, has been developed and has generated jobs in food manufacturing, aircraft disassembly and storage, telemarketing and state government. Biotech has sprung up on southern Maine soil and Maine exports not just paper and lumber and seafood, but also computer and aircraft parts. Tourism continues to be the biggest business here, and Bath Iron Works, long the state's largest private employer, has a long-term contract to build 21 *Arleigh Burke* Class Naval destroyers. Maine politicians rallied when the Pentagon in May 2005 recommended closing down the Portsmouth Naval Shipyard, which repairs submarines; the base closing commission took it off its list and doubled the employment in an accounting office in Aroostook County, but ordered the shutdown of Brunswick Naval Air Station, the state's second largest employer. But Maine, its economic development director insists, has "the best work force on the planet," and Governor John Baldacci's Pine Tree Zones have generated 3,000 new jobs.

Now in effect there are two Maines—booming coastal Maine and declining interior Maine, one symbolized by the lobster and the other by the moose. Growth is greatest in York County and along the coast east of Portland to the Penobscot River; population is stable in the North Woods and declining in the northern and eastern edges of the state. Demographically, Maine is like Western Europe, with an aging population and the lowest birth rate in the United States; the U.S. as a whole grew by 18% from 1990 to 2004, but Maine grew by just 7%, as young people in their early 20s continue to leave the state. An aging population has its advantages (Maine has one of the nation's lowest crime rates) and disadvantages (health care costs are high and the percentage with employer-provided health insurance low). Maine has the highest high school graduation rate in the country, but its high schools and colleges have not been providing enough graduates to fill its job openings. There has been little immigration here (in 2004 Maine tourist businesses couldn't get enough visas for summer employees): Maine is the whitest state in the nation, 1% Hispanic and less than 1% black or Asian. But it treasures what diversity it has. French-Canadian immigrant children were once chided when they spoke French; now the legislature has a French-American day each year, with business conducted and the Pledge of Allegiance recited in French, with French and English verses of "The Star-Spangled Banner."

In politics, Maine is contrary-minded. Until 1958, Maine held state elections in September, a date originally chosen because it followed the state's early harvest; in the days before polls, the results here were taken as a gauge of national partisan movement—hence the saying, "As Maine goes, so goes the nation." However, in September 1936, Maine voted 56% for Republican Governor Lewis Barrows and in November only Maine and Vermont voted for Alf Landon over Franklin D. Roosevelt, prompting Roosevelt's campaign manager to observe, "As Maine goes, so goes Vermont." Maine's adherence to flinty Yankee Republicanism and Prohibition was echoed almost nowhere else in the nation. Since then, it has voted for the loser in the close presidential elections of 1948, 1960, 1968, 1976, 2000 and 2004—a record equaled by no other state. Maine cast the nation's highest percentages for Ross Perot, 30% in 1992 and 14% in 1996. In 1994 and 1998 it elected Angus King, an Independent and former Democrat, as governor, as it had elected Independent and former Republican James Longley in 1974. Thus in the past eight gubernatorial elections Maine voted twice for Republicans, four times for Democrats and twice for Independents.

If Maine's tradition-minded Yankees kept the state Republican long after the nation embraced the New Deal, the sons and daughters of its ethnics—Irish, French Canadian, Greek and Arab immigrants have come to equal the numbers of pure WASPs (though these new Mainers in many ways share traditional Yankee traits and values)—made the Democrats competitive, perhaps even dominant, here in the 1980s as they were losing ground in the rest of the nation. Now, ticket-splitting is very much the norm here. In 2000 Maine voted 49%-44% for Al Gore, 69%-31% for Republican Senator Olympia Snowe and 66%-32% Democratic in its two House races. In 2002 Maine reelected Republican Senator Susan Collins 58%-42% and elected Democrat John Baldacci as governor by 47%-41%. In 2004 Maine voted 54%-45% for John Kerry but Republicans made gains in the state House. In 2006 Maine reelected Baldacci by 38%-30% over a Republican, with 22% for an Independent Maine Course candidate and 10% for the Green party nominee. Maine has more partisan turnover in state legislative seats than just about any other state; in its small seats (average population of a state House seat is 8,724) Mainers vote for the person, not the party. In 2004 Protestants voted 55%-43% for Bush and Catholics 58%-40% for Kerry—which looks like

Maine's politics of the past and is out of line with results elsewhere, and was good news for Democrats. But Bush also carried Mainers under 30—again contrary to the national trend, a good sign for Republicans.

As the economy changed, Maine moved toward a consensus on how to balance economic growth and preserve the environment. But there is disagreement raging about the North Woods. The big paper companies, long the biggest landowners in Maine, have been selling off huge acreage—7 million acres between 1998 and 2004. As Conservation Commissioner Patrick McGowan put it, "For generations the paper companies sort of managed everything for us up here. They gave sportsmen pretty much free rein, and in turn people up here helped out as stewards of the land. But with all of these new buyers, nobody quite knows what will happen now, and people are getting nervous." Local Mainers want to keep using the land for hunting, trapping and snowmobiling. But a Concord, Massachusetts, group called Restore: The North Woods, with backing from Hollywood stars, wanted to create a huge national park, bigger than Yellowstone and Yosemite combined. Environmental-minded rich people are buying up land with a view toward donating it for a national park; Roxanne Quimby, a beeswax lip balm millionaire who spends much of the year in Palm Beach, bought 70,000 acres and has banned hunting and snowmobiling. Mainers reacted angrily to these folks "from away," as they say, and Governor John Baldacci called the national park proposal a "nonstarter," and has promoted alternatives. The Nature Conservancy in 2006 donated easements on 195,000 acres, with space for recreation and land available for sustainable timber harvests; Plum Creek Timber wants to build the state's largest subdivision on Moosehead Lake. To preserve salmon, one dam on the Kennebec River was dismantled in 1999 and in 2003 the power company agreed to dismantle two others on the Penobscot, while regulators voted down a wind farm near Rangeley.

The People		Race/Ethnic Origin			Military veterans: 154,590 (15.9%)	
Pop. 2006 (est):	1,321,574	1,230,297	96.5%	White	WWII: 19.8%	Korea: 14.1%
Pop. 2000:	1,274,923	6,440	0.5%	Black	Vietnam: 33.1%	Gulf War: 8.2%
Pop. 1990:	1,227,928	9,014	0.7%	Asian	**Most populous cities (2006):**	
Change 1990-2000:	Up 3.8%	6,911	0.5%	Native Am.	1. Portland	63,011
% of U.S. total:	0.5%	334	0.0%	Hawaiian	2. Lewiston	35,734
Pop. rank:	40th of 50	11,731	0.9%	Two+ races	3. Bangor	31,008
Area size:	35,385 sq. mi.	836	0.1%	Other	4. South Portland	23,784
State Native:	67.3%	9,360	0.7%	Hisp. Origin	5. Auburn	23,156
Non-citizen:	1.3%	**Ancestry**				
Language		English: 16.0%		Irish: 11.2%	Urban population: 40.2%	
English: 87.9%	Other Eur.:10.0%	French: 10.6%		USA: 7.0%	Rural population: 59.8%	
Spanish: 1.3%		Fr. Canadian: 6.4%				

Education		Work Sector			Legislature	
H.S. Grad:	85.4%	Private. 75.9%		Govt: 14.5%	Senate	18 D 17 R
College Grad:	22.9%	Self: 9.3%		Family: 0.3%	House	89 D 60 R 2 I
Industry		Unemployment: 4.7%			Legislative Term Limits: Yes	
Agri: 2.6%	Con: 6.9%	**Household Income**			**Registered Voters**	
Fin: 6.2%	Info: 2.5%	<15k: 17.8%		15-35k: 29.0%	D: 309,525	(31.1%)
Mfg: 18.5%	Prof: 30.1%	35-50k: 18.3%		50-100k: 27.7%	R: 279,641	(28.1%)
Public: 4.5%	Trade: 17.0%	100-150k: 4.7%		>150k: 2.4%	O: 404,582	(40.7%)
Other: 11.8%		Median: $37,240				
Occupation		Poverty status: 10.9%				
Blue collar: 25.6%	White collar: 57.4%	**Home Value**				
Gray collar: 17.0%		<50k: 15.4%	50-100k: 39.6%	100-200k: 34.6%	200-300k: 6.5%	
		300-500k: 2.7%	>500k: 1.2%	Median: $94,300		

Presidential politics   Maine has been a hard state to predict in recent presidential politics. It gave majorities to Republican George Bush in 1988 and Democrat Bill Clinton in 1996. In between, the 1992 race was very nearly a three-way tie, with Clinton in first place and Bush, who has spent nearly every summer of his life in Maine, in third place. In 2000, Al Gore won by a 49%-44% margin, with 6% for Ralph Nader. In 2004 Maine was a target state for both candidates. There were signs and stickers all over the state and turnout rose 14% in a state with population growth of 3% over the same period. But the result was more one-sided than expected earlier in the year: John Kerry won 54%-45%. Kerry's margin was larger than in two states

2004 Presidential Vote		
Kerry (D)	396,842	(54%)
Bush (R)	330,201	(45%)
Nader (BL)	8,069	(1%)
Other	5,640	(1%)
2000 Presidential Vote		
Gore (D)	319,951	(49%)
Bush (R)	286,616	(44%)
Nader (Green)	37,127	(6%)
Other	8,123	(1%)

that were on no one's target list, Delaware and Hawaii, and another, Washington, that had been conceded as safe for Kerry in August. It's not clear whether Maine will be on anyone's target list in 2008.

Maine is one of two states (Nebraska is the other) which gives two electors to the statewide winner and one elector to the winner in each congressional district. In 2004, Kerry carried the 1st District by nearly 50,000 votes and the 2d District by 20,762 votes.

Maine held its first-ever presidential primary on March 5, 1996, in an attempt to generate an early contest to which candidates would pay attention. But they didn't—at least not much. Maine abolished its presidential primary for 2004. In 2008, both parties will hold February caucuses.

Congressional districting   The lines in Maine are drawn by a 15-member bipartisan Legislative Apportionment Committee; the legislature can amend the plan and must approve it by a two-thirds vote. The governor has a veto, though presumably that's academic since there would be a two-thirds majority to override it. Under state law the committee sent its plan to the legislature in spring 2003. This arguably violates the Constitution, since the 2002 elections

110th Congress Lineup
2 D
109th Congress Lineup
2 D

were held within lines drawn on the basis of the 1990 Census. But no one has filed a lawsuit for the good reason that it makes no practical difference. There has been little change in the boundary between the two districts since Maine lost its third seat in the 1960 Census. In the 2003 session, however, the legislature failed to adopt a plan. On July 2, 2003, the state supreme court adopted a plan for the 2004 elections.

Governor

John Baldacci (D)

Elected 2002, term expires Jan. 2011, 2d term; b. Jan. 30, 1955, Bangor; home, Augusta; U. of ME, B.A. 1986; Catholic; married (Karen).

Elected Office: Bangor City Cncl., 1978-81; ME Senate, 1982-94; U.S. House of Reps., 1994-2002.

Professional Career: Restaurateur.

Office: 1 State House Station, Augusta, 04333, 207-287-3531; Fax: 207-287-1034; Web site: www.state.me.us/governor.

Election Results

2006 general	John Baldacci (D)	209,927	(38%)
	Chandler Woodcock (R)	166,425	(30%)
	Barbara Merrill (IMC)	118,715	(22%)
	Patricia LaMarche (Green)	52,690	(10%)
	Other	3,108	(1%)
2006 primary	John Baldacci (D)	40,314	(76%)
	Christopher Miller (D)	12,861	(24%)
2002 general	John Baldacci (D)	238,179	(47%)
	Peter Cianchette (R)	209,496	(41%)
	Jonathan Carter (Green)	46,903	(9%)

John Baldacci (pronounced *ball-DA-chee*) in 2002 became the first Democrat elected governor of Maine since 1986. Baldacci grew up in Bangor, then lived across the street from the house he grew up in and still attends the same church where he was christened. His family ran Momma Baldacci's, a restaurant started by his grandparents in 1933. He is of Italian and Lebanese descent, distantly related to former Senator George Mitchell, and the family restaurant used to get a daily delivery of rolls from former Senator William Cohen's father's bakery. Baldacci followed his father on the Bangor City Council in 1978, at 23; in 1982 he was elected to the state Senate, where he often dissented from Democrats and chaired the tax committee. When 2d District Congresswoman Olympia Snowe ran for the Senate in 1994, Baldacci ran for the House and campaigned by holding spaghetti dinners at $2 a head (children under 12 free). Maine's contrary-mindedness came out in the general election: Baldacci opposed the Clinton health care plan and pledged to oppose any new taxes; Republican nominee Richard Bennett was iffy about the Contract With America's defense spending increase. Baldacci won 46%-41%.

In the House, Baldacci had a mostly liberal voting record and was reelected three times with more than 70% of the vote. Maine's congressional districts are good springboards to statewide office, for each one is within both the Portland and Bangor television markets; Baldacci's three immediate predecessors in the 2d District were all elected to the Senate. But Baldacci's goal was the governorship, and he had pledged to serve only eight years in the House. From the time Independent Angus King was elected to a second and last term in 1998, Baldacci was recognized as the frontrunner for 2002. Yet there was plenty of competition. Baldacci said he was against tax increases; to spur economic development, he wanted to increase state aid to public schools (to hold down property taxes), slow down the growth of state spending and eliminate the property tax on business equipment. He said a single-payer health care finance plan was unworkable and said he would set up an Office of Health Policy to coordinate changes in health care finance. Baldacci promised a "balanced economic strategy" with different approaches for rural and urban areas and reiterated his promise to limit spending increases to the rate of inflation. The leading Republican was former state Representative Peter Cianchette, who promised to cut the state tax burden by 20%; he said he would veto any tax increase and "any budget that grows faster than your paychecks." He called for a property tax cap, with no corresponding state aid. Independent candidate Jonathan Carter won the Green party nomination (there was actually a primary) and also qualified for the state's public financing system, which gave him $902,000 but limited his spending, almost as much as Baldacci's and Cianchette's $1.5 million. Carter called for single-payer health insurance and for a sales tax on professional services; like the others he was for eliminating the property tax on business equipment.

On Election Day, Baldacci won a 47%-41% plurality over Cianchette; Carter got only 9%. Baldacci won absolute majorities only in the counties north and east of Bangor, and they accounted for 26,000 of his 29,000-vote plurality; interestingly, these same counties were the strongest area that same day for Republican Senator Susan Collins, who is from Aroostook County: Hometown voting.

Facing a budget shortfall estimated at $1.2 billion, in 2003 Baldacci and the Democratic legislature managed to pass a balanced two-year budget without a tax increase. Baldacci also got enactment of his Pine Tree Opportunity Zones, to let economically ailing cities and towns offer business tax breaks. The legislature also passed Baldacci's ambitious Dirigo Health plan (*Dirigo*, the state motto, means "I lead"). Dirigo was designed to provide health insurance policies for low- and middle-income employees of small businesses and those with no employers, with state subsidies of individual premiums; it also authorized caps on medical expansion and fees for the state's 39 hospitals. In spring 2004 Baldacci sought bids from insurers; only one, Anthem Blue Cross Blue Shield, already Maine's largest health insurer, put in a bid. Anthem's DirigoChoice plan started taking enrollments in October 2004, but by spring 2005 enrollment was just over 5,000, representing about 1,200 self-employed people and 400 small businesses. Conservatives criticized the plan as not significantly cheaper than commercial alternatives. Anthem said that their target enrollment was only 10-15,000 by the end of 2005, considerably less than the 31,000 the state hoped to enroll. Maine's insurance superintendent determined in 2005 that insurers must pay nearly $44 million to Dirigo Health to account for reforms that were designed to reduce charges from hospitals and providers. The disputed payments have ended up in court and the legislature rejected two bills in 2006 to fix the problem. In May 2007, Baldacci proposed a host of changes to the program, including a provision for "shared responsibility." By 2008, employers not providing health insurance would have to pay a fee, and by January 2009, individuals without coverage would have to buy into Dirigo.

In 2004 Baldacci addressed the tax issue, made more pressing by the fact that two ballot propositions were going before the voters—one in June which would require the state to pay 55% of education costs, up from 43%, and the other in November which would limit property taxes to 1% of valuation. The legislature did not act in its spring session, but it did increase state education spending by $340 million in the years 2006-10, but not immediately. In June, 55% of voters approved the education cost requirement, while 63% rejected the property tax limit in November. In December Baldacci presented a tax package: limiting property taxes to 6% of income by state loans, capping spending at all levels at rises in income and inflation and proposing a constitutional amendment to allow towns and cities to freeze property taxes at current levels. Not included were recommendations of Baldacci's economic development commission in January 2004: abolish the personal property tax on new business equipment and reducing the business tax burden to the New England average. In 2003 another commission recommended consolidation of schools; Baldacci proposed that in 2004, but it was rejected 76-53 by the state House. In March 2005, the Democratic legislature approved Baldacci's request to borrow $450 million to balance the state budget. Republicans balked at the borrowing and began a drive to put the issue on the November ballot; Democrats responded by repealing the borrowing and made up the shortfall through spending cuts and targeted tax increases.

In January 2006, Baldacci signed a deal with Venezuela-owned Citgo Petroleum–in spite of Venezuelan President Hugo Chavez's fierce criticism of President Bush–to supply $5.5 million in home heating oil to low-income Mainers. Baldacci proposed an energy plan that would diversify the state's fuel use with tax breaks for bio-diesel and incentives for wind and hydroelectric power. He also signed an executive order for a plan to extend year-round passenger rail service past Portland to Brunswick and Lewiston-Auburn. Baldacci responded to the 2005 base closing commission's decision to close Brunswick Naval Air Station by proposing in 2006 to exempt the pensions of future military retirees from the state income tax.

Baldacci signed bills in 2006 to provide an additional $5 million for home heating assistance, raise the minimum wage to $7 an hour, eliminate property taxes on business equipment for new businesses and crack down on drivers who operate a vehicle with a suspended or revoked license. The legislature also amended the 2005 budget with a $219 million supplemental budget for school aid, prescription drugs, hospital payments and transportation projects. The legislature rejected raising the governor's salary, leaving Baldacci's annual pay at $70,000. Baldacci joined a lawsuit with four other states to fight a "clawback" provision that requires states to return Medicaid savings to the federal government that they realize by not having to pay for drugs now covered by the Medicare prescription drug program.

Republicans saw opportunity in 2006 as Baldacci's proposed borrowing and the problems with Dirigo contributed to the governor's low popularity ratings. State Senator Chandler Woodcock, a social conservative, won the three-way Republican primary in June by narrowly defeating a moderate Republican, whom Democrats viewed as a more formidable challenger in the November election. Baldacci faced three other candidates in the general election, including independent state Representative Barbara Merrill, a former Democrat. Woodcock campaigned on economic issues and supported a referendum also on the November ballot that would have imposed a state spending cap. But Maine had not ousted an incumbent from Blaine House, the governor's mansion, in 40 years. Baldacci carried 12 of 16 counties and won 38%, and he was again elected governor with a plurality. Woodcock finished second with 30%, followed by Merrill in third place with 22%. Voters also rejected 54%-46% a Taxpayer Bill of Rights, which would have imposed a state spending cap. Baldacci opposed the measure but after the election said he wanted to find a way to freeze increases in property valuations until a property is sold.

Democrats in 2006 increased their House majority in the 151-seat chamber from 74 to 89 seats, and held a narrow 18-17 majority in the state Senate. Baldacci shrugged off the results of his own close election and set out an ambitious agenda. In 2007 he proposed a two-year $6.4 billion budget that boosted state funding for public education by $178 million. The plan would seek savings in school administration costs by consolidating the number of school districts from 290 to 26, while also eliminating most of the 152 local school superintendents. It would also raise $130 million in new revenue by increasing cigarette taxes from $2 to $3 per pack.

Senior Senator

Olympia Snowe (R)

Elected 1994, seat up 2012, 3d term; b. Feb. 21, 1947, Augusta; home, Auburn; U. of ME, B.A. 1969; Greek Orthodox; married (John McKernan).

Elected Office: ME House of Reps., 1973-76; ME Senate, 1976-78; U.S. House of Reps., 1978-94.

Professional Career: Dir., Superior Concrete Co., 1969-78; Auburn Bd. of Voter Registration, 1971-73.

DC Office: 154 RSOB, 20510, 202-224-5344; Fax: 202-224-1946; Web site: snowe.senate.gov.

State Offices: Auburn, 207-786-2451; Augusta, 207-622-8292; Bangor, 207-945-0432; Biddeford, 207-282-4144; Portland, 207-874-0883; Presque Isle, 207-764-5124.

Committees: *Commerce, Science & Transportation* (5th of 11 R): Oceans, Atmosphere, Fisheries & Coast Guard (RMM); Interstate Commerce, Trade & Tourism; Aviation Operations, Safety & Security; Consumer Affairs, Insurance & Automotive Safety; Surface Transportation & Merchant Marine Infrastructure, Safety & Security. *Finance* (4th of 10 R): Health Care; International Trade & Global Competitiveness; Taxation & IRS Oversight & Long-Term Growth. *Intelligence (Select)* (6th of 7 R). *Small Business & Entrepreneurship* (RMM of 9 R).

Group Ratings

	ADA	ACLU	AFS	LCV	ITIC	NTU	COC	ACU	CFG	FRC
2006	45	50	38	86	75	39	75	36	9	37
2005	65	—	38	70	—	35	78	32	18	—

National Journal Ratings

	2005 LIB	—	2005 CONS	2006 LIB	—	2006 CONS
Economic	55%	—	44%	54%	—	45%
Social	53%	—	45%	55%	—	44%
Foreign	48%	—	51%	56%	—	43%

Key Votes of the 109th Congress

1. Bar ANWR Drilling	Y	5. Confirm Samuel Alito	Y	9. Limit Interstate Abortion	N
2. FY06 Spending Curb	N	6. Path to Citizenship	Y	10. CAFTA	N
3. Estate Tax Repeal	Y	7. Bar Same Sex Marriage	N	11. Urge Iraq Withdrawal	N
4. Raise Minimum Wage	Y	8. Stem Cell Research $	Y	12. Provide Detainee Rights	*

Election Results

2006 general	Olympia Snowe (R)	402,598	(74%)	($2,773,431)
	Jean Hay Bright (D)	111,984	(21%)	($126,823)
	William Slavick (I)	29,220	(5%)	($5,580)
2006 primary	Olympia Snowe (R)	unopposed		
2000 general	Olympia Snowe (R)	437,689	(69%)	($1,981,504)
	Mark Lawrence (D)	197,183	(31%)	($727,655)

Prior Winning Percentages: 1994 (60%); 1992 House (49%); 1990 House (51%); 1988 House (66%); 1986 House (77%); 1984 House (76%); 1982 House (67%); 1980 House (79%); 1978 House (51%)

Olympia Snowe, Maine's senior senator, is a Republican first elected to the House in 1978 and to the Senate in 1994. After losing her mother at age 8 and her father at age 9, Snowe grew up with her aunt and uncle in Auburn, and worked as a legislative staffer after college; in 1973, after her husband, state Representative Peter Snowe, died in an auto accident, she was elected to his seat. In 1978, when Congressman William Cohen ran for the Senate, she ran for the House in the northern 2d District, and won handily. She had a moderate record and won by large margins in the 1980s but more narrowly in the 1990s; in 1989 she married Governor John McKernan, her former House colleague. When Senator George Mitchell announced his retirement in March 1994, Snowe decided instantly to run. Immediately she went on the attack against her obvious Democratic opponent, 1st District Congressman Tom Andrews, whose winning margin two years before had been 107,000 votes, while hers was only 22,000. Snowe attacked him hard for voting for the bill that closed Loring Air Force Base in northern Maine and for opposing the balanced budget amendment. She won 60%-36%.

In the Senate, she was the least conservative of the 11 freshmen Republicans elected in 1994. Her voting record has been around the middle of the Senate; she has voted with Democrats on some economic and many cultural issues and has been more conservative on defense and foreign policy. She sees herself as a centrist; Snowe along with fellow Mainer Susan Collins in 2005 joined the "Gang of 14" senators that diffused a showdown over President Bush's judicial nominees and preserved the Democrats' ability to filibuster, but only under "extraordinary circumstances."

In early 2001, with the Senate equally divided, Snowe played a pivotal role on some issues. She insisted successfully on limiting the size of the Bush tax cut. In May 2001 she led a group of Finance Committee members who insisted that the child care tax credit would be refundable, so that money would go to those with low incomes who pay no income tax. Many Republicans opposed this as a form of welfare; Snowe argued that these people needed tax relief. The provision went into the Senate bill and while the conference committee was pending Snowe sponsored a nonbinding resolution insisting on it that passed 94–4: so the refundable credit became law. She was one of two Republicans voting with Democrats in July 2001 for a $7.5 billion farm aid bill; that was stopped by George W. Bush's veto threat. She and Collins voted for the 2002 farm bill after insertion of the $2 billion dairy program. In November 2002, the pair threatened to vote against the homeland security bill because of provisions, added quietly in the House, limiting liability of vaccine makers for additives, permitting overseas companies to compete for contracts and targeting one project to Texas A&M University. Snowe and Collins agreed to vote for the bill after Majority Leader Trent Lott gave them a commitment that the three provisions would be revisited early in 2003; in January 2003, new Majority Leader Bill Frist honored that commitment.

In the 2004 budget negotiations Snowe played a key role. She insisted on applying the pay-as-you-go rule to tax cuts as well as to spending increases; with John McCain and Lincoln Chafee taking the same stand, it was made part of the Senate budget resolution. House Republicans would not accept that, and so there was no binding budget resolution that year. From her seat on the Finance Committee, Snowe inserted into the corporate tax bill provisions for tax deferral for military shipbuilding yards (Bath Iron Works is Maine's largest employer), income averaging for fishermen, favorable accounting provisions for reforestation and favorable treatment for energy plants that burn wood chips. On prescription drugs, she was one of the sponsors of the Tripartisan plan, developed in the Finance Committee in 2001 and which became the chief alternative to the Democrats' plan in summer 2002. She favors reimportation of prescription drugs and sponsored a bill in May 2004 to regulate wholesalers who reimport drugs and to forbid pharmaceutical companies from refusing to sell to Canadian companies that export drugs to the U.S.; it was considered more favorable to reimportation than a competing measure sponsored by her Maine colleague Susan Collins. With Ron Wyden of Oregon, Snowe in November 2005 gathered 51 votes for an amendment allowing the government to negotiate lower drug prices with drug companies, though it fell short of the 60 votes needed to waive budget rules. With Hillary Rodham Clinton she sponsored a bill to provide kinship navigator programs and foster care funding for grandparents and other relatives taking care of children. Snowe has taken a lead role on many women's health care issues—more money for women's health research, more screening for osteoporosis, gender analysis in FDA clinical trials. She supports abortion rights and came out against George W. Bush's reinstatement of the Mexico City policy in 2001.

In January 2003 Snowe became chairman of the Small Business Committee and promised to work for more affordable health insurance, regulatory relief and access to foreign markets. She and John Kerry successfully sponsored the reinstatement of the Women's Business Center Sustainability program at SBA. In reauthorizing the SBA in 2004, Snowe opposed removing the subsidy from 7(a) programs, which were suspended briefly for want of funding in January 2004. But under pressure from the Bush administration, she and House Chairman Don Manzullo agreed to an end to the subsidy and higher fees, in return for increases in the loan guarantee and maximum loan amount. Her committee issued a report in September 2006 concluding the Small Business Administration failed to justify loans disbursed through a $3.7 billion program created to help small businesses weather the economic downturn after the 9/11 attacks.

On the Finance Committee, Snowe exercised great influence over the Bush administration's economic agenda. She joined Democrats in voting against the Australia Free Trade Agreement; she was opposed because it would increase dairy imports. She worked to extend the Milk Income Loss Compensation program. During the 2005 Social Security debate, Snowe opposed using payroll taxes for private accounts. By 2005, Snowe had grown wary of extending tax cuts in light of growing deficits and the cost of the Iraq war. After Hurricane Katrina, she opposed plans to cut Medicaid benefits while also cutting taxes. She cast a crucial vote to move a reconciliation bill out of committee after Finance Chairman Chuck Grassley dropped a capital gains and dividend provision, but in May 2006 she was one of three Republicans to vote against passage of the eventual $70 billion reconciliation tax cut package. In July 2006, Senate Republican leaders dropped plans to attach an estate tax repeal to the pension conference report after Snowe, a conferee, signaled she would oppose the conference report.

As chairman of the Oceans Subcommittee, she worked to reauthorize a lapsed 1996 fisheries law, but sought to drop the 10-year time frame for rebuilding fish stocks in return for limiting the catch on each stock according to scientific estimates. Snowe worked with Senate Commerce Chairman Ted Stevens in 2006 to revamp the 30-year-old Magnuson-Stevens fisheries act to prevent overfishing while aiding struggling fishing industries. With other members of the Maine delegation, she worked to save the Portsmouth Naval Shipyard from closure in the 2005 base-closing round; she and Trent Lott unsuccessfully tried to postpone the round by two years. When the Pentagon's recommendations were released in May 2005, Maine faced close to a worst case scenario: the shipyard was slated for closure and Brunswick Naval Air Station was to have all of its aircraft and half its military personnel eliminated. The base closing commission in August reversed the Pentagon's recommendations by voting to preserve the shipyard and an accounting center, but shuttering the naval air station. In March 2006, Snowe guided a bill through the Senate and won Bush's signature on a bill to direct $1 billion of funding to the Low Income Home Energy Assistance Program.

Snowe has enjoyed very high job ratings in Maine. She was reelected 69%-31% in 2000. In 2006 she easily turned back charges of being a "Bush enabler" to win reelection by a 74%-21% margin over Democrat Jean Hay Bright, an organic farmer, author and environmental activist.

Junior Senator

Susan Collins (R)

Elected 1996, seat up 2008, 2d term; b. Dec. 7, 1952, Caribou; home, Bangor; St. Lawrence U., B.A. 1975; Catholic; single.

Professional Career: Legis. Aide, U.S. Sen. Bill Cohen, 1975-87, Staff Dir., Oversight of Gov. Mgmt. Subcmte., 1981-87; Professional & Financial Regulation Comm., 1987-92; New England Regional Dir., U.S. Small Business Admin., 1992; ME Dpty. Treas., 1993; Exec. Dir., Ctr. for Family Business, Husson Col., 1994-96.

DC Office: 413 DSOB, 20510, 202-224-2523; Fax: 202-224-2693; Web site: collins.senate.gov.

State Offices: Augusta, 207-622-8414; Bangor, 207-945-0417; Biddeford, 207-283-1101; Caribou, 207-493-7873; Lewiston, 207-784-6969; Portland, 207-780-3575.

Committees: *Aging (Special)* (3d of 10 R). *Armed Services* (5th of 12 R): Personnel; Emerging Threats & Capabilities; Seapower. *Homeland Security & Governmental Affairs* (RMM of 8 R).

Group Ratings

	ADA	ACLU	AFS	LCV	ITIC	NTU	COC	ACU	CFG	FRC
2006	45	42	38	71	75	50	92	48	22	37
2005	65	—	38	70	—	40	78	32	22	—

National Journal Ratings

	2005 LIB	—	2005 CONS		2006 LIB	—	2006 CONS
Economic	53%	—	46%		51%	—	48%
Social	53%	—	45%		54%	—	45%
Foreign	51%	—	46%		51%	—	46%

Key Votes of the 109th Congress

1. Bar ANWR Drilling	Y	5. Confirm Samuel Alito	Y	9. Limit Interstate Abortion	N
2. FY06 Spending Curb	N	6. Path to Citizenship	Y	10. CAFTA	N
3. Estate Tax Repeal	Y	7. Bar Same Sex Marriage	N	11. Urge Iraq Withdrawal	N
4. Raise Minimum Wage	Y	8. Stem Cell Research $	Y	12. Provide Detainee Rights	N

Election Results

2002 general	Susan Collins (R)	295,041	(58%)	($3,961,167)
	Chellie Pingree (D)	209,858	(42%)	($3,806,798)
2002 primary	Susan Collins (R)	unopposed		
1996 general	Susan Collins (R)	298,422	(49%)	($1,621,475)
	Joseph Brennan (D)	266,226	(44%)	($976,805)
	Other	42,129	(7%)	

Susan Collins, Maine's junior Republican senator, was elected in 1996, the first time she won elective office. She grew up in Caribou, in potato-growing Aroostook County, about as far northeast as you can get in the United States, closer to the capitals of New Brunswick and Quebec than to the capital of Maine. Her family is in the lumber business, and also in politics: Her father was a state senator, her mother a mayor and her uncle a state Supreme Court justice. As a high school senior, she went to Washington on a Senate youth program, and Senator Margaret Chase Smith took her into her private office and talked to her for nearly two hours. (In November 2005, Collins surpassed Smith's voting streak by casting her 2,942th consecutive vote.) Right after college, she got a job as an intern with William Cohen, then a congressman on the Judiciary Committee who voted to impeach Richard Nixon. She was a Cohen staffer for 12 years and served as the staff director for the Senate Governmental Affairs Subcommittee on Oversight of Government Management, which Cohen chaired from 1981-87. After Republicans lost their majority, Collins returned to Maine to work five years for Governor John McKernan as a financial regulation commissioner. In 1992 she was New England administrator of the Small Business Administration, and by 1994 she had announced her candidacy for governor. It was a disastrous campaign: She won the Republican nomination, but was overshadowed by independent Angus King, and ran third, with only 23% of the vote. She then became the executive director of the Husson College Center for Family Business.

Then in January 1996 Cohen surprised almost everybody by announcing he would retire from the Senate—almost as big a surprise as his selection as Defense Secretary by Bill Clinton a year later. But there was a precedent in Maine for a third-place gubernatorial finisher to be elected senator: George Mitchell was similarly humiliated in 1974, then, after being appointed senator in 1980, won smashing victories in 1982 and 1988. In the Republican primary Collins played up her resemblance to Olympia Snowe and Cohen and called for a balanced budget amendment, line-item veto and term limits (she pledged to serve no more than two terms). She won with 56% of the vote. In the general election she was opposed by former Congressman and Governor Joseph Brennan. Brennan attacked Collins on economic issues and gun control but Collins raised much more money and won 49%-44%.

Collins has compiled a middle-of-the-Senate voting record; she has joined Democrats on issues including the 1999 tax cut, campaign finance regulation and the partial-birth abortion ban. She was one of the Republicans who called for cutting the 2003 Bush tax cut in half; it ended up being cut, but by considerably less. She also was one of the Republicans who insisted that the pay-as-you-go rule applies to tax cuts as well as spending increases in the budget in 2004, as a result of which the House and Senate never agreed on a budget resolution. Her first great cause in the Senate was campaign finance regulation; she was beaten by a millionaire in 1994, faced two of them in the 1996 primary and had only meager finances herself. She said that limitations on self-financing candidates were a "cornerstone" of any reform for her. But these have not been included because they were held unconstitutional under *Buckley v. Valeo*. In March 2001 she sponsored with Ron Wyden the amendment requiring negative ads to include a picture of the candidate running them or otherwise be ineligible for the lowest discounted advertising rate.

As chairman of the Permanent Subcommittee on Investigations Collins probed into Medicare fraud, investment scams, unsafe food, Internet ripoffs and fraudulent telephone billing—slamming and cramming—day trading, direct mail sweepstakes, property flipping, lead paint; as ranking minority member she participated in Chairman Carl Levin's careful and apolitical investigation into fraudulent corporate accounting.

In January 2003 she became chairman of the full Governmental Affairs Committee, on whose staff she had once served. Her highest-profile issue there was intelligence reorganization. She responded favorably to the 9/11 Commission's recommendations. Working closely with Joe Lieberman, she fashioned a bill that established a director of national intelligence and a new counterterrorism center. It was introduced in September 2004, and after a two-week debate in October was adopted by a 96–2 vote. With Lieberman's support, she beat back by 55-37 an amendment by Ted Stevens that would have kept secret the total amount of intelligence spending and by 62-29 another by Robert Byrd which would have limited the ability of the national intelligence director to shift funds and personnel. But grudges remained: on several separate votes, majorities denied the Governmental Affairs Committee oversight jurisdiction of various homeland security functions, though the committee was renamed Homeland Security and Governmental Affairs. There remained the matter of reconciling the bill with the House version, which included several provisions on immigration and homeland security not in the Senate bill and gave less control to the national intelligence director. Collins insisted the White House get involved in negotiations and ended up reviewing the language with Dick Cheney. The House's extra provisions were deleted and the White House agreed to draft guidelines that would ensure that the military chain of command remained in place. The bill was finally approved in December—a major victory for Collins.

Even before a dispute erupted over a proposed deal to lease operation of six U.S. ports to Dubai Ports World, Collins pressed for stricter port security. She joined Patty Murray of Washington on a bill requiring radiation screening for all cargo entering U.S. ports and a grant program to fund security improvements. Bush in October 2006 signed a law that authorized $400 million in port security grants and set up a pilot program in three foreign ports to test the feasibility of overseas cargo screening. Collins separately moved legislation out of her committee that would classify security threats at chemical facilities and require they implement security measures or use safer chemicals.

Building on work from the previous Congress, Collins and Democrat Thomas Carper moved a Postal Service reorganization bill through the Senate by voice vote. Congress ran out of time in 2004 to approve the postal overhaul; the bill faced a similar fate in 2006 until a compromise in the December lame-duck session cleared the way for the president's signature. The law caps postal increases to inflation, imposes a three-day waiting period for worker compensation claims, eliminates annual payments to an escrow fund and shifts the responsibility of military retirement benefits of postal employees to the Treasury. On civil service issues, Collins has generally supported Bush administration proposals to change federal work rules, but has said that the administration should preserve employees' rights.

In another lame duck finish, Collins won approval in late 2006 for a bill that allows minor league athletes and professional ice skaters to apply for P-1 immigration visas—many Canadian hockey players play for the Lewiston Maineiacs. In 2005, Collins also sponsored a bill to turn the Old Post Office Pavilion Annex in Washington into the National Women's History Museum.

Collins supported the Medicare/prescription drug bill which passed in November 2003. In June 2004 she sponsored a bill to allow reimportation of prescription drugs which had tighter restrictions than a similar measure, which she said she would also vote for, supported by Olympia Snowe. Her concern was with the safety of online pharmacies. In 2005 Collins, along with Snowe, joined the "Gang of 14" senators that agreed not to support any effort by their leadership to invoke the "nuclear option" to move President Bush's judicial nominees.

In 2001, Collins got Snowe's seat on Armed Services, from which she looks after Bath Iron Works, Maine's biggest private employer; in 2004 she got a commitment that at least some work will be done of the first new DD(X) destroyer at Bath. She worked to bring the 94th Military Police back from Iraq after an extended deployment. With the rest of the Maine delegation, Collins worked to save the state's military installations from the 2005 base closing round. The Pentagon recommended closing the Portsmouth Naval Shipyard, but the BRAC commission chose to keep it open while voting to close the Brunswick Naval Air Station. She has also worked on other local issues—she got fishermen included in Chapter 12 of the Bankruptcy Act, which covers farmers. Maine is a border state, so Collins also tends to border issues. She sought a National Weather Service office for her hometown of Caribou, pointing out that since it is surrounded by Canada it does not receive weather warnings from adjacent Weather Service offices as most other American communities do.

When Collins came up for reelection in 2002, national Democrats were optimistic about their chances. Their candidate, former Maine Senate Majority Leader Chellie Pingree, was energetic and politically creative, and was the chief sponsor of the state law authorizing the state to negotiate with pharmaceutical companies purchases of prescription drugs for the uninsured. Pingree raised $1 million by January 2002, more than Collins did during that period; eventually both spent over $2 million. Not widely known in the state, she ran a series of ads in the first months of 2001—positive spots on herself and tough attacks on Collins. The Senate debate over prescription drugs in July helped Collins: She could say that her amendment to make prescription drugs less expensive had passed the Senate by a wide margin and that she had voted for a couple of different prescription drug benefit programs. Pingree ads insisted that Collins was "siding with the big drug companies." Collins won by a solid 58%-42% margin.

Collins, who has enjoyed strong ratings at home, signaled in 2006 she would seek a third term. She will face questions about breaking a promise not to serve more than two terms; the Democratic takeover in the Senate will also cost her the visibility of chairing the Senate Homeland Security and Governmental Affairs Committee. Making clear that she would be a top target in 2008, Democrats opened the election cycle by criticizing Collins' vote in January 2007 for a minimum wage increase, noting that she had cast votes against wage increases two years earlier.

In May, six-term Democratic Congressman Tom Allen announced he would challenge Collins in 2008, and pointed to the Iraq war as a central issue in his campaign. He was the first Senate candidate in the 2008 election cycle to announce his candidacy online.

FIRST DISTRICT

Rep. Tom Allen (D)

Elected 1996, 6th term; b. Apr. 16, 1945, Portland; home, Portland; Bowdoin Col., B.A. 1967, Rhodes Scholar, Oxford U., B. Phil. 1970; Harvard U., J.D. 1974; Protestant; married (Diana).

Elected Office: Portland City Cncl., 1989-95; Portland Mayor, 1991.

Professional Career: Aide, U.S. Sen. Edmund Muskie, 1970-71; Practicing atty., 1974-94; Chmn., ME Clinton–Gore Campaign, 1992; Public Policy Consultant, 1995.

DC Office: 1127 LHOB, 20515, 202-225-6116; Fax: 202-225-5590; Web site: www.tomallen.house.gov.

District Offices: Portland, 207-774-5019; Saco, 207-283-8054.

Committees: *Budget* (5th of 22 D). *Energy & Commerce* (18th of 31 D): Environment & Hazardous Materials; Health; Energy & Air Quality.

Group Ratings

	ADA	ACLU	AFS	LCV	ITIC	NTU	COC	ACU	CFG	FRC
2006	95	95	100	100	71	13	47	8	7	0
2005	95	—	100	94	—	13	42	0	4	0

National Journal Ratings

	2005 LIB	—	2005 CONS		2006 LIB	—	2006 CONS
Economic	81%	—	18%		86%	—	11%
Social	92%	—	7%		74%	—	26%
Foreign	79%	—	20%		77%	—	20%

Key Votes of the 109th Congress

1. Estate Tax Repeal	N	5. Limit Interstate Abortion	N	9. Build Border Fence	N
2. Limit CAFE Standards	N	6. Extend Patriot Act	N	10. CAFTA	N
3. FY06 Spending Curb	N	7. Bar Same Sex Marriage	N	11. Oppose Iraq Withdrawal	N
4. Drilling in ANWR	N	8. Stem Cell Research	$	Y	12. Detainee Tribunals	N

Election Results

2006 general	Tom Allen (D)	170,949	(61%)	($656,455)
	Darlene Curley (R)	88,009	(31%)	($181,764)
	Dexter Kamilewicz (I)	22,029	(8%)	($43,934)
2006 primary	Tom Allen (D)	unopposed		
2004 general	Tom Allen (D)	219,077	(60%)	($727,772)
	Charles Summers (R)	147,663	(40%)	($505,698)

Prior Winning Percentages: 2002 (64%); 2000 (60%); 1998 (60%); 1996 (55%)

The People		Race/Ethnic Origin	Ancestry	
Area size:	5,400 sq. mi.	96.3% White	English: 16.2%	Irish: 12.1%
Urban population:	49.4%	0.6% Black	French: 9.5%	
Rural population:	50.6%	0.9% Asian	**2004 Presidential Vote**	
Pop. 2000:	637,450	0.3% Native Am.	Kerry (D) 211,703	(55%)
Pop. 2005 (est):	665,532	0.0% Hawaiian	Bush (R) 165,824	(43%)
Median income:	$42,044	0.9% Two+ races	Other 6,865	(2%)
Poverty status:	8.6%	0.1% Other	**2000 Presidential Vote**	
Military veterans:	15.8%	0.8% Hispanic Origin	Gore (D) 168,266	(50%)
			Bush (R) 144,013	(43%)
			Other 22,926	(7%)
			Cook Partisan Voting Index: D + 6	

Occupation   Blue collar: 23.0%   White collar: 61.5%   Gray collar: 15.6%

The 1st District of Maine stretches from southernmost Kittery and nearby Kennebunkport to the craggy-shored ancestrally Republican counties to the east. The historic center is Portland, Maine's largest city, home to the yuppies and lawyers that have revived and renovated its downtown landmarks. Portland's antique charm, mostly booming economy and tolerant lifestyle have made it a haven for singles, for lesbians and gays: the 2000 Census reported that Portland has the nation's third-largest concentration of women living together and is tenth in men living together. L.L. Bean, open 24/7/365, is not far away in Freeport. Former farm towns have transformed into suburbia, and old mill towns like Biddeford and Sanford have seen commercial development. The 2005 base-closing commission spared Portsmouth Naval Shipyard at Kittery from closure, but it voted to close down the Brunswick Naval Air Station, costing the area $211 million in annual wages and military contracts. Even as redevelopment authorities faced decisions about what to do with the station's 3,200 acres of real estate, two new runways and 700 empty housing units, the area enjoyed a minor boom in residential and commercial development.

Most voters in the 1st District live within a couple hours drive of the Maine Mall—just off the Maine Turnpike and I-295 and near the airport—the state's heaviest concentration of retail and office space. But in a lifestyle more reminiscent of the Alaska wilderness, those who live on the district's remote islands depend on ferries and Cessna aircraft as their lifeline to the mainland. In the summer, the air traffic includes the families of Fortune 500 executives traveling to their estates; in the winter, lobstermen and local business owners board most flights. Lobsters are not just a tradition here but an economic resource: Lobster fishing has been booming, even though fish stocks are down, and there's a new market in northern Europe for Maine shrimp. Politically, the 1st votes very much like the state as a whole, quirkily, often for independents, splitting tickets with abandon, more Democratic in presidential elections than the 2d. From 1968 to 1996 it elected three Democrats and three Republicans to the House, with each party holding the seat for 14 years.

The congressman from the 1st District is Tom Allen, a Democrat first elected in 1996. Allen grew up in Portland, where his grandfather and father served on the city council. He was class president in high school and college; at Bowdoin, he was captain of the football team and criticized fraternities because they wouldn't admit blacks. He was a Rhodes Scholar in Oxford the same years as Bill Clinton (who struck him as "one of the nicest, warmest people I ever knew"), Robert Reich and Strobe Talbott, and when he returned, he got a job on the staff of Senator Edmund Muskie. Then he dropped out of politics, went to Harvard Law School, practiced in Portland, and worked on charities and community service. In 1989 he was elected to the Portland City Council, and in 1991 rotated into the position of mayor. In 1994 he ran for governor, finishing a distant second to former Governor Joseph Brennan in the Democratic primary. The 1st District race in 1996 was an obvious next step, and an attractive opportunity. Freshman Republican James Longley had a well-known name as son of the independent governor elected in 1974, and he had won the 1994 race 52%-48%. But Longley's moderate record was overshadowed by his support for the Contract with America and more than $1 million in ads run against him by the AFL-CIO. Allen, with heavy support from Portland, won a 52%-48% primary victory over state Senator Dale McCormick. In the general, the candidates disagreed on capital punishment, partial-birth abortion, term limits and the balanced budget amendment. Allen called for scaling back Republicans' $10 billion increase in defense spending. Longley pointed out that it included a Navy destroyer to be built at the Bath Iron Works; Allen backtracked and said he would of course support Maine defense contracts. Allen won 55%-45%.

Allen has a liberal voting record. His first major initiative was a bipartisan campaign finance bill, proposed with other freshmen. After Allen launched a discharge petition, Speaker Newt Gingrich allowed the freshman bill to come to the floor as the vehicle for campaign finance bills. When the more stringent Shays-Meehan bill passed the House later that year, he became an active proponent. When a revised version was later enacted, Common Cause lauded his leadership. Allen and Republican Charles Bass offered legislation in 2006 that would exempt blogs and other Internet speech from campaign finance laws unless they spend more than $10,000. On the Energy and Commerce Committee, he was an outspoken foe of the Republicans' Medicare prescription drug bill. He became a strong advocate for government negotiation of drug prices and supported Maine's lawsuit against a "clawback" provision that requires states to return to the federal government the savings they get from no longer offering drug coverage. After 10 years in the minority, Allen said he was eager to legislate on health care policy in the majority. He opposed association health plans because he believes they would have the effect of increasing the number of uninsured people and instead has proposed incentives that would encourage private insurers to offer coverage for small businesses.

On other issues, Allen pushed to require coal-burning power plants and trash incinerators to cut mercury emissions 90%, and he feared the impact on fish in local lakes; he accused the Bush administration of reneging on promises to do its own scientific analyses. In 2005 he sponsored "Clean Smokestacks" legislation with California's Henry Waxman and New York's Sherwood Boehlert that would set emission standards for mercury and other pollutants. He helped to secure $2.8 billion for three Aegis destroyers with construction work divided by Bath Iron Works in Maine and Ingalls Shipyard in Mississippi, plus funds for projects at Saco Defense, Brunswick and Portsmouth. Allen worked to protect the two bases during the 2005 BRAC and voted in the minority against the base-closing commission's final report, which recommended keeping Portsmouth open and closing Brunswick. Allen backed the Bush administration's plan to dismantle MX missiles, but voiced alarm that the planned reduction in shipbuilding would reduce the Navy's fleet to 240 ships. He voted against the use of force in Iraq because the resolution gave President Bush "a blank check," and later called the war "a major miscalculation." Allen in February 2007 said he supported legislation to withdraw U.S. troops from Iraq by the end of the year and ban U.S. military bases in the country.

During the 2006 renewal of the Magnuson-Stevens act, Allen fought to protect smaller boat fleets in New England by establishing a quota system that requires skippers to seek a renewal every 10 years. He voted against offshore oil drilling because of fears an accident could harm fishing waters. Allen in 2007 helped author Oceans-21, a bill that would establish a comprehensive national oceans policy and a trust fund to implement it.

Allen appears to have a secure hold on this once competitive district. In 2006, Allen turned back Republican opposition from state Representative Darlene Curley by a 61%-31% margin. Republicans may get a better shot at the seat in 2008: Allen has boosted his profile around the state and in May 2007 announced he would challenge Senator Susan Collins. A number of Democrats announced or expressed interest in running, including former state Senate President Michael Brennan, former state Senate Majority Leader and unsuccessful 2002 U.S. Senate candidate Chellie Pingree, York County District Attorney Mark Lawrence, Portland City Councilor Jill Duson and Portland lawyer and Iraq war veteran Adam Cote. Potential Republican candidates included Curley, Collins's chief of staff Steve Abbott, businessman Dean Scontras, and former state Senator Phil Harriman. Charles Summers, a former state senator who unsuccessfully challenged Allen in 2004, declared his candidacy in July 2007; he is a lieutenant commander in the Navy Reserve, however, and was deployed to Iraq soon afterwards.

SECOND DISTRICT

Rep. Michael Michaud (D)

Elected 2002, 3d term; b. Jan. 18, 1955, Millinocket; home, East Millinocket; Schenck H.S., 1973; Catholic; single.

Elected Office: ME House, 1980-94; ME Senate, 1994-2001, Pres., 2001.

Professional Career: Mill worker, Great Northern Paper, 1973-2002.

DC Office: 1724 LHOB, 20515, 202-225-6306; Fax: 202-225-2943; Web site: michaud.house.gov.

District Offices: Bangor, 207-942-6935; Lewiston, 207-782-3704; Presque Isle, 207-764-1036; Waterville, 207-873-5713.

Committees: *Small Business* (6th of 18 D): Finance & Tax; Rural & Urban Entrepreneurship. *Transportation & Infrastructure* (20th of 41 D): Economic Development, Public Buildings & Emergency Management; Highways & Transit; Railroads, Pipelines & Hazardous Materials. *Veterans' Affairs* (4th of 16 D): Health (Chmn.).

Group Ratings

	ADA	ACLU	AFS	LCV	ITIC	NTU	COC	ACU	CFG	FRC
2006	90	82	100	75	43	18	40	12	9	14
2005	90	—	100	100	—	19	48	16	6	23

National Journal Ratings

	2005 LIB	—	2005 CONS		2006 LIB	—	2006 CONS
Economic	71%	—	28%		67%	—	33%
Social	67%	—	32%		71%	—	29%
Foreign	87%	—	12%		70%	—	28%

Key Votes of the 109th Congress

1. Estate Tax Repeal	N	5. Limit Interstate Abortion	N	9. Build Border Fence	N
2. Limit CAFE Standards	N	6. Extend Patriot Act	N	10. CAFTA	N
3. FY06 Spending Curb	N	7. Bar Same Sex Marriage	N	11. Oppose Iraq Withdrawal	N
4. Drilling in ANWR	N	8. Stem Cell Research $	Y	12. Detainee Tribunals	Y

Election Results

2006 general	Michael Michaud (D)	179,732	(71%)	($737,820)
	Laurence D'Amboise (R)	75,146	(29%)	($18,526)
2006 primary	Michael Michaud (D)	unopposed		
2004 general	Michael Michaud (D)	199,303	(58%)	($1,309,195)
	Brian Hamel (R)	135,547	(39%)	($667,464)
	Other	8,586	(3%)	

Prior Winning Percentages: 2002 (52%)

The People		Race/Ethnic Origin	Ancestry	
Area size:	29,985 sq. mi.	96.7% White	English: 15.8%	French: 11.7%
Urban population:	31.0%	0.4% Black	Irish: 10.3%	
Rural population:	69.0%	0.5% Asian	**2004 Presidential Vote**	
Pop. 2000:	637,473	0.8% Native Am.	Kerry (D) 185,139	(52%)
Pop. 2005 (est):	653,053	0.0% Hawaiian	Bush (R) 164,377	(46%)
Median income:	$32,600	0.9% Two+ races	Other 6,840	(2%)
Poverty status:	13.3%	0.1% Other	**2000 Presidential Vote**	
Military veterans:	15.9%	0.7% Hispanic Origin	Gore (D) 151,685	(48%)
			Bush (R) 142,603	(45%)
			Other 21,705	(7%)
			Cook Partisan Voting Index: D + 4	

Occupation	Blue collar: 28.5%	White collar: 53.0%	Gray collar: 18.5%

The 2d District of Maine is heavily forested, rough-hewn and enormous. It covers the northern three-quarters of the state's acreage; it is the largest congressional district east of the Mississippi,

larger than New Hampshire, Vermont and Massachusetts combined. The population is not evenly distributed, however: The district dips south to include the heavily Democratic mill town of Lewiston and east to Eastport, just across the bay and the Franklin D. Roosevelt Bridge from the Roosevelt Campobello International Park (Campobello is in New Brunswick, but is connected by bridge to the United States and not Canada). At Belfast on Penobscot Bay, art galleries and boutiques have replaced fish-processing plants. There are several different Maines here: The bays of coastal Maine, with their small fishing towns; the potato fields of far northern Aroostook County (at 6,543 square miles, Aroostook is so big that it covers an area greater than Rhode Island and Connecticut together); the mill towns on the fast-running streams of western Maine, penned in between mountains where there are more moose than people. This was one of America's frontiers in the 1850s, when Bangor on the Penobscot River was the lumber capital of the world; today tiny Bangor is the second-largest city in the district after Lewiston. This part of Maine has had its economic troubles, losing 22,000 jobs to neighboring Canada and other foreign markets after the 1993 passage of NAFTA, and further job losses in the shoe industry after that later. Potato production is only half what it was in 1980; a once-thriving sardine canning business is virtually gone; logging—long the largest business in Maine—has suffered job cutbacks as big paper companies sell off much acreage and a Massachusetts-based group seeks to create a North Maine Woods National Park. (Opponents' bumper stickers read: "If you don't like cutting trees, try using plastic toilet paper.") But there are also signs of life. Loring Air Force Base was closed in 1994, but new businesses from aircraft repair to telemarketing have replaced its civilian jobs and more. Despite a Pentagon recommendation to close a defense accounting office in Limestone, the 2005 base-closing commission voted to nearly double its workforce to at least 600. And some businesses persist: Washington County's sandy soil plains produce more than 90% of the nation's wild blueberry crop. Politically, this is protest country: This was Ross Perot's strongest congressional district in the United States in 1992 and 1996. The 2d was carried narrowly by Al Gore in 2000 and by a little wider margin by John Kerry in 2004.

The congressman from the 2d District is Mike Michaud *(me-SHOO)*, a Democrat first elected in 2002 when John Baldacci gave up the seat and was elected governor. Michaud grew up in East Millinocket in the North Woods; he comes from a blue collar family and is one of the few members of Congress who did not attend college. For 28 years, he was a mill worker at the Great Northern Paper; unhappily, this dominant employer in this economically depressed area closed its plant a month after his election. "I know what it's like to work the day shift, the midnight shift. I've been on strike. I know what it's like to worry about whether you will have a job or not." In 1980 he was elected to the state House and in 1994 to the state Senate, where he chaired the Appropriations Committee and became Senate President. Michaud has an eclectic mix of political views, which would have been popular several decades ago among House Democrats but no longer now. He is staunchly pro-labor, but opposes abortion rights. He opposes drilling for oil in the Arctic National Wildlife Refuge, but strongly supports gun ownership rights.

In the six-way Democratic contest for Baldacci's seat, Michaud's chief opponent was state Senator Susan Longley of Lewiston, the daughter of former Independent Governor James Longley and sister of the 1st District's former Republican Congressman James Longley Jr. She emphasized her support for abortion rights in a district that had not elected a pro-life candidate since the *Roe v. Wade* decision in 1973. But with support from organized labor, Michaud got 31% to Longley's 28% and 20% for former state Senator Sean Faircloth. It was a regional contest: Michaud carried the five most rural counties, and won 66% of the vote in Aroostook; Longley carried six counties chiefly in the southern part of the district, and won 59% in trendy coastal Waldo County.

In the general, Michaud faced Kevin Raye, the veteran chief of staff to Senator Olympia Snowe. Michaud attempted to turn Raye's experience into a liability. His campaign slogan was, "I'm One of Us, Working for Us"—an attempt to contrast his blue collar background and union membership with Raye's white collar Washington experience. Michaud, perhaps to appeal to feminists despite his opposition to abortion, set out a 10-point "women's equity agenda," including family planning, increased child care aid, breast cancer research, and equal pay for equal work; Raye won the support of abortion rights groups. Michaud won 52%-48%. He ran better than most Democrats in rural areas, winning 53% in the seven northern counties, where unions conducted a voter turnout drive in the mill towns.

In the House, Michaud's voting record was moderate for a Democrat and less liberal than that of Maine colleague Tom Allen. He opposed the Bush administration's new overtime rules, and he worked to create a caucus to join workers and environmentalists on issues such as trade. In June 2004, he welcomed the reopening of the Great Northern paper mill under new ownership, but with significantly less employees. Raising concerns about port security, Michaud joined John Murtha of Pennsylvania in leading the opposition to the Oman free trade agreement, which passed narrowly through the House in July 2006.

On the Veterans' Affairs Committee, Michaud advocated for more funding for the Togus VA Medical Center and sponsored a bill that sought to improve health care for rural veterans. After Democrats won the majority in 2006, Michaud vied to become the committee's full chairman and won the support of retiring Illinois Rep. Lane Evans, the panel's top Democrat. Evans in a letter to Democratic leaders wrote that Bob Filner, who had more seniority than Michaud, did not have the right temperament for the position. Filner had reportedly shouted obscenities to VA employees after revelations that a stolen laptop had put the personal data of millions of veterans at risk. To boost his bid, Michaud had donated liberally to Democratic candidates. In the Democratic steering committee, Michaud lost by a 24-20 vote, but the margin was close enough to force a vote in the full Democratic Caucus, which Filner won 112-69.

In 2004, Michaud faced Brian Hamel, a Republican with a record of job creation as the president of the Loring Development Authority. National Republicans took an early interest in the race; Hamel, who had never held elected office, had trouble getting noticed in this sprawling district with a presidential election and two controversial referendums on the ballot. Michaud was reelected 58%-39%. With continued strong support from organized labor, Michaud expanded his margin in 2006 and defeated eye care technician Laurence D'Amboise 71%-29%.

★ MARYLAND ★

Just south of the Mason-Dixon line and just north of the line between the Union and the Confederacy, the midpoint of the 13 colonies, Maryland has always been betwixt and between. It has a claim to be the typical American state, yet stands out for its particularities. This was the only one of the 13 colonies founded by Roman Catholics—the Calvert family—and its embrace of religious tolerance came less from abstract principle than from the Calverts' desire to protect their property from Protestant monarchs: A harbinger of Maryland's practical-mindedness. Similarly, although hot-blooded Baltimoreans wanted to secede in 1861 ("Maryland, My Maryland" condemns Abraham Lincoln's suppression of pro-Confederate rioters), practical heads prevailed.

The puritan impulse was never lively here: Prohibition was enforced only laxly in Baltimore, to the delight of its great journalist-cum-lexicographer H.L. Mencken, who called it Charm City; slot machines were legal in the rural counties of the Western Shore; horse-racing once thrived here, and has tried to escape its current problems by adding slots. An old state law guaranteeing blacks equal access to public accommodations specifically excluded the Eastern Shore. By not pursuing any one course rigorously, Maryland could be many things at once: Northern as well as Southern, moralistic as well as libertine, industrial as well as rural, leaving people to their own devices yet with a heavy government presence. Perhaps as a result, much of Maryland's political history reads like a chronicle of rogues. Maryland's genial tolerance may have given it a little too savory a history, but this state cherishes its sense of uniqueness. The Chesapeake Bay, for example, is the nation's largest estuary, with water saltier than a river but fresher than the ocean and with unique watermen and shellfish. The terrapin and Chesapeake oyster are rare today; oystermen harvested 5.6 million bushels in 1900 but only 148,000 in 2002, and, thanks in part to the cow-nosed ray, 26,000 in 2004. Rockfish and Chesapeake Bay blue crabs are much scarcer too.

Maryland has some reason to be proud of the economy, or economies, it has built over the years. Half a century ago, half the state's population lived in the city of Baltimore and only one-fifth in the suburbs. Now the proportions are the other way around, and then some: 11% Baltimore, 75% in the suburbs. The Census Bureau classifies Washington-Baltimore as a single metropolitan area, the nation's fourth largest, with 8 million people. But Baltimore and Washington are not fraternal twins like Dallas and Fort Worth or Minneapolis and St. Paul; they are two quite separate cities, with different economic bases and different attitudes toward public life. Baltimore started off as a port and an industrial city, and has managed to stay diversified and successful as it spread out into the countryside from its new central core at the Inner Harbor and the solidly built edifices of its downtown grid streets. With its large suburban population, Maryland ranks second in median household income, after similarly suburban New Jersey. It is home to the Orioles in their popular Oriole Park at Camden Yards, the first of the new-old ballparks of the 1990s, and to Johns Hopkins

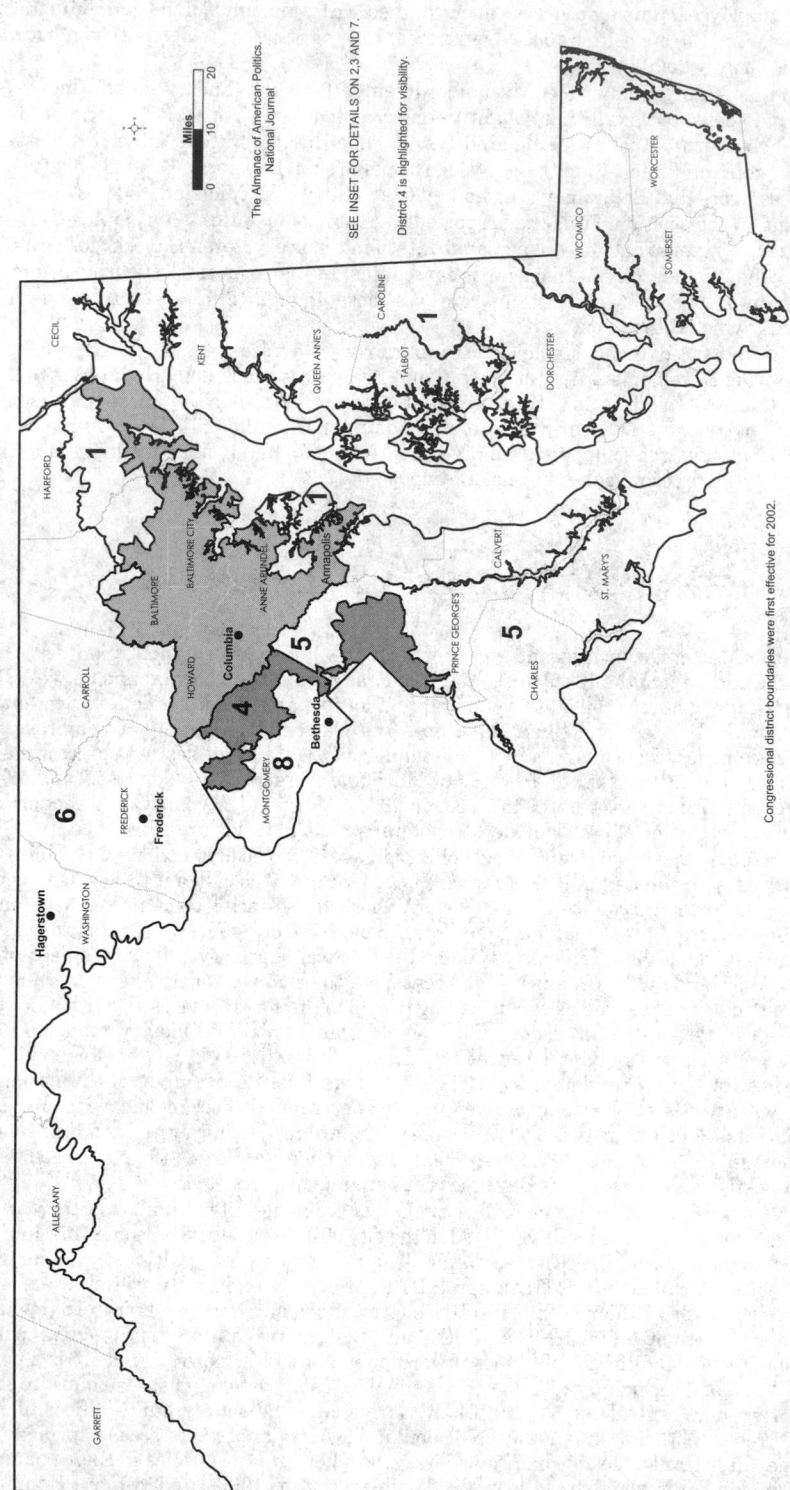

The Almanac of American Politics.
National Journal

SEE INSET FOR DETAILS ON 2,3 AND 7.

District 4 is highlighted for visibility.

Congressional district boundaries were first effective for 2002.

Miles
0   10   20

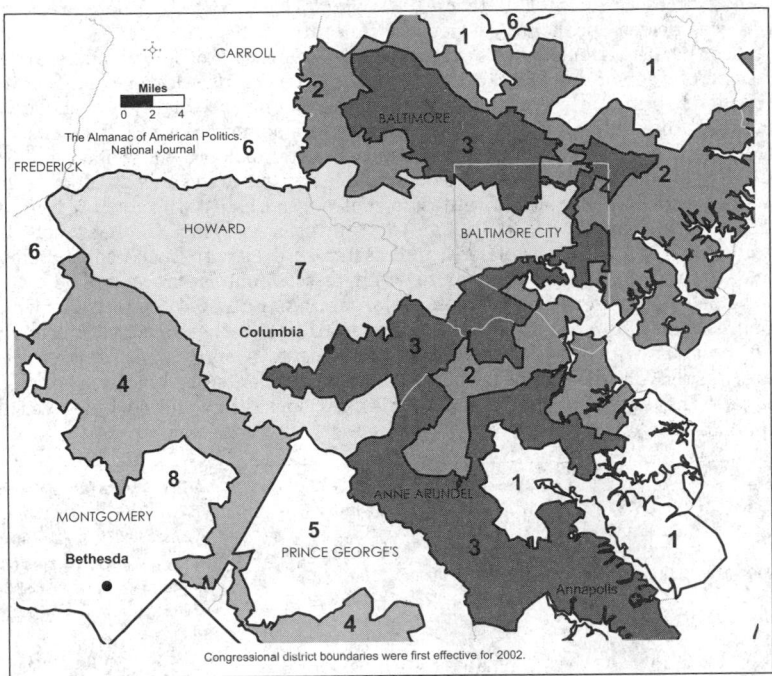

Congressional district boundaries were first effective for 2002.

University, with its Georgian buildings along the affluent corridor that runs directly north from downtown all the way to the developing edge city of Hunt Valley.

Baltimore remains the focus of Maryland's public life, for 47% of Marylanders still live in its metropolitan area, and its influence is far greater than Washington's on the Eastern Shore and in Western Maryland. For years, most of Maryland's successful statewide politicians came from Baltimore; today, both senators live there and commute to Washington. Baltimore has a long Democratic tradition, and most voters in the metropolitan area are registered Democrats; their default mode is to vote Democratic. Maryland did elect a Republican governor, Bob Ehrlich, in 2002, by a 52%-48% margin over Lieutenant Governor Kathleen Kennedy Townsend, who suffered from some of the accumulated resentments of outgoing Governor Parris Glendening. But Ehrlich, despite a job approval rating above 50% after long and constant wrangling with the heavily Democratic legislature, lost 53%-46% to Baltimore Mayor Martin O'Malley in 2006. Ehrlich's share of the vote dropped 9% in the Baltimore suburbs, despite his characteristic Bawlmer accent (you can hear it in Barry Levinson and John Waters movies) and fell 6% to 7% on the Eastern Shore and in Southern and Western Maryland. Republican statewide candidates need more than two-thirds of the non-black votes to win, and that's pretty hard to achieve when 17% of the votes are cast in the upscale and heavily liberal suburbs of Montgomery County, northwest of Washington.

That makes Maryland one of the nation's most Democratic states. It produced higher percentages for Al Gore and John Kerry than all but a handful of other states. Democrats held their 33-14 lead in the state Senate and picked up six seats in the House of Delegates in 2006, and have more than two-thirds of both houses. Top positions in the big counties' governments remain a near-monopoly of Democrats; Democrats picked up two Republican-held U.S. House seats in 2002, thanks to partisan redistricting—the best such pickup for Democrats in the entire nation. Maryland has not elected a Republican senator since Charles Mathias in 1980; Ehrlich was the first Republican governor since Spiro Agnew, elected in 1966. That gives Maryland some very long-lasting Democratic officeholders, with major influence over important issues, though it is often quietly exercised. Senator Barbara Mikulski was first elected to the Senate in 1986 and the House in 1976; Senator Paul Sarbanes retired in 2006 after 30 years in the Senate and served six years in the House before that. The new senator, Ben Cardin, served for 20 years in the House. All served in the same seat in the House (though redistricting changed its boundaries drastically), which is now represented by John Sarbanes, the senator's son. Maryland's most influential House member is

Majority Leader Steny Hoyer, first elected in 1981, who was elected state Senate President in 1975, at 35; Cardin was elected Speaker of the House of Delegates in 1979, also at 35.

One reason for this Democratic strength is that some 29% of Marylanders are black, the fifth-highest percentage of any state, after Mississippi, Louisiana, Georgia and South Carolina. Many of Maryland's blacks, especially in Prince George's County, are highly educated and economically upscale, but they vote almost as heavily Democratic as more downscale blacks. Lieutenant Governor Michael Steele, the Republican nominee for senator in 2006, who is black and from Prince George's County, hoped to make big inroads among blacks, but made only small ones: he got 25% from blacks statewide but only 50% of whites, in contrast to Ehrlich who got 15% from blacks and 54% of whites. Steele won 23% in Baltimore City and 24% in Prince George's, not much above George W. Bush's 17% in those jurisdictions, and essentially even with Bush's percentages in almost all the rest of the state—not nearly enough to win in a state John Kerry carried 56%-43%. Cardin beat Steele 54%-44%, a solid margin and notably larger than the 44%-41% margin by which he beat former Congressman and NAACP President Kweisi Mfume in the Democratic primary. Mfume carried Baltimore City with 64% of the vote and Prince George's County, which cast more votes, with 70%; he also carried Charles County, where most new residents are blacks moving south from Prince George's. That suggests some tension within the Democratic coalition, but it was not enough to give Republicans an upset victory.

The People		Race/Ethnic Origin			Military veterans: 524,230 (13.3%)	
Pop. 2006 (est):	5,615,727	3,286,547	62.1%	White	WWII: 17.6%	Korea: 12.1%
Pop. 2000:	5,296,486	1,464,735	27.7%	Black	Vietnam: 32.1%	Gulf War: 12.3%
Pop. 1990:	4,781,468	209,738	4.0%	Asian	**Most populous cities (2006):**	
Change 1990-2000:	Up 10.8%	13,312	0.3%	Native Am.	1. Baltimore	631,366
% of U.S. total:	1.9%	1,913	0.0%	Hawaiian	2. Rockville	59,114
Pop. rank:	19th of 50	82,946	1.6%	Two+ races	3. Frederick	58,882
Area size:	12,407 sq. mi.	9,379	0.2%	Other	4. Gaithersburg	57,934
State Native:	49.3%	227,916	4.3%	Hisp. Origin	5. Bowie	53,325
Non-citizen:	5.4%	**Ancestry**				
Language		German: 12.5%		Irish: 9.3%	Urban population: 86.1%	
English: 85.2%	Other Eur.: 5.4%	English: 7.1%		USA: 4.6%	Rural population: 13.9%	
Spanish: 5.2%		Italian: 4.0%				

Education		Work Sector		General Assembly	
H.S. Grad:	83.8%	Private: 72.1%	Govt: 22.3%	Senate	33 D 14 R
College Grad:	31.4%	Self: 5.4%	Family: 0.2%	House of Del.	106 D 35 R
Industry		Unemployment: 4.7%		Legislative Term Limits: No	
Agri: 0.6%	Con: 6.9%	**Household Income**		**Registered Voters**	
Fin: 7.1%	Info: 4.0%	<15k: 11.1%	15-35k: 20.2%	D: 1,733,126	(55.1%)
Mfg: 12.1%	Prof: 33.1%	35-50k: 15.4%	50-100k: 35.1%	R: 909,275	(28.9%)
Public: 10.5%	Trade: 13.3%	100-150k: 11.6%	>150k: 6.5%	O: 500,411	(15.9%)
Other: 12.4%		Median: $52,868			
Occupation		Poverty status: 8.5%			
Blue collar: 18.1%	White collar: 67.7%	**Home Value**			
Gray collar: 14.2%		<50k: 5.2% 50-100k: 20.6% 100-200k: 47.9% 200-300k: 15.5%			
		300-500k: 7.7% >500k: 3.0% Median: $143,300			

Presidential politics   With its large black population, concentrated in Baltimore City and Prince George's County, Maryland has become one of the most Democratic states in presidential elections. It was Bill Clinton's third-best state in 1992 and fifth-best in 1996, Al Gore's fourth-best in 2000 and John Kerry's fifth-best in 2004. In 2000 whites voted 51%-46% for George W. Bush, but blacks, casting one-quarter of the total, voted 92%-7% for Gore. In 2004 Bush did a little better with both groups, carrying whites 55%-44% and losing blacks 89%-11%.

Since 1992, Maryland has held its presidential primaries a week before Super Tuesday to try to get noticed, with limited success. The one notable result: In 1992, Paul Tsongas beat Clinton 41%-33%, with all his margin and more coming from suburban Baltimore and Montgomery County. In 2008, the primary will be held on February 12.

2004 Presidential Vote		
Kerry (D)	1,334,493	(56%)
Bush (R)	1,024,703	(43%)
Nader (POP)	11,854	(0%)
Other	13,188	(1%)

2004 Democratic Presidential Primary		
Kerry (D)	286,955	(60%)
Edwards (D)	123,006	(26%)
Sharpton (D)	21,810	(5%)
Dean (D)	12,461	(3%)
Kucinich (D)	8,693	(2%)
Other	28,551	(6%)

2000 Presidential Vote		
Gore (D)	1,145,782	(57%)
Bush (R)	813,797	(40%)
Nader (Green)	53,768	(3%)
Other	12,133	(1%)

Congressional districting   Maryland was the scene of the Democrats'

110th Congress Lineup	
6 D	2 R

109th Congress Lineup	
6 D	2 R

most successful partisan gerrymandering in the 2002 cycle. Gerrymandering is not too harsh a word: The convoluted shapes of the districts in the Baltimore area would have made Elbridge Gerry blush. The goal of the plan was to protect all four Democratic incumbents and to draw districts that would be impossible to win for 2d District Republican Bob Ehrlich and 8th District Republican Connie Morella. The Bush 2000 percentage in the 2d fell from 55% to 41% and in the 8th from 36% to 31%. Ehrlich ran for governor and had his revenge, though as it turned out only for four years. The 8th District attracted three Democratic challengers, each arguably a stronger candidate than any Morella had faced before, and she ended up losing narrowly to state Senator Chris Van Hollen. The four Democratic incumbents had no problems. The two other districts, the 1st, based in the Eastern Shore and the 6th, based in western Maryland, both snake into the Baltimore suburbs to take in heavily Republican precincts; they seem to be safely Republican.

Governor

Martin O'Malley (D)

Elected 2006, term expires Jan. 2011, 1st term; b. Jan. 18, 1963, Washington, D.C.; home, Baltimore; Catholic U., B.A. 1985; U. of MD, J.D. 1988; Catholic; married (Katie).

Elected Office: Baltimore City Cncl., 1992-99; Baltimore Mayor, 1999-2006.

Professional Career: Field dir., pres. candidate Gary Hart, 1982-84, Sen. Barbara Mikulski, 1986-88; Baltimore asst. state's atty., 1988-90; Practicing atty., 1991-99.

Office: 100 State Circle, Annapolis, 21401, 410-974-3591; Fax: 410-974-3275; Web site: www.gov.state.md.us.

Election Results

2006 general	Martin O'Malley (D)	942,279	(53%)
	Robert Ehrlich (R)	825,464	(46%)
	Other	20,573	(1%)
2006 primary	Martin O'Malley (D)	unopposed	
2002 general	Robert Ehrlich (R)	879,592	(52%)
	Kathleen Kennedy Townsend (D)	813,422	(48%)

Martin O'Malley, a Democrat, was elected governor in 2006. He was born in Washington, D.C., and grew up in the Maryland suburbs where his father was a trial lawyer who was active in Montgomery County, Maryland, politics and his mother worked as a receptionist for Democratic Senator Barbara Mikulski. O'Malley attended Gonzaga College High School in Washington, a private Jesuit academy in the shadow of the Capitol that also produced presidential candidate Pat Buchanan, former Secretary of Education William Bennett and former Virginia Lieutenant Governor Don Beyer, then graduated from Catholic University and the University of Maryland law school. He worked as a field organizer for Gary Hart's 1984 and 1988 presidential campaigns, and in between worked for Mikulski's 1986 run for Senate, where he met his future wife, Katie, the daughter of Joseph Curran, the longest-serving attorney general in state history. After law school O'Malley worked as a city prosecutor for two years then made his first bid for elected office, narrowly losing a state Senate race. In 1991, he ran for and won a seat on the Baltimore city council. He spent eight years as a city councilman, during which time he became known for his energy, ambition and his penchant for headlines. In 1999, at the age of 36, he ran for mayor with a reform message and won the first of two terms as a white candidate in a majority-black city.

O'Malley was the kind of mayor who rides on snow plows and fire engines and seemed to be everywhere. He approached the job with a sense of urgency, calling for zero-tolerance policing and demanding accountability from city officials. Baltimore's high crime, drug use and murder rates were a priority. He drew national acclaim for a reduction in crime and instituted a computerized system called CitiStat to track the performance of municipal government and make agencies and department heads more responsive and efficient. During this time, O'Malley cultivated a national image, appearing on the cover of *Esquire* magazine in 2002 as the "best young mayor in America", taking on a prime speaking role at the 2004 Democratic National Convention and winning notice from *Time* magazine in 2005 as one of the top five big-city mayors. He played a brief role as the mayor in the 2003 film *Ladder 49*, and fronted a Celtic rock band.

It was clear that the youthful and telegenic O'Malley envisioned office beyond City Hall, and in 2002 he considered but decided not to run for governor, saying he wanted to finish what he started in Baltimore. In 2003, when he sought reelection to a second term, both his Democratic opponents in Baltimore and the state Republican party accused him of using the city as a steppingstone to the governorship. In September 2005, O'Malley made the announcement that everyone in Maryland politics had been expecting: he would run against Robert Ehrlich, the first Republican governor of Maryland since Spiro Agnew. Ehrlich grew up in the Baltimore suburbs and served in the state House of Delegates and in Congress before his upset victory over Lieutenant Governor Kathleen Kennedy Townsend in 2002. Ehrlich had decent approval ratings but he had a stormy relationship with the Baltimore *Sun* and clashed with the legislature on many issues; there was little doubt that he entered the 2006 campaign as one of the most vulnerable governors in the nation.

O'Malley did not have a clear path to the Democratic nomination at first, as Montgomery County Executive Doug Duncan also entered the race. But in June 2006 Duncan, trailing O'Malley in both fundraising and in the polls, bowed out, citing a recent diagnosis of depression. This was a blow to Ehrlich's reelection chances for Ehrlich stood to gain from a hard-fought, cash-draining September Democratic primary which would have left little time for the victor to raise money and unite the party.

In a state where Democrats outnumber Republicans by 2-to-1 and where O'Malley led in the polls for virtually the entire campaign, Ehrlich nevertheless chose to run what he called a "noncampaign" that contrasted with the aggressive, energetic O'Malley effort. He touted his record of tackling budget deficits and his initiatives to restore the Chesapeake Bay but otherwise insisted that the election was about governing, not promises. "The governor has always said that governance comes first, and the best way to show Marylanders he is the better leader is by leading," a spokeswoman explained to the *Washington Post*. O'Malley offered a detailed agenda that called for, among other proposals, more funds for school construction, an affordable housing trust fund, a $1 increase in the minimum wage, tax incentives for small businesses to join health insurance purchasing pools. The two candidates spent freely—together they spent more than $46 million—and did not pull punches: Ehrlich consistently questioned O'Malley's record as mayor, pointing to its high level of violent crime and troubled school system, while O'Malley referred to the governor as "$3 billion Bob", a reference to what his campaign said was the cumulative effect of the state property tax increase and various other fees that were instituted during Ehrlich's time in office. O'Malley and state Democrats also sought to link Ehrlich to George W. Bush at every opportunity, ranging from mailers featuring photos of Ehrlich and Bush together to television ads; O'Malley referred to Ehrlich as "the George Bush Mini-Me of Maryland."

O'Malley won 53%-46%. Ehrlich, the only incumbent Republican governor to lose on Election Day, carried the Eastern Shore and Western Maryland but O'Malley won by landslide margins in Baltimore city (75%-23%) and in the populous Washington, D.C. suburbs of Montgomery (62%-37%) and Prince George's (79%-21%) counties. "It's clear in Maryland that there is a direction people are more comfortable with," said Ehrlich in a post-election radio interview. "It's the way it's always been. And then we had this four-year sort of off-course thing, and people are clearly more comfortable with a single party kind of deal here. They did not like the conflict."

O'Malley's first legislative session as governor was productive and marked by a cordial relationship with the legislature. He signed a formal apology for Maryland's role in slavery, a freeze on in-state tuition at public universities, legislation to impose tighter automobile emission standards and the nation's first statewide "living wage" law, requiring state contractors to pay employees more than the minimum wage. Maryland also became the first state to circumvent the electoral college by agreeing to deliver its electoral votes to the winner of the national popular vote, a measure that only takes effect if a number of other states agree to do the same.

Senior Senator

Barbara Mikulski (D)

Elected 1986, seat up 2010, 4th term; b. July 20, 1936, Baltimore; home, Baltimore; Mt. St. Agnes Col., B.A. 1958, U. of MD, M.S.W. 1965; Catholic; single.

Elected Office: Baltimore City Cncl., 1971-76; U.S. House of Reps., 1976-86.

Professional Career: Social worker, Baltimore Dept. of Social Svcs., 1965-70; Chmn., DNC Delegate Selection Comm., 1972; Adjunct prof., Loyola Col., 1972-76.

DC Office: 503 HSOB, 20510, 202-224 4654; Fax: 202-224-8858; Web site: mikulski.senate.gov.

State Offices: Annapolis, 410-263-1805; Baltimore, 410-962-4510; Greenbelt, 301-345-5517; Hagerstown, 301-797-2826; Salisbury, 410-546-7711.

Committees: *Appropriations* (5th of 15 D): Commerce, Justice, Science & Related Agencies (Chmn.); Transportation, Housing and Urban Development & Related Agencies; Homeland Security; State, Foreign Operations & Related Programs; Interior, Environment & Related Agencies; Defense. *Health, Education, Labor & Pensions* (4th of 11 D): Retirement & Aging (Chmn.); Employment & Workplace Safety. *Intelligence (Select)* (5th of 8 D).

Group Ratings

	ADA	ACLU	AFS	LCV	ITIC	NTU	COC	ACU	CFG	FRC
2006	100	83	100	100	50	9	42	0	0	0
2005	90	—	100	85	—	5	41	5	0	—

National Journal Ratings

	2005 LIB	—	2005 CONS		2006 LIB	—	2006 CONS
Economic	86%	—	13%		87%	—	0%
Social	82%	—	17%		80%	—	14%
Foreign	87%	—	10%		88%	—	8%

Key Votes of the 109th Congress

1. Bar ANWR Drilling	Y	5. Confirm Samuel Alito	N	9. Limit Interstate Abortion	N	
2. FY06 Spending Curb	N	6. Path to Citizenship	Y	10. CAFTA	N	
3. Estate Tax Repeal	N	7. Bar Same Sex Marriage	N	11. Urge Iraq Withdrawal	Y	
4. Raise Minimum Wage	Y	8. Stem Cell Research $	Y	12. Provide Detainee Rights	Y	

Election Results

2004 general	Barbara Mikulski (D) 1,504,691	(65%)	($5,997,093)
	E. J. Pipkin (R) 783,055	(34%)	($2,300,354)
	Other 33,989	(1%)	
2004 primary	Barbara Mikulski (D) 408,848	(90%)	
	Robert Kaufman (D) 32,127	(7%)	
	Other 13,901	(3%)	
1998 general	Barbara Mikulski (D) 1,062,810	(71%)	($3,014,312)
	Ross Z. Pierpont (R) 444,637	(30%)	($297,768)

Prior Winning Percentages: 1992 (71%); 1986 (61%); 1984 House (68%); 1982 House (74%); 1980 House (76%); 1978 House (100%); 1976 House (75%)

Barbara Mikulski, Maryland's senior senator, was first elected to the House in 1976 and to the Senate in 1986. She has deep roots in immigrant, urban America and a fascination for the new technology and jobs growing in edge cities and beyond; she is a person who doesn't look anything like a traditional politician but who has become a savvy Senate insider. Her roots are in east Baltimore, where her Polish immigrant grandparents ran a bakery and her father a grocery store; she graduated from Mount St. Agnes College and got a social work degree at the University of Maryland. Mikulski got a job as a social worker, helping at-risk children and educating seniors about Medicare. She entered politics by organizing community groups to stop a highway from going through the Highlandtown neighborhood where she grew up. She won, saving the now-thriving Inner Harbor, and in the process was elected to the Baltimore City Council in 1971. She ran for the Senate in 1974, and got a respectable 43% against incumbent Charles Mathias; when Paul Sarbanes ran for the other Senate seat in 1976, Mikulski ran for his 3d District House seat and won. Ten years later, she gave up that safe seat for what seemed like a chancy Senate race. She won handily, with 50% in the primary to 31% for Montgomery County Congressman Michael Barnes and 14% for Governor Harry Hughes. In the general, she beat Linda Chavez 61%-39%. She still lives in Baltimore and commutes to Washington; from her Baltimore office in Fells Point, the original port area, she can see where the highway she stopped would have gone through.

Mikulski is loud and brash, humorous and warm, brusque and aggressive when she feels it is necessary, curious and thoughtful when encountering another new part of the world. She was the first woman elected to the Senate whose husband or father did not serve in high office and every two years since 1992 she has held workshops for new women senators; now, the Senate has 16 women. She takes seriously her role as dean of the women, serving as a mentor to the newcomers. "When I came . . . .we were a bit of a novelty in the Senate," she said. "I think what we see now is that we're not viewed as a novelty. We're not viewed as celebrities. We're viewed as Senators." In her first term, she won a seat on the Appropriations Committee; within two years, she was chairman of a subcommittee, handling housing, space and veterans' programs. Now she chairs the revamped Commerce, Justice and Science Subcommittee, which also includes NASA. She has worked with other appropriators on projects in their states as well as her own. "When it comes to helping a senator who has an authentic need, I don't play politics. I solve problems."

Mikulski has been the Senate's chief superintendent of the space program and an enthusiast for space exploration. She has paid close attention to the Goddard Space Center, the Wallops Flight Facility and Johns Hopkins's Applied Science Lab in Maryland, and secured them additional funding on occasion. She has vowed to continue to raise funds for a mission to Pluto, the only unexplored plant in the solar system, stating, "Pluto is a bargain at less than $500 million." She called the Hubble space telescope "the most successful NASA program since Apollo," with the best telescope "since Galileo invented the first one," and in January 2004 attacked NASA Administrator Sean O'Keefe for his decision to let the project die; in September 2004 she and Kay Bailey Hutchison moved to add $800 million to NASA's appropriation to repair the Space Shuttle fleet and service the Hubble space telescope. In October 2006, she won a big victory when new NASA Administrator Michael Griffin announced that the mission to repair and upgrade Hubble could be accomplished safely and within budget, perhaps as soon as 2008. She promised to secure an additional $1 billion for NASA's shuttle fleet. The Hubble program provides about 1,000 jobs for Maryland. Her other funding for the state typically ranges from highways, housing, homeland security at the Port of Baltimore and Chesapeake Bay cleanup to research on oyster bed reseeding and a crab hatchery at the University of Maryland.

On domestic policy, Mikulski is a liberal but she voted for the Welfare Reform Act of 1996 and the Defense of Marriage Act in 1996. On the Health, Education, Labor and Pensions Committee, she chairs the Retirement and Aging Subcommittee, where she has taken a special interest in elder abuse, neglect and long-term care. She has battled against the Federal Activities Inventory Reform Act, which encourages the contracting out of government work to private firms. She voted against higher CAFE standards—there are still auto assembly plants in Maryland—and, mindful of her Polish heritage, urged that Poles be allowed into the United States without visas. In 2005, she and Mike DeWine insisted that House-Senate conferees on the pension bill strike a provision that required companies with poor credit to pay more into their pension funds, arguing that this provision hurt small businesses. She has fought to extend a visa program to permit more seasonal foreign workers to assist Maryland's seafood processors.

As the senior woman in the Senate, Mikulski has pushed many of what might be called women's issues—mammography clinic standards and homemaker IRAs, retaining a guaranteed benefit with inflation protection in Social Security reform. She was the chief Senate co-sponsor with John Chafee and then Lincoln Chafee for Medicaid financing of mammograms and Pap tests. Mikulski's skills are not just political. She coauthored *Capitol Offense* and *Capitol Venture*, mystery novels featuring freshman Senator Eleanor "Norie" Gorzack of Pennsylvania.

Mikulski's toughest Senate election was her first, which she won fairly easily against strong competition. In 2004 she faced a more serious challenger in state Senator E. J. Pipkin, a Dundalk native who made millions as a bond trader on Wall Street and returned to live on the Eastern Shore. He put $1 million of his own money into the race against Mikulski. He argued that Mikulski's voting record was far to the left ("Who knew?" asked his spots) and that she had not done enough for Chesapeake Bay. Mikulski still outspent him 2–1 in Maryland's most expensive Senate race and won 65%-34%. Pipkin carried his state Senate district, two counties in western Maryland and two exurban Baltimore counties. In 2005, she was briefly hospitalized for an irregular heartbeat. Some Maryland Democrats have speculated that she might retire in 2010, at 74. That likely would result in a wide-open Democratic primary, as happened after Paul Sarbanes retired in 2006.

Junior Senator

Ben Cardin (D)

Elected 2006, seat up 2012, 1st term; b. Oct. 5, 1943, Baltimore; home, Baltimore; U. of Pittsburgh, B.A. 1964, U. of MD, LL.B., J.D. 1967; Jewish; married (Myrna).

Elected Office: MD House of Delegates, 1966-86, Speaker, 1979-86; U.S. House of Reps., 1986-2006.

Professional Career: Practicing atty., 1967-86.

DC Office: 509 HSOB, 20510, 202-224-4524; Fax: 202-224-1651; Web site: cardin.senate.gov.

State Offices: Baltimore, 410-962-4436; Bowie, 301-860-0414; Salisbury, 410-546-4250.

Committees: *Budget* (10th of 12 D). *Environment & Public Works* (7th of 10 D): Transportation Safety, Infrastructure Security & Water Quality; Transportation & Infrastructure; Superfund & Environmental Health. *Foreign Relations* (9th of 11 D): African Affairs; European Affairs; Near Eastern & South & Central Asian Affairs. *Judiciary* (9th of 10 D): Constitution; Terrorism, Technology & Homeland Security; Human Rights & the Law; Antitrust, Competition Policy & Consumer Rights. *Small Business & Entrepreneurship* (9th of 10 D).

Group Ratings (as Member of U.S. House of Representatives)

	ADA	ACLU	AFS	LCV	ITIC	NTU	COC	ACU	CFG	FRC
2006	90	86	100	100	43	11	40	8	8	0
2005	95	—	100	94	—	13	40	0	3	0

National Journal Ratings (as Member of U.S. House of Representatives)

	2005 LIB	—	2005 CONS		2006 LIB	—	2006 CONS
Economic	91%	—	8%		94%	—	0%
Social	72%	—	27%		75%	—	24%
Foreign	67%	—	32%		83%	—	14%

Key Votes of the 109th Congress (as Member of U.S. House of Representatives)

1. Estate Tax Repeal	N	5. Limit Interstate Abortion	N	9. Build Border Fence	N
2. Limit CAFE Standards	N	6. Extend Patriot Act	Y	10. CAFTA	N
3. FY06 Spending Curb	N	7. Bar Same Sex Marriage	N	11. Oppose Iraq Withdrawal	N
4. Drilling in ANWR	N	8. Stem Cell Research $	Y	12. Detainee Tribunals	N

Election Results

2006 general	Ben Cardin (D)	965,477	(54%)	($8,676,056)
	Michael Steele (R)	787,182	(44%)	($8,219,686)
	Other...	28,480	(2%)	
2006 primary	Ben Cardin (D)	257,545	(44%)	
	Kweisi Mfume (D)	238,957	(41%)	
	Josh Rales (D)	30,737	(5%)	
	Other...	62,456	(11%)	
2000 general	Paul Sarbanes (D)	1,230,013	(63%)	($1,837,286)
	Paul H. Rappaport (R)	715,178	(37%)	($146,866)

Prior Winning Percentages: 2004 House (63%); 2002 House (66%); 2000 House (76%); 1998 House (78%); 1996 House (67%); 1994 House (71%); 1992 House (74%); 1990 House (70%); 1988 House (73%); 1986 House (79%)

The junior senator from Maryland is Ben Cardin, a Democrat elected in 2006 to succeed Senator Paul Sarbanes, a Democrat and the longest-serving Maryland senator in history. Both Cardin and Sarbanes are products of the Maryland House of Delegates Class of 1966; they served together with Spiro Agnew as governor. Cardin is one of the many bright politicos produced by the Jewish neighborhoods of northwest Baltimore, the son and nephew of state legislators, a man who was elected to the state House at the age of 23, the first time he was eligible to run. After serving four years as Ways and Means chairman, he became speaker in 1979, at 35. He had an interest in running for governor, but when Barbara Mikulski, now Maryland's senior senator, left her 3d District House seat to run for the Senate in 1986, he entered that race and was easily elected. In the House, Cardin got a seat on Ways and Means in his second term and became a productive and creative legislator. He supported NAFTA despite union opposition, backed a cap on medical malpractice damages despite trial lawyers' opposition, and voted for normal trade relations with China after securing for local consumption a rider designed to crack down on international dumping of subsidized steel in U.S. markets.

More than any Democrat at Ways and Means—and perhaps more than any Democrat in the House—he worked skillfully on bipartisan legislation at a time when few were sufficiently clever or independent to pursue such initiatives. Few House members of either party "can match his stature as legislative architect and master of bipartisan lawmaking," the Baltimore *Sun* editorialized. He was co-sponsor with Ohio Republican Rob Portman of the 1998 IRS reform law. Again with Portman, he produced in 2000 bipartisan legislation to expand 401(k) savings and other retirement plans. In 2001, when Congress enacted the Bush tax cut, it included his and Portman's measure to increase the limits for maximum IRA and 401(k) contributions. On Social Security, too, he has shown willingness to seek bipartisan reform with retirement accounts, but he was not receptive to George W. Bush's Social Security proposal; in March 2004 he told an audience of senior citizens to prepare for a benefit cut. Cardin also has been a workhorse on health care and welfare, but with less bipartisan success. He criticized the prescription drug coverage for Medicare beneficiaries that the House enacted in 2003 for failing to provide seniors what they needed, and he proposed an alternative to authorize HHS to negotiate lower drug prices.

In his 10 terms in the House representing parts of Baltimore and its suburbs, Cardin never won with less than 63%. But in April 2005, Cardin said he would run in 2006 for the seat being vacated by Sarbanes, a 30-year Senate veteran who announced his retirement after a career that followed a trajectory similar to Cardin's: state House to U.S. House and then to the Senate.

Maryland Senate seats don't come open very often so when this one did, Cardin and 17 other Democrats filed to run. An experienced campaigner and fundraiser, Cardin began as the frontrunner even though his earnest, low-key demeanor raised questions about his viability as a statewide candidate. His toughest primary opponent figured to be former Democratic Rep. Kweisi Mfume, who resigned his House seat in 1996 to chair the NAACP; other candidates included millionaire businessman Joshua Rales, college professor and cable television pundit Allan Lichtman, and former Baltimore County Executive Dennis Rasmussen. Mfume and Cardin were friends, both elected together to Congress in 1986, but Mfume and some other black leaders warned that the state Democratic establishment's support for Cardin could breed resentment among African-American voters.

The primary was expensive: Cardin, Rales and Mfume together spent more than $12 million. Cardin outspent Mfume by nearly 4-to-1 but Mfume had a compelling life story to tell and charisma that made Cardin pale by comparison. Rales spent heavily from his own pockets but barely registered in the polls. Cardin won 44%-41%, carrying all but two counties and Baltimore city. The win was powered in part by a nearly 2–1 margin over Mfume in suburban Washington's Montgomery County, the state's most populous. Mfume ran best among black voters, winning Baltimore by a more than 2–1 margin, black-majority Prince George's County, and southern Maryland's Charles County, increasingly a destination for African-Americans moving in from Prince George's.

The Republican nominee was Lieutenant Governor Michael Steele, the first African-American statewide officeholder in Maryland and a candidate exceptionally well-positioned to exploit Cardin's weaknesses, something that did not go unnoticed by the national Republican party when it recruited him. Steele combined his talent for retail politicking with quirky, unconventional ads designed to highlight his outsider status. Democrats, including Mfume, coalesced around Cardin and portrayed Steele as an inexperienced lightweight; Republicans criticized Cardin as a career pol who was closely tied to big money special interest groups. Without a legislative record, Steele made for an elusive target so Cardin sought to link him to President Bush and criticized Steele for his support for the Iraq war. Stem-cell research figured prominently. Cardin ran stark ads featuring actor Michael Fox, who suffers from Parkinson's disease, saying that "George Bush and Michael Steele would put limits on the most promising stem cell research"; Steele countered with an ad featuring his sister, a local doctor who revealed she had multiple sclerosis, saying Cardin was "using the victim of a terrible disease to frighten people all for his own political gain."

Cardin won 54%-44%, in what was a tough year for Maryland Republicans—aside from Steele's defeat, Governor Bob Ehrlich lost his reelection bid. Steele won 18 of 23 counties, carrying the Eastern Shore and western Maryland, but Cardin carried all the key suburban counties: 52%-47% in Baltimore County (which doesn't include the city); 54%-45% in Howard; 67%-32% in Montgomery. African-American voters voted overwhelmingly for Cardin: Cardin won by landslide margins in the city of Baltimore, 75%-23%, and in Steele's home base of suburban Prince George's County, 75%-24%.

In the Senate, Cardin requested a seat on the Finance Committee; he says Majority Leader Harry Reid's response was "Not gonna happen." Instead Cardin got seats on the Budget, Environment and Public Works, Foreign Relations, Judiciary and Small Business committees.

FIRST DISTRICT

Rep. Wayne Gilchrest (R)

Elected 1990, 9th term; b. Apr. 15, 1946, Rahway, NJ; home, Kennedyville; Wesley Col., A.A. 1971, DE St. Col., B.A. 1973, Loyola Col., 1984; Methodist; married (Barbara).

Military Career: Marine Corps, 1964-68 (Vietnam).

Professional Career: High schl. teacher, 1973-86; Natl. Forest Service worker, Bitterroot Natl. Forest, 1986.

DC Office: 2245 RHOB, 20515, 202-225-5311; Fax: 202-225-0254; Web site: gilchrest.house.gov.

District Offices: Bel Air, 410-838-2517; Chestertown, 410-778-9407; Salisbury, 410-749-3184.

Committees: *Natural Resources* (5th of 22 R): Fisheries, Wildlife & Oceans. *Transportation & Infrastructure* (6th of 34 R): Railroads, Pipelines & Hazardous Materials; Water Resources & Environment; Coast Guard & Maritime Transportation.

Group Ratings

	ADA	ACLU	AFS	LCV	ITIC	NTU	COC	ACU	CFG	FRC
2006	40	60	14	67	100	41	77	48	40	0
2005	25	—	0	50	—	48	89	42	44	38

National Journal Ratings

	2005 LIB	—	2005 CONS		2006 LIB	—	2006 CONS
Economic	48%	—	52%		48%	—	52%
Social	53%	—	47%		55%	—	45%
Foreign	47%	—	52%		56%	—	44%

Key Votes of the 109th Congress

1. Estate Tax Repeal	Y	5. Limit Interstate Abortion	N	9. Build Border Fence	Y
2. Limit CAFE Standards	N	6. Extend Patriot Act	Y	10. CAFTA	Y
3. FY06 Spending Curb	Y	7. Bar Same Sex Marriage	N	11. Oppose Iraq Withdrawal	Y
4. Drilling in ANWR	N	8. Stem Cell Research $	Y	12. Detainee Tribunals	N

Election Results

2006 general	Wayne Gilchrest (R)	185,177	(69%)	($182,375)
	Jim Corwin (D)	83,738	(31%)	($29,701)
2006 primary	Wayne Gilchrest (R)	unopposed		
2004 general	Wayne Gilchrest (R)	245,149	(76%)	($391,272)
	Kostas Alexakis (D)	77,872	(24%)	($113,435)

Prior Winning Percentages: 2002 (77%); 2000 (64%); 1998 (69%); 1996 (62%); 1994 (68%); 1992 (52%); 1990 (57%)

The People		Race/Ethnic Origin	Ancestry	
Area size:	3,702 sq. mi.	84.7% White	German: 15.5% Irish: 12.1%	
Urban population:	64.2%	11.2% Black	English: 10.7%	
Rural population:	35.8%	1.4% Asian	**2004 Presidential Vote**	
Pop. 2000:	662,062	0.2% Native Am.	Bush (R) 213,144	(62%)
Pop. 2005 (est):	714,699	0.0% Hawaiian	Kerry (D) 124,163	(36%)
Median income:	$51,918	0.9% Two+ races	Other 3,828	(1%)
Poverty status:	7.3%	0.1% Other	**2000 Presidential Vote**	
Military veterans:	15.2%	1.6% Hispanic Origin	Bush (R) 160,402	(57%)
			Gore (D) 111,807	(40%)
			Other 8,424	(3%)
			Cook Partisan Voting Index: R +10	
Occupation	Blue collar: 21.9%	White collar: 63.3% Gray collar: 14.8%		

Chesapeake Bay, technically not a bay but an estuary, was the central focus of the most thickly settled of the 13 colonies, and today remains a central focus for much of modern Maryland and a backwater where an older civilization lives on. The first British here were amazed at the Chesapeake's oysters and terrapin turtles and crabs and rockfish. But pollution, agricultural runoff and disease have vastly depleted their populations, and only a few watermen still make livings bringing them to shore. This was an estuary civilization in colonial days, with every little hamlet tied together by the highways of bays and creeks and inlets off the Chesapeake. The streets and docks of Chestertown, Oxford, St. Michaels and Cambridge still look something like what they did when George Washington slept there.

In post-colonial times, when most Americans were caught up in the romance of westward movement, these estuaries and peninsulas were mostly forgotten, off the main lines of railroads and highways, left behind by thousands moving west. In the 160 years between 1790 and 1950, the Eastern Shore counties of Maryland only doubled in population, perhaps the slowest growth rate on the Eastern Seaboard. Over the past half-century much of the Chesapeake has changed beyond recognition, as the Eastern Shore has grown vigorously, with second-home buyers, retirees and commuters across the Chesapeake Bay Bridge. This is a land of genteel estates fronting the water and of Frank Perdue's thriving chicken empire around Salisbury, of Easton's Waterfowl Festival and St. Michaels's Oysterfest, and the swarms of motorboats and sailing ships making their way up and down the inlets or under the twin spans of the Bay Bridge. This growth has forced people along the Bay to confront issues that once would have been unimaginable here, such as high-rise condominiums obscuring the sunrise in an old fishing village like Crisfield.

The 1st Congressional District of Maryland includes all nine counties of the Eastern Shore. It extends across the Bay and grabs parts of Harford, Baltimore and Anne Arundel Counties to strip Republican strongholds from the congressional districts which once contained them. The Baltimore and Harford County suburbs north of Baltimore are as solidly Republican as any part of Maryland. Although it is hard to avoid thinking of this district as the Eastern Shore district, nearly half the votes are cast on the west side of the Bay. This was one of only two districts in the state that twice voted for George W. Bush—and comfortably.

The congressman from the 1st District is Wayne Gilchrest, first elected in 1990. He is a Republican with political views that stamp him as an independent thinker, both on national and local issues. Gilchrest served in the Marine Corps in the Dominican Republic and then in Vietnam, where he was wounded in the chest as a platoon leader and received the Purple Heart and Bronze Star; he returned to study rural poverty in Appalachia, taught history in high school for 13 years and painted houses in the summer. In 1988 he ran for Congress and lost to incumbent Democrat Roy Dyson 50.4%-49.6%; Dyson spent vastly more money but was embarrassed by a *Washington Post* story on his personnel practices. In 1990, Gilchrest was again vastly outspent, but this time defeated Dyson 57%-43%, drawing on his genuineness and *Mr. Smith Goes to Washington* demeanor. The 1992 redistricting placed him in the same district with Democratic incumbent Tom McMillen, a former star athlete at the University of Maryland, Rhodes Scholar and pro basketball player. McMillen raised far more money, but Gilchrest won 52%-48%. Since then, he has not faced a competitive Democratic challenger.

Gilchrest's voting record in recent years has been almost precisely at the midpoint of the House, making him a crucial vote on many issues. His specialty, helpful in a district centered on the Chesapeake Bay, is environmental protection, without sacrificing economic development. His committee assignments—Transportation and Natural Resources—give him some leverage on these issues, though internal Republican politics deprived him of a top subcommittee position. With little notice, he has helped to enact several pro-environment laws, including a measure to assist in conservation of marine turtles and another to expand the Blackwater National Wildlife Refuge in Cecil County. He encouraged a federal program to restore oysters in the Bay by expanding their protected areas, and he secured additional funding for farm conservation on the Shore to reduce agricultural runoff into the Bay. He worked to enforce international treaties to conserve migratory fish, plus tigers and African elephants. But, under pressure from party leaders, he was a crucial vote in October 2005 for passage of a bill to expedite construction of new gasoline refineries. After initially clashing with Resources Committee chairman Richard Pombo on a measure to update federal oversight of fisheries, both joined a consensus agreement in December 2006. He has made multiple visits to post-Saddam Iraq to assess conditions.

He has been a maverick to the point of being courageous—and occasionally effective—in taking on economic and political powers, at home and in the Capitol. He opposed efforts backed by the Port of Baltimore to dredge the Chesapeake and Delaware Canal, which links the Chesapeake and Delaware Bays; his objections outraged powerful Marylanders, but the Army Corps of Engineers abandoned the plan. He opposed the National Rifle Association on its amendment to weaken restrictions on gun show sales—in a district where many are strongly opposed to gun control. In December 2005, he called for a House task force on ocean policy, which would impinge on the jurisdiction of several committees; he lost, 103-327. He called "ludicrous" the Pentagon's "don't ask, don't tell" policy, and said that gays serving in the military should be permitted out of the closet; he cited his brother, who is gay and "a rock-solid guy." The Democratic takeover of the House could leave this maverick at least as well-positioned to influence legislation.

In campaigns, Gilchrest says that he votes for issues, not with a party. He does not accept PAC contributions, and he has won the endorsements of the Sierra Club and League of Conservation Voters. His moderate voting record has led to competitive primary contests. In 2002, Baltimore County attorney and political unknown David Fischer loaned his campaign more than $300,000 and attracted support from the NRA and the Club for Growth. Fischer called Gilchrest out of step with the district's conservative views. "A safe Republican district deserves a congressman who actually votes like a Republican," said one of his newspaper ads, and he criticized Gilchrest for winning support from abortion rights and gay and lesbian groups. Gilchrest spent roughly $400,000 and won, 60%-36%. He ran much better on the Eastern Shore (67%-30%) than in the suburbs (52%-44%). The challenge in 2004 came from the Shore's conservative state Senator Richard Colburn, who ran unsuccessfully in the 1990 primary. Colburn ran billboards calling Gilchrest "the liberal incumbent." Gilchrest was backed by Speaker Dennis Hastert and the moderate Republican Main Street Partnership. He won more easily than expected, 62%-38%. His margins in the suburbs were bigger than in 2002 (60%-40%), and he narrowly lost two small counties on the Eastern Shore. In each case, he won the general with more than 75% of the vote.

Gilchrest escaped primary opposition in 2006 and won the general election with 69%. But in 2007 he was one of two Republicans to vote for the Democratic war funding bill vetoed by President Bush and one of 17 Republicans who backed a resolution disapproving of the President's troop "surge" and those votes helped revive conservative opposition back home. State Senator Andrew Harris filed to run against him in the Republican primary; on the Democratic side, Queen Anne's County State's Attorney Frank Kratovil announced his intent to run.

SECOND DISTRICT

Rep. Dutch Ruppersberger (D)

Elected 2002, 3d term; b. Jan. 31, 1946, Baltimore; home, Cockeysville; U. of MD, 1963-67, U of Baltimore, J.D. 1970; Methodist; married (Kay).

Elected Office: Baltimore Cnty. Cncl. 1986-94; Baltimore Cnty. Exec., 1994-2002.

Professional Career: Prosecutor, Baltimore Cnty. State's Atty. Office, 1970-75.

DC Office: 1730 LHOB, 20515, 202-225-3061; Fax: 202-225-3094; Web site: dutch.house.gov.

District Offices: Timonium, 410-628-2701.

Committees: *Appropriations* (34th of 37 D): Financial Services & General Government; Commerce, Justice, Science & Related Agencies; Legislative Branch. *Permanent Select Committee on Intelligence* (7th of 12 D): Technical & Tactical Intelligence (Chmn.); Intelligence Community Management; Oversight & Investigations.

Group Ratings

	ADA	ACLU	AFS	LCV	ITIC	NTU	COC	ACU	CFG	FRC
2006	85	82	86	92	83	15	67	24	21	0
2005	95	—	100	78	—	16	63	20	20	25

National Journal Ratings

	2005 LIB	—	2005 CONS		2006 LIB	—	2006 CONS
Economic	65%	—	35%		67%	—	33%
Social	65%	—	35%		65%	—	35%
Foreign	63%	—	36%		59%	—	40%

Key Votes of the 109th Congress

1. Estate Tax Repeal	Y	5. Limit Interstate Abortion	N	9. Build Border Fence	Y
2. Limit CAFE Standards	Y	6. Extend Patriot Act	Y	10. CAFTA	N
3. FY06 Spending Curb	N	7. Bar Same Sex Marriage	N	11. Oppose Iraq Withdrawal	N
4. Drilling in ANWR	N	8. Stem Cell Research $	Y	12. Detainee Tribunals	N

Election Results

2006 general	Dutch Ruppersberger (D) 135,818	(69%)	($590,984)
	Jimmy Mathis (R) 60,195	(31%)	($8,448)
2006 primary	Dutch Ruppersberger (D) 56,450	(82%)	
	Christopher Boardman (D) 12,118	(18%)	
2004 general	Dutch Ruppersberger (D) 164,751	(67%)	($648,488)
	Jane Brooks (R)................................... 75,812	(31%)	($76,897)
	Other.. 6,732	(3%)	

Prior Winning Percentages: 2002 (54%)

The People		Race/Ethnic Origin	Ancestry		
Area size:	359 sq. mi.	66.3% White	German: 15.6%	Irish: 10.4%	
Urban population:	98.3%	27.1% Black	English: 5.9%		
Rural population:	1.7%	2.4% Asian	**2004 Presidential Vote**		
Pop. 2000:	662,060	0.3% Native Am.	Kerry (D)	144,090	(54%)
Pop. 2005 (est):	686,894	0.0% Hawaiian	Bush (R)	118,429	(45%)
Median income:	$44,309	1.5% Two+ races	Other	3,103	(1%)
Poverty status:	9.8%	0.2% Other	**2000 Presidential Vote**		
Military veterans:	15.0%	2.2% Hispanic Origin	Gore (D)	127,510	(57%)
			Bush (R)	91,677	(41%)
			Other	5,285	(2%)
			Cook Partisan Voting Index: D + 8		

Occupation   Blue collar: 23.0%   White collar: 61.5%   Gray collar: 15.5%

The spokes of Baltimore's avenues spread out in all directions from the downtown centered on the Inner Harbor, connecting the central city with the suburbs where most residents of metropolitan Baltimore now live. The streets reach east to Dundalk and Essex, industrial suburbs where the tone of life was set for years by the giant Sparrows Point steel mill, long the biggest in the country. Northeastward, they extend to Havre de Grace and the oldest lighthouse in continuous use on the East Coast, and modest working-class suburbs in Harford County. The Aberdeen Proving Grounds has generated both military and civilian job growth, but the locale is now better known for its Ripken Stadium, the home of the Aberdeen Iron Birds, a Class A baseball team owned by hometown hero Cal Ripken, the Iron Man who set a baseball record by playing 2,632 consecutive games for the Baltimore Orioles. In an arc north of downtown are middle-income towns from Randallstown to White Marsh. A couple miles northwest of the county seat of Towson is Timonium, the site of the annual Maryland state fair.

The 2d Congressional District of Maryland is an irregularly shaped hodgepodge that includes much of this territory. Most of the district is not far from the Chesapeake Bay, running south from Havre de Grace past the Aberdeen Proving Grounds and the bustling Port of Baltimore, with its container facilities and large warehouses plus space for more than 500,000 new cars and trucks that annually move through the port. To the south is the busy Baltimore-Washington International Airport, a major hub for low-cost airlines. Close by is Fort Meade, the large Army base that houses the National Security Agency and that was a transit point for nearly four million soldiers in World War II. The district juts inland to include some Baltimore County suburbs, residential neighborhoods in northeast Baltimore and an industrial pocket in far southeast Baltimore. At that point, the district crosses the Harbor Tunnel to capture the row homes of Brooklyn and Curtis Bay, whose residents are mainly descendants of German and East European immigrants who arrived there to work on the docks and in the factories along the Patapsco River and the harbor. The Democrats who drew the district lines connected Democratic suburban and city neighborhoods while including as little Republican territory as possible. About 60% of its population is in Baltimore County, with the remainder divided roughly equally among Anne Arundel and Harford Counties and Baltimore City. The inclusion of Baltimore neighborhoods helped raise the district's black percentage from 8% to 27% and lowered the Bush 2000 percentage from 55% to 41%—one of the biggest changes in the nation.

The congressman from the 2d District is Dutch Ruppersberger, a Democrat first elected in 2002, for whom this district was drawn. Ruppersberger grew up in Baltimore, attended the University of Maryland and graduated from the University of Baltimore Law School; serving as Baltimore County assistant state's attorney, he had a near-fatal car accident while investigating a drug trafficking case. In 1986, he was elected to the Baltimore County Council; in 1994, he was elected Baltimore County executive, a position once held by a vice president of the United States, Spiro Agnew.

Barred from seeking a third term in 2002, Ruppersberger seriously considered running for governor but decided not to challenge Kathleen Kennedy Townsend. When Democratic redistricters produced a favorable district, he ran there. He faced some tough obstacles. In 2000, he backed a property condemnation plan to give him the power of eminent domain to redevelop large pieces of the county; the proposal was soundly rejected at the polls. In the 2002 Democratic primary, his little-known opponent, investment banker Osman "Oz" Bengur, spent more than $500,000 of his own money. But the state's Democratic establishment lined up behind Ruppersberger and he won 50%-36%. The fall campaign was no easier. This open seat attracted former Congresswoman Helen

Delich Bentley, who held the 2d District seat for a decade until she ran, unsuccessfully, for governor in 1994. At 78, Bentley was by far the oldest candidate in a seriously contested House race in 2002. But she remained feisty and energetic. With a strong record of constituent service, cross-party popularity and a willingness to buck her own party, she had a chance to overcome the new district's Democratic leanings. Both candidates supported additional dredging of shipping channels in the Bay plus increased port security. Ruppersberger won 54%-46%. His popular vote margin was more than 13,000 votes in the small part of the district in Baltimore City, which he carried 79%-21%, and only 3,000 votes in the rest of the district.

In the House Ruppersberger has had the least liberal voting record of Democrats from Maryland. With the help of Baltimore native Nancy Pelosi, he became the first freshman appointed to the Intelligence Committee. He initiated Operation Hero Miles, to facilitate the use of frequent-flyer miles to assist U.S. troops in Iraq flying home on civilian airlines during the Christmas season, and made the program permanent by including it in the Defense Department spending bill. Concerned about the potential sale of shipping operations at the Port of Baltimore to the United Arab Emirates, he helped to enact port-security legislation. In 2007, he took a seat on the Appropriations Committee, a useful assignment for his government-dependent district.

Ruppersberger has been reelected easily. His earlier statewide ambitions have dimmed with the election of other Baltimore-area Democrats to vacant seats for governor and the Senate, not to mention the increased opportunities in the House with Democrats in the majority.

THIRD DISTRICT

Rep. John Sarbanes (D)

Elected 2006, 1st term; b. May 22, 1961, Baltimore; home, Towson; Princeton, B.A. 1984, Harvard, J.D. 1988; Greek Orthodox; married (Dina).

Professional Career: Practicing atty., 1988-2006; Asst., MD Schls. Superintendent, 1998-2005.

DC Office: 426 CHOB, 20515, 202-225-4016; Fax: 202-225-9219; Web site: sarbanes.house.gov.

District Offices: Annapolis, 410-295-1679; Towson, 410-832-8890.

Committees: *Education & Labor* (18th of 27 D): Healthy Families & Communities; Early Childhood, Elementary & Secondary Education. *Natural Resources* (14th of 27 D): National Parks, Forests & Public Lands. *Oversight & Government Reform* (22d of 23 D): Federal Workforce, Postal Service & the District of Columbia.

Group Ratings and Key Votes: Newly Elected

Election Results

2006 general	John Sarbanes (D)	150,142	(64%)	($1,396,582)
	John White (R)	79,174	(34%)	($471,185)
	Other	5,170	(2%)	
2006 primary	John Sarbanes (D)	26,954	(32%)	
	Peter Beilenson (D)	21,481	(25%)	
	Paula Hollinger (D)	18,008	(21%)	
	Andy Barth (D)	7,561	(9%)	
	Kevin O'Keeffe (D)	4,084	(5%)	
	Oz Bengur (D)	3,774	(4%)	
	Other	2,592	(3%)	
2004 general	Ben Cardin (D)	182,066	(63%)	($1,011,951)
	Bob Duckworth (R)	97,008	(34%)	($140,972)
	Other	8,145	(3%)	

The People		Race/Ethnic Origin	Ancestry	
Area size:	293 sq. mi.	75.7% White	German: 14.3% Irish: 11.1%	
Urban population:	98.6%	16.2% Black	English: 7.7%	
Rural population:	1.4%	3.2% Asian	**2004 Presidential Vote**	
Pop. 2000:	662,062	0.3% Native Am.	Kerry (D) 163,088	(54%)
Pop. 2005 (est):	690,639	0.0% Hawaiian	Bush (R) 136,672	(45%)
Median income:	$52,906	1.5% Two+ races	Other 3,873	(1%)
Poverty status:	7.7%	0.2% Other	**2000 Presidential Vote**	
Military veterans:	13.0%	2.9% Hispanic Origin	Gore (D) 143,685	(55%)
			Bush (R) 107,481	(41%)
			Other 8,456	(3%)
			Cook Partisan Voting Index: D + 7	

Occupation   Blue collar: 15.7%   White collar: 71.7%   Gray collar: 12.5%

Baltimore, one of America's major cities since the Revolution, has been transformed into one of America's star cities. Its Inner Harbor and new ballpark at Camden Yards became national models. Its cuisine—steamed crabs with Chesapeake spices and crab cakes—became known beyond the watershed of the Chesapeake Bay. The city "prefers diners and taverns tucked into venerable row houses to newer, trendier spots," wrote *The New York Times*. The central city of Baltimore has had terrible problems—high crime, abandoned neighborhoods, poor schools—but the greater Baltimore that has grown far beyond the city and county lines retains a distinctive character. This is a city built solidly on commerce, and one that has always known how to reap its pleasures. To the south, Annapolis was laid out as a capital in 1694, with one circle planned for the Statehouse and one for the Church; the marble-halled Statehouse, built in 1772, where the Continental Congress ratified the Treaty of Paris, is the oldest state capitol in continuous use. Annapolis is also the home of the United States Naval Academy and its waterfront, though gentrified, is a waterman's as well as a yachter's port.

The 3d Congressional District of Maryland consists of three oddly disjointed portions that extend from the locus of the Inner Harbor area. Its boundaries were designed by Democrats with politics in mind: The 3d envelops on three sides the majority-black 7th District and is itself enveloped on three sides by the 2d District, which redistricters made more Democratic than the 3d. One spoke extends northeast from black city neighborhoods into mostly white suburbs. Another extends north and west from the city to the Baltimore County seat of Towson and the heavily Jewish suburbs of Pikesville and Owings Mills, past the array of temples and synagogues on Park Heights Avenue in Baltimore city. The largest bloc of voters is in the crooked spoke that extends southwest, past the old rowhouse neighborhoods overlooking Fort McHenry and out past blue-collar Arbutus into Linthicum in Anne Arundel County, and continuing to Annapolis. Just over one-third of the district population resides in Anne Arundel County (including all of Annapolis); a quarter resides within Baltimore city itself, in neighborhoods like Roland Park, and among the restaurants and bars of Little Italy and Fells Point. Another small slice in the 3d consists of parts of Elkridge and Columbia in Howard County. Redistricting left the new 3d District less Democratic than it had been; the Bush 2000 percentage vote increased from 34% to 41%; in 2004, his local vote share grew to 45%.

The new congressman from the 3d District is Democrat John Sarbanes, who replaces Ben Cardin, who won the Senate seat that Sarbanes's father had vacated. The younger Sarbanes graduated from Princeton and Harvard Law School (the same academic route as his dad), and returned to Baltimore to clerk for a federal district court judge. He then joined the Venable law firm, where he chaired the health care practice and represented non-profit hospitals and senior-living providers. He served seven years as special assistant to the Maryland superintendent of schools, where he was liaison to the Baltimore schools. Though this was his first bid for public office, Sarbanes enjoyed a considerable advantage because of his high name recognition. But the primary race was no cakewalk. Openings in the Maryland congressional delegation are rare, so when Cardin announced that he was giving up the seat he had held since 1986, eight candidates filed to run in the September primary. Contenders included veteran state Senator Paula Hollinger and former Baltimore Health Commissioner Peter Beilenson, the son of former California Democratic Congressman Anthony Beilenson. Cardin's nephew Jon Cardin, a Democrat in the House of Delegates, passed on the contest. Sarbanes issued lengthy, detailed proposals on health care and education, which he named as his top two legislative priorities. He supported repeal of the Bush tax cuts as "fundamentally unfair and leading us down a road to financial disaster." Beilenson emphasized his experience at managing a large government budget. Hollinger was endorsed by the teachers association; she had chaired the Senate Education, Health and Environmental Affairs Committee.

Sarbanes, who had a small fundraising advantage, won the Democratic primary with 32% to 25% for runner-up Beilenson and 21% for Hollinger. Although his customarily low-profile father mostly stayed in the background, John Sarbanes acknowledged that he benefited from name identification. He ran strongest in Anne Arundel County, which cast the most votes, and where he led Beilenson 40%-18%. Beilenson won more narrowly in Baltimore city, as did Hollinger in Baltimore County; Sarbanes finished second in each and also won the smaller vote in Howard County. Republican nominee John White, the founder and CEO of a marketing company, spent nearly a half-million dollars, most of it from his own pocket, but got little attention and lost 64%-34%.

FOURTH DISTRICT

Rep. Albert Wynn (D)

Elected 1992, 8th term; b. Sept. 10, 1951, Philadelphia, PA; home, Mitchellville; U. of Pittsburgh, B.S. 1973, Howard U., 1973-74, Georgetown U. Law Schl., J.D. 1977; Baptist; married (Gaines).

Elected Office: MD House of Delegates, 1982-87; MD Senate 1987-92.

Professional Career: Exec. Dir., Prince George's Cnty. Consumer Protection Comm., 1977-81; Chmn., Metro Wash. Cncl. of Consumer Agencies, 1980-81; Practicing atty., 1981-92.

DC Office: 2470 RHOB, 20515, 202-225-8699; Fax: 202-225-8714; Web site: www.wynn.house.gov.

District Offices: Gaithersburg, 301-987-2054; Largo, 301-773-4094.

Committees: *Energy & Commerce* (12th of 31 D): Environment & Hazardous Materials (Chmn.); Energy & Air Quality.

Group Ratings
	ADA	ACLU	AFS	LCV	ITIC	NTU	COC	ACU	CFG	FRC
2006	85	91	71	92	43	17	60	20	16	14
2005	95	—	100	67	—	18	70	24	10	31

National Journal Ratings
	2005 LIB	—	2005 CONS		2006 LIB	—	2006 CONS
Economic	60%	—	39%		65%	—	35%
Social	72%	—	28%		73%	—	27%
Foreign	70%	—	29%		75%	—	25%

Key Votes of the 109th Congress
1. Estate Tax Repeal	Y	5. Limit Interstate Abortion	N	9. Build Border Fence	N
2. Limit CAFE Standards	Y	6. Extend Patriot Act	N	10. CAFTA	N
3. FY06 Spending Curb	N	7. Bar Same Sex Marriage	N	11. Oppose Iraq Withdrawal	N
4. Drilling in ANWR	N	8. Stem Cell Research $	Y	12. Detainee Tribunals	N

Election Results
2006 general	Albert Wynn (D) 141,897	(81%)	($980,863)
	Michael Starkman (R) 32,792	(19%)	
	Other 1,214	(1%)	
2006 primary	Albert Wynn (D) 40,857	(50%)	
	Donna Edwards (D) 38,126	(46%)	
	George McDermott (D) 3,200	(4%)	
2004 general	Albert Wynn (D) 196,809	(75%)	($722,207)
	John McKinnis (R) 52,907	(20%)	($91,985)
	Theresa Dudley (Green) 11,885	(5%)	($6,084)

Prior Winning Percentages: 2002 (79%); 2000 (87%); 1998 (86%); 1996 (85%); 1994 (75%); 1992 (75%)

The People		Race/Ethnic Origin	Ancestry		
Area size:	318 sq. mi.	27.6% White	German: 5.3%		Irish: 5.0%
Urban population:	97.9%	56.8% Black	English: 4.0%		
Rural population:	2.1%	5.6% Asian	**2004 Presidential Vote**		
Pop. 2000:	662,062	0.2% Native Am.	Kerry (D) 217,549		(78%)
Pop. 2005 (est):	689,535	0.0% Hawaiian	Bush (R) 58,170		(21%)
Median income:	$57,727	2.0% Two+ races	Other 1,843		(1%)
Poverty status:	7.3%	0.2% Other	**2000 Presidential Vote**		
Military veterans:	12.2%	7.5% Hispanic Origin	Gore (D) 176,780		(77%)
			Bush (R) 49,202		(21%)
			Other 4,098		(2%)
			Cook Partisan Voting Index: D +30		

Occupation	Blue collar: 15.0%	White collar: 70.7%	Gray collar: 14.3%

In 1696, the proprietors of the colony of Maryland created a new county between the Potomac and Patuxent Rivers and named it after the husband of the heir to the throne, Prince George of Denmark. For 300 years Prince George's County has not often won national fame—maybe briefly when investigators chased the plotters of Abraham Lincoln's murder here—but it might now. Historically, Prince George's was tobacco country, rural and heavily settled, with blacks and Catholics and big property-owners who pretty much ran things. With its nearly two-thirds black population, Prince George's today is—or should be known as—the home of America's largest black middle class, a place that gives a hopeful glimpse of the future. The population of Prince George's grew as middle-class blacks moved out of Washington into modest suburbs at the county's edge and affluent subdivisions far to the east. In the 1960s this was one of the nation's fastest-growing suburban counties. Its black percentage increased from 14% in 1970 to 37% in 1980 to 63% by 2000, while the total population kept rising. Prince George's is affluent by national standards, with over 70% of women working, one of the highest percentages in the nation. With office and shopping mall growth, it has proved itself a far more commercially vibrant and culturally constructive community—including substantial home-schooling—than adjacent parts of the District of Columbia.

New economic projects include a 12-lane span across the Potomac to replace the crumbling Wilson Bridge and the huge National Harbor hotel and convention center going up at Oxon Hill near the bridge. The county's median household income of more than $55,000 compares favorably with the national median of about $43,000 and doubles the national median for black households. "The county ranks in the top two percent in the nation in income level, and in people who are employed in executive jobs," *Ebony* reported. Yet there are considerable problems amidst this success: Prince George's accounts for half of Maryland's car thefts, and homicides doubled from 2000 to 2004.

The 4th Congressional District of Maryland includes most of Prince George's County inside the Capital Beltway. It also includes a large portion of Montgomery County that is mostly outside the Beltway—starting in Silver Spring, heading up Georgia Avenue and covering a sizable rural area all the way to Clarksburg at the Frederick County line. This Montgomery area is heavily Democratic, though not so much so as the district's portion of Prince George's, and overall this is the most Democratic district in Maryland. George W. Bush got 21% here in both 2000 and 2004. The biggest industry here remains government: It has the highest percentage of federal employees of any congressional district in the nation;Suitland, inside the Beltway in Prince George's, is home of the Census Bureau.

The congressman from the 4th District is Albert Wynn, a Democrat first elected in 1992. Wynn grew up in Prince George's County, attending all-black schools there until integration began in his sophomore year. He went to the University of Pittsburgh on a debate team scholarship and received a law degree from Georgetown University. After directing the county's consumer protection commission, he served a decade in the Maryland legislature, first as a member of the House of Delegates and later the Senate. When the new black-majority 4th District was created in 1992, 20 candidates—13 Democrats and seven Republicans—ran for the seat; Wynn was endorsed by the major local newspapers and won the Democratic primary with 28% of the vote.

Although he is a loyal member of the Democratic Caucus, Wynn occasionally splits from the party line, especially on economic issues and in his work on the Energy and Commerce Committee. As Wynn himself has explained, many of his votes factor in his large Prince George's constituency of suburban small business owners—many of whom happen to be black Democrats. He worked with Republicans seeking to increase the profitability of electricity transmission systems, and was the only Maryland Democrat to support the energy bills in 2003 and 2005. When Democratic leaders strongly backed the Shays-Meehan campaign reform bill, Wynn felt that its ban on soft money would make it much harder to conduct voter registration and turnout drives in black districts. He was the lead Democratic sponsor of an unsuccessful amendment to strip out the soft money ban. He has been a steadfast ally of federal employees. On behalf of the American Federation of Government Employees, he took the lead in seeking to halt contracting out of federal jobs until Congress could improve its monitoring. After voting to authorize the use of force in Iraq, Wynn later voiced regret, especially when weapons of mass destruction could not be found. On the Commerce Committee, he has sought to ban automatic dialing systems that send recorded telephone messages; in his 2000 reelection campaign, his opponent had used such a tactic against him. In 2007, he became chairman of the Environment and Hazardous Materials Subcommittee, where he became a player in the global-warming debate.

At home, he has become an independent force in county and state politics, sometimes to the dismay of other local Democrats. In 2006, Wynn unexpectedly faced his most serious challenge since taking office, from a woman who had worked for him as a law clerk in the 1980s. Donna Edwards, a foundation executive with experience in lobbying Congress for nonprofit groups, surprised him with a well-funded and late-breaking primary campaign. She ran to his left, benefited from strong local opposition to the Iraq war and attacked Wynn's close ties to business interests. Wynn criticized Edwards for distorting his record; the dynamics of the contest resembled the 2006 Connecticut Democratic Senate primary between Joe Lieberman and Ned Lamont. *The Washington Post* endorsed Edwards and wrote that too often Wynn's "votes have been at odds with good government and the interests of his constituents." Nearly two weeks after the vote, Edwards conceded Wynn's stunningly close 49.7%-46.4% win. Wynn took his home county, by an unimpressive 57%-40%. In Montgomery County, which cast 32% of the vote and where Wynn had failed to devote sufficient attention, Edwards won 60%-35%, a result that nearly cost him his seat. Edwards announced she would seek a rematch in 2008; Wynn seemed to be taking this challenge more seriously than in 2006 by increasing his visibility in the district and co-sponsoring a resolution to impeach Vice President Dick Cheney.

FIFTH DISTRICT

Rep. Steny Hoyer (D)

Elected May 1981, 13th full term; b. June 14, 1939, New York, NY; home, Mechanicsville; U. of MD, B.S. 1963, Georgetown U., J.D. 1966; Baptist; widowed.

Elected Office: MD Senate, 1966-78, Pres., 1975-78.

Professional Career: Practicing atty., 1966-80; MD Bd. of Higher Educ., 1978-81.

DC Office: 1705 LHOB, 20515, 202-225-4131; Fax: 202-225-4300; Web site: hoyer.house.gov.

District Offices: Greenbelt, 301-474-0119; Waldorf, 301-843-1577.

Committees: *Majority Leader.*

Group Ratings

	ADA	ACLU	AFS	LCV	ITIC	NTU	COC	ACU	CFG	FRC
2006	90	91	100	100	57	10	40	4	7	0
2005	95	—	100	83	—	13	52	12	3	0

National Journal Ratings

	2005 LIB	—	2005 CONS		2006 LIB	—	2006 CONS
Economic	72%	—	26%		86%	—	11%
Social	74%	—	26%		82%	—	17%
Foreign	65%	—	35%		65%	—	34%

Key Votes of the 109th Congress

1. Estate Tax Repeal	N	5. Limit Interstate Abortion	N	9. Build Border Fence	N
2. Limit CAFE Standards	Y	6. Extend Patriot Act	Y	10. CAFTA	N
3. FY06 Spending Curb	N	7. Bar Same Sex Marriage	N	11. Oppose Iraq Withdrawal	N
4. Drilling in ANWR	N	8. Stem Cell Research $	Y	12. Detainee Tribunals	N

Election Results

2006 general	Steny Hoyer (D) 168,114	(83%)	($2,360,627)
	Steve Warner (Green) 33,464	(16%)	($10,424)
	Other 1,745	(1%)	
2006 primary	Steny Hoyer (D) .... unopposed		
2004 general	Steny Hoyer (D) 204,867	(69%)	($1,779,289)
	Brad Jewitt (R) 87,189	(29%)	($145,559)
	Other 6,279	(2%)	

Prior Winning Percentages: 2002 (69%); 2000 (65%); 1998 (65%); 1996 (57%); 1994 (59%); 1992 (53%); 1990 (81%); 1988 (79%); 1986 (82%); 1984 (72%); 1982 (80%); 1981 (55%)

The People		Race/Ethnic Origin	Ancestry	
Area size:	1,509 sq. mi.	60.4% White	German: 10.5% Irish: 9.9%	
Urban population:	75.2%	30.0% Black	English: 8.1%	
Rural population:	24.8%	3.7% Asian	**2004 Presidential Vote**	
Pop. 2000:	662,060	0.4% Native Am.	Kerry (D) 177,035	(57%)
Pop. 2005 (est):	737,203	0.0% Hawaiian	Bush (R) 128,861	(42%)
Median income:	$62,661	1.9% Two+ races	Other 2,692	(1%)
Poverty status:	5.6%	0.2% Other	**2000 Presidential Vote**	
Military veterans:	15.4%	3.5% Hispanic Origin	Gore (D) 139,068	(57%)
			Bush (R) 101,056	(41%)
			Other 5,871	(2%)
			Cook Partisan Voting Index: D + 9	

Occupation	Blue collar: 18.8%	White collar: 68.0%	Gray collar: 13.2%

Southern Maryland was first settled by Catholics, the Calvert family of the Lords Baltimore, who founded St. Mary's in 1634, not long after Jamestown and Plymouth Rock. Maryland became one of the two great Chesapeake tobacco colonies, and plantation houses were built on every inlet off the broad Potomac and Patuxent Rivers. For years, none of these towns grew much, and even today many people here are directly descended from the old families. This was never puritanical country: Liquor flowed even during Prohibition and slot machines were specifically allowed for years by Maryland law. But tobacco farming is nearing an end here, even if the area hasn't completely renounced its tobacco heritage: The highlight of the annual Charles County fair remains the crowning of Queen Nicotina, who must be a local high school senior. The area's economic base owes much to government installations like the Civil War Point Lookout prisoner-of-war camp and the Navy's Patuxent River complex, where many astronauts got their first training. And now metro Washington and Baltimore are spreading into southern Maryland, with rapid growth in Calvert County south of Annapolis—the fastest growing county in Maryland—and Charles County, with heavy African-American migration from Prince George's County; it is reaching even further south into St. Mary's County, which is home of the Naval Air Warfare Center.

The 5th Congressional District of Maryland includes those three counties, plus a large slice of Prince George's—most of the county beyond the Capital Beltway. Its lines were drawn to assure a large black percentage in the adjacent 4th District, but there are also large numbers of blacks in the 5th—30% of the population in 2002—both new suburbanites and descendants of old southern Maryland families. Many of its people live north of Washington, in College Park, home of the University of Maryland, and in Hyattsville, Greenbelt, Beltsville, Laurel and Bowie. The 5th also includes southern Prince George's, from Clinton south, southern Anne Arundel County and all of St. Mary's, Calvert and Charles Counties. Historically, this is a Democratic area, but southern Maryland voted heavily for Republican Governor Bob Ehrlich in 2002, and newcomers in fast-growing areas seem to be leaning Republican. In 2006, Democrat Martin O'Malley spent time here and carried Charles County, though Ehrlich ran strong in Calvert and St. Mary's.

The congressman from the 5th District is Steny Hoyer, a veteran Democrat and the Majority Leader, who was first elected to the House in 1981. In June 2007, he became the longest-serving congressman from Maryland. Hoyer graduated from the University of Maryland, where he was inspired by an on-campus campaign speech by John F. Kennedy, and he got his law degree at

Georgetown. He interned one summer with Senator Daniel Brewster, along with young Nancy D'Alesandro from Baltimore (more on her later). Hoyer was elected to the Maryland Senate in 1966, at 27, just after graduating from law school. He was Senate president from 1975-78, the youngest in Maryland history; he made a misstep running for lieutenant governor on a losing ticket in 1978. But in 1981, after incumbent Gladys Spellman went into an irreversible coma, the 5th District, then entirely in Prince George's, was declared vacant. Hoyer won the special election by edging out Spellman's husband and several other Democrats in the primary and beating a well-financed Republican in the general. That campaign launched Hoyer's long-standing friendship with Tony Coelho, who then chaired the DCCC.

Hoyer is of Danish descent, like the original Prince George; his first name, he says, was his parents' adaptation of the Danish name Steen, and the only other Steny he has encountered is a man from Milwaukee whose full first name is Stenerup. He has fine political instincts, works hard and can speak in an old-fashioned patriotic style that is genuinely moving. A fast riser in Maryland politics, he was also a fast riser in Congress. He excelled at constituency service and soon won a seat on the Appropriations Committee, where he worked with Republicans and became a key player for the whole D.C. metropolitan area. With Democrats in control, he chaired the Treasury, Postal Service and General Government subcommittee, which oversaw several major components of the federal work force and the White House budget. He has championed more spending for education programs, and worked for higher pay and benefits for federal workers. He was the chief House sponsor of the Americans with Disabilities Act of 1990. As ranking minority member on House Administration, he took the lead in hammering out bipartisan election reform legislation and in enhancing security in the Capitol complex. On September 11, 2001, it was Hoyer's idea to have rank and file members stand behind the leadership in front of the Capitol in the evening, when members long-locked in partisan battle sang out together, "God Bless America." In a not very bipartisan House, he has had monthly lunches with Minority Whip Roy Blunt.

Hoyer has pushed for funding for Chesapeake Bay cleanup and dredging the Bay for Baltimore harbor. He has worked endlessly and shrewdly to maintain and increase jobs at the Goddard Space Flight Center in Greenbelt, at Patuxent River Naval Air Station and the Naval Surface Warfare Center at Indian Head and to build the National Center for Weather and Climate Prediction in College Park. In March 2004, work began on a $21 million complex at Pax River to test and develop the Joint Strike Fighter; in July, Hoyer helped deliver $40 million for the Presidential Helicopter Program there. He also secured funding for local military bases in anticipation of the round of base closings scheduled for 2005. When the Pentagon issued base closing recommendations in May 2005, Hoyer's efforts paid off: Pax River ended up gaining 87 jobs and Indian Head lost just 95 jobs out of 3,600. Citizens Against Government Waste rated him, not admiringly, among the top 10 members in obtaining local projects, noting earmarks such as $50,000 for the Agricultural Research Service in Beltsville to study the health benefits of barley.

His voting record is relatively moderate among Democrats, and less liberal than when he represented a near-black-majority district in the 1980s. He broke with party lines by supporting the balanced budget amendment in 1995; he backed NAFTA, GATT, fast track and normal trade relations with China. In October 2002, he voted to authorize military action in Iraq. Later he argued that the administration didn't send enough troops to Iraq and that the United Nations "has shirked its own responsibility." He is a former chairman of the Helsinki commission and has been a champion of human rights around the world.

Hoyer has long been on the leadership track. In 1989, he was elected chairman of the Democratic Caucus, a term-limited position that he left in 1994. When he tried to move up in 1991, he was beaten for Majority Whip by David Bonior, who had the support of liberals and committee chairmen, 160-109. He became chairman of the Democratic Steering Committee and has been Parliamentarian at four Democratic conventions. During much of 2000 he conducted a campaign for Majority Whip against Nancy (nee D'Alesandro) Pelosi, all premised on the notion that Democrats would win control of the House. He ran as the candidate with the more moderate voting record, but that contest was mooted by the 2000 election. In 2001 Bonior, faced with unfavorable redistricting, began running for governor of Michigan; Hoyer and Pelosi both sought to replace him as Minority Whip. Hoyer argued that he had greater experience in leadership positions and could do a better job of unifying the caucus; he cited his support from such diverse members as John Dingell, John Lewis and Charles Stenholm. Pelosi had more publicly committed votes going into the October 2001 caucus, and she won 118-95 (both did less well than predicted, as often happens in secret ballot leadership races).

Looking ahead after the crushing loss of two leadership contests, Hoyer wisely concluded that there might be another opportunity soon. After Democrats failed to win a majority in 2002, Dick Gephardt stepped down as minority leader. With Pelosi running to succeed Gephardt, Hoyer had collected commitments for months and was unanimously elected Minority Whip. In that position, it was his job to be partisan and he often was. In 2004, after 11 Democrats voted for the rule to consider the corporate tax bill, Hoyer sent a letter to all House Democrats admonishing them for supporting a procedure that prevented Democrats from offering amendments. This was standard: in the majority, both House Democrats and Republicans have taken a dim view of members of their party who buck their leadership on procedural issues. Since 1997, the two parties had an ethics truce in which they promised not to file politically inspired ethics complaints against the other parties' members and particularly leaders. But in 2004, Hoyer called for consideration of complaints that Tom DeLay or other GOP leaders offered undue inducement to Nick Smith to vote for the Medicare/ prescription drug bill. In the 2004 campaign, Hoyer once again contributed to and campaigned tirelessly for Democratic House candidates and denounced the Bush administration. He made it clear that he was willing to raise taxes to finance more government programs. "Unlike John Kerry, I am not prepared to make an absolute pledge" not to raise middle class taxes, he said.

The 2006 election rated as a stellar moment for Hoyer. It marked the culmination of four decades of political efforts and left him well-positioned to wield great influence in the House and within the party. In Maryland, he could claim some credit for the successful Senate campaign—both the primary and general—of long-time friend Ben Cardin, for whom he was an early backer, to the dismay of former House colleague Kweisi Mfume and his backers. And voters in his district showed more support for Democrat Martin O'Malley in the governor's race than they had for the Democratic nominee in 2002. Nationally, Hoyer worked closely with DCCC Chairman Rahm Emanuel and was an indefatigable fundraiser and ally for candidates, especially those running against Republican incumbents; in the two years preceding the election, he made at least 316 campaign stops in 80 districts in 33 states, and raised more than $8 million for members, candidates and the DCCC. In September 2006, he predicted a gain of 30 House seats; that turned out to be right on the money. "We have close to 50 extraordinarily good candidates," he told *Congress Daily*. "I don't know which of the 50 will win, but I absolutely believe the American public by an overwhelming majority believes we are moving in the wrong direction in this country." Many of the freshmen subsequently cited the help that Hoyer provided, especially those from swing districts where liberal Democratic leaders are not always welcome. Lost amid the euphoria were the occasional criticisms from liberal activists that Hoyer was an old-style pol and a Washington insider, with close ties to the lobbying community.

Following the election, he endured a bitter 10-day contest for Majority Leader with John Murtha, the defense hawk who had become an outspoken opponent of the Iraq war. Adding to the intrigue was the role played by the Speaker-in-waiting, Nancy Pelosi, a prominent Murtha ally, whom Hoyer had known since their summer interning for Senator Brewster. Murtha contended that he could work better with Pelosi; Hoyer had little choice but to speak positively about his long-standing relationship with her—he calls her a "favorite daughter" of Maryland—and their success in largely unifying an often unruly party. But he left no doubt about his dismay over her arm-twisting for Murtha. In a powerful endorsement for him (and a stunning rebuke and warning to Pelosi that many Democrats opposed strong-arm rule), Hoyer won 149-86. Members responded well to his "ability, patience, know-how and experience," explained one Democratic lobbyist. More impressively, Hoyer won the support of many California Democrats who previously had been unified behind Pelosi, and from numerous prospective committee chairmen who doubted Murtha's ability to do the job. "Nancy thought she could put these people away because of pressure," Coelho told *The New York Times*. "But these people that got elected understand relationships, and they're not going to flip away because of pressure. [Hoyer] has a tremendous capacity for friendship, and when you have that, people don't flake off on you." Following the vote, Pelosi and Hoyer were a picture-perfect symbol of unity; the dour Murtha was less than gracious. It remained to be seen when, and how, Hoyer would assert his autonomy. In one of his first steps, he announced that the House would be in session five days a week—occasionally, at least.

At home, after the 1992 redistricting added southern Maryland counties to his district and subtracted black precincts in Prince George's, Hoyer had some serious Republican competition; he won by only 53%-44% in 1992. But he has increased his margins since then and is now firmly entrenched. Although he keeps close attention to his political base, that hasn't interfered with his national responsibilities and continuing ambitions. He clearly is number two to Pelosi, but he probably has the best sense among Democratic leaders of competing demands within the Caucus.

SIXTH DISTRICT

Rep. Roscoe Bartlett (R)

Elected 1992, 8th term; b. June 3, 1926, Moreland, KY; home, Frederick; Columbia Union Col., B.A. 1947, U. of MD, M.S. 1949, Ph.D. 1952; Seventh Day Adventist; married (Ellen).

Professional Career: Farmer; Prof., U. of MD, 1948-52; Asst. Prof., Loma Linda Schl. of Medicine, 1952-54; Asst. Prof., Howard U. Medical Schl., 1954-56; Research scientist, N.I.H., 1956-58; Research scientist, U.S. Naval Aerospace Medical Inst., 1958-62; Research scientist, Johns Hopkins U., 1962-67; Research Mgr., IBM, 1967-74; Pres., Roscoe Bartlett & Assoc., 1974-86.

DC Office: 2412 RHOB, 20515, 202-225-2721; Fax: 202-225-2193; Web site: bartlett.house.gov.

District Offices: Cumberland, 301-724-3105; Frederick, 301-694-3030; Hagerstown, 301-797-6043; Westminster, 410-857-1115.

Committees: *Armed Services* (5th of 29 R): Seapower & Expeditionary Forces (RMM); Oversight & Investigations. *Science & Technology* (5th of 20 R): Research & Science Education; Energy & Environment. *Small Business* (2d of 15 R): Contracting & Technology; Rural & Urban Entrepreneurship.

Group Ratings

	ADA	ACLU	AFS	LCV	ITIC	NTU	COC	ACU	CFG	FRC
2006	25	36	0	58	86	63	80	84	67	100
2005	5	—	0	39	—	73	85	84	94	100

National Journal Ratings

	2005 LIB	—	2005 CONS		2006 LIB	—	2006 CONS
Economic	45%	—	55%		46%	—	53%
Social	49%	—	51%		44%	—	55%
Foreign	46%	—	53%		51%	—	48%

Key Votes of the 109th Congress

1. Estate Tax Repeal	Y	5. Limit Interstate Abortion	Y	9. Build Border Fence	Y
2. Limit CAFE Standards	N	6. Extend Patriot Act	N	10. CAFTA	Y
3. FY06 Spending Curb	Y	7. Bar Same Sex Marriage	Y	11. Oppose Iraq Withdrawal	Y
4. Drilling in ANWR	N	8. Stem Cell Research $	N	12. Detainee Tribunals	N

Election Results

2006 general	Roscoe Bartlett (R)	141,200	(59%)	($422,097)
	Andrew Duck (D)	92,030	(38%)	($210,533)
	Other	6,223	(3%)	
2006 primary	Roscoe Bartlett (R)	45,474	(79%)	
	Joseph Krysztoforski (R)	11,889	(21%)	
2004 general	Roscoe Bartlett (R)	206,076	(67%)	($436,891)
	Kenneth Bosley (D)	90,108	(29%)	
	Other	9,673	(3%)	

Prior Winning Percentages: 2002 (66%); 2000 (61%); 1998 (63%); 1996 (57%); 1994 (66%); 1992 (54%)

The People		Race/Ethnic Origin	Ancestry	
Area size:	3,094 sq. mi.	91.5% White	German: 20.1%	Irish: 10.6%
Urban population:	60.5%	4.8% Black	English: 8.4%	
Rural population:	39.5%	1.0% Asian	**2004 Presidential Vote**	
Pop. 2000:	662,060	0.2% Native Am.	Bush (R) 209,764	(65%)
Pop. 2005 (est):	724,685	0.0% Hawaiian	Kerry (D) 110,821	(34%)
Median income:	$50,957	0.9% Two+ races	Other 3,635	(1%)
Poverty status:	6.7%	0.1% Other	**2000 Presidential Vote**	
Military veterans:	14.0%	1.4% Hispanic Origin	Bush (R) 160,263	(61%)
			Gore (D) 95,282	(36%)
			Other 8,029	(3%)
			Cook Partisan Voting Index: R +13	

Occupation   Blue collar: 23.9%   White collar: 61.5%   Gray collar: 14.6%

One of America's first frontiers was in western Maryland, where the Appalachian ridges that cross the state diagonally from northeast to southwest cut through the long green sloping fields. These wheat fields were settled first by Pennsylvania Dutch and Scots-Irish hill people, not Chesapeake Bay tobacco growers. Maryland is where the fall line comes closest to an ocean port, where the 19th century's great paths to the interior were staked out: The Chesapeake and Ohio Canal, which began operating in 1828, primarily to haul coal from western Maryland to the port of Georgetown in Washington; the National Road; and then the nation's first railroad, the Baltimore & Ohio, crossed the wide valleys of bounteous farms and climbed over the Catoctin Mountains. Towns grew up on narrow streets lined with row houses that today are overhung with telephone and streetcar wires, overlooking long vistas of cornfields, pastureland and mountains of ancient stone rising above the plains. Across this placid land moved vast armies during the Civil War. In Frederick, city officials paid Confederates $200,000 not to burn down the town, and near Sharpsburg, blue and gray-clad soldiers fought the Battle of Antietam, on the bloodiest day in American military history. A century later, on the steps of City Hall in Cumberland—near the western edge of the district in the coal-laced hills of Appalachia—President Lyndon Johnson declared his War on Poverty. Poverty fell here in the 1970s, but local conditions worsened in the 1980s with the closure of several large factories; recently, Cumberland has attempted to refashion itself as an arts community with dozens of studios. To the east, Carroll County in metro Baltimore, and Frederick County in metro Washington, have grown rapidly in recent years and have become new hubs for outward expansion.

The 6th Congressional District includes all of western Maryland, takes in a small part of northern Montgomery County and runs eastward across the northern farmlands and hunt country of Baltimore and Harford Counties all the way to the Susquehanna River. The political tradition in most of this area, unlike the rest of Maryland, is Republican. This was Union country in the Civil War and has been mostly Republican ever since. The new rush of settlement—which made this the fastest growing district in Maryland in the 1990s—is mostly made up of young families of modest incomes seeking respite from metropolitan life, strengthening the area's already conservative leanings. Only eight of 24 counties in Maryland have more registered Republican voters than Democrats, and five of them are in this district.

The congressman from the 6th District is Roscoe Bartlett, a Republican "citizen legislator" first elected in 1992. He is a curious character, a descendant of a signer of the Declaration of Independence and a Seventh Day Adventist with 10 children (he and his wife each have four children from previous marriages). He was born in Kentucky and grew up in poverty in western Pennsylvania, where his father was a tenant farmer; but his family would not take welfare. After getting a bachelor's degree in theology and biology, he earned a Ph.D. in physiology at the University of Maryland, where he also taught and wrote more than 100 scientific articles; over the years he has also operated a 145-acre dairy farm, where he still milks his goats. He was awarded 20 patents for inventing life-support equipment for pilots, astronauts, fire fighters, and respiratory patients needing oxygen supplies, and ran his own business. In 1999, the Aeronautics and Astronautics Institute gave him an award for his career contributions to the advancement of medical knowledge and technologies. When Bartlett was first elected, he was a 65-year-old retired University of Maryland professor who seemed to have no chance of winning. Democrat Beverly Byron had represented the district for 14 years and had a conservative voting record; when Bartlett challenged her in 1982, he lost 74%-26%. But in 1992 Byron was upset in the primary by a liberal who favored national health insurance and abortion rights. Bartlett's conservative views and his attacks on his opponent's perks in the state legislature won him a 54%-46% victory.

Bartlett has proved a surprisingly durable politician, though iconoclastic to the point of being quirky. Profiled in *The Washington Post* as Maryland's Mr. Right, he described a visit to Iraq in 2004 when he visited the spider hole where Saddam Hussein was captured. "I was probably the only Congressman who laid down there. It's very interesting dirt—it doesn't collapse. The water table is at 17 feet throughout most of Iraq." Bartlett is the most conservative member of the state's congressional delegation, but his conservative views have sometimes not been consistent with Republican orthodoxy. "I'm not interested in politics," he says. "I am a conservative who wants to help restore the limited federal government envisioned and established in the Constitution by our nation's founders." He sometimes objects to Republican big spending, including George W. Bush's education act, but he voted for the 2003 Medicare/prescription drug bill He voted against normal trade relations with China, against trade promotion authority, and against renewal of the Patriot Act because he saw it as a threat to civil liberties. His fiscal prudence was reflected in his opposition to expanded federal funds for the local Interstate highway. He was one of 33 House Republicans to oppose renewal of the Voting Rights Act. "He believes that when a disease is cured, you don't have to keep taking the same medicine," a spokeswoman said. In July 2006, President Bush signed his bill to prohibit a condominium or other residential group from barring a member from displaying the American flag. As chairman of an Armed Services subcommittee, he claimed credit for a study on increasing efficiency in the shipbuilding industry and steps to review potential changes in the Navy fleet. As George Wilson wrote in *Congress Daily*, he suffers from sticker shock and has urged new thinking by the defense establishment, including smaller and cheaper ships. "He believes the Navy is not only pricing itself out of a fleet large enough to cover the world's hotspots but also is making it easy for the bad guys to sink it by having so few ships." In 2007, he became ranking member of the Seapower and Expeditionary Forces Subcommittee.

Bartlett has been reelected by solid margins. In 2004 he faced an unusual primary challenge from Frederick County State's Attorney Scott Rolle, who criticized Bartlett for not supporting the Bush administration strongly enough. Bartlett responded by calling out a big gun. Before more than 700 loyalists at a breakfast in Hagerstown four days before the vote, Vice President Cheney said, "In this time of testing, the president and I have been grateful to have Congressman Bartlett at our side." Bartlett won 70%-30% and carried Rolle's Frederick County base 60%-40%.

Bartlett is the oldest member of the Maryland delegation but says he has no plans to retire. Republican Frank Nethken, a former mayor of Cumberland, announced he would challenge Bartlett in the 2008 primary, saying "God told me I'm going to be the next congressman." Democrat Andrew Duck, an Iraq War veteran who lost 59%-38% to Bartlett in 2006, is expected to seek a rematch.

SEVENTH DISTRICT

Rep. Elijah Cummings (D)

Elected April 1996, 6th full term; b. Jan. 18, 1951, Baltimore; home, Baltimore; Howard U., B.S. 1973, U. of MD, J.D. 1976; Baptist; divorced.

Elected Office: MD House of Delegates, 1982-96, Speaker Pro–Tem, 1995-96.

Professional Career: Practicing atty., 1976-96.

DC Office: 2235 RHOB, 20515, 202-225-4741; Fax: 202-225-3178; Web site: www.house.gov/cummings.

District Offices: Baltimore, 410-685-9199; Catonsville, 410-719-8777; Ellicott City, 410-465-8259.

Committees: *Armed Services* (31st of 34 D): Readiness. *Joint Economic Committee* (5th of 10 D). *Oversight & Government Reform* (6th of 23 D): Domestic Policy; Federal Workforce, Postal Service & the District of Columbia. *Transportation & Infrastructure* (11th of 41 D): Coast Guard & Maritime Transportation (Chmn.); Railroads, Pipelines & Hazardous Materials; Highways & Transit.

Group Ratings

	ADA	ACLU	AFS	LCV	ITIC	NTU	COC	ACU	CFG	FRC
2006	100	95	100	100	43	12	33	8	12	0
2005	100	—	100	83	—	13	41	4	3	8

National Journal Ratings

	2005 LIB	—	2005 CONS	2006 LIB	—	2006 CONS
Economic	80%	—	20%	86%	—	11%
Social	77%	—	23%	79%	—	20%
Foreign	86%	—	13%	80%	—	18%

Key Votes of the 109th Congress

1. Estate Tax Repeal	N	5. Limit Interstate Abortion	N	9. Build Border Fence	N
2. Limit CAFE Standards	Y	6. Extend Patriot Act	N	10. CAFTA	N
3. FY06 Spending Curb	N	7. Bar Same Sex Marriage	N	11. Oppose Iraq Withdrawal	N
4. Drilling in ANWR	N	8. Stem Cell Research $	Y	12. Detainee Tribunals	N

Election Results

2006 general	Elijah Cummings (D)	unopposed		($560,956)
2006 primary	Elijah Cummings (D)	unopposed		
2004 general	Elijah Cummings (D)	179,189	(73%)	($877,808)
	Tony Salazar (R)	60,102	(25%)	($109,426)
	Other	4,892	(2%)	

Prior Winning Percentages: 2002 (74%); 2000 (87%); 1998 (86%); 1996 (83%); 1996 (81%)

The People		Race/Ethnic Origin	Ancestry	
Area size:	296 sq. mi.	34.2% White	German: 7.9%	Irish: 6.0%
Urban population:	94.9%	58.8% Black	English: 4.6%	
Rural population:	5.1%	3.5% Asian	**2004 Presidential Vote**	
Pop. 2000:	662,060	0.2% Native Am.	Kerry (D) 192,081	(73%)
Pop. 2005 (est):	651,355	0.0% Hawaiian	Bush (R) 69,545	(26%)
Median income:	$38,885	1.3% Two+ races	Other 2,830	(1%)
Poverty status:	17.6%	0.2% Other	**2000 Presidential Vote**	
Military veterans:	12.0%	1.7% Hispanic Origin	Gore (D) 166,410	(73%)
			Bush (R) 57,262	(25%)
			Other 5,766	(3%)
			Cook Partisan Voting Index: D +25	

Occupation	Blue collar: 16.2%	White collar: 66.7%	Gray collar: 17.1%

At the junction of North and South, terminus of America's first railroad and the East Coast port closest to the great West, Baltimore is one of the few American cities to have had large numbers of both blacks and European immigrants throughout its history. Its black community has a rich and notable history. The *Afro-American* newspaper has been published here for more than 100 years and there was once a black symphony orchestra. Eubie Blake, the famous black musician and one of the founders of ragtime music, grew up here and now has a museum in his honor on Charles Street. Jazz great Billie Holliday was born here; these were the stomping grounds of the great musician Cab Calloway and the great legal advocate Thurgood Marshall. Near downtown on the west side is the childhood home of Babe Ruth and the home of H.L. Mencken, two great white Baltimoreans. For years this side of town had a biracial, bipartisan politics in which Democrats like Governor Albert Ritchie and Republicans like Mayor and Governor Theodore McKeldin competed zestfully for black and white votes.

Baltimore has been a black majority city since the late 1970s, and most of its west side neighborhoods are heavily black. In the 1990s Baltimore had a terrible crime wave, with open drug markets on both the west and east sides. Martin O'Malley, elected in 1999, took a different approach as mayor, promising to build "a new Baltimore" with "zero tolerance" of crime; he went on to win the governorship in 2006. But many of the city's problems remained, with almost 20% of the city's residential areas classified as distressed.

Maryland's 7th Congressional District includes most of Baltimore's black neighborhoods, reaches into the heavily black suburbs running west from the city, to Catonsville along the old Baltimore National Pike, and extends west to include most of suburban Howard County. The boundaries have removed some black Baltimore neighborhoods to strengthen Democrats' chances of capturing the mostly suburban 2d District. About 40% of the district's votes are cast in Baltimore city's precincts, largely north of Pratt Street, in places like Druid Heights, Charles Village (home to Johns Hopkins University), Harlem Park and poverty-stricken Sandtown-Winchester. Howard County is quite a different area: It grew 32% in the 1990s and its largest community, Columbia, is a planned town that attracts a culturally liberal population. It tends to vote Democratic, and in 2004 cast 13% of the district's votes. There is a sharp socioeconomic contrast between these two parts of the district: In Howard County, 32% of families earned more than $100,000 in 2000 and 4% of children under five lived in poverty status; in Baltimore City, only 6% earned more than $100,000 and 32% of children were poor.

The congressman from the 7th District is Elijah Cummings, who won a 1996 special election after Kweisi Mfume resigned to become president of the NAACP. Cummings grew up in Baltimore, graduated from Howard University and the University of Maryland law school, practiced law in Baltimore, and in 1982, at 31, was elected to the Maryland House of Delegates. His main competition for the seat came from the Reverend Frank Reid III, stepbrother of Mayor Kurt Schmoke, who raised $255,000. Cummings had support from community development organizations and from businessmen and lobbyists. He raised $450,000, and won 37% of the vote to 24% for Reid. He has not been seriously challenged in a primary or general since then.

Cummings lives in troubled west Baltimore, where urban realities have made him a crusader against drug abuse and a death-penalty foe; he favors strict gun control. His voting record has been mostly liberal; he was the only Marylander to oppose the 1996 welfare act. But he has acquired a pragmatic streak, evidenced by a friendship and working alliance to promote local economic development with Wayne Gilchrest, the Republican who represents Maryland's Eastern Shore. As ranking Democrat on the Criminal Justice subcommittee on the Government Reform Committee, he worked with Republican Mark Souder to reauthorize the White House drug control office. He also used that panel to tend to the interests of his many federal employees. In the majority, he gained a seat on the Armed Services Committee. He also became chairman of the Coast Guard and Maritime Transportation Subcommittee at Transportation and Infrastructure, a useful niche for his port-dependent district and an opportunity to play a role in the debate on homeland security. He is the only Maryland Democrat on the Transportation committee.

Cummings was chairman of the Congressional Black Caucus in 2003 and 2004. He spoke out on issues ranging from the presidential succession crisis in Haiti to the ouster of Trent Lott as Senate majority leader to the appointment of federal judges. Redistricting changes led to a reduction in Cummings's winning percentage, but he still wins by landslide margins. In 2002 and 2004, he carried Howard County only narrowly, but garnered more than 90% of the votes in Baltimore City. In 2006, he was unopposed. He backed Mfume in the primary for the open Senate seat that year, and then played a constructive role in coalescing Democrats behind nominee Ben Cardin and raising questions about where Republican Michael Steele stood on the issues.

EIGHTH DISTRICT

Rep. Chris Van Hollen (D)

Elected 2002, 3d term; b. Jan. 10, 1959, Karachi, Pakistan; home, Kensington; Swarthmore Col., B.A. 1982, Harvard U., M.P.P. 1985, Georgetown U., J.D. 1990; Protestant; married (Katherine).

Elected Office: MD House of Delegates, 1990-94; MD Senate, 1994-2002.

DC Office: 1707 LHOB, 20515, 202-225-5341; Fax: 202-225-0375; Web site: vanhollen.house.gov.

District Offices: Hyattsville, 301-891-6982; Rockville, 301-424-3501.

Committees: *DCCC Chairman. Oversight & Government Reform* (19th of 23 D): National Security & Foreign Affairs. *Ways & Means* (21st of 24 D): Income Security & Family Support; Trade.

Group Ratings

	ADA	ACLU	AFS	LCV	ITIC	NTU	COC	ACU	CFG	FRC
2006	90	91	100	100	57	14	40	4	12	0
2005	100	—	100	100	—	14	37	0	7	0

National Journal Ratings

	2005 LIB	—	2005 CONS		2006 LIB	—	2006 CONS
Economic	92%	—	6%		86%	—	11%
Social	81%	—	19%		78%	—	21%
Foreign	85%	—	15%		83%	—	14%

Key Votes of the 109th Congress

1. Estate Tax Repeal	N	5. Limit Interstate Abortion	N	9. Build Border Fence	N
2. Limit CAFE Standards	N	6. Extend Patriot Act	N	10. CAFTA	N
3. FY06 Spending Curb	N	7. Bar Same Sex Marriage	N	11. Oppose Iraq Withdrawal	N
4. Drilling in ANWR	N	8. Stem Cell Research $	Y	12. Detainee Tribunals	N

Election Results

2006 general	Chris Van Hollen (D)	168,872	(77%)	($676,816)
	Jeffrey Stein (R)	48,324	(22%)	($31,845)
	Other	3,489	(2%)	
2006 primary	Chris Van Hollen (D)	73,544	(91%)	
	Deborah Vollmer (D)	6,989	(9%)	
2004 general	Chris Van Hollen (D)	215,129	(75%)	($1,235,488)
	Chuck Floyd (R)	71,989	(25%)	($352,644)

Prior Winning Percentages: 2002 (52%)

The People		Race/Ethnic Origin	Ancestry	
Area size:	307 sq. mi.	56.1% White	German: 8.2%	Irish: 7.9%
Urban population:	98.8%	16.4% Black	English: 6.6%	
Rural population:	1.2%	10.9% Asian	**2004 Presidential Vote**	
Pop. 2000:	662,060	0.2% Native Am.	Kerry (D) 205,660	(69%)
Pop. 2005 (est):	700,364	0.0% Hawaiian	Bush (R) 90,108	(30%)
Median income:	$68,306	2.4% Two+ races	Other 3,196	(1%)
Poverty status:	6.2%	0.3% Other	**2000 Presidential Vote**	
Military veterans:	9.6%	13.7% Hispanic Origin	Gore (D) 177,475	(66%)
			Bush (R) 84,088	(31%)
			Other 9,382	(3%)
			Cook Partisan Voting Index: D +20	

Occupation   Blue collar: 10.6%   White collar: 77.1%   Gray collar: 12.3%

Along an old road, down which colonial farmers rolled barrels of tobacco to the port of Georgetown 200 years ago, has grown one of America's most affluent and best-educated communities. The old road, now called Wisconsin Avenue and Rockville Pike, is the commercial spine of Montgomery County, Maryland. And this suburban jurisdiction just northwest of Washington, D.C., has for several decades ranked at or near the top counties in income and education. Today's Montgomery County is in large part a creation of the federal government, which has placed huge facilities there—Bethesda Naval Hospital, the National Institutes of Health, the Food and Drug Administration, the National Institute of Standards and Technology—and it has become the center of America's biotech industry, the home of firms like Celera and Human Genome Sciences which, in parallel with the Human Genome Project, are pioneering the study of the human gene. Some of the federal labs have gained high-security classification because of their research on bio-hazards and infectious diseases in the war on terrorism.

Wisconsin Avenue and Rockville Pike have become traffic-choked strip highways, with 1950s commercial development and 1960s shopping centers like so many in the country. But the stores are upscale, some *very* upscale, and the skyscrapers and dining scene of downtown Bethesda have become genuinely impressive. Author David Brooks mocked Bethesdans as "urban exiles" who frequent "anti-chain chain stores...that cater to people who consider themselves too refined and individualistic to shop at the mall or the mass-market big-box stores." Historically, the typical Montgomery County voter was a high-ranking civil servant. "A candidate knocking on doors in the 8th District can reasonably expect to be questioned about a government regulation by the person who wrote it," explained *The Washington Post*. As growing private-sector employment outpaces government work, the picture has changed. The growth here is out the I-270 and Metro corridors past Rockville to Gaithersburg and Germantown. Montgomery County also has become racially diverse: in 2000, it was 15% black, 12% Hispanic and 11% Asian. And not all of the county is exclusively high-income. There are some modest neighborhoods in Silver Spring and Wheaton, plus one of the nation's largest Asian populations. The district has the largest share of Latinos in Maryland.

The 8th Congressional District of Maryland includes most of the heavily populated parts of Montgomery County, which accounts for more than 90% of the population. In 2002, redistricting added a slice of strongly Democratic territory in Prince George's County. Perhaps the 8th's most unique precinct is Leisure World in Silver Spring, whose 6,000-plus senior citizens have one of Maryland's largest, most partisan and highest voter turnouts; Democratic candidates practically camp out there during primaries. This is the most Democratic white-majority district in the state.

The congressman from the 8th District is Chris Van Hollen, first elected in 2002 in one of the nation's most competitive congressional races and now a major player in the House. The son of a Foreign Service officer, Van Hollen was born in Pakistan, graduated from Swarthmore, got a master's from Harvard and a law degree from Georgetown University. He worked on the staff of the Senate Foreign Relations Committee in the late 1980s, and he co-authored a report on Iraq's use of chemical weapons. In 1990 he was elected to the House of Delegates and in 1994 to the state Senate. Wonky and telegenic, Van Hollen's legislative accomplishments earned him the moniker, "Mr. Fix-It" from the *Washington Post*.

The 2002 race attracted strong Democratic candidates: Van Hollen; Delegate Mark Shriver, a Kennedy cousin who had extensive labor support; and Ira Shapiro, a former Clinton administration trade official who stressed his familiarity with federal policy issues as a senior Senate aide. Bolstered by a crucial endorsement from the *Post*, Van Hollen defeated Shriver, 43%-41%, with 13% for Shapiro. Van Hollen had only eight weeks to take on Republican incumbent Connie Morella, who was widely viewed as hard working, cooperative with colleagues, congenial with constituents, and with a liberal voting record that was largely out of step with the Republican-controlled House. Morella once again proved her independence from her party by voting against military force in Iraq and as the lead House sponsor of the amendment, opposed by the Bush administration, insisting on strict civil service protections for Department of Homeland Security employees. Van Hollen refrained from directly attacking Morella, but argued that her vote to organize the House with Republicans kept in power a conservative leadership out of line with the views of most district voters: She was an enabler of the Republican majority. Morella criticized Van Hollen's record in Annapolis, including his decision to quit a Senate subcommittee over proposed budget cuts. The *Washington Post* and the Baltimore *Sun* endorsed Morella, but it wasn't enough. In a race in which the two candidates together spent nearly $6 million, Van Hollen won 52%-47%. Democrats had redrawn the district for the express purpose of defeating Morella; the gambit worked. Nearly half of Van Hollen's popular vote margin came in the small sliver of the district in Prince George's (which is 55% black), which he carried 78%-21%. If the contest had been held in the old district, Morella clearly would have won.

In the House, Van Hollen has been an activist liberal on most issues. In his first term, he scored an unexpected victory when he got the House—including 26 Republicans, some of them conservatives—to approve his amendment to limit a Republican plan to outsource more federal jobs. Despite that vote, the Bush administration eventually got its way. With his experience as a former Capitol Hill aide, he said that Congress had an obligation to "do our oversight, to get the facts, to ask the hard questions." He also worked on lobbying legislation to eliminate conflicts of interests in congressional budget earmarks. In early 2006, he turned his attention to party leadership activities, notably his appointment by Rahm Emanuel as a co-chairman of the Democratic Congressional Campaign Committee, with added responsibility for candidate recruitment and execution of the "Red to Blue" campaign plan. Working closely with Emanuel, the lower-key Van Hollen traveled to many battleground districts during the final months for hands-on candidate mentoring.

In 2007, he gained his rewards with a seat on the Ways and Means Committee and an appointment to chair the DCCC from Speaker Nancy Pelosi. As a party leader, he played a role in shaping the House Democrats' policy agenda. With former top Pelosi aides serving as senior DCCC officials, Van Hollen expected to work closely with the Speaker on campaign strategy. In contrast to Emanuel's strained relations with the DNC, Van Hollen sought a harmonious relationship with party chairman Howard Dean.

At home, where Van Hollen's earnest approach has made him nearly unassailable, he has been reelected easily in what now is a safe Democratic district. Following the retirement of Senator Paul Sarbanes in early 2005, he gave serious thought to entering the multi-candidate Democratic primary. But at the urging of then-Minority Whip Steny Hoyer, with the likely prospect of advancement in the House, he decided against it. Now, his influence in the House has expanded, and he is likely to have other opportunities to run statewide in coming years.

★ MASSACHUSETTS ★

It would be a city on a hill, John Winthrop wrote of the Massachusetts Bay colony his Puritans were building, an example to the entire world. And Massachusetts, in the nearly four centuries since, has always assumed it has a lot to teach others. The New World Puritans' austere creed taught that only the select would be saved and that they must extirpate the forces of Satan—Indians, Papists, tolerationists. For 150 years, New England was partial to learning, but also insular, hostile to outsiders and economically stagnant. Then, after the American Revolution, the international war between royal Britain and revolutionary and Napoleonic France allowed New England ship owners to cross enemy lines to become the world's leading merchants. They made vast profits and invested the money in textile mills, then railroads, then coal mines and steel mills, providing much of the capital that made industrial America.

Massachusetts made a new America in other ways. Intellectually, New England flowered in the 19th century: Writers from Boston, Cambridge and Concord—Ralph Waldo Emerson, Henry Wadsworth Longfellow, Henry David Thoreau, John Greenleaf Whittier, Nathaniel Hawthorne—created an American literature and popularized an American philosophy, more than 200 years after Plymouth Rock: Hawthorne was as far away in time from the Salem witch trials as he is to us. Demographically, New England Yankees surged across the continent: Long blocked from Upstate New York by mountains and the British-Iroquois alliance, they only reached Syracuse in the 1820s. By the 1850s, they were in Iowa and Kansas and Oregon's Willamette Valley, and by the 1870s in Los Angeles. They helped start the Republican Party and did much to start—and win—the Civil War. They planted their economic system and their values, articulated in the *McGuffey Readers*, across the continent.

In the meantime, Massachusetts itself and Boston, the hub of the universe, were being remade. The potato famine of the 1840s and an economy that continued imploding for decades sent Irish immigrants across the Atlantic, and many came to Boston, looking for work in the mills, docks and factories. Yankee Protestants had seen Catholics as their great political and cultural enemy since the 17th century; they felt their commonwealth was under siege. As Catholics became a majority, first in Boston and then statewide, Protestants feared the Irish would use their political clout to ladle out government jobs and benefits to their own—and the Irish had a much better flair for politics than instinct for commerce. But they encountered such bigotry and rejection by the Yankees that even as successful an Irish Catholic as Joseph Kennedy felt obliged to move from Boston to New York in 1927. Politics in Massachusetts for years was a kind of culture war between Yankee Republicans and Irish Democrats, an argument not so much over the distribution of income or the provision of services as over whose vision of Massachusetts should be honored, and whose version of history should be taught—not unlike battles being fought between cultural liberals and conservatives today.

Sometimes, the stakes were concrete—control of patronage jobs, command of the Boston Police Department—but more often they were symbolic. Yankee Republicans tended to back activist government programs: Public works and protective tariffs to help business, the Civil War and Reconstruction to help suitably distant oppressed people like Southern blacks, uplifting (and productivity-enhancing) social movements like temperance. The Irish found 19th century Democrats—a party promoting *laissez-faire*—more congenial. The Irish had come from a place where the government was the enemy and didn't want government spending money to help the rich or to stimulate commerce. They also didn't want government to restrict immigration, to advance blacks (potential competitors in the labor market) or to ban alcohol.

The Irish and Catholic percentages slowly rose over the years. Yankees had smaller families, moved west, intermarried with people of immigrant stock and lost their Yankee identity. The Irish mostly stayed put, raised large families and maintained their Catholic identity. Slowly but surely Massachusetts moved from being one of the most Republican states to one of the most Democratic. Economically, early 20th century Massachusetts did not make much progress. The descendants of the Yankees who had been so venturesome in the early 19th century became the most cautious investors in the early 20th, while the predominance of the textile mills in their home state meant that for a century beginning in the 1820s, Massachusetts imported low-skill labor and exported high-skill people. As textile mills started moving south in the 1920s, Massachusetts started exporting low-skill people as well. From the waning of Yankee authority until the national rise of the Kennedys, Massachusetts seemed to run out of things to teach the rest of the nation. The state's Yankee Republicans were backward looking, out of power in Washington, on the defensive at home,

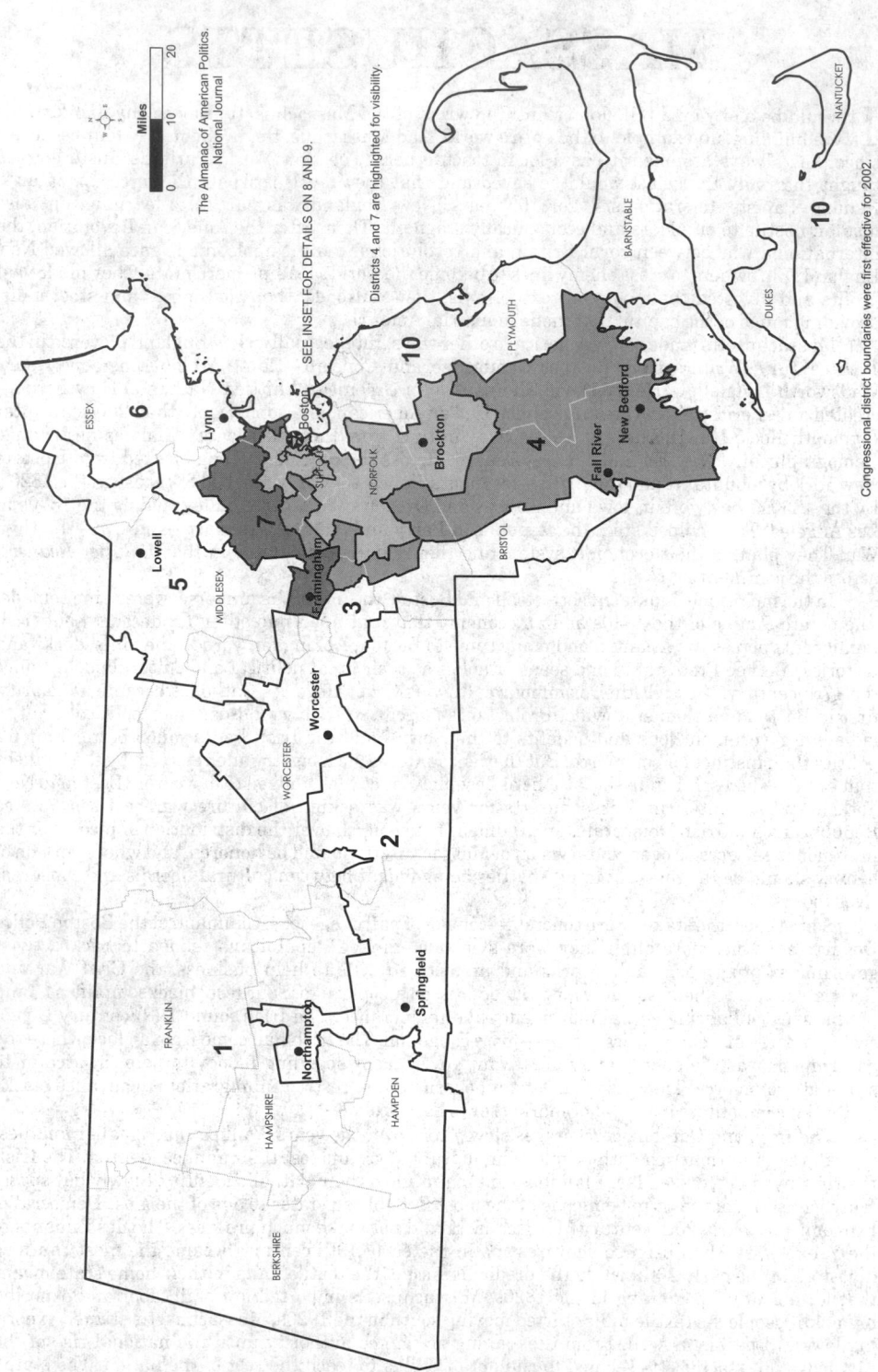

The Almanac of American Politics.
National Journal

SEE INSET FOR DETAILS ON 8 AND 9.

Districts 4 and 7 are highlighted for visibility.

Congressional district boundaries were first effective for 2002.

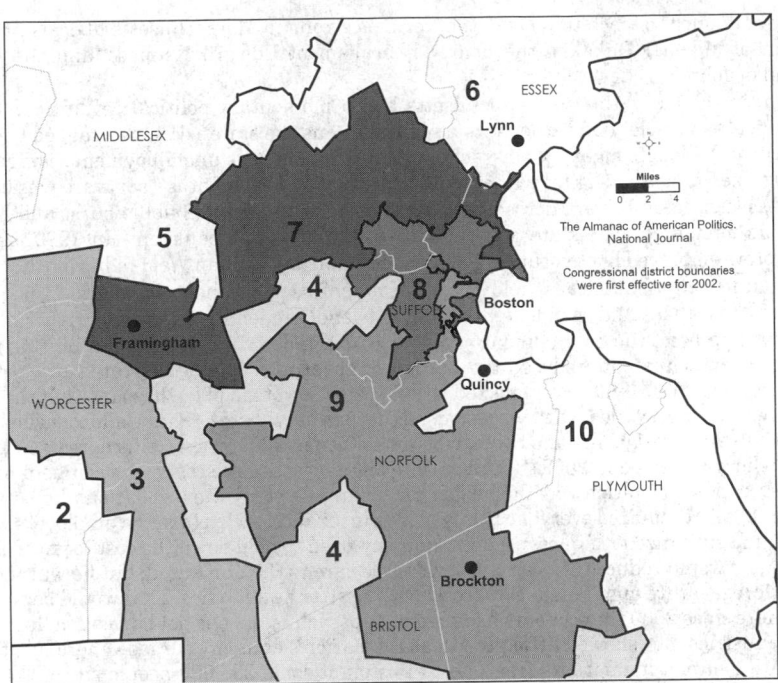

without a cause to champion. The Irish Democrats were hostile to Franklin Roosevelt's pro-British internationalism and receptive to the anti-Communism of the very Irish Joe McCarthy.

Then came the Kennedys. Rose Kennedy was born in 1890 (and died in 1995), the daughter of John "Honey Fitz" Fitzgerald, who was elected to Congress at 31 and was mayor of Boston in 1906-07 and 1910-14. Her husband Joseph Kennedy, first chairman of the Securities and Exchange Commission in the 1930s and ambassador to the Court of St. James from 1937-40, was perhaps the richest Catholic in the world and a shrewd and ruthless political operator. Their only residence in Massachusetts after 1927 was their summer home in Hyannis Port. In 1946 Joseph Kennedy moved his oldest surviving son, John, to Boston, and engineered his election to the House that year, to the Senate in 1952 and to the presidency in 1960. The Kennedys, with their elegant manners and great achievements, seemed like royalty to the Irish Catholics of Massachusetts, and John Kennedy's election in 1960 certified to U.S. Catholics, 78% of whom voted for him, and quickly to everybody else that they too were Americans. Joseph and John Kennedy were, on many issues, conservative or skeptical. But Kennedy's administration was increasingly, even before his untimely death, identified as liberal, and his example and that of his brother, Edward, elected to the U.S. Senate in 1962, moved Massachusetts Catholics to the left. At the same time, Massachusetts Protestants were influenced by the leftward direction on the state's elite campuses in the 1960s. The universities also provided the basis for a surging high-tech economy, to the point that Massachusetts started importing high-skill people even as it exported those with low skills.

In the 1970s and 1980s, Massachusetts, with one interval, had the most liberal governance and national politics of any state in the country. Massachusetts was the only state to vote for George McGovern in 1972 and, although it voted twice for Ronald Reagan, the son of an Irish Catholic, its Democratic percentage in presidential contests from 1968-88 was 53%, just 0.4% behind Rhode Island and well ahead of every other state. The state's senators included Edward Kennedy, liberal Republican Edward Brooke, and Democrats Paul Tsongas and John Kerry. Liberal governors such as Republican Francis Sargent and Democrat Michael Dukakis vastly increased spending and endorsed policies that helped sink Dukakis's 1988 presidential campaign, notably the law that granted weekend furloughs to prisoners sentenced to life without parole. As historian David Hackett Fischer points out in *Albion's Seed*, the mindset of the original settlers remains strong even when the ethnic origin of current residents is far different, and the spirit of the Puritans, the faith that they had much to teach the rest of the world, is strong in Massachusetts liberals: In the smug liberalism of Michael Dukakis, the hearty liberalism of Edward Kennedy and the combative liberalism of John Kerry.

Then, in the early 1990s, Massachusetts had a momentary political revolution. The 1980s "Massachusetts miracle" had turned into a nightmare, as the state's economy sagged badly, as the defense cutbacks long sought by Massachusetts politicians sent unemployment rising and high-tech firms like Wang and Digital withered and Cambridge-based Lotus's software was eclipsed by Redmond, Washington-based Microsoft's. The Northeast real estate bubble burst and Massachusetts banks foundered. The state government essentially went bankrupt. In 1990, as Dukakis retired, voters embraced big tax cuts and elected Republican William Weld in his place.

Four different Republicans held the governorship for the next 16 years. Weld favored a government that taxes and spends lightly, that is friendly to feminism and gay rights, that exerts some effort to protect the environment and that is tough on crime. Referenda limiting taxes and Weld's sharp spending cuts reduced the burden of government, and the state's private economy began recovering. Weld, who was reelected with 71% of the vote in 1994, has since left the state, but his basic approach prevailed, with variations, under his successors—Paul Cellucci, who took office in 1997 when Weld resigned, Jane Swift, who took office in 2001 when Cellucci resigned, and Mitt Romney, who was elected in 2002. But they were able to reduce the cost of government only so far; the biggest policy innovation was the health care plan passed by the legislation and supported by Romney in 2006. It required everyone to buy health insurance, levied taxes on employers who do not provide it and subsidized it for low earners. Romney tried to hold down the cost to government and argued that it would reduce the need to provide free care to the uninsured; but he warned that the Democratic legislature might make it more expensive after he left office. That would be a problem in a state where since 2000 the economy has sagged. Massachusetts has held its own in high-tech and defense industries, but showed little growth as the nation's economy surged. There has been a net out-migration of non-immigrants from metro Boston of some 265,000 people since 2000, most of them young, many professionals, many with fewer skills and unable to afford Massachusetts's high housing costs: the state's work force declined by nearly 2%. They have been only partly replaced by about half as many immigrants, about half of them Brazilians; Massachusetts has many descendants of Portuguese and Azorean immigrants and the Brazilians have evidently been attracted to the most Lusophone part of the United States. Massachusetts's population declined between 2003 and 2005, and increased only 1.4% between 2000 and 2006, the sixth lowest of any state, ahead only of industrial Pennsylvania, Ohio and West Virginia, rural North Dakota and hurricane-stricken Louisiana.

At the same time the cultural liberalism which Weld championed has prevailed. Weld was one of America's first politicians to endorse gay rights, and he appointed Supreme Judicial Court Chief Justice Margaret Marshall, who pushed through the 4–3 decisions in November 2003 requiring the legislature to give equal marriage rights to gays and then, when the legislature declined, in May 2004 declaring that same-sex couples have the right to marry. There was an initial rush of same-sex couples to clerk's offices, though not out-of-state couples, barred from marrying in Massachusetts by a 1913 law; there were some 2,500 same-sex marriages the week after the court's decision and in the next six months only 1,700. (In heavily gay Provincetown and heavily lesbian Northampton same-sex marriages outnumbered opposite-sex marriages during that period.) Romney opposed the decision, and House Speaker Thomas Finneran pushed the legislature, acting in joint session in March 2004, to vote 105-92 to send to the voters a constitutional amendment banning same-sex marriage and endorsing civil unions. But under the Massachusetts Constitution, the legislature must vote for an amendment twice before it goes on the ballot. In Democratic primaries and in the general election, opponents of same-sex marriage fared poorly, while Speaker Finneran was ousted by Salvatore DiMasi, a same-sex marriage backer from the once heavily Italian and now gentrified North End of Boston. In June 2005, Romney announced he would support a proposed constitutional amendment in the form of a citizen's initiative, which would ban same-sex marriage without creating civil unions; the earliest it could end up on the ballot would be 2008. Signatures were gathered but the state Constitution provides that it doesn't go on the ballot if it gets fewer than one-quarter of the votes in the bicameral session. Throughout 2006 DiMasi refused to let it come to a vote, and the state Senate refused to vote on it November 9. Romney, who had not run for reelection, told a rally November 19, "The issue before us is not whether same-sex couples should marry. The issue before us today is whether 109 legislators will follow the Constitution. Let us not see the state which first established constitutional democracy become the first to abandon it." He filed a suit in the Supreme Judicial Court; on December 27 the court unanimously said that the legislature was required to vote, but said it couldn't compel it to do so. On January 2 the legislature voted 134-62 against the amendment, but since it got more than the needed 50 votes it survived. In early 2007 it was not clear whether the legislature would vote again. Same-sex marriage advocates said they had gained seven seats in the legislature, but that appeared not to be enough to kill it; incoming Governor Deval Patrick, a strong advocate of same-sex marriage, seemed certain not to apply the pressure Romney did. Then on June 14, the legislature voted 151-45 against the amendment, five votes shy of the 50 needed to place the measure on the ballot, ensuring the right of same-sex couples to wed in the state until at least 2012. Ironically, given all the energy same-sex marriage advocates have put into their drive to keep the issue off the ballot, polls suggest that same-sex marriage may now be supported by most Massachusetts voters.

In other states ballot propositions opposing same-sex marriage have brought Republicans and religious conservatives to the polls to the detriment of Democrats. That is not a problem in Massachusetts, where there are very few of either. With Patrick's 56%-35% victory over Romney's lieutenant governor, Kerry Healey, Democrats now hold all six statewide offices, all twelve U.S. House and Senate seats and 176 of the 200 seats in the state legislature (whose official name is the Great and General Court). Republicans failed to contest seven of the U.S. House and 130 of the state legislative seats. The state voted 62%-37% for its own John Kerry in the 2004 presidential election and 69%-31% for Edward Kennedy in 2006 for a term which will bring him to his 50th year in the Senate. In recent elections the most heavily Democratic parts of the state have not been the blue collar wards of Boston (they're mostly either gentrified or heavily black or immigrant), but the university towns like Cambridge, the Berkshires and the college-rich Pioneer Valley in the west and variously fashionable resort areas like Martha's Vineyard, Nantucket and Provincetown. The most heavily Republican (or less Democratic) areas are what political scientist Robert David Sullivan called the "Offramps," towns near the I-495 ring road and "cranberry country" in Plymouth County and Cape Cod, working class Worcester County in the center of the state and high-income Essex County in the northeast.

The People		**Race/Ethnic Origin**			**Military veterans:** 558,933 (11.5%)	
Pop. 2006 (est):	6,437,193	5,198,359	81.9%	White	WWII: 25.7%	Korea: 15.7%
Pop. 2000:	6,349,097	318,329	5.0%	Black	Vietnam: 28.4%	Gulf War: 6.6%
Pop. 1990:	6,016,425	236,786	3.7%	Asian	**Most populous cities (2006):**	
Change 1990-2000:	Up 5.5%	11,264	0.2%	Native Am.	1. Boston	590,763
% of U.S. total:	2.3%	1,706	0.0%	Hawaiian	2. Worcester	175,454
Pop. rank:	13th of 50	110,338	1.7%	Two+ races	3. Springfield	151,176
Area size:	10,555 sq. mi.	43,586	0.7%	Other	4. Lowell	103,229
State Native:	66.1%	428,729	6.8%	Hisp. Origin	5. Cambridge	101,365
Non-citizen:	6.9%	**Ancestry**				
Language		Irish: 16.8%		Italian: 10.1%	Urban population: 91.4%	
English: 78.8%	Other Eur.:11.4%	English: 8.5%		French: 6.0%	Rural population: 8.6%	
Spanish: 6.3%		German: 4.4%				

Education		**Work Sector**		**General Court**	
H.S. Grad:	84.8%	Private: 80.0%	Govt: 13.5%	Senate	35 D 5 R
College Grad:	33.2%	Self: 6.4%	Family: 0.2%	House	141 D 19 R
Industry		Unemployment: 4.6%		Legislative Term Limits: No	
Agri: 0.4%	Con: 5.5%	**Household Income**		**Registered Voters**	
Fin: 8.2%	Info: 3.7%	<15k: 14.4%	15-35k: 20.5%	D: 1,472,707	(37.2%)
Mfg: 17.0%	Prof: 35.3%	35-50k: 14.5%	50-100k: 32.9%	R: 498,962	(12.6%)
Public: 4.3%	Trade: 14.4%	100-150k: 10.9%	>150k: 6.8%	O: 1,987,053	(50.2%)
Other: 11.2%		Median: $50,502			
Occupation		Poverty status: 9.3%			
Blue collar: 18.7%	White collar: 67.0%	**Home Value**			
Gray collar: 14.3%		<50k: 1.5%	50-100k: 10.2%	100-200k: 45.1%	200-300k: 23.6%
		300-500k: 14.0%	>500k: 5.6%	Median: $182,800	

Presidential politics   Over the last ten presidential elections, Massachusetts has been the most Democratic state, giving Democratic nominees an average margin of 55%-38%. It was Bill Clinton's best state in 1996, Al Gore's second best in 2000 and, not surprisingly, John Kerry's best in 2004. What is also striking about Massachu-
setts is how many serious presidential candidates it has produced over the last three decades: Edward Kennedy in 1980, Michael Dukakis in 1988, Paul Tsongas in 1992, John Kerry in 2004, Mitt Romney in 2008. Only California and Texas have produced more serious candidates over that period, but they are the number one and two states in population and Massachusetts was number 13, but seemed likely to fall behind Indiana, Washington and Arizona to be number 16 when the 2010 Census is taken. Some credit must be given to the fact that the first primary is in New Hampshire, just north of Massachusetts and most of it picking up Boston TV; but even more credit must go to the hyperpolitical culture of Boston. Only Chicago seems as preoccupied by its local political figures, but Boston also believes that they are capable of national leadership.

2004 Presidential Vote		
Kerry (D).................... 1,803,800	(62%)
Bush (R) 1,071,109	(37%)
Badnarik (Lib)................ 15,022	(1%)
Other.......................... 22,457	(1%)

2004 Democratic Presidential Primary		
Kerry (D)....................... 440,964	(72%)
Edwards (D) 108,051	(18%)
Kucinich (D) 25,198	(4%)
Dean (D) 17,076	(3%)
Sharpton (D)..................... 6,123	(1%)
Other........................... 17,776	(3%)

2000 Presidential Vote		
Gore (D)...................... 1,616,487	(60%)
Bush (R) 878,502	(33%)
Nader (Green) 173,564	(6%)
Other.......................... 32,389	(1%)

Massachusetts's presidential primary has long been held in early March and was once the scene of great commotion. It produced victories for native sons like Dukakis, Tsongas and Kerry (though at one point in late 2003 Kerry trailed Howard Dean in Massachusetts primary polls). In 2000, it voted solidly for Al Gore and John McCain, as many independents reregistered as Republicans. Candidates contesting New Hampshire always buy time on Boston TV stations, which reach much of the Granite State (most of the cost of which does not have to be charged against the low limit on spending in New Hampshire), and so their ads are widely seen in Massachusetts. But they don't usually bother campaigning here.

Congressional districting   Massachusetts's convoluted congressional district lines deserve their own biographer, someone with a sure political instinct and a touch of whimsy. This is, after all, the state whose Governor Elbridge Gerry gave name to the term "gerrymander" in the early 19th century. The state lost two seats in the 1960 Census, one each in 1980 and 1990; it survived the 2000 Census without losing another but appears likely to lose one in the 2010

110th Congress Lineup	
9 D	1 V

109th Congress Lineup
10 D

count. Secretary of State William Galvin has already begun urging the Census to count all students to avoid that. The redistricting process after the 2000 Census was a ruckus nonetheless. Many legislators wanted simply to protect all 10 incumbents, but that was hard to do because the districts were already convoluted. In July 2001, House Speaker Thomas Finneran advanced a plan to smooth out the district lines and create a district that would unite southeastern Massachusetts—the congressmen who represent the area live in Boston and next-door Newton and Quincy and far off Worcester—and a Boston-based district with large percentages of blacks and Hispanics and to eliminate the district of Martin Meehan, who was contemplating running for governor. But other politicians complained loudly and Meehan opted out of the race for governor; state senators, helped by senior incumbent Edward Markey, came up with a plan to protect incumbents. Republican Governor Jane Swift came up with her own plan, which of course didn't pass in the heavily Democratic state House. In January 2002, both houses agreed on an incumbent protection plan and passed it over Swift's veto. Looking ahead, perhaps in part to 2010, senior Massachusetts incumbents Edward Markey and Barney Frank have amassed huge campaign treasuries; Meehan in early 2007 announced he was retiring. But he seemed certain to be replaced by another Democrat who will not be eager to lose his or her seat and, unless one member retires after the 2010 Census, there could be another free-for-all redistricting fight.

Governor

Deval Patrick (D)

Elected 2006, term expires Jan. 2011, 1st term; b. July 31, 1956, Chicago, IL; home, Milton; Harvard U., A.B. 1978, J.D. 1982; Presbyterian; married (Diane).

Professional Career: Michael Clark Rockefeller Memorial Traveling Fellow, Sudan, 1978-79; Law clerk, 9th Circuit Court of Appeals, 1982-83; Practicing atty., 1983-94, 1997-99; Asst. U.S. Atty. Gen. for Civil Rights, 1994-97; Vice president and general counsel, Texaco, 1999-2001; Executive vice president and general counsel, Coca-Cola, 2001-04; ACC Capital Holdings, 2004-06.

Office: State House, Rm. 360, Boston, 02133, 617-725-4005; Fax: 617-727-9725; Web site: www.mass.gov/gov.

Election Results

2006 general	Deval Patrick (D)	1,234,984	(56%)
	Kerry Healey (R)	784,342	(35%)
	Christy Mihos (I)	154,628	(7%)
	Other	45,825	(2%)
2006 primary	Deval Patrick (D)	452,229	(50%)
	Christopher Gabrieli (D)	248,301	(27%)
	Thomas Reilly (D)	211,031	(23%)
2002 general	Mitt Romney (R)	1,091,988	(50%)
	Shannon O'Brien (D)	985,981	(45%)
	Jill Stein (Green)	76,530	(4%)
	Other	38,379	(2%)

Deval Patrick, elected in 2006, is the first Democrat in 20 years to win the Massachusetts governor's office. He is the state's first African-American governor and only the second elected in U.S. history, after Virginia's Douglas Wilder. Patrick grew up in a tough South Side Chicago neighborhood, and lived in an apartment where he shared a single room with his mother and sister; his father left the family when he was a child. As early as grade school he showed tremendous promise and a teacher recommended him to A Better Chance, an organization that identifies and sends gifted minority students to college preparatory schools. Patrick received a scholarship and was sent far from home to the tony Milton Academy in Massachusetts. "[It] was like coming to a different planet," Patrick would later say. He attended Harvard College and after graduating spent a year working in Africa on a United Nations project in the Darfur region of Sudan. When he returned, he enrolled at Harvard Law School and then clerked for a federal appeals court judge in Los Angeles. In 1983, he joined the NAACP Legal Defense Fund in New York and in 1986 Patrick went into private law practice; in 1994, he was appointed as the Justice Department's Assistant Attorney General for Civil Rights by President Bill Clinton. After three years in that post, Patrick returned to private practice in 1997 and later served as general counsel for Texaco and Coca-Cola.

Since Democrat Michael Dukakis left office in 1991, Massachusetts has had four Republican governors, the latest of which was Mitt Romney. Romney, running as an outsider in 2002, defeated state Treasurer Shannon O'Brien by 50%-45%. He faced large Democratic majorities in the statehouse; after a single term he decided not to seek reelection but instead to run for president. The open governor's race attracted a formidable Democratic primary field that included Attorney General Thomas Reilly and venture capitalist Christopher Gabrieli. Patrick was a long-shot in his first-ever run for elected office but his grassroots campaign quickly built support among liberal activists who liked his outsider message and his criticism of the state's "backroom" political culture. He won the state party endorsement at its June 2006 convention, and after holding a steady lead in the polls throughout the summer, won the nomination decisively in the September 19 primary. Despite speculation that, as the most liberal of the three candidates, he would prove to be the weakest nominee, Patrick won 50% to Gabrieli's 27%. Reilly finished third with 23%. The Republican nominee was Lieutenant Governor Kerry Healey, who sought to become the state's first female governor. Also running a competitive campaign was Christy Mihos, a wealthy businessman and former director of the Massachusetts Turnpike Authority, who left the Republican party to run as an Independent. Mihos never gained traction and Healey struggled to generate enthusiasm about her campaign. One reason was Romney, who was no asset in Healey's bid to succeed him. He had failed to build the state party in his four years; his frequent out of state travel and the jibes he directed at Massachusetts while preparing to run for president left him with low job approval ratings. Patrick consistently referred to the "Romney-Healey administration" and ran television ads featuring photos of Romney and Healey. In his role as chairman of the Republican Governors Association, Romney even admitted that the GOP would likely lose seats this year—including his own. Healey said Patrick was soft on crime and insisted he would raise taxes and increase state spending. Patrick pointed to his credentials as a Justice Department prosecutor and highlighted his executive-level experience at two Fortune 500 companies as evidence of his business-friendly background. Late in the campaign, Patrick was put on the defensive when Healey's campaign ran tough ads criticizing him for his advocacy on behalf of convicted rapist Benjamin LaGuer. Patrick declined to respond with an aggressive counterattack, insisting that his success so far was the result of avoiding such conventional political tactics. His instincts proved correct: the ensuing publicity surrounding the negative ads—which featured a woman walking alone in a parking garage—muted the charges that Patrick would weaken criminal justice laws. He won a sweeping 56%-35% victory, with 7% for Mihos.

In office, Patrick set about unraveling Romney's initiatives. He restored $383.6 million in budget cuts made by Romney, rescinded an agreement with the federal government that empowered the state police to arrest illegal immigrants, and put the brakes on a Romney administration plan to revamp the state's automobile insurance system. He refused to sign a proclamation commemorating February 6, the late president's birthday, as "Ronald Reagan Day." But Patrick's honeymoon period ended quickly as a series of missteps tarnished his image. Lavish spending on his official state car, helicopter travel, a renovation of the governor's office that included $12,000 drapes and the hiring of a chief of staff for his wife led to weeks of bad press and harsh criticism. In March, Patrick acknowledged making a telephone call to Robert Rubin of Citigroup, which has significant business interests in the state, on behalf of the controversial mortgage lender Ameriquest; Patrick had served on Ameriquest's parent company's board of directors as recently as 2006. The state Republican party filed a complaint with the State Ethics Commission but in June the commission decided against reprimanding Patrick. Amidst all this, in mid-March Patrick was forced to scale back his public appearances after his wife, a prominent local lawyer, was revealed to be suffering from exhaustion and depression.

Senior Senator

Edward Kennedy (D)

Elected 1962, seat up 2012, 8th full term; b. Feb. 22, 1932, Boston; home, Hyannis Port; Harvard U., B.A. 1956, The Hague Intl. Law Schl., 1958, U. of VA, LL.B. 1959; Catholic; married (Vicki).

Military Career: Army, 1951-53.

Professional Career: Western states coord., John F. Kennedy Pres. Campaign, 1960; Asst. Dist. Atty., Suffolk Cnty., 1961-62.

DC Office: 315 RSOB, 20510, 202-224-4543; Fax: 202-224-2417; Web site: kennedy.senate.gov.

State Office: Boston, 617-565-3170.

Committees: *Armed Services* (2d of 13 D): Seapower (Chmn.); Emerging Threats & Capabilities; Personnel. *Health, Education, Labor & Pensions* (Chmn. of 11 D). *Joint Economic Committee* (2d of 10 D). *Judiciary* (2d of 10 D): Immigration, Refugees & Border Security (Chmn.); Constitution; Crime & Drugs; Terrorism, Technology & Homeland Security; Human Rights & the Law.

Group Ratings

	ADA	ACLU	AFS	LCV	ITIC	NTU	COC	ACU	CFG	FRC
2006	100	92	100	100	50	10	36	0	0	0
2005	95	—	100	95	—	7	28	0	0	—

National Journal Ratings

	2005 LIB	—	2005 CONS	2006 LIB	—	2006 CONS
Economic	95%	—	0%	87%	—	0%
Social	90%	—	0%	88%	—	11%
Foreign	95%	—	0%	98%	—	0%

Key Votes of the 109th Congress

1. Bar ANWR Drilling	Y	5. Confirm Samuel Alito	N	9. Limit Interstate Abortion	N
2. FY06 Spending Curb	N	6. Path to Citizenship	Y	10. CAFTA	N
3. Estate Tax Repeal	N	7. Bar Same Sex Marriage	N	11. Urge Iraq Withdrawal	Y
4. Raise Minimum Wage	Y	8. Stem Cell Research $	Y	12. Provide Detainee Rights	Y

Election Results

2006 general	Edward Kennedy (D)	1,500,738	(69%)	($7,043,877)
	Ken Chase (R)	661,532	(31%)	($853,730)
2006 primary	Edward Kennedy (D)	unopposed		
2000 general	Edward Kennedy (D)	1,889,494	(73%)	($3,662,652)
	Jack E. Robinson III (R)	334,341	(13%)	($150,430)
	Carla A. Howell (Lib)	308,860	(12%)	($1,055,186)
	Other	66,725	(3%)	

Prior Winning Percentages: 1994 (58%); 1988 (65%); 1982 (61%); 1976 (69%); 1970 (62%); 1964 (74%); 1962 (55%)

Edward Kennedy has served more than 44 years in the Senate—longer than all but two other senators in American history—and he is still going strong. He has served with nine presidents of the United States and ten governors of Massachusetts, most of them Republicans; the only senators who have served longer are Strom Thurmond of South Carolina and Robert Byrd of West Virginia. Kennedy has had the highs and lows of his personal life followed by millions and criticized vitriolically by many. "I've made mistakes. Certainly there are things I'm not proud of," he admits. He has been a presidential candidate and, while still in his 30s, was widely assumed to be the next president. He is second in seniority in the Senate, behind Byrd. His reputation as an idealistic champion of the poor has been burnished by the praise of first-rate celebrators that no American political family has attracted before, and the nation has watched him cope impressively time and again with family tragedy. To others, he is a symbol of personal immorality and unpunished criminal behavior, a man who has gotten away with things that would have ended the public career of almost anyone else. There is some basis for both views, but neither is an entirely fair picture of this politician, who was reelected without much fuss in 2006 to a term which will take him to his 50th year in the Senate, and both in the minority and, once again, in the majority, he has done much to set national policy on any number of issues.

In most of America and even in much of Massachusetts the luster of the Kennedys has worn off, and most Americans have no memory of the years when John Kennedy was president. But Edward Kennedy has remained a major political force. There was little in the early life of this youngest of the Kennedy siblings to suggest he would be a major politician, much less for so long. He grew up in Bronxville, New York, a rich suburb with many other rich Catholics, was thrown out of Harvard for cheating on a Spanish exam and served in the Army, returned to earn degrees at Harvard and Virginia Law School, and married a Bronxville girl who never developed a taste for politics. Then his brother was elected president of the United States at 43, and the 28-year-old Edward Kennedy was a national celebrity. His father insisted that he run for the Senate; a JFK college roommate was found to hold the seat until Kennedy reached the constitutional age of 30, in 1962. His family money and the enthusiasm among Massachusetts Catholics for this seeming royalty enabled him to beat strong candidates with good political names: Attorney General Edward McCormack, nephew of Speaker John McCormack, in the Democratic primary; George Cabot Lodge, son and great-grandson of senators, in the general. "He can do more for Massachusetts" was his slogan, as it had been John F. Kennedy's in his first Senate race 10 years before. Two years later, his brother Robert Kennedy was elected senator from New York, regarded generally as a carpetbagger although he had grown up from age two in the state; Robert Kennedy ran for president and was murdered just after winning the California primary in June 1968.

After his brothers' assassinations, Edward Kennedy was seen by many as their natural heir, and he could have been nominated for president in 1968, at 36, or in 1972, had he chosen to run. But after the accident at Chappaquiddick in July 1969, for which he pleaded guilty to leaving the scene his poll ratings dropped and he became a polarizing figure. In 1972, he delivered the first of many stirring convention speeches promoting his trademark liberalism. In 1979, he did run for president, and began the race against incumbent Jimmy Carter far ahead in the polls. But he was unable to articulate his reasons for running, and his candidacy was greeted with adverse reaction to him personally as well as to his policies. It ended in a crushing defeat, relieved only by another stirring convention speech, after which he pointedly refused to raise Carter's hand on the podium. In retrospect, it is plain that Edward Kennedy's presidential chances were ended by Chappaquiddick. But he has always been reelected with solid margins in Massachusetts, and received his toughest competition from Mitt Romney, then a venture capitalist and later governor, in the Republican year of 1994.

Kennedy has been a hardworking and practical politician who, after his brothers' deaths, took up liberal causes and attention to the poor, which had been the focus of Robert Kennedy in the last years of his life. He was elected Senate majority whip in 1967, but lost the post to Robert Byrd in 1971. He worked hard for a quarter century without friendly support from a Democratic administration, until the election of Bill Clinton. Among the laws which he played an important role in enacting were the National Teachers Corps, bilingual education, low-income heating assistance, the WIC nutrition program, the Job Training Partnership Act (on which he worked with freshman Dan Quayle), and the Americans With Disabilities Act. As chairman of the Judiciary Committee in 1979-80 (his chief aide was a young lawyer named Stephen Breyer, now on the U.S. Supreme Court), he supported abortion rights and feminist groups with energy and enthusiasm. He immediately pounced on Judge Robert Bork's nomination in 1987, but played a lesser role in the Clarence Thomas hearings, which came shortly after an incident in which his nephew William Kennedy Smith was arrested and charged with rape in Palm Beach, Florida. As chairman of the Health, Education, Labor and Pensions Committee from 1987-94, Kennedy supported the higher spending sought by teachers' unions.

In 1992, Kennedy supported Bill Clinton and basked as Clinton gave repeated homage to the Kennedy family. Legislatively, Kennedy was productive, though not as much as he wished. He worked to pass direct student loans, AmeriCorps, Goals 2000 and the School-to-Work Opportunity Act. He again sponsored the Family and Medical Leave Act which George H. W. Bush had vetoed; it was the first law Clinton signed. After Republicans won a Senate majority in 1994, Kennedy shifted his focus from expanding government to protecting it from downsizing. In 1996, he went on the offensive. He pushed the Kassebaum-Kennedy health care bill, an incremental measure to provide portability of health insurance and to limit exclusions for pre-existing conditions; he worked to keep Medical Savings Accounts out, and the bill passed. He worked on the CHIP children's health insurance act, passed as part of a grand compromise between Clinton and the Republican leadership in 1997, and on the minority health disparities law.

Kennedy did not quit legislating when George W. Bush took office in 2001. Kennedy goes back a long time with the family; sworn in in November 1962, he was technically a colleague of George W. Bush's grandfather Prescott Bush, whose last term ended in January 1963. He got on well with George H. W. Bush in 1989-93. George W. Bush started off his term by inviting Kennedy to the White House frequently and to view *Thirteen Days*, the film about the Cuban missile crisis. Kennedy played a major role in producing Bush's first major bipartisan achievement, the education bill passed by the Senate in June 2001 and signed in January 2002. This represented a change in course by Kennedy and by George Miller, ranking Democrat on the House committee; they agreed to accept the accountability measures Bush sought, though opposed by many in the teachers' unions, which were designed especially to raise test scores among minority and disadvantaged pupils.

Kennedy broke with Bush, after initial cooperation, on the Medicare/prescription drug bill passed in November 2003. Kennedy succeeded in getting a version to his liking through the Senate, but the House produced quite a different version that largely prevailed in the conference committee. But he pursued other bipartisan causes—automated exit and entry customs systems with biometric identifiers with Sam Brownback and Saxby Chambliss, strengthening defenses against biological warfare with Bill Frist, HMO regulation with John Edwards and John McCain, colon cancer screening with Jesse Helms, hate crimes legislation with Gordon Smith, FDA regulation of tobacco with Mike DeWine. Most of these bills did not become law, but no one doubts that Kennedy will persist. Even his partisan opponents admit that he has become a superb legislator. And one deeply involved in local issues. In 2005 and 2006 he worked closely with Governor Mitt Romney, his 1994 opponent, on the universal health care program passed by the Massachusetts legislature. Romney conceded that it could probably never have passed without Kennedy's active involvement.

In 2005 and 2006 Kennedy was an increasingly sharp critic of the Bush administration, but continued to work on a bipartisan basis on many issues. He worked with HELP Chairman Mike

Enzi on an electronic health records bill in 2005, to reconcile it with a version sponsored by Bill Frist and Hillary Clinton. He worked with Sam Brownback on a bill to require doctors to provide up-to-date information on Down syndrome to expectant parents and support services for them. He worked with Enzi to block a proposal by House Democrat Maurice Hinchey to ban scientists with business ties from serving on FDA panels; Enzi and Kennedy instead favored disclosure and clarification by the FDA of when such ties constitute a conflict of interest. He worked with John McCain to develop the version of the immigration bill, with guest worker and law enforcement as well as border security provisions, which passed the Senate in May 2006. He worked with George Miller and House Republican Tom Petri to encourage more government direct student loans and fewer subsidized bank loans. He pushed through an amendment to stop universities from running school-as-lender programs, from which they pocketed the proceeds, and pressed Education Secretary Margaret Spellings to enforce it. On a local matter, he opposed the Cape Wind project of creating a 130-turbine wind farm in the Horseshoe Shoal in Nantucket Sound, one of the two places where state waters are surrounded by federal waters; he pushed for a bill that would allow governors to veto such projects, knowing that Mitt Romney was prepared to do so.

On some issues Kennedy has continued to issue clarion calls for liberalism. On the Judiciary Committee he opposed the nominations of John Roberts and Samuel Alito to the Supreme Court. He pressed Alberto Gonzales on interrogation of unlawful combatant detainees. On Iraq, he voted against the Iraq war resolution, while his colleague John Kerry voted for it, and later called the case for the war "a fraud . . . cooked up in Texas." "Iraq is George Bush's Vietnam," he said in April 2004 at the sober Brookings Institution. "This is the pattern and the record of the Bush administration [on] Iraq, jobs, Medicare, schools, issue after issue—mislead, deceive, make up the needed facts, smear the character of any critics. Again and again we see this cynical, despicable strategy playing out." In January 2005 he presented a five-point plan for Iraqi self-government and a definite timetable for a phased withdrawal of U.S. troops.

After the 2006 elections, as he prepared to become chairman of the HELP Committee for the third time, he said the first items in the Democrats' agenda should be raising the minimum wage, getting federal financing of embryonic stem cell research and reducing interest rates on college loans. On education, he worked with Republicans, including Enzi and Secretary Margaret Spellings, on reauthorizing the No Child Left Behind Act. He has long maintained that the administration promised to fully fund the act, that is, to appropriate the full amount authorized, although administration officials remembered no such promise.

Kennedy played a key role in securing the 2004 Democratic National Convention for Boston—its first national convention ever—and campaigned heavily for Kerry in the Democratic primaries. In 2005 he said he would support Kerry again if he ran in 2008; in December 2006, however, after Kerry's "stuck in Iraq" remark, he said he might support another candidate unless Kerry made a decision on running soon; Kerry bowed out in January 2007.

Kennedy was reelected with 73% of the vote in 2000 and with 69% in 2006; he carried all but two towns in Hampden County, losing those by a combined 69 votes. Over the years there was speculation that he would like to pass the seat on to one of his younger relatives, but he has indicated no desire to retire and has continued to be more active legislatively than many much younger senators. At the end of his current term he will have served 50 years, longer than anyone has ever served in the Senate, although Robert Byrd if he serves out his term will reach that milepost before him, in 2008.

Junior Senator

John Kerry (D)

Elected 1984, seat up 2008, 4th term; b. Dec. 11, 1943, Denver, CO; home, Boston; Yale U., A.B. 1966, Boston Col., LL.B. 1976; Catholic; married (Teresa Heinz).

Military Career: Navy, 1966-70 (Vietnam), Naval Reserves, 1972-78.

Elected Office: MA Lt. Gov., 1982-84.

Professional Career: Organizer, Vietnam Veterans Against the War; Asst. Dist. Atty., Middlesex Cnty., 1976-81; Practicing atty., 1981-82.

DC Office: 304 RSOB, 20510, 202-224-2742; Fax: 202-224-8525; Web site: kerry.senate.gov.

State Offices: Boston, 617-565-8519; Fall River, 508-677-0522; Springfield, 413-785-4610; Worcester, 508-831-7380.

Committees: *Commerce, Science & Transportation* (3d of 12 D): Science, Technology & Innovation (Chmn.); Aviation Operations, Safety & Security; Space, Aeronautics & Related Sciences; Oceans, Atmosphere, Fisheries & Coast Guard; Surface Transportation & Merchant Marine Infrastructure, Safety & Security; Interstate Commerce, Trade & Tourism. *Finance* (5th of 11 D): Social Security, Pensions & Family Policy (Chmn.); Health Care; Energy, Natural Resources & Infrastructure. *Foreign Relations* (3d of 11 D): Near Eastern & South & Central Asian Affairs (Chmn.); Western Hemisphere, Peace Corps & Narcotics Affairs; East Asian & Pacific Affairs; International Development & Foreign Assistance, Economic Affairs & International Environmental Protection. *Small Business & Entrepreneurship* (Chmn. of 10 D).

Group Ratings

	ADA	ACLU	AFS	LCV	ITIC	NTU	COC	ACU	CFG	FRC
2006	95	83	100	71	50	15	55	12	4	0
2005	100	—	100	95	—	7	33	8	0	—

National Journal Ratings

	2005 LIB	—	2005 CONS		2006 LIB	—	2006 CONS
Economic	91%	—	8%		87%	—	0%
Social	90%	—	0%		89%	—	8%
Foreign	72%	—	25%		72%	—	26%

Key Votes of the 109th Congress

1. Bar ANWR Drilling	Y	5. Confirm Samuel Alito	N	9. Limit Interstate Abortion	N
2. FY06 Spending Curb	N	6. Path to Citizenship	Y	10. CAFTA	N
3. Estate Tax Repeal	N	7. Bar Same Sex Marriage	N	11. Urge Iraq Withdrawal	Y
4. Raise Minimum Wage	Y	8. Stem Cell Research $	Y	12. Provide Detainee Rights	Y

Election Results

2002 general	John Kerry (D)	1,605,976	(80%)	($9,305,860)
	Michael Cloud (Lib)	369,807	(18%)	($207,684)
2002 primary	John Kerry (D)	unopposed		
1996 general	John Kerry (D)	1,334,135	(52%)	($12,619,152)
	William Weld (R)	1,143,120	(45%)	($8,002,123)
	Other	78,687	(3%)	

Prior Winning Percentages: 1990 (57%); 1984 (55%)

John Kerry, Massachusetts's junior senator and the Democratic nominee for president in 2004, has been a figure in national politics going back to 1971. The son of a Foreign Service officer, he grew up in many places and at one point attended boarding school in Switzerland. He graduated from Yale in 1966 and, after exploring alternatives, enlisted in the Navy. He served on a swift boat in Vietnam—hazardous duty—and was awarded a Silver Star and three Purple Hearts. He attended the Winter Soldier hearings in Detroit in April 1971 which veterans testified (some of them falsely, it turned out) about atrocities and became one of the leaders in Vietnam Veterans Against the War. He attracted much attention for his articulateness and for his background, unusual for a Vietnam veteran, when he testified before the Senate Foreign Relations Committee in April 1971. "How do you ask a man to be the last to die for a mistake?" he asked in congressional testimony—a good question, and one that also suggested his future political ambitions. He condemned "war crimes committed in Southeast Asia," which, he said, were "not isolated incidents, but crimes committed on a day-to-day basis with the full awareness of officers at all levels of command." Kerry became familiar enough to be featured in *Doonesbury* and plunged quickly into politics. He ran for Congress in 1972, after some widely observed district-shopping, and lost in a district carried by George McGovern. Chastened, he went to law school, worked as top aide to the Middlesex County district attorney, was elected lieutenant governor on a ticket with Michael Dukakis in 1982, and ran for senator in 1984. In both races, he upset a favored rival for the Democratic nomination; in the 1984 general election he beat Republican state chairman Raymond Shamie 55%-45%.

Kerry came to the Senate with a reputation as a strong liberal. He has had a similar voting record to fellow Senator Edward Kennedy, but there have been differences of nuance and interest: For some years Kerry seemed respectful of economic free markets and more inclined to support an expansive U.S. foreign and military policy. In his first 20 years in the Senate Kerry was not a visibly active legislator—during the 2004 campaign factcheck.org said that only 11 of his bills became law—but was arguably more influential behind the scenes. One reason may have been his senior colleague: Edward Kennedy has been active on many legislative issues, as well as Massachusetts causes, and did not invite junior colleagues to play on his turf.

Kerry made his name more as an investigator, spending some time up blind alleys with klieg lights but also producing some important information. He used his Foreign Relations Western Hemisphere, Peace Corps, Narcotics and Terrorism Subcommittee chairmanship to investigate the infamous Bank of Credit & Commerce International scandal. Kerry's other great investigation was as chairman of the Select Committee on POW/MIA Affairs, on whether Americans were left behind in Vietnamese hands in 1973. Kerry and Republican Bob Smith of New Hampshire went to Vietnam and attempted to turn up new evidence. He concluded that there is evidence "that indicates the possibility of survival, at least for a small number," after 1973, but also said, "There is at this time no compelling evidence that any American remains alive in captivity in Southeast Asia." By May 1995, Kerry and fellow Vietnam veteran Senator John McCain were convinced that Hanoi was fully cooperating and, aware they had standing on this issue that Bill Clinton conspicuously lacked, they convinced him to normalize relations with Vietnam. Kerry has remained close with McCain and other Vietnam veterans in the Senate. Like McCain, he spoke out strongly in favor of the bombing of Serbia in April 1999.

His toughest race came in 1996, when he was opposed by Republican Governor William Weld, who had been reelected in 1994 with 71% of the vote. Earlier, the two had worked together on some state problems and emphasized the similarity of their views, but the campaign inevitably produced disagreements and some gentlemanly acrimony. They held eight debates altogether, literate rounds of accusations and one-liners. They both spent liberally—Kerry, $12.6 million, the second highest of any Senate candidate that year; Weld, $8 million. It got more coverage than any other Senate race that year, but the outcome in retrospect was unsurprising. Democratic Massachusetts voted 52%-45% for its junior Democratic senator.

When Clinton was president, Kerry took some interesting positions on issues that put him at odds with Democratic interest groups. He supported the balanced budget amendment and voted for the welfare act of 1996. In June 1998, he decried the "implosion" of public education and said it was caused not just by overcrowded classrooms but also by the "stifling bureaucracy" of school systems. His list of reforms, co-sponsored with Oregon Republican Gordon Smith, included some strongly opposed by the teachers' unions—important backers of the Democratic Party—ending teacher tenure, changing certification requirements to end the education school monopoly and allow lateral entry into teaching. He favored normal trade relations with China and led the floor fight against the Thompson-Torricelli amendment, which would have required review of China's human rights practices.

After George W. Bush became president, Kerry turned to sharp-edged opposition to administration policy. The Bush tax cut, he said, was "unfair, unaffordable and unquestionably ineffective in growing our economy." On the environment, he was one of the most outspoken opponents of oil drilling in the Arctic National Wildlife Refuge and threatened a filibuster on the issue. He criticized the administration for its rejection of the Kyoto Protocol, although he was one of 95 senators who voted in 1997 to reject Kyoto so long as it exempted developing nations like China and India—a main feature of the treaty then and now. On foreign policy, in June 2002 he said it was a "catastrophic mistake" not to press the Israelis to negotiate with the Palestinians; he said at the same time he would not negotiate with Yasir Arafat but would not support the calls that he be removed. He criticized the administration for letting Afghan troops take the lead in Tora Bora in late 2001 and said that may have allowed Al Qaeda and Taliban leaders to escape. Despite considerable criticism of administration policy on Iraq, he voted for the Iraq war resolution in October 2002 but said shortly afterward, "I'm going to keep asking tough questions to hold the President accountable for his promise to insist on arms inspections first, act multilaterally and only go to war as a last resort."

Many senators want to run for president; Kerry's peers have felt he had presidential ambitions since he was in prep school. He did not run in 1988, in his first term in the Senate. He did not run in 1992, presumably because he felt his vote against the Gulf war resolution in January 1991 would be a liability. With Bill Clinton in office there was no opening in 1996. In February 1999, with Clinton obviously smoothing the way for his choice, Al Gore, Kerry announced he would not run in 2000. There were no such obstacles in his way to running in 2004. He had an additional advantage: money. His wife Teresa Heinz Kerry, inherited $600 million when her first husband, Pennsylvania Republican Senator John Heinz, died in a 1991 plane crash. Her net worth in 2004 was estimated at around $1 billion, making Kerry the richest member of Congress according to *Roll Call*. In 1996, when Kerry was hard-pressed by Weld and by his practice of not taking PAC contributions, he borrowed $1.9 million against his and his wife's joint assets. In December 2003, when he was trailing Howard Dean in the polls, Kerry borrowed $6.4 million against his share of their Beacon Hill townhouse.

Kerry entered the presidential race in 2003 as the favorite to win the nomination. But by July 2003 he was trailing in the polls far behind Dean, whose outspoken opposition to the Iraq war attracted the left half of the Democratic electorate and whose innovative use of the Internet generated an unprecedented amount of small contributions. Kerry, who had voted for the war, began to criticize Bush's conduct of it, often in harsh terms. But at year's end he was still behind. Then, in mid-January, Dean's poll numbers in Iowa and New Hampshire started dropping. Kerry, well organized in Iowa and well known in New Hampshire, was the Democrat best positioned to fill the vacuum. His record in Vietnam, he suggested, would protect him against criticisms that he was too soft on foreign and military policy. "Bring it on!" he said at the end of his speeches. He won a solid though not overwhelming victory in the Iowa caucuses and, eight days later, an impressive victory in New Hampshire, the one state where primary turnout zoomed upward. Kerry won all the primaries but three and clinched the Democratic nomination on March 2, exactly seven months before the general election.

As early as May pollster John Zogby said the election was "Kerry's to lose." The Kerry campaign raised far more money than anyone expected; it was helped as well by 527 organizations which spent more than $200 million to defeat Bush. Bush's job approval hovered under 50% and he trailed Kerry in polls for much of the seven-month campaign. Kerry performed well in debates, being judged the winner in snap polls in all three. Yet he lost. One reason may have been encapsulated by his March 16 defense of his November 2003 vote against the supplemental appropriation for Iraq: "I actually did vote for the $87 billion before I voted against it." The Bush campaign painted Kerry as a flip-flopper, and in fact he has a propensity, common in politicians, to try to please those on all sides of an issue. More important, he was trying to rally a Democratic party split between fiercely anti-war Bush haters on the one hand and, on the other, more moderate Democrats who hoped for the best in Iraq but preferred a Democrat to Bush on the issues.

Second, the credential which the Kerry campaign emphasized at the Democratic National Convention, his decorated service in Vietnam, was undermined by the ads and book sponsored by Swift Boat Veterans for Truth. Kerry had claimed, in the *Boston Herald* in 1979, on the Senate floor in 1986 and to the Associated Press in 1992 to have served on secret missions in Cambodia in Christmas season 1968. But those claims were withdrawn by his campaign in August, and no one, including the boat mates who supported him, came forward to corroborate his claim to have served in Cambodia in later months.

Finally, Kerry was vulnerable to attack as a Massachusetts liberal. The Bush campaign highlighted his rating by *National Journal* as the number one liberal in the Senate in 2003— arguably unfairly, since he skipped many roll call votes that year while campaigning for president. But over his 20-year Senate career the *National Journal* rated him as the 11th most liberal senator—well to the left of midpoint. And the Massachusetts Supreme Judicial Court's legalization in May 2004 of same-sex marriage provided a vivid illustration of the difference between opinion in Massachusetts and majority opinion in the rest of the country. Democratic voter turnout efforts were successful; Kerry won 59 million votes, 16% more than Al Gore, and the second-highest total in American history. But Republican voter turnout efforts were even more successful; George W. Bush won 62 million votes, 23% more than he had four years before, and won the popular vote 51%-48%.

Kerry in 2005 was the first senator to return to the Senate as a defeated presidential nominee since George McGovern in 1973. He proceeded to stake out stands on important issues. He proposed a Kids First bill, to provide health insurance for every child; his colleague Edward Kennedy, to whom he had usually deferred on health care issues, agreed to be the lead co-sponsor. He followed up with a proposal that would require all Americans to have health insurance by 2012. With John McCain, he pressed the administration to make periodic assessments of how rising temperatures can affect the environment. In a June 2006 speech at Faneuil Hall he called for reducing oil consumption by 2.5 million barrels a day by 2015, for requiring that all gas stations have ethanol pumps by 2010 and all cars be fitted for E85 ethanol fuel; beyond that, he called for freezing carbon dioxide emissions by 2010 and decreasing their levels to 65% below the 2000 figure in 2050. As ranking Democrat on the Small Business Committee, he recognized the problems caused by military callups by calling for up to $21,000 in tax credits for businesses with 50 or fewer employees to cover salary shortfalls for mobilized reservists or hiring costs for replacements and up to $25,000 in disaster grants when a crucial employee is called for active duty. He criticized the administration for failing to produce proper paperwork for most Katrina loans.

Kerry supported the administration on one foreign policy issue in 2006, the agreement on India's civilian nuclear program, provided it pushed India to agree on IAEA standards of safeguarding civilian nuclear plants. But he increasingly opposed the administration's course in Iraq. In June 2006, as the Senate considered an amendment by Carl Levin and Jack Reed calling for redeployments from Iraq with no set date, Kerry and Russ Feingold insisted on bringing up an amendment to withdraw all combat forces by July 2007. It was defeated 86-13. For some observers, this was reminiscent of Kerry's performance on the nomination of Samuel Alito. Minority Leader Harry Reid asked colleagues not to filibuster this nomination, but in January 2006, while visiting Switzerland, Kerry called for a filibuster; it was defeated 72-25, a much wider margin than that by which Alito was confirmed.

Kerry's course during 2005 and 2006—his continued sharp criticisms of the administration, his new proposals on major issues, his heavy travel and fundraising schedule in support of Democratic candidates—suggested he was interested in running for president again in 2008. Criticized by some Democrats for having left $15 million in his presidential account in November 2004, he contributed more than $1 million to Democratic candidates and the House and Senate Democratic campaign committees. Of his 2002 vote for the Iraq resolution, he wrote on the left-wing Huffington Post blog, "There's nothing—nothing—in my life in public service I regret more, nothing even close." Then, on October 30, 2006, at Pasadena City College, he told a crowd of students, "Education: If you make the most of it, you study hard, you do your homework, and you make an effort to be smart, you can do well. If you don't, you get stuck in Iraq." This sounded to many like a disparaging comment about American military troops, and to some it was reminiscent of his 1971 Foreign Relations Committee testimony. In Seattle the next day, Kerry refused to apologize and said that demands he do so were a dirty trick by Karl Rove. When criticism continued, and Democratic candidates began to ask Kerry to skip scheduled campaign appearances, Kerry and his staffers said that the comment was "a botched joke," and that he had meant to say that "you get us stuck in Iraq"—an attack on George W. Bush and his supposedly weak academic record, although in fact Bush's marks at Yale were satisfactory and just slightly better than Kerry's. That explanation did not prevent the cancellation of all his appearances in the last week of the campaign, and as Democrats rejoiced at the results they noted that Kerry's ratings in the polls, not strong during most of 2005, had weakened. Edward Kennedy, who in March 2005 had said that "My man is John Kerry" for 2008, on December 11 said that he would not wait "indefinitely" for Kerry to make a decision on a presidential candidacy. Kerry had no public events in the seven weeks after the election and on January 24, 2007, announced he was not running for president.

It was widely presumed that he would run for reelection to the Senate in 2008 and would be reelected about as easily as he was in 2002, when he had no Republican opponent. This came no doubt as a disappointment to many ambitious Massachusetts politicians. The last time the state has had an open seat was in 1984, when Kerry won; the last open seat before that was in 1966, on the retirement of Leverett Saltonstall, who was born in the 19th century. The last time before that was in 1962, when the seat was reserved for Edward Kennedy.

FIRST DISTRICT

Rep. John Olver (D)

Elected June 1991, 8th full term; b. Sept. 3, 1936, Honesdale, PA; home, Amherst; Rensselaer Polytechnic Inst., B.S. 1955, Tufts U., M.A. 1956, M.I.T., Ph.D. 1961; no religious affiliation; married (Rose).

Elected Office: MA House of Reps., 1968-72; MA Senate, 1972-91.

Professional Career: Chemistry Prof., U. of MA, Amherst, 1961-69.

DC Office: 1111 LHOB, 20515, 202-225-5335; Fax: 202-226-1224; Web site: www.house.gov/olver.

District Offices: Fitchburg, 978-342-8722; Holyoke, 413-532-7010; Pittsfield, 413-442-0946.

Committees: *Appropriations* (11th of 37 D): Transportation, HUD & Related Agencies (Chmn.); Interior, Environment & Related Agencies; Energy & Water Development.

Group Ratings

	ADA	ACLU	AFS	LCV	ITIC	NTU	COC	ACU	CFG	FRC
2006	95	100	100	100	29	16	40	4	10	0
2005	95	—	100	94	—	17	33	0	3	0

National Journal Ratings

	2005 LIB	—	2005 CONS		2006 LIB	—	2006 CONS
Economic	94%	—	0%		91%	—	6%
Social	93%	—	7%		97%	—	0%
Foreign	96%	—	0%		92%	—	5%

Key Votes of the 109th Congress

1. Estate Tax Repeal	N	5. Limit Interstate Abortion	N	9. Build Border Fence	N
2. Limit CAFE Standards	N	6. Extend Patriot Act	N	10. CAFTA	N
3. FY06 Spending Curb	N	7. Bar Same Sex Marriage	N	11. Oppose Iraq Withdrawal	N
4. Drilling in ANWR	N	8. Stem Cell Research $	Y	12. Detainee Tribunals	N

Election Results

2006 general	John Olver (D)	158,057	(76%)	($670,481)
	William Szych (I)	48,574	(23%)	($46,497)
2006 primary	John Olver (D)	unopposed		
2004 general	John Olver (D)	unopposed		($460,462)

Prior Winning Percentages: 2002 (68%); 2000 (68%); 1998 (72%); 1996 (53%); 1994 (100%); 1992 (52%); 1991 (50%)

The People		Race/Ethnic Origin	Ancestry	
Area size:	3,192 sq. mi.	88.8% White	Irish: 13.5%	French: 10.7%
Urban population:	69.3%	1.6% Black	English: 9.0%	
Rural population:	30.7%	1.7% Asian	**2004 Presidential Vote**	
Pop. 2000:	634,479	0.2% Native Am.	Kerry (D) 185,377	(63%)
Pop. 2005 (est):	640,984	0.0% Hawaiian	Bush (R) 103,990	(35%)
Median income:	$42,570	1.2% Two+ races	Other 4,352	(1%)
Poverty status:	10.5%	0.1% Other	**2000 Presidential Vote**	
Military veterans:	13.5%	6.3% Hispanic Origin	Gore (D) 150,418	(56%)
			Bush (R) 88,690	(33%)
			Other 27,700	(10%)
			Cook Partisan Voting Index: D +15	

Occupation   Blue collar: 23.9%   White collar: 59.8%   Gray collar: 16.4%

The stony hills and green-clad mountains of western Massachusetts, with more trees today than when Henry David Thoreau was writing in the 1840s, where stone wall fencing once bounded one working farm from another, probably do not look much different from 300 years ago. This was the frontier in the 17th century, where Puritan preachers founded new towns in the wilderness, farming the rocky soil and preaching against declension. This was also the site of the Indian uprising known as King Philip's War in 1676, and the Indian raid, supported by the French in Quebec, at Deerfield in 1704. This was Yankee New England's western frontier for nearly 200 years. In the 19th century, the area was the home of writers and artists: Emily Dickinson lived quietly in Amherst, Edith Wharton grandly on her estate in Lenox and Herman Melville struck a friendship with Nathaniel Hawthorne after purchasing a farm near Hawthorne's Pittsfield home, not far from where the Boston Symphony plays at the Tanglewood Festival each summer. There were mill towns here as well, jammed in mountain crevasses or along the wide Connecticut River; but as the 20th century went on, and trees grew up on stony land once farmed, western Massachusetts came to look less settled, except near giant factories like General Electric's now-closed electric transformer plant in Pittsfield and the Crane paper factory in nearby Dalton, since 1879 the only company used by the U.S. Treasury to print money, with armed guards to protect the secret plating process. The region's rolling hills and charming New England towns attract a tourist trade, with destinations such as Tanglewood and Jacob's Pillow, the only dance institution to be named a National Historic Landmark, and there are year-round weekend and vacation homes in the Berkshires.

Western Massachusetts has also changed politically. For many years it was a heartland of the Republican Party—flinty, thrifty and chilly just like the area's most famous politician, Calvin Coolidge. But by the end of the 20th century, the area contained some of the most left-wing parts of America. Stockbridge attracted liberal artist Norman Rockwell and baby boom radical Arlo Guthrie, whose Alice's Restaurant was there. The concentration of colleges and universities in the Pioneer Valley brought together a critical mass of liberal scholars and an even more leftish graduate student proletariat; the University of Massachusetts in Amherst is the largest. The results show up in the election returns: John Kerry carried Amherst 85%-13% over George W. Bush. Western Massachusetts voted heavily for Democrat Shannon O'Brien for governor in 2002, even as she lost the rest of Massachusetts to Mitt Romney.

The 1st Congressional District covers most of western Massachusetts—all of Berkshire and Franklin Counties and their small towns not replicated elsewhere in the state, most of Hampshire County, Holyoke and West Springfield on the Connecticut River, the more working-class areas of northern Worcester County—and extends east to Pepperell in Middlesex County, about 40 miles from Boston. It is the state's largest congressional district (it borders four states) and covers about 40% of the land area of Massachusetts. Over time, the solidly Democratic voting base has shifted from low-income mill workers in places like Holyoke and Pittsfield to liberal and radical academics in the college towns.

The congressman from the 1st District is John Olver, a Democrat first chosen in a June 1991 special election after the death of longtime Republican Congressman Silvio Conte. Olver was educated at Tufts and MIT and came to UMass as a chemistry professor in 1961, at 25; his wife Rose is a professor of psychology and women's and gender studies at Amherst College. In 1968, he began a 22-year career in the legislature. In the special election to replace Conte, his Pioneer Valley base helped him win 31% in the fragmented Democratic primary. In the general, he faced Steven Pierce, former state House Republican leader and Governor William Weld's conservative opponent in the 1990 primary. With Massachusetts liberalism in disrepute after the loss by Governor Michael Dukakis in the 1988 presidential campaign, the contest was close; Weld scheduled it after students' summer vacation began. Olver eked out a 50%-48% win, becoming the first Democrat to hold the seat since the Spanish-American War.

Olver has one of the most liberal voting records in the House. He has voted against the kind of international trade deals that decades ago would have added manufacturing jobs in the 1st District, and he favors Canadian-style single-payer health insurance. Olver has worked quietly to fund local projects on the Appropriations Committee. Olver now chairs the Transportation, Housing and Urban Development Subcommittee, where he has sought expanded Amtrak service and subsidies in the Northeast Corridor. He also has advocated increased support for bicyclists, for both recreational and transportation purposes. Local projects that he has funded include the Main Street Mercado in Holyoke, an intermodal parking facility in Fitchburg, reconstruction of the Coolidge Bridge in Northampton, and an information system kiosk program along Route 2—routine stuff, but still welcomed by local users. In November 2005, he worked to reduce from $250,000 to $15,000 the ceiling on government credit cards issued after Hurricane Katrina; he cited the potential for fraud and abuse. With Wayne Gilchrest of Maryland, he formed the House's bipartisan Climate Change Caucus and filed legislation to cap greenhouse gas emissions. Outside of his Appropriations work, he has had few legislative accomplishments and he rarely seeks attention. He introduced a total of 29 bills during his first 14 years in the House. Olver does not seem a natural politician and dislikes fundraising. He likes to rock climb, a solitary and meticulous business. In a delegation filled with natural-born politicos, Olver is notably shy. An exception came in April 2006 when he and four other House Democrats were handcuffed, arrested and briefly jailed for protesting the violence in Darfur at the Sudanese Embassy in Washington. Some Massachusetts Democrats have complained that as the state's only Appropriations member, he hasn't done much for the Boston area. In the majority, he warned against expectations that there is an "easy pot of money."

Olver has only had one close contest for reelection; in 1996 he beat Jane Swift, then a state representative and later governor, by 53%-47%. He has been reelected easily since then. In 2005, he was hospitalized with a brain infection but he rebounded with a 76%-23% win in 2006 against Billy Szych, the former Hatfield town administrator, who challenged Olver as influenced by political action committees and part of the problem with the "squabbling" in Washington. With Massachusetts facing the likely loss of a seat in the 2010 reapportionment, Olver and his rambling district are obvious targets for Boston-area pols.

SECOND DISTRICT

Rep. Richard Neal (D)

Elected 1988, 10th term; b. Feb. 14, 1949, Springfield; home, Springfield; Amer. Intl. Col., B.A. 1972, U. of Hartford, M.A. 1976; Catholic; married (Maureen).

Elected Office: Springfield City Cncl., 1978-83; Springfield Mayor, 1984-88.

Professional Career: Staff Asst., Springfield Mayor William C. Sullivan, 1973-78; High Schl. & Col. teacher, 1978-83.

DC Office: 2208 RHOB, 20515, 202-225-5601; Fax: 202-225-8112; Web site: www.house.gov/neal.

District Offices: Milford, 508-634-8198; Springfield, 413-785-0325.

Committees: *Ways & Means* (6th of 24 D): Select Revenue Measures (Chmn.); Oversight.

Group Ratings

	ADA	ACLU	AFS	LCV	ITIC	NTU	COC	ACU	CFG	FRC
2006	95	95	100	100	50	16	36	4	10	0
2005	85	—	100	89	—	12	41	0	3	8

National Journal Ratings

	2005 LIB	—	2005 CONS		2006 LIB	—	2006 CONS
Economic	88%	—	12%		94%	—	0%
Social	82%	—	18%		84%	—	15%
Foreign	85%	—	14%		92%	—	5%

Key Votes of the 109th Congress

1. Estate Tax Repeal	N	5. Limit Interstate Abortion	N	9. Build Border Fence	N
2. Limit CAFE Standards	N	6. Extend Patriot Act	N	10. CAFTA	N
3. FY06 Spending Curb	N	7. Bar Same Sex Marriage	N	11. Oppose Iraq Withdrawal	N
4. Drilling in ANWR	N	8. Stem Cell Research $	Y	12. Detainee Tribunals	N

Election Results

2006 general	Richard Neal (D)	.... unopposed	($552,127)
2006 primary	Richard Neal (D)	.... unopposed	
2004 general	Richard Neal (D)	.... unopposed	($427,864)

Prior Winning Percentages: 2002 (100%); 2000 (100%); 1998 (100%); 1996 (72%); 1994 (59%); 1992 (53%); 1990 (100%); 1988 (80%)

The People		Race/Ethnic Origin	Ancestry	
Area size:	952 sq. mi.	82.5% White	Irish: 13.4%	French: 10.8%
Urban population:	84.8%	5.5% Black	Italian: 8.9%	
Rural population:	15.2%	1.3% Asian	**2004 Presidential Vote**	
Pop. 2000:	634,444	0.2% Native Am.	Kerry (D) 169,460	(59%)
Pop. 2005 (est):	658,425	0.0% Hawaiian	Bush (R) 113,284	(40%)
Median income:	$44,386	1.2% Two+ races	Other 3,324	(1%)
Poverty status:	10.8%	0.1% Other	**2000 Presidential Vote**	
Military veterans:	13.3%	9.2% Hispanic Origin	Gore (D) 150,148	(58%)
			Bush (R) 89,775	(35%)
			Other 19,588	(8%)
			Cook Partisan Voting Index: D +13	

Occupation	Blue collar: 24.1%	White collar: 60.6%	Gray collar: 15.4%

As American as apple pie, the place where basketball was invented, the city where the Webster's unabridged dictionaries (2d and 3d editions) were edited and published, the site of the armory where M-1 rifles were manufactured during World War II: This is Springfield, Massachusetts. Springfield is the third largest city in the Bay State, but far from Boston. Historically overshadowed by Hartford as the center of the Connecticut River Valley, it is a medium-sized American city built by New England Yankees, where immigrants from a dozen different countries have worked their way up. Today, blacks and Hispanics make up nearly half its population. Like other New England cities, Springfield's downtown has emptied and its tax base has shrunk. Business leaders have tried to revive it, in part with the expansion of the Basketball Hall of Fame. But the once-powerful city has suffered from corruption and serious crime, and was forced to submit to state control in 2004 in a financial bailout. Local companies, too, have been forced to adapt. The gun manufacturer Smith & Wesson in the 1990s embraced the marketing restrictions sought by gun control advocates, and then saw its sales sag, as gun control opponents—its natural market—shunned its products. Under new ownership, it abandoned that stance and sales rose again.

Springfield is the largest city in the 2d Congressional District of Massachusetts, which stretches east from Springfield to a point 30 miles southwest of Boston. Its irregular boundaries stretch north to South Hadley and Northampton (Hamp to oldsters; NoHo to the younger artsy crowd), the homes of Mount Holyoke and Smith Colleges; since the downturn in the 1970s, these tourist destinations have revived with trendy restaurants and avant-garde liberalism. To the east it stretches across stony hills and east of Worcester to the antique center of Brimfield and the factory towns of the Blackstone Valley just north of Woonsocket, Rhode Island. Historically, this was a Yankee Republican district for much of the 20th century, then a solidly Catholic Democratic district. Now it is more diverse culturally, and even more solidly Democratic.

The congressman from the 2d District is Richard Neal, a Democrat first elected in 1988. Neal grew up in Springfield, graduated from American International College and got a master's in public administration from the University of Hartford. In Springfield, he worked for the mayor, and was elected to the city council in 1978, while teaching high school and college history. As mayor from 1984-88, Neal worked to rehabilitate downtown and revitalize neighborhoods. His predecessor, 36-year incumbent Edward Boland, a longtime pal of Tip O'Neill, essentially bequeathed him the House seat. Boland announced his retirement just before the filing deadline, and after Neal had traveled the district for a year. Unopposed in the Democratic primary, Neal won 80% in the general.

Neal has a generally liberal voting record but has favored enough moderate initiatives to separate himself from more liberal Massachusetts colleagues. He voted for the final version of welfare reform, the partial-birth abortion ban and the Defense of Marriage Act; he refused to support Bill Clinton's health care plan. On the issue of embryonic stem cell research, he reversed his earlier opposition. Neal serves on Ways and Means, where he voted for NAFTA and GATT and—after considerable hand wringing—for normal trade relations with China. But he opposed trade promotion authority and voted against the Iraq war resolution. Neal decries the complications of the tax code and has crusaded for repeal of the alternative minimum tax and its growing bite on middle-income taxpayers. He was first alerted to the problem by a local accountant; later he discovered that stock options had forced many workers at EMC Corporation, a Hopkinton-based software maker, into paying the AMT. Republicans have complicated the tax code to mask the impact of their changes, he contends. So far, tax-writers have punted rather than raise the hundreds of billions of dollars that would be required to "fix" the AMT. But, as he warns, the problem is not going away. He knows first-hand about Social Security: He and his younger sisters received monthly survivor benefits after both of his parents died when he was a teenager.

Neal took the lead for House Democrats on a popular proposal to clamp down on companies that incorporate in Bermuda and other offshore havens to avoid U.S. taxes. He gave the initiative an additional bite when he directed its fire at companies that moved offshore after September 11, terming it "The Corporate Patriot Enforcement Act." Neal showed a proclivity for making a point on behalf of futile causes when he called on House members to publicly reveal the details of pork-barrel projects that they embedded in highway legislation. In 2006, he forced a vote in the Budget Committee on President Bush's proposed budget; it lost, 39–0. Why did Neal do that? "To be a pain in the neck," he replied. Plus, he made the political point that not a single Republican would vote for the proposal.

Like many other Irish Catholic brethren over the years, Neal has encouraged American attempts at reconciliation in Northern Ireland, both as a city council member and in the House. He personally lobbied President Clinton to grant a visa for Gerry Adams of Sinn Fein to visit the U.S. In 2005, he urged Adams to disband the IRA "sooner rather than later" and he was optimistic about the prospect for peace in Ireland. At home, he has focused on the economic problems of Springfield, including a proposal to convert the abandoned Union Station into a multi-modal transportation hub.

Neal had serious primary challenges in 1990 and 1992, but won by satisfactory margins. Republicans have never mounted credible opposition; he last faced a GOP challenger in 1996. With his secure local seat, he is rising in seniority at Ways and Means, where the more senior Democrats are at least nine years older; he chairs the Select Revenue Measures Subcommittee, which handles many tax and tariff bills.

THIRD DISTRICT

Rep. Jim McGovern (D)

Elected 1996, 6th term; b. Nov. 20, 1959, Worcester; home, Worcester; American U., B.A. 1981, M.P.A. 1984; Catholic; married (Lisa).

Professional Career: Aide, U.S. Sen. George McGovern, 1977-80; Sr. Aide, U.S. Rep. Joseph Moakley, 1982-96.

DC Office: 438 CHOB, 20515, 202-225-6101; Fax: 202-225-5759; Web site: mcgovern.house.gov.

District Offices: Attleboro, 508-431-8025; Fall River, 508-677-0140; Marlborough, 508-460-9292; Worcester, 508-831-7356.

Committees: *Budget* (13th of 22 D). *Rules* (2d of 9 D): Rules & Organization of the House (Chmn.).

Group Ratings

	ADA	ACLU	AFS	LCV	ITIC	NTU	COC	ACU	CFG	FRC
2006	95	95	100	100	29	14	40	4	7	0
2005	100	—	100	100	—	17	35	0	3	8

National Journal Ratings

	2005 LIB	—	2005 CONS		2006 LIB	—	2006 CONS
Economic	94%	—	0%		91%	—	6%
Social	90%	—	9%		93%	—	6%
Foreign	96%	—	0%		92%	—	5%

Key Votes of the 109th Congress

1. Estate Tax Repeal	N	5. Limit Interstate Abortion	N	9. Build Border Fence	N
2. Limit CAFE Standards	N	6. Extend Patriot Act	N	10. CAFTA	N
3. FY06 Spending Curb	N	7. Bar Same Sex Marriage	N	11. Oppose Iraq Withdrawal	N
4. Drilling in ANWR	N	8. Stem Cell Research $	Y	12. Detainee Tribunals	N

Election Results

2006 general	Jim McGovern (D) .... unopposed		($705,491)
2006 primary	Jim McGovern (D) .... unopposed		
2004 general	Jim McGovern (D) 192,036	(71%)	($1,184,239)
	Ron Crews (R) 80,197	(29%)	($152,853)

Prior Winning Percentages: 2002 (100%); 2000 (100%); 1998 (57%); 1996 (53%)

The People		Race/Ethnic Origin	Ancestry	
Area size:	612 sq. mi.	86.2% White	Irish: 16.1%	Italian: 9.5%
Urban population:	93.4%	2.6% Black	English: 8.5%	
Rural population:	6.6%	3.2% Asian	**2004 Presidential Vote**	
Pop. 2000:	634,585	0.2% Native Am.	Kerry (D) 167,402	(59%)
Pop. 2005 (est):	658,865	0.0% Hawaiian	Bush (R) 112,957	(40%)
Median income:	$50,223	1.5% Two+ races	Other 3,667	(1%)
Poverty status:	9.0%	0.3% Other	**2000 Presidential Vote**	
Military veterans:	11.7%	6.0% Hispanic Origin	Gore (D) 153,044	(59%)
			Bush (R) 90,375	(35%)
			Other 17,711	(7%)
			Cook Partisan Voting Index: D +13	

Occupation	Blue collar: 20.6%	White collar: 65.5%	Gray collar: 13.8%

Worcester (its name still pronounced with a particularly pungent Massachusetts accent making it sound as if it had no *R*s), for more than 200 years has been one of the nation's centers of tinkering, contriving and inventing, even though it is one of the few active industrial cities not located on a river, lake or seacoast. In the mid-19th century, the city won renown as the valentine-making capital of the U.S. for its production of lavish valentines and greeting cards. Fifty years ago, Worcester's biggest industries were wire-making, textiles, grinding wheels and envelopes. It is where the birth control pill was invented and where Worcester native and Clark University professor Robert Goddard shot off experimental rockets before relieved locals saw him off to New Mexico.

In the 1970s and 1980s, electronics and computer firms sprouted along I-495—the circumferential highway 20 miles east of Worcester, as they had earlier around Route 128, closer to Boston. The high-tech boom brought prosperity, labor shortages, new residents and higher housing prices to central Massachusetts. Then, in the early 1990s, the minicomputer industry slumped, bringing a recession. But Worcester's ingenious entrepreneurs and skilled labor force hustled, and local leaders set up a Biotechnology Research Institute to draw on the city's nine colleges and the University of Massachusetts medical center to place the city back on course. Just as the city's economy has changed, so has its face, with a 78% increase in Asians, 55% increase in blacks and a 61% increase in Hispanics (mainly Puerto Ricans) in the 1990s. Overall, population declined by 20% between 1950 and 1980, but increased by 7% from 1980 to 2000 and another 2% since then, as the area attracted Hmong and Albanians as well as Africans, many fleeing Liberia after civil war. That rebound contrasts to nearby Springfield and Hartford, and placed Worcester as New England's third-largest city, behind Boston and Providence. Since 2000, Worcester County has been the fastest-growing in the state.

The 3d Congressional District of Massachusetts has Worcester as its largest city, but not its geographic center. A little more than half its people live in Worcester and a cluster of adjacent towns. The other population cluster is 60 miles away, in and around the old textile mill town of Fall River, east of Rhode Island. The two are connected by a string of towns which reaches almost to Buzzards Bay. In national elections since 1992 this district has been solidly Democratic. In recent Massachusetts governor elections, however, the district has been mixed. Worcester and Fall River (only a portion of which is in the district) voted by significant margins for Democrat Shannon O'Brien in 2002. But the Interstate 495 corridor and the towns northeast of Rhode Island gave even larger margins to Republican Mitt Romney. In 2006, Democrat Deval Patrick won by close to 3–1 margins in Worcester and Fall River and lost only a handful of towns here.

The congressman from the 3d District is Jim McGovern, a Democrat first elected in 1996. McGovern grew up in Worcester, where his parents owned a package store. He went to American University in Washington, and while in graduate school worked in the office of former South Dakota Senator George McGovern (no relation). He ran McGovern's 1984 campaign in the Massachusetts presidential primary, where he finished third with 21% of the vote, and nominated him at the San Francisco convention. After that he got a job in Boston Congressman Joe Moakley's office and became chief of staff as Moakley became chairman of the Rules Committee. McGovern got into the spotlight himself, leading a 1989 investigation of the murders of six Jesuits and two lay women in El Salvador, which led to a cutoff of aid. In 1994, he ran for the House and lost in the Democratic primary 38%-30%. In 1996 he ran again, this time with no primary opposition. In the general election, two-term Republican Congressman Peter Blute stressed his "independence" from the House leadership and attacked McGovern for liberal stands on abortion and Cuba. McGovern ran a humorous spot that asked, "If you wouldn't vote for Newt, why would you ever vote for Blute?" McGovern won 53%-45%.

With deft maneuvers reflecting his Capitol Hill experience, McGovern has positioned himself to become a power broker now that Democrats have regained their majority in the House. In 2001, the dying Moakley made a personal request to Minority Leader Dick Gephardt that McGovern get a seat on Rules, which schedules most legislation for the House floor; the next seat went to Florida's Alcee Hastings, a member of the Congressional Black Caucus, but McGovern got a commitment for the next available Democratic seat, with seniority over Hastings. On Rules, he immediately showed familiarity with House procedures. Following the defeat of ranking member Martin Frost of Texas in 2004, McGovern became the number-two Democrat behind 75-year-old Louise Slaughter of New York. In the majority for the first time, he said he gladly moved from "being a pain in the ass [in the minority] to more of an advocate for respect, inclusion, and fairness." But with the roles reversed, he showed a sharp partisan edge as he embraced parliamentary maneuvers that led to cries of outrage from House Republicans. He also took a seat on the Budget Committee. With his considerable leverage, he became a party leader on Iraq war strategy.

McGovern has a solid liberal voting record. He is a member of the Cuba Working Group, which has called for easing sanctions against Fidel Castro's regime. He has won bipartisan House votes to lift the travel ban to the island. He contends that the U.S. embargo has not achieved its goal of improving the human rights and economic situation in Cuba, and that only a change in policy—not continued sanctions—will improve living conditions and foment democratic reforms in Cuba. In December 2006, he was part of a congressional delegation to Cuba that concluded that Castro's death likely would not result in major changes on the island.

Although Republicans held this seat not long ago, they have given up on it. McGovern was unopposed in three of the past four elections.

FOURTH DISTRICT

Rep. Barney Frank (D)

Elected 1980, 14th term; b. Mar. 31, 1940, Bayonne, NJ; home, Newton; Harvard U., B.A. 1962, J.D. 1977; Jewish; single.

Elected Office: MA House of Reps., 1972-80.

Professional Career: Exec. Asst., Boston Mayor Kevin White, 1967-71; A.A., U.S. Rep. Michael Harrington, 1971-72; Teaching Fellow, Harvard JFK Schl. of Govt., 1978-80.

DC Office: 2252 RHOB, 20515, 202-225-5931; Fax: 202-225-0182; Web site: www.house.gov/frank.

District Offices: New Bedford, 508-999-6462; Newton, 617-332-3920; Taunton, 508-822-4796.

Committees: *Financial Services* (Chmn. of 37 D).

Group Ratings

	ADA	ACLU	AFS	LCV	ITIC	NTU	COC	ACU	CFG	FRC
2006	95	100	100	100	29	19	29	12	9	0
2005	100	—	100	94	—	19	33	0	7	0

National Journal Ratings

	2005 LIB	—	2005 CONS	2006 LIB	—	2006 CONS
Economic	94%	—	0%	90%	—	9%
Social	94%	—	5%	82%	—	17%
Foreign	81%	—	18%	92%	—	5%

Key Votes of the 109th Congress

1. Estate Tax Repeal	N	5. Limit Interstate Abortion	N	9. Build Border Fence	Y
2. Limit CAFE Standards	N	6. Extend Patriot Act	N	10. CAFTA	N
3. FY06 Spending Curb	N	7. Bar Same Sex Marriage	N	11. Oppose Iraq Withdrawal	N
4. Drilling in ANWR	N	8. Stem Cell Research $	Y	12. Detainee Tribunals	N

Election Results

2006 general	Barney Frank (D) .... unopposed			($1,159,692)
2006 primary	Barney Frank (D) .... unopposed			
2004 general	Barney Frank (D) 219,260	(78%)		($1,290,341)
	Charles Morse (I) 62,293	(22%)		($21,985)

Prior Winning Percentages: 2002 (100%); 2000 (75%); 1998 (100%); 1996 (72%); 1994 (100%); 1992 (68%); 1990 (66%); 1988 (70%); 1986 (89%); 1984 (74%); 1982 (60%); 1980 (52%)

The People		Race/Ethnic Origin	Ancestry	
Area size:	844 sq. mi.	87.9% White	Irish: 13.5%	Portuguese: 13.4%
Urban population:	88.2%	2.0% Black	English: 9.0%	
Rural population:	11.8%	3.2% Asian	**2004 Presidential Vote**	
Pop. 2000:	634,624	0.2% Native Am.	Kerry (D) 194,914	(65%)
Pop. 2005 (est):	636,916	0.0% Hawaiian	Bush (R) 99,878	(33%)
Median income:	$53,169	1.9% Two+ races	Other 3,502	(1%)
Poverty status:	8.4%	1.6% Other	**2000 Presidential Vote**	
Military veterans:	11.0%	3.3% Hispanic Origin	Gore (D) 178,354	(65%)
			Bush (R) 79,201	(29%)
			Other 18,067	(7%)
			Cook Partisan Voting Index: D +19	

Occupation	Blue collar: 19.2%	White collar: 67.6%	Gray collar: 13.2%

The political transformation of Massachusetts is nowhere better illustrated than in the Boston suburbs of Brookline and Newton. These were Yankee enclaves a century ago, with avenues built to resemble the sweep of Haussmann's Grand Boulevards in Paris, and villages of giant clapboard houses clustered within a few blocks of commuter railroad stations. Brookline, which celebrated its 300th anniversary in 2005, was where The Country Club (the very first one) was established in 1882, and where Joseph Kennedy, an Irish Catholic 20-something banker seeking respectability, moved his family in 1914. Brookline and Newton then were solidly Republican in politics, the political base of leading politicians like Christian Herter, governor of Massachusetts and U.S. secretary of state in the 1950s; as late as 1960, Brookline and Newton and adjacent wards of Boston were electing a Republican congressman. Then came the transformation, personified by the election in 1962 of Michael Dukakis at 29 to the Great and General Court (the legislature). As Massachusetts's university-educated classes became more liberal, as Brookline's and Newton's Jewish populations grew, and as young liberal-minded families refurbished the graceful old houses, these towns became Democratic bastions. Now there are an increasing number of Russian Jews and of Orthodox and Hasidic synagogues. Brookline and Newton, are part of the liberal heart of Massachusetts: They voted 73%-19% for Al Gore in 2000 and 77%-22% for John Kerry in 2004.

The 4th Congressional District of Massachusetts includes Brookline and Newton, which are the political home bases for its congressman, Barney Frank. Anchoring the hook-like northern tip of the district, they account for less than one-quarter of the district's votes. The shape results from successive redistrictings: In 1982, Frank's district was extended south to the old textile mill city of Fall River; in 1992, it lost much of Fall River and gained New Bedford, the great 19th century whaling port; in 2002, it kept New Bedford and regained most of Fall River. New Bedford and Fall River are close to the sea and New Bedford is proud of the Greek Revival architecture of its great whaling days, when it was one of the richest cities in the country; it stages a 25-hour reading of *Moby Dick* every January 3, the day that Ishmael and his friend Queequeg sailed out under the command of Captain Ahab. Today it is the center of the largest concentrations of Portuguese-Americans, many of them fishermen, who haul in groundfish and scallops. Fall River was famous for years as the home of Lizzie Borden, who supposedly killed her father and mother in 1892 with 40 and 41 whacks of an axe; today it's resisting a proposed liquefied natural gas port which seems unusually close to a built-up area. New Bedford and Fall River have long been working-class Democratic. Connecting the two sets of Democratic cities, sometimes by a corridor only a mile wide, is an attenuated series of towns—Wellesley, Dover, Sherborn, Millis, Norfolk, Sharon. There is a bit of most kinds of America here: high-income WASPy Wellesley, French-Canadian mill-worker Fall

River, Foxborough with its Patriots football stadium, Sharon with a middle-income Jewish population and countrified Dover. This is a very Democratic district, although a handful of the suburban towns voted for Republican Lieutenant Governor Kerry Healey for governor in 2006 over Democrat Deval Patrick.

The congressman from the 4th District is Barney Frank, chairman of the House Financial Services Committee and one of the intellectual and political leaders of the Democratic party in the House. Frank grew up in Bayonne, New Jersey, and went to Harvard, where he got to know local politicians as well as political scientists. In 1967, he went to work for newly-elected Boston Mayor Kevin White; in 1971, he went to Washington to work for Massachusetts Congressman Michael Harrington. In 1972, Frank was elected to the Massachusetts House from the Back Bay of Boston, in his school years still a fusty Republican bastion and then just starting to be a liberal singles neighborhood. In 1980, when Congressman Robert Drinan retired after Pope John Paul II commanded Jesuits to leave elective office, Frank moved to Brookline and ran in the 4th District. With a strong base in Brookline and Newton, he won. After redistricting threw him in with Republican incumbent Margaret Heckler in 1982, he beat her 60%-40%. He has been reelected by wide margins since.

In the House, Frank quickly gained a reputation as one of the smartest talkers and best debaters in the chamber—maybe one of the best of all time. Frank listens to others' arguments and engages them in his inimitable rapid-fire delivery. In the 2006 *Washingtonian* poll of staffers he was voted the brainiest, the funniest and the most eloquent member of the House. He is admired even by Republicans for his intellectual rigor and honesty; at the same time he is a wily political operator. He does not profess to be a political theoretician, though few in the House exceed him as such. "My job is to be the mediator between people who have policy ideas and public policy. My strength is to be able to understand policy ideas and decide how best to implement them. I am about the political process. I know the rules of the House as much as anybody. I am a wonk about how to get things done, more than about what to do." In his early years in the House, he worked hard, often behind the scenes, on many substantive issues. He worked on the immigration acts of 1986 and on the issue since, seeking to expand legal immigration, to allow HIV-positive people to enter the country, to bar states from excluding children of illegal aliens from school and to change the 1996 law that required mandatory deportation of immigrants convicted of a crime carrying a one-year sentence even if the offense occurred many years ago; this had been hurting Azorean and Cape Verdean immigrants in New Bedford. After Republicans won a majority of seats in the House, Frank started spending much time on the floor, pouncing on the new majority's mistakes, noting that it was not keeping its promises of fair treatment of the minority and criticizing its policies.

In 1999, after four years of Republican control, Frank became ranking minority member on the Housing Subcommittee of the Banking Committee; in 2003 he became ranking minority member on the full committee, renamed Financial Services, of which he became chairman in 2007. This committee has proved to be one of the less partisan committees in Congress, and Frank has worked with Republican members on many issues. He worked with Spencer Bachus, now ranking minority member, on debt relief for very poor countries. With the late Paul Gillmor he worked to prevent Wal-Mart from using industrial loan companies to get into the banking business; with characteristic attention to detail, he sought copies of Wal-Mart leases of space to banks when there was conflicting testimony about them. He mastered parts of the Banking Committee's jurisdiction with which he was unfamiliar—securities, corporate governance, accounting issues, insurance, flood insurance. The regulatory issues before the committee are complex, and heavily lobbied, the negative effects of bad decisions can be enormous (remember the savings and loan crisis?) and many issues do not break down on party lines; in that atmosphere, bipartisan cooperation may seem appropriate.

Unlike some Democrats who have chaired this committee—notably Wright Patman in the 1960s and 1970s—Frank acknowledges the efficiency and productivity of markets. "I think people may misunderstand what being a liberal means. I really do believe in the free market. You need inequality in the capitalist system, but we are at a point now where we are getting more inequality than is necessary for efficiency or socially helpful. The role of government should put some limits on that inequality, through raising the minimum wage, encouraging unions, providing public sector programs that help people go to college." He argues that the U.S. economy is at an "inflection point" where it is easier to create wealth than create jobs. During and after the 2006 election he spoke frequently about the need for a "grand bargain" between business and liberals. "Pro-growth policies are necessary, but . . . they are insufficient for improving the quality of life for most Americans." And pro-growth policies like free trade agreements and tax cuts, in his view, have tended to widen economic inequality and produce creative destruction which increases opposition to those very policies. His "grand bargain" would have Republicans accept an increased minimum wage, a tax increase on high earners, union certification as bargaining agents after obtaining signatures of a majority of workers rather than by secret ballot election. And it would have Democrats accept free trade agreements with labor and environmental standards meeting "minimal standards of civility" and continued trade promotion authority, accepting foreign direct investment in the U.S. without restriction and "controlling health care costs in a responsible way." "I want to get the people who have been concerned about equity to support growth policies and the people who have been chafing that we aren't doing enough for growth to support policies that provide equity." Of course not all this agenda would go through Frank's committee; this was more in the nature of a general strategy, one which Frank and perhaps Ways and Means Chairman Charles Rangel felt more comfortable with than did incoming Speaker Nancy Pelosi, and very large majorities of Republicans opposed the 2007 minimum wage and card check bills. But Frank can claim that he has already been carrying out his side of the grand bargain. He has supported many free trade agreements, though not CAFTA, and has trenchantly criticized and voted against farm subsidies backed by most Democrats. He argues that "employer-paid health care is a mistake," which "depresses wages"—a point made in George W. Bush's 2007 State of the Union speech.

Affordable housing has been a longtime Frank cause, and he has called the Bush administration policy of allowing old Section 8 units and others to go out of the subsidized inventory "the worst failure of this administration."

Long a supporter of the GSEs (government-sponsored enterprises) Fannie Mae and Freddie Mac, he joined committee chairman Michael Oxley in June 2004 in supporting higher funding for their regulator OFHEO and in September joined Oxley in seeking power to subpoena top Fannie executives. In May 2005 Oxley accepted Frank's amendment setting higher affordable housing goals and requiring the GSEs to contribute 5% of their after-tax income to an affordable housing fund. The Oxley-Frank measure replaced OFHEO with an independent agency outside of Treasury, provided looser limits on the GSEs' portfolios than the Bush administration version; it passed the committee in May 65–5, with Frank's amendment approved 53-17. In October 2005 Frank complained when House Republican leaders rejected the affordable housing provisions and limited the political activity of housing sponsors, many of them community agencies serving low earners. Frank offered an amendment to an appropriation in June 2006 to stop HUD from limiting the issuance of new vouchers to replace the lost Section 8 units; it was rejected on a 214-214 tie only after Republican leaders twisted arms. The Senate did not act on the GSE issue, and after the 2006 election Frank came forward with another version, with unexpectedly strict limits on the GSEs' portfolios, plus his affordable housing fund—his version of "getting the federal government back in the business of housing."

Frank has worked on a wide variety of other issues. He sponsored a predatory lending bill, modeled after a North Carolina law, in April 2005, with Tarheels Mel Watt and Brad Miller, and he sought out data showing discrimination against blacks on mortgage rates. With Oxley and Bachus, he sponsored a bill in March 2005 to require all U.S. bank regulators to take a unified position when negotiating with foreign regulators on the Basel accord new international capital standards scheduled for 2008. With Oxley he sponsored a bill in May 2005 to allow national banks to engage in real estate brokerage and management, a position opposed by Senate Banking Chairman Richard Shelby. With Oxley he got a provision in the 2006 budget resolution to merge the two FDIC insurance funds. He opposed the SEC regulation, opposed also by Massachusetts-based Fidelity, requiring mutual funds to have independent directors, and in April 2006 he cautioned during the Dubai Ports furor that it would be unwise to put too many limits on foreign direct investment in the United States.

Frank does not always opt for more regulation. In December 2006 he declined to sponsor any regulation on hedge funds and said he might hold hearings with no "predisposition one way or another." When it appeared that the 2003 Sarbanes-Oxley Act and especially its Section 404 were discouraging U.S. IPOs and imposing huge costs on small firms, Frank admitted there may be problems; he said he didn't think it needed "statutory adjustments," but promised hearings on IPOs and encouraged SEC Chairman Christopher Cox, a law school classmate as well as former House colleague, to come up with regulations to make the law "less burdensome." He and Cox had both voted for the 1995 law limiting securities class action lawsuits, which was passed over Bill Clinton's veto, and worked together to privatize the National Helium Reserve. Frank promised hearings on predatory lending and consumer credit bureaus, which might lead to more regulation, and he said he would seek to make it harder for non-financial companies (i.e., Wal-Mart) to own banks if the

FDIC doesn't extend its moratorium on the practice. Like many Democrats, Frank has been dismayed at the widening ratio between executives' and workers' pay, but he opposes having government set limits. He sponsored a bill in November 2005 requiring shareholder approval of public companies' executive compensation plans, with disclosure of performance targets for compensation and corporate jet use, plus recapture of bonuses that later financial results show weren't warranted. He criticized Cox when the SEC plan did not have shareholder approval and noted that Fannie Mae CEO (and Clinton administration OMB director) Franklin Raines was paid millions in bonuses based on accounting which Fannie later conceded was erroneous. "I don't think the government should be telling people what to pay. I think the shareholders should."

For all his professional accomplishments, Frank's personal life once threatened to end his career. In May 1987, in a seemingly casual answer to a reporter's question, Frank disclosed that he is gay. Then in August 1989, the conservative *Washington Times* reported that Frank had employed as a personal aide a male prostitute and convicted drug possessor, Steve Gobie, and let him live in his apartment. When faced with a scandal that threatened to end his career, Frank told the truth. He admitted paying Gobie, but was careful never to use official or campaign funds; he denied that he tolerated prostitution in his apartment and said he had thrown the man out when he suspected it was going on. Frank called on the ethics committee to investigate. It did and dismissed all but two minor charges. The committee recommended a reprimand, but not censure; Frank agreed in a contrite appearance before the House in July 1990 and the House voted 287-141 against censure. The vote for reprimand was 408-18. "I think members will agree that I have always had a reputation for honesty, not always tact or tolerance," Frank said to the House. That reputation was one reason he survived and has thrived in the House; his brains, liberal stands, hard work and constituency service helped him not only survive, but become overwhelmingly popular in the 4th District. In 1998, as the House debated the impeachment of Bill Clinton, Frank acknowledged that Clinton lied in his deposition in the Paula Jones case, but ridiculed the case against him. But he was harshly critical of Bill Clinton's last minute pardons and in February 2001 proposed a constitutional amendment to prevent the president from using the pardoning power from a month before the presidential election until inauguration day.

Frank has been the House's leading legislator on gay rights issues. One was the issue, raised in the 1992 campaign by Bill Clinton and not by Frank or by gay advocacy groups, of gays in the military. To the disappointment of many in the gay community, Frank admitted that allowing open homosexuals to serve in the military would not be accepted by most in Congress or the Pentagon. In the years since, Frank has criticized the military when the number of service members discharged for homosexuality increased, and he helped persuade Al Gore to come out against "Don't ask, Don't tell" in 1999. Frank and Republican Christopher Shays have sponsored a bill to prohibit employment discrimination on account of sexuality, which gained a surprising degree of support in the Republican House. He has long sponsored a bill to allow benefits for same-sex partners of federal employees.

Frank hailed the Massachusetts Supreme Judicial Court's decision in November 2003 that led to the legalization of same-sex marriage. But he was critical of San Francisco Mayor Gavin Newsom's promotion of what turned out to be illegal same-sex marriages there. "I was against pretend marriage," he explained later. It was "political hoopla with no gain." After George W. Bush's reelection victory and the passage of same-sex marriage bans in 11 states in November 2004, he reflected further, "The thing that agitated people were the mass weddings. It was a mistake in San Francisco, compounded by people in Oregon, New Mexico and New York. What it did was provoke a lot of fears. He created a sense there was chaos rather than give us a chance to show, as we have in Massachusetts, that this doesn't mean anything to anyone else." But he took satisfaction in the fact that the House fell far short in September 2004 of approving the Family Marriage Amendment.

Through all his work on national issues, Frank has not neglected the home front. He has worked especially hard on projects in Fall River and New Bedford. All of this seems to have paid off in the polls. In 2004 he was opposed by a former radio talk show host who claims that changes Frank made in the immigration laws in the 1980s allowed the legal entry of the 9/11 hijackers; Frank said that was nonsense and that they could and should have been barred under existing law. In the last weeks of the campaign Frank spent $350,000 on television—not because he was at risk of losing, but to give him more exposure should John Kerry be elected president and should he run for Kerry's Senate seat. Frank won his House race 78%-22%; he carried every city and town, including four towns which voted for George W. Bush. He had no opposition in 2006.

FIFTH DISTRICT
Vacant

Election Results

2006 general	Martin Meehan (D) .... unopposed			($452,780)
2006 primary	Martin Meehan (D) .... unopposed			
2004 general	Martin Meehan (D) 179,652	(67%)		($459,977)
	Thomas Tierney (R) 88,232	(33%)		($30,406)

The People		Race/Ethnic Origin	Ancestry	
Area size:	582 sq. mi.	79.7% White	Irish: 16.6%	Italian: 9.8%
Urban population:	93.5%	1.7% Black	English: 8.9%	
Rural population:	6.5%	5.2% Asian	**2004 Presidential Vote**	
Pop. 2000:	635,326	0.1% Native Am.	Kerry (D) 158,455	(57%)
Pop. 2005 (est):	657,896	0.0% Hawaiian	Bush (R) 114,874	(41%)
Median income:	$56,217	1.4% Two+ races	Other 3,813	(1%)
Poverty status:	8.9%	0.2% Other	**2000 Presidential Vote**	
Military veterans:	10.9%	11.6% Hispanic Origin	Gore (D) 145,277	(57%)
			Bush (R) 93,406	(36%)
			Other 18,433	(7%)
			Cook Partisan Voting Index: D +11	

Occupation   Blue collar: 20.9%   White collar: 66.9%   Gray collar: 12.1%

The Merrimack River Valley at the northern edge of Massachusetts has had an erratic history: High-tech boom, bust, boom, bust, boom. When Massachusetts was a kind of maritime republic in the 19th century, with its farmers struggling to scratch out a living from the stony soil, a few clever Yankees used their profits from the sea trade to try to tame the rapidly flowing Merrimack and build cotton-spinning mills. Creating the cities of Lowell and Lawrence, they built model dormitories and recreation programs for their women workers. This was the center of America's textile industry for more than a century, long after the maritime industry faded. But in the 1920s, the price of labor rose and newly-built mills in the Carolinas, much closer to the cotton supply, decimated the industry that Lawrence and Lowell built. Many residents—by then, rather elderly—waited forlornly for an upturn in the local economy.

It came eventually, largely due to an unexpected source. High-tech industry drove the growth, beginning in the 1960s around MIT, then moving out to the Route 128 ring road and then I-495, which passes through Lowell and Lawrence. Wang, headquartered in Lowell, grew spectacularly, and Senator Paul Tsongas—the local kid who made it big before his early death to cancer—spearheaded a national historic restoration of the old mill area. This was the Massachusetts miracle of the 1980s. Then came the bust: Wang's word processors and minicomputers slumped as businesses purchased personal computers and hooked them together in networks. But Lowell revived again. Its new immigrants—mostly from Cambodia and Puerto Rico—provide vitality and entrepreneurial creativity; the old Wang buildings are filled with health care, banking, telecommunications and Internet companies. Old mills have been converted to pricey condos with upscale owners.

The 5th Congressional District of Massachusetts includes Lawrence and Lowell, which along with next-door towns account for about two-thirds of the district's population. The remainder of the district is the high-tech corridor south on 495. The district also includes tony suburbs like the Revolutionary War battleground of Concord where the Minutemen stood their ground in 1775, the mountains along the New Hampshire state line and the small towns west of Lowell that once hosted Fort Devens; the base closed in 1996, though part of it survives as a training site for New England Army Reserve and National Guard soldiers. Except for Lowell and Lawrence, it is ancestrally Yankee Republican. It is culturally liberal, with pockets of big wealth, and trended toward the Democrats in the early 1970s. Back then, the 5th produced two Democratic candidates who would later run for president: John Kerry, who lost the general election in 1972, and Tsongas, who won the seat two years later. In the 1980s and early 1990s, amid the high-tech boom, it went Republican in national and even statewide elections: A kind of Baja New Hampshire. In 1992, it gave Bill Clinton his lowest percentage in the state, while a big vote went to high-tech pioneer Ross Perot. But its cultural liberalism has moved it toward Democrats, though not as far as some Massachusetts districts: Al Gore carried the 5th District by 57%-36%, John Kerry by 57%-41%.

The 5th District seat was temporarily vacant after Democrat Martin Meehan resigned on July 1, 2007, to become chancellor of the University of Massachusetts's Lowell campus. Meehan, who was in his eighth term, had voiced interest in running statewide and had accrued a campaign bank account of $4.9 million. But the state's two senators gave no indication that they would soon depart, and Meehan had turned down opportunities to run for governor. Some Democratic leaders grumbled that that they wanted him to spend some of his money to help elect candidates to the House. As a member of Congress, Meehan's most significant cause was campaign finance reform; he co-sponsored the landmark proposal that was enacted in 2002 but that the Supreme Court subsequently limited.

In this comfortably Democratic district, Niki Tsongas, the winner of the September 4, 2007, Democratic special primary election, was expected to be Meehan's successor. Tsongas, the widow of former Senator Paul Tsongas, won 36% in a five-way contest to finish ahead of runner-up Eileen Donoghue, a Lowell city councilor who won 31%. Tsongas, whose husband held this House seat from 1975 to 1979, was endorsed by EMILY's List and had a substantial fundraising advantage over Republican nominee James Ogonowski, a retired Air Force lieutenant colonel who won 89% in the Republican special primary election.

The special general election was scheduled for October 16.

SIXTH DISTRICT

Rep. John Tierney (D)

Elected 1996, 6th term; b. Sept. 18, 1951, Salem; home, Salem; Salem St. U., B.A. 1973, Suffolk U., J.D. 1976; no religious affiliation; married (Patrice).

Professional Career: Practicing atty., 1976-96.

DC Office: 2238 RHOB, 20515, 202-225-8020; Fax: 202-225-5915; Web site: www.house.gov/tierney.

District Offices: Lynn, 781-595-7375; Peabody, 978-531-1669.

Committees: *Education & Labor* (9th of 27 D): Higher Education, Lifelong Learning & Competitiveness; Health, Employment, Labor & Pensions. *Oversight & Government Reform* (9th of 23 D): National Security & Foreign Affairs (Chmn.); Domestic Policy. *Permanent Select Committee on Intelligence* (8th of 12 D): Oversight & Investigations.

Group Ratings

	ADA	ACLU	AFS	LCV	ITIC	NTU	COC	ACU	CFG	FRC
2006	100	100	100	100	29	17	33	8	9	0
2005	100	—	100	100	—	19	30	0	7	0

National Journal Ratings

	2005 LIB	—	2005 CONS		2006 LIB	—	2006 CONS
Economic	92%	—	6%		91%	—	6%
Social	92%	—	8%		78%	—	21%
Foreign	96%	—	0%		92%	—	5%

Key Votes of the 109th Congress

1. Estate Tax Repeal	N	5. Limit Interstate Abortion	N	9. Build Border Fence	N
2. Limit CAFE Standards	N	6. Extend Patriot Act	N	10. CAFTA	N
3. FY06 Spending Curb	N	7. Bar Same Sex Marriage	N	11. Oppose Iraq Withdrawal	N
4. Drilling in ANWR	N	8. Stem Cell Research $	Y	12. Detainee Tribunals	N

Election Results

2006 general	John Tierney (D) 168,056	(70%)	($497,514)
	Richard Barton (R) 72,997	(30%)	($65,688)
2006 primary	John Tierney (D) .... unopposed		
2004 general	John Tierney (D) 213,458	(70%)	($415,117)
	Stephen O'Malley (R) 91,597	(30%)	($48,633)

Prior Winning Percentages: 2002 (68%); 2000 (71%); 1998 (55%); 1996 (48%)

The People		Race/Ethnic Origin	Ancestry	
Area size:	805 sq. mi.	89.8% White	Irish: 18.6%	Italian: 13.1%
Urban population:	94.9%	1.9% Black	English: 10.6%	
Rural population:	5.1%	2.5% Asian	**2004 Presidential Vote**	
Pop. 2000:	636,554	0.1% Native Am.	Kerry (D) 185,264	(58%)
Pop. 2005 (est):	641,197	0.0% Hawaiian	Bush (R) 130,924	(41%)
Median income:	$57,826	1.1% Two+ races	Other 3,970	(1%)
Poverty status:	6.3%	0.2% Other	**2000 Presidential Vote**	
Military veterans:	12.6%	4.4% Hispanic Origin	Gore (D) 172,840	(57%)
			Bush (R) 107,415	(36%)
			Other 20,760	(7%)
			Cook Partisan Voting Index: D +11	
Occupation	Blue collar: 17.2%	White collar: 69.7%	Gray collar: 13.1%	

The North Shore of Massachusetts Bay has a number of times been at the leading edge of the nation's economy. In 1640, the Saugus Iron Works was built here—the beginning of American heavy industry. When Europe's great powers were convulsed in international war from 1792 to 1815, American ship owners suddenly became the richest in the world, and traders from Boston and Salem accumulated the capital needed to build textile mills and railroads and to finance much of the American industrial revolution. From the small port of Salem, ships left for China, bringing back porcelain and artifacts, which helped change American styles forever. Salem, first settled in 1626, had the nation's first millionaire, Elias Hasket Derby; in 1900, it was the richest city per capita in the nation. Today, the North Shore is a quiet place, from Boston Harbor north to the mouth of the Merrimack River, a collection of ethnic factory towns from Lynn on up through next-door Peabody (once one of the world's great leather producers with over 100 tanneries) to the former ship-building Newburyport, alternating with the high-income enclaves of Marblehead with its yachts and Beverly with its estates, and artsy Rockport. Salem's House of the Seven Gables is a popular site; built in 1668, it inspired the novel by Nathaniel Hawthorne and is the oldest surviving wooden mansion in New England. The Salem witch trials are probably the town's most famous legacy; more than two centuries later, they inspired Arthur Miller's play *The Crucible*, which used the trials as an allegory for the hearings of Senator Joseph McCarthy. Moviegoers will recognize the fishing town of Gloucester as the homeport of the *Andrea Gail*, the 72-foot swordfishing boat whose tragic plight was dramatized in the novel and film *The Perfect Storm*. Although the ports were hard hit by overfishing of mackerel and herring in the 1970s and cod in the 1990s, pleasure boating has surged. Lynn is the district's largest city and its General Electric jet engine plant is the largest employer, though with about one-third as many jobs as the 13,000 at its peak in the late 1970s and with payrolls threatened by offset deals to produce some engines in the countries purchasing them.

The 6th Congressional District of Massachusetts includes the North Shore from Saugus and Lynn northward, plus towns and cities inland west to Burlington. Its high-income Yankee towns were historically liberal Republican, while Lynn, Salem, Peabody and the Merrimack mill towns are still Irish working-class Democratic. The Hanscom Air Force Base in Bedford survived the base closing review in 2005, though hopes for additional high-tech aerospace research were dashed. The 6th typically has been a Democratic district since the 1960s, though only marginally in the 1980s and in the early 1990s. While this is the site of the original gerrymander—named after Elbridge Gerry—the current 6th District boundaries are hardly grotesque by current national standards.

The congressman from the 6th District is John Tierney, a Democrat first elected in 1996. Tierney grew up in Salem in modest circumstances; he worked his way through Salem State College and Suffolk University Law School as a janitor on the night shift and clerk in a Boston law firm. For nearly 20 years, he practiced law in Salem. In 1994, he spied a political opening and ran for Congress. The incumbent, Peter Torkildsen, was a Republican elected in 1992 by beating veteran Democrat Nicholas Mavroules, who had been indicted for tax evasion and bribery. But in Republican 1994, Torkildsen won 51%-47%. In 1996, Tierney ran again. His ads, along with the AFL-CIO's, assailed Newt Gingrich and Republican Medicare "cuts." He called for health care insurance for children and criticized Torkildsen for not bringing enough defense dollars to the district. Torkildsen spent $1.1 million, while keeping his promise to accept no PAC money. Tierney held his $776,000 spending mostly until the end. The result was one of the closest races in the country. After several recounts, which stretched into December, Tierney won by 371 votes.

In the House, Tierney has been a solid ally of the unions on the renamed Education and Labor Committee and a consistent liberal vote. His work on that panel has included support for alternative paths to teaching, schools and communities that are gang and drug-free, and strengthened vocational education. He has been a leader among Democrats seeking to reduce prescription drug costs for senior citizens. Tierney has worked with Bill Delahunt and Republican Jim Saxton to support a ban on big fishing trawlers from Georges Bank and he has raised questions with federal regulators about security procedures at the nearby Seabrook nuclear plant in New Hampshire. He is well-connected to Speaker Nancy Pelosi: For several years, his top aide was her daughter Christine.

Torkildsen challenged Tierney in a 1998 rubber match, but Tierney won 55%-42%. He has faced token opposition since then. He has been mentioned as a possible contender in the event of a Senate opening. In 2007, he joined the Intelligence Committee and also became chairman of the National Security and Foreign Affairs Subcommittee at the Oversight and Government Reform panel.

SEVENTH DISTRICT

Rep. Edward Markey (D)

Elected 1976, 16th full term; b. July 11, 1946, Malden; home, Malden; Boston Col., B.A. 1968, J.D. 1972; Catholic; married (Susan Blumenthal).

Military Career: Army Reserves, 1968-73.

Elected Office: MA House of Reps., 1973-76.

DC Office: 2108 RHOB, 20515, 202-225-2836; Fax: 202-226-0092; Web site: markey.house.gov.

District Offices: Framingham, 508-875-2900; Medford, 781-396-2900.

Committees: *Energy & Commerce* (3d of 31 D): Telecommunications & the Internet (Chmn.); Energy & Air Quality; Commerce, Trade & Consumer Protection. *Homeland Security* (3d of 19 D): Transportation Security & Infrastructure Protection. *Natural Resources* (16th of 27 D). *Select Committee on Energy Independence and Global Warming* (Chmn. of 9 D).

Group Ratings

	ADA	ACLU	AFS	LCV	ITIC	NTU	COC	ACU	CFG	FRC
2006	100	100	100	100	14	18	20	4	8	0
2005	100	—	100	100	—	18	30	0	7	0

National Journal Ratings

	2005 LIB	—	2005 CONS		2006 LIB	—	2006 CONS
Economic	94%	—	0%		91%	—	6%
Social	97%	—	2%		96%	—	3%
Foreign	91%	—	7%		95%	—	0%

Key Votes of the 109th Congress

1. Estate Tax Repeal	N	5. Limit Interstate Abortion	N	9. Build Border Fence	N
2. Limit CAFE Standards	N	6. Extend Patriot Act	N	10. CAFTA	N
3. FY06 Spending Curb	N	7. Bar Same Sex Marriage	N	11. Oppose Iraq Withdrawal	N
4. Drilling in ANWR	N	8. Stem Cell Research $	Y	12. Detainee Tribunals	N

Election Results

2006 general	Edward Markey (D) .... unopposed		($913,564)
2006 primary	Edward Markey (D) .... unopposed		
2004 general	Edward Markey (D) 202,399	(74%)	($1,181,782)
	Kenneth G. Chase (R) 60,334	(22%)	($62,022)
	James Hall (I) 12,139	(4%)	

Prior Winning Percentages: 2002 (100%); 2000 (100%); 1998 (71%); 1996 (70%); 1994 (64%); 1992 (62%); 1990 (100%); 1988 (100%); 1986 (100%); 1984 (71%); 1982 (78%); 1980 (100%); 1978 (85%); 1976 (77%)

The People		Race/Ethnic Origin	Ancestry	
Area size:	188 sq. mi.	83.5% White	Irish: 18.5%	Italian: 16.9%
Urban population:	99.5%	3.3% Black	English: 7.5%	
Rural population:	0.5%	5.7% Asian	**2004 Presidential Vote**	
Pop. 2000:	634,287	0.1% Native Am.	Kerry (D) 192,133	(66%)
Pop. 2005 (est):	613,339	0.0% Hawaiian	Bush (R) 96,374	(33%)
Median income:	$56,110	1.9% Two+ races	Other 3,880	(1%)
Poverty status:	6.7%	0.5% Other	**2000 Presidential Vote**	
Military veterans:	10.5%	4.8% Hispanic Origin	Gore (D) 181,417	(64%)
			Bush (R) 82,250	(29%)
			Other 20,891	(7%)
			Cook Partisan Voting Index: D +19	

Occupation   Blue collar: 14.3%   White collar: 72.9%   Gray collar: 12.8%

The Yankee Protestants and Irish Catholics who settled Massachusetts arrived by boat, the Yankees to a cold stony land with a few Indians, the Irish to a crowded city with Yankees who seemed no more welcoming. The Yankees whose ancestors once farmed the soil had, by the early 20th century, founded suburbs filled with solid brick and white frame houses, furnished in Early American furniture. As the years went on, their local public schools were emptied as young people with children moved out, and attendance at Protestant churches went down. The Irish, for decades heavily concentrated in the crowded wards of Boston, started moving out into the Yankee suburbs 50 years ago. There were other ethnic groups here and there (Jews, Italians, French-Canadians) but the major conflict—fought out in neighborhood playgrounds, in school committee meetings and not least in political campaigns—was between Protestant Yankee Republicans and Catholic Irish Democrats.

The 7th Congressional District of Massachusetts is made up of Boston's northern and western suburbs, where vestiges of this conflict can still be seen. Geographically, it forms an arc around Boston, starting with the clapboard beach towns of Winthrop and Revere just beyond Logan Airport, going north as far as working-class Woburn (where Charles Goodyear developed the art of vulcanizing rubber) and west as far as modest-income Natick and Framingham. Framingham is home to many Brazilian immigrants who began arriving after World War II, when Boston-based mining companies began extracting mica from an area near the Brazilian city of Governador Valadares. The 7th also includes the university towns of Medford, home of Tufts University, and Waltham, home of Brandeis University, the patriot town of Lexington, where Minute Men fired the shots heard 'round the world in 1775, and high-income Lincoln and Weston. Many of these towns were Yankee Republican through the 1950s, but by the late 1960s they were solidly Democratic; the high-tech suburbs trended Republican again in the 1980s but swung against Republicans in the 1990s. The highest income areas seem to run across the grain of their ethnic experience: Weston, with many Catholics, sometimes votes Republican (though it went 58%-41% for John Kerry in 2004), while WASPy Lincoln has been liberal Democratic since it voted for George McGovern in 1972. But in state politics, the suburbanites of the 7th District have been less liberal: This district was close in the gubernatorial election of 1998 and again in 2002, when Republican Mitt Romney won 51%-49%, but Democrat Deval Patrick carried every town and city in the district in 2006.

The congressman in the 7th District is Edward Markey, first elected in 1976 at age 30, and now dean of the Massachusetts House delegation. He grew up in Malden, where his father was a milkman; he went to Malden Catholic High, Boston College and Boston College law school, then immediately to the state House, at 26. In 1976, he ran for the House and won a 12-candidate primary with 22% of the vote; he had never been to Washington. Now he ranks number 13 in House seniority, and in February 2007 became the 12th current member to have served more than half his life in Congress.

In his first years in the House, Markey made his name as a fierce opponent of nuclear power plants and in the early 1980s was a leading political crusader for the nuclear freeze. In 1984, he announced he was running for the Senate seat being vacated after one term by Paul Tsongas; but he withdrew from the race, which was won by then-Lieutenant Governor John Kerry. One reason he may have withdrawn is that seniority—and Speaker Tip O'Neill—put him in a position to be a serious legislator in the House from early on, and he has long since become one of the House's most legislatively productive and creative members. With O'Neill's help, he got on the Commerce Committee; impressed by the high-tech boom around Route 128, he joined the old Communications Subcommittee early. Then, after only eight years in the House, he became chairman of the Energy Conservation and Power Subcommittee; after the 1986 election, with help from Chairman John Dingell, who liked aggressive and loyal younger Democrats, Markey became chairman of the Telecommunications Subcommittee. This is one of the plum positions in the House, with fabulous possibilities for campaign fundraising, and with subject matter that is intellectually more demanding (and, in lobbying terms, more fiercely contested) than almost anything else in Congress. He has been the lead Democrat on, and since 2007 once again the chairman of, this subcommittee ever since.

Markey has been a major shaper of public policy, often working with Republicans, often coming up with original initiatives, knowledgeable about the workings of these industries and inclined often toward deregulation, but also casting himself as the defender of consumers. He combined his penchant for regulation with political shrewdness to produce the 1992 cable TV re-regulation bill on which both houses overrode George H. W. Bush's veto—the only bill passed over his veto in his four-year term. Markey's influence was not greatly reduced when he became ranking minority member; bills in these areas are hard to pass without bipartisan consensus, and he was in a key position to create or withhold it. He was a major player in the passage of the landmark Telecommunications Act of 1996.

Markey was less successful in opposing the Tauzin-Dingell bill to revise the 1996 act by allowing the Bell phone companies—Verizon, SBC, BellSouth and Qwest—to offer broadband services without opening up their lines to competitors, including the CLECs which came into existence after the 1996 law and first soared and then thudded on the stock market. He and Republican ally Chris Cannon were defeated in a rare parliamentary vote in February 2002. Markey continued to press for digital television, seeking to force the FCC to require cable companies to carry digital TV before the required date of 2007. He and John Dingell pressed in 2005 to have the government pay for the $75 converter boxes which will be required on old sets after digital television becomes universal in February 2009.

On the big telecom issues of 2005 and 2006, Markey found himself in the minority. He favored allowing regional Bell and satellite companies to compete with cable companies locally (and cable companies compete with others nationally) in providing broadband and other Internet services, but only with a "build-out" requirement that new entrants must serve all video customers in a geographic areas; he favored "net neutrality," which would prohibit Internet carriers from charging higher fees to big-volume users like Google, Yahoo, Amazon and eBay. "If we don't protect the openness of the Internet for entrepreneurial activity, we're ruining a wonderful model for low-barrier entry, innovation and job creation. Once they start making money by leveraging that bottleneck position in the marketplace, will a future Congress really stare them down and take that revenue stream away?" Markey lost a subcommittee net neutrality vote in April 2006 27–4 and lost on a similar amendment on the floor in June, 269-152. The House passed the bill, sponsored by Chairman Joe Barton and Democrat Bobby Rush, 321-101. But there was no agreement with the Senate.

Markey promised to press his views as chairman in 2007. He bypassed the chairmanship of the full Resources Committee (as he had given up the ranking minority member position on it in 2001) in order to retain the Telecommunications chairmanship; despite his seniority, he ranks behind Chairman John Dingell and Henry Waxman on the full Energy and Commerce Committee. By remaining at the head on Telecom, he blocked Rick Boucher, who opposes net neutrality and build-out requirements; but was willing to leave Boucher, who represents a coal-producing district, as chairman of the Energy and Air Quality Subcommittee. But Markey may be in a position to sidestep Boucher and Dingell on one air quality issue, carbon emissions. Speaker Nancy Pelosi appointed Markey chairman of a select committee on climate change. Under pressure from Dingell, she announced it would not have authority to propose legislation, but she gave Markey a July deadline on recommendations.

There may be some irony here, since the energy source producing the least in carbon emissions—zero—is nuclear power, of which Markey has long been a critic and a proponent of tougher regulation. In November 2001, he sponsored a bill to require that guards at nuclear plants be federal employees; in a March 2002 report, he pointed out that the NRC doesn't require plant guards to be U.S. citizens and limits its background criminal checks to the U.S. In another report, he pointed out that the number of security guards at nuclear facilities declined 40% between 1992 and 2001. Markey has a gift for memorable phrases. "We have a 'loose nuke' problem right here at home," he said in May 2002, because some 1,500 types of radioactive material had been lost in five years and only half traced down; he estimated that the loose material, put together, could create a "dirty bomb." In June 2002, he called for a permanent end to the testing of nuclear weapons. In March 2006 he attacked an Energy Department program as "a reckless and dangerous boondoggle" to increase nuclear energy production here and abroad. He was one of the House's leading opponents of exempting India from the Nuclear Nonproliferation Act. He passed an amendment saying that the United States should urge the IAEA to rule that nations withdrawing from the Nonproliferation Treaty must return nuclear materials. Markey was one of three Massachusetts House members to vote for the Iraq war resolution in October 2002. By 2004 he said he regretted the vote and he sponsored a bill to bar the CIA from "extraordinary renditions"—turning terrorists to be interrogated by countries that use torture.

In April 2005 his and Mike Castle's amendment to give localities vetoes over liquefied natural gas facility construction was defeated 237-194. On other energy issues, Markey has pressed unsuccessfully for higher CAFE auto mileage standards and for windfall taxes on oil. He lost on mileage standards in committee in 2005 and 2006 by 36-10 and 36-17; on the floor he lost 254-177 in April 2005. He proposed a bill to stop the favorable treatment of SUVs under the mileage standards (they're classified as light trucks, and indeed the SUV category seems to have emerged as a response to the CAFE regulations). In November 2005 he sponsored a windfall tax on oil when prices are above $60 per barrel and he sought a reduction in federal royalties on oil and gas when prices rise. He has waged a battle to force oil and gas companies to pay increased royalties when prices rise in the case of contracts negotiated in 1998 and 1999 by the Clinton administration, in which Clinton administration negotiators inadvertently or negligently failed to seek such provisions.

From his seat on the Homeland Security Committee, Markey has worked hard on air cargo security issues; he pointed out that while passenger luggage is x-rayed, commercial cargo went unscreened on passenger planes. In 2003, his amendment to require screening of all air cargo passed the House easily, but was opposed by the Bush administration and went nowhere in the Senate. A similar amendment was rejected by the House in 2004. His amendment for 100% screening of maritime cargo for both density and radiation was defeated in committee; similar measures to inspect all cargo on commercial planes were also defeated in committee. But in January 2007, with Democrats in the majority, these measures were included in the first bill passed by the House implementing the recommendations of the 9/11 Commission and the final version also reflected Markey's efforts to require chlorine and other hazardous gases to be shipped by truck or rail around rather than in urban areas. He succeeded in forcing some changes in nuclear plant safety procedures: force-on-force exercises every three years; a prohibition on using Wackenhut, which provides safety for many plants, as the adversary force in them; an upgrade of the Design Basis Threat. In response to a TSA relaxation of rules, Markey and Joe Crowley got a Homeland Security subcommittee in April 2006 to reimpose the ban on sharp blades on commercial planes: so much for nail clippers, and some more serious threats as well. And he has been pressing for increased funding of the Metropolitan Medical Response System.

Other Markey causes include financial privacy—he and Republican Joe Barton got a provision into the financial services deregulation—and de-monopolizing the electric power industry. He and Republican Joe Pitts pushed through committee in March 2006 a bill requiring that cellphone numbers be unpublished. He has sponsored a bill for FTC regulation of the buying and selling of personal information. The IRS, prompted by Markey, issued a Tax Guidance letter in December 2005 requiring taxpayer consent before tax records are sent for preparation in other countries, where private protections are often weaker. But his attempt to allow states' more stringent protections of privacy to prevail lost 222-198.

Markey has weighed in on all manner of issues. He called for a CDC investigation of the effect of electronic media on children and on hearing loss from portable music players. He opposed the FDA approval of Ketek, a prescription drug, and charged it was an abuse of the accelerated approval process. He has pressed for vast increases in low-income heating funding. He persuaded Armed Services Chairman Duncan Hunter to stop the practice by which military pay was cut for some of those wounded in combat. He has opposed oil drilling in the Arctic National Wildlife Refuge and has a bill to declare it a wilderness area. He has pressed for federal regulation of amusement parks. Perhaps most momentously for most Americans, he and Fred Upton introduced a bill which became law in August 2005, extending daylight savings time by four weeks a year.

Markey has made a couple of runs at the Senate, both involving John Kerry. In 1984 he was one of several Democrats who started running for the Senate seat being vacated by Paul Tsongas; Kerry was another. Kerry stayed in the race, and won the seat; Markey bowed out, and ran for the House again, after several other Democrats were off and running for the seat. But with help from his campaign manager, Mary Beth Cahill, he beat the one who stayed in, state legislator Sam Rotondi, by a 54%-41% margin—his closest call since he was first elected in 1976. Fast forward to fall 2003, when Kerry's presidential campaign was faltering. At the suggestion of Edward Kennedy, Kerry named Cahill as his campaign manager and Markey, who had already endorsed Kerry, went to work to persuade colleagues in the House not to endorse anyone, especially Howard Dean, until the voters in Iowa and New Hampshire had a chance to speak. Markey predicted, correctly, that Dean would fade and Kerry would rally to victory, and he was mostly successful in keeping House members off the Dean team. Markey supported Kerry actively in the winter primaries and in October 2004 he spent $300,000 on ads in the Boston media market trumpeting his work against nuclear terrorism and, oddly, his support back in the days of the Cold War of the nuclear freeze. Congressman Barney Frank of the 4th District, similarly unthreatened by opposition for reelection, also put up ads in October. Both obviously had some interest in the Senate seat. But Kerry's defeat and his subsequent withdrawal meant that there would be no opening—as there usually isn't in hyperpolitical Massachusetts. The last open Senate race before 1984 was in 1966, when Leverett Saltonstall, born in 1892, retired. Technically, there was an open seat in 1962, but that was reserved for Edward Kennedy. The last open seat before that was in 1944, when John Kerry was an infant and Edward Kennedy a child.

EIGHTH DISTRICT

Rep. Michael Capuano (D)

Elected 1998, 5th term; b. Jan. 9, 1952, Somerville; home, Somerville; Dartmouth Col., B.A. 1973, Boston Col., J.D. 1977; Catholic; married (Barbara).

Elected Office: Somerville Alderman Ward 5, 1977-79; Somerville Alderman-At-Large, 1985-89; Somerville Mayor, 1989-98.

Professional Career: Chief Legal Cnsl., MA Legislature Taxation Cmte., 1978-84; Practicing atty., 1984-90.

DC Office: 1530 LHOB, 20515, 202-225-5111; Fax: 202-225-9322; Web site: www.house.gov/capuano.

District Offices: Cambridge, 617-621-6208.

Committees: *Financial Services* (13th of 37 D): Oversight & Investigations; Capital Markets, Insurance & Government Sponsored Enterprises. *House Administration* (3d of 6 D). *Transportation & Infrastructure* (17th of 41 D): Highways & Transit; Water Resources & Environment; Aviation.

Group Ratings

	ADA	ACLU	AFS	LCV	ITIC	NTU	COC	ACU	CFG	FRC
2006	90	100	100	100	43	14	40	8	11	0
2005	95	—	100	94	—	16	37	4	7	0

National Journal Ratings

	2005 LIB	—	2005 CONS	2006 LIB	—	2006 CONS
Economic	85%	—	15%	83%	—	16%
Social	87%	—	12%	88%	—	11%
Foreign	91%	—	7%	83%	—	14%

Key Votes of the 109th Congress

1. Estate Tax Repeal	N	5. Limit Interstate Abortion	N	9. Build Border Fence	Y
2. Limit CAFE Standards	N	6. Extend Patriot Act	N	10. CAFTA	N
3. FY06 Spending Curb	N	7. Bar Same Sex Marriage	N	11. Oppose Iraq Withdrawal	N
4. Drilling in ANWR	N	8. Stem Cell Research $	Y	12. Detainee Tribunals	N

Election Results

2006 general	Michael Capuano (D) 125,515	(91%)	($626,795)
	Laura Garza (SW) 12,449	(9%)	
2006 primary	Michael Capuano (D) .... unopposed		
2004 general	Michael Capuano (D) .... unopposed		($953,342)

Prior Winning Percentages: 2002 (100%); 2000 (100%); 1998 (82%)

The People		Race/Ethnic Origin	Ancestry	
Area size:	92 sq. mi.	48.9% White	Irish: 9.9%	Italian: 7.3%
Urban population:	100.0%	21.9% Black	West Indian: 5.2%	
Rural population:	0.0%	8.1% Asian	**2004 Presidential Vote**	
Pop. 2000:	634,835	0.2% Native Am.	Kerry (D) 168,264	(79%)
Pop. 2005 (est):	603,883	0.1% Hawaiian	Bush (R) 40,885	(19%)
Median income:	$39,300	3.5% Two+ races	Other 3,683	(2%)
Poverty status:	19.9%	1.5% Other	**2000 Presidential Vote**	
Military veterans:	5.5%	15.9% Hispanic Origin	Gore (D) 142,500	(73%)
			Bush (R) 28,903	(15%)
			Other 23,374	(12%)
			Cook Partisan Voting Index: D +33	

Occupation	Blue collar: 12.4%	White collar: 70.6%	Gray collar: 17.0%

The "Hub of the Solar System" is what the elder Oliver Wendell Holmes called the Massachusetts State House in the 19th century, though over time, his statement has come to be remembered as referring to Boston as the "Hub of the Universe." Either way, this most political of cities often has been the focal point of essential moments in American history. These streets, originally laid out as 17th century cowpaths, are where Samuel Adams and Paul Revere plotted revolution, where the abolitionist movement helped ignite the Civil War and are the sites of rallies and headquarters of the various Kennedy campaigns. Today's Boston is a different city from the Boston of John Kennedy's time. Boston then was a gray city with no new buildings and dust on every windowsill; the sky was dark with pollution and the air was thick with ancient Yankee and Irish animosity. The old office buildings were full of Yankees seeking safe investments for their antique family fortunes; the State House and City Hall were full of Irishmen, scampering after good patronage jobs and regaling each other with political battle stories. Today that Boston is mostly gone. The new skyscrapers are full of well-educated venture capitalists, lawyers and management consultants, many working for high-tech companies radiating from Cambridge out into the countryside. Of the roughly 200 U.S. cities with more than 160,000 people, only four (Boulder, Madison, San Jose and Stamford) have a larger share of residents with college degrees than does Boston. Most of the city's neighborhoods have changed. Minorities and young singles increasingly populate the central city. The city's population is down from 801,000 in 1950 to 560,000 in 2005; more than 80% of people in the metropolitan area live in the suburbs.

A long generation ago, students from suburbs across the country who were exploring Boston from their dormitories and campuses felt they were pawing through the living remnants of 1920s America, a quaint place where people called traffic circles "rotaries" and milk shakes "frappes." Massachusetts has since changed, and nowhere more than in Cambridge. As universities and high tech and biotech have become driving forces of economic growth, Cambridge has gone glitzy, with trendy restaurants and high-priced hotels, boutiques and upscale condominiums; the Central Square retains some of its edginess. Greater Boston may well have the heaviest concentration of graduate students and post-graduate hangers-on of any major city, and this graduate student proletariat's world is centered on Cambridge, with outposts in lower-income Somerville, Boston's tonier Back Bay, plus funky Allston and more family-oriented Brighton near Harvard's Business School.

These communities are part of Massachusetts's 8th Congressional District, a district rich with historic sites, from the Paul Revere house in the North End to the frigate *U.S.S. Constitution* in the Charlestown docks. The district, with MIT and the software concentration in Cambridge's once downscale Lechmere Square, is one of the high-tech capitals of America. The 8th includes all of

Cambridge, Somerville and economically revived Chelsea and many Boston neighborhoods—newly upscale East Boston around Logan Airport, Brighton and the Back Bay, Fenway, Mattapan, Mission Hill, the South End. It shares Hyde Park, Roxbury, Dorchester and Jamaica Plain with the neighboring 9th District. For the first time in its history, whites are a minority of Boston's population. As they replace the many Irish and Italians who left in the 1970s because of court-ordered busing in the schools, Hispanics have caused a population boom in Chelsea and in Dorchester, which annually celebrates one of the nation's largest Caribbean festivals. This is by far the most Democratic district in Massachusetts.

The congressman from the 8th District is Michael Capuano, the winner of a 10-candidate brawl in the 1998 primary who has been safe since then. It has been said that over the last 60-odd years this district has been represented alternately by townies and Kennedys: James Michael Curley, the scampish five-term mayor of Boston and one-term governor; followed by John F. Kennedy in 1946, then from 1952, Tip O'Neill, the most successful House speaker of this half-century; succeeded on his retirement in 1986 by Joe Kennedy; and now Capuano. He was born and raised in Somerville; his paternal grandfather emigrated from Italy, and his father was the first Italian-American elected official in Somerville; his mother is the granddaughter of Irish immigrants. Capuano graduated from Dartmouth and Boston College Law School. He returned to Somerville to raise his family, practice law and get into politics. By day, he worked for the legislature's Joint Committee on Taxation and practiced law; in off-hours, he served as alderman in the 5th Ward, like his father before him. He was elected alderman-at-large from 1985-89, then won election five times as the city's mayor. For decades an Irish and Italian town, Somerville now attracts many grad students and yuppies. Capuano seems to have been the right politician for this mix, with deep Somerville roots and a penchant for innovation and reform. So he had a solid base to run for the 8th District seat when Joe Kennedy announced that he wouldn't seek re-election. In a 10-candidate field, Capuano led with 23%, with former Boston Mayor (1983-93) Ray Flynn the runner-up at 17%.

In the House, Capuano is well to the left on the national political spectrum, though relatively centrist within the Massachusetts delegation: For same-sex marriage, against the partial-birth abortion ban and opposed to the flag-burning amendment. He sponsored a proposal to expand federal terrorism risk insurance coverage to include group life insurance; the Financial Services Committee, on which he serves, approved a modified version. On the Transportation Committee, he got his share of goodies in the 2005 highway law, including funding for the North Washington Street Bridge near North Station plus several rapid-transit extensions.

Capuano has not been shy about moving beyond local politics. When Catholic bishops across the nation said in 2004 that they would deny communion to John Kerry because of his support for abortion, Capuano replied that all Catholics should vote their conscience. He was a cofounder of the Congressional Caucus on Sudan, and traveled to the region in February 2006 in support of United Nations peacekeeping forces. Even before Democrats won back the House, Nancy Pelosi identified Capuano as somebody who could take an assignment and quietly get the job done without posing a threat to some old-style ways of doing business. She assigned him to lead the effort to rewrite the Caucus rules, including those surrounding gifts and financial disclosure, just after the *Boston Globe* reported that his December 2005 corporate-sponsored trip to Brazil was one of the most expensive that year. And, following the 2006 election, Pelosi tapped him to take charge of the myriad tasks in the transition to the majority. In many ways, it was a rocky exercise; with Pelosi, he backed John Murtha's ill-fated challenge to Steny Hoyer for Majority Leader. Some of the rules changes had to be rewritten, and his task to revise ethics enforcement was deferred until months later. "There are no axes out, no blacklist," he said. "That is not the way we are going to approach things." He conceded that many tasks were daunting and "disjointed" and that he had a lot to learn, but—in the style of Tip O'Neill—he emphasized inclusion and reform.

Since 1998 Capuano has not faced major-party opposition in either primary or general elections.

NINTH DISTRICT

Rep. Stephen Lynch (D)

Elected Oct. 2001, 3d full term; b. Mar. 31, 1955, Boston; home, South Boston; Wentworth Inst., B.S. 1988, Boston Col. Schl. of Law, J.D. 1991, Harvard U. JFK Schl. of Gov., M.A. 1998; Catholic; married (Margaret).

Elected Office: MA House of Reps., 1994-96; MA Senate, 1996-2001.

Professional Career: Structural ironworker, 1973-91; Practicing atty., 1991-2001.

DC Office: 221 CHOB, 20515, 202-225-8273; Fax: 202-225-3984; Web site: www.house.gov/lynch.

District Offices: Boston, 617-428-2000; Brockton, 508-586-5555.

Committees: *Financial Services* (18th of 37 D): Oversight & Investigations; Housing & Community Opportunity; Capital Markets, Insurance & Government Sponsored Enterprises. *Oversight & Government Reform* (12th of 23 D): National Security & Foreign Affairs; Federal Workforce, Postal Service & the District of Columbia.

Group Ratings

	ADA	ACLU	AFS	LCV	ITIC	NTU	COC	ACU	CFG	FRC
2006	90	76	100	100	29	11	27	20	5	28
2005	90	—	100	94	—	11	37	12	5	46

National Journal Ratings

	2005 LIB	—	2005 CONS		2006 LIB	—	2006 CONS
Economic	75%	—	25%		83%	—	16%
Social	69%	—	31%		68%	—	31%
Foreign	71%	—	29%		64%	—	35%

Key Votes of the 109th Congress

1. Estate Tax Repeal	N	5. Limit Interstate Abortion	Y	9. Build Border Fence	Y
2. Limit CAFE Standards	N	6. Extend Patriot Act	N	10. CAFTA	N
3. FY06 Spending Curb	N	7. Bar Same Sex Marriage	N	11. Oppose Iraq Withdrawal	Y
4. Drilling in ANWR	N	8. Stem Cell Research $	Y	12. Detainee Tribunals	N

Election Results

2006 general	Stephen Lynch (D)	169,420	(78%)	($868,163)
	Jack Robinson (R)	47,114	(22%)	($138,092)
2006 primary	Stephen Lynch (D)	75,323	(77%)	
	Philip Dunkelbarger (D)	22,048	(23%)	
2004 general	Stephen Lynch (D)	unopposed		($591,797)

Prior Winning Percentages: 2002 (100%); 2001 (66%)

The People		Race/Ethnic Origin	Ancestry	
Area size:	319 sq. mi.	79.3% White	Irish: 23.2%	Italian: 10.3%
Urban population:	98.4%	8.1% Black	English: 7.0%	
Rural population:	1.6%	3.7% Asian	**2004 Presidential Vote**	
Pop. 2000:	634,062	0.2% Native Am.	Kerry (D) 188,439	(63%)
Pop. 2005 (est):	630,745	0.0% Hawaiian	Bush (R) 106,734	(36%)
Median income:	$55,407	2.4% Two+ races	Other 3,378	(1%)
Poverty status:	7.5%	1.8% Other	**2000 Presidential Vote**	
Military veterans:	11.6%	4.6% Hispanic Origin	Gore (D) 167,059	(60%)
			Bush (R) 93,529	(33%)
			Other 19,051	(7%)
			Cook Partisan Voting Index: D +15	

Occupation   Blue collar: 17.3%   White collar: 68.9%   Gray collar: 13.7%

The Irish remain the dominant political tribe in Boston and in Massachusetts, though even in South Boston, long the center of Irish Boston, vestiges of the old Irish neighborhoods are starting to gentrify. Southie's influence endures in the memory of two Irish Democrats who represented the area for all but two years from the Great Depression to the start of the 21st century. The first was John McCormack, an old-style backroom dealmaker who served as House Speaker during the 1960s, when he arguably had passed his political prime; the second was Joe Moakley, a close pal of Tip O'Neill, who got his former seat on the Rules Committee and chaired the panel before Democrats lost their House majority in 1994.

The 9th Congressional District, historically anchored in Boston, has followed the move of the Irish to the suburbs. Today, less than one-third of its residents are in Boston, mostly in still-Irish areas of South Boston, Hyde Park (shared with the 8th) and West Roxbury. Completion of the transformational Big Dig highway construction, with a new tunnel under Boston Harbor, has spurred economic development along the waterfront, including office buildings, hotels, condominiums and a huge new convention center—which, in turn, have reduced some of the parochialism in South Boston. At long last, the ugly Central Artery, the North-South expressway that for five decades divided the city, has been moved underground and traffic moves far more efficiently, though with huge cost over-runs driving the Big Dig bill to $15 billion. In the traditionally Italian North End, the result has been likened to taking down the Berlin Wall, encouraging residents to walk the Freedom Trail to downtown. The 9th district also includes much of Beacon Hill, including the gold-domed State House facing Boston Common. From there, the 9th heads west to comfortable suburbs of Needham and Medfield and southeast to Braintree, ancestral home of the presidential Adamses, and Brockton, the old shoe manufacturing town. Ethnically, this remains a heavily Irish congressional district, with Southie as home to an annual St. Patrick's Day parade preceded by a political breakfast/roast that is a must-attend for state politicians. Only the neighboring 10th District has more residents of Irish ancestry—further evidence of the Irish move out of Boston to the far suburbs.

The congressman from the 9th District is Stephen Lynch, who won a special election in October 2001 to replace Joe Moakley, who was beloved by many House Democrats as a link between the party's old and new generations. Lynch grew up in Boston's housing projects and took pride in succeeding by the old ethnic codes of hard work, family loyalty and personal determination. After graduating from South Boston High School, he joined his father in working full-time as an ironworker while attending Wentworth Institute; eventually, he became the youngest president ever of the 2,000-member Local 7 of the Ironworkers union. After a fall on the job cut short his work on the iron, he graduated from Boston College law school and opened a legal practice representing working people. In 1994, he was elected to the state House. Fourteen months later, he won a special election for a seat in the state Senate.

Lynch built a political base in South Boston and had strong union ties, advantages that led him to seek the seat when Moakley announced in February 2001 that he would not seek reelection; Moakley died in May. Lynch was one of several Democrats who had expressed interest in the race. The most prominent was Max Kennedy, son of Robert and Ethel Kennedy, but his campaign never gathered any traction. When Kennedy bowed out, Lynch became the frontrunner. He stumbled following the *Boston Globe*'s revelations of his student loan defaults years earlier, plus a tax lien that was resolved in 1998; he also had been twice arrested two decades earlier, once for striking an anti-American student demonstrator and the other for smoking marijuana at a concert. Three other state senators opposed Lynch: Cheryl Jacques, Brian Joyce, and Marc Pacheco. The strongest foe was Jacques, who is openly gay and had support from EMILY's List and other national feminist groups, which criticized Lynch's anti-abortion views. But her switch to opposing capital punishment stirred controversy. Joyce, the most prolific fundraiser of the four, sought to rally suburban support. Pacheco vied with Jacques for the liberal vote, and was endorsed by teachers' unions. Moakley's two brothers, who wielded much influence, endorsed Lynch. Despite the Boston-based terror attacks on the September 11 primary day, Governor Jane Swift decided not to postpone balloting; Lynch won with 39%, to 29% for Jacques. In the anti-climactic general election five weeks later, he defeated another state senator, Jo Ann Sprague. 66%-33%.

In the House, Lynch votes roughly in the middle of the Democratic Caucus but has had the most conservative voting record in the Massachusetts delegation, especially on cultural issues. "That's like being called the slowest of the Kenyans in the marathon," he once quipped to the *Boston Herald*. Initially he turned his attention to security, both at the nation's airports and in the war on terrorism. In 2006, he helped to secure $25 million for rail security in the homeland security spending bill. He was one of three Massachusetts House members to vote for the Iraq war resolution, and joined the first congressional delegation to Iraq after the overthrow of Saddam Hussein; later, he criticized contractors' "disgraceful" abuse of war funding. In June 2006, he was one of 42 House Democrats to vote for a Republican resolution backing President Bush's policies in Iraq. He was the only Massachusetts Democrat to vote for federal intervention on behalf of Terri Schiavo. He showed unexpected support for gay-rights causes, developing a political alliance with Barney Frank to educate himself. At the March 2005 hearings on steroid use in baseball, he criticized the game's officials for a policy that "facilitates steroid abuse" and he threatened additional congressional action. At home, he established the Cushing House, a residential drug-rehab center for adolescents.

Lynch has been reelected without difficulty. In 2006, he was challenged by Jack E. Robinson, who had run two statewide races. Robinson supported Bush's Social Security reform plan and cuts in capital gains and income taxes, and called for dividing Iraq into three territories. Lynch had little reason for concern and won 78%-22%.

TENTH DISTRICT

Rep. Bill Delahunt (D)

Elected 1996, 6th term; b. July 18, 1941, Quincy; home, Quincy; Middlebury Col., B.A. 1963, Boston Col., J.D. 1967; Catholic; divorced.

Military Career: Coast Guard, 1963; Coast Guard Reserves, 1963-71.

Elected Office: Quincy City Cncl., 1971; MA House of Reps., 1972-75.

Professional Career: Practicing atty., 1967-75; Asst. Clerk, Norfolk Superior Court, 1969-71; Norfolk Cnty. Dist. Atty., 1975-96.

DC Office: 2454 RHOB, 20515, 202-225-3111; Fax: 202-225-5658; Web site: www.house.gov/delahunt.

District Offices: Hyannis, 508-771-0666; Quincy, 617-770-3700.

Committees: *Foreign Affairs* (9th of 27 D): International Organizations, Human Rights & Oversight (Chmn.); Western Hemisphere. *Judiciary* (10th of 23 D): Crime, Terrorism & Homeland Security; Commercial & Administrative Law; Immigration, Citizenship, Refugees, Border Security & International Law. *Standards of Official Conduct* (5th of 5 D).

Group Ratings

	ADA	ACLU	AFS	LCV	ITIC	NTU	COC	ACU	CFG	FRC
2006	90	95	86	92	43	16	53	12	9	0
2005	85	—	100	78	—	15	35	0	5	8

National Journal Ratings

	2005 LIB	—	2005 CONS		2006 LIB	—	2006 CONS
Economic	91%	—	9%		74%	—	23%
Social	83%	—	16%		86%	—	13%
Foreign	91%	—	7%		75%	—	23%

Key Votes of the 109th Congress

1. Estate Tax Repeal	N	5. Limit Interstate Abortion	N	9. Build Border Fence	Y
2. Limit CAFE Standards	N	6. Extend Patriot Act	N	10. CAFTA	N
3. FY06 Spending Curb	N	7. Bar Same Sex Marriage	N	11. Oppose Iraq Withdrawal	N
4. Drilling in ANWR	N	8. Stem Cell Research $	Y	12. Detainee Tribunals	N

Election Results

2006 general	Bill Delahunt (D)	171,812	(64%)	($974,422)
	Jeffrey Beatty (R)	78,439	(29%)	($107,734)
	Peter White (I)	16,808	(6%)	($4,709)
2006 primary	Bill Delahunt (D)	unopposed		
2004 general	Bill Delahunt (D)	222,013	(66%)	($843,755)
	Michael Jones (R)	114,879	(34%)	($262,798)

Prior Winning Percentages: 2002 (69%); 2000 (74%); 1998 (70%); 1996 (54%)

The People		Race/Ethnic Origin	Ancestry	
Area size:	2,969 sq. mi.	92.2% White	Irish: 23.9%	English: 11.9%
Urban population:	92.2%	1.5% Black	Italian: 9.9%	
Rural population:	7.8%	2.7% Asian	**2004 Presidential Vote**	
Pop. 2000:	635,901	0.3% Native Am.	Kerry (D) 194,092	(56%)
Pop. 2005 (est):	661,826	0.0% Hawaiian	Bush (R) 151,209	(43%)
Median income:	$51,928	1.3% Two+ races	Other 3,910	(1%)
Poverty status:	5.9%	0.6% Other	**2000 Presidential Vote**	
Military veterans:	15.1%	1.3% Hispanic Origin	Gore (D) 175,426	(54%)
			Bush (R) 124,956	(39%)
			Other 22,722	(7%)
			Cook Partisan Voting Index: D + 9	

Occupation	Blue collar: 18.1%	White collar: 66.7%	Gray collar: 15.2%

The South Shore of Massachusetts Bay, from Boston southward to Plymouth and then down Cape Cod (there is a lot of dispute about which way is up and down on the Cape), is Massachusetts's oldest-settled territory. The Pilgrims landed here at Plymouth Rock in 1620; this stony land was farmed by John Adams's father, who was anything but the aristocrat some later members of the Adams family would have had you believe. Daniel Webster lived in the South Shore town of Marshfield, today a high-income suburb of Boston far out on the usually clogged Southeast Expressway. Joseph P. Kennedy used to summer with his young family on Nantasket Beach in Hull, before moving out of Massachusetts when the Yankees wouldn't let them into their beach club in Cohasset in the 1920s; but the Kennedys continue to summer at their Hyannis Port compound on the Cape. Provincetown, at the tip of the Cape, is still a fishing port, one of the major gay vacation areas in the country; the islands of Martha's Vineyard and Nantucket, rich whaling ports in the early 19th century, are favored summer resorts for the liberal rich of Boston, New York and Washington. Half the nation's cranberry growers are clustered among the bogs along Cape Cod Bay. But the Cape is also filled with retirees who enjoy the beauty and quiet pace. To some dismay, this is the fastest-growing part of Massachusetts; the Cape's Barnstable County grew 19% in the 1990s, though the pace has slowed considerably since then.

The 10th Congressional District of Massachusetts follows the South Shore from Quincy (pronounced *quin*zee), with its large Asian population, to the Cape. It juts inland almost, but not quite to Brockton, and includes Martha's Vineyard and Nantucket, where the glitterati have generated a "not in my backyard" fury over a proposed windmill farm in the nearby channel waters. The South Shore and the Cape were once exclusively Protestant and Yankee, but in the Massachusetts way they have changed over the years, with Irish and Italian surnames as common as Yankee ones (this is the nation's most heavily Irish congressional district), and the descendants of Portuguese-Azorean fishermen have fanned out into the countryside. Liberal politics, well established on the Vineyard and Nantucket, have spread inland as well. Although Republican Mitt Romney carried the area in 2002, the South Shore is generally Democratic territory; in 2004 George W. Bush fell well short of John Kerry there.

The congressman from the 10th District is Bill Delahunt, a Democrat first elected in 1996. Delahunt is a lifelong resident of Quincy at the northern tip of the district; he graduated from Middlebury College and Boston College Law School and served in the Coast Guard. He practiced law and served on the Quincy Council. In 1972, he was elected to the state House; Governor Michael Dukakis in 1975 appointed him district attorney of Norfolk County, a job that Delahunt held for two decades. He ran for the House in 1996 when 24-year incumbent Gerry Studds retired, and faced serious primary competition from former state Representative Philip Johnston and self-financed environmentalist Ian Bowles. The initial results showed 38% each for Delahunt and Johnston, with Johnston ahead by 266 votes; a recount declared Johnston still ahead by 175 votes. But Delahunt sued, and on October 4, a judge ruled that more than 900 punch card votes in Weymouth had not been properly tabulated. In shades of another election challenge four years later, the judge ordered a recount of every ballot with an indentation, dimple or other mark: Only in this district and in 14 counties in Texas had dimpled chads ever been counted as votes in the U.S. until the Broward, Palm Beach and Miami-Dade County canvassing boards started counting them in November 2000. On October 10, Delahunt was declared the winner by 108 votes, even as Johnston was being hailed at a Quincy rally by Ted Kennedy and Hillary Rodham Clinton. Johnston called the result a "travesty," and Delahunt had less than a month to campaign for the general against conservative state House Minority Leader Edward Teague. Both ran million-dollar campaigns. Eight years earlier, George H.

W. Bush carried this district over Governor Michael Dukakis. But reaction here to the new Republican majority in the House was hostile; Delahunt won 54%-42%.

Delahunt has been an active legislator with a very liberal voting record, and has kept a pledge to wear Cape Cod ties in the House and hand them out to colleagues of both parties. As the father of an adopted daughter who escaped Vietnam in the 1975 Operation Babylift, he has written laws to ease international adoptions. His positions on abortion offer a window on Massachusetts's move to the left: In 1974 as a state legislator he called *Roe v. Wade* "a tragic decision," but he switched to a pro-abortion rights position before running for the House and then voted against the partial-birth abortion ban as a congressman. His experience with contested elections made him an enthusiast for abolishing the Electoral College. With Illinois Republican Ray LaHood, he filed the Innocence Protection Act, which includes federal funding to the states for DNA testing of the accused; the House passed the measure, 393-14, and it became law in 2004. On the Judiciary Committee, he wants to increase the number of temporary visas, partly to boost the seasonal work force on the Cape.

Delahunt has generated controversy with his hands-on diplomatic efforts. He has met frequently with Venezuela president Hugo Chavez, partly with the goal of securing cheaper oil for low-income constituents; critics accuse him of supporting a despot. Delahunt also joined several congressional delegations to visit Cuba—to encourage democratic reforms, he has said. He wants to remove travel restrictions, and may now be in a position to do something about it: In the majority, he became chairman of the International Organizations, Human Rights and Oversight Subcommittee on Foreign Affairs. Speaker Nancy Pelosi named him to the ethics committee.

Delahunt has easily won his reelection bids, with no need to count dimpled chads. On Capitol Hill, he is the fourth tenant in a house with the better-known Senators Chuck Schumer and Richard Durbin plus the landlord, Representative George Miller. He shares the living room with Schumer in conditions best described as ramshackle, and he reportedly provides much of the fraternal humor.

★ MICHIGAN ★

When Alexis de Tocqueville on his travels to America in 1831 wanted to visit the frontier, he went to the Michigan Territory. He traveled in a boat across Lake Erie, as other Frenchmen had for nearly 200 years. French explorers and missionaries sailed the Great Lakes and slapped their version of Indian names on the landscape, which is why Michigan's *ch* is pronounced like *sh* and why Mackinac is pronounced with a silent final *c* (but Michiganians don't carry it to extremes: Detroit ends with a robust English *oit*). Michigan was not effectively occupied by the United States until 1796, and was bypassed in the initial westward rush into Ohio, Indiana and Illinois. Tocqueville was still able to travel through virgin woods occupied by Indian tribes, but only barely; in the 1830s Michigan was settled in a rush by Yankee migrants from Upstate New York, who cut down trees and built farms and neat New Englandish towns complete with schools and colleges. Politically, Michigan was full of Yankee reformers who hated slavery, manned the Underground Railroad, promoted temperance and in 1855 gave Michigan a constitution that banned (as it does to this day) capital punishment. Michigan was one of the birthplaces of the Republican Party, which was founded in Jackson in 1854 (Ripon, Wisconsin, also stakes a claim as the party's birthplace) and swept the state in the elections later that year. Until 1929, Michigan was one of the most Republican states in the nation.

After the Civil War, Michigan developed an industrial economy. Its Lower Peninsula was mostly covered with trees, and lumber was the first boom industry on which Michigan overrelied; forests were clear-cut or swept by blazes like the 1881 fire that burned out half the Thumb. In the late 1800s, huge copper deposits were discovered on the Keweenaw Peninsula, which juts from the Upper Peninsula into icy Lake Superior; immigrants from Italy and Finland, Cornwall and Croatia came to work in the mines. Then came the auto industry. A combination of accident and shrewdness, of bankers willing to finance auto startups and the prickly genius of Henry Ford, ensured that America's fastest-growing industry for the first 30 years of the 20th century was centered in Michigan. Detroit became a boomtown—the nation's fastest-growing major metropolitan area after Los Angeles—zooming from 426,000 in 1900 to 2.2 million in 1930 (it was 4.2 million in 2000). The auto industry drew labor from the Outstate Michigan, from southern Ontario and from the farms of Ohio and Indiana. It attracted Poles and Italians, Hungarians and Belgians, Greeks and Jews. During World War II and after, it brought whites from the Kentucky and Tennessee mountains and

Miles
0   20   40

The Almanac of American Politics.
National Journal

SEE INSET FOR DETAIL ON 9, 11-14.

Congressional district boundaries were first effective for 2002.

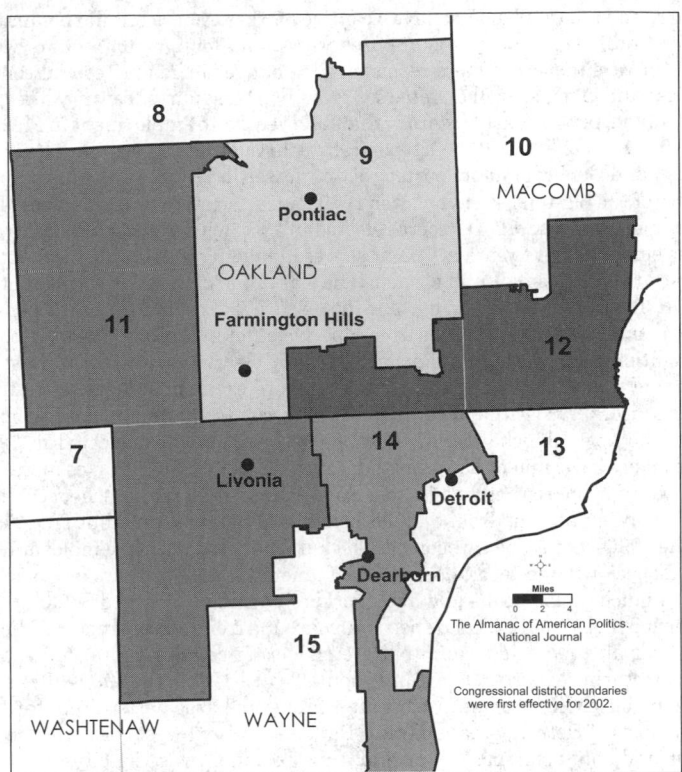

blacks from Alabama and Mississippi. This influx of a polyglot proletariat eventually changed Michigan's politics. The catalyst was the Great Depression of the 1930s and the company managers' desire to use machines efficiently, treating employees as extensions of machines and with great distrust. The results were the 1937 sit-down strikes organized by the new United Auto Workers (UAW); management and labor fought, sometimes literally, for pieces of what both sides feared was a shrinking pie. The UAW won and organized most of the companies after Democratic Governor Frank Murphy refused to send in troops to break the illegal strikes. In the years that followed, autoworkers became a heavily Democratic voting bloc.

Michigan politics became a kind of class warfare, conducted with a bitterness that split families and neighbors. The union mostly won, because demographics benefited the Democrats: autoworkers and post-1900 immigrants produced more children than did Outstate Yankees or management. After Walter Reuther's election as UAW president in 1947, voters elected young, liberal G. Mennen Williams governor in 1948. By 1954, the Democrats, closely tied to the UAW, seemed to have become the natural majority in the state. As growth continued, economic issues became less bitter; by the early 1960s, the class-warfare atmosphere had dissipated. A Republican former auto executive, George Romney, was narrowly elected governor in 1962, and Henry Ford II joined Reuther in backing Lyndon B. Johnson in 1964. Romney and his successor, William Milliken, accepted the welfare-state policies endorsed by the UAW leadership and the Democrats. The state government was one of the nation's most generous, and not just to the poor and the unemployed: it supported one of the nation's most distinguished and extensive higher education systems, built state parks and recreation areas, and pioneered efforts to end racial discrimination.

This system, which had seemed eternal, came crashing down with the collapse of the domestic auto industry after the oil shocks of the 1970s. Union-management relations had been static since 1941, and there had been no major technological changes in American autos since the automatic transmission in 1940. Michigan incomes had grown as Americans grew more affluent; the one-car household became the two-car household, and consumers enjoyed the tail fins and chrome of new car styling. But in 1979, this big-unit economy went bust. It became startlingly clear that the Big

Three automakers and the UAW did not have a captive market, Americans did not have to buy a new full-sized American-made car every two or three years, and foreign competitors were producing better and cheaper cars that were more responsive to changes in gas prices and consumer preference. Big business and labor, so well adapted for growth in the quarter century after World War II, proved poorly adapted for the quarter century that followed. Auto employment in Michigan fell from 437,000 in October 1978 to 289,000 in October 1982. Chrysler nearly went bankrupt, Ford was in financial distress, and General Motors posted its first losses in years.

The collapse of the big-unit economy after 1979 forced the state to experiment. The first to try was Governor James Blanchard, a Democrat elected in 1982 with a record of supporting big units. His major achievement in eight years in Congress was managing the Chrysler bailout in the House. Blanchard worked to build a small-unit economy; he was proud of his efforts to stimulate high-skill, capital-intensive, flexible manufacturing, and he used $750 million of state pension funds as venture capital for manufacturers of items from tape drives for microcomputers to fiberglass coffins. Dodging his traditional labor allies, Blanchard made it clear that Michigan must learn how to nurture growth and that workers, instead of seeking more vacation and earlier retirement, would have to hustle and work harder than ever before. The second experiment came from John Engler, the Republican who beat Blanchard in 1990 and was resoundingly reelected in 1994 and 1998. Engler believed in less government activism and industrial policy; he cut taxes more than 30 times; welfare rolls were cut by more than two-thirds. Engler pressed for public school choice and charter schools, changing state pensions from defined benefits to defined contributions. Throughout the second half of the 1990s, the economy boomed. The auto industry, once an employer of thousands of low-skill workers, became high-tech; the number of unionized auto workers fell to 250,000 in 2000, but jobs required much higher skills and auto workers' earnings averaged $60,000. With the auto companies requiring high standards and speedy turnaround from subcontractors, Michigan became the home of almost all the nation's auto parts engineering centers and of much of the nation's large-scale manufacturing experts. Michigan's population rose 7% in the 1990s after staying even in the 1980s; median household incomes rose 5% after inflation. Large parts of the state—the western and northern suburbs of Detroit, greater Grand Rapids, the northwest corner of the Upper Peninsula—were unmistakably booming. The one glaring exception was the city of Detroit. Detroit's population fell to 951,000 in 2000, almost exactly half its 1,849,000 in 1950. Starting with the riot of 1967, crime rates in Detroit were enormously high for 25 years, and much of the city simply vanished—houses abandoned or burned down, commercial frontage with nearly 100% vacancy rates, the downtown a beleaguered fortress surrounded by blasted-out square miles. Detroit began rebounding in the 1990s and after: crime and welfare rolls were down, new stadiums and gambling casinos, even some new housing, were built downtown and old theaters refurbished.

But since 2000 Michigan has been in economic trouble again. The first signs came in 2000, when the state's unemployment rate rose above the national average for almost the first time in seven years; employment peaked at 4.93 million in January 2001. But while most of the rest of the country recovered from the brief 2001 recession, Michigan hasn't. Employment rose only to 4.74 million in September 2005 and sagged to 4.72 million in December 2006: 200,000 below that five years before. Unemployment spiked to 7.2% in December 2006. The number of unemployed more than doubled from February 2000 (165,000) to December 2006 (366,000). The problem can be pinpointed: the woes of the Big Three auto companies. From 2000 to 2007, the state lost 275,000 manufacturing jobs—a 26% loss. The losses came as the Big Three, facing big losses, squeezed their Tier 1 and Tier 2 subcontractors hard; many of these companies, which had grown more supple and adaptive in the 1990s, cut their payrolls and some went bankrupt—notably Delphi, a spinoff from General Motors. Then as SUV sales plummeted, the Big Three started cutting jobs as well. In 2006 GM announced a 35,000 cutback; Ford announced it was closing 14 factories; Ford and Chrysler started wringing concessions on work rules from the United Auto Workers. The auto manufacturing sector accounted for just 5% of Michigan's jobs in 2006, but produced 75% of job losses. With Ford facing record losses and GM and Chrysler restructuring in early 2007, more seemed in store. Governor Jennifer Granholm, a Democrat elected by a narrow margin in 2002, encouraged "cool cities" developments and arranged for tax breaks for new Big Three facilities, but was unable to rescue the economy from the damage done by the implosion of the Big Three; still she was reelected by a robust 56%-42% margin in 2006 over former Amway CEO Dick DeVos, who called for lower taxes and a more business-friendly climate. She blamed the state's economic woes on the Bush administration's unwillingness to do anything for the auto industry and on foreign trade agreements.

Michigan's unemployment since 2000 has not been nearly as high as in the early 1980s, or in the recessions of 1970 and 1958. But that's partly because a lot of people, as in the early 1980s, aren't sticking around. Michigan's rate of net internal migration was a negative 3.8% between 2000 and 2006—higher than any other state except Louisiana, New York and Massachusetts. Educated young adults in particular seem to be leaving; Michigan has a higher than average percentage of high school graduates but lower than average percentage of college grads. Nor has it attracted large numbers of immigrants; the population is 4% Hispanic and 2% Asian. The old UAW-Big Three model—high pay and exceedingly generous health insurance, strict work rules and huge retirement costs—seems clearly to be unsustainable, yet many who remain in Michigan seem to yearn for its golden days to return. As a report of the liberal Brookings Institution put it, "What was once the most dynamic, innovative economy in the country is now a change-averse economic culture, with low entrepreneurship and new business creation levels, and sticky attitudes of entitlement and belief that things should stay as they were." Much more than coastal Americans, they continue overwhelmingly to buy Big Three cars (45% own a GM car, 39% Ford, 22% Chrysler) and put lots of mileage on them; some 725,000 hunters drive up north every November for the start of the deer season and Detroit's three casinos and the 17 tribal casinos Outstate have made Michigan the fourth largest casino state. But plunging real estate prices and half-empty restaurants leave little doubt that Michigan is in trouble; polls in 2006 showed three-quarters of voters believed the state was moving in the wrong direction. But there seemed to be no consensus on how to turn things around.

From the 1930s through the 1980s, politics divided Michigan between labor and management, and between the Detroit metro area and Outstate. In 1960, John Kennedy carried three-county metro Detroit 62%-38% and Richard Nixon carried Outstate 60%-39%, for a 51%-49% Kennedy victory. In 2004 John Kerry carried the three-county metro area 56%-43% while George W. Bush carried the rest of the state, which now casts 61% of the vote, by only 52%-47%, for a 51%-48% Kerry victory. Kerry's lead in the metro area came almost entirely from the city of Detroit, which cast only 7% of the state's votes but voted 94% for Kerry. In the industrial Michigan of 1960, economic status—and more specifically, union membership or non-membership—tended to drive party preference. In the Michigan of 2004, economics played some role, but more often cultural attitudes drove voting behavior. Kerry carried affluent Oakland County, where many upscale voters moved toward the Democrats in the 1990s on cultural issues. Bush carried Macomb County, historically more blue collar and Democratic, though pretty affluent now, which in the 1970s and 1980s trended away from Democrats on cultural issues. The Grand Rapids area, with its large Dutch-American population and many Christian conservatives, voted heavily Republican. The industrial Flint, Saginaw and Bay City areas, where unions remain relatively strong, voted heavily Democratic, as did the areas around Lansing, the state capital, and Ann Arbor, home of the University of Michigan. The Upper Peninsula, historically Democratic, voted for Bush. In Detroit and heavily Democratic areas, turnout in 2004 increased relatively little over 2000; it increased most in the suburban ring around Detroit, but not enough for Bush to overtake Kerry. In 2006, despite DeVos's expensive self-financed campaign, a beleaguered Michigan turned to the Democrats. Granholm's 56%-42% win was echoed by the 57%-41% reelection margin of Democratic Senator Debbie Stabenow. Democrats recaptured a majority in the state House, held by Republicans since 1994, and ran what turned out to be competitive races in four Republican congressional districts. Senator Carl Levin, Michigan Democrats' most popular statewide official, announced shortly after the 2006 election that he would run for a sixth term in 2008. Even so, there was one discordant result. The ballot measure banning racial quotas and preference in state government and state universities, which was opposed and shunned by politicians of both parties, passed by a resounding 58%-42% margin, trailing only in the counties that include Detroit, the University of Michigan and Michigan State University. Michigan may still be a battleground state in the years ahead.

The People		Race/Ethnic Origin			Military veterans: 913,573 (12.4%)	
Pop. 2006 (est):	10,095,643	7,806,691	78.6%	White	WWII: 21.3%	Korea: 14.0%
Pop. 2000:	9,938,444	1,402,047	14.1%	Black	Vietnam: 31.4%	Gulf War: 8.4%
Pop. 1990:	9,295,297	175,311	1.8%	Asian	**Most populous cities (2006):**	
Change 1990-2000:	Up 6.9%	53,421	0.5%	Native Am.	1. Detroit	871,121
% of U.S. total:	3.5%	2,145	0.0%	Hawaiian	2. Grand Rapids	193,083
Pop. rank:	8th of 50	163,487	1.6%	Two+ races	3. Warren	134,589
Area size:	96,716 sq. mi.	11,465	0.1%	Other	4. Sterling Heights	127,991
State Native:	75.4%	323,877	3.3%	Hisp. Origin	5. Flint	117,068
Non-citizen:	2.9%	**Ancestry**				
Language		German: 14.9%		Irish: 7.9%	Urban population: 74.7%	
English: 89.2%	Other Eur.: 4.8%	English: 7.3%		Polish: 6.3%	Rural population: 25.3%	
Spanish: 3.5%		USA: 3.8%				

Education		Work Sector		Legislature	
H.S. Grad:	83.4%	Private: 83.1%	Govt: 11.4%	Senate	21 R 17 D
College Grad:	21.8%	Self: 5.2%	Family: 0.3%	House	58 D 52 R
Industry		Unemployment: 5.8%		Legislative Term Limits: Yes	
Agri: 1.1%	Con: 6.0%	**Household Income**		**Registered Voters**	
Fin: 5.3%	Info: 2.1%	<15k: 14.1%	15-35k: 24.8%	No party registration	
Mfg: 26.7%	Prof: 27.9%	35-50k: 16.5%	50-100k: 32.0%		
Public: 3.6%	Trade: 15.2%	100-150k: 8.6%	>150k: 4.1%		
Other: 12.2%		Median: $44,667			
Occupation		Poverty status: 10.5%			
Blue collar: 27.6%	White collar: 57.1%	**Home Value**			
Gray collar: 15.3%		<50k: 14.3%	50-100k: 30.3%	100-200k: 38.8%	200-300k: 10.6%
		300-500k: 4.4%	>500k: 1.5%	Median: $110,300	

Presidential politics   For three elections in a row—1984, 1988 and 1992—Michigan voted within 1% of the national average for all major presidential candidates. In the last three elections—1996, 2000 and 2004—Michigan voted 3% more Democratic than the nation as a whole. This despite the fact that Al Gore and John Kerry both backed higher gas mileage standards, opposed by both the Big Three auto companies and the United Auto Workers, and despite John Kerry's wobble on diversion of Great Lakes water ("It's a delicate balancing act. There are different ways of managing water rights with remunerations and the appropriate respect to states' rights"). Most of the difference can be accounted for by the move toward Demo-

2004 Presidential Vote		
Kerry (D)	2,479,183	(51%)
Bush (R)	2,313,746	(48%)
Nader (NPA)	24,035	(0%)
Other	22,288	(0%)

2000 Presidential Vote		
Gore (D)	2,170,418	(51%)
Bush (R)	1,953,139	(46%)
Nader (Green)	84,165	(2%)
Other	24,779	(1%)

crats on cultural issues in the nation's largest metro areas, including Detroit. Republicans used to be able to count on big margins in affluent Oakland County, but it voted by narrow margins for Bill Clinton, Gore and Kerry. Macomb County, somewhat less affluent, heavily Democratic in the 1950s and 1960s, then trended Republican in the 1970s and 1980s, and is now closely divided, voting for Gore in 2000 and George W. Bush in 2004. Voters in union households voted 61%-37% for Kerry—a sign that union loyalty is not entirely a thing of the past—but they comprised just 37% of the electorate, down from around half in the 1970s. Michigan was a battleground state throughout the 2004 campaign, and both sides made great efforts to get out the vote. Both sides had their successes—Democratic turnout surged in Ann Arbor, Republican turnout surged in exurban Livingston County and northern Macomb County. But both had their disappointments as well. Turnout in Detroit, which voted 94% for Kerry, rose only 9%; the Republican margin in heavily Republican metro Grand Rapids declined, as the central city voted for Kerry. As in Ohio, the winning party's 2000 margin was reduced, but not enough for Kerry to carry Ohio or for Bush to carry Michigan.

Michigan has had problems getting influence in the presidential selection process. One reason is that it does not have party registration, which is required by Democratic party rules. So Michigan Democrats have to select their delegates through caucuses. In 2003, the Michigan Democratic party, led by Senator Carl Levin, attempted to challenge New Hampshire's first-in-the nation status by moving the 2004 Michigan Democratic caucuses to the same January date as the New Hampshire primary. Levin questioned why Iowa and New Hampshire should always vote first. But national Democrats threatened not to recognize the Michigan delegation, and Michigan Democrats backed down. Levin and Debbie Dingell, wife of Congressman John Dingell, did extract a promise of a new commission to reexamine the delegate selection process after the 2004 election. It was duly appointed and the Democratic National Committee voted to allow two new early contests, a Nevada caucus and a South Carolina primary: not the result Michigan Democrats hoped for. In December 2006 Michigan Republican Chairman Saul Anuzis said that he and Democratic state Chairman Mark Brewer agreed that Michigan should hold simultaneous primaries; in September 2007, Governor Jennifer Granholm signed a bill setting a January 15 primary date, the earliest in state history.

Michigan Democrats held their 2004 caucus on February 7, after the primaries that came one week after New Hampshire. Some 46,000 Democrats voted by Internet and 24,000 by mail, in addition to the 94,000 who managed to find the polling sites, which were different from and fewer than the precincts used in primary and general elections. John Kerry, supported by former Governor Jim Blanchard and Granholm's husband Dan Mulhern, won by a large margin.

Republicans can hold primaries in Michigan, though they didn't bother in 2004, when George W. Bush was unopposed. But the Republican primary in 2000, held February 22, did attract lots of attention. Governor John Engler hoped to deliver the state's delegates to Bush, whose candidacy he had backed early on. But John McCain, aroused after his defeat in South Carolina February 19, contested the state vigorously. In a stinging rebuke to Engler, McCain won 51%-43%. The national press hailed this as a great breakthrough, but it turned out to be atypical and an augury of nothing. Turnout was a huge 1.3 million, far higher than the 524,000 of 1996 or the 437,000 of 1992; indeed, even Bush got more votes than were cast for all candidates in those primaries. But the VNS exit poll showed that 18% of the votes were cast by self-identified Democrats (almost double the percentage in any other primary that year) and only 47% by self-identified Republicans. Bush won solidly among Republicans, as he did everywhere except in a few Northeast states, but lost by 2–1 among self-identified Independents and 8–1 among Democrats. Nothing barred Democrats from voting; when Democrats held caucuses in March, only 22,000 bothered to vote or mail in ballots. In no other state would self-identified Democrats be such a large proportion of the electorate, and so Michigan's Republicans proved no more consequential in 2000 than the Democrats in 2004.

Congressional districting   Michigan has now lost four seats in the last three censuses—one after the 1980 Census, two after the 1990 Census, another one after the 2000 Census. In 2001, for the first time since the 1930s, redistricting was controlled by Republicans, with majorities in both houses of the legislature and with Governor John Engler determined to use the power to reverse the Democrats' 9–7 edge to a 9–6 Republican edge: He succeeded. There was no

110th Congress Lineup
9 R   6 D

109th Congress Lineup
9 R   6 D

pretense of bipartisanship: bills were introduced in the House and Senate abruptly in June 2001 and passed on near party-line votes. The plan ended the 26-year congressional career of House Democratic Whip David Bonior, by removing just about every Macomb County precinct he carried heavily; he ran for governor and lost in the Democratic primary. It put two pairs of Democratic incumbents in the same districts; Jim Barcia of the 5th District decided to return to the state Senate, where he used to serve, while John Dingell, the dean of the House, slugged it out with liberal Lynn Rivers in the new 15th District. The 1st District, held by Democrat Bart Stupak, seems likely to go Republican if he is not running. A new Republican district was created in western Wayne and Oakland Counties, and shaky Republican incumbents Mike Rogers and Joe Knollenberg were strengthened.

This was arguably the most successful partisan redistricting plan in the nation. In a state carried by Bill Clinton and Al Gore, only five of the 15 seats are now safely Democratic. But it may go the other way after 2010. Michigan is projected to lose one seat in the reapportionment following the

2010 Census. If Democrats can hold the governorship and capture the state Senate by then, they will have a chance to increase the number of Democratic seats and pare down the Republican delegation.

Governor

Jennifer Granholm (D)

Elected 2002, term expires Jan. 2011, 2d term; b. Feb. 5, 1959, Vancouver, BC; home, Northville; U. of CA, B.A. 1984, Harvard U., J.D. 1987; Catholic; married (Daniel Mulhern).

Elected Office: MI Atty. Gen., 1998-2002.

Professional Career: Prosecutor, U.S. Atty.'s Office, 1991-94; Corporation Cnsl., Wayne Cnty., 1994-98.

Office: P.O. Box 30013, Lansing, 48909, 517-373-3400; Fax: 517-335-6863; Web site: www.michigan.gov/gov.

Election Results

2006 general	Jennifer Granholm (D)	2,142,513	(56%)
	Dick DeVos (R)	1,608,086	(42%)
	Other	50,657	(1%)
2006 primary	Jennifer Granholm (D)	unopposed	
2002 general	Jennifer Granholm (D)	1,633,796	(51%)
	Dick Posthumus (R)	1,506,104	(47%)
	Other	37,665	(1%)

Jennifer Granholm, a Democrat, was elected governor of Michigan in 2002. She was born in British Columbia, a Canadian citizen and so not eligible for the presidency, and moved to California at age 4 when her father's work as a bank teller and branch manager took him there. She lived in Anaheim in the 1960s, where she could watch the fireworks over Disneyland, and then in San Jose and San Carlos, a middle-class suburb on the Peninsula south of San Francisco. She was a popular student in San Carlos High School and won the Miss San Carlos beauty/talent pageant. At 18 she became a U.S. citizen. That year she also moved to Los Angeles to try her luck as an actress even though her parents wanted her to be the first in the family to graduate from college. She graduated from the American Academy of Dramatic Arts with Nick Cassavetes but never got a part; she once was a contestant on *The Dating Game*. She made her living as a tour guide at Universal Studios, took delivery complaints for the *Los Angeles Times* and was the first female tour guide at Marine World Africa USA in Redwood City, piloting boats with 25 tourists aboard. She returned to San Carlos and in 1980 won admission to the University of California at Berkeley. In 1984 she went off to Harvard Law School where she demonstrated in favor of disinvestment in South Africa and edited the Civil Rights and Civil Liberties Law Review. In Cambridge she met her husband, Dan Mulhern, from Inkster, Michigan, a working class suburb near Detroit's Metro Airport. After law school, they moved to Michigan. Thus was a star of Michigan politics born.

Granholm worked as a law clerk for federal appeals court Judge Damon Keith, then got a job in the U.S. Attorney's office in Detroit. In 1994 she got what turned out to be her great political break when she was appointed corporation counsel to Wayne County Executive Ed McNamara. McNamara, who obviously has an eye for political talent, has called Granholm a "child of destiny." In 1998 Frank Kelley, Michigan's attorney general since January 1962, announced that he was retiring (the "Eternal General," some called him). McNamara pushed Granholm forward to run for the office. She won the Democratic nomination at the state party convention in August 1998 and was elected in November—the only Democrat to win statewide, as Republican Governor John Engler and Secretary of State Candice Miller were reelected by wide margins. She might not have won except that conservatives at the Republican state convention nominated a little known candidate rather than Engler's choice, Scott Romney, son of former Governor George Romney and brother of former Massachusetts Governor Mitt Romney.

Suddenly Granholm was the most visible Democrat in Michigan state government and an obvious candidate to succeed Engler in 2002, when he would be barred from running by term limits.

What made her an attractive candidate was less her record than her persona. She is articulate, poised, always able to connect with her audience, enthusiastic, almost always striking a note of consensus rather than confrontation. Granholm had serious competition in the Democratic primary from former Governor Jim Blanchard and Congressman David Bonior. Much of the primary was a battle for endorsements. Bonior was endorsed by the state AFL-CIO and the United Auto Workers—endorsements that in the 1960s or 1970s would have clinched the nomination for him. But Granholm was endorsed in 2002 by the Teamsters and the Michigan Education Association—now at least as important factors in Democratic politics. In December 2001, Granholm was endorsed by EMILY's List, which had raised $1.4 million in bundled contributions for Senator Debbie Stabenow in 2000. The legislature passed a law that month limiting bundled contributions to $34,000, the limit for PACs. But it did not take effect until April 2002, by which time EMILY's List had raised more than $400,000 for Granholm. Blanchard and Bonior decided to take state matching funds and accept a spending limit of $2 million in the primary; Granholm rejected the matching funds and raised and spent $5.7 million. By early 2002, Granholm was leading in polls both for the primary and the general election against the presumed Republican nominee Lieutenant Governor Dick Posthumus. Michigan does not have party registration, so voters can vote in either party's primary; in August 2002, 1.8 million voted, 58% of them in the Democratic primary, which was much more seriously contested. Granholm won 48% of the vote, Bonior 28% and Blanchard 24%.

Posthumus, Granholm's general election opponent, was not well known to voters. A farmer from Grand Rapids's Kent County with solid conservative credentials, he insisted he was a blue-collar candidate. He called for tax cuts and ending the single business tax. He split with Engler to oppose slant oil drilling under the Great Lakes and opposed school vouchers, which had been beaten in a 2000 referendum. He attacked Granholm for saying she favored "tweaking" Proposal A—evidently allowing school districts to raise property taxes more than the measure allowed—and for opposing changes in welfare. But he concentrated much of his fire on her out-of-state origins. He portrayed himself as "raised in Michigan, went to Michigan public schools." "Let's just say I've got different values than come from Hollywood, Berkeley and Harvard." But most voters did not seem to care that Granholm grew up somewhere else; after all, she chose to live in Michigan.

Granholm won by a closer-than-expected 51%-47%. Only 220,000 Detroiters voted, but they cast more than 92% of their votes for Granholm and accounted for all of her popular vote margin and more. Granholm carried Oakland County and suburban Wayne County but lost Macomb County. She carried the Upper Peninsula, the Flint-Saginaw-Bay City corridor and the counties containing Lansing, Battle Creek and Kalamazoo; she lost Outstate by only 51%-47%—a good showing for a Democrat.

Granholm's first term was a time when most of the nation recovered from the 2001 recession—but not Michigan. Job losses continued, as the Big Three auto companies squeezed their subcontractors and still faced serious losses themselves. In her first year she faced a $3 billion shortfall in a $39 billion budget. She set to work cutting spending: her first budget cut aid to universities and cities, sold 2,500 state cars, rescinded $220 million in contracts and adult education by 70% and arts spending 50%. More cuts followed in fall 2003 and in 2004 she persuaded the legislature to raise the cigarette tax 75 cents but not to replace the expiring estate tax with an inheritance tax. She cut or froze revenue sharing grants to local governments by $523 million and got the legislature to increase the casino tax from 18% to 24%. After some balking from the state House, the legislature voted to allow local governments to collect property taxes five months earlier than scheduled. She and the legislature put through $600 million in property tax relief for manufacturers moving to or expanding in Michigan. The single business tax was considered by many to discourage job formation, and its phaseout became an issue. In October 2004 Granholm called for sweeping tax reform. In 2005 she proposed to replace it with a tax on insurance; the legislature refused, and in March 2006 voted to schedule its abolition at the end of 2007 rather than 2009. Granholm vetoed the bill on the grounds that it provided no replacement taxes. In response Oakland County Executive Brooks Patterson got signatures on a petition requiring a November vote on single business tax repeal unless the legislature acted. The legislature voted repeal in August 2006—a law Granholm could not repeal under the terms of the referendum. After the November election, Granholm proposed as a replacement a business income tax and a small tax increase on insurance premiums, plus some reduction of business property taxes; the legislature did not take action in its lame duck session. With Democrats in the majority in the House, in June 2007 Granholm reached agreement with House and Senate leaders on a business tax to replace the 30-year-old system repealed in 2006. Granholm said the plan called for a tax cut of 70% for in-state businesses and had provisions for new companies to pay lower taxes during their first five years. The plan also called for a higher premium tax on out-of-state companies and insurance firms.

In the meantime Michigan continued to lose jobs—the only state in 2005 to do so, except for hurricane-ravaged Louisiana and Mississippi. She accelerated spending on building roads and bridges. She welcomed new or expanded facilities by Hino Motors, Hyundai, Nissan, Suzuki, Aisin Seiki and Toyota, but Michigan failed to attract big new production plants from foreign automakers. She got the legislature to raise the minimum wage and to raise high school graduation requirements. She assigned Lieutenant Governor John Cherry to come up with ways to double the state's percentage of college graduates in a decade. Granholm joined with eight other Great Lakes states in July 2004 in a water compact requiring eight-state approval of withdrawals of 1 million gallons a day and a three-state veto of withdrawals over 5 million gallons a day; all this evidently to prevent shipping water to thirsty southwestern states. She signed some conservative legislation—a bill giving pregnant women considering abortion the option of viewing ultrasound pictures, a bill limiting welfare recipients able to work to four years of benefits, a bill opening up cable TV to competition—but vetoed a bill allowing motorcyclists not to wear helmets. A July 2006 budget deal increased spending on K-12 and higher education, and the legislature adopted Granholm's proposal for $4,000 Promise Grants to college students who maintain a 2.5 average their first two years.

Granholm's job approval remained high her first two years but sagged in 2005 as Michigan's economy failed to grow. In June 2005 Republican Dick DeVos, son of the co-founder of Amway and president of the company (now called Alticor) until 2002, entered the race for governor. DeVos's ability to self-finance his campaign moved others out of the race, and he began a heavy television advertising buy in February 2006; altogether he spent $42 million, $35 million of it his own money, while Granholm spent $14 million. He stressed his business experience and offered some detailed programs on his website. "We have gone backward while the country has gone forward," DeVos said. Granholm's response: "My opponent began advertising way back in February trying to put the blame for Michigan's economic contraction on me, when most people who work in the plants know that the shift of jobs to India or China is much more the result of federal policy and these trade agreements." She favored "as robust an industrial policy as we can to keep those jobs here. My tools can do only so much." Democrats attacked DeVos for his conservative stands on cultural issues; he attacked Granholm for her veto of a partial-birth abortion ban. From the start Democrats charged that Amway had moved jobs from Michigan to China; DeVos said that the company had to build plants and create new jobs in China to serve the market there, which accounted for something like one-third of Amway sales. Democrats also attacked DeVos for sponsoring a school voucher initiative which lost 69%-31% in 2000 after teacher unions spent millions in opposition. Polls showed DeVos running about even with Granholm in April and somewhat ahead by July. In the August primary, in which voters can choose to vote in either primary and neither candidate had opposition, DeVos won 52% of the votes to Granholm's 48%. Immediately after the primary she began running ads. The first one promised action against gouging by gas stations; she also had an online petition calling on George W. Bush to put a cap on oil company profits.

DeVos's inexperience showed in his performance in debates, which was generally considered weak; he claimed he was frustrated by Granholm's distortions. His businesslike demeanor contrasted with Granholm's ebullience and her charm in interacting with voters. He may also have been hurt by his proposal to cut business property taxes, which threatened to deprive local governments of $1.7 billion in revenues. By October Granholm was leading in the polls, and she won by a solid 56%-42% margin—a much better showing than indicated by polls, in contrast to 2002 when she won by much less than they suggested. At the same time the Michigan Civil Rights Initiative, prohibiting the state from using racial preferences and quotas, was approved 58%-42%, even though both Granholm and DeVos opposed it. Turnout was 3.8 million, up 20% from the 3.1 million in 2002; it rose less than that in Detroit and Wayne County, which were losing population, and the highest rises were mostly in traditionally Republican areas. This was a dividend, probably, of the big turnout drives by both the Bush and Kerry campaigns in 2004, but it appears that many of the new voters who had voted for Bush that year now in 2006 voted Democratic. DeVos won 1.6 million votes, up 7% from the 1.5 million Posthumus had won in 2002. But Granholm won 2.1 million votes, up 31% from the 1.6 million she had won four years before. Granholm carried 55 of 83 counties, including many counties that have long voted Republican; she ran 9% or more ahead of John Kerry's showing in 29 rural counties. DeVos carried about half the counties in western Michigan, the Republican counties in the Thumb and Livingston County, the fastest-growing county in the state.

Senior Senator

Carl Levin (D)

Elected 1978, seat up 2008, 5th term; b. June 28, 1934, Detroit; home, Detroit; Swarthmore Col., B.A. 1956, Harvard U., J.D. 1959; Jewish; married (Barbara).

Elected Office: Detroit City Cncl., 1969-77, Pres., 1973-77.

Professional Career: Practicing atty., 1959-64, 1971-73, 1978-79; MI Asst. Atty. Gen. & Gen. Cnsl., MI Civil Rights Comm., 1964-67; Detroit Chief Appellate Defender, 1967-69.

DC Office: 269 RSOB, 20510, 202-224-6221; Fax: 202-224-1388; Web site: levin.senate.gov.

State Offices: Detroit, 313-226-6020; Escanaba, 906-789-0052; Grand Rapids, 616-456-2531; Lansing, 517-377-1508; Saginaw, 989-754-2494; Traverse City, 231-947-9569; Warren, 586-573-9145.

Committees: *Armed Services* (Chmn. of 13 D). *Homeland Security & Governmental Affairs* (2d of 9 D): Investigations (Permanent) (Chmn.); Federal Financial Management, Government Information, Federal Services & International Security; Oversight of Government Management, the Federal Workforce & the District of Columbia. *Small Business & Entrepreneurship* (2d of 10 D).

Group Ratings

	ADA	ACLU	AFS	LCV	ITIC	NTU	COC	ACU	CFG	FRC
2006	100	92	100	57	50	13	50	8	5	0
2005	100	—	100	80	—	7	39	17	0	—

National Journal Ratings

	2005 LIB — 2005 CONS	2006 LIB — 2006 CONS
Economic	78% — 19%	75% — 22%
Social	77% — 18%	96% — 0%
Foreign	95% — 0%	79% — 16%

Key Votes of the 109th Congress

1. Bar ANWR Drilling	Y	5. Confirm Samuel Alito	N	9. Limit Interstate Abortion	N
2. FY06 Spending Curb	N	6. Path to Citizenship	Y	10. CAFTA	N
3. Estate Tax Repeal	N	7. Bar Same Sex Marriage	N	11. Urge Iraq Withdrawal	Y
4. Raise Minimum Wage	Y	8. Stem Cell Research $	Y	12. Provide Detainee Rights	Y

Election Results

2002 general	Carl Levin (D)	1,896,614	(61%)	($4,133,866)
	Andrew Raczkowski (R)	1,185,545	(38%)	($849,501)
2002 primary	Carl Levin (D)	unopposed		
1996 general	Carl Levin (D)	2,195,738	(58%)	($6,223,409)
	Ronna Romney (R)	1,500,106	(40%)	($3,208,968)
	Other	66,731	(2%)	

Prior Winning Percentages: 1990 (57%); 1984 (52%); 1978 (52%)

Carl Levin, first elected in 1978, is a member of one of Michigan's most respected political families and the longest-serving senator in Michigan's history. He is rumpled, unfashionable, speaks articulately but without apparent political artifice and takes unpopular stands on issues he cares about. He grew up in Detroit, graduated from Swarthmore and Harvard Law School, worked for the state Civil Rights Commission and the appellate public defender's office, and was elected to Detroit's city council in 1969 and 1973, with substantial support from both blacks and whites. In 1978 he ran for the Senate and was helped when incumbent Robert Griffin got out of the race and then back in; Levin won 52%-48%. In 1984 he won by a similar margin against a former astronaut who had given a public testimonial for his Japanese car; in 1990, 1996 and 2002 he was reelected by wide margins.

Levin is chairman of the Armed Services Committee, as he was from June 2001 to January 2003. He brought to the Senate the skepticism about defense spending and military involvements common among Democrats in the 1970s, and has built up an impressive expertise in military affairs. For a time he opposed the B-2 and he voted against the Gulf War resolution in 1991—on the advice of Colin Powell, he has said, and added that he was mistaken. On taking the chair in 2001, he said he would not concentrate on major weapons systems, but on military pay, health care and housing, plus purchasing systems; unlike his predecessor and successor, John Warner, he favored another round of base closings—one issue on which he agreed with Defense Secretary Donald Rumsfeld. Where he disagreed most strongly with Rumsfeld was on missile defense, of which he has been the Senate's most persistent critic. In June 2001, on becoming chairman, he said more testing was needed and a system was unlikely to be fielded until after the next presidential election. On defense bills he worked to freeze any money that might conceivably conflict with ABM Treaty. On September 7, 2001, he got the committee to move $1.3 billion from missile defense to anti-terrorism programs. On September 16 Warner said he was ready to file his own defense bill. On September 21 Levin backed down, saying he did not wish to "create dissent where we need unity." In December 2001 Levin was outflanked when George W. Bush invoked the clause in the ABM Treaty allowing him to abrogate it with six months warning. Still, in May 2002 he got the committee to approve a defense authorization bill that cut the Bush administration missile defense request by $812 million; in June, a Senate compromise was struck on the final version that gave Bush the authority to restore the cuts. In March 2004 Levin said he opposed $500 million in the defense authorization for missile defense and argued that the Pentagon would break a 1986 law if it spends certain monies before operational tests.

Levin was very skeptical about the need for military action in Iraq and argued fervently that any such action must be taken multilaterally. He argued in September 2002 that military action was not necessary now because Saddam Hussein would be deterred from using weapons of mass destruction and that the United States should not act without first receiving the approval of the United Nations. In October 2002 he offered an alternative resolution on military action in Iraq, calling on the administration to get the UN to vote a more vigorous weapons inspection program, but not authorizing military action until it was approved by the UN. It was defeated 75-24. In February 2003 he continued to argue that the United States should not take military action without another resolution from the United Nations. In October 2004 he issued a report charging that Pentagon official Douglas Feith deliberately exaggerated ties between Saddam Hussein's Iraq and al Qaeda and ignored corrections requested by the CIA; in November 2005 he cited a Pentagon report describing one source of information on Iraq as unreliable as another indication of misuse of prewar intelligence. In March 2006 he said, "My main message to the Iraqi people was that the American people are impatient and want the leadership to stop squabbling and put together a government of national unity." In June 2006 he and Jack Reed sponsored an amendment calling for a "phased redeployment" in six months, with no deadline for complete withdrawal; it also called for U.S. forces to transition to training Iraqi security forces. The more extreme alternative, John Kerry's amendment calling for withdrawal by July 2007, was defeated 86-13; the Levin-Reed amendment lost 60-39, with six Democrats and one Republican, Lincoln Chafee, crossing party lines. In November 2006 Levin described the situation in Iraq as "a low-grade civil war" and called for a bipartisan resolution supporting phased redeployment; committee colleagues John McCain and Lindsey Graham immediately sharply disagreed. "We have to force the Iraqis to take responsibility for their own nation, that we cannot save them from themselves," he said. "The president himself believes that what I'm saying is a useful thing for the Iraqis to hear." In December 2006, he called for implementation of the Iraq Study Group report, which he said could be "the beginning of a development of a new, realistic, bipartisan and hopefully successful approach." Despite his disagreements with administration policy, he voted to confirm the nomination of Defense Secretary Robert Gates and said he was a "welcome break of honest, candid realism." In May 2007, Levin opposed a redeployment measure sponsored by Russ Feingold and Harry Reid that set a deadline for troops to be out of Iraq. "I can't support a cutoff on funding and I cannot support a fixed date for removing all troops," he said.

Levin joined Armed Services colleague John McCain in strongly questioning the Pentagon's leasing, rather than purchase, of KC-767 refueling tankers from Boeing. After emails obtained by McCain revealed improper negotiations between the Air Force and Boeing, Levin, McCain and Warner passed in November 2003 a proposal to lease only 20 of the aircraft and purchase 80 others, to keep the total cost down to $23.5 billion. In March 2004 Levin, McCain and Warner, disturbed by a Pentagon audit, imposed a hold on the project; in October 2004, they demanded an investigation of everyone who participated in awarding the contract. Levin also expressed concern about the condition of the Army. In November 2004, in hearings on the nominee for secretary of the Army, he said that the Army was stretched too thin, that there were not enough soldiers and protective gear in Iraq, that too many personnel were held in the service by stop loss orders and that the Army was not adequately replacing old equipment. In July 2005 he and Warner pressed for a $100,000 death gratuity for all killed on active duty, not just those killed in combat. Levin and Lindsey Graham worked together on a bill to authorize military tribunals in November 2005. In 2006 Levin and Graham got an additional $100 million for acquisition of Cougar and Buffalo blast-protective vehicles.

Levin has also weighed in on intelligence matters. He obtained passage of an amendment to the intelligence reorganization bill requiring the national intelligence director to be independent of the White House. He got passage of another amendment barring the national intelligence director from shifting uniformed military personnel in defense intelligence agencies to agencies outside the Defense Department. In October 2004 he declined to sign the conference committee report on the grounds that the bill didn't contain enough safeguards against politicization of intelligence. He voted for the final bill in December though he said he was "mystified" that the Senate dropped language on the independence of the NID objected to by the White House. He objected to the NSA surveillance of communications between al Qaeda suspects abroad and persons in the United States.

Levin is chairman of the Permanent Investigations Subcommittee of Governmental Affairs. There he worked on laws for whistleblower protection, competition in government contracting and lobbying disclosure. He has also focused over the years on money laundering, phony tax shelters and, in November 2004, the UN Oil for Food program. After the November 2006 election, he announced he would concentrate on credit card company practices, tax haven abuse and currency manipulation.

Levin generally has one of the most liberal records in the Senate, with some Michigan accents. He opposed NAFTA and has complained about Japanese auto-parts and Korean car trade restrictions. When John Kerry and John McCain proposed raising CAFE auto mileage standards to 36 miles per gallon by 2015, Levin and Christopher Bond responded with an amendment requiring NHTSA to raise the standard for light trucks (including SUVs) within 15 months and for cars within two years; it passed 62-38. In May 2006 he called for the Department of Transportation rather than Congress to set fuel mileage standards and said the Bush administration's new light truck standards were "reasonable." Levin was angry when the Republican majority blocked votes on Michigan appointees to federal judgeships when Bill Clinton was president, and for four years blocked all Bush appeals court nominees for the 6th Circuit, which includes Michigan, Ohio, Kentucky and Tennessee; in June 2005, he relented and voted to confirm Richard Griffin and David McKeague. In 2006 he worked with Ohio's Mike DeWine to reauthorize the Great Lakes Fish and Wildlife Restoration Act, first passed in 1990; in October 2006 he celebrated the return after eight decades of whitefish to the Detroit River. He criticized George W. Bush for cancelling a meeting with the CEOs of the Big Three automakers and called for stopping tax avoidance by foreign automakers, cracking down on foreign trade barriers and Chinese and Japanese currency manipulation and backing research and development of new generation fuels.

Michigan touches on all but one of the Great Lakes, which have been threatened by invasive species; the zebra mussel has wiped out many native species and Asian carp are making their way up the Illinois River and threatening to enter the Great Lakes. With Mike DeWine he sponsored a $6 billion Great Lakes trust fund, to pay for cleaning up the Lakes, restoring wetlands and repelling invasive species. Some 415 truckloads of Canadian trash are dumped in Michigan daily; Levin called for enforcement of a 1992 treaty requiring notice of such shipments and allowing the U.S. to stop them. In August 2006 he and Michigan colleague Debbie Stabenow negotiated an agreement with Ontario officials to stop the trash shipments by 2010; a House bill to stop it earlier passed the same week but it did not pass the Senate. Levin has also stepped forward to question why New Hampshire should always be the site of the first presidential primary. In March 2003 he proposed the Michigan Democrats caucus on the same day as the New Hampshire primary. He and other Michigan Democrats were persuaded not to, but national Democrats promised to appoint a commission after November 2004 to reconsider the caucus and primary schedule. The Democratic National Committee voted to add a Nevada caucus and a South Carolina primary shortly after the Iowa and New Hampshire contests, but the move of states with a majority of the nation's population to vote just weeks after Iowa and New Hampshire may make Democrats more amenable to the kind of changes Levin has championed.

Levin's reputation for candor and hard work, and his rumpled persona have given him great political strength in Michigan. Every six years his percentage has crept a little higher. In December 2006 he announced he would run again in 2008. Republican state Chairman Saul Anuzis said his party would field a strong candidate, but Representatives Candice Miller and Mike Rogers, mentioned as candidates if the seat were open, were unlikely to run. Other possibilities: Secretary of State Terri Lynn Land and Attorney General Mike Cox, who would not have to give up their jobs to run in 2008.

Junior Senator

Debbie Stabenow (D)

Elected 2000, seat up 2012, 2d term; b. Apr. 29, 1950, Gladwin; home, Lansing; MI St. U., B.A. 1972, M.S.W. 1975; United Methodist; married (Tom Athans).

Elected Office: Ingham Cnty. Comm., 1975-78, Chair, 1976-78; MI House of Reps., 1978-90; MI Senate, 1990-94; U.S. House of Reps 1996-2000.

Professional Career: Consultant & Co–founder, MI Leadership Inst., 1995-96.

DC Office: 133 HSOB, 20510, 202-224-4822; Fax: 202-228-0325; Web site: stabenow.senate.gov.

State Offices: Detroit, 313-961-4330; East Lansing, 517-203-1760; Flint, 810-720-4172; Grand Rapids, 616-975-0052; Marquette, 906-228-8756; Traverse City, 231-929-1031.

Committees: *Agriculture, Nutrition & Forestry* (6th of 11 D): Rural Revitalization, Conservation, Forestry & Credit (Chmn.); Nutrition and Food Assistance, Sustainable and Organic Agriculture & General Legislation; Domestic & Foreign Marketing, Inspection, & Plant & Animal Health. *Budget* (7th of 12 D). *Finance* (9th of 11 D): International Trade & Global Competitiveness; Taxation & IRS Oversight & Long-Term Growth; Health Care.

Group Ratings

	ADA	ACLU	AFS	LCV	ITIC	NTU	COC	ACU	CFG	FRC
2006	90	67	100	71	25	14	50	16	6	0
2005	100	—	88	85	—	6	44	12	0	—

National Journal Ratings

	2005 LIB	—	2005 CONS		2006 LIB	—	2006 CONS
Economic	71%	—	28%		67%	—	29%
Social	90%	—	0%		68%	—	31%
Foreign	90%	—	5%		66%	—	33%

Key Votes of the 109th Congress

1. Bar ANWR Drilling	Y	5. Confirm Samuel Alito	N	9. Limit Interstate Abortion	N
2. FY06 Spending Curb	N	6. Path to Citizenship	N	10. CAFTA	N
3. Estate Tax Repeal	N	7. Bar Same Sex Marriage	N	11. Urge Iraq Withdrawal	Y
4. Raise Minimum Wage	Y	8. Stem Cell Research $	Y	12. Provide Detainee Rights	Y

Election Results

2006 general	Debbie Stabenow (D)	2,151,278	(57%)	($11,220,506)
	Mike Bouchard (R)	1,559,597	(41%)	($6,050,148)
	Other	69,267	(2%)	
2006 primary	Debbie Stabenow (D)	unopposed		
2000 general	Debbie Stabenow (D)	2,061,952	(49%)	($7,892,518)
	Spencer Abraham (R)	1,994,693	(48%)	($13,028,636)
	Other	111,040	(3%)	

Prior Winning Percentages: 1998 House (57%); 1996 House (54%)

Michigan's junior senator is Debbie Stabenow, a Democrat elected in 2000. Stabenow grew up in the small Outstate town of Clare, where her father was an Oldsmobile dealer and her mother a nurse. She went to Michigan State, where she got a master's degree in social work, counseled kids in public schools, and made money singing folk songs in coffeehouses. She marched in antiwar rallies and volunteered for George McGovern in 1972, when her then-husband ran an unsuccessful race for Ingham County Commissioner. Provoked when the commission closed a nursing home, she ran for the commission two years later and, at 24, beat an incumbent who referred to her as "that young broad." She was elected to the state House in 1978, at 28, and was elected to the state Senate in 1990. In 1994, while running for governor, she was at the storm center of state politics and policy. In response to Republican Governor John Engler's call for changes in education finance, she proposed to zero out the property tax and start over, apparently calculating that he would reject such a drastic tax cut. Instead he accepted her proposal and passed a plan reducing property taxes vastly and increasing the sales tax, which was approved by voters 70%-30% in March 1994. In the August primary for governor, the major forces in the Democratic Party opposed Stabenow: the Michigan Education Association, the UAW and AFL-CIO. She won 30% of the vote, ahead of Larry Owen's 26% but behind former Congressman Howard Wolpe's 35%. She was chosen as Wolpe's running mate, but the ticket lost to Engler by a 61%-38% margin.

Undaunted, Stabenow almost immediately began running for Congress. The 8th District seat, which included Lansing's Democratic Ingham County and heavily Republican Livingston County to the east, was held by freshman Republican Dick Chrysler. For the 1996 race, Stabenow raised more than $1 million in individual contributions, a tribute to her industriousness and the fundraising prowess of the feminist left; overall each spent $1.5 million. She won impressively, 54%-44%. In the House, Stabenow had a fairly liberal voting record. She opposed trade promotion authority and the partial-birth abortion ban. In March 1999 she announced she was running against first-term Senator Spencer Abraham in 2000; the same day Abraham ran full-page ads calling her a liberal.

This turned out to be one of the critical races in the 2000 Senate cycle. The first barrage of ads in the race came not from either candidate or party, but from the Federation for American Immigration Reform, which in early 2000 spent $700,000 attacking Abraham for his stands on immigration and charging that his stands cost Michigan workers jobs. In summer 2000 Abraham used his money advantage—he ultimately spent $13 million, to Stabenow's nearly $8 million—to run ads spotlighting his own program for prescription drugs for seniors and attacked Stabenow as a free-spending liberal favoring increased bureaucracy and opposing tax cuts, opposing welfare reform and supporting more lenient sentences for criminals. Stabenow resisted pressure and hoarded her money for an October ad buy. This proved to be a good strategy: Stabenow was down by 17% in one mid-October poll. But she answered charges that she was a liberal by citing her votes for a balanced budget and ending the marriage penalty; she kept herself in the good graces of labor by voting against normal trade relations with China. Stabenow said Abraham was beholden to corporations and special interests and attacked his stands on prescription drug and HMO regulation. This race was heavy on ads by outside groups—the Sierra Club, Peace Action and EMILY's List for Stabenow, the Chamber of Commerce, Business Roundtable, Americans for Job Security, National Rifle Association and Michigan Right to Life for Abraham. This was the most expensive Senate race in Michigan history, and the first since 1942 in which neither candidate won a majority of the vote. Stabenow won 49%-48%, carrying only 13 of the state's 83 counties.

Senate Democrats made Stabenow head of the prescription drug task force. She organized bus trips of seniors to Canada and pressed for measures allowing reimportation of drugs from Canada and permitting states to continue to negotiate prices with pharmaceutical companies on Medicaid drug purchases, and barring the U.S. trade negotiators from including drug patent-related provisions in future trade deals. In September 2006, the Senate approved the trade proposal, which she proposed with David Vitter.

Stabenow has sponsored measures on Michigan's environment. In 2003 Toronto began shipping all its trash to a landfill southwest of Detroit: 180 truckloads a day, 1.1 million tons a year. By November 2004, 415 truckloads a day of Canadian trash were entering Michigan, most of it over the Blue Water Bridge in Port Huron. Stabenow opposed this and argued that it violated a 1992 treaty. She began an online campaign to amass signatures to demand that EPA enforce the treaty, which required notification of each shipment and allowed the U.S. to decline any shipment. She presented 165,000 signatures to EPA Administrator Mike Leavitt. Leavitt said that only hazardous waste violated the treaty; Stabenow argued that all waste was covered. Leavitt said he would establish a pilot program to ask Canadian shippers for notification and promised he would fund the state's efforts to stop shipments that violate state standards; a law took effect in October 2004 requiring out-of-state shipments to meet state standards. But the shipments continued, as did the fight on this issue. In August 2006, Stabenow and Carl Levin announced an agreement with Ontario's Environment Minister to end the shipment of municipal garbage by 2010. "This is real. It's concrete. It cannot be challenged in court," she said. Some skeptics were dubious that it was comprehensive or legally binding. Stabenow also sponsored an amendment for $2 billion in corporate tax cuts for manufacturers who create jobs in the U.S.; this act did pass. In 2006, she was one of only four Senate Democrats to vote against passage of the immigration reform bill.

Stabenow has proved to be an effective partisan. In November 2004, when Barbara Mikulski stepped down from the position of Secretary of the Democratic Conference, Stabenow called Mikulski and asked for her support; they worked the phones and Stabenow got the job, the number three position in the leadership. It gave her a seat and a voice at leadership meetings, though her performance was limited. Other senior Senate Democrats quietly discussed replacing her after the 2006 election. Ultimately, all sides reached a satisfactory agreement: Stabenow got a much-sought seat on the Senate Finance Committee; she became chair of the Democratic Steering and Outreach Committee, a liaison to grass-roots groups across the nation, and Patty Murray took over as Conference Secretary.

Facing reelection in 2006, Stabenow got early breaks when two Republican House members, Candice Miller and Mike Rogers, said that they would not run. Several second-tier candidates emerged, including wealthy Reverend Keith Butler, a former Detroit councilman, and Jerry Zandstra, a director at a Grand Rapids religious think tank. National Republicans encouraged Oakland County sheriff Mike Bouchard, who initially demurred but later announced his candidacy in October 2005 after addressing some health problems. When Zandstra dropped out, Bouchard and Butler agreed on most issues but they had personal animosities. Bouchard won the August primary, 61%-39%. The general was overshadowed by the more competitive race for governor, and Bouchard struggled for attention and fundraising. Republicans ran an ad on the mercidebbie.com website that mocked Stabenow for caving to Canadian interests on trash shipments; Bouchard called her ineffective. But more concerned with salvaging their own struggling incumbents, Republicans did not make this a high-priority contest. Stabenow won 57%-41%, and took 65 of the 83 counties.

FIRST DISTRICT

Rep. Bart Stupak (D)

Elected 1992, 8th term; b. Feb. 29, 1952, Milwaukee, WI; home, Menominee; NW MI Comm. Col., A.A. 1972, Saginaw Valley St. Col., B.S. 1977, Thomas Cooley Law Schl., J.D. 1981; Catholic; married (Laurie).

Elected Office: MI House of Reps., 1988-90.

Professional Career: Escanaba Police Officer, 1972-73; MI St. Trooper, 1974-84; Practicing atty., 1981-92.

DC Office: 2352 RHOB, 20515, 202-225-4735; Fax: 202-225-4744; Web site: www.house.gov/stupak.

District Offices: Alpena, 989-356-0690; Crystal Falls, 906-875-3751; Escanaba, 906-786-4504; Houghton, 906-482-1371; Marquette, 906-228-3700; Petoskey, 231-348-0657; West Branch, 989-345-2258.

Committees: *Energy & Commerce* (10th of 31 D): Oversight & Investigations (Chmn.); Environment & Hazardous Materials; Telecommunications & the Internet.

Group Ratings

	ADA	ACLU	AFS	LCV	ITIC	NTU	COC	ACU	CFG	FRC
2006	75	81	100	42	33	9	33	28	5	42
2005	80	—	100	78	—	13	46	25	3	46

National Journal Ratings

	2005 LIB	—	2005 CONS		2006 LIB	—	2006 CONS
Economic	68%	—	32%		77%	—	23%
Social	60%	—	40%		63%	—	36%
Foreign	77%	—	22%		73%	—	26%

Key Votes of the 109th Congress

1. Estate Tax Repeal	N	5. Limit Interstate Abortion	Y	9. Build Border Fence	Y
2. Limit CAFE Standards	Y	6. Extend Patriot Act	N	10. CAFTA	N
3. FY06 Spending Curb	N	7. Bar Same Sex Marriage	N	11. Oppose Iraq Withdrawal	N
4. Drilling in ANWR	N	8. Stem Cell Research $	Y	12. Detainee Tribunals	N

Election Results

2006 general	Bart Stupak (D)	180,448	(69%)	($833,135)
	Don Hooper (R)	72,753	(28%)	($5,362)
	Other...	6,726	(3%)	
2006 primary	Bart Stupak (D) .... unopposed			
2004 general	Bart Stupak (D)	211,571	(66%)	($771,354)
	Don Hooper (R)	105,706	(33%)	($11,070)
	Other...	5,397	(2%)	

Prior Winning Percentages: 2002 (68%); 2000 (58%); 1998 (59%); 1996 (71%); 1994 (57%); 1992 (54%)

The People		Race/Ethnic Origin	Ancestry	
Area size:	27,809 sq. mi.	93.8% White	German: 15.8%	English: 7.7%
Urban population:	33.4%	1.0% Black	Irish: 7.2%	
Rural population:	66.6%	0.4% Asian	**2004 Presidential Vote**	
Pop. 2000:	662,563	2.4% Native Am.	Bush (R)............ 177,315	(53%)
Pop. 2005 (est):	671,874	0.0% Hawaiian	Kerry (D) 151,450	(46%)
Median income:	$34,076	1.4% Two+ races	Other 3,623	(1%)
Poverty status:	11.2%	0.0% Other	**2000 Presidential Vote**	
Military veterans:	16.9%	0.9% Hispanic Origin	Bush (R)............ 154,772	(52%)
			Gore (D) 135,503	(45%)
			Other 9,371	(3%)
			Cook Partisan Voting Index: R + 2	

Occupation   Blue collar: 28.8%   White collar: 50.7%   Gray collar: 20.5%

Michigan's Upper Peninsula, commonly known as the UP, is a land apart. Surrounded on three sides by frigid Lakes Superior, Huron and Michigan, the UP is no farther north than Montreal or Seattle, but there are places here that have some of the coldest climates in settled parts of North America. The area surrounding Keweenaw County, which juts into Lake Superior, often ranks high in the nation's heaviest snowfall. "In October, usually, the first snow falls steady on the northland," writes Dixie Lee Franklin in *A Most Superior Land*, "whispering teasing promises of more to come"—for six or even eight months more. Far away from any major city, with ground too frozen and stony and a growing season too short for most crops, the Upper Peninsula was explored by French voyagers and missionaries more than 300 years ago but was never thickly settled until prospectors found rich veins of ore here. The mineral veins of the Keweenaw Peninsula produced 13.3 billion pounds of copper; the Marquette, Menominee and Gogebic iron ranges have produced more than one billion tons of iron ore. Starting in the 1840s, immigrants flocked here to work the mines: Irish, Italians, Swedes, Norwegians, miners' sons from Wales and Cornwall, and most prominently Finns, who must have found this cold land with its lakes and hills much like their home. Many were Roman Catholic, and they remain predominantly anti-abortion. Before 1900, the UP was a northern industrial belt, with a few bosses and some absentee overlords and a work force disposed to radical ideas and union movements. Timber was another major industry a century ago.

A major strike in 1913-14 and falling ore prices after World War I—events that would be long forgotten elsewhere—are remembered in the UP as accelerating the copper decline: The UP's population peaked at 332,000 in 1920. The accessible copper veins were mostly depleted by then, mining iron ore became less labor-intensive, and lumber and farming provided only a few thousand jobs. Other industries have grown since then: Marinette Marine, which builds Coast Guard cutters and military ships just across the state border in Wisconsin, is important to Menominee County. Enstrom Helicopter, founded in Menominee in the 1950s by a lumberman who wanted a helicopter suited for the rugged UP, sells models that are popular overseas and with law enforcement. But in the last half century, there has been great migration to Detroit for auto jobs, and to the West for mining; the UP's population has hovered around 300,000, rising to 315,000 in 2004. But "Yoopers"— who some say have their own dialect, "Yoopanese"—remain devoted to their land.

The 1st Congressional District of Michigan includes the Upper Peninsula and 16 northern counties in the Lower Peninsula: nearly half of all Michigan. Nearly half the people live in the UP, in small towns spread across heavily forested distances; Marquette, with 21,000 people, is the largest city in the district, followed by the "Soo", Sault Ste. Marie, with 14,000. The other half lives south of the breathtaking Mackinac Bridge. This is a vast area, in sheer size the second-largest district east of the Mississippi (after Maine's 2d), and it has the most shoreline of any district; it is a 490-mile drive from Ironwood at the western end of the UP to the edge of Bay City on the southern tip of Saginaw Bay. The Lower Peninsula counties have two different personalities. On Lake Huron—the sunrise side—are smaller industrial towns and middle-class resorts. On Lake Michigan are affluent resort areas around Petoskey and Charlevoix, long summer places for people from Chicago (this is Ernest Hemingway's "up in Michigan"). Politically, the UP had long been Democratic, some parts more than others, but it can be contrarian; this is one part of Michigan that has not liked many national Democrats' environmental and gun control stands. The Lake Michigan shore of the Lower Peninsula is growing fast and heavily Republican, the sunrise side is growing more slowly and politically marginal. The 1st District voted solidly for Bush in 2000 and 2004 and narrowly for Republican governor candidate Dick Posthumus in 2002, even as both lost statewide. But in 2006, Democratic Governor Jennifer Granholm carried the 1st, winning every county in the UP and 61% farther south in Bay County.

The congressman from the 1st District is Bart Stupak, a Democrat and a "Yooper" from Menominee on the Wisconsin border, just a short jaunt from Green Bay. He was a police officer in Escanaba, then became a Michigan state trooper in 1974 and also earned a law degree; in 1984 he was injured in the line of duty and retired from the force. In 1988 he was elected to the Michigan House; in 1990 he lost a race for the state Senate. Stupak got into the 1992 House race when incumbent Republican Bob Davis, with 878 overdrafts in the House bank, decided to drop out. In the general he beat Republican Philip Ruppe, who had represented the district from 1966-78, by 54%-44%.

Stupak's voting record has been toward the center for House Democrats, though he is more conservative than most of them on cultural issues. He is a founder of the Congressional Law Enforcement Caucus. He is strongly opposed to abortion, and spoke out against it at the 1996 Democratic National Convention; he used his speaking slot in 2000 to talk about his district. In 2003, the House passed the bill he cosponsored to prohibit cloning, including for the production of embryos intended for research, but the bill stalled in the Senate. In 2006, he supported Bush's veto of the bill to expand embryonic stem cell research.

In the House, Stupak has paid great attention to local issues. He claims to be the first elected official to oppose drilling for oil and gas under the Great Lakes and worked on the successful bill to permanently kill it in 2005. He was a leading Democratic proponent of a September 2005 measure to crack down on oil-price gouging.

On Mother's Day 2000, Stupak suffered a personal tragedy, which for a time raised questions about his political future. His 17-year-old son B.J., a high school football player and class president, killed himself on the morning after his prom; more than 60 House members attended the funeral in Menominee. In coping with the tragedy, Stupak and his wife Laurie focused on their son's use of Accutane, a prescription-drug for acne treatment; the Food and Drug Administration had issued warnings about adverse psychological effects, including suicide attempts. Stupak went public with his concerns and he organized a House hearing about Accutane. He and his wife console other grieving families, and he devotes part of his congressional website to Accutane. In December 2004, the FDA responded to calls for an advisory panel to tighten restriction on the drug, including creation of a mandatory registry for individuals who dispense or use it.

During the 2000 campaign, Stupak faced a vigorous challenge from Chuck Yob, a Republican national committeeman, who criticized Stupak for taking more than 80% of his campaign money from special interest groups; the NRA endorsed Yob. Stupak argued that voters favored common-sense gun laws, and voters seemed to be in no mood for controversy after the family tragedy. Stupak won 58%-40%, losing only one county, and hasn't had a competitive race since. Republicans hope to win the seat if Stupak does not run, but there is little chance as long as he does. Republicans were floating state Representative Tom Casperson of Escanaba as a potential 2008 candidate; Casperson defeated Stupak's wife Laurie, who had been mayor of Menominee since 1996, 52%-48% to win his state House seat in 2002.

With the Democratic takeover of the House, Stupak pledged to serve as an aggressive chairman of the Oversight and Investigations Subcommittee at Energy and Commerce, which has long been a platform for committee chairman John Dingell, a home-state ally. An early focus was security breaches at the Los Alamos labs.

SECOND DISTRICT

Rep. Pete Hoekstra (R)

Elected 1992, 8th term; b. Oct. 30, 1953, Groningen, Netherlands; home, Holland; Hope Col., B.A. 1975, U. of MI, M.B.A. 1977; Christian Reformed; married (Diane).

Professional Career: Furniture Exec., Herman Miller Co., 1977-92.

DC Office: 2234 RHOB, 20515, 202-225-4401; Fax: 202-226-0779; Web site: hoekstra.house.gov.

District Offices: Cadillac, 231-775-0050; Holland, 616-395-0030; Muskegon, 231-722-8386.

Committees: *Education & Labor* (3d of 22 R): Early Childhood, Elementary & Secondary Education; Health, Employment, Labor & Pensions. *Permanent Select Committee on Intelligence* (RMM of 8 R).

Group Ratings

	ADA	ACLU	AFS	LCV	ITIC	NTU	COC	ACU	CFG	FRC
2006	5	11	0	0	71	64	93	92	79	100
2005	0	—	0	6	—	63	89	100	71	83

National Journal Ratings

	2005 LIB	—	2005 CONS	2006 LIB	—	2006 CONS
Economic	24%	—	74%	9%	—	90%
Social	26%	—	73%	6%	—	92%
Foreign	11%	—	86%	33%	—	63%

Key Votes of the 109th Congress

1. Estate Tax Repeal	Y	5. Limit Interstate Abortion	Y	9. Build Border Fence	Y
2. Limit CAFE Standards	Y	6. Extend Patriot Act	Y	10. CAFTA	Y
3. FY06 Spending Curb	Y	7. Bar Same Sex Marriage	Y	11. Oppose Iraq Withdrawal	Y
4. Drilling in ANWR	Y	8. Stem Cell Research $	N	12. Detainee Tribunals	Y

Election Results

2006 general	Pete Hoekstra (R)	183,006	(66%)	($676,667)
	Kimon Kotos (D)	86,950	(32%)	($9,622)
	Other	5,438	(2%)	
2006 primary	Pete Hoekstra (R)	unopposed		
2004 general	Pete Hoekstra (R)	225,343	(69%)	($498,230)
	Kimon Kotos (D)	94,040	(29%)	($14,779)
	Other	5,622	(2%)	

Prior Winning Percentages: 2002 (70%); 2000 (64%); 1998 (69%); 1996 (65%); 1994 (75%); 1992 (63%)

The People		Race/Ethnic Origin	Ancestry	
Area size:	5,508 sq. mi.	87.5% White	German: 15.3% Dutch: 14.8%	
Urban population:	56.2%	4.5% Black	English: 7.1%	
Rural population:	43.8%	1.0% Asian	**2004 Presidential Vote**	
Pop. 2000:	662,563	0.6% Native Am.	Bush (R)	203,051 (60%)
Pop. 2005 (est):	691,599	0.0% Hawaiian	Kerry (D)	131,552 (39%)
Median income:	$42,589	1.2% Two+ races	Other	2,904 (1%)
Poverty status:	8.9%	0.1% Other	**2000 Presidential Vote**	
Military veterans:	13.2%	5.2% Hispanic Origin	Bush (R)	172,428 (59%)
			Gore (D)	111,739 (38%)
			Other	6,550 (2%)
			Cook Partisan Voting Index: R + 9	
Occupation	Blue collar: 33.1%	White collar: 51.3%	Gray collar: 15.6%	

Lining the eastern shoreline of Lake Michigan, where the lake winds temper the frigid Michigan winters, are some of the nation's longest and highest sand dunes. In the late 19th century, this shoreline was America's greatest lumber country; the ports on the small rivers were choked with logs and full of lumbermen from Norway and Sweden, Ireland and Scotland, Quebec and New England. During the timber boom, the shoreline just to the south was the locus of America's largest migration from the Netherlands and still has the nation's largest concentration of Dutch-Americans. Wooden shoes are now seen only in the Tulip Festival in Holland, but here conscientious Dutch work habits have produced some of the most highly skilled workers in America, and this has become a busy manufacturing area, with products ranging from baby food at Gerber in Fremont to self-dimming car mirrors at Gentex in Zeeland. With Herman Miller in Zeeland, Haworth in Holland and Steelcase in Grand Rapids, it is the center of the American office furniture industry. The lands just behind the shore are fruit-growing country, with some of the nation's largest cherry orchards to the north and blueberry patches to the south.

The 2d Congressional District of Michigan occupies the Lake Michigan shoreline counties, plus a tier of counties inland including a small part of Grand Rapids's Kent County. It stretches from the lumber country around Manistee south to Holland and the resort town of Saugatuck. For years Dutch-American voters have been America's most Republican ethnically identifiable group (the only competitor: Cuban-Americans), and the 2d and 3d Districts centered on Grand Rapids are the two most Republican districts in Michigan. Holland and surrounding Ottawa County voted 72% for George W. Bush in 2004.

The congressman from the 2d District is Pete Hoekstra (pronounced *HOOK-stra*), first elected to the House in 1992. He emigrated from the Netherlands at 3, graduated from Hope College in Holland (with a semester in Washington during Watergate) and got an MBA at the University of Michigan. Hoekstra went to work at Herman Miller, where he helped develop the "Equa Chair" seat and became vice president for marketing. In 1992, he decided to run what seemed an improbable campaign for Congress against Guy Vander Jagt, 26-year incumbent and chairman of the NRCC since 1975. Hoekstra saved up vacation time and took a county-by-county bicycle tour of the district. With an earnestness that rang true, Hoekstra called for citizen, not career, politicians; refused PAC money and supported abolishing PACs; advocated 12-year term limits; promised to uphold family values and to oppose abortion. Hoekstra spent only $55,600 to Vander Jagt's $725,000. But on primary day, he carried the heavily Dutch Ottawa and Allegan Counties, 53%-31%; they cast 59% of the primary vote, and Hoekstra won 46%-40%. He won the general election easily and has not been threatened since.

Hoekstra brought to Washington a mistrust of government and a desire to apply the participatory management ideas he had developed at Herman Miller; he still works at a standup Herman Miller desk and sleeps on the office's black leather couch. In early 1994 he was asked by Newt Gingrich to plan how to manage a Republican House, something few others thought they would live to see. Only a few of his reforms were adopted: the House barred former members from lobbying on the floor, and it passed (though the Senate didn't) a ban on pensions to former members convicted of a felony.

In 1995, Hoekstra got the chair of the Oversight and Investigations Subcommittee of the Education and Workforce Committee. In summer 1997 he started on two major assignments from the leadership. The first was an investigation of labor law. Republican leaders hoped he would investigate the role of unions in the 1996 campaigns, but instead he conducted what he called the American Worker at a Crossroads project. Another assignment was investigating problems with the Teamsters Union but the Teamsters were unforthcoming with evidence. Hoekstra chose not to hold publicized hearings. In early 1999 the leadership took the issue away from Hoekstra and gave it to committee chairman Bill Goodling. In May 2001 he was one of 52 Republicans voting against the annual testing provisions in George W. Bush's education bill. He was the only Michigan member to vote against the bill in December 2001, when it passed overwhelmingly; he was unhappy that vouchers had been voted down.

In 1996 Hoekstra began a campaign to limit Federal Prison Industries, which employs prisoners at China-level prices to produce office furniture and auto components; for years it was the mandatory source for federal purchases of office furniture. Hoekstra stepped up his campaign after 2001, when office furniture manufacturers faced a slump; in November 2003, the House passed Hoekstra's bill phasing out the mandatory source requirement over five years. It eventually passed the Senate and became law in December 2004. Hoekstra continued working the issue, sponsoring after negotiations with the Justice Department a bill that eliminates the requirement that agencies buy furniture from FPI, caps FPI sales at 20% of government purchases and creates new training programs for prisoners; it passed the House 362-57 in September 2006. On other issues with a local impact, Hoekstra hailed the end of the steel tariffs in December 2003 (office furniture manufacturers buy a lot of steel) and joined with Illinois Democrat Rahm Emanuel to cosponsor the Great Lakes

Financing Act, to authorize funding for combating invasive species and cleaning up the lakes. He sponsored a bill in April 2006 with grants to local communities, like Muskegon, that provide money for private health insurance to the uninsured. He has opposed Indian gambling casinos and criticized the Justice Department for approval of an Indian land trust in Allegan County.

For several years Hoekstra was frustrated in his attempts to move up in the leadership, perhaps because of his less than perfect record of supporting leadership positions on issues like missile defense and normal trade relations with China; he has proposed a constitutional amendment to establish recall for members of Congress, nonbinding national referenda on issues and a "none of the above" choice in elections. In November 1998 he ran for vice chairman of the House Republican Conference but he was eliminated on the second ballot. After the 2000 election, he expressed interest in succeeding John Kasich as Budget chairman. But the position went to Jim Nussle instead. He sought the chairmanship of the Education and the Workforce Committee, but he lost to John Boehner in the Republican Steering Committee.

Hoekstra got a seat on the Intelligence Committee in 2001 and sponsored the bill to improve intelligence sharing between law enforcement and intelligence agencies that passed overwhelmingly in June 2002. In October 2003, when weapons inspector David Kay delivered his interim report, Hoekstra stressed Kay's finding that the Saddam Hussein regime had maintained weapons of mass destruction program capability. In August 2004, after Porter Goss was confirmed as CIA Director, Speaker Dennis Hastert and the Steering Committee had to select a new Intelligence chairman. Hoekstra was third in seniority but got the job. The most senior member, Ray LaHood, insisted on keeping his seat on Appropriations; that was evidently unacceptable to Hastert. Jim Gibbons, a rough-hewn Westerner and now governor of Nevada, was apparently unacceptable too. So Hoekstra was named chairman. His appointment was hailed by ranking Democrat Jane Harman. When George W. Bush issued executive orders increasing the authority of the CIA director, Hoekstra and Harman issued a joint statement saying that they needed to be supported by legislation, and promised to advance it. Hoekstra supported intelligence reorganization along the lines recommended by the 9/11 Commission, although the House passed a somewhat different bill. He hailed final passage of the bill in December 2004 and said the committee would monitor "whether this person [the national intelligence director] is getting the support that's needed, whether there are elements elsewhere in the bureaucracy that are trying to undercut it."

But not all was comity on the committee in the 109th Congress. After opposition from Democrats and the administration, Hoekstra in June 2005 withdrew an amendment limiting transfer of personnel from one agency to another. In February 2006 he criticized a legal analysis by the Congressional Research Service of the program of NSA surveillance of contacts between al Qaeda suspects abroad and persons in the United States; Harman sharply disagreed. Hoekstra has pressed for publication and translation of material captured in the invasion of Iraq, which he argued might shed light on the state of Saddam's weapons of mass destruction programs: in December 2005 he and Pat Roberts called for declassifying 35,000 boxes of documents and for posting them on the Internet; in March 2006 he pressed DNI John Negroponte to get 2,500 hours of secret audio recordings transcribed (only 12 hours had been). He did not always support the administration: in a May 2006 letter to George W. Bush he complained about not being informed of certain unspecified secret programs and repeated his criticism in July. Also in May he opposed the nomination of General Michael Hayden to be head of the CIA on the grounds that there were too many military men in top intelligence positions; he was "the wrong person at the wrong place at the wrong time." In October he pressed the administration to "pursue illegal disclosures of classified information," including the NSA surveillance program and the terrorist finance tracking program which had been revealed by newspapers. In October 2006 he suspended a Democratic staffer suspected of leaking a National Intelligence Estimate in September, shortly after it was made available to the committee; the staffer denied the leak and Harman protested vociferously. Also Harman criticized him for being in touch with imprisoned former committee member Duke Cunningham about testifying and for refusing to release an outside investigator's report on Cunningham. After Democrats won their majority and Speaker Nancy Pelosi appointed Silvestre Reyes as committee chairman, Hoekstra as ranking minority member said, "I think Silvestre and I are going to have the same kind of relationship. I get the sense that he is going to reach out to me as I did to Jane [Harman]."

In 1992, as term limits on state legislators passed in Michigan, Hoekstra pledged to serve only 12 years. By 2002 he had changed his mind and announced he would run again in an open letter to his constituents. He also communicates with his district by posting a daily travel diary from his foreign trips and by summer bike tours through the district; the theme of the latter in 2006 was "energy diversity equals energy independence." Hoekstra speaks Dutch and in May 2006 he and

Dutch-American Democrat Chris Van Hollen created a Dutch Caucus. He has opposed comprehensive immigration bill and cherishes his own naturalization papers, which he carries to naturalization ceremonies. "I describe it as one of the most valuable pieces of paper in the world. I really end up having a problem with giving one of the most valuable pieces of paper in the world to people who came here illegally." Hoekstra, who has been reelected without serious competition, has said he is considering a bid for governor in 2010, when term limits will prohibit Democrat Jennifer Granholm from running again.

THIRD DISTRICT

Rep. Vernon Ehlers (R)

Elected Dec. 1993, 7th full term; b. Feb. 6, 1934, Pipestone, MN; home, Grand Rapids; Calvin Col., 1952-55; U. of CA, A.B. 1956, Ph.D. 1960, U. of Heidelberg, Germany, 1961-62; Christian Reformed; married (Johanna).

Elected Office: Kent Cnty. Comm., 1974-82, Chmn., 1978-81; MI House of Reps., 1982-86; MI Senate, 1986-93, Pres. Pro Tem, 1990-93.

Professional Career: Prof., Calvin Col., 1966-82.

DC Office: 2182 RHOB, 20515, 202-225-3831; Fax: 202-225-5144; Web site: www.house.gov/ehlers.

District Offices: Grand Rapids, 616-451-8383.

Committees: *Education & Labor* (6th of 22 R): Early Childhood, Elementary & Secondary Education; Higher Education, Lifelong Learning & Competitiveness. *House Administration* (RMM of 3 R). *Science & Technology* (6th of 20 R): Research & Science Education (RMM); Technology & Innovation. *Transportation & Infrastructure* (7th of 34 R): Water Resources & Environment; Aviation.

Group Ratings

	ADA	ACLU	AFS	LCV	ITIC	NTU	COC	ACU	CFG	FRC
2006	10	45	0	75	100	50	80	68	49	85
2005	15	—	0	50	—	50	85	64	40	77

National Journal Ratings

	2005 LIB	—	2005 CONS		2006 LIB	—	2006 CONS
Economic	46%	—	54%		46%	—	53%
Social	55%	—	45%		48%	—	52%
Foreign	52%	—	47%		55%	—	44%

Key Votes of the 109th Congress

1. Estate Tax Repeal	Y	5. Limit Interstate Abortion	Y	9. Build Border Fence	Y
2. Limit CAFE Standards	N	6. Extend Patriot Act	Y	10. CAFTA	Y
3. FY06 Spending Curb	Y	7. Bar Same Sex Marriage	Y	11. Oppose Iraq Withdrawal	Y
4. Drilling in ANWR	N	8. Stem Cell Research $	N	12. Detainee Tribunals	Y

Election Results

2006 general	Vernon Ehlers (R)	171,212	(63%)	($458,540)
	James Rinck (D)	93,846	(35%)	($24,122)
	Other	6,294	(2%)	
2006 primary	Vernon Ehlers (R)	unopposed		
2004 general	Vernon Ehlers (R)	214,465	(67%)	($308,785)
	Peter Hickey (D)	101,395	(31%)	($1,054)
	Other	6,243	(2%)	

Prior Winning Percentages: 2002 (70%); 2000 (65%); 1998 (73%); 1996 (69%); 1994 (74%); 1993 (67%)

The People		Race/Ethnic Origin	Ancestry	
Area size:	1,897 sq. mi.	82.2% White	German: 14.6%	Dutch: 13.1%
Urban population:	77.1%	7.9% Black	Irish: 7.9%	
Rural population:	22.9%	1.6% Asian	**2004 Presidential Vote**	
Pop. 2000:	662,563	0.4% Native Am.	Bush (R) 197,493	(59%)
Pop. 2005 (est):	691,531	0.0% Hawaiian	Kerry (D) 133,460	(40%)
Median income:	$45,936	1.5% Two+ races	Other 1,964	(1%)
Poverty status:	8.6%	0.1% Other	**2000 Presidential Vote**	
Military veterans:	11.4%	6.2% Hispanic Origin	Bush (R) 170,622	(60%)
			Gore (D) 110,121	(38%)
			Other 5,942	(2%)
			Cook Partisan Voting Index: R + 9	

Occupation	Blue collar: 29.5%	White collar: 56.7%	Gray collar: 13.8%

Grand Rapids is Michigan's second-largest city, the center of its most prosperous and confident metropolitan area. The city's roots are in trees: It grew as a center for processing and turning into furniture the hardwood forests of northern Michigan. By the early 20th century, Grand Rapids was the leading furniture manufacturer in the nation. The Depression of the 1930s knocked the bottom out of the residential furniture market, and many manufacturers moved to cheaper-labor North Carolina. So Grand Rapids had to reinvent itself, and did. It went into office furniture, and today, three of the nation's largest office furniture manufacturers (Steelcase, Haworth and Herman Miller) are located in or near here. It capitalized also on a knack for sales. Rich DeVos and Jay Van Andel started Amway, the direct sales empire, which now has half of its sales abroad, and Frederik and Hendrik Meijer started Meijer's Thrifty Acres, combining supermarkets with discount stores in a way that even Wal-Mart has not been able to equal. Grand Rapids is also the center of a machine tool empire; the home of Wolverine World Wide, maker of Hush Puppy shoes; and the headquarters of Bissell and its carpet sweepers. Fifty years ago Grand Rapids and its up-and-coming businesses were outshined by Detroit and the auto industry. Today, the Grand Rapids region has been outpacing the rest of the state in growth and has been a major engine in Michigan's economy.

One ingredient in Grand Rapids's success is its unique ethnic mix. It was founded by New England Yankees, but much of its character was set by the Dutch immigrants who began arriving in western Michigan in the 1870s, and are still coming today; 13% of people here claim Dutch ancestry (probably no other American city has such a high proportion of "V" pages in the phone book). The Dutch brought with them a piety witnessed in their Reform and Christian Reform churches, and a culture of hard work and precision craftsmanship; their cultural conservatism and belief in market economics runs deep. Dutch tradition and entrepreneurial success have been the ingredients of a civic activism that has given Grand Rapids a host of creative civic institutions—and an Alexander Calder stabile—that are the match of any city in the country. Currently Grand Rapids's downtown has been thick with construction cranes, as the city prepares to open a new Grand Rapids Art Museum with triple the space of the old, as well as a new hotel and medical buildings. Years ago Grand Rapids commissioned an Alexander Calder sculpture for the plaza outside its city hall, and now it has others by Calder, Andy Goldsworthy and Maya Lin. Other attractions: the Gerald R. Ford Presidential Library and Museum and the outdoor Meijer Gardens.

Politically, Grand Rapids has been the center of Michigan Republicanism for much of the last century. It has also produced national Republican leaders. Arthur Vandenberg, originally a newspaper editor, was U.S. senator from 1928-51; once an isolationist, he provided key support for the bipartisan internationalist foreign policies of Franklin D. Roosevelt and Harry Truman. Another was Gerald Ford, who rose to House Republican leader in 1965, vice president in 1973, and then president after Richard Nixon resigned in 1974. Nixon got a bit of a nudge from the Grand Rapids area when, in a February 1974 special election, it voted to replace Ford with a Democrat, a clear sign that the Republican heartland was turning on Nixon. Since then, however, the area became more Republican than ever; Grand Rapids and Kent County voted 59% for George W. Bush in 2000 and 2004.

The 3d Congressional District of Michigan includes Grand Rapids and almost all of Kent County, plus Ionia and Barry Counties to the east and south. It is one of the two most Republican districts in Michigan, indeed one of the most Republican in the Midwest.

The congressman from the 3d District is Vern Ehlers, first chosen in a December 1993 special election. Ehlers grew up in small-town Minnesota, the son of a Christian Reform minister, attended Calvin College in Grand Rapids, got a Ph.D. in physics at Berkeley and then returned to Calvin to teach for 17 years. In 1974, concerned about local waste management, he was elected Kent County commissioner; in 1982 he won a seat in the state House and in 1986 the state Senate. After Congressman Paul Henry died in July 1993, Ehlers ran to succeed him, as he had in both houses of the legislature. He won the November primary with 33% of the vote; a month later he whipped the Democrat 67%-23%.

Ehlers brought to House Republicans, then entering their 40th year in the minority, a majority mindset. That brought him to the attention of Newt Gingrich, who named him to his transition team after the 1994 election. He assigned Ehlers, the first research physicist in Congress, to lead efforts to revamp the House's computer system (there were 11 different email systems). In 1995 Ehlers responded with a system making available vote tallies, public hearing transcripts and texts of amendments and bills, plus the Thomas Library of Congress website; he was responsible for convincing the House to migrate from one-time market leader Lotus Notes to the now ubiquitous Microsoft Exchange email program. His religious faith and scientific training have left Ehlers with a middle-of-the-House voting record. Ehlers often insists on the need for research to determine public needs. In February 2004 he passed an amendment to the transportation bill pegging future research at 1.08% of total spending. When controversy arose over the composition of National Academy of Science advisory panels, he said, "A single, guiding principle should be applied—select the most qualified person for the job." But he added that on presidential appointments, "It is important that the scientists be in tune with the philosophy of the appointing president."

As chairman of the Science subcommittee overseeing EPA and NOAA, he has sponsored several laws that have won widespread backing. With Senator Carl Levin, he has sponsored measures to study invasive species, and in October 2004 he helped pass $9 million for an electric barrier in the Illinois River to prevent Asian carp from getting into the Great Lakes. He has continued to press with some success for more spending on Great Lakes problems. With Carl Levin, he proposed a $23 billion program, with most of the money for rebuilding old sewer systems, plus a requirement that oceangoing ships treat ballast water by 2011 to keep out invasive species and a tripling of funding to clean up contaminated areas and reduce mercury levels. In the 109th Congress he worked with the Transportation and Environment committees to get agreement on an organic act for NOAA. When he took over the chairmanship of House Administration, he said he still wanted to chair the Science Committee, but after the 2006 election the ranking minority member position was given to Ralph Hall. Ehlers is now ranking minority member on the Research and Science Education Subcommittee. At one subcommittee hearing, he acknowledged that he was a nerd in high school and said he told students that "they shouldn't look down on nerds because if they are not a nerd they are going to end up working for one."

Ehlers has a penchant for compromise. As head of a three-member task force on Robert Dornan's challenge to his 984-vote defeat in 1996, Ehlers looked over the evidence and announced that it showed "a large amount" of vote fraud but not enough to vacate the seat. That may help explain why Speaker Dennis Hastert bypassed him and selected Bob Ney to chair the House Administration Committee after the 2000 election. But after Hastert pressed Ney to resign in January 2006, Ehlers got the chairmanship; now he is ranking minority member. He has worked with the Congressional Management Foundation on a 10-year strategic technological program for the House. He supported the March 2006 measure to exclude the Internet from the definition of public communication under the campaign finance laws. He argues that voting machines should have auditability, but "there's also other issues, a lack of security and hacking. I could hack a voting computer." He led the debate on the bill to require photo ID for voting which was passed 228-196 in September 2006. The House has passed his bill for grants and scholarships to help small manufacturers. He persuaded Bill Young to put in the defense appropriations bill $2 million for a Navy study of water-free urinals.

Like most other Michigan Republicans, he opposed George W. Bush's steel tariffs, and he was one of the Republicans who voted to repeal the section of the Patriot Act allowing agents access to library records. He has been one of the House Republicans who opposed oil drilling in the Arctic National Wildlife Refuge and who forced the Republican leadership to take the issue out of must-pass appropriation bills. He was the only member of the Michigan delegation to decline to sign a letter calling on George W. Bush to pressure the oil companies to set targets for the number of ethanol pumps in gas stations.

Ehlers refuses to take more than 30% of his campaign money from outside the district. He has been re-elected by very wide margins.

FOURTH DISTRICT

Rep. Dave Camp (R)

Elected 1990, 9th term; b. July 9, 1953, Midland; home, Midland; Albion Col., B.A. 1975, U. of San Diego, J.D. 1978; Catholic; married (Nancy).

Elected Office: MI House of Reps., 1988-90.

Professional Career: Practicing atty., 1978-90; MI Special Asst. Atty. Gen., 1980-84; A.A., U.S. Rep. Bill Schuette, 1984-87.

DC Office: 137 CHOB, 20515, 202-225-3561; Fax: 202-225-9679; Web site: camp.house.gov.

District Offices: Midland, 989-631-2552; Traverse City, 231-929-4711.

Committees: *Ways & Means* (3d of 17 R): Health (RMM); Income Security & Family Support.

Group Ratings

	ADA	ACLU	AFS	LCV	ITIC	NTU	COC	ACU	CFG	FRC
2006	0	15	0	8	100	58	100	84	53	85
2005	10	—	13	6	—	55	89	83	56	85

National Journal Ratings

	2005 LIB	—	2005 CONS		2006 LIB	—	2006 CONS
Economic	23%	—	77%		15%	—	85%
Social	17%	—	83%		17%	—	79%
Foreign	34%	—	61%		38%	—	59%

Key Votes of the 109th Congress

1. Estate Tax Repeal	Y	5. Limit Interstate Abortion	*	9. Build Border Fence	Y
2. Limit CAFE Standards	Y	6. Extend Patriot Act	Y	10. CAFTA	Y
3. FY06 Spending Curb	Y	7. Bar Same Sex Marriage	Y	11. Oppose Iraq Withdrawal	Y
4. Drilling in ANWR	Y	8. Stem Cell Research $	N	12. Detainee Tribunals	Y

Election Results

2006 general	Dave Camp (R)	160,041	(61%)	($1,111,769)
	Mike Huckleberry (D)	100,260	(38%)	($62,030)
	Other	3,944	(2%)	
2006 primary	Dave Camp (R)	unopposed		
2004 general	Dave Camp (R)	205,274	(64%)	($521,658)
	Mike Huckleberry (D)	110,885	(35%)	($83,217)
	Other	2,765	(1%)	

Prior Winning Percentages: 2002 (68%); 2000 (68%); 1998 (91%); 1996 (65%); 1994 (73%); 1992 (63%); 1990 (65%)

The People		Race/Ethnic Origin	Ancestry	
Area size:	8,053 sq. mi.	92.8% White	German: 19.5%	English: 8.9%
Urban population:	41.4%	2.1% Black	Irish: 8.2%	
Rural population:	58.6%	0.7% Asian	**2004 Presidential Vote**	
Pop. 2000:	662,563	0.8% Native Am.	Bush (R) 181,314	(55%)
Pop. 2005 (est):	686,660	0.0% Hawaiian	Kerry (D) 145,774	(44%)
Median income:	$39,020	1.1% Two+ races	Other 2,697	(1%)
Poverty status:	10.5%	0.1% Other	**2000 Presidential Vote**	
Military veterans:	13.6%	2.4% Hispanic Origin	Bush (R) 154,539	(54%)
			Gore (D) 126,282	(44%)
			Other 7,468	(3%)
			Cook Partisan Voting Index: R + 4	

Occupation	Blue collar: 28.7%	White collar: 53.5%	Gray collar: 17.8%

Flat and treeless for miles, the central reaches of Michigan's Lower Peninsula are farm country, exposed to bitter winds and snow drifts in winter and shining sun for precious weeks in summer. Like the steppes of Eastern Europe, these are farmlands that produce hearty crops: potatoes, navy beans, sugar beets. The little cities here are often small factory towns, with neat tree-lined streets on a grid layout that suddenly end and turn to bare fields. Each city has some distinction. Midland in 1891 was a declining lumber town when Herbert Dow perfected an electrolytic process to extract chemicals from northern Michigan's extensive brine wells; that was the start of Dow Chemical, still headquartered in this now upscale town. Owosso in 1902 was the birthplace of Thomas E. Dewey, later New York governor and Republican nominee for president in 1944 and 1948. It was also the home of novelist James Oliver Curwood and his Curwood Castle writing studio; today it hosts the Curwood Festival, lovingly chronicled by Thomas Mallon in *Rockets and Rodeos,* and is the site of Mallon's novel *Dewey Defeats Truman.* Mount Pleasant, to the north, is the home of Central Michigan University.

The 4th Congressional District of Michigan, the state's second largest, includes much of this territory north of Lansing and Grand Rapids and west of Flint and Saginaw. It stretches north up the freeways, hemmed in between U.S. 131 to the west and I-75 to the east; thousands drive up the routes in the fall to hunt and in winter to ski, into the rolling country around Houghton Lake, once lumber country and now a retirement and resort area, with trailers and condominiums between knotty-pine cottages clustered around icy green lakes. It has more farms than any other district in Michigan. The district reaches Traverse City, which has the world's largest concentration of red tart cherry orchards and is burgeoning with vacation homes, resorts and more than two dozen wineries: Michigan leads the nation in production of tart cherries, blueberries and dry edible beans. Politically, the district remains mostly Republican territory, especially in the Midland and Traverse City areas, though some counties vote Democratic on occasion. George W. Bush won 54% and 55% here in 2000 and 2004.

The congressman from the 4th District is Dave Camp, a Republican first elected in 1990. Camp grew up in Midland and returned there after school to practice law. In 1984 he managed the successful congressional campaign of his boyhood friend Bill Schuette; in 1990 Schuette unsuccessfully ran against Senator Carl Levin, and Camp ran for Congress after having served two years in the state House. His key victory was in the Republican primary, where he beat former legislator and Pat Robertson supporter Al Cropsey, 33%-30%. He has won since without difficulty.

Camp has a generally conservative voting record, especially on cultural issues, and is influential on the Ways and Means Committee, where he has become the third-ranking Republican. He played a key role in passing the welfare bill in 1996, helping to write the two bills vetoed by Bill Clinton. In response to attacks from Democrats, he defended a provision that he added to the Medicare/prescription drug bill in 2003 permitting nursing homes to restart nurse aide training programs even if the facility has recently violated federal nursing home standards. Suspending the programs "exacerbates the nurse aide shortage," Camp said. As enacted, that bill also included an amendment by Camp to cover cholesterol screening for all beneficiaries. Separately, he pushed legislation to assist patients with kidney disease. He has advocated changes in the federal Hope scholarships to direct more benefits to low-income students. In 2007, he became the ranking minority member of the Health Subcommittee.

Camp has worked on other issues. In 2000, he helped win enactment of the International Adoption Act, which designates the State Department to help adoptive parents in dealing with officials in other nations. Since then, he has pushed for ratification by the Senate of a treaty on international adoption, which would remove additional obstacles; as a state legislator in Michigan, he had worked with parents and children in the foster-care system. He authored the Organ Donor Card Insert Act, under which 70 million taxpayers received organ donor information with their income tax refunds, and he has sought expansion of trade-adjustment assistance for workers. He won enactment of his bill to protect the state's 120 lighthouses, the most in the nation. In 2006, he was the only House Republican who belonged to both the conservative Steering Committee and the moderate Main Street Partnership.

Camp has had minimal opposition in the 4th District. He keeps in close touch with the district by signing every constituent letter that leaves his office, often with a personal note—a total of roughly 30,000 each year.

FIFTH DISTRICT

Rep. Dale Kildee (D)

Elected 1976, 16th term; b. Sept. 16, 1929, Flint; home, Flint; Sacred Heart Seminary, B.A. 1952, U. of MI, M.A. 1961, Rotary Fellow, U. of Peshawar, Pakistan; Catholic; married (Gayle).

Elected Office: MI House of Reps., 1964-74; MI Senate, 1974-75.

Professional Career: H.S. teacher, 1954-64.

DC Office: 2107 RHOB, 20515, 202-225-3611; Fax: 202-225-6393; Web site: www.house.gov/kildee.

District Offices: Bay City, 989-891-0990; Flint, 810-239-1437; Saginaw, 989-755-8904.

Committees: *Education & Labor* (2d of 27 D): Early Childhood, Elementary & Secondary Education (Chmn.); Health, Employment, Labor & Pensions. *Natural Resources* (2d of 27 D): Fisheries, Wildlife & Oceans; National Parks, Forests & Public Lands.

Group Ratings

	ADA	ACLU	AFS	LCV	ITIC	NTU	COC	ACU	CFG	FRC
2006	80	86	100	100	29	7	27	20	4	42
2005	80	—	100	89	—	13	33	20	3	46

National Journal Ratings

	2005 LIB	—	2005 CONS		2006 LIB	—	2006 CONS
Economic	74%	—	25%		86%	—	11%
Social	66%	—	33%		67%	—	32%
Foreign	74%	—	25%		80%	—	18%

Key Votes of the 109th Congress

1. Estate Tax Repeal	N	5. Limit Interstate Abortion	Y	9. Build Border Fence	Y
2. Limit CAFE Standards	Y	6. Extend Patriot Act	N	10. CAFTA	N
3. FY06 Spending Curb	N	7. Bar Same Sex Marriage	N	11. Oppose Iraq Withdrawal	N
4. Drilling in ANWR	N	8. Stem Cell Research $	N	12. Detainee Tribunals	N

Election Results

2006 general	Dale Kildee (D)	176,171	(73%)	($593,816)
	Eric Klammer (R)	60,967	(25%)	($638)
	Other	4,553	(2%)	
2006 primary	Dale Kildee (D)	unopposed		
2004 general	Dale Kildee (D)	208,163	(67%)	($608,283)
	Myrah Kirkwood (R)	96,934	(31%)	($281,615)
	Other	4,818	(2%)	

Prior Winning Percentages: 2002 (92%); 2000 (61%); 1998 (56%); 1996 (59%); 1994 (51%); 1992 (54%); 1990 (68%); 1988 (76%); 1986 (80%); 1984 (93%); 1982 (75%); 1980 (93%); 1978 (77%); 1976 (70%)

The People		Race/Ethnic Origin	Ancestry	
Area size:	1,780 sq. mi.	75.0% White	German: 15.3% Irish: 7.6%	
Urban population:	79.4%	18.5% Black	English: 7.4%	
Rural population:	20.6%	0.7% Asian	**2004 Presidential Vote**	
Pop. 2000:	662,563	0.5% Native Am.	Kerry (D)	187,671 (59%)
Pop. 2005 (est):	653,755	0.0% Hawaiian	Bush (R)	129,457 (41%)
Median income:	$39,675	1.7% Two+ races	Other	1,889 (1%)
Poverty status:	13.7%	0.1% Other	**2000 Presidential Vote**	
Military veterans:	13.2%	3.6% Hispanic Origin	Gore (D)	174,788 (61%)
			Bush (R)	106,445 (37%)
			Other	5,811 (2%)
			Cook Partisan Voting Index: D +12	

Occupation   Blue collar: 31.4%   White collar: 51.0%   Gray collar: 17.6%

The flat plains south of Saginaw Bay, the inlet of Lake Huron that separates Michigan's Thumb (people really call it that) from the mitten of the Lower Peninsula, is one of the nation's premier industrial areas. Some 130 years ago it was the nation's premier lumber country, with huge stands of virgin trees being cut down and 36 sawmills in Bay City, with logs piled high along both banks of the Saginaw River in the 15 miles between Bay City and Saginaw. When the land was clear, it was sown with beans—the navy beans that are the primary ingredient of Senate bean soup—and sugar beets. A century ago, heavy industry followed. Flint, a small town on a minor branch of the Saginaw River, was the home base of W. C. Durant, the investor who merged several young auto firms and formed General Motors. GM put its Chevrolet and Buick factories in Flint and its power steering facility in Saginaw, chosen because it was already a center of precision machinery manufacturing. From 1910 through the 1960s, Flint grew lustily as it built Chevys and Buicks, attracting workers from the mountains of Kentucky and Tennessee and the Black Belt of Alabama; country music, blues and soul and Southern accents became common in an area originally settled by New England Yankees. There was turmoil, too. Flint was the scene in January 1937 of the great sit-down strike that, when Governor Frank Murphy refused to send the National Guard to enforce a court order, forced GM to recognize the United Auto Workers as the bargaining agent for all its workers. Yet in many ways the GM company towns built good lives for their citizens. The UAW-GM contracts produced the world's highest wages for industrial workers and lavish fringe benefits, including a generous health care plan.

Then disaster struck. Auto sales plummeted with the oil shocks of the 1970s. Imports, especially from Japan, that were higher-quality and lower-price than American cars, took an increasing share of the market. In 1979 GM employed more than 70,000 workers in its Flint plants, a huge share of the labor force in a metro area of 430,000 people. Eventually, thousands left Flint as GM closed 12 of its 15 factories; by 2006 the GM payroll fell below 12,000. Flint's brave attempts to spruce up its downtown failed, and many storefronts have been boarded-up; its economic woes forced the state to take control of the city government. One-third of Flint households are in poverty, and many skilled workers have fled. Michael Moore, the prolific and partisan filmmaker, has used his hometown of Flint as the locale for much of his work about deteriorating life in America. Gritty Saginaw suffered with cutbacks by Delphi, its largest employer. But there has been some upturn. American car manufacturers have grown more adaptable and resilient, and small high-skill manufacturing operations in the Saginaw area have grown up in old factory buildings once considered worthless. This is part of southern Michigan's industrial belt with the expertise to sustain just-in-time manufacturing. In 2004, after the state announced jobs initiatives, GM said that it would invest $450 million to expand and refurbish engine and truck assembly operations in Flint. Two years later, it began production at the Flint Engine South plant of the new V6 engine, with improved fuel economy and lower emissions; Flint's old V8 engine plant had closed in 1992.

The 5th Congressional District of Michigan includes Flint and surrounding Genesee County, Saginaw and eastern Saginaw County, Bay City and eastern Bay County and rural Tuscola County, which is part of the Thumb. Flint, evenly divided between the parties when the sit-down strikes divided the community in the 1930s, is now heavily Democratic; Saginaw and Bay City somewhat less so. Tuscola continues to vote Republican.

The congressman from the 5th District is Dale Kildee, a Democrat first elected in 1976. Kildee grew up in Flint, studied for the priesthood, taught at a Catholic high school in Detroit and at Flint Central. His door-to-door campaigning got him elected to a state legislative seat in 1964, at 35, and enabled him to beat a 26-year veteran of the state Senate in 1974. He won the House seat in 1976. Kildee has an intensity of conviction derived from the liberal tradition lively in the American Catholic church—a tradition with little regard for market economics, a strong sense of obligation to care for the needy and a cultural conservatism. He is always pro-union, opposes abortion, and is something of a stickler on ethics. On the Education and the Workforce Committee, he is a strong ally of teachers' unions, a backer of increased federal aid for education and an opponent of school choice.

Kildee was the first House member to argue imported minivans should be subject not to the 2.5% tariff for cars but to the 25% tariff for trucks, which has been on the books since the early 1960s. The truck tariff has become a sticking point in U.S. negotiations with several countries, which led to his fierce opposition to a bilateral trade deal with Thailand; he also was a strong opponent of NAFTA and CAFTA. On the Resources Committee, he has concentrated on Indian issues; Kildee carries with his copy of the Constitution a copy of the 1832 Supreme Court decision that recognized Indian sovereignty. His efforts to clean up the Great Lakes have produced commendations by environmentalists. When Republican leaders confessed inadequate oversight of the House page program, Kildee complained about their failure to alert him; he has served more than two decades on the page board. In the majority, he took over as chairman of the Subcommittee on Early Childhood, Elementary and Secondary Education at Education and Labor and conducted extensive oversight, while demanding adequate funding of the No Child Left Behind Act, which was up for renewal in 2007.

Kildee has been easily reelected, except for a couple of tight races in the 1990s. In 2002, redistricting put him in the same heavily Democratic district with Bay City Democrat Jim Barcia, one of the more conservative Democrats in the House and, like Kildee, an opponent of abortion. Barcia evidently found the prospect of taking on Kildee daunting, and ran successfully for the state Senate. If the seat becomes open, Barcia is a possible candidate.

SIXTH DISTRICT

Rep. Fred Upton (R)

Elected 1986, 11th term; b. Apr. 23, 1953, St. Joseph; home, St. Joseph; U. of MI, B.A. 1975; Protestant; married (Amey).

Professional Career: Project coord., U.S. Rep. David Stockman, 1975-80; Legis. Affairs, O.M.B., 1981-83, Dir., 1984-85.

DC Office: 2183 RHOB, 20515, 202-225-3761; Fax: 202-225-4986; Web site: www.house.gov/upton.

District Offices: Kalamazoo, 269-385-0039; St. Joseph, 269-982-1986.

Committees: *Energy & Commerce* (4th of 26 R): Telecommunications & the Internet (RMM); Energy & Air Quality.

Group Ratings

	ADA	ACLU	AFS	LCV	ITIC	NTU	COC	ACU	CFG	FRC
2006	10	14	14	50	100	46	100	80	48	71
2005	10	—	13	6	—	52	89	80	48	85

National Journal Ratings

	2005 LIB	—	2005 CONS		2006 LIB	—	2006 CONS
Economic	42%	—	57%		48%	—	52%
Social	36%	—	64%		41%	—	58%
Foreign	48%	—	51%		50%	—	49%

Key Votes of the 109th Congress

1. Estate Tax Repeal	Y	5. Limit Interstate Abortion	Y	9. Build Border Fence	Y
2. Limit CAFE Standards	Y	6. Extend Patriot Act	Y	10. CAFTA	Y
3. FY06 Spending Curb	Y	7. Bar Same Sex Marriage	Y	11. Oppose Iraq Withdrawal	Y
4. Drilling in ANWR	Y	8. Stem Cell Research $	Y	12. Detainee Tribunals	Y

Election Results

2006 general	Fred Upton (R)	142,125	(61%)	($972,296)
	Kim Clark (D)	88,978	(38%)	($145,039)
	Other	3,480	(1%)	
2006 primary	Fred Upton (R)	unopposed		
2004 general	Fred Upton (R)	197,425	(65%)	($678,684)
	Scott Elliott (D)	97,978	(32%)	($46,185)
	Other	6,755	(2%)	

Prior Winning Percentages: 2002 (69%); 2000 (68%); 1998 (70%); 1996 (68%); 1994 (73%); 1992 (62%); 1990 (58%); 1988 (71%); 1986 (62%)

The People		Race/Ethnic Origin	Ancestry	
Area size:	3,420 sq. mi.	84.3% White	German: 17.2%	English: 8.3%
Urban population:	58.3%	8.8% Black	Irish: 8.3%	
Rural population:	41.7%	1.1% Asian	**2004 Presidential Vote**	
Pop. 2000:	662,563	0.5% Native Am.	Bush (R) 164,595	(53%)
Pop. 2005 (est):	673,966	0.0% Hawaiian	Kerry (D) 143,906	(46%)
Median income:	$40,943	1.6% Two+ races	Other 2,759	(1%)
Poverty status:	11.4%	0.1% Other	**2000 Presidential Vote**	
Military veterans:	12.8%	3.6% Hispanic Origin	Bush (R) 138,658	(52%)
			Gore (D) 119,740	(45%)
			Other 7,413	(3%)
			Cook Partisan Voting Index: R + 2	

Occupation Blue collar: 31.3% White collar: 53.0% Gray collar: 15.7%

The southwest corner of Michigan is at the western end of the overland trail from Detroit, over which the state's two southern tiers of counties were settled by New England Yankees and Upstate New Yorkers in the 1830s and 1840s. They built small towns with schools and churches and colleges, supported temperance and opposed capital punishment, and in 1854 started the Republican party. There are towns in southwest Michigan that still recall proudly their past as termini of the Underground Railroad, and black families with ancestors who made their way north out of slavery to freedom. Later, big industries transformed some of the small towns into significant cities. Kalamazoo, started by Dutch-Americans who introduced celery to this country, became the home of Upjohn pharmaceuticals, which went through several corporate changes and is now part of Pfizer. Predominantly black and struggling Benton Harbor and predominantly white and prosperous St. Joseph, twin towns on Lake Michigan originally known for cherry and peach orchards, remain the home of Whirlpool appliances. Many other local companies and other famous industrial names have moved out, along with their thousands of jobs. This southwest corner is where the influence of Michigan recedes: People here watch Chicago television and root for the Cubs or White Sox rather than the Tigers.

The 6th Congressional District of Michigan occupies this southwest corner of the state, with Kalamazoo and Benton Harbor-St. Joseph its two major urban areas, and three smaller counties and parts of two others besides. It was for many years arch-Republican territory, represented by a succession of congressmen who deplored federal spending and welfare state measures: New Deal opponent Clare Hoffman (1935-63), Nixon defender Edward Hutchinson (1963-77), and pork barrel critic and later Reagan Office of Management and Budget Director David Stockman (1977-81). In the 1990s, Kalamazoo trended toward the Democrats, and the 6th (with slightly different boundaries) cast small pluralities for Bill Clinton. George W. Bush carried the district twice but lost Kalamazoo County in 2000 and 2004, thanks in part to the influence of the Western Michigan University community and its 25,000 students; Democrat Governor Jennifer Granholm won Kalamazoo County by a 59%-39% margin over western Michigan Republican Dick DeVos in 2006.

The congressman from the 6th District is Fred Upton, a Republican first elected in 1986. The grandson of one of the founders of Whirlpool, Upton grew up in St. Joseph, attended the University of Michigan and worked for David Stockman, first on his House staff, then from 1981-85 at OMB. He returned home and ran in the 1986 Republican primary against Congressman Mark Siljander, a conservative and evangelical Christian, and won 55%-45%. Upton is less like the congressional David Stockman, a scourge of federal spending, and more like the OMB Stockman, who rued the Reagan tax cuts.

Upton has a moderate voting record and he has often flaunted his independence in the Republican House. He has sought, with limited success, to use his leverage to reduce the size of tax cuts during the Bush presidency. He has backed more transparency to spending earmarks, an increase in the minimum wage and increased funding for Amtrak. He voted for the constitutional amendment to ban same-sex marriage, but he supports embryonic stem cell research.

Upton is the 4th most senior Republican on the Energy and Commerce Committee. As chairman of the Oversight and Investigations Subcommittee, he investigated the Salt Lake City Olympics scandal and defects in Firestone-Bridgestone tires; he worked to pass a package of safety reforms in 2000. As chairman of the Telecommunications Subcommittee for the next six years, he endorsed the Tauzin-Dingell bill to allow regional telephone companies to provide broadband service more easily. He criticized the recording industry for its inadequate parental advisory labels on music that contains sex, violence or strong language, but he took the view that the First

Amendment bars Congress from such regulation. Bush signed his bill to create a "safe playground for kids" on the Internet—a "kids" space free of pornography and other inappropriate materials. After the Janet Jackson "wardrobe malfunction" in a Super Bowl halftime show in 2004, he helped to secure stiff increases in fines for broadcast indecency, from $32,500 to $325,000, though the legislation kept the existing standards. He won House approval of the Junk Fax Prevention Act, which gave an opt-out notice to recipients. Overall, he has backed deregulation of the broadcast industry, including the lifting of cross-ownership media bans in the same market. Upton could be in line for the committee chairmanship, presuming Republicans regain their majority. In the minority, he continued as top Republican on the Telecommunications subcommittee.

Upton has been reelected by wide margins. But his 61% in the 2006 general against theater owner and former television producer Kim Clark was his lowest since 1990, and was reflective of his gradually declining winning percentages in Berrien and Kalamazoo Counties.

SEVENTH DISTRICT

Rep. Tim Walberg (R)

Elected 2006, 1st term; b. Apr. 12, 1951, Chicago, IL; home, Tipton; Attended Western IL U., Attended Moody Bible Institute, Fort Wayne Bible Col., B.S. 1975, Wheaton Col. Graduate Schl., M.A. 1978; Christian; married (Sue).

Elected Office: MI House of Reps., 1982-98.

Professional Career: Minister, 1973-82; Pres., Warren Reuther Center for Education and Community Impact, 1999-2000; Division manager, Moody Bible Institute, 2000-05.

DC Office: 325 CHOB, 20515, 202-225-6276; Fax: 202-225-6281; Web site: walberg.house.gov.

District Offices: Battle Creek, 1-877-846-6407; Jackson, 517-780-9075.

Committees: *Agriculture* (21st of 21 R): Conservation, Credit, Energy & Research; Livestock, Dairy & Poultry. *Education & Labor* (21st of 22 R): Higher Education, Lifelong Learning & Competitiveness; Health, Employment, Labor & Pensions.

Group Ratings and Key Votes: Newly Elected

Election Results

2006 general	Tim Walberg (R)	122,348	(50%)	($1,225,137)
	Sharon Renier (D)	112,665	(46%)	($55,794)
	Other	10,013	(4%)	
2006 primary	Tim Walberg (R)	33,245	(53%)	
	Joe Schwarz (R)	29,330	(47%)	
2004 general	Joe Schwarz (R)	176,053	(58%)	($750,290)
	Sharon Renier (D)	109,527	(36%)	($8,742)
	Other	16,062	(5%)	

The People		Race/Ethnic Origin	Ancestry	
Area size:	4,365 sq. mi.	88.5% White	German: 17.4% English: 9.7%	
Urban population:	54.0%	5.6% Black	Irish: 8.3%	
Rural population:	46.0%	0.8% Asian	**2004 Presidential Vote**	
Pop. 2000:	662,563	0.4% Native Am.	Bush (R)	176,624 (54%)
Pop. 2005 (est):	691,095	0.0% Hawaiian	Kerry (D)	145,979 (45%)
Median income:	$45,181	1.4% Two+ races	Other	2,322 (1%)
Poverty status:	7.9%	0.1% Other	**2000 Presidential Vote**	
Military veterans:	13.5%	3.2% Hispanic Origin	Bush (R)	141,647 (51%)
			Gore (D)	127,344 (46%)
			Other	6,682 (2%)
			Cook Partisan Voting Index: R + 2	
Occupation	Blue collar: 31.3%	White collar: 53.6% Gray collar: 15.1%		

The small cities and towns spotting the southern-tier farmland counties of Michigan have been incubators of innovation since they were settled by Yankees from New England 150 years ago. The state's public school system was established by two politicians from Marshall, whose hopes to make it the state capital were dashed. A few miles away, in Battle Creek, sanitarium operator W.K. Kellogg invented corn flakes as a health food; he and his one-time patient, C.W. Post, both established factories in the late 19th century and created the American breakfast cereal industry. Kellogg, a prospering firm that has increased jobs through corporate acquisitions, delivered its CEO, Carlos Gutierrez, to George W. Bush's second-term Cabinet. To the south is Hillsdale, where conservative Hillsdale College has been proudly admitting blacks and women since the 1850s and refusing all federal aid. Politically, this area has been Republican territory since 1854, when the party was founded in the manufacturing and prison town of Jackson as a kind of reformist institution out of the same activist impulse that produced local support for women's rights and Prohibition, and opposition to the death penalty. Southern Michigan mostly rejected New Deal tinkering and was hostile to the UAW, but the people here were receptive to moral claims made by later 20th century reformers challenging racial segregation, the Vietnam War and the Watergate cover-up.

The 7th Congressional District of Michigan covers all of five counties and parts of two others in Michigan's southern tiers. Although Battle Creek retains strong Republican enclaves, local ancestral ties have become a bit shaky: Bill Clinton carried the district by small pluralities in 1992 and 1996. George W. Bush won it back with 51% in 2000 and 54% in 2004.

The new congressman from the 7th District is Tim Walberg, who ousted first-term incumbent Joe Schwarz in the Republican primary. Walberg was born in Chicago and grew up on the south side, working for a time as union steel mill worker. He attended several colleges before getting degrees from Fort Wayne Bible College and Wheaton College. He served as a pastor, then won election to the Michigan House in 1982 by knocking off a moderate Republican incumbent. He spent 16 years there, was a strong advocate for gun ownership rights and was part of a group known as the "No" Caucus for its unflinching opposition to raising taxes or increasing spending. Term limits forced him from office in 1998; after that, he served as president of a conservative-minded education foundation and think tank and as a division manager and fundraiser for the Moody Bible Institute of Chicago.

For Walberg, it took two tries to win the 7th District seat. His first bid came in 2004, when he finished third in the Republican primary behind Schwarz and Brad Smith, the son of retiring Republican Congressman Nick Smith. At the time, Schwarz had the benefit of running as the only moderate in a field where five conservatives splintered the conservative vote. Schwarz won with 28% of the vote to 22% for Smith and 18% for Walberg—a clear warning that Schwarz needed to expand his base. But he did not, and was imperiled in 2006 when he faced Walberg in a head-to-head contest. On the campaign trail, Walberg emphasized that he never once voted for a tax increase as a state legislator and that he planned to continue his streak in Congress. The clear contrasts attracted the support of the Club for Growth, which spent some $500,000 on television ads attacking Schwarz; its members delivered about $600,000 on top of that in campaign contributions. The incumbent was poorly positioned to weather the onslaught, despite assistance from the national GOP establishment, which included robo-calls to voters on his behalf from President Bush and Sen. John McCain. Walberg hammered the incumbent for his "liberal" voting record, including support for "pork-barrel" spending and "amnesty" for illegal immigrants, while emphasizing his own opposition to abortion and gay rights; with his pre-primary vote against the constitutional amendment to ban same-sex marriage, Schwarz held firm to his beliefs. Schwarz outspent Walberg by 2-to-1, but Walberg's formidable grassroots operation—powered in part by Christian conservatives attracted to his socially conservative message—negated Schwarz's spending advantage. In his 53%-47% victory, Walberg ran strongly in the three counties of the district's southern tier, where he won 67% of the vote. Schwarz won in his home base in Battle Creek-based Calhoun, plus Eaton and Washtenaw Counties, but with a total of only 56%. Jackson, the most populous county in the district, proved to be the key: Walberg took it 54%-47%. The defeat of Schwarz marked the first time that a candidate backed by the Club for Growth, a national anti-tax group, defeated a sitting Republican member. Schwarz wrote in September 2006 that his setback showed that, as a moderate, "I am the political equivalent of a woolly mammoth, a rarity headed for extinction."

Residual bitterness for the primary led to a general election that was much closer than expected. Democratic nominee Sharon Renier, an organic farmer from Jackson County who called for an international peace-keeping force to replace the U.S. military in Iraq, had lost to Schwarz 58%-36% in 2004. Her prospects in 2006 didn't seem much brighter as she had little money and scant national party assistance. But Walberg, who outspent Renier $1.2 million to $56,000, only managed a 49.9%-46.0% win. Schwarz, who filed as a write-in candidate six days before the election, got 1%; he denied that he was seeking to reduce the Republican vote for Walberg and said he filed to ensure that write-in votes for him were tallied and not discarded. Like Schwarz in the primary, Renier won narrowly in Calhoun, Eaton and Washtenaw Counties. Walberg took the rest, including Jackson County by 51%-46%.

Walberg's weak performance prompted Democrats to make him a prime target in 2008 in what once had been a safe Republican seat. Two Democrats were making moves to run: state Senate Minority Leader Mark Schauer and Renier. Schwarz also was considering running again, possibly as a Democrat.

EIGHTH DISTRICT

Rep. Mike Rogers (R)

Elected 2000, 4th term; b. June 2, 1963, Livingston Cnty.; home, Brighton; Adrian Col., B.A. 1985; Methodist; married (Diane).

Military Career: Army, 1985-88.

Elected Office: MI Senate, 1995-2000, Maj. Floor Ldr., 1999-2000.

Professional Career: Co-founder, E.B.I. Builders, 1985; FBI Spec. Agent, 1988-94.

DC Office: 133 CHOB, 20515, 202-225-4872; Fax: 202-225-5820; Web site: mikerogers.house.gov.

District Offices: Lansing, 517-702-8000.

Committees: *Energy & Commerce* (21st of 26 R): Health; Environment & Hazardous Materials; Energy & Air Quality. *Permanent Select Committee on Intelligence* (7th of 8 R): Terrorism, Human Intelligence, Analysis & Counterintelligence (RMM).

Group Ratings

	ADA	ACLU	AFS	LCV	ITIC	NTU	COC	ACU	CFG	FRC
2006	5	9	0	8	86	60	93	88	58	85
2005	5	—	0	6	—	62	93	92	75	92

National Journal Ratings

	2005 LIB	—	2005 CONS		2006 LIB	—	2006 CONS
Economic	24%	—	74%		21%	—	77%
Social	0%	—	89%		11%	—	85%
Foreign	11%	—	86%		17%	—	73%

Key Votes of the 109th Congress

1. Estate Tax Repeal	Y	5. Limit Interstate Abortion	Y	9. Build Border Fence	Y
2. Limit CAFE Standards	Y	6. Extend Patriot Act	Y	10. CAFTA	Y
3. FY06 Spending Curb	Y	7. Bar Same Sex Marriage	Y	11. Oppose Iraq Withdrawal	Y
4. Drilling in ANWR	Y	8. Stem Cell Research $	N	12. Detainee Tribunals	Y

Election Results

2006 general	Mike Rogers (R)	157,237	(55%)	($1,863,914)
	Jim Marcinkowski (D)	122,107	(43%)	($552,220)
	Other	5,127	(2%)	
2006 primary	Mike Rogers (R)	41,839	(84%)	
	Patrick Flynn (R)	7,784	(16%)	
2004 general	Mike Rogers (R)	207,925	(61%)	($797,146)
	Robert Alexander (D)	125,619	(37%)	($79,392)
	Other	6,879	(2%)	

Prior Winning Percentages: 2002 (68%); 2000 (49%)

The People		Race/Ethnic Origin	Ancestry	
Area size:	2,288 sq. mi.	87.7% White	German: 17.3%	English: 9.6%
Urban population:	70.0%	4.8% Black	Irish: 9.2%	
Rural population:	30.0%	1.9% Asian	**2004 Presidential Vote**	
Pop. 2000:	662,563	0.4% Native Am.	Bush (R) 191,287	(54%)
Pop. 2005 (est):	703,972	0.0% Hawaiian	Kerry (D) 161,282	(45%)
Median income:	$52,510	1.6% Two+ races	Other 2,668	(1%)
Poverty status:	8.4%	0.1% Other	**2000 Presidential Vote**	
Military veterans:	11.0%	3.5% Hispanic Origin	Bush (R) 153,798	(51%)
			Gore (D) 141,770	(47%)
			Other 8,426	(3%)
			Cook Partisan Voting Index: R + 2	

Occupation	Blue collar: 23.0%	White collar: 62.6%	Gray collar: 14.4%

Lansing is Michigan's state capital, chosen in 1847 because of its geographic position halfway between Lake Huron and Lake Michigan and away from the border with Canada and the threat of invasion by British forces, but in ignorance of the fact that it has fewer days with sunshine than any place else in the state. But it is a tidy and pleasant city with more than its share of amenities. It has a beautifully restored Capitol and a fine state history museum and is neighbor to Michigan State University in East Lansing, started in 1855 as America's first land-grant college. Its Oldsmobile plant stimulated growth in the first half of the 20th century, and state government did the same in the second half. GM closed its Olds line in 2004, but two new highly efficient GM assembly plants have been constructed in the Lansing area and the Oldsmobile name remains alive at two local museums and at the baseball stadium where the Lansing Lugnuts play. Historically, the Lansing area voted Republican, up through the 1960s. But as public employee unions have grown in membership and strength, Lansing like some other state capitals has become heavily Democratic, as is university-influenced East Lansing.

Just east of Lansing's Ingham County is quite another part of Michigan, Livingston County (most of the counties in these parts were named for members of President Andrew Jackson's Cabinet; Livingston was secretary of state and Ingham secretary of the Treasury). Thirty years ago, Livingston County was mostly rural, known mainly for its many lakes. But in the years since then, thousands of Detroit area residents have driven out I-96 to Brighton and Howell and other Livingston townships, and subdivisions, schools and shopping malls have sprouted up. Most of these people are conservatives, happy to leave the problems of Detroit behind them, angry at high taxes and annoyed by government regulations and hewing to traditional religious faiths. They have made Livingston Michigan's fastest-growing county—its population rose 59% from 1990 to 2006—and one of its most Republican. In 1970 Livingston had 58,000 people to Ingham's 261,000; in 2006 Livingston had 185,000 to Ingham's 277,000. So as Ingham has grown more Democratic, Livingston has been casting bigger Republican margins to counterbalance Ingham's Democratic margins. In the close presidential election of 1968, 19,000 people voted in Livingston and gave Richard Nixon a 3,000-vote margin, while 90,000 voted in Ingham and gave Nixon a 9,000-vote margin (this was before East Lansing went Democratic). In the close presidential election of 2004, 93,000 people voted in Livingston and gave George W. Bush a 25,000-vote margin—up from 16,000 in 2000. By comparison, 133,000 voted in Ingham and gave John Kerry a 22,000 vote-margin, up from 21,000 in 2000.

The 8th Congressional District of Michigan includes all of Ingham and Livingston Counties, Shiawassee County south of Owosso, plus Clinton County directly north of Lansing and northern Oakland County.

The congressman from the 8th District is Mike Rogers, a Republican first elected in 2000 (He is one of two Republican Mike Rogers in the House; the other hails from Alabama). He grew up in Brighton, in Livingston County, and graduated from Adrian College in southeastern Michigan. He was commissioned by the ROTC as commander of an Army rapid deployment unit. He graduated from the FBI Academy, and focused on public corruption cases as an FBI special agent in Chicago for six years. In 1994 he returned to Michigan, started a family home construction business and was elected to the state Senate, where in 1999 he became majority floor leader. In 2000, when Democrat Debbie Stabenow gave up the 8th District seat to run successfully for the Senate, Rogers and Democrat Dianne Byrum, a fellow state senator, both ran in the 8th. Each candidate raised about $2 million; this turned out to be the closest race in the country. It took six weeks to count the final tally, and Rogers won by 111 votes.

Rogers describes his political philosophy as consistent with President Bush's "compassionate conservatism," with a bit more conservative record on cultural issues than on the economy. With his military, law enforcement and legislative backgrounds, Rogers was well-positioned to advise colleagues on policies to respond to the September 11 attacks. He provided expertise on the high-tech tools used to track terrorists and on the use of wiretaps, sought federal aid to pay for National Guard troops at Michigan's borders with Canada, and urged that airport screeners have federal supervision. On other issues, he has been an activist member of the Energy and Commerce Committee. He sought more authority for Michigan to limit its flow of trash from other states and Canada. Citing the fact that only a few hundred gas stations nationwide have the requisite equipment, he won bipartisan House approval in 2006 of a bill to create a grant program for independent businesses to purchase equipment for ethanol gas pumps. The House also passed his committee bill to eliminate state food-safety warnings that are stronger than comparable federal warnings. His aggressive approach has made Rogers a rising star among House Republicans. With his significant fundraising skills, Republican leaders have tapped him for prime fundraising assignments in contested races. He positioned himself to run for House Republican whip in 2006, but Roy Blunt did not relinquish the post.

At home, Rogers has won reelection without problems. In 2006, he won 55%-43% against Royal Oak deputy city attorney Jim Marcinkowski, a former CIA agent who voiced disappointment when DCCC chairman Rahm Emanuel failed to deliver on promises of support. Rogers lost Lansing's Ingham County by 10,000 votes, but he took Republican Livingston County by 22,000 and his opponent's Oakland County base by 14,500. Political insiders in Michigan have speculated that he might make a strong statewide candidate, though the recent climate has not been hospitable for Republican candidates.

NINTH DISTRICT

Rep. Joe Knollenberg (R)

Elected 1992, 8th term; b. Nov. 28, 1933, Mattoon, IL; home, Bloomfield Township; E. IL U., B.S. 1955; Catholic; married (Sandie).

Military Career: Army, 1955-57.

Professional Career: Insurance agent, 1958-92.

DC Office: 2349 RHOB, 20515, 202-225-5802; Fax: 202-226-2356; Web site: knollenberg.house.gov.

District Offices: Farmington Hills, 248-851-1366.

Committees: *Appropriations* (8th of 29 R): Transportation, HUD & Related Agencies (RMM); State, Foreign Operations & Related Programs.

Group Ratings

	ADA	ACLU	AFS	LCV	ITIC	NTU	COC	ACU	CFG	FRC
2006	5	18	0	0	100	58	100	75	57	71
2005	0	—	0	6	—	53	93	84	55	75

National Journal Ratings

	2005 LIB	—	2005 CONS		2006 LIB	—	2006 CONS
Economic	34%	—	65%		4%	—	94%
Social	41%	—	59%		43%	—	56%
Foreign	40%	—	58%		17%	—	73%

Key Votes of the 109th Congress

1. Estate Tax Repeal	Y	5. Limit Interstate Abortion	Y	9. Build Border Fence	Y
2. Limit CAFE Standards	Y	6. Extend Patriot Act	Y	10. CAFTA	Y
3. FY06 Spending Curb	Y	7. Bar Same Sex Marriage	N	11. Oppose Iraq Withdrawal	Y
4. Drilling in ANWR	Y	8. Stem Cell Research $	N	12. Detainee Tribunals	Y

Election Results

2006 general	Joe Knollenberg (R) 142,390	(52%)	($3,105,161)
	Nancy Skinner (D) 127,620	(46%)	($403,726)
	Other... 6,170	(2%)	
2006 primary	Joe Knollenberg (R) 46,713	(70%)	
	Patricia Godchaux (R)........................... 20,211	(30%)	
2004 general	Joe Knollenberg (R) 199,210	(58%)	($1,412,320)
	Steven Reifman (D) 134,764	(40%)	($120,386)
	Other... 6,825	(2%)	

Prior Winning Percentages: 2002 (58%); 2000 (56%); 1998 (64%); 1996 (61%); 1994 (68%); 1992 (58%)

The People		Race/Ethnic Origin	Ancestry	
Area size:	323 sq. mi.	81.4% White	German: 13.6%	Irish: 9.2%
Urban population:	99.3%	8.0% Black	English: 8.5%	
Rural population:	0.7%	5.6% Asian	**2004 Presidential Vote**	
Pop. 2000:	662,563	0.2% Native Am.	Bush (R) 180,073	(51%)
Pop. 2005 (est):	669,855	0.0% Hawaiian	Kerry (D) 174,078	(49%)
Median income:	$65,358	1.6% Two+ races	**2000 Presidential Vote**	
Poverty status:	5.4%	0.1% Other	Bush (R) 164,149	(51%)
Military veterans:	10.6%	3.0% Hispanic Origin	Gore (D) 151,996	(47%)
			Other 5,987	(2%)
			Cook Partisan Voting Index: R + 0	

Occupation   Blue collar: 14.7%   White collar: 75.2%   Gray collar: 10.1%

Oakland County, Michigan, long considered just a suburban adjunct of Detroit, is now the center of a giant, spread-out, affluent urban area. It is only minutes on the Lodge or Chrysler Freeways from the empty, abandoned blocks of inner-city Detroit; but suddenly, north of the Eight Mile Road boundary, there are giant office buildings and multiplying small businesses, expensive houses on large lots and one shopping mall after another, high education levels and low crime rates. Even physically there is a distinction between the two areas: Detroit is on almost perfectly flat land, while much of Oakland County lies on a line of hills and lakes that marks the southernmost advance of an Ice Age glacier. Like most large suburban counties, Oakland is a mixture of communities, more diverse than the standard critique of suburbs suggests and, in this case, it is the heart of the metropolitan area. I-75 in eastern and northern Oakland County is now the nerve center of tier one and two auto company suppliers, many in the big office centers and near the upscale malls in Troy, others north into Auburn Hills, near Daimler Chrysler's North American headquarters. Near the center of Oakland is Bloomfield Hills, metro Detroit's wealthiest community; just to the north is the old factory town of Pontiac, with a black majority and a new postal facility going up downtown. Birmingham and Royal Oak, little suburbs set among farm fields half a century ago, are now upscale gentrified nodes amid a vast suburban expanse. Booming growth came in the 1990s to Rochester Hills, north of Troy, and West Bloomfield, west of Bloomfield Hills; the latter is increasingly the focus of metro Detroit's Jewish community and has a large number of Asians, many from India and Pakistan; others are Chaldeans, descended from Iraqi Catholics, numerous enough to have their own chamber of commerce. Oakland County has become the population center of metro Detroit. In 1950, the city of Detroit had 1,849,000 million people and Oakland County 396,000. In 2005, Detroit had 887,000 and Oakland 1,214,000.

The 9th Congressional District of Michigan includes a little more than half the population of Oakland County. It does not include Southfield, Oak Park, Ferndale, Hazel Park or Madison Heights in the southeast—all heavily Democratic and part of the 12th District. It does include almost all of Royal Oak, all of Birmingham and Bloomfield Hills, Rochester Hills and Auburn Hills, Farmington Hills (you begin to see the prestige value of hills to people who grew up in the flatlands of Detroit) and West Bloomfield, Pontiac and Waterford Township. It is Michigan's most affluent congressional district, and also one that trended toward the Democrats because of cultural issues starting in the 1990s. This has created problems for Republicans, for there is a strong Right to Life movement in Michigan, and as pro-life activists win Republican conventions and nominations, voters have moved toward Democrats. Republicans no longer win huge majorities in Birmingham and Bloomfield Township, and run no better in fast-growing Troy and Rochester Hills. Royal Oak, Farmington Hills and West Bloomfield, once solidly Republican, now lean Democratic; while

Waterford Township, with a more working class population, leans Republican. This is one part of Michigan where George W. Bush lost ground: he carried the 9th District 51%-47% in 2000 but by only 51%-49% in 2004.

The congressman from the 9th District is Joe Knollenberg, a Republican first elected in 1992. Knollenberg grew up the fifth child in a family of 13 on a farm in Downstate Illinois, went to college in Illinois and became an insurance agent. He moved to Oakland County in 1967 and became involved in civic affairs and Republican politics. When Republican William Broomfield retired in 1992 after 36 years in office—every one of them in the minority—Knollenberg ran to succeed him. With Broomfield's support and that of Michigan Right To Life, he was able to win the primary with 43% of the vote. He won the general election easily.

Knollenberg entered the House as a junior member of the minority. But in two years, with a change in control, he became a member of Appropriations advancing some cutting-edge ideas. He moved to zero out funding for the statistics required for CAFE standards and managed to zero out funding for implementation of the 1997 Kyoto treaty pending Senate ratification (which never came). Knollenberg was a strong supporter of NAFTA, normal trade relations with China and trade promotion authority; Michigan is the sixth-largest exporter among states. He opposed George W. Bush's tariffs on steel imports in March 2002, as automakers and auto suppliers were faced with 20% to 50% price increases for steel; he hailed their repeal in December 2003. He sponsored a bill to require counterfeiters of machinery to forfeit not only their earnings but the machinery they used to make fake goods after conviction; the auto parts industry estimates that counterfeits bring in more than $12 billion a year. George W. Bush signed the bill he sponsored in March 2006. He is the co-chairman of the Congressional Armenian Caucus, and pressed successfully for equal amounts of military aid for Armenia and Azerbaijan and to increase aid to Armenia from the $33 million requested by the Bush administration to $68 million, plus $6 million for Artsakh (the Armenian enclave formerly known as Nagorno-Karabakh). "It's my job to make sure Armenia gets heard," he says.

In 2001 Knollenberg became chairman of the District of Columbia Subcommittee, and hence one of Appropriation's 13 "cardinals." In 2003 he became chairman of the Military Construction Subcommittee. His main goal was to raise the $850 million cap on privatized housing construction, supported by both Democrats and Republicans, to allow the Pentagon to hire private construction companies for military housing improvements. Knollenberg got the Appropriations Committee to increase the cap from $850 million to $1.35 billion, but did not persuade the Rules Committee to preclude its being scored as a spending increase, exceeding the subcommittee's $10 billion allocation of discretionary funds. The military construction appropriation is usually uncontroversial, but when the measure came to the floor in July 2004 the Republican leadership opposed the cap increase, and Budget Chairman Jim Nussle raised a point of order against it; Nussle and the leadership prevailed after a long roll call 212-211. But Knollenberg and ranking Democrat Chet Edwards continued to argue that without the higher cap, 50,000 military families would have to wait for housing. The cap was lifted in the defense authorization passed in October 2004; Knollenberg and Edwards and their Senate counterparts were ready to raise it in the appropriation had that not happened.

In January 2005 the number of Appropriations subcommittees was reduced from 13 to 10 and Military Construction's jurisdiction was given to Defense. But Knollenberg came out a winner. He was given the chairmanship of the Transportation Subcommittee, whose previous (and more senior) chairman, Ernest Istook, had antagonized the Republican leadership. Transportation handles much more money and many more politically sensitive—and locally important—projects than the subcommittees Knollenberg previously chaired. But he was criticized for earmarking $8.3 million to Amtrak to purchase premium freight cars, which are manufactured by a firm in the district owned by a major financial supporter of Knollenberg; at first he defended the earmark, but withdrew it in December 2005.

Oakland County became steadily more Democratic since the late 1990s. Redistricting in 2001 removed heavily Democratic Southfield and made the district slightly more Republican, but it also meant that nearly two-thirds of the district was new territory for Knollenberg. In 2002 he had vigorous and well-financed opposition from politically-connected lawyer David Fink, who spent $1.2 million of his own money on his campaign. Fink said Knollenberg was beholden to the gun and pharmaceutical industries and he reminded voters that Knollenberg had promised in 1992 to retire in 2004. Knollenberg replied that he no longer believed in term limits. This was a big-spending race in an affluent metropolitan district but Knollenberg won 58%-40%, an uptick from his 2000 showing. In 2004 against an indifferently financed challenger, Knollenberg won by the same 58%-40% margin.

He had more difficulty in 2006. Publicity about the freight car earmark and a trip to Hawaii paid for by the American Association of Airport Executives (allowed by House rules) spurred opposition. In December 2005 WDTW radio talk show host Nancy Skinner announced she was running as a Democrat; a newcomer to Michigan, she had run in the 2004 Illinois Democratic primary for U.S. senator and finished sixth, with 1% of the vote, far behind the winner, Barack Obama. Then in January 2006 former state Representative Pan Godchaux announced she was running in the Republican primary. She argued that Knollenberg was too conservative, and highlighted her stands for abortion rights, against the Iraq war, against school vouchers and for funding embryonic stem cell research. Michigan does not have party registration, and Godchaux urged Democrats to vote for her in the primary; Skinner had no Democratic opposition, and Godchaux argued that Skinner couldn't win. A Knollenberg spokesman called this "a silly strategy by a silly candidate," but two weeks before the primary Knollenberg unveiled a six-figure television buy. He beat Godchaux by a convincing 70%-30% margin, but won only 50% of the votes cast for all three candidates. Skinner did not get national Democratic financing and spent only $404,000 to Knollenberg's $3.1 million. But Knollenberg won by only a 52%-46% margin, well below his previous showings. To be sure, that was well above what Bush would have gotten in the district if he were up in 2006, but Democrats started talking about seriously targeting Knollenberg in 2008, when he will be 74.

In early 2007, Knollenberg seemed to be gearing up for the next campaign: He paid for a billboard along I-75 featuring a photo of California Governor Arnold Schwarzenegger that read, "Arnold to Michigan: Drop Dead!", a reference to Schwarzenegger's role in promoting legislative initiatives that Knollenberg says are bullying the U.S. auto industry. State Lottery Commissioner Gary Peters, a Democrat, announced he would run in 2008; Skinner was also considering running again in 2008.

TENTH DISTRICT

Rep. Candice Miller (R)

Elected 2002, 3d term; b. May 7, 1954, Detroit; home, Harrison Twnshp.; Macomb Cnty. Community Col., 1973-74, Northwood U.; Presbyterian; married (Donald).

Elected Office: Trustee, Harrison Twnshp. Bd., 1979-80; Harrison Twnshp. Supervisor, 1980-92; Macomb Cnty. Treasurer, 1992-94; MI Secy. of State, 1994-2002.

Professional Career: Secy.-Treas., D.B. Snider Inc. marina, 1972-79

DC Office: 228 CHOB, 20515, 202-225-2106; Fax: 202-226-1169; Web site: candicemiller.house.gov.

District Offices: Shelby Twnshp., 586-997-5010.

Committees: *Armed Services* (20th of 29 R): Air & Land Forces; Readiness. *Select Committee on Energy Independence and Global Warming* (6th of 6 R). *Transportation & Infrastructure* (31st of 34 R): Water Resources & Environment; Highways & Transit.

Group Ratings

	ADA	ACLU	AFS	LCV	ITIC	NTU	COC	ACU	CFG	FRC
2006	10	18	14	17	71	57	93	84	50	85
2005	5	—	0	11	—	52	89	84	43	92

National Journal Ratings

	2005 LIB	—	2005 CONS		2006 LIB	—	2006 CONS
Economic	37%	—	62%		30%	—	70%
Social	0%	—	89%		37%	—	63%
Foreign	34%	—	61%		0%	—	94%

Key Votes of the 109th Congress

1. Estate Tax Repeal	Y	5. Limit Interstate Abortion	Y	9. Build Border Fence	Y
2. Limit CAFE Standards	Y	6. Extend Patriot Act	Y	10. CAFTA	N
3. FY06 Spending Curb	Y	7. Bar Same Sex Marriage	Y	11. Oppose Iraq Withdrawal	Y
4. Drilling in ANWR	Y	8. Stem Cell Research $	N	12. Detainee Tribunals	Y

Election Results

2006 general	Candice Miller (R)	179,072	(66%)	($692,651)
	Robert Denison (D)	84,689	(31%)	($14,077)
	Other	6,660	(2%)	
2006 primary	Candice Miller (R)	unopposed		
2004 general	Candice Miller (R)	227,720	(69%)	($442,297)
	Rob Casey (D)	98,029	(30%)	($16,585)
	Other	6,119	(2%)	

Prior Winning Percentages: 2002 (63%)

The People		Race/Ethnic Origin	Ancestry	
Area size:	3,663 sq. mi.	93.6% White	German: 19.1%	Polish: 10.5%
Urban population:	66.0%	1.5% Black	Irish: 8.2%	
Rural population:	34.0%	1.2% Asian	**2004 Presidential Vote**	
Pop. 2000:	662,562	0.3% Native Am.	Bush (R) 193,727	(57%)
Pop. 2005 (est):	718,799	0.0% Hawaiian	Kerry (D) 147,288	(43%)
Median income:	$52,690	1.2% Two+ races	Other 1,748	(1%)
Poverty status:	6.0%	0.1% Other	**2000 Presidential Vote**	
Military veterans:	12.6%	2.1% Hispanic Origin	Bush (R) 152,780	(53%)
			Gore (D) 127,640	(45%)
			Other 6,242	(2%)
			Cook Partisan Voting Index: R + 4	

Occupation Blue collar: 31.5%   White collar: 55.2%   Gray collar: 13.4%

Macomb County, Michigan, on the billiard-table-flat shore of Lake St. Clair just northeast of Detroit, has been one of the nation's most closely watched political battlegrounds, a place where it once seemed the electoral fate of Michigan and even the entire country might be determined. It owes much of that to its reputation as blue collar suburbia, but that is no longer quite accurate: more people hold white-collar jobs than blue-collar these days and far fewer work in auto plants than in earlier generations. There are plenty of affluent subdivisions now, and boat ownership is close to the highest in the country. Macomb County is the product of the post-World War II boom: In 1940 it had 107,000 residents, many in the old sulphur-water spa town of Mount Clemens; Macomb passed the 400,000 mark in 1960 and 600,000 by 1970; in 2005, it reached 821,000. Many people came here from the east side of Detroit: These new suburbanites were heavily Catholic, often blue-collar, at least modestly affluent and ancestrally Democratic. They accepted the New Deal as part of their natural heritage but resented the efforts of Detroit politicians to tax them to pay for welfare, and they were fearful of the high crime rates in Detroit's black neighborhoods.

In 1960, Macomb County was the most Democratic major suburban county in the United States, voting 63% for America's first Catholic president, John F. Kennedy. For three decades afterwards Macomb moved away from national Democrats—in 1962 because they would let Detroit tax suburbanites, in 1972 because they didn't vehemently oppose a metropolitan school busing plan. From 1976 through 1992, no Democratic presidential candidate got more than 40% of the vote here. In 1996, after great effort and with the advice of pollster Stan Greenberg, who has studied Macomb closely, Bill Clinton carried Macomb County by a 49%-39% margin; in 2000 Al Gore carried it by 50%-48%, nearly the national average. But the Democratic tide receded a little. Central and northern Macomb County have been filling up with expensive subdivisions that have been growing rapidly—some by more than 40% in the 1990s—and are not as culturally liberal as affluent parts of Oakland County. In 2002 Macomb County voted 52%-47% for Republican governor candidate Dick Posthumus, even as he was losing statewide, and it elected more Republican state legislators than Democrats. In 2004 George W. Bush carried Macomb 50%-49%, even while losing more affluent Oakland County next door. But as Republicans suffered nationwide in 2006, they suffered in Macomb too: In her successful reelection, Governor Jennifer Granholm defeated Republican Dick DeVos in Macomb 52%-46%.

The 10th Congressional District of Michigan includes the northern two-thirds of Macomb County, with nearly half its voters. It also includes fast-growing Lapeer County, north of Macomb and Oakland and east of Flint; St. Clair County, with Port Huron and its Blue Water Bridge to Canada, and two rural counties in Michigan's Thumb. Northern Macomb has become increasingly Republican, Lapeer and St. Clair have long been pretty Republican and the Thumb has long been very Republican. Overall this is a comfortably Republican district—53% for George W. Bush in 2000 and 57% in 2004.

The congresswoman from the 10th District is Candice Miller, a Republican elected in 2002. Miller grew up in Macomb County. In 1979, at 25, she was elected Harrison Township trustee. A year later, she was elected as the youngest and first female supervisor in the township. In 1986 she ran against David Bonior and lost 66%-34%. In 1992, she won an upset bid to become Macomb County treasurer. In 1994, she defeated 24-year incumbent Richard Austin and was elected Michigan secretary of state. In 1998 she carried all of Michigan's counties and set a state record for total votes.

Armed with huge name recognition as secretary of state but prevented from running for reelection by term limits, Miller was the favorite to succeed Bonior, who ran for governor in 2002. Democrats were enthusiastic about Macomb County Prosecutor Carl Marlinga; he had held office 20 years and had been mentioned several times as a candidate for statewide office. But he could not keep pace with her fundraising and failed to do much to increase his name recognition north of Macomb. He called himself a "Hubert Humphrey Democrat"—not a big advantage in this district. Miller called herself a "George W. Bush Republican." She opposed abortion and supported NAFTA, trade promotion authority and favored making the Bush tax cuts permanent—all positions opposite to Marlinga. Both candidates supported gun rights. Citing her daughter's membership in the United Auto Workers, Miller reached out to unions, and was endorsed by the Teamsters (but not the AFL-CIO). Marlinga was hurt by allegations that he accepted campaign contributions from supporters of a convicted rapist who benefited from the prosecutor's handling of his case. Miller won by a huge 63%-36% margin; she carried Macomb County 61%-37%. She has been reelected easily.

In the House, Miller had a moderate-to-conservative voting record, more conservative on cultural issues. On the Armed Services Committee, she worked to protect the Selfridge Air National Guard Base, and sought additional Pentagon contracts for local firms, including the General Dynamics plant in Sterling Heights that manufactures the Army Stryker armored vehicle; the base closing commission closed the Army garrison at Selfridge but the base gained new aircraft. In 2004, she joined the first congressional delegation to Libya, where she met Moammar Gadhafi and said that the trip reflected a Bush foreign policy success because Gadhafi "only has to look to Iraq to see what regime change can mean." By 2007, Miller's support for the Iraq war had softened and she opposed the President's "surge" strategy. But she refused to support the Democratic resolution condemning the buildup because of concerns it would demoralize the troops.

Miller has filed a proposed constitutional amendment to exclude illegal aliens from the decennial congressional reapportionment process, calling it "absolutely outrageous" that non-citizens had "a profound impact on our political system." The Ethics Committee admonished her after it reviewed charges that Majority Leader Tom DeLay sought to influence the vote of Representative Nick Smith on the 2003 Medicare/prescription drug bill. Dismissing the committee's claim that she intimidated Smith to vote for the bill, she referred to Smith's skills in martial arts when she told the *Detroit Free Press,* "If a black belt can be intimidated by an overweight, middle-age woman, that's too bad."

Despite strong encouragement from George W. Bush to run in 2006 against Senator Debbie Stabenow, Miller decided against it. She also has been mentioned as a possible candidate against 30-year Senate veteran Carl Levin in 2008 or as a candidate for governor in 2010 when Governor Jennifer Granholm is term-limited.

ELEVENTH DISTRICT

Rep. Thaddeus McCotter (R)

Elected 2002, 3d term; b. Aug. 22, 1965, Detroit; home, Livonia; U. of Detroit, B.A. 1987, J.D. 1990; Catholic; married (Rita).

Elected Office: Schoolcraft Community Col. Trustees Bd., 1989-92; Wayne Cnty. Commission, 1992-98; MI Senate, 1998-2002.

DC Office: 1632 LHOB, 20515, 202-225-8171; Fax: 202-225-2667; Web site: mccotter.house.gov.

District Offices: Livonia, 734-632-0314; Milford, 248-685-9495.

Committees: *Republican Policy Committee Chairman. Financial Services* (32d of 33 R): Housing & Community Opportunity; Capital Markets, Insurance & Government Sponsored Enterprises.

Group Ratings

	ADA	ACLU	AFS	LCV	ITIC	NTU	COC	ACU	CFG	FRC
2006	15	18	14	17	71	49	93	83	44	100
2005	20	—	0	17	—	58	81	88	54	85

National Journal Ratings

	2005 LIB	—	2005 CONS		2006 LIB	—	2006 CONS
Economic	42%	—	57%		40%	—	60%
Social	32%	—	66%		23%	—	74%
Foreign	40%	—	58%		45%	—	54%

Key Votes of the 109th Congress

1. Estate Tax Repeal	Y	5. Limit Interstate Abortion	Y	9. Build Border Fence	Y
2. Limit CAFE Standards	Y	6. Extend Patriot Act	Y	10. CAFTA	N
3. FY06 Spending Curb	Y	7. Bar Same Sex Marriage	Y	11. Oppose Iraq Withdrawal	P
4. Drilling in ANWR	Y	8. Stem Cell Research $	N	12. Detainee Tribunals	Y

Election Results

2006 general	Thaddeus McCotter (R)	143,658	(54%)	($875,708)
	Tony Trupiano (D)	114,248	(43%)	($134,142)
	Other	7,878	(3%)	
2006 primary	Thaddeus McCotter (R)	unopposed		
2004 general	Thaddeus McCotter (R)	186,431	(57%)	($735,845)
	Phillip Truran (D)	134,301	(41%)	($43,255)
	Other	6,484	(2%)	

Prior Winning Percentages: 2002 (57%)

The People		Race/Ethnic Origin	Ancestry		
Area size:	413 sq. mi.	89.5% White	German: 15.5%	Irish: 10.8%	
Urban population:	97.0%	3.7% Black	Polish: 9.8%		
Rural population:	3.0%	3.0% Asian	**2004 Presidential Vote**		
Pop. 2000:	662,563	0.3% Native Am.	Bush (R)	183,835	(53%)
Pop. 2005 (est):	707,850	0.0% Hawaiian	Kerry (D)	164,037	(47%)
Median income:	$59,177	1.4% Two+ races	**2000 Presidential Vote**		
Poverty status:	4.3%	0.1% Other	Bush (R)	150,692	(51%)
Military veterans:	12.1%	2.0% Hispanic Origin	Gore (D)	138,735	(47%)
			Other	6,022	(2%)
			Cook Partisan Voting Index: R + 1		

Occupation	Blue collar: 23.4%	White collar: 64.8%	Gray collar: 11.8%

The inexorable pattern of growth and its consequences is a vivid tale in the western suburbs of Wayne County, 15 and 25 miles from downtown Detroit. Consider the case of Livonia, just west of Northwest Detroit. Sixty years ago the 36 square miles of Livonia had 17,000 people; by 1960 there were 66,000 and by 2000 100,000. Similar growth occurred just to the south in Westland, named after a shopping center. To the west, around the old towns of Plymouth and Northville, affluent subdivisions sprang up; to the southwest, Canton Township grew 34% with more modest subdivisions. To the northwest Novi, in Oakland County, has emerged as one of the metro area's highest-income suburbs; Lyon Township just to the west looks to be the next boom area. Livonia is aging now—its school-age population was 38,000 in the 1970s and 17,000 in 2002—with some vacant factories and closed malls, but these newer places are young, and all have been thriving while the central city of Detroit is terribly troubled. Tying these areas together was I-275, which runs along the western edge of Livonia and Westland and provides easy access to Metro Airport, the Northwest hub with nonstop flights to just about every big city in the country, as well as major European cities and Tokyo and Beijing. From affluent areas in Oakland County you have to budget an hour to drive to Metro; from I-275 it's more like 15 minutes.

Livonia was originally the political base of longtime Wayne County Executive Ed McNamara (1986-2002), an old-style political boss who built the beautiful new midfield terminal at Metro (which is named after him). Livonia, originally settled by Detroiters, was long closely divided between the two parties, but the recent affluent influx into western Wayne County, plus Novi and other Oakland towns has made those areas more Republican. Racial minorities have become a majority in Wayne County; that's due partly to the rapid growth of Hispanics and Asian-Americans, many of them doing high-tech work in what local officials trumpet as the Automation Alley, the long miles of open road between Detroit and Ann Arbor.

The 11th Congressional District of Michigan covers much of this territory in western Wayne and Oakland Counties—Livonia and Redford Township just to the east, Westland and Canton Township, Northville and Plymouth, Novi and several fast-growing townships to the north and west. The lines were carefully drawn to produce a district that voted 51% for George W. Bush in 2000 and with the clear intention of electing a Republican congressman.

The congressman from the 11th District is Thaddeus McCotter, a Republican first elected in 2002. He grew up in Livonia, where his mother Joan McCotter was city clerk. He graduated from Detroit's Catholic Central High School, where he was a first-team all-Catholic football player, and from the University of Detroit and its law school. He was elected to the Wayne County Commission in 1992, at 27, and became the driving force to change the county's charter to require a new tax to win approval of two-thirds of the commissioners and 60% of the voters in a referendum. In 1998, he was elected to the state Senate where, critically, he was vice-chairman of the Senate's reapportionment committee. He helped to design the new 11th District, which included his entire senate district, and became the early frontrunner in 2002. He received pre-primary endorsements and contributions from House Republican leaders and won the primary 69%-31%. But McCotter did not win the seat without a contest. Democrat Kevin Kelley, Redford Township Supervisor and son of longtime Detroit Councilman Jack Kelley, was unopposed in the primary. Kelley called himself a "centrist Democrat"; both candidates supported the Bush tax cuts, authorization of military force in Iraq and opposed individual investment accounts in Social Security. McCotter defined himself as a conservative who opposed abortion and gun control; Kelley supported abortion rights and restrictions on gun ownership. They drew sharp distinctions on trade policy. McCotter favored NAFTA, trade promotion authority and normal trade relations with China; Kelley opposed all three. Kelley hoped to benefit from governor candidate Jennifer Granholm's local popularity and hoped that his outgoing personality would be more appealing than McCotter's more reserved persona. But McCotter raised more money, much of it at a mid-October fundraiser with Bush. His 57%-40% margin was larger than expected.

In the House, McCotter had a moderate-to-conservative voting record, with streaks of independence. He is an avid rock and roll fan, with a quirky sense of humor, prone to quoting song lyrics. He has a large poster of John Lennon hanging on the wall in his congressional office. Less outgoing and more cerebral than many of his colleagues, he enjoys playing the guitar; with four other House members, he formed the Second Amendments, a bipartisan rock and country band, which performed for U.S. forces in Iraq and Afghanistan.

In June 2006, he voted "present" on a Republican leadership resolution supporting the war in Iraq and rejecting a timetable for withdrawal; he called the resolution "strategically nebulous, morally obtuse and woefully inadequate." He urged the Bush administration to eliminate the steel tariffs imposed in March 2002. McCotter was an early supporter of John Boehner for Majority Leader in early 2006 and has joined his inner circle. That may have helped him defeat Darrell Issa in a November 2006 contest for chairman of the Republican Policy Committee; he had finished second in a four-candidate race for the same post nine months earlier. Within the House, he believes Republicans should take a less centralized approach and should do a better job of engaging rank-and-file members.

In this competitive district, McCotter has twice won reelection but by unimpressive margins against underfinanced opponents. In 2006, he won 54%-43% against Tony Trupiano, an outspoken syndicated radio talk show host who was the first House Democrat endorsed by ImpeachPAC.org. A well-funded, top tier Democratic opponent might give McCotter a tough race.

TWELFTH DISTRICT

Rep. Sander Levin (D)

Elected 1982, 13th term; b. Sept. 6, 1931, Detroit; home, Royal Oak; U. of Chicago, B.A. 1952, Columbia U., M.A. 1954, Harvard U., LL.B. 1957; Jewish; married (Vicki).

Elected Office: Oakland Bd. of Supervisors, 1961-64; MI Senate, 1964-70.

Professional Career: Practicing atty., 1957-64, 1970-76; Fellow, Harvard JFK Schl. of Govt., 1975; A.A., Agency for Intl. Devel., 1977-81.

DC Office: 1236 LHOB, 20515, 202-225-4961; Fax: 202-226-1033; Web site: www.house.gov/levin.

District Offices: Roseville, 586-498-7122.

Committees: *Joint Committee on Taxation* (3d of 5 D). *Ways & Means* (3d of 24 D): Trade (Chmn.); Social Security.

Group Ratings

	ADA	ACLU	AFS	LCV	ITIC	NTU	COC	ACU	CFG	FRC
2006	90	95	100	100	43	9	40	8	7	0
2005	95	—	100	89	—	12	48	4	3	0

National Journal Ratings

	2005 LIB	—	2005 CONS	2006 LIB	—	2006 CONS
Economic	75%	—	24%	86%	—	11%
Social	86%	—	14%	76%	—	23%
Foreign	77%	—	22%	77%	—	20%

Key Votes of the 109th Congress

1. Estate Tax Repeal	N	5. Limit Interstate Abortion	N	9. Build Border Fence	N
2. Limit CAFE Standards	Y	6. Extend Patriot Act	N	10. CAFTA	N
3. FY06 Spending Curb	N	7. Bar Same Sex Marriage	N	11. Oppose Iraq Withdrawal	N
4. Drilling in ANWR	N	8. Stem Cell Research $	Y	12. Detainee Tribunals	N

Election Results

2006 general	Sander Levin (D)	168,494	(70%)	($742,094)
	Randell Shafer (R)	62,689	(26%)	
	Other	8,932	(4%)	
2006 primary	Sander Levin (D)	unopposed		
2004 general	Sander Levin (D)	210,827	(69%)	($869,446)
	Randell Shafer (R)	88,256	(29%)	
	Other	5,051	(2%)	

Prior Winning Percentages: 2002 (68%); 2000 (64%); 1998 (56%); 1996 (57%); 1994 (52%); 1992 (53%); 1990 (70%); 1988 (70%); 1986 (76%); 1984 (100%); 1982 (67%)

The People		Race/Ethnic Origin	Ancestry	
Area size:	160 sq. mi.	81.7% White	German: 14.1%	Polish: 11.4%
Urban population:	100.0%	12.0% Black	Irish: 8.0%	
Rural population:	0.0%	2.3% Asian	**2004 Presidential Vote**	
Pop. 2000:	662,563	0.3% Native Am.	Kerry (D) 193,894	(61%)
Pop. 2005 (est):	646,265	0.0% Hawaiian	Bush (R) 125,460	(39%)
Median income:	$46,784	2.1% Two+ races	**2000 Presidential Vote**	
Poverty status:	7.3%	0.2% Other	Gore (D) 175,524	(61%)
Military veterans:	12.5%	1.5% Hispanic Origin	Bush (R) 106,628	(37%)
			Other 5,940	(2%)
			Cook Partisan Voting Index: D +13	

Occupation   Blue collar: 26.7%   White collar: 59.7%   Gray collar: 13.6%

The flat expanse of land just north of Eight Mile Road, Detroit's northern city limit, was mostly vacant in the years just after World War II. A string of suburbs in Oakland County ran along Woodward Avenue, Detroit's main street, where Henry Ford drove his first prototype in 1896, and which led to the Shrine of the Little Flower church in Royal Oak. There, in the 1930s, Father Charles Coughlin made his radio broadcasts backing and then opposing Franklin D. Roosevelt and denouncing bankers and Jews. In the 1950s and 1960s, Woodward was one of America's greatest cruising highways, where teenagers drove big Detroit cars up and down the eight lanes where the lights were timed at 42 miles per hour and zoomed into its drive-in restaurants—an era commemorated since 1994 with the Woodward Dream Cruise of old cars, a mega-celebration that annually draws more than 1 million for the one-day event. To the east in Macomb County was some industrial development along Van Dyke Road, but this was mostly empty land, too. Then Polish-Americans began marching out Van Dyke from Hamtramck to Warren; Italian-Americans headed out Gratiot from Detroit's east side to Roseville and Clinton Township; Belgian-Americans from the Mack corridor moved out farther to St. Clair Shores. Today, these areas are well-settled suburbs, long since built up, a few neighborhoods edging toward seediness, many others continually renovated. Almost half of metro Detroit's population is now north of Eight Mile, in communities drawing on old traditions but crackling with economic creativity.

The 12th Congressional District of Michigan is in this suburban territory, with two-thirds of its population in Macomb. On the Oakland County side are the southern part of Royal Oak and other Woodward Avenue suburbs, which have been economically revitalized, and attract singles and gays as well as families; Oak Park, heavily Jewish in the 1950s and now perhaps the only small city in America with sizable numbers of Jews, Arabs and blacks; Hazel Park and Madison Heights, mostly peopled with descendants of the Appalachian migrants of a few decades ago; Southfield, Michigan's largest office space center (far ahead of Detroit), with a black middle class majority in 2000; and Ferndale, one of the original bedroom communities for autoworkers that has been revived with help from bonds to modernize downtown and is viewed as a model to rescue aging suburbs. On the Macomb side are the county's more Democratic neighborhoods: Warren and the southern part of Sterling Heights, site of the General Motors Technical Center, a big Chrysler plant and the now-privatized M-1 tank plant. Farther east are blue-collar communities of Macomb: Eastpointe (formerly known as East Detroit, it voted to change its name to make it sound less like Detroit and more like Grosse Pointe), Roseville, St. Clair Shores, Clinton Township and Mount Clemens. George W. Bush narrowly carried Macomb County in 2004, but not this part of it. This district is solidly Democratic.

The congressman from the 12th District is Sander Levin, a Democrat first elected in 1982, an influential lawmaker, and a member of one of Michigan's most respected political families; he is the older brother of Senator Carl Levin. Levin grew up in Detroit and got degrees from the University of Chicago, Columbia and Harvard Law School. He settled in the Woodward Avenue suburb of Berkley after school and was elected state senator in 1964; in 1970 and 1974 he ran for governor and lost narrowly each time to Republican William Milliken. In the Carter administration he was a top appointee at the Agency for International Development. In 1982, a House seat suddenly opened up in redistricting. Levin won a spirited primary and held the seat without difficulty. The 1992 redistricting moved him east, into Macomb County, and placed him in the same district with Democrat Dennis Hertel, who decided to retire; Levin easily won the nomination.

Levin is a hard worker, a details man, willing to spend endless hours with others working out solutions. Based on his work with local communities to create coalitions to combat drug and alcohol abuse, he co-authored the federal Drug Free Communities Act. On Ways and Means, he has played an important role on major issues. On welfare, Levin opposed the 1995 bills passed by Republicans but helped shape the bill enacted in August 1996. Like most Democrats, he split with Republicans when the House sought to extend the welfare law. After the death of Robert Matsui in January 2005, Levin became the ranking Democrat on the Social Security Subcommittee; in that year's major debate, his outspoken opposition to personal retirement accounts put Republicans on the defensive and helped to stymie serious action on the proposal. He said that Bush's initial warnings about the threats to the Social Security system were exaggerated, and he downplayed the need for Democrats to offer their own alternative.

In the majority, he became chairman of the Trade Subcommittee. For years, Levin has been at the center of trade debates—seeking ways, as he often says, to shape globalization. He favored the Free Trade Agreement with Canada, which was designed in large part by auto manufacturers and the United Auto Workers. But he was wary of Japanese trade barriers and pushed unsuccessfully for stringent measures on Japanese minivans. He was a strong opponent of NAFTA in 1993, but supported GATT and normal trade relations with China, on which he played an instrumental role in crafting details with the Clinton administration. He opposed trade promotion authority in both the Clinton and Bush years. He supported agreements that the Bush administration reached with Australia and Morocco, but he raised concerns over the impact on auto imports from a potential agreement with Thailand. In discussion of a bilateral trade deal with South Korea, a high priority of the Bush administration, he demanded "measurable benchmarks" for opening that market. He wants trade agreements to contain provisions on workers' rights, fair ways of settling workers' disagreements and environmental provisions. In opposing the use of force in Iraq, he consulted extensively with his brother, who is chairman of the Senate Armed Services Committee. Each offered alternatives reflecting what they view as a more internationalist approach, but each was defeated.

After the 1992 redistricting, which removed much of metro Detroit's Jewish community from Levin's district and added unfamiliar territory in Macomb County, Levin had serious competition from Republican John Pappageorge, a retired Army colonel and M-1 tank executive. In the anti-incumbent atmosphere of 1992, Levin outspent Pappageorge by $1.18 million to $190,000 and won by just 53%-46%. In 1994, when Clinton was affirmatively unpopular, Levin again greatly outspent Pappageorge and won by 52%-47%. But in the more pro-incumbent environment of 1996, Levin won by a larger 57%-41%. Since then, the local tide has shifted his way and Levin has won easily.

THIRTEENTH DISTRICT

Rep. Carolyn Cheeks Kilpatrick (D)

Elected 1996, 6th term; b. June 25, 1945, Detroit; home, Detroit; Ferris St. U., 1968-70, W. MI U., B.S. 1972, U. of MI, M.S. 1977; African Methodist Episcopal; divorced.

Elected Office: MI House of Reps., 1978-96.

Professional Career: Teacher, Detroit public schls., 1970-78.

DC Office: 2264 RHOB, 20515, 202-225-2261; Fax: 202-225-5730; Web site: www.house.gov/kilpatrick.

District Offices: Detroit, 313-965-9004; Wyandotte, 734-246-0780.

Committees: *Appropriations* (21st of 37 D): Financial Services & General Government; Homeland Security.

Group Ratings

	ADA	ACLU	AFS	LCV	ITIC	NTU	COC	ACU	CFG	FRC
2006	100	100	100	100	29	12	27	4	7	0
2005	100	—	100	83	—	16	32	4	3	0

National Journal Ratings

	2005 LIB	—	2005 CONS	2006 LIB	—	2006 CONS
Economic	77%	—	22%	86%	—	11%
Social	88%	—	11%	91%	—	9%
Foreign	94%	—	4%	86%	—	13%

Key Votes of the 109th Congress

1. Estate Tax Repeal	N	5. Limit Interstate Abortion	N	9. Build Border Fence	N
2. Limit CAFE Standards	Y	6. Extend Patriot Act	N	10. CAFTA	N
3. FY06 Spending Curb	N	7. Bar Same Sex Marriage	N	11. Oppose Iraq Withdrawal	*
4. Drilling in ANWR	N	8. Stem Cell Research $	Y	12. Detainee Tribunals	N

Election Results

2006 general	Carolyn Cheeks Kilpatrick (D)	.... unopposed		($551,497)
2006 primary	Carolyn Cheeks Kilpatrick (D)	.... unopposed		
2004 general	Carolyn Cheeks Kilpatrick (D)	 173,246	(78%)	($591,551)
	Cynthia Cassell (R)	 40,935	(18%)	
	Other	 7,472	(3%)	

Prior Winning Percentages: 2002 (92%); 2000 (89%); 1998 (87%); 1996 (88%)

The People		Race/Ethnic Origin	Ancestry	
Area size:	108 sq. mi.	28.9% White	German: 5.4% Polish: 4.2%	
Urban population:	100.0%	60.5% Black	Irish: 4.2%	
Rural population:	0.0%	1.2% Asian	**2004 Presidential Vote**	
Pop. 2000:	662,563	0.3% Native Am.	Kerry (D) 188,555	(81%)
Pop. 2005 (est):	609,907	0.0% Hawaiian	Bush (R) 45,019	(19%)
Median income:	$31,165	1.8% Two+ races	**2000 Presidential Vote**	
Poverty status:	24.4%	0.2% Other	Gore (D) 167,830	(80%)
Military veterans:	10.7%	7.2% Hispanic Origin	Bush (R) 39,024	(19%)
			Other 1,975	(1%)
			Cook Partisan Voting Index: D +32	

Occupation	Blue collar: 29.3%	White collar: 50.7%	Gray collar: 20.1%

Few central cities in America had as vibrant a 20th century history, and as sad a recent past, as Detroit. This was America's first automobile city, not just because it manufactured so many of the nation's cars but also because it was built to automobile scale. Detroit started the century as a second-rank city, no bigger than Milwaukee, with less than half a million people and extending no farther than four or five miles out from the site where the French built Fort Pontchartrain on the Detroit River in 1701. As the Motor City boomed, it grew outward along wide avenues and, starting in the 1950s, freeways; the auto companies put their factories and headquarters near the edge of urban settlement. As early as 1954, the nation's first big suburban shopping center, with parking for 10,000 cars, was drawing retail trade from downtown. Metro Detroit expanded to four million people, each generation moving out the roadways rapidly in many directions, leaving behind the previous generation's neighborhoods and civic institutions.

Today, that rapid movement has left large parts of Detroit literally empty. The central city had nearly 1.85 million people in 1950, but dropped below 1 million in 2000; in 2006 the population was estimated to be 871,000. The reason is obvious: crime. For 30 years Detroit had a murder rate drastically higher than in the suburbs, and naturally those who could afford to leave did so. Downtown, formerly iconic buildings have been torn down and others are all but empty while officials struggle to create new population centers and a business district. General Motors and Ford have been losing billions of dollars each year. There have been some positive developments. GM bought for $72 million the 70-story Renaissance Center, built in the 1970s for $350 million, and the company moved several thousand employees there. Beyond downtown, some of the city's jewels have been maintained: the Detroit Institute of Arts, the hospital center, the old Fox Theater. New baseball and football stadiums have opened just north of downtown—in 2006, they hosted the World Series and the Super Bowl. Three gambling casinos have opened in nearby Greektown, where most Greek immigrants have moved out though their businesses remain. Residential and commercial projects have risen and more are planned on the long-neglected riverfront, with encouragement from a new shopping plaza and promenade at the Renaissance Center. But beyond these well-policed enclaves lie acres of vacant fields and half-empty blocks where there were once five-story apartments or brick houses. The continuing job losses at the auto makers showed no sign of abating.

Detroit's fate is all the more tragic because it comes in a city where liberal reformers hoped to create model anti-poverty and anti-discrimination programs. Coleman Young, Detroit's mayor from 1973 to 1993, spent his energy on courting the Big Three; he bulldozed the viable Poletown neighborhood for a new Cadillac plant. Dennis Archer, who served the next eight years, took a more constructive and intelligent approach, and the city began to turn around, with lower crime, more jobs, new housing permits and a start at a growing private sector. In 2001, Kwame Kilpatrick, a former state legislator, brought young blood when he was elected mayor, at age 31, as the self-styled "America's first hip-hop mayor." He styled himself a national leader of urban America but was reelected only narrowly.

The 13th Congressional District of Michigan includes more than half of Detroit, plus a few adjacent suburbs, from the affluent Grosse Pointes with nearly 50,000 people looking out toward Lake St. Clair to the Downriver industrial towns of River Rouge, Ecorse, Lincoln Park and Wyandotte. It includes practically all of the east side of Detroit and the west side up to about five miles north of the Detroit River—the entire riverfront and downtown, the old General Motors and Fisher Buildings, most of Detroit's auto factories. At 108 square miles, this is the smallest district in the state, with the biggest problems: the state's highest rates of poverty, unemployment and percentages of residents on public assistance. Between 2000 and 2005, the district population declined by 53,000, one of the biggest hemorrhages in the nation. Politically, the 13th is overwhelmingly Democratic, but voter turnout is low—126,323 in the House race in 2006, far below the 276,180 in the high-income 9th District. This is one of Michigan's 2 black-majority seats and one of the safest Democratic districts in the nation.

The congresswoman from the 13th District is Carolyn Cheeks Kilpatrick, a Democrat first elected in 1996 and the mother of Detroit Mayor Kwame Kilpatrick. She was born and raised in Detroit, attended Ferris State and graduated from Western Michigan University and the University of Michigan. She taught business education in Detroit public schools and was elected to the state House in 1978. She lost a race for the Detroit City Council, but won the 1996 Democratic primary for the congressional seat by a solid 51%-31% margin against her one-time political partner, incumbent Barbara-Rose Collins.

Kilpatrick, whose voting record once was among the most liberal in the House, has moderated slightly. She made a point of visiting the suburbs in her district, meeting local officials and assigning staffers to work with them—a contrast to Collins. On the Appropriations Committee, she has taken credit for funding Detroit-area transportation projects and for funding Detroit water treatment and sewage facilities. She spurred the creation of the Detroit Area Regional Transportation Authority as an essential first step to increased national support for local funding. Her other chief focus at Appropriations has been increased foreign aid for needy areas in Africa, including additional hundreds of millions of dollars to combat HIV/AIDS overseas. Kilpatrick has had no problems winning reelection, and she has focused her local political energy on boosting her son, the Detroit mayor.

In January 2007, as part of the House majority for the first time, Kilpatrick took over as chair of the record-high, 43-member Congressional Black Caucus. She said that the Caucus will "create new ways to address the challenges facing our community so that we can ensure future generations have access to power and prosperity in America."

FOURTEENTH DISTRICT

Rep. John Conyers (D)

Elected 1964, 22d term; b. May 16, 1929, Detroit; home, Detroit; Wayne St. U., B.A. 1957, LL.B. 1958; Baptist; married (Monica).

Military Career: National Guard, 1948-50; Army, 1950-54 (Korea), Army Reserves, 1954-57.

Professional Career: Legis. Asst., U.S. Rep. John Dingell, 1958-61; Practicing atty., 1959-61; Referee, MI Workmen's Comp. Dept., 1961-63.

DC Office: 2426 RHOB, 20515, 202-225-5126; Fax: 202-225-0072; Web site: www.house.gov/conyers.

District Offices: Detroit, 313-961-5670; Trenton, 734-675-4084.

Committees: *Judiciary* (Chmn. of 23 D): Commercial & Administrative Law; Courts, the Internet & Intellectual Property; The Constitution, Civil Rights & Civil Liberties.

Group Ratings

	ADA	ACLU	AFS	LCV	ITIC	NTU	COC	ACU	CFG	FRC
2006	100	100	100	100	14	16	20	4	4	0
2005	95	—	100	89	—	23	35	13	12	8

National Journal Ratings

	2005 LIB	—	2005 CONS		2006 LIB	—	2006 CONS
Economic	75%	—	25%		83%	—	16%
Social	98%	—	0%		97%	—	0%
Foreign	96%	—	0%		95%	—	0%

Key Votes of the 109th Congress

1. Estate Tax Repeal	N	5. Limit Interstate Abortion	N	9. Build Border Fence	N
2. Limit CAFE Standards	Y	6. Extend Patriot Act	N	10. CAFTA	N
3. FY06 Spending Curb	N	7. Bar Same Sex Marriage	N	11. Oppose Iraq Withdrawal	N
4. Drilling in ANWR	N	8. Stem Cell Research $	Y	12. Detainee Tribunals	N

Election Results

2006 general	John Conyers (D)	158,755	(85%)	($913,514)
	Chad Miles (R)	27,367	(15%)	($6,963)
2006 primary	John Conyers (D)	unopposed		
2004 general	John Conyers (D)	213,681	(84%)	($534,363)
	Veronica Pedraza (R)	35,089	(14%)	
	Other	5,809	(2%)	

Prior Winning Percentages: 2002 (83%); 2000 (89%); 1998 (87%); 1996 (86%); 1994 (82%); 1992 (82%); 1990 (89%); 1988 (91%); 1986 (89%); 1984 (89%); 1982 (97%); 1980 (95%); 1978 (93%); 1976 (92%); 1974 (91%); 1972 (88%); 1970 (88%); 1968 (100%); 1966 (84%); 1964 (84%)

The People		Race/Ethnic Origin	Ancestry	
Area size:	123 sq. mi.	32.1% White	German: 5.0%	Polish: 4.8%
Urban population:	100.0%	61.1% Black	Arab: 4.7%	
Rural population:	0.0%	1.2% Asian	**2004 Presidential Vote**	
Pop. 2000:	662,563	0.3% Native Am.	Kerry (D) 219,075	(83%)
Pop. 2005 (est):	618,274	0.0% Hawaiian	Bush (R) 46,240	(17%)
Median income:	$36,099	3.3% Two+ races	**2000 Presidential Vote**	
Poverty status:	19.7%	0.2% Other	Gore (D) 198,687	(81%)
Military veterans:	11.2%	1.8% Hispanic Origin	Bush (R) 44,345	(18%)
			Other 2,449	(1%)
			Cook Partisan Voting Index: D +33	

Occupation	Blue collar: 28.4%	White collar: 53.0%	Gray collar: 18.5%

Detroit's early auto factories—Packard, Hudson, Ford Highland Park, Dodge Main, Briggs, Ford Rouge, Cadillac, Kelsey-Hayes, Chrysler, Plymouth, DeSoto—were built between 1905 and 1925 in an arc about five miles from the city's center, in green fields at what was then the edge of urban development. Almost instantly the flat farmlands all around were platted in grid streets and filled with wooden bungalows and brick prairie-style houses, often with a driveway at the side and a single elm in front. Commercial strips lined the mile-square and radial main streets, stretching straight as far as the eye could see. Detroit's neighborhoods filled up with factory workers and civil servants, professionals and maintenance men, corner store owners and management personnel, Catholics and Protestants and Jews: a middle-class melting pot. With one exception: Detroit in those days had few blacks; they did not begin their big migrations here from the South, especially Alabama, until around 1940, when defense plants began hiring blacks in large numbers.

The history of black Detroit is one of conflict and uplift, inspiration and tragedy. The wartime mixture of Appalachian mountain whites and Deep South blacks proved volatile: there was a violent race riot in June 1943. During the war years, blacks were pent up in a few severely overcrowded neighborhoods like the Black Bottom, most of it now covered by the Chrysler Freeway. After 1945, when blacks began moving outward, real estate agents played on racial fears, and in the 1950s whole square miles of Detroit changed racial composition in months. In the 1960s there was hope that the civil rights movement, encouraged by Walter Reuther's UAW, and antipoverty programs would improve blacks' fortunes, and in fact many black Detroiters found good jobs and made good incomes, bought their own homes and built community institutions. Then came the riot of July 1967, followed by extensive white flight and terrible increases in crime. Detroit's first black mayor, Coleman Young, elected in 1973, responded with policies that may have seemed appropriate in the 1960s but had disastrous results in the 1970s and 1980s: He pressured major employers like the Big Three auto companies to build facilities in Detroit, raised taxes to support a vast army of city employees, and attributed city problems to white racism. Violent crime became a part of everyday life and arson became common.

Detroit took on a garrison atmosphere. Crime reduced the value of residential real estate to near zero, and the city's population dropped from 1.7 million in 1960 to 886,000 in 2005. In political dialogue, most black politicians called for, and most black voters seemed to support, an ever-increasing public sector. Yet the existing public sector, which took a larger share of residents' income than almost anywhere else in the country, served citizens very poorly. Turnaround came agonizingly late in the 1990s, as Mayor Dennis Archer, elected in 1993, worked to fight crime and encourage private-sector growth. Incomes rose and the median housing value doubled from $32,000 to $63,000.

The 14th Congressional District of Michigan consists of nearly half of Detroit (though not the downtown) and some disparate suburbs. Its part of Detroit is north and west of where the old auto plants were built and is mostly residential—square mile after square mile of grid streets, some always working class, some middle class, a few—Palmer Woods, Sherwood Forest, Rosedale Park—upscale. In most of them, abandoned houses and empty lots are commonplace where houses once stood, and yet in many neighborhoods, residents struggle to maintain their houses and patrol their streets. Commercial frontage on Detroit's straight-line avenues is still patchy and often vacant. Politically, this is one of the most Democratic districts in the United States.

The suburbs of the 14th are diverse. Highland Park is like much of Detroit; Hamtramck still retains the flavor of its original Polish immigrants (on Fat Tuesday, this is where to find the best paczki) who made it America's fastest-growing city in 1910-20; it had 56,000 people in 1930 but only 22,000 in 2006. The 14th District now includes most of Dearborn, including the Ford headquarters, the Ford Rouge plant and Henry Ford's Greenfield Village. Dearborn was known from the 1940s to the 1970s as an adamantly all-white town under longtime Mayor Orville Hubbard, although it is open to blacks today. It is more famous now as the home of the nation's largest Arab-American community with 30% claiming Arab ancestry, among them Lebanese, Iraqis and Yemenis; you can see signs in Arabic and find mosques and Arab community centers. There was a parade in Dearborn when the statue of Saddam Hussein fell in April 2003 and Iraqi citizens came there to vote absentee two times in 2005. From Dearborn, the district extends south, to take in working-class suburbs—Melvindale, Allen Park, Southgate, Riverview, Trenton and Gibraltar. The last three are on the Detroit River, and the district also includes the island of Grosse Ile, a high-income community that works to keep some of its space open.

The congressman from the 14th District is John Conyers, the second most senior member of the House and chairman of the House Judiciary Committee. First elected in 1964, he was a founder of the Congressional Black Caucus. The son of a left-wing UAW operative, he grew up in Detroit. He played cornet in Northwestern and Cass Technical High Schools and, underage, watched jazz greats at Baker's Keyboard Lounge; in 1987 he passed a resolution declaring "the sense of Congress that jazz is [a] rare and valuable American national treasure." He served in the Army in Korea, practiced law and worked as a staffer for a young congressman named John Dingell. Conyers was one of six blacks in the House when first elected to Congress in 1964 and the only one to take a militant approach to politics; he won his primary, in which 60,000 votes were cast, by 108 votes. The civil rights heroine Rosa Parks, who had moved to Detroit, worked in his 1964 campaign and then worked in his Detroit office until her retirement in 1988; on her death he sponsored the resolution that she lie in state in the Capitol Rotunda, the first woman so honored. His response to the 1967 riots was to introduce the first bill for a guaranteed annual income. He first sponsored a Martin Luther King holiday bill days after the civil rights leader was murdered in 1968, and persevered until it passed in 1983. Since 1989 he has sponsored bills to establish a commission to examine slavery and its lingering effects, and for consideration of whether reparations should be paid to descendants of slaves. He opposed most controversial parts of the crime bills of the past three decades and welfare changes in the 1990s and calls for single-payer health plans and massive public works projects.

After September 11, Conyers as ranking minority member worked together with the new Judiciary chairman, James Sensenbrenner, on terrorism legislation. In October 2001 they agreed that the government could detain immigrants suspected of terrorism without bringing charges, but only for seven days, and they introduced the antiterrorism bill together. In April 2002 Sensenbrenner got Conyers's support for splitting the INS into two agencies by agreeing to add counsel positions. Conyers opposed the Iraq war resolution. He opposed the House version of the intelligence reorganization bill. He cosponsored Charles Rangel's bill to reinstitute the military draft and then, along with Rangel, voted against it on the floor. In December 2004 he asked for an FBI investigation of election procedures into "inappropriate and likely illegal election tampering" in Hocking County, Ohio, and also asked television networks to turn over raw exit poll data. In January 2005 he said there were "massive and unprecedented voter irregularities in Ohio" and voted to challenge the Ohio electoral votes. In September 2005, over Sensenbrenner's objection, the House passed 223-199 a Conyers amendment expanding hate crimes categories to sexual orientation, gender and disability and to allow separate criminal counts to be based on them. On telecom issues he has taken a bipartisan course: in December 2005 he and Sensenbrenner cosponsored a bill to require that analog-to-digital video conversion devices maintain digital rights management invisible coding; in May 2006 they passed through committee an amendment to prohibit telecom and cable companies from blocking or degrading Internet services. In April 2006 he was one of 11 House members to sue to invalidate the 2006 deficit reduction bill on the ground that the House and Senate versions were not identical.

Conyers is the only member of the House ever to have served on two committees handling presidential impeachment, in 1974 and 1998. In May 1972, a month before the Watergate burglary, he called for impeaching Richard Nixon because of his conduct of the Vietnam War. As the hearings on Bill Clinton's impeachment opened in 1998, some Democrats were queasy about Conyers, sharing the judgment of Judiciary Committee Republican George Gekas that he was "predictably unpredictable." But Conyers, the ranking Democrat, performed ably. For all his criticisms of Clinton, Conyers rallied behind him; he managed to craft an alternative investigation resolution that Republicans wouldn't accept, the start of partisan divisions on the issue. In 2005 Conyers suggested that impeachment of George W. Bush might be in order. In June 2005 he held a public forum on the Downing Street memo reported in the *Sunday Times* of London. In December 2005 he called on Congress to censure Bush and Dick Cheney for misleading Congress and the American people on Iraq and called for creation of a special committee to investigate. After the *New York Times* that month revealed the NSA surveillance of contacts between al Qaeda suspects abroad and persons in the United States, Conyers called for an independent committee to investigate the program. During the 2006 campaign Republicans charged that Conyers, as chairman of the Judiciary Committee, would bring impeachment proceedings. After Minority Leader Nancy Pelosi said that impeachment should not be considered, Conyers agreed that it would be "off the table." (But not for his wife, Detroit City Councilmember Monica Conyers, who sponsored a resolution calling for the impeachment of Bush and Cheney; the council approved the symbolic measure 7–0 in May 2007). After the 2006 election, he noted that, "Investigations into what went on are completely different from whether there should be an impeachment proceeding."

Over the years, Conyers—described by the *Detroit News* as "part showman, part junkyard dog, part evangelist"—has mostly been reelected without difficulty. He made two runs for mayor of Detroit, in 1989 and 1993. But he ran a desultory campaign the first time and almost no campaign the second, and came in far behind. He had two serious primary opponents in the 1994 House race, but finished well ahead of both with 51% of the vote. In recent years, he suffered some unfavorable publicity. In November 2003 the *Detroit Free Press* after a two-month investigation reported that Conyers and his top staffers assigned congressional staff to work on political campaigns, including the city council campaign of former staffer JoAnn Watson and Conyers's wife's state Senate campaign. In December, the House ethics committee began an investigation into the matter, which was later expanded after former staffers claimed Conyers also made them run his personal errands and baby-sit his two children. In December 2006, the ethics committee concluded its investigation and stated Conyers must take "a number of additional, significant steps to ensure that his office complies with all rules and standards regarding campaign and personal work by congressional staff," including sending a memo to all staff members stating what duties they are prohibited from performing.

In 2006 Conyers was reelected without difficulty. As incoming chairman of the Judiciary Committee, he promised to concentrate on voter suppression, racial disparities in sentencing, harsh penalties for first-time drug offenders, the impact of the 2005 bankruptcy law on the poor, corporate antitrust violations, violence against women, hate crimes and putting more policemen on the beat.

With almost all the members of the committee classifiable as liberal Democrats and conservative Republicans, he seemed to have clear majorities on most issues.

FIFTEENTH DISTRICT

Rep. John Dingell (D)

Elected Dec. 1955, 26th full term; b. July 8, 1926, Colorado Springs, CO; home, Dearborn; Georgetown U., B.S. 1949, J.D. 1952; Catholic; married (Deborah).

Military Career: Army, 1944-46 (WWII).

Professional Career: Practicing atty., 1952-55; Wayne Cnty. Asst. Prosecuting Atty., 1953-55.

DC Office: 2328 RHOB, 20515, 202-225-4071; Fax: 202-226-0371; Web site: www.house.gov/dingell.

District Offices: Dearborn, 313-278-2936; Monroe, 734-243-1849; Ypsilanti, 734-481-1100.

Committees: *Energy & Commerce* (Chmn. of 31 D).

Group Ratings

	ADA	ACLU	AFS	LCV	ITIC	NTU	COC	ACU	CFG	FRC
2006	95	95	100	100	43	10	33	13	8	0
2005	95	—	100	89	—	16	52	12	3	0

National Journal Ratings

	2005 LIB	—	2005 CONS		2006 LIB	—	2006 CONS
Economic	69%	—	29%		86%	—	11%
Social	75%	—	25%		72%	—	28%
Foreign	81%	—	18%		59%	—	41%

Key Votes of the 109th Congress

1. Estate Tax Repeal	N	5. Limit Interstate Abortion	N	9. Build Border Fence		N
2. Limit CAFE Standards	Y	6. Extend Patriot Act	N	10. CAFTA		N
3. FY06 Spending Curb	N	7. Bar Same Sex Marriage	N	11. Oppose Iraq Withdrawal		*
4. Drilling in ANWR	N	8. Stem Cell Research $	Y	12. Detainee Tribunals		N

Election Results

2006 general	John Dingell (D)	181,946	(88%)	($1,400,145)
	Aimee Smith (Green)	9,447	(5%)	
	Gregory Stempfle (Lib)	8,410	(4%)	
	Other	7,065	(3%)	
2006 primary	John Dingell (D)	unopposed		
2004 general	John Dingell (D)	218,409	(71%)	($1,127,151)
	Dawn Reamer (R)	81,828	(27%)	
	Other	7,726	(3%)	

Prior Winning Percentages: 2002 (72%); 2000 (71%); 1998 (67%); 1996 (62%); 1994 (59%); 1992 (65%); 1990 (67%); 1988 (97%); 1986 (78%); 1984 (64%); 1982 (74%); 1980 (70%); 1978 (77%); 1976 (76%); 1974 (78%); 1972 (68%); 1970 (79%); 1968 (74%); 1966 (63%); 1964 (73%); 1962 (83%); 1960 (79%); 1958 (79%); 1956 (74%); 1955 (76%)

The People		Race/Ethnic Origin	Ancestry	
Area size:	981 sq. mi.	79.2% White	German: 15.0% Irish: 8.4%	
Urban population:	87.7%	11.7% Black	Polish: 6.7%	
Rural population:	12.3%	3.7% Asian	**2004 Presidential Vote**	
Pop. 2000:	662,563	0.4% Native Am.	Kerry (D) 191,091	(62%)
Pop. 2005 (est):	680,070	0.0% Hawaiian	Bush (R) 118,217	(38%)
Median income:	$48,963	2.0% Two+ races	Other 573	(0%)
Poverty status:	10.3%	0.2% Other	**2000 Presidential Vote**	
Military veterans:	11.1%	2.8% Hispanic Origin	Gore (D) 161,913	(60%)
			Bush (R) 101,607	(38%)
			Other 7,086	(3%)
			Cook Partisan Voting Index: D +13	

Occupation   Blue collar: 26.2%   White collar: 59.0%   Gray collar: 14.7%

The southeast corner of Michigan is a part of the country most Americans don't think about much, and it doesn't look very interesting out the plane window as you approach Metro Airport. The flat marshlands along the shore of Lake Erie give way to flat farm lands, with rivers flowing lazily in summer and flashing with ice in winter. Here and there you see power plants with giant smokestacks and factories. Out on the horizon you can get a glimpse of the sprawl of metro Detroit, of the great auto and steel and chemical plants along the Detroit River; over on the other side is Ann Arbor, home of the University of Michigan.

The 15th Congressional District of Michigan includes much of this southeastern corner of the state. It owes its shape to Republican redistricters, who in July 2001 devised the nation's most successful partisan redistricting plan of the decennial cycle. The district includes industrial parts of Wayne County, all of Monroe County and the Ann Arbor and Ypsilanti areas in Washtenaw County. In Wayne County, the 15th includes the western part of Dearborn and most of Dearborn Heights; the most heavily Arab-American parts of Dearborn were put in the 14th District, and these are more middle class, even affluent areas; the line cuts through Dearborn Heights and put one trailer park in two districts. To the south are working class suburbs: Taylor, Romulus (home of Metro Airport), and Woodhaven, site of a big Ford plant. Flat Rock is home to a joint Ford-Mazda auto plant, one of the few Japanese plants in Michigan. Monroe was the boyhood home of General George Armstrong Custer, and in his day agricultural; now it is more industrial, and the southern part is in many ways an extension of Toledo, Ohio. (Michigan and Ohio almost went to war over the Toledo land in the 1830s; Ohio got Toledo and Michigan got the Upper Peninsula as recompense.) Ann Arbor is one of the nation's largest university towns, oriented to the university but also full of people, from auto executives to perennial graduate students, who like the atmosphere of a town with plenty of book stores, coffee houses and liberal neighbors; it voted 74% to legalize medical marijuana in November 2004. In 2006, it landed the headquarters of Google's AdWords unit, which operates the company's "pay-per-click" advertising method—its main revenue source. Ypsilanti, though it also has a university (Eastern Michigan), is less bookish and more industrial. All of these areas tend to vote Democratic, though Monroe is sometimes marginal, but they house very different kinds of Democrats. In Wayne County, union political operatives have dominated Democratic party politics for 50 years. In Ann Arbor, Democratic politics is dominated by leftist peace activists, environmentalists and feminists.

The congressman from the 15th District is John Dingell, the dean of the House of Representatives and chairman of the Energy and Commerce Committee. His father, John Dingell, Sr., was first elected to the House in 1932, from a district created as a result of the Detroit area's auto boom. The first Congressman Dingell was one of the most productive urban liberals of his day, a sponsor of Social Security and, starting in 1943, of national health insurance. John Dingell Jr. has been around Capitol Hill almost as long. He was a House page from 1938-43 and served in the Army in World War II; he graduated from Georgetown and its law school, paying his way by working as an elevator operator in the Capitol; he practiced law in Detroit and served as an assistant prosecutor in Wayne County. After his father died in September 1955, Dingell was elected to succeed him in December, at 29, from a district entirely within Detroit with large Polish, black and Jewish populations. He still uses his father's office furniture and every session continues to introduce as H.R. 15 (the number matches the district) the national health insurance bill his father co-sponsored in 1943. He is the only member of the House who served in the 1950s; indeed only two others served in the 1960s (John Conyers and David Obey); it is a measure of his seniority that the second most senior member of the House, Conyers, once served on his staff. He has an interesting personal life, raising his children after his divorce and marrying in 1981 a granddaughter of one of General Motors' Fisher brothers. Debbie Dingell is vice-chairman of the General Motors Foundation and a Democratic national committeewoman, and an encourager of bipartisan amity as well; she headed the Michigan campaigns for Al Gore in 2000 and John Kerry in 2004, and helped each win 51% of the vote in this battleground state.

Dingell served as chairman of Energy and Commerce for 14 years, from 1981 to 1995, and was also chairman of its Investigative and Oversight Subcommittee; by common consent he was one of the most powerful and effective chairmen ever. It had wide jurisdiction, handled up to 40% of all House bills, and had the largest budget and staff of any House committee. As institutions will, the committee took on the character of its leader, widely known as "the truck": bright, aggressive, domineering, determined. Dingell and his committee superintended the breakup of AT&T and the sale of Conrail by public offering; Commerce's cable reregulation law of 1992 was the only bill on which Congress overrode George H.W. Bush's veto. After a decade of sparring over clean air legislation, Dingell worked together with Health Subcommittee Chairman Henry Waxman to produce the 1990 Clean Air Act.

On other issues, Dingell backed organized labor's agenda against NAFTA and trade promotion authority. An avid outdoorsman (he hunts deer, elk, caribou and moose), he long opposed gun control but voted for the 1994 crime bill and resigned from the National Rifle Association board. On the old Merchant Marine and Fisheries Committee, he was responsible for wildlife refuge legislation, and one of his proudest accomplishments is the creation in 2001 of the Detroit River International Wildlife Refuge, on both sides of the river from Zug Island in River Rouge south to Lake Erie. This is not publicly owned land; Dingell has worked to get donations of land or easements from private landowners, land preservation groups and the Army Corps of Engineers, and the refuge has expanded from 394 to 4,399 acres. In many ways, he is an old-fashioned Franklin D. Roosevelt Democrat, supporting big government and strenuous regulation, taking a conservative line on some cultural issues and backing an assertive foreign policy; he was the only Michigan Democrat to vote for the Gulf War resolution in January 1991, although he voted against the Iraq war resolution in October 2002.

When the Republican majority took over, Dingell, as the senior House member, swore in Newt Gingrich with good grace and proceeded to work with Republicans and produce legislation. Dingell's goal remains national health insurance; asked what is a desirable system, he says, "Canada's, right across the river." He opposed the Republicans' Medicare/prescription drug bill in 2003 and went out on the road to criticize it in 2004. "HMOs, foreign diplomats and the mentally insane are the only people in this country who are exempt from the consequences of their decisions." In 2004 Dingell and the new Energy and Commerce chairman, Joe Barton, asked the FCC for an investigation of a la carte cable channels (customers would pay for only those channels they wanted). Dingell tended toward opposition.

Dingell has sprung into action when Michigan has been adversely affected. In January 2003 the city of Toronto started transporting all its trash—180 truckloads a day, 1.1 million tons a year—in a landfill in southwest Wayne County, in Dingell's district. Dingell had long complained of Canadian trash dumping, and he and Senator Debbie Stabenow insisted that EPA enforce a 1992 treaty which, they said, required that Canada give notice of each shipment and which allowed the U.S. to reject each one. EPA Administrator Mike Leavitt argued that only hazardous waste was covered by the treaty, but Dingell persisted and got a 12–4 subcommittee vote demanding enforcement. After voters in Romulus approved an Indian casino, Dingell put an amendment approving it on the transportation bill in March 2004, though it was later removed. Dingell has long opposed raising CAFE gas mileage standards, but has not followed the industry lead uncritically. In October 2003 the House accepted his amendment to require NHTSA to raise fuel economy standards enough to save 5 billion gallons of gasoline. He was also pushing an amendment with incentives for the auto companies to develop diesel engines with low sulfur emissions and to offer more diesel cars and trucks. He promised in December 2006 to hold hearings on efforts to create energy-efficient vehicles and viable alternatives to gasoline, including biofuels, electric power trains and diesel engines, and to push for more ethanol pumps at gas stations, next-generation batteries, clean-burning diesel engines and plug-in hybrids.

After Democrats won the House majority in 2006, Dingell prepared to take over as chairman again. "It's been a long 12 years, and the work has been piling up," he said. "We will kill the closest snake first. That is what we will do—try to do things in the best order possible and get as much done in the public interest." He listed as priorities CAFE standards, the decline in manufacturing jobs, health care. To the *New Republic*, he set out a formidable agenda: "Privacy. Social Security number protection. Outsourcing protection. Unfair trade practices. Currency manipulation. Air quality. We'll look at the implementation of the Energy Policy Act of 2005. We'll take a look at climate change. We'll take a look at the nuclear waste program, where literally billions of dollars are being dissipated. We'll look at port security and nuclear smuggling, where there's literally nothing being done. We'll look at the Superfund program. We'll take a look at EPA enforcement. On health, we'll take a look at Medicaid and waivers. The Food and Drug Administration. Generic drug approval. Medical safety. We'll also take a look at food supplements, where people are being killed. We will look at Medicare Part D. Telecom. We'll look at FCC actions. . . . Media ownership. Adequate spectrum for police, fire, public safety and addressing the problems of terrorism. . . . We will look also at the overall question of Katrina recovery efforts." He said he would handle the spectrum issue before considering a major telecom bill, that he would introduce a bill reauthorizing the SCHIP children's health insurance program and would reexamine the issue of net neutrality. He criticized Republicans for having excluded Democrats from consideration of issues and promised extensive hearings and a willingness to listen to the minority. His predecessor, ranking minority member Joe Barton, said, "As chairman, he had a lot of authority and he used that authority. He was never arbitrary. He was never mean to be mean or ruthless just to be ruthless. He was always fair in the application of the rules. But in his mind, in hindsight, he was a lot fairer than those of us in the minority remember him being."

In some respects Dingell does not have as much power as he did in his earlier stint as chairman. He no longer chairs the Investigative subcommittee, but can be expected to have considerable influence over its new chairman, fellow Michiganian Bart Stupak. The House Republican leadership, in order to settle a dispute over the chairmanship, ceded Energy and Commerce's jurisdiction over securities, accounting and insurance legislation to the Financial Services Committee; Barney Frank, the new Financial Services chairman, got Speaker Nancy Pelosi to say that she would not revisit the jurisdiction issue. In early 2007 Dingell and Frank sparred briefly over data security legislation, then promised to cooperate. Despite Dingell's statement in November 2006 that he would hold hearings on carbon emissions, Pelosi also created a select committee to consider legislation to address carbon emissions, over Dingell's objections; its chairman was Edward Markey, an Energy and Commerce member usually allied with Dingell but with different views on the emissions issue. "These committees," Dingell said, "are as useful in relevance as feathers on a fish." Moreover, unlike some other major committees, Energy and Commerce has several moderate Democrats who may not back Dingell on some important issues.

Since his first election in December 1955, Dingell has had only two serious challenges, both in Democratic primaries after being redistricted in with another incumbent. In 1964 he ran in a district mostly new to him against another incumbent who had followed his father to the House, John Lesinski of Dearborn, who was the only northern Democrat to vote against the Civil Rights Act of 1964. With strong support from the UAW, Dingell won 54%-46%. Then in July 2001 the Republican legislature put him in the same district with Lynn Rivers, an Ann Arbor liberal first elected in 1994, who was born in 1956, Dingell's first full year in the House. Democratic leaders urged Rivers to run in the neighboring 11th District, but she decided on what she called a "David vs. Goliath match up." Their voting records were similar, though not identical, but their cultural backgrounds were as different as the working class suburbs of Wayne County and the university town of Ann Arbor. Rivers campaigned as a congresswoman who knew what the ordinary person went through and cast her votes accordingly. Dingell campaigned as a congressman who had gotten many things done and was in a position to do much more. On September 10, 2001, the day before the redistricting bill was to be signed, Nancy Pelosi, then running for minority whip, sent Rivers $10,000—"a minor annoyance," Dingell said. Rivers emphasized their differences on the partial-birth abortion ban, particular gun control proposals and environmental standards; Dingell voted for the first, opposed the second and tended to support the auto companies (and the UAW) on the third. Dingell parried by pointing to the women's issues he had been instrumental on—breast and cervical cancer screening, minimum hospital stays after childbirth, children's health insurance. This was an expensive election; as Dingell recalled, he spent $35,000 against Lesinski in 1964 and $2.5 million against Rivers in 2002; she raised $1.5 million, much of it in bundled contributions from EMILY's List, making this Michigan's most expensive House primary ever.

In June, Rivers started running spots in which she recounted her personal struggles. Her plainspoken, perky manner evidently got through: by late July, two polls showed the race even. Dingell fired back with a spot praising his effectiveness on prescription drugs, HMO regulation, children's health insurance and the Clean Air Act. In contrast, he said, "She's never authored a single piece of legislation that's been signed into law." For him the race came down to the question,

"Are you going to replace one of the most effective members of the House of Representatives with one of the least effective members?" In the August primary Dingell won 59%-41%. He won 74%-26% in Wayne County, which cast 43% of the votes, even though part of it was in Rivers's old district, and 80%-20% in Monroe County, which cast 19% of the votes. Rivers won Washtenaw County 69%-31%. The general election was anticlimactic; Dingell won easily in this Democratic district.

In July 2006 he attracted some criticism when he voted against a resolution supporting Israel against Hezbollah attacks and told a Detroit TV station, "I don't take sides for or against Hezbollah, for or against Israel." Days later he wrote in the *Detroit News*, "I believe the United States has no truer friend in the Middle East than Israel. . . . There is no doubt that Hezbollah is a terrorist organization. . . . There is no room in politics, in Lebanon or anywhere, for groups that use violence and terror to achieve their political ends." He called for the U.S. to push for a "cessation of hostilities" and to try to get Syria to stop supporting Hezbollah. He was reelected without difficulty.

In December 2005 Dingell marked the 50th anniversary of his election to the House. At the National Building Museum he was feted by Democrats including Bill Clinton and Nancy Pelosi, and Republicans Dick Cheney and Joe Barton. On the anniversary he and Debbie Dingell lunched with George and Laura Bush at the White House. He has had two heart operations and an artificial hip. "I creak a little more each year," he admitted, "but I keep going"—and with an iPod, which he got after his press secretary explained that podcasts were something like Franklin Roosevelt's fireside chats. "I will burn out when I burn out. I don't know when the hell it will come. It probably will come in time. But I still give my people a full day's work. I still give them seven days a week. I still travel the district. I still work hard on legislation." In February 2009, Dingell will have been the longest-serving House member in history; in January 2013 he will have served longer in Congress than anyone else. A man who persevered in 12 frustrating years in the minority seemed prepared to keep charging ahead as chairman once again.

★ MINNESOTA ★

Minnesota has long been a distinctive commonwealth, set far in America's frozen North, a state which in commerce, culture and politics has set one example after another for the rest of the nation. It is the node of transcontinental railroads that linked the winter wheat fields of the northern prairies to the greatest grain-milling center in the world and the great Pacific ports of Puget Sound. It is also the birthplace of Scotch tape, Betty Crocker, Target and the Mall of America, the home base of dyspeptic chroniclers of small town America from Sinclair Lewis to Garrison Keillor. Politically, Minnesota for much of the 20th century provided the nation with some of its most articulate and honorable leaders—Harold Stassen, Hubert Humphrey, Eugene McCarthy, Walter Mondale—and with traditions of probity, civic-mindedness and innovation which are second to none. Yet while commercially and culturally Minnesota has never been stronger, its recent political history has been unusual. After a dozen years in which the two political parties, the Democratic-Farmer-Labor and Republican, were dominated by activists of left and right who were stubbornly out of touch with ordinary people, the voters in 1998 elected as governor a former professional wrestler and suburban mayor, Jesse "The Body" Ventura. What had been one of the nation's more heavily Democratic states became a target very much up for grabs. Ventura retired from politics in 2002, and Republicans seemed to seize the tide. Tim Pawlenty was elected governor and Norm Coleman senator by impressive margins. In 2004 Minnesota was a target state, carried by John Kerry by a 51%-48% margin. Then in 2006 the DFL seized the tide. Pawlenty was reelected by only a 47%-46% margin and the DFL's Amy Klobuchar was elected to the Senate by a huge margin. The DFL, already holding the state Senate, gained control of the state House and picked up the 1st Congressional District seat as well. Has Minnesota become a solidly DFL state again, as it was during much of the 1950s, 1960s and 1970s?

Minnesota's distinctive traditions come from a distinctive history. The far northern states were ignored by most Yankee immigrants, who headed straight west into Iowa, Nebraska and Kansas. But others saw opportunity in Minnesota's icy lakes and ferocious winters. James J. Hill, the builder of the Great Northern Railroad ("You can't interest me in any proposition in any place where it doesn't snow"), and others operating out of Minneapolis and St. Paul—already twin cities by 1860—worked to attract Norwegian, Swedish and German migrants who would find the terrain and climate congenial. By 1890, the Twin Cities—rivals that year in a Census competition—were the

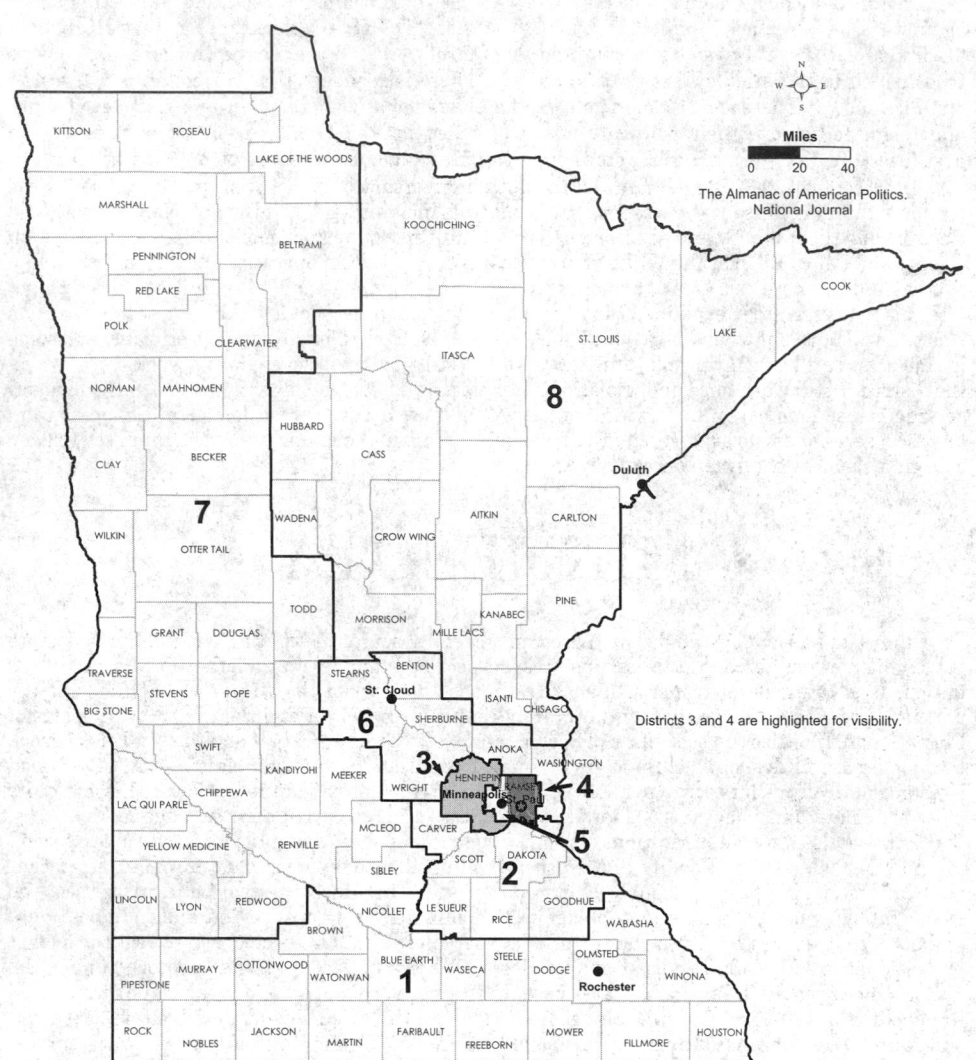

Districts 3 and 4 are highlighted for visibility.

The Almanac of American Politics.
National Journal

Congressional district boundaries were first effective for 2002.

nerve center of a sprawling and rich agricultural empire stretching west from Minnesota through the Dakotas and into Montana and beyond. Minneapolis and St. Paul became the termini of its rail lines and the site of its grain-milling companies.

The Twin Cities also became the center of a three-party politics and an economic radicalism reminiscent of the politics of Scandinavia. For our American regions seem a mirror image of the geography of Europe, with the East Coast resembling the British Isles and France, the industrial Midwest reminiscent of Germany and Poland, the relatively poor and always hawkish South a Baptist Mediterranean, and the Upper Midwest of Minnesota, Wisconsin and North Dakota as North American versions of Scandinavia. The Scandinavian flavor of life lives on: You can get lutefisk (smelly lye-soaked cod) around Christmastime in Minneapolis restaurants (though you probably don't want to). It extends also to politics. Like Scandinavia, these Upper Midwestern commonwealths pioneered their continent's welfare states, with an effect on public policy far out of proportion to their numbers. Alarmed by the unprecedented concentration of economic power and wealth into the hands of just a few identifiable millionaires who lived on St. Paul's Summit Avenue or the hill above Minneapolis's Hennepin Avenue, the immigrants drew on their native traditions of cooperative activity and bureaucratic socialism.

As in Wisconsin and North Dakota, a strong third party developed here in the years after the Populist era. This Farmer-Labor Party elected senators in the 1920s and dominated state politics in the 1930s. Hurt by their ties to Communists, the Farmer-Laborites were beaten by Harold Stassen's Republicans in 1938. But this was still a New Deal state, and by 1944 the bedraggled local Democrats were merged with the anti-Communist faction of Farmer-Laborites to form the Democratic-Farmer-Labor Party. A key role was played by Hubert Humphrey—mayor of Minneapolis in 1945, and the dazzling advocate of the civil rights plank at the 1948 Democratic National Convention. Humphrey's DFL—clean, idealistic, closely tied to labor, backed by many farmers—attracted dozens of talented politicians, including Eugene McCarthy, Orville Freeman and Walter Mondale. In 1948 Humphrey's speech helped put the Democrats on record for civil rights, and he was elected to the Senate at age 37.

In the years that followed, the DFL dominated Minnesota politics, while a series of progressive companies led the development of a strong, diversified economy. The DFL stood for a generous, compassionate government, for strong labor unions and high wages, for an expansionist fiscal policy to encourage consumer-led economic growth, for civil rights, and for an anti-Communist, but not bombastic, foreign policy. Its base was among blue-collar workers in the Twin Cities, in Duluth and the Iron Range, and among farmers of Scandinavian origin. Minnesota's business leaders were conservative politically and innovation-minded in their work. New entrepreneurs rose in the 1990s, and Minnesota's incomes rose to 11th in the nation; the slowdown after 2000 was less severe than in many other states. It is part of a long pattern: Minnesota's economy hums along, growing robustly in prosperous years and not falling behind in recessions, and squeaky-clean if sometimes eccentric Minnesota has levels of crime, divorce and aberrant behavior most states should envy. From 1990 to 2006, Minnesota's population grew by 18%, significantly more than any other Midwestern state though behind the national rate of 20%.

Minnesota has more social connectedness than any other large state, Robert Putnam notes in *Bowling Alone*, and this spirit of civic participation is echoed in the party precinct caucuses and party conventions. The early DFLers were proud of this system, which allowed plenty of political participation and ended control by party bosses. But by the 1980s the conventions came to be dominated not by laborite Humphrey followers or the wives of management Republicans, but by left-wingers and counterculturites, right-wing abortion opponents and religious hardliners. The result was the nomination of left-wing and right-wing candidates often rejected by the voters in primaries or general elections and in shrill, off-putting political rhetoric. All this left Minnesota open to the appeal of Jesse Ventura, candidate of the Independence party in 1998. Ventura was already known to Twin Cities television viewers—nearly three-quarters of the state's voters—and his clever ads tended to overshadow his more conventional rivals, Attorney General Skip Humphrey and DFL-turned-Republican St. Paul Mayor Norm Coleman. Ventura scored in the low teens in most polls, but he sparked a huge rise in turnout—Minnesota has Election Day registration—and won with 37% of the vote, to 34% for Coleman and only 28% for Humphrey—less than half the 60% his father won in his first electrifying election for senator exactly 50 years earlier.

Ventura pulled out a new electorate in the Minneapolis-St. Paul media market beyond the Twin Cities core of Hennepin and Ramsey Counties. In 2002 this area went heavily Republican, voting 51%-30% for Pawlenty and 56%-41% for Coleman over former Vice President and Senator Walter Mondale, who had been nominated to run in the late Paul Wellstone's place. In 2004 George

W. Bush carried the area 54%-45%, not quite enough to overcome the big DFL margins in Hennepin and Ramsey Counties and on the Iron Range. In 2006 Pawlenty carried the area 54%-39%, which was barely enough. This is family country and by far the fastest growing part of Minnesota—most counties outside it lost rather than gained population between 2000 and 2006. But the DFL constituency in the Iron Range has deep roots and Hennepin and Ramsey County, which have relatively few children, have by that fact a higher proportion of adults who can be rallied to the polls by DFL activists. That leaves Minnesota in something of a balance. The DFL won big victories in 2006, but has not elected a governor since 1986. DFL leaders in the legislature are aware that they hold majorities only because of seats won in the suburbs and so promised to proceed cautiously and not to the rhythm of their left-wing activists. So national Republicans, when they assemble for their national convention in St. Paul in 2008 (the second in the area; they met in Minneapolis in 1892), will not be on entirely hostile turf, and the DFL mayors of St. Paul and Minneapolis have been careful to be Minnesota nice.

The People		Race/Ethnic Origin			Military veterans: 464,968 (12.8%)	
Pop. 2006 (est):	5,167,101	4,337,143	88.2%	White	WWII: 20.2%	Korea: 14.6%
Pop. 2000:	4,919,479	168,813	3.4%	Black	Vietnam: 32.8%	Gulf War: 7.6%
Pop. 1990:	4,375,099	141,083	2.9%	Asian	**Most populous cities (2006):**	
Change 1990-2000:	Up 12.4%	52,009	1.1%	Native Am.	1. Minneapolis	372,833
% of U.S. total:	1.8%	1,714	0.0%	Hawaiian	2. St. Paul	273,535
Pop. rank:	21st of 50	70,304	1.4%	Two+ races	3. Rochester	96,975
Area size:	86,939 sq. mi.	5,031	0.1%	Other	4. Duluth	84,167
State Native:	70.2%	143,382	2.9%	Hisp. Origin	5. Bloomington	80,869
Non-citizen:	3.3%	**Ancestry**				
Language		German: 25.2%		Norwegian: 11.8%	Urban population: 70.9%	
English: 89.6%	Other Eur.: 3.9%	Irish: 7.7%		Swedish: 6.8%	Rural population: 29.1%	
Spanish: 3.6%		English: 4.3%				

Education		Work Sector		Legislature	
H.S. Grad:	87.9%	Private: 80.4%	Govt: 12.4%	Senate	44 D 23 R
College Grad:	27.4%	Self: 6.9%	Family: 0.3%	House	85 D 49 R
Industry		Unemployment: 4.1%		Legislative Term Limits: No	
Agri: 2.6%	Con: 5.9%	**Household Income**		**Registered Voters**	
Fin: 7.2%	Info: 2.5%	<15k: 12.1%	15-35k: 23.8%	No party registration	
Mfg: 21.4%	Prof: 29.7%	35-50k: 17.0%	50-100k: 34.5%		
Public: 3.4%	Trade: 15.5%	100-150k: 8.3%	>150k: 4.4%		
Other: 11.8%		Median: $47,111			
Occupation		Poverty status: 7.9%			
Blue collar: 23.3%	White collar: 62.3%	**Home Value**			
Gray collar: 14.4%		<50k: 11.1%	50-100k: 27.6%	100-200k: 45.8%	200-300k: 10.1%
		300-500k: 4.0%	>500k: 1.3%	Median: $118,100	

Presidential politics   Minnesota has the longest consecutive streak of voting Democratic for president of any state: the last time it voted Republican was in 1972, and even then it gave Richard Nixon his lowest percentage margin over George McGovern. But in 2000 and 2004 Minnesota was seriously contested, and gave Al Gore and John Kerry only 48%-46% and 51%-48% margins over George W. Bush. One might attribute the increasing Democratic margin to the decision of 2000 Ralph Nader voters to back John Kerry, but that was only part of the reason. Total turnout was up 15% in a state that allows new voters to register on Election Day, and the DFL seems to have turned out more new voters. Bush's popular vote margin increased by 44,000

2004 Presidential Vote		
Kerry (D)	1,445,014	(51%)
Bush (R)	1,346,695	(48%)
Nader (BL)	18,683	(1%)
Other	17,995	(1%)

2000 Presidential Vote		
Gore (D)	1,168,266	(48%)
Bush (R)	1,109,659	(46%)
Nader (Green)	126,696	(5%)
Other	34,064	(1%)

votes in the Twin Cities media market counties outside the metropolitan core. But in the core counties of Hennepin and Ramsey, John Kerry's popular vote margin was 71,000 votes more than Al Gore's. Whether Republicans can continue to increase their popular vote margin in fast-growing counties outside the metro core and whether the DFL can continue to increase their popular vote margin in the slow-growing Hennepin and Ramsey Counties core are both unclear.

Incidentally, one DFL elector cast his votes for both president and vice president for John Edwards. But neither reporters nor Secretary of State Mary Kiffmeyer could determine which elector had done so, and all 10 said they had voted for Kerry. Evidently it was just a mistake.

Minnesota has a tradition of selecting national convention delegates in caucuses. But caucus turnout has been low. In the 1998 DFL caucuses, an average of 4.4 voters showed up in each precinct, and in one-fourth of the precincts, no one showed up at all. DFL leaders, reeling from their party's third-place finish in 1998, tried to attract more voters to the March 2000 presidential precinct caucuses by moving them from Tuesday night to Saturday and by holding a presidential preference vote, with national convention delegates assigned proportionately. It made little difference: By the time Minnesotans caucused, the nomination was already clinched. Governor Tim Pawlenty sought in 2003 to move the caucus date to February, but his effort failed. In 2004, Minnesota was one of 10 states holding contests on March 2. Kerry carried 51% of the 55,000 votes cast in the presidential preference vote, Edwards took 27% and Dennis Kucinich finished third with 17%. The Republican and DFL precinct caucuses for 2008 were set for February 5.

Minnesota competed for both parties' 2008 national conventions, with politicians of both parties gamely pitching in. Both parties were impressed by the Twin Cities and the possible venues, but the Minnesotans made it clear that they could only hold one of the conventions and promised to go with whichever party chose it first. The Republicans, meeting on a Wednesday, picked St. Paul's Xcel Energy Center, a hockey arena that was a key project of Senator Norm Coleman when he was mayor, and Coleman gave Minneapolis Mayor R. T. Rybak the news at noon. Rybak called Democratic National Chairman Howard Dean, who asked him to hold off for an hour. But Dean could not get Democrats to make a decision before the Friday meeting, and chose Denver instead.

Congressional districting

110th Congress Lineup
5 DFL   3 R

109th Congress Lineup
4 DFL   4 R

After the 2000 Census it never seemed likely that Minnesota's Republican House, DFL Senate and Independence party governor would agree on congressional redistricting, and they didn't—the new plan was drawn by a special panel of five judges appointed by Chief Justice Kathleen Blatz. The Republicans wanted to combine Minneapolis and St. Paul into one heavily Democratic district, in the hope of winning three or four of four suburban districts. Democrats designed a plan that would continue the longstanding practice of having predominantly rural districts anchored in each corner of the state; the result would be four rural districts, two dominated by Minneapolis and St. Paul and two in the suburbs. Governor Jesse Ventura submitted a plan with two urban, three suburban and three rural districts, with one of them stretching along the western side of the state from Iowa to Canada.

The special panel drew its own plan and, when Republicans, Democrats and Ventura couldn't agree by the March 19, 2002, deadline, it was publicly revealed and put into effect. Minneapolis and St. Paul would each continue to dominate a district. Three suburban and three rural districts were created, one running along the southern end of the state from Wisconsin to South Dakota. Republican and Democratic leaders and Ventura all said they were pleased with the plan: It is probably what they might have agreed to if someone had put a gun to their heads. The homes of two incumbents, DFLer Bill Luther and Republican Mark Kennedy were placed in the new 6th District. Luther, after pondering the decision for two months, decided to run in the new 2d District, much of which he had represented; he lost in November. The southernmost district, expected to be safely Republican, fell to the DFL in 2006.

Minnesota seems to be on the cusp of losing a House seat after the 2010 election. Polidata estimates, based on extrapolation of 2000-06 growth to 2010, that Minnesota's eighth seat will be number 436 in the formula used to apportion seats, and the House is limited to 435 seats. So if Minnesota's population growth speeds up for the rest of the decade, it will probably hold the seat; if not, it won't. Loss of a seat would increase the pressure to move the central cities of Minneapolis and St. Paul into a single district; 2006 estimates show them together with less than the population required in a seven-district plan. Party control depends on the outcome of the 2010 governor race and the 2008 and 2010 races for legislative seats. If the DFL were in control, it would presumably extend the Minneapolis 5th and St. Paul 4th Districts further out into the suburbs and protect the 7th and 8th Districts represented by Agriculture and Transportation Committee Chairmen Collin

Peterson and Jim Oberstar. If the Republicans were in control, they'd probably consolidate Minneapolis and St. Paul and try to draw an additional suburban district.

Governor

Tim Pawlenty (R)

Elected 2002, term expires Jan. 2011, 2d term; b. Nov. 27, 1960, St. Paul; home, Eagan; U. of MN, B.A. 1983, J.D. 1986; Protestant; married (Mary).

Elected Office: Eagan Planning Comm., 1988-89; Eagan City Cncl., 1990-92; MN House of Reps., 1992-2002, Maj. Ldr., 1999-2002.

Professional Career: Practicing atty., 1986-92.

Office: 130 State Capitol, 75 Rev. Dr. Martin Luther King Jr. Blvd., St. Paul, 55155, 651-296-3391; Fax: 651-296-2089; Web site: www.governor.state.mn.us.

Election Results

2006 general	Tim Pawlenty (R)	1,028,568	(47%)
	Mike Hatch (DFL)	1,007,460	(46%)
	Peter Hutchinson (Ind)	141,735	(6%)
	Other	25,174	(1%)
2006 primary	Tim Pawlenty (R)	147,622	(89%)
	Sue Jeffers (R)	18,490	(11%)
2002 general	Tim Pawlenty (R)	999,473	(44%)
	Roger Moe (DFL)	821,268	(36%)
	Tim Penny (I)	364,534	(16%)
	Other	67,198	(3%)

Tim Pawlenty, a Republican, was elected governor of Minnesota in 2002 and reelected in 2006. Pawlenty grew up in South St. Paul near the stockyards and a meatpacking plant; when he was 16 his mother died and his father lost his job at a trucking company. He worked his way through college and law school at the University of Minnesota, the first college graduate in his family. At first he wanted to be a dentist, but he got involved in politics when interning for Senator David Durenberger. He practiced law and in 1992 was elected to the state House from Eagan in suburban Dakota County. Soon he became recognized as one of his party's leaders. Pawlenty started running for governor in 1998, but was persuaded to step aside for St. Paul Mayor Norm Coleman, who had switched parties and become a Republican. In 1999 Pawlenty was elected Majority Leader in the state House. In 2001 he set out to run against Senator Paul Wellstone, but White House political strategist Karl Rove thought Coleman would be a stronger candidate. Dick Cheney then called Pawlenty and said that it would be better if he got out of the Senate race and ran for governor. For the second time, Pawlenty deferred to Coleman.

Running for governor in 2002 was a formidable task. And the incumbent governor was Jesse Ventura, the former professional wrestler who as the Reform Party candidate was elected in 1998 over Coleman and Democrat Skip Humphrey and who for his first three years had high job ratings. Pawlenty set his own agenda and put forward his own persona. He talked constantly of his South St. Paul roots and said he wanted Republicans to be "the party of Sam's Club, not the country club." He promised never to raise taxes and took conservative stands on abortion and other cultural issues; he had voted for a gay rights measure as a freshman legislator, but now said that was a mistake. Brian Sullivan, a conservative and a self-financing businessman, was in the lead; a straw poll of those attending the March 2002 precinct caucuses showed him leading Pawlenty 51%-37%. But Pawlenty's organizational work left him even when the state convention assembled in June. Almost every state House Republican showed up wearing a Pawlenty blue shirt, and he ended up winning 58%-42%. The DFL nomination had already been settled. Roger Moe, the state Senate President since 1981, first elected to the legislature in 1970, had been poised to run for governor several times, but had always drawn back. Democrats chose him at their May convention. For the first time since 1978, no serious candidate challenged the candidate endorsed by either party's nominating convention.

The guiding assumption in both parties was that Ventura would run for another term. But on June 18 Ventura announced he wasn't running. Into that void stepped Tim Penny, a former Democratic congressman from a Republican-leaning district who retired in 1994, disgusted with the partisanship of Washington; several of his former aides had been appointed to top jobs by Ventura. On June 26 Penny announced that he was switching to the Independence Party, Ventura's vehicle, and running for governor. He chose a Republican state senator as his running mate and Ventura supported him. Ventura had not cared about making friends in politics, but the three men running to succeed him had. Just about everyone in Minnesota politics agreed that Pawlenty, Moe and Penny were decent, likeable people: a Minnesota Nice campaign. Of course there were differences on issues. Pawlenty pledged no tax increase. "The last thing I want to do is raise your taxes," Moe said. But also: "You pay a high income tax because you have high incomes in this state and we enjoy a higher quality of life." Penny said he "would keep taxes on the table as a last resort," and suggested there would have to be tax increases and spending cuts, and that he was the only candidate leveling with the voters. Pawlenty favored restrictions on abortion; Moe and Penny opposed them. Pawlenty and Penny favored a concealed weapons law; Moe was against. Moe said that Pawlenty's regret at his gay rights vote showed that he had moved "incredibly far to the right." Penny said he represented "the sensible center."

For most of the campaign, polls showed the three in a three-way tie. Then in October it suddenly seemed that Pawlenty might be knocked out of the race. All three had accepted public financing of up to $400,000, which required them to limit spending to $2.2 million. The parties were allowed to spend money for their candidates, but not in "cooperation or concert." The Pawlenty campaign in the summer shot footage of the candidate talking about growing up in South St. Paul and making humorous comments and then sold the footage to the state Republican party. On October 9, the Campaign and Finance Disclosure Board ruled that this violated the law. Board Chairman Doug Kelley, a friend of Pawlenty, said that the cost of those ads had to be counted against Pawlenty's $2.2 million; initial estimates of that cost were $1 million, and Pawlenty had already spent $1 million. On October 12 Pawlenty appeared before cameras and said that while he disagreed with the ruling he would defer to the Board's "higher authority" and not appeal, but would negotiate with the Board on the amount of the fine. On October 14 the Board fined the campaign $100,000 and charged it with $500,000 in ad spending; that left Pawlenty with about $600,000 to spend. Pawlenty, who had raised more money than his competitors, remained even with them in polls and in late October pulled ahead. He won with 44% of the vote to 36% for Moe and 16% for Penny.

Pawlenty may also have been helped by the fact that he was the only candidate committed to opposing a tax increase. For this was a Republican victory up and down the ballot. Walter Mondale failed to carry Minnesota for the first time in his long political career, and Norm Coleman was elected senator. Republicans won narrow victories for secretary of state and auditor. The only statewide DFL winner was Attorney General Mike Hatch, who calmly and fairly handled the issue of replacing Paul Wellstone on the ballot after his death in a plane crash. Republicans increased their majority in the state House to 82-52 and narrowed the DFL margin in the state Senate to 35-31–1.

Pawlenty took office with a budget shortfall estimated at $4.2 billion. He started off with good relations with legislative leaders of both parties, but much of that goodwill dissipated after an acrimonious budget battle. Pawlenty held to his no-new-taxes pledge and cut spending by more than $2 billion, explaining, "The days of a program for every problem and a state government that leads by blank check are over." There were small increases in health and human services, public education and criminal justice funding but overall state spending fell by .03% in from 2003 to 2004 and increased by just 2.3% in 2005, the lowest increase in a consecutive two-year period in more than 40 years. "We're transitioning from a classic liberal state to a swing or transition or center-right state," Pawlenty told the Minneapolis *Star Tribune*. "That's not to say we are going to become North Carolina, nor should we be. We want the traditions of Minnesota, the heritage of Minnesota, the priorities of Minnesota updated for the times. There's more than one way to better health care, more than one way to better schools." Among Pawlenty's other accomplishments in 2003: a 24-hour waiting period for abortions, a conceal weapons law, repeal of the state's Profiles of Learning standards, establishment of tax-exempt zones in distressed rural areas, a bill requiring recitation of the Pledge of Allegiance in public schools. He proposed an ambitious mail-order program to buy cheaper prescription drugs from Canada through a state-sponsored website. In 2004, when the legislature could not agree on a plan to close the state's $160 million budget deficit, Pawlenty balanced the budget largely by tapping a windfall of federal dollars that had been designated for the state's subsidized health insurance plan. Failed measures included Pawlenty's education initiatives, a bill for stricter penalties for sexual predators, a stadium bill, and Pawlenty's $740 million bonding bill, casualties of a partisan impasse over a proposed same-sex marriage constitutional amendment. Democrats in November 2004 reduced the Republican majority in the state House from 81-53 to a tenuous 68-66—the first time in 12 years the DFL gained seats in the House. In 2005 polarization increased. After Pawlenty and the legislature could not agree on a budget, there was a partial shutdown of the state government in July, the first in Minnesota's history. Pawlenty got the legislature to impose a 75 cent "health impact fee" on cigarettes—a retreat from his no-new-taxes pledge, many charged; Democrats charged that he was responsible for higher property taxes because of reductions in state aid. In 2006 he and the legislature reached accord on bonding for a new University of Minnesota stadium and a ballpark for the Minnesota Twins. He vetoed only $1 million in spending and approved measures to conserve duck lands and reduce mercury levels in coal-fired plants and arranged for toll lanes on the Twin Cities' congested freeways.

Pawlenty entered campaign year 2006 with the most polarized job ratings in SurveyUSA's 50-state polls: Republicans loved him, DFLers hated him. His DFL opponent was Attorney General Mike Hatch, who ran for governor in the primaries in 1990 and 1994 and was elected attorney general in 1998. Hatch attacked HMOs and declared that "health care is a right, not a privilege." He charged that property taxes and college tuition had increased 50% in Pawlenty's term and called for better roads. Also running, on Ventura's Independence Party line, was former Minneapolis school superintendant Peter Hutchinson. He also called for better roads and for a gas tax increase, which Pawlenty had vetoed; he favored modernizing and standardizing medical records. Pawlenty charged that Hatch's health care bill would encourage lawsuits against insurers and called for health savings accounts, price transparency and patient incentives. He favored the death penalty, defining marriage as between a man and a woman and performance pay for teachers. "The future doesn't belong to the tax increasers or the education-without-accountability promoters and the folks who want to have government take over the health care system . . . and to the people who want to ignore illegal immigration." Polls showed the race between Pawlenty and Hatch close, with Hutchinson far behind. In the last week Hatch was embarrassed when his running mate, Judi Dutcher, said she had never heard of E-85, the ethanol fuel that is sold at many Minnesota gas pumps. On November 2, when a reporter asked Hatch to speak to Dutcher about that, Hatch said, "You're nothing but a Republican whore." This got widespread publicity in the land of Minnesota Nice; Hatch said he had called her a "Republican hack," but that was not widely accepted.

Pawlenty beat Hatch 47%-46%, with 6% for Hutchinson, in what was otherwise a good election day for the DFL. They unseated 1st District Congressman Gil Gutknecht and picked up many legislative seats, giving them a 44-23 majority in the state Senate and 85-49 advantage in the state House. DFL candidates were elected attorney general, secretary of state and auditor. DFL Senate nominee Amy Klobuchar won 58%-38%, a margin exceeded only once by Hubert Humphrey. In the Twin Cities core counties of Hennepin and Ramsey, Hatch led 51%-39%; Pawlenty won 54%-39% in the outer counties in the Twin Cities media market. In the remainder of the state it was a standoff: Hatch led 48%-46% because of his big margins in the traditionally DFL Iron Range. Turnout was down 2% from 2002 and up only 5% from the exciting 1998 three-way race, despite greater population growth during that eight-year period. But turnout was up 4% from 2002 in the area of Pawlenty's strength, the Twin Cities area outside the core, while it was down 6% in the Twin Cities core and 5% in the rest of the state. The demographic shift which produced an across-the-board victory for Republicans in the Republican year of 2002 was, just barely, enough to reelect Pawlenty in the Democratic year of 2006.

After the election, Pawlenty sounded rather different than he had in 2003. After election: "Republicans love to talk about markets. Well, the market just told Republicans something. The market just told them, 'We're not much interested in your product, and we're choosing to go to your competitor.' We need to hear that message." He said that people want certain basic things from government but "other than that" they say "get out of my face." Incoming DFL Speaker Margaret Anderson Kelliher, noting that her party had won many seats in the Republican-leaning suburbs, announced her "stick to the basics agenda": improve public education, increase access to health care, provide property tax relief. Pawlenty still called for more accountability in education and, with a $2.2 billion budget surplus in sight, continued to stand against tax increases but promised little in the way of tax cuts. He called for health insurance for all children and an energy initiative including more E-85 pumps, energy efficient buildings and for 25% of electricity to be produced by renewable sources by 2025.

Even with his narrow reelection margin, Pawlenty was on the list of possible Republican vice presidential nominees in 2008. He became chairman of the National Governors Association in 2007. As governor, he will welcome Republican delegates to St. Paul; early on he endorsed John McCain and became a national co-chairman for his campaign. "I am committed to serving out my term as governor," he said in January 2007. "That's what I am going to do." He is eligible to run for a third term in 2010; in early 2007 Ramsey County Attorney Susan Gaertner said she might run, and in May former Senator Mark Dayton said he might also.

Senior Senator

Norm Coleman (R)

Elected 2002, seat up 2008, 1st term; b. Aug. 17, 1949, Brooklyn, NY; home, St. Paul; Hofstra U., B.A. 1971, U. of IA, J.D. 1976; Jewish; married (Laurie).

Elected Office: St. Paul Mayor, 1993-2001.

Professional Career: MN Atty. Gen.'s office, 1976-93.

DC Office: 320 HSOB, 20510, 202-224-5641; Fax: 202-224-1152; Web site: coleman.senate.gov.

State Offices: Grand Rapids, 218-327-9333; Mankato, 507-625-6800; St. Paul, 651-645-0323.

Committees: *Aging (Special)* (7th of 10 R). *Agriculture, Nutrition & Forestry* (7th of 10 R): Nutrition and Food Assistance, Sustainable and Organic Agriculture & General Legislation (RMM); Production, Income Protection & Price Support; Energy, Science & Technology. *Foreign Relations* (3d of 10 R): Near Eastern & South & Central Asian Affairs (RMM); African Affairs; Western Hemisphere, Peace Corps & Narcotics Affairs. *Homeland Security & Governmental Affairs* (4th of 8 R): Investigations (Permanent) (RMM); State, Local & Private Sector Preparedness & Integration. *Small Business & Entrepreneurship* (3d of 9 R).

Group Ratings

	ADA	ACLU	AFS	LCV	ITIC	NTU	COC	ACU	CFG	FRC
2006	25	17	38	29	100	58	100	68	44	87
2005	30	—	50	35	—	51	88	64	59	—

National Journal Ratings

	2005 LIB	—	2005 CONS		2006 LIB	—	2006 CONS
Economic	49%	—	50%		49%	—	50%
Social	39%	—	58%		40%	—	59%
Foreign	0%	—	74%		47%	—	50%

Key Votes of the 109th Congress

1. Bar ANWR Drilling	Y	5. Confirm Samuel Alito	Y	9. Limit Interstate Abortion	Y
2. FY06 Spending Curb	Y	6. Path to Citizenship	Y	10. CAFTA	Y
3. Estate Tax Repeal	Y	7. Bar Same Sex Marriage	Y	11. Urge Iraq Withdrawal	N
4. Raise Minimum Wage	Y	8. Stem Cell Research $	N	12. Provide Detainee Rights	N

Election Results

2002 general	Norm Coleman (R)	1,116,697	(50%)	($10,035,279)
	Walter Mondale (DFL)	1,067,246	(47%)	($1,833,029)
	Other	70,696	(3%)	
2002 primary	Norm Coleman (R)	195,630	(94%)	
	Jack Shepard (R)	11,678	(6%)	
1996 general	Paul Wellstone (DFL)	1,098,493	(50%)	($7,459,878)
	Rudy Boschwitz (R)	901,282	(41%)	($4,385,982)
	Dean Barkley (Ref)	152,333	(7%)	($37,240)

Norm Coleman, a Republican, was elected to the Senate after a tumultuous and tragic campaign in 2002. Coleman grew up in a modest neighborhood in Brooklyn and graduated from James Madison High School, as did New York Senator Charles Schumer and Supreme Court Justice Ruth Bader Ginsburg. An anti-war activist, he graduated from Hofstra University on Long Island and the

University of Iowa law school; he was student-body president at each. In 1975 he went to work in the attorney general's office in St. Paul and became chief prosecutor and solicitor general, working closely with DFL Attorney General Skip Humphrey. In 1989 he ran for mayor of St. Paul but withdrew after losing the DFL endorsement. In 1993 he ran again and won by challenging the DFL endorsee in the primary. As mayor, Coleman was credited with leading a downtown revitalization; he boasted of attracting 18,000 new jobs and not raising property taxes for his last seven years. Coleman's opposition to abortion and his bargaining stance toward public employee unions made him many enemies among the liberals who dominate DFL caucuses, and in December 1996 he switched to the Republican party; he has the unusual distinction of having served as 1996 state co-chairman for Bill Clinton and 2000 state chairman for George W. Bush. In 1997 he ran for reelection and defeated the DFL candidate, and became the first Republican mayor of St. Paul since 1960. In 1998 he ran for governor. He won the Republican nomination but finished second, behind Reform Party nominee Jesse Ventura, by a 37%-34% margin; but he ran ahead of his old boss, DFL nominee Skip Humphrey, who won only 28% of the vote. Coleman did not run for reelection in 2001, and was considering running for governor again. But George W. Bush called and asked him to run for the Senate, and in February 2002 he announced he was running against Senator Paul Wellstone.

Wellstone was first elected in a major upset in 1990, when he was a Carleton College political science professor. He had the most liberal voting record of any senator and delivered stirring orations on many issues. In his first campaign Wellstone promised to accept no PAC money or contributions over $100 and to serve only two terms. In 1996 he dropped the $100 limit and in January 2001 he announced he would run for a third term. Wellstone's greatest political asset was his authenticity: You might not like the positions he took, but you knew he did so sincerely and without regard to political consequences. Going back on his two-term promise evidently made him seem insincere to some voters, and polls showed him under 50% of the vote.

Coleman's strategy was to portray Wellstone as an obstructionist and himself as someone who gets things done; an attempt to turn Wellstone's strength, his authenticity, into a weakness. Coleman took care to oppose Bush on some issues: he opposed oil drilling in the Arctic National Wildlife Refuge and favored an increase in the minimum wage. But he also called for making the 2001 tax cuts permanent, opposed Senate Democrats' union provisions in the homeland security bill and called for individual investment accounts for Social Security, though he ran an ad in October opposing "privatization." Wellstone, as always, campaigned as the tribune of the little guy, opposed to "Robin Hood in reverse" tax cuts. Using the fundraising system he had criticized in 1990, he raised more money than Coleman, though both campaigns were well-funded. After Bush's speech to the United Nations September 12, Coleman came out in favor of authorizing military action in Iraq. Wellstone was opposed and favored action only with the approval of the UN. Polls showed the race exceedingly close.

On Friday, October 25, 11 days before the election, Wellstone, his wife and daughter and five others died in a plane crash in northern Minnesota. As the news became known about noon, Coleman suspended his campaign. Coleman after a meeting with supporters decided not to drop out of sight, as Missouri's John Ashcroft had done in October 2000 when his opponent died in a plane crash, but to participate publicly in the mourning process. But behind the scenes, leaders of both parties were pondering what to do next. Minnesota has a law that allows parties to substitute a new nominee in these circumstances. On Saturday Wellstone's son David, his campaign treasurer Rick Kahn and his campaign manager met with Walter Mondale and asked him to run. Mondale, though 74, was obviously the strongest candidate. He had been elected to the Senate by solid margins in 1966 and 1972 and after serving as Jimmy Carter's vice president had returned to Minnesota, run his 1984 presidential campaign from St. Paul and had been practicing law and serving on civic and charitable boards. Mondale declined to say he would run, and said he would not decide until after the funeral and memorial service, but let the Wellstone supporters tell reporters he was "highly likely to run."

Coleman and his advisers decided not to resume campaigning until after the memorial service, but to be ready to campaign vigorously beginning the morning after. Coleman would not attack Mondale, but speak respectfully of him and campaign around the clock across the state as the candidate of 21st century ideas. In the meantime he would appear on TV and talk only about mourning. On Monday the Wellstones were buried after a private funeral. On Tuesday night, one week before the election, the memorial service was held at the Williams Arena at the University of Minnesota. It was broadcast statewide and across the country; most Minnesota voters were watching. Suddenly the memorial service turned into a campaign rally. Kahn spoke about Wellstone, then launched into campaigning. "We are begging you to help us win this election for Paul Wellstone," he thundered. Many in the crowd of more than 20,000 booed Republican senators who had come to show their respect. The next morning, Wellstone's campaign manager apologized for the tone of the memorial.

Coleman boarded a plane at 6:15 the next morning to campaign around the state, while the DFL met and nominated Mondale. Mondale and his staff were amazed when DFL pollster Paul Harstad reported that an overnight survey had shown 73% of voters agreeing that the memorial service went overboard, with 52% agreeing strongly. Mondale's Sunday night lead of 52%-39% had vanished and the race was suddenly at 43%-43%. Seldom if ever has political polling shown such an overnight shift. On Thursday, Coleman continued campaigning across the state while Mondale campaigned in Minneapolis. On Monday morning Mondale and Coleman appeared in their one televised debate. Coleman treated Mondale with great respect, always referring to him as Vice President, but argued that he was the candidate of the future. Mondale debated aggressively, referring to Coleman as Norman; he may have reflected the contempt DFL insiders have for Coleman as a party-switcher when he asked, "Who do you trust?" On the issues Mondale was clearly well-informed, but he sounded antique and abstract, while Coleman sounded contemporary and concrete. Afterwards, Coleman embarked on an 18-hour bus tour.

Coleman won 50%-47%, with a popular vote margin of 49,000; 11,000 absentee votes were counted for Wellstone. It was the first time Mondale had lost an election in Minnesota. This was a different Minnesota than the one that had reelected him to the Senate in 1972, 30 years before. In the Twin Cities core, Hennepin and Ramsey Counties, Mondale won 53%-44%. In the counties outside the Twin Cities media market, Mondale won 50%-46%; the city-based Coleman did not have as strong an appeal as George W. Bush in 2000 in rural areas. But the difference was the Ventura Belt, the counties in the Twin Cities media market beyond the core. In 1972 they had cast 481,000 votes; in 2002 they cast 906,000, a rise of 88%. In 1972 Mondale had carried those counties 53%-47%. In 2002 Coleman carried them 56%-41%.

In the Senate Coleman achieved high visibility for a freshman and voted toward the center, though more conservative on foreign policy. He chaired two high-profile subcommittees, the Permanent Subcommittee on Investigations and the Foreign Relations subcommittee on the Western Hemisphere. On Investigations, he held hearings on the safety of Internet drugs, on tax loopholes, on the recording industry's crackdown on Internet piracy, on the Pentagon's purchases of first and business class airline tickets, on credit counseling abuses. In November 2004 he held hearings on corruption in the UN Oil for Food program; he called for the resignation of UN Secretary General Kofi Annan and for "tough love" by the U.S. In 2005, his panel's investigation found that at least 27,000 Pentagon contractors owed about $3 billion in taxes, and he filed a bill directing the Pentagon to create a registry of contractors for tax purposes. He criticized the Australian Wheat Board for paying illegal kickbacks to Saddam's government. Citing problems with Hurricane Katrina, the failed Supreme Court nomination of Harriet Miers, and the Dubai Ports controversy, he criticized the White House in March 2006 for its political "tin ear."

Coleman took care to look to Minnesota interests. He supported energy bill provisions increasing the ethanol producer tax credit and providing a biodiesel tax credit, and inserted into the energy bill $800 million in loan guarantees for a coal gasification plant in the Iron Range. He voted against ANWR oil drilling, but said he might vote for an energy bill that allowed it if it contained the above provisions; when he voted for the big energy bill in 2005, it did not include ANWR. That was in line with his general approach: "What I tried to accomplish was to be part of a coalition that got things done. Working with the president, not against him. I try to find ways to get things done." He co-sponsored $3 billion in disaster relief for farmers, an extension of the Milk Income Loss Contract program. He also sponsored an amendment requiring the Pentagon to pay for servicemen's trips home on leave. He voted for the Central America Free Trade Agreement only after Agriculture Secretary Mike Johanns promised to study the cost of producing ethanol from sugar. In February 2007, he abandoned his earlier plan to prevent states from fighting carbon dioxide emissions and said that he was "passionate" about reducing the risk of global warming.

Coleman was disappointed when he ran for the chairmanship of the NRSC in November 2004 and lost to Elizabeth Dole 28-27 on a secret ballot. Coleman comes up for reelection in 2008. Al Franken, the Minnesota-raised comedian and talk show host returned to Minnesota and said that he will run against Coleman. Attorney Michael Ciresi, who ran unsuccessfully for the Senate in 2000, also joined the contest, and other Democrats were contemplating running. The outcome in this competitive state seemed likely to be close and Coleman seemed to be seeking some distance from the Bush administration. In January 2007 Coleman said he opposed Bush's plan to send more troops to Iraq; he opposed a Republican filibuster against a resolution critical of the plan.

Junior Senator

Amy Klobuchar (DFL)

Elected 2006, seat up 2012, 1st term; b. May 25, 1960, Plymouth; home, Minneapolis; Yale U., B.A. 1982, U. of Chicago, J.D. 1985; Protestant; married (John Bessler).

Elected Office: Hennepin Cnty. Atty., 1998-2006.

Professional Career: Practicing atty., 1985-98.

DC Office: 302 HSOB, 20510, 202-224-3244; Fax: 202-228-2186; Web site: klobuchar.senate.gov.

State Offices: Fort Snelling, 612-727-5220; Rochester, 507-288-5321.

Committees: *Agriculture, Nutrition & Forestry* (11th of 11 D): Nutrition and Food Assistance, Sustainable and Organic Agriculture & General Legislation; Production, Income Protection & Price Support; Energy, Science & Technology. *Commerce, Science & Transportation* (12th of 12 D): Oceans, Atmosphere, Fisheries & Coast Guard; Science, Technology & Innovation; Consumer Affairs, Insurance & Automotive Safety; Surface Transportation & Merchant Marine Infrastructure, Safety & Security; Aviation Operations, Safety & Security. *Environment & Public Works* (8th of 10 D): Transportation Safety, Infrastructure Security & Water Quality; Public Sector Solutions to Global Warming, Oversight & Children's Health Protection. *Joint Economic Committee* (4th of 10 D).

Group Ratings and Key Votes: Newly Elected

Election Results

2006 general	Amy Klobuchar (DFL)	1,278,849	(58%)	($9,095,671)
	Mark Kennedy (R)	835,653	(38%)	($10,347,739)
	Other	88,270	(4%)	
2006 primary	Amy Klobuchar (DFL)	294,671	(93%)	
	Darryl Stanton (DFL)	23,872	(7%)	
2000 general	Mark Dayton (DFL)	1,181,553	(49%)	($11,957,114)
	Rod Grams (R)	1,047,474	(43%)	($6,024,866)
	Jim Gibson (I)	140,583	(6%)	
	Other	49,910	(2%)	

Amy Klobuchar, a Democrat elected in 2006, is Minnesota's junior senator and the fourth occupant of this Senate seat in as many elections. She was born in the Minneapolis suburb of Plymouth, the daughter of longtime Minneapolis *Star Tribune* columnist Jim Klobuchar. She attended Yale University, where she wrote a senior paper on the machinations behind the building of the Hubert H. Humphrey Metrodome, then graduated from the University of Chicago law school. After returning home, she worked primarily as a lawyer and was registered as a lobbyist. In 1994, she ran for Hennepin County Attorney but left the race when Mike Freeman, the officeholder at the time, unsuccessfully sought the Democratic endorsement for governor and decided to run for reelection. In 1998, Freeman ran for governor again and Klobuchar sought to succeed him; she defeated the sister of 3d District Congressman Jim Ramstad in the general election. Klobuchar won election to two terms as Hennepin County Attorney, served as president of the Minnesota County Attorneys Association and took credit for spearheading a crackdown on gun crimes and securing nearly 300 homicide convictions.

Minneapolis's Hennepin County is home to almost a quarter of the state's population, so it provided an excellent springboard for Klobuchar to run for Senate in 2006, when Democratic Sen. Mark Dayton declined to run for a second term. Dayton had spent $11.9 million, almost all of it his own money, to defeat Republican incumbent Rod Grams in 2000. But he attracted unflattering national attention in October 2004, after Congress had recessed for the election, when he announced that he was closing his Washington office because of security threats. No other member took such a position, and Dayton was attacked and ridiculed by Democrats as well as Republicans. The *Star-Tribune*, often a Dayton defender, editorialized that many were "scratching their heads at Mark Dayton's preemptive shuttering of his Senate office." It went on, "In staking out this Cassandra position, Dayton has added considerably to unfortunate aspects of his reputation: loner, loose cannon, flake."

Dayton's action resulted in low poll showings and raised doubts about his ability to win reelection in 2006. Money was another problem. Back in July 2003 he said, "I'm telling people I can't afford to spend my own money next time." In June 2004 he reported his net worth as between $5 million and $15 million—not enough to enable him to spend $12 million as he had in 2000. He estimated that it would take $15 million to run but raised only $1.7 million in 2004. In November 2004 incoming NRSC Chairman Elizabeth Dole named Dayton as one of her top targets. Congressman Mark Kennedy, fresh from defeating a well-known and well-financed Democrat, made it no secret that he was running.

In February 2005, Dayton announced he would not run and issued a brief statement. "Everything I've worked for, and everything I believe in, depends upon this Senate seat remaining in the Democratic Caucus in 2007. I do not believe I am the best candidate to lead the party to victory next year." Kennedy confirmed he was running; he was soon supported by Senator Norm Coleman and 26 of the 31 Republican state senators. While Minnesota Republicans quickly united behind Kennedy's candidacy—a comeback attempt by Grams was brusquely dismissed—the Democratic field took time to shake out. On the DFL side, many prominent possibilities quickly took themselves out of the race: Walter Mondale, Justice Alan Page, Buck Humphrey (grandson of the senator), Attorney General Mike Hatch, radio talk show host (and Minnesota native) Al Franken. Klobuchar was the first to formally announce her candidacy in April; also making moves to run were child safety advocate Patty Wetterling (who lost to Kennedy in 2004), and Minnesota Heart Institute Research Foundation president Ford Bell.

Wetterling, however, left the race in early 2006 to run for Kennedy's open seat in the 6th District. Bell dropped out in July, one month after Klobuchar received the party endorsement at the Democratic-Farmer-Labor Party state convention. With a clear path to the party nomination, Klobuchar was able to conserve her resources and focus her sights on Kennedy. Kennedy, meanwhile, struggled in his effort to distance himself from an unpopular Republican president, the war in Iraq and from his national party. In one television ad, Kennedy offered a list of issues on which he voted against the Bush administration and crossed party lines. He claimed he was an independent, bipartisan leader who would not "take up Senator Dayton's place on the fringe." He sought to portray Klobuchar as an ineffective liberal by linking her to the unpopular outgoing incumbent, questioned the number of cases she actually prosecuted herself and highlighted the increasing rate of violent crime in Minneapolis.

When Dayton first announced his retirement, this open Senate race figured to be one of the Republican party's best opportunities to pick up a Democratic-held seat. But in her first bid for statewide office, Klobuchar built an early lead in the polls and never relinquished it. She referred to Kennedy as a "rubber stamp for President Bush" who supported Bush's policies more than 90 percent of the time. She talked about middle-class tax relief and called for an increase in the minimum wage. She emphasized her tough-on-crime credentials and ran on a more fiscally conservative platform than Dayton and the late Minnesota Democrat Paul Wellstone.

Klobuchar won 58%-38%, the biggest Minnesota Senate margin since 1978—only twice did Hubert H. Humphrey win a margin this big. She swept the Iron Range and won by 2–1 margins in the Twin Cities core counties, carrying Hennepin County (64%-32%) and St. Paul's Ramsey County (66%-29%). She also showed strength in the eastern Twin Cities suburbs, winning Dakota County (56%-40%), Anoka County (55%-42%) and Washington County (55%-41%).

In the Senate, where she promised a focus on ethics issues, Klobuchar said she would not accept gifts, meals or trips from private groups or individuals, regardless of what congressional rules allow. She instituted "Minnesota Mornings", where every Thursday the Senate is in session she meets with visiting Minnesotans for coffee and "potica"—a traditional Slovenian holiday nut roll that highlights Klobuchar's ethnic heritage and Iron Range family roots.

FIRST DISTRICT

Rep. Tim Walz (DFL)

Elected 2006, 1st term; b. Apr. 6, 1964, West Point, NE; home, Mankato; Chadron St. Col., B.S. 1989, MN St. U., M.S. 2001; Lutheran; married (Gwen).

Military Career: Army Natl. Guard, 1981-2005.

Professional Career: Teacher, Pine Ridge Indian Reservation, SD, 1984; Teacher, People's Republic of China, 1989-90; Founder, Educational Travel Adventures, 1991-2006; High school teacher, 1989-2006.

DC Office: 1529 LHOB, 20515, 202-225-2472; Fax: 202-225-3433; Web site: walz.house.gov.

District Offices: Mankato, 507-388-2149; Rochester, 507-206-0643.

Committees: *Agriculture* (17th of 25 D): Conservation, Credit, Energy & Research; General Farm Commodities & Risk Management. *Transportation & Infrastructure* (32d of 41 D): Economic Development, Public Buildings & Emergency Management; Railroads, Pipelines & Hazardous Materials; Highways & Transit. *Veterans' Affairs* (16th of 16 D): Oversight & Investigations.

Group Ratings and Key Votes: Newly Elected

Election Results

2006 general	Tim Walz (DFL) 141,556	(53%)	($1,281,136)
	Gil Gutknecht (R) 126,486	(47%)	($1,723,707)
2006 primary	Tim Walz (DFL) .... unopposed		
2004 general	Gil Gutknecht (R) 193,132	(60%)	($666,410)
	Leigh Pomeroy (DFL) 115,088	(36%)	($58,826)
	Gregory Mikkelson (Ind) 15,569	(5%)	($7,472)

The People		Race/Ethnic Origin	Ancestry	
Area size:	13,521 sq. mi.	93.2% White	German: 31.7%	Norwegian: 14.3%
Urban population:	56.5%	1.0% Black	Irish: 7.1%	
Rural population:	43.5%	1.7% Asian	**2004 Presidential Vote**	
Pop. 2000:	614,935	0.2% Native Am.	Bush (R) 171,952	(51%)
Pop. 2005 (est):	627,278	0.0% Hawaiian	Kerry (D) 159,776	(47%)
Median income:	$40,941	0.8% Two+ races	Other 5,043	(2%)
Poverty status:	8.5%	0.1% Other	**2000 Presidential Vote**	
Military veterans:	13.0%	3.0% Hispanic Origin	Bush (R) 146,212	(49%)
			Gore (D) 133,078	(45%)
			Other 17,501	(6%)
			Cook Partisan Voting Index: R + 1	
Occupation	Blue collar: 26.8%	White collar: 56.7%	Gray collar: 16.5%	

The Mississippi River flows majestically southeast from Minneapolis and St. Paul, cutting through rolling hills and, where it widens, forming calm lakes lapping at the bottomlands: one of the finest river landscapes of North America, exemplified by the river towns of Wabasha and Winona, with their 19th century stone storefronts and mountain-like rock outcroppings above the river. This far north, the westward tide of Yankee migrants thinned out. After the Civil War, most settlers following the railroads on the flood plains west of the river were Germans and Scandinavians, bringing their families to this terrain so much like the Rhineland, and to the rolling uplands beyond, which resemble the northern European plain.

Southern Minnesota is a borderland between Yankee and German settlements. Along the Mississippi River, tourism spiked upward (from a nonexistent base) after the old St. Paul and Milwaukee Railroad was converted into a hiker-biker nature trail during the 1990s; "Historic Bluff Country" now draws enough visitors to support not one but two former jails that have been converted, with Minnesota practicality, into upscale bed-and-breakfasts. A little to the west is Rochester, home to the Mayo Clinic, founded in 1863 when English-born physician William Mayo set up a practice to examine inductees into the Union Army. In 2007 the Mayo Clinic hailed the Federal Railroad Administration for denying a $2.3 billion loan request by the Dakota, Minnesota and Eastern Railroad to upgrade tracks that would allow for larger coal shipments across southern

Minnesota and right past the clinic. Rochester, with its large professional population, is prosperous and the growth center of southern Minnesota. Austin, a county away, is headquarters of the Hormel meatpacking firm that beat a bitter strike in the 1980s; its huge plant produces "miracle meat" Spam, Hormel chili, Dinty Moore stew and, say critics, too much ammonia-loaded waste. This is one place where class-conscious politics survives, though all sides are proud of their Spam Museum. The farther west you go, the more frequently you find communities with a German heritage, like New Ulm, where the "Hermann the German" monument guards the town and the Concord Singers—30 men decked out in lederhosen, red vests and white shirts—are described as one of the best male choruses in the nation. Further south is dairy country, with a sprinkling of small industry. In tiny Ormsby, North County Seed breeds soybeans to match the wishes of its international customers.

The 1st Congressional District of Minnesota includes the state's two southern tiers of counties, running along Interstate 90 just north of the Iowa border. It stretches 280 miles from the South Dakota border at Sioux Falls to the Wisconsin border at LaCrosse. Historically, this was a political borderland, with Civil War Republicans in the east and Farmer-Laborites more common in the west. Rochester has long been a Republican stronghold, though not by much in 2004; like many communities with large numbers of professionals, it has been trending toward Democrats. Austin with its working class tradition has long been solidly Democratic-Farmer-Labor. To the west, Mankato voted narrowly for John Kerry and the population-losing farm counties between Mankato and the South Dakota border voted solidly Republican.

The new congressman from the 1st District is Tim Walz, a Democrat first elected in one of the biggest upsets of 2006. Walz grew up in Nebraska and joined the Army National Guard when he was 17. When he retired 24 years later in 2005, he held the rank of command sergeant major. Walz earned his teaching degree in Nebraska, taught school in China for a year through a Harvard University program, and later established an educational travel company that helped high school students study in China. He and his wife moved to Minnesota in 1996 to accept teaching jobs in Mankato. There he taught high school geography and coached the high school football team to two state championships. Walz might not have not have entered politics if he had not attempted to enter a 2004 campaign event for President Bush along with two students. He said campaign staffers demanded to know whether he supported the president, and barred the students from entering after they discovered one of them had a John Kerry sticker on his wallet. Walz had just returned from eight months service in Italy, where he was supporting operations in Afghanistan, and he suggested the Bush campaign would not want to arrest a veteran. Walz was allowed into the event but the campaign kept a close eye on him. Walz had never run for office before and said the experience sparked his interest in politics, first as a volunteer for the Kerry campaign and then as a congressional candidate in 2006. "I don't know if I'd necessarily call it an epiphany, but it was definitely one of those things that pushed me into that," Walz said.

The incumbent was six-term Republican Gil Gutknecht, an affable conservative who won reelection in 2004 with 60%—running 9 points ahead of Bush. The district had sent Republicans to Washington for 100 of the last 114 years, and Gutknecht was not considered especially vulnerable in 2006. Walz was not a polished campaigner: his speaking style was didactic compared to the smooth-talking Gutknecht, a former auctioneer. But Walz decried declining middle class wages, tax cuts for the wealthy and Congress's failure to hold Bush accountable on Iraq war. He ran as a political outsider and painted Gutknecht as too closely tied to Bush.

By October, Republicans began to take the threat against Gutknecht seriously. Walz had raised $870,000 by then, which kept pace with Gutknecht, who had raised $1.2 million. Walz enjoyed independent support from VoteVets, a Democratic-oriented group of Iraq and Afghanistan war veterans, and labor support from AFSCME. The DCCC ran ads that criticized Gutknecht for votes against increasing military benefits while raising his own pay. Gutknecht sought to halt his slide by attacking Walz on taxes and illegal immigration and by characterizing him as a liberal who was out of sync with this socially conservative district. Walz's support for abortion rights and his opposition to a constitutional amendment against same-sex marriage fell outside district norms, but his opposition to gun control put him squarely in the mainstream; his military experience and football coaching gave an aura of authenticity to his campaign that made it harder to attack (Eleven days before the election, Walz took a break from campaigning to help a carful of rival Independence Party campaign workers replace a flat tire).

On Election Day, Walz defeated Gutknecht 53%-47%. Walz carried Democratic areas around Mankato and Austin and won Rochester's Olmsted County by more than 1,800 votes (52%-48%). Despite encouragement from some activists, Walz quickly ruled out a 2008 Senate run against Norm Coleman. By August 2007, former state Senate Minority Leader Dick Day, state Representative Randy Demmer, radiation oncologist Brian Davis and Mark Meyer, a Lake Crystal School Board member had lined up to challenge Walz; the NRCC was already running ads against Walz claiming he was tied too closely to Speaker Nancy Pelosi.

SECOND DISTRICT

Rep. John Kline (R)

Elected 2002, 3d term; b. Sept. 6, 1947, Allentown, PA; home, Lakeville; Rice U., B.A. 1969, Shippensburg U., M.P.A. 1988; Christian; married (Vicky).

Military Career: Marine Corps, 1969-94 (Vietnam).

Professional Career: Vice-pres., Cntr. of the American Experiment, 2001-02.

DC Office: 1429 LHOB, 20515, 202-225-2271; Fax: 202-225-2595; Web site: kline.house.gov.

District Offices: Burnsville, 952-808-1213.

Committees: *Armed Services* (19th of 29 R): Military Personnel; Terrorism, Unconventional Threats & Capabilities. *Education & Labor* (11th of 22 R): Health, Employment, Labor & Pensions (RMM); Workforce Protections. *Standards of Official Conduct* (4th of 5 R).

Group Ratings

	ADA	ACLU	AFS	LCV	ITIC	NTU	COC	ACU	CFG	FRC
2006	0	9	0	8	100	63	100	88	70	100
2005	0	—	0	0	—	60	93	100	68	100

National Journal Ratings

	2005 LIB — 2005 CONS		2006 LIB — 2006 CONS	
Economic	19% —	79%	7% —	91%
Social	0% —	89%	28% —	70%
Foreign	40% —	58%	17% —	73%

Key Votes of the 109th Congress

1. Estate Tax Repeal	Y	5. Limit Interstate Abortion	Y	9. Build Border Fence	Y
2. Limit CAFE Standards	Y	6. Extend Patriot Act	Y	10. CAFTA	Y
3. FY06 Spending Curb	Y	7. Bar Same Sex Marriage	Y	11. Oppose Iraq Withdrawal	Y
4. Drilling in ANWR	Y	8. Stem Cell Research $	N	12. Detainee Tribunals	Y

Election Results

2006 general	John Kline (R)	163,269	(56%)	($1,478,465)
	Coleen Rowley (DFL)	116,343	(40%)	($690,132)
	Douglas Williams (Ind)	10,802	(4%)	
2006 primary	John Kline (R)	unopposed		
2004 general	John Kline (R)	206,313	(56%)	($1,610,055)
	Teresa Daly (DFL)	147,527	(40%)	($1,182,465)
	Other	12,105	(3%)	

Prior Winning Percentages: 2002 (53%)

The People		Race/Ethnic Origin	Ancestry	
Area size:	3,154 sq. mi.	91.8% White	German: 28.4%	Norwegian: 11.3%
Urban population:	80.1%	1.6% Black	Irish: 9.2%	
Rural population:	19.9%	2.3% Asian	**2004 Presidential Vote**	
Pop. 2000:	614,934	0.4% Native Am.	Bush (R) 203,538	(54%)
Pop. 2005 (est):	701,104	0.0% Hawaiian	Kerry (D) 169,704	(45%)
Median income:	$61,344	1.1% Two+ races	Other 4,105	(1%)
Poverty status:	3.9%	0.1% Other	**2000 Presidential Vote**	
Military veterans:	12.1%	2.6% Hispanic Origin	Bush (R) 150,366	(51%)
			Gore (D) 131,414	(44%)
			Other 14,526	(5%)
			Cook Partisan Voting Index: R + 3	

Occupation   Blue collar: 22.3%   White collar: 65.0%   Gray collar: 12.6%

Drive south from the Twin Cities and you will encounter new housing developments and big-box store parking lots inhabited by youngish families working in managerial, business and technical careers. Many come from elsewhere, attracted by Minnesota's strong economy and pleasant living (if you don't mind winter). They have turned such places as Eagan, Lakeville, Apple Valley, Mendota Heights and Burnsville in Dakota County into fast-growing, "mallified" suburbs. More upscale are the suburbs of Scott and Carver Counties; Scott County was the 15th fastest-growing county in the nation between 2000 and 2005. In recent years, these suburban areas have begun to see the migration of lower-income residents attracted by the same good schools and low crime rates. Drive farther south on Interstate 35—a little farther every year—and suddenly you are surrounded by farm country, as well as modest towns such as Northfield, the idyllic home of Carleton College and its late professor-turned-Senator, Paul Wellstone. Northfield is only 40 miles from Minneapolis and St. Paul, and some people there commute to the Twin Cities core on I-35.

These places make up the 2d Congressional District of Minnesota. Historically, Dakota County, just south of St. Paul, which casts nearly half the votes in the district, was marginally Democratic, while the other counties were fairly heavily Republican. But in 1998 this was Jesse Ventura Country: in that three-way race he carried each of the counties in the district, with a sharply increased turnout. As the suburbs have continued growing, Ventura country has become more Republican. George W. Bush narrowly carried Dakota County in 2000 and 2004, and it produced big margins for Republican Senator Norm Coleman and Governor Tim Pawlenty in 2002. But in 2006 Democrat Amy Klobuchar showed Democrats can still compete in Dakota County: she captured 56% while Pawlenty won 52%. The only remaining DFL stronghold here is Rice County, home of Northfield.

The congressman from the 2d District is John Kline, a Republican first elected in 2002 and one of only four challengers to defeat an incumbent that year: Kline's third try at beating DFL incumbent Bill Luther proved a charm. Kline grew up in Corpus Christi, Texas, where his father owned a small hometown newspaper and his mother managed the Corpus Christi Symphony Orchestra for more than 40 years. After graduating from Rice University he served 25 years in the Marine Corps. He served in Vietnam, commanded Marine aviation forces in Somalia and his headquarters duties included responsibility for the Corps's $50 billion program objective memorandum, a budget and planning analysis. He was assigned to the White House when Jimmy Carter was president and he carried the nuclear "football"—the package containing the launch codes—for Carter and for Ronald Reagan: he surely has had more face time with presidents than any other member of Congress. When he retired in 1994, he settled in Lakeville, in Dakota County, where he managed his wife's family farm.

In 1998, Kline challenged Luther, a Democrat first elected in 1994 who had a history of expensive and fierce campaigns in the old 6th. Kline favored tax cuts, more military spending and the resignation of Bill Clinton, and opposed abortion. He spent only $283,000; Luther, who raised $1.1 million in the cycle, spent only $412,000. That might have been a mistake: Luther won by only 50%-46%. Kline hardly stopped running; more experienced and better financed in 2000, he made the rematch one of the nation's high-profile House contests. The result was closer across the board, but Luther survived 50%-48%. Discouraged, Kline said he was unlikely to run again. Then the unexpected happened. The redistricting plan ordered into effect by the state supreme court in March 2002 placed Kline's home in a new 2d District that contained the home of no incumbent. Republican leaders in Minnesota and Washington urged Kline to run again, and a few days later he announced his candidacy. Luther, whose home was in the new 6th District, a dozen miles north of the 2d, waited two months before announcing which district he would run in, or whether he would retire. He didn't have a good choice: In contrast to his old 6th District, where George W. Bush got only 48% of the vote in 2000, majorities in both the new 2d and 6th Districts had voted for Bush.

Luther finally decided to run in the 2d and started with some advantages: 28 years of experience in elected office, $1.2 million in cash on hand. The acrimonious campaign resumed where it left off in 2000. Luther called Kline an extremist who held "Texas values." Luther's campaign manager encouraged Sam Garst, a Sierra Club activist and Luther supporter, to enter the race as a candidate of a new "No New Taxes" party—a purposefully deceptive banner designed to siphon votes from the Republican column. At first the Luther campaign denied all connection with Garst, but the facts came out: Luther had not discouraged the action. Even liberal local media harshly criticized the scheme as "un-Minnesotan" and characterized it as a cynical dirty trick in a hotly contested race where a few votes might make the difference. Kline got further mileage out of the issue by refusing to debate Luther unless Garst was included; Garst left town in the weeks before the election. What had twice been a close race turned out to be no contest in 2002. Kline won by a comfortable 53%-42%. Luther later said that the controversial memorial service for Paul Wellstone cost him independent and Republican support and conceded that he suffered from anger over the Garst candidacy.

In the House, Kline's voting record made him the most conservative member of the Minnesota delegation. Kline won a seat on Armed Services, plus the Education and Labor Committee. Kline was a conferee on pension legislation signed into law in 2006. He worked to include relief for struggling airlines, including Minnesota-based Northwest Airlines, by giving them more time to make contributions to employee pensions. Kline also passed through the House a bill that would require states to adopt policies that prevent schools from forcing parents to medicate children with behavioral problems. He sponsored legislation to replace Ulysses S. Grant with Ronald Reagan on the $50 bill. Backed by Minnesota corn growers, he sponsored legislation requiring that gasoline contain 10% blended ethanol by 2010. He helped delay a plan by Defense Secretary Donald Rumsfeld to overhaul the officer management program; Kline worried that it would politicize the appointment of senior officers and hurt morale among young officers.

Democrats in 2006 appeared to have found in retired FBI agent Coleen Rowley a challenger uniquely suited to exploit the twin Republican liabilities of ethics and Iraq war. *Time* magazine named Rowley one of three "Persons of the Year" in 2002 for going public with the FBI's decision to ignore recommendations to investigate Zacarias Moussaoui, a figure in the September 11 attacks. Though initially touted by national Democrats, Rowley, a first-time candidate, struggled to find her footing and the party lost interest in her campaign. She was forced to apologize to Kline for portraying him on her website as the incompetent Colonel Klink, a Nazi prison camp commandant from the TV series "Hogan's Heroes." While other Republicans distanced themselves from Bush and the Iraq war, the former marine and father of an Army Blackhawk helicopter pilot in Iraq, did not. Kline won reelection by 56%-40% against Rowley, identical to his margin two years earlier.

THIRD DISTRICT

Rep. Jim Ramstad (R)

Elected 1990, 9th term; b. May 6, 1946, Jamestown, ND; home, Minnetonka; U. of MN, B.A. 1968, George Washington U., J.D. 1973; Protestant; married (Kathryn Mitchell).

Military Career: Army Reserves, 1968-74.

Elected Office: MN Senate, 1980-90.

Professional Career: Special Asst., U.S. Rep. Tom Kleppe, 1970; Practicing atty., 1973-80; Adjunct Prof., American U., 1975-78.

DC Office: 103 CHOB, 20515, 202-225-2871; Fax: 202-225-6351; Web site: www.house.gov/ramstad.

District Offices: Minnetonka, 952-738-8200.

Committees: *Ways & Means* (4th of 17 R): Oversight (RMM); Health.

Group Ratings

	ADA	ACLU	AFS	LCV	ITIC	NTU	COC	ACU	CFG	FRC
2006	35	27	29	83	86	54	87	68	50	57
2005	35	—	38	61	—	51	81	46	46	69

National Journal Ratings

	2005 LIB	—	2005 CONS		2006 LIB	—	2006 CONS
Economic	52%	—	48%		52%	—	48%
Social	43%	—	57%		49%	—	50%
Foreign	51%	—	48%		55%	—	44%

Key Votes of the 109th Congress

1. Estate Tax Repeal	Y	5. Limit Interstate Abortion	Y	9. Build Border Fence	Y
2. Limit CAFE Standards	N	6. Extend Patriot Act	Y	10. CAFTA	Y
3. FY06 Spending Curb	Y	7. Bar Same Sex Marriage	Y	11. Oppose Iraq Withdrawal	Y
4. Drilling in ANWR	N	8. Stem Cell Research $	Y	12. Detainee Tribunals	Y

Election Results

2006 general	Jim Ramstad (R)	184,333	(65%)	($1,424,365)
	Wendy Wilde (DFL)	99,588	(35%)	($67,861)
2006 primary	Jim Ramstad (R)	unopposed		
2004 general	Jim Ramstad (R)	231,871	(65%)	($921,476)
	Deborah Watts (DFL)	126,665	(35%)	($36,064)

Prior Winning Percentages: 2002 (72%); 2000 (68%); 1998 (72%); 1996 (70%); 1994 (73%); 1992 (64%); 1990 (67%)

The People		Race/Ethnic Origin	Ancestry	
Area size:	513 sq. mi.	88.6% White	German: 22.8%	Norwegian: 11.3%
Urban population:	95.8%	3.8% Black	Irish: 8.6%	
Rural population:	4.2%	4.0% Asian	**2004 Presidential Vote**	
Pop. 2000:	614,935	0.3% Native Am.	Bush (R) 190,339	(51%)
Pop. 2005 (est):	640,640	0.0% Hawaiian	Kerry (D) 179,488	(48%)
Median income:	$63,816	1.4% Two+ races	Other 3,735	(1%)
Poverty status:	3.5%	0.1% Other	**2000 Presidential Vote**	
Military veterans:	12.4%	1.8% Hispanic Origin	Bush (R) 161,999	(50%)
			Gore (D) 149,277	(46%)
			Other 13,483	(4%)
			Cook Partisan Voting Index: R + 1	

Occupation   Blue collar: 16.7%   White collar: 73.1%   Gray collar: 10.1%

Over the past half century, Minnesota's great twin metropolis has spread out from the neat streets inside the city limits of Minneapolis and St. Paul into the countryside all around. People have sorted themselves out geographically. In the lower lands along the Mississippi and Minnesota Rivers, where rail lines fan out from the Twin Cities heading toward the great farmlands of America, are the blue-collar suburbs, with modest houses on grid streets and warehouses and factories near the tracks. Inland, around the lakes Minnesota is so proud of, in subdivisions with curved streets hugging the hills, are the Twin Cities' more affluent neighborhoods, quiet and unflashy in the Minnesota way, but comfortable whether blanketed with snow or when the lake is glinting in the summer sun. At the edge of Lake Minnetonka is Wayzata, the monied suburb that is the top ZIP code in Minnesota for political donations. In between are the freeway interchanges where some of the Twin Cities' great innovations can be seen—Southdale Shopping Center in Edina, the first enclosed mall and site of the first B. Dalton store, which begat the national book chains; huge indoor water parks; and the giant Mall of America, with its 4.2 million square feet, 520 stores, 86 eating options, 14 theaters, 8 nightclubs and 13,000 employees; there are plans to add 5.7 million square feet on an additional 42 acres, including a 5,000 seat performing arts center and a rail connection to downtown Minneapolis. The mall, the nation's number one tourist attraction, attracting 40 million people annually, is unmatched as a symbol of American consumerism; security was quickly heightened after the September 11 attacks.

The 3d Congressional District of Minnesota takes in Hennepin County suburbs north, south and west of Minneapolis. On the north side of the 3d is working-class Brooklyn Park, long a DFL stronghold but more famous now for its former mayor, later governor, Jesse Ventura; on the south is middle-income Bloomington, home of the Mall of America; to the west are Edina, Plymouth,

Wayzata and other towns around Lake Minnetonka, traditionally Republican but marginal in the 2004 presidential election. This is the largest lake and these are the most affluent communities in the Twin Cities area. The area is home to the headquarters of such diverse companies as Cargill and Radisson Hotels, and large biotech facilities in Brooklyn Park and Maple Grove. This area trended Democratic in the 1990s, as Bill Clinton twice won pluralities here. The 3d may be the home of Minnesota's traditional Republican establishment, but it voted just 51% for George W. Bush in 2004.

The congressman from the 3d District is Jim Ramstad, a Republican first elected in 1990. He has been in politics since childhood: Raised in North Dakota, he used to go with his grandfather to visit Republican Senator Milton Young. He saw President Eisenhower in 1956 and met President Kennedy in 1963 at the same Rose Garden ceremony where a young Bill Clinton was photographed shaking Kennedy's hand (Ramstad is in the background of the now famous photo). He was an intern to Young and a staffer to Congressman Tom Kleppe while in his 20s. He moved to Minnesota and in 1980, at 34, he unseated a Democratic state senator (spending the then record-breaking sum of $77,932). In 1990, when Representative Bill Frenzel retired after 20 years, Ramstad ran for the House. The crucial contest was the Republican convention. Ramstad was pro-choice on abortion while most delegates were anti-abortion, but he had useful endorsements, from Senator Rudy Boschwitz and Congressman Vin Weber, both anti-abortion, and won the party convention on the eighth ballot.

Ramstad's voting record has been slightly right of the middle of the House, a bit more conservative on economic issues. On the Ways and Means Committee, he has strongly supported free trade. Ramstad also talked about his mother's Alzheimer's disease when he urged George W. Bush to support stem cell research. He has been an enthusiastic backer of Bush's faith-based initiative and of tax cuts. He split with Republican leaders on campaign finance regulation, federalizing security agents at the airports and the Cuban trade embargo. He called the 2002 farm bill "a horrendous hit on taxpayers." In 2005, Ramstad gained the seniority to become chairman of the Ways and Means Oversight Subcommittee and now serves as the panel's ranking Republican.

Ramstad has been a recovering alcoholic since 1981, when he awoke in jail after a night of drinking ended in a brawl; he has backed measures for both discipline and therapy for substance abusers. With Patrick Kennedy, he organized a caucus to educate lawmakers on addiction and treatment, and in 2006 became Kennedy's recovery sponsor after Kennedy checked himself into the Mayo Clinic in Rochester for treatment of prescription drug abuse. Ramstad drove two hours from his home to meet with Kennedy on four consecutive Saturdays. In memory of the late Paul Wellstone, Ramstad and Kennedy pushed for equal coverage of mental and physical illness, but he said that Speaker Dennis Hastert blocked the bill. "I've spoken to him until I'm blue in the face," he told the *Associated Press*. The bill by 2006 had over 230 House sponsors, but opposition from the insurance industry kept it from reaching the floor. Ramstad and Kennedy in 2007 launched a six-city tour to promote the parity bill.

Ramstad has been easily reelected every two years in this high-turnout district. Despite token opposition in 2006, Ramstad spent $1.4 million on his re-election. He has been listed among the best-dressed members of Congress, and the longtime bachelor returned to the gossip pages after he married in October 2005. After Democrats took control of Congress, Ramstad's centrist record stood out prominently. He was one of three Republicans to vote for all six bills on the Democrats' first 100-hour agenda. Initially a supporter of the war in Iraq, he was one of 17 Republicans to vote for the Democrats' February 2007 resolution opposing a troop increase. With Rahm Emanuel, he sponsored legislation to provide health care access for uninsured children.

In September 2007, citing exhaustion in public life, Ramstad announced he would not seek reelection. Although Republicans have long had a lock on this district, the open seat race figures to be one of the most competitive House contests of 2008.

FOURTH DISTRICT

Rep. Betty McCollum (DFL)

Elected 2000, 4th term; b. July 12, 1954, Minneapolis; home, St. Paul; Inver Hills Comm. Col., A.A. 1980, Col. of St. Catherine, B.A. 1987; Catholic; divorced.

Elected Office: N. St. Paul City Cncl., 1986-92; MN House of Reps., 1992-2000.

Professional Career: Teacher; Retail sales & management.

DC Office: 1714 LHOB, 20515, 202-225-6631; Fax: 202-225-1968; Web site: mccollum.house.gov.

District Offices: St. Paul, 651-224-9191.

Committees: *Appropriations* (31st of 37 D): Legislative Branch; State, Foreign Operations & Related Programs; Labor, HHS, Education & Related Agencies. *Oversight & Government Reform* (17th of 23 D): National Security & Foreign Affairs.

Group Ratings

	ADA	ACLU	AFS	LCV	ITIC	NTU	COC	ACU	CFG	FRC
2006	95	95	100	100	57	13	33	4	8	0
2005	95	—	100	100	—	17	33	0	0	0

National Journal Ratings

	2005 LIB	—	2005 CONS		2006 LIB	—	2006 CONS
Economic	94%	—	0%		85%	—	14%
Social	89%	—	10%		84%	—	16%
Foreign	94%	—	4%		92%	—	5%

Key Votes of the 109th Congress

1. Estate Tax Repeal	N	5. Limit Interstate Abortion	N	9. Build Border Fence	N
2. Limit CAFE Standards	N	6. Extend Patriot Act	N	10. CAFTA	N
3. FY06 Spending Curb	N	7. Bar Same Sex Marriage	N	11. Oppose Iraq Withdrawal	N
4. Drilling in ANWR	N	8. Stem Cell Research $	Y	12. Detainee Tribunals	N

Election Results

2006 general	Betty McCollum (DFL)	172,096	(70%)	($611,908)
	Obi Sium (R)	74,797	(30%)	($75,617)
2006 primary	Betty McCollum (DFL)	unopposed		
2004 general	Betty McCollum (DFL)	182,387	(57%)	($707,384)
	Patrice Bataglia (R)	105,467	(33%)	($194,717)
	Peter Vento (Ind)	29,099	(9%)	

Prior Winning Percentages: 2002 (62%); 2000 (48%)

The People		Race/Ethnic Origin	Ancestry		
Area size:	220 sq. mi.	77.7% White	German: 22.0%	Irish: 9.5%	
Urban population:	99.9%	6.5% Black	Norwegian: 7.7%		
Rural population:	0.1%	7.5% Asian	**2004 Presidential Vote**		
Pop. 2000:	614,935	0.7% Native Am.	Kerry (D)	205,467	(62%)
Pop. 2005 (est):	594,709	0.0% Hawaiian	Bush (R)	123,313	(37%)
Median income:	$46,811	2.2% Two+ races	Other	4,341	(1%)
Poverty status:	9.6%	0.1% Other	**2000 Presidential Vote**		
Military veterans:	11.8%	5.2% Hispanic Origin	Gore (D)	166,919	(57%)
			Bush (R)	109,670	(37%)
			Other	18,146	(6%)
			Cook Partisan Voting Index: D +13		

Occupation	Blue collar: 19.2%	White collar: 67.0%	Gray collar: 13.7%

Above the Mississippi River bluffs, forested when the first settlers arrived in the 1850s and one of America's great urban vistas today, stand the two great landmarks of St. Paul: the Minnesota Capitol and Archbishop Ireland's Cathedral. This is the older and smaller of the Twin Cities, settled mainly by Catholic Irish and German immigrants, while Minneapolis was attracting Protestant Swedes and Yankees. St. Paul became a major transportation hub, a railroad center and river port, while Minneapolis, farther up river at the Falls of St. Anthony, became the nation's largest grain milling center; both industries stoked the ire of farmers in the Dakotas who had no choice but to deal with them to make a living. Beneath the Capitol and the cathedral, the city's skywalk-linked downtown is home to the Ordway Music Theater, the headquarters of Minnesota Public Radio and an active pop music industry; the Winter Carnival is an annual highlight. Beyond the cathedral is Summit Avenue, on which capitalists like the Great Northern Railway's James J. Hill built grandiose Romanesque houses, and which, with Monument Avenue in Richmond and Meridian Street in Indianapolis, remains one of America's grand 19th century residential boulevards. The parallel Grand Avenue is home to a pleasant commercial strip with a walkable, urban feel; more modest neighborhoods elsewhere are notable for their grid streets lined with sturdy houses.

Minnesota's 4th Congressional District is made up of St. Paul, the Ramsey County suburbs to the north, and the southern suburbs of West St. Paul and South St. Paul. When a special panel of judges drew the new districts in 2002, they rejected a Republican proposal to combine Minneapolis and St. Paul into one district and made only modest changes in the boundaries. St. Paul was one of the most Democratic parts of Minnesota even before the Democratic-Farmer-Labor Party was formed in 1944, and it remained proudly DFL for a half-century. It voted to reelect Mayor Norm Coleman in 1997 after he switched to the Republican party, but he failed to carry a single precinct in the city when he ran successfully for the Senate in 2002. The area has become home to more than 24,000 Hmong immigrants, the largest concentration in any American city. The Hmong had been recruited by the CIA and U.S. Special Forces during the Vietnam War and resettled here after Laos fell to the Communists in 1975; another 5,000 refugees arrived from Thailand in 2004 and 2005. The 4th District seat has been held by the DFL since it elected Eugene McCarthy in 1948, and remains the second-most Democratic district in the state.

The congresswoman from the 4th District is Betty McCollum, a Democrat first elected in 2000. The daughter of a military intelligence officer, she grew up in North St. Paul and graduated from the College of St. Catherine. For 11 years she taught high school social studies and then she was a retail sales manager for 14 years at Dayton's department store. After her daughter was hurt on the slide in a city park, McCollum ran and was elected in 1986 to the North St. Paul City Council. She served on the council until 1992, when she was elected to the state House of Representatives after defeating incumbents in both the primary and general.

The 4th District had been represented since 1976 by Bruce Vento, a Democrat with an almost perfectly liberal voting record. In February 2000 Vento announced he would not seek reelection and that he had malignant mesothelioma; he died on October 10, 2000. In the September primary, McCollum, who was endorsed by Minnesota's Democratic-Farmer-Labor Party and EMILY's List, faced three opponents. The primary at first appeared wide open, but in this race, unlike some statewide contests, the DFL convention endorsement counted for something, and McCollum won easily with 50% to 23% for state Senator Steve Novak. Republicans nominated state senator Linda Runbeck, a vigorously anti-abortion candidate. McCollum backed prescription drug coverage under Medicare and opposed large tax cuts before Congress paid down the debt. Runbeck, who opposed gun control and took conservative positions on health care and education, attacked McCollum and her Democratic allies for running "hateful, vicious attack ads" that distorted her positions on guns. This was a three-way race, thanks to the candidacy of former Ramsey County prosecutor Tom Foley, a long-time DFLer who ran on the ticket of Governor Jesse Ventura's Independence party. Once again, McCollum won unexpectedly easily, 48%-31%, with 21% for Foley. She was the first woman elected to the House from Minnesota since Coya Knutson was famously called home by her estranged husband in 1958 (see 7th District).

In the House, McCollum has a consistently liberal voting record. Although she worked on the No Child Left Behind Act as a member of the Education and Labor Committee and backed the House version of the bill, she was one of six Democrats who voted against the final agreement and the only committee Democrat to do so. She made the national news when Fox News Channel showed footage of her leading the House in the Pledge of Allegiance and omitting the words "under God." McCollum cited faulty intelligence in strongly opposing the war in Iraq. Despite bitter divisions among local Hmongs, she called for normal trade relations with Laos, and the measure was enacted after the 2004 election. McCollum secured $2 million to promote the Central Corridor, an 11-mile light rail link between downtown St. Paul and Minneapolis and passed legislation in the House to start the process of establishing a national trail along the Mississippi River from Minnesota to the Gulf of Mexico. She also sponsored legislation that would crack down on diploma mills that sell worthless degrees. McCollum quickly became an ally of Nancy Pelosi, whom she calls a mentor, and delivered the speech formally nominating her as party whip in October 2001. In return, McCollum has won some leadership assignments, including a seat on the steering committee. After the 2006 election, McCollum lobbied for and won the Appropriations Committee seat that had been held by former Representative Martin Sabo. She was also appointed to the House Oversight and Government Reform Committee, but in exchange had to give up her slots on the Education and Labor and Foreign Relations committees. Pelosi also named McCollum to a task force to consider how to enforce House ethics rules.

McCollum has been reelected easily. In 2004, Peter Vento, son of the late congressman, ran as the Independent Party nominee, though he did not campaign much; he got 9% of the vote. McCollum is sometimes mentioned as a possible statewide candidate, but she declined to run for Mark Dayton's open Senate seat in 2006. Comfortable in her safe district and rewarded with choice committee assignments, McCollum has said she has no plans to challenge Republican Senator Norm Coleman in 2008.

FIFTH DISTRICT

Rep. Keith Ellison (DFL)

Elected 2006, 1st term; b. Aug. 4, 1963, Detroit, MI; home, Minneapolis; Wayne St. U., B.A. 1985, U. of MN, J.D. 1990; Muslim; married (Kim).

Elected Office: MN House of Reps., 2002-06.

Professional Career: Practicing atty., 1990-2002.

DC Office: 1130 LHOB, 20515, 202-225-4755; Fax: 202-225-4886; Web site: ellison.house.gov.

District Offices: Minneapolis, 612-522-1212.

Committees: *Financial Services* (28th of 37 D): Domestic and International Monetary Policy, Trade & Technology; Housing & Community Opportunity; Financial Institutions & Consumer Credit. *Judiciary* (22d of 23 D): The Constitution, Civil Rights & Civil Liberties; Immigration, Citizenship, Refugees, Border Security & International Law.

Group Ratings and Key Votes: Newly Elected

Election Results

2006 general	Keith Ellison (DFL)	136,060	(56%)	($786,127)
	Alan Fine (R)	52,263	(21%)	($198,621)
	Tammy Lee (Ind)	51,456	(21%)	($226,398)
	Other	5,126	(2%)	
2006 primary	Keith Ellison (DFL)	29,003	(41%)	
	Mike Erlandson (DFL)	21,857	(31%)	
	Ember Reichgott Junge (DFL)	14,454	(21%)	
	Paul Ostrow (DFL)	3,795	(5%)	
	Other	1,265	(2%)	
2004 general	Martin Olav Sabo (DFL)	218,434	(70%)	($497,073)
	Daniel Nielsen Mathias (R)	76,600	(24%)	($11,504)
	Jay Pond (Green)	17,984	(6%)	

The People		Race/Ethnic Origin	Ancestry	
Area size:	130 sq. mi.	71.2% White	German: 17.6%	Norwegian: 9.3%
Urban population:	100.0%	12.8% Black	Irish: 7.6%	
Rural population:	0.0%	5.1% Asian	**2004 Presidential Vote**	
Pop. 2000:	614,935	1.5% Native Am.	Kerry (D) 237,418	(71%)
Pop. 2005 (est):	590,654	0.1% Hawaiian	Bush (R) 92,797	(28%)
Median income:	$41,569	3.0% Two+ races	Other 5,060	(2%)
Poverty status:	12.7%	0.2% Other	**2000 Presidential Vote**	
Military veterans:	10.8%	6.0% Hispanic Origin	Gore (D) 185,874	(63%)
			Bush (R) 85,447	(29%)
			Other 24,577	(8%)
			Cook Partisan Voting Index: D +21	

Occupation	Blue collar: 17.9%	White collar: 67.2%	Gray collar: 14.9%

From almost nowhere in Minneapolis today can you see the geographic feature that put the city here—the Falls of St. Anthony, the head of navigation on the Mississippi River, where waters rush in rapids beneath low downtown bridges. In olden days, every riverboat had to stop here, and the waterpower generated by the falls was the energy source first for pioneers' grist mills and then for the giant grain mills that processed the wheat of the northern Great Plains into food for the United States and the world. By 1890 Minneapolis and St. Paul made up one of America's largest urban areas, living mainly off grain. Today, Minneapolis is a center of high-tech industry, banking and finance. It is a regional railroad center, home of Northwest Airlines, and the center of an economic region that extends almost 1,000 miles to the Rocky Mountains in Montana.

The city of Minneapolis, plus a few of its older, adjoining suburbs, comprise the 5th Congressional District. In the southwest corner are the affluent neighborhoods around Lake Calhoun and Lake Harriet—long built-up and proudly maintained, amidst trees that turn beautifully golden in early autumn. Not far away are Minneapolis's skywalk-laced downtown skyscrapers, the museum quarter up on the hill above Hennepin Avenue, and the Hubert H. Humphrey Metrodome, nick-named (inaccurately, say some) the "Homerdome" but still unloved by baseball fans. Straddling the Mississippi River is the University of Minnesota, which has fostered the area's cutting-edge biotech research and medical innovations, and nearby Dinkytown, a student area where Robert Zimmerman discovered folk music and reinvented himself as Bob Dylan. Most of the 5th District is low on the income scale. Many of the working-class neighborhoods of small frame houses on grid streets with ample parks are now kept up by elderly homeowners, while new immigrants live in small communities of their own. Minneapolis does not have the endless stretches of abandoned blocks commonly seen in Chicago or Detroit, but all is not well, and crime rates are uncomfortably high.

For a place often thought of as monochromatically white and Scandinavian, the city is a place of surprising diversity. To the northeast, behind the railroad and warehouse district along the Mississippi, are many Hmongs from Laos. Hennepin County is home to the largest number of African immigrants in the state, following a decade in which African immigrants to Minnesota jumped sevenfold. The Jewish community here has increased with immigrants from the former Soviet Union. Ticket machines on the new Hiawatha Avenue light-rail line, from downtown to the airport and Mall of America, do business in four languages—English, Spanish, Hmong and Somali.

The 5th is the most heavily Democratic district in the state. Minneapolis's political liberalism is drawn from the Yankee tradition of clean government, the Scandinavian tradition of cooperative enterprise and the industrial-labor tradition of economic redistribution. To this has been added in recent years, by feminists and the graduate student proletariat, a more antic cultural liberalism that is alien to both. George W. Bush got only 29% of the vote here in 2000, his worst performance in the state's eight districts. Al Gore and John Kerry carried this district by more than 2–1 margins.

The new congressman from the 5th District is Keith Ellison, a Democrat elected in 2006. Ellison, a relatively unknown state legislator, garnered international attention when he was elected as the first Muslim to serve in Congress and as the first black representative from Minnesota. He was raised Catholic in Detroit, the son of a psychiatrist and the third of five boys. (Four became lawyers and the other a doctor.) Ellison studied economics at Wayne State University and it was there that he converted to Sunni Islam. He moved to Minnesota in 1987 to study law at the University of Minnesota, worked in private practice, and ran a nonprofit criminal defense firm, while also hosting a public affairs radio show. Ellison ran unsuccessfully for the DFL nomination for the state House in 1998, then won the first of two terms in the state House in 2002.

The surprise retirement of Democrat Martin Olav Sabo, who had held the seat since 1978, unleashed a torrent of pent-up political ambition. Nearly a dozen Democrats sought the party endorsement at the May 6 DFL district convention, but the main contenders were Ellison, former DFL chairman and longtime Sabo aide Mike Erlandson, and former state Senator Ember Reichgott Junge. Ellison, a charismatic legislator who strongly opposed the war in Iraq, attracted support from war opponents and key backers of the late Paul Wellstone. "I have the passion of a Wellstone and the practicality of a Sabo," he told convention activists. Ellison easily won the DFL endorsement, but Erlandson and Reichgott Junge did not abide by the party endorsement and competed for the Democratic nomination in a seven-way September 12 primary.

In the majority-white 5th, Ellison talked little about race or religion and emphasized issues that animated the district's liberal voters: peace, environmental justice, and government-funded universal health care. Ellison's campaign confronted a series of disturbing personal revelations: unpaid parking tickets and moving violations that led to multiple suspensions of his driver's license; $25,000 he once owed in back taxes; twice being fined by the state campaign finance board for late filings. But it was his ties to the controversial Nation of Islam leader Louis Farrakhan and accusations of anti-Semitism that proved to be the most damaging. Ellison said his association with the group was limited to 18 months during which he helped to organize the 1995 Million Man March, although his writings about Farrakhan were traced back to the *Minnesota Daily* newspaper during his law school days. Ellison denied being a member of Farrakhan's group and reached out to local Jewish leaders, insisting that he was unaware of its anti-Semitic views. In the primary, Ellison relied on direct mail and grassroots campaigning and reached out to traditionally low-turnout voters. Reichgott Junge courted suburban voters, while Erlandson, backed by Sabo, courted seniors. Despite the personal baggage, Ellison won the primary with 41%, followed by Erlandson with 31%, and Reichgott Junge with 21%.

Heavily favored in the general election, Ellison faced two third-party candidates and Republican Alan Fine, who described Ellison as "an embarrassment to our district, our state, our country, and our world." In October, Ellison accused a local Democratic activist of blackmailing him over an extramarital relationship that he denied having with her. Ellison had obtained a restraining order against the woman in May 2005; one week before the 2006 primary, the woman requested a restraining order against Ellison in connection with an incident that allegedly occurred more than a year before. After the election, a judge denied the woman's request for a restraining order and issued a gag order preventing her from repeating the allegations. Ellison agreed to drop his restraining order. During the general election campaign, Ellison observed Ramadan by not eating or drinking during the day. On Election Day, he won 56% of vote, while Fine and Independence Party candidate Tammy Lee each won 21%.

Controversy followed Ellison after the election. A conservative commentator stirred up opposition to Ellison's plan to take the oath of office with the Quran, rather than the Bible. "If you are incapable of taking an oath on that book, don't serve in Congress," radio talk show host Dennis Prager wrote on the Internet. In a letter to constituents, Republican Congressman Virgil Goode of Virginia said that without tighter immigration limits, more Muslims would be elected to Congress and would also insist on using the Quran. In a smart move, Ellison borrowed a Quran from the Library of Congress that was once owned by Thomas Jefferson. He got a seat on the Judiciary Committee, but said he had no immediate plans to offer an impeachment resolution of President Bush as he had in the Minnesota House a year earlier. In July 2007, before a gathering of Minneapolis-area atheists, Ellison again sparked controversy by comparing 9/11 to the burning of the Reichstag building in Nazi Germany, an event used by Adolph Hitler to suspend civil liberties. Several House Republicans wrote to Speaker Nancy Pelosi asking her to reprimand Ellison over the remarks; Ellison backed away from the comparison and said, "It was probably inappropriate to use that example, because it's a unique historical event, without any clear parallels."

SIXTH DISTRICT

Rep. Michele Bachmann (R)

Elected 2006, 1st term; b. Apr. 6, 1956, Waterloo, IA; home, Stillwater; Winona State U., B.A. 1978, Oral Roberts U., J.D. 1986, Col. of William and Mary, LL.M. 1988; Lutheran; married (Marcus).

Elected Office: MN Senate, 2000-06.

Professional Career: Practicing atty., 1995-2000.

DC Office: 412 CHOB, 20515, 202-225-2331; Fax: 202-225-6475; Web site: bachmann.house.gov.

District Offices: St. Cloud, 320-253-5931; Woodbury, 651-731-5400.

Committees: *Financial Services* (29th of 33 R): Oversight & Investigations; Domestic and International Monetary Policy, Trade & Technology; Capital Markets, Insurance & Government Sponsored Enterprises.

Group Ratings and Key Votes: Newly Elected

Election Results

2006 general	Michele Bachmann (R)	151,248	(50%)	($2,694,789)
	Patty Wetterling (DFL)	127,144	(42%)	($3,179,222)
	John Binkowski (Ind)	23,557	(8%)	($17,261)
2006 primary	Michele Bachmann (R)	unopposed		
2004 general	Mark Kennedy (R)	203,669	(54%)	($2,649,747)
	Patty Wetterling (DFL)	173,309	(46%)	($1,935,813)

The People		Race/Ethnic Origin	Ancestry		
Area size:	3,237 sq. mi.	94.9% White	German: 29.9%	Norwegian: 10.0%	
Urban population:	63.8%	0.9% Black	Irish: 8.0%		
Rural population:	36.2%	1.4% Asian	**2004 Presidential Vote**		
Pop. 2000:	614,935	0.4% Native Am.	Bush (R)	216,574	(57%)
Pop. 2005 (est):	707,195	0.0% Hawaiian	Kerry (D)	161,601	(42%)
Median income:	$56,862	1.0% Two+ races	Other	4,576	(1%)
Poverty status:	4.7%	0.1% Other	**2000 Presidential Vote**		
Military veterans:	12.4%	1.3% Hispanic Origin	Bush (R)	152,977	(52%)
			Gore (D)	123,247	(42%)
			Other	15,954	(5%)
			Cook Partisan Voting Index: R + 5		

Occupation	Blue collar: 26.9%	White collar: 60.3%	Gray collar: 12.8%

The earliest settlers to the Twin Cities of Minneapolis and St. Paul came up the Mississippi River, or up the rail lines that were soon built on the bottomlands beside. They lived within walking distance of the mills and factories and railyards; as the first streetcars and then automobiles allowed them to live farther from work, they spread out in St. Paul and Minneapolis and then all around the lake-strewn countryside. The flatlands are bleak here when the winter sun struggles to shine through gray clouds. The lakes are often surrounded by, and sometimes indistinguishable from, swamps. Stillwater, an old lumber mill town built by pioneers on the hills above the St. Croix River, once nearly became Minnesota's capital, but later turned into an economic backwater, its Victorian structures ill-tended. Even so, the creativity and productivity of Minnesotans have turned this superficially grim countryside into some of the nation's most pleasant suburbs. Taking maximum advantage of their lakes, they refurbished old towns and farmhouses and built comfortable homes in new subdivisions.

The 6th Congressional District of Minnesota is a suburban and exurban district north of St. Paul and Minneapolis. It dips as far south and east as Stillwater, with new riverfront housing developments along the St. Croix. It spreads north over Washington and Anoka Counties, just north of the Twin Cities, with a mix of upscale and working class suburbs. To the northwest, along the Mississippi River, are Wright, Sherburne and Benton Counties, which have grown rapidly, from 140,000 in 1990 to 238,000 in 2006. These were once rural areas, with here and there a small town and a small city as the county seat. Now this lake country is filling with new subdivisions and shopping centers, and young voters usually from ancestrally DFL families who have become the key swing voters in the state. Farther to the northwest, the district also includes the eastern half of St. Cloud-based Stearns County, a heavily German Catholic area and a stronghold of anti-abortion sentiment. The 1990s saw an influx of Vietnamese, Chinese and Japanese people into St. Cloud; since then, many Somalis have moved in. In 1998 the district, especially the fast-growing counties, was Jesse Ventura Country. At the same time, the newcomers tended to vote Republican for other office, and ever since. George W. Bush carried the district 52%-42% in 2000 and 57%-42% in 2004, the latter his best showing in any Minnesota district. In 2002 it produced big margins for Republican Senator Norm Coleman and Governor Tim Pawlenty. In 2006, Pawlenty again swept the district although in the Senate race Democrat Amy Klobuchar won four of the six counties here against Republican Mark Kennedy, the 6th District's congressman at the time.

The new congresswoman for the 6th District is Michele Bachmann, a Republican elected in 2006. Bachmann grew up in cities across the Midwest and attended Winona State University, where she met her husband while working on Jimmy Carter's 1976 presidential campaign. She became disillusioned with Carter and his party's position on abortion, and gravitated toward Ronald Reagan and the Republican Party. Bachmann and her husband, both born-again Christians, moved to Tulsa, where she earned a degree at Coburn Law School at Oral Roberts University. After studying tax law at the College of William and Mary, Bachmann landed a job as a U.S. Treasury Department attorney in St. Paul arguing criminal and civil tax cases. Her political career began in 1999 with a losing bid for the Stillwater school board. A year later, she won a seat in the state Senate by defeating a moderate Republican incumbent for the party endorsement and then in the primary. In 2002, she defeated a ten-year Democratic incumbent when redistricting put them in the same Senate district. In the Legislature, Bachmann sought to protect private-property rights, limit government spending, and cut taxes. She was a prominent abortion opponent, and gained notoriety in 2004 for leading the Senate fight for a state constitutional amendment to ban same-sex marriage.

When Republican incumbent Mark Kennedy gave up the 6th District seat to run for Senate, Bachmann entered the Republican race as the candidate to beat; she clinched the nomination at the party convention by defeating three other candidates. She had a following among social conservatives, but her stances also made her a polarizing political figure. There were clear ideological differences separating Bachmann and her Democratic opponent, Patty Wetterling, who was defeated by Kennedy 54%-46% two years earlier. Wetterling, a nationally recognized advocate for missing children after her 11-year-old son Jacob was abducted in 1989 and never found, originally had announced she was running for Senate, but returned to the House race after Democrats rallied behind Amy Klobuchar. Her support for abortion rights, her call for the withdrawal of U.S. troops from Iraq, and opposition to a constitutional amendment outlawing same-sex marriage allowed Republicans to portray her as too liberal for this suburban and exurban seat.

Neither candidate lacked money: Wetterling spent more than $3 million to Bachmann's $2.7 million. President Bush helped Bachmann raise more than $500,000 at an August fundraiser, while Wetterling enjoyed support from EMILY's List; the NRCC spent nearly $2.5 million in the race, more than double its Democratic counterpart. Bachmann downplayed her social positions and instead emphasized her opposition to taxes. Wetterling trailed in polls until October, when the Mark Foley congressional page scandal suddenly thrust her into the national spotlight. With her background in child advocacy, Wetterling emerged as a top party spokeswoman on the scandal. Four days after Foley resigned, she ran the first ad in the country mentioning the scandal. Democratic leaders tapped her to deliver the party's weekly radio address. But Bachmann was well-positioned to weather the political fallout. She is the mother of 5 children and she had sponsored legislation in the state Senate to establish a task force on Internet crimes against juveniles; she was also a foster parent to 23 children. Polls showed that Wetterling had surged ahead after the scandal broke, but the lead was fleeting. In a political atmosphere that could not have been more hostile for Republicans, Bachmann won a decisive 50%-42% victory.

Bachmann won widespread notice in January 2007 during the State of the Union address. Like many other members, she had staked out a prime aisle seat in the House so she could greet President Bush. On his exit from the House chamber after the speech, Bush signed two autographs for Bachmann. The freshman clutched his shoulder for nearly 30 seconds, even as he greeted other members, and the president kissed her on the cheek. Video of the awkward encounter played repeatedly on the Internet. Democrat Bob Olson, an attorney, dropped his 2008 Senate bid against Norm Coleman and announced in July 2007 that he would instead run against Bachmann in the 6th District; attorney Bob Hill, also a Democrat, had already declared his intention to run.

SEVENTH DISTRICT

Rep. Collin Peterson (DFL)

Elected 1990, 9th term; b. June 29, 1944, Fargo, ND; home, Detroit Lakes; Moorhead St. U., B.A. 1966; Lutheran; divorced.

Military Career: Army Natl. Guard, 1963-69.

Elected Office: MN Senate, 1976-86.

Professional Career: Accountant, 1966-90.

DC Office: 2211 RHOB, 20515, 202-225-2165; Fax: 202-225-1593; Web site: collinpeterson.house.gov.

District Offices: Detroit Lakes, 218-847-5056; Marshall, 507-537-2299; Montevideo, 320-269-8888; Red Lake Falls, 218-253-4356; Redwood Falls, 507-637-2270; Willmar, 320-235-1061.

Committees: *Agriculture* (Chmn. of 25 D).

Group Ratings

	ADA	ACLU	AFS	LCV	ITIC	NTU	COC	ACU	CFG	FRC
2006	35	36	57	17	71	29	73	72	31	100
2005	65	—	75	50	—	32	70	56	28	83

National Journal Ratings

	2005 LIB	—	2005 CONS	2006 LIB	—	2006 CONS
Economic	54%	—	46%	55%	—	45%
Social	50%	—	50%	44%	—	55%
Foreign	55%	—	45%	53%	—	46%

Key Votes of the 109th Congress

1. Estate Tax Repeal	Y	5. Limit Interstate Abortion	Y
2. Limit CAFE Standards	Y	6. Extend Patriot Act	N
3. FY06 Spending Curb	N	7. Bar Same Sex Marriage	Y
4. Drilling in ANWR	Y	8. Stem Cell Research $	N

9. Build Border Fence	Y
10. CAFTA	N
11. Oppose Iraq Withdrawal	Y
12. Detainee Tribunals	Y

Election Results

2006 general	Collin Peterson (DFL)	179,164	(70%)	($645,285)
	Michael Barrett (R)	74,557	(29%)	($41,375)
	Other	3,473	(1%)	
2006 primary	Collin Peterson (DFL)	33,732	(86%)	
	Erik Thompson (DFL)	5,476	(14%)	
2004 general	Collin Peterson (DFL)	207,628	(66%)	($523,484)
	David Sturrock (R)	106,349	(34%)	($127,271)

Prior Winning Percentages: 2002 (65%); 2000 (69%); 1998 (72%); 1996 (68%); 1994 (51%); 1992 (51%); 1990 (54%)

The People		Race/Ethnic Origin	Ancestry	
Area size:	33,745 sq. mi.	93.1% White	German: 28.5%	Norwegian: 20.3%
Urban population:	34.0%	0.3% Black	Swedish: 7.0%	
Rural population:	66.0%	0.5% Asian	**2004 Presidential Vote**	
Pop. 2000:	614,935	2.4% Native Am.	Bush (R) 180,743	(55%)
Pop. 2005 (est):	620,958	0.0% Hawaiian	Kerry (D) 140,332	(43%)
Median income:	$36,453	0.9% Two+ races	Other 4,917	(2%)
Poverty status:	10.3%	0.0% Other	**2000 Presidential Vote**	
Military veterans:	13.7%	2.6% Hispanic Origin	Bush (R) 155,794	(54%)
			Gore (D) 116,099	(40%)
			Other 18,706	(6%)
			Cook Partisan Voting Index: R + 6	

Occupation	Blue collar: 29.2%	White collar: 53.3%	Gray collar: 17.5%

Mark Twain's fabled Mississippi River begins so modestly in Minnesota's Itasca State Park, 2,552 miles from the Gulf of Mexico, that it can be crossed by foot on steppingstones. The lake-strewn country in which the river is born has made its own contributions to American literature: A century ago, Sinclair Lewis grew up in the town of Sauk Centre, which provided grist for his critical but affectionate portrayals of small-town America in Main Street and Babbitt. In those years, this seemingly placid country was seething with rage, as WASPy nationalists banned German from schools, renamed sauerkraut "liberty cabbage," and boycotted German-American businesses. This fed the bitter isolationism of the 1930s and 1940s, led by Charles Lindbergh, who grew up in Little Falls as the son of an isolationist congressman who voted against declaring war on Germany in 1917. This part of Minnesota is probably also the home of Lake Wobegon; Garrison Keillor says he was inspired by small towns in Stearns County that were evenly divided between German Catholics and Norwegian Lutherans. Farther south, where the plains rise above the river-cut gorges, is great farming country, settled more than 100 years ago by Yankees, Germans and Scandinavians. Even today, farmers still toil against the elements to make a profitable living, so productively that their lands are slowly but surely depopulating; 100,000 acres of farmland in the Minnesota River watershed has been taken out of production by the Conservation Reserve Program. This area is the nation's leading producer of sugar beets and a leading producer of turkeys; it also produces wheat, soybeans and oilseeds. On the shores of Plum Creek, near Walnut Grove, is where Laura Ingalls Wilder's family came on the way west to the "Little House on the Prairie" in South Dakota; after all their struggles, Laura's family left the farm for town as soon as they could. Their pain would be all too familiar to contemporary residents along the Red River of the North, which overflowed its banks in April 1997, inundating Grand Forks, North Dakota, and East Grand Forks, Minnesota, and dislocating 50,000 residents of the region—America's largest mass evacuation between the Civil War and Hurricane Katrina.

The 7th Congressional District of Minnesota covers almost all of the western part of the state. Its southeastern end is just 30 miles from Minneapolis, just beyond the zone of rapid exurban growth; most of its counties have lost population since 2000. It takes in the wheat-farming plains adjoining North Dakota as well as the German Catholic areas strewn with farm villages named for saints. Many political traditions coexist here: some wheat counties are heavily DFL while heavily Norwegian Otter Tail County leans Republican. The 7th's political history reads like something out of *Lake Wobegon Days*. Back in 1958, DFL Congresswoman Coya Knutson was defeated for reelection when her husband Andy issued a plaintive statement urging her to come home and make his breakfast again; she was the only incumbent Democrat to lose in that heavily Democratic year. Other Scandinavian names followed, of varying partisan affiliations; for three decades this was one of America's prime marginal districts. In 2000 the unpopularity of Clinton administration environmental and gun control policies produced a 54%-40% margin for George W. Bush, his best showing in a Minnesota district. In 2004 ancestral Democratic loyalties resurfaced a bit, and Bush's 55%-43% margin here was smaller than in the fast-growing suburban 6th District.

The congressman from the 7th District is Collin Peterson, a Democrat who after four unsuccessful tries won the seat in 1990 and now is chairman of the House Agriculture Committee. Peterson was born in Fargo, North Dakota, grew up across the Red River of the North on a farm in Baker, went to Moorhead State College, then started a CPA office in Detroit Lakes; all are within 50 miles of each other. In 1976 he was elected to the state Senate. He also started running for the House. He lost a DFL caucus in 1982; he lost to Republican Arlan Stangeland in 1984 and 1986 (by only 121 votes the second time; he declared victory and went to Washington to set up an office); he lost the DFL primary in 1988. But in 1990, when the *St. Cloud Times* reported that Stangeland made 341 credit card calls to a woman not his wife, Peterson won with a robust 54%. In office, he has been known as a free spirit, wearing cowboy boots and playing guitar in a band called The Second Amendments (the other four members are Republicans), acting as his own campaign consultant and pilot on flights within the district, and until the rules changed enjoying a cigar—often with Republicans—in the Speaker's Lobby off the House floor. He has a small staff, with community economic development professionals rather than Washington policy wonks. He opposes abortion and gun control; backs farm subsidies and labor unions; voted for the Iraq war resolution in 2002, for the Republicans' border security bill and for extending the Bush tax cuts. In October 2006 he said his vote on Iraq "was a mistake, and I would vote against it today, knowing what I now know." But he said withdrawal "would be more dangerous than anything we could do," and voted against the supplemental with a timetable.

In the House Peterson has been something of a populist, with conservative leanings on social issues and definitely a maverick. His political fortune was bolstered by the Republican takeover in 1994, which made him a visibly different kind of Democrat. In 1995, while voting for parts of the Contract with America, he founded with Gary Condit the Blue Dog Democrats for "common sense legislation that embraces the ideas and values of mainstream America." He sided with Republicans on HMO regulation and was one of 16 Democrats to vote for the Medicare/prescription drug bill in November 2003. When Minority Whip Steny Hoyer complained about his vote, Peterson said that the vote meant "life or death" for rural doctors and hospitals in his district. He opposed trade promotion authority, and said that his local farmers are furious about the Bush administration's trade deals.

Peterson is the opposite of many middle-of-the-House Republicans, who favor heavy environmental restrictions; he takes the view of his constituents, who hunt and fish as a way of life and see environmentalists' policies as hindrances. He expressed reservations that the 1996 Freedom to Farm Act would cause low prices and joined the bipartisan majority on the committee in restoring market controls when the farm program was renewed in 2002.

When Charles Stenholm of Texas was defeated in 2004, Peterson was next in line to be ranking minority member on the Agriculture Committee. But the Democratic leadership demanded that he pay $70,000 in back dues to the Democratic Congressional Campaign Committee. He agreed to be more of a team player and to raise money for other Democrats, although he still says, "We have a lot of very liberal people in our caucus. They're misguided in my opinion in a lot of areas." But he supported Nancy Pelosi on the theory that only a liberal can tell liberals what to do. He invited her to attend Farm Fest in Redwood County in August 2006, where she wore cowboy boots and ate pork chops on a stick and got a warm reception. He supported Pelosi's platform of raising the minimum wage, supporting ethanol and reinstituting paygo rules. After the Democrats won their majority in 2006, there was no question about his becoming chairman. "She gets it," Peterson said. "She's going to govern from the center, and she will work with Republicans. There will be no getting even."

Peterson came to the chairmanship just as the 2002 farm act was coming up for reauthorization. The previous Republican chairman, Bob Goodlatte, represented a district with few subsidized crops and took a more free market approach, while Peterson said he was "more protective of commodity programs"; nevertheless, they cooperated in holding hearings around the country in 2006. As incoming chairman, Peterson added one subcommittee, added new subjects to their titles—Energy and Organic Farming—and shuffled jurisdiction; he urged them to get to work drafting their portions of the farm act so that a bill could be passed and on the president's desk in September. In the 109th Congress Peterson worked unsuccessfully to advance supplemental disaster aid; he said that he wanted permanent disaster aid in the reauthorization. But "what's really going to drive this farm bill is renewable fuels." On ethanol, he said, "Frankly, there's not a lot that needs to be done there, other than stay out of the way and don't screw it up." He called for extending the Conservation Reserve Program to keep millions of additional acres of farmland idle to produce switchgrass and plant waste that could be used to make ethanol. His idea is that that would encourage the building of three or four cellulosic ethanol plants to show that they could be as profitable as the ethanol plants springing up all over the Midwest. "This would revolutionize rural America." He was skeptical of limiting farm subsidies to $200,000, a limit strongly opposed by Southern cotton and rice farmers. "Lots of people want to clamp down on payment limits, but if we do that, we are not going to pass a bill." On other agricultural issues, he pushed for including a one-month extension of the Milk Income Loss Contract in the Iraq supplemental, so that it would be included in the baseline for the 2007 farm bill, a baseline reduced by the fact that subsidies under the 2002 act have run $17 billion less than CBO projections. On a trip to Brazil, this representative of the nation's number one sugar beet district, listened to pleas for reductions in trade barriers that keep Brazil's sugar-based ethanol out of the United States. "I made it pretty clear to them that we're not interested." He promised oversight on the administration's program for mandatory animal identification of livestock; he had backed it but said it was badly administered. He called for freer trade for Cuba and said that the Democratic leadership would not allow appropriations to be amended to postpone the country-of-origin meat labeling provisions of the 2002 farm act. He called for changing the tax code to allow buyers of farmland a tax exemption from gains made selling other land only available to those paying with money earned by selling other farmland; this was in response to claims that farmland prices were being bid up by taxpayers seeking exemptions within the 180-day period from sale of other land.

Peterson's politics have been a smash hit with 7th District voters and an irritant to local DFL activists, while local Republicans have not produced well-financed opposition. He has not had a close contest since 1994; in 2004 and 2006 he carried all 35 counties in the district. The new House rule prohibiting flying in private planes prevented Peterson from claiming reimbursement for flights in his Beechcraft Bonanza; he had to lease aircraft at a higher cost of $7,500 a month. Naturally, he protested. "I threatened to put in a bill to make it illegal for any member to drive their own car until we got this fixed. And I told Nancy Pelosi that if she didn't get this fixed, I was going to quit and there was going to be a Republican in my place, that if I couldn't fly I wasn't going to do this any more. She just kind of looked at me—she said it'll be fixed." In May 2007 the rule was changed to accommodate Peterson and other members who fly their own planes.

EIGHTH DISTRICT

Rep. James Oberstar (DFL)

Elected 1974, 17th term; b. Sept. 10, 1934, Chisholm; home, Chisholm; St. Thomas Col., B.A. 1956, Col. of Europe, Bruges, Belgium, M.A. 1957; Catholic; married (Jean).

Professional Career: Navy civilian language teacher, Haiti, 1959-63; A.A., U.S. Rep. John Blatnik, 1963-74; A.A., U.S. House Public Works Cmte., 1971-74.

DC Office: 2365 RHOB, 20515, 202-225-6211; Fax: 202-225-0699; Web site: www.house.gov/oberstar.

District Offices: Brainerd, 218-828-4400; Chisholm, 218-254-5761; Duluth, 218-727-7474; North Branch, 651-277-1234.

Committees: *Transportation & Infrastructure* (Chmn. of 41 D).

Group Ratings

	ADA	ACLU	AFS	LCV	ITIC	NTU	COC	ACU	CFG	FRC
2006	80	90	100	67	57	11	27	22	4	42
2005	90	—	100	83	—	18	31	20	0	31

National Journal Ratings

	2005 LIB	—	2005 CONS		2006 LIB	—	2006 CONS
Economic	79%	—	20%		72%	—	27%
Social	70%	—	30%		65%	—	35%
Foreign	96%	—	0%		95%	—	0%

Key Votes of the 109th Congress

1. Estate Tax Repeal	N	5. Limit Interstate Abortion	Y	9. Build Border Fence	N
2. Limit CAFE Standards	N	6. Extend Patriot Act	N	10. CAFTA	N
3. FY06 Spending Curb	N	7. Bar Same Sex Marriage	N	11. Oppose Iraq Withdrawal	N
4. Drilling in ANWR	N	8. Stem Cell Research $	N	12. Detainee Tribunals	N

Election Results

2006 general	James Oberstar (DFL)	180,670	(64%)	($1,422,123)
	Rod Grams (R)	97,683	(34%)	($546,121)
	Other	5,663	(2%)	
2006 primary	James Oberstar (DFL)	unopposed		
2004 general	James Oberstar (DFL)	228,586	(65%)	($972,916)
	Mark Groettum (R)	112,693	(32%)	($41,187)
	Other	9,204	(3%)	

Prior Winning Percentages: 2002 (69%); 2000 (68%); 1998 (66%); 1996 (67%); 1994 (66%); 1992 (59%); 1990 (73%); 1988 (75%); 1986 (73%); 1984 (67%); 1982 (77%); 1980 (70%); 1978 (87%); 1976 (100%); 1974 (62%).

The People		Race/Ethnic Origin	Ancestry	
Area size:	32,419 sq. mi.	94.6% White	German: 20.2%	Norwegian: 10.8%
Urban population:	37.4%	0.5% Black	Swedish: 9.6%	
Rural population:	62.6%	0.4% Asian	**2004 Presidential Vote**	
Pop. 2000:	614,935	2.5% Native Am.	Kerry (D) 191,228	(53%)
Pop. 2005 (est):	643,193	0.0% Hawaiian	Bush (R) 167,439	(46%)
Median income:	$37,911	1.0% Two+ races	Other 4,890	(1%)
Poverty status:	10.4%	0.0% Other	**2000 Presidential Vote**	
Military veterans:	16.2%	0.8% Hispanic Origin	Gore (D) 153,962	(49%)
			Bush (R) 136,884	(44%)
			Other 22,302	(7%)
			Cook Partisan Voting Index: D + 4	

Occupation   Blue collar: 28.9%   White collar: 52.9%   Gray collar: 18.2%

In the 1860s, prospectors in the Arrowhead region of the new state of Minnesota, northwest of Lake Superior in the low hills of the Mesabi Range, happened upon the nation's largest veins of iron ore; they moved on, looking for gold. But in the 1880s, Duluth banker George Stone and Philadelphia financier Charlemagne Tower started mining the Iron Range and created the northern end of the lifeline of American heavy industry. South from the Range run rail lines to the port of Duluth, nestled on dramatic bluffs over the always cold and, for long months every winter, frozen waters of Lake Superior—one of the most beautiful settings for a city in North America, and there is similar beauty on the North Shore of Lake Superior for the 150 miles from Duluth to the Canadian border. Duluth was a grain-shipping rival of Chicago and the premier iron ore port. Its city plan was drawn up by Daniel Burnham and its splendid turn-of-the-century buildings still celebrate the triumph of technology and civilization over wilderness and the elements. Millions of tons of ore have been dug out of the Range, loaded into rail cars for the ride to Duluth, and into Great Lakes freighters for shipment to Cleveland, Gary, Detroit, Chicago, Pittsburgh and Buffalo.

For most of the last century, in this land where the Arctic winds blow down over the Canadian Shield's thousands of inland lakes, about 100,000 people have lived on the Iron Range and another 100,000 in Duluth, most of them the products of America's 1880-1924 wave of immigration: Italians, Poles, Serbs and Croats, Jews, Swedes and Finns. In this punishing environment, they worked to the point of exhaustion, built solid houses with staunch central heating and wore layers of warm clothing to survive the winter: it got down to 54 below on the Range in January 2005. Life was rough: The work was hard, the hours long and the pay low. The churches, a separate one for each ethnic group, were the main community institutions. Living conditions improved vastly in the decades of great economic growth after World War II, but life remains rough-hewn today, and there is still economic distress. As iron mines and steel factories got more efficient they needed fewer workers; employment is well below its 1970s peak. As water fills abandoned open-pit mines and factories close and mines are shut down, the Iron Range looks bleaker. Duluth's population was down to 85,000 in 2005, and the Iron Range's was about the same. But all is not moribund. Northwest Airlines, with an $840 million investment from state government in 1993, built a repair facility in Duluth and a reservations center in the Iron Range. The port of Duluth still ships large quantities of grain, and in the late 1990s a new taconite and steelmaking factory was built—the first big new plant in more than 20 years. And up in Chisholm in the Range, Cleveland Cliffs, after settling a strike, announced a plant expansion in September 2004, the first one in these parts since the 1970s. There is a Greyhound Museum in Hibbing, where in 1914 an entrepreneur started transporting people in unsaleable open-air Hupmobiles, an enterprise that eventually became the Greyhound Bus Company. People here have made the best of the frozen climate: Nearby Eveleth boasts the world's longest hockey stick, 107 feet long, carved from aspen and aimed at a 700-pound puck; the severe winters of International Falls in Koochiching County have given rise to a cold weather testing industry—this is where automakers test a car's performance under extreme winter conditions.

The 8th Congressional District of Minnesota includes Duluth and the Iron Range, plus much of the north woods and lake country to the west and south; it moves all the way south to the boundaries of the Twin Cities metro area, to Isanti and Chisago Counties, where young families are building new homes near pleasant old lakeside towns. While the Iron Range grows only sluggishly, there has been vigorous population growth in the southern and western counties in the district, as young families move out farther from the Twin Cities core and older Minnesotans move farther north to enjoy life on the lakes. This district has been a bulwark of Minnesota's Democratic-Farmer-Labor Party since it was formed in 1944, and has been considered safely Democratic for years. But there are signs of change. The fast-growing counties in the south and west have trended toward Republicans, while Duluth and the Iron Range remain Democratic though issues like gun control and environmental restrictions have sometimes moved opinion toward the Republicans. George W. Bush lost the 8th District to Al Gore by only 49%-44%, a much smaller margin than his father's 60%-40% loss 12 years earlier. Bush campaigned on the Iron Range in July 2004 but the DFL came back some distance: John Kerry won here 53%-46%.

The congressman from the 8th District is Jim Oberstar, a Democrat first elected in 1974—"part scholar and part Iron Range street fighter, part pothole-filling ward healer and part workaholic," in the words of the *St. Paul Pioneer Press*—and chairman of the House Transportation and Infrastructure Committee. Oberstar grew up in the Iron Range city of Chisholm, where his father was an iron miner and union official, who sent him off to St. Thomas College with $2,500 saved in quarters at the Slovenian National Benefit Society; Oberstar has been known to sing polka songs in Slovenian at a House Democratic retreat. He studied French in college and in Belgium; for four years he was a civilian employee of the U.S. Naval Mission to Haiti, teaching French and Creole to Marines, and French and English to Haitians (he also speaks Serbo-Croatian, Italian and Spanish). Then, in 1963, at 29, he landed a job as chief of staff to Congressman John Blatnik in Washington: he has been working for the 8th District for more than four decades. When Blatnik retired in 1974, Oberstar won a primary over Tony Perpich, brother of Governor Rudy Perpich.

Oberstar's views are in the liberal Catholic tradition. He believes in an economically active government and has little faith in economic markets. He was long dubious about American military involvement abroad, especially in Central America, but favored the 1994 deployment in Haiti. He voted against the Iraq war resolution in October 2002 and has decried the results of U.S. intervention there since. He is an opponent of abortion and a backer of adoption, sponsoring bills to insure family and medical leave and dependent deductions for families in the process of adopting; when he first proposed a $1,500 adoption tax deduction in the 1970s he was laughed out of Ways and Means, but now, thanks in large part to his effort, there is a $5,000 tax credit.

From this North Country district, Oberstar has been a supporter of local hunting and fishing activities and of the steel industry. When normal trade relations with China came before the House, he tried to get an amendment of the 1974 trade act that would treat steel slab imports as a direct threat to taconite miners; when the administration wasn't interested, he voted against the bill. He was disappointed by George W. Bush's steel tariffs in March 2002, because imported semi-finished slab steel, which competes with Minnesota's taconite, was not subject to the 30% top duty until imports reached 5.4 million tons, 77% of previous levels.

From October 1995 to January 2007, Oberstar was ranking minority member on Transportation and Infrastructure—a position of real power. The committee has a long tradition of bipartisanship, and of sponsoring members' roads (and, since 1994, other transportation) projects; it has 75 members, the largest in the House and maybe the largest legislative committee anywhere. For six years Oberstar and Chairman Bud Shuster worked to make it more powerful than ever. Their great monument was the May 1998 TEA-21 transportation bill, with $217 billion in spending, including $10 billion in projects earmarked by members. Back when Oberstar's boss John Blatnik was chairman, the committee's power was threatened by an alliance of environmentalists and fiscal conservatives; by 1998 it was carrying all before it. Another reason: the 1991 ISTEA, of which 1998's TEA-21 was the reauthorization, included spending for mass transit, bicycle trails and pollution control research, at the option of states or House members. This has helped win the support of many liberals; Oberstar himself is a bicycling enthusiast, proud of logging 2,700 miles a year in Washington, Duluth, on the Range and in the Tour de Frog in St. Cloud. One special project is Safe Routes to School, grants for sidewalks, bike paths and safe crossings to encourage kids to walk to school; Oberstar had relentlessly pushed for more and has pushed spending up from an initial $20 million to $612 million over five years in 2006. The purpose is to encourage fitness and reduce childhood obesity. "I would say in time it will be the best thing I've ever done." In April 2004 Oberstar and the new Transportation Chairman, Don Young, persuaded the House to pass a $275 billion, six year bill; the Senate in February 2004 passed a $318 billion bill. The White House insisted on capping spending at $256 billion, and the result was that no bill was passed in 2003 and 2004. Oberstar and Young were unfazed. In March 2005, after Bush threatened to veto a bill calling for more than $284 billion, the House passed a bill for that amount by a vote of 417–9. Finally, in July 2005 both houses passed a $286 billion act, with $24 billion for more than 6,000 earmarked projects and Bush signed it two weeks later. He defended the earmarks when they came under criticism. "They were part of the committee record for everybody to see. They weren't put in at midnight." And he defended Don Young's "bridge to nowhere." "That was his determination," said Oberstar. "It came out of Alaska's allocation, not out of the general revenues of the federal government."

Oberstar once chaired Transportation's Aviation Subcommittee and remains involved in aviation issues. He was one of the architects of the airline bailout bill in fall 2001 and strongly pushed for federal employees in airport security. He worked hard for the state investment in Northwest Airlines, but criticized the company when it cut jobs in Duluth below the agreed on level in early 2004; by December most of the jobs were restored. Despite Northwest's Minnesota presence, he came out in December 2006 for awarding a new route to China to United, flying out of Washington, rather than Northwest, flying out of Detroit. In June 2006 the House adopted an Oberstar amendment by 291-137 to continue barring foreign companies from owning more than 25% of U.S. airline stock. In November 2006 he came out against plans backed by the Bush administration and many airlines to fund the FAA entirely on user fees based on miles flown, with a quasi-governmental commission making spending decisions on air traffic control management and other matters. "There are some functions government must undertake in the public interest." After a 70-year-old bicyclist left his vintage Raleigh in a Minneapolis-St. Paul airport terminal and maintenance personnel destroyed it, Oberstar called for bicycle parking spaces in airports and said he would insert "bicycle storage" grants in the next FAA authorization. After JetBlue left dozens of passenger-filled planes on the ground for 10 hours in February 2007, Oberstar called for hearings on flight delays.

The 2005 transportation act included $495 million in earmarks in Minnesota, about one-quarter in the 8th District, and overall a 41% increase in federal aid. But not all of it has been spent as he would like. He was angered when Governor Tim Pawlenty vetoed a gas tax increase and in February 2007 he urged the legislature, with both houses controlled by the DFL, to raise it. Since 2001 he has worked to upgrade U.S. 53, which runs from Duluth through the Iron Range to the Canadian border. He succeeded in getting a dangerous interchange and railroad overpass rebuilt. But the state DOT has been unwilling to spend the $50 million he earmarked to widen 20 miles north of the Iron Range to four lanes and to add passing lanes in the remaining 70 miles to the Canadian border at International Falls. He was aroused particularly by the account of a former aide who witnessed a fatal crash on the road in the 1990s. "People in greater Minnesota have a right to live and have safe highways, and if the state DOT won't see to those needs, then I am their state representative and I am going to take care of them, by God." On another issue, he has called for more dredging of the Great Lakes, since lake levels have fallen in recent years, and called for a new fleet of short ships on the Great Lakes.

Oberstar won tough primaries in 1980 and 1984, the latter after briefly running for the Senate. Oberstar's one political setback came in 1984, when he ran for the Senate but was denied endorsement by the liberal DFL convention. In the 8th District he has been re-elected by very wide margins; longtime DFL voters may be moving away from Democrats higher up on the ticket, but they remain faithful to Oberstar. Former 6th District Congressman and one-term Senator Rod Grams, a resident of Isanti County in the southern part of the district, challenged him in 2006 and ran slightly better than other Republicans, but Oberstar won 64%-34%, carrying every county. He is the longest-serving member of Congress from Minnesota ever.

★ MISSISSIPPI ★

Mississippi, burdened with a tragic history, has been taking quickening steps toward the future—and quickly got up off the ground and started rebuilding after the central force of Hurricane Katrina hit the Gulf Coast. This green land was settled in a rush in Jacksonian America, mostly by small farmers heading west from Georgia and south from Tennessee—and also by a few big planters, who made and sometimes lost vast fortunes, built grand mansions and sent their sons to fight in the Civil War. For a century afterward, as planters and engineers drained the Delta lands, Mississippi with its racial segregation, subsistence farmers and sharecroppers and low wages, lived apart from most of America. Faulkner's Mississippi never knew the Homestead Act, the giant factories, the rushes of immigration, the rise of suburbs that were the indispensable backdrop of most of 20th century American life. Mississippi never developed great cities—its two commercial metropolises are just outside its borders, Memphis and New Orleans. But if it did not excel at commerce, it did produce great art. Mississippi gave us the music of the blues and Elvis Presley. It gave the world William Faulkner and Eudora Welty, Walker Percy and Shelby Foote; the state with the highest illiteracy rate has also produced the most Pulitzer Prizes for literature. Their work was informed by a sense of the tragic missing or forgotten in most of America, where life is a triumphant sales pitch or a labor-saving invention. For years no other state had such a painful contrast between image and reality, between an ideal sincerely strived for and the tawdry facts of everyday life. Magnolia trees on the lawns of antebellum mansions, golden-haired young women in white dresses on the veranda, faithful black servants and retainers: This was once the ideal. And behind it stood loose-jointed frame houses and unpainted back-country stores, cabins without indoor plumbing and poor white crossroads clustered with askew advertising signs. As David Sansing writes, "We at one time have the scent of magnolias and the smell of burning crosses."

Today Mississippi still ranks 49th or 50th on many scales, but the gulf between Mississippi and the rest of America has narrowed enormously. In 1940, Mississippi had an economy based on low-wage, subsistence or sharecropper agriculture and a system of racial segregation enforced often by violence. If history is, as Sir Henry Maine wrote, the story of the progress from status to contract, then old Mississippi was still at the beginning, for status—race—meant just about everything. In the years since, Mississippi has moved, not always willingly, from status to contract, in its economy and in race relations. Per capita income in Mississippi was 36% of the national average in 1940; in 1990 it was 67% and in 2005 it was 73%, well below average but, given the lower cost of living here, a level recognizably American. Most Mississippians of 50 years ago would be astonished by the physical comforts and mechanical marvels their grandchildren take for granted today: Nearly every classroom in the state is air-conditioned and is being wired to the Internet. They would be astonished as well by relations between whites and blacks, who are 36% of the population, the highest of any state. As Mississippi native William Raspberry wrote in the Washington Post, "There is an easiness to relationships, a mutual respect and a willingness to move beyond race that, quite frankly, didn't exist during my years in the state. Mississippi is finally a good place to be." Forty years ago, blacks held no public offices in Mississippi; now the state has more black elected officials than any other, including 47 of 174 state legislators; black mayors have been elected in Vicksburg, Jackson, Hattiesburg, Greenville and Natchez. The Mississippi traditions of friendliness and courtesy seem to be trumping the historical tradition of racism: Mississippi may rank 50th in per capita income, but for a decade it has ranked number one or two in charitable giving. Mississippi has not forgotten the past, and in April 2001 65% of voters chose to retain the Confederate battle cross in the state flag. But prosecutors have also hunted down the KKK members who killed civil rights activists in the 1960s: one was convicted in June 2005 and another charged in January 2007. Governor Haley Barbour joined Jackson state Senator Hillman Frazier in support of building a Mississippi civil rights museum.

Mississippi's economy once depended on cotton; now its growth comes from other things. Manufacturing jobs have declined here, as elsewhere, in recent years, but northeast Mississippi around Tupelo remains the center of the nation's upholstered furniture industry, and there has been rapid growth along the new Interstate 22 from Tupelo to the fast-growing suburbs of DeSoto County just south of Memphis. Growth has also been rapid around the $1.4 billion Nissan auto plant opened in May 2003 in Canton, just north of Jackson, attracted by $363 million in state aid and incentives, with 4,000 jobs and thousands more from nearby suppliers, building 278,000 vehicles a year. Highland Colony Parkway heading north from Jackson in Madison County and Lakeland Drive heading east into Rankin County have become boom areas. In February 2007 Toyota announced

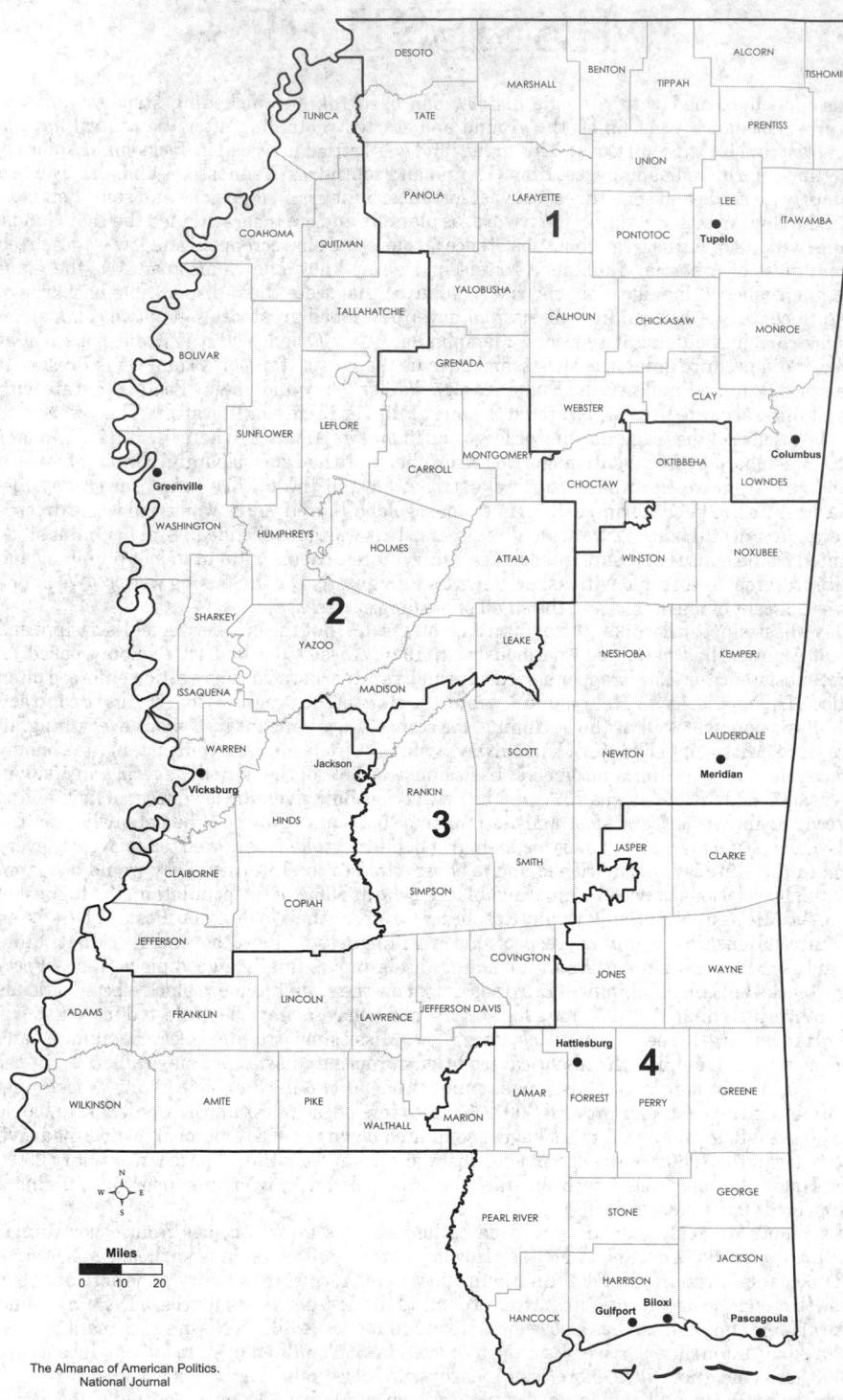

The Almanac of American Politics.
National Journal

Congressional district boundaries were first effective for 2002.

that it would build a new plant in Blue Springs, 10 miles northwest of Tupelo, with 2,000 jobs, to produce 150,000 Highlanders a year starting in 2010. That state offered $296 million in incentives and a sales pitch by Governor Haley Barbour, as described by a Toyota official: "He described to me the character and the resiliency of the folks who were involved in the Katrina disaster and it showed a strength of character where they came together and helped each other in a way that obviously makes the workforce very desirable." Other sources of growth: Northrop Grumman's huge shipyard in Senator Trent Lott's hometown of Pascagoula and the Richton salt dome, which is being developed for the Strategic Petroleum Reserve at a cost of $1 billion, generating 1,000 jobs.

Then there is gambling. Mississippi approved gambling in 1990, and in 1992 riverboat and dockside casinos started to open. Big gambling companies built some 29 casinos, 9 in once-impoverished Tunica County, just south of Memphis, 12 on the Gulf Coast and the rest scattered along the Mississippi River, all technically on boats and barges but tied to land. Mississippi is number three in gambling revenue, behind Nevada and New Jersey; gambling has produced 40,000 service jobs, at above-average wages, and some $500 million in state revenues a year. Then in August 2005 Hurricane Katrina struck the Gulf Coast. The main force of the hurricane was directed at Hancock County, Mississippi, not New Orleans, and the towns of Waveland, Bay St. Louis and Pass Christian were totally wiped out. In a few hours waves up to 55 feet destroyed one-quarter of the structures in Biloxi and Gulfport; the homes of Congressman Gene Taylor in Bay St. Louis and Senator Trent Lott in Pascagoula, the latter more than a century old, were totally swept away, as were many houses a quarter mile away from the Gulf. Floodwaters swept 10 miles inland. Some casinos, connected to the shore by plankways, were utterly destroyed and others severely damaged. Federal emergency plans rest on the assumption that local officials and first responders will cope for the first three days, but city halls were without power and the roads to hospitals blocked by felled trees. In New Orleans many first responders fled; in Mississippi they went to work, on 24-hour shifts and with Barbour quickly taking charge. Biloxi Mayor A. J. Holloway later described his people's response. "Our people have been good, too. You know, they shed some tears, work a little bit, cry again and go back to work. We're not sitting on our behinds and waiting for someone to give us a hand."

Recovery was helped by federal money secured by the Mississippi delegation, and it did not hurt that Senator Thad Cochran was chairman of the Appropriations Committee. Barbour administered grants and low interest loans to home and business owners who suffered uninsured losses, even as FEMA shelled out $1.8 billion for National Flood Insurance Program claims. In September and October, as the closed casinos were costing the state $500,000 a day in revenue, the state House and Senate changed the gambling law to allow casinos to be built on land within 800 feet of the shore. The casino owners moved in rapidly to rebuild and some did groundbreaking for new casinos. Hispanic workers streamed in to clean up the damage and work on new construction. By June 2006 the state had gained 30,000 jobs over 2005 and wages were up, despite Katrina; many of the casinos were back in business, generating state revenue. Developers made plans for gentrifying what used to be low-income Gulf Coast neighborhoods.

Politically, Mississippi is increasingly a Republican state, carried by Republicans in the last seven presidential elections. Republicans have held both U.S. Senate seats since John Stennis retired in 1988 and have generally done well in House elections. But Mississippi Democrats with good old boy personas can be competitive, like Gene Taylor who was elected in the heavily Republican Gulf Coast House seat in 1989 and has won by wide margins ever since. In 2002 Haley Barbour returned to Yazoo City, where he had always kept a home during a career as a Washington lobbyist and Republican national chairman during the first Clinton term, to run against Democratic Governor Ronnie Musgrove. One big issue was tort law. By 2002 the state had become a trial lawyer's paradise, with seven product liability judgments of $100 million or more in six years; medical malpractice lawsuits raised insurance premiums so much that 73 doctors left the state, an obstetric clinic in the Delta closed down temporarily and there was only one neurosurgeon left on the Gulf Coast. Hundreds of cases were brought in tiny, impoverished Jefferson County where juries awarded huge judgments; there were more plaintiffs in court than the county had people. Musgrove, though supported by trial lawyers, called a special session of the legislature in September 2002 which placed some limits on medical malpractice and product liability cases and on forum-shopping. Barbour promised more and won 53%-46%. Barbour called a special session in May 2004 and in June signed a bill capping pain and suffering damages generally to $1 million and to $500,000 in medical malpractice cases, further limiting forum-shopping and protecting "innocent sellers" of faulty products.

In August 2005, before Katrina hit, Barbour's positive job rating in a SurveyUSA poll was 43%. In September it zoomed to 58% and up through November 2006 it averaged 55% in monthly

SurveyUSA polls. There was a clear contrast here with Louisiana, where Governor Kathleen Blanco's job rating zoomed downward in September 2005 and stayed there, to the point that she declined to seek a second term. Barbour, also approaching a 2007 election, seemed in much better political shape. He took credit for converting a $700 million deficit to a $70 million surplus by cutting spending requests. Republicans seem to be on the rise as well in state politics. In 2003 Tim Ford, the Democratic Speaker of the House for 16 years, retired, and Lieutenant Governor Amy Tuck, who presides over the Senate, switched to the Republican party in December 2002. In January 2007, Republicans trailed Democrats 27-25 in the state Senate but after two Democrats switched parties, Republicans led 27-25 going into the 2007 election. However, Democrats still led (75-47) in the state House.

The People		Race/Ethnic Origin			Military veterans: 249,431 (12.0%)	
Pop. 2006 (est):	2,910,540	1,727,908	60.7%	White	WWII: 18.7%	Korea: 13.5%
Pop. 2000:	2,844,658	1,028,473	36.2%	Black	Vietnam: 31.0%	Gulf War: 13.1%
Pop. 1990:	2,573,216	18,349	0.6%	Asian	**Most populous cities (2006):**	
Change 1990-2000:	Up 10.5%	11,224	0.4%	Native Am.	1. Jackson	176,614
% of U.S. total:	1.0%	569	0.0%	Hawaiian	2. Gulfport	64,316
Pop. rank:	31st of 50	17,272	0.6%	Two+ races	3. Hattiesburg	45,202
Area size:	48,430 sq. mi.	1,294	0.0%	Other	4. Biloxi	44,342
State Native:	74.3%	39,569	1.4%	Hisp. Origin	5. Southaven	41,295
Non-citizen:	0.8%	**Ancestry**				
Language		USA: 12.7%		Irish: 6.1%	Urban population: 48.8%	
English: 94.4%	Spanish: 3.1%	English: 5.4%		German: 4.1%	Rural population: 51.2%	
Other Eur.: 1.6%		French: 2.1%				

Education		Work Sector		Legislature	
H.S. Grad:	72.9%	Private: 75.6%	Govt: 17.6%	Senate	27 R 25 D
College Grad:	16.9%	Self: 6.4%	Family: 0.4%	House	75 D 47 R
Industry		Unemployment: 7.3%		Legislative Term Limits: No	
Agri: 3.4%	Con: 7.6%	**Household Income**		**Registered Voters**	
Fin: 4.8%	Info: 1.8%	<15k: 24.9%	15-35k: 29.9%	No party registration	
Mfg: 23.7%	Prof: 25.3%	35-50k: 16.4%	50-100k: 22.8%		
Public: 5.1%	Trade: 15.2%	100-150k: 3.9%	>150k: 2.2%		
Other: 13.1%		Median: $31,330			
Occupation		Poverty status: 19.9%			
Blue collar: 31.6%	White collar: 52.3%	**Home Value**			
Gray collar: 16.1%		<50k: 36.4%	50-100k: 38.9%	100-200k: 19.1%	200-300k: 3.7%
		300-500k: 1.3%	>500k: 0.7%	Median: $64,700	

Presidential politics   Mississippi voted 59%-40% for George W. Bush in 2004—almost the same as his 58%-41% margin four years before or his father's 60%-39% margin in 1988. There is no way of avoiding the conclusion that this is a racially polarized electorate: whites voted 85%-14% for Bush, blacks 90%-10% for John Kerry. White evangelical or born again Protestants made up 48% of the electorate and voted 88%-12% for Bush. Yet it should also be said that few Mississippi whites yearn for a return of racial segregation; they line up with Republicans on a whole raft of other issues—defense, crime, cultural attitudes, taxes—just as most blacks line up with Democrats on the same issues. And on some issues they are on the same page: whites voted 89% and blacks 77% for a constitutional amendment banning same-sex marriage in November 2004.

Mississippi holds a presidential primary on Southern Super Tuesday, which fell on March 9 in

2004 Presidential Vote
Bush (R)	684,981	(59%)
Kerry (D)	457,766	(40%)
Nader (Ref)	3,175	(0%)
Other	6,223	(1%)

2004 Democratic Presidential Primary
Kerry (D)	59,815	(78%)
Edwards (D)	5,582	(7%)
Sharpton (D)	3,933	(5%)
Dean (D)	1,997	(3%)
Clark (D)	1,878	(2%)
Other	3,093	(4%)

2000 Presidential Vote
Bush (R)	572,844	(58%)
Gore (D)	404,614	(41%)
Nader (Green)	8,122	(1%)
Other	8,604	(1%)

2004, one week after the race for the Democratic nomination was over. In 2008, the state will hold its presidential primary on March 11, long after the rest of the South has voted.

Congressional districting   Mississippi lost one of its five House districts in the 2000 Census; this is the first time Mississippi has had just four congressmen since the 1840s. In 2001 Democrats held the governorship and both houses of the legislature, and one might have expected that they would draw a plan ousting one of the state's two Republican congressmen. But the state House, led by Speaker Tim Ford, and the state Senate, led by Lieutenant Governor Amy Tuck, could not agree on a plan. Ford wanted to draw a plan connecting northeast Mississippi, home of Republican incumbent Roger Wicker, and DeSoto County, just south of Memphis, with part of Rankin County, just east of Jackson and home of Republican incumbent Chip Pickering. Republicans called this the "tornado district" because it was shaped something like a funnel cloud. This plan would leave Pickering with the choice of running against Wicker in a primary where he would be at a great geographic disadvantage or running in a new 3d District against incumbent Democrat Ronnie Shows in a district that was 38% black. Tuck (who in December 2002 switched parties and became a Republican), Republicans and northeast Mississippians in the Senate favored a plan that would combine most of the old 3d and 4th Districts, represented by Pickering and Shows and would be 34% black. Governor Ronnie Musgrove called a special session in November 2001, and on the first day, the Senate and House passed versions of Ford's and Tuck's plans. Negotiations for a compromise went nowhere, and Ford moved to adjourn the session.

| 110th Congress Lineup |
| 2 D   2 R |
| 109th Congress Lineup |
| 2 D   2 R |

Action shifted to the courts. Democrats filed a lawsuit in state court and Republicans filed one in federal court. The Mississippi Supreme Court left the Democrats' case to Hinds County Chancery Judge Patricia Wise, elected from a heavily Democratic district. On December 21 she adopted a plan put forward by Democrats with a 38% black 3d District. On December 26 Attorney General Mike Moore forwarded it to the U.S. Justice Department for the preclearance required by the Voting Rights Act. On January 15, the three-judge federal court in the case brought by Republicans took the issue away from the Chancery Court on the ground that the Justice Department might not finish its review by Mississippi's March 1 filing deadline; the federal judges put forward a plan with a 30% black 3d District, similar to the state Senate's. On February 14 the Justice Department sent a five-page letter to Mississippi officials asking them to "explain the state's view of the legal basis for the Mississippi Supreme Court to vest a chancery court with jurisdiction to create and implement a statewide redistricting plan." Democrats complained that that was not an issue pertinent to the Voting Rights Act and that the three federal judges, all appointed by Republican presidents, were improperly trying to impose a plan favoring Pickering, who is the son of federal Judge Charles Pickering, whose nomination to a federal appeals court judgeship was rejected on party lines by the Senate Judiciary Committee in March 2002. On February 25 the federal court ordered its own plan into effect; Supreme Court Justice Antonin Scalia rejected an emergency appeal by Democrats.

Democrats were furious. They claimed that DOJ dragged its feet during the preclearance process and that Scalia, a friend of the Pickering family, should have recused himself from the case. But the districts in the federal court plan were about as compact as possible given the state's geography and the imperative, which everyone agreed on, of retaining a black-majority 2d District. Democrats persisted in their appeal of the federal court decision even though it was obvious its lines would be in effect for the November 2002 election. On March 31, the Supreme Court ruled against their claim, holding that a federal court may impose a congressional redistricting plan when a state fails to properly enact its own plan.

Mississippi is not expected to lose a seat in the reapportionment following the 2010 Census, and Census population estimates suggest that the state's current districts could be redesigned to meet the equal population standard by just a minor tweaking of the lines. Democrat Gene Taylor's 4th District, very safe for him, would probably go Republican if he were not to run.

Governor

Haley Barbour (R)

Elected 2003, term expires Jan. 2008, 1st term; b. Oct. 22, 1947, Yazoo City; home, Yazoo City; Attended U. of MS; U. of MS, J.D. 1973; Presbyterian; married (Marsha).

Professional Career: State Dir., US Census Bureau, 1969-70; RNC Committeeman, 1984-98; Dir., White House Office of Political Affairs, 1985-87; CEO, Founder, Barbour, Griffith & Rogers, 1991-present; Chmn., RNC, 1993-97.

Office: State Capitol, P.O. Box 139, Jackson, 39205, 601-359-3150; Fax: 601-359-3741; Web site: www.governor.state.ms.us.

Election Results

2003 general	Haley Barbour (R)	470,404	(53%)
	Ronnie Musgrove (D)	409,787	(46%)
	Other	14,296	(2%)
2003 primary	Haley Barbour (R)	158,284	(83%)
	Mitch Tyner (R)	31,762	(17%)
1999 general	Ronnie Musgrove (D)	379,034	(50%)
	Mike Parker (R)	370,691	(49%)
	Other	14,213	(2%)

Haley Barbour was elected governor in 2003, only the second Republican to win the office since Reconstruction. He was born and grew up in Yazoo City in the Mississippi Delta. His father was a local lawyer who died of a heart attack when Haley was 2 years old, leaving his 31-year-old mother to raise the three Barbour boys. A star athlete and class valedictorian, Barbour was voted Mr. Yazoo High School and won scholarship money to attend Ole Miss but he left his senior year before graduating to take a job on Richard Nixon's 1968 campaign. He returned to Ole Miss and graduated from its law school in 1973; then he ran Gerald Ford's 1976 campaign in the Southeast and worked on John Connally's campaign for president in 1980. In 1982 he was the Republican nominee for Senate against Senator John C. Stennis, then the senior member of the Senate, a chairman of Armed Services from 1969-81 and later chairman of the Appropriations Committee. Stennis had not faced a serious challenge since 1947, when he was elected to replace Theodore G. Bilbo, and some expected that the octogenarian would not seek reelection in 1982. But he did and Barbour approached the issue of Stennis' advanced age gingerly. He ran with the slogan, "A senator for the '80s," knowing that it would remind voters that he was running against a senator who was actually in his 80s. The strategy didn't work; Stennis won 64%-36%, carrying 80 of 82 counties despite being outspent by Barbour. But at age 35, Barbour showed a sophisticated understanding of the nexus between money and politics: in what was then the most expensive race in state history, he raised and spent more than $1 million at a time when that amount could buy a great deal of attention in Mississippi.

It also got him noticed in Washington, where he became Ronald Reagan's White House political director in 1985 and later an adviser to George H.W. Bush's presidential campaign. In 1991 he took advantage of his Republican connections and hung out his own shingle, founding Barbour, Griffith & Rogers, now one of D.C.'s powerhouse lobbying firms; then he served as Republican National Committee chairman from 1993-97. He chaired the party when it won a congressional majority for the first time in 40 years and he shared in the credit. When he left the RNC and returned to his lobbying firm, he was positioned as one of Washington's most powerful lobbyists, well-connected to key members of the House and Senate and much sought-after by big corporate clients with interests before the Republican Congress.

In all his time in Washington, Barbour had maintained his ties back home. He served as a Republican national committeeman from 1984 until 1998 and regularly commuted back to Yazoo City where his wife and sons resided. He was approached in 2001 about running for governor and a year later announced he would challenge Governor Ronnie Musgrove in 2003.

Musgrove had been elected governor by the Mississippi House of Representatives in January 2000, after leading the popular vote in November 1999 by a 49.6%-48.5% margin. But winning the popular vote was not decisive under Mississippi law. The law said that if no candidate won a majority of the popular vote the winner would be determined by which candidate won the most state House districts. After the tedious tabulation, it appeared that 61 districts voted for Musgrove and 61 for Parker. Under the 1890 law, the decision then went to the state House of Representatives, where Democrats had a big margin. On January 4, 2000, Musgrove was finally elected by a margin of 86-36.

In his first legislative session, Musgrove achieved his biggest goal, a six-year, $338 million teacher pay raise, up to the Southeastern state average. The issue of the Mississippi flag was kindled in May 2000, when the state Supreme Court ruled that the flag, which features the Confederate battle cross in the upper left corner, was not legally the state flag, because the 1894 law authorizing it was not included in the full codification in state laws in 1906. Musgrove appointed a commission to design a new flag which he and four other statewide officials endorsed, but legislators decided to send the issue to voters in a referendum in April 2001. Most blacks and many business leaders support the new design, but there was vocal opposition from many whites, and many feared—or hoped—that a large majority of white voters would choose that in the privacy of the voting booth. The new flag design was defeated by a resounding 65%-35%.

The big issue of 2002 was the civil justice system. Mississippi had become a trial lawyers' paradise, with huge verdicts awarded by juries in tiny impoverished counties. Musgrove was supported by and generally friendly to trial lawyers. Musgrove vetoed a second time a bill opposed by trial lawyers capping damages from fraudulent lending. Meanwhile, there were newspaper reports that investigators were looking into allegations that two prominent trial lawyers Paul Minor and Richard Scruggs paid off debts owed by two judges and were looking into the pattern of Musgrove receiving big contributions from trial lawyers just before he made judicial appointments.

Musgrove's own survival was also in doubt. He was the last remaining Democratic governor in the Deep South after incumbents in Alabama, Georgia and South Carolina failed to win second terms in 2002. There was widespread speculation that he was seeking to be named president of Delta State University, rather than stand for reelection. Musgrove, though known for his hyperkinetic energy, seemed to lack a sense of urgency, raising money but not starting his campaign in earnest until a few months before the election. By that time, Barbour already had been touring the state for a year promising voters that he would use his Washington connections to help create jobs in Mississippi and had spent more than $2 million, much of it on television ads.

Musgrove won the August primary with 76% against four minor opponents; Barbour won 83%-17% against Mitch Tyner, a trial lawyer who pounded on him as a "fat cat" lobbyist and whose campaign created a website called WashingtonFatCat.com. Barbour ignored him; there was speculation that Tyner was a stalking horse for the trial lawyers lobby, which didn't like Barbour's calls for additional limits on civil lawsuits. Tyner denied it, but was revealed to be a donor to Musgrove's 1999 campaign.

Musgrove picked up where Tyner left off and both candidates sounded economic themes in the general election. "I've put Mississippi first. Haley Barbour has spent the last 20 years in Washington, D.C., putting special interests first," Musgrove said after winning the primary. He framed Barbour as an outsider who was closely tied to big tobacco and pharmaceutical companies. He called Barbour a "hired gun for Mexico" who lobbied for passage of NAFTA which, Musgrove said, cost Mississippi 41,000 jobs. Barbour denied lobbying for passage of NAFTA and said he didn't start lobbying for the Mexican government until 2000 or 2001, long after NAFTA had passed in 1993, and he focused only the issue of Mexican trucks entering the U.S.

In a September debate, Barbour claimed Musgrove mismanaged the state economy and wasn't serious enough about fixing the civil justice system. Musgrove responded that Barbour was "running down Mississippi, talking about what we haven't done and what we couldn't do. Now that may be the way they do it in Washington, but that's not the way we do it here." Musgrove said Mississippi was faring better than most states despite a weak national economy; he pointed to the opening of the new Nissan auto plant in Madison County and took credit for creating 56,000 new jobs across the state. Attending the debate, in the front row of the Barbour section, was Melanie Musgrove, from whom the governor got divorced in 2001 after 24 years of marriage. She left afterwards without answering questions; Ronnie Musgrove said he hadn't noticed her in the audience.

Musgrove sought to keep his distance from the national Democratic party. His television ads referred to him as an "independent conservative" but Barbour sought to remind voters of Musgrove's endorsement of Al Gore in 2000 by airing a commercial with footage of Gore and Musgrove embracing. Musgrove was not helped by Senate Democrats' October 2003 filibuster of the nomination of Mississippi Judge Charles Pickering to the 5th Circuit Court of Appeals. Musgrove publicly backed Pickering's nomination, and sent senators a letter urging them to confirm Pickering, who was criticized for his record on civil rights issues. Barbour, also a strong Pickering supporter, was no bystander: His D.C. lobbying firm was heavily involved in the campaign supporting Pickering's nomination.

The Democratic nominee for lieutenant governor, trial lawyer and state Senator Barbara Blackmon, was no asset either. In October Blackmon drew widespread criticism for signing a sworn statement saying she had never had an abortion and then challenging Lieutenant Governor Amy Tuck to sign a similar affidavit. Barbour attacked the "liberal" Musgrove-Blackmon "ticket," though in Mississippi both offices are elected separately. The state Republican party sent mailers featuring photos of the two candidates inside a valentine heart. Some Democrats called that a thinly-veiled appeal to racism since Blackmon is African-American; they pointed also to Republican use of the state flag issue against Musgrove.

Money was not a problem for either candidate: Barbour raised $10.6 million to Musgrove's $8.5 million, in what was the most expensive race in state history. Barbour won 53%-46%. He carried 51 of 82 counties and won big margins amid heavy turnout in key Republican counties like fast-growing DeSoto County, just south of Memphis, and suburban Rankin County, just east of Jackson. That offset high black voter turnout, which Democrats had counted on because of the presence of two African-American statewide nominees, Blackmon and state treasurer candidate Gary Anderson. Both lost; Blackmon by a wide 61%-37% margin and Anderson by a narrower 52%-47%. Exit polls (the first live run conducted for the National Election Pool in preparation for 2004) showed a racially polarized electorate: black voters went 94% for Musgrove and white voters went 77% for Barbour.

Barbour took office facing Democratic majorities in the House and Senate and said job creation was his top priority. He unveiled a budget that called for $709 million in spending cuts over 2 years, threatened to veto any new tax increases and proposed a package of comprehensive changes to the civil justice system that included a lowering of the caps on pain-and-suffering damages. Barbour called a special session in May 2004 and in June signed a bill capping pain and suffering damages generally to $1 million and to $500,000 in medical malpractice cases, further limiting forum-shopping and protecting "innocent sellers" of faulty products. He took credit for several economic development deals—a 500-job Textron Fastening Systems plant in Greenville and a 400-job FedEx Ground facility in Olive Branch. The legislature approved a nursing home bed tax increase to help fund the state's ailing Medicaid program but his attempt to cut rising costs by eliminating coverage for 50,000 recipients was stalled by a federal judge.

In 2005, he proposed cutting most agency budgets by 5%. The legislature failed to pass a budget in regular session but Barbour managed to address the state's Medicaid crisis by calling a special session in mid-March that restored the program to solvency by borrowing $240 million from the state's health care trust fund and instituting tighter restrictions on the number of prescriptions, emergency room visits and home health care visits. Barbour was not entirely forgotten in Washington. In November 2004, his office denied rumors he was under consideration for a Cabinet position under George W. Bush. And some Republicans listed him as a possible candidate for president in 2008.

Then came Hurricane Katrina. Katrina struck the Gulf Coast on August 29, 2005, causing what Barbour referred to as "nuclear destruction." The main force of the hurricane was directed at Hancock County, Mississippi, not New Orleans, and the towns of Waveland, Bay St. Louis and Pass Christian were totally wiped out. Some casinos were utterly destroyed while others suffered severe damage, costing the state $500,000 a day in revenue. The shrimping and shipbuilding industries were also disrupted by the extensive storm damage to the state's 90-mile coastline. All in all, 47 of the state's 82 counties were declared disaster areas.

In the days afterwards Barbour struggled to keep his emotions in check but quickly took charge and drew national notice for his decisive leadership. He quickly appointed a commission to coordinate the recovery, led by by former Netscape CEO Jim Barksdale. "We will rebuild bigger and better than ever," Barbour said. "It's going to take some time, and people have to be patient." The state's recovery was assisted by federal money secured by the powerful Mississippi congressional delegation, and it did not hurt that Senator Thad Cochran was chairman of the Appropriations Committee. Soon $5.1 billion was authorized for Mississippi, $3 billion of it for housing. Barbour administered grants and low interest loans to home and business owners who suffered uninsured losses, even as FEMA shelled out $2.4 billion for National Flood Insurance Program claims. The state House and Senate changed the gambling law to allow casinos to be built on land within 800 feet of the shore. The casino owners moved in rapidly to rebuild and some did groundbreaking for new casinos. By June 2006 the state had gained 30,000 jobs over 2005 and wages were up, despite Katrina; many of the casinos were back in business, generating state revenue. Developers made plans for gentrifying what used to be low-income Gulf Coast neighborhoods.

Mississippi's recovery efforts stood in contrast to neighboring Louisiana. While Barbour declined to criticize the federal government's response, Louisiana Democrats and the Bush administration battled to affix blame. Then Louisiana state officials stunned Congress by requesting a $250 billion package of spending and tax relief. Barbour pursued a strikingly different strategy for securing federal aid, working through back channels and stressing the importance of the private sector in the rebuilding effort. Here, Barbour's political connections in Washington paid off, as D.C. lobbyists and friends of the governor sent supplies in the first days following the hurricane and later assisted by holding fundraising events for the Mississippi Hurricane Recovery Fund, created by Barbour not long after Katrina landed.

In August 2005, before Katrina hit, Barbour's positive job rating in a SurveyUSA poll was 43%. In September it spiked to 58% and he remained above 50% for the rest of the year. In 2006, he was forced to delay release of his budget until March when he said there would be a better idea of how much federal aid was forthcoming. Twice he vetoed measures to raise the cigarette tax and lower the grocery tax, calling it a "risky tax swap." In July, touting his job creation efforts and fiscal restraint, Barbour announced the state's first budget surplus in years. "In just two budget years, we have gone from a deficit of $700 million to a surplus of approximately $70 million," he said.

In his 2007 State of the State address, Barbour told lawmakers, "There's no doubt in my mind that the future of Mississippi is brighter than it's ever been in our history. As strange as it might seem, that awful catastrophe Katrina is part of the reason." He might as well have been discussing his own political future. Though in February 2006 he made clear that he would not run for president in 2008 because hurricane recovery demanded his full attention, his post-Katrina leadership made him an even more attractive national candidate. He had been stockpiling dollars for his 2007 reelection campaign and began the year with $3.5 million. Democrats had no obvious top-tier candidate to run against him, but the party began running ads in January that criticized Barbour as a flip-flopper on education funding and for his opposition to eliminating the grocery tax. Barbour was taking no chances. He began running his own ads touting his record in February; he got a boost when not long afterwards Toyota announced it had chosen Tupelo as the site of a new 2,000-job assembly plant. The winner of the August Democratic primary was wealthy attorney John Arthur Eaves, whose father had run unsuccessfully for governor three times. Eaves, who had lost a bid for Congress himself, had run in the 2003 Democratic primary for governor but dropped out. In the Republican primary, Barbour won 93% against a little-known opponent.

Senior Senator

Thad Cochran (R)

Elected 1978, seat up 2008, 5th term; b. Dec. 7, 1937, Pontotoc; home, Jackson; U. of MS, B.A. 1959, J.D. 1965, Rotary Fellow, Trinity Col., Ireland, 1963-64; Baptist; married (Rose).

Military Career: Navy, 1959-61.

Elected Office: U.S. House of Reps., 1972-78.

Professional Career: Practicing atty., 1965-72.

DC Office: 113 DSOB, 20510, 202-224-5054; Fax: 202-224-9450; Web site: cochran.senate.gov.

State Offices: Gulfport, 228-867-9710; Jackson, 601-965-4459; Oxford, 662-236-1018.

Committees: *Agriculture, Nutrition & Forestry* (3d of 10 R): Production, Income Protection & Price Support; Nutrition and Food Assistance, Sustainable and Organic Agriculture & General Legislation; Rural Revitalization, Conservation, Forestry & Credit. *Appropriations* (RMM of 14 R): Homeland Security (RMM); Agriculture, Rural Development, Food and Drug Administration & Related Agencies; Defense; Energy & Water Development; Labor, Health and Human Services, Education & Related Agencies; Interior, Environment & Related Agencies. *Rules & Administration* (4th of 9 R).

Group Ratings

	ADA	ACLU	AFS	LCV	ITIC	NTU	COC	ACU	CFG	FRC
2006	10	8	13	14	100	65	92	67	56	87
2005	0	—	0	0	—	70	100	88	79	—

National Journal Ratings

	2005 LIB — 2005 CONS		2006 LIB — 2006 CONS	
Economic	6%	90%	36%	63%
Social	23%	64%	32%	67%
Foreign	0%	74%	36%	60%

Key Votes of the 109th Congress

1. Bar ANWR Drilling	N	5. Confirm Samuel Alito	Y	9. Limit Interstate Abortion	Y
2. FY06 Spending Curb	Y	6. Path to Citizenship	N	10. CAFTA	Y
3. Estate Tax Repeal	Y	7. Bar Same Sex Marriage	Y	11. Urge Iraq Withdrawal	N
4. Raise Minimum Wage	N	8. Stem Cell Research $	Y	12. Provide Detainee Rights	N

Election Results

2002 general	Thad Cochran (R)	533,269	(85%)	($1,453,688)
	Shawn O'Hara (Ref)	97,226	(15%)	
2002 primary	Thad Cochran (R)	unopposed		
1996 general	Thad Cochran (R)	624,154	(71%)	($1,305,680)
	James W. Hunt (D)	240,647	(27%)	
	Other	13,861	(2%)	

Prior Winning Percentages: 1990 (100%); 1984 (61%); 1978 (45%); 1976 House (76%); 1974 House (70%); 1972 House (48%)

Thad Cochran was elected to the House in 1972 and the Senate in 1978, where he sits at Jefferson Davis's old desk. He grew up in small towns in northern Mississippi and near Jackson, the son of a principal and a teacher, graduated with high grades from Ole Miss (where he was a cheerleader, which is a very big deal) and its law school, served in the Navy, spent a year abroad and practiced law in Jackson. In 1968 he worked on the Nixon-Agnew campaign in Mississippi, where Nixon ran third. Four years later, when Nixon was sweeping Mississippi, he ran for Congress and was elected as a Republican from the Jackson-area district with a plurality against a white Democrat and black independent. After three terms, he was ready to step down; when Senator James Eastland retired, Cochran jumped into the race and once again won with a plurality over a white Democrat and a black independent. In the House and in the Senate he has managed to amass a generally conservative record with little controversy or acrimony. His pleasant personal demeanor, his refusal to engage in racial politics and his Republican Party label, in a state where most whites have been voting Republican for president for three decades, have made him broadly acceptable to voters at home. His toughest race came in 1984, when he was opposed by popular former Governor William Winter. Winter could make a case for himself but not against Cochran; Cochran outraised him $2.7 million to $738,000, and won 61%-39%. In 2002 he had no Democratic opponent and won with 85% of the vote.

Cochran is the ranking minority member on the Appropriations Committee; from 2005 to 2007 he was chairman. He serves on the Defense Appropriations Subcommittee, where he has been a key proponent of missile defense, and he has worked to fund projects big and small which are based in Mississippi. Timely amendments to appropriations that make major policy are a Cochran specialty. In 2003 and 2004 Cochran chaired the new Homeland Security Subcommittee, which sharply increased spending over what the agencies in the new department had spent before. He got additional screening technologies for the TSA, accelerated funding of the Coast Guard's Deepwater long-term recapitalization program and worked for funding of NOAA research vessels. With ranking minority member Robert Byrd he secured Senate passage of the New Shippers Review, to help Customs and Border Protection collect anti-dumping and countervailing duties on imports from countries evading payment.

In January 2005 Cochran succeeded Ted Stevens as chairman of the full committee. "We're not going to have runaway spending on the Appropriations Committee when I'm chairman," he said. "I won't tolerate it." Stevens noted that "he's less confrontational, perhaps, more deliberate." Cochran said he would not encourage earmarks. "If it's not agreed upon by all who are concerned, then it doesn't get included in the bill. I'm not going to engage in a practice of putting things in bills without consultation with other senators." And he sought to tamp down expectations that he would provide for Mississippi as Stevens had for Alaska. "I think Mississippi can be assured that our needs will be carefully considered, but it will be a tough budget year, and I don't want to enlarge expectations too much." And he warned that some Mississippi military bases could end up on the 2005 base closing list, which indeed happened. In May 2005, the Pentagon recommended closing Pascagoula Naval Station, shrinking Keesler Air Force Base and redistributing airplanes from the 186th Refueling Wing at Key Field in Meridian. Cochran said he wanted to avoid omnibus bills in which multiple subcommittees' bills are rolled into one huge piece of legislation. "It's my plan to have us stay on a schedule that will cause us to pass 13 individual appropriation bills." Later, when the House Appropriations Committee reduced the number of its subcommittees from 13 to 10, the Senate committee reduced its number from 13 to 12, with jurisdictions congruent with those of the House panels. In June 2005 he allocated $843 billion to subcommittees, switching $7 billion from defense to domestic spending. The committee took action on 5 bills by June 24.

Then came Hurricane Katrina on August 29. Cochran viewed the devastation by helicopter on August 31. On September 1 he persuaded the Senate to vote $10.5 billion in disaster relief. A week later he persuaded it to vote for $51.8 billion more. In late October George W. Bush called for an additional $17 billion. Cochran, working closely with Governor Haley Barbour and with others in the Mississippi and Louisiana delegations, pushed for $35 billion, with Community Development Block Grants available for homeowners and business owners with uninsured losses. This was a new policy, suggested by Barbour and not included in the administration request. In early December he targeted Iraq reconstruction and Millennium Challenge Account funds for Katrina. On December 21, Congress passed a $29 billion package, with $11.5 billion for CDBG loans and grants. Mississippi received $5.1 billion of the CDBG funds—as Barbour said, "unprecedented amounts of money and unprecedented latitude in how we can spend that money." In the meantime, work on other appropriations continued. Cochran worked with House Chairman Jerry Lewis to avoid an omnibus bill but in December they resigned themselves to a continuing resolution for nine bills they couldn't pass. In 2006 Cochran worked to restore funds cut from the Coast Guard's Deepwater program. In February 2006, Bush asked for a supplemental bill with Iraq funding and $19.8 billion for Katrina recovery. The House voted $19 billion for the latter; Cochran sought as much as $27 billion. Cochran's bill included some controversial provisions: $700 million for building a CSX rail line inland, to replace the line on the Gulf Coast; $500 million for Northrop Grumman, which was in litigation with the insurers of its Pascagoula shipyard; $1 billion for Katrina cottages, 400-square-foot manufactured housing considered preferable to FEMA trailers; $176 million to rebuild the Gulfport Armed Services Retirement Home. The CSX line was labeled "the railroad to nowhere," but survived by 50-47 Tom Coburn's attempt to kill it. Speaker Dennis Hastert and House Majority Leader John Boehner called Cochran's bill a "special interest shopping cart." In June the conference committee agreed on a bill with $19.8 billion for Katrina recovery; the railroad was dropped, but remaining was $140 million for shipyard infrastructure, the Armed Services Retirement Home, repairs to the Stennis Space Center, $150 million for Gulf Coast fisheries and $4 million for community health center satellite phones.

On the regular appropriations, Cochran again worked to avoid an omnibus bill. All 12 appropriations were approved by the committee by July 21, the first time in 18 years they were all passed before the August recess. They included some policy changes: lifting some restrictions on flights out of Dallas's Love Field, barring banks from the real estate business, lifting the ban on agricultural sales to Cuba and raising the mandatory retirement age for pilots to 65, but continuing the limits on foreign ownership of U.S. airlines. The appropriations ran into trouble in September. The defense and homeland security appropriations were passed by both houses in late September and the homeland security appropriation in early October. But there were objections to the 10 others by opponents of congressional earmarks and critics of high government spending. Majority Leader Bill Frist declined to bring the appropriations to the floor before the November election. Then Democrats won majorities in both houses, and on November 17, when a continuing resolution expired, Frist and other leaders decided to pass another and not try to bring either the individual appropriations or an omnibus forward. Democrats said the Republicans were feckless. Cochran said, "I'm terribly disappointed with the failure of this Congress to have passed the spending bills. The judgment was wrong." In the 110th Congress he is the ranking minority member on Appropriations and on its Homeland Security Subcommittee, positions of considerable influence since business on Appropriations is usually conducted on a bipartisan basis.

On the Agriculture Committee Cochran played an important role in shaping the very different 1996 and 2002 farm bills. In 1996 he supported the move to phase out most crop subsidies over seven years, but insisted on maintaining the cotton marketing loan plan that he largely wrote in 1985. In

2002 he supported the strategy of reviving annual crop payments through the marketing loan program and the target price mechanism, which was abolished in 1996, and of vastly increasing the Conservation Reserve Program to provide money for producers of non-program crops, thus producing more support for the bill. The bill also required country-of-origin labeling for beef, pork, lamb and fish—the last being very important for Mississippi's big catfish farm industry; Cochran has worked hard to get the Senate to prevent a similar Vietnamese fish from being labeled catfish. After the bill passed Cochran argued that it was weaning farmers from subsidies. In January 2003 Cochran moved swiftly to fashion a $3.1 billion drought relief measure, about half the size of Tom Daschle's, which spread money not just to the drought-stricken Great Plains but to most of the South, with special aid for tobacco and catfish producers; he got it into the omnibus appropriation with a coalition of all Republicans and seven southern Democrats. In 2004 he pushed through reauthorization of nutrition programs like WIC and the school lunch program, providing more access to the poor. In November 2005 he defeated 53-46 Charles Grassley's move to limit farm subsidies to $250,000. "You just can't change the rules from one year to the next and expect to have a dependable source of revenue to sustain an economy, a farm economy that is so important to the nation." In February 2006 he opposed the Bush budget's 5% cut in farm subsidies and called for more disaster aid. Over the years he has built up a National Writing Project, to instruct teachers how to teach writing; for only $21.5 million it sends 137,000 teachers to summer programs on 197 campuses.

Going into the 110th Congress, Cochran and Trent Lott had combined congressional service of 68 years; both were first elected to the House in 1972. Their relations have not always been harmonious. They clashed over judgeships and vied for White House favor in the 1980s and mixed it up in leadership fights in the 1990s. In 1990 Cochran challenged the more moderate John Chafee of Rhode Island for the chairmanship of the Senate Republican Conference, the number three leadership position, and won 22-21. When Lott challenged Alan Simpson for majority whip, the number two position, Cochran pointedly endorsed Simpson; Lott won anyway, with the support of junior conservatives, and thus leapfrogged Cochran. When Bob Dole announced in May 1996 that he would resign from the Senate in June, Cochran and Lott both entered the race for majority leader; Lott had the contest sewed up, but Cochran stayed in and lost 44–8. In January 2001, Cochran appeared by John McCain's side as a new cosponsor of the latest version of the McCain-Feingold campaign finance bill; this had been strongly opposed by Lott, and Cochran's vote made the bill apparently filibuster-proof. It gave McCain leverage in his drive to get it early consideration. But Cochran spoke sympathetically about Lott after he relinquished the majority leadership in December 2002. They seem to have worked smoothly together in responding to Hurricane Katrina and with the two very different and very much less senior Louisiana senators, Democrat Mary Landrieu and Republican David Vitter, as well. In March 2007 Lott sponsored a bill naming the new Jackson federal courthouse after Cochran.

Cochran holds what seems to be one of the safest seats in the Senate. In 1990 he was unopposed and in 1996 he was reelected 71%-27%. In 2002 he beat a Reform party candidate 85%-15%. He comes up for reelection in 2008. In December 2006 some wondered whether he would run again; he had built a lakefront house near Oxford and hadn't raised much money. In August 2007, a spokeswoman said Cochran was planning to seek reelection and was expected to make his official announcement in November.

On February 8, 2007, he became the 28th senator to have cast a 10,000th vote, something which he had not noticed but for which Robert Byrd organized a celebration on the floor. Cochran is considered a shoo-in if he runs. If he doesn't, Republican Congressmen Chip Pickering, who announced he would not run for reelection to the House in 2008, or Roger Wicker might run. Mentioned as possible Democratic candidates were former Attorney General Mike Moore and former Governor Ronnie Musgrove; Democratic Congressman Gene Taylor said he would prefer to stay in the House.

Junior Senator

Trent Lott (R)

Elected 1988, seat up 2012, 4th term; b. Oct. 9, 1941, Grenada; home, Pascagoula; U. of MS, B.A. 1963, J.D. 1967; Baptist; married (Tricia).

Elected Office: U.S. House of Reps., 1972-88.

Professional Career: Practicing atty., 1967-68; A.A., U.S. Rep. William Colmer, 1968-72.

DC Office: 487 RSOB, 20510, 202-224-6253; Fax: 202-224-2262; Web site: lott.senate.gov.

State Offices: Gulfport, 228-863-1988; Jackson, 601-965-4644; Oxford, 662-234-3774; Pascagoula, 228-762-5400.

Committees: *Commerce, Science & Transportation* (3d of 11 R): Aviation Operations, Safety & Security (RMM); Space, Aeronautics & Related Sciences; Oceans, Atmosphere, Fisheries & Coast Guard; Surface Transportation & Merchant Marine Infrastructure, Safety & Security; Consumer Affairs, Insurance & Automotive Safety. *Finance* (3d of 10 R): Taxation & IRS Oversight & Long-Term Growth; Social Security, Pensions & Family Policy; Energy, Natural Resources & Infrastructure. *Rules & Administration* (5th of 9 R).

Group Ratings

	ADA	ACLU	AFS	LCV	ITIC	NTU	COC	ACU	CFG	FRC
2006	5	17	13	0	100	76	92	88	71	87
2005	5	—	0	0	—	70	100	91	80	—

National Journal Ratings

	2005 LIB	—	2005 CONS		2006 LIB	—	2006 CONS
Economic	11%	—	88%		31%	—	68%
Social	0%	—	77%		27%	—	72%
Foreign	0%	—	74%		18%	—	76%

Key Votes of the 109th Congress

1. Bar ANWR Drilling	N	5. Confirm Samuel Alito	Y	9. Limit Interstate Abortion	Y
2. FY06 Spending Curb	Y	6. Path to Citizenship	N	10. CAFTA	Y
3. Estate Tax Repeal	Y	7. Bar Same Sex Marriage	Y	11. Urge Iraq Withdrawal	N
4. Raise Minimum Wage	N	8. Stem Cell Research $	Y	12. Provide Detainee Rights	N

Election Results

2006 general	Trent Lott (R)	388,399	(64%)	($2,088,465)
	Erik Fleming (D)	213,000	(35%)	($38,495)
	Other	9,522	(2%)	
2006 primary	Trent Lott (R)	unopposed		
2000 general	Trent Lott (R)	654,941	(66%)	($3,663,052)
	Troy Brown (D)	314,090	(32%)	($40,349)
	Other	25,113	(3%)	

Prior Winning Percentages: 1994 (69%); 1988 (54%); 1986 House (82%); 1984 House (85%); 1982 House (79%); 1980 House (74%); 1978 House (100%); 1976 House (68%); 1974 House (73%); 1972 House (55%)

Trent Lott, Senate Majority Leader from June 1996 until June 2001 and Minority Leader from then until January 2003, was first elected to the House in 1972 and to the Senate in 1988. He grew up in Pascagoula, the son of a shipyard worker and a teacher, went to Ole Miss (where he was a cheerleader, like his Mississippi colleague Thad Cochran) and worked his way through law school by running the Ole Miss alumni affairs office, accumulating good contacts along the way. After a year of law practice, he got a job with Democratic Gulf Coast Congressman William Colmer, chairman of the House Rules Committee, who was from his hometown and served in the House for 40 years. When Colmer retired in 1972, Lott ran for the House seat with Colmer's encouragement and endorsement—as a Republican. He was elected with 55% in what was the strongest Nixon district in the country that year. In 1974, Lott was the youngest member of the Judiciary Committee, loyally defending Richard Nixon in the impeachment hearings. In 1980, he was elected Republican whip, and he ran the Republican National Convention's platform committees in 1980 and

1984. In the House he was an ally of Jack Kemp and Newt Gingrich. He supported Kemp for president in 1988, and his decision to run for the Senate that year opened the way for Gingrich's rise: Lott was succeeded as whip by Dick Cheney; when Cheney became Defense secretary in March 1989, Gingrich was elected whip 87-85.

There is a discernible hard core of beliefs in Lott's career, and yet he is less a hard-edged ideologue than an instinctive deal-maker, not much interested in quixotic gestures, an orderly and well-organized man who is dismayed by the dilatoriness of others. As one colleague put it in 2001, "After pork, Trent's default position is conservative—but he likes to compromise." His beliefs are reminiscent of the mostly unarticulated beliefs of the coalition of Southern conservative Democrats and small-town conservative Northerners which had controlled the House for most of the 35 years prior to when he arrived there: Against increased taxes, hostile to federal regulation of business and local government, for an assertive foreign policy and strong defense, for traditional rules of moral conduct. On one issue, civil rights, he has moved from Colmer's support for racial segregation to the small town Republicans' backing for equal rights—although doubts were raised about that by comments he made at Strom Thurmond's 100th birthday party in December 2002, comments that cost him the majority leadership. He can be sharp in debate, aggressively partisan and combative, but he is gregarious and personable, striving to keep on good terms with most other members and careful to cultivate those whose support he needs.

In the Senate, as in the House, Lott seemed less interested in committee work than in moving into a leadership position. After the 1992 election, he ran for Conference secretary, the number four leadership post, and won. In 1994, after he had been reelected 69%-31%, he challenged Republican Whip Al Simpson. Majority Leader Bob Dole and most Republican moderates backed Simpson, but Lott won most of the younger conservatives elected in 1992 and 1994 and won 27-26—the first Republican ever elected whip in both houses. In the process he leapfrogged over his Mississippi colleague Thad Cochran, who held the number three leadership position. As whip for 17 months, Lott was careful not to usurp the prerogatives of Dole, who kept many decisions close to the chest. Then in May 1996 Dole surprised almost everyone when he announced he would resign from the Senate in June. Lott immediately began canvassing for votes for Majority Leader and found himself far ahead of Cochran, who ran anyway and lost 44-8. During the summer, Lott moved adroitly, pushing for a vote on welfare reform, disposing of the minimum wage issue, pushing for the compromise health care bill and the Safe Drinking Water Act. He gave Senate Republicans a solid record to run on—but left Dole with fewer issues on which to attack Clinton. He established a smooth working relationship with Democratic Leader Tom Daschle. After Dole lost and Gingrich faced ethics charges that threatened to topple him, Lott was suddenly the most visible Republican leader in Congress.

Then came the Clinton impeachment, which tested both his influence among Republican senators and his close working relationship with Daschle. In 1999 and 2000, Lott tried to bar non-germane amendments on appropriations bills, arguing that Democrats were using them to hurt Republicans in elections and that it was better procedure to have "clean votes" on issues. Democrats were immensely irritated, and in spring 2000 relations between Lott and Daschle turned very sour. In June 2000 Nebraska's Chuck Hagel said there could be changes in the leadership if Republicans lost seats in November; Hagel had contemplated running against Lott after the November 1998 elections, and ran unsuccessfully against campaign chairman Mitch McConnell instead. In July 2000 Lott steered estate tax repeal through, but at the cost of allowing votes on many Democratic amendments. In fall 2000 Lott followed a "no veto" strategy and tried to negotiate with the Clinton administration on appropriations; House Republican Whip Tom DeLay, who wanted to set clear conservative markers and get members out of town, opposed this. The result was relatively high spending, and a delay in many appropriations until after the November elections and, as seemed sensible, after the Florida recounts as well.

By late 2000, almost everyone seemed angry with Lott for one reason or another. But no one—not even Majority Whip Don Nickles, a frequent critic—moved to run against him. With the Senate divided 50-50, Democrats demanded equal numbers of members on each committee; some Republican conservatives strongly opposed that, though some committee chairmen offered equal membership. On January 5, 2001, after negotiations with Daschle, Lott surprised many by agreeing to equal membership. There was a strong theoretical argument for that—committee membership should reflect the balance on the floor—but even stronger practical arguments. Lott wanted to make sure that no Democratic senator would challenge the Florida electoral votes on January 6, and thereby trigger debate on that issue. There was always the possibility that control could shift to the Democrats. Most observers pointed to 98-year-old Strom Thurmond as one senator who might leave office, but there were 45 senators with governors of a different party, 26 Democrats and 19 Republicans, whose departure could change the partisan balance. While there was some hope that Georgia's Zell Miller might cross the aisle and strengthen this fragile majority, it was not much suspected until May 2001 that James Jeffords would defect and unravel it. The visibly angry Lott called it a "coup of one."

Even as minority leader, Lott had sharp elbows. When it became clear in 2002 that Senate Democrats would pass no budget resolution, he said, "The Senate is becoming dysfunctional, the Daschle Democrat dysfunctional process." In the fall, things seemed to be going very much his way. In October 2002 Don Nickles announced he would not challenge Lott for the leadership, even though term limits would force him to leave his position as Whip. On election night, the returns revealed that the president's party for the first time in history went from a minority to a majority in the Senate in an off-year election. Lott would be majority leader again.

Then came Thurmond's 100th birthday party. Speaking from notes Lott said, "I want to say this about my state. When Strom Thurmond ran for president, we voted for him. We're proud of it. And if the rest of the country had followed our lead, we wouldn't have had all these problems over the years, either." There were audible gasps and silence, but Lott went on. Major media did not mention the comment over the next 24 hours. Asked about it, Lott's spokesman the next day said, "Senator Lott's remarks were intended to pay tribute to a remarkable man who led a remarkable life. To read anything more into these comments is wrong." But bloggers noticed. By Monday, December 9, conservative bloggers were writing about Lott's comments, and not favorably. It was not surprising that liberals like Al Gore and Jesse Jackson called on Lott to resign the majority leadership, but it was noteworthy that demands for his resignation resounded over the conservative blogosphere. On December 9 Lott, on vacation in Key West, Florida, three hours' drive from the nearest television studio, issued a statement saying, "A poor choice of words conveyed to some the impression that I embraced the discarded policies of the past. Nothing could be further from the truth, and I apologize to anyone who was offended by my statement." Tom Daschle downplayed the remarks and Lott's sometime adversaries—Jeffords and former Democratic Senator Paul Simon—came forward to testify that he was not a racist. But others poking through old clippings found similar comments. On Thursday, December 12, George W. Bush spoke to an inner city group in Philadelphia. "Any suggestion that the segregated past was acceptable or positive is offensive, and it is wrong. Recent comments by Senator Lott do not reflect the spirit of this country. He has apologized, and rightly so. Every day our nation was segregated was a day that America was unfaithful to our founding ideals."

On December 13 Lott held a press conference in Pascagoula and announced that he would appear on Black Entertainment Television the next week. "I apologize for opening old wounds and hurting many Americans who feel so deeply in this area. I take full responsibility for my remarks. . . . I only hope people will find it in their heart to forgive me for that grievous mistake on that occasion." Lott's hearty endorsement of affirmative action on BET December 16 dismayed some conservatives who opposed racial quotas and preferences precisely because they believe they violate the civil rights laws which Lott's old boss William Colmer strongly opposed. Lott had been elected Majority Leader at a November 14 Republican Conference meeting, and that could not be reconsidered until the next scheduled meeting January 6, unless five members called for a special meeting. Nickles was one such vote, and it quickly became clear that there would be others. On December 19 Bill Frist stepped forward and said he would accept the job of majority leader if his colleagues voted for him. On the morning of December 20 Lott stepped down. By the end of the day, Frist had the votes to become majority leader, and was elected by a Conference meeting held by conference call. Lott said later that he had no "vengeance in his heart" but noted a little tartly, "You can't just lay this at the door of the Democrats—some of the Republicans didn't do me any good either. I plan to look to the future, to be very sensitive to everything I say."

Some observers thought Lott would sulk in a corner or display bitterness at every turn, but he did neither. "I still think those comments were misinterpreted, but I made a mistake and I have no one else to blame but myself," he said. "I take a few licks now and then, but I get back up and keep fighting." He retained enough of a sense of humor about the incident to say, when John Kerry made his "botched joke" about people "stuck in Iraq" in November 2006, Lott said, "I kind of felt sorry for John Kerry yesterday. I almost felt like calling John Kerry and saying, 'John, apologize and go home.' " He became chairman of the Rules Committee, which handles campaign finance and internal Senate matters, and started exploring changes in the filibuster rule and the presidential succession law. Freed from leadership responsibilities, he made some public criticisms of the Bush administration and of Bill Frist. In July 2003 he criticized Frist for taking up the Medicare/

prescription drug bill, which he opposed, rather than the energy bill and for taking too much time for debate on judicial nominations. In September he said the administration should provide more details on what was happening in Iraq. He opposed the administration on media ownership limits. His opposition to the Medicare/prescription drug bill, a priority for the administration and one on which Frist put his personal stamp, was strong. "What I have always wanted to see was a prescription program for the low-income elderly only," he said. It "will cost more than $400 billion minimum in the first 10 years. We put more furniture on the deck of a ship that's already listing, Medicare." But on November 24, two days after it was passed by the House, the Senate leadership was one vote short of the 60 required under the rules to bring it to the floor. Republican colleagues huddled around Lott, urging him to vote yes; he gestured angrily, then went forward, voted yes and stomped out of the chamber. That brought the bill forward and, "the worst damn thing I have ever seen Republicans do," passed 54-44. Lott was still angry later. He said it was one of his worst two votes, the other being in favor of the 1986 tax bill.

But even as he was criticizing the leadership, he was working behind the scenes with both Senate and House members to solve problems. Lott pressed Frist and the White House to accept a deal with Frank Lautenberg on privatization of air traffic controller jobs to get the FAA authorization through. In March 2004 he switched and supported prescription drug reimportation from Canada and he was the only Republican to vote against the budget resolution (because it didn't have enough room for tax cuts). He refused to give money to the National Republican Senatorial Committee, chaired by George Allen, and gave it directly to candidates instead. In September 2004 he criticized Frist for concentrating on homeland security and appropriations and not breaking deadlocks on the energy, transportation and corporate tax bills (only the last one passed). He criticized the administration for not accepting a deal on nominations he concocted with Tom Daschle (Charles Pickering was on the list). But before the election he got the Rules Committee to eliminate the eight-year term limit on Intelligence Committee members and afterwards he got the Republican Conference, by a 27-26 vote, to give the Majority Leader power to choose half the new "A" committee members.

Lott was also active legislatively on several fronts. In May 2004 his bill to postpone the 2005 round of base closings was beaten by only 49-47; he argued that the Pentagon should close bases abroad first. He warned Mississippians that Naval Station Pascagoula was in jeopardy because it had only interdiction missions; in May 2005, it appeared on the Defense Department's list of recommended closures. He put a hold on a Commerce Department nomination to prevent money for a study of billfish—a matter of some interest in Pascagoula—from being sent to a firm in Brownsville, Texas. He pushed successfully to block a tax change that would have U.S.-based automakers paying less than Nissan, which has a big new plant in Canton, Mississippi. After Donald Rumsfeld made controversial statements in December, he said, "I'm not a fan of Secretary Rumsfeld. I don't think he listens enough to his uniformed officers. I would like to see a change in that slot in the next year or so." In January 2005 he criticized Mitch McConnell for allowing too much in committee spending. And he joined with John McCain in sponsoring legislation to subject 527 organizations to the same campaign finance regulations as PACs. As Senate Rules chairman, he presided over the inauguration ceremonies at the Capitol.

In August 2005 his book *Herding Cats: A Life in Politics* was published. He recalled his years at Ole Miss, when its first black student had to be escorted by federalized National Guard troops, as idyllic and said that he believed then that "segregation was wrong and that it was cruel, but we were living in a world our ancestors had created for us." Of his remarks about Thurmond, he wrote, "My innocent and thoughtless remark was treated by most of the media as a hanging offense." He was in Alabama promoting the book when Hurricane Katrina hit the Gulf Coast on August 29. His wife called him later and told him that their house in Pascagoula had totally disappeared; only an oak tree was left. Lott immediately began working with his Mississippi colleague Thad Cochran and others in the Mississippi and Louisiana delegations on recovery efforts. It was something of a balancing act. Cochran as chairman of the Senate Appropriations Committee was well positioned to channel funds, and did so promptly. The Louisiana senators, Democrat Mary Landrieu and Republican David Vitter, had little seniority. Gulf Coast Democratic Congressman Gene Taylor, whose house in Bay St. Louis was destroyed, was ready to pitch in, as well as Louisiana Republican Bobby Jindal. The Mississippians had the advantage of having a governor, Haley Barbour, who came to them with a specific plan and concrete requests, while Louisiana's Kathleen Blanco was preoccupied by the chaos of New Orleans. But Lott seems to have held them all together and to have made considerable contributions of his own. "We need thoughtful things," he said on September 6. "We need innovative things, but we do need speed." Four days before, he had already helped bring in $50 million of Labor Department money to hire cleanup crews. On September 21 he and John Cornyn sponsored a bill to limit the liability of volunteers in recovery efforts. He was not afraid to be sharply critical of federal efforts in public; in early December he said, "Mr. President, the recovery is not going exactly right. Three months after Katrina, 42% of the travel trailers required for those still homeless have not been delivered by FEMA. Winter is coming to Mississippi, and too many people are still living in tents or carports. Three months after the hurricane, only an estimated one-quarter of the storm's debris has been removed in most areas, and too many neighborhoods have had none removed." His Gulf Zone Opportunity Act, reminiscent of Jack Kemp's enterprise zones, became law in December 2005 and provided $8.7 billion in tax breaks over 10 years for Gulf Coast businesses. He worked hard to see that shipyards were repaired and defense contractors got back into business and for a $520 million Medicaid installment that came in March 2006. He supported Cochran's spring 2006 supplemental with its controversial $700 million for CSX to relocate its Gulf Coast railroad and helped get $44 million for reopening the Gulfport-Biloxi airport. On the first anniversary of the hurricane, he summed up: "If Katrina has taught Mississippians anything, it is that true recovery and relief begin with those willing to go beyond convention. We further have learned that relief begins locally. It is a function of our community, not of Washington. While government agencies failed to push the envelope—paralyzed by the status quo and oblivious to Katrina's magnitude—Mississippians acted."

At one point Lott rationalized the loss of his house as the way the Lord let him know what other homeowners were going through. He was incensed that State Farm refused to pay a claim on his house on the grounds that it was covered only for wind damage and not for destruction by flood; this was only one of thousands of claims the company refused to pay on that theory. Lott agreed to support Gene Taylor's bill to allow homeowners not on federally designated floodplains to retrospectively buy flood insurance if their insurers refused to pay for wind damage. He filed a lawsuit himself against State Farm; his attorney was his brother-in-law, Richard Scruggs, the trial lawyer who brought some of the first tobacco class actions. In January 2007, while the state attorney general was considering criminal charges, State Farm settled many of the claims (including Lott's), and withdrew from the property insurance market in Mississippi. "The amount of insensitivity and greed by the industry has stunned me," he said, and cosponsored a bill with Cochran, Landrieu and Florida's Bill Nelson to create a bipartisan commission to recommend changes in the insurance business. With Patrick Leahy, Arlen Specter and Landrieu, he sponsored a bill to repeal the insurance industry's antitrust exemption, established by the McCarran-Ferguson Act of the 1940s. He sponsored another bill to require insurance companies to label damaged cars they might sell to otherwise unaware consumers.

During 2005 and spring 2006 Lott said that he had no intention of seeking a leadership position again, although it was obvious that there would be at least one opening: Bill Frist was retiring and Conference Chairman Rick Santorum was trailing badly in the polls in Pennsylvania. Viewing the impasse between the Senate and the House on immigration, he was almost visibly itching to make a deal. In fall 2006 an old adversary, John McCain, urged him to run for Whip. The two go back a long way; both are of Scots descent and have ancestors from Carroll County, Mississippi; Lott recalls that McCain's ancestors were known as inveterate fighters. They clashed on campaign finance and other issues, and Lott endorsed George W. Bush over McCain in 2000. But in early 2006 he endorsed McCain for president with considerable vigor. The results of the November 2006 elections left Lott competing for a different position than he had originally sought, Minority Whip. In a Conference meeting he beat Lamar Alexander of Tennessee by a 25-24 vote. In early 2007 he seemed careful to let Minority Leader Mitch McConnell have the spotlight and to operate mainly behind the scenes.

Lott's standing in Mississippi has remained very high over the years. He gave up a safe House seat to run for the Senate in 1988, and was elected over Democratic Congressman Wayne Dowdy 54%-46%. In 1994 and 2000 Lott did not have serious competition and won easily. Some thought he might resign after losing the majority leadership; in July 2004 he suggested that his decision might hinge on his chances to chair a major committee. "Odds are I'll end up being chairman of Finance or Commerce, depends on the years." Katrina seems to have erased any doubts about running. In January 2006 he announced for reelection, saying, "This is no time for me or any of us to think about quitting." He spent some $2 million and his Democratic opponent almost nothing. Lott won 64%-35%, carrying all but 17 majority-black counties; he carried seven other black-majority counties.

FIRST DISTRICT

Rep. Roger Wicker (R)

Elected 1994, 7th term; b. July 5, 1951, Pontotoc; home, Tupelo; U. of MS, B.A. 1973, J.D. 1975; Baptist; married (Gayle).

Military Career: Air Force, 1976-80; Air Force Reserve, 1980-present.

Elected Office: Tupelo City Judge Pro Tem, 1986-87; MS Senate, 1987-94.

Professional Career: Staff, U.S. House Rules Cmte., 1980-82; Practicing atty., 1982-94; Lee Cnty. Public Defender, 1984-87.

DC Office: 2350 RHOB, 20515, 202-225-4306; Fax: 202-225-3549; Web site: www.house.gov/wicker.

District Offices: Columbus, 662-327-0748; Grenada, 662-294-1321; Southaven, 662-342-3942; Tupelo, 662-844-5437.

Committees: *Appropriations* (11th of 29 R): Military Construction, Veterans Affairs & Related Agencies (RMM); Defense.

Group Ratings

	ADA	ACLU	AFS	LCV	ITIC	NTU	COC	ACU	CFG	FRC
2006	0	5	0	0	100	56	100	88	52	100
2005	5	—	0	0	—	53	93	96	53	83

National Journal Ratings

	2005 LIB	—	2005 CONS		2006 LIB	—	2006 CONS
Economic	6%	—	94%		4%	—	94%
Social	0%	—	89%		11%	—	85%
Foreign	23%	—	73%		16%	—	83%

Key Votes of the 109th Congress

1. Estate Tax Repeal	Y	5. Limit Interstate Abortion	*	9. Build Border Fence	Y
2. Limit CAFE Standards	Y	6. Extend Patriot Act	Y	10. CAFTA	Y
3. FY06 Spending Curb	Y	7. Bar Same Sex Marriage	Y	11. Oppose Iraq Withdrawal	Y
4. Drilling in ANWR	Y	8. Stem Cell Research $	N	12. Detainee Tribunals	Y

Election Results

2006 general	Roger Wicker (R)	95,098	(66%)	($746,938)
	James Hurt (D)	49,174	(34%)	($16,398)
2006 primary	Roger Wicker (R)	unopposed		
2004 general	Roger Wicker (R)	219,328	(79%)	($426,024)
	Barbara Washer (Ref)	58,256	(21%)	

Prior Winning Percentages: 2002 (71%); 2000 (70%); 1998 (67%); 1996 (68%); 1994 (63%)

The People		Race/Ethnic Origin	Ancestry	
Area size:	11,647 sq. mi.	71.3% White	USA: 16.6%	Irish: 7.1%
Urban population:	38.5%	26.2% Black	English: 6.1%	
Rural population:	61.5%	0.4% Asian	**2004 Presidential Vote**	
Pop. 2000:	711,160	0.2% Native Am.	Bush (R) 187,979	(62%)
Pop. 2005 (est):	750,233	0.0% Hawaiian	Kerry (D) 111,509	(37%)
Median income:	$32,535	0.5% Two+ races	Other 2,439	(1%)
Poverty status:	16.4%	0.0% Other	**2000 Presidential Vote**	
Military veterans:	11.4%	1.4% Hispanic Origin	Bush (R) 146,197	(59%)
			Gore (D) 98,350	(40%)
			Other 3,690	(1%)
			Cook Partisan Voting Index: R +10	

Occupation   Blue collar: 38.6%   White collar: 48.5%   Gray collar: 12.9%

The university town of Oxford, the "Jefferson" of William Faulkner's fictional Yoknapatawpha County, sits on a divide between the hill country of Mississippi and the flat farmlands of the Mississippi Delta. Named for Oxford, England, it is the home of the Center for the Study of Southern Culture and of Ole Miss, the University of Mississippi, which saw violence when James Meredith integrated the school in 1962 but now houses his papers in its library; Senator Thad Cochran was at the law school then and Senator Trent Lott a senior in college. To the west is the Delta, with a large black majority, and also DeSoto County, just south of Memphis, Mississippi's fastest-growing county and one of its most affluent and Republican. East of Oxford is the hill country, which stretches up to where the Tennessee River nicks the northeast corner of Tishomingo County. The Tennessee Valley Authority brought electricity here, the Tennessee-Tombigbee Waterway provided construction jobs for years and a shipping canal when it was completed in 1985; the Tenn-Tom is the largest water resource project built in the U.S. This was traditional farming country, now more engaged in small manufacturing. The Golden Triangle in the Starkville area has become a center for aerospace research, including unmanned air vehicle designs for improved surveillance and communications. The biggest town here is Tupelo, a stronghold of private enterprise and traditional values. It is home to an upholstered furniture industry that is the largest manufacturing sector in the state and has survived more prosperously than furniture centers elsewhere; Donald Wildmon's American Family Association, based in Tupelo, is an outspoken pro-family group. Elvis Presley was born in Tupelo in 1935, in a two-room house that is open to visitors, as is the Elvis Presley Museum with a modest collection of memorabilia. In February 2007, Toyota decided to build a plant near Tupelo that eventually will employ 2,000 workers and produce 150,000 vehicles each year.

The 1st Congressional District of Mississippi includes Oxford, Tupelo, most of the hill country and DeSoto County. This is the descendant of the district represented by Jamie Whitten, the long-time chairman of the Appropriations Committee and the longest-serving House member in history, from his special election victory in November 1941 until January 1995: 53 years and 62 days; John Dingell would surpass the mark in February 2009. Historically this was hell-of-a-fellow Democratic territory; in an April 2001 referendum it voted overwhelmingly to keep the 1894 state flag with the Confederate battle cross. It voted solidly for Democratic Governor Ronnie Musgrove in 1999 but in 2003 favored his Republican successor Haley Barbour. In national politics it is solidly Republican, 59% for George W. Bush in 2000 and 62% in 2004.

The congressman from the 1st District is Roger Wicker, a Republican first elected in 1994. He grew up in Pontotoc, 20 miles west of Tupelo, the son of a state senator and circuit judge, attended public schools and was a House page in 1967: The first of the 1994 freshmen to get on the House floor. Wicker went to college and law school at Ole Miss, where he was student body president; he served in the Air Force and in 1980 became a staffer to Trent Lott. In 1987, at 36, he was the first Republican elected to the state Senate from northern Mississippi since Reconstruction. When Whitten retired, he was one of six Republicans and three Democrats to run for the seat. Carrying his home base around Tupelo, Wicker led the primary 27%-19% over Grant Fox, a former aide to Thad Cochran. In the runoff, Wicker campaigned as a conservative, but Fox, just 27, hammered him for voting to override Governor Kirk Fordice's sales tax increase veto. Wicker won by 53%-47%. State Representative Bill Wheeler, the Democratic nominee, had support from blacks, unions and teachers—an advantage in the primary but not the general. The result wasn't close: A district held for 53 years by a Democratic titan voted 63%-37% Republican.

In the House, Wicker was elected president of the 73-member freshman class, one of the largest in the 20th century, and has compiled a solidly conservative voting record. He followed Whitten to the Appropriations Committee and moved up the seniority ladder so that he likely will be a subcommittee chairman—a "cardinal"—if Republicans regain control; in 2007, he became senior Republican on the Military Construction subcommittee. He became part of "The Group," an informal network of Speaker Dennis Hastert's close legislative advisers. Despite his New South style, in some ways Wicker has acted like an old-style Democrat. He worked on local projects and supported funding of the Natchez Trace Parkway (started in the 1930s, and completed in May 2005) and Yalobusha River flood control. He sought to route a new Interstate highway through DeSoto County. He passed a bill to establish academies for teachers and students of American history and delivered research dollars to Mississippi universities. Although his district was not badly affected by Hurricane Katrina, he worked hard to direct federal aid elsewhere in the state. In 2006, he objected to efforts to restrict spending earmarks in the House. He urged the Pentagon to spend in the United States its procurement funds to rebuild Iraq. In 2004, he filed a resolution with 60 co-sponsors calling for Kofi Annan to resign as Secretary General of the United Nations because of fraud and mismanagement in the Oil for Food program in Saddam Hussein's Iraq.

Wicker has consistently been reelected with 2–1 margins and more. He could be a candidate for the Senate if Lott or Cochran steps down.

SECOND DISTRICT

Rep. Bennie Thompson (D)

Elected April 1993, 7th full term; b. Jan. 28, 1948, Bolton; home, Bolton; Tougaloo Col., B.A. 1968, Jackson St. U., M.S. 1972; Methodist; married (London).

Elected Office: Bolton Bd. of Aldermen, 1969-73; Bolton Mayor, 1973-79; Hinds Cnty. Supervisor, 1980-93.

DC Office: 2432 RHOB, 20515, 202-225-5876; Fax: 202-225-5898; Web site: www.house.gov/thompson.

District Offices: Bolton, 601-866-9003; Greenville, 662-335-9003; Greenwood, 662-455-9003; Jackson, 601-946-9003; Marks, 662-326-9003; Mound Bayou, 662-741-9003.

Committees: *Homeland Security* (Chmn. of 19 D).

Group Ratings

	ADA	ACLU	AFS	LCV	ITIC	NTU	COC	ACU	CFG	FRC
2006	90	86	100	50	29	14	60	30	16	28
2005	95	—	100	78	—	13	52	12	5	15

National Journal Ratings

	2005 LIB	—	2005 CONS		2006 LIB	—	2006 CONS
Economic	65%	—	34%		61%	—	39%
Social	75%	—	25%		68%	—	32%
Foreign	81%	—	18%		70%	—	28%

Key Votes of the 109th Congress

1. Estate Tax Repeal	N	5. Limit Interstate Abortion	N	9. Build Border Fence	N
2. Limit CAFE Standards	Y	6. Extend Patriot Act	N	10. CAFTA	N
3. FY06 Spending Curb	N	7. Bar Same Sex Marriage	Y	11. Oppose Iraq Withdrawal	Y
4. Drilling in ANWR	Y	8. Stem Cell Research $	Y	12. Detainee Tribunals	N

Election Results

2006 general	Bennie Thompson (D)	100,160	(64%)	($1,393,496)
	Yvonne Brown (R)	55,672	(36%)	($122,769)
2006 primary	Bennie Thompson (D)	58,941	(64%)	
	Chuck Espy (D)	31,906	(35%)	
	Other	743	(1%)	
2004 general	Bennie Thompson (D)	154,626	(58%)	($724,653)
	Clinton LeSueur (R)	107,647	(41%)	($331,464)
	Other	2,596	(1%)	

Prior Winning Percentages: 2002 (55%); 2000 (65%); 1998 (71%); 1996 (60%); 1994 (54%); 1993 (55%)

The People		Race/Ethnic Origin	Ancestry	
Area size:	13,937 sq. mi.	34.5% White	USA: 6.8%	Irish: 3.7%
Urban population:	62.8%	63.2% Black	English: 3.3%	
Rural population:	37.2%	0.4% Asian	**2004 Presidential Vote**	
Pop. 2000:	711,164	0.2% Native Am.	Kerry (D) 153,786	(59%)
Pop. 2005 (est):	695,616	0.0% Hawaiian	Bush (R) 104,749	(40%)
Median income:	$26,894	0.5% Two+ races	Other 2,217	(1%)
Poverty status:	27.3%	0.0% Other	**2000 Presidential Vote**	
Military veterans:	10.0%	1.2% Hispanic Origin	Gore (D) 134,513	(57%)
			Bush (R) 97,979	(41%)
			Other 4,464	(2%)
			Cook Partisan Voting Index: D +10	

Occupation	Blue collar: 28.8%	White collar: 52.2%	Gray collar: 19.0%

"The Mississippi Delta," wrote Delta native David Cohn, "begins in the lobby of the Peabody Hotel in Memphis and ends on Catfish Row in Vicksburg." For centuries, the flooding Mississippi and Yazoo Rivers left their sediments here, producing a fertile dark soil. Ironically, what may well be America's richest agricultural land has been home for more than a century to many of its poorest people. The Delta, crisscrossed by rivers and famously disease-ridden, wasn't much settled until after the Civil War; the tradition here is not of paternal masters and gracious mansions, but of sharp, profit-seeking operators who used late 19th century technology to drain the land, line the river with levees and build railroads on tracks above the rise of the river. Black sharecroppers and field hands worked here in conditions almost of bondage. From this episode of industrial farming came both great misery and great art: Clarksdale in Coahoma County was the real birthplace of blues music, the home of W.C. Handy and Muddy Waters, John Lee Hooker, Ike Turner and Sam Cooke; Greenville on the Mississippi has produced writers of the caliber of Walker Percy and Shelby Foote; Yazoo City produced author Willie Morris and bluesman Skip James. Now Vicksburg's antebellum mansions, battlefield monuments and riverboat gambling bring in 1.5 million tourists annually.

Twentieth century technology changed life in the Delta. The mechanical cotton-picking machine, invented in 1944, came along just as northern factories were seeking low-wage workers; the great exodus to Chicago began, and the Delta's population has been declining ever since. Income levels remain very low, poverty is over 50% in some areas and infant mortality is at Third World levels; the crime and drugs of urban Chicago have been brought back by Delta migrants returning home. Commercial development was long stifled by the state's reputation as a haven for lawsuits and large jury awards. Yet, there are signs of hope: Soybeans have become a big dollar crop here; poultry farms have become a major enterprise, and the Delta produces most of the nation's catfish. Riverboat gambling operates in Tunica County, by some measures long the nation's poorest county, perhaps best known for its Sugar Ditch, the open sewer in the town of Tunica's black section. About 12 million people annually enter Tunica County's nine casinos (which have more square footage than Atlantic City's), and runways at the regional airport have been extended to accommodate Boeing 747s bearing even more tourists and players in national poker tournaments; a golf and tennis resort is going up. The casinos have led to a local increase in per capita income and a decrease in welfare rolls, but there is still a gulf between the races, culturally and economically, and the Delta has been slow to develop a self-propelling market economy. At the edge of the Delta there are other economic stories. In 2003, just north of fast-growing affluent suburbs of Jackson, Nissan opened a $1.4 billion, 5,000-job factory in Canton, historically a heavily African-American area, where it builds the flexfuel Titan and Armada vehicles; one consequence was the tripling of land values, as thousands more jobs were created for suppliers, and property moved from agriculture to residential or commercial use. A few miles southwest in Clinton, just west of Jackson, is the former headquarters of WorldCom, which filed the largest bankruptcy in U.S. history in July 2002; now there are plans to put a new nuclear power plant in the area.

The 2d Congressional District of Mississippi includes the entire Delta, indeed the whole Mississippi riverfront from Tunica almost to Natchez. It includes most of heavily black and low-income Jackson and surrounding Hinds County except for the affluent Bellehaven neighborhood. This is Mississippi's one black-majority district, first created as such in 1984. The 2d includes a few counties in the east that are majority-white and vote Republican, but the political tone of the district is set by the black neighborhoods in Jackson and the black counties of the Delta. Before the Voting Rights Act of 1965, these were run politically by segregationists like Senator and Delta landowner James Eastland, Judiciary Committee chairman from 1955 to 1979. In 1986, the district elected its first black congressman since Reconstruction, Mike Espy, whose grandfather and father built a chain of funeral homes and were among the biggest landowners in the state.

The congressman from the 2d District is Bennie Thompson, who grew up in Bolton, in Hinds County outside Jackson, graduated from Tougaloo College and Jackson State. He was elected alderman in Bolton in 1969, at 21, and mayor four years later; he was the first person in Mississippi to get a street named after Martin Luther King Jr. and he got the first fire engine for Bolton; he was a volunteer fire fighter himself for 26 years. In 1980 he became a Hinds County supervisor. A life-long grass-roots activist and labor organizer, he successfully encouraged other blacks to run for office. After Mike Espy resigned in 1993 to become Secretary of Agriculture, Thompson ran for the House, and in an all-party primary, he ran ahead of Henry Espy, Mike Espy's brother and mayor of Clarksdale, by a 28%-20% margin. Republican Hayes Dent, an aide to Governor Kirk Fordice, led with 34%. Voting in the runoff was mostly along racial lines, and Thompson won 55%-45%, with his margin coming mostly from Hinds County.

Unlike Espy, Thompson has a solidly liberal voting record and initially made no particular attempt to win white votes, making almost as few concessions across the racial divide as had Eastland in his day. In time, he moderated his votes and reached out to the white community, including some large farmers. His bill for a National Center for Minority Health and Health Care was enacted in 2000. He voted for the constitutional amendment to prohibit same-sex marriage; 77% of Mississippi blacks voted for a similar amendment in November 2004. In 2005, he left the Agriculture Committee to replace the retiring Jim Turner as ranking minority member on the Homeland Security Committee; this was in effect an appointment by Minority Leader Nancy Pelosi. But he continued to press for the Agriculture Department to hire an ombudsman to investigate complaints by minority farmers, and said that attempts by the WTO to eliminate farm subsidies—like the 2005 decision in a case brought by Brazil against the U.S. cotton program—would be a "travesty." On homeland security, he called for more attention to the needs of first responders; but he caused turmoil inside the committee by firing some Democratic staffers, cutting the pay of others and hiring more minority aides. After the Democrats' victory in November 2006, he became chairman in January 2007.

Hurricane Katrina did not strike Jackson or the Delta with anything like the force that devastated the Gulf Coast, but it did inflict considerable damage. Four days afterwards, Thompson said, "We have the capacity to respond in a timely manner, but that hasn't happened so far. It's like they brought a squirt gun to put out a forest fire." He found the federal assistance lines so tied up that he sent a staffer with a cellphone to the Mississippi Emergency Management Agency. Six days later, he said, "I think Hurricane Katrina has really shone a light on a FEMA independent agency versus FEMA in a bureaucracy." When Don Young in June 2006 proposed to set up FEMA as an entirely independent agency, Thompson and committee Chairman Peter King instead called for keeping it in the Department of Homeland Security, but with the kind of autonomy the Coast Guard has there. DHS Secretary Michael Chertoff had already taken the disaster preparedness function away from FEMA and limited it to disaster response. Thompson worked with King on the first authorization bill for DHS, but his amendment to increase authorized funding from $34.7 billion to $40.8 billion was defeated on a 16-13 party line vote. Thompson negotiated with King an agreement on restructuring FEMA, but in September 2006 Thompson demanded an additional $3.1 billion for state and local governments to develop interoperable communications. King said he never brought that up in negotiations; Thompson staffers said they had brought it up with King staffers before Labor Day. In any case Thompson said he wouldn't support King's measure without that money. Later in September 2006 Thompson listed a series of complaints about the Republicans' performance on homeland security: a failure to enact risk-based funding allocations, inaction on interoperable communications, insufficient funding of the Nunn-Lugar program to round up loose nuclear weapons (though this is outside the committee's jurisdiction), targeting the BioShield program against only two biological agents when researchers identified many more, and inaction on inspecting air cargo.

As chairman, Thompson promised greater oversight and lamented that Chertoff had appeared before the committee only twice in 2006. In January 2007, the first measure brought forward in the Democrats' 100 hours program was a bill purporting to follow all the recommendations of the 9/11 Commission. It included a requirement to screen all passenger jet and ship cargo, though it authorized only $250 million for a checkpoint screening security fund. When asked where additional funding could be found, and in light of the fact that Homeland Security Appropriations Subcommittee Chairman David Price was not committed to funding all this, Thompson said, "In the spirit of 'let's get it done,' we'll work it out." Another looming problem was that Transportation and Infrastructure Chairman Jim Oberstar was claiming jurisdiction for port security. In any case, the bill passed 299-128. Thompson has said his priorities on homeland security include encouraging awards of contracts to minority firms, making sure that contractors hire minorities, delivering research money to historically black colleges and universities and ensuring that border security and TSA officers don't single out travelers because of race or ethnicity. In January 2007 in a talk to elected officials in the Delta, he said, "There are a number of research facilities around homeland security; there are a number of educational facilities that we will be building over the next few years. . . . I plan to make sure that we get our apportioned share. . . . There's nothing that politics doesn't control, so don't let anybody try to divorce you from politics. Politics is the determining factor in whatever our status in life is. People say, 'I'm apolitical.' Well, you may be apolitical, but politics still controls us."

Thompson's arguably confrontational politics has produced significant but far from overwhelming opposition in the 2d District. In 2002 he was reelected by a less than impressive 55%-43% margin against Republican challenger Clinton LeSueur, a former aide to the District of Columbia city council and consultant to the Yazoo Community Action Agency. LeSueur ran again in 2004, and spent three times the money he had in 2002. He emphasized personal responsibility and took culturally conservative views on abortion and gay rights. But LeSueur received little support from national Republicans and Thompson increased his majority to 58%-41%. In 2005, state Representative Chuck Espy, nephew of former Congressman Mike Espy, launched a primary challenge to Thompson. Thompson, in a staff memo to Nancy Pelosi, requested assistance in snuffing out Espy's potential candidacy because he did not want to end up like other black members who had "come under successful attack from 'younger' leaders," presumably meaning the challengers who in Democratic primaries defeated Earl Hilliard in Alabama and Cynthia McKinney in Georgia in 2002. Perhaps coincidentally, a 15-member delegation of the Congressional Black Caucus came to Jackson and the Delta to study issues in August 2005. Espy started running ads on Super Bowl Sunday in February 2006; some Democrats charged that he was receiving Republican support and brought a lawsuit challenging the state law that allowed any voter to vote in the Democratic primary and to enjoin the holding of the primary in June 2006. That didn't succeed and Thompson won the primary 64%-35%. He carried Jackson's Hinds County and the three counties to the south by the overwhelming margin of 71%-28%. In the rest of the district, Espy carried four counties, including his base in Clarksdale, Espy carried four counties and ran behind by only a 62%-37% margin—not overwhelming for an incumbent in a primary. Thompson won the general election, in which his Republican opponent complained about lack of support from the national party, by a solid 64%-36% margin. The 2d District's population declined by 2% between 2000 and 2005, but redistricting after the 2010 Census is unlikely to change the boundaries in any politically significant way.

THIRD DISTRICT

Rep. Chip Pickering (R)

Elected 1996, 6th term; b. Aug. 10, 1963, Laurel; home, Hebron; MS Col., 1981-82, U. of MS, B.A. 1986, Baylor U., M.B.A. 1988; Baptist; married (Leisha).

Professional Career: Baptist missionary, Budapest, Hungary, 1986-87; Spec. Asst. to the Admin. & Asst. Coord., East European & Soviet Secretariat, U.S. Dept. of Agriculture, 1989-90; Legis. Aide, U.S. Sen. Trent Lott, 1990-94.

DC Office: 229 CHOB, 20515, 202-225-5031; Fax: 202-225-5797; Web site: www.house.gov/pickering.

District Offices: Brookhaven, 601-823-3400; Meridian, 601-693-6681; Natchez, 601-442-2515; Pearl, 601-932-2410; Starkville, 662-324-0007.

Committees: *Energy & Commerce* (12th of 26 R): Commerce, Trade & Consumer Protection; Energy & Air Quality; Telecommunications & the Internet.

Group Ratings

	ADA	ACLU	AFS	LCV	ITIC	NTU	COC	ACU	CFG	FRC
2006	0	9	0	17	83	54	100	84	52	100
2005	10	—	13	0	—	53	92	92	54	92

National Journal Ratings

	2005 LIB	—	2005 CONS	2006 LIB	—	2006 CONS
Economic	35%	—	65%	34%	—	65%
Social	12%	—	88%	28%	—	70%
Foreign	23%	—	73%	14%	—	86%

Key Votes of the 109th Congress

1. Estate Tax Repeal	Y	5. Limit Interstate Abortion	Y
2. Limit CAFE Standards	Y	6. Extend Patriot Act	*
3. FY06 Spending Curb	Y	7. Bar Same Sex Marriage	Y
4. Drilling in ANWR	Y	8. Stem Cell Research $	N

9. Build Border Fence	Y
10. CAFTA	Y
11. Oppose Iraq Withdrawal	Y
12. Detainee Tribunals	Y

Election Results

2006 general	Chip Pickering (R)	125,421	(78%)	($726,303)
	Jim Giles (I)	25,999	(16%)	
	Lamonica Magee (Ref)	10,060	(6%)	
2006 primary	Chip Pickering (R)	unopposed		
2004 general	Chip Pickering (R)	234,874	(80%)	($832,981)
	Jim Giles (I)	40,426	(14%)	($300)
	Lamonica Magee (Ref)	18,068	(6%)	

Prior Winning Percentages: 2002 (64%); 2000 (73%); 1998 (85%); 1996 (61%)

The People		Race/Ethnic Origin	Ancestry	
Area size:	13,310 sq. mi.	63.7% White	USA: 13.5%	Irish: 6.1%
Urban population:	40.3%	33.1% Black	English: 6.0%	
Rural population:	59.7%	0.6% Asian	**2004 Presidential Vote**	
Pop. 2000:	711,115	0.9% Native Am.	Bush (R) 203,376	(65%)
Pop. 2005 (est):	732,202	0.0% Hawaiian	Kerry (D) 106,455	(34%)
Median income:	$31,907	0.5% Two+ races	Other 1,827	(1%)
Poverty status:	19.2%	0.0% Other	**2000 Presidential Vote**	
Military veterans:	11.5%	1.2% Hispanic Origin	Bush (R) 173,434	(64%)
			Gore (D) 93,454	(35%)
			Other 2,752	(1%)
			Cook Partisan Voting Index: R +14	

Occupation	Blue collar: 28.9%	White collar: 56.7%	Gray collar: 14.5%

Mississippi, old and new: The old Mississippi is the Neshoba County fair, held every August since 1889 in the town of Philadelphia. What started as a farmer's picnic has become the traditional place where Mississippi politicians announce their candidacies, with the crowds watching to take their measure and watch races on the state's only legal horse track. When Ronald Reagan came here in 1980 and Michael Dukakis in 1988, neither mentioned what Philadelphia and Neshoba County are best known for nationally, nor is there any memorial except engraved stones at two black churches. It was here during the "Freedom Summer" of 1964 that three civil rights workers, two white and one black, were murdered for the crime of urging black American citizens to register and vote. In June 2005, a jury of nine whites and three blacks convicted Edgar Ray Killen, an 80-year old preacher and saw mill operator, of manslaughter in the murders. The new Mississippi is some 80 miles away, in Rankin and Madison Counties east and north of Jackson, where subdivisions, shopping centers and office complexes are sprouting up in the countryside, as well as the big Nissan plant operating in Canton since 2003.

The 3d Congressional District of Mississippi includes the Rankin and south Madison County suburbs of Jackson, plus the affluent neighborhoods of northeast Jackson in Hinds County. It stretches north to Starkville, home of Mississippi State University, and south almost to Laurel. In the southwest it reaches over to include Natchez, where 600 antebellum mansions and other properties with live oaks sit on the bluffs overlooking the Mississippi River. In the middle are Neshoba County and Meridian, a small city that may go down in history as the site of departures of two White House chiefs of staff: Here Richard Nixon in April 1973 informed Bob Haldeman that he was out and here John Sununu penned his letter of resignation to George H. W. Bush in December 1991. In January 2007, the Justice Department for the first time under the Voting Rights Act sued a black Democratic party leader for discriminating against the voting rights of minority whites in the small town of Macon. The political tradition here was Southern Democratic, but the area's recent preference has been strongly Republican: Mississippi, old and new.

The congressman from the 3d District is Chip Pickering, a Republican first elected in 1996. He grew up in Laurel where he worked on the family dairy and catfish farm and attended public schools. His father, Judge Charles Pickering, was defeated for reelection as prosecutor in the 1968 after testifying against a Ku Klux Klan leader—something that took great courage in those days. The senior Pickering later was a state senator and state Republican chairman, and was nominated by George H. W. Bush to be a federal district judge and then confirmed without controversy by the Democratic-controlled Senate. When George W. Bush nominated him to be a federal appeals court judge, the Senate Judiciary Committee voted him down on party lines in March 2002. Bush renominated Charles Pickering again in 2003, and Chip Pickering worked hard to convince members of the Congressional Black Caucus to go along, but he was unsuccessful; in early 2004, Bush gave him a recess appointment, but Pickering had to step down at the end of the year. When Bush offered another appointment in 2005, Pickering turned him down and then wrote a book about his experience: *Supreme Chaos.*

Chip Pickering was more interested in football than politics at college; after that, he spent 17 months as a Southern Baptist missionary, the first such full-time presence in then-Communist Hungary. He worked on Eastern European development at the Agriculture Department in the administration of Bush the elder, and worked on telecommunications issues for Senator Trent Lott. In 1996, Sonny Montgomery, a Democrat who mostly voted with Republicans, retired after 30 years in the House. Chip Pickering returned to Mississippi and ran for the seat. Against nine Republicans and three Democrats, he made use of his party ties: His father's executive director at the state party had been Halcy Barbour, Republican National Committee chairman from 1993 to 1997 and now governor. In the primary Pickering won 27% of the vote; former state Representative Bill Crawford, with 24%, was second. Pickering won the runoff 56%-44% with big margins in the Jackson suburbs. Against 29-year-old John Arthur Eaves Jr., son of a well-known lawyer and Democratic politician, Pickering, age 33, spent more than $1 million in the general, twice what Eaves spent, and won 61%-36%.

In the House, Pickering has a voting record that is relatively moderate for a Deep South Republican. His Capitol Hill contacts led to assignment on the Energy and Commerce Committee. As co-chairman of the Congressional Wireless Caucus, he sought increased focus on the industry's concerns: Competition, public safety, privacy and the spectrum. Although an opponent of the bill to enable the regional Bells to offer broadband service, he backed off when House passage became certain. On the Telecommunications and the Internet Subcommittee, Pickering sought to preempt state regulation of the growing Internet phone industry; after Congress failed to act, he praised the FCC when it asserted exclusive control in November 2004. After Hurricane Katrina, he criticized the Bush administration's slow response, and helped investigate contracting practices at FEMA as part of the government's emergency response. He won approval for a 160 million barrel oil reserve at the Richton salt domes in south Mississippi under the federal government's plan to increase its strategic reserve.

Redistricting placed Pickering in the same district with two-term Democrat Ronnie Shows in 2002. Democratic strategists hoped Shows could run as a populist, denouncing the executives of WorldCom, the bankrupt telecommunications giant that was headquartered just west of Jackson. He called for trade protections, attacked Republicans on Social Security, and distanced himself from national Democrats on gun control and abortion. But the new 3d District, though 33% black, had voted 64% for George W. Bush in 2000; 59% of its voters had been represented by Pickering and just 41% by Shows. Pickering raised twice as much money and ran the more skillful campaign. And Pickering wasn't shy about criticizing Shows for his lukewarm support for his father's nomination. In the end, it wasn't close. Pickering won 71%-28% in his old territory and 53%-45% in Shows's—a final outcome of 64%-35%. Otherwise, he has not been seriously challenged. Pickering's success raised the possibility he might some day run for the Senate. In 2003, he revealed that he rejected a $1 million job offer to become president of the Cellular Telecommunications and Internet Association.

In August 2007, Pickering announced that he would not seek reelection. He remains a possible successor to either Lott or his colleague Thad Cochran and he also suggested he might one day be interested in running for governor. Pickering's seat is likely to remain in Republican hands; former Democratic Congressman Ronnie Shows said he is considering running.

FOURTH DISTRICT

Rep. Gene Taylor (D)

Elected Oct. 1989, 9th full term; b. Sept. 17, 1953, New Orleans, LA; home, Bay St. Louis; Tulane U., B.A. 1974; Catholic; married (Margaret).

Military Career: Coast Guard Reserve, 1971-84.

Elected Office: Bay St. Louis City Cncl., 1981-83; MS Senate, 1983-89.

Professional Career: Sales rep., Stone Container Corp., 1977-89.

DC Office: 2269 RHOB, 20515, 202-225-5772; Fax: 202-225-7074; Web site: www.house.gov/genetaylor.

District Offices: Bay St. Louis, 228-469-9235; Gulfport, 228-864-7670; Hattiesburg, 601-582-3246; Laurel, 601-425-3905; Ocean Springs, 228-872-7950.

Committees: *Armed Services* (4th of 34 D): Seapower & Expeditionary Forces (Chmn.); Readiness. *Transportation & Infrastructure* (10th of 41 D): Water Resources & Environment; Coast Guard & Maritime Transportation.

Group Ratings

	ADA	ACLU	AFS	LCV	ITIC	NTU	COC	ACU	CFG	FRC
2006	40	14	71	42	57	26	53	68	21	100
2005	60	—	75	56	—	38	59	60	25	92

National Journal Ratings

	2005 LIB	—	2005 CONS	2006 LIB	—	2006 CONS
Economic	55%	—	44%	56%	—	44%
Social	27%	—	73%	41%	—	58%
Foreign	54%	—	45%	52%	—	47%

Key Votes of the 109th Congress

1. Estate Tax Repeal	N	5. Limit Interstate Abortion	Y	9. Build Border Fence	Y
2. Limit CAFE Standards	Y	6. Extend Patriot Act	*	10. CAFTA	N
3. FY06 Spending Curb	N	7. Bar Same Sex Marriage	Y	11. Oppose Iraq Withdrawal	Y
4. Drilling in ANWR	Y	8. Stem Cell Research $	N	12. Detainee Tribunals	Y

Election Results

2006 general	Gene Taylor (D)	110,996	(80%)	($320,183)
	Randy McDonnell (R)	28,117	(20%)	
2006 primary	Gene Taylor (D)	unopposed		
2004 general	Gene Taylor (D)	179,979	(64%)	($426,134)
	Michael Lott (R)	96,740	(35%)	($89,085)
	Other	3,663	(1%)	

Prior Winning Percentages: 2002 (75%); 2000 (79%); 1998 (78%); 1996 (58%); 1994 (60%); 1992 (63%); 1990 (81%); 1989 (65%)

The People		Race/Ethnic Origin	Ancestry	
Area size:	9,536 sq. mi.	73.5% White	USA: 13.4%	Irish: 7.3%
Urban population:	53.7%	22.1% Black	English: 6.3%	
Rural population:	46.3%	1.2% Asian	**2004 Presidential Vote**	
Pop. 2000:	711,219	0.3% Native Am.	Bush (R) 188,880	(68%)
Pop. 2005 (est):	741,519	0.0% Hawaiian	Kerry (D) 86,010	(31%)
Median income:	$33,023	0.9% Two+ races	Other 1,697	(1%)
Poverty status:	16.9%	0.1% Other	**2000 Presidential Vote**	
Military veterans:	15.3%	1.8% Hispanic Origin	Bush (R) 154,997	(65%)
			Gore (D) 78,224	(33%)
			Other 4,152	(2%)
			Cook Partisan Voting Index: R +16	

Occupation	Blue collar: 29.7%	White collar: 51.9%	Gray collar: 18.4%

The strand where Mississippi faces the Gulf of Mexico has gone through several transformations. French explorers here founded Biloxi in 1699, before New Orleans or St. Louis, and made it the capital of an empire extending to what is now Yellowstone National Park. Two hundred years later, rich people from New Orleans came to this Gulf Coast in summer to get away from yellow fever and to rest on Victorian verandas; six American presidents have vacationed here. More recently the Gulf Coast, with the help of riverboat casinos since 1992, grew more than any other major part of Mississippi; along much of the strand, new 1,000-room hotels rose as part of Mississippi's boom and about 50,000 jobs were created. There is a military flavor to the Gulf Coast: Biloxi's Keesler Air Force Base was once one of the four largest in the country. Pascagoula, once a small town, has been home of the more than 12,000 employees at Ingalls Shipyard, whose gray hangar-like buildings and skeletons of ships under construction loom over the flat landscape. The Pentagon's 2005 base closing actions hit hard here: Pascagoula Naval Station was listed for closure, with its equipment and personnel shifted to Mayport Florida; Keesler was scheduled to shrink by about 400 military jobs.

That blow, though severe, was trifling compared to the direct hit that the coastal communities took from Hurricane Katrina on August 29, 2005. From Waveland to Pascagoula, about 80 miles were obliterated: beach-front cottages, fishing villages, hotel casinos, oil drilling platforms and refineries all were cruelly swamped and many were washed away. Status meant nothing: The homes of Confederate president Jefferson Davis in Biloxi and Senator Trent Lott in Pascagoula were lost. With the eye of the monster storm passing over this area, the devastation was, if anything, worse than from the collapsed levees of New Orleans. In an instant, the storm ruined countless livelihoods, caused losses in the tens of billions of dollars, and laid waste to a way of life. If there was a saving grace, many of these communities were left with a clean slate to restart development, with more managed control over the high-rise condos and strip malls that had started to overwhelm more distinctive properties. With more organization and speed than in Louisiana, the state's officials planned for the future and quickly spent the money available from Washington and insurance proceeds. It helped to have Haley Barbour, a well-connected national Republican insider, as governor and Thad Cochran as Senate Appropriations Committee chairman. Even while the clean-up continued, important decisions were made, especially in Biloxi: condominium projects were more carefully managed; shrimp boaters got docks for their boats and places to sell their catch; casinos were permitted to be built on land, instead of the barges they were restricted to in the past. In Pascagoula, five new buildings were planned for the site of the naval station.

This is the heart of the 4th Congressional District of Mississippi. Prior to Katrina, half of its people lived on the Gulf Coast; the rest are inland, in farm counties or around Hattiesburg and Laurel. This was mostly scrub land, not much good for plantations. With its low black percentage, the 4th District has been prime Republican territory. In close to its current form, it gave Richard Nixon his highest percentage in all 435 districts in 1972, voted five times against fellow Southerners Jimmy Carter, Bill Clinton and Al Gore, and was represented for 16 years in the House by Lott until he was elected to the Senate in 1988.

The congressman from the 4th District is Gene Taylor, a Democrat chosen in a 1989 special election. Taylor graduated from Tulane and served in the Coast Guard Reserves as skipper of a search and rescue boat for 10 years. He was elected to the Bay St. Louis Council in 1981 and in 1983, at 30, was elected to the state Senate. In 1988, when Lott ran for the Senate, Taylor ran for his House seat, won the Democratic primary, but lost to Republican Larkin Smith 55%-45%. When Smith died in an August 1989 plane crash, Lott brushed aside Smith's widow and backed his own longtime aide Tom Anderson, who had spent little time in the district and proved to be an abrasive candidate. Taylor, combining a barely reined-in aggressiveness with a down-home manner, won the special 65%-35%.

In the House, Taylor has been among the most conservative Democrats, especially on cultural issues, and has bluntly criticized the leadership of both parties. Taylor is a peppery populist with a reasonably consistent view on issues. He is against abortion, gun control, foreign aid and federal deficits. He is strongly pro-defense and boasts of bringing defense contracts to the area. As a senior Democrat on the Armed Services Committee, he has participated actively in expanding health benefits for military retirees. In 2007, he became chairman of the Seapower and Expeditionary Forces Subcommittee, which remains a useful assignment for this district.

Taylor has tended to oppose any U.S. military commitment that stops short of assured and total victory. In the 1990s, he voted against the Gulf War resolution, lifting the arms embargo on Bosnia, and sending troops to Haiti, and won House passage of limits on forces in Colombia. Since then, he has become more willing to use military power. When faced with apparently ineffective American military involvement in Serbia in 1999, he called for a declaration of war; in 2002 he voted for the use of force in Iraq. He is a protectionist, loudly opposing NAFTA, CAFTA, and normal trade relations with China. If anything holds his record together, it is boats. He promotes Ingalls and other shipyards, succeeded in widening and deepening the Gulfport shipping channel, promotes the Merchant Marine fleet, champions the seafood industry, and wants to prohibit foreign-flag ships from conducting passenger "voyages to nowhere" from U.S. ports. With Jo Ann Davis of Virginia, he organized the Shipbuilding Caucus to expand the Navy fleet. He vigorously opposed the 2005 base-closing round, arguing that Congress was surrendering its constitutional authority, that it was the wrong time because the nation was at war—and out of concern that facilities in his district would be on the closing list; he lost and Pascagoula Naval Station was indeed slated to be closed. In 2006, he added an amendment to the defense bill requiring the Pentagon to equip all vehicles in Iraq and Afghanistan with technology to jam improvised explosive devices. He has fought to give the National Guard membership in the Joint Chiefs of Staff.

Katrina focused the attention of Taylor, who lost his home in Bay St. Louis and joined a lawsuit against State Farm for unpaid claims. He added links to his website to aid constituents seeking Social Security checks and missing persons. Despite opposition from Democratic Leader Nancy Pelosi to a Republican-led select committee investigation, Taylor participated. At a hearing a month after the storm, he grilled former FEMA director Michael Brown about the inadequate response: "I was there, and I don't recall seeing you . . . .You get an F minus in my book." He filed a bill for retroactive federal compensation for homes and businesses without flood insurance. "After the storm, so many people who normally ask very little of their nation were now looking at losing everything, and they needed our help," he told a local reporter in April 2006. Two months later, the House passed his amendment requiring the Homeland Security Department to investigate whether insurance companies had wrongly denied claims after Katrina.

Taylor is hardly ever a reliable Democratic vote. But he has rebuffed all importunings to switch parties. "I personally would feel like a prostitute. I still believe the average working person's best interest is best served by the Democratic Party." Facing the possibility that the House would decide the 2000 presidential election, he said that he would vote for George W. Bush to reflect the views of his constituents. After voting for John Murtha for Speaker in 2001, 2003 and 2005, when it mattered in 2007 he voted for Nancy Pelosi. At home, he faced serious opposition only in 1996, when Republican Dennis Dollar opposed him. Taylor won with a solid 58%-40%, even as Bob Dole was carrying the district by a similar margin. If Taylor departs, Republicans would have an excellent chance to capture this seat. But he shows no signs of accommodating them.

★ MISSOURI ★

When Meriwether Lewis and William Clark set out on their expedition across the Louisiana Purchase to the Pacific in May 1804, the place they embarked from was St. Louis. On high ground just below the point where the Missouri River swirls into the Mississippi, St. Louis was at the time the one well-established city in America's interior, with an aristocracy of French merchants, a brawling bourgeoisie of Yankee and Southern frontiersmen and fur traders and a proletariat of black slaves. Part of the Louisiana Purchase in 1803, St. Louis by 1821 was part of the new state of Missouri, and for decades St. Louis and Missouri were the gateways to the frontier. In Missouri Daniel Boone finally found elbow room. Here were the eastern termini of the Pony Express, in St. Joseph, and the Santa Fe Trail, in Westport, now part of Kansas City; here were railroads reaching across the continent, connecting the farmers of vast prairies with their markets. Here also were the Mississippi River steamboats, and the boyhood home of their great chronicler, Mark Twain.

For Missouri was not just the gateway to the frontier; it was also a focus of the furious battle over slavery. Missouri was the northernmost slave state in 1850; it was Missouri ruffians crossing the border and killing antislavery settlers in the Kansas Territory that led proximately to the Civil War, and Missouri had its own mini-civil war in the hilly counties along the Missouri River. Throughout the 19th century, both before and after the Civil War, Americans turned away from their oceans and headed inward to settle the great interior of the continent. They found Missouri at its heart, with farmland and mines, rivers and railroads, a major manufacturing state—and in the days before tractors, the nation's leading breeder and trader of mules. In 1874 the Eads Bridge opened, one of very few across the Mississippi, and St. Louis' Cupples Station was the largest rail hub in the world. At the turn of the 20th century, Missouri was the fifth largest state and St. Louis

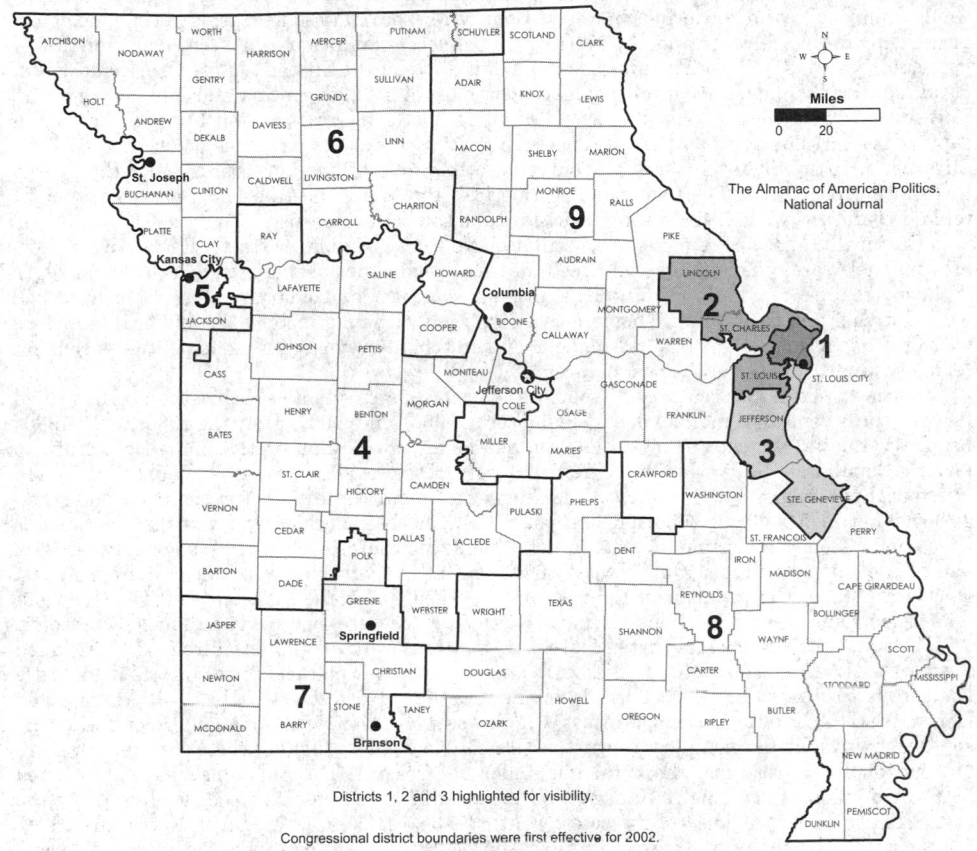

Districts 1, 2 and 3 highlighted for visibility.

Congressional district boundaries were first effective for 2002.

was the fourth largest city, site of the 1904 World's Fair, and one of the few cities with two major league baseball teams, the Cardinals and the Browns; Missouri after the 1900 Census had 16 congressional districts.

Today, Missouri does not loom as large in the national consciousness, yet it is in some ways still central. In the 20th century, Americans—like the Browns who moved to Baltimore in the 1950s and the football Cardinals who moved to Phoenix in the 1980s—increasingly headed toward the coasts, to the big cities of the East and West, and eventually to Florida and Texas. Missouri has had below average population growth since 1900, and today it is the 17th largest state, with just nine congressional districts. But Missouri was the geographic center of the nation's population in the 2000 Census: an imaginary, flat map of the United States population, if everyone weighed the same, would balance near Edgar Springs in Phelps County, Missouri. Missouri started perking up demographically in the 1990s, growing by 9% (its greatest decennial increase in a century); growth was particularly strong in the outer suburbs of St. Louis and Kansas City and in the Ozarks; dozens of rural counties that have been losing population for most of the 20th century started growing again. The state economy, long sluggish, was showing signs of solid growth. And Missouri has again captured Americans' imaginations: if Americans in 1904 flocked to St. Louis on the banks of the Mississippi, in the 1990s their vans and buses were jamming the two-lane road through the Ozarks to Branson, population 7,010, now one of America's top tourist destinations (with nearly eight million visitors a year), with country music stars and soft rock veterans.

Culturally, Missouri remains more conservative than most bigger states. Its relatively slow-growing metro areas have not overwhelmed the countryside; the only big growth is at the far edges of the metro areas and in the Ozarks. This rural Missouri is a land of farms and small towns, thick with churches and free of glitzy shopping centers, laced with man-made lakes and boat launches, with only one town over 150,000 (Springfield) and 103 counties where life—and politics—seem not to have changed much over the past half-century.

For most of the 20th century, Missouri was one of America's political bellwethers: it has voted for every presidential winner but one (Eisenhower in 1956) since 1900. From the 1960s to the 1990s it mirrored national trends by moving its congressional politics from pretty solidly Democratic to leaning Republican. Starting with the excruciatingly close presidential year of 2000, the results in Missouri have been very close as well. Missouri had eight contests for president, senator and governor between 2000 and 2006, and only one of them has been decided by a wide margin, Senator Christopher Bond's reelection in 2004. In the other seven contests, Republicans got between 47% and 53% of the vote, Democrats between 46% and 50%. Republicans won four of those contests, Democrats three. The Republicans' percentages averaged 49.7%, the Democrats' 48.4%. The popular vote margins in seven elections in which 16 million votes were cast was less than 260,000 votes.

The patterns of support in these 21st century elections were very different from what prevailed for most of the 20th century. Then Missouri's ancient Civil War political divisions still held: Little Dixie in the northeast, first settled by Virginians, and the northwest, settled by Southerners, voted Democratic; the Ozarks in the southwest, which was pro-Union, was unusually Republican; the southeast was split, like next-door Downstate Illinois. Now the real divide is between the state's two big metropolitan areas and the rural remainder of Missouri. The St. Louis metro area voted 54%-45% for John Kerry; metro Kansas City, about half as big, voted 52%-47% for Kerry. But the rest of Missouri, casting 43% of the votes, went 63%-36% for George W. Bush. Kerry carried St. Louis city, St. Louis County, Kansas City's Jackson County and just one of the 112 other counties in the state; Bush carried 111. The 2006 Senate race was a contest between incumbent Republican Jim Talent and Democratic Auditor Claire McCaskill, who lost a race for governor in 2004. McCaskill won 50%-47%, carrying metro St. Louis 55%-43% and metro Kansas City, her home area, 57%-40%; she lost the rest of the state 52%-42%. Ancestrally Democratic rural counties have taken to electing Republican congressmen and legislators. Only one Democrat, House Armed Services Committee Chairman Ike Skelton, represents a congressional district that is predominantly rural. Missouri remains closely divided between the parties, just as it is uniquely divided in another way: this is the only state whose name is pronounced differently in different regions: in metro St. Louis they say Missouree, in the rest of the state Missouruh.

The People		Race/Ethnic Origin			Military veterans: 592,271 (14.2%)	
Pop. 2006 (est):	5,842,713	4,686,474	83.8%	White	WWII: 20.3%	Korea: 14.4%
Pop. 2000:	5,595,211	625,667	11.2%	Black	Vietnam: 31.6%	Gulf War: 9.2%
Pop. 1990:	5,117,073	61,041	1.1%	Asian	**Most populous cities (2006):**	
Change 1990-2000:	Up 9.3%	23,302	0.4%	Native Am.	1. Kansas City	447,306
% of U.S. total:	2.0%	2,939	0.1%	Hawaiian	2. St. Louis	347,181
Pop. rank:	17th of 50	71,905	1.3%	Two+ races	3. Springfield	150,797
Area size:	69,704 sq. mi.	5,291	0.1%	Other	4. Independence	109,400
State Native:	67.8%	118,592	2.1%	Hisp. Origin	5. Columbia	94,428
Non-citizen:	1.6%	**Ancestry**				
Language		German: 17.9%		Irish: 9.7%	Urban population: 69.4%	
English: 92.9%	Spanish: 3.1%	USA: 8.0%		English: 7.2%	Rural population: 30.6%	
Other Eur.: 2.8%		French: 2.7%				

Education		Work Sector			General Assembly	
H.S. Grad:	81.3%	Private: 80.0%		Govt: 12.8%	Senate	21 R 13 D
College Grad:	21.6%	Self: 6.9%		Family: 0.4%	House	92 R 71 D
Industry		Unemployment: 5.3%			Legislative Term Limits: Yes	
Agri: 2.2%	Con: 6.9%	**Household Income**			**Registered Voters**	
Fin: 6.7%	Info: 3.0%	<15k: 17.1%		15-35k: 28.9%	No party registration	
Mfg: 20.5%	Prof: 27.9%	35-50k: 17.5%		50-100k: 27.7%		
Public: 4.6%	Trade: 15.5%	100-150k: 5.7%		>150k: 3.0%		
Other: 12.8%		Median: $37,934				
Occupation		Poverty status: 11.7%				
Blue collar: 26.0%	White collar: 58.3%	**Home Value**				
Gray collar: 15.7%		<50k: 21.3%	50-100k: 38.6%	100-200k: 29.9%	200-300k: 6.3%	
		300-500k: 2.6%	>500k: 1.2%	Median: $86,900		

Presidential politics   Missouri's peculiar balance of North and South, urban and rural, has helped to make it a presidential bellwether and explains its one deviation in the 20th century, in 1956 when it voted for Adlai Stevenson. He capitalized on farmer discontent and his lukewarmness on civil rights helped him carry traditional Southern Democrats. In the 1990s Missouri saw the two countervailing national trends—toward Democrats in major metropolitan areas, toward Republicans in rural areas—but in different proportions: the rural areas count for more here. Bill Clinton carried Missouri by 10% in 1992 and by 7% in 1996. In 2000 Al Gore could carry only a handful of counties outside Missouri's two big metropolitan areas, and lost by a 3% margin; John Kerry, despite big turnout in St. Louis, lost by 7%. Issues like gun control and abortion, which worked for him in the largest states, worked against him in Missouri. It did not help him that St. Louis's Archbishop Raymond Burke in June said that voting for Kerry would be a "grave" sin; Bush carried Catholics 50%-49%.

2004 Presidential Vote

Bush (R)	1,455,713	(53%)
Kerry (D)	1,259,171	(46%)
Badnarik (Lib)	9,831	(0%)
Other	6,649	(0%)

2004 Democratic Presidential Primary

Kerry (D)	211,745	(51%)
Edwards (D)	103,088	(25%)
Dean (D)	36,288	(9%)
Clark (D)	18,340	(4%)
Lieberman (D)	14,727	(4%)
Other	34,151	(8%)

2000 Presidential Vote

Bush (R)	1,189,924	(50%)
Gore (D)	1,111,138	(47%)
Nader (Green)	38,515	(2%)
Other	20,315	(1%)

The Kerry campaign cut its ad budget by three-quarters in July and stopped advertising here altogether after the Republican National Convention. In November Democrats did widen their margin in metro St. Louis by 22,000 votes, but it was reduced by 23,000 in metro Kansas City and Bush's margin outside the two big metro areas increased by 116,000.

Missouri joined the Super Tuesday primary for 1988, then went back to multi-tiered caucuses to elect delegates in 1992 and 1996. In 2000 Missouri went back to the Super Tuesday primary. In 2000 Bush and Gore won easy victories, even though Gore's rival Bill Bradley grew up in Jefferson County, Missouri. In 2004 Missouri was not much contested, because it was assumed Missouri's

Dick Gephardt would win there; but he dropped out before the February 3 primary. Kerry won with 51% of the vote; John Edwards, apparently unable to make a connection with Missouri's many southern-accented voters, won only 25%.

Congressional districting   Missouri did not lose any seats in the 2000 Census, and control of redistricting was split between the parties: Democrats held

110th Congress Lineup
5 R   4 D

109th Congress Lineup
5 R   4 D

the governorship and had a majority in the state House; Republicans, by winning two special elections in January 2001, had an 18-16 margin in the state Senate. The main problem was how to adjust for the declining population of St. Louis. Back in 1950 the city of St. Louis had 856,000 people, enough for almost three congressional districts; in 2000 it had 348,000 people, not enough for half a district. But it is heavily Democratic, and in early 2001 1st District Congressman William Lacy Clay was demanding more of the city, to keep the black percentage in his district well above 50%. That was resisted by 3d District Congressman Dick Gephardt, who didn't want his district moved farther out into Republican suburbs. On April 23 Gephardt and Clay met at the St. Louis Labor Central headquarters and made a deal; the city would be divided roughly along I-44.

In early May, Democrats passed a plan in the House which protected all incumbents and pretty well followed the Gephardt-Clay deal. In Senate committee Republicans prepared a plan that would have given Gephardt a much more Republican district, but Democrats filibustered to keep it from the floor. On May 11, a deal was reached. Gephardt got the agreed on portion of St. Louis and the close-in, increasingly Democratic suburbs of Maplewood, Richmond Heights, Clayton and University City. Clay got the increasingly black northern suburbs of Florissant, Hazelwood, Bridgeton and St. Ann plus affluent Creve Coeur and Ladue. Republican Todd Akin of the 2d District lost all those areas and got Sunset Hills, Sappington and Concord from Gephardt's old district and new territory in suburban St. Charles and rural Lincoln Counties. Akin was the only incumbent who didn't like the plan, but said he wouldn't challenge it in court. It was signed by Governor Bob Holden June 1. Some Republicans complained that it did not make the 3d District more Republican. But otherwise it was a success for Republicans, especially considering that their sole leverage was an 18-16 margin in the state Senate. They have a 5–4 lead in the delegation, and it is generally agreed that the 4th District, safe for conservative Democrat Ike Skelton, will probably elect a Republican when he retires.

Missouri's population rose only 4% between 2000 and 2006, and the state seems likely to lose a House seat in the reapportionment following the 2010 Census. Control is not clear. Republican Governor Matt Blunt will probably have serious competition in 2008, and the state's last two governor races have been decided by narrow margins. Republicans currently hold majorities in both houses of the legislature, but it's not clear whether they will hold on to them in the 2008 and 2010 elections. Demographically, the St. Louis area is even more at risk of losing a seat than it was in 2001. Population has been declining not only in St. Louis City but also in St. Louis County, which together would be entitled, under the Census's 2006 population estimates, to just under two seats in an eight-district plan. The surrounding counties—Jefferson, Franklin, Warren, Lincoln, St. Charles—would be entitled to precisely one district. Redistricters, aware of the Voting Rights Act, will presumably create a black majority district in the St. Louis area and a Kansas City district consisting of Jackson County plus some suburban territory. Beyond that one can only speculate.

Governor

Matt Blunt (R)

Elected 2004, term expires Jan. 2009, 1st full term; b. Nov. 20, 1970, Strafford; home, Springfield; U.S. Naval Academy, B.S. 1993; Baptist; married (Melanie).

Military Career: Navy, 1993-98; Naval Reserve, 1998-present.

Elected Office: MO House, 1998-2000; MO Secy. of State, 2000-04.

Professional Career: Naval officer, 1993-98.

Office: State Capitol Bldg., Rm. 216, Jefferson City, 65101, 573-751-3222; Fax: 573-751-1495; Web site: gov.mo.gov.

Election Results

2004 general	Matt Blunt (R)	1,382,419	(51%)
	Claire McCaskill (D)	1,301,442	(48%)
	Other	35,738	(1%)
2004 primary	Matt Blunt (R)	534,393	(88%)
	Karen Lee Dee Skelton-Memhardt (R)	26,089	(4%)
	Other	44,275	(7%)
2000 general	Bob Holden (D)	1,152,752	(49%)
	Jim Talent (R)	1,131,307	(48%)
	Other	62,771	(3%)

Matt Blunt was elected governor of Missouri in 2004. He was born in the town of Strafford in southwest Missouri, the first child of House Majority Whip Roy Blunt; at the time, Roy Blunt was a high school teacher. After a decade as Greene County Clerk, Roy Blunt in 1984 was elected secretary of state and the family moved to Jefferson City, where Matt Blunt attended and graduated high school. Matt Blunt won an appointment to the Naval Academy in Annapolis, spent a summer interning in the office of Governor John Ashcroft, then went on active duty in the Navy for five years, serving as an engineering, administrative and navigation officer aboard various ships. One frigate he served on was assigned to the UN-authorized blockade of Haiti and conducted anti-drug missions off the South American coast.

When his tour ended, Blunt returned home to Missouri where he immediately he joined the family business by winning a state House seat in 1998. His grandfather, Leroy Blunt, had been elected to the Missouri House in 1978 (his opponent was Betty McCaskill, whose daughter Claire would one day figure prominently in his grandson's political career). Matt Blunt's father Roy was twice elected secretary of state, lost in the Republican primary for governor in 1992 and won election to the House in 1996, where he rose to become the second-ranking Republican in the House.

Matt Blunt served one term in the state House before winning election as secretary of state in 2000 at age 29. As a lieutenant commander in the Naval Reserves, he was called up for six months active duty in the United Kingdom after September 11. With the assistance of his deputy secretary of state, he performed some official duties from his overseas post; he even conducted a telephone interview with reporters, though he could not disclose his location.

It was clear even then that Matt Blunt had his eye on the governor's office. He did not consider his age a problem; he pointed out that if elected in November 2004 he would be several months older than Senator Christopher Bond was when he was first elected governor in 1972 and that he would have had more experience in elective office. In the August primary, Blunt won 88% against five other Republican challengers.

On the Democratic side, there was a serious question as to whether incumbent Governor Bob Holden would be the nominee. Holden's administration started off on the wrong foot, holding a $1 million inaugural, the largest in state history, and then confessing that the committee was $417,000 in debt. In January 2001 he discovered he needed to cut state spending by $200 million and, thanks to Republican victories in special elections, he had to deal with a Republican state Senate, which killed his plan for a $500 million tax increase for roads. In the 2002 regular session the legislature resisted his proposal to dip into the rainy day fund and found enough revenue, but for the first time since 1997 did not provide full school funding. In November 2002 Republicans gained seats in the state Senate and had a 20-14 majority and gained control of the state House for the first time since 1948, with a 90-73 margin.

In early 2003 Holden's prospects for reelection in 2004 looked iffy. The *St. Louis Post-Dispatch* called him "a luckless politician who has encountered one problem after another since taking office." State Auditor Claire McCaskill, a Kansas City-area Democrat who was reelected 60%-37% in 2002, had in 2001 said, "I would never run against Bob Holden in a Democratic primary and I don't think anyone would be wise to do that." But she did and defeated Holden by 52%-45%.

After his defeat, Holden graciously conceded to McCaskill and the party and the state's major labor unions, which backed Holden, quickly united behind her. Blunt ran his first television ads after the primary and promised to make state government more accountable and efficient. He called for limiting awards in civil suits and restricting workers compensation insurance payments. He supported concealed-carry legislation, a state constitutional amendment banning same sex marriage and opposed abortion. McCaskill supported abortion rights, though she opposed late term abortions, with an exception for the life of the mother; she opposed the concealed-carry gun law and the amendment banning same sex marriage. McCaskill, 51, a former state legislator and prosecutor, sought to take advantage of the 33-year-old Blunt's youth and relative inexperience in state government, noting that she would not need on-the-job training. In one debate, she congratulated Blunt and his wife, who were expecting their first child, then mentioned her 17-year-old son and said, "It's something we have in common. I was expecting my first child when I was 33 years old." In her closing statement she said, "I've learned an awful lot since I was 33 years old."

Blunt won 51%-48%, running 2% behind George W. Bush and 5% behind Senator Christopher Bond. Outstate Missouri proved pivotal. McCaskill carried metro St. Louis 55%-44% and ran 5% ahead of John Kerry in metro Kansas City, winning there 57%-42%. But Blunt carried 90 of 97 counties in the rest of Missouri and won there 61%-38%. In his home area, in the counties of his father's congressional district, he led 67%-32%.

Blunt became governor as Missouri entered its fifth straight year of budget deficits. With a 23-11 Republican advantage in the Senate and a 97-66 margin in the House, it was the first time in eight decades that Republicans controlled all three branches of government. Blunt faced close to a billion-dollar shortfall for the next fiscal year and set about cutting the budget. He closed the state's Washington, D.C., office and called for paring spending by $362 million, a reduction of more than 1,000 state jobs, and for deep cuts in Medicaid spending, saying that "Missourians can no longer afford the second most expensive Medicaid program in the United States." He worked harmoniously with the legislature and got much of what he wanted, including a scaling back of the state's overextended Medicaid system with tightened eligibility requirements that cut more than 90,000 people from the Medicaid rolls. He won restrictions on medical malpractice and personal injury lawsuits with a $350,000 limit on damages for pain and suffering, changes to workers' compensation eligibility rules and a new K-12 education funding formula. His second year in office was less ambitious and productive, reflecting election year imperatives, but this time Blunt was working with a $245 million budget surplus, a development he attributed to job creation sparked by his pro-business accomplishments in 2005. He followed through on a campaign promise by signing an ethanol mandate bill requiring most fuel to contain 10% ethanol. But he failed in his effort to pass a $450 million spending plan that called for selling off Missouri Higher Education Loan Authority (MOHELA) assets to fund building projects on college campuses, new scholarships and to commercialize existing research; some legislators complained the proposal caught them by surprise and others said it was half-baked.

In 2007, health care and MOHELA again dominated the headlines. With the state's Medicaid program scheduled to expire in July 2008, Blunt proposed a new health care delivery system called Missouri HealthNet and offered proposals to encourage preventive approaches, give low-income residents better access to doctors, provide more funding for community centers and to subsidize insurance premiums for private employers. Not all of his plans were adopted, but the basics were and Blunt was able to claim he had transformed the state's health care safety net. Democrats countered that, since there was another budget surplus, the legislative session represented a blown opportunity to restore health care to many of those who had been cut off in 2005. Blunt also managed to enact his MOHELA college construction proposal, though in a watered-down form after it got caught up in the state's volatile stem cell research politics; abortion opponents argued that proceeds from the asset sales would go to life sciences research that would involve embryonic stem cell research.

While Blunt's Medicaid cuts helped balance the budget in 2005, his tightfisted approach left many voters with cool feelings toward him that lasted long past his first year on office. In 2006, he alienated his conservative base by supporting Amendment 2, the constitutional amendment that provided protections for embryonic stem cell research in Missouri; the amendment passed narrowly. By November 2006 his job approval rating was at 38%, according to a SurveyUSA poll, ranking him as one of least popular governors in the nation and among a class of politicians who were either enmeshed in scandal or so unpopular that they'd lost reelection bids or couldn't realistically hope to win again. Through mid-2007, Blunt had not officially announced he was running for reelection in 2008, but he continued to fundraise aggressively. Through July 2007, he had $5.8 million cash on hand. Longtime Democratic Attorney General Jay Nixon was already in the race, having announced his intentions in 2005; there also was talk that state Treasurer Sarah Steelman might challenge Blunt in the Republican primary.

Senior Senator

Christopher (Kit) Bond (R)

Elected 1986, seat up 2010, 4th term; b. Mar. 6, 1939, St. Louis; home, Mexico; Princeton U., B.A. 1960, U. of VA, LL.B. 1963; Presbyterian; married (Linda Pell).

Elected Office: MO Auditor, 1970-72; MO Gov., 1972-76, 1980-84.

Professional Career: Practicing atty., 1964-69, 1977-80; MO Asst. Atty. Gen., 1969-70.

DC Office: 274 RSOB, 20510, 202-224-5721; Fax: 202-224-8149; Web site: bond.senate.gov.

State Offices: Cape Girardeau, 573-334-7044; Columbia, 573-442-8151; Jefferson City, 573-634-2488; Kansas City, 816-471-7141; Springfield, 417-864-8258; St. Louis, 314-725-4484.

Committees: *Appropriations* (5th of 14 R): Transportation, Housing and Urban Development & Related Agencies (RMM); Financial Services & General Government; Agriculture, Rural Development, Food and Drug Administration & Related Agencies; Defense; State, Foreign Operations & Related Programs; Energy & Water Development. *Environment & Public Works* (9th of 9 R): Transportation Safety, Infrastructure Security & Water Quality; Public Sector Solutions to Global Warming, Oversight & Children's Health Protection. *Intelligence (Select)* (Vice Chmn. of 7 R). *Small Business & Entrepreneurship* (2d of 9 R).

Group Ratings

	ADA	ACLU	AFS	LCV	ITIC	NTU	COC	ACU	CFG	FRC
2006	5	17	0	14	100	67	92	80	56	87
2005	0	—	0	0	—	69	100	88	74	—

National Journal Ratings

	2005 LIB	—	2005 CONS	2006 LIB	—	2006 CONS
Economic	6%	—	90%	20%	—	77%
Social	23%	—	64%	18%	—	74%
Foreign	26%	—	65%	18%	—	76%

Key Votes of the 109th Congress

1. Bar ANWR Drilling	N	5. Confirm Samuel Alito	Y	9. Limit Interstate Abortion	Y
2. FY06 Spending Curb	Y	6. Path to Citizenship	N	10. CAFTA	Y
3. Estate Tax Repeal	Y	7. Bar Same Sex Marriage	Y	11. Urge Iraq Withdrawal	N
4. Raise Minimum Wage	N	8. Stem Cell Research $	Y	12. Provide Detainee Rights	N

Election Results

2004 general	Christopher (Kit) Bond (R)	1,518,089	(56%)	($7,848,506)
	Nancy Farmer (D)	1,158,261	(43%)	($3,548,116)
	Other	30,052	(1%)	
2004 primary	Christopher (Kit) Bond (R)	541,998	(88%)	
	Mike Steger (R)	73,354	(12%)	
1998 general	Christopher (Kit) Bond (R)	830,625	(53%)	($6,229,649)
	Jay Nixon (D)	690,208	(44%)	($2,568,879)
	Other	56,024	(4%)	

Prior Winning Percentages: 1992 (52%); 1986 (53%)

Christopher Bond was first elected to statewide office in 1970 and was first elected to the Senate in 1986. Bond grew up in the town of Mexico, Missouri, where his family were part owners of the largest business, A.P. Green, makers of heat-resistant bricks, which was sold to another firm in 1998. He graduated from Princeton and the University of Virginia law school, then clerked for Judge Elbert Tuttle, one of the great pioneers on civil rights in the Fifth Circuit in Atlanta. He returned to Missouri, practiced law and ran for Congress in 1968, at age 29, and narrowly lost. He was elected state auditor in 1970 and then elected governor at 33 in 1972, and became one of the youngest governors in the nation's history. He lost in an upset to Democrat Joseph Teasdale in 1976 and won a comeback victory against Teasdale in 1980. After two years in private life he ran for the Senate against Harriett Woods, who had come close to beating Bond's longtime ally, then-Senator John Danforth, in 1982. Woods ran a three-part ad showing a farmer breaking into tears as he and his wife told Woods about their foreclosure and named Bond as a board member of the insurance company that foreclosed; evidently this struck voters as either demagoguery or an invasion of privacy, and Woods fell in the polls. Bond won, 53%-47%.

Bond has a moderate voting record in the Senate, but can also be a strong partisan; he does much of his work behind the scenes. He was the chief Republican sponsor of the Family and Medical Leave Act, vetoed by George H.W. Bush and signed by Bill Clinton. For years he was the lead Republican senator on housing issues, starting on the Banking Committee and then for years as chairman and ranking member of the VA-HUD Appropriations Subcommittee. There he worked in bipartisan fashion with ranking Democrat Barbara Mikulski, funding the space program in which she takes an interest and projects affecting Missouri. Bond has sponsored many amendments aiding inner city organizations and encouraging small businesses in troubled urban areas and has worked cooperatively with many black community leaders in St. Louis and Kansas City, to the point that Kansas City's mayor declined to endorse his Democratic opponent in 1998. He has opposed companies and European nations which have sought to ban genetically modified food, of which the chief producer is St. Louis-based Monsanto, and has sought tougher FDA regulation of compounded medicines in pharmacies.

On the Defense Appropriations Subcommittee, he has worked hard to keep in operation the F-15 production line at Boeing's (formerly McDonnell Douglas's) plant next to the St. Louis airport. In 2004 he got $120 million to build two more F-15s, keeping the production line open until 2008. Other Missouri interests have prompted Bond initiatives. He was the co-sponsor with Carl Levin of the amendment, passed 62-38 in March 2002, that delayed any increase in CAFE auto mileage standards for two years; Missouri has auto assembly plants. In January 2003 he became chairman of the Environment and Public Works Subcommittee that has jurisdiction over reauthorization of highway and other transportation spending; he declined the chairmanship of the Small Business Committee to keep this one. He held hearings around Missouri on road issues in 2002 and pushed hard for a $318 billion transportation bill in 2003 and 2004 and he held out in the 2004 conference committee against a lower figure. He hailed the passage of the transportation act in August 2005 and said it had $1.3 billion for projects in Missouri. In August 2006 the Senate passed a water resources bill with $900 million for new locks and $1.6 billion for ecosystem restoration on the Mississippi, Missouri and Illinois Rivers, but the House did not act; in January 2007 Bond and the two Illinois senators were back with another bill. When the Appropriations subcommittees were reorganized in February and March 2005 he did not oppose the breaking up of the VA-HUD Subcommittee; he ended up with the chairmanship of the Transportation, Treasury, the Judiciary, HUD, and Related Agencies Subcommittee.

In September 2003 Bond sponsored an amendment to bar states from imposing on small engines emission standards stricter than federal standards. At issue in his view were 1,750 jobs at two Briggs & Stratton lawn mower factories in Missouri which would be jeopardized by a strict

California standard. It passed in November 2003 when Bond reduced the horsepower of affected engines from 175 to 50. But California Governor Arnold Schwarzenegger objected and began making calls around Capitol Hill. In conference committee Bond agreed to exempt California from the bill. In 2005 he passed an amendment barring EPA from issuing new rules without conducting safety tests; he declined to push a similar amendment in July 2006, saying he would monitor the administrative process. Bond worked with Kansas City Mayor Kay Barnes to move 6,000 IRS employees to the main post office in Missouri; Democratic Congressman Dennis Moore, who represents Kansas City's Kansas suburbs, objected to the removal of jobs from his district but admitted he didn't have the clout to stop it.

Bond got his political start as part of a group of young reform-minded Republicans—his former Senate colleague John Danforth was another—working against the Democratic political establishment in Missouri, and he can be a strong partisan on occasion. On election night 2000 he was furious when St. Louis Democrats persuaded a state judge to order the polls opened three extra hours in the city; an appeals court overturned the order within 45 minutes, but Bond, who charged that Democrats tried to keep the St. Louis polls open till midnight to defeat him in 1972, said the election had been stolen, and indeed Republicans Jim Talent and John Ashcroft lost by narrow margins. In Washington Bond became heavily involved in the election procedures bill that was an obvious item of business after the 2000 Florida controversy. The centerpiece of the bill was its national standards for voting equipment coupled with $3.5 million in federal aid and statewide voter registries. Bond argued that the motor voter act had installed and kept on the rolls many names of those not entitled to vote, and insisted on a provision requiring mail-in registrants to vote in person the first time they vote and to present a driver's license or photo identification. He negotiated this with lead Democrat Christopher Dodd; "I've told him [Dodd] that I will agree with his concept that we need to make it easier to vote, if he agrees with my concept that we need to make it harder to cheat." The bill was eventually passed in October 2002.

In 2005 and 2006 Bond surprised some observers by vigorously defending the Bush administration on the Dubai Ports purchase, on NSA surveillance of contacts between al Qaeda suspects abroad and persons in the United States, on enhanced interrogation of unlawful combatants. On the Intelligence Committee he strongly defended the nomination of Michael Hayden at CIA and pushed for more authority for the Director of National Intelligence. He sponsored a bill with criminal penalties for government employees or contractors who leak classified information. He supported the immigration bill in May 2006. "As a practical problem, you can't treat 11 million people as felons. We have to give them some way to pay their dues." He is co-Chairman of the National Guard Caucus, and with Patrick Leahy has sponsored legislation to give four-star status to the head of the National Guard, with a seat on the Joint Chiefs of Staff and budgetary power to research and procure equipment. So far this has not passed muster with the Armed Services Committee. He has generally supported the Bush administration on Iraq, but in January 2007 said, "Count me very skeptical about a surge." His son, Marine Lieutenant Sam Bond, has served two tours in Iraq.

Bond was reelected 52%-45% in 1992, a year in which Missouri Republicans lost every other major race. In 1998, against Attorney General Jay Nixon, he was reelected 53%-44%. Democrats hoped to target Bond in 2004, but their most prominent candidates did not run. Congressman Dick Gephardt was running for president, and Governor Bob Holden was running for reelection; Auditor Claire McCaskill was running against Holden in the Democratic primary (she lost the general election in 2004 but was elected to the Senate in 2006). Attorney General Jay Nixon had already lost two Senate races, and Lieutenant Governor Joe Maxwell declined to run. But Treasurer Nancy Farmer stepped forward; DSCC Chairman Jon Corzine talked up her chances. But unlike Corzine, she was not capable of self-financing a campaign, and Bond outspent her $7.9 million to $3.5 million. Bond ran ads claiming that he had saved Missouri jobs and brought more in: 1,800 jobs at Briggs & Stratton and "thousands more" to Missouri suppliers, 5,000 at Boeing with "800 new jobs on the way." His ads claimed that as treasurer Farmer invested $1 billion out of state, "costing communities 10,000 lost Missouri jobs." Bond won only 14% of the black vote this time and lost metro St. Louis 52%-47%. But he carried usually Democratic metro Kansas City 51%-48% and carried the rest of the state 67%-33%, for a 56%-43% victory, his widest percentage margin ever in a Senate or governor's race.

Junior Senator

Claire McCaskill (D)

Elected 2006, seat up 2012, 1st term; b. July 24, 1953, Rolla; home, St. Louis; U. of MO, B.S. 1975, J.D. 1978; Catholic; married (Joseph Shepard).

Elected Office: MO House of Reps., 1982-88; Jackson Cnty. Legislature, 1990-92; Jackson Cnty. Prosecutor, 1992-98; MO Auditor, 1998-2006.

Professional Career: Law clerk, MO Court of Appeals, 1978; Asst. Jackson Cnty. Prosecutor, 1978-82; Practicing atty., 1983-92.

DC Office: 717 HSOB, 20510, 202-224-6154; Fax: 202-228-6326; Web site: mccaskill.senate.gov.

State Offices: Cape Girardeau, 573-651-0964; Columbia, 573-442-7130; Kansas City, 816-421-1639; Springfield, 417-291-1475; St. Louis, 314-367-1364.

Committees: *Aging (Special)* (10th of 11 D). *Armed Services* (13th of 13 D): Personnel; Readiness & Management Support; Airland. *Commerce, Science & Transportation* (11th of 12 D): Interstate Commerce, Trade & Tourism; Science, Technology & Innovation; Consumer Affairs, Insurance & Automotive Safety; Surface Transportation & Merchant Marine Infrastructure, Safety & Security; Aviation Operations, Safety & Security. *Homeland Security & Governmental Affairs* (8th of 9 D): Federal Financial Management, Government Information, Federal Services & International Security; Investigations (Permanent); State, Local & Private Sector Preparedness & Integration. *Indian Affairs* (7th of 8 D).

Group Ratings and Key Votes: Newly Elected

Election Results

2006 general	Claire McCaskill (D)	1,055,255	(50%)	($11,705,967)
	Jim Talent (R)	1,006,941	(47%)	($14,340,762)
	Other	66,263	(3%)	
2006 primary	Claire McCaskill (D)	282,767	(81%)	
	Bill Young (D)	67,173	(19%)	
2002 general	Jim Talent (R)	935,032	(50%)	($8,322,003)
	Jean Carnahan (D)	913,778	(49%)	($12,293,579)
	Other	28,810	(2%)	

Claire McCaskill, a Democrat, was elected as Missouri's junior senator in 2006. She was born in Rolla, Missouri, located about halfway between St. Louis and Springfield, and grew up in various small towns in southern Missouri. She comes from a political family: Her father served for a time as state insurance commissioner and her mother was the first female city council member in Columbia. Claire McCaskill got degrees from the University of Missouri and its law school, clerked for the state Court of Appeals in Kansas City and worked as an assistant prosecutor. In 1982, at the age of 29, she was elected to the Missouri House, where she notes she was the first woman to give birth as an active member of the legislature. In 1990 she was elected to the Jackson County legislature. Two years later, McCaskill ran for county prosecutor and won; in 1998 she decided to run statewide and was elected state auditor.

In 2004, halfway through her second term as auditor, McCaskill challenged incumbent Governor Bob Holden in the Democratic primary. Holden's administration had started off on the wrong foot, holding a $1 million inaugural, the largest in state history, and it turned out the inaugural committee was $417,000 in debt. Things didn't get much better as a tough economic climate necessitated deep spending cuts and Holden battled with the legislature over education funding. Despite roots in the Ozarks, he was hurt in outstate Missouri by his 2003 veto of a concealed-carry gun law, his maneuvering to move a constitutional amendment to ban same-sex marriage to the August primary ballot (where it passed overwhelmingly 71%-29%) rather than the general election and by his handling of education spending.

McCaskill, who was reelected 60%-37% in 2002, had in 2001 said, "I would never run against Bob Holden in a Democratic primary and I don't think anyone would be wise to do that." But she did and defeated him by 52%-45%. Holden graciously conceded to McCaskill, and the party and the state's major labor unions, which backed Holden, quickly united behind her against Republican Secretary of State Matt Blunt, the 33-year-old son of House Majority Whip Roy Blunt. This was not the first contest between the McCaskills and Blunts: Blunt's grandfather, Leroy Blunt, had been elected to the Missouri House in 1978 by defeating McCaskill's mother, Betty McCaskill.

Blunt ran his first television ads after the primary and promised to make state government more accountable and efficient. He supported concealed-carry legislation and the constitutional amendment banning same sex marriage and opposed abortion. McCaskill supported abortion rights, though she opposed late term abortions, with an exception for the life of the mother; she opposed the concealed-carry gun law and the constitutional amendment banning same sex marriage. McCaskill sought to take advantage of Blunt's youth and relative inexperience in state government, noting that she would not need on-the-job training. She lost 51%-48%. McCaskill easily carried the Kansas City and St. Louis metropolitan areas but lost big in outstate Missouri where Blunt won 90 of the 97 counties outside the two metro areas.

Despite the narrow loss, with three previous statewide races under her belt McCaskill was a prize Senate recruit for the national party in 2006. She was viewed as the only top-tier Democratic candidate, certainly capable of winning a seat that had changed hands twice between 2000 and 2002. In 2000, Republican John Ashcroft had lost 51%-48% to Mel Carnahan, the sitting governor whose name remained on the ballot after his death 22 days before the election. Carnahan's wife Jean was appointed to the vacancy; in the 2002 election for the remaining four years of the term, she lost 50%-49% to Republican Jim Talent.

In almost any other election year, Talent would have been well-positioned for reelection. He had avoided ethics missteps, was attentive back home and had quietly built a solid legislative record. But the war in Iraq and the unpopularity of the Bush administration was not helpful to a politician elected to the Senate with a thin 21,000 vote margin.

McCaskill announced her candidacy in August 2005 on the steps of the feed mill where her father once worked—a backdrop that telegraphed her heightened focus on the rural counties that cost her the governor's election. Touting her country upbringing, McCaskill promised to "never forget rural Missouri." She ran as a populist and traveled the state in a 31-foot recreational vehicle though the rural region she once called "Ashcroftland" for its religious conservatism. She denounced tax breaks for oil companies and called for an increase in the minimum wage and tax credits for first-time home purchases, child care, and college education. In December, McCaskill was forced to take a temporary leave from the campaign trail to deal with a family tragedy: her ex-husband, whom she divorced in 1995, was shot and killed in Kansas City.

Throughout the campaign, McCaskill linked Talent to George W. Bush—"He agrees with President Bush more than I agree with my husband," McCaskill quipped—but it was the issue of stem cell research that generated the most attention. A controversial proposed constitutional amendment forced both candidates to address the issue, with McCaskill supporting the measure and Talent weighing in against it. His opposition was not without risk and it exposed a rift among Missouri Republicans: state business leaders backed the Missouri Stem Cell Research and Cures Initiative for its potential to attract biomedical research to the state, while religious conservatives opposed it, considering the destruction of embryos tantamount to the destruction of human life.

In October, Talent flayed McCaskill over her family's personal finances and demanded that she release the tax returns of her husband, Joseph Shepard, a millionaire developer who filed his taxes separately from her. Talent also suggested that they hadn't paid all their taxes and accused McCaskill's husband of owning an offshore tax shelter. Through late October, polls showed this race to be a dead heat. On Election Day, McCaskill won 50%-47%, a difference of just 48,000 votes out of 2.1 million cast. This was the third consecutive election for this seat that was decided by less than 50,000 votes. Just as in the 2004 governor's race, McCaskill won big margins in the Kansas City and St. Louis metro areas but unlike 2004, McCaskill held her own in outstate Missouri and even carried 11 counties she lost in 2004.

FIRST DISTRICT

Rep. William Lacy Clay (D)

Elected 2000, 4th term; b. July 27, 1956, St. Louis; home, St. Louis; U. of MD, B.S. 1983; Catholic; married (Ivie).

Elected Office: MO House of Reps., 1983-90; MO Senate, 1991-2000.

Professional Career: Asst. Doorkeeper, U.S. House of Reps, 1976-83; Paralegal, 1982-2000; Real estate agent, 1986-2000.

DC Office: 434 CHOB, 20515, 202-225-2406; Fax: 202-226-3717; Web site: lacyclay.house.gov.

District Offices: St. Louis, 314-367-1970; St. Louis County, 314-383-5240.

Committees: *Financial Services* (15th of 37 D): Housing & Community Opportunity; Domestic and International Monetary Policy, Trade & Technology; Financial Institutions & Consumer Credit. *Oversight & Government Reform* (10th of 23 D): Information Policy, Census & National Archives (Chmn.); Federal Workforce, Postal Service & the District of Columbia.

Group Ratings

	ADA	ACLU	AFS	LCV	ITIC	NTU	COC	ACU	CFG	FRC
2006	90	95	86	92	57	19	67	16	17	0
2005	85	—	100	83	—	18	44	21	12	23

National Journal Ratings

	2005 LIB	—	2005 CONS		2006 LIB	—	2006 CONS
Economic	67%	—	33%		69%	—	31%
Social	84%	—	16%		75%	—	25%
Foreign	89%	—	10%		83%	—	14%

Key Votes of the 109th Congress

1. Estate Tax Repeal	Y	5. Limit Interstate Abortion	Y	9. Build Border Fence	N
2. Limit CAFE Standards	Y	6. Extend Patriot Act	N	10. CAFTA	N
3. FY06 Spending Curb	N	7. Bar Same Sex Marriage	N	11. Oppose Iraq Withdrawal	N
4. Drilling in ANWR	N	8. Stem Cell Research $	Y	12. Detainee Tribunals	N

Election Results

2006 general	William Lacy Clay (D)	141,574	(73%)	($464,665)
	Mark Byrne (R)	47,893	(25%)	($72,558)
	Other	4,768	(2%)	
2006 primary	William Lacy Clay (D)	unopposed		
2004 general	William Lacy Clay (D)	213,658	(75%)	($262,648)
	Leslie Farr (R)	64,791	(23%)	
	Other	5,322	(2%)	

Prior Winning Percentages: 2002 (70%); 2000 (75%)

The People		Race/Ethnic Origin	Ancestry	
Area size:	227 sq. mi.	45.8% White	German: 13.6%	Irish: 7.8%
Urban population:	99.2%	49.7% Black	English: 4.3%	
Rural population:	0.8%	1.5% Asian	**2004 Presidential Vote**	
Pop. 2000:	621,690	0.2% Native Am.	Kerry (D) 216,372	(75%)
Pop. 2005 (est):	597,251	0.0% Hawaiian	Bush (R) 71,367	(25%)
Median income:	$36,314	1.3% Two+ races	**2000 Presidential Vote**	
Poverty status:	15.8%	0.1% Other	Gore (D) 182,323	(72%)
Military veterans:	13.6%	1.3% Hispanic Origin	Bush (R) 65,686	(26%)
			Other 5,022	(2%)
			Cook Partisan Voting Index: D +26	

Occupation	Blue collar: 20.7%	White collar: 61.9%	Gray collar: 17.4%

For a century or more, St. Louis seemed the center of America: the starting point for the Lewis and Clark expedition in 1804; the locus half a century later of the *Dred Scott* case, a Supreme Court ruling that helped split the nation; the site of the 1904 World's Fair that introduced the hot dog and the ice cream cone and got 19 million people to *Meet Me in St. Louis*. Its 630-foot-high Gateway Arch is just below the point where the waters of the Missouri surge into the Mississippi, about halfway between New Orleans and Lake Superior, the Atlantic and the Pacific. This first major American city west of the Mississippi River was the final resting place of Daniel Boone and for many years was Chicago's rival as the transportation hub of America. In 1904 St. Louis already had the Eads Bridge, one of America's first suspension bridges; the Wainwright Building, one of Louis Sullivan's first skyscrapers; and Union Station, the world's largest passenger train station when it opened in 1894. Some 600,000 people lived then in densely packed brick houses on old street grids radiating outward from downtown. This was a heavily German city, with a Teutonic solidity and orderliness that distinguished it from the surrounding Southern-accented rural terrain; and from Mitteleuropa came the founders of St. Louis's great businesses—the Anheuser-Busch brewery, May Company department stores, Joseph Pulitzer's *St. Louis Post-Dispatch*—and its first great politician and a friend of Abraham Lincoln, Senator and Interior Secretary Carl Schurz. There is almost a European aura to Forest Park, the site of the 1904 fair, and the dozen mansion-lined private streets nearby, like Portland Place.

St. Louis is still one of the nation's 20 largest metro areas, but today it does not occupy as central a place in the national consciousness, and the central city itself has largely emptied out. The German order that made so many people comfortable living in close quarters and commuting by streetcar seems to have yielded to an American desire for Daniel Boone's wide open (suburban) spaces and the less restrictive automobile. St. Louis' population peaked at 856,000 in 1950; it was down to 343,000 in 2004, less than its 350,000 in 1880 and far less than the 1,000,510 now in suburban (and juridically separate) St. Louis County. Indeed, more blacks live in St. Louis County than St. Louis City. Downtown St. Louis has been spruced up admirably: the Gateway Arch was finished in 1965; Union Station has been redeveloped; Laclede's Landing and the former garment district are stocked with shops; a new Busch Stadium opened with a panoramic view of the Arch and downtown. But most of St. Louis's old factories have closed and many of its once tight neighborhoods are only a memory.

Missouri's congressional districts have followed the people out of St. Louis, where the Democratic organization has been weakened by the loss of patronage and state approval of term limits. The 1st District of Missouri, historically based on the north side of the city, now has three-quarters of its residents in suburban St. Louis County. It includes St. Louis City north of I-44 and the northern and some central portions of St. Louis County. The district includes all the predominantly black suburbs to the north of the city, including Bellefontaine Neighbors, Ferguson, Spanish Lake and Black Jack. It also includes along I-70 working-class St. Ann and Bridgeton and, just west of the city, parts of the affluent suburbs of University City, Ladue and Creve Coeur. In the 1990s, the population of the district was 60% black; now it is 50% black. But blacks account for far more than 50% of the votes in Democratic primaries that, in this heavily Democratic district, are the contests that matter.

The congressman from the 1st District is William Lacy Clay, a Democrat first elected in 2000 to the seat that his father Bill Clay had held for 32 years. Lacy Clay's whole life bears the imprint of his father's politics. Born in St. Louis, he moved to the Washington, D.C. area at age 12 after his father's election in 1968 and grew up as a congressman's son. He attended Silver Spring, Maryland, public schools and then the University of Maryland, studying by night for seven years while he worked as a House staffer by day. He had started law classes at Howard University when a special election for the state House in 1983 drew him back to St. Louis, and party leaders appointed him the Democratic nominee. Eight years later, Lacy Clay was again picked by party leaders to run in a special election for a safely Democratic state Senate seat, after the incumbent got a job with a congressional subcommittee. In 1999 Bill Clay decided to retire after having helped to enact many labor and education laws. Lacy Clay had a serious primary. St. Louis Councilman Charlie Dooley, his most credible opponent, raised nearly $400,000 and, though black, built up a base of support in the mostly white suburbs of St. Louis County. Dooley campaigned that the office should not be "inherited" and he attacked what he called Clay's old-style tactics of political threats and bossism. To make sure voters knew he was not challenging the incumbent, Dooley's billboards said, "Congressman Bill Clay is retiring this year." The St. Louis Labor Council and Missouri AFL-CIO, long allied to Bill Clay, declined to endorse his son, but he was endorsed by more than 30 locals. Lacy Clay played up his father's name and revved up the still reliable machine. He won the primary 61%-28% over

Dooley, winning St. Louis City 76%-12% and St. Louis County, where twice as many votes were cast, 49%-39%. In the general, Lacy Clay won 75%-22%, which was better than his father's recent elections.

In the House, Clay was president of the Democrats' freshman class. His mostly liberal voting record has turned centrist on economic issues. He has worked to protect voting rights for blacks and the reliability of electronic voting equipment. On the reorganized Oversight and Government Reform Committee, Clay chairs the Information Policy, Census and National Archives Subcommittee, with jurisdiction ranging from the Freedom of Information Act to the Census Bureau, a useful post for blacks concerned about maximizing rights and their House seats following the next redistricting. In his March 2006 call to withdraw U.S. troops from Iraq, he called President Bush an "incompetent chickenhawk."

Clay has not been seriously challenged for reelection. His biggest concern may be the declining population in his district, and its implications for the next round of redistricting; the 1st District was the only one in the state to lose population between 2000 and 2005.

SECOND DISTRICT

Rep. Todd Akin (R)

Elected 2000, 4th term; b. July 5, 1947, New York, NY; home, Town and Country; Worcester Polytech Inst. (MA), B.S. 1971, Covenant Theological Seminary (MO), M. Div. 1985; Presbyterian; married (Lulli).

Military Career: Army Reserves 1972-80.

Elected Office: MO House of Reps., 1988-2000.

Professional Career: Marketing Mgr., IBM, 1974-78; Mgmt. Dir., Laclede Steel, 1977-80; Instructor, Maryville U.

DC Office: 117 CHOB, 20515, 202-225-2561; Fax: 202-225-2563; Web site: akin.house.gov.

District Offices: St. Charles, 636-949-6826; St. Louis, 314-590-0029.

Committees: *Armed Services* (11th of 29 R): Oversight & Investigations (RMM); Air & Land Forces. *Science & Technology* (9th of 20 R): Energy & Environment. *Small Business* (4th of 15 R): Contracting & Technology.

Group Ratings

	ADA	ACLU	AFS	LCV	ITIC	NTU	COC	ACU	CFG	FRC
2006	0	5	0	8	100	71	100	92	84	100
2005	0	—	0	0	—	71	89	100	100	100

National Journal Ratings

	2005 LIB	—	2005 CONS	2006 LIB	—	2006 CONS
Economic	0%	—	97%	16%	—	81%
Social	0%	—	89%	6%	—	92%
Foreign	0%	—	89%	0%	—	94%

Key Votes of the 109th Congress

1. Estate Tax Repeal	Y	5. Limit Interstate Abortion	Y	9. Build Border Fence	Y
2. Limit CAFE Standards	Y	6. Extend Patriot Act	Y	10. CAFTA	Y
3. FY06 Spending Curb	Y	7. Bar Same Sex Marriage	Y	11. Oppose Iraq Withdrawal	Y
4. Drilling in ANWR	Y	8. Stem Cell Research $	N	12. Detainee Tribunals	Y

Election Results

2006 general	Todd Akin (R)	176,452	(61%)	($698,050)
	George Weber (D)	105,242	(37%)	
	Other	5,923	(2%)	
2006 primary	Todd Akin (R)	41,464	(88%)	
	Sherman Parker (R)	5,597	(12%)	
2004 general	Todd Akin (R)	228,725	(65%)	($702,232)
	George Weber (D)	115,366	(33%)	
	Other	5,776	(2%)	

Prior Winning Percentages: 2002 (67%); 2000 (55%)

The People		Race/Ethnic Origin	Ancestry		
Area size:	1,288 sq. mi.	93.2% White	German: 26.7%	Irish: 12.7%	
Urban population:	91.7%	2.2% Black	English: 8.2%		
Rural population:	8.4%	2.0% Asian	**2004 Presidential Vote**		
Pop. 2000:	621,690	0.2% Native Am.	Bush (R) 215,123	(60%)	
Pop. 2005 (est):	683,109	0.0% Hawaiian	Kerry (D) 142,824	(40%)	
Median income:	$61,416	0.9% Two+ races	Other 155	(0%)	
Poverty status:	3.6%	0.1% Other	**2000 Presidential Vote**		
Military veterans:	13.5%	1.4% Hispanic Origin	Bush (R) 179,633	(59%)	
			Gore (D) 119,907	(39%)	
			Other 6,744	(2%)	
			Cook Partisan Voting Index: R + 9		

Occupation	Blue collar: 17.5%	White collar: 71.3%	Gray collar: 11.2%

Just as the U.S. population's geographic center has moved west from the St. Louis area to rural Phelps County, so the center of metropolitan St. Louis area continues to move farther west from the Gateway Arch on the Mississippi River. The fulcrum point now is in St. Louis County, established in 1876 when the city, tired of paying for dusty back roads, separated itself from the sticks. There were then about 350,000 people in the city and 31,000 in the county. In 2006, the city had 344,000 and St. Louis County 1,000,510. By the 1960s, the center of office employment had moved from downtown across the county line to Clayton; now, the focus is fast moving out the Daniel Boone Expressway (U.S. 40) to Chesterfield, west of the I-270 ring road.

The 2d Congressional District of Missouri is made up of central and western St. Louis County, most of St. Charles County northwest across the Missouri River and rural Lincoln County to the north. In the center of St. Louis County, along the Daniel Boone Expressway, are the long-settled suburbs of Kirkwood, most of high-income Town and Country and Ladue, fast-growing Chesterfield and, to the south, Sunset Hills—all Republican areas, even more so in the newer family-oriented subdivisions than in the leafy precincts of the old rich. St. Charles County, where the supply of available land and affordable housing has become tight, now casts more votes than the city of St. Louis and is the most Republican suburban county in Missouri; the county council in May 2004 added a statement to its marriage licenses that the recipients are a man and a woman. This is a Republican district that voted 60% for George W. Bush in 2004.

The congressman from the 2d District is Todd Akin, a Republican first elected in 2000. He continues to live in his boyhood home, a 60-year-old farmhouse that rests in what has become an upscale neighborhood in Town and Country. He graduated from Worcester Polytechnic Institute and got a divinity degree at Covenant Seminary. After service as an Army combat engineer, he worked for IBM in the Boston area and then at Laclede Steel in Alton, Illinois, the same company where his father once worked. He was elected to the state House in 1988. Akin is an avid student of American history and the Constitution, on which he lectures at various public and private institutions. While a state legislator, he sold standardized tests to parents who home school their children; he and his wife have home schooled their six children. State House reporters noted that he sometimes played gospel tunes on his guitar in the Capitol late at night. When Jim Talent announced in early 1999 that he was running for governor, Akin ran for his House seat. He started off as the underdog to Gene McNary, the former Bush administration INS commissioner and well known from his 15 years as St. Louis County Executive, and as a three-time loser in statewide races between 1972 and 1984. Akin called himself "a conservative with a soft edge." He emphasized that he had never voted to raise taxes, and he had strong support from religious conservatives. In a low-turnout, rainy day Republican primary, Akin rallied his committed cadre to win the five-candidate contest by 56 votes over McNary. In the general election against state Senator Ted House, Akin focused on their differences on taxes. House, whose TV ads did not identify himself as a Democrat, depicted Akin as a narrow ideologue who was an ineffective legislator. Akin carried St. Louis County 57%-40% and won overall 55%-42%.

In the House, Akin has one of the most strongly conservative voting records, with an emphasis on free enterprise. On the Armed Services Committee he emphasized what he said was the essential role played by special operation forces in fighting terrorism and supported production of electronic attack aircraft at Boeing's local plant. With Dana Rohrabacher, he passed in the House a bill to promote development of the commercial human space flight industry, to encourage entrepreneurship especially in suborbital rockets. After a federal appeals court in California ruled that the reference to "one nation under God" in the Pledge of Allegiance was unconstitutional, Akin twice passed in the House a bill that would strip the lower courts of jurisdiction over challenges to the Pledge; but it went nowhere in the Senate. He sponsored the Parents' Right to Know Act, which bars funding to family planning projects that provide contraceptive drugs and devices to minors before getting parental consent. He burned some bridges with Republican leaders when he voted against the Medicare/prescription drug bill; he worried that it would be a "budget buster" and would attract more illegal immigrants. In 2007, he became ranking Republican on the Armed Services Subcommittee on Oversight and Investigation. One of his sons was a Marine in Iraq.

Back home, Akin has been easily reelected. In 2006, Republican primary challenger Sherman Parker—a moderate African American and state representative—was arrested a week before the contest for failing to register his car or appear in court for a speeding ticket. Akin won 88%-12%.

THIRD DISTRICT

Rep. Russ Carnahan (D)

Elected 2004, 2d term; b. July 10, 1958, Columbia; home, St. Louis; U. of MO, B.S. 1979, J.D. 1983; Methodist; married (Debra).

Elected Office: MO House of Reps., 2000-04.

Professional Career: Practicing atty., 1988-96; Consultant, BJC HealthCare, 1996-2004.

DC Office: 1710 LHOB, 20515, 202-225-2671; Fax: 202-225-7452; Web site: carnahan.house.gov.

District Offices: Crystal City, 636-937-8039; St. Louis, 314-962-1523.

Committees: *Foreign Affairs* (13th of 27 D): International Organizations, Human Rights & Oversight; Middle East & South Asia. *Science & Technology* (20th of 24 D): Research & Science Education. *Transportation & Infrastructure* (22d of 41 D): Aviation; Water Resources & Environment.

Group Ratings

	ADA	ACLU	AFS	LCV	ITIC	NTU	COC	ACU	CFG	FRC
2006	90	86	100	100	71	13	53	12	12	14
2005	95	—	100	89	—	12	41	0	3	8

National Journal Ratings

	2005 LIB	—	2005 CONS		2006 LIB	—	2006 CONS
Economic	82%	—	16%		79%	—	18%
Social	73%	—	27%		73%	—	27%
Foreign	66%	—	33%		69%	—	30%

Key Votes of the 109th Congress

1. Estate Tax Repeal	N	5. Limit Interstate Abortion	N	9. Build Border Fence	N
2. Limit CAFE Standards	N	6. Extend Patriot Act	Y	10. CAFTA	N
3. FY06 Spending Curb	N	7. Bar Same Sex Marriage	N	11. Oppose Iraq Withdrawal	N
4. Drilling in ANWR	N	8. Stem Cell Research $	Y	12. Detainee Tribunals	N

Election Results

2006 general	Russ Carnahan (D)	145,219	(66%)	($1,184,962)
	David Bertelsen (R)	70,189	(32%)	($8,300)
	Other	6,040	(2%)	
2006 primary	Russ Carnahan (D)	37,200	(76%)	
	Jim Frisella (D)	11,517	(24%)	
2004 general	Russ Carnahan (D)	146,894	(53%)	($1,392,248)
	Bill Federer (R)	125,422	(45%)	($1,367,643)
	Other	5,600	(2%)	

The People		Race/Ethnic Origin	Ancestry	
Area size:	1,266 sq. mi.	85.7% White	German: 23.1%	Irish: 11.6%
Urban population:	86.7%	9.1% Black	English: 5.9%	
Rural population:	13.3%	1.6% Asian	**2004 Presidential Vote**	
Pop. 2000:	621,690	0.2% Native Am.	Kerry (D) 168,740	(57%)
Pop. 2005 (est):	634,102	0.0% Hawaiian	Bush (R) 127,668	(43%)
Median income:	$41,091	1.4% Two+ races	Other 657	(0%)
Poverty status:	10.1%	0.1% Other	**2000 Presidential Vote**	
Military veterans:	13.2%	1.8% Hispanic Origin	Gore (D) 140,954	(54%)
			Bush (R) 112,460	(43%)
			Other 7,972	(3%)
			Cook Partisan Voting Index: D + 8	

Occupation	Blue collar: 24.2%	White collar: 60.4%	Gray collar: 15.4%

Middle America, it could be said, lies somewhere on the south side of metropolitan St. Louis. The geographical center of the country's population was here in 1980, just south of St. Louis in once rural and now mostly suburban Jefferson County; while that point has moved southwest, St. Louis is still the metro area nearest the demographic midpoint of a country most of whose people live in million-plus metro areas. Geographically, this is a node where some of the nation's main arteries come together. The Missouri River flows into the Mississippi a few miles north of St. Louis's Gateway Arch; the National Road and its successors, U.S. 40 and Interstate 70, cross the Mississippi just below the Arch. And the great tides of Southerners migrating west up the Mississippi and Germans migrating overland met here to create one of the nation's largest and most bustling cities out of a town founded by the French before the Revolutionary War. The south side of St. Louis is famous for its pleasant parks and tight-knit, neat neighborhoods, including "Little Bosnia" in the Bevo Mill neighborhood; its most famous symbols are the Anheuser-Busch brewery just south of downtown and Grant's Farm, where Ulysses S. Grant lived in the 1850s and where Anheuser-Busch now keeps the Budweiser Clydesdales. But many more people now live in the suburbs heading out all directions, well into Jefferson County to the south. In St. Louis County and south St. Louis, the Catholic Church has closed more than 20 parishes and eight schools since 1970, and the number of registered parishioners has dropped by half to about 115,000, while suburban parishes have been growing.

The 3d Congressional District of Missouri consists of the south side of St. Louis, part of suburban St. Louis County and, to the south, Jefferson County and rural Ste. Genevieve County, the site of Missouri's oldest permanent settlement, where the nation's largest cement plant is now being planned. Its St. Louis County portions are mostly suburbs close to the St. Louis City line—Clayton, Maplewood, Richmond Heights, Webster Groves, Affton, Lemay, Oakville. This is the descendant of districts dominated by St. Louis voters, but today the city casts less than 25% of its votes, fewer than in Jefferson County, where local Republicans have been making inroads; almost half are cast in St. Louis County. Ethnically, this has been a heavily German-American area since the mid-19th century. Politically, it has been Democratic since the New Deal of the 1930s. The district voted 57% for John Kerry in 2004; Ste. Genevieve was the only non-metropolitan Missouri county Kerry carried.

The congressman from the 3d District is Russ Carnahan, a Democrat elected in 2004. He succeeded Richard Gephardt, who retired after serving 28 years as a tireless party strategist, including nearly six years as majority leader and eight years as minority leader, and twice unsuccessfully sought the Democratic nomination for president. Carnahan is the son of the late governor Mel Carnahan and former Senator Jean Carnahan, who was appointed to the Senate seat that her husband won after he died in an airplane crash two weeks before the 2000 election. Russ Carnahan grew up in Rolla and graduated from the University of Missouri and its law school. He practiced law with his wife Debra until 1996, when he took a job as a lobbyist and consultant with BJC Health System, now BJC HealthCare, a non-profit that operates several nursing homes and hospitals. In 1990 he ran unsuccessfully against Republican Bill Emerson in the old 10th Congressional District in southeast Missouri. In 2000 he was elected to the state House and after the 2002 election became chairman of the House Democratic Caucus. In 2003, when Gephardt was running for president and not for reelection, Carnahan ran to succeed him.

Carnahan was among four current or former state legislators in the primary. Opponents ganged up on him, claiming he had a thin legislative record and was trading on his family name. His toughest opponent turned out to be Jeff Smith, a youthful political science instructor at Washington

University in St. Louis, who volunteered for Bill Bradley's presidential campaign in 2000 and Howard Dean's in 2004. He was endorsed by Dean and by the *St. Louis Post-Dispatch* and assembled a large corps of volunteers. Gephardt remained neutral, but many of his allies backed state Senator Steve Stoll, who supported gun rights and opposed abortion. This turned out to be a very close race. Carnahan won with 23% of the vote, Smith finished a close second with 21% and Stoll had 18%. Smith led in St. Louis City and County; Stoll led by a wide margin in Jefferson and Ste. Genevieve Counties; Carnahan ran second or third in each—a sign that he had greater name recognition but lacked a committed core of supporters. In the general election, Carnahan faced Republican author Bill Federer, who had lost twice to Gephardt. Federer spent heavily; he opposed all abortions and criticized Carnahan for supporting the national assault weapon ban. Carnahan called for increased funding for education and said that he would "retarget" Bush's tax cuts to the middle class. Carnahan won 53%-45% on the same day his sister Robin Carnahan was elected Missouri's secretary of state. Federer led 50%-48% in Jefferson County, but Carnahan carried St. Louis County 52%-46%, and St. Louis City 61%-36%.

In the House, he voted near the center of his party but a bit more conservative on foreign policy. He helped to whip support for the bill to provide federal funding for embryonic stem cell research. On the Transportation Committee, he took credit for $42 million in earmarks for local highway projects. He worked with colleagues to enact the Combat Meth Act, with tough restrictions on production of the drug. He had an easy reelection. Smith, runner-up in the 2004 primary, thought about another run but instead sought and won a state Senate seat.

FOURTH DISTRICT

Rep. Ike Skelton (D)

Elected 1976, 16th term; b. Dec. 20, 1931, Lexington; home, Lexington; Wentworth Military Acad. Jr. Col., 1949-51, U. of MO, A.B. 1953, LL.B. 1956; Disciples of Christ; widowed.

Elected Office: MO Senate, 1970-76.

Professional Career: Lafayette Cnty. Prosecuting atty., 1957-60; MO Special Asst. Atty. Gen., 1961-63; Practicing atty., 1963-76.

DC Office: 2206 RHOB, 20515, 202-225-2876; Fax: 202-225-2695; Web site: www.house.gov/skelton.

District Offices: Blue Springs, 816-228-4242; Jefferson City, 573-635-3499; Lebanon, 417-532-7964; Sedalia, 660-826-2675.

Committees: *Armed Services* (Chmn. of 34 D).

Group Ratings

	ADA	ACLU	AFS	LCV	ITIC	NTU	COC	ACU	CFG	FRC
2006	55	50	86	50	86	23	80	50	35	71
2005	75	—	88	56	—	19	70	38	23	69

National Journal Ratings

	2005 LIB	—	2005 CONS		2006 LIB	—	2006 CONS
Economic	57%	—	42%		61%	—	39%
Social	52%	—	48%		54%	—	46%
Foreign	53%	—	47%		54%	—	46%

Key Votes of the 109th Congress

1. Estate Tax Repeal	Y	5. Limit Interstate Abortion	Y	9. Build Border Fence	Y
2. Limit CAFE Standards	N	6. Extend Patriot Act	Y	10. CAFTA	Y
3. FY06 Spending Curb	N	7. Bar Same Sex Marriage	Y	11. Oppose Iraq Withdrawal	N
4. Drilling in ANWR	Y	8. Stem Cell Research $	Y	12. Detainee Tribunals	N

Election Results

2006 general	Ike Skelton (D)	159,303	(68%)	($1,044,003)
	Jim Noland (R)	69,254	(29%)	($21,027)
	Other	6,968	(3%)	
2006 primary	Ike Skelton (D)	unopposed		
2004 general	Ike Skelton (D)	190,800	(66%)	($703,768)
	Jim Noland (R)	93,334	(32%)	
	Other	4,092	(1%)	

Prior Winning Percentages: 2002 (68%); 2000 (67%); 1998 (71%); 1996 (64%); 1994 (68%); 1992 (70%); 1990 (62%); 1988 (72%); 1986 (100%); 1984 (67%); 1982 (55%); 1980 (68%); 1978 (73%); 1976 (56%)

The People		Race/Ethnic Origin	Ancestry	
Area size:	14,825 sq. mi.	92.4% White	German: 17.4%	USA: 11.0%
Urban population:	39.9%	3.2% Black	Irish: 8.6%	
Rural population:	60.1%	0.6% Asian	**2004 Presidential Vote**	
Pop. 2000:	621,690	0.5% Native Am.	Bush (R) 187,111	(64%)
Pop. 2005 (est):	651,589	0.1% Hawaiian	Kerry (D) 102,652	(35%)
Median income:	$34,541	1.3% Two+ races	Other 1,622	(1%)
Poverty status:	12.1%	0.1% Other	**2000 Presidential Vote**	
Military veterans:	16.1%	1.9% Hispanic Origin	Bush (R) 147,694	(58%)
			Gore (D) 100,171	(39%)
			Other 6,024	(2%)
			Cook Partisan Voting Index: R +11	

Occupation	Blue collar: 31.9%	White collar: 51.4%	Gray collar: 16.7%

Missouri was the first state settled entirely west of the Mississippi, and the folks who settled it were a picture of pioneer diversity. Virginians and other Southerners made their way to counties north of the Missouri River, while Germans settled around the still small capital city of Jefferson City. A taste of that diversity can be found in the Capitol, with its mural by Thomas Hart Benton, great-grandnephew and eponym of one of Missouri's first senators, who championed hard money and westward expansion for 30 years and lost his seat for opposing the expansion of slavery. The painting shows dance hall girls, black coal miners and a mother diapering an infant—all reminders that pioneer life was less homogeneous than many imagine.

The 4th Congressional District of Missouri occupies much of this early-settled part of central and western Missouri. It includes part of Blue Springs and Oak Grove in Jackson County east of Kansas City, but the overall atmosphere here is rural and small-town, with political traditions dating back to the community's early days. The rural counties around Kansas City were full of pro-slavery-expansion Bushwhackers who rode across the Kansas line to thwart the Yankee Jayhawks, and these areas today vote Democratic. The German area around Jefferson City was anti-slavery and remains among the most Republican parts of Missouri, and the growing resort areas around Lake of the Ozarks are mixed. The southern portion of the district, near Springfield, was Union country during the Civil War but is Republican now. There are two big military bases here: Fort Leonard Wood in Pulaski County, where Marines, sailors and airmen train in joint exercises with Army troops, and Whiteman Air Force Base, near Knob Noster in Johnson County, from which B-2s took off and flew across the world to drop precision-targeted bombs in Afghanistan. There are three rapidly growing parts of the district, Cass County, just south of Kansas City; the Lake of the Ozarks area; and Webster County, northeast of Springfield, where the 4th of July parade in Marshfield is the oldest-running parade west of the Mississippi, running past the courthouse lawn where there is a replica of the Hubble telescope, invented by Marshfield native Edwin Hubble.

Much of this region is Truman country: Harry Truman was born in Barton County, at the southern end of the district, and lived in Independence, just a few miles from Blue Springs. He spent much of election night 1948, when just about everyone thought he would lose, in Excelsior Springs, on the border of Ray County, the district's one county north of the Missouri River. In his long life Truman spanned the gaps between country and city, South and North: his mother could remember her house being attacked by Yankee soldiers, and she remained pro-Confederate even when her son was in the White House; he got his political start in urban Independence and Kansas City and desegregated the military services.

The congressman from the 4th District is Ike Skelton, chairman of the House Armed Services Committee, who in many ways can be called a Harry Truman Democrat. His father met Truman in 1928, when he was Lafayette County prosecutor and the future president was Jackson County judge, and they remained friends for life; his father supported Truman when he was nearly defeated in the 1940 Senate primary, and he took 17-year-old Ike to Washington for Truman's inaugural in 1949. In 1952 Skelton and a friend talked their way past the Secret Service in Jackson County and spoke with Truman himself. Skelton is from a military family: his father served in the Navy, he and his brothers went to military academies and he has sons in the Army and Navy; a teenage bout with polio made him ineligible for military service, but he was treated in Warm Springs, Georgia, and recovered enough to run in two-mile races on his high school track team. He grew up in Lexington, of old Missouri stock; he is a distant cousin through the Boone family of New York Congresswoman Louise Slaughter. He remembers walking down the street in 1944 watching C-47s droning overhead pulling gliders, training pilots for D-Day. Skelton graduated from the University of Missouri and its law school and returned to Lexington to practice law. He became county prosecutor in 1957, at 25; in 1962 Harry Truman urged him to run for Congress, but he continued practicing law with his father. He was elected to the Missouri Senate in 1970. In 1976 he ran for Congress and won rather easily; Bess Truman, remembering the 1940 primary, endorsed him. Skelton looks and votes like an old-fashioned rural Missouri Democrat: his voting record puts him near the midpoint of this Republican House on economics and foreign issues, slightly to the right on cultural issues. He has tended to support the same expansive, assertive foreign and defense policies the preponderance of Democrats supported in the days of Truman.

Skelton became chairman of the Armed Services Committee in 2007; he served as ranking minority member from 1999 to 2006. Over the years he has made significant contributions to military policy. He played a key role in passing the Goldwater-Nichols Act in 1986, which created the joint commands which have proved so successful. In 1987 and 1988 he chaired a panel on professional military education, which revamped the intermediate and senior officer schools; he has drawn up his own National Security List of 50 books on military history and analysis and has read them all. Since he came to Congress, he has filled blank books with quotes from military thinkers from Sun Tzu on; he is now on his sixth book. He has said that the first Bush administration and the Clinton administration both cut the military too much, and he has criticized the current Bush administration for not seeking higher force levels. In February 2005 he told Donald Rumsfeld that to prevent "a hollow army . . . a permanent addition to the force is needed. You're wearing 'em out, secretary, that's the bottom line." He has worked hard to improve housing and facilities for service members and their families and has proposed offering 18-month enlistments plus four years of Reserve duty to get more recruits. He warned the Clinton and Bush administrations that troops could be worn out by multiple deployments. He supported the air war in the former Yugoslavia in March 1999.

In September 2002, after a meeting in the White House, he wrote George W. Bush a letter arguing that the occupation of Iraq would be difficult. As he wrote in *The Hill*, "I have no doubt that our military would decisively defeat Iraq's forces and remove Saddam. But like the proverbial dog chasing the car down the road, we must consider what we would do after we caught it." With apparent reluctance he voted for the Iraq war resolution in October 2002. On the eve of military action, in March 2003, he wrote Bush another letter, saying that there was "great potential for a ragged ending to a war as we deal with the aftermath." In August 2004 he said that the Iraq war caused "a stretching and straining of the U.S. military like I have not seen before" and that the Pentagon was pushing Reservists "nearly to the breaking point." He supported resolutions of inquiry to obtain the Joint Chiefs of Staff's "lessons learned" reports on pre-war Iraq intelligence. In December 2004 he urged the Pentagon to use M-113 armored personnel carriers in Iraq pending delivery of armored humvees. After a trip to Iraq in November 2006 he said, "We are now, I think, strategically lost." He listed as strategic errors the lack of a plan for the occupation, failure to deploy an adequate number of troops, allowing looting, disbanding Iraqi army, kicking Baathists out of teacher and other government jobs, lack of a strategy for dealing with militias, lack of an accounting of weapons given to Iraqi forces or failure to place guards around Iraqi ammunition dumps. He said he hoped for a "bipartisan way forward" and hoped the Iraq Study Group would provide one. He floated a plan to withdraw one U.S. brigade every time the Iraqi army stands up three brigades judged ready to fight. When George W. Bush announced his surge in January 2007, he said, "What is the military mission? I don't think it will change a thing." He said the surge was "three-and-a-half years late and several hundred thousand troops short." Sun Tzu, he argued, "said never begin a war without its end in sight, and never have so many enemies that you cannot defeat all of them. We have violated both of these precepts in the Iraqi war." In February 2007 he introduced a nonbinding resolution "disapproving of the decision of the President announced on January 10, 2007, to deploy more than 20,000 additional U.S. combat troops to Iraq." But he did not call for cutting off funds for the fighting and in May 2007 voted against a resolution favoring that.

Armed Services is one of the House's least partisan committees; most members are strong defense supporters and it usually reports bills with bipartisan support. Skelton is greatly respected by Republicans as well as Democrats on the committee. He can be cautious about change. When Donald Rumsfeld proposed major changes in Pentagon procedures and personnel rules in 2003, Skelton said, "I went from shock and awe to disbelief." But he was not troubled by the intelligence reorganization bill that centralized spending control over intelligence in a national director of intelligence. Looking ahead in January 2005, he said, "I am convinced that the straits of Taiwan are the most dangerous part of the world. The way to deter problems is to have a strong capability. We can't have signs that we're weakening." That would suggest support for sophisticated weaponry like the F-22. As the incoming chairman, he said that Iraq was not the major challenge before the committee. "The major challenge is larger than that. It's making sure our armed forces will be ready for future contingencies," and provided a list of 12 unanticipated crises that the military had to deal with since he came to the House in 1977.

Naturally Skelton looks out for the interests of Fort Leonard Wood and Whiteman Air Force Base which, as he points out, are both major bases with unique functions and thus were spared from the May 2005 base closing recommendations list. He encouraged joint operations at Leonard Wood and was instrumental in getting Whiteman, with its 12,400-foot runway, designated in 1987 as the home of the first wing of B-2s; the base had been used for the Minuteman II missile which was about to be phased out. The 2006 Defense authorization included $10.6 million for a vehicle maintenance facility at Fort Leonard Wood, $3.8 million to build a Military Working Dog kennel at Whiteman Air Force Base, $9.3 million for M915A3 tractor trailer trucks for the Missouri National Guard and $9.3 million for an air traffic control system for the Missouri National Guard.

On non-military issues, Skelton tends to stick with other Democrats on taxes and economic issues, though he was one of only 20 Democrats who voted for trade promotion authority in 2001 and 2002: "For me it was the right thing to do. I represent a rural area. We have a lot of farms—a lot of soybeans, wheat and corn. And one-fourth of all that depends on foreign markets."

Skelton's toughest race came in 1982, when he was redistricted in with a Republican incumbent; he won 55%-45%. He has won by very large margins in recent years; in 1999 citizens in Lexington and Lafayette Counties began raising money to build the Ike Skelton Museum of the American Armed Forces. He regards his constituents warmly. "Wonderfully warm people. Conservative. Religious. Hardworking. Patriotic." They seem to reciprocate. In 2004, when George W. Bush was carrying the district 64%-35%, Skelton was reelected 66%-32%—more ticket-splitting than just about anywhere in America. In 2006 he won 68%-29%. It is widely assumed that when he retires, the 4th District will elect a Republican to replace him; in the 2006 primary more people voted in the contested Republican primary than in the Democratic primary in which Skelton was unopposed. Missouri seems likely to lose a House seat after the 2010 Census, and the 4th may be eliminated if Skelton chooses not to run in 2012, when he will be 80.

FIFTH DISTRICT

Rep. Emanuel Cleaver (D)

Elected 2004, 2d term; b. Oct. 26, 1944, Waxahachie, TX; home, Kansas City; Prairie View A&M U., B.S. 1968, St. Paul Schl. of Theology, M.Div. 1974; Methodist; married (Dianne).

Elected Office: Kansas City Cncl., 1979-91; mayor, 1991-99.

Professional Career: Pastor, 1970-present; radio talk-show host, 2002-04.

DC Office: 1641 LHOB, 20515, 202-225-4535; Fax: 202-225-4403; Web site: www.house.gov/cleaver.

District Offices: Independence, 816-833-4545; Kansas City, 816-842-4545.

Committees: *Financial Services* (22d of 37 D): Housing & Community Opportunity; Financial Institutions & Consumer Credit. *Select Committee on Energy Independence and Global Warming* (7th of 9 D).

Group Ratings

	ADA	ACLU	AFS	LCV	ITIC	NTU	COC	ACU	CFG	FRC
2006	95	100	100	75	57	10	50	8	9	0
2005	100	—	100	89	—	12	48	8	3	0

National Journal Ratings

	2005 LIB	—	2005 CONS		2006 LIB	—	2006 CONS
Economic	74%	—	26%		74%	—	26%
Social	82%	—	18%		74%	—	25%
Foreign	81%	—	18%		77%	—	23%

Key Votes of the 109th Congress

1. Estate Tax Repeal	N	5. Limit Interstate Abortion	N	9. Build Border Fence	*
2. Limit CAFE Standards	Y	6. Extend Patriot Act	N	10. CAFTA	N
3. FY06 Spending Curb	N	7. Bar Same Sex Marriage	N	11. Oppose Iraq Withdrawal	*
4. Drilling in ANWR	N	8. Stem Cell Research $	Y	12. Detainee Tribunals	*

Election Results

2006 general	Emanuel Cleaver (D)	136,149	(64%)	($617,748)
	Jacob Turk (R)	68,456	(32%)	($31,796)
	Randall Langkraehr (Lib)	7,314	(4%)	
2006 primary	Emanuel Cleaver (D)	unopposed		
2004 general	Emanuel Cleaver (D)	161,727	(55%)	($1,521,741)
	Jeanne Patterson (R)	123,431	(42%)	($3,207,825)
	Other	7,867	(3%)	

The People

Area size:	519 sq. mi.
Urban population:	96.1%
Rural population:	3.9%
Pop. 2000:	621,691
Pop. 2005 (est):	632,312
Median income:	$38,311
Poverty status:	12.4%
Military veterans:	14.0%

Race/Ethnic Origin

66.3% White
24.2% Black
1.3% Asian
0.4% Native Am.
0.2% Hawaiian
1.9% Two+ races
0.1% Other
5.6% Hispanic Origin

Ancestry

German: 13.5%   Irish: 8.8%
English: 7.5%

2004 Presidential Vote

Kerry (D)	175,352	(59%)
Bush (R)	118,915	(40%)
Other	714	(0%)

2000 Presidential Vote

Gore (D)	149,621	(60%)
Bush (R)	91,626	(37%)
Other	6,625	(3%)

Cook Partisan Voting Index: D +12

Occupation

Blue collar: 22.7%   White collar: 61.8%   Gray collar: 15.4%

Kansas City, named after a state it isn't in and a river it doesn't touch, is the center of one of America's large metro areas, the biggest on the central Great Plains. The first pioneers here started little towns on the bluffs above the Missouri River—Independence, Kansas City, Westport—that coalesced a few decades later. Here traders on the Santa Fe Trail set out to cross the Sand Hills of Kansas and reach Mexican territory; here Jayhawks and Bushwhackers set out to fight for control of Bleeding Kansas. Kansas City was a rail center and, in the 1920s, had one of the largest stockyards in the country, a major commercial center with lean skyscrapers and the Country Club Plaza, the first shopping center in America. It is famous for Harry Truman, who grew up on a farm now in the suburb of Grandview and who lived in his wife's family's house in Independence, the old county seat just to the east. It is famous also for its black community, its National Negro Leagues Baseball Museum, its historic jazz district that has been home to musicians like Scott Joplin, Charlie Parker and Count Basie, and for its much-praised barbecue.

The 5th Congressional District of Missouri includes most of Kansas City, the largest city in Missouri, plus Grandview and the bulk of Independence. The more suburban slices of Jackson County to the east have been filled with new subdivisions. It also includes fast-growing Belton and Raymore along U.S. 71 in Cass County just to the south. Most of the metro area's landmarks, including the Truman home, are here but much of the metropolitan area growth is across the state line in Kansas, where there has been more resistance to tax increases. One-quarter of the district's residents are black, the second highest percentage among Missouri districts. Politically, the seat has been solidly Democratic. John Kerry carried it 59%-40%.

The congressman from the 5th District is Emanuel Cleaver, a Democrat elected in 2004. He grew up in Waxahachie, Texas, in a three-room shack with no plumbing or electricity. He graduated from Prairie View A&M, moved to Kansas City and earned a divinity degree, then became pastor of St. James United Methodist Church. He was elected to the city council in 1979 and elected mayor in 1991. As mayor, Cleaver voiced support for the Clinton administration welfare reforms, which he described as "corrective surgery." He backed expansion of downtown's Bartle Hall Convention Center and supported the renovation of the deteriorating Liberty Memorial, the country's largest World War I memorial. After leaving office he hosted a radio talk show.

In December 2003, Democratic Congresswoman Karen McCarthy announced that she would not run for reelection, and Cleaver was widely expected to succeed her. Few expected just how tough Cleaver's road to Congress would be. In the primary he faced former National Security Council aide Jamie Metzl, who raised substantial funds. Metzl hammered Cleaver on ethics issues. He questioned the propriety of a loan that Cleaver took out to purchase a car wash business and criticized Cleaver for his failure to pay $36,000 in back taxes that he owed on the business. Cleaver won the primary by 60%-40%. Metzl carried Cass County 59%-41% and ran 178 votes ahead in suburban Jackson County. But Cleaver led 68%-32% in Kansas City, where 57% of the votes were cast. In the general, Cleaver faced Republican businesswoman Jeanne Patterson, who said she would spend whatever it took to make the race competitive. Patterson spent more than $3.2 million of her own money on the contest. Like Metzl, she made an issue of Cleaver's ethics. She talked about the bribery and fraud convictions of Cleaver's allies, though there was no evidence that he was involved in their crimes. Cleaver said that Patterson was politically inexperienced and was trying to buy the seat. He called himself a "hundred-aire" and criticized Patterson as a hypocrite for promising to create local jobs while her husband's company reportedly was outsourcing work to India. "Money does talk, and it is talking quite eloquently," he said in one debate. Cleaver won 55%-42%; Cleaver ran 4% behind John Kerry. In his Kansas City base, which cast 48% of the vote, he led 71%-27%. Patterson took Jackson County 54%-43%.

In the House, Cleaver's voting record fit in the center of the Democrats. He got a seat on the Financial Services Committee. In his relatively low-profile start, he led Congressional Black Caucus members seeking to play a role on environmental issues. Speaker Nancy Pelosi designated Cleaver to act as a liaison with mayors and faith communities on global warming and energy independence, and appointed him to the House select committee on global warming. Having promised to bring more civility to Congress, he stirred the waters with a proposal to change House rules to require members to lease energy-efficient vehicles in their districts. "The public would rather see a sermon than hear one," he preached, with little evident response. His own auto runs on used cooking grease. Cleaver continued preaching regularly at his church in Kansas City, and he has presided over the annual National Prayer Breakfast in Washington. He called it "the highest profile congregation" of his career. In 2006, his reelection was a breeze.

SIXTH DISTRICT

Rep. Sam Graves (R)

Elected 2000, 4th term; b. Nov. 7, 1963, Tarkio; home, Tarkio; U. of MO, B.S. 1986; Baptist; married (Lesley).

Elected Office: MO House of Reps., 1992-94; MO Senate 1994-2000.

Professional Career: Farmer.

DC Office: 1415 LHOB, 20515, 202-225-7041; Fax: 202-225-8221; Web site: www.house.gov/graves.

District Offices: Liberty, 816-792-3976; St. Joseph, 816-233-9818.

Committees: *Agriculture* (7th of 21 R): General Farm Commodities & Risk Management; Conservation, Credit, Energy & Research. *Small Business* (3d of 15 R): Contracting & Technology. *Transportation & Infrastructure* (17th of 34 R): Economic Development, Public Buildings & Emergency Management (RMM); Aviation; Railroads, Pipelines & Hazardous Materials.

Group Ratings

	ADA	ACLU	AFS	LCV	ITIC	NTU	COC	ACU	CFG	FRC
2006	0	0	0	8	100	62	100	88	57	100
2005	0	—	0	0	—	61	93	92	72	92

National Journal Ratings

	2005 LIB	—	2005 CONS		2006 LIB	—	2006 CONS
Economic	36%	—	63%		27%	—	71%
Social	0%	—	89%		16%	—	84%
Foreign	39%	—	60%		0%	—	94%

Key Votes of the 109th Congress

1. Estate Tax Repeal	Y	5. Limit Interstate Abortion	Y	9. Build Border Fence	Y
2. Limit CAFE Standards	Y	6. Extend Patriot Act	Y	10. CAFTA	Y
3. FY06 Spending Curb	Y	7. Bar Same Sex Marriage	Y	11. Oppose Iraq Withdrawal	Y
4. Drilling in ANWR	Y	8. Stem Cell Research $	N	12. Detainee Tribunals	Y

Election Results

2006 general	Sam Graves (R)	150,882	(62%)	($1,215,978)
	Sara Jo Shettles (D)	87,477	(36%)	($130,313)
	Other	6,436	(2%)	
2006 primary	Sam Graves (R)	unopposed		
2004 general	Sam Graves (R)	196,516	(64%)	($1,741,133)
	Charlie Broomfield (D)	106,987	(35%)	($887,833)
	Other	4,352	(1%)	

Prior Winning Percentages: 2002 (63%); 2000 (51%)

The People		Race/Ethnic Origin	Ancestry	
Area size:	13,124 sq. mi.	92.4% White	German: 17.1%	Irish: 9.8%
Urban population:	66.3%	2.8% Black	USA: 8.9%	
Rural population:	33.7%	0.8% Asian	**2004 Presidential Vote**	
Pop. 2000:	621,690	0.4% Native Am.	Bush (R) 178,669	(57%)
Pop. 2005 (est):	650,837	0.1% Hawaiian	Kerry (D) 132,007	(42%)
Median income:	$41,225	1.1% Two+ races	Other 2,001	(1%)
Poverty status:	8.7%	0.1% Other	**2000 Presidential Vote**	
Military veterans:	14.5%	2.4% Hispanic Origin	Bush (R) 143,954	(53%)
			Gore (D) 119,861	(44%)
			Other 7,380	(3%)
			Cook Partisan Voting Index: R + 5	

Occupation	Blue collar: 25.9%	White collar: 58.6%	Gray collar: 15.5%

The rolling, surging fields along the Missouri River in northwest Missouri were settled in a rush in the late 19th century and they lost people for most of the 20th century. Fewer hands were needed on farms than half a century ago, far fewer than a century ago. In 1940, this area had one of the largest meatpacking operations in the world, but the meatpacking business for years generated no new jobs here. Barge traffic on the Missouri has all but disappeared, a victim of drought, low levels (because of recreational uses upstream) and court rulings in favor of environmentalists. Just as Kansas City was the starting place for many wagon trains heading west, the river town of St. Joseph was the starting point for the Pony Express and its roughly 10-day transport of mail to Sacramento. Today, St. Joe is the biggest town north of Kansas City, with 73,000 people in 2005; it recently spent more than $1 million for a port to service the barges, though it has rarely been used. The counties of northwest Missouri, aside from those in the Kansas City metro area, had 508,000 people in 1900, 452,000 in 1940 and 318,000 in 1990. But in the 1990s, the local economy began to perk up a little, and the number climbed to 330,000; some counties that had been losing population since 1900 started to gain. Biopharming—the use of genetically modified crops, such as rice, to grow medications—has become a growth industry in some of these rural communities.

The 6th Congressional District of Missouri takes in all these counties plus part of metro Kansas City—Clay and Platte Counties and a small portion of Jackson County east of Independence, including Blue Springs. The Kansas City area casts about half the district's votes. The historic political tradition here was mostly Democratic, but it has been tempered by dislike for national Democrats' cultural liberalism. This was strong Perot country in 1992; Bill Clinton carried it with a plurality in 1992 and 1996. But the rural vote here, as across the nation has moved toward Republicans. George W. Bush carried the district with 53% in 2000 and 57% in 2004.

The congressman from the 6th District is Sam Graves, a Republican first elected in 2000. He is a lifelong resident of Tarkio in the northwest corner of the state. He graduated from the University of Missouri with a degree in agronomy, farmed with his father and brother, and joined the Farm Bureau. He ran for the state House in 1992 and beat a longtime Democratic incumbent; in 1994 he was elected to the state Senate. He attracted attention in 1998 with a five-hour filibuster against a school desegregation bill he said was slanted against rural areas; but the bill eventually passed. Graves got his opportunity to run for the U.S. House when Congresswoman Pat Danner, 22 minutes before the May withdrawal deadline and without a public announcement, delivered to the secretary of state her withdrawal from the race. Not by accident, the immediate favorite to succeed her was her son, state Senator Steve Danner. Graves entered the race within the short window provided by state law and drew support from national Republicans. Teresa Loar, a moderate Republican on the Kansas City Council, attacked Graves as the darling of extremist and sexist party leaders. Graves beat her 68%-17%. Against three weak Democratic alternatives, Steve Danner was held to 56% in the Democratic primary—a bad omen for November. In the general, Danner called himself a conservative Democrat and the candidates agreed on some issues: the death penalty, repeal of the marriage penalty tax and trade relations with China. But they differed on education funding, abortion rights (Danner switched from pro-life to pro-choice), gun control and the performance of Bill Clinton. Graves called Danner a "tax and spend liberal" and said that when this acorn fell from the tree, "it rolled to the left." In an editorial endorsing Graves, the *Kansas City Star* said that Danner's campaign switch on abortion showed that he "engaged in raw opportunism at the slightest opportunity," and that his central principle was "me first." Graves won 51%-47%.

In the House, Graves showed some moderate instincts, especially on foreign policy, and has usually been a party loyalist. He supported the 2002 farm bill and tended mostly to local issues. In 2005 the House passed his amendment to the transportation bill to preempt state laws on liability for damages involving rental cars, a measure of interest to St. Louis-based Enterprise Rent-A-Car.

In this previously competitive district, Graves has had no trouble with reelection; local Democrats and a few Republicans have complained about his hard-nosed political tactics. In 2006, the *Star* endorsed his opponent Sara Jo Shettles, who chaired the Clay County Democrats, and criticized Graves as "reluctant to acknowledge serious problems facing the country." Graves won 62%-36%.

In May 2007, Kansas City Mayor Kay Barnes, long sought after by national Democrats as a candidate in the 6th, announced she would challenge Graves in 2008. A month later, the Graves family was in the news again: the congressman's brother, Todd, a former U.S. attorney, testified before Congress that he had been forced to resign by high-ranking Justice Department officials. It was reported that Senator Kit Bond had urged Justice to replace Graves; Bond had also raised eyebrows in April when he publicly praised Barnes's record in office at the same time she was being recruited to run against Sam Graves.

SEVENTH DISTRICT

Rep. Roy Blunt (R)

Elected 1996, 6th term; b. Jan. 10, 1950, Niangua; home, Strafford; SW Baptist U., B.A. 1970, SW MO St. U., M.A. 1972; Baptist; married (Abigail Perlman).

Elected Office: MO Secy. of State, 1984-93.

Professional Career: H.S. teacher, 1970-73; Greene Cnty. Clerk, 1973-85; Adjunct Instructor, Drury Col., 1976-82; Pres., SW Baptist U., 1993-96.

DC Office: 217 CHOB, 20515, 202-225-6536; Fax: 202-225-5604; Web site: blunt.house.gov.

District Offices: Springfield, 417-889-1800.

Committees: *Minority Whip.*

Group Ratings

	ADA	ACLU	AFS	LCV	ITIC	NTU	COC	ACU	CFG	FRC
2006	0	5	0	0	100	60	100	88	65	100
2005	0	—	0	6	—	59	93	96	63	100

National Journal Ratings

	2005 LIB	—	2005 CONS	2006 LIB	—	2006 CONS
Economic	13%	—	87%	2%	—	98%
Social	19%	—	80%	28%	—	70%
Foreign	14%	—	85%	17%	—	83%

Key Votes of the 109th Congress

1. Estate Tax Repeal	Y	5. Limit Interstate Abortion	Y	9. Build Border Fence	Y
2. Limit CAFE Standards	Y	6. Extend Patriot Act	Y	10. CAFTA	Y
3. FY06 Spending Curb	Y	7. Bar Same Sex Marriage	Y	11. Oppose Iraq Withdrawal	Y
4. Drilling in ANWR	Y	8. Stem Cell Research $	N	12. Detainee Tribunals	Y

Election Results

2006 general	Roy Blunt (R)	160,942	(67%)	($3,301,391)
	Jack Truman (D)	72,592	(30%)	
	Other	7,589	(3%)	
2006 primary	Roy Blunt (R)	47,758	(80%)	
	Clendon Kinder (R)	5,197	(9%)	
	Midge Potts (R)	4,294	(7%)	
	Bernard Kennetz (R)	2,498	(4%)	
2004 general	Roy Blunt (R)	210,080	(70%)	($3,527,363)
	Jim Newberry (D)	84,356	(28%)	($214,240)
	Other	3,769	(1%)	

Prior Winning Percentages: 2002 (75%); 2000 (74%); 1998 (73%); 1996 (65%)

The People		Race/Ethnic Origin	Ancestry	
Area size:	5,555 sq. mi.	92.9% White	German: 13.5%	USA: 10.8%
Urban population:	59.1%	1.2% Black	Irish: 9.2%	
Rural population:	40.9%	0.7% Asian	**2004 Presidential Vote**	
Pop. 2000:	621,690	1.0% Native Am.	Bush (R) 202,486	(67%)
Pop. 2005 (est):	664,214	0.1% Hawaiian	Kerry (D) 97,557	(32%)
Median income:	$32,929	1.5% Two+ races	Other 1,705	(1%)
Poverty status:	13.0%	0.1% Other	**2000 Presidential Vote**	
Military veterans:	14.4%	2.6% Hispanic Origin	Bush (R) 153,453	(62%)
			Gore (D) 87,663	(35%)
			Other 6,124	(2%)
			Cook Partisan Voting Index: R +14	

Occupation   Blue collar: 28.5%   White collar: 55.0%   Gray collar: 16.5%

One of the biggest tourist destinations in America today is Branson, Missouri—something almost no one predicted 30 years ago. Even today Branson has only 7,010 residents, is served by two-lane roads, is nowhere near a major airport; but it thrives, paralleling the surging popularity of country and western music. Branson was put on the map early in the century by Harold Bell Wright's novel, *The Shepherd of the Hills*, about the hardy people of the mountains, hills and meadows of southwest Missouri, just north of Arkansas. More tourists came in with completion of the Ozark Beach Dam that created Bull Shoals Lake in 1913, lured by the native bass and stocked trout. Then in the 1960s, new lakes were formed, a Shepherd of the Hills pageant and Silver Dollar City were started, and entertainers—the five Maybe brothers performing as "The Baldknobbers" and Box Car Willie from the Grand Ole Opry—started performing. Today Branson has nearly 8 million visitors a year, 80% of whom have visited before, and more than two dozen theaters with 56,000 seats—more than Broadway. What do people like about Branson? The non-stop entertainment and fishing and boating; country music and family style entertainment; plenty of shopping and a safe atmosphere. These are also the things that have made southwest Missouri the fastest growing part of the state in the past 20 years, generating new businesses and attracting retirees as well as vacationers.

Workers come to Branson from as far away as Springfield, the biggest city in southwest Missouri and the self-styled "buckle of the Bible Belt." Springfield is home to more than 200 churches as well as the headquarters of such middle American institutions as the Bass Pro Shops

Outdoor World, probably the nation's largest fishing equipment store; the Assemblies of God, one of the nation's and the world's largest and fastest-growing Protestant denominations; and two of the nation's three largest coachbuilders (stretch limousine manufacturers), Springfield Coach and DaBryan Coach Builders, with a third nearby in Seymour, Executive Coach, run by a Nigerian immigrant. Southwest Missouri is dairy country with a growing poultry industry; Latinos have been moving into McDonald County to work in chicken processing plants. The Ozarks, long considered a backwater, are on the cutting edge of many trends in today's America.

The 7th Congressional District of Missouri includes Branson and Springfield in the southwest corner of Missouri. Historically, this area has been Republican since it opposed secession in 1861: pro-Union Springfield changed hands several times as Missouri staged its own civil war. Its conservative response to the big-spending government of the 1960s and cultural liberalism of the 1970s reinforced its allegiance, and now this is the most Republican part of Missouri.

The congressman from the 7th District is Roy Blunt, a Republican first elected in 1996 and the House Republican Whip. Blunt grew up on a dairy farm near Springfield, in a political family; his father was a state representative who won election in 1978 by defeating Senator Claire McCaskill's mother. He graduated from Southwest Baptist University, 25 miles north of Springfield, and taught high school and college history and government. He got his start in politics by volunteering for John Ashcroft's unsuccessful campaign for Congress in 1972; the story goes that he showed up at campaign headquarters in his pickup truck, Ashcroft asked, "Have you got gas in this truck?" Blunt said yes and became his driver. In 1973, 33-year-old freshman Governor Christopher Bond, in his second appointment, named the 23-year-old Blunt to be Greene County clerk. In 1980 Senator John Danforth asked him to run for lieutenant governor; he did and lost. In 1984, at 34, Blunt was elected Missouri secretary of state, the first Republican to win that office in half a century; he was reelected with 60% of the vote in 1988. In 1992 he ran for governor and lost the Republican primary to William Webster, 44%-39%. Blunt then became president of Southwest Baptist University. In 1996 Congressman Mel Hancock kept his pledge to serve only four terms and retired. In the primary Blunt faced Gary Nodler, businessman and one-time staffer to Congressman Gene Taylor, and won 56%-44%. In the general election Blunt won 65%-32%, running ahead of the Republican ticket and carrying every county with at least 62% of the vote. He has been reelected easily since.

Blunt's voting record has been solidly conservative, with an occasional move toward the center on social issues. He has on occasion pursued a bipartisan approach, as with his proposal to increase charitable giving. In 2006, he sponsored the Combat Meth Act, the first comprehensive approach enacted to fighting the supply of methamphetamines. With Senator Barack Obama, he passed a measure that year to set up an Internet database of federal spending. In 1999, Blunt was among the original 10 members of then-Governor Bush's presidential exploratory committee. Bush has called him "a leader who knows how to raise his sights and lower his voice."

With his considerable political skills, he wanted to run for freshman class president. But at then-Majority Whip Tom DeLay's suggestion, he ran for the freshman spot on the Republican Steering Committee, where he worked to get good committee assignments for freshmen. After the 1998 election Blunt won a seat on the Commerce Committee. Then, in January 1999, DeLay plucked him from the ranks of 48 deputy whips and appointed him chief deputy whip, the position Dennis Hastert held until his astonishing elevation to speaker. Blunt has said that he never lobbied for the job and didn't even know he was being considered until he read it in a newspaper. On a number of issues Blunt was given the job of making more palatable to core Republicans measures that were going through in any case.

As chief deputy whip, Blunt spent much time meeting with lobbyists, organizing groups interested in various issues like trade, taxes and energy. He developed a reputation as a good listener with a soft touch and took care to pay attention to party moderates. Hastert assigned Blunt to mediate disputes between Republicans and to win over votes on critical issues. Blunt also weighed in on some local issues. After Democrat Rob Andrews complained that New Jersey-licensed limousines were not allowed into New York without paying a tax, Blunt, representing the number one stretch-limousine-producing district, sponsored a bill limiting local regulation of limousines that cross state lines. It was opposed by New York officials eager for revenue and Nevada limousine drivers, worried about competition from California drivers; but it was enacted by wide margins.

In 2000 Blunt began keeping a list of members who would back him for a higher leadership position. He headed the Battleground 2002 operation, which contributed $5.6 million to Republican House candidates. When Majority Leader Dick Armey announced that he would retire in 2002, DeLay immediately began to run for majority leader and Blunt said he would run for majority whip. Ray LaHood of Illinois announced he was running for whip too. Within weeks, he said he would not run and was supporting Blunt; he found that Blunt had the support not only of most Republicans but of most moderates. In November 2002 both DeLay and Blunt were elected to their new positions without opposition; DeLay presented Blunt with a velvet-covered hammer.

As whip, Blunt made two decisions that showed he was not DeLay's puppet. One was his decision to name as his chief deputy whip Eric Cantor, who had served only one term in the House; Cantor was as surprised as everyone else. And he proposed to change House rules by repealing the eight-year term limit Newt Gingrich had imposed on speakers; that was agreed to by the whole House. Speculation grew that Blunt might some day run for Speaker, perhaps against DeLay. Blunt was for the most part successful as whip, but stumbled a couple of times. In June 2003 the leadership had to pull a compensatory time bill from the floor when it became apparent there were not enough votes to pass it. *The Washington Post* reported that Blunt in November 2002 had inserted into the homeland security bill a provision benefiting Philip Morris. He met his toughest challenge in passing the 2003 Medicare/prescription drug bill. In June he assembled a huge coalition and helped to produce a one-vote victory on the floor. In November on the vote on the conference report the leadership went to the floor without the needed 218 votes; the roll call started at 3 a.m. and lasted a record two hours and 53 minutes. Finally conservatives Trent Franks and Butch Otter were persuaded to switch their votes by the possibility that if the Republican bill failed the Democrats would get a vote on a bill with much more government involvement; they switched and the bill passed 220-215. In December 2004, after Republicans increased their majority to 232-203, Blunt worried that more Republicans would feel free to go off the reservation.

But that soon became the least of his worries. When DeLay was forced to step down as Majority Leader after he was indicted by a Texas grand jury in September 2005, Hastert initially planned to give the job to David Dreier for a temporary period. Just before the decision was to be announced, Blunt changed Hastert's mind in a one-on-one meeting and he got the job while retaining his Majority Whip post. That was a heavy burden, especially with the House struggling to deal with the impact of Hurricane Katrina. During the next three months, Republicans struggled to pass bills in the House. In January 2006, DeLay announced that he would permanently give up his post as Leader. Blunt positioned himself as the Healer to replace the Hammer, but faced spirited month-long challenges from John Boehner and John Shadegg. After a week, Blunt claimed that he had the votes to win. But many members doubted his inevitability, and Boehner pushed ahead with his insurgent campaign. Scarred by multiple DeLay controversies and fearful of the November election, many worried that Blunt and his connections to Washington's K Street would be a burden. In a dramatic second-ballot showdown, Boehner prevailed, 122-109. Blunt remained as Whip, and developed what appeared to be a smooth working relationship with Boehner. When House Republicans lost their majority in November, he received a new challenge: Shadegg challenged him for the downsized post of Minority Whip. Blunt won by an unexpectedly wide margin, 137-57. In the minority, he became more outspoken in criticizing Democrats' management of the House and their efforts to "embarrass the president."

Blunt has been reelected by wide margins. In January 2004, his son Matt Blunt announced his candidacy for governor with his father at his side in the high school gym in Strafford in Greene County. But the two then parted ways: Matt Blunt campaigned all over Missouri, while Roy Blunt did most of his campaigning for House Republicans across the nation. In November Matt Blunt was elected governor by a 51%-48% margin; he won 67%-32% in the counties in the 7th District.

Roy Blunt's future is uncertain. In July 2007, amid speculation that he would retire at the end of the 110th Congress, Blunt said he would run for reelection in 2008. His goal to become Speaker of the House seems less likely to come to fruition. Some Republicans predicted that his loss to Boehner would lead him to quit the House but he has shown surprising resilience and remains an active Republican leader.

EIGHTH DISTRICT

Rep. Jo Ann Emerson (R)

Elected 1996, 6th full term; b. Sept. 16, 1950, Washington, D.C.; home, Cape Girardeau; Ohio Wesleyan U., B.A. 1972; Presbyterian; married (Ron Gladney).

Professional Career: Deputy Communications Dir., Natl. Repub. Cong. Cmte., 1984-91; Dir., State Relations & Grassroot Programs, Natl. Restaurant Assn., 1991-94; Sr. Vice Pres., Pub. Affairs, American Insurance Assn., 1994-96.

DC Office: 2440 RHOB, 20515, 202-225-4404; Fax: 202-226-0326; Web site: www.house.gov/emerson.

District Offices: Cape Girardeau, 573-335-0101; Farmington, 573-756-9755; Rolla, 573-364-2455.

Committees: *Appropriations* (16th of 29 R): Agriculture, Rural Development, FDA & Related Agencies; Energy & Water Development; Interior, Environment & Related Agencies.

Group Ratings

	ADA	ACLU	AFS	LCV	ITIC	NTU	COC	ACU	CFG	FRC
2006	15	19	29	8	100	50	93	72	37	85
2005	15	—	13	11	—	50	89	88	46	85

National Journal Ratings

	2005 LIB	—	2005 CONS		2006 LIB	—	2006 CONS
Economic	38%	—	60%		44%	—	56%
Social	32%	—	68%		34%	—	66%
Foreign	50%	—	50%		33%	—	63%

Key Votes of the 109th Congress

1. Estate Tax Repeal	Y	5. Limit Interstate Abortion	Y	9. Build Border Fence	Y
2. Limit CAFE Standards	Y	6. Extend Patriot Act	Y	10. CAFTA	Y
3. FY06 Spending Curb	Y	7. Bar Same Sex Marriage	Y	11. Oppose Iraq Withdrawal	Y
4. Drilling in ANWR	Y	8. Stem Cell Research $	Y	12. Detainee Tribunals	Y

Election Results

2006 general	Jo Ann Emerson (R)	156,164	(72%)	($1,129,359)
	Veronica Hambacker (D)	57,557	(26%)	($59,493)
	Other	4,268	(2%)	
2006 primary	Jo Ann Emerson (R)	unopposed		
2004 general	Jo Ann Emerson (R)	194,039	(72%)	($1,163,588)
	Dean Henderson (D)	71,543	(27%)	($17,801)
	Other	3,129	(1%)	

Prior Winning Percentages: 2002 (72%); 2000 (69%); 1998 (63%); 1996 (50%); 1996 (63%)

The People		Race/Ethnic Origin	Ancestry		
Area size:	18,818 sq. mi.	92.5% White	USA: 13.7%	German: 12.7%	
Urban population:	39.6%	4.3% Black	Irish: 8.5%		
Rural population:	60.4%	0.4% Asian	**2004 Presidential Vote**		
Pop. 2000:	621,690	0.6% Native Am.	Bush (R)	173,378	(63%)
Pop. 2005 (est):	639,236	0.0% Hawaiian	Kerry (D)	97,778	(36%)
Median income:	$27,865	1.1% Two+ races	Other	1,886	(1%)
Poverty status:	18.2%	0.0% Other	**2000 Presidential Vote**		
Military veterans:	15.1%	1.0% Hispanic Origin	Bush (R)	143,511	(59%)
			Gore (D)	93,244	(38%)
			Other	5,635	(2%)
			Cook Partisan Voting Index: R +11		

Occupation	Blue collar: 34.5%	White collar: 47.7%	Gray collar: 17.8%

Mark Twain might not recognize life on the Mississippi below St. Louis today, where the Ozark mountains to the west flatten out and the river is hidden behind levees, which ordinarily, except during the terrible flood of 1993, screen small towns and river roads from the sight of rows of barges tethered together, full of coal and corn and soybeans. The Mississippi today is an industrial waterway. But it was never really all that romantic. Twain's steamboats, as he was at pains to point out, were dangerous, noisy contraptions, forever blowing up or getting embedded in roots and branches in the swirling river currents. This is one of the older settled parts of the U.S.: French settlers founded Missouri towns like Cape Girardeau in the late 1700s. The big influx started a few years after the 1811 earthquake centered on New Madrid; the spongy Mississippi valley land is seismically very active, and this was the site of one of the most devastating earthquakes in U.S. history.

The southeast quadrant of Missouri—the river valley and the hills to the west, with coal and lead mines with their miles of tunnels, plus the Bootheel that hangs down in the far southeast—has not seemed to change much in 50 years. For years there has been a population outflow from the Bootheel, as machines replaced low-wage farm workers and crops shifted from cotton to rice, corn and soybeans. Dairy cattle, pigs, apples, and berries—plus, some timber—are among the area's other products. But this is also home to Missouri's Lead Belt, a mining region rich in ore minerals such as lead, zinc, copper, silver and cadmium. Reynolds and Iron Counties produce about 80% of the nation's lead; the EPA has ordered a cleanup of massive piles of lead waste. An aluminum smelting plant in New Madrid provides more than 1,000 jobs. Still, the only big growth here has been around the retail and medical hub of Cape Girardeau and along I-44; the poverty rate in the Bootheel is the highest in the state. At a point 20 miles south of Rolla in Phelps County is Edgar Springs, the home to 190 residents and the population center of the nation, according to the 2000 Census; 10 years earlier, that designation was 35 miles to the northeast in Steelville.

The sprawling 8th Congressional District, the largest in Missouri, covers the state's southeast corner. The political heritage is mixed. The Bootheel was as solidly Democratic as the Mississippi Valley around Memphis once was, and some mining counties show traces of Democratic sentiment. Cape Girardeau is heavily Republican and an incubator of Republican talent: it is the hometown of Rush Limbaugh, Lieutenant Governor Peter Kinder, and Jack Oliver, George W. Bush's chief fundraiser in 2004. Once a safely Democratic district, it has been represented since 1980 by Republicans. This was one of the rural areas that trended to Republicans in the Clinton years; George W. Bush won 59% of the vote here in 2000 and 63% in 2004.

The congresswoman from the 8th District is Jo Ann Emerson, first elected in 1996 to replace her late husband Bill Emerson, who died that June. Jo Ann Emerson grew up in Bethesda, Maryland, in a Republican family (her father was executive director of the Republican National Committee) but next door to Democrats Hale and Lindy Boggs, who served in Congress nearly a half-century. In 1975 she married Republican Bill Emerson, then a Washington lobbyist. In 1979, spotting the vulnerability of the Democratic incumbent in the Bootheel district, he went home to Missouri to run, and won with 55% of the vote. In 1995 he was diagnosed with cancer, but missed few votes during radiation therapy. After Bill's death, Jo Ann Emerson decided to run. She had worked for the American Insurance Association and National Restaurant Association, and was a press aide at the National Republican Congressional Committee. Her views were conservative, and leading state and national Republicans quickly endorsed her. But Missouri law bars reopening the filing deadline if an incumbent dies less than 11 weeks before the primary, so she ran as an independent. Democrat Emily Firebaugh, a timber company owner, attacked Emerson as a product of the Washington suburbs. Firebaugh spent $831,000, slightly more than Emerson. The Republican nominee Richard Kline was less trouble: In 1995 he had used pepper spray to try to place a Veterans Administration doctor under citizen's arrest. Bill Emerson's record, Jo Ann Emerson's conservative views, and the poignancy of the situation all worked toward an Emerson victory. She won 50%, with 37% for Firebaugh and 11% for Kline.

In the House, Emerson has had a moderate-leaning voting record though sometimes conservative on cultural issues. On the Appropriations Committee and its Agriculture Subcommittee, her priority was addressing low prices for farm commodities. She has worked with other members from farm districts to open agricultural trade with Cuba and made visits to Cuba to encourage deals. She demanded protection of U.S. food aid programs from international trade restrictions and has crusaded for hunger relief, an issue that Bill Emerson popularized.

Emerson occasionally straddles the center line. She cast the deciding vote in June 2003 on the House version of the Medicare/prescription drug bill. She opposed the measure but changed her vote in exchange for a promise from Speaker Dennis Hastert for a floor vote on reimportation of prescription drugs (she complained that her mother-in-law paid $11,000 a year for drug coverage) and assurance that Majority Whip Roy Blunt wouldn't whip Republicans to vote against it. She got the vote; Blunt did not do any whipping but Majority Leader Tom DeLay did. Emerson's side won, but the provision failed to become law. In November, she was one of 25 House Republicans who voted against the conference report on the Medicare bill. In January 2007, she voted for five of the six bills in the House Democrats' opening "100-hour" agenda. Emerson has a personal connection to the Iraq war: Her stepdaughter served with the First Infantry Division in Iraq. She reluctantly opposed the Democratic non-binding resolution opposing President Bush's surge policy in Iraq because she said it wouldn't accomplish anything. Her independence has not seemed to affect her influence among House Republicans, perhaps because she has been upfront with party leaders about her views, and it has not affected her electoral prospects—she has won reelection without difficulty.

NINTH DISTRICT

Rep. Kenny Hulshof (R)

Elected 1996, 6th term; b. May 22, 1958, Sikeston; home, Columbia; U. of MO, B.S. 1980, U. of MS, J.D. 1983; Catholic; married (Renee).

Professional Career: Asst. Pub. Defender, 32d Judicial Circuit, 1983-86; Asst. Prosecuting Atty., Cape Girardeau, 1986-89; Spec. Prosecutor, MO Atty. Gen., 1989-96.

DC Office: 409 CHOB, 20515, 202-225-2956; Fax: 202-225-5712; Web site: hulshof.house.gov.

District Offices: Columbia, 573-449-5111; Hannibal, 573-221-1200; Washington, 636-239-4001.

Committees: *Ways & Means* (8th of 17 R): Health; Trade.

Group Ratings

	ADA	ACLU	AFS	LCV	ITIC	NTU	COC	ACU	CFG	FRC
2006	0	14	0	8	100	54	100	80	53	100
2005	0	—	0	0	—	56	92	92	58	100

National Journal Ratings

	2005 LIB	—	2005 CONS		2006 LIB	—	2006 CONS
Economic	35%	—	64%		30%	—	68%
Social	23%	—	76%		32%	—	66%
Foreign	42%	—	55%		46%	—	53%

Key Votes of the 109th Congress

1. Estate Tax Repeal	Y	5. Limit Interstate Abortion	Y	9. Build Border Fence	Y
2. Limit CAFE Standards	Y	6. Extend Patriot Act	Y	10. CAFTA	Y
3. FY06 Spending Curb	Y	7. Bar Same Sex Marriage	Y	11. Oppose Iraq Withdrawal	Y
4. Drilling in ANWR	Y	8. Stem Cell Research $	N	12. Detainee Tribunals	Y

Election Results

2006 general	Kenny Hulshof (R)	149,114	(61%)	($1,363,653)
	Duane Burghard (D)	87,145	(36%)	($253,380)
	Other	6,412	(3%)	
2006 primary	Kenny Hulshof (R)	unopposed		
2004 general	Kenny Hulshof (R)	193,429	(65%)	($1,017,285)
	Linda Jacobsen (D)	101,343	(34%)	($130,908)
	Other	4,675	(2%)	

Prior Winning Percentages: 2002 (68%); 2000 (59%); 1998 (62%); 1996 (49%)

The People		Race/Ethnic Origin	Ancestry	
Area size:	14,082 sq. mi.	92.6% White	German: 21.7%	Irish: 9.3%
Urban population:	45.8%	3.9% Black	USA: 9.2%	
Rural population:	54.2%	0.9% Asian	**2004 Presidential Vote**	
Pop. 2000:	621,690	0.3% Native Am.	Bush (R) 180,362	(59%)
Pop. 2005 (est):	641,318	0.0% Hawaiian	Kerry (D) 124,965	(41%)
Median income:	$36,693	1.1% Two+ races	Other 2,008	(1%)
Poverty status:	11.8%	0.1% Other	**2000 Presidential Vote**	
Military veterans:	13.5%	1.1% Hispanic Origin	Bush (R) 145,604	(55%)
			Gore (D) 112,239	(42%)
			Other 7,093	(3%)
			Cook Partisan Voting Index: R + 7	

Occupation   Blue collar: 29.7%   White collar: 54.4%   Gray collar: 15.9%

Little Dixie, the swath of northeast Missouri along the Mississippi River, was settled by Southerners from Kentucky and Virginia. Its most famous native son is Mark Twain, born Sam Clemens in Hannibal, then as now a little town on bluffs overlooking the river. Hannibal was the thinly disguised St. Petersburg of Tom Sawyer and Huckleberry Finn, lovingly created years later complete with Pike County and other dialect by Twain, then living in New England. Little Dixie was pro-Confederate during the Civil War; Callaway County declared its independence from the Union. For many years faithfully Democratic, Little Dixie has reared some notable politicians as well. One was Champ Clark, speaker of the House from 1911 to 1919 and candidate for the Democratic presidential nomination in 1912; another was Clarence Cannon, author of the definitive text on the House's parliamentary procedures and chairman of the House Appropriations Committee from 1941 to 1964 except for four years of Republican control.

The 9th Congressional District of Missouri is the descendant of the Little Dixie districts that elected Clark and Cannon, but slow population growth has expanded it far to the south and into the foothills of the Ozarks. It includes Columbia, home of the University of Missouri, and Fulton, home of Westminster College, where Winston Churchill, accompanied by President Harry Truman, told the world in 1946 that "from Stettin on the Baltic to Trieste on the Adriatic, an iron curtain has descended across the continent." The district includes the western edge of the St. Louis metro area, western St. Charles County and Franklin County south of the Missouri River. Its grain fields have become a center for ethanol production, including a new $220 million plant in Monroe City. Despite its Democratic heritage, it votes mostly Republican now, 55% for George W. Bush in 2000 and 59% in 2004.

The congressman from the 9th District is Kenny Hulshof (pronounced *HULLZ-hoff*), a Republican first elected in 1996. He grew up on a farm in far southeast Missouri. After getting his bachelor degree in agriculture economics at the University of Missouri and his law degree from the University of Mississippi, he joined the public defender's office in Cape Girardeau. In 1989, he became a special prosecutor for the Missouri attorney general's office and traveled to 53 counties, obtaining 60 violent felony convictions and seven death sentences; he is certified as a specialist instructor in criminal law. In 1994, he became the Republican nominee in the 9th District. This was a surprise: challenger Rick Hardy had held Democratic Congressman Harold Volkmer to a 48%-46% win in 1992 and was running again; but after the filing deadline he withdrew from the race due to depression and exhaustion. Party leaders named Hulshof to run. He was far outspent, but made a respectable showing and lost 50%-45%. In 1996 Hulshof ran again. Volkmer's combative temperament and irritation with the new Republican majority made him one of its most persistent antagonists. Volkmer ran an ad showing Hulshof in a Porsche driven by Newt Gingrich and attacking him for signing away his independence in the Contract with America. Hulshof replied that Volkmer had voted to raise taxes 20 times in 20 years and had voted for 40% pay raises. The key moment came in October when Volkmer, in response to a question, said voters were not overtaxed and that he would not mind paying $1 million in taxes. Hulshof ran radio ads quoting Volkmer all over the district. Volkmer carried Little Dixie 53%-46%, but Hulshof led elsewhere for a 49%-47% win.

In the House, Hulshof has a voting record near the center of his party. He was elected president of the Republican freshman class. With Democratic freshman president Jim Davis, he supported the 1997 balanced budget agreement; he helped organize the civility retreats in Hershey and backed Shays-Meehan campaign finance reform. The Republican leadership gave him a prized seat on Ways and Means as a freshman and he used the platform to back repeal of the estate tax, scaling back taxation of dividend and interest income, and favorable tax treatment of ethanol. He helped to enact Bush's proposal to create education savings accounts, and he has been a leader for making permanent the tax cuts of 2001. On the Social Security Subcommittee, he praised Bush's reform initiative but said that he was open to other approaches. With a district crisscrossed by many long-distance rail lines, he proposed to cut the excise tax on rail fuel.

On the ethics committee, Hulshof chaired the subcommittee that investigated allegations of undue pressure on members during the 2003 vote on the Medicare/prescription drug bill and he joined the unanimous committee votes in October 2004 to admonish Majority Leader Tom DeLay on two counts; he praised its efforts as "the least partisan committee work I've ever been involved with." In January 2005, Speaker Hastert dropped him from the panel and Hulshof reportedly was miffed that he was given no explanation; later, he called for tightened ethics rules and disclosure, and he donated to charity campaign funds that he had received from DeLay. He has played drums in the bipartisan "Second Amendments" band that has entertained troops in Iraq.

Hulshof has been reelected by wide margins. In May 2007, Hulshof acknowledged he was a finalist to take over as president of the University of Missouri, his alma mater. But the university passed him over in June.

★ MONTANA ★

Just a little more than 200 years ago, in April 1805, Meriwether Lewis and William Clark and their pirogues wended up the Missouri River just past the Yellowstone into what now is Montana. It was wild, open country, under a big sky—and most of it still is. To celebrate July 4, 1976, the late historian Stephen Ambrose took his family to Lemhi Pass at the other end of Montana, nearly 500 miles west, where Lewis was the first American to cross the Continental Divide—and noted that the land was little different from when Lewis and Clark passed through. Ambrose later retold the Lewis and Clark story in *Undaunted Courage* and he and his family settled in Montana; they are far from the only outsiders who have moved, part-time or full, into the Big Sky State in recent years.

Yet American civilization has touched down only lightly on Montana. It is still a land of great empty vistas, with mountains in the west and vast expanses of plateaus and plains in the east—the 4th largest state in area and 44th in population. Almost nowhere in the state are wilderness and empty land out of sight. Montana sits atop the continental United States, spanning the Rockies so that on I-15 you can cross the Continental Divide three times. But since the time of Lewis and Clark, it has not been much of a crossroads. The first Americans here were itinerant trappers seeking fur and miners seeking gold, silver and copper, who built ramshackle towns where outlaws battled vigilantes—and in a few cases gained sudden riches, which would make them kings not of this barren land but of the metropolises back East. Then came the workers who built and serviced the Northern Pacific and Great Northern railroads, followed by wheat farmers and ranchers.

Statehood came less than a century after the first white Americans, Lewis and Clark and their men, came here as agents of the government. The mining economy gave Montana a radical, class warfare political tradition. On one side was the Anaconda Mining Company, which until 1959 owned five of Montana's six daily newspapers, the Montana Power Company and many of its politicians. It had strong allies in the Stockmen's Association and the Farm Bureau. On the other side were progressives like Senators Thomas Walsh, who exposed the Teapot Dome scandal, and Burton Wheeler, a New Dealer who broke with Franklin D. Roosevelt over court packing and isolationism, the labor unions (Montana has no right-to-work law and may be the most pro-union state in the Rockies), and pork barrel beneficiaries (for a while in the 1930s, Montana received more federal money per capita than almost any other state). The locus of all this was Butte, with its gold and copper mines on "The Richest Hill on Earth," with its gamblers and bootleggers, company goons and union thugs, IWW organizers and Socialist mayor, and millionaires who bought seats in the U.S. Senate. Today the mines are closed, the ore depleted, and the stone temples of commerce are grim; looming mineheads are being restored to a cleanliness they never enjoyed in the boom days.

Butte's population peaked in 1920, mines gradually closed all over the state, and agriculture—wheat growing and cattle grazing—became the mainstays of the economy. Class warfare died down. Other towns grew, though none is over 100,000 yet: Billings with its agricultural marketing in the east, the university town of Missoula, Great Falls just east of the Rockies, Kalispell near Flathead Lake, the university and resort town of Bozeman, and the state capital of Helena. The muscular tone of a land settled by ranch hands, miners and railroad workers, of cowboy hats, boots and blue

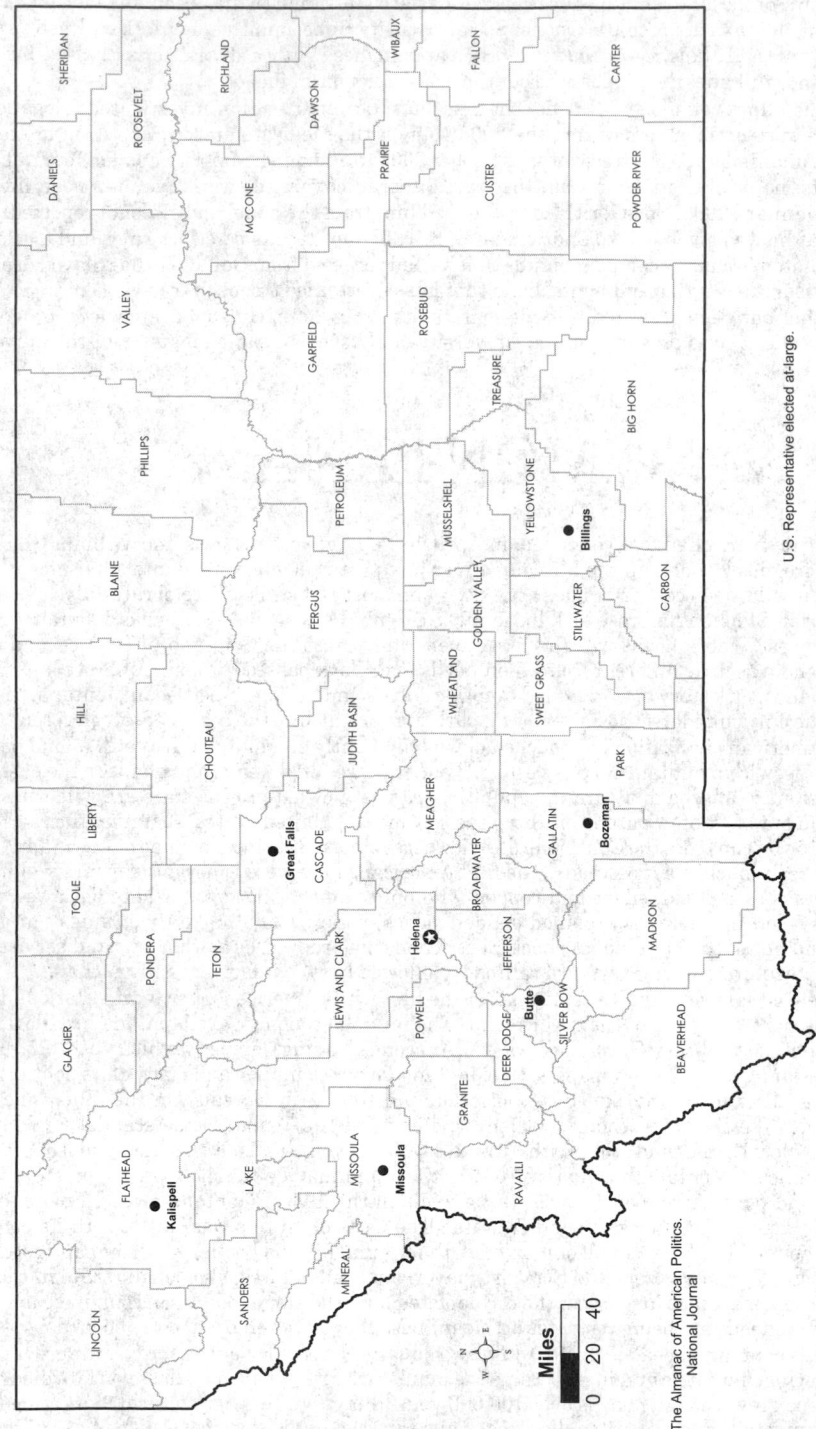

U.S. Representative elected at-large.

jeans, of men who do hard physical work and relax hard afterwards, remains a link with Montanans going back to the mountain men, miners and cowboys who drove herds of Texas longhorns across the open range. And there is still the sense of space. Hunting and fishing are never far away; development in the small cities and resort areas has not been enough to drive the game away.

Over the past quarter-century, the Big Sky country attracted at first a trickle and then a flood of affluent Americans who purchased second homes here—high-visibility movie stars and billionaires like Ted Turner, but also just ordinary people buying small spreads near Big Sky or McLeod, near Bozeman, or around Flathead Lake or Big Timber or the Big Mountain ski resort in Whitefish. Many newcomers, from California and other urban states, set down roots here, as computers, modems and fax machines make it possible for small businessmen and entrepreneurs to work in Montana, far from their customers and clients, but in an environment they love—and not far from the coffee houses and gambling parlors you find on every highway. These new Montanans have added a spark of energy and inventiveness to a state much of which consisted of those left behind when others moved elsewhere. Montana's population grew 13% in the 1990s, despite losses in the eastern plains; its economy, fueled by construction, continued to grow during the national recession of 2001-02. Growth was especially vigorous around Bozeman and Big Sky, in Missoula and Ravalli County to the south, and around Kalispell and Lake Flathead to the north. Fueled by construction and strong agricultural and petroleum prices, the state's economy continued to grow during 2003-04. Thanks to an oil boom, Blaine County in northern Montana and Richland and Fallon Counties to the east posted the fastest economic growth. But the northern and southeastern plains counties almost all lost population.

Sometimes there are conflicts between newcomers' expectations and the hardness of Montana life. The DeLorme Montana Road Atlas gives advice on what you should do if you encounter a bear. There are lively political arguments over the grizzly bears and gray wolves reintroduced to Montana in the 1990s. The American Prairie Foundation, funded by Manhattan and Silicon Valley millionaires, is buying up land in the northern plains to create a reserve where buffalo and prairie dogs can roam, and attract tourists and hunters; the Nature Conservancy has been persuading ranchers in Phillips County to change their practices. The state conducted a lottery in 2006 for 50 licenses (Indian tribes were allotted 16 of them) to hunt buffalo north and west of Yellowstone National Park because ranchers fear that the buffalo will transmit brucellosis, which causes cows to abort, to their herds.

There are two lively political traditions in Montana today. One draws on its heritage of class warfare politics, radical miners and angry labor unions, which made Montana for many years the most Democratic of the Rocky Mountain states. From 1952 to 1984 it elected only Democratic U.S. senators, and after the 2006 election it has two Democratic senators again. In 1992 it voted 38%-35% for Bill Clinton, with 26% for Ross Perot. The other, more recent tradition is in line with conservative activist Grover Norquist's "Leave-Us-Alone-Coalition"—a fierce opposition to higher taxes and federal government dictates. Montana has not elected a Democrat to the U.S. House since 1994, and Montana voted for George W. Bush 58%-33% in 2000 and 59%-39% in 2004. The Democratic tradition is strongest in the old mining towns like Butte and Anaconda, Indian reservations (7% of Montanans are Indians), old railroad towns like Great Falls and Havre, university towns like Missoula and Bozeman, and the state capital of Helena. The Republican tradition is strongest in the population-losing eastern plains counties and in fast-growing Flathead and Ravalli Counties in the west.

In 2004 and 2006 both traditions were apparent. In 2004 Bush carried the state by a smaller margin (evidently the Nader vote went for John Kerry) and Republican Congressman-at-Large Denny Rehberg was reelected with 64%. But Democrat Brian Schweitzer was elected governor and Democrats won a majority in the state Senate and a tie in the state House. This Democratic surge owed much to the unpopularity of Republican Governor Judy Martz, who in 2003 announced she would not seek a second term. But it was also the result of corporate malfeasance. In 1997 the legislature deregulated electricity rates and in 2000 Montana Power, the state's largest corporation, sold its power facilities for $2.1 billion and put all the money into a fiber optics firm. Bad timing: the fiber optics firm went bankrupt, and so did the buyer of the power facilities; the results were big local job losses, higher utility rates, big payouts to a few corporate executives and a rash of highly publicized lawsuits. Republican business-friendly policies were discredited and Schweitzer, a politically appealing rancher with longtime Montana roots who ran a strong race for U.S. Senate in 2000, argued convincingly for change.

In 2006 the Democrats won the most important victory, when rancher and state Senator Jon Tester beat three-term U.S. Senator Conrad Burns 49%-48%. That victory owed much to the fact that Burns received more contributions from Indian tribe clients of disgraced lobbyist Jack Abramoff than any other member of Congress. But Rehberg was reelected 59%-39%. And, despite Schweitzer's high job approval, Republicans actually made gains in the state legislature. Initial returns showed the Senate tied at 50-50, but Republican Sam Kitzenberg switched parties, putting Democrats in control by 26-24. Initial returns showed the House evenly split, with one race a 1,971–1,971 tie. But a recount gave that race to the Republicans and with the vote of one Constitution party member they prevailed 51-49.

The People		Race/Ethnic Origin			Military veterans: 108,476 (16.1%)	
Pop. 2006 (est):	944,632	807,823	89.5%	White	WWII: 19.7%	Korea: 13.4%
Pop. 2000:	902,195	2,534	0.3%	Black	Vietnam: 34.2%	Gulf War: 9.5%
Pop. 1990:	799,065	4,569	0.5%	Asian	**Most populous cities (2006):**	
Change 1990-2000:	Up 12.9%	54,426	6.0%	Native Am.	1. Billings	100,148
% of U.S. total:	0.3%	425	0.0%	Hawaiian	2. Missoula	64,081
Pop. rank:	44th of 50	13,768	1.5%	Two+ races	3. Great Falls	56,215
Area size:	147,042 sq. mi.	569	0.1%	Other	4. Bozeman	35,061
State Native:	56.1%	18,081	2.0%	Hisp. Origin	5. Butte	32,801
Non-citizen:	0.8%	**Ancestry**				
Language		German: 18.8%		Irish: 10.3%	Urban population: 54.0%	
English: 92.0%	Other Eur.: 3.3%	English: 8.8%		Norwegian: 7.4%	Rural population: 46.0%	
Spanish: 2.6%		USA: 3.6%				

Education		Work Sector		Legislature	
H.S. Grad:	87.2%	Private: 69.2%	Govt: 18.3%	Senate	26 D 24 R
College Grad:	24.4%	Self: 11.8%	Family: 0.7%	House	50 R 49 D 1 I
Industry		Unemployment: 6.3%		Legislative Term Limits: Yes	
Agri: 7.9%	Con: 7.4%	**Household Income**		**Registered Voters**	
Fin: 5.5%	Info: 2.2%	<15k: 20.2%	15-35k: 32.5%	No party registration	
Mfg: 11.4%	Prof: 28.2%	35-50k: 18.2%	50-100k: 23.5%		
Public: 5.9%	Trade: 15.8%	100-150k: 3.6%	>150k: 1.9%		
Other: 15.6%		Median: $33,024			
Occupation		Poverty status: 14.6%			
Blue collar: 22.0%	White collar: 58.6%	**Home Value**			
Gray collar: 19.4%		<50k: 19.4%	50-100k: 33.8%	100-200k: 34.5%	200-300k: 7.2%
		300-500k: 3.1%	>500k: 2.0%	Median: $95,800	

Presidential politics   Montana, with its 3 electoral votes, doesn't see much of presidential candidates. Its presidential primary is in early June, far too late to affect any results; in 2004, Dennis Kucinich campaigned here and finished second with 10% of the vote. But in 1992 and 1996, Montana was closely divided. Ross Perot won 26% in Montana in 1992 and 13.6% in 1996, which was his second-best showing that year. Almost all those votes seem to have gone for George W. Bush in 2000, as he carried the state by a wider margin than Ronald Reagan or Richard Nixon in 1984 and 1972. Ralph Nader won 6% in 2000, and those votes seem to have gone for John Kerry in 2004, who cut Bush's margin but still ran 20% behind. Democrats may target the Mountain West in 2008, but winning Montana will be tough—unless Brian Schweitzer winds up on the ticket.

2004 Presidential Vote

Bush (R)	266,063	(59%)
Kerry (D)	173,710	(39%)
Nader (I)	6,168	(1%)
Other	4,493	(1%)

2004 Democratic Presidential Primary

Kerry (D)	63,611	(68%)
Kucinich (D)	9,686	(10%)
Edwards (D)	8,516	(9%)
No Preference (D)	6,899	(7%)
Clark (D)	4,081	(4%)
Other	750	(1%)

2000 Presidential Vote

Bush (R)	240,178	(58%)
Gore (D)	137,126	(33%)
Nader (Green)	24,437	(6%)
Other	9,245	(2%)

Congressional districting   Montana's population grew at a lower percentage rate than the national average in 2000-06, which makes it unlikely that Montana will regain a second House seat in the reapportionment following the 2010 Census.

Governor

Brian Schweitzer (D)

Elected 2004, term expires Jan. 2009, 1st term; b. Sept. 4, 1955, Havre; home, Whitefish; CO St. U., B.S. 1978; MT St. U., M.S. 1980; Catholic; married (Nancy).

Professional Career: Farm developer, 1980-86; Farmer, rancher, 1986-present; Committee Member, Montana Farm Service Agency, 1993-99.

Office: P.O. Box 200801, State Capitol, Helena, 59620, 406-444-3111; Fax: 406-444-4151; Web site: www.state.mt.us/governor.

Election Results

2004 general	Brian Schweitzer (D)	225,016	(50%)
	Bob Brown (R)	205,313	(46%)
	Other	15,817	(4%)
2004 primary	Brian Schweitzer (D)	68,738	(73%)
	John Vincent (D)	26,057	(27%)
2000 general	Judy Martz (R)	209,135	(51%)
	Mark O'Keefe (D)	193,131	(47%)
	Other	7,926	(2%)

Brian Schweitzer, a Democrat elected governor of Montana in 2004, grew up on his family's ranch in the Judith Basin, east of Great Falls; his Irish grandparents had homesteaded in Hill County, near the Great Northern rail line. He graduated from Colorado State and Montana State with degrees in soil science and in the early 1980s went off to the Middle East. He developed a 15,000-acre farm in the Sahara in Libya and dairy, grain and vegetable farms in Saudi Arabia on irrigated cropland. In 1986 he returned to Montana and bought two farms. He raised cattle and exported bull semen and, innovation-minded, grew mint and dill. In 1993, when the Clinton administration took office, he was appointed to the three-member, part-time Farm Service Agency that helps distribute federal payments to farmers.

With minimal political experience, he embarked on a race against two-term Senator Conrad Burns in 2000. In fall 1999, he organized the first busload of seniors to Canada to buy prescription drugs at lower prices. With armed guards, he strode into the Capitol in Helena and poured out $47,000 in cash—the amount, he said, of contributions to Burns from tobacco PACs. He attacked Burns for supporting a bill that would limit compensation to those with asbestos-related disease and shut down the giant asbestos tort cases. Burns, who had reneged on a 1988 promise to serve only two terms, outspent Schweitzer by 2–1 but won by only a 51%-47% margin.

The Senate race made Schweitzer a formidable political figure and an obvious candidate for governor in 2004. The incumbent, Republican Judy Martz, elected in 2000 by only a 51%-47% margin, had a rocky tenure. In August 2001 the state House majority leader was killed in the crash of a car driven by Martz's chief policy advisor, who was intoxicated; Martz took him from the hospital at 4 a.m. and washed his bloodstained clothes. She endured months of unfavorable publicity over a personal land purchase from a company involved in a lawsuit with the state until she was exonerated. Her job rating plunged in 2002 and in August 2003, one month after Republican Secretary of State Bob Brown entered the race, she announced she would not run for a second term.

Schweitzer entered the race for governor as the clear frontrunner in the Democratic primary. He campaigned against one-party rule—Montana had had Republican governors since 1988—and championed small businesses against out-of-state corporations. He said Montana had a "salmon economy" ("all our young leave the state and then they come home to die") and that Republicans were to blame for high property taxes and for the state's low wage levels. He made common cause with both environmental advocates and hunters and fishermen by championing hunting and fishing rights on private lands and opposing sale of public lands. He called for low-tuition technical colleges to provide training so young people can qualify for jobs in Montana and for a pharmacy purchasing pools to buy prescription drugs in Canada. He named Republican state Senator John Bohlinger as his lieutenant governor candidate and named him head of a Corps of Recovery (echoing Lewis and Clark's Corps of Discovery) to come up with $60 million of spending cuts without cutting services. He won the June 2004 Democratic primary 73%-27%.

Republicans, long the dominant party, had a four-candidate primary. The winner, with 39% of the vote, was Bob Brown, a Helena veteran: he had been elected to the legislature in 1970, at 23, and served 26 years; for four years he was a lobbyist for USWest, Columbia Falls Aluminum Company and the state university system. Brown's three opponents were all more conservative and all from Yellowstone County (Billings); Brown, like Schweitzer, declined to take the Americans for Tax Reform pledge not to raise taxes. Brown favored limited oil and gas exploration on the Rocky Mountain Front and the ballot proposition to repeal the state's ban on cyanide mining; Schweitzer took the opposite stand on both issues.

Schweitzer raised more money than Brown, some of it from out-of-state contributors to his 2000 Senate race. With his flair for promoting new ideas and his invocation of his homesteader Montana roots, he seemed a more vibrant candidate than the reserved Brown. A self-described "pickup-driving, God-fearing, gun-toting, red-meat-eating, take-responsibility-for-my-actions, invest-in-education kind of Democrat," he showed shrewd political instincts. Like Brown, he backed the referendum banning same-sex marriage (it passed with 67% of the vote). Schweitzer won by a 50%-46% margin, and Democrats swept to a 27-23 majority in the state Senate and a 50-50 tie in the state House (thus giving them control because state law requires that, in the case of a tie, the speaker must come from the governor's party). Schweitzer carried not only the usual Democratic areas (Butte, the Indian reservations, Missoula) but also Billings, the state's largest city, and Helena, the capital.

Schweitzer announced an open door policy in the governor's office, and brought his border collie Jag there every day. In early 2005 he faced a rosy fiscal situation, with a projected $300 million surplus. He and the legislature froze the business equipment tax at 3% and eliminated it for 13,000 businesses that own $20,000 worth of equipment or less. But the legislature refused to pass Schweitzer's proposal for capturing unpaid taxes on business and property sales. He signed a bill requiring country of origin meat labeling. On energy, Schweitzer proposed a bill to require 10% of motor fuel to be a certain form of ethanol after state ethanol production reaches 55 million gallons a year; most Republicans preferred tax incentives for the ethanol industry. The Senate passed Schweitzer's bill 34-16 in March 2005, but there was resistance in the House, where with three Republican votes it passed 52-48 in April. Schweitzer predicted new ethanol plants would be built, with 10,000 jobs. He promoted more coal mining and proposed a coal liquefaction plant, although he admitted that any synfuels production would require federal subsidy. He also promoted wind power and required a minimum percentage of renewable energy to be produced by utilities. His goals include energy independence. And he wants to deliver Montana electricity to Las Vegas and Los Angeles. On environmental issues, he took some risks. When the Bush administration opened up national forest land to new logging roads, Schweitzer pressed local officials to request that none be built. He proposed to buy up grazing rights near Yellowstone National Park to prevent the spread of brucellosis from the local buffalo to cattle.

In March 2005 the state Supreme Court ruled that Montana's school funding laws were "constitutionally deficient." The legislature did not come up with a new formula in its regular session, and Schweitzer called a short special session in December 2005. He unveiled a plan to spend some $31 million on building maintenance, energy costs and the Indian Education for All program. It passed the two chambers by 54-42 and 31-19. In addition, Schweitzer and the legislature put $125 million into the teacher and state employee pension funds, which were figured to be $1.4 billion short because of investment losses and benefit increases.

Schweitzer has had very high job ratings, although he says, "They like my dog better than me, but in politics you kind of ride the wave." He traveled widely to promote investment in Montana. He set up a Montana Ambassadors program, getting Montana natives in Seattle and other big cities to sing the state's praises. He campaigned for Senate candidate Jon Tester, who won, and for two ballot initiatives, an ethics measure that got 76% of the vote and a minimum wage increase that got 73%. But Democrats, contrary to the national trend, lost seats in both houses: the Senate went from 27-23 Democratic to 25-25, after which a Republican switched parties and made it 26-24; the House, after all the votes were counted went from 50-50 to 49-50 (with one Constitution party member caucusing with Republicans), and Republican Scott Sales became Speaker. Still, Schweitzer seems in a strong position to win reelection in 2008. And there has been talk that he might have national potential. "I am just a Montana farmer," he has said. "I don't know if what I say or do is exportable. It is a long way from the Little League to playing for the Yankees." But he did go to New York to campaign for successful governor candidate Eliot Spitzer, and he did come out early in opposition to U.S. military action in Iraq. Some Democratic bloggers have argued that a plain-spoken Montana rancher may be just what the party needs to balance its ticket.

Senior Senator

Max Baucus (D)

Elected 1978, seat up 2008, 5th term; b. Dec. 11, 1941, Helena; home, Helena; Stanford U., B.A. 1964, LL.B. 1967; Protestant; married (Wanda).

Elected Office: MT House of Reps., 1973-74; U.S. House of Reps., 1974-78.

Professional Career: Staff atty., Civil Aeronautics Bd., 1967-69; Legal Asst., Securities & Exchange Comm., 1969-71; Practicing atty., 1971-74.

DC Office: 511 HSOB, 20510, 202-224-2651; Fax: 202-224-0515; Web site: baucus.senate.gov.

State Offices: Billings, 406-657-6790; Bozeman, 406-586-6104; Butte, 406-782-8700; Great Falls, 406-761-1574; Helena, 406-449-5480; Kalispell, 406-756-1150; Missoula, 406-329-3123.

Committees: *Agriculture, Nutrition & Forestry* (4th of 11 D): Domestic & Foreign Marketing, Inspection, & Plant & Animal Health (Chmn.); Rural Revitalization, Conservation, Forestry & Credit; Production, Income Protection & Price Support. *Environment & Public Works* (2d of 10 D): Transportation & Infrastructure (Chmn.); Private Sector & Consumer Solutions to Global Warming & Wildlife Protection; Superfund & Environmental Health. *Finance* (Chmn. of 11 D): Taxation & IRS Oversight & Long-Term Growth; International Trade & Global Competitiveness. *Joint Committee on Taxation* (Vice Chmn. of 5 D).

Group Ratings

	ADA	ACLU	AFS	LCV	ITIC	NTU	COC	ACU	CFG	FRC
2006	70	83	86	71	50	20	70	8	17	12
2005	90	—	86	55	—	23	71	24	12	—

National Journal Ratings

	2005 LIB	—	2005 CONS		2006 LIB	—	2006 CONS
Economic	54%	—	45%		60%	—	39%
Social	63%	—	35%		66%	—	33%
Foreign	63%	—	36%		71%	—	28%

Key Votes of the 109th Congress

1. Bar ANWR Drilling	Y	5. Confirm Samuel Alito	N	9. Limit Interstate Abortion	N
2. FY06 Spending Curb	N	6. Path to Citizenship	Y	10. CAFTA	N
3. Estate Tax Repeal	Y	7. Bar Same Sex Marriage	N	11. Urge Iraq Withdrawal	Y
4. Raise Minimum Wage	Y	8. Stem Cell Research $	Y	12. Provide Detainee Rights	Y

Election Results

2002 general	Max Baucus (D)	204,853	(63%)	($6,189,970)
	Mike Taylor (R)	103,611	(32%)	($1,839,020)
	Other	18,073	(5%)	
2002 primary	Max Baucus (D)	unopposed		
1996 general	Max Baucus (D)	201,935	(50%)	($4,280,747)
	Denny Rehberg (R)	182,111	(45%)	($1,358,165)
	Becky Shaw (Reform)	19,276	(5%)	

Prior Winning Percentages: 1990 (68%); 1984 (57%); 1978 (56%); 1976 House (66%); 1974 House (55%)

Max Baucus is from a well-known Montana ranching family; in 1897 his great-grandfather Henry Sieben started the huge Sieben Ranch, including the land in *A River Runs Through It*. Baucus grew up on a 125,000-acre (195 square miles) ranch near Helena, graduated from college and law school at Stanford, then worked four years at the now-abolished Civil Aeronautics Board and the Securities and Exchange Commission in Washington. He returned to Montana in 1971 and was executive director of the state constitutional convention in 1972. In 1973, he served in the state House. In 1974, at 32, he won the western House seat (Montana had two House seats until 1992) by walking 600 miles along highways through the district and beating three past or future holders of it (Democrats Pat Williams and Arnold Olsen in the primary and Republican Richard Shoup in the general). He won his Senate seat in 1978 by easily beating an appointed senator in the primary and a conservative Republican investment adviser in the general. Reelected easily in 2002, he became in March 2005 the longest-serving senator from Montana, though he has spent only four years of his adult life living full-time in the state.

Since Daniel Patrick Moynihan retired in 2000, Baucus has been the senior Democrat on the Senate Finance Committee, chairman from June 2001 to January 2003 and again since January 2007, and ranking minority member for the first six months of 2001 and in 2003-07. In that position he has been subject to competing influences. Finance has jurisdiction over tax, trade and Medicare issues—all controversial in this decade—and the Senate Democratic leadership has wanted a chairman loyal to party positions. But passing a bill in the Senate often requires 60 votes, and they are much more easily obtained when Baucus works out an agreement with his Republican counterpart, Charles Grassley. This has been a tradition on Finance, adhered to by Moynihan and William Roth in the 1990s and Bob Dole and Russell Long in the 1980s. Also, as a Democratic senator from a generally Republican state—although one that has seemed less so since the victories of Governor Brian Schweitzer in 2004 and Senator Jon Tester in 2006—Baucus has political incentives to take a moderate course on some issues.

On taxes in 2001, Baucus, starting off in the minority, unveiled a $1.3 trillion tax cut package with Grassley in May, with specific provisions tailored to moderate Republicans and Democrats on the committee. The bill passed the committee 14-6 and the Senate 62-38 (with 12 Democrats, including Baucus). Key members of the coalition Grassley and Baucus assembled insisted they would not accept major changes from the Senate bill; so something very much like it came out of the conference committee. So, just as Jim Jeffords was in the process of leaving the Republican party, the first domestic priority of the Bush administration was passed into law. Tom Daschle, who became majority leader in June, was reportedly furious that Baucus refused to consult with the Democratic Caucus before markup; he presumably wanted the 50 Democrats to hold out for a much more Democratic tax cut that would have left the government with much more revenue in the out-years. Pressure from Daschle may have reined in Baucus in October 2001, when Baucus introduced a $70 billion stimulus package and Republicans urged him to negotiate a compromise with Grassley; Baucus instead called on Bush to step in. A smaller Baucus plan passed the committee 11-10 in November (with Jeffords as the swing vote). Similarly, on welfare, Baucus was unable to come up with a united Democratic position; the 1996 law was not reauthorized until 2006. In September 2002, Baucus summoned all Finance members and told them that Daschle would allow no prescription drug bill to come out of committee and, according to some reports that Baucus denied, said that Daschle would strip him of his chairmanship if he marked one up; instead Daschle brought his own bill to the floor. That month Baucus also cancelled the markup on a small business tax cut after Daschle, the third-ranking Democrat on Finance, filed 78 amendments—one of four markups cancelled because Baucus could not assemble a majority.

After Republicans won the Senate majority in November 2002, Baucus began working closely again with Grassley on major legislation. Pressure to replace the export subsidy ruled illegal by the WTO was strong as the European Union imposed $4 billion in retaliatory tariffs, and Grassley and Baucus came up with a corporate tax bill that passed the Senate 92-5 in May 2004. "This is the biggest loophole-closing bill in my memory," Baucus said. Baucus was one of six Democrats on the conference committee, a narrow majority of which acquiesced in the House's removal of FDA regulation of tobacco from the bill. Baucus has favored extension of some of the Bush tax cuts, but not the 2003 cuts on capital gains and dividends.

Baucus also worked with Grassley in drawing up in June 2003 a Medicare/prescription drug bill that won a majority in the Finance Committee and in the Senate. Baucus supported provisions sought mostly by Republicans for a larger role for private health insurance in Medicare but got Republicans to drop provisions that would allow greater prescription drug coverage in private plans than in Medicare. He and Grassley also got what they wanted on rural health care. This bill got its final shape in the conference committee dominated by House Ways and Means Chairman Bill Thomas, who allowed no House Democrats to participate; Baucus and John Breaux were the only Senate Democrats present. Thomas could argue that concessions to him were necessary in the

House, where the conference bill was approved by one vote only after a three-hour roll call. But the final product was attacked bitterly by Edward Kennedy and other liberal Democrats who had been favorable to the concept when Baucus and Grassley were marking up their bill in Finance.

Trade issues had been Baucus's main concentration on Finance before 2001. Although he, like other Democrats, called for stronger labor and environmental standards in trade agreements, he has generally been more favorable to lowering trade barriers than most congressional Democrats: Montana is an exporting state. He was a leading advocate of normal trade relations with China, a potentially huge market for Montana wheat. In 2000, he led the fight for approval of PNTR with China and later PNTR with Vietnam. After that Baucus called for an end to the trade embargo on Cuba. After Japan banned U.S. beef in December 2003 Baucus negotiated directly with the Japanese to open up their market again; Japan announced in October 2004 that it would. Baucus supported the U.S.-Australia Free Trade Agreement in 2004, but opposed the Central American FTA in 2005; he criticized but supported the Oman FTA. In January 2006 he criticized "politically motivated trade agreements with very small countries of little economic significance that create few jobs at home" and called for a position of chief trade prosecutor in the U.S. Trade Representative's office. In January 2007 he called for reauthorizing Trade Promotion Authority, but suggested that he would insist on stronger labor and environmental provisions, which were arguably necessary for passage in the Democratic House.

On Social Security, Baucus joined Grassley and other moderates in 2004 to discuss changes in the system. But in spring 2005 Baucus proved to be a trusted point man for Minority Leader Harry Reid by sticking to the party line and rejecting personal retirement accounts. "Privatization has to be off the table because it exacerbates or makes more difficult [achieving] Social Security solvency," he said. He refused to discuss any proposal that included personal investment accounts and pressed other Democratic senators to do likewise. In 2005 he told AARP that "I'm the lead guy on this end, the person in charge of preventing privatization, and I love it. I've never had so much fun fighting for something that's right. This is one of the biggest battles I've confronted in all the years I've been in Congress." He admitted that Social Security faces long-term solvency questions. "But Social Security will be there for Americans for the next 50 years, so we should not be frightened into believing we need to privatize it just to save Social Security." He appeared to be taking a similar position as chairman in early 2007.

Baucus has sponsored a bill to impose a 25% tax on Internet pornography sites and to create a new .xxx domain for pornography—and set up cyber crime task forces in Great Falls and Missoula. He got into a tussle with his Republican colleague Conrad Burns in 2006 over getting $50 million in funding for rebuilding Going-to-the-Sun Road in Glacier National Park. Baucus held up a Federal Highway Administration nominee because the agency wouldn't fund the project; the agency and Burns said that the language Baucus put in the transportation bill—he is the most senior Democrat on the Environment and Public Works Committee—didn't authorize that. Baucus sponsored an amendment to the supplemental to clarify that, then refused to accept Burns as a co-sponsor, before relenting when Republican Christopher Bond insisted on it. Overall he boasted that Montana got an increase of 44% in the 2005 transportation act. "Frankly, I'm very proud of the highway dollars I got for Montana. We're a highway state and we really depend on our highway dollars. I think that's more than appropriate, frankly, it's what I'm elected to do."

When Baucus was first elected to the Senate in 1978, Montana had been represented there only by Democrats since 1952. As the state trended Republican in the 1980s and 1990s, he was reelected nonetheless, but was pressed in 1996 when he beat Dennis Rehberg, then lieutenant governor and since 2000 congressman-at-large, by only 50%-45%. Resentment over Clinton administration environment programs and George W. Bush's big victory margin here in 2000 suggested he might have a serious challenge in 2002.

But Baucus has worked hard to maintain a presence in Montana. In 1995-96 he walked 820 miles across the state and shook thousands of hands. He has run 50- and 100-mile races as well as marathons. He has a "day in the life" program of working a day a month at an ordinary job.

In early 2001, Baucus nonetheless seemed vulnerable. One Republican who could clearly beat him was Marc Racicot, who had high job ratings as governor from 1992 to 2000. But Racicot, having been the lowest-salaried governor in the nation, wanted to make money and refused to run, despite pleas from Bush; in December 2001 Bush made him Republican National Committee chairman. That left the Republican nomination to state Senator Mike Taylor. Taylor had made millions in a hair salon and cosmetology school business and eventually spent $1 million of his own money on the campaign.

But Baucus had much more money. As chairman of the Senate Finance Committee, his fundraising capacity was enormous, and in all he spent over $6 million—almost four times as much as Taylor. Baucus ran ads showing how he helped Montana small businesses and showing George W. Bush thanking him at bill-signing ceremonies. Then, on October 10, Taylor announced he was dropping out of the race, because of an ad run by the Montana Democratic party that slyly suggested he was homosexual. The ad showed 1980s footage of Taylor, with open front shirt and gold chains, massaging a man's face applying facial cream; it stated that Taylor had failed to refund student loan money when students dropped out. Taylor claimed that his wife made paperwork errors and a Taylor aide said, "They're playing off the old stereotype of men who work in the hair-care profession." In any case, the race was already probably over. Taylor had only raised $658,000 from others and was unwilling or unable to put more of his own money in; he was still far behind Baucus in public polls, and national Republicans had decided this was not a priority race. In late October, Taylor resumed his campaign. It didn't matter. Baucus won 63%-32%, carrying all but two small counties.

Baucus, always fit and physically active, has had a few health problems. In November 2003 he took a bad fall in a 50-mile race in Maryland and two months later had surgery to relieve pressure on his brain. In June 2004 he had a pacemaker installed, and in July 2004 he suffered minor injuries in a motorcycle crash in Montana. He suffered a tragic personal loss in July 2006 when his nephew, Corporal Phillip Baucus, was killed in Iraq.

Baucus cast his 10,000th vote in the Senate in September 2006, and after the November election he said that he would probably run for reelection in 2008. "It helps us in Montana, my being chairman of the Finance Committee. It helps us a lot." The best known of the possible Republican candidates were Marc Racicot and Dennis Rehberg. Racicot seemed unlikely to leave his job at the American Insurance Association. Baucus and some of his current and former staffers made a point of contributing to Rehberg's opponent in the 2006 House race; Rehberg in July 2007 said he would run for reelection to the House. One Republican had announced as of summer 2007: state Representative Michael Lange, the former Majority Leader who lost his post after he made vulgar remarks about Governor Brian Schweitzer that were caught on videotape.

Junior Senator

Jon Tester (D)

Elected 2006, seat up 2012, 1st term; b. Aug. 21, 1956, Havre; home, Big Sandy; U. of Great Falls, B.S. 1978; Christian; married (Sharla).

Elected Office: Big Sandy Schl. Bd., 1982-92; MT Senate, 1998-2006; MT Senate Pres., 2005-06.

Professional Career: Music teacher, Big Sandy Schl. Dist., 1978-80; Custom butcher, T-Bone Farms, 1978-98; Farmer, T-Bone Farms, 1978-present.

DC Office: 204 RSOB, 20510, 202-224-2644; Fax: 202-224-8594; Web site: tester.senate.gov.

State Offices: Billings, 406-252-0550; Bozeman, 406-586-4450; Butte, 406-723-3277; Glendive, 406-365-2391; Great Falls, 406-452-9585; Helena, 406-449-5401; Kalispell, 406-257-3360; Missoula, 406-728-3003.

Committees: *Banking, Housing & Urban Affairs* (11th of 11 D): Financial Institutions; Housing, Transportation & Community Development; Securities, Insurance & Investment. *Energy & Natural Resources* (11th of 12 D): National Parks; Water & Power; Energy. *Homeland Security & Governmental Affairs* (9th of 9 D): Federal Financial Management, Government Information, Federal Services & International Security; Investigations (Permanent); State, Local & Private Sector Preparedness & Integration. *Indian Affairs* (7th of 8 D). *Small Business & Entrepreneurship* (10th of 10 D). *Veterans' Affairs* (6th of 8 D).

Group Ratings and Key Votes: Newly Elected

Election Results

2006 general	Jon Tester (D)	199,845	(49%)	($5,588,292)
	Conrad Burns (R)	196,283	(48%)	($8,516,022)
	Other	10,377	(3%)	
2006 primary	Jon Tester (D)	65,757	(61%)	
	John Morrison (D)	38,394	(35%)	
	Other	4,047	(4%)	
2000 general	Conrad Burns (R)	208,082	(51%)	($4,337,961)
	Brian Schweitzer (D)	194,430	(47%)	($2,033,530)
	Other	9,089	(2%)	

Jon Tester, a Democrat, was elected Montana's junior senator in 2006. He grew up in a farm family, on the same prairie land his grandparents homesteaded almost a century ago near the small town of Big Sandy. His family ran a custom butcher shop behind the barn; at the age of 9, he lost three fingers on his left hand in a meat grinder. The accident, he says, changed him from a saxophone player to a trumpet player; he earned a music degree from the College of Great Falls and later taught music at a local elementary school before devoting himself to farming. He served on the local Soil Conservation Service Committee and raised organic wheat, alfalfa, barley, buckwheat, lentils, millet, and peas. In 1982, he was elected to the Big Sandy School Board, where he served for a decade. In 1998, when his neighbor, a Republican state senator, decided not to run for reelection, Tester ran for and won the seat.

Tester was one of the few Montana Democrats who represented a rural district and in 2002 he was elected minority leader; after Democrats won a Senate majority, he became Senate president in 2005. When the 2005 legislative session had adjourned, he announced he would challenge three-term Republican Senator Conrad Burns. Tester was one of five Democrats seeking the party nomination; the only real opposition came from two-term state Auditor John Morrison. Morrison was a former president of the Montana Trial Lawyers Association, the son of a state Supreme Court justice who ran for governor and the grandson of a former Nebraska governor; he outspent Tester by nearly 2-to-1. But in a campaign that figured to focus on Burns' ethics, Morrison was weakened by the disclosure that he had an extramarital affair in 1998 with the fiancée of a businessman who was later investigated by the auditor's office. This enabled Tester to rebut claims that Morrison was the more electable candidate and led him to say he was the only Democrat who could go "belly to belly and toe to toe" with Burns. He ran as an unabashed populist, which made him a darling of liberal Internet activists, and he assembled a formidable grass roots operation with hundreds of volunteers. He won in a 61%-35% rout over Morrison.

In Burns, Tester was taking on the only Republican senator Montana voters had ever reelected. After ousting Democratic Senator John Melcher in 1988, Burns had won reelection easily enough in 1994. But he had a surprisingly hard time defending his seat in 2000 against Democrat Brian Schweitzer, who was later elected governor in 2004, winning by only 51%-47%. In 2006, the 71-year-old conservative incumbent had two serious problems. The first was his connection to disgraced and later convicted lobbyist Jack Abramoff. Burns was the largest congressional recipient of campaign donations from Abramoff, a fact that national Democrats relentlessly hammered him on, beginning as early as 2005. He faced campaign accusations that he had "sold his vote" and betrayed Montana's Native American population by earmarking funds for Abramoff's Indian clients in other states; Burns urged Attorney General Alberto Gonzales to fully investigate the donations so that "these outrageous and wrongful allegations may be put to rest."The broader theme, one used by Tester, was that Burns was not the same down-to-earth Westerner Montanans had sent to Washington 18 years earlier.

Burns's second handicap was a gaffe-prone style ill-suited for the YouTube era. His proclivity for making inappropriate or intemperate statements was one trait that had not changed in his two decades in Congress. In February 1999, he was forced to make a quick apology after referring to Arabs as "ragheads." In 2006, while discussing the war on terrorism, he spoke of enemies who "drive taxicabs in the daytime and kill at night." In July, he admonished a group of firefighters for doing a "piss-poor job" of battling a wildfire. A month later, he referred to his handyman as a "nice little Guatemalan man" and joked about the man's immigration status. "I can self-destruct in one sentence," he admitted. "Sometimes in one word." In past elections, those blunders might have been overlooked as part of Burns's folksy appeal but they were harder to dismiss now that some of them were memorialized on video and posted on numerous websites for all to see.

This was a bare-knuckled campaign. Burns spent $8.5 million, roughly twice as much as in 2000 and $3 million more than Tester. Burns was pummeled over his link to Abramoff while Republicans sought to portray Tester as too liberal for Montana, criticizing his opposition to the Patriot Act and linking him to "radical environmentalists" and liberal extremist bloggers. But Tester was not so easily caricatured. His signature $8 flattop haircut, highlighted in a television ad filmed at the Riverview Barbershop in Great Falls, his down-to-earth demeanor, beefy farmer's build and agricultural background worked to temper the criticism. He also had the support of Governor Schweitzer, Burns's former foe, who taped an ad saying, "Senator Burns and his crooked pals in Washington are lying about my friend Jon Tester."

The race was decided by just 3,562 votes. Burns carried 41 of 56 counties, including Yellowstone County, home to agriculture industry-oriented Billings, the state's largest city. But Tester carried the counties including Great Falls and the state capital of Helena, and won 64%-34% in Missoula County.

In Washington, Tester's victory was hailed by Democrats as a signal of a new political direction in the Mountain West. His distinctive look—he's tall, barrel-chested, wears a flattop and cowboy boots—won him immediate notice in the Senate, as did his practice of prominently posting his daily schedule on the Internet, a Senate first.

Representative-At-Large

Denny Rehberg (R)

Elected 2000, 4th term; b. Oct. 5, 1955, Billings; home, Billings; WA St. U., B.A. 1977; Episcopalian; married (Jan).

Elected Office: MT House of Reps., 1984-90; MT Lt. Gov., 1991-96

Professional Career: Leg. Asst., U.S. Rep. Ron Marlenee, 1979-82; Rancher, 1982-present.

DC Office: 516 CHOB, 20515, 202-225-3211; Fax: 202-225-5687; Web site: www.house.gov/rehberg.

District Offices: Billings, 406-256-1019; Great Falls, 406-454-1066; Helena, 406-443-7878; Missoula, 406-543-9550.

Committees: *Appropriations* (26th of 29 R): Financial Services & General Government; Labor, HHS, Education & Related Agencies.

Group Ratings

	ADA	ACLU	AFS	LCV	ITIC	NTU	COC	ACU	CFG	FRC
2006	0	18	0	0	86	55	100	83	52	85
2005	10	—	0	11	—	51	89	92	37	92

National Journal Ratings

	2005 LIB	—	2005 CONS		2006 LIB	—	2006 CONS
Economic	14%	—	83%		4%	—	94%
Social	32%	—	66%		26%	—	73%
Foreign	23%	—	73%		6%	—	86%

Key Votes of the 109th Congress

1. Estate Tax Repeal	Y	5. Limit Interstate Abortion	Y	9. Build Border Fence	Y
2. Limit CAFE Standards	Y	6. Extend Patriot Act	Y	10. CAFTA	N
3. FY06 Spending Curb	Y	7. Bar Same Sex Marriage	Y	11. Oppose Iraq Withdrawal	Y
4. Drilling in ANWR	Y	8. Stem Cell Research $	N	12. Detainee Tribunals	Y

Election Results

2006 general	Denny Rehberg (R) 239,124	(59%)	($1,132,530)
	Monica Lindeen (D) 158,916	(39%)	($512,425)
	Other... 8,085	(2%)	
2006 primary	Denny Rehberg (R) .... unopposed		
2004 general	Denny Rehberg (R) 286,076	(64%)	($608,199)
	Tracy Velazquez (D) 145,606	(33%)	($127,716)
	Other... 12,548	(3%)	

Prior Winning Percentages: 2002 (65%); 2000 (51%)

Dennis Rehberg, a Republican first elected in 2000, is a rancher from Billings who raises cattle and cashmere goats on his family ranch, flies his helicopter across the state and who has been involved in politics most of his life. His father was a state legislator who ran against Democratic Congressman John Melcher in 1970, and Denny Rehberg was an intern in Helena.

After college, he worked in real estate, moved to Washington while his wife attended law school and then worked for Montana Republican Congressman Ron Marlenee. He returned to Montana in 1982 and ran the family ranch. He was elected to the state House in 1984, at 29; he managed Marlenee's campaign in 1986 and Conrad Burns' first campaign for the Senate in 1988. He served as Burns' state director for two years, then was appointed lieutenant governor by Republican Stan Stephens, and was elected to that post on the ticket headed by Marc Racicot in 1992. In 1996, he ran against Senator Max Baucus. Rehberg backed term limits, promised to forego pay increases and attacked Baucus for backing the 1993 tax increase and the assault weapons ban. Baucus called Rehberg a "special interest" candidate backing billions in tax cuts for the rich and argued against Republican Medicare "cuts." Rehberg was outspent by $4.3 million to $1.4 million, but made it a close race: Baucus won 50%-45%.

Rehberg (pronounced *REE-berg*) returned to ranching. The opportunity to run for the House arose in September 1999 when incumbent Republican Rick Hill, reelected by only 53%-44% and facing vigorous opposition from Democratic Superintendent of Public Instruction Nancy Keenan, announced he would not run because of complications from eye surgery. Rehberg was unopposed for the Republican nomination. The general race against Keenan was a classic contest between a liberal Democrat and a conservative Republican. But Rehberg and Keenan agreed on opposing gun control, repealing the marriage penalty and letting patients sue HMOs.

Naturally there was more discussion of their disagreements—on abortion rights, on inheritance taxes, a prescription drug benefit (Rehberg favored it for the needy, Keenan for all), and individual investment accounts in Social Security. The tone got testier, as outside groups—the AFL-CIO, the NEA, the Chamber of Commerce, the NFIB—spent over $100,000 each; something like $20 million was spent in this state with seriously contested races for Senate and House. Rehberg ran ads with strong endorsements from Governor Racicot and often showing his family, especially his two-year-old daughter—an implicit contrast with Keenan, a former copper smelter worker and special education teacher who had never married. Rehberg won 51%-46%, almost precisely the same margin as in the races for governor and senator that year; all the Republicans were surely helped by George W. Bush's 58%-33% margin over Al Gore.

As a freshman, Rehberg concentrated on issues with impact in Montana. He worked with Conrad Burns in 2002 to get $5 billion in drought relief for farmers in addition to the farm bill; they were frustrated by Bush's opposition, and had to settle for $752 million in farm bill funds. He sought repeal of the Clinton administration's restrictions on snowmobiling in Yellowstone National Park; after a hearing Rehberg organized, the Bush administration changed the policy. In his second term Rehberg took up the cause of preserving mandatory country of origin labeling of meat, a provision of the 2002 farm bill set to go into effect in September 2004. In a law signed in January 2004 Congress delayed implementation by two years. In July 2004 the Agriculture Committee rejected Rehberg amendments to leave mandatory country of origin labeling intact and to make the labeling voluntary. In 2005 he sponsored an amendment to tariff law requiring country of origin labeling of imported livestock, to assure Japan and South Korea, which had banned U.S. beef exports because of mad cow disease, that U.S. beef was safe. This was opposed by Texas cattlemen, who import many calves from Mexico, and by the Bush administration. Japan agreed to repeal its ban in July 2006.

Rehberg has supported the Bush administration strongly on Iraq, and after a trip there in December 2005 sharply disagreed with John Murtha's statement that the Army was "broken down and worn out." "To a person over there, the morale of our fighting men and women is high." He disagrees with the administration on other issues. He voted against the Central American FTA. He favors reimportation of prescription drugs from Canada, backed the House's $318 billion transportation bill and opposed putting guest worker and legalization provisions in the immigration bill. He has harshly criticized the Endangered Species Act and says it leads farmers and ranchers to "shoot, shovel and shut up"—to kill animals that may be labeled endangered because of onerous enforcement. He has pushed for expedited federal testing of an additive which is believed to make it impossible to make methamphetamine from anhydrous ammonia, a common fertilizer.

Rehberg declined a repeat run against Senator Max Baucus in 2002, though polls suggested he would be competitive. He was reelected with 65% and 64% of the vote in 2002 and 2004. In 2006 he was opposed by Billings-area state Representative Monica Lindeen, whose family started Montana's largest Internet service provider and sold it in 2000. Like Montana's two senators, he had received contributions from Indian tribes represented by disgraced lobbyist Jack Abramoff, some $1¾000, plus $2,000 from Abramoff himself. He returned the former to the tribes and donated the $2,000 to domestic violence centers on Montana reservations. Lindeen raised $518,000, with notable contributions from Senator Max Baucus and former Baucus staffers. Rehberg raised $1.2 million, but didn't spend it all. He won by the reduced margin of 59%-39%, but it was his most serious challenge for reelection in a pretty good year for Montana Democrats. Had Burns retired and Rehberg run for the seat, he might well have been elected to the Senate.

Rehberg was mentioned as a possible candidate against Baucus in 2008, but in July 2007 he said he would run for reelection to the House. In 2005 he won a seat on the Appropriations Committee—a sign he may be settling in for a long House career—and after Democrats won back control he noted that in Montana and in Washington he had "worked in virtually every combination" of partisan balance.

★ NEBRASKA ★

"The sea of Nebraska" is what the first settlers coming west called the Platte River—not actually a single river, but a braid of streams that weaves a silver chain around sandbars and islands, flooding the level floor of the great plain—a mile wide, as the saying goes, and six inches deep. Nebraska was formed in one rush of settlement in the 1880s, when its population increased from 452,000 to 1,062,000; it increased less than that, to 1,578,000, in the next 100 years. In the 1880s Omaha became a major railroad center, Lincoln the state capital, and farming and food products the main businesses. And for about 100 years, Nebraska remained pretty much that way. This is not what its founders intended: They hoped Nebraska would develop a diversified farming, industrial and commercial economy like Ohio, Illinois, Missouri or Minnesota. But while the 1880s were a time of plentiful rain here, the 1890s were a decade of drought, and Nebraska stopped growing. Many rural counties and even Omaha lost population, and Nebraska exported people for 100 years: 48% of Nebraskans in 1890 were children; in 2000, only 26% were. For a long time the creative energies in the economy seem to have skipped over the Great Plains and moved far to the West.

The sudden boom of the 1880s and the bust of the 1890s produced the most colorful—and atypical—politics of Nebraska's history: The populist movement and William Jennings Bryan, the "silver tongued orator of the Platte." Bryan was only 36 when he delivered his Cross of Gold speech at the 1896 Democratic National Convention and was swept to the Democratic nomination. He was so radical that Democratic President Grover Cleveland wouldn't support him, but he still won 47% of the popular vote in the first of three attempts at the presidency. Since Bryan's time, Nebraska's most notable politician has been George Norris, who led the House rebellion against Speaker Joseph Cannon in 1911, and in the 1930s championed the state's unicameral, nonpartisan legislature (in which every bill gets a public hearing) and pushed through the Norris-LaGuardia Anti-Injunction Act (the first federal pro-union legislation) and the Tennessee Valley Authority. But most Nebraskans were repelled by the New Deal, which seemed to threaten their way of life. Although it often elects Democratic governors and senators, Nebraska over the past half-century has been the second-most Republican state in presidential elections.

Since 1990, Nebraska has been growing robustly for the first time in decades. Its population grew 12%, to 1,768,000 between 1990 and 2006, less than the national average but more than Nebraska has grown since the 1910s. The age tilt has changed too: Nebraska's percentages of old people and children are now within 1% of the national average. The growth has not been even. In 68 of its 93 counties, population has declined since 2000. In tiny county seats stores are closing, across the plains farmhouses are shuttered up, small school buildings are half-empty. The acreage of

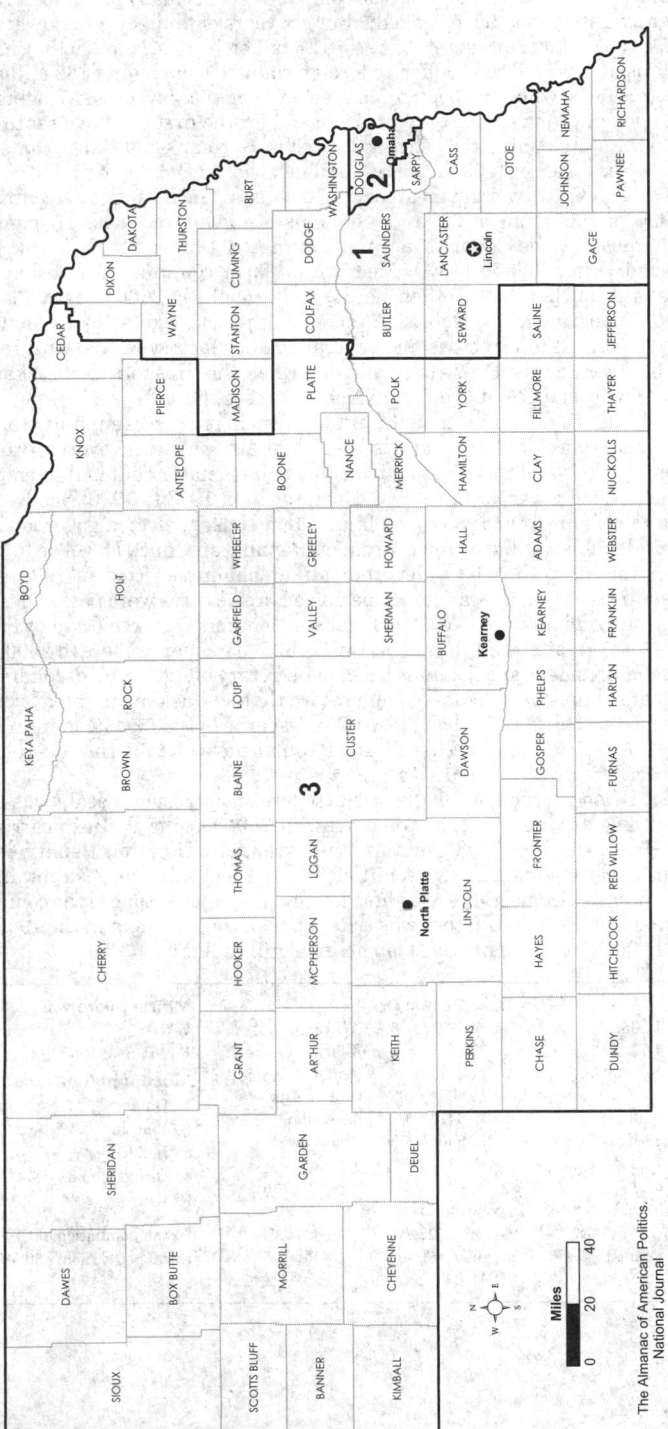

Congressional district boundaries were first effective for 2002.

The Almanac of American Politics.
National Journal

irrigated land has been rising, but a state law passed in 2004 seems likely to reduce irrigation from wells. Groundwater irrigation may have peaked; after six years of drought groundwater was down 30 feet in fall 2006. Even so, farm incomes hit a record $4 billion in 2004, though they have declined since; in 2004, Nebraska exported $2.3 billion to foreign countries, including $88 million to China. The number of jobs rose 18% when the population rose 8%. For years Nebraska's aging population was not producing enough young people to fill its jobs, and for the first time in a century there has been migration into the state. A hundred years ago, Czechs, Germans and Danes came to work the farms on the plains—Willa Cather tells the story—and factories in Omaha. Now Latinos have been coming from Texas and Mexico to work in meatpacking factories: The Hispanic percentage rose from 2% to 7% from 1990 to 2005, and in 2000, 8% of the state's children were Hispanic. Hispanic percentages are highest in the counties around Lexington (30%), South Sioux City (29%), Scottsbluff (19%) and Grand Island (18%). Meanwhile, farm counties keep losing population; drought in 2002 caused ranchers to cull their herds, and drought in 2006 caused $342 million in agricultural losses. Demographically, Nebraska increasingly looks like a Rocky Mountain state, with population concentrated in two cities and several smaller factory towns, with relatively few people spread out over farmlands. Every fall Saturday when the 'Huskers (Nebraskans don't say Cornhuskers) play in Lincoln, one out of every 25 Nebraskans is there.

Nebraska may be heavily Republican, but it is also a small enough community that attractive Democrats can win high office. The pattern has been this: A Republican governor raises taxes, a Democrat defeats him or her and then goes on to serve in the Senate. That is the template for the careers of Jim Exon, elected governor in 1970 and senator from 1978 to 1996; Bob Kerrey, elected governor in 1982 and senator from 1988 to 2000; and Ben Nelson, elected governor in 1990 and senator in 2000. But Republicans have grown stronger. Republican Chuck Hagel beat Nelson when Nelson first ran for the Senate in 1996. Governor Mike Johanns, elected in 1998, opposed tax increases; temporary increases in the sales, income and cigarette taxes were passed over his veto in 2002. But the old pattern did not hold. In 2002 Hagel and Johanns were reelected by 83%-15% and 69%-28% margins—even greater than George W. Bush's 62%-33% margin here in 2000; Hagel then considered running for president and Johanns became Secretary of Agriculture. Johanns's replacement, Dave Heineman, compiled a popular enough record that he was renominated over 3d District Congressman (and former 'Huskers football coach) Tom Osborne by a 50%-44% margin and won the general election by a 73%-24% margin. That means Republicans will hold the governorship for 12 years, the longest such stretch since the 1950s.

The last time a Democrat won one of Nebraska's three congressional seats was in 1992 and Republicans hold all five downballot statewide offices. In 2004 George W. Bush carried the state 66%-33%, winning 92 of the state's 93 counties (the exception, Thurston County, is an Indian reservation); he ran under 60% in only five counties, two of them the counties containing Omaha and Lincoln. But Nebraska's Democrats are a game lot, and they include one of the country's richest men, investor Warren Buffett, whose father was a Republican congressman in the 1940s and early 1950s; in this mostly flat state, they have a steep political hill to climb.

The People		Race/Ethnic Origin			Military veterans: 173,189 (13.7%)	
Pop. 2006 (est):	1,768,331	1,494,494	87.3%	White	WWII: 20.0%	Korea: 15.0%
Pop. 2000:	1,711,263	67,537	3.9%	Black	Vietnam: 32.3%	Gulf War: 10.8%
Pop. 1990:	1,578,385	21,677	1.3%	Asian	**Most populous cities (2006):**	
Change 1990-2000:	Up 8.4%	13,460	0.8%	Native Am.	1. Omaha	419,545
% of U.S. total:	0.6%	647	0.0%	Hawaiian	2. Lincoln	241,167
Pop. rank:	38th of 50	17,696	1.0%	Two+ races	3. Bellevue	47,594
Area size:	77,354 sq. mi.	1,327	0.1%	Other	4. Grand Island	44,632
State Native:	67.1%	94,425	5.5%	Hisp. Origin	5. Kearney	29,385
Non-citizen:	3.0%	**Ancestry**				
Language		German: 27.7%		Irish: 9.6%	Urban population: 69.7%	
English: 90.4%	Spanish: 5.4%	English: 6.9%		Swedish: 3.5%	Rural population: 30.3%	
Other Eur.: 2.9%		USA: 3.2%				

Education		Work Sector		Unicameral	
H.S. Grad:	86.6%	Private: 77.1%	Govt: 13.7%	Senate	49 I
College Grad:	23.7%	Self: 8.7%	Family: 0.5%	Legislative Term Limits: Yes	
Industry		Unemployment: 3.5%		**Registered Voters**	
Agri: 5.6%	Con: 6.5%	**Household Income**		D: 370,600	(32.6%)
Fin: 7.7%	Info: 2.5%	<15k: 14.9%	15-35k: 29.5%	R: 572,869	(50.3%)
Mfg: 18.4%	Prof: 28.0%	35-50k: 18.4%	50-100k: 29.2%	O: 194,600	(17.1%)
Public: 3.9%	Trade: 15.7%	100-150k: 5.5%	>150k: 2.6%		
Other: 11.9%		Median: $39,250			
Occupation		Poverty status: 9.7%			
Blue collar: 24.4%	White collar: 59.4%	**Home Value**			
Gray collar: 16.2%		<50k: 21.3%	50-100k: 40.2%	100-200k: 30.4%	200-300k: 5.3%
		300-500k: 2.0%	>500k: 0.7%	Median: $86,900	

Presidential politics   Over the last 50 years, Nebraska has voted more Republican in presidential elections than all but one other state—61.1% to Utah's 61.6%. It was appropriate, perhaps, that this was the last state Bill Clinton visited as president, in December 2000. Greater Omaha usually goes Republican, while Lincoln is more closely divided; rural western counties are heavily Republican—Bush's 2004 percentages there ranged up to 90%. In the NEP exit poll, no statistically significant demographic group came close to voting for John Kerry. Nebraska law allows its electoral votes to be split, with one going to the winner of each congressional district and two to the statewide winner. But this has never made any difference. In spring 2004 Kerry backers hoped he would carry the 1st Congressional District; it voted 63%-36% for Bush. Nebraska's May presidential primary once attracted attention; the whole national press followed Robert Kennedy and Eugene McCarthy out here in 1968 and took note when Frank Church won in 1976. In recent years, the

2004 Presidential Vote		
Bush (R)	512,814	(66%)
Kerry (D)	254,328	(33%)
Nader (I)	5,698	(1%)
Other	5,346	(1%)

2004 Democratic Presidential Primary		
Kerry (D)	52,479	(73%)
Edwards (D)	10,031	(14%)
Dean (D)	5,400	(8%)
Kucinich (D)	1,490	(2%)
Sharpton (D)	1,367	(2%)
Other	805	(1%)

2000 Presidential Vote		
Bush (R)	433,862	(62%)
Gore (D)	231,780	(33%)
Nader (Green)	24,540	(4%)
Other	6,837	(1%)

primary hardly mattered. Nominations are now sewn up long before May, and Nebraska voted as unnoticed then as in November. Hoping to play a more prominent role in 2008, Nebraska Democrats decided to hold caucuses on February 9; state Republicans stuck with the traditional primary in May.

Congressional districting   Nebraska has had three congressional districts since the 1960 Census. Redistricting made only marginal changes for 2002; Democrats were angered when traditionally Democratic Saline County was moved from the 1st to the 3d District. No Democrat has been elected from a Nebraska district since 1992.

110th Congress Lineup
3 R

109th Congress Lineup
3 R

Governor

Dave Heineman (R)

Assumed office Jan. 2005, term expires Jan. 2011, 1st full term; b. May 12, 1948, Falls City; home, Fremont; U.S. Military Acad., B.S. 1970; Eastern Orthodox; married (Sally Ganem).

Military Career: Army, 1970-75.

Elected Office: Fremont City Cncl., 1990-94; NE Treasurer, 1994-2001; Lt. Gov., 2001-05.

Professional Career: Ex. Dir., NE Republican party, 1979-81; Chief of Staff, U.S. Rep. Hal Daub, 1983-88.

Office: P.O. Box 94848, Lincoln, 68509, 402-471-2244; Fax: 402-471-6031; Web site: www.gov.state.ne.us.

Election Results

2006 general	Dave Heineman (R)	435,507	(73%)
	David Hahn (D)	145,115	(24%)
	Other	12,735	(2%)
2006 primary	Dave Heineman (R)	138,216	(50%)
	Tom Osborne (R)	121,973	(44%)
	Dave Nabity (R)	14,786	(5%)
2002 general	Mike Johanns (R)	330,349	(69%)
	Stormy Dean (D)	132,348	(28%)
	Paul Rosberg (NEB)	18,294	(4%)

Dave Heineman became governor of Nebraska in January 2005, when Mike Johanns resigned to become George W. Bush's secretary of agriculture. Heineman was born in Falls City (pop. 4,375) in the state's southeastern corner, 100 miles equidistant from Omaha and Lincoln. He grew up in a handful of small towns across the state, the son of an itinerant J.C. Penney's store manager, before graduating from Wahoo High School. He went east to attend the United States Military Academy at West Point and expected to see action in Vietnam but the war ended first. He served five years in the Army, graduating from the Army's Airborne and Ranger schools and rising to the rank of captain. When his tour ended in 1975, he returned to Nebraska and immediately dove into politics as an envelope-stuffing volunteer for the Republican party in Omaha.

Heineman was named the party's executive director in 1979, held the position for two years and for the rest of the decade he worked in politics and government: as campaign manager and aide to Congressman Hal Daub, political consultant to Governor Kay Orr's reelection campaign, local office manager for Congressman Doug Bereuter. In 1990, he won his first elective office, a seat on the Fremont City Council, and then was elected state treasurer in 1994 and reelected in 1998. In 2001 he was chosen by Johanns to replace Lieutenant Governor David Maurstad, who resigned to become a regional director for the Federal Emergency Management Agency. He ran for lieutenant governor in 2002 on a ticket with Johanns; they won by 69%-28%.

As treasurer, Heineman modernized the state's money management system and its methods of returning unclaimed property to residents. As lieutenant governor, he served as the state's official lobbyist in Washington, its homeland security director and as chairman of Nebraska's Information Technology Commission, where he helped create a telecommunications backbone for state government, medical facilities and the University of Nebraska. All the while, he had his eye on the governorship. When Bereuter announced he would not seek reelection to Congress in 2004, Heineman declined to run for the open 1st District seat, saying he was focused on running for governor in 2006 when term limits would prevent Johanns from running again. "I would rather pursue my dream of becoming governor, even if that opportunity never materializes, than to pursue another office that I am not committed to." But he also said that if Congressman Tom Osborne, the former University of Nebraska football coach and the state's most popular politician, decided to run for governor, it was unlikely he would challenge him.

Johanns' next move seemed obvious: speculation that he would run against Senator Ben Nelson in 2006 began almost immediately after his 2002 reelection. According to some reports, Republicans tried to persuade Nelson to switch parties to stave off what was expected to be a tough challenge. Another option for Nelson: Ten days after the 2004 election, according to the *Omaha*

World-Herald, White House strategist Karl Rove offered him the position of secretary of agriculture; the paper said Nelson considered it for five days before declining. If he had accepted, Johanns would have appointed his successor.

But Johanns' surprise Cabinet appointment reordered the 2006 political landscape. Nelson's reelection prospects suddenly grew brighter and the governor's race suddenly became a lot more complicated. By spring 2005, the picture was clearer. In March, Attorney General Jon Bruning announced he would not run for governor and would instead seek a second term as attorney general. On April 11, Heineman signaled his intention to run for governor by filing papers to form a campaign committee; Senator Chuck Hagel endorsed Heineman's candidacy the same day. On April 30, Osborne said he would run for governor but only intended to serve a single term if elected. After Osborne announced for governor, national party officials were hoping to convince Heineman to run against Ben Nelson, but Heineman told the Lincoln *Journal Star* in May that his interest in the Senate, on a scale of zero to 100, was "minus-1000 and dropping."

Heineman's first year as governor began on solid footing. Nebraska is the only state with a unicameral legislature, the Senate, often called the Unicam, and some of its 49 members were still angry over Johanns' heavy involvement in the 2004 campaign; they welcomed a new face in the governor's office because Johanns had leveled tough criticisms of a 2003 tax increase that was passed over his veto. After four lean years marked by contentious budget cuts and tax increases, the state's revenue outlook began to pick up. In August, Heineman led a 10-member trade delegation to Cuba to encourage the purchase of various Nebraska-grown products; despite tough criticism of his trip from several Florida congressional Republicans, Heineman came back with an agreement to sell 5,000 metric tons of dry beans, with the future prospect of exporting 25,000 metric tons of corn, 25,000 metric tons of wheat and 15,000 metric tons of soybeans and soy meal. Heineman met for four hours with Cuban President Fidel Castro and said Castro "knew quite a bit about Nebraska and what we were there for." Later that month Heineman signed an agreement with Cuban government officials to sell a total of $30 million in Nebraska agricultural products.

In 2006 Heineman vetoed a pay raise for the state's top elected officials, a separate measure to improve retirement benefits for state workers and a bill to allow children of illegal immigrants to qualify for in-state tuition rates at state colleges and universities; all three vetoes were overridden by the legislature, which saw its first class of lawmakers forced to depart because of term limits. More controversial was an ongoing boundary dispute involving the Omaha public schools. In June 2005, Omaha school officials announced a "one city, one school district" initiative to expand the school district boundaries and take over 21 schools in Millard and 4 in Ralston that are inside Omaha city limits. The Millard and Ralston school superintendents resisted and were joined in opposition by two other suburban districts; the matter ended up in the legislature in 2006, where a bill passed dividing OPS into three racially-identifiable districts—one largely Latino, one largely black and one largely white. The bill attracted national and international attention, with critics claiming it was state-sanctioned resegregation. Heineman, who had sided with the suburban schools in the dispute, signed the measure into law in April. "It is a new beginning for a community dialogue that needed to occur before, but could not. While neither side won everything they sought, this bill, particularly with recent amendments, secures both boundaries and future cooperation. This bill is far from perfect, and I'll be honest, there are parts that make me less than comfortable, and parts that would make me pause as a parent," he said. "It is clear to me that the motivation behind this proposal is neither segregation, nor separation, but instead the goal of improving student achievement and the responsiveness of schools."

Overshadowing all this was the looming showdown the next month in the May primary. Heineman trailed badly in some early 2005 polls but by April 2006 he had drawn even with Osborne while Omaha businessman David Nabity, who played up his private sector experience, was a distant third. An aggressive ribbon-cutter and campaigner, Heineman's hard-charging approach contrasted with the 69-year-old Osborne, who had never been seriously challenged in his brief political career. Heineman had key endorsements from the state Farm Bureau, Nebraska Right to Life and the National Rifle Association. Osborne had endorsements from the state employees and teachers' unions. Heineman gained traction with criticism of Osborne's support for the in-state college tuition law for illegal immigrants' children; Osborne explained that he didn't believe that children should be penalized for their parents' actions. Without a top-tier Democratic candidate in the race, the high-profile Republican primary drew heightened interest. As many as 10,000 voters switched parties so that they could vote; famed investor and Omaha resident Warren Buffett, a Democrat, said he would switch parties and vote for Osborne. Osborne said that if he won the governorship, Buffett would oversee a top-to-bottom review of state government operations. But

Heineman won 50%-44%, with Nabity finishing third with 5%. Osborne carried the state's two most populous counties, Omaha's Douglas County (47%-44%) and Lincoln's Lancaster County (53%-43%), but not by enough to erase Heineman's margins elsewhere. Heineman's position on the Omaha schools proposal boosted him with suburban voters; he carried the central and eastern parts of the state and also won 54 of the 69 counties in Osborne's western Nebraska-based congressional district (selecting the Chimney Rock landmark as the design for Nebraska's quarter helped, as did his 2005 veto of a bill to eliminate elementary-only school districts).

The general election was largely an afterthought against Democrat David Hahn, an attorney and Internet entrepreneur from Lincoln. Hahn scoffed at talk of tax cuts and supported abortion rights; even before the Republican nomination was settled, he was forced to deny he was a "sacrificial lamb"—not a good sign. In a year that featured competitive Senate and congressional races, a long-shot governor's race was a low Democratic priority. Hahn trailed badly in the polls and Heineman won 73%-24%, the largest winning margin in a Nebraska governor's race since Dwight Griswold won reelection in 1944 with 76% of the vote. No Nebraska governor has ever served more than 8 years; if Heineman seeks and wins a second term in 2010, he could leave office as the longest-serving governor in state history.

Senior Senator

Chuck Hagel (R)

Elected 1996, seat up 2008, 2d term; b. Oct. 4, 1946, North Platte; home, Omaha; U. of NE, B.A. 1971; Episcopalian; married (Lilibet).

Military Career: Army, 1967-68 (Vietnam).

Professional Career: Newscaster & Talk Show Host, KBON & KLNG Radio, 1969-71; Admin. Asst., U.S. Rep. John Y. McCollister, 1971-77; Mgr., Govt. Affairs, Firestone Tire & Rubber Co., 1977-80; Dpty. Admin., Veterans' Admin., 1981; U.S. Dpty. Commissioner General, World's Fair, 1982; Pres., Collins, Hagel & Clarke Inc., 1983-84; Co–founder, Dir. & Exec. V.P.., Vanguard Cellular Systems Inc., 1984-87; Pres. & CEO, World USO, 1987-90; Pres. & CEO, Priv. Sector Cncl., 1990-92; Pres., McCarth & Co., 1992-95.

DC Office: 248 RSOB, 20510, 202-224-4224; Fax: 202-224-5213; Web site: hagel.senate.gov.

State Offices: Kearney, 308-236-7602; Lincoln, 402-476-1400; Omaha, 402-758-8981; Scottsbluff, 308-632-6032.

Committees: *Banking, Housing & Urban Affairs* (5th of 10 R): Financial Institutions (RMM); Securities, Insurance & Investment; Housing, Transportation & Community Development. *Foreign Relations* (2d of 10 R): International Development & Foreign Assistance, Economic Affairs & International Environmental Protection (RMM); Near Eastern & South & Central Asian Affairs; African Affairs; East Asian & Pacific Affairs. *Intelligence (Select)* (3d of 7 R). *Rules & Administration* (7th of 9 R).

Group Ratings

	ADA	ACLU	AFS	LCV	ITIC	NTU	COC	ACU	CFG	FRC
2006	5	36	13	14	100	82	100	75	87	62
2005	10	—	0	5	—	76	94	96	99	—

National Journal Ratings

	2005 LIB	—	2005 CONS		2006 LIB	—	2006 CONS
Economic	12%	—	86%		13%	—	82%
Social	43%	—	56%		47%	—	52%
Foreign	35%	—	64%		18%	—	76%

Key Votes of the 109th Congress

1. Bar ANWR Drilling	N	5. Confirm Samuel Alito	Y	9. Limit Interstate Abortion	Y
2. FY06 Spending Curb	Y	6. Path to Citizenship	Y	10. CAFTA	Y
3. Estate Tax Repeal	Y	7. Bar Same Sex Marriage	*	11. Urge Iraq Withdrawal	N
4. Raise Minimum Wage	N	8. Stem Cell Research $	N	12. Provide Detainee Rights	N

Election Results

2002 general	Chuck Hagel (R)	397,438	(83%)	($1,394,770)
	Charlie Matulka (D)	70,290	(15%)	
	Other	12,489	(3%)	
2002 primary	Chuck Hagel (R)	unopposed		
1996 general	Chuck Hagel (R)	379,933	(56%)	($3,564,316)
	Ben Nelson (D)	281,904	(42%)	($2,159,653)
	Other	14,952	(2%)	

Chuck Hagel, first elected in 1996, is Nebraska's senior senator. Hagel grew up in the Sand Hills and small towns of Nebraska; his father died when he was 16, and Chuck Hagel started supporting his family. He dropped out of college, worked as a radio DJ, then with his younger brother Tom volunteered for service in Vietnam. Promoted to sergeant because so many were dying, Chuck and Tom served together; in March 1968, when their armored personnel carrier hit a mine, Chuck, his body on fire, dragged Tom from the APC to safety. Chuck Hagel returned home, worked his way through the University of Nebraska in Omaha, then got a job in Omaha Congressman John McCollister's office. He rose to administrative assistant; after McCollister lost a Senate race in 1976, Hagel became a lobbyist for Firestone. He later got the number two position in the Reagan Veterans' Affairs Administration, but resigned after only one year. He was one of two main speakers at the 1982 groundbreaking of the Vietnam Veterans' Memorial. Then he made his great break, using all of his savings—$5,000—and starting Vanguard Cellular Systems, which became the second largest independent cell phone company in the nation; Hagel traveled on business to 60 countries and installed cell phone systems in Costa Rica, Saudi Arabia and Britain. Then he became head of World USO and then deputy director of the 1990 G-7 Summit. In 1992 he returned to Omaha, to work in investment banking; the McCarthy Group, of which he was a partner, owned a share of a company that is now known as Election Systems & Software, which manufactures nearly half of American voting machines. He was criticized later for naming in his disclosure forms the McCarthy Group, and not the firms in which it has an interest.

In 1995, when Senator Jim Exon announced his retirement, Hagel started running for the Senate, very much the underdog. His platform was solidly conservative, sometimes riskily so: He backed school choice, opposed racial quotas and preferences, backed the Freedom to Farm Act, opposed the estate tax. In the primary he called state Attorney General Don Stenberg a "career politician"; Stenberg hit him for living 20 years in Virginia and for contributing to Bob Kerrey's 1992 presidential campaign. Hagel won the May primary 62%-37% and in the general faced Governor Ben Nelson, who had won re-election in 1994 by a 73%-26% margin. Nelson had a record of tax-cutting and supported the balanced budget amendment. He led consistently in polls, though by lower margins in the fall, and raised far more PAC money—$909,000, nearly half of his campaign funds—but Hagel spent $1 million of his own money and $3.5 million altogether. Hagel resisted advice from Republican campaign committee head Alfonse D'Amato to go negative; Nelson in the last weeks charged that Hagel had engaged in fraudulent franchising practices with Vanguard. Newspapers hit Nelson, and Hagel responded, "This is a guy who lies. This is a guy who cheats. This is a guy who will do anything." Hagel won 56%-42%, carrying 88 of 93 counties.

In the Senate, Hagel sought a seat on Foreign Relations and got it—because no other freshman Republican wanted it. He quickly became, in columnist David Broder's words, "the freshman who probably has made the deepest impression on his colleagues of both parties." Hagel's opposition to the Vietnam war—arrived at after long study afterwards—and his extensive travels overseas and his involvement in the G-7 summit seem to have left him inclined to agree with criticisms of assertive American policies. Hagel called on his military experience in 1997 to support the treaty against land mines, which was opposed by the Clinton administration; he spoke for the chemical weapons treaty ratified by the Senate in 1997 over the objections of Foreign Relations Chairman Jesse Helms; he voted against the Comprehensive Test Ban Treaty in October 1999 but joined Democrats and the administration in trying to prevent the vote when it became clear the treaty would be rejected. He supported the bombing of Serbia in spring 1999, but decried the Clinton policy of ruling out the use of ground troops. In George W. Bush's first full month as president, Hagel joined Christopher Dodd in sponsoring a resolution to open Cuba to all U.S. exports and to end all restrictions on travel and credit. He was one of two senators to vote against extending trade sanctions on Iran and Libya, and in 2006 he called for direct negotiations with Iran and North Korea. He has said that he is for "principled realism."

After September 11, he has been one of the Republicans most cautious against taking action against states that sponsor terrorism and most eager to work in tandem with international organizations. "Great powers remain great powers if they, too, recognize they have limitations to that power." In February 2002 he accused the Bush administration of a "cavalier approach" to the rest of the world and said that the axis of evil part of George W. Bush's first State of the Union speech was "name calling." Before Bush's September 12, 2002, speech to the United Nations, Hagel said he had "a completely open mind" on military action in Iraq. He backed Joseph Biden and Richard Lugar in their efforts to draft a resolution endorsing military action only after diplomatic efforts were exhausted in the United Nations; that was put aside after Bush got agreement on his draft from congressional Republican leaders and House Minority Leader Richard Gephardt. He voted for the Iraq war resolution, but insisted, "Actions in Iraq must come in the context of an American-led, multilateral approach to disarmament, not as the first case for a new American doctrine involving the preemptive use of force." In February 2003 he said that the United States stood "nearly alone" on using force in Iraq. In a *Foreign Affairs* article in July 2004, he wrote that U.S. policy should not be ruled by a sense of "divine mission," but should inspire allies to work with us on "making a better world." He argued for expanding free trade agreements, seeking long-term security through alliances, coalitions and international institutions like the United Nations and NATO and advancing democracy with an eye on realities in the Middle East, particularly anger toward the U.S. stance on Israel-Palestinian issues. "We're in deep trouble in Iraq," he told the press in September 2004. "It's beyond pitiful, it's beyond embarrassing. It is now in the zone of dangerous." Some of his comments were quoted by John Kerry in one of the presidential debates, and Hagel's comments on his fellow Vietnam veteran suggested he might be closer to him on Iraq than to Bush. In June 2005 he said the White House was "disconnected from reality" on Iraq and that America was "losing" the war. "I don't want the president to lose," Hagel said. "I want him to win. But I can't just go along with the sheep here and say 'Everything is fine, just be patient.' We did that once." In October 2006, in the midst of the campaign, he said, "The American people are not going to continue to support, sustain a policy that puts American troops in the middle of a civil war. . . . We need to find a new strategy, a way out of Iraq, because the entire Middle East is more combustible than it's been probably since 1948, and more dangerous, and we're in the middle of it." He said after the November election that the forthcoming Baker-Hamilton Iraq Study Group report would give Bush a "a new opportunity to form a bipartisan consensus to get out of Iraq," but when the report came out he expressed "caution" about its recommendation to embed more U.S. troops in Iraqi units. He said that Iraq wouldn't become a terrorist haven if U.S. troops left. "A terrorist nation, a terrorist state, is certainly not in the interest of the Syrian government or the interests of the Iranian government, or of Jordan, or of any of those governments there." On December 7, he called for a substantial withdrawal of U.S. troops beginning in 2007. "I believe America is coming dangerously close to isolating itself in the Muslim world. . . . We cannot make the training of Iraqi troops a prerequisite for our withdrawal from Iraq." In January 2007 he co-sponsored with Joseph Biden a resolution disapproving of Bush's surge of U.S. troops; it passed the Foreign Relations Committee 12–9.

Hagel has a mostly conservative voting record in the Senate. He opposes abortion, favors school prayer, and has taken stands in favor of school vouchers. But he has been critical of his party's leaders on occasion. When in July 1999 Majority Leader Trent Lott and others put holds on the nomination of Richard Holbrooke to be U.N. ambassador, he said that was "an irresponsible way to govern." He spent much of his time that year and in early 2000 campaigning for John McCain for president. The two had often met with other senators who were Vietnam veterans and had developed a strong bond; they worked together on opening up trade with Vietnam. He sharply criticized George W. Bush's campaign tactics in South Carolina, but he also was one of the few who would talk back to McCain. After McCain lost, Hagel was on Bush's short list of vice presidential prospects.

Hagel did not agree with McCain on campaign finance. He favored reducing soft money contributions but not limiting them; his amendment to do that was rejected 60-40 in March 2001. He supported oil drilling in the Arctic National Wildlife Refuge and opposed limits on drilling, logging and grazing in national forests. He opposed the farm bill passed in 2002 and criticized its conservation sections for interfering with water rights under state law.

Hagel voted against the 2001 education bill and the Medicare/prescription drug bill in 2003, calling it "a sham and a ripoff for everybody . . . and actually it's going to make our problems worse." On immigration, in January 2004 he sponsored an immigration bill with Tom Daschle to let illegal immigrants achieve "earned legalization" on demonstrating four years of work and mastery of the English language; willing workers would be matched with willing employers. In 2006, when the Senate appeared headed for deadlock on overhauling the nation's immigration policy, Hagel and Mel Martinez of Florida brokered a compromise that allowed the Senate debate to proceed by establishing different requirements for illegal immigrants to legalize their status depending on their length of time in the country. The Senate passed the bill but it clashed with the House's border enforcement approach and the two chambers never reconciled their differences.

In September 2004 he proposed to waive the $1,200 enrollment fee for G.I. Bill of Rights benefits and to increase the death benefit for soldiers from $12,000 to $50,000; in January 2005 he raised that to $100,000. In March 2005 he introduced the first bill that session to change Social Security by adding voluntary personal retirement accounts.

In March 2003 Hagel and the entire Nebraska delegation sponsored a bill to double the use of ethanol in gasoline and to mandate five billion gallons of renewable fuels, mainly ethanol, by 2015. In October 2003 he voted against the McCain-Lieberman bill to impose limits on carbon dioxide emissions, but later promised his own bill on the subject in 2005. He and Nebraska colleague Ben Nelson co-sponsored the $2.9 billion drought and hurricane relief package that passed the Senate in September 2004. When the White House made and then withdrew the nomination of Columbus, Nebraska, businessman Tony Raimondo as a "jobs czar," Hagel was furious that he had not been notified. Raimondo was a friend of Ben Nelson, Hagel's opponent in 1996, whose stands on the 2001 tax cuts, the 2002 farm bill and Department of Homeland Security labor regulations he had criticized in blunt terms. Asked if there was bad feeling between them, Hagel said, "We're not friends, we're colleagues. That's not unusual." They have nonetheless worked together on many Nebraska and some national issues.

In 2002 Hagel's Democratic opponent couldn't afford the $1,500 filing fee and filed as a pauper. Hagel raised $3.5 million, but spent only $2 million, and won 83%-15%, by a considerable margin the biggest percentage victory ever in a Nebraska Senate race. He won 78% or more in 91 of 93 Nebraska counties, and as much as 94% in one.

Hagel has long been mentioned as a possible presidential candidate. When asked the day after the 2004 election whether he would run, he said, "I've not reached that point yet; I don't need to reach that point yet." In spring 2005 he made a swing around New Hampshire; in the fall he gave a speech in Iowa. Speculation that he would not run against his friend McCain diminished as it became apparent that they had sharply different positions on Iraq. Still, his stand on Iraq and his approach to foreign policy generally could be liabilities among Republican electorates, and so was his unwillingness to take a pledge never to raise taxes and his suggestion that more revenues will be needed to solve the problems of Social Security and Medicare. The November 2006 exit poll showed that only 37% of Nebraskans said Hagel would be a good president; that low showing can be attributed to Republicans who disagreed with some of his positions. Hagel's response to the election was that the message "is the American people saying you failed" and that Republicans had been so focused on maintaining power that "we came loose of our moorings."

In March 2007, Hagel called a much-anticipated press conference in Omaha for "an announcement on [his] political future," only to declare in front of the local and national media that he would make a decision on his political future later in the year. In May, he said he would make a decision in the next few months about whether to pursue a third-party bid for the presidency or run for reelection to a third term. By then, however, Hagel's drawn out decision-making process was beginning to wear thin back home. Former Omaha Mayor and 2d District Congressman Hal Daub and state Attorney General Jon Bruning went forward with exploratory committees after initially showing some deference to Hagel. Bruning later announced he was running even if it meant challenging Hagel in the Republican primary; Daub would not rule out running in the primary as he had previously. In June, Raimondo said he was assembling a campaign, though he said he would not challenge Hagel.

In September, Hagel finally made his intentions clear. He announced that he would not seek reelection nor would he run for president in 2008. With Bruning and Daub already in the race, former Governor Mike Johanns resigned from his post as Agriculture Secretary and returned to Nebraska, with plans to run for the seat; Daub subsequently droopped out. On the Democratic side, Omaha Mayor Mike Fahey, Scott Kleeb, the 3d District nominee in 2006, and former Senator Bob Kerrey were mentioned.

Junior Senator

Ben Nelson (D)

Elected 2000, seat up 2012, 2d term; b. May 17, 1941, McCook; home, Omaha; U. of NE, B.A. 1963, M.A. 1965, LL.B. 1970; Methodist; married (Diane).

Elected Office: NE Gov., 1990-98.

Professional Career: Gen. Cnsl., Central Natl. Group Insurance, 1972-74, Pres. & CEO, 1977-81; NE Insurance Dir., 1975-76; Exec. V.P., Natl. Assn. of Insurance Commissioners, 1982-85; Practicing atty., 1985-90.

DC Office: 720 HSOB, 20510, 202-224-6551; Fax: 202-228-0012; Web site: bennelson.senate.gov.

State Offices: Kearney, 308-293-5818; Lincoln, 402-441-4600; Omaha, 402-391-3411; Scottsbluff, 308-631-7614; South Sioux City, 402-209-3595.

Committees: *Agriculture, Nutrition & Forestry* (7th of 11 D): Energy, Science & Technology; Domestic & Foreign Marketing, Inspection, & Plant & Animal Health; Rural Revitalization, Conservation, Forestry & Credit. *Appropriations* (15th of 15 D): Legislative Branch; Financial Services & General Government; Agriculture, Rural Development, Food and Drug Administration & Related Agencies; Military Construction, Veterans Affairs & Related Agencies; Homeland Security; Interior, Environment & Related Agencies. *Armed Services* (8th of 13 D): Personnel (Chmn.); Strategic Forces; Emerging Threats & Capabilities. *Rules & Administration* (7th of 10 D).

Group Ratings

	ADA	ACLU	AFS	LCV	ITIC	NTU	COC	ACU	CFG	FRC
2006	35	17	38	43	100	57	83	64	49	87
2005	55	—	63	30	—	41	94	60	35	—

National Journal Ratings

	2005 LIB	—	2005 CONS		2006 LIB	—	2006 CONS
Economic	50%	—	49%		53%	—	46%
Social	51%	—	48%		29%	—	69%
Foreign	46%	—	52%		51%	—	46%

Key Votes of the 109th Congress

1. Bar ANWR Drilling	Y	5. Confirm Samuel Alito	Y	9. Limit Interstate Abortion	Y
2. FY06 Spending Curb	N	6. Path to Citizenship	N	10. CAFTA	Y
3. Estate Tax Repeal	Y	7. Bar Same Sex Marriage	Y	11. Urge Iraq Withdrawal	N
4. Raise Minimum Wage	Y	8. Stem Cell Research $	Y	12. Provide Detainee Rights	N

Election Results

2006 general	Ben Nelson (D)	378,388	(64%)	($6,992,058)
	Pete Ricketts (R)	213,928	(36%)	($13,417,690)
2006 primary	Ben Nelson (D)	unopposed		
2000 general	Ben Nelson (D)	353,093	(51%)	($2,794,887)
	Don Stenberg (R)	337,977	(49%)	($1,795,402)

Ben Nelson, two-term Democratic governor of Nebraska, was elected to the Senate in 2000 in his second try. Nelson grew up in McCook, the hometown of Senator George Norris and novelist Willa Cather; his high school principal, Ralph Brooks, a Democrat, was elected governor in 1958, by a 50.2%-49.8% margin. Nelson graduated from the University of Nebraska, practiced law, served as state insurance director and headed a major insurance company. He has collected several hundred clocks and is an avid hunter of turkeys and bears. In 1990 he ran for governor, taking on former Bob Kerrey staff aide Bill Hoppner in the primary, and won by all of 42 votes. In the general he beat Governor Kay Orr 50%-49%, because she raised taxes and her political consultants failed to place many of her paid-for TV spots in October. He built more prisons, trimmed workmen' comp and reorganized the human services department. He cut property taxes and reduced the income and sales taxes. His record won him high job ratings and re-election by a 73%-26% margin in the Republican year of 1994. When he ran for the Senate in 1996, he led in polls most of the way, but then fell behind in October and lost to Republican Chuck Hagel by a 56%-42% margin.

In 2000 Nebraska's other Senate seat came up. Senator Bob Kerrey, one of the Democratic Party's national stars, shocked just about everyone when he said that he would not seek reelection that fall. Nelson, a lawyer in Omaha with an interest in a Republican-leaning public affairs firm in Washington, was obviously the strongest possible Democratic nominee and entered the race in February 2000. Attorney General Don Stenberg won the Republican primary, with 50% of the vote against five opponents. Nelson and Stenberg both opposed abortion and backed tax cuts. But they had significant differences in style and a long history of clashes. Stenberg ran as part of the "Bush-Hagel-Stenberg Team," sometimes bringing in Governor Mike Johanns as well. Nelson led from the start in the polls, and raised and spent more money. Nelson was helped also by active campaigning by Bob Kerrey; George W. Bush, in a close national race, couldn't afford to spend time in locked-up (for him) Nebraska. Nelson's poll leads narrowed in October, and memories went back to 1996, when it vanished altogether. This time that didn't quite happen. Nelson won 51%-49%.

Nelson turned out to be, after Zell Miller, the Senate Democrat most likely to support Bush and to differ from most Democrats. He helped to broker the big tax cuts of 2001 and 2003. He was one of three Democrats to vote against the McCain-Feingold campaign finance bill. On the labor relations sections of the homeland security bill, he sought to stake out a middle position. But his version was unacceptable to the Bush administration, and the bill was not passed before the November 2002 election. A week after the election, Nelson was one of the senators who put together a compromise to permit the president to cancel collective bargaining rights but allow that decision to be overturned by a future president. His Democratic colleagues tolerated these apostasies; as one said, "He needs to do what he needs to do to keep his seat" in one of the most Republican states in the nation. He supported Bush generally on Iraq; when the Abu Ghraib prison abuses were exposed, Nelson called for tearing down the prison. He voted against the Family Marriage Amendment, arguing that same-sex marriage was a state issue after passage of the Defense of Marriage Act.

Many of Nelson's legislative initiatives have been aimed squarely at doing "what is right for Nebraska." He voted for country of origin meat labeling. He voted for the farm bill in 2002, saying that it provided $1.1 billion for Nebraska. When the Great Plains were hit by a drought that year, Nelson argued that affected areas should get disaster relief, in the same way that places hit by hurricanes and floods do; the compensation would be for crops or livestock lost, rather than property destroyed. Twice he got the Senate to pass disaster relief; both times it was rejected in the House. In January 2003, he started applying a name to each drought, as names are applied to hurricanes, and filed his bill again for relief from "Drought David." In September 2004, when a bill for hurricane relief came up, Nelson and Hagel attached $2.9 billion in drought relief; the House accepted that but only by reducing farm bill conservation spending as an offset. He co-sponsored a bill to double the use of ethanol; it was approved by the Senate in June 2003. He got into the 2003 Medicare prescription drug bill a pilot provision providing 100% reimbursement for Nebraska rural hospitals too small to qualify for higher reimbursement and too large to qualify for another provision requiring 100% reimbursement. Nelson's relationship with colleague Chuck Hagel is not warm. "We're not friends, we're colleagues," Hagel said. Nelson responded, "He said we are not friends, we are colleagues. That's fine with me." Evidently there was bitterness left over from the 1996 campaign, when Nelson challenged Hagel's business ethics. Nelson said, "I've gotten over losing in 1996. I don't know if Senator Hagel has gotten over winning."

Republicans tried to persuade Nelson to switch parties several times during his first term. Ten days after the 2004 election, according to the *Omaha World-Herald*, White House strategist Karl Rove offered Nelson the position of secretary of agriculture; the paper said Nelson considered it for five days before declining. If he had accepted, Republican Governor Mike Johanns would have appointed his successor. In Bush's second term, Nelson continued to cooperate. On Social Security, Nelson said in 2005 he was not opposed to personal retirement accounts "in principle," but added, "I don't know how the economics of that can work." He declined to sign the letter signed by 42 Democratic senators opposing personal retirement accounts. He helped to create the "Gang of 14" senators who sought a middle ground on judgeships, thus scuttling possible filibusters against Bush's judicial nominees while preserving the Senate's ability to filibuster other nominations in the future.

In the 2006 campaign, it was generally assumed that Johanns would run against Nelson. But in December 2004 Bush announced he was appointing Johanns as secretary of agriculture. Soon after, Congressmen Lee Terry and Tom Osborne said that they would not run for the Senate. This left the race for the Republican nomination wide open. National party officials were hoping to convince Governor Dave Heineman to run, but Heineman told the Lincoln *Journal Star* that his interest, on a scale of zero to 100, was "minus-1000 and dropping." Former Attorney General Don Stenberg, the Republican nominee in 2000, announced he would seek a rematch. But Stenberg created little enthusiasm, and Republicans rallied behind Pete Ricketts, a self-financing multimillionaire who was an executive with Ameritrade. Running on a platform of tax cuts and smaller government, Ricketts sought to appeal to traditional red-state values. He won the primary with 48% to 36% for Stenberg and 16% for former state Republican chairman David Kramer. In the general, he supported a guest-worker program for immigration, which allowed Nelson to position himself to the right of Ricketts with demands to seal the border. Ricketts supported private accounts as a first step in "modernizing" Social Security; Nelson opposed such accounts. Ricketts opposed spending earmarks in the federal budget, but Nelson backed them as useful for sparsely-populated states. Ricketts spent more than $13 million, most of it from his deep pockets. The combined $20 million-plus spending for the two candidates was roughly three times the previous record for a Nebraska contest. But the result wasn't close. With his 64%-36% win, Nelson took Omaha's Douglas County 65%-35% and Lincoln's Lancaster County 70%-30%. Ricketts took 13 counties, all of them sparsely populated and west of North Platte.

Moving into the majority could prove a mixed blessing for Nelson. His new seat on the Appropriations Committee enables him to direct more federal dollars to Nebraska. But he is under greater pressure to toe the line for his party, from which he has enjoyed independence. His priorities include making drought aid a permanent part of the new farm bill, and allowing small businesses to join together to buy health insurance for their employees.

FIRST DISTRICT

Rep. Jeff Fortenberry (R)

Elected 2004, 2d term; b. Dec. 27, 1960, Baton Rouge, LA; home, Lincoln; LA St. U., 1982, Franciscan U. of Steubenville, M.A. 1985, Georgetown U., M.P.P. 1986; Catholic; married (Celeste).

Elected Office: Lincoln City Cncl., 1997-2001.

Professional Career: Staffer, U.S. House Comm. on Ag., 1986; Research assoc., Gulf South Research Inst., 1987-89; Asst. Dir., Baton Rouge Downtown Dev. District, 1989-92; Sales rep., Sandhills Publishing, 1995-2004.

DC Office: 1517 LHOB, 20515, 202-225-4806; Fax: 202-225-5686; Web site: www.house.gov/fortenberry.

District Offices: Fremont, 402-727-0888; Lincoln, 402-438-1598; Norfolk, 402-379-2064.

Committees: *Agriculture* (17th of 21 R): Conservation, Credit, Energy & Research; Specialty Crops, Rural Development & Foreign Agriculture. *Foreign Affairs* (18th of 23 R): Africa & Global Health; Middle East & South Asia. *Small Business* (8th of 15 R): Rural & Urban Entrepreneurship (RMM).

Group Ratings

	ADA	ACLU	AFS	LCV	ITIC	NTU	COC	ACU	CFG	FRC
2006	5	9	0	25	86	53	93	84	50	100
2005	5	—	0	0	—	54	93	92	53	92

National Journal Ratings

	2005 LIB	—	2005 CONS		2006 LIB	—	2006 CONS
Economic	14%	—	83%		34%	—	65%
Social	27%	—	72%		6%	—	92%
Foreign	23%	—	73%		38%	—	62%

Key Votes of the 109th Congress

1. Estate Tax Repeal	Y	5. Limit Interstate Abortion	Y	9. Build Border Fence	Y
2. Limit CAFE Standards	Y	6. Extend Patriot Act	Y	10. CAFTA	Y
3. FY06 Spending Curb	Y	7. Bar Same Sex Marriage	Y	11. Oppose Iraq Withdrawal	Y
4. Drilling in ANWR	Y	8. Stem Cell Research $	N	12. Detainee Tribunals	Y

Election Results

2006 general	Jeff Fortenberry (R) 121,015	(58%)	($1,134,332)
	Maxine Moul (D) 86,360	(42%)	($994,032)
2006 primary	Jeff Fortenberry (R) .... unopposed		
2004 general	Jeff Fortenberry (R) 143,756	(54%)	($1,224,266)
	Matt Connealy (D).............................. 113,971	(43%)	($989,884)
	Other... 7,345	(3%)	

The People		Race/Ethnic Origin	Ancestry	
Area size:	12,034 sq. mi.	90.5% White	German: 30.8% Irish: 8.7%	
Urban population:	65.1%	1.4% Black	English: 6.8%	
Rural population:	34.9%	1.5% Asian	**2004 Presidential Vote**	
Pop. 2000:	570,325	1.2% Native Am.	Bush (R) 169,888	(63%)
Pop. 2005 (est):	594,581	0.0% Hawaiian	Kerry (D) 96,314	(36%)
Median income:	$40,021	1.1% Two+ races	Other 3,896	(1%)
Poverty status:	9.2%	0.1% Other	**2000 Presidential Vote**	
Military veterans:	12.9%	4.2% Hispanic Origin	Bush (R) 138,799	(59%)
			Gore (D) 85,634	(36%)
			Other 12,242	(5%)
			Cook Partisan Voting Index: R +12	

Occupation	Blue collar: 26.2%	White collar: 57.7%	Gray collar: 16.1%

The eastern half of Nebraska, between the Missouri River and the 98th parallel, was laid out in relentless Midwestern mile-square grids and became some of America's prime farmland in the single decade of the 1880s. The land here has contours just regular enough and weather just favorable enough to make farming economically viable. The plains here have completed most of their gentle decline from the Rockies to sea level; above the river bottoms the land is open to the winds. This land was settled by Yankee-descended Midwestern farmers and immigrants from Germany and other countries. The immigrant heritage is not often remembered now, but traces of it can still be found. Many immigrants from Luxembourg, for example, settled along the Platte River in Butler County, where St. Mary's Presentation Parish still has a statue of Our Lady of Luxembourg. Not far away are villages with names that recall other immigrants' heritage—Prague (Czechs), Malmo (Swedes), Aloys (Germans). Now a new wave of immigrants is coming to eastern Nebraska, Latinos from Mexico and the southwest United States, to work in the meatpacking factories in the area. Wakefield (Dixon County) had the highest percentage increase in Hispanic population in the country in the 1990s, 8,700%—though that's a little less impressive when you realize that the Hispanic population went from 4 to 348. But there are larger numbers in other towns, and Nebraska's face is changing.

The 1st Congressional District of Nebraska is made up of 22 counties and parts of two others in the eastern part of the state; Omaha and most of its suburbs are in the 2d District. The 1st District's largest city is Lincoln, the state capital and home of the University of Nebraska Cornhuskers. Lincoln, with the state government, the university and telemarketing, has been growing rapidly. It is affluent, with above-national-average incomes and unemployment that is among the lowest in the United States. Local planners hope that their Antelope Valley public-works project, with an estimated $238 million cost, will spur economic development and improve flood control. In smaller towns there are significant farm equipment and meatpacking factories; population growth has been robust around Schuyler, Norfolk and Dakota City. Politically, Lincoln is fond of moderate Democrats but is still on balance Republican in national contests; the district voted 59% for George W. Bush in 2000 and 63% in 2004.

The congressman from the 1st District is Jeff Fortenberry, a Republican elected in 2004. Fortenberry grew up in Baton Rouge, Louisiana, the son of a life insurance salesman and a mother who worked as a 4-H extension agent. He graduated from Louisiana State University, got a master's degree in theology from Franciscan University of Steubenville, Ohio, and then another one in public policy from Georgetown. For a time, he studied for the priesthood. He worked as assistant director for the Baton Rouge Downtown Development District and in 1995 moved to Nebraska to take a public relations position with Sandhills Publishing, a publisher of trade magazines for the trucking, aircraft and computer industries. He then moved into publishing sales at the company, working on what he called a "truckers' eBay." His first foray into local politics came in 1997, two years after his arrival in Nebraska, when he won a seat on the Lincoln City Council. He served for four years, focusing on neighborhood concerns, and worked to increase the number of police officers.

When Congressman Doug Bereuter, first elected in 1978, announced he would not run again in 2004, seven candidates ran for the Republican nomination. But only three mounted competitive campaigns: Fortenberry; Curt Bromm, the speaker of the state's unicameral legislature; and Greg Ruehle, a former executive vice president of the Nebraska Cattlemen's Association. Bromm, a moderate whom Bereuter endorsed, began as the front-runner. But he quickly lost momentum after a barrage of negative television ads financed by the Club for Growth, an anti-tax group that supported Ruehle. Fortenberry, a social conservative, drew criticism from his opponents as a single-issue candidate but his superior grass roots operation and fundraising carried him to victory in the primary. He won just seven of the 24 counties but in Lincoln's Lancaster County, which cast 43% of the votes, he got 52% to 29% for Bromm and 13% for Ruehle. The vote in the rest of the district was closer: 29% for Fortenberry, 36% for Bromm and 27% for Ruehle. Overall, Fortenberry won with 39% of the vote, to 33% for Bromm and 21% for Ruehle.

Some national Republicans worried that Fortenberry would not be able to hold the seat in November. He faced state Senator Matt Connealy, a farmer from Decatur who sought to exploit Republican divisions (Bromm refused to endorse Fortenberry after the primary) and characterized Fortenberry as a stranger to Nebraska farm issues, a potent charge in a state where one in four jobs is connected to agriculture. "If you want a guy in a slick suit with slick answers, I'm probably not your guy," he said. Fortenberry responded by promising to help families retain control of their farms by improving trade policies and by supporting ethanol development. He also promised to stand up to trial lawyers. His main message, however, focused on socially conservative themes: opposition to abortion, support of capital punishment and for a constitutional amendment defining marriage as between a man and a woman. Connealy gained traction briefly by hammering Fortenberry's city council attendance record but his advance came to a halt when the Fortenberry campaign responded with an emotional ad explaining that the absences were connected to his infant daughter's open-heart surgery. He won 54%-43%, losing only two small Indian reservation counties. In Lancaster County, which cast 46% of the votes, he won by only 49%-47%.

In the House, Fortenberry became a reliable backbencher who sought to expand his portfolio. More conservative than Bereuter, he voted against expanded embryonic stem-cell research, saying it "poses profound ethical dilemmas." In planning for a new farm bill in 2007, he called for more support of renewable energy sources and new markets for farmers. On the International Relations Committee, he supported President Bush on the war in Iraq and worked on the deal to promote nuclear cooperation with India. In challenging his reelection, former Lieutenant Governor Maxine Moul cited the need for benchmarks in Iraq, and improved "ethical behavior" in Washington. Although her fundraising was competitive, Moul's late campaign attack ads did not catch fire in this district, which has not elected a Democrat since 1964. Fortenberry won 58%-42%, including 53% of the vote in Lancaster County. Moul won only in Burt County, where she was born and raised. Fortenberry had the biggest victory margin of Nebraska's three House Republicans.

SECOND DISTRICT

Rep. Lee Terry (R)

Elected 1998, 5th term; b. Jan. 29, 1962, Omaha; home, Omaha; U. of NE at Lincoln, B.A. 1984; Creighton U., J.D. 1987; Methodist; married (Robyn).

Elected Office: Omaha City Cncl., 1991-98, Pres., 1995-96.

Professional Career: Practicing atty., 1988-98.

DC Office: 1524 LHOB, 20515, 202-225-4155; Fax: 202-226-5452; Web site: leeterry.house.gov.

District Offices: Omaha, 402-397-9944.

Committees: *Energy & Commerce* (19th of 26 R): Commerce, Trade & Consumer Protection; Environment & Hazardous Materials; Telecommunications & the Internet.

Group Ratings

	ADA	ACLU	AFS	LCV	ITIC	NTU	COC	ACU	CFG	FRC
2006	0	9	0	8	100	71	100	92	72	85
2005	0	—	0	0	—	63	89	92	78	92

National Journal Ratings

	2005 LIB	—	2005 CONS	2006 LIB	—	2006 CONS
Economic	41%	—	59%	16%	—	81%
Social	38%	—	61%	23%	—	74%
Foreign	0%	—	89%	6%	—	86%

Key Votes of the 109th Congress

1. Estate Tax Repeal	Y	5. Limit Interstate Abortion	Y	9. Build Border Fence	Y
2. Limit CAFE Standards	Y	6. Extend Patriot Act	Y	10. CAFTA	Y
3. FY06 Spending Curb	Y	7. Bar Same Sex Marriage	Y	11. Oppose Iraq Withdrawal	Y
4. Drilling in ANWR	Y	8. Stem Cell Research $	N	12. Detainee Tribunals	Y

Election Results

2006 general	Lee Terry (R)	99,475	(55%)	($998,578)
	Jim Esch (D)	82,504	(45%)	($420,010)
2006 primary	Lee Terry (R)	52,890	(84%)	
	Steve Laird (R)	10,380	(16%)	
2004 general	Lee Terry (R)	152,608	(61%)	($1,454,559)
	Nancy Thompson (D)	90,292	(36%)	($899,399)
	Other	6,864	(3%)	

Prior Winning Percentages: 2002 (63%); 2000 (66%); 1998 (66%)

The People		Race/Ethnic Origin	Ancestry	
Area size:	421 sq. mi.	79.6% White	German: 22.1%	Irish: 11.6%
Urban population:	97.8%	10.2% Black	English: 6.6%	
Rural population:	2.2%	1.8% Asian	**2004 Presidential Vote**	
Pop. 2000:	570,421	0.5% Native Am.	Bush (R) 153,041	(60%)
Pop. 2005 (est):	600,877	0.1% Hawaiian	Kerry (D) 97,858	(38%)
Median income:	$45,235	1.5% Two+ races	Other 3,525	(1%)
Poverty status:	8.8%	0.1% Other	**2000 Presidential Vote**	
Military veterans:	14.4%	6.3% Hispanic Origin	Bush (R) 125,973	(57%)
			Gore (D) 85,853	(39%)
			Other 10,183	(5%)
			Cook Partisan Voting Index: R + 9	

Occupation   Blue collar: 19.5%   White collar: 66.8%   Gray collar: 13.7%

Omaha, the commercial metropolis of Nebraska, the largest city on the Great Plains north of Kansas City and west of Minneapolis, got its start from government: Abraham Lincoln picked it as the eastern terminus of the Union Pacific railroad, from which emerged the stockyards and livestock exchange that made it a top livestock town. Over the years, Omaha filled up with cattle hands from the West and European immigrants, especially Germans and Czechs; it developed fine civic institutions from the Joslyn Art Museum to Boys Town, founded by Father Flanagan in 1917, the subject of a 1938 movie, and today gender-neutral as Boys and Girls Town but still innovative and thriving in its promotion of traditional values. Though a major city by the 1880s, Omaha has remained small enough (and famous on Wall Street as the place where Warren Buffett lives and works) to be readily comprehensible; you don't feel distant, physically or psychologically, from the other side of town, and you usually know people from a broader range of backgrounds than you would in a large homogeneous neighborhood within a big metropolitan area. The older, less affluent part of Omaha is near the river and Iowa. Downtown and the riverfront have been in a construction boom; the Tower at First National Center became the tallest structure between Minneapolis and Denver. To the west, the city has been quietly booming, with affluent neighborhoods and new shopping malls. Omaha's economy has been changing. It remains dependent on overseas trade of meat and has many processors of food products, like the hard-charging ConAgra company, Omaha Steaks and Nebraska Beef, but it also has the giant Peter Kiewit construction firm. It has become the nation's telecommunications center, handling 20 million '800' and '900' calls a day and employs more than 30,000 people in over three dozen telemarketing centers. It is also ethnically diverse: 31% of students in the Omaha public schools are black and 23% Hispanic.

The 2d Congressional District of Nebraska includes most of metropolitan Omaha: Douglas County with Omaha and its western suburbs, and the eastern part of fast-growing Sarpy County with Bellevue and the Offutt Air Force Base. The U.S. Strategic Air Command is headquartered there; leading the Defense Department's global intelligence operations, it opened a foreign language training center in 2005. Politically, Omaha has long had competitive politics, with Democrats strong on the south side around the stockyards and the northeast and Republicans strong to the west. But as Omaha and Nebraska have boomed, they have become more Republican, and increasingly it is the Republican primary that decides elections here.

The congressman from the 2d District is Lee Terry, a Republican first elected in 1998. Terry grew up in Omaha, and became interested in politics at 14 when his father, TV anchor Lee Terry Sr., ran for the House in 1976; a conservative, he lost 55%-45% to 31-year-old Democrat John Cavanaugh. Terry Sr. remained a prominent local commentator on politics; Terry Jr. went off to college and law school, practiced law, and was elected to the Omaha Council from an affluent west side district in 1991, at 29. When Congressman Jon Christensen ran for governor, Terry announced for the House seat; his chief opponents were Brad Kuiper, owner of a pest control business, and Steve Kupka, former chief of staff to Mayor Hal Daub and an official in Ronald Reagan's OMB. The contrast between the three was less on issues—all were for lower taxes and against abortion—than on style and approach. Kuiper, with less money than the other two, targeted religious conservatives and emphasized cultural issues. Kupka assembled Washington endorsements and, spending the most money, went on the attack. He criticized Terry for not opposing a 1991 garbage fee and said Terry had increased the city budget. Terry won 40% to 30% for Kupka and 26% for Kuiper. The general election was anticlimactic. Despite the fact that Democrats had won open seats here in 1976 and 1988, Terry won 66%-34% against Democrat Michael Scott. In April 1999, shortly after taking office, he reneged on his pledge to serve only three terms.

In Washington, Terry has had a moderate-to-conservative voting record. He attracted attention in 1999 when he purposely bundled Bill Clinton tax increases and user fees into one $19 billion bill and brought it to the floor; it lost 419–5. He became co-chairman of the Impact Aid Coalition to protect the interests of Offutt Air Force Base, and he reversed his previous opposition to mandatory trigger locks for guns "after a year of reflection." He got a seat on the Energy and Commerce Committee, where he became an advocate of pro-business legislation. He sponsored a bill to expedite review of applications for offshore liquefied natural gas terminals. He has worked with Democrat Rick Boucher of Virginia on efforts to overhaul the federal universal service fund for telecommunications services in low-income and rural areas. He was one of eight House members who voted against "do not call" restrictions on telemarketers. The sales call is a "minor annoyance that puts bread on the tables of many people in my congressional district," he said.

With his low-key style, Terry has survived easily against well-funded reelection opponents. In 2004, state Senator Nancy Thompson ran an aggressive campaign with ads criticizing his support for budget deficits and failure to give adequate support to veterans. Democrats mocked him for contradicting his "decency" values when he held a Washington fundraiser at a Madonna concert; a spokesman for Terry called her a legitimate entertainer and said that he does not necessarily subscribe to her lyrics. Despite polls indicating a tight contest, Terry won 61%-36%. But against the less well-financed political newcomer Jim Esch, who had worked for the Omaha Chamber of Commerce, he was held to a 55%-45% win in 2006; he got only 53% in Douglas County, which cast 82% of the vote. Terry attributed the closer outcome to discontent over the war in Iraq, which was "deeper than I perceived it to be, honestly." After the election, he leased billboards across the district that featured his photo along with the message, "Thank You for Your Trust." Terry has served the 2d District longer than anyone since 1970. After having been largely ignored by national and state Democrats, Esch plans to run again in 2008.

THIRD DISTRICT

Rep. Adrian Smith (R)

Elected 2006, 1st term; b. Dec. 19, 1970, Scottsbluff; home, Gering; Attended Liberty U., 1989-90, U. of NE, B.S. 1993; Evangelical Free; single.

Elected Office: Gering City Council, 1994-98, NE Unicameral, 1998-2006.

Professional Career: Realtor, Buyer Realty, 1997-2006; Owner, My Other Garage, 2003-06.

DC Office: 503 CHOB, 20515, 202-225-6435; Fax: 202-225-0207; Web site: adriansmith.house.gov.

District Offices: Grand Island, 308-384-3900; Scottsbluff, 308-633-6333.

Committees: *Agriculture* (19th of 21 R): Specialty Crops, Rural Development & Foreign Agriculture; Livestock, Dairy & Poultry. *Budget* (16th of 17 R). *Science & Technology* (19th of 20 R): Technology & Innovation.

Group Ratings and Key Votes: Newly Elected

Election Results

2006 general	Adrian Smith (R)	113,687	(55%)	($1,242,661)
	Scott Kleeb (D)	93,046	(45%)	($975,392)
2006 primary	Adrian Smith (R)	42,218	(39%)	
	John Hanson (R)	30,501	(29%)	
	Jay Vavricek (R)	29,224	(27%)	
	Other	4,954	(5%)	
2004 general	Tom Osborne (R)	218,751	(87%)	($63,654)
	Donna Anderson (D)	26,434	(11%)	($10,867)
	Other	4,951	(2%)	

The People		Race/Ethnic Origin	Ancestry	
Area size:	64,899 sq. mi.	91.9% White	German: 30.3% Irish: 8.5%	
Urban population:	46.1%	0.3% Black	English: 7.2%	
Rural population:	53.9%	0.5% Asian	**2004 Presidential Vote**	
Pop. 2000:	570,517	0.7% Native Am.	Bush (R) 189,885	(75%)
Pop. 2005 (est):	562,336	0.0% Hawaiian	Kerry (D) 60,156	(24%)
Median income:	$33,866	0.6% Two+ races	Other 3,623	(1%)
Poverty status:	11.1%	0.0% Other	**2000 Presidential Vote**	
Military veterans:	13.9%	6.0% Hispanic Origin	Bush (R) 169,090	(71%)
			Gore (D) 60,293	(25%)
			Other 8,952	(4%)
			Cook Partisan Voting Index: R +24	

Occupation	Blue collar: 27.6%	White collar: 53.5%	Gray collar: 18.8%

West of Grand Island, Nebraska is wheat and livestock country. For miles on end you can see nothing but rolling brown fields, sectioned off here and there by barbed wire fences, and in the distance a grain elevator towering over a tiny town and its miniature railroad depot. The winds, rain and tornadoes that come suddenly out of the sky remind you that the original settlers likened this part of the country to an ocean and thought themselves in their wooden wagons almost as helpless as passengers at sea in a rowboat. Settlers passed through here on the Oregon Trail in the 1840s, then set down roots in the 1880s, but the rain they hoped for fell too unreliably, and wheatlands gave way to pasture and open range. It is a beautiful but hard land, exacting much from its people, as the novels of western Nebraska's Willa Cather make poignantly clear. Chimney Rock—a clay and sandstone spire that marked a good camping spot and offered reliable spring water for travelers and their animals—was the landmark that travelers on the Oregon Trail most frequently mentioned in their journals; this symbol of westward expansion now graces the Nebraska quarter, released in 2006. Dozens of small counties today have fewer people than they did in 1940 or 1900. Severe droughts in recent years have seemed a kind of endpoint, as ranchers sold off their herds that were thinning and sickening as the grasslands turned dry and brown, and reservoirs and aquifers were running dry. In North Platte, Bailey Yard is the world's largest railroad classification yard, covering 2,850 acres and handling 10,000 rail cars every 24 hours. The Union Pacific line from North Platte east to Gibbon is the busiest freight rail corridor in the world. Farther west on I-80 is the town of Sidney, home of Cabela's, the world's largest mail-order and Internet business for hunting, fishing and camping gear.

The 3d Congressional District of Nebraska has one-third of the state's people spread out over nearly 85% of its acreage and two time zones. At nearly 65,000 square miles, it is one of the nation's largest congressional districts, bigger than the state of New York and with more counties. Except along the interstate and around Scottsbluff, the 3d has been losing population for decades and several of the western ranching counties are among the poorest in the nation; one such is Loup County, in the center of the state, which has the nation's fifth-lowest per capita income. But nearby Valley County has fought back, creating a "business coach" to assist local firms in selling on the Internet; its population will likely increase this decade for the first time since the 1920s. The district includes 69 of Nebraska's 93 counties, and has moved so far east that it's on the outskirts of Lincoln. Still, it remains one of the nation's top-ranked ag districts, with more farms than all but one other congressional district and more cattle and calves than any other place in the nation. Geographically and politically, the 3d District is where the Midwest becomes the West. For years people here welcomed farm subsidies even as they angrily opposed federal interference. Politically, it is heavily Republican and sometimes ornery: In 1992 Ross Perot got more votes than Bill Clinton. It voted 71% for George W. Bush in 2000 and 75% in 2004.

The new congressman from the 3d District is Adrian Smith, a Republican who struggled in November after winning a contentious primary. The youngest of the 13 freshman House Republicans, his political resume belies his youth. He comes from a politically active family—his father is a former county Republican chairman and his mother is the state party secretary—and he served as an intern in the Nebraska governor's office and as a page in the state's unicameral legislature. At 23, shortly after graduating from the University of Nebraska, he won election to the Gering City Council. Four years later, he knocked off a Democratic incumbent to win the first of two terms in the unicam. As a state lawmaker, Smith devoted his efforts to opposing abortion, protecting Nebraskans' right to bear arms, fighting tax increases, and blocking efforts to expand casino gambling. He also worked as a realtor and storage business owner. In May 2005, two weeks after Tom Osborne announced his ultimately unsuccessful primary bid for governor, Smith joined the race to win his House seat.

The crowded Republican primary field included Grand Island Mayor Jay Vavricek and John Hanson, Osborne's former district director. The contest focused on economic development and agricultural issues. Smith championed tax incentives to attract new residents and encourage investment in the district, which some fear will be eliminated after the next census because of a decline in population. He also promised to expand markets globally for Nebraska farmers. Still, his opponents suggested that he betrayed rural Nebraska by accepting more than $300,000 in contributions from members of the Club for Growth, a national anti-tax group that was originally founded by Wall Street financiers and opposes farm subsidies. Smith said he supported limited farm subsidies, but pointed to his support from the Nebraska Farm Bureau as evidence of his strong record on agriculture. Smith opposed in-state college tuition rates for children of illegal immigrants. In the May 9 primary, Smith carried 39 of the 69 counties to win the nomination with 39%. Hanson, who finished second with 29%, was strongest in the Republican River valley south of North Platte while Vavricek's 27% came mainly from the Grand Island area.

The Democratic Party fielded an unusually strong nominee, Yale-educated cattle rancher Scott Kleeb. He accused Smith of "distorting the truth" about the Club for Growth's opposition to farm subsidies. Smith responded that the group backed him because of his record on taxes. He sought to link Kleeb to Democrats who supported a timetable for withdrawal from Iraq, and called him a political carpetbagger who grew up overseas on military bases and attended schools in Colorado and Connecticut before settling in Nebraska on a family-owned ranch. Kleeb replied, "You don't run as a Democrat in the 3d District because you thought it would be easy." Kleeb called for changes in farm policy to emphasize niche markets, and made the contest much closer than anybody expected. Each candidate raised more than $1 million. After late October polling showed a virtual toss-up, the Democratic Congressional Campaign Committee ran an ad attacking Smith for accepting campaign money from "Washington special interests." President Bush made one of his final campaign stops here—an atypical last-minute campaign stop for a Republican president. Smith won 55%-45%, though Kleeb won a dozen counties in the eastern portion of the district.

With a seat on the Agriculture Committee, Smith pledged to focus on the farm bill, to expand rural development programs and to seek international markets for American crops.

★ NEVADA ★

A pyramid rising from the desert, New York skyscrapers across the street from the sphinx-like lion, a not-too-miniature Eiffel Tower and the gondolas of Venice, a flaming pirate ship next door to Roman ruins: this is what you see as the plane descends to the runway at Las Vegas. All these surrealistic monuments, and miles of spreading subdivisions, are set in one of North America's most forbidding landscapes, a bowl-shaped desert valley rimmed by barren peaks. "Geologically Nevada is a gigantic, post-oceanic ditch between the Rockies and the Sierras, filled with rough, secondary mountain ranges that stack and twine across the naked landscape like ranks of FEMA house trailers in a storage lot," writes Las Vegas art critic Dave Hickey. The first settlers came to mine lodes of silver and gold, starting with the Comstock Lode silver mine in 1859, which produced $500 million in the next 20 years. Abraham Lincoln's Republicans made Nevada a state in 1864, even though Nevada did not meet the population requirement for statehood, because Republicans thought they needed an extra three electoral votes. But Nevada was not really a viable state; its population dropped by the early 20th century, and in the early 1930s there were only 91,000 Nevadans and the state government was about to go bankrupt. So Nevada decided to roll the dice. The state reduced its residency requirement for divorce to six weeks and legalized gambling. Catering to what most Americans considered sin—casinos, pawnshops, divorce mills, quick wedding chapels, even legal brothels—turned out to be good business. Nevada was America's fastest-growing state between 1960 and 2005, though its growth in 2005-06 (3.45%) was topped by Arizona (3.58%). Nevada's population has more than doubled, from 1.2 million to 2.5 million, from 1990 to 2006.

Las Vegas, a mere spot on the map when gambling was legalized, now is the center of a metro area of 1.7 million. Reno, known as "the biggest little city in the world," now has, together with Lake Tahoe and the capital of Carson City, another 492,000. Gaming—the Nevada word for gambling—generates most of this growth: Las Vegas's had 151,000 hotel rooms in 2007 and insiders expect another 44,000 to be built by 2010, requiring 100,000 new workers. Las Vegas's tourists spend more than $33 billion a year, Reno's about $4 billion, and not just in casinos and hotels but in increasingly upscale restaurants and malls. They come from all over the United States and from foreign countries, especially Japan. Though at least one form of gambling is now available in 48 states, Las Vegas has made itself a destination; it has more than twice as much convention exhibit space as the number two city, Chicago. This is a service economy—of the more than 1 million people employed, nearly 90% produce services rather than goods. The 6.75% gambling receipts tax has generated enough revenue so that Nevada has no income, corporate or inheritance tax; even in a fiscal crisis in early 2003 no one proposed one. The cost of living is low, housing is relatively inexpensive and a newcomer doesn't stand out in the crowd. Some 5,000 people move in every month, and the unemployment rate is among the nation's lowest.

From mining to gaming, Nevada has been a second chance state, a place for outcasts to succeed and misfits to rebound. With Alaska, it is one of the few states with more men than women. At 14%, Nevada has the highest percentage of divorced residents in the nation. Only 21% of Nevadans were born in the state, the lowest of any state; in Stateline, on Lake Tahoe, just 5% were born in Nevada. Nevada has been an avenue of success for ethnic groups who faced roadblocks elsewhere. The four owners of the Comstock Lode—MacKay, Fair, Flood, O'Brien—were Irishmen; the first big hotel on the Las Vegas strip, the Flamingo, was built in 1946 by Jewish gangster Bugsy Siegel, later gunned down in his Beverly Hills home; most of the big casinos were owned by mobsters until Howard Hughes—a different kind of outcast—bought them up in the late 1960s. Since 1990 Latinos moved here in large numbers, attracted by the plentiful jobs; Nevada's population in 2004 was 23% Hispanic, 7% black and 5% Asian. Some 4% of Nevadans told the 2000 census takers they were of multiple races, the fourth highest of any state. Nevadans tend to be unchurched and not highly educated: only 34% belonged to a church in 2000, lower than in any state but Oregon and Washington; only 17% of adults in Las Vegas and Clark County had college degrees, one of the lowest numbers for any big metropolitan area. For years, the casinos catered to older tastes in entertainment, from Frank Sinatra to girlie shows, and depended on gamblers for all their trade. For a time in the 1990s, as riverboat and Indian casinos opened in many states, Las Vegas billed itself as a family-friendly destination resort. In this decade it has marketed itself by proclaiming that "what happens in Vegas stays in Vegas." Either way, its huge and flashy hotels have glittering attractions: Caesars Palace has an upscale shopping center with Roman-style storefronts, the pyramid-shaped Luxor that looms over this desert has an amusement park and huge obelisk inside, New York New

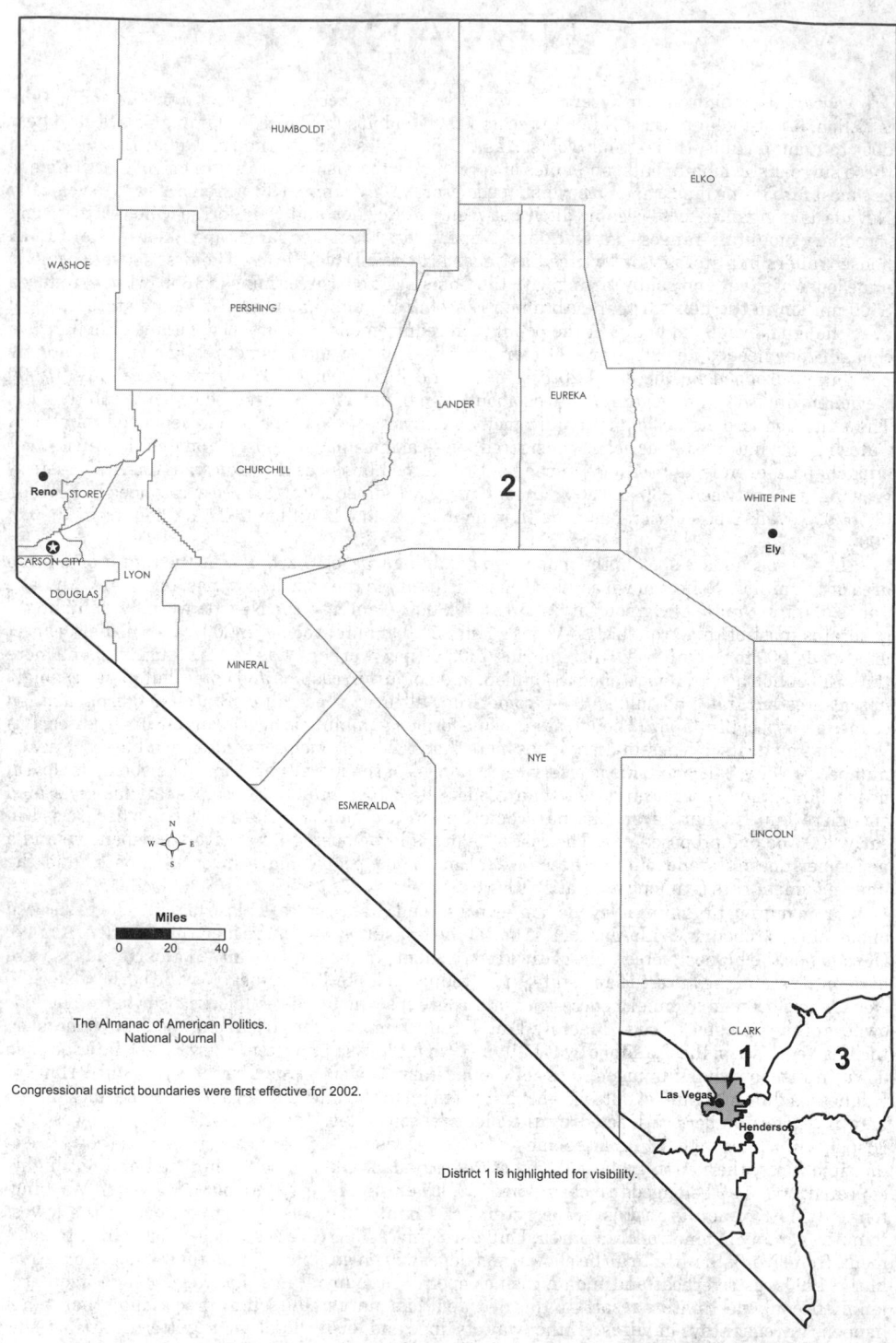

HUMBOLDT

ELKO

WASHOE

PERSHING

LANDER

EUREKA

WHITE PINE

Reno STOREY

CHURCHILL

2

Ely

CARSON CITY

LYON

DOUGLAS

MINERAL

NYE

ESMERALDA

LINCOLN

N
W E
S

Miles
0　20　40

The Almanac of American Politics.
National Journal

CLARK

1

3

Las Vegas

Congressional district boundaries were first effective for 2002.

Henderson

District 1 is highlighted for visibility.

York imitates Gotham, and the Bellagio has a museum-class art gallery and an eleven-acre lake with 1,000 fountains. Las Vegas has become decorous enough to attract the American Booksellers and Southern Baptist conventions. It seems unlikely that either political party will dare to hold its national convention here, but in 2006 the Democratic National Committee awarded Nevada one of its early slots in the primary schedule, just after the Iowa caucuses; its attractions included the large number of racial minorities (in comparison with almost all-white Iowa and New Hampshire), the strength of the state's labor unions (growing here while declining almost everywhere else) and the clout of Senate Democratic leader Harry Reid.

There are other things in Nevada besides gambling and other places besides Las Vegas (though 71% of Nevadans live in Clark County). The state's low taxes have made it a regional distribution and credit card operations center and it has attracted warehouses and factories from California, though taxes were raised by a July 2004 order of the state Supreme Court. There is still some mining—mostly gold mining—which has been booming since Clinton administration mining regulations were scrapped and the price of gold rose. Nevada also mines the less glamorous diatomaceous earth, used for swimming pool filters and kitty litter. And a lot of older Californians cash out their expensive homes and come to low-tax Nevada to retire. A Wild West atmosphere remains in the "Cow Counties" beyond Las Vegas and Reno; half of the 37,000 wild horses that roam the American West can be found in Nevada.

For the past two decades, Nevada politics have been volatile. Historically, it was Democratic, sending politically shrewd Democrats to Washington and keeping them there to protect the interests of a state always heavily dependent on the federal government. The most powerful were Key Pittman, chairman of the Senate Foreign Relations Committee, who backed FDR's foreign policy only after Roosevelt agreed to buy absurdly large amounts of Nevada's silver, and Pat McCarran, author of the repressive McCarran Act, who shamelessly pushed aid for Reno and Las Vegas (the airport there is named for him) and became suddenly solicitous of civil liberties when mobsters and casino owners were called to testify before the Kefauver committee investigating racketeering. In the 1980s, Nevada trended sharply Republican, primarily because of newcomers. In the 1990s, the dice rolled both ways. Bill Clinton, to the surprise of managers on both sides, carried Nevada in 1992, by 37%-35%, and again in 1996, by 44%-43%. The key here was his promise to veto any bill that moves toward building the national nuclear waste repository in Yucca Mountain, some 90 miles north of Las Vegas. But that was not enough for Al Gore, who carried Clark County, but lost by wide margins in Reno and the Cow Counties; George W. Bush, without promising a veto on nuclear waste, carried the state 50%-46%. In 2004, despite Bush's approval of the repository in 2002, he once again carried the state, by a narrower 50%-48%. The state has a bipartisan congressional delegation, united by devotion to the gaming industry; incumbent Democrat Harry Reid beat Congressman John Ensign by only 428 votes in 1998, but two years later Ensign won the other Senate seat 55%-40%; they have something in the nature of a nonaggression pact, and both have since won reelection by wide margins. Republicans have held the governorship since 1998 but Democrats won more downballot statewide offices in 2006; Republicans continue to control the state Senate, Democrats the Assembly. Republicans hold two of the three U.S. House seats, but carried both with lower than usual margins in 2006.

Nevada voters on balance seem to lean Republican, with a libertarian but sometimes culturally conservative streak. This is not the cultural liberalism of college-educated baby boomers. One reason that Gore and John Kerry lost the state is that they didn't win the margins here that they did in larger states among unmarried people without children, people who never attend church and people with graduate degrees. Yet Nevadans voted in 2006 to ban smoking in bars and restaurants, despite opposition from the gaming industry. Another unique feature of Nevada politics: since 1975 voters can vote for "none of these candidates." "None" finished second in the 1998 Democratic primary for lieutenant governor and has occasionally finished first in races for minor offices, but the law is unfortunately toothless: even when there is a plurality for "none of the above," the top-running candidate wins. And some observers say that Nevada has a third party that always wins, the gaming party, closely allied with the Culinary Union, which has seen its membership increase to 60,000; Las Vegas casinos are the one private sector business with fast-growing union membership. Las Vegas gaming interests have backed every recent governor, from Democrat Bob Miller, who first won in 1990, to Republicans Kenny Guinn and Jim Gibbons, who won in 1998 and 2006. Harry Reid has been close to the gaming industry over a political career that goes back to the 1960s; his colleague John Ensign's stepfather was until 2005 chairman of the company that owns the Mandalay Bay Resort and Casino.

One issue that has long preoccupied Nevada is the proposed Yucca Mountain nuclear waste repository. The federal government took responsibility for nuclear waste in 1982 and the Yucca Mountain site was singled out by chosen by Congress in 1987, when the Nevada delegation was unusually weak: Harry Reid was in his first year in the Senate and Republican Chic Hecht seemed to be facing sure defeat in 1988. The plan is to bury the waste deep within the mountain, 1,300 feet above the water table, in reinforced steel containers in a 1,400-acre maze with 100 miles of storage tunnels. Many in Nevada argue that rainwater will flush the radioactive material out of the depository and into the water table. More recently, Yucca Mountain opponents have charged that the site is geologically flawed and within an earthquake zone, and that transportation of nuclear waste across the country would be hazardous, especially after September 11. Bill Clinton promised to veto a temporary site but veto-proof majorities in the House voted for a temporary site in Nevada. Senators Richard Bryan and Reid lobbied furiously to get enough votes to prevent a veto override in the Senate and succeeded in 1995, 1997 and 2000. In 2000, George W. Bush pledged not to place a temporary storage site in Nevada. But he refrained from promising to veto a permanent repository, saying that his decision would be based on "sound science and not politics." In February 2002 Bush, on the recommendation of Energy Secretary Spencer Abraham, designated Yucca Mountain as the permanent site. The law provided for a veto by the governor, which could be overridden by majorities in both houses of Congress. In April 2002, with great ceremony, Governor Kenny Guinn issued his veto. In May 2002 the House cast a large majority for Yucca Mountain. In the Senate, Reid and Ensign lobbied furiously for votes, but in July 2002 the designation of Yucca Mountain was affirmed 60-39. Many Nevadans cheered when the D.C. Circuit Court of Appeals ruled in July 2004 that the EPA's health and safety standards were insufficient. But the court also upheld the selection of the site and the standards can be changed. The permanent site is not supposed to open until 2012, and could be delayed more by regulatory proceedings and lawsuits. The Nevada delegation in Congress have vowed not to work for concessions on the building of the repository but to fight it every step of the way. With the Democratic victory in November 2006, Harry Reid became majority leader and promised that any legislation advancing Yucca Mountain would never get to the floor of the Senate.

The People		Race/Ethnic Origin			Military veterans: 238,128 (16.0%)	
Pop. 2006 (est):	2,495,529	1,303,001	65.2%	White	WWII: 16.0%	Korea: 13.9%
Pop. 2000:	1,998,257	131,509	6.6%	Black	Vietnam: 34.8%	Gulf War: 10.4%
Pop. 1990:	1,201,833	88,593	4.4%	Asian	**Most populous cities (2006):**	
Change 1990-2000:	Up 66.3%	21,397	1.1%	Native Am.	1. Las Vegas	552,539
% of U.S. total:	0.7%	7,769	0.4%	Hawaiian	2. Henderson	240,614
Pop. rank:	35th of 50	49,231	2.5%	Two+ races	3. Reno	210,255
Area size:	110,561 sq. mi.	2,787	0.1%	Other	4. North Las Vegas	197,567
State Native:	21.3%	393,970	19.7%	Hisp. Origin	5. Sparks	83,959
Non-citizen:	10.0%	**Ancestry**				
Language		German: 10.9%		Irish: 8.5%	Urban population: 91.6%	
English: 76.0%	Spanish: 14.6%	English: 7.8%		Italian: 5.1%	Rural population: 8.4%	
Asian: 4.3%		USA: 3.7%				

Education		Work Sector		Legislature	
H.S. Grad:	80.7%	Private: 82.4%	Govt: 12.5%	Senate	11 R 10 D
College Grad:	18.2%	Self: 4.9%	Family: 0.3%	Assembly	27 D 15 R
Industry		Unemployment: 6.2%		Legislative Term Limits: Yes	
Agri: 1.6%	Con: 9.2%	**Household Income**		**Registered Voters**	
Fin: 6.5%	Info: 2.2%	<15k: 12.4%	15-35k: 25.4%	D: 494,092	(40.2%)
Mfg: 10.1%	Prof: 21.7%	35-50k: 18.1%	50-100k: 32.8%	R: 482,948	(39.3%)
Public: 4.5%	Trade: 14.0%	100-150k: 7.4%	>150k: 3.9%	O: 252,189	(20.5%)
Other: 30.3%		Median: $44,581			
Occupation		Poverty status: 10.5%			
Blue collar: 21.8%	White collar: 53.3%	**Home Value**			
Gray collar: 24.9%		<50k: 7.7%	50-100k: 19.4%	100-200k: 55.0%	200-300k: 11.3%
		300-500k: 4.5%	>500k: 2.1%	Median: $132,500	

Presidential politics   In the 1940s, Nevada was a Democratic state; in the 1960s, it was divided much as the nation was, voting narrowly for John Kennedy in 1960 and Richard Nixon in 1968. In the 1980s, it was heavily Republican, voting more than 60% twice for Ronald Reagan and 59%-38% for George Bush in 1988. In the 1990s, it voted twice for Bill Clinton; critical to his margin was his pledge to veto bills moving nuclear waste to Yucca Mountain or temporary storage sites. But the basic Republican proclivity of the state produced a 50%-46% margin for George W. Bush in 2000, who promised only to block a temporary storage site and to make a decision on the permanent repository based on "sound science." In 2004 Nevada Democrats charged that Bush had broken his promise. John Kerry came several times to the state and proclaimed, "When John Kerry is president, there is going to be no nuclear waste at Yucca Mountain, period." But some doubt was cast on his resolve when Senator John Ensign highlighted seven pro-repository votes by Kerry and when Kerry selected as his running mate John Edwards, who voted for the permanent repository. Democrats made the obvious point that Kerry, not Edwards, would make the decision, and Senator Harry Reid said that the seven votes were on amendments he and Richard Bryan sponsored and which hardly anybody else voted for. But Bush said Kerry was using the issue as "a political poker chip" and the Bush campaign ran ads claiming Kerry had flip-flopped on the issue. Bush's narrow victory preserved Nevada's string of voting for the winners of the last seven presidential elections and indeed for every winner starting in 1912 except Jimmy Carter in 1976.

2004 Presidential Vote		
Bush (R)	418,690	(50%)
Kerry (D)	397,190	(48%)
Nader (I)	4,838	(1%)
Other	8,869	(1%)
2000 Presidential Vote		
Bush (R)	301,575	(50%)
Gore (D)	279,978	(46%)
Nader (Green)	15,008	(2%)
Other	12,409	(2%)

For many years Nevada saw little of presidents and presidential campaigning, but it saw plenty in 2004. Democrats ran strong organizational efforts in Las Vegas and Reno; they reduced Bush's margin in traditionally Republican Reno and Washoe County and produced a slight increase in their majority in Las Vegas and Clark County. But some of their efforts may have been misdirected. Union members cast 25% of Nevada's votes (Nevada ranks fifth among states in percentage of private sector union members), but they gave Kerry only a 56%-42% margin. Latinos cast 10% of the votes, and voted only 60%-39% for Kerry. But the Bush campaign seems to have out-organized the Democrats in the Cow Counties. In these lightly populated places Bush's popular vote margin increased from 35,000 in 2000 to 41,000 in 2004. Some 40% of the voters thought Yucca Mountain was a very important issue, and 73% of them voted for Kerry. But 26% thought it was only somewhat important, and 56% of them voted for Bush.

Nevada's late March presidential primary attracted little attention for years. In 2004 some 9,000 Nevada Democrats caucused on February 14, with just one voting place per county, and produced a majority for John Kerry; Republicans held a state convention in April. But it appears that Nevada will be a key early voting state in 2008 after the Democratic National Committee voted to allow Nevada and South Carolina to have a caucus and a primary just after the Iowa and New Hampshire contests. Nevada's cause may have been helped by Senator Harry Reid's praise for Chairman Howard Dean's 50 state strategy; also, organized labor pushed for a Nevada contest, because of the strength of unions there, and many Democrats like the prospect of an early race in a state with many Hispanic, black and Asian voters. The state Democratic party planned to raise $1 million to staff some 1,000 caucus sites and hired the Iowa Democrats' election director to run the project. Potential presidential candidates thronged to Nevada to support local Democrats in fall 2006 and their staffs started boning up on issues important in Nevada but unfamiliar in Iowa or New Hampshire: the Yucca Mountain nuclear waste depository; water rights; mining laws; management of federal lands (90% of Nevada is owned by the feds); the gaming industry; traffic-jammed highways. In April 2007, Nevada Republicans decided to move their caucuses to the same day as the Democratic contest.

Congressional districting   Nevada gained a second congressional district in the 1980 Census and a third congressional district in the 2000 Census. If growth continues at the present percentage rate, it will likely gain a fourth and maybe even a fifth in the 2010 Census. Redistricting was easy in the 1980s and 1990s: the 1st District was the inner part of Clark County, politically marginal and won by both parties in the 1990s; the 2d District was the rest of the state, heavily Republican.

110th Congress Lineup
2 R   1 D
109th Congress Lineup
2 R   1 D

It was a little more difficult in 2001, with a third district and control of redistricting split between a Republican governor and state Senate and a Democratic Assembly. Clark County, with 69% of the Census population, was entitled to two of the seats and a small part of the third. For a time Republicans argued that two or all three of the districts should combine part of Clark County with part of the rest of the state. But that idea was dropped in the June 2001 special session. Eventually agreement was reached on a plan with an inner city Las Vegas 1st District, a 2d District including all the rest of the counties plus much of outer Clark County and a Y-shaped 3d District including much of the Las Vegas suburbs. The 1st District was safe for Democrat Shelley Berkley, the 2d safe for Republican Jim Gibbons and the 3d was drawn so that it was exactly even in party registration; it cast narrow pluralities for Al Gore in 2000 and George W. Bush in 2004.

Governor

Jim Gibbons (R)

Elected 2006, term expires Jan. 2011, 1st term; b. Dec. 16, 1944, Sparks; home, Reno; U. of NV, B.S. 1967, M.S. 1973; Southwestern U., J.D. 1979; Mormon; married (Dawn).

Military Career: Air Force, 1967-71 (Vietnam), NV Air Natl. Guard, 1975-96 (Persian Gulf).

Elected Office: NV Assembly, 1988-94; U.S. House of Reps., 1996-2006

Professional Career: Pilot, Western Airlines, 1979-87, Delta Airlines, 1987-96.

Office: 101 N. Carson St., Carson City, 89701, 775-684-5670; Fax: 775-684-5683; Web site: gov.state.nv.us.

Election Results

2006 general	Jim Gibbons (R)	279,003	(48%)
	Dina Titus (D)	255,684	(44%)
	None of these candidates	20,699	(4%)
	Other	26,772	(5%)
2006 primary	Jim Gibbons (R)	67,717	(48%)
	Bob Beers (R)	40,876	(29%)
	Lorraine Hunt (R)	25,161	(18%)
	Other	6,761	(5%)
2002 general	Kenny Guinn (R)	344,001	(68%)
	Joe Neal (D)	110,935	(22%)
	None of these candidates	23,674	(5%)
	Other	25,469	(5%)

Jim Gibbons was elected governor of Nevada in 2006, the first from northern Nevada since Republican Robert List won election in 1978 and the first Nevada-born governor since Republican Paul Laxalt in 1966. Gibbons grew up in Sparks, next door to Reno, and like White House political strategist Karl Rove, was a graduate of Sparks High School. He graduated from the University of Nevada and served in the Air Force in Vietnam. He went to law school and has practiced law, but he also was a mining geologist, a hydrologist, a pilot for Delta and Western Airlines and vice commander of the Nevada Air National Guard. In 1988 he was elected to the Assembly; in 1990 he was called up to active duty in the Gulf War. While he was flying unarmed air reconnaissance missions of enemy targets in Kuwait, his wife took his place in the legislature. After his celebrated return, he proposed a ballot initiative to require a two-thirds supermajority to raise any state tax; it passed with more than 70% of the votes in 1994; this was suspended in July 2003 when the state Supreme Court required the legislature to pass Governor Kenny Guinn's tax increase by majority vote. In 1994, Gibbons ran for governor. He beat Secretary of State Cheryl Lau 52%-32% in the primary, but lost the general to Democratic incumbent Bob Miller, 53%-41%. In 1996, after Congresswoman Barbara Vucanovich retired, Gibbons ran in the 2d District and won the general election, 59%-35%.

In Congress, he easily won reelection in the sprawling and heavily Republican 2d Congressional District, which covers most of the state's land and just a tiny part of Las Vegas's Clark County. In his five terms, he opposed federal intrusion on local rights and was a tough opponent of the nuclear repository at Yucca Mountain and the proposed temporary storage at the Nevada Test Site. He showed an independent streak that placed him toward the center of the House on cultural issues. In November 2004, Gibbons sponsored an initiative to force funding of the education budget before any other part of Nevada government; it passed with 57 percent of the vote in 2004. In August 2005, he announced he would run for governor to replace term-limited Republican Kenny Guinn and appeared to be the frontrunner. His wife Dawn sparked controversy by running to replace her husband in Congress, raising objections that she would not be able to fulfill her duties as First Lady; she lost in the Republican primary.

Gibbons faced state Senator Bob Beers, Lieutenant Governor Lorraine Hunt and adult movie star Melody Damayo in the Republican primary. Beers ran a hard-hitting campaign with an anti-tax focus; Hunt spent nearly $800,000 of her own money on the campaign. (Damayo, using her nom de porn, Mimi Miyagi, posted a racy campaign website). Gibbons campaigned as a fiscal conservative who promised to make education a priority and won with 48%. Beers finished second with 29%, followed by Hunt, who had 18%. Damayo won 1%.

The Democratic nominee was state Senate Minority Leader Dina Titus, a political science professor who had defeated Henderson Mayor Jim Gibson 54%-36% in the primary. In Titus and Gibbons, the governor's race featured candidates who were approximate versions of the two Nevadas. Titus was born outside the state—much attention was paid to her Southern accent—and represented a southern Nevada Senate district that included the dazzling and gaudy Las Vegas Strip; Gibbons was a native-born northern Nevadan who in Congress represented less glitzy Reno and the "Cow Counties" north of Las Vegas.

Titus sought to portray Gibbons as an "inconsequential" Washington backbencher and offered a campaign platform featuring her five "E's": economic development, education, energy, environment and ethics. She criticized his support for the federal No Child Left Behind education law and said full-day kindergarten would be one of her first priorities in office. Gibbons advocated merit pay for teachers and touted his Education First initiative, which Titus had opposed. He called Titus a tax-and-spend liberal—he referred to her as "Dina Taxes" and ran ads on Reno television reminding voters of disparaging remarks Titus had made about northern Nevada some years before. "Dina Titus called Washoe County a sponge and called us rascals who want handouts," said one of the ads. "Jim Gibbons calls Washoe County home and calls us neighbors and friends."

In the final weeks of the campaign, Gibbons suffered through a stretch of publicity so negative it is a wonder he won the governorship. In mid-October, a casino cocktail waitress filed a complaint alleging that Gibbons propositioned and threatened to sexually assault her in a parking garage after an evening of drinking at a restaurant. Gibbons denied her account, contending that he merely caught her when she tripped and called for the release of tapes from video cameras at the garage. The video tapes failed to show either of them in the garage. In early December, the Las Vegas police recommended that no charges be filed against Gibbons and at the end of the month, the Clark County district attorney declined to pursue the case but continued to investigate whether there had been attempts to influence the waitress's statements to the police.

On the heels of that heavily-publicized incident, also in late October, came reports that the Gibbons family had hired an illegal immigrant as a housekeeper and nanny in the late 1980s; in 1995, Dawn Gibbons had filed a police report accusing the woman of attempting to extort money. The Gibbons campaign said the Titus campaign was behind the assertions. Then, less than one week before Election Day, *The Wall Street Journal* reported that Gibbons in 2005 took a lavish, weeklong Caribbean cruise that was paid for by a friend and contributor whom the congressman had helped to win classified federal software contracts.

Naturally, Gibbons's lead in the polls dwindled but he still managed to win, 48%-44%, outspending Titus $5.7 million to $3.6 million. He lost Las Vegas's Clark County, where he trailed by 23,000 votes, but won everywhere else. He won enough votes in the capital of Carson City, in Reno's Washoe County, and in fast-growing Douglas County by Lake Tahoe, to overcome Titus's advantage in southern Nevada; she failed to break 41% anywhere outside of Clark County. Titus, who was later reelected as Senate Minority Leader, did not take the defeat well. "I wouldn't be surprised if he got indicted while in office," she told the *Las Vegas Sun* after the election. "Personally, I will never forgive him for telling outright lies about me." His relationship with Titus was not the only contributing factor to what turned out to be an unsteady start. Citing unspecified homeland security concerns, he was sworn in 12 seconds after midnight on January 1, a move widely viewed as an attempt to prevent a key appointment by his Republican predecessor Kenny Guinn, with whom he had a strained relationship. In February, the *Wall Street Journal* reported that a federal corruption inquiry had been opened; Gibbons publicly speculated that the newspaper had been paid by Democrats to write the damaging stories about him.

Senior Senator

Harry Reid (D)

Elected 1986, seat up 2010, 4th term; b. Dec. 2, 1939, Searchlight; home, Searchlight; S. UT St. Col., A.S. 1959, UT St. U., B.S. 1961, George Washington U., J.D. 1964, U. of NV, 1969-70; Mormon; married (Landra).

Elected Office: NV Assembly, 1968-70; NV Lt. Gov., 1970-74; U.S. House of Reps., 1982-86.

Professional Career: Practicing atty., 1969-82; Henderson City Atty., 1964-66; Chmn., NV Gaming Comm., 1977-81.

DC Office: 528 HSOB, 20510, 202-224-3542; Fax: 202-224-7327; Web site: reid.senate.gov.

State Offices: Carson City, 775-882-7343; Las Vegas, 702-388-5020; Reno, 775-686-5750.

Committees: *Majority Leader. Rules & Administration* (8th of 10 D).

Group Ratings

	ADA	ACLU	AFS	LCV	ITIC	NTU	COC	ACU	CFG	FRC
2006	90	67	100	57	50	14	50	12	3	12
2005	100	—	100	100	—	5	50	4	0	—

National Journal Ratings

	2005 LIB — 2005 CONS	2006 LIB — 2006 CONS
Economic	92% — 6%	79% — 18%
Social	65% — 29%	72% — 27%
Foreign	72% — 25%	79% — 16%

Key Votes of the 109th Congress

1. Bar ANWR Drilling	Y	5. Confirm Samuel Alito	N	9. Limit Interstate Abortion	Y
2. FY06 Spending Curb	N	6. Path to Citizenship	Y	10. CAFTA	N
3. Estate Tax Repeal	N	7. Bar Same Sex Marriage	N	11. Urge Iraq Withdrawal	Y
4. Raise Minimum Wage	Y	8. Stem Cell Research $	Y	12. Provide Detainee Rights	Y

Election Results

2004 general	Harry Reid (D)	494,805	(61%)	($7,040,588)
	Richard Ziser (R)	284,640	(35%)	($647,500)
	Other	30,623	(4%)	
2004 primary	Harry Reid (D)	unopposed		
1998 general	Harry Reid (D)	208,650	(48%)	($4,939,010)
	John Ensign (R)	208,222	(48%)	($3,490,256)
	Other	18,918	(4%)	

Prior Winning Percentages: 1992 (51%); 1986 (50%); 1984 House (56%); 1982 House (58%)

Harry Reid, a Democrat first elected to the House in 1982 and to the Senate in 1986, is the Senate Majority Leader. He grew up in Searchlight, Nevada, in the scorching desert south of Las Vegas, where his father was a hardrock miner and the family lived in a house without indoor plumbing. It was a hard life: his mother did laundry for a bordello; his father killed himself. Reid hitchhiked 40 miles to high school in Henderson, where his civics teacher and boxing coach Mike O'Callaghan became his political mentor. Henderson businessmen helped him pay for college, and he graduated from Southern Utah State (where he and his wife decided to become Mormons) and George Washington law school. He was an amateur boxer and at nights during law school he worked as a Capitol Police officer; he likes to say, "I would rather dance than fight, but I know how to fight." He returned to Henderson and practiced law. Reid was elected to the Assembly in 1968, at age 28; he filed more bills than any other member. In 1970, O'Callaghan was elected governor and Reid, running separately, was elected lieutenant governor. In 1974 he came within 624 votes of beating Paul Laxalt in the race for senator, lost for mayor of Las Vegas in 1976, and then became head of the Gaming Commission from 1977 to 1981—as sensitive a post as any in Nevada. His life was threatened and mobsters put a bomb in his car. In 1982, when Nevada got two House seats for the first time and Congressman-at-Large Jim Santini ran for the Senate, Reid ran in the Las Vegas-based 1st District and won. Laxalt retired in 1986 and Reid ran for the Senate again; his opponent turned out to be Santini, who had switched parties at the last minute and was running as a Republican. Reid's ads depicted him as David to Santini's Goliath, and he won 50%-45%.

Over the years Reid has had a voting record more moderate than those of many Senate Democrats. He voted for the partial-birth abortion ban and against resolutions endorsing *Roe v. Wade*. He co-sponsored the constitutional amendment to allow the outlawing of flag burning. He was one of the few Democrats to vote for the Gulf War resolution in 1991 and he voted for the Iraq war resolution in 2002. He has consistently and effectively opposed environmental groups on mining issues and blocked attempts by environmentalists and the Clinton administration to impose higher fees on hardrock miners. He has opposed most gun control measures. He has steered counterterrorism money to Nevada and has worked to get the old Nevada nuclear test site, with its hundreds of underground tunnels, made into a $250 million center for training first responders how to cope with acts of terrorists. He has been a strong supporter of the gaming industry; when Bill Clinton proposed a 4% gaming tax, Reid promised, "I will become the most negative, the most irresponsible, the most obnoxious person of anyone in the Senate." He has worked to block the bill, backed by John McCain and others, to prohibit betting on college and amateur sports, which is legal only in Nevada; to block action he introduced many amendments, including one to ban gambling in all states but Nevada.

The key federal issue for Nevada during his years in the Senate has been the proposed nuclear waste repository in Yucca Mountain. The federal government assumed responsibility for nuclear waste in 1982 and a bill passed in 1987, Reid's first year in the Senate, named Yucca Mountain and one other contender as the only two sites; the other one was later ruled out. Reid has stubbornly and persistently opposed the repository with every parliamentary and political tool at his command but other senators with nuclear waste piling up in their states (and 39 states have it) and especially Larry Craig of Idaho, where the government established a temporary nuclear waste site, have pressed hard for designation of Yucca Mountain. Bill Clinton carried Nevada by narrow margins in 1992 and 1996 largely because he promised to veto even a temporary site in Yucca Mountain, and so during his presidency Reid's task was to assemble enough votes to prevent an override of his veto. He did so in 1997, then prevented a vote in 1998 and 1999, then kept 34 votes in line in April 2000—just barely enough. George W. Bush in 2000 pledged not to support a temporary site, but he also refrained from promising to veto a permanent site, saying that his decision would be based on "sound science and not politics." In February 2002 Bush, on the recommendation of Energy Secretary Spencer Abraham, designated Yucca Mountain as the permanent site. The law provided for a veto by the governor, which could be overridden by majorities in both houses of Congress. In April 2002, Governor Kenny Guinn issued his veto. In May 2002 the House cast a large majority for Yucca Mountain. Reid lobbied furiously for Democratic votes, while John Ensign, his 1998 opponent and now his Republican colleague, lobbied desperately for Republican votes.

Reid argued that the site was geologically flawed and that transporting nuclear waste to it would be hazardous, especially after September 11. He spoke passionately when the issue was debated in July, enough so to convert Debbie Stabenow, who had voted for the Yucca Mountain site in the House. Altogether he got 35 Democrats and Jim Jeffords to vote his way. Ensign, opposed by the Bush administration, could get only two other Republicans, Lincoln Chafee and Ben Nighthorse Campbell. So the site was approved 60-39. But for Reid the fight was not over. Lawsuits had been filed against the plan, and the Energy Department must get approval from the Nuclear Regulatory Commission, which could take many years. Reid chaired the Appropriations subcommittee with jurisdiction over the Energy Department; in 2002 it cut $189 million from the Yucca Mountain budget. Reid fiercely opposed the Bush administration proposal to finance work at Yucca Mountain from a nuclear waste trust fund funded by utility industry fees, on the ground that this would remove it from congressional supervision; when that resulted in the non-funding of the work in

November 2004, appropriators scrambled to find cuts in other programs to pay for the $577 million price tag. Reid threw in a provision allowing Nevada counties to use Energy Department funding to take part in NRC licensing procedures. Also in November 2004 Reid, elected to be the new minority leader, negotiated with the Bush administration over appointments; he agreed to approve 175 Bush nominees in return for the recess appointment of his aide Gregory Jaczko to the Nuclear Regulatory Commission, where he is likely to vote against the Yucca Mountain repository. In November 2006, after it became apparent he would be Senate Majority Leader, Reid said, "Yucca Mountain will be protected better than ever because I control what we take up on the floor."

Reid had a close political call in his 1998 race against then-Congressman John Ensign, but he still spent much time seeking the votes of Democratic colleagues to replace Wendell Ford, who retired, as minority whip. After the election he got the job without opposition. For the next six years he was a constant presence on the floor, advancing the cause of his party and maintaining civil relations with Republican leaders. He played a key role in persuading Jim Jeffords to leave the Republican party in May 2001 and make the Democrats the majority party in the Senate again.

He worked closely and cooperatively with Democratic Leader Tom Daschle. Reid's combativeness came out when Republicans ran all-night sessions in November 2003 to protest Democratic filibusters of nominees for appellate judgeships. Reid spoke for nine hours, reading from his book about his upbringing in Searchlight, Nevada. In 2004 Reid contributed generously to other Democrats; he gave $1 million to the Democrats' Senate campaign committee in September and in October, as Daschle's chances for winning reelection in South Dakota seemed to be waning, gave money to other colleagues as well. After Daschle lost on November 2, Reid already had enough votes lined up to become Minority Leader; Christopher Dodd, who was interested in the post, declined to run. He was officially selected on November 16 and after some talk of working with Republicans seemed to indicate that he would be as tough a partisan as Daschle had been. Reid is not inclined to boast. "I know my limitations. I haven't gotten where I am by my good looks, my athletic ability, my great brain, my oratorical skills." But he seems quick to take offense and is sometimes ready with insults: Alan Greenspan was "a political hack," Clarence Thomas "an embarrassment," George W. Bush a "loser," a "liar" and "King George."

Reid worked deftly behind the scenes, giving up his seat on the Environment Committee to accommodate other Democrats and pledging to rely on committee chairmen on policy. In January 2005 he and House Minority Leader Nancy Pelosi gave a "prebuttal" of Bush's State of the Union speech two days before he delivered it; they also presented a Democratic response afterwards, in which Reid called for a Marshall Plan for America. In February Reid prevented nongermane amendments from coming forward on the class action bill, which many Democrats and all Republicans supported. He was plainly irritated when the Republican National Committee shortly thereafter sent out an e-mail attacking him as "chief Democratic obstructionist," pointing out that his son and son-in-law were lobbyists (both had let their lobbyist registrations drop) and mentioning his $750,000 Washington condominium (Republicans had reminded South Dakotans that Daschle had bought a $1.7 million house in Washington). At a dinner at the White House that night Reid and Bush talked about the e-mail (neither disclosed what he said), and Reid told reporters afterwards, "When you have a real bad chafe—is that what they call it?—it's hard to get soothed." He staunchly opposed George W. Bush's proposal for individual retirement accounts in Social Security, and in March 2005 got 42 Democratic senators to sign a letter opposing them. Bush's efforts to get Democratic support got nowhere. "President Bush should forget about privatizing Social Security. It will not happen," he said. "They are trying to destroy Social Security by giving this money to the fat cats on Wall Street, and I think it's wrong." When Bush renominated several filibustered judicial appointees, he promised to filibuster them again and threatened to bring the business of the Senate to a halt if Republicans changed the rules by majority vote. In May 2005 he acquiesced in the agreement of the bipartisan Gang of 14 to allow some of the nominees to come to a vote. He voted to confirm John Roberts as Chief Justice but joined most Democrats in opposing the nomination of Samuel Alito; he did not threaten a filibuster.

In the 2006 political cycle, he contributed heavily to Democratic candidates' campaigns and was delighted when Democrats gained the six seats needed for a Senate majority. After the election he deftly juggled committee and leadership posts, giving Debbie Stabenow a seat on Finance and giving her post as conference secretary to Patty Murray; Charles Schumer was given another term as head of the campaign committee, chairmanship of the Joint Economic Committee and the new leadership post as vice-chairman of the conference, the moderate Ben Nelson was switched from Commerce to Appropriations and the liberals Ben Cardin and Sheldon Whitehouse got seats on Judiciary. All these moves seemed designed to increase resistance to Bush administration proposals; the one exception was that Joe Lieberman—whose vote would be crucial to keeping the majority—was given the chairmanship of Homeland Security and Governmental Affairs. When the Iraq Study Group called for a U.S. withdrawal, Reid said, "It is up to President Bush to implement the recommendations of his commission." When Bush didn't do so, Reid worked for approval of a non-binding resolution condemning Bush's troop surge.

Reid started off as Democratic leader politically strengthened because in November 2004 he won by a large margin in Nevada for the first time. He was elected in 1986 by 50%-45%. In the 1992 primary he won 53%-39% over Charles Woods, a businessman badly wounded and scarred in World War II; in the general, he beat rancher Demar Dahl 51%-40%. In 1998, against Congressman John Ensign, he was very hard pressed. Ensign's stepfather Mike Ensign was head of the Mandalay Resort Group, one of the big Las Vegas casino operations, and Ensign raised plenty of money from the gaming industry, as did Reid: Reid spent $4.9 million and Ensign $3.5 million. Reid in his feisty way attacked Ensign harshly as an "extremist" who called environmentalists "socialists," and would gut Social Security. Reid carried Clark County, which casts two-thirds of the vote and is normally more Democratic than the rest of the state, by only 53%-44%; he may have won because he ran ahead of party lines in the usually Republican Reno area, where his work on local projects was appreciated, and lost there by only 48%-46%. The election night tally showed Reid ahead by 459 votes; Ensign called for a recount, and a hand count in Reno's Washoe County took weeks. Ensign finally conceded December 9, with Reid ahead by 428 votes. Two years later Ensign was elected by a wider margin to Nevada's other Senate seat after Reid's Democratic colleague Richard Bryan retired. Despite his strong partisanship and the bitterness and the closeness of the 1998 campaign, Reid and Ensign have become friendly colleagues who work together on many Nevada projects and have something in the nature of a political non-aggression pact; like Oregon's Ron Wyden and Gordon Smith, they know that after one bitter race they will never have to run against each other again.

Going into the 2004 cycle Reid had a problem and found a solution. The problem was that there are so many newcomers to Nevada, most of them Republicans unfamiliar with his work in almost 40 years of public life. About 5,000 people have been moving to the Las Vegas area every month—which means nearly 300,000 Nevadans in 2004 were not in the state the last time Reid ran. Some 436,000 Nevadans voted in 1998, when Reid faced Ensign; 830,000 would vote in November 2004, which means that roughly half the voters (because some 1998 voters died or dropped out) never saw Reid's name on a November ballot before. The solution was to preclude serious opposition from 2d District Congressman Jim Gibbons or one of Nevada's several Republican statewide officeholders by show-ing strong support from Las Vegas big hitters. They are thoroughly bipartisan and have been the motivating force in Nevada state politics, smoothing the election of Democratic Governor Bob Miller in 1990 and 1994 and Republican Governor Kenny Guinn in 1998 and 2002. Reid got early support from Governor Guinn, former Reagan appointee Sig Rogich and gaming executives Terry Lanni and Mike Ensign. The Republican nominee, Richard Ziser, an evangelical Christian who led the drive to ban same-sex marriages on the 2000 and 2002 ballots, got little financial support in Nevada or from national Republicans. Reid won 61%-35%; he carried Las Vegas's Clark County 65%-31% and Reno's Washoe County 58%-38%; he lost the usually Republican Cow Counties, which George W. Bush carried 2–1, by exactly 137 votes. He had the additional satisfaction of seeing his son Rory Reid elected chairman of the Clark County Commission.

Reid has been criticized for lapses in ethics; he has argued that none of the charges had merit. A June 2003 *Los Angeles Times* story pointed out that his son and a son-in-law were lobbying in Washington for Nevada companies; Reid then banned relatives from lobbying his office. Reid was a leading recipient of contributions from Indian tribe clients of disgraced lobbyist Jack Abramoff, and in January 2006, 3d District Congressman Jon Porter called on him to return the money. Reid refused and pointed out that he had always opposed expansion of Indian gambling (as any member from Nevada would). Later in 2006 he raised money for Porter's opponent Tessa Hafen, a former Reid staffer in the Senate. Between 2003 and 2005 Reid accepted free seats at Las Vegas boxing matches from the Nevada Athletic Commission (John McCain paid $1,400 for tickets to the same matches); in December 2006 the Ethics Committee said that violated no rule because the money came from a state government agency. In October 2006 it was reported that Reid had not disclosed a transaction on a land deal in 2001 that netted him $1.1 million in 2004. Reid said that he had purchased the land in 1998 at market price, then sold it to a friend's corporation in 2001 in return for a stake in that corporation and then got his share of the proceeds in 2004 when the property was sold to a shopping center developer. Reid reported the 1998 and 2004 transactions and said he would revise his disclosure form to report the 2001 transaction as well.

Junior Senator

John Ensign (R)

Elected 2000, seat up 2012, 2d term; b. Mar. 25, 1958, Roseville, CA; home, Las Vegas; OR St. U., B.S. 1981, CO St. U., D.V.M. 1985; Christian; married (Darlene).

Elected Office: U.S. House of Reps. 1994-98.

Professional Career: Veterinarian, 1987-93; Gen. Mgr., Gold Strike Hotel, 1991-93.

DC Office: 119 RSOB, 20510, 202-224-6244; Fax: 202-228-2193; Web site: ensign.senate.gov.

State Offices: Carson City, 775-885-9111; Las Vegas, 702-388-6605; Reno, 775-686-5770.

Committees: *Budget* (9th of 11 R). *Commerce, Science & Transportation* (7th of 11 R): Science, Technology & Innovation (RMM); Interstate Commerce, Trade & Tourism; Aviation Operations, Safety & Security. *Finance* (10th of 10 R): Social Security, Pensions & Family Policy (RMM); Energy, Natural Resources & Infrastructure; Health Care. *Veterans' Affairs* (6th of 7 R).

Group Ratings

	ADA	ACLU	AFS	LCV	ITIC	NTU	COC	ACU	CFG	FRC
2006	5	17	13	43	100	91	92	100	94	75
2005	5	—	0	20	—	82	88	100	94	—

National Journal Ratings

	2005 LIB	—	2005 CONS		2006 LIB	—	2006 CONS
Economic	28%	—	71%		40%	—	59%
Social	0%	—	77%		0%	—	82%
Foreign	0%	—	74%		36%	—	60%

Key Votes of the 109th Congress

1. Bar ANWR Drilling	N	5. Confirm Samuel Alito	Y	9. Limit Interstate Abortion	Y
2. FY06 Spending Curb	Y	6. Path to Citizenship	N	10. CAFTA	Y
3. Estate Tax Repeal	Y	7. Bar Same Sex Marriage	Y	11. Urge Iraq Withdrawal	N
4. Raise Minimum Wage	N	8. Stem Cell Research $	N	12. Provide Detainee Rights	N

Election Results

2006 general	John Ensign (R)	322,501	(55%)	($4,456,881)
	Jack Carter (D)	238,796	(41%)	($2,264,708)
	Other	21,275	(4%)	
2006 primary	John Ensign (R)	127,023	(90%)	
	None of these candidates	6,754	(5%)	
	Edward Hamilton (R)	6,649	(5%)	
2000 general	John Ensign (R)	330,687	(55%)	($4,872,176)
	Ed Bernstein (D)	238,260	(40%)	($2,449,093)
	Other	31,303	(5%)	

Prior Winning Percentages: 1996 House (50%); 1994 House (48%)

John Ensign was elected to the Senate in 2000, in his second try for the office. Ensign grew up in northern Nevada and moved to Las Vegas at 16. For a time his mother was a change girl at a Reno casino, supporting three children with no help from her ex-husband. Then she married Mike Ensign, who became a top executive at Circus Circus and was chairman of the Mandalay Resort Group until 2005. John Ensign graduated from Oregon State in 1981 and in 1985 graduated from veterinary school at Colorado State, where he became a born-again Christian. He built a successful veterinary practice in Las Vegas, with the first 24-hour clinic, and managed a family hotel, became involved in civic affairs and at his wife's suggestion became active in Promise Keepers. Disturbed at trends in national life, they decided he would run for the House in 1994, against 1st District incumbent James Bilbray. This was the more Democratic of Nevada's then two seats, and Bilbray was an eight-year incumbent. But 1994 was also a Republican year, and with the help of Ensign's stepfather's connections in the gaming industry he was able to raise substantial funds. On election night, Bilbray claimed victory, but when the votes came in Ensign had won by 1,436 votes. In the House, Ensign compiled a generally conservative voting record and got a seat on the Ways and Means Committee. In the summer of 1996 he and colleague David Camp persuaded Newt Gingrich to separate the welfare and Medicaid issues and present Bill Clinton with a welfare bill, which he signed 11 weeks before the election; Ensign can reasonably claim to be one of the fathers of the 1996 Welfare Act. He was reelected in 1996 by 50%-44%.

Ensign decided to run against Senator Harry Reid in 1998. This was a hard-fought, high-spending race, targeted by both national parties and fought with intensity by the candidates; Reid spent $4.9 million and Ensign $3.5 million. Reid attacked Ensign harshly as an "extremist" who called environmentalists "socialists," and would gut Social Security. "You send Ensign to the Senate, you send nuclear waste to Nevada," he proclaimed. The election night tally showed Reid ahead by 459 votes; Ensign called for a recount, and it turned out that the Washoe County ballots had been misprinted, preventing some from being read by machines. The hand count there took weeks, and Ensign finally conceded December 9, with Reid ahead by 428 votes.

Then just two months later, in February 1999, Bryan announced that he would not run for reelection in 2000. Ensign, who had said he would not run against Bryan, announced his candidacy the next day. Democrats tried to enlist their strongest candidate, Bob Miller, who had just completed eight years as governor, but he preferred to remain in the private sector in Las Vegas. Then Attorney General Frankie Sue Del Papa launched her candidacy; an April poll showed Ensign with a narrow 45%-40% lead, but he was much farther ahead in money: $1.1 million to $250,000 by the end of June. In September Del Papa abruptly withdrew from the race, as she had withdrawn from the 1998 race for governor, citing difficulties in fundraising; her bad relations with Las Vegas unions did not help. Democratic efforts to recruit Brian Greenspun, owner of the *Las Vegas Sun*, failed. What appears to have happened is that the gaming industry, developers and other leading funders in Las Vegas, who had supported Miller and then Republican Kenny Guinn to succeed him, decided that Ensign was on the road to victory and that it might suit their interests to have in a Republican Senate one Democratic and one Republican senator.

That left the Democratic banner in the hands of Ed Bernstein, a personal injury lawyer who had run ads on Las Vegas TV for years. Bernstein put in $1.1 million of his own money; his main issues were prescription drugs for seniors and abortion. The candidates engaged in six debates; one highlight came when Ensign quizzed Bernstein about a water project in northern Nevada of which Bernstein obviously had never heard. Naturally both candidates promised to fight nuclear waste storage in Nevada; Ensign was careful to return a contribution from a Yucca Mountain contractor. Bernstein managed to tighten the race for a while, but Ensign ended up winning by a large 55%-40%. Ensign carried Las Vegas and Clark County 51%-45%, Reno and Washoe County 58%-35% and the Cow Counties 68%-27%.

Ensign and Reid, bitter rivals in 1998, quickly became cooperative colleagues. In December 2000 they announced that their first priority was blocking the move by John McCain and Sam Brownback to prohibit betting on college and amateur sports—they argue that sports books are well regulated by Nevada state authorities—and Ensign tried to gut the bill in the Commerce Committee in May 2001 but his amendment to do so failed 10-10. They co-sponsored a bill to make permanent the Social HMOs permitted in Nevada under Medicare.

As a freshman senator, Ensign did much of his work by sponsoring amendments. To the HMO regulation bill he sponsored amendments to prohibit genetic discrimination, to make sure its protections were available to union members and to protect doctors doing pro bono work in poor areas from lawsuits. He sponsored an amendment to ban interstate transportation of cockfighting paraphernalia and increase to two years the sentence for interstate transportation of cockfighting roosters; he failed to get it into the 2002 farm bill and it was stripped out of the forestry bill in November 2003. He sponsored another bill to outlaw the slaughter of horses in the U.S. for human consumption in other countries. After Hurricane Katrina hit the Gulf Coast in 2005, Ensign traveled to Louisiana to review FEMA's efforts at rescuing pets displaced by the storm.

Ensign had supported the Bush guest worker immigration proposal but in May 2006 he voted against the Senate's immigration bill because he said it would not penalize illegal immigrants that fraudulently used another individual's Social Security number to collect benefits. He announced in January 2004 he would support the filibuster of the energy bill because of its new subsidies for the nuclear power industry. He got Budget Chairman Don Nickles to delete from the 2004 budget resolution a proposal requiring casinos to withhold winnings from gamblers behind on child support payments. With Lindsey Graham, he sponsored a bill to cut U.S. dues to the United Nations 10%

unless the UN cooperates with American investigations of the Oil For Food program; in December 2004 he called for the resignation of UN Secretary General Kofi Annan.

In July 2006, Ensign won Senate passage, by a 65-34 vote, of a bill making it a federal crime to assist minors across state lines to avoid parental notification laws on abortion. Democrats said the vote was engineered to motivate social conservatives for the midterm elections, but Ensign said the bill represented "reasonable restrictions" on abortion that a majority could accept. Richard Durbin of Illinois blocked the Senate from negotiating a final bill with the House. Rather than take up Ensign's bill, the House in September passed a modified version. Ensign, the only member of Congress in Iraq when Saddam Hussein was captured in December 2003, also has sought to increase the tools available to U.S. military and intelligence forces. He opposed limits on enemy interrogation methods that fall short of torture, including sleep deprivation and "waterboarding," in which the detainee is dunked in water nearly to the point of drowning. He moved through Congress an amendment that permits the president to authorize the military to use tear gas against an enemy, as domestic police departments can use to control a riot. Opponents argued the Chemical Weapons Convention prohibits the use of riot control agents in war.

One important federal issue for Nevada is the proposed nuclear waste repository in Yucca Mountain, 90 miles northwest of Las Vegas. The federal government assumed responsibility for nuclear waste in 1982 and a bill passed in 1987 named Yucca Mountain and one other contender as the only two sites; the other one was later ruled out. Ensign strongly opposed Yucca Mountain when he was in the House, but there the odds were very heavily against him. Creation of a temporary storage site in Yucca Mountain was prevented during the Clinton years by Clinton's promise to veto it—probably the reason he carried Republican-leaning Nevada twice by narrow margins—and by Harry Reid's success in getting at least 34 senators to oppose it, enough to prevent an override of Clinton's veto. George W. Bush in 2000 also pledged not to support a temporary site, but at the same time he refrained from promising to veto a permanent site. In February 2002 Bush, on the recommendation of Energy Secretary Spencer Abraham, designated Yucca Mountain as the permanent site. The law provided for a veto by the governor, which could be overridden by majorities in both houses of Congress. In April 2002, Governor Kenny Guinn issued his veto. In May 2002, the House cast a large majority for Yucca Mountain. In the Senate Reid lobbied furiously for votes among Democrats, most of whom had stood with him before on the issue, while Ensign lobbied desperately for Republican votes. This was much more difficult because of the opposition of the Bush administration. Reid got 35 Democrats and Jim Jeffords to vote his way. Ensign could get only two other Republicans, so the site was approved 60-39. But the fight was not over. Lawsuits had been filed against the plan, and the Energy Department must get approval from the Nuclear Regulatory Commission, which could take many years. And Ensign has worked with Harry Reid to block funding of Yucca Mountain outside the congressional appropriations process.

Ensign's reelection in 2006 was not seriously contested, but Democratic nominee Jack Carter, the eldest son of former President Jimmy Carter, attracted a level of national interest not usually afforded to a longshot candidate. Carter, an investment consultant who moved into the state in 2002, benefited from his father's famous name and campaign appearances, as well as a national donor base, but that was about all. Jimmy Carter had lost Nevada in both 1976 and 1980, the latter election by 36 points. At the urging of Reid and DSCC Chairman Charles Schumer, Las Vegas Mayor Oscar Goodman considered challenging Ensign but he declined in April and his potential candidacy prevented Carter from locking up donors and building his campaign early.

When Ensign launched his campaign in March, he commended Bush for fighting the war on terrorism. He called for adding 10,000 new Border Patrol agents, incentives to help children study math and science and cuts in taxes and government spending. Ensign was better funded and had been running television ads for the general election since Labor Day. Carter was forced off the campaign trail for two weeks in September after he was hospitalized for colitis. Ensign criticized Carter as a carpetbagger, but softened some of the blows by reminding voters of his past career as a veterinarian. One campaign ad showed Ensign in white coat and stethoscope, holding a small dog. Carter assailed Ensign for supporting a failed strategy in Iraq and the Bush agenda; he largely ignored such critical state issues as Yucca Mountain and water resources and his admitted youthful use of marijuana, which got him discharged from the Navy 36 years earlier, continued to linger as a campaign sidenote. During an October debate, Ensign noted his good working relationship with Reid, and said that resulted in $3 billion in state receipts from federal public land sales in Nevada, $300 million for Lake Tahoe preservation and a new veterans hospital in Las Vegas. Ensign won reelection by a 55%-41% margin over Carter.

On election night, Ensign said voters reelected him because of his work on Nevada issues and his cooperation with Reid. "He works his side of the aisle, and I work mine. Because of that working relationship and trust, we are able to get things done that frankly, members of the same party in some states can't get done." That bipartisanship could be tested in the 110th Congress as Ensign assumes the chairmanship of the National Republican Senatorial Committee, the party's political arm charged with the task of returning Republicans to the Senate majority. Ensign committed himself to seeking the position before the 2006 election results after Senator John Thune opted not to seek the job. Republicans began the 2008 election cycle with the challenge of defending 21 Republican Senate seats, while Democrats have just 12 senators up for reelection.

FIRST DISTRICT

Rep. Shelley Berkley (D)

Elected 1998, 5th term; b. Jan. 20, 1951, South Fallsburg, NY; home, Las Vegas; U.N.L.V., B.A. 1972; U. of San Diego Law Schl., J.D. 1976; Jewish; married (Larry Lehrner).

Elected Office: NV Assembly, 1982-84; Regent, U. Commun. Col. System of NV, 1990-98.

Professional Career: Cnsl., SW Gas Corp., 1977-82; VP, Sands Hotel, 1989-98; Chair, NV Hotel & Motel Assn., 1994.

DC Office: 405 CHOB, 20515, 202-225-5965; Fax: 202-225-3119; Web site: berkley.house.gov.

District Offices: Las Vegas, 702-220-9823.

Committees: *Veterans' Affairs* (10th of 16 D): Disability Assistance & Memorial Affairs; Health. *Ways & Means* (19th of 24 D): Trade; Income Security & Family Support.

Group Ratings

	ADA	ACLU	AFS	LCV	ITIC	NTU	COC	ACU	CFG	FRC
2006	80	90	100	100	57	15	54	13	11	0
2005	90	—	100	100	—	21	54	13	14	31

National Journal Ratings

	2005 LIB	—	2005 CONS		2006 LIB	—	2006 CONS
Economic	74%	—	26%		77%	—	22%
Social	71%	—	29%		74%	—	26%
Foreign	58%	—	41%		62%	—	37%

Key Votes of the 109th Congress

1. Estate Tax Repeal	Y	5. Limit Interstate Abortion	N	9. Build Border Fence	Y
2. Limit CAFE Standards	N	6. Extend Patriot Act	N	10. CAFTA	N
3. FY06 Spending Curb	N	7. Bar Same Sex Marriage	N	11. Oppose Iraq Withdrawal	N
4. Drilling in ANWR	N	8. Stem Cell Research $	Y	12. Detainee Tribunals	N

Election Results

2006 general	Shelley Berkley (D)	85,025	(65%)	($1,674,409)
	Kenneth Wegner (R)	40,917	(31%)	($96,534)
	Other	5,182	(4%)	
2006 primary	Shelley Berkley (D)	29,655	(90%)	
	Asimosondra Lawlor (D)	3,267	(10%)	
2004 general	Shelley Berkley (D)	133,569	(66%)	($1,248,297)
	Russ Mickelson (R)	63,005	(31%)	($17,662)
	Other	5,862	(3%)	

Prior Winning Percentages: 2002 (54%); 2000 (52%); 1998 (49%)

The People		Race/Ethnic Origin	Ancestry	
Area size:	177 sq. mi.	51.5% White	German: 8.8%	Irish: 7.1%
Urban population:	99.9%	11.9% Black	English: 5.9%	
Rural population:	0.1%	4.6% Asian	**2004 Presidential Vote**	
Pop. 2000:	666,088	0.6% Native Am.	Kerry (D) 121,453	(57%)
Pop. 2005 (est):	764,054	0.4% Hawaiian	Bush (R) 89,800	(41%)
Median income:	$39,480	2.6% Two+ races	Other 3,457	(2%)
Poverty status:	13.9%	0.1% Other	**2000 Presidential Vote**	
Military veterans:	14.4%	28.2% Hispanic Origin	Gore (D) 87,345	(56%)
			Bush (R) 63,163	(41%)
			Other 4,801	(3%)
			Cook Partisan Voting Index: D + 9	

Occupation   Blue collar: 23.0%   White collar: 47.8%   Gray collar: 29.2%

Las Vegas, a city whose garishness and sheer improbability is literally awesome, had a fittingly colorful beginning. It began as a Paiute Indian settlement that in the late 1700s served as a watering stop for Spanish priests making the 1,200-mile trek between New Mexico and California. By the 1800s, the Old Spanish Trail, as it came to be known, was used by horse and mule smugglers, by white explorers like John Fremont and by Mormon emigrants heading west. Las Vegas was still a small crossroads when Nevada, its mining industry a shambles, legalized gambling in the 1930s. The *WPA Guide* to Nevada, published in 1940, when the city had 10,000 people, describes a prim Las Vegas: "Relatively little emphasis is placed on the gambling clubs and divorce facilities—though they are attractions to many visitors—and much effort is being made to build up cultural attractions. No cheap and easily parodied slogans have been adopted to publicize the city, no attempt has been made to introduce pseudo-romantic architectural themes, or to give an artificial glamour or gaiety."

All that changed big-time after World War II, when gangster Bugsy Siegel built the Flamingo hotel on what became The Strip south of the city limits. Pseudo-romantic architectural themes became the order of the day (you find flamingoes in the waters of Florida, not in the deserts of Nevada) and one casino followed another. Organized crime provided much of the money and muscle for Las Vegas, and investment capital came from Teamsters pension funds. That changed in the late 1960s, when the eccentric billionaire Howard Hughes moved into the Desert Inn, bought most of the casinos and hired Mormons to run them. Then Hughes abruptly left town, most of his hotels eventually were torn down, and other operators built casinos like Caesars Palace and Circus Circus, the Mirage and Excalibur, the lavish Bellagio and Venetian. In the 1970s, the casinos were the haven of flashy high rollers, of Frank Sinatra and girl shows. Since the 1990s, diversification has been the buzz. Las Vegas produced more family-oriented entertainment, shopping, and even high art, with the Bellagio's museum-quality art collection on view, and Las Vegas built the biggest convention center in the country. But recent promotions have sounded a naughtier theme, "What happens in Vegas stays in Vegas." The scent of the underworld has not entirely disappeared; the flashy Oscar Goldman, a former Mob lawyer who was hired for his first job by Arlen Specter in the Philadelphia district attorney's office, was elected mayor and actively promoted the city. After September 11, 15,000 casino workers were laid off in the downturn but bolstered by a surge in convention business and its draw as a tourist destination, the gaming industry posted record profits in 2005; it remains one of the great leisure destinations in the world. Since the 1960s, Las Vegas has grown faster than any other metropolitan area in the nation.

The 1st Congressional District of Nevada consists of the inner core of Las Vegas that visitors are most likely to see. They cross into it as soon as they drive their rental cars out of the lot at McCarran International Airport and remain in the 1st as they cruise down Las Vegas Boulevard. On the three-mile Strip you can find 8 of the world's 10 largest hotels, each with thousands of rooms. North of Sahara Avenue, Las Vegas Boulevard enters the city of Las Vegas, the older and less glamorous part of town. The 1st continues north for another dozen miles through the housing developments and scrubland that follow the U.S. 95 and Interstate 15 diagonals, to include the sizable Hispanic and black communities of North Las Vegas. The 1st is home to the University of Nevada-Las Vegas and includes the Clark County Government Center, a circular sandstone complex whose beautiful Indian-inspired architecture is a testament to the power of the gambling dollar. The population of the 1st in 2000 was 12% black and 28% Hispanic, with a high percentage of union members; more than 80,000 Jews live in the area, supporting 18 synagogues and a Kosher supermarket. Overall, this is a safely Democratic district.

The congresswoman from the 1st District is Shelley Berkley, a Democrat first elected in 1998. Berkley was born on the Lower East Side of New York, and moved to Las Vegas as a child. "I am not a politician who happens to be Jewish. I am a Jew who happens to be in politics." Her parents emigrated from eastern Europe before World War II, and her father worked at the Sands and rose to maitre d'; she waited tables and was a keno runner as she made her way through the UNLV, where she was student body president, and the University of San Diego law school. She chaired the Nevada Hotel and Motel Association, was government and legal affairs vice president at the Sands and in-house counsel at Southwest Gas. She was elected to one term in the state House. In 1990, she was appointed to the University of Nevada Board of Regents and then was elected to two terms.

After the 1996 election, she decided to run in the 1st District. Incumbent Republican John Ensign, reelected by only 50%-44% after spending $1.9 million, decided to run against Senator Harry Reid, and Berkley—brassy, direct, effusive—seemed headed for victory. Republicans lacked a serious candidate until filing day in May 1998; 15 minutes before the deadline, Judge Donald Chairez resigned his post and filed for the seat. Then in June came a bombshell. The *Las Vegas Review-Journal* reported on tapes of Berkley's May 1997 telephone conversations to a friend and texts of a memo she sent the Sands's owner Sheldon Adelson when he was seeking approvals for his Venetian megahotel. They showed her advising him to make campaign contributions to local judges to curry favor and to grant concessions to Clark County commissioners to get their votes for approval. Adelson fired Berkley. She quickly apologized; the Clark County district attorney saw no cause for prosecution. But Chairez made his slogan, "Fairness, not favors!" With strong support from the gaming industry, Berkley outspent Chairez by $1.2 million to $554,000. She won narrowly, 49%-46%.

In the House, Berkley's voting record has been moderate. She keeps a close watch on the interests of the gaming industry. She led opposition in the House to a proposal by the National Collegiate Athletic Association to bar Nevada casinos from accepting bets on college sports, and opposed passage of an Internet gambling ban; the bill passed the House but died in the Senate. With the state's bipartisan delegation, she fought the plan to store nuclear waste at Yucca Mountain, and in 2006 led an unsuccessful effort to dump a cartoon miner that appeared on a taxpayer-funded website to promote the repository among children. Berkley in 2006 authored a bill that would repeal subsidies and tax breaks for the nuclear power and oil and gas industries, in favor of incentives for renewable energy. She has shown a strong interest in Middle East affairs and is an advocate for Israel. She forcefully backed George W. Bush on the use of force in Iraq, but later in July 2004 said that she was misled by phony intelligence and called for Defense Secretary Donald Rumsfeld's resignation. She also fought for homeland security money for Las Vegas as a terrorist target. The new Democratic majority immediately opened up new opportunities for Berkley as she won a seat on the House Ways and Means Committee in December 2006.

Berkley has faced tough reelection contests. In 2000, state Senator Jon Porter revived the 1998 Adelson controversy but Berkley won 52%-44%; Porter then ran and won in the state's newly-created 3d District in 2002. That year, Berkley faced Las Vegas Councilwoman Lynette Boggs-McDonald, a former Miss Oregon and former Democrat who hoped to become the first Republican black woman elected to the House. But redistricting had removed many suburban precincts, and Berkley won with 54%. Since then, she has faced weak opposition. Republicans criticized Berkley in 2005 for missing votes on Hurricane Katrina aid while she was home recovering from complications to cosmetic surgery performed on her neck; her 2006 Republican opponent, an Army veteran and bail enforcement agent, ran on border security issues and criticized Berkley for not doing enough to preserve veterans benefits. Berkley countered by noting her efforts to open a veterans hospital in southern Nevada and won 65%-31%.

SECOND DISTRICT

Rep. Dean Heller (R)

Elected 2006, 1st term; b. May 10, 1959, Castro Valley, CA; home, Carson City; U. of S. CA, B.A. 1985; Mormon; married (Lynne).

Elected Office: NV Assembly, 1990-94, NV Sec. of State, 1994-2006.

Professional Career: Stockbroker, 1983-88; Chief Deputy State Treas., 1988-90; Public Funds Rep., Bank of America, 1990-95.

DC Office: 1023 LHOB, 20515, 202-225-6155; Fax: 202-225-5679; Web site: heller.house.gov.

District Offices: Elko, 775-777-7920; Las Vegas, 702-255-1651; Reno, 775-686-5760.

Committees: *Education & Labor* (22d of 22 R): Healthy Families & Communities; Early Childhood, Elementary & Secondary Education. *Natural Resources* (18th of 22 R): Water & Power; Energy & Mineral Resources; National Parks, Forests & Public Lands. *Small Business* (11th of 15 R): Finance & Tax (RMM); Rural & Urban Entrepreneurship.

Group Ratings and Key Votes: Newly Elected

Election Results

2006 general	Dean Heller (R)	117,168	(50%)	($1,674,281)
	Jill Derby (D)	104,593	(45%)	($1,594,051)
	Other	10,963	(5%)	
2006 primary	Dean Heller (R)	24,770	(36%)	
	Sharron Angle (R)	24,349	(35%)	
	Dawn Gibbons (R)	17,317	(25%)	
	Other	2,556	(4%)	
2004 general	Jim Gibbons (R)	195,466	(67%)	($1,171,994)
	Angie Cochran (D)	79,978	(27%)	
	Janine Hansen (IAP)	10,638	(4%)	
	Other	4,997	(2%)	

The People		Race/Ethnic Origin	Ancestry	
Area size:	105,635 sq. mi.	74.8% White	German: 12.8%	Irish: 9.7%
Urban population:	78.5%	2.4% Black	English: 9.6%	
Rural population:	21.5%	2.8% Asian	**2004 Presidential Vote**	
Pop. 2000:	666,087	2.1% Native Am.	Bush (R) 172,422	(57%)
Pop. 2005 (est):	770,973	0.3% Hawaiian	Kerry (D) 123,490	(41%)
Median income:	$43,879	2.1% Two+ races	Other 5,641	(2%)
Poverty status:	10.1%	0.1% Other	**2000 Presidential Vote**	
Military veterans:	17.1%	15.3% Hispanic Origin	Bush (R) 134,540	(57%)
			Gore (D) 87,705	(37%)
			Other 12,493	(5%)
			Cook Partisan Voting Index: R + 8	

Occupation   Blue collar: 24.3%   White collar: 54.9%   Gray collar: 20.9%

Outside of metro Las Vegas, huge, empty, and mountainous Nevada has only one sizable population cluster, located much further north near the border with California—the casino cities of Reno and Sparks; the small capital of Carson City; the restored Comstock Lode boomtown of Virginia City and the resort areas that surround (and endanger) the deep, impossibly blue waters of Lake Tahoe. Reno is so remote from Las Vegas that the only practical way to get there is by air; it takes more than nine hours to drive, eight of which are on two-lane highways that pass through just a handful of towns, none bigger than 7,000 people. Ghost towns that once bustled with miners dot the parched, sandswept deserts of Nevada; in some places, these lands remain distinctly rutted from the wagon trains that crossed them more than 100 years ago. Today these towns survive on mining, ranching and in some cases, servicing the human sins of greed and lust (it is in the small counties that you find Nevada's legal brothels). Immigrant Basque shepherds once tended their flocks in remote portions of northern Nevada and made carvings on aspen trees to pass the time; today, Basque festivals, social clubs and restaurants can be found in Winnemucca, Ely and Elko, while Reno is home to the national sheepherder's monument and the nation's only Basque Studies Department, at the University of Nevada-Reno.

The military has vast holdings in the Nevada interior: the Fallon Naval Air Station, home to the Navy Fighter Weapons ("Top Gun") School; the 3.1 million-acre Nellis Air Force Gunnery Range; and the Energy Department's Nevada Test Site, where more than 800 underground tests of nuclear weapons were held, as well as 100 above-ground tests, all before July 1962. These explosions have left the Rhode Island-sized facility pockmarked with unstable "subsidence craters" as far as the eye can see. Many places in Nevada are dependent on other federal government programs: the Newlands Irrigation Project near Fallon was among the first projects of its kind, and Nevada's gold mining operations, booming since 2000, do not have to pay royalties to the federal government thanks to the Mining Act of 1872. Some 87% of the land in Nevada is owned by the federal government—a constant source of tension with local officials, ranchers, loggers and miners, whose pursuits, frequently solitary and often ornery, shaped Nevada's culture from its earliest days. On the desolate frontier, speculation runs wild: Art Bell used to broadcast his popular radio show about the paranormal, aliens and other unexplained phenomena from tiny Pahrump, while the government's top-secret aviation experiments at places like Area 51 on the Nellis Gunnery Range have stoked UFO lore to the point that adjoining Route 375 was rededicated as the Extraterrestrial Highway in 1996. Anti-establishment views also flourish here in more mainstream ways. Nevada residents have long opposed a nuclear waste repository 1,000 feet beneath Yucca Mountain, 90 miles northwest of Las Vegas. Congress finally approved the project in 2002, with a scheduled opening of 2012, but stubborn opponents continued their battle.

The 2d Congressional District of Nevada takes in all of this and the vast majority of Nevada's land. Excluding single-member states, this is the largest congressional district in the nation. After the 2000 Census results came in, two districts were created entirely within Clark County, which had 69% of the state's population; the 2d consisted of all the other counties, plus small slices of Clark County. About one-half of the 2d's population is in Washoe County, which contains Reno and Sparks. Half a century ago, Reno was Nevada's largest city ("the Biggest Little City in the World," reads the neon sign across downtown Virginia Street). Local features include the National Automobile Museum and the National Bowling Stadium. It has grown vastly, but vastly less than Las Vegas, and is now overshadowed by it, and has become the state's third-largest city behind Henderson; its casinos were hit hard by Indian casinos in California. Its growth has been matched and more by growth around Lake Tahoe just to the west. People here are from all over: the Tahoe communities of Stateline, Zephyr Cove and Incline Village were three of the top eight American cities with the smallest percentage of residents born in the state. Historically, Reno has been Republican and Las Vegas Democratic. In the 1990s, when the federal government was widely viewed as unfriendly to mining, grazing and timber interests, the Cow Counties, as the counties outside Reno and Las Vegas are called, became even more Republican. All that has made the 2d District heavily Republican.

The new congressman from the 2d District is Dean Heller, a Republican elected in 2006. Heller was a political fixture in Carson City long before he ran for this seat, left vacant when five-term Republican Jim Gibbons ran for governor. Heller got his first taste of politics during childhood when his newspaper route included deliveries at the state Capitol. He graduated from the University of Southern California in 1985 with a degree in business administration, then worked as a stockbroker and traded on the Pacific Stock Exchange. In 1990, he won the first of two terms in the Nevada House and in 1994 he was elected to the first of three terms as Nevada secretary of state. During his 12-year tenure, Heller streamlined the corporation registration process and revenues increased tenfold. He has supported increased public access to government records and greater transparency in the state campaign finance system. Nevada was seen as a national model in 2004 when it became the first to create a paper trail for its electronic voting machines.

Heller faced competition for the Republican nomination from Assemblywoman Sharron Angle and former Assemblywoman Dawn Gibbons, the outgoing congressman's wife. Heller and Gibbons began with the strongest name recognition, but Gibbons' candidacy was underfunded and never took off. Angle, a Christian conservative, emerged as a serious primary rival after she picked up the endorsement and financial support of the anti-tax Club for Growth. Angle ran as the race's true conservative, while Heller campaigned on his record in state office and called for cuts in taxes and government spending. Heller won 36% of the vote, giving him a 421-vote victory over Angle, who placed second with 35%. Gibbons finished third with 25% (she later became the state's First Lady when her husband was elected governor in November). Instead of requesting a recount, Angle filed a lawsuit seeking a new election because some polling locations in Washoe County had opened late. A judge denied her request, and she conceded two weeks after the primary had ended.

Heller entered the general election campaign with a depleted campaign treasury and faced Democrat Jill Derby, an 18-year veteran of the Nevada Board of Regents. He ran the race as a referendum on President Bush and his policies. He sided with the White House on the Iraq war, making Bush tax cuts permanent and support for private Social Security accounts for younger workers. While many Republican candidates elsewhere considered Bush a liability in 2006, the president stumped twice for Heller in the last five weeks of the campaign, including a visit to the Elko airport that drew an estimated crowd of 5,000. Bush's stops helped Heller rebuild his campaign reserves and motivate the traditionally Republican-leaning rural vote. Derby emphasized her rural roots, criticized Heller for his Iraq war stance and framed the election as a chance for voters to reject Republican control in Washington. Polls in September showed Derby was running competitively for the open seat; the Democratic Congressional Campaign Committee in October mounted a late attack on Heller. Democrats insinuated the Drug Enforcement Administration in 2005 had seized Heller's race car (he is a stockcar racing enthusiast) in connection with a drug case involving Heller's friend Eddie Floyd, a former Reno talk show host who was also a convicted sex offender. Heller said he did not own the car, but had been helping Floyd's son to build it. The controversy wasn't enough to overcome the district's wide Republican voter registration advantage; Heller defeated Derby by 50%-45%. This seat has not elected a Democrat since it was created after the 1980 census.

THIRD DISTRICT

Rep. Jon Porter (R)

Elected 2002, 3d term; b. May 16, 1955, Ft. Dodge, IA; home, Henderson; Attended Briar Cliff College, 1974-78.; Catholic; divorced.

Elected Office: Boulder City Cncl., 1983-93; Boulder City Mayor, 1987-91; NV Senate, 1994-2002.

Professional Career: Indep. contractor, Farmers Insurance Group Corp., 1982-2000.

DC Office: 218 CHOB, 20515, 202-225-3252; Fax: 202-225-2185; Web site: porter.house.gov.

District Offices: Henderson, 702-387-4941.

Committees: *Budget* (14th of 17 R). *Ways & Means* (17th of 17 R): Income Security & Family Support.

Group Ratings

	ADA	ACLU	AFS	LCV	ITIC	NTU	COC	ACU	CFG	FRC
2006	10	23	0	8	100	54	100	80	50	71
2005	5	—	0	0	—	56	93	84	57	85

National Journal Ratings

	2005 LIB	—	2005 CONS	2006 LIB	—	2006 CONS
Economic	28%	—	71%	32%	—	67%
Social	46%	—	53%	46%	—	53%
Foreign	27%	—	71%	38%	—	59%

Key Votes of the 109th Congress

1. Estate Tax Repeal	Y	5. Limit Interstate Abortion	Y	9. Build Border Fence	Y
2. Limit CAFE Standards	Y	6. Extend Patriot Act	Y	10. CAFTA	Y
3. FY06 Spending Curb	Y	7. Bar Same Sex Marriage	Y	11. Oppose Iraq Withdrawal	Y
4. Drilling in ANWR	Y	8. Stem Cell Research $		12. Detainee Tribunals	Y

Election Results

2006 general	Jon Porter (R)	102,232	(48%)	($3,036,311)
	Tessa Hafen (D)	98,261	(47%)	($1,501,465)
	Other	10,486	(5%)	
2006 primary	Jon Porter (R)	unopposed		
2004 general	Jon Porter (R)	162,240	(54%)	($2,653,136)
	Tom Gallagher (D)	120,365	(40%)	($2,372,518)
	Other	15,313	(5%)	

Prior Winning Percentages: 2002 (56%)

The People		Race/Ethnic Origin	Ancestry	
Area size:	4,749 sq. mi.	69.3% White	German: 11.1%	Irish: 8.7%
Urban population:	96.3%	5.5% Black	English: 7.7%	
Rural population:	3.7%	5.9% Asian	**2004 Presidential Vote**	
Pop. 2000:	666,082	0.5% Native Am.	Bush (R) 156,335 (50%)	
Pop. 2005 (est):	879,929	0.4% Hawaiian	Kerry (D) 152,150 (49%)	
Median income:	$50,749	2.7% Two+ races	Other 4,608 (1%)	
Poverty status:	7.5%	0.1% Other	**2000 Presidential Vote**	
Military veterans:	16.4%	15.6% Hispanic Origin	Gore (D) 104,772 (49%)	
			Bush (R) 103,720 (48%)	
			Other 6,119 (3%)	
			Cook Partisan Voting Index: D + 1	

Occupation	Blue collar: 18.4%	White collar: 56.8%	Gray collar: 24.8%

Las Vegas means The Meadows, and was the name of a place on the Old Spanish Trail from Santa Fe to California. In the early 20th century it was one of the terminuses of the Las Vegas & Tonopah Railroad, a link to Nevada's silver mines. Even at the end of the 1930s, when gambling was legalized in Nevada, Las Vegas was still a town of less than 10,000. Then came decades of amazing growth, as Las Vegas became America's greatest center of gambling and one of its greatest centers of entertainment; it grew to a metropolitan area of 1.6 million people by 2000. For the past 15 years, Las Vegas has been the fastest-growing metropolitan area in America—up 123% from 1990 to 2004—and Clark County in 2006 was the nation's 15th largest county. Although the real estate market remains hot, this is still frontier country, one of the few places in the nation with more men than women. Las Vegas has spread from the few blocks around Fremont Street that it occupied in the 1930s all across the bleak desert, in every direction. It is an exuberant, undisciplined and chaotic American city, within its pattern of grid-street mile roads, all manner of curved-street subdivisions and gated communities, an America uncontrolled by traditional elites.

The 3d Congressional District is a Y-shaped segment of Nevada's Clark County made up of most of the suburbs of Las Vegas. It includes the south end of the Las Vegas Strip and McCarran International Airport and spreads west, northeast and south. It includes active retiree communities, blue-collar towns such as Blue Diamond that still have a rural flavor and a variety of planned (and often gated) areas like Summerlin that cater to young families drawn by the job opportunities. Southeast of Las Vegas, the district takes in two additional population hubs: Henderson, the fastest-growing city in the United States in the 1990s and the city ranked third in the nation in per capita online commercial activity by the auction site eBay, and Boulder City, originally built for federal workers at Hoover Dam. (Under an old agreement with the federal government, Boulder City is the only place in Nevada where gambling is prohibited). The 3d also includes the Nevada halves of Lake Mead and Lake Mohave, on the Arizona border, and the state's southernmost tip including Searchlight (hometown of Senator Harry Reid) and Laughlin, right across the Colorado River from Bullhead City, Arizona. The 3d District is a creature of redistricting, drawn after the 2000 Census so that the new district would have almost a precisely equal number of registered Democrats and registered Republicans. Clark County historically was the most Democratic part of Nevada, but the newcomers attracted to the state in the 1990s have tilted toward Republicans; the result is this closely divided district, with small pluralities for Al Gore in 2000 and George W. Bush in 2004.

The congressman from the 3d District is Jon Porter, a Republican first elected in 2002. He grew up in Humboldt, Iowa, and attended Briar Cliff College in Sioux City. After moving to Nevada, he managed an office with more than 40 agents for the Farmers Insurance Group. He was elected mayor of Boulder City in 1987 and in 1994 was elected to the state Senate, where he earned a reputation as a consensus-building moderate. In 2000 he ran against Democrat Shelley Berkley in the 1st District; he lost 52%-44%.

When the new district lines were adopted, Porter ran in the new 3d District. National Democrats were enthusiastic about their political *wunderkind* candidate, 28-year-old Clark County Commissioner Dario Herrera, who seemed to have the political skills and savvy that could make him in time a major statewide politician.

But Herrera turned out to have serious problems. He spent much of the campaign defending himself against a spate of charges over alleged ethics violations—such as his winning a no-bid consulting deal and taking a questionable loan. In turn, he sought to discredit Porter on the grounds that as an insurance agent he was furthering his own interests in restricting recoveries for medical malpractice, a raging issue in Nevada. Though both candidates strongly opposed shipping the nation's nuclear waste to the nearby Yucca Mountain site, Herrera attacked Porter for accepting contributions from House Republicans who supported the Nevada nuclear waste repository. It turned out to be no contest. Porter won 56%-37%, running far ahead of party lines—or perhaps it was Herrera running far behind party lines.

In the House, Porter has carved out a voting record near the center of House Republicans, and his votes on social issues were especially moderate. He proposed creation of a new undersecretary for local government and tourism in the Homeland Security Department; the House approved the proposal as part of its intelligence reorganization bill. He argued that his experience on tax issues and the underrepresentation of Western states should warrant a seat on the Ways and Means Committee; he got his wish in 2007. Before that he served as chairman of the Government Reform Subcommittee on Federal Workforce and Agency Organization, where he promised to devote attention to oversight of Energy Department contracts for the Yucca Mountain project. Porter has aided his district by securing federal transportation funding through the 2005 transportation bill, and has proposed voluntary toll lanes to speed traffic along portions of Interstate 15 outside Las Vegas. He has authored bills creating an electronic medical records system for federal employees and adding a real estate fund option to the federal employee Thrift Savings Plan. Porter voted against a ban on Internet gambling, but proposed a study to review the issue. Porter, who performed on keyboards, entertained U.S. troops in the Middle East and Europe during a 2005 holiday tour with a bipartisan musical group called the Second Amendments.

Even with the failure of Herrera, House Democrats held out hope for a serious challenger. Democrats in 2004 fielded former casino executive Tom Gallagher, who spent $940,000 of his own money. But Gallagher, who had little political experience and was not well known, lost by 14 points. Democrats did better in 2006 when Tessa Hafen, a former press secretary who had worked for Sen. Harry Reid for eight years, announced her candidacy with Reid at the podium. Porter criticized Hafen as inexperienced and portrayed her as a carpetbagger, even though she was a third-generation Nevadan and her father serves on the Henderson city council. Hafen criticized Porter for his support for the Iraq war and for various Republican ethics scandals—two lines of attack that proved successful for Democrats elsewhere. Porter responded that the Iraq war has kept terrorists out of the United States, and attacked Hafen as weak on illegal immigration. He also touted his success in passing a bill that allows schools to use national crime databases to run background checks on prospective teachers. Two weeks before Election Day, a former aide accused Porter of using his congressional offices to make fundraising calls, accusations which the FBI later declined to pursue. Porter's financial advantage and his attacks on Hafen proved enough to overcome the poor political environment for Republicans. The result was a 48%-47% Porter victory.

Hafen said she would not seek a rematch in 2008. Democratic state Senator Dina Titus, who lost in the 2006 gubernatorial race to Jim Gibbons, said she was considering a run against Porter but later bowed out. So did Larry Lehrner, husband to 1st District Congresswoman Shelley Berkley. But Clark County prosecutor Robert Daskas indicated he would seek the Democratic nomination; given Hafen's strong performance, the district is likely to remain a Democratic target in 2008.

★ NEW HAMPSHIRE ★

New Hampshire, in an odd corner of the country, with 44 one-hundredths of 1% of the nation's population, with unusual public policies, becomes every four years the epicenter of the political universe, the site where the contest for the presidency of the most powerful nation in the history of the world is temporarily centered, where every vote is avidly sought and where members of the political press vie for access to candidates and for tables at the latest cycle's most fashionable bars and restaurants. New Hampshire has done much to change the political world—not just the United States, but the entire world: It gave a huge boost to Dwight Eisenhower's candidacy in 1952, it prompted the retirement of Lyndon Johnson in 1968, it sent on his way to power first Jimmy Carter in 1976, then Ronald Reagan in 1980 and George H. W. Bush in 1988. The lever by which this small state moves the world is New Hampshire's first-in-the-nation presidential primary, first seriously contested in 1952, then sanctioned as the first-in-the-nation primary by Democratic rules writers in the 1970s, and exploited by Republicans in the 1980s. And New Hampshire did all this when its public policies were atypical of the nation and its political terrain unusual if not eccentric. This is one of the few states that over the last half century has had more registered Republicans than Democrats, and of all the states it was for many years arguably the one with the most antipathy to taxes. Yet in the last dozen years, New Hampshire has changed. The last two presidents have both lost the New Hampshire primary. It gave Patrick Buchanan a surprising 37% of the vote in 1992 and a 27% victory in 1996, but he never did as well elsewhere and left the Republican party in 1999. It gave John McCain a thumping victory over George W. Bush in 2000, but that proved to be a harbinger for the Northeast and not the rest of the country. New Hampshire played a key role in nominating Al Gore in 2000 and John Kerry in 2004, but both lost the general election. That year New Hampshire was the only state that had a big increase in turnout in the Democratic primary—an increase that was a harbinger of its performance in November, when it was the only state that switched from George W. Bush in 2000 to John Kerry in 2004. That year it also elected a Democratic governor, John Lynch, by a narrow margin. In 2006 Lynch was reelected with 74% of the vote and Democrats swept the state, ousting two Republican congressmen and gaining 89 seats in the New Hampshire House. It was a startling result in a state that voted 58%, 69% and 62% for Republican presidents in the 1980s.

New Hampshire's distinctiveness started early. In a country that prides itself on its feistiness and freedom from outside direction, it has always been even feistier and lightly fettered by authority. Before the Revolutionary War, New Hampshire was almost an outlaw colony, its great fortunes made by poachers in the king's forests and smugglers avoiding taxes. It was the first colony with an independent government and was fighting the British before the Minutemen stood at Lexington and Concord. In this environment, 19th century entrepreneurs built textile mills along fast-flowing rivers; the Amoskeag Mills in Manchester, lining the Merrimack River for a mile, were once the largest cotton mills on the globe, employing 17,000 people and producing enough cloth every two months to put a band around the world (there's a Lego replica of them now at Manchester's SEE Science Center). Around the mills grew a city of red brick dormitories and three-family frame houses filled with immigrants from Quebec, Ireland, Poland and Greece, set down amid dirt-roaded villages of flinty Yankee farmers and mechanics. New Hampshire held to its traditions of local government and little external control, and for years its refusal to join most other states and enact an income or sales tax, or to provide statewide guidance of schools and social services, seemed to doom it to continued backwardness.

Instead low taxes proved to be New Hampshire's fortune. From the 1960s to the 1990s, New Hampshire had the fastest growth in the Northeast, attracting businesses from Massachusetts and other high-tax states. It became a location of choice for entrepreneurs and high-tech innovators, attracting an increasing number of people skeptical of government programs. From 1965 to 2000, Massachusetts grew from 5.5 million to 6.3 million, up 15%; New Hampshire grew from 676,000 to 1,236,000, up 83%. The bedraggled New Hampshire of 50 years ago, of poor Yankee farmers and French Canadian mill hands, has largely disappeared, and in its place one of the nation's most prosperous economic communities has arisen. The low taxes that spurred New Hampshire's growth would probably have been raised in the late 1960s or early 1970s, as they were in so many states at the time, but for the far from gentle advocacy of Manchester's *Union Leader* and its owner William Loeb. The *Union Leader* insisted that governors and legislators "take the pledge" to vote for no sales or income tax and, from 1970 to 1998, almost all did, and the two who didn't were defeated. That meant keeping education and welfare as local responsibilities and holding down spending. At the

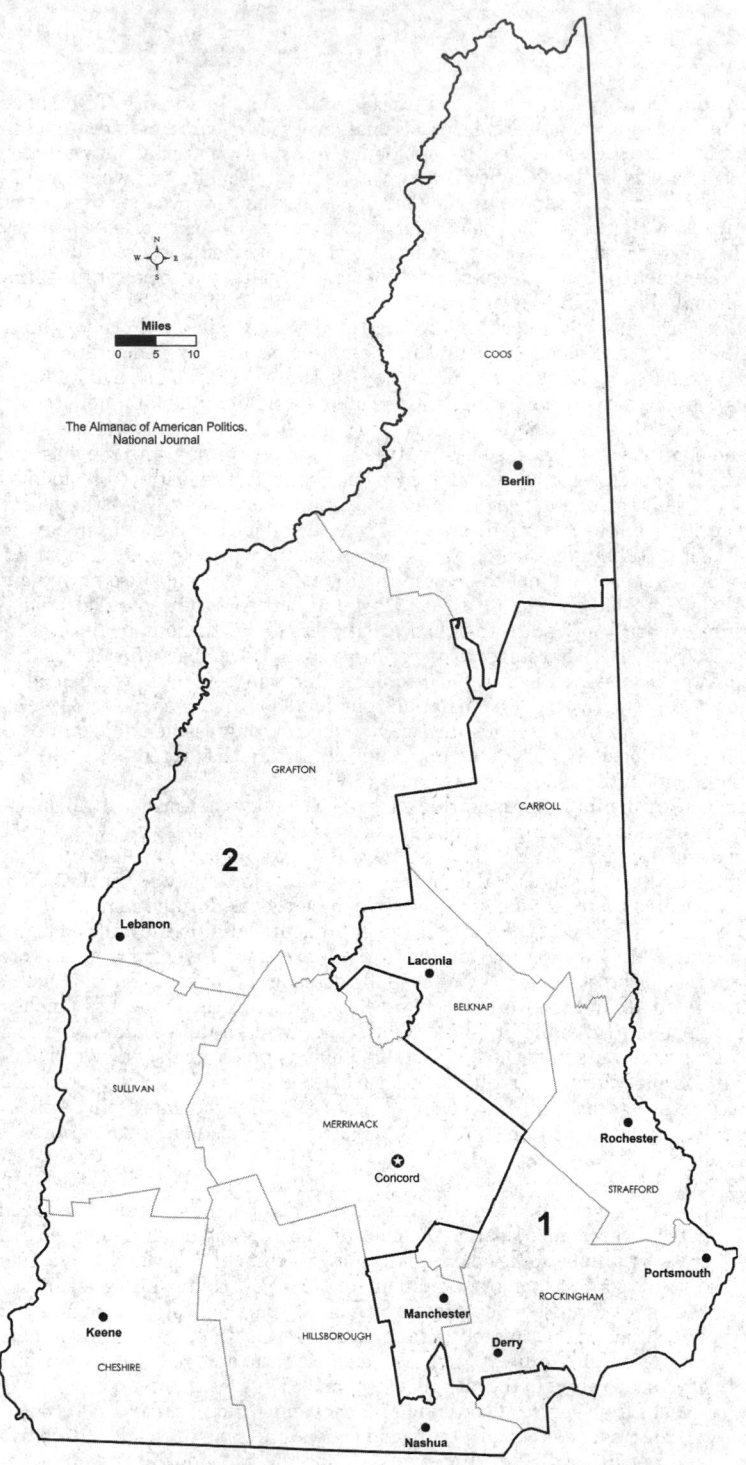

COOS

Berlin

The Almanac of American Politics.
National Journal

GRAFTON

CARROLL

2

Lebanon

Laconia

BELKNAP

SULLIVAN

MERRIMACK

Rochester

STRAFFORD

Concord

1

Portsmouth

ROCKINGHAM

Keene

Manchester

Derry

HILLSBOROUGH

CHESHIRE

Nashua

Congressional district boundaries were first effective for 2002.

same time, New Hampshire boasted the highest SAT scores in the country and had the brainpower to participate fully in New England's high-tech boom. The old Amoskeag Mills were converted to offices, and once grimy Manchester is now a high-tech center. Fidelity Investment, BAE Systems, Liberty Mutual and Timberland are big employers here, and New Hampshire has one of the nation's highest growth rates in information technology jobs.

This "Nouvelle Hampshire," to use *Washington Post* writer Henry Allen's term, has none of the architectural purity of Amoskeag. Its shopping centers and new subdivisions have a slapdash, half-built look, as if there were no time for details in the hurry to build. But it is also a state that claims to have the highest proportion of high-tech jobs, 8% of the total, and the highest percentage of citizens with Internet access. It also is a big center for financial services, with giant mutual fund campuses stuck out in the woods. This New Hampshire has not been without its problems. The booming New Hampshire priced itself out of the growth market: Its giddily high real estate prices in the late 1980s kept out the new workers its businesses needed to continue expanding. The recession of the early 1990s was harsher here than anywhere else. Thousands of jobs disappeared; real estate prices crashed so that ordinary people lost not only short-term income but also long-term wealth. By the mid-1990s growth returned again, and during the national recession of 2001-02 New Hampshire's unemployment stayed low, real estate prices were rising and incomes ranked seventh in the nation. It also has virtually no racial minorities; its population is 1% black, 2% Hispanic and 2% Asian. But there has been less in-migration in recent years, perhaps because Massachusetts and other states have lowered their taxes; the biggest in-migration since 2000 has been around Concord and the Lake Country, not along the Massachusetts border.

This helps to explain the state's political gyrations over the last dozen years. In 1992 in-migration had stopped and New Hampshire was reacting angrily to recession and rapidly declining house prices. It held George H.W. Bush to an unimpressive 53%-37% win over Patrick Buchanan in February and then voted for Bill Clinton over Bush in November. This turned out not to be a one-time fluke; like most states dominated by big metropolitan areas (most of New Hampshire gets Boston television) New Hampshire moved toward the Democrats in the 1990s, reassured by economic growth and comfortable with the Democrats' liberal stands on cultural issues. In 1996 New Hampshire voted 49%-39% for Clinton and elected Democrat Jeanne Shaheen as governor; Republican Senator Bob Smith came so close to losing that he was proclaimed the loser by the networks on election night.

Then New Hampshire's tax regime came under attack. The state Supreme Court in December 1997 ruled the state's school financing system unconstitutional because it leaves some districts with less taxable resources than others (the state provides only 10% of funding, far less than in the other 49 states) and gave the state an April 1999 deadline for coming up with a new system. The result was a statewide property tax—not anybody's first choice, but what the Democratic governor and Senate and the Republican House could agree on—and increases in business, cigarette and property sales taxes and a new tax on rental cars. In November 2002 voters had a clear choice: Republican Craig Benson took the pledge, while Democrat Mark Fernald supported an income tax. The verdict was clear: Benson won 59%-38%. But in 2004 Benson fared less well, after quarreling with the Republican legislature and facing an opponent, businessman John Lynch, who took the anti-tax pledge. Lynch won 51%-49%, as George W. Bush lost the state 50%-49%. Lynch kept his pledge even after the state Supreme Court once again rejected the legislature's school funding plan in September 2006. Republicans talked about amending the state constitution to bar the courts from reviewing school funding, but didn't act, and Democrats won a stunning victory across the board. The two incumbent congressmen lost their seats by almost precisely the same margins by which Bush had lost in their districts in 2004; Democrats won a 14-10 majority in the state Senate, a 239-161 majority in the state House and a 3–2 margin on the Executive Council (one of the winning Democrats was in Belgium on vacation on election night). This came despite, or because of, a 9% decline in turnout compared to 2002: New Hampshire has fewer newcomers seeking lower taxes than it used to, and elderly Yankees in the North Country may be dying out. Now, as New Hampshire hosts the two parties' presidential candidates, the new Democratic majorities must deal with the school funding issue and few seemed inclined to buck Lynch's opposition to an income or sales tax, despite a group set up by the New Hampshire Council of Churches to oppose the anti-tax pledge. They seem more inclined to ban smoking, raise the minimum wage, raise the school dropout age and join the 180 of 234 localities who voted in their town meetings on whether to call for federal action to address climate change.

The People		Race/Ethnic Origin			Military veterans: 139,038 (15.0%)	
Pop. 2006 (est):	1,314,895	1,175,252	95.1%	White	WWII: 18.4%	Korea: 13.6%
Pop. 2000:	1,235,786	8,354	0.7%	Black	Vietnam: 33.6%	Gulf War: 8.2%
Pop. 1990:	1,109,252	15,803	1.3%	Asian	**Most populous cities (2006):**	
Change 1990-2000:	Up 11.4%	2,698	0.2%	Native Am.	1. Manchester	109,497
% of U.S. total:	0.4%	330	0.0%	Hawaiian	2. Nashua	87,157
Pop. rank:	41st of 50	11,606	0.9%	Two+ races	3. Concord	42,378
Area size:	9,350 sq. mi.	1,254	0.1%	Other	4. Rochester	30,117
State Native:	43.3%	20,489	1.7%	Hisp. Origin	5. Dover	28,422
Non-citizen:	2.3%	**Ancestry**				
Language		Irish: 13.8%		English: 12.8%	Urban population: 59.2%	
English: 87.4%	Other Eur.: 9.0%	French: 10.4%		Fr.Canadian: 7.3%	Rural population: 40.8%	
Spanish: 2.3%		German: 6.1%				

Education		Work Sector		General Court	
H.S. Grad:	87.4%	Private: 79.4%	Govt: 12.8%	Senate	14 D 10 R
College Grad:	28.7%	Self: 7.6%	Family: 0.2%	House	239 D 161 R
Industry		Unemployment: 3.8%		Legislative Term Limits: No	
Agri: 0.9%	Con: 6.8%	**Household Income**		**Registered Voters**	
Fin: 6.3%	Info: 2.7%	<15k: 10.8%	15-35k: 22.4%	D: 221,549	(26.0%)
Mfg: 22.2%	Prof: 28.8%	35-50k: 17.2%	50-100k: 35.7%	R: 256,353	(30.1%)
Public: 3.8%	Trade: 17.3%	100-150k: 9.1%	>150k: 4.7%	O: 372,934	(43.8%)
Other: 11.2%		Median: $49,467			
Occupation		Poverty status: 6.5%			
Blue collar: 24.1%	White collar: 62.4%	**Home Value**			
Gray collar: 13.4%		<50k: 7.7%	50-100k: 24.8%	100-200k: 49.3%	200-300k: 12.2%
		300-500k: 4.5%	>500k: 1.4%	Median: $127,500	

Presidential politics   Since 1920, New Hampshire has held the first-in-the-nation primary, and since 1952, when candidates' names were first put on the ballot, it has had extraordinary influence on the presidential selection process—a fact that will surely strike 23rd century historians as bizarre. To be sure, there are arguments for having early contests in small states that provide a venue for "retail politics," in which candidates meet voters in person, listen and talk to them, exchange ideas and allow them to gauge their character. New Hampshire is small enough physically (unlike Iowa) that candidates can efficiently meet voters; everything except the lightly populated North Country is within an hour's drive of Manchester, and for all the state's abstract dislike of government, New Hampshire does an excellent job of keeping its roads clear of snow. New Hampshire's retail politics offers little-known candidates the ability to propel themselves into the national spotlight, though over the last 25 years none of those candidates has gone on to win his party's nomination. The last to do so were George McGovern and Jimmy Carter in the 1970s.

2004 Presidential Vote		
Kerry (D)	340,511	(50%)
Bush (R)	331,237	(49%)
Nader (I)	4,479	(1%)
Other	1,435	(0%)

2004 Democratic Presidential Primary		
Kerry (D)	84,377	(38%)
Dean (D)	57,761	(26%)
Clark (D)	27,314	(12%)
Edwards (D)	26,487	(12%)
Lieberman (D)	18,911	(9%)
Other	4,937	(2%)

2000 Presidential Vote		
Bush (R)	273,559	(48%)
Gore (D)	266,348	(47%)
Nader (Green)	22,188	(4%)
Other	5,700	(1%)

In any case, New Hampshire retains its first-in-the-nation status not on its merits but because of threats. Democrats tried in the 1970s to confine primaries to a "window" period in which New Hampshire would have competition. But New Hampshire, with its outlaw tradition, insisted it would hold its primary before the window if necessary, confident that candidates and reporters would pay it heed even if its tiny delegation were threatened with not being seated at the national convention. Republicans made no such rules, but in 1996 let Iowa Governor Terry Branstad and New Hampshire Governor Steve Merrill, both Republicans, threaten voter retaliation against candidates who took part in caucuses or primaries held before their states' or even during the week afterwards. Democratic Governor Jeanne Shaheen continued the tradition in December 1998, demanding candidates take a pledge not to participate in such contests. In 2000 the Democrats imposed a *five-week* window of no contests after New Hampshire, which made Al Gore's 50%-46% victory here decisive; Bill Bradley's candidacy effectively died through inattention before he could reach Super Tuesday. Fortunately for George W. Bush, the *laissez faire* Republicans did not restrict other states as much as the rule-bound Democrats, and he could recover 19 days later in South Carolina. John McCain's smashing 49%-30% victory in New Hampshire knocked the wind out of the Bush campaign for about a week, but it turned out to be a template not for contests in other states, but for other contests in the Northeast.

In 2003, the Michigan Democratic Party, led by Senator Carl Levin, attempted to challenge New Hampshire's first-in-the nation status by moving the 2004 Michigan Democratic caucuses to the same January date as New Hampshire's; after a noisy debate, Michigan backed down. But Levin got the national party to promise to convene another commission in 2005 to study the nomination process. New Hampshire Democrats predictably were threatening ostracism to any 2008 candidate who did not promise to campaign first in their state. This time New Hampshire may be in weaker position than before. Former Governor Jeanne Shaheen notes that if John Kerry had won, he would surely have kept New Hampshire first, out of gratitude; but he didn't, and other Democrats may not feel so warmly about the state. New Hampshire may have to fight hard to stay first.

New Hampshire is still one of the few states with more registered Republicans than Democrats, but it effectively chose, or ratified Iowa caucusgoers' choice of, the Democratic nominee in both 2000 and 2004. Once upon a time New Hampshire's registered Democrats were mill workers in Manchester and other factory towns, ethnics who rejected the Yankee Republican consensus of the state. Those days are long gone. Democratic turnout is not concentrated in the two largest cities, Manchester and Nashua, which often vote Republican, but in the state capital of Concord and clusters of towns around universities—the area around Durham (the University of New Hampshire) and Dover in southeast New Hampshire, the area around Keene (Keene State College) in the southwest and the area around Hanover (Dartmouth University). Once upon a time the typical Democratic primary voter here was a textile mill worker; now she is more likely to be an assistant professor. In 2000 the upscale character of this electorate was already clear. Al Gore, with strong support from labor unions, had won a wide victory in Iowa. But in New Hampshire he was fortunate to squeeze out a 50%-46% victory against Bill Bradley, who ran to his right on some economic issues and to his left on cultural issues.

In the 2004 cycle, New Hampshire was the first venue in which Howard Dean raced to a lead, far ahead of New Hampshire's Massachusetts neighbor John Kerry. Some voters in the western part of the state were perhaps familiar with Dean's somewhat moderate record as governor of Vermont. But his real appeal—what kept volunteers buzzing at their computers in his crowded Manchester headquarters, earnest Democrats turning out at his public appearances and his poll numbers rising above 50% in a multicandidate field—came from his vitriolic denunciations of George W. Bush, especially on the war in Iraq. About half of Dean's support evaporated after his third-place showing in Iowa and his election night scream. But he had already set the tone of the campaign and stirred the enthusiasm of New Hampshire Democrats. Turnout was up a huge 42%, from 154,000 in 2000 to 219,000 in 2004. The mainstream media reported this as a huge outpouring of enthusiasm, as indeed it was, and continued to make similar comments on subsequent contests although, as it happened, none had a similar increase in Democratic turnout. Kerry argued, as he had in Iowa, that he was the Democrat best able to defeat Bush; New Hampshire gave him 38% of its votes, to 26% for Dean, 12.4% for Wesley Clark (who skipped Iowa), 12.1% for John Edwards (who had done much better in Iowa) and 9% for Joseph Lieberman (who also skipped Iowa). In retrospect, New Hampshire nailed the nomination for Kerry: Lieberman soon dropped out and Dean did not long after; Clark was never able to make himself Kerry's chief rival; Edwards did, but never overtook him.

What do the New Hampshire primary electorates look like for 2008? The Democratic primary electorate seems likely to be leftish on cultural issues and not terrifically interested in economic issues. The larger Republican electorate seems likely to be moderate, perhaps even liberal on cultural issues, perhaps less supportive of George W. Bush on Iraq and foreign policy than Republican electorates in other states; less fixated on tax cuts than in the 1970s and 1980s, more secular and with a much smaller segment of religious conservatives than Republican primary electorates in most other states.

Up through 1992 political reporters left New Hampshire the day after the primary and never returned in the fall; it was assumed that the state would go Republican in November. But Bill

Clinton carried it twice, and in 2000 it was close again; Al Gore unaccountably visited the state just once in the general election campaign and George W. Bush carried it 48%-47%, with a popular vote margin of 7,211. In 2004 New Hampshire was a target state for both campaigns, and the enthusiasm evoked by the Dean campaign and transferred to Kerry in New Hampshire seems to have carried over into the fall: this was the only Bush 2000 state that went for Kerry. Again the margin was close, 50%-49%, with a popular vote margin of 9,274—without which it would not have mattered whether Bush carried Ohio. Interestingly, Bush won majorities among both Protestants and Catholics—New Hampshire's old sectarian political divide was gone—but Kerry won 69% among those of no religion and 63% who never attended religious services, the latter comprising 24% of the electorate, outnumbering the 18% who attend services weekly. Total turnout was up 19% over 2000, not much more than the national average; Bush's popular vote total was up 21%, nearly his national average, but Kerry's was up 28% over Gore's, much more than his national average. The common myth about New Hampshire is that it has become more Democratic because of the people moving across the line from Massachusetts. The vote totals tell a different story. Bush carried Manchester and almost all the towns in Rockingham and Hillsborough Counties just over the Mass line, and he increased his percentage there from 2000 as well. People here are still voting against Taxachusetts. But Bush lost most of western New Hampshire and saw his percentage drop there, sometimes sharply, not just in college towns like Keene and Hanover, but in rural areas and mill towns; the same phenomenon was apparent around Concord (where the liberal *Concord Monitor* overshadows the conservative *Union Leader*) and around trendily restored Portsmouth. A similar phenomenon was apparent in the Democrats' sweep of the state elections in 2006.

Congressional districting   With only slight changes, New Hampshire's two congressional districts basically have had the same boundaries since 1881, neatly separating the Merrimack River mill towns of Manchester and Nashua, the state's largest cities. That was done originally to split the Catholic Democratic vote, but now both cities are high-tech towns. If the split has given Republicans an edge in both districts in recent years, it has also given Democrats a chance for upset victories in both, which they achieved in 2006.

110th Congress Lineup
2 D
109th Congress Lineup
2 R

Governor

John Lynch (D)

Elected 2004, term expires Jan. 2009, 2d term; b. Nov. 25, 1952, Waltham, MA; home, Hopkinton; U of NH, B.A., 1974; Harvard U., M.B.A., 1979; Georgetown U., J.D., 1984; Catholic; married (Susan).

Professional Career: Ex. Dir., NH Dem. party, 1975-77; Dir. of Admissions, Harvard Bus. Schl., 1982-86; Partner, consulting firm, 1987-94; Pres. and CEO, Knoll Inc., 1994-2001, Pres., Lynch Group, 2001-04.

Office: State House, 25 Capitol St., Concord, 3301, 603-271-2121; Fax: 603-271-2130; Web site: www.state.nh.us/governor.

Election Results

2006 general	John Lynch (D)	298,677	(74%)
	Jim Coburn (R)	104,223	(26%)
2006 primary	John Lynch (D)	unopposed	
2004 general	John Lynch (D)	339,925	(51%)
	Craig Benson (R)	325,614	(49%)

John Lynch, a Democrat, was elected governor of New Hampshire in 2004 in his first run for political office. Lynch grew up in Waltham, Massachusetts, the fifth of six children; his father ran a local Boys Club and his mother was a schoolteacher. He graduated from the University of New

Hampshire in 1974, got his MBA from Harvard Business School in 1979 and a law degree from Georgetown in 1984. He took an interest in politics in college, interned for Senator Tom McIntyre in 1975 and not long after became executive director of the Democratic state committee. He left state politics to attend business school and later became the school's admissions director; in 1994, he became president and CEO of Knoll, Inc., a Pennsylvania-based high-end office furniture maker. All the while, he nurtured his New Hampshire connections. He commuted from Knoll's headquarters in East Greenville, Pennsylvania, to his home in Hopkinton and served as president of the University of New Hampshire alumni association. In the mid-1980s and 1990s he dabbled in state and local politics by working for the Merrimack County Democratic party, contributing to various campaigns and working to establish a New Hampshire chapter of the centrist Democratic Leadership Council. In 2001, he left Knoll and later opened his own management consulting firm on Elm Street in Manchester. In 2000 Governor Jeanne Shaheen appointed Lynch to the University System of New Hampshire's Board of Trustees, where he served as chairman from 2001 to 2004, when he resigned to run for governor.

Lynch was seeking to oust Craig Benson, a wealthy political outsider who won his first term in 2002 in the state's most expensive gubernatorial race ever. Benson, a high-tech entrepreneur, was one of three Republican former CEO's elected to New England governorships that year (Massachusetts' Mitt Romney and Rhode Island's Donald Carcieri were the others) and the only one with the advantage of a Republican-controlled legislature. But he had a tough time making the transition to the public sector; his brusque and heavy-handed style alienated legislators from both parties. Benson fared well in polls in his first year, as voters gave him high approval ratings for his hard-charging style and his call for a constitutional amendment to limit tax increases. But Benson's popularity began to fade after frequent missteps and controversies. Several of his appointees were forced to step down from office for ethical lapses; Benson and his state safety commissioner were accused of interfering with an investigation that eventually cleared Attorney General Peter Heed of allegations that he sexually harassed a woman. In October, the prosecutor cleared Benson and recommended that the safety commissioner be disciplined. Lynch made the ethics issue a cornerstone of his campaign and promised in his campaign kickoff speech that he would "restore integrity, trust and a bipartisan spirit" to state government. He faced lawyer and former legislator Paul McEachern, a twice-unsuccessful gubernatorial nominee making his fourth run for governor, in the September primary. McEachern argued that he was the only real Democrat in the race and called for a low-rate income tax to address the state's chronic education funding problem. Lynch took the pledge not to support a sales or income tax and won 75%-25%. The general election was dominated by two issues, taxes and ethics. Lynch highlighted his opposition to a sales or income tax but did back an increase in the cigarette tax; he said he would provide targeted aid to schools while phasing out the state property tax adopted in 1999. Benson hewed to a hard anti-tax position and insisted that Lynch's plan to repeal the statewide property tax would lead to a "back-door income tax." Lynch denied Benson's charges, insisting that existing revenues would enable him to pay for his spending priorities; he focused on the "culture of corruption" that he said marked the Benson administration and pointed out that Benson himself had been cited twice for having illegal landscaping in front of his beachfront home. The two candidates, both millionaires, largely self-financed their campaigns. Benson, after spending more than $9 million out of pocket in 2002, put up $3.3 million of his own money in 2004, out of a total of $4.1 million raised. Lynch raised $3 million, $2.1 million of it his own money. That was enough to keep him competitive through Election Day when he won 51%-49%. The governor's vote closely tracked presidential returns: John Kerry ran just 600 votes ahead of Lynch, winning the state by 50% to George W. Bush's 49%. Lynch and Kerry won the same six counties, both carrying western New Hampshire and Concord's Merrimack County and both losing in Manchester's Hillsborough County and Rockingham County. Benson became the first freshman governor in 78 years to be denied a second term; ever the outsider, he failed to give a concession speech or speak to campaign supporters on election night.

In Lynch's first act in office, he issued an executive order requiring everyone who works in the governor's office, regardless of title or pay grade, to file a financial disclosure form that details their sources of income, loans of $5,000 or more, the location of real estate other than homes worth $2,500 or more and businesses they or their spouses are involved in if the investment is 1% or more of the outstanding stock or securities issued by the business. His mild-mannered and cautious style offered a marked contrast to Benson and enabled him to work productively with the Republican-controlled legislature. Lynch stressed the importance of a bipartisan approach. "Being bipartisan is exactly the right way to conduct myself as governor of New Hampshire," he said. "I was not elected to represent a party." In October, Lynch drew praise for his leadership when severe flooding devastated parts of southwestern New Hampshire; he flew back from a European trade mission to oversee flood recovery efforts and surprised homeowners and local officials by handing them laminated cards that included phone numbers of key state and National Guard officials, as well as his own personal cell phone number. Lynch failed to achieve everything he wanted in his first year—he was unable to repeal the statewide property tax, among other things—but his work with the state's congressional delegation to help keep the Portsmouth Naval Shipyard open and his flood response led to high approval ratings. In 2006, Lynch had to deal with more flooding problems. He was able to establish an ethics commission for the executive branch; he signed a tough law cracking down on child sexual predators and "Michelle's Law", named for a cancer-stricken college student who was forced to continue attending classes so she could keep her insurance benefits, which required heath insurers to continue covering severely ill college students if doctors have certified that they are unable to maintain their status as full-time students.

Vermont and New Hampshire are the last two states with two-year gubernatorial terms and, Benson aside, voters in both states are inclined to grant their governors a second term. So with approval ratings in excess of 70% according to a May 2006 Granite State Poll, Lynch was solidly positioned for reelection in 2006. No well-known Republican stepped forward to run; little-known state Representative Jim Coburn, a successful businessman, had the party nomination to himself. Coburn and Lynch both opposed sales and income taxes but Coburn went a step beyond Lynch, arguing that fees and surcharges were also taxes. He said he didn't support tax increases of any kind. In September, in the latest installment of New Hampshire's long-running school funding saga, the state Supreme Court again ruled that the state's system of funding education is unconstitutional; the court set a June 2007 deadline before it would impose its own financing system. Coburn supported a constitutional amendment to remove control of the education financing system from the courts. Lynch argued that the state could fund the public schools without a sales or income tax and indicated he would consider a narrowly-crafted constitutional amendment designed to give the state more flexibility; Coburn said Lynch's position left open the possibility of broad-based taxes. The result wasn't close. It was Lynch in a landslide, 74%-26%, the largest margin ever for a gubernatorial candidate in New Hampshire. Democrats won a stunning across the board victory, gaining 89 seats in the New Hampshire House to give them a 239-161 majority, along with a 14-10 majority in the state Senate and a 3–2 margin on the Executive Council. For the first time since the Civil War era, New Hampshire had a Democratic legislature and governor. In 2007 the legislature enacted one of Lynch's priorities, an increase in the school dropout age from 16 to 18 and was active in ways that would have seemed unthinkable not so long ago. While it failed to accept the governor's education funding plan, the minimum wage was increased, cigarette taxes increased by 28-cents per pack and the state's parental notification abortion law was repealed. Lynch also signed a measure that made New Hampshire the fourth state to allow civil unions. One thing remained unchanged: a measure to make the state join the 49 others with a mandatory seat belt law failed in the Senate.

Senior Senator

Judd Gregg (R)

Elected 1992, seat up 2010, 3d term; b. Feb. 14, 1947, Nashua; home, Rye; Columbia U., A.B. 1969, Boston U., J.D. 1972, LL.M. 1975; Protestant; married (Kathleen).

Elected Office: NH Exec. Cncl., 1978-80; U.S. House of Reps., 1980-88; NH Gov., 1988-92.

Professional Career: Practicing atty., 1976-80.

DC Office: 393 RSOB, 20510, 202-224-3324; Fax: 202-224-4952; Web site: gregg.senate.gov.

State Offices: Berlin, 603-752-2604; Concord, 603-225-7115; Manchester, 603-622-7979; Nashua, 603-577-3823; Portsmouth, 603-431-2171.

Committees: *Appropriations* (8th of 14 R): State, Foreign Operations & Related Programs (RMM); Commerce, Justice, Science & Related Agencies; Homeland Security; Labor, Health and Human Services, Education & Related Agencies; Interior, Environment & Related Agencies; Defense. *Budget* (RMM of 11 R). *Health, Education, Labor & Pensions* (2d of 10 R): Retirement & Aging; Children & Families.

Group Ratings

	ADA	ACLU	AFS	LCV	ITIC	NTU	COC	ACU	CFG	FRC
2006	15	33	0	43	75	88	100	72	92	62
2005	5	—	0	30	—	78	72	72	99	—

National Journal Ratings

	2005 LIB	—	2005 CONS		2006 LIB	—	2006 CONS
Economic	41%	—	58%		3%	—	96%
Social	39%	—	58%		36%	—	63%
Foreign	42%	—	57%		46%	—	53%

Key Votes of the 109th Congress

1. Bar ANWR Drilling	N	5. Confirm Samuel Alito	Y	9. Limit Interstate Abortion	Y
2. FY06 Spending Curb	Y	6. Path to Citizenship	Y	10. CAFTA	Y
3. Estate Tax Repeal	Y	7. Bar Same Sex Marriage	N	11. Urge Iraq Withdrawal	N
4. Raise Minimum Wage	N	8. Stem Cell Research $	Y	12. Provide Detainee Rights	N

Election Results

2004 general	Judd Gregg (R)	435,846	(66%)	($1,897,466)
	Doris Haddock (D)	221,544	(34%)	($177,199)
2004 primary	Judd Gregg (R)	60,597	(92%)	
	Tom Alciere (R)	2,682	(4%)	
	Michael Tipa (R)	2,563	(4%)	
1998 general	Judd Gregg (R)	213,477	(68%)	($904,448)
	George Condodemetraky (D)	88,883	(28%)	($28,547)
	Other	12,596	(4%)	

Prior Winning Percentages: 1992 (48%); 1986 House (74%); 1984 House (76%); 1982 House (71%); 1980 House (64%)

Judd Gregg, a Republican, was first elected governor in 1988 and senator in 1992. He grew up in Nashua and was involved in politics early: in 1952, when he was 5, his father Hugh Gregg was elected governor. Hugh Gregg remained a power in presidential primary politics for many years and in 1988 provided crucial backing to George H.W. Bush; he died in September 2003. Judd Gregg was a student at Columbia during the student riots of 1968, but stayed true to New Hampshire Republicanism; he graduated from Boston University law school and returned to Nashua and practiced law. In 1978, at 31, he was elected to the Executive Council, which dates to the colonial era and approves state appointments and expenditures. In 1980 he was elected to the U.S. House, where he was an eager participant in the Reagan revolution. In 1988, he ran for governor and won handily; he was easily reelected in 1990.

In 1992, Gregg ran for the Senate when Warren Rudman retired, and in his taciturn way seemed sure he would win. But the New Hampshire economy had turned sour, and the race turned close. In the September primary he beat a construction company owner by only 50%-38%. In the general, he faced retired businessman John Rauh, who backed the line-item veto and balanced budget amendment and attacked Gregg for opposing abortion rights. He won by an unimpressive 48%-45% margin.

Gregg was chairman of the Health, Education, Labor and Pensions Committee for five months in 2001 and again from 2003 to 2005; he was the ranking minority member after Jim Jeffords left the Republican party in May 2001. In 2001 he was the lead Senate supporter of the Bush education bill. He worked with Edward Kennedy on the details; his amendment to allow private school choice in 10 cities was rejected in June 2001 by a 58-41 vote. In November 2001 he and Kennedy and House members John Boehner and George Miller reached a final compromise; it left in place the Bush proposal for annual testing in math and reading from grades three to eight and flexibility for states and school districts; it included allowing disadvantaged students to use federal funds for private tutoring and summer school. In September 2005 he proposed cash grants that parents of New Orleans area schoolchildren could use in public or private schools; as a result a larger percentage of New Orleans children are in charter schools than in any other district in the country. And he worked with Edward Kennedy on the Gulf Coast Recovery and Disaster Preparedness Act. Gregg worked on consensus health legislation with Democrats and other Republicans—a law requiring the FDA to test drugs' effects on children, a bill limiting pharmaceutical companies to one 30-month stay of an application to sell a generic drug. He got the Senate to approve FDA regulation of tobacco together with a buyout of tobacco quotas in the 2004 corporate tax bill, but the former was taken out in conference committee; Gregg voted against the overall bill on the grounds it cost too much. He has put together drug reimportation legislation which would allow imports first from Canada and later from the European Union, with licensing of Internet pharmacies; some Democrats opposed the bill as too restrictive. He co-sponsored the Biodefense Act of 2005 that promoted the development of vaccines and a bill setting down strict criteria for plaintiffs seeking punitive damages from health care providers or medical product manufacturers. In 2003 Gregg and his New Hampshire colleague John Sununu voted against the energy bill because it banned the state of New Hampshire's lawsuit against the manufacturers of the fuel additive MTBE, which was found to be polluting. They effectively blocked the energy bill from passing.

In November 2004 Gregg decided to leave the chairmanship of the HELP Committee to become chairman of the Budget Committee. He promised "very strong enforcement measures" and sought to "put the brakes on the growth of entitlements." In April 2005 he pushed through a budget resolution but failed to get the tight limits on Medicaid spending he sought. He worked to hold the cost of the Medicare/prescription drug bill to the $400 billion over 10 years that was forecast when it was passed. When the Senate's transportation bill was $11 billion higher than the House's, he protested the evasion of budget limits, asking, "Are we going to pass budgets that mean something, or are we going to pass budgets for show?" In March 2006 he proposed "a standard, vanilla budget" and in June 2006 he advanced a provision to slow the growth of entitlements as well as discretionary spending if annual deficit targets were not met, with line-item rescission authority for the president. Gregg passed up a chance to get on the Finance Committee to remain on Appropriations, where he has been somewhat more tightfisted than many of his colleagues. He has procured federal money to buy land to preserve Lake Tarleton, expand the Hubbard Brook Experimental Forest, purchase a conservation easement in the Ossipee Mountains, and maintain the Great Bay Estuarine Research Reserve, the Mount Washington Observatory Weather Discovery Center, and the University of New Hampshire aquaculture program. He has gotten funding for the purchase of easement rights on the extensive lands owned by paper companies in New Hampshire and northern New England—a major conservation project. In 2005, when subcommittee jurisdictions were changed, he moved from chairing the Commerce-State-Justice Subcommittee to the new Homeland Security Subcommittee. In June 2006 he acceded to White House plans to spend more on border security and less on the Coast Guard, but later sought to channel more money to the Coast Guard.

After Democrats won their majority in the Senate, Gregg became active on the floor in trying to stop what he considered bad legislation. In December 2006 he raised points of order against the $39 billion end-of-session spending package, opposing its $4 billion assumption of insurance liability from coal companies, the $184 million rum excise revenue sharing with Puerto Rico and the $3 million for the Music Writers of America. In January 2007 he introduced an amendment to the ethics bill giving the president line-item rescission power on earmarks; he withdrew that when Robert Byrd threatened a filibuster but said he'd bring it up on the minimum wage. Minority Leader Mitch McConnell invited him to sit in on leadership meetings; Majority Leader Harry Reid called him "the designated 'see-if-we-can-mess-up-the-legislation' guy this year." Gregg responded, "I don't think I came here to be a potted plant." In March 2007, when Democrats allowed Republicans a floor vote on one alternative to their nonbinding resolution calling for withdrawal from Iraq, Republicans chose Gregg's resolution calling for fully funding the troops; it passed 82-16.

Gregg has maintained a network of supporters in New Hampshire, but the Gregg organization that was so effective for George H.W. Bush in 1988 was unable to deliver a victory for George W. Bush in the 2000 primary. Gregg played Al Gore in candidate Bush's debate preparation; whether he anticipated Gore's loud sighs in the first debate is not clear. Gregg's standing in New Hampshire seems strong. In 1998 he was opposed by a low-spending Democrat who called him a "draft dodger" and a "wimp" and who said at one rally that he would like to get Gregg between a dog and a fire hydrant. Gregg won 68%-28%. In 2003 he seemed to face opposition in the primary from former state Representative Tom Alciere and in the general election from state Senator Burt Cohen. But Alciere, who had posted messages on the Internet condoning the killing of police officers, did not run. Cohen, who supported a state income tax in the legislature, had a campaign up and running for 18 months. But just before the filing date he discovered that his campaign manager and much of his campaign treasury was missing, and he took himself out of the race. New Hampshire Democrats, eager for a nominee, found Doris "Granny D" Haddock, a 94-year-old longtime leftish activist who in 2000 walked 3,225 miles across America to support campaign finance regulation. Granite Staters may have admired her pluck, but not very many voted for her; Gregg won 66%-34% and became the first New Hampshire senator elected to a third term since Norris Cotton in 1968. Gregg comes up for reelection in 2010.

Junior Senator

John Sununu (R)

Elected 2002, seat up 2008, 1st term; b. Sept. 10, 1964, Boston, MA; home, Bedford; M.I.T., B.S. 1986, M.S. 1987, Harvard U., M.B.A. 1991; Catholic; married (Kitty).

Elected Office: U.S. House of Reps., 1996-2002.

Professional Career: Design Engineer, Remec Inc., 1987-89; Mgr. & Operations Specialist, Pittiglio, Rabin, Todd & McGrath, 1990-92; C.F.O. & Dir. of Operations, Teletrol Systems Inc., 1993-95; Consultant, JHS Associates, 1995-96.

DC Office: 111 RSOB, 20510, 202-224-2841; Fax: 202-228-4131; Web site: sununu.senate.gov.

State Offices: Berlin, 603-752-6074; Claremont, 603-542-4872; Manchester, 603-647-7500; Nashua, 603-577-8960; Portsmouth, 603-430-9560.

Committees: *Banking, Housing & Urban Affairs* (8th of 10 R): Securities, Insurance & Investment; Financial Institutions; Housing, Transportation & Community Development. *Commerce, Science & Transportation* (8th of 11 R): Consumer Affairs, Insurance & Automotive Safety (RMM); Space, Aeronautics & Related Sciences; Oceans, Atmosphere, Fisheries & Coast Guard; Science, Technology & Innovation; Interstate Commerce, Trade & Tourism; Aviation Operations, Safety & Security. *Foreign Relations* (5th of 10 R): African Affairs (RMM); Near Eastern & South & Central Asian Affairs; Western Hemisphere, Peace Corps & Narcotics Affairs. *Homeland Security & Governmental Affairs* (8th of 8 R): State, Local & Private Sector Preparedness & Integration (RMM); Federal Financial Management, Government Information, Federal Services & International Security; Investigations (Permanent). *Joint Economic Committee* (9th of 10 R).

Group Ratings

	ADA	ACLU	AFS	LCV	ITIC	NTU	COC	ACU	CFG	FRC
2006	20	42	0	43	67	89	91	88	100	75
2005	10	—	0	40	—	91	64	83	100	—

National Journal Ratings

	2005 LIB	—	2005 CONS		2006 LIB	—	2006 CONS
Economic	44%	—	55%		8%	—	89%
Social	44%	—	55%		33%	—	64%
Foreign	51%	—	46%		47%	—	50%

Key Votes of the 109th Congress

1. Bar ANWR Drilling	N	5. Confirm Samuel Alito	Y	9. Limit Interstate Abortion	Y
2. FY06 Spending Curb	Y	6. Path to Citizenship	N	10. CAFTA	Y
3. Estate Tax Repeal	Y	7. Bar Same Sex Marriage	N	11. Urge Iraq Withdrawal	N
4. Raise Minimum Wage	N	8. Stem Cell Research $	N	12. Provide Detainee Rights	Y

Election Results

2002 general	John Sununu (R)	227,229	(51%)	($3,545,925)
	Jeanne Shaheen (D)	207,478	(47%)	($5,821,219)
	Other	12,428	(3%)	
2002 primary	John Sununu (R)	81,920	(53%)	
	Bob Smith (R)	68,608	(45%)	
	Other	2,694	(2%)	
1996 general	Bob Smith (R)	242,257	(49%)	($1,929,468)
	Dick Swett (D)	227,355	(46%)	($1,558,563)
	Ken Blevens (Lib)	22,261	(5%)	

Prior Winning Percentages: 2000 House (53%); 1998 House (67%); 1996 House (50%)

John E. Sununu, a Republican elected in 2002 when he defeated the state's senior senator and its governor, remains the youngest member of the Senate. He grew up in Salem, on the Massachusetts border, one of eight children of John H. Sununu, who was elected to the first of three terms as governor in 1982 and served as White House chief of staff from 1989 to 1991. The younger Sununu graduated from M.I.T, where he also got a master's degree, and got an M.B.A. at Harvard. He worked as an engineer for a microwave manufacturer, a high-tech consulting firm, the building automation manager Teletrol and as a consultant for JHS Associates. In 1996, when Congressman Bill Zeliff announced for governor, eight Republicans got into the House race; Sununu won with 28% of the vote. In the general, he faced Joe Keefe, former state Democratic chairman, who had run twice before in the district and who, with help from PACs, raised more money than Sununu. This was a close race, but Sununu won 50%-47%.

In the House, Sununu compiled a conservative voting record and climbed to important positions on the Appropriations and Budget committees. In 2002, Republican Senator Bob Smith was obviously vulnerable in the primary and seemed likely to lose the general election. How a New Hampshire Republican got himself into this predicament is an interesting tale. Smith, a fervent opponent of abortion, ran for an open Senate seat in 1990 and won 65%-32%. In 1996 Smith had well-financed competition from former Democratic Congressman Dick Swett. Smith won by only 49%-46%. Astonishingly, Smith proceeded to run for president. He had no executive experience in government and no major legislative achievement. His standing with New Hampshire voters was shaky and support from his colleagues was nonexistent. He spent much time on the road in 1997 and 1998 and became the first candidate to formally announce for the presidency in February 1999. Much of the buzz in New Hampshire was hostile, and many feared his presence would drive out other presidential contenders, and thus reduce the importance of New Hampshire's first-in-the-nation primary. In July 1999 Smith rose on the Senate floor and made a 50-minute speech announcing that he was leaving the Republican party and would run for president as an independent or third-party candidate. Senate Republican leaders allowed him to keep his committee seats and seniority. Then in October 1999 Senator John Chafee died; he was chairman of the Environment and Public Works Committee and Smith held the next-ranking Republican seat. Four days later Smith abandoned his presidential candidacy, saying he could not raise enough money, and then he announced he was a Republican again. A day later he became chairman of the Environment Committee. Previously, his record on the committee had been solidly conservative. Now he took liberal stands on environmental issues, including opposing oil drilling in the Arctic National Wildlife Refuge.

By early 2001 New Hampshire polls showed Smith trailing Governor Jeanne Shaheen in the general election and Sununu in the primary; they also showed Sununu ahead of Shaheen. The Bush White House was officially on Smith's side: Dick Cheney assured him in March 2001 that the White House backed all incumbent Republican senators. But Republican consultants believed that only a Sununu win in the primary could save the seat, and the White House appeared to make no attempt to persuade Sununu not to run. Smith argued that with his seniority it would be a "serious matter" for Republicans to reject him. Sununu's argument was that he was the only one who could win. It is highly unusual for leaders of both parties to refuse to support, much less oppose, one of their incumbents in a primary. But even leaders officially on Smith's side were lukewarm in their support. Presidential adviser Karl Rove attended a Smith fundraiser, but White House Chief of Staff Andrew Card, who knew the Sununus for 30 years, endorsed Sununu. GOP Leader Trent Lott attended two Smith fundraisers but in April 2002 attended a Sununu fundraiser. Senate Republican campaign committee chairman Bill Frist said he supported Smith, but in October 2001 Smith upbraided him in the cloakroom for not supporting him strongly enough. Judd Gregg, Smith's New Hampshire colleague for 10 years, said he was neutral. The House Republican leadership held a fundraiser for Sununu. The Manchester *Union Leader* endorsed Sununu. Despite all his support from leading Republicans, Sununu raised far less money than Smith, who raised much by direct mail; altogether Smith raised $3.8 million and Sununu $1.5 million.

The candidates disagreed on only a few issues—normal trade relations with China and ANWR oil drilling, both of which Smith opposed and Sununu favored. A few other differences surfaced during the long campaign up to the September primary. One was policy in the Middle East. Sununu is of Lebanese descent, and was one of the few Republicans to vote against recognizing Jerusalem as the capital of Israel. The weekend before the primary, Smith ran an ad saying that Sununu voted to let terrorist suspects stay in the United States; Sununu replied that someone granted permanent residency status has rights under the Constitution. New Hampshire polls often produce conflicting results, as close observers of New Hampshire presidential primaries know. In the weeks before the September 10 primary, one New Hampshire poll showed the race even and one showed Sununu with a 22% lead. Both turned out to be wrong. Turnout was a record high and Sununu won 53%-45%. Sununu carried every county and even carried Smith's hometown. Smith made a gracious concession statement and endorsed Sununu.

Now, having beaten New Hampshire's senior senator, Sununu faced New Hampshire's governor, Jeanne Shaheen. The Senate Republican campaign committee had been running ads against

Shaheen since the spring, focusing especially on education funding. This had been the central issue of her governorship. She was proud of extending kindergarten, regulating HMOs and joining the tri-state pool (with Maine and Vermont) to purchase prescription drugs at discount. But her real problem was how to respond to the state supreme court decision outlawing New Hampshire's local-based school financing. In 2000 Shaheen declined to take the pledge to oppose income and sales taxes and was whipsawed on both sides. She beat state Senator (and former U.S. Senator) Gordon Humphrey by only 49%-44%. Shaheen ran as a moderate on some issues. She said she supported the 2001 Bush tax cut and in October 2002 came out staunchly for the Iraq war resolution. She emphasized her support of abortion rights and with help from EMILY's List and other feminist groups and from likely presidential candidates she raised far more money than Sununu. She attacked Sununu for supporting "privatization" of Social Security. He responded with an articulate advocacy of voluntary individual investment accounts as part of Social Security—"modernization", as he put it.

The polls tightened in late October and national Democrats started to count this seat as a pickup. But the New Hampshire tax issue may have hurt Shaheen. She was on record in support of a sales tax and she was supporting gubernatorial nominee Mark Fernald, an outspoken advocate of an income tax. Fernald was defeated 59%-38% and Sununu defeated Shaheen 51%-47%. His margin was nearly 20,000 votes—eight times as great as the number of write-ins that resulted from a campaign by supporters of Bob Smith. (Now president of the Everglades Foundation, Smith mulled running for the Senate from Florida in 2004.)

In the Senate Sununu's voting record has moved closer to the center than during his House years. He has not always supported the Bush administration. In 2003 he voted against the Medicare/prescription drug bill as overexpensive and opposed the energy bill, partly because it barred a lawsuit by New Hampshire against the manufacturers of the gasoline additive MTBE, which has caused environmental damage. With Congressman Paul Ryan he sponsored a version of voluntary personal retirement accounts as part of Social Security; he remained a stalwart booster, even as Bush's initiative fizzled, and he criticized Democrats for their failure to offer an alternative. On the Commerce Committee he was active on telecom and other regulatory issues. The New Hampshire and Vermont senators sponsored a bill to change TV market definitions in small states so that satellite TV could carry more local stations. Sununu pushed for a bill providing federal and eliminating state regulation of Voice over Internet Protocol phone service. But in the July 2004 markup, the panel amended it with provisions allowing states to enact universal service fees, requirements to carry 911 and taxes on providers. In 2005, Sununu predicted that the Senate would pass a major telecom bill, and hoped it would create a framework to encourage Internet and voice data transmission. But telecom issues saw very little movement in 2006. Sununu's strong support for a tougher federal regulator for government sponsored enterprises Fannie Mae and Freddie Mac also fell flat. With Senator Tim Johnson, he filed a dramatic overhaul of regulation of the insurance industry. In January 2007, he called for a permanent ban on taxes of Internet connections and online sales.

Sununu surprised some cultural conservatives when he twice voted against the constitutional amendment to ban same-sex marriage (he said it should be a state issue unless courts overturn the Defense of Marriage Act) and opposed the House's uniform driver's license standards in the intelligence reorganization bill (he said there shouldn't be federal standards). With Larry Craig and Lisa Murkowski, he delayed renewal and in March 2006 forced revisions in the PATRIOT Act, including sunsets to several provisions, limits on access by law-enforcement officials to library and business records, plus the right to court appeals. In 2004, he was one of three senators to vote against a resolution commending Israel's Prime Minister Ariel Sharon's proposed withdrawal from the Gaza strip; in July 2006, he disapproved of Israel's attacks on public buildings and utilities in Lebanon.

In November 2006, Sununu got an early warning of the perils he faces when he comes for reelection in 2008. Both House Republicans from New Hampshire were defeated and Democrats took control of the state legislature. Another cause for concern: the state was the only one to vote against George W. Bush in 2004 after voting for him in 2000. In early 2007, MoveOn.org ran ads criticizing his vote against the Senate resolution opposing deployment of additional troops to Iraq. Early candidates who stepped forward included Katrina Swett, wife of 1996 Senate challenger Dick Swett and daughter of California Congressman Tom Lantos, former astronaut Jay Buckey and Portsmouth Mayor Steve Marchand. But when Jeanne Shaheen announced in September 2007 that she would seek a rematch in 2008, Swett and Marchand dropped out. It seems likely that this contest will be at least as close as Sununu's first Senate run.

FIRST DISTRICT

Rep. Carol Shea-Porter (D)

Elected 2006, 1st term; b. Dec. 1952, New York, NY; home, Rochester; U. of NH, B.A. 1975, M.P.A. 1979; Catholic; married (Gene).

Professional Career: Social worker; Comm. col. instructor; Lecturer.

DC Office: 1508 LHOB, 20515, 202-225-5456; Fax: 202-225-5822; Web site: shea-porter.house.gov.

District Offices: Dover, 603-743-4813; Manchester, 603-641-9536.

Committees: *Armed Services* (25th of 34 D): Military Personnel; Readiness. *Education & Labor* (27th of 27 D): Healthy Families & Communities; Workforce Protections.

Group Ratings and Key Votes: Newly Elected

Election Results

2006 general	Carol Shea-Porter	100,691	(51%)	($291,663)
	Jeb Bradley (R)	95,527	(49%)	($1,062,132)
2006 primary	Carol Shea-Porter (D)	12,497	(54%)	
	James Craig (D)	7,944	(34%)	
	Gary Dodds (D)	1,125	(5%)	
	Peter Sullivan (D)	1,021	(4%)	
	Other	563	(2%)	
2004 general	Jeb Bradley (R)	204,836	(63%)	($1,055,083)
	Justin Nadeau (D)	118,226	(37%)	($530,364)

The People		Race/Ethnic Origin	Ancestry	
Area size:	2,688 sq. mi.	95.1% White	Irish: 14.6%	English: 12.7%
Urban population:	66.6%	0.7% Black	French: 10.5%	
Rural population:	33.4%	1.2% Asian	**2004 Presidential Vote**	
Pop. 2000:	617,575	0.2% Native Am.	Bush (R) 171,013	(51%)
Pop. 2005 (est):	661,698	0.0% Hawaiian	Kerry (D) 163,191	(48%)
Median income:	$50,135	0.9% Two+ races	Other 2,749	(1%)
Poverty status:	6.7%	0.1% Other	**2000 Presidential Vote**	
Military veterans:	15.0%	1.6% Hispanic Origin	Bush (R) 136,474	(49%)
			Gore (D) 128,278	(46%)
			Other 11,545	(4%)
			Cook Partisan Voting Index: R + 0	
Occupation	Blue collar: 23.6%	White collar: 62.7%	Gray collar: 13.7%	

The greatest growth in New Hampshire over the past two decades has been in the southeast and south central parts of the state—the Seacoast and the Manchester area. Manchester was once famous for the Amoskeag Mills, the world's largest textile mill complex, and in the first half of the 20th century was the quintessential mill town, with a few mansions for mill owners and managers and close packed neighborhoods of frame houses for mill workers, many of them immigrants—from Quebec, Ireland and Greece (Manchester has America's largest percentage of Greek Americans). By the beginning of the 21st century it was something quite different, a high-tech city, with big shopping malls at freeway interchanges, a spiffy new airport and downtown arena, spruced up neighborhoods and growth extending to the wooded suburbs all around. The Seacoast, within easy commuting distance of Massachusetts, is a collection of towns of ancient pedigree and high-tech growth. The biggest city on the coast is Portsmouth, the colonial capital of New Hampshire, with its busy Naval Shipyard and old seaport with well-preserved houses and a booming economy, including many galleries and bars. In the 2005 base closing round, the Pentagon recommended closing the shipyard. But Portsmouth did not immediately panic: The shipyard had been recommended for closure in two previous rounds and in August 2005 it again managed to get removed from the list during the hearing stage. There is a sign of hope nearby: The successful redevelopment of Pease Air Force Base after its 1991 closing and conversion to the Pease International Tradeport, with what developers termed high-end office buildings in an international trade environment (plus a convenient airport runway), has driven the Seacoast (sometimes called e-coast) economy with more than 160 businesses and nearly 10,000 jobs. Not far to the southwest is Stratham, where Swiss chocolate-maker Lindt is planning a multi-million-dollar expansion, and Exeter, home of Phillips Exeter Academy, on a campus most colleges would envy. Development leaders are also looking to Quebec for opportunities to attract Canadian businesses interested in a U.S. distribution hub. A quarter of New Hampshire residents claim French or French-Canadian ties, and the state in 2008 plans to take part in celebrating Quebec's 400th anniversary.

The 1st Congressional District of New Hampshire includes the Manchester area and the Seacoast from Manchester and next-door Bedford, its most affluent suburb, east to Portsmouth. It also extends north to Laconia and Lake Winnipesaukee, studded with summer resorts and Ossipee in Carroll County, which promotes rock and ice climbing. Politically, this is the more Republican of New Hampshire's two congressional districts: people came here from Massachusetts not to replicate its high-tax environment but to get away from it. Manchester, the largest city in the state, still has more registered Democrats than Republicans—a relic of its mill town days—but usually votes Republican in general elections. Portsmouth, with its trendy coffee shops, is Democratic, and so are Durham, home of the University of New Hampshire, and nearby Dover, once a mill town. Most of the smaller towns on the Seacoast and to the north have been solidly Republican though that is changing. George W. Bush carried the district 49%-46% in 2000 and 51%-48% in 2004.

The new congresswoman from the 1st District is Carol Shea-Porter, a Democrat elected in one of the biggest upsets of 2006. Shea-Porter ousted two-term Republican Jeb Bradley to become the first woman elected to Congress from New Hampshire. She was born in New York City and grew up in a large extended family in New Hampshire. After her high school guidance counselor recommended she go to secretary school, Shea-Porter enrolled in the University of New Hampshire, and worked her way through college and grad school. She moved to Colorado with her husband, an Army officer stationed at the medical center. There she witnessed soldiers returning from the Vietnam War in need of medical and psychological care, an experience that would contribute to her anti-war candidacy decades later. She and her family moved to New Orleans, and then to the Washington, D.C. area, before returning to New Hampshire. Shea-Porter worked as a social worker, directed programs for senior citizens, and lectured at a community college. She worked on former Gen. Wesley Clark's 2004 presidential primary campaign and served as chair of the Rochester Democrats; afterward, she cultivated a network of liberal activists and began the practice of following Bradley from event to event, asking pointed questions and learning about the issues. In February 2005, Shea-Porter was escorted from a town hall meeting with President Bush when she removed her sweater to reveal a T-shirt that read, "Turn your back on Bush." On relief trips to New Orleans, she concluded the federal government had failed to help its citizens recover from Hurricane Katrina and decided to run for Congress.

Shea-Porter launched her campaign in February 2006 with an unwavering anti-war platform. She advocated the creation of a federal institute dedicated to reducing dependence on foreign oil and for a nationalized health care system. She originally called for all troops to be withdrawn from Iraq six months after the November 7 election, before adjusting her position to call on the Bush administration to set a timetable. National Democrats questioned her viability in a general election and three months before the September 12 primary, the Democratic Congressional Campaign Committee announced it would back state House Minority Leader Jim Craig in the four-way primary. Craig proved to be a disappointing candidate; he ran well in his Manchester base, but lost nearly everywhere else in the district. Shea-Porter had assembled a deeply committed grassroots network that turned out many voters that the state party had failed to identify. Her 54%-34% victory stunned many political observers and even the candidate herself: "Oh my God, I think I'm going to faint," she told supporters on primary night.

Feisty, quirky (she is the only member of Congress who refuses to disclose her exact date of birth) and seemingly indefatigable, Shea-Porter entered the general election a decided underdog: she was outspent by a more than 3-to-1 margin. Her elderly mother, a lifelong Republican, recorded a TV spot. "We can't fire the president, but we can vote out his supporters in Congress," she said. "Please vote for my daughter, Carol Shea-Porter. She's a hard worker and I know she'll do a great job." Bradley defended Bush on the Iraq war and argued that withdrawing troops would destabilize the Middle East; polls showed Bradley leading narrowly but hampered by Bush's unpopularity. The largest union at the Portsmouth Naval Shipyard, which Bradley helped protect during the 2005 base-closing round, endorsed Shea-Porter.

Three weeks before the election, national Republican strategists recognized Shea-Porter's late surge and dispatched help to Bradley. National Democrats remained skeptical and instead pumped $1.1 million into the neighboring 2d District in a successful campaign to elect Paul Hodes, leaving Shea-Porter to pull off her improbable victory alone. Aided by Bush's negative ratings, a shift in favor of Democratic registrations and the landslide reelection of Democratic Governor John Lynch, Shea-Porter won 51%-49%. The victory surprised even Democratic National Committee Chairman Howard Dean, the former governor of neighboring Vermont, who could not remember Shea-Porter's name in a morning-after press conference.

Bradley said he got caught up in a "perfect storm" in 2006, and signaled early that he was planning on a rematch. John Stephen, who lost to Bradley in the 2002 Republican primary, resigned as the state's health and human services commissioner in July 2007 and seemed to be preparing for a run as well. Shea-Porter, spurned by national Democrats in 2006, didn't seem too worried. She turned down a chance to participate in the DCCC's "Frontline" program for vulnerable members, explaining that she wanted to run a low-budget campaign similar to her 2006 race.

SECOND DISTRICT

Rep. Paul Hodes (D)

Elected 2006, 1st term; b. Mar. 21, 1951, New York, NY; home, Concord; Dartmouth Col., A.B. 1972, Boston Col., J.D. 1978; Jewish; married (Peggo Horstmann Hodes).

Professional Career: NH Asst. Atty. Gen., 1979-82; NH Special Prosecutor, 1982-83; Practicing atty., 1983-2006; Musician and founder, Peggosus, 1985-present.

DC Office: 506 CHOB, 20515, 202-225-5206; Fax: 202-225-2946; Web site: hodes.house.gov.

District Offices: Concord, 603-223-9814; Keene, 603-358-1023; Littleton, 603-444-8967; Nashua, 603-579-6913.

Committees: *Financial Services* (27th of 37 D): Capital Markets, Insurance & Government Sponsored Enterprises; Financial Institutions & Consumer Credit. *Oversight & Government Reform* (20th of 23 D): Information Policy, Census & National Archives; National Security & Foreign Affairs.

Group Ratings and Key Votes: Newly Elected

Election Results

2006 general	Paul Hodes (D)	108,743	(53%)	($1,638,729)
	Charles Bass (R)	94,088	(46%)	($1,237,271)
	Other	3,461	(2%)	
2006 primary	Paul Hodes (D) .... unopposed			
2004 general	Charles Bass (R)	191,187	(58%)	($717,749)
	Paul Hodes (D)	124,275	(38%)	($625,062)
	Other..	11,726	(4%)	

The People		Race/Ethnic Origin	Ancestry	
Area size:	6,662 sq. mi.	95.1% White	Irish: 13.0%	English: 12.9%
Urban population:	51.7%	0.6% Black	French: 10.3%	
Rural population:	48.3%	1.3% Asian	**2004 Presidential Vote**	
Pop. 2000:	618,211	0.2% Native Am.	Kerry (D) 177,320	(52%)
Pop. 2005 (est):	646,327	0.0% Hawaiian	Bush (R) 160,224	(47%)
Median income:	$48,762	0.9% Two+ races	Other 3,165	(1%)
Poverty status:	6.4%	0.1% Other	**2000 Presidential Vote**	
Military veterans:	15.0%	1.7% Hispanic Origin	Gore (D) 134,343	(48%)
			Bush (R) 132,336	(47%)
			Other 12,801	(5%)
			Cook Partisan Voting Index: D + 3	

Occupation	Blue collar: 24.7%	White collar: 62.1%	Gray collar: 13.2%

Political reporters covering New Hampshire's first-in-the-nation political primary usually stay in Manchester, the state's largest city and within an hour or so of driving time from the rest of the state except for the North Country. Yet there are other noteworthy cities and towns in New Hampshire. Concord, north of Manchester, is the state capital; on one side of Main Street is the handsome, small, granite Capitol, and on the other you can usually find the headquarters of the two political parties and many candidates: an entire state's politics within 100 yards. Nashua, south of Manchester and on the Massachusetts line, is the state's second largest city, a high-tech and financial services center that has been booming for two decades. To the east is prosperous and growing Salem, first chartered in 1750 and the largest of the border suburbs. To the west of Nashua, past the pleasant country around Mount Monadnock, is Keene, the hub of southwest New Hampshire. To the north are the towns along the Connecticut River, some mill towns and others in vacation home territory; New Hampshire prosperity has spread to most of these, just across the river from Vermont. Hanover, home of Dartmouth College, is an unbearably picturesque tiny town amid the mountains. And every political reporter's itinerary has to include a trip, usually by plane, to the little lumber mill city of Berlin in the midst of the North Country – now suffering from the closing of Fraser Mill in 2006 – and perhaps also to Dixville Notch, where the town's roughly two dozen voters cast their votes a minute past midnight and provide the first reported returns in every presidential election; Neil Tillotson, the town moderator in every election from 1960 to 2000, was unhappily not there in 2004; he died in 2002 at 102. (Hint for election analysts: if Dixville Notch doesn't go heavily Republican, the Republicans are in trouble.)

The 2d Congressional District of New Hampshire includes Concord, Nashua, Salem, Keene, the Connecticut River counties, Hanover, Berlin and Dixville Notch. It also includes Mount Washington, with its spectacularly violent weather, with winds measured up to 231 miles per hour, and the Bretton Woods resort where the world monetary system was established at a conference in 1944. Politically this is mixed country, but much of it has been trending Democratic. Nashua is more Democratic than Manchester, Salem more Republican. The area between Mount Monadnock and Keene and the territory running north along the Connecticut River to Hanover and Dartmouth has become very Democratic: much like Vermont across the river. Overall, this is the more Democratic of New Hampshire's two districts, and it got more so in 2004, after heavy campaigning for a year by backers of Howard Dean: it voted 48%-47% for Al Gore in 2000 and 52%-47% for John Kerry in 2004.

The new congressman from the 2d District is Paul Hodes, a Democrat elected in a 2006 upset over Republican Charles Bass. He grew up in New York City, the grandson of Russian and Hungarian Jewish immigrants. His younger brother died of Hodgkins disease in his childhood. Hodes became disillusioned by the Vietnam War before graduating from Dartmouth College, his father's alma mater. After college, Hodes worked as an actor, playwright, musician (he began playing guitar at 15) and documentary filmmaker, before he accepted his grandmother's advice to have a fallback plan and studied law at Boston College. Fresh out of law school, Hodes was hired by then-New Hampshire Attorney General David Souter as a state prosecutor, then went into private practice in Concord. He continued to pursue musical interests: He and his wife, Peggo, founded Peggosus, a children's rock group whose repertoire includes the songs "If My School Was a Zoo" and "Cheerios in My Kazoo" (President Clinton invited the duo to perform at the White House in 1996).

Hodes first ran for Congress in 2004 and lost badly to Bass, 58%-38%—the six-term incumbent's biggest margin of victory ever. But Hodes came again in 2006 when the political environment was far more hostile to Republicans. This time he had more support from the national party and raised much more money, outspending Bass $1.6 million to $1.2 million. Bass claimed he was an "independent voice for New Hampshire" in an attempt to distance himself from the unpopular Republican congressional leadership and the Bush administration. His claim was not entirely unfounded: In January 2006, Bass helped launch the petition for new House Republican leadership elections that prompted former Majority Leader Tom DeLay to relinquish any plans to retake his post. Bass also cast maverick votes against drilling in the Arctic National Wildlife Refuge and against the same-sex marriage ban. Hodes nevertheless sought to tie his opponent to President Bush, calling for a "new course for this country." The two candidates sparred over the Iraq war; national Democrats said Bass stood "toe-to-toe with [the president] on the war."

Bass appeared to be in reasonably good shape in the summer, but the Democratic Congressional Campaign Committee nevertheless signaled it would target the race; the liberal MoveOn.org also began running a television ad suggesting Bass had voted for wasteful Iraq reconstruction funds, including payments to Halliburton. Bass did not appear to be vulnerable until late in the campaign, starting with the Congressman Mark Foley congressional page scandal. As the incumbent's polling lead started to fade, both national parties took an interest in the race and began pouring in money. The National Republican Congressional Committee spent $450,000 on the race and ran television ads charging that "liberal Paul Hodes wants to raise taxes."

The NRCC lobbed automated telephone calls into the district, but discontinued them after they ran afoul of state law and under pressure from the state attorney general. The DCCC returned fire by pumping $1.1 million into ads accusing Bass of voting to raise his own salary and to increase the national debt. Bass never recovered; Hodes won 53%-46%. After the election, Hodes won a seat on the Financial Services Committee and was elected president of the Democratic freshman class. In Congress, Hodes sponsored a bill to create the Northern Border Regional Development Commission to invest federal money into economic development and job creation in the Northeast. This district leans Democratic but only slightly, so Hodes can expect that Republicans will attempt to recruit a top tier challenger in 2008. Venture capitalist Stephen Gray was among those considering a run for the Republican nomination.

★ NEW JERSEY ★

"A valley of humility between two mountains of conceit": That is what Benjamin Franklin called New Jersey, which even in colonial days was overshadowed by the metropolises of New York and Philadelphia. New Jersey was named by King James II, then Duke of York, for the Channel Island on which he was sheltered during the English Civil War. New Jersey was plagued in its early years by rival claims from its neighbors and, still defensive, went to the Supreme Court in the 1980s to argue that it and not New York owns the Statue of Liberty and Ellis Island; New Jersey eventually got most of the islands' acreage, but New York got the immigrant museum and Great Hall which are built on fill land. But New Jersey has much to say for itself. It is "a sort of laboratory in which the best blood is prepared for other communities to thrive on," Woodrow Wilson said when he was governor, just a tad defensively.

Today, New Jersey is the nation's eleventh most populous state: It boomed in the 1980s, suffered sharply in the early 1990s recession, came back strongly, then fell back by the tech bust of 2000. New Jersey was the home of Thomas Edison and of the old Bell Labs, and a decade ago it was one of the centers of the telecommunications business. But Lucent, the successor to Bell Labs, was burned in the high tech bust; its stock fell from $65 to $3 and it was acquired by the French firm Alcatel in 2006; its former parent AT&T shut down its Basking Ridge campus in 2002. New Jersey is the home of several of the nation's biggest pharmaceutical firms—Merck, Johnson & Johnson, Bristol-Myers Squibb, Novartis, Schering-Plough—with complexes spread out through north and central Jersey. But they have been troubled by class action lawsuits and by the threat of policies—reimportation of drugs from Canada, government negotiation of drug prices—which would destroy their business model and force sharp cuts in research on new drugs. These industries have given the state a high-income, high-education work force, but one ill at ease in an economy whose creative destruction richly rewards those who anticipate the future but imposes harsh penalties on those who, by mistake or misfortune, don't. New Jersey is by most measures exceedingly prosperous: in 2000 it passed Connecticut and posted the nation's highest median household income. But its hold on that position seems tenuous. It still trailed in per capita income and wealth and has a lower percentage of college graduates than Colorado, Connecticut, Maryland, Massachusetts, Virginia, and the District of Columbia; this is the home not only of high-income Ph.D.'s, but also of The Sopranos. This is prosperous middle-income country, with more two-car than one-car families but fewer limousines than Manhattan, with an estimated 13,500 $1 million houses but not the multi-million dollar co-ops of Manhattan or mansions of Greenwich, Connecticut.

Within New Jersey's close boundaries is great diversity, geographically from beaches to mountains, demographically from old Quaker stock to new Hispanics, economically from inner city slums to hunt country mansions. Though New York writers are inclined to look on New Jersey as a land of 1940s diners and 1970s shopping malls, this state much more closely resembles the rest of America than does Manhattan, though drivers will find some peculiarities: horizontal traffic lights, jughandle intersections (you turn off to the right, and then wait for the light to make a left turn), a ban on self-service gas stations. The Jersey City row houses seen on emerging from the Holland Tunnel, many renovated by Wall Street commuters and Latin immigrants, give way within a few miles to the skyscrapers of Newark and its new Performing Arts Center. Farther out are comfortably packed middle-income suburbs and the horse country around Far Hills, the university town of Princeton, old industrial cities like Paterson and Trenton, and dozens of suburban towns and small

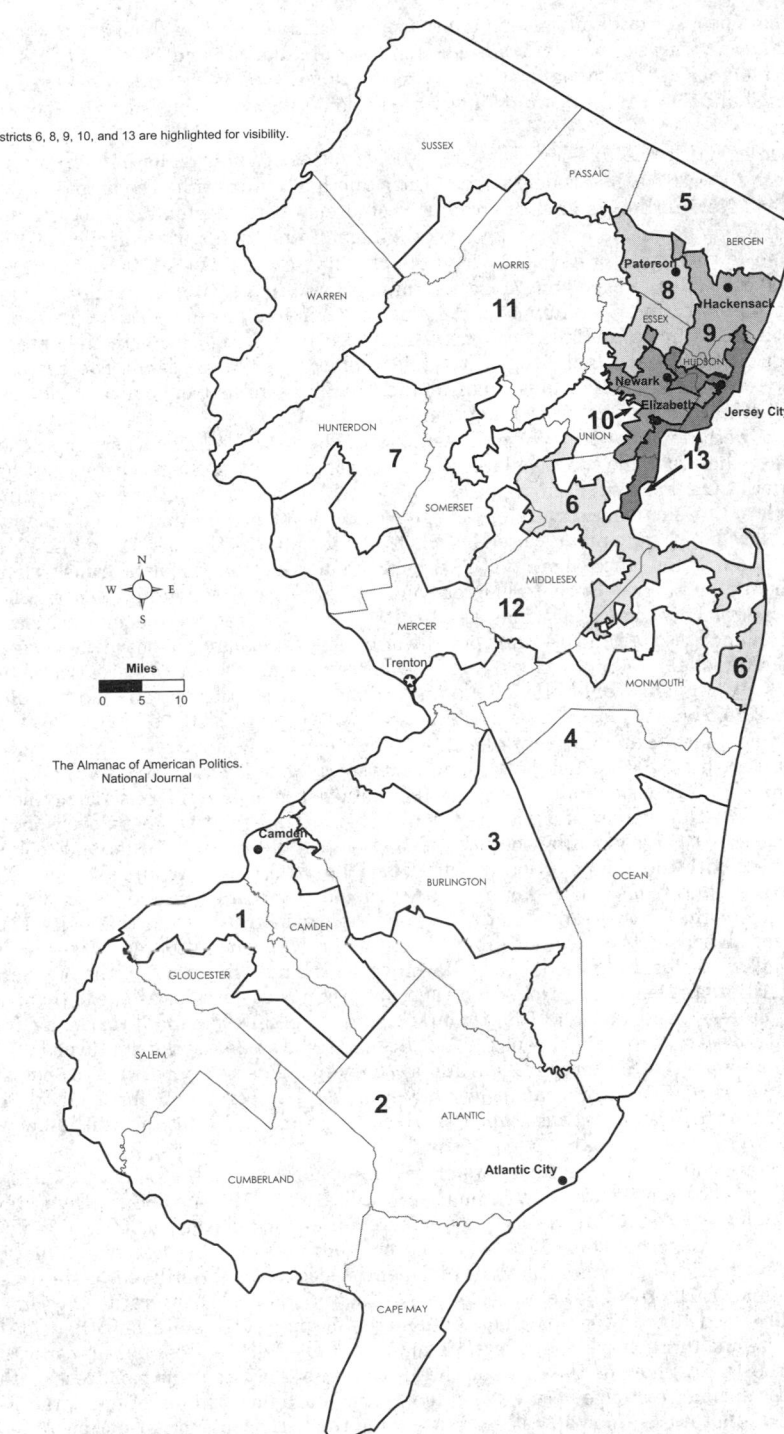

Districts 6, 8, 9, 10, and 13 are highlighted for visibility.

SUSSEX

PASSAIC

5

MORRIS

BERGEN

Paterson

8

Hackensack

WARREN

11

ESSEX

9

HUDSON

HUNTERDON

Newark

Elizabeth

Jersey City

7

10

UNION

13

SOMERSET

6

N
W   E
S

6

MIDDLESEX

Miles

12

0   5   10

MERCER

MONMOUTH

Trenton

The Almanac of American Politics.
National Journal

4

Camden

3

BURLINGTON

OCEAN

CAMDEN

1

GLOUCESTER

SALEM

2

ATLANTIC

CUMBERLAND

Atlantic City

CAPE MAY

Congressional district boundaries were first effective for 2002.

factory cities where people work and raise families over generations. Among them are commuter towns like Middletown, whose commuter trails lead to Lower Manhattan, and which lost dozens of neighbors on September 11. A year later, only 37% of New Jersey citizens said their lives had returned to normal and 29% said they would never be the same; 43% said they thought about the attacks every day.

Whoever has legal title to Ellis Island, New Jersey has long been a magnet for immigrants, and it is again today. In 2000, 29% of its residents were born in another country or had a parent who was; only California and New York have larger percentages of foreign-born residents. Hudson County, the land along the ridge opposite Manhattan, was the home to hundreds of thousands of Irish, Italian, Polish and Jewish immigrants in the early 20th century; in 2003 it was 41% Hispanic, with Cubans, Puerto Ricans, Dominicans and Mexicans. Immigrants are plentiful in the little middle-American towns of Bergen County, Filipinos in Bergenfield, Guatemalans in Fairview, Koreans in Leonia, Indians in Lodi, Chinese in Palisades Park. The old central cities of Elizabeth and Paterson were half-Hispanic in 2000 and Camden, opposite Philadelphia, was 39% Hispanic. There is still a black majority in Newark, but that includes many of the Brazilians in the Ironbound district. New Jersey has all the ethnic variety that America offers.

In the last two decades, a new New Jersey has sprouted. The oil tank farms and swamplands of the Jersey Meadows have become sports palaces and office complexes; the Singer factory in Elizabeth, the Western Electric factory in Kearny, the Ford plant in Mahwah, the Shulton plant in Clifton are all gone, replaced by shopping centers or hotels or other development, and the GM plant in Linden, the last New Jersey auto plant, closed in April 2005; the intersection of I-78 and I-287 has become a major shopping and office edge city; U.S. 1 north from Princeton to North Brunswick has become one of the nation's high-tech centers. Even some of New Jersey's long-ailing central cities are perking up. New Jersey increasingly has an identity of its own. It is the home of big league football, basketball and hockey franchises and of the world's longest expanse of boardwalks on the Jersey Shore from Cape May to Sandy Hook. And New Jersey is one of America's great gambling centers: Atlantic City, an hour from Philadelphia and two hours from Manhattan, had gambling revenues in 2006 of $5.5 billion, a close second behind the Las Vegas strip's $6.7 billion.

State government played an important role in building New Jersey identity and pride. Governor Brendan Byrne in the 1970s started the Meadowlands sports complex and got casino gambling legalized in Atlantic City. Governor Tom Kean in the 1980s started education reforms and promoted the state shamelessly ("New Jersey and you: perfect together"). The revolt against Governor Jim Florio's tax increase in 1990 was led by the first all-New Jersey talk radio station and took on national significance with the 1993 election of Christine Todd Whitman, who later became EPA administrator. In the 1990s crime and welfare rolls dropped, but auto insurance and property taxes remain the highest in the nation—and health insurance is expensive as well, thanks to state mandates requiring all policies to cover all manner of treatments. New Jersey, contained within two of the nation's biggest metropolitan areas, was a harbinger of the national trend in the big metro areas toward Bill Clinton's Democrats. Not so long ago, suburban New Jersey was one of the most Republican of big states: It voted 56%-42% for the first George Bush in 1988 and it turned against Florio in 1993 and moved toward Republicans in 1994. But in 1996 New Jersey voters, turned off by the congressional Republicans' Southern leaders and by the national party's opposition to abortion and gun control, voted 54%-36% for Clinton and 53%-43% for Democrat Bob Torricelli for the Senate. In 1997 Whitman, despite cutting taxes, was reelected by only 47%-46% over little-known Democrat Jim McGreevey.

In the years since 2000, the balance in New Jersey politics has favored the Democrats. In two elections each for governor and senator New Jersey has voted between 53% and 56% for Democrats and between 42% and 44% for Republicans. The numbers tell a story. Governor 2001: 56%-42%. Senator 2002: 54%-44%. Governor 2005: 53%-43%. Senator 2006: 53%-44%. In these years, surprisingly, the worst Democratic result was in the 2004 presidential election, when still reasonably fresh memories of September 11 probably helped George W. Bush: 53%-46% Democratic. On a map showing the results by city and townships, Democrats carry the spine of the state, on either side of the Metroliner route and through the South Jersey suburbs of Philadelphia; Republicans carry the outliers, most of the Jersey Shore on the east and the affluent suburban and exurban areas on the northwest. Democrats' margins have been augmented by the steady absorption of immigrants—some 40,000 take out naturalization papers every year—and the outflow of modest-income Americans from the formerly middle American suburbs within close range of the Metroliner spine.

Democrats have been helped by a number of factors. First, the fact that New Jersey is the second most expensive political state in the nation, because candidates who hope to compete have to buy New York and Philadelphia television, which reach more people than live in the number two population state, Texas. That has helped Democrats because Jon Corzine, who amassed a fortune of $300 million when Goldman Sachs went public, spent more than $100 million on his races for senator in 2000 and for governor in 2005 and has generously subsidized other Democratic campaigns in between. Second is the habit of high-income, highly-educated New Jersey politics to defer to the choices of county and city political machines, of varying degrees of competence, cronyism and corruption. It is, astonishingly, a great advantage in both parties to have the designation of the local county party on the primary ballot. A 1993 campaign finance law allowed county parties to take contributions 18 times as large as candidates could, so money is increasingly raised by chairmen of parties that have control of local government and can dole out contracts—the Jersey term is "pay to play"—and then "wheeled," or doled out, to favored candidates all over the state. Corzine has given hundreds of thousands of dollars to county Democratic machines which has enabled him to wield the power once held by the bosses of yore. Third has been the readiness of Democrats to pitch losers aside and the willingness of the legal and political establishments to go along. In September 2002 Senator Bob Torricelli, plagued by scandals, dropped out of his race for reelection and the state Supreme Court, in a bipartisan decision, upheld the right of Democrats to substitute on the ballot former Senator Frank Lautenberg (whose relations with Torricelli were famously acerbic). In August 2004 Governor Jim McGreevey, already in trouble because of his ties to later-convicted fundraiser Charles Kushner, announced that he would resign November 15; this was prompted by the revelation that he had appointed a gay lover as his homeland security advisor. McGreevey's delayed announcement prevented a special election in 2004 (which a Republican might have won), installed in office as successor state Senate President Richard Codey (an amiable man who gets along with most New Jersey politicians) and allowed Corzine, with his capacity to spend unlimited amounts, to muscle Codey aside and seize the gubernatorial nomination, which proved to be tantamount to election.

What New Jersey gets out of this is a state with significant achievements and significant handicaps. McGreevey, Codey and Corzine all pushed for state subsidy of stem cell research, and in 2006 the legislature voted for a $270 million to subsidize this research at the New Jersey Institute of Technology in Newark, the Rutgers campuses in New Brunswick and Camden, and several other facilities. The Highlands Water Protection and Planning Act, passed in 2004, sealed off one-ninth of the state's land in the northwestern hills from development, with delayed if any compensation to landowners. The legislature, given an ultimatum by the state Supreme Court—one of the most activist state courts over the last half-century—passed a civil unions law in December 2006. Corzine, over the opposition of Speaker Joe Roberts, in 2006 pushed through an increase in the sales tax, with an assurance that half the revenues would be spent on property tax relief. He pledged to support all-day kindergarten, community health clinics, rehabilitation of Port Newark and low-interest loans for first-time homebuyers. New Jersey, for many years the site of vibrant suburban growth, has seen since 2006 a domestic outflow of 3% of its 2000 population, matched only a little by a 4% immigrant inflow; can its pharmaceutical and telecom sectors continue to support a government that is growing as a percentage of the private sector economy? New Jersey honors its recent past with 9/11 memorials, a statute of an eagle in flight on the Eagle Rock Reservation in West Orange, on a ridge overlooking the Manhattan skyline 15 miles away, and an American eagle grasping a beam of the World Trade Center in Monmouth County, where so many residents left their cars in the parking lots that bright September morning never to return. New Jersey is headed to a different future, with the outcome uncertain.

The People		Race/Ethnic Origin			Military veterans: 672,217 (10.6%)	
Pop. 2006 (est):	8,724,560	5,557,209	66.0%	White	WWII: 26.3%	Korea: 15.8%
Pop. 2000:	8,414,350	1,096,171	13.0%	Black	Vietnam: 28.1%	Gulf War: 6.2%
Pop. 1990:	7,730,188	477,012	5.7%	Asian	**Most populous cities (2006):**	
Change 1990-2000:	Up 8.6%	11,338	0.1%	Native Am.	1. Newark	281,402
% of U.S. total:	3.0%	2,175	0.0%	Hawaiian	2. Jersey City	241,789
Pop. rank:	9th of 50	133,689	1.6%	Two+ races	3. Paterson	148,708
Area size:	8,721 sq. mi.	19,565	0.2%	Other	4. Elizabeth	126,179
State Native:	53.4%	1,117,191	13.3%	Hisp. Origin	5. Trenton	83,923
Non-citizen:	9.4%	**Ancestry**				
Language		Italian: 13.8%		Irish: 12.2%	Urban population: 94.3%	
English: 73.0%	Spanish: 11.7%	German: 9.7%		Polish: 5.3%	Rural population: 5.7%	
Other Eur.: 10.4%		English: 4.8%				

Education		Work Sector		Legislature	
H.S. Grad:	82.1%	Private: 80.8%	Govt: 13.9%	Senate	22 D 18 R
College Grad:	29.8%	Self: 5.0%	Family: 0.2%	G. Assembly	49 D 31 R
Industry		Unemployment: 5.8%		Legislative Term Limits: No	
Agri: 0.3%	Con: 5.6%	**Household Income**		**Registered Voters**	
Fin: 8.9%	Info: 4.4%	<15k: 11.7%	15-35k: 19.4%	D: 1,150,184	(23.7%)
Mfg: 17.9%	Prof: 31.3%	35-50k: 14.3%	50-100k: 33.3%	R: 890,118	(18.3%)
Public: 4.5%	Trade: 15.7%	100-150k: 12.8%	>150k: 8.6%	O: 2,820,977	(58.0%)
Other: 11.3%		Median: $55,146			
Occupation		Poverty status: 8.5%			
Blue collar: 19.7%	White collar: 66.5%	**Home Value**			
Gray collar: 13.8%		<50k: 3.0% 50-100k: 14.4% 100-200k: 46.1% 200-300k: 20.4%			
		300-500k: 11.7% >500k: 4.4% Median: $167,900			

Presidential politics   For most of the 20th century New Jersey was a close state in close presidential elections, giving small margins to winners in 1960 and 1968 and to losers in 1948 and 1976, but no more. In the 1980s the vast suburban expanses of New Jersey leaned toward the Republicans; since 1995 they have leaned to the Democrats, though a little less so in 2004. This is a state with relatively few strong-belief Christians and with a high number of seculars and Jews; sophisticated and cynical, it reacted strongly against the Southern-accented Republicans of Newt Gingrich's revolution.

In 2004 Bush campaign strategists kept an eye on New Jersey polls to see if for some reason— the impact of September 11, for example—it might qualify for target status. A few public polls showed the race close or tied, but others showed John Kerry well ahead. South Jersey saw all the spots aimed at target state Pennsylvania on Philadelphia TV; but the campaigns never bought

2004 Presidential Vote
Kerry (D)	1,911,430	(53%)
Bush (R)	1,670,003	(46%)
Nader (I)	19,418	(1%)
Other	10,840	(0%)

2004 Democratic Presidential Primary
Kerry (D)	198,213	(92%)
Kucinich (D)	9,251	(4%)
LaRouche (D)	4,514	(2%)
Ballard (D)	2,826	(1%)

2000 Presidential Vote
Gore (D)	1,788,850	(56%)
Bush (R)	1,284,173	(40%)
Nader (Green)	94,554	(3%)
Other	19,649	(1%)

time on the New York stations that reach 70% of the state. The Kerry campaign, wisely as it turned out, did not flinch and spend much time or money in New Jersey. Kerry carried the state 53%-46%, a solid margin but considerably smaller than Gore's, indeed smaller than Kerry's margin in the target state of Maine. The NEP exit poll showed interesting differences from 2000. Bush carried Catholics with 58%, up 7% from 2000; Archbishop John Myers of Newark said in May 2004 that any elected official who supports abortion rights was not worthy to receive communion. Bush won 24% among Jews (7% of the electorate, one of the highest figures in the nation), up 8% from 2000. The Bush campaign did much organizing work among Latinos, and they voted for Kerry by only 56%-43%; Bush's percentage among Latinos was much closer to his percentage among whites (54%) than among blacks (17%). And his percentages among blacks and Latinos were up 6% and 8% from 2000. New Jersey looks to be on the verge of being a competitive state in presidential elections again. Geographically, Bush's greatest gains over 2000 came in Monmouth County, many of whose residents died on 9/11, and in Ocean County, New Jersey's fastest-growing county, with many retirees from the metro New York area.

For years, New Jersey's June presidential primary was overshadowed by California's on the same day. In 1996 California voted in March, and New Jersey did not get to the polls until two months after the nominations were sewn up. In 1998 the state Senate refused to move the primary to March. But in April 2007, with the approval of Governor Jon Corzine, the New Jersey primary was moved, like so many others, to February 5, 2008. This may make the state less of a focus of campaigning than many hoped. Hillary Clinton, from across-the-river New York, led in early primary polls (and got Corzine's endorsement in April 2007). And New Jersey Republicans, alert to the consequences for their county party organizations' clout, swiftly moved to make New Jersey a winner-take-all state, knowing that Rudolph Giuliani was leading in polls of New Jersey Republicans. So one prospect is that, if New York as well as New Jersey votes on February 5, that other candidates will concede these contests to Clinton and Giuliani—and save the money they would otherwise have to spend on New York TV.

Congressional districting   New Jersey has a Congressional Redistricting Commission, made up of 12 members appointed by the legislative and party leaders of both parties; they pick a 13th as arbiter, and in both 1991 and 2001 chose Professor Alan Rosenthal of the Eagleton Institute at Rutgers. He can break a tie, produce a compromise plan of his own and see if a majority will accept it or forward two plans to the state Supreme Court. In 1991 Rosenthal picked the

110th Congress Lineup
7 D   6 R
109th Congress Lineup
7 D   6 R

Republican plan, with grotesquely shaped districts. But given New Jersey's post-1994 Democratic trend, by 2000 it yielded the Republicans only 6 of the state's 13 seats. The commission first met in July 2001, two days after the 13 incumbents had agreed on a bipartisan congressional delegation plan. The biggest changes were in the 12th District, which Democrat Rush Holt had won three times by narrow margins, and by just 651 votes in 2000, and the 7th District, which freshman Republican Mike Ferguson had won by just 52%-46% in 2000. Furious attempts were made to change the plan by Republican Finn Caspersen Jr., who wanted to challenge Holt, and Democrat Susan Bass Levin, who had run unsuccessfully in the 3d in 2000 and wanted to have Cherry Hill, where she was mayor, placed in the heavily Democratic 1st so she could run if incumbent Rob Andrews should retire. But Camden County Democratic Chairman George Norcross had other candidates in mind, and Ferguson was bound to resist the major changes needed to put Caspersen's very Republican hometown of Bedminster into the 12th. Anyway, Rosenthal liked the incumbent-protection plan, and in October it was adopted with slight changes. The result is a map with very erose district lines and oddly shaped districts, drawn explicitly to protect incumbents and blessed by an esteemed political scientist. The partisan tilt is plain from the presidential election returns. Within these lines, George W. Bush carried only three of these districts in 2000, when he won 40% of the vote in New Jersey. But in 2004, when he won 46%, he carried all six of the districts represented by Republicans.

New Jersey is likely to lose a seat after the 2010 Census, as it did after the Censuses of 1970 and 1980; it has grown slowly, and was passed in population by Georgia in 2002 and North Carolina in 2005. Any new plan will surely maintain the majority-black 10th and the heavily Hispanic 13th Districts in their current form (though the latter will presumably have to be renumbered), and the lines are unlikely to be disturbed much in South Jersey, which has grown more than the rest of the state. That means squeezing out a North Jersey seat. One candidate is the 7th District, where incumbent Republican Mike Ferguson won by only 49%-48% in 2006, but Democrats may not want to eliminate it if they capture it in 2008 or 2010. For Republicans the favored target would probably be the 8th, centered on Paterson; its Democratic towns could be added to the 9th, 10th and 13th Districts, which will have to be expanded due to low population growth.

Governor

Jon Corzine (D)

Elected 2005, term expires Jan. 2010, 1st term; b. Jan. 1, 1947, Taylorville, IL; home, Summit; U. of IL (Urbana-Champaign), B.A. 1969; U. of Chicago, M.B.A. 1973; Christian; divorced.

Military Career: Marine Corps Reserve, 1969-75.

Elected Office: U.S. Senate, 2000-05.

Professional Career: Officer, Continental IL Natl. Bank, 1970-73; Asst. V.P., BancOhio, 1973-75; Goldman Sachs, Bond Trader 1975-80, Partner 1980-99, Chmn. & CEO 1994-99.

Office: P.O. Box 001, Trenton, 08625, 609-292-6000; Fax: 609-292-3454; Web site: www.state.nj.us/governor.

2005 general	Jon Corzine (D)	1,224,493	(53%)
	Douglas Forrester (R)	985,235	(43%)
	Other	80,277	(4%)
2005 primary	Jon Corzine (D)	207,670	(88%)
	James Kelly (D)	19,512	(8%)
	Francis Tenaglio (D)	8,596	(4%)
2001 general	James McGreevey (D)	1,256,853	(56%)
	Bret Schundler (R)	928,174	(42%)

Jon Corzine was elected senator from New Jersey in 2000 and governor of New Jersey in 2005, after two campaigns in which he spent record amounts of money. Corzine grew up on a family farm in Downstate Illinois, far from New Jersey; he went to college at the University of Illinois, business school at the University of Chicago and served six years in the Marine Corps Reserve. In 1975 he joined Goldman Sachs in New York; his entry-level position included fetching coffee for his superiors. Corzine was a successful bond trader and a protege of Robert Rubin, who became Treasury Secretary in the Clinton administration. In 1980 Corzine was made a general partner and in 1994 he became co-chairman and CEO. In May 1999 Goldman Sachs went public, and the $3.6 billion initial public offering netted Corzine more than $300 million; he retired in 1999 after a management shakeup. Aside from contributing to Democratic (and some Republican) candidates, he was not involved in politics, indeed did not vote in primary elections from 1988 to 1998 or in the 1991, 1995 and 1998 general elections; in 1997 he co-chaired a presidential commission on increasing investment in technology, infrastructure and schools.

In early 1999 a Senate race was probably the farthest thing from Corzine's mind. Then, in February 1999, Senator Frank Lautenberg announced he would not run again in 2000 (Lautenberg later returned to win election to Senator Bob Torricelli's seat in 2002). Plunging immediately into the race was former Governor Jim Florio, still unpopular for the $2.8 billion tax increase he secured in 1990. In April, Governor Christine Todd Whitman, presumably the strongest possible Republican candidate, announced she was running; she came close to beating Senator Bill Bradley in 1990 and defeated Florio in 1993. Many Democratic leaders, including Torricelli, feared that Whitman would win the seat, and scurried around to find other contenders. They found Corzine, with $300 million and without a job. He started running, going around the state to meet leaders of the county Democratic organizations, who are considered vital in the primary, and, it was revealed much later, contributing generously to them and to community organizations. His great wealth and willingness to spend it cleared the field; Whitman withdrew in September 1999. Corzine's money talked even while most New Jersey voters had never heard of him.

Still, Florio campaigned aggressively. He attacked Corzine's inexperience and spotty voting record. Even so, New Jersey Democratic leaders dreaded that Florio would lose to even the little-known candidates running for the Republican nomination. In March, three months before the primary, Corzine went up with TV ads in the New York and Philadelphia markets. Corzine's investment—he spent $35 million up to the June primary—paid off. He won a 58%-42% victory.

After the primary, Corzine cut back on spending—for a while. The Republican primary, with a pathetically low turnout, was won by 7th District Congressman Bob Franks—a member of the same church as Corzine. Corzine's ads talked about his big-government positions in appealing terms, but he made a political neophyte's mistakes and got some bad publicity. In early September he told the Sierra Club he had voted for an open space referendum in 1998; but he had not voted at all that year. Still stuck below 50% in the polls, he started running negative ads against Franks two weeks later. He had been refusing to make his income tax returns public, on the ground that they violated a confidentiality agreement with Goldman Sachs. Then in mid-September he released records showing that in 1996-99 he made $145 million, paid $43 million in taxes and contributed $25 million to charity. But when reporters started investigating which charities, they found that he had stepped up giving to New Jersey groups in 1999, and that he gave hundreds of thousands to groups whose leaders and sponsors later endorsed him.

Franks, like Florio, argued that Corzine was trying to buy a Senate seat and attacked him for failing to disclose the tax returns and for backing "universal" government programs that were unrealistic and costly. When Corzine's numbers stalled, Franks held onto his money and spent $2.5 million in the last two and a half weeks, when he also benefited from endorsements by the *New York Times* and *Philadelphia Inquirer*. Corzine spent $7.4 million on turnout efforts including busing in residents of Philadelphia homeless shelters and halfway houses to work on his campaign. In total Corzine spent $63 million, an all-time record. He won 50%-47%, with big margins in the central cities. But he ran behind Al Gore's 56%-40% margin and his showing was the weakest of any winning statewide Democratic candidate in the state between 1994 and 2006.

September 11 hit New Jersey especially hard—10 people from Corzine's home town of Summit died—and his major initiative in response was a chemical security bill that would require businesses to conduct vulnerability assessments and consider safer security technology. He was a co-sponsor of the Terrorism Risk Insurance Act which became law in November 2002. On the Banking Committee he worked on what became the Sarbanes-Oxley Act of 2003. Corzine and Lautenberg voted against the Medicare/prescription drug bill in November 2003, though it was supported by New Jersey pharmaceutical firms. He fought successfully in November 2003 to delay for a year the Education Department's reductions in deductions for state taxes when calculating Pell grants; this would hurt most in high-income, high-tax states like New Jersey. He worked to raise the maximum penalty for willful work safety violations that result in an employee's death from six months to 10 years. He sought to increase the guaranty in VA home mortgage loans to $83,000; this would allow veterans to buy houses worth up to $333,000, which are pretty numerous in New Jersey.

A newcomer to politics, Corzine became a strong and active partisan. He supported the election of Governor Jim McGreevey in 2001, who won by 56%-42%, the best margin for a statewide Democrat in New Jersey between 1994 and 2006. He showed his skills at handling difficult political situations in the imbroglio over whether Bob Torricelli should drop out of the 2002 Senate race. He had backed Torricelli all along, but helped to negotiate his departure and the selection of Frank Lautenberg to replace him. In 2003 he liberally supported county Democratic organizations, which helped Democrats win majorities in both houses of the legislature. Throughout the 2002 cycle he let it be known he would like to become DSCC chairman in 2003-04; in December 2002, Tom Daschle accommodated him. He did an excellent job of fundraising, outraising the Republicans' Senate committee. He sought out candidates capable of self-financing their races and recruited candidates who ran well ahead of Democratic party lines in Alaska, Colorado and Oklahoma. He discouraged primary competition in four of the five southern states where Democrats were retiring. Through much of the spring and summer he said, not unreasonably, that Democrats had a chance to gain seats. But in the end the close races went the other way, and Democrats lost all five southern seats plus Tom Daschle's seat in South Dakota.

Even before November 2004, Corzine was thinking about another goal: the governorship. Democrats in the state had become used to jettisoning losing candidates, as they did Torricelli in September 2002; in summer 2004, when Jim McGreevey's job rating was low, there was talk of replacing him with another candidate. Hanging over all this were images of corruption. U.S. Attorney Christopher Christie obtained indictments of many local officials and of prominent McGreevey fundraisers Charles Kushner and David D'Amiano. Kushner was charged with trying to thwart a federal investigation by luring a grand jury witness into a tryst with a prostitute; D'Amiano's indictment said "State Official 1" would signal his agreement in an extortion scheme by using the word "Machiavelli," and there was testimony that McGreevey referred to Machiavelli in a meeting. When asked if he was interested in running for governor, Corzine said, "Why would I work so hard to take back the majority in the Senate if I were leaving?" But he also said he missed being in an executive position. At the Democratic National Convention in July 2004, Corzine, not McGreevey, was head of the New Jersey delegation. Then, on August 12, McGreevey announced that he had had an extramarital affair with a man whom he had appointed, despite lack of any visible qualifications, as his homeland security advisor; he said he was resigning effective November 15. Under New Jersey law, if he should resign before September 3 there would be a special election on November 2, and the rules would enable state party organizations to exercise significant influence in picking a candidate. Camden County Democratic Chairman George Norcross and Middlesex County Democratic Chairman John Lynch, both staunch supporters of McGreevey and Corzine (who had given $4 million to county Democratic organizations) and adversaries of state Senate President Richard Codey, who would become acting governor on McGreevey's resignation, urged McGreevey to resign before September 3. They didn't want Codey to be governor 14 months, as he would be if McGreevey resigned in November, and possibly for five or nine years, if he won the job in his own right. Corzine made it clear, despite his Senate campaign duties, that he would run for governor if McGreevey resigned before the deadline, and no one in either party seemed to have the name recognition and fundraising ability to beat him in November. On August 18 McGreevey and Corzine spoke on the phone and, as Corzine put it, "The governor made it clear in our conversation his absolute intent to serve until November 15, 2004. I accept that decision as final."

"If I really want to get things done, I need to be in the majority," Corzine has said. On election night 2004 it was clear he would not be in the majority in the Senate for the next two years. The ability of a New Jersey governor to get things done is not in doubt. He or she is the strongest governor in the nation, the only statewide elected official who appoints all others, including the attorney general and the 21 county district attorneys. On November 4 Corzine held meetings of political advisers and supporters. The one obstacle was Richard Codey. After he took office November 16 (McGreevey insisted on remaining governor for all 24 hours of November 15), Codey started to make appearances around the state and seemed to cast off his earlier reluctance to run for the job in 2005. Meanwhile, 1st District Congressman Rob Andrews, who narrowly lost the 1997 gubernatorial primary to McGreevey, indicated that he might be interested in running for governor too; with his base in South Jersey, he looked like a formidable contender. Codey made moves to demonstrate his own support, but Corzine, Norcross and Lynch had lined up endorsements from dozens of Democrats—Congressmen Bob Menendez and Frank Pallone (both interested in being appointed to Corzine's Senate seat), Speaker Albio Sires and many others whom Corzine had supported generously over the years. On December 2 Corzine announced he was running. He said his wealth insured that he would be "unbought and unbossed." "It's his right to run," Codey said. "He considers me a friend of his. So be it. It is what it is." Codey held a rally of Essex County Democrats on December 9 and he prepared meticulously for his State of the State speech January 11. But it became clear that Corzine had much more support. On January 31 Codey announced he was not running and backed Corzine. Codey noted that he would still remain Senate President throughout 2005 and after, assuming a Democratic majority; Corzine or a Republican governor would have to deal with him in 2006 and beyond.

The Republicans had a primary contest. Former Jersey City Mayor Bret Schundler, who upset Congressman Bob Franks in the June 2001 primary and then lost 56%-42% to McGreevey, started running in July 2004 on a platform of limiting state and local spending to 1.3 times the inflation rate, with a view toward reducing property tax rates. But organization Republicans disliked him for his maverick ways and conservative views on abortion. Another candidate was Doug Forrester, a health benefits administrator who ran against Senator Bob Torricelli in the 2002 Senate race and was leading in the polls when Torricelli withdrew; he lost in November 2002 to his replacement, Frank Lautenberg, 54%-44% after spending $8 million of his own money. In 2005 Forrester again spent $10 million of his own money and defeated Schundler in June 36%-31%.

New Jersey property taxes are the highest in the country, and both parties' nominees presented property tax relief plans. Forrester called for a 30% cut over three years and said he would pay for it by spending cuts and layoffs of state employees. Corzine called for graduated rebates over four years averaging 10%, with higher rates for those with lower incomes and for seniors. Corzine charged that Forrester's plan would end senior citizen rebates. Forrester charged that Corzine's spending programs would be unsustainable. Soon the arguments over policy were overshadowed by personal attacks. Forrester charged that Corzine sought a government subsidy as part of a group seeking to buy the New Jersey Nets; Corzine said Forrester's firm benefited from government contracts made by officials to whom he gave campaign contributions; both charges were based on flimsy evidence. Forrester trumpeted the revelation that Corzine had loaned $470,000 to Carla Katz, then his girlfriend, who was also head of the largest state public employee union, and that he had forgiven the loan around the time he announced for governor. Newspapers reported that Corzine's 89-year-old mother had given $37,000 to Bergen County Democrats since 2003. In the last week of the campaign Forrester ran an ad that quoted what Corzine's former wife of 33 years told the *New York Times*: "When I saw the campaign ad where Andrea Forrester said, 'Doug never let his family down and he won't let New Jersey down,' all I could think was that Jon did let his family down and he'll probably let New Jersey down too." But this was not enough to turn the tide. Corzine won 53%-43%; he had big margins in the central cities. Forrester carried only three counties on the Shore and five counties from affluent Morris and Somerset west to the state line. The margin was almost the same as John Kerry's 53%-46% in 2004 and Bob Menendez's 53%-44% in the 2006 Senate race. Interestingly, Corzine's old hometown of Summit split evenly, 3,328 to 3,328.

Corzine took office pledging to take only $1 a year in salary and soon started wearing what became his trademark navy blue sweater-vest. One of his first orders of business was to appoint his successor in the Senate. He chose 13th District Congressman Bob Menendez, the dominant political figure in Hudson County and a member of the House leadership. His other major Hispanic appointee, Attorney General Zulima Farber, did not turn out so well. In May 2006 she came to the aid of her boyfriend, in a police car with sirens flashing, when he was stopped at a seat belt checkpoint and found to have no registration and a suspended driver's license; troopers let him drive home with her, but an special counsel appointed by Corzine in July found that she violated three ethics rules and she resigned in August.

In January Corzine faced a projected $4 billion budget deficit, and his $30.9 billion budget evoked cries of protest. Hospitals were hit with a $620 monthly per bed fee, state aid to poor school districts was frozen and he proposed to increase the sales tax from 6% to 7%. Speaker Joe Roberts, a Camden County ally of George Norcross, balked and forced an impasse in July 2006. The state government was shut down and so were the Atlantic City casinos, which require state monitoring to stay open. Corzine threatened to spend his own money on ads targeting Roberts; the Assembly backed down after five days and the sales tax was increased, with a promise that half of the proceeds would go to property tax relief. The legislature voted $270 million for stem cell research, with $150 million to a stem cell institute at Rutgers; this built on the stem cell initiatives of Codey and McGreevey. In October 2006 the state Supreme Court ruled that barring same-sex couples from marrying violated the state Constitution and ordered the legislature to give them equal treatment, beyond the existing domestic partnership law; in December the legislature passed a civil unions law, similar to those in Vermont and Connecticut. In December Corzine ignited a kerfuffle when he asked the legislature to change the state pension system; he said the shortfall was much larger than the official estimate of $18 billion. But a few days later he said the legislators couldn't consider any pensions that would be covered in union negotiations the next year. In January 2007 he asked the legislature to cap property taxes at 4% a year, rather than the current 7%. When the legislature missed a deadline, he threatened to call for a constitutional convention in the fall. He added that he would not accept a bill that did not ban double office-holding—New Jersey, like France, has allowed its legislators to hold local office as well. The ban passed the legislature in June. In April the legislature came up with a bill that met his specifications, with graduated property tax rebates up to 20% and a 4% cap on increases. But local governments would be able to apply for exemptions from the cap with the support of voters. He was less successful at "asset monetization." He said he did not want to sell, but might be willing to lease, the often jammed New Jersey Turnpike, which has had only one toll increase in 55 years. "I'm not sure we're pricing it right for the marketplace." And he looked toward monetizing other assets—the lottery, site elements, air rights, naming rights (will they change the Joyce Kilmer rest stop to the Continental Airlines rest stop?).

In April 2007 Corzine made national news when he was seriously injured in an auto accident. A state trooper driving him on the Garden State Parkway from Atlantic City to a meeting in New Brunswick between radio talk show host Don Imus and the Rutgers women's basketball team was traveling at 91 miles per hour when a truck veered into its path; the governor's SUV crashed into a guard rail. Corzine, who was in the front seat and not wearing a seat belt (though he has championed mandatory seat belt laws), suffered a broken breastbone, collarbone and leg and many broken ribs; he was on a ventilator for several days and returned weeks later to conduct business at the governor's mansion, Drumthwacket. He publicly apologized for not wearing his seat belt, paid a $46 fine, and filmed a 30-second public service announcement where he said, "I'm New Jersey Governor Jon Corzine, and I should be dead."

Senior Senator

Frank Lautenberg (D)

Elected 2002, seat up 2008, 4th term; b. Jan. 23, 1924, Paterson; home, Cliffside Park; Columbia U., B.S. 1949; Jewish; married (Bonnie).

Military Career: Army Signal Corps, 1942-46 (WWII).

Elected Office: U.S. Senate, 1982-2000.

Professional Career: Co–founder, Automatic Data Processing, 1952-82; NY & NJ Port Authority Comm., 1978-82.

DC Office: 324 HSOB, 20510, 202-224-3224; Fax: 202-228-4054; Web site: lautenberg.senate.gov.

State Offices: Camden, 856-338-8922; Newark, 973-639-8700.

Committees: *Appropriations* (14th of 15 D): Financial Services & General Government; Homeland Security; Labor, Health and Human Services, Education & Related Agencies; Commerce, Justice, Science & Related Agencies; Energy & Water Development; Transportation, Housing and Urban Development & Related Agencies. *Budget* (9th of 12 D). *Commerce, Science & Transportation* (8th of 12 D): Surface Transportation & Merchant Marine Infrastructure, Safety & Security (Chmn.); Oceans, Atmosphere, Fisheries & Coast Guard; Consumer Affairs, Insurance & Automotive Safety; Aviation Operations, Safety & Security. *Environment & Public Works* (6th of 10 D): Transportation Safety, Infrastructure Security & Water Quality (Chmn.); Private Sector & Consumer Solutions to Global Warming & Wildlife Protection; Superfund & Environmental Health.

Group Ratings

	ADA	ACLU	AFS	LCV	ITIC	NTU	COC	ACU	CFG	FRC
2006	100	83	100	86	33	11	42	0	0	0
2005	100	—	100	100	—	7	29	0	0	—

National Journal Ratings

	2005 LIB	—	2005 CONS		2006 LIB	—	2006 CONS
Economic	95%	—	0%		87%	—	0%
Social	90%	—	0%		89%	—	8%
Foreign	75%	—	24%		67%	—	29%

Key Votes of the 109th Congress

1. Bar ANWR Drilling	Y	5. Confirm Samuel Alito	N	9. Limit Interstate Abortion	N
2. FY06 Spending Curb	N	6. Path to Citizenship	Y	10. CAFTA	N
3. Estate Tax Repeal	N	7. Bar Same Sex Marriage	N	11. Urge Iraq Withdrawal	Y
4. Raise Minimum Wage	Y	8. Stem Cell Research $	Y	12. Provide Detainee Rights	Y

Election Results

2002 general	Frank Lautenberg (D)	1,138,193	(54%)	($2,929,206)
	Douglas Forrester (R)	928,439	(44%)	($10,606,843)
	Other	45,972	(2%)	
1996 general	Robert G. Torricelli (D)	1,519,154	(53%)	($9,134,854)
	Dick Zimmer (R)	1,227,351	(43%)	($8,238,181)
	Other	136,961	(5%)	

Prior Winning Percentages: 1994 (50%); 1988 (54%); 1982 (51%)

Frank Lautenberg is New Jersey's senior senator. He was elected in 1982, 1988 and 1994 and retired in 2000, then returned to run again in October 2002 after Bob Torricelli withdrew from the race. When Jon Corzine, who succeeded Lautenberg in the Senate, was sworn in as governor in January 2006, he resigned his Senate seat and Lautenberg assumed the title of senior senator. With his personal wealth and name recognition, Lautenberg was an obvious choice to succeed Torricelli; New Jersey Democrats persuaded the state supreme court to let them put Lautenberg's name on the ballot. Lautenberg grew up in Paterson, the son of an immigrant silk worker. He served in the Army Signal Corps in World War II and says he never would have gone to college without the G.I. Bill of Rights. He graduated from Columbia and in 1952 started a company called Automatic Data Processing, which by the mid-1990s had almost 30,000 employees and processed the payroll for nearly 10% of private sector jobs in the United States—a brilliant success story. When ADP went public in 1961, Lautenberg's stock was worth $50,000; now his net worth is in the vicinity of $40 million. Lautenberg was a contributor to Democratic campaigns and got on Richard Nixon's enemies list when he contributed $90,000 to George McGovern in 1972.

But no one thought of him as a candidate until, not for the last time, scandal provided an opening: Democratic Senator Harrison Williams resigned in March 1982 as the Senate was considering his expulsion after his conviction in the Abscam case, and his appointed successor, Republican Nicholas Brady, made it clear he was not running for a full term (he became the first George Bush's Treasury Secretary). Lautenberg ran and spent $5 million of his own money and boasted of his high-tech experience. He beat several professional politicians in the primary and upset Republican Congresswoman Millicent Fenwick in the general 51%-48%. During the campaign he referred to the 72-year-old Fenwick, who was satirized in *Doonesbury*, as "eccentric" and a "national monument" and questioned her "fitness" and "ability to do the job."

Lautenberg believes government helped him and others work their way up, and in his first three terms had a solidly liberal voting record. He bucked the party only occasionally. As chairman and ranking Democrat on the Transportation Appropriations Subcommittee, he got Congress to ban smoking first on two-hour flights, then on all domestic flights. In 2006 he wrote to the Senate's food service management asking to ban the sale of tobacco products in the Senate complex. He is a strong backer of gun control and author of the 1996 law barring those convicted of domestic abuse from possessing firearms.

New Jersey is the second most expensive state to campaign in, because candidates must buy New York and Philadelphia TV, and Lautenberg's willingness to spend large amounts of his own money helped him win reelection over retired General Pete Dawkins in 1988 by 54%-46% and Assembly Speaker Chuck Haytaian in 1994 by 50%-47%. In 1998 he seemed primed to run again, and no well-known Republican seemed eager to challenge him. But in February 1999 he announced that he would retire in 2000.

One thing he surely did not miss was dealing with his colleague Bob Torricelli. Relationships between senators of the same state and party are often frayed and acrimonious; but the relationship between Lautenberg and Torricelli was probably more hostile than any since 1859, when California Senator David Broderick was killed in a duel with his colleague William Gwin's best friend. In March 1999, as Torricelli, the chairman of the Senate Democrats' campaign committee, was briefing colleagues, Lautenberg accused him of being too friendly with Republican Governor Christine Todd Whitman; Torricelli was enraged and in full view after the meeting approached Lautenberg and, as *The New York Times* daintily put it, "made a vulgar threat on his manhood." So Lautenberg was one New Jersey Democrat who was not unhappy when Torricelli fell into disfavor with voters in his 2002 reelection campaign.

In most respects, Torricelli seemed a clear favorite to win. The three candidates in the June primary were mostly unknown—businessman Doug Forrester, South Jersey state Senators Susan Allen and John Matheussen. Money made the difference: Forrester, who started BeneCard, a manager of prescription drug benefits, was worth some $50 million and spent $3 million in the primary and beat Allen by a 45%-37% margin.

But scandal loomed over Torricelli. For three years the U.S. Attorney's office in Manhattan had been investigating charges that businessman David Chang had given lavish gifts and cash to Torricelli and that Torricelli had worked to advance Chang's business interests in Korea. Torricelli did give such assistance, but denied receiving gifts; he said he reimbursed Chang. In January 2002 U.S. Attorney Mary Jo White announced that Torricelli would not be prosecuted. But White had sent information about the charges to the Senate Ethics Committee; on July 30 the committee "severely admonished" Torricelli for violating the Senate rule against receiving gifts over $50 but did not release the evidence to the public.

Forrester made much of Torricelli's problems and, as details poured out, Torricelli plummeted in the polls. On Saturday, September 28, a *Star-Ledger* poll showed Forrester ahead 47%-34%—a devastating result. On Sunday Governor Jim McGreevey, Senator Jon Corzine and other New Jersey Democratic leaders met in Trenton and patched in Majority Leader Tom Daschle over the phone: Obviously they were trying to get Torricelli to withdraw from the race. On Monday Torricelli's office announced he would hold a press conference at 11 a.m.; he finally appeared around 5 p.m. and, in a lugubrious speech, withdrew.

New Jersey Democrats were now in need of a well-known candidate to replace Torricelli. Congressman Bob Menendez, seeking a leadership position in the House, wasn't interested. Congressman Rob Andrews was presumably vetoed by McGreevey, who had narrowly beaten him in the 1997 gubernatorial primary. Congressman Frank Pallone, after giving it some thought, decided not to run. The risk of giving up a safe House seat to seek a nomination that might be rejected by a court may have seemed too great. Former Senator Bill Bradley let it be known he had no interest. But Lautenberg, now evidently missing life in the Senate, said he would "seriously consider serving again if asked." It seems unlikely that Torricelli would have withdrawn if he had known that Lautenberg would get the nomination. But there was nothing he could do to stop him. Lautenberg was well known and capable of self-financing. McGreevey and the other Democrats quickly agreed on him.

New Jersey law does not contain a provision for substituting a new candidate so late in the campaign unless a candidate has died; ballots had already been printed with Torricelli's name. But the New Jersey Supreme Court is made up of judicial activists of both parties with a propensity to accommodate the insiders of both major parties. In October 2002 it quickly approved state Democrats' request to substitute Lautenberg for Torricelli and ordered the state Democratic party to pay the $800,000 needed to print new ballots. The Lautenberg campaign moved into the Torricelli headquarters and Lautenberg was again a candidate for the Senate, without having to spend months fundraising. The easiest source of funds proved unavailable: Torricelli would not send over a dime from his $5 million campaign treasury.

Now Forrester could no longer introduce himself as "the guy running against Bob Torricelli." He did run a cute ad on cable TV, showing a kid slamming his desk and saying, "I can't do this. I quit! If I fail this test, can I have Frank Lautenberg take it for me?" Forrester attacked Lautenberg as soft on defense and terrorism, citing his 1991 vote against the Gulf War resolution and he questioned whether Lautenberg at 78—six years older than Millicent Fenwick was when Lautenberg questioned her ability to do the job—was too old. Lautenberg attacked Forrester on Social Security, prescription drugs, abortion and gun control: Forrester was against state-paid abortions and had written a 1992 column in the *West Windsor-Plainsboro Chronicle* on owning semiautomatic guns. "Liberty is all about the government allowing citizens to do weird things unless there is a compelling documented public purpose which should preclude them." On October 30 they appeared together for 30 minutes on News 12 New Jersey, a cable channel available to 55% of state households; Lautenberg seemed a little ragged, but was plainly still up to the job. Forrester spent $10 million altogether, $7.5 million of it his own money; the Senate Republican campaign committee did not make New Jersey a top priority. Lautenberg spent $1.5 million of his own money, and those funds, plus $1.2 million from national and New Jersey Democrats, turned out to be enough in this Democratic state. Unsurprisingly, Lautenberg won 54%-44%, a better showing than in 1994; but then New Jersey has become more Democratic than it was in 1994.

Lautenberg was disappointed when Senate Democrats did not give him credit for all his seniority; his previous service only entitled him to seniority over other freshmen. But he quickly directed his ire away from his fellow Democrats and toward the Bush administration. He moved aggressively to stop privatization of the air traffic control system, holding up the FAA reauthorization in summer 2003 by demanding that the FAA refrain from even studying privatization. He got Trent Lott to agree to a one-year moratorium on privatizing any jobs, but that was unacceptable to the administration; passage of the bill waited until FAA Administrator Marion Blakey sent over a letter stating that no jobs "directly related to our air traffic control system" would be privatized during the fiscal year. Lautenberg voted against the Medicare/prescription drug bill, even though it was supported by many New Jersey pharmaceutical companies, and in 2004 tried to stop HHS from sending out letters explaining the new benefit. He spoke out stringently in November 2003 after George W. Bush signed the partial-birth abortion ban.

During 2004 Lautenberg kept up a drumbeat of criticism of the Pentagon for awarding sole-source contracts to Halliburton. He sponsored an amendment, aimed at Halliburton, to prevent foreign subsidies of U.S. corporations to do business with nations on the terrorist watch list; it was defeated in the Senate 50-49 in May 2004 when Max Baucus changed his vote. In October he tried to attach the amendment to a must pass bill and threatened a filibuster. In April 2004 he took to the floor of the Senate with an object he called a chicken hawk and made a thinly veiled attack on Dick Cheney. He requested a hearing after Disney refused to distribute director Michael Moore's film *Fahrenheit 9/11*. In June 2004 he urged Attorney General John Ashcroft to authorize a special counsel investigation of the Halliburton contract. That month he sponsored an amendment to allow the media to photograph coffins of servicemen at Dover Air Force Base and another for a $2,000 bonus for troops subject to stop loss orders. When Bush made a campaign stop in New Jersey in October 2004, Lautenberg said, "President Bush, time and time again, has made decisions that made New Jersey more vulnerable to terrorism. He's here because of November 2, not 9/11." When asked why Lautenberg was more outspoken than in his first three Senate terms, his colleague Jon Corzine said, "He's less risk-averse. I think Frank couldn't care less." Lautenberg said, "I do feel unconstrained." To protest the Iraq war, Lautenberg in 2005 used a foyer outside his Senate office to display the photos of U.S. soldiers killed in Iraq and Afghanistan. Lautenberg in January 2006 introduced Samuel Alito, a New Jersey native, to the Senate Judiciary Committee for his Supreme Court confirmation hearings, but he later voted against him.

From his seat on the Commerce committee, Lautenberg has looked after his state's transportation needs with particular attention to guarding against terrorist threats. He pressed for better security at airports, ports and railroads. He advocated that the Port Authority of New York and New Jersey break its lease with Dubai Ports World if the foreign-owned company was allowed to assume operations of the Newark port. Lautenberg secured $8.4 million to begin engineering work on a new rail tunnel from northern New Jersey to Manhattan, and a $700,000 federal grant to fund improvements at Lakewood Airport. In 2007, Lautenberg introduced with Trent Lott a six-year reauthorization of AMTRAK that provided $3.2 billion in annual funding, while also requiring better efficiency and more state aid. With Robert Menendez, Lautenberg introduced a bill requiring chemical plans to use safer chemicals whenever possible, and he opposed a move by the Bush administration that would allow the federal government to preempt the state's tougher chemical safety rules.

In June 2005, Lautenberg cast his 7,000th vote, a milestone made only by two other New Jersey senators. After the 2006 elections, Lautenberg won a seat on the Appropriations Committee after giving up his seat on Homeland Security and Governmental Affairs Committee. He had sought to chair the latter panel by recouping his years of previous experience and leapfrogging Joe Lieberman. But Democratic leaders—who had abandoned Lieberman after he lost the Democratic primary but won the general as an independent—had an incentive to keep Lieberman happy in the Democratic Caucus.

Lautenberg's seat comes up in 2008, when he turns 84, and he shows little sign of slowing down. Lautenberg regretted his first retirement, and in November 2006 he told the Bergen *Record* he would run again in 2008. "There is a lot that remains to be done," he said. "The people respect what I do, they know I'm straightforward in my efforts for my state. And I want to continue doing it." If Lautenberg does not carry through on his plans for reelection, Congressman Robert Andrews and Frank Pallone are the most likely Democratic contenders. The Republican field for 2008 is unclear, though polls in 2007 revealed voters are less than enamored with Lautenberg and that his advanced age is an issue. U.S. Attorney Christopher Christie effectively ruled out a run, and state Senator Tom Kean Jr., who lost to Menendez in 2006, showed no interest in challenging Lautenberg. Among the Republicans mentioned as potential candidates were Anne Evans Estabrook, a Summit developer, and state Assemblyman Joseph Pennacchio.

Junior Senator

Robert Menendez (D)

Appointed Jan. 2006, seat up 2012, 1st full term; b. Jan. 1, 1954, New York, NY; home, Union City; St. Peter's Col., B.A. 1976, Rutgers Law Schl., J.D. 1979; Catholic; married (Jane Jacobsen-Menendez).

Elected Office: Union City Bd. of Ed., 1974-82; Union City Mayor, 1986-92; NJ Assembly, 1987-91; NJ Senate, 1991-92; U.S. House of Reps., 1992-2006.

Professional Career: Practicing atty., 1980-92.

DC Office: 317 HSOB, 20510, 202-224-4744; Fax: 202-228-2197; Web site: menendez.senate.gov.

State Office: Bayonne, 201-823-2900.

Committees: *Banking, Housing & Urban Affairs* (7th of 11 D): Securities, Insurance & Investment; Financial Institutions; Housing, Transportation & Community Development. *Budget* (8th of 12 D). *Energy & Natural Resources* (9th of 12 D): National Parks; Energy; Public Lands & Forests. *Foreign Relations* (8th of 11 D): International Development & Foreign Assistance, Economic Affairs & International Environmental Protection (Chmn.); International Operations & Organizations, Democracy & Human Rights; European Affairs; Western Hemisphere, Peace Corps & Narcotics Affairs.

Group Ratings (Only Served Partial Term)

	ADA	ACLU	AFS	LCV	ITIC	NTU	COC	ACU	CFG	FRC
2006	90	67	100	100	100	17	55	4	0	0
2005	—	—	—	—	—	—	—	—	—	—

National Journal Ratings (Only Served Partial Term)

	2005 LIB	—	2005 CONS		2006 LIB	—	2006 CONS
Economic	*	—	*		79%	—	18%
Social	*	—	*		80%	—	14%
Foreign	*	—	*		84%	—	15%

Key Votes of the 109th Congress (Only Served Partial Term)

1. Bar ANWR Drilling	*	5. Confirm Samuel Alito	N	9. Limit Interstate Abortion	N
2. FY06 Spending Curb	*	6. Path to Citizenship	Y	10. CAFTA	*
3. Estate Tax Repeal	N	7. Bar Same Sex Marriage	N	11. Urge Iraq Withdrawal	Y
4. Raise Minimum Wage	Y	8. Stem Cell Research $	Y	12. Provide Detainee Rights	Y

Election Results

2006 general	Robert Menendez (D)	1,200,843	(53%)	($13,328,665)
	Thomas Kean Jr. (R)	997,775	(44%)	($7,762,373)
	Other	51,452	(2%)	
2006 primary	Robert Menendez (D)	159,604	(84%)	
	James Kelly (D)	30,340	(16%)	
2000 general	Jon Corzine (D)	1,511,237	(50%)	($63,209,506)
	Bob Franks (R)	1,420,267	(47%)	($6,389,936)
	Other	84,158	(3%)	

Prior Winning Percentages: 2004 House (76%); 2002 House (78%); 2000 House (79%); 1998 House (80%); 1996 House (79%); 1994 House (71%); 1992 House (64%)

Robert Menendez, New Jersey's junior senator, was appointed by Governor Jon Corzine in January 2006 and won election to a full term 10 months later. His ascension to the Senate was no lucky break, but rather the culmination of a career marked by an ability to adapt to and thrive in the most demanding and bruising political arenas. He is of Cuban descent and grew up in Union City, America's most densely populated city (in 2000 it had 60,000 people in 1.3 square miles), and got into politics early. He was elected to the school board in 1974, at 20. He worked for Union City Mayor William Musto in the 1970s, but quit and testified against Musto in a corruption trial (Menendez later said that he wore a bulletproof vest due to death threats), and ran against him and lost in 1982. Menendez was elected mayor in 1986, to the Assembly in 1987 and Senate in 1991; he served both as mayor and legislator (a common practice in New Jersey) until his 1992 election to Congress. He was the first New Jersey Latino in the legislature and Congress. When new district lines were created and incumbent Frank Guarini retired, Menendez won the 1992 primary 68%-32% and the general election 64%-31%.

In the House, Menendez was a strong supporter of anti-Castro legislation—the 1992 Cuban Democracy Act, the 1996 Helms-Burton Act. He sponsored a bill in 2004 to put illegal immigrants on the path to permanent worker status and citizenship. Noting the increasing importance of the financial services industry in Hudson County, his home base, he broke with many Democrats to support the bankruptcy bill and financial services deregulation; one Blue Dog Democrat called him "the pro-business member of the leadership." In 2004 he sponsored a bill aimed at improving railroad security, with $5 billion for capital equipment and $800 million for operating expenses.

Menendez heads the Democratic party organization in Hudson County and is a major player in state politics. He has shown fine political skills—and, at times, sharp elbows—both at home and in Washington. Some have called him the political boss of Hudson County. "I bristle at the term," Menendez said. But he did admit to the existence of what some would call political bosses. "I think there are people with very significant influence in certain parts of the state." In the House, he aggressively supported Loretta Sanchez against the election challenge brought by Robert Dornan, whom she ousted in November 1996; in November 1998, his party colleagues elected him vice chairman of the Democratic Caucus.

When Senator Frank Lautenberg announced his retirement in February 1999, Menendez was widely expected to run for the Senate. But support was not forthcoming from New Jersey Senator Bob Torricelli, the DSCC Chairman, who wanted a deep-pockets candidate and found him in Jon Corzine, whom Menendez endorsed in November 1999. One reason Menendez decided not to run for the Senate in 2000 is that Minority Leader Dick Gephardt urged him to stay in the House, arguing that as a leader of a Democratic majority he could be more important than a junior senator. Democratic caucus chairmen and vice-chairmen are limited to two two-year terms, so Menendez in 2001 began running for caucus chairman. He raised more than $1 million for House Democrats in the 2000 cycle and $3 million in the 2002 cycle and traveled around the country campaigning. His Hispanic background was an asset, and not just within the 20-member Hispanic Caucus. "There are 50 to 60 members who are not Hispanic but have significant Hispanic communities in their districts," he pointed out. He issued a Latino Leadership Link every week in English and Spanish.

Menendez announced his candidacy for chairman of the Democratic Caucus in October 2001, just after the caucus picked Nancy Pelosi over Steny Hoyer to replace David Bonior as minority whip. Also running was Rosa DeLauro, who had been Assistant to Minority Leader Richard Gephardt. In February 2002 Menendez charged that DeLauro backers were saying, wrongly, that he did not support abortion rights; he argued that the caucus, having chosen Pelosi for the number one post, would be better off with an Hispanic than another woman in the number three post. In an unusual turn, Pelosi openly endorsed DeLauro and Hoyer openly endorsed Menendez. Then, on September 30, came another opportunity to run for the Senate: Bob Torricelli dropped out of the race and Governor Jim McGreevey and other Democratic leaders sought another candidate. Menendez, with more than $2 million in his campaign treasury, probably could have had the nomination for the asking. He pondered the situation for a day, and then decided not to run; he said he was too committed to getting a Democratic majority in the House and becoming caucus chairman. On November 5 he failed to achieve the first goal and on November 14, the day of the caucus election, he very nearly failed to achieve the second. Menendez walked into the caucus with a list of 107 members who had agreed to openly support him. He won the secret ballot 104-103.

As caucus chairman, Menendez continued to show his fundraising prowess. By June 2003 he had $2.8 million in his campaign fund, more than any other House member; over the 2003-04 cycle he raised $3.6 million.

In July 2004, when McGreevey's job rating was low, Menendez was one Democrat speculating about pushing him aside in favor of Senator Jon Corzine. Of Corzine, he said, "He's popular, and if people would think about where to turn outside of Governor McGreevey, he has the relationships, good will and good standing to attract support." On August 12 McGreevey announced that he had had an affair with a man and would resign, but not until November 15. Menendez, along with Camden County Democratic Chairman George Norcross and Middlesex County Chairman John Lynch, urged McGreevey to resign before September 3, which would trigger a November special election in which Corzine could run and which he would probably win, at which point he could appoint Menendez senator. But McGreevey refused and Senate President Richard Codey, a political adversary of Norcross's and Lynch's, became acting governor from November 15 until January 2006.

To be sure, Menendez continued to be active in the House. In October 2004 he announced he would be running for majority whip if Democrats regained a majority in the House. But he also clearly hankered to run for the Senate. In December 2004, after Corzine announced he would run for governor and before Acting Governor Richard Codey took himself out of the race, Menendez made it known that, if Corzine were elected, he would run for the Senate even if Corzine named someone else to the seat. As the presumed frontrunner to succeed Corzine, Menendez had amassed more than $4 million for a statewide campaign, which was far more than his two leading rivals—Congressmen Robert Andrews and Frank Pallone—had on hand. By May 2005, Menendez began spending time on the Senate side of the Capitol at news conferences and developing relationships with senators. Menendez, Pallone and Andrews all actively campaigned for Corzine's gubernatorial bid, while at the same time positioning themselves for a Senate campaign.

After Corzine won the election in November 2005, he waited a month before revealing his chosen successor, leading to speculation that he had reservations about choosing Menendez. State Senator Tom Kean Jr., the son and namesake of popular former Republican Governor Thomas Kean Sr., was already viewed as the likely Republican nominee. Codey was the favorite of DSCC Chairman Charles Schumer because of his popularity and name recognition, but Codey took his name out of consideration before Thanksgiving. Democrats worried about Menendez's Hudson County political baggage, and had questions about Menendez's relationship with former aide Kay LiCausi and his efforts to steer lobbying and consulting work her way. In December, Corzine announced he would appoint Menendez as his replacement, and did so in January after he was sworn in as governor. Menendez joined Senators Mel Martinez of Florida and Ken Salazar of Colorado as the chamber's Hispanic members.

In February 2006, Menendez ran afoul of John McCain when he insisted on a roll call vote rather than a voice vote on a non-binding amendment urging an extension of a tax break for the alternative minimum tax. Menendez said he was unaware that McCain was scheduled to leave for Europe and was pressed for time. Menendez recounted McCain rushing across the Senate floor to him, "And he goes, 'You're a jerk, you're a jerk. This is no way to introduce yourself to the Senate. You're a jerk. You don't need a roll call vote.'" Menendez had his successes. He won $2.6 million in additional funding for the New Jersey National Guard. He also passed a measure that would fund $60 million for a United Nations mission in the Darfur region in Sudan. Years earlier in the House, Menendez had won an exemption for the importation of gum arabic from Sudan in a trade sanctions bill. The leading importer of gum arabic, which is used in a range of products, had its headquarters in his district.

As he adjusted to the pace of the Senate, Menendez also prepared for the 2006 election for a full term. Andrews and Pallone each declared they would not challenge Menendez in the primary. Menendez and Kean had only token primary opposition and the general election campaign took shape early around national debates about the Iraq war and ethics. Menendez campaigned against the Iraq war, while Kean said he would have voted for the Iraq war resolution and opposed a timetable for withdrawing U.S. troops. But Kean also distanced himself from President Bush by criticizing his administration's handling of the war. In March, when Vice President Dick Cheney came to campaign for Kean, the candidate showed up at a fundraiser in Newark after Cheney had left. Kean's campaign blamed his tardiness on traffic congestion; Democrats said he wanted to avoid appearing with Cheney. Kean later called for the resignation of Defense Secretary Donald Rumsfeld, which Menendez called a "clumsy" attempt to find political cover for the unpopular war.

In the wake of a series of congressional scandals, congressional ethics played a prominent role in the 2006 elections; Kean attempted to capitalize by reminding voters of Menendez's influence in Hudson County, which has been long associated with political corruption. In June, Kean's campaign said it would make a campaign film about Menendez's early political career similar to the "Swift Boat Veterans for Truth" campaign waged during the 2004 presidential campaign against John Kerry's military record. Then, two months before the election, Christopher Christie, New Jersey's U.S. attorney and a Republican appointee, subpoenaed records from a lease arrangement between Menendez and the North Hudson Community Action Corp. The non-profit group, which received federal funding backed by Menendez, paid Menendez more then $300,000 over nine years to rent a building he owned in Union City.

Democrats condemned the subpoenas as politically motivated, and cried foul when a tape recording surfaced of a 1999 telephone call between Menendez confidant and fundraiser Donald Scarinci and psychiatrist Oscar Sandoval. In the call, Scarinci had urged Sandoval, who was under contract with Hudson County, to hire a physician supported by Menendez. Republicans circulated rumors that Menendez might drop out as the Democratic nominee as Bob Torricelli had in 2002. Menendez rejected the notion and responded with an attack ad linking Kean to contributors with their own ethics controversies. Kean's ethics offensive unraveled when it was revealed the Kean campaign had contacted former Hudson County Executive Robert Janiszewski in an attempt to dig up political dirt on Menendez. Janiszewski was serving time in federal prison on corruption charges. Experienced in political warfare, Menendez struck back with a television ad accusing Kean of a smear campaign: "Federal prisoner 25038-050. He's Tom Kean Jr.'s newest advisor." Polls late in the cycle showed Menendez with only a slight lead and for a moment it seemed Republicans had one of the few opportunities to contest a Democrat-held seat in 2006. But Menendez held on to win 53%-44%.

FIRST DISTRICT

Rep. Robert Andrews (D)

Elected 1990, 9th full term; b. Aug. 4, 1957, Camden; home, Haddon Heights; Bucknell U., B.A. 1979, Cornell U., J.D. 1982; Episcopalian; married (Camille).

Elected Office: Camden Cnty. Bd. of Chosen Freeholders, 1987-90.

Professional Career: Practicing atty., 1982-90; Adjunct Prof., Rutgers Law Schl., 1985-86, 1989-90.

DC Office: 2439 RHOB, 20515, 202-225-6501; Fax: 202-225-6583; Web site: www.house.gov/andrews.

District Offices: Haddon Heights, 856-546-5100; Woodbury, 856-848-3900.

Committees: *Armed Services* (13th of 34 D): Terrorism, Unconventional Threats & Capabilities; Oversight & Investigations. *Budget* (14th of 22 D). *Education & Labor* (4th of 27 D): Health, Employment, Labor & Pensions (Chmn.); Higher Education, Lifelong Learning & Competitiveness.

Group Ratings

	ADA	ACLU	AFS	LCV	ITIC	NTU	COC	ACU	CFG	FRC
2006	85	82	86	100	43	14	40	16	11	0
2005	90	—	100	83	—	18	42	8	9	8

National Journal Ratings

	2005 LIB	—	2005 CONS		2006 LIB	—	2006 CONS
Economic	77%	—	23%		82%	—	17%
Social	74%	—	26%		76%	—	23%
Foreign	68%	—	31%		66%	—	33%

Key Votes of the 109th Congress

1. Estate Tax Repeal	N	5. Limit Interstate Abortion	N	9. Build Border Fence	Y
2. Limit CAFE Standards	*	6. Extend Patriot Act	Y	10. CAFTA	N
3. FY06 Spending Curb	N	7. Bar Same Sex Marriage	N	11. Oppose Iraq Withdrawal	N
4. Drilling in ANWR	N	8. Stem Cell Research $	Y	12. Detainee Tribunals	Y

Election Results

2006 general	Robert Andrews (D) ....unopposed		($1,450,582)
2006 primary	Robert Andrews (D) ....unopposed		
2004 general	Robert Andrews (D) 201,163	(75%)	($848,616)
	Daniel Hutchison (R) 66,109	(25%)	($176,791)

Prior Winning Percentages: 2002 (93%); 2000 (76%); 1998 (73%); 1996 (76%); 1994 (72%); 1992 (67%); 1990 (54%); 1990 (55%)

The People		Race/Ethnic Origin	Ancestry	
Area size:	352 sq. mi.	71.2% White	Irish: 16.8%	Italian: 14.8%
Urban population:	98.6%	16.3% Black	German: 13.0%	
Rural population:	1.4%	2.6% Asian	**2004 Presidential Vote**	
Pop. 2000:	647,258	0.2% Native Am.	Kerry (D) 170,786	(61%)
Pop. 2005 (est):	664,488	0.0% Hawaiian	Bush (R) 111,073	(39%)
Median income:	$47,473	1.3% Two+ races	**2000 Presidential Vote**	
Poverty status:	9.9%	0.1% Other	Gore (D) 144,226	(63%)
Military veterans:	12.4%	8.2% Hispanic Origin	Bush (R) 77,367	(34%)
			Other 7,261	(3%)
			Cook Partisan Voting Index: D +14	

Occupation	Blue collar: 22.8%	White collar: 62.4%	Gray collar: 14.8%

The closely built streets of the little city of Camden, New Jersey, across the Delaware River from Philadelphia's skyline, have seen a fair amount of history. This was where the poet Walt Whitman lived when he wrote some of the versions of his *Leaves of Grass*. It was an immigrant-jammed industrial city then, with tinkerers and inventors. In 1894, a Camden machinist named Eldridge Johnson produced the Victor Talking Machine—the birth of the company that became RCA Victor in 1929 and the beginning of the recorded music industry. In 1897, Camden was the site of the invention of condensed soup, and the Campbell Soup Company was founded soon afterwards. Camden remained for years afterward a major industrial locus on the Jersey side of the Delaware River, not the broadest and certainly not the most picturesque of our Atlantic estuaries, but probably the East Coast's premier industrial waterway, with a concentration of steel factories, chemical plants and oil tank farms equal to any in the country. The flat lands of South Jersey all around, mostly ignored in the 19th century, had easy access to cheap water transport and plenty of skilled labor from the Philadelphia area. For a quarter-century starting in the 1940s, they became one of the country's fastest-growing industrial areas.

In the 1980s and 1990s, Camden emptied out, many of its factories closed and fewer than 10,000 manufacturing jobs remained. Its neighborhoods were beset by crime, its mostly minority residents were heavily dependent on public assistance, and its mayor was convicted for doing favors for Philadelphia's organized crime leaders. Camden, which has been ranked the second-poorest city in America, continues to struggle: the state pays for much of the budget for the nearly bankrupt city and national crime data showed that Camden in 2005 remained the nation's most dangerous city. But it also has a few attractions: A newly-developed riverfront park, the New Jersey Aquarium and the Sony Music/Pace amphitheater; an aerospace complex and a Campbell Soup office tower have gone up. The port of Camden has rebounded, spurred by Del Monte's largest fruit processing plant, plus large imports of foreign steel and exports of scrap metal.

The 1st Congressional District is, more or less, greater Camden, the Delaware riverfront from Riverton south to a point across from the Delaware state line, and suburbs running southeast to the flat vegetable fields of South Jersey. It is traversed by Black Horse Pike and White Horse Pike. Both routes dates back two centuries; today, they connect Philadelphia and its middle class South Jersey suburbs. Many of these boroughs and townships developed over the past half-century as a result of flight from Camden; a few, like Gloucester City, emerged on their own rather than as an outgrowth of the city. The PATCO High-Speed Line to Philadelphia is just a quick trip over the Delaware River from here, making for an easy commute from places such as prosperous Haddonfield. The district includes a growing number of Hispanics, primarily Puerto Ricans in Camden, though many Mexicans from Puebla, in central Mexico, have settled in the region. Politically, this is an area with a Democratic heritage.

The 1st District is represented by Rob Andrews, first elected in 1990. Andrews grew up in Bellmawr, the son of a shipyard worker, made a splendid record in college and law school, returned home and with then-Congressman Jim Florio's support was elected to the Camden County Board of Chosen Freeholders before he was 30. When Florio left Congress to become governor in January 1990, he postponed the special election to replace him until November; he supported Andrews, though Andrews was silent on Florio's controversial state tax increase. Andrews had other help: a Republican opponent who switched positions on abortion and claimed to have attended a college he hadn't. Even so, in the anti-Florio climate, Andrews won by only 54%-43%.

Andrews has a mostly moderate record, particularly on foreign policy. After Democrats lost House control, Andrews remained a legislative activist, often by working with Republicans. He typically introduces more than 100 bills every two years, the most for any House member. As the ranking Democrat on the Employer-Employee Relations Subcommittee, he worked with committee Chairman John Boehner to expand its focus on pension and retirement issues. As an ardent proponent of the use of force in Iraq, Andrews joined other House Democratic supporters in several meetings with George W. Bush. Even when conditions in Iraq worsened after the overthrow, this Armed Services Committee member remained convinced that conditions were "better than leaving Saddam Hussein in power." But in 2006, he second-guessed Bush's handling of post-Saddam Iraq and he called for a stronger presence by Iraqi soldiers.

In the majority, Andrews gained the influential post as chairman of the Education and Labor Subcommittee on Health, Employment, Labor and Pensions. With George Miller, he spearheaded House approval of the controversial "employee free choice" bill, a labor-backed measure that passed the House 241-185, with 13 Republicans in favor. His ambitious plans included expanded health coverage for the uninsured, perhaps paid for by higher taxes on the top 1% of taxpayers. Andrews said that is a realistic goal. "My confidence is grounded in the ability of our leaders to be pragmatic."

Andrews has been reelected to the House by overwhelming margins and he has continued to live with his family in Haddon Heights, commuting by train to the Capitol and occasionally sleeping overnight in his office. After the 1996 election, he announced he was running for governor. Andrews was initially favored to win the primary in June 1997, but he ran into stiff competition from then-state Senator James McGreevey, who won 39%-37%. After McGreevey was elected in 2001, he refused to support Andrews as the successor to Senator Bob Torricelli. When McGreevey announced in August 2004 that he would resign, Andrews seemed even more interested in running. But after Jon Corzine announced his candidacy, Andrews declined to run and endorsed Corzine, with the hope of winning appointment as his successor in the Senate. That didn't happen. Andrews has made clear his plan to run for the Senate in 2008 if Frank Lautenberg retires. If that happens, it is likely that another Democrat would win this House seat.

SECOND DISTRICT

Rep. Frank LoBiondo (R)

Elected 1994, 7th term; b. May 12, 1946, Bridgeton; home, Vineland; St. Joseph's U., B.A. 1968; Catholic; married (Tina).

Elected Office: Cumberland Cnty. Bd. of Chosen Freeholders, 1985-88; NJ Assembly, 1987-94.

Professional Career: Operations Mgr., LoBiondo Bros. Motor Express Inc., 1968-94.

DC Office: 2427 RHOB, 20515, 202-225-6572; Fax: 202-225-3318; Web site: www.house.gov/lobiondo.

District Offices: Mays Landing, 609-625-5008.

Committees: *Armed Services* (15th of 29 R): Air & Land Forces; Readiness. *Transportation & Infrastructure* (10th of 34 R): Water Resources & Environment; Coast Guard & Maritime Transportation; Aviation.

Group Ratings

	ADA	ACLU	AFS	LCV	ITIC	NTU	COC	ACU	CFG	FRC
2006	25	23	14	83	57	42	73	68	30	85
2005	30	—	13	78	—	48	70	60	39	85

National Journal Ratings

	2005 LIB — 2005 CONS		2006 LIB — 2006 CONS	
Economic	53% —	47%	52% —	48%
Social	46% —	53%	40% —	59%
Foreign	40% —	58%	49% —	50%

Key Votes of the 109th Congress

1. Estate Tax Repeal	Y	5. Limit Interstate Abortion	Y	9. Build Border Fence	Y
2. Limit CAFE Standards	N	6. Extend Patriot Act	Y	10. CAFTA	N
3. FY06 Spending Curb	Y	7. Bar Same Sex Marriage	Y	11. Oppose Iraq Withdrawal	Y
4. Drilling in ANWR	N	8. Stem Cell Research $	N	12. Detainee Tribunals	Y

Election Results

2006 general	Frank LoBiondo (R)	111,245	(62%)	($1,648,220)
	Viola Thomas-Hughes (D)	64,279	(36%)	($26,903)
	Other	5,051	(3%)	
2006 primary	Frank LoBiondo (R)	unopposed		
2004 general	Frank LoBiondo (R)	172,779	(65%)	($872,384)
	Timothy Robb (D)	86,792	(33%)	($6,325)
	Other	5,871	(2%)	

Prior Winning Percentages: 2002 (69%); 2000 (66%); 1998 (66%); 1996 (60%); 1994 (65%)

The People		Race/Ethnic Origin	Ancestry	
Area size:	2,683 sq. mi.	71.7% White	Irish: 13.9%	Italian: 13.0%
Urban population:	79.0%	13.8% Black	German: 12.5%	
Rural population:	21.0%	2.4% Asian	**2004 Presidential Vote**	
Pop. 2000:	647,258	0.3% Native Am.	Bush (R) 141,123	(50%)
Pop. 2005 (est):	680,382	0.0% Hawaiian	Kerry (D) 138,797	(49%)
Median income:	$44,173	1.4% Two+ races	Other 2,578	(1%)
Poverty status:	10.3%	0.1% Other	**2000 Presidential Vote**	
Military veterans:	13.0%	10.3% Hispanic Origin	Gore (D) 134,345	(54%)
			Bush (R) 105,630	(43%)
			Other 7,906	(3%)
			Cook Partisan Voting Index: D + 4	
Occupation	Blue collar: 23.0%	White collar: 53.6%	Gray collar: 23.4%	

The builders of the Camden & Atlantic Railroad in 1852 may not have known it, but when they extended their line to the little inlet town of Absecon, they were starting America's biggest beach resort, Atlantic City. Like all resorts, it was a product of developments elsewhere: Of industralization and spreading affluence, of railroad technology and the conquest of diseases which used to make summer a time of terror for parents and doctors. In the years after the Civil War, first Atlantic City and then the whole Jersey Shore from Brigantine to Cape May became America's first seaside resort, and Atlantic City developed its characteristic features: The Boardwalk in 1870, the amusement pier in 1882, the rolling chair in 1884, salt water taffy in the 1890s, Miss America in 1921. By 1940, when 16 million Americans visited every summer, Atlantic City was a common man's resort of old traditions; it declined in the years after World War II as people could afford nicer vacations. By the early 1970s, Atlantic City was grim, with a bedraggled convention hall (site of the 1964 Democratic National Convention), empty hotels and bleak streets of rowhouses built in the ugliest Philadelphia style.

Then in 1977, New Jersey voters legalized casino gambling in Atlantic City and gleaming new hotels sprang up, big name entertainers came in and Atlantic City became more glamorous than it had been in 90 years. But not for all of its residents: casino and hotel jobs tend to be low-wage, and the slums begin just feet from the massive parking lots of the casinos. Atlantic City's gambling business has been thriving—its dozen casinos have net annual revenues of more than $5 billion, nearly as much as in Las Vegas, and the $5 blackjack table has become a relic–and huge new casinos were built on both the Boardwalk and bayside. Atlantic City now has one of the nation's largest tourism economies and may be growing into what Las Vegas has become, not just a collection of gaudy casinos but also a gaggle of theme parks, with entertainment for the family as well as adults. Gone is the Miss America pageant; the casinos are more interested in legalizing sports gambling.

The Jersey Shore south of Atlantic City is a string of different resorts. There is the old Methodist town of Ocean City, where Gay Talese grew up the son of Italian immigrants, as he told movingly in *Unto the Sons*. There is Wildwood, with its refurbished 1950s motels and the Doo Wop revival, and Cape May, with its beautifully preserved Victorian houses and a "ghosts of Cape May" trolley tour. Behind the Shore are swamp and flatland, the Pine Barrens and vegetable fields that gave New Jersey the name "Garden State." Growth has been slow in these small towns and gas station intersections, communities in whose eerie calmness in the summer you can hear mosquitoes whining. In the flatness, you can also find towns clustered around low-wage apparel factories or petrochemical plants on the Delaware estuary; the Northeast high-tech and service economy has not reached this far south in Jersey yet.

The 2d Congressional District covers this part of South Jersey. Politically, it has strong Democratic presences in the chemical industry towns along the Delaware River and in Vineland and a strong Republican presence in Cape May; Atlantic City often votes Democratic but has an antique Republican machine that goes back generations. Al Gore carried this district by a 54%-43% margin in 2000. But in 2004 it swung back toward the Republicans and George W. Bush, 50%-49%. This remains prime marginal territory, off the beaten track of Northeast politics.

The congressman from the 2d District is Frank LoBiondo, a Republican first elected in 1994. He grew up in Vineland, went to college in Philadelphia and worked for the family trucking firm, LoBiondo Brothers Motor Express, which originally carried produce from Jersey farms. In 1987 he was elected to the Assembly, where he stoutly opposed new taxes. LoBiondo also opposes gun control, and was backed by the National Rifle Association. In 1992 LoBiondo ran against veteran Congressman William Hughes, and lost 56%-41%. After Hughes decided to retire in 1994, LoBiondo ran again and in the primary faced state Senator William Gormley; LoBiondo attacked him as a taxer and NRA ads called him "a liberal in Republican clothing." LoBiondo won 54%-35%, an impressive margin. LoBiondo then easily won the 1994 general, 65%-35%. Since then, he has never fallen short of 60%—an impressive feat in a nationally competitive district.

In the House, LoBiondo has compiled a moderate voting record, especially on economic and labor issues, that is in sync with his district but has made few ripples in Washington. He is a founder of the Congressional Gaming Caucus. He remains a friend of the NRA—one of two House members from New Jersey to vote for John Dingell's amendment that ended the push for gun control in 1999. He is the state's only member on the Transportation and Infrastructure Committee; he chaired the Coast Guard and Maritime Transportation Subcommittee, a useful assignment for New Jersey, but he lost the top GOP position in the minority. He opposes oil drilling within 125 miles of the Jersey coast, and worked against the proposal by the Bush administration to reduce the federal contribution to beach replenishment. When Congress passed the intelligence reform bill, it included his provision to authorize Atlantic City's federal air marshal center to train foreign law enforcement officers serving on overseas air carriers serving the United States. With Steve LaTourette, he pushed a bill to require the FAA resume contract talks with the air traffic controllers union, but it failed to win two-thirds support in a June 2006 House vote. He helped to enact the Delaware River Protection Act, increasing the liability for single-hull oil tankers on the rivers. He worked with Democrats to increase the minimum wage.

LoBiondo announced in 2003 that he would not keep his pledge to serve only 12 years, contending that it was "unfair" to hold him to a promise that other members had broken. Secure at home where he has never won reelection with less than 60%, he seems content to climb the seniority ladder at the Transportation and Infrastructure Committee

THIRD DISTRICT

Rep. Jim Saxton (R)

Elected 1984, 12th full term; b. Jan. 22, 1943, Nicholson, PA; home, Mt. Holly; E. Stroudsburg St. Col., B.A. 1965, Temple U., 1967-68; United Methodist; divorced.

Elected Office: NJ Assembly, 1975-82; NJ Senate, 1982-84.

Professional Career: Jr. High schl. teacher, 1965-68; Real estate broker, 1968-84.

DC Office: 2217 RHOB, 20515, 202-225-4765; Fax: 202-225-0778; Web site: www.house.gov/saxton.

District Offices: Mt. Holly, 609-261-5800; Ocean County, 732-914-2020.

Committees: *Armed Services* (2d of 29 R): Air & Land Forces (RMM); Terrorism, Unconventional Threats & Capabilities. *Joint Economic Committee* (RMM of 10 R). *Natural Resources* (2d of 22 R): Fisheries, Wildlife & Oceans.

Group Ratings

	ADA	ACLU	AFS	LCV	ITIC	NTU	COC	ACU	CFG	FRC
2006	20	23	14	83	71	41	67	68	31	85
2005	20	—	13	72	—	49	81	60	45	85

National Journal Ratings

	2005 LIB	—	2005 CONS		2006 LIB	—	2006 CONS
Economic	50%	—	50%		50%	—	49%
Social	43%	—	57%		40%	—	59%
Foreign	34%	—	61%		6%	—	86%

Key Votes of the 109th Congress

1. Estate Tax Repeal	Y	5. Limit Interstate Abortion	Y	9. Build Border Fence	Y
2. Limit CAFE Standards	N	6. Extend Patriot Act	Y	10. CAFTA	Y
3. FY06 Spending Curb	Y	7. Bar Same Sex Marriage	Y	11. Oppose Iraq Withdrawal	Y
4. Drilling in ANWR	N	8. Stem Cell Research $	N	12. Detainee Tribunals	Y

Election Results

2006 general	Jim Saxton (R).................................	122,559	(58%)	($1,314,846)
	Rich Sexton (D).................................	86,113	(41%)	($161,186)
	Other..	1,179	(1%)	
2006 primary	Jim Saxton (R).................................	unopposed		
2004 general	Jim Saxton (R).................................	195,938	(63%)	($919,338)
	Herb Conaway (D).............................	107,034	(35%)	($42,334)
	Other..	5,890	(2%)	

Prior Winning Percentages: 2002 (65%); 2000 (57%); 1998 (62%); 1996 (64%); 1994 (66%); 1992 (59%); 1990 (58%); 1988 (69%); 1986 (65%); 1984 (61%); 1984 (62%)

The People		Race/Ethnic Origin	Ancestry	
Area size:	1,180 sq. mi.	83.4% White	Irish: 15.8%	Italian: 15.0%
Urban population:	96.2%	8.5% Black	German: 13.5%	
Rural population:	3.8%	2.7% Asian	**2004 Presidential Vote**	
Pop. 2000:	647,257	0.1% Native Am.	Bush (R) 167,254	(51%)
Pop. 2005 (est):	698,414	0.0% Hawaiian	Kerry (D) 159,041	(49%)
Median income:	$55,282	1.3% Two+ races	**2000 Presidential Vote**	
Poverty status:	5.1%	0.1% Other	Gore (D) 141,964	(54%)
Military veterans:	15.6%	3.8% Hispanic Origin	Bush (R) 114,621	(43%)
			Other 8,208	(3%)
			Cook Partisan Voting Index: D + 3	

Occupation   Blue collar: 18.6%   White collar: 67.6%   Gray collar: 13.7%

The Pine Barrens of New Jersey are one of the last vacant spots on the eastern seaboard; not quite *terra incognita*, but still not thickly populated. Encroached by the Philadelphia suburbs of South Jersey on the west and burgeoning retirement developments of the Jersey Shore on the east, they are crossed even today mostly by narrow two-lane roads; there are only a few small towns here, plus Fort Dix and McGuire Air Force Base. For years, the Barrens were seen as a barrier to civilization; only recently have environment-minded Jerseyites come to see them as a natural treasure.

The 3d Congressional District of New Jersey spans the Pine Barrens, thousands of acres of farmland and includes large parts of Burlington and Ocean Counties and Cherry Hill in Camden County. Most of its residents live in the South Jersey suburbs of Philadelphia, in spread-out Cherry Hill with its 1960s and 1970s shopping centers, or in the older towns along the Delaware River and newer ones inland toward McGuire. This is comfortable, but not hugely affluent, suburban country. Lockheed Martin in Moorestown is a big employer here, with its naval electronic and surveillance system plant: the birthplace of the Aegis radar. Curiously, in 2007 Internet auction site eBay reported that, on a per capita basis, Lumberton had more activity in its online marketplace than anywhere else in the nation. Politically it is competitive territory, with big Democratic margins in Willingboro and Cherry Hill.

East of the Pine Barrens is Ocean County, including the barrier islands from Normandy Beach south to Little Egg Harbor, with older beachfront communities and larger clusters of new subdivisions and condominium complexes inland. Ocean County has been the fastest-growing part of New Jersey, a kind of Frost Belt Florida, with many retirees from New York and North Jersey eager to leave the urban areas' high crime and high taxes. The two big military bases have remained active, with Fort Dix especially busy after September 11 training troops for new assignments and sending war materials to their destination. Ocean County has been Republican, and seems to have become more so after September 11. This district voted 54%-43% for Al Gore in 2000, but George W. Bush carried it 51%-49% in 2004—a pronounced 9/11 effect.

The congressman from the 3d District is Jim Saxton, a Republican first elected in 1984. He grew up in South Jersey, worked as a teacher for three years, then became a real estate broker. In 1975 he was elected to the New Jersey Assembly and later to the state Senate. In 1984 he ran to fill a vacancy in the House caused by the death of a Republican incumbent, won the Republican primary 45%-41%, and easily won the special election.

In the House, Saxton has compiled a moderate to conservative voting record, which leans to the right on foreign issues. When Republicans won the House, he became chairman of the Fisheries Conservation, Wildlife and Oceans Subcommittee, a useful post when representing a coastal district. But his environment-friendly record became an obstacle when he sought to become chairman of the Resources Committee in 2003. Although he was the most senior member seeking the position, most Western Republicans on the panel united against him. Saxton floated the idea of splitting the Resources panel so that he could chair a panel dealing with Merchant Marine issues, but Republican leaders had eliminated the Merchant Marine and Fisheries Committee in 1995 and weren't about to bring it back. Instead, Saxton got to chair the newly-created Subcommittee on Terrorism, Unconventional Threats and Capabilities at Armed Services. He remained active on environmental issues, winning enactment in 2004 of his program to encourage volunteer programs in national wildlife refuges; in 2006, he expanded that program to cover national fish hatcheries.

Saxton is now the second-ranking Republican on Armed Services and has been a consistent supporter of strong anti-terrorism efforts and aid to Israel. An ardent supporter of the war in Iraq, he filed bills to prevent French companies from receiving any U.S. funds spent rebuilding post-war Iraq and to prevent U.S. officials from participating in the annual Paris Air Show. He worked to protect Dix and McGuire from base closing review panels; both ended up gaining jobs under the 2005 review, and McGuire remains the home of the C-17 Globemaster. He strongly opposed the Dubai Ports World takeover of U.S. seaports. With Duncan Hunter planning to retire in 2008, Saxton is in line to become the top Republican on Armed Services. On the Joint Economic Committee, he defended the Bush administration plan to return most of the tax cut to higher-income taxpayers. As JEC chairman, he warned the Federal Reserve against undue increases in interest rates. He was one of 22 House Republicans who opposed the Bush administration's proposed changes in overtime-pay rules.

Saxton has had just one serious challenge. Democrats targeted him early in the 2000 campaign with strong support for Cherry Hill Mayor Susan Bass Levin. Levin was well-funded; she depicted Saxton as too conservative and out of the mainstream locally. But he was helped by endorsements from the local Sierra Club and the New Jersey Environmental Federation and won 57%-41%. In 2006, Saxton faced the similarly-named Democrat Richard Sexton. "It's not about 'e' and 'a.' It's about 'D' and 'R,'" said the challenger. Their names were closer than the 58%-41% outcome.

FOURTH DISTRICT

Rep. Chris Smith (R)

Elected 1980, 14th term; b. Mar. 4, 1953, Rahway; home, Hamilton; Trenton St. Col., B.S. 1975; Catholic; married (Marie).

Professional Career: Sales exec., family–owned sporting goods business, 1975-80; Exec. Dir., NJ Right to Life, 1976-78.

DC Office: 2373 RHOB, 20515, 202-225-3765; Fax: 202-225-7768; Web site: chrissmith.house.gov.

District Offices: Hamilton, 609-585-7878; Whiting, 732-350-2300.

Committees: *Foreign Affairs* (2d of 23 R): Africa & Global Health (RMM); Western Hemisphere.

Group Ratings

	ADA	ACLU	AFS	LCV	ITIC	NTU	COC	ACU	CFG	FRC
2006	30	27	14	92	71	37	67	68	33	100
2005	30	—	25	78	—	42	70	60	28	92

National Journal Ratings

	2005 LIB — 2005 CONS		2006 LIB — 2006 CONS	
Economic	53%	— 46%	52%	— 48%
Social	48%	— 52%	47%	— 53%
Foreign	33%	— 66%	53%	— 46%

Key Votes of the 109th Congress

1. Estate Tax Repeal	Y	5. Limit Interstate Abortion	Y	9. Build Border Fence	Y
2. Limit CAFE Standards	N	6. Extend Patriot Act	Y	10. CAFTA	N
3. FY06 Spending Curb	N	7. Bar Same Sex Marriage	Y	11. Oppose Iraq Withdrawal	Y
4. Drilling in ANWR	N	8. Stem Cell Research $	N	12. Detainee Tribunals	Y

Election Results

2006 general	Chris Smith (R)	124,482	(66%)	($471,992)
	Carol Gay (D)	62,905	(33%)	($94,172)
	Other	2,153	(1%)	
2006 primary	Chris Smith (R)	unopposed		
2004 general	Chris Smith (R)	192,671	(67%)	($533,725)
	Amy Vasquez (D)	92,826	(32%)	($34,687)
	Other	2,056	(1%)	

Prior Winning Percentages: 2002 (66%); 2000 (63%); 1998 (62%); 1996 (64%); 1994 (68%); 1992 (62%); 1990 (63%); 1988 (66%); 1986 (61%); 1984 (61%); 1982 (53%); 1980 (57%)

The People		Race/Ethnic Origin	Ancestry	
Area size:	762 sq. mi.	81.3% White	Italian: 15.9%	Irish: 15.2%
Urban population:	93.2%	7.5% Black	German: 11.8%	
Rural population:	6.8%	2.3% Asian	**2004 Presidential Vote**	
Pop. 2000:	647,258	0.1% Native Am.	Bush (R) 172,369	(56%)
Pop. 2005 (est):	689,202	0.0% Hawaiian	Kerry (D) 134,220	(44%)
Median income:	$54,073	1.1% Two+ races	**2000 Presidential Vote**	
Poverty status:	6.6%	0.1% Other	Gore (D) 123,764	(50%)
Military veterans:	13.3%	7.6% Hispanic Origin	Bush (R) 114,309	(46%)
			Other 8,301	(3%)
			Cook Partisan Voting Index: R + 1	

Occupation	Blue collar: 20.1%	White collar: 65.3%	Gray collar: 14.5%

An invisible and not very well defined line lies across central New Jersey dividing North Jersey and South Jersey. North of the line people watch New York TV stations, eat hero sandwiches and root for the Yankees; south of the line they watch Philadelphia TV, eat hoagies and root for the Phillies. The state capital of Trenton lies south of the line, which passes east somewhere around Six Flags Great Adventure and Wild Safari in the Pine Barrens and heads southeast past Lakewood and Bricktown to the little village of Mantoloking on the Jersey Shore. But on both sides of the line there has also developed over the last two decades a stronger New Jersey identity. The big cities are, after all, far away, particularly when traffic is heavy, and the economy of central New Jersey has its own special character, with big pharmaceutical companies and Fort Dix and McGuire Air Force Base. New Jersey politics is also centered here: Trenton is the state capital and also the home of the first New Jersey-oriented talk radio station, started in 1989. Some parts of this area are old: Trenton has been a manufacturing center since the 19th century, with the Lenox and Boehm china factories, the old Roebling ironworks which produced parts for many of our great bridges (the reason for the sign, refurbished in 2005, that you see across the Delaware River, "Trenton Makes, the World Takes"). But much of this area is also spanking new, with growing subdivisions just west of the Shore and office buildings stretching north from Princeton. Even Trenton has had some growth: preservationists are eyeing its antique buildings and, long the only state capital without a hotel, it now has the Marriott Lafayette Yard Conference Hotel near the War Memorial.

The 4th Congressional District of New Jersey covers much of the central part of the state and the invisible line separating North Jersey and South Jersey. It stretches from the eastern part of Trenton to Mantoloking, Point Pleasant, Sea Girt and Spring Lake on the Shore. It includes the old colonial town of Burlington on the Delaware River and the new spacious subdivisions of Colts Neck just west of the Shore. It includes the Lakehurst air terminal where the zeppelin *Hindenburg* exploded in 1937 and where the Navy launched an airship in 2006. This is one part of America where population movement has been eastward, away from the old neighborhoods of Trenton and its close-in suburbs and toward the new subdivisions of Ocean County and Wall Township. Politically, it is a mixed area. The Trenton area has long been solidly Democratic, but the Pine Barrens and Shore have leaned Republican. A Republican trend and increasing turnout in Ocean and Monmouth Counties carried this Gore 2000 district for George W. Bush in 2004.

The congressman from the 4th District is Christopher Smith, a youthful-looking Republican first elected in 1980. Smith grew up in the Trenton area, worked in his family's sporting goods business, and after graduating from college became executive director of the New Jersey Right to Life Committee in 1976. In 1980 he ran for the House in a more Trenton-centered 4th District and beat 26-year incumbent Frank Thompson, a convicted Abscam defendant. A fluke, it seemed, but Smith proceeded to beat several additional serious Democrats, winning more than 60% each time.

On abortion, Smith has worked to stop abortions in military hospitals and to reinstate the Reagan-era restrictions that would deny federal funds to family planning organizations that promote abortions abroad; George W. Bush restored the family-planning restrictions in an executive order in his first full day in office. Smith also has been a prime mover of legislation to ban partial-birth abortions.

He has fought not only Democrats but the House Republican leadership on the abortion issue. In July 2002 the bankruptcy bill, strongly backed by the leadership, came out of conference committee; the House had passed it 306-108 in March 2001. But it contained a provision, negotiated by Senator Charles Schumer and longtime abortion opponent Henry Hyde, providing that court judgments or fines could not be wiped out in bankruptcy: Schumer inserted this as a favor to abortion rights groups, after some abortion protesters declared bankruptcy to avoid paying fines.

Smith and Joe Pitts led a group of abortion opponents and said they would vote against the bill unless the provision was removed. In November the leadership brought forward the rule to vote on the bill. Smith and Pitts stood their ground despite furious efforts by Whip Tom DeLay, and the rule went down 243-172, with 87 Republicans voting against. It was only the second rule defeated during Dennis Hastert's first four years as speaker, and Hastert called Smith into his office to scold him in January 2003. Smith won a victory in 2004 when a provision stating that state and local governments could not force hospitals and care providers to perform abortions was put in the omnibus appropriation. His Unborn Child Pain Awareness Act, requiring doctors to inform pregnant women that some experts say fetus can feel pain after 20 weeks, finally got a floor vote in December 2006, the Republicans' last month of control, but is unlikely to go anywhere in the Democratic House. Neither is his bill to revoke the FDA approval of the abortifacient RU-486—"baby pesticide," to Smith, and "poison to the women themselves." Smith has opposed funding embryonic stem-cell research. But he has been a champion on other stem-cell research. His bill to authorize $265 million for research and therapy with umbilical cord stem-cells and bone marrow transplant stem-cells passed the House 431–1 in May 2005.

Smith has brought his strong moral views and his indefatigable energy to work against abuses of human rights and human dignity abroad and at home. He has strongly criticized China for its forced sterilizations and abortions and its persecution of Christians and other religious minorities, and opposed normal trade relations with China. Smith has condemned Russia for barring entry of foreign Catholic priests and Saudis for treating foreign servants as slaves. He sponsored an embassy protection act before September 11. In 2000 he had the signal success of pushing to passage a bill combating sex trafficking around the world, including a provision opposed by the Clinton administration requiring yearly reports on each nation's record; Clinton signed it anyway. In 2003 he succeeded in extending it to 2005. He got a third extension passed in 2005, with $361 million for prosecution of domestic trafficking and aid to young women and children victims. He cut short a trip to Africa for the signing in January 2006 and afterwards appeared on the Oprah Winfrey Show.

As chairman of the Africa, Global Human Rights and International Operations Subcommittee, he traveled to Sudan to talk with government leaders and visit the refugee camps in Darfur. Smith has also taken action on the subject: When he heard about Ukrainian girls being held against their will in brothels in Montenegro, he called the Montenegran prime minister, who ordered a raid on the operation. In July 2004 the House passed 323-45 his bill to bar increased aid to Vietnam unless the administration finds substantial progress toward releasing political prisoners and fostering religious freedom and democratic government and he sought to block WTO membership for Vietnam until it improves its human rights record. He held a hearing in February 2006 on the cooperation of Yahoo, Google, Microsoft and Cisco with Chinese government censorship and compared Chinese bloggers to Anne Frank; he sponsored a bill to regulate Internet companies abroad. He cosponsored the 2005 reauthorization that included a doubling of U.S. contributions to international peacekeeping, support of democracy in Haiti, permanent funding for Radio Free Asia and an Advance Democracy Act setting up a separate division in the State Department. He sponsored the 2005 law allowing U.S. participation in the Regional Emerging Diseases Intervention Center in Singapore. When Republicans lost their majority, he became ranking member of the renamed Africa and Global Health Subcommittee and promised to keep working on his causes. "Maybe if I hadn't been in the minority for 14 years, I wouldn't have that sense, but you just make it work."

In January 2001 Smith became chairman of the Veterans Committee and there pushed for policies opposed by the Republican leadership—which resulted in his losing the chairmanship in January 2005, two years short of the ordinary six-year limit. Over four years, Smith's veterans bills increased VA disability payments by $2.5 billion, increased G.I. Bill of Rights spending 46%, authorized $1 billion in aid to homeless veterans and added $100 million in health care benefits for surviving spouses of veterans. Smith's 2004 bill increased from 18 to 24 months the coverage of the Uniformed Services Employment and Reemployment Act, set up a pilot program for recruitment of nurses and authorized a new research center of veterans with multi-trauma combat injuries. By no means were all of these programs authorized by Smith's committee funded by the Appropriations Committee, and for three years Appropriations explicitly forbade spending on Smith's four research centers to develop responses to chemical, biological and radiological attacks. In early 2003 Smith called for making veterans benefits an entitlement—mandatory spending that would not have to go through Appropriations. This the leadership opposed and there were threats he'd lose the chair. In 2003 he voted for the Republican budget resolution that included a $1.8 billion increase in veterans spending, but in July 2003 appropriators did not include the money; Smith opposed that but disappointed Democrats by not voting against the rule sending the measure to the floor. In 2004,

Smith voted against the Republican resolution and for the Democratic budget resolution because the latter included more spending on veterans programs.

Over the last 30 years in both Republican and Democratic Houses the leadership of the majority party does not expect a committee chairman to vote against the party's budget resolution. It did not help that Smith ranked eighth lowest among House Republicans in party-line voting (though that was still 81%). It seems that Smith did not expect a challenge for the chair. But Steve Buyer, the fourth ranking Republican on the committee, asked for an interview with the Republican Steering Committee, and on January 5, 2005, it voted to make him chairman. That decision was ratified by the Republican Conference January 6; Smith was off the committee altogether. New Jersey Republicans expressed dismay, and New Jersey Democrats and the leaders of just about every veterans group expressed outrage. His warning that veterans' programs were being underfunded by $2.6 billion was proved true in June 2005, when Veterans Secretary Jim Nicholson announced that the agency had underestimated the number of return Iraq veterans by a factor of four and that the department needed another $2.6 billion. In November 2005, after Henry Hyde announced his retirement, Smith sought the chairmanship of the International Affairs Committee. He ranked behind the liberal Jim Leach in seniority, but ahead of Dan Burton, Elton Gallegly and Ileana Ros-Lehtinen. "The budget proved we were right," he said, referring to the veterans issue. "That should count for something. I never sought attention. I didn't run out and do press conferences." But the leadership was not persuaded and when it came time to pick the ranking minority member, it was Ros-Lehtinen who got the job.

Smith tends to the needs of his district, which was particularly hard hit by the September 11 attacks: 57 residents of the 4th District were killed, and later in September, the anthrax letters sent to New York and Washington passed through the post office sorting facility in Hamilton, just east of Trenton. The facility was closed and some 800,000 pieces of mail delayed. Smith introduced a bill to waive financial penalties for people whose mail was delayed; the banking industry agreed to do that voluntarily. He voted to postpone the 2005 base closing round by two years and over 10 years worked to bring in $50 million for the Naval Air Engineering Station in Lakehurst; the station, which designs and builds aircraft carrier catapults and arresting gear, was spared when the Pentagon released its base closing recommendations in May 2005, though it was slated to lose 186 jobs. Smith's devotion to principle and his reputation for tending to constituent problems have made him very popular in the 4th District. In 2004, Smith was reelected 67%-32%, and 66%-33% in the not very Republican year of 2006.

FIFTH DISTRICT

Rep. Scott Garrett (R)

Elected 2002, 3d term; b. July 9, 1959, Englewood; home, Wantage; Montclair St. U., B.A. 1981, Rutgers U., J.D. 1984; Protestant; married (Mary Ellen).

Elected Office: NJ Assembly, 1990-2002.

Professional Career: Practicing atty., 1984-2002.

DC Office: 1318 LHOB, 20515, 202-225-4465; Fax: 202-225-9048; Web site: garrett.house.gov.

District Offices: Newton, 973-300-2000; Paramus, 201-712-0330.

Committees: *Budget* (4th of 17 R). *Financial Services* (18th of 33 R): Housing & Community Opportunity; Financial Institutions & Consumer Credit; Capital Markets, Insurance & Government Sponsored Enterprises.

Group Ratings

	ADA	ACLU	AFS	LCV	ITIC	NTU	COC	ACU	CFG	FRC
2006	20	19	0	25	57	77	87	100	91	100
2005	5	—	0	11	—	74	85	100	87	92

National Journal Ratings

	2005 LIB	—	2005 CONS		2006 LIB	—	2006 CONS
Economic	14%	—	83%		42%	—	57%
Social	17%	—	82%		41%	—	59%
Foreign	39%	—	61%		45%	—	55%

Key Votes of the 109th Congress

1. Estate Tax Repeal	Y	5. Limit Interstate Abortion	Y	9. Build Border Fence	Y
2. Limit CAFE Standards	N	6. Extend Patriot Act	Y	10. CAFTA	N
3. FY06 Spending Curb	Y	7. Bar Same Sex Marriage	Y	11. Oppose Iraq Withdrawal	Y
4. Drilling in ANWR	Y	8. Stem Cell Research $	N	12. Detainee Tribunals	Y

Election Results

2006 general	Scott Garrett (R)	112,142	(55%)	($1,081,990)
	Paul Aronsohn (D)	89,503	(44%)	($554,555)
	Other	2,597	(1%)	
2006 primary	Scott Garrett (R)	23,760	(86%)	
	Michael Cino (R)	3,747	(14%)	
2004 general	Scott Garrett (R)	171,220	(58%)	($1,268,289)
	Anne Wolfe (D)	122,259	(41%)	($475,949)
	Other	3,946	(1%)	

Prior Winning Percentages: 2002 (59%)

The People		Race/Ethnic Origin	Ancestry	
Area size:	1,130 sq. mi.	86.3% White	Italian: 16.2%	Irish: 15.3%
Urban population:	82.7%	1.5% Black	German: 13.2%	
Rural population:	17.3%	6.6% Asian	**2004 Presidential Vote**	
Pop. 2000:	647,258	0.1% Native Am.	Bush (R) 184,530	(57%)
Pop. 2005 (est):	672,970	0.0% Hawaiian	Kerry (D) 137,019	(43%)
Median income:	$72,781	1.0% Two+ races	**2000 Presidential Vote**	
Poverty status:	3.6%	0.1% Other	Bush (R) 140,132	(52%)
Military veterans:	11.6%	4.5% Hispanic Origin	Gore (D) 120,142	(45%)
			Other 9,431	(3%)
			Cook Partisan Voting Index: R + 4	
Occupation Blue collar: 16.3%		White collar: 72.9%	Gray collar: 10.8%	

The northern edge of New Jersey was first settled three centuries ago by the Dutch, for whom this plateau of land behind the Hudson River Palisades seemed a natural part of Nieuw Amsterdam. The Dutch influence is seen in old steep-roofed farmhouses and in many of the place names—Bergen County, Cresskill, Closter. And some "Dutchness" remains in local communities. But overall, northernmost New Jersey has the well-settled look of so many northeastern suburbs, with touches both of affluence and small-town hominess, criss-crossed at its edges with limited access highways lined with shopping centers. Not far away are Saddle River and Franklin Lakes, with million-dollar houses on multi-acre lots, and Park Ridge, with office buildings and condominiums. This area may look like WASP suburbia on the surface, but in fact it is home to successful people of all ethnic groups, many descended from those who first saw the Statue of Liberty from the steerage deck and passed through the inspection queues at Ellis Island. A curiosity: Asian women in Bergen County have the nation's longest life expectancy: age 91.

The 5th Congressional District of New Jersey consists of most of northern Bergen County, plus a swath of North Jersey stretching west to the hill-enclosed upper reaches of the Delaware River, crossing one ridge of mountains after another, then running south to I-78. About 60% of its population is in Bergen County; to the west, little subdivisions set amid the lakes of western Passaic County are filling up with young families; farther west are once rural, now more or less suburban, Sussex and Warren Counties. Politically, this area has long been solidly Republican, although like all of New Jersey it moved toward Democrats in the 1990s. It was one of the state's three districts carried by George W. Bush in 2000 and one of six in 2004, when his vote in the 5th grew from 52% to 57%. But not all is well for local Republicans: In Bergen, the party's headquarters were padlocked because of failure to pay rent. In 2006 Senate contest, Republican Tom Kean Jr. lost the county 53%-45%.

The congressman from the 5th District is Scott Garrett, a Republican elected in 2002. Garrett graduated from Montclair State College and Rutgers law school and became a trial lawyer in Sussex

County. He's a born-again Christian who meets most Saturday mornings for three hours with a small group that calls itself Joshua Men. In 1989, he was elected to the state House, where he quickly became one of the most conservative members. In 1998 and 2000, he challenged veteran Congresswoman Marge Roukema in the Republican primary. He attacked her for supporting abortion rights and gun control; she pointed to her conservative votes on economic issues and was supported by the Republican leadership. Each time, Garrett carried the western part of the district but Roukema ran strongly in her Bergen County base; she won by only 53%-47% in 1998 and 52%-48% in 2000. In 2001, Roukema announced that she would not seek another term.

Garrett ran again in 2002. His challenge in the primary was to sell his views in Bergen County, where Sussex County is viewed as a distant province somewhere near Idaho. Garrett supported tax cuts and smaller bureaucracy, and opposed abortion and gun control; the American Conservative Union and the Club for Growth endorsed him. Two well-known Republicans from Bergen entered the race: state Senator Gerald Cardinale and Assemblyman David Russo. They argued that nominating Garrett would put the seat at risk. But Garrett won the primary with 41% to 26% for Russo and 25% for Cardinale. Garrett won a stunning 81% of the vote in Sussex, and 68% in Warren. But in Bergen County, he won just 25%, raising Republican fears and Democratic hopes. The Democratic nominee was Anne Sumers, a former Republican who switched parties in early 2002 and stressed her agreement with Roukema on most issues. With help from the national Democrats, Sumers attacked Garrett as an "extremist," pointing to his support for only limited federal aid to education. Roukema, recovering from surgery and chemotherapy, remained notably silent. Garrett pounced on Sumers's failure to vote in local school board elections and her musings on a liberal website where she characterized American patriotism as "jingoistic." At the urging of the House Republicans' campaign committee, he soft-pedaled some of his more conservative views. Sumers outspent Garrett, $1.6 million to $1.3 million, including nearly $400,000 of her own money. But national Republicans spent heavily on issue ads on Garrett's behalf. This turned out to be less of a contest than many people expected; Garrett won 59%-38%. In Bergen County, which cast 64% of the total, he led 55%-43%.

In the House, Garrett is the most conservative member of the New Jersey delegation and a tight-fisted spender. His vote against the Medicare/prescription drug bill angered Republican leaders and limited Garrett's influence in the House. When the state delegation sent a letter to George W. Bush opposing oil exploration off the New Jersey shore, Garrett was the only member who did not sign on. In 2005, he strongly supported UN Ambassador John Bolton. He took credit for delivering $50 million to safeguard New Jersey against terrorist attacks and advanced his tight fiscal views as a member of the Republican Study Committee. In April 2006, the House passed his amendment to require disclosure of earmarks on tax as well as spending bills. He lost on an amendment to require Fannie Mae and Freddie Mac to reduce their investment portfolios.

After winning reelection 58%-41%, Garrett faced a more serious challenge in 2006. Paul Aronsohn, who was communications director for Governor Jim McGreevey and a State Department adviser in the 1990s, called Garrett "too extreme, too disconnected to the people he represents," raised nearly $600,000 and reduced Garrett's margin. Garrett took Bergen by only 51%-48%. But with more than 60% in both Sussex and Warren, he was reelected 55%-44%.

SIXTH DISTRICT

Rep. Frank Pallone (D)

Elected 1988, 10th full term; b. Oct. 30, 1951, Long Branch; home, Long Branch; Middlebury Col., B.A. 1973, Fletcher Schl. of Law & Diplomacy, M.A. 1974, Rutgers U., J.D. 1978; Catholic; married (Sarah).

Elected Office: Long Branch City Cncl., 1982-88; NJ Senate, 1983-88.

Professional Career: Asst. prof., Rutgers U., 1979-80; Practicing atty., 1981-83; Instructor, Monmouth Col., 1984-86.

DC Office: 237 CHOB, 20515, 202-225-4671; Fax: 202-225-9665; Web site: www.house.gov/pallone.

District Offices: Long Branch, 732-571-1140; New Brunswick, 732-249-8892.

Committees: *Energy & Commerce* (6th of 31 D): Health (Chmn.); Environment & Hazardous Materials; Telecommunications & the Internet. *Natural Resources* (6th of 27 D): Fisheries, Wildlife & Oceans.

Group Ratings

	ADA	ACLU	AFS	LCV	ITIC	NTU	COC	ACU	CFG	FRC
2006	100	91	100	100	14	16	27	4	8	0
2005	100	—	100	100	—	14	30	4	9	15

National Journal Ratings

	2005 LIB	—	2005 CONS	2006 LIB	—	2006 CONS
Economic	85%	—	13%	91%	—	6%
Social	82%	—	17%	91%	—	8%
Foreign	77%	—	22%	75%	—	23%

Key Votes of the 109th Congress

1. Estate Tax Repeal	N	5. Limit Interstate Abortion	N	9. Build Border Fence	N
2. Limit CAFE Standards	N	6. Extend Patriot Act	N	10. CAFTA	N
3. FY06 Spending Curb	N	7. Bar Same Sex Marriage	N	11. Oppose Iraq Withdrawal	N
4. Drilling in ANWR	N	8. Stem Cell Research $	Y	12. Detainee Tribunals	N

Election Results

2006 general	Frank Pallone (D)	98,615	(69%)	($874,194)
	Leigh-Ann Bellew (R)	43,539	(30%)	($15,289)
	Other	1,619	(1%)	
2006 primary	Frank Pallone (D)	unopposed		
2004 general	Frank Pallone (D)	153,981	(67%)	($1,038,217)
	Sylvester Fernandez (R)	70,942	(31%)	($66,473)
	Other	5,228	(2%)	

Prior Winning Percentages: 2002 (66%); 2000 (68%); 1998 (57%); 1996 (61%); 1994 (60%); 1992 (52%); 1990 (49%); 1988 (52%); 1988 (52%)

The People		Race/Ethnic Origin	Ancestry	
Area size:	388 sq. mi.	61.7% White	Italian: 12.7%	Irish: 12.6%
Urban population:	99.7%	16.1% Black	German: 8.1%	
Rural population:	0.3%	8.3% Asian	**2004 Presidential Vote**	
Pop. 2000:	647,257	0.1% Native Am.	Kerry (D) 144,105	(57%)
Pop. 2005 (est):	654,790	0.0% Hawaiian	Bush (R) 109,729	(43%)
Median income:	$55,681	1.7% Two+ races	**2000 Presidential Vote**	
Poverty status:	9.1%	0.3% Other	Gore (D) 132,583	(61%)
Military veterans:	10.2%	11.7% Hispanic Origin	Bush (R) 74,828	(35%)
			Other 8,638	(4%)
			Cook Partisan Voting Index: D +12	

Occupation	Blue collar: 20.1%	White collar: 66.1%	Gray collar: 13.8%

For generations great transportation arteries have brought people out of the huge central cities of New York and Philadelphia and into the long-empty flatlands and hills of New Jersey—to vacation, to raise families and to work toward affluence and build communities. The railroads of the late 19th century created the towns of the Jersey Shore, from 1874, when the first train from New York City reached Long Branch, which quickly became the summer home of seven presidents from Grant to Wilson (Garfield, convalescing after he was shot, died there in 1881) and of New York racehorse owners and socialites. But the ambiance became honky-tonk, and the fishing pier plus much of the boardwalk went up in flames in 1987; only recently have developers sought to revive it. The great freight rail lines in the New York-Philadelphia corridor sparked electrical and chemical industries here; they built on the inventions of Thomas Edison, many of them produced in his Menlo Park laboratory just off the rail lines, where a 131-foot tower now marks a memorial to the inventor. The same corridor was the site of America's first cloverleaf intersection, at the junction of U.S. 1 and U.S. 9, and the intersection of two of America's great post-World War II highways, the New Jersey Turnpike and the Garden State Parkway. The Turnpike, now 12 lanes wide, roars past oil tank farms and petrochemical plants, major rail lines, Newark Airport and the oily waters of Raritan Bay; the Parkway links leafy affluent suburbs a dozen miles west of the Hudson with the Jersey Shore.

The 6th Congressional District inelegantly ties together these great transportation nodes, and the upward mobility and economic progress that have taken place around them. The district is shaped something like an overturned capital F, with a long string of towns running from Piscataway to Sandy Hook, and two appendages running south: One along the Middlesex-Monmouth county line, the other along the Atlantic Ocean. Middlesex and Monmouth Counties account for 90% of the district's population. It includes the central core of Middlesex County: New Brunswick, Highland Park, Metuchen, Sayreville, parts of Edison Township and surrounding communities—a heavy industry area that also, since the time of Thomas Edison, has housed some of America's great research and development facilities, plus Rutgers, the state university of New Jersey. In recent years, Edison has seen an influx of immigrants from India, many of them engineers and doctors. The 6th also includes Monmouth County territory overlooking Lower New York Bay, with spacious estates on highlands above little port towns from Sandy Hook, home to the nation's oldest operating lighthouse (1764), south to the mile-long boardwalk of Belmar. Between them are Asbury Park, founded as a Christian resort and immortalized by a Bruce Springsteen album but now with a high poverty rate, and Ocean Grove, founded in 1869 as a square-mile Methodist resort "free from the dissipation and follies of fashionable watering places," still dry for teetotalers who throng to its 10,000-seat 1894 Great Hall and with the nation's greatest concentration of Victorian homes; the revival of Ocean Grove began in 1978 when the state Supreme Court overturned a Sunday ban on wheeled vehicles. The Shore has remained a summer vacation area that attracts millions, but also hosts year-round communities, with their own upward-striving families.

The congressman from the 6th District is Frank Pallone, a moderate-to-liberal Democrat elected in 1988. Pallone is the son of a disabled Long Branch policeman; he has been an environmentalist since 1969, when as a Middlebury College freshman in Vermont he worked for that state's first-in-the-nation bottle deposit law. After getting a master's in international relations from Tufts and a law degree from Rutgers, he was elected to the Long Branch city council in 1982, at 31, and to the New Jersey Senate in 1983. Following the death of Representative Jim Howard, who chaired the Public Works and Transportation Committee, Pallone ran for the House. The district leaned Republican, but residents were angry about untreated sludge, plastic containers and medical waste washing up on the beach. Pallone's bumper sticker, without mentioning party affiliation, said, "Stop Ocean Dumping." That, combined with conservative stands on taxes and crime, helped him to win 52% in both the special and general elections.

Pallone started as a political maverick but became more partisan after Democrats lost control of the House. With the district's many Indian-Americans (the most in the country, he says), he formed the Congressional Caucus for India and Indian-Americans; he is also a co-founder of the Congressional Armenian Caucus and helped to approve normal trade relations for Armenia. After the September 11 attacks, he said that U.S. defense relations with India had improved and he called for increased democracy in Pakistan and controls on its nuclear weapons technology. At home, Pallone's environmental focus turned to the ever-lively border war with New York, opposing offshore dumping near Sandy Hook of highly contaminated material dredged from New York harbor; the Army Corps of Engineers, he complained, failed to respond to New Jersey objections. He enacted in 2006 a bill for a program to reduce and prevent debris in the marine environment. In 2007, he became chairman of the influential Energy and Commerce Subcommittee on Health, where he criticized shortfalls in children's health funding and attacked President Bush's plan to permit insured workers to switch to lower-cost health coverage. He has been a harsh foe of the Medicare/prescription-drug program, and he helps to coordinate the House Democrats' message as the policy committee's communications chairman.

With redistricting and time, his district became more safely Democratic. Since 1994, Pallone has been reelected with at least 60% of the vote—with one exception. It came in 1998, when he had a tough challenge from 28-year-old Republican Mike Ferguson, an education reformer close to former Governor Thomas Kean. An insurance group unhappy with Pallone's support for Clinton's HMO regulation plan spent nearly $2 million in an independent expenditure campaign, but Pallone won 57%-40%. Two years later, Ferguson won in the next-door 7th District. Pallone's ambition for statewide office has run into obstacles. When Senator Frank Lautenberg announced his retirement in 1999, Pallone formed an exploratory committee but did not run. When Senator Bob Torricelli quit the 2002 Senate race on September 30, and Governor Jim McGreevey offered the nomination to Pallone, he reportedly agreed to run. But Pallone quickly withdrew, reportedly because his wife opposed the move. If so, she was shrewd: He would have given up a safe House seat for a candidacy that could have been abruptly ended by either state or federal judges. When Jon Corzine ran for governor in 2005, Pallone endorsed him and said that he would like to fill Corzine's Senate seat. But he was again the bridesmaid as Corzine, after his victory, appointed Robert Menendez. Pallone might have another chance for the Senate in 2008 if Lautenberg decides to retire at 84.

SEVENTH DISTRICT

Rep. Michael Ferguson (R)

Elected 2000, 4th term; b. July 22, 1970, Ridgewood; home, Warren; U. of Notre Dame, B.S. 1992, Georgetown U., M.P.P. 1994; Catholic; married (Maureen Malloy).

Professional Career: H.S. teacher, Mount St. Michael Acad., 1992-93; Exec. Dir., Better Schools Fndt., 1994; Dir., Save Our Schoolchildren, 1994; Exec. Dir., Catholic Campaign for America, 1995-97; Adjunct Prof., Brookdale Com. Col., 1997-2000; Founder & Pres., Strategic Educ. Initiatives, 1997-present.

DC Office: 214 CHOB, 20515, 202-225-5361; Fax: 202-225-9460; Web site: www.house.gov/ferguson.

District Offices: Warren, 908-757-7835.

Committees: *Energy & Commerce* (20th of 26 R): Oversight & Investigations; Health; Telecommunications & the Internet.

Group Ratings

	ADA	ACLU	AFS	LCV	ITIC	NTU	COC	ACU	CFG	FRC
2006	20	18	14	83	86	47	80	64	44	85
2005	5	—	0	17	—	55	89	76	54	92

National Journal Ratings

	2005 LIB	—	2005 CONS	2006 LIB	—	2006 CONS
Economic	43%	—	56%	51%	—	49%
Social	42%	—	58%	46%	—	53%
Foreign	34%	—	61%	43%	—	55%

Key Votes of the 109th Congress

1. Estate Tax Repeal	Y	5. Limit Interstate Abortion	Y	9. Build Border Fence	Y
2. Limit CAFE Standards	N	6. Extend Patriot Act	Y	10. CAFTA	Y
3. FY06 Spending Curb	Y	7. Bar Same Sex Marriage	Y	11. Oppose Iraq Withdrawal	Y
4. Drilling in ANWR	N	8. Stem Cell Research $	N	12. Detainee Tribunals	Y

Election Results

2006 general	Michael Ferguson (R)	98,399	(49%)	($3,043,589)
	Linda Stender (D)	95,454	(48%)	($1,932,510)
	Other	5,222	(3%)	
2006 primary	Michael Ferguson (R)	unopposed		
2004 general	Michael Ferguson (R)	162,597	(57%)	($2,847,822)
	Steve Brozak (D)	119,081	(42%)	($792,575)
	Other	4,169	(1%)	

Prior Winning Percentages: 2002 (58%); 2000 (52%)

The People		Race/Ethnic Origin	Ancestry	
Area size:	603 sq. mi.	79.0% White	Italian: 15.3%	Irish: 13.0%
Urban population:	90.4%	4.4% Black	German: 11.7%	
Rural population:	9.6%	8.2% Asian	**2004 Presidential Vote**	
Pop. 2000:	647,257	0.1% Native Am.	Bush (R) ... 164,176	(53%)
Pop. 2005 (est):	672,996	0.0% Hawaiian	Kerry (D) ... 144,767	(47%)
Median income:	$74,823	1.2% Two+ races	**2000 Presidential Vote**	
Poverty status:	3.4%	0.2% Other	Bush (R) ... 127,702	(49%)
Military veterans:	10.6%	6.9% Hispanic Origin	Gore (D) ... 124,699	(48%)
			Other ... 9,099	(3%)
			Cook Partisan Voting Index: R + 1	

Occupation	Blue collar: 15.7%	White collar: 74.5%	Gray collar: 9.8%

The transportation arteries beneath the curve of the First Watchung Mountain are among New Jersey's historic lines of development. The rail lines of the late 19th century opened up commuter suburbs; in the 1940s the four lanes of U.S. 22 created an automobile civilization; and finally I-78, completed in the mid-1980s, put Newark only an hour's distance from the Pennsylvania line.

Interstate 78 stimulated the development of an Edge City called Bridgewater Commons—halfway between Philadelphia and Manhattan—where an enormous shopping mall and office developments that included the headquarters of AT&T rose up amid horse country around Far Hills and Bernardsville, where the likes of Malcolm Forbes and Charles Engelhard owned huge estates in horse country (New Jersey claims more horses per square mile than any other state). These are in Somerset County, one of the nation's top counties in per capita income.

The 7th Congressional District of New Jersey, with its contorted boundaries, covers these several generations of suburban development. It ranges across the breadth of the state, from the edge of Pennsylvania's Lehigh Valley in the west almost to Staten Island in the east. It is an agglomeration of places, some of affluence, not a district with a distinct character—the 7th includes parts of four counties, and parts of places such as Edison, Woodbridge, Bridgewater, Linden and Union. Its easternmost points are in Union County, just shy of Newark International Airport. It includes Summit, Scotch Plains and North and South Plainfield, but not heavily Democratic Plainfield. It follows I-78 and the Watchung Mountains to western Somerset County and most of fast-growing Hunterdon County, where the county seat of Flemington was the site of the "trial of the century" for the kidnapping and murder of the 20-month-old son of Charles Lindbergh. There is, of course, a political imperative behind the weird shape of the district: The 7th was designed as part of the bipartisan incumbents' plan to put heavily Democratic areas into the adjacent 12th, 6th and 10th Districts while moving Republican areas formerly in those districts, to this one. As a result, the Bush 2000 percentage in the 7th rose from 43% to 49%—the biggest partisan change in any New Jersey district.

The congressman from the 7th District is Michael Ferguson, a Republican first elected in 2000. He grew up in Ridgewood, in Bergen County; after graduating from Notre Dame, he taught history as an unpaid volunteer and coached basketball at Mount St. Michael Academy in the Bronx. He served as executive director of the Catholic Campaign for America and of the Better Schools Foundation in Washington; during that time, he focused on education issues while earning a master's degree in public policy from Georgetown. He returned to New Jersey to found Strategic Education Initiatives, an education consulting firm, and became an ally of Jersey City's Republican mayor Bret Schundler and a backer of school choice. In 1998, Ferguson challenged Frank Pallone in the 6th District, spending $1 million but losing 57%-40%.

When Bob Franks decided to give up the 7th District seat to run for the Senate in 2000, Ferguson moved to the district and entered the contest. He faced serious opposition in the primary, notably from Tom Kean Jr., son of the popular former governor, who had the highest name recognition and the most early endorsements, and Assemblyman Joel Weingarten. Ferguson focused on cutting taxes and won with 41% of the vote, to 28% for Kean and 23% for Weingarten. In the general, Ferguson faced Fanwood Mayor Maryanne Connelly, who in 1998 lost to Franks by 53%-44%. Ferguson barely mentioned his conservative views—for school prayer and a constitutional amendment banning abortion—but emphasized centrist positions on the environment and health care. His centerpiece issue was education: strong backing of school vouchers and increased accountability for public schools. Against the 55-year-old Connelly, a widow without children, Ferguson highlighted his youthfulness and two children. He won 52%-46%. In 2003, the Federal Election Commission ordered him to pay a $210,000 fine for an improper campaign loan to himself from a trust created by his parents during the 2000 campaign.

In the House, Ferguson has been near the center on economic and cultural issues but more conservative on defense. He voted against oil drilling in the Arctic National Wildlife Refuge but for the Bush tax cuts, trade promotion authority, and authorization for war in Iraq. With a seat on the Energy and Commerce Committee, he appealed to constituent interests by supporting an overhaul of telecommunications laws. He opposed Edward Markey's "net neutrality" restrictions on broadband providers as "a solution in search of a problem." In 2006, he won enactment of his Lifespan Respite Care Act, for states to train volunteers and provide other services to the estimated 50 million families caring at home for adults and children with special needs.

Ferguson's voting record plus the redistricting changes strengthened him at home. But Democrats continue to place him in their top tier of targets. In 2004, Democratic challenger Stephen Brozak spent a bit short of $1 million; he ran on his service as an Iraq war veteran and sought to make the Bush administration's handling of the war his central issue. Ferguson emphasized tax cuts and support for the troops in Iraq. National Democrats sought to highlight Brozak's candidacy by giving him a speaking slot at the national convention in Boston. But the first-time candidate's campaign skills were disappointing and national Democrats lost enthusiasm. Ferguson won 57%-42%. Two years later, Democrats fared better with Linda Stender, an experienced assemblywoman and former mayor of Fanwood. In the toxic climate for Republicans, she was an energetic candidate familiar with the issues and emphasized "It's time for a change." But she was in the second tier of the House Democrats' select candidates. Ferguson emphasized his partisan independence and the slogan, "Stender is a Spender." Ferguson won 49%-48%. Stender took the eastern part of the district: narrowly in Union County and comfortably in Middlesex; Ferguson's victory margin came in Hunterdon, where he led 56%-40%. Stender planned for a 2008 rematch.

EIGHTH DISTRICT

Rep. Bill Pascrell (D)

Elected 1996, 6th term; b. Jan. 25, 1937, Paterson; home, Paterson; Fordham U., B.A. 1959, M.A. 1961; Catholic; married (Elsie).

Military Career: Army, 1961; Army Reserves, 1962-67.

Elected Office: Pres., Paterson Bd. of Ed., 1979-82; NJ Assembly, 1987-97, Minority Ldr. Pro-Tem; Paterson Mayor, 1990-97.

Professional Career: High Schl. teacher, 1960-74; Dir., Paterson Dept. of Public Works, 1974-77; Dir., Paterson Dept. of Policy, 1977-87.

DC Office: 2464 RHOB, 20515, 202-225-5751; Fax: 202-225-5782; Web site: www.pascrell.house.gov.

District Offices: Paterson, 973-523-5152.

Committees: *Ways & Means* (18th of 24 D): Trade; Oversight.

Group Ratings

	ADA	ACLU	AFS	LCV	ITIC	NTU	COC	ACU	CFG	FRC
2006	95	86	100	100	43	10	27	12	7	0
2005	100	—	100	89	—	10	37	0	4	8

National Journal Ratings

	2005 LIB	—	2005 CONS		2006 LIB	—	2006 CONS
Economic	82%	—	16%		94%	—	0%
Social	76%	—	24%		75%	—	24%
Foreign	75%	—	24%		70%	—	28%

Key Votes of the 109th Congress

1. Estate Tax Repeal	N	5. Limit Interstate Abortion	N	9. Build Border Fence	Y
2. Limit CAFE Standards	N	6. Extend Patriot Act	N	10. CAFTA	N
3. FY06 Spending Curb	N	7. Bar Same Sex Marriage	N	11. Oppose Iraq Withdrawal	N
4. Drilling in ANWR	N	8. Stem Cell Research $	Y	12. Detainee Tribunals	N

Election Results

2006 general	Bill Pascrell (D)	97,568	(71%)	($1,098,407)
	Jose Sandoval (R)	39,053	(28%)	($234,505)
	Other	1,018	(1%)	
2006 primary	Bill Pascrell (D)	unopposed		
2004 general	Bill Pascrell (D)	152,001	(69%)	($948,047)
	George Ajjan (R)	62,747	(29%)	($137,886)
	Other	4,072	(2%)	

Prior Winning Percentages: 2002 (67%); 2000 (67%); 1998 (62%); 1996 (51%)

The People		Race/Ethnic Origin	Ancestry	
Area size:	110 sq. mi.	53.7% White	Italian: 15.3%	Irish: 8.0%
Urban population:	100.0%	12.7% Black	German: 6.0%	
Rural population:	0.0%	5.3% Asian	**2004 Presidential Vote**	
Pop. 2000:	647,258	0.1% Native Am.	Kerry (D) 142,081	(59%)
Pop. 2005 (est):	654,271	0.0% Hawaiian	Bush (R) 99,239	(41%)
Median income:	$51,954	2.1% Two+ races	**2000 Presidential Vote**	
Poverty status:	10.7%	0.3% Other	Gore (D) 129,906	(60%)
Military veterans:	8.3%	25.8% Hispanic Origin	Bush (R) 78,446	(36%)
			Other 6,784	(3%)
			Cook Partisan Voting Index: D +12	

Occupation   Blue collar: 22.4%   White collar: 64.1%   Gray collar: 13.5%

Paterson, New Jersey, is one of few American cities that have turned out pretty much as planned. The planner was Alexander Hamilton, who in the 1790s journeyed 20 miles from Manhattan into the interior of New Jersey to the Great Falls of the Passaic River. Watching the water surge down 72 feet—the highest falls along the East Coast—he predicted an industrial city would rise on this site. He formed the Society for Establishing Useful Manufactures, which opened a calico factory in 1794, and got Pierre L'Enfant, the designer of Washington, D.C., to design Paterson (named after then-Governor William Paterson). In 1836, Samuel Colt began manufacturing revolvers here; one of the first American locomotives, the Sandusky, was built here in 1837; a walkout of Paterson cotton workers in 1828 was America's first factory strike. Paterson ultimately became America's "Silk City," employing 25,000 silk mill workers before the great strike of 1913 led by the radical Industrial Workers of the World. Paterson kept producing locomotives and, after the silk mills started closing down following another unsuccessful strike in 1924, became a cloth-dying center. Throughout, it attracted immigrants from England, Ireland and, after 1890, Italy and Poland. And it continues to attract them today, even if its economy produces more service and fewer manufacturing jobs. In 2000 Paterson's population was 50% Hispanic (up 30% since 1990); downtown's "Little Palestine" reflects the city's sizable Arab community—Turks, Palestinians, Lebanese, Syrians, and Jordanians. Overall, this area lost population and reported an increase in poverty in the 1990s; since then, the population rebounded slightly.

The 8th Congressional District of New Jersey includes Paterson as its largest city and much suburban and industrial territory west and south of Paterson and north of Newark. More than half the population lives in Passaic County; the rest are in Essex County. It includes the mixed factory and middle-class towns south of Paterson on the Passaic River—Clifton, Nutley, Belleville, Bloomfield, majority Hispanic and fast-growing Passaic. In some of these towns you can see vestiges of the gritty Republicanism that prevailed in North Jersey in the 1940s and 1950s. On higher ground is affluent Montclair, with large populations of well-off blacks and Manhattan-oriented Boomers, the most Democratic part of the district except for Paterson. Over the Watchung Mountain are affluent West Orange and South Orange, both heavily Democratic, and the small Republican towns of Cedar Grove and Verona. In the 1980s the district leaned Republican, in the 1990s it became heavily Democratic; it remains Democratic, but somewhat less so since the September 11 attacks.

The congressman from the 8th District is Bill Pascrell, a Democrat elected in 1996. He grew up in Paterson, the grandson of Italian immigrants, graduated from Fordham, served in the Army, then taught high school for 14 years. From there he went into politics, as director of Paterson's department of public works, school board president, then in 1987 to the New Jersey Assembly. In 1990 he was elected mayor of Paterson, but continued to serve in the Assembly—a common practice in New Jersey (and also in France) until the legislature voted in 2007 to stop the practice. Meanwhile, he watched as the 8th District seat changed hands. After Public Works Committee chairman Robert Roe retired in 1992, liberal Democrat Herb Klein won, only to be replaced by Bill Martini in the Republican sweep in 1994. Pascrell ran in 1996 and attacked him as a tool of an "extremist" Republican leadership—one ad even showed Martini's face on a puppet operated by Speaker Newt Gingrich. Despite Martini's support from the Sierra Club and some labor unions, Pascrell rode the coattails of the Clinton-Gore campaign. In a district that went 58% for Clinton, Pascrell won 51%-48%. Since then, he has won at least 62% of the vote against weak challengers.

In the House, Pascrell has compiled a liberal record on economics, more moderate on cultural and foreign issues. He voted for the partial-birth abortion ban and for parental-notification requirements for abortions across state lines. He voted to authorize the use of force in Iraq. On the

Homeland Security Committee, he was a voice for strengthening homeland defense, calling for improved communications among first responders. "How is it we can talk to people on the moon, but we can't talk one block away?" Pascrell asked. In 2005, a House-Senate conference committee stripped his House-passed amendment to ban state highway contractors from "pay to play" contributions to gubernatorial candidates or state parties. For years, he has fought to designate Paterson's Great Falls as a 120-acre national park. After earlier unsuccessful bids for a seat on the Ways and Means Committee and a vigorous lobbying effort, he finally got on the committee in 2007. Pascrell is New Jersey's first member on the panel in a decade; he pledged to work on fair trade.

Like others in the House delegation, Pascrell has had ambitions for statewide office. He expressed interest in running for governor in 2001. But his support for Jim Florio in the 2000 Senate primary against Jon Corzine left him on the losing side of the New Jersey party establishment. In 2005 he supported Corzine for governor and said he would be interested in succeeding him in the Senate. With his Ways and Means seat, he is less likely to seek a move elsewhere. An eventual replacement could be his son, Passaic County Counsel Bill Pascrell III.

NINTH DISTRICT

Rep. Steven Rothman (D)

Elected 1996, 6th term; b. Oct. 14, 1952, Englewood; home, Fair Lawn; Syracuse U., B.A. 1974, Washington U., J.D. 1977; Jewish; married (Jennifer Beckenstein).

Elected Office: Englewood Mayor, 1983-89; Bergen Cnty. Surrogate Court Judge, 1993-96.

Professional Career: Practicing atty., 1977-93.

DC Office: 2303 RHOB, 20515, 202-225-5061; Fax: 202-225-5851; Web site: rothman.house.gov.

District Offices: Hackensack, 201-646-0808; Jersey City, 201-798-1366.

Committees: *Appropriations* (24th of 37 D): State, Foreign Operations & Related Programs; Agriculture, Rural Development, FDA & Related Agencies; Defense. *Science & Technology* (15th of 24 D): Space & Aeronautics; Investigations & Oversight.

Group Ratings

	ADA	ACLU	AFS	LCV	ITIC	NTU	COC	ACU	CFG	FRC
2006	90	86	100	100	29	13	27	8	4	0
2005	95	—	100	94	—	10	48	5	0	8

National Journal Ratings

	2005 LIB	—	2005 CONS		2006 LIB	—	2006 CONS
Economic	74%	—	26%		78%	—	21%
Social	76%	—	24%		80%	—	19%
Foreign	70%	—	30%		87%	—	13%

Key Votes of the 109th Congress

1. Estate Tax Repeal	N	5. Limit Interstate Abortion	*	9. Build Border Fence	N
2. Limit CAFE Standards	N	6. Extend Patriot Act	N	10. CAFTA	N
3. FY06 Spending Curb	N	7. Bar Same Sex Marriage	N	11. Oppose Iraq Withdrawal	N
4. Drilling in ANWR	N	8. Stem Cell Research $	Y	12. Detainee Tribunals	N

Election Results

2006 general	Steven Rothman (D)	105,853	(71%)	($912,808)
	Vincent Micco (R)	40,879	(28%)	($52,114)
	Other	1,363	(1%)	
2006 primary	Steven Rothman (D)	unopposed		
2004 general	Steven Rothman (D)	146,038	(68%)	($630,160)
	Edward Trawinski (R)	68,564	(32%)	($17,532)
	Other	1,649	(1%)	

Prior Winning Percentages: 2002 (70%); 2000 (68%); 1998 (65%); 1996 (56%)

The People		Race/Ethnic Origin	Ancestry	
Area size:	100 sq. mi.	61.3% White	Italian: 16.2%	Irish: 9.0%
Urban population:	100.0%	6.6% Black	German: 6.6%	
Rural population:	0.0%	10.7% Asian	**2004 Presidential Vote**	
Pop. 2000:	647,257	0.1% Native Am.	Kerry (D) 144,723	(59%)
Pop. 2005 (est):	660,294	0.0% Hawaiian	Bush (R) 101,229	(41%)
Median income:	$52,437	2.1% Two+ races	**2000 Presidential Vote**	
Poverty status:	7.6%	0.3% Other	Gore (D) 135,406	(63%)
Military veterans:	8.6%	18.8% Hispanic Origin	Bush (R) 72,695	(34%)
			Other 6,110	(3%)
			Cook Partisan Voting Index: D +13	

Occupation	Blue collar: 20.3%	White collar: 66.8%	Gray collar: 12.9%

The George Washington Bridge, one of several wondrous suspension bridges completed in America in the 1930s, strides the Hudson, its west tower almost up against the green cliff of New Jersey's Palisades. It is one of the glories of modern engineering, enabling people and goods to be transported through the irregular terrain of metropolitan New York—tidal rivers and cliffs and broad expanses of swamp. For a century the dramatic beauty of the Palisades contrasted with the ugly sprawl of the Hackensack River Valley and the Jersey Meadowlands not far to the west. This giant swamp was the image of New Jersey for many—a landscape of gas station signs, oil tank farms, truck terminals and 12 lanes of New Jersey Turnpike—a smelly, ugly place that meant you were still not where you wanted to go, full of garbage and pig farms, briefly famous when Secaucus tavern owner Henry Krajewski ran for president in 1956. But the Meadowlands—which survive as 8,400 acres of wetlands and home to thousands of species of animals and plants—were the largest hunk of empty real estate near such a huge city center, and eventually they were developed. In the 1970s, the state built in East Rutherford the Meadowlands Sports Complex—Giants Stadium (where the Giants and Jets play), the Meadowlands Racetrack, the Brendan Byrne Arena (later Continental Airlines Arena, but with the hockey Devils departing for downtown Newark and the basketball Nets planning a move to a new arena in Brooklyn). Private development followed—hotels, warehouses, light industry, shopping centers (including a huge Wal-Mart)—in what became a small city. Now, a generation later, the state plans to build a new $1.4 billion stadium at the Meadowlands for the two football teams, and pollution control has restored aquatic life to the former wasteland. But the GW Bridge has acquired a new form of pollution: billboard advertising atop the toll booths.

The 9th Congressional District of New Jersey includes much of the Palisades and the Meadowlands. The scenery here is familiar to fans of the cable television series, *The Sopranos*: Jersey City, Kearny, North Arlington, Lodi (home to the fictitious Bada Bing; the actual strip club uses a different name). The 9th runs from the high-rise towers of Fort Lee, Cliffside Park and fast-growing Edgewater, where dwellers in luxury apartment houses brag about their views of New York City, west and north to the leafy suburbs of Englewood and Teaneck, and southwest to the high land overlooking the Meadowlands and the Passaic River in old towns like Rutherford, with Polish-, German- and Italian-Americans. Blue-collar Palisades Park has become a center for Korean-Americans. Teaneck and Englewood are home to middle-class blacks and young, Orthodox Jewish families.

Fairview, Bergenfield and Hackensack, an old industrial town and the Bergen County seat, are home to growing numbers of Hispanics; from 2000 to 2005, Hispanic population in the county soared 30% to 120,000. This was a growth area in the 1950s and 1960s, as New Yorkers moved out of the City; it lost population in the 1970s and 1980s, as young people moved farther out and left empty nesters behind. Now the population in some towns is rising due to new immigrants. Conservative families griping about taxes, who grew up in Bergen County, are being replaced by heavily Democratic immigrants and "tower dwellers," who have eviscerated the GOP's former stranglehold on the county. George W. Bush lost the county twice: in 2000 with 43%, and in 2004 with 47%.

The congressman from the 9th District is Steve Rothman, a Democrat first elected in 1996. Rothman grew up in Englewood and Tenafly, went off to school at Syracuse University and Washington University law school in St. Louis, then practiced law. From 1983-89 he was mayor of Englewood; in 1993 he became a judge in the Bergen County Surrogate's Court. When Congressman Bob Torricelli ran for the Senate in 1996, Rothman resigned his judgeship and ran for the House. With the party endorsement, Rothman faced Republican Kathleen Donovan—Bergen County Clerk, former Assemblywoman, and chairman of the New York-New Jersey Port Authority, who was endorsed by the New Jersey Education Association and Cuban-American leader Jorge Mas Canosa.

But this part of New Jersey swung sharply to the Democrats following the 1994 Republican takeover of Congress. The 9th District voted overwhelmingly for Bill Clinton and 56%-42% for Rothman.

In the House, Rothman often has been more liberal on economic issues than on defense. He voted for the Iraq war resolution; in 2006, he called for a pullout in six months and opposed federal funds for permanent military bases in Iraq. In 2004, he sought unsuccessfully to extend the assault weapons ban. On local issues, his most innovative work has been to limit further development and gain protections for the Meadowlands. He secured $5.2 million more to help create an 8,400-acre state park in the one-third of the Meadowlands that had not been developed and ultimately hopes to turn the area into an environmental park. "From an industrial waste dump to a nature preserve," Rothman exulted. He fought proposals to expand the Teterboro airport and the House in September 2003 approved his provision to ban 737s at Teterboro; in October 2006, he brokered a noise-control agreement for the airport, including a weight limit for jets and an overnight curfew. He has claimed delivery of hundreds of millions of dollars for local highways, including ever-congested Route 17, and worked to pass a measure that would enable states like New Jersey to adopt more stringent chemical plant security regulations than required by the federal government.

Rothman has won reelection by wide margins. He has said he will run for the Senate in 2008, if Frank Lautenberg retires; he likely would face a competitive primary.

TENTH DISTRICT

Rep. Donald Payne (D)

Elected 1988, 10th term; b. July 16, 1934, Newark; home, Newark; Seton Hall, B.A. 1957; Baptist; widowed.

Elected Office: Essex Cnty. Bd. of Chosen Freeholders, 1972-78, Dir. 1977-78; Newark Municipal Cncl., 1982-89.

Professional Career: Elem. & High Schl. teacher, 1957-64; Exec., Prudential Insurance Co., 1964-72; Pres., YMCAs of the U.S., 1970; Vice Pres., Urban Data Systems Inc., 1975-88.

DC Office: 2209 RHOB, 20515, 202-225-3436; Fax: 202-225-4160; Web site: www.house.gov/payne.

District Offices: Elizabeth, 908-629-0222; Jersey City, 201-369-0392; Newark, 973-645-3213.

Committees: *Education & Labor* (3d of 27 D): Workforce Protections; Early Childhood, Elementary & Secondary Education. *Foreign Affairs* (5th of 27 D). Africa & Global Health (Chmn.); International Organizations, Human Rights & Oversight; Western Hemisphere.

Group Ratings

	ADA	ACLU	AFS	LCV	ITIC	NTU	COC	ACU	CFG	FRC
2006	85	100	100	92	17	16	14	4	5	0
2005	85	—	100	83	—	17	29	0	4	0

National Journal Ratings

	2005 LIB	—	2005 CONS	2006 LIB	—	2006 CONS
Economic	94%	—	0%	89%	—	11%
Social	95%	—	5%	94%	—	5%
Foreign	96%	—	0%	95%	—	0%

Key Votes of the 109th Congress

1. Estate Tax Repeal	N	5. Limit Interstate Abortion	N	9. Build Border Fence	N
2. Limit CAFE Standards	N	6. Extend Patriot Act	N	10. CAFTA	N
3. FY06 Spending Curb	N	7. Bar Same Sex Marriage	N	11. Oppose Iraq Withdrawal	N
4. Drilling in ANWR	N	8. Stem Cell Research $	Y	12. Detainee Tribunals	N

Election Results

2006 general	Donald Payne (D)............................. unopposed		($495,562)
2006 primary	Donald Payne (D)............................. unopposed		
2004 general	Donald Payne (D)............................... 155,697	(97%)	($483,000)
	Other.. 5,016	(3%)	

Prior Winning Percentages: 2002 (84%); 2000 (88%); 1998 (84%); 1996 (84%); 1994 (76%); 1992 (78%); 1990 (81%); 1988 (77%)

The People		Race/Ethnic Origin	Ancestry	
Area size:	69 sq. mi.	21.4% White	West Indian: 6.4% Italian: 4.2%	
Urban population:	100.0%	56.6% Black	Irish: 3.6%	
Rural population:	0.0%	3.6% Asian	**2004 Presidential Vote**	
Pop. 2000:	647,258	0.2% Native Am.	Kerry (D) 167,707	(82%)
Pop. 2005 (est):	658,040	0.0% Hawaiian	Bush (R) 36,660	(18%)
Median income:	$38,177	2.8% Two+ races	**2000 Presidential Vote**	
Poverty status:	17.5%	0.5% Other	Gore (D) 147,112	(83%)
Military veterans:	8.1%	15.0% Hispanic Origin	Bush (R) 27,718	(16%)
			Other 3,004	(2%)
			Cook Partisan Voting Index: D +34	

Occupation	Blue collar: 23.6%	White collar: 58.0%	Gray collar: 18.4%

Newark has been the hollow core of New Jersey, the city to which main transportation arteries once led and whose corporate headquarters buildings were the tallest in the state. In 1930, 442,000 people lived here, one of every nine in New Jersey; in 2000, there were 273,000, one of every 30. Even so, Newark's core has recently been perking up; new office buildings have joined the Prudential and Public Service Electric & Gas headquarters, and the New Jersey Performing Arts Center has been a big hit. There are new restaurants and hip bars, a new downtown arena will house the hockey Devils and an assortment of condominium projects are on the drawing board. There has been industrial development around Newark Airport, and immigrant neighborhoods are showing new vitality following the devastation that lingered after riots in 1967. The glass and aluminum airport has greatly expanded for international carriers and is prospering as a hub for Continental, the most thriving of the legacy airlines.

Port Newark-Elizabeth Marine Terminal is the largest container port on the East Coast and ranks nationally behind only Los Angeles and Long Beach; old warehouses there have been cleared for more modern facilities. What hurt Newark for so many years was the plague of horrendous schools and high crime; large parts of the city were dominated by criminals and deserted by most law-abiding residents who could get out. Now crime rates have declined, the state has taken over the schools and life is returning to deserted streets. Young and charismatic Mayor Cory Booker brought energy to the city and has made war against gang crime a central campaign theme. The question is whether finances will stabilize, progress will continue and Newark can become once again the vital center of New Jersey.

The 10th Congressional District of New Jersey is centered in Essex County and is made up of most of Newark—the Central, South and West Wards—plus Irvington, most of the Oranges and part of Montclair to the west, and much of Elizabeth, Rahway, and Linden to the south. Its boundary lines wiggle around to include African-Americans in Jersey City, Montclair and Elizabeth, while leaving Hispanics in the next-door 13th District. Overall the district is 57% black; it is by far the most Democratic district in New Jersey.

The congressman from the 10th District is Donald Payne, a Democrat first elected in 1988. He grew up in Newark, worked as a teacher and for Prudential, served on the Essex Board of Chosen Freeholders in the 1970s and was vice president of Urban Data Systems for 13 years. In 1980 and 1986, he ran against Congressman Peter Rodino, chairman of the House Judiciary Committee when it voted to impeach President Richard Nixon; Payne lost, even as an African-American in a district with a black majority. But when Rodino retired in 1988, Payne, at age 54, won 73% in the Democratic primary and easily won the general. He has not faced a serious reelection challenge.

Payne has a strongly liberal voting record. He served as chairman of the Congressional Black Caucus in 1995 and 1996, just as Republicans were defunding the caucuses. He rescued the Africa Subcommittee from abolition, and attacked cuts in aid to African countries. But he did not lionize all of Africa's leaders. He sponsored a resolution to cut off new investment in Sudan because of its practice of slavery—though he criticized as "unconscionable" the pullout of international private-aid agencies from Sudan. As ranking Democrat on the Africa Subcommittee, roughly half the bills he sponsored dealt with Africa. He criticized foreign aid as insufficient to meet the needs of United Nations peacekeeping operations, and has pointed out that the more than 700 million people of Africa receive far less aid from the United States than do the six million of Israel. In 2003, George W. Bush named him as one of two members of Congress to serve as a delegate to the United Nations. But he was one of 22 House members who voted "present" on the March 2003 resolution of "unequivocal support" for the war in Iraq, calling the war "ill-conceived" and one that "could have been avoided through diplomacy." He criticized Secretary of State Colin Powell as not tough enough in stopping the war in Sudan; in July 2004, the House passed his resolution condemning the conflict and terming it "genocide," and the Bush administration agreed. Payne came to the defense of UN Secretary-General Kofi Annan in December 2004 when Republicans called for his resignation amid allegations concerning corruption in the Iraq oil-for-food program. In 2006, Payne helped to package a bipartisan deal in the House to expand presidential authority to promote peace and accountability in Darfur, and he joined a delegation led by Nancy Pelosi to Darfur and elsewhere in Africa. In the majority, he chairs the expanded Foreign Affairs Subcommittee on Africa and Global Health. On the Education and Labor Committee, Payne won bipartisan support to add poverty reduction as a basic purpose of welfare reform.

Payne has been reelected by very wide margins. Alone among New Jersey Democratic congressmen in recent years, he has not drawn frequent mention as a possible candidate for statewide office. He remains the only African-American to have represented New Jersey in Congress, and he is well-connected in Newark: His brother is a state assemblyman and his son, Donald Payne Jr., was elected at-large to the Newark city council in 2006 as an ally of Mayor Cory Booker. By fall 2007, however, Payne the congressman and Booker were at odds and there were rumors Booker would back a primary challenger.

ELEVENTH DISTRICT

Rep. Rodney Frelinghuysen (R)

Elected 1994, 7th term; b. Apr. 29, 1946, New York City; home, Harding; Hobart Col., B.A. 1969; Episcopalian; married (Virginia).

Military Career: Army, 1969-71 (Vietnam).

Elected Office: Morris Cnty. Bd. of Freeholders, 1974-83; NJ Assembly, 1983-94.

Professional Career: Aide, Morris Cnty. Bd. of Freeholders, 1972-74.

DC Office: 2442 RHOB, 20515, 202-225-5034; Fax: 202-225-3186; Web site: frelinghuysen.house.gov.

District Offices: Morristown, 973-984-0711.

Committees: *Appropriations* (10th of 29 R): Commerce, Justice, Science & Related Agencies (RMM); Defense.

Group Ratings

	ADA	ACLU	AFS	LCV	ITIC	NTU	COC	ACU	CFG	FRC
2006	25	23	0	67	100	50	80	60	43	42
2005	15	—	0	33	—	51	89	60	54	67

National Journal Ratings

	2005 LIB	—	2005 CONS		2006 LIB	—	2006 CONS
Economic	46%	—	53%		46%	—	54%
Social	49%	—	51%		47%	—	52%
Foreign	11%	—	86%		17%	—	73%

Key Votes of the 109th Congress

1. Estate Tax Repeal	Y	5. Limit Interstate Abortion	Y	9. Build Border Fence	Y
2. Limit CAFE Standards	N	6. Extend Patriot Act	Y	10. CAFTA	Y
3. FY06 Spending Curb	Y	7. Bar Same Sex Marriage	N	11. Oppose Iraq Withdrawal	Y
4. Drilling in ANWR	N	8. Stem Cell Research $	Y	12. Detainee Tribunals	Y

Election Results

2006 general	Rodney Frelinghuysen (R)	126,085	(62%)	($1,187,427)
	Tom Wyka (D)	74,414	(37%)	($12,107)
	Other	2,572	(1%)	
2006 primary	Rodney Frelinghuysen (R)	unopposed		
2004 general	Rodney Frelinghuysen (R)	200,915	(68%)	($801,784)
	James Buell (D)	91,811	(31%)	($3,406)
	Other	3,276	(1%)	

Prior Winning Percentages: 2002 (72%); 2000 (68%); 1998 (68%); 1996 (66%); 1994 (71%)

The People		Race/Ethnic Origin	Ancestry	
Area size:	628 sq. mi.	82.9% White	Italian: 16.8% Irish: 14.4%	
Urban population:	93.5%	2.6% Black	German: 11.8%	
Rural population:	6.5%	6.3% Asian	**2004 Presidential Vote**	
Pop. 2000:	647,258	0.1% Native Am.	Bush (R)	186,993 (58%)
Pop. 2005 (est):	675,968	0.0% Hawaiian	Kerry (D)	135,578 (42%)
Median income:	$79,009	1.0% Two+ races	Other	1,847 (1%)
Poverty status:	3.5%	0.1% Other	**2000 Presidential Vote**	
Military veterans:	10.4%	6.8% Hispanic Origin	Bush (R)	151,617 (54%)
			Gore (D)	121,036 (43%)
			Other	9,763 (3%)
			Cook Partisan Voting Index: R + 6	

Occupation	Blue collar: 14.0%	White collar: 76.2%	Gray collar: 9.8%

New Jersey's Morris County, west of the Watchung Mountain ridges, was one of the first settled parts of the interior United States west of the seaboard. It has long been a place of comparative affluence, the home of skilled craftsmen during the Revolutionary War, with plenty of water mills and iron forges by the 19th century. But only in the late 20th century did it come into its own, as one of the most affluent parts of the United States. And it is not just a collection of country estates with huddled small towns for the servants to live in, but a well-rounded community with all the appurtenances of urbanity except high crime and poverty rates. The very rich have lived here for some time, connected to Manhattan by commuter rail lines. But starting in the 1970s, new residents rushed out the newly completed I-80 and I-280 or the ring road I-287. Prompted by court-required zoning changes, old farms and woods have been cleared to make way for new subdivisions. And this is not just a bedroom community. Much of New Jersey's economic energy, entrepreneurial creativity and research expertise is out here. New office complexes and corporate headquarters have been rising though large forested areas of state parkland remain, including the Wildcat Ridge Wildlife Management Area. The Bush administration has cited preservation of the state's Highlands region, a 1,000-square-mile forest- and lake-filled stretch from Ringwood southwest to Warren County, as a national priority.

The 11th Congressional District of New Jersey includes all of Morris County plus small slices of Sussex, Passaic, Essex and Somerset Counties. It is one of the most affluent districts in the country. It ranks second in the nation in median household income. It is family territory, with relatively few singles; not a strongly cultural conservative area, but not aggressively liberal either. It has few blacks but a larger share of Hispanics, many of whom arrived as day laborers and some of whom have settled comfortably; one of its biggest immigrant populations is of Indians, whose household incomes are double the national average. Politically, it is the most Republican district in New Jersey, and one of the most Republican in the Northeast. It was one of only three New Jersey districts to vote for George W. Bush in 2000, and gave him a comfortable 58% in 2004.

The congressman from the 11th District is Rodney Frelinghuysen (pronounced *FREE-ling-high-zen*), a Republican and scion of one of New Jersey's most durable political families, which moved from Germany near the Dutch border in 1720 and settled in what is now the 11th District. Four Frelinghuysens served as senator from New Jersey, starting in 1793 and as recently as 1923; Theodore Frelinghuysen was the candidate for vice president in 1844 (leading to the memorable chant, "Hurrah! Hurrah! The country's risin'/ For Henry Clay and Frelinghuysen"); Frederick Frelinghuysen was Chester Arthur's secretary of state; Peter Frelinghuysen, Rodney's father, was elected to the House in 1952 and served until his retirement in 1974. History tends to repeat itself, and Frelinghuysens have been involved in every presidential impeachment: Rodney Frelinghuysen's great-great-grandfather Frederick voted to convict Andrew Johnson in 1868; his father Peter, after the revelations of July 1974, would have voted to impeach Richard Nixon if the president had not resigned; and this generation's Frelinghuysen voted to impeach Bill Clinton in December 1998. As a child, Rodney Frelinghuysen lived in the large brick house on Georgetown's N Street now owned by former *Washington Post* editor Ben Bradlee and his wife Sally Quinn; he attended St. Albans prep school with Al Gore. After college, the congressman's son was drafted and served in the Army in Vietnam, where he built roads in the Mekong Delta. In 1972 he was appointed an aide by then-Morris County Freeholder (and later 11th District Congressman) Dean Gallo; he served as a freeholder himself from 1974-83 and was elected to the Assembly in 1983.

Frelinghuysen ran for Congress in 1990 in what is now the 12th District; he lost the primary to Dick Zimmer. In August 1994, after the primary, Gallo retired because of illness; he died two days before the election. Frelinghuysen was chosen to be the Republican nominee at a September party convention and was elected with 71% of the vote. He showed his insider skills by winning a seat as a freshman on the Appropriations Committee, where he worked to cut spending on many programs but delivered on New Jersey interests for members of both parties. New Jersey had no senator on Appropriations between 2000-06, and Frelinghuysen became the go-to guy for the entire delegation. He concentrated on big projects—construction of the Hudson-Bergen light rail, dredging of channels in the Port of New York and New Jersey, millions to slow erosion on the faraway Jersey Shore.

Frelinghuysen has taken moderate or even liberal stands on some issues, but is more conservative on defense. He twice won House passage of his "Know Your Caller" bill, which bars telemarketers from interfering with caller-ID systems of customers seeking to avoid such solicitations. He has said that he has more Superfund sites in his district than any other congressman and "we need to continue the cleanup and the remediation;" he tours the sites annually with environmental and local officials to get updates on clean-up progress. In 2004, he won enactment of legislation to protect the New Jersey Highlands. On Iraq, he said that it was vital for the United States to stay the course and he condemned European nations that have not sent troops there. In 2003, he became an Appropriations cardinal at the Subcommittee on the District of Columbia. He sought to avoid additional strings on local activities but was unable to remove restrictions that conservatives previously added, including limits on abortion services and distribution of needles. But that panel was eliminated in 2005 when the number of subcommittees was reduced from 13 to 10, and Frelinghuysen did not get a chairmanship. In the minority in 2007, he became senior Republican at the Commerce-Justice-Science subcommittee.

Frelinghuysen has not been seriously challenged for reelection. In 2006, he was among the House Republicans targeted by MoveOn.org for supporting the war in Iraq. Against first-time candidate Tom Wyka, who hammered him on Iraq, he was reelected with his smallest margin since he took office: a still-comfortable 62%-37%. He has shown no interest in running statewide. This patrician evidently believes that his gritty work in the House is more important than taking a chance on gaining the glamour of serving in the Senate from a state that has not elected a Republican senator since 1972.

TWELFTH DISTRICT

Rep. Rush Holt (D)

Elected 1998, 5th term; b. Oct. 15, 1948, Weston, WV; home, Hopewell Township; Carleton Col., B.S. 1970, N.Y.U., PhD. 1981; Protestant; married (Margaret Lancefield).

Professional Career: Prof., Swarthmore Col., 1981-89; Asst. Dir., Princeton Plasma Physics Lab., 1989-98.

DC Office: 1019 LHOB, 20515, 202-225-5801; Fax: 202-225-6025; Web site: www.holt.house.gov.

District Offices: West Windsor, 609-750-9365.

Committees: *Education & Labor* (12th of 27 D): Health, Employment, Labor & Pensions; Early Childhood, Elementary & Secondary Education. *Natural Resources* (9th of 27 D): Energy & Mineral Resources; National Parks, Forests & Public Lands. *Permanent Select Committee on Intelligence* (6th of 12 D): Intelligence Community Management (Vice Chmn.); Technical & Tactical Intelligence.

Group Ratings

	ADA	ACLU	AFS	LCV	ITIC	NTU	COC	ACU	CFG	FRC
2006	95	100	100	100	43	16	20	5	9	0
2005	100	—	100	100	—	13	33	0	4	0

National Journal Ratings

	2005 LIB	—	2005 CONS		2006 LIB	—	2006 CONS
Economic	92%	—	6%		91%	—	6%
Social	90%	—	10%		90%	—	10%
Foreign	88%	—	11%		87%	—	12%

Key Votes of the 109th Congress

1. Estate Tax Repeal	N	5. Limit Interstate Abortion	N	9. Build Border Fence	N
2. Limit CAFE Standards	N	6. Extend Patriot Act	N	10. CAFTA	N
3. FY06 Spending Curb	N	7. Bar Same Sex Marriage	N	11. Oppose Iraq Withdrawal	N
4. Drilling in ANWR	N	8. Stem Cell Research $	Y	12. Detainee Tribunals	N

Election Results

2006 general	Rush Holt (D)	125,468	(66%)	($1,055,244)
	Joseph Sinagra (R)	65,509	(34%)	($2,272)
2006 primary	Rush Holt (D)	unopposed		
2004 general	Rush Holt (D)	171,691	(59%)	($1,651,175)
	Bill Spadea (R)	115,014	(40%)	($341,354)
	Other	3,080	(1%)	

Prior Winning Percentages: 2002 (61%); 2000 (49%); 1998 (50%)

The People

Area size:	642 sq. mi.
Urban population:	93.2%
Rural population:	6.8%
Pop. 2000:	647,258
Pop. 2005 (est):	694,103
Median income:	$69,668
Poverty status:	5.2%
Military veterans:	10.6%

Race/Ethnic Origin

72.4% White
11.4% Black
9.1% Asian
0.1% Native Am.
0.0% Hawaiian
1.4% Two+ races
0.2% Other
5.5% Hispanic Origin

Ancestry

Italian: 13.7%   Irish: 12.1%
German: 9.3%

2004 Presidential Vote

Kerry (D)	165,776	(54%)
Bush (R)	138,454	(46%)

2000 Presidential Vote

Gore (D)	141,568	(56%)
Bush (R)	101,145	(40%)
Other	9,188	(4%)

Cook Partisan Voting Index: D + 8

Occupation   Blue collar: 13.8%   White collar: 75.7%   Gray collar: 10.4%

It was once the main East Coast arterial highway, carrying the nation's highest volume of truck traffic. Today it is crowded with cars taking high-salaried workers and clerical help to one of the East Coast's thickest concentrations of office buildings in one of the bigger edge cities spawned in the 1980s. This is U.S. 1, which once just connected the industrial cities of Trenton and New Brunswick on its way from Philadelphia to New York; now it is better thought of around here as connecting the university towns around Princeton and Rutgers, and is a locus of telecommunications and pharmaceutical research. This had been empty bucolic country, looked out on by F. Scott Fitzgerald's undergraduates from their Gothic Princeton towers; now it is filled with postmodern office campuses and hotels and restaurants clamoring for attention.

The 12th Congressional District of New Jersey meanders across the breadth of New Jersey, from the Delaware River in the west to the Atlantic Ocean. It extends several dozen miles on either side of U.S. 1 as it slices through Mercer and Middlesex Counties; it is home to both an Englishtown and a Frenchtown. To the west, it takes some of the rolling country of Hunterdon County. On the other side of U.S. 1, the 12th takes in Princeton and then some modest-income suburbs—Franklin in Somerset County, East Brunswick in Middlesex County—and some fast-growing Monmouth County areas such as Rumson, part of Middletown, and Holmdel; Monmouth, Marlboro and Manalapan have been rated among the best small towns on the East Coast. Redistricting made the 12th, represented for most of the 1990s by a Republican, more Democratic—virtually taking it off the table for effective competition.

The congressman from the 12th District is Rush Holt, a Democrat first elected in 1998. He has an impressive political pedigree that is, however, of no importance to this district. His father Rush D. Holt, a favorite of United Mine Workers leader John Lewis, was elected as the "boy senator" from West Virginia in 1934 when he was 29; he could not take his seat until June 1935 when he turned 30.

But he clashed early and often with Franklin D. Roosevelt and lost the Democratic primary to Harley Kilgore in 1940. Former Senator Holt died when the young Rush Holt was 6, and he grew up in Washington, D.C., where his mother Helen, who had been West Virginia secretary of state, was an official in the Federal Housing Agency. He went off to Carleton College in Minnesota and to New York University, where he earned advanced degrees in physics and researched alternative energy, eventually becoming assistant director of the Princeton Plasma Physics Laboratory. Holt—the only five-time *Jeopardy!* champion to serve in Congress—also was an arms-control expert for the State Department.

Holt entered politics in 1996, when Republican Congressman Dick Zimmer ran for the Senate against Bob Torricelli and lost. Holt finished third in the Democratic primary; cultural conservative Mike Pappas won the Republican primary, then the general election but by only 50%-47%. Pappas immediately became a top Democratic target in 1998. Holt decided early in the year that Bill Clinton's State of the Union message gave him an agenda to appeal to suburban voters. Princeton Town Committeeman Carl Mayer ran again, but national and local Democrats favored Holt, who won the endorsements of all five county Democratic organizations; he won the primary 64%-36%. Then, in July, Pappas took to the House floor to recite a poem: "Twinkle, Twinkle Kenneth Starr, now we see how brave you are. We could not see which way to go, if you did not lead us so." New Jersey was pro-Clinton, anti-impeachment territory, and Pappas's ditty, replayed on network newscasts and incorporated into a Holt TV spot, proved a great liability. Holt won in a 50%-47% upset.

He has compiled a solidly liberal voting record. As the second research physicist in the House, he worked with the other, Republican Vern Ehlers, to promote science education, trying to give science equal standing with reading and math in Title I. He sponsored an assortment of gun control measures, including one to require licensing and registration of all handguns (it attracted no cosponsors). Locally, he has secured funding for open space and helped to get added protection for the lower Delaware River.

Holt is perhaps the House's most prominent crusader on election reform, his interest sparked in part by a belief that his father's close defeat in West Virginia resulted from ballot fraud. "One of my earliest memories is the talk in the family about votes being stolen and ballot boxes being found on the riverbanks," he told *Roll Call*. He has proposed the Voter Confidence and Increased Accessibility Act, which calls for an improved paper trail for voting machines. When the vote count was challenged in Florida's 13th District in 2006, Holt became an advocate of Democratic nominee Christine Jennings and her demand for a House review. On the House Intelligence Committee, he became an outspoken critic of the Bush administration's failure to disclose sufficient information to Congress and sought more details about disclosure of the identity of CIA agent Valerie Plame. In 2007, after failing to get a seat on the Appropriations Committee, he became chairman of the new Select Intelligence Oversight Panel, a hybrid group of members from the appropriations and authorizing committees with intelligence expertise. In the fall of 2005, he advocated withdrawal of U.S. troops from Iraq.

In 2000, the seat was fiercely contested. After flirting with another Senate bid, Zimmer declared for his old House seat; Pappas did too. Zimmer won the Republican primary 62%-38%. He immediately became the target of some $2 million of Democratic Congressional Campaign Committee negative ads. Zimmer acknowledged that the political terrain had changed. "There's a cultural divide between the Northeast and what's become the Republican base," he said during the primary. "The world looks different from suburban New Jersey than it does from Texas." In one of the closest races in the nation, Holt won by a bit more than 1,000 votes. In 2001, he focused heavily on redistricting. Holt was alone among the congressional delegation in his sharp opposition to the state redistricting commission's plan. But the new boundaries ended up suiting him fine. In 2002, Holt's Republican opponent was former New Jersey Secretary of State DeForest "Buster" Soaries, a black minister with a 6,000-member Baptist church. With little financial support from national Republicans, he lost 61%-37%. Holt has made this a safe Democratic seat.

THIRTEENTH DISTRICT

Rep. Albio Sires (D)

Elected 2006, 1st full term; b. Jan. 26, 1951, Bejucal, Cuba; home, West New York; St. Peter's Col., B.A. 1974, Middlebury Col., M.A. 1985; Catholic; married (Adrienne).

Elected Office: West New York Mayor, 1995-2006; NJ Assembly, 1999-2006; NJ Assembly Speaker, 2002-06.

Professional Career: High schl. Spanish and ESL teacher, 1975-85; Special Asst., NJ Dept. of Community Affairs, 1985; Part-owner, A.M. Title Agency, 1986-2006.

DC Office: 1024 LHOB, 20515, 202-225-7919; Fax: 202-226-0792; Web site: www.house.gov/sires.

District Offices: Bayonne, 201-823-2900; Carteret, 732-969-9160; Jersey City, 201-222-2828; West New York, 201-558-0800.

Committees: *Financial Services* (26th of 37 D): Housing & Community Opportunity; Capital Markets, Insurance & Government Sponsored Enterprises. *Foreign Affairs* (25th of 27 D): Western Hemisphere; Asia, the Pacific & the Global Environment; Europe.

Group Ratings and Key Votes: Newly Elected

Election Results

2006 general	Albio Sires (D)	77,238	(78%)	($1,884,679)
	John Guarini (R)	19,284	(19%)	
	Other	3,108	(3%)	
2006 primary	Albio Sires (D)	24,661	(72%)	
	Joseph Vas (D)	9,486	(28%)	
2006 spec. gen.	Albio Sires (D)	75,403	(97%)	
	Other	2,592	(3%)	
2006 spec. primary	Albio Sires (D)	24,216	(90%)	
	James Geron (D)	2,647	(10%)	
2004 general	Robert Menendez (D)	121,018	(76%)	($3,941,956)
	Richard Piatkowski (R)	35,288	(22%)	
	Other	3,235	(2%)	

The People		Race/Ethnic Origin	Ancestry	
Area size:	74 sq. mi.	32.3% White	Italian: 7.3%	Irish: 5.3%
Urban population:	100.0%	11.3% Black	Polish: 3.8%	
Rural population:	0.0%	5.5% Asian	**2004 Presidential Vote**	
Pop. 2000:	647,258	0.1% Native Am.	Kerry (D) 127,168	(69%)
Pop. 2005 (est):	640,330	0.0% Hawaiian	Bush (R) 57,278	(31%)
Median income:	$37,129	2.4% Two+ races	**2000 Presidential Vote**	
Poverty status:	18.0%	0.6% Other	Gore (D) 114,586	(72%)
Military veterans:	5.4%	47.6% Hispanic Origin	Bush (R) 39,554	(25%)
			Other 4,338	(3%)
			Cook Partisan Voting Index: D +23	

Occupation	Blue collar: 28.4%	White collar: 55.7%	Gray collar: 15.9%

The Statue of Liberty, standing in New York Harbor since 1886, has been the great symbol of America welcoming immigrants to its shores. Actually, the statue is on the New Jersey side of the harbor, and so (as the Supreme Court ruled in 1998) is most of Ellis Island, where they were processed. The towns sitting on the granite and gneiss ridge of Hudson County, overlooking the harbor, have been immigrant territory. When immigration was shut off in 1924, many children and grandchildren of the Irish and Italian immigrants stayed in Hudson County, living in the same neighborhoods, working on the same docks or factories and voting the dictates of the same political machine. Hudson County was the setting of one of America's classic political machines, undisciplined by any metropolitan elite. From 1917-49, the boss of Hudson County was Frank ("I am the law") Hague; his machine chose governors and U.S. senators, prosecutors and judges, and had influence in the White House of Franklin D. Roosevelt. Hague collected high taxes from industries clustered here—who then passed them on to consumers everywhere—and in return gave them an orderly city, free of most crime and vice, and a work force insulated against racketeers and militant unions. Hague's successor, John V. Kenny, was boss from 1949-71—continuous power for 54 years.

But Hudson County began changing again. New immigrants were coming in—refugees from Castro's Cuba, other Latinos and Asians after the 1965 immigration act. Union City became predominantly Cuban, Jersey City neighborhoods became heavily Latino. Upscale young singles looking for lower rents moved into Hoboken's five-story Victorian apartments that sparkle with light off the Hudson, and were a quick commute through the PATH tubes to Wall Street or Greenwich Village. Starting in the 1980s, huge new condominium and office developments went up in Jersey City with back-office buildings for big banks and securities firms. In Hoboken, the home of Frank Sinatra and the Oreo Cookie, shopping and apartment complexes have taken waterfront sites where Maxwell House Coffee and Lipton Tea had great factories (and where the movie classic, *On the Waterfront*, was filmed on location). Bayonne has become a cruise-ship port. Aiding this private sector growth was public sector reform, but old times seemed to return in 2004 when electronic cartridges containing some 2,000 votes went missing in a close special election for mayor. Meanwhile, new immigrants continue to arrive. As middle-class Cubans move to Bergen County suburbs and the Jersey mainstream, Union City is less Cuban and more Colombian, Ecuadoran, Peruvian, Dominican and Filipino. Hudson County, which seemed to be dying a generation ago, is now pulsing with new life.

The 13th Congressional District of New Jersey includes most of Hudson County plus most of the immigrant entry ports along the water, from West New York and Weehawken, where Alexander Hamilton was killed in a duel with Vice President Aaron Burr in 1804, south past Jersey City and Bayonne (where you can still find bocce courts), past the Port of New York and New Jersey to the waterfront areas of Elizabeth, Linden, Carteret (with its Sikh community), Woodbridge and Perth Amboy. The district's population is 48% Hispanic and also includes the Ironbound district of Newark, with its Portuguese and Brazilian immigrants; working-class Harrison, an aging factory town where European immigrants have been replaced by Hispanic immigrants; and part of industrial Kearny. The 13th is heavily Democratic.

The new congressman from the 13th District is Albio Sires, a Democrat who replaced Robert Menendez, who was appointed to the Senate in January 2006. Born in Cuba, he remembers the book-burning following the revolution and he arrived in the United States at age 10 after his family fled Fidel Castro's regime in 1962. With a bachelor's from St. Peter's College, where he received a four-year basketball scholarship, and a master's from Middlebury, he became a high school Spanish teacher. On his fourth try, he became mayor of West New York as a Republican in 1995 and held that post until 2006. He focused on the creation of more affordable housing in the small but densely populated town and won praise for merging the fire department with three neighboring departments. He switched parties in 1999 and, with support of party leaders, defeated a veteran Democratic incumbent in the primary to win a state House seat (dual office-holding has been a common practice in New Jersey). With strong support from newly-elected Governor Jim McGreevey in 2002, he became Speaker of the Assembly, as a compromise candidate.

After Governor Jon Corzine appointed Menendez to take his Senate seat, Sires immediately became the frontrunner for the House seat. But it remained vacant for 10 months because the special election was not scheduled until the day of the November 2006 general election. In the primary, Sires faced a fierce challenge from Joe Vas of Perth Amboy, who likewise was a state House member and a mayor. Vas assailed Sires as a puppet of the powerful Hudson County Democratic machine. He also questioned whether Sires—who began his political career as a Democrat, ran for Congress in 1986 as a Republican, and was later elected to local office as an independent before rejoining the Democratic Party—is a true Democrat. Sires responded with harsh attacks that depicted Vas as soft on crime and won the support of most leading Democrats except for long-time rival Menendez, who remained neutral. Vas accused Sires of ties to organized crime; Sires linked Vas to drug dealers. But the shrill tenor of the campaign made little difference. Vas carried his home base of Middlesex County, 76%-24%. Sires crushed him 80%-20% in Hudson County, which cast 74% of the total vote. Overall, Sires won 72%-28%. In the general election for a full-term, Republicans nominated John Guarini, a second cousin of former Democratic Rep. Frank Guarini—who in 1986 overwhelmed Sires—to run for the full House term. Guarini didn't raise money, however, and posed no threat. Sires won 78%-19%. He also won the special election that day without major party opposition, and served in the final weeks of the Republican-controlled House. He succeeded Menendez as the only Cuban-American House member from a state other than Florida; in 2007, he allied himself with South Florida members who want to keep U.S. sanctions on Cuba in place.

★ NEW MEXICO ★

The oldest and the newest of America, some of our oldest settlements and some of our newest technologies can be found, in surrealistic proximity, in New Mexico. The oldest permanently inhabited city in the United States is not Plymouth or Jamestown or St. Augustine; it is probably Acoma, New Mexico, which apparently thrived long before the Spanish conquistadors arrived in 1540 and seems to have been continuously inhabited for the nearly 470 years since. While the settlers of Jamestown and Plymouth were building flimsy wood houses, the Indians in New Mexico were living in extensive dwellings hundreds of years old, made with the adobe that is still the characteristic building material here, and on this rocky desert land used small pebbles as mulch to retain scarce moisture. Nearly five centuries later, much of what makes New Mexico distinctive derives from the people found here by the first European explorers—something true of no other state but Hawaii. The cultures in other states are mostly an outgrowth of what early white settlers brought to the land; natives have mostly disappeared, been killed off by diseases or driven onto reservations. Not so in New Mexico. New Mexico is the northernmost salient of the great Indian-Spanish civilizations of the Cordillera, which extend along the mountain chain through Mexico and Central and South America, to the southern Chile. The Spanish settled in Santa Fe in 1609, and though their hold on the town was often tenuous, their imprint remains. There are still 19 Indian pueblos in New Mexico today, plus the reservations of the Navajo and the Jicarilla and Mescalero Apache. Today a very substantial minority of New Mexicans are descendants of those Indians or the Spanish, or both. New Mexico's population is 43% Hispanic in 2006, the highest percentage of any state, and 10% American Indian. Almost one-third of the people in this state speak Spanish in everyday life, but relatively few are recent immigrants from Mexico; only 8% of New Mexicans are foreign-born, less than the national average.

Yet New Mexico also is a civilization built on modern technology. It was to a remote mesa called Los Alamos that General Leslie Groves brought his Manhattan Project scientists during World War II to build a secret town and develop a secret weapon that would in two explosions end World War II and change the course of history. Los Alamos is still a government high-tech laboratory, and a source of controversy since 1999 when it was revealed that Chinese spies had obtained hundreds of computer files from there. New Mexico has other high-tech sites as well—the White Sands Missile Range near Alamogordo, where the first atomic bomb was detonated, and the Sandia Laboratories near Albuquerque, run by Lockheed-Martin for the government, a non-nuclear high-tech weapons research facility, with one of the fastest computers in the world, used to simulate nuclear explosions. Near Carlsbad is the federal Waste Isolation Pilot Plant (WIPP), where the Energy Department deposits transuranic radioactive waste. And at the western edge of White Sands near Upham is the Virgin Galactic spaceport, where British entrepreneur Richard Branson is planning to base his space tourism business. With the state and federal government financing the runways, and investors paying $200,000 each for rights to early rides, Branson plans to launch his SpaceShipTwo crafts from the bellies of aircraft at 55,000 feet, fly them at 3,000 miles per hour on an arc 70 miles into space, where passengers can float in glassed-in cabins for six minutes and then glide back down to earth below. The first rides are planned for late 2009 or early 2010. "This sends a message," Governor Bill Richardson, a big booster and prospective early passenger, proclaimed, "that will be heard around the world—that New Mexico is a state that embraces entrepreneurs, adventurers and pioneers."

New and old New Mexico intermingle in varying proportions in this land of majestically vast vistas. The Hispanic and Indian cultures predominate north and west of Albuquerque, with picturesque old towns and still-functioning pueblos, backward Indian reservations and lavish casino resorts. "Little Texas," in the south and east, has small cities, plenty of oil wells, vast cattle ranches and desolate military bases, and resembles, economically and culturally, the adjacent west Texas High Plains. Here, as everywhere in New Mexico, government is a prime employer (accounting for 23% of jobs, one of the highest figures in the country) and often the moving force in the local economy. In the middle is Albuquerque, which, with the arrival of air conditioning, grew from a small desert town of 35,000 in 1940 into a Sun Belt metropolis of 800,000 today; it has a large Hispanic minority. Its economy is based heavily on high tech, especially nuclear power, but it has relatively low income and education levels: New Mexico ranks high among states in the percentage living in poverty and low in income—the downscale Sun Belt. It also has high rates of drunk driving (and a state law requiring ignition interlocks for DWI offenders), teenage pregnancies and drug overdoses. But over the years its amazing scenery and unique culture have attracted writers like D.

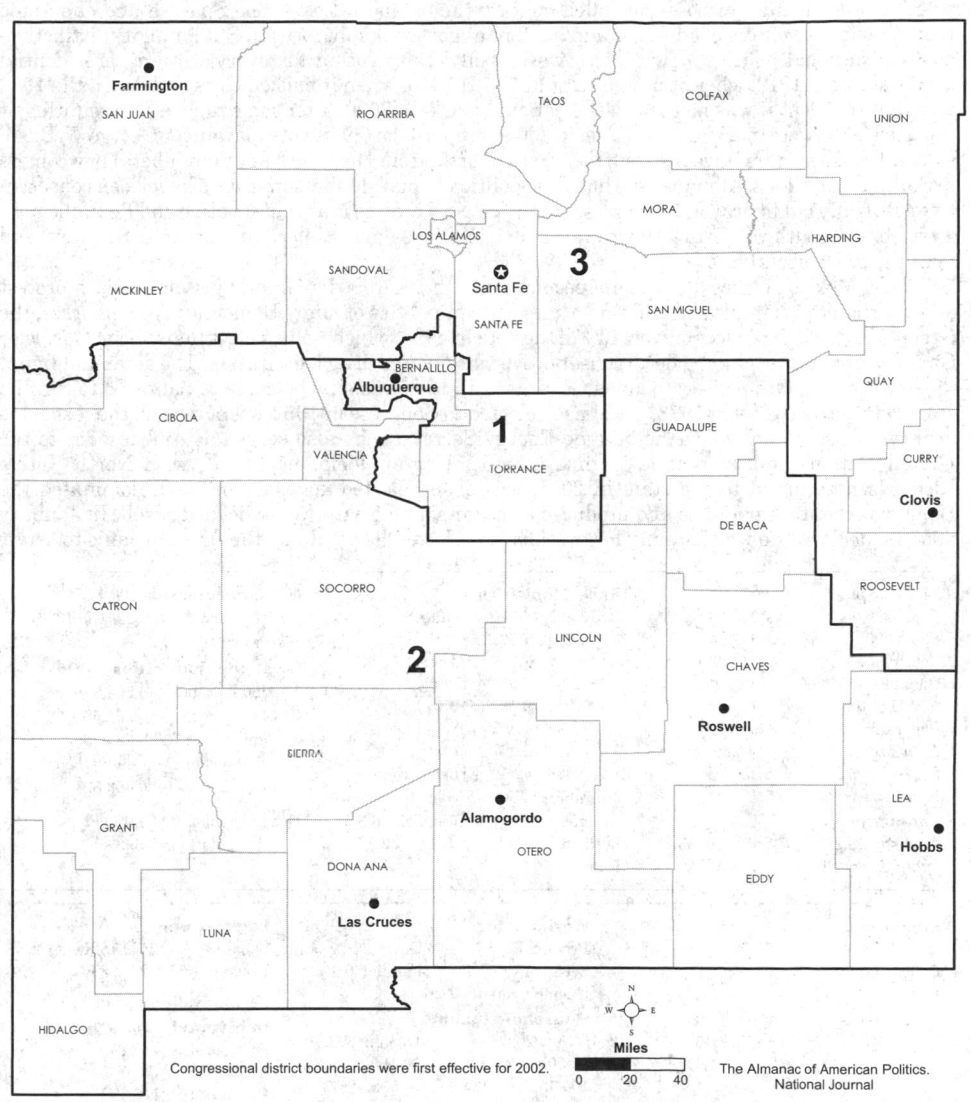

Congressional district boundaries were first effective for 2002.

Miles
0   20   40

The Almanac of American Politics.
National Journal

H. Lawrence and painters like Georgia O'Keefe, and Santa Fe today is a magnet for young people with a taste for alternative lifestyles and trust funds to comfortably finance them. Different kinds of outsiders are attracted by the ten or so destination golf courses built by Indian tribes next to their reservation casinos.

For many years, New Mexico politics was a somnolent business. Local bosses—first Republican, later Democratic—controlled the large Hispanic vote. Elections in many counties featured irregularities that would have made a Chicago ward committeeman blush. New Mexico had for years another feature of boss-controlled politics: the balanced ticket, one Spanish and one Anglo senator, with the offices of governor and lieutenant governor split as well. But for all its distinctiveness, in national politics New Mexico was a bellwether, voting for every winning presidential candidate from 1912, when it became a state, until 1976, when it backed Gerald Ford. In the 1988 and 1996 elections it was just 1% off the national mark. In 2000, after some ragged vote counting, it reported a 365-vote margin for Al Gore; in 2004, it reported a 5,988-vote margin for George W. Bush. Currently, Democrats have a strong base in the north, from Hispanics and from liberal newcomers in Santa Fe and Taos. Albuquerque has been politically marginal; its migrants have been conservative culturally but liberal on economics. Southeast New Mexico is as conservative and Republican as west Texas. Southwest New Mexico, around Las Cruces and Silver City, is more Hispanic and marginally Democratic.

New Mexico politics also has its peculiarities. In the 1990s a Green Party formed, in protest against the practical-minded and sometimes corrupt politics of many Democratic wheelhorses; the Green candidate for governor won 10% of the vote in 1994, which helped elect Republican Governor Gary Johnson, an original, a fiscal conservative who favored drug legalization. The dominant figure in New Mexico state politics today is Governor Bill Richardson, who came to Santa Fe to run the state Democratic party in 1978, got himself elected to Congress in 1982, spent most of the rest of his years in Washington, where he became Energy Secretary; he also served as Ambassador to the United Nations and from time to time as official or unofficial negotiator with North Korea. Richardson returned to the state in 2001, was easily elected governor in 2002, dominated the Democratic state legislature and produced a record popular with Republicans as well. In January 2007 he declared he was running for president; if elected he would be the first Hispanic to serve.

The People		Race/Ethnic Origin			Military veterans: 190,718 (14.5%)	
Pop. 2006 (est):	1,954,599	813,495	44.7%	White	WWII: 18.0%	Korea: 13.2%
Pop. 2000:	1,819,046	30,654	1.7%	Black	Vietnam: 34.7%	Gulf War: 10.7%
Pop. 1990:	1,515,069	18,257	1.0%	Asian	**Most populous cities (2006):**	
Change 1990-2000:	Up 20.1%	161,460	8.9%	Native Am.	1. Albuquerque	504,949
% of U.S. total:	0.7%	992	0.1%	Hawaiian	2. Las Cruces	86,268
Pop. rank:	36th of 50	25,793	1.4%	Two+ races	3. Santa Fe	72,056
Area size:	121,589 sq. mi.	3,009	0.2%	Other	4. Rio Rancho	71,607
State Native:	51.5%	765,386	42.1%	Hisp. Origin	5. Roswell	45,582
Non-citizen:	5.4%	**Ancestry**				
Language		German: 8.2%		English: 6.3%	Urban population: 75.0%	
English: 58.2%	Spanish: 33.3%	Irish: 6.1%		USA: 4.2%	Rural population: 25.0%	
Other Eur.: 2.1%		Italian: 2.0%				

Education		Work Sector		Legislature	
H.S. Grad:	78.9%	Private: 68.5%	Govt: 22.7%	Senate	24 D 18 R
College Grad:	23.5%	Self: 8.4%	Family: 0.4%	House	42 D 28 R
Industry		Unemployment: 7.2%		Legislative Term Limits: No	
Agri: 4.0%	Con: 7.9%	**Household Income**		**Registered Voters**	
Fin: 5.5%	Info: 2.4%	<15k: 20.8%	15-35k: 30.2%	D: 538,471	(49.4%)
Mfg: 11.2%	Prof: 31.1%	35-50k: 17.0%	50-100k: 24.3%	R: 358,825	(33.0%)
Public: 8.0%	Trade: 14.9%	100-150k: 5.0%	>150k: 2.6%	O: 191,681	(17.6%)
Other: 14.9%		Median: $34,133			
Occupation		Poverty status: 18.4%			
Blue collar: 22.2%	White collar: 59.9%	**Home Value**			
Gray collar: 17.9%		<50k: 22.7%	50-100k: 31.1%	100-200k: 33.4%	200-300k: 7.7%
		300-500k: 3.6%	>500k: 1.6%	Median: $94,600	

Presidential politics   New Mexico's near-bellwether status seems more accidental than anything else; it's hard to think of a state more atypical of the nation, yet it keeps on voting at or near the national average. It voted Republican for president in the 1980s, Democratic in the 1990s. It gave Al Gore a 365-vote margin in 2000 when he did, after all, win the popular vote, and it gave George W. Bush a 5,988-vote margin in 2004. New Mexico was as closely contested as any state in 2004, with constant visits from the nominees and huge doses of advertising. It was also organized to the gills. During the campaign most of the coverage focused on Governor Bill Richardson's efforts to register new Democrats, and a plurality of new voters registered Demo-

2004 Presidential Vote		
Bush (R)	376,930	(50%)
Kerry (D)	370,942	(49%)
Nader (I)	4,053	(1%)
Other	4,379	(1%)

2000 Presidential Vote		
Gore (D)	286,783	(48%)
Bush (R)	286,418	(48%)
Nader (Green)	21,251	(4%)
Other	4,154	(1%)

cratic. The rolls may have swelled partly because the Democratic-dominated New Mexico Supreme Court ruled that people didn't need to show identification to register. But Bush's volunteer-based organization quietly matched and perhaps exceeded their effort. Turnout was up 26% in a state where the population grew 5% in four years. Turnout was up 34% in Santa Fe County, which grew 7% and voted 71% for John Kerry. But in Lea County in Little Texas, which grew only 1%, turnout was up 28% and the county voted 79% for Bush. Democrats increased their nominees' margins by 13,000 in Santa Fe and Taos Counties and 6,500 in Albuquerque's Bernalillo County. But in the 10 counties of Little Texas, Bush's margin increased by 18,000 and in San Juan County, mining country around Farmington, it increased by another 5,000. In 2000 Bush's popularity among Texas Latinos didn't travel across the state border and he won only 32% of the Hispanic vote. In 2004 there were Viva Bush movements in all 33 counties and heavy emphasis on Bush's cultural conservatism, and he won 44% of the Hispanic vote. Bush led among white Anglos 56%-43%, and that was enough for a 50%-49% win. New Mexico had less trouble counting votes than in 2000, but it still took some time and in December the Green and Libertarian parties called for a recount. But they failed to put up the $1.4 million the state said it would cost.

New Mexico traditionally held its presidential primary in June, long after every major party nomination since 1984 has been settled. But in 2003 Governor Richardson signed a bill allowing parties to hold caucuses in lieu of the presidential primary, and the Democrats held caucuses February 3.

Congressional districting   The boundaries of New Mexico's three congressional districts have been substantially the same since 1982. Control of the redistricting process in 2001 was split between the Democratic legislature and Republican Governor Gary Johnson. In June 2001 the legislature passed a plan that would make the 1st District, held by Republican Heather Wilson, more Democratic. Johnson vetoed it. In September 2001 the legislature passed a plan that would make the 2d District, held by Republican Joe Skeen, more Democratic. Johnson vetoed it. Republicans had already taken the issue to court. A federal court decided to let the state court handle the issue. In January 2002, state District Judge Frank Allen, a Democrat, imposed his own plan. He said he was reluctant to make major changes and his plan shifted only 22,000 people into different districts. Democrats were disappointed; Republicans were pleased.

110th Congress Lineup	
2 R	1 D

109th Congress Lineup	
2 R	1 D

In February 2003 state Senate President Richard Romero, who lost to Wilson in 2002 and 2004, pressed the legislature to redistrict the House seats once again. But national Democrats urged caution and Governor Bill Richardson seemed uninterested, perhaps because a new plan might jeopardize his good relations with Senator Pete Domenici, who would be miffed if a new plan hurt Heather Wilson. In December 2006, after Wilson was very narrowly reelected, state Senator Jerry Ortiz y Pino called for a redistricting plan that would make the 1st District more Democratic; Richardson said he was willing to listen to the proposal but it never went anywhere.

Governor

Bill Richardson (D)

Elected 2002, term expires Jan. 2011, 2d term; b. Nov. 15, 1947, Pasadena, CA; home, Santa Fe; Tufts U., B.A. 1970, Fletcher Schl. of Law and Diplomacy, M.A. 1971; Catholic; married (Barbara).

Elected Office: U.S. House of Reps., 1982-97.

Professional Career: Congressional rel., U.S. Dept. of State, 1973-75; Staff, Senate Foreign Relations Subcmte., 1975-78; Exec. Dir., NM Dem. Party, 1978; Pres., Richardson Trade Group, 1978-82; U.S. Ambassador to U.N., 1997-98; Secy., U.S. Dept. of Energy, 1998-2000.

Office: Office of the Governor, 490 Old Santa Fe Trail, Room 400, Santa Fe, 87501, 505-476-2200; Fax: 505-576-2226; Web site: www.governor.state.nm.us.

Election Results

2006 general	Bill Richardson (D)	384,806	(69%)
	John Dendahl (R)	174,364	(31%)
2006 primary	Bill Richardson (D)	unopposed	
2002 general	Bill Richardson (D)	268,674	(55%)
	John Sanchez (R)	189,090	(39%)
	David Bacon (Green)	26,465	(5%)

Bill Richardson, a Democrat, was elected governor of New Mexico in 2002, 20 years after he was first elected to Congress. Richardson is a unique politician—an Hispanic with an Anglo name, a newcomer when he was first elected in New Mexico where many families go back 300 years, an adept politician who has also been an international negotiator. He was born in California and grew up in the Coyoacan neighborhood of Mexico City, where the family lived behind high walls but Bill played baseball outside with the neighborhood kids. His father was a banker from Boston who became head of Citibank in Mexico City, and his mother is Mexican; she still lives in Mexico and votes in elections there. Richardson attended Middlesex School in Concord, Massachusetts and he graduated from his father's alma mater, Tufts, in Medford; there he stood out as a baseball player. For many years he claimed that he was drafted by the Kansas City Athletics and Los Angeles Dodgers; but after the *Albuquerque Journal* investigated the story, he conceded it was not true. In any case, an elbow injury wrecked his pitching arm in his junior year, and after raising his grades he went on to Tufts's Fletcher School of Law and Diplomacy where he earned a master's degree. This was the era of campus unrest over the Vietnam war, but Richardson did not take part in protests; he received a medical draft deferment. After graduation he went to Washington, where his first job was working for the liberal Republican Wednesday Group; he went on to the State Department's congressional relations office and the Senate Foreign Relations Committee's staff on human rights. That led to a job as a "sort of go-fer" at the State Department and a stint on Senator Hubert Humphrey's staff.

In 1975 Richardson visited New Mexico for the first time in his life, where he met with state Democratic leaders and told them he was interested in moving to the state and running for Congress. Most were nonplussed, but in 1978 the outgoing governor's state party chairman hired him to be his executive director. But the winner of the 1978 Democratic primary for governor, former and future Governor Bruce King, got Richardson fired within a month. He managed to get a job with the Bernalillo County Democratic party in Albuquerque, then after the election hung out his shingle as a consultant. In February 1980, he filed to run against Republican Congressman Manuel Lujan. This was a Republican year, Lujan had deep roots in Albuquerque and had been in office since 1968. But Richardson held him to a 51%-49% victory. New Mexico got a third congressional district from the 1980 Census, and the legislature drew a new, heavily Hispanic 3d District in northern New Mexico. Richardson, based in Santa Fe, had already carried much of this territory in the 1980 race, and he ran for the new seat. He had substantial competition in the Democratic primary, from Lieutenant Governor Roberto Mondragon and Tom Udall, who was later state attorney general and now holds the 3d District seat. Richardson was accused of exaggerating the importance of some of his Washington jobs, but won 36% to 31% for Mondragon; he won the general election 64%-35%. At age 35, after four years in New Mexico, he had a safe seat in the House.

In the House Richardson had a somewhat moderate voting record. He got a seat on Energy and Commerce in his first term and filed an unusually large number of amendments. He favored abortion rights, opposed gun control, favored the death penalty, voted for the amendment to allow criminalization of flag burning and for the 1986 immigration law. He voted against the Gulf war resolution—a mistake, he said in his 2005 autobiography. He was passed over for the job of interior secretary by Bill Clinton, but he lobbied hard for ratification of NAFTA in 1993. In the 1990s he spent more time on foreign policy issues. In July 1994 he traveled to Haiti and met with General Raoul Cedras and in a five-hour conversation tried to get him to cede power, unsuccessfully. In December 1994 he was traveling to North Korea when two U.S. helicopter pilots were gunned down for allegedly trespassing into North Korean airspace. He negotiated for the release of the surviving pilot but ended up returning with the remains of the one who died; the other pilot was soon released. In 1995 he met with Saddam Hussein to seek the release of two Americans who had crossed the Iraqi border. In 1996 he met with Fidel Castro and obtained the release of three dissidents. He took to calling himself the Undersecretary of Thugs and described his negotiating technique. "I listen a lot. I try not to impose my views. It's important to listen, but it's important to be forceful too."

In January 1997 Richardson was nominated as ambassador to the United Nations. Here was an opportunity to be a major player in foreign policy, although Richardson was cabined in by the close supervision of his predecessor, Secretary of State Madeleine Albright. But he did negotiate agreements between the Taliban regime in Afghanistan and opposition forces and secured the release of Red Cross workers held hostage in Sudan, and the foreign policy experience he was gaining seemed likely to make him a plausible vice presidential candidate in 2000 or later. The only embarrassing thing about his service was the fact, later disclosed, that at the request of a White House staffer and without asking why, he offered a job to Monica Lewinsky; she rejected it as insufficiently grand. Then in June 1998 Energy Secretary Federico Pena resigned and Bill Clinton, eager to have at least one Hispanic in an official cabinet position, shifted Richardson to the post. This was not really a promotion: Energy is a department that is made up of several unrelated agencies, some of them with deep troubles at the time. One of those was the Los Alamos National Laboratory, from which, it seemed, secret documents about the assembly of nuclear weapons made their way to China. Richardson was much criticized in Congress for his work on improving security in the national laboratories, and his connection to the Wen Ho Lee security case was a political liability. Later, in May 1999, two hard drives with designs of the nation's nuclear labs were found to be missing after a fire; in June 1999 he decided not to appear at a Senate committee hearing on the issue, on the grounds he had no answers; at a later Armed Services Committee hearing he was lambasted by Robert Byrd, who said he would never be confirmed for another job (the hard drives were later found behind a copying machine). He was mentioned as a possible vice presidential candidate in 2000—the Democrats would have loved to run a Hispanic—but his name soon fell off the list.

After Al Gore's defeat, Richardson returned to Santa Fe; he did some work for Kissinger McClarty Associates and served on corporate boards, but it was obvious he was running for governor. He had considered running before, especially in 1994, but decided not to. The governor elected that year, Republican Gary Johnson, had been reelected in 1998 and was ineligible to run again. Richardson announced his candidacy in January 2002 and pledged to shake 600 hands a day; on September 16 he broke Theodore Roosevelt's record of 8,513, set on New Year's Day 1908, by shaking 13,392 hands at the New Mexico State Fair and a tailgate party at the University of New Mexico (his campaign flew in a representative of the Guinness Book of World Records to document the feat). He faced opposition from two Democrats, but at the state Democratic convention in March Richardson won 1,288 of 1,705 votes, and the others failed to get enough to qualify for the ballot. With his energy and his national contacts, Richardson raised and spent large sums, eventually $6.8 million, more than twice as much as both parties' candidates spent in 1998, and began running ads showing his vision for the state.

The Republican nominee was state Representative John Sanchez, a roofing contractor from Albuquerque's North Valley, who in 2000 beat by 206 votes the 30-year Speaker of the New Mexico House. Sanchez called for vouchers, merit pay for teachers and better testing; he ran a series of ads recounting his rise from poverty under the theme of "Dream Big." But Richardson had much more money and took many more specific stands on issues. He called for cutting the state income tax—New Mexico's 8.2% top rate was much higher than those of surrounding states—and eliminating the gross receipts tax. Amid news of drought and water conservation measures, he called for a statewide water policy and sketched one out in considerable detail. He opposed vouchers, but supported charter schools and tax credits for parochial schools. Like Sanchez he favored the death penalty and a concealed weapons law. Richardson ran a negative ad in September, despite a pledge not to do so. Sanchez criticized Richardson for serving on the board of a company which misstated its earnings; Richardson ran ads criticizing Sanchez for absenteeism in the legislature and for doctoring his resume. Sanchez said he started his roofing business in 1980, but in the mid-1980s was also working as a flight attendant. "While Bill Richardson was cutting taxes for New Mexico, John Sanchez was serving orange juice at 30,000 feet." There was little suspense about the result: Richardson won 55%-39%. He was the only one of four Clinton cabinet members running in 2002 who won. Inevitably, he was asked whether he had ambitions for national office. "I've always wanted to run for governor. I love this state, and I think the governor can make an enormous difference in people's lives—more so than any job I have held. I see this as a sort of culmination of my career. I am not interested in going back to Washington."

In office, he did not act like a governor whose horizon ended at the state line. He frequently traveled out of state—to Davos, Switzerland, for the 2003 World Economic Forum; to Chicago, to talk businesses into relocating to New Mexico; to Hollywood, to promote the state as a good location for shooting movies; to Mexico City, where he once lived, to meet with President Vicente Fox. Days after his swearing in, he met with a North Korean delegation in Santa Fe, with Secretary of State Colin Powell's permission, for three days of discussions about nuclear weapons; it became known as "green chile diplomacy." Other foreign dignitaries would follow: Spain's Prime Minister Jose Maria Aznar, Saudi Arabian Ambassador Prince Bandar bin Sultan, Prince Andrew of Great Britain. He was a familiar face in the national media and in Times Square too, where his picture appeared on a giant billboard advertising the virtues of New Mexico and its tax policy. In September 2003, he hosted the first party-sanctioned presidential debate in Albuquerque.

Richardson's first year in office was among the most productive and successful of all governors elected in his Class of 2002. "We will move so fast! You're not going to see us," he said in his address to the opening of the 2003 legislature. Move fast he did. He immediately started lobbying legislators of both parties for his tax cut. Unusually in New Mexico, they brought the issue up before the budget and on Valentine's Day 2003 Richardson signed a bill cutting the top income tax rate from 8.2% in steps to 4.9% and cutting the capital gains tax in half over five years. He signed a bill to crack down on drunken drivers, an especially vexing problem in New Mexico, and signed an executive order that extended employee benefits to the domestic partners of gay and lesbian state workers. In September, voters approved two constitutional amendments strongly backed by Richardson: one to create a Cabinet-level education secretary appointed by the governor and another to permit the state to increase the annual payout from the state's Land Grant Permanent Fund for public schools.

Less successful was a fall special session where Richardson called for more fundamental changes in tax laws. There he supported a failed bill that offered further tax cuts but with a net increase of $135 million in state and local taxes and fees; among the proposed increases was a hike in alcohol taxes, already among the highest in the nation. Critics said it would hurt the tourism and hospitality industry. The session did produce a tougher sex offender law and a $1.6 billion transportation package.

The even-year, legislative short session in New Mexico is generally limited to budget issues, though the governor can add to the agenda; in 2004 Richardson pushed the limit. He got the food tax cut he wanted after threatening to call the legislature back into session, though the gross receipts tax on other goods and services increased and Republicans complained about his "bullying tactics". The legislature also passed tougher DWI penalties, a tougher truancy law and facilitated the school bureaucracy changes approved by voters in 2003.

Richardson played a highly visible role in state and national Democratic politics in 2004. At home, he used his $2 million PAC, Moving America Forward, to register new voters and influence state and local elections. He was the driving force in 2003 behind a bill allowing parties to hold caucuses in lieu of the presidential primary and state Democrats held their presidential nominating caucus in February 2004; New Mexico traditionally held its presidential primary in June, usually long after the party nomination had been settled. At the Democratic National Convention in Boston, he served as chairman. As chairman of the Western Governors Association, he pushed governors to agree to work toward establishing a single date for western presidential primary and caucuses in 2008 to give the region more clout in the nominating process and to focus attention on issues like water rights, energy, the environment and immigration.

In 2005 Richardson got the legislature to require that DWI offenders install ignition interlocks in their vehicles to prevent drunk driving, to give National Guard members $250,000 life insurance policies and to cut the income tax up through 2008. Richardson called for a huge increase in pre-kindergarten education funding and urged that schools have more physical education and less junk food, more security cameras and GPS systems for school buses. In 2006 he got $12.5 million for pre-K. In the short session of early 2006, the legislature voted a solar energy tax credit but failed to pass other Richardson energy proposals. In March 2006 the state entered the Chicago Climate Exchange's cap-and-trade system for reducing carbon dioxide emissions. In October he called for reducing carbon dioxide emissions from new cars and trucks by 22% by 2012 and for tax credits and a tax holiday for buying Energy Star appliances. But for all his desire to cut emissions, Richardson has so far been unable to stop the Navajo Nation from building a coal-fired plant on their reservation. Richardson has been a big booster of Richard Branson's Virgin Galactic space tourism business, and got $30 million from the legislature to help pay for the runways near the White Sands Missile Range site from which space travelers will take off in space vehicles which will be released by aircraft at 55,000 feet to fly at 3,000 miles per hour outside the atmosphere and then glide back down to earth. "This sends a message that will be heard around the world that New Mexico is a state that embraces entrepreneurs, adventurers and pioneers." Flights are expected to begin in late 2009 or early 2010; Richardson has signed on to be a passenger.

In the 2006 legislative session a budget was passed with raises of 5% for teachers and 16% for state police. In March 2006 Richardson vetoed $269 million of spending, but finances were boosted by skyrocketing oil and natural gas royalties enough to allow spending $400 million on a commuter train from Belen to Santa Fe and $225 million on the spaceport. Richardson opposed George W. Bush's order sending the National Guard to patrol the border and said there was "no consultation—zero, zero, zero" with border state governors.

In 2006 Richardson was up for reelection, with the result never in doubt. His opponent was former Republican state Chairman John Dendahl, an ally of former Governor Gary Johnson, who got some attention when he said that teachers shortchange the basics because they are too interested in "the three Ss—sexuality, self-esteem and socialism." Richardson raised $14 million and won 69%-31%, the highest percentage for a governor in New Mexico history. He lost only one county, and that by only 6 votes. He also raised $13 million for the Democratic Governors Association, which he headed, and which had a very successful year.

For 2007, Richardson said his legislative goals were more tax cuts, another minimum wage increase and a $250 million road improvement package. But his sights seemed also trained beyond New Mexico. In his first term he spent more than 200 days out of state, and in January 2007 he was involved in negotiations between the Sudanese government and rebel factions that led to a 60-day ceasefire in Darfur. In 2002 he had said he had no interest in office beyond New Mexico, and in 2004 he said repeatedly that he would not accept the vice presidential nomination. In 2005 he took another tack. "I'm not ruling anything out," he told the *Albuquerque Journal*. "But I'm not focused on it, really." In January 2007 he announced on his website, in English and Spanish, that he was running for president. "I wouldn't run as a Hispanic candidate; I would run as an American, proud to be Hispanic," he said. "Most importantly, I can bring this country together. I'm a negotiator. I've brought countries together, closer, on peace treaties. I've rescued American hostages and servicemen. What we have right now is an opportunity to deal with major issues that really are dividing this country. I have the experience, I've been in Iraq. I've negotiated with Saddam Hussein. I was Secretary of Energy, I increased energy efficiency in our country. I've been a governor. I created 86,000 jobs in four years. I've cut taxes. I've brought economic growth to our state. I've made our schools better. I've got the strongest record on the environment and dealing with clean energy and fighting global warming." But once again he said he was not interested in the vice presidency. "I got a better job as governor of New Mexico. If I don't get the nomination, I'll come back" to Santa Fe.

Senior Senator

Pete Domenici (R)

Elected 1972, seat up 2008, 6th term; b. May 7, 1932, Albuquerque; home, Albuquerque; U. of NM, B.S. 1954, Denver U., LL.B. 1958; Catholic; married (Nancy).

Elected Office: Albuquerque City Comm., 1966-70, Mayor Ex–Officio, 1967-70.

Professional Career: Practicing atty., 1958-72.

DC Office: 328 HSOB, 20510, 202-224-6621; Fax: 202-228-3261; Web site: domenici.senate.gov.

State Offices: Albuquerque, 505-346-6791; Las Cruces, 505-526-5475; Roswell, 505-623-6170; Santa Fe, 505-988-6511.

Committees: *Appropriations* (4th of 14 R): Energy & Water Development (RMM); Commerce, Justice, Science & Related Agencies; Defense; Interior, Environment & Related Agencies; Homeland Security; Transportation, Housing and Urban Development & Related Agencies. *Budget* (2d of 11 R). *Energy & Natural Resources* (RMM of 11 R). *Homeland Security & Governmental Affairs* (6th of 8 R): Disaster Recovery; Investigations (Permanent); Federal Financial Management, Government Information, Federal Services & International Security; State, Local & Private Sector Preparedness & Integration. *Indian Affairs* (5th of 7 R).

Group Ratings

	ADA	ACLU	AFS	LCV	ITIC	NTU	COC	ACU	CFG	FRC
2006	0	17	13	14	100	64	100	75	54	87
2005	15	—	13	5	—	66	94	91	70	—

National Journal Ratings

	2005 LIB	—	2005 CONS		2006 LIB	—	2006 CONS
Economic	39%	—	59%		24%	—	75%
Social	36%	—	63%		37%	—	61%
Foreign	0%	—	74%		8%	—	85%

Key Votes of the 109th Congress

1. Bar ANWR Drilling	N	5. Confirm Samuel Alito	Y	9. Limit Interstate Abortion	Y
2. FY06 Spending Curb	Y	6. Path to Citizenship	Y	10. CAFTA	Y
3. Estate Tax Repeal	Y	7. Bar Same Sex Marriage	Y	11. Urge Iraq Withdrawal	N
4. Raise Minimum Wage	N	8. Stem Cell Research $	N	12. Provide Detainee Rights	N

Election Results

2002 general	Pete Domenici (R)	314,193	(65%)	($4,144,286)
	Gloria Tristani (D)	168,863	(35%)	($836,604)
2002 primary	Pete Domenici (R)	unopposed		
1996 general	Pete Domenici (R)	357,171	(65%)	($3,435,164)
	Art Trujillo (D)	164,356	(30%)	($155,213)
	Abraham Gutmann (Green)	24,230	(4%)	($12,025)

Prior Winning Percentages: 1990 (73%); 1984 (72%); 1978 (53%); 1972 (54%)

Pete Domenici, New Mexico's senior senator, was first elected to the Senate in 1972. He grew up in Albuquerque, the son of Italian immigrants who ran a wholesale grocery business. He played baseball for the Albuquerque Dukes, practiced law and was elected to the city commission in 1966. In 1970 he ran for governor and lost 51%-46% to Democrat Bruce King. In 1972, when a Senate seat opened up in a Republican year, he ran and won 54%-46%, beating a Democrat named Jack Daniels. Since 1984, he has been reelected by wide margins.

Domenici is the longest-serving senator from New Mexico and over the years has served as chairman of the Budget Committee and of the Energy and Natural Resources Committee; he is a senior member of Appropriations as well. Domenici joined the Budget Committee in his first year in the Senate, 1973; from 1981 to 2003 he was either the chairman or the ranking member of the committee. After supporting the 1981 Reagan tax cuts, Domenici was appalled at budget deficits and pushed for entitlement cuts and tax increases, but Democrats fought the first and Republicans the second. In May 1985, Domenici and Bob Dole got Republican senators to pass a freeze on Social Security cost-of-living adjustments; then Ronald Reagan dropped the COLA freeze in a compromise with House Speaker Tip O'Neill, and Senate Republicans, left exposed, lost their majority in 1986. After Republicans became the majority party in 1995, Domenici's ideas—a consumption tax; more in spending on education and defense than tax cuts—were initially overruled by Speaker Newt Gingrich. But the tax increase he opposed in 1993 and the spending standstill in the budget eventually passed in early 1996 put the deficit on a downward trajectory. Domenici was the impresario in the negotiations that produced the May 1997 balanced budget agreement. He helped to shape the budget resolutions in 1999 and 2000, but as an appropriator helped work out the arrangements that resulted in exceeding the budget caps.

In February 2001 he worked to pass the $1.6 trillion Bush tax cut and charged that Democrats had "anti-tax cut fever." In June 2001 Domenici lost the chairmanship, but the budget resolution had already passed and in 2002 the Democrats were not able to pass one. After the 2002 election, with only two more years under Republican rules as Budget chairman, he decided to move to the chairmanship of Energy and Natural Resources; for 12 years he had passed up the top Republican slot on this committee to keep that slot in Budget.

Domenici took over the Energy chairmanship from his Democratic New Mexico colleague, Jeff Bingaman, who became ranking minority member; this was the first time in history senators from the same state held the top two positions on a committee. Among the reasons he did so were his continuing interest in New Mexico's Los Alamos and Sandia National Laboratories and in promoting the expansion of nuclear power. After the controversy over security lapses at Los Alamos, he sponsored the creation of a new Undersecretary of Energy for Nuclear Stewardship. In 2001 he got the appropriation for the labs up to $5.8 billion, the highest ever and $500 million above the administration request. In 2003 he battled with House appropriator David Hobson who had cut funding for Sandia and Los Alamos. His knowledge of the labs' work made him interested in other programs. He favors development of new nuclear weapons and in 2003 prevailed over Dianne Feinstein in moving forward on bunker buster bombs. The labs also made him aware of homeland security problems before September 11; the Sandia Lab has one of the world's most comprehensive anthrax databases. In 2001 he called for bringing back the Price-Anderson Act, which protected the nuclear power industry from liability for catastrophic accidents. In 2005 he published a book, *A Brighter Tomorrow: Fulfilling the Promise of Nuclear Energy*.

In his first three years as Energy chairman Domenici tried to put together an omnibus energy bill similar to Bush administration proposals. He allowed votes on increasing CAFE auto mileage standards—that was rejected—and put in tax incentives for renewable energies, but not the requirement that utilities get 10% of their energy from such sources by 2020 that Bingaman favored. He put in plenty of provisions for nuclear power. In July 2003 the Senate passed the bill and most differences with the House seemed bridgeable. But several Northeastern Republican senators joined many Democrats in opposing a provision relieving oil companies from liability for MTBE, an additive that government fuel standards encouraged them to use. House Majority Leader Tom DeLay and Energy and Commerce Chairman Joe Barton both said they wouldn't accept a bill without the MTBE provision. In April 2004 the tax provisions of the energy bill were added to the corporate tax bill, and in May Domenici thought about putting the entire energy bill in that must-pass legislation. But Majority Leader Bill Frist said he wouldn't bring the energy bill to the floor unless Democrats agreed to limit debate to two or three days, and Minority Leader Tom Daschle said Democrats needed more time than that to propose amendments on climate change and fuel efficiency.

In January 2005 Domenici reached out to Bingaman in order to produce a less contentious energy bill. At Domenici's suggestion Arctic National Wildlife Refuge drilling was put into the budget resolution and passed 51-49 in March 2005. That eliminated one controversial issue; another set aside was increasing the CAFE standards. As Domenici said, "You cannot order Americans to buy little tiny cars." Domenici and Bingaman, together with House counterparts, were able to come up with a bill that passed the House 275-156 and the Senate 74-26 in July 2005. George W. Bush signed it in August in the Sandia National Laboratories' National Solar Thermal Test Facility. Provisions included the first federal electric transmission standards, incentives to build electric lines and natural gas pipelines, startup design for three advanced design nuclear plants, federal authority over liquefied natural gas terminals, more clean coal research, incentives for wind and solar power, new efficiency standards for appliances, requirements for increased use of ethanol, a four-week extension of Daylight Saving Time and creation of an Office of Indian Energy Policy and Programs at the Energy Department. Domenici said it was his greatest accomplishment in 33 years in the Senate; Bingaman said it "is not perfect, but it's a good bill." In August 2006 Domenici credited the 2005 law with stimulating plans to build up to 25 nuclear power plants in 20 years, groundbreaking for 29 new ethanol plants with almost 150 more planned, and a stronger renewable energy sector.

Other energy issues remained. In summer 2005 Domenici started talks with Bingaman on a bill to reduce carbon dioxide emissions, stimulated by a commission report calling for cutting them by 2.4% a year starting in 2010. But in March 2006, when Environment Committee Chairman Jim Inhofe said he would block the bill from the floor, Domenici said the Energy Committee wouldn't consider one. In October 2005 Domenici urged the administraton to grant new leases for natural gas drilling on the Outer Continental Shelf in the Gulf of Mexico, and supported a House move to put this in the budget, with a share of royalties going to the states. In July 2006 the Senate took up such a bill and after much controversy OCS drilling, with 37.5% of the royalties going to the states, was approved in December. In March 2006 Domenici opposed Alaska Congressman Don Young's amendment to the Coast Guard bill banning wind farms 1.5 miles from shipping lanes; this would have barred the proposed Cape Wind farm in Nantucket Sound opposed by Senator Edward Kennedy. In April the conference committee agreed on a provision letting governors veto such projects; Domenici and Bingaman threatened to block the bill in May, and House leaders backed down and removed the amendment in June. On a local issue, Domenici was neutral in September 2006 when 3d District Democrat Tom Udall moved to ban oil and gas drilling in the Valle Vidal area of Carson National Forest; when Domenici backed it in November it cleared the Senate floor.

Domenici has been one of the leaders in the Senate to extend health insurance coverage for mental illness. He became interested in the issue after his daughter Clare, the fourth of his eight children, was diagnosed with atypical schizophrenia. He uses his Appropriations seat to help New Mexico projects. With Dianne Feinstein he sponsored a bill to allow Indian tribes to contract with the federal government to take care of forests on reservations. When New Mexico's Supreme Court—"partisan Democrats," Domenici said—were preparing to allow people to register to vote without identification in September 2004, Domenici sponsored a bill to require identification. Domenici and Bingaman got into the omnibus appropriation $10 million to the descendants of Hispanic homesteaders who had been paid only a few dollars an acre in the 1940s for land that became part of the Los Alamos Laboratory. When the U.S. Attorney for New Mexico said that the Pueblo Act of 1924 left certain pueblo areas "prosecution-free zones," Domenici and Bingaman in 2005 sponsored a bill to amend the 1924 law.

Domenici has not been successful in seeking Senate leadership positions. He lost the majority leadership to Bob Dole in 1984 and the post of Republican Policy Committee chairman to Don Nickles in November 1990. In December 2000 he made a last-minute race against Policy Committee Chairman Larry Craig and lost 26-24.

Domenici has remained highly popular in New Mexico and has won reelection easily. In 2002 he was opposed by Gloria Tristani, granddaughter of longtime (1935-62) Senator Dennis Chavez and former state corporation commissioner and FCC member. He campaigned heavily across the state and was endorsed by 74 mayors, including dozens of Democrats. Some raised questions about his health; he has been stricken with acute pain in two fingers in his right hand since a touch football accident in 1999, but has reportedly reduced the pain by physical therapy and medication. On Election Day Domenici won 65%-35%; he lost only three counties, and those narrowly. He reached out immediately to Governor-elect Bill Richardson, of whom he had been critical in the past. In late 2004 he seemed uncertain whether he would run again in 2008. But in December 2006 he insisted he would. "I love being a senator. Thirty-four years is a pretty long time. I'm still going to run again, and win again."

At that point, Domenici would have been considered a lock for reelection. But in February 2007, the state political landscape was roiled by allegations that Domenici and Congresswoman Heather Wilson had pressured David Iglesias, one of eight U.S. attorneys asked in early December 2006 to resign, to pursue public corruption cases before the November elections. Domenici waited several days to respond to the accusations; he then admitted that he had telephoned Iglesias to inquire about the status of the case but denied threatening or pressuring him. "In retrospect, I regret making that call and I apologize," Domenici said. Iglesias claimed that Domenici had attempted to exert political influence over a federal investigation. "[Domenici] said, 'Are [the corruption cases] going to be filed before November?' And I said I didn't think so, to which he replied, 'I'm very sorry to hear that.' And then the line went dead," Iglesias testified before the Senate Judiciary Committee.

In the wake of the controversy, Democrats promised a stiff challenge to Domenici in 2008. But in October 2007, Domenici announced he would not seek reelection. Among the Democratic candidates mentioned as possible candidates were Lieutenant Governor Diane Denish, former Attorney General Patricia Madrid, wealthy businessman Don Wiviott and Albuquerque Mayor Martin Chavez. On the Republican side, Heather Wilson made plans to run and Congressman Steve Pearce also was mentioned as a possible candidate.

Junior Senator

Jeff Bingaman (D)

Elected 1982, seat up 2012, 5th term; b. Oct. 3, 1943, El Paso, TX; home, Santa Fe; Harvard U., B.A. 1965, Stanford U., LL.B. 1968; United Methodist; married (Anne).

Military Career: Army Reserves, 1968-74.

Elected Office: NM Atty. Gen., 1978-82.

Professional Career: NM Asst. Atty. Gen., 1969; Practicing atty., 1970-78.

DC Office: 328 HSOB, 20510, 202-224-5521; Fax: 202-224-2852; Web site: bingaman.senate.gov.

State Offices: Albuquerque, 505-346-6601; Las Cruces, 505-523-6561; Las Vegas, 505-454-8824; Roswell, 505-622-7113; Santa Fe, 505-988-6647.

Committees: *Energy & Natural Resources* (Chmn. of 12 D). *Finance* (4th of 11 D): Energy, Natural Resources & Infrastructure (Chmn.); Health Care; International Trade & Global Competitiveness. *Health, Education, Labor & Pensions* (5th of 11 D): Children & Families; Retirement & Aging. *Joint Economic Committee* (3d of 10 D).

Group Ratings

	ADA	ACLU	AFS	LCV	ITIC	NTU	COC	ACU	CFG	FRC
2006	100	100	100	100	100	16	36	8	1	12
2005	95	—	100	70	—	17	72	13	13	—

National Journal Ratings

	2005 LIB	—	2005 CONS		2006 LIB	—	2006 CONS
Economic	65%	—	34%		87%	—	0%
Social	63%	—	35%		76%	—	23%
Foreign	66%	—	29%		85%	—	12%

Key Votes of the 109th Congress

1. Bar ANWR Drilling	Y	5. Confirm Samuel Alito	N	9. Limit Interstate Abortion	N
2. FY06 Spending Curb	N	6. Path to Citizenship	Y	10. CAFTA	Y
3. Estate Tax Repeal	N	7. Bar Same Sex Marriage	N	11. Urge Iraq Withdrawal	Y
4. Raise Minimum Wage	Y	8. Stem Cell Research $	Y	12. Provide Detainee Rights	Y

Election Results

2006 general	Jeff Bingaman (D)	394,365	(71%)	($2,628,276)
	Allen McCulloch (R)	163,826	(29%)	($555,511)
2006 primary	Jeff Bingaman (D)	unopposed		
2000 general	Jeff Bingaman (D)	363,744	(62%)	($2,568,649)
	Bill Redmond (R)	225,517	(38%)	($639,424)

Prior Winning Percentages: 1994 (54%); 1988 (63%); 1982 (54%)

Jeff Bingaman, a Democrat first elected in 1982, is New Mexico's junior senator. He has a good political lineage: His father was a professor at Western New Mexico University in Silver City, and his uncle was campaign manager for longtime (1949-73) Senator Clinton Anderson. He graduated from Harvard and Stanford Law School, then returned to New Mexico. A year out of law school, Bingaman was counsel to the state constitutional convention; later he went into law practice in Santa Fe with former Governor Jack Campbell. Bingaman's wife, Anne, started a highly successful law practice of her own that helped finance his first campaigns; she was assistant attorney general for antitrust in the first Clinton term. In a small state, bright young people like Jeff Bingaman can rise fast. He ran for attorney general in 1978 and won; in 1982, he ran against Senator Harrison Schmitt, the former astronaut, also from Silver City, and won with 54%, partly because it was a recession year, but also because of Schmitt's misleading and negative ads.

Bingaman has followed a course in the Senate much like that of Clinton Anderson, who used his influence behind the scenes to great effect but shunned national publicity—so much so that *Roll Call* called Bingaman "preternaturally reticent." As the top-ranking Democrat since 1999 on the Energy and Natural Resources Committee, where he returned as chairman in January 2007, he has protected the interests of New Mexico's Los Alamos and Sandia labs. That influence has been especially strong since 2003 when his colleague Pete Domenici became the senior Republican on the Energy Committee, the first time in history that the two top members on a Senate committee were from the same state. Even though they have clashed on national energy policy, they understand each other when they disagree and they work well on local issues. Bingaman has aggressively sought alternative sources of energy. "I think we need to assume the [worst] and work aggressively to develop alternatives to oil . . . and also work aggressively to reduce our consumption of oil," he told the *Santa Fe New Mexican* after the 2006 election. "The period of cheap oil is largely behind us." His top priorities include action to deal with global warming, notably a "cap and trade" program to curb greenhouse gas emissions by allowing companies to buy and sell emission credits based on their pollution exhaust. Not surprisingly for a New Mexican, he is a vocal supporter of nuclear power and is willing to provide incentives for the industry to develop new types of reactors. He supports energy efficiency plus conservation, especially with vehicles, appliances and buildings. Bingaman praised the incentives for conservation included in the 2005 Energy Policy Act, a model for his deliberate and consensus-building style, but he said that the legislation should have gone further. "We did way too little in my view and we need to look at what more can be done," he said.

On that bill, Bingaman showed persistence and shrewd parliamentary maneuvering. When he became chairman in June 2001, he had the responsibility of coming up with an energy bill in response to President's Bush energy proposals. The House passed an energy bill in August, but Bingaman did not present his own version until September. It ignored the controversial proposal for oil drilling in the Arctic National Wildlife Refuge and left the issue of raising CAFE auto mileage standards to the Commerce committee. He wanted to encourage more nuclear energy and reauthorize the Price-Anderson Act, which shields plant operators from liability, to require reporting of emissions from so-called greenhouse gases and to give FERC authority over electricity transmission systems; he said the administration and House version leaned too much toward production incentives and had too little for renewable energy and energy efficiency. But the administration's approach, including ANWR drilling, seemed to have majority support on the committee and in October he withdrew his bill. Republicans, including Domenici, were furious at this and at the Democrats' subsequent decision to bring the issue to the floor without committee consideration—a highly unusual tactic for such complex legislation. Floor debate began in February 2002 and went on for six weeks. Bingaman was beaten by a 62-38 margin on his proposal to increase CAFE mileage standards in cars and SUVs to 35 miles per gallon but kept his proposal to require that 10% of electricity be produced by renewable energy sources by 2020. Bingaman accepted amendments on pipeline safety and maintained his provisions, opposed by environmental restriction groups, to increase the use of nuclear power and promote research in clean coal technology in New Mexico labs. He preserved his provisions to encourage more oil and gas development on Indian reservations. After Senate passage, the conference committee with the House met periodically, but never reached agreement; the bill died after the November election.

When Democrats lost their majority in the 2002 election, Domenici became chairman and Bingaman ranking minority member. This time Domenici put together an energy bill which, without ANWR drilling, passed the Senate in July 2003. When Domenici went into one-on-one negotiations with House Energy and Commerce Committee chairman Billy Tauzin before the conference committee met, Bingaman said this procedure was "deeply flawed." That fall the Senate and House remained in conflict over protecting oil companies from liability for the MTBE gas additive; the House insisted on it and prevailed in the conference committee. But the Senate fell two votes short in a vote to break a filibuster on the agreement. Domenici said Bingaman was to blame for the failure of the bill; Bingaman said it was Domenici's fault for keeping conference committee members out of negotiations. In 2005, Bingaman and Domenici made a point of emphasizing areas of agreement from the start. House Republicans agreed to drop the provision to protect MTBE manufacturers. Plus, there was bipartisan agreement on new federal transmission standards and incentives to build more electricity lines to avert major blackouts, the start-up of advanced-design nuclear power plants, and federal authority over liquefied natural gas terminals. Though he was disappointed in the bill's "failure" to fully address fuel efficiency and greenhouse gas emissions, Bingaman praised Domenici's cooperation.

As a member of the Senate Finance Committee, Bingaman sponsored a bill to bar the selection of New Mexico as a premium support site under the 2003 Medicare prescription drug act. He disappointed organized labor when he backed the Central American Free Trade Agreement after gaining White House support for tougher enforcement of labor standards. He voted against the confirmation of Attorney General Alberto Gonzales because, he said, Gonzales had tolerated or encouraged loosening the definition of torture.

Many of his bills have a New Mexico angle. With Domenici he has sought more money to improve border security and infrastructure. They directed $10 million to the descendants of Hispanic homesteaders who had been paid only a few dollars an acre in the 1940s for land that became part of the Los Alamos Laboratory. After previously opposing a long fence along the border with Mexico, Bingaman in 2006 joined passage of an alternative version because it no longer dictated the location. Bingaman and Domenici successfully collaborated to bar the Air Force from retiring 10 F-117s assigned to New Mexico's Holloman Air Force Base. With Tom Udall, the two senators in November 2006 enacted the Valle Vidal Protection Act, which covered 102,000 acres of Forest Service lands in the Raton Basin of northeast New Mexico.

Now in his fifth term, Bingaman faced his most serious challenge in the Republican year of 1994, when Republican Colin McMillan, a rancher and former assistant Defense secretary, spent over $1 million of his own money and attacked Bingaman's vote for Clinton's 1993 tax increase and for what McMillan said was a vote to increase grazing fees. Bingaman ads boasted of his work on defense conversion, national education standards and education technology. Bingaman won 54%-46%. In 2000 he faced former Congressman Bill Redmond, who won the heavily Democratic 3d District in a 1997 special election and then lost to Tom Udall in 1998. Bingaman spent $2.56 million to Redmond's $639,000. Bingaman won 62%-38%; he lost only six counties and ran 14% ahead of Al Gore. His reelection in 2006 barely attracted attention. Little-funded political neophyte Allen McCulloch, a Farmington urologist, called himself a "dirt under the fingernails" candidate who would pay particular attention to health care, farming, and the oil and gas industry. But most of his publicity came three weeks before the election when he was cited for careless driving after he lost control of his GMC Yukon during icy weather and slammed into a pickup truck parked along the highway near the town of Cuba. The truck burst into flames and one of its passengers suffered significant burns; McCulloch kicked out the rear window of the truck so that the passengers could escape. In what became an afterthought, Bingaman won the contest 71%-29%, and carried every county. He has surpassed Clinton Anderson in Senate longevity, and may eclipse his Senate influence.

FIRST DISTRICT

Rep. Heather Wilson (R)

Elected June 1998, 5th full term; b. Dec. 30, 1960, Keene, NH; home, Albuquerque; U.S. Air Force Acad., B.S. 1982, Rhodes Scholar, Oxford U., M.A. 1984, Ph.D. 1985; Methodist; married (Jay Hone).

Military Career: Air Force, 1978-89.

Professional Career: Dir., European Defense Policy & Arms Control, White House NSC, 1989-91; Pres. Keystone Intl. Inc., 1991-95; NM Secy. of Children, Youth & Families, 1995-98.

DC Office: 442 CHOB, 20515, 202-225-6316; Fax: 202-225-4975; Web site: wilson.house.gov.

District Offices: Albuquerque, 505-346-6781.

Committees: *Energy & Commerce* (10th of 26 R): Health; Environment & Hazardous Materials; Telecommunications & the Internet. *Permanent Select Committee on Intelligence* (3d of 8 R): Technical & Tactical Intelligence (RMM); Oversight & Investigations.

Group Ratings

	ADA	ACLU	AFS	LCV	ITIC	NTU	COC	ACU	CFG	FRC
2006	25	24	43	17	100	39	93	67	39	71
2005	25	—	38	22	—	46	96	75	42	75

National Journal Ratings

	2005 LIB	—	2005 CONS	2006 LIB	—	2006 CONS
Economic	49%	—	51%	49%	—	50%
Social	55%	—	45%	50%	—	50%
Foreign	47%	—	52%	45%	—	54%

Key Votes of the 109th Congress

1. Estate Tax Repeal	Y	5. Limit Interstate Abortion	*	9. Build Border Fence	Y
2. Limit CAFE Standards	Y	6. Extend Patriot Act	Y	10. CAFTA	Y
3. FY06 Spending Curb	N	7. Bar Same Sex Marriage	Y	11. Oppose Iraq Withdrawal	*
4. Drilling in ANWR	Y	8. Stem Cell Research $	Y	12. Detainee Tribunals	Y

Election Results

2006 general	Heather Wilson (R)	105,986	(50%)	($4,906,596)
	Patricia Madrid (D)	105,125	(50%)	($3,386,538)
2006 primary	Heather Wilson (R) .... unopposed			
2004 general	Heather Wilson (R)	147,372	(54%)	($3,401,887)
	Richard Romero (D)	123,339	(46%)	($2,106,588)

Prior Winning Percentages: 2002 (55%); 2000 (50%); 1998 (48%); 1998 (45%)

The People		Race/Ethnic Origin	Ancestry	
Area size:	4,720 sq. mi.	48.5% White	German: 9.6%	English: 7.0%
Urban population:	91.3%	2.3% Black	Irish: 6.9%	
Rural population:	8.7%	1.7% Asian	**2004 Presidential Vote**	
Pop. 2000:	606,400	2.9% Native Am.	Kerry (D) 139,820	(51%)
Pop. 2005 (est):	651,979	0.1% Hawaiian	Bush (R) 130,946	(48%)
Median income:	$38,413	1.6% Two+ races	Other 2,896	(1%)
Poverty status:	14.0%	0.2% Other	**2000 Presidential Vote**	
Military veterans:	15.2%	42.6% Hispanic Origin	Gore (D) 106,572	(48%)
			Bush (R) 103,770	(47%)
			Other 10,385	(5%)
			Cook Partisan Voting Index: D + 2	

Occupation　　Blue collar: 18.9%　　White collar: 65.2%　　Gray collar: 16.0%

The future and the past of New Mexico come together in its single metropolis, Albuquerque. Its Spanish and Indian past is memorialized in its name (for a 17th century Spanish grandee) and age (founded in 1706) and its quaint Old Town, but Albuquerque's future is decidedly high-tech. For decades, the Sandia National Laboratories, Kirtland Air Force Base and the University of New Mexico have attracted scientists and engineers to Albuquerque and promoted private sector technology growth. When rocket scientist Robert Goddard moved here in 1930 and nuclear scientist J. Robert Oppenheimer reconnoitered the site in 1940, Albuquerque was still a town of 35,000 sitting at the junction of the Rio Grande and the old U.S. 66 that paralleled the Santa Fe Railroad—"a dirty red sod-hut tortilla desert highway city," Tom Wolfe wrote. Now, metro Albuquerque, spreading out from Bernalillo County into Sandoval and Valencia Counties, has more people (817,000 in 2006) than all New Mexico did when the scientists first arrived. Here in 1975, Bill Gates founded a little company called Micro-Soft; although the software maker moved its 16 employees to Seattle in 1979. Intel now employs nearly 5,000 people here in an advanced chip-making facility. Albuquerque's prosperous neighborhoods have climbed the gently rising heights to the east; poorer residents have spread north and south along the Rio Grande; in the Old Town Plaza, some of the adobe buildings date to the 18th century. Hemmed in by the Sandia mountains and by federal installations, growth is moving west and north, especially to the new town of Rio Rancho, home of the Intel plant and facilities for Sprint PCS and Victoria's Secret. Despite its cold winters, Albuquerque is counted as part of the Sun Belt. Its economy also differs from those of other Sun Belt cities; despite the tech base, it has lower income levels than Phoenix or Denver. While Albuquerque has seen some growth in tourism—it is home of the International Balloon Fiesta every October, and includes many resident balloonists—it is heavily dependent on federal jobs.

The 1st Congressional District of New Mexico includes Albuquerque and some of its suburbs, and is 43% Hispanic. It takes in most of Bernalillo County and stretches into the desert to include sparsely populated Torrance County. But the 1st does not include most of big-growth suburbs Corrales and Rio Rancho to the north in Sandoval County, and Isleta and Las Lunas to the south in Valencia County. Despite the fact that Democrats outnumber Republicans here, the district always has elected a Republican to Congress since it was carved out of the rest of the state in 1968. This is one of the nation's most competitive districts: It voted 48%-47% for Al Gore in 2000 and 51%-48% for John Kerry in 2004. Kerry visited Albuquerque six times during his campaign.

The congresswoman from the 1st District is Heather Wilson, a Republican first elected in a June 1998 special election. She is wonky, ambitious, a national security expert, sometimes partisan but willing to go her own way. She grew up in New Hampshire, and learned to fly before she learned to drive. She graduated from the Air Force Academy, then became a Rhodes Scholar at Oxford. She served in the Air Force until 1989, and worked two years for President George H.W. Bush on the National Security Council in charge of NATO and European affairs before turning 30. In 1991 she moved to New Mexico, to marry her former Air Force Academy law instructor; she started a consulting firm, and then Governor Gary Johnson appointed her secretary of the Children, Youth and Families Department.

In January 1998, Republican Congressman Steven Schiff announced he would not run again; he died two months later. Senator Pete Domenici backed Wilson strongly; she defeated a conservative state senator for the state central committee endorsement by winning 55 votes, the minimum required. The Democratic nomination was captured by Phil Maloof, a young state senator from a wealthy family that made its fortune through beer distribution, casinos, banking interests, hotels and sports franchises. Also running was Green Party candidate Bob Anderson. Wilson's first ad showed her two-year-old daughter running into her arms; she concluded speeches by talking about reading to her four-year-old son on the roof of their house. Maloof favored raising the minimum wage, opposed school vouchers and ran soft-focus ads playing on his family's 100-year history in New Mexico (next to Wilson's seven). Maloof spent $3.1 million, almost all of it his own. Wilson won 45% to 40% for Maloof and 15% for Anderson, though he spent less than $10,000. She thus became the second woman veteran and first woman service academy graduate to serve in Congress; the first woman veteran was Cathy Long who served in the Navy in the 1940s and represented the 8th District of Louisiana from 1985 to 1987. All three candidates ran again in November and the margin was similar: Wilson 48%, Maloof 42%, Anderson 10%. Wilson has always faced competitive reelections.

In the House, Wilson's voting record has become more moderate and she has been one of its reliable—though not always predictable—centrists. When she complained that Republicans planned to bring a bill to the House floor that would have moved the nuclear weapons program from the Energy Department to the Pentagon, party leaders made changes. Republican leaders tapped her as a leading advocate for George W. Bush's energy plan, and she sponsored the successful amendment to limit oil drilling in the Arctic National Wildlife Refuge to 2,000 acres. On the Energy and Commerce Committee, with Democrat Gene Green, she won enactment of a bill to toughen anti-spam restrictions on commercial email. She worked to defend Kirtland in the base-closing procedure and sponsored additional criteria to the procedures; she also called for an increase in military troop levels. In 2005, she was forced to give up her seat on the Armed Services Committee in order to remain on Energy and Commerce. That move followed threats by Chairman Joe Barton to remove her from Energy and Commerce after she joined Democrats in questioning the cost of the 2003 Medicare/prescription drug law. But she got a consolation prize, a seat on the Intelligence Committee, where she became chairman of the Technical and Tactical Intelligence Subcommittee. She harshly criticized aspects of the Bush administration's electronic surveillance program and demanded a thorough congressional investigation, then became a chief sponsor of legislation that would have placed significant restrictions on the warrantless surveillance program while granting it legal status; the bill passed the House in September 2006 but was never considered by the Senate. "The President has his duty to do, but I have mine too, and I feel strongly about that," she said. In February 2005, she was one of eight Republicans to vote against barring illegal immigrants from getting driver's licenses; she said it was a state matter. The House passed her bill to prohibit price-gouging in the sale of gasoline and oil products.

Against well-financed challengers, Wilson has benefited from a warm campaign style. "This is not a typical Republican district, and I'm not a typical Republican," she said. John Kelly, the former U.S. Attorney in New Mexico and a friend of Bill Clinton since both were undergraduates at Georgetown, ran in a 2000 campaign filled with controversial advertising by outside groups. Wilson won 50%-43%. In 2002, the challenger was Richard Romero, a state senator who was elected Senate president in 2001 in a coalition that ousted the Democratic incumbent. Romero had been rated a top-tier challenger by national Democrats, but he suffered from local Democratic divisions; one Democratic state senator called him Benedict Arnold. Wilson won with her largest majority, 55%-45%. In 2004, Romero ran again. His negative ads ran side-by-side photos of Wilson and Osama bin Laden to highlight her vote against cargo screening on airline security legislation. The result was a nearly identical 54%-46% win for Wilson. During the campaign she said that House Democratic leaders had invited her to switch parties; Minority Leader Nancy Pelosi dismissed that.

In 2006, she faced state Attorney General Patricia Madrid, one of Rahm Emanuel's top campaign recruits; the two candidates spent more than $8 million in a bruising contest. Madrid, who grew up in a modest Las Cruces family and became a labor lawyer, attacked Wilson for being close to lobbyist Jack Abramoff and ethically-challenged House Republicans. Wilson's campaign took the offensive with criticism that Madrid, as attorney general, failed to investigate claims that former state treasurer Robert Vigil had accepted kickbacks—charges on which he was later indicted. A crucial turning point came in a late campaign debate when Madrid froze in response to Wilson's question, "Can you cite something that would give people of New Mexico some kind of reassurance that you will prevent a tax increase?" Wilson immediately turned the sequence into a television ad telling voters not to "take the risk" with Madrid. The campaign went down to the wire, with Wilson winning by less than 900 votes in one of the last House contests to be resolved. Her victory margin came from the southern portion of the district where she won 61%-39% in Torrance County and 53%-47% in Valencia County. Madrid carried Bernalillo County, the district's most populous, 50.3%-49.7%; she also won Sandoval County 51%-49%.

After the 2006 election, there was talk Domenici might retire in 2008 and Wilson figured to be a contender for his Senate seat. But New Mexico's political landscape shifted considerably in February 2007, when allegations surfaced that Wilson and Domenici had pressured David Iglesias, one of the eight U.S. attorneys asked to resign in early December 2006, to expedite indictments in a public corruption case for political purposes. Wilson waited several days to respond to the accusations; she then admitted that she had contacted him about the cases but denied that the call was "motivated by politics or partisanship." "I did not ask about the timing of any indictments and I did not tell Mr. Iglesias what course of action I thought he should take or pressure him in any way," she said.

Hoping to take advantage of the controversy, the DCCC began airing attacks against Wilson in April. In October 2007, Domenici announced he would not seek reelection; Wilson made plans to run for his Senate seat.

SECOND DISTRICT

Rep. Steve Pearce (R)

Elected 2002, 3d term; b. Aug. 24, 1947, Lamesa, TX; home, Hobbs; NM St. U., B.B.A. 1970, E. NM U. M.B.A. 1991; Baptist; married (Cynthia).

Military Career: Air Force, 1970-76 (Vietnam).

Elected Office: NM House of Reps., 1996-2000.

Professional Career: Owner, Lea Fishing Tools.

DC Office: 1607 LHOB, 20515, 202-225-2365; Fax: 202-225-9599; Web site: pearce.house.gov.

District Offices: Hobbs, 505-392-8325; Las Cruces, 505-522-2219; Roswell, 505-622-0055; Socorro, 505-838-7516.

Committees: *Financial Services* (22d of 33 R): Housing & Community Opportunity; Financial Institutions & Consumer Credit. *Natural Resources* (9th of 22 R): Energy & Mineral Resources (RMM); National Parks, Forests & Public Lands.

Group Ratings

	ADA	ACLU	AFS	LCV	ITIC	NTU	COC	ACU	CFG	FRC
2006	5	18	0	0	100	64	100	92	70	100
2005	0	—	0	0	—	55	96	96	53	92

National Journal Ratings

	2005 LIB — 2005 CONS	2006 LIB — 2006 CONS
Economic	19% — 79%	0% — 98%
Social	37% — 63%	37% — 63%
Foreign	31% — 67%	6% — 86%

Key Votes of the 109th Congress

1. Estate Tax Repeal	Y	5. Limit Interstate Abortion	Y	9. Build Border Fence	Y
2. Limit CAFE Standards	Y	6. Extend Patriot Act	Y	10. CAFTA	Y
3. FY06 Spending Curb	Y	7. Bar Same Sex Marriage	Y	11. Oppose Iraq Withdrawal	Y
4. Drilling in ANWR	Y	8. Stem Cell Research $	N	12. Detainee Tribunals	Y

Election Results

2006 general	Steve Pearce (R)	92,620	(59%)	($1,349,394)
	Albert Kissling (D)	63,119	(40%)	($183,160)
2006 primary	Steve Pearce (R)	unopposed		
2004 general	Steve Pearce (R)	130,498	(60%)	($1,997,549)
	Gary King (D)	86,292	(40%)	($1,143,705)

Prior Winning Percentages: 2002 (56%)

The People		Race/Ethnic Origin	Ancestry	
Area size:	69,598 sq. mi.	44.3% White	German: 7.4%	English: 5.9%
Urban population:	71.0%	1.6% Black	Irish: 5.7%	
Rural population:	29.0%	0.5% Asian	**2004 Presidential Vote**	
Pop. 2000:	606,406	4.8% Native Am.	Bush (R) 127,391	(58%)
Pop. 2005 (est):	625,204	0.0% Hawaiian	Kerry (D) 91,073	(41%)
Median income:	$29,269	1.2% Two+ races	Other 2,281	(1%)
Poverty status:	22.4%	0.2% Other	**2000 Presidential Vote**	
Military veterans:	14.9%	47.3% Hispanic Origin	Bush (R) 96,161	(54%)
			Gore (D) 76,868	(43%)
			Other 5,667	(3%)
			Cook Partisan Voting Index: R + 6	

Occupation	Blue collar: 26.7%	White collar: 52.9%	Gray collar: 20.4%

Southern and eastern New Mexico is a disparate landscape: endless sagebrush-strewn acreage and then, suddenly, 9,000-foot mountain peaks rising along the Continental Divide. The eastern part of this region—places like Clovis and Portales, Lovington and Hobbs—speaks with a Texas twang rather than a northern New Mexico lilt. In Little Texas, oil has long been the economic mainstay; cattle ranching is common and cotton is grown on irrigated land. One of the larger towns is Roswell, site of a supposed flying saucer landing in 1947 and now home of the International UFO Museum and Research Center. Further west is White Sands National Monument, with its immaculate gypsum dunes and animals with specially evolved white coloration that allows them to survive predators in the harsh environment; close by is Alamogordo, where the first atomic bomb was exploded at 5:29:45 a.m. Mountain War Time on July 16, 1945. Near White Sands, a new generation of entrepreneurs hopes to build a spaceport, where millionaires can pay to go into orbit. Like many places on America's high plains, population here is thinning and old economic pillars are crumbling; Carlsbad, once reliant on potash mining, aggressively sought the Waste Isolation Pilot Plant, a nuclear waste repository. East of Carlsbad, a uranium enrichment plant is under construction in Eunice, the first such facility licensed by the Nuclear Regulatory Commission. In central and western New Mexico, the scrub land shades into desert, and people are crammed into small cities, protected from summer's burning heat and winter's deathly cold. The Hatch Valley, in the desert adjoining Interstate 25, is home to perhaps the world's finest chili peppers—the traditional cornerstone of the Southwest's spicy cuisine. Places like Silver City and Bayard were built on mining, and occasional discord; the story of a strike by Mexican-American workers at a zinc mine here in 1950 and 1951 was told in *Salt of the Earth*, a movie with such a volatile message that it was blacklisted. Now home to miners, artists, ranchers and outdoor enthusiasts alike, Silver City lacks the polish of Santa Fe or Taos but locals like to say it offers "the real New Mexico experience."

This is also an international frontier—the tiny town of Columbus was the site of a raid by Pancho Villa and his irregular band of soldiers in 1916. Las Cruces, now New Mexico's second-largest city, whose Robledo Mountains were hailed by the Smithsonian Institution as the world's greatest repository of pre-dinosaur era fossil tracks, has grown at rates well above the statewide average, thanks to migrants from Mexico coming up the Rio Grande. For decades, Anglo and Mexican ranchers across the border spoke "the common language of cattle"; communities frequently shared public services with their cross-border neighbors and left the gates open at night for stragglers stuck too late on the wrong side of the border. But rapid development due to NAFTA, a surge in illegal immigration and drug trafficking have brought enormous strains. Still, the New Mexico portion of the U.S.-Mexico border remains far sleepier than elsewhere and the border posts that dot New Mexico's largely empty 150-mile frontier apprehend considerably fewer illegal immigrants than those in Arizona. The national training center for Border Patrol agents has been consolidated in Artesia.

The 2d Congressional District of New Mexico covers this southern part of the state, going as far north as the suburb of Las Lunas and the Isleta Pueblo south of Albuquerque and the Acoma Pueblo to the west. Demographically and politically, it is diverse. It includes most of New Mexico's Little Texas—majority Anglo and solidly conservative, though with a Democratic heritage. It includes Las Cruces and the mining counties in the southwest corner of the state; Las Cruces is politically marginal and the mining counties Democratic. And it includes the Indian country around the pueblos, which is strongly Democratic. The district was 47% Hispanic in 2000, the highest of any New Mexico district, and 5% Indian. But more of the Hispanics are ineligible to vote here than in the 1st or 3d Districts.

The congressman from the 2d District is Steve Pearce, a Republican first elected in 2002. He grew up in Hobbs, near the Texas line, and graduated from New Mexico State in Las Cruces; he served in the Air Force and flew missions during the Vietnam War. He returned to Hobbs and started an oil-field service company. In 1996 he was elected to the state House. In 2000 he ran for the Senate, but lost the Republican primary to former Congressman Bill Redmond. In 2002, when Republican Congressman Joe Skeen, stricken with Parkinson's disease, announced he would not run again, Pearce sought to succeed him. He had two major competitors in the Republican primary: former state representative Phelps Anderson of Roswell, the son of former Arco chairman Robert Anderson, and Ed Tinsley, the owner of the K-BOBS USA steakhouse chain, who got Skeen's endorsement. Pearce ran a deft primary campaign. Using youth volunteers, he maximized his vote in Little Texas. He built on his ties to Las Cruces, where he had gone to college, and carried its Dona Ana County with 38% of the vote. Tinsley carried ten counties, but with no geographic base won only 27% of the vote. Anderson, without much support outside his home county, won 24%. In the general, there did not seem to be much difference between Pearce and the Democratic nominee, state Senator John Arthur Smith of Deming. Smith was an opponent of abortion rights, a believer in Second Amendment rights, a conservative who had often split from liberal Democrats in the legislature. Pearce piloted his own plane around the district; Smith drove his own car (this matters in a district that covers 69,598 square miles). Despite polls showing a close race, Pearce won by a solid 56%-44% margin. He won large percentages, from 58% to 77%, in Little Texas. Smith's margins in his home county and in the mining and Indian counties were not enough to offset this.

In the House, Pearce usually votes with conservatives, though he has been a bit more moderate on social issues. The House passed his bill to eradicate water-depleting tamarisks in Western states, including New Mexico. He also won House approval of his bill to cut in half royalties paid to the federal government by the potash industry, a substantial source of jobs in New Mexico; most potash is used as fertilizer, and the decline in production during the past decade had raised costs for farmers. In 2005, Pearce took over as chairman of the National Parks subcommittee and launched a sweeping review of Park Service operations. He made parks accessibility a priority, and proposed giving states and counties broad authority over rights of way on federal land. But he made little progress on the measure before Democrats took back House control with a very different environmental agenda. Pearce tended to his district's substantial military facilities, calling for the Air Force to locate its new F-22 Raptor fighter at Holloman Air Force Base, which has been home to the aging F-117 Nighthawk stealth fighters. He voiced doubts when House Republicans in 2006 sought to accelerate construction of a fence along the Mexican border to curb illegal immigration. Citing opposition from most local law enforcement officers, Pearce said, "If the people on the border don't believe that the wall will have the effect that people [in Washington] think, then we ought to reconsider it."

In 2004 New Mexico was a target state in the presidential election, and George W. Bush appeared often with Pearce. Bush's success in increasing his district vote from 54% in 2000 to 58% four years later was crucial to swinging the state his way. Pearce ran a bit ahead of Bush, winning 60%-40% in an expensive contest against Gary King, a Clinton Energy Department official and son of former three-term Democratic governor Bruce King. In the more hostile political climate two years later, he faced Albert Kissling, a little-known retired minister, and was held to 59%; Democratic Dona Ana County Commissioner Bill McCamley was actively fundraising for 2008. After Senator Pete Domenici said he would retire in 2008, Pearce drew mention as a possible Senate candidate.

THIRD DISTRICT

Rep. Tom Udall (D)

Elected 1998, 5th term; b. May 18, 1948, Tucson, AZ; home, Santa Fe; Prescott Col., B.A. 1970; Cambridge U., B.L. 1975; U. of NM, J.D. 1977; Mormon; married (Jill Cooper).

Elected Office: NM Atty. Gen., 1990-98.

Professional Career: Law clerk, 10th Circuit Court of Appeals, 1977; Asst. U.S. Atty, 1978-81; Practicing atty., 1981-83, 1985-90; Chief Cnsl., NM Health & Environment Dept., 1983-84.

DC Office: 1410 LHOB, 20515, 202-225-6190; Fax: 202-226-1331; Web site: tomudall.house.gov.

District Offices: Clovis, 505-763-7616; Farmington, 505-324-1005; Gallup, 505-863-0582; Las Vegas, 505-454-4080; Rio Rancho, 505-994-0499; Santa Fe, 505-984-8950.

Committees: *Appropriations* (28th of 37 D): Legislative Branch; Interior, Environment & Related Agencies; Labor, HHS, Education & Related Agencies.

Group Ratings

	ADA	ACLU	AFS	LCV	ITIC	NTU	COC	ACU	CFG	FRC
2006	95	100	100	100	17	14	29	4	7	0
2005	95	—	100	94	—	12	41	0	5	0

National Journal Ratings

	2005 LIB — 2005 CONS		2006 LIB — 2006 CONS	
Economic	77%	— 23%	83%	— 16%
Social	80%	— 20%	84%	— 15%
Foreign	84%	— 16%	88%	— 10%

Key Votes of the 109th Congress

1. Estate Tax Repeal	N	5. Limit Interstate Abortion	N	9. Build Border Fence	N
2. Limit CAFE Standards	N	6. Extend Patriot Act	N	10. CAFTA	N
3. FY06 Spending Curb	N	7. Bar Same Sex Marriage	N	11. Oppose Iraq Withdrawal	N
4. Drilling in ANWR	N	8. Stem Cell Research $	Y	12. Detainee Tribunals	N

Election Results

2006 general	Tom Udall (D)	144,880	(75%)	($396,860)
	Ronald Dolin (R)	49,219	(25%)	($23,572)
2006 primary	Tom Udall (D)	unopposed		
2004 general	Tom Udall (D)	175,269	(69%)	($452,489)
	Gregory Tucker (R)	79,935	(31%)	($56,051)

Prior Winning Percentages: 2002 (100%); 2000 (67%); 1998 (53%)

The People		Race/Ethnic Origin	Ancestry	
Area size:	47,271 sq. mi.	41.4% White	German: 7.4%	English: 6.0%
Urban population:	62.8%	1.1% Black	Irish: 5.6%	
Rural population:	37.2%	0.7% Asian	**2004 Presidential Vote**	
Pop. 2000:	606,240	18.9% Native Am.	Kerry (D)	139,336 (54%)
Pop. 2005 (est):	646,324	0.1% Hawaiian	Bush (R)	118,350 (45%)
Median income:	$35,058	1.4% Two+ races	Other	2,653 (1%)
Poverty status:	19.0%	0.1% Other	**2000 Presidential Vote**	
Military veterans:	13.4%	36.3% Hispanic Origin	Gore (D)	102,809 (52%)
			Bush (R)	86,004 (43%)
			Other	9,676 (5%)
			Cook Partisan Voting Index: D + 6	

Occupation   Blue collar: 21.7%   White collar: 60.3%   Gray collar: 18.0%

"The dancing ground of the sun," the Pueblo Indians called the land of northern New Mexico, where the long vistas, dotted with low-lying scrub, are painted in pastel hues in the cold light and clear air. For 100 years, artists have been coming here, attracted by the scenery and by a unique civilization that is part Indian, part Anglo, part Spanish, and only a little Mexican (northern New Mexico was under Mexican control only from 1821-46). The region's long-surviving traditions, however, hide the instabilities of this blended civilization. The adobe pueblos, including some of the world's earliest apartment buildings, were built in spurts; the Spanish conquistadors and priests brought the Catholic religion, the baroque architectural accents and the Spanish language in a rush. Successive waves of American settlement have changed New Mexico in multiple ways. The Indian crafts that thrive today nearly died out in the 1880s, while the Palace of the Governors, built in Santa Fe in 1610, had its Victorian balustrade torn off in 1913 to restore its original appearance. Yet up the back roads in Rio Arriba or Taos Counties, one can find a religion that mixes Catholicism with adaptations of Indian festivals, buildings not that much different from the old pueblos and a standard of living reminiscent of the Indian past, sometimes punctuated by high rates of drug abuse—quite a contrast to the chi-chi ski lodges in the Taos Valley, the high security research facilities of Los Alamos or the affluent, bohemian activity in modern-day Santa Fe, where zoning laws decree that the color of all buildings must be adobe brown.

The 3d Congressional District of New Mexico contains most of the state's historic Spanish-speaking and Indian parts. The district's largest and dominant city is Santa Fe, where Georgia O'Keeffe was a major cultural force and local spas have encouraged the tourism boom. But the 3d also runs from the High Plains along the Texas border, past the haunting Sangre de Cristo Mountains, through the vast ridges and isolated buttes in the center, to the windy and dusty desert-like plains. Its Hispanic population is 36%, the lowest of the state's three districts, but in the central part of the district it ranges from almost half in Santa Fe County to nearly 80% in Mora County. Another 19% of the district population is Indian, mostly in and around the Navajo Reservation in the west, which is hard hit by poverty and poor health. The politics of northern New Mexico is unique. For years, debate was conducted and votes bartered in Spanish, not by separatists, but by Republicans and Democrats, often cynically, sometimes corruptly; loyalties ran to families and communities more than to principles or parties. In the backcountry, you can still find more than just vestiges of the old communities and old politics—though no one is going to let you in on them, even if you speak good Spanish. Although the Little Texas counties, the Albuquerque suburb of Rio Rancho, the mining and ranching country around Farmington, and the nuclear scientists of Los Alamos tend to vote Republican, this is on the whole a Democratic district; both Hispanics and Indians are very Democratic, and in Santa Fe and Taos, the affluent and hippie migrants have produced a strong leftist tilt. Politically, this is a sharply divided district. Santa Fe, Taos and San Miguel Counties voted more than 70% for John Kerry in 2004. But Bush won 65% to 77% in the counties on the Texas border and 66% in Farmington's San Juan County. Overall the district, after voting 52%-43% for Al Gore in 2000, voted 54%-45% for Kerry in 2004.

The congressman from the 3d District is Tom Udall, a Democrat first elected in 1998, the son of Arizona Congressman (1955-61) and Interior Secretary (1961-69) Stewart Udall, nephew of Arizona Congressman (1961-91) Morris Udall, first cousin of Colorado Congressman Mark Udall, and distant cousin of Oregon Senator Gordon Smith, the only Republican in the bunch—sometimes called the "Kennedys of the West." Tom Udall grew up in Tucson and in McLean, Virginia, went to college in Arizona, got a degree at Cambridge University in England, and went to law school in New Mexico. He worked as a law clerk to a federal judge, then as a lawyer in New Mexico state government and went into private law practice. Politics was obviously on his mind. He ran for Congress in 1982 when the 3d District was newly created, and finished last among four candidates, with 13% of the vote; the winner was Bill Richardson, now governor. In 1988 he ran in the open Albuquerque-based 1st District, won the Democratic nomination but lost the general to Steven Schiff 51%-47%. In 1990 he was elected state attorney general.

In 1997, when Richardson resigned and the 3d District seat opened up, Udall did not run. Republican Bill Redmond, an independent Christian minister from Los Alamos, won in a shocking upset, assisted by a Green Party candidate nominee who won 17%. In 1998, Udall ran for the seat. He worked to consolidate the Democratic and leftist vote; drawing on lawyers, the arts community and friends of the Udall family, he raised daunting sums. The Sierra Club and the League of Conservation Voters criticized Redmond and ran waves of ads against him. As for the third party threat, Udall said, "I intend to make peace with the Greens." He was utterly successful. Udall won

53% of the vote, Redmond got the same 43% he had won 18 months before, while Green Party nominee Carole Miller saw her 17% evaporate to 4%. He has not been seriously challenged since then.

In the House, Udall has proudly preserved his family's legacies. He had a seat on the Resources Committee, on which his father served and which his uncle chaired, and helped to enact a bill to explore establishment of a national historical park at Los Alamos. With Republican Roscoe Bartlett, he formed the Peak Oil Caucus to seek alternatives to high-priced and finite petroleum resources; locally, he called for a ban on oil drilling in the Valle Vidal area of the Carson National Forest, which was enacted in the 2006 lame-duck session. As a leading Democratic proponent of forest health, he opposed Republican attempts to permit salvage logging. With his largely liberal voting record, he voted against creation of the Homeland Security Department, opposed the use of force in Iraq, and called "misguided" a bill to restrict illegal immigrants from obtaining drivers' licenses. He proposed revisions in the Patriot Act, to limit authority to obtain search warrants and restore protections for libraries and bookstores. He also called for an independent agency to monitor civil liberties abuses in the war on terrorism. With the rest of the New Mexico delegation, he protested the Pentagon's recommendation to close Cannon Air Force Base in Clovis, which would have meant the loss of roughly 20 percent of the local work force. Instead, the Pentagon decided to move its Special Operations Wing to Cannon.

When Democrats took control of the House, Udall left the Natural Resources Committee because he landed a seat on Appropriations. He has been mentioned as a possible Interior Secretary if Democrats win the White House in 2008.

★ NEW YORK ★

It was a beautiful fall morning, the sunshine lighting a blue sky above the skyscrapers of Manhattan, commuters hurrying through the streets and subways to work, at 8:45 a.m. on September 11, 2001. Then, one minute later, the first plane hit the North Tower of the World Trade Center, and everything changed. When the second plane hit the South Tower 16 minutes later, it was clear that America was under attack, at war, even as office workers fled the burning buildings and New York fire fighters streamed in. The terrorists had chosen to attack Washington—the Pentagon and the building United Flight 93 was heading toward when heroes brought it down—and New York, the greatest city in the nation and the world, to inflict the greatest possible damage on our country. Yet the people of New York, like those at the Pentagon and on United 93, responded with the courage and determination, the devotion to duty and the willingness to take the initiative that made this city and this country great. Fire fighters and police officers and rescue workers risked death to help others. Strangers helped strangers. People who had no experience with disaster figured out how to cope and help others. Millions volunteered to give blood, send in money, or provide food and supplies. The *Wall Street Journal*, headquartered across the street from the World Trade Center, scrambled to put out a newspaper that was distributed at the regular time across the nation the next day. In less than a week the New York Stock Exchange was reopened. Mayor Rudolph Giuliani worked tirelessly to share with the nation the tragic news of deaths and to assert the determination to recover.

The bravery, the determination, the generosity that the world saw on that terrible day and the days after were some of the same qualities that had, over the centuries, made New York what it is—America's largest city, its financial capital, its center of arts and letters and media and its largest immigrant destination. New York's achievements were not inevitable. They happened because New Yorkers—and not least those people from elsewhere who opted to become New Yorkers—worked to make them happen. They did it in a city that has a certain enduring character that goes back to its birth as the 17th century Dutch colony of Nieuw Amsterdam. Simon Schama's *The Embarrassment of Riches* paints a picture of the old world Amsterdam: the richest city in the world; full of people who work hard all day and stay up late at night, smoke too much tobacco and drink too much coffee and gin, but are dazzlingly smart and shrewd; people who know their way around every corner of the globe and can make fine aesthetic discriminations, but are attached to their uncomfortable, crowded, bad-smelling city. They were merchants and manipulators with no aristocratic pedigree, welcoming any religious or ethnic group who can achieve and accumulate and show good taste, cherishing education and culture but indifferent to credentials. Probably fewer than 2% of today's New Yorkers are descended from the Dutch of Nieuw Amsterdam, but the

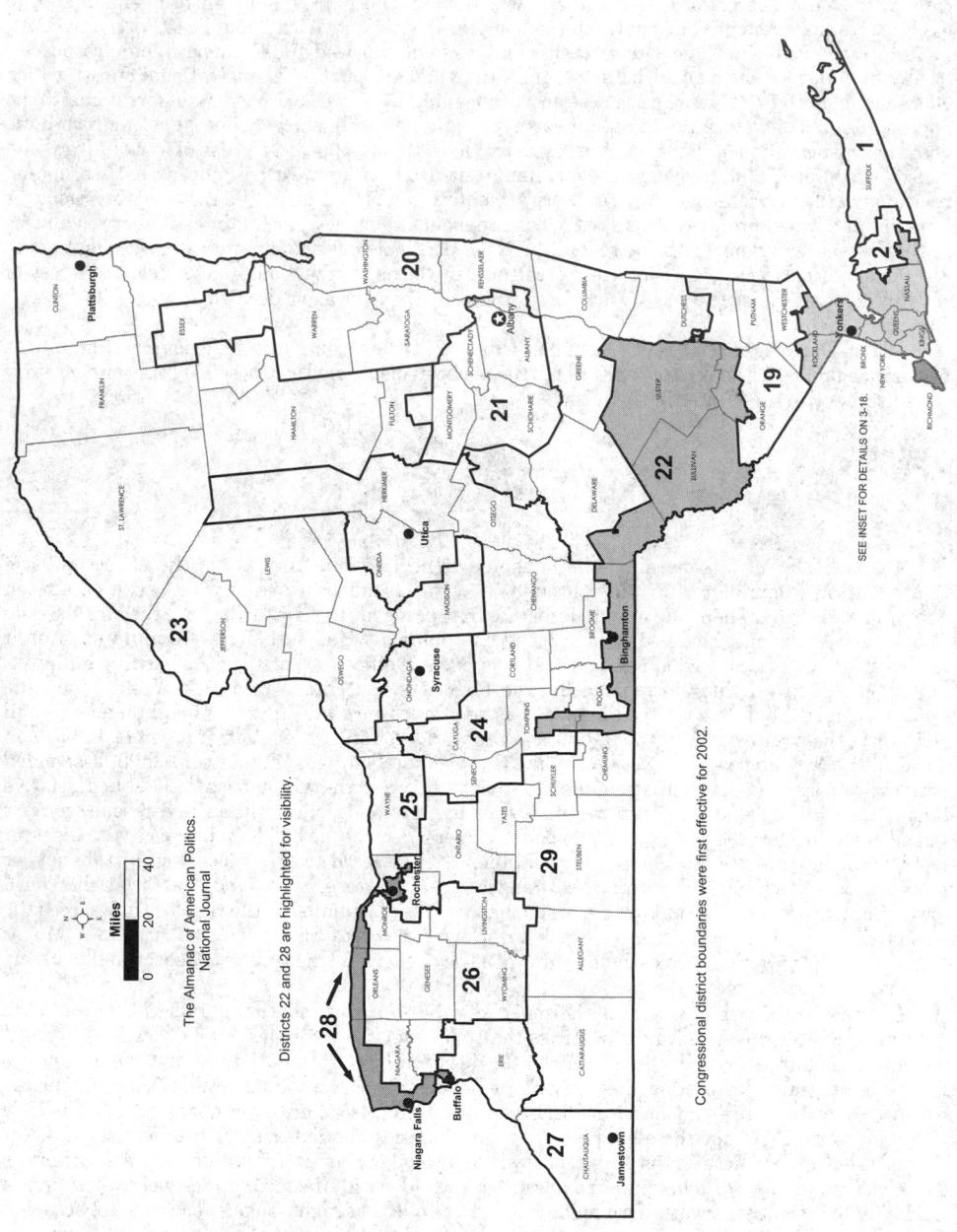

The Almanac of American Politics.
National Journal

Districts 22 and 28 are highlighted for visibility.

Congressional district boundaries were first effective for 2002.

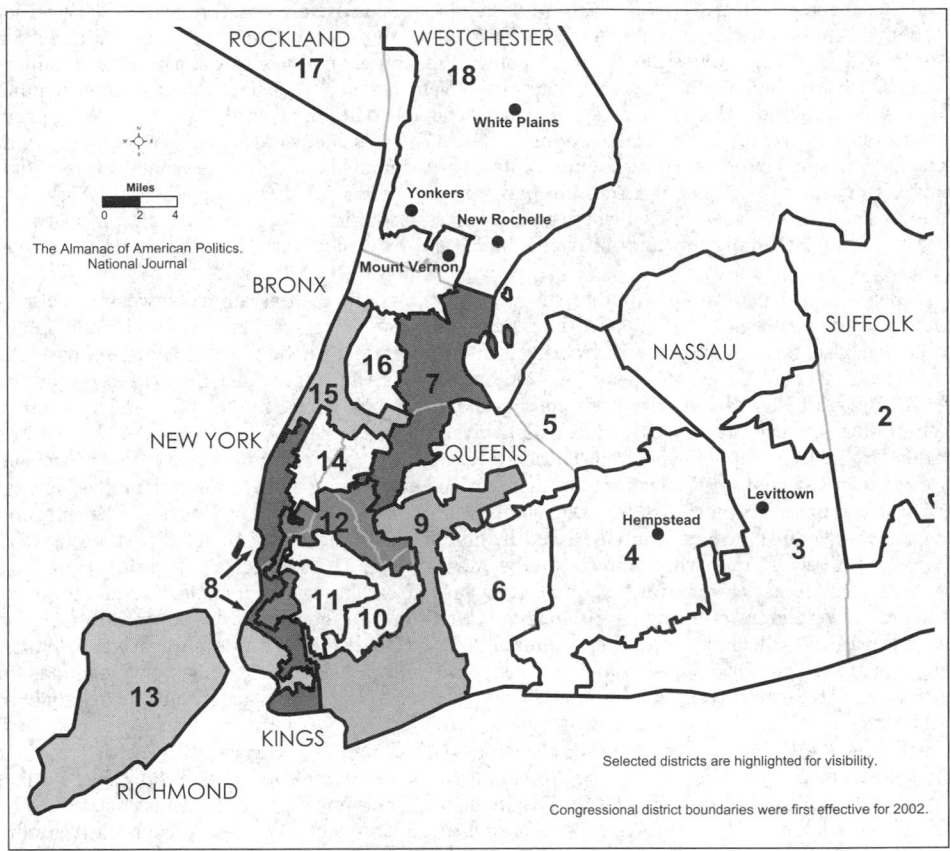

ROCKLAND
17

WESTCHESTER
18

White Plains

Miles
0   2   4

The Almanac of American Politics.
National Journal

Yonkers

New Rochelle

BRONX

Mount Vernon

16
15
7
14
QUEENS
5
12
9
8
11
10
6

NEW YORK

NASSAU

SUFFOLK

2

Levittown

Hempstead
4

3

13

KINGS

Selected districts are highlighted for visibility.

RICHMOND

Congressional district boundaries were first effective for 2002.

character of the place endures in daily life and in the workings of its great institutions, and helps explain its miraculous growth. Combine Amsterdam and America: Dutch character with British-born political freedoms and American military strength and you have the opportunity to build a city-state that can lead the world—and be the natural target of terrorists who hate that civilization.

New York was not always the nation's leader. In 1776 it was only the seventh most populous colony. Only in the 19th century did the descendants of Dutch patroons, Huguenot refugees, British West Indies traders and Yankee farmers become the nation's most successful merchants and capitalists, forging the first routes to the great American interior through the valleys of the Hudson and the Mohawk, and building grand brownstone mansions on broad midtown Manhattan avenues. That early diversity provides one clue to New York's success: if New York has been cynical, ready to cooperate with Loyalists and Revolutionaries, depending on who was ahead, it has also been tolerant, ready to accept anyone smart or rich enough to be counted a success. It has been propelled upward at each stage—forging ahead of London as a financial and manufacturing center by World War I, and staying ahead of surging Chicago—by incorporating every wave of immigrants and consistently rewarding intelligence and hard work, with no concern about preserving hierarchies.

New York's success has been a product not only of market economics, but of government—and politics. The English saw New York as a pivotal point in North America, a connecter of its northern and southern colonies and an avenue to the interior: that is why the Lord High Admiral, 30-year-old James, Duke of York, ordered the fleet to take Nieuw Amsterdam in 1664; the city and state are named for the man who was later King James II. The Iroquois, the most deeply-rooted and militarily strong Native Americans, were kept in place for 100 years by an alliance with British troops, then were driven out of most of Upstate New York after the Revolution. The Erie Canal, which connected western New York State with the Hudson River, was the project of Governor DeWitt Clinton's state government. And New York led the nation in political innovation: Martin Van Buren's Albany Regency was the first state political machine, an ally of New York City's Tammany Hall; Van Buren invented or institutionalized the Democratic party, the national convention and the inaugural parade. His adversaries, Thurlow Weed and William Seward, formed the Whig party and ultimately became Republicans; noting that Van Buren's Democrats were winning large margins from Irish Catholics and other immigrants, they too made bids for the newcomers' votes. Both parties served the function of mediating between the divergent interests of the New York City masses and Upstate New York's farmers and burghers, a conflict still evident in New York between city and country, immigrant and native, Catholic and Protestant, the Big Apple and the apple-knockers.

Both parties also worked to protect New Yorkers against the untrammeled workings of free economic and political markets. Old-line Democrats embarked on an unprecedented, labor-intensive building of infrastructure, of bridges and tunnels that made Greater New York possible, from the time of Mayor Abram Hewitt, elected in 1886 over the single-taxer Henry George and the young Theodore Roosevelt, up through the time of Governor Al Smith in the 1920s and his protégé Robert Moses, who built bridges, tunnels, highways, beaches and two World's Fairs up through the 1960s. Progressive Republicans, from Theodore Roosevelt through Elihu Root and Henry Stimson, worked to create civil service laws and bureaucratized purchasing and spending to protect taxpayers from corrupt party machines. The Democratic Tammany machine led by Charles F. Murphy and the talented young men he advanced, Al Smith and Robert Wagner, responded to the shocking 1911 Triangle Shirtwaist fire (when hundreds of women jumped 11 floors to their death because fire escapes were blocked) by passing labor and safety measures. The results included minimum wages, maximum work hours, working-conditions regulations, encouragement of unions and state-owned electric utilities—the prototype 20 years later of the New Deal and the first American welfare state. In years after, New York pioneered public housing and fair housing laws, industry-wide unions (in the garment trades), increased minimum wages, rent control and dairy price controls to help both New York City tenants and Upstate farmers.

Statewide elections were exceedingly close, with Democrats carrying the New York City Catholic vote and Republicans winning Protestants Upstate. Swing votes were cast by the 2 million Jewish immigrants and their children, who supported a generous welfare state but mistrusted the Tammany machine and valued civil rights. The politician who combined these appeals most cannily was Fiorello LaGuardia: a nominal Republican but almost a socialist, an Episcopalian who was half-Jewish as well as Italian, and who, as mayor of New York City from 1933 to 1945, built much of the public housing and many of the civic monuments that still stand. But both parties produced politicians whose positions appealed to these swing voters, politicians who became nationally prominent and often presidential candidates at a time when the national media was much more concentrated in Manhattan than today: Democrats Al Smith, Robert Wagner, Franklin D. Roosevelt and Averell Harriman; Republicans Thomas Dewey, Wendell Willkie, Dwight Eisenhower (a New Yorker as president of Columbia University when he was elected president in 1952) and Nelson Rockefeller.

The polity that these men built was productive, generous, tolerant and closely regulated. In an America where people were becoming used to working in big units—employed by big corporations, represented by big unions, regulated by big government—this kind of New York was a natural leader. The financial dominance of Wall Street and the big banks was protected by federal regulation. The high-tech thrust of America in the mid-20th century was directed by big companies headquartered in New York's suburbs or Upstate: General Electric and IBM, Eastman Kodak and Xerox. This New York took for granted the productivity of its thousands of entrepreneurs and the high skills of its largely immigrant-born, public and Catholic school-educated work force. It was blasé about its own miraculous infrastructure—the bridges and subways, electronic cables and electric wires connecting it better than any place else with every corner of the world.

But in the last quarter of the 20th century New York's public strengths became weaknesses. The state that was clearly the national leader of a big-unit America lost the leadership of a country where growth now occurs in small economic units, where flexibility and adaptability are more important than centralized planning. The institutions, practices and infrastructure which helped produce its successes became ossified and brittle and in decline. Welfare-state benefits became too expensive, measures meant to protect against corruption stifled innovation, and both failed to achieve their objectives—ghettos throbbed with the pains of disorganization, and payoffs and rackets remained part of the everyday cost of doing business in New York as in no other place in the country. The noble aim of creating a public sector which would guarantee cheap rents, top-notch public schools and colleges, and public hospitals, instead guaranteed that none of these will be readily available: Rent control kept housing scarce, school bureaucracies stifled good teaching, public hospitals rationed care down. The attempt to create a fail-safe government produced a government that was sure to fail. The government that intended to aid growth seemed to be cutting it off—not completely, but enough to explain why New York state, which grew 32% in population from 1940 to 1965, grew only 2% from 1965 to 1997, while California was growing 74% and Texas 87%, making both much larger now than New York.

People and businesses started voting with their feet, especially during the terms of Mayor John Lindsay, a liberal Republican who caved into municipal unions' demands and borrowed against next year's revenues to pay this year's bills. That brought the city to the brink of bankruptcy in 1975, two years after he left office. In the 1970s, the population of New York, city and state, dropped by 1 million—an unprecedented hemorrhage of talent and productivity. Retrenchment followed the mid-1970s bankruptcy crisis. Private financiers and the state government took control of city government, cut spending and negotiated cutbacks in jobs and salaries with public employees' unions. Wall Street boomed in the 1980s and Manhattan once again brimmed over with confidence. Some taxes were cut under Mayor (1978-90) Edward Koch and Governor (1983-95) Mario Cuomo, public employee unions were for a time reined in, rational management was installed. But institutional problems remained. New York's legislature remained unusually tightly controlled by the two chambers' leaders, the Democratic Assembly Speaker from New York City and the Republican state Senate President from Upstate or the suburbs, and these leaders engaged in classic political logrolling, lavishing taxpayers' dollars on each other's pet projects. Public employee unions reestablished their stranglehold. The mild recession of the early 1990s struck New York with great force: A private sector that had grown little if at all outside Wall Street could no longer finance the countercyclically growing demands of its oversized welfare state, while big companies Upstate—Xerox, Kodak, IBM—suffered serious reverses.

By the end of the 1990s New York seemed to have adapted and changed. Mayor Rudolph Giuliani, first elected in 1993, cut crime and welfare rolls in half and cut hard deals with the unions. Governor George Pataki, first elected in 1994, came into office and imposed huge tax and spending cuts in 1995. Wall Street and the financial services industry boomed in the late 1990s, to the point that the jobs lost in the 1990-94 recession were replaced. Then came September 11. Giuliani, under a cloud in his last months in office as his marriage collapsed publicly and he withdrew from the 2000 Senate race against Hillary Rodham Clinton, became a national hero. Pataki also performed well in the national spotlight. But New York faced an economic downturn and a turn in the course of government. Despite heroic efforts at recovery, Manhattan and New York lost 200,000 jobs in 2001 and 2002. Downtown real estate values tumbled, as financial services firms decentralized and sought office space elsewhere. Giuliani was term-limited, and all the leading contestants were well to his left. Media billionaire Michael Bloomberg, long a Democrat, became a Republican and spent $70 million of his own money on the campaign, and beat Public Advocate Mark Green 45.1%-44.5%. Pataki, running for reelection in 2002, made a $1.8 billion deal with the hospital workers' union and insured that he would be reelected without serious opposition. Bloomberg, faced with a fiscal crunch in 2002, increased property taxes 18% and raised other taxes as well. In his third term as governor, Pataki tried to hold down spending, but big tax increases, supported by Assembly Democrats and Senate Republicans, were passed over his veto. The lessons of the 1970s, 1980s and 1990s seemed to have been forgotten.

New York does continue to grow, but only sluggishly. New York City had more than 8 million people in the 2000 Census—8,008,000, more than the previous high, in 1950, of 7,984,000; that was up to 8,214,000 in the 2006 Census estimate. But this small change masked much greater movements: in those six years there was an immigrant inflow of 12% of the 2000 population and a domestic outflow of 8%—at least 1.5 million people moving in or out. Moving out were descendants of pre-1924 immigrants, the elderly to Florida, middle-income workers to the suburbs, young blue-collar workers all over. Moving in were immigrants, streaming into outer borough neighborhoods, creating new businesses, churches and neighborhood institutions—Caribbean blacks in Flatbush, Chinese in Flushing and Borough Park, Colombians and Mexicans in Corona, Pakistanis in Jackson Heights, Greeks in Astoria, Russians in Brighton Beach. In 2000 36% of City residents were born in other countries—almost as high as the 1910 peak of 41%. But they come to a different City. New York has long since lost most of its manufacturing jobs and many big corporate headquarters have moved elsewhere. The financial services industry thrives and pays enormous salaries and bonuses to those at the top and generates a lot of service sector jobs for those who tend to the needs of the very rich. But as historian Fred Siegel points out, the outer boroughs are increasingly dependent on public sector jobs, with one-third of jobs in Brooklyn and half in the Bronx directly dependent on the city or state governments. An especially heavy burden is New York's Medicaid program, designed by Nelson Rockefeller in 1966 to be far more generous than any other state's and requiring local governments to spend money as mandated by the state, with caps on increases only imposed in 2005. The good news is that this Medicaid spending provides a lot of jobs, including many for immigrants: hospitals are major employers in the outer boroughs. The bad news is that it tends to squeeze the life out of the private sector. New York spends some $44 billion a year on Medicaid, more than California, which is nearly twice as large. Spending has tripled since the 1980s, while the fraud investigation unit has been cut in half. New Yorkers are good at gaming the system, and a single dentist in Brooklyn ripped off Medicaid to the tune of $5 million in 2003. New York has more public sector hospitals per head than any other state and an oversupply of 20,000 beds. But Dennis Rivera, the head of the hospital workers' union, is the most politically important union leader in the state and has adamantly opposed cuts.

The suburbs have similar problems, exacerbated by much higher property taxes than in the City. The immigrant inflow is smaller here, 3% in 2000-06, but they also had a domestic outflow of 3%. Places like Levittown, buzzing with young families moving in from Brooklyn in the 1950s, are now aging and losing population; the high property taxes are in effect tuition to good suburban school districts, but become a heavy burden when the kids go off to college. Long Island is additionally burdened with some of the nation's highest utility rates. The suburbs are not attractive to new businesses—the burgeoning hedge fund sector has gone across the line to Greenwich, Connecticut—and population is growing more sluggishly than in the City.

Upstate New York has greater problems. Burdened with a state tax system constructed to support New York City's welfare state, it has been at a substantial disadvantage with nearby Northeastern states, not to mention the Sun Belt, in attracting jobs. Medicaid mandates have forced Upstate counties to raise property taxes as much as 70%. Large companies, formally paternalistic, have been shedding jobs. The big steel companies in Buffalo cut back in the 1980s. IBM cut back heavily in the 1990s in the Hudson Valley and farther Upstate. Kodak, hard hit by competition from digital cameras, employed 60,000 people in the Rochester area in 1981; it cut back 30,000 jobs between 2004 and 2007. Xerox jobs in the area fell from 16,000 to 8,000. The Carrier air conditioning plant in Syracuse was closed in 2004. General Electric, which employed 40,000 in Schenectady in the 1950s, cut the payroll there to 3,000 in 2006. Upstate's population actually declined from 2000 to 2006, something that has happened in only one state, North Dakota; 27 of 50 counties lost population and only one, Saratoga, gained more than 4%. Increasingly the population left behind is old; natural increase, the excess of births, has been only 1% in Upstate, and in many counties more people are dying than are being born. Governor Eliot Spitzer was criticized for comparing Upstate to Appalachia in his 2006 campaign. But the comparison was uncomfortably close to the mark.

In the first half of the twentieth century, New York politics was a battle between the Democratic city, with more than half the state's population then, and Republican Upstate. As previously noted, Jewish voters, concentrated in the city and moored to neither party, provided critical swing votes. In the post-World War II period, the suburbs grew and tended to produce small Republican majorities. Today the picture is different. In national politics, George W. Bush, even with his improved 2004 showing here, lost New York City 75%-24% and trailed very narrowly in the suburbs (47%-51%) and Upstate (48.5%-49.5%). Large numbers of Jewish and black voters have turned Westchester from a Republican to a Democratic county; Nassau County voters threw out a corrupt and high-spending Republican regime and the county leans Democratic. The Upstate counties containing Buffalo, Rochester, Syracuse, Albany and Binghamton produced Democratic margins to counterbalance Republican margins in smaller counties. New York voters turned to Republicans amid the economically straitened and crime-ridden early 1990s—Rudolph Giuliani in the City in 1993, George Pataki as governor, defeating Mario Cuomo for governor in 1994. But they left no political heirs unless you count Michael Bloomberg, a Democrat who changed his party registration so that he could run for mayor without the inconvenience of going through a left-wing gauntlet in a Democratic primary (he changed his party registation once again in 2007 to unaffiliated). Senator

Charles Schumer, who defeated Republican incumbent Alfonse D'Amato in a close-run race in 1998, was reelected in 2004 by a 71%-24% margin; he won 86% of the vote in the City, 66% in the suburbs and 63% Upstate. That was the pattern again in 2006. Eliot Spitzer, who narrowly defeated a Republican incumbent attorney general in 1998, used the office to bring charges of wrongdoing against corporate executives and Wall Street figures, and in the process restructured securities market regulation. Even before Pataki announced he would not seek a fourth term, it was apparent that Spitzer was the next governor, and he won 70%-29%. Senator Hillary Rodham Clinton, the 55%-43% winner in a vigorously contested Senate race in 2000, did not draw a serious opponent and was reelected 67%-31%, a margin only slightly smaller than Schumer's. Republicans have been reduced to only six of the state's 29 House seats, only one each in the suburbs (Peter King in Nassau County) and in the City (Vito Fossella in Staten Island); they lost three seats in 2006 and held three Upstate seats with only 51% or 52% of the vote. Democrats hold a better than 2–1 margin in the Assembly, and a special election caused by Spitzer's appointment of a Republican senator to state homeland security chief resulted in the Democrats capturing a Long Island state Senate seat and narrowing the seemingly perpetual Republican hold on the Senate (every year since 1939 except 1965) to 33-29. Albany in early 2007 was full of talk that two Republicans might switch parties, in which case Lieutenant Governor David Paterson would give control to the Democrats; in any case, it's entirely possible for Democrats to win two seats in 2008.

The future of one-party politics in New York depends on the performance of Governor Eliot Spitzer—and on whether the Republicans nominate a presidential candidate more in harmony with New York's tastes than George W. Bush. Spitzer has a strong hand to play in budgetary negotiations with Assembly Speaker Sheldon Silver and Senate President Joseph Bruno, thanks to a court ruling Pataki obtained that strengthened the governor's budget powers. But at the same time he must lighten the burden that big government puts on New York, especially Upstate, and placate the union leaders and other interests whose power is so deeply rooted in the present system. New York is now a pretty solidly Democratic state. But as the 1990s showed, if government becomes unbearably overlarge the voters may call the Republicans in.

The People		Race/Ethnic Origin			Military veterans: 1,361,164 (9.5%)	
Pop. 2006 (est):	19,306,183	11,760,981	62.0%	White	WWII: 25.4%	Korea: 15.5%
Pop. 2000:	18,976,457	2,812,623	14.8%	Black	Vietnam: 27.7%	Gulf War: 7.1%
Pop. 1990:	17,990,455	1,035,926	5.5%	Asian	**Most populous cities (2006):**	
Change 1990-2000:	Up 5.5%	52,499	0.3%	Native Am.	1. New York	8,214,426
% of U.S. total:	6.7%	5,230	0.0%	Hawaiian	2. Buffalo	276,059
Pop. rank:	3rd of 50	366,116	1.9%	Two+ races	3. Rochester	208,123
Area size:	54,556 sq. mi.	75,499	0.4%	Other	4. Yonkers	197,852
State Native:	65.3%	2,867,583	15.1%	Hisp. Origin	5. Syracuse	140,658
Non-citizen:	11.0%	**Ancestry**				
Language		Italian: 11.4%		Irish: 10.2%	Urban population: 87.5%	
English: 70.4%	Spanish: 13.3%	German: 8.9%		English: 4.8%	Rural population: 12.5%	
Other Eur.: 11.4%		Polish: 4.1%				

Education		Work Sector			Legislature	
H.S. Grad:	79.1%	Private: 76.8%		Govt: 17.0%	Senate	33 R 29 D
College Grad:	27.4%	Self: 6.0%		Family: 0.2%	Assembly	108 D 42 R
Industry		Unemployment: 7.1%			Legislative Term Limits: No	
Agri: 0.6%	Con: 5.2%	**Household Income**			**Registered Voters**	
Fin: 8.8%	Info: 4.1%	<15k: 17.9%		15-35k: 23.1%	D: 5,507,928 (47.2%)	
Mfg: 15.5%	Prof: 34.5%	35-50k: 14.8%		50-100k: 29.0%	R: 3,130,122 (26.8%)	
Public: 5.2%	Trade: 13.8%	100-150k: 9.1%		>150k: 6.2%	O: 3,031,523 (26.0%)	
Other: 12.3%		Median: $43,393				
Occupation		Poverty status: 14.6%				
Blue collar: 19.3%	White collar: 63.8%	**Home Value**				
Gray collar: 16.9%		<50k: 9.1%	50-100k: 25.3%	100-200k: 32.0% 200-300k: 18.5%		
		300-500k: 10.0%	>500k: 5.1%	Median: $147,600		

Presidential politics   In the first half of the 20th century, New York was the most pivotal—indeed, sometimes it seemed the dominant—state in presidential politics. It had the most electoral votes—45 from 1912-28, 47 from 1932-48, 45 from 1952-60—and of all the large states it was usually the most evenly divided between the two parties. But New York had just 33 electoral votes in 2000 and just 31 in 2004, and is, among the largest states, the most heavily Democratic. How has this come to pass? One reason is that Jewish voters, who did not identify strongly with either major party in the first half of the 20th century, became strong Democrats in the second. Increases in the percentages of black and Puerto Rican voters raised the Democratic percentage. White Catholic voters took conservative positions on cultural issues like crime and foreign policy in the 1970s and 1980s, which was one reason Senator James Buckley was elected on the Conservative party line in 1970, Ronald Reagan won New York's electoral votes narrowly in 1980 and 1984 and

2004 Presidential Vote		
Kerry (D-WF)	4,314,280	(58%)
Bush (R-C)	2,962,567	(40%)
Nader (I-PJ)	99,873	(1%)
Other	71,546	(1%)

2004 Democratic Presidential Primary		
Kerry (D)	437,754	(61%)
Edwards (D)	143,960	(20%)
Sharpton (D)	57,456	(8%)
Kucinich (D)	36,680	(5%)
Dean (D)	20,471	(3%)
Other	19,312	(3%)

2000 Presidential Vote		
Gore (D)	4,107,697	(60%)
Bush (R)	2,403,374	(35%)
Nader (Green)	244,030	(4%)
Other	66,898	(1%)

George H. W. Bush was beaten by only a 52%-48% margin in 1988. But these voters now, or their descendants, were more likely to take liberal stands on cultural issues salient in the 1990s, gun control and abortion. So Bill Clinton carried New York by 50%-34% in 1992 and 61%-31% in 1996 and Al Gore by 60%-35% in 2000.

In 2004 George W. Bush ran better, losing the state 58%-40%. His percentage jumped 6% in the city and suburbs, and 4% Upstate. It jumped even more among some specific groups—11% among Catholics (he carried them 51%-48% over the Catholic John Kerry), 6% among Latinos, about the same percentage among Jews. Bush's percentage rose 11% in Staten Island, which probably has more police officers and fire fighters per capita than anywhere else in America; 10% in Rockland County, which has large Orthodox Jewish communities which vote unanimously for favored candidates; 9% in Brooklyn, which also has large Orthodox communities and 8% in Nassau County. In parts of metro New York with more seculars and Protestants, the Bush percentage rose very little—3% in Manhattan and Westchester County. In metro New York City, Bush's percentage rose 6%—a percentage exceeded in only two states (Hawaii, 8%; Rhode Island, 7%) and equaled in four others (nearby New Jersey and Connecticut and Jacksonian Tennessee and Alabama). The metro New York-New Jersey-Connecticut numbers seem to reflect a rallying to the president prompted by his leadership on and after September 11, big enough to make New Jersey and Connecticut, but not New York, conceivably competitive in national elections.

For years New York had boss politics, and it never had a presidential primary until 1968. Turnout is low. Democratic turnout was 1.1 million in 2000, well below the peak of 1.5 million in 1988, when Mayor Ed Koch's shrill support of Al Gore won him few votes as Michael Dukakis beat Jesse Jackson; on March 7, 2000, Gore beat Bill Bradley by a 2–1 margin. As for the Republican primary, the rules for qualifying for the ballot are so convoluted that no one but party insiders can master them; there were no contests here in the 1980s and Steve Forbes qualified in 1996 only after spending $1 million. In 2000 Republican state Chairman William Powers maneuvered to keep John McCain off the ballot, to give an uncontested victory to Bush, Governor George Pataki's candidate. But McCain went to court and got on the ballot. Voting was limited to registered Republicans, and McCain did not have the appeal here he showed in New England; he carried affluent parts of Manhattan and the suburbs, but Bush won just about everywhere else. Voters voted for delegates, not presidential candidates; Bush delegates got 50% of the vote, McCain delegates 44%. In 2004 New York's Democrats voted on March 2, the last day on which the race for the nomination was securely contested; John Kerry prevailed in every congressional district. New York has moved its 2008 primary to February 5. But it is only one of more than a dozen states voting that day, including California and New Jersey, and Florida was scheduled to vote January 29. In New York the clear favorites in early polls were hometowners Hillary Clinton and Rudolph Giuliani, and if they lead in New Jersey as well, other candidates may decide not to spend the money to buy New York City television.

New York's minor parties no longer matter much. The Liberal Party and its predecessor, the American Labor Party, were founded to give Jewish garment workers a line on which to vote for Franklin D. Roosevelt and against local Tammany Hall candidates; the Liberal line was a help to Giuliani in the 1993 and 1997 mayoral elections. But in 2002 the Liberals endorsed Andrew Cuomo for governor, and he bowed out of the race a week before the Democratic primary. He got only 16,000 votes in November—far fewer than the 50,000 the Liberals needed to keep their position on the ballot. The Conservative Party was founded to withhold votes from liberal Republicans like Nelson Rockefeller and John Lindsay and encourage the Republican Party to nominate more conservative candidates. Lack of the Conservative line was a problem for Giuliani when he was running for senator, but the party did support the not-very-conservative Rick Lazio. It was quite comfortable with George Pataki, the first and so far only Conservative-backed governor, who got 177,000 votes on the Conservative line in 2002. The newest third party is the Working Families party, formed by the Communications Workers and United Auto Workers unions, which takes liberal views on economic issues and ignores cultural issues. It endorses Democratic candidates statewide but has had some distinctive local successes: its nominee was elected Albany County district attorney in 2004, and it determined the outcome of a couple of legislative races.

Congressional districting   When John Kennedy was elected president in 1960, New York elected 43 congressmen, California 30 and Texas 22. Now New York elects 29 congressmen, California 53 and Texas 32. Reapportionment is carnage time for New York: the state lost five districts in the 1980 Census, another three in 1990 and two more in 2000. In 2002, as in 1992, New York produced a convoluted redistricting plan. New York has more than 200 state legislators, but legislative decisions are made by three men; in 2002, they were Governor George Pataki, Republican state Senate President Joseph Bruno and Democratic Assembly Speaker Sheldon Silver. Party discipline is so strong that Bruno and Silver can always deliver majorities in their chambers, and Pataki had a veto. New York lost two seats in the 2000 Census, and before the Census numbers came in, it was assumed that the final plan would cut one Democratic district in the City and one Republican district Upstate. But the Census figures showed that, for the first time in more than 50 years, most of the state's growth had come in New York City; its population was up 9%, the suburbs up 6% and Upstate up only 1%. So congressmen hired well-wired lobbyists and negotiations began.

110th Congress Lineup	
23 D	6 R
109th Congress Lineup	
20 D	9 R

Negotiators usually don't reach agreement until they have to; in this case, the deadline was in June 2002, when candidates have to start circulating their petitions. In April 2002 a three-judge court appointed Frederick Lacey, a former federal judge, as a special master with orders to draft a plan that could be adopted if the legislature failed to act. To that court Pataki in May submitted a plan that targeted Democrats Maurice Hinchey and Carolyn Maloney: an obvious negotiating ploy, since Silver would never accept it. Senate Republicans prepared a plan putting two pairs of Democrats in the same districts; Assembly Democrats prepared a plan putting two pairs of Republicans in the same districts: more negotiating ploys. On May 13 Lacey presented a plan placing two pairs of Upstate members—Republican Sherwood Boehlert and Democrat Maurice Hinchey, Republican Jack Quinn and Democrat John LaFalce—in the same districts. On May 23, the court adopted the plan, but gave the legislature more time to act and said it would gladly accept its plan if it did so.

The pressure was on. Silver wanted to protect Hinchey and other Democrats discommoded by the plan. Bruno got a call from Dick Cheney urging him to deal, since the Lacey plan seemed to put some Republican seats at risk. The three decision-makers decided to target Rochester Democrat Louise Slaughter and Republican Benjamin Gilman, though Slaughter said she would run in the primary against LaFalce and Gilman threatened to switch parties and run against Republican Sue Kelly. The last hitch was on Long Island. State Senate Republicans there didn't like the incumbent-protection plan agreed on by the Island's two Democratic and two Republican incumbents; they wanted a better shot at Democrat Carolyn McCarthy's district. But they were brought in line. The new plan was passed and signed June 5. Slaughter went into court and asked it to adopt the Lacey plan. On June 25 the court accepted the legislature's plan and the Justice Department gave it clearance under the Voting Rights Act. On June 26 LaFalce announced that he would not run against Slaughter, who is now chairman of the House Rules Committee. On July 2, Gilman, who was 79 and was serving his 30th year in the House, announced that he would retire. All the incumbents running were easily reelected, except for 1st District Republican Felix Grucci, who lost for reasons having nothing to do with redistricting.

In 2005, Democrats began talking about redrawing the congressional map before the next census. The party seemed likely to win the governorship in 2006 and some were hopeful it could pick up the two seats needed to control the state Senate. In that case, a new map would be drawn. But in January 2007 incoming Governor Eliot Spitzer called for the creating of an independent redistricting commission and said he would veto any partisan redistricting plan. But the lead sponsor of such legislation, Republican state Senator Nicholas Spano, lost to a Democrat in November 2006. And Bruno and Silver seemed less than enthusiastic about the proposal. Each seemed concerned more about maintaining control of his own chamber than about congressional redistricting. New York is expected to lose two seats again after the 2010 Census.

Governor

Eliot Spitzer (D)

Elected 2006, term expires Jan. 2011, 1st term; b. June 10, 1959, Bronx; home, Albany; Princeton, B.A. 1981, Harvard, J.D. 1984; Jewish; married (Silda Wall).

Elected Office: NY Atty. Gen., 1998-2006.

Professional Career: Clerk, U.S. Dist. Ct. Judge Robert Sweet, 1984-85; Practicing atty., 1985-86, 1992-98; Manhattan Asst. Dist. Atty., 1986-92.

Office: State Capitol, Albany, 12224, 518-474-8390; Fax: 518-474-1513; Web site: www.ny.gov/governor.

Election Results

2006 general	Eliot Spitzer (D-Ind-WF)	3,086,709	(70%)
	John Faso (R-C)	1,274,335	(29%)
	Other	76,176	(2%)
2006 primary	Eliot Spitzer (D)	624,684	(82%)
	Tom Suozzi (D)	138,263	(18%)
2002 general	George Pataki (R-C)	2,262,255	(49%)
	Carl McCall (D-WF)	1,534,064	(34%)
	Thomas Golisano (Ind)	654,016	(14%)
	Other	128,743	(3%)

Eliot Spitzer was elected, virtually without competition, governor of New York in 2006. Spitzer grew up in the comfortable Riverdale neighborhood in the Bronx. His father Bernard Spitzer, whose parents immigrated from Austria in the 1920s, started off with nothing and made a fortune developing apartment buildings; he met his wife at a Catskill resort: a New York story. Eliot Spitzer went to the Horace Mann School in the Bronx, where he played tennis and faced rival Trinity's best player, John McEnroe. He graduated from Princeton, where he was elected president of the student body as a sophomore, and from Harvard Law School, where he worked for Professor Alan Dershowitz on the defense of Claus von Bulow. After law school he clerked for the liberal federal judge Robert Sweet. From 1986 to 1992 he worked in the office of Manhattan District Attorney Robert Morgenthau and became head of the labor-racketeering bureau. There he helped to force the Gambino mob out of the trucking business in the garment district; as in his later work, there was no prison time but a $12 million fine. From 1992 to 1994 he worked at the high-powered Skadden, Arps law firm. In 1994 he ran for attorney general of New York. The appointed incumbent, Oliver Koppell, was seeking a full term and Spitzer was one of three challengers; he finished fourth. He financed his campaign by a $4.3 million bank loan and spent most of it on television advertising; Koppell brought a lawsuit, which came to nothing, but Spitzer later conceded that after the election his father lent him money to repay the loan.

This was not an auspicious beginning for a political career and few imagined then that 12 years later Spitzer would stand like a colossus over New York state politics. But he had at least one lucky break. Even in New York, 1994 was a Republican year, and George Pataki defeated Mario Cuomo 49%-45%, and the Republican nominee for attorney general, former U.S. Attorney Dennis Vacco, beat the winner of the Democratic primary, former state Senator Karen Burstein, by 49%-47%. It would have been awkward to take on an incumbent Democrat in the 1998 primary, but winning the nomination to face Vacco was easier. This time Spitzer did enough campaigning across the state to wear out a pair of dress shoes and bought plenty of ads on TV as well. While Pataki was cruising to reelection by a 54%-33% margin, Vacco trailed behind. Spitzer won by a 25,000-vote margin out of 4.3 million votes cast, 48.2%-47.6%. He carried New York City 73%-24%, ran not far behind in the suburbs 45%-52% and was walloped Upstate by Upstater Vacco 34%-61%. It was the only close election of his career, at least so far.

Spitzer had criticized Vacco for making political patronage hires. Once in office he hired highly able lawyers without political ties, the practice in the Morgenthau office. He started off by aggressively bringing cases against coal-burning Midwestern and Southern power plants and predatory lenders. He sued gun makers unsuccessfully for selling unsafe weapons. He called for stronger laws to prosecute Medicaid fraud, a major industry in New York, which has by far the nation's most expensive Medicaid program. He made creative use of the Martin Act, an obscure state law, which gave him authority to subpoena documents, compel testimony and conduct public investigations into vaguely defined fraud. His investigators used those powers to subpoena emails from Merrill Lynch and other brokerage firms and hit pay dirt when they found among many other things an email from ace technology analyst Henry Blodget describing a firm called 24/7 Media as "a pos" (a piece of excrement) even as the firm's brokers were urging clients to buy the stock. There was a near-stumble when this was made public in April 2002; it could have triggered a federal law which would have shut down much of the nation's largest brokerage firm and caused chaos in the markets, and Spitzer asked the court to suspend an order which would have done that. But he got Merrill Lynch, under threat of prosecution, to agree to change its practices and pay a $100 million fine. That caught the attention of Wall Street—and New York voters. Other firms scurried to change their practices and to avoid recommending stocks that would subject them to similar action. A global settlement modeled on Spitzer's settlement with Merrill Lynch was reached, involving the SEC, the NASD and the New York Stock Exchange, in December 2002: Spitzer had effectively made significant changes in the securities industry. To critics who said that he was usurping the powers of the SEC, he replied, "Critics of state action overlook the absence of federal action that made the Merrill Lynch investigation and reforms necessary." Interestingly, Spitzer was not one of the state attorneys general who challenged the consent decree in the federal government's antitrust case against Microsoft, a cause he could have joined if his only concern was publicity.

As this was going on, Spitzer was reelected by a 66%-30% margin while Pataki was winning reelection with just 49% of the vote. Pataki had cut a generous deal for the 1199 Hospital Workers union, headed by the influential Dennis Rivera, who gave him tacit support; but he seemed unlikely to be able to do that again in 2006, and Spitzer began to look like the next governor. As attorney general, he continued to bring high-profile cases. He charged mutual fund executives with engaging in illegal market timing or late trading in shares and got 11 guilty pleas and $4 billion in settlements. He accused the giant insurer Marsh & McLennan of bid-rigging and announced that he would not negotiate with its CEO Jeffrey Greenberg; this left the firm with the choice of ousting him or being faced with a criminal indictment, and Greenberg stepped down. The new CEO was Michael Cherkasky, who had been Spitzer's boss in the Morgenthau office and had contributed to his campaigns. Spitzer negotiated a settlement that required significant changes in business practices and an $850 million fine. Spitzer brought a case against the pharmaceutical firm GlaxoSmithKline for not disclosing information from clinical trials. As journalist Joe Conason wrote, "He is less concerned with notching convictions than with changing corporate behavior. His success has relied at least as much on public shaming of executives, and the consequences of falling stock prices, as on sending malefactors to prison." He accused giant insurer AIG of manipulating financial statements to bolster its stock price; longtime CEO Maurice Greenberg, accused of fraud, was forced out by the board. For his handling of this case former Goldman Sachs Chairman John Whitehead publicly criticized Spitzer; as Whitehead recounted in a *Wall Street Journal* opinion article, Spitzer called him and said, "It's now a war between us and you've fired the first shot. I will be coming after you. You will pay the price." Spitzer did not deny the words and conceded, "It was a call that could have been handled more judiciously." He obtained a $5 million settlement with the Warner Music Group for payments to radio programmers for playing their music. He sued New York Stock Exchange compensation committee chairman Kenneth Langone and former NYSE CEO Richard Grasso for approving Grasso's $190 million pay package. Grasso, who had resigned and who presumably could afford the cost of litigation, fought the charges and in May 2007 four of the counts, the major portion of the case, were dismissed by an appeals court. But by then Spitzer was governor.

In July 2005 Pataki announced he would not seek a fourth term as governor. Spitzer's candidacy was a foregone conclusion. He compared himself to Theodore Roosevelt, who as a young assemblyman and governor took on New York's machine politicians, and with Alexander Hamilton. To those who said he was too brash, he replied, "You don't change the world by whispering." The day after Pataki's announcement, Spitzer said would tackle "massive fraud" in Medicaid, lack of strategic investments in higher education and a state debt load "rampantly out of control." He seemed unafraid to antagonize established politicians and to take liberal positions on cultural issues. He declared forthrightly that he would preserve the choice of late-term abortion options and that he favored same-sex marriage (a stand not taken by the state's two Democratic senators). He called for a nonpolitical redistricting process, something that would strike at the root of the power of Democratic Assembly Speaker Sheldon Silver and Republican Senate President Joseph Bruno, who cemented their tight control of their chambers by mutually agreeing to each other's redistricting plans. In January 2006 he chose state Senator David Paterson from Harlem as his lieutenant governor candidate over Leecia Eve from Buffalo, backed by Congressman Charles Rangel and longtime Harlem power broker Percy Sutton. Rangel's response: "When Eliot Spitzer, the world's smartest man, is telling me that he has picked his candidate and knows that his candidate can win, who am I to question the world's smartest man?" He helped to defeat a constitutional amendment which would have restored to legislators budgetary powers that they had lost in a lawsuit initiated by Pataki, even though Assembly Speaker Sheldon Silver, who had long backed Spitzer for governor, supported the amendment. He pointedly refrained from asking for the endorsement of the 1199 health care union and Dennis Rivera. Yet he had no trouble raising $19 million by January 2006.

New York went through the motions of holding elections in 2006, but the results were predictable: Democrats would hold the Assembly, Republicans would hold the Senate, Senator Hillary Clinton would be reelected and Eliot Spitzer would be elected governor. Some opposition did appear. Former Massachusetts Governor William Weld set out to be a candidate, with the support of Pataki. But there was criticism of his work as head of a for-profit Kentucky college, and he dropped out of the race in June 2006. Nassau County Executive Thomas Suozzi, with a record of cutting spending and opposing a corrupt Republican machine, made a game try at running in the primary. But Spitzer won 82%-18%. Former Assemblyman John Faso became the Republican nominee, but he was little known and attracted little financing.

The general election was anticlimactic. Spitzer won 70%-29%, running 3% ahead of Hillary Clinton. He carried New York City 84%-14%, the suburbs 65%-34%, Upstate 63%-35%. The one embarrassment was that Comptroller Alan Hevesi was reelected after it was revealed that he had used state employees to drive his wife around; this was considered a criminal violation, and he resigned in December 2006. Also in December Joseph Bruno revealed that the FBI was investigating his business interests, but he stayed in his powerful position; for many years now negotiations on the budget and other major issues have been conducted by three men, the governor, the Senate president and the Assembly speaker, the latter with the power to compel their chambers to do their bidding. Spitzer seemed to challenge this and other Albany arrangements. "On day one," he proclaimed, "everything changes." He was going to be, as he told the Assembly minority leader, "a [expletive] steamroller." In January 2007 he presented a $120.6 billion budget and got the legislative leaders to agree to drop a $200 million catchall for "member items" and to list each of them individually. He approached health care with an advantage: Pataki had gotten the legislature to agree to a commission that could close hospitals unless the legislature overrode it; its list appeared in November 2006. Spitzer called for a 1.7% increase in Medicaid spending, which had been going up 8% a year, and whose mandated spending was causing Upstate counties to raise property taxes by as much as 70%. He called at the same time for extending health insurance to all children and enrolling all eligible adults in Medicaid. He made proposals to cut subsidies to hospitals and nursing homes, slashed Medicaid reimbursement rates and called for stepped up efforts to prevent Medicaid fraud. He unveiled a new education formula, with $3.2 billion more for New York City, and a new municipal aid formula, with $350 million less for New York City and more for impoverished Upstate cities. He called for a $1,000-per-child tuition tax deduction. He proposed $1.5 billion in property tax reductions. He called for a commission, similar to Pataki's health care commission, to close prisons—a major source of jobs in many Upstate areas. He called for $2 billion in bonds to support medical research over 10 years, with at least half to go to stem-cell research. He called for building a second bridge in Buffalo and overhauling the Tappan Zee Bridge across the Hudson.

On some things the legislative leaders pushed back. They had promised to elect a new comptroller from a list of financial experts submitted by former comptrollers. But in February 2007 the leaders broke this promise and in joint session elected Nassau County Assemblyman Thomas DiNapoli. "We have just witnessed an insider's game of self-dealing that unfortunately confirms every New Yorker's worst fears and image of all that goes on in the legislature of this state," Spitzer responded, and went on to criticize individual members while speaking in their districts. By April he had retreated somewhat on school and hospital spending, dropped a proposal to apply the bottle-deposit law to water and juice containers and dropped his promise to bring negotiations with legislative leaders out in the open. When Spitzer called for a limit on campaign contributions, Bruno pushed for the Senate to pass a bill imposing term limits on the governor and other statewide elected officials, but not on sitting officials so Spitzer is not affected. The leaders resisted his proposal for redistricting. But he succeeded in getting the legislature to overhaul workers' compensation, to pass a law keeping some sexual predators locked up after their sentences expired and to promote ethics in government.

Spitzer seems determined to change the operation of state politics. He appointed a Republican state senator as the state homeland security chief, triggering a February 2007 special election which the Democrat won. That reduced the Republican margin in the Senate to 33-29 and threatened to upset the balance of power that has prevailed in Albany for what seems like generations: the Republicans have held the Senate every year since 1939 except 1965, the Democrats have held the Assembly since 1975. There was talk in Albany that two Republican senators might switch parties and give control to the Democrats (Lieutenant Governor David Paterson would cast the deciding vote), and political observers believed that in increasingly Democratic New York it was possible that voters would oust enough Republicans to give Democrats control in 2008 or 2010. This would shake up New York's carefully calibrated political system, in which powerful interests cultivate the Democratic speaker and Republican state Senate president with the assurance that they could deliver their chambers.

Once upon a time, every New York governor was considered a potential candidate for president. Many were nominated—Horatio Seymour, Samuel Tilden, Grover Cleveland, Theodore Roosevelt, Charles Evans Hughes, Al Smith, Franklin Roosevelt, Thomas Dewey. This was from 1820 until 1963 the largest state and it was until the 1960 election a swing state in every close election since the Civil War. It has been less the case since the 1970s, when New York has become a safe Democratic state in any close election. Hugh Carey, who enabled New York City to recover from threatened bankruptcy, only briefly considered a national candidacy. Mario Cuomo seriously considered one, but didn't make a move to run in 1988, when another ethnic Northeasterner won the nomination, and decided not to in December 1991 as his plane waited on the runway in Albany to fly him to New Hampshire. George Pataki toured Iowa and New Hampshire in 2005 and 2006 but found little support and quietly abandoned any plans to run in early 2007. Spitzer's rise to national prominence and his electoral success raise the question of whether he will some day run. In early 2007 any such day seemed far off. He faced major challenges as governor and at least two New Yorkers, Hillary Clinton and Rudolph Giuliani (and possibly even Michael Bloomberg), were running in 2008. If either of them wins and serves two terms, it seems unlikely that the nation would be ready for another New Yorker. And presumably there would be no opening until 2016 if any Democrat wins in 2008 and runs for reelection in 2012. A Spitzer candidacy may depend, as his second and successful run for attorney general did, on a Republican winning. Certainly Spitzer seems to have ambition and energy, but it's not clear whether he is motivated to run for president. When asked whether he would, his wife Silda Wall Spitzer said, "That would not be my choice, that he run."

Senior Senator

Charles Schumer (D)

Elected 1998, seat up 2010, 2d term; b. Nov. 23, 1950, Brooklyn; home, Brooklyn; Harvard U., B.A. 1971, J.D. 1974; Jewish; married (Iris Weinshall).

Elected Office: NY Assembly, 1974-80; U.S. House of Reps., 1980-1998.

DC Office: 313 HSOB, 20510, 202-224-6542; Fax: 202-228-3027; Web site: schumer.senate.gov.

State Offices: Albany, 518-431-4070; Binghamton, 607-772-6792; Buffalo, 716-846-4111; Manhattan, 212-486-4430; Melville, 631-753-0978; Peekskill, 914-734-1532; Rochester, 585-263-5866; Syracuse, 315-423-5471.

Committees: *DSCC Chairman. Banking, Housing & Urban Affairs* (4th of 11 D): Housing, Transportation & Community Development (Chmn.); Securities, Insurance & Investment; Financial Institutions. *Finance* (8th of 11 D): Social Security, Pensions & Family Policy; Taxation & IRS Oversight & Long-Term Growth; International Trade & Global Competitiveness. *Joint Economic Committee* (Chmn. of 10 D). *Judiciary* (7th of 10 D): Administrative Oversight & the Courts (Chmn.); Immigration, Refugees & Border Security; Antitrust, Competition Policy & Consumer Rights; Terrorism, Technology & Homeland Security; Crime & Drugs. *Rules & Administration* (5th of 10 D).

Group Ratings

	ADA	ACLU	AFS	LCV	ITIC	NTU	COC	ACU	CFG	FRC
2006	100	83	100	71	75	15	64	4	3	0
2005	100	—	88	100	—	13	39	8	2	—

National Journal Ratings

	2005 LIB	—	2005 CONS		2006 LIB	—	2006 CONS
Economic	85%	—	14%		71%	—	28%
Social	77%	—	18%		80%	—	14%
Foreign	66%	—	29%		67%	—	29%

Key Votes of the 109th Congress

1. Bar ANWR Drilling	Y	5. Confirm Samuel Alito	N	9. Limit Interstate Abortion	N
2. FY06 Spending Curb	N	6. Path to Citizenship	Y	10. CAFTA	N
3. Estate Tax Repeal	*	7. Bar Same Sex Marriage	N	11. Urge Iraq Withdrawal	Y
4. Raise Minimum Wage	Y	8. Stem Cell Research $	Y	12. Provide Detainee Rights	Y

Election Results

2004 general	Charles Schumer (D-Ind-WF)	4,769,824	(71%)	($15,467,530)
	Howard Mills (R)	1,625,069	(24%)	($628,578)
	Other	307,982	(5%)	
2004 primary	Charles Schumer (D)	unopposed		
1998 general	Charles Schumer (D-Ind-L)	2,551,065	(55%)	($16,671,877)
	Al D'Amato (R-C-RTL)	2,058,988	(44%)	($24,195,287)
	Other	60,752	(1%)	

Prior Winning Percentages: 1996 House (75%); 1994 House (73%); 1992 House (89%); 1990 House (80%); 1988 House (78%); 1986 House (93%); 1984 House (72%); 1982 House (79%); 1980 House (77%)

Charles Schumer is New York's senior senator, first elected to the House in 1980 and to the Senate in 1998. Schumer grew up in Flatbush, Brooklyn, and graduated first in his class at James Madison High School, alma mater also of Justice Ruth Bader Ginsburg and Minnesota Senator Norm Coleman. He graduated from Harvard College and Law School and, with the latter diploma fresh in his hand in June 1974, immediately began running for an open Assembly seat. He won, at 23. In 1980 he was elected to the House from an open Brooklyn seat, just before he turned 30. Through energy, imagination, hard work, good humor and a certain amount of chutzpah, he became a skilled legislator, and one noted—and sometimes resented—for his knack for getting publicity: Bob Dole was one of the first to say that the most dangerous place in Washington was in between Schumer and a television camera.

From the unlikely venue of the Banking Committee, a panel that most talented members lobby to get off of, Schumer spotted the perverse incentives set up by the combination of deposit insurance and letting S&Ls make risky investments. On Judiciary and, eventually, as chairman of its Crime Subcommittee, he ranged far afield, contributing key provisions to immigration acts in 1986 and 1990, leading attacks on farm subsidies, and a nearly successful assault on sugar programs. Schumer sponsored the 1994 crime bill and got the House to pass the Brady bill, with its waiting period for handgun purchases, over strong opposition from the National Rifle Association.

The idea of running for statewide office was surely never far from his mind. In 1997 he pondered running for governor, but by April Governor George Pataki's strong job rating, and especially his overwhelming strength Upstate, convinced Schumer to use his $5 million treasury to run for Alfonse D'Amato's Senate seat instead. It was by no means obvious that Schumer would win. D'Amato was known for his assiduous constituent service and for his ability to win the tabloid wars that dominate campaigning in metropolitan New York. D'Amato was chairman of the Banking Committee and excelled at raising money. Schumer started off largely unknown outside his district and faced serious primary opposition from 1984 vice presidential nominee Geraldine Ferraro and Mark Green, New York City Public Advocate and D'Amato's opponent in 1986. By summer, Schumer was leading in polls and was much better financed, and in September he won the primary with 51% of the vote.

Schumer immediately launched an attack on D'Amato, saying he had told "too many lies for too long"; it echoed D'Amato's attacks on earlier opponents as "too liberal for too long." Schumer claimed he was tougher on crime; he emphasized his support of abortion rights and gun control. D'Amato concentrated heavily on Schumer's missed votes while running for Senate, but the implication that Schumer was lazy was implausible. Still, by mid-October, Schumer's poll leads were mostly less than the statistical margin of error. But in a closed meeting before a Jewish group D'Amato called Schumer a "putzhead"; when that became public, he denied it, then backtracked unconvincingly after his own supporter, former Democratic Mayor Edward Koch, confirmed it. D'Amato lost confidence and momentum, and by early November was sagging in polls. Schumer, who announced in October that he would vote against impeachment though he believed Bill Clinton lied under oath, was the beneficiary of two visits from Clinton and no less than four from Hillary Rodham Clinton (the rousing receptions she got may have encouraged her to run for the Senate in New York two years later). Though outspent, Schumer won 55%-44%.

In the Senate, Schumer has had a solidly liberal voting record. He holds regular Sunday press conferences, to get in the Monday papers. He has made a practice of visiting all 62 counties each year, and regularly spends Mondays on Upstate swings that get him on Buffalo, Rochester, Syracuse and Albany television. He is one of three Americans in history who have cast two votes on the impeachment of the same president (the other two are Mike Crapo of Idaho and Jim Bunning of Kentucky, also congressmen elected to the Senate in 1998); Schumer voted against impeaching Clinton in the House in December 1998 and against conviction in the Senate in February 1999.

An ally of the securities industry on both the House and Senate Banking Committees, he played a key role in the scuttling of the bankruptcy bill in 2002. He persuaded the Senate to pass an amendment that made fines and penalties for blocking access to or attacking abortion clinics not dischargeable in bankruptcy in May 2002; some abortion opponents had taken to declaring bankruptcy to avoid paying fines. But abortion opponents in the House refused to vote for the bill as long as it had Schumer's amendment. Leaders in both houses got Schumer and Henry Hyde, with whom he had long worked on the House Judiciary Committee, to negotiate a compromise amendment. But that too was unacceptable to the abortion opponents, and when the House leadership introduced a rule to consider the bill in November 2002 it was defeated 243-172 and the bankruptcy bill died. Schumer tried again in March 2005, but this time the abortion amendment was voted down, 53-46, in the Senate, and the bill was quickly passed, sent to the House and enacted. He has opposed bills to strengthen regulation of the government sponsored enterprises Fannie Mae and Freddie Mac, cited the increasing rate of homeownership under the current arrangements and the possibility of increased interest rates; in April 2005 he urged "a great deal of caution and maybe some humility" in making any changes. He has proposed establishing an Office of Identity Theft in the FTC, to set minimum security standards. Despite his opposition to many Bush administration policies, he strongly supported some Bush nominees—Christopher Cox for the SEC in July 2005, Kevin Warsh for the Federal Reserve Board of Governors in April 2006, Goldman Sachs CEO Hank Paulson as Treasury Secretary in June 2006. He blocked approval of Special Trade Representative nominee Susan Schwab for her position on China; he lifted the hold in June 2006, saying, "She has convinced me that she will be a very strong voice on opening markets."

In January 2004 he and paleoconservative commentator Paul Craig Roberts wrote an article arguing the "new developments," chiefly global competition, "call into question some of the key assumptions supporting the doctrine of free trade." In February 2005 he and Lindsey Graham sponsored a bill to impose a 27.5% tariff on all Chinese goods until the Chinese government revalues its currency, then tied to the dollar. They agreed to delay a vote in June 2005. In July the Chinese devalued their currency by 2% and suggested that it would periodically be adjusted; Schumer and Graham were not satisfied. They allowed a delay on the vote in September 2006, but in December said they would press the issue in the new Congress.

Schumer serves on Judiciary, where he has argued that senators should reject Bush appointees on "purely ideological grounds." Starting with the nomination of Miguel Estrada, he has led the opposition to at least 10 Bush judicial nominees whom he and liberal lobbying groups have said were out of the mainstream, and together with other Democrats has been using the filibuster to prevent the confirmation of federal judges with majority support. He took strong exception to Senate Republicans who have advocated changing the rules to allow nominations to be considered by majority vote. In 2005, he tried to pin John Roberts down in committee hearings and was one of 22 senators who voted against him and noted later, "Roberts was quite stealthy, but he was so brilliant he could pull it off." He met with nominee Harriet Miers in October 2005 and revealed that she declined to answer questions about the landmark cases *Griswold v. Connecticut* and *Meyer v. Nebraska*; later he predicted that her nomination would fail. When George W. Bush nominated Samuel Alito at the end of October 2005, he said he was "sad that the President felt he had to pick a nominee likely to divide America" and wondered "whether [Alito] would use that seat to reverse much of what Rosa Parks and so many others fought so hard and for so long to put in place." Schumer and Charles Grassley have co-sponsored bills to allow the chief justice and chief judges of the courts of appeals to televise hearings.

On September 11 Schumer was in Washington; his daughter was in school a few blocks from the World Trade Center. Amid the terrible news, Schumer and others in the New York delegation conferred and agreed to seek $20 billion in aid for New York. In the Oval Office on September 13 Schumer and Clinton met with George W. Bush. Bush asked how much New York needed. Schumer paused and said $20 billion. Bush's reaction: "You got it." The usually voluble Schumer's reaction? "My mouth dropped open." Of course there was more to it than that. The New Yorkers understood that some of the money would not be forthcoming immediately, since no one had decided how to reconstruct the World Trade Center site and its transportation facilities. Schumer worked to prevent OMB and House Republicans from putting off as much of the spending as they wanted and dealt with the backlash against Pataki's calling for $54 billion. The Bush administration turned to Schumer to get support for what became the USA Patriot Act, and Schumer and Clinton backed the proposal to let the FBI share information on terrorism with state and local police.

Channeling the flow of money into New York state and city has been part of Schumer's job. In 2004 he sought $7.1 billion in transit money over six years in the transportation bill. In 2005 he called for an additional $61 million for housing in New York City when inflation had increased costs. He secured grants for all manner of projects, ranging from an ambulance for the volunteer fire department in Hermon in St. Lawrence County to funding for tritium cleanup at the Brookhaven National Laboratory. Schumer did not have close ties to Governor George Pataki; for much of 2004 he was rumored to be interested in running for governor himself. He got along much better with nominally Republican Mayor Michael Bloomberg. Schumer's wife Iris Weinshall was Bloomberg's transportation commissioner and in late October 2004 Bloomberg endorsed Schumer for reelection.

When Hillary Rodham Clinton was elected in November 2000, many thought there would be friction between the aggressive Schumer and the more famous Clinton. There mostly hasn't been, not in public anyway. Clinton was probably irritated after Schumer criticized Bill Clinton's January 2001 pardon of Marc Rich. And they must have had some disagreements as they struggled to help New York after September 11: the more earthy Schumer seemed to get along better with Bush, the more disciplined Clinton seemed to get along better with some Republican senators. Relations between two senators of the same party from the same state are very often fractious, especially when both are seeking plenty of home state publicity; Schumer may be the senior senator, but Clinton is the better-known and the one regarded by many as her party's likeliest presidential nominee in 2008. And there is some lifestyle difference. While Clinton holds fundraisers in her $2.8 million house in Washington, Schumer shares a Capitol Hill townhouse with Senator Dick Durbin and Congressmen Bill Delahunt and George Miller.

Schumer has been a prodigious fundraiser since his early days in the House. Over the 2004 cycle Schumer raised $11.9 million. Speculation abounded that he was interested in running for governor in 2006; in the meantime his Senate race proved easy. Constant travels in Upstate New York made him as well known there as in New York City. The Republican nominee, Assemblyman Howard Mills, was little known and poorly financed; he was ignored by Schumer and hectored by Conservative nominee Marilyn O'Grady. No Democratic incumbent senator has been defeated in New York since direct election of senators began (although seven incumbent Republicans have lost). Schumer won 71%-24%, exceeding the 67%-31% record set by Daniel Patrick Moynihan in 1988; he won 66% of the vote in the suburbs, 63% Upstate and 86% in New York City. That only increased the rumors that Schumer would run for governor; some thought there was a game of chicken between him and highly publicized Attorney General Eliot Spitzer.

That issue was settled in in mid-November, when Schumer agreed to accept Harry Reid's appointment as chairman of the Democratic Senatorial Campaign Committee (and got a seat on Finance to boot). That committed Schumer to a continuing Senate career and left Spitzer free to run for governor. The work ahead looked difficult. The lineup of Senate seats up in 2006 seemed to leave Republicans with more target seats than Democrats. As Schumer put it later, "Our goal then was preserving North Dakota, Nebraska and Florida and keeping the Democrats at 45 seats." He did a brilliant job of fundraising; the DSCC outraised its Republican counterpart $119 million to $87 million. By July, Schumer raised $20 million from contributors writing single checks for $25,000. He concentrated first on persuading incumbent Democrats not to retire: Jeff Bingaman in New Mexico, Kent Conrad of North Dakota, Ben Nelson in Nebraska, Bill Nelson in Florida, Robert Byrd in West Virginia—all states George W. Bush carried in 2004. They all ran. Then he worked on getting strong challenger candidates. In Pennsylvania he aggressively recruited state Treasurer Bob Casey, Jr., son of the late governor who had not been allowed to speak at the 1992 Democratic National Convention in part because of his strong opposition to abortion. Schumer calculated that Casey would make inroads in the cultural conservative base of incumbent Rick Santorum and would be acceptable to pro-choice voters in suburban Philadelphia. Governor Ed Rendell, who won big margins in the Philly suburbs, joined in the effort; pro-choice groups with which Schumer worked closely on Judiciary protested, to no avail. Casey ran and won by a wide margin. He made a pitch over dinner in London to Claire McCaskill and her new husband to run in Missouri, where she had shown some strength while losing the 2004 governor race. She ran and narrowly won. He had some failures: Congressman Jim Langevin refused to run in Rhode Island, but Sheldon Whitehouse beat incumbent Lincoln Chafee anyway. In Montana he stayed out of the Democratic primary but spent money on ads against incumbent Conrad Burns, reminding voters that he had received more contributions from the clients of disgraced lobbyist Jack Abramoff than any other member of Congress. He encouraged Iraq war veteran Paul Hackett, who nearly won a special election in a heavily Republican district, to run against Mike DeWine in Ohio. But when Congressman Sherrod Brown entered the race, and after Hackett made some offputting statements, Schumer switched and supported Brown; Hackett bowed out, with some angry words for Schumer. Campaign committee chairmen rarely make endorsements in seriously contested primaries, but Schumer effectively did in Ohio and also in Virginia. There he backed Reagan administration Navy Secretary and decorated Vietnam veteran Jim Webb over liberal lobbyist Harris Miller. Webb won a narrow victory in the primary and an even narrower one in the general election, upsetting George Allen, who spent part of the campaign period exploring his presidential chances in Iowa and New Hampshire. The count in that race became final only on the Thursday after the election, and Virginia gave the Democrats their 51st seat. "We pulled an inside straight," Schumer said and recounted his congratulatory phone call from George W. Bush. "The president called and said jokingly, 'I wish you were on my team.'"

He declined all the credit for the Democratic takeover—"I'd say it was 65% Republican mistakes and 35% Democratic successes"—but his aggressive fundraising, recruitment and endorsements surely made the difference between 51 and 49. He was adept at raising issues. The award of a contract to manage major ports to Dubai Ports World aroused little interest at first, but Schumer held a press conference in New York in February 2006, and then got Republicans like Senator Tom Coburn and House Homeland Security Chairman Peter King to express their reservations. "I had an instinct about this situation, and it was to keep it as bipartisan as possible. So I went first to Coburn and he was very concerned." During the campaign he was working on a book, published as *Positively American: Winning Back the Middle-Class Majority One Family at a Time*, in which he urged Democrats to offer 50% solutions—increase math and reading scores by 50%, cut property taxes by 50%, reduce illegal immigration 50% and so forth. But he didn't press his candidates to raise these issues. Instead he advised them to campaign against the perceived incompetence of the Bush administration and to avoid much in the way of alternative policies. "The whole issue of Iraq will be how well George Bush is doing in Iraq, not if Democrats have a substitute plan or not." His advice served Democrats well. Harry Reid, delighted to be the incoming Majority Leader, got Schumer to agree to chair the campaign committee for the 2008 cycle. The lineup going into the cycle looked this time very favorable for Democrats. But Schumer cautioned, that 2006 would be an aberration "unless we stop listening to the special interest groups—and those are on the left as well as the right."

In New York politics Schumer is in a strong position. His performance in the 2006 elections makes it easy for him to persuade appropriators to support New York projects, particularly while Hillary Clinton is busy running for president. He endorsed her heartily in December 2006, before she declared. His relations with Governor Eliot Spitzer may be dicey, since he seemed to be giving serious consideration to running for governor himself in 2004 and he refused, citing his DSCC duties, to make an endorsement in the primary between Spitzer and Nassau County Executive Thomas Suozzi. But these three politicians, winning between 67% and 71% of the vote in their most recent elections, must live with each other, and while it is unclear whether Hillary Clinton will be elected president in 2008, it seems as clear as anything ever has been in New York politics that Schumer and Spitzer will be reelected in 2010.

Junior Senator

Hillary Rodham Clinton (D)

Elected 2000, seat up 2012, 2d term; b. Oct. 26, 1947, Chicago, IL; home, Chappaqua; Wellesley Col., B.A. 1969; Yale U., J.D. 1973; Methodist; married (Bill).

Professional Career: Atty., Children's Defense Fund, 1973-74; Council, U.S. House of Reps. Judiciary Committee, 1974; Asst. professor, U. of AR School of Law, 1974-77, 1979-80; Practicing atty., 1977-92; Chair, Pres. Task Force on Health Care Reform, 1993.

DC Office: 476 RSOB, 20510, 202-224-4451; Fax: 202-228-0282; Web site: clinton.senate.gov.

State Offices: Albany, 518-431-0120; Buffalo, 716-854-9725; Hartsdale, 914-725-9294; Lowville, 315-376-6118; Melville, 631-249-2825; New York City, 212-688-6262; Nyack, 845-613-0076; Rochester, 585-263-6250; Syracuse, 315-448-0470.

Committees: *Aging (Special)* (7th of 11 D). *Armed Services* (10th of 13 D): Airland; Readiness & Management Support; Emerging Threats & Capabilities. *Environment & Public Works* (5th of 10 D): Superfund & Environmental Health (Chmn.); Clean Air & Nuclear Safety; Transportation & Infrastructure. *Health, Education, Labor & Pensions* (8th of 11 D): Employment & Workplace Safety; Children & Families.

Group Ratings

	ADA	ACLU	AFS	LCV	ITIC	NTU	COC	ACU	CFG	FRC
2006	95	83	100	71	50	17	67	8	8	0
2005	100	—	88	95	—	9	35	12	0	—

National Journal Ratings

	2005 LIB	—	2005 CONS	2006 LIB	—	2006 CONS
Economic	84%	—	15%	63%	—	35%
Social	83%	—	10%	80%	—	14%
Foreign	66%	—	29%	62%	—	35%

Key Votes of the 109th Congress

1. Bar ANWR Drilling	Y	5. Confirm Samuel Alito	N	9. Limit Interstate Abortion	N
2. FY06 Spending Curb	N	6. Path to Citizenship	Y	10. CAFTA	N
3. Estate Tax Repeal	N	7. Bar Same Sex Marriage	N	11. Urge Iraq Withdrawal	Y
4. Raise Minimum Wage	Y	8. Stem Cell Research $	Y	12. Provide Detainee Rights	Y

Election Results

2006 general	Hillary Rodham Clinton (D-Ind-WF)	3,008,428	(67%)	($34,358,255)
	John Spencer (R-C)	1,392,189	(31%)	($5,660,688)
	Other	89,436	(2%)	
2006 primary	Hillary Rodham Clinton (D)	640,955	(84%)	
	Jonathan Tasini (D)	124,999	(16%)	
2000 general	Hillary Rodham Clinton (D-L-WF)	3,747,310	(55%)	($41,469,898)
	Rick Lazio (R-C)	2,915,730	(43%)	($40,576,273)
	Other	116,799	(2%)	

Hillary Rodham Clinton, First Lady of the United States from 1993 to 2001, was elected junior senator from New York in November 2000. Clinton grew up in Park Ridge, Illinois; her father owned and ran a drape and curtain factory. She excelled at her studies and was elected to student government at Maine South High School. Park Ridge is a solidly Republican Chicago suburb, near O'Hare Airport, and the young Hillary Rodham was a Goldwater girl in 1964. She went to Wellesley College, where she became a Democrat in the turbulent election year of 1968: she wrote her senior thesis (kept under lock and key by the college since 1993) on applying the theories of radical Chicago organizer Saul Alinsky and argued that antipoverty programs did not give enough power to the poor. She was elected student government president, and pushed successfully for admission of more black students and admission of men to women's dorms. At the 1969 commencement she gave a speech that won notice in *Life* magazine. She went on to Yale Law School, where she worked with the attorney for Black Panthers accused of murder and clerked for a summer with Communist attorney Robert Treuhaft in Berkeley. At Yale she met Bill Clinton, and they became partners for life.

Bill Clinton was anything but reticent about his political ambitions in his native Arkansas. He showed her around the state and together they went to Austin in 1972 to run the McGovern campaign in Texas. After graduation in 1973, Bill Clinton moved to Fayetteville to teach law at the University of Arkansas. In 1974 Hillary Rodham moved to Washington to work for the House Judiciary Committee's special counsel John Doar on the impeachment of Richard Nixon; Bill Clinton ran for Congress and came close to unseating a Republican incumbent. After Nixon resigned, she returned to Arkansas to teach law, and in October 1975 she and Clinton were married. In 1976 he was elected attorney general of Arkansas; she worked for Jimmy Carter's campaign. After that she worked for the Rose Law Firm in Little Rock and in 1977 was appointed part-time chairman of the Legal Services Corporation. Under her leadership, the Legal Services budget increased dramatically, including contributions to local political campaigns and conducting campaigns against ballot propositions. In 1978 Bill Clinton ran for governor, and after he won the Democratic nomination, tantamount to victory that year, Hillary Rodham invested $1,000 in commodities future and, with the help of a friend who was general counsel of Tyson Foods, one of the state's biggest businesses, saw that turned into $100,000.

In 1980 Bill Clinton was defeated for re-election. He promptly took up a more moderate line and his wife began to call herself Hillary Clinton; in 1982 he beat the incumbent and became governor again. Hillary Clinton continued her law practice and service on the board of the Children's Defense Fund and other organizations. She served on the boards of Wal-Mart, TCBY and in 1988 and 1991 was named by the *National Law Journal* as one of the 100 most influential lawyers in the country. It was in these years also that she and her husband invested in the Whitewater real estate project and that she performed legal work for the Morgan Guaranty Savings and Loan, which invested in the project and whose failure cost the federal government $73 million. Whitewater later became the subject of congressional hearings and an independent counsel investigation, both of which were impeded when Rose Law Firm billing records were subpoenaed in July 1994 but were not found until they turned up in the residential quarters of the White House in January 1996. Independent Counsel Robert Ray in September 2000 ended the investigation, saying he could not prove that the Clintons had been involved in criminal activity or that they concealed information from investigators or obstructed justice. In his final report in March 2002 Ray noted that Rose Law Firm records were found in the family quarters of the White House in January 1996 and that three witnesses told investigators they saw her "carrying records that had the appearance of the billing records in July 1995"; but he said that that evidence was insufficient to obtain and sustain a conviction beyond a reasonable doubt.

In 1991 Bill Clinton ran for president. It was widely rumored that he had had many extramarital affairs; at a Washington press breakfast the Clintons admitted that their marriage had not been without problems. After the election, Clinton announced that the leader of his task force on health care reform would be the first lady, Hillary Rodham Clinton—the first time her maiden name was featured. The task force under her direction and that of Ira Magaziner met secretly and without input from members of Congress; a complicated plan was finally produced after a couple of deadlines were not met. Clinton eventually did testify before Congress; there and in other public forums she was crisp, articulate, and knowledgeable. But she was unable to persuade Congress to adopt her plan. It never came to the floor in either house, and was abandoned in September 1994. In the meantime, the first lady had other problems. In May 1993 the members of the White House Travel Office were fired, and director Billy Ray Dale was later prosecuted—and acquitted by a jury within minutes. Clinton denied that she had any role in the firings, or in apparent plans to replace the charter service with one owned by Clinton friends and Hollywood producers Harry Thomason and Linda Bloodworth-Thomason. In June 2000 Independent Counsel Ray concluded that Clinton had given "factually false" testimony in a sworn deposition, but declined to prosecute her.

Clinton persevered through the humiliations of the health care fiasco and the scandals with an aplomb that showed great discipline and determination. She wrote *It Takes a Village* and donated the proceeds to children's hospitals. In January 1998, when Bill Clinton denied the charge that he had had an affair with then-White House intern Monica Lewinsky, Hillary Rodham Clinton flew to New York to appear on the Today show and charged that the allegations were the product of "a vast right-wing conspiracy." She continued to support him, though with obvious frostiness, when he was forced to admit in August 1998 that the charges were true.

Meanwhile, she campaigned gamely for Democratic candidates in the 1998 elections, and was particularly moved by the warm applause she received in her four appearances in New York for Senate candidate Charles Schumer. Three days after the 1998 election, Senator Daniel Patrick Moynihan announced that he would not run for re-election in New York in 2000. Moynihan, the nation's best thinker among politicians since Lincoln and its best politician among thinkers since Jefferson, a man whose public career extended back into the 1950s and included many prescient warnings and original insights, who had served four terms in the Senate after serving in the cabinet or sub-cabinets of four successive presidents, obviously was not going to be replaced by a politician of similar magnitude; there aren't any. But there also weren't any obvious Democratic successors in New York. Moynihan, who passed away in March 2003, himself suggested state comptroller Carl McCall; Congresswoman Nita Lowey of Westchester County was interested in the race, though it was not clear that either had the stature to beat the likely Republican nominee, New York City Mayor Rudolph Giuliani. In early 1999 Bob Torricelli, the aggressive head of the Senate Democrats' campaign committee, called for Clinton to run. She said she was giving "careful thought" to it. She started making more trips to New York, and Lowey said she would be glad to step aside if Clinton ran. In July 1999 she appeared at Moynihans' Upstate farm and then began a "listening tour" across Upstate New York. Giuliani responded with an appearance in Arkansas.

Clinton's early campaign was not without troubles. There was widespread ridicule of the idea of someone with no previous connection with the state running for senator from New York. In August 1999 Bill Clinton granted clemency to four Puerto Rican terrorists who never expressed remorse for their violent crimes—an obvious pitch for the Puerto Rican vote. Embarrassed, she came out against the move, without giving a heads-up to Puerto Rican leaders. That same month the Clintons left their favorite vacation spot, fashionable Martha's Vineyard, for a sojourn in Skaneateles, a pleasant town in the Finger Lakes they would probably never have visited otherwise. In October the Clintons bought a house in woodsy Chappaqua in Westchester County and were then embarrassed because they borrowed most of the purchase price from Democratic fundraiser Terry McAuliffe; later they got more conventional financing. In November 1999 on a trip to Israel, Clinton embraced and kissed the wife of Yasir Arafat after a speech in which she lambasted the Israelis; Clinton explained later that she was acting in a diplomatic capacity, but her act brought back memories of her endorsement of an independent Palestinian state when that was not yet U.S. policy. In February 2000 she formally announced her candidacy, with her husband standing silently by, from a venue in Westchester. By that point her poll ratings had slipped, and she was running no better than even with Giuliani.

Carpetbagging is not necessarily a political crime in New York. Voters there in 1964 elected Robert Kennedy, though he lived in Virginia and had a technical residence in Massachusetts. Robert Kennedy won in 1964 not just because of Lyndon Johnson's coattails, but because he ran virtually even in usually Republican Upstate New York; national celebrities may be commonplace in New York City, but when they show up in Upstate towns and cities it is noted and appreciated. Hillary Rodham Clinton's strategy was similar. With her usual hard work, perseverance and intensity, she criss-crossed Upstate New York, listened to its voters' many complaints, learned about local issues and adopted appealing positions on them: the same slogging persistence she had shown in the dreary days in Arkansas and the tumultuous days after the failed health care initiative and scandal charges in Washington. In April Giuliani announced that he had prostate cancer; in May he announced that he was seeking a separation from his wife. Days later, in a dramatic press conference, he announced he was leaving the Senate race.

Within 24 hours the Republicans had another candidate, Long Island Congressman Rick Lazio. He had talked of running in summer 1999, until Governor George Pataki announced suddenly in August that he was backing his longtime rival Giuliani. Lazio had a moderate voting record in the House; like Giuliani he backed abortion rights. He raised plenty of money: Hillary haters from all over the country sent in contributions large and small, and he ended up spending $40 million. But his campaign was less than perfect. Lazio was vulnerable to attacks, made often by Clinton, that he had supported Newt Gingrich, a *bete noire* to most New York voters. And there were unforced errors. In the first debate on September 13, Lazio walked over to Clinton and presented her a paper with a pledge to eschew soft money ads. In a time when voters were eager for consensus, Lazio was providing them with confrontation, and this in-your-face behavior was especially repugnant to women. Nine days later they both agreed to not run ads financed by soft money, that is, contributions to parties; but this was unenforceable, since parties and others can spend what they want to, and the assumption that campaign finance was a vote-moving issue proved ill-founded. In the second debate, Lazio declined to say that he would vote for any Supreme Court nominee who opposed the key abortion rights decision of *Roe v. Wade*, a defensible position intellectually, but one difficult to sustain politically in New York; Clinton pounded him on it.

For a race that was close almost all the way in the polls, this Senate election—surpassing the 1998 New York Senate race as the most expensive in history not involving a self-financing candidate—was decided by a surprisingly wide margin. Clinton won 55%-43%, almost the same as Schumer's 55%-44% two years earlier. "Sixty-two counties, 16 months, three debates, two opponents and six black pantsuits later—here we are!" exulted Clinton on election night. She was helped, of course, by the fact that Al Gore was carrying New York 60%-35%. But she ran well on her own. She carried New York City by 74%-25%, the same margin as Schumer's in 1998. She trailed in the suburbs by only 53%-45%, despite Lazio's suburban provenance; he carried his Long Island base, but she carried her now native Westchester. And Lazio won Upstate by only 50%-47%; Clinton carried most of the large counties there, and her percentages in county after county, not usually 50% but seldom under 40%, were impressive evidence of her hard work in campaigning and mastering Upstate issues. Clinton carried the Jewish vote, according to the VNS exit poll, by only 53%-45%, which would usually mean disaster for a Democrat in New York, and she did far less well than Schumer and other Democrats among those with graduate degrees, a large percentage of whom are Jewish. But she carried Upstate women by 55%-43%, an excellent showing for a Democrat: the work paid off.

A few days after the election, Clinton took a victory lap around Upstate New York. But her standing fell in the months after the election. In December 2000 she signed a book contract with Simon & Schuster for $8 million—$4.5 million more than the book contract for which Newt Gingrich was so roundly attacked in 1995. In departing the White House, the Clintons took $190,000 in gifts—far above the Senate's $50 limit—and many had to be returned when it was revealed that they included items donated to the White House, not the Clintons. Among the gifts were $7,375 worth of coffee tables and chairs donated by Denise Rich, former wife and advocate of Marc Rich, the fugitive financier pardoned by Bill Clinton on his last day in office, despite the opposition of New York U.S. Attorney Mary Jo White. Hillary Rodham Clinton said she had no opinion on the pardon. Nor, she said, did she have any role in the pardon of four Hasidic Jews from the Rockland County community of New Square who were convicted of fleecing the federal government of millions of dollars—a pardon White also opposed. But Clinton had visited New Square in August 2000, had won the community's vote by a margin of 1,400 to 12 and had been present at a White House Map Room meeting between their leaders and Bill Clinton on December 21, 2000, where they asked for the pardons. She said she had no knowledge as well that her brother Hugh Rodham had, while living at the White House, pushed for and obtained the pardon of two other felons for which he had been paid $400,000.

Many expected that Clinton would be greeted grudgingly and suspiciously by other senators because of her obvious presidential ambitions. In fact she has worked hard at the often tedious business of being a senator. She continued to travel around New York, especially Upstate: by June 2002 she had made 130 trips to Upstate New York. She worked on the arcana of dairy price supports and turned down many opportunities for national appearances; only after September 11 did she appear again on *Meet the Press*, in December 2001. She worked hard in the Senate, attending just about every committee and subcommittee hearing, spending time on the floor, approaching Republican colleagues to ask if she could cosponsor their bills. At Democratic caucus meetings, she would get coffee for other senators. Republicans found themselves sheepishly admitting they liked her. At the same time, by all accounts she took a hard partisan line behind closed doors. She advised Tom Daschle that Senate Democrats should have a war room, as the Clinton campaign and White House did. She supported George W. Bush in the war on terrorism and voted for the Iraq war resolution, and told him in their meeting on September 13, 2001, that she was one of the few who understood the loneliness of the White House, but she advised down-the-line opposition to his domestic policies. Occasionally in public she sounded a partisan note. In May 2001 she cast the single vote against the Justice Department confirmation of Michael Chertoff, who had worked on the Whitewater independent counsel investigation. HILLPAC, her leadership PAC, raised $3.2 million in the 2002 cycle and contributed more than $1 million to Democrats across the country; she put on fundraisers for fellow Democrats in her Washington house.

Clinton's propensity for bipartisanship and her partisanship were both on display at the opening of the 108th Congress in January 2003. In December she had gotten agreement with Don Nickles on a compromise proposal to extend unemployment benefits. It was the first item of business in the new Congress. But unexpectedly Clinton rose and offered an amendment to extend coverage to 1 million people whose benefits had expired. This triggered several hours of debate on parliamentary motions—a tough initiation for the new Majority Leader Bill Frist. Eventually Clinton's amendment was rejected and a compromise was passed. In the new Congress, Clinton was elected head of the Democrats' Steering and Coordination Committee, a job that has never generated much publicity for its incumbent; it gave her an institutional base for her behind-the-scenes partisan strategizing. She got a seat on the Armed Services Committee, on which no New York senator had ever served, and worked methodically on defense issues. Republican Lindsey Graham, who cosponsored benefit increases with her, said, "People may think she has an antimilitary bias or is not strong on defense. But I find her to be very reasonable. I think she has been responsible in making sure the men and women in the military are well taken care of."

Clinton voted for the Iraq war resolution in October 2002 and did not flinch from supporting it later; she voted for the $87 billion supplemental in November 2003. "The fact is we're in Iraq and we're in Afghanistan, and we have no choice but to be successful," she said in December 2003. In spring 2004, when other Democratic senators were flocking to the premiere of Michael Moore's "Fahrenheit 9/11," she said Saddam Hussein was "a potential threat" who "was seeking weapons of mass destruction, whether or not he actually had them." She was critical of the conduct of operations, however. After a trip to Iraq in December 2003, she said, "Everybody told me we don't have enough intelligence, civil affairs, MPs, engineers." She said that the Bush administration wasn't "leveling with the American people about what it is we're up against, how long it's going to take, how much it's going to cost."

On domestic policy she described the administration as "radical," bent on dismantling the "central pillars of progress in our country during the 20th century" and seeking "to undo the New Deal." But her specific proposals were more incremental and less confrontational. On homeland security, Clinton got passed in September 2004 amendments providing $50 million for nonprofits and community organizations vulnerable to terrorist threats and $570 million to safeguard New York's trains and tunnels. Clinton had cast lone votes against Michael Chertoff, the onetime Whitewater investigator, for a Justice Department position and a judgeship, but when he was nominated for Homeland Security secretary in January 2005 she said coolly, "I look forward to meetings with Judge Chertoff in the very near future to discuss many important issues, including the specific homeland security needs of New York as well as the many homeland security challenges confronting our nation." She voted for his confirmation: working for homeland security for New York and the nation was evidently more important than any personal grudge.

Clinton made it plain after the November 2004 election that she took a different approach than John Kerry. When Kerry's defeat was blamed on values issues, she commented, "I don't think you can win an election or even run a successful campaign if you don't acknowledge what is important to people. We don't have to agree with them. But being ignored is a sign of such disrespect. And therefore I think we should talk about these issues." In January 2005, speaking to abortion rights supporters in Albany, she surprised many in the audience by saying, "Yes, we do have deeply held differences of opinion about the issue of abortion, and I, for one, respect those who believe with all their hearts and conscience that there are no circumstances under which any abortion should ever be available. There is an opportunity for people of good faith to find common ground in this debate.

We should be able to agree that we want every child born in this country to be wanted, cherished and loved. We can all recognize that abortion in many ways represents a sad, even tragic choice to many, many women." She continued to support a partial-birth abortion ban only with an exception for the health of the mother and parental notification only with a judicial bypass. She supported an informed consent law for New York and voted in the Senate against a bill penalizing those who help girls cross state lines to get abortions and in October 2006 taped automated calls against a California parental notification ballot proposition. While many Democrats were skeptical of government aid to faith-based service providers, Clinton, a regular participant in the National Prayer Breakfast, said, "There is no contradiction between support for faith-based initiatives and upholding our constitutional principles."

She continued to work on defense issues major and minor. "She's very industrious. She does her homework very carefully. She's very respectful of how the committee does its business," said Armed Services Chairman John Warner. With committee Republicans she worked to improve the living conditions of military personnel and for better health care for National Guard troops. She visited soldiers in Afghanistan and Iraq, on one trip accompanied by John McCain. She demanded an inquiry in January 2006 on body armor. In March 2007 she told the Human Rights Campaign that she opposes the ban on openly gay service members. Over several years she worked with Republican Congressman Tom Reynolds to get $17 million in earmarks for the Niagara Falls Air Reserve Station; when it showed up on the Pentagon's base closing list in May 2005, she obtained an internal Pentagon document showing that closure would cost $190 million more than the official estimate. She called the head of the base closing commission, former Veterans Secretary Tony Principi, with whom she had worked on veterans issues, on the day the commission made its decision, and the commission recommended it be kept open. Similarly the commission rejected the Pentagon recommendation that personnel in Stratton Air National Guard Base in Glenville be moved to Arkansas.

On Iraq her tone, if not her position, evolved. In a November 2005 letter to constituents she said, "I voted for [the resolution] on the basis of the evidence presented by the administration, assurances they gave that they would first seek to resolve the issue of weapons of mass destruction peacefully through United Nations sponsored inspections...Their assurances turned out to be empty ones." When Democrats were divided in June 2006 on Russ Feingold's amendment for U.S. withdrawal, she opposed it and said, "Although unity is important, it is not the most important value." In August 2006 she called for the resignation of Defense Secretary Donald Rumsfeld for his "failed policy" in Iraq. In October 2006 she said flatly, "If we knew then what we know now there never would have been a vote and there would never have been a war." In January 2007 she called George W. Bush's surge "a losing strategy," but added, "I'm not for imposing a date-certain withdrawal date. But don't be mistaken, I am for ending this war as soon as possible." She continued to refuse to apologize for her October 2002 vote; campaigning in New Hampshire in February 2007 she said, "If the most important thing to any of you is choosing someone who did not cast that vote or has said his vote was a mistake, then there are others to choose from." In March 2007 she voted for the nonbinding resolution that sets a "goal" of March 31, 2008, for withdrawal from Iraq. In May 2007 she voted for a resolution sponsored by Feingold to de-fund the war after March 31, 2008, saying, "we, as a united party, must work together with clarity of purpose and mission to begin bringing our troops home and end this war."

Clinton voted against several prominent Bush administration nominees: John Roberts and Samuel Alito, Lester Crawford at the FDA, Alberto Gonzales, Porter Goss at the CIA. She and Patty Murray blocked a vote on FDA nominee Andrew von Eschenbach pending approval of over-the-counter sales of the Plan B abortifacient; when it was approved for adults in August 2006 they withdrew their objection and he was confirmed. She pursued several cross-aisle initiatives. With Newt Gingrich outside the Congress and with Bill Frist in the Senate, she pressed for legislation improving the use of information technology in health care; their bill passed the Senate in November 2005. She worked with Trent Lott on improving FEMA, with Tom DeLay on foster children care, with Rick Santorum and other conservatives on children's exposure to graphic images, with Mike DeWine on asthma, with Wayne Allard on barring banks from the real estate business. In September 2005 she sponsored with Barack Obama a bill to encourage providers to disclose medical errors early, issue apologies if warranted, offer immediate compensation and analyze errors; this was offered as an alternative to the medical malpractice bill supported by most Republicans. In February 2007 she and Charles Schumer sponsored a bill to create a process in the FDA to approve generic biotech drugs. In May 2006 she sponsored a bill to put an extra tax on oil company profits and repeal some oil company tax breaks and use the money for a Strategic Energy Fund to reduce the consumption of foreign oil 50% by 2025. On immigration, in March 2006 she cited the Bible in criticizing the provision in the House-passed bill criminalizing the offering of aid to illegal immigrants. She voted for the bill passed by the Senate in May 2006 and for the border fence bill passed in September 2006; with an eye on the labor needs of Upstate farmers, she urged the Senate to pass Larry Craig's AgJobs bill, with its guest worker provisions. She continued to work on Upstate projects. She and Tom Reynolds arranged $30 million in federal funds for expansion of the Buffalo Niagara Medical Campus. She got funding for fiber optic wiring for St. Lawrence County. She worked for disaster aid for dairy farmers and apple and grape growers.

No Democratic senator from New York has been defeated for reelection since the institution of popular election of senators, and no one thought Hillary Clinton would fail to win reelection in 2006. She refrained from making the usual promise to serve out the full term (which her husband had made in his 1990 campaign for reelection in Arkansas), serene in her confidence that voters wouldn't mind. They didn't. She had an anti-war primary opponent who rode his bicycle from Manhattan to Buffalo; she won 84%-16%. She lost in the college town of Ithaca and a township next door but won everywhere else. Republicans tried to find a suitable candidate. Edward Cox, Manhattan lawyer and son-in-law of Richard Nixon, traveled around the state but in November 2005 withdrew from the race. Former Yonkers Mayor John Spencer declared his candidacy in June 2005, although his star was dimmed by the revelation that he had carried on an affair with his chief of staff for many years and had two out-of-wedlock children with her. Westchester County District Attorney Jeanine Pirro declared for statewide office in 2005 and said she was running for senator until December, when she declared for attorney general instead; her star was dimmed by her husband's tax fraud conviction. Reagan administration appointee K. T. McFarland ran a game campaign against Spencer but lost 61%-39%. In October, Spencer made the tabloids when he charged that Clinton had had cosmetic surgery; Clinton, showing a light touch, tilted back her head and asked reporters to look for scars. Clinton raised some $34 million for this campaign, a figure so high that some Democrats complained she was taking money away from other candidates. But in October she had given $1.1 million to the DSCC, $250,000 to the DCCC and $150,000 to the New York Democratic primary. She appeared at fundraisers and campaigned for Upstate Democratic House candidates who won or came unexpectedly close to winning. Statewide she won 67%-31%, a margin a little smaller than Eliot Spitzer's in 2006 or Charles Schumer's in 2004, but very impressive indeed. She won 83% of the vote in New York City, 62% in the suburbs and 60% Upstate.

She proceeded to do what everyone expected her to do: run for president. It turned out to be a different kind of contest than many expected. In early 2006 it looked like she might have ideological opposition on the left from Russ Feingold and on the right from Mark Warner. In such a contest her firm stand on Iraq and her familiarity with military and defense issues, together with her leadership on domestic issues and her ability to work with Republicans on some issues all seemed like assets. But both Feingold and Warner decided not to run. So did 2004 presidential nominee John Kerry. In the race, however, were 2004 vice presidential nominee John Edwards and 2004 national convention keynoter Barack Obama, and in mid-2007 they were Clinton's strongest competitors in the polls. Edwards had barely stopped stumping in Iowa after the 2004 campaign; Obama in the fall of 2006 rocketed to popularity among Democrats and all voters as well. Obama's rise in the polls seems to have prompted Clinton to formally announce her candidacy earlier than planned, in January 2007. Obama's opposition from the beginning to the Iraq war—he spoke out against it while an Illinois state senator—and John Edwards's apology for his war vote and calls for immediate withdrawal put Clinton on the defensive in a race among a Democratic electorate almost unanimously and usually bitterly opposed to the war. At the same time some Democrats wondered whether a candidate who polarizes the electorate as much as Clinton, at least in summer 2007, could win the presidency. But she has assets no other candidate brings to the race: actual day-to-day experience in the White House, and she has shown the grace under pressure and the persistence in the face of daunting setbacks that are qualities most voters seek in a president.

FIRST DISTRICT

Rep. Tim Bishop (D)

Elected 2002, 3d term; b. June 1, 1950, Southampton; home, Southampton; Holy Cross Col., A.B. 1972; Long Island U., M.P.A. 1981; Catholic; married (Kathy).

Professional Career: Admin., Southampton College, 1973-2002.

DC Office: 225 CHOB, 20515, 202-225-3826; Fax: 202-225-3143; Web site: www.house.gov/timbishop/.

District Offices: Coram, 631-696-6500; Southampton, 631-259-8450.

Committees: *Budget* (20th of 22 D). *Education & Labor* (16th of 27 D): Workforce Protections; Higher Education, Lifelong Learning & Competitiveness. *Transportation & Infrastructure* (19th of 41 D): Water Resources & Environment; Coast Guard & Maritime Transportation; Highways & Transit.

Group Ratings

	ADA	ACLU	AFS	LCV	ITIC	NTU	COC	ACU	CFG	FRC
2006	85	86	100	92	43	14	40	16	10	0
2005	95	—	100	94	—	12	41	0	7	8

National Journal Ratings

	2005 LIB	—	2005 CONS		2006 LIB	—	2006 CONS
Economic	88%	—	9%		94%	—	0%
Social	67%	—	32%		71%	—	29%
Foreign	67%	—	33%		82%	—	17%

Key Votes of the 109th Congress

1. Estate Tax Repeal	N	5. Limit Interstate Abortion	N	9. Build Border Fence	Y
2. Limit CAFE Standards	N	6. Extend Patriot Act	N	10. CAFTA	N
3. FY06 Spending Curb	N	7. Bar Same Sex Marriage	N	11. Oppose Iraq Withdrawal	*
4. Drilling in ANWR	N	8. Stem Cell Research $	Y	12. Detainee Tribunals	N

Election Results

2006 general	Tim Bishop (D-Ind-WF)	104,360	(62%)	($1,065,866)
	Italo Zanzi (R-C)	63,328	(38%)	($321,495)
2006 primary	Tim Bishop (D)	unopposed		
2004 general	Tim Bishop (D-Ind-WF)	156,354	(56%)	($1,908,440)
	William Manger (R-C)	121,855	(44%)	($1,385,362)

Prior Winning Percentages: 2002 (50%)

The People		Race/Ethnic Origin	Ancestry	
Area size:	1,944 sq. mi.	84.5% White	Italian: 21.1% Irish: 17.5%	
Urban population:	94.0%	4.0% Black	German: 13.7%	
Rural population:	6.0%	2.4% Asian	**2004 Presidential Vote**	
Pop. 2000:	654,360	0.3% Native Am.	Bush (R) 154,249	(49%)
Pop. 2005 (est):	689,853	0.0% Hawaiian	Kerry (D) 152,165	(49%)
Median income:	$61,884	1.2% Two+ races	Other 5,991	(2%)
Poverty status:	6.0%	0.1% Other	**2000 Presidential Vote**	
Military veterans:	12.1%	7.5% Hispanic Origin	Gore (D) 139,490	(52%)
			Bush (R) 116,308	(44%)
			Other 10,705	(4%)
			Cook Partisan Voting Index: D + 3	

Occupation	Blue collar: 20.3%	White collar: 64.4%	Gray collar: 15.3%

Long Island—"the Island" to most New Yorkers—is America's largest, most populous and in some ways most troubled island. Long Island stretches 103 miles, from the two-century-old Montauk Point lighthouse on a crumbling bluff at its eastern extremity to Fort Hamilton at the foot of the Verrazano Narrows Bridge. Between 12 and 20 miles wide, Long Island is ringed by gentle hills and cliffs above Long Island Sound and sandspit beaches that front the Atlantic Ocean. Including Brooklyn and Queens, some 7.5 million people live on Long Island, more than in all but 11 states. Brooklyn, at the western end of the island, is urban and thickly settled, while the Hamptons in the east are carefully manicured countryside, preserved as a playground by a style-conscious New York elite. Demographically, the Hamptons are only a small (though growing) part of Long Island. More important are the (slower growing) suburbs created in the post-World War II rush out of the city.

Developers looking for cheaper land for aircraft factories, shopping centers, subdivisions or office parks found them first in Nassau County, just east of Queens, and then further out in Suffolk County. Suffolk attracted young families, of Irish and Italian descent more often than Jewish or black, looking for more space, less crime and other opposites of what the city could offer. More recently Suffolk County has been attracting Latinos (13% of total population), Salvadorans as well as Puerto Ricans, in many of its lower income areas. In the last two decades of the 20th century, life in Long Island turned sour, as defense plants were decimated by the end of the Cold War, cost overruns on nuclear plants led to electricity rate increases and older suburbs began maturing. The Bush administration's defense buildup has resulted in more defense jobs at Northrop Grumman and at newer firms with computer-controlled machine tools, and the Long Island Power Authority wants to build wind farms, underwater cables and a floating natural gas plant to bring more energy across Long Island Sound from Connecticut and elsewhere. But high taxes and expensive housing remain endemic problems.

Such upheavals, combined with partisan rivalries, have fed political turbulence. The 1st Congressional District of New York, consisting of the eastern end of Long Island, ousted its incumbent congressmen in both 2000 and 2002, the only district to do so. The 1st covers eastern Suffolk County, now more populous (1.48 million people) and faster growing (12% growth from 1990 to 2004) than Nassau County, its neighbor to the west. The district runs as far west as Smithtown on the North Shore and Patchogue on the South Shore. It includes Shelter Island, located between the north and south fork of Long Island's "fishtail," and Plum Island, which houses the nation's only animal infection research site; the research facility was recently acquired by the Department of Homeland Security from the Department of Agriculture. Some farmers continue to grow sweet corn and pumpkins. The 1st includes two areas frequented in the summer by urban sophisticates: all of the Hamptons, with their ever-soaring prices, and most of Fire Island National Seashore, the only federal wilderness area in New York state, and a magnet for gay vacationers for decades. Politically, the more important areas are the Brookhaven National Laboratory and the defense plants in the center of the Island. Suffolk County was long one of the most conservative parts of New York, though not very conservative by today's national standards. Republican voter registration remains high, and Suffolk voted strongly for Governor George Pataki's reelection in 2002 and for county native Rick Lazio in the 2000 Senate race, but in 2006 it voted comfortably for Hillary Rodham Clinton in her landslide reelection and it elected mostly Democrats at the county and town level. It voted solidly for Al Gore in 2000 but made a big swing toward George W. Bush in 2004—a September 11 effect—giving him a narrow winning margin.

The congressman from the 1st District is Tim Bishop, a Democrat first elected in 2002. He grew up in Southampton and graduated from Holy Cross College and Long Island University. He spent his entire professional career at Southampton College, where he began in 1973 as an admissions counselor and in 1986 became provost. He chaired the town of Southampton's board of ethics and was on the board of the Eastern Long Island Coastal Conservation Alliance. Few paid much attention when Bishop announced he would oppose Felix Grucci, the first-term Republican congressman, who had won the seat in a bizarre contest in 2000: Mike Forbes, a Republican elected in 1994 as part of the Gingrich revolution, switched parties in July 1999, then lost the low-turnout Democratic primary by 35 votes to Regina Seltzer, a 71-year-old retired librarian, and Grucci easily won the general, 56%-41%. Grucci seemed headed for reelection when, in late September, he ran an ad accusing Bishop of falsifying rape statistics at Southampton College and "turning his back on rape victims." This turned out to be untrue. The basis for the allegations had been several articles in the college newspaper that turned out to be so riddled with inaccuracies that the editors voluntarily retrieved every copy of the newspaper they could find. Grucci's campaign refused to repudiate the ad, on the ground that no correction had ever appeared in print. House Democrats' campaign committee quickly saw an opportunity to pick up a seat. Soon the airwaves became saturated with ads attacking Grucci both for the rape commercial and for his environmental voting record. In one spot, the Grucci family's famed fireworks enterprise was linked to the chemical contamination of local drinking water. Republican operatives privately fumed that Grucci had failed to tell them about the college rape ad and that he had blundered in failing to offer a positive message. The official result was delayed a week by a recount and Grucci did not concede until ten days after the election; Bishop won 50%-49%.

In the House, Bishop has a voting record that is more liberal on economics than on other issues. He opposed the war in Iraq and supported abortion rights and a rollback of the Bush tax cuts. Speaking knowledgeably, he played a leading role on the Education and the Workforce Committee during the higher education reauthorization debate. With Hilda Solis, he passed an amendment in May 2005 to bar the Environmental Protection Agency from testing pesticides on humans. He fought proposed cutbacks at Brookhaven and sought funds for a third track on the Long Island Railroad.

Republicans have identified Bishop as a prime target. In 2004, their nominee was Bill Manger, who served four years as a village trustee in Southampton and was a top adviser to Rick Lazio in his Senate race; he emphasized his independence from national Republicans and attacked Bishop for opposing tax cuts. That wasn't nearly enough. Bishop won handily, 56%-44%. In 2006, he increased the margin to 62%-38% against Major League Baseball official Italo Zanzi, a political neophyte. Voting trends in the state and on the Island are going Bishop's way.

SECOND DISTRICT

Rep. Steve Israel (D)

Elected 2000, 4th term; b. May 30, 1958, Brooklyn; home, Dix Hills; George Wash. U., B.A. 1983; Jewish; married (Marlene Budd).

Elected Office: Huntington Town Bd., 1993-2000, Maj. Ldr., 1997-2000.

Professional Career: Legis. Asst., U.S. Rep. Richard Ottinger, 1980-83; Fundraising Dir., Touro Law Ctr., 1985-88; Pres., Steve Israel Assoc., Inc., 1992-98; Pres. & CEO, Inst. on Holocaust and Law, 1998-2000.

DC Office: 432 CHOB, 20515, 202-225-3335; Fax: 202-225-4669; Web site: www.house.gov/israel.

District Offices: Hauppauge, 631-951-2210.

Committees: *Appropriations* (32d of 37 D): State, Foreign Operations & Related Programs; Energy & Water Development.

Group Ratings

	ADA	ACLU	AFS	LCV	ITIC	NTU	COC	ACU	CFG	FRC
2006	90	91	100	92	67	14	50	12	11	0
2005	90	—	100	94	—	18	52	8	10	8

National Journal Ratings

	2005 LIB	—	2005 CONS		2006 LIB	—	2006 CONS
Economic	69%	—	29%		74%	—	23%
Social	70%	—	30%		75%	—	24%
Foreign	62%	—	38%		66%	—	33%

Key Votes of the 109th Congress

1. Estate Tax Repeal	Y	5. Limit Interstate Abortion	N	9. Build Border Fence		Y
2. Limit CAFE Standards	N	6. Extend Patriot Act	N	10. CAFTA		N
3. FY06 Spending Curb	N	7. Bar Same Sex Marriage	N	11. Oppose Iraq Withdrawal		N
4. Drilling in ANWR	N	8. Stem Cell Research $	Y	12. Detainee Tribunals		N

Election Results

2006 general	Steve Israel (D-Ind-WF) 105,276	(70%)	($1,167,026)
	John Bugler (R-C) 44,212	(30%)	
2006 primary	Steve Israel (D) .... unopposed		
2004 general	Steve Israel (D-Ind-WF) 161,593	(67%)	($1,077,719)
	Richard Hoffmann (R-C) 80,950	(33%)	($11,679)

Prior Winning Percentages: 2002 (58%); 2000 (48%)

The People		Race/Ethnic Origin	Ancestry	
Area size:	330 sq. mi.	71.5% White	Italian: 18.8%	Irish: 14.1%
Urban population:	99.7%	9.8% Black	German: 10.3%	
Rural population:	0.3%	3.0% Asian	**2004 Presidential Vote**	
Pop. 2000:	654,360	0.2% Native Am.	Kerry (D) 148,625	(53%)
Pop. 2005 (est):	673,287	0.0% Hawaiian	Bush (R) 127,626	(45%)
Median income:	$71,147	1.4% Two+ races	Other 5,569	(2%)
Poverty status:	5.9%	0.2% Other	**2000 Presidential Vote**	
Military veterans:	10.6%	13.9% Hispanic Origin	Gore (D) 146,723	(57%)
			Bush (R) 100,708	(39%)
			Other 8,165	(3%)
			Cook Partisan Voting Index: D + 8	

Occupation	Blue collar: 20.1%	White collar: 66.3%	Gray collar: 13.6%

Shortly after World War II, hundreds of thousands of New York City residents, many of them young veterans and their families, moved to detached suburban homes built on the former potato fields of central Long Island. Those in the first wave of postwar migration settled in Nassau County, and they included a cross-section of all but the poorest New Yorkers: roughly half Catholic, a quarter Protestant and a quarter Jewish. As Long Island developed its own employment base, another wave moved further east into Suffolk County. This group was more Catholic, less Jewish and more blue-collar. Ancestrally Democratic, these voters were culturally conservative, and in the 1970s and 1980s, they tended to vote Republican. Since then, voters in Suffolk County have joined the rest of the New York metro area in shunning a Republican party that has been run increasingly by politicians with southern accents.

The 2d Congressional District of New York includes most of western Suffolk County, part of the town of Islip and a small portion of Nassau County—Plainview, Woodbury and part of Jericho. For the most part, the 2d is the humbler part of Long Island: further east than most of the fashionable commuter suburbs, well south of the picturesque North Shore, not as far east as the ritzy Hamptons, and, aside from a handful of ferry-only resort towns on Fire Island, located inland from the southern shore. With some of the lowest-priced housing on the Island, this part of Long Island has been attracting young families and minorities. Brentwood, settled in 1851 as part of a free-love social experiment that lasted 13 years, is now more than half Hispanic; once a destination for Puerto Ricans, it has been populated by Salvadorans, Guatemalans and Mexicans. Illegal immigration has been a divisive issue in Suffolk County; in 2006, officials barred day laborers from loitering on public roads while looking for work. Though the 2d is historically Republican, it voted for Al Gore and John Kerry. George W. Bush's performance spiked here in 2004, but not by enough to carry the district. In 2005, corruption-plagued Republicans lost influence in their long-time bastion of Islip.

The congressman from the 2d District is Steve Israel, a Democrat first elected in 2000. He grew up in Wantagh and graduated from George Washington University in 1983. While in college, he worked full-time on Capitol Hill, first as a constituent correspondent for Robert Matsui of California, then as a legislative assistant for Richard Ottinger of New York. After college Israel returned to Long Island, where he was Suffolk director for the American Jewish Congress, fundraising director for Touro Law School and assistant for intergovernmental relations to Suffolk County Executive Patrick Halpin for three years. Then he started his own public relations and marketing firm and was president and CEO of the Institute on the Holocaust and the Law. In 1993 Israel was the only Democrat elected to the Huntington Town Council, where he made a reputation as a bipartisan leader who helped revive the town's finances.

Israel had not been planning to run until May 2000 when Rudolph Giuliani suddenly dropped out of the Senate race against Hillary Rodham Clinton and 2d District incumbent Rick Lazio announced he was running for the Senate. In the September primary, Israel squeaked out a 45%-41% victory. In the general, he faced Republican Joan Johnson, who had an appealing story. A 66-year old Florida native who grew up in segregated areas and moved to New York to become a schoolteacher, she would have been the first black Republican woman elected to Congress. As the elected town clerk of Islip since 1991, she had the Suffolk County party's supposed organizational muscle behind her. But, despite help from Lazio, Johnson was a disappointing candidate. She pulled a TV ad attacking Israel for voting to raise taxes after Israel protested that he had opposed tax increases. Israel won by a surprisingly easy 48%-35%.

In the House, Israel's voting record is moderate but a tad more liberal on cultural issues. In an early sign of his connections and knowledge of House politics, he was elected as the freshman on the

Democratic Steering Committee. Israel joined the Blue Dogs and was one of 28 House Democrats who voted for the House-Senate agreement on George W. Bush's tax cuts; he supported the use of force in Iraq, but said in April 2006 that the case for war was based on a "false pretense." After irritating Democratic leaders by voting for the Republicans' prescription drug bill in 2002 because of a provision that increased annual Medicare payments to HMOs on Long Island, he partly redeemed himself with Democratic leaders by voting against the Medicare/prescription drug bill in 2003. But he burned some bridges when he favored Steny Hoyer over Nancy Pelosi for minority whip.

Israel's legislative interests have ranged widely. He has sought to prohibit "coercive and abusive religious proselytizing" at the Air Force Academy; in 2006, he joined a compromise directing the academies to reinstate previous policies. To promote civility and bipartisanship, he joined with Illinois Republican Tim Johnson in February 2005 to form the Center Aisle Caucus; its impact seemed minimal. Israel believes that national Democrats can learn something from the successes of centrist Democrats on Long Island. They prevailed locally, he said, by protecting national security, balanced budgets, and civil and human rights. The party icon, Israel added, should be former Senator Scoop Jackson of Washington, whose views are hardly in today's Democratic mainstream.

When Lazio decided not to run again for this seat in March 2002, local Republicans grumbled about his delay in deciding, and quietly threw in the towel. Israel won 58%-40% and since then, he has become entrenched. His position was further secured in 2007 with a seat on Appropriations, useful for delivering federal dollars back home and a sign that he had mended fences with Pelosi.

THIRD DISTRICT

Rep. Peter King (R)

Elected 1992, 8th term; b. Apr. 5, 1944, Manhattan; home, Seaford; St. Francis Col., B.A. 1965, U. of Notre Dame, J.D. 1968; Catholic; married (Rosemary).

Military Career: Army Natl. Guard, 1968-73.

Elected Office: Hempstead Town Cncl., 1977-81; Nassau Cnty. Comptroller, 1981-92.

Professional Career: Practicing atty., 1968-72, 1978-81; Dep. Atty., Nassau Cnty., 1972-74; Exec. Asst., Nassau Cnty. Exec., 1974-76, Gen. Cnsl., 1977.

DC Office: 436 CHOB, 20515, 202-225-7896; Fax: 202-226-2279; Web site: peteking.house.gov.

District Offices: Massapequa Park, 516-541-4225; Suffolk County, 631-541-4225.

Committees: *Financial Services* (5th of 33 R): Housing & Community Opportunity; Capital Markets, Insurance & Government Sponsored Enterprises; Financial Institutions & Consumer Credit. *Homeland Security* (RMM of 15 R).

Group Ratings

	ADA	ACLU	AFS	LCV	ITIC	NTU	COC	ACU	CFG	FRC
2006	5	9	14	8	100	49	100	76	44	85
2005	0	—	0	11	—	52	89	83	52	83

National Journal Ratings

	2005 LIB	—	2005 CONS		2006 LIB	—	2006 CONS
Economic	47%	—	52%		40%	—	60%
Social	36%	—	64%		39%	—	60%
Foreign	23%	—	73%		17%	—	73%

Key Votes of the 109th Congress

1. Estate Tax Repeal	Y	5. Limit Interstate Abortion	Y	9. Build Border Fence	Y
2. Limit CAFE Standards	N	6. Extend Patriot Act	Y	10. CAFTA	Y
3. FY06 Spending Curb	Y	7. Bar Same Sex Marriage	Y	11. Oppose Iraq Withdrawal	Y
4. Drilling in ANWR	Y	8. Stem Cell Research $	N	12. Detainee Tribunals	Y

Election Results

2006 general	Peter King (R-C-Ind) 101,787	(56%)	($2,075,502)
	David Mejias (D-WF) 79,843	(44%)	($908,135)
2006 primary	Peter King (R) 11,077	(84%)	
	Robert Previdi (R) 2,110	(16%)	
2004 general	Peter King (R-C-Ind) 171,259	(63%)	($536,345)
	Blair Mathies (D) 100,737	(37%)	($212,580)

Prior Winning Percentages: 2002 (72%); 2000 (60%); 1998 (64%); 1996 (55%); 1994 (59%); 1992 (50%)

The People		Race/Ethnic Origin	Ancestry	
Area size:	393 sq. mi.	86.9% White	Italian: 23.1%	Irish: 17.7%
Urban population:	99.6%	2.1% Black	German: 12.0%	
Rural population:	0.4%	3.0% Asian	**2004 Presidential Vote**	
Pop. 2000:	654,361	0.1% Native Am.	Bush (R) 162,181	(52%)
Pop. 2005 (est):	639,679	0.0% Hawaiian	Kerry (D) 147,317	(47%)
Median income:	$70,561	1.0% Two+ races	Other 4,332	(1%)
Poverty status:	4.3%	0.1% Other	**2000 Presidential Vote**	
Military veterans:	11.8%	6.9% Hispanic Origin	Gore (D) 150,165	(52%)
			Bush (R) 127,869	(44%)
			Other 10,251	(4%)
			Cook Partisan Voting Index: D + 2	

Occupation	Blue collar: 17.0%	White collar: 69.3%	Gray collar: 13.6%

September 1947 was a pivotal moment in American history—the month when 300 families moved into 750-square-foot houses that sold for $6,990, with no money down for veterans. This was Levittown—America's first mass-produced suburb, where delivery trucks dropped off piles of pre-fabricated materials 60 feet apart, so that roving teams of specialized workers could assemble them with power tools. By the time the final house was sold for $9,500 in November 1951, Levittown, a onetime potato field, had become synonymous with instant suburbanization. Southern State Parkway, the road that drew New York City's working- and middle-class families out to Long Island, was originally constructed in the 1920s by the legendary city-builder Robert Moses as a way of linking New Yorkers (at least those affluent enough to own a car) with the newly constructed Jones Beach State Park, which has been visited since 1929 by more than 500 million people (and it's not true that all were there on the same day!). Three decades later, Moses widened the parkway to accommodate the growing ranks of long-distance commuters who populated Long Island's bedroom communities and worked in New York City. More than a half-century later, aging Nassau County is all but built out; it is sometimes referred to as the nation's "first mature suburb." Nassau County's population, 450,000 in 1940, zoomed to 1.3 million in 1960 and 1.4 million in 1970. In recent years it has stabilized at 1.3 million.

In this first modern suburb, Nassau County created what may have been the nation's premier county Republican machine—among other pols, it produced former Hempstead supervisor and later three-term Senator Alfonse D'Amato. This was one of the highest-salaried, highest-spending local governments in America—one that thrived until the late 1990s, when fiscal laxity dropped the county's credit rating to near junk-bond status, despite tax rates that were among the highest in the country. Voters rebelled in 1999, giving Democrats their first-ever majority in the county legislature, and in 2001 elected Democrat Thomas Suozzi as county executive. He has shaken up local government, and criticized New York state government for its imposition of costly mandates and tax increases, agreed to by Assembly Democrats and Senate Republicans; he not only opposed Republican incumbents but also Democrats in primaries. But he fared poorly against Eliot Spitzer in the 2006 Democratic primary for governor.

The 3d Congressional District of New York includes roughly half of Nassau County. It covers much of the southern shoreline of Long Island, taking in the old railroad resort of Long Beach, plus Baldwin, Merrick and Massapequa in Nassau County and Amityville, Lindenhurst, most of Babylon, Bay Shore and Islip in Suffolk County. From there, the 3d runs north all the way to Long Island Sound, where old estates—including Sagamore Hill, the home Theodore Roosevelt built on Cold Spring Harbor in 1885—alternate with more modest homes built for servants and newer subdivision mansions. Most of the people in the district live in towns strung along either side of Sunrise Highway or just off the Southern or Northern State Parkways: Levittown, Syosset, Hicksville, home to Billy Joel, and Bethpage, home to a major Northrop Grumman facility. While few of greater New York's wealthiest live in the 3d, the overall level of affluence is high. September

11 seemed to affect voting here in 2004: Al Gore carried this suburban district by 52%-44% in 2000, but it broke sharply toward George W. Bush in 2004, giving him a 52%-47% win.

The congressman from the 3d District is Peter King, a Republican first elected in 1992. King grew up in Sunnyside, Queens; his parents were Irish immigrants and Democrats, his father an NYPD detective. He went to St. Francis College and law school at Notre Dame, and clerked one summer at Richard Nixon's law firm with a Long Islander named Rudolph Giuliani. After school he followed the trek to the suburbs and became part of the Nassau County Republican machine. He started working as a lawyer and staffer in county government in 1972, at 28; in 1981 he became county comptroller. When 22-year Republican Congressman Norman Lent retired in 1992, King won the Republican primary 2–1. In the general, King ran as a political insider, fiscal conservative and abortion opponent; he won by just 50%-46%. He has not faced a close reelection since then.

King has a middle-of-the-House voting record, more conservative on foreign issues, but with distinctive interests and accents. He is against abortion, racial quotas and preferences, bilingual education, gun control and the National Endowment for the Arts. He is for English-only laws and against aid to illegal immigrants. He came to the House as one of the nation's strongest supporters of the Irish Republican Army; within days of his election in 1992 he flew to Belfast to meet with leaders of Sinn Fein, the IRA's political arm. In the 1998 negotiations finale, King carried messages between the IRA and the Irish government. His cooperation with President Clinton may help to explain why King in 1998 voted against impeachment. But in March 2005, after Sinn Fein/IRA's suspected involvement in a recent bank robbery and a highly-publicized murder, King called for the IRA to disband. He often seems more comfortable with Democrats and labor leaders—the kind of people he dealt with in Nassau County, than with southern or western Republicans.

After the September 11 attacks, in which 160 of his constituents died, King became more of a party regular. He hailed Bush's $20 billion spending pledge for New York City and state, and attacked Democrats' criticism of how that was handled. He stuck with President Bush in his opposition to labor protections at the new Homeland Security Department. His focus on preventing a repeat of 9/11 led to his big opportunity to move into the power ranks of the House: After Christopher Cox resigned to become chairman of the Securities and Exchange Commission, GOP leaders in September 2005 tapped King to succeed him as chairman of the Homeland Security Committee. A major part of his job, he said, was to "articulate the Republican view on homeland security." In February 2006, he was the first House Republican to attack the Bush administration's plan to give control of six major U.S. ports to a company in Dubai, and he subsequently helped to enact tighter controls on port security. He called for a criminal investigation of *The New York Times* after its June 2006 report on an international financial monitoring program that seeks terrorists. In the minority in 2007, he criticized the failure of Democrats to pursue bipartisanship.

Over the years, King has been a provocative presence on broadcast chat shows. He also gained attention with two novels about politics and diplomacy in Northern Ireland; Bill Clinton wrote a flattering blurb for *Deliver Us from Evil*, in which a thinly-disguised Long Island congressman is the protagonist. His latest novel, *Vale of Tears,* focused on Muslim extremists and their control of many mosques in the United States; some Democrats condemned his comments as inflammatory. After the 2004 election, he decried the woes of the New York Republican Party, including its loss of local offices in Nassau County, and said that it had "no overwhelming vision or course." After Suffolk County legislator David Bishop decided not to run against King in 2006 because national Democrats would not commit to sufficient funding, freshman Nassau County legislator David Mejias stepped forward, got an endorsement from the AFL-CIO and sought to link King to Bush and "special interests." But in a dismal year for Republicans in New York, King won 56%-44%—solid evidence that he keeps a close eye on his district.

FOURTH DISTRICT

Rep. Carolyn McCarthy (D)

Elected 1996, 6th term; b. Jan. 5, 1944, Brooklyn; home, Mineola; Glen Cove Nursing Schl., L.P.N. 1964; Catholic; widowed.

Professional Career: Nurse, 1964-93; Gun control activist, 1993-96.

DC Office: 106 CHOB, 20515, 202-225-5516; Fax: 202-225-5758; Web site: carolynmccarthy.house.gov.

District Offices: Garden City, 516-739-3008.

Committees: *Education & Labor* (8th of 27 D): Healthy Families & Communities (Chmn.); Health, Employment, Labor & Pensions. *Financial Services* (16th of 37 D): Oversight & Investigations; Capital Markets, Insurance & Government Sponsored Enterprises; Financial Institutions & Consumer Credit.

Group Ratings

	ADA	ACLU	AFS	LCV	ITIC	NTU	COC	ACU	CFG	FRC
2006	90	81	100	100	71	10	47	20	8	0
2005	90	—	100	94	—	16	50	8	11	17

National Journal Ratings

	2005 LIB	—	2005 CONS	2006 LIB	—	2006 CONS
Economic	71%	—	28%	79%	—	18%
Social	69%	—	30%	70%	—	30%
Foreign	61%	—	38%	70%	—	28%

Key Votes of the 109th Congress

1. Estate Tax Repeal	Y	5. Limit Interstate Abortion	N	9. Build Border Fence	Y
2. Limit CAFE Standards	N	6. Extend Patriot Act	N	10. CAFTA	N
3. FY06 Spending Curb	N	7. Bar Same Sex Marriage	N	11. Oppose Iraq Withdrawal	Y
4. Drilling in ANWR	N	8. Stem Cell Research $	Y	12. Detainee Tribunals	N

Election Results

2006 general	Carolyn McCarthy (D-Ind-WF)	101,861	(65%)	($1,368,799)
	Martin Blessinger (R-C)	55,050	(35%)	($112,122)
2006 primary	Carolyn McCarthy (D)	unopposed		
2004 general	Carolyn McCarthy (D-Ind-WF)	159,969	(63%)	($1,688,005)
	James Garner (R-C)	94,141	(37%)	($304,521)

Prior Winning Percentages: 2002 (56%); 2000 (61%); 1998 (53%); 1996 (57%)

The People		Race/Ethnic Origin	Ancestry	
Area size:	103 sq. mi.	62.3% White	Italian: 17.5%	Irish: 12.4%
Urban population:	100.0%	17.6% Black	German: 8.0%	
Rural population:	0.0%	4.5% Asian	**2004 Presidential Vote**	
Pop. 2000:	654,360	0.1% Native Am.	Kerry (D) 153,546	(55%)
Pop. 2005 (est):	664,857	0.0% Hawaiian	Bush (R) 124,617	(44%)
Median income:	$66,799	1.6% Two+ races	Other 3,178	(1%)
Poverty status:	6.4%	0.3% Other	**2000 Presidential Vote**	
Military veterans:	9.9%	13.6% Hispanic Origin	Gore (D) 156,276	(59%)
			Bush (R) 99,263	(38%)
			Other 8,612	(3%)
			Cook Partisan Voting Index: D + 9	

Occupation   Blue collar: 16.6%   White collar: 67.9%   Gray collar: 15.5%

By the mid-20th century, Nassau County changed from almost entirely rural to almost entirely suburban. One of its first suburbs was Garden City, with its wide avenues and single-family homes, laid out more than a century ago by New York retailer A.T. Stewart at a time when reformers were urging that new communities retain the commercial vitality and social interaction of the city within a setting that preserved the healthful openness of the countryside. After World War II, freeways replaced strip highways and shopping centers sprang up at intersections, but many of the middle- and upper-income residents here continue to depend on the Long Island Railroad, with new construction planned to speed them to jobs in New York City. Garden City has maintained high real estate prices and is surrounded by some of Nassau County's key institutions: the county seat of Mineola; Hofstra University in Hempstead; Roosevelt Field, where Charles Lindbergh took off for Paris, now a shopping center; and the inelegant Nassau Coliseum that county leaders hope to turn into a "town square."

The 4th Congressional District of New York includes Garden City and the towns all around. It has several suburbs just north of the Jericho Turnpike—New Hyde Park, Mineola, Westbury—as well as a large swath of southern Nassau County east of the Queens County line. This territory includes communities like the surviving Republican citadel of Hempstead, Uniondale, Rockville Center and ethnically diverse Valley Stream, as well as the "Five Towns"—the railway suburbs of Lawrence, Inwood, Cedarhurst, Hewlett and Woodmere—many of which have more students at private schools (mostly yeshivas) than in public schools. Nassau County has traditionally been Republican, and both Garden City and heavily Catholic East Meadow remain that way. But the Five Towns are heavily Democratic, and about one-third of the district's residents are black or Hispanic. Elmont, near the Queens line, once heavily white, now has a large Caribbean and Latin American population. The traditional Republican heritage in the 4th District is becoming a dim memory; the county legislature is now led by a Democratic majority, something that would have seemed unimaginable just a few decades ago.

The congresswoman from the 4th District is Carolyn McCarthy, a Democrat first elected in 1996. She was born in Brooklyn, trained as a nurse, married and raised a family on Long Island; originally, she was a Republican. In 1993 her husband was killed and her son seriously injured in the "Long Island Railroad Massacre," when a gunman opened fire on passengers as the train crossed the Nassau County line. McCarthy spoke movingly at the killer's trial and her strength in tragedy won many admirers. She began campaigning for gun control, and in 1995 lobbied her Congressman Daniel Frisa to vote against repeal of the assault weapons ban, unsuccessfully. McCarthy inquired about running against Frisa in the primary, but Nassau County Republicans discouraged this. Democrats had been eyeing the seat for some time and recruited her. McCarthy initially knew little about politics. When told that Minority Leader Dick Gephardt wanted to meet her, she reportedly asked, "Who's Dick Gephardt?" But she learned quickly. As the Democratic nominee, she called for gun control and attacked Frisa as too close to Newt Gingrich. Frisa disappeared in the campaign's final week, did not show up at his election night party and never made a concession statement. McCarthy won 57%-41%.

In the House, McCarthy compiled a voting record among the least liberal of New York Democrats. Passionately in favor of gun control measures, she called for childproof locks on handguns, fines for parents if a child gets a handgun and shows it in public, and jail terms if a crime is committed with a gun. With support from the NRA, the House approved her bill to assist states to gain more access to the federal background check system for gun buyers. The sniper spree in the Washington D.C. area gave her the opportunity to gain approval in the House of her bill—the Our Lady of Peace Act—to strengthen laws prohibiting the mentally ill from buying guns, again with NRA backing. In 2004, she led the unsuccessful effort to force a House vote on extending the assault weapon ban. Majority Leader Tom DeLay said that there were not enough votes to extend the ban and refused to schedule a vote; McCarthy criticized George W. Bush for "winking" at the NRA on the issue, but she also blamed Democrats for their lack of support. She continued her crusade with a call to ban .50 caliber sniper rifles. In 2005, she successfully opposed part of an amendment to an anti-gang bill that inadvertently would have permitted grade-schoolers to pack a pistol while they were with a parent.

With only limited success on gun issues, McCarthy has broadened her portfolio, using her experience as a mother and nurse to take an interest in education and health-care issues. She stood at Bush's side in 2002 when he signed her bill to give incentives to hospitals in hiring more nurses and remedy the acute shortages. She surprised people on some votes, opposing the partial-birth abortion ban and backing the use of force in Iraq; in 2006, she was one of two New York Democrats to vote for a Republican resolution supporting the war in Iraq. In 2007, she chaired the revamped Education and Labor Subcommittee on Healthy Families and Communities, with issues ranging from child nutrition and gang violence to low-income home energy assistance.

At home, Republicans have thrashed around to line up opposition. She had a tough time in 2002, when she was challenged by ophthalmologist Marilyn O'Grady, who took a hard line on terrorism and immigration, opposed abortions, and ran ads that attacked McCarthy for taking a 1998 contribution from Barbra Streisand. Although O'Grady received little national attention or party support, McCarthy's margin shrunk to 56%-43%. In 2004, James Garner, the mayor of Hempstead and head of the U.S. Conference of Mayors, sought to rally support as a black Republican and called McCarthy a one-issue lawmaker. But Garner was criticized for local problems in Hempstead, and national Republicans showed no indication that they viewed this district as an opportunity. McCarthy won, 63%-37%. In 2006, she had her biggest win, 65%-35%, against retired Nassau County police sergeant Martin Blessinger.

FIFTH DISTRICT

Rep. Gary Ackerman (D)

Elected Mar. 1983, 12th full term; b. Nov. 19, 1942, Brooklyn; home, Jamaica Estates; Queens Col., B.A. 1965; Jewish; married (Rita).

Elected Office: NY Senate, 1978-83.

Professional Career: Jr. High schl. teacher, 1966-70; Editor & publisher, *Queens Tribune*, 1970-78; Pres., advertising agcy., 1972-78.

DC Office: 2243 RHOB, 20515, 202-225-2601; Fax: 202-225-1589; Web site: www.house.gov/ackerman.

District Offices: Bayside, 718-423-2154.

Committees: *Financial Services* (8th of 37 D): Capital Markets, Insurance & Government Sponsored Enterprises; Financial Institutions & Consumer Credit. *Foreign Affairs* (3d of 27 D): Middle East & South Asia (Chmn.); Asia, the Pacific & the Global Environment.

Group Ratings

	ADA	ACLU	AFS	LCV	ITIC	NTU	COC	ACU	CFG	FRC
2006	95	100	100	92	43	15	47	8	14	0
2005	95	—	100	94	—	12	37	4	3	0

National Journal Ratings

	2005 LIB	—	2005 CONS		2006 LIB	—	2006 CONS
Economic	94%	—	0%		73%	—	26%
Social	92%	—	7%		96%	—	3%
Foreign	71%	—	28%		75%	—	23%

Key Votes of the 109th Congress

1. Estate Tax Repeal	N	5. Limit Interstate Abortion	N	9. Build Border Fence	N
2. Limit CAFE Standards	N	6. Extend Patriot Act	N	10. CAFTA	N
3. FY06 Spending Curb	N	7. Bar Same Sex Marriage	N	11. Oppose Iraq Withdrawal	N
4. Drilling in ANWR	N	8. Stem Cell Research $	Y	12. Detainee Tribunals	N

Election Results

2006 general	Gary Ackerman (D-Ind-WF) .... unopposed		($844,526)
2006 primary	Gary Ackerman (D) .... unopposed		
2004 general	Gary Ackerman (D-Ind-WF) 119,726	(71%)	($675,631)
	Stephen Graves (R-C) 46,867	(28%)	
	Other 1,248	(1%)	

Prior Winning Percentages: 2002 (92%); 2000 (68%); 1998 (65%); 1996 (64%); 1994 (55%); 1992 (52%); 1990 (100%); 1988 (100%); 1986 (77%); 1984 (69%); 1983 (49%)

The People		Race/Ethnic Origin	Ancestry	
Area size:	85 sq. mi.	44.2% White	Italian: 9.7%	Irish: 5.8%
Urban population:	100.0%	5.1% Black	German: 3.7%	
Rural population:	0.0%	24.5% Asian	**2004 Presidential Vote**	
Pop. 2000:	654,361	0.1% Native Am.	Kerry (D) 128,252	(63%)
Pop. 2005 (est):	649,880	0.0% Hawaiian	Bush (R) 74,635	(36%)
Median income:	$51,156	2.1% Two+ races	Other 1,834	(1%)
Poverty status:	12.1%	0.4% Other	**2000 Presidential Vote**	
Military veterans:	6.7%	23.5% Hispanic Origin	Gore (D) 127,288	(67%)
			Bush (R) 56,027	(30%)
			Other 6,256	(3%)
			Cook Partisan Voting Index: D +18	

Occupation   Blue collar: 18.2%   White collar: 65.2%   Gray collar: 16.6%

Queens is to most Americans the mystery borough, little known even to many Manhattanites, though it contains both LaGuardia and Kennedy airports. Some of it is almost suburban: Bayside, Douglaston and Little Neck are upper-middle income neighborhoods far beyond the subway lines, with detached houses with driveways and views across the water. Other Queens neighborhoods are more modest, with crowded houses on side streets and apartment buildings on avenues. In the past two decades, Queens has become the number one immigrant destination in New York City and quite possibly the most diverse place in the world. Corona was once predominantly Italian and black (Louis Armstrong, Duke Ellington and Malcolm X lived here); today, there is a large Latin American community, with many Dominican immigrants and also many Asians—a modern-day melting pot. Flushing, long a modest-income Jewish and white ethnic neighborhood, is now the biggest Asian neighborhood in New York. West of 138th Street it is dominated by Taiwanese and ethnic Chinese from Malaysia, Vietnam and Thailand; shops there have a more urban "Chinatown" feel, and feature an amazing variety of delicacies. (New York has three Chinatowns—one each in Manhattan, Brooklyn and the largest in Queens.) East of 138th Street is predominantly Korean, with development following a more suburban pattern. As Chinese businesses moved into Flushing's Main Street commercial strip, Korean storeowners moved east to Union Street, a major north-south artery, and Northern Boulevard. In 2004, Chinese businessman Jimmy Meng from Flushing defeated long-time machine incumbent Barry Grodenchik in a Democratic primary for the state Assembly, an indication that local Asian political power was rising; the city's most ambitious Asian politician may be City Councilman John Liu of Flushing. Just east of Flushing is Flushing Meadow, the huge drainage basin and former dumping ground that hosted two World's Fairs (1939 and 1964) and now is home to the U.S. Open tennis tournament, and countless informal soccer games played among Queens' many immigrant groups.

Just a few miles but a world away is the North Shore of Long Island. For a century it has had an upper-crust ambiance—peninsulas jutting out into Long Island Sound, the vast green lawns, and the great capitalist mansions that inspired East Egg and West Egg in *The Great Gatsby*. In the 19th century, millionaires used steam yachts to commute from Manhattan to their estates here. During Prohibition, the richest people in business and entertainment spent their leisure time playing croquet while their servants unloaded bootleggers' shipments at private docks. Inland, behind the expansive lawns, Long Island was still farm country, with little villages clustered at railroad stations, occasional colonial era houses, and acres of billboard-strewn wasteland along the highways to New York City. By the middle of the 20th century, the city grew out, and the Great Neck and Sands Point peninsulas became affluent, predominantly Jewish suburbs with thick hedges enveloping stately Tudor homes. Lately, many wealthy Asians have moved here.

The 5th Congressional District of New York takes in this territory in Queens and suburban Nassau County. Roughly half the population is Asian or Hispanic. The district includes most of Queens east of Flushing Meadow and north of Union Turnpike—Flushing, Bayside, Douglaston, Little Neck (but not the airports). And it includes the northwest corner of Nassau County—Great Neck, super-rich Sands Point, Lake Success, Port Washington, and Kings Point, home of the U.S. Merchant Marine Academy. Both the Queens and Nassau County portions of the district have long voted heavily Democratic.

The congressman from the 5th District is Gary Ackerman, a Democrat first elected in 1983. Ackerman grew up in Flushing, taught junior high school, ran an advertising agency, started the weekly *Queens Tribune* in 1970 and sold it to publisher Jerry Finkelstein in 1978 (and then was part of an investment group that repurchased it in 2002). That same year he was elected to the New York

Senate. He won his seat in the House in a special election from a district that was then centered in the heavily Jewish apartment complexes in central Queens. Ackerman is a colorful character, who always wears a white carnation and lives on a houseboat in Washington (the *Unsinkable II*, successor to the *Unsinkable I*, which sunk); he hosts an annual "Taste of New York" fundraiser, featuring pastrami sandwiches and stuffed cabbage, with waiters imported from New York. Acerbic but humorous, he is a pungent speaker, with a humor that makes even opponents smile.

Ackerman has a penchant for taking on worthy but neglected causes; his once solidly liberal voting record has moderated on foreign policy issues. Despite opposition from many constituents, including his wife, Ackerman defended his vote to authorize war in Iraq; by 2005, he said that he regretted it. He backed the Bush administration's handling of the Israeli-Palestinian conflict; as ranking Democrat on the Middle East and Central Asia Subcommittee, he met frequently with leaders in the region. A long-time supporter of India (Queens is home to a large and fast-growing Indian-American population), he urged Bush not to sell sophisticated weapons and F-16s to Pakistan but he's been willing to offer counter-narcotics, anti-terrorism and peacekeeping aid to Pakistan. He enthusiastically supported the nuclear energy deal with India. In the majority, he became chairman of the Middle East and South Asia Subcommittee, a panel of great interest to his constituents—and renamed from its previous incarnation as the Middle East and *Central* Asia Subcommittee. On domestic issues, he helped to pass the "Baby AIDS" bill requiring HIV testing of newborns and disclosure of the results to the mother; the bill also bars insurers from terminating coverage because of AIDS test results. Still, he occasionally stands out as a lonely liberal, as when he was one of only three members to vote against a House resolution criticizing a federal appeals court that ruled unconstitutional the phrase "under God" in the Pledge of Allegiance. Ackerman became knowledgeable on "mad cow" disease, and pushed for a ban on the commercial slaughter of downer cows. In July 2003, the House defeated his amendment, 199-202; the White House later took regulatory action to adopt the ban.

Ackerman survived redistricting in 1992 when it moved him farther out on Long Island and into a district where two other incumbents also lived; both of them retired. He regularly wins reelection by large margins; the chief threat that he faces is a candidacy from immigrant communities—with or without redistricting.

SIXTH DISTRICT

Rep. Gregory Meeks (D)

Elected Feb. 1998, 5th full term; b. Sept. 25, 1953, Harlem; home, Far Rockaway; Adelphi U., B.A., 1975, Howard U., J.D., 1978; Baptist; married (Simone-Marie).

Elected Office: NY Assembly, 1992-98.

Professional Career: Asst. Dist. Atty., Queens Co., NY, 1978-84; NY St. Comm. of Investigations, 1984-85; Judge, NY St. Workers Compensation Bd., 1985-92.

DC Office: 2342 RHOB, 20515, 202-225-3461; Fax: 202-226-4169; Web site: www.house.gov/meeks.

District Offices: Far Rockaway, 718-327-9791; Jamaica, 718-725-6000.

Committees: *Financial Services* (11th of 37 D): Capital Markets, Insurance & Government Sponsored Enterprises; Domestic and International Monetary Policy, Trade & Technology. *Foreign Affairs* (10th of 27 D): Western Hemisphere; Asia, the Pacific & the Global Environment; International Organizations, Human Rights & Oversight.

Group Ratings

	ADA	ACLU	AFS	LCV	ITIC	NTU	COC	ACU	CFG	FRC
2006	90	100	100	83	100	18	57	8	20	0
2005	90	—	100	72	—	16	59	12	20	0

National Journal Ratings

	2005 LIB	—	2005 CONS		2006 LIB	—	2006 CONS
Economic	65%	—	35%		66%	—	34%
Social	91%	—	9%		83%	—	16%
Foreign	85%	—	14%		67%	—	31%

Key Votes of the 109th Congress

1. Estate Tax Repeal	N	5. Limit Interstate Abortion	N	9. Build Border Fence	N
2. Limit CAFE Standards	Y	6. Extend Patriot Act	N	10. CAFTA	Y
3. FY06 Spending Curb	N	7. Bar Same Sex Marriage	N	11. Oppose Iraq Withdrawal	N
4. Drilling in ANWR	N	8. Stem Cell Research $	Y	12. Detainee Tribunals	N

Election Results

2006 general	Gregory Meeks (D) .... unopposed	($935,949)
2006 primary	Gregory Meeks (D) .... unopposed	
2004 general	Gregory Meeks (D-WF) .... unopposed	($537,089)

Prior Winning Percentages: 2002 (97%); 2000 (100%); 1998 (100%); 1998 (57%)

The People		Race/Ethnic Origin	Ancestry	
Area size:	46 sq. mi.	12.8% White	West Indian: 15.9% Italian: 3.4%	
Urban population:	100.0%	52.1% Black	USA: 3.0%	
Rural population:	0.0%	8.9% Asian	**2004 Presidential Vote**	
Pop. 2000:	654,361	0.5% Native Am.	Kerry (D) 154,468	(84%)
Pop. 2005 (est):	661,299	0.1% Hawaiian	Bush (R) 27,352	(15%)
Median income:	$43,546	6.1% Two+ races	Other 1,128	(1%)
Poverty status:	14.5%	2.6% Other	**2000 Presidential Vote**	
Military veterans:	6.2%	16.9% Hispanic Origin	Gore (D) 145,684	(87%)
			Bush (R) 17,632	(10%)
			Other 4,874	(3%)
			Cook Partisan Voting Index: D +38	
Occupation	Blue collar: 20.5%	White collar: 57.4%	Gray collar: 22.1%	

The eastern edge of Queens has been an important transportation hub for New York for almost 250 years. In the 1750s, the British laid out what is now Jamaica Avenue to help them defend Long Island. In the 1830s—nearly a century before most present-day commuters would have guessed—the Long Island Rail Road was built here. Today, this corner of Queens is sliced by the Belt Parkway and the Van Wyck Expressway two integral parts of Robert Moses' mid-century highway network—and is home to John F. Kennedy International Airport, a leading port of entry for air travelers entering the United States. Jamaica is so well situated with transportation links that officials have worked mightily to improve its commercial vitality. The old elevated subway line on Jamaica Avenue has been removed and buried underground, so that shoppers could have a less claustrophobic experience. Now, billions of dollars are being spent for a Long Island Rail Road line from Queens to Grand Central Station in Manhattan.

This part of Queens—rather than Harlem or Brooklyn—is home to New York City's largest collection of middle-class black homeowners; their median income is higher than in white households in Queens. The neighborhoods of Springfield Gardens and Laurelton, St. Albans and Rosedale, Cambria Heights and Queens Village consist of block upon block of low-rise, frame and brick houses built mostly from the 1920s to the 1950s. There was a small black community in South Jamaica half a century ago, and since then many black families have bought houses and raised their families in neighborhoods that fan east from Jamaica. They fought to maintain the relatively spacious streets, relishing the light in their windows, the safe schools and the good neighborhood stores; these areas never experienced the kind of riots that damaged Harlem and parts of Brooklyn.

The 6th Congressional District of New York contains all of these southeast Queens neighborhoods, plus others less affluent and orderly, in southern Queens. It is bounded on the north, more or less, by the Jackie Robinson Parkway, on the east by the Nassau County line and on the west by Cross Bay Boulevard; to the south it includes part of the Rockaway Peninsula across Jamaica Bay from the rest of Queens. Richmond Hill and Ozone Park, previously white ethnic neighborhoods, now have sizable numbers of Latinos and South Asians. South Ozone Park is home to many immigrants from Guyana, Jamaica, Haiti, the Dominican Republic and Trinidad and Tobago.

The Rockaway portions of the district, despite being just a few blocks from the beach, are a relatively undeveloped backwater, leveled by urban renewal in the late 1960s but never rebuilt, and now home to many of Queens' nursing homes; one area, called Almost Paradise, was a popular scuba diving spot until a developer moved in. As a whole, the 6th is 52% black, 17% Hispanic and 9% Asian; if there is a common denominator, it is the amount of time 6th District residents spend traveling to work. The district is ranked as the nation's worst for commuters—at 48 minutes of mean travel time to work. Politically, the district is overwhelmingly Democratic.

The congressman from the 6th District is Gregory Meeks, a Democrat first elected in 1998 to replace Floyd Flake, who resigned to devote more time to his church. Meeks grew up in Harlem, in public housing projects. After graduating from college and law school, he moved to Far Rockaway and pursued a public sector career. He became an assistant district attorney in 1978, a staffer for the state Committee on Investigations in 1984, a workmen's comp judge in 1985; after losing a race for City Council in 1991, he was elected assemblyman in 1992. He became an ally of Flake, a minister whose Allen A.M.E. Church congregation grew from 1,400 members in 1976 to 12,000 in 2000. At the January 1998 endorsement meetings, Meeks won a bare majority of committeemen and thus became the Democratic nominee. Democratic State Senator Alton Waldon ran on the Conservative and Independence lines, and spent $100,000; Assemblywoman Barbara Clark ran an independent candidacy and Republicans had a candidate as well. But Meeks had support from Flake, Congressman Charles Rangel, Al Sharpton and Jesse Jackson. He won with 57%, to 21% for Waldon, 13% for Clark, and 9% for Republican Celestine Miller.

Meeks got Flake's seat on the Financial Services Committee and has a liberal voting record on social issues. But his record on economic issues makes him arguably the most pro-business member among New York City Democrats. In 2000, Meeks emerged as a player. As one of the final undecideds on normal trade relations with China, both sides lobbied him furiously. Among the factors that finally convinced him to support the deal: vigorous advocacy by Rangel and Bill Clinton; support by United Parcel Service, a major employer at Kennedy airport; a White House-sponsored trip to China where he met with senior officials and saw first-hand the economic growth; and a last-minute agreement by the White House and Speaker Dennis Hastert to extend tax breaks and public investment to distressed urban and rural areas. In July 2005, Meeks voted for the Central American Free Trade Agreement, which also was approved in a squeaker vote; Meeks cited increased traffic for JFK Airport, but Democratic Leader Nancy Pelosi voiced unhappiness. He has made many overseas trips, and has ranked in the top 10 of congressional travelers. All trips were cleared by the Ethics Committee, he said.

Meeks has shown a desire to advance within the party. When several House Democratic leadership positions opened after the 2002 election, he campaigned to be vice-chairman of the Democratic Caucus but was bested by James Clyburn of South Carolina. In early 2003, he was one of the first members of Congress to endorse John Kerry for president. Kerry rewarded Meeks by naming him a national co-chairman. Meeks spent considerable time with Kerry on his campaign, especially during the closing weeks, and advised him on relationships with minority groups across the nation. After the election, Meeks sought a leadership post at the Democratic National Committee, but he lost to California Congressman Mike Honda. He has been active in the centrist Democratic Leadership Council.

Locally, Meeks has sought to bring business deals to Queens by meeting with leaders of other nations, including India. He has not faced major party opposition for reelection. Some expect him to run some day for mayor, or perhaps for a Senate seat if there is an opening.

SEVENTH DISTRICT

Rep. Joseph Crowley (D)

Elected 1998, 5th term; b. Mar. 16, 1962, Elmhurst, NY; home, Elmhurst; C.U.N.Y. Queens College, B.A. 1985; Catholic; married (Kasey).

Elected Office: NY Assembly, 1986-98.

DC Office: 312 CHOB, 20515, 202-225-3965; Fax: 202-225-1909; Web site: www.crowley.house.gov.

District Offices: Bronx, 718-931-1400; Jackson Heights, 718-779-1400.

Committees: *Chief Deputy Majority Whip. Foreign Affairs* (18th of 27 D): International Organizations, Human Rights & Oversight; Terrorism, Nonproliferation & Trade. *Ways & Means* (20th of 24 D): Trade; Oversight.

Group Ratings

	ADA	ACLU	AFS	LCV	ITIC	NTU	COC	ACU	CFG	FRC
2006	95	95	100	92	50	13	57	8	17	0
2005	95	—	100	100	—	10	44	8	0	8

National Journal Ratings

	2005 LIB	—	2005 CONS	2006 LIB	—	2006 CONS
Economic	80%	—	20%	68%	—	31%
Social	78%	—	22%	86%	—	13%
Foreign	75%	—	24%	67%	—	31%

Key Votes of the 109th Congress

1. Estate Tax Repeal	N	5. Limit Interstate Abortion	N	9. Build Border Fence	N
2. Limit CAFE Standards	Y	6. Extend Patriot Act	N	10. CAFTA	N
3. FY06 Spending Curb	N	7. Bar Same Sex Marriage	N	11. Oppose Iraq Withdrawal	N
4. Drilling in ANWR	N	8. Stem Cell Research $	Y	12. Detainee Tribunals	N

Election Results

2006 general	Joseph Crowley (D-WF)	63,997	(84%)	($1,505,477)
	Kevin Brawley (R-C)	12,220	(16%)	
2006 primary	Joseph Crowley (D)	unopposed		
2004 general	Joseph Crowley (D-WF)	104,275	(81%)	($1,160,532)
	Joseph Cinquemain (R-C)	24,548	(19%)	($26,337)

Prior Winning Percentages: 2002 (73%); 2000 (72%); 1998 (69%)

The People		Race/Ethnic Origin	Ancestry	
Area size:	42 sq. mi.	27.6% White	Italian: 9.6%	Irish: 5.0%
Urban population:	100.0%	16.5% Black	West Indian: 3.6%	
Rural population:	0.0%	12.8% Asian	**2004 Presidential Vote**	
Pop. 2000:	654,360	0.2% Native Am.	Kerry (D) 129,909	(74%)
Pop. 2005 (est):	666,488	0.0% Hawaiian	Bush (R) 44,607	(25%)
Median income:	$36,990	2.7% Two+ races	Other 1,367	(1%)
Poverty status:	17.7%	0.6% Other	**2000 Presidential Vote**	
Military veterans:	6.4%	39.5% Hispanic Origin	Gore (D) 114,365	(75%)
			Bush (R) 31,682	(21%)
			Other 6,236	(4%)
			Cook Partisan Voting Index: D +28	

Occupation   Blue collar: 21.1%   White collar: 57.4%   Gray collar: 21.6%

Over the last two decades, hundreds of thousands of immigrants have been moving into many of New York City's modest neighborhoods—neighborhoods that had been emptying out as the children of the immigrants who came to New York between 1890 and 1924 died or moved to the suburbs or Florida. These are places which affluent New Yorkers and traveling journalists seldom see as they whiz by on freeways to destinations in Manhattan—rather, these are the neighborhoods pop star Jennifer Lopez sings about. Most of the housing here was built in the decades after 1910, when the subways first started connecting these neighborhoods with job sites in Manhattan. You can find many of these neighborhoods in the East Bronx, off the Bruckner Expressway and near the cluster of highways north of the Bronx-Whitestone Bridge—places like Bruckner, Morris Park, Schuylerville, and Throgs Neck, which is named after Dutchman John Throgmorton, who settled the area and farmed the land. The district includes the Hunts Point meat and produce markets, where some of the nation's toniest restaurants handpick their daily provisions from the city's largest supplier. Increasingly these neighborhoods are full of Latinos, many from Puerto Rico, but many also from the Dominican Republic and other Caribbean and Latin American countries. Lopez hails from Castle Hill; her *On the 6* album is a reference to the Number 6 train that whisked her to Manhattan auditions. Here are two massive apartment projects: Parkchester, built just before World War II by Metropolitan Life Insurance in the center of the Bronx, and sprawling Co-op City—35 buildings and more than 50,000 residents in 15,000 apartments that were built in the late 1960s by a consortium of labor unions on marshy land near Eastchester Bay. Out past the bay is City Island, a Cape Cod-like resort area with boatmakers and plenty of fish restaurants; it is hard to believe here that you are in New York City.

Across the bridges in Queens are Jackson Heights, home to Little India and a sizable Latino community; Elmhurst, a place so diverse that one local hospital counted more than 100 different languages and dialects; and Woodside, a long-settled Irish enclave with residents from 49 nations who speak 34 languages. These are the places serviced by the Number 7 elevated line—you can find Pakistanis and Peruvians, Koreans and Dominicans, Indians and Filipinos, Mexicans and Bangladeshis.

These Bronx and Queens neighborhoods are all in the 7th Congressional District of New York. The district is polyglot indeed: its population in 2000 was 17% black, 40% Hispanic and 13% Asian. Politically, the 7th District votes heavily Democratic. But more important for its political future may be those who don't vote at all. In 2006 only 76,000 people voted in this district of 661,000, less than half the 157,000 who voted in the nearby suburban 4th District.

The congressman from the 7th District is Joseph Crowley, a Democrat first elected in 1998 and effectively chosen by one man, his predecessor Tom Manton, who remained the boss of the efficient Queens County Democratic Party. Crowley grew up in Woodside, where his family was involved in politics; his uncle Walter Crowley was elected to succeed Manton on the City Council in 1984. When Walter Crowley died in 1985, Crowley wanted to succeed him, though he was only 23; Manton chose his chief of staff, Walter McCaffrey, instead. In 1986 Assemblyman Ralph Goldstein from Elmhurst died; fresh from Queens College, Crowley ran and won at 24, with support from Manton. Crowley was interested in Irish affairs and sponsored the law that requires public school students to be taught about the Irish potato famine. He played guitar and sang tenor with the Budget Blues Boys, a group of assemblymen who performed on cold Albany nights.

Crowley's elevation to Congress came suddenly. In 1998, Manton filed for reelection by the July 16 filing deadline. Then at 11:00 a.m. on July 21, he convened a meeting of Queens Democratic committeemen, announced he was retiring and got them to vote in Crowley as the Democratic nominee. Other potential candidates were not notified ahead of time and were naturally miffed, but quickly accepted the reality. Manton argued that Crowley, at 36, was in a good position to accumulate seniority and power in Washington. Crowley was plainly delighted. "What you're hearing is not so much about the process, but sour grapes. What happened here is simply that I was offered an ice cream cone, and I took it." His Republican opponent had no money and no chance. Crowley won in November 69%-26%.

Once elected, Crowley voted as a centrist Democrat and demonstrated leadership ambition. He served six months as the freshman Democrats' class president. He arrived in Congress as an abortion opponent but by 2006 he was endorsed by NARAL Pro-Choice America. The September 11 attacks struck a grievous blow to Crowley's community, with the loss of many local firefighters, including his first cousin, who was a battalion chief; he passed in the House an amendment to issue the Public Safety Officers Medal of Valor to 414 who died on September 11. He fought to change funding formulas for homeland security, which he said shortchanged New York. On the Financial Services Committee, he advocated Wall Street interests. There is a sizable Indian-American community in Queens, many of whom are foreign-born; Crowley has responded by urging the State Department to permit India to buy Patriot missile systems from the Army, and in 2006 he was an active proponent of the U.S.-India agreement on nuclear energy. He worked with Republican leaders on behalf of business interests in gaining approval of bilateral free-trade agreements; Roy

Blunt praised his efforts to secure Democratic votes. He also was prominent in securing bipartisan approval of stricter rules on foreign investment following the flap over the initial purchase of American facilities by Dubai Ports World. But he opposed the Central American free trade deal as "a step backward" for labor rights.

The earlier bitterness about how Crowley was elected in 1998 seems to have dissipated. At home, he has not faced serious opposition from either party. Redistricting radically reshaped his constituency. In the old district, Queens cast 74% of the votes; now, the Bronx casts 62% (he remains a Mets fan, though). He also has worked to help Democrats win more House seats from New York by assisting the campaigns of Tim Bishop in Suffolk County in 2002 and Brian Higgins in an open Buffalo-area seat in 2004. In 2006, Crowley initially focused on electing Michael Arcuri to the open seat of Sherwood Boehlert; that effort was successful, and Crowley also claimed a role in defeating two other upstate Republicans.

After the 2004 election, Crowley sought to chair the Democratic Congressional Campaign Committee, highlighting his fundraising connections to New York's financial community. But he suffered from having been an active supporter of Minority Whip Steny Hoyer, and the post went to Rahm Emanuel. He was named instead to lead the DCCC's Business Council, a key fundraising post, and he expressed again his interest in a leadership position. That happened a year later when the Caucus vice-chairmanship opened. Crowley campaigned aggressively as one of three candidates. But allies of Minority Leader Nancy Pelosi switched their support from Jan Schakowsky to John Larson, and Crowley lost on the second ballot. This was yet another case of bad blood between the Pelosi and Hoyer camps. Crowley remained a team player, and did some bridge-building with Pelosi and her allies. He finally got his reward after the 2006 election when she named him to a Ways and Means Committee seat. Crowley also expanded his influence as a vice-chairman of the New Democrat Coalition, while retaining his DCCC Business Council post. Back home, he became Queens Democratic chairman after Manton died in July 2006. His enthusiasm and ambition, plus his relative youth, give him plenty of opportunity to be a player in the party and the House.

EIGHTH DISTRICT

Rep. Jerrold Nadler (D)

Elected 1992, 8th full term; b. June 13, 1947, Brooklyn; home, Manhattan; Columbia U., B.A. 1970, Fordham U., J.D. 1978; Jewish; married (Joyce Miller).

Elected Office: NY Assembly, 1976-92.

Professional Career: Legis. Asst., NY Assembly, 1972; Law Clerk, 1976.

DC Office: 2334 RHOB, 20515, 202-225-5635; Fax: 202-225-6923; Web site: www.house.gov/nadler.

District Offices: Brooklyn, 718-373-3198; Manhattan, 212-367-7350.

Committees: *Judiciary* (4th of 23 D): The Constitution, Civil Rights & Civil Liberties (Chmn.); Crime, Terrorism & Homeland Security. *Transportation & Infrastructure* (6th of 41 D): Railroads, Pipelines & Hazardous Materials; Highways & Transit.

Group Ratings

	ADA	ACLU	AFS	LCV	ITIC	NTU	COC	ACU	CFG	FRC
2006	100	100	100	100	29	11	27	4	4	0
2005	100	—	100	94	—	14	35	0	3	0

National Journal Ratings

	2005 LIB	—	2005 CONS		2006 LIB	—	2006 CONS
Economic	94%	—	0%		94%	—	0%
Social	94%	—	5%		97%	—	0%
Foreign	90%	—	9%		87%	—	13%

Key Votes of the 109th Congress

1. Estate Tax Repeal	N	5. Limit Interstate Abortion	N	9. Build Border Fence	N
2. Limit CAFE Standards	N	6. Extend Patriot Act	N	10. CAFTA	N
3. FY06 Spending Curb	N	7. Bar Same Sex Marriage	N	11. Oppose Iraq Withdrawal	N
4. Drilling in ANWR	N	8. Stem Cell Research $	Y	12. Detainee Tribunals	N

Election Results

2006 general	Jerrold Nadler (D-WF)	108,536	(85%)	($764,960)
	Eleanor Friedman (R)	17,413	(14%)	
	Other	1,673	(1%)	
2006 primary	Jerrold Nadler (D)	unopposed		
2004 general	Jerrold Nadler (D-WF)	162,082	(81%)	($867,427)
	Peter Hort (R-Ind-C)	39,240	(19%)	($142,401)

Prior Winning Percentages: 2002 (76%); 2000 (81%); 1998 (86%); 1996 (82%); 1994 (82%); 1992 (81%); 1992 (100%)

The People		Race/Ethnic Origin	Ancestry	
Area size:	28 sq. mi.	68.7% White	Italian: 8.7%	Russian: 7.2%
Urban population:	100.0%	5.4% Black	Irish: 5.7%	
Rural population:	0.0%	11.0% Asian	**2004 Presidential Vote**	
Pop. 2000:	654,360	0.1% Native Am.	Kerry (D) 180,080	(72%)
Pop. 2005 (est):	707,145	0.0% Hawaiian	Bush (R) 66,948	(27%)
Median income:	$47,061	2.5% Two+ races	Other 2,723	(1%)
Poverty status:	18.7%	0.5% Other	**2000 Presidential Vote**	
Military veterans:	5.1%	11.7% Hispanic Origin	Gore (D) 162,240	(74%)
			Bush (R) 39,280	(18%)
			Other 18,448	(8%)
			Cook Partisan Voting Index: D +28	

Occupation	Blue collar: 10.1%	White collar: 79.2%	Gray collar: 10.7%

Over the course of the 20th century, New York City spread so far beyond its origins in lower Manhattan that, for a while, it became easy to forget how pivotal the southern end of the island had been in making the city what it is today. That all changed in an instant, on the morning of September 11, 2001, when Al Qaeda terrorists flew two hijacked jets into the twin towers of the World Trade Center, killing approximately 2,800 people, and laying waste to at least 13 blocks. The target was chosen deliberately: The terrorists struck the tallest buildings in America's biggest city, toppling a complex whose name embodied the reach of American capitalism. Lower Manhattan has long been home to Wall Street and the Financial District, but over the years it has embodied America's striving spirit in other ways as well. The Brooklyn Bridge, begun in 1867 just a few blocks east of the Twin Towers site and completed in 1883, was half again as long as any bridge then standing, and seven times higher than any buildings in the adjoining boroughs. The Holland Tunnel, built in 1927, was the first underwater vehicular tunnel built anywhere in the world. Just offshore stand Ellis Island, where members of the great immigration wave first set foot on American soil, and the Statue of Liberty, the symbol of freedom they saw as they sailed in.

The 8th Congressional District of New York includes all of these places. From the Battery, at the very southern tip of Manhattan Island, the 8th spreads out in two directions, north and south. As the 8th District moves up the west side of Manhattan, it takes in the Financial District; Battery Park City, the attractive modern apartments and parks built on 32 acres of infill west of the now-torn down West Side Highway; the artist lofts of sophisticated TriBeCa and shoppers' paradise of SoHo, in former warehouses and factories; Greenwich Village and the art galleries of Chelsea, New York's leading gay areas and strong voting blocs; Clinton, the new, economically diverse incarnation of the old slum Hell's Kitchen; the economically-revived Theater District and the cleaned-up Times Square, where neon signs have been replaced by digital screens; the huge Port Authority bus terminal; and long stretches of the Upper West Side, including Lincoln Center and the American Museum of Natural History, as far north as West 89th Street. Mayor Michael Bloomberg wanted to build a new $2 billion stadium near the Javits Convention Center to house the NFL Jets and the 2012 Olympics, but the state Public Authorities Control Board in 2005 rejected the plan; the Jets are staying in New Jersey and London got the Games. South from the Battery, the 8th crosses into Brooklyn, running along the Brooklyn waterfront before taking in the inland neighborhood of Borough Park and the waterside enclaves of Sea Gate, Brighton Beach and Coney Island, once known as the world's largest playground.

In both halves of the 8th District, there is a strong Jewish heritage. The city's Dutch founders came from the European country then most tolerant of Jews. German Jews came to New York in large numbers in the 19th century, with many considering themselves more German than Jewish; a few founded merchant banking, retail and clothing empires. Around 1890, Ashkenazi Jews from Eastern Europe began arriving from Poland, Lithuania, Belarus, Ukraine, Hungary and Romania. In the years after World War I, as many as 400,000 Jews a year debarked at Ellis Island until a 1924 law virtually shut down immigration. Had a malapportioned, rural-dominated, nativist Congress not done that, perhaps two million of the six million who perished in the Holocaust would instead have become Americans. Ashkenazi Jews initially lived on the Lower East Side but moved out to Brooklyn and the Bronx almost as soon as the subways were built. Their children moved up faster than any new group in memory, despite widespread prejudice in the professions and in educational institutions. They invented new businesses, from the rag trade to show biz: second-caste people from third-rate countries almost immediately becoming elite in the world's foremost country. Their descendants live all over the country, but New York has the largest Jewish population of any city in the world.

One big voting area of the 8th is the Upper West Side: the venerable apartments along Central Park West, West End Avenue and Riverside Drive, and the brownstones on the cross streets which house some of America's most idealistic and dedicated liberals (and radicals). These professional people—lovingly satirized on *Seinfeld,* the long-running sitcom that resonated far beyond Manhattan—include a mix of the wealthy and less-affluent intellectuals. In the 1950s, West Siders took up the reform banner and eviscerated the old Tammany Hall Democratic machine; in the 1960s, they fought the Vietnam War and helped oust a Democratic administration. Another big voting area is Greenwich Village, which in the 1910s was America's original Bohemia, now with a mix of expensive apartments and cheaper dwellings. Politically, the Village has long had a taste for what it regards as radical, though some of its ideas are now mainstream, such as the historic preservation and urbanist policies developed in the Village's successful fight against a proposed lower Manhattan expressway, led by *The Death and Life of Great American Cities* author Jane Jacobs. Downtown in the Financial District, the real-estate market has improved but endless infighting has frustrated redevelopment at Ground Zero.

The Brooklyn part of the district is probably more Jewish than the Manhattan part. Brighton Beach ("Little Odessa") and Coney Island house the largest concentration of recent Russian Jewish immigrants in New York. Here you can see Cyrillic as well as Roman letters on store signs; Borough Park has one of the nation's largest Orthodox communities, with Yiddish-language ATM's, plus saunas and massages in Russian bathhouses. The eight-block shopping district along Brighton Beach Avenue hosts a handful of furriers catering to the decided preference among Russian women for fur coats. The political attitudes in these neighborhoods are quite different from those of most American Jews, who are liberal on both cultural and economic issues. The Russians, many of whom live close to poverty, favor free enterprise and are anti-socialist. The Hasidic Jews of Borough Park are conservative, hostile to racial preferences and favor tough police treatment of crime. Still, voters in these areas tend to register as Democrats and vote Democratic in most elections. The district voted 74%-18% for Al Gore in 2000, but gave John Kerry a smaller 72%-27% margin in 2004; this resulted from a sharp increase for Bush in Brooklyn and especially in Borough Park, where Bush won 66%.

The congressman from the 8th District is Jerrold Nadler, a West Side liberal Democrat first elected in 1992. He was born in Brooklyn and moved around; his father was a chicken farmer in New Jersey, ran a gas station on Long Island and owned a traveling auto parts store. At Columbia University, Nadler campaigned for Eugene McCarthy with his roommate Dick Morris and was there during the 1968 campus riots. He worked as a legislative staffer and ran for the Assembly in 1976, at 29; in the primary he beat Ruth Messinger (the Democratic nominee for mayor in 1997) by 73 votes. In 1992 he was suddenly presented with the opportunity to run for Congress. Ted Weiss, long an Upper West Side icon, died the day before the September primary, which he won anyway. The nomination was decided by a convention of almost 1,000 county Democratic committee members, many of them involved in acerbic ideological and personal squabbles for decades. In a system of weighted voting, Nadler won 62% of the votes and Councilwoman Ronnie Eldridge 21%; opponents decried this system, after they lost. Nadler became the Democratic nominee and thus congressman. He has not been seriously challenged since.

Nadler's voting record has been among the most liberal in the House, with a strong civil libertarian bent. As ranking Democrat on the Constitution Subcommittee, he opposed Republican constitutional amendments to overturn court rulings and abortion restrictions, including legislation designed to give legal standing to the fetus. He led the fight in the House against the proposed Federal Marriage Amendment, and he proposed to give same-sex domestic partners the same immigration rights and benefits as heterosexual spouses. Although his district includes Wall Street, Nadler strongly opposes individual investment accounts in Social Security.

On local issues, he successfully fought developer Donald Trump's attempts to alter the West Side Highway to accommodate his luxury housing project on old rail yards between 59th and 72d Streets. (In a book, Trump termed Nadler "one of the most egregious hacks in contemporary politics.") He fought to get more rail competition east of the Hudson, and worked to save Amtrak. His greatest project is a rail-freight tunnel under the Hudson, from the 65th Street rail yard in Bay Ridge to little-used rail yards in either Bayonne, New Jersey or Staten Island. Lack of a rail-freight line means that New York gets only a tiny share of its freight by rail; cheaper freight could lower consumer prices, help rebuild small manufacturing in New York and could revive the Brooklyn docks, which Governor Nelson Rockefeller abandoned in the 1960s when vessels began the switch to container cargo. The cost would be billion of dollars, but it could provide a way upward for the city's economy and its waves of new immigrants. Nadler's proposal was ridiculed for years, but he persisted and got $12 million for a two-year design and environmental study of the tunnel. Mayor Rudolph Giuliani endorsed it, and others have come to appreciate it as well. But Mayor Michael Bloomberg sided with neighborhood groups in Queens that objected to the plan because it would increase noise.

As the representative of Ground Zero, in the aftermath of the September 11 attacks Nadler found that his work life became both sad and frenetic. When the second airplane struck the tower, he rushed to catch a 10 a.m. train from Washington to Manhattan; after delays en route, he finally arrived at 6 p.m. to view a scene of emptiness that he later called "surrealistic." He worked with city, state and federal officials and local business leaders to identify immediate needs and then to secure $20 billion for the clean-up and eventual rebuilding. He spearheaded numerous actions on behalf of affected families, local communities and small business. But he remained true to his liberal views. He vigorously opposed the USA Patriot Act and the Iraq war resolution. In June 2005, he had a nasty showdown with James Sensenbrenner after the then-Judiciary Committee chairman cut short a hearing on renewal of the Patriot Act. Nadler said that he "abused his power to stifle debate," but the House rejected his bid to sanction Sensenbrenner. In 2007, he became chairman of the Constitution, Civil Rights and Civil Liberties Subcommittee, where he worked to narrow the definition of "enemy combatants" and to remove restrictions on detainees to protect their habeas corpus rights.

NINTH DISTRICT

Rep. Anthony Weiner (D)

Elected 1998, 5th term; b. Sept. 4, 1964, Brooklyn; home, Brooklyn; S.U.N.Y. Plattsburgh, B.A. 1985; Jewish; single.

Elected Office: NY City Cncl., 1991-98.

Professional Career: Aide, U.S. Rep. Charles Schumer, 1985-91.

DC Office: 1122 LHOB, 20515, 202-225-6616; Fax: 202-226-7253; Web site: www.house.gov/weiner.

District Offices: Brooklyn, 718-743-0441; Kew Gardens, 718-520-9001; Rockaway, 718-318-9255.

Committees: *Energy & Commerce* (26th of 31 D): Environment & Hazardous Materials; Commerce, Trade & Consumer Protection; Energy & Air Quality; Health. *Judiciary* (18th of 23 D): Crime, Terrorism & Homeland Security; Courts, the Internet & Intellectual Property.

Group Ratings

	ADA	ACLU	AFS	LCV	ITIC	NTU	COC	ACU	CFG	FRC
2006	95	100	100	100	43	13	40	8	10	0
2005	95	—	100	89	—	15	37	0	7	0

National Journal Ratings

	2005 LIB	—	2005 CONS	2006 LIB	—	2006 CONS
Economic	94%	—	0%	86%	—	11%
Social	81%	—	18%	78%	—	21%
Foreign	84%	—	16%	73%	—	26%

Key Votes of the 109th Congress

1. Estate Tax Repeal	N	5. Limit Interstate Abortion	N	9. Build Border Fence	Y
2. Limit CAFE Standards	N	6. Extend Patriot Act	N	10. CAFTA	N
3. FY06 Spending Curb	N	7. Bar Same Sex Marriage	N	11. Oppose Iraq Withdrawal	N
4. Drilling in ANWR	N	8. Stem Cell Research $	Y	12. Detainee Tribunals	N

Election Results

2006 general	Anthony Weiner (D-WF) .... unopposed			($837,956)
2006 primary	Anthony Weiner (D) .... unopposed			
2004 general	Anthony Weiner (D-WF) 113,025	(71%)	($1,329,530)
	Gerard Cronin (R-Ind-C) 45,451	(29%)	($8,093)

Prior Winning Percentages: 2002 (66%); 2000 (68%); 1998 (66%)

The People		Race/Ethnic Origin	Ancestry	
Area size:	103 sq. mi.	64.0% White	Italian: 12.3%	Irish: 7.5%
Urban population:	100.0%	4.0% Black	Russian: 7.2%	
Rural population:	0.0%	14.5% Asian	**2004 Presidential Vote**	
Pop. 2000:	654,360	0.1% Native Am.	Kerry (D) 111,850	(56%)
Pop. 2005 (est):	640,987	0.0% Hawaiian	Bush (R) 87,449	(44%)
Median income:	$45,426	3.0% Two+ races	Other 1,658	(1%)
Poverty status:	12.2%	0.7% Other	**2000 Presidential Vote**	
Military veterans:	7.1%	13.6% Hispanic Origin	Gore (D) 123,763	(67%)
			Bush (R) 54,699	(30%)
			Other 6,649	(4%)
			Cook Partisan Voting Index: D +14	
Occupation	Blue collar: 17.6%	White collar: 68.4%	Gray collar: 14.0%	

Forty years ago, most of the neighborhoods in New York's outer boroughs were almost all-white. A few were WASPy and high-income—Forest Hills in Queens, with its famous tennis stadium and large Tudor houses on winding lanes within view of massive high-rises, is a notable example—but most of them were filled by descendants of the great mass of immigrants who came over from eastern and southern Europe between 1890 and 1924 and from northern Europe earlier—Irish and Italians, Jews and Hungarians, Poles and Czechs and Greeks. The great pitched battles of city politics in the 1960s were between John Lindsay, a liberal Manhattan Republican, and his mostly outer borough opponents. Lindsay won big margins in Manhattan from Harlem blacks, Upper East Side Republicans, Upper West Side and Greenwich Village liberal Democrats, but he lost the other four boroughs collectively both times he ran, and was elected each time with only a plurality of the votes. Lindsay's attitudes and policies—soft on law enforcement, high on taxes, disregard for middle class taxpayers who wanted low taxes and safe neighborhoods—fueled an exodus of middle class New Yorkers, and the city lost 1 million people in the 1970s. Some of this neighborhood change would have happened anyway: neighborhoods settled by immigrants in the 1920s were full of old people, and increasing numbers of blacks were bound to move out of the old ghettoes anyway. Unnoticed, increasing numbers of immigrants started coming to the United States after the 1965 changes in immigration law, and eventually large numbers came to New York.

Some white upper-middle and lower-middle class neighborhoods remain in the outer boroughs, though they are ethnically more diverse than those of 40 years ago. Many of these neighborhoods are gathered within the convoluted boundaries of the 9th Congressional District, which includes parts of Queens and Brooklyn. Its population is only 4% black and 14% Hispanic, and some of its neighborhoods, like the Italians of Howard Beach on Jamaica Bay, have remained remarkably parochial and seemingly unaffected by changes swirling elsewhere. The 9th begins in Queens near Fresh Meadows, just inside Nassau County; it then runs west through Pomonok and the old rail suburbs of Kew Gardens and Forest Hills, built to resemble English cottage neighborhoods. The district continues west to Rego Park ("Regostan"), with its 1950s high-rise apartments for many central Asian groups, where Wal-Mart abandoned plans for a store because of community opposition; Middle Village; the old German (and now more Eastern European) neighborhood of Glendale;

and part of Maspeth. From there, the 9th heads south, taking in Woodhaven, Lindenwood and Howard Beach. It then crosses over open parkland to include the shoreline areas of Bergen Beach, Mill Basin, Mill Island, Marine Park and Sheepshead Bay. It takes in Broad Channel, the only inhabited island in Jamaica Bay's Gateway National Recreation Area, where many descendants of the original fishing families still live. On the Rockaway Peninsula, the 9th includes the neighborhoods of Seaside, Rockaway Park, Belle Harbor, Roxbury and the tight-knit enclave of Breezy Point, once referred to as the "Irish Riviera," a clannish, white ethnic middle class enclave where the bungalows and brick homes often change hands by word of mouth alone. The 9th has a large and diverse Jewish population, with politically conservative Orthodox neighborhoods and liberal voters. This is unquestionably a Democratic district, but conservative by New York City standards: it voted 67%-30% for Al Gore in 2000 but in 2004, after George W. Bush's response to September 11, it gave John Kerry only a 56%-44% margin. The 25-percentage point erosion in the Democratic margin of victory marked the greatest swing of any congressional district in the nation.

The congressman from the 9th District is Anthony Weiner, a Democrat first elected in 1998. Weiner grew up in Brooklyn, went to school Upstate at SUNY-Plattsburgh, then returned to work in the House for the energetic Charles Schumer. In 1991 Weiner was elected to the City Council, at 27, the youngest member ever. In 1997, as Schumer prepared to run for the Senate, Weiner began running for the House. In the Democratic primary, he faced two members of the Assembly and another councilman. This was mainly a battle of organizations and endorsements. In the final weeks, Schumer endorsed Weiner. The primary was so close that the results weren't certified for two weeks. In a turnout of 45,000, Weiner won with 28.1%, to 27.5% for the runner-up. He won the general election easily.

In the House, Weiner usually votes with liberals but styles himself a moderate on issues dealing with business and crime. Except for his eagerness to appear on cable talk shows—as befits a Schumer protégé—Weiner has had few moments in the congressional spotlight and he worked mostly as a backbencher on local issues. He sought to protect local pharmacies from the invasion of chain drug stores by permitting them to negotiate collectively with insurance and drug companies, and he filed a bill to bar pharmaceutical firms from owning a controlling interest in a pharmacy benefit management company. In July 2004, the House passed his amendment, on a 217-191 vote, to prohibit U.S. foreign aid to Saudi Arabia; he cited Saudi support of terrorists, including within their own nation. In June 2006, he won 312-97 on a similar amendment, which permitted some funds for the Saudi military.

In 2002, redistricting moved the 9th more into Queens and left Weiner with 30% new territory, but the basic character of the district remained the same and he has been easily reelected. In 2005, Weiner sought the Democratic nomination for mayor; other candidates included former Bronx borough president Fernando Ferrer, Manhattan borough president Virginia Fields, and city council Speaker Gifford Miller. Weiner featured his trademark self-deprecating humor and sought to build an outer borough base that focused on the needs of working people and he called for a new football stadium in Queens instead of Manhattan. He called for a 10% cut in income taxes for persons earning less than $150,000, which would be financed by a tax increase on millionaires. He pledged more government support for religious schools. In the campaign, he tried to avoid racial conflicts or alliances. In the September primary, Weiner finished second with 29% to Ferrer's 40% but generated political goodwill by choosing not to seek a runoff when it first appeared that Ferrer had fallen short of the percentage necessary to win outright. Michael Bloomberg then trounced Ferrer to win a second term. In February 2007, Weiner made clear what was already apparent: He filed papers to run for mayor in 2009.

When Democrats took the House majority, he got a prized seat on the Energy and Commerce Committee, where he said he would focus on issues from "fixing Medicaid to dealing with 9/11 health issues and lowering gas prices."

TENTH DISTRICT

Rep. Edolphus Towns (D)

Elected 1982, 13th term; b. July 21, 1934, Chadbourn, NC; home, Brooklyn; NC A&T, B.S. 1956, Adelphi U., M.S.W. 1973; Baptist; married (Gwendolyn).

Military Career: Army, 1956-58.

Professional Career: Baptist Minister; Social Worker; Prof., Medgar Evers Col.; NY public schl. teacher; Dpty. Hospital Admin., 1965-71; Brooklyn Dpty. Borough Pres., 1976-82.

DC Office: 2232 RHOB, 20515, 202-225-5936; Fax: 202-225-1018; Web site: www.house.gov/towns.

District Offices: Brooklyn, 718-855-8018; Brooklyn, 718-272-1175; Brooklyn, 718-774-5682; Brooklyn, 718-434-7931.

Committees: *Energy & Commerce* (5th of 31 D): Health; Telecommunications & the Internet; Commerce, Trade & Consumer Protection. *Oversight & Government Reform* (3d of 23 D): Government Management, Organization & Procurement (Chmn.).

Group Ratings

	ADA	ACLU	AFS	LCV	ITIC	NTU	COC	ACU	CFG	FRC
2006	95	95	100	83	57	15	53	8	12	14
2005	70	—	100	44	—	22	60	14	26	17

National Journal Ratings

	2005 LIB	—	2005 CONS	2006 LIB	—	2006 CONS
Economic	67%	—	33%	66%	—	33%
Social	80%	—	20%	82%	—	17%
Foreign	79%	—	21%	83%	—	14%

Key Votes of the 109th Congress

1. Estate Tax Repeal	Y	5. Limit Interstate Abortion	N	9. Build Border Fence	N
2. Limit CAFE Standards	N	6. Extend Patriot Act	N	10. CAFTA	Y
3. FY06 Spending Curb	N	7. Bar Same Sex Marriage	N	11. Oppose Iraq Withdrawal	N
4. Drilling in ANWR	N	8. Stem Cell Research $	Y	12. Detainee Tribunals	N

Election Results

2006 general	Edolphus Towns (D)	72,171	(92%)	($1,339,964)
	Jonathan Anderson (R)	4,666	(6%)	
	Other	1,470	(2%)	
2006 primary	Edolphus Towns (D)	19,469	(47%)	
	Charles Barron (D)	15,345	(37%)	
	Roger Green (D)	6,237	(15%)	
2004 general	Edolphus Towns (D-WF)	136,113	(91%)	($757,121)
	Harvey Clarke (R)	11,099	(7%)	
	Other	1,554	(1%)	

Prior Winning Percentages: 2002 (98%); 2000 (90%); 1998 (92%); 1996 (91%); 1994 (89%); 1992 (96%); 1990 (93%); 1988 (89%); 1986 (89%); 1984 (85%); 1982 (84%)

The People		Race/Ethnic Origin	Ancestry		
Area size:	18 sq. mi.	16.2% White	West Indian: 14.8% USA: 3.9%		
Urban population:	100.0%	60.2% Black	Subsaharan: 2.5%		
Rural population:	0.0%	2.7% Asian	**2004 Presidential Vote**		
Pop. 2000:	654,361	0.2% Native Am.	Kerry (D)	166,840	(86%)
Pop. 2005 (est):	676,384	0.0% Hawaiian	Bush (R)	25,359	(13%)
Median income:	$30,212	2.6% Two+ races	Other	1,195	(1%)
Poverty status:	29.0%	0.9% Other	**2000 Presidential Vote**		
Military veterans:	5.3%	17.2% Hispanic Origin	Gore (D)	149,018	(88%)
			Bush (R)	13,058	(8%)
			Other	8,029	(5%)
			Cook Partisan Voting Index: D +41		

Occupation   Blue collar: 17.5%   White collar: 60.4%   Gray collar: 22.1%

Bedford, a century ago one of Brooklyn's fashionable neighborhoods, has given its name to half of what is Brooklyn's best known black neighborhood, Bedford-Stuyvesant. African-Americans began settling here in the 1930s, with the opening of the new subway line that was celebrated in Duke Ellington and Billy Strayhorn's "Take the A Train." After World War II, the pace accelerated, as crime and crowding in Harlem—as well as a large migration of blacks from the South—drove black New Yorkers to the aging but solid brownstones of "Bed-Stuy." When job growth slowed, Bed-Stuy, like New York's other black neighborhoods, faced more than its share of poverty and crime. But after a 1966 visit by Robert F. Kennedy and Jacob Javits, New York's two senators, Bed-Stuy won a Model Cities designation, which brought federal development funds and the establishment of the Bedford-Stuyvesant Restoration Corporation, the first such community development organization in the United States. Even as the black community expanded across Brooklyn, Bed-Stuy grew to become almost as powerful a symbol of black New York as Harlem. As an NYU film student in 1983, Brooklyn native Spike Lee made *Joe's Bed-Stuy Barbershop: We Cut Heads*, about a tonsorial parlor that fronts for the numbers racket; five years later, he shot *Do the Right Thing* on Stuyvesant Avenue between Lexington Avenue and Quincy Street, a film that succinctly captured the racial tensions then brewing in the old neighborhood. From a different perspective, Billy Joel in the 1980s sang, "I've been stranded in the combat zone. I walked through Bed-Stuy alone." But by the new century, Bed-Stuy was in better shape than many other areas of Brooklyn. The neighborhood's stately, Hopperesque architecture largely avoided the wrecking ball, and community vigilance kept the streets maintained. The revitalized residential area has developed a Caribbean flavor which, combined with the modest prices for handsome brownstones, has led to a noticeable wave of gentrification.

The 10th Congressional District of New York takes the shape of a sideways "V" as it zigzags across Brooklyn. It takes in several neighborhoods near, but not on, the East River, including part of affluent Brooklyn Heights; downtown Brooklyn, with Borough Hall and the $670 million courthouse complex; the rising arts area of Fort Greene; and part of Williamsburg (shared with the 12th), inhabited by Hasidic families with large numbers of children. From there, it runs southeasterly through Bed-Stuy, Clinton Hill and East New York, until it hits the Queens border and turns to the southwest to take in three communities along Jamaica Bay: Spring Creek, the huge middle-income apartment complex of Starrett City, and Canarsie, the site of Jonathan Rieder's classic sociological study of Jewish and Italian flight from increasingly black neighborhoods. In the 1990s, Canarsie again experienced significant demographic change, as the neighborhood's black population grew from 10% to 60%, mainly due to an influx of Caribbean immigrants who prize the backyards and single-family homes. The 10th also includes Remsen Village, Flatlands and part of East Flatbush. The economic boom and the drop in crime rates improved even the borough's most hopeless areas, such as East New York, as gutted blocks were torn down and in many cases rebuilt. The district is 60% black—the highest of any New York district—and 17% Hispanic. Politically, it is overwhelmingly Democratic, one of the most Democratic districts in the nation.

The congressman from the 10th District is Edolphus Towns, first elected in 1982 to an open seat that resulted from redistricting and retirement. He is a Democrat from East New York who is as experienced in government as in politics. He was born in North Carolina, the son of a tobacco sharecropper, graduated from North Carolina A&T, served two years in the Army and soon moved to Brooklyn, where he taught in the public schools and at Medgar Evers College. He became a social worker and hospital administrator, and was active in community affairs. In 1976, he became Brooklyn's deputy borough president, a position he held for six years.

In the House, Towns's voting record has lost some of its liberal edge, especially on economic issues, where he occasionally sides with business. Starting out he worked on the Student Athlete Right-to-Know Act, which requires colleges to report the graduation rates of student athletes, and on strengthening the National Health Service Corps and the Minority Health Initiative. He has demonstrated an ability to work across party lines. With Energy and Commerce Committee Chairman Joe Barton and the support of several large auto parts suppliers, he introduced the Right to Repair Act, to require automakers to give more information about their vehicles to repair shops. With Mike Rogers of Michigan, he got the House to pass a bill to impose uniform safety rules on food and to limit the reach of state laws. In July 2005, his vote for the Central American Free Trade Agreement infuriated Minority Leader Nancy Pelosi, not only because Towns holds a safe Democratic seat and sits on an exclusive committee but also because his vote—and the 217-215 final tally—permitted an additional Republican to play to local sentiments. She demanded an explanation, and threatened to deprive Towns (and a few other maverick Democrats) of their committee seats. In the majority, Towns did not take a subcommittee chairmanship at Energy and Commerce where he was the fifth most-senior Democrat; perhaps that decision resulted from Pelosi's unhappiness over his CAFTA vote. Instead, he became chairman of the Government Management, Organization, and Procurement Subcommittee at Oversight and Government Reform. He planned to investigate no-bid contracts that have been issued by the Pentagon, especially for the war in Iraq.

For years Towns was reelected without difficulty. In 1997 he endorsed Rudolph Giuliani for mayor; this took some courage, or showed bad judgment, since Giuliani got only 15% of the vote in two Bedford-Stuyvesant assembly districts. In 1998 Kings County Democratic Chairman Clarence Norman recruited a primary opponent in Barry Ford, a Harvard-educated Wall Street lawyer. Towns' critics concentrated on his opposition to anti-tobacco legislation on the ground it would hurt farmers. The Campaign for Tobacco-Free Kids put up billboards reading, "Representative Towns: Big Tobacco or Kids?" Towns beat Ford, but by only 52%-36%. Emboldened by that result, Ford barely stopped campaigning for the next two years. In 2000, he appeared to have a real prospect of ousting Towns. But the incumbent campaigned much harder. Towns defended his support for Giuliani by pointing to the mayor's support for commercial development. He did not take campaign contributions from tobacco companies. Towns won this time, 57%-43%. In 2006, his opponents in the primary were councilman Charles Barron, who said that Towns had been "missing in action for years," and Assemblyman Roger Green, who cited his accomplishments in Albany. But the challengers had their own problems: Green had pleaded guilty in 2004 to petty larceny for his phony travel expenses in office, and Barron's call for reparations for descendants of slaves was controversial. In the closing weeks, the two of them discussed the possibility that one would drop out; neither did. Towns campaigned as the incumbent seeking to rise above the electioneering and he had a huge fundraising advantage. Towns won with 47% to 37% for Barron and 15% for Green—less than impressive for a 12-term incumbent.

There has been speculation that the incumbent would like to pass the district to his son, Assemblyman Darryl Towns, when he retires. Towns turns 74 in 2008.

ELEVENTH DISTRICT

Rep. Yvette Clarke (D)

Elected 2006, 1st term; b. Nov. 21, 1964, Brooklyn; home, Brooklyn; Attended Oberlin Col.; Protestant; single.

Elected Office: NY City Cncl., 2001-06.

Professional Career: Childcare specialist, Erasmus Neighborhood Fed., 1987-89; leg. aide, state Sen. Velmanette Montgomery, 1989-91; exec. asst., NY Workers' Compensation Bd., 1992-93; youth program dir., Hospital League/Local S.E.I.U. 1199 Training and Upgrading Fund, 1993-97; bus. devel. dir., Bronx Overall Devel. Corp., 1997-2001.

DC Office: 1029 LHOB, 20515, 202-225-6231; Fax: 202-226-0112; Web site: clarke.house.gov.

District Offices: Brooklyn, 718-287-1142.

Committees: *Education & Labor* (25th of 27 D): Healthy Families & Communities; Health, Employment, Labor & Pensions. *Homeland Security* (16th of 19 D): Management, Investigations & Oversight; Transportation Security & Infrastructure Protection. *Small Business* (13th of 18 D): Contracting & Technology; Rural & Urban Entrepreneurship.

Group Ratings and Key Votes: Newly Elected

Election Results

2006 general	Yvette Clarke (D-WF)	88,334	(90%)	($622,247)
	Stephen Finger (R-Lib)	7,447	(8%)	
	Other	2,321	(2%)	
2006 primary	Yvette Clarke (D)	15,711	(31%)	
	David Yassky (D)	13,928	(27%)	
	Carl Andrews (D)	11,685	(23%)	
	Chris Owens (D)	9,971	(19%)	
2004 general	Major Owens (D-WF)	144,999	(94%)	($474,168)
	Other	9,199	(6%)	

The People		Race/Ethnic Origin	Ancestry	
Area size:	12 sq. mi.	21.4% White	West Indian: 23.2% USA: 4.1%	
Urban population:	100.0%	58.5% Black	Italian: 2.8%	
Rural population:	0.0%	4.1% Asian	**2004 Presidential Vote**	
Pop. 2000:	654,361	0.2% Native Am.	Kerry (D) 172,654	(86%)
Pop. 2005 (est):	657,101	0.0% Hawaiian	Bush (R) 26,172	(13%)
Median income:	$34,082	3.0% Two+ races	Other 1,616	(1%)
Poverty status:	23.2%	0.6% Other	**2000 Presidential Vote**	
Military veterans:	4.1%	12.1% Hispanic Origin	Gore (D) 149,740	(83%)
			Other 15,828	(9%)
			Bush (R) 15,652	(9%)
			Cook Partisan Voting Index: D +40	

Occupation   Blue collar: 15.7%   White collar: 61.2%   Gray collar: 23.1%

Brooklyn. The single word used to arouse laughter in a comedian's monologue, applause when someone said that's where they were from. It evoked an accent that twisted the English language almost to non-recognition, a raucous and brusque confrontational style, a sense of humor with an edge, the chip-on-the-shoulder assertiveness of those sure they will always be in second place. Brooklyn would never be more important than Manhattan; the Dodgers would always lose the World Series to the Yankees or the pennant to the Giants, and when they finally did win, in 1955, they moved to Los Angeles two years later. Brooklyn, as its Dutch name testifies, was a separate community from the 17th century on, one of the largest cities in the country in the 19th century, with its own celebrities (Henry Ward Beecher, Walt Whitman, John Roebling). By 1898, when the five boroughs were welded into Greater New York, one million people lived in Brooklyn, but the Brooklyn of the comedians really came into being as the subways were built in the early 20th century. In 1913, a transit agreement was struck to interlink the city's then-independent lines and triple the track to 619 miles; this agreement helped Brooklyn expand well beyond its established neighborhoods near the Brooklyn Bridge and into then-rural southwestern Brooklyn.

Suddenly, Manhattan factory workers no longer had to live in the Lower East Side tenements that social reformer Jacob Riis had exposed in the 1890s; they moved in droves into neighborhoods of three- to five-story apartments and four-family houses. Brooklyn grew from 1.1 million in 1900 to 1.6 million in 1910 to 2 million in 1920 and 2.6 million in 1930. The old Brooklynites were mostly Protestant—Dutch, Yankee, German—plus some Catholic Irish. The new Brooklynites were heavily Italian and Jewish, and peopled the sports and entertainment businesses for a long generation, making their hometown nationally famous. In 1940, Brooklyn had 2.7 million people: one of every 49 Americans lived in Brooklyn. But in 2000, Brooklyn had 2.47 million people—one of every 119 Americans—and it is no longer a staple of national comedy. Some of its old neighborhoods have been ravaged by crime, but there is also great vitality among upwardly mobile Hispanic, Asian, Caribbean and Russian immigrants, among the hard-working black middle class, and among new generations of Italians and Jews. A change in zoning laws in 2004 resulted in a burst of new residential and office space construction that has reinvigorated Brooklyn's commercial district; one measure of Brooklyn's new vigor is a controversial $4 billion project to build a new arena for the New Jersey Nets basketball team as part of a large office and residential complex. In late 2006, state regulators gave approval to move ahead with the plans but pending lawsuits threatened to interfere with the project.

The heart of the old Brooklyn was Ebbets Field, where the Dodgers played. Around the time Jackie Robinson suited up for the Brooklyn Dodgers in 1947 as the first black player in Major League Baseball, Brooklyn was experiencing an influx of blacks into Brownsville and Crown Heights near Ebbets Field. Just as rapid was the flight of ethnic whites, driven away by "blockbusting," in which hard-nosed real estate brokers stoked white fears, then bought their homes cheaply and re-sold high. After "Dem Bums" left for Los Angeles in 1958 and Ebbets Field was knocked down to be replaced by an apartment complex, Brooklyn's black neighborhoods continued to grow. Many of New York's black families came from the American South, but large numbers, particularly in Flatbush and Crown Heights, come from "the Islands"—Jamaica, Haiti, the Dominican Republic, Barbados, Trinidad and Tobago. Speaking deeply accented English, French, Spanish or various forms of Creole, they bring aromatic cooking (jerk chicken, spiced bread, peanut punch and Matouk's Special Hot Calypso Sauce) and reggae and calypso music—as well as strong families and an entrepreneurial spirit. The annual Labor Day West Indian Carnival reflects this strong local Caribbean presence.

The 11th Congressional District of New York begins at the edge of downtown Brooklyn and includes some of the borough's jewels—the Grand Army Plaza, the Parisian-style Eastern Parkway (the world's first six-lane parkway), and Prospect Park, home to the Brooklyn Library, the Brooklyn Museum and the Brooklyn Botanic Garden, with its Japanese landscaping and placid duck ponds. Park Slope, on Prospect Park's west side, has become increasingly affluent, filling up with professionals who appreciate the easy commute to downtown Manhattan. On the east side of Prospect Park is Crown Heights, with its mix of modest apartment buildings and nicely restored row houses; it was the scene of violent clashes between blacks and Hasidic Jews in 1991 (the Lubavitch Hasids, the largest Hasidic sect in the world, has its headquarters in Crown Heights). Prospect Park South, also adjoining the park, is another affluent neighborhood whose suburban feel, once enforced by restrictive covenants, contrasts sharply with the vibrant Caribbean street life just around the corner on Flatbush's Church Avenue and with struggling, depopulated Brownsville to the east. Most of these neighborhoods are places of great ethnic diversity: One minute you are in "La Saline," a center of the Haitian community in the East Flatbush-Crown Heights area, nicknamed for the slum district of Port-au-Prince; the next, you are in "Little Pakistan" in Midwood, home to the largest concentration of Pakistanis living in America. From the 1920s to the 1960s the area defined by the 11th District had the largest concentration of Jews in America but today the population is 59% black and 12% Hispanic. Politically, the district is overwhelmingly Democratic, but the borough's party organization has been weakened by allegations of corruption.

The new congresswoman from the 11th District is Yvette Clarke, a Democrat elected in 2006. She was born in Brooklyn to immigrant parents; as a young girl, she tagged along to political meetings and events with her mother, Una Clarke, who in 1991 became the first Jamaican elected to the New York City Council. Yvette Clarke attended Oberlin College in Ohio, came close to graduating but fell short by six credit hours. She returned to New York, helped train child care workers, worked as a state legislative aide and served as business development director for the Bronx Overall Economic Development Corp. When term limits forced her mother off the New York City Council, Clarke defeated four other candidates in 2001 to succeed her in the predominately Caribbean area of Flatbush and East Flatbush.

Since its creation in 1968, the 11th District had been represented by just two people, both Democrats—trailblazer Shirley Chisholm, the first black woman elected to Congress and a 1972 presidential candidate, and Major Owens, who succeeded her in 1982. Owens had announced in 2004 that he would serve just one more term before stepping down, with the hope that his son Chris, his campaign manager and an HMO administrator, would succeed him. But Clarke was also part of a political family that had designs on the seat. Her mother Una had run against Owens in the 2000 Democratic primary, a bitter contest that exposed divisions between the local Caribbean-American and African-American communities. Although Una Clarke and Owens had long been friends and he had helped her win her city council seat, their relationship became rancorous, and she accused Owens of being ineffective and anti-immigrant. Owens accused Clarke of betraying their friendship; he won 54%-46%.

Four years later, Yvette Clarke, who had replaced her mother on the city council, and fellow city councilwoman Tracy Boyland, challenged Owens in the Democratic primary, both with the knowledge that his son would likely run for the seat two years later. Owens won the low-turnout primary with an unimpressive 45% to 29% for Clarke and 22% for Boyland. When Clarke faced reelection to the council in 2005, Major Owens retaliated by backing, unsuccessfully, her primary election opponent.

The 2004 primary gave Clarke a test run for the 2006 race, but first she had to navigate through a competitive primary field. New York City Councilman David Yassky, who is white, pushed racial politics to the front of the debate when he announced he would run for the seat. Major Owens called him a "colonizer" for running in a majority-black district originally designed in 1968 in response to a Voting Rights Act lawsuit. The black community feared that the well-financed Yassky, who moved three blocks into the district to run for the seat, would be the beneficiary if the black vote was splintered among the three prominent black candidates: Yvette Clarke, Chris Owens and state Senator Carl Andrews.

By the end of August, Yassky had raised over $1.3 million, more than the other three candidates combined. But Yassky had an awkward campaign style that made it difficult for him to connect with voters. Clarke worked the racial angle, but her status as the only woman and her support among Caribbean-Americans was at least as helpful. On the leading local issue, Clarke supported a plan to build a Nets arena and other development in Brooklyn, while Owens vigorously opposed it. She stumbled when she was forced to backtrack from her claim that she graduated from

Oberlin, when she had not. But Clarke picked up the endorsement from the Service Employees International Union's powerful healthcare local 1199, which worked to turn out crucial votes, and had support from Queens Democrat Anthony Weiner and from Democrat John Murtha. In the September 12 primary, the only election that mattered in this heavily Democratic district, Clarke defeated Yassky 31%-27%, while Andrews finished third with 23% and Owens last with 19%.

After the election, Clarke dismissed any idea that she felt entitled to the seat, and said no one questions the Bush, Kennedy or Gore family dynasties in politics. "But when it's just Yvette and Una from Brooklyn, it's like 'You think you're owed this,' and blah, blah, blah. No, I have to work every single day for each and every vote I can possibly get," she told the *New York Observer*.

TWELFTH DISTRICT

Rep. Nydia Velazquez (D)

Elected 1992, 8th term; b. Mar. 28, 1953, Yabucoa, PR; home, Brooklyn; U. of PR, B.A. 1974, N.Y.U., M.A. 1976; Catholic; married (Paul Bader).

Elected Office: NY City Cncl., 1984-86.

Professional Career: Instructor, U. of PR, 1976-81; Adjunct prof., Hunter Col., 1981-83; Special Asst., U.S. Rep. Edolphus Towns, 1983; Migration Dir., PR Dept. of Labor & Human Resources, 1986-89; Secy., PR Dept. of Community Affairs in the U.S., 1989-92.

DC Office: 2466 RHOB, 20515, 202-225-2361; Fax: 202-226-0327; Web site: www.house.gov/velazquez.

District Offices: Brooklyn, 718-599-3658; Brooklyn, 718-222-5819; Manhattan, 212-673-3997.

Committees: *Financial Services* (6th of 37 D): Housing & Community Opportunity; Oversight & Investigations; Capital Markets, Insurance & Government Sponsored Enterprises. *Small Business* (Chmn. of 18 D).

Group Ratings

	ADA	ACLU	AFS	LCV	ITIC	NTU	COC	ACU	CFG	FRC
2006	100	100	100	92	29	14	27	4	5	0
2005	100	—	100	72	—	21	48	0	4	0

National Journal Ratings

	2005 LIB	—	2005 CONS		2006 LIB	—	2006 CONS
Economic	75%	—	25%		79%	—	18%
Social	98%	—	0%		93%	—	6%
Foreign	94%	—	6%		95%	—	0%

Key Votes of the 109th Congress

1. Estate Tax Repeal	N	5. Limit Interstate Abortion	N	9. Build Border Fence	N
2. Limit CAFE Standards	N	6. Extend Patriot Act	N	10. CAFTA	N
3. FY06 Spending Curb	N	7. Bar Same Sex Marriage	N	11. Oppose Iraq Withdrawal	N
4. Drilling in ANWR	N	8. Stem Cell Research $	Y	12. Detainee Tribunals	N

Election Results

2006 general	Nydia Velazquez (D-WF)	62,847	(90%)	($698,615)
	Allan Romaguera (R-C)	7,182	(10%)	
2006 primary	Nydia Velazquez (D)	unopposed		
2004 general	Nydia Velazquez (D-WF)	107,796	(86%)	($551,994)
	Paul Rodriguez (R-C)	17,166	(14%)	

Prior Winning Percentages: 2002 (96%); 2000 (87%); 1998 (84%); 1996 (85%); 1994 (92%); 1992 (77%)

The People		Race/Ethnic Origin	Ancestry	
Area size:	20 sq. mi.	23.3% White	Italian: 4.7%	Polish: 4.4%
Urban population:	100.0%	8.8% Black	Irish: 3.4%	
Rural population:	0.0%	15.9% Asian	**2004 Presidential Vote**	
Pop. 2000:	654,360	0.2% Native Am.	Kerry (D) 130,019	(80%)
Pop. 2005 (est):	628,489	0.0% Hawaiian	Bush (R) 29,942	(19%)
Median income:	$29,195	2.5% Two+ races	Other 1,750	(1%)
Poverty status:	28.3%	0.7% Other	**2000 Presidential Vote**	
Military veterans:	4.0%	48.5% Hispanic Origin	Gore (D) 102,465	(77%)
			Bush (R) 19,604	(15%)
			Other 11,268	(8%)
			Cook Partisan Voting Index: D +34	

Occupation	Blue collar: 27.5%	White collar: 50.9%	Gray collar: 21.5%

In 1957, amid a vast wave of migration that seemed destined to make Puerto Ricans the majority in New York, Leonard Bernstein wrote his musical, *West Side Story*, with Romeo as an Italian-American and Juliet as a Manhattan Puerto Rican. But New York never became majority Puerto Rican. Before World War II, there were 60,000 Puerto Ricans in New York City; three decades later, there were 800,000. But they were among the first immigrants to arrive in a city whose industrial base was stagnant. With cheap airfares and no need to go through passport control, the inflow and outflow of Puerto Ricans balanced out by the early 1960s, and in the late 1990s the number of Puerto Ricans in New York was declining, as young New Yorkers of Puerto Rican descent increasingly moved to Puerto Rico. But by then, New York City was experiencing a vast influx of Latinos from places not under the U.S. flag, and today most New York Hispanics come not from Puerto Rico but from the Dominican Republic, Colombia, Mexico, Panama and Peru.

The 12th Congressional District of New York was designed to stitch many of these diverse people together. More than two-thirds of the people here live in Brooklyn, and most of the rest in Queens, with some in Manhattan. In Brooklyn the district hugs the waterfront and dips inward to include areas with large Hispanic populations—but this is New York, so it gets many others as well. Overall the district in 2000 was 49% Hispanic, 16% Asian and 9% black. The 12th includes the upscale Brooklyn Heights waterfront, with its stunning but, after September 11, haunting views of Lower Manhattan, and nearby Carroll Gardens with young professionals intermingled with Italian immigrants. To the south is Sunset Park, once the home of Irish, Polish and Norwegian immigrants, now filled with Chinese, Puerto Ricans, Colombians and Ecuadorans. North of Brooklyn Heights is DUMBO (Down Under the Manhattan Bridge Overpass), with artists in old industrial lofts, and just above it, Vinegar Hill. North of the Brooklyn Navy Yard, a major base for the Navy until it was shuttered in 1966, and now an industrial park, is Williamsburg, with Orthodox Jews and recent Latino arrivals and some hip young people as well. Inland is Bushwick, with low-income Latinos and a lot of new housing thanks to longtime Assemblyman Vito Lopez. Just a few streets away, across the Brooklyn-Queens border, is Ridgewood, once mostly Irish, then Polish, now filled with new arrivals from Poland, Romania, Albania, Serbia and Bosnia. Nearby is industrial Maspeth. In Manhattan, the 12th District includes parts of the Lower East Side, Chinatown and Little Italy. In 1910, 373,000 people lived there, mostly Jewish and Italian immigrants. Today there are only a few Jews and virtually no Italians (only Italian restaurants remain); its population of 91,000 is mostly Chinese, with some Latinos and some young professionals renting newly converted apartments. Politically, the 12th District is heavily Democratic.

The congresswoman from the 12th District is Nydia Velazquez, chosen by a narrow margin in the 1992 Democratic primary and reelected ever since. She grew up in Puerto Rico, taught at the University of Puerto Rico in the 1970s and at Hunter College in the 1980s, worked for Congressman Ed Towns in 1983 and served on the New York city council, the first Hispanic woman there, in 1984. Then she worked for Puerto Rico's government offices in New York. She was one of three major contenders when the district was created in 1992. The others were liberal Elisabeth Colon and incumbent Stephen Solarz; he decided to run here rather than in the Manhattan-dominated 8th or in the 9th District in which Charles Schumer had a heavy advantage. Velazquez got the endorsements of Mayor David Dinkins and of Jesse Jackson, and in a light turnout beat Solarz 34%-28%, with 26% for Colon. After the primary, confidential hospital records were leaked to a New York tabloid showing that in September 1991, Velazquez had attempted suicide, was hospitalized and later underwent counseling. Evidently, that was of little concern to voters: she won in November with 77%.

In the House she has a solidly liberal voting record. Velazquez is chairman of the Small Business Committee; from 1998 to 2007 she was its ranking minority member. Citing the 2 million minority-owned and 9 million woman-owned businesses, she spoke out for repeal of the estate tax in June 2000 and voted for it. But when Bill Clinton vetoed the bill, she voted to uphold his veto after a phone call from him. More recently she has opposed repeal but called for lower rates and a higher exemption. In 2001 she called for repeal of the 1996 welfare law, and wants no time limits on welfare and benefits for legal immigrants. After September 11, she and Jerrold Nadler got $550 million in Community Development Block Grant aid for businesses impacted by the attacks; in 2003 she called for a GAO investigation on why more than half the New York small businesses applying for disaster loans after September 11 did not receive them. When funding for the SBA's 7(a) loan program lapsed in January 2004, she joined Small Business Chairman Don Manzullo demanding reinstatement of the program; the SBA had previously guaranteed lenders 75% if the borrower defaulted on loans up to $750,000. But the Bush administration insisted on abolishing the SBA subsidy and funding the program with higher fees to borrowers and lenders. In June 2004 Manzullo and Velazquez got the House, 281-137, to add $79 million to the SBA budget but the funds would not go straight to 7(a). The SBA reauthorization foundered on this issue, but in November 2004 Manzullo and Senate Chairman Olympia Snowe got the administration to agree on increased fees, with increases in the amounts of loans; Manzullo was agreeable since 7(a) lending remained strong after the authorization expired on October 1; the administration argued that the authority to back loans rose from $9.5 billion in 2001 to $16 billion in 2005 even as the agency's budget fell. As chairman, Velazquez has called for lower 7(a) fees.

As ranking minority member, Velazquez initiated an annual scorecard to show whether the federal government has met its goal of granting 23% of contracts to small businesses. In 2005 the SBA Office of Advocacy found significant miscoding of loans to small divisions of large firms counted as small business loans. Velazquez said the administration was "cooking the books." In 2006 her scorecard showed that the government miscoded $12 billion of contracts and that only 22% of contracts went to small businesses. She also charged that the SBA repeatedly fell short of its goal of granting 5% of loans to women. After Hurricane Katrina, the SBA received many applications for loans. In December 2005, Velazquez said it was rejecting 82% of loan applicants referred by FEMA; in contrast, she said, 60% of loans were granted after Hurricane Andrew in 1992. That month she called for SBA Director Hector Barreto to resign and in April he did. In January 2007 a GAO report criticized SBA for chaotic service, a failure to plan for increased staff and office space, an untested computer system and a loan approval process that lagged behind demand. Velazquez said, "At this point, SBA has given us no reason to believe it can adequately respond to another Katrina, and that is simply not acceptable." As incoming chairman, she sponsored bills to ease tax rules on small businesses and helped to pass a temporary reauthorization bill requested by Steven Preston, Barreto's successor.

Velazquez has been a major voice on issues relating to Puerto Rico. She once favored independence; by 1997 she favored continuation of the current commonwealth status (more accurately described in the Spanish term, *estado liberado asociado*, free associated state). She attacked the March 1998 bill setting the terms for a referendum on status as "a one-sided bill that is biased in favor of Puerto Rican statehood" that shows "a lack of respect for the people of Puerto Rico." She said its definition of commonwealth was biased, because it did not guarantee U.S. citizenship to future generations of Puerto Ricans (citizenship is now based not on the Fourteenth Amendment, but on a law Congress passed in 1917, which could be repealed). Velazquez strongly advocated clemency for members of the FALN terrorist group—which was responsible for the deaths of six people—who had been imprisoned for 19 years after being convicted on seditious conspiracy and weapons charges and who had not expressed regret. When Bill Clinton granted clemency in August 1999 conditioned on a renunciation of violence, she said that the clemency should have been unconditional; she was dismayed when the House condemned the clemency by a 311-41 vote. In September 2005 Filiberto Ojeda Rios, member of an independence group that killed two U.S. Navy sailors in 1979 and robbed a bank in 1983 who was sentenced to 55 years, then paroled, broke his electronic basis and then was surrounded by 20 FBI agents and killed. Velazquez, together with Jose Serrano and Luis Gutierrez, demanded the FBI investigate; Director Robert Mueller said it would.

Velazquez has been one of many combatants in New York City's political wars but she has won reelection easily. In 2005 she put a $18.25 million earmark in the transportation bill for the Brooklyn Greenway and worked with Anthony Weiner to get an EPA study of a huge 1950 oil spill which has apparently left a 55-acre underground plume of oil in Newtown Creek in Greenpoint. She participated in April 2006 in a Brooklyn march protesting immigration restriction proposals. "Si se puede," she cried, adding, "We should not be in the business of criminalizing undocumented immigrants." In November 2006 Velazquez ran for chairman of the Hispanic Caucus, but Joe Baca, the incumbent first vice chairman, won; Baca, like all chairmen of the caucus since 1995, is of Mexican descent.

THIRTEENTH DISTRICT

Rep. Vito Fossella (R)

Elected Nov. 1997, 5th full term; b. Mar. 9, 1965, Staten Island; home, Staten Island; U. of PA., B.S. 1993, Fordham U., J.D. 1994; Catholic; married (Mary Pat).

Elected Office: NY City Cncl., 1994-97.

Professional Career: Practicing atty., 1994.

DC Office: 2453 RHOB, 20515, 202-225-3371; Fax: 202-226-1272; Web site: www.house.gov/fossella.

District Offices: Brooklyn, 718-630-5277; Staten Island, 718-356-8400.

Committees: *Energy & Commerce* (13th of 26 R): Commerce, Trade & Consumer Protection; Environment & Hazardous Materials; Telecommunications & the Internet.

Group Ratings

	ADA	ACLU	AFS	LCV	ITIC	NTU	COC	ACU	CFG	FRC
2006	10	14	0	17	100	66	100	75	71	71
2005	5	—	0	11	—	60	93	84	72	85

National Journal Ratings

	2005 LIB —	2005 CONS	2006 LIB —	2006 CONS
Economic	38% —	60%	43% —	56%
Social	32% —	66%	45% —	55%
Foreign	17% —	79%	17% —	73%

Key Votes of the 109th Congress

1. Estate Tax Repeal	Y	5. Limit Interstate Abortion	Y	9. Build Border Fence	Y
2. Limit CAFE Standards	N	6. Extend Patriot Act	Y	10. CAFTA	Y
3. FY06 Spending Curb	Y	7. Bar Same Sex Marriage	Y	11. Oppose Iraq Withdrawal	Y
4. Drilling in ANWR	Y	8. Stem Cell Research $	Y	12. Detainee Tribunals	Y

Election Results

2006 general	Vito Fossella (R-C-Ind)	59,334	(57%)	($1,639,598)
	Stephen Harrison (D-WF)	45,131	(43%)	($132,454)
2006 primary	Vito Fossella (R)	unopposed		
2004 general	Vito Fossella (R-C)	112,934	(59%)	($1,134,213)
	Frank Barbaro (D-Ind-WF)	78,500	(41%)	($423,793)

Prior Winning Percentages: 2002 (70%); 2000 (65%); 1998 (65%); 1997 (61%)

The People		Race/Ethnic Origin	Ancestry	
Area size:	113 sq. mi.	70.9% White	Italian: 29.5%	Irish: 11.5%
Urban population:	100.0%	6.3% Black	German: 4.3%	
Rural population:	0.0%	9.1% Asian	**2004 Presidential Vote**	
Pop. 2000:	654,361	0.1% Native Am.	Bush (R) 118,370	(55%)
Pop. 2005 (est):	679,819	0.0% Hawaiian	Kerry (D) 96,474	(45%)
Median income:	$50,092	2.3% Two+ races	Other 1,916	(1%)
Poverty status:	11.9%	0.2% Other	**2000 Presidential Vote**	
Military veterans:	9.0%	11.0% Hispanic Origin	Gore (D) 101,079	(52%)
			Bush (R) 85,119	(44%)
			Other 6,538	(3%)
			Cook Partisan Voting Index: D + 1	

Occupation	Blue collar: 18.3%	White collar: 65.0%	Gray collar: 16.7%

Staten Island is part of New York City, yet a land apart, closer geographically to New Jersey than to Brooklyn. The sixth largest island in the continental U.S., its inclusion in Greater New York as part of the great 1898 consolidation was something of an afterthought. It was connected to the rest of the City only by ferry or through Bayonne, New Jersey, until the Verrazano Narrows Bridge—one of Robert Moses's last and most impressive infrastructure achievements—opened to traffic in 1965. Hilly Staten Island (or Richmond County) is the state's southernmost county, one-tenth as densely populated as Manhattan—and that's after it grew 22% between 1990 and 2004, the fastest growth rate of any county in New York state. Ethnically, the 13th District has the highest percentage of residents of Italian ancestry in the nation; the signs on coffee shops here read *Caffe* and on delicatessens *Salumeria*. The Staten Island Ferry docks at St. George, the government hub and home of the Staten Island Yankees' new ballpark. The north and south shores that spread out from there are notable for their pleasant Victorian homes, while the island's west shore is industrial marshland, with plans for the eventual development of a 2,200-acre park (more than twice as large as Central Park) on the landfill of the now-closed Fresh Kills dump. Staten Island's interior consists of blocks of suburbia alternating with scrubland that's rapidly being turned into suburbia; this growth, plus a shortage of mass transit, has brought significant traffic congestion to this spacious island.

Culturally, Staten Islanders are deeply conservative—more so than in most of New York's suburbs, and quite a contrast from Manhattanites who live a 20-minute ferry ride away. Taking a cue from Fresh Kills, their motto is apt: "Don't dump on us." Not many people here read the *New York Times*; the local paper is the *Staten Island Advance* (emphasis on the first syllable, please), the foundation of the Newhouse publishing empire. Fed up with New York City's high income taxes and social programs, Staten Island residents voted in 1993 for secession, but the legislature never acted. That same election, Staten Islanders provided the margin of victory for Mayor Rudolph Giuliani, whose agenda of cutting crime and welfare rolls soothed the secessionist fervor. The Giuliani years produced an economic boom, with a new ferry terminal, additional shops and hundreds of new homes near cleaned-up beaches. The biggest victory was the closing of Fresh Kills in March 2001, though it opened again temporarily for the cleanup of the World Trade Center site. The September 11 attacks killed nearly 250 Staten Islanders—nearly 10% of the dead, including nearly one-quarter of all the fire fighters who died.

The 13th Congressional District of New York is made up of Staten Island plus a few adjacent neighborhoods with similar demographics over the Verrazano Narrows Bridge in Brooklyn. These include heavily Catholic and Italian Bay Ridge and Bensonhurst—middle-class enclaves with large single-family brownstones and small apartment buildings. The entertainment industry has found in these two neighborhoods some memorable characters: The Three Stooges (Moe, Curly and Shemp) grew up in Bensonhurst; it was also home to the fictional Ralph Kramden of *The Honeymooners*. And it was on the streets of Bensonhurst and Bay Ridge that John Travolta danced to fame in *Saturday Night Fever*. The district includes Fort Hamilton, the only active-duty military base in New York City and one of the oldest military posts still in operation in the United States. The 13th is seeing a rising number of immigrants—growing numbers of Muslims in Bay Ridge, plus an influx of newcomers from West Africa, Mexico, South America, Southeast Asia, and Russia in a few white ethnic neighborhoods near St. George. But Staten Island remains New York's whitest borough and home to families who have lived there for generations; the 13th is only 6% black and 11% Hispanic. State Senator John Marchi, a local legend, retired in 2006 after 50 years in Albany; Republicans kept the seat. Voters here solidly backed Republicans George Pataki for governor and Rick Lazio for senator and gave Mayor Michael Bloomberg his slim winning margin in 2001. The district voted 52%-44% for Al Gore in 2000. But it snapped back and voted 55%-45% for George W. Bush in 2004, one of his biggest increases in the country and strong evidence of a September 11 effect at the polls.

The congressman from the 13th District is Vito Fossella, a Republican who won a 1997 special election. Fossella comes from a political, and Democratic, Staten Island family: his great-grandfather, James O'Leary, was a New Deal congressman from this area in 1935-44; his father, Vito Fossella Sr., chaired the city's Board of Standards under Mayor Edward Koch; his uncle, Frank Fossella, was elected to the city council and was beaten in 1985 by Republican Susan Molinari, Vito Jr.'s predecessor in Congress. Despite the party difference, the families became close. Vito Fossella graduated from Penn and Fordham law school and became a Republican in 1990, at 25, because of his conservative philosophy; he switched from pro-choice to pro-life in 1995, after the birth of his son. He worked on the campaigns of Susan Molinari, who succeeded her father, Guy Molinari, in the House. In 1994, less than a year after finishing law school, Fossella was elected to the city council to fill a vacancy, with the help of the Molinaris. He was elected to Congress in 1997 after Susan

Molinari's surprise resignation. Democrats picked Eric Vitaliano, a 15-year assemblyman, an abortion opponent and sponsor of New York's death penalty. Vitaliano criticized Fossella as inexperienced and constantly tried to link Fossella with House Speaker Newt Gingrich. Fossella hit Vitaliano for supporting needle exchanges and for not taking Americans for Tax Reform's anti-tax-raise pledge. Fossella was helped by $750,000 in independent expenditures by the national Republican Party, attacking Vitaliano for supporting tax increases. Also helpful was the reelection campaign of Giuliani, in a district where few local Democratic officeholders would admit they supported their liberal nominee Ruth Messinger. On Election Day, Giuliani carried the district 3–1 and Fossella won 61%-39%.

In the House, Fossella serves on the Energy and Commerce Committee and has one of the most conservative voting records in the New York delegation, though he leans centrist on social and economic issues. He worked on interstate waste issues, pushed for rerouting Newark Airport flights away from Staten Island, helped to save Fort Hamilton from base-closing, and sponsored the law that designates September 11 as Patriot Day, a day of reflection. He was an outspoken critic of the proposed purchase of U.S. seaports by Dubai Ports World. In 2007, after Republicans lost their majority, Fossella was to forced to choose between his seats on the Financial Services Committee and Energy and Commerce; he gave up his seat on Financial Services, noting that he had more seniority on Energy and Commerce.

Fossella faced a serious challenge in 2004, when 76-year-old former Assemblyman Frank Barbaro ran an aggressive campaign with help from organized labor. Barbaro ran ads that attacked Fossella as anti-union and too conservative even for this district. Fossella defended his record of helping to rebuild lower Manhattan and tending to local health problems after the September 11 attacks, plus his support for tax cuts. He won 59%-41%, with 63% in Staten Island; Barbaro got 53% of the vote in Brooklyn, his home, which cast only 24% of the total. In the more difficult 2006 cycle, Fossella won 57%-43% against poorly-funded Bay Ridge lawyer Stephen Harrison after several better-known prospects declined to run. Harrison announced he would run again in 2008; several other more prominent candidates also were considering the race. An early supporter of Rudy Giuliani's campaign for president, Fossella has been mentioned as a possible mayoral candidate in 2009.

FOURTEENTH DISTRICT

Rep. Carolyn Maloney (D)

Elected 1992, 8th term; b. Feb. 19, 1948, Greensboro, NC; home, Manhattan; Greensboro Col, A.B. 1968; Presbyterian; married (Clifton).

Elected Office: NY City Cncl., 1982-92.

Professional Career: NYC Bd. of Ed., 1970-77; Legis. aide, NY Assembly & NY Senate, 1977-82.

DC Office: 2331 RHOB, 20515, 202-225-7944; Fax: 202-225-4709; Web site: maloney.house.gov.

District Offices: Astoria, 718-932-1804; Manhattan, 212-860-0606.

Committees: *Financial Services* (4th of 37 D): Financial Institutions & Consumer Credit (Chmn.); Domestic and International Monetary Policy, Trade & Technology; Housing & Community Opportunity. *Joint Economic Committee* (Vice Chmn. of 10 D). *Oversight & Government Reform* (5th of 23 D): National Security & Foreign Affairs; Information Policy, Census & National Archives; Government Management, Organization & Procurement.

Group Ratings

	ADA	ACLU	AFS	LCV	ITIC	NTU	COC	ACU	CFG	FRC
2006	85	95	86	92	43	12	43	8	4	0
2005	100	—	100	100	—	15	37	0	4	0

National Journal Ratings

	2005 LIB	—	2005 CONS		2006 LIB	—	2006 CONS
Economic	94%	—	0%		71%	—	28%
Social	87%	—	12%		86%	—	13%
Foreign	79%	—	21%		70%	—	28%

Key Votes of the 109th Congress

1. Estate Tax Repeal	N	5. Limit Interstate Abortion	N	9. Build Border Fence	Y
2. Limit CAFE Standards	N	6. Extend Patriot Act	N	10. CAFTA	N
3. FY06 Spending Curb	N	7. Bar Same Sex Marriage	N	11. Oppose Iraq Withdrawal	N
4. Drilling in ANWR	N	8. Stem Cell Research $	Y	12. Detainee Tribunals	N

Election Results

2006 general	Carolyn Maloney (D-WF-Ind)	119,582	(84%)	($1,030,382)
	Danniel Maio (R)	21,969	(16%)	($82,425)
2006 primary	Carolyn Maloney (D)	unopposed		
2004 general	Carolyn Maloney (D-Ind-WF)	186,688	(81%)	($918,162)
	Anton Srdanovic (R-C)	43,623	(19%)	($23,217)

Prior Winning Percentages: 2002 (75%); 2000 (74%); 1998 (77%); 1996 (72%); 1994 (64%); 1992 (50%)

The People		Race/Ethnic Origin	Ancestry	
Area size:	15 sq. mi.	65.9% White	Irish: 8.1%	Italian: 7.7%
Urban population:	100.0%	4.8% Black	German: 6.1%	
Rural population:	0.0%	11.4% Asian	**2004 Presidential Vote**	
Pop. 2000:	654,361	0.1% Native Am.	Kerry (D) 201,782	(74%)
Pop. 2005 (est):	662,128	0.0% Hawaiian	Bush (R) 66,494	(24%)
Median income:	$57,152	3.1% Two+ races	Other 3,160	(1%)
Poverty status:	12.4%	0.6% Other	**2000 Presidential Vote**	
Military veterans:	6.0%	14.0% Hispanic Origin	Gore (D) 168,842	(70%)
			Bush (R) 56,055	(23%)
			Other 16,908	(7%)
			Cook Partisan Voting Index: D +26	

Occupation   Blue collar: 7.8%   White collar: 82.1%   Gray collar: 10.2%

The Upper East Side of Manhattan, the home today of people with more accumulated wealth than anywhere else in the world, began as much of New York City did—as farmland. Its eastern border was established at Fifth Avenue when work began on Central Park in 1857, but most of the area was still farmland when the park was completed in 1873. During the 1880s, the avenues—Fifth, Madison, Park, Lexington, Third, Second, First—were paved, and rich New Yorkers and many who had made their money elsewhere—Pittsburgh steel baron Andrew Carnegie, Montana mining magnate William Clark—built mansions on Fifth Avenue. Third Avenue, with its elevated train line, was lined with walkups for working class commuters, while the side streets off Fifth Avenue were lined with massive brownstone houses shielded from the industrial haze along the East River. The Upper East Side began taking on its present character in 1913, when Grand Central Terminal was opened and the New York Central rail line was buried under Park Avenue: what had been a filthy railroad cut became a broad boulevard lined with grand apartment buildings. The federal income tax, passed the same year, had the unintended consequence of encouraging New York's rich to dispense with grand mansions and live, quietly and out of sight, in apartment buildings where doormen protected their privacy.

The emergence of the modern Upper East Side represented yet another iteration of the pattern noticed by the mid-19th century New York diarists Philip Hone and George Templeton Strong: On such a compact island, it took only a generation or so before buildings were torn down and rebuilt. Even today, New York is being transformed by gleaming postmodern skyscrapers and high-priced storefronts, though its most enduring landmarks were products of the first half of the 20th century: the Flatiron Building in 1901; the Woolworth Building and Grand Central in 1913; the Chrysler Building, Empire State Building and Rockefeller Center in the 1920s and 1930s; and the United Nations headquarters, the world's first glass-fronted skyscraper, after World War II. This area holds the more humble distinction as site of the first public housing project in America—the First Houses, built in lower Manhattan in 1935 by Mayor Fiorello LaGuardia.

The 14th Congressional District of New York includes within its irregular borders the Upper East Side and nearly all of these buildings. The district begins at East 96th Street, the historic dividing line between Manhattan's wealthiest and poorest neighborhoods, near where the railroad emerges from its tunnel and comes out in the middle of Park Avenue, and runs all the way down to East 9th Street in the East Village. It includes all of Central Park; much of the midtown corporate district; Murray Hill in the 30's and Gramercy Park to the south; and parts of the East Village, with its pricey lofts and remnants of addiction, and the Lower East Side. Midtown Manhattan's skyscrapers and the Garment District are also here. The 14th takes in Roosevelt Island, a 147-acre expanse in the East River that was transformed in the 1970s from a hospital-and-prison complex to an ethnically diverse residential neighborhood (and stripped of its old name, Welfare Island). The 14th also includes part of Queens across the East River: blue-collar Long Island City; Steinway, part of historically Irish Sunnyside; and vibrantly Greek Astoria, now with many Asians, Latinos and Arabs. The institutions of the 14th are famous and powerful—from the United Nations to the New York Public Library to St. Patrick's Cathedral—and its stores of culture are among the world's finest: the Metropolitan Museum of Art, the Guggenheim, the Whitney and the Frick, but also a rising arts cluster in Long Island City with the contemporary art gallery P.S. 1 and the American Museum of the Moving Image adjoining the old Astoria movie studios, where most movies were made before the industry moved to sunnier Hollywood.

The 14th District is the latest version of the Upper East Side-based Silk Stocking district, originally created in 1918. The district has always been dominated by its affluent and highly educated voters, leaders in securities, publishing, advertising, entertainment, broadcasting and communications. Historically, the Silk Stocking creed was confidence in its duty to lead the nation and mistrust of the city's (usually Democratic) immigrant masses—the politics of Theodore Roosevelt, the old *New York Herald Tribune* and Henry Luce's *Time* magazine. While it did not trust union leaders and Democratic Party politicians, it accepted much of the New Deal. This district believed the nation should be led by the well-educated Protestant gentlemen one saw strolling down Madison Avenue to their clubs, who held high government posts from Theodore Roosevelt's day and past Franklin's. But the attitude of the Manhattan elite was transformed from liberal Republican to leftish Democratic in a way personified by the Silk Stocking district's most famous congressman, John Lindsay. He was elected in 1958 as a liberal Republican, an advocate of civil liberties full of mistrust of machine Democrats and unions, and in 1965 he was elected mayor of New York. While mayor, he ran up huge debts that led the city to the brink of bankruptcy in 1975, while neighborhoods deteriorated and the city lost 1 million people in the 1970s. He was succeeded as congressman and ultimately as mayor by Edward Koch, whose political travels were the reverse: Koch started as a liberal reform Democrat and became more conservative, and in the process lost the support of elite Manhattan by backing capital punishment, opposing racial quotas and questioning poverty programs. Since then, Rudolph Giuliani and his successor Michael Bloomberg, who lives in his town house on East 79th Street, have been cultural liberals on abortion, gay rights and gun control. To the national Republican party of Newt Gingrich in the 1990s and now George W. Bush, who brought the Republican Convention of 2004 to a less than enthralled Manhattan, the Upper East Side is unremittingly hostile: these are people that seem to come from another country. The Upper East Side reacted with similar disdain to Barry Goldwater in 1964, and voted for Lyndon Johnson by a wide margin, as did the entire country; but, when the rest of the country narrowly favored George W. Bush over Al Gore and then John Kerry, the Upper East Side voted for the Democrats by wider margins than it had voted for Johnson. In American politics today, cultural issues trump economics: the affluent Upper East Side votes heavily Democratic (the 10021 zip code was the nation's top zip code for Democratic campaign contributions in the 2004 election cycle) while low-income Mississippi votes heavily Republican.

The congresswoman from the 14th District is Carolyn Maloney, a Democrat first elected in 1992. Born and educated in North Carolina, she visited New York in 1970 at the age of 22, loved it and "just stayed." She worked on welfare education programs on behalf of teachers during the 1970s, and from 1977 to 1982 was an influential legislative staffer in Albany. She was elected to the New York City Council in 1982. For 1992, redistricting made the Silk Stocking district more Democratic and Maloney ran against incumbent Bill Green, an independent Republican who shared Manhattan's cultural liberalism but could not compete with the enthusiasm of a Democratic Party dominated by the feminist left. He was poorly positioned to appeal to voters in the outer borough neighborhoods that were added to the district, who preferred Republicans conservative on cultural issues but liberal on economics. Maloney lost the Manhattan part of the district 50%-44%, but carried Queens heavily and won 50%-48% overall.

Maloney started off in the House with an outsider's enthusiasm and a mostly liberal voting record, and stayed to make serious contributions on important issues. On the Financial Services

Committee, she worked to keep banks from controlling other businesses, sought more oversight of the Federal Reserve, and added some privacy provisions to the Gramm-Leach-Bliley financial modernization law. She worked on data-collection and security rules, and has helped to craft reforms tightening rules for foreign investment. With an eye to Astoria, she helped found the Congressional Caucus on Hellenic Issues; with an eye to the corporate suites, she voted for normal trade relations with China. A leader of the Women's Caucus, she demanded that the FDA permit over-the-counter sales of morning-after birth control pills, and opposed separating men and women in basic training; her bill to restrict allegedly deceptive advertising by anti-abortion "crisis pregnancy centers" led to an unusual conflict with the ACLU. She filed a bill to create an office within the IRS to prosecute sex traffickers who violate tax laws. In the majority, she became chairman of the Financial Services Subcommittee on Financial Institutions and Consumer Credit, and vice-chairman of the Joint Economic Committee to chairman Charles Schumer; in 2009, she could chair JEC. Her priorities include limits on predatory loans and protections from inaccurate credit reports.

With part of her district in Lower Manhattan and close to Ground Zero, the aftermath of the September 11 attacks kept her busy. She was among the most outspoken House Democrats urging George W. Bush to quickly send New York the $20 billion that Congress approved for cleanup and recovery and she urged him to appoint a coordinator to work with the city. Her proposal to give a $1,000 tax credit to visitors to the city went nowhere.

Any doubts that Maloney had a firm lock on the district were dispelled in the Republican year of 1994. Manhattan Councilman Charles Millard spent almost $1 million against her; but the 14th District voted 78% for Mario Cuomo (who lost his bid that year for a fourth term as governor) and Maloney won 64%-35%. Aside from the perils of redistricting, she has not had to worry about reelection since then.

FIFTEENTH DISTRICT

Rep. Charles Rangel (D)

Elected 1970, 19th term; b. June 11, 1930, New York City; home, Harlem; N.Y.U., B.S. 1957, St. John's U., LL.B. 1960; Catholic; married (Alma).

Military Career: Army, 1948-52 (Korea).

Elected Office: NY Assembly, 1966-70.

Professional Career: Asst. U.S. Atty., S. Dist. of NY, 1959-64; Legal Cnsl., NYC Housing & Redevel. Bd., Neighborhood Conservation Bureau, 1963-68; Gen. Cnsl., Natl. Advisory Comm. on Selective Svc., 1966.

DC Office: 2354 RHOB, 20515, 202-225-4365; Fax: 202-225-0816; Web site: www.house.gov/rangel.

District Offices: Manhattan, 212-663-3900.

Committees: *Joint Committee on Taxation* (Chmn. of 5 D). *Ways & Means* (Chmn. of 24 D).

Group Ratings

	ADA	ACLU	AFS	LCV	ITIC	NTU	COC	ACU	CFG	FRC
2006	95	100	100	100	67	15	40	4	7	0
2005	100	—	100	94	—	15	38	0	3	0

National Journal Ratings

	2005 LIB	—	2005 CONS		2006 LIB	—	2006 CONS
Economic	88%	—	12%		94%	—	0%
Social	92%	—	7%		96%	—	3%
Foreign	85%	—	14%		83%	—	14%

Key Votes of the 109th Congress

1. Estate Tax Repeal	N	5. Limit Interstate Abortion	N	9. Build Border Fence	N
2. Limit CAFE Standards	Y	6. Extend Patriot Act	N	10. CAFTA	N
3. FY06 Spending Curb	N	7. Bar Same Sex Marriage	N	11. Oppose Iraq Withdrawal	N
4. Drilling in ANWR	N	8. Stem Cell Research	$	12. Detainee Tribunals	N

Election Results

2006 general	Charles Rangel (D-WF) 103,916	(94%)	($2,047,116)
	Edward Daniels (R) 6,592	(6%)	
2006 primary	Charles Rangel (D) .... unopposed		
2004 general	Charles Rangel (D-WF) 161,351	(91%)	($1,728,867)
	Kenneth Jefferson (R) 12,355	(7%)	
	Other... 3,345	(2%)	

Prior Winning Percentages: 2002 (88%); 2000 (92%); 1998 (93%); 1996 (91%); 1994 (97%); 1992 (95%); 1990 (97%); 1988 (97%); 1986 (96%); 1984 (97%); 1982 (97%); 1980 (96%); 1978 (96%); 1976 (97%); 1974 (97%); 1972 (96%); 1970 (87%)

The People		Race/Ethnic Origin	Ancestry	
Area size:	16 sq. mi.	16.4% White	West Indian: 2.8% German: 2.0%	
Urban population:	100.0%	30.5% Black	Irish: 2.0%	
Rural population:	0.0%	2.8% Asian	**2004 Presidential Vote**	
Pop. 2000:	654,361	0.2% Native Am.	Kerry (D) 194,186	(90%)
Pop. 2005 (est):	671,634	0.0% Hawaiian	Bush (R) 20,049	(9%)
Median income:	$27,934	1.8% Two+ races	Other 2,255	(1%)
Poverty status:	30.5%	0.4% Other	**2000 Presidential Vote**	
Military veterans:	4.6%	47.9% Hispanic Origin	Gore (D) 165,002	(87%)
			Other 13,292	(7%)
			Bush (R) 12,430	(7%)
			Cook Partisan Voting Index: D +43	

Occupation   Blue collar: 14.8%   White collar: 63.8%   Gray collar: 21.4%

Harlem, for many years America's most famous black ghetto, is now rebounding from decades of grim times. Harlem's development came relatively late in New York City's history. When Alexander Hamilton and Roger Morris built mansions in northern Manhattan, they were far out in the countryside. Early critics of Central Park questioned the necessity of setting aside open land when picnickers could always go to Harlem. By the late 19th century, Harlem had become a commuter neighborhood for Germans and then Jews and Italians. After the turn of the century, real-estate speculators began constructing blocks of impressive brownstones, hoping to capitalize on the impending arrival of the subway. But overbuilding led to high vacancy rates, and some landlords, in desperation, agreed to rent to African-Americans as long as they were willing to pay a premium. After generations of being shunted from one neighborhood to the next as the city developed, enough black residents were willing to do so that the neighborhood soon turned into the locus of New York City's African-American community. Harlem expanded from its nucleus around Lenox Avenue and 125th Street, while the Italian neighborhood to the east later known as Spanish Harlem grew outward from 116th Street and Pleasant Avenue. In northwest Harlem's Sugar Hill lived many of the greatest black Americans—W.E.B. DuBois, Thurgood Marshall, Ralph Ellison, Joe Louis.

For a long moment Harlem was a wondrous place, a center of writers and professionals and entertainers; the rosters of the Apollo Theater on 125th Street in the 1920s and 1930s were filled with the names of great artists still remembered today. Back then, the *WPA Guide* described Harlem as "the spiritual capital of Black America." But starting with the summer 1964 riot, Harlem faced decades of deterioration. Hundreds of brownstones were abandoned or pulled down. As successful black families moved outward—to Springfield Gardens in Queens or Williamsbridge in the Bronx or to the Westchester or New Jersey suburbs—Harlem was increasingly left with welfare mothers and criminal gangs, and its population dropped by one-third between 1970 and 1990.

But starting in the 1990s things turned better. The federal government gave $300 million in investment capital, and the huge drop in crime under Mayor Rudolph Giuliani made Harlem real estate valuable again. Brownstones were renovated, vacant city buildings sold off; neighborhood schools upgraded; commercial frontage repaired; arts spaces opened. Harlem was made an Enterprise Zone, with favorable federal and state tax treatment, and the Metropolitan Economic Revitalization Fund pumped money into new developments, as did Calvin Butts's Abyssinian Baptist Church. Younger African-Americans are returning, while visitors from overseas, especially Japan and Europe, flock to the area for historical tours, prompting a boomlet in niche hotels and guest houses. The façade of the Apollo Theater has been restored, a new Harlem pier has been constructed, supermarkets and chain drug stores have opened, and there is a big shopping center on 125th Street, with the same stores found in suburban malls. In July 2001, Bill Clinton opened his post-presidential office at 55 West 125th Street. Harlem and Upper Manhattan now account for nearly 10% of Manhattan condominium and co-op sales.

Politically, Harlem has been heavily Democratic ever since the 1930s, when black voters switched from the Republican party of Abraham Lincoln to the Democratic party of Franklin Roosevelt. Oddly, Harlem did not get its own congressional district until 1944; the lines, previously drawn in 1918, were based on the 1910 Census, when Harlem had far fewer people. The new congressman was Adam Clayton Powell Jr., minister at the Abyssinian Baptist Church and a brilliant orator who became the most famous (and infamous) black politician of his time: chairman of the Education and Labor Committee when it passed the Great Society programs in 1965, then excluded from Congress in 1967 (illegally, the Supreme Court ruled) for refusing to honor a New York decree in a libel case brought by a plaintiff he called a "bag woman."

Today, the 15th Congressional District of New York includes not just Harlem but all of northern Manhattan, down to 89th Street on the west side and 96th Street on the east side. On the west side, the district's southern reaches include portions of the white-liberal Upper West Side as well as the Morningside Heights precincts around Columbia University. On the east side, 96th Street is where the railroad comes out of the tunnel that runs under Park Avenue to Grand Central Station and the Upper East Side gives way to Harlem. Spanish Harlem, just to the north, was once Italian (it was Fiorello LaGuardia's political base), and later heavily Puerto Rican; today, "El Barrio" has fewer Puerto Ricans and more Mexicans and Dominicans and some gentrifying whites. Still further north, the district includes Washington Heights, once mainly Jewish, and Inwood, once heavily Italian. Now both are heavily Latino, the center of Dominican life in New York as Dominicans replace Puerto Ricans as New York's most numerous Latino group. Washington Heights was hit especially hard by the crack epidemic in the late 1980s and early 1990s, but now it too is recovering thanks to reduced crime and immigrant vitality. The district also includes imposing parts of New York's infrastructure—the huge Con Edison plant on the East River, Wards Island, home to the Triborough Bridge, and the city prison on Rikers Island: but there are no voters here. Overall, the district in 2000 was 31% black and 48% Hispanic—figures that testify to decades of black flight from Harlem and the continuing in-rush of immigrants from the Western Hemisphere. Since 2000 there has been an outmigration of blacks from New York City, mostly to the South, to the point that in 2005 a white candidate finished second in a council race in a Harlem-dominated district. In 2004 this was the most heavily Democratic congressional district in the nation, 90% for John Kerry and 9% for George W. Bush.

The congressman from the 15th District is Charles Rangel, first elected to the House in 1970, now chairman of the House Ways and Means Committee, the first New Yorker to chair the committee since Fernando Wood in 1877-81. Rangel grew up in Harlem and served in the Army in Korea, where he rescued 40 men from behind the lines in Kunu-ri and was awarded the Bronze Star. He graduated from New York University and St. John's University law school, served as legal counsel in several government agencies and was elected to the Assembly in 1966; he was part of a group of young black politicians, with Basil Paterson, Carl McCall and Percy Sutton, who for many years dominated Harlem and greatly influenced New York politics. In 1970 Rangel challenged Powell in the Democratic primary and narrowly won. After the 1974 election, he got Governor-elect Hugh Carey's seat on Ways and Means. Like most Harlem politicians, he has long argued that government aid and racial preferences are needed to solve Harlem's problems. Yet much in his own career suggests otherwise.

Rangel's main emphasis for a decade was denunciation of the drug trade. From 1983 until it was abolished in 1993 with the other House select committees, Rangel chaired the Select Committee on Narcotics Abuse and Control, and seldom missed a chance to relate other problems to drugs; after all, he has seen how they can destroy a community. On Ways and Means Rangel worked, with success, to protect state and local income tax deductibility in the 1986 tax reform and is an author of the Federal Empowerment Zone demonstration, the Low Income Housing tax credit and the Targeted Jobs tax credit. He was a key sponsor of the 1993 increases in the Earned Income Tax Credit. All those are aimed at turning around places like Harlem and enabling people there to rise on the economic ladder. Looking abroad, he sponsored a 1987 act that eliminated the deductibility of taxes paid to the apartheid regime in South Africa; this induced many firms to pull out of the country.

Rangel combines political shrewdness with a winning personality, but when Republicans took control of the House he indulged in some extravagant rhetoric. When a bipartisan majority voted to end racial preferences in broadcasting in 1995, Rangel lashed out in a letter to Ways and Means Chairman Bill Archer: "Mr. Chairman, in America we cannot afford to be colorblind. Just like under

Hitler, people say they don't mean to blame any particular individuals and groups, but in the U.S. those groups always turn out to be minorities and immigrants." Archer refused to speak to Rangel, who became ranking minority member in 1997, except in public committee meetings and refused to meet with him in private until June 1999, when Archer and Rangel were working on Social Security. Rangel defended Bill Clinton against impeachment with great vigor, but he did not always get along with Clinton. He resented it when the administration negotiated directly with Republicans, leaving congressional Democrats out of the loop.

Rangel favors eliminating all sanctions on trade with Cuba; he favors allowing Haitian and Dominican immigrants into the United States on the same basis as refugees from Cuba. Rangel voted against the Iraq war resolution in October 2002 and in November 2003 called for the resignation of Donald Rumsfeld. In March 2004, he had discussions with Haiti's ousted President Jean-Bertrand Aristide; he relayed Aristide's claim that "the so-called resignation was dictated to him over the phone by representatives of the United States embassy," but added, "I'm not in a position to contradict Secretary Powell. But this information about Aristide asking to leave the country, or that his life was in danger, was never shared with us." He was arrested after protesting outside the Sudanese Embassy in 2004, as he had been outside the South African Embassy in 1984. In his travels abroad over the years Rangel encountered few black diplomats, so in 2003 he set up fellowships with $28,000 stipends for two years of graduate study in preparation for the Foreign Service; ten Rangel Fellows were sworn into the Service by Secretary of State Condoleezza Rice in November 2006. On the last day of 2002 he called for a revival of the military draft, contending that "a disproportionate number of the poor and members of minority groups make up the enlisted ranks of the military, while the most privileged Americans are underrepresented or absent." He introduced a bill in 2003 to require some form of national service, military or civilian, from Americans from 18 to 26, and found 13 cosponsors. When House Republican leaders brought it to a vote in October 2004, he called it a "political maneuver to kill rumors of the president's intention to reinstate the draft after the November election," and voted against it, saying it had had no committee hearings; it was voted down 402–2. Nevertheless he reintroduced bills to reinstate the draft in 2006 and 2007.

Ways and Means Chairman Bill Archer was crisp and to the point; Bill Thomas, who succeeded him in 2001, was acerbic and uncollegial and made few if any moves to bipartisanship. Rangel's frustration came out when he was asked in October 2002 about a Thomas tax proposal. "It's almost accepted now that all Thomas has to do is to talk to DeLay and Armey, and then his bills come to the floor. I am embarrassed that I would hear about [the tax proposal] from you, [but] it is not unusual." In July 2003, a Ways and Means markup of pension legislation ended in chaos after Democrats walked out in protest; they charged that they hadn't had enough time to review a substitute amendment that the committee had met to mark up. Thomas called on Capitol Police to remove them from the library where they had gathered; in their absence, Republicans approved the bill by voice vote. Rangel later offered a resolution to nullify the markup and chastise Thomas but dropped it after Thomas took to the House floor and gave an emotional apology for his actions. Rangel also protested when he was excluded by Thomas from the conference committee on the 2003 Medicare prescription drug bill; at one point in October he, Stephanie Tubbs Jones and Marion Berry showed up at the room where the conference was meeting. But the only Democrats Thomas allowed to participate were Senators Max Baucus and John Breaux.

In 2000, Rangel worked hard for a bill to cut tariffs on apparel and other imports from sub-Saharan Africa, despite opposition by unions and textile interests and from other members of the Congressional Black Caucus. His leadership on the Africa free trade agreement was not accidental, and its effects seem to have prompted him to take a more favorable view of trade agreements than most House Democrats. During 2004 Rangel did not take a position on the Central American-Dominican Republic Free Trade Agreement, perhaps because there are many Dominican and Central American immigrants in New York. But in March 2004 he did praise the administration for including the Dominican Republic in the agreement, though in October 2004 criticized the administration for threatening to exclude the Dominican Republic if it didn't repeal its tax on soft drinks with high-fructose corn syrup; Rangel said that issue should be taken to the WTO. In May 2005 he signed a letter protesting CAFTA's labor provisions and as Minority Leader Nancy Pelosi declared it a party-line issue, he offered a substitute in committee that predictably failed and then watched as administration inducements produced just enough votes for it to pass in July. He noted ruefully that New Yorkers Ed Towns and Gregory Meeks, with many constituents from the region, supplied two of the 15 Democratic votes that helped pass the measure. In November 2005 he spoke more enthusiastically about the Bahrain free trade agreement but said he was concerned about the labor provisions. After meeting with Peruvian President Alejandro Toledo in March 2006 he said he was "optimistic" about the Peru FTA. On becoming chairman, he said he wanted the full committee, not the Trade Subcommittee chaired by Sander Levin, who has taken a harder line on labor and environmental provisions, to handle trade agreements. In June, he and ranking Republican Jim McCrery agreed on provisions that enabled them to support the Peru and Panama FTAs. Negotiations continued over the FTA with Colombia, which is much larger, and the terms and conditions for renewing the president's trade promotion authority, which ultimately expired at the end of June 2007.

"I came to the Congress to close up all the tax loopholes," Rangel said in June 2005. "How little did I know that so many of them would be incentives." In December 2005 he unsuccessfully opposed extensions of the 2003 capital gains and dividends tax cuts. But even in the minority he was looking ahead to the larger issue of broad tax changes. He said in March 2006 that he wouldn't use a broad-based tax bill to gain more revenue, but would take the revenue-neutral approach that Ways and Means Chairman Dan Rostenkowski used on the 1986 act, the last broad-based changes. In September 2006 he said he would consider scrapping the Bush tax cuts to limit the Alternative Minimum Tax, which has been threatening huge percentages of taxpayers in high-income, high-tax states like New York. In November 2006 he said he wanted a permanent change on the AMT and would try to pay for the $1 trillion cost by restricting foreign tax shelters or narrowing the gap between taxes owed and taxes paid. But he has made it plain many times over the years, as he did in the debates leading to the 1986 tax act, that he would always oppose eliminating the deduction for state and local taxes—a deduction worth a great deal to New Yorkers whose state and local taxes are so high, and to New York public employee unions, who might face downward pressure on taxes and spending if voters couldn't deduct those taxes any longer. Asked just before the election whether he would extend the Bush tax cuts, he replied in a New York minute, "Forget about it." But he added that he didn't intend to legislate that they end before 2010. "I think it would be ridiculous for us in 2007 to be talking about 2010 tax cuts. I don't want to go retroactive in terms of any of the tax cuts. I think retroactive tax increases are bad tax policy."

Rangel opposed George W. Bush's proposal for individual investment accounts in Social Security. "There's no guarantee the market's going to work for you. I don't think the president's going to give us a bill," he said in March 2005. He was right: Bush never did produce a text, even as he kept pressing for individual accounts. Looking ahead after Bush's proposal had become moot in March 2006, he said, "It's not going to be easy for anyone to raise taxes or cut benefits, delay the age of benefits. All of these are necessary and difficult—it's just a question of coming together and doing it."

By the summer of 2006, as Republicans fell in the polls, it became clear that Rangel had a good chance to be in the majority again. In August 2006 he vowed to leave the House if Republicans kept their majority. When Republicans warned against Rangel as a tax raiser, he replied good-naturedly, "Republicans have to say these things. If I was down in the polls as they are, I'd knock Charlie Rangel too." When asked if he would want to be addressed as Mr. Chairman, he said, "If I become the chairman of the Ways and Means Committee, I don't want to be treated any differently than any other world leader." In October Dick Cheney said, "Charlie is losing it. I think Charlie is a lot older than I am, and it shows." Rangel replied with some asperity, "I was flattered that he knew I was this old. I knew all I had to do was challenge him to a psychiatric examination, to take a lie-detector test over the reasons we went to war. And I would have fun doing it. But then I realized that I could be showing disrespect for my country and the office." After the Democratic victory, he said, "One of my biggest jobs is to convince Democrats that it's not in our best interests to get even if we want to get something done. I'm convinced the Republican losses wasn't because of this country's love of the Democrats. It was frustration with the war, with Katrina, with corruption. Now we get a two-year window." He said he would conduct bipartisan retreats, as Rostenkowski used to do; the first one was held in January 2007 and described by some as "the Kumbaya meeting." He found ranking Republican Jim McCrery much more friendly and respectful than Thomas. In February 2007 he worked with McCrery on a bipartisan package of small business tax breaks to attach to the minimum wage bill, as an alternative to the Senate's package. And he conducted extensive negotiations with McCrery on trade.

Rangel has long been a major player in New York city and state politics. He strongly backed his old friend Carl McCall for governor, and in December 2001 said he would vote for George Pataki if the nomination went to McCall's rival, Andrew Cuomo. In October 2002 Rangel attacked the DNC for not backing McCall strongly enough. In March 2005 he backed Mayor Michael Bloomberg's plans for a Jets stadium on the West Side and in May he endorsed Virginia Fields for the Democratic nomination for mayor. He gave a hearty endorsement of Andrew Cuomo for attorney general in 2006. He was frostier toward governor candidate Eliot Spitzer after he chose a running mate who was not Rangel's first choice: "When Eliot Spitzer, the world's smartest man, is telling me that he has picked his candidate and knows that his candidate can win, who am I to question the world's smartest man?"

Rangel himself has been easily reelected. In 1994 he faced primary opposition from the son of his predecessor, the Puerto Rican-raised Councilman Adam Clayton Powell IV (Adam Clayton Powell III, another son, is a respected media expert). Rangel spent $1.4 million and won 61%-33%. Rangel had no primary opposition in 2006, when it appeared he was in position to become Ways and Means chairman. He won the general election 94%-6%.

SIXTEENTH DISTRICT

Rep. Jose Serrano (D)

Elected Mar. 1990, 9th full term; b. Oct. 24, 1943, Mayaguez, PR; home, Bronx; Lehman Col.; Catholic; married (Mary).

Military Career: Army Medical Corps, 1964-66.

Elected Office: Dist. 7 Schl. Bd., 1969-74; NY Assembly, 1974-90.

Professional Career: Banker, 1961-69.

DC Office: 2227 RHOB, 20515, 202-225-4361; Fax: 202-225-6001; Web site: www.house.gov/serrano.

District Offices: Bronx, 718-620-0084.

Committees: *Appropriations* (8th of 37 D): Financial Services & General Government (Chmn.); Homeland Security; Energy & Water Development.

Group Ratings

	ADA	ACLU	AFS	LCV	ITIC	NTU	COC	ACU	CFG	FRC
2006	90	100	100	100	29	15	15	4	8	0
2005	100	—	100	94	—	15	33	4	0	8

National Journal Ratings

	2005 LIB	—	2005 CONS		2006 LIB	—	2006 CONS
Economic	94%	—	0%		82%	—	18%
Social	91%	—	9%		96%	—	3%
Foreign	96%	—	0%		88%	—	10%

Key Votes of the 109th Congress

1. Estate Tax Repeal	N	5. Limit Interstate Abortion	N	9. Build Border Fence	N
2. Limit CAFE Standards	N	6. Extend Patriot Act	N	10. CAFTA	N
3. FY06 Spending Curb	N	7. Bar Same Sex Marriage	N	11. Oppose Iraq Withdrawal	N
4. Drilling in ANWR	N	8. Stem Cell Research $	Y	12. Detainee Tribunals	N

Election Results

2006 general	Jose Serrano (D-WF)	56,124	(95%)	($314,380)
	Ali Mohamed (R-C)	2,759	(5%)	
2006 primary	Jose Serrano (D)	unopposed		
2004 general	Jose Serrano (D-WF)	111,638	(95%)	($351,845)
	Ali Mohamed (R-C)	5,610	(5%)	

Prior Winning Percentages: 2002 (92%); 2000 (96%); 1998 (95%); 1996 (96%); 1994 (96%); 1992 (91%); 1990 (93%); 1990 (92%)

The People		Race/Ethnic Origin	Ancestry		
Area size:	13 sq. mi.	2.9% White	West Indian: 3.9% Subsaharan: 3.1%		
Urban population:	100.0%	30.3% Black	USA: 2.3%		
Rural population:	0.0%	1.6% Asian	**2004 Presidential Vote**		
Pop. 2000:	654,360	0.3% Native Am.	Kerry (D) 130,109	(89%)	
Pop. 2005 (est):	672,918	0.0% Hawaiian	Bush (R) 14,766	(10%)	
Median income:	$19,311	1.6% Two+ races	Other 799	(1%)	
Poverty status:	42.2%	0.5% Other	**2000 Presidential Vote**		
Military veterans:	3.9%	62.8% Hispanic Origin	Gore (D) 112,786	(92%)	
			Bush (R) 6,634	(5%)	
			Other 2,630	(2%)	
			Cook Partisan Voting Index: D +43		

Occupation	Blue collar: 23.6%	White collar: 46.4%	Gray collar: 30.0%

It may not quite be "the beautiful Bronx," as borough historian Lloyd Utlan calls it, but The Bronx seems to have rebounded from rock bottom. The beautiful days were in the 1930s and 1940s, when Presidents Roosevelt and Truman rode down 138th Street, when Babe Ruth, Lou Gehrig and Joe DiMaggio knocked home runs out of Yankee Stadium, when Art Deco apartment buildings were built along the Grand Concourse, when shoppers thronged Tremont Avenue stores, and when Bronx County Democratic Chairman Ed Flynn was chairman of the Democratic National Committee. As early as the 1880s, the Bronx (then known as the Northside and only recently annexed from Westchester County) was linked to the level eastern half of Manhattan by elevated steam locomotives. The borough really took off in 1906 with the arrival of the first subway, which allowed the children of immigrants to move from grim Lower East Side tenements to spacious walkup apartments flooded with light. The Bronx's population grew from 200,000 in 1900 to 430,000 in 1910—enough, had the borough been independent, to rank as America's sixth largest city—and 1.2 million in 1930. The Bronx's population peaked at nearly 1.5 million in 1950. After a quarter-century of deterioration, the population shrunk to 1.2 million by 1990. Now it's up again, to 1.3 million, as new immigrants revive neighborhoods that had been given up for dead.

The downfall began in the mid-1960s, with multiple failures leading to destruction of neighborhoods. Rent control, insisted upon by tenants, guaranteed that many owners of low-rent property wouldn't maintain it; once empty, buildings were torched for the insurance money, sometimes as many as four blocks a week. At the same time, a drop in low-income, low-skill jobs in Manhattan and the Bronx—abetted by high, union-enforced wages and organized crime—led to a rise in welfare dependency and crime, with empty building shells becoming the perfect venue for drug dealing. And the 13-year, $250 million effort to build the Cross-Bronx Expressway—a brainchild of Robert Moses that crossed 113 streets and avenues, hundreds of utility mains and ten mass-transit lines—made things worse. As workers plowed through acres of tough bedrock, the project shredded entire neighborhoods, forcing 40,000 people to move from their homes and forever changing the landscape. In the upheaval, longtime residents fled in droves—whites to the suburbs or the Sun Belt, Puerto Ricans to their homeland, African Americans to the South or other cities—and the rapid turnover strained PTAs and other civic institutions. A vicious cycle emerged: Crime drove away jobs, which drove away fathers, which produced more crime. When Tom Wolfe imagined the "wrong turn" that sunk a high-flying Wall Street career in *Bonfire of the Vanities*, he set it in the South Bronx; the movie version filmed the scene under the Bruckner Expressway.

Presidents and presidential candidates came in—Jimmy Carter in 1977, Ronald Reagan in 1980—promising help. Ironically, the South Bronx was never the worst slum in New York; it just looked the worst. The borough's saviors were churches and creative community groups that built single-family pastel bungalows and small-scale apartment projects for the elderly, single-parent families and former homeless. With their help, the South Bronx turned a corner; local enthusiasts want to move beyond its reputation by renaming the area Downtown Bronx. A building spree created the Bronx's first new wave of housing starts since the 1950s, and the first new cluster of private residences since the 1930s. As immigrants from Dominican Republic, Jamaica, Ecuador, and Central America settled in, the population again rose; 32% are foreign-born and 47% speak Spanish. A few corners of the South Bronx, such as Mott Haven, have even seen yuppies and artists colonizing old industrial space where gang wars prevailed not long ago. Charlotte Street, which Carter and Reagan visited as the worst of the slums, is now Charlotte Gardens, with owner-occupied houses worth more than $180,000. After decades of decay, some businesses have begun to move back in: warehouses, distribution centers, small industrial parks—all fueled by declining and more expensive space nearby. But this remains a low-income area, with many still on public assistance, and check-cashing outlets remain easier to find than banks.

The 16th Congressional District of New York includes most of the South Bronx. It is bounded by the Harlem River on the west, the East River on the south, the Bronx River and Bronx Park (home of the Bronx Zoo) on the east, and goes just past Fordham Road on the north. It includes the Parisian-style Grand Concourse, where single-family homes for the wealthy were replaced in the 1930s by stylish Art Deco apartment buildings; this was one of America's biggest Jewish neighborhoods up through the 1960s. It also includes Belmont, a "Little Italy" and site of an old-fashioned food market on Arthur Avenue, though few Italians actually live there. The 16th also includes the industrial flatlands of Bruckner Boulevard and Hunts Point (though not the meat and produce markets). The 16th is 30% black, 63% Hispanic—the latter, the highest percentage in any New York district. This has long been New York's largest concentration of Puerto Ricans, but an increasing number of Hispanics here now are from other parts of Latin America. Measured by median income and percentage of families below poverty status, it ranks as the most impoverished congressional district in the nation. This was the most heavily Democratic district in the nation in 2000 (92%-5% for Al Gore) and the second most heavily Democratic in 2004 (89%-10% for John Kerry).

The congressman from the 16th District is Jose Serrano, first chosen in a 1990 special election. A native of Mayaguez, Puerto Rico, he grew up in the Mill Brook project in Mott Haven. After serving in the Army, he worked at a bank and as a school administrator. Serrano moved up while other Bronx politicians fell by the wayside because of corruption. He was elected to the Assembly in 1974 and chaired its Education Committee. In 1985, he ran for Bronx borough president, bucking the Democratic organization, and nearly won. Then in January 1990 South Bronx Congressman Robert Garcia was convicted for accepting money from the minority contractor Wedtech; his conviction was later reversed, but his resignation led to Serrano's election to the House.

Serrano has one of the most liberal voting records in the House. Much of his focus has been south of the border. In 1997, Dick Gephardt passed over him for the less senior Robert Menendez of New Jersey—a better fundraiser, with his Cuban-American connections—to be chief deputy whip. In 1998 Serrano ran for Democratic Caucus vice-chairman as "the candidate who refuses to raise money to buy your vote for leadership." But he withdrew in favor of Menendez. In stark contrast to Menendez, Serrano has been known as Fidel Castro's greatest champion in the House. He has sought repeal of economic sanctions on Cuba and of the Helms-Burton Act. When questions arose about Castro's future after major surgery in July 2006, Serrano issued a press release warning President Bush, "Hands Off Cuba." The pro-statehood Serrano has devoted much time to the cause of Puerto Rico, which he calls an American "colony." He backs a referendum to determine the status of the island. In 2000, he was arrested for blocking passage at the White House to protest the Navy's bombing range at Vieques, Puerto Rico. He took credit for working with Venezuelan president Hugo Chavez and former Congressman Joe Kennedy's Citizen Energy Corp. to get cheaper oil for the South Bronx. He has criticized the reluctance of House Democratic leaders to deal with immigration reform.

Serrano has used his position on the Appropriations Committee to address past injustices by the FBI and to monitor law enforcement excesses after September 11; he strongly opposes the PATRIOT Act. In the majority, he is one of the Appropriations Committee "cardinals", as chair of the new Subcommittee on Financial Services and General Government, which oversees many federal regulators. Given his humble background, he says, that's "quite an honor." A local priority has been to deliver money to clean up the Bronx River.

In New York politics, Serrano backed former Bronx Borough President Fernando Ferrer for mayor in 2001 and 2005; he backed Al Sharpton for president in 2004. His son Jose, a former city councilman, ousted a Republican incumbent in 2004 to win a state Senate seat. Serrano the elder remains secure in his district.

SEVENTEENTH DISTRICT

Rep. Eliot Engel (D)

Elected 1988, 10th term; b. Feb. 18, 1947, Bronx; home, Bronx; Hunter-Lehman Col., B.A. 1969, C.U.N.Y., Lehman Col., M.A. 1973, NY Law Schl., J.D. 1987; Jewish; married (Patricia).

Elected Office: NY Assembly, 1977-88.

Professional Career: Teacher, guidance counselor, NYC public schl., 1969-77.

DC Office: 2161 RHOB, 20515, 202-225-2464; Fax: 202-225-5513; Web site: www.house.gov/engel.

District Offices: Bronx, 718-796-9700; Mt. Vernon, 914-699-4100; West Nyack, 845-735-1000.

Committees: *Energy & Commerce* (11th of 31 D): Health; Telecommunications & the Internet. *Foreign Affairs* (8th of 27 D): Western Hemisphere (Chmn.); Europe; Middle East & South Asia.

Group Ratings

	ADA	ACLU	AFS	LCV	ITIC	NTU	COC	ACU	CFG	FRC
2006	95	100	100	100	33	11	36	4	7	0
2005	95	—	100	94	—	12	41	0	3	8

National Journal Ratings

	2005 LIB	—	2005 CONS		2006 LIB	—	2006 CONS
Economic	85%	—	13%		86%	—	11%
Social	79%	—	21%		89%	—	10%
Foreign	61%	—	39%		65%	—	35%

Key Votes of the 109th Congress

1. Estate Tax Repeal	N	5. Limit Interstate Abortion	N	9. Build Border Fence	N
2. Limit CAFE Standards	N	6. Extend Patriot Act	N	10. CAFTA	N
3. FY06 Spending Curb	N	7. Bar Same Sex Marriage	N	11. Oppose Iraq Withdrawal	N
4. Drilling in ANWR	N	8. Stem Cell Research $	Y	12. Detainee Tribunals	N

Election Results

2006 general	Eliot Engel (D-WF)	93,614	(76%)	($945,640)
	Jim Faulkner (R-C-Ind)	28,842	(24%)	($3,359)
2006 primary	Eliot Engel (D)	26,564	(83%)	
	Jessica Flagg (D)	5,430	(17%)	
2004 general	Eliot Engel (D-WF)	140,530	(76%)	($961,863)
	Matt Brennan (R)	40,524	(22%)	
	Other	3,482	(2%)	

Prior Winning Percentages: 2002 (63%); 2000 (90%); 1998 (88%); 1996 (85%); 1994 (78%); 1992 (80%); 1990 (61%); 1988 (56%)

The People		Race/Ethnic Origin	Ancestry	
Area size:	146 sq. mi.	41.3% White	West Indian: 10.1% Irish: 8.7%	
Urban population:	99.9%	30.4% Black	Italian: 8.4%	
Rural population:	0.1%	4.5% Asian	**2004 Presidential Vote**	
Pop. 2000:	654,360	0.2% Native Am.	Kerry (D)	149,727 (67%)
Pop. 2005 (est):	671,934	0.0% Hawaiian	Bush (R)	73,896 (33%)
Median income:	$44,868	2.6% Two+ races	Other	584 (0%)
Poverty status:	16.0%	0.5% Other	**2000 Presidential Vote**	
Military veterans:	7.7%	20.4% Hispanic Origin	Gore (D)	141,525 (69%)
			Bush (R)	54,362 (27%)
			Other	8,438 (4%)
			Cook Partisan Voting Index: D +21	

Occupation   Blue collar: 16.0%   White collar: 64.9%   Gray collar: 19.1%

The Bronx, settled mostly in the early 20th century, was originally a collection of middle-class neighborhoods clustered around subway stops, places where the children of immigrants left behind

Manhattan's gloomy tenements and walkups and basked in the sunlight, wide avenues and hilly vistas. Different ethnic groups collected here and there: Irish in Kingsbridge, in the valley between Riverdale and the Grand Concourse; well-to-do WASPs and Jews in Riverdale, on the palisades above the Hudson River; middle-class blacks in Williamsbridge in the north central part of the borough. When neighboring areas in the South Bronx began to deteriorate, many of those residents fled, many to the southern cities of Westchester County on the Bronx border, some of which have taken on a central-city character. Others drove over the Tappan Zee Bridge to the pleasant suburbs of Rockland County, just north of Bergen County, New Jersey.

The 17th Congressional District of New York includes the bulk of these Bronx neighborhoods, plus Baychester, Eastchester and Spuyten Duyvil, and the century-old Van Cortlandt Park—at 1,146 acres, New York City's third-largest. It also includes leafy Woodlawn, still a magnet for Irish immigrants and more like neighboring Westchester County than the Bronx. The district skips around Marble Hill, an African-American and Latino enclave on the Bronx mainland that, eccentrically, was kept as part of Manhattan after engineers diverted the Harlem River around it in 1895, hoping to improve shipping flow. The 2002 redistricting extended the 17th deep into the suburbs. It takes in black-majority Mount Vernon and financially-troubled Yonkers—Dutch for "young squire," in honor of its founder in the mid-1600s—and a narrow strip of land running north from Yonkers along the Hudson River. Across the Tappan Zee, the district includes the southern half of Rockland County, including Nyack, Orangetown, Suffern, Ramapo and part of Clarkstown. Rockland casts 40% of the vote, the Bronx casts 37% and Westchester 23%. This is a strongly Democratic district.

The congressman from the 17th District is Eliot Engel, a son of the Bronx who now lives in Riverdale, a political junkie who memorized the names of all 100 senators when he was a boy, who was first elected to the House in 1988. He graduated from Hunter-Lehman College, got a master's in guidance and counseling from the City University of New York, and 14 years later received a law degree from New York Law School. He was a New York City teacher and guidance counselor who replaced incumbents struck by scandal. He was elected to the New York Assembly in a 1977 special election, at 30, to replace a convicted incumbent, and to the House in 1988 to replace Democrat Mario Biaggi after he was convicted in two tawdry bribery cases.

Engel's once strongly liberal voting record has become more moderate, especially on foreign policy. On what is now the Foreign Affairs Committee, he made his name as the backer of one ethnic cause after another; members of just about any ethnic group can be found in the Bronx. He has been a prime sponsor of the resolution to recognize Jerusalem as the capital of Israel, headed the Congressional Albanian Issues Caucus, called for investigation of the internment of Italian nationals and other harsh restrictions during World War II, and has co-chaired the Congressional ad hoc Committee on Irish Affairs, to foster the peace process. Engel is not a 1970s-style dove: He supported the Gulf War resolution, the bombing of Serbia to get a settlement in Bosnia, and the use of force in Iraq, though he criticized George W. Bush's handling of that conflict following the ouster of Saddam Hussein. In 2007, he became chairman of the Western Hemisphere Subcommittee. He focused on slave labor in Brazil as a priority.

With Jack Kingston, he worked across the aisle to promote alternative and renewable sources of energy. He has called for a national education campaign for digital television. An Engel tradition: Since 1989 he has staked out an aisle seat hours before each State of the Union speech, so that he can shake the president's hand or give an occasional hug. At home, Engel is a relentless constituency service congressman.

When his district was mostly in the Bronx and almost 80% black and Hispanic, he faced constant primary challenges. In the 2000 primary, Assemblyman Larry Seabrook, with support from Bronx Democratic Chairman Roberto Ramirez, argued that the district needed "real leadership" and attacked Engel for living in suburban Maryland. Seabrook had a meeting with Congressional Black Caucus members, which brought angry comments from other Jewish members who argued that all Democrats should support their incumbent colleagues; Engel won 50%-41%. After redistricting made his district more suburban, Engel had vigorous competition in 2002 from Rockland County Executive Scott Vanderhoef, a Republican who criticized Engel for voting against tax cuts and defense spending. Vanderhoef carried Rockland County by 53%-45%. But Engel won big in Westchester and the Bronx, for a 63%-34% victory—far from marginal. In 2004, New York City firefighter Kevin McAdams challenged Engel in the primary for his support of the war in Iraq and for not spending more time in his district. Engel won easily: 59%-20%. In 2006, against progressive Jessica Flagg, who criticized his support for "Bush war policies," he got 83% of the vote in the Democratic primary. This incumbent who seemed an endangered species during the past decade now looks stronger than ever.

EIGHTEENTH DISTRICT

Rep. Nita Lowey (D)

Elected 1988, 10th term; b. July 5, 1937, Bronx; home, Harrison; Mt. Holyoke Col., B.A. 1959; Jewish; married (Stephen).

Professional Career: Asst. for Econ. Devel. & Neighborhood Preservation, NY Secy. of State; Dep. Dir., Division of Econ. Opportunity, 1975-85; NY Asst. Secy. of St., 1985-87.

DC Office: 2329 RHOB, 20515, 202-225-6506; Fax: 202-225-0546; Web site: www.house.gov/lowey.

District Offices: Rockland, 845-639-3485; White Plains, 914-428-1707; Yonkers, 914-779-9766.

Committees: *Appropriations* (7th of 37 D): State, Foreign Operations & Related Programs (Chmn.); Labor, HHS, Education & Related Agencies; Homeland Security. *Homeland Security* (7th of 19 D): Emergency Communications, Preparedness & Response.

Group Ratings

	ADA	ACLU	AFS	LCV	ITIC	NTU	COC	ACU	CFG	FRC
2006	95	95	100	100	43	11	40	4	10	0
2005	95	—	100	94	—	11	41	0	4	0

National Journal Ratings

	2005 LIB — 2005 CONS		2006 LIB — 2006 CONS	
Economic	88%	9%	94%	0%
Social	87%	12%	86%	13%
Foreign	74%	26%	75%	23%

Key Votes of the 109th Congress

1. Estate Tax Repeal	N	5. Limit Interstate Abortion	N	9. Build Border Fence	N
2. Limit CAFE Standards	N	6. Extend Patriot Act	N	10. CAFTA	N
3. FY06 Spending Curb	N	7. Bar Same Sex Marriage	N	11. Oppose Iraq Withdrawal	N
4. Drilling in ANWR	N	8. Stem Cell Research $	Y	12. Detainee Tribunals	N

Election Results

2006 general	Nita Lowey (D-WF)	124,256	(71%)	($1,555,658)
	Richard Hoffman (R-C)	51,450	(29%)	($65,824)
2006 primary	Nita Lowey (D)	unopposed		
2004 general	Nita Lowey (D-Ind-WF)	170,715	(70%)	($1,742,423)
	Richard Hoffman (R)	73,975	(30%)	($96,662)

Prior Winning Percentages: 2002 (92%); 2000 (67%); 1998 (83%); 1996 (64%); 1994 (57%); 1992 (56%); 1990 (63%); 1988 (50%)

The People		Race/Ethnic Origin	Ancestry	
Area size:	270 sq. mi.	67.1% White	Italian: 17.2%	Irish: 11.0%
Urban population:	99.3%	9.5% Black	German: 6.2%	
Rural population:	0.7%	5.2% Asian	**2004 Presidential Vote**	
Pop. 2000:	654,360	0.1% Native Am.	Kerry (D) 164,342	(58%)
Pop. 2005 (est):	657,650	0.0% Hawaiian	Bush (R) 119,981	(42%)
Median income:	$68,887	1.6% Two+ races	**2000 Presidential Vote**	
Poverty status:	7.8%	0.3% Other	Gore (D) 155,700	(58%)
Military veterans:	9.2%	16.2% Hispanic Origin	Bush (R) 103,248	(38%)
			Other 9,268	(3%)
			Cook Partisan Voting Index: D +10	

Occupation   Blue collar: 12.8%   White collar: 73.2%   Gray collar: 13.9%

The great granite ridges that form the spine of Manhattan and the Bronx move north into lower Westchester County, the thin peninsula of land between Long Island Sound and the Hudson River. This was active territory from early on. Washington Irving, the first fully professional writer in America, has his headless horseman chase schoolmaster Ichabod Crane through Sleepy Hollow, a fictionalized version of Tarrytown, on the east bank of the Hudson. Revolutionary War battles were fought here, and figures like John Peter Zenger, Alexander Hamilton and John Jay lived here. Blessed with some of America's loveliest scenery, and easily accessible from Manhattan by train since the mid-19th century, this became some of America's first suburban terrain, with grand estates built by great millionaires—Jay Gould's Gothic revival Lyndhurst and John D. Rockefeller's spectacular Kykuit, with villages for retainers clustered around the railroad stations. Today, Westchester still looks suburban, perhaps more than ever now that it has a nice patina of age. It has little commuter railroad stations across from faux Tudor drugstores, soda fountains and cobblestone post offices; it also has shopping malls and gallerias and plenty of corporate headquarters, from IBM and Texaco to PepsiCo and Reader's Digest (as well as corporate watchdogs: *Consumer Reports* magazine is based in Yonkers). Intensive development slows north of White Plains, for Westchester is crossed by the first of several mountain ridges just to the north—the closest the Appalachians come to the ocean. The county does have its share of homeless people and racial ghettos; to the north, in Ossining, on the Hudson River, looms the famed Sing Sing maximum security prison.

The 18th Congressional District of New York contains the heart of suburban Westchester County and also crosses the Hudson River into Rockland County to Haverstraw. It includes a host of affluent suburbs, many within easy reach of Grand Central via the Metro North rail lines—Bronxville, Tuckahoe, Eastchester, New Rochelle, Scarsdale, White Plains, Larchmont, Mamaroneck, Rye, Harrison, Armonk and Chappaqua, where Bill and Hillary Rodham Clinton reside, for now. Historically, Westchester was a Republican county, with a successful Republican machine and an electorate of affluent professionals who naturally preferred the party opposed to big city political bosses and labor union leaders. But Westchester today is mostly Democratic, after a heavy influx of Jews who broke down many legal restrictions and other barriers to residence after World War II. These Jewish voters, long Democratic, became even more so thanks to the visibility of Christian conservatives in the Republican party. Another reason is that on the cultural issues of greatest import, gun control and abortion, affluent suburbanites in America's biggest metropolitan area have been strongly on the liberal side. Westchester County is more diverse than one might imagine and the 18th District reflects this: it is 10% black, 16% Hispanic and 5% Asian. George Pataki, who began his political career as mayor of Peekskill in northern Westchester, carried the county by handsome margins in 1998 and 2002. But the county gave strong support to Al Gore and John Kerry in 2000 and 2004 and, unlike the Long Island suburbs, voted for Hillary Rodham Clinton in 2000. In 2006, Eliot Spitzer took the governor's race in Westchester, 69%-29%; Clinton also won the county, 66%-32%.

The congresswoman from the 18th District is Nita Lowey, a Democrat first elected in 1988. She was born in the Bronx, raised her family in Queens, and lives in upper-crust Harrison in Westchester County. After graduating from Mount Holyoke, she later went to work for Mario Cuomo in 1975 after he was appointed secretary of state, and became assistant secretary of state. In the 1988 Democratic primary, she faced Hamilton Fish III, son and grandson of Republican Hudson River congressmen, but as a former publisher of *The Nation* considerably to the left of Lowey; she won 44%-36%. Her opponent in the general was Joseph DioGuardi, a two-term incumbent who trumpeted his experience as a CPA but was dogged by charges of illicit contributions; she won 50%-47%. Each spent over $1 million, with Lowey spending $657,000 of her own money.

In the House, Lowey's voting record is liberal, though she is more moderate on foreign policy. She was a Clinton loyalist when it was tough to be so, voting for the 1993 budget and tax package in this high-income district, splitting with most New York Democrats and organized labor to support both NAFTA and normal trade relations with China; she recalls receiving high-pressure tactics from then-Clinton aide Rahm Emanuel. When Clinton proposed to change the health care finance system, she organized 72 members who demanded that it cover abortions. Much of Lowey's legislative work has been on Appropriations. On domestic issues, she has actively supported the National Endowment for the Arts, been a big supporter of biomedical research, and she has helped to increase spending for cancer research at the National Institutes of Health. Pursuing her interest in feminist issues, she backed funds for international family planning, and led the unsuccessful opposition to George W. Bush's reversal of the policy when he took office. On homeland security, she worked to implement recommendations of the 9/11 Commission, and pursued a grant program for interoperable communications for local governments. She has been a strong advocate of aid to Israel, voted for the Iraq war resolution, and against trade promotion authority for Bush. Now an Appropriations Committee "cardinal" as the chairwoman of the expanded State, Foreign Operations Subcommittee,

Lowey rivals Secretary of State Condoleezza Rice as the most powerful woman in U.S. foreign policy. In early 2007, she opposed Bush's call to increase troops in Iraq, but urged more money for Afghanistan.

Since Lowey first won, the boundaries of her district have been twice sharply changed by redistricting, but she has been reelected by wide margins. She thought about a Senate bid in 2000, but deferred to her new constituent, the then-First Lady. Her party loyalty and avid fundraising led Minority Leader Dick Gephardt in 2001 to appoint her chairman of the Democratic Congressional Campaign Committee. In early 2002 she optimistically said that Democrats' recruiting efforts, their fundraising, their apparent success in preventing Republican gains in redistricting, and their attacks on Republicans for "privatizing" Social Security would enable the party to recapture the House. Ultimately, Democrats defeated only three Republican incumbents, while losing five of their own. The GOP's six-seat gain was an acute disappointment to Lowey, who quietly bowed out of the chairmanship. But the 2006 campaign success of Emanuel gave her the chairmanship that she wanted most.

NINETEENTH DISTRICT

Rep. John Hall (D)

Elected 2006, 1st term; b. July 23, 1948, Baltimore, MD; home, Dover Plains; Attended U. of Notre Dame, Loyola Col. (MD); Protestant; married (Pamela).

Elected Office: Ulster Cnty. Legislature, 1989-91; Saugerties Bd. of Educ., 1996-99.

Professional Career: Singer/songwriter.

DC Office: 1217 LHOB, 20515, 202-225-5441; Fax: 202-225-3289; Web site: johnhall.house.gov.

District Offices: Carmel, 845-225-3641x371; Goshen, 845-291-4100.

Committees: *Select Committee on Energy Independence and Global Warming* (8th of 9 D). *Transportation & Infrastructure* (37th of 41 D): Aviation; Water Resources & Environment. *Veterans' Affairs* (7th of 16 D): Disability Assistance & Memorial Affairs (Chmn.); Economic Opportunity.

Group Ratings and Key Votes: Newly Elected

Election Results

2006 general	John Hall (D)	100,119	(51%)	($1,629,865)
	Sue Kelly (R-C-Ind)	95,359	(49%)	($2,519,164)
2006 primary	John Hall (D)	11,231	(49%)	
	Judy Aydelott (D)	6,110	(27%)	
	Ben Shuldiner (D)	3,568	(16%)	
	Darren Rigger (D)	1,799	(8%)	
2004 general	Sue Kelly (R-Ind-C)	175,401	(67%)	($1,250,053)
	Michael Jaliman (D)	87,429	(33%)	($67,453)

The People		Race/Ethnic Origin	Ancestry	
Area size:	1,470 sq. mi.	83.5% White	Italian: 17.6%	Irish: 16.5%
Urban population:	78.7%	5.0% Black	German: 10.6%	
Rural population:	21.3%	2.2% Asian	**2004 Presidential Vote**	
Pop. 2000:	654,361	0.2% Native Am.	Bush (R) 162,960	(54%)
Pop. 2005 (est):	691,648	0.0% Hawaiian	Kerry (D) 137,432	(45%)
Median income:	$64,337	1.2% Two+ races	Other 2,097	(1%)
Poverty status:	6.4%	0.2% Other	**2000 Presidential Vote**	
Military veterans:	11.8%	7.7% Hispanic Origin	Bush (R) 133,157	(49%)
			Gore (D) 126,785	(47%)
			Other 11,698	(4%)
			Cook Partisan Voting Index: R + 1	

Occupation   Blue collar: 18.5%   White collar: 67.2%   Gray collar: 14.3%

The great interior of America can be said to begin where the Hudson River squeezes through the series of Appalachian ridges at the Hudson Highlands. This choke point was the barrier to British military power during the Revolutionary War, when American forces built a chain across the river to keep the British from sailing north. It was over control of this part of the Hudson that Benedict Arnold betrayed his country, and it was here that the new nation built its Military Academy high on the cliffs at West Point. The Hudson was the impetus for the builders of the Erie Canal and the water-level New York Central Railroad, the great projects that made New York City the port of the American interior, as well as for the builders of the Croton Aqueduct not far away, which provided the water without which New York could not grow—and which provided a way for the first cockroaches to reach the city. Some distant day the great aqueduct may crumble, but the cockroaches will remain.

The 19th Congressional District of New York covers much of the lower Hudson Valley, sprawling across parts of five counties. West of the Hudson, the district takes in much of Orange County, New York's second-fastest growing county from 1990 to 2004, where old farming villages like Warwick adjoin mountains, farms and new, middle-income subdivisions on the nation's biggest deposit of muck soil outside the Everglades. The district includes Kiryas Joel, a politically controversial Satmar Hasidic settlement that became embroiled in a long-running battle over whether it could establish a government-funded but religiously run school district for disabled children. Its 20,000 residents function almost as a single voting unit, without much regard to partisan affiliation, a fact that has not escaped the notice of the state's top politicians, who regularly court local leaders. When Mayor Abraham Wieder backed President Bush in 2004, Bush won 92% here.While the district excludes two of Orange County's biggest population centers, Middletown and Newburgh, it takes in portions of northern Rockland County, including Stony Point, the home of James A. Farley, Franklin D. Roosevelt's campaign manager in 1932 and 1936. The district crosses the Hudson where the rebels' chain did, near West Point. East of the river, the district begins in northern Westchester County, including Peekskill, where George Pataki was mayor before becoming governor; Croton-on-Hudson; Yorktown; and Mount Kisco. Farther north, the 19th takes in all of Putnam County and part of Dutchess County, including the suburbs (but not the center city) of Poughkeepsie, and Wappingers Falls; Putnam has become popular for first-time homebuyers who take the 80-minute commute to Grand Central Station. The region also has proved attractive to middle- and higher-income public and corporate employees seeking reasonably priced housing in safe areas, a trend that has led to robust growth at a time when other areas of New York state are losing population; immigrants from Ecuador who have settled here find the mountains and farm land similar to home. Politically, this area moved toward Democrats in the 1990s, but voted for George W. Bush in 2004.

The new congressman from the 19th District is John Hall, a Democrat elected in 2006. The singer-songwriter Hall is the first professional rock musician to serve in Congress. (Singer Sonny Bono did not play an instrument on stage.) Hall was raised in Upstate New York and began playing the piano at four. His father was a Westinghouse engineer, and his mother a college professor. He entered Notre Dame University at 16 and studied physics for just a year, and later attended Loyola College in Baltimore. Hall dropped out of school to pursue a music career, performing in the West Village and writing music for Broadway musicals. He recorded with such top artists as Janis Joplin, Bonnie Raitt, and Jackson Browne. In 1972, he helped found the soft rock band Orleans, which performed the smash hits "Still the One" and "Dance With Me." Even then Hall was a budding policy wonk and activist, occasionally holding forth on the dangers of plutonium production. Hall became an accomplished session guitarist and played with Bob Dylan during a short-lived music project. In 1977, Hall left Orleans to pursue a solo career but the group reunited in 1984. Hall also became an activist for anti-nuclear and environmental causes. He founded the anti-nuclear group Musicians United for Safe Energy and in 1979 organized a series of "No Nukes" concerts.

Hall won his first elected office in the early 1990s when he served two years in the Ulster County legislature, and then four years on the Saugerties School Board. In October 2004, he attracted fleeting national attention for noisily protesting the Bush campaign's use of "Still the One" at events. The Bush campaign did not have Hall's permission and stopped using the song, but the incident served to stoke Hall's interest in politics. Hall entered the race against Republican Sue Kelly at the urging of Congresswoman Debbie Wasserman Shultz, who overheard Hall complaining backstage about the Iraq war after a Florida concert, and also from Maurice Hinchey, who represents an adjoining congressional district. But in the Democratic primary, party strategists preferred lawyer Judy Aydelott, a former Republican, because of her seeming crossover appeal and fundraising skills. Hall, who was viewed as too liberal for the district, nevertheless had considerable grassroots strength, and his star power and music industry contacts won him enough attention and money to remain competitive. He defeated Aydelott 49%-27% in the four-way primary held on September 12.

Kelly first won the district in 1994 and initially faced stiff opposition, but had since won reelection easily, bolstered by her moderate record and endorsements from the New York League of Conservation Voters and local labor groups. This time, Hall had the support of organized labor and worked to tie Kelly to President Bush. Kelly portrayed herself as an "independent voice" and attacked Hall as a tax-raising liberal who would vote to impeach Bush, advocate for socialized medicine and withdraw U.S. troops from Iraq. During the general election, a mailer surfaced showing the reprinted cover of the Orleans' 1976 "Waking and Dreaming" album, in which Hall appeared bearded and bare-chested along his bandmates. "John Hall, wrong for America" read the mailer, which was in contrast to Hall's usual campaign appearances in pinstripes and wingtips. Hall wasn't a completely buttoned-down candidate: Against the advice of his advisers, he sang an impromptu duet of "Dance With Me" with cable TV talk show host Stephen Colbert, a scene that played repeatedly on the Internet.

Republicans have an 18,000-voter enrollment advantage in the district and Kelly appeared well-positioned for another term, until late in the campaign when she became tarred by the congressional page scandal involving Florida Republican Mark Foley. Kelly had previously served on the page board; she faced questions about her awareness of Foley's behavior. A television crew filmed her running away from questions about the Foley scandal. Hall won the general election 51%-49%, by less than 5,000 votes, with the winning margin coming from Westchester County.

Hall is a likely Republican target in this swing district, a fact he seemed to acknowledge when he told the *Washington Post* after the election that he had met with Raytheon lobbyists and criticized their missile system. "Maybe they'll write checks to my next opponent. I don't care. I got into this race because my wife told me to stop yelling at the TV," Hall said. Republican Andrew Saul, a wealthy businessman and philanthropist, declared his candidacy in April 2007; Kieran Lalor, an Iraq war veteran, was also making moves to run.

TWENTIETH DISTRICT

Rep. Kirsten Gillibrand (D)

Elected 2006, 1st term; b. Dec. 9, 1966, Albany; home, Hudson; Dartmouth Col., A.B. 1988, U.C.L.A., J.D. 1991; Catholic; married (Jonathan).

Professional Career: Practicing atty, 1991-2006; special counsel, HUD, 2000.

DC Office: 120 CHOB, 20515, 202-225-5614; Fax: 202-225-1168; Web site: gillibrand.house.gov.

District Offices: Glen Falls, 518-743-0964; Hudson, 518-828-3109; Saratoga Springs, 518-581-8247.

Committees: *Agriculture* (18th of 25 D): Livestock, Dairy & Poultry; Horticulture & Organic Agriculture; Conservation, Credit, Energy & Research. *Armed Services* (28th of 34 D): Seapower & Expeditionary Forces; Terrorism, Unconventional Threats & Capabilities.

Group Ratings and Key Votes: Newly Elected

Election Results

2006 general	Kirsten Gillibrand (D-WF) 125,168	(53%)	($2,595,659)
	John Sweeney (R-C-Ind) 110,554	(47%)	($3,425,841)
2006 primary	Kirsten Gillibrand (D) .... unopposed		
2004 general	John Sweeney (R-Ind-C) 188,753	(66%)	($1,392,817)
	Doris Kelly (D) 96,630	(34%)	($22,823)
	Other 1,353	(0%)	

The People		Race/Ethnic Origin	Ancestry	
Area size:	7,200 sq. mi.	93.4% White	Irish: 15.1%	German: 11.8%
Urban population:	44.9%	2.4% Black	Italian: 9.8%	
Rural population:	55.1%	0.8% Asian	**2004 Presidential Vote**	
Pop. 2000:	654,360	0.2% Native Am.	Bush (R) 170,307	(54%)
Pop. 2005 (est):	682,472	0.0% Hawaiian	Kerry (D) 145,289	(46%)
Median income:	$44,239	0.9% Two+ races	Other 2,635	(1%)
Poverty status:	7.9%	0.1% Other	**2000 Presidential Vote**	
Military veterans:	14.3%	2.2% Hispanic Origin	Bush (R) 146,792	(51%)
			Gore (D) 127,419	(44%)
			Other 15,232	(5%)
			Cook Partisan Voting Index: R + 3	

Occupation   Blue collar: 22.7%   White collar: 61.1%   Gray collar: 16.2%

The Hudson River, an avenue of commerce in colonial days, an inspiration to artists in the federal republic, is still one of America's great sights, though it is no longer central, as it was not so long ago, to the nation's consciousness and politics. The classic mansions overlooking the river, like Clermont, whose builder Robert Livingston financed Robert Fulton's first steamboat, and Montgomery Place, built by Janet Livingston Montgomery, widow of the general who attacked Quebec in 1775, are reminders of the cool serenity of the 18th century mind and the daring nature of its spirit. Robert Livingston (whose descendants include Eleanor Roosevelt, former Governor Thomas Kean of New Jersey and former Congressman Bob Livingston of Louisiana) administered the first oath of office to George Washington in 1789 and helped negotiate the Louisiana Purchase in 1803. It was on a visit to his lands in the 1790s that James Madison and Aaron Burr welded the Virginia-New York alliance that set the course of American political history. The Hudson was also a center of America during the Romantic Era: From Frederick Church's Moorish mansion, Olana, you can see the still unspoiled river landscape that inspired his art and that of others of the Hudson River school of painters. Later, the photographer Alfred Stieglitz and his wife, the painter Georgia O'Keeffe, drew inspiration from the mountains and placid waters in Lake George, where they had a summer home.

The Hudson gave birth to America's passionate party politics. Nearby is Kinderhook, home of Martin Van Buren, the innkeeper's son who in alliance with Andrew Jackson invented the torch-light parade, the national party convention and, some argue, the Democratic party itself. Later in the 19th century, the Hudson was lined with the palaces of the nation's first great millionaires and the comfortable country homes of New York's gentry. One of the latter, Springwood in Hyde Park, was the birthplace and home of Franklin D. Roosevelt; this politician, who expanded government at home and was the victorious commander-in-chief of American military forces throughout the world, was most comfortable looking out over his sloping lawn down to the river on which he remembered iceboating during the winters of the 1880s.

The sprawling 20th Congressional District of New York clamps around the Albany metro area and includes much of the Hudson Valley—the grand river south of Albany and the smaller river, freshly fed by the Adirondacks, to the north. It includes four full counties (Warren, Washington, Columbia and Greene), most of Saratoga County, and parts of five others (Dutchess, Essex, Rens-selaer, Delaware and Otsego). The northern extreme of the 20th extends right up to Lake Placid in the Adirondacks, site of the 1980 Winter Olympics. The southern extreme in Dutchess County is close enough for commuters from New York to travel back and forth regularly. Just to the north is Columbia County, where urban New Yorkers go to introduce their children to "the country." The district extends west just short of Cooperstown, home of the National Baseball Hall of Fame, but it includes Oneonta, home of the less well-known National Soccer Hall of Fame; it also includes Saratoga Springs with its grand race track and the nearby battlefield where the British were decisively stopped in 1777. Despite Van Buren and Roosevelt, this has been a Republican area since the birth of the Republican Party; indeed, Roosevelt never carried his home territory except when he ran for state Senate in 1910. The 20th was one of only six New York districts to vote for George W. Bush in 2000 and one of nine to vote for him in 2004.

The new congresswoman from the 20th District is Kirsten Gillibrand, a Democrat elected in 2006. She comes from a politically sophisticated family: her father was an attorney and lobbyist with ties to George Pataki; her grandmother was a prominent Democratic activist in Albany who brought Gillibrand along with her on the campaign trail. Gillibrand attended an all-girls prep school in Troy and graduated from Dartmouth College, where she majored in Asian studies. She traveled widely, worked a summer for Republican Senator Alfonse D'Amato, went to law school at

UCLA, and did a United Nations internship in Vienna, Austria. After law school, Gillibrand clerked for a federal appeals court judge and served briefly as special counsel under Housing and Urban Development Secretary Andrew Cuomo, before going to work for a major New York City law firm.

Gillibrand's run for Congress appeared improbable when she launched her campaign for Congress in 2005. The incumbent was four-term John Sweeney, a rising Republican star with a seat on the Appropriations Committee, who had never had a serious reelection challenge. As the campaign progressed, Sweeney showed signs of rust and faced other distractions. Sweeney took leave from House voting for several weeks after he was hospitalized in February 2006 for treatment of vasculitis, a brain inflammation condition. He also had to contend with negative press surrounding two ski trips, a fundraising event in Utah that included dinner at the home of a pharmaceutical lobbyist and another that he took at state expense. In April 2006, he drew unflattering headlines after making a convivial visit to a college fraternity party; Sweeney denied college newspaper reports that he had been intoxicated. The state Democratic party issued a press release asking, "What is a 50-year-old congressman doing at a frat party at 1 a.m.?"

As late as August, polls showed Sweeney with a solid lead. But Gillibrand's aggressive campaign put Sweeney on the defensive. In TV ads, Sweeney accused her campaign of making anonymous and intimidating phone calls to his wife. Underscoring his charge that Gillibrand was a carpetbagger, he claimed that her actual residence was a Manhattan high-rise. Gillibrand demanded that he release police reports from his two prior arrests—one in 1977 and one in 1978—and from a 2001 automobile accident; he called on her to release her income-tax records. In August, the liberal group MoveOn.org weighed in with ads against Sweeney. Sweeney emphasized his independence and contrasted his working class background with Gillibrand's prep school pedigree.

In October, Sweeney faced the specter of the Jack Abramoff lobbying scandal, when it was revealed that he had asked the House Ethics Committee for guidance on whether to amend a disclosure report for a 2001 trip he took to the Northern Mariana Islands with Tony Rudy, who pleaded guilty to conspiracy charges in the scandal. In a year in which Hillary Clinton and Eliot Spitzer were heading to landslide statewide victories and Republicans struggled under the drag of the unpopular Bush administration, Sweeney had little margin for error; then came a late-breaking revelation of a domestic disturbance that doomed his campaign. One week before the election, the Albany *Times Union* reported that Sweeney's wife had called local police in December 2005 to complain that the congressman was "knocking her around." Sweeney's campaign at first insisted that the police report on the incident was "false and concocted by our opposition," but local newspapers had pursued the story for 10 months and the campaign conceded that state police were called to their home.

Sweeney had spent $3.4 million to Gillibrand's $2.6 million; Gillibrand came out on top and won 53%-47%. After the election, Gillibrand began posting the "Sunlight Report" of her daily schedule, which included meetings with lobbyists (though her schedule was not quite so prominently displayed as freshman Montana Democratic Senator Jon Tester, who followed a similar practice). Anticipating a competitive reelection challenge, she raised $668,000 in her first 3 months in office and launched aggressive constituent outreach efforts that included holding office hours outside grocery stores. Colleagues close to Sweeney said after the election the Democrats' personal attacks and his health problems had drained him, but through mid-2007 Sweeney had not ruled out a comeback attempt. Other potential Republican candidates included former New York Republican Party Chairman Alexander Treadwell and Richard Wager, an aide to New York City Mayor Michael Bloomberg and the son of a former *Poughkeepsie Journal* publisher.

TWENTY-FIRST DISTRICT

Rep. Michael McNulty (D)

Elected 1988, 10th term; b. Sept. 16, 1947, Troy; home, Green Island; Holy Cross Col., B.A. 1969; Catholic; married (Nancy Ann).

Elected Office: Green Island Town Supervisor, 1969-77; Green Island Mayor, 1977-82; NY Assembly, 1982-88.

DC Office: 2210 RHOB, 20515, 202-225-5076; Fax: 202-225-5077; Web site: www.house.gov/mcnulty.

District Offices: Albany, 518-465-0700; Amsterdam, 518-843-3400; Johnstown, 518-762-3568; Schenectady, 518-374-4547; Troy, 518-271-0822.

Committees: *Ways & Means* (7th of 24 D): Social Security (Chmn.); Income Security & Family Support.

Group Ratings

	ADA	ACLU	AFS	LCV	ITIC	NTU	COC	ACU	CFG	FRC
2006	75	79	100	100	17	12	27	20	7	28
2005	95	—	100	94	—	16	41	12	10	38

National Journal Ratings

	2005 LIB	—	2005 CONS		2006 LIB	—	2006 CONS
Economic	78%	—	21%		94%	—	0%
Social	67%	—	33%		67%	—	33%
Foreign	85%	—	15%		80%	—	18%

Key Votes of the 109th Congress

1. Estate Tax Repeal	N	5. Limit Interstate Abortion	Y	9. Build Border Fence	N
2. Limit CAFE Standards	N	6. Extend Patriot Act	N	10. CAFTA	N
3. FY06 Spending Curb	N	7. Bar Same Sex Marriage	N	11. Oppose Iraq Withdrawal	N
4. Drilling in ANWR	N	8. Stem Cell Research $	Y	12. Detainee Tribunals	N

Election Results

2006 general	Michael McNulty (D-Ind-C-WF)	167,604	(72%)	($562,751)
	Warren Redlich (R)	46,752	(20%)	
	Other	17,554	(8%)	
2006 primary	Michael McNulty (D)	26,246	(86%)	
	Thomas Raleigh (D)	4,341	(14%)	
2004 general	Michael McNulty (D-Ind-C-WF)	194,033	(71%)	($442,149)
	Warren Redlich (R)	80,121	(29%)	($41,497)

Prior Winning Percentages: 2002 (75%); 2000 (74%); 1998 (74%); 1996 (66%); 1994 (67%); 1992 (63%); 1990 (64%); 1988 (62%)

The People		Race/Ethnic Origin	Ancestry	
Area size:	1,962 sq. mi.	85.5% White	Irish: 15.0%	Italian: 12.4%
Urban population:	84.3%	7.5% Black	German: 11.8%	
Rural population:	15.7%	2.1% Asian	**2004 Presidential Vote**	
Pop. 2000:	654,361	0.2% Native Am.	Kerry (D) 169,693	(55%)
Pop. 2005 (est):	663,797	0.0% Hawaiian	Bush (R) 133,016	(43%)
Median income:	$40,254	1.3% Two+ races	Other 5,182	(2%)
Poverty status:	11.2%	0.2% Other	**2000 Presidential Vote**	
Military veterans:	13.1%	3.2% Hispanic Origin	Gore (D) 165,003	(56%)
			Bush (R) 114,979	(39%)
			Other 15,101	(5%)
			Cook Partisan Voting Index: D + 9	
Occupation	Blue collar: 18.9%	White collar: 66.0%	Gray collar: 15.0%	

Albany, as readers of its novelist laureate William Kennedy know, is within living memory an antique city. Its solid rowhouses show its 19th century prosperity; its once teeming lumberyards and railroad car shops, old restaurants and hotels, have the patina of age and the accumulated grime of decades of coal smoke burned during six-month-long winters. Its history goes back to 1624, when the Dutch built Fort Orange on the banks of the Hudson so seagoing ships could dock at the edge of the great gloomy forests near the confluence of the Hudson and the Mohawk—the natural crossroads of Upstate New York even before the building of the Erie Canal and the New York Central Railroad. This was one of America's early industrial centers. Troy, a few miles upriver, was a steel town rivaling Pittsburgh in the 1840s, and later the leading producer of detachable collars; Cohoes, at the junction of the Hudson and the Mohawk, became a leading textile producer; Schenectady, a few miles up the Mohawk, was the site of Charles Steinmetz's fabled General Electric laboratories (with help from Thomas Edison) and long remained a GE town. Albany was one of America's biggest lumber towns as well as the state capital.

Albany, with a state capitol completed in 1899 after 32 years, for the then-staggering sum of $25 million, has one of the nation's most famed Democratic political machines, dating back to 1921, when Daniel O'Connell and his brothers and local aristocrat Edwin Corning took control of City Hall. They never really relinquished it: O'Connell died in 1977 at age 91, still boss after 56 years, and his early partner's son, Erastus Corning II, was mayor from 1942 until his death in 1983. The machine was sustained by legions of city and county employees, by a certain creativity when it came to counting votes, and by the raffish atmosphere that was found in the speakeasies of so many cities during Prohibition and lingered in Albany for decades after: read Kennedy and you are there. Curiously, the machine made possible the transformation of antique Albany into the shinier metropolis it is today. Mayor Corning and Nelson Rockefeller collaborated on a smorgasbord of civic-improvement projects: the Empire State Plaza with 11,000 employees in 10 government buildings on 98 acres; the distinctive, ovoid performing arts center known as the Egg; expressways; and a renovated Union Station.

The 21st Congressional District of New York includes most of the Albany metro area: all of Albany County, Schenectady County (including Schenectady, where the industrial base has faded and the population has dropped by one-third from its 1950 level of 92,000), Montgomery County (including Amsterdam, a carpet-making town until the mills moved south in 1955), and rural Schoharie County; parts of Rensselaer (including the gentrified Troy, with its bustling antique shops), Fulton and Saratoga Counties. Times have been tough here: Albany lost 5% of its population during the 1990s, Schenectady 6% and Troy 9%. While the outer counties lean modestly Republican, the Democratic machine vote in Albany makes this a comfortably Democratic district. Even Democrat Carl McCall, who lost every other county in the state outside New York City, beat incumbent Governor George Pataki in Albany County in 2002. Eliot Spitzer and Hillary Rodham Clinton each took more than 70% of the vote there in 2006.

The congressman from the 21st District is Michael McNulty, a Democrat first elected in 1988. McNulty's roots in Albany politics go back to his grandfather, who served as Albany County sheriff; his father was mayor of the industrial suburb of Green Island for 30 years (not consecutively) until he retired in 2002, when he was succeeded by Michael's sister, Ellen McNulty-Ryan. Michael McNulty was first elected to office in 1969, at 22, and served 13 years as town supervisor and mayor in Green Island; while also serving as an insurance broker, he was elected to the Assembly in 1982, at 35. The opening in Congress came without much warning. In 1988, four days after the July filing deadline and on the last day for withdrawal, 30-year incumbent Democrat Samuel Stratton announced he was retiring for health reasons, giving the Democratic machine a chance to name a replacement, who turned out to be McNulty. He won the general by 62%-38% against a venture capital specialist who attacked him for having been chosen by party bosses. Since then, he has had no trouble in general elections.

McNulty's voting record is usually like that of an old-style ethnic Democrat: liberal on economics, less so on foreign and cultural issues. He is one of the few New York Democrats endorsed by the Conservative Party. He opposes abortion and voted for the amendment allowing penalties for flag desecration. But he supported campaign finance regulation, even though some abortion foes opposed it. He strongly opposed welfare reform and wants to increase payments to unemployed adults, legal immigrants and families with high shelter costs. On Ways and Means, where he usually has operated independently of both parties, he became chairman in 2007 of the Social Security subcommittee; he has strongly opposed President Bush's plan for private accounts, and early expectations were that this would not be a busy assignment.

McNulty keeps a close eye on the interests of Watervliet Arsenal, known as "America's Cannon Factory" for its manufacture of tank and artillery cannons and home to the Army's Benet Laboratories, a research, development and engineering facility. On Iraq, after initially voting to authorize the use of force, he voiced regret that his decision was based on false information; in January 2007, he joined local activists protesting the increase in American troops.

In 1996 he had primary opposition on the left from Lee Wasserman, head of Environmental Advocates, a statewide lobbying firm, and won by only 57%-43%. Since then, McNulty seems to have solidified his base. In 2006, he actively backed Kirsten Gillibrand's campaign in the neighboring 20th District. He has suffered from post-polio syndrome, and his declining energy level and his perennially low profile have spurred retirement rumors.

TWENTY-SECOND DISTRICT

Rep. Maurice Hinchey (D)

Elected 1992, 8th term; b. Oct. 27, 1938, New York, NY; home, Saugerties; S.U.N.Y. New Paltz, B.S. 1968, M.A. 1969; Catholic; married (Allison Lee).

Military Career: Navy, 1956-59.

Elected Office: NY Assembly, 1974-92.

Professional Career: Cement plant worker, 1959-64; NY St. Thruway toll collector, 1959-68; Analyst, NY St. Dept. of Educ., 1971-74.

DC Office: 2431 RHOB, 20515, 202-225-6335; Fax: 202-226-0774; Web site: www.house.gov/hinchey.

District Offices: Binghamton, 607-773-2768; Ithaca, 607-273-1388; Kingston, 845-331-4466; Middletown, 845-344-3211; Monticello, 845-791-7116.

Committees: *Appropriations* (17th of 37 D): Agriculture, Rural Development, FDA & Related Agencies; Interior, Environment & Related Agencies; Financial Services & General Government. *Joint Economic Committee* (2d of 10 D). *Natural Resources* (18th of 27 D): Energy & Mineral Resources; National Parks, Forests & Public Lands.

Group Ratings

	ADA	ACLU	AFS	LCV	ITIC	NTU	COC	ACU	CFG	FRC
2006	100	100	100	100	14	11	27	4	5	0
2005	100	—	100	89	—	15	30	4	5	8

National Journal Ratings

	2005 LIB	—	2005 CONS		2006 LIB	—	2006 CONS
Economic	88%	—	9%		90%	—	9%
Social	86%	—	14%		85%	—	14%
Foreign	96%	—	0%		80%	—	18%

Key Votes of the 109th Congress

1. Estate Tax Repeal	N	5. Limit Interstate Abortion	N	9. Build Border Fence	N
2. Limit CAFE Standards	N	6. Extend Patriot Act	N	10. CAFTA	N
3. FY06 Spending Curb	N	7. Bar Same Sex Marriage	N	11. Oppose Iraq Withdrawal	N
4. Drilling in ANWR	N	8. Stem Cell Research $	Y	12. Detainee Tribunals	N

Election Results

2006 general	Maurice Hinchey (D-Ind-WF) .... unopposed			($685,751)
2006 primary	Maurice Hinchey (D) .... unopposed			
2004 general	Maurice Hinchey (D-Ind-WF) 167,489	(67%)		($631,944)
	William Brenner (R) 81,881	(33%)		($6,497)

Prior Winning Percentages: 2002 (64%); 2000 (62%); 1998 (62%); 1996 (55%); 1994 (49%); 1992 (50%)

The People		Race/Ethnic Origin	Ancestry	
Area size:	3,334 sq. mi.	79.9% White	Irish: 13.2%	German: 11.8%
Urban population:	67.8%	7.7% Black	Italian: 11.1%	
Rural population:	32.2%	2.5% Asian	**2004 Presidential Vote**	
Pop. 2000:	654,361	0.2% Native Am.	Kerry (D) 151,890	(54%)
Pop. 2005 (est):	671,332	0.0% Hawaiian	Bush (R) 127,253	(45%)
Median income:	$38,586	1.7% Two+ races	Other 3,629	(1%)
Poverty status:	14.3%	0.2% Other	**2000 Presidential Vote**	
Military veterans:	12.3%	7.8% Hispanic Origin	Gore (D) 131,421	(51%)
			Bush (R) 108,460	(42%)
			Other 17,578	(7%)
			Cook Partisan Voting Index: D + 6	

Occupation	Blue collar: 21.4%	White collar: 60.8%	Gray collar: 17.8%

In colonial days, the Catskills looming over the mid-Hudson River Valley were a great barrier—a mysterious place where Rip Van Winkle was said to have fallen asleep for 20 years after drinking with nine pipe-playing dwarfs, and where Indians lurked in the days of James Fenimore Cooper. Eventually, the area became part of a great pathway west, along the Erie Lackawanna and Delaware & Hudson Railroad lines, with engines steaming over giant viaducts and along narrow river valleys through the hills and mountains. Later in the 19th century, huge kosher hotels were built in Sullivan County in the Catskills—the Jewish resort area popularly known as the Borscht Belt. These thrived when Jews were excluded from other resorts, but fell on hard times in the late 20th century, as discrimination ended; some survive to cater to nearby Russian Jewish immigrants and a kosher clientele. Today, the Catskills are no longer on great transportation lines; there is little passenger train service and the area is bypassed by major airlines. But the pace in the area is expected to accelerate with a Mohawk casino outside Monticello in Sullivan County, near an old horse track.

The sprawling 22d Congressional District of New York includes all of Sullivan and Ulster Counties and most of the Catskills area; it covers part of the Hudson Valley and part of the Southern Tier counties along the New York-Pennsylvania border. Its two population centers are on its east and west ends. On the east are Newburgh, Poughkeepsie and Kingston, old towns in the Hudson Valley. Poughkeepsie is the home of Vassar College and Kingston, in Ulster County, was the political base of long-time Governor and two-term Vice President George Clinton. This area has been growing relatively rapidly, with new residents from metro New York. In the west, connected to the rest of the district by a narrow corridor of Southern Tier townships, is the technology-dependent town of Binghamton and the university town of Ithaca, where Cornell University sits high above the Cayuga's waters and is by far the largest employer in Tompkins County. The Binghamton area has been losing population, like much of Upstate New York. In between are the Catskills, including Bethel, site of the misnamed 1969 Woodstock music festival. Most of this territory voted Republican for many years, though Sullivan County, with the only large rural Jewish population in the U.S., has long been Democratic. Today most of the area is Democratic, especially the university towns of Ithaca, Poughkeepsie and New Paltz in Ulster County and the actual Woodstock (not where the festival was held), a favorite country house place for liberal New Yorkers.

The congressman from the 22d is Maurice Hinchey, a Democrat first elected in 1992. Hinchey grew up in humble circumstances, enlisted in the Navy at 18, labored in a cement factory for five years, then worked his way through college as a New York State Thruway toll collector. He was an analyst for the state education department. Then in the Democratic year of 1974, at 36, he was elected as the first Democrat from Ulster County to the Assembly since 1912, and served for nine terms. When he ran for Congress, Hinchey called for national health insurance, a repeal of Reagan-Bush tax cuts for the rich and corporations, and "reindustrializing America." His Republican opponent Bob Moppert, a Binghamton moving company owner, called for less government spending and bureaucracy. In a contest that was not only partisan but geographic, Hinchey beat Moppert 50%-47%.

Hinchey has one of the most liberal voting records for a non-urban member in the House. One issue that caused Hinchey discomfort is gun control. He backed the Brady Bill on handguns. But in 1994, as he faced a tough reelection campaign, he agonized over the assault weapons ban, deciding at the last minute to vote against it, despite a call from Bill Clinton. Frequently in the minority of the House minority, he often took on lost causes. He sparked a House debate with his proposal to prohibit the private donation of food and beverages for official events at the Vice President's residence; his amendment was defeated, with 54 Democrats opposed. After the September 11 attacks, he criticized the White House for spending disaster relief money on national security. Hinchey was a vocal opponent of the war in Iraq, and condemned the "deplorable" humanitarian conditions that the United States had created there. In September 2004, he was one of 16 House members voting against a resolution of sympathy for the victims of September 11; he objected to the Republicans' inclusion of "political" language with the "destruction of two terrorist regimes" in Afghanistan and Iraq, and called the measure "back-slapping, self-congratulatory." In the minority, he was prolific in offering on the House floor amendments hostile to the Bush administration, mostly unsuccessfully. With Dana Rohrabacher, he backed state laws that authorize the use of medical marijuana.

Hinchey has been a frequent traveler: it was revealed that between 2000 and 2005 Hinchey took more than 20 privately-funded foreign trips to many exotic places, ranking him among the top members of Congress who received travel gifts and leading the *New York Post* to call him a "junket junkie." When *The Ithaca Journal* suggested his trips were a conflict of interest, Hinchey responded that it was "a result of the paper falling victim to Republican spin." Recent reports have shown a cutback in trips. With other Democrats, he organized the Future of American Media Caucus to "address critical media policy issues," where he has advocated a return of the Fairness Doctrine. In March 2007, he criticized the television networks, contending that they continued to give disproportionate air time to conservatives on their Sunday morning talk shows. "When network news shows favor one political point of view over others, the American people are cheated out of an open, honest, and fair discussion," Hinchey said.

On the Appropriations Committee, his focus has included assuring the independence of the Food and Drug Administration from the pharmaceutical industry, and demanding that owners of oil and gas leases pay "fair market prices." In 2007, he stirred controversy in Utah when he sought to limit the sale of oil and gas leases in wilderness areas there. At home, he directed several appropriations grants to the revitalization of downtown Poughkeepsie. With other local lawmakers, he voiced concern over safety of the Indian Point Nuclear Power Plant.

Early in his House tenure Hinchey was a Republican target, but since the mid-1990s he has won reelection easily; his district became more secure after redistricting with the help of Assembly Speaker Sheldon Silver, a friend of Hinchey's from their time in the Assembly. In 2006, he ran unopposed.

TWENTY-THIRD DISTRICT

Rep. John McHugh (R)

Elected 1992, 8th term; b. Sept. 29, 1948, Watertown; home, Pierrepont Manor; Utica Col., B.A. 1970, S.U.N.Y. Albany, M.P.A. 1977; Catholic; divorced.

Elected Office: NY Senate, 1984-92.

Professional Career: Confidential Asst., Watertown City Mgr., 1971-76; Research & Liaison Chief, NY Sen. Douglas Barclay, 1976-84.

DC Office: 2366 RHOB, 20515, 202-225-4611; Fax: 202-226-0621; Web site: www.mchugh.house.gov.

District Offices: Canastota, 315-697-2063; Mayfield, 518-661-6486; Plattsburgh, 518-563-1406; Watertown, 315-782-3150.

Committees: *Armed Services* (3d of 29 R): Military Personnel (RMM); Readiness. *Oversight & Government Reform* (4th of 18 R): Federal Workforce, Postal Service & the District of Columbia; National Security & Foreign Affairs. *Permanent Select Committee on Intelligence* (5th of 8 R): Terrorism, Human Intelligence, Analysis & Counterintelligence; Oversight & Investigations.

Group Ratings

	ADA	ACLU	AFS	LCV	ITIC	NTU	COC	ACU	CFG	FRC
2006	15	18	29	25	57	42	86	75	36	85
2005	20	—	25	17	—	48	81	80	33	85

National Journal Ratings

	2005 LIB	—	2005 CONS		2006 LIB	—	2006 CONS
Economic	44%	—	55%		48%	—	52%
Social	27%	—	72%		34%	—	65%
Foreign	42%	—	55%		33%	—	63%

Key Votes of the 109th Congress

1. Estate Tax Repeal	Y	5. Limit Interstate Abortion	Y	9. Build Border Fence	Y
2. Limit CAFE Standards	Y	6. Extend Patriot Act	Y	10. CAFTA	N
3. FY06 Spending Curb	N	7. Bar Same Sex Marriage	Y	11. Oppose Iraq Withdrawal	Y
4. Drilling in ANWR	Y	8. Stem Cell Research $	N	12. Detainee Tribunals	Y

Election Results

2006 general	John McHugh (R-Ind-C) 106,781	(63%)	($744,416)
	Robert Johnson (D-WF) 62,318	(37%)	($160,193)
2006 primary	John McHugh (R)............................... unopposed		
2004 general	John McHugh (R-Ind-C) 160,079	(71%)	($471,790)
	Robert Johnson (D) 66,448	(29%)	($21,141)

Prior Winning Percentages: 2002 (100%); 2000 (74%); 1998 (79%); 1996 (71%); 1994 (79%); 1992 (61%)

The People		Race/Ethnic Origin	Ancestry	
Area size:	14,739 sq. mi.	92.9% White	Irish: 12.0%	German: 9.9%
Urban population:	34.7%	2.6% Black	French: 9.9%	
Rural population:	65.3%	0.6% Asian	**2004 Presidential Vote**	
Pop. 2000:	654,361	0.9% Native Am.	Bush (R) 134,174	(51%)
Pop. 2005 (est):	663,223	0.0% Hawaiian	Kerry (D) 123,216	(47%)
Median income:	$35,434	0.8% Two+ races	Other 4,810	(2%)
Poverty status:	13.5%	0.1% Other	**2000 Presidential Vote**	
Military veterans:	14.3%	2.1% Hispanic Origin	Bush (R) 119,472	(49%)
			Gore (D) 115,611	(47%)
			Other 10,520	(4%)
			Cook Partisan Voting Index: R + 0	

Occupation　Blue collar: 27.4%　White collar: 52.4%　Gray collar: 20.2%

Some early 19th century visionaries believed that the North Country of Upstate New York—a battleground in both the Revolutionary War and the War of 1812—was the land of the future. Financier Gouverneur Morris, French slave trader James Leray, and Dutch silver speculator David Parish bought up thousands of acres between the Adirondacks and the St. Lawrence River and tried to unload them on farmers unaware of the shortness of the growing season and the unnavigability of the river. These developers left behind grand mansions, but their hopes for huge profits were frustrated when the Erie Canal turned the stream of settlement westward, and Canadians built their new capital of Ottawa far north of the river (Queen Victoria picked the site, and put it as far from the U.S. border as possible). But northern New York was not without its business successes: It was in Watertown in 1878 that 26-year-old Frank Woolworth put a sign over a table of odds and ends that read "Any Article 5 Cents," starting America's first retail chain and inventing the concept of discount stores.

More recently, the North Country has looked to government for help. The St. Lawrence Seaway proved too small for most oceangoing freighters and remains frozen three months of the year; the locks are slow and icebreakers would wreck the shoreline. The state government has built prisons in Ogdensburg and Cape Vincent and Malone. North Country and Vermont members of Congress tried to get Lake Champlain declared one of the Great Lakes, to qualify for funding for various programs; the gambit failed as Michigan members bellowed in protest. The biggest initiative has been the enlargement of Fort Drum, near Watertown and adjacent to Lake Bonaparte, where despite the Army's preference for warm weather training sites, a 10,000-person light infantry division, the 10th Mountain Division, has been stationed since 1985; the 10th Mountain has performed valiantly in difficult environs in Afghanistan and Iraq. Private developers have built big malls in Watertown and Massena (attracting Canadians, as even New York has lower taxes than Ontario).

The 23d Congressional District of New York covers most of the North Country, starting at Lake Champlain, running westward along the St. Lawrence Seaway and over the Adirondacks Forest Preserve to Lake Ontario. It includes Madison County to the south. The district has only a few population centers, including Plattsburgh on Lake Champlain and Watertown and Oswego on Lake

Ontario; Oswego, which occasionally docks ocean-going bulk vessels, bills itself as the first U.S. port of call on the Great Lakes from the Seaway. Geographically it is the largest district in New York state, and one of the largest in the East. Politically, it is mostly ancestral Republican country; it gave George W. Bush a small plurality in 2000 and a small majority in 2004.

The congressman from the 23d District is John McHugh, a Republican first elected in 1992. McHugh has long been in government. He worked for the Watertown city manager for five years and was a state senate staffer for nine years. In 1984, he was elected to succeed his boss Douglas Barclay in Albany. McHugh specialized in dairy issues (New York has long price-fixed dairy products to help farmers) and military bases—both part of the North Country's economic lifeblood. When incumbent David Martin announced his retirement, McHugh ran, with plenty of financing plus Martin's endorsement. He won the Republican primary with 70%, then won the general 61%-24%.

McHugh combines a relatively moderate voting record with a focus on local economic development, which in his district is closely tied to the dairy industry and military installations. In 1993 he got a seat on Armed Services and hired Martin, his predecessor, to monitor the base closing commission. But that yielded little return. The commission voted to close Plattsburgh Air Force Base, a major employer in McHugh's district, plus Griffiss Air Force Base, to the south. McHugh was more successful in his efforts to preserve Fort Drum, the largest employer in northern New York, in the 2005 base closing round; it got an expansion of another 6,000 troops. With $500 million of earlier improvements that he had encouraged, McHugh called it the nation's "most modern military installation." In 2006, he stuck in the defense bill another $202 million for housing at Fort Drum.

His efforts were facilitated by his chairmanship of the Military Personnel Subcommittee, where he had jurisdiction over a broad range of issues dealing with benefits and the demands placed on military officers. He sought a permanent increase of nearly 40,000 Army and Marine troops; the Pentagon preferred to keep the changes temporary, but he eventually got most of what he wanted. He worked with the Army brass to develop new incentives for recruitment. In 2005, he helped to broker a deal with the Pentagon to assert congressional oversight over the role of women in combat, with a requirement that Congress approve any of the 191 military positions closed to women. In January 2007, he joined Hillary Rodham Clinton in a delegation to Iraq. That country's leaders understood that "the clock is ticking," he said. Now the third-ranking Republican on Armed Services, he is positioned to wield broad influence, especially if Republicans regain House control.

McHugh takes a parochial view on trade issues. He opposed trade promotion authority because of fear that the dairy industry would not be adequately protected; he styles himself as a "champion of dairy farmers."

After Republicans won control of the House in 1994, McHugh chaired the Government Reform subcommittee with jurisdiction over the Postal Service, and had to deal with one of Congress's perennial headaches. He worked on what would have been the biggest reform of Postal Service law since the 1970s; with help from committee chairman Tom Davis, he kept the issue alive even after he gave up the subcommittee chairmanship. In one of the final actions of the 2006 lame-duck session, as Republicans were giving up House and Senate control, McHugh finally got the bill enacted with bipartisan backing. The final measure overcame the Bush administration's insistence that the Postal Service absorb $27 billion in disputed pension costs for postal retirees who have had military service; the compromise required it to use $6 billion in escrow funds to pay some benefits, with the Treasury absorbing the remainder. The law creates a new Postal Regulatory Commission, gives the Postal Service greater competitive flexibility to set rates and reduce its costs, and includes provisions to assure that it does not abuse its monopoly status in dealing with private competitors carrying first-class mail. Without major reform, McHugh had warned, the alternatives were steep increases in postal rates or a taxpayer bailout.

McHugh has been reelected against modest opposition. His win in 2006 was his closest since he was first elected, though he barely broke a sweat. Democrat Robert Johnson, a Watertown surgeon making his second run at McHugh, campaigned for national health insurance and opposed the war in Iraq. McHugh highlighted his accomplishments for the district, criticized Johnson for backing socialized medicine, and said that the war in Iraq is winnable. He won 63%-37%, taking all 11 counties. He led by more than 2-to-1 in the Watertown area, but his vote slipped below 60% in the Syracuse outskirts.

TWENTY-FOURTH DISTRICT

Rep. Michael Arcuri (D)

Elected 2006, 1st term; b. June 11, 1959, Utica; home, Utica; S.U.N.Y. Albany, B.A. 1981; NY Law Schl., J.D. 1984; Catholic; married (Sabrina).

Elected Office: Oneida Cnty. D.A., 1993-2006.

Professional Career: Practicing atty., 1984-93.

DC Office: 327 CHOB, 20515, 202-225-3665; Fax: 202-225-1891; Web site: arcuri.house.gov.

District Offices: Auburn, 315-252-2777; Cortland, 607-756-2470; Utica, 315-793-8146.

Committees: *Rules* (8th of 9 D): Rules & Organization of the House. *Transportation & Infrastructure* (34th of 41 D): Economic Development, Public Buildings & Emergency Management; Highways & Transit; Water Resources & Environment.

Group Ratings and Key Votes: Newly Elected

Election Results

2006 general	Michael Arcuri (D-Ind-WF)	109,686	(54%)	($2,197,558)
	Ray Meier (R-C)	91,504	(45%)	($1,586,397)
	Other	2,134	(1%)	
2006 primary	Michael Arcuri (D)	unopposed		
2004 general	Sherwood Boehlert (R-Ind)	143,000	(57%)	($1,524,703)
	Jeffrey Miller (D)	85,140	(34%)	($32,965)
	David Walrath (C)	23,228	(9%)	($234,640)

The People		Race/Ethnic Origin	Ancestry	
Area size:	6,356 sq. mi.	92.2% White	Irish: 12.3%	German: 11.9%
Urban population:	50.5%	3.3% Black	Italian: 10.9%	
Rural population:	49.5%	0.9% Asian	**2004 Presidential Vote**	
Pop. 2000:	654,361	0.2% Native Am.	Bush (R) 147,509	(53%)
Pop. 2005 (est):	647,900	0.0% Hawaiian	Kerry (D) 130,568	(47%)
Median income:	$36,082	1.1% Two+ races	Other 2,367	(1%)
Poverty status:	12.6%	0.1% Other	**2000 Presidential Vote**	
Military veterans:	14.2%	2.3% Hispanic Origin	Bush (R) 129,050	(48%)
			Gore (D) 126,021	(47%)
			Other 12,639	(5%)
			Cook Partisan Voting Index: R + 1	

Occupation	Blue collar: 24.4%	White collar: 57.3%	Gray collar: 18.3%

One of the first American frontiers was the Mohawk River Valley of Upstate New York—a frontier that remained static for 150 years. From the establishment of Fort Orange in 1624 in what now is Albany until the Revolutionary War, white settlers did not dare move west along the Mohawk. The British used their Iroquois allies as a buffer against the French and in return kept New England Yankees from moving westward. Only after the French were driven from the colonies in 1759 did the pressures for westward settlement prevail; the British tried to keep their word to the Indians, but once the Revolutionary War started, the Iroquois dominion ended.

This is the background of *Drums Along the Mohawk* and of James Fenimore Cooper's *Leatherstocking Tales*. But there is little in these rolling hills today to evoke the bloody violence whose conclusion made possible the digging of the Erie Canal and the building of the New York Central Railroad. The canal was a staggering engineering feat. In 1811, it cost more to ship goods 30 miles inland from New York City than it cost to send them to England. But after eight years of work by 9,000 men, the canal opened in 1825, ahead of schedule and on budget, effectively tying together the nation and cementing the importance of New York City to America's future. Then the New York Central built its water-line route, and the Mohawk Valley became one of the nation's early industrial centers. The little Oneida County hamlets of Utica and Rome, where the canal builders had to dig through the route's highest ground, became sizable factory towns. Even the utopian Oneida

Community, with its believers in plural marriage and communal ownership, operated a stainless steel factory. First settled by New England Yankees, these towns attracted a new wave of immigration from the Atlantic coast in the early 20th century, including many Italian- and Polish-Americans.

The 24th Congressional District of New York sprawls through parts of 11 counties in central New York, few of them heavily populated. The biggest centers are Utica and Rome in Oneida County and Auburn in Cayuga County, which sits amidst the narrow Finger Lakes and was the home of Governor, Senator and Secretary of State William Seward. Nearby Seneca Falls was the birthplace of the women's movement in 1848, when Boston transplant Elizabeth Cady Stanton and Lucretia Mott produced a Declaration of Sentiments that initiated the push for women's suffrage. Abolition and temperance were also popular here. Today, this is a part of Upstate New York that feels itself bypassed by more recent economic growth and in need of government assistance. Young people increasingly see their futures in larger cities like Albany or Syracuse, rather than Utica. Oneida County's population fell 6% between 1990 and 2004, and in the latter year the county lost jobs at Rome Cable, Remington Arms, and Union Tools. After the September 11 attacks, new security restrictions reduced demand for Oneida Ltd. stainless steel flatware (the airline industry removed it from planes), accelerating the decline of what has been a local economic mainstay for decades. Six of the district's other 10 counties also experienced population declines; the booming business here is the Oneida Indians' Turning Stone Resort Casino, which generates $440 million in annual revenue for the region. At the south end of Otsego Lake is Cooperstown, where baseball was supposedly invented in 1839 and which is the home of the Baseball Hall of Fame. Like much of Upstate New York, the 24th District is historically Republican, but trended to Democrats in the 1990s. George W. Bush carried it only narrowly in 2000 and by a wider margin in 2004.

The new congressman from the 24th District is Michael Arcuri, a Democrat elected in 2006. Arcuri grew up in Utica and went to college at SUNY Albany, where he distinguished himself as a Division III football star. He got his law degree at New York Law School in Manhattan and returned home to open a law practice. In 1993, Arcuri was elected Oneida County district attorney, the first Democrat elected to the position in 40 years. During his tenure, violent crime decreased and he boasted of a conviction rate above 90%. Arcuri sometimes pursued unpopular prosecutions, including the convictions of a veteran local politician and an assistant fire chief.

Arcuri replaces veteran incumbent Sherwood Boehlert, a leading Republican centrist who announced in March 2006 that he would retire after 12 terms. Boehlert had nearly lost his party's nomination in 2002 to a conservative candidate and in 2006 faced the prospect of his third straight competitive primary. In 2004 he had undergone successful triple bypass surgery. After his announcement, Democrats united behind Arcuri and Republicans also cleared the field for 10-year Republican state Senator Ray Meier. Republicans had nearly 40,000 more registered voters than Democrats but the district's nearly 72,000 unaffiliated voters and Upstate Democratic voting trends made this a highly competitive race.

Arcuri and Meier hewed to the ideological center, but it was Arcuri who most closely reflected Boehlert's viewpoints. "I've been calling myself, much to my opponent's chagrin, a Boehlert Democrat," Arcuri said during the campaign. Meier opposed abortion, while Arcuri supported abortion rights, as did Boehlert. Meier, who actually had Boehlert's endorsement, said he was more conservative than the incumbent, but would stand up to his party and seek bipartisan compromises in Congress.

Arcuri won endorsements from organized labor and enjoyed one other critical advantage: unlike his opponent, Arcuri had no legislative record to defend, making it difficult for Republicans to argue that he was too liberal. Arcuri and Meier were both veterans of Oneida County politics; they remained relatively civil for much of the campaign, even as the national parties spent millions attacking the candidates. The Democratic Congressional Campaign Committee sponsored one direct-mail piece, titled "Spending like a Drunken Sailor," that showed Meier holding a champagne bottle. The National Republican Congressional Committee ran a racy ad featuring the silhouette of a dancing woman that accused Arcuri of calling a phone sex line and charging Oneida County taxpayers for it. Seven TV stations rejected the ad, and the basis for the attack was later discredited.

The NRCC spent $2.2 million on the race to the DCCC's $1.8 million, but it wasn't enough to overcome the political damage from the late-breaking Mark Foley congressional page scandal and landslide victories by Democrats Eliot Spitzer and Hillary Rodham Clinton at the top of the ticket. Arcuri won decisively 54%-45%. After the election, Arcuri won a seat on the exclusive Rules Committee, a prominent posting for a freshman. Although the district has grown more favorable to Democrats, the district remains winnable territory for the right Republican candidate.

TWENTY-FIFTH DISTRICT

Rep. James Walsh (R)

Elected 1988, 10th term; b. June 19, 1947, Syracuse; home, Syracuse; St. Bonaventure U., B.A. 1970; Catholic; married (Dede).

Elected Office: Syracuse Common Cncl., 1978-88, Pres. 1986-88.

Professional Career: Peace Corps, Nepal, 1970-72; Social worker, Onondaga Cnty. Social Svcs. Dept., 1972-74; Marketing exec., NYNEX, 1974-88.

DC Office: 2372 RHOB, 20515, 202-225-3701; Fax: 202-225-4042; Web site: www.house.gov/walsh.

District Offices: Palmyra, 315-597-6138; Syracuse, 315-423-5657.

Committees: *Appropriations* (6th of 29 R): Labor, HHS, Education & Related Agencies (RMM); Transportation, HUD & Related Agencies.

Group Ratings

	ADA	ACLU	AFS	LCV	ITIC	NTU	COC	ACU	CFG	FRC
2006	25	20	29	58	100	44	79	63	30	85
2005	0	—	0	22	—	51	89	65	42	69

National Journal Ratings

	2005 LIB	—	2005 CONS		2006 LIB	—	2006 CONS
Economic	43%	—	57%		46%	—	54%
Social	40%	—	59%		50%	—	50%
Foreign	30%	—	69%		33%	—	63%

Key Votes of the 109th Congress

1. Estate Tax Repeal	Y	5. Limit Interstate Abortion	Y	9. Build Border Fence		Y
2. Limit CAFE Standards	Y	6. Extend Patriot Act	Y	10. CAFTA		Y
3. FY06 Spending Curb	Y	7. Bar Same Sex Marriage	Y	11. Oppose Iraq Withdrawal		Y
4. Drilling in ANWR	N	8. Stem Cell Research $	N	12. Detainee Tribunals		Y

Election Results

2006 general	James Walsh (R-C-Ind)	110,525	(51%)	($1,787,552)
	Dan Maffei (D-WF)	107,108	(49%)	($918,270)
2006 primary	James Walsh (R)	unopposed		
2004 general	James Walsh (R-Ind-C)	189,063	(90%)	($656,874)
	Howie Hawkins (PJ)	20,106	(10%)	

Prior Winning Percentages: 2002 (72%); 2000 (69%); 1998 (69%); 1996 (55%); 1994 (58%); 1992 (56%); 1990 (63%); 1988 (57%)

The People		Race/Ethnic Origin	Ancestry		
Area size:	2,561 sq. mi.	86.6% White	German: 13.9%	Irish: 13.9%	
Urban population:	79.0%	7.1% Black	Italian: 12.4%		
Rural population:	21.0%	1.8% Asian	**2004 Presidential Vote**		
Pop. 2000:	654,361	0.6% Native Am.	Kerry (D)	158,063	(50%)
Pop. 2005 (est):	661,570	0.0% Hawaiian	Bush (R)	150,098	(48%)
Median income:	$43,188	1.5% Two+ races	Other	5,935	(2%)
Poverty status:	10.4%	0.1% Other	**2000 Presidential Vote**		
Military veterans:	12.7%	2.3% Hispanic Origin	Gore (D)	148,623	(51%)
			Bush (R)	132,126	(45%)
			Other	12,619	(4%)
			Cook Partisan Voting Index: D + 3		

Occupation   Blue collar: 20.8%   White collar: 65.0%   Gray collar: 14.2%

Syracuse is a middle American city in the middle of Upstate New York, halfway between Albany and Buffalo on the Erie Canal and the old New York Central Railroad, which were for years the nation's major east-west transportation routes. Built on a swamp that was a salt spring, Syracuse is the home of many practical-minded inventions—the dental chair, Stickley mission furniture, the drive-in bank teller, the serrated knife, the foot measuring devices used in shoe stores—and was an early manufacturer of typewriters. It is the site of the New York State Fair, which attracts 1 million visitors annually, and of Syracuse University, which plays basketball inside the Carrier Dome, the only domed stadium in the Northeast. The agricultural hinterland is rich with specialty crops like wine grapes, and its industrial jobs are mostly high-skill. But Onondaga County has been losing population since 1990, with a big loss in the 20-35 age group. Manufacturing jobs are being lost, and the Carrier air conditioner factory laid off 1,200 workers, but there are job gains in business services, education and health care, and unemployment has run below the national average.

The 25th Congressional District of New York includes all of Syracuse and Onondaga County. West of Syracuse it includes territory just south of Lake Ontario, northern Cayuga County and Wayne County, where in the village of Palmyra Joseph Smith had his vision of the angel Moroni and saw the golden tablets that led him to found the Mormon Church. The district's western end is in the suburbs of Rochester in Monroe County, which is split up between four districts. Historically, Syracuse and Rochester have been heavily Republican, partly out of antipathy to New York City. But in the 1990s, economically ailing Upstate New York trended sharply toward national Democrats (to bring in federal dollars) even as it voted for Republican Governor George Pataki (to hold down taxes). This district voted 51% for Al Gore in 2000 and 50% for John Kerry in 2004.

The congressman from the 25th District is James Walsh, a Republican first elected in 1988. He grew up in Syracuse, the son of Syracuse mayor and Congressman (1973-79) William Walsh. He came to the House as almost a professional civic activist: He was a volunteer in the Peace Corps in Nepal, a social worker, then worked for New York Telephone and NYNEX, which detailed him to a local university. He was elected five times to the Syracuse common council, then ran for Congress in 1988 when a Republican incumbent nearly beaten two years earlier decided to retire. He won by a solid 57%-42%. Like other Republicans from economically sluggish Upstate areas, he is open to government intervention in the economy.

Walsh serves on the Appropriations Committee, and has been part of the "college of cardinals"—chairman of four different subcommittees and now ranking minority member on a fifth. In 1995 and 1996 he chaired the District of Columbia Subcommittee, just as Marion Barry was returned to the mayor's office after serving time in prison. In 1997 and 1998 Walsh chaired the Legislative Branch Subcommittee, which sets Congress's own budget. He suffered the embarrassment in spring 1997 of seeing his appropriation defeated because of defections by 11 Republicans, who were determined to uphold promises to cut Congress's budget. From 1999 to 2004 Walsh was chairman of the VA-HUD-Independent Agencies Subcommittee. In his first two years he battled with HUD Secretary Andrew Cuomo, attacking Cuomo for using anti-drug money to fund a gun buy-back program. Walsh has not been shy about supporting what some call pork barrel projects, many for the Syracuse area. "Our economy's in tough shape right now, so we're not bashful at all in helping our own state."

In November 2001 Walsh and Democrat Nita Lowey pushed for $11 billion in aid to New York in the defense supplemental. This was opposed by the Bush administration, and Dick Cheney brought Walsh to the White House to ask him to defer the money until later. Walsh refused. Although Walsh and Upstater John Sweeney crossed party lines, their amendment, reduced to $9.7 billion, was defeated by two votes in committee. Walsh continued fighting and threatened to vote against the rule unless it allowed a vote on his amendment. But in a meeting with OMB Director Mitch Daniels and Chief Deputy Whip Roy Blunt, he gave way, and agreed to accept $1.75 billion. Sweeney and New York Democrats were furious, but Walsh said, "I was concerned that we could lose everything if we just went right at the president and drew a veto." Walsh complained to Dennis Hastert in August 2002 about the level of spending allowed, but worked doggedly and in October 2002 the subcommittee approved a $90.9 billion appropriation, under both the Senate level and the president's request, though funding for some programs, like AmeriCorps, were eliminated, which Walsh said would probably be added in conference. In 2003 the subcommittee's appropriation was held to $90.8 billion; in 2004 it was $92.9 billion. This was above the Bush budget, to which Walsh's response was, "It looks to me as if the president's budget is very, very tight for what I do."

In November 2002 House Republicans changed their rules to make Appropriations subcommittee chairmen, previously chosen by the full committee chairmen, subject to veto by the Steering Committee—clipping the cardinals' wings. In October 2004 Walsh asked Speaker Dennis Hastert for a waiver from the six-year Republican term limit on Appropriations subcommittee chairmanships. Incoming Appropriations Chairman Jerry Lewis decided to reduce the number of subcommittees from 13 to 10. Walsh ended up with the chairmanship of the Military Quality of Life Subcommittee, which meant he retained jurisdiction over veterans programs and gained military construction, but lost HUD and NASA. In 2005 he steered $63 million to Central New York projects—$5.6 million for a Hancock Field Air National Guard facility, $38.5 million for a barracks at Fort Drum, $9.7 million for an airfield vehicle support facility and $6.8 million for a physical fitness facility there, $850,000 for a Griffiss Northeast Air Defense support sector facility. In May 2006, when the Republican Study Committee sought to cut $500 million from Walsh's appropriation, he said he would get it back in conference with the Senate. He adjusted the deficit reduction package in November 2005 to soften the restrictions on food stamp eligibility. In June 2005 he said he would find the money to adjust for an embarrassing $1 billion shortfall in Veterans Administration health programs. In April 2006 he noted that Congress had blocked administration plans to raise co-payments and fees in the Veterans Administration. In July 2006 he raised the appropriation for the Syracuse VA Medical Center spinal cord injury center from $54 million to $78 million. A decade earlier, Walsh voted for the version of the line-item veto passed in 1996 (and later ruled unconstitutional); in 2006, with the advantage of 10 years' experience as an appropriator, he voted against another version.

Walsh has been co-chairman of the congressional Friends of Ireland and a strong supporter of the Easter peace accords signed in 1998. That year he sponsored the "Walsh Visas" to allow 4,000 unemployed young people a year from Northern Ireland and adjacent counties in the Irish Republic to live and work in Pittsburgh, Boston, Washington, Colorado Springs and, yes, Syracuse. As the peace process progressed and Northern Ireland's economy improved the program began to be phased out; the last Walsh visas were issued for Colorado Springs in 2003 and for Washington and Syracuse in 2006. In March 2004 he hosted Sinn Fein's Gerry Adams at Syracuse's St. Patrick's Day Parade. In March 2005, when Adams was shunned by George W. Bush, Edward Kennedy and others who had received him in the past because of IRA/Sinn Fein participation in a bank robbery and the murder of Robert McCartney, Walsh met with him anyway; he also met with McCartney's five sisters, who were demanding justice for their brother's murderers. In February 2006 he took advantage of a meeting at the White House to ask George W. Bush that Adams be given a visa that allowed him to do fundraising. Walsh has also taken an interest in Nepal, where he served in the Peace Corps, and has kept tabs on the Maoist insurgency there; in December 2005 he gave a telephone press conference to reporters in Nepal, speaking in Nepali.

Over most of his career in Congress Walsh has won reelection without difficulty. In 2004, he had no opposition at all. After that election Dan Maffei, former press secretary to Ways and Means ranking Democrat Charles Rangel, noticed that Walsh was the only Republican in a district carried by John Kerry who had no Democratic opponent. Maffei is a Syracuse native who worked as a TV reporter there and in 1996 went off to Washington and worked as a press aide to Senator Daniel Patrick Moynihan and presidential candidate Bill Bradley before his job with Rangel. In 2005 he launched his campaign and raised $100,000 by January 2006—the kind of fundraising the campaign committees and PACs look for before committing their support. He raised $380,000 by March 2006, and Walsh felt it necessary to run $100,000 of TV ads in June. Maffei depicted Walsh as a Bush clone and capitalized on opposition to and weariness with the military struggle in Iraq. Walsh emphasized the money and projects he had brought to the district. Hillary Rodham Clinton and Eliot Spitzer were expected to carry the district by wide margins, and Walsh was put very much on the defensive. Maffei was aided when a Democratic primary opponent withdrew in July and when in the September primary he won the Working Families line by a vote of 50-16 (those are not percentages, they are numbers of votes) and got 6,503 votes on that line in November. Maffei brought in leading Democrats—Bill Bradley, Wesley Clark, DCCC Chairman Rahm Emanuel and, twice, Bill Clinton. Walsh refrained from inviting Bush administration members. Toward the campaign's end he called Maffei a carpetbagger and said he shared voters' frustrations with the war. In late October 2006 the *Wall Street Journal* reported that Walsh and John McHugh got meals from defense contractors on a trip to Europe; Walsh said he had not violated the rules and pointed out that Maffei as a staffer took trips paid for by nonprofits to Paris, Geneva and China. Overall Walsh spent $1.8 million, Maffei $920,000. National Democrats seriously contested five Upstate New York districts in the cycle, of which Walsh's gave George W. Bush the lowest percentage (48%) in 2004; in the others Bush had won between 53% and 56% of the vote. Two of these districts fell to Democrats, but this one didn't, by the narrowest of margins. Election night returns showed Walsh with a narrow lead, with 13,000 absentee votes uncounted. It took a week to count them. Walsh came out ahead 51%-49%, and Maffei conceded November 17. Walsh was saved by the two small counties in the district, where he won 60% and 62% of the vote. He trailed by 283 votes in the Rochester suburbs in Monroe County and lost Syracuse's Onondaga County 51%-49%. He responded, "I've worked harder for the city of Syracuse than I have in any other part of the district. I have given my heart and soul to that city. And I'll continue to do that, but I've got a little hole in my heart."

Both Walsh and Maffei set out for a rematch in 2008; the DCCC considered the seat as one of its top 10 targets. Walsh called for defeated Republican Jim Leach, who had voted against the Iraq war resolution, to be appointed ambassador to the United Nations, and he voted for the nonbinding resolution opposing the surge in Iraq—though he voted against the supplemental with a timeline for withdrawal despite TV ads anti-war groups were running in Syracuse and Rochester. He became ranking minority member on the Labor-HHS Subcommittee which handles $600 billion in federal spending and on which, given appropriators' bipartisan way of doing business, he would be able to funnel federal monies to the district.

TWENTY-SIXTH DISTRICT

Rep. Tom Reynolds (R)

Elected 1998, 5th term; b. Sept. 3, 1950, Belfonte, PA; home, East Amherst; Springville-Griffith Inst., Kent St. U.; Presbyterian; married (Donna).

Military Career: NY Air Natl. Guard, 1970-76.

Elected Office: Concord Town Bd., 1974-82; Erie Cnty. Legislature, 1982-88; NY Assembly, 1988-98, Min. Ldr., 1995-98.

Professional Career: Real estate & insurance broker; Erie Cty. Repub. Chmn., 1990-96.

DC Office: 332 CHOB, 20515, 202-225-5265; Fax: 202-225-5910; Web site: www.house.gov/reynolds.

District Offices: Greece, 585-663-5570; Williamsville, 716-634-2324.

Committees: *Ways & Means* (11th of 17 R): Select Revenue Measures; Trade.

Group Ratings

	ADA	ACLU	AFS	LCV	ITIC	NTU	COC	ACU	CFG	FRC
2006	5	15	0	8	100	53	100	87	52	85
2005	0	—	0	11	—	55	93	83	53	75

National Journal Ratings

	2005 LIB	—	2005 CONS	2006 LIB	—	2006 CONS
Economic	36%	—	63%	32%	—	68%
Social	41%	—	58%	34%	—	65%
Foreign	34%	—	61%	33%	—	67%

Key Votes of the 109th Congress

1. Estate Tax Repeal	Y	5. Limit Interstate Abortion	Y	9. Build Border Fence	Y
2. Limit CAFE Standards	Y	6. Extend Patriot Act	Y	10. CAFTA	Y
3. FY06 Spending Curb	Y	7. Bar Same Sex Marriage	Y	11. Oppose Iraq Withdrawal	Y
4. Drilling in ANWR	Y	8. Stem Cell Research $	N	12. Detainee Tribunals	Y

Election Results

2006 general	Tom Reynolds (R-C)	109,257	(52%)	($5,275,474)
	Jack Davis (D-Ind-WF)	100,914	(48%)	($2,386,358)
2006 primary	Tom Reynolds (R)	unopposed		
2004 general	Tom Reynolds (R-Ind-C)	157,466	(56%)	($2,522,713)
	Jack Davis (D-WF)	125,613	(44%)	($1,356,713)

Prior Winning Percentages: 2002 (74%); 2000 (69%); 1998 (57%)

The People		Race/Ethnic Origin	Ancestry	
Area size:	2,749 sq. mi.	92.3% White	German: 20.6%	Irish: 12.3%
Urban population:	71.2%	3.0% Black	Italian: 11.9%	
Rural population:	28.8%	1.5% Asian	**2004 Presidential Vote**	
Pop. 2000:	654,361	0.3% Native Am.	Bush (R) 176,235	(55%)
Pop. 2005 (est):	667,804	0.0% Hawaiian	Kerry (D) 137,543	(43%)
Median income:	$46,653	0.8% Two+ races	Other 4,384	(1%)
Poverty status:	6.9%	0.1% Other	**2000 Presidential Vote**	
Military veterans:	12.9%	1.9% Hispanic Origin	Bush (R) 144,516	(51%)
			Gore (D) 126,693	(44%)
			Other 14,188	(5%)
			Cook Partisan Voting Index: R + 3	

Occupation　　Blue collar: 23.4%　　White collar: 61.7%　　Gray collar: 14.8%

The destination of the Erie Canal—the great state engineering project that made New York the Empire State—is Lake Erie, and for its last hundred miles the canal passed through the rolling countryside of western New York. This was land scarcely settled, except by Indians, when the canal was begun in 1817, and in many ways it is part of the Midwest: water here flows not into the Atlantic but into the Great Lakes; people speak not in the pungent accents of New York City but in a flat Midwestern tone. The economy, based originally on farming fertile land, by the late 19th century became dominated by heavy industry. This land was settled mostly by New England Yankees, with cultural folkways quite different from those of New York City; later they were joined by Irish, Italian and Polish immigrants who came to work in the factories of Buffalo and Rochester. For most of its history, western New York had an economy more prosperous than that of the rest of the country, as you can still see in the solid houses and schools, stores and factories built to weather the Upstate winter. But economic growth here in the past three decades has lagged behind the rest of the nation. Many of Buffalo's factories have closed, and the large Delphi plant in Lockport—where the locks of the Erie Canal are near Main Street—had major cutbacks following the company's bankruptcy in 2005; Rochester's premier industries, Kodak and Xerox, fell on hard times and laid off thousands.

The 26th Congressional District of New York covers much ᴏ̲̲̲̲̲̲̲̲̲̲̲̲̲̲̲ ᴏ̲̲. .lf its people are in the suburbs of Buffalo in Erie and Niagara Counties, though none in the city of Buffalo itself. It extends from the city limits of Buffalo to the city limits of Rochester and includes that city's northwestern suburbs. In between is rural and small town territory, with many towns bearing the classical names sprinkled by state commissioners across Upstate New York. One such is Attica, scene of the terrible prison riot in 1970. Politically, this is ancestrally Republican territory. For a long time this was due to Upstaters' distrust of Democratic New York City. But as economic growth has lagged, Upstate New York has moved toward the Democratic party. Not enough to make the 26th District Democratic, however: it is one of six New York districts that voted for George W. Bush in both 2000 and 2004.

The congressman from the 26th District is Tom Reynolds, a Republican first elected in 1998. Reynolds grew up in Springville, in southern Erie County, and became an insurance and real estate broker there. He got into politics early: in 1973 he was aide to an assemblyman and that same year, at 23, he was elected to the Concord town council. In 1982 he was named to a vacant seat in the Erie County Legislature. In 1988 he was elected to the Assembly and also helped run the congressional campaign of Bill Paxon, who was elected to succeed Jack Kemp in Congress from the Buffalo suburbs. From 1990 to 1996 he was Erie County Republican chairman, from 1995 to 1998 the Assembly minority leader. In early 1998, Paxon unexpectedly announced he would not run for reelection. At his side when he made his announcement was his long-time friend and ally Reynolds, who announced the next morning he was running for the House. No serious Republican opposition appeared; Democrats nominated a professor at SUNY-Geneseo. It was not a suspenseful or eventful campaign. Reynolds won 57%-43%.

In the House, Reynolds has had the most conservative voting record in the New York delegation. With help from Paxon, he quickly won the favor of the Republican leadership and became only the second Republican freshman in a century to win a seat on the Rules Committee. That assignment gave him quick entry into the House's leadership circles and the Capitol's back rooms. Like Paxon, Reynolds proved a skillful fundraiser, gaining appointment to chair the National Republican Congressional Committee's Battleground 2000 program, which raised $21 million from House members. In 2001 Speaker Dennis Hastert gave Reynolds a slot on the leadership-friendly House Administration Committee, which has responsibility for campaign finance legislation. As a further sign of the leadership's gratitude to Reynolds for his campaign service and a mark of his growing influence, Hastert got him a seat on the Ways and Means Committee; technically he did not join the committee until four years later, after the retirement of Ways and Means Upstate neighbor Amo Houghton. In the meantime, Reynolds showed his legislative savvy. When the House took up campaign finance regulation, he said that the Shays-Meehan bill had a loophole allowing Democrats to use their $40 million soft money building fund for hard money purposes; the language was fixed. After September 11, some Democrats criticized Reynolds as more interested in the priorities of the White House than the needs of New York, but Reynolds responded that he played an essential role as honest broker in getting money to his home state; many champions of New York City agreed. In 2005, Reynolds voiced frequent doubts about President Bush's plan for Social Security reform, in part because of his concern that it would backfire politically on Republicans. He spoke out frequently against the alternative minimum tax and its growing bite on middle-income taxpayers in New York.

In November 2002, Reynolds and Jerry Weller ran vigorous campaigns to chair the NRCC. Weller's district is adjacent to that of Hastert, who said he was neutral; other leadership members, notably Tom DeLay, backed Reynolds. He won 123-91. As NRCC chairman, Reynolds worked closely with Hastert, with whom he shared many qualities: beefy, former state legislators with an everyman style, who gained influence by their backroom skills rather than their public personality; the two of them talked frequently. He was an active fundraiser for George W. Bush's campaign and built close relationships with top officials of the Bush administration, including Dick Cheney and Karl Rove. Throughout the 2004 cycle, Reynolds insisted that relatively few seats were in play and that incumbent Republicans would do fine. He suffered setbacks in February and June 2004 when Democrats captured two previously Republican-held seats in special elections in Kentucky and South Dakota. But in November, with a boost from DeLay's redistricting plan in Texas, Republicans gained a net three seats and saw only two incumbents lose. This increased Reynolds's already considerable influence in Republican ranks, and some mentioned him as a possible future leader. His rapid rise in House influence is "not bad for a kid from Springville," he often says. But he publicly denied any ambition to move up the leadership ladder.

His second term as NRCC chairman did not go so well. Democrats were able to point to several ethically-tainted Republican incumbents as evidence of a "culture of corruption" in the Republican-controlled House, Majority Leader Tom DeLay was indicted and later resigned, there were deepening problems with the war in Iraq, and the botched federal response to Hurricane Katrina raised troubling questions about Bush administration competence. Reynolds insisted that Republicans would retain their majority in the House. "These are local contests," was his constant refrain. After the 2006 election, he confidently predicted, "We will be in the majority." He continued to predict that only a handful of House seats would be in play, and he dismissed suggestions that 2006 would parallel the 1994 wipeout of congressional Democrats.

Whether or not he was trying to reassure nervous colleagues and Republican donors, his forecasts ultimately proved far too optimistic. He got a break in June 2006 when Republicans narrowly held the California seat left vacant by Duke Cunningham after he pleaded guilty to corruption and resigned, but that momentum proved illusory. In September, Reynolds and House Republicans suffered what became a near-fatal blow when Congressman Mark Foley unexpectedly resigned amid reports that he had inappropriate communications with male House pages. The saga affected Reynolds directly when it was learned that his chief of staff Kirk Fordham previously held the same job with Foley; questions were raised of whether Reynolds should have known of Foley's problems. In July 2006, Foley had given $100,000 to the NRCC. When Reynolds said that he had referred reports about Foley to Hastert, his previously close confidant, the Speaker said he could not recall such warnings. This highly unusual and public disagreement became a burden for both Hastert and Reynolds during the final weeks of the campaign. In the end, 22 Republican incumbents were defeated and House Republicans suffered a net 30-seat loss. Reynolds cast some blame on incumbents who did not take their challengers seriously.

Meanwhile, he faced problems at home. The 2002 redistricting appeared to leave Reynolds with a relatively safe district. But in 2004 he got surprisingly tough competition from Jack Davis, a businessman and former Republican who spent $1.25 million of his own money on his campaign. Davis ran ads depicting Reynolds as a free trader who outsourced American jobs—an effective line of attack in Upstate New York, where manufacturing job losses have been steep—but he received little help or attention from national Democrats. Reynolds won by an unexpectedly close 56%-44%. Davis ran again in 2006, and again conducted a maverick, self-financed campaign focused on Upstate economic woes. This time, the Foley scandal breathed life into his campaign as Reynolds struggled to defend his activities and his disagreements with Hastert, and local Democrats pointed out his failure to protect the pages. A freakish mid-October snow storm that dumped nearly two feet of snow on the Buffalo area proved to be a serendipitous event; his role in quickly mobilizing the federal response gave Reynolds an opportunity to remind voters of his clout in Washington. The campaign committees of both parties spent heavily here; Republicans might have used that money to attempt to rescue their fading prospects in other Upstate New York contests, where they lost three seats. Reynolds survived, but by only 52%-48% in his once-safe seat. Davis led in the Erie and Niagara County portions of the district, with 55% of the vote. But Reynolds had big margins in the small towns and led 57%-43% in Monroe County.

Back in Washington, Reynolds chose not to seek another leadership post and burrowed into his Ways and Means work at the beginning of the 110th Congress. Although he seemed likely to retain his House seat, he faced a steeper challenge in rebuilding his standing after what otherwise had been a remarkably swift and steep ascent in the House. Democrat Jonathan Powers, a 29-year-old Iraq war veteran, announced he would challenge Reynolds in 2008.

TWENTY-SEVENTH DISTRICT

Rep. Brian Higgins (D)

Elected 2004, 2d term; b. Oct. 6, 1959, Buffalo; home, Buffalo; S.U.N.Y. Buffalo, B.A. 1984, M.A. 1985, Harvard U. M.P.A. 1996; Catholic; married (Mary Jane).

Elected Office: Buffalo City Cncl., 1987-93; NY Assembly, 1998-2004.

Professional Career: Chief of Staff, Erie Cnty. Leg., 1994-98; Lecturer, Buffalo State College, 2000-03.

DC Office: 431 CHOB, 20515, 202-225-3306; Fax: 202-226-0347; Web site: house.gov/higgins.

District Offices: Buffalo, 716-852-3501; Jamestown, 716-484-0729.

Committees: *Oversight & Government Reform* (13th of 23 D): National Security & Foreign Affairs; Domestic Policy. *Transportation & Infrastructure* (21st of 41 D): Coast Guard & Maritime Transportation; Water Resources & Environment; Highways & Transit.

Group Ratings

	ADA	ACLU	AFS	LCV	ITIC	NTU	COC	ACU	CFG	FRC
2006	85	73	100	92	67	9	43	20	4	0
2005	95	—	100	94	—	11	52	16	10	31

National Journal Ratings

	2005 LIB	—	2005 CONS		2006 LIB	—	2006 CONS
Economic	71%	—	28%		79%	—	18%
Social	61%	—	39%		67%	—	32%
Foreign	65%	—	34%		59%	—	40%

Key Votes of the 109th Congress

1. Estate Tax Repeal	N	5. Limit Interstate Abortion	N	9. Build Border Fence	N
2. Limit CAFE Standards	N	6. Extend Patriot Act	Y	10. CAFTA	N
3. FY06 Spending Curb	N	7. Bar Same Sex Marriage	N	11. Oppose Iraq Withdrawal	Y
4. Drilling in ANWR	N	8. Stem Cell Research $	Y	12. Detainee Tribunals	Y

Election Results

2006 general	Brian Higgins (D-Ind-WF)	140,027	(79%)	($854,559)
	Michael McHale (R)	36,614	(21%)	
2006 primary	Brian Higgins (D)	unopposed		
2004 general	Brian Higgins (D-Ind-WF)	143,332	(51%)	($1,372,162)
	Nancy Naples (R-C)	139,558	(49%)	($1,581,433)

The People		Race/Ethnic Origin	Ancestry	
Area size:	2,444 sq. mi.	88.8% White	German: 19.2%	Polish: 14.7%
Urban population:	81.5%	4.0% Black	Irish: 12.5%	
Rural population:	18.5%	0.7% Asian	**2004 Presidential Vote**	
Pop. 2000:	654,361	0.8% Native Am.	Kerry (D) 158,433	(53%)
Pop. 2005 (est):	643,885	0.0% Hawaiian	Bush (R) 132,416	(45%)
Median income:	$36,884	1.0% Two+ races	Other 6,709	(2%)
Poverty status:	12.0%	0.1% Other	**2000 Presidential Vote**	
Military veterans:	14.0%	4.6% Hispanic Origin	Gore (D) 149,840	(53%)
			Bush (R) 114,859	(41%)
			Other 16,090	(6%)
			Cook Partisan Voting Index: D + 7	

Occupation   Blue collar: 25.3%   White collar: 57.9%   Gray collar: 16.8%

Buffalo, with its massive 1920s skyscraper City Hall overlooking the Niagara River and Lake Erie, has gone through rough times. The butt of many jokes about the snow that piles up at the eastern end of Lake Erie and that supposedly keeps it immobilized half the year, Buffalo also should be credited with building a heavy industrial base in the late 19th and early 20th centuries, as America's number one grain milling center and as a major steel producer. Today, the Lackawanna steel mills are cold, and grain milling waned after the St. Lawrence Seaway opened in the 1950s. Buffalo is eclipsed economically by the bigger Great Lakes industrial cities of Cleveland, Detroit and Chicago, and its architecturally bold downtown skyscrapers are far overshadowed by the high-rise horizon of Toronto, not many miles away. Buffalo was the nation's 15th largest city in 1950 when it had a population of 580,000; in 2006 it was number 66, with a population down to 276,000, less than it had in 1900. Surrounding Erie County, once well over 1 million, was down to 921,000 in 2006. The downward spiral of what some call the Incredible Shrinking City intensified in the 1980s when the Bethlehem Steel plants were shuttered. Buffalo, which remains the second-largest city in the state, still has considerable assets: a high-skill labor force and inexpensive real estate, including a gentrified and handsome waterfront on a now-cleaner Lake Erie and some impressive cultural institutions.

Right across Buffalo's Peace Bridge is the richest part of Canada, the golden horseshoe from Niagara Falls through Hamilton to Toronto. But Buffalo's hopes of becoming Toronto's back office have faded and New York taxes are still high enough to leave Buffalo at a serious competitive disadvantage. Local boosters have criticized state capital powerbrokers for lavishing excessive attention on New York City as the state's economic engine; it doesn't help that Buffalo is closer to Detroit than Albany.

The 27th Congressional District of New York consists of the eastern and southern two-thirds of Buffalo, plus most of the Erie County suburbs east and south of the city—from working-class Cheektowaga and Lackawanna to higher-income Hamburg and Orchard Park. The 27th also includes Chautauqua County, the famed birthplace of a movement to promote high-minded discourse; in 2006, Al Gore drew a big crowd for a lecture on global warming. It was there that a training camp for Methodist Sunday school teachers was founded in 1874, attracting some 25,000 people to educational talks and inspirational lectures from the likes of Ralph Waldo Emerson and William Jennings Bryan; rounds of lectures continue every summer. Although some Buffalo suburbs are Republican, this district is solidly Democratic. But as Buffalo struggled, it became politically volatile. In 1992 Buffalo gave Ross Perot 28% of the vote, his best showing in a central city anywhere; in 1994, Mario Cuomo lost Erie County to George Pataki, who carried it again in 1998 and 2002. But in recent contests for president and statewide offices, Buffalo and Erie County have returned to solidly Democratic.

The congressman from the 27th District is Brian Higgins, a Democrat elected in 2004 in the last contest to determine a winner that year. Higgins grew up in Buffalo and graduated from Buffalo State College, and got a master's degree more than a decade later at Harvard. His father was a skilled tradesman who was prominent in local politics; he served on the city council and later as commissioner of the New York State Workers Compensation Board under Governor Hugh Carey; his mother was a school teacher. His uncle was president of the Buffalo Federation of Labor in the 1950s. Brian Higgins was a political junkie, securing staff jobs in the Erie County sheriff's office, the state Assembly, and the county Legislature. In 1993, after six years on the Buffalo city council, he ran for county comptroller and lost to Republican Nancy Naples. In 1998, he was elected to the

Assembly and served three terms. In a district crowded with unionized workers, Higgins often reminded voters that his father and uncle were bricklayers and he stressed his Irish immigrant heritage.

Both parties were stunned when Jack Quinn, a Republican who was first elected in 1992 and had support from local unions, announced his retirement in April 2004. That included Tom Reynolds, who represents the adjacent district and chaired the National Republican Campaign Committee. The 27th District immediately became a hotly contested race. Naples, a former Merrill Lynch executive in Manhattan and a popular local figure with strong name recognition, quickly wrapped up the Republican nomination, while five Democrats battled for their party's nomination. Higgins was the favorite of local and national Democratic leaders, organized labor and the *Buffalo News*, which called him "an unusually productive member of a largely dysfunctional legislative body" in Albany. He won the primary with 44% to 26% for West Seneca supervisor and certified public accountant Paul Clark, who appealed to the large base of Polish voters in the district. In the contentious general election, Higgins reminded voters that Naples supported many of George W. Bush's policies, including his handling of national security. He criticized Republicans for shifting the tax burden from the rich to the middle class, and promised that he would make health care more available and protect Social Security. Naples criticized Higgins for his record in Albany, including support for tax increases. Higgins won 51%-49%; Naples took 57% of the vote in Chautauqua County, which cast 20% of the district's votes; Higgins won 53% in Erie County. It took 16 days of recounts and a court challenge before Naples conceded the nearly 3,800-vote victory.

In the House, Higgins had a centrist voting record and was the most conservative Democrat in the state delegation. On the Transportation and Infrastructure Committee, he gave a tour of the Buffalo waterfront to ranking Democrat Jim Oberstar, and he got $42 million for local projects in the highway bill. He helped to broker an agreement with the New York Power Authority for local financial aid, including waterfront improvements, in exchange for its long-term right to operate the Niagara Power Project. The *Buffalo News* said that he was "the Lone Ranger in the fight" and that he "gets the most credit from players in the power game." The issue strained his relationship with Louise Slaughter in the adjoining district, who disagreed with his strategy but was credited with behind-the-scenes work on the agreement. His support for the Patriot Act and opposition to a deadline for withdrawal of troops in Iraq led to complaints from some liberals, but those positions may have been a net plus for him in the district.

Reynolds had said that would try to defeat Higgins in 2006. But he couldn't find a credible challenger, and he had to deal with more pressing challenges to upstate Republican seats, including his own. Higgins initially got the endorsement of local conservative leaders, but the state Conservative Party chairman overruled it. Still, he won 79%-21% against assistant district attorney Michael McHale. He appears safe, at least until redistricting. He failed in a bid for a seat on the Appropriations Committee.

TWENTY-EIGHTH DISTRICT

Rep. Louise Slaughter (D)

Elected 1986, 11th term; b. Aug. 14, 1929, Harlan Cnty., KY; home, Fairport; U. of KY, B.S. 1951, M.S. 1953; Episcopalian; married (Robert).

Elected Office: Monroe Cnty. Legislature, 1976-79; NY Assembly, 1982-86.

Professional Career: Regional Coord., Lt. Gov. Mario Cuomo, 1976-79.

DC Office: 2469 RHOB, 20515, 202-225-3615; Fax: 202-225-7822; Web site: www.louise.house.gov.

District Offices: Buffalo, 716-853-5813; Niagara Falls, 716-282-1274; Rochester, 585-232-4850.

Committees: *Rules* (Chmn. of 9 D): Legislative & Budget Process; Rules & Organization of the House.

Group Ratings

	ADA	ACLU	AFS	LCV	ITIC	NTU	COC	ACU	CFG	FRC
2006	85	89	100	92	20	11	29	9	5	0
2005	95	—	100	89	—	12	41	4	5	8

National Journal Ratings

	2005 LIB	—	2005 CONS		2006 LIB	—	2006 CONS
Economic	76%	—	23%		94%	—	0%
Social	78%	—	22%		88%	—	12%
Foreign	89%	—	11%		88%	—	10%

Key Votes of the 109th Congress

1. Estate Tax Repeal	N	5. Limit Interstate Abortion	N	9. Build Border Fence	N
2. Limit CAFE Standards	N	6. Extend Patriot Act	N	10. CAFTA	N
3. FY06 Spending Curb	N	7. Bar Same Sex Marriage	N	11. Oppose Iraq Withdrawal	N
4. Drilling in ANWR	N	8. Stem Cell Research $	Y	12. Detainee Tribunals	N

Election Results

2006 general	Louise Slaughter (D-Ind-WF)	111,386	(73%)	($675,787)
	John Donnelly (R-C)	40,844	(27%)	($24,468)
2006 primary	Louise Slaughter (D)	unopposed		
2004 general	Louise Slaughter (D-WF)	159,655	(73%)	($353,874)
	Michael Laba (R-C)	54,543	(25%)	($14,725)
	Other	5,678	(3%)	

Prior Winning Percentages: 2002 (62%); 2000 (66%); 1998 (65%); 1996 (57%); 1994 (57%); 1992 (55%); 1990 (59%); 1988 (57%); 1986 (51%)

The People		Race/Ethnic Origin	Ancestry	
Area size:	2,282 sq. mi.	62.0% White	German: 13.4%	Italian: 11.0%
Urban population:	93.5%	28.7% Black	Irish: 9.7%	
Rural population:	6.5%	1.4% Asian	**2004 Presidential Vote**	
Pop. 2000:	654,360	0.5% Native Am.	Kerry (D) 162,319	(63%)
Pop. 2005 (est):	607,634	0.0% Hawaiian	Bush (R) 92,627	(36%)
Median income:	$31,751	1.7% Two+ races	Other 4,581	(2%)
Poverty status:	18.7%	0.1% Other	**2000 Presidential Vote**	
Military veterans:	12.2%	5.5% Hispanic Origin	Gore (D) 151,402	(60%)
			Bush (R) 88,461	(35%)
			Other 14,160	(6%)
			Cook Partisan Voting Index: D +15	

Occupation   Blue collar: 23.2%   White collar: 58.3%   Gray collar: 18.5%

Rochester, with a metro area of just over one million, is one of the major cities of Upstate New York. Located where the Erie Canal, the backbone of Upstate, crosses the Genesee River, Rochester became a major industrial city—the "Flour City" in the 1830s, as it milled the wheat produced by western New York farmers; then, a high-tech city, after a bank clerk named George Eastman began making photographic dry plates and marketed the first still camera and film for Thomas Edison's motion picture camera. Later, Bausch & Lomb developed its lens business here. Rochester, the home of Susan B. Anthony and Frederick Douglass, has lived on high-tech interpretations of the eye, and the optics and imaging industry continues to be a significant regional employer. Its great industries—Bausch & Lomb, Eastman Kodak, and Xerox (which started here as Haloid)—have thrived on technical innovation, precision workmanship, high reliability and customer service, lending Rochester an affluent and well-educated population as well as fine civic institutions, including the George Eastman House, one of the world's leading repositories of photographic and motion-picture history. This was the city that in 1918 invented the Community Chest and at one time had the nation's highest United Way contributions. Unhappily, Rochester's big employers have fallen on hard times, and young professionals have been leaving the area. Kodak, hard hit by competition from digital cameras, employed 60,000 people in the Rochester area in 1981; by 2005 that was down to 16,300. Xerox jobs in the area fell from 16,000 to below 7,700.

Not far west of Rochester is a very different part of Upstate New York, the Niagara Frontier—the local name for the Buffalo-Niagara Falls area. The Niagara Frontier was once an armed frontier, between the United States and British-held Upper Canada, where American troops crossed the raging Niagara River during the War of 1812 to fight the Battle of Lundys Lane. Later in the 19th century Niagara Falls became a prime vacation spot—a must-see sight for European tourists and American honeymooners. Few tourists today notice the huge water intakes farther up the river or the hydroelectric power lines strung out on giant pylons fanning out in every direction, providing cheap public power for the chemical and steel factories that made the Niagara Frontier one of the heavy industry capitals of America. But the city of Niagara Falls has suffered hard times. Tourists tend to stay on the Canadian side, which has better views of the Falls and loose enforcement of sex and gambling laws that make it, as some say, the "Las Vegas of the North." Niagara Falls has lost 70% of its manufacturing since the 1960s and had the nation's third-lowest rate of job growth in the late 1990s; it has suffered double-digit unemployment and population losses. The downtown, leveled by urban renewal, remains troubled but there is hope: the Seneca Nation of Indians converted the city's faded convention center into a casino and 604-room hotel, one of three Indian casinos on the Niagara Frontier.

The 28th Congressional District of New York was created by redistricting in 2002. It includes Rochester, Niagara Falls and part of Buffalo, all connected by a thin strip of land along Lake Ontario and the Niagara River. Most of Rochester's suburbs are in three other districts, but the 28th includes Grand Island, Tonawanda and the northeast quadrant of Buffalo, where it includes much of the city's downtown and its fine cultural institutions. This is mainly a central city district, and 29% of its residents are black, by far the highest percentage in any Upstate district. Politically, this is a solidly Democratic district.

The congresswoman from the 28th District is Louise Slaughter, a Democrat first elected in 1986. A coal miner's daughter and a descendant of Daniel Boone (which makes her a cousin of Armed Services Committee chairman Ike Skelton), she grew up in Kentucky and still speaks with the accent and pungent phraseology of the mountains. Slaughter worked as a local staffer for Mario Cuomo when he was lieutenant governor in the 1970s and she won a seat on the Monroe County Legislature in 1976; she was elected to the New York Assembly in 1982. In 1986 she beat a one-term conservative Republican congressman 51%-49%, after charging that he did nothing to free *Associated Press* reporter Terry Anderson, a Rochester native held hostage in Lebanon. She secured what had been a marginal seat by tending carefully to local problems, by winning the support of area businessmen and the local *Democrat & Chronicle* newspaper—ironically, the flagship of Gannett, a chain founded by a diehard Upstate Republican.

Slaughter, the first woman to chair the influential Rules Committee, has regularly posted a liberal voting record. She is a prime supporter of the National Endowment for the Arts and has sponsored bills for free broadcast time for candidates. A microbiologist by training, and consistent with the Rochester-area research mindset, Slaughter opposed proposals to ban human cloning and was an outspoken proponent of stem-cell research. She backs feminist causes and is active on health issues. In 1991 she was one of the seven women House members who marched on the Senate to protest its treatment of Anita Hill. The Lewinsky scandal and impeachment left Slaughter uncomfortable. In March 1998 she said defensively, "I have not changed a bit from my days with Anita Hill. Sexual harassment in the workplace is a terrible thing and should not be tolerated." She said she was ready to call for Bill Clinton's resignation in August, but backed away when she saw the videotape of his testimony in which she thought his rights were abridged.

It took Slaughter many years to gain a higher position. In 1994 she lost to Barbara Kennelly in the race for vice chairman of the Democratic Caucus, and in 1996 she was defeated by John Spratt for the ranking Democrat post on the Budget Committee. In 2005, she finally became the ranking Democrat on the Rules Committee after Martin Frost lost in Texas. As a loyal lieutenant of Nancy Pelosi, Slaughter became an outspoken critic of Republican policies and their management of the House. She released a 147-page report that highlighted what Democrats said was "profound abuse" of House rules by Republicans in 2003-04. She was among the most outspoken critics of the Republican "culture of corruption," a prime talking point in Pelosi's campaign message; a chief target was the breakdown of the ethics process in the House. "Enough is enough," she said. "The ethics committee deserves more than partisan political power plays." She accused Republicans of "strong-arm tactics" and a "win at all costs mentality" to move legislation. In January 2007, she helped to bring the first legislation to the House floor for the new majority: an overhaul of House rules, largely dictated and massaged by Pelosi and her lieutenants. The loyal Slaughter hailed the result as "a Congress people can be proud of again." But Republicans quickly cried foul when Democrats next moved to the floor 6 bills from their campaign agenda, without committee action and with no opportunity for amendments on the House floor. When former Republican chairman David Dreier complained that reporters saw the details of the Rules package before it was given to the new minority party, Slaughter backhandedly said that "years of hurt" were on display. "What I sense from them is that they feel we will treat them as they treated us," she said, while rejecting the possibility. To a Rochester newspaper, the gentlewoman said of Dreier, "he's a prick." Slaughter was nearly as outspoken in attacking what she called a conservative bias in the national news media, claiming that liberals did not get sufficient time on television talk shows.

At home, she quickly developed an unexpectedly testy relationship with Democrat Brian Higgins in the Buffalo-based district. When he sought to mediate a dispute between the New York Power Authority and local users over rights to operate the Niagara Power Project, Slaughter objected: "I think federalizing this issue would be a disaster." But the upstart largely got his way, though Slaughter reportedly worked behind the scenes on the final deal.

In 2002, redistricting was a perils-of-Pauline nightmare for Slaughter. Sluggish population growth meant that Upstate New York had to lose one congressional district, and after much political maneuvering Slaughter was placed in the same district as Democrat John LaFalce, the party's ranking member on the Banking Committee. LaFalce sent clear signals that he would run against Slaughter, but three weeks later he announced his retirement. In the general, Slaughter campaigned in much new territory, but most of it was Democratic. She won 73% of the vote in Monroe County and 60% in Erie County, for a 62%-38% victory against an inexperienced Republican challenger. In 2006 her biggest problem was being bedridden with shingles in the closing weeks of the 2006 campaign. In this solidly Democratic district, Slaughter's chief threat is a primary challenge.

TWENTY-NINTH DISTRICT

Rep. Randy Kuhl (R)

Elected 2004, 2d term; b. Apr. 19, 1943, Bath; home, Hammondsport; Union College, B.S. 1966, Syracuse U., J.D. 1969; Episcopalian; divorced.

Elected Office: NY Assembly, 1980-86; NY Senate, 1986-2004.

Professional Career: Practicing atty., 1970-2005.

DC Office: 1505 LHOB, 20515, 202-225-3161; Fax: 202-226-6599; Web site: www.kuhl.house.gov.

District Offices: Bath, 607-776-9142; Fairport, 585-223-4760; Olean, 800-562-7431.

Committees: *Agriculture* (14th of 21 R): Horticulture & Organic Agriculture. *Education & Labor* (18th of 22 R): Higher Education, Lifelong Learning & Competitiveness; Early Childhood, Elementary & Secondary Education. *Transportation & Infrastructure* (27th of 34 R): Economic Development, Public Buildings & Emergency Management; Water Resources & Environment; Aviation.

Group Ratings

	ADA	ACLU	AFS	LCV	ITIC	NTU	COC	ACU	CFG	FRC
2006	5	14	14	33	100	55	100	83	58	100
2005	15	—	0	6	—	58	89	92	61	100

National Journal Ratings

	2005 LIB — 2005 CONS		2006 LIB — 2006 CONS	
Economic	38%	— 60%	45%	— 55%
Social	37%	— 62%	32%	— 66%
Foreign	31%	— 67%	17%	— 73%

Key Votes of the 109th Congress

1. Estate Tax Repeal	Y	5. Limit Interstate Abortion	Y	9. Build Border Fence	Y
2. Limit CAFE Standards	Y	6. Extend Patriot Act	Y	10. CAFTA	Y
3. FY06 Spending Curb	Y	7. Bar Same Sex Marriage	Y	11. Oppose Iraq Withdrawal	Y
4. Drilling in ANWR	Y	8. Stem Cell Research $	N	12. Detainee Tribunals	Y

Election Results

2006 general	Randy Kuhl (R-C-Ind) 106,077	(51%)	($1,475,289)
	Eric Massa (D-WF) 100,044	(49%)	($1,501,716)
2006 primary	Randy Kuhl (R) .... unopposed		
2004 general	Randy Kuhl (R) 136,883	(51%)	($937,340)
	Samara Barend (D-WF) 110,241	(41%)	($612,443)
	Mark Assini (C) 17,272	(6%)	($267,016)
	Other 5,819	(2%)	

The People		Race/Ethnic Origin	Ancestry	
Area size:	5,761 sq. mi.	92.5% White	German: 16.3% Irish: 12.2%	
Urban population:	58.4%	2.7% Black	English: 11.1%	
Rural population:	41.6%	1.8% Asian	**2004 Presidential Vote**	
Pop. 2000:	654,361	0.5% Native Am.	Bush (R) 171,317	(56%)
Pop. 2005 (est):	662,939	0.0% Hawaiian	Kerry (D) 127,481	(42%)
Median income:	$41,875	1.0% Two+ races	Other 4,660	(2%)
Poverty status:	9.9%	0.1% Other	**2000 Presidential Vote**	
Military veterans:	14.2%	1.4% Hispanic Origin	Bush (R) 152,004	(53%)
			Gore (D) 121,596	(43%)
			Other 11,318	(4%)
			Cook Partisan Voting Index: R + 5	

Occupation	Blue collar: 23.0%	White collar: 61.3%	Gray collar: 15.7%

The Southern Tier of New York is one of the nation's forgotten stretches of territory, yet it has an interesting and distinctive history. Elmira was the hometown of Mark Twain's beloved wife, Olivia, and is where Twain is buried. Corning is the headquarters of Corning Glass Works, a company successful over the years not only in manufacturing but in its artistic distinction, which is show-cased at a well-visited glass museum. This area has an Indian presence—some small reservations as well as the Seneca-Iroquois National Museum in Salamanca—plus miles and miles of dairy farms and much of New York's wine country. Sheltered by hills, the lands at the edge of Upstate's deep lakes constitute the nation's largest grape-growing area outside California, the leader in Concord grapes, with headquarters of prime New York State wineries and a major Welch's grape juice plant. But this area is isolated, and ill-served by air travel or Interstate highways. Cat-taraugus County, slightly inland from Lake Erie, is actually 110 miles closer to Washington, D.C., than it is to New York City, though getting to either destination requires considerable patience. The cruelest cut was the Internet bust. Corning's prospects grew dramatically when fiber optics and other high-tech components were being installed at a feverish pace, but the reduction in orders following the bust forced the company to lay off more than 1,000 of its local workers, in a town of only 11,000 people. In March 2007, it was making a comeback, according to *Forbes,* "as fiber products rejuvenate and as liquid crystal display (LCD) glass goes everywhere," especially in new television screens.

The 29th Congressional District of New York includes much of the state's Southern Tier, from Elmira to Cattaraugus County; to the north it includes the westernmost of the Finger Lakes and the southern suburbs of Rochester. Politically, this has been Republican country since the party's founding. These towns and the countryside are no longer homogeneously Protestant and the trend in Upstate New York has been toward national Democrats, but the 29th remains comfortably Republican for now. This was George W. Bush's best congressional district in New York in both 2000 and 2004.

The congressman from the 29th District is Randy Kuhl, a Republican elected in 2004. He grew up in western New York and graduated from Union College and Syracuse University law school. He worked ten years as a lawyer before winning election to the state Assembly in 1980; in 1986, he was elected to the state Senate. In April 2004 Amo Houghton, former CEO of Corning and one of the richest members of Congress, announced he was retiring after 18 years in the House after being assured that the district would not be sacrificed in redistricting. Kuhl was the early frontrunner to succeed him.

Even with the endorsement of Houghton, who wanted a successor from the Southern Tier, Kuhl was forced to endure two tough campaigns. He kicked off his campaign with an attempt to inoculate himself by apologizing for a 1997 drunk driving conviction, but that issue turned out to be the least of his worries. He drew heavy criticism for his service in Albany, in a legislature that is widely regarded as the most dysfunctional in the nation. Shortly before the Republican primary, his conservative challenger, Monroe County legislator Mark Assini, turned up the heat by releasing a radio ad that accused Kuhl of being a bigot. The attack, based on an 11-year-old comment about groups with "genetic traits," did not seem effective. Assini carried his base in the Rochester suburbs of Monroe County with 69% of the vote, but only 19% of the votes were cast there. Kuhl won just about everywhere else in the district and beat Assini by 64%-33%. The general election was expected to be anticlimactic in this solidly Republican district. Kuhl called for lowering taxes to attract more investment to western New York and said that he would work to ensure that the local agricultural sector remained competitive. The Democratic nominee, Samara Barend, 27, had never held elected office; she had served briefly as an aide to former Senator Daniel Patrick Moynihan and had worked on Senator Hillary Rodham Clinton's 2000 campaign. Kuhl, with his extensive political experience, was endorsed by the national and state AFL-CIO as "a strong advocate for working men and women and their families." But his campaign was rocked in late October by the unauthorized release of his sealed divorce records, which included charges of excessive drinking and womanizing and an accusation that Kuhl had pulled out two shotguns at a dinner party and threatened to shoot his wife. Both Kuhl and his ex-wife denounced the release of the records, which had been obtained by Barend's campaign manager after a staffer got them from a county clerk's office; apparently the documents were inadvertently released. Barend initially denied any role in the incident and refused demands to fire her campaign manager. In the end, the damaging documents weren't enough to overcome widespread distaste for the manner in which they were made public. Kuhl's win was narrower than had been expected, 51%-41%, with 6% to Assini on the Conservative Party line. In Monroe County, which cast 36% of the total vote, Barend led 48%-39%. Kuhl carried the other counties, including 67% in Corning-based Steuben County.

In the House, Kuhl has been a centrist Republican, with a slightly more conservative voting record on foreign policy. He has seats on three constituent-oriented committees: Agriculture, Education and Labor, and Transportation and Infrastructure. He helped to enact a dam-safety bill, requiring the Army Corps of Engineers to maintain and update a national inventory of dams, including information on federal and state inspections; the federal government owns only about 5% of the nation's 78,000 dams. On the Education Committee, he bucked party leaders by opposing a proposal to give parents of students displaced by Hurricanes Katrina and Rita access to an account of $6,700 to cover the cost of public, private or parochial school.

Kuhl's first reelection campaign was even more competitive than his open seat race. Democratic nominee Eric Massa was a Navy veteran and had been a top aide to Wesley Clark, the former NATO Supreme Allied Commander and 2004 Democratic presidential aspirant. After retiring from the Navy, Massa worked at Corning. He said that the war in Iraq was "never defined" and "misbegotten," and criticized Kuhl's support for the Central American Free Trade Agreement. He was boosted by ads from MoveOn.org that depicted Kuhl as "caught red-handed" in sending billions of dollars to Iraq to benefit companies like Halliburton. Kuhl criticized the partisanship in Washington, and said that he had delivered on his promise of an annual town hall meeting in each of the district's 145 towns and villages. Massa had the fundraising advantage late in the campaign. Kuhl won 51.5%-48.5%. He won every county, except for Monroe in the Rochester suburbs, which cast 36% of the total vote; Massa won 57%-43% there. Massa announced he would seek a rematch in 2008.

★ NORTH CAROLINA ★

North Carolina, in its third century as a state, has become one of the leading-edge parts of the nation, a state whose growing economy, booming demography and vibrant culture are in many ways typical of the way the nation is going—or would like to go. This was mostly unanticipated. Few people 30 years ago picked North Carolina as a state that would chart a path to the future. It had no great central city, no Atlanta primed to become another Chicago or Los Angeles, but rather a series of small metropolitan areas spaced out over thickly settled countryside. It did not have what seemed to be cutting-edge industries: the biggest employer was textiles, typically an underdeveloped nation's first industry, and the next two were stolid furniture and soon-to-be-disfavored tobacco. Geographically, it seemed to be off the nation's main lines of commerce—too steamy to be business-like in the summer, too cold to be a resort in the winter. It did not seem socially advanced, with a population made up almost entirely of native-born Anglo-Saxons and African-Americans and with an attachment to traditional and sometimes fundamentalist religion.

Yet North Carolina has emerged as one of America's leading growth states. Its population grew by 51% from 1980 to 2006, from just under 6 million to nearly 9 million; it ranks just behind also-fast-growing Georgia and passed New Jersey to become the 10th largest state in September 2005. Its economy has diversified and grown steadily. The number of textile and tobacco jobs is down, but Research Triangle Park, between Raleigh, Durham and Chapel Hill, has become one of the world's leading pharmaceutical and high-tech research centers: semiconductors, photonics, nanotechnology and security technology. GlaxoSmithKline has headquarters here, and Cisco, IBM, Nortel, and Sony Ericsson have big facilities. And the Triangle's success has been echoed by the Centennial Campus at Raleigh's North Carolina State University and the Piedmont Research Triad in Winston-Salem, which attracted a 2,000-job Dell facility in 2004. North Carolina has become one of the nation's leading banking centers, the headquarters of Bank of America (formerly NationsBank and NCNB) and Wachovia, both of which have been buying up other banks; Winston-Salem's Wachovia merged with Charlotte's First Union in 2003. The Charlotte and Raleigh-Durham metro areas accounted for more than half the state's population growth from 1990 to 2006, and they are now not just regional centers but major metro areas, with national sports franchises and huge hub airports. Nearly half the state's population—and more than half its affluent population—are in the Charlotte, Raleigh-Durham and Greensboro-Winston-Salem metro areas which have spread out into formerly rural counties. North Carolina is not just Mayberry any more.

Not all of North Carolina is upscale. The state is the nation's number two hog producer; some people are worried about the state's decline in manufacturing jobs, as low-wage factories close and work moves to lower-wage factories in less affluent states or abroad. The furniture industry is pressed by competition from China. The October 2004 tobacco buyout, ending tobacco allotments, is spurring farmers to shift to other crops like blueberries and pumpkins, even sheep and goats; some, free to compete in the market, are shifting from flue leaf to burley leaf, but the old tobacco economy will never be the same. North Carolina, number one in the percentage of workers in manufacturing jobs in 1993, was number eight in 2004. But other businesses have been moving in: Site Selection magazine rated North Carolina number one as a place to relocate a business in five of the six years from 2000 to 2006. As Governor Mike Easley says, "Our biggest advantage over who we compete with—San Diego, San Francisco, Massachusetts and the Maryland-Virginia area—is that we can do everything they can do, if not more, but we can do it 20 to 25% cheaper when you look at labor and capital investment." Manufacturing job losses have been overwhelmed by the rise in service and high-tech jobs, and the unemployment rate is low enough that thousands of Latinos moved into North Carolina seeking jobs in construction and meat and chicken factories. The state's Hispanic population rose from 77,000 in 1990 to 553,000 in 2005. Yet for all its metropolitan growth, life in North Carolina has not lost its rural tone. This has always been thickly settled rural land, and if one is never out of sight of others there is also plenty of green space and reminders of rural roots, from barbecue stands to country Baptist churches to stock car tracks.

Change has not been directed from any single establishment; the forces that have produced it are diverse and sometimes hostile. North Carolina historically had a small and articulate elite, which looked for guidance from the University of North Carolina at Chapel Hill and the liberal editors of the state's newspapers, most prominently the Raleigh *News & Observer* and the *Charlotte Observer*. Quite different attitudes are nurtured by tradition-minded churches in a state where churchgoing is deeply ingrained, endorsed for years through Sunday blue laws and strengthened periodically by religious revivals. When North Carolina was an economically backward state, infant

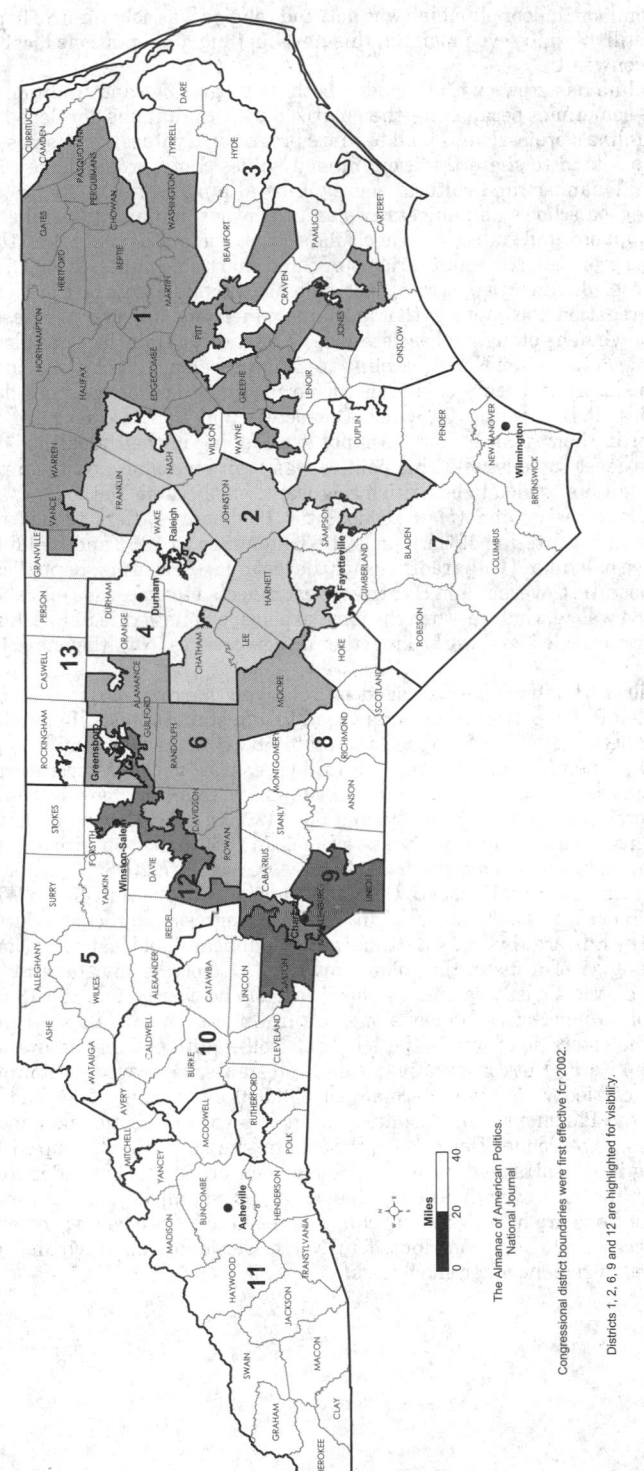

The Almanac of American Politics.
National Journal

Congressional district boundaries were first effective for 2002.

Districts 1, 2, 6, 9 and 12 are highlighted for visibility.

mortality was common, indoor plumbing was not, and religion was a fountain of hope and a source of discipline; it is still, perhaps even more, in this now bustling air-conditioned, cable- and Internet-connected commonwealth.

North Carolina has grown with the aid of both its progressive and tradition-minded citizens, and in spite of—sometimes because of—the polarized politics that has developed between the two sides. North Carolina's professionals tend to share progressive values; its businessmen and conservative Protestants tend to share tradition-minded values. Both groups have contributed to the state's economic dynamism and cultural energy. Liberal progressivism has provided an impetus toward building good schools and universities and highways and amenities like the nation's first state-funded symphony and state high schools for science and mathematics and the arts. Religious conservatism has provided a communitarian spirit and charitable impulses, and a moral undertone that anchors those who might go astray. Each side also has its excesses: the historic racism that undergirded segregation, the impulses that led black leaders and university professors to cheer on a rogue prosecutor when he brought a baseless case against three Duke lacrosse players.

From these two strands of North Carolina tradition developed a polarized, increasingly party-line politics that is pretty evenly balanced, waged partly on economic issues but even more on cultural attitudes. It is a politics in which Democrats and Republicans have been distinctive, sometimes bitter in their rivalries, for years not overlapping in their ideas but by the mid-1990s converging on at least some issues. This politics was built on historic partisan patterns. Coastal North Carolina settlers tended to be British Anglicans who became Methodists, slaveholders who supported the Confederacy and voted Democratic; Piedmont settlers tended to be Scots-Irish Presbyterians with a scattering of German sects, Union men in 1861 and Republicans ever after. The most effective paladins of both traditions for the last quarter century, Republican Senator Jesse Helms and Democratic Governor Jim Hunt, were each elected to statewide office five times over 25 years, and in 1984 waged what was then the most expensive Senate race in U.S. history; once bitter rivals, they later reconciled, and worked together on some issues. Now they have both retired from office.

Most elections here have been decided by relatively narrow margins. Since 2000, election results have fallen into a pattern: Democrats tend to win state contests, Republicans tend to win federal elections. George W. Bush carried the state 56%-43% in 2000 and by a nearly identical 56%-44% in 2004, when North Carolina's John Edwards was on the Democratic ticket. Democrat Mike Easley from east Carolina—traditionally Democratic country where Jesse Helms ran well—won the governorship in 2000 by 52%-46% and 56%-43% in 2004. Democrats have held the state Senate through his governorship, won the state House in 2000, ended up with a 60-60 tie there after the 2002 election, then won a majority in 2004 and increased it in 2006. North Carolina's two U.S. senators are now Republicans. Elizabeth Dole won her seat in 2002 over Clinton White House Chief of Staff Erskine Bowles by a 54%-45% margin. In 2004 Congressman Richard Burr beat Bowles for the seat vacated by Edwards by a 52%-47% margin. Republicans hold just six of North Carolina's 13 House seats, because of a districting plan drawn by Democrats and because three moderate Democrats hold districts easily carried by Bush; in 2004 he carried 9 of the 13 current districts.

North Carolina's electorate breaks along cultural, not economic lines. In the 2004 exit poll blacks, 21% of the voters according to the NEP exit poll—quite possibly an oversampling—voted 85%-14% for John Kerry. But conservative white Protestants, 24% of the electorate, voted 95%-5% for Bush. Bush carried voters with incomes of $30,000 on up (only 28% had lower incomes). Geographically, the Piedmont urban counties, filling up with professionals and with significant black populations, have trended Democratic; the counties farther out, filling up with middle-income families working in decentralized businesses, have been producing large Republican majorities. Coastal east Carolina, once overwhelmingly Democratic, is now mixed; smaller counties in and near the western mountains are heavily Republican. The result is a close balance between two cultural and political blocs which have contributed to North Carolina's unanticipated growth—though neither is inclined to give the other much credit.

The People		Race/Ethnic Origin			Military veterans: 792,646 (13.0%)	
Pop. 2006 (est):	8,856,505	5,647,155	70.2%	White	WWII: 17.3%	Korea: 12.5%
Pop. 2000:	8,049,313	1,723,301	21.4%	Black	Vietnam: 32.3%	Gulf War: 13.3%
Pop. 1990:	6,628,637	112,416	1.4%	Asian	**Most populous cities (2006):**	
Change 1990-2000:	Up 21.4%	95,333	1.2%	Native Am.	1. Charlotte	630,478
% of U.S. total:	2.9%	3,165	0.0%	Hawaiian	2. Raleigh	356,321
Pop. rank:	11th of 50	79,965	1.0%	Two+ races	3. Greensboro	236,865
Area size:	53,819 sq. mi.	9,015	0.1%	Other	4. Durham	209,009
State Native:	63.0%	378,963	4.7%	Hisp. Origin	5. Winston-Salem	196,990
Non-citizen:	3.9%	**Ancestry**				
Language		USA: 11.7%		English: 8.1%	Urban population: 60.2%	
English: 90.7%	Spanish: 5.4%	German: 8.0%		Irish: 6.3%	Rural population: 39.8%	
Other Eur.: 2.4%		Scotch-Irish: 2.7%				

Education		Work Sector			General Assembly	
H.S. Grad:	78.1%	Private: 78.8%		Govt: 14.5%	Senate	31 D 19 R
College Grad:	22.5%	Self: 6.4%		Family: 0.3%	House	68 D 52 R
Industry		Unemployment: 5.2%			Legislative Term Limits: No	
Agri: 1.6%	Con: 8.2%	**Household Income**			**Registered Voters**	
Fin: 6.0%	Info: 2.3%	<15k: 16.9%		15-35k: 27.7%	D: 2,533,424	(45.5%)
Mfg: 24.4%	Prof: 26.9%	35-50k: 17.7%		50-100k: 28.3%	R: 1,923,047	(34.5%)
Public: 4.1%	Trade: 14.9%	100-150k: 6.0%		>150k: 3.4%	O: 1,110,953	(20.0%)
Other: 11.6%		Median: $39,184				
Occupation		Poverty status: 12.3%				
Blue collar: 29.7%	White collar: 56.0%	**Home Value**				
Gray collar: 14.3%		<50k: 18.0%	50-100k: 35.1%	100-200k: 33.7%	200-300k: 8.2%	
		300-500k: 3.6%	>500k: 1.5%	Median: $95,800		

Presidential politics   North Carolina was not a competitive state in the 2000 and 2004 campaigns, despite the presence of North Carolina Democratic Senator John Edwards on the Democratic ticket in 2004. He was the first North Carolinian on a major party national ticket since William A. Graham was nominated by the Whigs in 1852. The Kerry-Edwards campaign gamely ran ads in the state in July, but took them off the air in August when polls showed the state out of reach. Edwards came back in October to vote early, but otherwise was not much of a presence in his home state. Did Edwards help the Democratic ticket? Probably a little. In 2004 Bush won the same 56% of the vote he had in 2000, in an electorate 20% larger.

2004 Presidential Vote
Bush (R)	1,961,166	(56%)
Kerry (D)	1,525,849	(44%)
Badnarik (Lib)	11,731	(0%)
Other	2,261	(0%)

2000 Presidential Vote
Bush (R)	1,631,163	(56%)
Gore (D)	1,257,692	(43%)
Other	26,135	(1%)

In contrast, Bush's percentage went up in 2004 in Virginia, South Carolina and Georgia. The Kerry-Edwards ticket won higher percentages in the metropolitan counties containing (in order of increase) Durham, Chapel Hill, Asheville, Charlotte, Raleigh, Winston-Salem and Greensboro. But Bush made larger gains in East Carolina counties, including those with large black percentages, and especially those around Fort Bragg and Camp Lejeune.

North Carolina's presidential primary has been crucial only once, in 1976, when after five straight losses, Ronald Reagan started denouncing the Panama Canal Treaty and won his first victory over Gerald Ford. It has been part of the Super Tuesday primary since 1988, but has been overshadowed by the even larger states that vote that day.

Congressional districting   North Carolina won a 12th House seat in the 1990 Census and,
quite unexpectedly, a 13th seat in the 2000 Census. It beat out

110th Congress Lineup
7 D   6 R
109th Congress Lineup
7 R   6 D

Utah for the latter by just 856 people, and because its apportionment population includes some 18,000 U.S. troops and diplomats who claim North Carolina as their home, Utah filed a
lawsuit arguing that its apportionment population should be
credited with Mormon missionaries overseas who claim Utah as
their home. But in April 2001 a three-judge federal panel ruled unanimously against Utah and in
November 2001 the Supreme Court affirmed that decision without opinion.

In the 1990s, North Carolina was the epicenter of race-based redistricting litigation, home to a
legal controversy that went to the U.S. Supreme Court four times. Democratic legislators created
their plans for 2002 with this litigation in mind. The state House and Senate passed the same plan
in November 2001; in North Carolina the governor does not have a veto on redistricting bills. The
plan created a new 13th District seat in the northern Piedmont which leaned Democratic in state
elections, though it was even in the 2000 presidential race; the district ended up electing Democrat
Brad Miller, not coincidentally the chairman of the Senate redistricting committee. The plan
significantly weakened 8th District Republican Congressman Robin Hayes. It created six heavily
Republican districts and three solidly Democratic districts, with the other four districts tailored to
the needs of local Democrats. Republicans filed suit even before the plans were passed. But while
their arguments about the Democratic plans for redistricting state legislative seats prevailed in the
state Supreme Court, their case against the congressional district lines was dropped after the
Justice Department approved the maps and the U.S. Supreme Court refused to intervene.

Governor

Michael Easley (D)

Elected 2000, term expires Jan. 2009, 2d term; b. Mar. 23, 1950, Nash
County; home, Southport; U. of N.C. (Chapel Hill), B.A. 1972; N.C. Central
U., J.D. 1975; Catholic; married (Mary).

Elected Office: NC Atty. Gen., 1992-2000.

Professional Career: Asst. D.A., N.C. 13th Dist., 1976-78, 1979-82;
N.C. Dist. Atty., 1982-90; private practice, 1978-79, 1990-92.

Office: Office of the Governor, 20301 Mail Service Center, Raleigh,
27699,   919-733-4240;   Fax: 919-715-3175;   Web   site:
www.governor.state.nc.us.

Election Results

2004 general	Michael Easley (D)	1,939,154	(56%)
	Patrick Ballantine (R)	1,495,021	(43%)
	Other	52,513	(2%)
2004 primary	Michael Easley (D)	379,498	(85%)
	Rickey Kipfer (D)	65,061	(15%)
2000 general	Michael Easley (D)	1,530,324	(52%)
	Richard Vinroot (R)	1,360,960	(46%)
	Other	50,778	(2%)

Mike Easley, a Democrat, was elected governor of North Carolina in 2000, the first time either party
won a third consecutive term since 1968. Easley grew up on a tobacco farm near Rocky Mount, 50
miles east of Raleigh, and graduated from the University of North Carolina and North Carolina
Central University Law School. He has spent his whole adult life in government. He served as an
assistant district attorney and in 1982, at 31, became district attorney in three southeast counties.
In 1992 he took a big step upward by winning election statewide as attorney general. He backed the
death penalty and supported gun rights. He appeared in $1 million worth of public service ads,
many warning about predatory lending to old people; his constant appearances irritated Republicans, who pushed through a law banning such appearances in election years.

Reelected in 1996, Easley started running for governor in 1999, obviously a strong candidate but by no means the favorite. His main Democratic primary opponent, Lieutenant Governor Dennis Wicker, was endorsed by teachers' unions, feminist groups and black leaders. But Easley won the May primary by 59%-36%. Meanwhile, the Republican nomination went to former Charlotte Mayor Richard Vinroot. Easley called for prescription drugs for seniors and HMO regulation, improvements in public schools and a lottery to fund education. He avoided the national Democratic Party and didn't attend the convention in Los Angeles. Vinroot opposed the lottery but said he would allow a referendum; he pledged not to raise taxes and called for school vouchers for low-income children in failing schools.

For most of the campaign, Easley ran about 10% ahead in polls. Then, when the presidential candidates debated at Wake Forest University in Winston-Salem on October 11, Vinroot tied Easley to Al Gore. One ad called Easley an "Al Gore liberal." Easley attacked Vinroot for his support of vouchers and opposition to a lottery. Easley had more money, and in the last week ran an ad with an endorsement from North Carolina's Andy Griffith. That helped portray him as a down-home, rural Carolinian, running against a city slicker. Even as George W. Bush was carrying North Carolina, Easley won 52%-46%.

Easley came to the governorship at a time when voters were used to an expanding economy and used to the leadership talents of Jim Hunt, elected in 1976 and 1980 and again in 1992 and 1996, and at a time when North Carolina's booming economy was slowing down. As the first North Carolina governor never to have been a legislator in nearly 50 years, he lacked the horsetrading skills that are useful in dealing with a legislature and did not spend much time negotiating with legislative leaders. He attracted more attention dealing with emergencies—three ice storms and seven hurricanes in his first term—and when he slammed into the speedway wall at 120 m.p.h. at Lowes's Motor Speedway in Concord in 2003 (he was unhurt). In his first years Easley had some success. In September 2001 he persuaded the legislature to pass his budget with money for his More at Four academic preschool program and smaller class sizes for grades K-3; he proposed a 1% increase in the sales tax and the legislature passed that and an income tax increase as well. But as time went on he faced severe fiscal problems. In May 2002 he presented a budget which cut overall spending and depended on receipts from an as yet unapproved lottery, but provided money for More at Four and more teachers in early grades and cut aid to local governments; they could increase their sales taxes by a half-percent if they liked. In June 2002 the state Senate rejected his education spending increases; in July 2002 the House, with Republicans solidly against, blocked his plan to cut local aid. In September the House rejected putting the lottery on the ballot 69-50. But a budget agreement was reached that month protecting Easley's More at Four and class size proposals and gave state agency heads greater flexibility in making cuts.

In November 2002 Republicans gained seven seats in the state Senate and emerged with a 61-59 majority in the House (though a January 2003 party switch left the House evenly divided). The next day Easley astonished legislators by vetoing his first bill. The Founding Fathers of North Carolina, suspicious of executive tyranny, had written a state constitution in which the governor had no veto; only in 1996 did the voters grant the governor a limited veto. Hunt had never used it; Easley did, on a bill designating appointments to boards and commissions. The legislature, summoned to the required special session to consider override, let it stand: The first veto by a governor of North Carolina since Josiah Martin vetoed a bill in 1774. Faced with another budget shortfall, Easley got the legislature to extend the 2001 tax increase, but later called for a small cut in the corporate tax rate. In 2004, as revenues started coming in more generously, Easley got $60 million for More for Four and reducing K-3 class sizes. Easley also pushed through $3 billion in bonds for university and community college facilities and $700 million in bonds for transportation and infrastructure.

Easley entered the 2004 campaign year with good but not stellar job ratings and there was a serious contest for the Republican nomination. The favorite was Richard Vinroot, running in his third straight gubernatorial race; he directed most of his fire at Easley. "I told you this fellow would raise taxes." Former one-term Congressman Bill Cobey ran with the endorsement of former Senator Jesse Helms; he and Vinroot represented the two wings of the party that had clashed in many primaries before. But the nomination went to the third candidate, state Senator Patrick Ballantine, who resigned in April and campaigned as a strong conservative. Ballantine won, with 30.4% of the votes to 30.0% for Vinroot—much lower than his 2000 showing—and 27% for Cobey. When the results were announced, Vinroot declined to ask for the runoff he was entitled to under state law since no candidate got 40%.

Ballantine tried to break into Easley's area of strength in east Carolina and campaigned in all 100 counties. "Mike Easley is a big tax-and-spender," he said. "First he blamed Jim Hunt, then it was George W. Bush, then it was 9/11, then it was the legislature, then it was the drought and then it was the rain." And he said he was in favor of teacher salary increases and literacy programs. Easley came scorching back in debate. "If Patrick Ballantine is a champion of education, then Saddam Hussein is a champion of civil rights." Easley ran on his record. "Every other state said, 'We've got to cut. We've got to cut everything, including education.' We all got together, and we said, 'We've got to cut, but we're not going to cut education.'" He raised $9 million to Ballantine's $4.5 million, and his campaign ran many negative ads, suggesting Ballantine was way off to the right. Easley conspicuously declined to attend the Democratic National Convention (though he had campaigned for John Edwards in North Carolina) and supported a constitutional amendment to ban same-sex marriage. He ran ads with Andy Griffith and boasted of his endorsement by the National Rifle Association.

Easley won 56%-43%. Easley carried all of east Carolina except for three counties on the coast and Johnston County outside Raleigh; he carried all the big metropolitan counties but lost in the Piedmont textile counties and in several mountain counties.

Backed by Democratic majorities in both chambers, Easley in his second term won approval for a state lottery in 2005 with revenues directed toward expanding More at Four, reducing classroom sizes, college scholarships and school construction, although lottery sales by 2007 had fallen short of expectations. For the first time in seven years, the state entered 2006 without a budget deficit and had the luxury of a $2 billion surplus. Easley and the legislature reduced sales and income taxes and capped the gas tax, increased the minimum wage by a $1 to $6.15 an hour, placed limits on eminent domain powers, increased spending for mental health programs and gave state employees an average 5.5% pay increase. After a series of scandals forced House Speaker Jim Black (he narrowly won reelection in 2006) to step down after eight years in leadership, the legislature also overhauled ethics and lobbying rules. After the 2006 elections, Democratic increased their legislative majorities to 68-52 in the House and 31-19 in the Senate. However, the bill for the tax breaks and spending came due in 2007, when the state faced an estimated $500 million shortfall.

Easley has a blue-collar appeal, in part because he looks to popular culture for political insight; he has instructed his pollster to ask respondents whether they watch Fox television's animated series "King of the Hill." Easley is a fan of the show and its main character Hank Hill, a conservative propane salesman in a small Texas town who likes guns and NASCAR. Hill's character doesn't identify with a political party, but Easley has said Democrats have had difficulty winning these voters and likes to know whether his proposals appeal to this audience. Easley's success in this traditionally conservative state has caught the notice of national Democrats, whose successful Democratic presidential candidates over the past 40 years have come from the ranks of Southern governors. However, Easley has made no moves to run for president. When his wife was asked about his political future in October 2004, she said, "What else would he run for? He's happy being in North Carolina." Easley is prevented by term limits from running for a third term in 2008 and Democrats have talked about him as a candidate against Republican Senator Elizabeth Dole. He has expressed little interest in a Senate run, leading Democrats to suggest his wife Mary Easley, a former prosecutor and law professor, could run against Dole. The race to replace Easley began taking shape in early 2007. Lieutenant Governor Beverly Perdue, who would be the state's first female governor, and state Treasurer Richard Moore were actively raising money for a potential run at the Democratic nomination. Among Republicans, former state Supreme Court Justice Bob Orr, state Senator Fred Smith and wealthy trial lawyer Bill Graham announced in early 2007.

Senior Senator

Elizabeth Dole (R)

Elected 2002, seat up 2008, 1st term; b. July 29, 1936, Salisbury; home, Salisbury; Duke U., B.A. 1958, Harvard U., M.A. 1960, J.D. 1965; Methodist; married (Robert).

Professional Career: Deputy Asst., U.S. Consumer Affairs, 1969-73; Fed. Trade Commission, 1973-79; Public liason, U.S. Pres. Ronald Reagan, 1981-83; Secy., U.S. Dept. of Trans., 1983-87; Secy., Dept. of Labor, 1989-90; Pres., Amer. Red Cross, 1991-95, 1997-99.

DC Office: 555 DSOB, 20510, 202-224-6342; Fax: 202-224-1100; Web site: dole.senate.gov.

State Offices: Greenville, 252-329-1093; Hendersonville, 828-698-3747; Raleigh, 919-856-4630; Salisbury, 704-633-5011.

Committees: *Aging (Special)* (6th of 10 R). *Armed Services* (8th of 12 R): Emerging Threats & Capabilities (RMM); Personnel; Readiness & Management Support. *Banking, Housing & Urban Affairs* (9th of 10 R): Housing, Transportation & Community Development; Security & International Trade & Finance; Financial Institutions. *Small Business & Entrepreneurship* (5th of 9 R).

Group Ratings

	ADA	ACLU	AFS	LCV	ITIC	NTU	COC	ACU	CFG	FRC
2006	5	17	13	0	100	79	83	96	80	87
2005	5	—	0	0	—	68	94	96	77	—

National Journal Ratings

	2005 LIB	—	2005 CONS		2006 LIB	—	2006 CONS
Economic	29%	—	69%		13%	—	82%
Social	0%	—	77%		0%	—	82%
Foreign	0%	—	74%		33%	—	66%

Key Votes of the 109th Congress

1. Bar ANWR Drilling	N	5. Confirm Samuel Alito	Y	9. Limit Interstate Abortion	Y
2. FY06 Spending Curb	Y	6. Path to Citizenship	N	10. CAFTA	Y
3. Estate Tax Repeal	Y	7. Bar Same Sex Marriage	Y	11. Urge Iraq Withdrawal	N
4. Raise Minimum Wage	N	8. Stem Cell Research $	Y	12. Provide Detainee Rights	N

Election Results

2002 general	Elizabeth Dole (R)	1,248,664	(54%)	($13,735,220)
	Erskine Bowles (D)	1,047,983	(45%)	($13,306,317)
	Other	34,534	(1%)	
2002 primary	Elizabeth Dole (R)	342,631	(80%)	
	Jim Snyder (R)	60,477	(14%)	
	Other	22,998	(5%)	
1996 general	Jesse Helms (R)	1,345,833	(53%)	($14,589,266)
	Harvey B. Gantt (D)	1,173,875	(46%)	($7,992,980)

Elizabeth Dole, former Secretary of Transportation and Secretary of Labor, former president of the American Red Cross and candidate for president, was elected senator from North Carolina in 2002. She grew up in Salisbury, in the Piedmont textile country between Charlotte and Greensboro; her father was a wholesale florist and her mother had the pleasure of attending, at 101, her daughter's election night celebration. Elizabeth Hanford, as she then was, graduated from Duke, got a master's in education at Harvard and taught school in Boston. She spent the summer of 1960 working in the office of North Carolina Senator B. Everett Jordan; in the fall, she worked on Lyndon Johnson's campaign train through the South. In 1962 she went to Harvard Law School, one of 29 women in a class of 550; her classmates included future Congresswomen Patricia Schroeder and Elizabeth Holtzman. In summers she worked at the Peace Corps headquarters, the United Nations and Oxford University. After graduation she practiced law briefly in Washington. With help from Democratic Governor Terry Sanford she got a job at HEW, then at the White House Office of Consumer Affairs. She stayed on after the change in administrations in 1969 and changed her registration from Democratic to Independent. In 1973 she was nominated to a six-year term on the Federal Trade Commission. In 1975 she married Senator Bob Dole and campaigned with him when he was nominated for vice president in 1976.

In all these jobs she was a hard-working perfectionist with no sharp ideological edge. She always maintained her gracious Southern manners and showed an enthusiasm and friendliness that was off-putting to some but which served her well in a series of positions that few or no women had held. In 1981 she headed Ronald Reagan's Public Liaison office and in 1983 she was appointed Secretary of Transportation; in that capacity, she likes to point out, she was the first woman to head a branch of the armed services, the Coast Guard. In 1989 George H. W. Bush appointed her Secretary of Labor. In 1991 she became head of the American Red Cross, which had grave organizational problems and whose blood bank program was in trouble. She restructured the organization and put in place new blood bank procedures. She took a leave of absence to work on her husband's presidential campaign from November 1995 to January 1997; many will remember her speech about her husband at the San Diego convention, in which she walked about and spoke fluently and fervently. In 1999 she resigned from the Red Cross to run for president. She placed third in the August 1999 Iowa straw poll, but dropped out of the race in October. She did not endorse George W. Bush at that point and did not take a job in the Bush administration.

In early 2001 it was not clear whether North Carolina Senator Jesse Helms would run for reelection. White House political strategists were already looking at Dole as a possible candidate; in August 2001 Helms announced his retirement. Dole moved back to her mother's house in Salisbury and registered to vote. She started out with very high ratings from the public. But some Republican insiders worried that Dole would be a brittle candidate. Her perfectionism and insistence on tight control of every public event would keep her distant to the voters, they feared, and a campaign based on her Washington resume would seem out of touch with North Carolina.

Dole did not make these mistakes. Instead she made two very shrewd decisions. One was to conduct a tour of all of North Carolina's 100 counties. Everywhere she drew crowds, not just in the big metro areas but also in small towns. People mobbed her, asked for autographs, and clicked photos of her. Sometimes they also noticed Bob Dole, traveling with her over back roads. She said that she had a religious renewal in the early 1980s and that her religious faith was the center of her life and that she hoped that September 11 would cause a "spiritual renewal." In November 2001, former Charlotte Mayor Richard Vinroot dropped out of the race; her other primary competitors were little-known and attracted little attention or support. When they questioned her conservatism, she said, "Just to set the record straight, in case there is any misunderstanding, I am pro-life and I am a strong supporter of the Second Amendment of the Constitution, protecting the constitutional rights of law-abiding citizens." In February 2002 Helms endorsed her. Their connections went back a long way: Helms had been a friend of her mother since his first campaign in 1972; Bob Dole had asked for Helms to vouch for him with her when he was wooing her daughter.

Dole's other wise decision was to develop a set of specific stands on issues and distribute them as the "Dole Plan." She set out a detailed plan for individual investment accounts in Social Security. On taxes she called for higher depreciation, more flexibility for Medical Savings Accounts and permanent repeal of the estate tax. On gun control she switched her positions from her 1999 campaign, this time opposing background checks on individuals' sales of guns at gun shows and a ban on assault weapons. Tobacco and textiles have long been political issues in North Carolina: Dole presented a plan for buying out tobacco quotas and called for electronic labeling of U.S.-manufactured cloth to enable duties to be laid on imports of cloth falsely labeled Made in U.S.A. But she favored trade promotion authority, which was opposed by all the other three Republicans and six Democrats running for the seat. It was widely believed that North Carolina had lost many textile jobs since NAFTA went into effect in 1995. Secretary of State Elaine Marshall, the first candidate in the race, strongly criticized NAFTA and opposed trade promotion authority. So did state Representative Dan Blue, who had been the first black Speaker of North Carolina's House. And so did former White House Chief of Staff Erskine Bowles. Though he had supported NAFTA and had lobbied Congress to give Bill Clinton trade promotion authority, he opposed it now.

Bowles was an investment banker from a prominent family. His father, Hargrove "Skipper" Bowles was the Democratic nominee for governor in 1972 who lost in a Republican year but was still remembered fondly. His wife, Crandall Close, was CEO of Springs Industries, a large textile firm started by her family. Bowles, as Clinton's chief of staff, negotiated the 1997 budget package that led to a balanced budget; he had been trusted by Republican leaders when they seethed with mistrust of Clinton. But it didn't help Bowles that Blue and Marshall continued to hammer him on trade and that, because of a lawsuit against the Democratic legislature's state legislative redistricting plans, the primary was delayed from May to September 10.

Dole won the Republican primary with 80% of the vote; Bowles won the Democratic primary with 43% of the vote, to 29% for Blue and 15% for Marshall. This was a heavy-spending race. Dole raised and spent $13.7 million, Bowles spent nearly as much; he put in $2.9 million of his money before October 15 and then another $3.6 million. Some of the ads got personal. A Dole ad criticized Bowles's wife for laying off workers in North Carolina and creating new jobs in Mexico and China; Bowles responded in an angry face-on ad and ran an ad showing racecar driver Junior Johnson saying he wouldn't let the Republicans "run Erskine Bowles into the wall." One debate was videotaped behind locked doors in accordance with the candidates' demands. Bowles attacked Dole on trade and Social Security. She stood her ground on both issues, arguing for free trade and promoting her Dole plan for Social Security: she would hold up papers with her plan written out and then say she would show Bowles's plan—and hold up a blank sheet of paper. Dole ads often mentioned Bill and Hillary Rodham Clinton; Bowles's ads avoided mentions of the Clintons. The late surge of Bowles's spending enabled him to close the gap in the polls, but this seems mostly to have been a matter of the coalescence of the usual party constituencies.

Dole won 54%-45%, just shy of Bush's 56%-43% lead in 2000. She carried two of the three big metro areas by wide margins—Charlotte (57%-42%) and Greensboro-Winston Salem—and finished just behind Bowles in Raleigh-Durham (49%-50%), where the Democratic margins in Durham and Chapel Hill are balanced by the Republican margins in much faster-growing areas in Wake County like Cary. In the other half of the state, Dole led 54%-46%. West of Raleigh-Durham, Dole carried all but a few mountain and sand hill counties. She carried the central part of eastern North Carolina but lost in heavily black counties to the north and south.

Dole started off quietly in the Senate, as Hillary Rodham Clinton had two years before; she turned down requests to appear on television shows and instead traveled around North Carolina to places like Flat Rock (pop. 1,690) and Winterville (4,791). She accepted Barbara Mikulski's gracious offer to give up her desk, which had been Bob Dole's. She got seats on Armed Services, Banking and Agriculture: "I chose the committees that would be most beneficial to North Carolina." Her first bill was to give full federal recognition to the Lumbee Indians, recognized as a tribe by the state in 1885 and by Congress in 1956, but denied tribal benefits. This was opposed by those who feared the Lumbees would build a casino off Interstate 95—Republican Congressman Walter Jones, the North Carolina Family Council, the Eastern Band of Cherokees who have their own casino in East Tennessee. Dole's bill passed the Indian Affairs Committee, but was kept off the floor by parliamentary maneuvers.

On broader national issues, she had a conservative voting record and generally supported the Bush administration. She was the only woman senator to vote against a resolution declaring *Roe v. Wade* "appropriate." One big issue was the tobacco buyout. In 2003 Dole cosponsored a bill to end the 1938 tobacco quota system and to spend $10.1 billion over 10 years to buy out quota-holders and tobacco farmers. She argued that tobacco quotas were being reduced sharply and stood to be reduced even more, and that the cost of renting quotas (many quota holders treat them as an investment) raised the U.S. price of tobacco above the world price. It was widely believed that the buyout could succeed only if it was tied to giving the FDA regulatory power over tobacco, a position taken by the largest tobacco company, Altria, but opposed by the others. Dole tried to put the buyout without FDA regulation on the November 2003 omnibus, but failed. Political pressure built as Democrats seemed more favorable to the buyout than Republicans: John Kerry endorsed the buyout while George W. Bush in May 2004 said there should be no changes in tobacco law; Erskine Bowles, running for the Senate again, attacked his opponent Congressman Richard Burr for not doing enough to get a buyout. In October the buyout, without FDA regulation, was attached to the corporate tax bill; House Ways and Means Chairman Bill Thomas saw it as a way to attract 13 southern Democrats. In the Senate Dole overcame opposition from those who sought FDA regulation, and the buyout was included in the corporate tax bill signed by Bush.

On other North Carolina issues, Dole weighed in against EPA approval of a wood treatment which, she said, would cost North Carolina jobs (though Bob Dole was lobbying for the other side) and hailed the International Trade Commission decision in December 2004 to uphold tariffs on government-subsidized furniture from China. She continued her fight for recognition of the Lumbees, and a bill was passed by the Indian Affairs Committee in August 2006, but did not come to the floor. With Hillary Clinton, she co-sponsored a bill to institute 211 numbers, to connect volunteers and those in need with nonprofit agencies; she cited her experience in the Red Cross and the 211 call centers that already existed in 15 North Carolina counties. She and colleague Richard Burr voted for an amendment to block an inventory of offshore oil and gas resources; they said it threatened the North Carolina coast. She sponsored a bill to provide job training in colleges and community colleges for laid-off manufacturing workers. She worked on the Armed Services Committee to improve the quality of life of soldiers and to restrict predatory lending to them.

After the 2004 election, Dole ran for the chairmanship of the NRSC and beat Norm Coleman 28-27. Previous NRSC Chairmen, Bill Frist in 2002 and George Allen in 2004, helped Republicans pick up Senate seats and went on to higher things—Frist as Senate Majority Leader, Allen as a leading conservative candidate for president until he was defeated in the 2006 election. Dole enlisted for what turned out to be a tougher term. She was criticized because the DSCC, under Chairman Charles Schumer, outraised the NRSC, $119 million to $87 million. But the Democrats' Senate committee has outraised the Republicans' for some time, in part because Democratic senators give more support to their colleagues than Republicans. Her bigger problem was the political climate. Recruits like Mike McGavick in Washington, Michael Bouchard in Michigan and Michael Steele in Maryland might have been strong challengers in the climate of 2002 or 2004, but they were not in 2006. Nor did Dole have any targets in Southern states, as Frist and Allen did; by 2006 Republicans held all but four Senate seats in the 11 states of the Old Confederacy, and the only Democratic seat up in 2006 was Bill Nelson's in Florida. Karl Rove had promised Congresswoman Katherine Harris, who got bad job ratings for her performance as Secretary of State in the 2000 Florida controversy, that she could run in 2006 if she would step aside and not run in the open 2004 race. Dole's behind-the-scenes efforts to find another candidate proved unavailing. There also were incumbents who, at the beginning of the cycle, seemed to be in no trouble but got into trouble by mid-2006. Conrad Burns in usually Republican Montana insisted on running again even though he was the number one recipient of contributions from clients of disgraced lobbyist Jack Abramoff. Mike DeWine and Jim Talent, running in states where George W. Bush had won narrowly in 2000 and 2004, attracted strong challengers and lost. And George Allen, touring Iowa and New Hampshire when his seat was up in Virginia, uttered the word "macaca" in Breaks, Virginia, an incident which ultimately left him vulnerable to Jim Webb. Other incumbents who lost were Lincoln Chafee in heavily Democratic Rhode Island and Rick Santorum whose controversial comments on cultural issues netted him negative ratings in Pennsylvania. Like Jon Corzine, head of the DSCC in 2004, Dole played a losing hand pretty deftly, but still lost.

During the 2005-06 cycle Dole spent relatively little time in North Carolina and ended the year with only $245,000 cash on hand. State and national Democrats targeted her seat for 2008. But many well-known North Carolina Democrats seemed uninterested in running. Governor Mike Easley said he was not interested in the Senate; neither, evidently, was his wife Mary Easley, a former prosecutor. Erskine Bowles, after two expensive losses, seemed uninterested. Lieutenant Governor Beverly Perdue and Treasurer Richard Moore were busy running for governor; Attorney General Roy Cooper was running for reelection. The state's Democratic congressmen were looking forward to serving in the majority in a chamber where the majority tends to get its way. In April 2007, 13th District Congressman Brad Miller said he was considering running but in June announced he would not challenge Dole.

Junior Senator

Richard Burr (R)

Elected 2004, seat up 2010, 1st term; b. Nov. 30, 1955, Charlottesville, VA; home, Winston-Salem; Wake Forest U., B.A. 1978; Methodist; married (Brooke).

Elected Office: U.S. House of Reps., 1994-2004.

Professional Career: Natl. Sales Mgr., Carswell Distributing, 1978-94.

DC Office: 217 RSOB, 20510, 202-224-3154; Fax: 202-228-2981; Web site: burr.senate.gov.

State Offices: Asheville, 828-350-2437; Gastonia, 704-833-0854; Rocky Mount, 252-977-9522; Wilmington, 910-251-1058; Winston-Salem, 336-631-5125.

Committees: *Energy & Natural Resources* (4th of 11 R): National Parks (RMM); Energy; Public Lands & Forests. *Health, Education, Labor & Pensions* (4th of 10 R): Retirement & Aging (RMM); Employment & Workplace Safety. *Indian Affairs* (7th of 7 R). *Intelligence (Select)* (7th of 7 R). *Veterans' Affairs* (5th of 7 R).

Group Ratings

	ADA	ACLU	AFS	LCV	ITIC	NTU	COC	ACU	CFG	FRC
2006	10	17	0	0	75	80	67	92	75	87
2005	5	—	13	5	—	76	94	92	85	—

National Journal Ratings

	2005 LIB — 2005 CONS		2006 LIB — 2006 CONS	
Economic	36%	— 61%	23%	— 76%
Social	0%	— 77%	18%	— 74%
Foreign	26%	— 65%	42%	— 54%

Key Votes of the 109th Congress

1. Bar ANWR Drilling	N	5. Confirm Samuel Alito	Y	9. Limit Interstate Abortion	Y
2. FY06 Spending Curb	Y	6. Path to Citizenship	N	10. CAFTA	Y
3. Estate Tax Repeal	Y	7. Bar Same Sex Marriage	Y	11. Urge Iraq Withdrawal	N
4. Raise Minimum Wage	N	8. Stem Cell Research $	Y	12. Provide Detainee Rights	N

Election Results

2004 general	Richard Burr (R)	1,791,450	(52%)	($12,853,110)
	Erskine Bowles (D)	1,632,527	(47%)	($13,359,764)
	Other	48,105	(1%)	
2004 primary	Richard Burr (R)	302,319	(88%)	
	John Hendrix (R)	25,971	(8%)	
	Albert Wiley (R)	15,585	(5%)	
1998 general	John Edwards (D)	1,029,237	(51%)	($8,331,382)
	Lauch Faircloth (R)	945,943	(47%)	($9,375,771)
	Other	36,963	(2%)	

Prior Winning Percentages: 2002 House (70%); 2000 House (93%); 1998 House (68%); 1996 House (62%); 1994 House (57%)

North Carolina's junior senator is Richard Burr, first elected to the House in 1994 and to the Senate in 2004. Burr, a distant relative to Vice President Aaron Burr, grew up a minister's son in Winston-Salem, was a star football player at Reynolds High and Wake Forest, then worked in sales for a wholesaling firm. In 1992 Burr ran against Congressman Steve Neal, a Democrat first elected in 1974; Burr was outspent 3–1 and lost 53%-46%. Neal retired in 1994 and Burr ran again, this time winning a solid 57% of the vote. He did not have a serious challenge in the next four House elections.

In the House Burr had a mostly conservative voting record. On the Commerce committee, his early cause became streamlining the FDA drug and medical device approval process, which he claimed kept life-saving products from patients. At first Burr took a radical approach that aroused much opposition, but then for over two years worked with the agency, doctors, patients, consumer groups and the pharmaceutical industry to come up with a consensus. With broad bipartisan support his FDA Modernization Act became law in 1997. He helped to set up the National Institute for Biomedical Imaging and Bioengineering in NIH. After September 11 he sponsored amendments incorporated into law to improve defenses against bioterrorism and to compensate people injured by smallpox vaccination. He inserted into the 2003 energy bill a provision allowing two firms that supply 60% of the world's isotopes for medical diagnoses to continue receiving U.S. bomb grade uranium. He strongly opposed FDA regulation of tobacco. With others from North Carolina, he later called for an optional buyout of tobacco quotas. He sought a crackdown on illegal textile imports and he opposed normal trade relations with China. But he backed George W. Bush's call for trade promotion authority after securing what he said were promises that the local textile industry would have a seat at the table; this was not an easy vote, he said, but it gave U.S. textile companies an opportunity to become more competitive internationally.

By 1999 Burr made no secret of his interest in running for the Senate. He had promised to serve only five terms in the House, and it looked like there would be opportunities in 2002, when Jesse Helms would turn 80, and in 2004, when Democrat John Edwards's seat would come up. In 2002, he deferred to Elizabeth Dole when it became apparent that the Bush White House was pushing her and that she was very popular with voters. In early 2003, he moved toward a bid even before Edwards, running for president, said that he wouldn't seek reelection; he had $2 million in his campaign account and got encouragement from White House political strategist Karl Rove.

Unlike the 2002 Senate race, there were no seriously contested primaries: Burr won 88% of the Republican vote and Erskine Bowles, the 2002 nominee, was unopposed in the Democratic primary.

Bowles was an investment banker from a prominent family. His father, Hargrove "Skipper" Bowles was the Democratic nominee for governor in 1972 who lost in a Republican year; his wife, Crandall Close, was CEO of Springs Industries, a large textile firm started by her family. Bowles, as Bill Clinton's chief of staff, negotiated the 1997 budget package that led to a balanced budget; he had been trusted by Republican leaders when they seethed with mistrust of Clinton. Bowles, well known from the 2002 campaign, led by about 10% in most polls until September. He started running ads six months before the election and had the resources to continue. Burr didn't run ads until September, hoping to match whatever Bowles could spend in the final weeks. In the end they spent about the same, Burr $12.7 million and Bowles $13.2 million; this was the third-most expensive Senate campaign in 2004.

Bowles presented a 10-point economic program and, pointing to recent losses of furniture and textile jobs, said he was "the only candidate with a real jobs plan." He called for expanding health insurance for children and providing tax credits for health insurance for small businesses. He said that he had shown the ability when in government to work with both parties. He depicted Burr as a fighter for special interests, especially pharmaceutical and tobacco companies; one ad called Burr the king of the special interests, and indeed Burr raised $2.8 million from corporate PACs, more than any other Senate candidate in 2004. One major issue was the tobacco buyout. The issue was before Congress, and the entire North Carolina delegation favored ending the tobacco quota system in place since 1938; tobacco quotas had been cut back in recent years and seemed likely to be again. At issue was whether the buyout should be coupled with FDA regulation of tobacco. The Senate passed its corporate tax bill—must-pass legislation, because it was needed to avoid European trade sanctions—with both the buyout and FDA regulation. In the House Burr voted for the buyout without FDA regulation. "I'm not opposed to new regulation for the industry. But the FDA's the wrong agency, if you truly want to do it right," he said. He argued that the toxicity of cigarettes should be regulated by the Center for Disease Control, and packages and labeling by the Federal Trade Commission. Bowles charged that Burr had voted against a $13 billion buyout with FDA regulation and for only a $10 billion buyout without because Winston-Salem-based R.J. Reynolds opposed FDA regulation; Altria, the biggest cigarette manufacturer, favored it. In the fall, Bowles interrupted his campaign to lobby for the buyout; he claimed he persuaded Senate Democrats not to filibuster.

Burr was appointed by House Republican leaders to the conference committee on the corporate tax bill. When the House side held out for the buyout without FDA regulation, the Senate yielded and the bill was enacted. Republicans made much of Burr's role. Senate Majority Leader Bill Frist came to North Carolina and proclaimed, "It took monumental leadership, and without Richard Burr providing that monumental leadership, this bill would not have occurred." This may have been the turning point of the campaign. Burr had pulled even with Bowles in polls by late September. His ads linked Bowles to Bill Clinton and to his policies on tax increases, welfare for immigrants, trade with China and trade policy generally; one, dubiously, called Bowles Clinton's "chief negotiator" on NAFTA. Both candidates skittered back from previous free trade positions. A Burr ad said Bowles "doesn't have the courage to stand up for traditional marriage."

George W. Bush carried North Carolina 56%-44%; Burr beat Bowles 52%-47%. Burr ran 4% behind Bush in the state's three big metropolitan areas, which cast just over half the votes; he ran 5% behind Bush in the rest of the state. Bowles won big majorities in rural black-majority counties and in the counties with Durham and Chapel Hill. Burr carried almost every rural county in the Piedmont and the mountains.

In the Senate, Burr leaned conservative on cultural issues and toward the center on foreign policy. At the top of his agenda, he said, was changing NIH as he had worked to change the FDA in the 1990s. "Given the sheer volume of research money we're running through NIH, I think it makes sense to look at NIH from top to bottom to see if it's structured right. You've had a ramp-up of 100% in research dollars. Given that that's supposed to be chasing the best potential research items, is the NIH structured in a way to do that?" Unlike George W. Bush, he supported using frozen embryos in fertility clinics in stem-cell research. Burr resumed his focus on bioterrorism, winning enactment of a bill to create a new agency—the Biomedical Advanced Research and Development Authority—to develop vaccines and other countermeasures to biological terrorism or a pandemic. Opponents criticized the bill for its secret operations and for protecting companies that make ineffective or harmful medicines. Burr responded that the agency would become the "venture capitalist" for private-sector initiatives, and would have complete access to their data. Biotech firms applauded the bipartisan deal.

After pledging to vote against CAFTA during his 2004 campaign, Burr voted for the agreement in June 2005, stating "new side agreements" that would boost the state's economy convinced him to support it. In May 2006, he voted against the Senate immigration overhaul because it called for "blanket amnesty" for illegal immigrants. During negotiations on the compromise bill in June 2007, he supported the "touchback" amendment sponsored by Lindsey Graham that would force illegal immigrants to return to their home countries before applying for a Z visa; when the amendment was voted down, he voted against allowing the compromise bill to advance. In January 2007, he supported Bush's plan for a troop surge in Iraq, citing the need for "security and stability."

In 2007, Burr was named a deputy whip. He does not come up for reelection until 2010, and is a Republican in a Republican-leaning state. But there seems to be a jinx on this seat. Since Sam Ervin retired in 1974, none of its holders has won a second term: Democrat Robert Morgan lost in 1980, Republican James Broyhill lost in 1986, Democrat Terry Sanford lost in 1992, Republican Lauch Faircloth lost in 1998 and Democrat John Edwards, running for president, did not seek reelection in 2004.

FIRST DISTRICT

Rep. G.K. Butterfield (D)

Elected July 2004, 2d full term; b. Apr. 27, 1947, Wilson; home, Wilson; NC Central U., B.A. 1971, J.D. 1974; Baptist; divorced.

Military Career: Army, 1968-70.

Elected Office: NC Superior Ct., 1988-2001, 2002-04; NC Sup. Ct., 2001-02.

Professional Career: Practicing atty., 1974-88.

DC Office: 413 CHOB, 20515, 202-225-3101; Fax: 202-225-3354; Web site: www.house.gov/butterfield.

District Offices: Weldon, 252-538-4123; Williamston, 252-789-4939; Wilson, 252-237-9816.

Committees: *Chief Deputy Majority Whip. Energy & Commerce* (28th of 31 D): Energy & Air Quality (Vice Chmn.); Commerce, Trade & Consumer Protection; Environment & Hazardous Materials.

Group Ratings

	ADA	ACLU	AFS	LCV	ITIC	NTU	COC	ACU	CFG	FRC
2006	95	95	100	75	43	13	47	16	9	14
2005	85	—	100	89	—	14	56	12	10	15

National Journal Ratings

	2005 LIB	—	2005 CONS		2006 LIB	—	2006 CONS
Economic	77%	—	23%		65%	—	34%
Social	68%	—	32%		68%	—	31%
Foreign	59%	—	40%		73%	—	26%

Key Votes of the 109th Congress

1. Estate Tax Repeal	Y	5. Limit Interstate Abortion	N	9. Build Border Fence	N
2. Limit CAFE Standards	N	6. Extend Patriot Act	Y	10. CAFTA	N
3. FY06 Spending Curb	N	7. Bar Same Sex Marriage	N	11. Oppose Iraq Withdrawal	N
4. Drilling in ANWR	N	8. Stem Cell Research $	Y	12. Detainee Tribunals	N

Election Results

2006 general	G.K. Butterfield (D)	unopposed		($359,758)
2006 primary	G.K. Butterfield (D)	unopposed		
2004 general	G.K. Butterfield (D)	137,667	(64%)	($403,957)
	Greg Dority (R)	77,508	(36%)	($39,130)

Prior Winning Percentages: 2004 (71%)

The People		Race/Ethnic Origin	Ancestry	
Area size:	7,664 sq. mi.	44.4% White	USA: 10.7%	English: 6.1%
Urban population:	47.7%	50.5% Black	Irish: 3.6%	
Rural population:	52.3%	0.5% Asian	**2004 Presidential Vote**	
Pop. 2000:	619,178	0.7% Native Am.	Kerry (D) 128,129	(57%)
Pop. 2005 (est):	618,817	0.0% Hawaiian	Bush (R) 94,738	(42%)
Median income:	$28,410	0.8% Two+ races	Other 554	(0%)
Poverty status:	21.1%	0.1% Other	**2000 Presidential Vote**	
Military veterans:	12.3%	3.1% Hispanic Origin	Gore (D) 111,558	(57%)
			Bush (R) 82,204	(42%)
			Cook Partisan Voting Index: D + 9	

Occupation	Blue collar: 34.8%	White collar: 45.5%	Gray collar: 19.7%

Eastern North Carolina in colonial days was a smaller version of the Chesapeake Bay colonies of Virginia and Maryland—a fertile land laced by dozens of rivers and inlets, with tobacco plantations and farms with docks on the water accessible to the ocean and so to London. North Carolina was settled later than the Chesapeake colonies, and was poorer, with smaller landholdings. But vestiges of its 18th century past can still be seen in New Bern with its Tryon Palace, the governor's house when this was the capital, and the tiny, well-preserved town of Edenton on Albemarle Sound, where 51 Edenton women in 1774 protested the taxing of tea and cloth—an act considered the first women's political protest on these shores.

Today, east Carolina is still tobacco country, and is still largely inhabited by the descendants of the original white settlers and black slaves of 250 years ago. They live in small towns and cities and in some of the most thickly settled rural land in the United States. Tobacco is a labor-intensive crop that for many years produced yields of $4,000 an acre;a family lucky enough to have a tobacco quota could make a living off 40 acres. In 2004 Congress voted a $10 billion buyout of quota holders, and many old east Carolina tobacco fields are now planted with cucumbers, sweet potatoes, blueberries, and especially cotton. There have been socioeconomic troubles in this region: several of the rural counties have had high HIV infection rates. Seven counties in northeast North Carolina lost population from 2000 to 2006; Perdue closed a chicken-processing plant, and even fast-food giant Hardee's, founded here in Rocky Mount, decamped to St. Louis. In Beaufort County, more than one-third of African-Americans live in poverty.

The 1st Congressional District of North Carolina, which is among the poorest in the nation, covers much of the old tobacco country of east Carolina. It touches Albemarle and Pamlico Sounds in the east and juts inland to reach black neighborhoods in Greenville and Goldsboro. It includes Halifax County, the state's number one deer hunting county. Together, the 1st and the 3d Districts blanket the eastern quarter of the state, with intricately drawn boundaries whose fingers reach deep into each other's territory, like hands in a tight embrace. There is a political reason for this. The 1st is 52% percent black, the highest percentage of any district in the state, and solidly though not overwhelmingly Democratic. The 3d is only 17% black and, with retirees and new residents in fast-growing coastal counties, votes heavily Republican. The 1st is also notable for its unique and curious gender ratio: There are 56,000 more female voters here than male voters—a far greater disparity than in any other congressional district in the state.

The congressman from the 1st District is G.K. (George Kenneth) Butterfield, a Democrat who won a special election in July 2004 to replace incumbent Frank Ballance, who had announced his retirement after less than one term and then resigned in June 2004; Ballance cited medical problems, but he pleaded guilty five months later to federal fraud charges in the operation of his anti-drug foundation and was sent to prison for money laundering. Butterfield grew up in Wilson County, where his father was a dentist and the first black elected official in Wilson in the 20th century and his mother was a school teacher for 48 years; he got his bachelor's and law degrees from North Carolina Central University. A civil-rights lawyer who represented poor people, Butterfield took on many voting rights cases. As a Superior Court judge for 12 years, he handled thousands of civil and criminal cases in 46 counties until February 2001, when Governor Mike Easley appointed him to the state Supreme Court. After Butterfield lost election in 2002 to a full term, Easley appointed him as a special superior court judge. In the July 2004 special election to fill the remainder of Ballance's term, which was held on the same date as the primary, party caucuses selected the nominees, and the six-week contest in this safe Democratic district received little local or national attention. Butterfield said that his priorities would be strengthening the rural economy and halting U.S. job losses. He won 71%-27%.

In the House, where his voting record was moderate, he urged the Federal Communications Commission to move slowly to all-digital cable television. "In poor rural places like eastern North Carolina, this could leave a lot of people in the dark when it comes to watching television," he said. He filed a bill to create an exhibit in the new Capitol Visitors Center to depict the use of slave labor in building the Capitol, and describe the careers of the 22 blacks who served in Congress during and following Reconstruction. "African Americans have played an active and important role in Congress' history, and that must not be forgotten." In calling for renewal of the Voting Rights Act, he noted that his father lost his seat on the local city council in 1957 because of a discriminatory voting law change. A friend of Representative James Clyburn for 30 years, Butterfield managed his successful campaign for Majority Whip in 2006 and the two were virtually inseparable for 12 days before the November election—in South Carolina and at campaign events across the nation. "I was his conscience and insisted that he make his calls," Butterfield said. "He called about 200 members, with the help of four or five cell phones and an occasional staffer. Now he is grateful to me."

With his influential connections, he got a seat in 2007 on the Energy and Commerce Committee. He wants to prohibit states from passing on their Medicaid costs to the counties; in his district, many counties spend more of their property tax revenues on Medicaid than on the schools. In 2006, Butterfield was reelected without opposition.

SECOND DISTRICT

Rep. Bob Etheridge (D)

Elected 1996, 6th term; b. Aug. 7, 1941, Turkey; home, Lillington; Campbell U., B.S. 1965; Presbyterian; married (Faye).

Military Career: Army, 1965-67.

Elected Office: Harnett Cnty. Comm., 1973-76, Chmn., 1975-76; NC House of Reps., 1978-88; NC Superintendent of Public Instruction, 1988-96.

Professional Career: Farmer, 1965-present; V.P. Sales, Sorensen Industries, 1968-87; Owner, Layton Hardware, 1973-90; Co–owner, WLLN Radio, 1979-91.

DC Office: 1533 LHOB, 20515, 202-225-4531; Fax: 202-225-5662; Web site: www.house.gov/etheridge.

District Offices: Lillington, 910-814-0335; Raleigh, 919-829-9122.

Committees: *Agriculture* (4th of 25 D): General Farm Commoditico & Risk Management (Chmn.); Horticulture & Organic Agriculture. *Budget* (16th of 22 D). *Homeland Security* (12th of 19 D): Emerging Threats, Cybersecurity & Science and Technology; Emergency Communications, Preparedness & Response.

Group Ratings

	ADA	ACLU	AFS	LCV	ITIC	NTU	COC	ACU	CFG	FRC
2006	80	64	100	75	43	16	60	44	17	42
2005	95	—	100	89	—	13	52	16	3	31

National Journal Ratings

	2005 LIB	—	2005 CONS		2006 LIB	—	2006 CONS
Economic	78%	—	21%		63%	—	36%
Social	63%	—	37%		61%	—	39%
Foreign	56%	—	44%		58%	—	41%

Key Votes of the 109th Congress

1. Estate Tax Repeal	N	5. Limit Interstate Abortion	Y	9. Build Border Fence	Y
2. Limit CAFE Standards	N	6. Extend Patriot Act	Y	10. CAFTA	N
3. FY06 Spending Curb	N	7. Bar Same Sex Marriage	Y	11. Oppose Iraq Withdrawal	Y
4. Drilling in ANWR	N	8. Stem Cell Research $	Y	12. Detainee Tribunals	Y

Election Results

2006 general	Bob Etheridge (D)	85,993	(67%)	($918,522)
	Dan Mansell (R)	43,271	(33%)	($61,689)
2006 primary	Bob Etheridge (D) .... unopposed			
2004 general	Bob Etheridge (D)	145,079	(62%)	($989,599)
	Billy Creech (R)	87,811	(38%)	($137,820)

Prior Winning Percentages: 2002 (65%); 2000 (58%); 1998 (57%); 1996 (53%)

The People		Race/Ethnic Origin	Ancestry	
Area size:	3,979 sq. mi.	59.1% White	USA: 12.3%	English: 6.7%
Urban population:	49.5%	30.1% Black	German: 5.7%	
Rural population:	50.5%	0.9% Asian	**2004 Presidential Vote**	
Pop. 2000:	619,178	0.6% Native Am.	Bush (R) 128,220	(54%)
Pop. 2005 (est):	669,031	0.1% Hawaiian	Kerry (D) 107,912	(46%)
Median income:	$36,510	1.2% Two+ races	Other 777	(0%)
Poverty status:	14.3%	0.1% Other	**2000 Presidential Vote**	
Military veterans:	13.1%	7.9% Hispanic Origin	Bush (R) 98,607	(53%)
			Gore (D) 85,552	(46%)
			Other 1,378	(1%)
			Cook Partisan Voting Index: R + 3	

Occupation	Blue collar: 32.6%	White collar: 52.1%	Gray collar: 15.3%

The coastal plain of North Carolina was long bypassed by history. It was settled after Virginia and South Carolina, and only filled in with English settlers as Scots-Irish families were streaming down the valley of Virginia to the western Piedmont. This has always been tobacco country, a high-yield crop that for many years could support a family on 40 acres. Tobacco, an important colonial crop, became even more so after James B. Duke created Bull Durham tobacco and Lucky Strike cigarettes. But this was long a backward area. Its small farms and little cities were homes mainly to tenant farmers and mill hands, people raising families in thin-walled frame houses, often with no electricity or running water.

In many ways, life here has improved, in large part because this region adjoins one of the nation's fastest-growing metropolitan areas, Raleigh-Durham. The population of Wake County, which includes Raleigh, grew 86% from 1990 to 2006; there has been similar growth in surrounding Franklin (55%), Johnston (87%), Harnett (57%) and Chatham (55%) Counties. The dynamic local economy has generated tens of thousands of jobs, with subdivisions and retirement communities sprouting up all around. While counties to the east have seen denim mills close and tobacco plots replaced with less lucrative crops, other parts of the region have boomed. Raleigh combines North Carolina State University and glitzy new cultural institutions with country-cured hams and collard greens at such culinary destinations as Big Ed's City Market Restaurant. In Chatham County, a co-op in 2006 opened the state's first biodiesel production plant.

The 2d Congressional District of North Carolina consists of an irregular loop south of Raleigh, taking in parts of nine counties, including Wake County, which is split among three congressional districts. It covers all of Johnston County, the state's top tobacco-producing county, and parts of hog-producing Sampson County and Cumberland County, including portions of the Army's Fort Bragg and Pope Air Force Base. The district has an 8% Hispanic population, the highest of any in North Carolina; Latinos have been coming to work in meat and chicken processing factories, but most are not registered to vote. This is by and large the blue-collar, country music part of the booming Raleigh-Durham metro area, a place where most voters have a Democratic heritage but many have gotten into the habit of voting Republican for major offices. In 2000 it voted for George W. Bush and for Democratic Governor Mike Easley. In 2002 it voted for Republican Senator Elizabeth Dole. Despite the presence of John Edwards on the Democratic ticket, the 2d voted for Bush again in 2004.

The congressman from the 2d District is Bob Etheridge, a Democrat first elected in 1996. His biography seems tailored to the district: He was born in the hamlet of Turkey in Sampson County, grew up in Johnston County, went to Campbell University in Harnett County, where he was a basketball star, and he owned a hardware store in Lillington, the county seat. He is a tobacco farmer; he served four years on the Harnett County Commission in the 1970s, was elected to the North Carolina House in 1978 and served 10 years, eventually chairing the Appropriations Committee. In 1988 and 1992 he was elected state superintendent of public instruction. In the mid-1990s, Governor Jim Hunt called for abolishing the superintendent post and transferred 300 employees to the state Board of Education. Etheridge, spying an opportunity, decided to run for the House in 1996 against freshman David Funderburk, a longtime ally of Jesse Helms. When Funderburk tried to tie Etheridge to FDA Commissioner David Kessler's announcement that tobacco could be regulated as a drug, Etheridge responded by citing his own tobacco credentials: "I own tobacco allotments and have for years. I'd like to know how many days Mr. Funderburk spent priming tobacco, setting tobacco, and how many days he spent under the hot sun in the tobacco fields." Etheridge won 53%-46%.

In the House, Etheridge has compiled a voting record a bit to the left of center and generally more liberal on economic issues. The only tobacco farmer in Congress, Etheridge vigorously opposed all attempts to regulate the crop and worked for years on the tobacco buyout bill, which finally was enacted in 2004 and reportedly paid him and his wife $31,000. Utilizing his previous experience as an educator, he won a provision in the Higher Education Reauthorization Act to teach values in public schools, and sought federal funds to research and implement "character education" programs. He has pushed legislation to allow states to obtain interest-free loans to build schools. He supported the flag burning amendment and partial-birth abortion ban, and voted to override Bill Clinton's veto of estate tax repeal. He belongs to the New Democrats, and split with his party when he was among 21 House Democrats—and the only one from North Carolina—voting for trade promotion authority; North Carolina high-tech and farm interests supported the measure. The state has suffered setbacks from expanded trade, he said, but "we've been a net winner." Etheridge also split with most House Democrats to support the use of force in Iraq. He won enactment of his bill to assist weather forecasters to improve hurricane warnings for inland areas; his district was devastated by Hurricane Floyd in 1999. On the first anniversary of Katrina, he joined other Democrats in New Orleans and criticized the lack of planning and the wasteful spending on no-bid contracts. He passed a measure to name the post office in Smithfield for actress Ava Gardner, who "did live the American dream, but never forgot her beginnings in Johnston County." In the majority, he joined the Budget Committee and became chairman of the Agriculture Subcommittee on General Farm Commodities and Risk Management, which positioned him to influence the farm bill. He is an enthusiast for production of renewable fuels.

The Democratic legislature's redistricting plan, by adding a part of Raleigh, made this district more Democratic. Since then, Etheridge has won easily. He twice thought about running for an open Senate seat, but was preempted by self-financing Erskine Bowles. Etheridge seems safe, but an open seat contest in this district could be competitive.

THIRD DISTRICT

Rep. Walter Jones (R)

Elected 1994, 7th term; b. Feb. 10, 1943, Farmville; home, Farmville; NC St. U., 1962-65, Atlantic Christian Col., B.A. 1967; Catholic; married (Joe Anne).

Military Career: NC Natl. Guard, 1967-71.

Elected Office: NC House of Reps., 1982-92.

Professional Career: Mgr., Walter B. Jones Office Supply Co., 1967-73; Salesman, Dunn Assoc., 1973-82; Pres., Benefit Reserves Inc., 1989-94; Pres., Judson Co., 1990-94.

DC Office: 2333 RHOB, 20515, 202-225-3415; Fax: 202-225-3286; Web site: jones.house.gov.

District Offices: Greenville, 252-931-1003.

Committees: *Armed Services* (8th of 29 R): Readiness; Oversight & Investigations; Military Personnel. *Financial Services* (11th of 33 R): Domestic and International Monetary Policy, Trade & Technology; Financial Institutions & Consumer Credit.

Group Ratings

	ADA	ACLU	AFS	LCV	ITIC	NTU	COC	ACU	CFG	FRC
2006	45	36	50	50	17	57	50	79	43	100
2005	45	—	0	50	—	62	58	80	53	100

National Journal Ratings

	2005 LIB	—	2005 CONS	2006 LIB	—	2006 CONS
Economic	51%	—	49%	57%	—	42%
Social	44%	—	56%	45%	—	54%
Foreign	52%	—	48%	57%	—	42%

Key Votes of the 109th Congress

1. Estate Tax Repeal	Y	5. Limit Interstate Abortion	Y	9. Build Border Fence	Y
2. Limit CAFE Standards	Y	6. Extend Patriot Act	Y	10. CAFTA	N
3. FY06 Spending Curb	*	7. Bar Same Sex Marriage	Y	11. Oppose Iraq Withdrawal	P
4. Drilling in ANWR	Y	8. Stem Cell Research $	N	12. Detainee Tribunals	N

Election Results

2006 general	Walter Jones (R) 99,519	(69%)	($674,917)
	Craig Weber (D) 45,458	(31%)	($58,650)
2006 primary	Walter Jones (R) .... unopposed		
2004 general	Walter Jones (R) 171,863	(71%)	($586,012)
	Roger Eaton (D) 71,227	(29%)	($15,265)

Prior Winning Percentages: 2002 (91%); 2000 (61%); 1998 (62%); 1996 (63%); 1994 (53%)

The People		Race/Ethnic Origin	Ancestry	
Area size:	10,048 sq. mi.	76.3% White	USA: 12.9%	English: 9.9%
Urban population:	53.2%	16.6% Black	German: 7.6%	
Rural population:	46.8%	0.9% Asian	**2004 Presidential Vote**	
Pop. 2000:	619,178	0.4% Native Am.	Bush (R) 169,674	(68%)
Pop. 2005 (est):	643,554	0.1% Hawaiian	Kerry (D) 79,936	(32%)
Median income:	$37,510	1.2% Two+ races	Other 839	(0%)
Poverty status:	12.4%	0.1% Other	**2000 Presidential Vote**	
Military veterans:	15.7%	4.4% Hispanic Origin	Bush (R) 134,471	(64%)
			Gore (D) 73,035	(35%)
			Other 1,589	(1%)
			Cook Partisan Voting Index: R +15	

Occupation	Blue collar: 27.3%	White collar: 55.9%	Gray collar: 16.8%

Nearly 500 years ago, Giovanni da Verrazano sailed past the Gulf Stream and landed on a sand spit island he thought was the outer edge of China. He was wrong: It was the Outer Banks of North Carolina. These are probably America's most unstable barrier islands, constantly changing shape and cut by new inlets as they are battered by ocean currents and storm winds, as recently as 2003 when 30-foot waves from Hurricane Isabel pounded the beaches. They were settled early by Europeans: Sir Walter Raleigh's Roanoke colony was founded here in 1587, then vanished shortly thereafter; Edward Teach—Blackbeard—and other pirates lurked in Pamlico and Albemarle Sounds behind the islets. History is still very much alive on the Outer Banks. An antique form of English is spoken on Ocracoke Island, reachable only by ferry; the 208-foot lighthouse on Cape Hatteras, America's tallest, looks out on some of the most treacherous currents in the Atlantic. The sands along Kitty Hawk, with their constant winds, are where the Wright Brothers made mankind's first heavier-than-air flight in December 1903. The Outer Banks has become prime vacation and retirement country, with affluent beachfront communities around Kitty Hawk, Nags Head and Duck and, much farther south, on the "Crystal Coast" around Beaufort (BOWfort, not BEWfort as in South Carolina) and Morehead City. Inland, amid swamps, is the Marine Corps' Camp Lejeune, home base of one-fifth of the Marine Corps, many of whom have served in Iraq; on the other side of the Croatan National Forest is Cherry Point, the world's largest Marine Corps Air Station. The flat lands of east Carolina have long been tobacco and peanut-growing country, and are now also hog-raising land.

The 3d Congressional District of North Carolina covers the Outer Banks and much of the coastal plain of North Carolina, though the northeastern tier—from the desolate Great Dismal Swamp to the affluent oceanside resort communities—move more in the orbit of Virginia's Hampton Roads than North Carolina's Research Triangle. The 3d exists in balance with the 1st, with which it shares most of eastern North Carolina. Fingers of the 3d go deep inland to include mostly white portions of Goldsboro and Greenville, where tobacco farms are fading and a pharmaceutical company is the largest industrial employer. The 3d is predominantly white and Republican, compared to the 1st, which is half-black and heavily Democratic. Party registration here is misleading, an artifact of the past. There are 27,000 more registered Democrats than Republicans here but the district voted for George W. Bush by 68%-32 in 2004.

The congressman from the 3d District is Walter Jones, a Republican first elected in 1994. He grew up in eastern North Carolina, attended North Carolina State and Atlantic Christian College, and served in the National Guard. His father, Walter Jones Sr., was a Democratic congressman from the old 1st District; he served a quarter-century and chaired the Merchant Marine and Fisheries Committee. The younger Jones was elected in 1982 to the state House, where he voted to oust the Democratic speaker and often broke with Democratic leaders. In 1992 he ran as a Democrat in the new black-majority 1st District after his father decided to retire, led the primary with 38%, but lost the runoff to Eva Clayton 55%-45%. In April 1993, he switched to the Republican Party, and soon announced he was running in the 3d. This pitted Jones against four-term Congressman Martin Lancaster, a Democrat who had worked hard on local projects. But Lancaster voted for the Clinton budget and tax package plus the crime bill, and failed to persuade the Clintons to drop the cigarette tax from their health care package. Jones ran an ad showing Lancaster jogging with Bill Clinton: "How'd Martin Lancaster get so out of touch? Well, look who he's running around with in Washington." Jones won 53%-47%.

In the House, Jones got seats on Armed Services and on Resources, which absorbed his father's Merchant Marine panel. His voting record began as consistently conservative and hawkish but has moderated on non-cultural issues as he has taken issue with President Bush's policies. Jones has favored more defense spending, and he passed a bill for a $500 tax credit for military personnel on food stamps. He opposed normal trade relations with China which, he said, "steals technology and sells it to our enemies, steals our nuclear secrets and tries to influence our election process," and joined Democrats at press conferences opposing the Central America Free Trade Agreement.

Following crashes of the Osprey helicopter, including one near Camp Lejeune, Jones defended it as "the fighting machine that the Marines say they need." Jones, who posted the Ten Commandments in his Capitol Hill office, supported politically active churches with his proposal to permit them to endorse candidates without losing their tax-exempt status. The bill generated lots of traffic on the Internet, but the House defeated it 178-239 in 2002. On the Resources Committee, he has sought water quality improvements.

In North Carolina, Jones has generated controversy by intervening in conflicts outside his district. He called for the state school superintendent to remove from an elementary school in Wilmington a book about two gay princes who got married, opposed full recognition to the Lumbee Indians for fear that they would build a big casino on Interstate 95, and called for a federal review of the Durham County District Attorney's prosecution of three Duke University lacrosse players for an alleged sexual attack. He opposes oil drilling on the North Carolina coast and opposed a Bush administration proposal to shift to local governments a greater share of the cost for beach restoration.

Jones voted to authorize the use of force in Iraq and even led the 2003 effort to rename House cafeteria French fries "Freedom fries." But not long afterward, he was profoundly affected by a local Marine's funeral, setting the stage for an unlikely conversion from conservative war supporter to Bush administration antagonist. He began writing letters to the families of every serviceman and woman killed in Iraq; he told *Mother Jones*, the liberal opinion magazine whose cover he graced in January 2006, that he had written more than 2,000 by that time, penning them every Saturday while sitting alone in his Greenville office. By June 2005, he had joined with some of the most liberal members of the House to cosponsor a resolution calling for the Bush administration to publish a timetable for withdrawing troops from Iraq. At the same time, Jones expressed regret over his 2003 effort to rename House cafeteria French fries "Freedom fries." The London *Guardian* ran the headline, "French fries protester regrets war jibe." He voted "present" on a 2006 Republican resolution calling for victory in the war on terror and in Iraq and in January 2007 he sponsored a resolution seeking to ensure that the President receive specific authorization from Congress before initiating the use of military force against Iran. In February, Jones was one of only two Republicans to cosponsor the Democrats' non-binding resolution opposing Bush's military surge in Iraq. His position on Iraq cost him the top Republican post on the Readiness Subcommittee at Armed Services in January 2007. Jones says that after Armed Services ranking member Duncan Hunter told him the news, he asked Hunter for a slot on the oversight subcommittee. Jones got it, but the denial of ranking member status on Readiness led various Democrats to approach him about switching parties. "I think at the present time, because of the pro-life issue primarily, I am where I need to be," Jones told *The Hill* in March 2007.

Jones has easily won reelection but his outspoken criticism of Iraq war policy has generated serious 2008 primary opposition from Onslow County Commissioner Joe McLaughlin, a former Army officer who announced his candidacy in May 2007.

FOURTH DISTRICT

Rep. David Price (D)

Elected 1996, 10th term; b. Aug. 17, 1940, Erwin, TN; home, Chapel Hill; U. of NC, B.A. 1961, Yale U., B.D. 1964, Ph.D. 1969; Baptist; married (Lisa).

Elected Office: U.S. House of Reps., 1986-94.

Professional Career: Legis. Aide, U.S. Sen. Bartlett, 1963-67; Prof., Yale U., 1969-73, Duke U., 1973-present; Exec. Dir., NC Dem. Party, 1979-80, Chmn., 1983-84; Staff Dir., DNC Comm. on Pres. Nominations, 1981-82.

DC Office: 2162 RHOB, 20515, 202-225-1784; Fax: 202-225-2014; Web site: price.house.gov.

District Offices: Chapel Hill, 919-967-7924; Durham, 919-688-3004; Raleigh, 919-859-5999.

Committees: *Appropriations* (13th of 37 D): Homeland Security (Chmn.); Transportation, HUD & Related Agencies; Commerce, Justice, Science & Related Agencies.

Group Ratings

	ADA	ACLU	AFS	LCV	ITIC	NTU	COC	ACU	CFG	FRC
2006	95	100	100	92	43	10	47	4	7	0
2005	100	—	100	94	—	12	48	4	3	0

National Journal Ratings

	2005 LIB	—	2005 CONS		2006 LIB	—	2006 CONS
Economic	85%	—	13%		69%	—	30%
Social	79%	—	20%		79%	—	20%
Foreign	79%	—	20%		77%	—	20%

Key Votes of the 109th Congress

1. Estate Tax Repeal	N	5. Limit Interstate Abortion	N	9. Build Border Fence	N
2. Limit CAFE Standards	N	6. Extend Patriot Act	N	10. CAFTA	N
3. FY06 Spending Curb	N	7. Bar Same Sex Marriage	N	11. Oppose Iraq Withdrawal	N
4. Drilling in ANWR	N	8. Stem Cell Research $	Y	12. Detainee Tribunals	N

Election Results

2006 general	David Price (D)	127,340	(65%)	($800,298)
	Steve Acuff (R)	68,599	(35%)	($53,697)
2006 primary	David Price (D)	39,637	(89%)	
	Kent Kanoy (D)	2,768	(6%)	
	Oscar Lewis (D)	1,886	(4%)	
2004 general	David Price (D)	217,441	(64%)	($1,192,561)
	Todd Batchelor (R)	121,717	(36%)	($49,474)

Prior Winning Percentages: 2002 (61%); 2000 (62%); 1998 (57%); 1996 (54%); 1992 (65%); 1990 (58%); 1988 (58%); 1986 (56%)

The People		Race/Ethnic Origin	Ancestry	
Area size:	1,298 sq. mi.	68.8% White	English: 10.2%	German: 9.8%
Urban population:	83.2%	20.6% Black	Irish: 7.7%	
Rural population:	16.8%	3.9% Asian	**2004 Presidential Vote**	
Pop. 2000:	619,178	0.3% Native Am.	Kerry (D) 193,126	(55%)
Pop. 2005 (est):	714,334	0.0% Hawaiian	Bush (R) 154,743	(44%)
Median income:	$53,847	1.3% Two+ races	Other 1,833	(1%)
Poverty status:	9.2%	0.2% Other	**2000 Presidential Vote**	
Military veterans:	10.3%	5.0% Hispanic Origin	Gore (D) 131,532	(53%)
			Bush (R) 112,885	(46%)
			Other 3,180	(1%)
			Cook Partisan Voting Index: D + 6	

Occupation	Blue collar: 14.3%	White collar: 74.8%	Gray collar: 10.9%

Back in the 1950s, few people would have predicted that the countryside around Raleigh and Durham, North Carolina, would become one of America's high-tech boom areas. But Governor Luther Hodges did, when he started the 6,900-acre Research Triangle Park as an R&D industrial park between the musty state capital of Raleigh, the Lucky Strike-manufacturing city of Durham and the small university town of Chapel Hill. With the drawing power of three universities—North Carolina State in Raleigh, Duke in Durham and the University of North Carolina in Chapel Hill—Research Triangle Park slowly began attracting top-tier R&D organizations, which in turn spawned a dynamic entrepreneurial sector. Today, IBM, GlaxoSmithKline, Cisco, Nortel, RTI International, EPA and BASF are big employers here, but there are small businesses too; 42% of Triangle employers have less than 10 employees. A sleepy metro area which once trailed the nation in income is now a fast-growing, vibrant, affluent metropolis—the prime engine of North Carolina's growth. The Raleigh-Durham airport, which had four gates in the 1970s, now has 49 and is tripling the size of Terminal C.

Three decades of vibrant economic growth have made the Triangle affluent, but it still prides itself on its homier touches, from slow-cooked pit barbecue to a minor-league baseball stadium in Durham that features a smoke-snorting replica of a bull, a prop made famous by the movie *Bull Durham*. This combination of upscale and down-home has proved to be a popular draw. From 1990 to 2006, the Raleigh-Durham metro area grew by 71%, from 855,000 to 1.46 million: The fastest metropolitan growth north and east of Atlanta. Growth has been slow in Durham and Chapel Hill, rapid in Raleigh and Wake County and in Chatham County to the southwest. College basketball makes the headlines here, and UNC, NC State and Duke have fielded more March Madness contenders than any similarly sized area. But for much of 2006 and 2007 more headlines were made by lacrosse, as Durham prosecutor Mike Nifong charged three Duke lacrosse players with rape—charges of which they were "innocent," ruled North Carolina Attorney General Roy Cooper in April 2007, the product of a "rogue" prosecutor.

The 4th Congressional District of North Carolina covers much of the fast-growing Research Triangle area. It includes Durham County and Chapel Hill's Orange County, part of Chatham County to the south and a little less than half of Wake County. Politics here revolves around cultural issues. The Democratic base here is made up of two parts, the black community, with 21% of the district's population, and whites with post-graduate degrees. This part of the Triangle has one of the highest concentrations of Ph.D.s in the nation, and their livelihoods—in academia, in the sciences, in the social services—tend to depend on government. Durham and Orange Counties are heavily Democratic, the strongest areas in North Carolina for Erskine Bowles and against Elizabeth Dole and Richard Burr in 2002 and 2004 Senate elections except for a few rural counties with large black percentages. The burgeoning suburbs of Wake County are pretty heavily Republican, like so many fast-growing areas at the edge of metropolitan development across the nation, and provide some counterweight. On balance, though, this is a district that votes for Democrats, not only local moderates but also for Al Gore and John Kerry.

The congressman from the 4th District is David Price, a Democrat first elected in 1986; he lost his seat in 1994 and regained it in 1996. Price grew up in east Tennessee, the son of a school principal and an English teacher. He is an interesting blend of political scientist, practical politician, and a lay Baptist preacher. He came to Chapel Hill to go to college, worked as a young aide on Capitol Hill, earned a degree in divinity and a Ph.D. in political science at Yale and taught there for four years, then became a political science professor at Duke in 1973. He was executive director of the North Carolina Democratic Party in the 1980 election cycle and chairman from 1983-84—both, in effect, appointments of Governor Jim Hunt; he helped develop North Carolina's robust straight-ticket politics. He worked for Hunt when he headed a commission on revising the Democratic party's nominating rules. In 1986 he ran for the House and beat Republican Bill Cobey, who had won in the 1984 sweep. In 1994 Price lost 50.4%-49.6% to Fred Heineman, a former New York City cop and Raleigh police chief in the 1970s. In 1996 Heineman made unforced errors and was outspent by Price, who regained the seat 54%-44%. Price has written four books, including *The Congressional Experience*, about his observations on Congress.

In the House, his voting record typically places him near the center of House Democrats. During his first years, Price helped pass laws increasing the percentage of a home's value the FHA can insure, aiding technical education at community colleges and setting up an Advanced Techno-logical Education program at the National Science Foundation. When he returned, Price rejoined the Appropriations Committee on which, had he not lost in 1994, he would have had enough seniority to be ranking minority member of a subcommittee. His Education Affordability Act, "my personal centerpiece," on which he had been working for a dozen years, was folded into the 1997 Balanced Budget Act; it made interest on student loans tax deductible and allowed penalty-free withdrawals from IRAs for education expenses.

Price has combined strong opposition to Bush administration policies in Iraq and elsewhere with his work on homeland security on Appropriations. He voted against the Iraq war resolution in October 2002 and later called the administration "out of touch and out of control." In October 2005 he and North Carolina neighbor Brad Miller sponsored a resolution to require withdrawal of troops from Iraq as soon as possible; in 2006 they sponsored another requiring the administration to specify an exit strategy from Iraq; in January 2007 they sponsored a bill to dissolve the administra-tion's ability to prosecute the military effort after December 2007. In 2006 he and Zoe Lofgren called for an independent counsel to investigate the NSA surveillance of communications between al Qaeda suspects abroad and persons in the United States. Price was one of the founders of the House Democracy Assistance Commission, which has worked with leaders of emerging democracies, and in that effort he was in Lebanon on July 4, 2006, just before the Hamas attacks on Israel. He voted for the resolution supporting Israel's response to Hamas's attack. On a trip to Afghanistan in December 2006, he said, "What's happening is, basically, the Taliban is back," and said we can't abandon the fight. "Finding Osama bin Laden, there's no more basic objective to the pursuit of al Qaeda. It's a major failure, but it's indicative of the diversion in Iraq."

In January 2007 Price became chairman of the Homeland Security Appropriations Subcom-mittee, on which he had served quietly under Republican Harold Rogers. He pledged to take a bipartisan approach, as he said Rogers had, and he has directed much less funding to his district than Rogers to his. His first priority, he said, was to strengthen disaster assistance and to aid first responders. When the Bush administration in 2007 proposed, as it had the year before, to reduce spending on first responders from $3.4 billion to $2.2 billion, he said that was "particularly disappointing." In 2006 he called the bill to build a border fence "bumper sticker legislation." He later said that he was skeptical of barriers in remote areas that might be served better by new technologies and when asked about the fence, he asked, "Is this the best possible use of these funds? That's the bottom line." He planned to hold 22 hearings, one each for the 22 agencies that had been folded into the Department of Homeland Security.

In the appropriations process, Price has nurtured local projects ranging from $272 million for a new EPA complex in Research Triangle Park to $750,000 for electronic arrival signs at 14 bus stops in Chapel Hill. With Republican Steve Horn, a fellow political scientist formerly in the House, Price sponsored the "stand by your ad" requirement for candidates to appear in the full frame of TV ads reading their disclaimers on the air, so they would more likely be held responsible for negative ads. This became part of the campaign reform law in 2002; he wants a similar requirement for Internet ads. In January 2007 he sponsored a bill to double the amount of public financing presidential candidates could receive if an opponent outside the public financing scheme spends more than 120% of the public financing limit; it would be financed by increasing the checkoff on the tax returns to $10.

Since his return to the House in 1996, Price has been reelected by wide margins. In 2006 he won 65%-35%. In the fastest-growing part of the district, Wake County, he campaigned hard and won just 54% of the votes. He ran much better in the areas dominated by universities: 76% in Durham County, 79% in Orange County and 70% in Chatham County.

FIFTH DISTRICT

Rep. Virginia Foxx (R)

Elected 2004, 2d term; b. June 29, 1943, Bronx, NY; home, Banner Elk; U. of NC, A.B. 1968, M.A.C.T. 1972, U. of NC-Greensboro, Ed.D. 1985; Catholic; married (Thomas).

Elected Office: Watauga Bd. of Ed., 1976-88; NC Senate, 1994-2004.

Professional Career: Owner, Grandfather Mountain Nursery, 1976-present; Asst. Dean of General College, Appalachian St. U., 1976-1984; Pres. Mayland CC, 1987-1994.

DC Office: 430 CHOB, 20515, 202-225-2071; Fax: 202-225-2995; Web site: foxx.house.gov.

District Offices: Boone, 828-265-0240; Clemmons, 336-778-0211.

Committees: *Agriculture* (15th of 21 R): Horticulture & Organic Agriculture; Livestock, Dairy & Poultry. *Education & Labor* (17th of 22 R): Higher Education, Lifelong Learning & Competitiveness; Health, Employment, Labor & Pensions. *Oversight & Government Reform* (15th of 18 R): National Security & Foreign Affairs.

Group Ratings

	ADA	ACLU	AFS	LCV	ITIC	NTU	COC	ACU	CFG	FRC
2006	5	0	0	8	71	69	93	96	74	100
2005	5	—	0	11	—	70	78	100	88	100

National Journal Ratings

	2005 LIB	—	2005 CONS		2006 LIB	—	2006 CONS
Economic	0%	—	97%		19%	—	80%
Social	0%	—	89%		0%	—	94%
Foreign	17%	—	79%		17%	—	73%

Key Votes of the 109th Congress

1. Estate Tax Repeal	Y	5. Limit Interstate Abortion	Y	9. Build Border Fence	Y
2. Limit CAFE Standards	Y	6. Extend Patriot Act	Y	10. CAFTA	N
3. FY06 Spending Curb	Y	7. Bar Same Sex Marriage	Y	11. Oppose Iraq Withdrawal	Y
4. Drilling in ANWR	Y	8. Stem Cell Research $	N	12. Detainee Tribunals	Y

Election Results

2006 general	Virginia Foxx (R)	96,138	(57%)	($797,491)
	Roger Sharpe (D)	72,061	(43%)	($97,747)
2006 primary	Virginia Foxx (R)	unopposed		
2004 general	Virginia Foxx (R)	167,546	(59%)	($1,182,132)
	Jim Harrell (D)	117,271	(41%)	($383,579)

The People		Race/Ethnic Origin	Ancestry	
Area size:	4,424 sq. mi.	87.9% White	USA: 15.7%	English: 9.9%
Urban population:	42.9%	6.7% Black	German: 9.5%	
Rural population:	57.1%	0.8% Asian	**2004 Presidential Vote**	
Pop. 2000:	619,178	0.2% Native Am.	Bush (R) 191,034	(66%)
Pop. 2005 (est):	650,127	0.0% Hawaiian	Kerry (D) 95,811	(33%)
Median income:	$39,710	0.7% Two+ races	Other 1,140	(0%)
Poverty status:	9.5%	0.1% Other	**2000 Presidential Vote**	
Military veterans:	12.3%	3.6% Hispanic Origin	Bush (R) 163,705	(66%)
			Gore (D) 81,704	(33%)
			Other 2,147	(1%)
			Cook Partisan Voting Index: R +15	

Occupation   Blue collar: 33.2%   White collar: 54.1%   Gray collar: 12.7%

From the Atlantic Ocean, the terrain of North Carolina rises slowly through the Piedmont—a transitional land of modest hills that lies between the coastal plain and the Blue Ridge mountains. The Blue Ridge, named for the mysterious blue haze that blankets it, provides the headwaters of the New River, which cuts majestic crevasses—alternately lush and mined-out—as it flows north to

West Virginia. The lower Piedmont lands of North Carolina were first settled by independent-minded Scots-Irish farmers and by followers of British and German sects like the Moravians. This was hardscrabble farm country before the Civil War, with few slaves. By the late 19th century, it was becoming industrialized, with textile mills alongside streams, furniture factories not far from hardwood forests and R. J. Reynolds's cigarette factories in Winston-Salem. The Piedmont economy was hailed as the basis of a progressive New South, although textile mills paid low wages and tobacco employed fewer workers.

North Carolina's present-day affluence owes more to pharmaceuticals, banking and high-skill Piedmont factories. Lowe's, the $31 billion home improvement giant, is based in Wilkesboro, population 3,200. The merger of banking giants Wachovia and First Union proved bittersweet for Winston-Salem, Wachovia's home base since 1879: First Union let the new company keep Wachovia's name but shifted its headquarters to Charlotte. In 2005, Dell opened a plant in Winston-Salem that produced 2 million computers and 1,100 jobs in its first year. Yet large swaths of the region remain rural, from chicken-raising Wilkes County to Appalachian State University in Boone (named for Daniel), a center for resurgent pride in the culture of Appalachia, a region toward which the rest of America has so often displayed condescension. This was one of the birthplaces of stock car racing.

All these places lie within the boundaries of the 5th Congressional District. The 5th begins in the heart of the Piedmont: The suburbs of Winston-Salem (though not the city, which is in the 12th). From there, it drops south just short of the outer fringes of metropolitan Charlotte; then heads west and north to the Tennessee line, taking in mountain communities like Boone. The core of its population base is the Winston-Salem suburbs in Forsyth County, plus small industrial cities in Stokes and Surry Counties, including Mount Airy, the model for Mayberry in *The Andy Griffith Show*. The district is solidly Republican.

The congresswoman from the 5th District is Virginia Foxx, a Republican who won a fiercely contested Republican primary in 2004. She graduated from the University of North Carolina and had a diverse professional and political background before winning election to Congress at age 61. She owned a nursery and landscape company, taught sociology and was assistant dean of the General College at Appalachian State University; later, she became president of Mayland Community College. She served 12 years on the Board of Education of Watauga County, on the western edge of the district (nearly as close to Knoxville as to Winston-Salem), and in 1994 was elected to the state Senate. In the legislature she sponsored a constitutional amendment to ban same-sex marriage and a bill to deny Social Security to illegal aliens. She actively supported gun rights and home schools, and opposed abortion rights.

Foxx was one of eight candidates in the Republican primary, five of whom ran serious campaigns; collectively they spent more than $6 million. Ed Broyhill, the son of former Senator James Broyhill, started off as the early front-runner. Broyhill was endorsed by his father's onetime colleague Jesse Helms, but was hurt by stories about business reverses. Aggressively on the attack was Winston-Salem Councilman Vernon Robinson, a retired Air Force officer, who campaigned as a staunch conservative, "the black Jesse Helms," as he put it. Robinson finished first in the primary, with 24% of the vote. Foxx unexpectedly finished second, with 22%, just 511 votes ahead of Broyhill. Foxx had big leads in three mountain counties in her home area; Robinson carried Forsyth and one adjacent county. The four-week campaign for the runoff was heatedly contested. Robinson said that Foxx was "fighting the cultural war on the wrong side," and he aired several controversial ads targeting his tougher position on illegal aliens. Foxx warned voters that Robinson's aggressive style would make him a weak general election candidate who could lose, although that seemed unlikely in a district that twice voted 66% for George W. Bush. Foxx won 55%-45%, with between 73% and 82% in her home area in the three mountain counties. Robinson carried Forsyth County, which cast 40% of the vote, but by only 38 votes. Mountain Republicans evidently rejected Robinson not because he was black but because of a long coolness toward Jesse Helms's brand of Republicanism. Some Democrats argued that the general election would be close because of the local appeal of vice presidential nominee John Edwards. But the Kerry-Edwards ticket carried none of the counties in the district, and Foxx won 59%-41%.

In the House, Foxx had a solidly conservative voting record. She reinforced her reputation as a tight-spender when she was 1 of 11 members voting against House passage of the $52 billion relief package following Hurricane Katrina. "The real issue for me was accountability," Foxx said. She was more generous for local projects, taking credit for $500,000 for a teapot museum in Sparta, which President Bush later criticized as wasteful spending. She wrote a letter to *The Wall Street Journal* protesting an article that called Wilkes County the "least highly educated" in the nation, and she emphasized its "strong and knowledgeable workforce."

In 2006, she was reelected 57%-43% against weakly-funded Roger Sharpe, a former state senator.

SIXTH DISTRICT

Rep. Howard Coble (R)

Elected 1984, 12th term; b. Mar. 18, 1931, Greensboro; home, Greensboro; Appalachian St. U., 1949-50, Guilford Col., B.A. 1958, U. of NC, J.D. 1962; Presbyterian; single.

Military Career: Coast Guard, 1952-56, 1977-78, Coast Guard Reserves, 1960-81.

Elected Office: NC House of Reps., 1968-70, 1978-84.

Professional Career: Claims Rep., State Farm Ins., 1961-67; Asst. Guilford Cnty. Atty., 1967-69; Asst. U.S. Atty., NC Middle Dist., 1969-73; Secy., NC Dept. of Revenue, 1973-77; Practicing atty., 1979-83.

DC Office: 2468 RHOB, 20515, 202-225-3065; Fax: 202-225-8611; Web site: coble.house.gov.

District Offices: Asheboro, 336-626-3060; Graham, 336-229-0159; Granite Quarry, 704-209-0426; Greensboro, 336-333-5005; High Point, 336-886-5106.

Committees: *Judiciary* (3d of 17 R): Courts, the Internet & Intellectual Property (RMM); Crime, Terrorism & Homeland Security. *Transportation & Infrastructure* (4th of 34 R): Aviation; Coast Guard & Maritime Transportation; Highways & Transit.

Group Ratings

	ADA	ACLU	AFS	LCV	ITIC	NTU	COC	ACU	CFG	FRC
2006	10	5	0	8	71	70	93	92	67	71
2005	10	—	0	6	—	59	78	84	58	83

National Journal Ratings

	2005 LIB	—	2005 CONS		2006 LIB	—	2006 CONS
Economic	34%	—	66%		10%	—	89%
Social	24%	—	74%		11%	—	85%
Foreign	42%	—	55%		38%	—	59%

Key Votes of the 109th Congress

1. Estate Tax Repeal	Y	5. Limit Interstate Abortion	Y	9. Build Border Fence	Y
2. Limit CAFE Standards	Y	6. Extend Patriot Act	Y	10. CAFTA	N
3. FY06 Spending Curb	Y	7. Bar Same Sex Marriage	Y	11. Oppose Iraq Withdrawal	Y
4. Drilling in ANWR	Y	8. Stem Cell Research $	Y	12. Detainee Tribunals	Y

Election Results

2006 general	Howard Coble (R)	108,433	(71%)	($552,271)
	Rory Blake (D)	44,661	(29%)	($14,004)
2006 primary	Howard Coble (R)	unopposed		
2004 general	Howard Coble (R)	207,470	(73%)	($400,493)
	William Jordan (D)	76,153	(27%)	($12,223)

Prior Winning Percentages: 2002 (90%); 2000 (91%); 1998 (89%); 1996 (73%); 1994 (100%); 1992 (71%); 1990 (67%); 1988 (62%); 1986 (50%); 1984 (51%)

The People		Race/Ethnic Origin	Ancestry	
Area size:	2,989 sq. mi.	85.3% White	USA: 15.3%	German: 10.1%
Urban population:	51.6%	8.6% Black	English: 8.9%	
Rural population:	48.4%	1.0% Asian	**2004 Presidential Vote**	
Pop. 2000:	619,178	0.4% Native Am.	Bush (R) 200,942	(69%)
Pop. 2005 (est):	667,696	0.0% Hawaiian	Kerry (D) 87,295	(30%)
Median income:	$43,503	0.7% Two+ races	Other 1,202	(0%)
Poverty status:	8.2%	0.1% Other	**2000 Presidential Vote**	
Military veterans:	13.8%	3.9% Hispanic Origin	Bush (R) 160,141	(67%)
			Gore (D) 76,315	(32%)
			Other 1,727	(1%)
			Cook Partisan Voting Index: R +17	

Occupation	Blue collar: 32.3%	White collar: 55.8%	Gray collar: 11.9%

For more than half a century, furniture store managers and owners from all over the country twice a year have converged on the huge Furniture Mart in High Point, the center of the U.S. furniture business, for the giant trade show put on by manufacturers; it now attracts about 70,000 visitors. High Point sits amidst rolling farmland originally settled by Quakers; it was the site of the Battle of Guilford Courthouse in the Revolutionary War. The furniture business grew here early in the 20th century because of the hardwoods in the mountains not far west and the abundance of low-wage labor in the flatlands not far east. For many years the furniture business has proven more resilient than textiles and tobacco, but lately it has faced serious competition from China and many furniture jobs have been lost. The Triad area—Greensboro, High Point, and Winston-Salem—has been forced to scramble for new engines of economic growth to keep pace with booming Raleigh-Durham and Charlotte. Some seem to be coming. FedEx is building a new hub at Piedmont Triad airport, between Winston-Salem and Greensboro, with some 1,500 workers; that has led other firms to plan distribution centers to utilize the new facility. At the same time, the region's Hispanic population is growing. The town of Robbins in Moore County—the childhood home of former Senator John Edwards—is now 48% Hispanic, as Latinos moved in to seek jobs in chicken processing and furniture making.

The 6th Congressional District of North Carolina is centered on greater Greensboro and High Point, which collectively cast about one-third of the votes. The Furniture Mart itself is not physically located within the 6th, but the district takes in other parts of High Point, which calls itself "North Carolina's International City," plus Quaker-settled Randolph County with its pottery craftsmen, golf-course-sprinkled Moore County to the south, parts of furniture-manufacturing Davidson County, most of textile-making Alamance County, much of populous Guilford County (though not central Greensboro) and the eastern half of Rowan County. Many of these areas are historically Republican, and others have moved that direction in the past generation; this is one of North Carolina's most Republican districts.

The congressman from the 6th District is Howard Coble, a Republican first elected in 1984. He grew up in Guilford County, went to Guilford College, then after wrecking his father's car joined the Coast Guard, in which he started off collecting garbage and served for five years. He was an insurance claims representative, went to law school and became an assistant U.S. attorney, state revenue commissioner and served in the state House for eight years. Coble was elected to Congress in what was then a swing district; it was the third time the 6th had changed parties in three elections. Coble won reelection in 1986 by just 79 votes—in a contest that Democrats complained was decided by the Guilford County election board's refusal to hold a recount. But his personal popularity and redistricting made this a safe seat.

Coble is a friendly man who asks visitors if they mind if he smokes his cheap cigars; he likes bluegrass music and eats pork brains and eggs for breakfast. He is solidly conservative, with interesting twists. He is tightfisted, and since his first term he has tried to pass legislation to abolish pensions or health coverage for congressional retirees; he hasn't found many co-sponsors, but he has refused to back down on his pledge to boycott the program himself. Like many of his constituents, he is leery of free trade. He opposed fast track for NAFTA, but finally voted for it in 1993; but he opposed GATT and normal trade relations with China. He was one of three House Republicans from North Carolina to oppose trade promotion authority, and in 2005 was one of 27 Republicans who voted against the Central America Free Trade Agreement. With Democratic colleague Mel Watt, he launched a House caucus to inform members of job losses in the furniture industry.

"I see my role more as one of keeping bad legislation off the books," Coble once said. But as a subcommittee chairman he was legislatively productive. In 1997 he became chairman of the Courts and Intellectual Property Subcommittee of Judiciary. Arguing that copyright industries produce more GDP than manufacturing and that patent protection is essential to technological progress, Coble supported greater protection for intellectual property. When the Bush administration sought budget cuts from the Patent and Trademark Office, Coble told the appropriators to "keep their grubby paws out of the PTO's coffers." In 2002, he shepherded the enactment of additional changes in the patent law, including the development of an electronic system for the filing and processing of patent and trademark applications. In 2004, the Judiciary Committee approved his bill to protect commercial databases from piracy.

Despite his own limitations in operating a computer, Coble says that has not been an obstacle to dealing with the digital revolution and that he has come to appreciate the Internet. In 2003, Coble became chairman of the Crime, Terrorism and Homeland Security Subcommittee. The House passed his bill to modernize the Bureau of Alcohol, Tobacco and Firearms, with new investigative powers against rogue dealers who fail to follow rules on firearms sales. But gun-control advocates worried that his proposal set too high a standard to impose sanctions. He was in line to become senior Republican on the Judiciary Committee in 2007, but GOP leaders gave the post to Lamar Smith, a more prolific party fundraiser. Coble, instead, regained the top Republican post on the Subcommittee on Courts, the Internet and Intellectual Property. He planned to focus on some patent disputes plus copyright-law changes to accommodate new technologies. Though he voted to authorize force in Iraq, by 2005 he began to distance himself from the party position and raised questions about war policy.

When Coble faces a Democratic opponent, which isn't very often, he typically exceeds 70% of the vote. Democrats view this seat as possibly competitive once Coble departs, but that may be a stretch.

SEVENTH DISTRICT

Rep. Mike McIntyre (D)

Elected 1996, 6th term; b. Aug. 6, 1956, Lumberton; home, Lumberton; U. of NC, B.A. 1978, J.D. 1981; Presbyterian; married (Dee).

Professional Career: Practicing atty., 1981-96.

DC Office: 2437 RHOB, 20515, 202-225-2731; Fax: 202-225-5773; Web site: www.house.gov/mcintyre.

District Offices: Fayetteville, 910-323-0260; Lumberton, 910-735-0610; Wilmington, 910 815-4959.

Committees: *Agriculture* (3d of 25 D): Specialty Crops, Rural Development & Foreign Agriculture (Chmn.). *Armed Services* (10th of 34 D): Terrorism, Unconventional Threats & Capabilities; Air & Land Forces.

Group Ratings

	ADA	ACLU	AFS	LCV	ITIC	NTU	COC	ACU	CFG	FRC
2006	50	41	57	67	43	23	73	64	30	100
2005	70	—	75	67	—	27	62	48	22	85

National Journal Ratings

	2005 LIB	—	2005 CONS	2006 LIB	—	2006 CONS
Economic	56%	—	44%	59%	—	40%
Social	49%	—	50%	55%	—	45%
Foreign	51%	—	48%	57%	—	43%

Key Votes of the 109th Congress

1. Estate Tax Repeal	Y	5. Limit Interstate Abortion	Y	9. Build Border Fence	Y
2. Limit CAFE Standards	Y	6. Extend Patriot Act	Y	10. CAFTA	N
3. FY06 Spending Curb	N	7. Bar Same Sex Marriage	Y	11. Oppose Iraq Withdrawal	Y
4. Drilling in ANWR	N	8. Stem Cell Research $	N	12. Detainee Tribunals	Y

Election Results

2006 general	Mike McIntyre (D)	101,787	(73%)	($1,006,381)
	Shirley Davis (R)	38,033	(27%)	($41,222)
2006 primary	Mike McIntyre (D)	unopposed		
2004 general	Mike McIntyre (D)	180,382	(73%)	($758,418)
	Ken Plonk (R)	66,084	(27%)	

Prior Winning Percentages: 2002 (71%); 2000 (70%); 1998 (91%); 1996 (53%)

The People		Race/Ethnic Origin	Ancestry	
Area size:	6,510 sq. mi.	63.0% White	USA: 11.1%	English: 7.7%
Urban population:	45.1%	23.1% Black	German: 6.1%	
Rural population:	54.9%	0.5% Asian	**2004 Presidential Vote**	
Pop. 2000:	619,178	8.5% Native Am.	Bush (R) 141,459	(56%)
Pop. 2005 (est):	671,253	0.0% Hawaiian	Kerry (D) 110,589	(44%)
Median income:	$33,998	0.9% Two+ races	Other 858	(0%)
Poverty status:	16.7%	0.1% Other	**2000 Presidential Vote**	
Military veterans:	14.1%	3.9% Hispanic Origin	Bush (R) 108,091	(52%)
			Gore (D) 100,025	(48%)
			Other 1,420	(1%)
			Cook Partisan Voting Index: R + 3	

Occupation   Blue collar: 32.4%   White collar: 50.5%   Gray collar: 17.2%

Southernmost North Carolina was long a somnolent part of America. Its one port, Wilmington, was far overshadowed by Charleston and Norfolk; its miles of beaches seemed too hot in the summer and too cold in the winter to attract many tourists; its farmlands inland were mainly planted in tobacco. Tobacco was America's first export crop, and one that can be cultivated profitably in only a few places in the world. Under the quota system established in 1938, tobacco farmers could make a living off small plots; it produced more voters per federally assisted acre than any other crop. But tobacco became disfavored in recent decades, as smoking declined and tobacco companies were hit by lawsuits; in 2004, North Carolina politicians managed to pass a $10 billion buyout and in the process abolish the quota system. So tobacco farmers are diversifying; some have switched to blueberries.

The coastal counties of southernmost North Carolina and some inland counties have been growing fast. One reason is the military. Wilmington is home of the World War II battleship *U.S.S. North Carolina*, and a little further south the Army runs the 16,000-acre Military Ocean Terminal at Sunny Point—the largest ammunition port in the U.S., and the Army's main deep-water port on the east coast, built securely amidst enormous sand berms. The state has been reviewing options for a new deep-water port in Brunswick County near Southport. Condominiums have sprouted along and near the beaches north and south of Wilmington, and tourism has boomed. This area also has some of the busiest American movie and television-production facilities outside of Los Angeles; the state legislature in 2006 approved new incentives to further boost the business. In Sampson and Duplin Counties, the growth industry is hog farming—vertically integrated factory farming, loved by the industry for its robotic efficiency, criticized by environmentalists for its enormous output of hog waste. One Smithfield Foods facility has a slaughter limit of 8.48 million animals a year and is believed to be the largest slaughterhouse in the world.

The 7th Congressional District of North Carolina covers much of this territory. The district consists of three main areas: the Wilmington region, with affluent condo-dwellers along the beach and retiree subdivisions reclaimed from timbered-out pinelands further inland; the outskirts of Fayetteville, heavily dependent on Fort Bragg and Pope Air Force Base, even when the servicemen have been shipped overseas; and economically disadvantaged Robeson County, the home of the Lumbee Indians, whose origins have been lost to antiquity but who were treated by state segregation laws as a race distinct from whites and blacks and were recognized as a tribe by the state in 1885. For many years, this was a solidly Democratic district. Robeson County—with 20% of the district's population, and where whites, blacks and Lumbees each comprise about a third of the population—remains heavily Democratic in both national and state elections. But the Wilmington area and the hog-farming counties are now pretty heavily Republican, voting for George W. Bush and Senator Richard Burr in 2004. The Fayetteville area and the old tobacco counties are politically marginal. The result is a district Republican in national contests but still Democratic in some state races; it voted strongly for former area district attorney Mike Easley for governor in 2000 and 2004.

The congressman from the 7th District is Mike McIntyre, a Democrat first elected in 1996. McIntyre grew up in Lumberton, in Robeson County, graduated from college and law school at Chapel Hill and practiced law in Lumberton, where his family has been prominent for 200 years. When he was an intern in the office of Congressman Charlie Rose, where he watched the Watergate hearings and President Nixon's resignation speech, he whispered to his father that he would like one day to run for Rose's seat. McIntyre was active in civic affairs and in his church and was often asked to run for office. In 1995, McIntyre decided to run. When Rose four months later decided to retire, seven Democrats and four Republicans filed. McIntyre's chief opposition in the primary was Rose Marie Lowry-Townsend, a Lumbee and a liberal, who had support from the National Education Association, labor PACs and national women's groups. Lowry-Townsend led McIntyre 30%-23% in the primary. In the runoff McIntyre called for smaller government, cited his close ties to the district and involvement in community activities, and won 52%-48%. McIntyre's platform was almost as conservative as that of his Republican opponent, who ridiculed McIntyre's emphasis on his community ties: "While it's all well and good to coach Little League, that doesn't mean you're ready to go to Congress." McIntyre won 53%-46%.

McIntyre joined the conservative Blue Dog Democrats and got seats on Armed Services and Agriculture. His voting record—conservative among Democrats, especially on cultural issues—stands slightly left of the middle of the House. He voted for the anti-flag burning amendment, the partial-birth abortion ban, and constitutional ban on same-sex marriage, and he placed the Ten Commandments in his office. But he supported racial quotas and preferences and opposed school vouchers.

McIntyre has co-chaired the Rural Health Care Coalition and co-chaired caucuses on fatherhood and Special Operations Forces. He opposed normal trade relations with China and trade promotion authority, and he sought to impose a higher tariff on new imports of Caribbean Basin footwear; Converse's plant west of Lumberton was once the country's largest shoe factory. He proposed additional subsistence payments and job-training assistance for workers who have lost their jobs because of NAFTA; he estimated the loss at nearly 10,000 jobs in Robeson and Columbus Counties. With support from Senators Elizabeth Dole and Richard Burr, McIntyre sought to break the deadlock in the century-old battle for federal recognition of the Lumbees, which other tribes have opposed as too costly. As many of the troops based in the district headed to the Persian Gulf, McIntyre voted to authorize the use of force in Iraq, but he later criticized the Bush administration for its post-Saddam planning and its slowness in giving more control to the Iraqis.

McIntyre has won endorsements from the U.S. Chamber of Commerce, Gary Bauer's Campaign for Working Families and the VFW; Republicans have not seriously challenged him. McIntyre says that he is not interested in switching parties, having been active in the Democratic Party since high school. He has been reelected without serious opposition. He now chairs the Specialty Crops, Rural Development and Foreign Agriculture Subcommittee, and was expected to play a big role on the new farm bill.

EIGHTH DISTRICT

Rep. Robin Hayes (R)

Elected 1998, 5th term; b. Aug. 14, 1945, Concord; home, Concord; Duke U., B.A. 1967; Presbyterian; married (Barbara).

Elected Office: Concord Bd. of Aldermen, 1978-81; NC House of Reps., 1992-96, Maj. Whip, 1995-96.

Professional Career: Owner, Mt. Pleasant Hosiery Mill, 1988-present.

DC Office: 130 CHOB, 20515, 202-225-3715; Fax: 202-225-4036; Web site: hayes.house.gov.

District Offices: Concord, 704-786-1612; Rockingham, 910-997-2070.

Committees: *Agriculture* (5th of 21 R): Livestock, Dairy & Poultry (RMM); Specialty Crops, Rural Development & Foreign Agriculture; Conservation, Credit, Energy & Research. *Armed Services* (9th of 29 R): Terrorism, Unconventional Threats & Capabilities; Readiness. *Transportation & Infrastructure* (13th of 34 R): Water Resources & Environment; Highways & Transit; Aviation.

Group Ratings

	ADA	ACLU	AFS	LCV	ITIC	NTU	COC	ACU	CFG	FRC
2006	5	9	0	17	86	58	93	88	50	100
2005	0	—	0	0	—	55	89	92	46	92

National Journal Ratings

	2005 LIB	—	2005 CONS		2006 LIB	—	2006 CONS
Economic	30%	—	68%		32%	—	67%
Social	0%	—	89%		11%	—	85%
Foreign	16%	—	84%		17%	—	73%

Key Votes of the 109th Congress

1. Estate Tax Repeal	Y	5. Limit Interstate Abortion	Y	9. Build Border Fence	Y
2. Limit CAFE Standards	Y	6. Extend Patriot Act	Y	10. CAFTA	Y
3. FY06 Spending Curb	Y	7. Bar Same Sex Marriage	Y	11. Oppose Iraq Withdrawal	Y
4. Drilling in ANWR	Y	8. Stem Cell Research $	N	12. Detainee Tribunals	Y

Election Results

2006 general	Robin Hayes (R)	60,926	(50%)	($2,475,169)
	Larry Kissell (D)	60,597	(50%)	($803,841)
2006 primary	Robin Hayes (R) .... unopposed			
2004 general	Robin Hayes (R)	125,070	(56%)	($1,611,679)
	Beth Troutman (D)	100,101	(44%)	($225,675)

Prior Winning Percentages: 2002 (54%); 2000 (55%); 1998 (51%)

The People		Race/Ethnic Origin	Ancestry	
Area size:	3,318 sq. mi.	61.8% White	USA: 10.8%	German: 7.6%
Urban population:	69.4%	26.6% Black	English: 5.9%	
Rural population:	30.6%	1.7% Asian	**2004 Presidential Vote**	
Pop. 2000:	619,178	1.7% Native Am.	Bush (R) 126,041	(54%)
Pop. 2005 (est):	655,810	0.1% Hawaiian	Kerry (D) 105,248	(45%)
Median income:	$38,390	1.4% Two+ races	Other 815	(0%)
Poverty status:	12.4%	0.2% Other	**2000 Presidential Vote**	
Military veterans:	14.0%	6.6% Hispanic Origin	Bush (R) 105,484	(54%)
			Gore (D) 89,672	(46%)
			Other 1,568	(1%)
			Cook Partisan Voting Index: R + 3	
Occupation Blue collar: 31.8%	White collar: 53.3%	Gray collar: 14.9%		

In the Carolina Piedmont, ranging from Atlanta to Durham along Interstate 85, lies the thickest concentration of America's once-mightytextile industry. Within North Carolina, I-85 brushes past Concord and Kannapolis, the latter named for its founding company, Cannon Mills. While eastern Carolina was settled by Englishmen from the coast, this Piedmont land was settled mainly by Scots and diverse groups like Quakers and Moravian sects, coming down the Blue Ridge from Pennsylvania through Virginia. These migratory patterns were reflected in Civil War divisions and continue in current voting habits. The coastal counties all the way up through the Sand Hills were Confederate and are now Democratic. The textile mill towns along I-85 were anti-secession and are now Republican.

Parts of both these areas are in the 8th Congressional District. The most populous county in the district is Cabarrus County, which includes the southern end of the textile corridor around Kannapolis and Concord. In recent years, Cabarrus, fed by migration from Charlotte, has moved beyond its textile and small town roots and become an exurban county, growing by 58% from 1990 to 2006; it now casts one-fourth of the district's votes. The bankruptcy of Pillowtex (once known as Cannon Mills) in 2003 eliminated some 4,800 jobs in Cabarrus and Rowan Counties; it was a major setback to the old way of life. The 8th extends east to include part of Fayetteville's Cumberland County, which casts 19% of the vote, but stops short of the military neighborhoods just outside the gates of Fort Bragg. Democratic redistricters included as much of the Democratic Sand Hills as they could, and removed most of Union County, a fast-growing and heavily Republican area just east of

Charlotte. And they added central city precincts in Charlotte with some blacks and some affluent white liberals. This split-personality district has usually been carried by Republican presidential candidates and by North Carolina Democrats in close statewide contests. Both parties have long targeted it as a marginal district, though over the past three decades it has only changed political hands twice, in 1974 and 1998.

The congressman from the 8th District is Robin Hayes, a Republican elected in 1998. He grew up in Concord, the grandson of Cannon Mills founder Charles Cannon, a legendary figure in textile country, once the dominant economic and political force in this part of North Carolina. Hayes graduated from Duke and returned to Concord, where he ran several businesses—selling Mack trucks, building highways, running the Mount Pleasant Hosiery Mills. He coached football at a local college and worked in the Prison Fellowship movement. He was elected a Concord alderman and in 1991 he switched to the Republican Party. In 1992 Hayes was elected to the North Carolina House, and became majority whip. In 1996 he ran for governor, won the Republican primary, but lost to Jim Hunt 56%-43%.

In November 1997 Hayes announced he was running against Democratic Congressman Bill Hefner; two months later, Hefner surprised just about everyone by announcing that he would retire. After several better-known Democrats decided not to run, Mike Taylor, a Stanly County lawyer with an attractive biography but little name recognition, emerged as the nominee. Hayes campaigned on a standard conservative platform, stressing the issues he had pushed in the legislature and calling for "top-to-bottom comprehensive tax reform." Taylor's military record helped him win the endorsement of the VFW, but Hayes outspent him by 3–1. Hayes won 51%-48%.

One of the wealthiest members of Congress, Hayes has compiled a conservative voting record, with an occasional populist streak, devoting much of his energy to getting federal money for the folks back home. In December 2001, he became the focal point in the dramatic House vote on trade promotion authority. The Republican leadership took the issue to the floor without having a majority of votes in hand and held the vote open until they could squeeze them out. Hayes delayed casting his vote and, with the outcome still in doubt, he found himself surrounded by Republican leaders pleading for his vote. After his "aye" vote produced a 215-214 victory for Bush, Hayes broke down in tears in the House chamber after what he called "a very intense experience." Later, he said that he got no projects for his district in exchange for the vote, but that George W. Bush had assured him that he would treat the textile industry fairly in future trade agreements, and that textiles imported from the Caribbean would have to be finished and dyed in the United States. When the final House-Senate agreement came for a vote in July 2002, Hayes voted against it because it permitted additional textile and apparel imports; others provided the majority this time. Republicans embraced him as a hero for putting his career on the line, and Democrats vowed that Hayes would pay the price in the next election. On the Central America Free Trade Agreement in 2005, the scenario seemed familiar: Republican leaders were barely short of a majority; they appealed to Hayes, who initially was opposed. Days before the vote he told the *Charlotte Observer* that he was "flat out, completely, horizontally opposed to CAFTA." But he changed his vote at the last minute to help the bill pass by a one-vote margin. In response to reports that U.S. Border Patrol agents wear uniforms made in Mexico, he sponsored legislation requiring the Homeland Security Department to buy American -made materials only.

Democrats have regularly targeted Hayes but he has hung on with at least 54% each time. In 2006, Democratic efforts to recruit Iraq war veteran Tim Dunn fell short and party leaders all but wrote off the contest. But this turned out to be a good year for Democrats, and challenger Larry Kissell, a former textile worker who became a high-school teacher, had some attention-grabbing gimmicks. Kissell targeted Hayes for his trade votes, including appearances with a pygmy goat named CAFTA. He sold gasoline to voters for $1.22 a gallon, the price when Hayes took office. But when he called for campaign help from Washington, he didn't get much response. Four weeks after the votes were cast, Hayes was declared the winner by 329 votes: 50.14%-49.86%. Kissell took Mecklenberg County with 68%, but Hayes won 60% in Cabarrus, 61% in Stanly, and 54% in Cumberland. This was a missed opportunity, as DCCC chairman Rahm Emanuel ruefully conceded. Kissell said that he will run again in 2008, and the DCCC in 2007 was providing him with support for the expected rematch.

NINTH DISTRICT

Rep. Sue Myrick (R)

Elected 1994, 7th term; b. Aug. 1, 1941, Tiffin, OH; home, Charlotte; Heidelberg Col., 1959-60; Methodist; married (Ed).

Elected Office: Charlotte City Cncl., 1983-85; Charlotte Mayor, 1987-91.

Professional Career: Pres. & CEO, Myrick Advertising, 1985-94; Pres. & CEO, Myrick Enterprises, 1992-94.

DC Office: 230 CHOB, 20515, 202-225-1976; Fax: 202-225-3389; Web site: myrick.house.gov.

District Offices: Charlotte, 704-362-1060; Gastonia, 704-861-1976.

Committees: *Energy & Commerce* (22d of 26 R): Health; Commerce, Trade & Consumer Protection; Energy & Air Quality.

Group Ratings

	ADA	ACLU	AFS	LCV	ITIC	NTU	COC	ACU	CFG	FRC
2006	0	5	0	0	100	71	100	92	81	100
2005	0	—	0	6	—	71	87	96	99	100

National Journal Ratings

	2005 LIB	—	2005 CONS		2006 LIB	—	2006 CONS
Economic	8%	—	92%		19%	—	80%
Social	15%	—	84%		0%	—	94%
Foreign	11%	—	86%		6%	—	86%

Key Votes of the 109th Congress

1. Estate Tax Repeal	Y	5. Limit Interstate Abortion	Y	9. Build Border Fence	Y
2. Limit CAFE Standards	Y	6. Extend Patriot Act	Y	10. CAFTA	Y
3. FY06 Spending Curb	*	7. Bar Same Sex Marriage	Y	11. Oppose Iraq Withdrawal	Y
4. Drilling in ANWR	Y	8. Stem Cell Research $	N	12. Detainee Tribunals	Y

Election Results

2006 general	Sue Myrick (R)	106,206	(67%)	($1,262,588)
	Bill Glass (D)	53,437	(33%)	($11,692)
2006 primary	Sue Myrick (R)	unopposed		
2004 general	Sue Myrick (R)	210,783	(70%)	($991,241)
	Jack Flynn (D)	89,318	(30%)	($36,080)

Prior Winning Percentages: 2002 (72%); 2000 (69%); 1998 (69%); 1996 (63%); 1994 (65%)

The People		Race/Ethnic Origin	Ancestry	
Area size:	1,018 sq. mi.	82.9% White	German: 11.2% USA: 9.5%	
Urban population:	84.2%	10.3% Black	English: 9.0%	
Rural population:	15.8%	2.0% Asian	**2004 Presidential Vote**	
Pop. 2000:	619,178	0.3% Native Am.	Bush (R)	193,419 (63%)
Pop. 2005 (est):	740,132	0.0% Hawaiian	Kerry (D)	110,769 (36%)
Median income:	$55,059	0.8% Two+ races	Other	1,134 (0%)
Poverty status:	6.2%	0.1% Other	**2000 Presidential Vote**	
Military veterans:	12.4%	3.5% Hispanic Origin	Bush (R)	157,734 (63%)
			Gore (D)	91,353 (36%)
			Other	2,066 (1%)
			Cook Partisan Voting Index: R +12	
Occupation	Blue collar: 20.4%	White collar: 69.5%	Gray collar: 10.2%	

"An agreeable village but in a damn rebellious country," recorded General Cornwallis when, before the unpleasantness at Yorktown, he visited Charlotte, North Carolina. "A veritable nest of hornets." This town, settled by Scots-Irish and German colonists who came down the Blue Ridge from Pennsylvania, is now a rapidly-growing metropolitan area of 1.5 million people. Before the California gold rush, Charlotte was the gold mining capital of the country; in 1837, the U.S. Mint established a branch here. Now, Charlotte is headquarters to two of the nation's biggest banks: Bank of America, formed from the 1998 merger of Charlotte-based NationsBank and San Francisco's Bank of America; and Wachovia, created by the 2001 merger of Charlotte's First Union and Winston-Salem's Wachovia. All told, $1.8 trillion in banking resources are headquartered in Charlotte—more than in any American city except New York. Charlotte is also home to nine companies in the Fortune 500, including Duke Energy, Sonic Automotive, B.F. Goodrich and Nucor; it is the center of the nation's biggest textile manufacturing region, and serves as a hub for troubled USAirways.

The past two decades have brought Charlotte cultural growth worthy of its growing business stature. It now boasts a $50 million performing arts center across from the 60-story Bank of America tower, and is home to the NFL Panthers and the NBA Bobcats franchise owned by Black Entertainment Television founder Robert Johnson. The rebelliousness Cornwallis noted can be seen in this region's passion for the booming stock-car circuit: One of the nation's biggest auto-racing tracks is here, and just up the road is Mooresville, home of the sport's giant, the late Dale Earnhardt, and the family's racing business. In 2010, the NASCAR Hall of Fame is scheduled to open in Charlotte. The city has built a boosterish pride in its capacity for accommodation. It is proud that it responded amicably to a busing order approved in a landmark Supreme Court case in 1971; that it twice elected Harvey Gantt, who is black, then replaced him with Sue Myrick, a Republican whose grievance wasn't race but traffic. Charlotte's metro area is projected to equal Atlanta's by 2030, and environmental critics said it had the worst sprawl of the 15 fast-growing metro areas.

The 9th Congressional District of North Carolina includes about half of Mecklenburg County; it extends west to include most of Gaston County, long a textile center, and south to take in upscale bedroom communities in Union County, North Carolina's fastest-growing county from 1990 to 2006 (population up 108%), where one-seventh of the population is employed in construction. Mecklenburg County as a whole is politically marginal, but the 9th District is overwhelmingly Republican. With 20% growth between 2000 and 2005, this is the state's fastest-growing congressional district.

The congresswoman from the 9th District is Sue Myrick, a Republican first elected in 1994. Myrick grew up and went to college in Ohio, raised her family in Charlotte, owned an advertising agency and Amway distributorship. In 1981 she ran for the Charlotte city council and lost. She ran again and won in 1983, ran for mayor and lost in 1985, then beat Harvey Gantt in 1987. Despite nasty personal charges, she was reelected in 1989; she is proud of making infrastructure improvements and preventing property tax increases for four years. Myrick ran for the Senate in 1992, but was beaten by Lauch Faircloth in the primary 48%-30%. In 1994 Charlotte Congressman Alex McMillan, passed over for the ranking position on the House Budget Committee, retired. In the first round of the primary, against State House Minority Leader David Balmer, Myrick led 34%-28%. Before the runoff three weeks later, it was revealed that he had falsely claimed on his resume to have graduated in the top 20% of his law school class and to have played varsity soccer. Myrick won 68%-32%, then easily won the general. Myrick was a leader of the 1994 Republican freshman class. She served on Newt Gingrich's transition team and was freshman liaison to the leadership. But she communicated with leaders of the unsuccessful coup against Gingrich in July 1997, and later that month lost the post of Conference secretary by 110-65 to Deborah Pryce, whom Gingrich backed.

Myrick, a reliable conservative, has taken a lead role on many Republican initiatives. Representing a prosperous and growing district, she turned down the Transportation Committee's offer of $15 million for Charlotte's outerbelt because she felt the transportation bill would bust the budget: "I said when I ran for this job, 'If you want somebody to bring home the bacon, don't send me.'" With relatively few textile workers in her district, she voted for trade promotion authority. After apparent congressional leaks of post-September 11 intelligence data, Myrick proposed that members of Congress undergo the same background checks as non-elected security officials. Not surprisingly, the bill was not passed. A vocal opponent of illegal immigration, she won House approval in December 2005 of a measure to deport illegal immigrants convicted of drunk-driving. On the proposal for Dubai Ports World to purchase several U.S. ports, she wrote President Bush: "Not just NO—but HELL NO!"

Myrick had surgery for breast cancer in 1999 and underwent three months of chemotherapy and another six weeks of radiation treatment. After that, she sponsored the law to provide Medicaid coverage for low-income women for mammograms and pap smears. Myrick co-chaired the Cancer Caucus, and cosponsored with Nita Lowey a bill to require the National Institutes of Health to explore the connection between the environment and cancer. Myrick was declared cancer-free. In

January 2005, after eight years on the leadership-controlled Rules Committee, she switched to Energy and Commerce, where she focused on health care, including mental health.

After the 2002 election, Myrick filed a change in the rules of the House Republican Conference to require that each Appropriations subcommittee chairman secure party approval; Speaker Dennis Hastert modified the proposal to give the review power to the leadership's Steering Committee, and it was approved. In 2003, she became chairman of the expanded Republican Study Committee, activist conservatives who have urged spending restraint. She said that she felt "betrayed" by Senate Republicans for halving President Bush's proposed tax cuts, and that they needed to "get a handle on the deficit." Myrick considered, but quickly decided against, Senate bids in 2002 and 2004. She also turned down calls to run for governor in 2008. She has won reelection easily.

TENTH DISTRICT

Rep. Patrick McHenry (R)

Elected 2004, 2d term; b. Oct. 22, 1975, Charlotte; home, Cherryville; Attended NC St. U., Belmont Abbey Col., B.A. 1999; Catholic; single.

Elected Office: NC House of Reps., 2002-04.

Professional Career: Real estate broker, 2000-02.

DC Office: 224 CHOB, 20515, 202-225-2576; Fax: 202-225-0316; Web site: mchenry.house.gov.

District Offices: Hickory, 828-327-6100; Shelby, 704-481-0578; Spruce Pine, 828-765-2729.

Committees: *Budget* (9th of 17 R). *Financial Services* (26th of 33 R): Oversight & Investigations; Domestic and International Monetary Policy, Trade & Technology; Financial Institutions & Consumer Credit. *Oversight & Government Reform* (14th of 18 R): National Security & Foreign Affairs.

Group Ratings

	ADA	ACLU	AFS	LCV	ITIC	NTU	COC	ACU	CFG	FRC
2006	10	5	0	0	71	75	93	92	86	100
2005	5	—	0	11	—	70	89	100	96	100

National Journal Ratings

	2005 LIB	—	2005 CONS	2006 LIB	—	2006 CONS
Economic	0%	—	97%	9%	—	91%
Social	12%	—	86%	0%	—	94%
Foreign	17%	—	79%	17%	—	73%

Key Votes of the 109th Congress

1. Estate Tax Repeal	Y	5. Limit Interstate Abortion	Y	9. Build Border Fence	Y
2. Limit CAFE Standards	Y	6. Extend Patriot Act	Y	10. CAFTA	N
3. FY06 Spending Curb	Y	7. Bar Same Sex Marriage	Y	11. Oppose Iraq Withdrawal	Y
4. Drilling in ANWR	Y	8. Stem Cell Research $	N	12. Detainee Tribunals	Y

Election Results

2006 general	Patrick McHenry (R)	94,179	(62%)	($1,339,776)
	Richard Carsner (D)	58,214	(38%)	($22,724)
2006 primary	Patrick McHenry (R)	unopposed		
2004 general	Patrick McHenry (R)	157,884	(64%)	($936,071)
	Anne Fischer (D)	88,233	(36%)	($10,710)

The People		Race/Ethnic Origin	Ancestry	
Area size:	3,362 sq. mi.	84.9% White	USA: 16.5%	German: 10.4%
Urban population:	49.9%	9.2% Black	English: 6.9%	
Rural population:	50.1%	1.5% Asian	**2004 Presidential Vote**	
Pop. 2000:	619,178	0.2% Native Am.	Bush (R) 169,484	(67%)
Pop. 2005 (est):	652,606	0.0% Hawaiian	Kerry (D) 82,965	(33%)
Median income:	$37,649	0.7% Two+ races	Other 1,043	(0%)
Poverty status:	10.6%	0.1% Other	**2000 Presidential Vote**	
Military veterans:	12.8%	3.5% Hispanic Origin	Bush (R) 143,124	(65%)
			Gore (D) 75,592	(34%)
			Other 1,693	(1%)
			Cook Partisan Voting Index: R +15	

Occupation	Blue collar: 41.9%	White collar: 45.4%	Gray collar: 12.6%

Steeped in the hues that gave them the name "Blue Ridge," the heavily wooded mountains of North Carolina seem placid and ancient. Geologically, they are some of the oldest ranges in the world; economically, the region is blue collar and oriented towards manufacturing, though there is some cotton farming, too. During the 1990s, residents here benefited from investment in fiber-optic factories, which, along with the general economic boom, helped reduce the local unemployment rate to near-record lows. But the Internet bust hurt the fiber-optic business; textiles and furniture were also troubled, and the local unemployment rate rose. At the same time, this corner of North Carolina is adapting—as are so many other rural areas in the U.S.—to growing diversity. County seats like Morganton in Burke County are now home not just to Hispanics but to newcomers from Laos; the influx of recent arrivals has prompted some anti-immigrant backlash in this previously insular region, including the occasional rejection of school bond proposals on the grounds that they could help immigrants disproportionately. Ironically, the area desperately needs more education: The region around Hickory, in Catawba County, ranked last among the state's 11 metropolitan areas in education rates. A Census report found almost a third of adults in this districtlacked a high-school degree. The Catawba Valley has produced about one-third of the nation's hosiery and remains a furniture center, but it has suffered major job losses due to international competition and is at risk of more competitive threats, especially from China.

The 10th Congressional District of North Carolina stretches across the state from Tennessee, where the mountains are high enough to support a modest ski industry, to the South Carolina border. It is a district comprised mostly of small towns; it is still predominantly white, ranges throughout 10 counties, and is bisected by Interstate 40. The largest population center in the 10th is Hickory in Catawba County, which accounts for just over 20% of the district's population. This remains a very Republican area—home to a rough-hewn, hill variety of Republicanism that is unsympathetic to government regulators, from factory inspectors to revenuers on the lookout for illegal stills. Despite job losses and worries about international competition that increasingly have made this a service economy, it remains one of North Carolina's most Republican districts, and George W. Bush got 67% here in 2004.

The congressman from the 10th District is Patrick McHenry, a Republican elected at age 29 in 2004—since then, the youngest member of Congress. He grew up in Cherryville, graduated from Belmont Abbey College and served as president of the state College Republicans. After college, he became a real estate broker. In 1997, after Bill Clinton was accused of rewarding big contributors with nights in the Lincoln bedroom and then made a trip to North Carolina, McHenry stood along the motorcade route dressed in a Abraham Lincoln costume with a sign reading, "Who's been sleeping in my bed?" In 2000 he ran a web site, *www.notHillary.com*, opposing Hillary Rodham Clinton's Senate candidacy in New York. At the start of the Bush administration, he was appointed to a job in the Labor Department. In 2002 he was elected to the state House.

When 10th District Congressman Cass Ballenger announced his retirement, McHenry was one of four Republicans running to succeed him. In a district ranking first among 435 in percentage of manufacturing and blue-collar jobs, trade policy and job creation issues seemed likely to dominate the debate. But the two candidates who made conservative "Christian values" their focal point— McHenry and Catawba County Sheriff David Huffman—were the leading vote-getters in the primary. Huffman finished first with 35%, but was forced to a runoff against McHenry with 26%. Retired cable television executive Sandy Lyons, a self-financing millionaire who was endorsed by Ballenger, ran an unexpectedly poor third, with 20%. In the four-week runoff, the campaign took a negative turn. Huffman questioned McHenry's record as a businessman and accused him of having noisy all-night parties at his house, which also served as his campaign headquarters and residence for some of his campaign staffers; six of McHenry's neighbors later insisted Huffman's claim was untrue. McHenry accused Huffman of campaign finance irregularities and called him a friend of Bill Clinton. McHenry said he and his energetic grassroots campaign knocked on more than 60,000 doors and made 100,000 phone calls. In television ads, he billed himself as a "pro-life, pro-gun, anti-gay-marriage," Christian conservative. He was endorsed by the Wall Street-based Club for Growth. McHenry won the runoff by 85 votes, after a recount. Huffman carried Catawba County 59%-41%. But McHenry rolled up huge majorities in the counties south of I-40 and close to his Gaston County home. He easily won the general against Anne Fischer, who lost her home to foreclosure during the campaign and described herself as a part-time stress release facilitator.

In the House, McHenry is a sharp-edged and gleeful partisan, always eager to needle Democrats, and has the most conservative record in the North Carolina delegation. He cites former Senator Jesse Helms as his role model. His top legislative priorities have been job creation, allowing small business owners to form pools to purchase health insurance and Social Security reform, including personal retirement accounts. The House passed his amendment to limit foreign aid to nations that refuse to extradite suspects accused of killing U.S. law enforcement officers. He is vigorously anti-abortion and pro-gun, and voted against the Central America Free Trade Agreement and extension of the Voting Rights Act. On the Financial Services committee, he pushed a bill to ease requirements on credit unions seeking to convert to a mutual savings bank or association; many credit unions opposed the measure. When Tom DeLay was asked in 2006 who might be "the next Tom DeLay" in Congress, he listed McHenry, along with Mike Pence and Adam Putnam. McHenry said that he was "honored that such a strong leader of the conservative movement would say that." On the opening of the new Congress in 2007, he accused Speaker Nancy Pelosi of "hypocrisy" for shutting Republicans out of the legislative process. He joined the NRCC's executive committee to oversee spending of independent expenditures.

At home, where some hard feelings still linger from the hard-fought 2004 primary, Hickory Mayor Rudy Wright thought about a Republican primary challenge to McHenry in 2006, but backed off after he was told that "some heavyweight people" in Washington would make sure that he did not win. McHenry was reelected easily and should have plenty of freedom to gain influence in the House.

ELEVENTH DISTRICT

Rep. Heath Shuler (D)

Elected 2006, 1st term; b. Dec. 31, 1971, Bryson City; home, Waynesville; U of TN, B.A. 2001; Baptist; married (Nikol).

Professional Career: Pro football player, 1994-98; Owner, Heath Shuler Real Estate, 1998-2003; Property development investor.

DC Office: 512 CHOB, 20515, 202-225-6401; Fax: 202-226-6422; Web site: shuler.house.gov.

District Offices: Asheville, 828-252-1651.

Committees: *Natural Resources* (27th of 27 D): National Parks, Forests & Public Lands. *Small Business* (2d of 18 D): Rural & Urban Entrepreneurship (Chmn.). *Transportation & Infrastructure* (33d of 41 D): Water Resources & Environment; Highways & Transit.

Group Ratings and Key Votes: Newly Elected

Election Results

2006 general	Heath Shuler (D)	124,972	(54%)	($1,804,365)
	Charles Taylor (R)	107,342	(46%)	($4,425,482)
2006 primary	Heath Shuler (D)	29,921	(75%)	
	Michael Morgan (D)	10,180	(25%)	
2004 general	Charles Taylor (R)	159,709	(55%)	($2,083,993)
	Patsy Keever (D)	131,188	(45%)	($1,224,306)

The People		Race/Ethnic Origin	Ancestry	
Area size:	6,088 sq. mi.	89.8% White	USA: 13.2%	English: 9.8%
Urban population:	43.9%	4.6% Black	German: 8.7%	
Rural population:	56.1%	0.5% Asian	**2004 Presidential Vote**	
Pop. 2000:	619,177	1.5% Native Am.	Bush (R) 169,872	(57%)
Pop. 2005 (est):	651,897	0.0% Hawaiian	Kerry (D) 126,979	(43%)
Median income:	$34,720	0.9% Two+ races	Other 1,747	(1%)
Poverty status:	12.0%	0.1% Other	**2000 Presidential Vote**	
Military veterans:	15.6%	2.6% Hispanic Origin	Bush (R) 150,004	(58%)
			Gore (D) 102,321	(40%)
			Other 4,514	(2%)
			Cook Partisan Voting Index: R + 7	

Occupation	Blue collar: 31.5%	White collar: 51.9%	Gray collar: 16.6%

Western North Carolina, the protrusion of the Tar Heel state deep into the eastern United States' highest and oldest mountains, is a land of long and ornery traditions. First settled by whites not long after the Revolutionary War, it still has Indian communities and hollows where people are descended from the first white settlers. Its biggest city, Asheville, memorialized in Thomas Wolfe's novels, was a retreat for lung patients. Asheville was also the home of the brilliant eccentric George Vanderbilt, who built the chateau-like Biltmore mansion amidst vast forests on which he pioneered scientific forestry. A dozen miles east was Black Mountain College, frequented by such innovators as Buckminster Fuller and minimalist composer John Cage. Asheville's historic structures, from Gothic Revival to Art Deco, remain well preserved and are a magnet for tourists, who in turn support some of the few coffeehouses, microbreweries and artsy cinemas within hours of here. Not far to the west is the Eastern Band of Cherokee's gambling casino, which has given the tribe a yearly budget of $130 million and considerable political influence. Over a ridge is the Great Smoky Mountains National Park, the nation's most heavily visited, 20 degrees cooler in the summer than the lowland towns an hour or so away. The climate and the forested, green, fog-wisped mountains have attracted millions of tourists to this area—so many that, every summer, the park's one transverse road becomes hopelessly clogged with traffic. And many Americans bring a little bit of western North Carolina home with them each winter: the Fraser fir trees that grow on private land in the mountains are America's favorite Christmas trees ("incomparable needle retention", boosters say), and North Carolina is the number two state in the business.

The 11th District of North Carolina includes the western end of the state, including Asheville's Buncombe County, which accounts for one-third of the votes. Less than 5% of the voters in the district are black, the lowest percentage in any district in North Carolina. The orneriness of the mountain country has been manifest in its politics. This part of the state was reluctant to secede in the Civil War. There were few slaves and many small farmers loyal to the Union, and those who took up the Confederate cause did so out of loyalty to Governor Zebulon Vance, an Asheville native and reluctant secessionist. For a long time, the partisan balance here was close, and for a dozen years the 11th was one of the nation's most closely contested districts, throwing out incumbents in five of six elections between 1980 and 1990. But in the last dozen years, coinciding with an influx of retirees in the mountains south of Asheville, it has tilted Republican. In 2004, however, it was one North Carolina district which gave George W. Bush a slightly lower percentage than it did in 2000.

The new congressman from the 11th District is Heath Shuler, a Democrat elected in 2006. Shuler, the son of a mailman, grew up on Toot Hollow Road in tiny Bryson City, closer to the Tennessee line than to Asheville. Shuler led Swain County High School to three state football championships and starred as quarterback at the University of Tennessee, where he was the 1993 runner-up for the Heisman Trophy. The Washington Redskins picked Shuler, then a college junior, third in the 1994 draft and first among quarterbacks. He played three disappointing seasons before being traded to the New Orleans Saints, where he injured his left foot when a 334-pound defensive tackle fell on him. He attempted a comeback but was reinjured while playing for the Oakland Raiders. Shuler was a bust in pro football, but he remained a hero in Swain County and western North Carolina. He founded a successful real estate business in Knoxville, Tennessee, with his brother, and returned to North Carolina with his family in 2003. Shuler still cuts the figure of a professional athlete, wears his NFL alumni ring and, like in his playing days, does not smoke or drink alcohol or soda. All of this made him an attractive candidate for public office and Democrats aggressively recruited him in 2006. Rahm Emanuel allayed Shuler's fears about missing time with his children by persistently calling Shuler on his cell phone each time he dropped his own children off at school or attended their events. This wasn't the first time Shuler was sought as a candidate: Republicans in 2002 also had tried to get Shuler to run in Tennessee, but he declined.

Shuler's opponent was eight-term incumbent Charles Taylor, a Republican who had faced competitive races the past three elections. Democrats had attacked Taylor for his business dealings. Two associates at a bank Taylor controlled pleaded guilty to bank fraud charges; Taylor's business relationship with a former Russian KGB general also attracted attention. Although Taylor had survived those controversies, the Democratic Congressional Campaign Committee again tried to make them liabilities by running newspaper ads in July 2005. Shuler announced his candidacy later that same month. Taylor provided Democrats with fresh controversies: he did not record a vote in 2005 for the Central America Free Trade Agreement, which was passed only narrowly by 217-215 vote. This was no small matter, for trade pacts are unpopular in North Carolina, where they are blamed for the loss of textile jobs. Taylor explained that he had actually cast a no vote, but said a computer glitch with the House's electronic voting system did not register his vote. He received additional unflattering attention when, as chairman of the Interior Appropriations Subcommittee, in 2006 he opposed a $10 million request to buy land in Shanksville, Pennsylvania, for a permanent memorial for the hijacked United Airlines flight 93 that crashed there on September 11, 2001. Taylor said he was opposed in principle to the government owning more land and he also worried that taxpayers would have to pick up the cost of the project if private donations fell short. He later relented, but his opposition made him appear out of touch.

Taylor sought to tie Shuler to national Democrats. "Rookie Heath Shuler is following the playbook of San Francisco liberal Nancy Pelosi," claimed one radio ad, as stadium crowd noises buzzed in the background. "The Pelosi game plan: Elect Heath Shuler and others like him, and take over Congress with the votes of illegal immigrants." Shuler was not an easy target: he had no legislative record to mine for controversial votes and his politics are in line with the socially conservative district. He campaigned on "mountain values" and he opposes abortion rights, gay marriage and gun control. Shuler stumped on health care, education, expanding economic opportunities, reducing the federal deficit and a change in Iraq war policies. He spent $10,000 to emblazon his name on a car at a NASCAR race. Taylor, who was an Appropriations Committee "cardinal," campaigned on his ability to bring home federal money and its positive impact in the district. In October, with polls showing Taylor trailing, the *Wall Street Journal* ran a story about earmarks sought by Taylor that had the effect of benefiting many of his own business interests. Shuler never actually met the incumbent over the course of the campaign: Taylor hadn't debated an opponent since 1994, and a joint radio debate fell apart after Taylor opted to call in rather than appear at the station.

The incumbent poured $2.5 million of his own money into his race, and spent $4.4 million overall, compared to Shuler's $1.8 million. But Shuler won 54%-46%, an impressive showing for a novice candidate against an incumbent in a conservative district. Most of his margin came in Asheville's Buncombe County, but he carried 9 of the district's 15 counties overall. After the election, Shuler joined the Blue Dog Coalition of conservative Democrats and became chairman of the Small Business Rural and Urban Entrepreneurship Subcommittee. He voted for the Democrats' 100-hour legislative agenda, except for lifting the ban on federal funding for embryonic stem-cell research. As a freshman in a Republican-leaning district in a presidential election year, Shuler could face strong Republican opposition in 2008; through September 2007, possible candidates were awaiting Taylor's decision on whether to seek a rematch.

TWELFTH DISTRICT

Rep. Melvin Watt (D)

Elected 1992, 8th term; b. Aug. 26, 1945, Mecklenburg; home, Charlotte; U. of NC, B.S. 1967, Yale U., J.D. 1970; Presbyterian; married (Eulada).

Elected Office: NC Senate, 1984-86.

Professional Career: Practicing atty., 1971-92; Co–owner, East Town Manor nursing home, 1989-present; Campaign Mgr., Harvey Gantt Senate Campaign, 1990.

DC Office: 2236 RHOB, 20515, 202-225-1510; Fax: 202-225-1512; Web site: watt.house.gov.

District Offices: Charlotte, 704-344-9950; Greensboro, 336-275-9950.

Committees: *Financial Services* (7th of 37 D): Oversight & Investigations (Chmn.); Financial Institutions & Consumer Credit. *Judiciary* (6th of 23 D): Courts, the Internet & Intellectual Property; Commercial & Administrative Law; The Constitution, Civil Rights & Civil Liberties.

Group Ratings

	ADA	ACLU	AFS	LCV	ITIC	NTU	COC	ACU	CFG	FRC
2006	95	100	100	92	57	14	47	4	4	0
2005	100	—	100	94	—	15	35	0	3	0

National Journal Ratings

	2005 LIB	—	2005 CONS	2006 LIB	—	2006 CONS
Economic	88%	—	9%	74%	—	23%
Social	90%	—	9%	90%	—	10%
Foreign	96%	—	0%	92%	—	5%

Key Votes of the 109th Congress

1. Estate Tax Repeal	N	5. Limit Interstate Abortion	N	9. Build Border Fence	N
2. Limit CAFE Standards	Y	6. Extend Patriot Act	N	10. CAFTA	N
3. FY06 Spending Curb	N	7. Bar Same Sex Marriage	N	11. Oppose Iraq Withdrawal	N
4. Drilling in ANWR	N	8. Stem Cell Research $	Y	12. Detainee Tribunals	N

Election Results

2006 general	Melvin Watt (D)	71,345	(67%)	($535,743)
	Ada Fisher (R)	35,127	(33%)	($446,779)
2006 primary	Melvin Watt (D)	unopposed		
2004 general	Melvin Watt (D)	154,908	(67%)	($519,881)
	Ada Fisher (R)	76,898	(33%)	($104,667)

Prior Winning Percentages: 2002 (65%); 2000 (65%); 1998 (56%); 1996 (71%); 1994 (66%); 1992 (70%)

The People		Race/Ethnic Origin	Ancestry	
Area size:	827 sq. mi.	44.6% White	USA: 8.0%	German: 6.5%
Urban population:	88.5%	44.6% Black	English: 4.6%	
Rural population:	11.5%	2.1% Asian	**2004 Presidential Vote**	
Pop. 2000:	619,178	0.4% Native Am.	Kerry (D) 149,940	(63%)
Pop. 2005 (est):	656,214	0.0% Hawaiian	Bush (R) 88,955	(37%)
Median income:	$35,775	1.1% Two+ races	Other 871	(0%)
Poverty status:	15.9%	0.1% Other	**2000 Presidential Vote**	
Military veterans:	11.3%	7.1% Hispanic Origin	Gore (D) 115,445	(57%)
			Bush (R) 85,950	(42%)
			Other 1,495	(1%)
			Cook Partisan Voting Index: D +11	
Occupation	Blue collar: 32.1%	White collar: 51.9%	Gray collar: 16.0%	

"This is perhaps the Negro's temporary farewell to Congress," said George White, a Tarboro, North Carolina lawyer and Republican, in his last days in the House of Representatives in 1901. Segregation was being imposed by law, and blacks informally but effectively were being stricken from the voting rolls in the rural South. It was 28 years until another black candidate was elected to

Congress (from Chicago), and 72 years until another African-American won in the South (in Atlanta). When George White said farewell, most North Carolina blacks lived on farms or in tiny towns. As the 20th century went on, few moved to the textile towns, where most mills hired only whites, but some blacks did move to North Carolina's larger cities. In the years after the Voting Rights Act of 1965, these blacks were numerous enough to elect members to the state legislature, and some black candidates managed to appeal to enough whites to win in white-majority constituencies, notably Charlotte Mayor Harvey Gantt. But North Carolina blacks were not concentrated in high enough numbers either in the rural areas or in the cities to constitute geographically regularly shaped black-majority constituencies, and no North Carolina black followed George White to Congress until the Democratic legislature after the 1990 Census drew two irregularly shaped black-majority districts. That resulted in the election in 1992 of Eva Clayton in the mostly rural and small-town 1st District—and Mel Watt in the 12th District, whose original boundaries connected blacks in such far-flung cities as Charlotte, Winston-Salem, Greensboro and Durham.

This 12th Congressional District of North Carolina was the most litigated district in the country during the 1990s, and was the focus of no less than four Supreme Court cases. Its original shape—a series of scattered black precincts connected in some places by nothing wider than the lanes of Interstate 85—stretched 160 miles from Gastonia, west of Charlotte, through Winston-Salem and Greensboro all the way to Durham. In the current version, drawn in 2001, the 12th remains a 100-mile-long, snake-like agglomeration that roughly parallels I-85 and includes black voters in and near Charlotte, Winston-Salem, Greensboro, Lexington, Salisbury and High Point, the international furniture center. A near-majority, 45%, of its residents are black. The Charlotte-area precincts account for a bit more than one-third of the district population, the Greensboro area is slightly more than 20%, while the Winston-Salem portion accounts for a little under 20%. This is North Carolina's most urban district, and includes the nation's second-largest banking center in downtown Charlotte. Politically it is reliably though not overwhelmingly Democratic.

The congressman from the 12th District is Mel Watt, a Democrat first elected in 1992. Watt grew up in a place called Dixie outside Charlotte, now overgrown with woods, in a tin-roofed house with no electricity or running water. His dream was to attend the University of North Carolina, and he was one of the first black students there; he made a fine academic record, went on to Yale Law School, and then to a civil rights law practice in Charlotte. He served one term in the state Senate, then decided not to seek office again until his sons completed high school. He managed Harvey Gantt's campaigns for city council and mayor in the 1980s and for the U.S. Senate in 1990.

In 1992 Watt decided to run in the 12th District. The contest turned out to be the kind of friends-and-neighbors Democratic primary common in the old segregated South. Watt won 47% in a four-way race; his base in Charlotte was bigger than those of his rivals, and he made inroads in other counties as well. He won the general election easily.

In the House, Watt has compiled a voting record among the most liberal of southern Democrats. He voted against crime bills because of death penalty provisions, against increased prison sentences for crimes against children because he said that would interfere with the U.S. Sentencing Commission's autonomy, and against the constitutional amendment to prohibit desecration of the flag. He vehemently opposed the 1996 Welfare Reform Act; and he cast the only vote in the House against Megan's Law requiring registration of convicted sex offenders because, he said, individuals ought to be able to get on with their lives once they have paid their debt to society. When the Judiciary Committee debated George W. Bush's plan to assist faith-based social services, Watt said that he was made nauseous by a resolution that Patrick Kennedy offered to honor George Washington for his letter to a Rhode Island synagogue in support of religious tolerance. "For us to be applauding the statements discussing bigotry that were written by a person who owned slaves is a little bit more than I can, without a churning stomach, be able to tolerate," Watt told the committee. When the faith-based bill reached the House floor, Watt tried unsuccessfully to remove provisions that permit religious groups to receive federal funds to hire people only of their own faith.

In 2005, Watt became chairman of the Congressional Black Caucus. He showed his independence by voting against a formal challenge by several Black Caucus members to the November 2004 presidential vote count in Ohio. He led the CBC members to a meeting with George W. Bush, where they gave him a copy of the Caucus agenda and voiced hope that this would be "the first of many" discussions; Bush included what appeared to be a couple of the CBC's proposals in his State of the Union address. But other than the broadly backed 25-year extension of the Voting Rights Act, the two sides reached little common ground. His chairmanship was marked by frequent clashes with Nancy Pelosi, notably his vigorous objection to her successful effort to oust William Jefferson from the Ways and Means Committee. Watt criticized the "political expediency" of taking on a Black Caucus member when Pelosi did not take comparable action against ethically-tainted white Democrats.

Despite the many twists and turns in the 12th District since he was first elected, Watt has shown the ability to entrench himself with voters regardless of their race. His toughest reelection contest came in 1998, when the black share of the population had shrunk to 36%. Republican Scott Keadle called for major tax cuts, attacked Watt as an "extreme liberal," and concentrated on his vote against Megan's Law. In their final debate, Watt defended his vote by saying, "Would the next step be to register everyone who commits a murder?" But later he conceded that his vote had been wrong and he voted funds for state compliance with the law. Watt won 56%-42%, with support from the district's many white liberals. In 2007, he chaired the oversight subcommittee on Financial Services—a useful opportunity for a skilled advocate who has criticized high interest rates by his banker constituents. He began with a review of the insurance industry's response to Hurricane Katrina.

THIRTEENTH DISTRICT

Rep. Brad Miller (D)

Elected 2002, 3d term; b. May 19, 1953, Fayetteville; home, Raleigh; U. of NC, B.A. 1975, London Schl. of Economics, M.S.C. 1978, Columbia U., J.D. 1979; Episcopalian; married (Esther Hall).

Elected Office: NC House of Reps., 1992-94; NC Senate, 1996-2002.

Professional Career: Clerk, Judge J. Dickson Phillips Jr., U.S. Fourth Circuit Ct. of Appeals, Durham, 1979-80; Practicing atty., 1980-2002.

DC Office: 1722 LHOB, 20515, 202-225-3032; Fax: 202-225-0181; Web site: www.house.gov/bradmiller.

District Offices: Greensboro, 336-574-2909; Raleigh, 919-836-1313.

Committees: *Financial Services* (19th of 37 D): Capital Markets, Insurance & Government Sponsored Enterprises; Financial Institutions & Consumer Credit. *Foreign Affairs* (21st of 27 D): Europe; Africa & Global Health. *Science & Technology* (8th of 24 D): Investigations & Oversight (Chmn.).

Group Ratings

	ADA	ACLU	AFS	LCV	ITIC	NTU	COC	ACU	CFG	FRC
2006	90	82	100	92	43	11	47	17	4	0
2005	100	—	100	94	—	9	41	0	3	0

National Journal Ratings

	2005 LIB	—	2005 CONS		2006 LIB	—	2006 CONS
Economic	92%	—	6%		74%	—	23%
Social	71%	—	29%		66%	—	34%
Foreign	69%	—	30%		67%	—	33%

Key Votes of the 109th Congress

1. Estate Tax Repeal	N	5. Limit Interstate Abortion	N	9. Build Border Fence	Y
2. Limit CAFE Standards	N	6. Extend Patriot Act	Y	10. CAFTA	N
3. FY06 Spending Curb	N	7. Bar Same Sex Marriage	N	11. Oppose Iraq Withdrawal	P
4. Drilling in ANWR	N	8. Stem Cell Research $	Y	12. Detainee Tribunals	N

Election Results

2006 general	Brad Miller (D)	98,540	(64%)	($1,766,708)
	Vernon Robinson (R)	56,120	(36%)	($2,207,519)
2006 primary	Brad Miller (D)	unopposed		
2004 general	Brad Miller (D)	160,896	(59%)	($1,181,327)
	Virginia Johnson (R)	112,788	(41%)	($350,395)

Prior Winning Percentages: 2002 (55%)

The People		Race/Ethnic Origin	Ancestry	
Area size:	2,294 sq. mi.	63.3% White	USA: 10.0%	English: 8.7%
Urban population:	73.7%	26.9% Black	German: 6.8%	
Rural population:	26.3%	2.0% Asian	**2004 Presidential Vote**	
Pop. 2000:	619,178	0.3% Native Am.	Kerry (D) 147,144	(52%)
Pop. 2005 (est):	673,451	0.0% Hawaiian	Bush (R) 132,581	(47%)
Median income:	$41,060	1.2% Two+ races	Other 1,180	(0%)
Poverty status:	11.6%	0.2% Other	**2000 Presidential Vote**	
Military veterans:	11.3%	6.0% Hispanic Origin	Bush (R) 113,600	(50%)
			Gore (D) 112,953	(49%)
			Other 2,429	(1%)
			Cook Partisan Voting Index: D + 2	

Occupation	Blue collar: 25.7%	White collar: 60.5%	Gray collar: 13.8%

Metropolitan growth has come to some of the long humble countryside of North Carolina. A generation ago, Raleigh, Durham, Burlington and Greensboro were a string of small cities connected by I-85 across the central Piedmont, moderately prosperous, with textile, tobacco and furniture factories, but not very big: just a few miles from the center of town, farm fields started, dotted by country towns with barbecue restaurants and churches. The counties to the north were almost purely rural, with a few factory towns. Today, many of the old tobacco fields are used for growing other crops. The booming metropolitan areas of North Carolina have spread far beyond the old city and county lines into the adjacent counties. Wake County, which includes Raleigh, grew 86% between 1990 and 2006, and the surrounding counties grew between 42% and 87%. Rural roads are clogged in the morning with commuters headed for jobs in new office parks, and income levels have risen far above what they once were.

Much of this territory now makes up the 13th Congressional District of North Carolina, a district created after the 2000 Census. Almost half of its residents live in Wake County, including the center of Raleigh, a tangent going off to North Carolina State University and much of the northern part of the county, but few of the affluent new subdivisions that are mostly in the 4th District. Another 18% of its residents live in Guilford County, with black neighborhoods and the University of North Carolina's Greensboro campus. The rest of the district includes all or most of four counties up to the Virginia border—Granville, Person, Caswell, Rockingham—with fairly large black percentages. The district lines were drawn by the Democratic legislature to produce a new Democratic district, one of the few created in the South in recent decades which does not have a majority or near-majority of blacks; only 27% of its residents are black. But the rural counties have a historical Democratic heritage, and university neighborhoods are heavily Democratic. The district has been closely divided in presidential races, with George W. Bush winning narrowly in 2000 and John Kerry winning by a slight margin in 2004.

The congressman from the 13th District is Brad Miller, a Democrat first elected in 2002. Born and raised in Fayetteville by his widowed mother, a school cafeteria bookkeeper, he graduated from the University of North Carolina, and got a master's degree at London School of Economics and a law degree from Columbia. After clerking for a federal appeals court judge, he began practicing law in Raleigh. In 1992, he was elected to the state House. But he was swept away in the 1994 Republican landslide. He was elected in 1996 to the state Senate where, like many members of the House, he had a hand in drawing his own congressional district as chairman of the Senate's redistricting committee.

Miller drew a district very much in his own political interest, but he couldn't be sure that he could run in the seat he had drawn for himself. Utah brought a lawsuit against the Census Bureau, arguing that because the census counted servicemen with legal residence in a state but serving overseas, it should also count Mormon missionaries domiciled in a state but serving overseas. North Carolina has a lot of servicemen, but Utah has many Mormon missionaries, and such a count would have increased Utah's population enough that it, rather than North Carolina, would have gotten the 435th district. Utah lost in federal court. With the Supreme Court's affirmation, four experienced Democrats launched an 11-week sprint to the September primary, which seemed likely to determine the winner in November. Miller raised the most money and got early endorsements from teachers and other labor unions, plus the League of Conservation Voters. In the primary, Miller led with 40% (enough to avoid a runoff) to 24% for former Congressman Robin Britt, who won the four western counties where his name was familiar. In Wake County, which cast 49% of the vote, Miller won 58% to only 10% for Britt. In the general, Miller faced Carolyn Grant, a commercial real-estate broker and former head of the Raleigh Chamber of Commerce. Grant called Miller a tax-and-spend Democrat, but also criticized him for voting to cut prescription drug assistance for the elderly. Miller said that North Carolina had the second-best record of any state in cutting taxes during the prior six years. Grant got little help from national Republicans and Miller won 55%-42%.

In the House, Miller has a relatively liberal record, especially on economics. He joined the Financial Services Committee, a useful post for home-state interests. He filed a bill to prohibit anti-predatory lending practices, including the abuse of fees charged by mortgage brokers. By 2007, he was hopeful that a comparable bill would become law. In November 2006, Raleigh's *News & Observer* wrote that Miller "remains somewhat uncomfortable with the rituals of Congress" and often sits alone on the House floor reading memos while colleagues chat up each other in the aisles. "He doesn't make a lot of noise, but he's doing the work," colleague Bob Etheridge told the newspaper. In the majority, he became chairman of the Science and Technology Subcommittee on Investigations and Oversight, where he planned to explore the politicizing of scientific research in the Bush administration. In January 2007, he filed a bill with David Price to terminate by the end of the year the President's authority to wage war in Iraq.

Back home, he appeared to entrench himself, at least until the next redistricting. In 2006, his Republican challenger was Vernon Robinson, an outspoken and conservative African-American, who ran in the 5th District in 2004 and criticized Miller as soft on illegal immigration and gays. "If Miller had his way, America would be nothing but one big fiesta for illegal aliens and homosexuals." Robinson was well-funded, but he received little national party assistance. Miller won 64%-36%.

Miller showed a puckish sense of humor following a congressional delegation visit to Antarctica in 2006. Of his trip to the magnetic South Pole, he said, "I thought, 'Every other politician who thinks the world is revolving around them is wrong. It actually revolves around me.'"

★ NORTH DAKOTA ★

Two hundred years ago, in late 1804, the Lewis and Clark expedition paddled up the Missouri River and reached what is now North Dakota. There they bivouacked for the winter across the river from what is now the state capital of Bismarck. Lewis and Clark, North Dakota proudly proclaims, spent more nights in North Dakota, 146, than in any other state. And here you can still see on the Lewis and Clark Trail much of the pristine land that the expeditioners saw. North Dakota has long been the state least visited by other Americans, but some 3.9 million visitors stopped along the state's Lewis and Clark Trail between 2002 and 2005, and some 54,000 copies of Lewis and Clark and Sacagaweacookbooks were sold. The Three Affiliated Tribes—Mandan, Arikara, Hidatsa—sold pottery, basketry, quill and bead work and the traditionally crafted leather pouches commissioned by the U.S. Mint to hold the commemorative Lewis and Clark Westward Journey nickels.

What Lewis and Clark and later venturers into this territory—George Armstrong Custer, Theodore Roosevelt—saw was Indian country, a vast unfenced land where the Indians built a civilization based on the buffalo and, a Spanish import, the horse. The history of North Dakota is short: Roosevelt did not arrive until nearly 80 years after Lewis and Clark, and bicentennial tourists came just a little more than 120 years after Roosevelt. There are still a few North Dakotans alive today who knew the men and women that settled this land and saw the state enter the Union in 1889. As children, they walked in the ruts left by the early settlers' wagon trains; they saw the Indians, recently defeated, herded onto reservations. This was some of the best wheat land in the world, empty by then of buffalo, connected to markets by rail, ready to become a cog in the industrial world.

And so, in a sudden rush of settlement during the 20 years before World War I, North Dakota filled up to pretty much its present population. There were 632,000 people here in 1920 and in counts since the number has fluctuated between 617,000 and 680,000. In the 2000 Census it was 642,000—when it was the state with the lowest growth rate since 1950—and the Census estimate for 2006 is 636,000. Wheat—mostly spring wheat but also durum used to make pasta—is the biggest crop here but not the only one: North Dakota ranks number one in sunflowers, barley, dry edible beans, oats, and dry peas, and ranks high in sugar beets and rye; there is plenty of cattle ranching and livestock grazing in the arid plains in the western half of the state.

Its dependence on agriculture shaped North Dakota's politics. Farmers, as much as they like to extol their way of life, are seldom content with the workings of the market. When prices are high, it

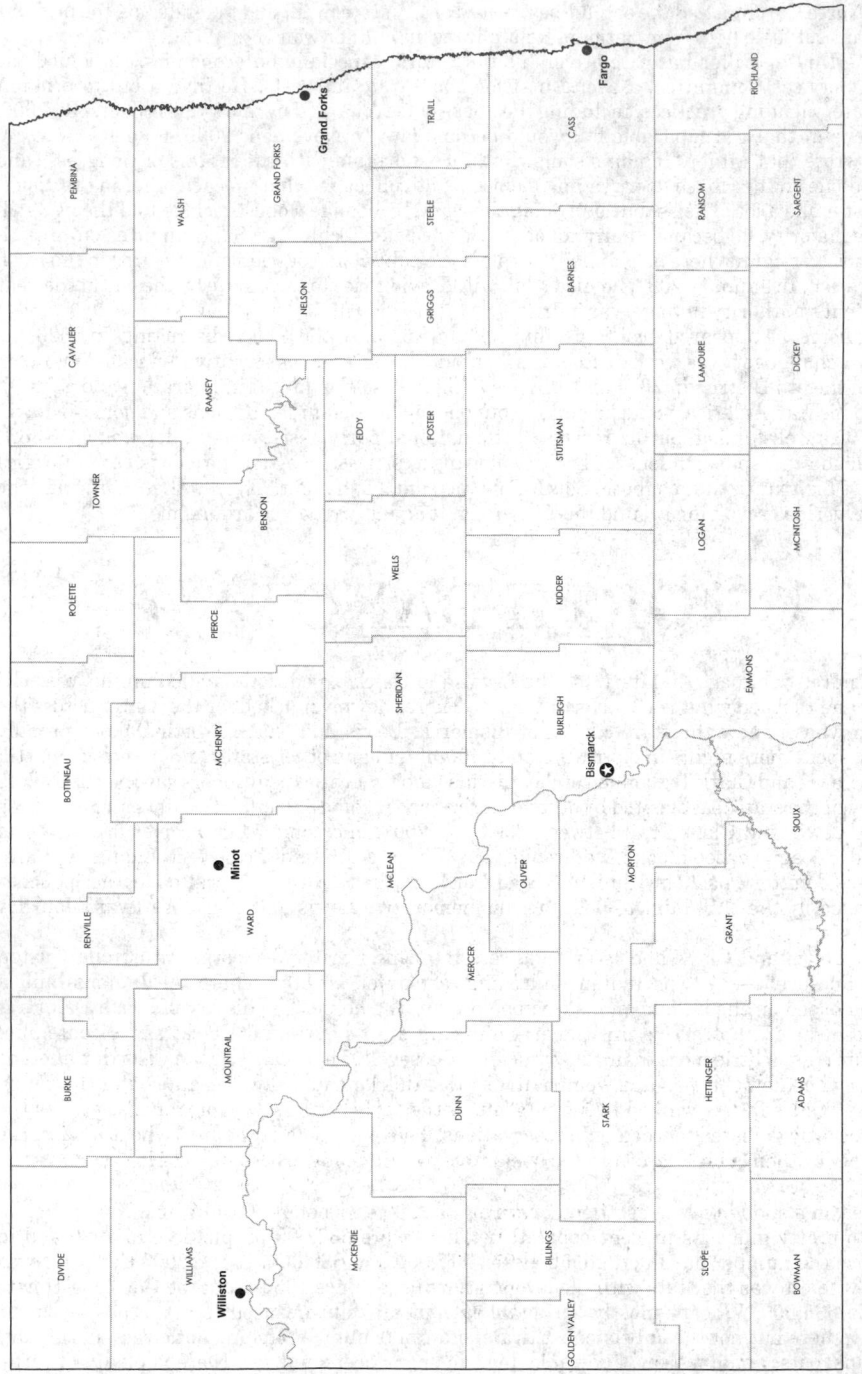

The Almanac of American Politics.
National Journal

Miles

0 10 20

U.S. Representative elected at-large.

PEMBINA

WALSH

CAVALIER

GRAND FORKS

Grand Forks

TRAILL

CASS

Fargo

RICHLAND

NELSON

STEELE

RAMSEY

BARNES

RANSOM

SARGENT

TOWNER

BENSON

EDDY

FOSTER

GRIGGS

STUTSMAN

LAMOURE

DICKEY

ROLETTE

PIERCE

WELLS

KIDDER

LOGAN

MCINTOSH

BOTTINEAU

MCHENRY

SHERIDAN

BURLEIGH

Bismarck

EMMONS

MCLEAN

OLIVER

MORTON

SIOUX

Minot

WARD

RENVILLE

MERCER

GRANT

BURKE

MOUNTRAIL

DUNN

STARK

HETTINGER

ADAMS

DIVIDE

WILLIAMS

MCKENZIE

BILLINGS

SLOPE

BOWMAN

Williston

GOLDEN VALLEY

N
W   E
S

is often because of low production; when they are low, farmers seek protection. The boosterish optimism of the first settlers was soon followed by cries reverberating with varying intensity for government protection against market forces. Since commodity prices tend to fall during periods of economic growth, there has been a countercyclical element in North Dakota politics, a tendency to vote against the national trends, and a radical strain going back to the 1910s and still lively in recent decades. That radical strain also owes much to the immigrant origins of so many of North Dakota's early settlers: Norwegians in the eastern part of the state, Canadians along the northern border, colonies of Poles and Czechs and Icelanders, and Germans throughout the state. German is still spoken on the streets of some towns, and the state is proud of its Nordic Initiative which welcomed Princess Martha Louise of Norway to Grand Forks in April 2006.

These immigrants produced orderly small towns and grain and other cooperatives; they also provided support for the Non-Partisan League, which flourished from its founding in 1915 to its alliance with the Democratic Party in 1956. It appealed to marginal farmers, cut off in many cases from the wider American culture by language barriers and seemingly at the mercy of the grain millers in Minneapolis, the railroads of St. Paul, the banks of New York and the commodity traders of Chicago. The NPL's program was socialist—government ownership of railroads and grain elevators—and, like most North Dakota ethnics, it opposed going to war with Germany. The NPL often determined the outcome of the usually decisive Republican primary and sometimes swung its support to the otherwise heavily outnumbered Democrats, instituting reforms and creating a state-owned bank and grain elevator. By 1960, the NPL had more or less merged into the Democratic Party, a merger symbolized by the election of the late Democratic Senator Quentin Burdick, whose father, Usher Burdick, served 20 years in the House as an NPL-endorsed Republican. North Dakota's leading Democrats of recent decades, Senators Kent Conrad and Byron Dorgan, have championed a politics clearly of NPL lineage: For government farm programs, wary if not hostile to American military involvement abroad, and cheerfully championing the little guy from North Dakota against out-of-state corporations.

This is a place where everyone knows everyone else; for years there has been no voter registration because people obviously spot anyone not eligible. People have been around practically forever: the 2000 Census reported that North Dakota had the highest proportion of any state, and tiny McIntosh County the highest proportion of any county, of residents 85 and older. This communal closeness has produced an innate conservatism in North Dakota. Divorce is as uncommon here as anywhere in the United States, the two-parent family is still very much the norm and abortions are available in only one clinic in the state. Politics is personal, too, in a state where every politician is known to many voters. North Dakota is one of four states with an all-Democratic congressional delegation (Massachusetts, Rhode Island and Hawaii are the others: the four don't have much else in common). The two senators and one congressman are all allies who have worked together for years.

Yet there are signs of change even in this settled commonwealth. The land, it seems, is emptying out. Increasing agricultural productivity has meant fewer farmers living directly off the land, and more people living in towns and off other industries. Out-of-staters are buying up farmland for vacation hunting: North Dakota sits below the North American Flyway. Bison have been reintroduced, and the idea circulated two decades ago that North Dakota would become a "buffalo commons" may be coming true. But energy is also a North Dakota product: the lignite coal fields in the west fuel enough power plants that North Dakota exports much of its electricity to other states, and the unproven Bakken oil formation in the west may prove to be one of the nation's biggest oilfields.

All the same, North Dakota's small cities have grown. Back in 1955 North Dakota-born sociologist Carl Kraenzel predicted in *The Great Plains in Transition* that "sutland" communities (places on transportation lines) would grow and "yonland" communities (places away from transportation lines) wane; and so it has happened. North Dakota's four biggest counties, containing Fargo, Grand Forks, Bismarck and Minot, grew from 134,000 in 1930 to 329,000 in 2006, while the state's other 49 counties dropped from 546,000 to 307,000; in 2004, these four counties cast 52% of the state's votes. In effect, North Dakota is developing the demographics of the Rocky Mountain states, with population concentrated in a few cities and towns. And these are the engines of its economic growth. Microsoft bought Great Plains Software in 2000 for $1.1 billion and the Microsoft Fargo campus is the headquarters of its business systems division and is the state's third largest employer. Alien Technology has a plant in Fargo that produces the tiny radio frequency tags used by Wal-Mart and the military. Grand Forks, devastated by flood in 1997, generously provided its "lessons learned" to its sister city Biloxi, Mississippi, in 2005. It is the home of the University of

North Dakota and its splendid Ralph Engelstad hockey rink; its president defended its Fighting Sioux sports team against outsider protest, and pointed out that they're strongly supported by North Dakota Indians and that UND graduates more Indian professionals than any other school in America. North Dakota is number two in academic research and development dollars per $1,000 of gross state product, after Maryland and ahead of Massachusetts. North Dakota may even be solving the problem it has agonized about for years: how to retain its young people. North Dakota spends more per capita on state colleges than any other states, and a smaller proportion of graduates seem to be heading off to to Minneapolis and Denver, Chicago and California. Fargo and Bismarck, Grand Forks and Minot still have the coldest winters of American cities, but they are also spouting hip restaurants and Starbucks, industrial parks and office buildings. The Census Bureau estimates that North Dakota's population started rising after years of decline in 2003. The declining number of farmers seems to be yielding place to another story: economic success. North Dakota's unemployment rate lately has been one of the lowest in the nation; its wages and incomes have been rising more than the national average, with per capita income rising from 81% of the nation's in 1997 to 91% in 2005; its farm incomes are among the highest ever; its state government faced the problem of dealing with a $500 million surplus in a $2 billion budget.

You can make the case that these developments are undermining the state's radical tradition. If the typical elderly North Dakotan is a hard-working retired farmer, with fond memories of NPL agitation and a belief in government programs (those over 60 voted only 52% for George W. Bush in 2004), the typical young North Dakotan is a family person with a college education more trusting of markets and the private sector (those under 45 voted 69% for Bush). Bush carried the state 63%-35% and Republican Governor John Hoeven was reelected 71%-27%. Yet the heirs of that radical tradition continue to do well. The state's two Democratic senators continue to be reelected by wide margins—Byron Dorgan by 68%-32% in 2004, Kent Conrad by 69%-30% in 2006—and Democratic Congressman Earl Pomeroy won by 66%-34% in 2006. These were consensus elections: Hoeven in 2004, Dorgan and Conrad carried all 53 counties, and Pomeroy carried 52, losing Billings County by 5 votes. Republicans hold most of the downballot statewide offices and have majorities, reduced in 2006, in both houses of the legislature. North Dakota prizes frugality in government, and values Senate Budget Committee Chairman Conrad's denunciations of federal budget deficits. But it was happy to receive some $10 billion in farm subsidies in 1995-2005 and fought against Air Force base cutbacks in Grand Forks. The issues here can be intensely local. Consider Devils Lake. It sits in a basin with drainage neither to the Mississippi nor to the Red River of the North, which flows north to Manitoba and Hudson Bay. Starting in 1993, water began to accumulate and Devils Lake rose 26 feet, expanded in size and inundated farms, roads and houses. North Dakotans' solution was to drain the water through an outlet to the Sheyenne River and then to the Red. Canada and Minnesota objected: the water might be impure or contain invasive species; it might flood parts of their territory. Governor Hoeven proposed that the state build a $28 million outlet to the Sheyenne, with crude rock filtering of the water; objections would go to the International Joint Commission set up by the U.S. and Canada. Dorgan and Conrad objected: ILC review could take years, and there might be objection to introducing Missouri River water to the Red River basin. Hoeven agreed and got Minnesota and Canada to go along in August 2005; testing of the pumps began and North Dakota would be open to more intensive sand filtering of the water if someone else—the federal government or Canada—was willing to put up the necessary $18 million. North Dakota seems to have gained a certain confidence from its recent successes, and its economic transition. Case in point: In 2006 the North Dakota Farmers Union opened a restaurant, Agraria, on the Washington, D.C., waterfront, with decor suggesting the plains of North Dakota and a sophisticated menu and wine list. North Dakota, which successfully navigated a turn of the century 100 years ago, seems to be turning a century successfully again.

The People

Pop. 2006 (est):	635,867
Pop. 2000:	642,200
Pop. 1990:	638,800
Change 1990-2000:	Up 0.5%
% of U.S. total:	0.2%
Pop. rank:	47th of 50
Area size:	70,700 sq. mi.
State Native:	72.5%
Non-citizen:	1.1%

Language

English: 90.1%	Other Eur.: 6.5%
Spanish: 2.1%	

Race/Ethnic Origin

589,149	91.7%	White
3,761	0.6%	Black
3,566	0.6%	Asian
30,772	4.8%	Native Am.
218	0.0%	Hawaiian
6,666	1.0%	Two+ races
282	0.0%	Other
7,786	1.2%	Hisp. Origin

Ancestry

German: 30.6%	Norwegian: 20.9%
Irish: 5.4%	Swedish: 3.5%
English: 3.4%	

Military veterans: 61,365 (12.7%)

WWII: 19.8%	Korea: 14.1%
Vietnam: 32.7%	Gulf War: 11.3%

Most populous cities (2006):

1. Fargo	90,056
2. Bismarck	58,333
3. Grand Forks	50,372
4. Minot	34,745
5. West Fargo	21,508

Urban population: 55.8%
Rural population: 44.2%

Education

H.S. Grad:	83.9%
College Grad:	22.0%

Industry

Agri: 8.2%	Con: 6.2%
Fin: 5.9%	Info: 2.3%
Mfg: 12.8%	Prof: 30.2%
Public: 4.8%	Trade: 16.4%
Other: 13.1%	

Occupation

Blue collar: 22.2%	White collar: 59.4%
Gray collar: 18.4%	

Work Sector

Private: 72.2%	Govt: 16.5%
Self: 10.7%	Family: 0.6%

Unemployment: 4.5%

Household Income

<15k: 19.0%	15-35k: 31.5%
35-50k: 18.6%	50-100k: 25.2%
100-150k: 3.8%	>150k: 1.9%

Median: $34,604
Poverty status: 11.9%

Home Value

<50k: 34.5%	50-100k: 41.2%	100-200k: 20.8%	200-300k: 2.4%
300-500k: 0.8%	>500k: 0.3%	Median: $68,300	

Legislative Assembly

Senate	26 R 21 D
House	61 R 33 D

Legislative Term Limits: No

Registered Voters

No state voter registration

Presidential politics   Massachusetts, Rhode Island and Hawaii, the other states with all-Democratic congressional delegations, are heavily Democratic in presidential elections; North Dakota is heavily Republican. In olden days, North Dakota veered toward Democrats when farm prices fell; in 2000, though prices were low, it voted heavily 61%-33% for George W. Bush. In 2004, when farm prices were high, Bush won 63%-35%. John Kerry carried four counties, three of them with Indian reservations.

North Dakota chooses its national convention delegates in party caucuses. With a tiny number of delegates, an out-of-the-way location and frigid weather in the early primary season, they attract little attention.

2004 Presidential Vote

Bush (R)	196,651	(63%)
Kerry (D)	111,052	(35%)
Nader (I)	3,756	(1%)
Other	1,374	(0%)

2000 Presidential Vote

Bush (R)	174,852	(61%)
Gore (D)	95,284	(33%)
Nader (Green)	9,486	(3%)
Other	8,634	(3%)

Governor

John Hoeven (R)

Elected 2000, term expires Dec. 2008, 2d term; b. Mar. 13, 1957, Bismarck; home, Bismarck; Dartmouth, B.A. 1979; Northwestern U., Kellogg Grad. Schl., M.B.A. 1981; Catholic; married (Mikey).

Professional Career: Exec. V.P., First Western Bank, 1986-93; Pres. & CEO, Bank of ND, 1993-2000.

Office: State Capitol, 600 E. Boulevard, Bismarck, 58505, 701-328-2200; Fax: 701-328-2205; Web site: www.governor.state.nd.us.

Election Results

2004 general	John Hoeven (R)	220,803	(71%)
	Joseph Satrom (D)	84,877	(27%)
	Other	4,193	(1%)
2004 primary	John Hoeven (R)	unopposed	
2000 general	John Hoeven (R)	159,255	(55%)
	Heidi Heitkamp (D)	130,144	(45%)

John Hoeven, the Republican governor of North Dakota, is the longest serving governor in the United States. He was first elected in November 2000 and was sworn into office on December 15, 2000—six days before the second-longest serving governor, Rick Perry of Texas, who took office when President-elect George W. Bush announced his resignation on December 21. Hoeven was born in Bismarck and grew up in Minot; he graduated from Dartmouth College and received an MBA from Northwestern. In 1981, he entered the family business, First Western Bank in Minot and became executive vice president. He was active in many civic endeavors. In 1993 he was chosen to be head of the state-owned Bank of North Dakota—a Non-Partisan League creation—by a board that included his predecessor as governor, Republican Ed Schafer, and his 2000 Democratic opponent, Attorney General Heidi Heitkamp. Under Hoeven's stewardship, the bank's worth rose from $990 million to $1.6 billion and its loan portfolio increased from $200 million to $1 billion; it returns $50 million into the state's biannual budget. Hoeven was not always a Republican; in 1996, he thought out loud about running as a Democrat against Schafer. He gave serious consideration to running in 2000 only when Schafer announced in October 1999 he would not run again. In November Hoeven, who had never won elective office, announced his candidacy.

This was a generally civil campaign, between two candidates who knew each other well. Bismarck is a small town, where officeholders can scarcely avoid each other, and North Dakotans are a civil people. Hoeven cited his work in attracting jobs by founding Minot's Magic Fund, a city sales tax used for business development, and by organizing to keep Minot Air Force Base off the base-closure list, as well as his work at the Bank of North Dakota. He called for economic development with high-paying jobs in technology and said that education was crucial in preparing future workers; he pledged more money for teacher training and salaries. Heitkamp, who grew up in the town of Mantador (population 77), was elected tax commissioner in 1984 and 1988 and attorney general in 1992 and 1996. She said she would try to keep young people in the state through a recruitment and mentoring program, by reinstating a living wage for employees of companies receiving financial assistance and by giving tax incentives to companies guaranteeing high-wage jobs. But in September 2000 Heitkamp announced that she had breast cancer. She underwent a mastectomy September 25, and Hoeven suspended his ads for two days. Quickly she returned to the campaign trail. For several weeks, she led in polls, but the momentum went back to Hoeven, and he won 55%-45%. Voters over the age of 60 backed the Democrat, voters under 60 the Republican: A familiar North Dakota pattern. At the same time, Republicans won seven of nine of the statewide offices and increased their majorities in the legislature. North Dakota's skyscraper Capitol, towering over neatly-kept Bismarck and the rolling plains beyond, now contained more Republicans in high office than at any time since the NPL allied with the Democrats around 1960.

As governor, Hoeven began Phase 2 of the North Dakota Telecommunications Network and combined several state agencies—tourism, economic development, finance, job training—into a

Department of Commerce. In December 2002, Hoeven presented a budget that drew $50 million from two trust funds and borrowed $20 million to complete the Telecommunications Network and which provided for teacher salary increases and $10 million for a Devils Lake outlet. Legislators resisted earmarking teacher salary increases; Hoeven vetoed their budget and, in a three-day special session, got 70% of education funds earmarked for salary increases. Altogether, teachers got $75 million in salary increases in his first term. In 2004 Hoeven promoted GoE! ethanol fuel and required its use in state vehicles. He proposed a Centers of Excellence program, borrowing $50 million to generate $150 millionin economic development centered on the state's universities. He brought suit to roll back the Burlington Northern Santa Fe Railroad's rate increases and eliminated the sales tax on used farm machinery and parts.

Water is a controversial issue in river-crossed North Dakota. For years there was concern about the rising water level in land-locked Devils Lake, which was submerging farmland, and houses and after heavy rains threatened local roads. North Dakotans in Congress tried to get the federal government to act, but Hoeven stepped in and construction began in October 2003 on a channel to divert the water through the Sheyenne River which drains into the northward-flowing Red River of the North. This generated protests from Minnesota and Manitoba officials, worried about water quality and other environmental risks, and Manitoba threatened a lawsuit; North Dakota retaliated by suing Manitoba over high roads that act as dikes on the Red River. As the 14-mile-long open channel came close to completion in 2005, Canadian officials mounted a lobbying campaign against the project in Washington and sought to have the State Department send the matter to the International Joint Commission, an entity designed to resolve boundary waters disputes with Canada. An agreement was reached to install a filter to prevent invasive species and pollutants from moving downstream but Canada remained unsatisfied; in June 2007, the House of Commons passed a motion calling for the Canadian government "to continue to employ every means possible to have the flow of water from Devils Lake into the Canadian water system stopped immediately." That same month, the Manitoba Premier protested by notifying Hoeven in a letter that he would no longer work with North Dakota on flooding issues in Pembina County, which shares a border with Canada.

In 2004 Hoeven was opposed by former state Senator Joseph Satrom, who had low name identification and little money. Hoeven pointed to the state's economic growth and indications that the state was finally gaining population and not losing young people. It didn't help Satrom that he opposed the constitutional amendment banning same-sex marriage, which was approved by 73% of the voters. Hoeven won 71%-27%, the biggest percentage victory since C. Norman Brunsdale was reelected in 1952. Democratic Agriculture Commissioner Roger Johnson held on to his job with 50.3% of the votes, but Republicans swept other partisan offices with percentages ranging up to 73% and increased their majorities in the legislature. In December 2004, Hoeven submitted a $5.5 billion budget with spending increases on education (more teacher salary increases) and corrections, and $5 million in bonuses to North Dakota soldiers; he projected a $200 million surplus.

By July 2005, Hoeven ranked as the nation's most popular governor, according to a SurveyUSA poll, with an approval rating hovering over 70%. He was probably the only candidate who could oust Democratic Senator Kent Conrad in 2006 and national Republicans, including presidential adviser Karl Rove, pressed him to run. Conrad took Hoeven's potential candidacy seriously; he raised $2.7 million by June 2005, more than he had ever spent over the course of an entire election cycle. He began running ads in September 2005 touting his accomplishments in the Senate. Later that month, Hoeven announced he would not run. "A day may come when we ask the people of North Dakota to allow us to serve them in a different capacity, but that time is not now," he said in a statement. The relieved state Democratic chairman said, "This race, between Conrad and Hoeven, would have been Armageddon. I think that we've averted a race here that would have involved the expenditure of millions of dollars, and the people of North Dakota will be better off not having to be subjected to it."

North Dakota is one of six states where the legislature meets biennially and for most of the state's history the governor delivered the State of the State speech only in the years the legislature convened. Hoeven's predecessor, Ed Schafer, had changed that tradition and gave the speech every January even when the legislature was not in session. But in 2006, after following Schafer's lead for his first five years in office, Hoeven felt secure enough to dispense with the speech. Other issues preoccupied him, among them the state's harsh weather. Within a one-year period beginning in 2005, the state was hit by two big snowstorms and severe summer weather, leading Hoeven to seek and win approval of three separate Presidential Disaster Declarations. The weather-related woes continued. In March 2006, Hoeven issued a flood emergency declaration after rapid snowmelt and rainfall led to Red River Valley flooding; in June, in response to dry conditions in the south central part of the state and its effects on farmers and ranchers, Hoeven declared an agricultural drought emergency. Also in June, Hoeven traveled to Iraq to visit North Dakota soldiers.

When the legislature next met in 2007, it achieved a productive session that enacted much of Hoeven's agenda for the year. Flush with revenues, Hoeven signed off on the largest tax relief measure in state history, the biggest increase in higher education funding in state history, a renewable energy package and a landmark K-12 education funding bill that featured a more equitable school aid formula and funding for statewide all-day kindergarten. Hoeven is up for reelection in 2008. He said in September 2007 that he would seek a third term in 2008.

Senior Senator

Kent Conrad (D)

Elected 1986, seat up 2012, 4th full term; b. Mar. 12, 1948, Bismarck; home, Bismarck; Stanford U., B.A. 1971, George Washington U., M.B.A. 1975; Unitarian; married (Lucy Calautti).

Elected Office: ND Tax Commissioner, 1981-86.

Professional Career: Asst., ND Tax Commissioner, 1974-80; Dir., Mgmt. Planning & Personnel, ND Tax Dept., 1980.

DC Office: 530 HSOB, 20510, 202-224-2043; Fax: 202-224-7776; Web site: conrad.senate.gov.

State Offices: Bismarck, 701-258-4648; Fargo, 701-232-8030; Grand Forks, 701-775-9601; Minot, 701-852-0703.

Committees: *Agriculture, Nutrition & Forestry* (3d of 11 D): Energy, Science & Technology (Chmn.); Domestic & Foreign Marketing, Inspection, & Plant & Animal Health; Production, Income Protection & Price Support. *Budget* (Chmn. of 12 D). *Finance* (3d of 11 D): Taxation & IRS Oversight & Long-Term Growth (Chmn.); Energy, Natural Resources & Infrastructure; Social Security, Pensions & Family Policy. *Indian Affairs* (3d of 8 D). *Joint Committee on Taxation* (3d of 5 D).

Group Ratings

	ADA	ACLU	AFS	LCV	ITIC	NTU	COC	ACU	CFG	FRC
2006	85	67	88	43	75	16	45	33	15	25
2005	85	—	86	60	—	17	69	21	7	—

National Journal Ratings

	2005 LIB	—	2005 CONS		2006 LIB	—	2006 CONS
Economic	62%	—	37%		59%	—	40%
Social	58%	—	40%		58%	—	41%
Foreign	57%	—	42%		77%	—	21%

Key Votes of the 109th Congress

1. Bar ANWR Drilling	Y	5. Confirm Samuel Alito	Y	9. Limit Interstate Abortion	Y
2. FY06 Spending Curb	N	6. Path to Citizenship	Y	10. CAFTA	N
3. Estate Tax Repeal	N	7. Bar Same Sex Marriage	N	11. Urge Iraq Withdrawal	Y
4. Raise Minimum Wage	Y	8. Stem Cell Research $	Y	12. Provide Detainee Rights	Y

Election Results

2006 general	Kent Conrad (D)	150,146	(69%)	($3,532,732)
	Dwight Grotberg (R)	64,417	(30%)	($259,081)
	Other	3,589	(2%)	
2006 primary	Kent Conrad (D)	unopposed		
2000 general	Kent Conrad (D)	176,470	(62%)	($2,312,543)
	Duane Sand (R)	110,420	(38%)	($399,584)

Prior Winning Percentages: 1994 (58%); 1992 (63%); 1986 (50%)

Kent Conrad, North Dakota's senior senator, was first elected to the Senate in 1986. He grew up in North Dakota; his parents were killed in an auto accident when he was five, and he was raised by his grandparents. One grandfather owned a bi-weekly newspaper in Bismarck and had been North

Dakota chairman for Progressive Robert LaFollette in 1924; another was the physician for longtime Governor and Senator William Langer: a family full of connections in the small world of North Dakota politics. Conrad's first political effort was to lead, in 1968, a campaign to grant voting rights to 19-year-olds. He graduated from Stanford, and then returned in 1974 to work on Byron Dorgan's unsuccessful House campaign. When Dorgan ran for Congress again in 1980, Conrad ran for tax commissioner and won; when Dorgan declined to run against Senator Mark Andrews in 1986, Conrad ran and won 50%-49%. In 1986 Conrad earnestly promised not to run again unless "the federal deficit, the trade deficit and real interest rates will be brought under control." By 1992 the latter two arguably were, and he could argue that he had worked to cut the budget deficit. Early 1992 polls showed Conrad well ahead, but in April 1992, after ruminating on the issue and after his wife had been mugged and dragged down the street near their Capitol Hill home, Conrad announced he was retiring because he had not kept his pledge, and Dorgan ran for his seat.

Then, in September 1992, the elderly Senator Quentin Burdick, no ally of Dorgan and Conrad, died. State law said a special election had to be held after November but before January, so Conrad ran for this seat while serving his last month in the other. He was nominated unanimously at the Democratic state convention. His Republican opponent Jack Dalrymple, now lieutenant governor, called for a very expensive $5 per bushel wheat program, and an anti-abortion independent lambasted Conrad; Conrad had far more money and won easily, 63%-34%. For a few hours in December 1992, Conrad technically held both Senate seats: he was sworn in December 14 to fill Burdick's term, and a few hours later Dorgan was sworn in to fill his. In 1994 Conrad's new Senate seat came up again. Republican Ben Clayburgh, 70-year-old former head of the state medical association, accused Conrad of voting most of the time with Bill Clinton; Conrad responded with an ad saying he voted with Bob Dole more than 50% of the time. Dole endorsed Clayburgh, but in a Republican year Conrad won by a reduced margin of 58%-42%.

Conrad is the chairman of the Senate Budget Committee. He became the ranking Democrat on the committee in January 2001 and became chairman when Democrats gained a majority through Jim Jeffords's party switch in June 2001 and then again after the Democratic victory of November 2006. Throughout his career he has always called for balanced budgets and decried budget deficits. From the 1930s to the 1970s, Republicans were the great critics of deficits, calling, usually ineffectually, for lower spending. Since the 1980s Democrats have increasingly taken that stand, Conrad foremost among them, often calling for higher tax rates. One reason is that deficits put downward pressure on spending, and surpluses, like those of the 1998-2000 period, tend to relieve that pressure. In spring 2001 Conrad worked to get in the budget resolution $73 billion for farm programs over the next 10 years: This left room for the farm bill passed in 2002. But he also called for a continued surplus. Once chairman, he started lambasting the Bush administration and, using his trademark charts (he became known as "the chart man" in the Senate), argued that the tax cut passed in May 2001 and lower than expected revenue would lead to deficits. But he did not seek to undo the tax cut. In March 2002 Conrad presented a $2.1 trillion dollar budget with a $90 billion deficit; it would pay off more of the national debt than the Bush budget. His plan passed in committee but in the 51-49 Senate there were not enough senators willing to constrain appropriators, and Conrad's resolution never came to a vote. For the first time since the Budget Committees were set up in 1974, no budget resolution passed Congress; there was no agreement on a budget in 2004 or 2006 either.

The Republicans won back a Senate majority in November 2002 and in January 2003 Conrad became ranking minority member again. The Republicans dropped the paygo rule, in place since 1990 and supported by Conrad, that required that spending increases and tax cuts be "paid for" by corresponding spending decreases or tax increases. This made possible passage of the 2003 Bush tax cuts on dividends and capital gains, and the extension of various Bush tax cuts later. Conrad continued to press, unsuccessfully, for restoration of the paygo rule. In 2005 Republicans managed to pass a budget resolution, including funds for oil drilling in the Arctic National Wildlife Refuge; but that was blocked by moderate Republicans in the House. In March 2006 Conrad failed to get restoration of paygo rules on a 50-50 floor vote. That spring he attacked Republican provisions requiring automatic cuts in mandatory spending and new caps on discretionary and emergency spending. He pointed out repeatedly that the surplus in Social Security revenues over benefits was reducing the nominal federal budget deficit, but that that would no longer be the case within a decade or so, when Social Security benefits would exceed revenues. He called repeatedly for a crackdown on uncollected taxes. After the 2006 election, he said, "Raising taxes would certainly be an option. The president, this is his policy. He's got an obligation to pay for it." In March 2007 Conrad presented a budget resolution that put the budget into balance by 2012, ended the supplemental appropriations and bridge funds used heavily by the Bush administration, and provided biennial fixes of the Alternative Minimum Tax. It called for cutting in half interest rates on student loans, more spending on homeland security, extending the child tax credit and the 10% bracket, and eliminating the marriage penalty. Republicans charged that this amounted to a tax increase, but Democrats envisioned that Bush tax cuts set to expire in 2010 or sooner would be either allowed to expire or offset at that time. Conrad and House Budget Committee Chairman John Spratt pushed similar packages through the two chambers in April 2007, and the conference report passed both the House and Senate on May 17.

On the Finance Committee, Conrad voted against the Bush tax cuts and against repeal of the estate tax. But he has been willing to work with Republicans on other issues. He was one of 11 Democratic senators to vote for the 2003 Medicare/prescription drug bill—not perfect, in his view, but a step forward in providing help for many North Dakota seniors. He sponsored bills that in his view would improve it, to allow federal negotiation of prices with pharmaceutical companies, reimportation of drugs and removal of incentives for private Medicare insurers. In 2005 some in the Bush White House, noting Conrad's continual warnings about the fiscal difficulties facing Social Security as baby boomers reach retirement age, hoped that he would join in discussions on a long-term Social Security fix. Conrad did sponsor a bill with Republican Gordon Smith in June 2005 giving employees automatic enrollment in 401(k) accounts unless they opted out and extending tax credits for voluntary savings accounts. But he, like other Finance Committee Democrats, steered clear of any public discussions or negotiations, and House Republicans, leery of the issue, were happy to see it disappear from the agenda in September 2005 after Hurricane Katrina.

On the Agriculture Committee, Conrad worked on putting together a generous 2002 farm bill, which abandoned the 1996 act's promise of getting rid of subsidies, a promise undermined anyway by the voting of annual farm disaster relief. He was one of four Senate conferees and helped insure that the bill required country of origin labeling for meat and better treatment of pulses—peas, lentils and other crops planted in rotation on wheat fields. As he said later, "No one did better than North Dakota under the current bill": the state received $2,368 per person in payments, more than any other state. But North Dakota farm interests, particularly its sugar beet farmers and processors, have been increasingly impacted by trade agreements, on which Conrad has a voice on the Finance Committee. His objections helped ensure that sugar was not included in the Australia Free Trade Agreement, but his effort to give House and Senate committees vetoes over waiver of limits on Australian beef imports was characterized as unconstitutional and failed. In March 2004 Special Trade Representative Robert Zoellick included limited imports from the Dominican Republic in the Caribbean Free Trade Agreement. Conrad spoke out strongly against any increases in sugar imports, lest they lead to more. "This is about whether we have sugar in our future. This is whether we have 30,000 jobs in the valley. This is about whether we have a strong and vibrant economy in the Red River Valley of North Dakota and Minnesota." However surprising it may be to some that North Dakota is a sugar producer, it is not in any way a cotton producer. Yet Conrad reacted sharply when the WTO in May 2004 ruled, in a case brought by Brazil, that the cotton program in the 1996 and 2002 farm bills was an illegal subsidy with effect on world markets. As he noted, that threatened the treatment of other crops, including those produced in North Dakota, like wheat. In the meantime, Conrad worked with his North Dakota colleague Byron Dorgan and successfully sponsored a $3.9 billion farm disaster relief package to the Senate version of the May 2006 emergency supplemental. The House resisted that, but Conrad and Dorgan persevered, trying to attach it to the military construction appropriation in November 2006. His pressure got a floor vote on which he prevailed 56-38 in December; but that was short of the 60 votes needed to overcome a point of order. But as Budget chairman and Agriculture member, Conrad was well positioned in 2007 to help reauthorize a farm bill similar to the 2002 measure and to find ways to avoid adverse impacts by WTO decisions.

Conrad has worked on many North Dakota issues. He inserted into the 2004 intelligence bill an amendment authorizing a project that would put softball-sized balls with infrared motion sensors all along the Canadian border; they would have nanoblock integrated circuits developed by North Dakota State University and would be run by a computer program developed by the University of North Dakota. In October 2006 he moved to block a Pentagon plan to cut 50 of 500 Minuteman III nuclear missile sites; Minot Air Force Base is home to 150 of them. In April 2006 Conrad presented his own BOLD energy bill (Breaking Our Long-term Dependence), which would raise ethanol use from 4.7 billion gallons in 2007 to 30 billion gallons in 2025, raise biodiesel use from 250 million gallons in 2008 to 2 billion gallons in 2015, spend $500 million on 10 coal liquification plans, provide rebates for purchases of electric vehicles, $2.5 billion for hydrogen research and extend the tax credit for wind energy. North Dakota produces corn used to make ethanol, has major coal deposits suitable for liquification and has more wind energy potential than any other state.

Conrad was reelected 62%-38% in 2000 against Annapolis graduate and Navy veteran Duane Sand, who returned to North Dakota and campaigned door-to-door in every city and town with a post office. Conrad spent far more money, $2.3 million, and ran 29% ahead of Al Gore. In early 2005, the Bush White House encouraged Governor John Hoeven, just reelected by a 71%-27% margin, to run against Conrad in 2006; Conrad ran ads in 2005 touting his Senate accomplishments and Hoeven decided not to run. In 2006, against Barnes County farmer Dwight Grotberg, Conrad spent $3.5 million and won 69%-30%, carrying every county.

Junior Senator

Byron Dorgan (D)

Elected 1992, seat up 2010, 3d term; b. May 14, 1942, Dickinson; home, Bismarck; U. of ND, B.S. 1965, U. of Denver, M.B.A. 1966; Lutheran; married (Kimberly).

Elected Office: ND Tax Commissioner, 1969-80; U.S. House of Reps., 1980-92.

Professional Career: Martin–Marietta Exec. Develop. Prog., 1966-68; ND Dpty. Tax Commissioner, 1968-69.

DC Office: 322 HSOB, 20510, 202-224-2551; Fax: 202-224-1193; Web site: dorgan.senate.gov.

State Offices: Bismarck, 701-250-4618; Fargo, 701-239-5389; Grand Forks, 701-746-8972; Minot, 701-852-0703.

Committees: *Appropriations* (8th of 15 D): Energy & Water Development (Chmn.); Agriculture, Rural Development, Food and Drug Administration & Related Agencies; Interior, Environment & Related Agencies; Defense; Commerce, Justice, Science & Related Agencies; Transportation, Housing and Urban Development & Related Agencies. *Commerce, Science & Transportation* (4th of 12 D): Interstate Commerce, Trade & Tourism (Chmn.); Aviation Operations, Safety & Security; Space, Aeronautics & Related Sciences; Science, Technology & Innovation; Surface Transportation & Merchant Marine Infrastructure, Safety & Security. *Energy & Natural Resources* (3d of 12 D): Energy (Chmn.); National Parks; Water & Power. *Indian Affairs* (Chmn. of 8 D).

Group Ratings

	ADA	ACLU	AFS	LCV	ITIC	NTU	COC	ACU	CFG	FRC
2006	95	67	100	43	25	12	33	12	5	12
2005	100	—	100	65	—	10	33	17	0	—

National Journal Ratings

	2005 LIB	—	2005 CONS		2006 LIB	—	2006 CONS
Economic	70%	—	29%		67%	—	29%
Social	65%	—	29%		57%	—	42%
Foreign	87%	—	10%		95%	—	2%

Key Votes of the 109th Congress

1. Bar ANWR Drilling	Y	5. Confirm Samuel Alito	N	9. Limit Interstate Abortion	Y
2. FY06 Spending Curb	N	6. Path to Citizenship	N	10. CAFTA	N
3. Estate Tax Repeal	N	7. Bar Same Sex Marriage	N	11. Urge Iraq Withdrawal	Y
4. Raise Minimum Wage	Y	8. Stem Cell Research $	Y	12. Provide Detainee Rights	Y

Election Results

2004 general	Byron Dorgan (D)	211,843	(68%)	($2,676,756)
	Mike Liffrig (R)	98,553	(32%)	($381,125)
2004 primary	Byron Dorgan (D)	unopposed		
1998 general	Byron Dorgan (D)	134,747	(63%)	($1,681,842)
	Donna Nalewaja (R)	75,013	(35%)	($152,183)
	Other	3,598	(2%)	

Prior Winning Percentages: 1992 (59%); 1990 House (65%); 1988 House (71%); 1986 House (76%); 1984 House (79%); 1982 House (72%); 1980 House (57%)

Byron Dorgan, North Dakota's junior senator, was first elected to the House in 1980 and to the Senate in 1992. Dorgan grew up in Regent, North Dakota (population 268), where his family had a farm equipment and petroleum business and raised cattle and horses; he was one of nine students in his high school graduating class. After college and business school he worked for a Denver aerospace firm; then in 1969, at 26, he was appointed state tax commissioner. His politics are very much out of the Non-Partisan League tradition: He has a strong mistrust of economic markets, a deep belief that government should intervene to protect the family farmer and small businessman, and a capacity to frame issues in a popular and unthreatening way. His first big issue, as tax commissioner, was taxing out-of-state corporations, which struck a chord in a state always hostile to big out-of-state money. To his work Dorgan brought the zest and cornball good humor that New Deal enthusiasts liked to summon up when liberals thought they represented the ordinary, inarticulate little guy, in contrast to the conservatives seen as old stuffed shirts.

Dorgan ran for the House in 1974, and lost to Republican Mark Andrews. In 1980, when Andrews ran for the Senate, Dorgan was elected to the House. His lowest reelection percentage in a House race was 65%, in 1990 against Ed Schafer, who was elected governor in 1992 and 1996. The cautious Dorgan declined to challenge Andrews for the Senate in 1986, a race his successor as tax commissioner, Kent Conrad, won, and he declined to take on 80-year-old fellow-Democrat Quentin Burdick in 1988. Only with Conrad's surprise decision not to run for reelection in 1992 did Dorgan finally run for the Senate. He and his Republican opponent both backed normal trade relations with China (a major buyer of North Dakota wheat), but remained wary of free trade otherwise. Dorgan won by a solid 59%-39% margin.

In the Senate, Dorgan's voting record has been similar to Conrad's—generally moderate to liberal, and more centrist on cultural issues; this is one case where senators of the same party from the same state have worked harmoniously together. They call themselves and Congressman Earl Pomeroy "Team North Dakota." Dorgan strongly backed fellow Dakotan Tom Daschle for Senate Democratic leader in 1994, and became an assistant floor leader. In 1998, he considered running for whip against Harry Reid, but withdrew and became co-chairman of the Democratic Policy Committee. In 2004, when Daschle was defeated and it became apparent that Reid had the votes to succeed him as minority leader, Dorgan started running for whip, but quickly dropped out when it was clear Richard Durbin had the votes. "It seemed to me that a number of our members felt that, for our two top spots, at least one should be from a blue state," he said. Unhappy with the Republican-controlled Senate's lack of oversight of the Bush administration, he used the policy committee to hold quasi-hearings on topics ranging from post-Katrina relief to contracting abuses in Iraq. With the Democrats' return to the majority, Dorgan made his Policy Committee chairmanship more visible in setting the agenda.

Dorgan continues to be a champion of family farms, even as their numbers decline. He has been a leading proponent of crop insurance and disaster relief packages. On the 2002 farm bill, he and Charles Grassley led the move to limit farm subsidies. He argued that too much would go to a few rich farmers and feared that such payments would build opposition to the farm bill as a whole; anyway, not many North Dakota or Iowa farmers qualify for huge payments. It failed in committee, opposed by senators from states with big cotton and rice farms, but the Senate passed by voice vote a limit of $275,000 per farmer.

Throughout Dorgan's record one sees a traditional North Dakota distrust of economic markets. During the 1990s he often criticized Alan Greenspan for backing high interest rates and he was one of four senators to vote against his reconfirmation as Federal Reserve chairman in 2000. He wants a more vigorous antitrust policy, with temporary bans on agribusiness and airline mergers. He opposes individual investment accounts for Social Security and full repeal of the estate tax. He has sought to expand broadband access in rural communities. In July 2006, he promoted his new book, *Take This Job and Ship It: How Corporate Greed and Brain-Dead Politics Are Selling Out America*.

To promote North Dakota grain sales, Dorgan has been a prime mover in scaling back the embargo on Cuba. He attacked the Bush administration proposal to require Cuban purchasers to make payments before goods were shipped. Dorgan has worked closely with Conrad on water issues and he has been a backer of wind energy projects, in which North Dakota is a leader. He has worked for several years to create a Red River Valley Research Corridor, to link North Dakota colleges and businesses with federal research contracts. On the Indian Affairs Committee's investigation of the abuses of lobbyist Jack Abramoff, Dorgan worked with John McCain to document the bilking of Indian tribes. When news reports documented that he had received large campaign contributions from some of those tribes, Dorgan heatedly replied that he had long backed the Indian projects and that others "will try to spin a web of deception to smear and discredit those of us who are investigating the wrongdoing." As the new chairman of Indian Affairs, he planned to focus on health problems. "We spend twice as much on health services for federal prisoners as we do on health services for American Indians." He also has targeted the need for economic development and youth centers, and wants to encourage the settlement of long-running litigation over Interior Department mismanagement of Indian trust funds.

Dorgan has been easily re-elected. In 1998 he beat state Senator Donna Nalewaja 63%-35%, carrying every county but one in which the vote was tied. For 2004, national Republicans tried to recruit former Governor Ed Schafer, but he declined to run. The Republican nominee, rancher Mike Liffrig attacked Dorgan for supporting human cloning (he altered a bill he sponsored in response); another ad portrayed couples at the altar and then showed two men in black ties about to kiss each other and pairs of men and women getting married. "You can kiss our North Dakota values goodbye or you can kiss Senator Dorgan goodbye," the voiceover said. Dorgan ran editorials condemning the Liffrig ads by the Fargo *Forum* and *Grand Forks Herald*. With far more money and more than three decades of winning statewide races, Dorgan won 68%-32%. This time he carried every county.

Representative-At-Large

Earl Pomeroy (D)

Elected 1992, 8th term; b. Sept. 2, 1952, Valley City; home, Valley City; U. of ND, B.A. 1974, J.D., 1979; Presbyterian; married (Laurie Kirby).

Elected Office: ND House of Reps., 1980-84; ND Insurance Commissioner, 1984-92.

Professional Career: Practicing atty., 1979-84; Natl. Assn. of Insurance Commissioners., Vice Pres. 1989, Pres. 1990.

DC Office: 1501 LHOB, 20515, 202-225-2611; Fax: 202-226-0893; Web site: www.house.gov/pomeroy.

District Offices: Bismarck, 701-224-0355; Fargo, 701-235-9760.

Committees: *Agriculture* (20th of 25 D): Department Operations, Oversight, Nutrition & Forestry; Specialty Crops, Rural Development & Foreign Agriculture; General Farm Commodities & Risk Management. *Ways & Means* (11th of 24 D): Social Security; Health.

Group Ratings

	ADA	ACLU	AFS	LCV	ITIC	NTU	COC	ACU	CFG	FRC
2006	80	67	100	67	57	16	50	38	18	14
2005	90	—	100	56	—	18	67	36	13	38

National Journal Ratings

	2005 LIB	—	2005 CONS		2006 LIB	—	2006 CONS
Economic	60%	—	39%		66%	—	34%
Social	60%	—	40%		60%	—	39%
Foreign	60%	—	40%		62%	—	37%

Key Votes of the 109th Congress

1. Estate Tax Repeal	N	5. Limit Interstate Abortion	Y	9. Build Border Fence	Y
2. Limit CAFE Standards	N	6. Extend Patriot Act	Y	10. CAFTA	N
3. FY06 Spending Curb	N	7. Bar Same Sex Marriage	N	11. Oppose Iraq Withdrawal	N
4. Drilling in ANWR	N	8. Stem Cell Research $	Y	12. Detainee Tribunals	Y

Election Results

2006 general	Earl Pomeroy (D)	142,934	(66%)	($1,378,061)
	Matt Mechtel (R)	74,687	(34%)	($79,554)
2006 primary	Earl Pomeroy (D)	unopposed		
2004 general	Earl Pomeroy (D)	185,130	(60%)	($1,809,046)
	Duane Sand (R)	125,684	(40%)	($1,007,576)

Prior Winning Percentages: 2002 (52%); 2000 (53%); 1998 (56%); 1996 (55%); 1994 (52%); 1992 (57%)

Earl Pomeroy, North Dakota's lone House member, is a Democrat first elected in 1992. Pomeroy grew up in Valley City and after college served as Byron Dorgan's driver during the 1974 campaign, then went to law school and practiced law in Valley City. In 1980, when Dorgan and Kent Conrad won statewide elections, Pomeroy at 28 won a seat in the legislature; in 1984 and 1988 he was elected insurance commissioner. In 1992, he was planning to retire from politics and serve in the Peace Corps in Russia; then Dorgan ran for Conrad's seat in the Senate and Pomeroy decided to run for Dorgan's seat in the House. Articulate, cheerful and sincere, a critic of insurance companies yet unabrasive, he was the obvious choice for the House seat and was nominated unanimously by the Democratic convention. He won the general 57%-39%, almost exactly Dorgan's margin in the Senate race.

Pomeroy has compiled a moderate to liberal voting record, defending North Dakota interests and working with Republicans as well as Democrats on some issues. In the Republican Congress, he strongly supported the adoption tax credit and brought his two-year-old daughter, adopted from Korea, onto the floor for the vote. He strongly supported normal trade relations with China and has pushed for more exports of North Dakota wheat there. In 2001 he got a seat on the Ways and Means Committee, where he voted against repeal of the estate tax. When Republican leaders brought up a bill to make it permanent in June 2002, Pomeroy offered an amendment to raise the $1 million exemption to $3 million; in April 2005 he proposed a $3.5 million exemption; both were rejected. In 2003 Pomeroy supported the Medicare/prescription drug bill, which among other things increased the Medicare reimbursement rate for rural and small city hospitals; this brought in $48 million to Bismarck hospitals alone and $183 million statewide. In 2005 and 2006 he co-chaired the House Democrats' Social Security Task Force, but did not engage in public discussions with Republicans on George W. Bush's proposal for individual retirement accounts. In 2007 he tried to revive the wind energy production tax credit, enacted in 1992 but allowed to expire in 2003; he argued that North Dakota was the number one state in wind energy production potential.

In 2003 Democrats, noting that Pomeroy was attacked in the 2002 election for leaving the Agriculture Committee, allowed him to regain a seat there even while staying on Ways and Means—something they don't allow for most other members. He opposed the 1996 Freedom to Farm Act, supported the crop insurance and disaster relief bills that have provided the rough equivalent of the old subsidies that the Freedom to Farm Act tried to phase out; he backed the 2002 farm act that vastly altered its terms and expanded the Conservation Reserve Program, in which North Dakota is the third largest participant, with 3.3 million acres. In that bill he pressed successfully for country-of-origin meat labeling; in 2004 he opposed the postponement of the effective date for that from 2004 to 2006. He and ranking Democrat Collin Peterson, from adjoining northwest Minnesota, opposed the Budget Committee's $3.7 billion cuts over 5 years, and unsuccessfully resisted them in committee; Pomeroy supported a $4 billion farm disaster relief bill in 2006, with a drought package that included $6 million for Devils Lake. But with the Democratic victory, Peterson, from a district with farm interests very similar to North Dakota's, becomes chairman, and Pomeroy seems likely to be a key ally in the reauthorization of the farm bill in 2007.

In the meantime, the biggest agricultural issues are related to trade, over which Ways and Means has jurisdiction. When Special Trade Representative Robert Zoellick negotiated an allowance of sugar imports from the Dominican Republic as part of the Central American Free Trade Agreement in March 2004, Pomeroy protested vigorously and said that the only way to settle sugar issues should be through worldwide WTO negotiations, not regional free trade agreements. North Dakota has a thriving sugar beet industry; Pomeroy said, "Granting subsidized foreign sugar access to our markets in an incremental fashion amounts to 'death by a thousand cuts' for our sugar industry." He voted against the Australian Free Trade Agreement in July 2004, arguing that the Australian Wheat Board provided subsidies; it passed anyway. He led the fight in July 2005 against ratification of the Central American-Dominican Republic Free Trade Agreement, opposed by the Red River Valley Sugarbeet Growers Association but backed by the North Dakota Wheat Commission. When Agriculture Secretary Mike Johanns said that the sugar provisions amounted to only two little packets of sugar being let in per consumer per week, Pomeroy replied, "Those two little packets of sugar cost us $180 million in lost income to farmers." But CAFTA passed narrowly.

During the devastating Grand Forks flooding in April 1997, Pomeroy helped man the dikes and slept in a nearby Air Force shelter in order to help residents deal with the disaster; later he worked and got nearly $500 million in flood relief, and has worked for a $300 million system of levees and walls to prevent future floods. He worked to get federal funding for an emergency outlet for Devils Lake, which has no natural outlet and whose water has risen to record levels and flooded more than 100,000 acres. But he was foiled by the Republican leadership, and in 2003 work was begun by the state government on a channel connecting Devils Lake with the Sheyenne River and through it the Red River of the North; the first waters started flowing out in August 2005.

Pomeroy had a serious challenges in 2002 from Tax Commissioner Rick Clayburgh, who argued that North Dakota would do better with a Republican congressman. He repeatedly attacked Pomeroy for leaving the Agriculture Committee just before it was going to consider the farm bill in order to take the seat on Ways and Means. Republicans hit Pomeroy for voting against estate tax repeal and trade promotion authority and for backing "privatization" of Social Security. In October Pomeroy ran an ad showing him near George W. Bush at the signing of a bill of which he was one of 39 co-sponsors continuing a tax exemption for clergy housing expenses. "President Bush signed Pomeroy's bill to stop a $2 billion tax on our rural churches," the announcer intoned. Pomeroy won 52%-48%; he carried Fargo, Minot and Grand Forks, Clayburgh's hometown; Clayburgh carried Bismarck. In 2004 Pomeroy was opposed by Duane Sand, a 15-year Navy officer who returned to North Dakota and in 2000 lost to Senator Kent Conrad by a 62%-38% margin. He was reinforced by a late October appearance by Speaker Dennis Hastert, who said, "When we're talking about water policy, when we talk about farm policy, there's really nobody there to represent North Dakota"—a reference to the Devils Lake outlet issue. Pomeroy's campaign replied that he had delivered on Medicare reimbursement, disaster relief legislation and agricultural policy. The result was Pomeroy's widest victory margin yet, 60%-40%, even as George W. Bush was carrying the state 63%-35%. In 2006 Pomeroy was opposed by Cass County farmer Matt Mechtel, a political newcomer. Pomeroy won by an impressive 66%-34%, carrying 52 counties and losing the 53d, Billings County, by 5 votes.

★ OHIO ★

Ohio was the first entirely American state, and one which ever since has seemed an epitome of American normalcy. The original 13 states started as British colonies, and the next three, Vermont, Kentucky and Tennessee, were spun off from them. But Ohio sprung Athena-like from the head of Congress, as the first state formed from the Northwest Territory. The Northwest Ordinance of 1787 established 6-by-6 mile square townships, which imposed geometric order on diverse American landscapes west to the Pacific; it set aside one square mile per township for public schools, and the landscape was soon peppered with schoolhouses and small colleges, the foundation stones of a literate republic. The Ordinance prohibited slavery, opening the way for free labor to clear fields, raise crops, build mills and factories, and in less than half a century, make this wilderness one of the most productive parts of western civilization. Ohio in the years after the Civil War became one of the great industrial states, the original headquarters of John D. Rockefeller's Standard Oil, the site of major steel mills along the narrow and languidly flowing Cuyahoga and Mahoning Rivers, and home of the biggest soap companies, machine tool makers, tire manufacturers and producers of safety glass. Dayton was the home of the Wright brothers, of James Ritty and James Patterson, the inventor and manufacturer of the cash register, of Charles Kettering, who invented the automobile starter and many other things. Akron was the home of Harvey Firestone, B. F. Goodrich and F. A. Seiberling, founder of Goodyear—the great tire manufacturers. They invented their devices and built their factories in a state that was culturally split, settled by New Englanders in the northeast in the Western Reserve and by Virginians in the south, split between the Southern-accented counties south of the National Road and U.S. 40 and the Northern-accented cities and towns to the north; between Butternut and Copperhead territory that didn't want to fight the Civil War and Yankee territory that fiercely prosecuted the War and Reconstruction afterwards.

This split heritage made Ohio politically a closely divided state—and a nationally pivotal one. A little more than a century ago Ohio produced the candidate and campaign manager—Governor and former Ways and Means Chairman William McKinley and iron and coal industrialist Mark Hanna; McKinley won the presidency in 1896 and 1900 and inaugurated a 34-year period of Republican national majorities. McKinley's Republicans were for high tariffs and hard money, had a friendly regard for workers and even some unions, but no patience with large union combinations and nascent socialism. They preached a nationalist Americanism tempered by a wariness about making major commitments abroad. Republicans were the majority in this increasingly industrial Ohio, losing rural Butternut counties but carrying the big industrial cities of the north.

Then came the Depression of the 1930s, and Ohio became the scene of something like class warfare, with sit-down strikes and victories for the CIO industrial unions in autos, steel and tires. CIO cities—Cleveland, Akron, Youngstown, Toledo—moved sharply toward the Democrats, while places with few CIO members—Cincinnati, Columbus, the dozens of small factory towns dotting the

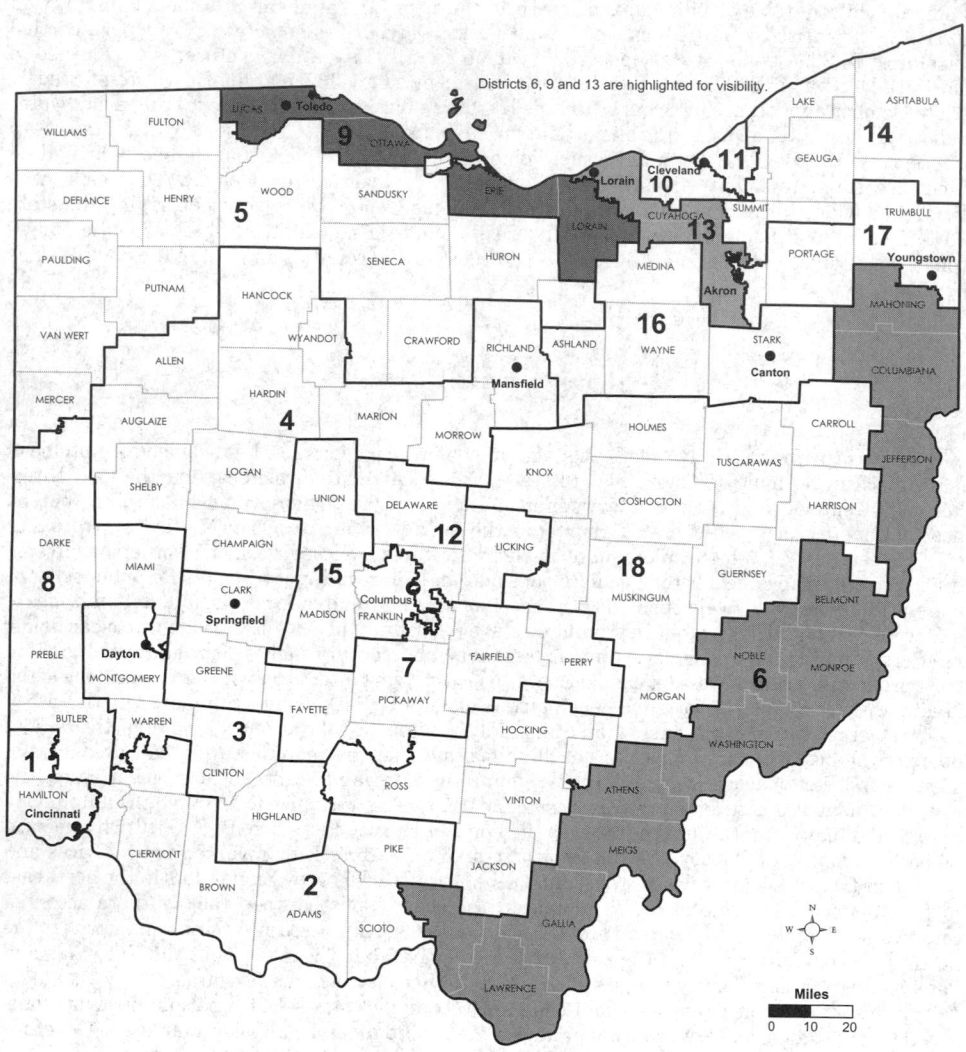

Districts 6, 9 and 13 are highlighted for visibility.

Congressional district boundaries were first effective for 2002.

The Almanac of American Politics.
National Journal

Miles
0   10   20

flat limestone plains of northern Ohio—stayed Republican. The political fighting was fierce and the stakes seemed high. CIO leaders hoped to organize the entire work force and build a Scandinavian-style welfare state; Republican leaders like Ohio's Senator Robert Taft feared union control of business would imperil freedoms and throttle the economy. In the 1930s and 1940s the unions made great gains. But Taft held them off, reducing union power with the Taft-Hartley Act of 1947, his own reelection to the Senate in 1950, and the election of his rival Dwight Eisenhower as president in 1952.

In the years since, Ohio has oscillated and been courted by national campaigns. In the 1990s Ohio swung to the Republicans. Bill Clinton did carry the state twice, but by the narrowest of his margins in any large state—40%-38% in 1992, 47%-41% in 1996—and Al Gore lost here 50%-46% in 2000. Ohio Republicans won smashing victories in 1994 and 1998 and held their own in 1996 and 2000. The leading figure was George Voinovich, elected governor in 1990 by 56%-44%, reelected in 1994 by 72%-25%—by far the biggest margin since 1826, when neither Republican nor Democratic parties existed—and elected senator by 56%-44% in 1998. But this has not just been a personal victory. From 1976 to 1994 Ohio was represented by two Democrats in the Senate, but when they retired they were replaced by Republicans: Mike DeWine and Voinovich, both of whom had run unsuccessfully for the Senate before. In 1998 Republican Bob Taft, bearer of a great Ohio name, was elected governor over Democrat Lee Fisher by 50%-45%. Until Taft's 1998 victory, Ohio's governorship had been passed back and forth between the two parties, with neither holding it for more than eight years, since George K. Nash won in 1899. By 2006 Republicans held it for a longer period than any party since 1803-22. Republicans also held every downballot statewide office, most of which were held by Democrats between 1970 to 1994, seemingly impervious margins in both houses of the legislature, and the majority of the U.S. House delegation. Despite the state's lagging economy, George W. Bush carried Ohio 51%-49% in 2004, as turnout surged as much as 20% in a state with very little population growth.

Then in 2006 came a great turnaround toward the Democrats. Ohio, unused to having one party in control for more than a decade, recoiled against the Republicans. It did not help that the supposedly fiscally responsible party had raised taxes several times, and that was not mitigated by cuts in the income tax made by Taft and the legislature in 2005 or by the $2 billion bond issue passed by voters that year. As often happens when a party is in power for many years, there was scandal. In August 2005 Taft pleaded no contest to criminal violations of state ethics laws: he had failed to report some $6,000 of gifts—free golf outings, meals, hockey tickets. Minor stuff, but the first time an Ohio governor had been found to have violated criminal law. At the same time the state Bureau of Workmen's Compensation, controlled by Republicans, was under investigation for placing $50 million in investments in a rare coin business run by major Republican contributor Tom Noe; the story was broken by the *Toledo Blade* in April 2005, and in May it was reported that as much as $13 million of the state's assets were missing. The state had made money on the investments, but so did Noe: his 20% share of profits amounted to nearly $2.6 million. And a couple of coins were lost in the mail, including an 1855 $3 gold piece, one of two in existence. Noe was indicted in February 2006 for stealing from the coin investment fund and in May 2006 pleaded guilty to violating federal campaign finance laws. His trial on state charges took place from mid-October until the week after the election. Democrats swept the 1970 election here after the Republican state treasurer was charged with making improper investments through a firm called Crofters. The rare coin scandal produced similar results in 2006.

Democratic Congressman Ted Strickland, a former prison psychologist, was elected governor by a 61%-37% margin over Secretary of State Ken Blackwell, a Taft critic from the right. Strickland carried 72 of 88 counties and won more popular votes than Voinovich had in 1994; the only major metro area Blackwell carried was his home base of Cincinnati. Democrats won the offices of attorney general, secretary of state and treasurer. Democratic Congressman Sherrod Brown beat Senator Mike DeWine by a solid 56%-44%. Democrats did not quite sweep the board, however. A Republican won the race for auditor narrowly; one Republican won a seat on the state Supreme Court and another Republican justice was reelected; Republicans held on to majorities in the legislature, losing just one seat in the state Senate and seven in the House. And Democrats gained only one U.S. House seat, that vacated by Bob Ney, who was later sentenced to jail for doing favors for lobbyist Jack Abramoff. Turnout was up 25% over 2002, perhaps partly because of the minimum wage referendum Democrats put on the ballot, which passed 57%-43%; Ohioans also voted 57% against slot machines and 59% to bar smoking in public places. High turnout in a sweep year seems to be an Ohio tradition; turnout spiked in the 1962 and 1990 Republican sweeps and the 1970 and 1982 Democratic sweeps.

The Republican trend of the 1990s and the Democratic trend of 2006 occurred in a state that is still more industrial than post-industrial, a state changed by the immigration of the early 20th century but little touched by the immigration of the late 20th century, a state where cultural liberalism has a far smaller constituency than it does on the East or West Coasts or even in nearby Illinois and Michigan. It used to be said that Ohio was a typical state, a great test market, for in income levels, urban-rural balance, and ethnic mix, as well as presidential percentages, it is not very far from the national average. But economically and culturally, it is different, a template perhaps for Indiana and Missouri but not for Oregon and Arizona. There are few immigrants here; the population is only 2% Hispanic. Ohio's median household income is only 6% below the national average, but the median housing value is 23% below. Ohio trails only California and Texas, which are three and two times as large, in manufacturing jobs, yet it has 400,000 fewer of them than it did in the peak year, 1969, and its population and income have been increasing at less than the national average; from 2000 to 2004 it had a lower rate of population growth than any state but West Virginia and North Dakota. The Ohio economy seems stuck in the 2001-02 recession. Employment peaked at 5,585,000 in February 2000, fell to 5,502,000 in February 2004 and didn't overcome its peak 2000 employment until February 2006. The unemployment rate rose from 3.9% in March 2001 to 6.0% in January 2003, 6.1% in March 2005 and 5.6% in July 2006—far lower than in the recession years of 1958 and 1982, but still uncomfortably above the national average. The unemployment is worst not in the Cleveland metro area, which hasn't gained much population in decades, but in Youngstown and Dayton and in rural counties in the eastern, southern and western parts of the state. Pretty much gone is the old tradition of heading straight from high school and perhaps military service to a high-wage factory job. General Motors and Ford have been shutting down plants and permanently laying off thousands of workers in Ohio, while Honda decided in 2006 not to build a fourth plant in Ohio but to go to Indiana instead; the state's encouragement of bioscience and high-tech businesses has not generated nearly as many offsetting job gains.

Politically, there are two distinct parts of Ohio. One, call it Northeast Ohio, is the part where the CIO unions organized the big factories, the heavy industry area along Lake Erie and reaching south to the coal-mining counties across the Ohio River from West Virginia. In Northeast Ohio giant steel mills closed in Cleveland and the Mahoning Valley around Youngstown in the 1980s, and population declined as young people moved out. Politically, the Democratic voting habits instilled by the CIO unions are still evident, though there was no movement toward Democrats on cultural issues in the 1990s here, as there was in larger metro areas. George W. Bush lost the area 55%-41% in 2000 and 54%-46% in 2004. But it has swung in both directions in recent gubernatorial elections, 49%-48% for Republican Bob Taft in 2002, a huge 68%-29% for Democrat Ted Strickland in 2006. The rest of the state, call it Southwest Ohio, is a more diversified industrial area, never so dependent on big industries like steel, tires and autos. It did not lose so many jobs or suffer such population loss in the early 1980s as Northeast Ohio. Parts of it began building a new, more supple and adaptable manufacturing economy, with smaller factories, less rigid management and fewer union members, an economy which did reasonably well in the 1990s but has had little growth since 2000. In this part of Ohio the cultural atmosphere in small towns and even its big cities has become culturally quite conservative, with the possible exception of Columbus, Ohio's fastest-growing metro area, with something of a post-industrial, information-based economy. Politically, this area has long been heavily Republican; the old Butternut Democratic tradition for many years seemed to have disappeared by the 1990s. Bush carried this part of the state 56%-40% in 2000 and 60%-40% in 2004 and Taft carried it 65%-31% in 2002. But in 2006 Southwest Ohio swung Democratic: 56%-42% for Strickland, who comes from the farthest south part of the state, and 51%-49% for Senator Sherrod Brown. The shift to the Democrats was bigger here, where the electorate has been growing faster than in northeast Ohio. Between 1980 and 2000 turnout in Northeast Ohio rose only 3%, while it rose 16% in Southwest Ohio; in 2004 the Democrats' heroic efforts increased turnout in Northeast Ohio 18% over 2000, but the Bush campaign's efforts helped increase turnout in Southwest Ohio 21%. Similarly, turnout between 2002 and 2006 rose 22% in Northeast Ohio and 26% in Southwest Ohio.

So where does Ohio stand in history? Is it New Deal Ohio, with ethnic factory workers arranged against small town businessmen, ethnic Catholics versus rural Protestants, all engaged in a contest to see how far and in what ways government should be enlarged? Or is it McKinley's Ohio, with mechanical tinkerers and can-do manufacturers, adaptive businessmen and employees, striving to work hard, raise families and serve communities that feel little class conflict or economic envy? For a decade or so it seemed to be McKinley's Ohio. The 2006 election results suggest that happy days are here again for the Democrats and that it may be once again New Deal Ohio.

A footnote on Ohio politics. Since the 1950s, no one has been elected governor or senator here without losing a race for one of those offices first, with the single exception of William Saxbe, elected to the Senate in 1968. In 2006 the jinx seemed to be broken as Congressman Sherrod Brown was elected to the Senate and Congressman Ted Strickland was elected governor. But Brown had a losing statewide race in his past, when he lost a bid for reelection as Secretary of State in 1990.

The People		**Race/Ethnic Origin**			**Military veterans:** 1,144,007 (13.5%)	
Pop. 2006 (est):	11,478,006	9,538,111	84.0%	White	WWII: 21.7%	Korea: 13.7%
Pop. 2000:	11,353,140	1,290,662	11.4%	Black	Vietnam: 30.7%	Gulf War: 8.8%
Pop. 1990:	10,847,115	131,670	1.2%	Asian	**Most populous cities (2006):**	
Change 1990-2000:	Up 4.7%	21,985	0.2%	Native Am.	1. Columbus	733,203
% of U.S. total:	4.0%	2,336	0.0%	Hawaiian	2. Cleveland	444,313
Pop. rank:	7th of 50	137,770	1.2%	Two+ races	3. Cincinnati	333,252
Area size:	44,825 sq. mi.	13,483	0.1%	Other	4. Toledo	298,446
State Native:	74.7%	217,123	1.9%	Hisp. Origin	5. Akron	209,704
Non-citizen:	1.5%	**Ancestry**				
Language		German: 18.8%		Irish: 9.5%	Urban population: 77.3%	
English: 91.4%	Other Eur.: 4.1%	English: 6.9%		USA: 6.5%	Rural population: 22.7%	
Spanish: 3.0%		Italian: 4.4%				

Education		**Work Sector**		**General Assembly**	
H.S. Grad:	83.0%	Private: 82.0%	Govt: 12.2%	Senate	21 R 12 D
College Grad:	21.1%	Self: 5.5%	Family: 0.3%	House	53 R 46 D
Industry		Unemployment: 5.0%		Legislative Term Limits: Yes	
Agri: 1.1%	Con: 6.0%	**Household Income**		**Registered Voters**	
Fin: 6.3%	Info: 2.4%	<15k: 15.6%	15-35k: 26.9%	No party registration	
Mfg: 25.0%	Prof: 27.8%	35-50k: 17.3%	50-100k: 30.4%		
Public: 4.1%	Trade: 15.5%	100-150k: 6.5%	>150k: 3.3%		
Other: 12.0%		Median: $40,956			
Occupation		Poverty status: 10.6%			
Blue collar: 27.8%	White collar: 57.3%	**Home Value**			
Gray collar: 14.9%		<50k: 12.2%	50-100k: 37.5%	100-200k: 38.6%	200-300k: 7.8%
		300-500k: 2.9%	>500k: 1.0%	Median: $100,500	

Presidential politics   With 20 electoral votes and a tradition of close partisan competition, Ohio is a crucial state in presidential politics. Of the large industrial states—Pennsylvania, Ohio, Michigan, Illinois—Ohio has been consistently the most Republican for 50 years, with the single exception of 1976, when Jimmy Carter ran well in the Southern-accented counties below U.S. 40 and carried the state by 11,000 votes. Ohio matched the national average in 1984 and 1988, came close to doing so in 1996 and was only 2% off in 2000. In 2004 George W. Bush matched his national percentage here and John Kerry ran 1% ahead of his. No Republican has ever been elected president without carrying Ohio; no Democrat, in today's electoral vote arithmetic, can be sure of winning without it. On election night 2004, after it became clear that Bush had won Florida, all eyes were on Ohio: if Bush's lead held up here, he would be president again; if not, John Kerry would be elected even though trailing in the popular vote by 3 million.

2004 Presidential Vote		
Bush (R)	2,859,764	(51%)
Kerry (D)	2,741,165	(49%)
Badnarik (Lib)	14,676	(0%)
Other	12,298	(0%)

2004 Democratic Presidential Primary		
Kerry (D)	632,590	(52%)
Edwards (D)	416,104	(34%)
Kucinich (D)	110,066	(9%)
Dean (D)	30,983	(3%)
Lieberman (D)	14,676	(1%)
Other	16,595	(1%)

2000 Presidential Vote		
Bush (R)	2,350,363	(50%)
Gore (D)	2,183,628	(46%)
Nader (Green)	117,799	(3%)
Other	50,208	(1%)

The dynamics of the presidential race in Ohio were quite different in 2000 and 2004. In 2000 Bush, despite holding narrow leads in polls, made Ohio a priority state from start to finish, while the Gore campaign, looking to opportunities elsewhere, pulled out much of its advertising in mid-October—perhaps its greatest strategic mistake. Bush carried Ohio by only 50%-46%. In 2004 both campaigns recognized that Ohio was a major, perhaps the major, target state. Job losses, especially manufacturing job losses, seemed to make the atmosphere especially favorable to Democrats on economic issues. The 527 organizations spent $9.7 million on ads in Ohio markets, more than in any other state, and the top five media markets in ad exposures included Toledo, Dayton, Columbus and Cleveland. Democrats and anti-Bush 527 organizations ran a classic industrial era registration and turnout drive aimed especially at black neighborhoods in central cities and at university communities. By all measures it was spectacularly successful. The Democratic popular vote margin was increased by 60,000 votes in Cleveland's Cuyahoga County, and Democratic margins were increased as well in the counties containing Columbus, Cincinnati, Akron, Toledo, Lorain, Youngstown and Warren and in a five-county cluster centered on the university town of Athens. Overall, in the 18 counties where the Democratic margin was increased or the Republican margin reduced (or in the case of Canton's Stark County, which had a 6% job loss, a Bush margin was converted to a Kerry margin), the Democratic margin increased by 183,000. If the Bush margin in the remaining 70 counties had remained static, Kerry would have erased Bush's 2000 margin of 165,000 votes and carried the state by some 17,000.

But the Bush margin did not remain static. The Bush campaign ran a post-industrial registration and turnout organization, with some 65,000 volunteers, networking with evangelical and Catholic churches, farmers, doctors and community organizations. It made 3.9 million phone calls to voters, 1.8 million in the last five days. Not all of these were obvious targets. In a tier of seven counties on the western edge of the state which had no population growth or population decline from 2000 to 2004, the Bush margin went up by 13,000 in those four years. In Cincinnati's population-losing Hamilton County, the Bush margin declined by 19,000 votes, but in the three population-gaining counties surrounding it the Bush margin increased by 37,000. The Bush campaign converted a Gore margin into a Bush margin in Springfield's Clark County, transatlantically famous as the target of a letter-writing campaign by readers of Britain's left-wing *Guardian* newspaper.

Job losses and economic issues were not the primary movers of votes. Bush carried 10 of the 12 counties, most of them small, with the largest percentage of job losses. A 43%-38% plurality preferred Bush over Kerry on the issue of economic recovery, and he held larger leads on moral values and the war on terrorism. Members of union households, one-third of voters, preferred Kerry 58%-42%, while those in other households favored Bush by a similar margin. But there was a starker difference along the lines of religion. Bush won 56% among Protestants and 55% among Catholics, the latter a 5% gain from 2000. Those attending religious services weekly preferred Bush 65%-35%, with no appreciable difference between Protestants and Catholics, while occasional attenders favored Kerry 57%-43% and the 14% who never attend religious services preferred Kerry 63%-35%. In states like New York and California, voters with graduate school degrees vote overwhelmingly Democratic, but in Ohio they were evenly split between the two candidates. Cultural liberalism has not made the inroads among the highly educated and those with high incomes here in the heartland that it has made on the coasts.

The initial count showed Bush 136,000 votes ahead of Kerry—many times the margin that any candidate has ever successfully challenged. There was some controversy over the provisional ballots. Secretary of State Kenneth Blackwell, a Republican and Bush backer, had been backed up by the courts in his ruling that provisional ballots had to be cast in the voter's precinct, not just anywhere in the same county as the Democrats wanted. When the 155,000 provisional ballots were counted, the Bush margin was reduced to 119,000. Still there were cries of vote fraud and charges that lines were longer in Democratic areas and that the voting machines had been programmed to produce overly Republican results. The Green and Libertarian parties sued to get a recount, and Jesse Jackson alleged that 130,000 votes were switched from Kerry to Bush. But no substantial evidence was brought forward to substantiate these charges, and Ohio's electoral votes were cast a second time for George W. Bush.

In 1996 Ohio switched its presidential primary from May to March 19, and voted on the same day as Illinois, Michigan and Wisconsin. But even then, just four weeks after New Hampshire, the race was already over. In May 1999 the state legislature voted to move the date to March 7, and Ohio was seriously contested. George W. Bush and Al Gore, with serious organizational support, won overwhelming victories as they clinched their parties' nominations. In 2004 Ohio held its primary on March 2, with seven other states; John Kerry won easily here and elsewhere and clinched the Democratic nomination exactly nine months before the general election, which was held, appropriately for Ohio, on the birthday of Warren G. Harding, Ohio's most recent president.

Congressional districting

110th Congress Lineup
10 R   7 D   1 V
109th Congress Lineup
12 R   6 D

Ohio lost one House seat in the 2000 Census and now has a House delegation of 18 members, its smallest since the 1820s. Republicans had majorities in the legislature and held the governorship, and so had control of the process for the first time since 1960. It was clear that the Republicans could eliminate the seat of 13th District Democrat Sherrod Brown and imperil the chances of 6th District Democrat Ted Strickland. But Strickland threatened to run against 18th District Republican Bob Ney and Brown made it clear that if his seat was eliminated he would run for governor. Governor Bob Taft, even though he had ousted Brown as secretary of state in 1990, did not want to face a well-financed and politically adept challenger, and asked Republican legislators not to target him. The legislature did not act in 2001.

Then, in January 2002, the Republicans effectively lost control. Ohio's filing deadline for the May primary was February 21, and under the Ohio Constitution, a law passed in 2002 could take immediate effect only if it had a two-thirds vote in both houses. This meant the Republicans had to get the votes of at least one Democrat in the Senate and seven in the House. In the circumstances, the Republicans constructed a pretty ingenious plan, which they unveiled January 16. All 11 Republican incumbents got districts very similar to their current ones. So did the two Cleveland Democrats. Every other Democrat got a significantly different district. The incumbent put into the most parlous position was the 17th District's Jim Traficant. But he was facing trial on bribery charges (he was convicted in April and expelled from the House in July), and had been voting with Republicans on many issues; if one Democrat had to go, Democrats obviously preferred to sacrifice him. The 3d District was made significantly more Republican, but incumbent Tony Hall had long run far ahead of party lines; so long as he continued to run the seat seemed safe Democratic. The 14th District's Tom Sawyer had been given much of Traficant's old territory, but he had cast some free trade votes and organized labor didn't care if he was discomfited. Ted Strickland, given a seat stretching 325 miles along the Ohio River and up to Youngstown, was happy, even though he might have to face Traficant in a primary; the seat was much more Democratic than his previous district. Brown, given a safe Democratic seat, was pleased too. So on January 17 Democrats made a deal: they would provide the votes to give the plan immediate effect and avoid having to reschedule the congressional primary for August or September at a cost to taxpayers of $7 million. The plan passed on January 22.

Then on January 26 Tony Hall said he might give up his seat for a humanitarian job and George W. Bush offered him the ambassadorship to the Food and Agriculture Organization in Rome. Republican Dayton Mayor Mike Turner had already announced he would run for the seat; Hall did not file for reelection and resigned when he was confirmed by the Senate, and Turner easily won the seat. The upshot was that the legislature's plan, and Hall's well-timed appointment, increased the Republican edge in the delegation from 11–8 to 12–6. In 2003 longtime Republican state Chairman Robert Bennett, noting that his party controlled the legislature and the governorship, suggested that Ohio might want to redistrict once again, as Texas did in 2003 and Georgia would in 2005. But Republicans evidently concluded that they had little to gain and that the current district lines suited them just fine.

In 2006 Republicans lost scandal-plagued Bob Ney's seat and came within 3% of losing three more; had they lost these Democrats would have had a 10–8 edge. And Sherrod Brown, spared by the 2002 redistricting compromise, ran for the Senate and beat incumbent Republican Mike DeWine 56%-44%. The possibility of intra-decade redistricting now seems to be zero, since the Democratic governor faces a Republican legislature, and the Republicans' 21-12 edge in the state Senate seems unlikely to be reversed in 2008. But after the 2010 Census the balance could well shift. Census estimates show Ohio's population up only 1.1% from 2000 to 2006, a lower rate than any other state except West Virginia (North Dakota and Louisiana have lost population), and demographers estimate that Ohio may lose two seats. If Democrats hold the governorship and gain control of the legislature in 2010, they could pass a plan that would remove at least three Republicans and elect one or more new Democrats.

Governor

Ted Strickland (D)

Elected 2006, term expires Jan. 2011, 1st term; b. Aug. 4, 1941, Lucasville; home, Bexley; Asbury Col., B.A. 1963, M.Div. 1967, U. of KY, Ph.D. 1980; Methodist; married (Frances).

Elected Office: U.S. House of Reps., 1992-94, 1996-2006.

Professional Career: Assoc. Minister, Trinity Methodist Church, 1967-68; Dir. of Soc. Svcs., KY Methodist Home, 1968-70; Consulting psychologist, Southern OH Correctional Facility, 1985-92, 1995-96; Prof., Shawnee St. U., 1988-92, 1995-96.

Office: Governor's Office, Riffe Center, 30th Floor, 77 S. High Street, Columbus, 43215-6108, 614-466-3555; Fax: 614-466-9354; Web site: governor.ohio.gov.

Election Results

2006 general	Ted Strickland (D)	2,435,384	(61%)
	Kenneth Blackwell (R)	1,474,285	(37%)
	Other	113,085	(3%)
2006 primary	Ted Strickland (D)	634,114	(79%)
	Bryan Flannery (D)	166,253	(21%)
2002 general	Bob Taft (R)	1,865,007	(58%)
	Timothy Hagan (D)	1,236,924	(38%)
	John Eastman (I)	126,686	(4%)

Ted Strickland in 2006 became the first Democrat elected governor of Ohio since 1986. He was born and raised in Lucasville in Appalachian Ohio, the son of a steelworker with a sixth-grade education and the eighth of nine children. His family lived a hardscrabble existence, briefly living in a chicken coop after their home burned down, and religion played a significant role in his early life. College did not seem within the realm of possibilities but a high school teacher took him on a trip to visit Asbury College and Theological Seminary in Kentucky and he ended up graduating from there with degree in history in 1963 and a master's in divinity in 1967. He served as a Methodist minister and then in various roles at the Methodist Home for Children in Versailles, Kentucky; in 1980, he got a Ph.D. in counseling psychology from the University of Kentucky. After that, he worked as a prison psychologist and a psychology professor at Shawnee State University.

His path to the governorship was long and there was little in his early political career to suggest he might one day end up there. Strickland ran for the House unsuccessfully in 1976, 1978 and 1980, and then ran again in 1992 when redistricting placed two Republican incumbents in the district. One lost in the primary 50.2%-49.8% and Strickland defeated the other 51%-49%. In his first term Strickland voted for the Clinton budget and tax package, but against the 1994 crime bill because of its gun control provisions and against NAFTA. As the 1994 election neared, Strickland suggested there might be a need for tax increases to pay for health care programs; Republican challenger Frank Cremeans seized on this and won 51%-49%. In a 1996 rematch, Strickland attacked Cremeans for Medicare "cuts" and scaling down the Earned Income Tax Credit, which he called a tax increase on the poor. Strickland won 51%-49%.

In Congress, Strickland's voting record was generally moderate but a bit more liberal on foreign policy. After the 2004 election, Strickland was mentioned as a possible candidate for governor or senator; in January 2005 he appeared to rule out a run for governor. But in May, after Columbus Mayor Michael Coleman, the leading Democratic candidate, seemed to falter, Strickland changed his mind and said he would run.

The governor at the time, Republican Bob Taft, was ineligible for a third term and likely could not have won anyway as he suffered from extremely low job ratings. In any case, Ohio Democrats were well positioned to argue that Republicans had been in office too long: the only party controlling the governorship longer was Thomas Jefferson's Democratic Republicans, who held it from 1803 to 1822. It did not help that the supposedly fiscally responsible party had raised taxes several times, and that was not mitigated by cuts in the income tax made by Taft and the legislature in 2005 or by the $2 billion bond issue passed by voters that year. As often happens when a party is in power for many years, there was scandal. In August 2005 Taft pleaded no contest to criminal violations of state ethics laws: he had failed to report some $6,000 of gifts—free golf outings, meals, hockey tickets—marking the first time an Ohio governor had been convicted of a crime. At the same time the state Bureau of Workmen's Compensation, controlled by Republicans, was under investigation for placing $50 million in investments in a rare coin business run by major Republican contributor Tom Noe; the story was broken by the *Toledo Blade* in April 2005, and in May it was reported that as much as $13 million of the state's assets were missing. The state had made money on the investments, but so did Noe: his 20% share of profits amounted to nearly $2.6 million. And a couple of coins were lost in the mail, including an 1855 $3 gold piece, one of two in existence. Noe was indicted in February 2006 for stealing from the coin investment fund and in May 2006 pleaded guilty to violating federal campaign finance laws. His trial on state charges took place from mid-October until the week after the election.

Strickland, who won a 79%-21% victory over former state Representative Bryan Flannery in the May primary, faced Secretary of State Kenneth Blackwell, a strong fiscal and cultural conservative. Like Strickland, Blackwell had a compelling life story: The son of a meatpacker, he lived in a Cincinnati housing project until he was six, attended Xavier University on a football scholarship—he tried out for the Dallas Cowboys upon graduation but didn't make the cut—and rose to serve as Cincinnati councilman and mayor, U.S. Department of Housing and Urban Development undersecretary, ambassador to the United Nations Human Rights Commission, and Ohio treasurer and secretary of state. He would have been Ohio's first African-American governor. Blackwell had some distance from the state party, having criticized Taft and Republican legislative leaders often for raising taxes and overspending. With assistance from the anti-tax political action committee Club for Growth and religious conservatives, Blackwell defeated moderate Ohio Attorney General Jim Petro by 56%-44% in what was an expensive and divisive Republican primary.

Strickland campaigned on a platform called "Turnaround Ohio", a plan to strengthen the state's economy, improve education, retrain workers for the global economy and increase access to health care. Blackwell called for repeal of the sales tax increase and a constitutional amendment limiting the growth of state spending. Both candidates opposed gun control and legalizing same-sex marriage, though Strickland supported legal benefits for gay partners. Faith played an unusually prominent role; both candidates incorporated biblical verses into their speeches. Blackwell carried a Bible to campaign events but Strickland gave no ground to Blackwell, running ads on Christian radio saying that "biblical principles" would guide his actions as governor.

Strickland led in the polls by large margins for much of the campaign and won 61%-37%. He carried 72 of 88 counties and won more popular votes than George Voinovich had in 1994; the only major metro area Blackwell carried was his home base of Cincinnati. In 1970, Democrats swept the election here after the Republican state treasurer was charged with making improper investments through a firm called Crofters. The rare coin scandal produced similar results in 2006. Democrats won the offices of U.S. senator, attorney general, secretary of state and treasurer. Republicans held on to majorities in the legislature, losing just one seat in the state Senate and seven in the House.

Senior Senator

George Voinovich (R)

Elected 1998, seat up 2010, 2d term; b. July 15, 1936, Cleveland; home, Cleveland; Ohio U., B.A. 1958, Ohio St. U., J.D. 1961; Catholic; married (Janet).

Elected Office: OH House of Reps., 1966-71; Cuyahoga Cnty. Auditor, 1971-76; Cuyahoga Cnty. Commissioner, 1977-78; OH Lt. Gov., 1979; Cleveland Mayor, 1979-89; OH Gov., 1990-98.

Professional Career: OH Asst. Atty. Gen., 1963-64.

DC Office: 524 HSOB, 20510, 202-224-3353; Fax: 202-228-1382; Web site: voinovich.senate.gov.

State Offices: Cincinnati, 513-684-3265; Cleveland, 216-522-7095; Columbus, 614-469-6697; Nelsonville, 740-441-6410; Toledo, 419-259-3895.

Committees: *Environment & Public Works* (3d of 9 R): Clean Air & Nuclear Safety (RMM); Transportation & Infrastructure; Transportation Safety, Infrastructure Security & Water Quality. *Foreign Relations* (6th of 10 R): International Operations & Organizations, Democracy & Human Rights; European Affairs; Near Eastern & South & Central Asian Affairs. *Homeland Security & Governmental Affairs* (3d of 8 R): Oversight of Government Management, the Federal Workforce & the District of Columbia (RMM); State, Local & Private Sector Preparedness & Integration; Federal Financial Management, Government Information, Federal Services & International Security.

Group Ratings

	ADA	ACLU	AFS	LCV	ITIC	NTU	COC	ACU	CFG	FRC
2006	20	17	50	43	75	59	75	56	40	87
2005	15	—	25	15	—	60	100	68	56	—

National Journal Ratings

	2005 LIB	—	2005 CONS	2006 LIB	—	2006 CONS
Economic	46%	—	53%	47%	—	51%
Social	39%	—	58%	45%	—	54%
Foreign	46%	—	52%	26%	—	67%

Key Votes of the 109th Congress

1. Bar ANWR Drilling	N	5. Confirm Samuel Alito	Y	9. Limit Interstate Abortion	Y
2. FY06 Spending Curb	Y	6. Path to Citizenship	Y	10. CAFTA	Y
3. Estate Tax Repeal	N	7. Bar Same Sex Marriage	Y	11. Urge Iraq Withdrawal	N
4. Raise Minimum Wage	N	8. Stem Cell Research $	N	12. Provide Detainee Rights	N

Election Results

2004 general	George Voinovich (R)	3,464,356	(64%)	($8,956,380)
	Eric Fingerhut (D)	1,961,171	(36%)	($1,166,538)
2004 primary	George Voinovich (R)	640,082	(77%)	
	John Mitchel (R)	195,476	(23%)	
1998 general	George Voinovich (R)	1,922,087	(56%)	($6,756,712)
	Mary O. Boyle (D)	1,482,054	(44%)	($2,236,137)

George Voinovich, Ohio's senior senator, is a Republican, who was first elected to public office in 1966. He is of Serbian and Slovenian descent and grew up in the heavily ethnic, working class neighborhood of Collinwood in Cleveland, where he still lives. He graduated from Ohio State and its law school, then practiced law in Cleveland. He was elected to the state House in 1966 at the age of 30, elected Cuyahoga County auditor in 1971 and county commissioner in 1977. In 1978 he was selected by 69-year-old Governor James Rhodes to be lieutenant governor. In 1979, after Cleveland went into bankruptcy under Mayor (now Congressman) Dennis Kucinich, Voinovich ran for mayor. It was a strenuous campaign, running as a Republican in a heavily Democratic city, and one touched by tragedy: his nine-year-old daughter was killed in an auto accident at the time. But he won, and in 10 years in office, he fixed the budget and sparked the city's renaissance. His one defeat came in 1988, when he lost 57%-43% to Senator Howard Metzenbaum. In 1990 Voinovich ran for governor and beat Attorney General Anthony Celebrezze Jr., 56%-44%; in 1994 he was reelected by the spectacular margin of 72%-25%. Voinovich got the state government's fiscal house in order, with the help of a tax increase in 1992.

In February 1997 Senator John Glenn announced he would retire in 1998, and Voinovich, not eligible to run for reelection as governor, was the obvious favorite; he led in polls for nearly two years. His Democratic opponent was another Clevelander (as a boy Voinovich delivered newspapers to her family's house), Cuyahoga County Commissioner Mary Boyle, who lost the 1994 Senate primary but this time had no competition for the nomination. Boyle campaigned on education, blaming Voinovich for allowing Ohio schools to decline; she called for HMO regulation and a minimum wage increase. Voinovich mostly ignored her attacks and outspent her by almost 3–1, running ads that highlighted his record as governor. In November his margin over Boyle was a decisive but not overwhelming 56%-44%.

Voinovich came to the Senate, after 32 years in public office, as a big government Republican, willing to back tax increases as he did in 1992 but dubious about cutting them, as he was in 1999 and 2000. In his previous positions he had been required to balance budgets, and he seemed viscerally repelled by deficits. In April 2000 he was one of two Republicans to vote against the Republican budget. In July 2000 he was one of four Republicans to vote against estate tax repeal and the only Republican to vote against marriage penalty relief. He did support the Bush tax cuts in May 2001, when it looked as if the surplus would be permanent. In October 2001 he worked to scale back the tax cuts in House Republicans' stimulus package. In February 2003 he came out against the $700 billion Bush tax cut and in April he and Olympia Snowe insisted they would back no cut higher than $350 billion. That led Finance Chairman Charles Grassley and Majority Leader Bill Frist to say they would insist on that figure from conference, to the rage of the House Republican leadership. When George W. Bush came to Ohio in April 2003, Voinovich was cordial but refused to budge; he voted for the $350 billion cut. In 2004 Voinovich declined to back the "paygo" amendment, requiring all tax cuts and spending increases to be offset by tax increases or spending cuts elsewhere, but in

March 2005 he did back a paygo amendment, along with Lincoln Chafee and John McCain, but they did not have enough votes to prevail in the Senate and agreement on a budget resolution was reached.

In March 2005 he voted against the Republican budget resolution because it would extend earlier tax cuts, one of four Republicans to do so; it passed anyway. In September 2005 he continued to argue against extending the tax cuts. "Hopefully, we won't hear any more about making the tax cuts permanent." In May 2006 he was one of three Republicans to vote against the tax bill extending the capital gains and dividend tax cuts and providing a one-year fix of the Alternative Minimum Tax. In June he voted against allowing permanent estate tax repeal to come to a vote; he also opposed the compromise limiting it to estates over $5 million. He joined most Democrats in voting against the Republican leadership's trifecta bill in August 2006, which included estate tax reductions, a minimum wage increase and extensions of other tax cuts. He explained his position in an impassioned speech in May: "Instead of making the tax cuts permanent, we should be leveling with the American people about the fiscally shaky ground we are on. . . . I have to say this, and I know it is controversial, but if you look at the extraordinary costs that we have had with the war and homeland security and Katrina, the logical thing that one would think about is to ask for a temporary tax increase to pay for them." He has advanced his own solutions to budget and Social Security problems. For the budget he favors "accrual accounting." On Social Security he said he was favorable to individual investment accounts, but did not think the issue should be addressed in early 2005. In September he called for using payroll taxes not to purchase Treasury bonds but to buy municipal or corporate bonds or mortgage-backed securities, to be cashed in ultimately to pay benefits; he called for similar "lock box" devices for the Civil Service Retirement and Disability Fund, Medicare trust funds, Military Retirement Funds. But on major changes in Social Security, he said in September 2005, after Katrina, "That's not going to happen now."

Voinovich has shown interest not only in maintaining government's revenue flow, but in how government works. As chairman of the Government Reform subcommittee on Government Management, Restructuring and the District of Columbia, he found that agencies could not say how much they spend on training. In October 2001 he introduced a bill that he hoped would lead to the first major change in civil service laws since 1978. It provided for chief human capital officers at each agency; hiring from a wider pool of applicants rated either basically qualified, highly qualified or superior (current practice is to choose among those rated, often arbitrarily, the top three); greater leeway for demonstration projects; allowing agencies to buy out workers for $25,000 to reshape their work forces. In July 2002 Voinovich and then-subcommittee Chairman Daniel Akaka got a version of this bill inserted as the personnel section in the homeland security bill. There it became law in December 2002. This was a major achievement: the new department has 173,000 employees and, together with Defense, which has been seeking its own civil service changes, accounts for most federal government employees. Voinovich submitted another version of his bill to cover the rest in January 2003.

As an Environment and Public Works subcommittee chairman, he steered to passage in September 2000 a giant energy and water authorization, which included the $1.1 billion Everglades restoration project estimated to eventually cost $7.8 billion. But a month later he voted against a water and power appropriation, which included many Ohio projects, arguing that it spent too much money: authorizing committee members like to keep appropriators on a short leash. In January 2003 Energy Committee Chairman James Inhofe asked him to manage George W. Bush's Clear Skies Initiative providing a cap-and-trade system to limit emissions of sulfur dioxide, nitrogen oxide and mercury. In June he rejected calls for carbon dioxide controls. "Regulation of carbon is not going to happen." In November 2003 Voinovich and Inhofe increased the first-year mercury emissions, bringing target dates closer and providing for one-year extensions if needed to maintain a reliable supply of electricity. But this did not satisfy committee Democrats and Republican Lincoln Chafee. In March 2005 Voinovich floated a compromise, with a voluntary carbon dioxide emissions program; it was rejected in committee 9–9 because of Chafee's opposition.

Voinovich has sometimes surprised colleagues by his stands on foreign issues. He is the only Serbian-American in the Senate, and as a college freshman wrote a paper on how the United States sold out Yugoslavia at the February 1945 Yalta conference; in 1991 his Serbian relatives were forced out of their homes in the newly independent Croatia. In March and April 1999 he strongly opposed the bombing of Serbia, but he called Slobodan Milosevic a "war criminal" and tried to convince the State Department to support forces to depose him. In April 2006 he said that Kosovo was moving too rapidly toward independence and that if we pulled out 1,900 U.S. troops too quickly "this problem will continue to fester and we'll have a continuation of the problems that we've had for centuries." In

April 2005, after not attending earlier hearings on the subject, he held up the confirmation of John Bolton as ambassador to the United Nations; in May 2005 he spoke out strongly against Bolton in committee but voted with other Republicans to send the nomination to the floor without recommendation. On the floor he spoke, as he often does, emotionally to the point of tears and said that Bolton was "the poster child of what someone in the diplomatic corps should not be." He voted against cloture, and Bolton was not confirmed; in August Bush gave him a recess appointment that lasted until January 2007. In July 2006, when another attempt was made to confirm him, Voinovich did a volte-face and supported Bolton, "While Bolton is not perfect, he has demonstrated his ability, especially in recent months, to work with others and follow the president's lead by working multilaterally." He took a hard line against Iranian President Ahmadinejad in September 2006. "I think he's a Hitler-type of person. He has made it clear that he wants to destroy Israel. He's made it clear that he doesn't believe in the Holocaust."

As governor, Voinovich opposed gambling referenda in 1996 and 1998; he and Mike DeWine sponsored a bill in 2005 to bar Indian tribes from operating casinos on land where it is not permitted by state law. When gambling promoters moved in 2005 to put a "Learn and Earn" initiative on the November 2006 ballot to allow slot machines at racetracks and two casinos in Cleveland, Voinovich said, "If this thing raises its head, we're going to go out there and chop it off." In May 2006 he led a campaign against the initiative, which was joined by Republican statewide officials and Democratic governor candidate Ted Strickland. The measure was defeated 57%-43%. During 2006 Voinovich was called on to answer questions about scandals. His personal brokers were indicted in June for bribing an official of the Ohio Bureau of Workmen's Compensation; newspaper accounts recalled that the OBWC made its first $25 million investment with coin dealer and Republican fundraiser Tom Noe in 1998, when Voinovich was governor. Noe was later convicted on campaign finance and fraud charges; Voinovich refused to disclose his personal brokerage accounts and said that he had been mistaken in believing the Noe and the OBWC officials were honest.

Voinovich came up for reelection in 2004. In early 2003 he had $2.5 million in his campaign treasury and was getting high job ratings. In March 2003 state Senator Eric Fingerhut, who was elected to one term in the House in 1992 and defeated in 1994, announced he was running. For several months the Democrat getting the most attention was Jerry Springer, the successful host of a talk show aimed at unsuccessful people, who had a political career in the 1970s and 1980s as councilman and mayor in Cincinnati; at one point he resigned after it was revealed he had paid for a prostitute with a credit card, but he was later returned to office. But in August 2003, with some apparent reluctance, he took himself out of the race. That left Fingerhut as the only serious Democratic candidate. In 2004 he embarked on a hike across Ohio. But Voinovich outspent him by $9 million to $1.1 million and won the election 64%-36%, just shy of beating John Glenn's record percentage in a Senate race set in 1974. Voinovich carried all 88 counties. Voinovich comes up for reelection in 2010. If Ohio Democrats should follow up their big 2006 victories with a successful record in office, he could face serious opposition.

Junior Senator

Sherrod Brown (D)

Elected 2006, seat up 2012, 1st term; b. Nov. 9, 1952, Mansfield; home, Avon; Yale U., B.A. 1974, OH St. U., M.A. 1979, M.A. 1981; Lutheran; married (Connie Schultz).

Elected Office: OH House of Reps., 1974-82; OH Secy. of State, 1982-90, U.S. House of Reps., 1992-2006.

Professional Career: Prof., OH St. U. at Mansfield, 1979, 1981, 1991.

DC Office: 455 RSOB, 20510, 202-224-2315; Fax: 202-228-6321; Web site: brown.senate.gov.

State Office: Cleveland, 216-522-7272.

Committees: *Agriculture, Nutrition & Forestry* (9th of 11 D): Nutrition and Food Assistance, Sustainable and Organic Agriculture & General Legislation; Energy, Science & Technology; Production, Income Protection & Price Support. *Banking, Housing & Urban Affairs* (9th of 11 D): Economic Policy; Security & International Trade & Finance; Housing, Transportation & Community Development. *Health, Education, Labor & Pensions* (10th of 11 D): Retirement & Aging; Employment & Workplace Safety. *Veterans' Affairs* (5th of 8 D).

Group Ratings (as Member of U.S. House of Representatives)

	ADA	ACLU	AFS	LCV	ITIC	NTU	COC	ACU	CFG	FRC
2006	75	90	86	100	29	14	40	25	7	0
2005	100	—	100	100	—	12	33	4	1	8

National Journal Ratings (as Member of U.S. House of Representatives)

	2005 LIB — 2005 CONS	2006 LIB — 2006 CONS
Economic	82% — 16%	74% — 23%
Social	79% — 21%	68% — 32%
Foreign	90% — 9%	70% — 28%

Key Votes of the 109th Congress (as Member of U.S. House of Representatives)

1. Estate Tax Repeal	N	5. Limit Interstate Abortion	N	9. Build Border Fence	Y
2. Limit CAFE Standards	N	6. Extend Patriot Act	N	10. CAFTA	N
3. FY06 Spending Curb	N	7. Bar Same Sex Marriage	*	11. Oppose Iraq Withdrawal	N
4. Drilling in ANWR	N	8. Stem Cell Research $	Y	12. Detainee Tribunals	Y

Election Results

2006 general	Sherrod Brown (D)	2,257,369	(56%)	($10,752,665)
	Mike DeWine (R)	1,761,037	(44%)	($14,161,402)
2006 primary	Sherrod Brown (D)	583,776	(78%)	
	Merrill Keiser (D)	163,628	(22%)	
2000 general	Mike DeWine (R)	2,665,512	(60%)	($5,699,889)
	Ted Celeste (D)	1,595,066	(36%)	($477,176)
	Other	188,223	(4%)	

Prior Winning Percentages: 2004 House (67%); 2002 House (69%); 2000 House (65%); 1998 House (62%); 1996 House (60%); 1994 House (49%); 1992 House (53%)

Sherrod Brown, Ohio's junior senator, is a Democrat first elected to the House in 1992 and to the Senate in 2006. He grew up in Mansfield, the son of a doctor, graduated from Yale in 1974, won a seat in the state House later that year (another House member, mistaking him for an intern, gave him a dollar to get her a cup of coffee), and later got master's degrees in education and public administration from Ohio State. He has spent more than half his life in public office. In 1982 he was elected secretary of state at the age of 29 and worked hard to increase voter registration and turnout. In 1990, after serving two terms, he lost that office to Bob Taft, who was later elected governor. In 1992 Brown ran for the open 13th District House seat. With solid labor support, he campaigned loud and hard against NAFTA and championed universal health care. He won 53%-35%.

In the House, Brown had a consistently liberal voting record and proved to be a politically adept member of the Energy and Commerce Committee. On trade he was one of the most voluble pro-labor and "fair-trade" members from the Great Lakes area attacking NAFTA, GATT, normal trade relations with China and trade promotion authority. In 2004, he added an amendment to an appropriation bill clarifying that fast-food workers are not part of the nation's manufacturing sector. He focused his attention on health care when he became ranking Democrat on the Health Subcommittee; he sponsored bus trips to Canada for consumers to buy prescription drugs. Brown had some legislative successes while in the minority, notably helping to enact the Children's Health Act, which created a new Pediatric Research Institute. In 2003, he helped to secure an increase in Medicaid funding. He urged a ban on the use of antibiotics on farm animals, including penicillin and tetracycline. He called for enforcement of laws against importing goods made with slave labor in China and helped to increase funding for international programs to fight tuberculosis. He authored *Congress from the Inside*, a book that reviews why House Democrats lost their majority in 1994, including his conclusion "we were blamed for everything the voters did not like." Later, he authored a book titled *Myths of Free Trade*.

Brown had a serious challenge in his initial reelection campaign but won easily after that. Still, he never took his eye off statewide office. After the 2000 election, he made it known that he would run again for governor if his congressional district was threatened in redistricting. He continued to draw attention as a possible gubernatorial candidate until May 2005, when he announced he would not seek the governorship in 2006. Several months later, Brown also said he would not challenge two-term Republican Senator Mike DeWine, which left Iraq war veteran Paul Hackett as the Democratic frontrunner. Hackett, who had won some fame after nearly pulling off a major upset in an August 2005 House special election, was an attractive candidate but there were questions about whether he could raise enough money to be competitive and his shoot-from-the-hip style led to concerns about how well he would play in a statewide race. Brown then reconsidered and entered the race in October. "The culture of corruption plaguing state and federal government has led our state down the wrong path, and it is time for a change," Brown said in a statement announcing his Senate candidacy. Hackett reacted angrily—he accused Brown of reneging on a promise of support—and in February 2006 Hackett withdrew from the race, claiming that the national party was undermining his candidacy. With Hackett out of the picture, Brown breezed to the Democratic nomination.

DeWine, meanwhile, won a lackluster 72% in the May primary against two little-known opponents, a reflection of conservative dissatisfaction with his votes on several high-profile issues, including his support for gun restrictions and his role in the bipartisan compromise to end Senate filibusters on federal judicial nominees. This was a troubling sign, for DeWine also had the misfortune of running for reelection in an unusually hostile political environment for Ohio Republicans. DeWine had to contend with undertow from various scandals associated with Republican-controlled state government, though he was not implicated in any of them, in addition to the drag from the unpopular Bush administration. Brown charged that DeWine was a "rubber stamp" for President George W. Bush and tied him to Bush's Iraq war policy. For his own part, Brown campaigned as a populist progressive. He called for an increase in the minimum wage, railed against free trade agreements and criticized the 2003 Medicare/prescription drug law as a windfall for the pharmaceutical industry. While Brown sought to nationalize the race, DeWine pursued a more localized approach. He focused on his accomplishments and ability to work across party lines, hoping to contrast himself against the more sharply partisan Brown, whose legislative effectiveness had been limited under Republican rule. "Both of us have been in politics for a long time. Both of us have been in Washington working for a long time. The question is, which one of us is the most likely in the future to get things done on a bipartisan basis and make things happen for the state? I have a record of doing that."

Brown won 56%-44%. He won nearly all of Ohio's population centers: Cleveland's Cuyahoga County (71%-29%); Toledo's Lucas County (66%-33%); Akron's Summit County (64%-36%); Columbus's Franklin County (59%-41%); and Dayton's Montgomery County (53%-47%). DeWine carried Cincinnati's Hamilton County, but by just 2,000 votes—in his 2000 reelection win, he won Hamilton by 94,000 votes. DeWine carried much of the state west of Interstate 75, where the tone is more Midwestern; Brown carried everything east of Interstate 77, where the coal and steel counties look toward Pennsylvania and West Virginia and his high-profile opposition to free trade resonated.

FIRST DISTRICT

Rep. Steve Chabot (R)

Elected 1994, 7th term; b. Jan. 22, 1953, Cincinnati; home, Cincinnati; William & Mary Col., B.A. 1975, N. KY U., J.D. 1978; Catholic; married (Donna).

Elected Office: Cincinnati City Cncl., 1985-90; Hamilton Cnty. Comm., 1990-94.

Professional Career: Elem. Schl. teacher, 1975-76; Practicing atty., 1978-94.

DC Office: 129 CHOB, 20515, 202-225-2216; Fax: 202-225-3012; Web site: www.house.gov/chabot.

District Offices: Cincinnati, 513-684-2723.

Committees: *Foreign Affairs* (8th of 23 R): Middle East & South Asia; Asia, the Pacific & the Global Environment. *Judiciary* (6th of 17 R): Crime, Terrorism & Homeland Security; Courts, the Internet & Intellectual Property. *Small Business* (RMM of 15 R).

Group Ratings

	ADA	ACLU	AFS	LCV	ITIC	NTU	COC	ACU	CFG	FRC
2006	10	14	0	8	100	74	93	96	86	100
2005	0	—	0	11	—	70	89	96	98	100

National Journal Ratings

	2005 LIB	—	2005 CONS	2006 LIB	—	2006 CONS
Economic	19%	—	79%	34%	—	65%
Social	0%	—	89%	34%	—	65%
Foreign	0%	—	89%	30%	—	67%

Key Votes of the 109th Congress

1. Estate Tax Repeal	Y	5. Limit Interstate Abortion	Y	9. Build Border Fence	Y
2. Limit CAFE Standards	Y	6. Extend Patriot Act	Y	10. CAFTA	Y
3. FY06 Spending Curb	Y	7. Bar Same Sex Marriage	Y	11. Oppose Iraq Withdrawal	Y
4. Drilling in ANWR	Y	8. Stem Cell Research $	N	12. Detainee Tribunals	Y

Election Results

2006 general	Steve Chabot (R)	105,680	(52%)	($2,991,572)
	John Cranley (D)	96,584	(48%)	($2,021,495)
2006 primary	Steve Chabot (R)	unopposed		
2004 general	Steve Chabot (R)	173,430	(60%)	($479,225)
	Greg Harris (D)	116,235	(40%)	($86,663)

Prior Winning Percentages: 2002 (65%); 2000 (53%); 1998 (53%); 1996 (54%); 1994 (56%)

The People		Race/Ethnic Origin	Ancestry	
Area size:	420 sq. mi.	68.6% White	German: 23.6%	Irish: 9.8%
Urban population:	94.8%	27.4% Black	English: 5.4%	
Rural population:	5.2%	1.3% Asian	**2004 Presidential Vote**	
Pop. 2000:	630,730	0.2% Native Am.	Bush (R) 152,441	(51%)
Pop. 2005 (est):	601,620	0.0% Hawaiian	Kerry (D) 149,180	(49%)
Median income:	$37,414	1.2% Two+ races	**2000 Presidential Vote**	
Poverty status:	13.9%	0.2% Other	Bush (R) 136,372	(51%)
Military veterans:	12.5%	1.1% Hispanic Origin	Gore (D) 120,927	(46%)
			Other 8,463	(3%)
			Cook Partisan Voting Index: R + 1	

Occupation	Blue collar: 23.1%	White collar: 60.5%	Gray collar: 16.5%

From its seven hills, Cincinnati, dubbed the Queen City of the West in the 19th century, looks down on the curves of the Ohio River. Ohio's first major metropolis and a heavily German beehive of riverboats and sausage factories, known in the 1850s as Porkopolis, this was the nation's fourth-largest city and a chief destination for slaves on the Underground Railroad at the outbreak of the Civil War. Cincinnati has long given off an air of the recent past; Mark Twain said he'd like to be there for the apocalypse because everything in Cincinnati is 10 years behind. Growing slowly over many decades, Cincinnati has long-settled good looks and urbanity somehow consistent with its natural terrain: the bottomlands along the river, the hills and rolling terrain above. In the middle of Cincinnati is Mill Creek, lined with factories; on the hills to the west, above the restored Union Terminal with the children's, historic, and natural history museums, are the modest streetcar suburbs of the 19th century and the early years of the 20th. On Mount Adams and toward the northeast are set a string of affluent neighborhoods, with stately mansions like the William Howard Taft house, and the comfortable Tudors and colonials of the 20th century bourgeoisie—Reform Jewish as well as WASP and German. Families have lived for generations in the same neighborhoods, though typically not ethnic enclaves.

Cincinnati was the site of great innovations: the first iron suspension bridge, in 1867, connecting Cincinnati to northern Kentucky and designed by John Roebling, who later built the Brooklyn Bridge; the first baseball team, the Red Stockings, in 1869; the country's leading Reform Jewish seminary, Hebrew Union College, in 1875. Cincinnati has not had the growth spurts of cities like Cleveland or Houston; it spawned not flashy but solid industries, America's biggest concentration of machine tool makers (now a fraction of its once-robust size), plus the Procter & Gamble soap business, with its twin-towered headquarters at the edge of downtown and its Ivorydale manufacturing facility, which has made soap since the 1880s. Downtown Cincinnati's spruced-up Fountain Square shows off well-maintained skyscrapers of the past plus a revival of museums, arts institutions and retail shops; its first-class restaurants still attract a dressy clientele. Old ethnic neighborhoods on the west side, crowded with brick row houses on steep hills, keep their thick local accents and special local foods, from German sauerbraten to Cincinnati chili in Price Hill and Camp Washington. Baseball's career hitting (and betting) leader Pete Rose grew up here, and many

Catholic schools remain. Yet the city has faced tough times. Crime has raged and there has been a flight to the suburbs; in the low-income Over-the-Rhine community (originally named because its residents crossed the canal that ran through downtown), riots broke out and racial tensions lingered after a white police officer shot an unarmed young black man in 2001. With fewer recent immigrants than comparable northern cities, Cincinnati's population declined in the 1990s. But there are some encouraging signs. Census Bureau figures show a gain from 2000 to 2006; recent corporate expansions by Procter & Gamble, Federated Department Stores and Chiquita Brands have added local jobs.

The 1st Congressional District of Ohio includes almost all of Cincinnati, except for parts of its affluent eastern edge, plus most of the middle-class suburbs that cling to the woody hills west of I-71 and south of I-275. It covers the southwest quarter of Butler County plus the western parts of Hamilton County all the way to the Indiana border, including North Bend, the home of President William Henry Harrison. Ancestrally Republican, Cincinnati was a German anti-slavery island in a Southern-stock pro-Confederate sea. City elections here were for years competitive between old-line Republicans and a combination of Democrats and Charterites (the latter started by Charles Taft, liberal brother of Senator Robert Taft Sr. and great-uncle of recent Governor Bob Taft). As its population declined Cincinnati became noticeably more Democratic, but the suburbs, which now cast more votes than the city, remain pretty heavily Republican. This leaves the 1st a closely divided district, one which George W. Bush carried with just 51% of the vote in 2000 and 2004.

The congressman from the 1st District is Steve Chabot (pronounced *SHAB-butt*), a Republican first elected in 1994 and one of the few nationwide who represents a large urban district. Like so many of the local congressmen here over the decades, he grew up in Cincinnati and served on the city council. He graduated from William and Mary, taught elementary school for a year, then graduated from Northern Kentucky law school and started a family law practice. In 1985, at 32, he was elected to the council, and in 1990 he was elected to the Hamilton County Commission. Chabot ran for Congress in odd circumstances. In 1992, first term Democrat Charles Luken (son of longtime incumbent Tom Luken) retired suddenly after the June primary; he later became mayor of Cincinnati. In the special primary to replace him, moderate Democratic Councilman David Mann defeated liberal state Senator William Bowen, by 416 votes, and won the general 51%-43%. In the House, Mann voted against the Clinton tax package and for NAFTA, which infuriated local unions. In 1994, Chabot backed the balanced budget amendment, strongly opposed abortion, and attacked Mann's support of Bill Clinton. Chabot won comfortably, 56%-44%.

Chabot has a generally conservative voting record in the House, but he has been a tight-spending maverick willing to split from his party and take political risks for principle. He voted against the Appalachian Regional Commission, a $2 million study of light rail in the Cincinnati area and a bill containing $6 million for the National Underground Railroad Freedom Center in Cincinnati; he argued that the city should solve problems with local resources and not depend on Washington. Despite a 5 a.m. phone call from George W. Bush, he was the only Ohio Republican to oppose the Medicare/prescription drug bill in 2003.

Most of his committee work has been on Judiciary. As chairman of the Constitution Subcommittee, he was a House leader for a constitutional amendment to protect the rights of crime victims. In 2003 he helped to enact the partial-birth abortion ban by specifying its policy findings and narrowing its terms in an attempt to comply with Supreme Court decisions. He pushed measures to impose restrictions on minors who cross state lines to get an abortion and to make violence against an unborn child a crime, as well as a bill to require physicians to inform women seeking an abortion that the fetus will feel pain. He led House passage of a bill to reverse a Supreme Court ruling that restricted property rights in eminent domain cases. He supported extension of the Voting Rights Act. On the Foreign Affairs Committee, he is a founder of the Taiwan Caucus. Chabot showed his independence as a successful co-sponsor with Rob Andrews of an amendment in the House to prohibit federal funds from being used to construct a road for harvesting timber in the Tongass National Forest. In 2007, he unexpectedly became ranking Republican on the Small Business Committee, where he pledged to "foster an environment where entrepreneurs and their employees can prosper."

In his first years in the House Chabot was a prime Democratic campaign target. In 1996 the AFL-CIO spent over $1 million, running nearly 2,000 television ads against him, but Chabot won 54%-43%. In 1998 Chabot was opposed by Cincinnati Mayor Roxanne Qualls. Qualls argued that Chabot's views were too conservative for the district. In one of the nation's most expensive contests, Chabot won 52%-48%. Redistricting made the district safer, but in 2006 he faced another high-profile challenge from Cincinnati city councilor John Cranley, who ran against the "culture of corruption," Social Security "privatization" and the Iraq war. Chabot emphasized his independence, with a TV ad that said he "follows his heart, not the crowd" and he attacked Cranley's council votes. With a strong grass-roots campaign, he won 52%-48%; he led by 5,600 votes in Hamilton County, which cast 95% of the vote. His victory was all the more impressive given the tough political climate for Republicans, especially in Ohio. For 2008, national Democrats were touting state Representative Steve Driehaus as a strong challenger to Chabot.

SECOND DISTRICT

Rep. Jean Schmidt (R)

Elected Aug. 2005, 1st full term; b. Nov. 29, 1951, Cincinnati; home, Miami Township; U. of Cincinnati, B.A. 1974; Catholic; married (Peter).

Elected Office: Miami Township Bd. of Trustees, 1989-2000; OH House of Reps., 2000-04.

Professional Career: Branch mgr., Midwest Savings Assoc., 1971-78; Fitness instructor, Elaine Powers, 1984-86; Teacher, 1986-90; President, Right to Life of Greater Cincinnati, 2004-05.

DC Office: 238 CHOB, 20515, 202-225-3164; Fax: 202-225-1992; Web site: www.house.gov/schmidt.

District Offices: Cincinnati, 513-791-0381; Portsmouth, 740-354-1440.

Committees: *Agriculture* (18th of 21 R): Conservation, Credit, Energy & Research; Livestock, Dairy & Poultry. *Transportation & Infrastructure* (30th of 34 R): Water Resources & Environment; Highways & Transit.

Group Ratings (Only Served Partial Term)

	ADA	ACLU	AFS	LCV	ITIC	NTU	COC	ACU	CFG	FRC
2006	0	13	0	8	100	58	100	88	54	85
2005	—	—	0	0	—	—	82	88	—	100

National Journal Ratings (Only Served Partial Term)

	2005 LIB	—	2005 CONS	2006 LIB	—	2006 CONS
Economic	*	—	*	16%	—	81%
Social	*	—	*	17%	—	79%
Foreign	*	—	*	0%	—	94%

Key Votes of the 109th Congress (Only Served Partial Term)

1. Estate Tax Repeal	*	5. Limit Interstate Abortion	*	9. Build Border Fence		Y
2. Limit CAFE Standards	*	6. Extend Patriot Act	*	10. CAFTA		*
3. FY06 Spending Curb	Y	7. Bar Same Sex Marriage	Y	11. Oppose Iraq Withdrawal		Y
4. Drilling in ANWR	Y	8. Stem Cell Research $	N	12. Detainee Tribunals		Y

Election Results

2006 general	Jean Schmidt (R)	120,112	(50%)	($2,078,564)
	Victoria Wulsin (D)	117,595	(49%)	($1,041,185)
2006 primary	Jean Schmidt (R)	33,938	(48%)	
	Bob McEwen (R)	30,297	(43%)	
	Deborah Kraus (R)	4,433	(6%)	
	James Constable (R)	2,526	(4%)	
2005 special	Jean Schmidt (R)	59,671	(52%)	
	Paul Hackett (D)	55,886	(48%)	

The People		Race/Ethnic Origin	Ancestry	
Area size:	2,630 sq. mi.	91.7% White	German: 21.3% Irish: 11.1%	
Urban population:	73.0%	4.7% Black	USA: 8.6%	
Rural population:	27.0%	1.3% Asian	**2004 Presidential Vote**	
Pop. 2000:	630,730	0.2% Native Am.	Bush (R) 211,489	(64%)
Pop. 2005 (est):	655,004	0.0% Hawaiian	Kerry (D) 119,139	(36%)
Median income:	$46,813	0.9% Two+ races	Other 476	(0%)
Poverty status:	8.4%	0.1% Other	**2000 Presidential Vote**	
Military veterans:	13.0%	1.0% Hispanic Origin	Bush (R) 175,382	(63%)
			Gore (D) 96,027	(34%)
			Other 8,187	(3%)
			Cook Partisan Voting Index: R +13	

Occupation	Blue collar: 23.2%	White collar: 63.7%	Gray collar: 13.1%

The most Republican major metro area in the nation over the longest time span has been Cincinnati. Back in the 1850s, when Harriet Beecher Stowe wrote *Uncle Tom's Cabin* here, Cincinnati was an island of German, pro-Union, Republican sentiment in a Southern, Democratic, pro-slavery sea. Later Cincinnati attracted fewer southern and eastern European immigrants than Great Lakes industrial cities like Cleveland, Detroit and Chicago; its ethnic character (like its physical appearance) and its political preference have remained pretty well fixed. Even many of the Appalachians here are Republicans, from Civil War Republican counties in the hills. Democratic constituencies here never got very large: economically, it was never a strong CIO town; culturally, its conservatism was revealed in a strong anti-pornography movement that made this the site of obscenity charges filed against *Hustler* publisher Larry Flynt. The local Republican record remains intact: It was the only million-plus metro area that George H.W. Bush and Bob Dole carried by more than 50% in 1992 and 1996, and George W. Bush twice won it handily.

For 140 years after 1852, Cincinnati and surrounding Hamilton County were divided by a north-south line into two congressional districts. But by 1990 Hamilton County no longer had enough people for two full districts, and today both Cincinnati-based districts include territory in other counties. Ohio's 2d Congressional District includes the eastern edge of Cincinnati and the boutiques of Hyde Park Square, a more transient area than the west side neighborhoods; the mostly affluent suburban subdivisions of eastern Hamilton County; and the fast-growing suburbs of Clermont County and southern Warren County. In once-rural Clermont, Miami Township has become a bedroom community and a center of commercial development along the I-275 loop. The district also ranges farther east on the Ohio River, all the way to the old industrial city of Portsmouth and the hills of rural Pike County, the site of a former nuclear weapons facility in Piketon that the Energy Department was considering as a long-term storage facility for nuclear waste. These are distinctly different places. The metropolitan parts of the district, with roughly 80% of the people, are mostly affluent and Republican. The counties farther east are less well off, with most of the old factories gone, and pockets of long-term unemployment and poverty. They are close to marginal in most elections, and Pike County has an historical Democratic tradition, though Bush won each of these counties in his reelection, including Adams County, which lost a six-year battle to place Ten Commandments monuments on local school grounds. Portsmouth, on the district's western fringe, has a depressed economy and an Appalachian frame of mind. Overall, this is a very Republican district, delivering 64% for Bush in 2004.

The congresswoman from the 2d District is Jean Schmidt, who won an August 2005 special election after Republican Rob Portman resigned to become the United States Trade Representative and later President Bush's director of the Office of Management and Budget. A lifelong resident of Clermont County, she grew up on the family farm. Her father, a well-known local banker, owned a motor-car racing team and she spent time on the racing circuit. "I'd rather smell ethanol than Chanel No. 5," Schmidt told the *Cincinnati Enquirer.* Also, she has competed in more than 60 marathons and continues to run in long-distance races across the country. Schmidt majored in political science at the University of Cincinnati and entered public life as an anti-abortion activist, served 10 years as a Miami Township trustee and two terms in the state House. In 2004, she lost a state Senate primary by 22 votes. Subsequently, she has prevailed in close contests.

In the special primary for Portman's seat, the early favorite was Pat DeWine, the son of Republican Mike DeWine, the state's two-term senator. He had the highest name identification and the most lavish financing, with the help of his father plus the Cincinnati corporate establishment. But his election the previous November as Hamilton County commissioner led many to believe that he was too eager to move up the political ladder; he had three small children and recently divorced his wife after having an affair with a local business lobbyist. The other leading contenders were former Congressman Bob McEwen, who became a Washington-based lobbyist after he was defeated in 1992; state Representative Tom Brinkman, and Schmidt. The contest demonstrated the perils of negative campaigning. As DeWine's support dropped, he made a heavy ad buy against McEwen. The Club for Growth ran ads against Schmidt for her backing of tax hikes proposed by Governor Bob Taft. Conservatives ended up dividing their votes between McEwen, Brinkman and Schmidt. Benefiting from her strong base in Clermont County, Schmidt was the surprise winner with 31% to 26% for McEwen and 20% for Brinkman; DeWine was a distant fourth with 12%. Democrats nominated attorney and Iraq war veteran Paul Hackett for the August special general election; it was expected to be a mere formality. Instead, it became a harbinger of the 2006 national midterm elections. Hackett gained national attention as he raised hundreds of thousands of dollars on the Internet from liberal activists. The Marine Corps Reserve major called President Bush a "chicken hawk" for his failure to serve in Vietnam, and strongly attacked Bush's decision to invade Iraq. But his TV ad began with a clip of Bush praising American soldiers and his brochures emphasized, "He just got back from Iraq." Schmidt squeaked by with 51.6% to Hackett's 48.4%. Her entire margin of victory came from her Clermont base, which cast 26% of the vote and where she led by 4,893 votes. She won just 51% in Republican Hamilton County, which cast 43% of the vote, and 58% in Warren County. Hackett won handily in the four down-river counties. The next day, Democratic Congressional Campaign Committee chairman Rahm Emanuel called the outcome a "wake-up call" to Republicans.

As the most junior member of the House, Schmidt gained much attention, not all of it positive. Her biggest moment came in November 2005, when she told the House about a letter she received from a local Marine urging Congress to stay the course on Iraq. Then, she cited his view on Democratic advocates of withdrawal: "He also asked me to send Congressman [John] Murtha a message: That cowards cut and run. Marines never do." Across the aisle, Democrats exploded in shouts and boos. Schmidt quickly retracted her comments and apologized, and apparently did not know that Murtha was a ribboned veteran who served in Vietnam. The speech instantly made "Mean Jean" an object of ridicule. The *Enquirer* editorialized that she was "way out of line." Local Democrats drove a "billboard on wheels" across the district that said: "Shame on you, Jean Schmidt. Stop attacking veterans." She later conceded that she would have changed the words of her House speech, but not the message.

That incident all but assured a competitive reelection. Schmidt got a break when Hackett, who had declared and then abandoned his challenge to Senator Mike DeWine, decided not to challenge her. But she did face a competitive rematch with Bob McEwen, the runner-up in the 2005 special election primary. He cited his 12 years of congressional experience and called for a start to withdrawing U.S. forces from Iraq. Schmidt claimed that McEwen was a resident of Virginia and had voted illegally in Ohio. She won the contest by an unimpressive 48%-43%; without her 4,000-vote lead in Clermont County, she would have lost. Democrats nominated Victoria Wulsin, a local physician who had finished a distant second to Hackett a year earlier and was not expected to pose a serious challenge. Campaigning for Wulsin, Murtha said Schmidt's attack on him was "embarrassing," but "she didn't know me from Adam." Wulsin ran the "cowards" speech in a TV ad. Schmidt got unwelcome attention when she said that it might be a good idea to send nuclear waste from around the world to a storage facility in Pike County. Again in this firmly Republican district, Schmidt won narrowly. But it took three weeks before absentee and provisional ballots were counted and for Wulsin to concede. Schmidt won 50.5%-49.4%. She carried Clermont by 7,900 votes and Warren by 5,700 votes, but lost Hamilton County by nearly 5,800 votes and ran poorly in three of the four down-river counties. The outcome fueled speculation that 2008 would feature additional competitive challenges, in both the Republican primary and the general. Wulsin announced in April 2007 that she would run again in 2008; former Hamilton County Commissioner Phil Heimlich was the first Republican to announce he would challenge Schmidt in the primary. Schmidt appears to have turned a once-solid Republican district into a battleground.

THIRD DISTRICT

Rep. Mike Turner (R)

Elected 2002, 3d term; b. Jan. 11, 1960, Dayton; home, Dayton; OH N. U., B.A. 1982, Case Western Reserve U., J.D. 1985, U. of Dayton, M.B.A. 1992; Protestant; married (Lori).

Elected Office: Dayton Mayor, 1994-2001.

Professional Career: Practicing atty.

DC Office: 1740 LHOB, 20515, 202-225-6465; Fax: 202-225-6754; Web site: www.house.gov/miketurner.

District Offices: Dayton, 937-225-2843; Wilmington, 937-383-8931.

Committees: *Armed Services* (18th of 29 R): Strategic Forces; Air & Land Forces. *Oversight & Government Reform* (10th of 18 R): Information Policy, Census & National Archives (RMM); National Security & Foreign Affairs. *Veterans' Affairs* (9th of 13 R): Disability Assistance & Memorial Affairs.

Group Ratings

	ADA	ACLU	AFS	LCV	ITIC	NTU	COC	ACU	CFG	FRC
2006	5	14	0	8	86	49	93	80	51	100
2005	5	—	0	6	—	52	96	80	48	85

National Journal Ratings

	2005 LIB	—	2005 CONS		2006 LIB	—	2006 CONS
Economic	45%	—	55%		29%	—	71%
Social	32%	—	66%		32%	—	66%
Foreign	23%	—	73%		17%	—	73%

Key Votes of the 109th Congress

1. Estate Tax Repeal	Y	5. Limit Interstate Abortion	Y	9. Build Border Fence	Y
2. Limit CAFE Standards	Y	6. Extend Patriot Act	Y	10. CAFTA	Y
3. FY06 Spending Curb	Y	7. Bar Same Sex Marriage	Y	11. Oppose Iraq Withdrawal	Y
4. Drilling in ANWR	Y	8. Stem Cell Research $	N	12. Detainee Tribunals	Y

Election Results

2006 general	Mike Turner (R)	127,978	(59%)	($1,112,107)
	Richard Chema (D)	90,650	(41%)	($417,577)
2006 primary	Mike Turner (R)	unopposed		
2004 general	Mike Turner (R)	197,290	(62%)	($1,019,127)
	Jane Mitakides (D)	119,448	(38%)	($565,435)

Prior Winning Percentages: 2002 (59%)

The People		Race/Ethnic Origin	Ancestry	
Area size:	1,610 sq. mi.	79.5% White	German: 17.9% Irish: 9.1%	
Urban population:	84.7%	16.9% Black	USA: 8.5%	
Rural population:	15.3%	1.1% Asian	**2004 Presidential Vote**	
Pop. 2000:	630,730	0.2% Native Am.	Bush (R) 178,323	(54%)
Pop. 2005 (est):	650,299	0.0% Hawaiian	Kerry (D) 148,978	(45%)
Median income:	$41,591	1.2% Two+ races	Other 134	(0%)
Poverty status:	10.2%	0.1% Other	**2000 Presidential Vote**	
Military veterans:	14.3%	1.1% Hispanic Origin	Bush (R) 130,446	(52%)
			Gore (D) 112,102	(45%)
			Other 6,874	(3%)
			Cook Partisan Voting Index: R + 3	

Occupation   Blue collar: 26.0%   White collar: 59.7%   Gray collar: 14.3%

Dayton, a medium-sized city once known as the home of the typical American voter, became the name of the international peace agreement reached in November 1995 that stopped the slaughter in the former Yugoslavia. The 21 days of negotiating took place at nearby Wright-Patterson Air Force Base, and the people of Dayton played a role. "From the time we landed at the airport," wrote U.S.

negotiator Richard Holbrooke, "until the time we left, we felt that we were in a community that was literally praying for us. People were lighting candles in their windows, there were signs all over the airport and on the byways. That would never have happened in New York or in Washington. And it made a tremendous impression on people."

Dayton has made a difference in people's lives in America and around the world for many years. Here, just south of the old National Road that spans the Midwest, was the home of James Ritty, who in 1879 invented the cash register—that indispensable instrument of mass retail trade—and of John Henry Patterson, who bought it from Ritty for $6,500 in 1884 and established the National Cash Register company (NCR). It was the home of a former Patterson employee, Tom Watson Sr., who feuded with him and went off to found IBM. It was in Dayton in the 1890s that Wilbur and Orville Wright, tinkering in their bicycle shop and observing the horseless carriages driven through Dayton's streets, experimented with kites and gliders and constructed the first wind tunnel in the world and the first heavier-than-air flying machine, which they took to ever-windy Kitty Hawk, North Carolina, to fly in December 1903. A few years later, Dayton's Charles Kettering invented the automatic starter for cars, and became a father of the automobile industry. At the confluence of four rivers, the city suffered a calamitous flood in 1913, which breached levees, destroyed many buildings and sparked major fires; the disaster led to construction of five dams. In the 1970s and 1980s, Dayton's economy seemed to be sputtering. General Motors, then the area's largest employer, was in trouble; NCR was taken over in a merger. Manufacturing jobs continue to exit, especially with the bankruptcy of GM parts supplier Delphi Corp, but the local economy has turned around. Now, Wright-Pat is the biggest employer, and is the Air Force's largest site for analyzing intelligence about foreign aerospace and weapons technology. DHL has invested $350 million in its local air-cargo hub at the Wilmington Air Park in Clinton County, which has more than 100 nightly flights. Today there are more scientists, engineers, computer specialists and technicians here than GM workers. The area's small manufacturers and suppliers are home to more patents per capita than any other city in the nation. They have shown that Dayton's spirit of tinkering and innovation, practical organization and mechanical dreaming continue to thrive, as much as its neighborliness and compassion. The revived Wright-Dunbar business village (named for the Wright brothers and African-American poet Paul Laurence Dunbar), with buildings that are more than a century old, is a source of local pride. The spiritual has its place, too: In Monroe, a 62-foot styrofoam and fiberglass sculpture of Christ welcomes parishioners at Solid Rock, a nondenominational mega-church; it is believed to be the largest such sculpture in the world.

Politically, the area has been known as a bellwether since Richard Scammon and Ben Wattenberg's *The Real Majority* of 1970 profiled the Dayton housewife. Since then, the area has mostly voted for statewide and national winners, leaning a bit more Democratic than Ohio as a whole; Dayton's Montgomery County is the fourth-largest county in Ohio and the most evenly divided politically of its big counties. Democrats comfortably won the county in the 2006 races for governor and senator.

The 3d Congressional District of Ohio includes most of Dayton and all but the northeast corner of Montgomery County. The 2002 redistricting added the northern half of fast-growing suburban Warren County to the southeast, and mostly rural and small town Clinton and Highland Counties. Those changes made the district distinctly more Republican; George W. Bush won 54% here in 2004.

The congressman from the 3d District is Mike Turner, a Republican first elected in 2002. Turner grew up in Dayton, where his father worked 42 years for GM. He graduated from Ohio Northern University, Case Western law school and the University of Dayton business school and became a corporate lawyer. In 1993, at age 33, he narrowly defeated a scandal-touched Democratic incumbent to win the first of two terms as mayor of Dayton. Although he narrowly lost for reelection in 2001, Ohio and national Republican leaders considered him a prime challenger in the 3d District, which had been marginal in national contests but where Democratic Congressman Tony Hall had served 12 terms. On January 24, 2002, Turner announced he was running for Congress, the same day the Ohio legislature passed the redistricting plan that made the district more Republican. A week later, Bush nominated Hall as ambassador to the Food and Agriculture Organization in Rome. Hall had a long and fervent interest in anti-hunger programs at home and abroad, and the Bush administration long before had been sounding him out for the job: here was a chance to appoint a liberal Democrat to a position where his strongly held views were congruent with administration policy and at the same time pick up a House seat that had long been safely Democratic.

In the Republican primary Turner had fierce opposition from newspaper publisher Roy Brown, grandson and son of Congressmen Clarence Brown and Clarence Brown Jr., who represented the neighboring 7th District from 1938 to 1982. Brown spent $1.3 million of his own money in the primary, largely on ads attacking Turner's record on taxes and crime and lambasting him for being insufficiently conservative. Brown owned more than 50 newspapers, 10 in the 3d District; Turner contended that Brown's campaign guided his newspapers' coverage of the race. The Montgomery County Republican party censured Brown as "unfit to hold public office" for allegedly misleading voters. A few days before the primary, the Ohio Election Commission ruled by a 5–2 vote that Brown violated state law with false statements in a televised ad. Voters evidently took the same view. Turner beat Brown 80%-14%; Brown spent more than $160 for each vote that he received. NRCC chairman Tom Davis, who supported Turner in the primary, said that Brown should have sued his consultants for malpractice. The general election was comparatively sedate. The Democratic nominee was Rick Carne, Hall's chief of staff. He had little support from the national party but he raised nearly $600,000, with help from a local appearance by Dayton native Martin Sheen, President Bartlet on *The West Wing*. Turner spent about the same amount. Turner won 59%-41%.

In the House, Turner's voting record placed him toward the center of his party. He got a seat on Armed Services and worked successfully to keep Wright-Pat off the base-closing list and to expand its jobs, including a new center for research on fixed-wing aircraft. In December 2005, he visited the Balkans to celebrate the 10th anniversary of the Dayton peace accords. As chairman of the Federalism and the Census Subcommittee on Government Reform, he held hearings on urban issues including planning for the 2010 Census. He worked on House-passed legislation to accelerate clean-up of brownfields by making it easier for communities to apply for federal grants for revitalization efforts. As chairman of Speaker Dennis Hastert's Saving America's Cities working group, Turner promoted the kind of public-private partnerships that he used for economic development in Dayton. His interest in Dayton-area projects led him to co-found, with Brad Miller of North Carolina, the Congressional Historic Preservation Caucus. He also formed a caucus of former mayors serving in Congress.

Turner seems entrenched in what had been a safe Democratic district. In 2006, he had to wait until late in the campaign to learn his Democratic opponent. Three months after veterinarian Stephanie Studebaker won the Democratic nomination, both she and her husband were arrested at their home and charged with domestic violence. She withdrew as a candidate and federal prosecutor Richard Chema in September won a special primary to replace her. Chema criticized the Bush administration's handling of the Iraq war, but he couldn't keep pace with Turner's fundraising; Turner won easily.

FOURTH DISTRICT

Rep. Jim Jordan (R)

Elected 2006, 1st term; b. Feb. 17, 1964, Troy; home, Urbana; U. of WI, B.A. 1986, OH St. U., M.Ed. 1991, Capital U., J.D. 2002; Christian; married (Polly).

Elected Office: OH House of Reps., 1994-2000; OH Senate, 2000-06.

Professional Career: Asst. wrestling coach, OH St. U., 1987-95; Wrestling camp coach, clinician, 1987-2006.

DC Office: 515 CHOB, 20515, 202-225-2676; Fax: 202-226-0577; Web site: jordan.house.gov.

District Offices: Findlay, 419-423-3210; Lima, 419-999-6455; Mansfield, 419-522-5757.

Committees: *Judiciary* (17th of 17 R): Commercial & Administrative Law; The Constitution, Civil Rights & Civil Liberties. *Oversight & Government Reform* (18th of 18 R): Federal Workforce, Postal Service & the District of Columbia. *Small Business* (15th of 15 R): Finance & Tax; Regulations, Healthcare & Trade.

Group Ratings and Key Votes: Newly Elected

Election Results

2006 general	Jim Jordan (R)	129,958	(60%)	($1,348,197)
	Rick Siferd (D)	86,678	(40%)	($161,767)
2006 primary	Jim Jordan (R)	38,017	(51%)	
	Frank Guglielmi (R)	22,504	(30%)	
	Kevin Nestor (R)	8,460	(11%)	
	Other	6,193	(8%)	
2004 general	Michael Oxley (R)	167,807	(59%)	($1,909,844)
	Ben Konop (D)	118,538	(41%)	($178,197)

The People		Race/Ethnic Origin	Ancestry	
Area size:	4,642 sq. mi.	91.7% White	German: 23.4%	USA: 9.7%
Urban population:	58.6%	5.2% Black	Irish: 8.1%	
Rural population:	41.4%	0.6% Asian	**2004 Presidential Vote**	
Pop. 2000:	630,730	0.2% Native Am.	Bush (R) 193,875	(65%)
Pop. 2005 (est):	634,878	0.0% Hawaiian	Kerry (D) 102,332	(34%)
Median income:	$40,100	1.0% Two+ races	Other 1,384	(0%)
Poverty status:	9.4%	0.1% Other	**2000 Presidential Vote**	
Military veterans:	14.0%	1.2% Hispanic Origin	Bush (R) 158,862	(62%)
			Gore (D) 88,760	(35%)
			Other 8,244	(3%)
			Cook Partisan Voting Index: R +14	

Occupation   Blue collar: 37.5%   White collar: 47.1%   Gray collar: 15.5%

Central Ohio looks mostly like farmland to the traveler. Yet this is manufacturing country, indeed one of America's premier manufacturing areas, where the economy is based on factories in small towns and on rural highways. These places seem far from anywhere important, yet are on one of the great east-west routes—the old rail lines and newer highways—that cross the country. They seem old-fashioned and rooted in an older technological time, yet here is Wapakoneta, a typically Ohioan-Indian name, the hometown of Neil Armstrong, first man on the moon and home of the Neil Armstrong Air and Space Museum. A county away is Bellefontaine, site of the first concrete street in America. Politically, this crossroads on the flat limestone plains of northern Ohio is one of the Republican heartlands of the United States. On the B&O tracks from Dayton to Toledo that intersect the east-west rail lines used by Richard Nixon in 1968, Ronald Reagan in 1984, George Bush in 1992 and Bill Clinton in 1996 to make whistle-stop campaign tours, one can summon up memories of past campaign styles and loyalties.

Much of central Ohio makes up the 4th Congressional District. It includes Lima, whose name was pulled from a hat; Findlay, where a museum holds the captain's bathtub from the *U.S.S. Maine*, sunk in the Havana harbor in 1898; Marion, where young Socialist-to-be Norman Thomas delivered newspapers edited by President-to-be Warren Harding; and Mansfield, home of John Sherman, one of Ohio's great 19th century Republican statesmen, and his brother General William Tecumseh Sherman, who marched his troops through Georgia for the Union and refused to be considered for president. This has been a Republican stronghold since the Civil War, industrial since the late 19th century, quietly prosperous most of the years since World War II, though shaken by the collapse of the auto-steel-coal industries after the oil shock of 1979 and troubled by recent manufacturing job losses. Lima had reason to be optimistic when Procter & Gamble decided to build a massive new warehouse to distribute liquid Tide detergent, which is produced in a factory a mile away. George W. Bush carried the district 62%-35% in 2000 and 65%-34% in 2004; he increased his popular vote margin over four years by 21,000 in a district that has had little population growth in that time—one of the reasons he carried Ohio, and the presidency, a second time.

The new congressman from the 4th District is Jim Jordan, elected in 2006. Jordan grew up in Champaign County and graduated from Graham High School in 1982, after earning four state wrestling championships and a 150–1 record. At the University of Wisconsin, Jordan won two NCAA wrestling championships in the 134-pound weight class and was inducted into the Badger Hall of Fame. After graduating in 1986 with an economics degree, Jordan worked as an assistant wrestling coach at Ohio State University, where he earned a master's degree in education before completing a law degree from Capital University. Jordan ran for the state House in 1994, won re-election twice, and then won a tough primary in 2000 for the state Senate. During his time in the legislature, Jordan compiled a solidly conservative voting record on fiscal and social issues. He sponsored legislation creating Ohio's "Choose Life" license plates, backed a ban on same-sex marriage, supported vouchers and charter schools and a constitutional amendment to limit government spending. When Jordan announced he was running to succeed Republican Michael Oxley, who decided not to seek a 13th term, *The Columbus Dispatch* referred to him as "one of the best-known conservative Republicans in the Ohio legislature."

Jordan entered the six-way Republican primary with the most name recognition and had support from Ohio Right to Life, the National Rifle Association and the Club for Growth. His frontrunner status made him the prime target of his primary opponents. Findlay real estate developer Frank Guglielmi spent $1.6 million of his own money and saturated the television airwaves with ads from late March onward. Jordan raised plenty of money, but did not break the $1 million mark until a month after the May primary. While money mattered, so did geography. Jordan won with 51%, carrying 8 of 11 counties. He ran far ahead of Guglielmi, who carried only his home county and one other to finish second with 30%. Kevin Nestor, president of the Mansfield-Richland Area Chamber of Commerce, came in third with 11%; he won only in Richland County.

Despite Ohio's tough political environment for Republicans in 2006, Democrats never mounted a competitive campaign for the seat. Jordan raised almost 10 times as much money as his Democrat opponent, Lima attorney and Vietnam veteran Rick Siferd, and won 60%-40%. Jordan's comfortable primary and general election wins make him a solid bet for reelection.

FIFTH DISTRICT
Vacant

Election Results

2006 general	Paul Gillmor (R) 129,813	(57%)	($723,408)
	Robin Weirauch (D) 98,544	(43%)	($115,664)
2006 primary	Paul Gillmor (R) .... unopposed		
2004 general	Paul Gillmor (R) 196,649	(67%)	($440,891)
	Robin Weirauch (D) 96,656	(33%)	($77,145)

The People		Race/Ethnic Origin	Ancestry		
Area size:	6,158 sq. mi.	93.7% White	German: 29.9% Irish: 7.5%		
Urban population:	48.9%	1.1% Black	USA: 7.3%		
Rural population:	51.1%	0.4% Asian	**2004 Presidential Vote**		
Pop. 2000:	630,730	0.2% Native Am.	Bush (R) 188,935	(61%)	
Pop. 2005 (est):	630,856	0.0% Hawaiian	Kerry (D) 119,308	(39%)	
Median income:	$41,701	0.7% Two+ races	Other 1,558	(1%)	
Poverty status:	7.6%	0.1% Other	**2000 Presidential Vote**		
Military veterans:	12.8%	3.8% Hispanic Origin	Bush (R) 158,037	(59%)	
			Gore (D) 99,818	(37%)	
			Other 9,383	(4%)	
			Cook Partisan Voting Index: R +10		

Occupation   Blue collar: 39.8%   White collar: 46.0%   Gray collar: 14.2%

Undergirded by limestone, as flat and fertile as any place in America, northwest Ohio sits astride the land routes in parts of the country that were economically the most productive in the years they were settled. Here were the "Firelands," reserved for Connecticut Yankees whose farms were burned in the Revolution, and the neat and substantial small towns built by German Protestants in the mid-19th century. Northwest Ohio is the beginning of the great corn and hog belt that stretches through Indiana and Illinois into Iowa, and has long been a Republican heartland. Fremont, settled by abstemious Yankees, was the home of President Rutherford B. Hayes, whose wife Lucy served only lemonade in the White House. Nearby Sandusky, settled by Germans who built big wineries and breweries, has its own Merry-Go-Round Museum.

This is also prime industrial country. Its limestone, rail connections and location near the Great Lakes have spurred the growth of a factory economy that financially is far more important than agriculture. After the first settlement, northwest Ohio grew steadily for many decades, surging ahead in the 1950s and 1960s as its small factories supplied the big auto plants in Detroit and Ohio. Growth lagged noticeably in the 1980s, when the domestic auto industry collapsed, but returned in the 1990s as small firms sold not only to the Big Three but to foreign customers. That gave this area the highest percentage of blue-collar workers in the state. Van Wert was a finalist for a giant new Honda plant, which instead went across the state line in Indiana. Honda still has dozens of suppliers in the area, though many parts companies continue to cut back with the shrinkage of the domestic auto industry.

The 5th Congressional District of Ohio sweeps across northwest Ohio, from northern Ashland County, almost within the ambit of metro Cleveland, across the limestone plains through Sandusky County and Fremont, past the university town of Bowling Green and the Toledo suburb of Perrysburg, to the towns of Defiance and Napoleon and on to the northwest corner where Ohio borders Michigan and Indiana. Its factories include the aromatic Heinz ketchup plant in Fremont—the world's largest, with the equivalent of 4 million 14-ounce bottles produced every day—and the largest Whirlpool washing machine plant in Clyde, both in Sandusky County. In Seneca County is the Arm and Hammer Baking Soda plant—which is, of course, the world's largest. Historically, this has been a solidly Republican district since the Civil War; as part of his big push in western Ohio, George W. Bush increased his lead here from 59%-37% in 2000 to 61%-39% in 2004.

The 5th District was temporarily vacant after the death of Republican Paul Gillmor. Gillmor, who was in his 10th term, was found dead in his Arlington, Virginia, townhouse on September 5, 2007. As a member of Congress, Gillmor had a relatively moderate voting record. On Energy and Commerce, he chaired the Subcommittee on Environment and Hazardous Materials and drafted a section of the energy bill enacted in 2005 that would permit greater flexibility in use of the trust fund for cleaning up leaking underground gasoline storage tanks. He enacted the Fair and Accurate Credit Transactions (FACT) Act, requiring credit agencies to disclose when inquiries on a consumer's report are considered adversely. With Barney Frank, he sponsored a bill to prevent Wal-Mart and other commercial companies from owning state-chartered industrial loan companies. In September 2006, the House passed his bill to permit states to restrict solid wastes from other nations; the bill was aimed primarily at Canada. In 2007, he switched to the top Republican spot on the Financial Services Subcommittee on Financial Institutions and Consumer Credit.

In this reliably Republican district, the GOP nominee in the special election will be heavily favored to succeed Gillmor. The special primary election was scheduled for November 6, 2007, with the special general election to be held on December 11. State Senator Steve Buehrer and state Representative Bob Latta, the son of Gillmor's predecessor, Congressman Delbert Latta, both filed to run for the vacant seat; Bob Latta lost to Gillmor in the 1988 primary by 27 votes. On the Democratic side, former Bowling Green University official Robin Weirauch, who ran unsuccessfully in 2004 and 2006, announced she would run.

SIXTH DISTRICT

Rep. Charlie Wilson (D)

Elected 2006, 1st term; b. Jan. 18, 1943, Martins Ferry; home, St. Clairsville; Cincinnati Col. of Mortuary Science, 1967, OH U., B.A. 1980; Catholic; divorced.

Elected Office: OH House of Reps., 1996-2004; OH Senate, 2004-06.

Professional Career: Welder, painter, assembly-line worker, 1963-64; Owner, Wilson Funeral and Furniture Co., 1966-2006; Owner, Wilson Realty Co., 1978-2006.

DC Office: 226 CHOB, 20515, 202-225-5705; Fax: 202-225-5907; Web site: charliewilson.house.gov.

District Offices: Bridgeport, 740-633-5705; Canfield, 330-533-7250; Marietta, 740-376-0868.

Committees: *Financial Services* (31st of 37 D): Domestic and International Monetary Policy, Trade & Technology; Housing & Community Opportunity; Financial Institutions & Consumer Credit. *Science & Technology* (24th of 24 D): Technology & Innovation.

Group Ratings and Key Votes: Newly Elected

Election Results

2006 general	Charlie Wilson (D)	135,628	(62%)	($1,800,909)
	Chuck Blasdel (R)	82,848	(38%)	($1,066,716)
2006 primary	Charlie Wilson (D)	43,687	(66%)	
	Robert Carr (D)	14,900	(23%)	
	John Luchansky (D)	7,459	(11%)	
2004 general	Ted Strickland (D) .... unopposed			($215,879)

The People		Race/Ethnic Origin	Ancestry		
Area size:	5,236 sq. mi.	95.2% White	German: 15.2%	Irish: 9.9%	
Urban population:	50.0%	2.4% Black	USA: 8.4%		
Rural population:	50.0%	0.5% Asian	**2004 Presidential Vote**		
Pop. 2000:	630,730	0.2% Native Am.	Bush (R)	153,983	(51%)
Pop. 2005 (est):	616,878	0.0% Hawaiian	Kerry (D)	149,080	(49%)
Median income:	$32,888	0.8% Two+ races	Other	938	(0%)
Poverty status:	14.0%	0.1% Other	**2000 Presidential Vote**		
Military veterans:	14.5%	0.8% Hispanic Origin	Bush (R)	129,689	(49%)
			Gore (D)	125,292	(47%)
			Other	11,969	(4%)
			Cook Partisan Voting Index: D + 0		
Occupation	Blue collar: 31.3%	White collar: 51.7%	Gray collar: 17.0%		

In the years after the American Revolution, the Ohio River was one of the great highways west. From Pittsburgh, where the Allegheny and Monongahela meet and form the Ohio, the river led south and west toward the Mississippi and the great port of New Orleans. Shipping goods downriver by raft was cheaper than sending them over the Appalachian chains, and so the Ohio became a great highway of commerce. For hundreds of miles, the Ohio twisted this way and that through rounded-off mountains and rolling hills, land that marked the boundary between post-Revolutionary Virginia and the Northwest Territory, between slaveholding territory and soil that the Confederation Congress decided in 1787 should be free. Across this boundary settlers made their way in those years—Yankees in 1788 to Marietta, Ohio's first town, and, in larger numbers, Virginians from those parts of Virginia that became Kentucky in 1792 and West Virginia in 1863. By the late 19th century the Ohio was an industrial river; coal was nearby, barge transportation was available and railroads were built in the narrow valleys between the hills, steel mills went up on the riverfront. This produced prosperity for a while, but it also produced pollution—Steubenville on the Ohio River once had the nation's dirtiest air—and after the old-line steel industry fell on hard times, the Ohio River was lined with some of the least prosperous parts of America. Even with mandates from the Clean Air Act, the pollution in much of this area from coal-fired power plants remains so bad that many residents have considered moving.

The 6th Congressional District of Ohio is made up of a string of counties running 325 miles along the Ohio River plus part of the Mahoning Valley, named after a narrow tributary of the Ohio. In the north it includes the Youngstown suburbs of Boardman, Canfield and part of Poland in Mahoning County, and East Liverpool and Steubenville on the Ohio. It curves along the lightly populated stretch of the river south from Marietta, the old industrial town of Ironton and it extends to the city limits of Portsmouth, not quite in the Cincinnati metropolitan area, where the Scioto River empties into the Ohio. Much of this area is part of poverty-ridden Appalachia. Historically, the northern part of the district was Republican and the southern part Democratic, but that was a long time ago. The steel and coal areas in the north became Democratic during the 1930s and the southern counties started trending Republican in the 1960s. This mix makes for a Democratic-leaning district but the cultural conservatism of this region, much like that of West Virginia and eastern Kentucky across the river, put it narrowly in George W. Bush's column, by 49%-47% in 2000 and 51%-49% in 2004.

The new congressman from the 6th District is Charlie Wilson, elected in 2006, just the fifth person to reach Congress by running a write-in campaign. Wilson was born in Martins Ferry, across the Ohio River from Wheeling, West Virginia; he worked as a UAW welder, painter and assembly line worker before earning his mortician's license from Cincinnati College of Mortuary Science in 1967. He started the Wilson Funeral and Furniture Company in 1967 and the Wilson Realty Company in 1979 and, as a 37-year-old businessman, got his bachelor's degree from Ohio University. In 1996, Wilson won the first of four terms in the Ohio House, where he served as Democratic whip and assistant leader. In 2004, he was term-limited in the House and won a seat in the state Senate. Wilson worked in the legislature to improve health care, spur job creation and promote economic development in the Ohio Valley. When Democratic incumbent Ted Strickland announced he would run for governor, Democrats touted Wilson as their top candidate to run for the seat.

But Wilson, despite a decade in the legislature, made a classic rookie mistake that nearly cost him his chance to win this seat. He failed to file the nominal 50 valid signatures to register his candidacy. His son, acting as campaign manager, submitted 96 signatures collected from Belmont and Scioto Counties. The problem was that not all of the signatures came from within the district nd, as it turned out, only 46 were valid. The campaign discovered the mistake before candidate filing closed, but state law prevented Wilson from updating his original filing. The bungled filing was an enormous embarrassment and it stunned national Democrats, who figured that a proven vote-getter like Wilson was their best chance of holding the seat. Two other little-known Democrats made the primary ballot, but they would be at a disadvantage against the likely and eventual Republican nominee, Chuck Blasdel, the speaker pro tempore of the Ohio State House.

Wilson had two options available to him at that point. He could run as an independent in November, or mount a write-in campaign for the Democratic nomination; he chose the latter. A write-in candidacy is an uphill endeavor, but Republicans recognized that if Wilson failed to win the nomination this seat was a potential pick-up; the National Republican Congressional Committee spent $500,000 to run attack ads that accused Wilson of allowing raw sewage to flow into the Ohio River and covering it up while he served as chairman of the Eastern Ohio Regional Wastewater Authority in the mid-1990s. "Wilson demanded it be kept secret because it would hurt his career," the NRCC ad said. "Charlie Wilson. Dirty secrets. We just can't trust him to do what's right."

The Democratic Congressional Campaign Committee also understood the high stakes in the primary and insisted on installing a professional manager in Wilson's campaign. The DCCC backed the write-in effort with radio and television ads while the Ohio AFL-CIO mobilized the district's union members by making 120,000 phone calls and putting 300 volunteers in the field. Wilson knocked on 40,000 doors and wrote 4,000 personal letters. The field work paid off—Wilson won with an astounding 66%, with 43,687 write-in votes. That was 4,500 more votes than were cast for the four candidates in the Republican primary. Blasdel won a lackluster 47% in the Republican primary, and by the fall the district had fallen off the Republicans' list of targeted Democratic seats. Wilson defeated Blasdel 62%-38% in the general election.

SEVENTH DISTRICT

Rep. David Hobson (R)

Elected 1990, 9th term; b. Oct. 17, 1936, Cincinnati; home, Springfield; OH Wesleyan U., B.A. 1958, OH St. U., J.D. 1963; Methodist; married (Carolyn).

Military Career: OH Air Natl. Guard, 1958-63.

Elected Office: OH Senate, 1982-90, Majority Whip, 1986-88, Pres. Pro-Tem, 1988-90.

Professional Career: Real estate agent, 1969-90; Restaurant owner, 1977-93.

DC Office: 2346 RHOB, 20515, 202-225-4324; Fax: 202-225-1984; Web site: www.house.gov/hobson.

District Offices: Lancaster, 740-654-5149; Springfield, 937-325-0474.

Committees: *Appropriations* (7th of 29 R): Energy & Water Development (RMM); Defense.

Group Ratings

	ADA	ACLU	AFS	LCV	ITIC	NTU	COC	ACU	CFG	FRC
2006	10	18	14	0	100	53	93	76	49	71
2005	0	—	0	6	—	51	96	83	51	85

National Journal Ratings

	2005 LIB	—	2005 CONS		2006 LIB	—	2006 CONS
Economic	27%	—	72%		30%	—	68%
Social	32%	—	66%		32%	—	66%
Foreign	31%	—	67%		33%	—	63%

Key Votes of the 109th Congress

1. Estate Tax Repeal	Y	5. Limit Interstate Abortion	Y	9. Build Border Fence	Y
2. Limit CAFE Standards	Y	6. Extend Patriot Act	Y	10. CAFTA	Y
3. FY06 Spending Curb	Y	7. Bar Same Sex Marriage	N	11. Oppose Iraq Withdrawal	Y
4. Drilling in ANWR	Y	8. Stem Cell Research $	N	12. Detainee Tribunals	Y

Election Results

2006 general	David Hobson (R)	137,899	(61%)	($2,157,850)
	William Conner (D)	89,579	(39%)	($17,119)
2006 primary	David Hobson (R)	unopposed		
2004 general	David Hobson (R)	186,534	(65%)	($1,049,259)
	Kara Anastasio (D)	100,617	(35%)	($25,807)

Prior Winning Percentages: 2002 (68%); 2000 (68%); 1998 (67%); 1996 (68%); 1994 (100%); 1992 (71%); 1990 (62%)

The People		Race/Ethnic Origin	Ancestry	
Area size:	2,866 sq. mi.	88.7% White	German: 17.6%	USA: 10.1%
Urban population:	71.3%	7.5% Black	Irish: 9.3%	
Rural population:	28.7%	1.0% Asian	**2004 Presidential Vote**	
Pop. 2000:	630,730	0.3% Native Am.	Bush (R) 176,365	(57%)
Pop. 2005 (est):	654,846	0.0% Hawaiian	Kerry (D) 132,124	(43%)
Median income:	$43,248	1.3% Two+ races	Other 1,306	(0%)
Poverty status:	8.8%	0.1% Other	**2000 Presidential Vote**	
Military veterans:	15.3%	1.1% Hispanic Origin	Bush (R) 137,548	(55%)
			Gore (D) 102,846	(41%)
			Other 7,644	(3%)
			Cook Partisan Voting Index: R + 6	

Occupation	Blue collar: 28.1%	White collar: 57.1%	Gray collar: 14.8%

The hills and plains of central Ohio are dotted with towns and small cities that have been manufacturing centers almost since they were settled in the early 19th century, when the dominant technologies were the waterwheel and the open forge. In the decades since, they have been replaced by one new technology after another—the automobile and the airplane—and the local manufacturing economy, sometimes with uncomfortable fits and starts, has adjusted and advanced. This has been the story of Springfield, oft studied as a typical American city. In the early 1980s, International Harvester, the city's largest employer, went bankrupt, downsized dramatically and was renamed Navistar. In 1996, the company cut 3,000 jobs from its Springfield plant, and after more cuts, the workforce was pared down to 2,800 in 2000, though it remained Clark County's largest employer. More recently, there have been smaller job losses at other manufacturing facilities, as the Vining Broom plant was moved out of town. But amid these highly publicized and visible examples of capitalism's creative destruction there have been less noticed examples of its creativity. Small manufacturing businesses have grown up in empty factory space, diesel-electric hybrid truck engines are being produced in the old Navistar plant and service employment has grown.

Politically Springfield and Clark County became a highly competitive battleground in the 2004 election. Al Gore carried the county in 2000, and Democrats hoped that local job losses would increase their margin. So did the editors of the British left-wing newspaper the *Guardian*, which obtained the addresses of 14,000 Clark County voters and called on its readers to write personal letters urging them to throw out the iniquitous George W. Bush. But the letters aroused fierce resentment, and while Democrats concentrated their turnout efforts on Springfield's black precincts, Bush campaign volunteers scoured the whole county and turned a 324-vote Gore plurality in 2000 into a 1,406-vote Bush majority in 2004.

The 7th Congressional District of Ohio is made up of a portion of the south central part of Ohio, which is shaped like a horseshoe south of Columbus. It includes Springfield and Clark County and, just to the south, the growing Greene County suburbs of Dayton around Wright-Patterson Air Force Base, whose name recalls the fathers of the airplane and the cash register, both from Dayton. Although Wright-Pat gained a few hundred jobs in the base-closing review of 2005, Springfield's Air National Guard station lost its F-16 training unit. Other population centers are in Fairfield County, southeast of Columbus, and a slice of Columbus's Franklin County, including part of the east side of Columbus, Whitehall, Blacklick Estates, Canal Winchester and Lockbourne. Fairfield is home to the 5200-seat World Harvest Church, where politically active Pastor Rod Parsley is one of the nation's leading evangelicals and a prominent opponent of abortion and gay marriage. Farther east in Perry County, coal mining has revived with rising energy prices. The district has always been Republican territory. It backed the policies of Ohio Republican President William McKinley—tariff protection, railroad regulation, antitrust suits against monopolies, discouragement of labor unions—and of Governor James Rhodes—low taxes, promotion of new businesses and jobs. It is culturally conservative and economically mostly satisfied with free markets. It has given healthy margins to recent Republican presidential contenders.

The congressman from the 7th District is Dave Hobson, a savvy Republican often at the center of legislative action. He grew up in Springfield, graduated from Ohio Wesleyan and Ohio State law school, served on active duty overseas with the Ohio Air National Guard during the 1961 Berlin crisis, and worked in commercial real estate in Springfield. In 1982 he was elected to the state Senate and in 1990, when Congressman Mike DeWine ran for lieutenant governor, he was elected to the House. He is a practical-minded politician who in his second term got a seat on Appropriations and has a moderate to conservative voting record, which includes support for abortion rights. Hobson's steady demeanor and backroom skills continue to make him a resource for House Republican leaders; he worked on health issues with Dennis Hastert long before he became Speaker. But Hobson does not seek the spotlight on Capitol Hill: When leadership meetings break up and many head for the ever-present microphones and television cameras, Hobson typically passes them by. For the most part he has supported the Republican leadership. But not always: twice, he raised objections when Republican leaders sought House approval of restrictions on health care equipment—specifically, oxygen tanks manufactured by a local firm. He is loyal to his neighbors, notably Republican Leader John Boehner, who represents an adjoining district and entered the House with Hobson. He is especially solicitous of jobs for his own district.

In 1999 Hobson became chairman of the Military Construction Appropriations Subcommittee, a body known for legislating on a bipartisan basis and with due regard to members' local concerns; there he was able to look after the interests of Wright-Patterson Air Force Base. In 2003, Hobson became chairman of the Energy and Water Appropriations Subcommittee. There he worked on projects for his district and those of many other members, and he also set national policy. He pressed for funding the Yucca Mountain nuclear waste repository, and in 2003 his bill provided $765 million for it. In conference he was sharply opposed by Nevada's Harry Reid, ranking member of the Senate subcommittee and a strong opponent of Yucca Mountain. Still Hobson ended up with $580 million, $155 million more than the Senate bill. He also worked to slow down development of new nuclear weapons. "We have too much of a Cold War arsenal." He scaled back spending on the bunker buster weapon and, in 2005, zeroed out its funds. He said the development of the bunker buster and other weapons were "very provocative and overly aggressive policies that undermine our moral authority to argue that other nations should forgo nuclear weapons." For single-handedly killing this proposed weapon, "It's no exaggeration to call [Hobson] a giant killer within the military-industrial complex," George Wilson wrote in *Congress Daily*. His success "seems to come from his amateur eyes that see through the smoke of the experts, from his willingness to shout out that the king has no clothes and from his support of military programs that make sense to him." Since the Hurricane Katrina disaster, Hobson has turned his attention to overhaul of the Army Corps of Engineers, which he has been critical of. Relegated to the minority in 2007, he lost his chairmanship but he likely will benefit from his close relationship with senior Appropriations Democrats, including Defense Subcommittee chairman John Murtha.

Hobson has always been elected with at least 60% of the vote. There has been speculation that Hobson will retire in 2008. If so, Republicans would be favored to retain the seat.

EIGHTH DISTRICT

Rep. John Boehner (R)

Elected 1990, 9th term; b. Nov. 17, 1949, Cincinnati; home, West Chester; Xavier U., B.S. 1977; Catholic; married (Debbie).

Military Career: Navy, 1969.

Elected Office: Union Township Bd. of Trustees, 1981-85, Pres., 1984; OH House of Reps., 1984-90.

Professional Career: Pres., Nucite Sales Inc., 1976-90.

DC Office: 1011 LHOB, 20515, 202-225-6205; Fax: 202-225-0704; Web site: www.johnboehner.house.gov.

District Offices: Troy, 937-339-1524; West Chester, 513-779-5400.

Committees: *Minority Leader.*

Group Ratings

	ADA	ACLU	AFS	LCV	ITIC	NTU	COC	ACU	CFG	FRC
2006	5	18	0	0	100	59	100	88	59	100
2005	0	—	0	0	—	65	88	100	74	92

National Journal Ratings

	2005 LIB	—	2005 CONS	2006 LIB	—	2006 CONS
Economic	3%	—	94%	2%	—	98%
Social	27%	—	72%	35%	—	63%
Foreign	16%	—	83%	17%	—	73%

Key Votes of the 109th Congress

1. Estate Tax Repeal	Y	5. Limit Interstate Abortion	Y	9. Build Border Fence	Y
2. Limit CAFE Standards	Y	6. Extend Patriot Act	Y	10. CAFTA	Y
3. FY06 Spending Curb	Y	7. Bar Same Sex Marriage	Y	11. Oppose Iraq Withdrawal	Y
4. Drilling in ANWR	Y	8. Stem Cell Research $	N	12. Detainee Tribunals	Y

Election Results

2006 general	John Boehner (R)	136,863	(64%)	($2,952,525)
	Mort Meier (D)	77,640	(36%)	
2006 primary	John Boehner (R)	unopposed		
2004 general	John Boehner (R)	201,675	(69%)	($1,407,907)
	Jeff Hardenbrook (D)	90,574	(31%)	($41,184)

Prior Winning Percentages: 2002 (71%); 2000 (71%); 1998 (71%); 1996 (70%); 1994 (100%); 1992 (74%); 1990 (61%)

The People		Race/Ethnic Origin	Ancestry	
Area size:	2,031 sq. mi.	91.8% White	German: 22.0%	USA: 9.8%
Urban population:	78.1%	4.4% Black	Irish: 8.9%	
Rural population:	21.9%	1.2% Asian	**2004 Presidential Vote**	
Pop. 2000:	630,730	0.2% Native Am.	Bush (R) 199,265	(64%)
Pop. 2005 (est):	644,530	0.0% Hawaiian	Kerry (D) 109,374	(35%)
Median income:	$43,753	1.1% Two+ races	Other 439	(0%)
Poverty status:	8.8%	0.1% Other	**2000 Presidential Vote**	
Military veterans:	13.8%	1.3% Hispanic Origin	Bush (R) 155,132	(61%)
			Gore (D) 91,744	(36%)
			Other 7,371	(3%)
			Cook Partisan Voting Index: R +12	

Occupation	Blue collar: 29.9%	White collar: 56.0%	Gray collar: 14.0%

The far west end of Ohio—where U.S. 40, the old National Road, heads straight as an arrow in its last miles across Ohio to Indiana, and the rail lines crisscross the land from Cincinnati to Dayton— has since the early 20th century housed some of the nation's prime industrial country. Here the Great and Little Miami rivers drain south into the Ohio; U.S. 40 jogs southward twice to go over the Miami and Stillwater River dams, built after the great flood of 1913 that killed 361 people in Dayton and caused $1 billion in damage. Around Dayton and Cincinnati, in large factory towns like Middletown and Hamilton and smaller factory towns like Troy and Piqua, Ohioans, after the recession of the early 1980s, adapted to new conditions and began to produce exports to Europe, Latin America and Asia as well as for the American market. At the same time people leaving the central cities of Dayton and Cincinnati moved into new subdivisions amid new shopping malls and office parks in Butler County, between those two cities. Hamilton, the Butler County seat founded in 1791 and named after the Treasury Secretary then, lost jobs when International Paper shut down a plant, but many more were created all around it. Hamilton has rallied: In the 1950s it refused to let I-75 through town, but it got the state to build Route 129 to link it with I-75 and the growth it has brought. The result has been retail development and a new hospital satellite center.

The 8th Congressional District of Ohio covers much of this territory. It includes all of Butler County (except four lightly populated townships), two counties to the north on the Indiana line and part of a third. It also includes Miami County north of Dayton and the northeastern corner of Montgomery County, including part of Dayton, all of Huber Heights and part of Wright-Patterson Air Force Base. Politically, this is very Republican territory; the district voted 61% for George W. Bush in 2000 and 64% in 2004. In September 2004 Bush appeared at a rally here that attracted 50,000 people; some called it the largest political rally in Ohio history.

The congressman from the 8th District is John Boehner (pronounced *BAY-ner*), a Republican first elected in 1990 and now the House Minority Leader. Boehner grew up in Cincinnati, the second oldest of 12 children in a home with two bedrooms; his father ran Andy's Café, a neighborhood bar. Playing at a much heavier weight than he is now, he was a linebacker for Cincinnati's Archbishop Moeller high school on a team coached by Gerry Faust, before Faust went to Notre Dame.

Boehner graduated from Xavier University, the first college graduate in his family. He moved to Butler County and became financially comfortable after working for and eventually taking over a small business that sold plastics for packaging; he had a knack for attracting new customers. He served on the Union Township Board of Trustees, and in 1984, at 34, was elected to the Ohio House. He won the congressional seat in the 1990 primary, by beating not one but two of his predecessors— incumbent Buz Lukens, who inexplicably ran after he was convicted of having sex with a 16-year-old girl, and Tom Kindness, who gave up the seat to run against Senator John Glenn in 1986 and then, as Boehner put it, deserted the district to become a Washington lobbyist. Boehner won 49%, to 32% for Kindness and 17% for Lukens. Boehner has since been reelected without difficulty.

In the House, Boehner joined the Gang of Seven, young freshman Republicans who insisted on revealing the names of all 355 members who had overdrafts at the House bank, and then went on to assail Democratic leaders and Republican go-alongers on the pay raise and the House Post Office scandal. Boehner's Gang of Seven infuriated House veterans, but they struck a chord around the nation. In the process Boehner became a top lieutenant of Minority Whip Newt Gingrich, raising money for Republican candidates and managing Gingrich's campaign for Republican leader. He was a major player in drafting and championing the 10-point Contract With America. After the 1994 election, he ran for chairman of the Republican Conference and, with Gingrich's backing, beat California's Duncan Hunter 122-102.

That made Boehner number four in the Republican leadership, and he worked hard to prepare the party message and to enforce discipline on issues from repealing the assault weapons ban to fielding ethics charges against Gingrich. Boehner also pushed for the Freedom to Farm bill in 1996, which sought to phase out most subsidies. But in 1998 Congress started voting disaster relief for farmers; Boehner led the fight against the House's 2002 farm bill, which restored subsidies.

The Gingrich years were a turbulent time for Boehner. The ethics investigation of Gingrich placed Boehner in the middle of a legal altercation after a Florida couple taped Boehner's cell phone conversation with Republican leaders while he was driving through the state. The couple, Democratic activists, presented the tape to their congresswoman, Karen Thurman, who suggested they turn it over to Jim McDermott of Washington, senior Democrat on the House ethics committee, who then made the contents available to *The New York Times*. In 1998 Boehner sued McDermott in federal court for invasion of privacy; the trial judge ruled that the suit would infringe First Amendment rights, but the D.C. Circuit Court of Appeals reversed the decision. McDermott appealed to the Supreme Court, which decided another case instead and sent this one back to the D.C. Circuit, which sent it to District Court. Despite attempts to settle the case, the two could not agree on terms. In October 2004 the judge ruled that McDermott must pay Boehner $60,000 plus attorney's fees; the next month the 7th District's Dave Hobson filed an ethics committee complaint against McDermott. In December 2006, the committee concluded that McDermott's actions were "not consistent with the spirit of the [ethics] rules," but it did not call for sanctions. In July 2007, after the D.C. appeals court ruled 5–4 in favor of Boehner, McDermott said that he would take his case to the Supreme Court on the grounds that it raises First Amendment issues.

After Republicans lost five seats in the 1998 election, Boehner was challenged for the conference chairmanship by J.C. Watts of Oklahoma. Some Republicans believed that Boehner had been part of the July 1997 coup attempt against Newt Gingrich, and Boehner's fate was probably sealed when Dick Armey held the majority leadership even though he had misled members about his role in the coup. Even though Gingrich had resigned, someone else had to go; it was Boehner, who lost 121-93. After such a loss many members withdraw from legislative work. But Boehner plunged into action as chairman of the Employer-Employee Relations Subcommittee. In six months, the subcommittee passed eight bills restructuring managed care and health insurance; Speaker Dennis Hastert, pleased by Boehner's initiative and dismayed that other committees had not acted, adopted these as the Republican health care agenda.

After the 2000 election Boehner sought the chairmanship of the Education and the Workforce Committee. Incumbent William Goodling was retiring; also seeking the job were second ranking Republican Tom Petri and the less senior Pete Hoekstra. Boehner got Armey's support and Hastert told him, "If I were you, I'd go ahead." Boehner, like many others, had long considered the committee a "partisan pit." Since 1960 Democrats had assigned only union loyalists to the committee and most Republican members took stands on employment issues opposed by industrial unions and stands on education opposed by teachers' unions. The basic education bill was up for reauthorization. Boehner knew that that would be the committee's first order of business and that George W. Bush's education proposals were one of his top priorities. So he tried to encourage a sense of bipartisanship. Miller had been teaching school dropouts and believed that current programs weren't teaching disadvantaged children what they should, and he became convinced that Bush and Boehner shared his concern. So Boehner and Miller worked together on the House bill, which ended up including Bush's principles of annual testing and accountability. It passed committee with six Republicans and one Democrat opposed and passed on the floor 384-45.

Negotiations continued during summer and fall between Boehner, Miller, Senator Edward Kennedy and ranking Senate Republican Judd Gregg. The final agreements came in November, and in December the House passed the bill 381-41, with most of the nays from Republicans (including Tom DeLay), and the Senate 87-10. Bush came to Hamilton High School to sign the bill in January 2002. As a sign of Boehner's enduring partnership with Kennedy, the two sponsored an annual dinner in Washington that raised more than a million dollars for underfunded Roman Catholic schools in Washington, D.C., and featured motivational speakers (including Laura Bush) and good-natured ribbing between the two hosts.

In 2003 and 2004 Boehner worked on reauthorization of IDEA, the special education act. This again was a bipartisan undertaking. Teacher's unions were seeking a relaxation of IDEA's requirement that administrators take special ed students' disabilities into account when disciplining them and that Individualized Education Programs be submitted annually for each special ed student. The House version relaxed the discipline requirement; the Senate version didn't. The differences were ironed out in conference committee after the November 2004 election. The final bill retained the requirement that disabilities be taken into account on discipline, provided stronger certification requirements and withholding of state funds if local districts fail to comply with the act. Waivers were authorized for 15 states on paperwork requirements. To complaints that Congress has funded only 19% of special ed costs, rather than the 40% authorized by IDEA in 1975, Boehner agreed to discretionary increases through 2011.

The committee also tackled the complex issue of pensions. In 2003, Boehner steered bipartisan passage of a bill requiring employers to use a blend of corporate bond rates when calculating payments funding their pension plans; the Senate passed the measure in January 2004 and Bush signed it into law in April. As bankrupt airlines handed over their pension obligations to the Pension Benefit Guaranty Corporation, Boehner in January 2005 said, "We have a huge pension underfunding problem," and called for bipartisan action. But when the AFL-CIO encouraged unions to keep pension funds away from financial service firms that backed the Bush Social Security changes, Boehner charged the unions would be making illegal investment decisions based on politics. With bipartisan support, he renewed his push for a comprehensive plan. Months of painstaking House-Senate negotiations were required, with Boehner playing an instrumental role. The eventual reforms, passed in summer 2006, "represent the most sweeping changes to American pension laws in more than 30 years," he said. The legislation closed loopholes that had permitted many companies to underfund their plans by an estimated $450 billion, and set deadlines for them to make payments, with additional time for financially-strapped airlines. It also included provisions such as automatic enrollment in 401(k) plans for many workers, and Boehner-backed steps to make information more available to employees. It was one of the rare moments in recent legislative history when a party leader was instrumental in enacting his own major legislation, which had been several years in the making.

On student loans, Boehner set out to reauthorize the Higher Education Act, on a budget-neutral basis. He and Miller showed little interest in George W. Bush's proposal to extend the No Child Left Behind approach to high schools. But they failed to reach their own agreement while Boehner was chairman.

When a Texas grand jury indictment forced Tom DeLay to step aside as Majority Leader in September 2005, Boehner publicly remained mum as Hastert tapped Majority Whip Roy Blunt to serve as acting leader. But he quietly stepped up his planning for a showdown that he had been expecting for many months. His contest against Blunt officially began on Jan. 7, 2006, when DeLay announced that he would abandon efforts to regain his leadership post. Blunt had styled himself as heir apparent, but Boehner believed that restiveness among House Republicans might support an insurgency-type challenge. "You have to know where you are going," he said in a veiled challenge to increasingly reactive GOP leadership. He offered a 37-page campaign manifesto, "A Majority that Matters," on which he had worked with aides and advisers for more than a year. It included a call for "one big, bold goal" each year, plus more deference to committees by GOP leaders. He sought to invigorate a tired—and, as became clear later that year, defensive—leadership. In the three-candidate race, John Shadegg was forced out after the first ballot when he got 40 votes to 110 for Blunt and 79 for Boehner. But Boehner got most of the Shadegg vote plus some of Blunt's first-ballot support and won 122-109.

Profiles often focus on his stylistic differences with Dennis Hastert and Tom DeLay, and tend to depict Boehner as a Barclay-smoking, eternally-tanned golfer—true enough, including the fact that his Ohio home backs onto the tenth green of his golf course. Indeed, he is more outgoing than Hastert and less of an ideologue than DeLay. But Boehner is at least as much of a partisan and legislative activist as either of them. As Majority Leader, after taking some time to establish a working relationship with Hastert, Boehner soon focused on lobbying reform legislation. Like many Republicans, he was less enthusiastic about Hastert's call for strict limits on privately-funded travel for lawmakers. Instead, Boehner wanted to restrict the explosion of spending earmarks, especially from the Appropriations Committee. He proudly noted that he had never sought an earmark for his own district, though he did not seek to impose that standard for the entire House. On immigration reform, he dropped his earlier advocacy of a middle ground rather than buck most House Republicans, who insisted on a harder line. He remained an ardent supporter of the war in Iraq as part of the fight against terrorism, and he told reporters in September 2006, "I wonder if [Democrats] are more interested in protecting terrorists than protecting the American people." After the resignation of Congressman Mark Foley following revelations of his e-mails with House pages, Boehner got into an awkward situation when he told reporters that he was "99 percent" sure he had earlier relayed to Hastert a warning about Foley from another House Republican. In October, he visited the districts of many endangered House Republicans and made numerous national media appearances, largely in a bid to turn out the Republican vote. Although he was disappointed by the party's loss of House control, he took some satisfaction that Ohio's House Republicans kept their losses to one seat. After Hastert said that he was stepping down from GOP leadership, Boehner was challenged by Mike Pence for Minority Leader. Despite Pence's efforts to appeal to grass-roots conservatives, Boehner won in a breeze, 168-27. "To earn our majority back, House Republicans must rededicate ourselves to the spirit of reform and we must regain our confidence and courage to tackle the big issues the American people care about," he said following his selection.

NINTH DISTRICT

Rep. Marcy Kaptur (D)

Elected 1982, 13th term; b. June 17, 1946, Toledo; home, Toledo; U. of WI, B.A. 1968, U. of MI, M.A. 1974, M.I.T., 1981-82; Catholic; single.

Professional Career: Urban planner, Lucas Cnty. Planning Comm., 1969-75; Urban planning consultant, 1975-77; White House Asst. Dir. for Urban Affairs, 1977-80; Dpty. Secy., Natl. Consumer Coop. Bank, 1980-81; Author.

DC Office: 2186 RHOB, 20515, 202-225-4146; Fax: 202-225-7711; Web site: kaptur.house.gov.

District Offices: Toledo, 419-259-7500.

Committees: *Appropriations* (5th of 37 D): Transportation, HUD & Related Agencies; Defense; Agriculture, Rural Development, FDA & Related Agencies. *Budget* (7th of 22 D).

Group Ratings

	ADA	ACLU	AFS	LCV	ITIC	NTU	COC	ACU	CFG	FRC
2006	85	91	100	100	43	8	33	21	7	14
2005	95	—	100	89	—	12	41	24	3	31

National Journal Ratings

	2005 LIB — 2005 CONS		2006 LIB — 2006 CONS	
Economic	78%	— 21%	68%	— 31%
Social	67%	— 33%	66%	— 34%
Foreign	80%	— 20%	70%	— 28%

Key Votes of the 109th Congress

1. Estate Tax Repeal	N	5. Limit Interstate Abortion	N	9. Build Border Fence	P
2. Limit CAFE Standards	N	6. Extend Patriot Act	N	10. CAFTA	N
3. FY06 Spending Curb	N	7. Bar Same Sex Marriage	N	11. Oppose Iraq Withdrawal	N
4. Drilling in ANWR	N	8. Stem Cell Research $	N	12. Detainee Tribunals	N

Election Results

2006 general	Marcy Kaptur (D)	153,880	(74%)	($495,351)
	Bradley Leavitt (R)	55,119	(26%)	
2006 primary	Marcy Kaptur (D)	unopposed		
2004 general	Marcy Kaptur (D)	205,149	(68%)	($615,506)
	Larry Kaczala (R)	95,983	(32%)	($255,894)

Prior Winning Percentages: 2002 (74%); 2000 (75%); 1998 (81%); 1996 (77%); 1994 (75%); 1992 (74%); 1990 (78%); 1988 (81%); 1986 (78%); 1984 (55%); 1982 (58%)

The People		Race/Ethnic Origin	Ancestry	
Area size:	1,244 sq. mi.	79.6% White	German: 21.3%	Irish: 8.9%
Urban population:	86.0%	13.6% Black	Polish: 6.4%	
Rural population:	14.0%	1.0% Asian	**2004 Presidential Vote**	
Pop. 2000:	630,730	0.2% Native Am.	Kerry (D) 181,889	(58%)
Pop. 2005 (est):	619,854	0.0% Hawaiian	Bush (R) 129,825	(42%)
Median income:	$40,265	1.5% Two+ races	Other 133	(0%)
Poverty status:	12.0%	0.1% Other	**2000 Presidential Vote**	
Military veterans:	13.6%	4.0% Hispanic Origin	Gore (D) 134,907	(55%)
			Bush (R) 100,704	(41%)
			Other 7,894	(3%)
			Cook Partisan Voting Index: D + 9	

Occupation	Blue collar: 29.2%	White collar: 54.9%	Gray collar: 15.8%

Toledo was one of America's boomtowns in the 1920s, "a decade of fabulous figures," as historian Harlan Hatcher wrote. The Willys-Overland plant employed 25,000 workers and turned out an automobile every 30 seconds; the Libbey-Owens-Ford merger made Toledo, with local supplies of natural gas and sand, the nation's largest glass manufacturer; the city built $20 million coal and iron ore docks and a transcontinental airport. Toledo had long been well-situated, where the Maumee River empties into Lake Erie, where two dozen rail lines connected it with the East Coast, Chicago, and the coal fields of Kentucky and West Virginia. It was well positioned to be a center of the brash auto industry, a national leader when it first produced the Jeep in the 1940s. During World War II, it also produced aircraft parts, rockets and other military equipment. But by the early 1980s auto company management had allowed the unions to bid wages and benefits too high while watching quality decline. Subsidies, beyond the temporary Chrysler loan and a few small trade barriers, were not forthcoming, so Toledo and other auto-dependent cities went through tough times.

But revival was on the way. Toledo's small manufacturers in search of markets showed energy and ingenuity. Sport utility vehicles were invented here. They produced one of America's hottest vehicles, the Jeep Cherokee; the old plant was set to close, but the city offered Chrysler $300 million in incentives to stay, and a new plant was built along I-75. Since then, DaimlerChrysler has built new Jeep Liberty and Jeep Wrangler factories here, and is barely able to meet growing demand as it expands those operations plus the additional parts and services that accompany them. That led the company in 2002 to begin demolishing what had been the 62 buildings of the Jeep Parkway plant, which had been the nation's longest-operating auto plant. Some workers from Jeep Parkway began work on a third shift to manufacture the Dodge Nitro.Other auto companies are developing the Toledo-to-Ann Arbor corridor as a major auto research area. Still, the continuing loss of other manufacturing jobs has left Toledo near the bottom of the nation's metropolitan areas in job growth, ahead of only several other areas in Ohio and Michigan.

The 9th Congressional District of Ohio is centered on Toledo, spreading east through the flatlands of Ottawa and Erie Counties on the Lake Erie shore and inland to southern Lorain County southwest of Cleveland, including Oberlin, home of Oberlin College, founded in 1833 and the first American college to admit women as well as men and blacks as well as whites. Port Clinton, on Lake Erie, bills itself as the "Walleye Capital of the World" and drops a walleye on New Year's Eve to rival Times Square. Sandusky is home of the giant Cedar Point amusement park, which surprisingly hires about 1,000 seasonal employees (about one-fourth of its total) from eastern Europe and Asia. Not far away is Milan, birthplace of the great inventor and capitalist Thomas Edison. Politically, Toledo has been heavily Democratic since CIO unions organized the plants in the late 1930s; the collapse of the auto industry so unnerved the district that in 1980 it voted for Ronald Reagan and elected a Republican congressman, but it switched back to the Democrats in 1982 and stayed with them in almost all elections ever since. But the suburbs and the countryside around are mostly Republican, and one survey showed that the Toledo media market had more campaign ads than anywhere else in the nation in 2004.

The congresswoman from the 9th District is Marcy Kaptur, a plain-spoken, old-fashioned Democrat who is a dedicated opponent of free trade. First elected in 1982, she is now the senior female Democrat in the House, a distinction not lost on her. She has pushed for more portraits and statues of women in the Capitol and authored a book on women in Congress. Always a loyal daughter of Toledo, Kaptur grew up there in a blue-collar neighborhood, her Polish-American parents worked at local auto plants. The family also operated a small grocery store, but her father sold it to get a job with health benefits. "It broke his heart," she said. She has spent almost her entire career in public service; she and her brother Steve live in the house where they grew up. She graduated from the University of Wisconsin, the first in her family to attend college, got a master's degree from the University of Michigan and then spent eight years as an urban planner in Toledo. She worked on urban revitalization in the Carter White House and was shrewd enough to return home in 1980. That year Republican Ed Weber defeated 26-year incumbent Thomas Ashley. In 1982, when no other Democrat would run against Weber, she did and won 58%-39% despite being outspent 3–1.

Kaptur's great cause is trade. She has long been convinced that Toledo and places like it have lost jobs and industry because of unfair trade practices and low wage competition in countries like Mexico and China. She pressured the Japanese to buy more American auto parts, but has been leery of Japanese investment in the United States. Kaptur was probably Congress's most vocal and dedicated opponent of NAFTA. She became something of a national figure in 1995, when she appeared before Ross Perot's United We Stand and made a rousing speech, mostly on trade, that had delegates cheering. Perot praised her and offered his vice presidential nomination a year later; she turned it down. She argued that 100,000 jobs had been transferred from Ohio to Mexico, and criticized Bill Clinton for doing nothing for sagging U.S. industries and for ignoring Democrats opposed to NAFTA. She was a vocal opponent of normal trade relations with China and trade promotion authority, and predicted that the Central American Free Trade Agreement would destroy jobs in Ohio. She backed a resolution calling for the United States to withdraw from the World Trade Organization, citing "the $600 billion trade deficit and the fact that these trade agreements are hollowing out our country." She co-chairs the Congressional Ukrainian Caucus.

Kaptur has a liberal voting record but departs from party orthodoxy on abortion—she opposes funding for abortion and favored the partial-birth abortion ban. She keeps close tabs on her district: a constituent gave her the idea to sponsor the legislation that authorized the World War II Memorial on the Washington Mall. For her district, she has focused on improvements in bridge, road, rail and port facilities. On the Appropriations Agriculture Subcommittee, where she was the ranking Democrat, she sought to limit farm payments, which led Republicans to threaten her favorite projects; she backed off, saying, "I may be blockheaded sometimes, but I'm not stupid." She has become a strong advocate of alternative energy sources such as ethanol and biofuels for Ohio. She strongly opposed the war in Iraq. In 2005, Kaptur and Kay Granger became the first women to serve on the Defense Appropriations Subcommittee; Kaptur gave up the senior Democratic slot on the Agriculture Subcommittee to make the move. After the 2002 election she ran a quixotic one-day campaign for minority leader against Nancy Pelosi.

Kaptur, who has hosted a weekly radio show on nearly 100 stations, is exceedingly popular in Toledo and has not been seriously challenged in two decades. In 2004 her Republican opponent was Lucas County Auditor Larry Kaczala, who criticized Kaptur for comparing Osama bin Laden to American revolutionaries. But Kaptur won 68%-32%. In July 2006, she appeared in Connecticut to endorse Ned Lamont against Senator Joe Lieberman in that state's Democratic primary. "We have a responsibility within our own party," she said. Because of the high cost of campaigning and her accumulated seniority, she has declined opportunities to run for statewide office, including governor in 2006. With the Democratic takeover of the House, she and senior Republican Ralph Regula urged that the Ohio delegation seek more opportunities for bipartisanship.

TENTH DISTRICT

Rep. Dennis Kucinich (D)

Elected 1996, 6th term; b. Oct. 6, 1946, Cleveland; home, Cleveland; Cleveland St. U., 1967-70, Case Western Reserve U., B.A., M.A., 1973; Catholic; married (Elizabeth Harper).

Elected Office: Cleveland City Cncl., 1970-75, 1983-85; Cleveland Mayor, 1977-79; OH Senate, 1994-96.

Professional Career: Clerk, Municipal Courts, 1976-77; Radio Talk Show Host, 1979, 1989; Lecturer, 1980-83; Consultant, 1986-94; TV Reporter, Channel 8, 1989-92.

DC Office: 2445 RHOB, 20515, 202-225-5871; Fax: 202-225-5745; Web site: kucinich.house.gov.

District Offices: Lakewood, 216-228-8850; Parma, 440-845-2707.

Committees: *Education & Labor* (10th of 27 D): Early Childhood, Elementary & Secondary Education; Healthy Families & Communities. *Oversight & Government Reform* (7th of 23 D): Domestic Policy (Chmn.); Federal Workforce, Postal Service & the District of Columbia.

Group Ratings

	ADA	ACLU	AFS	LCV	ITIC	NTU	COC	ACU	CFG	FRC
2006	100	100	100	100	14	22	20	4	7	0
2005	100	—	100	100	—	23	30	0	0	0

National Journal Ratings

	2005 LIB	—	2005 CONS	2006 LIB	—	2006 CONS
Economic	88%	—	9%	74%	—	23%
Social	93%	—	6%	96%	—	3%
Foreign	96%	—	0%	88%	—	10%

Key Votes of the 109th Congress

1. Estate Tax Repeal	N	5. Limit Interstate Abortion	N	9. Build Border Fence	N
2. Limit CAFE Standards	N	6. Extend Patriot Act	N	10. CAFTA	N
3. FY06 Spending Curb	N	7. Bar Same Sex Marriage	N	11. Oppose Iraq Withdrawal	N
4. Drilling in ANWR	N	8. Stem Cell Research $	Y	12. Detainee Tribunals	N

Election Results

2006 general	Dennis Kucinich (D)	138,393	(66%)	($622,699)
	Michael Dovilla (R)	69,996	(34%)	($70,343)
2006 primary	Dennis Kucinich (D)	51,485	(76%)	
	Barbara Ferris (D)	15,890	(24%)	
2004 general	Dennis Kucinich (D)	172,406	(60%)	($406,033)
	Edward Herman (R)	96,463	(34%)	($298,082)
	Barbara Ferris (NP)	18,343	(6%)	($56,461)

Prior Winning Percentages: 2002 (74%); 2000 (75%); 1998 (67%); 1996 (49%)

The People		Race/Ethnic Origin	Ancestry	
Area size:	196 sq. mi.	87.2% White	German: 16.6%	Irish: 12.8%
Urban population:	99.4%	4.2% Black	Polish: 8.6%	
Rural population:	0.6%	1.7% Asian	**2004 Presidential Vote**	
Pop. 2000:	630,730	0.2% Native Am.	Kerry (D) 175,149	(58%)
Pop. 2005 (est):	621,443	0.0% Hawaiian	Bush (R) 125,102	(41%)
Median income:	$41,841	1.5% Two+ races	Other 1,363	(0%)
Poverty status:	9.1%	0.1% Other	**2000 Presidential Vote**	
Military veterans:	13.2%	5.0% Hispanic Origin	Gore (D) 122,219	(53%)
			Bush (R) 96,623	(42%)
			Other 11,540	(5%)
			Cook Partisan Voting Index: D + 8	

Occupation   Blue collar: 23.3%   White collar: 62.5%   Gray collar: 14.1%

Cleveland, one of America's great cities at the beginning of the 20th century, faced major hardships in the latter half of the century, but may be on its way back in the new century. It grew as a center of heavy industry: This was the original base of John D. Rockefeller's Standard Oil; the city's twisting and deep Cuyahoga River was the site of several of the nation's largest steel mills; great industrial fortunes here built civic institutions like the museums in Wade Park, Case Western University and the Cleveland Symphony, and financed the campaigns of northeast Ohio Republican Presidents James Garfield and William McKinley. On the old Public Square, designed like a New England town green by the Yankees who settled this Western Reserve (the northeast corner of Ohio) in the early 19th century, the two eccentric Van Sweringen brothers, trolley magnates of the early 20th century, built the Terminal Tower, for many years the highest skyscraper in interior America. This yeasty, ethnic city, with more than 40 nationalities—Hungarians, Czechs, Serbs, Croatians, Poles, Italians, Germans (the Hapsburg Empire and more)—and many distinct ethnic neighborhoods, produced a robust two-party politics. In the 1930s, after CIO unions organized steel factories and auto assembly plants, Cleveland became solidly Democratic, though with some affluent Republican suburbs.

Disgruntled by local taxes, Rockefeller and his corporate operations moved to New York, and Cleveland never led the nation as it hoped: America's fourth largest city in 1910, it was overtaken in size first by Detroit, eventually by the likes of Houston and Dallas; today, it's the center of the nation's 24th largest metropolitan area. The central city declined from 914,000 in 1950 to 444,000 in 2006, with a Census Bureau projection that it may soon fall below 400,000. As the children who grew up in the tightly packed neighborhoods made more money and moved to the close-in suburbs and then outer suburban counties, fewer new immigrants have taken their place. The 1970s were a bad decade for Cleveland, which became an object of ridicule by national sophisticates. Its heavy industries were fast declining, Lake Erie and the Cuyahoga River were badly polluted (the river caught fire in June 1969) and the city faced bankruptcy under the youthful Mayor Dennis Kucinich. The city government was rescued by George Voinovich, elected mayor in 1979 and later governor and senator. Downtown Cleveland revived, with the theater district center at Playhouse Square, the Jacobs Field baseball stadium, Gund Arena, and the Rock and Roll Hall of Fame. People swim in a clean Lake Erie (some hardy souls even "surf" it in winter); restaurants and pleasure boat docks line the Cuyahoga where diners can sip Burning River pale ale. Many corporate headquarters have departed, LTV shut down its steel plant and Ford has cut back its local auto manufacturing, but Cleveland remains home to several of the nation's largest law firms, and some businesses, like iron ore giant Cleveland-Cliffs, have sharply revived. In Brook Park, NASA's Glenn Research Center is developing the service module for the next generation of the space-shuttle.

The 10th Congressional District of Ohio includes most of the west side of Cleveland and the western and southern suburbs in Cuyahoga County. Excluded is one salient of mostly black Cleveland precincts attached to the 11th District across the river. Suburbs in the 10th include Lakewood, well-established by the 1920s and still comfortable middle-class territory, plus Rocky River and Bay Village, growing more affluent westward along the lake. Inland is Parma, a creation of the 1950s, when second- and third-generation ethnics moved out to subdivision houses set amid what was once America's densest concentration of bowling alleys. The district extends east of Cleveland on the southern edge of the county in Cuyahoga Valley suburbs. The political tradition in the 10th is primarily Democratic, though Voinovich has carried the area; George W. Bush got only 41% of the vote here in 2004.

The congressman from the 10th District is Dennis Kucinich, first elected in 1996, still unrepentant that he plunged the city into default and a long-shot presidential candidate in 2004 and 2008. Kucinich grew up as the oldest of seven children whose father was a truck driver; the family moved 21 times to various parts of Cleveland. Kucinich was a political prodigy who was elected to the city council in 1969, at 23; he saw himself as the champion of the working man, eager for confrontations with Cleveland's business establishment. He was elected mayor in 1977 when the city government was in terrible financial straits; at the time, he was the youngest-ever mayor of a major American city. Kucinich was unwilling or unable to balance the budget and meet obligations. When bankers demanded he sell city-owned properties, he refused and they called in their loans. The public verdict was negative: after surviving a recall petition by 236 votes of 120,000 cast, Kucinich was defeated in 1979. He argues that his primary goal was to preserve the city-owned Muny Light electric system, that he succeeded in that and has saved residents millions of dollars on their electric bills. He taught at Cleveland State and Case Western Reserve, hosted a radio talk show and was a TV reporter. In 1994 Kucinich staged a political comeback and was elected to the state Senate. In 1996 he ran for the House. Republican incumbent Martin Hoke was elected twice against Democrats with ethical problems. Kucinich campaigned against NAFTA and GATT and defended his ties with labor unions. Democrats, many of them former Kucinich critics, rallied around him: The Cleveland city council named a public power plant for him on the same day Bill Clinton campaigned for him in Parma. Kucinich won, but by only 49%-46%.

Kucinich's voting record has become mostly liberal, as he has acquired a national constituency and moved some distance from his earlier centrist approach on social issues such as gay rights and flag-burning. He has been a vocal foe of international trade agreements and bars his staff from parking foreign cars in congressional lots. A vegan since before he was elected to Congress, Kucinich attacked companies that produce genetically modified foods. He continues to emphasize his local roots, with a tab on his website dedicated to polka, bowling and Kielbasa; he is the only member of Congress who lists the addresses of all his district's bowling alleys. With Barbara Lee, he has co-chaired the Progressive Caucus—Democrats who believe their party should move to the left. His agenda includes a national health-care system, universal pre-kindergarten, abolition of all nuclear weapons, and repeal of the Patriot Act.

In early 2003, Kucinich decided to run for president. His motivating force was his opposition to American military action in Iraq and elsewhere. He voted to authorize the use of force in Afghanistan after the September 11 attacks, but after the defeat of the Taliban he focused on nonviolent responses and called for the creation of a Department of Peace. He joined five other House Democrats who filed a lawsuit to prevent George W. Bush from invading Iraq without an explicit declaration of war. In seeking the Democratic nomination, he called himself an "FDR Democrat" who wanted to "return the Democratic Party to its roots," with strong ties to organized labor. "Miracles occur," he claimed when he announced his candidacy. He spoke to enthusiastic audiences of peace activists on both coasts. Long an opponent of abortion, he voted present on two anti-abortion bills in 2002. After he launched his presidential campaign, he changed his position completely: "I want to state clearly that no one will be appointed to the U.S. Supreme Court if they don't commit to supporting *Roe v. Wade* and a woman's right to choose." Even though he did not come close to winning a single state as he trailed Howard Dean in seeking the affection of party leftists, Kucinich remained buoyant and enjoyed the attention. Long after John Kerry had clinched the nomination, he continued his campaign. At the Democratic convention in Boston, the 67 Kucinich delegates were a rump group for "peace and justice," and for shifting the party to the left. In December 2006, he announced his presidential candidacy for 2008.

At home, in 2006 the *Plain Dealer* endorsed his primary opponent Barbara Anne Ferris, a former Peace Corps and United Nations worker, in part because of Kucinich's failure to address local problems; he won 76%-24%. He has not faced a serious reelection challenge in the general. Back in the House, Kucinich gained a wide-ranging platform as chairman of the Government Reform's new Domestic Policy Subcommittee; he told *Congress Daily* he would focus on "monopolies in the grocery business" and wanted to investigate possible price-gouging by urban utility companies. It will be interesting to see how he collaborates with committee chairman Henry Waxman in pursuing oversight targets, and how the assignment fits with his presidential campaign. Rosemary Palmer, whose 23-year-old son was killed in the Iraq war, announced in June 2007 that she will challenge Kucinich in the 2008 Democratic primary.

ELEVENTH DISTRICT

Rep. Stephanie Tubbs Jones (D)

Elected 1998, 5th term; b. Sept. 10, 1949, Cleveland; home, Cleveland; Case Western Reserve U., B.A. 1971, J.D. 1974.; Baptist; widowed.

Elected Office: Cleveland Municipal Court Judge, 1981-83; Cuyahoga Cnty. Court of Common Pleas Judge, 1983-91; Cuyahoga Cnty. Prosecutor, 1991-98.

Professional Career: Asst. Gen. Cnsl. & EEO Admin., NE OH Regional Sewer Dist., 1974-76; Asst. Cuyahoga Cnty. Prosecutor, 1976-79; Equal Employment Opportunity Comm., 1979-81.

DC Office: 1009 LHOB, 20515, 202-225-7032; Fax: 202-225-1339; Web site: tubbsjones.house.gov.

District Offices: Shaker Heights, 216-522-4900.

Committees: *Standards of Official Conduct* (Chmn. of 5 D). *Ways & Means* (12th of 24 D): Oversight; Health; Social Security.

Group Ratings

	ADA	ACLU	AFS	LCV	ITIC	NTU	COC	ACU	CFG	FRC
2006	90	100	100	92	29	13	40	4	7	0
2005	100	—	100	83	—	17	38	4	0	0

National Journal Ratings

	2005 LIB	—	2005 CONS		2006 LIB	—	2006 CONS
Economic	81%	—	18%		79%	—	18%
Social	80%	—	19%		80%	—	20%
Foreign	85%	—	14%		82%	—	18%

Key Votes of the 109th Congress

1. Estate Tax Repeal	N	5. Limit Interstate Abortion	N	9. Build Border Fence	N
2. Limit CAFE Standards	Y	6. Extend Patriot Act	N	10. CAFTA	N
3. FY06 Spending Curb	N	7. Bar Same Sex Marriage	N	11. Oppose Iraq Withdrawal	N
4. Drilling in ANWR	N	8. Stem Cell Research $	Y	12. Detainee Tribunals	N

Election Results

2006 general	Stephanie Tubbs Jones (D)	146,799	(83%)	($781,721)
	Lindsey String (R)	29,125	(17%)	
2006 primary	Stephanie Tubbs Jones (D)	unopposed		
2004 general	Stephanie Tubbs Jones (D)	unopposed		($501,711)

Prior Winning Percentages: 2002 (76%); 2000 (85%); 1998 (80%)

The People		Race/Ethnic Origin	Ancestry		
Area size:	135 sq. mi.	38.8% White	German: 6.5%	Irish: 5.2%	
Urban population:	100.0%	55.5% Black	Italian: 4.9%		
Rural population:	0.0%	1.6% Asian	**2004 Presidential Vote**		
Pop. 2000:	630,730	0.1% Native Am.	Kerry (D) 237,469		(81%)
Pop. 2005 (est):	573,320	0.0% Hawaiian	Bush (R) 52,372		(18%)
Median income:	$31,998	1.4% Two+ races	Other 1,943		(1%)
Poverty status:	19.5%	0.2% Other	**2000 Presidential Vote**		
Military veterans:	11.9%	2.3% Hispanic Origin	Gore (D) 172,146		(79%)
			Bush (R) 38,382		(18%)
			Other 6,706		(3%)
			Cook Partisan Voting Index: D +33		

Occupation	Blue collar: 21.3%	White collar: 61.4%	Gray collar: 17.3%

Like most great American cities, Cleveland grew in great bursts of migration, when capitalists' investments suddenly were paying off beyond their wildest dreams and low-wage workers were attracted from ready corners of the country and the world. Cleveland's greatest surge of growth started in the 1890s and lasted through the 1920s, as tens of thousands of immigrants from central and southern Europe arrived here, looking for jobs in steel, auto and other factories. Bohemians came to the tightly packed neighborhoods along Broadway, Hungarians a bit to the northeast, Jews north of University Circle along East 105th Street, and Italians ran produce markets in Little Italy along Mayfield Road. As the nation's heavy industries geared up for World War II and enjoyed years of prosperous growth afterward, a second surge of immigrants came, this time blacks from the American South. From Cleveland's old ghetto, south of Carnegie Avenue downtown to East 105th, the rapidly increasing number of blacks covered most of the east side by the middle 1960s, with only a few Bohemian and Italian enclaves remaining east of the Cuyahoga. Migration stopped around 1965, but blacks continued to move beyond the city limits to the east side suburbs. These bursts of migration led to political changes. A string of ethnic mayors—Frank Lausche, Anthony Celebrezze, Ralph Locher—was followed by the election in 1967 of Carl Stokes, the nation's first black big-city mayor, and Cleveland had racially polarized politics for much of the 1970s. Even so, the west side stayed mostly white and Cleveland did not have a black majority until the 2000 Census, when its declining population was 51% black. The Census Bureau reported in 2006, for the second time in three years, that Cleveland is the poorest of the nation's big cities; nearly half of all children lived in poverty.

The 11th Congressional District of Ohio includes most of the east side of Cleveland, plus the suburbs just to the east, which together have about as many people as the city now. Some of these—East Cleveland, Warrensville Heights—are mostly black; some, notably Shaker Heights, have stable black percentages in carefully maintained neighborhoods where racial integration has succeeded. Near the campus of Case Western Reserve University on the east side, Severance Hall is one of the nation's grand symphony orchestra homes. Downtown, Cleveland State University has a large campus; nearly half of its roughly 16,000 students are at least 25 years old. The city's number one employer is health services, and the Cleveland Clinic is internationally renowned, especially for cardiac care.

Other suburbs are the destination of blacks seeking low-crime neighborhoods and middle-class schools not often found among Cleveland's impressive museums and medical centers. Still others have been the destination of Cleveland's relatively few new immigrants, most of them from eastern Europe—Russians in Mayfield Heights and Serbs in South Euclid. Overall, 56% of the people in the 11th District are African-American. Politically, this is by far the most Democratic district in Ohio.

The congresswoman from the 11th District is Stephanie Tubbs Jones, first elected in 1998. She grew up in Cleveland, the daughter of a Hopkins Airport skycap, graduated from college and law school at Case Western and worked as a local government lawyer. She served eight years as judge on the Court of Common Pleas of Cuyahoga County and in 1990 narrowly lost as a Democratic nominee for Ohio Supreme Court. In 1991 she was appointed by the county's Democratic Party as the first woman and first black prosecutor in Cuyahoga County; she easily won election with 79%. When Louis Stokes announced his retirement after 30 years in the House, she decided to run for the seat. Her chief opponents in the primary were state Senator Jeffrey Johnson and Reverend Marvin McMickle, minister of the Antioch Baptist Church, one of the city's largest black congregations. Tubbs Jones, the early favorite, campaigned in both black and white neighborhoods, unlike her opponents. Stokes was officially neutral, but helped her raise money in Washington. She won 51% of the vote, with 20% each to Johnson and McMickle. The general election was a formality in this district.

In the House, Tubbs Jones has a solidly liberal voting record. She showed her skills at internal party politics, winning election as president of the Democratic sophomore class. Under the Republican majority, she wisely sought ways to cooperate with influential Republicans in the Ohio delegation and worked successfully with others in the area to keep 1,000 jobs with the Pentagon's Defense Finance and Accounting Service in Cleveland. She offended the sizable bloc of Jewish voters in her district when she voted present in 2002 on a resolution to support Israel in the fight against terrorism, but she joined a local rally in July 2006 to support Israel in its conflict with Hezbollah forces. In 2003 she was one of 11 House Democrats who voted against the resolution supporting the troops and George W. Bush at the start of the Iraq war. The first African-American woman to serve on the Ways and Means Committee, she spoke out strongly against personal retirement accounts in Social Security. With Bush's proposal, she said, African-Americans "would run the risk of living in extreme poverty upon retirement." Instead, she proposed a tax incentive for retirees to annuitize a portion of their savings.

On the ethics committee, she served in 2006 on the four-member panel that investigated allegations surrounding Congressman Mark Foley and the House page program. The subcommittee criticized the inadequate response of House officials, but unanimously decided not to bring charges against members or aides. In the majority, Speaker Nancy Pelosi named Tubbs Jones to chair the Ethics Committee, and praised her for "steadfast and active leadership in a non-partisan and judicious way, holding Members to the highest ethical standard." Critics pointed out that Tubbs Jones had made more privately financed trips during the previous seven years than any other member of Congress. But she moved quickly to prepare the committee for an increased workload after the House passed measures tightening ethics regulations in January 2007. Clarifying an ambiguous provision in the ethics package, committee members warned colleagues in February that flying in private airplanes would constitute a violation of House rules; in May, they softened the rule to allow for exceptions. After Rep. William Jefferson was indicted in June 2007, Tubbs Jones and ethics committee ranking Republican Doc Hastings clashed publicly over the panel's investigation of his activities.

She has not faced serious opposition in the primary or general since she was elected. In 2004, she campaigned actively for John Kerry. She protested alleged voting irregularities, both before and after the November election. During the Electoral College count in January 2005, she lodged the formal complaint that resulted in a two-hour debate challenging the Ohio result, the first such debate of a state vote since 1969; the House sustained the result, 267-31, with four of Ohio's six Democrats voting in favor. Later, she proposed the "Count Every Vote Act" to set national standards for counting ballots.

TWELFTH DISTRICT

Rep. Pat Tiberi (R)

Elected 2000, 4th term; b. Oct. 21, 1962, Columbus; home, Columbus; OH St. U., B.A. 1985; Catholic; married (Denice).

Elected Office: OH House of Reps., 1992-2000, Maj. Ldr., 1999-2000.

Professional Career: Staff asst., U.S. Rep. John Kasich, 1984-92; Realtor, ReMax Achievers, 1995-2000.

DC Office: 113 CHOB, 20515, 202-225-5355; Fax: 202-226-4523; Web site: tiberi.house.gov.

District Offices: Columbus, 614-523-2555.

Committees: *Budget* (13th of 17 R). *Ways & Means* (16th of 17 R): Oversight.

Group Ratings

	ADA	ACLU	AFS	LCV	ITIC	NTU	COC	ACU	CFG	FRC
2006	0	18	0	8	100	62	100	84	62	85
2005	5	—	0	6	—	58	96	88	59	92

National Journal Ratings

	2005 LIB	—	2005 CONS		2006 LIB	—	2006 CONS
Economic	18%	—	82%		27%	—	71%
Social	27%	—	72%		17%	—	79%
Foreign	45%	—	55%		47%	—	51%

Key Votes of the 109th Congress

1. Estate Tax Repeal	Y	5. Limit Interstate Abortion	Y	9. Build Border Fence	Y
2. Limit CAFE Standards	Y	6. Extend Patriot Act	Y	10. CAFTA	Y
3. FY06 Spending Curb	Y	7. Bar Same Sex Marriage	Y	11. Oppose Iraq Withdrawal	Y
4. Drilling in ANWR	Y	8. Stem Cell Research $	N	12. Detainee Tribunals	Y

Election Results

2006 general	Pat Tiberi (R)	145,943	(57%)	($2,985,858)
	Bob Shamansky (D)	108,746	(43%)	($1,639,175)
2006 primary	Pat Tiberi (R) .... unopposed			
2004 general	Pat Tiberi (R)	198,112	(62%)	($853,384)
	Edward Brown (D)	122,109	(38%)	($29,540)

Prior Winning Percentages: 2002 (64%); 2000 (53%)

The People		Race/Ethnic Origin	Ancestry	
Area size:	1,031 sq. mi.	72.1% White	German: 16.8% Irish: 9.3%	
Urban population:	88.1%	21.7% Black	English: 7.5%	
Rural population:	11.9%	2.1% Asian	**2004 Presidential Vote**	
Pop. 2000:	630,730	0.2% Native Am.	Bush (R) 178,080	(51%)
Pop. 2005 (est):	684,455	0.0% Hawaiian	Kerry (D) 171,881	(49%)
Median income:	$47,289	1.9% Two+ races	Other 263	(0%)
Poverty status:	10.0%	0.2% Other	**2000 Presidential Vote**	
Military veterans:	12.5%	1.7% Hispanic Origin	Bush (R) 129,840	(51%)
			Gore (D) 115,083	(46%)
			Other 7,340	(3%)
			Cook Partisan Voting Index: R + 1	

Occupation   Blue collar: 18.0%   White collar: 68.4%   Gray collar: 13.6%

Columbus is on the verge of becoming a major metropolis. With city limits stretching toward farmland at each point of the compass, the central city of Columbus had 733,000 people in 2006, far more than Cleveland (444,000) or Cincinnati (332,000). The metropolitan area, though less populous than Cleveland and Cincinnati, is growing more rapidly; Columbus's Franklin County passed the one million mark in the 1990s. Columbus is centrally located, not only in the center of Ohio, but a one-day truck drive from more than one-half of the nation's population. With its growing jobs base, Columbus was the only one of the 15 largest cities in Ohio to gain population in the 1990s. It has the advantages of being a state capital, the home of Ohio State University, and a major white-collar employment town. It is the home of Nationwide Insurance, Wendy's International, and Red Roof Inns; The Limited is based at the Easton Town Center, a huge mall built in the 1990s on farmland. Columbus likes to brag that its airfreight operations at Port Columbus, the airport, make it the largest in the country dedicated to cargo. This economic base and civic infrastructure has attracted the kind of upscale, enterprising people who have produced much of America's growth in recent years. Its rapidly growing foreign-born population—Latinos, Asians, Ethiopians, Russian Jews, and 45,000 Somalis—exceeds that of Cleveland or Detroit. But the city also has suffered from traditional big-city problems more closely associated with places like Cleveland, which has spurred a big switch of students from public to private schools. The politics of Columbus have traditionally been Republican. It had few of the eastern European immigrants and CIO unions that made Cleveland so Democratic. But in 1999 Columbus elected African-American Democrat Michael Coleman as mayor, and in 2000 Franklin County was carried, though just barely, by Al Gore. In 2004 thanks to out-migration by whites and a vigorous registration and turnout drive by Democrats, John Kerry carried the county 54%-45%.

The 12th Congressional District of Ohio is one of two districts dominated by Columbus and Franklin County. It includes 39% of the city, including most of the east side, plus the affluent suburb of Bexley, home of the Governor's Mansion, and the northeastern suburbs in Franklin County. It also includes Delaware County directly north of Columbus, Ohio's fastest-growing county (up 113% from 1990 to 2004), and most of Licking County east of Columbus, including the small industrial town of Newark and the lovely college town of Granville. With big margins in Delaware and Licking Counties, George W. Bush won here 51%-49% in 2004.

The congressman from the 12th District is Pat Tiberi, a Republican first elected in 2000. The son of Italian immigrants, he grew up in Columbus and graduated from Ohio State. He worked as a real estate agent and for 8 years an assistant to Congressman John Kasich, who helped Tiberi win in 1992, at age 30, a seat in the state House. He became majority leader and supported business-friendly legislation and changes in tort law. In 1999 Kasich announced his retirement, after a brief run for the presidency and six years as chairman of the Budget Committee. Tiberi won support to replace his mentor from most of the Republican establishment plus the U.S. Chamber of Commerce. He faced a noisy but not very effective primary challenge from state Senator Gene Watts, who sought to rally the conservative base. Tiberi won 73%-21%. The resounding victory gave him a big boost heading into the general election against Maryellen O'Shaughnessy, a Columbus city council member. She told her personal story as the single mother of a 10-year-old son. Tiberi played up his Columbus roots and his membership in the Ohio State marching band, and attacked O'Shaughnessy for the negative Democratic party ads that labeled him as the defender of insurance companies on prescription drugs. This was one of the most-watched House races in the nation; with campaign help from Kasich, Tiberi won 53%-44%.

In the House, Tiberi's record has been conservative on economic and cultural issues but more centrist on foreign and defense policy. He called for scrapping the income tax code and creating a national commission to craft a new tax system. He called for lifting the embargo of Cuba. With other fiscal conservatives, he criticized the Appropriations Committee, and sought unsuccessfully to change House Republican rules to make it easier for the speaker to remove appropriators who signed a discharge petition. On the Financial Services Committee, he focused on housing and home ownership issues, including a bill to require an increase in zero-down-payment mortgages for first-time homebuyers, which he said would help 150,000 purchasers. The House passed his bill to change the loan insurance program for manufactured housing. In July 2006, he joined a group of Republican mavericks who urged a vote to increase the minimum wage, though he voted against it in 2007 while serving in the minority.

When Rob Portman resigned from the House in 2005, Tiberi was the Ohio delegation's choice to fill his seat on the Ways and Means Committee; after a bruising fight, the seat went to Devin Nunes of California. In January 2007, he finally won a Ways and Means seat, with a boost from Republican Leader John Boehner; Tiberi had been campaign manager for Boehner in his successful bid for Majority Leader in early 2006 against Roy Blunt and John Shadegg and remained a close adviser. Although he has been far more low-key than Kasich, Tiberi is positioned to emerge from the shadows of the influential Ohio delegation; he led Republicans in successfully fighting a November 2005 referendum to change the Ohio redistricting process.

Despite the district's narrow partisan balance, Tiberi has easily won reelection. In 2006, he faced an unusual challenge from 79-year-old Bob Shamansky, a lawyer and real-estate investor who held the seat for two years before Kasich defeated him in 1982. Shamansky criticized the Iraq war and congressional failure to allow the government to negotiate with pharmaceutical companies in the Medicare/prescription drug program; he loaned his campaign $1.4 million. Tiberi distanced himself from President Bush on Iraq and rejected criticism that he too closely embraced the Republican party line. In Franklin County, which cast 59% of the district vote, Shamansky won by a slim margin. But Tiberi won 69%-31% in Delaware County and 66%-34% in Licking, to win an overall 57%-43% victory.

THIRTEENTH DISTRICT

Rep. Betty Sutton (D)

Elected 2006, 1st term; b. July 31, 1963, Barberton; home, Copley Township; Kent St. U., B.A. 1985, U. of Akron, J.D. 1990; Methodist; married (Doug Corwon).

Elected Office: Barberton City Cncl., 1989-91; Summit Cnty. Cncl, 1991-92; OH House of Reps., 1992-2000.

Professional Career: Practicing atty., 2001-06.

DC Office: 1721 LHOB, 20515, 202-225-3401; Fax: 202-225-2266; Web site: sutton.house.gov.

District Offices: Akron, 330-865-8450; Lorain, 440-245-5350.

Committees: *Judiciary* (15th of 23 D). *Rules* (9th of 9 D): Legislative & Budget Process.

Group Ratings and Key Votes: Newly Elected

Election Results

2006 general	Betty Sutton (D)	135,639	(61%)	($1,278,960)
	Craig Foltin (R)	85,922	(39%)	($650,595)
2006 primary	Betty Sutton (D)	21,268	(31%)	
	Capri Cafaro (D)	16,915	(25%)	
	Thomas Sawyer (D)	14,837	(22%)	
	Gary Kucinich (D)	9,891	(14%)	
	Bill Grace (D)	3,537	(5%)	
	Other	2,474	(4%)	
2004 general	Sherrod Brown (D)	201,004	(67%)	($601,435)
	Robert Lucas (R)	97,090	(33%)	($7,518)

The People		Race/Ethnic Origin	Ancestry	
Area size:	537 sq. mi.	81.5% White	German: 17.3%	Irish: 10.1%
Urban population:	92.7%	12.1% Black	English: 6.7%	
Rural population:	7.3%	1.2% Asian	**2004 Presidential Vote**	
Pop. 2000:	630,730	0.2% Native Am.	Kerry (D) 177,472	(56%)
Pop. 2005 (est):	653,741	0.0% Hawaiian	Bush (R) 140,908	(44%)
Median income:	$44,524	1.3% Two+ races	Other 230	(0%)
Poverty status:	9.4%	0.1% Other	**2000 Presidential Vote**	
Military veterans:	14.0%	3.5% Hispanic Origin	Gore (D) 133,458	(53%)
			Bush (R) 110,812	(44%)
			Other 9,559	(4%)
			Cook Partisan Voting Index: D + 6	

Occupation	Blue collar: 26.3%	White collar: 59.2%	Gray collar: 14.4%

Fifty years ago most of the people of metro Cleveland were clustered in the city itself, in tightly packed blocks of houses on the limestone plains above the Cuyahoga River valley with its giant steel mills. Around the city there were some comfortable suburbs, then as you drove past them you found yourself amid miles of farm fields before you got to the nearby industrial cities—Akron, the "Rubber Capital" with its Firestone, B.F. Goodrich and Goodyear tire factories, or Lorain, a sort of mini-Cleveland, on Lake Erie with steel mills lining the narrow Black River. In the half-century since, the population of Cleveland has fallen by half and the metro area has spread out over the northern Ohio countryside. The suburbs have spread from Cleveland to Akron without interval; the shoreline from Cleveland to Lorain has been filled in. Medina County, between Lorain and Akron, has been transformed from farmland to suburbia; only the Cuyahoga River valley between Cleveland and Akron has been off limits to development, protected by the creation of the Cuyahoga Valley National Park. The economy has changed as well. In 1950, Cleveland depended on heavy manufacturing, especially steel, and Akron on tires. Today most of the steel mills have gone cold or been torn down, the old tire factories have mostly been converted to other uses, and Ford announced the closing of its assembly plant in Lorain. Akron has memorialized the past in the National Inventors Hall of Fame and has developed itself as the "Polymer Center of America," with 80% of the nation's polymer research and a first-class polymer engineering program at the University of Akron. Downtown Akron has been revived by entertainment areas, the University of Akron, and some upscale housing.

The 13th Congressional District of Ohio is made up of much of this area in metro Cleveland, but none of the city itself. It includes the west side of Akron and its western suburbs; the lines separating it from the 14th and 17th Districts in Akron's Summit County are absurdly convoluted. It includes the northern and eastern parts of Lorain County, including Lorain and Elyria just to the south; the southern tier of suburban townships in Cleveland's Cuyahoga County—Strongsville, North Royalton, Broadview Heights; and the northern tier of suburban townships in Medina County, including Brunswick. Fifty years ago this would have been a Republican area, with Democratic precincts in Akron and Lorain. Today, as Clevelanders have spread far and wide, the area is Democratic, though not overwhelmingly so: George W. Bush twice got 44% of the vote here.

The new congresswoman from the 13th District is Betty Sutton, elected in 2006. Sutton grew up in Barberton as the youngest of six children. Her mother was a library clerk and her father a boilermaker. Sutton graduated from Kent State University and then earned a law degree from the University of Akron. While still in law school, Sutton beat out incumbents in 1989 to win an at-large seat on the Barberton City Council, and in 1991 was elected to the Summit County Council. In 1992, at age 29, Sutton became the youngest woman to win a seat in the state House, where she worked on employment issues like health care, pensions and retirement benefits. Sutton testified in 1993 about her abusive first marriage and worked to pass domestic violence legislation. She fought passage of a Republican bill to cut workers compensation benefits and then led a referendum to repeal the law. She served in the legislature until term limits forced her out in 2000, and afterward worked as a labor lawyer.

When Democrat Sherrod Brown announced he would run for the Senate, Sutton entered the race for the Democratic nomination and quickly emerged as a leading contender. She faced significant opposition in the primary from former eight-term Congressman Tom Sawyer and shopping center heiress Capri Cafaro. The race also included Elyria Mayor Bill Grace and former Cleveland City Councilman Gary Kucinich, the brother of Democratic Congressman Dennis Kucinich. Sawyer had good name recognition but struggled to raise money and was dogged by his 1993 vote for the North American Free Trade Agreement, which was blamed for destroying many of the district's manufacturing jobs. Cafaro, who unsuccessfully ran in 2004 against Rep. Steven LaTourette, poured more than $2 million of her own money into the primary. Sutton ran aggressively as an anti-corruption crusader. She criticized Sawyer for taking privately financed trips while in Congress and Cafaro for her involvement in a federal investigation into former Democratic Congressman James Traficant, who was convicted of 10 counts of bribery in 2002. (Cafaro hired a lawyer and threatened to sue anyone who mischaracterized a 2001 immunity deal, in which she admitted no wrongdoing.) Sutton enjoyed strong backing from organized labor, but it was an endorsement from EMILY's List that proved just as decisive. The group's Ohio affiliate motivated grassroots support and ran mail pieces against Sawyer. Sutton won the eight-way primary with 31%, ahead of Cafaro with 25% and Sawyer with 22%.

Her Republican opponent in the general election was Lorain Mayor Craig Foltin, an accountant who campaigned on a record of sound fiscal management. National Republicans were attracted to his candidacy because he had won two races in a Democratic city and raised an impressive $250,000 for his last mayoral campaign. The Democratic Congressional Campaign Committee attacked Foltin early in the campaign by circulating news reports about a 2003 taped telephone conversation between Foltin and a police dispatcher that included sexually explicit banter. Democrats also attempted to tie Foltin to Republican scandals in Ohio and in Congress while Sutton referred to "rampant corruption" in Lorain. Sutton raised twice as much as Foltin, including more than $300,000 from EMILY's List donors. In another year, Foltin might have run competitively for the open seat, but the poor political environment and the district's large union presence proved too much to overcome. Sutton defeated Foltin 61%-39%. On election night, Sutton thanked unions for their support and revealed the depth of her commitment to organized labor. "You're not only a part of this campaign, but a part of who I am," Sutton said. As a freshman, Sutton impressed Democratic leaders and won a seat on the exclusive Rules Committee.

FOURTEENTH DISTRICT

Rep. Steven LaTourette (R)

Elected 1994, 7th term; b. July 22, 1954, Cleveland; home, Madison; U. of MI, B.A. 1976, Cleveland St. U., J.D. 1979; Methodist; married (Jennifer Laptook).

Elected Office: Lake Cnty. Prosecuting atty., 1988-94.

Professional Career: Lake Cnty. Asst. Public Defender, 1980-83; Practicing atty., 1983-88.

DC Office: 2371 RHOB, 20515, 202-225-5731; Fax: 202-225-3307; Web site: www.house.gov/latourette.

District Offices: Painesville, 440-352-3939.

Committees: *Financial Services* (9th of 33 R): Domestic and International Monetary Policy, Trade & Technology; Oversight & Investigations; Financial Institutions & Consumer Credit. *Transportation & Infrastructure* (8th of 34 R): Coast Guard & Maritime Transportation (RMM); Railroads, Pipelines & Hazardous Materials; Aviation.

Group Ratings

	ADA	ACLU	AFS	LCV	ITIC	NTU	COC	ACU	CFG	FRC
2006	20	36	14	33	86	43	93	72	39	71
2005	15	—	13	11	—	49	78	71	48	75

National Journal Ratings

	2005 LIB	—	2005 CONS		2006 LIB	—	2006 CONS
Economic	50%	—	50%		43%	—	56%
Social	45%	—	54%		43%	—	56%
Foreign	42%	—	55%		54%	—	45%

Key Votes of the 109th Congress

1. Estate Tax Repeal	Y	5. Limit Interstate Abortion	Y	9. Build Border Fence	Y
2. Limit CAFE Standards	Y	6. Extend Patriot Act	Y	10. CAFTA	Y
3. FY06 Spending Curb	N	7. Bar Same Sex Marriage	Y	11. Oppose Iraq Withdrawal	Y
4. Drilling in ANWR	Y	8. Stem Cell Research $	Y	12. Detainee Tribunals	N

Election Results

2006 general	Steven LaTourette (R)	144,069	(58%)	($1,446,269)
	Lewis Katz (D)	97,753	(39%)	($227,286)
	Other	8,500	(3%)	
2006 primary	Steven LaTourette (R)	unopposed		
2004 general	Steven LaTourette (R)	201,652	(63%)	($2,430,424)
	Capri Cafaro (D)	119,714	(37%)	($1,991,894)

Prior Winning Percentages: 2002 (72%); 2000 (69%); 1998 (66%); 1996 (55%); 1994 (48%)

The People		Race/Ethnic Origin	Ancestry	
Area size:	1,820 sq. mi.	93.8% White	German: 16.9%	Irish: 11.2%
Urban population:	74.1%	2.5% Black	Italian: 9.0%	
Rural population:	25.9%	1.1% Asian	**2004 Presidential Vote**	
Pop. 2000:	630,730	0.1% Native Am.	Bush (R) 178,510	(53%)
Pop. 2005 (est):	659,901	0.0% Hawaiian	Kerry (D) 159,929	(47%)
Median income:	$51,304	0.8% Two+ races	Other 1,190	(0%)
Poverty status:	5.7%	0.1% Other	**2000 Presidential Vote**	
Military veterans:	13.6%	1.3% Hispanic Origin	Bush (R) 147,148	(52%)
			Gore (D) 124,582	(44%)
			Other 11,360	(4%)
			Cook Partisan Voting Index: R + 2	
Occupation	Blue collar: 25.1%	White collar: 62.0%	Gray collar: 12.9%	

The imprint of the westward track of New England Yankee migration is still apparent today on the shores of Lake Erie in northern Ohio. The Yankees, cooped up in New England for 200 years, shot across the country through upstate New York, west across Ohio and Michigan to Chicago, and on to Kansas and southern California in just two or three generations, providing inspiration, manpower and technical might for the Union victory in the Civil War, and leaving their imprint along the way. One place they stopped was the Western Reserve, the northeast corner of Ohio, created for the excess population of Connecticut; its towns, colleges and cultural institutions were established by Yankees. This area produced some of the strongest opposition to slavery and support of the Union armies and Republican party in the nation; Lake Erie ports were prime transit points for the Underground Railroad to Canada. Its thrifty, hard-working, well-educated citizens built communities with fine schools and, with their accumulated savings, invested in what became some of the nation's leading industries. A century ago, that brought great masses of immigrants to Cleveland and the other cities of northeast Ohio. After the Great Depression and the bloody CIO organizing drives of the late 1930s, the Western Reserve was Democratic during Ohio's class-warfare politics. Now, like Connecticut and Massachusetts, it may be moving toward a post-industrial economy. Factory employment has dropped, but total jobs are rising again; small, adaptive business units with highly skilled workers are the growth sectors.

The 14th Congressional District of Ohio takes in parts or all of seven counties of northeast Ohio and the old Western Reserve. It includes Lake County, northeast of Cleveland, with abandoned industrial sites (including the former Diamond Shamrock factory that became known as Hiroshima because of its nasty wasteland) and the second-highest per capita income in the state, with fertile agriculture; and Geauga County, with prosperous suburbs amid Western Reserve villages that still participate in a maple syrup festival even though the loss of farmland has cut production. On the east end of the state are Ashtabula—home to 16 covered bridges and several wineries—and the northern part of Trumbull County: industrial country. It includes the affluent suburbs at the eastern edge of Cleveland's Cuyahoga County, comfortable suburbs in northern Summit County and the northern tier of townships in Portage County to the east. In the 19th century the Western Reserve was heavily Republican; the congressman from this area from 1863 to 1880 was James Garfield, also a general in the Civil War; in 1880 he was elected president and in 1881 was assassinated. In the 1930s this area grew politically competitive, as Cleveland became heavily Democratic, and it has been in most years since. But this district was designed to gather together Republican territory in the Western Reserve, and it voted 52%-44% for George W. Bush in 2000 and 53%-47% in 2004.

The congressman from the 14th District is Steven LaTourette, a Republican first elected in 1994. LaTourette grew up in the Cleveland area and went to law school at Cleveland State University; in the 1980s he worked as a public defender and in private practice in Lake County, and became Lake County district attorney in 1988, at 34. Well-known and well-liked, in 1994 he won a three-candidate Republican primary with 54%. In the general he faced Congressman Eric Fingerhut, a 35-year-old political prodigy who in 1992 was elected to replace two retiring Democratic incumbents. LaTourette attacked Fingerhut for backing the Clinton budget and tax increase, for being soft on crime and for hypocritically using his franking privileges. He won 48%-43%.

In the House, LaTourette has the most moderate voting record of Ohio's Republican members and he shows more irreverence than one might expect from a former prosecutor. He invited humorist Dave Barry to spend several days on his press staff, with predictably funny results. He was an ardent advocate of a minimum-wage hike and broke with many House Republicans to oppose normal trade relations with China, but he delivered crucial, last-minute support for the Central American Free Trade Agreement; he later said that he regretted that vote. As a senior member of the Transportation and Infrastructure Committee, his high-priority projects have included improvements of Ohio Routes 82 and 8, plus legislation to add Ashtabula, Mahoning and Trumbull Counties to the Appalachian Regional Commission. The House approved his amendment to restore $214 million in subsides for Amtrak. On the Ethics Committee in 2004, he joined the unanimous committee votes to admonish Majority Leader Tom DeLay on three charges. When Speaker Dennis Hastert without explanation removed LaTourette from the committee in 2005, he was privately unhappy but remained a loyal party soldier. On the Financial Services Committee in 2006, he won approval of a data-protection bill designed to combat identity theft; unresolved differences with other committees killed it.

In contrast to many members of the Class of 1994, LaTourette quickly secured his former Democratic seat without a competitive challenger. In 2004, he was pressed by Democratic challenger Capri Cafaro, a 26-year-old shopping center heiress who spent nearly $2 million of her own funds; her father had been granted immunity in exchange for his cooperation in the prosecution of Congressman Jim Traficant and was sentenced to probation. Cafaro struggled with the issues and in convincing voters of her maturity. He won 63%-37%. During the contest LaTourette acknowledged an affair with his former chief aide who had become a lobbyist, whom he soon married; Democrats had asked for a Justice Department investigation of possible violation of lobbying laws. His former wife endorsed Cafaro and complained, "Washington corrupts people." In the 2006 campaign, Democrats directed more attention at other Ohio Republicans.

Appeals Court Judge William O'Neill, a Democrat, announced in April 2007 that he would challenge LaTourette in 2008. He begins with some name recognition: O'Neill appeared on the ballot in 2006 when he made an unsuccessful bid for the state supreme court.

FIFTEENTH DISTRICT

Rep. Deborah Pryce (R)

Elected 1992, 8th term; b. July 29, 1951, Warren; home, Columbus; OH St. U., B.A. 1973, Capital U. Law Schl., J.D. 1976; Presbyterian; divorced.

Elected Office: Franklin Cnty. Municipal Court Judge, 1985-92.

Professional Career: Admin. Law Judge, OH Dept. of Insurance, 1976; Columbus City Asst. Prosecutor & Asst. City Atty., 1978-85; Practicing atty., 1992.

DC Office: 320 CHOB, 20515, 202-225-2015; Fax: ; Web site: www.house.gov/pryce.

District Offices: Columbus, 614-469-5614.

Committees: *Financial Services* (3d of 33 R): Capital Markets, Insurance & Government Sponsored Enterprises (RMM); Financial Institutions & Consumer Credit.

Group Ratings

	ADA	ACLU	AFS	LCV	ITIC	NTU	COC	ACU	CFG	FRC
2006	20	23	14	25	100	53	100	72	55	42
2005	15	—	13	6	—	54	88	83	56	77

National Journal Ratings

	2005 LIB	—	2005 CONS		2006 LIB	—	2006 CONS
Economic	17%	—	83%		37%	—	62%
Social	40%	—	59%		43%	—	56%
Foreign	34%	—	61%		17%	—	73%

Key Votes of the 109th Congress

1. Estate Tax Repeal	Y	5. Limit Interstate Abortion	Y	9. Build Border Fence	Y
2. Limit CAFE Standards	Y	6. Extend Patriot Act	Y	10. CAFTA	Y
3. FY06 Spending Curb	Y	7. Bar Same Sex Marriage	N	11. Oppose Iraq Withdrawal	Y
4. Drilling in ANWR	Y	8. Stem Cell Research $	Y	12. Detainee Tribunals	Y

Election Results

2006 general	Deborah Pryce (R)	110,714	(50%)	($4,696,772)
	Mary Jo Kilroy (D)	109,659	(50%)	($2,749,231)
2006 primary	Deborah Pryce (R)	unopposed		
2004 general	Deborah Pryce (R)	166,520	(60%)	($1,008,306)
	Mark Brown (D)	110,915	(40%)	

Prior Winning Percentages: 2002 (67%); 2000 (68%); 1998 (66%); 1996 (71%); 1994 (71%); 1992 (44%)

The People		Race/Ethnic Origin	Ancestry	
Area size:	1,182 sq. mi.	85.2% White	German: 18.5%	Irish: 10.4%
Urban population:	91.3%	7.2% Black	English: 8.0%	
Rural population:	8.8%	3.3% Asian	**2004 Presidential Vote**	
Pop. 2000:	630,730	0.2% Native Am.	Bush (R) 154,105	(50%)
Pop. 2005 (est):	649,132	0.0% Hawaiian	Kerry (D) 151,869	(50%)
Median income:	$43,885	1.7% Two+ races	Other 174	(0%)
Poverty status:	10.8%	0.2% Other	**2000 Presidential Vote**	
Military veterans:	11.6%	2.3% Hispanic Origin	Bush (R) 117,175	(52%)
			Gore (D) 98,204	(44%)
			Other 8,931	(4%)
			Cook Partisan Voting Index: R + 1	

Occupation	Blue collar: 19.8%	White collar: 66.3%	Gray collar: 13.9%

Columbus, smack in the center of Ohio, was founded in 1812 to be the state capital. Its flat-domed Capitol at Broad and High, with the statue of William McKinley out front, is surrounded by high-rises, public and private, old and new, while the city has grown in all directions into the countryside, and now is on the verge of becoming a large metropolis. It is the headquarters of state government and Ohio State, which, with more than 50,000 students, has the highest enrollment of any campus in the nation. It is the headquarters of the Batelle Memorial Institute, the think tank that helped invent compact discs, office copy machines and the universal product code; a major industry here is data retrieval. Columbus, after annexing many suburbs and doubling its geography since 1967, is now Ohio's largest central city by far, with 733,000 people in 2006; Franklin County topped one million in 2000 and the metro area extends into formerly rural counties. Columbus has built civic landmarks—the Center of Science and Industry on the riverfront, the Jerome Schottenstein Center for sports and concerts at OSU, a hockey stadium for the Columbus Blue Jackets and the nation's first stadium built for a professional soccer team, the Columbus Crew. There is residential building downtown in thriving entertainment districts, including jazz clubs. With the nation's highest proportion of residents age 25 to 34, Columbus has been attracting young professionals and immigrants more than any other Ohio city and continues to be a prime test market for commercial products of all kinds. With its suburban growth, more people in the seven-county metro area now live outside than inside the I-270 Outerbelt, which was completed in the 1980s.

The 15th Congressional District of Ohio includes all of Columbus except the east side, plus southern and western Franklin County and once-rural Madison and Union Counties directly to the west. Union County is where Honda built a motorcycle plant in 1979 and its Marysville auto plant in 1982; Honda has spent $6 billion there, recently added a new $123 million paint facility and employs about 16,000 workers locally. The 15th includes white working class areas on the south side of the city and in nearby Grove City. Politically, these Democratic areas have long been more than balanced by the heavily Republican suburb of Upper Arlington, across the Olentangy River from Ohio State, and by Republican subdivisions sprouting up in rural land between the old villages. But Columbus was the scene of a highly successful registration and turnout drive by Democrats in 2004, when Columbus and Franklin County went Democratic. The 15th District as a whole, 52% for George W. Bush in 2000, gave him only a 50.3% majority in 2004.

The congresswoman from the 15th District is Deborah Pryce, a Republican first elected in 1992. Pryce grew up in Warren, graduated from Ohio State and Capital University law school, worked in state government and as a city prosecutor, and was elected municipal court judge in 1985. In 1992, when incumbent Chalmers Wylie retired after 26 years, Pryce ran for the House. She was unopposed in the primary but had tough competition in the general from Democrat Richard Cordray and from anti-abortion independent Linda Reidelbach. Pryce talked much about congressional reform—term limits, rotating chairmanships, line-item veto—and called for limiting annual spending increases to 3%. She won with 44% of the vote to Cordray's 38% and Reidelbach's 18%.

In the House, Pryce has a voting record that is mostly conservative on economic and foreign issues, more moderate on cultural issues. In her first term she was elected interim president of her Republican class and helped to write the Contract with America. Pryce has been particularly interested in issues relating to children, adoption and cancer. Her adoptive daughter developed cancer in September 1998 and died at age nine in September 1999; she adopted a newborn in 2002. Pryce started Hope Street Kids, an organization to raise funds for cancer research, using funds donated in memory of her daughter. She is co-chairwoman of the House Cancer Caucus and sponsored a bill to require private insurers to provide coverage of routine patient costs of cancer patients who qualify to participate in a clinical trial. She won enactment of expanded grants for pediatric palliative care programs and to give parents of children with cancer access to both curative and palliative care.

From 2002 until 2006, Pryce chaired the Republican Conference, the number four position in the Republican leadership. Although in charge of the party's message, Pryce was not often seen on national television or quoted in national print media. "Controversy is part of politics, but not the part I like to participate in. Do I like being behind the scenes better than out in front? Yes. I work better. I'm more effective that way. I'm way more comfortable." She played more of an inside role, keeping Republicans, especially moderates, together; Pryce argued for maintaining party unity and accepting bills with conservative provisions, to keep the process moving, knowing that the Senate or the administration may modify things. In 2005, she urged quick House action on George W. Bush's Social Security reform so that it would not be a campaign issue. In February 2006, she narrowly avoided a challenge by party renegades who wanted a new vote on all party leaders and who had complained that she was not sufficiently outspoken. Facing what looked to be certain competition, Pryce did not seek a third term as Conference chairman following the 2006 election.

In January 2005 Pryce left the Rules Committee and returned to the Financial Services Committee, which has major clout with the hefty Columbus-area banking business. She was credited for her former service and became chairman of the Domestic and International Monetary Policy Subcommittee. Although she had been mentioned as a possible successor to Financial Services Chairman Mike Oxley, she steered clear of the battle between Richard Baker and Spencer Bachus for the committee's top GOP post after the 2006 election.

Her lower profile in the House resulted, in part, from a grueling reelection campaign in 2006, which was her first serious challenge since 1992. Democrats nominated Mary Jo Kilroy, a Franklin County commissioner, who sought to link Pryce to unpopular Republican leaders and to the war in Iraq. Kilroy was a prime recruit of the DCCC; the labor-backed group Americans United launched an extensive anti-Pryce television campaign, with a focus on her promotion of Bush's Social Security plan, to which the Pryce campaign replied that the issue had become "ancient history." Pryce inadvertently created additional problems for herself when she told an interviewer for *Columbus Monthly* magazine in September 2006 that Congressman Mark Foley of Florida was among her close friends in Congress; that comment came shortly before revelations of his sexually explicit e-mails to House pages forced Foley to resign. "Apparently I did not know Mark Foley at all," she subsequently told reporters. Kilroy, in an attempt to undermine the Republican base, unleashed an attack ad on Christian and conservative radio stations that expanded on Pryce's remark. "What is going in Washington?" asked the female narrator. "Deborah Pryce's friend Mark Foley is caught using his position to take advantage of 16-year-old pages . . . Now Pryce is protecting [House Speaker Dennis] Hastert even though he protected a sex predator." In response, Pryce accused Kilroy of gay-baiting. In their one campaign debate, Pryce defended the Iraq war and the fight against terrorism, and touted the federal funds she had brought to the district. Kilroy called Iraq "a recruiting tool for terrorists," and criticized Pryce for budget deficits and the proliferation of spending earmarks. Pryce won, but barely: 50.2%-49.7%. In Franklin County, which cast 86% of the vote, Kilroy led 52%-48%. But Pryce won 62% in Madison County and 66% in Union County to secure her 1,055-vote win.

Kilroy did not concede until after an official recount was finalized in mid-December; she quickly moved to challenge Pryce again in 2008. But in August 2007, Pryce announced she would not seek reelection, citing a desire to spend more time with her young daughter, who was about to enter kindergarten. Former Attorney General Jim Petro and several other top Republican prospects for the seat declined to run in the weeks following Pryce's announcement.

SIXTEENTH DISTRICT

Rep. Ralph Regula (R)

Elected 1972, 18th term; b. Dec. 3, 1924, Beach City; home, Navarre; Mt. Union Col., B.A. 1948, William McKinley Law Schl., LL.B. 1952; Episcopalian; married (Mary).

Military Career: Navy, 1944-46 (WWII).

Elected Office: OH House of Reps., 1964-66; OH Senate, 1966-72.

Professional Career: Teacher & schl. principal, 1948-52; Practicing atty., 1952-73; OH Bd. of Educ., 1960-64.

DC Office: 2306 RHOB, 20515, 202-225-3876; Fax: 202-225-3059; Web site: www.house.gov/regula.

District Offices: Canton, 330-489-4414; Medina, 330-722-3793.

Committees: *Appropriations* (3d of 29 R): Financial Services & General Government (RMM); Labor, HHS, Education & Related Agencies.

Group Ratings

	ADA	ACLU	AFS	LCV	ITIC	NTU	COC	ACU	CFG	FRC
2006	15	14	14	8	86	48	80	71	35	71
2005	5	—	0	0	—	51	93	76	42	77

National Journal Ratings

	2005 LIB	—	2005 CONS		2006 LIB	—	2006 CONS
Economic	30%	—	68%		42%	—	58%
Social	38%	—	61%		35%	—	63%
Foreign	34%	—	61%		17%	—	73%

Key Votes of the 109th Congress

1. Estate Tax Repeal	Y	5. Limit Interstate Abortion	Y	9. Build Border Fence	Y
2. Limit CAFE Standards	N	6. Extend Patriot Act	Y	10. CAFTA	Y
3. FY06 Spending Curb	Y	7. Bar Same Sex Marriage	Y	11. Oppose Iraq Withdrawal	Y
4. Drilling in ANWR	Y	8. Stem Cell Research $	Y	12. Detainee Tribunals	Y

Election Results

2006 general	Ralph Regula (R)	137,167	(58%)	($1,016,885)
	Thomas Shaw (D)	97,955	(42%)	
2006 primary	Ralph Regula (R)	32,526	(58%)	
	Matt Miller (R)	23,170	(42%)	
2004 general	Ralph Regula (R)	202,544	(67%)	($606,430)
	Jeff Seemann (D)	101,817	(33%)	($59,667)

Prior Winning Percentages: 2002 (69%); 2000 (69%); 1998 (64%); 1996 (69%); 1994 (75%); 1992 (64%); 1990 (59%); 1988 (79%); 1986 (76%); 1984 (72%); 1982 (66%); 1980 (79%); 1978 (78%); 1976 (67%); 1974 (66%); 1972 (57%)

The People		Race/Ethnic Origin	Ancestry	
Area size:	1,741 sq. mi.	92.4% White	German: 21.9% Irish: 9.5%	
Urban population:	73.6%	4.8% Black	English: 7.3%	
Rural population:	26.4%	0.6% Asian	**2004 Presidential Vote**	
Pop. 2000:	630,730	0.2% Native Am.	Bush (R) 171,561	(54%)
Pop. 2005 (est):	643,308	0.0% Hawaiian	Kerry (D) 146,066	(46%)
Median income:	$41,801	1.1% Two+ races	Other 1,085	(0%)
Poverty status:	8.3%	0.1% Other	**2000 Presidential Vote**	
Military veterans:	13.6%	0.9% Hispanic Origin	Bush (R) 141,311	(53%)
			Gore (D) 112,270	(42%)
			Other 10,908	(4%)
			Cook Partisan Voting Index: R + 4	
Occupation	Blue collar: 30.5%	White collar: 54.7% Gray collar: 14.8%		

A little more than a century ago, Canton, Ohio, was at the center of American politics. Canton was already an industrial city then, though not with the huge steel factories built in Youngstown or

Cleveland. Its high-skill workers were fashioning new kinds of plows and reapers, making watches and, beginning in 1899, roller bearings. Canton did not attract masses of immigrants. Its factories did not run on harsh stopwatch discipline; there were not the class warfare politics here that would be seen later in other northern Ohio industrial cities. Instead Canton was united in admiring its first citizen, William McKinley, who rose to the rank of major at 22 in the Civil War, was elected congressman and governor, and chaired the House Ways and Means Committee. As Republican nominee for president in 1896, McKinley campaigned from his front porch in Canton, meeting with delegations brought in by train from all over the country. This spectacle, with its display of technological virtuosity and personal modesty, sounds an appealing and reverberating note in American politics, as does the McKinley platform—the "full dinner pail," the gold standard, the enforcement of law and order in labor relations—which has long been viewed as antiquated but still provides useful instruction. A century later Canton is a community still based on manufacturing, but one troubled by manufacturing job losses. Its largest employer, locally-owned Timken, announced layoffs in 2004, but with business booming in early 2006 as it produced bearings exported to China the steelmaker reversed course and hired more workers; later n 2006, the slump of the Big Three auto companies brought more layoffs. Less widely reported were new jobs in smaller factories, like an Alliance casting plant reopened to make rail car parts with 420 jobs. Canton may be suffering a net loss of jobs, but this is nothing like the losses suffered in the Mahoning Valley in the late 1970s and the early 1980s.

The 16th Congressional District of Ohio includes all of Canton and Stark County, plus Wayne County to the west and most of Ashland and Medina Counties. Wayne County is home to the College of Wooster and the headquarters of Smuckers, which has acquired new brands from other food companies (Jif peanut butter, Hungry Jack pancakes, etc.) and doubled its sales and profits in recent years. In the southern part of the county (and in Holmes and Tuscarawas Counties to the south) is the largest Amish settlement in the world, where people drive horse-drawn tractors, eschew automobiles and electricity, quit school after the eighth grade and refuse to recognize daylight savings time. Tourism has been a growth industry in Amish country, with restaurants, bed and breakfasts and gift shops; on Sundays they are staffed by the "English" (i.e., non-Amish). Ashland is a smaller, non-metropolitan county; Johnny Appleseed once lived on what is now the campus of Ashland University, known for its Ashbrook Center for Public Affairs. Medina County, north of Wayne, is part of the Cleveland metropolitan area, as young families buy houses in new subdivisions off I-71; its most heavily suburbanized northern townships, however, are in the 13th District. Politically, this area is generally Republican, though not always by wide margins. Stark County was something like ground zero in the 2004 presidential campaign, and was the only Ohio county which George W. Bush carried in 2000 but lost in 2004, both times by narrow margins. But the other counties kept the district in the Republican column and Bush carried it 53%-42% in 2000 and 54%-46% in 2004.

The congressman from the 16th District is Ralph Regula, a Republican first elected in 1972; he is second in seniority among House Republicans, after Florida's Bill Young. Regula grew up in rural Stark County, the son of a farmer and coal mine operator; he served in the Navy in World War II, then worked his way through the William McKinley School of Law while teaching elementary school. He was elected to the Ohio legislature in 1964, just before turning 40. He still has a cattle farm near Canton. When incumbent Frank Bow, first elected in 1950, retired in 1972, Regula ran for the House and was easily elected.

Regula is now the third ranking Republican on the Appropriations Committee. From 1995 to 2001 he chaired the Interior Subcommittee. On the Interior Subcommittee, Regula was a counterweight to the Resources Committee and its chairman, Don Young of Alaska, who added riders to Regula's appropriations strongly opposed by environmental groups and the Clinton administration. Regula resisted these, and often gave them up in end-of-session conference committees when Clinton threatened a veto. Young and Regula also got into a fight over Mount McKinley. Young introduced a bill to rename the mountain Denali, an Alaska Native name; Regula, McKinley's successor in the House, replied heatedly that that controversy had already been settled in 1980, when the McKinley name stayed on the mountain but the park was renamed Denali National Park. In each Congress he has filed bills reaffirming the McKinley name; the Board of Geographic Names, which won't change a name if it's the subject of legislation, has been prevented from changing it to Denali. In his last year as Interior chairman, Regula increased the appropriation by 26%, added a ban on the Interior Department moving callers into voice mail between 7:30 a.m. and 4:30 p.m. and designated the Cuyahoga Valley National Recreation Area a national park, but not subject to national park air standards. In 2000 he created the First Ladies National Historic Site in Canton;

his wife Mary Regula is the founding president of the National First Ladies' Library, which operates the site. He has put $4.5 million into the site over the years; she takes no salary for her work. In 1996 he established visitors' fees at recreation areas run by the Forest Service, the Bureau of Land Management, the Fish and Wildlife Service and the National Park Service. These have sparked resentment in the West, but in the November 2004 omnibus appropriation he extended them for 10 years.

In January 2001 Regula took over the Labor-HHS-Education Subcommittee, whose appropriation is second in size only to Defense. There he worked harmoniously with ranking Democrat David Obey and produced a $123 billion appropriation approved in October 2001. In summer 2002, Speaker Dennis Hastert was under pressure from conservative Republican Study Committee members to bring forward the Labor-HHS bill before any other appropriations; they wanted to hold it to the president's $129.9 billion level, while the Senate had voted $136.4 billion and Regula struggled to reconcile the demands of education and health constituencies. Regula argued that an appropriation under the Bush limit couldn't win a majority on the floor, and as a result all appropriations except Defense and Military Construction were postponed until after the election. In February 2003, when the appropriations were finally passed, Regula's bill provided increases for Title I and special education $500 million under the Bush figure. In February 2004 Regula said he was looking to see where programs weren't serving their purpose, but he did not impose major cuts.

In 2005 the subcommittee produced a $142.5 billion appropriation, below the previous year's level. It defunded 49 programs with a savings of $2.3 billion. "We had to make tough choices by reconciling competing priorities with the resources available." The bill included a 46% cut in public broadcasting funds, reducing the Corporation for Public Broadcasting by $100 million. Congressional scholar Norman Ornstein charged that Regula had a plan to zero out public broadcasting by 2009. Regula argued that the rationale for funding was obsolete. "Keep in mind that this was created at a time, some 30-plus years ago, when we didn't have the huge variety of programming that's available today." But the public broadcasters had a strong constituency, and the House voted 284-140 to restore $100 million to public broadcasting and to reduce the 46% cut to 25%. In 2006 Regula and his subcommittee removed $1.5 billion that the administration wanted to use to extend the No Child Left Behind Act to high schools and rerouted it to the Perkins loan program and drop-out prevention programs. The $141.9 billion appropriation passed in subcommittee, after Democrats took the unusual move of demanding a roll call vote, on a 9–7 party line vote. When the subcommittee dissolved into hubbub, Regula quieted things down by saying, "This is not the Ways and Means Committee." This bill froze NIH funding and cut by one-third funds for the low income heating program; maximum Pell grants were raised $100, rather than the usual $50; it added funds over administration requests for community health centers, immunization and special education grants. Regula said that he would accept no more earmarks than were already in the bill. But this proved moot as the Republican leadership never took the appropriation to the floor; it was left to the incoming Democratic Congress to pass a continuing resolution which largely left the previous appropriation in place. This was Regula's sixth and last year as the leading Republican on this subcommittee; in 2007 he became ranking minority member on the Financial Services and General Government Subcommittee.

In November 2002 the Republican Conference chose to give the Steering Committee a veto over the selection of Appropriations subcommittee chairmen; this tended to make cardinals more amenable to the demands of the Republican leadership and more assiduous in raising funds for other Republicans. Appropriations Chairman Bill Young would reach the end of his six-year term limit in January 2005, and Regula, first in line in seniority, competed hard for the position. His CARE PAC gave $553,000 to 87 Republican candidates, $15,000 to the House Republican campaign committee and $91,000 to 18 state Republican parties. He said that he would consider changing earmarks for Democrats and revamping the committee staff, a target of criticism by fiscally conservative Republicans. But all of this proved in vain. In January 2005, 26 of the 34 votes on the Republican Steering Committee were cast for Jerry Lewis of California. Regula, like the other competitor, Hal Rogers of Kentucky, was a good sport. "That is the way of elections. You win some, you lose some and you move on." This was a blow to both Regula and the Ohio delegation and Lewis named him vice chairman of the full committee; Speaker Dennis Hastert named him to the NATO Parliamentary Assembly and the Smithsonian Board of Regents.

Regula claims credit for bringing $125 million of federal funding for projects in northeast Ohio, including, in 2005-06, $1 million for a Wadsworth industrial park, $1.2 million for the Tremont Avenue Bridge and $6 million for the Orville truck bypass. In 2005 he placed a rider in the appropriation preventing the Army Corps of Engineers from spending money on evaluations of proposals to build landfills in Tuscarawas and Stark Counties; that prevented EPA approval of a project opposed by local residents.

In 2004 Regula ran 13% ahead of George W. Bush and was reelected 67%-33%. In 2006, a very bad year for Ohio Republicans, he did less well. He was challenged in the primary by 29-year-old Matt Miller, a member of the Ashland County Commission. Miller spent only $91,000, about one-tenth of Regula's spending, but Regula won by only 58%-42%, a weak performance in a primary by a longtime incumbent. Miller won his home county 82%-18% and lost by only 57%-43% in Medina County, which Regula hadn't represented before 2002. Regula carried Stark County 65%-35%, a solid but not overwhelming margin. Regula's response: "I was very aware of the level of effort that this young man made and of course he tried to play up the difference in age and the need to change." Regula's Democratic opponent was a Methodist minister from Wooster who spent so little money that he was not required to file a report with the FEC. Regula won 58%-42%, a solid majority for a general election, but Regula's lowest reelection percentage ever. Regula turns 84 in 2008; he did not miss a day of work in the 108th Congress. But in early 2007 some were speculating that he might decide to retire; he no longer has a subcommittee chairmanship, the subcommittee on which he has ranking status provides less opportunity for programs that aid his district and the moves against earmarks may make it harder to do so. In 2004 there was talk that Regula wanted his son, former Stark County Commissioner Richard Regula, to succeed him. But in 2006 the Medina County Republican chairman said, "When Ralph retires, that open seat will bring people out of the woodwork."

Noting that in 2006 Democratic Governor Ted Strickland and Senator Sherrod Brown carried Stark County by 64% and 57%—the same place where George W. Bush lost with 49% in 2004— national Democratic strategists considered targeting the district. Democratic state Senator John Boccieri, an Air Force Reserve major who served in Iraq, announced his candidacy in June 2007. Miller said he would run again in the Republican primary. Republican state Senator Kirk Schuring formed an exploratory committee, but said he would run only if Regula retires; state Representative Scott Oelslager also indicated interest in the seat if Regula retires.

SEVENTEENTH DISTRICT

Rep. Tim Ryan (D)

Elected 2002, 3d term; b. July 16, 1973, Niles; home, Niles; Bowling Green St. U., B.A. 1995, Franklin Pierce Law Ctr., J.D. 2000; Catholic; divorced.

Elected Office: OH Senate, 2000-02

Professional Career: Aide, U.S. Rep. Jim Traficant, 1995-97.

DC Office: 1421 LHOB, 20515, 202-225-5261; Fax: 202-225-3719; Web site: timryan.house.gov.

District Offices: Akron, 330-630-7311; Warren, 330-373-0074; Youngstown, 330-740-0193.

Committees: *Appropriations* (33d of 37 D): Energy & Water Development; Labor, HHS, Education & Related Agencies.

Group Ratings

	ADA	ACLU	AFS	LCV	ITIC	NTU	COC	ACU	CFG	FRC
2006	80	81	86	92	43	12	47	28	9	28
2005	95	—	100	89	—	14	48	25	10	33

National Journal Ratings

	2005 LIB	—	2005 CONS		2006 LIB	—	2006 CONS
Economic	69%	—	31%		77%	—	23%
Social	64%	—	35%		63%	—	37%
Foreign	71%	—	28%		77%	—	20%

Key Votes of the 109th Congress

1. Estate Tax Repeal	Y	5. Limit Interstate Abortion	Y	9. Build Border Fence	Y
2. Limit CAFE Standards	Y	6. Extend Patriot Act	N	10. CAFTA	N
3. FY06 Spending Curb	N	7. Bar Same Sex Marriage	N	11. Oppose Iraq Withdrawal	N
4. Drilling in ANWR	N	8. Stem Cell Research $	Y	12. Detainee Tribunals	N

Election Results

2006 general	Tim Ryan (D)	170,369	(80%)	($642,773)
	Don Manning (R)	41,925	(20%)	
2006 primary	Tim Ryan (D)	unopposed		
2004 general	Tim Ryan (D)	212,800	(77%)	($495,122)
	Frank Cusimano (R)	62,871	(23%)	($9,700)

Prior Winning Percentages: 2002 (51%)

The People		Race/Ethnic Origin	Ancestry	
Area size:	1,033 sq. mi.	84.5% White	German: 15.5%	Irish: 10.3%
Urban population:	84.3%	11.6% Black	Italian: 9.2%	
Rural population:	15.7%	0.7% Asian	**2004 Presidential Vote**	
Pop. 2000:	630,730	0.2% Native Am.	Kerry (D) 188,531	(63%)
Pop. 2005 (est):	614,164	0.0% Hawaiian	Bush (R) 111,663	(37%)
Median income:	$36,705	1.2% Two+ races	**2000 Presidential Vote**	
Poverty status:	12.3%	0.1% Other	Gore (D) 150,748	(60%)
Military veterans:	14.6%	1.6% Hispanic Origin	Bush (R) 88,184	(35%)
			Other 10,767	(4%)
			Cook Partisan Voting Index: D +14	

Occupation   Blue collar: 31.8%   White collar: 51.6%   Gray collar: 16.6%

For nearly a century, the Mahoning Valley, between the Lake Erie docks that unload iron ore from Great Lakes freighters and the coalfields of western Pennsylvania and West Virginia, was one of the steel capitals of the United States. The first coal mine here opened in 1826, canals followed, and in 1892 the first steel mill was built in Youngstown. The valley soon filled up with mills, converters, and furnaces. Now the steel mills stand empty, smokeless and silent—except those that have been dynamited or torn down. Big steel management allowed foreign producers to gain a technological edge in the 1950s and 1960s; worldwide overcapacity in steel grew as almost every developing country decided it needed its own steel mill, while cooperation between the United Steelworkers and management after the 119-day strike in 1959 boosted wages and fringe benefits to price domestic steel out of the market. Import restrictions kept the furnaces hot for a while, but the oil shock of the 1970s produced sharply higher energy prices and a collapse in the U.S. auto and steel markets. Every plant in the Mahoning Valley closed, with a loss of 40,000 jobs, and in the early 1980s metro Youngstown had one of the nation's highest unemployment rates; from 1990 to 2004 the population of Youngstown's Mahoning County declined by 6% and next-door Trumbull County's by 3%. Steel has since revived, but not here: in decentralized mini-mills around the country or in huge new rolling plants in northern Indiana. The high-wage living standard vanished, though not all work: several aluminum plants opened in nearby Warren, but young people looking for opportunities routinely leave. Youngstown's population was 82,000 in 2006, less than half of its size in the 1950s. Organized crime, it seems, has deeply infiltrated local government; a federal investigation led to more than 70 convictions, including a prosecutor, a sheriff and a congressman. Instead of looking for growth, local officials have responded to rampant abandoned property by deliberately downsizing local infrastructure and creating parks and open space, as they go from "gray to green."

The 17th Congressional District of Ohio includes most of the Mahoning Valley industrial area—Youngstown, but not its southern Mahoning County suburbs, Warren and almost all of Trumbull County. It includes nearly all of Portage County to the west and part of eastern Summit County and Akron. It contains two loci of 1970s protest—Kent State University, where four war-protesting students were killed by National Guardsmen, and Lordstown, site of the General Motors plant where workers purposely built shoddy cars to protest the tedium of the assembly line. The division of Akron and Summit County among three districts in the 2002 redistricting caused local controversy, but was essential to a compromise between Republican and Democratic legislators. This is a Democratic district, 63% for John Kerry in 2004, his second best district in Ohio, even though the Democratic mayor of Youngstown endorsed George W. Bush, who held a rally at the Youngstown-Warren Airport in late October. In 2006, Democrat Ted Strickland got 76% in Mahoning County in the governor's election.

The congressman from the 17th District is Tim Ryan, a Democrat first elected in 2002 at age 29 when he beat two incumbents, one in the Democratic primary and one in the general election. Ryan grew up in Niles and graduated from Bowling Green State University. His first job was with 17th District Congressman James Traficant. In 2000, after graduating from Franklin Pierce Law Center, Ryan was elected to the state Senate. His opening to run for Congress came from Traficant's downfall. For years Traficant was a colorful figure in the House, whose ranting orations and retro haircut ("I do my hair with a weed whacker," he said; it turned out to be a wig) entertained C-SPAN viewers. The Democratic leadership scorned him and he voted for Dennis Hastert for speaker. Traficant was convicted on 10 counts of bribery in April 2002.

After Traficant did not file for reelection, most insiders thought the 17th District would be won by Akron-based incumbent Tom Sawyer, first elected in 1986. Ryan's opponents seized on his two years on Traficant's staff and accused him of everything short of wearing his denim suits. After one exchange Ryan exclaimed, "Would you guys let it go about Jim Traficant?" By standard measures, Sawyer should have won easily. He outspent Ryan by nearly 6–1. But his record on issues gave Ryan an opening. After much public agonizing Sawyer had voted for NAFTA in 1993, and he was one of the few Rust Belt Democrats to vote for normal trade relations for China in 1999 after Bill Clinton visited Akron a few days before the vote. Ryan hammered on these votes in the Mahoning Valley, where it is gospel writ that free trade exported its high-paying jobs abroad. Ryan also got the endorsement of the National Rifle Association in a district with more blue-collar hunters than upscale suburban women who abhor guns. In Summit and Portage Counties, Sawyer led Ryan 62%-16%. But that produced a margin of only 6,846 votes. In Mahoning and Trumbull Counties, which had a greater share of the population and where Sawyer had never run before, Ryan led 48%-18%. That produced a popular vote margin of 16,521. Overall Ryan beat Sawyer 41%-27%. The Republican nominee was state Representative Ann Womer Benjamin. Ryan slammed her and the Ohio Republican legislature for votes that led to higher tuitions at state universities. Republicans fired back with ads highlighting several disorderly conduct charges lodged against Ryan while he attended college. Traficant ran as an independent. But in July he was expelled from the House by a 420–1 vote, and in August he was sentenced and taken off to federal prison. The district's Democratic leanings and Ryan's labor support proved decisive. He won 51% of the vote to 34% for Womer Benjamin and 15% for Traficant.

Ryan has leaned to the left on economic and foreign policy, while his splits with Democrats on abortion and guns placed him in the center on social issues. With abortion rights advocate Rosa DeLauro, he filed the "Reducing the Need for Abortion and Supporting Parents Act"; Democratic activists depicted this as a move toward party consensus on a difficult issue. Under local pressure to keep the Youngstown Air Reserve Station, with its C-130 Hercules aircraft and 2,000 employees and reservists, off the base-closing list, he co-chaired the Domestic Industrial Base Congressional Caucus; the station was a net gainer under the Pentagon's recommendations. Worried about the loss of local call center jobs, he was one of seven members who voted against the national do-not-call list. With Armed Services Committee chairman Duncan Hunter in April 2005, he sponsored the Chinese Currency Act seeking to counter China's alleged manipulation and undervaluation of its currency. He was the youngest Democrat in the 108th Congress and worked loyally on party initiatives; Ryan often discussed issues on the House floor with Kendrick Meek in their self-styled "30-Something Working Group." In late-night House talk-fests, he was an outspoken opponent of President Bush's Social Security reform. But he sided with Republicans on repealing the estate tax, and on building a fence along the border with Mexico. Following the 2006 election, he was a chief backer of John Murtha in his unsuccessful bid for Majority Leader. That support helped Ryan win a seat on the Appropriations Committee, with Murtha's backing.

Ryan has not faced serious reelection problems in the primary or general. He considered a run for the Senate in 2006, but decided against it. His interest suggested a possible bid for the seat of George Voinovich, whose term expires in 2010.

EIGHTEENTH DISTRICT

Rep. Zack Space (D)

Elected 2006, 1st term; b. Jan. 27, 1961, Dover; home, Dover; Kenyon Col., B.A. 1983, OH St. U., J.D. 1986; Greek Orthodox; married (Mary).

Elected Office: Dover law director, 2000-06.

Professional Career: Public defender, 1986-87; Practicing atty., 1986-2006; Hotel developer, 1995-2004.

DC Office: 315 CHOB, 20515, 202-225-6265; Fax: 202-225-3394; Web site: space.house.gov.

District Offices: Chillicothe, 740-779-1636; Dover, 330-364-4300; Zanesville, 740-452-6338.

Committees: *Agriculture* (16th of 25 D): Conservation, Credit, Energy & Research; General Farm Commodities & Risk Management. *Transportation & Infrastructure* (28th of 41 D): Railroads, Pipelines & Hazardous Materials; Aviation; Highways & Transit. *Veterans' Affairs* (15th of 16 D): Oversight & Investigations.

Group Ratings and Key Votes: Newly Elected

Election Results

2006 general	Zack Space (D)	129,646	(62%)	($1,611,369)
	Joy Padgett (R)	79,259	(38%)	($851,149)
2006 primary	Zack Space (D)	18,251	(39%)	
	Jennifer Stewart (D)	12,071	(26%)	
	Joe Sulzer (D)	11,340	(24%)	
	Ralph Applegate (D)	5,514	(12%)	
2004 general	Bob Ney (R)	177,600	(66%)	($1,484,643)
	Brian Thomas (D)	90,820	(34%)	($18,417)

The People		Race/Ethnic Origin	Ancestry	
Area size:	6,876 sq. mi.	95.9% White	German: 16.7%	USA: 10.2%
Urban population:	43.3%	1.9% Black	Irish: 8.7%	
Rural population:	56.7%	0.3% Asian	**2004 Presidential Vote**	
Pop. 2000:	630,730	0.2% Native Am.	Bush (R) 163,121	(57%)
Pop. 2005 (est):	646,498	0.0% Hawaiian	Kerry (D) 121,495	(43%)
Median income:	$34,462	1.0% Two+ races	Other 1,216	(0%)
Poverty status:	12.6%	0.1% Other	**2000 Presidential Vote**	
Military veterans:	14.3%	0.6% Hispanic Origin	Bush (R) 132,709	(55%)
			Gore (D) 98,328	(41%)
			Other 9,810	(4%)
			Cook Partisan Voting Index: R + 6	
Occupation	Blue collar: 37.5%	White collar: 45.8%	Gray collar: 16.7%	

The hills of eastern Ohio are one of those obscure parts of America, seen by most Americans, if they are at all, from speeding cars on the Interstates or U.S. highways on their way to some place else. They were settled early on in our history, in the 1790s, mostly by Virginians (there was no West Virginia until 1863), and for the most part sparsely: this was hard land to clear and hard land to farm, better suited for dairy cattle than the plains that lay beyond. In some places near the Ohio River there was industrial development early on. The local clay was used to make pottery, the coal that lies near the surface was dug up, a green vitriol works was built, and a nail factory went into operation, all before 1814, and in time the area became dotted with small factory towns and some coal mines. Farther south there was little industrial development and the landscape has a timeless feel today. This is a part of America little affected by the flow of immigrants from Europe in 1880-1924, southern blacks in 1940-65 or Latino and Asian immigrants since 1970. Some counties have seen sharp job losses, as coal mines and factories shut down; others have benefited from local economic development and construction of a gasoline pipeline from the Ohio River to Columbus. As the price of oil and natural gas has risen, the coal industry has begun to rebound, reopening some mines and returning jobs. This passes over scenic country, much of it forest lands opened up to hunters by MeadWestvaco. The most distinctive people here are the Amish, driving their horses and buggies over covered bridges in Holmes, Tuscarawas and Wayne Counties, the largest concentration of Amish in the world; they run shops now as well as farm and no longer eschew all farm machinery.

The 18th Congressional District of Ohio covers much of this hill country, from Holmes and Tuscarawas Counties in the north to Ross and Jackson Counties in the south. Geographically, it is the largest district in the state, spanning 5 media markets, including 2 in West Virginia. It includes such cities as New Rumley, the birthplace of General George Custer; Zanesville, the birthplace of writer Zane Grey and architect Cass Gilbert and home of a famous Y-shaped bridge; and Chillicothe, the first capital of Ohio, on the Scioto River, beneath Mount Logan, which is stamped on the Great Seal of the state of Ohio. Politically, much of this area was ancestrally Democratic, but in the last two decades it has become more Republican. George W. Bush won 55% of the vote here in 2000 and 57% in 2004.

The new congressman from the 18th District is Zack Space, who was first elected in 2006. He was born in Dover and named after his grandfather Zacharias, a Greek immigrant who won U.S citizenship for his World War I service. Space attended Kenyon College, where he distinguished himself as a Division III All-American football player, earned a law degree from Ohio State University and started Space & Space Company, a law practice with his father Socrates Space. While practicing consumer rights law for two decades, Space also served as a public defender and as the business manager of a local hotel company. He was appointed Dover law director in 2000, and was twice elected to the position.

In 2006, Space was one of a handful of Democrats seeking to oust six-term Republican Rep. Bob Ney, chairman of the House Administration Committee. Ney had been firmly entrenched in the district, but he began to look more vulnerable after the November 2004 election when reports about his relationship with lobbyist Jack Abramoff began to surface. In January 2006, Ney gave up his chairmanship, saying that he had become a distraction for the party. Still, for the first half of 2006, Ney told voters and his House colleagues that he was innocent and would be exonerated, and he worked to convince prosecutors that he had been tricked by Abramoff.

The Democratic Congressional Campaign Committee initially favored Chillicothe Mayor Joe Sulzer in the primary, but he proved unable to expand his base outside the southern part of the sprawling district. Space campaigned against corruption and signed an ethics pledge saying he would not accept gifts from lobbyists. He also talked about economic issues like lost manufacturing jobs and health care. Space won the May primary with 39%, defeating Ohio Board of Education member Jennifer Stewart with 26% and Sulzer with 24%.

In August, Ney bowed to House Republican leadership pressure and withdrew his candidacy for reelection; in October, he would plead guilty to corruption charges. But Ney did not resign the seat until November 3, 2006, four days before the election, ensuring that the specter of scandal would linger over the campaign until the end.

Republicans had to move quickly to replace Ney; party leaders anointed state Senator Joy Padgett, who was also Ney's preferred successor. She easily won a five-way September 14 special election primary but her late start gave Space an advantage. Padgett campaigned on pocketbook and national security issues; she attacked Space for taking contributions from MoveOn.org and other liberal groups, while the National Republican Congressional Committee poured in over $2 million to defend the seat. Despite being tagged as a liberal, Space's positions on tax cuts, gun ownership rights, trade and illegal immigration were not all that different from Padgett's. Democrats emphasized Padgett's ties to unpopular Governor Bob Taft, who had appointed her director of the Office of Appalachia. They also noted the 2005 bankruptcy of her family's office-supply business and that Padgett and her husband had filed for personal bankruptcy protection as recently as 2006. Space spent over $1.6 million to Padgett's $850,000 and won 62%-38%.

The circumstances surrounding Space's election and the Republican lean of this district led Republicans to refer to Space as "the accidental congressman." Possible challengers in 2008 included former state Department of Agriculture Director Fred Dailey, attorney and Air Force veteran Paul Phillips, and Jeannette Moll, a former magistrate from Zanesville.

★ OKLAHOMA ★

Oklahoma, our fifth-newest state, celebrating its centennial in 2007, is proud of its history of rising from humble beginnings, but not sure whether it is keeping pace with the growth and growing sophistication of the American economy. The fact that it is one of only five states admitted to the Union in the 20th century may come as a surprise to most Americans, but not to Oklahomans; the Capitol dome, left unconstructed when the Capitol was opened in 1917, was finally finished in 2002. But all of Oklahoma's history has been a story of stops and sudden starts. Oklahoma was settled in a rush, first by the Five Civilized Tribes driven west by Andrew Jackson's troops over the Cherokees' Trail of Tears in the 1830s. Then came white settlers one morning in April 1889 when, in the great land rush memorialized in an Edna Ferber novel and half a dozen Hollywood movies, thousands of would-be homesteaders drove their wagons across the territorial line at the sound of a gunshot, the most adventurous or unscrupulous of them literally jumping the gun—the Sooners. In 1905, a convention of the Civilized Nations, as they became known, sought to have eastern Oklahoma admitted as a separate state of Sequoyah. Washington instead ended the tribal government and admitted what had been the Indian and Oklahoma Territories as a single state.

The heritage of these rushes remains. Oklahoma has the second-largest Indian population in the country, after California—273,000 in the 2000 Census—though there is just one reservation and the status of many other tribal entities is often disputed. Some Indian tribes here have unsuccessfully sought a return of native lands and face high unemployment rates. But there has been much intermarriage over the years, and many Oklahomans—and not a few of its politicians—proudly claim Indian blood. Assimilation into everyday life, plus commemoration of historic traditions and efforts to keep the Cherokee, Choctaw, Chickasaw and Seminole languages from dying out—you can see street signs in the Cherokee alphabet in Tahlequah—seem to have provided a better life for most Native Americans here than other approaches have elsewhere. The counties with a large Indian heritage in the eastern part of the state have been growing smartly, even as the Great Plains farm and oil counties west of Oklahoma City and Tulsa have lost population, and Indians own 6% of businesses in Oklahoma, about equal to their 7% share of the popualtion.

The Rodgers and Hammerstein musical recalled an Oklahoma on the brink of statehood—an event that came late, in 1907, at which point the territory filled up with farmers, rising from 1.5 million people in 1907 to 2.4 million in 1930. Oil helped: The first well was drilled here in 1897 and by 1920, Tulsa was an oil boom town. Then in the 1930s came a decade of bust—or dust—as soil loosened by erosion was whipped into giant swirling clouds: The Dust Bowl. "On a single day, I heard, 50 million tons of soil were blown away," John Gunther reported later. "People sat in Oklahoma City, with the sky invisible for three days in a row, holding dust masks over their faces and wet towels to protect their mouths at night, while the farms blew by." Okies headed in droves west on U.S. 66 to the green land of California, and Oklahoma's population sank to 2.3 million in 1940 and 2.2 million in 1950, not to reach its 1930 level again until 1970.

Then oil brought another boom: As the oil shocks of 1973 and 1979 sent oil prices up, Oklahoma's population rose from 2.5 million in 1970 to 3 million in 1980 and 3.3 million in 1983. Then, with the collapse of oil prices and of Oklahoma's farm economy as well, it was bust again. A giddy rise was followed by a giddier fall: The rig count fell from 882 in January 1982 to 232 in February 1983 and was just 186 in May 2007. The 1990 Census reported just 3.1 million Oklahomans, after more than a decade of population increases. But in the 1990s, Oklahoma began building a more diversified economy, with high-tech employers as well as oil and gas firms. Population rose 10% in the decade, to 3.45 million in 2000, and another 4% to 3.58 million in 2006. High oil prices made it worthwhile to squeeze more of its marginal wells, and Oklahoma's natural gas—it's the second state in production, after Texas—has commanded high prices given strong demand. Oklahoma continues to have above-average rates of divorce, teenage pregnancy and crime, and a low rate of college graduates, but unemployment has been low and a Chinese company is building a plant to produce British-style MGs near Ardmore. Oklahoma knows it has risen far, but still has some distance to go.

In federal elections, Oklahoma is a safely Republican state—George W. Bush carried all 77 counties in 2004—but in state politics there is vigorous two-party competition and Democrats still have an edge in party registration. But they are conservative Democrats: the NEP exit poll showed Republicans leading Democrats by only 43%-40% in party identification, but conservatives outnumbered liberals 43%-13%. The state's congressional delegation includes only one Democrat, Congressman Dan Boren, son of former Governor David Boren, the only Democrat elected here to the U.S. Senate since 1966. Democratic Governor Brad Henry was reelected in 2006 by a 67%-33%

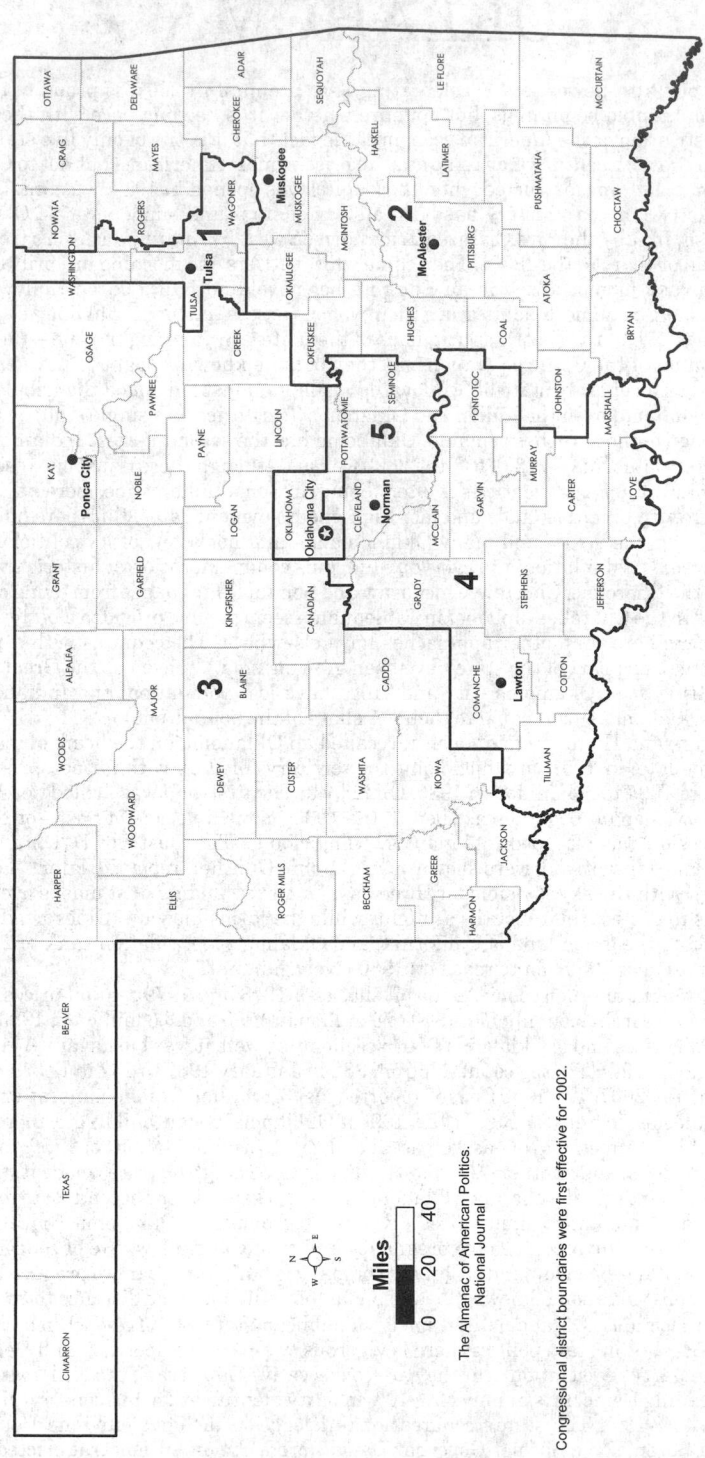

The Almanac of American Politics.
National Journal

Congressional district boundaries were first effective for 2002.

margin, and Democrats won all but one statewide race that year. Republicans captured a 57-44 majority in the state House in 2004 and held it in 2006; they gained two seats the latter year in the state Senate for a 24-24 tie. The parties agreed to share control, with equal numbers on each committee, but the tie-breaking vote will be cast by Democratic Lieutenant Governor Jari Askins.

For many years Oklahoma politics was a struggle between Oklahoma City and Tulsa Republicans and rural Democrats, and that was the dynamic between 1994 and 2002, when Tulsa-based Republican Frank Keating was governor and the legislature was run by rural-based Democrats. Keating prevailed on many issues and got voters to pass a right-to-work law, long opposed by the legislature, by a 54%-46% margin in September 2001. But another, quite different ballot proposition helped to elect Democrat Brad Henry governor in November 2002. The issue was cockfighting: Oklahoma was one of three states that allowed it (the others, Louisiana and New Mexico, banned the practice in 2007); the issue split voters not on party, but on urban/rural lines. Keating favored the ban; rural Democrats opposed it. It passed by 2–1 in metro Oklahoma City and Tulsa and by a 56%-44% margin statewide. But rural areas voted against, 55%-45%, and in Little Dixie (southeast and east central Oklahoma), where cockfighting is part of local culture, voters turned out in large numbers to oppose it. These are, as it happens, counties with an historic Democratic tradition, the home of U.S. House Speaker (1971-76) Carl Albert, a tradition that still carries over into state politics. Increased Democratic turnout in anti-cockfighting counties was probably responsible for Henry's 6,866-vote victory.

The People		Race/Ethnic Origin			Military veterans: 376,062 (14.7%)	
Pop. 2006 (est):	3,579,212	2,556,368	74.1%	White	WWII: 18.6%	Korea: 13.2%
Pop. 2000:	3,450,654	257,981	7.5%	Black	Vietnam: 34.6%	Gulf War: 11.5%
Pop. 1990:	3,145,585	46,172	1.3%	Asian	**Most populous cities (2006):**	
Change 1990-2000:	Up 9.7%	266,158	7.7%	Native Am.	1. Oklahoma City	537,734
% of U.S. total:	1.2%	2,100	0.1%	Hawaiian	2. Tulsa	382,872
Pop. rank:	27th of 50	140,249	4.1%	Two+ races	3. Norman	102,827
Area size:	69,898 sq. mi.	2,322	0.1%	Other	4. Lawton	87,540
State Native:	62.6%	179,304	5.2%	Hisp. Origin	5. Edmond	76,644
Non-citizen:	2.5%	**Ancestry**				
Language		German: 10.1%		USA: 9.1%	Urban population: 65.3%	
English: 90.8%	Spanish: 5.0%	Irish: 8.2%		English: 6.7%	Rural population: 34.7%	
Other Eur.: 1.8%		French: 1.8%				

Education		Work Sector		Legislature	
H.S. Grad:	80.6%	Private: 74.6%	Govt: 16.8%	Senate	24 D 24 R
College Grad:	20.3%	Self: 8.2%	Family: 0.5%	House	57 R 44 D
Industry		Unemployment: 5.2%		Legislative Term Limits: Yes	
Agri: 4.1%	Con: 6.9%	**Household Income**		**Registered Voters**	
Fin: 6.0%	Info: 2.7%	<15k: 20.7%	15-35k: 31.3%	D: 1,045,490	(50.4%)
Mfg: 18.1%	Prof: 27.8%	35-50k: 17.1%	50-100k: 24.3%	R: 805,607	(38.8%)
Public: 5.9%	Trade: 15.4%	100-150k: 4.3%	>150k: 2.3%	O: 224,464	(10.8%)
Other: 13.0%		Median: $33,400			
Occupation		Poverty status: 14.7%			
Blue collar: 26.7%	White collar: 56.9%	**Home Value**			
Gray collar: 16.4%		<50k: 33.9%	50-100k: 40.6%	100-200k: 20.3%	200-300k: 3.3%
		300-500k: 1.3%	>500k: 0.6%	Median: $67,700	

Presidential politics   Oklahoma has been a solidly Republican state in presidential elections since the 1950s. There are no large blocs of voters here who back national Democrats and most Oklahomans find national Republicans acceptable. It has been a long time since Oklahoma has been on anyone's list of target states, and seems unlikely ever to be. Interestingly, even as Democrats were winning state elections because of their strength in rural areas, George W. Bush's percentages increased sharply more in rural counties than in the state's two big metro areas; in 2004 for the first time in memory the Republican percentage was identical, at 66%, in the two big metro areas and in the rest of Oklahoma.

2004 Presidential Vote		
Bush (R)	959,792	(66%)
Kerry (D)......................	503,966	(34%)

2004 Democratic Presidential Primary		
Clark (D)	90,526	(30%)
Edwards (D)	89,310	(30%)
Kerry (D)......................	81,073	(27%)
Lieberman (D)	19,680	(7%)
Dean (D)	12,734	(4%)
Other...........................	9,062	(3%)

2000 Presidential Vote		
Bush (R)	744,337	(60%)
Gore (D).......................	474,276	(38%)
Other...........................	15,616	(1%)

Nor has Oklahoma's presidential primary attracted much attention. For years it was held in March, as one of many Super Tuesday primaries, and was ignored. In 2001 one Democratic legislator tried to abolish the primary; instead the legislature rescheduled it for February 3, 2004, a week after New Hampshire. As one of two primaries in a southern-accented state that day (the other was South Carolina), Oklahoma was targeted by John Edwards and Wesley Clark, desperate for a win after John Kerry's triumphs in Iowa and New Hampshire. Clark won here—his first and only electoral victory—but with just 29.9%, to 29.5% for Edwards and 27% for John Kerry. Kerry carried the counties including Oklahoma City, Tulsa and Norman (home of the University of Oklahoma), and not much else; Clark got big pluralities in the counties around Fort Sill and Altus Air Force Base, and not much else; Edwards carried most suburban and rural counties, but seldom by big pluralities. Edwards's failure to win Oklahoma the same day he won South Carolina may have hurt him; in any case he won no more contests. Clark's failure to win big may have hurt him too. Kerry's third-place finish proved no problem for him, as he won nearly all the other Democratic contests. But his anemic percentage here was a harbinger of his Oklahoma performance in November.

Congressional districting   Oklahoma lost one of its six House seats in the 2000 Census, and for months there was a deadlock over redistricting between Republican Governor Frank Keating and the Democratic legislature. Keating wanted to keep a Tulsa-centered district, especially before the December 2001 special election in which his wife Cathy Keating ran for the Tulsa-centered 1st District seat vacated by Steve Largent. But she lost the Republican nomination. In 2002, the solution appeared after 3d District Congressman Wes Watkins announced he was retiring. Watkins was a Republican (and a former Democrat) and the 3d District was centered in Little Dixie; the seat was safe for Watkins, but Democrats carry the area in state elections and would have a good chance to win an open seat contest. The issue went to court, and in May 2002, a county judge ordered the adoption of a plan that eliminated Watkins's district and gave the other incumbents safe seats; it also had the virtue of creating an Oklahoma City-centered district rather than splitting the city between several districts as it had been since 1981. Democrats, happy that Democratic incumbent Brad Carson got a safe seat, let the matter drop. Carson ran for the Senate in 2004 and lost to Tom Coburn, but Democrat Dan Boren easily held the seat.

110th Congress Lineup	
4 R	1 D

109th Congress Lineup	
4 R	1 D

Governor

Brad Henry (D)

Elected 2002, term expires Jan. 2011, 2d term; b. July 7, 1963, Shawnee; home, Shawnee; U. of OK, B.S. 1985, J.D. 1988; Baptist; married (Kim).

Elected Office: OK Senate, 1992-2002.

Professional Career: Practicing atty., 1989-2002; Atty., City of Shawnee, 1990-2002.

Office: State Capitol Bldg., 2300 N. Lincoln Blvd., Rm. 212, Oklahoma City, 73105, 405-521-2342; Fax: 405-521-3353; Web site: governor.state.ok.us.

Election Results

2006 general	Brad Henry (D)	616,135	(67%)
	Ernest Istook (R)	310,327	(33%)
2006 primary	Brad Henry (D)	226,957	(86%)
	Andrew Marr (D)	37,510	(14%)
2002 general	Brad Henry (D)	448,143	(43%)
	Steve Largent (R)	441,277	(43%)
	Gary Richardson (I)	146,200	(14%)

Brad Henry, a Democrat, was elected governor of Oklahoma in an upset in 2002. Henry grew up in Shawnee, one county east of Oklahoma City; he was the kind of boy who built a tree house with multiple floors and 20 rooms and whose Future Farmers of America project was to borrow $10,500 from a bank to buy 15 crossbred cow-calf pairs. He graduated from the University of Oklahoma and its law school and returned home to practice law. In 1992, at 29, he was elected to the state Senate. There he achieved little statewide notice. He opposed right-to-work, but voted to put the issue on the ballot; when his committee bottled up Governor Frank Keating's covenant marriage bill, Keating called him "anti-family." At the beginning of the 2002 race for governor, Henry was not on anyone's political radar screen. The candidate considered most likely to win was Republican Congressman Steve Largent, a football star at the University of Tulsa and with the Seattle Seahawks, who resigned from the House in February 2002 to make the race; the favorite for the Democratic nomination was Oklahoma City area restaurateur Vince Orza, a former Republican who lost the 1990 Republican runoff for governor by a 51%-49% margin. Henry was not sure whether to run; he did not announce until the breathtakingly late date of June 24.

But he had a good campaign plan. He had one big issue (a lottery to fund education), one big vehicle (an RV in which he traveled around the state) and one big endorser (former University of Oklahoma and Dallas Cowboys football coach Barry Switzer). Voters may not be much interested in meeting politicians, but Oklahoma voters are very interested in meeting football coaches. Henry's folksy, aw-shucks manner appealed to rural voters when the other major figures in gubernatorial politics—Keating, Largent, Orza—were from Oklahoma's two major cities. In the Democratic primary August 27, two months and three days after Henry announced, Orza led with 44% of the vote, short of the 50% needed to avoid a runoff, and Henry finished second with 29%; he carried only five counties. Orza called for ending reliance on the state income tax, which presumably meant a higher sales tax; Henry backed the lottery, plus an income tax exemption on seniors' retirement income. Henry had the support of third-place finisher state Senator Kelly Haney, a full-blooded Seminole-Creek; he took care to meet with tribal chiefs, who were conducting a big voter registration drive. Henry won the September 17 runoff by 52%-48%.

Against Largent in the general, there were clear contrasts. Largent opposed the lottery, called for moving from the income tax to consumption taxes over the next 10 years, and eliminating the sales tax on food. Henry was for across-the-board teacher salary increases and against merit pay—the teachers' union positions—while Largent took the other side on both. Largent, as Keating did, called for cutting administrative costs in schools; some rural Oklahomans feared that meant consolidating small school districts. And there was another issue that didn't qualify for the ballot until August 20: whether to ban cockfighting. In urban Oklahoma this was a popular stand; Keating endorsed it and so did Largent. But it was highly unpopular in Little Dixie in southeastern Oklahoma, where cockfighting is part of local culture. Henry came out against the cockfighting ban.

Another factor was the independent candidacy of businessman Gary Richardson, who spent $2 million of his own money on his campaign. Richardson also called for eliminating a whole raft of taxes and for replacing them with a tax on the gross revenues of all business operations. Polls showed Richardson with double-digit support, but his issue positions were less important than his ads attacking Largent. On September 11, 2001, though Congress was planning on going into session, Largent was bowhunting in Idaho and out of touch with his staff; he didn't hear about the attacks until two days later. In the meantime, his staff issued a statement from him, for which he had to apologize. Richardson's ads showed one of the World Trade Center towers collapsing and then asked about Largent's whereabouts, then showed Largent answering a reporter's aggressive question about the issue with an expletive. While all these things were working against Largent, Henry ran ads showing his young family and showcasing his folksy style. October polls showed the race closing. In November, Henry won by less than 7,000 votes of more than 1 million cast, 43.3%-42.6%, with 14% for Richardson. Largent led 46%-40% in the Oklahoma City area and 45%-39% in the Tulsa area—far less than the usual Republican leads there—while Henry carried the rest of Oklahoma, which cast 44% of the vote, 48%-39%. This, in many ways, was a victory for rural Oklahoma over urban Oklahoma.

Like many incoming governors in 2003, Henry faced budget shortfalls; he and the legislature avoided tax increases, cut projected spending and drew down the rainy day allowance to zero. In February 2004 Henry rolled out his program—a cigarette tax increase to pay for health care, the lottery for education, increased gambling at racetracks, plus a permanent cut in the top income tax rate from 7% to 6.65%, tax exemptions for retirees and zero capital gains tax on the sale of Oklahoma property. In May 2004 he achieved major victories on his platform; most legislators may have been unwilling to vote for them outright, but they voted to put them on the November ballot. All passed, most by handsome margins. One was expansion of tribal casinos and racetrack gambling, with proceeds for education; another was a lottery to provide insurance premiums for teachers and to raise their salaries to the average levels of surrounding states. A third was the cigarette tax increase, with proceeds for health care. Also there was an income tax exemption for retirees, the cut in the top income tax rate and elimination of capital gains taxes on sales of Oklahoma property.

Republicans captured the state House in the 2004 election, only the second time since statehood that Democrats failed to win control of that chamber. This made Henry's job more difficult but he still managed to pass key parts of his 2005 legislative agenda. His drug reimportation plan failed but he won creation of an "Oklahoma Smart Card" system that would help residents access existing pharmaceutical discounts and another program that gave low-income residents access to more affordable prescription drugs. He got a permanent reduction in the top income tax rate and several other tax cuts; the three bills comprising his "Operation Homefront" initiative also passed, providing assistance to military veterans and Oklahoma National Guard members. In a June special session, he signed compromise workers compensation legislation that was supported by the state business community. His tort reform plan died in the Democratic-controlled Senate when all 22 Republicans and a handful of Democrats opposed it; Republicans derided it as a "partisan, trial lawyer protection plan."

In January 2006, responding to cigarette tax revenue shortfalls, Henry signed emergency rules cracking down on tribal smoke shops that failed to collect enough taxes; Republicans had charged that the state was being shortchanged by as much as $75 million a year. He also signed a measure making Oklahoma the last state to legalize tattooing. High oil and gas prices gave the state a $1 billion surplus but the warring House and Senate were unable to come to an agreement on the budget and were forced into a special session. The budget accord, reached in June, reduced personal income tax rates from 6.25% to 5.25% over four years, eliminated the estate tax, gave pay raises to state workers and teachers, and gave an additional $130 million to higher education. Henry also signed a bill to allow the death penalty for repeat sex crimes involving children and several abortion-related measures, including one that required parental consent before a minor could have an abortion.

Going into the 2006 election campaign, Henry was in remarkably good shape for a Democratic governor elected with just 46% in a Republican state. His approval ratings were high and he could point to a record that seemed in line with Oklahoma values. He made Oklahoma one of only a few states to agree to having local police cooperate to enforce federal immigration laws. He opposed a federal constitutional amendment banning same-sex marriages, but firmly backed the current ban in Oklahoma law and signed a bill banning adoption by same-sex couples. He stood by as the state Senate rejected a bill for county-option cockfighting. He appointed the first black justice to the Oklahoma Supreme Court.

Republican Congressman Ernest Istook was the Republican nominee after winning 55% against state Senator Jim Williamson, Tulsa oil executive Bob Sullivan, and engineer Jim Evanoff, who said the state's biggest problem was the proliferation of attorneys in the legislative and executive branches. Istook, a conservative who considered running for governor in 2002 and Senate in 2004, had hit a wall in Congress. As chairman of the Appropriations Transportation Subcommittee, one of the "College of Cardinals", he had angered his Republican colleagues in 2004 when he without notice cut funds from transportation projects sought by 21 House Republicans who had signed a letter calling for increased Amtrak funding. That same year, Republicans were embarrassed by the disclosure that his appropriation had a provision that allowed the Appropriations chairman and designated staff to inspect individual tax returns; the Senate passed a resolution saying the provision had no effect, and the House quickly followed. He lost his cardinalship the next year when the number of subcommittees was reduced from 13 to 10.

History was against Istook. Only two U.S. House members had ever been elected governor of Oklahoma—"Alfalfa Bill" Murray in 1930 and maverick oilman E.W. Marland, who is said to have controlled one-tenth of the world's oil at one time, in 1934—and Henry won his office by defeating Steve Largent, the last congressman to run. Istook hammered Henry over illegal immigration, criticizing him for not doing enough to keep stop the influx and for signing into law a bill that made Oklahoma high school graduates eligible for in-state college tuition as long as they were working toward legal immigration status. Istook claimed he would repeal the law, if elected; he also ran a radio ad that included a western-style jingle with the lyrics, "If you sneak across the border, there's some help that you can get in a place called Oklahoma where you'll never have to fret. There a man they call Brad Henry has some gifts he'll give to you. Taxpayer money to pay for college and in-state tuition, too. If you re-elect Brad Henry, he'll never take a stand. Illegal immigration will continue in our land."

Henry defended himself with ads emphasizing that he instructed the state highway patrol to apprehend illegal immigrants; he said illegal immigration was a federal issue that Congress had failed to address. The two candidates clashed over education—Istook called for merit pay for teachers; Henry said teacher salaries were rising on his watch—a minimum wage increase and state spending. Henry outspent Istook and won in a 67%-33% landslide, making him just the third governor in state history to win back-to-back terms. He won all but the three panhandle counties. His rousing victory immediately sparked speculation that Henry would run for Senate in 2008 against Republican incumbent Jim Inhofe or in 2010 against Republican incumbent Tom Coburn. But in late 2006 a spokesman for the governor said, "He does not plan to run for the Senate in two years or four years."

Senior Senator

James Inhofe (R)

Elected 1994, seat up 2008, 2d full term; b. Nov. 17, 1934, Des Moines, IA; home, Tulsa; U. of Tulsa, B.A. 1973; Presbyterian; married (Kay).

Military Career: Army, 1957-58.

Elected Office: OK House of Reps., 1966-69; OK Senate, 1969-77, Repub. Ldr., 1975-77; Tulsa Mayor, 1978-84; U.S. House of Reps., 1986-94.

Professional Career: Businessman, land developer, 1962-86.

DC Office: 453 RSOB, 20510, 202-224-4721; Fax: 202-228-0380; Web site: inhofe.senate.gov.

State Offices: Enid, 580-234-5105; McAlester, 918-426-0933; Oklahoma City, 405-608-4381; Tulsa, 918-748-5111.

Committees: *Armed Services* (3d of 12 R): Strategic Forces; Readiness & Management Support; Airland. *Environment & Public Works* (RMM of 9 R).

Group Ratings

	ADA	ACLU	AFS	LCV	ITIC	NTU	COC	ACU	CFG	FRC
2006	0	8	0	0	75	89	91	100	94	100
2005	5	—	0	0	—	78	83	100	87	—

National Journal Ratings

	2005 LIB	—	2005 CONS		2006 LIB	—	2006 CONS
Economic	6%	—	90%		18%	—	80%
Social	23%	—	64%		0%	—	82%
Foreign	0%	—	74%		0%	—	92%

Key Votes of the 109th Congress

1. Bar ANWR Drilling	N	5. Confirm Samuel Alito	Y	9. Limit Interstate Abortion	Y
2. FY06 Spending Curb	Y	6. Path to Citizenship	N	10. CAFTA	Y
3. Estate Tax Repeal	Y	7. Bar Same Sex Marriage	Y	11. Urge Iraq Withdrawal	N
4. Raise Minimum Wage	N	8. Stem Cell Research $	N	12. Provide Detainee Rights	N

Election Results

2002 general	James Inhofe (R)	583,579	(57%)	($3,040,220)
	David Walters (D)	369,789	(36%)	($2,072,137)
	James Germalic (I)	65,056	(6%)	
2002 primary	James Inhofe (R)	unopposed		
1996 general	James Inhofe (R)	670,610	(57%)	($2,510,946)
	James Boren (D)	474,162	(40%)	($301,621)
	Other	38,378	(3%)	

Prior Winning Percentages: 1994 (55%); 1992 House (53%); 1990 House (56%); 1988 House (53%); 1986 House (55%)

James Inhofe (pronounced *IN-hoff*), Oklahoma's senior senator, was first elected to the Senate in 1994. He grew up in Tulsa, served in the Army, and worked in real estate, insurance and aviation. He has for years regularly flown planes and is one of Congress's few certified commercial pilots; he flew around the world following Wiley Post's route, but encountered problems in October 2006 when the small plane he was flying spun out of control and suffered significant damage after landing in Tulsa, though he and an aide escaped injury. Inhofe was elected to the Oklahoma House in 1966, at 31, and to the Oklahoma Senate in 1969; he ran for governor in 1974 and lost to David Boren, 64%-36%. In 1976, Inhofe ran for the U.S. House against Jim Jones and lost; from 1979-84, he was mayor of Tulsa. He won the heavily Republican 1st District House seat in 1986 when Jones ran unsuccessfully for the Senate, but held it with uninspiring margins. He was hurt by negative publicity about a family business lawsuit (he eventually was awarded $3.6 million) and charges of campaign finance irregularities, leveled often by the liberal-leaning *Tulsa World*. Inhofe's great achievement in the House was reforming the arcane discharge petition rule. For years, House rules kept secret the names of signers of petitions to discharge bills stuck in committees; members could say they had worked to bring legislation to the floor when they had done just the opposite. That was changed in 1993, and one of the first bills to benefit from the new rules was the aviation liability reform bill, co-sponsored by Inhofe, which limited the liability of small airplane manufacturers in lawsuits resulting from crashes.

Inhofe jumped into the 1994 Senate race when his onetime opponent Boren, a conservative Democrat who carried every precinct in 1990, announced he was retiring to become president of the University of Oklahoma. The Democratic nominee was moderate Dave McCurdy, congressman since 1980 from southwest Oklahoma. But in Oklahoma in 1994, the Clinton burden was too heavy for even McCurdy to carry. McCurdy had voted for the 1993 Clinton budget and tax package with its original Btu tax and for the 1994 crime bill with its assault weapons ban. Inhofe won by a solid 55%-40%. In the Senate, Inhofe was president of the conservative 11-member freshman class. He was elected to a full six-year term in 1996 over James Boren, David Boren's cousin, by 57%-40%.

Inhofe has a solidly conservative voting record, and is blunt and even acerbic in expressing his views. "I'm not afraid of controversy. I'm not afraid to say what's on my mind and what's on a lot of people's minds," he said after one controversy. "Philosophically, I'm very, very rigid in the things I believe in," he said after another. As a junior member of the Senate he spoke his mind in pungent terms. He compared Clinton EPA administrator Carol Browner to Tokyo Rose and said her agency used "Gestapo tactics." In a 2003 speech he said that the theory that man-made emissions have caused global warming was "the greatest hoax ever perpetrated on the American people." During the May 2006 debate on immigration reform, he got the Senate to pass his amendment to make English the national language. "This is not just about preserving our culture and heritage, but also about bettering the odds for our nation's newest potential citizens," he said. Also that year, he took a swipe at colleagues who posture against the congressional pay raise, which he called the "greatest single hypocrisy every year;" he proposed that any lawmaker voting against the pay raise should no longer take the dough.

Inhofe is now the third ranking Republican on the Armed Services Committee, after John McCain and John Warner. He has been a strong supporter of missile defense and one of the leaders of the successful fight to deny President Clinton's effort to ratify the Comprehensive Test Ban Treaty. He supported the Bush administration on Iraq and argued that the administration had not aggressively enough made the case that there were connections between Saddam Hussein and al Qaeda before September 11 and that some weapons of mass destruction—enough to kill 47 million people, Inhofe said—were found in Iraq after major military operations. In August 2006, he called the U.S. military results "nothing short of a miracle." He was one of two senators to vote against the intelligence reorganization in December 2004—hardly an unusual position for him, for he had also cast lonely votes against Richard Holbrooke for UN Ambassador, against the May 1997 budget deal and the October 1998 omnibus budget, and against the bipartisan Everglades bill in 2000.

In 2003 Inhofe became chairman of the Environment and Public Works Committee. For much of his time on the committee he has bucked environmental groups, favored oil drilling in the Arctic National Wildlife Refuge and more oil and gas drilling exploration in the United States generally. As for the Endangered Species Act, "America has adopted an attitude that places more value on the life of a critter than on a human being. We want to protect the Arkansas River shiner, a bait fish in Oklahoma, yet we will allow unborn babies to have their brains sucked out in a partial-birth abortion." He supported Bush's Clear Skies initiative, but complained that the administration failed to speak out more strongly for it. In March 2005, the committee deadlocked 9–9 on the bill, with Lincoln Chafee joining all Democrats. Later that year, after gasoline prices had soared because of Hurricane Katrina, he called for incentives to build refineries at shut-down military bases; the refinery bill also died in his committee on a 9–9 vote.

Yet much of Inhofe's tenure as chairman was devoted to an issue on which he was opposed by the Bush administration. This was the reauthorization of the transportation act, generally (though not entirely accurately) known as the highway bill, one of the main institutional responsibilities of the committee. By early 2004 Inhofe had hammered out agreement in the Senate on a $318 billion transportation bill; House Transportation Committee Chairman Don Young was seeking a $375 billion bill, while the Bush administration wanted to cap spending at $256 billion. Inhofe argued that money was needed to maintain the highway system and would be funded entirely by user fees (primarily the gas tax). With bipartisan support he got the Senate to pass the $318 billion bill (which would have increased Oklahoma spending by 42%) in 2004 by 76-21, but the White House renewed its veto threat, and the House bill was failing to get out of committee. Young got the House, cowed by the veto threat and pressured by Speaker Dennis Hastert, to pass a $275 billion bill. Inhofe was the chairman of the conference committee, and his goal was to get a bill passed in 2004. He did not succeed. With House Ways and Means Chairman Bill Thomas taking the lead, the House offered a $299 billion bill, with $284 billion guaranteed to be spent over its six-year life—and the veto threat withdrawn. Inhofe said, "I was not happy with that number." Later that month Inhofe proposed $301 billion, with $289 billion guaranteed. The numbers sound close together, but the political differences were significant: one goal of Inhofe's bill was to guarantee that every state got 95% of its gas tax money back, but when the total spending was decreased that meant that other states would lose projects. So, the issue was deferred to 2005. By that point, Republican leaders were eager to cut a final deal with Bush. Even Inhofe backed a scaled-down version of a transportation bill. "Get it done," was the ad campaign of the state transportation officials. The lawmakers failed in their initial goal of completing the bill before that summer's road-building season. In the Senate, Inhofe agreed to a six-year package of $284 billion, which he said would be underfunded. In a conference committee with the House, he wanted more but eventually agreed to $286 billion in funding. Oklahoma fared well, losing its status as a donor state. "I would challenge anyone to match my conservative performance and credentials," he said.

At the Environment committee, Inhofe has not been averse to sponsoring Oklahoma projects, like the Corps of Engineers projects at Arcadia Lake and Waurika Lake and the completion of the channel to the Port of Catoosa near Tulsa. In January 2007, Inhofe withstood a backroom challenge by John Warner and became the ranking minority member of the committee. Prospects for his cooperation with new chairman Barbara Boxer seemed dim. As she talked about the need for action on global warming, Inhofe stepped down as chairman with a swipe at news-media handling of the issue: "Hysteria sells."

Inhofe was reelected most recently in 2002. His Democratic opponent was former Governor David Walters, who in October 1993 pleaded guilty to a misdemeanor count of violating campaign finance laws in his 1990 campaign; the prosecution dropped eight felony counts. Oklahoma voters seem to have a fixed view of Inhofe: the result was almost identical to those in 1994 and 1996. He won statewide 57%-36%, winning big margins in metro Oklahoma City (62%-31%) and metro Tulsa (60%-34%) and winning more narrowly (52%-41%) in the rest of the state. His seat is up in 2008. After Governor Brad Henry seemed to rule out running against him, Inhofe looked to be a solid bet for reelection. One Democrat who announced for the race was state Senator Andrew Rice.

Junior Senator

Tom Coburn (R)

Elected 2004, seat up 2010, 1st term; b. Mar. 14, 1948, Casper, WY; home, Muskogee; OK St. U., B.S. 1970, OK U., M.D. 1983; Southern Baptist; married (Carolyn).

Elected Office: U.S. House of Reps., 1994-2000.

Professional Career: Mgr., Coburn Optical Industries, 1970-78; Practicing physician, 1983-present.

DC Office: 172 RSOB, 20510, 202-224-5754; Fax: 202-224-6008; Web site: coburn.senate.gov.

State Offices: Lawton, 580-357-9878; Oklahoma City, 405-231-4941; Tulsa, 918-581-7651.

Committees: *Health, Education, Labor & Pensions* (10th of 10 R): Employment & Workplace Safety. *Homeland Security & Governmental Affairs* (5th of 8 R): Federal Financial Management, Government Information, Federal Services & International Security (RMM); Investigations (Permanent); Oversight of Government Management, the Federal Workforce & the District of Columbia. *Indian Affairs* (3d of 7 R). *Judiciary* (9th of 9 R): Human Rights & the Law (RMM); Antitrust, Competition Policy & Consumer Rights; Crime & Drugs; Terrorism, Technology & Homeland Security.

Group Ratings

	ADA	ACLU	AFS	LCV	ITIC	NTU	COC	ACU	CFG	FRC
2006	5	8	0	29	75	86	64	100	100	100
2005	5	—	0	5	—	83	89	100	90	—

National Journal Ratings

	2005 LIB	—	2005 CONS		2006 LIB	—	2006 CONS
Economic	0%	—	94%		32%	—	65%
Social	0%	—	77%		0%	—	82%
Foreign	0%	—	74%		18%	—	76%

Key Votes of the 109th Congress

1. Bar ANWR Drilling	N	5. Confirm Samuel Alito	Y	9. Limit Interstate Abortion	Y
2. FY06 Spending Curb	Y	6. Path to Citizenship	N	10. CAFTA	Y
3. Estate Tax Repeal	Y	7. Bar Same Sex Marriage	Y	11. Urge Iraq Withdrawal	N
4. Raise Minimum Wage	N	8. Stem Cell Research $	N	12. Provide Detainee Rights	N

Election Results

2004 general	Tom Coburn (R)	763,433	(53%)	($5,078,647)
	Brad Carson (D)	596,750	(41%)	($6,172,076)
	Sheila Bilyeu (I)	86,663	(6%)	
2004 primary	Tom Coburn (R)	145,974	(61%)	
	Kirk Humphreys (R)	59,877	(25%)	
	Bob Anthony (R)	29,596	(12%)	
	Other	2,944	(1%)	
1998 general	Don Nickles (R)	570,682	(66%)	($2,415,565)
	Don E. Carroll (D)	268,898	(31%)	($8,618)
	Other	20,133	(2%)	

Prior Winning Percentages: 1998 House (58%); 1996 House (55%); 1994 House (52%)

Tom Coburn, a Republican who previously served six years in the House, was elected Oklahoma's junior senator in 2004. Coburn grew up in Muskogee, where his father started a company, Coburn Optical Services, which became the town's biggest employer. Coburn graduated from Oklahoma State, and while there married his childhood sweetheart, who was Miss Oklahoma 1967. His father moved his business to Virginia, and Tom Coburn joined him and worked there. These were years of campus and youth rebellions, but not for the Coburns. "I was focused on business, kind of driven. I was sort of aloof to the counterculture. I never even heard of marijuana." Coburn took over the lens division and raised sales from $100,000 to $40 million. In 1975 the company was sold to Revlon and Coburn, after being stricken with melanoma, decided to go to the University of Oklahoma Medical School. After graduating, at 35, he moved to Muskogee and opened Maternal and Family Practice Associates; he has delivered some 4,000 babies and went on medical missions around the world. In 1994 he read that 2d District Congressman Mike Synar was talking about nationalizing health care, and decided to run against him. Synar lost to a 71-year-old retired teacher in the Democratic runoff, and Coburn won the general election, in a district that leaned toward Democrats in state elections, 52%-48%.

Coburn was an outspoken member of Speaker Newt Gingrich's freshman class who arrived in Washington in 1995 determined to make changes. A strong opponent of abortion, he passed amendments requiring AIDS counseling for pregnant women and labels on condoms disclosing that they don't prevent infections which lead to cervical cancer. He passed a bill requiring HIV testing of infants if their mothers had not been tested. He regularly conducted slide shows for members and staffers on the effects of sexually transmitted diseases. Some of the 1994 freshmen accommodated to Washington; Coburn didn't. He was one of the leaders of the attempted coup against Gingrich in July 1997. He angered appropriators by opposing their bills and offering amendments. He got the ethics committee to reverse itself in March 1998 and rule that he could continue to practice medicine and he delivered nearly 500 babies while in office. In 1994 he had promised to serve only three terms; in 2000 he kept his promise and did not run for reelection, but returned to his medical practice in Muskogee. He wrote a book, *Breach of Trust: How Washington Turns Outsiders into Insiders,* in which he called members of Congress "Pharisees" and attacked Republican leaders by name.

In October 2003 Senator Don Nickles announced that he would not run for a fifth term in 2004. Several politicians soon entered the race—Oklahoma City Mayor Kirk Humphreys and state Corporation Commissioner Bob Anthony, both Republicans, and Democrat Brad Carson, who had been elected to Coburn's seat in 2000. Coburn was urged by many to run, but declined; he had been treated for colon cancer that year. In February 2004 he told his former colleague Steve Largent that he had prepared a press release announcing he would not run. But his mother told him, "If you're supposed to be a U.S. senator, you will. Put it in the Lord's hands and leave it there." After sleeping on it, he had "an impression in my spiritual life that I was supposed to do this." He called his mother, said he changed his mind and announced his candidacy publicly. He admitted the downsides. "Financially, it's terrible. For my family, it's terrible. And politically, it's stupid to get into a race six to nine months after everyone's already into it. But it's kind of been one of those things that's marked my life. I learned to be obedient to that still inner voice."

Leading Republicans had already lined up for Humphreys. He had been endorsed by Senators Nickles and Jim Inhofe, and Congressmen John Sullivan and Tom Cole; Coburn told them they should keep their commitments. Polls showed a close race, usually with Coburn just a bit ahead of Humphreys. Negative campaigning may have helped Coburn. Anthony accused Humphreys of "shady" business and land deals. Humphreys attacked Coburn for attending a Las Vegas fundraiser

(Coburn returned contributions from gambling figures) and ran an ad attacking Coburn for voting against intelligence and airport spending bills. The Club for Growth, supporting Coburn, replied with ads claiming the bills were loaded with pork. Coburn's cultural and fiscal conservatism, his opposition to Washington insiders and his keeping of his term limits promise made him many fans across the state, and he ended up winning the primary with 61% of the vote, to 25% for Humphreys and 12% for Anthony. Coburn carried 76 of 77 counties, losing one county by the margin of 19-13. In the counties of his old House district he won with between 73% and, in Muskogee County, 91% of the vote.

The winner of the Democratic nomination, with 79% of the primary vote, was Congressman Brad Carson. Part Cherokee, Southern Baptist, Carson had a sterling resume. He was an honors graduate at Baylor, a Rhodes Scholar at Oxford; he went to law school at Oklahoma, was a White House Fellow, then practiced with a big firm in Oklahoma City and returned to eastern Oklahoma. After replacing Coburn in the 2d District, he had one of the most moderate voting records of any House Democrat and favored gun rights, the death penalty and the war in Iraq. National Democrats, happy to have such a politically adept candidate with a chance in a heavily Republican state, eagerly supported him; he raised more money than Coburn. There were obvious contrasts between the two candidates' views on representation. Coburn described himself as a part-time lawmaker, determined to uphold principle and willing to take on his own party's leadership. Carson described himself as a practical-minded lawmaker, committed to a political career, "fight[ing] for Oklahoma" and eager for bipartisanship. Carson was aided by Coburn's penchant for impolitic statements and said, "We've got someone running for Congress, for the U.S. Senate right now in Tom Coburn, who's already made us a laughingstock all across not only the country but the whole globe." State Democratic Chairman Jay Parmley called Coburn "just flat crazy" and an "extremist."

September polls showed the race tight and some showed Carson ahead. Coburn brought in celebrities to campaign for him. Carson did not want national Democrats in, though he did say he supported John Kerry for president. Coburn made the point, "Brad Carson is a vote for Ted Kennedy and Hillary Clinton to run the Senate." Carson counterattacked: "Tom has opposed key bills that help our state. The road bill—Tom is opposed to it. The farm bill—Tom is opposed to it. The prescription drug benefit for seniors—Tom is opposed to it. The Patriot Act—Tom is opposed to it." The most incendiary issue was raised in September, when news broke of a lawsuit, long since settled, by a woman who claimed Coburn in 1990 sterilized her without her consent when operating on her ectopic pregnancy and then filed a false Medicaid claim; Coburn said she gave oral consent and never sought reimbursement for the sterilization. Coburn "sterilized an underage girl without her consent," a Carson ad said, then committed Medicaid fraud "to get paid for the illegal procedure." Coburn charged that Democrats had connived with reporters to raise the issue. Coburn was aided by ads run by the Club for Growth and a 527 organization that received $1 million from two Oklahoma City oilmen. He won by a solid 53%-41% margin. Carson carried all but two of the counties in his congressional district and won in some other rural, historically Democratic counties as well. But Coburn won 56%-37% in the Oklahoma City area and 55%-41% in the Tulsa area. In an increasingly straight ticket era, the Kerry candidacy was obviously a heavy weight on Carson's fortunes: he ran 7% ahead of Kerry. Interestingly, the NEP exit poll showed that more voters considered Carson too extreme than Coburn.

Returning to Washington, he initially said. "My goal in the Senate is I need to get done what I need to get done. And initially that means no confrontation." Maybe, but he did show an attitude. Senate rules give any one senator the ability to obstruct proceedings far more than Coburn was ever able to in the House. "I'll be sleeping every night" with the 1,500-page *Riddick's Senate Procedure*, he said. "My goal is to learn the rules as well as Robert Byrd." He quickly discovered, and lamented, that the Senate wastes lots of time. He was a quick study, turning his attention to the nation's "unsustainable course financially," and the need for accountability and transparency in federal spending. He would not seek earmarks for Oklahoma because "that earmark is coming out of the future standard of living of my grandchildren." And he became a self-appointed taxpayers' watchdog on the Senate floor. In 2005, he claimed that he offered more amendments during Senate debate than any other senator. He had a solidly conservative voting record. More than once, he was the only senator opposing passage of an appropriations bill. When he tried to delete $453 million that had been enacted for two bridges in Alaska and redirect the money to post-Katrina bridge repair in Louisiana, Alaska Senator Ted Stevens objected, "If the Senate decides to discriminate against our state . . . . I will resign from this body." Coburn lost that vote, 82-15, but he felt that he had made his point about priorities. Post-Katrina, he fought a $700 million proposal to relocate a rail line in Mississippi that recently had been repaired; he lost on a 49-48 Senate vote, but the money was dropped in the House-Senate conference committee. Pork isn't his only target. He complained that the Bush administration's handling of budget requests for the war in Iraq through "emergency" supplemental spending is a phony way to do business. With Barack Obama, Coburn won enactment in 2006 of a proposal to create a central database for citizens to track federal grants and contracts. "This bill is a small but significant step toward changing the culture in Washington," he said.

During the Judiciary Committee hearings on the nomination of John Roberts as Chief Justice, Coburn choked up as he decried "mindless partisanship which, at times, sounds almost hateful to the ears of Americans." Roberts turned down his invitation to declare that judges who cite precedents of other nations may be guilty of an impeachable offense. Pursuing his interest in health care, he filed a bill to fund research of embryonic stem cells so long as the research would not harm a human embryo. He unveiled a sweeping health care reform package designed to provoke debate, including a malpractice court that would be similar to the workers' compensation system, and revisions in international pricing for prescription drugs.

Coburn also challenged the Senate rule that bars senators from earning money practicing medicine. When the Rules and Administration Committee decreed that he must fold his medical practice because it poses a conflict of interest, Coburn adamantly objected and insisted that practicing medicine "will make me a better senator" who is more immersed with real problems. Senate Ethics Committee chairman George Voinovich objected that an exception would open the door for other Senators to earn income that might be subject to outside influence. In November 2005, on a procedural vote to permit him to see patients without making a profit, Coburn got 51 votes but that was short of the 60 required to prevail. The result was "a moral victory," he said, and he vowed to continue the fight.

Democrats believe that they could give Coburn a stiff reelection contest in 2010, especially with Governor Brad Henry as the challenger.

FIRST DISTRICT

Rep. John Sullivan (R)

Elected Jan. 2002, 3d full term; b. Jan. 1, 1965, Tulsa; home, Tulsa; Northeastern St. U., B.B.A., 1992; Catholic; married (Judy).

Elected Office: OK House of Reps., 1994-2001.

Professional Career: Trucking salesman, 1988-92, Gas and Fleet sales rep., 1991-98; Realtor, 1997-2002.

DC Office: 114 CHOB, 20515, 202-225-2211; Fax: 202-225-9187; Web site: sullivan.house.gov.

District Offices: Bartlesville, 918-336-6500; Tulsa, 918-749-0014.

Committees: *Energy & Commerce* (23d of 26 R): Health; Environment & Hazardous Materials; Energy & Air Quality. *Select Committee on Energy Independence and Global Warming* (4th of 6 R).

Group Ratings

	ADA	ACLU	AFS	LCV	ITIC	NTU	COC	ACU	CFG	FRC
2006	5	5	14	17	100	73	100	92	80	100
2005	5	—	13	0	—	63	85	100	76	92

National Journal Ratings

	2005 LIB	—	2005 CONS		2006 LIB	—	2006 CONS
Economic	3%	—	94%		24%	—	76%
Social	0%	—	89%		0%	—	94%
Foreign	15%	—	84%		6%	—	86%

Key Votes of the 109th Congress

1. Estate Tax Repeal	Y	5. Limit Interstate Abortion	Y	9. Build Border Fence	Y
2. Limit CAFE Standards	Y	6. Extend Patriot Act	Y	10. CAFTA	Y
3. FY06 Spending Curb	Y	7. Bar Same Sex Marriage	Y	11. Oppose Iraq Withdrawal	Y
4. Drilling in ANWR	Y	8. Stem Cell Research $	N	12. Detainee Tribunals	Y

Election Results

2006 general	John Sullivan (R)	116,920	(64%)	($767,488)
	Alan Gentges (D)	56,724	(31%)	($40,223)
	Bill Wortman (I)	10,085	(5%)	($6,785)
2006 primary	John Sullivan (R)	38,279	(87%)	
	Evelyn Rogers (R)	5,826	(13%)	
2004 general	John Sullivan (R)	187,145	(60%)	($1,019,758)
	Doug Dodd (D)	116,731	(38%)	($325,976)
	Other	7,058	(2%)	

Prior Winning Percentages: 2002 (56%); 2002 (54%)

The People		Race/Ethnic Origin	Ancestry	
Area size:	1,790 sq. mi.	73.8% White	German: 11.1%	Irish: 8.7%
Urban population:	89.6%	9.4% Black	English: 7.9%	
Rural population:	10.4%	1.4% Asian	**2004 Presidential Vote**	
Pop. 2000:	690,131	5.8% Native Am.	Bush (R) 206,744	(65%)
Pop. 2005 (est):	712,870	0.0% Hawaiian	Kerry (D) 109,486	(35%)
Median income:	$38,610	4.2% Two+ races	**2000 Presidential Vote**	
Poverty status:	11.3%	0.1% Other	Bush (R) 165,759	(62%)
Military veterans:	14.1%	5.3% Hispanic Origin	Gore (D) 99,283	(37%)
			Other 3,566	(1%)
			Cook Partisan Voting Index: R +13	

Occupation   Blue collar: 23.2%   White collar: 62.9%   Gray collar: 14.0%

The gushers of the 1905 Glenn Pool discovery made Tulsa one of America's oil boomtowns, settled not just by people from the immediate hinterland but by Midwesterners and New Englanders of Yankee stock. In the 1920s, as its art-deco skyscrapers rose in downtown on heights above the Arkansas River, it was a raw town, intent on culture. It was optimistic and ready to seek economic change, yet culturally and politically conservative, with a Yankee elite and an Indian heritage recalled today in the large collection of America West art of Gilcrease Museum—left by one-eighth Creek Indian oil millionaire Thomas Gilcrease—and an ethnic variety suggested by the Gershon & Rebecca Fenster Museum of Jewish Art. In the decades since, Tulsa has boomed and occasionally busted. It has remained cosmopolitan but conservative. Ordinary people here do not resent the oil companies or the new rich; they identify with them. As voters showed with their approval of the Vision 2025 economic development referendum—a $900 million package, with 32 projects—Tulsa is working to diversify from being solely one of America's leading petroleum centers. After Citgo Petroleum announced that it was moving its corporate headquarters to Houston, Tulsa persuaded American Airlines to move its maintenance and engineering center and over 7,000 jobs to Tulsa from Kansas City; that move spurred other aerospace-related development. In August 2005, a national magazine for small-business executives ranked the Tulsa-area as the most attractive commercial real estate market in the nation, and *Forbes* ranked the city fifth for its low cost of doing business. The city also is the headquarters of Oral Roberts University and its 60-story City of Faith hospital, and nearby is Catoosa, which was made a seaport by the federally-financed McClellan-Kerr Waterway.

The 1st Congressional District of Oklahoma includes Tulsa, Wagoner and Washington Counties and slices of Rogers and Creek Counties: just about all of the Tulsa metropolitan area. The political tradition here is heavily Republican, strengthened in recent decades by national Democrats' cultural liberalism. Even during the collapse of oil prices in the 1980s, Tulsa remained full of a contagious enthusiasm for new business enterprises and innovations. People here see not class conflict, but a coincidence of economic interests.

The congressman from the 1st District is John Sullivan, a Republican first elected in a January 2002 special election to replace Steve Largent, who resigned to run (unsuccessfully) for governor. Sullivan grew up in Tulsa and graduated from Northeastern Oklahoma State University. In Tulsa he worked in the transportation, oil and gas, and real estate industries. In 1994, at 29, he was elected to the state House, where he served as Republican whip. In the December 2001 primary for the seat, the best-known candidate was Cathy Keating, wife of Governor Frank Keating, who enthusiastically backed her campaign. She had a big fundraising advantage, but stumbled in the five-week campaign. Sullivan accused her of being too moderate for a conservative district; she had no legislative record to dispute his claims. Sullivan, meanwhile, built a strong grass-roots network among conservative activists. He led the first round of balloting, 46%-30%. Under state law,

Sullivan's failure to win 50% entitled Keating to a runoff. But his unexpectedly large lead, plus the unlikelihood that four weeks of campaigning during the Christmas and New Year seasons would capture voter attention, convinced her to drop her candidacy. So on January 8, Sullivan faced the Democratic nominee, Doug Dodd, a Tulsa attorney and former school board member. Dodd ran a spirited campaign and raised some money from labor PACs. Even though this is a district George W. Bush carried with more than 60% of the vote in 2000 and 2004, Sullivan only won 54%-44%. National Democrats may have regretted they did not target this race.

Sullivan has a very conservative voting record, and won a seat on the Energy and Commerce Committee, where oil and gas issues often are front and center. With help from Senator Jim Inhofe, who managed the highway bill across the Capitol, he fought for Tulsa's fair share of highway and transit funds; he sponsored a measure for a memorial to the 1921 Tulsa race riot, where more than 300 died. He pushed to build a huge refinery in nearby Cushing, which is home to nine pipelines. Contending that truckloads of illegal aliens were dumped into Tulsa neighborhoods, he pushed for tougher immigration enforcement; "catch and release" must give way to "deter and remove," he said. He warned Bush that he seemed insufficiently opposed to amnesty. After Hurricane Katrina, he joined other conservatives seeking other spending cuts to offset clean-up costs.

Sullivan has slowly entrenched himself. In two campaign rematches against Dodd, he increased his majority. In 2002, Dodd criticized him for missing a vote on increased subsidies for farmers, and noted that he misrepresented his arrest record on an application to coach youth soccer; still, Sullivan raised his margin to 56%-42%. In 2004, he faced a primary challenge from Bill Wortman, who attacked Sullivan's veracity on several issues and was backed by two disgruntled ex-consultants who complained that Sullivan had failed to pay for earlier services (Sullivan later reached agreement with the Federal Election Commission on a settlement); Sullivan won 70%-25%. In the fall campaign Dodd focused on the high cost of the "mess" in Iraq and the loss of U.S. jobs to outsourcing, but Sullivan ran as an insider and cited the accomplishments of the Bush administration and the Republican congressional majorities. He won 60%-38%. In 2006, he got 64% to 31% for Bartlesville attorney Alan Gentges and 5% for Wortman, running as an independent.

SECOND DISTRICT

Rep. Dan Boren (D)

Elected 2004, 2d term; b. Aug. 2, 1973, Shawnee; home, Paden; TX Christian U., B.S. 1997, U. of OK, M.B.A. 2000; Methodist; married (Andrea).

Elected Office: OK House of Reps., 2002-04.

Professional Career: Aide, OK Corp. Comm., 1997-98; Loan processor, Danc First Corp., 1999-2000; Staffer, U.S. Rep. Wes Watkins 2000-01.

DC Office: 216 CHOB, 20515, 202-225-2701; Fax: 202-225-3038; Web site: www.house.gov/boren.

District Offices: Claremore, 918-341-9336; McAlester, 918-423-5951; Muskogee, 918-687-2533.

Committees: *Armed Services* (20th of 34 D): Readiness; Air & Land Forces. *Financial Services* (37th of 37 D): Domestic and International Monetary Policy, Trade & Technology; Capital Markets, Insurance & Government Sponsored Enterprises. *Natural Resources* (13th of 27 D): Energy & Mineral Resources; National Parks, Forests & Public Lands.

Group Ratings

	ADA	ACLU	AFS	LCV	ITIC	NTU	COC	ACU	CFG	FRC
2006	25	27	43	0	71	43	100	72	52	71
2005	55	—	88	28	—	36	81	64	33	69

National Journal Ratings

	2005 LIB	—	2005 CONS		2006 LIB	—	2006 CONS
Economic	50%	—	49%		48%	—	52%
Social	48%	—	52%		49%	—	50%
Foreign	57%	—	42%		50%	—	50%

Key Votes of the 109th Congress

1. Estate Tax Repeal	Y	5. Limit Interstate Abortion	Y	9. Build Border Fence	Y
2. Limit CAFE Standards	Y	6. Extend Patriot Act	Y	10. CAFTA	N
3. FY06 Spending Curb	N	7. Bar Same Sex Marriage	Y	11. Oppose Iraq Withdrawal	Y
4. Drilling in ANWR	Y	8. Stem Cell Research $	Y	12. Detainee Tribunals	Y

Election Results

2006 general	Dan Boren (D) 122,347	(73%)	($1,000,638)
	Patrick Miller (R) 45,861	(27%)	
2006 primary	Dan Boren (D) .... unopposed		
2004 general	Dan Boren (D) 179,579	(66%)	($2,018,285)
	Wayland Smalley (R) 92,963	(34%)	($46,832)

The People		Race/Ethnic Origin	Ancestry	
Area size:	21,225 sq. mi.	70.2% White	USA: 10.2%	Irish: 7.8%
Urban population:	35.6%	4.0% Black	German: 7.2%	
Rural population:	64.4%	0.3% Asian	**2004 Presidential Vote**	
Pop. 2000:	690,130	16.8% Native Am.	Bush (R) 166,826	(59%)
Pop. 2005 (est):	703,943	0.0% Hawaiian	Kerry (D) 114,113	(41%)
Median income:	$27,885	6.2% Two+ races	**2000 Presidential Vote**	
Poverty status:	18.5%	0.0% Other	Bush (R) 123,952	(52%)
Military veterans:	15.4%	2.4% Hispanic Origin	Gore (D) 110,791	(47%)
			Other 3,438	(1%)
			Cook Partisan Voting Index: R + 5	

Occupation	Blue collar: 33.2%	White collar: 48.3%	Gray collar: 18.5%

The land that is now northeast Oklahoma a century ago was the Indian Territory, the place where in the 1830s the Five Civilized Tribes were driven from Georgia and Alabama over the Trail of Tears. Almost one in four people here report their race as American Indian, and in some counties one-third or more claim they are at least partly of Native American descent. The Indian percentage is highest in the hilly counties just west of the Ozarks of Arkansas, where county names—Cherokee, Osage, Sequoyah—recall the Civilized Tribes; the street signs in scenic Tahlequah, the Cherokee capital since 1839, are written in the Cherokee script as well as English. The Creek nation chose its tribal site in Okmulgee in the belief that tornadoes would not strike the area; history has proven them correct. In the northeast corner, Ottawa County has been the home to more Indian tribes than any other county in the nation. This pleasant land of gentle hills and man-made lakes recently has grown at a healthy pace, from overspill from Tulsa and also from retirees and young families moving into the land that became the home of the Civilized Tribes more than 150 years ago.

South of this Indian country is Oklahoma's Little Dixie, settled between 1889 and 1907 by white Southerners, most of them poor. Some of the county names—LeFlore, Pontotoc—are straight from Mississippi. Today, Interstate highways and turnpikes connect people to jobs in more vibrant metropolitan areas, while dam-made lakes have spurred the creation of resort and retirement communities. Still, traditional cultural attitudes and folkways remain strong. When Oklahoma voted in 2002 to outlaw cockfighting, voters in many towns in Little Dixie turned out in large numbers and voted to keep cockfighting by huge margins.

The 2d Congressional District includes most of the eastern third of Oklahoma, except for metropolitan Tulsa. It includes Muskogee, subject of Merle Haggard's song, "Okie from Muskogee," Will Rogers's hometown of Claremore in Rogers County and former Speaker of the House Carl Albert's home in McAlester in Little Dixie. McAlester, originally a rail center for the coal mining industry, is the site of a massive army ammunition plant that manufactures non-nuclear bombs ranging in size from 500 to 5,000 pounds (during the war in Iraq, it was forced to add a night shift), including one that killed terrorist leader Abu Musab al-Zarqawi. This area was ancestrally Democratic, but in the 1980s it trended Republican on cultural issues. In the late 1990s it moved back toward the Democrats, or at least Oklahoma Democrats; Brad Henry carried every county here in his two races for governor. Al Gore was competitive with a 52%-47% loss to George W. Bush, but John Kerry was defeated 59%-41%.

The congressman from the 2d District is Dan Boren, who was elected in 2004 and hails from one of Oklahoma's most prominent political families. His grandfather, Lyle Boren, represented southeastern Oklahoma in Congress from 1937 to 1947. His father, David Boren, was elected governor in 1974 and senator in 1978; he became chairman of the Senate Intelligence Committee before he resigned in 1994 to become president of the University of Oklahoma (Boren was breakfasting with CIA director and former Boren staffer George Tenet on September 11, 2001). Dan Boren grew up in Shawnee and in Longview, Texas, where he lived with his mother and stepfather. He graduated from Texas Christian University and the University of Oklahoma Business School; he worked as a college fundraiser, a staffer on the state Corporation Commission and a district aide to Republican Congressman Wes Watkins, who represented Little Dixie until he retired in 2002. Based in rural Okfuskee County, Boren ran for the state House in 2002, raised $200,000 and unseated a Republican who had switched from the Democratic party. He quickly became chairman of the Democratic Caucus. Then, just a year into his term, 2d District Congressman Brad Carson announced that he was running (unsuccessfully) for the Senate, and Boren announced he would run for the House seat.

The Democratic primary narrowed to a contest between Boren and former district prosecutor Kalyn Free. Boren, who had the backing of business and industry, was the more conservative candidate. At times, he sounded like a Republican. While Boren supported abortion rights, he opposed partial-birth abortion and favored requiring parental consent for minors wishing to have abortions. Unlike many other Democrats, Boren opposed repeal of the Bush tax cuts. And Boren said he "more than likely would have" voted to authorize the use of U.S. military force in Iraq. His positions aroused significant opposition from left-leaning interest groups. Free was endorsed by several labor unions, environmental groups and MoveOn.org. EMILY's List poured more than $500,000 into her campaign, but that wasn't enough. Boren won the Democratic primary 58%-36%,. He led in all 25 counties, with 71% in McAlester's Pittsburg County. In the general, Boren won 66%-34% over horse breeder Wayland Smalley.

His voting record placed Boren virtually at the center of the House. He was the only Democrat to oppose limits on the investigative authority under the Patriot Act for prosecutors to review library records, and he supported repeal of the estate and gift tax. On the Armed Services Committee, Boren filed a bill to ban the use of names and images of military members in anti-war commercial enterprises. Although he called himself a "very conservative Democrat" and he called Nancy Pelosi too partisan, he opposed the Central American Free Trade Agreement and favored reimportation of prescription drugs from Canada. After the 2006 election, he unsuccessfully sought a seat on the Energy and Commerce Committee.

Boren was reelected easily in 2006. Over the past 30 years, this has been a district that has sent young and little-experienced candidates to Washington— Democrat Mike Synar at age 28 in 1978; Republican Tom Coburn, after a career in obstetrics, in 1994; and Democrat Carson at 33 in 2000. Boren, at 31 and after only two years in the legislature, was in that tradition. He appears to have a safe House seat, but it seems possible that he may run some day for governor, as his father did, or for senator, as his two predecessors in this seat did in 2004. He dismissed the idea of a possible challenge to Senator Jim Inhofe in 2008.

THIRD DISTRICT

Rep. Frank Lucas (R)

Elected May 1994, 7th full term; b. Jan. 6, 1960, Cheyenne; home, Cheyenne; OK St. U., B.S. 1982; Baptist; married (Lynda).

Elected Office: OK House of Reps., 1988-94.

Professional Career: Farmer & rancher.

DC Office: 2311 RHOB, 20515, 202-225-5565; Fax: 202-225-8698; Web site: www.house.gov/lucas.

District Offices: Stillwater, 405-624-6407; Woodward, 580-256-5752; Yukon, 405-373-1958.

Committees: *Agriculture* (3d of 21 R): Conservation, Credit, Energy & Research (RMM); General Farm Commodities & Risk Management. *Financial Services* (7th of 33 R): Domestic and International Monetary Policy, Trade & Technology; Capital Markets, Insurance & Government Sponsored Enterprises. *Science & Technology* (7th of 20 R): Research & Science Education; Space & Aeronautics.

Group Ratings

	ADA	ACLU	AFS	LCV	ITIC	NTU	COC	ACU	CFG	FRC
2006	5	9	0	0	100	55	93	88	47	100
2005	0	—	0	0	—	56	92	92	57	92

National Journal Ratings

	2005 LIB	—	2005 CONS	2006 LIB	—	2006 CONS
Economic	17%	—	83%	4%	—	94%
Social	34%	—	65%	28%	—	70%
Foreign	0%	—	89%	6%	—	86%

Key Votes of the 109th Congress

1. Estate Tax Repeal	Y	5. Limit Interstate Abortion	Y	9. Build Border Fence	Y
2. Limit CAFE Standards	Y	6. Extend Patriot Act	N	10. CAFTA	Y
3. FY06 Spending Curb	Y	7. Bar Same Sex Marriage	Y	11. Oppose Iraq Withdrawal	Y
4. Drilling in ANWR	Y	8. Stem Cell Research $	N	12. Detainee Tribunals	Y

Election Results

2006 general	Frank Lucas (R)	128,042	(67%)	($507,637)
	Sue Barton (D).....................................	61,749	(33%)	($26,556)
2006 primary	Frank Lucas (R) .... unopposed			
2004 general	Frank Lucas (R)	215,510	(82%)	($371,139)
	Gregory Wilson (I)	46,621	(18%)	

Prior Winning Percentages: 2002 (76%); 2000 (59%); 1998 (65%); 1996 (64%); 1994 (70%); 1994 (54%)

The People		Race/Ethnic Origin	Ancestry	
Area size:	34,384 sq. mi.	81.0% White	German: 12.4%	USA: 10.0%
Urban population:	50.7%	3.8% Black	Irish: 8.2%	
Rural population:	49.3%	0.8% Asian	**2004 Presidential Vote**	
Pop. 2000:	690,131	6.0% Native Am.	Bush (R) 209,598	(72%)
Pop. 2005 (est):	690,274	0.1% Hawaiian	Kerry (D) 82,670	(28%)
Median income:	$32,098	3.0% Two+ races	**2000 Presidential Vote**	
Poverty status:	15.0%	0.1% Other	Bush (R) 163,302	(65%)
Military veterans:	14.0%	5.2% Hispanic Origin	Gore (D) 84,691	(34%)
			Other 2,805	(1%)
			Cook Partisan Voting Index: R +18	

Occupation	Blue collar: 28.2%	White collar: 54.1%	Gray collar: 17.7%

First settled just a century ago, western Oklahoma is a fertile land forever at the mercy of the elements. The western plains are scorching hot under the summer sun and snow-blown in winter; this is one of the windiest parts of America. Visitors to the Tallgrass Prairie Preserve, maintained by the Nature Conservancy near Pawhuska, can experience what settlers of untilled land found when they arrived here: a swaying ocean of 10-foot-high grasses filled with insects emitting a dull, incessant roar. Many rural counties here are not much more populous than they were during the virgin sod era. Far fewer people live here than did before the Dust Bowl hit in the 1930s, and fewer than during the Anadarko Basin oil and natural gas boom of the 1970s (now local planners hope to use the wind as an energy source). You can still see what the old towns looked like. In 1910, three years after statehood, Oklahoma moved its capital south 25 miles from Guthrie to Oklahoma City, leaving behind what has become one of the nation's largest historic preservation districts.

The 3d Congressional District includes Oklahoma's western plains and nearly half of the state's land, from the panhandle—an outlaw no man's land that did not officially join the Indian Territory until 1890—to the northern fringes of Oklahoma City. The 3d extends to north central Oklahoma, including Ponca City, the university town of Stillwater and Osage County, site of the state's one Indian reservation just west of Tulsa. A few of the southern counties, settled by farmers crossing the Red River from Texas, are ancestrally Democratic. But farmers coming south from Kansas settled most of these plains, and they have always been heavily Republican. In Kingfisher County, which harvests more rye than any other in the nation, George W. Bush won by more than 3-to-1 margins in both 2000 and 2004. Farther west in the panhandle are Beaver (home to the town that claims to be the cow-chip throwing capital of the world), Texas and Cimarron Counties, the only three counties Democratic Governor Brad Henry failed to carry in his landslide 2006 reelection. Those divisions have been as permanent as if Oklahoma had been split down the middle during the Civil War. There are few blacks in this part of Oklahoma, but an increasing number of Hispanics are moving here, as in other parts of the Great Plains, to work in hog farms and meatpacking plants. In October 2006, a business partnership announced plans for a $200 million beef-processing plant in Hooker, near the west end of the panhandle.

The congressman from the 3d District is Frank Lucas, a Republican chosen in a 1994 special election, which was a precursor to the party's takeover of the House later that year. Lucas's roots in western Oklahoma extend more than 100 years; he owns a farm and cattle ranch in Roger Mills County and was elected to the Oklahoma House in 1988, at 28. He got his chance to run for Congress when Glenn English, a 19-year conservative Democrat, resigned to head the National Rural Electric Cooperative Association. Lucas had serious competition in both the primary and general elections. In the primary, he trailed state Senator Brooks Douglass 36%-34%, who campaigned from his Oklahoma City base with a Western accent. In the runoff, Lucas ridiculed "some Johnny-come-lately dressed up like a drugstore cowboy" and carried all the rural areas to win 56%-44%. In the general, he faced Dan Webber, 27-year-old press secretary to outgoing Senator David Boren. Lucas ran an ad showing the U.S. Capitol ("this is where Dan Webber has worked his entire adult life") and Oklahoma farmland ("this is where Frank Lucas has worked his entire adult life"); he won 54%-46%. Since then, Lucas has been reelected by wide margins.

Lucas has a mostly conservative voting record, but less so on cultural issues. As the representative at the time of the site of the Oklahoma City bombing, he introduced the resolution condemning it, the bill for relief spending and the bill to authorize the bombing monument and make it part of the national parks system. After the Oklahoma City trial was moved to Denver, he sponsored the amendments to allow closed circuit broadcasting of out-of-town trials and to allow bombing victims, survivors and relatives to watch the trial and still testify in the sentencing hearing. On the 2002 farm bill, as a subcommittee chairman, he helped to unravel the 1996 Freedom to Farm Act that he had once embraced. He helped write the conservation incentives to control erosion, aid farmers suffering drought, and protect air and water quality, and he said that the package would be good for agriculture-dependent Oklahoma. He successfully fought a plan to reduce the number of Farm Service Agency field offices. On the energy bill in 2005, he helped to write the final provisions for rural grants and biodiesel tax credits. He has taken up the cause of numismatists with his measure allowing for the private sale of 1933 Double Eagle gold coins. Considered federal government property, most were destroyed when President Franklin Roosevelt took the U.S. off the gold standard.

Back home, Lucas's main challenge is the physical size of the district: From his home in Cheyenne, it extends 80 miles south, 240 miles west to the Panhandle, and 270 miles east to Tulsa's outskirts—more than 34,000 square miles in total. But the main trouble encountered by the easygoing Lucas seems to be on his ranch, which he operates: he broke his nose years ago when a cow slammed a gate on him and lost a tooth while trying to attach an identification tag to a 250-pound heifer. He has said he wants to stay in Congress long enough to become chairman of the Agriculture Committee, and he may be only a few years from achieving that goal.

FOURTH DISTRICT

Rep. Tom Cole (R)

Elected 2002, 3d term; b. Apr. 28, 1949, Shreveport, LA; home, Moore; Grinnell Col., B.A. 1971, Yale U., M.A. 1974, U. of OK, Ph.D. 1984; Methodist; married (Ellen).

Elected Office: OK Senate, 1988-91.

Professional Career: OK Repub. Party chmn, 1985-89; Exec. Dir. NRCC, 1991-95, OK Secy. of State, 1995-99; Pol. consultant, 2000-2002.

DC Office: 236 CHOB, 20515, 202-225-6165; Fax: 202-225-3512; Web site: www.house.gov/cole/.

District Offices: Ada, 580-436-5375; Lawton, 580-357-2131; Norman, 405-329-6500.

Committees: *NRCC Chairman. Armed Services* (16th of 29 R): Air & Land Forces; Readiness. *Natural Resources* (15th of 22 R): Fisheries, Wildlife & Oceans; National Parks, Forests & Public Lands.

Group Ratings

	ADA	ACLU	AFS	LCV	ITIC	NTU	COC	ACU	CFG	FRC
2006	0	5	0	8	100	57	100	84	61	100
2005	0	—	0	0	—	60	96	100	73	92

National Journal Ratings

	2005 LIB — 2005 CONS		2006 LIB — 2006 CONS	
Economic	19%	— 79%	12%	— 86%
Social	16%	— 83%	28%	— 70%
Foreign	11%	— 86%	17%	— 73%

Key Votes of the 109th Congress

1. Estate Tax Repeal	Y	5. Limit Interstate Abortion	Y	9. Build Border Fence	Y
2. Limit CAFE Standards	Y	6. Extend Patriot Act	Y	10. CAFTA	Y
3. FY06 Spending Curb	Y	7. Bar Same Sex Marriage	Y	11. Oppose Iraq Withdrawal	Y
4. Drilling in ANWR	Y	8. Stem Cell Research $	N	12. Detainee Tribunals	Y

Election Results

2006 general	Tom Cole (R)	118,266	(65%)	($1,059,124)
	Hal Spake (D).....................................	64,775	(35%)	($31,091)
2006 primary	Tom Cole (R)	unopposed		
2004 general	Tom Cole (R)	198,985	(78%)	($750,550)
	Charlene Bradshaw (I)	56,869	(22%)	

Prior Winning Percentages: 2002 (54%)

The People		Race/Ethnic Origin	Ancestry	
Area size:	10,409 sq. mi.	77.6% White	USA: 10.0%	German: 9.9%
Urban population:	63.3%	6.6% Black	Irish: 8.6%	
Rural population:	36.7%	1.7% Asian	**2004 Presidential Vote**	
Pop. 2000:	690,131	5.5% Native Am.	Bush (R) 194,977	(67%)
Pop. 2005 (est):	724,617	0.1% Hawaiian	Kerry (D) 96,100	(33%)
Median income:	$35,510	3.6% Two+ races	**2000 Presidential Vote**	
Poverty status:	13.1%	0.1% Other	Bush (R) 144,568	(61%)
Military veterans:	15.8%	4.8% Hispanic Origin	Gore (D) 91,078	(38%)
			Other 2,497	(1%)
			Cook Partisan Voting Index: R +13	

Occupation	Blue collar: 26.4%	White collar: 57.2%	Gray collar: 16.5%

In the years just after 1900, the brown hills west of Oklahoma City and north of the Red River suddenly filled up with farmers riding north from Texas, past the well-watered green lands of the east toward the bare pasture lands of the west. These were young people with large families, and in the years since, this land has emptied out, as children have grown up and moved elsewhere and fewer hands are needed for farming. The first settlers here arrived just as the buffalo were dying out: from an estimated 60 million animals to no more than 1,000. So in 1901, President William McKinley established the nation's first wildlife preserve in the Wichita Mountains, 25 miles northwest of Lawton. Fifteen bison were donated by the New York Zoological Society and arrived at the preserve via rail in 1907—a major factor in the survival of the species. Today this habitat supports grazing for Rocky Mountain elk, white-tailed deer and Texas longhorn cattle. Government has played a role in the survival of people, too, in this part of Oklahoma. Population in southwest Oklahoma clusters around major government institutions: The state capital in Oklahoma City; the University of Oklahoma in Norman, which was the world's first school of petroleum geology; the giant repair depot at Tinker Air Force Base, in southern Oklahoma City; the Army Field Artillery School at Fort Sill, in Lawton. Sill also is absorbing the Army Air Defense School from Fort Bliss, Texas.

The 4th Congressional District of Oklahoma begins a few miles from the oil-derrick-surrounded capitol in Oklahoma City, smack dab in the middle of the state, and proceeds south and west to cover half of Oklahoma's Red River Valley. Demographically, this district is becoming more suburban, but the cultural tone remains country. That is true even in the Oklahoma City suburbs, which stretch out over the mile-grid roads, where in new subdivisions dust may still get tracked indoors and people still prefer chicken-fried steak to stir-fried chicken (though they eat both) and watermelons from Rush Springs. Ancestrally, this is Democratic country, but Norman, Lawton and the Oklahoma City fringe have voted pretty solidly Republican since the 1990s.

The congressman from the 4th District is Tom Cole, a Republican first elected in 2002 after a long career trying to elect other politicians. Cole grew up in Moore, just south of Oklahoma City and north of Norman. He is a fifth-generation Oklahoman, and his mother was a state representative and senator (and a member of the Chickasaw Nation hall of fame); his father served in the Air Force and later worked at Tinker. With the retirement of Senator Ben Nighthorse Campbell, he is the only Native American in Congress; more than half of the nation's Chickasaws live in his district. He graduated from Grinnell College, took a masters degree at Yale, and got a Ph.D. in British history at the University of Oklahoma, studying for a year at the University of London. From 1985 to 1989, he was Oklahoma Republican party chairman. In 1988, he was elected to the state Senate. He moved to Washington in 1991 as executive director of the National Republican Congressional Committee, then returned to Oklahoma and was appointed Secretary of State—the first Republican to hold that office. He went back to Washington to serve as chief of staff at the Republican National Committee in the 2000 campaign. During much of this period he was president of a polling and political consulting firm in Oklahoma City, whose clients have included three Republican presidents, Governor Frank Keating and J.C. Watts.

In 2002, J. C. Watts, former college and professional football player and chairman of the House Republican Conference, announced that he would not seek reelection. Cole moved quickly to run. Despite his party connections and an endorsement from Watts, he faced formidable opposition. His chief opponent was attorney Marc Nuttle. The two shared positions on most issues and extensive party connections. Nuttle had been Cole's predecessor at the NRCC, and worked on Pat Robertson's 1988 campaign; Nuttle and Cole worked together to pass a right-to-work law in a September 2001 referendum. In the showdown between the strategists, Nuttle called himself a "grass-roots" activist and Cole a "party" activist who raised half his campaign funds from outside the state, much of it from other consultants. Cole won 60%-33%. He also had tough competition in the general election, from former state senate Majority Leader Darryl Roberts. He appealed to the "yellow dog" Democratic tradition that is particularly strong in the Red River counties. Cole countered by citing the Democratic presidential nominees Roberts had supported, and described him as "pro-tax," "pro-abortion," and "pro-lawsuit." Roberts had only limited national party support; Cole had much more and won 54%-46%.

In the House, Cole has a mostly conservative voting record. He serves on the Armed Services Committee, a seat of obvious importance to the district. He has made several trips to Iraq to monitor military operations. He took a leave from the panel in 2005 to serve on the Rules Committee, but that ended when Republicans lost the House majority. He has urged tribal leaders to educate all Americans about the importance of Indian sovereignty, and said that he is tired of being the only American Indian in Congress; in the wake of the Jack Abramoff lobbying scandal, he strongly opposed proposed limits on the right of tribes to contribute to political campaigns. As a member of the House Ethics Committee in 2005, he excused himself from investigation of Majority Leader Tom DeLay to avoid an appearance of impropriety; he had previously contributed to DeLay's legal defense fund.

Following the 2006 election, Cole won a second-ballot victory, 102 to 81, over Pete Sessions of Texas to become chairman of the NRCC. Phil English of Pennsylvania finished third on the first ballot and dropped out. His diverse background in Republican politics and campaigns, including at the NRCC, gives him unique experience for the job; his performance with party strategy, candidate recruiting and fundraising will be a major factor in determining whether Republicans regain House control in the 2008 election. Cole vowed to expand the playing field of competitive seats. "2008 will be a year to hunt with a shotgun, not a rifle," he said. The lack of an incumbent president or vice president on the next campaign ballot will make the presidential election "fundamentally different" and "probably the most intense" campaign in at least a generation. His initial targets will be the 30 freshman Democrats who defeated or replaced retiring House Republicans. "It's hard to imagine a cycle that will be worse" than 2006, he added.

FIFTH DISTRICT

Rep. Mary Fallin (R)

Elected 2006, 1st term; b. Dec. 9, 1954, Warrensburg, MO; home, Oklahoma City; Attended OK Baptist U., OK St. U., B.S. 1977, attended U. of Central OK; Christian; divorced.

Elected Office: OK House of Reps., 1990-94; Lt. Gov., 1994-2006.

Professional Career: OK Dept. of Tourism and Rec., OK Securities Comm., OK Office of Personnel Mgt., 1977-82; hotel mkting. and mgt., 1983-90.

DC Office: 1432 LHOB, 20515, 202-225-2132; Fax: 202-226-1463; Web site: fallin.house.gov.

District Offices: Oklahoma City, 405-234-9900; Shawnee, 405-273-1733.

Committees: *Natural Resources* (22d of 22 R): Water & Power. *Small Business* (13th of 15 R): Regulations, Healthcare & Trade; Contracting & Technology. *Transportation & Infrastructure* (33d of 34 R): Aviation; Highways & Transit.

Group Ratings and Key Votes: Newly Elected

Election Results

2006 general	Mary Fallin (R)	108,936	(60%)	($1,629,550)
	David Hunter (D)	67,293	(37%)	($400,837)
	Other	4,196	(2%)	
2006 runoff	Mary Fallin (R)	26,748	(63%)	
	Mick Cornett (R)	15,669	(37%)	
2006 primary	Mary Fallin (R)	16,691	(35%)	
	Mick Cornett (R)	11,718	(24%)	
	Denise Bode (R)	9,139	(19%)	
	Kevin Calvey (R)	4,870	(10%)	
	Fred Morgan (R)	4,493	(9%)	
	Other	1,376	(3%)	
2004 general	Ernest Istook (R)	180,430	(66%)	($1,371,961)
	Bert Smith (D)	92,719	(34%)	($11,292)

The People		Race/Ethnic Origin	Ancestry	
Area size:	2,089 sq. mi.	67.7% White	German: 9.7%	Irish: 7.7%
Urban population:	87.5%	13.6% Black	USA: 7.6%	
Rural population:	12.5%	2.5% Asian	**2004 Presidential Vote**	
Pop. 2000:	690,131	4.4% Native Am.	Bush (R) 181,644	(64%)
Pop. 2005 (est):	714,167	0.1% Hawaiian	Kerry (D) 101,595	(36%)
Median income:	$33,893	3.3% Two+ races	**2000 Presidential Vote**	
Poverty status:	15.8%	0.1% Other	Bush (R) 135,761	(62%)
Military veterans:	14.2%	8.3% Hispanic Origin	Gore (D) 82,584	(38%)
			Other 1,338	(1%)
			Cook Partisan Voting Index: R +12	
Occupation	Blue collar: 23.6%	White collar: 60.6%	Gray collar: 15.8%	

Oklahoma City, like many state capitals, was not the spontaneous creation of commerce but the deliberate creation of government, sited in the geographic center of the state, on what turned out to be oil lands. Oil rigs were pumping crude on the grounds of the then-domeless Capitol until 1989; a derrick still stands sentinel outside the governor's window. The land here is browner and more eroded by creeks than the greener, rolling Oklahoma farmland farther east. From its center Oklahoma City has grown far out into the countryside, followed, as in so many southwestern cities, by expanding city limits so that it extends into four counties and three congressional districts and covers 621 square miles. Oklahoma City became the center of the nation's attention in April 1995, when a bomb destroyed the Alfred P. Murrah Federal Building, killing 168 and injuring more than 500. The profound grief has persisted here, but was channeled into the construction of the Oklahoma City National Memorial on the site of the blast, movingly dedicated exactly five years later in April 2000. In 2006, fueled by the oil boom and sales tax revenues, the city moved to rebuild its downtown with condos, a baseball stadium, and a canal through the Bricktown area. A setback came in November 2005 when General Motors announced the closure of its local assembly plant.

The 5th Congressional District includes most of Oklahoma County and Oklahoma City, all except a small section of the county including Midwest City and Tinker Air Force Base. Also included are Pottawatomie and Seminole Counties to the east. These two counties partake of the ancestral Democratic leanings of most of Oklahoma. But Oklahoma City is solidly Republican in state as well as national politics and Oklahoma County casts roughly 90% of the district's votes.

The new congresswoman from the 5th District is Mary Fallin, a Republican who battled in the primary but breezed in the general. She was born in Missouri but raised in Tecumseh, where both her mother and father were Democrats who served as mayor. After graduating from Oklahoma State University, she managed hotel properties and was a commercial real estate broker. In 1990, she was elected to the state House, where she focused on victims' rights and health care reform. She became lieutenant governor four years later, making her the first Republican and the first woman ever to hold the office in her state. During her three terms as lieutenant governor, she expanded her reach well beyond the office's traditional ribbon-cutting responsibilities. With a focus on economic development, she compiled a pro-business record and played a key role in bringing the right-to-work issue to a successful statewide vote; in 2005, she failed to get the Democratic-controlled Senate to overhaul the state's worker compensation system. Her rising star dimmed a bit in 1998 when, in the course of a bitter divorce, she was accused of having a sexual relationship with a state trooper assigned to her security detail; both of them denied the charge. Democrats used the scandal to attack Governor Frank Keating for refusing to criticize Fallin, even though he had slammed President Clinton's relationship with White House intern Monica Lewinsky.

In June 2005, Fallin announced that she would seek a fourth term as lieutenant governor. But she changed her mind when Ernest Istook announced three months later that he would relinquish the House seat and run for governor. She joined a wide-open race for Istook's seat as one of six Republican candidates. Her chief opponents were state Corporation Commissioner Denise Bode and Oklahoma City Mayor Mick Cornett. The two statewide elected officials, Fallin and Bode, aggressively raised money through the end of 2005; Bode was criticized for being a former aide to Senator David Boren, a Democrat. Cornett didn't file until May 2006, but his late entry altered the landscape. He was backed by Christian conservatives, who were pleased that he had removed gay-themed books from the children's section of public libraries. In the initial July balloting, Fallin led with 35% and Cornett's Oklahoma City base propelled him to a second-place finish with 24%. Bode came in third with 19%. Since no candidate won a majority, Fallin and Cornett competed in an August runoff. Resentful of Cornett's late entry just two months after his reelection as mayor, the four unsuccessful candidates quickly endorsed Fallin. Cornett, a former local TV news anchor, responded that his opponent was a career politician. The two candidates had few differences on issues; Cornett was more specific in his support of the Hutchison-Pence immigration plan and a national sales tax. Fallin, who had a big fundraising advantage, easily defeated Cornett, 63%-37%; Oklahoma County cast 93% of the vote and Fallin won 63% there. In this solidly Republican district, the general election was an afterthought. Against Oklahoma City physician David Hunter, Fallin won 60%-37%.

★ OREGON ★

O regon is an experimental commonwealth and laboratory of reform on the Pacific Rim, a maker of national trends. It is far removed from where most Americans live, but closer in touch with the rest of America than it sometimes appears: Within minutes after a tree branch brushed a power line in Oregon in August 1996, the entire western power grid shut down all the way from the Canadian border to San Diego, where the Republican National Convention was opening two days later. Oregon has led the nation with bike trails and Nike sneakers, light rail trams and Pendleton shirts, with assisted suicide and mail-in ballots. Oregon is an affluent high-tech civilization where one can still see much the same land and water—and rain—that Lewis and Clark saw in 1805 when they came down the Columbia River gorge, past the Willamette River and what is now Portland, to the vast Pacific Ocean.

This Oregon was settled by Americans when John Jacob Astor set up his fur trading post at Astoria in 1811 and when New England Yankees in the 1840s rode the Oregon Trail and floated down the Columbia to the well-watered Willamette Valley. In this remote land, nearly 2,000 miles

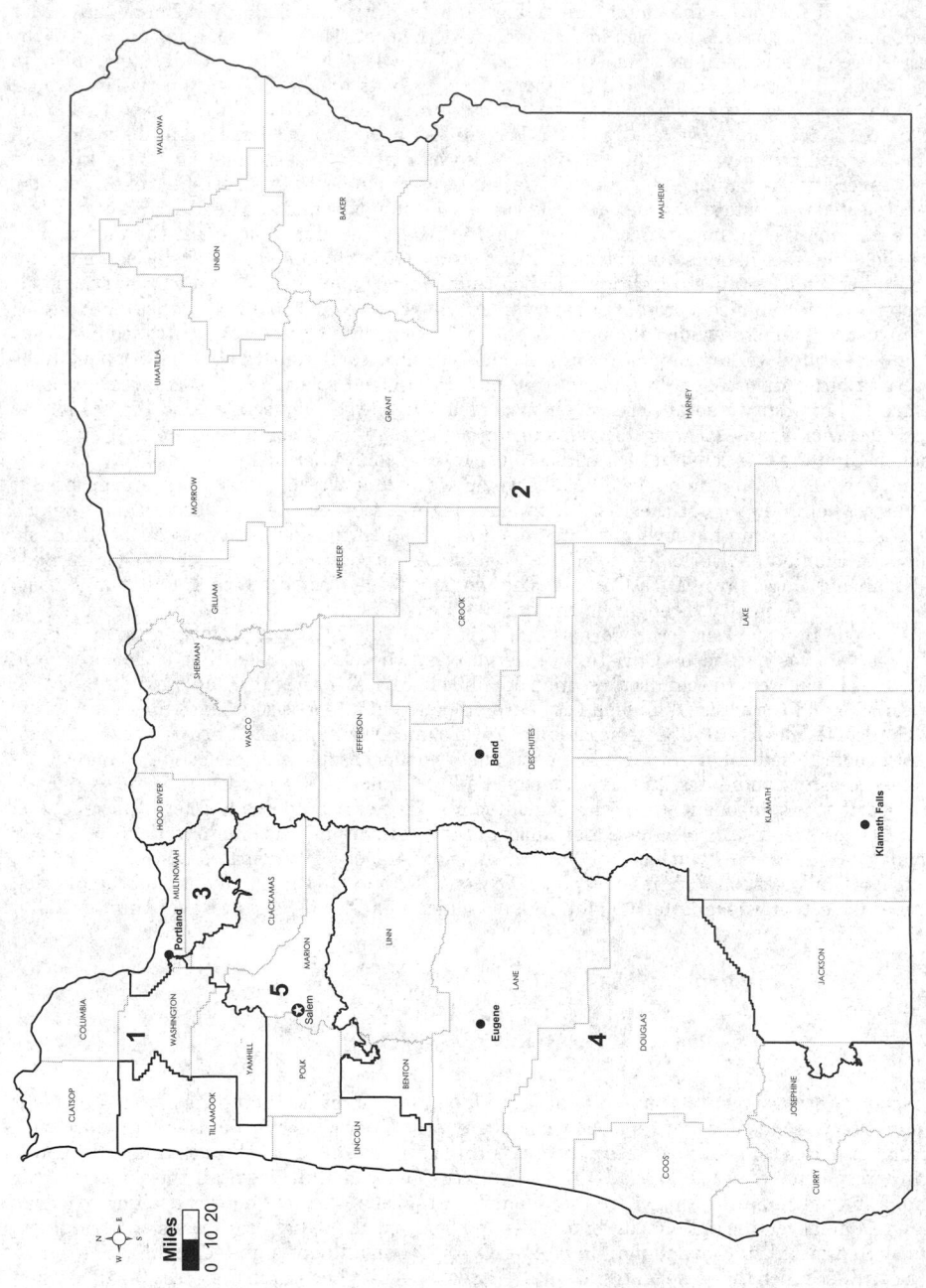

The Almanac of American Politics.
National Journal

Congressional district boundaries were first effective for 2002.

from the Mississippi River frontier and 700 miles from the small Mexican settlements in California, they built an orderly, productive society—a kind of western New England. It grew steadily over the years, with a few booms—when timber, until very recently its first industry, surged in 1900-10, during the war and after in the 1940s, and in the 1970s when home building skyrocketed and Oregon's natural environment began to be widely appreciated.

Newcomers find a state that has a distinctive culture. Founded by New England Yankees accustomed to town meeting government, Oregonians nearly a century ago pioneered in bringing the people closer to government: This was the first state to pass initiative and referendum, recall of elected officials, and election of U.S. senators by popular vote. It was also the first state to institute Labor Day, workmen's compensation and the eight-hour workday for women. In recent decades Oregon, founded by New England churchmen, has become America's most unchurched state, with the lowest rate of church membership, with large numbers of believers in astrology and New Age spiritualism; in the 2004 exit poll 28% of voters said they had no religion. To the innovations of this cultural left, the public voices of Oregon's big institutions, like those of New England, have been friendly. Oregon over the last two generations produced the first bottle-deposit law, decriminalized medical marijuana, legalized most abortions before *Roe v. Wade* and backed limits on development and use of property. It is one of two states that ban self-service gas (the other is New Jersey). It has had more ballot propositions than any other state—340 initiatives filed by citizens between 1902 and 2006, some 400 bills referred by the legislature; the November 2000 ballot had no less than 26 initiatives, more than any state since North Dakota in 1932, and the voters' guide ran 376 pages.

Oregon's population rose 26% between 1990 and 2004, the 11th fastest among the states, but not evenly. In the 1990s it thronged with newcomers in Portland's postmodern skyscrapers and high-tech offices in Silicon Forest to the west, and in the smaller cities and towns of the green Willamette Valley. More recently the fastest growth has been east of the Cascades, around Bend; land use restrictions have limited growth in Portland and its suburbs. Almost half of Oregon's population increase in 2000-05 was accounted for by Hispanics, who now account for 10% of the state's population, far more than blacks (2%), American Indians (1%) or Asians (3%). But lumber production was sharply curtailed in the 1990s (though Oregon is still number one in Christmas trees), and the high-tech bust of 2000-03 hit Oregon hard. Unemployment was the highest of any state, peaking at 8.1% in February 2002. State government revenues, heavily dependent on the income tax (Oregon has no sales tax) fell sharply, and political controversy ensued. In January 2003 voters rejected by a 54%-46% margin Measure 28, favored by retiring Governor John Kitzhaber and his newly elected successor Ted Kulongoski, which would have raised income taxes for three years. Kulongoski nonetheless got Democrats and moderate Republicans in the legislature to pass an $800 million tax increase later in the year. Anti-tax groups immediately sent out petitions, and the new taxes were submitted to the voters in February 2004; they were rejected 59%-41%.

Innovative health care policy has been an Oregon specialty. It legalized assisted suicide, in referenda in 1994 and 1997, to the point that doctors can prescribe but not administer lethal drugs; from 1997 to 2006, 292 people have killed themselves. Attorney General John Ashcroft angered many Oregonians by announcing in November 2001 that the federal government would prosecute doctors prescribing lethal drugs; a federal judge quickly blocked that, and the Supreme Court ruled 6–3 in January 2006 that the federal government had overstepped its powers. Another innovation was Kitzhaber's Oregon Health Plan that went into effect in 1994. State Medicaid officials draw up lists of some 700 medical treatments and rank them by effectiveness and importance to basic health. Then based on cost estimates, the state decides how many treatments it can afford, and draws a line—above the line, the state will pay; below, it won't. After voters rejected tax increases in referenda in 2003 and February 2004, the Oregon Health Plan took the brunt of the spending cuts.

Some issues arise unexpectedly. In March 2004 the Multnomah County Commission chair-woman ordered clerks to issue marriage licenses to same-sex couples. About 3,000 couples got licenses until a judge enjoined the clerks and referred the matter to the legislature. Attorney General Hardy Myers opined that the Oregon Supreme Court would probably find same-sex marriage constitutionally required. Governor Ted Kulongoski complained of being "blindsided" by the Multnomah licenses; he favored civil unions and said he hoped the issue would not divide the state. Across Oregon petitions were quickly circulated to put the issue on the ballot; a record 244,000 signatures were filed in July, far more than the 108,000 required. Local and national groups favoring same-sex marriage targeted Oregon for a full-fledged campaign; it was clearly the most culturally liberal of the 11 states voting on the issue in November 2004. In all $2.9 million was spent opposing this Measure 36, and very little in favor. It passed 57%-43%—a solid enough margin, but one indicating more widespread support than might have been expected for a position considered politically untenable not so long before.

If Oregon voters, by a relatively narrow margin in the national perspective, voted in 2004 to maintain the current definition of marriage, they also voted for a change in the longstanding trend of environmental policy in the state. Oregon pioneered state land use regulation and restriction; in 1973 it passed a state land use law that in many ways limited development and in the 1990s the Portland metro area sharply restricted growth and what many considered sprawl. These measures have been widely popular in Portland and the university towns and to a lesser extent in the suburbs. But environmental restrictions have raised hackles in non-metropolitan Oregon. Logging in the Pacific Northwest was largely wiped out because of restrictions imposed to protect the threatened spotted owl. This provoked sharp protests, and moves toward Republicans, in timber country. In 2001 the Interior Department cut off water to 1,000 farmers in the Klamath Basin, to protect the endangered and in any case unhappily named sucker fish. This became a major issue in the local media and helps explain why parched eastern Oregon, which once elected the Democratic chairman of the Ways and Means Committee, has become as heavily Republican as Portland is Democratic. In 2004 the discontent seemed to run statewide. State land use law prevented landowners from building houses on land without farming it, even if the land is unsuitable for farming. An aggrieved landowner sparked a petition drive that put on the November ballot Measure 37, requiring state and local governments to excuse property owners from rules enacted after they bought the land or compensate them for complying. In something of a surprise it passed 61%-39%, carrying even Portland's Multnomah County. It seems likely to make many land use restrictions nugatory, since state and local governments are not likely to be able to afford compensation for loss of value they have been happy to inflict on landowners.

Is there some common thread in Oregonians' votes on ballot issues? One common thread seems to be a regard for personal autonomy and a readiness to discard traditional rules and ways of doing things. Another seems to be a desire for putting some limits on the ability of officeholders to spend public money and to impose costs on citizens. Voting on most of these measures has followed similar patterns, with Portland and the university towns of Eugene and Corvallis taking liberal positions and counties east of the Cascades and outside the metro area taking more conservative stands.

These cultural and regional differences have been reflected increasingly in Oregon's partisan politics. In the 1980s and 1990s, the gulf between liberal Portland and Multnomah County and conservative eastern and southern Oregon widened and since 2000 it has been a chasm—and has left the state as a whole fairly close to evenly divided. In 2004 John Kerry carried Multnomah County 72%-27% and George W. Bush carried the counties east of the Cascades 63%-36%. The balance has generally tilted toward the Democrats, but not always. Oregon voted for Michael Dukakis in 1988 and for Bill Clinton twice. But Clinton's margin was smaller in 1996 than 1992, and in 2000 Al Gore won here by only 47.0%-46.5%; one reason was that Ralph Nader won 4% here in 1996 and 5% in 2000. In 2004 Nader was not on the ballot, and his votes seem to have gone to Kerry, who carried the state 51%-47%. Starting in 1986, Oregon has elected only Democratic governors, though only once by a wide margin; Kulongoski was reelected in 2006, but by only 51%-43%, an unimpressive showing in what was a Democratic year nationally. From 1994 to 2000 it elected Republican legislatures, but Democrats captured the state Senate in 2004 and the state House in 2006.

In 1998 Oregonians voted by referendum to hold all elections by mail. So there are no polls open on Election Day; voters have until that night to get their ballots to the election clerk. Proponents of mail-in ballots argue that they increase the percentage of eligibles who vote, which has always been high in Oregon anyway, and they give voters time to read over and think about the numerous ballot initiatives. Opponents fear they increase the possibility of fraud; Oregon has no statewide registry, so people might be able to cast votes in multiple counties.

The People

		Race/Ethnic Origin			Military veterans: 388,990 (15.1%)	
Pop. 2006 (est):	3,700,758	2,857,616	83.5%	White	WWII: 20.6%	Korea: 13.0%
Pop. 2000:	3,421,399	53,325	1.6%	Black	Vietnam: 33.9%	Gulf War: 8.5%
Pop. 1990:	2,842,321	100,333	2.9%	Asian	**Most populous cities (2006):**	
Change 1990-2000:	Up 20.4%	40,130	1.2%	Native Am.	1. Portland	537,081
% of U.S. total:	1.2%	7,398	0.2%	Hawaiian	2. Salem	152,239
Pop. rank:	28th of 50	82,733	2.4%	Two+ races	3. Eugene	146,356
Area size:	98,381 sq. mi.	4,550	0.1%	Other	4. Gresham	97,105
State Native:	45.3%	275,314	8.0%	Hisp. Origin	5. Beaverton	89,643
Non-citizen:	5.6%	**Ancestry**				
Language		German: 14.8%		English: 9.5%	Urban population: 78.7%	
English: 86.7%	Spanish: 6.7%	Irish: 8.6%		USA: 4.6%	Rural population: 21.3%	
Other Eur.: 3.5%		Norwegian: 3.1%				

Education

		Work Sector		Legislature	
H.S. Grad:	85.1%	Private: 76.3%	Govt: 14.4%	Senate	17 D 11 R 2 I
College Grad:	25.1%	Self: 8.9%	Family: 0.4%	House	31 D 29 R
Industry		Unemployment: 6.5%		Legislative Term Limits: No	
Agri: 3.2%	Con: 6.9%	**Household Income**		**Registered Voters**	
Fin: 6.1%	Info: 2.4%	<15k: 15.1%	15-35k: 27.3%	D: 763,301	(38.8%)
Mfg: 19.1%	Prof: 28.1%	35-50k: 17.7%	50-100k: 29.9%	R: 700,950	(35.7%)
Public: 4.4%	Trade: 16.5%	100-150k: 6.5%	>150k: 3.5%	O: 500,829	(25.5%)
Other: 13.2%		Median: $40,916			
Occupation		Poverty status: 11.6%			
Blue collar: 23.9%	White collar: 59.1%	**Home Value**			
Gray collar: 17.0%		<50k: 7.8%	50-100k: 16.5%	100-200k: 49.9%	200-300k: 16.2%
		300-500k: 7.2%	>500k: 2.4%	Median: $145,800	

Presidential politics   Oregon was once the most Republican state in the West, voting for Thomas Dewey over Harry Truman in 1948; in the 1980s and early 1990s it was one of the most Democratic. Now it seems more evenly balanced, significantly less Democratic than California, much less Republican than the Rocky Mountain states. Oregon was the closest West Coast state in 2000, when it backed Al Gore by only a 47.0%-46.5% margin. It remained a target state throughout the 2004 race, although ad volume started going down after mid-October when voters started mailing their ballots in. It got plenty of campaign appearances; on August 13 both George W. Bush and John Kerry held rallies in Portland.

Oregon once had an important presidential primary, scheduled in May. In 1948 Oregon ended Harold Stassen's serious presidential prospects, when he lost 52%-48% to Dewey; in 1968 Oregon gave Robert Kennedy his only defeat when it voted 44%-38% for Eugene McCarthy. Oregon in

2004 Presidential Vote

Kerry (D)	943,163	(51%)
Bush (R)	866,831	(47%)
Badnarik (Lib)	7,260	(0%)
Other	19,528	(1%)

2004 Democratic Presidential Primary

Kerry (D)	289,804	(79%)
Kucinich (D)	60,019	(16%)
Miscellaneous	10,150	(3%)
LaRouche (D)	8,571	(2%)

2000 Presidential Vote

Gore (D)	720,342	(47%)
Bush (R)	713,577	(47%)
Nader (Green)	77,357	(5%)
Other	22,692	(1%)

those days was part of a West Coast campaign swing, just before the California primary; at a time when campaigners were not used to flying all over the country they, like National Football League teams in the 1950s, scheduled West Coast contests together to minimize travel time. For 1992 and 1996, Oregon scheduled its primary for Super Tuesday in March, but it was overshadowed by bigger contests in the South. In 2000 and 2004 the primary was held again in May. That, of course, was well after the parties' nominees were determined. But in 2004 Ohio Congressman Dennis Kucinich spent four weeks campaigning in Oregon, hoping to inspire a New Age, Department of Peace, single payer health system constituency. Kerry beat him nonetheless by a 79%-16% margin.

Congressional districting

110th Congress Lineup	
4 D	1 R
109th Congress Lineup	
4 D	1 R

Oregon's latest congressional map looks a lot like the one it replaced. This was not what the Republican-controlled legislature originally set out to do. Republican redistricters intended to alter the boundaries of the marginal 1st District by shifting solidly Democratic western Multnomah County (1st District Congressman David Wu's political base) from the 1st to the 3d District—an attempt to pack Democratic voters into the 3d while making the 1st more competitive for a Republican challenger. But in June 2001 Democratic Governor John Kitzhaber vetoed the Republican plan. In the inevitable lawsuit, a Multnomah County judge in October chose the Democratic alternative, saying it was less disruptive and that it better preserved communities of interest: judicial incumbent protection. The decision left the old map largely in place with the exception of a few Multnomah County neighborhoods that were added to the 5th District. Oregon seems likely to gain an additional House seat in the reapportionment following the 2010 Census. If Democrats continue to hold the governorship and both houses of the legislature, they would probably try to create another safe Democratic district; that may prove difficult since the areas of the state growing fastest tend to be Republican.

Governor

Ted Kulongoski (D)

Elected 2002, term expires Jan. 2011, 2d term; b. Nov. 5, 1940, Missouri; home, Portland; U. of MO, B.A. 1967, J.D. 1970; Catholic; married (Mary).

Military Career: Marine Corps, 1959-63.

Elected Office: OR House of Reps., 1974-78; OR Senate, 1978-82; OR Atty. Gen., 1992-96; OR Sup. Ct., 1996-2001.

Professional Career: Practicing atty., 1971-87; OR Insurance Commissioner, 1982-92.

Office: 160 State Capitol, 900 Court St., Salem, 97301, 503-378-3111; Fax: 503-378-6827; Web site: www.governor.state.or.us.

Election Results

2006 general	Ted Kulongoski (D)	699,786	(51%)
	Ron Saxton (R)	589,748	(43%)
	Mary Starrett (CNP)	50,229	(4%)
	Other	39,892	(3%)
2006 primary	Ted Kulongoski (D)	170,944	(54%)
	Jim Hill (D)	92,439	(29%)
	Pete Sorenson (D)	51,346	(16%)
	Other	4,448	(1%)
2002 general	Ted Kulongoski (D)	618,004	(49%)
	Kevin Mannix (R)	581,785	(46%)
	Tom Cox (Lib)	57,760	(5%)

Ted Kulongoski (pronounced *koo-lun-GAW-ski*), elected governor of Oregon in 2002, comes from as humble a background as any governor. He was born in rural Missouri; after his father died he was raised by nuns in a Catholic boys' home from age 4 to 14. He joined the Marine Corps after high school and later saved enough money working in a steel mill and as a truck driver to attend the University of Missouri; he graduated from college and law school there at 26 and 29. He moved to Eugene, Oregon, and practiced labor law, representing mostly labor unions; as a legislative staffer he helped write a law giving public employee unions collective bargaining rights. He was elected to the Oregon House in 1974 and the Oregon Senate in 1978; he was regarded as a champion of labor unions. In 1980 he ran against Senator Bob Packwood and held him to a 52%-44% victory in a Republican year. In 1982 he ran against Governor Victor Atiyeh and lost by the humiliating margin of 61%-36%—the last time a Republican was elected governor here. He moved to Portland and practiced law. In 1987 he was appointed Insurance Commissioner by Governor Neil Goldschmidt and helped broker his workmen's compensation changes in 1990, which earned him resentment from some unions. In 1992, after a tough Democratic primary, he was elected attorney general; in 1996 he was elected to the Oregon Supreme Court. In 2001 he resigned to run for governor.

The overriding issue facing state government at the time was the budget shortfall which by November 2001was estimated at $720 million in a $16 billion budget. Oregon's revenue stream is especially volatile, because the state has no sales tax and relies heavily on the income tax; in addition, Measure 5, passed in 1990, limits property tax increases, so the state provides 80% of school funding. Budget problems kept making the news during the 2002 campaign cycle; altogether there were five special sessions of the legislature and constant news about shortfalls and cuts.

Of the six major candidates, three Democrats and three Republicans, Kulongoski was the best known: He had appeared on the statewide ballot four times in the preceding 22 years and had served in the legislative, executive and judicial branches of state government. He argued that he had the experience to solve the state's major problems—unemployment, the budget, school financing, the state employees' pension fund. Outgoing Governor John Kitzhaber and the preceding two Democratic governors, Barbara Roberts and Goldschmidt, quickly endorsed him. Against former state Treasurer Jim Hill and former Multnomah County Commission Chairman Bev Stein, Kulongoski depicted himself as the more moderate candidate. With late contributions from public employees unions, he outspent the others and won the May 2002 primary with 49% of the vote, to 26% for Hill and 22% for Stein.

The winner of the Republican primary was Kevin Mannix, a Democratic state representative from 1988 to 1996 and Democratic candidate for attorney general in 1996. He switched parties in 1997 and was elected to the state Senate as a Republican in 1998 and came close to winning as the Republican candidate for attorney general in 2000. Mannix was a prolific drafter of legislation—135 of his bills became law in 10 years—and a sponsor of ballot initiatives—his parental consent for abortion lost in 1992 but three tough on crime measures won in 1996. He ran as a "populist Republican," pledged to oppose new taxes and solidly opposed to abortion.

After the primaries, Kulongoski called Mannix "divisive" and criticized him for using the abortion issue in the primary. Mannix replied that he wouldn't focus on cultural issues as governor. The campaign focused more on fiscal issues. In September the legislature made more cuts in planned spending and authorized a January 2003 special referendum, on a three-year increase in the top income tax from 9% to 9.8%. Kulongoski supported the proposal, reluctantly he said; Mannix opposed it, and said he could make enough cuts to make it unnecessary. This Measure 28 was rejected 54%-46%.Kulongoski called for doubling car registration fees to $30 (which would still be the lowest in the nation) to pay for repairing bridges, and he said that localities should pay a greater share for education and that he would try to develop a consensus for a permanent, stable funding base for them, with everything on the table including a sales tax—long verboten in Oregon. He called for all children to be covered by the Oregon Health Plan and added that that would mean removing some adults now covered. He opposed the Bush forest plan, favored Vermont-style civil unions, and criticized Mannix for voting for a cigarette tax increase as part of a budget package. Mannix campaigned with gusto and good humor and seemed more articulate in debate; the tax issue was one that could unite Republicans and brought large contributions in the last weeks.

By all measures—party label, experience and familiarity, the positions on abortion—Kulongoski seemed to be an easy winner. But on election night Mannix was ahead in the count. In Oregon voters cast their votes by mail or at election clerks' offices, and have up to Election Day to get them to the clerks. It takes time to process and count the votes cast on Election Day, and the clerks' offices in big counties took time to count them. The big counties, especially Multnomah (Portland) and Lane (Eugene), took several days, and it was not until Wednesday evening that it was clear that Kulongoski was well ahead and Mannix conceded. When all the votes were in, Kulongoski won 49%-46%. Kulongoski carried only eight of 36 counties—Multnomah, the counties containing the state's two big universities, three on the Pacific coast and two on the Columbia River on either side of Portland.

Kulongoski had a stormy first term, marked by a recession that hit Oregon harder than almost any other state. After the rejection of Measure 28, spending had to be cut near the end of the two-year budget cycle, and some public schools had to shorten their school year. In May 2003 Multnomah County, putting its money where its mouth was, voted an income tax of its own, the first local income tax in the state. In August 2003 Kulongoski persuaded a majority of the divided legislature—Republicans had a majority in the House, the Senate was 15-15—to vote for a tax increase. Anti-tax increase groups quickly got out petitions and put Measure 30 on the ballot in February 2004. Kulongoski favored the increase but avoided full-throated support. This time the tax increase was rejected 59%-41%; even Multnomah County voters, apparently feeling taxed enough, voted against. Kulongoski let the scheduled $545 million cuts, phased in this time over the remaining 17 months of the budget cycle, go into effect; the Oregon Health Plan was particularly hard hit.

On other issues, in July 2003 Kulongoski got the legislature to pass a 10-year bill to borrow $2.5 billion to repair and replace bridges and roads; by December 2004 the state found that half the bridges were in good shape and the money could be used on road projects. In July 2003 he signed a law requiring the state pension plan to invest $100 million in Oregon venture capital projects and another levying a 1% lodging tax to pay for tourism promotion.

Kulongoski's political career was intertwined with that of Neil Goldschmidt, elected mayor of Portland in 1972 at 32, then Jimmy Carter's Transportation Secretary; he was elected governor in 1986 and appointed Kulongoski, his political career then in limbo, to a top post and relied on him heavily on his key issue, workmen's compensation. Goldschmidt, prominent in Portland civic life in the 1990s, had supported Kulongoski in his 1992, 1996 and 2002 campaigns. In November 2003 Kulongoski appointed Goldschmidt head of the state Board of Higher Education. It soon became a controversial appointment. It was disclosed that SAIF, the state-owned workmen's comp insurer, had paid Goldschmidt $1 million in lobbying fees and failed to report that. Also, Goldschmidt had agreed to head the board of PGE, the Portland utility, on completion of its acquisition by Texas Pacific. Then, on April 26, 2004, Goldschmidt abruptly resigned. The reason soon appeared. On May 6, after *Willamette Week* put the story on its website, Goldschmidt admitted to the Portland *Oregonian* that he had had an affair with a 14-year-old girl in 1975 and 1976 when he was mayor of Portland. This was a felony, though the statute of limitations had long ago passed. Kulongoski said he "had no knowledge" of the charge, but a Goldschmidt aide said he had told Kulongoski several times about it in the 1990s. Kulongoski said that the aide had only said that Goldschmidt had fathered an illegitimate child and said he felt that Goldschmidt had "betrayed" him. The story did not end there. Goldschmidt's wife Diana Goldschmidt, as a member of the Oregon Investment Council, had in October 2003 approved investing $300 million in state funds in Texas Pacific's acquisition of PGE. She said that she voted before Goldschmidt was approached by Texas Pacific to become involved in the deal, but in September 2004 Kulongoski demanded she resign and, when she refused, he fired her.

Going into his 2006 reelection campaign, Kulongoski looked to be one of the nation's most vulnerable governors. His job approval ratings were below 50%. He had followed a moderate course in an attempt to come to terms with a Republican House and a Democratic Senate but succeeded mainly in rousing opposition on both sides. Within his own party, there was considerable dissatisfaction with his performance, particularly from some labor groups, which resented his early efforts to reduce pension benefits of public employees and freeze state worker salaries. Republicans pointed to his support for two statewide income tax increases that were defeated by Oregon voters. Kulongoski had made some progress on creating jobs and created goodwill by attending the funeral of almost every Oregon soldier who died in the Iraq war but candidates on the left and the right were lining up against him.

Kulongoski got a break in January 2006 when his Democratic predecessor John Kitzhaber, a one-time political ally, announced he would not challenge him in the May primary. The state economy was also in better shape than when Kulongoski took office. But he still had serious opposition on the left from former State Treasurer Jim Hill, who finished second in the 2002 primary for governor, and Lane County Commissioner Pete Sorenson, both of whom who criticized him not doing enough on education and health care. Hill went so far as to refer to Kulongoski as a "bad Democrat." Kulongoski, however, had momentum from a successful April special session where he signed off on legislation that handed out stiffer penalties to sexual predators and "gap" funding authorization for the Portland public schools while filling a $136 million hole in the Department of Human Services budget. The next month, with Hill and Sorenson splitting the vote against him, Kulongoski won a low turnout affair with 54%, carrying all but two small counties and winning by 2–1 margins in Portland's Multnomah County and in suburban Portland's Washington and Clackamas Counties. Hill finished second with 29%, followed by Sorenson with 16%.

The nominee from the bruising Republican primary, which had a high turnout relative to party registration, was Ron Saxton, who had lost to Mannix in the 2002 primary but returned to defeat him in 2006. A former Portland School Board member, Saxton had run as a moderate in 2002 but this time he made a play for conservative votes, advocating tough immigration policies and courting abortion opponents on issues such as a late-term abortion ban and parental notification legislation. He did not have a clear shot at Kulongoski in the general election: state Senator Ben Westlund, a Republican who re-registered as an independent, announced in February he was running too. "I'm running against two Republicans, is how I look at it," Kulongoski said, though Westlund took some social policy positions that had appeal to Democrats.

Kulongoski talked about stabilizing school funding, providing more health insurance coverage for children and increasing the state's use of renewable energy. In early June, he generated controversy by suggesting that the state suspend its income tax "kicker" law, which sent rebate checks to taxpayers when there were excess revenues, and instead spend the money on schools, health care and other needs; he later backed away from that idea but did not rule out various tax increases. Saxton said "our views of government could not be more different" and insisted that the state had enough money for essential services. He called for tax cuts and more efficiency in state government. On the environment, there were also clear differences. Kulongoski touted his clean car initiative, similar to California's aggressive move to reduce car emissions; Saxton wanted to overturn it. Saxton said that wildfires were the most pressing environmental problem, an issue he said was exacerbated by Kulongoski policies. The governor wanted more funding for the state Department of Environmental Quality, which had experienced years of budget cuts; Saxton questioned whether DEQ deserved an increase and voiced concern over whether the agency had always been fair and even-handed in its regulatory approach to businesses.

In August, Westlund dropped out of the race, saying he could not win and did not want to be a spoiler candidate—a sign that Kulongoski had made considerable progress toward uniting Democrats behind his candidacy. In October, he endorsed Kulongoski and campaigned with him across the state. Kulongoski ended up winning 51%-43%. He carried just 12 of 36 counties and lost everything east of the Cascades but he won 68%-25% in Portland's Multnomah County, enough to power him to victory. Kulongoski won by 110,000 votes statewide; his 112,000-vote margin in Multnomah County made all the difference.

This was an unimpressive victory in what was a Democratic year nationally, but it hardly mattered. Republicans remained shut out of the governor's office, having last won it in 1982. Democrats captured the state House, giving them control of the governorship and the legislature for the first time in 16 years. Kulongoski quickly took advantage and in 2007 approved an 18% increase in K-12 education spending, funding for 100 more state troopers, domestic partnerships for same sex couples and the state's first "Rainy Day Fund." The session was widely described as the state's "greenest" in decades, with an expansion of Oregon's bottle bill to require deposits on bottled water containers and a plan to require utilities to generate a quarter of their electricity from renewable sources by 2025.

Senior Senator

Ron Wyden (D)

Elected Jan. 1996, seat up 2010, 2d full term; b. May 3, 1949, Wichita, KS; home, Portland; Stanford U., B.A. 1971, U. of OR, J.D. 1974; Jewish; married (Nancy Bass).

Elected Office: U.S. House of Reps., 1980-96.

Professional Career: Co–Dir. & Co–Founder, OR Gray Panthers, 1974-80; Dir., OR Legal Svcs. for the Elderly, 1977-79; Prof. of Gerontology, U. of OR, 1976, Portland St. U., 1979, U. of Portland, 1980.

DC Office: 223 DSOB, 20510, 202-224-5244; Fax: 202-228-2717; Web site: wyden.senate.gov.

State Offices: Bend, 541-330-9142; Eugene, 541-431-0229; LaGrande, 541-962-7691; Medford, 541-858-5122; Portland, 503-326-7525; Salem, 503-589-4555.

Committees: *Aging (Special)* (2d of 11 D). *Budget* (3d of 12 D). *Energy & Natural Resources* (4th of 12 D): Public Lands & Forests (Chmn.); Energy; Water & Power. *Finance* (7th of 11 D): Taxation & IRS Oversight & Long-Term Growth; Energy, Natural Resources & Infrastructure; Health Care. *Intelligence (Select)* (3d of 8 D).

Group Ratings

	ADA	ACLU	AFS	LCV	ITIC	NTU	COC	ACU	CFG	FRC
2006	100	92	100	100	75	13	42	8	0	0
2005	95	—	100	95	—	14	33	4	9	—

National Journal Ratings

	2005 LIB	—	2005 CONS	2006 LIB	—	2006 CONS
Economic	95%	—	0%	87%	—	0%
Social	77%	—	18%	80%	—	14%
Foreign	65%	—	34%	79%	—	16%

Key Votes of the 109th Congress

1. Bar ANWR Drilling	Y	5. Confirm Samuel Alito	N	9. Limit Interstate Abortion	N
2. FY06 Spending Curb	N	6. Path to Citizenship	Y	10. CAFTA	Y
3. Estate Tax Repeal	N	7. Bar Same Sex Marriage	N	11. Urge Iraq Withdrawal	Y
4. Raise Minimum Wage	Y	8. Stem Cell Research $	Y	12. Provide Detainee Rights	Y

Election Results

2004 general	Ron Wyden (D)	1,128,728	(63%)	($2,817,706)
	Al King (R)	565,254	(32%)	($32,930)
	Other	86,568	(5%)	
2004 primary	Ron Wyden (D)	unopposed		
1998 general	Ron Wyden (D)	682,425	(61%)	($2,866,368)
	John Lim (R)	377,739	(34%)	($413,187)
	Other	57,583	(5%)	

Prior Winning Percentages: 1996 (48%); 1994 House (73%); 1992 House (77%); 1990 House (81%); 1988 House (99%); 1986 House (86%); 1984 House (72%); 1982 House (78%); 1980 House (72%)

Ron Wyden, Oregon's senior senator, was first elected to the House in 1980 and to the Senate in January 1996. Wyden grew up in California, graduated from Stanford, and came to Oregon to attend the University of Oregon Law School. After graduating in 1974 he founded the Gray Panthers, an advocacy group for the elderly; his first foray into electoral politics was sponsoring a successful referendum reducing the price of dentures. In 1980, at 31, he challenged an incumbent in the heavily Democratic 3d District, which covers most of Portland, and won the primary 60%-40%. Wyden has a genius for coming up with sensible-sounding ideas no one else has thought of and a knack for making the counter-intuitive political alliances that proved helpful in passing unfamiliar measures through the House.

Wyden's way to the Senate was opened by the Senate Ethics Committee's recommendation in September 1995 that Oregon Senator Bob Packwood be expelled. Wyden, who had long been eyeing the seat, decided to run in the January 1996 special election to replace him—the first election Oregon conducted by mail-in ballot. With his home base in Portland, whose TV stations cover most of the state, he had greater name identification than any competitor. But he had spirited opposition in the primary from Eugene-based Congressman Peter DeFazio, who carried his own district overwhelmingly, holding Wyden to a 50%-44% win. The Republican nomination was won by state Senate President Gordon Smith, a frozen vegetable tycoon from eastern Oregon who ultimately spent $2 million of his own money. Most polls had the race in a dead heat and there were many negative ads; toward the end, Wyden said he would pull his negative spots. Wyden picked up strength the week before the January 30 deadline and won 48%-47%.

In the Senate, Wyden continued some of his crusades from the House. In April 1997 he and Republican Charles Grassley called for disclosure of the names of senators who place "holds" on legislation—a cause Wyden started working on in 1992 when a bill he backed was killed in the Senate by anonymous holds. Wyden and Grassley persevered, and have made slow progress. In March 1999 Trent Lott and Tom Daschle unveiled a new procedure: A senator putting a hold on a bill must inform the sponsor, the committee chairman and the two party leaders. In March 2006, the Senate voted 84-13 on a Wyden-Grassley amendment requiring senators to announce their opposition to legislation or a nominee in the Congressional Record within three days. The provision was included in the Senate version of the lobbying reform bill that passed in January 2007.

Another Wyden cause was the Internet. He and California Congressman Christopher Cox sponsored the three-year ban on Internet taxation that passed in October 1998. In 2001 they sought to extend it permanently, but also to set up a procedure to allow states to tax Internet sales if they adopt uniform sales tax rules, with one sales tax rate per state, and provide a means to file and remit sales taxes electronically; the ban was extended until 2005. In 2003 he worked with George Allen to extend it further; in 2004, the Senate passed a four-year extension that grandfathered in pre-1998 taxes and permitted states to apply telephone taxes to voice over Internet protocol (VOIP) services. The bill was signed in December 2004. Wyden has also worked on Internet privacy issues and on anti-spam ("Can-Spam") legislation which passed in 2003; as spam purveyors evolved, he moved to restrict spam messages over text-messaging systems and cell phones and to require notification and permission by distributors of spyware and adware. In 2006 he backed the "net neutrality" legislation which would bar Internet service providers from giving preference to websites which pay fees; when this was rejected in the Senate Commerce Committee, Wyden, with disclosure, put a hold on it.

In 2001 and 2002 he was chairman of the Science, Technology and Space Subcommittee. He has sought to require federal agencies to systematically develop checklists to fight cyberterrorism and encouraged the development of a volunteer force of programmers and engineers to reconstruct networks damaged by emergencies like September 11. He has called for changes in the 1996 telecom act. He was a sponsor of the campaign finance law provision requiring candidates to appear in their television ads, and has sought to extend that requirement to print, Internet and phone message ads.

On health care, Wyden voted against Oregon's assisted suicide law, but has defended it, threatening to filibuster against Don Nickles's attempts in 1999 and 2000 to repeal it and attacking Attorney General John Ashcroft's decision in 2001 to prosecute doctors who prescribe lethal drugs for terminally ill patients. That decision was challenged in court, and Wyden attended oral argument at the Supreme Court in October 2005. In January 2006 the Court ruled 6–3 against the federal government. But, as Wyden said after the oral argument, "I have long expected that I would have to go back to the floor of the Senate at some point to protect Oregon's right to make that choice." He also worked hard to get a waiver for the Oregon Health Plan and to bring the abortifacient RU-486 to the United States. And he has sponsored a bill with grants to states which decide to shift to vote by mail. He has praised FCC Chairman Kevin Martin's proposal for a "family-friendly tier" to be required on cable TV. "Why should sports fans and movie fans be treated any different from families and children?" In March 2006 he and Lindsey Graham proposed that senators be prohibited from raising and receiving campaign funds for the first 4 1/2 years of their terms, unless an opponent raises $100,000 or an issue advocacy group runs ads against them; this is one bipartisan proposal that got nowhere. In April 2006 Wyden held the floor for nearly five hours to get a vote on his amendment to bar the government from reducing oil royalties when the price of crude is over $55; at the time government regulations prohibited reduction of royalties when the price is over $35.86.

Health care has been an issue Wyden has addressed since before he was elected to Congress. He was one of 11 Senate Democrats to vote for the 2003 Medicare/prescription drug law, in the face of criticism from many Democrats and former allies. "It was clearly the toughest call I've ever had to make. It wasn't a bill I would have written. But I thought it was the right thing to do to get started." He got amendments creating his national commission to look at health care and to extend a managed care option for rural Oregon; he later worked to prevent Portland from becoming one of the markets selected for competition between Medicare and managed care and, with Olympia Snowe, sponsored a bill to allow HHS to negotiate prices with pharmaceutical companies. In July 2006 Wyden and Gordon Smith sponsored a bill for pilot projects for plans designed to combine universal coverage and private insurance; one would shield individuals from catastrophic out-of-pocket costs, another would help those with insurance but also with out-of-pocket costs over $10,500. In December 2006 Wyden announced a more comprehensive approach, a bill for a centrally financed system of private health insurance for all. Individuals would be required to buy private health insurance, with subsidies for low earners; Medicaid and employer-provided insurance would be abolished. Wyden hailed George W. Bush's State of the Union proposal to end the disparate treatment of employer-provided and individual-acquired health insurance. He canvassed senators of both parties and in February 2006 unveiled a letter from 10 senators, five from each party, calling for an end to preferential treatment of employer-provided insurance and for universal coverage through private insurance policies.

Wyden has also been trying to put together a bipartisan approach to taxes. He notes that since the last basic tax restructuring, in 1986, there have been some 14,000 changes in the tax code; and he notes that he, like Bill Bradley, one of the authors of the 1986 measure, was a basketball player in college (while conceding that Bradley had a more distinguished career in the sport). In December 2005, Congressman Rahm Emanuel joined Wyden on a bill they called the Fair Flat Tax, with three individual rates and a 35% corporate income tax rate with most deductions and credits eliminated.

Capital gains would be taxed at the individual rate rather than 15% and the measure would retain the home mortgage deduction and make it available to non-itemizers. In December 2006 he and Republican Larry Craig advanced a somewhat different Cleanse the Code initiative, calling for simplification, transparency and certainty. "It's very clear that the tax system is a monstrosity and abomination," he said, and consulted with Bradley and White House domestic advisor Al Hubbard.

Wyden voted against the Iraq war resolution. In July 2003 he criticized the Bush administration for using "any snippet of information to justify the decision they had made." He serves on the Intelligence Committee and in December 2004 was criticized for revealing allegedly classified information when he publicly referred to a "major acquisition program" that was "too necessary" and "unnecessary." A day later, *The Washington Post* said the program was a $9.5 billion spy satellite system; Wyden said his words were authorized by committee Chairman Pat Roberts.

Ten months after Wyden was elected, his opponent Gordon Smith won the state's other Senate seat: The first time two senators were elected who had run against each other in the same year. With the departure of Packwood and Mark Hatfield, Oregon had lost 56 years of Senate seniority and had gained two senators who everyone expected would be bitter enemies. But instead they became friends and collaborators. They have held dozens of town meetings together across Oregon and have met for lunch every Thursday with their chiefs of staff. After losing a bet with Smith, Wyden answered phones for him: "Senator Smith's office; this is Ron Wyden."

As chairman of the Forestry and Public Lands Subcommittee in 2001 and 2002, Wyden was thrust into national and local controversies. After the huge forest fires in the summer of 2002, he worked with Dianne Feinstein on a compromise national forest thinning plan. This resulted in passage of the Healthy Forests Restoration Act in 2003. Oregon Republican Congressman Greg Walden's similar bill passed the House in May 2003, and Wyden and Feinstein agreed to continuing limits on clear-cutting, limiting judicial review to those who participated in the initial process, reviewing injunctions after 45 days and requiring judicial decisions within 100 days. He added $760 million for thinning forests. Some environmental groups were unhappy, but this was popular in rural Oregon. In November 2006, noting the recession in the hardwood industry, he called for an investigation of China's timber subsidies, fraudulent labeling and illegal logging of hardwood.

His stands on many issues seem related to Oregon interests. He supported permanent repeal of the estate tax, pointing out the problems it caused for family businesses that own large stands of timber. In 2003 he worked to block welfare act reauthorization because it didn't extend the 1996 waiver for Oregon's welfare-to-work program which counts mental health treatment and drug treatment toward working hours. In November 2003 he filibustered the energy bill, because he said it did little to protect Oregon and Washington consumers from the double-digit increases in electricity rates seen in 2000 and 2001. Using a hold, in June 2006 he got into the fisheries bill a provision for federal disaster relief for Klamath River salmon fishermen after the federal government reduced catch limits and fishing days.

Wyden portrays himself as a bipartisan problem solver. "Look at my record. My record is based on the proposition that if you want to get anything done, it's got to be bipartisan. But sometimes you have to stand alone." He continues to hold open meetings in all 36 counties every year—a bit daring for a Democrat, perhaps, in a state where in 2004 George W. Bush carried 28 of them, with percentages ranging up to 79%—and even adds half a dozen high school forums. All this has paid off at election time. In November 1998 Wyden was elected to a full term by a 61%-34% margin. For his 2004 campaign Wyden raised $5 million but spent only $3.1 million of it; he donated $500,000 to other Democratic Senate campaigns. His Republican opponent was Klamath County rancher Al King, a former county GOP chairman who, while websurfing at a friend's house the day before the filing deadline, noticed that no well-known names had filed to run against Wyden and mouse-clicked his name in together with the filing fee; he won the six-candidate primary with 35% of the vote. Wyden won 63%-32%, carrying 33 of 36 counties; the three counties he lost have 26% of Oregon's land area but cast only 1% of its votes.

For nearly 10 years, Wyden had fought for a seat on the Finance Committee; in January 2005 he finally got it. Gordon Smith also serves on the committee, only the third time in history two senators from the same state have served on Finance.

Junior Senator

Gordon Smith (R)

Elected 1996, seat up 2008, 2d term; b. May 25, 1952, Pendleton; home, Pendleton; Brigham Young U., B.A. 1976, Southwestern U., J.D. 1979; Mormon; married (Sharon).

Elected Office: OR Senate, 1992-96, Pres., 1994-96.

Professional Career: Law Clerk, NM Supreme Court, 1979-80; Practicing atty., 1980-81; Pres., Smith Frozen Foods, 1980-96.

DC Office: 404 RSOB, 20510, 202-224-3753; Fax: 202-228-3997; Web site: gsmith.senate.gov.

State Offices: Bend, 541-318-1298; Eugene, 541-465-6750; Medford, 541-608-9102; Pendleton, 541-278-1129; Portland, 503-326-3386.

Committees: *Aging (Special)* (RMM of 10 R). *Commerce, Science & Transportation* (6th of 11 R): Surface Transportation & Merchant Marine Infrastructure, Safety & Security (RMM); Oceans, Atmosphere, Fisheries & Coast Guard; Interstate Commerce, Trade & Tourism; Science, Technology & Innovation; Aviation Operations, Safety & Security; Consumer Affairs, Insurance & Automotive Safety. *Energy & Natural Resources* (9th of 11 R): Water & Power; National Parks; Public Lands & Forests. *Finance* (6th of 10 R): International Trade & Global Competitiveness (RMM); Energy, Natural Resources & Infrastructure. *Indian Affairs* (6th of 7 R).

Group Ratings

	ADA	ACLU	AFS	LCV	ITIC	NTU	COC	ACU	CFG	FRC
2006	15	33	13	14	100	59	100	72	48	62
2005	20	—	13	45	—	54	88	58	46	—

National Journal Ratings

	2005 LIB	—	2005 CONS		2006 LIB	—	2006 CONS
Economic	48%	—	51%		45%	—	53%
Social	48%	—	51%		39%	—	60%
Foreign	51%	—	46%		51%	—	46%

Key Votes of the 109th Congress

1. Bar ANWR Drilling	Y	5. Confirm Samuel Alito		9. Limit Interstate Abortion	Y
2. FY06 Spending Curb	N	6. Path to Citizenship	Y	10. CAFTA	Y
3. Estate Tax Repeal	Y	7. Bar Same Sex Marriage	Y	11. Urge Iraq Withdrawal	N
4. Raise Minimum Wage	N	8. Stem Cell Research $	Y	12. Provide Detainee Rights	Y

Election Results

2002 general	Gordon Smith (R)	712,287	(56%)	($5,651,098)
	Bill Bradbury (D)	501,898	(40%)	($2,104,194)
	Other	53,036	(4%)	
2002 primary	Gordon Smith (R)	unopposed		
1996 general	Gordon Smith (R)	677,336	(50%)	($3,527,252)
	Tom Bruggere (D)	624,370	(46%)	($3,301,736)
	Other	58,524	(4%)	

Gordon Smith, Oregon's junior senator, was first elected to the Senate in 1996. Smith was born in Pendleton and grew up in the Washington suburbs, after his father sold his food processing business to serve as an aide to Eisenhower Agriculture Secretary Ezra Taft Benson. He is a cousin of former Congressmen Morris and Stewart Udall and of their sons, Congressmen Mark and Tom Udall. Smith served two years as a Mormon missionary in New Zealand, then graduated from Brigham Young and from law school in Los Angeles, was a law clerk in New Mexico and practiced law in Arizona. Then he bought the family frozen vegetable processing company in Pendleton, and guided it out of debt to profitability; Smith Frozen Foods is now one of largest private label packers of frozen vegetables in the country. In 1992 he was elected to the state Senate and in 1995 became Senate president, a fast rise. He ran against Ron Wyden for the Senate seat from which Bob Packwood resigned. He lost after a battle of negative ads, 48%-47% in January 1996. The month before, Mark Hatfield had announced his retirement after 30 years in the Senate. At first Smith was reluctant to run again—indeed, he is the only American in history to run for two Senate seats in the same year—but Republicans urged him to do so. Attacked during the Wyden race for being endorsed by the conservative Oregon Citizens' Alliance, Smith positioned himself closer to the center and turned down the OCA endorsement this time; when OCA head Lon Mabon ran against him in the primary, Smith beat him 78%-8%. Smith's opponent in the general was Tom Bruggere, another self-made millionaire who, like Smith, owned a Ferrari. In an ad shot in soft focus, Smith said he continued to oppose abortion, but promised not to back a constitutional amendment banning it and at the end of the campaign said he would vote for Medicaid to cover abortions in cases of rape, incest or threat to life of the mother; he promised to work for a balance of environmental protection, economic development and job creation. Smith won 50%-46%.

Against some expectations, Smith has compiled one of the more moderate voting records of Senate Republicans. "As a Republican senator from a politically divided state, Smith's Senate terms are six-year balancing acts in which he must please both conservatives in this party and enough liberal Oregonians to get reelected. In an increasingly polarized political world, Smith straddles a rare middle ground," *The Oregonian* wrote in August 2006. He frequently upsets ideologues on each side. He voted for mandatory background checks and for child safety locks on guns—both reversals of previous stands. He continued to oppose abortion, but backed the use of embryonic stem cells in medical research; the cells are used in research to combat Parkinson's disease, which has stricken several of his relatives. But he did not change his position on assisted suicide. While Wyden repeatedly threatened to filibuster legislation to overturn the assisted suicide law Oregon voters approved in referenda, Smith voted for it. "For me, it's an issue of principle on which I'm prepared to stake my political career," he said later. After the Supreme Court upheld the law in January 2006, Smith announced he would end his public opposition to it, though his personal position on the matter remained unchanged.

Smith has been Edward Kennedy's chief cosponsor of the hate crimes bill that adds penalties for crimes committed because of the victim's gender, sexual orientation or disability. He disappointed some of his admirers in gay rights groups by sponsoring a constitutional amendment banning same-sex marriage; he said he favors letting states decide whether to recognize civil unions. He voted against the McCain-Feingold campaign finance regulation bill when it passed with 59 votes in April 2001, but when it came back from conference committee in February 2002 he indicated he would provide a 60th vote against a filibuster, and thus assured its passage. He offered amendments to the 2003 Medicare/prescription drug bill to insure reimbursement of health clinics serving the poor and to require cost-based reimbursement for screening and diagnostic mammography. In voting for immigration reform, he cited his experience in hiring hundreds of Latino agricultural workers. He supported the Iraq war resolution in October 2002. By December 2006, he turned against the handling of the war; citing the growing attacks on U.S. soldiers, he told the Senate, "That is absurd. It may even be criminal."

Smith has tended to oppose measures sought by environmental restriction groups as undue limits on economic activity. He very strongly opposed breaching dams on the Snake River. He championed the cause of the Klamath Basin farmers who were denied irrigation water because it was said to be needed to protect the endangered sucker fish—a heavily publicized case in Oregon. He parted with most of his fellow Republicans to vote for higher CAFE auto gas mileage standards and against oil drilling in the Arctic National Wildlife Refuge. But he supported in 2005 a budget bill that included a provision to permit ANWR drilling, citing as a reason another part of the bill with his plan to prevent drastic Medicaid cuts; after the bill returned from a conference with the House, the ANWR provision had been stripped. He questioned Ron Wyden's proposal to double the wilderness area in the Mount Hood National Forest, and threatened to sponsor an amendment to end all legal challenges to salvage logging in the area affected by the 2002 Biscuit fire.

The election of Wyden in January 1996 and Smith in November 1996 was the first time two senators were elected who had run against each other in the same year. Surprisingly, considering the negative character of their campaign, they became friends. They have held dozens of joint town meetings across Oregon and have issued dozens of joint press releases; they lunch together every Thursday. They have cooperated when bills have special impact on Oregon. "When we vote the same, everyone seems delighted. When we vote differently, everyone feels represented," he said. Smith got a seat on the Finance Committee in 2003. Wyden got a seat there two years later, only the third time in history that a state has had both its senators on that committee. Smith was a lead sponsor of the main provision in the 2004 corporate tax bill reducing from 35% to 5.25% the tax on foreign profits returned to the United States; this resulted in a major repatriation of capital for many firms abroad, including some with big operations in Oregon, like Nike, Intel and Hewlett-Packard. In July 2006, he and Wyden filed an incremental bill to help uninsured families that face catastrophic medical costs.

In September 2003 Smith's 21-year-old son, afflicted with bipolar disease, killed himself. Smith announced this on the Senate floor six months later and said he would sponsor a bill to train childcare professionals and to develop screening for youth suicide prevention. He presented his bill, authorizing $60 million in grants to states and tribes and $22 million to colleges and universities, in July. Two months later, as Smith spoke tearfully on the floor, it was passed by both houses on the same day. In 2006, he wrote a book on his son, *Remembering Garrett*.

Smith faced reelection in 2002. Retiring Governor John Kitzhaber probably would have been the strongest potential opponent but he declined to run. That left Secretary of State Bill Bradbury. Bradbury attacked Smith's votes on environmental issues, abortion, tax cuts, education spending and assisted suicide. He had earlier revealed to voters that he has multiple sclerosis, which made it difficult for him to walk long distances; he carried a director's chair so he wouldn't have to stand for long periods. Smith had two strong assets. One was his work with Wyden. Wyden endorsed Bradbury and conducted fundraisers for him, but he also pledged not to attack Smith in any way and they continued to send out joint press releases. The other asset was money. By April 2002 Smith had raised $4 million—nearly twice as much as Bradbury would during the whole campaign. And, although Smith had spent none of his own money on his November 1996 campaign, Democrats knew that he could always get out his checkbook and match whatever they raised for Bradbury. In the spring, the DSCC ran some ads attacking Smith. But for most of the spring and summer and into October Smith had a monopoly on airtime. He ran ads on his accomplishments, stressing in the Portland media market his support of expanded health care benefits for women and children and his opposition to oil drilling in ANWR. In the Medford media market, he stressed his opposition to the cutoff of irrigation water to Klamath Basin farmers. On radio ads in rural areas, he called Bradbury an "environmental extremist." In September, he ran in the Portland market an ad featuring Judy Shepard, mother of murdered student Matthew Shepard, praising him for his support of including gays in the hate crimes bill—the first pro-gay rights TV ad run by any candidate, the Human Rights Campaign said. Lon Mabon, running as a third party candidate, said, "If you vote for Gordon Smith, you're voting for homosexuality." Bradbury went up with TV ads in October, attacking Smith for opposing assisted suicide and accusing him of preferring his own views to those of voters. But he couldn't come close to matching Smith, who ultimately spent $5.6 million to his $2.1 million. Smith won 56%-40%, carrying every county in the state but one, Multnomah (Portland).

After the 2006 election in which Republican Ron Saxton lost badly to Governor Ted Kulongoski and Democrats gained control of the state House, Smith seemed more vulnerable in his 2008 reelection. Democratic Congressmen Earl Blumenauer and Peter DeFazio both declined to run but in August 2007, state House Speaker Jeff Merkley announced he would challenge Smith. Merkley was heavily favored to win the Democratic nomination over Portland political activist Steve Novick.

FIRST DISTRICT

Rep. David Wu (D)

Elected 1998, 5th term; b. Apr. 8, 1955, Hsinchu, Taiwan; home, Portland; Stanford U., B.S. 1977; Harvard Med. Schl., 1978; Yale Law Schl., J.D. 1982; Presbyterian; married (Michelle).

Professional Career: Law clerk, 9th Circuit Court of Appeals, 1982-83; Campaign staff, Gary Hart for President, 1984; Practicing atty., 1984-98.

DC Office: 2338 RHOB, 20515, 202-225-0855; Fax: 202-225-9497; Web site: www.house.gov/wu.

District Offices: Portland, 503-326-2901.

Committees: *Education & Labor* (11th of 27 D): Higher Education, Lifelong Learning & Competitiveness; Health, Employment, Labor & Pensions. *Foreign Affairs* (20th of 27 D): Terrorism, Nonproliferation & Trade. *Science & Technology* (6th of 24 D): Technology & Innovation (Chmn.); Space & Aeronautics.

Group Ratings

	ADA	ACLU	AFS	LCV	ITIC	NTU	COC	ACU	CFG	FRC
2006	90	86	100	100	71	11	33	12	0	0
2005	100	—	100	100	—	15	50	8	5	0

National Journal Ratings

	2005 LIB	—	2005 CONS		2006 LIB	—	2006 CONS
Economic	69%	—	31%		69%	—	30%
Social	72%	—	28%		74%	—	26%
Foreign	69%	—	31%		69%	—	30%

Key Votes of the 109th Congress

1. Estate Tax Repeal	N	5. Limit Interstate Abortion	N	9. Build Border Fence	N
2. Limit CAFE Standards	N	6. Extend Patriot Act	N	10. CAFTA	N
3. FY06 Spending Curb	N	7. Bar Same Sex Marriage	N	11. Oppose Iraq Withdrawal	N
4. Drilling in ANWR	N	8. Stem Cell Research $	Y	12. Detainee Tribunals	N

Election Results

2006 general	David Wu (D)	169,409	(63%)	($1,130,617)
	Derrick Kitts (R)	90,904	(34%)	($144,469)
	Other	9,314	(3%)	
2006 primary	David Wu (D)	55,188	(87%)	
	Alexa Lewis (D)	4,795	(8%)	
	Other	3,411	(5%)	
2004 general	David Wu (D)	203,771	(58%)	($2,752,272)
	Goli Ameri (R)	135,164	(38%)	($2,327,527)
	Dean Wolf (CNP)	13,882	(4%)	
	Other	1,521	(0%)	

Prior Winning Percentages: 2002 (63%); 2000 (58%); 1998 (50%)

The People

Area size:	3,236 sq. mi.
Urban population:	86.7%
Rural population:	13.3%
Pop. 2000:	684,280
Pop. 2005 (est):	753,567
Median income:	$48,464
Poverty status:	8.7%
Military veterans:	13.4%

Race/Ethnic Origin

81.1% White
1.1% Black
5.0% Asian
0.7% Native Am.
0.2% Hawaiian
2.3% Two+ races
0.1% Other
9.4% Hispanic Origin

Ancestry

German: 15.0%   English: 9.5%
Irish: 8.4%

2004 Presidential Vote

Kerry (D)	200,489	(55%)
Bush (R)	161,738	(44%)
Other	4,507	(1%)

2000 Presidential Vote

Gore (D)	150,768	(50%)
Bush (R)	131,808	(44%)
Other	17,057	(6%)

Cook Partisan Voting Index: D + 6

Occupation   Blue collar: 20.6%   White collar: 65.3%   Gray collar: 14.1%

Postmodern skyscrapers rising above the riverfront and below a range of hills: This is downtown Portland. The city—which would have been named Boston if a coin toss had gone the other way—started here, along the Willamette River just before it flows into the Columbia. Downtown was built on the narrow margin of land west of the river and below the hills, not on the flat expanse that stretches east towards the snow-capped peak of Mount Hood. Downtown Portland was once a dowdy place, proper in a New Englandish way, with a few formal buildings above the warehouses and factories. But in the last 30 years there has been an explosion of affluence and creativity here, symbolized by handsome high-rises—the pyramid-crested brick KOIN Tower, the wedge-shaped Justice Center—restored Victorian storefronts, a downtown transit trolley and a light rail line known as MAX (Metropolitan Area Express), a free wireless network in Pioneer Courthouse Square and just across the river the Oregon Museum of Science and Industry. The affluent neighborhoods in the hills overlooking downtown are full of old lumber barons' mansions with splendid views.

Just over the hills are the valleys and interstices between green mountains of suburban Washington County. This was once farm country, with 39,000 people in 1940; now it has 514,000 and is an integral part of metro Portland. This is an affluent area, which grew 65% between 1990 and 2006, with clusters of towns and protected forest areas that feature a high-tech, healthy-lifestyle aura; major employers here are Tektronix, Intel, IBM, Columbia Sportswear and Adidas. Beaverton has the world headquarters of Nike, housed in 16 buildings over a 175-acre spread. Like Silicon

Valley, the Silicon Forest has an environment—at the foot of mountains, woodsy and even rustic, but outfitted with all the comforts and services of modern civilization—that appeals to a highly skilled work force. As they say locally, wood chips have been replaced by computer chips.

The 1st Congressional District of Oregon includes downtown Portland and its western hills, and all of suburban Washington County. The 1st also proceeds nearly 100 miles northwest from Portland along the Columbia River to the rain-swept port of Astoria on the Pacific Coast where Lewis and Clark spent the winter of 1805-06 at what is now the Fort Clatsop National Memorial, and southwest to Yamhill County, a prime site for turkey farms during the 1960s but where metro growth has been spreading. Like Oregon, the 1st District is historically New England Republican, electing only Republican congressmen from 1892 to 1972; like New England, it then trended sharply left on cultural issues, even as its high-tech economy brought new affluence, and starting in 1974 it has elected nothing but Democrats. In a district where no House candidate won more than 52% of the vote in the District in the 1990s, John Kerry won 55%-44% in 2004.

The congressman from the 1st District is David Wu, a Democrat first elected in 1998, the first Chinese-American to have served in the House. He was born in Taiwan in 1955 and came to the U.S. with his family to join his father, studying at Rensselaer Polytechnic Institute, in 1961. He grew up mostly in Orange County, California, graduated from Stanford, started medical school at Harvard (where he shared an apartment with Bill Frist), then switched to law school at Yale. He clerked for a federal judge in Portland and settled there; he worked on Jimmy Carter's campaign in 1980 and Gary Hart's in 1984. He started his own law firm in 1988 and served on the Portland Planning Commission. When the seat opened, the Democratic frontrunner was Linda Peters, who was well known as Washington County Board chairwoman and had the backing of EMILY's List. Wu left his law practice and spent $100,000 of his own money. He attacked Peters in ads for taking a personal loan from a developer and for misspending tax dollars while traveling on county business. He won the primary 52%-43%. The Republican nominee, 29-year-old Molly Bordonaro, the daughter of a prominent real estate man in Portland, came out of the primary with more money than Wu, a more united party behind her and was running even in the polls. With help from national Democrats and labor unions, he caught up in fundraising. Wu used his own life story to extol America's system of education and to call for more spending on Head Start (his wife was a Head Start teacher) and aid to college students. He won 50%-47%.

In the House, Wu joined the New Democrat Coalition and has had a centrist voting record. With one notable exception, he has usually been a reliable Democratic vote on education, health care, abortion and gun control. In votes that angered local tech firms, he voted against normal trade relations with China because of "our commitment to American values and the sacrifices of countless families like mine," and he opposed trade promotion authority. But in November 2003 he was one of 16 Democrats who voted for the Republican leadership's Medicare/prescription drug bill. On the extended three-hour roll call he sat stoically and silently on the House floor among acutely displeased Democrats, looking as though he preferred to be anywhere else in the world that night. He decided that the bill was good for his constituents, but he had promised party leaders that he would not cast his "yea" vote until a majority of House members had gone on record in support; he was the only member who had not cast a vote for much of that time, and he became the final and largely irrelevant supporter in the 220-215 passage of the bill. After the vote, he conceded that he needed to do fence-mending with Democrats on Capitol Hill and at home. Redemption was slow to arrive for Wu. As other Oregon Democrats gained added House influence, he remained mostly on the back bench. He was one of only seven House Democrats to favor increased campaign regulation of "527" nonprofit groups. He secured $8.7 million for a controversial project to widen the congested Highway 217 in Washington County. On the Education committee, he pushed for changes to permit students to seek the best deal on consolidated loans. In the majority, he became chairman of the Science Subcommittee on Technology and Innovation.

In the 2004 election Wu faced spirited competition from Goli Ameri, an Iranian-born communications consultant who was new to politics but showed a good grasp of local economic issues and raised lots of money. Ameri supported Bush on Iraq and tax cuts, but she differed on reimportation of prescription drugs, stem-cell research and oil drilling in the Arctic National Wildlife Refuge. In mid-October the Portland *Oregonian* published a lengthy article on which reporters had worked for many months, which set out in great detail charges that Wu had engaged in sexual harassment and a physical attack on a former girlfriend when they both were Stanford undergraduates. He was not arrested and no criminal charges were filed, but the university disciplined him and he privately apologized. Wu refused to cooperate with the newspaper's investigation. But after the story was published, he issued a statement taking responsibility and admitting to "inexcusable behavior."

Some Wu supporters questioned the newspaper's decision to publish the story so close to the election, just a few days after it had endorsed Ameri in an editorial. In a debate three days later, Ameri brought up the matter. "I cannot in good conscience stand here and pretend that violating the most fundamental human right, a woman's safety, is merely a wrongdoing." Wu replied that Ameri's attack was "unfortunate." She ran campaign ads on the incident, but the news story and extensive coverage appeared to cause little political harm to Wu. He won 58%-38%; he carried Washington County, which cast 63% of the vote, by a 55%-41% margin. By 2006, the issue had disappeared locally. Wu's 63%-34% reelection over state House Majority Whip and self-styled maverick Derrick Kitts was never in serious doubt. Kitts raised little money and Wu avoided debates.

SECOND DISTRICT

Rep. Greg Walden (R)

Elected 1998, 5th term; b. Jan. 10, 1957, The Dalles; home, Hood River; U. of OR, B.S. 1981; Episcopalian; married (Mylene).

Elected Office: OR House of Reps., 1988-94, Majority Ldr., 1991-93; OR Senate, 1994-96.

Professional Career: Press secy., U.S. Rep. Denny Smith, 1981-84, Chief of staff, 1984-86; Owner, Columbia Gorge Broadcasters Inc., 1986-present.

DC Office: 1210 LHOB, 20515, 202-225-6730; Fax: 202-225-5774; Web site: walden.house.gov.

District Offices: Bend, 541-389-4408; Medford, 541-776-4646.

Committees: *Energy & Commerce* (18th of 26 R): Oversight & Investigations; Energy & Air Quality; Telecommunications & the Internet. *Select Committee on Energy Independence and Global Warming* (3d of 6 R).

Group Ratings

	ADA	ACLU	AFS	LCV	ITIC	NTU	COC	ACU	CFG	FRC
2006	15	27	17	17	100	53	100	80	52	57
2005	20	—	0	11	—	57	93	76	64	67

National Journal Ratings

	2005 LIB	—	2005 CONS		2006 LIB	—	2006 CONS
Economic	14%	—	83%		34%	—	65%
Social	43%	—	56%		39%	—	60%
Foreign	23%	—	73%		17%	—	73%

Key Votes of the 109th Congress

1. Estate Tax Repeal	Y	5. Limit Interstate Abortion	Y	9. Build Border Fence	Y
2. Limit CAFE Standards	Y	6. Extend Patriot Act	Y	10. CAFTA	Y
3. FY06 Spending Curb	Y	7. Bar Same Sex Marriage	Y	11. Oppose Iraq Withdrawal	Y
4. Drilling in ANWR	Y	8. Stem Cell Research $	Y	12. Detainee Tribunals	Y

Election Results

2006 general	Greg Walden (R)	181,529	(67%)	($1,399,112)
	Carol Voisin (D)	82,484	(30%)	($65,266)
	Other	7,706	(3%)	
2006 primary	Greg Walden (R)	70,519	(90%)	
	Paul Daghlian (R)	7,401	(9%)	
2004 general	Greg Walden (R)	248,461	(72%)	($1,009,266)
	John McColgan (D)	88,914	(26%)	($30,874)
	Other	9,490	(3%)	

Prior Winning Percentages: 2002 (72%); 2000 (74%); 1998 (61%)

The People		Race/Ethnic Origin	Ancestry	
Area size:	70,227 sq. mi.	86.1% White	German: 13.6%	English: 9.9%
Urban population:	64.2%	0.4% Black	Irish: 8.7%	
Rural population:	35.8%	0.8% Asian	**2004 Presidential Vote**	
Pop. 2000:	684,280	1.9% Native Am.	Bush (R) 218,288	(61%)
Pop. 2005 (est):	738,136	0.1% Hawaiian	Kerry (D) 135,560	(38%)
Median income:	$35,600	1.8% Two+ races	Other 4,895	(1%)
Poverty status:	13.0%	0.1% Other	**2000 Presidential Vote**	
Military veterans:	17.3%	8.8% Hispanic Origin	Bush (R) 182,924	(60%)
			Gore (D) 105,971	(35%)
			Other 18,078	(6%)
			Cook Partisan Voting Index: R +11	

Occupation	Blue collar: 26.3%	White collar: 54.0%	Gray collar: 19.7%

The Cascade Mountains that wall off eastern Oregon from the rest of the state are a magnificent chain of once (and quite possibly still) active volcanic mountains that drain almost every drop of moisture out of the air coming in from the Pacific. They separate green, wet western Oregon from the brown, parched east. Eastern Oregon has 70% of the state's land, but only 477,000 of its 3.7 million people, most of whom still make their living off the land: Beef and dairy cattle, timber and lumber, fish from the Columbia River, and wheat and sugar beets from the irrigated plains. The effect of the Cascades can be felt in the one place they are breached—by the Columbia River Gorge. There, surrounded by brown hills on both sides, funneled winds pound in steadily from the west, making the confluence of the Columbia and Hood rivers the best windsurfing site in the United States. The world's largest wind farm opened here in 2002; it features 400 windmills capable of generating electricity for 60,000 homes.

The 2d Congressional District of Oregon covers all of the state east of the Cascades and the southernmost valley between the Cascades and the Coast Range. Much of this land is empty: Harney County, with a land area larger than that of nine states, has a population of 6,888. Population concentrations here are far apart: Pendleton, a genuine rodeo town amid the northeastern wheat fields; La Grande in the rich Grande Ronde Valley; The Dalles, where the Columbia River Gorge begins, and where housing prices spiked after Google purchased 30 acres of riverfront land for a 100-employee data center that is powered by cheap hydroelectricity; the town of Bend, the fastest-growing part of eastern Oregon, where saw mills have closed and the wilderness and high desert plateau have brought lots of outdoor activity, tourism, telecommuting and jobs; and nearby Crook County, which has seen an invasion of real estate developers. Until it voted for George H. W. Bush in 1992 Crook County was a bellwether, the only county in the country to have voted for the winning presidential candidate in every election in the 20th century; by 2004, with the local reaction against Democrats, it voted 68% for George W. Bush. In the district's southwestern corner west of the Cascades, near the once huge volcano whose blown-off cone is now the 1,932-foot deep Crater Lake (the deepest in the nation), is the lumber and pear orchard country around Klamath Falls, Ashland, Medford and Grants Pass.

Politically, the 2d District has grown very suspicious of the federal government and very Republican. The cultural liberalism of Portland isn't welcome here: This is part of the leave-us-alone Rocky Mountain basin, not the culturally hip West Coast. The federal government owns three-quarters of the district's land, with much of it fenced off from local use by various government decrees. Court decisions protecting the spotted owl eviscerated the logging industry here, and the cutoff of water in 2001 from the Klamath Basin to protect the endangered sucker fish threatened to destroy the livelihoods of 1,400 local farmers. The flow of water was restored, but logging still is endangered.

The congressman from the 2d District is Greg Walden, a Republican elected in 1998. He grew up on a cherry orchard near The Dalles in the Columbia gorge; his father served in the state House. Walden served as press secretary and chief of staff to Congressman Denny Smith from 1981-87, then returned to Hood River as a radio station owner. In 1988 he was elected to the state House, and soon became majority leader. He is conservative on economics but more moderate on cultural issues; he supports abortion rights and embryonic stem-cell research, but opposes federal funding of abortions.

When the district opened in 1998, Walden ran and faced substantial primary opposition. His opponents grumbled about outside interference, as Walden was backed by $130,000 in ads by Americans for Limited Terms and $50,000 in ads by Gary Bauer's Family Research Council.

Walden's wide support and the $500,000 he raised enabled him to win with 55% of the vote to 33% for religious broadcaster Perry Atkinson. In the anticlimactic general, against a conservative Democrat, Walden won 61%-35%.

In the House Walden has been an active legislator. Roy Blunt named him a deputy whip. On the Energy and Commerce Committee, he criticized the Food and Drug Administration for removing from prescriptions strong warning labels that might alarm users and their families; after a lengthy series in the Portland *Oregonian,* he urged the FDA to encourage development of cold remedies that cannot be converted to methamphetamines. As chairman of the Forests and Forest Health Subcommittee on the Resources Committee, Walden successfully sponsored measures to sell the Bend Pine Nursery, establish a forest research center in Prineville and promote Oregon's famous pears. He played a central role in 2003 in assembling bipartisan support for the Healthy Forests Restoration Act. This was a response to the wildfires that have raged in the West, caused by unlogged dry timber. Walden worked with Senator Ron Wyden on a similar measure that passed the Senate. He also successfully sought to reopen the flow of water to farmers in the Klamath Basin. Later, he pushed for legislation to expedite logging following natural disasters. In July 2006, the House passed his bill to expand the Mount Hood wilderness area, but the Senate did not act because of a controversial land swap for a local ski area. Walden worked to change the Endangered Species Act by encouraging a greater role for peer-reviewed science. He supported the Central American Free Trade Agreement, despite opposition from eastern Oregon sugar growers who worry the deal will drive down sugar prices.

Walden has been reelected easily. He has twice declined to run for governor, but may have other opportunities to run statewide in this swing state. "Greg Walden will be governor of Oregon one day," Senator Gordon Smith told the *Oregonian* in 2005.

THIRD DISTRICT

Rep. Earl Blumenauer (D)

Elected May 1996, 6th full term; b. Aug. 16, 1948, Portland; home, Portland; Lewis & Clark Col., B.A. 1970, J.D. 1976; no religious affiliation; married (Margaret).

Elected Office: OR House of Reps., 1972-78; Multnomah Cnty. Comm., 1978-86; Portland City Cncl., 1986-96.

Professional Career: Asst. to Pres., Portland St. U., 1970-77.

DC Office: 2267 RHOB, 20515, 202-225-4811; Fax: 202-225-8941; Web site: www.house.gov/blumenauer.

District Offices: Portland, 503-231-2300.

Committees: *Budget* (10th of 22 D). *Select Committee on Energy Independence and Global Warming* (2d of 9 D). *Ways & Means* (16th of 24 D): Trade; Select Revenue Measures.

Group Ratings

	ADA	ACLU	AFS	LCV	ITIC	NTU	COC	ACU	CFG	FRC
2006	90	95	100	92	50	18	27	8	14	0
2005	100	—	100	100	—	18	37	4	7	0

National Journal Ratings

	2005 LIB	—	2005 CONS	2006 LIB	—	2006 CONS
Economic	82%	—	16%	73%	—	27%
Social	89%	—	11%	90%	—	9%
Foreign	93%	—	7%	95%	—	0%

Key Votes of the 109th Congress

1. Estate Tax Repeal	N	5. Limit Interstate Abortion	*	9. Build Border Fence	N
2. Limit CAFE Standards	N	6. Extend Patriot Act	N	10. CAFTA	N
3. FY06 Spending Curb	N	7. Bar Same Sex Marriage	N	11. Oppose Iraq Withdrawal	N
4. Drilling in ANWR	N	8. Stem Cell Research $	Y	12. Detainee Tribunals	N

Election Results

2006 general	Earl Blumenauer (D)	186,380	(73%)	($676,028)
	Bruce Broussard (R)	59,529	(23%)	
	Other	7,701	(3%)	
2006 primary	Earl Blumenauer (D)	63,350	(91%)	
	John Sweeney (D)	6,338	(9%)	
2004 general	Earl Blumenauer (D)	245,559	(71%)	($701,713)
	Tami Mars (R)	82,045	(24%)	
	Other	18,956	(5%)	

Prior Winning Percentages: 2002 (67%); 2000 (67%); 1998 (84%); 1996 (67%); 1996 (68%)

The People		Race/Ethnic Origin	Ancestry	
Area size:	1,054 sq. mi.	77.2% White	German: 14.5% Irish: 8.7%	
Urban population:	93.1%	5.2% Black	English: 8.4%	
Rural population:	6.9%	5.4% Asian	**2004 Presidential Vote**	
Pop. 2000:	684,279	0.9% Native Am.	Kerry (D) 242,075	(67%)
Pop. 2005 (est):	709,029	0.3% Hawaiian	Bush (R) 118,442	(33%)
Median income:	$42,063	3.3% Two+ races	Other 568	(0%)
Poverty status:	11.7%	0.2% Other	**2000 Presidential Vote**	
Military veterans:	13.1%	7.6% Hispanic Origin	Gore (D) 176,831	(61%)
			Bush (R) 93,213	(32%)
			Other 20,264	(7%)
			Cook Partisan Voting Index: D +18	

Occupation   Blue collar: 24.6%   White collar: 59.4%   Gray collar: 16.0%

Portland, the Rose City set between Mount Hood to the east and the Tualatin Mountains to the west, spanning the Willamette River with its airport and industrial back to the Columbia, is still one of America's least known major cities—and one of its most distinctive. For most of its history Portland was a prosaic city in a magic setting; it was in many ways a muscular, blue-collar town, which piled Oregon lumber and Oregon pears into freight cars, or unloaded machines from back East or autos from Japan on its docks. But in the past three decades Portland has been transformed. Out on the Pacific Rim, it increasingly makes its living on foreign trade, seeing East Asians as customers more than competitors. It has become a home to high-tech industries, particularly in the Silicon Forest suburbs to the west. Government has also produced change. Oregon's land-use act, passed in 1973, required local governments to set geographic limits on growth; Metro, the regional government established in 1979 just as growth was accelerating, has created something of a counterweight against the endless spread outward of population into former farmland. With gentrification in the city, old neighborhoods have been revived with new names: "NoPo" refers to north Portland. With its first light-rail service, Portland encouraged the development of high-density commercial space and housing around transit stops. Bicycle paths wind throughout the metropolitan area, and downtown, west of the Willamette River, boasts proud postmodern structures amid classic masonry buildings. This is the nation's most bicycle-friendly large city, with the mileage on bikeways having tripled in a decade.

In the process, the central city of Portland, like San Francisco and Seattle, has attracted political and cultural liberals. And, like those two cities, Portland has its share of traffic congestion and high home prices. This "livable community" was rated the best city to live in by *Money* magazine in 2000 and its long-term approach to transportation, creating mixed-use neighborhoods and increasing development density, may ultimately pay off. But its national ranking has declined; for a time, the metropolitan region had one of the nation's highest unemployment rates, due partly to the dot-com bust and perhaps exacerbated by excessive controls on growth. *Money* dropped Portland from its top 100 list in 2006.

The 3d Congressional District of Oregon includes the large part of Portland and Multnomah County east of the Willamette River and some of suburban Clackamas County to the south. It extends over plains and hills to the splendid scenery of Mount Hood high in the Cascades and Bonneville Dam in the Columbia River Gorge. Politically, it remains dominated by cultural liberalism, which sets Portland apart from its suburbs and the rest of Oregon. In 2000 Multnomah County voted 64%-28% for Al Gore with 7% for Ralph Nader; in 2004, with turnout up 22%, it voted 72%-27% for John Kerry.

The congressman from the 3d District is Earl Blumenauer, who won a special election in May 1996 after Ron Wyden was elected to the Senate. Blumenauer grew up in Portland, graduated from

Lewis and Clark College and its Northwestern Law School. He was inspired by the civil rights and anti-Vietnam war movements while in his teens; in 1969, in college, he headed a statewide campaign to lower Oregon's voting age. He has held public office almost all his adult life. In 1972, at 23, he was elected to the Oregon House; in 1978 he was elected to the Multnomah County Board of Commissioners; in 1986 he was elected to the Portland City Council. In these offices he has championed many of the policies that have made Portland distinctive—regional light rail transit, curbside recycling, land use planning. He encouraged bike riding and Regional Rail Summits, which try to bring neighborhood residents into the planning for higher densities at transit nodes. Blumenauer has had some setbacks, notably when he lost the 1992 mayoral race. But he was the obvious successor to Wyden, and won the special election 68%-25%. His campaign slogan: "Vote Earl, Vote Often." He has been easily reelected.

In the House, Blumenauer has a liberal voting record and a distinctive agenda. Advocating that the federal government lead by example, he rides his bicycle everywhere from his Capitol Hill apartment, and formed a Bicycle Caucus with more than 100 members; he fought for showers for bike commuters on Capitol Hill and boasted that he has never driven a car in Washington, though he was forced to abandon his bike for a few months in 2006 after he broke his foot. He was astonished to find that the House subsidized parking for employees, but not mass transit; now, employees can get subsidized transit fares. A White House guard once questioned him when he showed up with his bike. He is interested in what seem like quixotic projects now, but may not be with time: An interstate highway system for bicycle paths and less dependence on driving as a tool to improve public health. In 2003, the House approved his amendment to the energy bill for a bicycling pilot program in the Transportation Department. Blumenauer has actively promoted trade across the Pacific—a key element of Portland's economy. He supported normal trade relations with China, but he joined most House Democrats in opposing trade promotion authority and the Central American Free Trade Agreement. With Jeff Flake of Arizona, he protested wasteful government spending. He demands that the Army Corps of Engineers show greater concern for the environment. In January 2005, concerned about flooding, he prophetically told the House that he feared New Orleans could suffer hurricane damages comparable to the tsunami in southeast Asia. In 2006, he and Greg Walden pushed through the House a bill to expand the Mount Hood wilderness area.

Blumenauer proudly terms Portland a model for the future of the city. And the sometimes nerdy policy wonk has taken his gospel of livability and civic values elsewhere, through his Livable Cities Task Force and his own political action committee. (His key components of livability: Simple, common-sense, low-tech, high-impact solutions.) He seriously considered running for mayor of Portland in 2004; he surprised some local Democrats when he decided against it. On Capitol Hill, he became a vigorous Democratic fundraiser. Following the 2006 election, in which he made campaign appearances in a dozen districts, he bolstered his influence with a seat on the Ways and Means Committee; he saw great opportunity there to pursue his bold concepts. Another sign of growing respect: He gained mention as a possible challenger to Senator Gordon Smith in 2008 (in May 2007, Blumenauer announced he would not run for Senate) or perhaps for governor in 2010.

FOURTH DISTRICT

Rep. Peter DeFazio (D)

Elected 1986, 11th term; b. May 27, 1947, Needham, MA; home, Springfield; Tufts U., B.A. 1969, U. of OR, M.S. 1977; Catholic; married (Myrnie).

Military Career: Air Force, 1967-71.

Elected Office: Lane Cnty. Bd. of Commissioners, 1982-86.

Professional Career: Dist. Dir., U.S. Rep. James Weaver, 1977-82.

DC Office: 2134 RHOB, 20515, 202-225-6416; Fax: 202-225-0032; Web site: www.defazio.house.gov.

District Offices: Coos Bay, 541-269-2609; Eugene, 541-465-6732; Roseburg, 541-440-3523.

Committees: *Homeland Security* (6th of 19 D): Management, Investigations & Oversight; Transportation Security & Infrastructure Protection. *Natural Resources* (17th of 27 D): National Parks, Forests & Public Lands. *Transportation & Infrastructure* (3d of 41 D): Highways & Transit (Chmn.); Railroads, Pipelines & Hazardous Materials; Aviation.

Group Ratings

	ADA	ACLU	AFS	LCV	ITIC	NTU	COC	ACU	CFG	FRC
2006	90	86	86	83	43	14	47	28	13	0
2005	100	—	100	100	—	16	37	12	6	8

National Journal Ratings

	2005 LIB	—	2005 CONS		2006 LIB	—	2006 CONS
Economic	78%	—	21%		74%	—	23%
Social	62%	—	37%		64%	—	36%
Foreign	74%	—	26%		88%	—	10%

Key Votes of the 109th Congress

1. Estate Tax Repeal	N	5. Limit Interstate Abortion	N	9. Build Border Fence	Y
2. Limit CAFE Standards	N	6. Extend Patriot Act	N	10. CAFTA	N
3. FY06 Spending Curb	N	7. Bar Same Sex Marriage	N	11. Oppose Iraq Withdrawal	N
4. Drilling in ANWR	N	8. Stem Cell Research $	Y	12. Detainee Tribunals	N

Election Results

2006 general	Peter DeFazio (D)	180,607	(62%)	($753,011)
	Jim Feldkamp (R)	109,105	(38%)	($473,235)
2006 primary	Peter DeFazio (D)	unopposed		
2004 general	Peter DeFazio (D)	228,611	(61%)	($909,241)
	Jim Feldkamp (R)	140,882	(38%)	($591,318)
	Other	5,416	(1%)	

Prior Winning Percentages: 2002 (64%); 2000 (68%); 1998 (70%); 1996 (66%); 1994 (67%); 1992 (71%); 1990 (86%); 1988 (72%); 1986 (54%)

The People		Race/Ethnic Origin	Ancestry	
Area size:	18,034 sq. mi.	89.7% White	German: 14.7%	English: 10.1%
Urban population:	69.2%	0.5% Black	Irish: 8.8%	
Rural population:	30.8%	1.5% Asian	**2004 Presidential Vote**	
Pop. 2000:	684,280	1.2% Native Am.	Kerry (D) 188,479	(49%)
Pop. 2005 (est):	706,676	0.1% Hawaiian	Bush (R) 187,292	(49%)
Median income:	$35,796	2.5% Two+ races	Other 5,801	(2%)
Poverty status:	13.7%	0.1% Other	**2000 Presidential Vote**	
Military veterans:	16.9%	4.2% Hispanic Origin	Bush (R) 156,362	(49%)
			Gore (D) 142,123	(44%)
			Other 22,601	(7%)
			Cook Partisan Voting Index: D + 0	

Occupation	Blue collar: 26.3%	White collar: 55.2%	Gray collar: 18.5%

Eugene is nestled in the southernmost bit of lowland at the end of Oregon's Willamette Valley, surrounded by mountains on three sides. It is a farming center, a lumber metropolis and, most notably, a leafy university town. Settlers first arrived here in 1846, farming in the valley and cutting timber in the hills. In 1876, the University of Oregon was established, a symbol of Oregon's strong Yankee cultural ethic and sparse settlement; its first graduating class had just five students. Thousands of miles from most Americans, Eugene and next-door Springfield, once a lumber town and now with computer chip factories, have grown into comfortable middle-sized towns. Eugene has bicycle paths along the riverbanks and on main streets and likes to bill itself as the Running Capital of the Universe; it is where Phil Knight and his former University of Oregon track coach, Bill Bowerman, started Nike—the first soles formed on a waffle iron. Now the third-largest city in Oregon (behind Portland and Salem) and one of the most livable in the nation, it offers the ambience of a small town and the counter-culture without the isolation, and its liberal voters have been vital to Democrats statewide.

Beyond Eugene and Springfield, southwestern Oregon is surrounded by green-clad mountains and for years cut more timber than any other place in the country. But demand for wood is volatile, dependent on the vagaries of interest rates; East Asia increasingly wants unprocessed logs rather than milled lumber, which means fewer jobs for Oregon. The 1980s were tough on this region:

recession reduced the demand for housing, and cutting of old-growth forests was banned to protect the spotted owl. But even as the lumber industry languished, a robust local economy and active job retraining resulted in local job gains in the 1990s. Recent development has been diverse, including health care, tourism, and retirement communities for California transplants. But Timber Country, including forest product businesses, continues to struggle, especially with the downturn in the housing market. With Weyerhaeuser's December 2006 closing of its Lane County plywood plant—the only such plant on the West Coast—the county's wood products sector employment had dropped by two-thirds since its 1977 peak of 14,000 jobs.

The 4th Congressional District of Oregon includes Eugene, Springfield and surrounding Lane County; it goes south on Interstate 5 to include Roseburg in Douglas County, once one of the premier logging counties in the United States. It extends north to Albany and includes most of Corvallis, but not Oregon State University. It includes the entire southern half of Oregon's stunning Pacific coastline down to the California border; the decline of commercial fishing has hit this area hard. Eugene is heavily Democratic. Roseburg and Albany and their surrounding counties vote heavily Republican, leaving a left-right clash in the district. The travails of the logging industry moved the area to the right: the 4th District (with only slightly different boundaries) voted 54%-44% against George H. W. Bush in 1988, but in 2000 it voted 49%-44% for George W. Bush. In 2004, the 4th voted narrowly for John Kerry, one of just two districts in the nation to flip from Bush to Kerry.

The congressman from the 4th District is Peter DeFazio (pronounced *da-FAH-zee-oh*), a Democrat first elected in 1986. He grew up in Massachusetts, came to Oregon for graduate school, was a bike mechanic, and went to work for 4th District Congressman Jim Weaver. In 1982 he moved to Springfield and won a seat on the county commission. When Weaver retired in 1986, DeFazio won the House seat in a tight race. He beat Bill Bradbury (the 2002 Democratic nominee for senator) by a 34%-33% margin and won the general election 54%-46%. DeFazio has compiled a record that seems to satisfy both Eugene and the rest of the district—liberal on most issues, moderate on social issues. An original founder of the loose-knit Progressive Caucus, he has not been shy to express his anger that millions of Americans were suffering during booming prosperity. He opposed the Clinton administration's NAFTA, GATT and trade promotion authority and was a leader of the fight against normal trade relations with China. Since the election of George W. Bush, DeFazio's populist criticism has grown more outspoken, and is sometimes directed at his own party.

DeFazio often takes idiosyncratic views. Unlike most Democrats, he has offered a specific proposal to fix Social Security: Remove the payroll deduction limitation that benefits the top wage earners. In June 2006, he was one of 17 House Democrats to oppose a resolution condemning news media disclosure of classified information. As the senior Democrat on the Aviation Subcommittee of Transportation and Infrastructure, he criticized inadequate security, poor oversight by the Federal Aviation Administration and he called for a more active role by Congress to stabilize the industry. He took the lead in the House with his amendment to permit airline pilots to carry guns in the cockpit. The Bush administration opposed this, and the Senate had avoided the issue. But DeFazio won by an astonishing 250-175; the Senate a few weeks later followed suit and Bush went along. After catastrophic wildfires in summer 2002, DeFazio teamed with Republican Greg Walden to seek a middle ground to speed the thinning of brush in the forests; DeFazio's environmental allies denounced him as a turncoat. Despite initial failure in committee, the bipartisan effort became law in 2003. He voted against the authorization of force in Iraq and criticized the Bush administration's lack of a strategy after the overthrow of Saddam Hussein. DeFazio now chairs the Highways Subcommittee, where he has played a major part in transportation reauthorization. In 2005, he tweaked the funding formula to benefit Oregon and added $200 million for bridge repair on Interstate 5.

DeFazio has won reelection impressively by more than 60% in a district that often had been marginal. Against former FBI agent Jim Feldkamp, who favored more local control of forests and spent a total of $1 million in the two contests, he won reelection with 61% in 2004 and 62% in 2006. The margin was close in the southern counties of Curry, Douglas and Josephine, but DeFazio exceeded two-thirds of the vote in Lane County. After Senator Bob Packwood resigned in 1995, DeFazio ran to succeed him. He had far less money than Portland Congressman Ron Wyden, whom he attacked for receiving money from Packwood contributors. His opposition to gun control, NAFTA and GATT provided clear contrasts with Wyden. But Wyden won a 50%-44% victory in the primary, and went on to win the seat. Since then, DeFazio has called for public financing of campaigns. In the 2002 cycle, DeFazio considered running for the Senate against Gordon Smith. But he said he would run only with the "strongest possible support" from Democratic leaders. The DSCC sent a message: No big money until DeFazio raised lots himself and rose in the polls. So he decided to remain in the

House, where his influence has grown. DeFazio again declined to take on Smith in 2008. Should DeFazio not run in this district, this might well be a seriously contested seat.

FIFTH DISTRICT

Rep. Darlene Hooley (D)

Elected 1996, 6th term; b. Apr. 4, 1939, Williston, ND; home, West Linn; OR St. U., B.S. 1961; Lutheran; divorced.

Elected Office: West Linn City Cncl., 1977-80; OR House of Reps., 1980-86; Clackamas Cnty. Comm., 1987-96.

Professional Career: Teacher, 1961-75.

DC Office: 2430 RHOB, 20515, 202-225-5711; Fax: 202-225-5699; Web site: hooley.house.gov.

District Offices: Salem, 503-588-9100; West Linn, 503-557-1324.

Committees: *Budget* (17th of 22 D). *Energy & Commerce* (25th of 31 D): Commerce, Trade & Consumer Protection; Energy & Air Quality; Health. *Science & Technology* (14th of 24 D): Investigations & Oversight; Research & Science Education.

Group Ratings

	ADA	ACLU	AFS	LCV	ITIC	NTU	COC	ACU	CFG	FRC
2006	90	91	86	92	71	17	53	24	11	0
2005	95	—	100	100	—	16	52	13	13	17

National Journal Ratings

	2005 LIB	—	2005 CONS		2006 LIB	—	2006 CONS
Economic	67%	—	32%		68%	—	32%
Social	66%	—	34%		64%	—	35%
Foreign	73%	—	26%		80%	—	18%

Key Votes of the 109th Congress

1. Estate Tax Repeal	Y	5. Limit Interstate Abortion	N	9. Build Border Fence	Y
2. Limit CAFE Standards	N	6. Extend Patriot Act	N	10. CAFTA	N
3. FY06 Spending Curb	N	7. Bar Same Sex Marriage	N	11. Oppose Iraq Withdrawal	N
4. Drilling in ANWR	N	8. Stem Cell Research $	Y	12. Detainee Tribunals	N

Election Results

2006 general	Darlene Hooley (D)	146,973	(54%)	($2,030,646)
	Mike Erickson (R)	116,424	(43%)	($1,798,733)
	Other	8,837	(3%)	
2006 primary	Darlene Hooley (D)	unopposed		
2004 general	Darlene Hooley (D)	184,833	(53%)	($2,054,417)
	Jim Zupancic (R)	154,993	(44%)	($1,291,211)
	Other	9,808	(3%)	

Prior Winning Percentages: 2002 (55%); 2000 (57%); 1998 (55%); 1996 (51%)

The People		Race/Ethnic Origin	Ancestry	
Area size:	5,829 sq. mi.	83.6% White	German: 16.0%	English: 9.7%
Urban population:	80.4%	0.6% Black	Irish: 8.1%	
Rural population:	19.6%	1.9% Asian	**2004 Presidential Vote**	
Pop. 2000:	684,280	1.1% Native Am.	Bush (R) 181,070	(50%)
Pop. 2005 (est):	730,192	0.2% Hawaiian	Kerry (D) 176,558	(49%)
Median income:	$44,409	2.2% Two+ races	Other 4,058	(1%)
Poverty status:	10.9%	0.1% Other	**2000 Presidential Vote**	
Military veterans:	14.8%	10.3% Hispanic Origin	Bush (R) 149,276	(48%)
			Gore (D) 144,657	(47%)
			Other 17,047	(5%)
			Cook Partisan Voting Index: D + 1	

Occupation	Blue collar: 22.1%	White collar: 60.6%	Gray collar: 17.4%

The Willamette Valley was the great Promised Land at the end of the Oregon Trail, shielded by the Coast Range from the cold storms of the Pacific but squeezing most of the moisture out of the clouds in the form of rain, fog and persistent mist. Here, New England Yankees planted small towns they called Salem and Oregon City, founded schools and colleges, built high-spired churches and eventually Salem's cylindrical-domed Art Deco state Capitol. This was one of the few valleys in the West that settlers found readily suitable for agriculture. The Willamette Valley's soil is fertile, the plain created by the waters of the Willamette sweeping down from the mountains is broad, but industrial runoff has made the river among the most polluted in the nation. Into this land metro Portland has spread, with young people leapfrogging over the lands protected from development and into Clackamas and Marion Counties to the south. In 2003, rapidly-growing Salem passed Eugene as the second-largest city in Oregon.

The 5th Congressional District of Oregon includes much of the northern Willamette Valley. Near Portland it has the old pioneer town of Oregon City, which was the end point of the Oregon Trail. It spreads south to the state capital of Salem, also home of Willamette University, the oldest university west of the Mississippi River. It includes part of Corvallis, home of Oregon State University and its renowned agricultural science department. Then the district hops over the Coast Range to take in Lincoln and Tillamook Counties, fishing and logging and cheese-making communities; it also includes all of rural Polk County. Although the area remains one of the nation's chief producers of processed vegetables, its crops of beans and berries have dropped significantly; nurseries have become a new growth industry. Historically, the Willamette Valley was Republican, like New England whence most of its settlers came, but, also like New England, it has been trending Democratic, and now is prime marginal territory. The Corvallis area is heavily Democratic, the Salem area more likely to be Republican while Clackamas County is competitive territory, more Republican than the more affluent Washington County west of Portland. This is a district that George W. Bush won by less than 5,000 votes in both the 2000 and 2004 presidential elections.

The congresswoman from the 5th District is Darlene Hooley, a Democrat first elected in 1996. Born in North Dakota, Hooley moved with her family to Salem at age 8. She majored in education at Oregon State, worked as a reading and physical education teacher in rural Woodburn Gervais and raised her family in West Linn, on the Willamette north of Oregon City. Angry when council members wouldn't replace the rugged asphalt after her son fell off a playground swing and cut his head, she served on the park district board and was elected to the city council in 1976, at 37. In 1980 she was elected to the Oregon House; in 1987 she was appointed to the Clackamas County Board of Supervisors. In 1996, Hooley challenged Republican Jim Bunn, elected 50%-47% in 1994; he combined religious conservatism with a moderate record on economic issues. With big fundraising help from EMILY's List, Hooley won the primary with 51%. She attacked Bunn for supporting Newt Gingrich and Medicare "cuts." Ultimately, she spent $1.1 million, twice as much as the incumbent. Working most strongly against Bunn was his divorce and subsequent marriage to his 31-year-old chief of staff, whom he was paying $97,500—more than any other staffer in Oregon's House delegation. Hooley won 51%-46%.

In the House, Hooley has a relatively moderate record. On the Financial Services Committee, she led a bipartisan group that enacted legislation in 2003 designed to reduce identity theft by permitting consumers a free annual credit report and requiring banks and credit agencies to keep an eye on fraud; Hooley called it the strongest consumer measure enacted in years, though some liberal activists disagreed. In 2006, she worked with Steve LaTourette on a bipartisan bill to require banks, credit bureaus and other businesses to notify consumer of data breaches that put their personal information at risk. She led the fight to preserve Oregon's assisted suicide law and argued for it on states' rights grounds. Curbing the growing problem of methamphetamines has been a top local priority. She joined the moderate New Democrats, contending that she wanted to work with business in a district dependent on trade; in contrast to David Wu in the adjacent suburban district, she voted for normal trade relations with China. But Hooley joined the other House Democrats from Oregon in opposing trade promotion authority for President Bush. She voted against the use of military force in Iraq, but later supported funds for the military and reconstruction. With little interest in gaining national attention, she is among the few House members without a press secretary. After repeated failure to get on the Appropriations Committee, she won a seat on Energy and Commerce in 2007.

In this marginal seat, which was represented by two Republicans and two Democrats during the 1990s, Hooley has had a series of competitive contests. In 2004 she faced Jim Zupancic, an entrepreneur in the voice-mail business and former school board chairman in Lake Oswego. Both candidates were well-funded. Zupancic called for changes in medical malpractice, attacked Hooley's "extreme liberal" record and said she did not support job creation. Hooley kept her distance from John Kerry and emphasized constituent services and her focus on consumer issues. Hooley won, 53%-44%. She carried all seven counties, though her home base of Clackamas, which cast one-third of the vote, was the closest: 51%-46%. In what Republicans billed as a sleeper race in 2006, the DCCC spent money here and Nancy Pelosi made a mid-October campaign visit as Hooley was challenged by Mike Erickson, a shipping entrepreneur whose ads depicted Hooley as a lazy career politician with a record more liberal than her rhetoric; he spent $1.8 million, nearly 90% from his own pocket. Hooley won 54%-43%, with 54%-44% in Clackamas; her margins in Polk and Salem-based Marion Counties were narrower.

★ PENNSYLVANIA ★

Pennsylvania started off as the center of America: Philadelphia was the 13 colonies' largest city when it hosted the Continental Congress in 1776 and the Constitutional Convention in 1787. This was one of the newer colonies, founded 52 years after Massachusetts and 75 years after Virginia. Under the benevolent rule of the early Penns and with its Quaker traditions, Pennsylvania soon became the major settlement in the Middle Colonies. Its tolerance attracted Englishmen of all religious sects and thousands of Germans as well: bordermen from Scotland, Yorkshire and Northern Ireland crossed the corduroy-like ridges of the Appalachians and settled the mountainous interior where General Braddock had been beaten by the French and Indians not long before, and where a decade later George Washington would again lead troops when the Whiskey Rebellion flared up. Pennsylvania, in the geometric lines William Penn had obtained from King Charles II, connected two major river systems—the golden triangle where the Allegheny and Monongahela Rivers joined to form the Ohio, George Washington's goal in 1754 and later, and the wide Delaware estuary, with its thriving commerce and rich hinterland. Philadelphia was, after London and Dublin, the largest Georgian city in the late 18th century, seemingly destined to be the London of America, the metropolis of government and commerce and culture; Pittsburgh was the frontier metropolis, the key to the great interior of North America, the fulcrum point of American expansion.

But Philadelphia—and Pennsylvania—failed to hold the central position the Founders had expected. The nation's capital was put on the Potomac rather than the Delaware as part of a political deal, and the Erie Canal and the water-level railroad from the Hudson to Lake Erie channeled trade away from Philadelphia to New York. Philadelphia lost its chance to be the nation's financial capital when Andrew Jackson in righteous rage vetoed the rechartering of the Second Bank of the United States. Philadelphia's Quaker tradition, tolerant of diversity and indifferent to others' behavior, was overshadowed in intellectual life by New England's Puritan tradition, angrily intolerant and ready to use the state to impose cultural values from abolition to prohibition. Instead, Pennsylvania became America's energy and heavy industry capital. The key was coal. Northeast Pennsylvania was the nation's primary source of anthracite, the hard coal used for home heating, and western Pennsylvania was laced with bituminous coal, the soft coal used in steel production. Connected with Philadelphia by the Pennsylvania Railroad, Pittsburgh was the center of the nation's steel industry

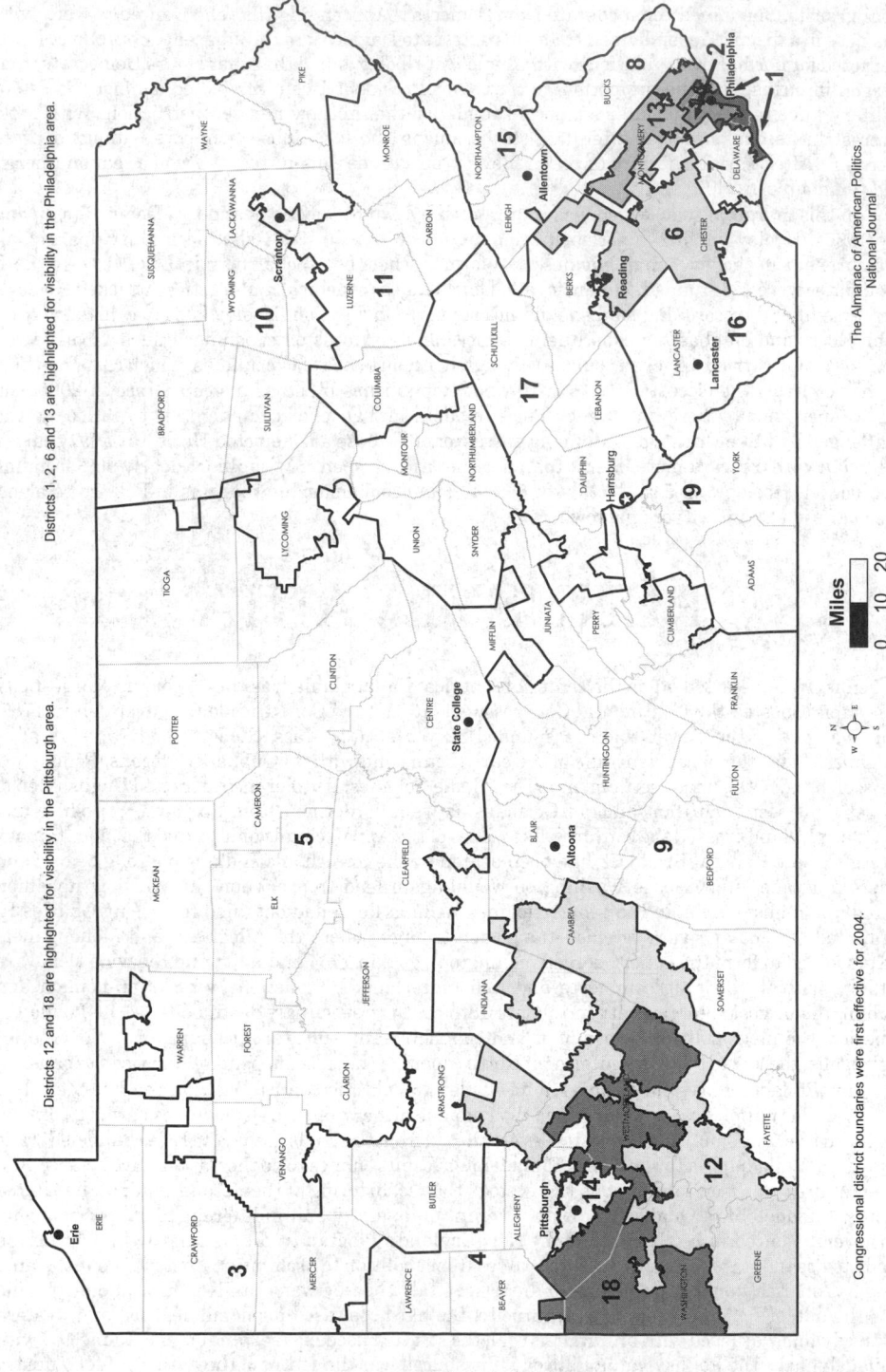

Districts 12 and 18 are highlighted for visibility in the Pittsburgh area.

Districts 1, 2, 6 and 13 are highlighted for visibility in the Philadelphia area.

The Almanac of American Politics.
National Journal

Congressional district boundaries were first effective for 2004.

Miles
0　10　20

by 1890. Immigrants poured in from Europe and from the surrounding hills to work in western Pennsylvania's mines and factories. Pittsburgh became synonymous with industrial prosperity, the inspiration behind the civic pride that celebrated huffing smokestacks. In 1900, Pennsylvania was the nation's second-largest state and growing rapidly. But the boom ended conclusively with the Depression of the 1930s, and in parts of Pennsylvania it has never returned. After World War II, both home heating and industry switched away from coal. John L. Lewis's United Mine Workers traded higher pay and benefits for payroll cuts. Even when coal prices boomed in the 1970s, strip mining created relatively few new jobs. Similarly, Pennsylvania steel began its decline three decades ago, when management decided not to keep up with new technology and agreed to big wage and benefit increases with the mistaken confidence they could pass the costs along. Big steel got import quotas as long ago as 1969—Pennsylvania has been the nation's most protectionist state since the first Bessemer converter furnaces were lit—but they didn't create jobs. By the time quotas lapsed in the 1990s, the industry had modernized, but mostly in huge new Indiana mills and small mini-mills scattered far from the factories that once lined the Monongahela.

The result has been the slowest population growth of any major state: There were 9.5 million Pennsylvanians in 1930, 12.4 million in 2006. Pennsylvania cast 36 electoral votes for Franklin Roosevelt in 1940 and 21 for John Kerry in 2004; it had 30 congressmen, as many as California, in 1960, but now has 19 to California's 53. People growing up here are as likely to leave the state as stay, and few out-of-staters move in. Pennsylvania looks and sounds today more like it did in the 1940s than any other major state. With the significant difference that Pennsylvania in 1940 had lots of young people, while the Pennsylvania of 2006 has the second largest elderly population (after Florida) of any state. Although Pennsylvania started off as our center of government, government has not been central to Pennsylvania for most of its history. During the Civil War, Pennsylvania was the site of the northernmost advance of the Confederate Army, at Carlisle, just north of Gettysburg; for generations after, it was the most Republican of the large states—for Lincoln and the Union, for the steel industry and the high tariff. Its malodorous Republican machines built parties which were not representative of one ethnic segment but had a place for just about everyone: in Philadelphia's huge City Hall, a knockoff of Paris' Hotel de Ville; in Pittsburgh's massive, Roman-columned City-County Building; in Harrisburg's grandiose Capitol with its rotunda modeled after St. Peter's in Rome and staircase modeled after the Paris Opera. In 1932, Pennsylvania was the only big state that stuck with Herbert Hoover and voted against Franklin Roosevelt. But the New Deal, John L. Lewis's United Mine Workers and the CIO industrial union movement, and a series of bloody strikes made industrial Pennsylvania almost as Democratic in the 1930s and 1940s as it had been Republican from the 1860s to the 1920s. Even then, parts of Pennsylvania not heavy with big steel factories and coal mines—the northern tier of counties along the New York border, the central part of the state around the Welsh railroad town of Altoona, and the Pennsylvania Dutch country around Lancaster, an area referred to by political consultants as the "T"—remained the strongest Republican voting bloc in the East. Philadelphia became a heavily Democratic city, but in the suburban counties, the antique Republican machines stayed in control. The result was a key marginal state in presidential elections from the 1950s to the 1990s.

In the 1980s, prosperous eastern Pennsylvania trended Republican and ailing western Pennsylvania trended Democratic. In the 1990s, culturally liberal eastern Pennsylvania trended Democratic and culturally conservative western Pennsylvania trended Republican. The east is larger—metro Philadelphia cast 33% of the state's votes in 2004 and metro Pittsburgh 20%—and the state has mostly gone its way: Pennsylvania voted Republican for president in 1980, 1984 and 1988 and Democratic in 1992, 1996, 2000 and 2004. Metro Philadelphia, which voted 50%-49% for Michael Dukakis in 1988, voted 59%-41% for John Kerry in 2004. Metro Pittsburgh, which voted 59%-40% for Dukakis, gave Kerry only a 52%-48% margin. In 1988, the senior George Bush carried Pennsylvania east of the first mountain ridge by 53%-46%, but lost the state west of the first ridge 48%-51%. In 2004, the regions were the other way around. George W. Bush lost Pennsylvania east of the first mountain ridge 44%-56% but carried west of the first ridge 53%-46%. These countervailing trends can best be explained by attitudes on cultural issues. Metro Philadelphia and eastern Pennsylvania are like the rest of the Northeast, liberal on issues like gun control and abortion; content with the economy, voters here moved toward Clinton-Gore Democrats in the 1990s. Pennsylvania west of the first mountain ridge, however, is full of strong-belief Catholics and Protestants and hunters who do not want their guns taken away. Relieved of economic stress, voters here moved toward Republicans in the 1990s.

In Pennsylvania, there is an unusually fine balance on cultural positions. Abortion is not political death here: The late Governor Bob Casey, a strong opponent of abortion, was reelected by a wide margin in 1990. And when Governor Tom Ridge first ran for the office in 1994, an anti-abortion independent got 13% of the vote, and Ridge won with only 45%. Republicans through 2006 held both of the state's U.S. Senate seats and, thanks to a partisan districting plan, a 12–7 edge in the House delegation. But for 2006 Governor Ed Rendell and Senate Democratic campaign committee head Charles Schumer had another strategy. To run against Republican Senator Rick Santorum they recruited state Treasurer Bob Casey, Jr., as solid an opponent of abortion as his father but on other issues content to identify with national Democrats. Santorum had taken his pro-life position to un-Pennsylvania-like theoretic extremes, leading the fight to provide a legislative reprieve for Terri Schiavo and interpreting the Supreme Court's decision in *Lawrence v. Texas* overturning a state anti-sodomy law as blocking any restrictions on polygamy or bestiality. This insistence on pressing cultural conservatism farther than voters would prefer was matched by the insistence of the Dover Area School District's anti-evolutionary "intelligent design" program, which was scornfully struck down by a Republican-appointed federal judge. Democrats were helped also by reaction against the Republican legislature's voting itself a pay raise—a decision which resulted in the primary defeats of 17 incumbents, including the two veteran leaders of the state Senate—and by the personal difficulties of some Republican congressmen. All of this puts Democrats in a good position going into the 2008 presidential election.

The People		Race/Ethnic Origin			Military veterans: 1,280,788 (13.7%)	
Pop. 2006 (est):	12,440,621	10,322,455	84.1%	White	WWII: 25.7%	Korea: 15.2%
Pop. 2000:	12,281,054	1,202,437	9.8%	Black	Vietnam: 28.7%	Gulf War: 6.8%
Pop. 1990:	11,881,643	218,296	1.8%	Asian	**Most populous cities (2006):**	
Change 1990-2000:	Up 3.4%	14,904	0.1%	Native Am.	1. Philadelphia	1,448,394
% of U.S. total:	4.4%	2,691	0.0%	Hawaiian	2. Pittsburgh	312,819
Pop. rank:	6th of 50	113,097	0.9%	Two+ races	3. Allentown	107,294
Area size:	46,055 sq. mi.	13,086	0.1%	Other	4. Erie	102,036
State Native:	77.7%	394,088	3.2%	Hisp. Origin	5. Reading	81,183
Non-citizen:	2.0%	**Ancestry**				
Language		German: 18.6%		Irish: 11.8%	Urban population: 77.0%	
English: 89.2%	Other Eur.: 5.4%	Italian: 8.5%		English: 5.8%	Rural population: 23.0%	
Spanish: 3.7%		Polish: 4.9%				

Education		Work Sector			General Assembly	
H.S. Grad:	81.9%	Private: 82.4%		Govt: 11.3%	Senate	29 R 21 D
College Grad:	22.4%	Self: 6.0%		Family: 0.3%	House	102 D 101 R
Industry		Unemployment: 5.7%			Legislative Term Limits: No	
Agri: 1.3%	Con: 6.0%	**Household Income**			**Registered Voters**	
Fin: 6.6%	Info: 2.6%	<15k: 16.7%		15-35k: 27.0%	D: 3,900,685	(47.7%)
Mfg: 21.4%	Prof: 30.4%	35-50k: 16.9%		50-100k: 29.0%	R: 3,300,894	(40.3%)
Public: 4.2%	Trade: 15.7%	100-150k: 6.6%		>150k: 3.7%	O: 981,297	(12.0%)
Other: 11.9%		Median: $40,106				
Occupation		Poverty status: 11.0%				
Blue collar: 25.2%	White collar: 59.5%	**Home Value**				
Gray collar: 15.3%		<50k: 17.9%	50-100k: 36.0%	100-200k: 34.4%	200-300k: 7.4%	
		300-500k: 3.1%	>500k: 1.2%	Median: $94,800		

Presidential politics For the last 70 years Pennsylvania has been a swing state in every close presidential election and even in some that were not close. Yet it is not typical of the country. With its older, deeply-rooted population, it tends to be culturally more conservative than the rest of the country; with its long-dying blue-collar communities, it tends to be economically more liberal—though both tendencies have been muted with time. But it does present a problem for political strategists of both parties: Combinations of issue positions which work for Democrats on the East and West Coasts or for Republicans in the South and the Heartland do not work well here. This was a state that was targeted by strategists for both parties in both 2000 and 2004; in his first term George W. Bush visited the state more than 30 times, more than any other state but Texas. During the campaign period, John Kerry visited just as often this state that is still the legal residence of his wife, Teresa Heinz Kerry. Both parties made yeoman

2004 Presidential Vote		
Kerry (D)	2,938,095	(51%)
Bush (R)	2,793,847	(48%)
Badnarik (Lib)	21,185	(0%)
Other	12,637	(0%)

2004 Democratic Presidential Primary		
Kerry (D)	585,683	(74%)
Dean (D)	79,799	(10%)
Edwards (D)	76,762	(10%)
Kucinich (D)	30,110	(4%)
Other	17,528	(2%)

2000 Presidential Vote		
Gore (D)	2,485,967	(51%)
Bush (R)	2,281,127	(46%)
Nader (Green)	103,392	(2%)
Other	41,699	(1%)

efforts to register and turn out voters, and with considerable success: turnout was up 23% in Philadelphia, despite declining population, and it was up as well in rural counties which are losing population. There are echoes, but rather faint ones, of the economically polarized politics of the past: the NEP exit poll showed John Kerry carrying large majorities of those with incomes under $30,000 and George W. Bush carrying large majorities of those with incomes over $150,000. But with the vast majority with incomes in between, 69% of the voters, the race was pretty much even. Voters in union households, 30% of the total, favored Kerry 62%-37%; but these are less likely to be steelworkers and more likely to be teachers today than a generation ago. There is a balancing here: 46% of Pennsylvania voters were gun owners, and they voted 62%-38% for Bush. There is relatively little evidence in the exit poll of traditional religious polarities. Protestants voted 55%-45% for Bush, Catholics only 51%-49% for Kerry, with Catholics attending mass weekly voting for Bush; those with other religions or none voted 71%-27% for Kerry.

Pennsylvania's April presidential primary has not been crucial since 1976, when Jimmy Carter clinched the Democratic nomination here by beating Henry Jackson and Morris Udall. In 1999 the legislature moved the primary date from April 25 to April 4, but it made little difference; both parties' nominations had already been cinched by then. In December 2004, Governor Ed Rendell started pushing for a primary in January or February but there wasn't much enthusiasm for the idea in the legislature.

Congressional districting Pennsylvania has 19 House members, the fewest since the 12th Congress assembled in 1811, when it had 18. It lost two seats in the reapportionment following the 2000 Census, just as it had after the seven preceding Censuses.

110th Congress Lineup
11 D   8 R

109th Congress Lineup
12 R   7 D

In 2001 and 2002 Republicans, with the governorship, a 29-21 majority in the state Senate and a 104-99 majority in the state House, were in firm control of redistricting and were determined to redraw the lines so as to transform an 11-10 margin in the House delegation to 13–6. Demographics suggested eliminating one district each from Philadelphia and the Pittsburgh area. In December 2001, state Senate Republicans unveiled their plan. Involved in drawing it were Senator Rick Santorum and Congresswoman Melissa Hart. Both had won Pittsburgh-area House seats previously held by Democrats—Santorum in 1990 and Hart in 2000—and both wanted to eliminate one Democratic and create one Republican district in the Pittsburgh area. Hart insisted she wanted to keep Democratic Beaver County in her 4th District. The Senate plan put three pairs of Democratic incumbents into the same districts: Tim Holden and

Paul Kanjorski, John Murtha and Frank Mascara, and Joe Hoeffel and Robert Borski. It created new Republican-leaning districts with no incumbents in metro Philadelphia and Pittsburgh. It seemed likely to raise the Republican edge to 13–6. The Senate passed it December 11, 27-22, basically along party lines.

But House Majority Leader John Perzel of Philadelphia had a different idea. Perzel is from Northeast Philadelphia, and had been reelected by only 92 votes in 2000, after Democrats put together a registration and voter turnout drive; he was eager to get even. He also cultivated a good relationship with Bob Brady, 1st District congressman and Philadelphia Democratic chairman. Perzel and Brady wanted to preserve three Philadelphia seats, which meant putting more Philadelphia than suburban Democrats in the new district pairing Philadelphian Bob Borski and suburbanite Joe Hoeffel. Perzel's House plan protected Murtha, the second-ranking Democrat on the House Appropriations Committee, and did not create a new Republican-leaning suburban Pittsburgh district. In the days that followed, Perzel got phone calls from NRCC Chairman Tom Davis and White House political strategist Karl Rove. Georgia Democrats had just passed a redistricting plan that seemed likely to cost Republicans seats they had counted on, and they asked Perzel to accept the Senate plan. He said there weren't enough votes to pass it in the House. But by early January 2002, House and Senate Republicans reached agreement. Their new plan made adjustments in western Pennsylvania to please Murtha; Mascara's house was placed across the street in the new Republican-leaning district in suburban Pittsburgh. Instead of pairing Democrats Holden and Kanjorski, it put Holden and Republican George Gekas in the same district. Overall it eliminated four Democratic seats and created two Republican-leaning seats.

Lawsuits were filed in both federal and state courts. Democrats argued that the plan was unconstitutional as an obvious partisan gerrymander. But the U.S. Supreme Court in racial redistricting cases in the 1990s had said that, while it was unconstitutional to draw contorted boundaries for racial reasons, it was permissible to do so for partisan reasons. The state Supreme Court rejected the Democrats' arguments. But on April 8, the three-judge federal court ruled that the plan was unconstitutional because there was a difference of 19 between the districts' population, and that the difference should have been 1; this was based on a 1980s U.S. Supreme Court case overturning a much larger population discrepancy. The court invited the legislature to amend its plan and said the election could be put off from May 21 to July 16. The legislature passed a new plan April 15 with a population discrepancy of only 1 and with minor changes, which transferred 0.6% of the state's population into different districts. But the primary season was already on; the filing deadline was March 12. Republicans asked the court to allow 2002 elections to take place under the first plan and some Democrats, afraid that their gubernatorial candidates Ed Rendell and Bob Casey Jr. would exhaust their funds in their primary fight while Republican Mike Fisher was unopposed, joined them. The court acceded.

The plan achieved some but not all of its partisan aims. Republicans took the new suburban districts. Mascara decided to run against Murtha in the primary; Murtha won handily. Borski decided to retire from the House. Democrat Holden beat Republican Gekas in the new Republican-leaning 17th District. The result was a 12–7 Republican delegation. But the results indicated that Republicans' hold on several districts was shaky and suggested they might change partisan hands some time between 2004 and 2010. In January 2003 a three-judge federal court approved the legislature's April 15 plan. In April 2004 the Supreme Court upheld the plan by a 5–4 vote stating, in effect, there is no way for a court to say when a political plan that meets the equal population standard is too political. Justice Anthony Kennedy, casting the swing vote, upheld the Pennsylvania plan but said that there still might be some role for judges in policing political gerrymanders. But Kennedy set forth no clear standard, and it seems unlikely that the courts will ever encounter a more plainly political plan than Pennsylvania's.

The shakiness of the Republicans' hold on the delegation became crystal clear when the results of the 2006 elections came in: Democrats gained 4 seats and emerged with an 11–8 edge in the delegation. Polidata estimates, based on extrapolating 2000-06 population growth to 2010, suggest that Pennsylvania will lose one seat in the apportionment following the 2010 Census. Democratic Governor Ed Rendell cannot run for reelection in 2010, and the two parties have alternated holding the governorship for eight year periods since the 1950s; Democrats had only a 102-101 margin in the state House, while Republicans despite dissatisfaction with a legislative pay raise continued to have a 29-21 edge in the state Senate. The 2005 Census estimates showed the two Philadelphia seats and the Pittsburgh area seats held by Democrats Mike Doyle and John Murtha losing population, while the only districts with a gain clearly large enough to meet the equal population standard in an 18-district plan were held by Republicans Jim Gerlach and Todd Platts. But there is enough room for manipulation of district lines in this large state to leave widely different partisan results possible.

Governor

Ed Rendell (D)

Elected 2002, term expires Jan. 2011, 2d term; b. Jan. 5, 1944, New York, NY; home, Harrisburg; U. of PA, B.A. 1965, Villanova U., J.D. 1968; Jewish; married (Marjorie).

Military Career: Army Reserve, 1968-74.

Elected Office: Dist. Atty., City of Philadelphia, 1977-85; Philadelphia Mayor, 1991-99.

Office: 225 Capitol Bldg., Harrisburg, 17120, 717-787-2500; Fax: 717-772-8284; Web site: www.governor.state.pa.us.

Election Results

2006 general	Ed Rendell (D)	2,470,517	(60%)
	Lynn Swann (R)	1,622,135	(40%)
2006 primary	Ed Rendell (D)	unopposed	
2002 general	Ed Rendell (D)	1,913,235	(53%)
	Mike Fisher (R)	1,589,408	(44%)
	Other	79,917	(2%)

Ed Rendell, a Democrat, was elected governor of Pennsylvania in 2002, the first Philadelphian elected to that position since 1914. He grew up in Manhattan, in an apartment overlooking the Hudson on Riverside Drive; his father was a middleman in the women's clothing business and an ardent New Dealer and his mother's family owned a big women's clothing manufacturer that clashed often with unions. That Rendell became a Democrat who, as mayor, clashed with unions is not perhaps a coincidence. After his father died when he was 14, he acted up and was thrown out of Riverdale Country School for a year. He graduated from the University of Pennsylvania and from the Villanova University law school, and never left Philadelphia. He got a job in Philadelphia District Attorney Arlen Specter's office prosecuting homicides. In 1977, at 33, he was elected district attorney himself, and reelected in 1981. The district attorney is a prominent figure not just in Philadelphia but also in the entire Philadelphia media market, where some 40% of Pennsylvania voters live; prominent enough that former Philadelphia district attorneys are now Pennsylvania's governor and senior U.S. senator. In 1985 he did not run for reelection but started running for governor; Pennsylvania law requires mayors and district attorneys to resign if they run for state-wide office. Since 1955 the two major parties have alternated in the governor's office every eight years; Republican Governor Richard Thornburgh was ineligible to run in 1986, and it seemed the Democrats' turn. In the Democratic primary he faced former Auditor General Bob Casey, who had lost in gubernatorial primaries in 1966, 1970 and 1978. This time Casey won, 51%-40%. Rendell carried the Philadelphia market, but in the rest of the state he seemed perhaps too young, too brash, too Philadelphian.

In 1987 Rendell ran unsuccessfully in the Democratic primary against Philadelphia's first black mayor, Wilson Goode. At 43, Rendell seemed to be through politically. But in 1991 he ran for mayor again. With Goode ineligible to run again and the city's finances in dreadful shape, Rendell, campaigning with his usual energy and ebullience, won the Democratic primary 49%-27%. In the general election he faced former Mayor Frank Rizzo, but Rizzo died of a heart attack in July 1991 and Rendell won easily in November, 64%-30%. Brash, energetic, cheerful, rumpled and a big sports fan, Rendell became a popular public figure in Philadelphia; he continues to serve as a cable television commentator for an Eagles football post-game show, a gig that began in 1998. In 2000 Rendell was named Democratic National Chairman. He campaigned for Al Gore, who had called him "America's mayor," but during the Florida controversy Rendell was readier to concede than Gore and his top advisers.

Immediately after the 2000 election Rendell set out to run for governor in 2002. Tom Ridge, the Republican governor elected in 1994 and 1998, was ineligible to run and became George W. Bush's homeland security adviser in October 2001; he was succeeded by Lieutenant Governor Mark Schweiker, who had previously announced he wanted to spend more time with his family and would not run for governor. In the 2002 Democratic primary, Rendell faced Auditor General Bob Casey Jr., whose father had defeated him 16 years earlier.

Early polls showed a close race in the Democratic primary, and many thought that this year, as in 1986, Rendell would be too Philadelphian for the rest of the state. There was a clear contrast between the candidates on issues. Casey, like his father, opposed abortion and said he would sign a ban on abortion if Roe v. Wade were reversed. He opposed gun control. Rendell favored abortion rights and gun control. There was a clear difference on economic issues as well. Rendell had an economic development initiative for parts of the state that missed the 1990s boom. Casey concentrated on extending government benefits; he advocated low-cost health insurance for unemployed workers and a $1 rise in the minimum wage. There was also a contrast in demeanor. Rendell embarked on a bus caravan traveling all over the state and campaigned with his usual brio; Casey was tightly scripted, polite and earnest.

Pennsylvania allows unlimited contributions to state campaigns, and this was a big money race: the two candidates spent more than $25 million on the primary. Rendell raised huge amounts from his Philadelphia and national contacts. Casey raised over $5 million from unions, including public employee unions still bitterly opposed to Rendell. Casey ran largely negative ads, calling Rendell's Philadelphia story a half-truth and blaming him for the conditions of the city's public schools, which had just been taken over by the state. Some of the Casey ads were scorching; a Philadelphia police officer was shown saying about Rendell, "He lies. Cops deal with liars all the time, and we have no respect for anybody who lies." The Democratic state committee endorsed Casey, and he counted on local endorsements, from influential state Senator Vince Fumo and union leaders, to dent Rendell's margin in Philadelphia.

Rendell spent $740,000 on Election Day activities, including $450,000 cash to be handed out in the city's 66 wards. But his popularity in the suburbs was even more decisive. Rendell won 79% of the vote in Philadelphia and even more in the suburbs. Altogether he carried the eight counties in the Philadelphia media market 79%-21%. Overall Rendell won 57%-43%, though he carried only two of the 59 counties outside the Philadelphia market (Lancaster and the county containing Penn State).

After the primary Rendell led conservative Attorney General Mike Fisher in the polls, but not by much. Pennsylvania's pattern of alternating parties in the governorship every eight years goes back to the 1954 election, but it is not a law of nature. Ridge and Schweiker had high job ratings. Pennsylvania elects judges in off-years, the auditor and treasurer in presidential years, and so there is a statewide partisan race every year, and Republicans had been winning almost all of them since 1990. Republicans held majorities in both houses of the legislature. Fisher had more experience in state government: he had been elected to the state House in 1974 and the state Senate in 1980 and as attorney general in 1996 and 2000; he had been the unsuccessful nominee for lieutenant governor in 1986 and an unsuccessful candidate in the 1994 primary for governor. His opposition to abortion was by no means a political liability in Pennsylvania. Nor was his platform—cutting the corporate income tax, expanding the state's prescription drug program with slots money, increased research and development tax credits, requiring school districts to give voters a choice between the property tax and an earned income tax. After the primary, Rendell was almost out of money; he had $1 million to Fisher's $5 million.

Rendell started off on a positive note, saying that Fisher had been a good attorney general and a good state senator. Fisher started more negatively, calling Rendell a "tax-and-spend liberal" and said his success as mayor was greatly exaggerated. Fisher got some bad publicity over the proposed sale of Hershey Foods by the trust that owns the company, when it was revealed that a Fisher aide had told trustees the sale, unpopular in central Pennsylvania, was a good idea. But Fisher fought the sale in court and got a judge to halt it, turning a minus into a plus. George W. Bush raised nearly $2 million for Fisher, who eventually raised $13.8 million. But Rendell vastly outraised him, with $42 million for the entire campaign, more than any other candidate in 2002 except California Governor Gray Davis, Texas Governor Rick Perry and New York Governor George Pataki. In the end, what elected Rendell was his popularity in the Philadelphia media market. In Pennsylvania, outside the two big media markets, Fisher led 58%-39%. But in the Philadelphia media market Rendell won a smashing 68%-30% victory. He won 84% of the vote in Philadelphia, but he also won huge margins in the suburbs where Republicans have a huge registration advantage and which they usually carry in statewide races. Turnout was again higher in the Philadelphia media market, which cast 41% of the state's votes.

Once in office, Rendell set about paring the state budget. He had problems with the Republican-controlled General Assembly, a far more partisan and far less malleable body than the overwhelmingly Democratic city council he had been accustomed to in Philadelphia. He proposed a 33% increase in the state income tax to help pay for early childhood education, but legislators scaled it down to just 10% and gave him less money than he wanted. His ambitious plan for slot machines to pay for property tax relief failed. The state got stuck in a bitter, nine-month budget stalemate after Rendell vetoed the $4 billion education appropriation.

But in his second year in office, Rendell won a victory on the most important piece of his agenda—slot machines. The fractious issue of legalizing gambling to pay for property tax relief created divisions within both parties; Rendell traveled the state in support of his legalized gambling plan and promised Republicans who supported his tax package, which included the slots proposal, he would not campaign against them. He said an expansion of gambling would staunch the flow of dollars to bordering states such as Delaware, New Jersey and West Virginia, all of which permit slots and other forms of wagering. The plan passed in July. The final deal authorized as many as 61,000 slot machines at 14 locations—more slots than any state other than Nevada. The 14 licenses would go to existing horse racing tracks, resorts and tracks and casinos that will be built later and were expected to bring in $1 billion per year in revenues to help the state reduce property taxes by an average of 20% statewide and pay for economic development.

Rendell had other successes in 2004. The legislature passed several items on his environmental agenda, including a bill requiring that 18% of the state's electricity come from renewable sources within 15 years and one that provided funding for rebuilding and repairing sewer and water systems. In November, Rendell won a Pittsburgh bailout package that gave the city new taxing authority. But he failed to secure a permanent funding solution for troubled transit systems in Philadelphia and Pittsburgh, caught between urban mass transit needs and those of rural areas seeking dollars for aging highways and bridges. His relations with the legislature remained stormy. When asked to assess his own performance after two years, Rendell used sports metaphors to give himself high marks. He said his achievements were an example of "winning ugly" and joked that he was "having a better year than Peyton Manning," the record-setting Indianapolis Colts quarterback. Ever the sports fan, he postponed the annual budget address in 2005 "in consideration of potential scheduling difficulties for those traveling out of state during the days immediately preceding Feb. 8." (Translation: The Eagles were in the Super Bowl and he was planning to attend).

But in May 2005, Rendell suffered a blow that threatened to kill his signature achievement. A companion bill to the legalized gambling legislation, known as Act 72, allowed school districts to opt in to the property tax relief system; districts that took that option would then receive a share of the gambling revenues in exchange for lowering property tax rates. A decision was required by May 30. The vast majority of the state's 501 school districts, it turned out, voted against participating in the distribution scheme, in part because opting in would make it more difficult for them to increase property taxes in the future.

The inability to enact property tax relief did not generate nearly as much controversy as a legislative pay raise that passed in July that year. Pennsylvania lawmakers already made a decent salary, with exceptionally generous perks and benefits, but nevertheless they voted to increase their base pay from $69,700 to about $81,000—a figure on the low end since many were entitled to even more than that because committee chairmen, vice chairmen and members of leadership receive extra pay. And they took their raise right away, despite a state constitutional clause that bars legislators from taking salary raises in the same term that they are passed in, by including a provision in the bill that allowed members to receive their raises immediately through something called "unvouchered expenses." Rendell signed the bill, which also provided raises for judges and executive branch officials, noting that the measure took away the power to grant future raises from the legislature and tied it to raises for comparable federal officials. Recognizing the volatility of the situation, he said he would not accept his own raise. Legislative pay raises are never popular with the voting public, but this one, with increases ranging from 15% to 34% and passed without debate at 2:30 a.m. as lawmakers prepared to leave for the summer, created a firestorm of outrage. In November 2005, at the first opportunity to register their anger, voters ousted state Supreme Court Justice Russell Nigro, who was seeking retention to a second 10-year term, and nearly ousted his colleague, Sandra Schultz Newman, who was also seeking retention. This jarring result, the first time a justice had lost a retention race, spurred the Republican legislature to action: eight days after the election, Rendell signed a bill repealing the raises that had passed both the House and Senate with just one vote in opposition.

Between the ill will surrounding the pay raise and his failure to enact statewide property tax relief, the cornerstone of his agenda, Rendell entered 2006 in a less than ideal position. His poll ratings were decent, but in May it became clear that the pay raise fiasco remained fresh in voters' minds as 17 legislators lost in primaries. In June though, Rendell got the silver bullet he had been seeking. He signed into law a $1 billion property tax cut, the largest in state history, with senior citizens slated to receive tax relief before gambling revenues begin to flow—an important consideration in a state with the second-largest elderly population after Florida.

By then, Republicans had settled on their nominee against Rendell: former professional football player Lynn Swann, a Hall of Famer who starred on the Pittsburgh Steelers Super Bowl champion teams of the 1970s and settled in the Pittsburgh suburbs. At first it looked as if Swann would have tough primary opposition from former two-term Lieutenant Governor Bill Scranton, the son of former Governor and 1964 presidential candidate William Scranton, but in February Scranton abruptly pulled out. That created a highly-anticipated matchup between two high-wattage candidates from opposite ends of the state. Swann dismissed Rendell's property tax plan as a "Band-aid solution" and promised "real property tax relief" pegged to passage of a constitutional amendment that would replace the current assessment-based system with one based on the purchase price of the home or other real property. After struggling with the issues in the early months of the campaign, he became defter as the campaign progressed. But Rendell, one of the most prolific fundraisers in American politics, had a large cash advantage. He began 2006 with $12 million in the bank and had $10 million more cash-on-hand than Swann through mid-September, enabling him to blanket the state in ads touting his administration's accomplishments. Rendell built a double-digit lead in the polls and ended up with a runaway 60%-40% victory, powered by huge margins in the Philadelphia media market. As expected, he won big in the city (89%-11%), but he also racked up remarkable margins in the vote-rich Philadelphia suburbs that once provided the foundation for Republican statewide victories. Rendell carried Bucks County (70%-30%), Chester County (65%-35%), Delaware County (74%-26%), and Montgomery County (72%-28%). In the west, Rendell also won Pittsburgh's Allegheny County (60%-40%).

Rendell said during the campaign that this, his 14th election, would be his last, and ruled out speculation that he was interested in running for president. When asked, Rendell said he would consider a request to run as vice president, a not so far-fetched scenario given his crushing reelection victory in a state with 21 electoral votes and his proven appeal to suburban voters. He has also been mentioned as a prospective Cabinet secretary.

Senior Senator

Arlen Specter (R)

Elected 1980, seat up 2010, 5th term; b. Feb. 12, 1930, Wichita, KS; home, Philadelphia; U. of PA, B.A. 1951, Yale U., LL.B. 1956; Jewish; married (Joan).

Military Career: Air Force, 1951-53.

Elected Office: Philadelphia Dist. Atty., 1965-73.

Professional Career: Practicing atty., 1955-56, 1974-80; Asst. Cnsl., Warren Comm., 1964; PA Asst. Atty. Gen., 1964-65.

DC Office: 711 HSOB, 20510, 202-224-4254; Fax: 202-228-1229; Web site: specter.senate.gov.

State Offices: Allentown, 610-434-1444; Erie, 814-453-3010; Harrisburg, 717-782-3951; Philadelphia, 215-597-7200; Pittsburgh, 412-644-3400; Scranton, 570-346-2006; Wilkes-Barre, 570-826-6265.

Committees: *Aging (Special)* (10th of 10 R). *Appropriations* (3d of 14 R): Labor, Health and Human Services, Education & Related Agencies (RMM); Agriculture, Rural Development, Food and Drug Administration & Related Agencies; Defense; State, Foreign Operations & Related Programs; Transportation, Housing and Urban Development & Related Agencies; Homeland Security. *Judiciary* (RMM of 9 R): Antitrust, Competition Policy & Consumer Rights; Constitution; Crime & Drugs. *Veterans' Affairs* (2d of 7 R).

Group Ratings

	ADA	ACLU	AFS	LCV	ITIC	NTU	COC	ACU	CFG	FRC
2006	30	58	33	14	67	51	100	43	40	37
2005	45	—	29	40	—	50	88	63	47	—

National Journal Ratings

	2005 LIB	—	2005 CONS		2006 LIB	—	2006 CONS
Economic	51%	—	48%		50%	—	49%
Social	52%	—	47%		56%	—	43%
Foreign	55%	—	44%		50%	—	49%

Key Votes of the 109th Congress

1. Bar ANWR Drilling	N	5. Confirm Samuel Alito	Y	9. Limit Interstate Abortion	N
2. FY06 Spending Curb	Y	6. Path to Citizenship	Y	10. CAFTA	N
3. Estate Tax Repeal	Y	7. Bar Same Sex Marriage	N	11. Urge Iraq Withdrawal	N
4. Raise Minimum Wage	Y	8. Stem Cell Research $	Y	12. Provide Detainee Rights	Y

Election Results

2004 general	Arlen Specter (R)	2,925,080	(53%)	($20,307,099)
	Joe Hoeffel (D)	2,334,126	(42%)	($4,540,209)
	James Clymer (CNP)	220,056	(4%)	($212,896)
	Other	79,843	(1%)	
2004 primary	Arlen Specter (R)	530,839	(51%)	
	Pat Toomey (R)	513,693	(49%)	
1998 general	Arlen Specter (R)	1,814,180	(61%)	($4,535,887)
	Bill Lloyd (D)	1,028,839	(35%)	($187,157)
	Other	114,753	(4%)	

Prior Winning Percentages: 1992 (49%); 1986 (56%); 1980 (50%)

Arlen Specter, one of the nation's most durable career politicians, has held public office and has been an important national figure off and on for more than four decades. Specter grew up in Russell, Kansas, also the hometown of Bob Dole; his father was an immigrant who worked as a tailor, owned a junkyard and sent four children through college. Specter came to Philadelphia at 17 to attend the University of Pennsylvania. After college he served in the Air Force, graduated from Yale Law School and practiced law in Philadelphia. In 1964 he was a top staffer for the Warren Commission investigating the Kennedy assassination and helped develop the single-bullet theory; at one point, he held Oswald's weapon and aimed it out the Texas Schoolbook Depository window toward Dealey Plaza. After the Warren Commission, he returned to his law practice, switched to the Republican Party, and was elected district attorney in Democratic Philadelphia in 1965 and again in 1969. As D.A. he gave his first job to a Penn law graduate from New York named Ed Rendell, who is now governor of Pennsylvania. Specter lost the race for D.A. in 1973, and was beaten in Republican primaries for senator in 1976 and governor in 1978. In 1980 he ran for the Senate again. He narrowly (36%-33%) edged a former state Republican chairman in the primary and beat a low-spending Democrat 50%-48% in the general. In 1986, he won reelection by a 56%-43% margin; in 1992 he was reelected 49%-46% after he became a target of feminists for his questioning of Anita Hill during the confirmation hearings of Clarence Thomas. He ran for president in 1995, but withdrew before the first caucus or primary.

Throughout this career of narrow victories and numerous defeats, Specter's assets have been brains and hard work. He is respected by colleagues and constituents, though not always well-liked. He sides with conservatives on some divisive issues, with liberals on others, building up no permanent credit with either. He is aggressive and prosecutorial, well-prepared and persuasive once he takes a stand. These traits are both his strengths and weaknesses; they explain why he was vulnerable in 1992, and why he won; why he ran for president in 1996, and why his campaign went nowhere. His voting record is almost precisely at the midpoint of the Senate, and he has played key roles on a variety of issues. Though he switched and voted to override Bill Clinton's partial-birth abortion veto, he is generally pro-choice on abortion—an issue he featured in his presidential campaign, infuriating many Republican activists. He pushes tough penalties for crime and supports capital punishment. On a closely divided and rancorous Judiciary Committee, he played a key role on several Supreme Court nominations. More than anyone else, he defeated Robert Bork in 1987 and, more than anyone but John Danforth, he secured the confirmation of Clarence Thomas in 1991. On many issues, Specter has been one of the few Republicans voting with Senate Democrats—on the Republican tax cut in August 1999, the Comprehensive Test Ban Treaty in October 1999, the minimum wage in November 1999, on the federal tobacco lawsuit in July 2000, HMO regulation in July 2000, on overtime regulations in September 2003 and March 2005.

He opposed George W. Bush's $250,000 limit on pain and suffering damages in medical malpractice cases, arguing that there should be no limit for egregious cases of severe bodily impairment, disfigurement or death; his son Shanin Specter is a Philadelphia malpractice lawyer who won a $49 million settlement in 2000. In 2003 he hired a former federal appeals judge to draw up specifications for a trust fund to handle asbestos claims. As chairman of the Judiciary Committee, he worked to create a trust fund to pay off asbestos claims and clear the dockets of the class action suits that have bankrupted dozens of companies. In April 2005 he proposed a $140 billion trust fund, to be financed by asbestos manufacturers and insurers, to compensate those who have asbestos-caused disease. This was opposed by Democrats like Richard Durbin, who opposed sending pending court cases to the trust fund, and Republicans like Jon Kyl and John Cornyn had reservations. In May 2005, after dealing with more than 100 amendments, the Judiciary Committee approved the bill; ranking Democrat Patrick Leahy joined Specter as cosponsor. But it was a complicated measure with serious financial implications and considerable opposition, and Majority Leader Bill Frist refused to bring it to the floor until January 2006. There Specter lashed out against Minority Leader Harry Reid's charge that it was a payoff to corporate lobbyists, and in February advocates fell one vote short of the 60 required to waive a budgetary point of order; it never came to the floor again.

Specter's elevation to the chairmanship did not come automatically. Senate Republicans' six-year term limit on chairmen meant that Orrin Hatch would be rotated out in January 2005. But Specter, fresh from a 51%-49% victory over conservative Congressman Pat Toomey in the April 2004 primary and a resounding victory in November, encountered opposition from cultural conservatives. Two days after the election he warned George W. Bush not to nominate judges who would try to overturn *Roe v. Wade*. In response, the Concerned Women of America, the Family Research Council and Dr. James Dobson were demanding that Republican senators deny Specter the chairmanship. Specter immediately sought to clarify his statement. "I did not warn the president about anything and was very respectful of his constitutional authority," he said. "I voted for every one of President Bush's nominees in committee and on the floor, every last one of them." Two days later White House chief strategist Karl Rove said, "Senator Specter's a man of his word. We'll take him at his word." But Majority Leader Bill Frist pointedly declined to endorse Specter for the chairmanship and said he would have to make his case to Republican senators. With his usual assiduousness, he did. On November 18 all the Republicans on the Judiciary Committee appeared with Specter and endorsed him. Specter read out a statement, "I have not and would not use a litmus test to deny confirmation to pro-life nominees. I have no reason to believe I will be unable to support any individual President Bush finds worthy of nomination." He met with leaders of cultural conservative organizations and said that there were "relevant recent precedents" to require only 51 votes to end the Democratic filibusters of judicial nominees. And he shepherded to passage the class action bill in February 2005.

"Our committee has the most liberal Democrats and, some might say, the most conservative Republicans," Specter said. "And I have to pull that group together." He held hearings and pressed successfully for approval on party lines of appeals court nominees Priscilla Owen and Janice Rogers Brown in April 2005. In May 2005 he refused to say whether he supported a change in rules, which required only 50 votes (plus Dick Cheney's tie-breaker) and was pressed by many Republicans, to prevent filibusters of judicial nominees—the so-called nuclear option. Instead he urged Frist to seek accommodation with Democrats. He attended early meetings of the bipartisan "gang of 14" which sought an agreement by enough senators to avoid a filibuster in the current composition of the Senate. When John Cornyn forced the issue by filing for cloture on nominations on May 24, the gang of 14 reached agreement, which allowed Specter to declare the nuclear option moot. In July, Justice Sandra Day O'Connor announced her retirement and George W. Bush nominated John Roberts. In his interview with Roberts, Specter asked him about televising Supreme Court arguments and pressed him on federalism—the Court in 1995 and 2000 had overturned as beyond Congress's powers to regulate interstate commerce, part of the Violence Against Women Act and the gun-free schools law. Specter backed the White House's refusal to turn over memos Roberts wrote while in the solicitor general's office (a stand endorsed by former solicitors generals of both parties). In Roberts's hearing he crisply grilled him about abortion and federalism, without the windy prefaces included by other committee members. He sharply admonished Edward Kennedy and Joseph Biden, both former chairmen of the committee, to let Roberts complete his answers without interruption. After the hearings he announced his support of Roberts and the committee approved him 13–5. In October, after Harriet Miers's nomination was withdrawn, he said she was the victim of a "one-sided debate" and could not survive "the heavy decibel level against her." When Samuel Alito was nominated, he sent him written questions and scheduled hearings for January 2006. On Alito, opinion split on party lines; Specter said, "There are too many senators who appear to have made up their minds." An attempt to filibuster fell far short of the needed votes, and Alito was approved 58-42. The Judiciary Committee does not hold oversight hearings on Supreme Court justices' opinions, but Specter has made a practice of lunching with each of them in the senators' dining room.

Specter worked for reauthorization of the Patriot Act, which the Senate passed in July 2005, with more restrictions than the House measure. Several Senate Republicans had qualms about the measure and blocked agreement on the conference report in December, but the bill passed in March 2006. When *The New York Times* reported in December 2005 that the NSA was conducting surveillance of communications between al Qaeda suspects abroad and persons in the United States, Specter said that that violated the Foreign Intelligence Surveillance Act of 1978. In February 2006 Intelligence Committee Chairman Pat Roberts said his committee could better handle the issue; Specter replied, "I would agree with him, and I would defer to him. Where's the legislation?" He introduced a bill requiring the FISA court to approve every surveillance every 45 days, and in April threatened to withhold funding of the program. In May 2006, when it was revealed that the NSA was engaged in data mining, he said he would request testimony from telephone companies which provided information. On the eve of the markup in May, he and Dianne Feinstein introduced another bill requiring that surveillance of U.S. citizens in the country must be conducted according to FISA, streamlining the approval process in the FISA court and requiring individual warrants for surveillance targets. But other committee Republicans failed to back Specter up, and in June he withdrew his request for information from the telephone companies and dropped the provision requiring mandatory FISA court approval. He criticized Dick Cheney for lobbying other committee Republicans on the latter issue; Cheney wrote a conciliatory letter in return. Because of objections, the bill did not come to the floor, and Specter produced a third version after the election, which Democrats blocked. Specter also has addressed the issue of illegal enemy combatants held in Guantanamo. In July 2006, he called for an independent commission to investigation incarceration policies. He visited Guantanamo in August 2005, but the Defense Department blocked him from holding a hearing there. In June 2006 the Supreme Court ruled that Congress must establish military tribunals to rule on Guantanamo detainees.

In February and March 2006 Specter introduced his own immigration bills, a guest worker bill with no limit on numbers and stays up to six years and a legalization bill providing for gold cards for eligible illegals that could be renewed every two years indefinitely. In April he urged George W. Bush to hold a "pre-conference" conference with Democrats and House members. In May immigration was taken up on the floor, and a compromise worked out by John McCain and Edward Kennedy passed. When the House leadership refused to go to conference and urged members to hold hearings across the country, Specter urged senators to hold hearings as well. The conference was never held, but in September the House and Senate passed a bill authorizing a 700-mile border fence. He weighed in on various issues, criticizing George W. Bush's signing statements, asking the FBI for information on the Able Danger intelligence, criticizing Deputy Attorney General Larry Thompson's 2003 memorandum requiring corporations to waive the attorney-client privilege in return for not being criminally prosecuted, opining that the Philadelphia Eagles's suspension of Terrell Owens was a violation of antitrust law. In February 2007, when some Democrats were urging rescission of the 2002 Iraq war resolution, he called for hearings on the president's commander-in-chief powers.

Specter has brought his legalistic approach to foreign policy. His May 1999 amendment to the defense authorization bill, invoking the War Powers Act to prevent the deployment of ground troops in the former Yugoslavia, failed 52-48. In July 2002 he called for a congressional vote on military action in Iraq. "We have a responsibility institutionally under the Constitution to declare war, and we have a responsibility to acquaint the American people as to what is involved." In debate on the resolution in October, he expressed doubts about whether Congress can delegate authority to president, but he voted for the resolution. In January 2003 he said it was not necessary for the United States to go back to the UN Security Council before taking action, but "realistically we should." He favors the International Criminal Court opposed by the Bush administration.

Specter has played a major role in encouraging medical research. He cited his own experiences with a brain tumor and with stage IV-B Hodgkin's lymphoma, for which he underwent chemotherapy for five months in 2005. (He never missed a session in that busy year and quipped later, "I think what I'm going to be most remembered for is having my hair grow back.") He and Tom Harkin, as their parties' leaders on the Labor-HHS Appropriations Subcommittee, strongly backed the process of doubling the NIH budget over five years. He has supported federal funding of embryonic stem cell research, together with Harkin and Orrin Hatch. In July 2005, as subcommittee chairman, he got an appropriation with a $1.1 billion increase for NIH approved by voice vote in the subcommittee. He said he might include funding for embryonic stem cell research, but dropped the idea in October; Congress in 2006 passed a freestanding stem cell bill which was vetoed by George W. Bush. Specter's attempt to provide flexibility for more funding of avian flu vaccine delayed approval. In July 2006 he led the subcommittee in approving an appropriation which, because of tight budget limits, in his opinion amounted to "the disintegration of the appropriate federal role in health, education and worker protections."

Specter is not shy about using his place on the committee to funnel money into Pennsylvania, from the Philadelphia Navy Yard to Lake Erie; he has traveled indefatigably to all over Pennsylvania's 67 counties and promoted projects in most or all of them. When Citizens Against Government Waste listed him in its "Pig Book," he said, "If they left me out, I'd be worried."

In politically marginal Pennsylvania, without a firm base in his own party, Specter has never had an entirely safe seat. Yet he has been, since November 2005, the longest-serving senator in Pennsylvania history. (The old record was held by Boies Penrose, who served from 1897 to 1921.) He has had opposition in each Republican primary. In 1986 he was renominated 76%-24% over a social studies teacher who said he had entered the race at God's urging; in 1992 he won 65%-35% over a state representative who opposed abortion; in 1998 he won with 67% against two candidates who won 18% and 15%. In February 2003 conservative Congressman Pat Toomey, an opponent of abortion and advocate of tax cuts, set out to run against him. White House political strategist Karl Rove made it clear to Toomey that George W. Bush would support Specter; White House Chief of Staff Andrew Card in February 2003 attended a fundraiser for Specter in Toomey's district. On Toomey's side was *National Review* (which called Specter "the worst Republican senator"), former Judge Robert Bork and former Attorney General Edwin Meese, former presidential candidate Steve Forbes and longtime conservative strategist Paul Weyrich. The Club for Growth raised $1 million for Toomey and spent $1 million of soft money on advocacy ads. But Specter had much more: in March 2003 he had $7 million in his campaign treasury and he spent $15 million up through the April 2004 primary. Specter campaigned on his seniority and his seat on the Appropriations Committee; his campaign slogan was "Courage. Clout. Convictions." "I would say it's an election to see if there's going to be any place in the Republican party for a big tent," he said. "It's more than the soul of the Republican party; it's to have some balance within the party and within the two-party system." Toomey's framing of the issues was directed at conservative Republicans. "Today we have complete control. And the question that I'm posing to Republican primary voters all across Pennsylvania is a simple one: Are we going to seize this opportunity to govern with a common sense conservative agenda, or are we going to let it slip away by reelecting a liberal who will fight our agenda?" Toomey's message was undercut by frequent appearances for Specter by his conservative colleague Rick Santorum and by Dick Cheney and George W. Bush. Specter had not backed Santorum in his 1994 primary, but had provided him critical help in the general election that year; the Bush White House has made it clear that it supports all incumbent Republicans and hopes that moderate incumbents will keep that in mind when casting key votes on priority issues. Toomey started off little known outside his own congressional district, but spent enough money to get his message across, and nearly won. After 24 years in the Senate Specter won the primary by only 51%-49%. He carried metro Philadelphia 57%-43%, but Toomey carried metro Pittsburgh 58%-42%. Toomey won 2–1 in his 15th District and carried Lancaster and York Counties in the Pennsylvania Dutch territory and several industrial counties in the ring around Pittsburgh. Perhaps decisive were Specter's large majorities in most of the state's small counties. "They know my footprint all over the northern tier," he said. "I have a very strong bond with the people of Pennsylvania. It comes from having visited every one of the counties." And certainly he would not have won without the vigorous support of Bush, Cheney and Santorum.

In the general election, against suburban Philadelphia Congressman Joe Hoeffel, Specter trumpeted his differences with the Bush administration on issues like overtime pay, vouchers and stem cell research. Hoeffel protested that Specter was "meek, a supporter of the Bush program, which has alarmed a lot of moderates, with the budget deficits growing and the deceptions in Iraq and all the rest." But Specter had much more money to deliver his message of clout and convictions. Overall, Specter spent $21.6 million to Hoeffel's $4.6 million; in the last three weeks of the campaign Specter outspent Hoeffel by $1.2 million to $450,000. National Democrats were reluctant to pour money into an iffy race in a large and expensive state. In September Specter was endorsed by the Philadelphia Black Clergy and the state AFL-CIO. In debates Specter relished taking the center position between Hoeffel, who had a very liberal voting record, and Constitution Party nominee James Clymer, who attacked him from the right and ended up winning 4% of the vote. Specter won 53%-42%, trailing 53%-47% in metro Philadelphia and leading 51%-49% in metro Pittsburgh. Specter won 25% among blacks, 48% in union households, and 23% among liberals. But his overall percentage of 53% was not much above Bush's 48%; though he ran 6% ahead of Bush in metro Philadelphia and more than that in the counties containing Scranton and Erie, he ran behind Bush in most of Pennsylvania west of Harrisburg except for the sparsely-populated northern tier.

In March 2007 Specter let it be known that he would run for reelection in 2010. "I'm right on the brink of being chairman of Appropriations," he said.

Junior Senator

Bob Casey (D)

Elected 2006, seat up 2012, 1st term; b. Apr. 13, 1960, Scranton; home, Scranton; Col. of the Holy Cross, B.A. 1982, Catholic U., J.D. 1988; Catholic; married (Terese).

Elected Office: PA Aud. Gen., 1996-2004; PA Treas., 2004-06.

Professional Career: Practicing atty., 1988-96.

DC Office: 383 RSOB, 20510, 202-224-6324; Fax: 202-228-0604; Web site: casey.senate.gov.

State Offices: Bellefonte, 814-357-0314; Erie, 814-874-5080; Harrisburg, 717-231-7540; Philadelphia, 215-405-9660; Pittsburgh, 412-803-7370; Scranton, 570-941-0930.

Committees: *Aging (Special)* (9th of 11 D). *Agriculture, Nutrition & Forestry* (10th of 11 D): Nutrition and Food Assistance, Sustainable and Organic Agriculture & General Legislation; Energy, Science & Technology; Domestic & Foreign Marketing, Inspection, & Plant & Animal Health. *Banking, Housing & Urban Affairs* (10th of 11 D): Housing, Transportation & Community Development; Security & International Trade & Finance; Securities, Insurance & Investment. *Foreign Relations* (10th of 11 D): International Operations & Organizations, Democracy & Human Rights; European Affairs; International Development & Foreign Assistance, Economic Affairs & International Environmental Protection. *Joint Economic Committee* (5th of 10 D).

Group Ratings and Key Votes: Newly Elected

Election Results

2006 general	Bob Casey (D)	2,392,984	(59%)	($17,592,210)
	Rick Santorum (R)	1,684,778	(41%)	($25,832,567)
2006 primary	Bob Casey (D)	629,271	(85%)	
	Chuck Pennacchio (D)	66,364	(9%)	
	Alan Sandals (D)	48,113	(6%)	
2000 general	Rick Santorum (R)	2,481,962	(52%)	($10,616,262)
	Ron Klink (D)	2,154,908	(46%)	($3,641,167)
	Other	98,246	(2%)	

Bob Casey Jr., a Democrat elected in 2006, is the junior senator from Pennsylvania. He was born in the former coal town of Scranton, the oldest son in a large Irish-Catholic political family that is often, and inaptly, referred to as Pennsylvania's equivalent of the Kennedys. Only one Kennedy, Kathleen Kennedy Townsend, has ever lost an election; the Caseys have lost almost as many as they have won. Casey's father, Robert Casey, lost in three Democratic primaries before winning the first of his two terms as governor in 1986. A brother, Pat Casey, twice ran unsuccessfully for the House with another Casey brother serving as his campaign manager. There is little glamour attached to the Caseys: Robert Casey was a feisty, tradition-minded practitioner of New Deal-style politics, known best nationally as a steadfast opponent of abortion. In 1992, he was prevented from speaking at the Democratic National Convention, a decision certainly related to his stance on abortion but also brought on by his skepticism about Bill Clinton.

Like his father, Bob Jr. graduated from the College of the Holy Cross in Massachusetts. He taught in an inner city Philadelphia school for the Jesuit Volunteer Corps and got his law degree from Catholic University in Washington, D.C. He practiced law in Scranton and then won election as state auditor general in 1996, a contest that marked the start of a brief but peripatetic career that landed him in the Senate exactly a decade later. He won reelection in 2000, ran unsuccessfully for governor in 2002, won the state treasurer's office in 2004, then defeated two-term Republican Senator Rick Santorum in 2006.

Just four years earlier, Casey's prospects did not seem so bright. Running as a cultural conservative with strong labor support, he lost a bitter and expensive 2002 governor's primary against former Philadelphia Mayor Ed Rendell. Casey's tightly-scripted campaign and negative ads tarnished his image, but he proved his resilience by returning two years later to win the treasurer's office with 3.4 million votes, more than any other candidate in Pennsylvania history. This of course caught the attention of the national party, which was looking for a top-tier challenger against Santorum, a high-profile social conservative with a red-state following and a blue-state electorate. First in the House and then in the Senate, Santorum showed a knack for winning elections against tough odds. But the state's political landscape had shifted considerably since his first election to the Senate in 1994. Pennsylvania has gone Democratic in the last four presidential elections; in 2002, Rendell captured the governorship and easily carried the populous and once-Republican Philadelphia suburbs.

The Democratic Senatorial Campaign Committee considered Casey the only prospective heavyweight challenger to Santorum and quickly moved to clear the field to avoid a bruising and cash-draining primary. There was one problem: Casey, like his father, opposes abortion, which made him anathema to the abortion-rights lobby. But expediency won over ideology as the DSCC calculated that Casey would make inroads into Santorum's culturally conservative and pro-life base yet still would be acceptable to pro-choice voters in suburban Philadelphia. The national party's heavy-handed involvement rankled many Democrats; for a time former NARAL Pro-Choice America President Kate Michelman contemplated running as an independent. Resistance to Casey's candidacy faded in the run-up to the election as Casey maintained a steady and sizable lead over Santorum in the polls.

Santorum began the campaign in a difficult position. Though he was mentioned as a potential presidential candidate, his standing back home was tenuous. As early as April 2005, he trailed Casey by double digits in the polls. That summer, he released a book titled, *It Takes a Family: Conservatism and the Common Good*—the year before he stood for reelection was perhaps not the best timing for a wide-ranging and frank discourse on some of the most divisive and controversial cultural issues. Nor was his high-ranking position in Senate Republican leadership and his support for the Bush administration helpful in 2006. Casey hammered him for voting "98 percent of the time" with Bush and characterized Santorum as an ideologue with close ties to special interests such as the oil, pharmaceutical and insurance industries. Democrats sought mileage from the issue of Santorum's residence—an issue Santorum had used against his opponent in his first House campaign in 1990—and questioned whether his Virginia home disqualified him from casting a vote in Penn Hills, the Pittsburgh suburb where Santorum owned a home and was registered to vote. Democrats also criticized him for using Penn Hills school district taxpayer dollars to educate his children in a Pennsylvania-based online charter school though they spent much of their time in Virginia.

Santorum did not run like an incumbent nor Casey like a challenger. Santorum, who trailed in the polls from beginning to end, campaigned aggressively across the state while Casey limited his public appearances in the early stages of the campaign. Santorum in November 2005 called for 10 debates—a typical challenger's move—while Casey declined to specify the number of debates they should have. Republicans accused Casey of not being ready to serve in the Senate; later, a Santorum ad would accuse Casey of constantly running for elected office rather than actually doing work. "Come out from behind the name and stand before the voters of Pennsylvania and talk about the issues that are important to the people of this state," Santorum said. The two candidates clashed over the war in Iraq, Social Security and immigration; Casey's socially conservative positions—he opposed abortion, gun control and same sex marriage (though he supported civil unions) and indicated he would have voted for George W. Bush's Supreme Court nominees, John Roberts and Samuel Alito—helped cut into Santorum's advantage outside the state's metropolitan areas.

This was an expensive campaign: together the two candidates raised $43 million. Santorum outspent Casey by more than $8 million, and it still wasn't nearly enough. Casey won in a 59%-41% rout, to become the first Pennsylvania Democrat elected to a full Senate term since Joe Clark in 1962 and the first senator elected from Northeastern Pennsylvania. Casey won by huge margins in Pittsburgh's Allegheny County (65%-35%) and in Philadelphia (84%-16%), while holding his own in the Republican "T" that stretches from Pennsylvania Dutch country around Lancaster to the northern tier of sparsely-populated counties along the New York border. Casey also swept the populous Philadelphia suburbs, winning 62% in Delaware and Montgomery Counties, 59% in Bucks County and 55% in Chester County.

In the Senate, despite concerns from abortion opponents who worried he would go wobbly, in April 2007 Casey was one of two Democrats to vote against a measure providing federal funding for embryonic stem cell research.

FIRST DISTRICT

Rep. Robert Brady (D)

Elected May 1998, 5th full term; b. Apr. 7, 1945, Philadelphia; home, Philadelphia; St. Thomas More H.S.; Catholic; married (Debra).

Elected Office: 34th Ward Dem. Exec. Cmte. Mbr., 1967-present, Ward Ldr., 1980.

Professional Career: Carpenter; Real estate salesman; Philadelphia Dpty. Mayor for Labor, 1984-87; Chmn., Philadelphia Dem. Party, 1986; Legis. Rep., Metro. Regional Cncl. of Carpenters & Joiners, 1987-98; Lecturer, U. of PA, 1997-present.

DC Office: 206 CHOB, 20515, 202-225-4731; Fax: 202-225-0088; Web site: www.brady.house.gov.

District Offices: Chester, 610-874-7094; Philadelphia, 215-389-4627; Philadelphia, 215-426-4616 .

Committees: *Armed Services* (12th of 34 D): Readiness; Air & Land Forces. *House Administration* (Chmn. of 6 D).

Group Ratings

	ADA	ACLU	AFS	LCV	ITIC	NTU	COC	ACU	CFG	FRC
2006	95	95	100	75	14	14	53	16	18	0
2005	100	—	100	72	—	12	35	4	10	8

National Journal Ratings

	2005 LIB	—	2005 CONS	2006 LIB	—	2006 CONS
Economic	71%	—	29%	66%	—	33%
Social	85%	—	15%	82%	—	18%
Foreign	76%	—	23%	70%	—	28%

Key Votes of the 109th Congress

1. Estate Tax Repeal	N	5. Limit Interstate Abortion	N	9. Build Border Fence	N
2. Limit CAFE Standards	Y	6. Extend Patriot Act	N	10. CAFTA	N
3. FY06 Spending Curb	N	7. Bar Same Sex Marriage	N	11. Oppose Iraq Withdrawal	N
4. Drilling in ANWR	Y	8. Stem Cell Research $	Y	12. Detainee Tribunals	N

Election Results

2006 general	Robert Brady (D) .... unopposed			($564,660)
2006 primary	Robert Brady (D) .... unopposed			
2004 general	Robert Brady (D) 214,462	(86%)		($361,532)
	Deborah Williams (R) 33,266	(13%)		

Prior Winning Percentages: 2002 (86%); 2000 (88%); 1998 (81%); 1998 (74%)

The People		Race/Ethnic Origin	Ancestry	
Area size:	68 sq. mi.	33.0% White	Irish: 8.9%	Italian: 7.8%
Urban population:	100.0%	44.9% Black	German: 5.0%	
Rural population:	0.0%	4.8% Asian	**2004 Presidential Vote**	
Pop. 2000:	646,357	0.2% Native Am.	Kerry (D) 227,327	(84%)
Pop. 2005 (est):	634,829	0.0% Hawaiian	Bush (R) 41,509	(15%)
Median income:	$28,261	1.8% Two+ races	Other 531	(0%)
Poverty status:	26.9%	0.2% Other	**2000 Presidential Vote**	
Military veterans:	10.2%	15.0% Hispanic Origin	Gore (D) 181,274	(84%)
			Bush (R) 31,722	(15%)
			Other 2,679	(1%)
			Cook Partisan Voting Index: D +36	

Occupation	Blue collar: 21.2%	White collar: 56.9%	Gray collar: 21.9%

In Center City Philadelphia, the 1680s look out on the 1780s, 1880s, 1980s and beyond. The statue of William Penn, who founded the city in 1682, stands 37 feet high atop the 548-foot tower of the 1880s Second Empire-style City Hall at Market and Broad. To the east is Independence Hall, where Americans in the 1780s drew up the nation's Constitution; to the west is the tower of One Liberty Place, with its "romantic modernist" spire, the 1980s building that broke tradition to rise above City Hall. Philadelphia is built on a certain order. Other American colonies were settled by practical men, out to make money or replicate a farm settlement back home. But Penn was a Quaker, a member of one of those rationalizing sects of the 17th century, who intended to impose order on his new environment, and did: no cowpath street patterns here, like those in Boston or Charleston, but a grid of numbered and named streets, with precisely spaced open squares. Penn's city of brotherly love has turned out to be a commercial and industrial metropolis that grew steadily over the years, spreading out over the countryside. Yet there are still places in which you can see the distant past: in the restored townhouses of Society Hill and the tree-shaded public buildings around Independence Hall and, on the way to the ornate City Hall, the Federal and Greek Revival buildings and the temples of commerce, built when Philadelphia was the nation's largest city. Interspersed are I.M. Pei's modernist Society Hill Towers (though the rich in Philadelphia, unlike New York or Chicago, don't much like apartments) and the 1920s masonry-faced skyscrapers and 1990s glass-and-steel towers built around City Hall and in Center City farther west.

For all the grandeur of its City Hall, with granite walls up to 22 feet thick, Philadelphia has seldom had a city government of which to be proud. "Corrupt beyond redemption" is how Lincoln Steffens described the city more than a century ago. Corruption and incompetence have reigned here off and on since then. While the city's private economy grew robustly in the 1980s, the city government lurched unknowingly toward bankruptcy under Mayor Wilson Goode. Then in 1991 Democrat Ed Rendell was elected mayor—and did well enough to become in 2002 the first former Philadelphia mayor to be elected governor since 1906. Unfortunately, Rendell's push for reform stalled in the mid-1990s. Philadelphia still has an inordinately expensive city government and neighborhoods, ravaged by crime, that have emptied out over the years. But there are signs of hope. Philadelphia has some of the nation's most vibrant and charitably active churches; its economy attracts some Latino and Asian immigrants, though many fewer than New York or Chicago; its Center City remains attractive to young professional residents, most of them white. The metropolitan area is still the sixth largest in the country, but most people live outside the city.

The 1st Congressional District of Pennsylvania contains much of Philadelphia east of Broad Street; City Hall is on the district line. The 1st includes all of 18th century Philadelphia—Independence Hall, the U.S. Mint, and Elfreth's Alley (the oldest continually occupied residential block in the country)—as well as Chinatown, Society Hill, Overbrook, the Northern Liberties village and Penn's Landing. It includes Philadelphia's four-square-block convention center, now the largest in the Northeast. North of Center City, the 1st takes in much of heavily black North Philadelphia, a couple of wards of Northeast Philadelphia (connected to the rest by irregular boundaries), Kensington and its closely packed 19th century homes, where descendants of Irish and Italian immigrants lived for years in tiny frame houses; now the neighborhood (as well as nearby Fairhill) is increasingly Hispanic. South of Center City, the 1st includes once-heavily Italian South Philadelphia, where families and their small stores and restaurants have been pressed tightly into narrow streets under a tangle of overhead wires; this is the neighborhood where the various *Rockys* were filmed and the original Philadelphia cheesesteaks are sold, as are some occasional politicians. Near there, the district takes in the city's stadium and arena complex, where the 2000 Republican convention was held, as well as the adjoining Navy Yard, established in 1762 and closed in 1996, with plans for commercial development. The 1st continues along the Delaware River shore southwest into Delaware County to impoverished Chester. The district includes three wards in heavily black West Philadelphia and a few small adjacent suburbs. The population of the minority-majority district in 2000 was 45% black, less than the 61% black 2d District, and 15% Hispanic (mainly Puerto Rican), the highest of any Pennsylvania district. This is a heavily Democratic district.

The congressman from the 1st District is Bob Brady, a Democrat first elected in May 1998. He is the personification of Philadelphia's old-fashioned urban politics, one of the last white ethnic machine bosses left in big-city America. He grew up in Overbrook Park in West Philadelphia, with an Irish father who was a policeman and an Italian mother; he depicts himself as a roll-up-your-sleeves guy who represents working class voters. After high school he went to work as a carpenter, quickly rose up the ranks of the carpenters' union leadership, and remains a dues-paying member. He entered politics in 1967, at 22, when the local ward leader wouldn't replace a burnt-out streetlight. Brady was elected to the 34th Ward Democratic Executive Committee, and in 1980 he was elected ward leader. In 1975 he became assistant sergeant-at-arms of the city council; he was a consultant to the state Senate and member of the Pennsylvania Turnpike Commission and on the board of the city's Redevelopment Authority. In 1986 he became chairman of the Philadelphia Democratic Party, where he has been a close ally of local powerbrokers like state Senator Vincent Fumo. Brady is proud to be the boss of what he calls the nation's largest big city machine—or, as he defines it, an "organization", one that mostly operates below the public's radar screen. Brady is known for making "arrangements" with others—"they're always arrangements, never deals," he insists—and that has enabled him to remain chairman for two decades.

In November 1997, Thomas Foglietta, a veteran of South Philly politics, resigned after being confirmed as ambassador to Italy, and Brady ran for the seat. In other cities, this might have led to a primary fight with black politicians but in Philadelphia, ward leaders in the district determined the Democratic nomination for the special election. That gave Brady a great advantage; former 2d District Congressman Lucien Blackwell, probably his strongest opponent, dropped out of the race even before Brady officially declared. With the endorsement of many black leaders and a strong Election Day organization, he won the special election with 74% of the vote. He is one of less than a handful of white members who represent an urban, primarily minority district.

Even after he was elected to the House, Brady's attention remained back home. He mediated the local teachers' strike in 2000, and he sought common ground between the mayor and city council on a deal for two new stadiums. His ties to City Hall and to local unions gave him credibility with both sides. As then-Mayor John Street won reelection in 2003, even as the feds were investigating city contracts, Brady worked to resolve local intra-party conflicts. According to the *Philadelphia Daily News,* he chewed out feuding city council Democrats at one memorable private meeting. "You are a [friggin'] embarrassment. You're embarrassing me, embarrassing yourselves. You're like a bunch of 10-year-old children. If you're not careful, you're not going to be here next year," he said, banging the table. "I've got 30 ward leaders who don't want to support you and 30 more who want to run against you."

In the House, where he has a mostly liberal voting record, his positions on national issues are not always set in stone; he decided that he was in favor of abortion rights after asking his mother. For "the most powerful man in Philadelphia," *Philadelphia* magazine wrote, "Washington gas-bagging is not his thing." His initiatives reflect his local orientation. His loyalty to unions led him to buck environmentalists and most Democrats, and vote to allow oil drilling in the Arctic National Wildlife Refuge. But these national issues and the aura of the Capitol are not what motivate Brady; his most important job remained running the party's city committee. "Ninety-five percent of my day is not Congress," he said in 2002.

After some hesitation, he ran for mayor in the May 2007 primary. He joined the field late and had significant opposition, including from three veteran local black officials who had operated largely outside the confines of Brady's organization—Congressman Chaka Fattah, state Representative Dwight Evans and former City Councilman Michael Nutter. Brady's platform was standard fare, including a call for cleaner and more open government, safer streets, improved schools and lower taxes—though the details were not always certain. "Don't lose hope. Help is on the way," he shouted as he declared his candidacy in January. Democratic ward leaders endorsed him, with varying enthusiasm. His campaign ran into an unusual stumbling block: a lawsuit seeking to remove Brady from the ballot because he did not include requisite information in a candidate disclosure form, most notably his union pension. When Brady revealed in court that his pension benefits were accruing as though he was working a full work week—a curiosity, given the fact that he was serving in Congress—the *Philadelphia Inquirer* reported that his "stumbling performance on the witness stand" raised "a harsh question: Is Bob Brady smart enough to be mayor?" He ended up finishing a distant third with 15%, well behind Nutter who won the nomination with 37% and wealthy businessman Thomas Knox, who had 25%. Fattah came in fourth, barely behind Brady, also with 15%.

Ever the party loyalist, Brady immediately dismissed the results as a "family squabble" and moved quickly to endorse Nutter. But in Philadelphia's Byzantine politics, Brady's weak performance—he won just 4 of 66 wards and lost even his home ward in Overbrook—raised questions about his political vulnerability. There was talk of a 2008 primary challenge from an African-American candidate, perhaps even from state Representative Thomas Blackwell, the son of former Congressman Lucien Blackwell. "I'm not going away anywhere," Brady told the *Inquirer*. "There's no blood in the water."

Despite the defeat, Brady ended up as a mayor of another kind. Shortly after his primary loss, Speaker Nancy Pelosi named Brady to replace the late Juanita Millender-McDonald as chairman of the House Administration Committee, making him the so-called as "Mayor of Capitol Hill."

SECOND DISTRICT

Rep. Chaka Fattah (D)

Elected 1994, 7th term; b. Nov. 21, 1956, Philadelphia; home, Philadelphia; Community Col. of Philadelphia, U. of PA, M.A. 1986, Harvard U. Kennedy Schl. of Gov., 1984; Baptist; married (Renee Chenault).

Elected Office: PA House of Reps., 1982-88; PA Senate, 1988-94.

Professional Career: Asst. Dir., House of Umoja, 1977-79; City of Philadelphia, Spec. Asst. to Dir. of Housing & Community Dev., 1980, Spec. Asst. to Managing Director, 1981.

DC Office: 2301 RHOB, 20515, 202-225-4001; Fax: 202-225-5392; Web site: www.house.gov/fattah.

District Offices: Philadelphia, 215-848-9386; Philadelphia, 215-387-6404.

Committees: *Appropriations* (23d of 37 D): Commerce, Justice, Science & Related Agencies; Energy & Water Development; Homeland Security.

Group Ratings

	ADA	ACLU	AFS	LCV	ITIC	NTU	COC	ACU	CFG	FRC
2006	100	95	100	100	0	11	40	8	11	0
2005	90	—	100	89	—	10	40	4	4	8

National Journal Ratings

	2005 LIB	—	2005 CONS		2006 LIB	—	2006 CONS
Economic	84%	—	15%		85%	—	15%
Social	82%	—	17%		81%	—	18%
Foreign	81%	—	18%		92%	—	5%

Key Votes of the 109th Congress

1. Estate Tax Repeal	N	5. Limit Interstate Abortion	N	9. Build Border Fence	N
2. Limit CAFE Standards	N	6. Extend Patriot Act	N	10. CAFTA	N
3. FY06 Spending Curb	N	7. Bar Same Sex Marriage	N	11. Oppose Iraq Withdrawal	N
4. Drilling in ANWR	N	8. Stem Cell Research $	Y	12. Detainee Tribunals	N

Election Results

2006 general	Chaka Fattah (D)	165,867	(89%)	($688,698)
	Michael Gessner (R)	17,291	(9%)	
	Other	4,125	(2%)	
2006 primary	Chaka Fattah (D)	unopposed		
2004 general	Chaka Fattah (D)	253,226	(88%)	($384,313)
	Stewart Bolno (R)	34,411	(12%)	($16,973)

Prior Winning Percentages: 2002 (88%); 2000 (98%); 1998 (87%); 1996 (88%); 1994 (86%)

The People		Race/Ethnic Origin	Ancestry	
Area size:	60 sq. mi.	29.9% White	Irish: 6.8%	Italian: 5.4%
Urban population:	100.0%	60.7% Black	German: 4.7%	
Rural population:	0.0%	4.3% Asian	**2004 Presidential Vote**	
Pop. 2000:	646,355	0.2% Native Am.	Kerry (D) 266,174	(87%)
Pop. 2005 (est):	598,266	0.0% Hawaiian	Bush (R) 37,811	(12%)
Median income:	$30,646	1.7% Two+ races	Other 759	(0%)
Poverty status:	23.8%	0.2% Other	**2000 Presidential Vote**	
Military veterans:	10.6%	3.0% Hispanic Origin	Gore (D) 221,517	(87%)
			Bush (R) 29,458	(12%)
			Other 3,529	(1%)
			Cook Partisan Voting Index: D +39	

Occupation	Blue collar: 14.6%	White collar: 65.8%	Gray collar: 19.5%

Looking out over the Schuylkill River north of Center City Philadelphia, you can still see the landscape painted 100 years ago by Philadelphia artist Thomas Eakins—the tightly-packed but formidable rowhouses, the old fieldstone houses of Germantown, the gray-blue water flowing past boat houses below the small Greek temples of the Water Works and the larger temple of the Philadelphia Museum of Art. On both sides of this romantic scene are some of Philadelphia's long-established black neighborhoods: West Philadelphia, across the Schuylkill on either side of Market Street; North Philadelphia, on either side of Broad Street; historic Germantown to the northwest, off the narrow diagonal of Germantown Avenue that ran through open fields in Benjamin Franklin's time, where the British prevailed in a 1777 battle. Many of these neighborhoods continue to suffer from poverty and blight, and the city has 600,000 fewer people today than in 1950.

The 2d Congressional District of Pennsylvania takes in much of the city of Philadelphia west of Broad Street, plus Cheltenham Township in suburban Montgomery County. It doesn't include the key colonial landmarks—they're in the neighboring 1st—but it does include most of the skyscrapers of Center City and well-heeled Rittenhouse Square, the Philadelphia Zoo (America's first), the University of Pennsylvania, Drexel University, and lush Fairmount Park, the largest landscaped urban park in the world, which climaxes at the grand Philadelphia Museum of Art, where a *Rocky*-like run up the steps became *de rigueur* for tourists. The 2d includes West Oak Lane, Strawberry Mansion and, further west, the distinguished old neighborhoods of Mount Airy, Chestnut Hill and East Falls, mostly pleasant these days with some grittier precincts replaced by open low-rise complexes. The 2d also covers Roxborough and the old mill area of Manayunk, now an artsy enclave with upscale boutiques. This is Pennsylvania's one black-majority district: 61% in 2000. Pennsylvania never had slavery—thanks to William Penn and his Quaker legacy—and Philadelphia has been home to a large black community since before the Civil War. That heritage is reflected in places like the John Coltrane House on North 33d Street, designated a national historic landmark in celebration of the jazz innovator's early years here. Suburban Cheltenham Township includes old, comfortable communities like Cheltenham, Melrose Park, Elkins Park and Glenside. The 2d was George W. Bush's 3d-worst performing district in the nation—he won just 12 percent here in 2004, the same as in 2000.

The congressman from the 2d District is Chaka Fattah (pronounced *SHOCK-ah Fa-TAH*), first elected in 1994. Fattah grew up in Philadelphia, and in 1982, at 25, was elected to the state House—the youngest member ever. In 1988 he was elected to the state Senate. In 1991, much to everyone's surprise, 2d District Congressman William Gray resigned to become head of the United Negro College Fund. In the special election to succeed him, local Democratic ward leaders nominated Councilman Lucien Blackwell, a former longshoreman, boxer and labor union stalwart. Fattah ran under the Consumer Party label while state Welfare Secretary John White ran as an independent. Blackwell won with 39% to 28% for Fattah and 27% for White. In 1994 Fattah ran again, this time in the Democratic primary, unafraid to take on the party establishment. Blackwell relied mostly on ward politicians; Fattah was endorsed by the Black Clergy of Philadelphia and Vicinity. This time Fattah won, 58%-42%.

Fattah's voting record has been mostly liberal. Unlike the parochial-minded Bob Brady, the city's other congressman, Fattah's focus has been more nationally-oriented, with an eye toward election of a Democratic House majority. "A policy wonk with savvy," the *Philadelphia Inquirer* called him. Much of his attention has been on education issues. He worked on the "Gear Up" program to prepare low-income students for college, and used his seat on the Appropriations Committee to push for more money for education. He also secured money to curb witness intimidation in Philadelphia, and combat the use of unsafe blood supplies that transmit HIV/AIDS in Africa. He talked up his proposal for a study to eliminate the federal tax code and replace all individual and corporate taxes with a system that would tax all individual transactions; this generated some interest among Republicans. But most Democrats were leery of something that looked like a consumption tax and were not much interested in broad tax changes so long as they remained in the minority. He got approval of a portrait in the Capitol for Joseph Rainey of South Carolina, the first black elected to Congress.

Since entering the House, Fattah has had no serious primary or general election challenge. Just before Thanksgiving 2006, he announced that he was running for mayor of Philadelphia in 2007. "I want to transform this city from a city of Brotherly Love to the city of Real Opportunity," he declared. This prompted grumbling among local Democrats planning to run for mayor that he was giving up his clout as an appropriator, and even some threats that Fattah could face a primary challenge for his House seat. In January, 1st District colleague Bob Brady entered the race, setting up the unusual spectacle of a primary contest involving two sitting House members; other serious candidates included former City Councilman Michael Nutter, wealthy businessman Thomas Knox and state Representative Dwight Evans. Fattah began the race in 2006 as the early frontrunner, but his campaign collapsed as he struggled to raise money and drew criticism over his refusal to release his income tax returns; he complained about biased news coverage (though his wife, Renee Chenault-Fattah, is a local television news anchor) and suggested the media was rooting for Nutter. Nutter was the eventual winner with 37%, followed by Knox who won 25%. Fattah finished fourth with 15%, less than 200 votes behind Brady, who also had 15%.

THIRD DISTRICT

Rep. Phil English (R)

Elected 1994, 7th term; b. June 20, 1956, Erie; home, Erie; U. of PA., B.A. 1978; Catholic; married (Christiane).

Elected Office: Erie City Controller, 1985-89.

Professional Career: Staff aide, PA Senate; 1980-84; Chief of Staff, PA Sen. Melissa Hart 1990-92; Exec. Dir., PA Senate Finance Cmte., 1990-94.

DC Office: 2332 RHOB, 20515, 202-225-5406; Fax: 202-225-3103; Web site: www.house.gov/english.

District Offices: Butler, 724-285-7005; Erie, 814-456-2038; Hermitage, 724-342-6132; Warren, 814-723-7282.

Committees: *Joint Economic Committee* (7th of 10 R). *Ways & Means* (6th of 17 R): Select Revenue Measures (RMM); Health; Income Security & Family Support.

Group Ratings

	ADA	ACLU	AFS	LCV	ITIC	NTU	COC	ACU	CFG	FRC
2006	15	18	14	25	86	53	100	80	53	71
2005	5	—	0	6	—	57	93	88	59	85

National Journal Ratings

	2005 LIB	—	2005 CONS	2006 LIB	—	2006 CONS
Economic	37%	—	62%	41%	—	59%
Social	31%	—	68%	44%	—	56%
Foreign	34%	—	61%	38%	—	59%

Key Votes of the 109th Congress

1. Estate Tax Repeal	Y	5. Limit Interstate Abortion	Y	9. Build Border Fence	Y
2. Limit CAFE Standards	N	6. Extend Patriot Act	Y	10. CAFTA	Y
3. FY06 Spending Curb	Y	7. Bar Same Sex Marriage	Y	11. Oppose Iraq Withdrawal	Y
4. Drilling in ANWR	Y	8. Stem Cell Research $	N	12. Detainee Tribunals	Y

Election Results

2006 general	Phil English (R)	108,525	(54%)	($1,390,914)
	Steven Porter (D)	85,110	(42%)	($233,034)
	Timothy Hagberg (CNP)	8,706	(4%)	
2006 primary	Phil English (R)	unopposed		
2004 general	Phil English (R)	166,580	(60%)	($1,595,195)
	Steven Porter (D)	110,684	(40%)	($224,002)

Prior Winning Percentages: 2002 (78%); 2000 (61%); 1998 (63%); 1996 (51%); 1994 (49%)

The People		Race/Ethnic Origin	Ancestry	
Area size:	4,777 sq. mi.	93.7% White	German: 20.8%	Irish: 10.5%
Urban population:	58.4%	3.5% Black	Italian: 7.1%	
Rural population:	41.6%	0.5% Asian	**2004 Presidential Vote**	
Pop. 2000:	646,311	0.1% Native Am.	Bush (R) 152,473	(53%)
Pop. 2005 (est):	643,141	0.0% Hawaiian	Kerry (D) 133,764	(47%)
Median income:	$35,884	0.8% Two+ races	Other 861	(0%)
Poverty status:	11.6%	0.1% Other	**2000 Presidential Vote**	
Military veterans:	14.6%	1.3% Hispanic Origin	Bush (R) 127,598	(51%)
			Gore (D) 116,118	(46%)
			Other 6,233	(2%)
			Cook Partisan Voting Index: R + 2	

Occupation   Blue collar: 30.7%   White collar: 52.3%   Gray collar: 17.0%

The best natural harbor on Lake Erie is in a state with the second-shortest Great Lakes shoreline. It is Erie, Pennsylvania, protected by the Presque Isle ("almost an island") peninsula—a cowlick-shaped, seven-mile-long sand spit blanketed by mature forest, with a lighthouse dating to 1872. Erie is in Pennsylvania's far northwest corner, only about 100 miles from Cleveland but 428 miles from Center City Philadelphia. There is farmland here, and even some woods, but this land between the Great Lakes and the basin of the Ohio River has been prime territory for heavy industry for more than a century. In the 1990s, under Governor Tom Ridge, an Erie native, the state invested $100 million in Erie's waterfront—a cruise ship terminal, a hotel and convention center, a ballpark for the single-A Erie SeaWolves baseball team, and restorations to the Warner Theatre—in an attempt to boost tourism. The effort spruced up a dying downtown, but it didn't buffer Erie from a subsequent economic downturn. International Paper, American Meter, Gunite/EMI and American Sterilizer laid off employees and closed plants. Local colleges document a brain drain as high as 70% from the region. After earlier cutbacks, General Electric, the area's largest employer, has been hiring again.

The 3d Congressional District of Pennsylvania occupies this northwest corner of the state—all of Erie County, most of Mercer, Crawford and Butler Counties and about half of Warren, Venango, and Armstrong Counties. Erie County has 43% of the district's population, and had almost no population gains from 1990 to 2005. Growth has been greater in Butler County, the northern edge of the Pittsburgh metropolitan area, while other parts of the district have lost population. Politically, the mix of industrial and rural voters makes for closely balanced territory. Erie and Mercer Counties vote Democratic in most national elections, but they have also voted for Republicans with working class appeal, like Ridge, from a Catholic working class family in Erie, and former Senator Rick Santorum. The other counties are culturally conservative and solidly Republican. This is a district that voted 51% for George W. Bush in 2000 and 53% in 2004; each time 5% better than the state as a whole.

The congressman from the 3d District is Phil English, a Republican first elected in 1994. English grew up in Erie and has worked at little else but politics and government. At 20, he was an alternate to the 1976 Republican National Convention, and he worked during the early 1980s as a Republican staffer in Harrisburg. In 1985 he became Erie controller; in 1988, he was the unsuccessful Republican nominee for state treasurer. In 1990 he helped produce Rick Santorum's upset win in the suburban Pittsburgh 18th District, the first step on Santorum's path to the Senate; he went on to become chief of staff to state Senator Melissa Hart, who later served three House terms in the adjacent 4th District. In 1994, when Ridge ran for governor, English ran for the House and won 66% in the Republican primary. In the general, English promised to reform welfare, cut wasteful spending and create jobs for northwestern Pennsylvania with an 18-point plan for revitalizing small business and manufacturing. Key to the outcome was Erie, English's home—and probably more important, Ridge's—which supported the Republican ticket, giving English a 49%-47% victory.

In the House, the obviously vulnerable English became one of the first freshman Republicans since George H. W. Bush in 1967 to win a seat on Ways and Means, an excellent spot from which to legislate and raise money. Early on, English made a record on local issues, working to stop Korea's dumping of steel pipe and tubing, and preserving spending on low income home heating. While he supports the Republican leadership on most votes, he has a moderate record on economic and social issues and has dissented prominently on occasion. He has been among the House Republicans most willing to support a minimum wage increase and was an early proponent of limiting the tax deduction for pay to corporate chief executives.

English worries about the collapse of manufacturing across the nation, including northwest Pennsylvania. He would impose tariffs on imports from China to respond to Beijing's alleged currency manipulation. In October 2003, he got House passage of his resolution calling on China to let market forces set its exchange rate; that was followed in July 2005 by the U.S. Trade Rights Enforcement Act to encourage increased use of countervailing duties to combat subsidies. "I think we have attracted the attention of the Chinese and Bush administration," he said. He also called for higher tariffs on imports from Vietnam. English supports major tax changes to replace individual and corporate income taxes with a consumption tax to promote savings and level the playing field for U.S. businesses and workers. He wants to repeal the alternative minimum tax on corporations. He voted for normal trade relations with China and trade promotion authority, and for the Central American free trade deal after winning concessions. In 2007, he became ranking member of the Select Revenue Measures Subcommittee at Ways and Means.

As chairman of the Steel Caucus, English welcomed President Bush's March 2002 decision to impose quotas on steel imports. When Bush agreed in December 2003 to go along with the World Trade Organization ruling against the action, English was conciliatory; the President had kept his promises, and the steel industry was "on stronger footing." He helped pass a resolution opposing any changes to U.S. anti-dumping laws in the Doha trade negotiations. In 2007, he called for permanent federal monitoring of steel imports.

English had a tough reelection challenge in 1996 from Democrat Ron DiNicola, who returned home from a law practice in Los Angeles to run in Erie. "California office. California driver's license. And a great tan," English's campaign proclaimed. English won 51%-49%. His next close challenge came a decade later, when he won 54%-42% against Steven Porter, a lightly-funded educator.

The loss in 2006 of seven House Republican seats in Pennsylvania and Upstate New York—in districts somewhat comparable to the one held by English—is a reminder both of his political skill and the long-term jeopardy that he faces. In November 2006, English lost to Tom Cole for the chairmanship of the National Republican Congressional Committee, but Cole retained him to work on fundraising. In February 2007, Porter filed a defamation suit against English for intentionally distorting and misquoting passages from Porter's 1991 book, titled *The Ethics of a Democracy*, which discusses arguments for government sterilization of alcoholics and welfare recipients. Porter insisted they were not his actual opinions and that they were used to provoke academic debate.

FOURTH DISTRICT

Rep. Jason Altmire (D)

Elected 2006, 1st term; b. Mar. 7, 1968, Kittanning; home, McCandless Twnshp.; FL. St. U., B.S. 1990, George Washington U., M.H.A. 1998; Catholic; married (Kelly).

Professional Career: Aide, U.S. Rep. Pete Peterson, 1991-96; Asst. VP, Fed. of American Hospitals, 1996-98; VP of Govt. Relations, U. of Pittsburgh Med. Ctr., 1998-2005.

DC Office: 1419 LHOB, 20515, 202-225-2565; Fax: 202-226-2274; Web site: altmire.house.gov.

District Offices: Aliquippa, 724-378-0928; Natrona Heights, 724-226-1304.

Committees: *Education & Labor* (22d of 27 D): Higher Education, Lifelong Learning & Competitiveness; Healthy Families & Communities. *Small Business* (11th of 18 D): Investigations & Oversight (Chmn.); Regulations, Healthcare & Trade. *Transportation & Infrastructure* (31st of 41 D): Economic Development, Public Buildings & Emergency Management; Highways & Transit.

Group Ratings and Key Votes: Newly Elected

Election Results

2006 general	Jason Altmire (D)	131,847	(52%)	($1,091,584)
	Melissa Hart (R)	122,049	(48%)	($2,235,952)
2006 primary	Jason Altmire (D)	32,322	(55%)	
	Georgia Berner (D)	26,596	(45%)	
2004 general	Melissa Hart (R)	204,329	(63%)	($1,368,946)
	Stevan Drobac (D)	116,303	(36%)	($14,082)
	Other	3,285	(1%)	

The People		Race/Ethnic Origin	Ancestry	
Area size:	1,318 sq. mi.	94.3% White	German: 20.7%	Irish: 12.4%
Urban population:	78.5%	3.4% Black	Italian: 11.7%	
Rural population:	21.5%	0.9% Asian	**2004 Presidential Vote**	
Pop. 2000:	646,609	0.1% Native Am.	Bush (R) 179,855	(54%)
Pop. 2005 (est):	652,639	0.0% Hawaiian	Kerry (D) 149,070	(45%)
Median income:	$43,547	0.7% Two+ races	Other 1,255	(0%)
Poverty status:	7.5%	0.1% Other	**2000 Presidential Vote**	
Military veterans:	14.7%	0.6% Hispanic Origin	Bush (R) 152,313	(52%)
			Gore (D) 134,688	(46%)
			Other 6,167	(2%)
			Cook Partisan Voting Index: R + 3	

Occupation	Blue collar: 22.4%	White collar: 63.7%	Gray collar: 13.9%

For a century, one of America's great industrial zones was near the intersection of the Beaver and Ohio Rivers in western Pennsylvania. This was steel country, with mills rising black and brooding from the bottomlands and filling the narrow river valleys with smoke. Immigrant families lived in small frame houses on hillsides, looking down on riverscapes lined with piles of iron ore, limestone and coal, and littered with cranes, stocks and furnaces. This was not an environmentalist's idea of perfection, but it was a land of opportunity for thousands whose lives were far worse before moving to steel country. One grandchild of a Hungarian immigrant steelworker in Beaver Falls grew up to be Joe Namath—one of many great quarterbacks produced by southwestern Pennsylvania (fellow Hall of Famers Jim Kelly, Joe Montana and Dan Marino are a few of the others). For a few heady years, high union wages and early retirement plans seemed to make working in the mills the way to affluence. But the industry crashed after the oil shock of 1979, when mills were closed and jobs vanished. Today, thousands of workers who long ago exhausted their unemployment benefits have given up and left the Beaver and Ohio valleys.

The 4th Congressional District of Pennsylvania includes much of this steel country and, equally important, a large swath of suburban Pittsburgh. The 4th begins around Farrell in Mercer County, located as close to Erie as to Pittsburgh, then travels south along Route 60 through steel-mill country in Lawrence and Beaver Counties; Aliquippa, a typically distressed former steel-mill city, was where composer Henry Mancini and football icon Mike Ditka grew up but then left for brighter futures elsewhere, like many others. The district then turns to the east, taking in a fast-growing tier of suburban southern Butler County and the longer-established Allegheny County suburbs north of Pittsburgh: old-money Fox Chapel and Sewickley, which is now attracting the region's high-tech wealth; affluent McCandless and middle-class Ross in the North Hills. It also takes in a tiny portion of Westmoreland County. The steel mill areas tend to be Democratic, with unions still capable of flexing some muscle. The suburbs of Butler County are tax-averse and strongly Republican, with solid growth in Cranberry and Seven Fields near the Turnpike. The older suburbs in Allegheny County, with some of the highest senior citizen populations in the country, are politically marginal—more Democratic than Butler, but much more Republican than the city of Pittsburgh. Overall, the district's heritage is Democratic but it has been trending modestly toward the Republicans. George W. Bush carried this district with 52% of the vote in 2000 and 54% in 2004.

The new congressman from the 4th District is Jason Altmire, a Democrat elected in a 2006 upset. Altmire grew up outside of Pittsburgh, and was a star high school athlete until he suffered a knee injury. He attended Florida State University, worked to rehabilitate himself and made the football team as a walk-on player; he suffered another injury as the team trained to play in the Sugar Bowl. Altmire volunteered for Florida Democrat Pete Peterson's successful congressional campaign, then worked as his legislative aide for 6 years, developing expertise in health care issues. Altmire earned a masters degree in health administration at George Washington University while working on the Hill, and at 25 was appointed to Bill Clinton's health care task force. Following a short stint with the Federation of American Hospitals, he returned home to western Pennsylvania in 1998 for a job with the University of Pittsburgh Medical Center, eventually becoming vice president for government relations. Sixteen months before the general election, Altmire quit his $130,000-a-year job and jumped into the race for Congress as a first-time candidate.

The incumbent was Republican Melissa Hart, a protege of Republican Rick Santorum, who had won an open seat in 2000 and had since compiled a conservative voting record. Hart was seen as one of the party's rising stars and had faced only light opposition in her congressional campaigns. Altmire faced businesswoman Georgia Berner in the Democratic primary. Both Democrats attacked Hart as a "rubber stamp" for the Bush administration, but they held divergent positions on key issues: Berner supported abortion rights, while Altmire opposed abortion and gun control. Altmire trailed Berner in fundraising, largely because of her $200,000 personal loan to her campaign, but he enjoyed support from key labor groups. In the May 16 primary, he won 55%-45% with strong support from his Allegheny County base, which he carried by nearly 10,000 votes.

Prior to winning the nomination, Altmire had criticized Hart for serving on the Ethics Committee but not doing enough to curtail Washington's "culture of corruption." He positioned himself as more socially conservative than the national Democratic Party, but also turned to two liberal lightning rods to help fill his coffers. In July, he went door-to-door with Democratic National Committee Chairman Howard Dean; in October, comedian Al Franken appeared at an Altmire fundraiser. In early October, Hart's responsibilities on the House Ethics Committee kept her off the campaign trail as the panel conducted its investigation into the Mark Foley congressional page scandal. In the last weeks of the campaign, Altmire had closed the gap enough to draw attention and funds from the Democratic Congressional Campaign Committee. One DCCC-backed ad tied the incumbent to the sinking popularity of Bush and Santorum. "Hart has sided with Bush and Santorum—and against us," the ad declared. An Altmire ad criticized Hart for voting to "raid" the Social Security trust fund and cut veterans benefits and student loans.

Hart outspent Altmire by more than $1 million, but she was also fighting an anti-Republican current in a traditionally Democratic district. Altmire won 52%-48%, narrowly losing Allegheny County but winning by large margins in traditionally Democratic Beaver County. Altmire appears likely to face significant Republican competition in 2008. Former Allegheny County Councilman Ron Francis announced he is preparing to run for Republican nomination, while Hart said she will seek a rematch against Altmire.

FIFTH DISTRICT

Rep. John Peterson (R)

Elected 1996, 6th term; b. Dec. 25, 1938, Titusville; home, Pleasantville; PA St. U., 1974-76; Methodist; married (Sandy).

Military Career: Army, 1958-64.

Elected Office: Pleasantville Borough Cncl., 1969-77; PA House of Reps., 1977-84; PA Senate, 1984-96.

Professional Career: Owner, Peterson's Golden Dawn Food Market, 1958-84.

DC Office: 123 CHOB, 20515, 202-225-5121; Fax: 202-225-5796; Web site: www.house.gov/johnpeterson.

District Offices: State College, 814-238-1776; Titusville, 814-827-3985.

Committees: *Appropriations* (18th of 29 R): Interior, Environment & Related Agencies; Labor, HHS, Education & Related Agencies; Homeland Security.

Group Ratings

	ADA	ACLU	AFS	LCV	ITIC	NTU	COC	ACU	CFG	FRC
2006	0	14	0	0	100	55	93	88	53	100
2005	0	—	0	0	—	56	92	92	62	85

National Journal Ratings

	2005 LIB	—	2005 CONS	2006 LIB	—	2006 CONS
Economic	32%	—	68%	6%	—	93%
Social	26%	—	73%	26%	—	73%
Foreign	29%	—	70%	29%	—	70%

Key Votes of the 109th Congress

1. Estate Tax Repeal	Y	5. Limit Interstate Abortion	Y	9. Build Border Fence	Y
2. Limit CAFE Standards	N	6. Extend Patriot Act	Y	10. CAFTA	Y
3. FY06 Spending Curb	Y	7. Bar Same Sex Marriage	Y	11. Oppose Iraq Withdrawal	Y
4. Drilling in ANWR	Y	8. Stem Cell Research $	N	12. Detainee Tribunals	Y

Election Results

2006 general	John Peterson (R)	115,126	(60%)	($668,336)
	Donald Hilliard (D)	76,456	(40%)	
2006 primary	John Peterson (R)	unopposed		
2004 general	John Peterson (R)	192,852	(88%)	($511,015)
	Thomas Martin (Lib)	26,239	(12%)	

Prior Winning Percentages: 2002 (87%); 2000 (83%); 1998 (85%); 1996 (60%)

The People		Race/Ethnic Origin	Ancestry	
Area size:	11,108 sq. mi.	96.0% White	German: 21.3% Irish: 9.1%	
Urban population:	46.0%	1.3% Black	English: 6.7%	
Rural population:	54.0%	1.1% Asian	**2004 Presidential Vote**	
Pop. 2000:	646,397	0.1% Native Am.	Bush (R)	165,343 (61%)
Pop. 2005 (est):	638,948	0.0% Hawaiian	Kerry (D)	105,295 (39%)
Median income:	$33,254	0.6% Two+ races	Other	1,031 (0%)
Poverty status:	13.5%	0.1% Other	**2000 Presidential Vote**	
Military veterans:	14.4%	0.8% Hispanic Origin	Bush (R)	137,837 (59%)
			Gore (D)	89,180 (38%)
			Other	6,197 (3%)
			Cook Partisan Voting Index: R +10	

Occupation   Blue collar: 32.5%   White collar: 51.1%   Gray collar: 16.4%

North central Pennsylvania—isolated from the rest of the country by chains of mountains, and off the main east-west rail and highway lines until the 1970s—is one of those empty spaces that make even the northeastern states seem lightly populated compared to the densely packed terrain of Western Europe or East Asia. Here you can find Forest and Cameron Counties, with fewer than 6,000 people each, dependent on tourism; Forest County has the highest percentage of second homes or cottages of any county in the nation. Pressed tightly by narrow valleys and fast-flowing rivers, roads here are often forced to switch back as they wind their way precariously over the mountains; Tioga County is home to Pine Creek Gorge, known as "Pennsylvania's Grand Canyon." This part of the state is a prime area for hunting (in 2006, 225 black bears were shot in Clinton County), fishing, all-terrain vehicles and snowmobiles, in wide-open spaces like the Allegheny National Forest, which sprawls across four counties and is a popular recreational area. To the west are Titusville, where Colonel Edwin Drake sank the first successful oil well in 1859, and Oil City, headquarters of Quaker State Oil from 1931 until it left for Texas in 1995; the last oil and natural gas wells were capped here in 1964. DuBois in Clearfield County is home to glass production and a powdered metal industry; timbering also remains important here. In Bradford, Zippo manufactures lighters; the company suffered because of 9/11 airline security restrictions but later won approval for them to be carried in airline luggage, so long as they are empty (30% of its business comes from souvenir sales to collectors). Elk County and the Elk State Forest feature a free-roaming herd of elk, of course, but also are home to a new trout hatchery that cleans polluted water. Neatly-preserved Ridgway, just outside the Allegheny National Forest, holds the largest chainsaw carving event in the world.

Punxsutawney in Jefferson County is home of the legendary groundhog Phil, who predicts the arrival of spring every year based on whether he sees his shadow on Gobbler's Knob on Feb. 2; the

1993 movie *Groundhog Day* sparked a tourism boomlet in this town of 6,000, even though the movie was filmed in Woodstock, Illinois. To the southeast is the Nittany Valley, home of State College and Pennsylvania State University. Penn State has long been known for its powerful football teams coached by iconic Joe Paterno ("JoePa," locally); the university's cutting-edge facilities have spawned a high-skills job market. There is something solid and grounded in this part of America. The sturdily built courthouses and banks in the center of each county seat testify to the long local history of hard work and thrift. Interstate 80 makes this part of Pennsylvania accessible to big markets, and there has been some modest population growth since 1990. In 2006, these northern tier counties launched the Pennsylvania Wilds campaign to promote the local economy and tourism.

The 5th Congressional District of Pennsylvania is the state's most rural and largest in area, taking in an enormous swath of north central Pennsylvania; it's one of the largest districts east of the Mississippi River. Politically, this area became Republican in the 1850s when the party was founded, and it has remained heavily Republican ever since. George W. Bush won 59% of the vote here in 2000 and 61% in 2004.

The congressman from the 5th District is John Peterson, a Republican first elected in 1996. Peterson grew up in Titusville, the son of a steelworker; he served in the Army as a cook, then opened a grocery store that eventually became Peterson's Golden Dawn Supermarket chain. He served on the Pleasantville Borough Council for eight years, then in 1977, at 39, was elected to the state House in a special election. In 1984 he was elected to the state Senate. In 1996, Peterson was an obvious candidate for the open House seat here; 3 other Republicans also ran. The one who attracted the most attention was Bob Shuster, the brother of current 9th District Congressman Bill Shuster and son of Bud Shuster, who then chaired the Transportation and Infrastructure Committee. But Shuster grew up outside the district and Peterson's chief competition was Daniel Gordeuk, a Centre County surgeon with strong local roots. Peterson won with 38%, to 28% for Gordeuk, and 18% for Shuster. In the general, he attacked the Democratic nominee as "an old-fashioned liberal" and won 60%-40%.

In the House, Peterson has been a Republican loyalist. He has been a critic of environmental restriction advocates, complaining about their "push for world government" in the Kyoto treaty and lawsuits to prevent logging in national forests. Curiously for an easterner, he has been a leader of the Western Caucus; he shares many of their concerns on private property rights and access to public lands. With a seat on the Appropriations Committee, he passed an amendment to block a cost-sharing requirement for the Essential Air Service program that would have forced many rural airports to pay tens of thousands of dollars in new fees. With Democrat Allen Boyd of Florida, Peterson co-chaired the Rural Caucus, to promote the interests of rural areas in national debates. In the 2003 Medicare/prescription drug bill, they got changes in payments to rural health care providers plus a multi-billion dollar package for health services in rural areas. At a Capitol Hill press conference on Groundhog Day 2005 with a groundhog alleged to be Punxsutawney Phil, Peterson defended $100,000 for the Punxsutawney Weather Discovery Center.

Peterson has become outspoken in advocating for more development of the nation's oil and natural gas resources and in criticizing what he views as the Bush administration's lack of a sustainable energy policy. He took some credit for enactment in 2006 of a relaxation of off-shore oil and gas exploration. "Our current energy crisis is self-imposed—the product of a failed national energy policy that for years has encouraged growth in demand for clean-burning natural gas, while at the same time working furiously to lock away supply," he said. Also in 2006, he got $1.5 billion to clean up Pennsylvania's most hazardous abandoned mine sites. No issue is too local: When constituent Jamie Dana was badly injured in Iraq by a roadside bomb, she survived with the help of a bomb-sniffing dog named Rex; the Air Force initially objected to her request to adopt the dog because the law requires that the dog be returned to active duty. But Peterson, along with Senator John Warner, pushed legislation changing the statute to allow the dog to be discharged under special circumstances and Dana was permitted to take custody of Rex.

In 2006, Peterson faced his first Democratic challenger since taking office. Former Jefferson County Commissioner Don Hilliard appealed to organized labor and criticized the incumbent for his ties to "special interests" but Hilliard raised little money, and Peterson won 60%-40%.

SIXTH DISTRICT

Rep. Jim Gerlach (R)

Elected 2002, 3d term; b. Feb. 25, 1955, Ellwood City; home, Upper Uwchlan Township; Dickinson Col., B.A. 1977, J.D. 1980; Presbyterian; divorced.

Elected Office: PA House of Reps., 1990-94; PA Senate, 1994-2002.

Professional Career: Practicing atty., 1980-2002.

DC Office: 308 CHOB, 20515, 202-225-4315; Fax: 202-225-8440; Web site: www.house.gov/gerlach/.

District Offices: Exton, 610-594-1415; Trappe, 610-409-2780; Wyomissing, 610-376-7630.

Committees: *Financial Services* (21st of 33 R): Capital Markets, Insurance & Government Sponsored Enterprises; Financial Institutions & Consumer Credit. *Transportation & Infrastructure* (20th of 34 R): Railroads, Pipelines & Hazardous Materials; Aviation; Highways & Transit.

Group Ratings

	ADA	ACLU	AFS	LCV	ITIC	NTU	COC	ACU	CFG	FRC
2006	45	29	29	67	71	37	79	62	30	57
2005	35	—	25	56	—	42	81	56	35	67

National Journal Ratings

	2005 LIB — 2005 CONS	2006 LIB — 2006 CONS
Economic	50% — 49%	52% — 47%
Social	45% — 54%	44% — 56%
Foreign	34% — 61%	50% — 50%

Key Votes of the 109th Congress

1. Estate Tax Repeal	Y	5. Limit Interstate Abortion	Y	9. Build Border Fence	Y
2. Limit CAFE Standards	N	6. Extend Patriot Act	Y	10. CAFTA	Y
3. FY06 Spending Curb	Y	7. Bar Same Sex Marriage	N	11. Oppose Iraq Withdrawal	Y
4. Drilling in ANWR	N	8. Stem Cell Research $	Y	12. Detainee Tribunals	Y

Election Results

2006 general	Jim Gerlach (R)	121,047	(51%)	($3,492,402)
	Lois Murphy (D)	117,892	(49%)	($4,097,663)
2006 primary	Jim Gerlach (R)	unopposed		
2004 general	Jim Gerlach (R)	160,348	(51%)	($2,231,609)
	Lois Murphy (D)	153,977	(49%)	($1,910,539)

Prior Winning Percentages: 2002 (51%)

The People		Race/Ethnic Origin	Ancestry	
Area size:	819 sq. mi.	86.3% White	German: 18.9% Irish: 12.6%	
Urban population:	85.8%	6.7% Black	Italian: 9.8%	
Rural population:	14.2%	2.0% Asian	**2004 Presidential Vote**	
Pop. 2000:	646,221	0.1% Native Am.	Kerry (D)	167,431 (51%)
Pop. 2005 (est):	707,551	0.0% Hawaiian	Bush (R)	156,634 (48%)
Median income:	$55,611	1.0% Two+ races	Other	1,064 (0%)
Poverty status:	6.1%	0.1% Other	**2000 Presidential Vote**	
Military veterans:	12.6%	3.7% Hispanic Origin	Gore (D)	130,472 (49%)
			Bush (R)	129,318 (49%)
			Other	5,589 (2%)
			Cook Partisan Voting Index: D + 2	
Occupation	Blue collar: 20.0% White collar: 68.1% Gray collar: 11.9%			

The gentle hills of southeastern Pennsylvania, settled in the 18th century by Quaker townsmen, Welsh farmers, German peasants, and members of pietistic sects who became known as the Pennsylvania Dutch, were America's first polyglot interior. Before and after independence, a diverse lot looking for tolerance in the area above Philadelphia and the Delaware River and below the first chains of the Appalachians found a land that yielded riches, first in crops, then in ironworking and other industry. Here are places like Valley Forge, where General George Washington and his men spent the terrible winter and spring of 1777-78, while the British luxuriated in Philadelphia 25 miles away. In Revolutionary times, this area was countryside, a long day's ride from the markets and docks of Philadelphia. In the years after, the great rail lines were built from Philadelphia: the Main Line of the Pennsylvania Railroad headed west to industrial Pittsburgh and the Midwest, and the Reading Railroad headed northwest to Reading and the anthracite coalfields beyond. Factories were built in some of the towns here, and many farms continued to thrive, but by the late 19th century some of this land had become commuter territory. The most lavish Philadelphia suburbs were built on the Main Line, where in mansions shaded by huge trees Philadelphia's captains of commerce could get respite from the rowhouses and narrow streets of the city. By the late 20th century highways spread over the area and giant shopping centers sprung up: this was affluent suburbia for the masses, or a large part of them. Prosperity even came to some of the factory towns. Reading, the decaying industrial town described in John Updike's *Rabbit* novels, in the 1970s was the site of the first factory outlet store, when a company called Vanity Fair began selling seconds and overruns of stockings and lingerie at wholesale prices in what had been the Berkshire Knitting Mills; it grew to more than 300 outlets there selling deeply-discounted goods on the polished wood floors of converted brick mills. But by 2004, most of the original shops were boarded up, and Vanity Fair had opened a smaller outlet center a couple of miles away. With hundreds of such outlets now spread across the countryside, the original had become a victim of its own success.

The 6th Congressional District of Pennsylvania includes parts of this countryside in Chester, Berks and Montgomery Counties. Chester County has the highest median income levels in Pennsylvania and is its fastest growing major county, though mushroom farming remains abundant. The boundaries of the 6th District are irregular. Geographically, the main body of the district is northern Chester County, including Coatesville, Downingtown and Phoenixville, and southern Berks County. The district also includes a salient that runs northward in eastern Berks County, with its rapidly growing exurbs. There is another salient, much more heavily populated, reaching south into Montgomery County from Pottstown to Lower Merion Township, which is home to some of Philadelphia's wealthiest people. The district includes Valley Forge, with its American Revolution Center, part but not all of Reading, and most of the Main Line suburbs—Ardmore, Bryn Mawr, part of Paoli—some old money, and some new. Until the 1990s the area had been heavily Republican, and this district was drawn for a Republican. But the suburbs of Philadelphia, like those in the nation's other very large metropolitan areas, have trended to the Democrats, especially since 2000. Al Gore won the district 49.2%-48.7% in 2000, Democratic Governor Ed Rendell twice carried it easily, and John Kerry carried it 51%-48% in 2004. With Montgomery leaning Democratic and Chester leaning Republican, Berks is the swing county that often determines the district outcome.

The congressman from the 6th District is Jim Gerlach, a Republican first elected in 2002. He grew up in Ellwood City, Pennsylvania, midway between Pittsburgh and Youngstown, Ohio. He graduated from Dickinson College and its law school, just west of Harrisburg. He continued moving east, settled in Chester County and practiced law. He was elected to the state House in 1990 and to the state Senate in 1994. When Republicans in 2002 created a new district in suburban Philadelphia, Gerlach was the obvious intended beneficiary. He had spirited competition from Democrat Dan Wofford, a former adviser to Governor Bob Casey. Wofford had not previously run for office, but his name was well known; his father Harris Wofford was elected to the Senate in a 1991 special election. Gerlach ran on his legislative accomplishments, including votes to expand Pennsylvania's prescription drug program for low-income seniors. Wofford attacked Gerlach as a career politician; they disagreed on abortion and Medicare. Polls showed the race close and national Republicans spent more than $1.5 million on ads for Gerlach. The outcome was not clear until the early morning hours; Gerlach won 51%-49%.

In the House, Gerlach's voting record was mostly moderate though more conservative on foreign policy. He was a strong supporter of middle-class tax cuts and eliminating the marriage penalty, but he opposed personal retirement accounts in Social Security. George W. Bush signed his bill to create a new veterans cemetery in the Philadelphia area, but officials subsequently struggled to find an acceptable site. In April 2005, the House passed his bill to improve access to services for non-members, as well as members, of federal credit unions. In October 2005, his late vote helped Republican leaders to win narrow passage of a bill to facilitate construction of new oil refineries.

In 2004, Gerlach was a prime Democratic target. After Dan Wofford decided not to run again, local Democrats settled on attorney Lois Murphy, who managed Rendell's 2002 campaign in Montgomery County. A former staffer in both Washington and Pennsylvania for NARAL ProChoice

America, she received strong support from EMILY's List and criticized Gerlach for his lack of leadership in Congress, especially on fiscal issues; she attacked him for being supported by Majority Leader Tom DeLay. Gerlach defended his support for the Republican agenda as consistent with the views of his constituents. Despite her initial low name identification, the well-financed Murphy made this an unexpectedly close contest; but, like Wofford, she fell just short. Gerlach won 51%-49% again, with 56% of the vote in Chester County, 52% in Berks County and 43% in Murphy's Montgomery County base. In 2006, Murphy ran again with strong encouragement from the DCCC and EMILY's List. She was better-known and the issues were similar, but the campaign rhetoric was even harsher than in 2004. Gerlach may have benefited from more aggressive attacks by his campaign on alleged inconsistencies in Murphy's agenda. His ads said that her "dirty little secret" was her support for a tax increase on the wealthy. For the third consecutive election, Gerlach won 51%-49%. He won 55% of the vote in Chester County, 54% in Berks County, and 41% in Montgomery County.

Democrats likely will give Gerlach another vigorous challenge in 2008, but Murphy voiced little interest in a third challenge.

SEVENTH DISTRICT

Rep. Joe Sestak (D)

Elected 2006, 1st term; b. Dec. 12, 1951, Secane; home, Edgemont; U.S. Naval Academy, B.S. 1974, Harvard U., M.P.A. 1980, Ph.D. 1984; Catholic; married (Susan).

Military Career: Navy, 1974-2005 (Kuwait, Afghanistan, Iraq)

Professional Career: Dir. for Defense Policy, National Security Council, 1994-97; Anti-terrorism Unit Dir., 2001-02; Commander, George Washington Aircraft Carrier Battle Group, 2002-03.

DC Office: 1022 LHOB, 20515, 202-225-2011; Fax: 202-226-0280; Web site: sestak.house.gov.

District Offices: Media, 610-892-8623.

Committees: *Armed Services* (29th of 34 D): Seapower & Expeditionary Forces; Oversight & Investigations; Air & Land Forces. *Education & Labor* (19th of 27 D): Health, Employment, Labor & Pensions; Early Childhood, Elementary & Secondary Education. *Small Business* (16th of 18 D): Finance & Tax; Contracting & Technology; Regulations, Healthcare & Trade.

Group Ratings and Key Votes: Newly Elected

Election Results

2006 general	Joe Sestak (D)	147,898	(56%)	($3,075,719)
	Curt Weldon (R)	114,426	(44%)	($2,940,608)
2006 primary	Joe Sestak (D)	unopposed		
2004 general	Curt Weldon (R)	196,556	(59%)	($678,444)
	Paul Scoles (D)	134,932	(40%)	($23,763)
	Other	3,039	(1%)	

The People		Race/Ethnic Origin	Ancestry	
Area size:	294 sq. mi.	88.4% White	Irish: 21.8%	Italian: 14.3%
Urban population:	98.6%	5.4% Black	German: 13.3%	
Rural population:	1.4%	3.7% Asian	**2004 Presidential Vote**	
Pop. 2000:	646,522	0.1% Native Am.	Kerry (D) 184,392	(53%)
Pop. 2005 (est):	659,581	0.0% Hawaiian	Bush (R) 163,095	(47%)
Median income:	$56,126	0.9% Two+ races	Other 233	(0%)
Poverty status:	5.4%	0.1% Other	**2000 Presidential Vote**	
Military veterans:	12.9%	1.3% Hispanic Origin	Gore (D) 150,805	(51%)
			Bush (R) 140,862	(47%)
			Other 6,945	(2%)
			Cook Partisan Voting Index: D + 4	

Occupation	Blue collar: 16.1%	White collar: 72.6%	Gray collar: 11.3%

The close-in suburbs of the great eastern cities were home to some of the most curious and long-lasting political machines in America. They were Republican; they conducted business in the accents of ordinary people, ethnic as well as WASP; they had a tolerance for patronage, and for what city reform liberals would call corruption, that was sharply at odds with their embodiment of middle-class morality; they were old, going back to the days when political machines were as much a part of the urban landscape as trolley lines or overhead electrical wires. One such machine was the War Board of Pennsylvania's Delaware County, a ruthlessly effective Republican organization that continues to influence local politics even in its current and greatly diminished form. But while Republicans have a decided advantage in party registration in Delaware County, in national races voters here recently have voted for Democrats. Delco voted for Bill Clinton, Al Gore and John Kerry by increasing margins, and it voted 2–1 for Democrat Ed Rendell for governor in 2002 and 2006. The reasons are partly demographic—in recent decades many Democrats have moved out to the suburbs from Philadelphia—and partly ideological. Republicans of the Newt Gingrich stripe are unfamiliar here, and Sun Belt Republicanism is not popular.

The 7th Congressional District of Pennsylvania includes almost all of Delaware County, except for a few towns with large black populations that are appended to Philadelphia's 1st District. The 7th extends north to include a few Montgomery County suburbs, such as modest Conshohocken, an old Schuylkill River factory town that is now the U.S. headquarters for Swedish home furnishings retailer Ikea, affluent Upper Merion Township and King of Prussia, an edge city where the Schuylkill Expressway intersects the Pennsylvania Turnpike. The 7th takes in southeastern Chester County, including the commercial hub of West Chester and a few further-out suburbs such as Malvern and part of Paoli. The 7th includes the elite small colleges of Haverford and Swarthmore, and the refined farm country of Chadds Ford, home to generations of Wyeths who used wheat-brown tones to limn the region's seasonal moods on canvas. Its housing is aging but well maintained; its population is above average in income but distinct from the inhabitants of more affluent commuter towns. People here have deep roots in greater Philadelphia, but many rarely venture into Center City.

The new congressman from the 7th District is Joe Sestak, a Democrat elected in 2006. Sestak, who retired as a two-star admiral after 31 years in the Navy, is the highest ranking former military officer ever elected to Congress and to serve in the House. (Navy Admiral Thomas Hart was appointed to the Senate from Connecticut.) He grew up in a large family in Delaware County, and followed his father, a World War II captain, into the Navy. He graduated from the U.S. Naval Academy second in his class, and rose through the ranks to become a three-star admiral; he holds a master's and doctoral degree from Harvard University. During his career, Sestak held various operational commands and high-level policy positions. He was a defense adviser for the National Security Council during the Clinton administration. He commanded the George Washington aircraft carrier battle group during combat operations in Afghanistan. After the September 11 terrorist attacks, Sestak became the first director of "Deep Blue," an anti-terrorism think tank within the Navy. In July 2005, he was reassigned following a shake-up of top leadership and shortly thereafter his young daughter was diagnosed with a malignant brain tumor, forcing his family to live in a Washington hospital for four months. He said his experience there with families lacking quality health insurance caused him to rethink his life priorities. After officially retiring from the Navy in January and after his daughter was declared free of cancer, in February 2006 Sestak launched his campaign for Congress.

The incumbent was 10-term Republican Curt Weldon, who had not been seriously challenged since he won the seat in 1986. A political novice, Sestak needed time to polish his retail campaigning skills. Weldon, on the other hand, struggled to shake off the cobwebs. In April Weldon drew criticism for suggesting that Sestak should have sent his daughter to a Pennsylvania hospital rather than to one in Washington, D.C. The comment reflected a broader Weldon strategy to portray Sestak, who had spent roughly three decades away from the suburban Philadelphia district, as an outsider. The Democratic Congressional Campaign Committee played up news reports that Weldon wanted to make a Memorial Day expedition to Iraq to dig up alleged weapons of mass destruction, contributing to the view that Weldon had indulged his interest in national security and conspiracy theories rather than tending to his district's economic needs.

The Democratic Party cleared the May 16 primary field for Sestak, and he established his credibility by raising $1.1 million by June 2006. Weldon responded by adopting a more energetic fundraising pace, relying heavily on contributions from defense industry PACs. Sestak vowed to run an issues-oriented campaign and ignored his consultants' advice against voicing his support for a U.S. withdrawal of troops from Iraq, which Weldon opposed. Weldon questioned Sestak's temperament, citing an August 2005 *Navy Times* report that he was relieved of his duties as deputy chief of naval operations a month earlier because of a "poor command climate."

While the Iraq war and Republican ethics scandals hurt Republicans elsewhere, it was a mid-October FBI raid on the homes of Weldon's daughter and a close associate that doomed the incumbent. The FBI was looking into whether Weldon improperly used his influence to win contracts for his daughter's lobbying firm. Weldon denied any wrongdoing and questioned the curious timing of the raid, which the FBI said was necessary to preserve evidence from destruction. But the news about a Justice Department investigation was too much to overcome in the tough 2006 election environment against an aggressive, well-funded challenger; the DCCC ran an ad putting Weldon in a "hall of shame" with Mark Foley, Randy (Duke) Cunningham and Tom DeLay, all of whom had resigned amid scandal and legal peril. The national Republican party pulled the plug on Weldon and scaled back its ad buys; Weldon himself canceled some of his scheduled ads, leading to unhelpful speculation that he was saving his money for a legal defense fund. Sestak won by 56%-44%—an impressive margin for a novice candidate.

Sestak's work ethic and fundraising ability, combined with suburban Philadelphia voting trends, make him perhaps better positioned for reelection than any of Pennsylvania's 4 Democratic House freshmen. The DCCC felt confident enough in 2007 about his reelection prospects to leave him off its Frontline list, which is designed to protect the most vulnerable incumbents. Still, the district remains politically competitive and Republicans will be eager to recruit a top-tier challenger, though one had not emerged through summer 2007.

EIGHTH DISTRICT

Rep. Patrick Murphy (D)

Elected 2006, 1st term; b. Oct. 19, 1973, Philadelphia; home, Bristol; Attended Bucks Cnty. Comm. Col., King's Col., B.A. 1996, Widener U., J.D. 1999; Catholic; married (Jennifer).

Military Career: Army, 1993-2004 (Iraq).

Professional Career: Asst. professor and staff atty., U.S. Military Academy, West Point, 1999-2004; Practicing atty., 2004-06.

DC Office: 1007 LHOB, 20515, 202-225-4276; Fax: 202-225-9511; Web site: www.patrickmurphy.house.gov.

District Offices: Bristol, 215-826-1963; Doylestown, 215-348-1194.

Committees: *Armed Services* (23d of 34 D): Military Personnel. *Permanent Select Committee on Intelligence* (12th of 12 D): Terrorism, Human Intelligence, Analysis & Counterintelligence; Intelligence Community Management; Technical & Tactical Intelligence.

Group Ratings and Key Votes: Newly Elected

Election Results

2006 general	Patrick Murphy (D)	125,656	(50%)	($2,410,530)
	Mike Fitzpatrick (R)	124,138	(50%)	($3,174,384)
2006 primary	Patrick Murphy (D)	17,889	(65%)	
	Andrew Warren (D)	9,812	(35%)	
2004 general	Mike Fitzpatrick (R)	183,229	(55%)	($1,046,153)
	Virginia Schrader (D)	143,427	(43%)	($613,850)
	Other	4,608	(1%)	

The People		Race/Ethnic Origin	Ancestry		
Area size:	634 sq. mi.	90.8% White	German: 18.5%	Irish: 18.1%	
Urban population:	90.8%	3.4% Black	Italian: 10.6%		
Rural population:	9.2%	2.4% Asian	**2004 Presidential Vote**		
Pop. 2000:	645,403	0.1% Native Am.	Kerry (D) 177,008	(51%)	
Pop. 2005 (est):	668,778	0.0% Hawaiian	Bush (R) 165,239	(48%)	
Median income:	$59,207	0.9% Two+ races	Other 1,997	(1%)	
Poverty status:	4.5%	0.1% Other	**2000 Presidential Vote**		
Military veterans:	12.9%	2.3% Hispanic Origin	Gore (D) 144,878	(51%)	
			Bush (R) 130,500	(46%)	
			Other 9,050	(3%)	
			Cook Partisan Voting Index: D + 3		

Occupation   Blue collar: 20.9%   White collar: 68.0%   Gray collar: 11.1%

Bucks County was one of William Penn's three original settlements and the launching point for George Washington's crossing of the frigid Delaware River to surprise English and Hessian forces on Christmas Day 1776. But it had a split personality from the start. Upper Bucks County was at once a paradise of bucolic hills and creeks running into the Delaware River and, after Penn's secretary James Logan built the Durham Furnace iron works in 1727, one of the nation's major industrial sites. In the 1920s, Bucks County's well-settled farmland, old fieldstone houses and covered bridges in its northern parts captured the imagination of writers and artists, attracting the New York theatrical crowd—Oscar Hammerstein, Moss Hart, Dorothy Parker, S. J. Perelman. After World War II, its location between Philadelphia and Trenton, New Jersey, brought industrial Lower Bucks County to the forefront. The ocean-navigable Delaware River and several rail lines resulted in huge new developments: U.S. Steel's Fairless Works, one of the few big postwar steel plants, down by the river, and the Levitt organization's second Levittown, in what had been farmland and swamp between U.S. 13 and U.S. 1. But most of the steel mill closed in 1991, and today Bucks County's largest employers are health care-oriented.

Bucks County's political tradition was heavily Republican and protectionist; more recently it has been marginally Republican and environmentalist. This was the home of Senator Joseph Grundy, longtime head of the Pennsylvania Manufacturers Association, who opposed the 1930 Smoot-Hawley tariff as insufficiently protectionist. Development in Bucks came after the New Deal, unlike other suburban Philadelphia counties where most blue-collar immigration occurred years earlier, when county political organizations were ready to enroll new residents in their party. So Lower Bucks around the Fairless Works and Levittown, with its tightly-packed homes filled with blue collar workers, became Democratic. In Upper Bucks, faster-growing and still attracting trendy New Yorkers, green space programs have kept large areas away from developers.

The 8th Congressional District of Pennsylvania includes all of Bucks County, a tiny finger of Montgomery County around Willow Grove and parts of two wards in Northeast Philadelphia. Bucks has the third highest income of any county in the state and the district as a whole has the highest percentage of married persons. Bucks County's population has been just slightly less than that of a full congressional district for several decades, and the 8th District has been virtually unchanged during the last three redistricting cycles. The 8th was marginal in elections during the 1980s; since then, it has moved like other Philadelphia suburbs toward national Democrats and voted for Democratic presidential candidates since 1992. It also joined the rest of southeastern Pennsylvania in voting decisively for Democrat Ed Rendell for governor in 2002 and 2006.

The new congressman from the 8th District is Patrick Murphy, a Democrat elected in 2006 and the only Iraq war veteran elected to Congress. Murphy grew up in Northeast Philadelphia, the son of a Philadelphia policeman and a legal secretary. He attended Bucks County Community College, enrolled as a cadet in the Army ROTC program at King's College, and after graduation earned a commission in the Army as a second lieutenant. He obtained his law degree at Widener University, got a job as a staff attorney at West Point, and later taught as a professor. Murphy trained as paratrooper with 82d Airborne Division and served four months in Bosnia in 2002 and seven months in Iraq beginning in mid-2003. In Iraq he worked as a JAG Corps attorney, handling court-martial cases and claims made against U.S. troops by Iraqis, and rebuilding the Iraqi justice system. He helped prosecute a deputy of Muqtada al-Sadr, and was awarded the Bronze Star. After returning from Iraq, he practiced law at a Philadelphia firm, lectured at universities and volunteered as a veterans' liaison in Pennsylvania for Democratic presidential nominee John Kerry's campaign in 2004.

Murphy announced his candidacy in May 2005 and reminded voters frequently of his Iraq war service. He spoke in opposition to Bush's handling of the war, but struck a different tone than other Democratic war opponents. "I'm not antiwar. I'm not pro-war. I'm pro-troops," Murphy told the *Philadelphia Inquirer*. A first-time candidate, he had a competitive primary with recent Democratic convert Andrew Warren, who was better known to voters after 4 terms as a Republican Bucks County commissioner. Warren called for rapid troop withdrawal from Iraq, while Murphy offered a three-phase troop redeployment that would bring American troops home by the end of 2007. Bucks County Democrats chose Murphy, who had voted for Bush in 2000 as a registered independent, over the former Republican; he won 65%-35%.

In the general election, Murphy faced first-term Congressman Mike Fitzpatrick, a Republican who was hurried onto the ballot in 2004 after moderate Republican incumbent Jim Greenwood announced he was leaving Congress to accept a job with the Biotechnology Industry Organization. Murphy, who turned 33 just before Election Day, cut a similar appearance to the boyish Fitzpatrick. But the incumbent had served 10 years as a Bucks County commissioner and his conservative positions on abortion rights and stem cell research differed from Murphy. Murphy's military credentials gave him credibility on Iraq and forced Fitzpatrick to stray from the party line; in one mailer the incumbent declared, "Mike Fitzpatrick to President Bush: 'America needs a better, smarter plan in Iraq.'" Fitzpatrick also distanced himself from the White House by noting he had voted against the Republican budget and a constitutional ban on same-sex marriage, while he earned endorsements from environmental groups. Fitzpatrick sought to localize the election by stressing his lifelong district residency and charging that Murphy had moved into the area to further his political ambitions. In one debate, he stumped Murphy, who hewed closely to national Democratic Party themes, by asking him how many school districts Bucks County had. When Fitzpatrick ran an ad questioning Murphy's claim that he worked as a Justice Department prosecutor, Murphy declared during a forum, "Mike, you are a liar and a coward." Kerry campaigned actively for Murphy, and at one point accused Republicans of an attempt at "Swift-boating" Murphy's military record.

Altogether, the National Republican Congressional Committee pumped $3.5 million in independent ads into the district, compared to the DCCC's $1.7 million; Fitzpatrick outspent Murphy $3.2 million to $2.4 million. But Murphy won a 50.3%-49.7% victory; Fitzpatrick's concession phone call didn't come until the next afternoon. Fitzpatrick actually carried Bucks County, which includes almost all the district, by just over 1,000 votes, but Murphy carried small areas of Northeast Philadelphia and Montgomery County by large enough margins to win the district by just over 1,500 votes.

After the election, Fitzpatrick said he was considering a rematch. In Congress, Murphy cut an unusually high profile for a freshman, especially one who had squeaked into office. He was a leading congressional voice against Bush's "surge" plan to send more combat troops to Iraq but generated some controversy by signing a book deal with a $100,000 advance shortly before taking office.

NINTH DISTRICT

Rep. Bill Shuster (R)

Elected May 2001, 3d full term; b. Jan. 10, 1961, McKeesport; home, Hollidaysburg; Dickinson Col., B.A. 1983; American U., M.B.A. 1987; Lutheran; married (Rebecca).

Professional Career: Mgr., Goodyear Tire & Rubber Co., 1983-87; District Mgr., Bandag Inc., 1987-90; Gen. Mgr., Shuster Chrysler, 1990-2001.

DC Office: 204 CHOB, 20515, 202-225-2431; Fax: 202-225-2486; Web site: www.house.gov/shuster.

District Offices: Chambersburg, 717-264-8308; Hollidaysburg, 814-696-6318; Indiana, 724-463-0516; Somerset, 814-443-3918.

Committees: *Armed Services* (24th of 29 R): Seapower & Expeditionary Forces; Terrorism, Unconventional Threats & Capabilities. *Natural Resources* (17th of 22 R): Energy & Mineral Resources. *Small Business* (5th of 15 R): Finance & Tax. *Transportation & Infrastructure* (18th of 34 R): Railroads, Pipelines & Hazardous Materials (RMM); Economic Development, Public Buildings & Emergency Management; Water Resources & Environment.

Group Ratings

	ADA	ACLU	AFS	LCV	ITIC	NTU	COC	ACU	CFG	FRC
2006	0	5	0	8	100	62	100	84	58	100
2005	5	—	0	0	—	63	93	100	75	100

National Journal Ratings

	2005 LIB	—	2005 CONS		2006 LIB	—	2006 CONS
Economic	3%	—	94%		21%	—	77%
Social	0%	—	89%		0%	—	94%
Foreign	0%	—	89%		14%	—	85%

Key Votes of the 109th Congress

1. Estate Tax Repeal	Y	5. Limit Interstate Abortion	Y	9. Build Border Fence	Y
2. Limit CAFE Standards	Y	6. Extend Patriot Act	Y	10. CAFTA	Y
3. FY06 Spending Curb	Y	7. Bar Same Sex Marriage	Y	11. Oppose Iraq Withdrawal	Y
4. Drilling in ANWR	Y	8. Stem Cell Research $	N	12. Detainee Tribunals	Y

Election Results

2006 general	Bill Shuster (R)	121,069	(60%)	($1,168,741)
	Tony Barr (D)	79,610	(40%)	($60,019)
2006 primary	Bill Shuster (R)	unopposed		
2004 general	Bill Shuster (R)	184,320	(69%)	($1,217,650)
	Paul Politis (D)	80,787	(30%)	($15,810)

Prior Winning Percentages: 2002 (71%); 2001 (52%)

The People		Race/Ethnic Origin	Ancestry	
Area size:	7,199 sq. mi.	96.4% White	German: 24.3%	Irish: 9.0%
Urban population:	40.5%	1.6% Black	USA: 7.5%	
Rural population:	59.5%	0.4% Asian	**2004 Presidential Vote**	
Pop. 2000:	646,628	0.1% Native Am.	Bush (R) 183,717	(67%)
Pop. 2005 (est):	650,591	0.0% Hawaiian	Kerry (D) 89,208	(33%)
Median income:	$34,910	0.6% Two+ races	Other 646	(0%)
Poverty status:	11.1%	0.0% Other	**2000 Presidential Vote**	
Military veterans:	14.6%	0.9% Hispanic Origin	Bush (R) 149,393	(64%)
			Gore (D) 80,008	(34%)
			Other 4,079	(2%)
			Cook Partisan Voting Index: R +15	

Occupation	Blue collar: 34.2%	White collar: 48.9%	Gray collar: 16.9%

Today, the old towns of south central Pennsylvania look much as they did 60 years ago: farmhouses and red barns set amidst rolling hills in the shadow of mountain ridges, seemingly isolated from the pulsing rhythms of 21st century America. But this tranquility was shattered on September 11, 2001, when United Airlines Flight 93, crashed into an empty former coalfield near Shanksville in Somerset County, killing all 40 passengers and crew on board. To Americans, the crash site became a symbol of both sadness and pride at the passengers' effort to wrest back control of the plane, initiated by the now-famous cry of "Let's roll!" The plane was headed to Washington; the bravery of the passengers prevented its reaching the hijackers' target, probably the Capitol or perhaps the White House. Just as Shanksville's 245 residents were grappling with the aftermath of Flight 93—the influx of visitors, the fears of commercialization—Somerset County was struck by another bolt of lightning, less than a year later and only 13 miles away. Nine miners at the Quecreek coal mine were trapped by rising waters 240 feet underground. As a breathless nation looked on as rescuers strained to dig rescue shafts, this outcome was more joyous. After 77 hours in confinement, the miners were lifted one by one to safety. In 2005, the National Park Service unveiled plans for a permanent memorial to Flight 93, with both public and private funding.

The area's usual placidity owes much to the Appalachian mountains, which run like a series of vertebrae up and down central Pennsylvania, long posing a formidable barrier. Up close, the mountains look tantalizingly low: you imagine that you could hike over them in an hour or so. But they are much more daunting than they seem. During the 18th century, the mountains provided Quaker Pennsylvania with a rampart against Indian attacks and allowed the commonwealth to become the richest and most populous of the colonies. But the colonials and British regulars led by General Braddock to defeat near Pittsburgh in 1754 found the mountains hard going, despite guidance from George Washington; 19th century pioneers in Conestoga wagons found it not much easier, for there are few gaps in the ridges. In the 19th century, when businessmen were ready to trade throughout the vast interior, the mountains proved to be a barrier, and people flocked to the easier routes through New York: the Erie Canal and the New York Central Railroad. It took the aggressive capitalists who built the Pennsylvania Railroad to get trains over these ridges. Conquering the mountains near Altoona required the work of several hundred Irish laborers, equipped with hand tools, gunpowder and pack animals, to build Horseshoe Curve between 1851 and 1854—one of the finest examples of railroad engineering anywhere, and today a National Historic Landmark that is celebrated by "railfans" who come from all over the world to visit it and a nearby railroaders museum; the local AA baseball team is called the Altoona Curve.

Though Pennsylvania's rail links remained important—the Nazis considered them key sabotage targets during World War II—the war-bound nation in 1940 opened the road of the future here: the Pennsylvania Turnpike, the first highway in America that was able to move vehicles dependably at high speeds over long distances. "The Pennsylvania Turnpike is a triumph of engineering," writes Tom Lewis in *Divided Highways*, a recent study of the Interstate highway system. "The road tunnels under the Allegheny Mountains and cuts about five hours off the journey between the cities. It is like no other road in America: a maximum rise at any point of just three feet in every 100; a minimum sight distance of 600 feet; bridges and underpasses that do away with cross traffic; and wide, banked curves that eliminate the need to slow down." Federal officials set a seemingly impossible 20-month deadline for construction, but the road was completed only three months late after 30,000 workers—five times the number that built the Hoover Dam—converged on western Pennsylvania during the project's final months.

Pennsylvania's 9th Congressional District takes in a wide swath of south and central Pennsylvania, including six full counties and parts of eight others. Most of the 9th is not coal country and was thus spared the boom-bust cycles of northeastern Pennsylvania and West Virginia. But this is a slow-growth, low-income area today. The largest city is Altoona, which withered from 82,000 people in 1930 to 47,000 in 2006 as the once-prosperous Pennsylvania Railroad succumbed to competition from truck traffic and became the bankrupt Penn Central and now privatized Conrail. Since the 1940s, Hollidaysburg near Altoona has been home to the small and scrupulously independent company that manufactures the Slinky, the inexpensive wire-coil toy invented accidentally by Navy engineer Richard James. Politically, this part of Pennsylvania has been solidly Republican since 1860, when Mercersburg native James Buchanan left the White House, and has not come close to electing a Democrat to Congress for decades. George W. Bush won 64% of the vote here in 2000 and 67% in 2004, both times his best performance in the state.

The congressman from the 9th District is Bill Shuster, a Republican first elected in a May 2001 special election. His father Bud Shuster, for six years the powerful chairman of the Transportation and Infrastructure Committee, announced his resignation in January 2001, after he failed to get an exemption from the Republicans' term limit on chairmanships. As Transportation chairman, Bud Shuster was a generous local benefactor: his work can be seen in the Bud Shuster Highway (as the lightly traveled Interstate 99 in Bedford and Blair Counties is known). Bill Shuster grew up in the Pittsburgh area, where his father started a successful business. After graduating from Dickinson College and American University's business school, he moved to Blair County, where he owned the family's car dealership, Shuster Chrysler in East Freedom, near Altoona. Although he was a newcomer to politics, he had plenty of experience observing his father.

The contest for the House seat was for all practical purposes decided at a district-wide Republican convention. Facing nine other contenders, Shuster—with back-room help from his father—ran an insider campaign that took advantage of the family's years of service. Although there was some local grumbling about a Shuster dynasty, opponents failed to coalesce behind a single candidate. In a key move, Shuster's allies obtained a state court injunction forcing a vote on a new slate of delegates for Blair County after claiming that the original slate supporting his opponent had been seated in violation of the rules. Shuster won 69 of the 133 votes, 2 more than the required majority. National Democrats ignored the race, which seemed to them hopeless; Governor Tom Ridge and Speaker Dennis Hastert came in for Shuster and George W. Bush cut a radio spot. But Democrat H. Scott Conklin campaigned vigorously as an opponent of abortion and gun control; Shuster won by a closer than expected 52%-44%. National Republicans attributed the narrow margin to residual intra-party ill will over his nomination; national Democrats said the district was just too Republican for a Democrat to win.

In the House, Bill Shuster has a conservative voting record, especially on social issues. Naturally, he ended up on the Transportation committee. He claimed credit for new local water and sewer projects that his father had earlier written into law; local officials call them "Shuster grants."

Following Hurricane Katrina, he questioned whether parts of New Orleans below sea level should be rebuilt. He called for removing FEMA from the Homeland Security, and restoring it as an independent agency. In 2007, Shuster was senior Republican on the Railroads, Pipelines, and Hazardous Materials Subcommittee at Transportation and Infrastructure.

Shuster had an unusually strong challenge in the 2004 primary from Michael DelGrosso, a management consultant whose family owns a Blair County tomato sauce company; he said that the district needed a new economic approach. DelGrosso carried Blair County and three nearby counties in the northern part of the district, but Shuster ran strongly enough elsewhere to squeeze out a 51%-49% win. Hanging over the campaign were allegations that Shuster ordered a staffer to spy on DelGrosso; after the primary, the House Ethics Committee criticized Shuster for improper handling of payroll records of a House aide but said the aide's activities were not done on official time.

TENTH DISTRICT

Rep. Christopher Carney (D)

Elected 2006, 1st term; b. Mar. 2, 1959, Cedar Rapids, IA; home, Dimock; Cornell College, B.S. 1981, U. of WY, M.A. 1983, U. of NE, Ph.D. 1993; Catholic; married (Jennifer).

Military Career: Naval Reserve, 1995-present.

Professional Career: Prof., PA St. U.-Worthington, 1992-2006.

DC Office: 416 CHOB, 20515, 202-225-3731; Fax: 202-225-9594; Web site: carney.house.gov.

District Offices: Clarks Summit, 570-585-9988; Williamsport, 570-327-1902.

Committees: *Homeland Security* (15th of 19 D): Management, Investigations & Oversight (Chmn.); Intelligence, Information Sharing & Terrorism Risk Assessment. *Transportation & Infrastructure* (36th of 41 D): Economic Development, Public Buildings & Emergency Management; Highways & Transit.

Group Ratings and Key Votes: Newly Elected

Election Results

2006 general	Christopher Carney (D)	110,115	(53%)	($1,530,004)
	Don Sherwood (R)	97,862	(47%)	($2,334,743)
2006 primary	Christopher Carney (D)	unopposed		
2004 general	Don Sherwood (R)	191,967	(93%)	($904,949)
	Veronica Hannevig (CNP)	14,805	(7%)	

The People		Race/Ethnic Origin	Ancestry	
Area size:	6,663 sq. mi.	95.5% White	German: 18.5%	Irish: 11.0%
Urban population:	44.6%	1.9% Black	Italian: 7.4%	
Rural population:	55.4%	0.5% Asian	**2004 Presidential Vote**	
Pop. 2000:	646,534	0.1% Native Am.	Bush (R) 170,880	(60%)
Pop. 2005 (est):	648,945	0.0% Hawaiian	Kerry (D) 112,923	(40%)
Median income:	$35,996	0.6% Two+ races	Other 1,196	(0%)
Poverty status:	10.3%	0.1% Other	**2000 Presidential Vote**	
Military veterans:	15.3%	1.4% Hispanic Origin	Bush (R) 140,387	(56%)
			Gore (D) 100,754	(40%)
			Other 7,887	(3%)
			Cook Partisan Voting Index: R + 8	
Occupation	Blue collar: 31.1%	White collar: 52.6%	Gray collar: 16.4%	

The northeast corner of Pennsylvania is a land of crevassed valleys and rugged mountains, crisscrossed by giant viaducts built for the railroads linking the East Coast with the Great Lakes and the mines to the big cities that heated their houses with the region's anthracite coal. Except for a row of anthracite coal cities from Scranton to Wilkes-Barre, this part of Pennsylvania still has a wild look to it: the superstructure of railroads and Interstate 80 pass through an area that seems otherwise little touched by recent prosperity. This is a land of numerous long-established small towns, with solidly built courthouses and banks and elderly citizens—a part of the Northeast that seems worlds away from the region's huge central cities and growing suburbs. The biggest towns here are Lewisburg, home of Bucknell University and a major federal penitentiary, and Williamsport, home of the Little League World Series. Only at the eastern edge is there significant growth. Pike County on the Delaware River grew 94% from 1990 to 2004, attracting many tired of paying high taxes in New Jersey and New York. The local Pocono mountains also are a destination for weekenders and, for a few days each November, for bear hunters. In the winter months, hunters in increasing numbers turn to tracking coyote in the fresh snow. Torrential rains hit the region particularly hard in July 2006 causing flood damage severe enough to designate much of the district as federal disaster areas.

The 10th Congressional District of Pennsylvania includes all of northeast Pennsylvania except for Scranton, Wilkes-Barre and fast-growing Monroe County, which are in the 11th District. The area's most consequential congressman was probably David Wilmot who in the 1840s introduced the Wilmot Proviso barring slavery from the New Mexico and California Territories acquired in the Mexican War; this raised the issue of slavery in the territories which led proximately to the Civil War. Wilmot was a founder of the Republican party and was elected to the Senate; most people in this part of Pennsylvania have been Republicans ever since.

The new congressman from the 10th District is Christopher Carney, a Democrat elected in 2006. Carney was born in Cedar Rapids, Iowa, studied at nearby Cornell College, the University of Wyoming and the University of Nebraska. In 1992 Carney moved his family to Pennsylvania to take a job as an associate professor at Penn State University's Scranton campus. After the September 11 terrorist attacks, Carney was called up to go to Afghanistan, but instead ended up at the Pentagon analyzing CIA intelligence for Undersecretary of Defense Douglas Feith in search of connections between al-Qaeda and Iraq. His conclusion, which he continues to defend, was that there were "high-level" contacts between the two, but he said the Bush administration took the evidence too far when Defense Secretary Rumsfeld declared the connection was "bulletproof." Carney told the Wilkes-Barre *Times Leader* he decided to run for Congress after he saw Republican Congressman Don Sherwood at a gas station, preparing to go to Washington to vote on the end-of-life case of Terri Schiavo. "This was the Republicans trying to capitalize on this family's misery and it made me mad. I'm Irish and I had a couple hundred more miles to go before I was home, and actually somewhere right around Wilkes-Barre I decided, 'Dammit, I'm going to do this.'"

Sherwood represented a reliably Republican district, but the seat was put into play after the *Times Leader* reported in April 2005 that D.C. police had been called to Sherwood's Capitol Hill apartment in September 2004 by a 29-year-old woman who accused him of punching and choking her. Sherwood said he was giving her a back rub. Sherwood's accuser later said she had a five-year affair with the married congressman. He described her as a "casual acquaintance," but issued an apology "for the pain and embarrassment I have caused my family and my supporters." In June 2005, the woman filed suit against Sherwood, seeking $5.5 million in damages, and the lawsuit was settled in November 2005, reportedly for $500,000. As a result of his indiscretion, Sherwood faced an unusually competitive challenge in the May Republican primary from an underfunded candidate who ran on family values and held the incumbent to just 56%-44%. "I got it. I got the message," Sherwood said afterward. In an attempt to steer the campaign back to safer territory in this conservative district, Sherwood portrayed Carney as a supporter of tax increases and accused Carney of deceiving voters on his position in favor of abortion rights. A cancer survivor, Carney also supported stem cell research. Carney criticized Bush's execution of the war and advocated the redeployment of a U.S. battalion for each equivalent Iraqi security force trained as a replacement. Because of Carney's opposition to the war, activists were willing to overlook his role in helping to make the White House case in Iraq; Pennsylvania Republicans, meanwhile, sent out a mailer in October blaming him for the war. "Chris Carney failed our nation once," the direct mail piece read. "Don't give Chris Carney a chance to FAIL us again."

Carney avoided direct mention of Sherwood's affair for most of the campaign until late September when he aired a TV ad that featured a one-time Sherwood supporter holding a photo of his 26-year-old stepdaughter. "How can I tell her I support Don Sherwood and feel good about myself?" he asked. The Mark Foley congressional page scandal that unfolded in late September also served to refocus attention on Sherwood's own scandal. In October Sherwood issued a direct apology to the district for the affair and denied that any abuse occurred. "Should you forgive me, you can count on me to continue fighting for you and your family," Sherwood said in a TV ad. The incumbent also sent out a mailer featuring his wife, Carol, criticizing Carney for being negative about their family.

John Boehner, Dick Cheney and George W. Bush all visited the district, with the latter telling voters that Sherwood was "the right man to represent" the 10th. Voters disagreed: Carney won 53%-47% with his winning margins coming from Lackawanna and Luzerne Counties. After his concession speech, Sherwood told reporters, "You won't see me again in politics."

John Murtha, who had campaigned with Carney, promised him a seat on the Appropriations Committee, on which Sherwood had also served, but Murtha's ability to deliver faded when he lost his bid for majority leader. Democrats instead named Carney as chairman of the Homeland Security oversight committee. Carney remains a lieutenant commander in the Navy Reserve and serves one weekend each month at the Pentagon.

Republicans are certain to target this district in 2008. The party's top recruit, U.S. Attorney Tom Marino, declined to run. But Dan Meuser, a wealthy wheelchair manufacturing company executive, and Luzerne County businessman Chris Hackett were seriously considering running.

ELEVENTH DISTRICT

Rep. Paul Kanjorski (D)

Elected 1984, 12th term; b. Apr. 2, 1937, Nanticoke; home, Nanticoke; Temple U., 1957-61, Dickinson Law Schl., 1962-65; Catholic; married (Nancy).

Military Career: Army Reserves, 1960-61.

Professional Career: Practicing atty., 1966-85; Nanticoke City Solicitor, 1969-81; Admin. Law Judge, 1971-80.

DC Office: 2188 RHOB, 20515, 202-225-6511; Fax: 202-225-0764; Web site: kanjorski.house.gov.

District Offices: Mount Pocono, 570-895-4176; Scranton, 570-496-1011; Wilkes-Barre, 570-825-2200.

Committees: *Financial Services* (2d of 37 D): Capital Markets, Insurance & Government Sponsored Enterprises (Chmn.); Domestic and International Monetary Policy, Trade & Technology; Financial Institutions & Consumer Credit. *Oversight & Government Reform* (4th of 23 D): Government Management, Organization & Procurement; Information Policy, Census & National Archives. *Science & Technology* (13th of 24 D): Energy & Environment.

Group Ratings

	ADA	ACLU	AFS	LCV	ITIC	NTU	COC	ACU	CFG	FRC
2006	70	71	100	67	57	20	43	29	15	28
2005	80	—	100	67	—	18	48	24	18	38

National Journal Ratings

	2005 LIB	—	2005 CONS	2006 LIB	—	2006 CONS
Economic	66%	—	34%	62%	—	37%
Social	58%	—	42%	61%	—	39%
Foreign	70%	—	29%	67%	—	33%

Key Votes of the 109th Congress

1. Estate Tax Repeal	N	5. Limit Interstate Abortion	Y
2. Limit CAFE Standards	Y	6. Extend Patriot Act	N
3. FY06 Spending Curb	N	7. Bar Same Sex Marriage	N
4. Drilling in ANWR	Y	8. Stem Cell Research $	Y

9. Build Border Fence	Y
10. CAFTA	N
11. Oppose Iraq Withdrawal	N
12. Detainee Tribunals	N

Election Results

2006 general	Paul Kanjorski (D)	134,340	(72%)	($652,549)
	Joseph Leonardi (R)	51,033	(28%)	($9,882)
2006 primary	Paul Kanjorski (D)	unopposed		
2004 general	Paul Kanjorski (D)	171,147	(94%)	($378,979)
	Kenneth Brenneman (CNP)	10,105	(6%)	

Prior Winning Percentages: 2002 (56%); 2000 (66%); 1998 (67%); 1996 (68%); 1994 (67%); 1992 (67%); 1990 (100%); 1988 (100%); 1986 (71%); 1984 (59%)

The People		Race/Ethnic Origin	Ancestry	
Area size:	2,249 sq. mi.	93.3% White	German: 14.5% Irish: 13.2%	
Urban population:	72.6%	2.5% Black	Italian: 12.0%	
Rural population:	27.4%	0.7% Asian	**2004 Presidential Vote**	
Pop. 2000:	646,209	0.1% Native Am.	Kerry (D) 143,205	(53%)
Pop. 2005 (est):	670,155	0.0% Hawaiian	Bush (R) 127,866	(47%)
Median income:	$34,979	0.7% Two+ races	Other 843	(0%)
Poverty status:	11.3%	0.1% Other	**2000 Presidential Vote**	
Military veterans:	15.3%	2.5% Hispanic Origin	Gore (D) 127,140	(54%)
			Bush (R) 101,629	(43%)
			Other 6,983	(3%)
			Cook Partisan Voting Index: D + 5	

Occupation   Blue collar: 29.8%   White collar: 54.0%   Gray collar: 16.1%

"Coal is the theme song of this city in the hills," the *WPA Guide* said of Scranton in 1940, but even as those words were written, the anthracite kingdom around Scranton and Wilkes-Barre was crumbling. In the 19th century anthracite had become America's main home heating fuel and the valley along the East Branch of the Susquehanna River and the creek that extends north was America's number one source of anthracite. Thousands of immigrants flocked to this valley, settling in a chain of little cities north and south of Wilkes-Barre (named for two backers of the American revolution) and Scranton (named for the leading founding family). There, they took honest jobs with long hours, modest pay, poor working conditions and high death rates—facts of life that made the violently pro-union Molly Maguires popular here, and which spawned periodic clashes between them and the Pinkerton security forces hired by the industrial moguls. While the supply of coal was endless—the area produced 40% of the world's hard coal—demand proved fleeting. Anthracite production peaked in 1917, with long strikes in 1922 and 1925 quickening the conversion to oil and gas. Demand for anthracite began to fall in the 1920s and plummeted in the 1940s; the counties containing Wilkes-Barre and Scranton, Luzerne and Lackawanna, had 755,000 people in 1930 and 523,000 in 2003. As the area's 50 collieries shut down, the once-ubiquitous coal dust vanished; the local ethnic mix—Irish and Polish, Ukrainian and Welsh—grew less distinctive; and former boomtowns full of young families became time-worn communities of senior citizens with modest household incomes.

Visitors can see how suddenly growth stopped here: at the edge of town streets with houses obviously built in the 1910s and 1920s suddenly end, with only open space beyond. In the 1960s and 1970s, textile and apparel mills brought low-wage, non-union jobs to a formerly high-wage, unionized area. But the anthracite kingdom, created by unbridled (and often exploitative) free enterprise, increasingly looked to the government for sustenance. Two longtime House Appropriations Committee members, Democrat Daniel Flood of Luzerne and Republican Joseph McDade of Lackawanna, specialized in funneling money and projects into the area, of which the most visible today is Scranton's $66 million Steamtown train historic site.

The 11th Congressional District of Pennsylvania is the anthracite district. It includes almost all of Luzerne County, plus Scranton and surrounding towns in Lackawanna County. It also includes Columbia County west of Luzerne, Carbon County to the south, and Monroe County to the east. Monroe is a different sort of place: it contains most of the Pocono resorts and the often congested Interstate 80 bridge to New Jersey; New Yorkers and New Jerseyites looking for lower taxes and pleasant scenery have moved here in large numbers and the county's population rose 66% from 1990 to 2004; a comparable increase is expected by 2030. More typical of the district are small towns like Centralia, site of a massive underground fire that has burned unchecked since 1962 and might burn for another 100 years, forcing out all but 11 stubborn and mostly elderly residents, and Jim Thorpe, created in 1953 from the unification of neighboring (and rival) Mauch Chunk and East Mauch Chunk. The cities changed their name after offering to provide a gravesite for the great football, baseball and Olympic track star when Thorpe's widow was shopping his remains to whichever town agreed to build him a suitable memorial. Downtown is lively today, with thousands of cyclists for regular enclaves, plus tourists drawn by Thorpe, the Oklahoma Indian who never came to Carbon County until his death. Hazleton gained national notoriety after passing a tough 2006 ordinance aimed at cracking down on illegal immigrants.

Since the 1930s, miners have been a large Democratic voting bloc, and this is a solidly Democratic district. But these Democrats tend to be cultural conservatives, pro-gun and anti-abortion. In 2004, John Kerry held his first rally in Scranton after the Democratic convention.

Kerry, George W. Bush and their running mates made 10 campaign appearances in the area. Bush closed the gap, but Kerry won the district 53%-47%.

The congressman from the 11th District is Paul Kanjorski, a Democrat first elected in 1984. Kanjorski grew up in Nanticoke, near Wilkes-Barre. As a 16-year-old page in the House of Representatives in 1954, he was on the floor when Puerto Rican terrorists started shooting from the gallery and wounded five congressmen; sprayed by dust from the gunfire, Kanjorski helped to bring stretchers into the chamber. He attended, but did not graduate from, college and law school, then passed the bar exam and returned home to practice law; he was a workmen's compensation administrative law judge for 9 years and Nanticoke city solicitor for 12. He ran for Congress and won the Democratic primary by pointing out the incumbent was in Central America while flood-soaked Wilkes-Barre area residents had to boil tap water because of contamination.

In the House, Kanjorski is a tough partisan whose voting record has been liberal on economics and moderate on cultural issues. He opposes abortion rights but has voted for international family planning aid. He voted to authorize force in Iraq, but later voiced regret and criticized the military for diverting funds from fighting al Qaeda. In 2005, he objected to the oversight hearing on steroid use in Major League Baseball. "Is this the most important issue for the U.S. Congress to spend its time on?" On the Financial Services Committee—where he is the number-two Democrat and chairman of the Subcommittee on Capitol Markets, Insurance and Government Sponsored Enterprises—Kanjorski helped to write the post-Enron bill to crack down on corporate fraud, and he pushed a "subprime lending" bill to protect consumers from predatory practices. With Republican Ken Calvert, he wants to keep banks out of the real estate business. In the majority, he sought regulatory flexibility for life insurance carriers.

Most important to Kanjorski is helping his economically ailing district. Abetted by Pennsylvania colleague John Murtha, he has directed millions of federal dollars into local projects; *The New York Times* has called him "a master of earmarking." But his eagerness to deliver money back home has gotten him some unwelcome notice. As reported in June 2007 by the Scranton *Times-Tribune*, since the late 1990s Kanjorski has earmarked nearly $10 million in federal funding to Cornerstone Technologies, a troubled high-tech research and development company controlled by his relatives. The company was supposed to turn coal into minute particles for use in carbon fibers but the end product was disappointing and Cornerstone filed for bankruptcy in 2006, with more than $1 million in debts. "It was just like the Three Stooges meet anthracite," a Penn State professor who worked with the firm told the *Times-Tribune*. Former employees charged that Kanjorski "often took an active role in its operations," according to the newspaper account.

Republicans targeted Kanjorski in 2002, when his involvement with Cornerstone first began to attract widespread attention. Their candidate was Hazleton Mayor Louis Barletta, who hammered him over his involvement with the company. Kanjorski said that his partisan opponents were manufacturing allegations to damage him politically. This was Kanjorski's closest contest since he was first elected, but he won decisively, 56%-42%. Kanjorski, who had triple bypass surgery in March 2007, seems politically secure, though Barletta said in mid-2007 that he might run again; Barletta's political stature has grown since his first challenge, largely due to his high-profile stance against illegal immigration, and national Republicans seem to think that renewed attention to Cornerstone Technologies might leave Kanjorski vulnerable.

TWELFTH DISTRICT

Rep. John Murtha (D)

Elected Feb. 1974, 17th full term; b. June 17, 1932, New Martinsville, WV; home, Johnstown; U. of Pittsburgh, B.A. 1962, Indiana U. of PA, 1963-64; Catholic; married (Joyce).

Military Career: Marine Corps, 1952-55, 1966-67 (Vietnam); Marine Corps Reserves, 1955-66, 1967-90.

Elected Office: PA House of Reps., 1969-74.

Professional Career: Owner, Johnstown Minute Car Wash.

DC Office: 2423 RHOB, 20515, 202-225-2065; Fax: 202-225-5709; Web site: www.house.gov/murtha.

District Offices: Johnstown, 814-535-2642.

Committees: *Appropriations* (2d of 37 D): Defense (Chmn.).

Group Ratings

	ADA	ACLU	AFS	LCV	ITIC	NTU	COC	ACU	CFG	FRC
2006	65	77	100	58	67	23	50	28	14	28
2005	75	—	100	56	—	21	62	40	11	31

National Journal Ratings

	2005 LIB	—	2005 CONS		2006 LIB	—	2006 CONS
Economic	60%	—	40%		58%	—	42%
Social	62%	—	38%		62%	—	37%
Foreign	64%	—	36%		59%	—	40%

Key Votes of the 109th Congress

1. Estate Tax Repeal	N	5. Limit Interstate Abortion	Y	9. Build Border Fence	N
2. Limit CAFE Standards	Y	6. Extend Patriot Act	N	10. CAFTA	N
3. FY06 Spending Curb	N	7. Bar Same Sex Marriage	N	11. Oppose Iraq Withdrawal	N
4. Drilling in ANWR	Y	8. Stem Cell Research $	Y	12. Detainee Tribunals	N

Election Results

2006 general	John Murtha (D)	123,472	(61%)	($3,254,226)
	Diana Irey (R)	79,612	(39%)	($852,811)
2006 primary	John Murtha (D)	unopposed		
2004 general	John Murtha (D)	unopposed		($1,559,185)

Prior Winning Percentages: 2002 (73%); 2000 (71%); 1998 (68%); 1996 (70%); 1994 (69%); 1992 (100%); 1990 (62%); 1988 (100%); 1986 (67%); 1984 (69%); 1982 (61%); 1980 (59%); 1978 (69%); 1976 (68%); 1974 (58%); 1974 (50%)

The People		Race/Ethnic Origin	Ancestry	
Area size:	2,781 sq. mi.	95.0% White	German: 17.3% Irish: 9.8%	
Urban population:	62.5%	3.3% Black	Italian: 9.2%	
Rural population:	37.5%	0.3% Asian	**2004 Presidential Vote**	
Pop. 2000:	646,249	0.1% Native Am.	Kerry (D) 141,046	(51%)
Pop. 2005 (est):	629,676	0.0% Hawaiian	Bush (R) 133,088	(49%)
Median income:	$30,612	0.7% Two+ races	Other 119	(0%)
Poverty status:	13.6%	0.1% Other	**2000 Presidential Vote**	
Military veterans:	15.3%	0.6% Hispanic Origin	Gore (D) 131,960	(55%)
			Bush (R) 105,451	(44%)
			Other 3,595	(1%)
			Cook Partisan Voting Index: D + 5	

Occupation	Blue collar: 30.5%	White collar: 51.4%	Gray collar: 18.1%

The mountains and valleys within a 100-mile radius of Pittsburgh comprise one of America's most beautiful—and economically troubled—regions. This has been tough, hard-working country ever since Scots-Irish farmers settled here in the 1790s. Their first big product was whiskey—this was the site of the Whiskey Rebellion of 1794—but historically the most important product was bituminous coal. Discovered in the 19th century, it was the basic energy source for the production of iron and steel. The offspring of the original settlers were joined by immigrants from Italy, Poland and Czechoslovakia, living in little frame houses packed into the towns on interstices between hills and rivers, within walking distance of steel factories, foundries and coal mine shafts. It is an industrial landscape and yet there are spots of natural beauty, like the swirling waters of the Youghiogheny River, now much enjoyed by rafters. But the water coming down from the mountains can be dangerous. Its best known community is Johnstown, where on May 31, 1889, floodwater from the ruptured South Fork Dam, gaining speed during an 18-mile trip down steep-walled valleys, poured into the little industrial city with a force equal to Niagara Falls. During 10 awful minutes buildings crumpled like paper, the tumbling hearths and gaslights ignited the wreckage, a flaming pile of debris converged on a 30-acre expanse, and 2,209 people died. This was the worst single-day civilian loss of life in American history until September 11, 2001, when airliners crashed into the World Trade Center and the Pentagon and came down in a field just 50 miles southwest of Johnstown near Shanksville. The 1889 flood and its class overtones (the dam, built at a rural retreat owned by western Pennsylvania's richest families, had been negligently maintained) are documented thoughtfully by the Johnstown Flood Museum in the old Carnegie Library. The museum provides an offset to the economic woes of Johnstown, whose population fell from 67,000 in 1920 to 22,000 in

2006—a decline similar to that of many communities in this region. Life was never easy here; after some prosperous years in the 1960s and 1970s, the "Cradle of the American Steel Industry" was hit hard by the recession that followed the 1979 oil shock. Young people have been leaving the area for years, downtown has been deserted and this district now has the highest elderly percentage in the state. Yet there are some signs of revival. The Johnstown area gained jobs in 2005 and 2006, and in Washington County in 2005 Consol Energy announced a $500 million expansion of the Enslow Fork Mine, with 400 new jobs. But they're not drawing newcomers: Johnstown ranks number one among 318 metro areas in the percentage of residents born in the state, 90%.

The 12th Congressional District of Pennsylvania, with highly irregular boundaries, contains much of this coal and steel country. It includes all of Greene County and parts of Fayette, Somerset, Cambria, Indiana, Armstrong, Washington and Westmoreland Counties. The boundaries were drawn by Republican legislators who wanted to create a new Republican-leaning 18th District in the southern suburbs of Pittsburgh while also accommodating Democratic Congressman John Murtha, then second ranking minority member on the Appropriations Committee, who has worked assiduously to help Pennsylvania. The district unites Murtha's home base of Johnstown and Democratic territory in the southwestern corner of the state.

Politically, this was one of the most Republican parts of America from the Civil War up to the 1930s. Republican policies, including high tariffs and hostility to labor unions, were seen as protecting jobs and increasing growth in the steel economy centered on Pittsburgh. With the coming of the New Deal, and success of the United Mine Workers and the United Steelworkers, the area began voting mostly Democratic. Since 1945, on the Monday before primary and general elections, Democratic pols from across southwestern Pennsylvania have attended the "rally in the valley" held at the Slovak Home in the mill town of Monessen, whose high school is known for producing NFL players (as is nearby McKeesport's). But this area has not followed the national Democratic Party on all issues. Voters here have strongly favored trade restrictions on steel imports, even when most other Democrats were free traders in the 1960s and 1970s; more recently most House Democrats have been opposing free trade measures. Voters here also tend to take conservative stands on cultural issues and foreign policy. This carefully carved district voted 55%-44% for Al Gore in 2000. But after George W. Bush imposed import quotas on steel and boosted clean coal technology, the district voted only 51%-49% for John Kerry.

The congressman from the 12th District is John Murtha, a Democrat first elected in a February 1974 special election that signaled the political weakness of Richard Nixon; he was the first Vietnam veteran elected to Congress. Murtha grew up in the Johnstown area, attended Washington and Jefferson College, then in 1952 enlisted in the Marine Corps; he became a drill instructor at Parris Island and was selected for officer candidate school in Quantico. He graduated from the University of Pittsburgh and re-enlisted in the Marines in 1966, at 34 and served in Vietnam. For his service there he was awarded the Bronze Star, two Purple Hearts and the Vietnamese Cross for Gallantry. Murtha is a member of the Appropriations Committee and chairman of the Defense Appropriations Subcommittee, his party's key man on the defense budget. His voting record over the years—hawkish on foreign policy, interventionist on economics and usually tradition-minded on cultural issues—seemed perfectly suited to the steel and coal country. Murtha is also one of those old-time politicians who operate best in secret, holding court in the back corner of the House chamber, "the Murtha corner," where he trades gossip and votes to colleagues who crowd around him as if they were kissing his ring. For most of his career, he spoke for attribution to few national or local reporters, hardly ever appeared on television, and rarely spoke in the House chamber except for the annual defense spending bill, which often passes with little debate. He wields power not only on his committee work but also on many back-room issues dear to his colleagues, including pay raises, committee assignments and, after the trial and acquittal of Pennsylvania Republican Joseph McDade, a provision requiring the Justice Department to reimburse members of Congress who are indicted but acquitted. He has opposed abortion and gun control and supported oil drilling in the Arctic National Wildlife Refuge.

As ranking minority member of the Defense Appropriations Subcommittee, Murtha was caught sometimes between Democratic demands for lower defense spending and Republican desires to spend even more on defense, but in the bipartisan culture of the Appropriations Committee he exerted major influence even while in the minority. Appropriations Chairman David Obey has called him a man "who likes to get things done with virtually no spoken words." Murtha voted for the Gulf War resolution in 1991, but opposed intervention in Bosnia and deployment in Somalia, arguing that UN officials lacked the know-how to command U.S. troops. Inside the Democratic Caucus, he wielded considerable clout, and became an ally of Nancy Pelosi in her quest for a leadership position. In 2001, after David Bonior resigned as Minority Whip, Murtha managed Pelosi's campaign for that post against the more senior Steny Hoyer, and Pelosi won 118-95—a victory that put Pelosi on the road to the speakership. Murtha played a similar role to that played by coal-country Democrat Wayne Hays for San Francisco's Phil Burton in his quest for the majority leadership in 1976, providing assurance to more conservative and traditional Democrats that a West Coast liberal would provide the kind of leadership they wanted. Murtha's admiration for Pelosi is unbounded; in January 2007 he said, "The Speaker has the best political mind I've ever seen."

Murtha voted for the Iraq war resolution in October 2002, contrary to Pelosi and most members of the Democratic Caucus. But he seems to have had reservations about the war early on. He complained loudly that troops in Iraq were poorly equipped, with both personal gear and machines, and he questioned the civilian decision-making. In May 2004, he said, "We cannot prevail in this war as it is going today. We either have to mobilize or we have to get out." In October 2004, he was one of two House members who voted to reinstate the military draft, advanced on the theory that Congress would be less willing to support wars if their constituents were subject to conscription. In May 2005 he supported a defense appropriation with a $45.3 billion bridge fund for Iraq and Afghanistan. In early November 2005 he signaled his dissatisfaction by calling CIA secret prisons "absolutely outrageous" and by saying he would put a ban on torture in the defense appropriation. On November 17, to much publicity, he called for withdrawal from Iraq. "It is time for a change in direction," he said, and decried "a flawed policy wrapped in illusion." This was treated in the press as the sudden conversion of a military hawk, but Murtha's previous statements about the stress on the troops suggest that his thinking was moving in this direction for some time. When Dick Cheney criticized his statement, he dismissed "people with five deferments." Ohio Republican Jean Schmidt, recently sent to Congress in a special election, said on the floor that she had received a call from a Marine. "He asked me to send Congress a message: stay the course. He also asked me to send Congressman Murtha a message, that cowards cut and run, Marines never do." Democrats protested furiously and Schmidt apologized. Murtha became a hero to many House Democrats, but not to all; Steny Hoyer, by then Minority Whip, said that a premature withdrawal from Iraq would be a "disaster." House Republicans insisted on a vote on a resolution stating that "deployment of United States forces be terminated immediately" and it failed 403–3.

Murtha continued his criticism of the conduct of the war. In May 2006 he said that everything in Iraq had deteriorated, and that month he said that "there has to have been a cover-up" in the case of Marines who killed 24 civilians in Haditha in November 2005; the military had been investigating the charges since they were aired in *Time* earlier in the year. One Marine sued him for libel, but the case was dismissed. In June 2006 he was asked on *Meet the Press* where troops now in Iraq should be deployed. He mentioned Kuwait, Qatar and Bahrain, and then added, "We can go to Okinawa. We can deploy there almost instantly." When Tim Russert suggested that Okinawa is far from Iraq (it's 4,899 miles), Murtha said, "When I say a timely response, you know, our fighters can fly from Okinawa very quickly."

In June 2006 Murtha announced that he would run against Hoyer for majority leader in the event, increasingly likely as the year went on, that Democrats won a majority in the House. He said Pelosi was aware of his intention and didn't encourage or discourage him. But days later, after some Democrats said this would hurt party unity, Pelosi convinced him to set aside his campaign until November and released a statement in his name, "For the unity of the party and to focus on Democratic victory in November, I have suspended my campaign for majority leader until after the election." But this genie was not to be put back in the bottle, and in October Murtha said, "We're back campaigning again." Five days after the election Pelosi backed Murtha. Hoyer responded mildly. "Nancy told me some time ago that she would personally support Jack. I respect her decision as the two are very close." But most of the Blue Dogs backed Hoyer and so did senior incoming committee chairmen like John Dingell, Henry Waxman and Barney Frank. Democrats had run against a "climate of corruption" in 2006, but some Democrats thought Murtha's record was in tension with that theme. Videotape was unearthed of Murtha's interchange with a purported sheik, actually an undercover FBI agent, in the Abscam case in 1980. It showed the "sheik" offering Murtha $50,000. Murtha said he wasn't interested "at this point," but "I want to get [expletive] jobs in the area, you know, a few bank deposits. . . .Later on, after we've dealt a while . . . we might want to do more business." The ethics committee voted not to bring charges against Murtha, after which its special counsel resigned in protest; Murtha was a cooperating witness against two other members. Murtha explained himself to MSNBC's Chris Matthews, "Listen, I wanted to negotiate with them about investment in the district; that's what I was interested in. It's the only thing I was interested in." In October, *The New York Times* ran an article on how Murtha "often delivers Democratic votes to Republican leaders in a tacit exchange for earmarks for himself and his allies." It cited votes blocking investigation of contract fraud in Iraq, enacting lobbying reform, financing flood control, adding $150 million to veterans health care and job training, exempting middle class families from the Alternative Minimum Tax and a proposal to spend base closing funding on prosthetic limbs for veterans. With some precision (perhaps provided by Hoyer backers), it said he sided with Republicans on close votes 169 times since 1994, more than all but three other Democrats. Despite confident statements that he would win, Murtha lost to Hoyer on the secret ballot 149-86.

Despite this loss, Murtha continued to be a leading spokesman for House Democrats as Defense Appropriations chairman. In January 2007 he said that the military faced a $100 billion shortfall in equipment because of Iraq. "We have no ability to deploy and sustain a deployment in Iran or Korea, and the enemy knows this." He said he would force the closing of the detention center for illegal combatants at Guantanamo. He defended his intervention on getting military aircraft for Pelosi (which her predecessor Dennis Hastert also used): "All I did was call the Air Force and say let's take care of this." In February he began work on the defense supplemental, saying, "We're supporting the troops, we're protecting the troops, but on the other hand we're going to stop this surge." He said that he planned to attach readiness conditions to the supplemental: troops must have at least one year between deployments, no deployment must last more than one year, the stop-loss program must be ended. He made his intentions clear and publicized them on an antiwar website. "They know they can't sustain the surge if it passes the House and the Senate. And the president could veto it. But then he wouldn't have any money." This got a harsh reaction from many Democrats, and Appropriations Chairman David Obey handled the framing of the supplemental.

The Democrats' promises to change the way the House does business were in conflict with the practice of appropriators of placing programs in their districts. Murtha, after a close primary race in 1990, worked at this assiduously. Johnstown has a Murtha highway, a Murtha airport and Murtha health centers. Murtha persuaded the University of Pittsburgh to set up a nonprofit, now called Concurrent Technologies, which could use Navy money to establish a Center for Excellence in Metalworking in Johnstown. Between 1999 and 2006 military and other federal agencies spent nearly $1 billion on contracts and grants to Concurrent; Concurrent executives donated $114,000 to Murtha's 2000, 2002 and 2004 campaigns, and Concurrent paid about $500,000 a year to a lobbying firm, PMA Group, whose executives and clients contributed more than $1 million to Murtha since 1999. Other firms represented by Murtha's brother got substantial contracts. On May 1, 2007 Murtha submitted a $23 million earmark to the Intelligence Committee for the National Drug Intelligence Center in Johnstown, which OMB recommended defunding; this was five weeks after the deadline for earmarks, but it may have been unclear that it deserved that designation. Michigan Republican Mike Rogers objected to the $23 million, and on May 17 Murtha approached him on the floor and said, according to Rogers, "I hope you don't have any earmarks in the appropriations bill because they are gone and you will not get any earmarks now and forever." Rogers accused him of violating a new House rule Democrats had passed in January, barring members from considering the inclusion of any earmarks on the basis of a member's vote on other matters, and brought a privileged resolution that he be reprimanded. The matter came to the floor on May 22 and the Democratic leadership moved to table; all but two Democrats so voted. On May 23 Murtha sent a written apology to Rogers.

Murtha's work on district matters has paid off handsomely at the polls. In 2001 Pennsylvania Republicans consulted Murtha during the redistricting process and made adjustments to the boundaries to suit him. In February 2006 Washington County Commissioner Diana Irey, roused by Murtha's accusations against the Marines in Haditha, launched a campaign, and in May brought Marines to Washington demanding he apologize. She put the Abscam tapes on the web. Murtha's opposition to the war may have disturbed some of his constituents, but many rallied to him; former Senator Max Cleland went to Johnstown to campaign for him. Murtha won 61%-39%, a convincing margin but one considerably smaller than in 2002, when he faced much less visible opposition.

THIRTEENTH DISTRICT

Rep. Allyson Schwartz (D)

Elected 2004, 2d term; b. Oct. 3, 1948, Queens, NY; home, Jenkintown; Simmons Col., B.A. 1970, Bryn Mawr Col., M.S.W. 1972; Jewish; married (David).

Elected Office: PA Senate, 1990-2004.

Professional Career: Exec. Dir., Elizabeth Blackwell Center, 1975-88; Dep. Comm., Philadelphia Human Rights Dept., 1988-90.

DC Office: 423 CHOB, 20515, 202-225-6111; Fax: 202-226-0611; Web site: schwartz.house.gov.

District Offices: Jenkintown, 215-517-6572; Philadelphia, 215-335-3355.

Committees: *Budget* (6th of 22 D). *Ways & Means* (23d of 24 D): Social Security; Select Revenue Measures.

Group Ratings

	ADA	ACLU	AFS	LCV	ITIC	NTU	COC	ACU	CFG	FRC
2006	85	82	100	100	57	17	47	16	15	0
2005	90	—	100	94	—	10	44	4	4	0

National Journal Ratings

	2005 LIB	—	2005 CONS		2006 LIB	—	2006 CONS
Economic	78%	—	21%		73%	—	27%
Social	70%	—	30%		73%	—	27%
Foreign	70%	—	29%		77%	—	20%

Key Votes of the 109th Congress

1. Estate Tax Repeal	N	5. Limit Interstate Abortion	N	9. Build Border Fence	N
2. Limit CAFE Standards	N	6. Extend Patriot Act	Y	10. CAFTA	N
3. FY06 Spending Curb	N	7. Bar Same Sex Marriage	N	11. Oppose Iraq Withdrawal	N
4. Drilling in ANWR	N	8. Stem Cell Research $	Y	12. Detainee Tribunals	N

Election Results

2006 general	Allyson Schwartz (D)	147,368	(66%)	($2,248,091)
	Raj Bhakta (R)	75,492	(34%)	($477,960)
2006 primary	Allyson Schwartz (D)	unopposed		
2004 general	Allyson Schwartz (D)	171,763	(56%)	($4,572,500)
	Melissa Brown (R)	127,205	(41%)	($1,927,499)
	Other	9,156	(3%)	

The People		Race/Ethnic Origin	Ancestry	
Area size:	258 sq. mi.	85.7% White	Irish: 19.5%	German: 15.6%
Urban population:	98.5%	5.9% Black	Italian: 10.4%	
Rural population:	1.5%	4.0% Asian	**2004 Presidential Vote**	
Pop. 2000:	647,435	0.1% Native Am.	Kerry (D) 182,552	(56%)
Pop. 2005 (est):	652,003	0.0% Hawaiian	Bush (R) 140,900	(43%)
Median income:	$49,319	1.0% Two+ races	Other 1,345	(0%)
Poverty status:	7.1%	0.1% Other	**2000 Presidential Vote**	
Military veterans:	12.8%	3.1% Hispanic Origin	Gore (D) 155,903	(56%)
			Bush (R) 117,773	(42%)
			Other 5,972	(2%)
			Cook Partisan Voting Index: D + 8	

Occupation	Blue collar: 19.3%	White collar: 68.1%	Gray collar: 12.6%

Montgomery County, Pennsylvania, is the proximate hinterland of Philadelphia: rolling hills cut on one side by the Schuylkill River and at intervals by the Pennsylvania and Reading Railroad lines radiating outward from Center City. Older suburbs, both rich and modest, grew up around rail stations, with comfortable houses within walking distance for commuters. Further out are 18th and 19th century villages, once surrounded by farm fields, now encroached by subdivisions where people depend on cars, not rail lines, to get to work. Montgomery County has its shopping malls and office parks, but not many freeways; most of the traffic here is along roads on the area's diagonal grid or along the old pikes laid out when Pennsylvania was a colony. It is the most populous and second most affluentcounty in metropolitan Philadelphia, with solid job growth prospects.

Quite a different place, though adjacent to southern Montgomery County, is Northeast Philadelphia. This is relatively new urban territory, with more than half its houses built after 1950. When the alley-wide streets of North and South Philadelphia and the river wards were already teeming and the Main Line suburbs were well-settled, the workers of Philadelphia's docks, factories and Center City offices were just starting to fill up vacant land here. They settled in neighborhoods like Bustleton, Somerton and Torresdale. Many of Philadelphia's Hispanics live in the industrial river wards along the Delaware River, but the other wards of Northeast Philadelphia are still mostly white and ethnic, the kind of places where city cops and firefighters live and that gave big margins to Mayor Frank Rizzo in the 1970s and 1980s. Federal Section 8 housing for low-income tenants and its effects on local real estate values has caused local consternation. More recently, outside investors and Hasidic Jews from New York looking for more space and opportunity have bid up residential prices.

The 13th Congressional District of Pennsylvania includes much of southeastern and central Montgomery County and most of Northeast Philadelphia. Historically Montgomery was quintessentially Republican, with a style of politics set for years by Ivy-educated Republican men, and with Republicans of more modest and sometimes ethnic backgrounds manning the precincts and staffing local offices. But the county, like other affluent suburbs in the Boston-Washington corridor, swung toward the Democratic Party in national politics in the 1990s, with abortion and other cultural issues usually trumping economic interests. The same county that voted by large margins for Ronald Reagan and George H.W. Bush in the 1980s has voted strictly and strongly for Democratic presidential candidates since then. In 2002 Montgomery County backed Democrat and former Philadelphia Mayor Ed Rendell for governor by a 2–1 margin, though Republicans in 2004 regained control of the county commission. Northeast Philadelphia has a different political heritage. Its feisty Republican organization has won some elections and shown facility in making deals to get its share of patronage. In 2006, 62% of the district's votes were cast in Montgomery County, 38% in Northeast Philly.

The congresswoman from the 13th District is Allyson Schwartz, a Democrat elected in 2004. Her mother fled Vienna as a teenager in 1938 after the Germans annexed Austria and traveled alone to America, where she settled at a Jewish foster home in Philadelphia. Her father was a dentist in Flushing, Queens, where she grew up. A graduate of Simmons with a master's in social work from Bryn Mawr, Schwartz started a women's health center in 1975 and worked on health care issues as first deputy commissioner for the Philadelphia Department of Human Services; her husband is a cardiologist. In 1990 she was elected to the state Senate, where she received some criticism for too eagerly seeking publicity. In 2000 she ran for the U. S. Senate and finished second in the Democratic primary, with 27% of the vote, behind Congressman Ron Klink, who had 41%.

The 13th District seat opened when Democrat Joe Hoeffel ran, unsuccessfully, against Senator Arlen Specter. Schwartz faced two rounds of serious competition. In the primary she faced Joe Torsella, an aide to then-Philadelphia Mayor Ed Rendell, and more recently head of the National Constitution Center. She was backed by EMILY's List, which spent $170,000 on her behalf, and raised other funds, phoned voters and sent out mailings that even a Torsella strategist said were the best he had ever seen. Torsella won 57% of the vote in Northeast Philadelphia, which had a larger turnout, but Schwartz carried the affluent suburbs of Montgomery County with 62%, for an overall win by 2,000 votes, 52%-48%. On the Republican side, Melissa Brown, an ophthalmologist who supports abortion rights and lost 51%-47% to Hoeffel in 2002, was nominated with 39% of the vote in a three-way primary.

In the general election, "the two opponents proved that women can sling mud as capably as any men," *The Philadelphia Inquirer* wrote. Schwartz called herself a "new Democrat," not a liberal; Brown called her a radical. Schwartz called the Republican "sleazy" because of her links to a bankrupt HMO and a lawsuit that the state insurance department filed against her. Both candidates emphasized health care. Schwartz emphasized her sponsorship of the state Children's Health Insurance Program, which provided health insurance for 133,000 children from low-income families. Brown, a physician with an M.B.A, called for changes in tort law, arguing that it would keep doctors' liability insurance down and lower the cost of health care. Schwartz benefited from her 14 years in the state Senate and her considerable fundraising advantage; she raised $3.7 million, with $500,000 after the primary from EMILY's List contributors. In the 2004 cycle, the only House candidate who raised more money was Speaker Dennis Hastert. Schwartz won 56%-41%, a bigger margin than Hoeffel scored as an incumbent; she won 60% of the vote in Northeast Philadelphia and 53% in Montgomery County.

In the House, Schwartz voted like a moderate suburban Democrat and had a surprisingly low profile, given her extensive experience. She worked on health care issues, joining with Rahm Emanuel to oppose a tax cut for Medicaid providers and to automatically enroll all children eligible for SCHIP. Schwartz was reelected easily against Republican Raj Bhakta, the son of an Indian father and Irish mother, who earned fleeting fame as an unsuccessful contestant on Donald Trump's "The Apprentice." The 66%-34% result belied Bhakta's showmanship. In an attempt to prove how easy it is to cross the U.S.-Mexican border, in October Bhakta rode an elephant along the banks of the Rio Grande River as a mariachi band played. Though he never crossed the river into Mexico and back, he claimed to have done so on the video he took of the event, which earned him national television notice.

In January 2007, Schwartz gained a seat on the Ways and Means Committee after Governor Ed Rendell wrote to Speaker Nancy Pelosi on her behalf.

FOURTEENTH DISTRICT

Rep. Mike Doyle (D)

Elected 1994, 7th term; b. Aug. 5, 1953, Pittsburgh; home, Swissvale; PA St. U., B.S. 1975; Catholic; married (Susan).

Elected Office: Swissvale Borough Cncl., 1977-81.

Professional Career: Insurance agent, 1975-77; Exec. Dir., Turtle Creek Valley Citizens Union, 1977-79; Chief of Staff, PA Sen. Frank Pecora, 1978-94; Co–Founder/Owner, Eastgate Insurance Agency, 1983-present.

DC Office: 401 CHOB, 20515, 202-225-2135; Fax: 202-225-3084; Web site: www.house.gov/doyle.

District Offices: Pittsburgh, 412-261-5091.

Committees: *Energy & Commerce* (16th of 31 D): Telecommunications & the Internet (Vice Chmn.); Oversight & Investigations; Energy & Air Quality. *Standards of Official Conduct* (4th of 5 D). *Veterans' Affairs* (9th of 16 D): Health.

Group Ratings

	ADA	ACLU	AFS	LCV	ITIC	NTU	COC	ACU	CFG	FRC
2006	85	77	100	75	29	15	47	12	14	28
2005	95	—	100	61	—	12	44	16	4	31

National Journal Ratings

	2005 LIB	—	2005 CONS	2006 LIB	—	2006 CONS
Economic	69%	—	29%	70%	—	29%
Social	68%	—	32%	71%	—	28%
Foreign	74%	—	25%	83%	—	14%

Key Votes of the 109th Congress

1. Estate Tax Repeal	N	5. Limit Interstate Abortion	Y	9. Build Border Fence	N
2. Limit CAFE Standards	Y	6. Extend Patriot Act	N	10. CAFTA	N
3. FY06 Spending Curb	N	7. Bar Same Sex Marriage	N	11. Oppose Iraq Withdrawal	N
4. Drilling in ANWR	N	8. Stem Cell Research $	Y	12. Detainee Tribunals	N

Election Results

2006 general	Mike Doyle (D)	161,075	(90%)	($829,745)
	Titus North (Green)	17,720	(10%)	
2006 primary	Mike Doyle (D)	54,213	(76%)	
	Mike Isaac (D)	17,193	(24%)	
2004 general	Mike Doyle (D)	unopposed		($745,788)

Prior Winning Percentages: 2002 (100%); 2000 (69%); 1998 (68%); 1996 (56%); 1994 (55%)

The People		Race/Ethnic Origin	Ancestry		
Area size:	170 sq. mi.	72.9% White	German: 15.5%	Irish: 12.1%	
Urban population:	99.8%	22.5% Black	Italian: 9.8%		
Rural population:	0.2%	1.7% Asian	**2004 Presidential Vote**		
Pop. 2000:	646,013	0.2% Native Am.	Kerry (D) 205,636	(69%)	
Pop. 2005 (est):	598,288	0.0% Hawaiian	Bush (R) 88,316	(30%)	
Median income:	$30,139	1.4% Two+ races	Other 2,325	(1%)	
Poverty status:	17.1%	0.3% Other	**2000 Presidential Vote**		
Military veterans:	14.1%	1.1% Hispanic Origin	Gore (D) 183,640	(70%)	
			Bush (R) 74,085	(28%)	
			Other 6,007	(2%)	
			Cook Partisan Voting Index: D +22		
Occupation	Blue collar: 18.6%	White collar: 61.7%	Gray collar: 19.7%		

The Golden Triangle is the inevitable focus of Pittsburgh, the tip of land where the Allegheny and Monongahela Rivers come together to form the Ohio. It has been a strategic site for more than 200 years. It was there, to Fort Duquesne during the French and Indian War, that Braddock's army was heading (with George Washington helping lead the way) when it was ambushed and defeated in 1754. A few years later, the first American city west of the Appalachian chain was carved out of the wilderness here and named after the English statesman William Pitt. Pittsburgh grew rapidly in the days when most of the nation's commerce moved over water. When railroads became ascendant, Pittsburgh still did nicely, since rail lines tend to run along the riverside rather than scaling the mountains. Then came Andrew Carnegie, a Scottish immigrant working as a telegrapher for the Pennsylvania Railroad who foresaw that steel would replace iron for railroad bridges; he built a steel factory in Pittsburgh, then not much more than a rail junction but blessed with ready deposits of coal and access to iron ore from the Great Lakes. With associates like Henry Clay Frick and Henry Phipps, Carnegie built his capacity to the point that when he sold out in 1901, the resulting U.S. Steel Corporation held a near-monopoly.

The Pittsburgh that Carnegie and his steel men built is one of giant mills in the bottomlands along the rivers and massive buildings downtown, such as H.H. Richardson's classic stone City-County Building. There were once 12 cable cars going up the Duquesne Incline and other routes, connecting mills with the neighborhoods above. Back then, the smog—a word used here before it was in Los Angeles—was so bad that street lights had to stay on all day downtown; a famous 1947 photograph shows a midnight-like darkness at nine in the morning. But then an alliance of local elected officials and corporate titans (including the leaders of such local Fortune 500 companies as USX, Heinz, Alcoa, and PPG) pushed through a series of forceful and visionary projects designed to improve the city's quality of life. Early on, this model produced tremendous successes: In the 1950s, Mayor David Lawrence and financier Richard King Mellon led efforts to cut air pollution, control river flooding, and construct an advanced network of highways and tunnels. They also turned a derelict industrial zone at the three-rivers confluence into Point State Park—a triangular gem that remains popular with office workers. Pittsburgh has become cleaner, but less crowded. In 1940, it was the nation's 10th largest city, with 672,000 people; by 2000, it ranked 53d with 335,000.

Pittsburgh is not just a downtown. It is a city of neighborhoods, built on or beneath vertiginous hills, with more bridges, it is often said, than any other city in the world except Venice; neighborhoods that look right next to each other on the map are in fact quite separate and distinct. There is the uptown neighborhood around Carnegie-Mellon University and the University of Pittsburgh with its neo-Gothic "cathedral of learning." These institutions have helped to spur robust high-tech and medical sectors that have replaced many of the manufacturing jobs lost in previous decades. Local universities and hospitals now have 10 times as many employees as the downsized U.S. Steel Corporation. Among and atop the hills are neighborhoods as different as the predominantly black Hill District, where the famed Pittsburgh Crawfords of baseball's Negro Leagues once played and playwright August Wilson set most of his chronicles, and WASPy Shady Side and Jewish Squirrel Hill, with fine mansions and fashionable shops. Along the Monongahela River are small industrial neighborhoods and towns, like Clairton (where the classic movie *The Deer Hunter* was set and filmed) with less than half as many residents as a half-century ago.

The 14th Congressional District of Pennsylvania includes all of Pittsburgh and mostly working class suburbs to the east, south and west. There is some verdant suburbia here, but much of the district is in the Monongahela (or Mon) Valley, where the old steel mills stand or once stood, and the hills above. More affluent suburbs to the north and south are in the 4th and 18th Districts. This is a heavily Democratic district.

The congressman from the 14th is Mike Doyle, a Democrat first elected in 1994. Of Irish and Italian descent, Doyle grew up in the Mon Valley town of Swissvale, worked in steel mills during summers off from Penn State, worked as an insurance agent, for a nonprofit agency and was elected to the Swissvale Borough Council in 1977, at 24. In 1978 he became chief of staff to state Senator Frank Pecora, who was then a Republican. Pecora switched parties in 1992 and briefly gave Democrats control of the state Senate. In 1994 Doyle, who had just switched to the Democratic Party, ran for the House seat vacated by Rick Santorum, who was running for the Senate; Doyle was one of seven Democrats and four Republican candidates. With endorsements from unions and community leaders, he won the primary with 20% of the vote; the next finisher had 18%. In the general, he faced John McCarty, an aide to the late Senator John Heinz; McCarty was pro-choice and Doyle anti-abortion. Doyle campaigned for sweeping health care changes, against the new General Agreement on Tariffs and Trade, and for rebuilding the Mon Valley's industrial base. In a Republican year, he won 55%-45%.

In the House, Doyle has a mixed voting record, toward the right on cultural issues, toward the left on economics. Doyle rarely seeks attention, nor has he caused much ruckus. An exception came in late October 2004, when he criticized White House national security adviser Condoleezza Rice for "transparently political appearances" on behalf of George W. Bush. As a Steel Caucus member, he worked to reduce foreign imports and pushed a bill to create a national historic site at the former U.S. Steel facilities along the Mon River as part of the local Rivers of Steel program. In June 2007 he was a co-founder of the Congressional Robotics Caucus with Zach Wamp; Pittsburgh is home not only to Carnegie Mellon, a leader in robotics technologies, but also to the National Center for Defense Robotics. Doyle, the manager of the Democrats in the annual congressional baseball game, lives on Capitol Hill with his bipartisan "family" of House colleagues and is one of the dwindling number of members who drive home after each week's final vote.

Redistricting attached Doyle's Mon Valley base to the city-based 14th District but he has since managed to avoid a serious primary challenge from a Pittsburgh Democrat. In the House, he has settled in to build seniority on the Energy and Commerce Committee, where his focus has been on high-tech initiatives, including increased availability of broadband. On the House floor, he often can be seen in the "Pennsylvania Corner," seated next to his close ally John Murtha.

FIFTEENTH DISTRICT

Rep. Charlie Dent (R)

Elected 2004, 2d term; b. May 24, 1960, Allentown; home, Allentown; PA St. U., B.A. 1982, Lehigh U., M.P.A. 1993; Presbyterian; married (Pamela).

Elected Office: PA House of Reps., 1990-98; PA Senate, 1998-2004.

Professional Career: Development officer, Lehigh U., 1986-90.

DC Office: 116 CHOB, 20515, 202-225-6411; Fax: 202-226-0078; Web site: www.dent.house.gov.

District Offices: Bethlehem, 610-861-9734; East Greenville, 215-541-4106.

Committees: *Homeland Security* (11th of 15 R): Emergency Communications, Preparedness & Response (RMM); Intelligence, Information Sharing & Terrorism Risk Assessment. *Transportation & Infrastructure* (23d of 34 R): Economic Development, Public Buildings & Emergency Management; Aviation; Highways & Transit.

Group Ratings

	ADA	ACLU	AFS	LCV	ITIC	NTU	COC	ACU	CFG	FRC
2006	30	27	14	17	86	51	93	72	54	57
2005	25	—	0	0	—	54	89	76	56	46

National Journal Ratings

	2005 LIB	—	2005 CONS	2006 LIB	—	2006 CONS
Economic	9%	—	88%	44%	—	56%
Social	49%	—	50%	46%	—	53%
Foreign	34%	—	61%	49%	—	50%

Key Votes of the 109th Congress

1. Estate Tax Repeal	Y	5. Limit Interstate Abortion	Y	9. Build Border Fence	Y
2. Limit CAFE Standards	Y	6. Extend Patriot Act	Y	10. CAFTA	Y
3. FY06 Spending Curb	Y	7. Bar Same Sex Marriage	Y	11. Oppose Iraq Withdrawal	Y
4. Drilling in ANWR	Y	8. Stem Cell Research $	Y	12. Detainee Tribunals	Y

Election Results

2006 general	Charlie Dent (R)	106,153	(54%)	($1,284,757)
	Charles Dertinger (D)	86,186	(43%)	($88,920)
	Other	5,802	(3%)	
2006 primary	Charlie Dent (R)	unopposed		
2004 general	Charlie Dent (R)	170,634	(59%)	($1,971,131)
	Joe Driscoll (D)	114,646	(39%)	($2,295,656)
	Other	5,854	(2%)	

The People		Race/Ethnic Origin	Ancestry	
Area size:	851 sq. mi.	86.4% White	German: 21.9% Irish: 9.0%	
Urban population:	87.2%	2.8% Black	Italian: 8.1%	
Rural population:	12.8%	1.7% Asian	**2004 Presidential Vote**	
Pop. 2000:	646,300	0.1% Native Am.	Kerry (D)	150,939 (50%)
Pop. 2005 (est):	687,053	0.0% Hawaiian	Bush (R)	150,213 (50%)
Median income:	$45,330	1.0% Two+ races	Other	1,404 (0%)
Poverty status:	8.2%	0.1% Other	**2000 Presidential Vote**	
Military veterans:	13.5%	7.9% Hispanic Origin	Gore (D)	119,393 (49%)
			Bush (R)	116,817 (48%)
			Other	8,865 (4%)
			Cook Partisan Voting Index: D + 2	
Occupation	Blue collar: 26.5%	White collar: 59.4%	Gray collar: 14.1%	

Allentown, Pennsylvania, has long been derided by show-biz songwriters, from "42nd Street" back in 1933, in which it was scorned as nowhere, the polar opposite of Broadway, to Billy Joel's "Allentown" in 1982, with its grim picture of closed factories and unemployment. Though both contain nuggets of truth, neither is an entirely fair portrait of Pennsylvania's Lehigh Valley today: Allentown and next-door Bethlehem did suffer when big employers—Mack Truck in Allentown and Bethlehem Steel in Bethlehem—closed down big plants in the 1980s. But the Lehigh Valley around Allentown and Bethlehem in recent years had solid growth and low unemployment rates, thanks to a mix of regional health care networks, telephone call-centers for insurance companies (Aetna) and banks (Wachovia), long-surviving industries (such as Air Products and Chemicals, energy utility PPL and the remnants of Mack Truck's local operations), and small startups that don't earn the visibility of the big closedowns but which together have created more new jobs than have been lost. In the Lehigh Valley, 43% of employees work for companies with 100 or fewer workers, and 10% for companies with 10 or fewer. Some 8% of the population here is Hispanic, higher than in any other Pennsylvania metro area—a sure sign that the area is generating new jobs, but a source of social and law enforcement tensions.

If the Lehigh Valley is off the main lines of traffic, it does have several features that make it attractive to people from the big city, which helps to explain why its population increased from 2000 to 2005. Commuters seeking less expensive housing and lower taxes are connected by I-78 to New York and by the Turnpike Extension to Philadelphia; it has a cluster of colleges (Lehigh, Muhlenberg, Moravian) and a strong regional newspaper (the Allentown *Morning Call*); and it has both Dorney Park, one of the nation's oldest amusement parks, and the delightful and child-friendly Crayola Crayon factory in Easton. Easton's old industrial buildings, just across the Delaware River from New Jersey, have become something of a magnet for artists seeking inexpensive loft and warehouse space.

The 15th Congressional District of Pennsylvania consists of the Lehigh Valley plus a small adjoining slice of northern Montgomery County. Politically, this has long been a classic swing area, located at the intersection of heavily Democratic industrial precincts and the Republican farmlands of the Pennsylvania Dutch Country. The valley backed Ronald Reagan twice, the elder George Bush in 1988 and Bill Clinton twice; it voted for Al Gore and John Kerry by miniscule margins. In the past six governors' races, it voted for the winner each time: twice for Democrat Robert Casey, twice for Republican Tom Ridge and twice for Democrat Ed Rendell.

The congressman from the 15th District is Charlie Dent, a Republican elected in 2004. Dent grew up in Allentown, graduated from Penn State and got a graduate degree at Lehigh, where he later worked as a development officer. In 1990 he was elected to the state House and in 1998 to the state Senate. When 15th District Republican Pat Toomey announced that he would keep his 1998 promise to serve only three terms and would run against Senator Arlen Specter in the 2004 Republican primary, Dent was the front-runner to succeed him. Dent's lifelong residence in the Lehigh Valley was in sharp contrast to the background of the Democratic nominee, businessman Joe Driscoll. Driscoll grew up in Massachusetts, where he went sailing with the Kennedys and made enough money to spend $2 million on this race. But he lived for years in posh Lower Merion Township in Montgomery County, just outside Philadelphia. In 2003, Driscoll considered running against Republican Jim Gerlach in the 6th District. But after Lehigh Valley Democrats failed to recruit a local candidate Driscoll announced he would run in the 15th; he bought a townhouse in Upper Macungie Township in September, though his wife and children continued living outside the district. In the April primary, Driscoll was opposed by a perennial candidate who sued to have Driscoll removed from the ballot for allegedly lying about his residence. The judge ruled that Driscoll could run here but that he must list his home in Lower Merion Township. He won, but by only 56%-44%. On the Republican side, Dent's two opponents charged he was too liberal, but he won with 51%.

Dent framed the campaign as a contest between a native son and a carpetbagging outsider. Aside from his college years and a stint in Washington as an aide to local Congressman Don Ritter, he had spent his entire life in the Lehigh Valley. He portrayed Driscoll as a Philadelphia outsider whom Democrats recruited because of his ability to self-finance his race. Dent said that Driscoll considered the Lehigh Valley "a speed bump on his way to Congress." Driscoll said that he would continue to live there, even if he lost the election. He sought to deflect the residency issue with aggressive criticism of the Bush administration; he claimed that a vote for Dent was an endorsement of Bush's policies. He blamed rising health care costs on Republicans, while Dent called for reform of medical malpractice insurance costs. When Driscoll criticized him for taking a $10,000 contribution from Majority Leader Tom DeLay's PAC, Dent responded, "99% of my opponent's campaign money comes from outside the 15th District." Dent's moderate record, which included support for abortion rights, made it difficult to tie him to Bush; he insisted he would be an independent voice in Washington. Dent won 59%-39%, a wider margin than Toomey had won in his three races. A few weeks after the election, Driscoll's real estate agent said that he put his townhouse here up for sale and moved back to Lower Merion Township.

In the House, Dent had a mostly centrist voting record. On Transportation and Infrastructure, he worked to deliver local pork—in contrast to the tight-fisted Toomey. He supported embryonic stem cell research and was one of only five Republicans to vote against allowing a federal court appeal of the Terri Schiavo case. He opposed "privatization" of Social Security, but said that he was open to personal retirement accounts; he was a last-minute supporter of the Central American Free Trade Agreement. Dent initially voiced skepticism about President Bush's troop "surge" in Iraq, but he voted against the House Democrats' non-binding resolution of opposition because: "It really didn't say anything about where to go from here. It only said what we were against." In 2007, he became co-chairman of the shrinking Tuesday Group of moderate House Republicans.

Democrats tried, but failed, to find a credible opponent to Dent in 2006. Northampton County Councilman Charles Dertinger got on the ballot as a write-in candidate for the Democratic nomination; in contrast to Driscoll two years earlier, he raised little money and got no national attention. But he made lots of noise in criticizing Dent for Bush's failures and "the culture of corruption." Dent won by a surprisingly narrow 54%-43%, with 56% in Lehigh County, 57% in Montgomery, and 50% in Northampton. The narrow margin led to some second-guessing among Democrats, both nationally and locally, for overlooking the race; it seems likely this district will be more seriously contested in 2008—possibly by state Sen. Lisa Boscola, who was unsuccessfully recruited in 2004, or Siobhan "Sam" Bennett, chair of the Allentown Democratic Committee.

SIXTEENTH DISTRICT

Rep. Joe Pitts (R)

Elected 1996, 6th term; b. Oct. 10, 1939, Lexington, KY; home, Kennett Square; Asbury Col., B.A. 1961, West Chester U., M.Ed. 1972; Protestant; married (Virginia).

Military Career: Air Force, 1963-69 (Vietnam).

Professional Career: High schl. teacher, 1969-72; PA House of Reps., 1972-96; Owner, Landscape & Nursery Co., 1974-90.

DC Office: 420 CHOB, 20515, 202-225-2411; Fax: 202-225-2013; Web site: www.house.gov/pitts.

District Offices: Lancaster, 717-393-0667; Unionville, 610-444-4581.

Committees: *Energy & Commerce* (16th of 26 R): Health; Commerce, Trade & Consumer Protection; Environment & Hazardous Materials.

Group Ratings

	ADA	ACLU	AFS	LCV	ITIC	NTU	COC	ACU	CFG	FRC
2006	5	14	0	8	86	73	92	86	79	100
2005	0	—	0	0	—	72	88	100	99	100

National Journal Ratings

	2005 LIB	—	2005 CONS		2006 LIB	—	2006 CONS
Economic	14%	—	83%		10%	—	90%
Social	19%	—	80%		15%	—	84%
Foreign	40%	—	58%		42%	—	57%

Key Votes of the 109th Congress

1. Estate Tax Repeal	Y	5. Limit Interstate Abortion	Y	9. Build Border Fence	Y
2. Limit CAFE Standards	Y	6. Extend Patriot Act	Y	10. CAFTA	Y
3. FY06 Spending Curb	Y	7. Bar Same Sex Marriage	Y	11. Oppose Iraq Withdrawal	Y
4. Drilling in ANWR	Y	8. Stem Cell Research $	N	12. Detainee Tribunals	Y

Election Results

2006 general	Joe Pitts (R)	115,741	(57%)	($579,161)
	Lois Herr (D)	80,915	(40%)	($320,016)
	John Murphy (Ind)	7,958	(4%)	($14,452)
2006 primary	Joe Pitts (R)	unopposed		
2004 general	Joe Pitts (R)	183,620	(64%)	($429,653)
	Lois Herr (D)	98,410	(34%)	($83,737)
	Other	3,269	(1%)	

Prior Winning Percentages: 2002 (88%); 2000 (67%); 1998 (71%); 1996 (59%)

The People		Race/Ethnic Origin	Ancestry	
Area size:	1,326 sq. mi.	84.5% White	German: 25.3%	Irish: 8.8%
Urban population:	76.0%	4.0% Black	English: 6.1%	
Rural population:	24.0%	1.4% Asian	**2004 Presidential Vote**	
Pop. 2000:	646,328	0.1% Native Am.	Bush (R) 182,856	(61%)
Pop. 2005 (est):	677,483	0.0% Hawaiian	Kerry (D) 113,193	(38%)
Median income:	$45,934	0.9% Two+ races	Other 1,472	(0%)
Poverty status:	9.4%	0.1% Other	**2000 Presidential Vote**	
Military veterans:	11.6%	9.0% Hispanic Origin	Bush (R) 144,862	(62%)
			Gore (D) 82,729	(35%)
			Other 5,713	(2%)
			Cook Partisan Voting Index: R +11	

Occupation   Blue collar: 29.7%   White collar: 54.5%   Gray collar: 15.8%

The Pennsylvania Dutch Country, settled by Germans in the 18th century when it was Pennsylvania's frontier, remains a distinctive part of America. These Germans were Amish and Mennonite, pietistic sects seeking religious liberty and determined to farm rich lands in the same intensive way they had in Germany. Today, many of their descendants—the Eisenhower family is the most famous example—have blended into mainstream America, but in the Dutch area around Lancaster, many "Plain People" still live in the old way. Though larger communities exist in Ohio and Indiana, tourists can still see families of Plain People clad in black, clattering over the back roads in horse-drawn carriages, with scrupulously tended farms set amid rolling hills and barns decorated with hex signs (the scene was captured memorably in the 1983 film *Witness*). Beneath the surface, Amish communities are facing the strains of modernity: In recent years, Amish teens have attracted public attention for using drugs and alcohol while participating in the "rumschpringes"—a period when adolescents are freed from their community's rigid rules and mores, before being given the choice of returning to the fold as an adult. In October 2006, five girls were killed and five others seriously wounded by a gunman at their one-room schoolhouse in Nickel Mines; the Amish quickly demolished that building and finished building a new one six months later. Still, the community remains robust, and tourism, much of it linked to interest in the Amish, brings in more than five million people annually. Agriculture is the other pillar of the local economy: Farmers here produce some of the highest per-acre yields on earth. Within an easy drive from Philadelphia, Baltimore and Washington, this area has also become home to outlet malls. Lancaster County and Chester County grew by double-digit rates in the 1990s—partly from religious families, partly from newcomers moving in—making this the heart of one of Pennsylvania's fastest-growing regions, though the pace is slowing.

The 16th Congressional District of Pennsylvania includes all of Lancaster County, plus parts of southwestern Chester County that adjoin the Maryland and Delaware borders, as well as a small slice of Berks County that reaches as far as Reading. Outside the regional hub of Lancaster, the 16th is mostly small-town territory, with numerous quaint and quirkily named, if somewhat touristy, villages, such as Bird-in-Hand, Blue Ball and Intercourse (the first two named for the posted logos of old pubs, the third for reasons that are obscure, but almost certainly non-sexual). Closer to Philadelphia, the district takes in the metropolis' spreading suburbs, including West Chester, Kennett Square, fragrant with the manure that makes it America's leading mushroom-growing center as well as the glorious perfumes of the flowers at Longwood Gardens, and the fringe of the Wyeth country west of Chadds Ford. During the 1990s, Reading and Berks County attracted a large number of Hispanics, who found jobs in a growing if not terribly affluent economy. But their inclusion in this district—now the second-most Hispanic in the state, at 9%—has not altered the political equation. This is one of the most Republican districts in Pennsylvania and, for that matter, in the whole Northeast. It has favored the party of Lincoln ever since it abandoned the party of Pennsylvania's only president, Lancaster resident James Buchanan, on the eve of the Civil War. In 2004, Karl Rove said a big vote in the county was key to a statewide win, and George W. Bush added 30,000 votes to his total in 2000. That wasn't enough for the Republicans, nor was Lynn Swann's 58% performance in Lancaster County in his unsuccessful 2006 run for governor.

The congressman from the 16th District is Joe Pitts, a Republican first elected in 1996. Pitts was born in Kentucky, spent time in the Philippines with his parents where they served as religious missionaries, joined the Air Force after college, served three tours of duty and flew 116 B-52 combat missions in Vietnam. He returned to become a math and science teacher in Malvern, in Chester County, and later owned a nursery near Kennett Square. He and his daughter have exhibited their artwork, everything from painting to sculpture and woodwork, at local galleries. In 1972, at 33, he was elected to the Pennsylvania House. In 1989 he became chairman of the Appropriations Committee; he oversaw the restoration of the glorious Pennsylvania Capitol. When Congressman Bob Walker, one of the conservative reformers close to Newt Gingrich who helped revolutionize the House, cited the "Pennsylvania Dutch tradition" of not serving over 20 years and said he was retiring, Pitts plunged into the primary. He spoke favorably of home-schooling and unfavorably of gambling, and ran as a "true conservative." He raised the most money and won with 45% to 26% for the runner-up, a moderate. In the general, Pitts easily defeated newspaper publisher James Blaine, a descendant of James G. Blaine, the "Plumed Knight" and Republican presidential nominee in 1884.

In the House, Pitts has a conservative record, though he has moved toward the center on foreign policy. He was an early advocate of repeal of the estate and gift tax, which was a core component of the first Bush tax cut. He led the Pro-Life Caucus and headed the Republicans' "values action team" that worked with the Christian Coalition and other family groups to promote a pro-family agenda. With his appreciation for both human rights and national defense, he founded two diverse groups: the Religious Prisoners' Congressional Task Force, to plead for human rights around the world, and the Electronic Warfare Working Group, to encourage more congressional support for military technology. He co-chairs the "Adopt a Country" caucus, which seeks improved relationships with other nations. He enacted a bill to make it easier for pharmaceutical companies to sell their products overseas. In 2004, he objected to plans by the UPN television network for "Amish in the City," a reality series about Amish teenagers; the program was dropped. Before the bankruptcy bill was enacted in 2005, he played a key role in scuttling a provision, added by Senator Charles Schumer, which would have made fines and criminal penalties for abortion protesters non-dischargeable under bankruptcy. He eagerly supported private accounts in Social Security, and voiced regret over congressional inaction on President Bush's plan. He was a chief proponent of legislation to ban human cloning.

Pitts has been reelected easily. In November 2002, several days before the election, he announced he was reneging on his 1996 pledge to serve only 10 years; it had little political effect since he had no major party opposition. In 2006, he had his closest election contest. In a rematch, former corporate executive Lois Herr said that Bush went after Saddam Hussein on "flimsy evidence," and she called for bringing home the troops from Iraq. Pitts led 60%-36% in Lancaster County, which cast 73% of the total vote. In the other counties, the vote was virtually even; Pitts won overall 57%-40%.

SEVENTEENTH DISTRICT

Rep. Tim Holden (D)

Elected 1992, 8th term; b. Mar. 5, 1957, Pottsville; home, St. Clair; U. of Richmond, 1976-78, Bloomsburg St. U., B.A. 1980; Catholic; married (Gwen).

Elected Office: Schuylkill Cnty. Sheriff, 1985-92.

Professional Career: Real estate agent; Insurance broker, Holden Insurance Agency, 1980-85; Probation Officer, 1980-85.

DC Office: 2417 RHOB, 20515, 202-225-5546; Fax: 202-226-0996; Web site: www.holden.house.gov.

District Offices: Harrisburg, 717-234-5904; Lebanon, 717-270-1395; Pottsville, 570-622-4212; Temple, 610-921-3502.

Committees: *Agriculture* (Vice Chmn. of 25 D): Conservation, Credit, Energy & Research (Chmn.); Livestock, Dairy & Poultry. *Transportation & Infrastructure* (14th of 41 D): Highways & Transit; Aviation.

Group Ratings

	ADA	ACLU	AFS	LCV	ITIC	NTU	COC	ACU	CFG	FRC
2006	60	52	100	50	43	19	53	64	18	71
2005	80	—	100	50	—	19	63	40	8	46

National Journal Ratings

	2005 LIB	—	2005 CONS		2006 LIB	—	2006 CONS
Economic	57%	—	43%		60%	—	40%
Social	52%	—	48%		57%	—	43%
Foreign	65%	—	34%		61%	—	38%

Key Votes of the 109th Congress

1. Estate Tax Repeal	N	5. Limit Interstate Abortion	Y	9. Build Border Fence	Y
2. Limit CAFE Standards	Y	6. Extend Patriot Act	Y	10. CAFTA	N
3. FY06 Spending Curb	N	7. Bar Same Sex Marriage	Y	11. Oppose Iraq Withdrawal	Y
4. Drilling in ANWR	N	8. Stem Cell Research $	N	12. Detainee Tribunals	Y

Election Results

2006 general	Tim Holden (D)	137,253	(65%)	($649,165)
	Matthew Wertz (R)	75,455	(35%)	($12,463)
2006 primary	Tim Holden (D)	unopposed		
2004 general	Tim Holden (D)	172,412	(59%)	($1,608,093)
	Scott Paterno (R)	113,592	(39%)	($1,057,940)
	Other	5,782	(2%)	

Prior Winning Percentages: 2002 (51%); 2000 (66%); 1998 (61%); 1996 (59%); 1994 (57%); 1992 (52%)

The People		Race/Ethnic Origin	Ancestry	
Area size:	2,378 sq. mi.	87.3% White	German: 26.0% Irish: 8.7%	
Urban population:	68.6%	7.3% Black	Italian: 5.1%	
Rural population:	31.4%	1.1% Asian	**2004 Presidential Vote**	
Pop. 2000:	646,420	0.1% Native Am.	Bush (R) 172,343	(58%)
Pop. 2005 (est):	650,157	0.0% Hawaiian	Kerry (D) 124,141	(42%)
Median income:	$40,473	0.9% Two+ races	Other 1,768	(1%)
Poverty status:	8.4%	0.1% Other	**2000 Presidential Vote**	
Military veterans:	14.8%	3.2% Hispanic Origin	Bush (R) 139,932	(56%)
			Gore (D) 103,603	(41%)
			Other 6,994	(3%)
			Cook Partisan Voting Index: R + 7	

Occupation	Blue collar: 30.2%	White collar: 55.1%	Gray collar: 14.8%

Through the center of Pennsylvania flows the Susquehanna, the longest river in the East if you include the Chesapeake Bay, which is actually the flooded lower Susquehanna Valley. Starting in Cooperstown, New York, emptying into the Chesapeake next to the antique town of Havre de Grace, Maryland, the Susquehanna is the one river strong enough to break through the Appalachian chains of central Pennsylvania. But few songs are written to celebrate the Susquehanna—it has not given a name to a fever (Potomac), a school of painting (Hudson) or economics (Charles), or to a state (Delaware, Connecticut, Ohio, Mississippi, Alabama, Illinois, Missouri, Colorado, Tennessee)—and its dams are silting up and threaten environmental havoc on the tenuously recovering Chesapeake, unless the unwieldy grouping of states through which the Susquehanna runs can find a solution; already, millions of fish and fish eggs are killed each year by power plants. In April 2005, American Rivers—a national conservation group—rated the Susquehanna the nation's "most endangered river," due mostly to sewer system discharge.

The 17th Congressional District of Pennsylvania includes two distinct areas: the agricultural lands adjoining the Susquehanna River, and the industrial areas of Schuylkill and Berks Counties. The first is centered on the state capital of Harrisburg; it includes Dauphin County, part of Perry County just across the river and Lebanon County to the east. Harrisburg features a string of mansions-turned-lobbying headquarters gracefully lining the banks of the Susquehanna and boasts Pennsylvania's marvelously restored Capitol building—its dome is modeled after St. Peter's in Rome, its stairway on the Paris Opera. Nearby is Hershey, the town erected by chocolate magnate Milton S. Hershey as a carefully planned, almost utopian village for his factory workers and their families. The surrounding area, fed by a steady flow of tourists to Hersheypark, with 10 roller coasters, has attracted top-flight hospitals and cultivated a prosperous air; the U.S. House of Representatives held "civility retreats" here during the 1990s (they lapsed due to insufficient interest). Directly south is Middletown, whose leafy, gridded streets and handsome homes give no hint that it is the location of the Three Mile Island nuclear plant, site in 1979 of the worst nuclear accident in American history.

The eastern half of the district has a grittier heritage. In Berks and Schuylkill Counties the farmers were rough-hewn and more violence-prone, and the towns existed solely to mine rich veins of anthracite coal, the primary energy source of late 19th and early 20th century America; although the big companies abandoned the mines long ago, some local entrepreneurs still go deep underground to blast their way into the anthracite. These mountain towns were less orderly, filled with tough-talking miners and factory workers who stayed menacingly in the background unless a character stumbled into the wrong roadhouse at night or the wrong diner at dawn—the Pennsylvania that John O'Hara grew up in and wrote about in the 1930s and 1940s. Pottsville, nestled amid mountains and the home of Yuengling lager (known locally as "Vitamin Y"), produced the Maroons, the team that may have won the 1925 National Football League championship (the league disputed the claim, to Pottsville's eternal chagrin) and whose ties to coal country are emblematic of the game's hardscrabble roots. Pottsville and its neighbors have never rebounded from the switch from anthracite coal to oil and natural gas for home heating: With a disproportionately aging population, Schuylkill County had 228,000 people in 1940 and 147,000 in 2006.

Politically, the 17th leans Republican. Harrisburg has been a Republican town from the days when the party seemed to conquer all in Pennsylvania; Republicans held the governorship for all but eight years from 1860 to 1934 and filled the ornate halls of the Capitol with Republican patronage hacks. Lebanon County is even more solidly Republican. Schuylkill County, in contrast, has a Democratic heritage from its mining days, though its Democrats tend to take conservative stands on cultural issues like abortion and guns. Berks County is somewhat more Republican. Overall, the district voted 56% for George W. Bush in 2000 and 58% in 2004.

The congressman from the 17th District is Tim Holden, a Democrat first elected from the old 6th District in 1992 and the winner of a 2002 battle between incumbents thrown together by redistricting. Holden comes from a political family from the coal mining hamlet of St. Clair; his great-grandfather was a coal miner who founded the forerunner to the United Mine Workers, and his father served four terms as Schuylkill County commissioner. Holden gained fame as a local football player, although tuberculosis cut short his college career. In 1985, at age 28, after selling insurance and real estate in the family business for five years, he was elected Schuylkill County sheriff. Holden's opponent in the 1992 race for an open seat was the better-financed John Jones III, a lawyer, but Holden's regular guy appeal played well in culturally conservative but economically polarized Schuylkill County; he won 52%-48%.

Holden has a moderate voting record, though a bit more conservative on cultural issues. He is one of the centrist Blue Dog Democrats and has consistently been near the center of the House. "The problems our country is facing need to be solved in a bipartisan manner," he says. "There's about 70 liberals and 70 ultraconservatives still in the House. They need to be left behind." He opposes abortion and opposed the FDA's approval of the RU-486 drug. But in January 2007, he supported embryonic stem cell research, after earlier voting against it. On the Agriculture Committee, where he is the number-two Democrat and chairman of the Conservation, Credit, Energy and Research Subcommittee, Holden looks after dairy programs. He also has gained influence as the senior Pennsylvanian on the Transportation and Infrastructure Committee. On the 2005 highway bill, he took credit for $10 million in local projects, far less than claimed by more influential or vulnerable members. Most of all, he has worked hard at home, talking issues and solving constituents' problems. As the Pottsville *Republican & Evening Herald* wrote, "It would be hard to imagine a legislator more precisely in tune with his county on virtually any and every issue that has come before Congress." He appears to relish his low profile and avoids the usual Capitol Hill partisanship.

Holden's constituent-oriented approach proved vital after redistricting in 2002. The new 17th District combined Holden's Schuylkill County base with the Harrisburg base of Republican incumbent George Gekas; the Republican edge in the district favored Gekas, but each was well-funded by additional expenditures by their party and interest groups. Holden spent many hours knocking on doors in Dauphin and Lebanon County emphasizing his independence, while Gekas was less organized and slower to introduce himself to voters in Schuylkill County. Holden won 51%-49%. In Dauphin County, which had the largest turnout, Gekas won 56%-44%; in Lebanon, he won 61%-39%. But Holden was far stronger in his base, winning Schuylkill 72%-28%.

Since then, well-known Republican officials have declined to run. In 2004, Republicans nominated Scott Paterno, a lawyer and the son of longtime Penn State football coach Joe Paterno; Holden won 59%-39%, with 74% in Schuylkill County and an impressive 58% in Dauphin County. In 2006, Republicans threw in the towel. Nominee Matthew Wertz raised little money and officially withdrew in September, though his name remained on the ballot. Wertz got 35%, which can be viewed as the Republican base.

EIGHTEENTH DISTRICT

Rep. Tim Murphy (R)

Elected 2002, 3d term; b. Sept. 11, 1952, Cleveland, OH; home, Upper St. Clair; Wheeling Jesuit U., B.S. 1974, Cleveland St. U., M.S. 1976, U. of Pittsburgh, Ph.D. 1979; Catholic; married (Nan Missig).

Elected Office: PA Senate, 1996-2002

Professional Career: Practicing psychologist, 1976-2002; author.

DC Office: 322 CHOB, 20515, 202-225-2301; Fax: 202-225-1844; Web site: murphy.house.gov.

District Offices: Greensburg, 724-850-7312; Pittsburgh, 412-344-5583.

Committees: *Energy & Commerce* (24th of 26 R): Oversight & Investigations; Health; Environment & Hazardous Materials.

Group Ratings

	ADA	ACLU	AFS	LCV	ITIC	NTU	COC	ACU	CFG	FRC
2006	10	18	14	17	86	51	93	80	48	100
2005	10	—	13	0	—	55	92	84	54	85

National Journal Ratings

	2005 LIB	—	2005 CONS		2006 LIB	—	2006 CONS
Economic	38%	—	60%		41%	—	59%
Social	42%	—	58%		32%	—	66%
Foreign	22%	—	77%		6%	—	86%

Key Votes of the 109th Congress

1. Estate Tax Repeal	Y	5. Limit Interstate Abortion	N	9. Build Border Fence	Y
2. Limit CAFE Standards	Y	6. Extend Patriot Act	Y	10. CAFTA	Y
3. FY06 Spending Curb	Y	7. Bar Same Sex Marriage	Y	11. Oppose Iraq Withdrawal	Y
4. Drilling in ANWR	Y	8. Stem Cell Research $	N	12. Detainee Tribunals	Y

Election Results

2006 general	Tim Murphy (R)	144,632	(58%)	($1,482,467)
	Chad Kluko (D)	105,419	(42%)	($81,321)
2006 primary	Tim Murphy (R)	unopposed		
2004 general	Tim Murphy (R)	197,894	(63%)	($1,103,313)
	Mark Boles (D)	117,420	(37%)	($149,356)

Prior Winning Percentages: 2002 (60%)

The People		Race/Ethnic Origin	Ancestry	
Area size:	1,437 sq. mi.	95.4% White	German: 19.4% Irish: 12.3%	
Urban population:	84.1%	2.0% Black	Italian: 11.8%	
Rural population:	15.9%	1.3% Asian	**2004 Presidential Vote**	
Pop. 2000:	646,374	0.1% Native Am.	Bush (R) 183,210	(54%)
Pop. 2005 (est):	652,995	0.0% Hawaiian	Kerry (D) 154,079	(46%)
Median income:	$44,938	0.6% Two+ races	Other 1,275	(0%)
Poverty status:	6.3%	0.1% Other	**2000 Presidential Vote**	
Military veterans:	14.9%	0.6% Hispanic Origin	Bush (R) 154,252	(52%)
			Gore (D) 139,346	(47%)
			Other 5,240	(2%)
			Cook Partisan Voting Index: R + 2	

Occupation	Blue collar: 13.7% White collar: 20.0% Gray collar: 63.3%

Pittsburgh was built on the unlikeliest terrain of any of our major cities. Just about the only level places in the city and its suburbs are the bottomlands along the rivers. Everything else is hills that approach the magnitude of mountains. Only a propitious location, where the Allegheny and Monongahela rivers join to form the Ohio, and the confluence of economically valuable natural resources, coal from the mountains and iron ore from the Great Lakes, can explain the fact that a vast metropolitan area has been built on such land. The great cities of California were built around and over mountains; but they are vast expanses of contiguous communities, most of them little distinguishable from the next. The cities and towns of greater Pittsburgh, in contrast, are discontinuous, separated from each other not just by miles but by altitude. So the region's high-income suburbs and its gritty factory towns are not concentrated in one quarter, but are scattered all around. This is long-settled country, with many more old towns than sparkling new suburbs. Since 2000, the population here has been declining, but with some increase in high-wage jobs and a continuing loss of blue-collar jobs.

The 18th Congressional District of Pennsylvania covers an irregularly shaped swath of the southern part of the Pittsburgh metropolitan area and was designed by Republican redistricters in Harrisburg to maximize the Republican vote. It includes most of southern Allegheny County, most of Westmoreland County to the east and most of Washington County to the west; it stretches from the Pittsburgh city limit to the West Virginia border. It contains the Pittsburgh International Airport in Moon Township, where the financial troubles of US Airways have cost thousands of jobs and reduced operations, but created opportunity by opening the gates to low-fare carriers; the merger of US Airways with America West in 2005 shifted more jobs away from the area. To the east are Monroeville, Greensburg and Ligonier, where a fort was an important frontier outpost in the French and Indian War, but the area is now green with prosperity and dotted with the vast estates of

Mellons and other scions of Pittsburgh's industrial elite; to the west is Canonsburg, which has unveiled a "singing sculpture" of its most famous son, the crooner Perry Como. The district's backbone is comprised of middle- to upper-middle-class bedroom suburbs, like Mount Lebanon and Upper St. Clair in Allegheny County and Penn Township and Greensburg in Westmoreland County. These areas lean Republican, but not overwhelmingly so. Democrats grumble that the Republican trend in Westmoreland reflects the local influence of the *Tribune-Review*, the Greensburg-based newspaper owned by conservative Richard Mellon Scaife, named by Clintonite conspiracy theorists as the mastermind of the vast right wing conspiracy. Although John Kerry spent some time at his wife Teresa Heinz Kerry's estate in Fox Chapel, the Democratic ticket has not done well here. George W. Bush carried the district with 52% of the vote in 2000 and 54% in 2004.

The congressman from the 18th District is Tim Murphy, a Republican first elected in 2002. He grew up in Cleveland in a family of 11 children. He graduated from Wheeling Jesuit University, got a Ph.D. from the University of Pittsburgh and became a child psychologist. He worked in several Pittsburgh area hospitals and was an adjunct faculty member in public health and pediatrics at the University of Pittsburgh. He became a public figure while offering medical advice as "Dr. Tim" in television appearances and on radio talk shows; he co-authored *The Angry Child: Regaining Control When Your Child is Out of Control*. After entering Congress, he co-authored another book titled, *Overcoming Passive-Aggression*, behavior that he now sees on a regular basis. In 1996 Murphy was elected to the state Senate, where he authored a new Patient Bill of Rights and increased funding for medical research. Redistricters drew the 18th with Murphy in mind. Even though the new district included the house of Congressman Frank Mascara, he ran in the primary against 12th District Democrat John Murtha and lost by a wide margin; Mascara's decision not to run here was an acknowledgement of Murphy's strength. Murphy, who was unopposed in the Republican primary, presented himself as an experienced and accomplished legislator who opposed abortion and supported gun rights. He had extensive support from Pennsylvania and national Republicans and outspent Democratic nominee Jack Machek, a school district administrator, $894,000 to $126,000. Murphy won 60%-40%—an impressive showing in an open seat race.

In the House, Murphy had a voting record that leaned conservative, especially on foreign policy issues. He quickly gained recognition as president of his freshman class. In January 2005, he made a giant step by winning a seat on the Energy and Commerce Committee. That gave him an opportunity to focus on health care issues, including medical malpractice reform, Medicaid restructuring, new medical technologies and steps to improve hospital care. He co-chaired with Patrick Kennedy the 21st Century Health Care Caucus, where they focused on improving communication among health information technology systems. He also co-chaired the Mental Health Caucus, where he focused in particular on veterans with mental illness and on improving security for their medical records. He opposed embryonic stem cell research and President Bush's call for personal retirement accounts in Social Security. In 2005, he sustained minor injuries when his military vehicle overturned during a Thanksgiving trip to Baghdad. During the base closing review, Murphy joined in the successful effort to keep the 911th Airlift Wing that is stationed at Moon Township off the Pentagon's closure list

In 2006, he escaped what likely would have been a competitive contest when former state Treasurer (and party-switcher) Barbara Hafer seriously explored but decided against a challenge. After several other prospective candidates bowed out, Democrats were left with Chad Kluko, a little-known and underfunded executive for Verizon Wireless. Murphy carried all four counties and won 58%-42%. Following the election, there were news reports that federal investigators were reviewing Murphy's possible use of government staff for campaign work. In June 2007, consultant and former teacher Beth Hafer—Barbara's Hafer's daughter—announced she would challenge Murphy in 2008.

NINETEENTH DISTRICT

Rep. Todd Platts (R)

Elected 2000, 4th term; b. Mar. 5, 1962, York; home, York; Shippensburg U., B.S. 1984, Pepperdine U., J.D. 1991; Episcopalian; married (Leslie).

Elected Office: PA House of Reps., 1992-2000.

Professional Career: Practicing atty, 1991-93.

DC Office: 1032 LHOB, 20515, 202-225-5836; Fax: 202-226-1000; Web site: www.house.gov/platts.

District Offices: Carlisle, 717-249-0190; Gettysburg, 717-338-1919; York, 717-600-1919.

Committees: *Education & Labor* (8th of 22 R): Healthy Families & Communities (RMM); Early Childhood, Elementary & Secondary Education. *Oversight & Government Reform* (7th of 18 R): Government Management, Organization & Procurement; National Security & Foreign Affairs. *Transportation & Infrastructure* (16th of 34 R): Railroads, Pipelines & Hazardous Materials; Water Resources & Environment; Highways & Transit.

Group Ratings

	ADA	ACLU	AFS	LCV	ITIC	NTU	COC	ACU	CFG	FRC
2006	25	19	14	42	86	48	93	72	47	71
2005	25	—	13	33	—	53	85	67	56	77

National Journal Ratings

	2005 LIB — 2005 CONS		2006 LIB — 2006 CONS	
Economic	49%	— 51%	49%	— 50%
Social	34%	— 65%	34%	— 65%
Foreign	31%	— 67%	52%	— 48%

Key Votes of the 109th Congress

1. Estate Tax Repeal	Y	5. Limit Interstate Abortion	Y
2. Limit CAFE Standards	N	6. Extend Patriot Act	Y
3. FY06 Spending Curb	Y	7. Bar Same Sex Marriage	Y
4. Drilling in ANWR	Y	8. Stem Cell Research $	Y

9. Build Border Fence	Y
10. CAFTA	Y
11. Oppose Iraq Withdrawal	Y
12. Detainee Tribunals	Y

Election Results

2006 general	Todd Platts (R)	142,512	(64%)	($374,579)
	Philip Avillo (D)	74,625	(33%)	($174,531)
	Other	5,640	(3%)	
2006 primary	Todd Platts (R)	unopposed		
2004 general	Todd Platts (R)	224,274	(91%)	($171,605)
	Charles Steel (Green)	8,890	(4%)	
	Other	11,930	(5%)	

Prior Winning Percentages: 2002 (91%); 2000 (73%)

The People		**Race/Ethnic Origin**	**Ancestry**	
Area size:	1,666 sq. mi.	92.2% White	German: 28.1% Irish: 9.0%	
Urban population:	71.4%	2.9% Black	USA: 6.7%	
Rural population:	28.6%	1.1% Asian	**2004 Presidential Vote**	
Pop. 2000:	646,389	0.1% Native Am.	Bush (R)	198,192 (64%)
Pop. 2005 (est):	691,369	0.0% Hawaiian	Kerry (D)	110,274 (36%)
Median income:	$45,345	0.9% Two+ races	Other	1,515 (0%)
Poverty status:	6.8%	0.1% Other	**2000 Presidential Vote**	
Military veterans:	14.3%	2.7% Hispanic Origin	Bush (R)	153,892 (61%)
			Gore (D)	90,125 (36%)
			Other	6,766 (3%)
			Cook Partisan Voting Index: R +12	

Occupation   Blue collar: 29.3%   White collar: 57.1%   Gray collar: 13.6%

The Mason-Dixon Line, the historic boundary between Maryland and Pennsylvania, runs through some of the country's most pleasant rolling farmlands, west of the Susquehanna River up through the first of the Appalachian chains. This area was home to the westernmost capital of the United States during the Revolutionary War: the small city of York, capital from September 1777 to June 1778. York is where the Continental Congress passed the Articles of Confederation, received word from Benjamin Franklin in Paris that the French would help the colonies with money and ships and issued the first proclamation calling for a national day of thanksgiving. A little more than four score years later, Robert E. Lee's Confederate troops crossed over this invisible line and were repulsed in the Battle of Gettysburg in July 1863. Not much today suggests that this region was either a frontier or the object of bloody struggle: The green farmland seems peaceful, prosperous and mostly undisturbed by the current era's commercial trappings and stylistic excesses; this is where Dwight D. Eisenhower, a man of Pennsylvania Dutch stock, chose to quietly spend his retirement years.

For more than 50 miles, the Mason-Dixon Line forms the southern boundary of the 19th Congressional District of Pennsylvania, which includes all of Adams and York Counties and part of Cumberland County to the north—relatively fast-growing areas in slow-growing Pennsylvania. The 19th takes in the fruit belt of Adams County, the Harrisburg suburbs across the Susquehanna and part of the old town of Carlisle, with Dickinson College, the Carlisle Barracks, and the U.S. Army War College, where free-wheeling discussions of military operations sometimes create consternation elsewhere. Hanover, in York County, is one of the world's snack headquarters—home to Snyder's of Hanover, which makes one of every four pretzels sold in the U.S. (people in this area take their pretzels seriously), as well as potato-chip giant Utz Quality Foods. The district's biggest city is York, the site of Harley-Davidson's largest manufacturing plant (with 2,800 production employees), the USA Weightlifting Hall of Fame at the York Barbell Company, and the 2008 World Horseshoe Pitching Tournament. York is a place where many residents commute less than an hour to work in Baltimore and where the Orioles, not the more distant Phillies, are the baseball team of choice; a few hardy souls who like the inexpensive housing commute from here to jobs in Washington. The city also hosts a rapidly growing Hispanic population, mainly Puerto Rican, but with increasing numbers of Mexicans; in Gettysburg, many Hispanics work the abundant orchards. Politically, the 19th is heavily Republican. George W. Bush won 61% of the vote here in 2000 and 64% in 2004.

The congressman from the 19th District is Todd Platts, a Republican first elected in 2000. Platts grew up in York, graduated from Shippensburg University and Pepperdine University School of Law. In 1992, at age 30, after practicing law in Lancaster, he was elected to the state House, where he served four terms. In 2000, he was the first to announce his candidacy after longtime Congressman Bill Goodling, chairman of the Education and the Workforce Committee, said that he would retire. Platts's chief primary opponents were state Representative Al Masland, attorney and Goodling-endorsed Dick Stewart and Charlie Gerow, head of the state Citizens Against Government Waste. The campaign motto for Platts, who refused contributions from political action committees and was outspent by his chief Republican rivals, was "Putting People First" (his conservative supporters apparently weren't bothered by the fact that the phrase had been the title of a book by Bill Clinton). Platts won with 33% to 29% for Masland and 19% for Stewart, rolling up huge margins in his home base of York County. In the general, Platts won 73%-26%, after spending about one-third the amount of the average House freshman that year.

In the House, Platts has a comparatively moderate voting record. In the majority, he chaired the Government Management, Finance and Accountability Subcommittee on the Government Reform Committee and took a special interest in oversight of federal agencies: He pushed legislation to require review of all government programs at least once every five years to evaluate their performance, and he chaired hearings where he demanded that the Homeland Security Department improve its accounting practices. He sponsored legislation to overturn a federal court ruling that he said created loopholes in the Whistleblower Protection Act. In the minority, he is now ranking member at the Healthy Families and Communities Subcommittee on Education and Labor.

Platts has not been afraid to challenge sacred cows in Congress: He filed with Jim Matheson a bill to repeal the automatic annual pay raises for members of Congress; he called for "real lobbying reform," including an Office of Public Integrity, and a cutoff of pensions for lawmakers convicted of crimes. On the Education Committee, he bucked most Republicans by opposing school-voucher proposals. Platts may hold the title for the longest daily commute to Congress: He drives the roughly 100 miles from his home in York to Washington nearly every day that the House is in session. Another distinction: In January 2007, he was one of 3 House Republicans who voted in favor of all 6 measures that House Democrats passed as part of their 100-hours agenda.

Platts has been reelected with only perfunctory opposition. In 2006, York College professor Philip Avillo, the Democratic challenger, called for a national health-care plan and criticized Platts for huge budget deficits. Platts won 64%-33%.

★ RHODE ISLAND ★

The tiny city-state with a mouthful of an official name, Rhode Island and Providence Plantations, has as turbulent a political history as any state in the Union. A successful trading community since the 1600s, a leader in manufacturing since Samuel Slater replicated from memory an English water-powered cotton textile mill in Pawtucket in 1791, Rhode Island also had its beginning as an upstart community, a refuge for religious dissenters, "the sewer of New England," as the orthodox Cotton Mather put it. Rhode Island profited from slavery (two-thirds of America's slaves arrived on ships owned by Rhode Islanders) and war (the state boomed during the Civil War), and carried its tradition of tolerating just about anything into its politics. Rhode Island refused to pay its share for the Revolutionary War, declined to send delegates to the 1787 Constitutional Convention and delayed joining the Union until the other 12 states had, prompting George Washington to say, "Rhode Island still perseveres in that impolitic, unjust—and one might add without much impropriety—scandalous conduct, which seems to have marked all her public counsels of late." The new nation's first bank failure occurred here in 1809, when a bank capitalized at $45 issued $800,000 in bank notes. In the 1840s, conflict between hard money merchants and soft money farmers resulted in two state governments and a conflict known as Dorr's War, with the outcome determined when merchant Dorr's two ancient cannons failed to fire.

Then, in the 1930s, Rhode Island had something resembling a political revolution. Thousands of immigrants from French Canada, Ireland and Italy came to Rhode Island to work in the textile mills and this colony of dissident Protestants became the most heavily Catholic state in the nation. Yankee Republicans tried to appeal to Catholics by running French Canadians for office. But national events—Al Smith's candidacy in 1928, when he carried Rhode Island, and Franklin Roosevelt's New Deal—moved the Catholics toward the Democrats. Then came the revolution: in 1935, the Democrats under Governor Theodore Green, although they had won only 20 of the 42 state Senate seats, refused to seat two Republicans. With the lieutenant governor's tie-breaker, they voted Democrats into the seats, and proceeded in 14 minutes to declare the state Supreme Court seats vacant, abolish state boards that controlled Democratic cities, strengthen the power of the governor and reorganize state government to purge Republicans. This ended the direct political control of Rhode Island's "Five Families"—the Browns, Metcalfs, Goddards, Lippitts and Chafees—who owned or ran many of the textile mills, the Rhode Island Hospital Trust (long the largest bank), the Providence *Journal-Bulletin*, Brown University, the Rhode Island School of Design and the state Republican Party. The Democrats have won most elections with the lion's share of votes from Rhode Island's Catholic majority, starting with Green's election in 1936, at age 69, to the first of his four terms as U.S. senator. From 1940 to 1980, Democrats won every election for U.S. House seats; its Democratic percentages in presidential elections from 1968 to 2004 are rivaled only by Massachusetts. Republicans have won when they've been able to capitalize on scandal or Democratic disarray, as Governors Lincoln Almond and Donald Carcieri did in 1994 and 2002. But the most durable Republican politician here was John Chafee, elected governor in 1962, 1964 and 1966, senator in 1976, 1982, 1988 and 1994, who also lost twice, in 1968 and 1972; he died in 1999.

Rhode Island has gone through a long and often painful economic transformation, from blue collar to white collar, from textiles to high-tech. It suffered economic problems in the early 1990s, as the submarine factory and Navy base at Quonset Point shed thousands of jobs, and employment in costume jewelry, Rhode Island's major manufacturer, fell from 32,500 in 1977 to 6,300 in 2000. But Republican Governor Lincoln Almond, elected in 1994 and 1998, persuaded the overwhelmingly Democratic legislature to gradually cut income taxes and eliminate the car tax, and Providence Mayor Buddy Cianci promoted brilliantly successful redevelopment in the state's capital and largest city. Tourism became Rhode Island's second largest industry, and computer data processing a major part of the economy. The state's population, after hovering around 1 million for decades, increased by more than 80,000 between 1990 and 2005. This new Rhode Island suffered only modest job losses in the 2001 recession; it recovered quickly as new jobs were generated faster than elsewhere in New England. Providence, after losing population for decades, grew 10% in that period, and its downtown has been enlivened with new buildings like the Gtech tower and events

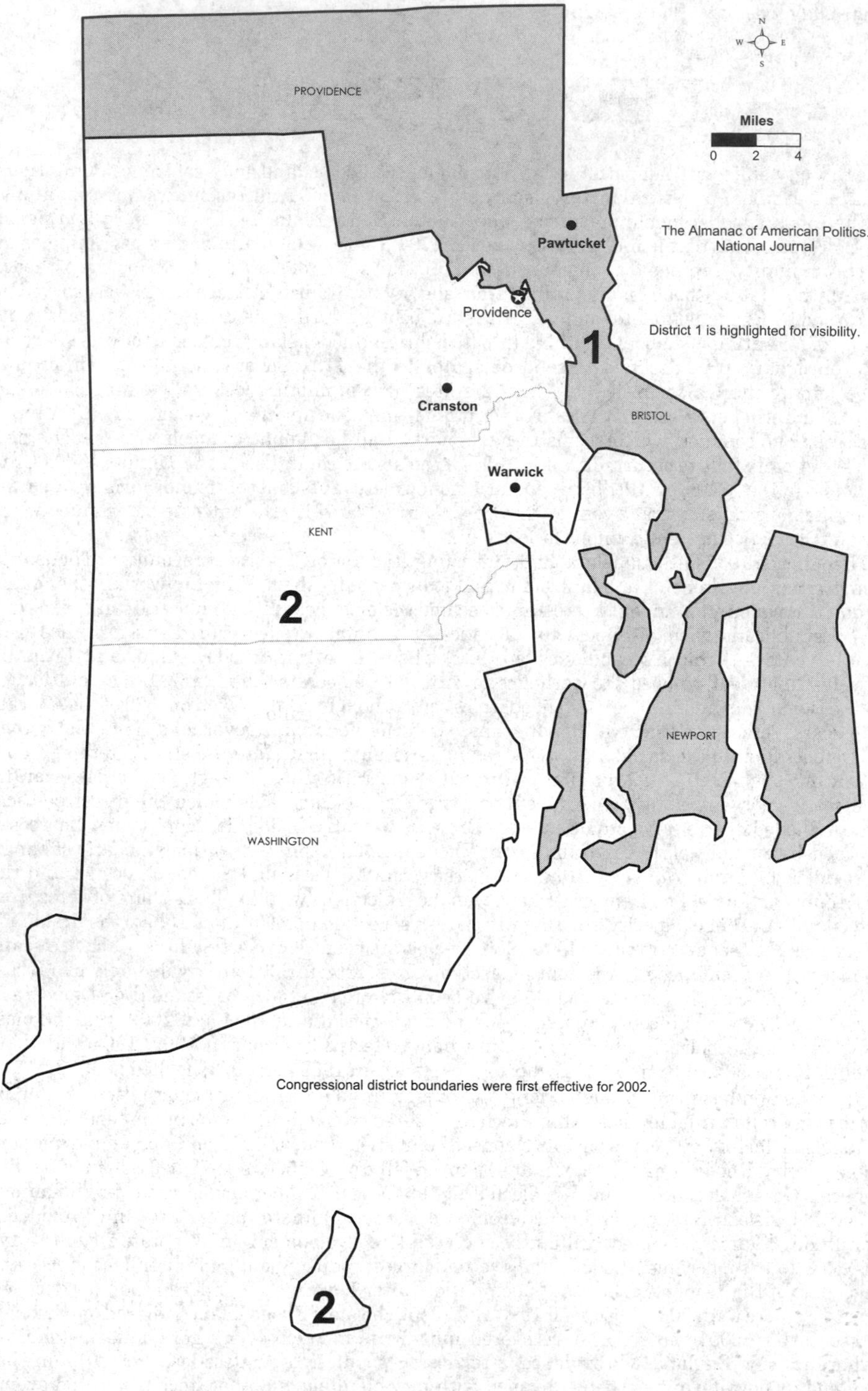

PROVIDENCE

N
W—E
S

Miles
0   2   4

Pawtucket

The Almanac of American Politics.
National Journal

Providence

District 1 is highlighted for visibility.

1

Cranston

BRISTOL

Warwick

KENT

2

NEWPORT

WASHINGTON

Congressional district boundaries were first effective for 2002.

2

like the SoundSession music festival and WaterFire, an art fair with 100 bonfires lit along the city's three rivers. In 2005 the legislature passed a 25% tax rebate for moviemakers, and Disney was given free rein to shoot *Underdog* film scenes in the State House; all 11 episodes of the *Brotherhood* series were shot in the state. To encourage economic growth the state halved the top income tax rate and voted a 30% tax credit for rehabilitation of historic buildings.

Still, problems remain. Rhode Island is one of the most elderly of states—it ranks fifth in percentage of population 75 and older—and housing is expensive; the state law requiring cities and towns to set aside 10% of new housing for low- and middle-income people may have thwarted some developments. Unemployment has remained relatively high despite job growth. The state is still mourning the 100 young people killed in the night club fire in West Warwick in 2003. Local lobstermen have faced a halving of the lobster population since 1999 due to shell disease but they've responded creatively. The settlement in an oil spill case financed a notching program, under which lobstermen were paid $8.50 each for carving notches in the shells of 1.2 million female lobsters and throwing them back into the ocean, not to be harvested until new shells grew in a few years. And lobstermen have proposed privatizing fishing rights, with transferrable shares of 800 lobster pots to lobstermen working in 2001-03. Massachusetts's same-sex marriage law has caused some legal problems, since many people commute between the two states. In September 2006 a Massachusetts judge said that same-sex couples living in Rhode Island could marry in Massachusetts, since in his view Rhode Island had no law holding such marriages illegal; Rhode Island Attorney General Patrick Lynch said that same-sex marriages in Rhode Island could only be legalized by the legislature or the courts. In February 2007, in response to a question from a state agency, Lynch concluded, "Rhode Island will recognize same-sex marriages lawfully performed in Massachusetts as marriages in Rhode Island" but maintained that same-sex couples cannot marry in Rhode Island.

Politically, Rhode Island continues to be heavily Democratic—although not always so. Republican Governor Donald Carcieri was reelected 51%-49% in 2006; Rhode Island has not elected a Democratic governor since 1992, the last time a governor was elected to a two-year term. Carcieri lost Providence and Pawtucket and some working class suburbs, but carried just about every other city and town. Senator Lincoln Chafee, who was appointed to succeed his father in 1999 and elected to a full term in 2000 by a 57%-41% margin, compiled the most liberal record of any Republican senator. He was opposed by conservative Cranston Mayor Steven Laffey in the Republican primary, and won by only 54%-46%; Chafee's campaign encouraged Independents and Democrats to reregister as Republicans, and turnout in the Republican primary ballooned from 26,000 in 2002 to 64,500—almost as many as the 85,000 who voted in the Democratic primary. Chafee ran strongest in Providence and in the affluent suburbs on either side of Narragansett Bay; Laffey carried most of the downscale suburbs north and west of Providence. But Chafee's crossover support was not enough for him to beat the Democratic nominee, former Attorney General Sheldon Whitehouse. (This is a small state: the two candidates' fathers were roommates at Yale.) Whitehouse won 54%-46%. Whitehouse won 72% in Providence, which had voted 63% for Chafee in the primary and had given him 44% of the vote six years before; his percentages declined similarly in other ethnic cities and by somewhat lesser margins in affluent suburbs. A Democratic trend was also observable in the 52%-48% approval of restoring felons' right to vote; that had been taken away by voters in 1986. But the biggest spending was on a proposition to allow Harrah's to build a casino in West Warwick; racetrack owners, fearful of losing slot machine revenues, financed an opposition campaign, and the proposition lost 63%-37%.

The People		Race/Ethnic Origin			Military veterans: 102,494 (12.8%)	
Pop. 2006 (est):	1,067,610	858,433	81.9%	White	WWII: 25.4%	Korea: 14.9%
Pop. 2000:	1,048,319	41,922	4.0%	Black	Vietnam: 29.6%	Gulf War: 7.0%
Pop. 1990:	1,003,464	23,416	2.2%	Asian	**Most populous cities (2006):**	
Change 1990-2000:	Up 4.5%	4,181	0.4%	Native Am.	1. Providence	175,255
% of U.S. total:	0.4%	320	0.0%	Hawaiian	2. Warwick	85,925
Pop. rank:	43rd of 50	20,816	2.0%	Two+ races	3. Cranston	81,479
Area size:	1,545 sq. mi.	8,411	0.8%	Other	4. Pawtucket	72,998
State Native:	61.4%	90,820	8.7%	Hisp. Origin	5. East Providence	49,123
Non-citizen:	6.0%	**Ancestry**				
Language		Italian: 14.1%		Irish: 13.7%	Urban population: 90.9%	
English: 77.2%	Other Eur.:12.8%	English: 8.9%		French: 8.1%	Rural population: 9.1%	
Spanish: 7.5%		Portuguese: 6.5%				

Education		Work Sector		General Assembly	
H.S. Grad:	78.0%	Private: 80.6%	Govt: 13.8%	Senate	33 D 5 R
College Grad:	25.6%	Self: 5.4%	Family: 0.2%	House	60 D 15 R
Industry		Unemployment: 5.6%		Legislative Term Limits: No	
Agri: 0.5%	Con: 5.4%	**Household Income**		**Registered Voters**	
Fin: 6.9%	Info: 2.3%	<15k: 17.7%	15-35k: 24.2%	D: 262,963	(35.1%)
Mfg: 20.3%	Prof: 31.3%	35-50k: 15.7%	50-100k: 30.8%	R: 110,464	(14.7%)
Public: 4.5%	Trade: 15.5%	100-150k: 7.6%	>150k: 3.9%	O: 375,563	(50.1%)
Other: 13.3%		Median: $42,090			
Occupation		Poverty status: 11.9%			
Blue collar: 22.9%	White collar: 61.1%	**Home Value**			
Gray collar: 16.0%		<50k: 2.0% 50-100k: 21.0% 100-200k: 59.6% 200-300k: 11.1%			
		300-500k: 4.5% >500k: 1.8% Median: $130,500			

Presidential politics   Rhode Island is almost always one of the most Democratic states in presidential elections—over the last generation, the most Democratic, though just a little bit less so lately. It voted 61%-32% for Al Gore in 2000—his best state in the country—but gave its neighbor John Kerry a somewhat smaller margin of 59%-39% in 2004, less than his margin in Massachusetts. Turnout in 2004 was 437,000, beating the record of 432,000 in 1980. Protestants, once the Republican base here, gave George W. Bush only a 52%-47% majority; Catholics, who made up 57% of the voters, went 59%-40% for Kerry. Rhode Island's Catholic majority is heavily Democratic and, interestingly, pro-choice on abortion: In states where Catholics are beleaguered minorities they may stand together and strongly oppose abortion; here, where they're the strong majority and where the mostly Mediterranean Catholics traditionally didn't pay strict attention to the mostly Irish priests, they come out against the church position.

2004 Presidential Vote		
Kerry (D)	259,760	(59%)
Bush (R)	169,046	(39%)
Nader (Ref)	4,651	(1%)
Other	3,677	(1%)

2004 Democratic Presidential Primary		
Kerry (D)	25,466	(71%)
Edwards (D)	6,635	(19%)
Dean (D)	1,425	(4%)
Kucinich (D)	1,054	(3%)
Uncommitted	415	(1%)
Other	764	(2%)

2000 Presidential Vote		
Gore (D)	249,508	(61%)
Bush (R)	130,555	(32%)
Nader (Green)	25,052	(6%)
Other	3,668	(1%)

Rhode Island holds a presidential primary the same day as Massachusetts, usually with the lowest turnout rate in the nation. It has not won much attention. In 2000, when the primary was held on March 7 and the outcomes were not entirely clear, 83,000 voted. Al Gore beat Bill Bradley 57%-41%—one of Bradley's better performances—and John McCain beat George W. Bush 60%-36%. In 2004, when the primary was held March 2 and the outcomes reasonably clear, 38,000 voted. The results mirrored those next-door: Kerry beat John Edwards 71%-19% here and 72%-18% in Massachusetts.

Congressional districting   Rhode Island legislators had a heck of a time redrawing the boundaries of their own districts in 2001 and 2002; voters in 1994 adopted a constitutional amendment reducing the size of the state House after the 2000 Census from 100 to 75 seats and the state Senate from 50 to 38. Redistricting the state's two congressional districts was much easier. Rhode Island's two congressional districts have remained pretty much the same since 1842, except for the period from 1912 to 1932 when the state had three districts. Providence is split and both districts are overwhelmingly Democratic. For 2002, 14,000 people needed to be moved from the 2d District to the 1st. Incumbents Patrick Kennedy and James Langevin agreed on a change in Providence that gave Kennedy his old state legislative district near Providence College.

110th Congress Lineup
2 D

109th Congress Lineup
2 D

Governor

Donald Carcieri (R)

Elected 2002, term expires Jan. 2011, 2d term; b. Dec. 16, 1942, East Greenwich; home, East Greenwich; Brown U., B.A. 1965; Catholic; married (Suzanne).

Professional Career: High schl. teacher, 1965-71; Banker, Old Stone Bank, 1971-81; Director, Catholic Relief Services, Jamaica, 1981-83; CEO, Cookson America, 1983-97.

Office: The State House, Room 115, Providence, 02903, 401-222-2080; Fax: 401-222-8096; Web site: www.governor.state.ri.us.

Election Results

2006 general	Donald Carcieri (R)	197,306	(51%)
	Charles Fogarty (D)	190,686	(49%)
2006 primary	Donald Carcieri (R)	unopposed	
2002 general	Donald Carcieri (R)	181,687	(55%)
	Myrth York (D)	150,147	(45%)

Donald Carcieri, elected governor of Rhode Island in 2002, grew up in East Greenwich, on Narragansett Bay, where his father was a teacher and coach at the town high school and a quahogger in the summer. East Greenwich today is one of Rhode Island's most affluent suburbs; in the 1950s, Carcieri says, it was a modest town of fishermen and farmers. Carcieri was class president and a top athlete in high school and attended Brown on scholarship and played varsity football and baseball. He taught high school math in Newport and then in Concord, Massachusetts. Then he went to work for Old Stone Bank and in 10 years became executive vice president. In 1981 he moved to Kingston, Jamaica, to be head of the Catholic Relief Service's West Indies operation. In 1983 he returned to Rhode Island and went to work for Cookson America, the U.S. branch of a London conglomerate that owns dozens of manufacturing, electronic and precious metals companies around the world. He rose to become CEO of Cookson America and a joint managing director of Cookson Group Worldwide. He moved Cookson America's headquarters to the former Providence train station, overlooking Burnside Park and the State House. He retired in 1997 and in 2002 started running for governor.

The incumbent, Republican Lincoln Almond, was ineligible to run for a third term. Three Democrats and two Republicans ran to succeed Almond; Carcieri was the only one with no experience in public office, though he did serve as the Bush chairman in Rhode Island in 2000. His primary opponent was James Bennett, former chairman of the Convention Center Authority and owner of Mitkem, an environmental testing laboratory. Carcieri and Bennett mostly agreed on priorities—rein in the legislature, cut spending increases, promote economic development. Both avoided Rhode Island's matching fund public financing and spent their own money on their campaigns—$600,000 for Carcieri and $275,000 for Bennett. Bennett spent much of his money on fierce negative ads against Carcieri, charging that under his leadership Cookson's debt rose, layoffs increased, and Carcieri was given a $2.6 million golden handshake. But Carcieri won the September primary 67%-33%.

Running again as the Democratic nominee was Myrth York, who lost to Almond in 1994 and 1998, with a liberal message. She had a new team of consultants and ran ads showing her family. Her father started a chemical equipment company, and she manages her family's money; she spent $2 million of her own money before the primary.

The *Providence Journal* post-primary poll showed York ahead 49%-35%, but she had led in early polls in 1994 and 1998 as well. Their differing stances were apparent in a September debate. York said, "I have a knowledge of government and a knowledge of how to get things done in government. Government is there to provide opportunity for folks." Carcieri said, "I believe if real change is going to happen in the state, it's going to have to come from somebody who owes nothing to the system, somebody from outside." Carcieri pledged not to raise taxes in his first year; York said she didn't want to but wouldn't make a pledge. York called for new prescription drug and education programs; Carcieri said economic development was his goal.

In mid-October York started running a series of negative ads about Cookson. One said the company brokered a "tin mining deal" that ravaged an Amazon rain forest, another that it owned a plant in Philadelphia that released hazardous lead into the neighborhood, a third with neighbors of the plant denouncing Carcieri. A radio ad talked about an accident in which 15 Amazon miners were killed. Carcieri's pollster said that his polls showed Carcieri behind after the primary, drawing even in mid-October and gaining rapidly as York's negative spots were airing. The *Providence Journal's* polls and the election result suggest this was accurate. Carcieri won 55%-45%. York won big in Providence but in the rest of the state carried only East Providence and the tiny textile mill town of Central Falls. Altogether York spent $3.8 million of her own money, Carcieri $1.5 million of his.

Carcieri faced an overwhelmingly Democratic legislature (32–6 in the Senate, 63-11–1 in the House) but posted early achievements. In January 2003 he won praise for scheduling monthly office hours for average citizens to meet the governor for a 10-minute private visit; he said he got the idea from former New Mexico Governor Gary Johnson. He was tested in February 2003, when a nightclub fire in West Warwick killed 100 people and injured many others. In a state with only one million residents, nearly everyone knew someone affected by the tragedy. At a Warwick church memorial service several days afterwards, Carcieri stood in the back of the church greeting mourners; his empathy, decisiveness and calm resolve in the days after the fire won him much acclaim. In July, he signed the Comprehensive Fire Safety Act, requiring most nightclubs to install sprinklers, banning pyrotechnics from all but the largest venues, and eliminating a grandfather clause that exempted buildings constructed before the state fire code was written. State officials called the new fire regulations the toughest in the nation.

He held a weekly deli lunch with legislators and got them to agree to send to the voters a measure strengthening the governor's appointment authority on commissions and boards. For more than three centuries dating back to the original colonial charter, the General Assembly has had wide-ranging powers, including the authority to appoint members to, and have legislators serve on, hundreds of boards and commissions that make state policy and control billions in state assets. Critics claim this has encouraged political patronage, cronyism and a culture of behind-the-scenes dealmaking; voters thought so too after a decade of assorted scandals that brought down a state supreme court justice, and sent former Governor Edward DiPrete and Providence Mayor Buddy Cianci to prison. In a referendum in 2004, the "separation of powers" measure passed 78%-22%.

The governor battled regularly with Democratic leaders on a stream of bills that often returned to the legislature for an override vote. Carcieri vetoed a bill that would have allowed home-based childcare providers to unionize and bargain with the state. He vetoed a medical marijuana bill, but was overridden by Democratic legislators. In the face of a likely override, Carcieri backed away from threats in 2006 to veto a minimum wage increase that allowed the minimum hourly rate to rise to $7.40 in January 2007. Carcieri in 2005 was unable to convince the legislature to reconvene in October to pass his proposals for home heating assistance and proposed sales tax holiday after Thanksgiving. He was also forced to back down from a plan to create a statewide system to evaluate teacher performance. On less partisan initiatives, Carcieri worked to increase the state's science and technology sectors through a state grant program. Citing security concerns, Carcieri signed a bill that prohibits large tankers from transporting liquefied natural gas through Narragansett Bay to a proposed $250 million facility at Fall River.

Like his predecessor Lincoln Almond, Carcieri also ran into resistance when it came time to limit spending. Almond had lost control of spending because of the Democrats' huge majorities in the legislature; Carcieri, also facing huge majorities, vetoed the budget in July 2003 but was overridden. In 2004, Carcieri again vetoed the $5.9 billion budget, and again the legislature overrode his veto, approving tax increases on hotel rooms, cell phone usage and on cigarettes, raising the price of cigarettes to the highest in the nation. Carcieri had more success in subsequent years in part because he worked more closely with Democrats including state House Speaker William J. Murphy. In 2006 the legislature approved a $6.66 billion tax and spending plan that restrained overall spending increases to 4.9%–palatable to Carcieri–and gradually reduced the cap on how much communities can raise property taxes annually from 5.5% to 4% over six years.

Lieutenant Governor Charles Fogarty, a Democrat barred by term limits from seeking a third term, announced his campaign against Carcieri in March 2006. An internal poll conducted for Fogarty three months earlier showed him starting with at a 22-point deficit to the governor. Fogarty was a career politician from a family of politicians: his father was a state senator and his uncle, the late Rep. John E. Fogarty, served in Congress for a quarter century. Fogarty ran on access to affordable health care and on government reform, while Carcieri touted his attempts to control government spending. Some Democrats questioned the wisdom of Fogarty's campaign on corruption because of Carcieri's already strong record on against public corruption. But after a series of recent scandals in the state legislature, corruption remained a salient issue; Carcieri sought to remind voters of Fogarty's 16 years in state government, including eight in the state Senate. On economic issues, Carcieri was considered more vulnerable. During a televised debate in October, Fogarty cited Rhode Island's high unemployment rate and pressed Carcieri on his failure to create 20,000 new private sector jobs, a goal he set during the 2002 campaign. "I think 15,000 is pretty good," Carcieri responded. "We are outperforming all of New England." Each candidate spent just over $2 million for the race. Fogarty had accepted public financing and was prohibited from outspending his opponent; Carcieri avoided spending any of his own money this time. Fogarty benefited from the Democrats' good voter turnout operation and from a strong Democratic current running through the state. But Fogarty still fell shy of victory and Carcieri clinched a second term by winning 51%-49%.

Senior Senator

Jack Reed (D)

Elected 1996, seat up 2008, 2d term; b. Nov. 12, 1949, Providence; home, Cranston; U.S. Military Acad., West Point, B.S. 1971, Harvard U., M.P.P. 1973, J.D. 1982; Catholic; married (Julia Hart).

Military Career: Army, 1967-79; Army Reserves, 1979-91.

Elected Office: RI Senate, 1984-90; U.S. House of Reps., 1990-96.

Professional Career: Assoc. Prof., U.S. Military Acad. at West Point, 1978-79; Practicing atty., 1982-90.

DC Office: 728 HSOB, 20510, 202-224-4642; Fax: 202-224-4680; Web site: reed.senate.gov.

State Offices: Cranston, 401-943-3100; Providence, 401-528-5200.

Committees: *Appropriations* (13th of 15 D): Military Construction, Veterans Affairs & Related Agencies; Labor, Health and Human Services, Education & Related Agencies; Agriculture, Rural Development, Food and Drug Administration & Related Agencies; Commerce, Justice, Science & Related Agencies; Energy & Water Development; Interior, Environment & Related Agencies; State, Foreign Operations & Related Programs. *Armed Services* (5th of 13 D): Emerging Threats & Capabilities (Chmn.); Strategic Forces; Seapower. *Banking, Housing & Urban Affairs* (3d of 11 D): Securities, Insurance & Investment (Chmn.); Housing, Transportation & Community Development; Financial Institutions. *Health, Education, Labor & Pensions* (7th of 11 D): Retirement & Aging; Children & Families.

Group Ratings

	ADA	ACLU	AFS	LCV	ITIC	NTU	COC	ACU	CFG	FRC
2006	100	83	100	100	75	11	42	4	0	0
2005	100	—	100	100	—	9	33	0	2	—

National Journal Ratings

	2005 LIB	—	2005 CONS		2006 LIB	—	2006 CONS
Economic	92%	—	6%		87%	—	0%
Social	90%	—	0%		89%	—	8%
Foreign	95%	—	0%		88%	—	8%

Key Votes of the 109th Congress

1. Bar ANWR Drilling	Y	5. Confirm Samuel Alito	N	9. Limit Interstate Abortion	N
2. FY06 Spending Curb	N	6. Path to Citizenship	Y	10. CAFTA	N
3. Estate Tax Repeal	N	7. Bar Same Sex Marriage	N	11. Urge Iraq Withdrawal	Y
4. Raise Minimum Wage	Y	8. Stem Cell Research $	Y	12. Provide Detainee Rights	Y

Election Results

2002 general	Jack Reed (D)	253,773	(78%)	($1,767,967)
	Robert Tingle (R)	69,808	(22%)	
2002 primary	Jack Reed (D)	unopposed		
1996 general	Jack Reed (D)	230,676	(63%)	($2,732,011)
	Nancy J. Mayer (R)	127,368	(35%)	($773,789)

Prior Winning Percentages: 1994 House (68%); 1992 House (71%); 1990 House (59%)

Jack Reed, Rhode Island's senior senator, was elected to the House in 1990 and the Senate in 1996. He grew up in working-class Cranston, the son of a school custodian; he graduated from West Point, served in the 82d Airborne, got a degree at Harvard's Kennedy School, then taught at West Point. In 1979 he retired from the Army and went to Harvard Law School. He practiced law briefly in Washington and then in Providence. In 1984, at 35, he beat an incumbent in the primary for state Senate, where he served for six years, was close to the party leadership and built a good reputation. When Republican Claudine Schneider left the House to run against Senator Claiborne Pell in 1990, Reed ran for the House seat, overcoming several better-known candidates in the primary, and winning the general election with 59%.

In 1995, when Pell announced his retirement after 36 years in the Senate, Reed almost immediately started running. Reed was easily nominated and faced state Treasurer Nancy Mayer in the general. National Republicans spent nearly $1 million on ads attacking Reed as a liberal for opposing workfare and for supporting labor unions; in liberal, heavily unionized Rhode Island these did not hurt him and may have helped. Mayer spent $773,000 and Reed $2.7 million. His biography was his message: Reed launched his campaign in a school conference room named after his late father, stressed how he came up from humble beginnings by hard work and called for education spending to help others rise as he had. That message, and his pleasant, unassuming demeanor evidently touched a chord. He won 63%-35%.

Reed is one of the few senators of his generation with military experience. He was appointed to the governing board of West Point in 1998; he was married in West Point's Catholic church in 2005 (he met his wife on a trip to Afghanistan). He got a seat on the Armed Services Committee in January 1999; he got a waiver to stay on Armed Services after he got a seat on Appropriations in 2007. He wants to consolidate the Naval War College and the Naval Undersea Warfare Center, two of the remaining Rhode Island military facilities; defense jobs in the state declined from 44,000 in 1970 to 8,000 in 1999. He supported Bill Clinton's bombing strikes in Afghanistan and Sudan in 1998, and in October 2002 voted against the Iraq war resolution. In December 2002 he led the successful fight in committee to cut $15 million off research into a bunker buster nuclear weapon and $812 million off the missile defense budget. He has sought to increase permanently the size of the Army. In October 2003 the Senate voted 52-45 for his amendment to increase the Army by 10,000 troops; it was dropped in conference. In March 2004 he and Chuck Hagel called for a permanent increase of 30,000, rather than the 30,000 increase for only four years announced by Defense Secretary Donald Rumsfeld. In June the Senate voted for an increase of 20,000; Reed sought to have the increase registered in the base budget, not in the supplemental appropriation. His 2006 amendment to add $65.4 million for buying more Predators passed 98–0. In 2006 he worked with the Republican leadership to add $3.7 billion for more soldiers and Marines in the regular budget, not the supplemental, and sponsored an amendment to add $10.2 billion to replace damaged or destroyed Army and Marines equipment and war reserve stocks. He also got $50 million more for Virginia class submarines.

Reed has been critical of the U.S. performance in Iraq after the initial military victory. In March 2004 he argued that the United Nations must approve a resolution to create an interim government. In September 2004 he found the reports of Army General George Fay and former Defense Secretary James Schlesinger incomplete on the subject of prison abuses. He opposed the nomination of Francis Harvey to be Secretary of the Army. In 2005, on his fifth trip to Iraq, he summarized his approach: "My job is to be critical about what's going on and what needs to be improved. I think my criticism has been accurate, certainly in the operations in this region, in that we didn't organize ourselves for the appropriate occupation and stabilization" after the overthrow of Saddam Hussein. He stressed the need to improve municipal services and spur economic development. When the Republican National Committee ran ads criticizing Democrats for their stance in December 2005, he said in a response to a Bush radio address, "Baseless partisan attacks won't help us win the war." In January 2006, after the Iraqi elections, he said the U.S. "has seized the military initiative," but warned there was "a real potential" for insurgents to regroup. In March he said it was time to "redeploy our forces as quickly as possible" to other parts of the Middle East. In June 2006 he and Carl Levin sponsored an amendment calling for a "phased redeployment" in six months, with no deadline for complete withdrawal; it also called for U.S. forces to transition to training Iraqi security forces. The more extreme alternative, John Kerry's amendment calling for withdrawal by June 2007, was defeated 86-13; the Levin-Reed amendment lost 60-39, with six Democrats and one Republican, Rhode Island's Lincoln Chafee, crossing party lines. In July 2006 he called the situation in Iraq a "low grade civil war," but pointed to gains in training Iraqis. He endorsed Israel's response to Hezbollah attacks but was concerned about possible coordination between Hezbollah and Hamas;

he also said that Israel should exercise restraint and that the U.S. should do more to stimulate negotiations between Israel and the Palestinians. In October 2006, after his ninth trip to Iraq, he said it was a "very, very difficult situation." He called for "laying out some red lines for the Iraqis" on disarming militias, holding provincial elections and spending money on economic development. In December 2006 he said the Iraq Study Group's report "may be the last chance to get it right" and noted that its recommendations were "strikingly similar" to the Levin-Reed amendment. In July 2007 he made his 10th trip to Iraq and co-sponsored with Levin an amendment to force a reduction and redeployment of troops by April 30, 2008. He voted to confirm the appointment of Robert Gates as secretary of defense. "He has struck me as a very thoughtful individual who studies the issues and makes good points. He's a listener who seeks information and then makes decisions."

On most issues Reed has had a solidly liberal voting record. He has championed the Low-Income Home Energy Assistance Program. He called the Senate's action in November 2005 classifying LIHEAP funding as emergency spending a "terrible precedent" and sponsored an amendment to raise spending from $2 billion to $5.1 billion. That amendment was put into the budget resolution in March 2006 by a 51-49 vote. His 2006 amendment to repeal the extension of the capital gains and dividend tax cuts and use increased revenue for military equipment was defeated 53-44. He was the lead opponent of the bill to bar victims from suing to hold gun manufacturers liable for crimes committed with their products. In December 2006 he blocked several bills to get the Senate to direct leftover CHIP funds in some states to those states with shortfalls, including Rhode Island. Reed voted against the nominations of Condoleezza Rice and opposed John Bolton; he voted against the confirmations of John Roberts and Samuel Alito. With a reported 10,000 Liberian immigrants in Rhode Island, Reed and Patrick Kennedy called in March 2006 for Liberian refugees to be given permanent immigrant status. "The Liberian community has been living, working and paying taxes in the United States, some for a decade or more, and has been ineligible for the benefits afforded to other taxpayers." He got such a provision into the immigration bill that passed the Senate in May 2006, but that went nowhere in the House, and in September 2006 the Department of Homeland Security ruled that because of the new democratic government in Liberia, Liberians would no longer have refugee status after October 2007.

In July 2001, after Democrats got their majority in the Senate, Reed got a seat on Appropriations. But when Democrats lost their majority in the 2002 election, he was rotated off the committee; when Democrats got their majority back in 2006, he got the Appropriations seat back; in the process he waived his seniority on the Joint Economic Committee in favor of Charles Schumer.

In Rhode Island politics, Reed has always been his own man, unentangled with the various machine politicians who come and go. In 2002, against a pit manager at Foxwoods Resort Casino, he was reelected 78%-22%. This is a Senate seat whose members have had long tenures. Theodore Green, elected at 69, served 24 years; Claiborne Pell, elected at 41, served 36 years. Reed, elected just before turning 47, has the prospect of long service before him.

Junior Senator

Sheldon Whitehouse (D)

Elected 2006, seat up 2012, 1st term; b. Oct. 20, 1955, New York City; home, Providence; Yale U., B.A. 1978, U. of VA, J.D. 1982; Protestant; married (Sandra).

Elected Office: RI Atty. Gen., 1998-2002.

Professional Career: RI Spec. Asst. Atty. Gen., 1984-90; Legal Counsel, Gov. Bruce Sundlun, 1991; Policy Director, Gov. Bruce Sundlun, 1992; Director, RI Dept. of Business Regulation, 1992-1994; U.S. Atty. for RI, 1994-1998; Practicing atty., 2003-2006.

DC Office: 502 HSOB, 20510, 202-224-2921; Fax: 202-228-6362; Web site: whitehouse.senate.gov.

State Office: Providence, 401-453-5294.

Committees: *Aging (Special)* (11th of 11 D). *Budget* (11th of 12 D). *Environment & Public Works* (9th of 10 D): Transportation Safety, Infrastructure Security & Water Quality; Public Sector Solutions to Global Warming, Oversight & Children's Health Protection. *Intelligence (Select)* (8th of 8 D). *Judiciary* (10th of 10 D): Administrative Oversight & the Courts; Human Rights & the Law.

Group Ratings and Key Votes: Newly Elected

Election Results

2006 general	Sheldon Whitehouse (D)	206,043	(54%)	($6,494,266)
	Lincoln Chafee (R)	178,950	(46%)	($5,381,488)
2006 primary	Sheldon Whitehouse (D)	69,290	(82%)	
	Christopher Young (D)	8,739	(10%)	
	Carl Sheeler (D)	6,755	(8%)	
2000 general	Lincoln Chafee (R)	222,588	(57%)	($2,265,221)
	Robert A. Weygand (D)	161,023	(41%)	($2,297,885)
	Other	7,742	(2%)	

The junior senator from Rhode Island is Sheldon Whitehouse, a Democrat elected in 2006. He is a wealthy descendant of Charles Crocker, one of California's "Big Four" men who built the Central Pacific Railroad, the eastbound section of railroad that connected with the Union Pacific line at Promontory Summit, Utah, to form the nation's first transcontinental railroad. His grandfather was a diplomat and so was his father Charles Whitehouse, a former World War II Marine Corps pilot who worked for the CIA, the Defense Department and the State Department before he became U.S. ambassador to Laos and Thailand in the 1970s. Sheldon Whitehouse was born in New York City and spent parts of his childhood in exotic locales; as a teenager, he taught English to Vietnamese children in Saigon. He attended the prestigious St. Paul's prep school before graduating from Yale University and the University of Virginia Law School. In 1985, Whitehouse began his ascent through state government as a special assistant attorney general. He moved to the governor's office after the 1990 election of Democrat Bruce Sundlun; he served as Sundlun's legal counsel and policy director and put in a stint as the state's top business regulator. In 1994, with support from family friend Senator Claiborne Pell, he was appointed U.S. Attorney for Rhode Island by President Bill Clinton.

Whitehouse ran for elected office for the first time in 1998, when he sought to become state attorney general, and the experience was a jarring one. In the three-way Democratic primary his opponents portrayed him as an inexperienced, fox-hunting patrician trying to buy his way into public office; the general election against state Treasurer Nancy Mayer wasn't much easier, as Mayer forced him to concede he had tried drugs as a student and questioned whether he was tough enough for the job. After his win he told the *Providence Journal Bulletin*, "The book on me was: 'Smart kid, works hard but, you know, has no common touch, can't relate to people, will be a disaster.' In fact, I got advice from some political types to run sort of a Rose Garden strategy—you know, 'Don't go out, don't let people see you, 'cause if they see you they're not going to like you. Just mail your resume around, you know, and spend a lot of money on television."

Almost immediately, Whitehouse was viewed as a contender for governor in 2002. He ran, but lost the Democratic primary by 926 votes to Myrth York, a wealthy liberal and a Federal Hill neighbor in Providence. She spent $2 million of her own money before the primary ("I was a real piker at $700,000," Whitehouse later quipped)and ultimately spent $3.8 million out-of-pocket in a 55%-45% loss to Republican Donald Carcieri. His primary election defeat, Whitehouse told a television reporter, "combines elements of losing a loved one, getting dumped by your girlfriend, having your house broken into, and losing the big game."

Prior to his unsuccessful run for governor, Whitehouse had considered running for Senate when Republican Senator John Chafee announced in 1999 that he would not run for a 5th term, but decided against it. But the Chafee seat came up again in 2006 and, after several years in private practice, Whitehouse decided to make a run for it.

John Chafee, who had roomed with Whitehouse's father at Yale University, died in office in October 1999; his son Lincoln was appointed to finish his term and won a full term in 2000 with 57%. He voted often with Democrats and there was frequent speculation that he would switch parties, but the national Republican party understood that he might be the only Republican in heavily Democratic Rhode Island who could hold the seat—he and his father were the only Republicans elected to the Senate from Rhode Island in the last 70 years. Still, Chafee had to fight for renomination against Cranston Mayor Steve Laffey, a fiscal conservative and a sharp-elbowed campaigner who was backed by the anti-tax Club for Growth. The National Republican Senatorial Committee under Elizabeth Dole vigorously defended Chafee, reasoning that he would be the stronger general election candidate; he won the bruising September primary 54%-46%. Chafee carried Providence by 789 votes and won 62% in Warwick; he got more than his 5,025-vote winning margin out of Warwick and the affluent communities on both sides of Narragansett Bay. Laffey won 53% in Cranston and carried the working class communities west and north of Providence.

Whitehouse also looked to have a competitive primary in 2006, but he won easily after Secretary of State Matt Brown dropped out of the race in April amid allegations of campaign finance violations. This gave Whitehouse a decided advantage over Chafee who had $700,000 cash on hand through mid-October while Whitehouse, who had raised $5.4 million by that time, still had more than $1 million in the bank. Chafee emphasized his willingness to work across party lines but Whitehouse urged voters to vote their party preference, a problem for Chafee in a state where registered Democrats outnumber Republicans by more than 2-to-1. There was little daylight between the candidates on issues—both backed an expansion of federal support for embryonic stem cell research, abortion rights and gun control—so Whitehouse hung the unpopular Bush administration and the national party around Chafee's neck, running ads with the tagline, "Finally, a Whitehouse in Washington you can trust."

Whitehouse won 54%-46% overall, with 72% in Providence, 66% in Pawtucket, 61% in East Providence, 64% in Woonsocket and 77% in Central Falls—mill towns and gentrifiers. Chafee won 54% in Warwick, carried Kingston and Westerly's Washington County, and ran not much better than even in Newport and Bristol Counties. As compared to his 2000 election, Chafee lost biggest in Providence, Central Falls and Jamestown (16%), Pawtucket (15%), Newport and Middletown, Woonsocket and Burrillville (14%).

In Washington, Whitehouse said his top legislative priority would be "finding a responsible way home from Iraq." He got seats on the Environment and Public Works, Budget and Intelligence committees and was also assigned to the Judiciary Committee, where he is the only WASP among the committee's ten Democrats.

FIRST DISTRICT

Rep. Patrick Kennedy (D)

Elected 1994, 7th term; b. July 14, 1967, Brighton, MA; home, Portsmouth; Providence Col., B.A. 1991; Catholic; single.

Elected Office: RI House of Reps., 1988-94.

DC Office: 407 CHOB, 20515, 202-225-4911; Fax: 202-225-3290; Web site: www.house.gov/patrickkennedy.

District Offices: Pawtucket, 401-729-5600.

Committees: *Appropriations* (16th of 37 D): Commerce, Justice, Science & Related Agencies; Military Construction, Veterans Affairs & Related Agencies; Labor, HHS, Education & Related Agencies. *Natural Resources* (19th of 27 D): Energy & Mineral Resources; Fisheries, Wildlife & Oceans.

Group Ratings

	ADA	ACLU	AFS	LCV	ITIC	NTU	COC	ACU	CFG	FRC
2006	85	95	100	33	29	12	31	10	7	0
2005	95	—	100	100	—	12	37	4	7	0

National Journal Ratings

	2005 LIB	—	2005 CONS		2006 LIB	—	2006 CONS
Economic	92%	—	6%		94%	—	0%
Social	79%	—	20%		82%	—	18%
Foreign	61%	—	39%		65%	—	35%

Key Votes of the 109th Congress

1. Estate Tax Repeal	N	5. Limit Interstate Abortion	N	9. Build Border Fence	N
2. Limit CAFE Standards	N	6. Extend Patriot Act	N	10. CAFTA	N
3. FY06 Spending Curb	N	7. Bar Same Sex Marriage	N	11. Oppose Iraq Withdrawal	N
4. Drilling in ANWR	*	8. Stem Cell Research $	Y	12. Detainee Tribunals	N

Election Results

2006 general	Patrick Kennedy (D) 124,634	(69%)	($2,155,761)
	Jonathan Scott (R) 41,836	(23%)	($9,542)
	Kenneth Capalbo (Ind) 13,634	(8%)	
2006 primary	Patrick Kennedy (D) .... unopposed		
2004 general	Patrick Kennedy (D) 124,923	(64%)	($1,958,492)
	David Rogers (R) 69,819	(36%)	($2,133,062)

Prior Winning Percentages: 2002 (60%); 2000 (67%); 1998 (67%); 1996 (69%); 1994 (54%)

The People		Race/Ethnic Origin	Ancestry	
Area size:	565 sq. mi.	82.6% White	Irish: 12.9%	Italian: 11.4%
Urban population:	95.5%	4.1% Black	Portuguese: 9.3%	
Rural population:	4.5%	1.9% Asian	**2004 Presidential Vote**	
Pop. 2000:	524,157	0.3% Native Am.	Kerry (D) 131,245	(62%)
Pop. 2005 (est):	533,326	0.0% Hawaiian	Bush (R) 77,480	(36%)
Median income:	$40,616	2.3% Two+ races	Other 3,900	(2%)
Poverty status:	11.9%	1.3% Other	**2000 Presidential Vote**	
Military veterans:	12.5%	7.5% Hispanic Origin	Gore (D) 125,174	(63%)
			Bush (R) 61,396	(31%)
			Other 12,705	(6%)
			Cook Partisan Voting Index: D +16	
Occupation	Blue collar: 23.2%	White collar: 61.3%	Gray collar: 15.5%	

The 1st Congressional District is the eastern half of Rhode Island, east of Narragansett Bay, a line that cuts through Providence and then proceeds west and north to the Massachusetts-Connecticut-Rhode Island border. It includes much of Providence (including elite East Side and College Hill around Brown University) and all of next-door Pawtucket whose Slater Mill is known as the birthplace of the American Industrial Revolution. The onetime textile mill towns of the Blackstone Valley, Woonsocket and Central Falls are also in the 1st, along with high-income Barrington and Bristol and, south on the ocean, the old city of Newport, with its restored 18th century houses and the summer "cottages" that are more like palaces. Newport was once home to the America's Cup races and now hosts a famous jazz festival; it is also the site of the oldest synagogue in North America, to whose congregation George Washington declared that the United States gives "to bigotry no sanction, to persecution no assistance." Ethnically, this district is the more French-Canadian and the less Italian of the two Rhode Island districts; politically, it is strongly Democratic.

The congressman from the 1st District is Patrick Kennedy, a Democrat first elected in 1994. Patrick Kennedy was born in 1967, his father Edward Kennedy's fifth year in the Senate; a week after his second birthday came the terrible accident at Chappaquiddick. He grew up in McLean, Virginia, and had a somewhat troubled youth, spending time in a drug rehabilitation clinic in 1986 before enrolling at Providence College, at 20, in 1987. Almost immediately, in 1988, he ran for a seat in the state House and beat the longtime incumbent John Skeffington as the tiny (population 9,800) district was inundated with visits by Kennedy family members and funds raised by the Kennedy national fundraising network. He became chairman of the Rules Committee in 1992, a year after spending the now-infamous Easter weekend in Palm Beach with his father and cousin William Kennedy Smith. In 1994, when the 1st District's Republican Congressman Ron Machtley ran for governor, Kennedy decided to run for Congress. Kennedy had an attractive and energetic Republican opponent, Kevin Vigilante, a doctor who worked with handicapped orphans in Romania and with female prison inmates infected with HIV. But Kennedy had the advantages of party, money and his family name, and won 54%-46% in a Republican year.

In the House Kennedy has a mostly liberal voting record and has proven an excitable if not always eloquent debater. He started off by avoiding national media and working on local issues, from the Naval Undersea Warfare Center in Newport to visas for Portuguese immigrants. He has been strongly opposed to Fidel Castro, whom he blames for the death of his uncle John F. Kennedy; he voted for the Helms-Burton Act, backed the 2000 bill that would have made Elian Gonzalez a U.S. citizen and for keeping the travel ban on Cuba in 2003. He has strongly supported gun control—another issue with family reverberations. He supported reauthorization of the assault weapons ban and in 2003 criticized presidential candidate Howard Dean for his statements that new gun control laws should be left to the states.

After winning re-election by 69%-28% in 1996, he took on a more combative role and seemed to be eyeing a race for the Senate seat held by John Chafee. He criticized Chafee sharply for several votes but Chafee fought back gamely, returning often to the state, working hard on local projects, and his standing in the polls, never weak, slowly rose. Meanwhile, the harshness of Kennedy's attacks evidently grated; his job approval fell from 62% to 44% during the year. In 1998 Kennedy's career took another turn. In April he said he wanted a seat on Appropriations—not a likely goal if he intended to seek only one more term in the House. He struck up a friendship with Minority Leader Dick Gephardt; Kennedy let it be known that he would support Gephardt for president against Al Gore. When Gephardt decided not to run for president, but rather to concentrate on helping Democrats win a House majority, he enlisted Kennedy as a key ally. In November 1998, after Kennedy easily won reelection, Gephardt named him chairman of the DCCC. A few days later Kennedy announced what was already pretty plain, that he would not run for the Senate.

As DCCC chairman, Kennedy excelled not as a strategist but as a fundraiser. He traveled indefatigably around the country to fundraisers, and made yeoman efforts to raise soft money, even while calling for campaign finance legislation that would outlaw it. As a result, the DCCC in 1999 and 2000 raised nearly $50 million in soft money, reaching parity with the Republicans' NRCC; the NRCC raised more hard money, but Kennedy vastly reduced the disadvantage his party labored under in the 1996 and 1998 cycles. But Democrats were unsuccessful in their efforts for a net gain of six seats to regain a majority in the House.

Instead he seemed to be moving from national politics to concentration on Rhode Island, where he had spent only 40 days in 1999 and 2000, and where his standing was in decline because of a series of imbroglios. In March 2000, he shoved an airport security guard in Los Angeles, sending her backward and jostling the metal detector archway. A police complaint was filed, but the Los Angeles city attorney decided against prosecution. In an informal hearing in May 2000, Kennedy apologized to the woman. But she sued him in March 2001, and Kennedy said his insurance company would handle the suit. The insurance company, it appeared, had already been busy settling multiple damage claims against Kennedy by owners of sailboats he had chartered. None of this hurt him in the 2000 election. Against a Republican who spent $9,000, he won 67%-33%. But his job approval in the district fell from 63% in February 2000 to 42% in September 2001.

In January 2001 Kennedy took back the seat on Appropriations to which he had been named in 1998, but from which he had taken a leave of absence to chair the DCCC. He worked on some other legislation, co-sponsoring the mental health parity bill which passed in the Senate but did not come to a vote in the House, but he mostly concentrated on getting federal money, especially defense dollars, for Rhode Island. Much of that was for hospitals, schools and bridges, but he also worked to bring in money for Rhode Island's military bases and defense industries. His involvement on these military issues may help to explain his differences with his father on the B-1 bomber and the Iraq war resolution, both of which Patrick Kennedy supported. As the insurgency against U.S. forces grew, Kennedy criticized the administration's policies and in 2004 said that the administration had deceived him by its statements on weapons of mass destruction.

Kennedy has taken distinctive stands on some other issues. One is parity for mental health treatments in insurance. In 2000 he appeared with Tipper Gore in Rhode Island and disclosed that he had been receiving treatment and therapy for manic depression. In 2004 he co-sponsored with his father and Republicans Pete Domenici and Jim Ramstad a bill extending Paul Wellstone's 1996 parity law by eliminating unequal limits on numbers of inpatient days and outpatient days in insurance policies. He has voted several times for the partial-birth abortion ban. In the 1990s he supported Indian gambling and in 2001 and 2002 was the House's top recipient of donations from Indian tribes; from 1999 to 2003 he received $42,500 from tribes which were clients of now disgraced Jack Abramoff. Rhode Island has 10,000 Liberian immigrants, and Kennedy joined Senator Jack Reed in seeking to give permanent residence status to Liberian refugees; in March 2006 he helped get Appropriations to vote $50 million in extra aid for Liberia. He has spoken favorably of same-sex marriage.

Kennedy claims that he has brought more than $400 million in projects to Rhode Island. The bulk of the money is in defense projects, but no cause seems too small or too local for this appropriator: $200,000 for equipment at the emergency operations center in Providence, $750,000 for the Norman Bird Sanctuary to buy 23 acres in Middletown, $25,000 for computers at the Leon Matthieu Senior Center in Pawtucket, $250,000 for juvenile justice programs in Bristol, $4 million for the Blackstone River Bikeway, $750,000 for the Thundermist Health Center in Woonsocket (which named its headquarters building for him). Kennedy sometimes presents the check personally. Handing a $150,000 check to the Smithfield police department, he said, "This is from me. This is one of those famous earmarks."

Kennedy has had some difficult personal problems. In July 2004 his brother was named temporary guardian of his mother, who suffers from alcoholism. After she broke her shoulder in a fall in March 2005 he and his two siblings sued to take legal custody of her affairs; a settlement was worked out in June, with two trustees managing her estate and a guardian supervising her personal affairs. In April 2006, in Rhode Island, a businessman demonstrating how a substance called Impact Gel was impervious to hammer blow, he lost control of the hammer which struck Kennedy in the mouth; he got six stitches in his lip. At 2:50 in the morning in May 2006 Kennedy drove his car into a security barrier outside the House office buildings. He told the Capitol Police that he needed to vote, but the House had adjourned hours before; they drove him home and, reportedly at the direction of supervisors, did not administer a sobriety check. In a statement later in the day he said he had not been drinking; in a second statement he said he was disoriented by prescription medicines he was taking, and experts said that was possible. The next day he announced he was checking into the Mayo Clinic for a one-month addiction treatment program; he had been there the previous Christmas for addiction to the painkiller OxyContin. Minnesota Republican Jim Ramstad, a recovering alcoholic, volunteered to be his sponsor; the two are now co-chairmen of the Addiction, Treatment and Recovery Caucus, which has almost 80 members (by no means all of them with such problems themselves). In June 2006 he pleaded guilty to driving under the influence of prescription medicines and was sentenced to one year of probation. This seems to have caused him no political problems in Rhode Island. A *Washington Post* reporter could find nary a constituent who said they were less likely to vote for him. One said, "Course not. You kidding me? Politicians drink like fish around here."

Certainly Kennedy has done well in elections. In 2002 Republican David Rogers, a former Navy Seal, raised $2 million, mostly by direct mail and ran hard-hitting ads. Kennedy won 60%-37%. In 2004 Rogers ran again; Kennedy won 64%-36%. In the runup to the 2006 election, many urged Kennedy to run against Senator Lincoln Chafee. Early in his career a Senate seat seemed his obvious goal; but he passed up the chance to run in 2000 to help his party in House races, and in December 2004 he said he wouldn't run because he wanted to keep working in the House and on the Appropriations Committee. He urged his 2d District colleague Jim Langevin to run. But in March 2005 Langevin said he wouldn't, and added that either Kennedy or former Attorney General Sheldon Whitehouse should be the party's candidate. Kennedy gave some further consideration to running for the Senate, but on March 30 said he would not; in April, he and Langevin endorsed Whitehouse, who beat Chafee 54%-46% in November. Kennedy's Republican opponent in 2006 spent some $10,000 against Kennedy's $2.2 million, and Kennedy won 69%-23%.

SECOND DISTRICT

Rep. Jim Langevin (D)

Elected 2000, 4th term; b. Apr. 22, 1964, Warwick; home, Warwick; RI Col., B.A. 1990, Harvard U., M.P.A. 1994; Catholic; single.

Elected Office: RI House of Reps., 1988-94; RI Sec. of State, 1994-2000.

DC Office: 109 CHOB, 20515, 202-225-2735; Fax: 202-225-5976; Web site: www.house.gov/langevin.

District Offices: Warwick, 401-732-9400.

Committees: *Homeland Security* (13th of 19 D): Emerging Threats, Cybersecurity & Science and Technology (Chmn.); Intelligence, Information Sharing & Terrorism Risk Assessment; Border, Maritime & Global Counterterrorism. *Permanent Select Committee on Intelligence* (11th of 12 D): Terrorism, Human Intelligence, Analysis & Counterintelligence; Technical & Tactical Intelligence.

Group Ratings

	ADA	ACLU	AFS	LCV	ITIC	NTU	COC	ACU	CFG	FRC
2006	75	77	86	100	29	14	33	16	10	28
2005	85	—	100	100	—	13	44	8	4	38

National Journal Ratings

	2005 LIB	—	2005 CONS		2006 LIB	—	2006 CONS
Economic	78%	—	21%		77%	—	23%
Social	66%	—	34%		68%	—	31%
Foreign	63%	—	36%		65%	—	34%

Key Votes of the 109th Congress

1. Estate Tax Repeal	N	5. Limit Interstate Abortion	Y	9. Build Border Fence	N
2. Limit CAFE Standards	N	6. Extend Patriot Act	N	10. CAFTA	N
3. FY06 Spending Curb	N	7. Bar Same Sex Marriage	N	11. Oppose Iraq Withdrawal	N
4. Drilling in ANWR	N	8. Stem Cell Research $	Y	12. Detainee Tribunals	N

Election Results

2006 general	Jim Langevin (D)	140,315	(73%)	($829,178)
	Rod Driver (Ind)	52,729	(27%)	($178,488)
2006 primary	Jim Langevin (D)	24,985	(62%)	
	Jennifer Lawless (D)	15,456	(38%)	
2004 general	Jim Langevin (D)	154,392	(75%)	($727,295)
	Chuck Barton (R)	43,139	(21%)	($49,633)
	Other	9,634	(5%)	

Prior Winning Percentages: 2002 (76%); 2000 (62%)

The People		Race/Ethnic Origin	Ancestry	
Area size:	980 sq. mi.	81.2% White	Italian: 16.7%	Irish: 14.4%
Urban population:	86.3%	3.9% Black	English: 9.8%	
Rural population:	13.7%	2.6% Asian	**2004 Presidential Vote**	
Pop. 2000:	524,162	0.5% Native Am.	Kerry (D) 128,515	(57%)
Pop. 2005 (est):	538,152	0.0% Hawaiian	Bush (R) 91,566	(41%)
Median income:	$44,129	1.6% Two+ races	Other 4,428	(2%)
Poverty status:	11.9%	0.3% Other	**2000 Presidential Vote**	
Military veterans:	13.1%	9.8% Hispanic Origin	Gore (D) 124,314	(60%)
			Bush (R) 69,076	(33%)
			Other 14,366	(7%)
			Cook Partisan Voting Index: D +13	

Occupation	Blue collar: 22.6%	White collar: 60.8%	Gray collar: 16.6%

The 2d Congressional District is the western half of Rhode Island. While the 1st includes many mill towns, the 2d has most of its population in towns like working-class Cranston and more upscale Warwick which, despite their British names, are inhabited mostly by people with Irish, Italian, French and Portuguese surnames. The 2d also includes the fastest-growing part of the state: South County, which is not an official place but the common name for Rhode Island south of East Greenwich, including the affluent suburbs and beachfront communities to the south along Narragansett Bay, the Kingston home of the University of Rhode Island, and the area around Westerly, where many residents work at the Electric Boat shipyards in Groton, Connecticut. The Base Realignment and Closure Commission spared Connecticut's submarine base in 2005, but Electric Boat announced that same year job cuts at Quonset Point, R.I. The district includes Rhode Island's rolling farm land, though there is not that much acreage, and the communities along the Bay and the Ocean, where many people still make their living building boats and catching fish. Although this remains a heavily Democratic district, George W. Bush cut the Democratic margin from 60%-33% in 2000 to 57%-41% in 2004.

The congressman from the 2d District is Jim Langevin, a Democrat first elected in 2000. Langevin grew up in Warwick, and as a boy hoped to become an FBI agent. But in 1980, at age 16, when he was a police cadet in the Boy Scout Explorer program, he was shot by a police officer when a gun accidentally discharged. The bullet went through his upper back and throat and damaged the upper part of his spinal column; ever since, he has been a quadriplegic, getting around in a wheelchair, the first to serve in Congress. He received $2.2 million in a settlement with the city of Warwick and currently hires a home health care aide; it takes him two and a half hours to get dressed each morning. This tragic accident focused attention on him, at first unwanted, but he says it made him determined to make something of his life. He worked as an intern in the State House and for Senator Claiborne Pell. In 1988, while he was a student at Rhode Island College, he was elected to the state House of Representatives, where he styled himself as a reformer; his 1st District colleague Patrick Kennedy was also elected that year to the state House as a college student. While in the state House Langevin graduated from college and received a master's degree from the Kennedy School at Harvard. In 1994 Langevin was elected Rhode Island's secretary of state.

When Congressman Bob Weygand ran for the Senate in 2000, Langevin decided to run for his House seat. It was a four-way race in the Democratic primary, and Langevin's most strenuous opposition came from Kate Coyne-McCoy, executive director of the Rhode Island Association of Social Workers. Langevin had support from many Democratic Party leaders and some unions, and won the party endorsement at the April convention, from which Coyne-McCoy angrily withdrew. But she waged an aggressive campaign, financed by unions, health care workers and EMILY's List. "There's no such thing as being too liberal," Coyne-McCoy said. Langevin called her positions "unrealistic and extreme." He favored less stringent forms of gun control and said, "No one has to tell me how dangerous weapons can be." Coyne-McCoy attacked Langevin for opposing abortion rights. He said, "because of what happened to me, I became aware of how precious life is . . . I'm pro-life." He spoke often of the accident that paralyzed him: "Certainly, being disabled is part of who I am, but it doesn't define me." In the primary, he led Coyne-McCoy 47%-29%. In the general, his chief opposition came from Rodney Driver, nominee of the Conscience for Congress Party, a retired mathematics professor who spent $300,000 of his retirement savings. Langevin won 62%-21%.

In the House, Langevin has been liberal on economic issues and more centrist on cultural and foreign issues: an apt representative of his district's ethnic communities. The House chamber was made wheelchair-accessible for Langevin, with two of the fixed seats in the front of the chamber removed to give him space to maneuver and talk to colleagues. Because he has only limited use of his hands, Langevin was unable to cast a secret ballot until Rhode Island purchased special voting machines. Despite the opposition of anti-abortion groups, he urged George W. Bush to support embryonic stem-cell research, arguing that it might alleviate suffering from certain diseases and injuries, and assist infertile couples to have children; he voted against the bill to permit therapeutic cloning. He sponsored several gun control bills. Langevin called universal health care coverage his overriding priority, and sponsored a bill to mandate the federal government to provide all Americans the health care choices available to federal employees to be financed by an increase in the payroll tax. In March 2005 he was one of two House Democrats from New England who supported federal judicial review in the Terri Schiavo case.

Langevin won passage in 2006 of a law that establishes a respite program that aids caregivers of individuals with special needs. He first introduced the bill in 2002 but had difficult advancing the measure in the GOP Congress until he asked a Republican, New Jersey Rep. Mike Ferguson, to become the bill's sponsor. Langevin has advocated on other health issues, most notably stem cell research. He protested the Bush administration's stem cell research policy by inviting Dana Reeve, the widow of actor and spinal repair research activist Christopher Reeve, to Bush's 2005 State of the Union address.

Langevin had the opportunity to run for Senate in 2006. One statewide poll in early 2005 showed him leading Republican Senator Lincoln Chafee. Rhode Island and national Democrats urged him to consider, but abortion rights groups objected to an anti-abortion candidate in Rhode Island. In March 2005 Langevin surprised many Democrats when he said he would not run for the Senate; he said he had important work to do in the House and did not rule out a later run for statewide office. Langevin opposed the Senate candidacy of Secretary of State Matt Brown, who later dropped out of the primary, and endorsed Democratic Sheldon Whitehouse, the state's former attorney general.

After Langevin announced he would not run for Senate, Brown University political scientist Jennifer Lawless announced in April 2005 she would challenge Langevin in the primary. Lawless, who had moved to Rhode Island two years earlier, drew support from national abortion rights groups, but never a formal endorsement from EMILY's List. She ran an aggressive and negative campaign that hit Langevin hard on his abortion stance and the war in Iraq. Lawless and Langevin ran dueling television ads on abortion: Lawless's spot featured a doctor talking about rape and cited 27 votes Langevin cast "against a woman's right to choose." Langevin countered that he supports abortion rights in case of rape. Lawless also accused Langevin of not mounting stronger opposition to the Iraq war and compared Langevin to Connecticut Senator Joe Lieberman, who lost his Democratic primary in August 2006 because of his support for the Iraq war. Langevin in December 2005 voted against a proposed timetable for U.S. troop withdrawal, but said he supported the redeployment of U.S. troops from Iraq. "The big difference between me and Joe Lieberman is that Joe Lieberman voted for the war and continued to defend it, and I voted against the war and have been a constant critic," Langevin told *The Providence Journal*. Langevin raised more than double what Lawless did and he defeated her by 62%-38% in the September primary. For the first time in 149 years, Republicans failed to field a candidate in the general election. Langevin faced only independent opposition and won reelection with 73%.

★ SOUTH CAROLINA ★

South Carolina, at times beleaguered and under attack, stands proud but not untroubled, a state that has made much progress but still feels it has some distance to go. Within living memory, this state looked like an underdeveloped country. Beneath a thin veneer of rich people, it was among the poorest of states, with income levels less than half the national average and with high levels of illiteracy and disease. South Carolina was founded by planters from Barbados and even today there are reminders of the West Indies—the semitropical climate, the lush foliage and trademark palmettos, and the billions in damage from hurricanes. But economically and culturally, South Carolina is now clearly part of the booming South Atlantic region from Maryland to Florida, filling up with new retirement condominiums, time shares (it ranks number two in the country), factories and office buildings, giant shopping centers, growing robustly for two decades now though not as rapidly as its neighbors Georgia and North Carolina.

South Carolina started off with a plantation economy built on the swampy Low Country below the Fall Line, where the great 18th and 19th century planters built rice paddies and cultivated exotic crops like indigo in the days before cotton was king. The great wealth of these Low Country planters was destroyed by the Civil War which they, more than any other Southerners, provoked. But their pride and way of life continued as did that of former slaves. As late as 1940, 43% of South Carolinians were black, most living in conditions inconceivable today. South Carolina's economic growth started only in the 1920s, with that lowest-wage of industries, textiles. Mills were built in the Up Country above Columbia, hiring poor whites (never blacks) from the hardscrabble farms in the area. Politics remained a rough business, with harsh appeals to racial fear and economic envy, and with limited participation: in 1940, just 99,000 South Carolinians voted for president, 96% of them Democratic—the highest Democratic percentage in the nation. In the 1946 Democratic primary, the year Strom Thurmond was elected governor, only 271,000 people voted in a state of more than 2 million.

Now this once underdeveloped country has joined the First World. Personal incomes have risen dramatically, up toward national levels, and factory productivity rose 59%. Poverty fell sharply; health standards are as good as those in the rest of the nation. Educational achievement still lags, though not nearly so much as before, with 80% of white and 65% of black adults classified as high school graduates; homeownership is well above the national average. Back in the 1970s much of South Carolina's economy depended on the military bases clustered around Charleston and by the big textile mills around Greenville and Spartanburg. Then South Carolina became the most aggressive state in the South in attracting new industry. It advertised its business climate (the nation's lowest rates of unionization), its taxes (low), its willingness to meet local employers' needs and tax breaks—set fees in lieu of property taxes, a $300 to $1,500 job creation income tax credit. From 1960 to 1990 international investment in the state grew from $80 million to $16.4 trillion. It enticed French and German firms to set up major operations in the Piedmont and the Low Country, a process capped when BMW in 1992 built its first U.S. assembly plant off I-85 in Spartanburg, now

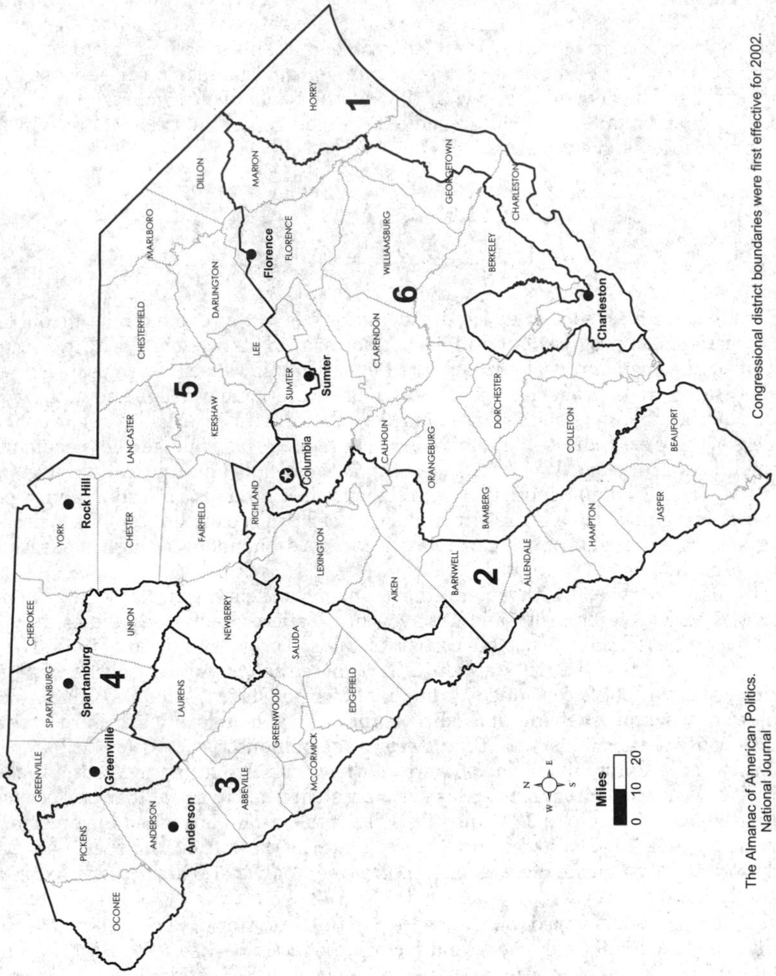

Congressional district boundaries were first effective for 2002.

The Almanac of American Politics.
National Journal

with 4,700 employees. Nearby are big Michelin and Fuji Photo plants. Vought Aircraft and Alenia Aeronautica's airplane plant in North Charleston is building aft parts of fuselages for Boeing's hugely successful 787 Dreamliner. Hilton Head and the Grand Strand around Myrtle Beach and Hilton Head bring in millions of tourists every year, and thousands of new residents, many of them affluent retirees. In Columbia, the University of South Carolina has been building a big Innovista research area in Columbia's Congaree Vista. Many of South Carolina's military bases have long since been closed, and much of the textile work has migrated elsewhere, with lower-income workers finding opportunities in the poultry industry, the number one agricultural product. This is a strong diversified economy that produces incomes only 13% below the national level—and just about at it or above when local costs of living are taken into account.

As South Carolina's economy grew, it slowly, sometimes grudgingly, overcame its heritage of slavery and racial segregation. Starting in the 1950s, fewer people were kept from voting by the poll tax, and turnout surged as South Carolina became competitive in the presidential elections of 1952, 1956 and 1960. Clemson University was peaceably desegregated during the governorship (1959-62) of Ernest Hollings; most South Carolina whites opposed integration, but not with the violence of Alabama and Mississippi. Then the Civil Rights Act of 1964 and the Voting Rights Act of 1965 ended legal segregation of public accommodations and workplaces and brought blacks suddenly into the electorate. This changed the political balance. Senator Strom Thurmond, who set a record filibustering a civil rights bill in 1957, started appointing black staffers and a black federal judge in the late 1960s and early 1970s. But politics still cleaves the electorate along racial lines: In 2004 whites voted 78%-22% for George W. Bush and blacks voted 85%-15% for John Kerry. For four years South Carolina grappled with a controversy over the Confederate battle flag, flown over the state Capitol since 1962. Successive governors—Republican David Beasley and Democrat Jim Hodges—favored taking it down; the NAACP organized a boycott of the state. Finally in May 2000 the legislature voted to fly the flag not from the Capitol, but from a 30-foot pole on the Capitol grounds, while an African-American history monument would rise nearby. The state NAACP was still not satisfied, and announced the boycott would continue.

Until the 1960s, South Carolina was an inward-looking state, with few people except military personnel moving in. That has changed as the economy has grown. Most of the newcomers are white, with conservative attitudes but less feeling for the state's ancient traditions; there have been only a few immigrants. The fastest growth in recent years has been in coastal resort areas around Hilton Head and Myrtle Beach and in suburban counties outside Columbia and just south of Charlotte, North Carolina. This growth reduced the state's black percentage to 30% in 2000, well above the national average of 12,but far below the near-majority of the 1940s. Politically, this change has helped move South Carolina toward the Republicans. But that change might not have occurred without the efforts of two individuals. One was Strom Thurmond, who had voted for Franklin D. Roosevelt at the 1932 Democratic National Convention, but who switched to the Republican party in September 1964 and provided critical votes to nominate Richard Nixon at the 1968 Republican National Convention. South Carolina voted for Barry Goldwater in 1964 and Nixon in 1968 and has only once voted for a Democrat since, Jimmy Carter in 1976, by a narrow margin. The other individual was Carroll Campbell, elected governor in 1986 and 1990, who with the aid of Lee Atwater built a Republican party capable of electing statewide officials and majorities in the legislature. In 1988 Campbell and Atwater, by then George H. W. Bush's campaign manager, set up the early Republican primary, on the Saturday before Super Tuesday, which enabled George H. W. Bush to clinch the Republican nomination that year; it did the same for Bob Dole in 1996 and, against John McCain's strong challenge, for George W. Bush in 2000. In 1989 Campbell and Atwater seemed to be Thurmond's heirs. But Atwater died of a brain tumor at 39 in 1991. In 1994 Campbell helped his protege David Beasley win the governorship. It was widely assumed that Campbell, making good money as a Washington lobbyist, would be appointed to fill Thurmond's seat if it should become vacant. But Beasley was defeated for reelection in 1998 and in 2001 Campbell announced that, at 61, he was battling Alzheimer's disease; he died in December 2005. Thurmond served out his eighth term as he had the other seven and as a United States senator celebrated his 100th birthday in December 2002.

South Carolina's other senator for years, Democrat Ernest Hollings, retired in 2004 after 38 years, 36 of them as a junior senator—a record. South Carolina politics now belongs to a new generation. The state continues to be heavily Republican, though Democrats have been competitive and cannot be counted out. But in 2002 the Republican trend continued. Former Congressman Mark Sanford, at odds with many organization Republicans, beat Hodges 53%-47%. Congressman Lindsey Graham won the race to succeed Thurmond, 54%-44%. In 2004 George W. Bush carried the state 58%-41%, Republican Congressman Jim DeMint beat Democrat Inez Tenenbaum for Hollings's Senate seat by the same margin as Graham had won in 2002, 54%-44%, and Republicans held their majority in the state Senate and gained one seat in the state House. Sanford was reelected 55%-45% in 2006 and Republicans held onto their legislative majorities. However, Sanford ran behind usual party lines in Columbia's Richland County (his skinflint ways are not popular among state employees), Republican school superintendent candidate Karen Floyd lost and Lieutenant Governor Andre Bauer almost lost.

The People		Race/Ethnic Origin			Military veterans: 420,971 (14.0%)	
Pop. 2006 (est):	4,321,249	2,652,291	66.1%	White	WWII: 16.1%	Korea: 12.0%
Pop. 2000:	4,012,012	1,178,486	29.4%	Black	Vietnam: 34.1%	Gulf War: 13.1%
Pop. 1990:	3,486,703	35,568	0.9%	Asian	**Most populous cities (2006):**	
Change 1990-2000:	Up 15.1%	12,765	0.3%	Native Am.	1. Columbia	119,961
% of U.S. total:	1.4%	1,270	0.0%	Hawaiian	2. Charleston	107,845
Pop. rank:	26th of 50	33,290	0.8%	Two+ races	3. North Charleston	87,482
Area size:	32,020 sq. mi.	3,266	0.1%	Other	4. Rock Hill	61,620
State Native:	64.0%	95,076	2.4%	Hisp. Origin	5. Greenville	57,428
Non-citizen:	1.8%	**Ancestry**				
Language		USA: 11.9%		German: 7.2%	Urban population: 60.5%	
English: 92.6%	Spanish: 4.0%	English: 7.0%		Irish: 6.8%	Rural population: 39.5%	
Other Eur.: 2.5%		Scotch-Irish: 2.5%				

Education		Work Sector			General Assembly	
H.S. Grad:	76.3%	Private: 78.1%		Govt: 15.9%	Senate	26 R 20 D
College Grad:	20.4%	Self: 5.7%		Family: 0.3%	House	73 R 51 D
Industry		Unemployment: 5.7%			Legislative Term Limits: No	
Agri: 1.1%	Con: 8.3%	**Household Income**			**Registered Voters**	
Fin: 5.6%	Info: 2.1%	<15k: 18.8%		15-35k: 28.3%	No party registration	
Mfg: 24.4%	Prof: 25.5%	35-50k: 17.6%		50-100k: 27.3%		
Public: 4.7%	Trade: 15.2%	100-150k: 5.3%		>150k: 2.8%		
Other: 13.0%		Median: $37,082				
Occupation		Poverty status: 14.1%				
Blue collar: 30.4%	White collar: 54.2%	**Home Value**				
Gray collar: 15.3%		<50k: 24.3%	50-100k: 38.3%	100-200k: 26.9%	200-300k: 6.1%	
		300-500k: 3.0%	>500k: 1.5%	Median: $83,100		

Presidential politics   In presidential general elections South Carolina is reliably Republican. It was the only Deep South state to vote for Richard Nixon over George Wallace in 1968 and since then has voted Democratic only once, for Jimmy Carter in 1976. In the 2004 general election, Democratic vice presidential candidate John Edwards did return to his hometown, Seneca, South Carolina, but took care not to linger long.

The presidential primaries are another matter: South Carolina has been important, indeed decisive, in determining the Republican nomination since 1988, and is now early on the schedule for the Democrats as well in 2008. Back in 1980 the state Republican chairman scheduled the South Carolina primary early, to help Ronald Reagan, and in 1987 Lee Atwater craftily scheduled the Republican primary here for the Saturday before Super Tuesday, a collection of mostly Southern primaries which Democrats hoped would move their party toward choosing a moderate Southerner. Instead, South Carolina moved Republicans toward choosing a moderate Southern Republican, George H.W. Bush of Texas, who won a 49%-21%-19% victory over Bob Dole and Pat Robertson, a foretaste of the Southern sweep

2004 Presidential Vote
Bush (R) 937,974   (58%)
Kerry (D) 661,699   (41%)
Nader (I) 5,520   (0%)
Other 14,705   (1%)

2004 Democratic Presidential Primary
Edwards (D) 132,660   (45%)
Kerry (D) 87,620   (30%)
Sharpton (D) 28,495   (10%)
Clark (D) 21,218   (7%)
Dean (D) 13,984   (5%)
Other 9,866   (3%)

2000 Presidential Vote
Bush (R) 786,892   (57%)
Gore (D) 566,039   (41%)
Nader (Green) 20,279   (1%)
Other 10,832   (1%)

that clinched his nomination four days later. Democrats chose their delegates by caucus; a Democratic primary would have had an electorate about 50% black and would surely have produced a victory for South Carolina native Jesse Jackson, which would not have been helpful to the party in state elections. In 1992 Bush beat Pat Buchanan 67%-26%, squashing Buchanan's claims to Southern support. Democrats held a primary the same day, which Bill Clinton won with 63% of the vote. In 1996 former Governor Carroll Campbell and Governor David Beasley led a grass-roots campaign that gave Bob Dole, after his disappointing showings elsewhere, an impressive 45%-29% victory over Buchanan: turnout was 276,000. And in 2000 Campbell and Beasley, both by then ex-governors, supported George W. Bush, as he beat John McCain 53%-42%: turnout was 573,000. Democrats chose their delegates by caucus in 1996 and 2000.

In 2004 Democrats held a primary on February 2, a week after New Hampshire, and attracted 292,000 voters, only about half of what Republicans attracted in 2000. Native son John Edwards won 45% of the vote, more than John Kerry's 30%, but perhaps not the landslide he wanted. Kerry had the endorsement of Congressman Jim Clyburn, South Carolina's most popular black politician, after Clyburn's early favorite, Dick Gephardt, dropped out. Al Sharpton hoped that a black-majority turnout would make him a contender; most voters appear to have been black, but Sharpton got only 10% of the vote. Edwards campaigned hard in South Carolina and spent little time in Oklahoma, which voted the same day; there he lost to Wesley Clark by 1,300 votes. That kept Clark in the race and gave Edwards a Southern rival who probably cost him some votes.

Presidential primaries in South Carolina are conducted and paid for by the state's two political parties, not by state government, and they can choose to hold them on different days. For 2008 the Republicans first chose February 2, the earliest date under the national party's rules and in the Atwater tradition held on a Saturday to set an example for the bunch of states voting the following Tuesday. But after Florida moved in May 2007 to schedule its primary on January 29, South Carolina Republicans responded in August 2007 by moving their primary to January 19 to protect the state's first-in-the-South status. As for the Democrats, the Democratic National Committee in August 2006 chose South Carolina as the only state allowed to hold a pre-February 5 primary except of course for New Hampshire, and South Carolina Democrats picked January 29.

But the candidates didn't wait for the date to be finally set. They started coming in more than two years before the contest. The two parties have rather different characters here. The dominant Republican party has several factions, in many ways represented by consultants Warren Tompkins (a Carroll Campbell ally for years and a Bush backer in 1988, 1992 and 2000), Richard Quinn (for John McCain in 2000 and Lindsey Graham in 2002) and Rod Shealy. John McCain in 2000 had the support of then Congressmen (and now Senator and Governor) Lindsey Graham and Mark Sanford; Graham was on board early for McCain '08, while Sanford, unpopular among Republican legislators, was keeping a low profile. Senator Jim DeMint endorsed Mitt Romney early on. Congressman Joe Wilson sided with George Allen, too early on; Allen lost his race for reelection in November 2006. The strongest political leader on the Democratic side is Congressman Jim Clyburn, now the House Majority Whip, who is widely popular among black South Carolina Democrats and white South Carolina Democrats as well. His summer Fish Fry event is a must-attend for Democratic presidential candidates.

Congressional districting

Control of the South Carolina redistricting process was split between Democratic Governor Jim Hodges and the Republican-controlled legislature. The legislature, after toying with proposals for major changes, passed in September 2001 a plan with no major changes. It expanded the black-majority 6th District, which extends from Columbia to Charleston and includes much of the Low Country and Pee Dee area, and increased its black percentage from 61% to 63%. Hodges vetoed the plan and Republicans failed to override. A three-judge federal court took over, and in March 2002 decided on a plan that smoothed out the lines considerably and reduced the black percentage in the 6th District to 57%.

110th Congress Lineup
4 R   2 D

109th Congress Lineup
4 R   2 D

Governor

Mark Sanford (R)

Elected 2002, term expires Jan. 2011, 2d term; b. May 28, 1960, Ft. Lauderdale, FL; home, Charleston; Furman U., B.A. 1983; U. of VA, M.B.A. 1988; Episcopalian; married (Jenny).

Elected Office: U.S. House of Reps., 1994-2000.

Professional Career: Real estate investor, 1988-92; Owner, Norton & Sanford real estate investment firm, 1992-2002.

Office: P.O. Box 12267, Columbia, 29211, 803-734-2100; Fax: 803-734-5167; Web site: scgovernor.com.

Election Results

2006 general	Mark Sanford (R)	601,868	(55%)
	Tommy Moore (D)	489,076	(45%)
2006 primary	Mark Sanford (R)	160,238	(65%)
	Oscar Lovelace (R)	87,043	(35%)
2002 general	Mark Sanford (R)	585,422	(53%)
	Jim Hodges (D)	521,140	(47%)

Mark Sanford, a Republican and something of a maverick, was elected governor of South Carolina in 2002. He grew up in Fort Lauderdale, the son of a heart surgeon; the family spent summers and vacations on 3,000-acre farm in Beaufort County, once known as Coosaw Plantation, and moved there permanently when Mark was 18. He graduated from high school in South Carolina and from Furman University in Greenville and the University of Virginia business school. He worked in real estate investment in New York where he met his wife, a Midwesterner; in 1992 he started a real estate investment firm in Charleston. He lives in the suburb of Sullivans Island and is perpetually tanned from windsurfing in the ocean. In 1994, 1st District incumbent Arthur Ravenel ran for governor, and Sanford, with no political experience, ran for the House. It was a family campaign, managed by his wife and financed by $100,000 of his own money. Sanford campaigned as an outsider: he pledged to serve only three terms, to take no PAC money, to vote for no tax increases and to refuse any salary increase until the budget was balanced. He finished second in the primary and then won the runoff 52%-48%. He carried the general election with 66%.

In the House Sanford voted more often than almost any other member against spending increases. He was one of the few members voting against measures passed by nearly unanimous votes and he opposed what he considered pork barrel spending, including projects in South Carolina. He spent much of late 1999 and early 2000 campaigning for John McCain across the state, as did Lindsey Graham, even though most state Republican insiders backed George W. Bush.

Back in South Carolina full-time in 2001 Sanford started running for governor. Well known and well liked in Charleston and the coast, he was unknown in the rest of the state, and he set about getting better acquainted. He was not the only Republican running. Lieutenant Governor Bob Peeler, originally from Cherokee County east of Greenville-Spartanburg, was traveling around the state in his trademark red pickup truck; he had backed George W. Bush in 2000 and was supported by most of the state Republican establishment, although former Governor Carroll Campbell endorsed Sanford. Attorney General Charlie Condon, who had won much publicity from his conservative stands on hot-button issues, had been running for the Senate, but switched abruptly to the governor race.

Their ultimate target was Governor Jim Hodges, the Democrat who had upset Republican incumbent David Beasley in 1998. Hodges was an obscure legislator whose main accomplishment was an all-day kindergarten bill. His chief plank was a lottery to pay for college scholarships, similar to Zell Miller's HOPE scholarships in Georgia, and for school construction and all-day kindergarten. Hodges played a major role in getting the legislature to vote in May 2000 to take the Confederate flag off the dome and put it up on the Capitol grounds; he also got the legislature to pass a Martin Luther King Holiday, plus a Confederate Memorial Day in May. Hodges's biggest success came when voters approved the lottery in November 2000 and it was passed by the legislature in

June 2001. His job ratings were not particularly high, and Republicans were confident they could beat "the accidental governor," as some called him, in this basically Republican state.

The three Republicans called for major changes in taxes and spending. Sanford proposed phasing out the income tax over 18 years and making up for fluctuations in revenues with a transition fund established by a sales tax on gas. He also called for school vouchers. Sanford raised more money and ran more ads than the other two. Peeler led in polls in the run up to the June 11 primary, and many expected that Condon would cut into Sanford's Low Country base. Instead, Sanford finished first with 39% of the vote, just ahead of Peeler's 38%; Condon was far behind with 16%.

Still, Sanford carried only 11 of 46 counties, and standard analysis would suggest that more of the culturally conservative Condon's votes would go to Peeler in the June 25 runoff. But the race was not defined ideologically. Peeler's strategists felt this "looks like more of a Bush-McCain thing" and that he would win if he could argue that Sanford was not a real conservative. Peeler criticized Sanford for votes on the breast cancer stamp, military housing and supporting military action; Sanford said these issues were taken out of context and were "negative." Sanford won 60%-40%.

Hodges approached the general election campaign much as Peeler had the runoff. The day after the runoff negative ads started running, spotlighting Sanford's votes in the House. Hodges played up his modest background and called Sanford a wealthy Charleston plantation owner from south Florida. But Hodges had embarrassments of his own. One of his ads attacked Sanford for having voted "against programs for disabled kids." But then it was revealed that Hodges had transferred $300,000 from the Continuum of Care for Emotionally Disturbed Children fund to the operating account for the governor's office. Hodges had also been embarrassed by his failure to keep an oft-repeated promise to block the shipment of spent plutonium to the Savannah River Site for reprocessing. Energy Secretary Spencer Abraham promised that the reprocessed fuel would be shipped out of state, but Hodges wanted a commitment in writing and in April 2002 brought a suit in federal court. This backfired: in June 2002, a week before the runoff, a federal judge ordered Hodges not to block the shipment; Hodges backed down on his promise to stand in the road in front of the convoy.

Hodges had more money, but Sanford seemed to attract more attention. Dressed usually in khakis and a plaid shirt, he talked about his plans for change and getting away from politics as usual. In November Sanford won 53%-47%. Metro Charleston and the coast, which had voted for Hodges in 1998, this time went 55%-45% for Sanford. So did metro Columbia-Aiken. The Greenville area gave Sanford a 60%-40% margin. Hodges carried the rest of the state by only 55%-45%.

As governor, Sanford continued to defy convention. He instituted an "open door at four" policy: citizens could line up to get five-minute audiences with the governor (they sometimes went longer). After the departure of his chief of staff, he brought in his wife Jenny, a former investment banker who ran her husband's campaigns, to temporarily fill the void though both denied she would be chief of staff. Sanford wondered out loud whether he should quit the Air Force Reserve, which he joined in 2002 just prior to running for governor, lest he be called to active duty; he decided to stay in and arranged that Lieutenant Governor Andre Bauer should become acting governor. He was not called up but did spend two weeks in the spring in training. In 2005, he spent two weeks in Texas training as a medical evacuation officer and missed the opening of the legislative session. He was later transferred to another unit, the Air Force's National Security Emergency Preparedness Agency.

From the legislature he asked some pretty major changes: abolishing the elective offices of secretary of state, treasurer, comptroller, adjutant general, superintendent of education and agriculture commissioner, and putting their functions under the governor; putting the state universities, accustomed to lobbying for themselves, under a single board of regents; enacting school vouchers ("education passports") for children in failing schools. Sanford managed to lower the DUI blood alcohol threshold to .08, win campaign finance changes that added more transparency and bring the Division of Motor Vehicles directly under the governor's office, but he failed to enact any of his major initiatives in his first year.

That was the beginning of a strained relationship with the Republican-controlled legislature. South Carolina's governorship is constitutionally weak and the legislature relatively strong; Sanford struggled to work within these confines. He frequently pointed out that he was the first governor in 50 years not to have come out of the legislature or state government, an observation that was obvious from his approach. After the failure of his plan in 2003 to swap a phase out of the income tax for an increase in the cigarette tax, Sanford promised to visit districts of lawmakers from both parties who did not support the plan and vetoed local issue bills that were routinely signed in the past. He angered legislators by commissioning a poll to measure his personal popularity against theirs. In 2004, Sanford again pursued an ambitious agenda, advocating tax credits for families who send their children to private schools, transfer them to another public school or home-school them. He called for worker's compensation reform, government restructuring, increasing the number of charter schools, containing health insurance costs and for a capital access program that would encourage financial institutions lend to small businesses. His tax plan drew the most attention; he proposed a 15 percent reduction in income taxes, offset by a 5-cent sales tax on lottery tickets and a 61-cent tax increase on a pack of cigarettes.

The General Assembly, primarily the Senate, again balked at his proposals. Sanford did little to placate recalcitrant legislators. He issued 106 budget vetoes to cut spending and the House overrode 105 of them. He also vetoed an economic development bill that began as the Life Sciences Act, offering tax incentives to biotech and medical research companies. Though he once supported the economic development initiative, he objected to various projects that legislators tacked onto the final bill; the legislature overwhelmingly overrode his veto. He angered legislators in the final week of the five-month legislative session by sneaking two piglets into the State House to symbolize the legislative appetite for pork. The pigs defecated on the carpet; the public, it turned out, loved the stunt. Another veto came in December, aimed at a property tax bill that would have capped valuation increases. Sanford cited the bill's unintended consequences and was applauded by the state Chamber of Commerce and the state School Boards Association.

Sanford's penchant for showmanship again surfaced in March 2005 when he brought a horse and buggy to the State House entrance to draw attention to his efforts to restructure government. "We have a system of government in this state that to a large extent is still stuck in 1895," he said. In May, he launched another round of vetoes, issuing 163 budget vetoes this time. In 2006, his battles with the legislature continued and so did the stunts: this time he stood in bank vaults across the state, holding up stacks of money, to emphasize his call for the House to rein in spending. Sanford ended up vetoing the entire budget in June—rather than utilize his line-item veto power—and legislators were faced with the dilemma of either overriding the veto or shutting down state government. They chose to override.

It was this contentious relationship that led *Time* magazine in November 2005 to name Sanford as one of the three worst governors in the nation, a stinging rebuke that listed as evidence Standard & Poor's 2005 lowering of South Carolina's bond rating, a 6.3% unemployment rate and the state's losing bid for a $500 million Airbus plant. Sanford dismissed the rating as the product of a liberal magazine; he pointed to *National Review*, a conservative publication, which had earlier described him as "one of the best new governors in the country," and to the Cato Institute, a libertarian think tank, which has also given him high ratings for his fiscal record. While little was fair about the ranking—it was accompanied by less than 200 words of explanation—and the methodology was suspect, it provided fuel to his many critics on the eve of his 2006 reelection campaign.

Sanford drew opposition in the primary from physician Oscar Lovelace, who talked about improving public education and criticized Sanford's inability to get along with the legislature. Sanford won 65%-35%, but there were troubling signs. He lost two counties, including the Republican stronghold of Lexington County where voters were angered over his veto of a bill that would have granted a license to create a new heart surgery center there. More ominously, the underfunded Lovelace had won more than one-third of the vote—more than the 28% protest vote lodged against Republican David Beasley in 1998, a precursor to Beasley's November loss to Jim Hodges. Republican hostility to Sanford still ran high weeks after the primary: State Senator Jake Knotts of Lexington County sought to get on the November ballot as a petition candidate—a maneuver which, by splitting the Republican vote, might have led to a Democratic victory—but in mid-July he dropped his bid, saying he wouldn't be able to raise the amount of money necessary to win.

The Democratic nominee was state Senator Tommy Moore of Aiken County, a veteran legislative dealmaker who touted his ability to bring people together. Sanford framed the race to the *The State* newspaper as a choice between his own outsider approach and the state's business-as-usual legislative culture. "I've not been a part of Columbia, and the way that things work around here. At times, that's been to my detriment. My competitor . . . has a 30-year tradition of working in Columbia." Moore wanted increased economic development in rural areas and focused on public education, though without much specificity. Sanford called for government restructuring, spending restraint and tax cuts and proposed school choice and merit pay for teachers. Sanford attacked Moore for accepting campaign contributions from trial lawyers while Moore criticized him for taking money from out of state interests who "want to dismantle public education."

Sanford led in the polls throughout the campaign and raised more than $8 million, far more than Moore, who raised just over $3 million; Moore wasn't able to run television ads until mid-October. On Election Day, Sanford won 55%-45%. Moore won in the Midlands and metro Columbia, but Sanford carried his Low Country base and won large margins Up Country in the Greenville and Spartanburg areas. He managed to win Lexington County 59%-41, but with a diminished margin from 2002 when he won 66%.

This was not the kind of sweeping victory that draws notice outside a state's border, but Sanford's fiscal record was popular with some national conservatives and there was still mention of him as a possible presidential candidate in 2008. Sanford vigorously denied it and made no moves in that direction. But unlike 2000, when he supported John McCain, he did not issue an early presidential endorsement. When *The Politico* asked in February 2007 whether he would accept the number two spot on the ticket, he said, "Anybody who says they wouldn't look at something of that magnitude isn't being honest."

Senior Senator

Lindsey Graham (R)

Elected 2002, seat up 2008, 1st term; b. July 9, 1955, Central; home, Seneca; U. of SC, B.A. 1977, J.D. 1981; Baptist; single.

Military Career: Air Force, 1982-88; SC Air Natl. Guard, 1989-94 (Operation Desert Storm); Air Force Reserves, 1995-present.

Elected Office: SC House of Reps., 1992-94; U.S. House of Reps., 1994-2002.

Professional Career: U.S. Air Forces Europe Circuit Trial Counsel, 1984-88; Asst. Oconee Cnty. Atty., 1988-92; Practicing atty., 1988-94; Judge Advocate, McEntire Air Natl. Guard Base, 1989-94; Central SC City Atty., 1990-94.

DC Office: 290 RSOB, 20510, 202-224-5972; Fax: 202-224-3808; Web site: lgraham.senate.gov.

State Offices: Columbia, 803-933-0112; Florence, 843-669-1505; Greenville, 864-250-1417; Mt. Pleasant, 843-849-3887; Rock Hill, 803-366-2828; Seneca, 864-888-3330.

Committees: *Agriculture, Nutrition & Forestry* (6th of 10 R): Domestic & Foreign Marketing, Inspection, & Plant & Animal Health (RMM); Energy, Science & Technology; Rural Revitalization, Conservation, Forestry & Credit. *Armed Services* (7th of 12 R): Personnel (RMM); Strategic Forces; Emerging Threats & Capabilities. *Budget* (11th of 11 R). *Judiciary* (6th of 9 R): Crime & Drugs (RMM); Administrative Oversight & the Courts; Constitution; Human Rights & the Law. *Veterans' Affairs* (4th of 7 R).

Group Ratings

	ADA	ACLU	AFS	LCV	ITIC	NTU	COC	ACU	CFG	FRC
2006	0	25	0	29	50	85	92	83	86	87
2005	20	—	0	20	—	74	83	96	72	—

National Journal Ratings

	2005 LIB	—	2005 CONS		2006 LIB	—	2006 CONS
Economic	39%	—	59%		32%	—	65%
Social	23%	—	64%		49%	—	49%
Foreign	36%	—	61%		0%	—	92%

Key Votes of the 109th Congress

1. Bar ANWR Drilling	N	5. Confirm Samuel Alito	Y	9. Limit Interstate Abortion	Y
2. FY06 Spending Curb	Y	6. Path to Citizenship	Y	10. CAFTA	N
3. Estate Tax Repeal	Y	7. Bar Same Sex Marriage	Y	11. Urge Iraq Withdrawal	N
4. Raise Minimum Wage	N	8. Stem Cell Research $	N	12. Provide Detainee Rights	N

Election Results

2002 general	Lindsey Graham (R)	600,010	(54%)	($6,213,563)
	Alex Sanders (D)	487,359	(44%)	($4,211,812)
2002 primary	Lindsey Graham (R)	unopposed		
1996 general	Strom Thurmond (R)	619,739	(53%)	($2,632,682)
	Elliott Close (D)	510,810	(44%)	($1,913,574)
	Other	30,419	(3%)	

Prior Winning Percentages: 2000 House (68%); 1998 House (100%); 1996 House (60%); 1994 House (60%)

Lindsey Graham, first elected to the House in 1994 and the Senate in 2002, is South Carolina's senior senator; Graham reached in two years a position it took his former colleague Ernest Hollings 36 years to reach. Graham grew up in Pickens County, where his parents owned a beer joint. His parents died after he went to college at the University of South Carolina; he became his younger sister's legal guardian. He was the first in his family to graduate from college, then received a master's and a law degree from the University of South Carolina, and then served in the Air Force as a prosecutor in Germany, Crete and other distant locales. In 1988 he returned home and practiced law in Seneca, the same town where former Senator John Edwards grew up; they were born in the same hospital two years apart. Graham also served as a judge advocate at McEntire Air National Guard Base. He was called up to active duty and served stateside during the Gulf War. In 1992 he was elected to the state House. He has served in the Air Force Reserves since 1995, as a senior instructor in the Air Force's JAG school and as a reserve judge on the Air Force Court of Criminal Appeals until in September 2006 the United States Court of Appeals for the Armed Services ruled it was the unconstitutional for him to serve as a judge.

In 1994, with the retirement of 20-year Congressman Butler Derrick, Graham ran for the House. Both parties had contested primaries, but the Republican contest attracted more votes—41,000 versus 35,000—and Graham won without a runoff with 52% of the vote. In the general he faced state Senator Jim Bryan. Graham called for term limits, supported more defense spending and opposed gays in the military. His attitude toward the Clinton administration and the Democratic leadership was unequivocal: "I'm one less vote for an agenda that makes you want to throw up." Graham won 60%-40%—a smashing victory in a district represented only by Democrats since Reconstruction. In the House Graham had a solidly conservative voting record but did not always support the Republican leadership. In July 1997 he helped organize the fight to overthrow Speaker Newt Gingrich. This coup soon foundered, and in a Republican Conference meeting, when Dick Armey said no member of the leadership was involved, Graham lunged to the microphone to contradict him.

As a member of the House Judiciary Committee, Graham played a major role in the impeachment of Bill Clinton. When Clinton defenders quibbled about the meaning of words and insisted that Clinton's deposition testimony was "legally accurate," Graham exploded in opposition. Yet he voted against impeaching Clinton for lying in the Paula Jones deposition, on the ground that it was later ruled immaterial by the judge. In the Senate trial Graham's folksy manner and clear description of Clinton's offenses—"Where I come from, a man who calls someone up at 2:30 in the morning is up to no good"—made him one of the most effective managers. He defied most South Carolina Republican leaders and supported John McCain in 2000 and was a tireless and highly visible supporter all over South Carolina.

Senator Strom Thurmond, reelected to his eighth term in 1996 one month before he turned 94, promised not to run again in 2002. It is not often that a Senate seat comes open in South Carolina; the last one before this was in 1941 (Thurmond and Ernest Hollings both won their seats by beating incumbent senators appointed to fill vacancies). Yet in this now heavily Republican state Graham had no opposition in the Republican primary: his work on impeachment and in the McCain campaign made him well-known and well-liked statewide. He was endorsed by three former governors and Bob Dole; Strom Thurmond added his endorsement in November 2001. Democrats portrayed him as lacking in substance, but had a hard time coming up with a candidate. Finally they found one, and an attractive one at that, Alex Sanders, president of the College of Charleston, with a colorful resume. Sanders ran off as a teenager and joined the circus, and was briefly a juggler and fire eater; in 1966 he was elected to the state House, in 1976 he was elected to the state Senate, in 1985 he was appointed to the state Court of Appeals and in 1992 he was named college president. Sanders was a folksy raconteur, gifted at telling hundreds of old stories, charming and well connected around the state.

Sanders was an active and energetic candidate. He dialed assiduously for dollars, even as he complained about being handed a script, and raised eventually $4.2 million, below Graham's $5.8

million, but a considerable achievement for a candidate who was always behind in the polls. He supported the Bush tax cuts and military action in Iraq. But he opposed the death penalty, on religious grounds. And he opposed a constitutional amendment to allow criminalization of flag burning. Graham hammered him on the death penalty and the flag amendment but most of all on his party. He said Sanders would advance the liberal agenda of Tom Daschle, Hillary Rodham Clinton and Edward Kennedy, and pointed to his contributions from Democratic celebrities. "Barbra Streisand, great singer, very liberal. My opponent is a nice guy, but he's getting Democratic support out the ying-yang." Democratic ads hit Graham for supporting individual investment accounts in Social Security. Graham stood his ground and argued that the system would be broke by 2040, when many of today's voters would be about to retire. In one of their four debates Sanders, perhaps weary of being attacked for associating with glamorous liberals, said of Graham's endorsement by Rudolph Giuliani, "He's an ultraliberal. His wife kicked him out and he moved in with two gay men and a Shih Tzu. Is that South Carolina values? I don't think so." But Sanders was put on the defensive by his own comment that South Carolinians could prove they were not racists by voting for him. Trying to explain, he said, "When I said I would show America that we are not ignorant, racist, redneck Dixiecrats, I was referring to the false stereotype many people in the North have of us in South Carolina. None of these terms are applicable to Senator Thurmond, and I most certainly was not referring to him."

Graham won 54%-44%, about the margin one might have projected from the polls. So Graham took the place of a senator first elected in the year before he was born. He has had a mostly conservative voting record but has disagreed with the Bush administration on important issues. He voted against the Medicare/prescription drug bill in June and November 2003 and in March 2005 called for annual ceilings on the program's costs. He called the medical malpractice bill "one of the worst pieces of legislation I have ever seen." He voted against it in July 2003 and February 2004 when Republicans tried to limit debate and failed. He and Richard Durbin sponsored a bill to ban punitive damages on doctors participating in Medicare and Medicaid. But he supported the class action bill that passed in February 2005 and cosponsored a bill requiring that the losing party pays the other side's legal fees in lawsuits between parties from different states. In March 2005 he proposed a federal law shielding reporters from having to disclose their sources in court.

To the surprise of some, Graham worked across the aisle with Democrats, including Hillary Rodham Clinton with he co-sponsored a bill to expand health care provision for Reservists and National Guard troops. "I readily look for opportunities to work with Democrats to solve problems important to my state and the nation. If Senator Clinton is willing to come to the middle to provide better benefits for the military, I will get a car and drive her." Graham has called for quotas on clothing imports from China and called for more aggressive trade policies toward countries that dump textiles. In February 2005 he and Charles Schumer sponsored a bill to impose a 27.5% tariff on all Chinese goods until the Chinese government revalues its currency, then tied to the dollar. They agreed to delay a vote in June 2005. In July the Chinese devalued their currency by 2% and suggested that it would periodically be adjusted; Schumer and Graham were not satisfied. They allowed a delay on the vote in September 2006, but in December said they would press the issue in the new Congress, and in March 2007 Schumer predicted that the bill would pass with a veto-proof majority.

Probably Graham's most prominent collaboration with Democrats was as part of the "Gang of 14," seven Democrats and seven Republicans who agreed in May 2005 not to filibuster judicial nominees except in "extraordinary circumstances." He voted without demur for John Roberts and predicted of Samuel Alito, "There's nothing to suggest that Alito is anything but a solid conservative judge. He's probably one of the most qualified. My belief is that during the hearings he will present himself in a very competent manner." After Democrats criticized Alito for membership in a college organization they characterized as bigoted, Graham asked Alito, "Are you really a closet bigot? No sir, you're not," at which point Alito's wife left the hearing room in tears. Graham was tougher on William Haynes, former Defense Department general counsel nominated for a seat on the Fourth Circuit Court of Appeals, which includes South Carolina. He grilled Haynes aggressively in his July 2006 hearing, and in August said, "To say the least, I have serious reservations about his nomination. This is not about being conservative. It's about being held accountable for what happened on your watch." Haynes asked that his name be withdrawn from consideration in December 2006.

Graham's disapproval of Haynes arose out of his work as a military lawyer. Like many others who have worked as military lawyers, he sought to ban procedures used in past wars but which in his view would give enemies an excuse to ignore the laws of war and would be a stain on the American character. On the NSA surveillance of communications between al Qaeda suspects abroad and persons in the United States, he said in February 2006, "When I voted for it, I never envisioned that I was giving to this president or any other president the ability to go around FISA carte blanche." He joined Judiciary Chairman Arlen Specter in urging George W. Bush to seek judicial review of the program in the FISA court. Graham was also a critic of the policy of holding unlawful combatants in Guantanamo Bay without offering them an array of rights. When the Bush administration in response to a June 2006 Supreme Court ruling proposed procedures for trying these detainees, Graham criticized them for not allowing detainees to see all the evidence against them and for defying Geneva Convention protections (though he conceded that such unlawful combatants were not entitled to full Geneva Convention protections). Working with Armed Services Chairman John Warner and his frequent ally John McCain, Graham marshaled his expertise in military law and procedure to produce a bill allowing aggressive and classified interrogation techniques, defining what is a "grave breach" of the Geneva Conventions and establishing military tribunals allowing defendants to confront the evidence against them. The bill also prohibited habeas corpus suits by detainees and left up to the Annual Review Board at Guantanamo the amount of time enemy combatants can be held when they are acquitted. In March 2007, Graham and Carl Levin traveled to Guantanamo to watch, in a nearby room on closed-circuit television the military hearing of Khalid Sheikh Mohammed, who claimed responsibility for 30 attacks.

Graham talked about Social Security's impending fiscal problems and called for changes in his 2002 campaign. In November 2003 he unveiled his own plan: 4% of the payroll tax could go to personal retirement accounts, up to $1,300, with transition costs to come from cuts in government spending. He again proposed 4% personal retirement accounts, with higher taxes for workers who do not choose them; he would also raise the income limit subject to the payroll tax. This was sharply criticized by some conservatives, but Graham persisted. He participated in private meetings with both Democratic and Republican senators, and he insisted that raising the payroll tax limit was necessary if a plan was to get Democratic support. In February 2005 he said he would hold off introducing a bill until there was a "solution mix."

On local issues, in June 2004 he put into the defense authorization a provision allowing the Savannah River Site to reclassify nuclear waste; he said this would allow the waste to be disposed of more quickly and cheaply. In February 2005, after a fatal railroad accident in South Carolina, he sponsored a rail safety bill to increase fines, require a one-year review of all rail lines and a review of all 250,000 rail crossings, with rankings of the 10,000 most in need of improvement.

In May 2006 and in June 2007 Graham supported the McCain-Kennedy and Kennedy-Kyl immigration bills, positions which got him in considerable trouble with conservatives back home. Radio talk show host Rush Limbaugh belittled him as "Lindsey Grah-amnesty" and the Greenville County Republican party voted to censure him. Graham's public comments suggesting that immigration bill opponents were "bigots" did not help his cause.

After the November 2006 election gave Democrats a majority in the Senate, Graham analyzed the results: "Rather than Democrats winning, Republicans lost. Voters didn't pick a Democratic over Republican agenda. On many fronts, Republicans confused voters about what we stand for." Of his own position he said, "I think my political profile for the last four years fits the next two years very well. I think my stock and my ability has gone up and my ability to affect public policy is as great as it ever has been." But Graham's support of Senate immigration bills and opposition to the Bush administration on treatment of unlawful combatants have led to efforts to find a primary challenger for 2008. State Treasurer Thomas Ravenel was frequently mentioned until he was forced to resign his office in July after he was indicted on charges of conspiring to distribute cocaine. Among those listed as potential primary opponents are former Congressman Thomas Hartnett and Lieutenant Governor Andre Bauer.

Junior Senator

Jim DeMint (R)

Elected 2004, seat up 2010, 1st term; b. Sept. 2, 1951, Greenville; home, Greenville; U. of TN, B.S. 1973, Clemson U., M.B.A. 1981; Presbyterian; married (Debbie).

Elected Office: U.S. House of Reps., 1998-2004.

Professional Career: Sales Rep., Scott Paper, 1973-75; Acct. Rep., Henderson Advertising, 1975-81; V.P., Leslie Advertising, 1981-84; Pres., DeMint Marketing, 1983-98.

DC Office: 340 RSOB, 20510, 202-224-6121; Fax: 202-228-5143; Web site: demint.senate.gov.

State Offices: Charleston, 843-727-4525; Columbia, 803-771-6112; Greenville, 864-233-5366.

Committees: *Commerce, Science & Transportation* (9th of 11 R): Interstate Commerce, Trade & Tourism (RMM); Oceans, Atmosphere, Fisheries & Coast Guard; Surface Transportation & Merchant Marine Infrastructure, Safety & Security; Science, Technology & Innovation; Aviation Operations, Safety & Security. *Energy & Natural Resources* (5th of 11 R): Water & Power; Energy; Public Lands & Forests. *Foreign Relations* (8th of 10 R): European Affairs (RMM); International Operations & Organizations, Democracy & Human Rights; International Development & Foreign Assistance, Economic Affairs & International Environmental Protection. *Joint Economic Committee* (10th of 10 R).

Group Ratings

	ADA	ACLU	AFS	LCV	ITIC	NTU	COC	ACU	CFG	FRC
2006	0	17	0	14	100	92	92	100	100	100
2005	5	—	0	5	—	85	89	96	100	—

National Journal Ratings

	2005 LIB	—	2005 CONS		2006 LIB	—	2006 CONS
Economic	22%	—	76%		8%	—	89%
Social	0%	—	77%		0%	—	82%
Foreign	26%	—	65%		0%	—	92%

Key Votes of the 109th Congress

1. Bar ANWR Drilling	N	5. Confirm Samuel Alito	Y	9. Limit Interstate Abortion	Y
2. FY06 Spending Curb	Y	6. Path to Citizenship	N	10. CAFTA	Y
3. Estate Tax Repeal	Y	7. Bar Same Sex Marriage	Y	11. Urge Iraq Withdrawal	N
4. Raise Minimum Wage	N	8. Stem Cell Research $	N	12. Provide Detainee Rights	N

Election Results

2004 general	Jim DeMint (R)	857,167	(54%)	($9,036,086)
	Inez Tenenbaum (D)	704,384	(44%)	($6,265,786)
	Other	35,670	(2%)	
2004 runoff	Jim DeMint (R)	154,644	(59%)	
	David Beasley (R)	106,480	(41%)	
2004 primary	David Beasley (R)	107,847	(37%)	
	Jim DeMint (R)	77,567	(26%)	
	Thomas Ravenel (R)	73,167	(25%)	
	Charlie Condon (R)	27,694	(9%)	
	Other	8,394	(3%)	
1998 general	Ernest Hollings (D)	563,296	(53%)	($4,968,456)
	Bob Inglis (R)	488,217	(46%)	($2,143,278)
	Other	17,444	(2%)	

Prior Winning Percentages: 2002 House (69%); 2000 House (80%); 1998 House (58%)

South Carolina's junior senator is Jim DeMint, a Republican elected in 2004. DeMint was born in Greenville where his father was stationed in the Air Force; when his parents divorced, his mother earned money by turning their home into a dancing school, The DeMint Academy of Dance and Decorum. He graduated from the University of Tennessee and Clemson business school, and returned to Greenville to work as a paper salesman and in his father-in-law's advertising business.

In 1983 he founded DeMint Marketing, a research firm with businesses, schools, colleges and hospitals as clients. In 1992 he went to work for Bob Inglis's House campaign in the 4th District, honing the Inglis message using focus groups and advertising expertise. Inglis upset an incumbent Democrat by 50%-48%, and kept his promise to serve only three terms. In 1998 when Inglis ran for the Senate, DeMint ran to succeed him. Like Inglis, he pledged to serve only three terms and take no PAC money. He called for a national sales tax or flat tax, for individual retirement accounts in Social Security, and for the right-to-life amendment. The favorite was state Senator Mike Fair, a former University of South Carolina quarterback. In the primary Fair led with 32%, to 23% for DeMint. In the runoff, Fair bragged about his experience, but DeMint called him a "career politician." The result was a 53%-47% upset win for DeMint. He won the general election 58%-40%.

In the House, DeMint was elected president of the freshman class and joined other junior Republicans seeking to rein in spending by the appropriators. He resisted local pressures and was the only South Carolina House member to vote for permanent normal trade relations with China, arguing that the best way to remedy human rights abuses was "to export our products and principles." The libertarian Cato Institute ranked DeMint in the top 1% of "free traders" in the House. He sponsored an amendment to Bush's education bill to create a state-based block-grant program; to preserve his bipartisan coalition, Education and the Workforce Chairman John Boehner tried to discourage DeMint. Bush, in a meeting in the Oval Office, got DeMint to back down. On Social Security, he worked to advance individual investment accounts by getting 117 House members to sign a letter of support for the Social Security commission; he filed legislation in 2003 that allowed people under age 55 to set aside 3% to 8% of their Social Security withholding to personal investment accounts. DeMint's votes on trade provoked serious opposition in his textile-producing district. In 2002, Public Service Commissioner and former state Representative Phil Bradley challenged him in the primary. Bradley had the support of textile titan Roger Milliken, long a financer of conservative and protectionist candidates. But DeMint defended his support for free trade as beneficial for international investment in the district and won 62%-38%.

In 2003, DeMint said that he would keep his promise to serve only three terms in the House and that he would run for Democrat Ernest Hollings's Senate seat in 2004. DeMint couldn't be more different than the man he sought to replace. DeMint was from South Carolina's Up Country while Hollings was a Charleston native with a Low Country political base. Hollings was one of the Senate's leading protectionists; DeMint, an unwavering free trader. Where Hollings served in a variety of elected offices over a political career that spanned more than a half-century, DeMint's public service began in 1998, when he won his first House term. DeMint soon gained the backing of White House political strategist Karl Rove; in August 2003, Hollings announced he would not seek reelection. Commenting on South Carolina's increasingly Republican electorate, Hollings said, "It wouldn't be easy for anybody who's a Democrat in this state to get elected," he said. There were three competitive challengers to DeMint in the Republican primary: former Governor David Beasley, who lost for reelection in 1998, former state Attorney General Charlie Condon, and Thomas Ravenel, a millionaire Charleston developer and son of former Congressman Arthur Ravenel.

Trade policy is a consequential issue here; South Carolina had lost nearly 70,000 manufacturing jobs since 1999. DeMint and Ravenel ran as free traders; Beasley and Condon took protectionist positions. DeMint got money from the Club for Growth. Beasley's biggest contributor was Roger Milliken and he received contributions from many textile executives and political action committees. Beasley ran ads featuring an empty textile plant and talked about how unfair trade practices sent jobs to China; he claimed DeMint advocated trade policies that had cost the state more than 50,000 jobs. A Condon ad singled out DeMint's vote to allow China into the World Trade Organization and showed Red Army soldiers. DeMint responded with ads showing the BMW manufacturing plant near Greer and pointed to increased U.S. exports to China. Beasley was ahead in polls for much of the primary, but he was not close to the 50% requirement to win the nomination outright; the real battle was for second place, which would assure a spot in the runoff two weeks later. As expected, Beasley led the primary with 37%; DeMint came in second with 26%, 4,400 votes ahead of Ravenel, who had 25%. Condon finished fourth with 9%. In the runoff, DeMint picked up endorsements from Ravenel and Condon and won support from Republican voters still unhappy over Beasley's switches while governor on the Confederate battle flag and lottery issues; he won 59%-41%.

DeMint's general election opponent was State Superintendent of Education Inez Tenenbaum, a popular Democrat who had twice won statewide election. Tenenbaum ran on her record in education: South Carolina high school students, she said, were improving their SAT scores at the fastest rate in the nation. Her signature outfits were red dresses and suits and she campaigned around the state aboard the Red Dress Express, a recreational vehicle with an image of her on its sides. She picked up where the Republican contest left off, arguing that DeMint's House votes cost the state tens of thousands of jobs. She opposed the Central American Free Trade Agreement, which DeMint supported, and she was funded by textile interests. But it was taxes that gave traction to Tenenbaum. DeMint had cosponsored a bill to replace all federal taxes with a 23% national sales tax, explaining that trade and tax policy were the paths to creating an attractive business environment in South Carolina and the nation; he repeatedly described how Daimler-Chrysler might be Chrysler-Daimler were U.S. taxes more hospitable than German ones. Tenenbaum said DeMint's advocacy for a national sales tax would result in a tax hike on 95 percent of all South Carolina residents and hammered him on the issue in ads and in staged events; his standing in the polls began to drop in the fall and he ran radio and television ads accusing Democrats of misrepresenting his position. The Democratic Senatorial Campaign Committee spent $2.5 million through September for Tenenbaum; in October, the National Republican Senatorial Committee ran a $1.3 million ad campaign to shore up DeMint.

DeMint's campaign was also sidetracked by controversy over comments he made in a campaign debate: "folks teaching in schools need to represent our values." Afterwards, he said he would not require teachers to admit whether they were gay but if they were, "I do not think they should be teaching at public schools." Two days later, he suggested that unwed pregnant women also should not teach in the public schools. Overall, DeMint spent $9 million to Tenenbaum's $6.2 million. He won 54%-44%, the same as Lindsey Graham in 2002. DeMint lost Charleston County by 100 votes, but won big margins in his Up Country home turf: 63%-35% in Greenville County and 59%-38% in Spartanburg County. As recently as 2002, South Carolina's senior and junior senators, Strom Thurmond and Ernest Hollings, had 86 years of seniority between them. With DeMint's election, the state suddenly had two first-termers with only Graham's two years between them, though each was young enough to possibly accumulate decades of experience. South Carolina now has two Republican senators for the first time since 1877.

DeMint was the most conservative senator in 2006, according to *National Journal*'s ratings, and some partisans viewed him as a rising star. He advocated that Republicans take a hard-line approach in dealing with Democrats in the Senate. Unlike Lindsey Graham, he voted against the Senate plan for comprehensive immigration reform and he was a reliable ally of the Pentagon. He has been active on communications policy, including his proposal to reduce regulation of the telecom industry.

In 2007, as chairman of the Steering Committee, the informal group of Senate conservatives, DeMint joined Tom Coburn to limit earmarks in spending bills and to require increased earmark disclosure. With Graham, he called for elimination of the income tax and replacement with an 8.5 percent sales consumption tax plus a tax on business profits. He filed a proposal to assure a secret ballot election for workers in voting on whether to unionize. Among his successes was elimination of $25 million for spinach producers during a March 2007 vote on the spending bill for Iraq. He told Columbia's *The State* newspaper that Republicans "needed a good slap in the face" and voters gave it to them in November 2006.

FIRST DISTRICT

Rep. Henry Brown (R)

Elected 2000, 4th term; b. Dec. 20, 1935, Bishopville; home, Hanahan; The Citadel; Baptist Col.; Baptist; married (Billye).

Military Career: SC Natl. Guard, 1953-62.

Elected Office: Hanahan City Council, 1981-85; SC House of Reps., 1985-00.

Professional Career: V.P., Piggly Wiggly Carolina Co., 1958-85.

DC Office: 1124 LHOB, 20515, 202-225-3176; Fax: 202-225-3407; Web site: brown.house.gov.

District Offices: Myrtle Beach, 843-445-6459; N. Charleston, 843-747-4175.

Committees: *Natural Resources* (10th of 22 R): Fisheries, Wildlife & Oceans (RMM); National Parks, Forests & Public Lands. *Transportation & Infrastructure* (14th of 34 R): Railroads, Pipelines & Hazardous Materials; Water Resources & Environment; Highways & Transit. *Veterans' Affairs* (5th of 13 R): Health.

Group Ratings

	ADA	ACLU	AFS	LCV	ITIC	NTU	COC	ACU	CFG	FRC
2006	0	5	0	8	100	55	100	84	52	100
2005	0	—	0	6	—	56	93	96	59	83

National Journal Ratings

	2005 LIB	—	2005 CONS	2006 LIB	—	2006 CONS
Economic	9%	—	88%	4%	—	94%
Social	0%	—	89%	17%	—	79%
Foreign	23%	—	77%	17%	—	73%

Key Votes of the 109th Congress

1. Estate Tax Repeal	Y	5. Limit Interstate Abortion	Y	9. Build Border Fence	Y
2. Limit CAFE Standards	Y	6. Extend Patriot Act	*	10. CAFTA	Y
3. FY06 Spending Curb	Y	7. Bar Same Sex Marriage	Y	11. Oppose Iraq Withdrawal	Y
4. Drilling in ANWR	Y	8. Stem Cell Research $	N	12. Detainee Tribunals	Y

Election Results

2006 general	Henry Brown (R)	115,766	(60%)	($606,499)
	Randy Maatta (D-WF)	73,218	(38%)	($79,774)
	Other	4,391	(2%)	
2006 primary	Henry Brown (R)	unopposed		
2004 general	Henry Brown (R)	186,448	(88%)	($205,460)
	James Dunn (Green)	25,674	(12%)	

Prior Winning Percentages: 2002 (89%); 2000 (60%)

The People		Race/Ethnic Origin	Ancestry	
Area size:	3,419 sq. mi.	73.7% White	German: 9.6%	USA: 9.3%
Urban population:	78.4%	20.9% Black	English: 8.9%	
Rural population:	21.6%	1.2% Asian	**2004 Presidential Vote**	
Pop. 2000:	668,668	0.4% Native Am.	Bush (R) 172,836	(61%)
Pop. 2005 (est):	758,235	0.1% Hawaiian	Kerry (D) 109,790	(39%)
Median income:	$40,713	1.1% Two+ races	Other 1,353	(0%)
Poverty status:	11.5%	0.1% Other	**2000 Presidential Vote**	
Military veterans:	17.2%	2.5% Hispanic Origin	Bush (R) 139,758	(59%)
			Gore (D) 91,510	(38%)
			Other 6,849	(3%)
			Cook Partisan Voting Index: R +10	
Occupation	Blue collar: 23.0%	White collar: 59.7%	Gray collar: 17.3%	

Looking out across the harbor to Fort Sumter are the glorious mansions of the Battery, gazing on the same view that the hot-blooded young swells of Charleston saw in April 1861 when they fired the shots that began the Civil War. Today there are few more beautiful urban scenes in America than the pastel "single houses" of Charleston, built flush with the sidewalk, turning their shoulders to the streets, with open piazzas inside their iron gateways facing south to catch the breeze. Charleston, founded in 1670, was blessed with one of the finest harbors on the Atlantic, at the point where, Charlestonians say, the Ashley and Cooper Rivers meet to form the Atlantic Ocean. It was one of the South's two leading cities through the Civil War; across its docks went cargoes of rice, indigo, cotton and slaves, enriching the white planters and merchants who dominated the state's economic and political life. After the Civil War, Charleston became an economic backwater, enabling the old buildings to survive; more recently, prosperity and insurance payouts after Hurricane Hugo in 1989 have funded loving restorations making the center city look better than ever and attracting a considerable tourist trade.

This old society, descended from Barbados planters and French Huguenots, Sephardic Jews and the second sons of English gentry, was once a leading force in American political life. The hotheads in the gallery disrupted the 1860 Democratic National Convention here so boisterously that it was adjourned and reconvened in Baltimore, while Southern Democrats split off and nominated their own candidate, enabling Abraham Lincoln to win with 38% of the popular vote. The local accent seems to outsiders to have a touch of New Jersey and can be incomprehensible when rapidly spoken. The history of black South Carolinians, memorialized in George Gershwin's *Porgy and Bess*, is long and noteworthy, but the tale of slavery, once hidden under a blanket of politeness, is only now emerging, as many, though not all, plantations near Charleston add programs on the history of slavery to tours once dominated by romantic tales of the old South.

Some 30 years ago, Navy and Air Force bases accounted for 20% of payrolls in metropolitan Charleston. Many of these bases are now closed, but a vibrant private economy with lots of small companies has emerged, most notably at the 1,600-acre Charleston Naval Base, where, thanks to concerted efforts by regional officials, thousands of new jobs have been created since it closed in 1996. Ninety miles northeast, Myrtle Beach has bounced back impressively from the loss of an air force base in 1991; after years in which the site sat dormant, a mix of commercial and residential development has sparked a boom in retirees and vacationers. Myrtle Beach and the Grand Strand, the miles of beachfront and 123 golf courses, attract 14 million tourists annually and the population of Horry County has more than doubled since 1980. This popular resort area has moved to rein in its visual clutter, hoping to join the rest of the Low Country as one of the most gracefully growing regions of the United States.

The 1st Congressional District of South Carolina stretches along the coast from south of Charleston to north of Myrtle Beach, including Murrells Inlet, Pawleys Island and Litchfield Beach. It includes the heavily white Battery and the area west of the Ashley River but not the heavily black areas to the north and in North Charleston; still, the 1st District's population is 21% black. It also includes the burgeoning suburbs in Berkeley and Dorchester Counties; Google plans a $600 million data center in Berkeley. This is solidly Republican country, 61% for George W. Bush in 2004. The conservatism of the Low Country district is more economic and less cultural than the conservatism of Up Country South Carolina; many voters here favor environmental restrictions and efforts to curb sprawl. This area was strong for John McCain in the 2000 presidential primary and nearly unanimous for Mark Sanford, the former local congressman, when he sought the Republican nomination in 2002, the year he was first elected governor.

The congressman from the 1st District is Henry Brown, a Republican first elected in 2000. Brown grew up on a small farm in Cordesville in Berkeley County, worked at the Charleston Naval Shipyard as his father had, and then spent almost 30 years working for the Piggly Wiggly grocery chain, where he eventually became a vice president. In 1981, at age 45, Brown was elected to the city council in Hanahan, north of North Charleston. In 1985 he was elected to the state House in a special election; after the 1994 election he became chairman of the Ways and Means Committee, where he shepherded the largest tax cut in state history. When Sanford, first elected to the House in 1994, made clear he would keep his promise to serve only three terms in the House, Brown and other Republicans started running for the seat after the 1998 election. Brown stressed issues of concern to the district's many senior citizens—property tax relief and shoring up Social Security. To boost his name recognition, he distributed 20,000 "Oh! Henry" chocolate bars. Brown won endorsements from many legislators and from Christian conservatives. Buck Limehouse, his chief opponent and a Charleston developer, spent $790,000 to Brown's $315,000 and had the support of most party leaders. In the six-candidate primary Brown led 44%-34%. In the runoff two weeks later, he won 55%-45%. In the anticlimactic general election, Brown won 60%-36%.

In the House, Brown has usually had a conservative voting record. Responding to court decisions, he sponsored a constitutional amendment to ban child pornography, and the House passed his resolution expressing support for public schools that display "God Bless America." In March 2004, he fueled a local controversy when brush that he was burning on his property, with a permit, jumped to adjacent federal lands and burned 20 acres. When the Forest Service told him that he would be fined, Brown threatened to retaliate with congressional action; after the regulators agreed to clarify a regulation, he paid a $250 fine. He has lost bids for Appropriations and Ways and Means. In 2007, he became the ranking member of the Fisheries, Wildlife and Oceans Subcommittee at Resources, which oversees aquaculture programs at Fort Johnson. On the Veterans Affairs' Committee, he brokered a deal to add a VA facility next to a Medical University of South Carolina building that is under construction; the two hospitals will share equipment. On Transportation, he helped get $81 million to connect Interstate 73 into Myrtle Beach. In 2006, Brown defeated Randy Maatta 60%-38%; Maatta criticized his support for offshore gas drilling.

SECOND DISTRICT

Rep. Joe Wilson (R)

Elected Dec. 2001, 3d full term; b. July 31, 1947, Charleston; home, Springdale; Washington & Lee U., B.A., 1969, U. of S.C., J.D., 1972; Presbyterian; married (Roxanne).

Military Career: Army Reserves, 1972-75; SC Natl. Guard, 1975-2001.

Elected Office: SC Senate, 1985-2001.

Professional Career: Practicing atty., 1972-2001.

DC Office: 212 CHOB, 20515, 202-225-2452; Fax: 202-225-2455; Web site: joewilson.house.gov.

District Offices: Beaufort, 843-521-2530; West Columbia, 803-939-0041.

Committees: *Armed Services* (14th of 29 R): Air & Land Forces; Military Personnel; Seapower & Expeditionary Forces. *Education & Labor* (10th of 22 R): Workforce Protections (RMM); Early Childhood, Elementary & Secondary Education. *Foreign Affairs* (14th of 23 R): Europe; Middle East & South Asia.

Group Ratings

	ADA	ACLU	AFS	LCV	ITIC	NTU	COC	ACU	CFG	FRC
2006	5	5	0	0	86	65	91	91	67	100
2005	0	—	0	0	—	67	93	100	93	100

National Journal Ratings

	2005 LIB	—	2005 CONS	2006 LIB	—	2006 CONS
Economic	3%	—	94%	3%	—	97%
Social	0%	—	89%	8%	—	91%
Foreign	11%	—	86%	6%	—	86%

Key Votes of the 109th Congress

1. Estate Tax Repeal	Y	5. Limit Interstate Abortion	Y	9. Build Border Fence	Y
2. Limit CAFE Standards	Y	6. Extend Patriot Act	Y	10. CAFTA	Y
3. FY06 Spending Curb	Y	7. Bar Same Sex Marriage	Y	11. Oppose Iraq Withdrawal	Y
4. Drilling in ANWR	*	8. Stem Cell Research $	N	12. Detainee Tribunals	Y

Election Results

2006 general	Joe Wilson (R)	127,811	(63%)	($848,938)
	Michael Ellisor (D)	76,090	(37%)	
2006 primary	Joe Wilson (R)	unopposed		
2004 general	Joe Wilson (R)	181,862	(65%)	($944,659)
	Michael Ellisor (D)	93,249	(33%)	($12,990)
	Other	4,447	(2%)	

Prior Winning Percentages: 2002 (84%); 2001 (73%)

The People		Race/Ethnic Origin	Ancestry		
Area size:	5,237 sq. mi.	68.0% White	German: 10.0%	USA: 9.9%	
Urban population:	66.0%	26.2% Black	English: 7.9%		
Rural population:	34.0%	1.1% Asian	**2004 Presidential Vote**		
Pop. 2000:	668,668	0.3% Native Am.	Bush (R)	174,340	(60%)
Pop. 2005 (est):	737,272	0.0% Hawaiian	Kerry (D)	114,253	(39%)
Median income:	$42,915	0.9% Two+ races	Other	1,604	(1%)
Poverty status:	11.0%	0.1% Other	**2000 Presidential Vote**		
Military veterans:	15.1%	3.3% Hispanic Origin	Bush (R)	145,953	(58%)
			Gore (D)	97,985	(39%)
			Other	6,374	(3%)
			Cook Partisan Voting Index: R + 9		

Occupation   Blue collar: 22.6%   White collar: 63.1%   Gray collar: 14.3%

In 1786, soon after the Revolutionary War, the South Carolina legislature decided to move the state's capital away from the Charleston aristocracy and into the Up Country interior, away from a city named after a king to a new city named after a discoverer of America: so began Columbia. The

State House was built on high ground above the Congaree River in a town of one-and-a-half story houses with first floor porticoes, dormers and raised brick basements—"Columbia cottages." In 1865, General William Tecumseh Sherman's army burned almost everything here but the State House. Columbia recovered, but grew slowly, with state government and the university, the Army's Fort Jackson and local insurance companies providing steady employment. Manufacturing boomed in the 1970s and again in recent years, making Columbia a confident city, not just a village-capital. For a time, Columbia's politics was personified by Jimmy Byrnes, the Democrat who returned from top posts in Franklin D. Roosevelt's Washington to serve as governor and lament the *Brown v. Board of Education* decision in 1954. Since then, upwardly mobile South Carolinians, transplanted from underdeveloped rural areas to comfortable two-car-garage subdivisions, turned Republican, first in national and then in state and local elections. The Metro Columbia area has been mostly Republican: the increasing black percentage in Columbia's Richland County has helped Democrats carry it, but faster-growing Lexington County across the river has remained heavily Republican.

The 2d Congressional District of South Carolina includes most of metro Columbia, except for black neighborhoods in northern and western Columbia and the southern and eastern parts of Richland County that are in the black-majority 6th District. It contains the city's affluent white neighborhoods and the spread-out towns of Richland and Lexington Counties, with their shopping centers, churches and the Army's huge training center, Fort Jackson. The district extends south, taking in Barnwell County, which includes half of the Savannah River Site, one of the nation's nuclear weapons manufacturing complexes and still the site of a landfill for low-level nuclear waste; it takes in horse farm country around Aiken and several lightly populated, low-income, black-majority rural counties. The 2d also includes fast-growing Beaufort County on the coast, with the old county seat of Beaufort, the carefully manicured developments of Hilton Head Island and the Marine Corps's Parris Island training base and air station. This part of the district distinctively blends old and new: Beaufort's wonderful mansions and evocative Spanish moss provided the backdrop for the prose of Pat Conroy and the 1983 movie *The Big Chill*, while the posh condominium developments and golfing resorts around Hilton Head and the Sun City Hilton Head development helped drive up Beaufort County's population by 57% from 1990 to 2004, including a five-fold increase in Mexican immigrants—the state's highest growth rate. Neighboring Jasper County is less developed, but local officials expect a population surge of retirees and snowbirds. On nearby St. Helena Island slaveowners, hating the heat and mosquitoes, ran largely absentee operations, thus allowing Gullah culture—a fusion of English and African elements—to thrive. The current lines of the 2d make the district 26% black—enough to whittle down but not jeopardize its Republican margins. George W. Bush won 60% of the vote here in 2004.

The congressman from the 2d District is Joe Wilson, a Republican first chosen in a December 2001 special election. Wilson grew up in Charleston and graduated from Washington and Lee and the University of South Carolina law school. He worked as aide to 2d District Congressman Floyd Spence and Senator Strom Thurmond and was deputy general counsel at the Energy Department in the Reagan administration. He practiced law in West Columbia for 25 years and worked on many campaigns; in 1984, he was elected to the state Senate, where he chaired the Transportation Committee. He retired as a lawyer in the Army National Guard and his four sons all have been Eagle Scouts and served in the military; one has been an intelligence officer in Iraq. In 2001, when Spence died after more than 30 years in the House and after serving six years as chairman of the Armed Services Committee, Wilson became the frontrunner to replace his longtime ally and pledged to continue his focus on national defense. He won the Republican primary with 76% of the vote and defeated his Democratic opponent 73%-25%.

In the House, Wilson followed Spence to Armed Services and has had a mostly conservative voting record. He advocated a closer military relationship with India in the war on terrorism and he became co-chairman of the Caucus on India and Indian Americans. He joined most other Carolina Republicans in opposing trade promotion authority, but Wilson voted for CAFTA and was an early supporter of the Bush proposal to eliminate double taxation of dividends. On the Education and the Workforce Committee, where he has become ranking member of the Workforce Protections Subcommittee, he got the House to pass a bill to expand college loan forgiveness for math, science and special education teachers who work in impoverished areas. He has worked with Democrats to make permanent the child adoption tax credit.

Wilson, who makes an annual five-day bus tour across his district, has not faced a serious challenge for reelection. When he demanded in April 2004 that John Kerry apologize for criticizing soldiers in Vietnam in 1971 former senator Max Cleland said that Wilson was part of the "chicken hawks" who never went to war. Wilson attacked the name-calling and Kerry's accusation that the military was "complicit in war crimes." He strongly supported President Bush and Defense Secretary Donald Rumsfeld on Iraq.

THIRD DISTRICT

Rep. Gresham Barrett (R)

Elected 2002, 3d term; b. Feb. 14, 1961, Westminster; home, Westminster; The Citadel, B.S. 1983; Baptist; married (Natalie).

Military Career: Army, 1983-87.

Elected Office: SC House of Reps., 1996-2002.

Professional Career: Furniture store owner, 1987-96.

DC Office: 439 CHOB, 20515, 202-225-5301; Fax: 202-225-3216; Web site: barrett.house.gov.

District Offices: Aiken, 803-649-5571; Anderson, 864-224-7401; Greenwood, 864-223-8251.

Committees: *Budget* (2d of 17 R). *Financial Services* (20th of 33 R): Oversight & Investigations; Capital Markets, Insurance & Government Sponsored Enterprises; Financial Institutions & Consumer Credit. *Foreign Affairs* (16th of 23 R): Middle East & South Asia. *Standards of Official Conduct* (3d of 5 R).

Group Ratings

	ADA	ACLU	AFS	LCV	ITIC	NTU	COC	ACU	CFG	FRC
2006	10	0	0	8	86	76	93	96	78	100
2005	0	—	0	6	—	71	85	100	95	100

National Journal Ratings

	2005 LIB	—	2005 CONS		2006 LIB	—	2006 CONS
Economic	0%	—	97%		25%	—	74%
Social	0%	—	89%		0%	—	94%
Foreign	15%	—	84%		17%	—	73%

Key Votes of the 109th Congress

1. Estate Tax Repeal	Y	5. Limit Interstate Abortion	Y
2. Limit CAFE Standards	Y	6. Extend Patriot Act	Y
3. FY06 Spending Curb	Y	7. Bar Same Sex Marriage	Y
4. Drilling in ANWR	Y	8. Stem Cell Research $	N

9. Build Border Fence	Y
10. CAFTA	Y
11. Oppose Iraq Withdrawal	Y
12. Detainee Tribunals	Y

Election Results

2006 general	Gresham Barrett (R)	111,882	(63%)	($857,922)
	Lee Ballenger (D)	66,039	(37%)	($27,891)
2006 primary	Gresham Barrett (R)	unopposed		
2004 general	Gresham Barrett (R)	unopposed		($647,828)

Prior Winning Percentages: 2002 (67%)

The People		Race/Ethnic Origin	Ancestry	
Area size:	5,568 sq. mi.	76.0% White	USA: 15.0%	Irish: 8.0%
Urban population:	50.3%	20.5% Black	English: 7.3%	
Rural population:	49.7%	0.6% Asian	**2004 Presidential Vote**	
Pop. 2000:	668,669	0.2% Native Am.	Bush (R) 169,283	(66%)
Pop. 2005 (est):	697,985	0.0% Hawaiian	Kerry (D) 86,947	(34%)
Median income:	$36,092	0.7% Two+ races	Other 1,986	(1%)
Poverty status:	13.3%	0.1% Other	**2000 Presidential Vote**	
Military veterans:	13.5%	1.9% Hispanic Origin	Bush (R) 142,414	(63%)
			Gore (D) 77,694	(34%)
			Other 5,185	(2%)
			Cook Partisan Voting Index: R +14	

Occupation	Blue collar: 36.8%	White collar: 48.7%	Gray collar: 14.5%

The South Carolina Up Country, many days' travel by wagon from the Low Country plantations, was first settled by Scots-Irish farmers, including the family of John C. Calhoun around the time of the Revolutionary War. The pioneers wanted to make big plantations of these forests, but the land was too hilly for the labor-intensive rice crops grown in the Low Country and sometimes too cold for cotton. So relatively few slaves were brought here, and the land became mostly small farms owned by whites. Today, the racial and cultural tone of Up Country South Carolina shows traces of these roots. This is a mostly white part of the South, with a hell-of-a-fella tone to daily life and a tradition-minded slice of Middle America. Yet even this area has been touched by change. Aiken, with its horsey trappings for polo and steeplechase, has long attracted affluent transplants. The nearby Savannah River Site—a 310-square-mile federal weapons plant complex that for four decades produced tritium and plutonium that fueled America's nuclear arsenal—employed genera-tions of highly trained engineers (and produced nuclear waste), but more than 12,000 have been laid off; with federal support, local leaders plan to convert plutonium to mixed-oxide fuel there. Today, Interstate 85—once the Main Street of America's textile belt—sits amidst a booming southeastern corridor that runs from Raleigh-Durham to Atlanta. Clemson University, founded here by Calhoun's son-in-law and one of the state's two land-grant institutions, has helped attract European companies seeking sites for big plants.

The 3d Congressional District of South Carolina follows the Georgia border north from the Savannah River Site through the tree-harvesting country around McCormick County to mountains along the North Carolina border. The southern part of the 3d has a few heavily black areas, like Edgefield County, where Strom Thurmond grew up and first won public office in the 1930s; Edgefield County has grown significantly as it became part of the metropolitan area around Aiken and Augusta, Georgia. This part of South Carolina, ancestrally Democratic, began trending Repub-lican in the 1950s, first in Yankified Aiken, then in the Up Country as cultural issues became more important in this fervently religious area. The 3d has consistently voted Republican even when Democrats have won statewide elections. In 2004 George W. Bush won 66% of the vote here, his best showing in a South Carolina district.

The congressman from the 3d District is Gresham Barrett, a Republican first elected in 2002. Barrett grew up in Westminster in Oconee County and graduated from The Citadel in Charleston. After serving as an artillery captain in the First Cavalry Division at Fort Hood, he returned home to run his family's furniture store. In 1996 he was elected to the state House. In 2001 when Lindsey Graham, the first Republican to hold this seat since Reconstruction, started running for the Senate, Barrett became the frontrunner to succeed him. He opposed abortion, defended gun owner rights, called for a national missile defense system and new weapons technology as part of the effort to "hunt down scum like Osama bin Laden and wipe their kind from the face of the Earth." He told voters that government should operate more like a business—his business, specifically. Govern-ment should work "like Barrett's Furniture, where you get service, you get simplicity and people are there to help you." With a superior grass roots organization, he led the six-candidate primary with 43% of the vote. In the two-week runoff campaign, state Representative Jim Klauber argued that Barrett wasn't tough enough in cracking down on illegal immigrants; Barrett insisted that military issues were paramount. Barrett raised more money, won more endorsements and won the runoff 65%-35%. He won the general election 67%-31%.

In the House, Barrett hoped for a seat on Armed Services but instead got Budget, Ethics and Financial Services. Ever the Citadel graduate (his father, brother and two nephews are also grads), he drew attention for his crisp, military bearing. "With his pressed suits and posture as perfect as the Washington Monument's, Gresham Barrett is perhaps Congress' most starched member," wrote *The State* newspaper. Barrett joined the Republican Study Committee and had a conservative voting record, especially on cultural issues, with occasional maverick tendencies; he was one of the 15 House Republicans who voted against both the Medicare deal and the omnibus appropriations bill in late 2003. The House passed his amendment for the Energy Department to study the feasibility of commercial nuclear energy production at Savannah River. He has called for a Taxpayer Bill of Rights "to ensure that Washington will become more efficient and accountable to the taxpayers that pay for it." In 2006, he opposed expanded trade with Haiti because it would permit duty-free Chinese fabrics to the United States. He was the only lawmaker from South Carolina to vote against extension of the Voting Rights Act. He filed the Public Prayer Protection Act to permit public officials to pray in public as they see fit.

Barrett is safe in this district. He has expressed interest in running for governor in 2010, when Mark Sanford is term-limited.

FOURTH DISTRICT

Rep. Bob Inglis (R)

Elected 2004, 5th term; b. Oct. 11, 1959, Bluffton; home, Travelers Rest; Duke U., B.A. 1981, U. of VA Law Schl., J.D. 1984; Presbyterian; married (Mary Anne).

Elected Office: U.S. House of Reps., 1992-98.

Professional Career: Practicing atty., 1984-92.

DC Office: 330 CHOB, 20515, 202-225-6030; Fax: 202-226-1177; Web site: inglis.house.gov.

District Offices: Greenville, 864-232-1141; Spartanburg, 864-582-6422; Union, 864-427-2205.

Committees: *Foreign Affairs* (21st of 23 R): Europe; Middle East & South Asia. *Science & Technology* (13th of 20 R): Energy & Environment (RMM).

Group Ratings

	ADA	ACLU	AFS	LCV	ITIC	NTU	COC	ACU	CFG	FRC
2006	15	27	0	42	86	72	87	84	81	71
2005	5	—	0	28	—	67	85	80	82	85

National Journal Ratings

	2005 LIB	—	2005 CONS	2006 LIB	—	2006 CONS
Economic	38%	—	60%	34%	—	65%
Social	23%	—	76%	45%	—	55%
Foreign	40%	—	58%	46%	—	53%

Key Votes of the 109th Congress

1. Estate Tax Repeal	Y	5. Limit Interstate Abortion	Y	9. Build Border Fence	Y
2. Limit CAFE Standards	Y	6. Extend Patriot Act	Y	10. CAFTA	Y
3. FY06 Spending Curb	Y	7. Bar Same Sex Marriage	Y	11. Oppose Iraq Withdrawal	Y
4. Drilling in ANWR	N	8. Stem Cell Research $	N	12. Detainee Tribunals	Y

Election Results

2006 general	Bob Inglis (R)	115,553	(64%)	($397,946)
	William Griffith (D)	57,490	(32%)	($53,481)
	Other	6,888	(4%)	
2006 primary	Bob Inglis (R)	unopposed		
2004 general	Bob Inglis (R)	188,795	(70%)	($511,913)
	Brandon Brown (D)	78,376	(29%)	($15,778)
	Other	3,273	(1%)	

Prior Winning Percentages: 1996 (71%); 1994 (73%); 1992 (50%)

The People		Race/Ethnic Origin	Ancestry	
Area size:	2,165 sq. mi.	74.6% White	USA: 13.7%	English: 8.0%
Urban population:	73.5%	19.7% Black	Irish: 7.5%	
Rural population:	26.5%	1.3% Asian	**2004 Presidential Vote**	
Pop. 2000:	668,669	0.2% Native Am.	Bush (R) 181,255	(65%)
Pop. 2005 (est):	706,004	0.0% Hawaiian	Kerry (D) 94,760	(34%)
Median income:	$39,417	0.8% Two+ races	Other 3,232	(1%)
Poverty status:	11.4%	0.1% Other	**2000 Presidential Vote**	
Military veterans:	12.8%	3.2% Hispanic Origin	Bush (R) 151,975	(64%)
			Gore (D) 78,449	(33%)
			Other 5,843	(2%)
			Cook Partisan Voting Index: R +15	

Occupation	Blue collar: 30.8%	White collar: 56.0%	Gray collar: 13.2%

A century ago, Northern investors seeking sites for textile mills looked at the Up Country of South Carolina and found what was described then as "mild climate, abundant water power, proximity to the cotton fields and plenty of native [white] labor already accustomed to a low standard of living."

As mills fled New England, textile factories settled along the Southern Railway and Seaboard Coast Line tracks between Charlotte and Atlanta, especially in the Piedmont of South Carolina. The textile country might look bucolic, but Greenville, Spartanburg and the dozens of mill towns thick in the surrounding countryside became as industrial as Lancashire or the Ruhr, with mills rising up on what were once twisting woodland paths. In the days before child labor laws, factory work sometimes began at age six, condemning workers to a life of illiteracy; escapes to a brighter future, such as the brilliant but brief baseball career of West Greenville's Shoeless Joe Jackson, were rare.

Today, this same stretch of land along Interstate 85, which parallels the Southern Railway, remains one of the largest textile-producing areas in the United States, even though many mills have shut down and others are not likely to survive. But there is much more to the local economy than textiles. Although more than 30,000 textile and apparel jobs have been lost since 2000, with closings accelerated by the end of the Multifiber Agreement in 2005, many of those workers have taken jobs with the new companies that have moved in. So many other jobs have been created that the South Carolina Textile Manufacturers Alliance dropped "Textiles" from its name. Financial sweeteners, tax incentives, the absence of unions and solid infrastructure—airports, interstate highways, and the busy port of Charleston—have attracted an enormous BMW plant, the American headquarters of Michelin and a big Fuji Photo factory, among many others. Greenville's revitalized downtown now boasts fancy hotels and restaurants, including Korean, Thai and Vietnamese cuisine—each catering to the new corporate manager class.

The 4th Congressional District of South Carolina includes all of Greenville and Spartanburg Counties, plus much smaller Union County and a sliver of Laurens County. Culturally, the 4th ranges from conservative to very conservative, with strong influence from Greenville's many evangelical and fundamentalist churches. Bob Jones University is here; it has dropped its longtime ban on interracial dating but students are still prohibited from smoking, drinking, dancing and wearing jeans or shorts to class. Large new subdivisions have sprouted between Greenville and Spartanburg. Newcomers to the area have brought religious diversity. Greenville has growing populations not only of Catholics and Jews, but also Muslims, Buddhists, Hindus, Baha'is, and the only gay-oriented church within 60 miles. Still, this is a heavily Republican district, with the smallest black percentage in the state, and George W. Bush won 65% of the vote here in 2004. Here the real political divide is between religious and economic conservatives.

The congressman from the 4th District once again is Bob Inglis, who was elected in 2004 after having served from 1993 to 1999. He grew up in the Low Country, excelled at Duke and the University of Virginia law school and moved to Greenville to practice commercial law. He ran for the House against a Democratic incumbent in 1992 and pledged to serve only three terms, to take no money from political action committees and to oppose pork barrel projects even in South Carolina; he won 50%-48%. In the House, Inglis kept his promises. His calls for change went mostly unheeded in his first term, but when Republicans won the House they voted to apply all laws to Congress, cut staff and passed a gift ban. He resisted joining the Washington culture and slept in his office on an air mattress. In 1998 he ran against Senator Ernest Hollings and lost 53%-46%. He returned to practice law, specializing in commercial real estate and corporations.

In 2004, Inglis traded places with Jim DeMint, his House successor, who honored his own term-limits pledge and was elected to the Senate as Hollings retired. Inglis again ran as a citizen-politician, saying he was "reinvigorated" by his time in private life. But this time he refused to make another term limits pledge, which he said would be "unilateral disarmament" for local interests. He suggested that the Capitol Hill culture had changed, so that the same strategies that made sense after Republicans captured the House majority in 1994 no longer were required. Ever the budget hawk, Inglis enlisted his wife as his top campaign aide, eschewed political consultants, ran his race out of his home and refused PAC contributions. By getting an early start and raising large amounts of money, he scared off serious competition. He won 84% of the vote in the Republican primary. In November, he defeated funeral home executive Brandon Brown, 70%-29%. With two junior Republicans holding Senate seats, he settled in for what seemed to be a long career in the House. He was reassigned to the Judiciary Committee, with his accrued seniority, where he was a leader in opposing mandatory minimum sentences. On the Science Committee, he became ranking Republican on the Energy and Environment Subcommittee. His voting record moved toward the center from the more conservative stance that he took earlier, including opposition to oil drilling in the Arctic National Wildlife Refuge and renewal of rules for warrantless electronic surveillance. He joined a congressional delegation to Antarctica where scientific research convinced him of the risk of global warming. During his initial tenure, he told *The Greenville News*, "I just sort of reeked of sanctimony." No more, he pledged.

Inglis had an easy reelection in 2006. But his February 2007 support of the Democratic resolution opposing the military surge in Iraq, which he called "a vote of conscience," caused anger among many Republicans at home, including the chairman of the state party and some county leaders. Lieutenant Governor Andre Bauer and several other lawmakers were mentioned as possible primary challengers in 2008.

FIFTH DISTRICT

Rep. John Spratt (D)

Elected 1982, 13th term; b. Nov. 1, 1942, Charlotte, NC; home, York; Davidson Col., A.B. 1964, Oxford U., M.A. 1966, Yale U., LL.B. 1969; Presbyterian; married (Jane Stacy).

Military Career: Army Operations, U.S. Dept. of Defense, 1969-71.

Professional Career: Practicing atty., 1971-82; Pres., Bank of Ft. Mill, 1973-82; Pres., Spratt Insurance Agcy., 1973-82.

DC Office: 1401 LHOB, 20515, 202-225-5501; Fax: 202-225-0464; Web site: www.house.gov/spratt.

District Offices: Darlington, 843-393-3998; Rock Hill, 803-327-1114; Sumter, 803-773-3362.

Committees: *Armed Services* (2d of 34 D): Air & Land Forces; Oversight & Investigations; Strategic Forces. *Budget* (Chmn. of 22 D).

Group Ratings

	ADA	ACLU	AFS	LCV	ITIC	NTU	COC	ACU	CFG	FRC
2006	75	55	100	92	50	12	50	44	13	42
2005	90	—	100	89	—	14	52	12	3	15

National Journal Ratings

	2005 LIB	—	2005 CONS	2006 LIB	—	2006 CONS
Economic	72%	—	26%	71%	—	28%
Social	63%	—	36%	56%	—	44%
Foreign	58%	—	41%	57%	—	42%

Key Votes of the 109th Congress

1. Estate Tax Repeal	N	5. Limit Interstate Abortion	Y	9. Build Border Fence	Y
2. Limit CAFE Standards	N	6. Extend Patriot Act	Y	10. CAFTA	N
3. FY06 Spending Curb	N	7. Bar Same Sex Marriage	Y	11. Oppose Iraq Withdrawal	Y
4. Drilling in ANWR	N	8. Stem Cell Research $	Y	12. Detainee Tribunals	Y

Election Results

2006 general	John Spratt (D)	99,669	(57%)	($2,665,535)
	Ralph Norman (R)	75,422	(43%)	($1,431,802)
2006 primary	John Spratt (D)	unopposed		
2004 general	John Spratt (D)	152,867	(63%)	($757,151)
	Albert Spencer (R)	89,568	(37%)	($1,215)

Prior Winning Percentages: 2002 (86%); 2000 (59%); 1998 (58%); 1996 (54%); 1994 (52%); 1992 (61%); 1990 (100%); 1988 (70%); 1986 (100%); 1984 (92%); 1982 (68%)

The People		Race/Ethnic Origin	Ancestry	
Area size:	7,141 sq. mi.	64.1% White	USA: 14.8%	Irish: 5.6%
Urban population:	46.7%	32.2% Black	English: 5.6%	
Rural population:	53.3%	0.5% Asian	**2004 Presidential Vote**	
Pop. 2000:	668,668	0.6% Native Am.	Bush (R) 143,001	(57%)
Pop. 2005 (est):	707,115	0.0% Hawaiian	Kerry (D) 104,850	(42%)
Median income:	$35,416	0.7% Two+ races	Other 2,471	(1%)
Poverty status:	15.2%	0.1% Other	**2000 Presidential Vote**	
Military veterans:	13.0%	1.8% Hispanic Origin	Bush (R) 119,052	(55%)
			Gore (D) 93,637	(43%)
			Other 3,979	(2%)
			Cook Partisan Voting Index: R + 6	

Occupation   Blue collar: 37.5%   White collar: 48.5%   Gray collar: 14.1%

Some of the fiercest battles of the Revolutionary War were fought in South Carolina's Up Country, on hilly lands just being settled by Scots-Irish farmers moving up from the Low Country or down the Virginia Piedmont valley. This was a country of violent passions and unclear lines; Carolinians have long argued over which side of the North and South Carolina boundary Andrew Jackson was born in 1767. Ever since, the fighting spirit and Calvinist faith of Up Country Carolinians have never wavered. This "Olde English District" remains intensely religious and pro-military. But it is no longer impoverished. For many years, the dominant industry here was textiles, traditionally the first factory enterprise of industrializing countries, with low pay and poor working conditions. But in the 1980s and 1990s the number of textile jobs declined, and small business prosperity more recently has been barreling out the interstates from Greenville-Spartanburg and Columbia and Charlotte, to transform counties once dependent on tobacco fields and textile mills.

The 5th Congressional District of South Carolina consists of all or part of 14 counties, mostly in the Up Country. It includes fast-growing (up 17% from 2000 to 2006) York County, part of the Charlotte, North Carolina, metro area; growth accelerated here after settlement of the Catawba Indians' land claims in 1993. Just to the east is Lancaster County, where Del Webb's Sun City Carolina Lakes has plans for a retirement community of more than 3,600 new homes. Further east, the 5th includes Dillon County, site of the pink, orange and turquoise South of the Border tourist attraction heralded on 250 billboards on I-95, and Darlington, site of the Southern 500 stock car race every Labor Day. It also includes lowland tobacco country, including Marlboro and Chesterfield Counties. Politically, this homeland of Andrew Jackson is ancestrally Democratic. But Republicans are now competitive if not dominant here: the tobacco counties are heavily Democratic but York County is trending Republican. George W. Bush won 55% of the districtwide vote in 2000 and 57% in 2004.

The congressman from the 5th District is John Spratt, chairman of the House Budget Committee, a Democrat first elected in 1982. He comes from a prominent York County family and graduated from Davidson College, Oxford University and Yale Law School. He served two years in the Army, in the Operations Analysis Group in the office of the Pentagon comptroller. He first got involved in politics in Charles Ravenel's unsuccessful 1974 campaign for governor. In 1982 the 5th District incumbent announced his retirement a week before the filing deadline; Spratt put a campaign together fast and won 38% in the primary, 55% in the runoff against a high-spending candidate, and 68% in the general. And so a quickly improvised campaign a quarter-century ago has led to a long political career and has produced a member with a key role in shaping national legislation.

Spratt is the second-ranking Democrat on the Armed Services Committee. In the 1980s, he worked with Chairman Les Aspin and, in his thick Carolina accent and with impressive knowledge of details, stitched together compromises on the MX missile, binary nerve gas weapons, the Strategic Defense Initiative, and the Savannah River Site and other nuclear plants—keeping military projects flowing through the House, many of whose members were constantly looking to cut military spending. In the late 1990s Spratt was the House Democrats' lead man on missile defense; his amendment on the subject prevailed in February 1995 by 218-212, the first significant defeat of a Contract with America promise in the Republican House. Later he called for development of missile defense, but warned against hasty departure from the ABM treaty. After George W. Bush abrogated the treaty, Spratt moved in May 2004 to shift money from ballistic missile defense to theater defenses against tactical missiles, like the Navy's Area Missile Defense system and the Patriot missiles; that was defeated.

On the Iraq war resolution, Spratt played a key role for House Democrats. In September 2002, after Bush's speech at the United Nations, Minority Leader Dick Gephardt turned to Spratt and Ike Skelton, ranking Democrat on Armed Services, for help in drafting an alternative to the broad White House resolution authorizing the use of force. Spratt sought another round of weapons inspections and wanted Bush to ask for U.N. approval and suggested removing a phrase authorizing any action to ensure peace and security in the region; the administration agreed to delete it. He sought advice from Anthony Zinni, Joseph Hoar and other retired generals with experience in the region, and found that they were wary of military action against Iraq. When Gephardt went to the White House and agreed on a resolution, Spratt continued to prepare a Democratic alternative, working with Minority Whip Nancy Pelosi. He saw "no need to invoke preemptive intervention or to draw a tenuous connection between Iraq and Al Qaeda." His resolution authorized military action if the UN approved and left room for the administration to seek another resolution from Congress if the UN did not approve. "Iraq's defiance of Security Council resolutions is enough to warrant force, particularly if it does not comply with a new, tougher round of arms inspections," Spratt said, but he also argued that it was worth getting approval from others. He offered his resolution as an amendment and it was defeated 270-155; Democrats favored it 147-60 but Republicans opposed it 210–8. Spratt joined the majority and voted for the resolution sponsored by the administration and Gephardt, which passed 296-133. After the 2002 election, Gephardt stepped down and Pelosi was elected minority leader; one of her first acts was to appoint Spratt assistant to the leader and name him her designee on budget issues. Spratt in turn agreed to be a team player, and Pelosi could argue that Democratic budget policy was being driven by a member with a deserved reputation as a moderate.

Spratt had already has long involvement in the budget process. In 1991 he got a seat on the Budget Committee; his moderate voting record made him a natural point of contact between the parties, but Democrats did not see him as their leader: In their November 1992 caucus, he was beaten for Budget chairman by the more liberal Martin Sabo by 149-112. He rotated off the committee in 1992, then ran for the ranking Democrat position on Budget again in December 1996. Democrats, now in the minority, were more ready for his leadership; he beat the more liberal Louise Slaughter, now chairman of the Rules Committee, by 106-83. He played a major role in putting together the May 1997 agreement to reach a balanced budget. It required, he said, "Some stiff, tough bargaining. As a matter of process, it was a major accomplishment."

The bipartisanship of that period did not continue, and Spratt was given the role of offering Democratic alternatives which were beaten on party lines. After September 11, he issued a report predicting, accurately, that the budget surplus would disappear in 2002 and quite possibly for several years. In 2002 he called for negotiations like those that produced the 1997 budget agreement or the 1990 budget summit in which Bush's father agreed to break his promise and raise taxes. "He can take a page from his father's experience and hope it doesn't cost him what it cost his dad. But his dad did the right thing." In 2002 Republicans once again passed a budget resolution along party lines; surveying the deficits ahead, Spratt blamed them on the 2001 Bush tax cuts, but said that he would not urge their repeal. In September 2003 he presented forecasts that operations in Iraq could cost $418 billion over 10 years. In 2004 Nussle joined Spratt in expressing concern about the administration's practice of omitting from budget projections expenses for Iraq and Afghanistan provided for in supplemental appropriations. In January 2005, as Republicans continued their monopartisan approach, he complained that CBO forecasts of the deficit were unduly optimistic because they did not include all Iraq and Afghanistan costs.

Republicans continued to dominate the budget proceedings, and in October 2006 Spratt argued that while the administration approach of restraining domestic discretionary spending and waiting for a surge in revenues might shrink deficits in the short term, it would be inadequate for medium and long term fiscal challenges. "This is not a cyclical deficit. It's a structural deficit built into our budget." Looking ahead to the increasingly likely Democratic victory in November 2006, he endorsed the imposition of paygo rules and said Democrats would surely renew the 10% bracket, child tax credit, marriage penalty relief and $100,000 expensing for small businesses, but not other Bush tax cuts. He noted that there had been no "closet-cleaning in the tax codes since 1986."

After Democrats won majorities in both houses, he and Senate Budget Committee Chairman Kent Conrad called for a more realistic statement of war costs in the administration's budget. When the Bush budget was unveiled in February 2007, Spratt said, "If you look at the economic criteria on which their forecasts are based, what you'll see is in every case at the margins they're pushing for a little bit better, more favorable underlying circumstances."

He complained that the administration was counting on vastly increased revenues from the Alternative Minimum Tax, assuming that the 4.2 million taxpayers hit by the AMT would, without the one-year patch that had become routine, would balloon to 23 million—concentrated in high-income, high-tax states which vote heavily Democratic. Then came the hard work, unnecessary when Democrats were in the minority, of assembling 218 votes for the Democratic budget. "As I tell my Democratic colleagues, 'If you can't budget, you can't govern,'" he said, adding, "Nobody in the Democratic party is pushing me to come up with new taxes to pay for a balanced budget." Spratt's Democratic budget resolution passed the House in late March 2007. It assumed that the AMT would increase, that the children's health insurance program would be expanded and it included the administration's admittedly arbitrary estimate of the cost of the war in Iraq in 2009 at $50 billion. It assumed also that all the Bush tax cuts would stay in place until 2010 and then might disappear—prompting Republicans to label it the "biggest tax increase in American history." Looking ahead, Spratt opposed proposals for an entitlement commission and the base closing-like process to address entitlements on the ground that previous such efforts had had little or no effect. He said that on Social Security there could be "a supplemental savings account that you could opt into," but not individual investment accounts financed by a portion of current Social Security taxes.

On other issues, Spratt has a moderate record, a bit to the left of the middle of the House. He voted for NAFTA in 1993, but in 2005 opposed the Central America Free Trade Agreement. He has worked over the years to get more than $100 million in construction at Shaw Air Force Base in Sumter County, the largest base for F-16s; the 2005 base closing process moves the 3rd Army headquarters there from Fort McPherson, Georgia, and a $5 million education center there was named for Spratt in November 2005. He put into the 2006 defense authorization bill his amendment providing free life insurance for all troops in combat. He also passed two other interesting pieces of legislation, a bill setting up a study of Revolutionary War sites in the Up Country of South Carolina to be included in a Southern Campaign of the Revolution Heritage Area, and a law co-sponsored by Ed Whitfield, John Sweeney and Nick Rahall prohibiting the slaughter of horses for human consumption (the markets for this were primarily in France and Belgium).

Spratt has had two tough races, in 1994 and 1996, when he won by margins of 52%-48% and 54%-45%. From 1998 to 2004 he was reelected by wide margins. For 2006 Republicans targeted Spratt, and Karl Rove helped to recruit one-term Rock Hill legislator Ralph Norman, a residential and commercial real estate developer, and pushed aside another candidate who had won on the American Candidate reality television program. Senators Lindsey Graham and Jim DeMint, Governor Mark Sanford and Vice President Dick Cheney came in to campaign for Norman. Spratt responded with an ad calling Norman a hypocrite and claiming that he had been cited for hiring illegal immigrants. Actually, he was cited for his workers' actions but no mention was made of whether they were legal or illegal. Spratt sharply opposed the Dubai Ports deal while Norman, perhaps naively, initially endorsed it. In August 2006 2d District Congressman Joe Wilson said he was "personally ashamed" that Spratt didn't criticize House Democrats who had refused to vote for a resolution criticizing Hezbollah's attack on Israel; Spratt, who voted for the resolution, said Wilson was "crazy." In mid-October national Republicans, worried about their incumbents' chances, quit pouring money into Norman's campaign. Spratt outspent him nearly 2–1 and won 57%-43%—a solid margin, but the closest race he had encountered since 1996, despite the national Democratic trend.

South Carolina's early 2008 primary puts prominent local officials in a position to influence the presidential election. However, in early 2007 Spratt refused to endorse any candidate, perhaps a prudent move since none seemed capable of carrying the 5th District in the general election.

SIXTH DISTRICT

Rep. James Clyburn (D)

Elected 1992, 8th term; b. July 21, 1940, Sumter; home, Columbia; SC St. U., B.A. 1962; African Methodist Episcopal; married (Emily).

Professional Career: Teacher, 1962-66; Dir., Charleston Neighborhood Youth Corps, 1966-68; Exec. Dir., SC Comm. for Farm Workers, 1968-71; Asst., SC Gov. West, 1971-74; SC Human Affairs Comm., 1974-92.

DC Office: 2135 RHOB, 20515, 202-225-3315; Fax: 202-225-2313; Web site: clyburn.house.gov.

District Offices: Columbia, 803-799-1100; Florence, 843-622-1212; Santee, 803-854-4700.

Committees: *Majority Whip.*

Group Ratings

	ADA	ACLU	AFS	LCV	ITIC	NTU	COC	ACU	CFG	FRC
2006	95	95	100	100	67	11	50	12	9	0
2005	85	—	100	78	—	14	48	9	8	15

National Journal Ratings

	2005 LIB	—	2005 CONS		2006 LIB	—	2006 CONS
Economic	68%	—	32%		79%	—	21%
Social	73%	—	26%		72%	—	28%
Foreign	73%	—	27%		77%	—	20%

Key Votes of the 109th Congress

1. Estate Tax Repeal	N	5. Limit Interstate Abortion	N	9. Build Border Fence	N
2. Limit CAFE Standards	Y	6. Extend Patriot Act	Y	10. CAFTA	N
3. FY06 Spending Curb	N	7. Bar Same Sex Marriage	N	11. Oppose Iraq Withdrawal	N
4. Drilling in ANWR	N	8. Stem Cell Research $	Y	12. Detainee Tribunals	N

Election Results

2006 general	James Clyburn (D)	100,213	(64%)	($988,405)
	Gary McLeod (R)	53,181	(34%)	($3,155)
	Other	2,312	(1%)	
2006 primary	James Clyburn (D)	unopposed		
2004 general	James Clyburn (D)	161,987	(67%)	($725,832)
	Gary McLeod (R)	75,443	(31%)	($3,927)
	Other	4,157	(2%)	

Prior Winning Percentages: 2002 (67%); 2000 (72%); 1998 (73%); 1996 (69%); 1994 (64%); 1992 (65%)

The People		Race/Ethnic Origin	Ancestry	
Area size:	8,490 sq. mi.	40.3% White	USA: 9.0%	English: 4.1%
Urban population:	48.0%	56.7% Black	German: 3.7%	
Rural population:	52.0%	0.5% Asian	**2004 Presidential Vote**	
Pop. 2000:	668,670	0.3% Native Am.	Kerry (D) 151,061	(61%)
Pop. 2005 (est):	642,387	0.0% Hawaiian	Bush (R) 97,248	(39%)
Median income:	$28,967	0.7% Two+ races	Other 482	(0%)
Poverty status:	22.4%	0.1% Other	**2000 Presidential Vote**	
Military veterans:	12.4%	1.5% Hispanic Origin	Gore (D) 126,287	(58%)
			Bush (R) 87,252	(40%)
			Other 2,991	(1%)
			Cook Partisan Voting Index: D +11	

Occupation	Blue collar: 33.0%	White collar: 48.1%	Gray collar: 18.9%

South Carolina was first settled by planters from Barbados, bringing with them a tropical plantation economy, which they transferred to the not-quite-tropical climate of the Carolina coastal lowlands. Here the flat Low Country and many islands are laced with sluggish-flowing rivers and swamps, and here the planters brought thousands of slaves directly from Africa. Colonial South

Carolina was one of the richest parts of North America, with dazzling Georgian architecture in Charleston and classic plantation gardens; the planters built great irrigation systems and grew rice and cotton and the dye-plant indigo, all heavily in demand in Britain and elsewhere. All this wealth, of course, was built on the slave labor of countless African Americans. In colonial times, a majority of South Carolinians were slaves, as were a majority of lowlands residents when Fort Sumter was fired upon (although there were also many free blacks in Charleston, a few of whom owned slaves themselves). South Carolina's black heritage has left a lasting imprint on American culture. Gullah, a mixture of English, French and African dialects is still spoken on the sea islands, and Gullah customs survive—oyster roasts and sweet potato feasts at Christman, handmade dolls and sweetgrass baskets. The poverty that was the almost universal lot of lowland blacks after the Civil War has eased only in the last generation, as development came to the coast and long cultural isolation dissipated. But many blacks decided not to wait, abandoning South Carolina for opportunities in the North. Today, heavily black rural counties are suffering steeper losses in manufacturing jobs than urban areas.

The 6th Congressional District of South Carolina, created in 1992 as a black-majority district, includes only a bit of the South Carolina coast, which is increasingly lined with affluent retirement and recreational communities. The district's boundaries, less jagged since the 2002 redistricting, take in the black central city neighborhoods of Charleston, North Charleston and Columbia but leave their affluent white areas, both urban and suburban, in the adjacent 1st and 2d Districts. The 6th includes Orangeburg, home of the historically black South Carolina State University, and Florence, at the center of the Pee Dee tobacco-growing country in eastern South Carolina. Orangeburg was the scene of a massacre in February 1968, when three black students were killed and 27 wounded by police while protesting a segregated bowling alley; in April 2007 South Carolina State was the site of the first Democratic presidential debate in the 2007-08 cycle. The 6th's population in 2000 was 57% black, and in 2004 it gave George W. Bush only 39% of the vote—the only South Carolina district he failed to carry.

The congressman from the 6th District is James Clyburn, a Democrat first elected in 1992. Clyburn grew up in Sumter, the son of a minister. In 1960 he was one of seven young people who organized the state's first sit-ins, at a five-and-dime store in the Orangeburg town square; he met his wife while in jail for three days. Clyburn worked as a teacher, as an employment counselor and in government antipoverty programs. In 1970 he ran for the South Carolina House and went to bed on election night thinking he was the winner, only to find out the next morning that he had lost by a narrow margin. When asked for his reaction by a reporter, he said, "I lost because I didn't get enough votes." That prompted Governor-elect John West to ask him to join his administration. In 1974 West appointed him state Human Affairs commissioner and he served 18 years, under two Democratic and two Republican governors. Twice he ran for secretary of state, in 1978 and 1986, losing narrowly. Then the new, black-majority 6th District was created. The white incumbent, Democrat Robin Tallon, at the last minute decided not to run. Clyburn did, and in the Democratic primary won 56% of the vote against four black opponents, all with serious claims for the nomination. Clyburn, well known statewide, ran first or second in every part of the district and piled up 88% of the vote in his home county of Sumter.

Clyburn, the only black to represent South Carolina in Congress since George Washington Murray (a distant relative of his), left in 1897, has a moderate-to-liberal voting record. He was elected Chairman of the Congressional Black Caucus in 1998. He has good working relationships with leading businessmen and Republicans and—like many South Carolinians before him—has focused on local priorities first. He supported the balanced budget amendment and joined the moderate New Democrat Coalition at its inception in 1997, the only black House member to do so. When cigarette tax increases were proposed, he urged safeguards for tobacco farmers. He worked with Republican Sherwood Boehlert to pass a law in 2000 establishing whistleblower protection for airline employees. He voted for the partial-birth abortion ban in 2003. In September 2004 and March 2005, the House passed his bill to create a Gullah/Geechee Heritage Corridor from northern Florida to North Carolina.

On the Appropriations Committee from 1998 to 2006, he focused on local projects. He has sought to develop the corridor around I-95, which passes through rural counties in the district and to push for development of cellulosic ethanol. "We grow soybeans galore. Our energy alternative should be home-grown, American-owned. We can do sugar cane and sugar beets." As chairman of the Congressional Black Caucus in 1999, he urged the Democratic National Committee to become more responsive to blacks; he also sought to create a Policy and Leadership Institute for the Black Caucus to develop new liberal positions and protect black lawmakers in redistricting. After the 2002 election he won a three-candidate contest to become vice-chairman of the Democratic Caucus with 95 votes to 56 for Gregory Meeks and 53 for Zoe Lofgren. He said the leadership needed to reflect the party's diversity and not "just white men." In 2003, he demanded an apology after Tom DeLay said that minority Democrats in Texas were "more Democrat than they are minority" if they turn down his offer for additional minority districts from redistricting. "We have long and sordid experiences with policies and practices that are acted upon purportedly on our behalf without our inclusion in the process," he said. In January 2006 he was elected Democratic Caucus Chairman, the number four position in the party leadership. In November 2006 he was elected House Majority Whip; Rahm Emanuel, who was interested in the post and who as DCCC Chairman had done much to gain the majority for Democrats, succeeded him as Caucus Chairman. "For some reason people up here feel if you're going to get ahead in this environment you've got to learn how to elbow people aside and you've got to learn how to run over other people," he said after he was chosen. "I don't think so. That's not my style." He said he would delegate more than Steny Hoyer had as Minority Whip and described his approach: "When it comes to working with the Democratic Caucus, I have to fish in a lot of ponds. I go fishing with the Blue Dogs. I go fishing with the New Dems. I go fishing with the Hispanics and I go fishing with the Asian Pacific Islanders, trying to cobble together the 218 votes I need. But a lot of times I have to be a hunter, and they tell me, even though I never hunt, they tell me that a good hunter knows how to work both sides of the ditch. I fish among my caucus, Democratic members, and I go hunting sometimes, among my Republican members." Before the Democratic takeover he indicated his support for the seniority system. "I'm going to be leery of going away from seniority. African-Americans supported the seniority system and waited their turn. Now, we get nervous when people talk about changing the rules." In Febuary 2007, speaking to South Carolina pastors, he defeneded earmarks. "I've seen a lot of letters to the editor of the *Post and Courier* very critical of the earmarking I've been doing. Yet y'all are asking me this morning for earmarks. How many of you have written a letter in response to some of these letters? Have you ever written a letter to the *Post and Courier* or to any other newspaper saying you support what I'm doing? Not one of you ever have. We might lose this battle on earmarking because y'all are staying silent while you're sitting here telling me what you want."

Back home Clyburn has not faced serious opposition for reelection. He has relished his role as a major player and potential kingmaker in the state's often pivotal Democratic presidential primary. Blacks cast about half the votes in the primary, and Clyburn is the most prominent black politician in the state. In the 2004 presidential primary campaign, he first backed Dick Gephardt, with whom he had worked in the House. But Gephardt withdrew after the Iowa caucuses, and Clyburn endorsed frontrunner John Kerry rather than South Carolina native John Edwards. In 2007, his support was eagerly sought by Democratic contenders, who attended his annual Fish Fry in Columbia.

★ SOUTH DAKOTA ★

When the Census Bureau proclaimed the closing of the American frontier in 1890, one of the last places where it had closed was the southern part of the Dakota Territory, just admitted to the Union in 1889 as the state of South Dakota. For years this land had been the home of the Oglala Sioux, one of the largest Native American tribes, who had built a buffalo hunting civilization by becoming masters of the horses the Spaniards had imported to North America 350 years earlier. It was the Sioux warrior chief Sitting Bull, now buried on a bluff above the Missouri River, who destroyed Custer at Little Big Horn in 1876; it was Oglala Sioux who were the victims at the massacre of Wounded Knee in 1890. After half a century of horrifying disease and a decade of defeat, the Sioux were a traumatized people, and still are today, living on reservations with proud tradi-tions but in terrible poverty. They are isolated far from the mainstream economic marketplace, beset by high rates of crime, alcoholism and suicide, with life expectancy and disease rates like those of sub-Saharan Africa; on the Pine Ridge Reservation in Shannon County unemployment is 70% and incomes average $3,500 a year. But infant mortality has been reduced and the American Indian population has been growing rapidly. In 2004, 98 buffalo were rounded up on California's Catalina Island, the descendants of animals brought there to film a Western in the 1920s, and returned to the Lakota Reservation. Indians are in the process of getting a great monument, the late Korczak Ziolkowski's Crazy Horse sculpture, which—when and if finished; boosters are trying to raise $25 million—will dwarf Mount Rushmore (which was left unfinished itself at the start of World War II).

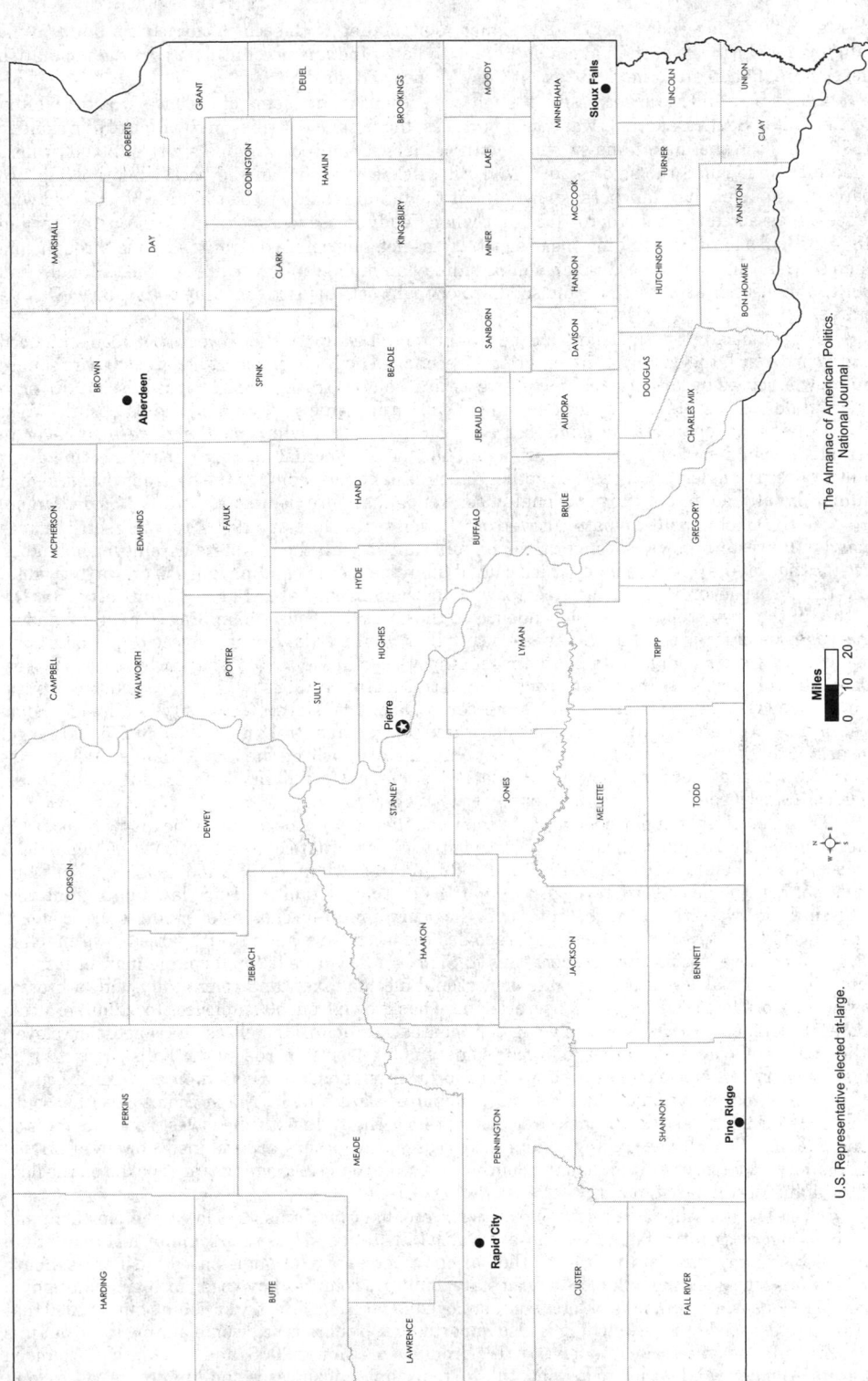

The Almanac of American Politics.
National Journal

U.S. Representative elected at-large.

In March 2007 Governor Mike Rounds signed a bill adding to the school curriculum units on the language and culture of the Lakota and other Indians; Indians account for 9% of the population here, more than in any other state except New Mexico and Alaska.

Less tragic and more successful, though not without its moments of violence, was the whites' settlement of South Dakota. It was a rapid process: the first gold strikes in the Black Hills came in 1876, and soon the mountains swarmed with settlers. Deadwood became a city of 20,000 where Calamity Jane ruled the saloons and Wild Bill Hickok was shot in the back while holding two pair—aces and eights. Ranchers, knowing that the buffalo could not be contained by barbed wire fences, massacred them so thoroughly that when Teddy Roosevelt got to the Dakota Territory in 1884, he had a hard time finding one to shoot. It was not long before the railroad came through, and then settlers, many of them German and Scandinavian immigrants recruited by the railroads, had built sodhouses, broken the land and set down enough roots to justify making both the two Dakota states.

Geographically, South Dakota has never entirely filled up. In the 25 years between statehood and World War I, the eastern third of the state, sectioned off Midwestern style into 640-acre square miles, was settled by farmers. But moving westward, before a traveler reaches the Missouri River in the middle of the state, green turns to brown, cultivation grows sparse and then stops; the West River plains are open grazing land, scarcely touched by the white men who were so eager to establish dominion over them a century ago. The land is punctuated, not by roads meeting every mile at precise angles, but by buttes, gullies and grasslands sweeping to the horizon with no sign of human habitation except the occasional missile silos that once pointed toward the Soviet Union.

South Dakota's political patterns were fairly well set by the early 1900s. Its early settlers were mostly Midwesterners who brought their Republicanism with them. Voters here never had much use for the Non-Partisan League, which caught on in the more Scandinavian soil of North Dakota, and there was never anything here comparable to the Farmer-Labor Party of Minnesota. But the nature of the farm economy—its dependence on the great railroads and milling companies, and on the vagaries of international markets—meant that South Dakota was subject to periodic farm revolts. It voted for Populists and William Jennings Bryan in the 1890s; it supported the early New Deal; it revolted against the Eisenhower administration in the 1950s by electing a young congressman named George McGovern, then a professor at Dakota Wesleyan University in Mitchell, home also of the Corn Palace, built in 1892 and decorated every year with 13 murals using 275,000 ears of corn. South Dakota shared the isolationist impulse of much of the Great Plains; McGovern's opposition to the Vietnam War in the late 1960s was not a liability here. In the early 1970s, Democrats seemed on the verge of becoming the majority party.

Then South Dakota moved sharply to the Republicans. This began with the angry response to the violence at Wounded Knee in 1975. And it was perpetuated by the policies of Republican Governor Bill Janklow, elected in 1978 and 1982 and then again in 1994 and 1998. In 1979 Sioux Falls banker Thomas Reardon suggested that the state get rid of its usury law limiting interest rates; inflation was driving market rates over the usury limits and choking off credit to the economy. Janklow and the legislature followed up, repealed the usury laws and in 1981 passed laws enabling Citibank to move its credit card operations to Sioux Falls, where it could charge market interest rates—all in a state with no corporate or personal income taxes, and community with a literate low-wage work force. The Citibank operation here has grown from 50 employees to 3,200, servicing some 118 million cardholders, replacing the meatpacker John Morrell as the biggest employer; other banks and telemarketing followed; some 15,000 people in the Sioux Falls area work in financial services. New firms started up, like NordicTrak and Gateway Computer (their executive offices have moved to San Diego but most employees are still in North Sioux City) as South Dakotans have proved to be an ideal work force; this is the state with the lowest rate of default on college loans. Some meatpacking plants have closed, but others are manned now by a largely Hispanic work force, recruited from the Southwest and beyond; 40 languages are spoken on the floor of the John Morrell plant in Sioux Falls.

South Dakota still has a relatively low-wage economy, but it also has low unemployment and low housing prices; its residents and those in North Dakota spend less time commuting to work than Americans in any other state. It leads the nation in percentage of home-based businesses. South Dakota has long been thought of as a farm state, but farm counties have been losing population; in the 1990 Census, 11% of the workforce was employed in farming, forestry or fishing but by 2000 that figure had dropped to 8%. Ranching is also important, and there is still some mining here, but it is tapering off. The state baked under a terrific drought in summer 2006, and speculation abounded that its economy would come to a standstill. Instead, small businesses and financial services kept humming, exports increased dramatically, unemployment stuck around 3% and the big news was that chemical and credit card entrepreneur T. Denny Sanford donated $400 million to Sioux Valley Hospitals and Health System and that a big anonymous investor, known locally as the Gorilla, was assembling a large plot of land for a big development in Union County south of Sioux Falls. Economically and demographically, South Dakota is coming to resemble the Rocky Mountain states, with most people concentrated around a few prosperous and growing cities and towns, while vast acreage remains vacant, punctuated with infrequent ranches and resort areas—a landscape that would not have been totally alien to Sitting Bull. South Dakotans have been adaptive in exploiting this acreage; the number of local hunters has been declining, but promoters are attracting record numbers of out-of-staters to hunt South Dakota's pheasants; some local meatpacking plants have closed, but the state is promoting the production of luxury beef, with computer tracking of each cow to guarantee its provenance and freedom from disease. Wide open spaces leave room for initiatives like the attempt by American Sign Language advocates to set up a town for the deaf in McCook County. South Dakota's major population centers have grown, while its farm counties continue to empty out. Lincoln County, just south of Sioux Falls, was the nation's 12th fastest-growing county from 2000 to 2006, and in 2006 Sioux Falls's Minnehaha County and Lincoln County together had 25% of the state's population. Politically, this growth has been a standoff between the parties: Democrats have benefited from growth and increased turnout on the reservations, while Republicans have benefited from growth in the Black Hills and the two parties have slugged it out in the Sioux Falls area.

South Dakota in recent years has been the scene of heated partisan fights. Briefly, from June 2004 to January 2005, it had an all-Democratic congressional delegation—Senators Tom Daschle and Tim Johnson and Congresswoman-at-Large Stephanie Herseth—for only the second time in its history (the other time was a period of five days in 1936-37). Johnson beat incumbent Republican Larry Pressler narrowly in 1996 and in 2002 held his seat against Congressman John Thune as a big turnout drive on the Pine Ridge Reservation enabled him to win by 524 votes. But in 2004 Thune came back and beat Daschle, then Senate Minority Leader and earlier Majority Leader, by a 51%-49% margin. Herseth won the state's single House seat in a special election after Bill Janklow resigned and held it in November 2004 by 53%-46%. This is a state where voters traditionally have expected to meet and talk with their representatives in Congress, and want them to bring back money—which has made Democrats more competitive in these races that they have been in presidential or state politics. Republicans have held the governorship since 1978 and have had wide margins in the state legislature.

State politics was marked with unexpected controversy after the legislature in February 2006 passed a law criminalizing abortion and providing no exceptions for rape and incest, the nation's most stringent abortion law. Governor Mike Rounds signed the bill in March 2006 and called it a "full frontal attack" on *Roe v. Wade*. Pro-life advocates outside the state criticized the South Dakotans for fashioning a test case of *Roe* when it seemed obvious that the votes were lacking on the Supreme Court to overturn it, but the strongest opposition came from inside the state. Petitions began circulating to put the bill on the ballot in November; Democrats suddenly found they had many more legislative candidates than in previous years; some Republicans opposed the bill as too restrictive and confrontational. It became an issue in Oglala Sioux politics as well: Cecelia Fire Thunder, the first woman elected tribal president in 2005, called for setting up an abortion clinic on the Pine Ridge Reservation, and was impeached and ousted from office in July 2006. The opponents of the abortion ban fared better. South Dakotans voted 56%-44% to repeal the bill. This must be counted as a major defeat for those who want to recriminalize abortion in the United States; even in this culturally conservative state, the people voted not to go so far. At the same time, it may undercut the claims of abortion rights advocates that an overturning of *Roe v. Wade* will result in the recriminalization of abortion in many jurisdictions. Not in South Dakota, it seems, and if not in South Dakota, then where?

The abortion issue did not totally overturn the political order here. Mike Rounds was reelected by 62%-36%, and voters did pass, though by a narrow margin, a constitutional amendment banning same-sex marriage and the establishment of domestic partnerships or civil unions. Democrats gained 5 seats in the state Senate but only 1 in the state House. Members of the state's congressional delegation seemed highly popular, and South Dakotans watched as Senator Tim Johnson, suffering a stroke in December 2006, made a slow but determined recovery into summer 2007.

The People

		Race/Ethnic Origin			Military veterans:	79,370 (14.4%)
Pop. 2006 (est):	781,919	664,585	88.0%	White	WWII: 19.3%	Korea: 16.1%
Pop. 2000:	754,844	4,563	0.6%	Black	Vietnam: 31.3%	Gulf War: 11.0%
Pop. 1990:	696,004	4,316	0.6%	Asian	Most populous cities (2006):	
Change 1990-2000:	Up 8.5%	60,988	8.1%	Native Am.	1. Sioux Falls	142,396
% of U.S. total:	0.3%	219	0.0%	Hawaiian	2. Rapid City	62,715
Pop. rank:	46th of 50	8,960	1.2%	Two+ races	3. Aberdeen	24,071
Area size:	77,116 sq. mi.	310	0.0%	Other	4. Watertown	20,526
State Native:	68.1%	10,903	1.4%	Hisp. Origin	5. Brookings	18,802
Non-citizen:	1.1%	Ancestry				
Language		German: 29.1%		Norwegian: 10.9%	Urban population: 51.9%	
English: 91.0%	Other Eur.: 3.8%	Irish: 7.4%		English: 5.0%	Rural population: 48.1%	
Spanish: 2.2%		Dutch: 3.4%				

Education

		Work Sector		Legislature	
H.S. Grad:	84.6%	Private: 72.9%	Govt: 15.3%	Senate	20 R 15 D
College Grad:	21.5%	Self: 11.0%	Family: 0.8%	House	50 R 20 D
Industry		Unemployment: 4.4%		Legislative Term Limits: Yes	
Agri: 8.1%	Con: 6.3%	Household Income		Registered Voters	
Fin: 7.4%	Info: 2.1%	<15k: 18.4%	15-35k: 31.2%	D: 190,905	(37.6%)
Mfg: 15.7%	Prof: 27.0%	35-50k: 19.0%	50-100k: 25.5%	R: 240,101	(47.3%)
Public: 4.8%	Trade: 15.3%	100-150k: 3.8%	>150k: 2.1%	O: 76,126	(15.0%)
Other: 13.3%		Median: $35,282			
Occupation		Poverty status: 13.2%			
Blue collar: 23.3%	White collar: 59.1%	Home Value			
Gray collar: 17.6%		<50k: 31.1%	50-100k: 39.4%	100-200k: 23.6%	200-300k: 3.7%
		300-500k: 1.4%	>500k: 0.7%	Median: $74,300	

Presidential politics   South Dakota has voted Democratic for president just four times since statehood, in 1896, 1932, 1936 and 1964. But it was fairly close in five of the seven elections between 1972, when South Dakota's George McGovern was the Democratic nominee, and 1996, when Bill Clinton came within 3% of winning. In 2000 the cultural liberalism and environmental policies of Al Gore were far from popular here, and George W. Bush carried the state 60%-38%. Gore carried only Indians, a rising but small percentage of the electorate, and ran even among the elderly, but the percentage of voters who remembered Franklin D. Roosevelt was on the wane. In 2004 Bush once again carried the state 60%-38%; he carried every county except those containing Indian reservations and the University of South Dakota. Bush's share of the vote declined by 0.4%, making South Dakota the only other state besides Vermont where his percentage fell. Bush's share of the vote increased in the Sioux Falls area and

2004 Presidential Vote

Bush (R)	232,584	(60%)
Kerry (D)	149,244	(38%)
Nader (I)	4,320	(1%)
Other	2,067	(1%)

2004 Democratic Presidential Primary

Kerry (D)	69,473	(82%)
Uncommitted (D)	5,105	(6%)
Dean (D)	4,838	(6%)
LaRouche (D)	2,943	(3%)
Kucinich (D)	2,046	(2%)

2000 Presidential Vote

Bush (R)	190,700	(60%)
Gore (D)	118,804	(38%)
Other	6,765	(2%)

most of eastern South Dakota, but fell in West River, where outrage against Clinton-Gore environmentalism had cooled. His biggest drops were in Indian reservation counties, where Democratic registration drives vastly increased turnout in 2002 and 2004. He lost Shannon County in the Pine Ridge Reservation by 1,415 votes in 2000 and 3,040 votes in 2004.

In 1988 South Dakota switched its presidential primary from the traditional June date to February, just one week after New Hampshire. It proved to be a booster of Great Plains candidates who did not fare well elsewhere: Bob Dole in 1988 and 1996, Dick Gephardt in 1988, Bob Kerrey and Tom Harkin in 1992. But in 1996 it attracted few candidates, and the South Dakota legislature decided to save the $400,000 it cost and went back to a June primary. In January 2007 there was a move in the legislature to hold the 2008 primary on February 5, but that was blocked by a 35-35 vote in the state House.

Governor

Mike Rounds (R)

Elected 2002, term expires Jan. 2011, 2d term; b. Oct. 24, 1954, Huron; home, Pierre; SD St. U., B.S. 1977; Catholic; married (Jean).

Elected Office: SD Senate, 1990-2000; Maj. Ldr. 1994-2000.

Professional Career: Practicing atty., 1979-2002.

Office: 505 E. Capitol Ave., Pierre, 57501, 605-773-3212; Fax: 605-773-5844; Web site: www.state.sd.us/governor.

Election Results

2006 general	Mike Rounds (R)	206,990	(62%)
	Jack Billion (D)	121,226	(36%)
	Other	7,292	(2%)
2006 primary	Mike Rounds (R)	unopposed	
2002 general	Mike Rounds (R)	189,920	(57%)
	Jim Abbott (D)	140,263	(42%)
	Other	4,376	(1%)

Mike Rounds, a Republican, was elected governor of South Dakota in 2002. He grew up the oldest in a family of 11 children in Pierre, the state's tiny capital; his father was director of the Office of Highway Safety and worked as a lobbyist for the petroleum industry. Rounds graduated from South Dakota State University, the first governor to do so. He worked as a partner in an insurance and real estate agency in Pierre and participated, as you would expect, in many civic activities. In 1990 he was elected to the state Senate and in 1996 he became Senate Majority Leader. He was prevented by term limits from running for reelection in 2000. In December 2001 he announced he was running for governor.

Rounds sought to replace the governor who had dominated state government for the past quarter-century, Bill Janklow. Janklow was elected attorney general in 1974; in 1978 and 1982 he was elected governor. Term-limited, he ran for the Senate and lost in 1986; in 1994, he returned and defeated Governor Walter Dale Miller in the Republican primary. He won the general election 55%-41% and was reelected 64%-33% in 1998.

In the Republican primary Rounds faced two much more well-financed opponents, former Lieutenant Governor Steve Kirby and Attorney General Mark Barnett. Rounds ran on property tax relief and opposition to an income tax and abortion. "No gimmicks, no grandstanding, just good government," read his fliers. He was willing to tell people what they didn't want to hear. He told a truckers' group that he was responsible for applying the sales tax to transportation services and said he might favor a higher gas tax if it would bring in much more federal money. He was the only candidate in either party to oppose mandated use of ethanol fuel, despite the state's many ethanol plants and corn growers. He told the South Dakota Education Association that there were "very limited funds" for education spending increases. He refused to pledge to oppose all tax increases.

At candidate forums and then in their ads and direct mail, Kirby and Barnett bitterly attacked each other, on economic development and on other substantive and character issues. They had plenty of money to launch these attacks: Kirby spent over $2.5 million and Barnett $1.75 million. Rounds spent just $147,000. But he had a strategy. In April 2002 he spelled it out. "For the time being, I haven't minded being considered by the other two candidates as this fly buzzing away over in the corner. I've heard several people say just stay out of the negative, there's enough of that. I'd like to run my spots right between Kirby and Barnett. Hopefully, people will see some differences."

Evidently they did. South Dakota is a small state in which voters expect to see candidates in person; candidate forums held in small towns can make some difference here. While Kirby and

Barnett attacked each other, Rounds always seemed to be smiling. In the June primary Rounds won 44% of the vote, to 30% for Barnett and 26% for Kirby. It was a classic illustration of the rule that it is not wise to launch a negative campaign in a multi-candidate race.

The Democratic nominee was Jim Abbott, a businessman who served in the legislature, lost races for lieutenant governor in 1994 and the House in 1996 and was on leave as president of the University of South Dakota. This was a gentlemanly race between old friends; after the primary Abbott said, "Mike Rounds is just a good guy. I really think the people of South Dakota like the idea of a positive message for the future, and this contest offers interesting options." Abbott called for state-sponsored research for economic development and for higher education to work with the private sector to create jobs. While negative ads were hitting the air in the Senate race, the dialogue in the governor race was positive. Rounds led in polls from the primary on and in November won 57%-42%.

After the election Rounds went to work on the state budget problems. In December Janklow presented figures showing spending requests $54 million higher than projected revenue, with $90 million in the state reserve. One problem was the state's structural deficit, exacerbated by the repeal of the state inheritance tax in 2000. In 2003 Rounds angered conservatives by proposing tax increases on cigarettes and alcoholic beverages and making more interstate phone calls subject to the sales tax. Though the legislature failed to pass his proposed tax on alcohol, it ended up passing 19 of the 22 bills requested by Rounds. Even without revenues from the tax measures he requested, he successfully cut the cost of prescription drugs for senior citizens and managed to increase state aid to school districts by $15.1 million. He also got a 2% pay raise for state workers, though it was 1% less than what he sought. But the big news story that year was Janklow. In August, Janklow, well known for his aggressive driving, blew through a stop sign in his car and killed a motorcyclist. In December, a jury in his hometown of Flandreau convicted him of felony manslaughter; he announced his resignation from Congress the same day, effective in January 2004.

Janklow wasn't the only national story in 2004. A restrictive abortion bill, which passed both the House and Senate, would have banned almost all abortions in the state; the only exception was to save the life of the mother. The bill's sponsor acknowledged that the measure would be challenged in court but had hoped for it to eventually reach the U.S. Supreme Court, where it might be used to overturn the *Roe v. Wade* decision. Abortion rights advocates, as expected, harshly criticized the bill. But many abortion opponents also opposed it, convinced that it could not survive legal scrutiny and might have the unintended effect of spurring a decision that strengthened abortion rights. Rounds said he supported overturning *Roe* but he issued a "form veto", which suggests changes and clarification of some of the bill's provisions. He issued the technical veto to ensure that existing abortion regulations remained in place during what state officials expected would be a lengthy court challenge; the Senate rejected the revisions and the bill died.

In 2006, strong economic growth enabled Rounds to propose a $3.2 million budget with a $130 million increase in spending. He outlined an ambitious education initiative designed to better prepare students to enter school, take more college-bound courses and continue their education or training after high school, all by the year 2010; one goal was to make South Dakota first in the nation in the percentage of students who go on to college, technical school or advanced training. But for a governor with high approval ratings and a legislature controlled by his own party, Rounds ran into considerable resistance on some high-profile initiatives. He called for raising the state's minimum wage $5.15 per hour to $6, the first raise since 1997, but it died in committee. He took a tough stance and vetoed a bill that eased the penalty on high school students caught using drugs—under an existing law, students were suspended for a year from high school activities—but the House and Senate voted to override the veto. Several of his 2010 education initiatives foundered, including a requirement to attend kindergarten and a raise in the age of mandatory school attendance from 16 to 18.

Abortion again dominated the headlines. In February 2006, the legislature revisited the issue, passing a law criminalizing abortion and providing no exceptions for rape and incest—the nation's most stringent abortion law. Rounds signed the bill in March and called it a "full frontal attack" on *Roe v. Wade*. Pro-life advocates outside the state criticized the South Dakotans for fashioning a test case of *Roe* when it seemed obvious that the votes were lacking on the Supreme Court to overturn it, but the strongest opposition came from inside the state. Petitions began circulating to put the bill on the ballot in November; Democrats suddenly found they had many more legislative candidates than in previous years; some Republicans opposed the bill as too restrictive and confrontational. There was an immediate affect on Rounds's poll ratings. For much of his time in office, his job approval ratings were at or above 70%, among the highest in the nation. In the aftermath of the bill signing, his approval rating spiked downward to 58% while his disapproval rating shot from 23% to 38%, according a SurveyUSA poll.

Even so, Rounds was in a solid position for reelection. His opponent was Jack Billion, a former state legislator and a retired Sioux Falls surgeon. Rounds touted his work on economic development and education. Billion criticized the "rigid, no exception" abortion law; Rounds reiterated his support and noted that the ban included an exception for the life of the mother and permitted the use of emergency contraception before a pregnancy is detected. Billion pointed to a delay in the scheduled August 29 execution of Elijah Page, convicted in 2000 in torture and murder case, as an example of the governor's "bad leadership." Rounds, who issued a reprieve just five hours before the death by injection was to be carried out—the state's first execution in 59 years—argued that state law and the Department of Corrections execution procedure were in conflict and that the legislature needed to settle it.

The abortion law roiled state politics, but not Rounds's reelection campaign. He held a steady lead in the polls throughout the campaign and won a landslide 62%-36% victory. Rounds carried all but four counties; just as in 2002, his Democratic opponent carried Indian reservations and the area around the University of South Dakota in Vermillion. Opponents of the abortion ban fared better than Billion as South Dakotans voted 56%-44% to repeal the abortion bill. Democrats gained five seats in the state Senate but only one in the state House.

Well before winning his second term, Rounds frequently drew mention as a possible Senate candidate against Democrat Tim Johnson in 2008. In April 2006, he called Johnson "my friend" and said in a televised interview, "I will tell you honestly that I really think at this stage of the game, this will probably be the last time that I actually run for a public office statewide within this state." But he declined to pledge to serve out a second full term if he was reelected. His remarks, closely scrutinized at the time, were revisited in December 2006 when Johnson was forced to undergo emergency surgery to stem bleeding in his brain and was listed in critical condition. In the event Johnson could not complete his term, Rounds was in a position to alter control of the Senate by his appointment of a replacement candidate; his intentions were the subject of much speculation. Johnson's condition stabilized, however, and he returned to the Senate in fall 2007. In the meantime, Rounds gave little indication he was planning to run for the seat, though if he was it was probably in his political interest not to announce before the recovering Johnson formally announced his plans for 2008. If Johnson does not run for reelection and Democrats, as is widely expected, look to popular Congresswoman Stephanie Herseth Sandlin to succeed him, Rounds will be under considerable Republican pressure to run.

Senior Senator

Tim Johnson (D)

Elected 1996, seat up 2008, 2d term; b. Dec. 28, 1946, Canton; home, Vermillion; U. of SD, B.A. 1969, M.A. 1970, J.D. 1975, MI St. U., 1970-71; Lutheran; married (Barbara).

Military Career: Army, 1969.

Elected Office: SD House of Reps., 1978-82; SD Senate, 1982-86; U.S. House of Reps., 1986-96.

Professional Career: Budget Analyst, MI Senate, 1971-72; Practicing atty., 1975-85; Clay Cnty. Dpty. Atty., 1985.

DC Office: 136 HSOB, 20510, 202-224-5842; Fax: 202-228-5765; Web site: johnson.senate.gov.

State Offices: Aberdeen, 605-226-3440; Rapid City, 605-341-3990; Sioux Falls, 605-332-8896.

Committees: *Appropriations* (11th of 15 D): Military Construction, Veterans Affairs & Related Agencies (Chmn.); Energy & Water Development; Agriculture, Rural Development, Food and Drug Administration & Related Agencies; State, Foreign Operations & Related Programs; Interior, Environment & Related Agencies; Transportation, Housing and Urban Development & Related Agencies. *Banking, Housing & Urban Affairs* (2d of 11 D): Financial Institutions (Chmn.); Securities, Insurance & Investment; Security & International Trade & Finance. *Energy & Natural Resources* (5th of 12 D): Water & Power (Chmn.); Public Lands & Forests; Energy. *Indian Affairs* (5th of 8 D).

Group Ratings

	ADA	ACLU	AFS	LCV	ITIC	NTU	COC	ACU	CFG	FRC
2006	85	42	88	71	75	16	50	12	3	37
2005	95	—	88	80	—	9	60	13	0	—

National Journal Ratings

	2005 LIB	—	2005 CONS		2006 LIB	—	2006 CONS
Economic	67%	—	32%		63%	—	35%
Social	60%	—	38%		61%	—	37%
Foreign	90%	—	5%		79%	—	16%

Key Votes of the 109th Congress

1. Bar ANWR Drilling	Y	5. Confirm Samuel Alito	Y	9. Limit Interstate Abortion	Y
2. FY06 Spending Curb	N	6. Path to Citizenship	Y	10. CAFTA	N
3. Estate Tax Repeal	N	7. Bar Same Sex Marriage	N	11. Urge Iraq Withdrawal	Y
4. Raise Minimum Wage	Y	8. Stem Cell Research $	Y	12. Provide Detainee Rights	Y

Election Results

2002 general	Tim Johnson (D)	167,481	(50%)	($6,152,991)
	John Thune (R)	166,957	(50%)	($5,989,043)
2002 primary	Tim Johnson (D)	65,438	(95%)	
	Herman Eilers (D)	3,558	(5%)	
1996 general	Tim Johnson (D)	166,533	(51%)	($2,990,554)
	Larry Pressler (R)	157,954	(49%)	($5,138,298)

Prior Winning Percentages: 1994 House (60%); 1992 House (69%); 1990 House (68%); 1988 House (72%); 1986 House (59%)

Tim Johnson, a Democrat, was first elected to the Senate in 1996. He grew up in Canton, Flandreau and Vermillion in southeast South Dakota, graduated from the University of South Dakota and served briefly in the Army (he was discharged because of a hearing problem). He graduated from Michigan State University business school and worked for the state Senate. Then he graduated from the University of South Dakota law school and started a law practice in Vermillion. He was elected to the state House in 1978, at 31, and served four years; in 1982, he was elected to the state Senate for another four years. When Congressman Tom Daschle ran for the Senate in 1986, Johnson ran for the House and won the general election by 59%-41%, and was reelected with larger percentages every two years.

In the House, Johnson compiled a generally liberal voting record, though he voted for the balanced budget amendment. In 1996 Johnson ran against Republican Senator Larry Pressler, then chairman of the Commerce committee. This was a high-spending, high-stakes race: Pressler spent $5.1 million, with over $1.7 million from PACs; Johnson spent almost $3 million, with $850,000 from PACs. TV ads began in August 1995, when the race was about even, and it stayed that way for 15 months. Since South Dakota TV is cheap, that meant one barrage of ads after another—plus seven debates. Pressler attacked Johnson as too liberal, going back to a 1981 vote in the legislature against workfare. Johnson attacked Pressler as a Newt-oid Medicare cutter and charged that he switched from opposition to support of maritime subsidies after receiving $29,000 from maritime PACs. Pressler spent much time in 1995 and 1996 on the telecommunications bill, a heavily lobbied and most complex bill. He succeeded in passing the bill, but back home Johnson was charging that phone and cable rates were going up. The final result was a 51%-49% Johnson victory, narrower than the final month's polls suggested.

In the Senate, Johnson's voting record has been toward the center of the Senate, though more liberal on foreign affairs issues. He supported the partial-birth abortion ban and cosponsored bills prohibiting meatpackers from owning, feeding or keeping livestock. He seldom got much publicity. "There are enough show horses in Washington to go around," he said.

By early 2001 it was apparent that Johnson would face a tough challenge in 2002. George W. Bush talked popular Republican Congressman John Thune into running for the Senate. Tom Daschle, majority leader starting in June 2001, said the race was "the most important political effort for me" in 2002. Daschle helped Johnson by getting him a seat on the Appropriations Committee, from which he could funnel money into South Dakota. And Johnson was careful to cast some moderate votes on important issues. Thune argued that the state would have been better off with a bipartisan Senate delegation. Of course, there was a caveat: a Thune victory could give the Republicans a Senate majority and make Daschle minority leader again. The two candidates spent record amounts for South Dakota—Johnson $6.1 million, Thune $6.0 million—and the national parties and independent expenditure groups on both sides spent much more. A week of TV ads cost only about $80,000 in South Dakota, as compared to about $1.5 million in Los Angeles. The ads started running in late 2001 and by November 2002 the average voter had seen more than 1,000 of them.

Thune was the more outgoing of the two, a candidate who loved shaking hands and seldom forgot a face. Johnson, more reserved, was nevertheless tenacious and moderate in demeanor. Of all the seriously contested Democratic senators in 2002, Johnson ran the most conservative-sounding campaign. "Tim Johnson has strongly supported President Bush, the war against terrorism, his tax cut and his education reform," one ad said. Thune attacked him for voting against making the tax cut permanent. Johnson replied that he supported eliminating the estate tax for family farmers and ranchers and family-owned businesses, and to increase the exemption to $4 million for individuals.

The biggest local issue was the drought that hit western South Dakota in 2002. Ranchers were selling off their herds for low prices; business losses were estimated at $1.8 billion. Daschle and Johnson responded by sponsoring $5 billion in disaster aid for farmers and ranchers, arguing that if floods and tornadoes triggered disaster relief, then droughts should too. But this was opposed by the Bush administration, which wanted any aid to come out of the federal dollars approved for farm spending. On August 15 George W. Bush came to South Dakota amid speculation that he would offer more. But, to the disappointment of the Thune campaign, he didn't. By this time, there seemed to be some improvement in Johnson's showing in the polls, though almost no polls throughout the campaign showed a margin for either candidate outside the statistical margin of error. In mid-September Agriculture Secretary Ann Veneman announced $750 million in aid for 30 states. Democrats grumbled that $750 million was a pittance, but Daschle's $5 billion, now raised to $6 billion, was stalled in the Senate.

On defense issues, Thune attacked Johnson for voting against the Gulf War resolution in January 1991 and for joining the group of Democratic members of Congress who sued George H.W. Bush challenging his conduct of the war. Johnson pointed out that his son, Brooks Johnson, served with the 101st Airborne Division in Afghanistan from December 2001 to June 2002 and could be sent to Iraq (which he later was) if the United States went in. With Daschle still publicly undecided, Johnson announced that he would vote for the Iraq war resolution.

There was one more issue blazing in October: fraudulent Indian voter registrations. The state Democratic party set up offices on each of the state's Indian reservations and paid bonuses to contractors who brought in signed voter registration cards. One such contractor was fired in October and charged with submitting scores of illegally filled out registration cards; state Attorney General Mark Barnett and the U.S. attorney launched investigations. On October 22, a consultant for the Sioux Tribes Voter Education and Registration Committee was indicted on five counts of forgery of voter registration cards. Johnson said that the voter registration operation was run by the state Democratic Party and that his campaign had nothing to do with it. At one debate Johnson challenged Thune to stop his negative ads. Thune said he would do so as soon as Johnson held a news conference to explain what he knew about this vote fraud.

This election turned out to be the closest in the nation. During most of election night and into the morning Thune led in the counting. The last two precincts came in from Shannon County, which includes most of the Pine Ridge Indian Reservation. Those two precincts put Johnson over the top, by a margin of 524 votes. In Shannon County, 3,118 votes were cast, as compared to 1,953 in the 2000 presidential election. The county voted 92%-8% for Johnson. In the six main reservation counties, turnout was 11,275, up from 7,500 in 2000. These six counties voted 78%-21% for Johnson. In 43 of the other 60 counties, including the 10 largest, Johnson's percentage declined from 1996, when he won 51% statewide. Many Republicans urged Thune to contest the election. But on November 13, he announced he would not. Johnson had won two full terms in the Senate by the smallest combined popular vote margin, 9,103, of any senator since George Malone of Nevada, elected by a combined margin of 7,970 in 1946 and 1952.

In his second term Johnson, back in the minority again, worked hard on South Dakota issues. He had helped put country of origin meat labeling into the 2002 farm bill. Congress later postponed it until 2006 and the House Agriculture Committee in 2004 voted to make it voluntary. He and Republican Mike Enzi sponsored a bill to bar the import of live cattle from Canada until country of origin labeling took effect.

Johnson passed a bill to provide more incentives and funding for housing on Indian reservations, and he proposed a series of tax credits for businesses on reservations and the building of wind-powered electricity plants there. In 2005, he sponsored a bill to make veterans health care an entitlement, not subject to annual appropriations. In 2006, he supported local funding for clean drinking water plus improved access to affordable health care, especially in rural communities. On the energy bill in 2005, he got commitments on the Energy and Natural Resources Committee for increases in ethanol and other renewable fuels:. South Dakota devotes more of its corn to ethanol than any other state. With John Sununu in 2006, he filed a bill to overhaul regulation of the insurance industry, giving companies the option of federal or state regulation. After an extensive lobbying campaign, Johnson was one of four Democratic senators in January 2006 who voted to confirm Samuel Alito to the Supreme Court; some local Democrats complained. In March 2006, Johnson may have balanced that by criticizing as "extreme and radical" a South Dakota law with a virtual ban on abortion. He was one of only two Senate Democrats in December 2005 who voted to force a vote on extension of the Patriot Act.

After Tom Daschle's narrow loss to John Thune in November 2004, Johnson convened a meeting of the new delegation with Thune and Democratic Congresswoman Stephanie Herseth Sandlin, and said they would work together on South Dakota projects. In 2005, their chief focus was the threat to close Ellsworth Air Force Base in the base-closing review. Johnson argued that studies showed no cost savings plus increased vulnerability for the B-1 fleet. When the commission unexpectedly voted to save Ellsworth, Johnson said that the delegation had worked closely together.

After the 2006 election, Johnson gained chairmanships of the Appropriations Subcommittee on Military Construction and Veterans Affairs, and the Banking Subcommittee on Financial Institutions. But his plans for the majority, and everything else, came to an abrupt halt on December 13, 2006, when he suffered a brain hemorrhage while at the Capitol. Within hours, he had extensive brain surgery. With prospects of his survival unclear and the assumption that Republican Governor Mike Rounds would appoint a GOP successor, speculation grew rampant that his departure from the Senate could reverse the Democrats' expected takeover. Although Johnson survived the immediate crisis, it became clear that he would be absent from the Senate for at least several months. Veteran Senate observers recalled that Republican Senator Karl Mundt, also of South Dakota, had a stroke in November 1969 and did not vote during the final three years of his Senate tenure. By March, Johnson's office released photographs of a smiling Johnson with his family, and Senate officials said that they were exploring steps to make his office more wheelchair-accessible. Even if he returned to the Senate, major questions lingered about Johnson's reelection in 2008. Other Democratic senators assisted on fundraising for him. Amid the uncertainty and also out of respect for Johnson, potential Republican candidates such as Mike Rounds delayed their decisions.

In late August 2007, Johnson held his first public appearance in South Dakota since his illness. On September 5, he returned to the Senate and made his first floor speech of the year. "My speech is not 100 percent," he said, referring to some slurring. "But my thoughts are clear and my mind is sharp." By then, Republican State Representative Joel Dykstra and Spearfish businessman Sam Kephart had already announced their intentions to run in 2008. If Johnson does not seek a third term, Herseth Sandlin is expected to become the Democratic nominee and Rounds will come under heavy pressure to run on the Republican side.

Junior Senator

John Thune (R)

Elected 2004, seat up 2010, 1st term; b. Jan. 7, 1961, Pierre; home, Sioux Falls; Biola U., B.A. 1983, U. of SD, M.B.A. 1984; Baptist; married (Kimberley).

Elected Office: U.S. House of Reps., 1996-2002.

Professional Career: Legis. Asst., U.S. Sen. James Abdnor, 1985-87; Special Asst., U.S. Small Business Admin., 1987-89; Exec. Dir., SD Republican Party, 1989-91; SD Railroad Dir., 1991-93; Exec. Dir., SD Municipal League, 1993-96.

DC Office: 493 RSOB, 20510, 202-224-2321; Fax: 202-228-5429; Web site: thune.senate.gov.

State Offices: Aberdeen, 605-225-8823; Rapid City, 605-348-7551; Sioux Falls, 605-334-9596.

Committees: *Agriculture, Nutrition & Forestry* (9th of 10 R): Energy, Science & Technology (RMM); Production, Income Protection & Price Support; Domestic & Foreign Marketing, Inspection, & Plant & Animal Health. *Armed Services* (10th of 12 R): Readiness & Management Support (RMM); Strategic Forces. *Commerce, Science & Transportation* (11th of 11 R): Science, Technology & Innovation; Consumer Affairs, Insurance & Automotive Safety; Surface Transportation & Merchant Marine Infrastructure, Safety & Security; Aviation Operations, Safety & Security. *Small Business & Entrepreneurship* (6th of 9 R).

Group Ratings

	ADA	ACLU	AFS	LCV	ITIC	NTU	COC	ACU	CFG	FRC
2006	0	17	13	14	75	78	92	100	80	87
2005	10	—	0	15	—	63	93	92	61	—

National Journal Ratings

	2005 LIB — 2005 CONS		2006 LIB — 2006 CONS	
Economic	33%	66%	25%	72%
Social	0%	77%	0%	82%
Foreign	40%	58%	15%	84%

Key Votes of the 109th Congress

1. Bar ANWR Drilling	N	5. Confirm Samuel Alito	Y	9. Limit Interstate Abortion	Y
2. FY06 Spending Curb	Y	6. Path to Citizenship	N	10. CAFTA	N
3. Estate Tax Repeal	Y	7. Bar Same Sex Marriage	Y	11. Urge Iraq Withdrawal	N
4. Raise Minimum Wage	N	8. Stem Cell Research $	N	12. Provide Detainee Rights	N

Election Results

2004 general	John Thune (R)	197,848	(51%)	($14,666,225)
	Tom Daschle (D)	193,340	(49%)	($19,991,369)
2004 primary	John Thune (R)	unopposed		
1998 general	Tom Daschle (D)	162,884	(62%)	($4,861,541)
	Ron Schmidt (R)	95,431	(36%)	($492,854)
	Other	3,796	(1%)	

Prior Winning Percentages: 2000 House (73%); 1998 House (75%); 1996 House (58%)

The junior senator from South Dakota is John Thune, a Republican elected in the most important Senate election held in 2004. He grew up in Murdo, on the dusty plains west of the Missouri River, where his father was a teacher and the family was Democratic; he went to college and business school at the University of South Dakota. As a high school freshman he met Congressman Jim Abdnor, when Abdnor spotted him at a grocery checkout counter and recalled that he had missed one of six free throws in the basketball game the previous night. They kept in touch and Thune got a job on by-then Senator Abdnor's staff in Washington in 1985; he stayed with Abdnor after he lost to Tom Daschle and was appointed to the Small Business Administration. Thune returned to South Dakota in 1989, at 28, to become executive director of the state Republican Party. In 1991 he became state railroad director under Governor George Mickelson and in 1993 director of the state Municipal League. Thune entered the 1996 race for the open House seat as very much an underdog. The favorite in the Republican primary was Lieutenant Governor Carole Hillard. But Thune attracted the support of religious conservatives, and won the primary 59%-41%. Against Democrat Rick Weiland, a former state director for Daschle, Thune opposed all tax increases (and opposed Bob Dole's tax cut, pending a balanced budget) and pledged to refuse the congressional pension; he promised to serve only three terms. He won 58%-37%.

In the House, Thune had a conservative voting record and served on the Agriculture and Transportation committees; he was chosen as freshman class representative to the Republican leadership. He was reelected 75%-28% in 1998, the largest vote margin ever for a statewide candidate in South Dakota.

After winning reelection in 2000, the question for Thune was whether he would run to replace Governor William Janklow or against Senator Tim Johnson. National Republicans hoped he would run for the Senate. Thune's wife and daughters, after trying life in metropolitan Washington, had chosen to live in Sioux Falls, and Thune seemed to be opting for a run for governor. But at a White House dinner in April 2001, George W. Bush urged Thune to run for the Senate. Within weeks, Thune agreed. Tom Daschle, majority leader starting in June 2001, said the race was "the most important political effort for me" in 2002. Daschle helped Johnson by getting him a seat on the Appropriations Committee, from which he could funnel money into South Dakota. But Thune argued that the state would be better off with a bipartisan Senate delegation. Of course, there was a caveat: a Thune victory could give the Republicans a Senate majority and make Daschle minority leader again. Johnson argued that he and Daschle made a uniquely powerful team. The two candidates spent record amounts for South Dakota—Johnson $6.2 million, Thune $6.0 million—and the national parties and independent expenditure groups on both sides spent much more.

The biggest local issue was the drought that hit western South Dakota for most of 2002. Daschle and Johnson responded by sponsoring $5 billion in disaster aid for farmers and ranchers, arguing that if floods and tornadoes triggered disaster relief, then droughts should too. But this was opposed by the Bush administration, which wanted any aid to come out of the $190 billion approved for farm spending. On August 15 George W. Bush came to South Dakota amid speculation that he would offer more. To the disappointment of the Thune campaign, he didn't. Defense was also a central issue. Thune attacked Johnson for voting against the Gulf War resolution in January 1991 and for joining the group of Democratic members of Congress who sued George H.W. Bush, challenging his conduct of the war. Johnson pointed out that his son served in the 101st Airborne Division in Afghanistan from December 2001 to June 2002 and could be sent to Iraq (which he later was) if the United States went in; Johnson announced that he would vote for the Iraq war resolution. There was one more issue blazing in October: fraudulent Indian voter registrations. The state Democratic party set up offices on each of the state's Indian reservations and paid bonuses to contractors who brought in signed voter registration cards. In October, a consultant for the Sioux Tribes Voter Education and Registration Committee was indicted on five counts of forgery of voter registration cards; Attorney General Mark Barnett and the U.S. attorney launched investigations. All of this made headlines in a state with a tradition of squeaky-clean voting and a memory of the violent Indian movement of the 1970s. Johnson said that the voter registration operation was run by the state Democratic party and that his campaign had nothing to do with it.

This election was the closest in the nation. During most of election night and into the morning, Thune led in the counting. Then the last two precincts came in, from Shannon County, which includes most of the Pine Ridge Indian Reservation. Those two precincts put Johnson over the top, by a margin of 524 votes—in percentage terms, 50.1%-49.9%. In Shannon County, 3,118 votes were cast; the vote was 92%-8% for Johnson. In the six main reservation counties, turnout was 11,275, up from 7,500 in 2000. These six counties voted 78%-21% for Johnson. Many Republicans urged Thune to contest the election. But on November 13, he announced he would not. "The people of South Dakota have been subjected to one of the longest and most expensive campaigns in South Dakota history. I choose not to subject them to more."

After the 2002 election, Thune opened his own lobbying firm and was a consultant to a D.C. law firm. But it wasn't long before he began thinking about seeking public office again. In December 2003, his successor in the House, Bill Janklow, announced he would resign after he was convicted in a fatal car crash; Thune was mentioned as a possible candidate. The other possibility was a challenge to Tom Daschle, who had been reelected by wide margins in 1992 and 1998 against lightly funded opponents. The emergence of a narrowly divided Senate and the election of George W. Bush made him one of the pivotal figures in American politics. But it seemed clear he would have trouble winning reelection. Thune's favorable ratings remained high after his defeat, and early Republican polls showed Thune 1% to 2% ahead of Daschle—the same kind of dead heat in almost every poll taken during the Johnson-Thune race. Thune figured to have the advantage of all-out support from the Bush White House and fundraising prowess as great as Daschle's, assets that none of Daschle's previous opponents had. And George W. Bush, who carried South Dakota 60%-38% in 2000, would be at the top of the ballot.

On Election Day 2002, a disappointed Daschle returned as Minority Leader. But, perhaps heeding some Democrats who argued that their party had not opposed Bush vociferously enough, he seemed determined to carry on from the minority, much as before. Senate Democrats embarked on a filibuster of a lower court nomination—the first in history. On March 17, 2003, as Bush was to address the nation that evening announcing a final 48-hour ultimatum to Saddam Hussein, Daschle said, "I'm saddened, saddened that this president failed so miserably at diplomacy that we're now forced to war. Saddened that we have to give up one life because this president couldn't create the kind of diplomatic effort that was so critical for our country." Republicans chastised him for criticizing the president at an inappropriate time. In January 2004, Thune announced that he would run against Daschle. "I had people encouraging me to run for House. But the House isn't where the problem is. The House is going to be just fine. I don't know of a place more in need of leadership than the U.S. Senate," he said.

With that statement, Thune was laying out the lead theme in his campaign—that Daschle was the chief obstructionist in the Senate, the leader of the Democratic forces that stood stubbornly in the way of the Bush administration agenda. To underscore this idea, Majority Leader Bill Frist broke with Senate tradition and traveled to South Dakota to campaign against Daschle. Daschle began running ads in the summer of 2003. His campaign revolved around the same theme used by Tim Johnson against Thune–Daschle's clout as a national party leader. He argued that a freshman senator could not hope to match his influence in Washington and he highlighted the various pork projects he delivered to South Dakota.

This was the most expensive election of the year, as both national parties and numerous third-party interest groups poured millions of dollars into South Dakota. By the end, they had spent $35 million. Almost nothing was off-limits. The state Republican party sent a mailer attacking the lobbying practices of Daschle's wife Linda, a former FAA official who later became an aviation industry lobbyist. The Club for Growth ran an ad called "Tom's House" that featured Daschle's $2 million house in a tony D.C. neighborhood; another showed Daschle as a bobble-head doll, nodding in unison with Ted Kennedy and Hillary Clinton bobble-head dolls. Daschle aired an ad that featured him embracing Bush; this infuriated Republicans who referred to Daschle as "the obstructionist-in-chief" to the Bush agenda. Thune boasted of his friendship and ability to work with the president. He said Daschle was out of touch with South Dakota values and priorities, and contended that the majority leader put the interests of the national party over the needs of the state. "He's not the same guy who put his suitcase in his station wagon and drove the family to Congress in 1978," Thune told *National Journal*. "He now is an inside-Washington, D.C., guy who lives in a multimillion-dollar mansion. The broader question is, who is more in touch with South Dakota?"

This was a closely fought race which brought out a huge turnout, up 23% from 2000 in a state with only modest growth. Thune won 51%-49%, marking the first defeat for a Senate party leader since Ernest McFarland lost to Barry Goldwater in 1952. The popular vote margin was 4,508—small, but more than eight times larger than the margin by which Thune lost to Johnson. The contours of the vote were very similar. Thune narrowly lost Sioux Falls's Minnehaha County, but won fast-growing Lincoln County next door by a bigger margin. He carried Mitchell, North Sioux City, Pierre and, by wide margins, Rapid City's Pennington Count y and the Black Hills counties around it. Daschle won most of the counties in eastern South Dakota. As compared to 2002, Thune's percentage rose in most eastern South Dakota counties and fell in most West River counties. But he increased his share of the vote significantly in the Pine Ridge and Rosebud Reservations, where his refusal to question the vote in November 2002 may have helped him.

Thune returned to Washington a conquering hero, celebrated by Republicans as a giant-killer. National Republican Senatorial Committee chairman George Allen put it this way: "When John Thune wins in South Dakota, that's like picking up three seats in itself." He became "a talk-show favorite, a fundraising star and a statesmen among freshmen Republicans," the Sioux Falls *Argus Leader* wrote in May 2005. Bill Frist named him to an informal group that met regularly over how to communicate the GOP message. But he conceded, "there are a lot of John Thune haters out there who are going to criticize whatever I do," especially in South Dakota.

Thune had a mostly conservative voting record, especially on cultural issues, but he showed some independence. In May 2005, he suffered a setback when the military base closings recommended by the Defense Department included Ellsworth Air Force Base, with nearly 4,000 local jobs and one-half of the nation's B-1 bombers. He had said during the 2004 campaign that a Republican senator with good relations with the Bush administration could better look out for Ellsworth's interests. When the base appeared on the closure list, Senate Democrats immediately used the opportunity to attack him. But Thune turned the initial setback to his favor by showing his independence in taking on the Bush administration. The initial news was "like a death in the family," he recounted. "In Washington, you can't count on anybody else to fight your battles." With Tim Johnson and Stephanie Herseth, he put aside the recent bitter partisanship at home, and made his case to the commission, the Pentagon, White House officials, and anybody else with clout about the high cost of closing Ellsworth. They generated a crowd of more than 10,000 and a pep-rally atmosphere when the base-closing commission held a hearing in Rapid City. The base survived. "It is a huge sense of relief," said Thune.

On other issues, Thune opposed the nomination of John Bolton as ambassador to the United Nations and voted against the Central American Free Trade Agreement, partly to show his independence from the White House. He joined Democrats to increase health care funding for veterans. He helped to get the Senate to agree to an annual mandate of 8 billion gallons of ethanol production by 2012, and he voiced concern in March 2007 when Bush visited Brazil to promote ethanol in that nation. He disappointed Senate Republicans in late 2006 when he decided against chairing the NRSC because he did not have enough time. Trent Lott tapped him as his chief deputy whip. With

Tim Johnson removed from Senate business because of his brain hemorrhage in December 2006, Thune was harder pressed to represent home-state interests on major issues, including the farm bill; the uncertainty over Johnson's future also postponed the focus on the prospects for a challenge to Thune in 2010.

Representative-At-Large

Stephanie Herseth Sandlin (D)

Elected June 2004, 2d full term; b. Dec. 3, 1970, Aberdeen; home, Brookings; Georgetown U., B.A. 1993, M.A. 1996, J.D. 1997; Lutheran; married (Max Sandlin).

Professional Career: Clerk, U.S. District Court, Judge Charles Kornmann 1998-99; Clerk, Judge Diana Gribbon Motz, U.S. Court of Appeals, 1999-2000; Practicing atty., 2000-01; Ex. Dir., SD Farmers Union Foundation, 2003; Legal cnsl., South Dakota Made Store, 2003.

DC Office: 331 CHOB, 20515, 202-225-2801; Fax: 202-225-5823; Web site: hersethsandlin.house.gov.

District Offices: Aberdeen, 605-626-3440; Rapid City, 605-394-5280; Sioux Falls, 605-367-8371.

Committees: *Agriculture* (10th of 25 D): Conservation, Credit, Energy & Research; General Farm Commodities & Risk Management. *Natural Resources* (26th of 27 D): National Parks, Forests & Public Lands. *Select Committee on Energy Independence and Global Warming* (6th of 9 D). *Veterans' Affairs* (5th of 16 D): Economic Opportunity (Chmn.).

Group Ratings

	ADA	ACLU	AFS	LCV	ITIC	NTU	COC	ACU	CFG	FRC
2006	65	52	71	50	71	22	80	60	30	42
2005	85	—	88	56	—	19	63	33	12	31

National Journal Ratings

	2005 LIB	—	2005 CONS		2006 LIB	—	2006 CONS
Economic	59%	—	41%		59%	—	40%
Social	57%	—	43%		59%	—	40%
Foreign	61%	—	39%		58%	—	41%

Key Votes of the 109th Congress

1. Estate Tax Repeal	N	5. Limit Interstate Abortion	N	9. Build Border Fence	Y
2. Limit CAFE Standards	Y	6. Extend Patriot Act	Y	10. CAFTA	N
3. FY06 Spending Curb	N	7. Bar Same Sex Marriage	Y	11. Oppose Iraq Withdrawal	Y
4. Drilling in ANWR	N	8. Stem Cell Research $	Y	12. Detainee Tribunals	Y

Election Results

2006 general	Stephanie Herseth Sandlin (D)	230,468	(69%)	($1,332,097)
	Bruce Whalen (R)	97,864	(29%)	($147,967)
	Other	5,230	(2%)	
2006 primary	Stephanie Herseth Sandlin (D)	unopposed		
2004 general	Stephanie Herseth (D)	207,837	(53%)	($4,026,661)
	Larry Diedrich (R)	178,823	(46%)	($2,526,515)
	Other	2,808	(1%)	

Prior Winning Percentages: 2004 (51%)

South Dakota's lone member of the House is Stephanie Herseth Sandlin, a Democrat first chosen in a June 2004 special election. She added to her name in March 2007 when she married Max Sandlin, who served eight years in the House as a Democrat from Texas until he became a victim of Tom DeLay's redistricting plan. Stephanie Herseth grew up on a farm near Brookings in northeastern South Dakota, in a family with a fine political pedigree. Her grandfather Ralph Herseth was governor from 1958 to 1960. Her grandmother Lorna Herseth was secretary of state from 1972 to 1978. Her father Lars Herseth served in the legislature from 1974 to 1986 and 1988 to 1996; in 1986 he ran for governor and lost by 52%-48%. In a state where voters expect to meet candidates the Herseths were well liked and well respected. Herseth graduated from Georgetown University and its law school, interned with Senator Tim Johnson (a college classmate of her father), clerked for federal judges in South Dakota and Maryland, taught at Georgetown law school and worked for a law firm in Washington. She turned down invitations to run against Attorney General Mark Barnett in 1998. In 2002 she decided to run for the House.

The seat was open because Republican incumbent John Thune, first elected in 1996, was running against Democratic Senator Tim Johnson. In the House race the clear favorite was Republican former Governor Bill Janklow. Blunt, plain-spoken and often tactless, Janklow pledged to be a "sledgehammer" in the House. In the June primary he beat former Senator Larry Pressler 55%-27%, while Herseth beat the 1996 Democratic House nominee, Rick Weiland, by a 58%-32% margin. She was in her own right a dynamic candidate, articulate and eager to meet people. She also proved to be a great fundraiser: with help from EMILY's List, she raised $1.5 million, more than Janklow's $1.3 million. Herseth, who started running when she was 30, argued that South Dakota had "a tradition of sending young passionate leaders to Congress," and cited Democrats Daschle and Johnson and Republicans Pressler and Thune, all first elected in their 30s. She avoided phrases that might be construed as "liberal," saying "that's not a term that's respected here." When asked about abortion, she would typically say she wanted to make it "as rare as possible." When asked about gun control she noted that she grew up on a farm in pheasant hunting country and saw no need for new restrictions on guns. Herseth was respectful of Janklow. "When I made the decision to seek office, I never thought I would be running against Bill Janklow. He is larger than life, especially for people of my generation." She noted that, while she was still in high school, then-Governor Janklow took time from his schedule to answer questions from her for a report she was writing.

The two candidates agreed on many local issues but they differed in their approaches to Iraq. In September 2002 Janklow said, "I'd love to have the support of our allies, but it's the American World Trade Center they flew the planes into. I'd love to have the support of our allies, but if we can't get the support of these people, then in this war they're not our allies, and we may have to go it alone." Herseth said, "We are looking at putting our men and women in urban warfare, hand-to-hand combat on the streets of Baghdad. I view it as a sliding scale. To the extent that we have little support from allies, the need goes way up for congressional approval. With more allied support, the bar goes down a little for congressional approval." Herseth was an attractive and energetic candidate, while some South Dakotans thought that Janklow had just run to block Pressler and was not really interested in the job. When the NRCC ran a spot attacking Herseth as a carpetbagger, Janklow insisted it be pulled. Janklow pulled ahead in the polls in October, as the nation contemplated military action in Iraq, and on Election Day he won 53%-46%.

But Janklow's House career was cut short. In August 2003 he sped through a stop sign in his Cadillac and killed a motorcyclist in Moody County. He was indicted, tried and, in December 2003, convicted of felony manslaughter, and immediately announced that he would resign. Governor Mike Rounds declared that the vacancy would be filled in a special election held in June 2004, the same day as South Dakota's primary. After the 2002 election Herseth taught at South Dakota State University and headed the South Dakota Farmers Union Foundation. She was the obvious and unanimous choice for the House race for the Democrats. The Republican nominee was state Senator Larry Diedrich, a corn, hog and soybean farmer who had headed the South Dakota and American Soybean Associations and served eight years in the legislature. Herseth campaigned as a "fiscally conservative and ideologically moderate" candidate; she called for changes in the 2003 Medicare/prescription drug act and a ban on meatpacker ownership of livestock. She supported abortion rights; he opposed abortion and criticized her for refusing to promise to vote for a constitutional amendment banning same-sex marriage. He also criticized her opposition to making some tax cuts permanent and focused attention on her lack of life experience. Herseth, who was single then, said, "A lot of people today know women, or even have women in their family, who have postponed marriage and family-raising for professional reasons. Some of the stereotypes that were once out there are not so strong any more." Herseth started off far ahead in the polls. But Diedrich campaigned hard and caught up by late May. Herseth won 51%-49%, with a popular vote margin of just 3,005. Turnout in the heavily Republican Black Hills area was low; Herseth carried the Indian reservations by wide margins.

For the November 2004 election, Diedrich was the Republican nominee and, after recovering from heart surgery in June, kept on running. As in the special election contest, the candidates debated frequently and civilly; Herseth even gave Diedrich credit for lobbying an Appropriations subcommittee chairman for the Lewis and Clark Water Project. But negative notes were also struck. Diedrich and national Republicans attacked Herseth for roll call votes—against making permanent the marriage penalty ban, the child tax credit and the deductibility of state sales taxes;

against EPA authority to waive state laws requiring low-pollution gasoline blends. National Democrats ran ads criticizing Diedrich's votes as a legislator to increase taxes on gasoline, cell phones and hospitals and opposing abolition of the inheritance tax. At one debate Herseth was asked how she would vote if the presidential election went to the House. "I represent South Dakota. And I'm going to put South Dakota first," she said. When Diedrich pressed her to say whom she would vote for, she said, "I guess Larry is parsing my words. I would vote for George Bush for president." This race was overshadowed by the hot and even closer race between John Thune and Tom Daschle. While Daschle lost, she managed to widen her margin to 53%-46%. In 2006, she finally had an easy contest, with a 69%-29% victory against Bruce Whalen, a member of the Oglala Sioux Tribe.

In the House, Herseth Sandlin's voting record ranks her among the more conservative Democrats. She cosponsored a bill that restricts victims of a shooting from filing a lawsuit against gun manufacturers and dealers. She worked closely with Senators Johnson and Thune in their successful effort in 2005 to remove Ellsworth Air Force Base from the base-closing list. Herseth Sandlin became a leader among the Blue Dogs, especially in their call for fiscal discipline; she co-chaired the Democrats' Rural Working Group while also serving on the Agriculture Committee, where she was an avid supporter of increased production of renewable fuels such as ethanol. On the farm bill, she hoped to add a permanent disaster-aid program—"one that removes politics from the process," she said. In the majority, she chaired the Veterans' Affairs Subcommittee on Economic Opportunity. She wants members of the National Guard and Reserves who have served extended periods of active duty since September 2001 to have benefits equivalent to those for active duty personnel. Speaker Pelosi tapped her for a seat on the Select Committee on Energy Independence and Global Warming—the only farm-state Democrat on the panel.

Many Democrats see Herseth Sandlin as a future national star. She was supportive of Tim Johnson following his brain hemorrhage in December 2006 and lengthy recuperation; she likely would run for his Senate seat if he retires in 2008. Other options include the governorship or a run against John Thune in 2010.

★ TENNESSEE ★

Tennessee is a battleground state, with a fighting temperament since it was settled 200 years ago by the likes of Andrew Jackson and went on to produce so many soldiers it came to be known as the Volunteer State. This was a frontier battleground in the 1790s, from which Jackson launched his wars on the Indians and the British. It was a military battleground in the 1860s, when Yankee troops swept down the Tennessee and Cumberland Rivers on their way to Mississippi and through Chattanooga's Lookout Mountain on their way to Atlanta and the sea. But a battleground with a certain civility: both Confederate and Union generals paid respectful calls on the widow of President James K. Polk, who stayed carefully neutral, in her Nashville mansion. Tennessee has been a cultural battleground for much of the 20th century. On one side were the Fugitives, writers like John Crowe Ransom and Allen Tate, who contributed to "I'll Take My Stand," a manifesto calling for retaining the South's rural economy and heritage. On the other side have been business leaders and politicians who have made Tennessee the fastest-growing state of the interior South: Tennessee has given birth to the first supermarket (a Piggly Wiggly), the Holiday Inn, FedEx and Goo-Goo Clusters.

This state has also been a marshaling ground for the music traditions that have a large place in Americans' lives. East Tennessee is one of the homes of bluegrass music and mountain fiddling, with string bands and vocal harmony; Knoxville's *Tennessee Barn Dance* has been broadcast since 1942. Gospel music has long been centered in Nashville, which is also the nation's leading center of religious publishing, the headquarters of Thomas Nelson, FaithWorks, Integrity Books and LifeWay's Broadman & Holman. Country music got its commercial start in Nashville, with broadcasts of the Grand Ole Opry from Ryman Auditorium starting in 1925; Nashville remains indisputably the capital of country music. The Mississippi lowlands around Memphis, economically and culturally the metropolis of the Mississippi Delta, gave birth to the blues in the years from the 1890s to 1920; and the blues were in turn the inspiration for the jazz musicians of Beale Street in the 1920s and Elvis Presley, whose Graceland mansion is now a major tourist destination, in the 1950s and 1960s.

Tennessee is and has long been a political battleground. Its political divisions have their roots in the Civil War, and many counties today still vote their 1860s loyalties: The Union counties,

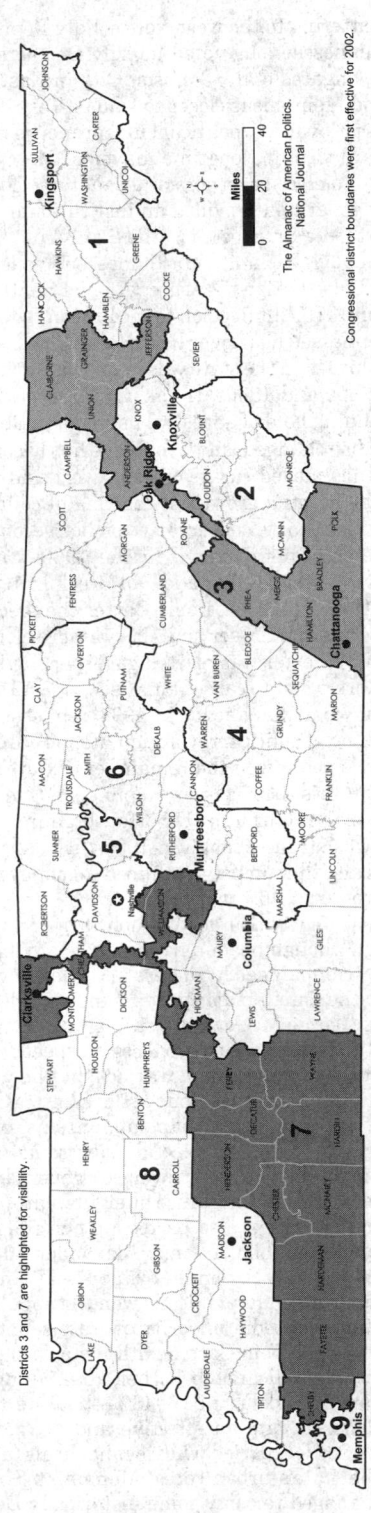

Districts 3 and 7 are highlighted for visibility.

The Almanac of American Politics.
National Journal

Congressional district boundaries were first effective for 2002.

mainly in the east but also a scattering to the west, vote solidly Republican, while the Confederate counties in middle and west Tennessee long voted heavily Democratic. There are long distances between these regions in this elongated state: Johnson City in East Tennessee is closer to Dover, Delaware, than to Memphis, and Memphis is closer to Dallas, Texas, than to Johnson City. Within the limits of these enduring party loyalties, political entrepreneurs have set the tone for the state. From the 1920s to 1948, Edward Crump, longtime mayor of Memphis, used his total control of Democratic primary votes there to elect governors and senators. The Tennessee Valley Authority and the cheap electric power it generated provided an institutional base for reform liberal Democrats Estes Kefauver and Albert Gore Sr., elected to the Senate in 1948 and 1952. They were soon national figures, with reliable enough backing from Tennessee's yellow-dog Democratic majority to vote for civil rights bills and to refuse to sign the segregationist Southern Manifesto. Kefauver died in 1963 and Gore was defeated in 1970, but lived on to see his son twice elected vice president before his death in December 1998. Tennessee has never had a large black population—16% today, half of whom live in and around Memphis—and the state was not riven by the racial animosity that seared so much of the South in the 1950s and 1960s, thanks in large part to the actions of its leading politicians, but also to the continuing hold of ancestral partisan preferences.

Today the political balance has changed, and Tennessee has become a mostly Republican state. Democrats' cultural liberalism has moved rural voters in west and middle Tennessee away from their ancestral loyalties, and the surging growth in the ring of counties around Nashville in the 1990s has created a new voting bloc that is conservative on both economic and cultural issues. The first movement toward the Republicans occurred in the 1960s and 1970s, symbolized by the elections of Republican Senators Howard Baker and Bill Brock in 1966 and 1970, and Republican Governor Lamar Alexander in 1978. Then, as Jimmy Carter changed the image of the Democratic Party, Democrats rallied; Democrats Jim Sasser and Al Gore were elected to the Senate in 1976 and 1984, and Democrat Ned Ray McWherter was elected governor in 1986. This movement was still strong enough for the Clinton-Gore ticket to carry Tennessee 47%-42% in 1992. But the narrowness of the margin was a warning of what was ahead. In 1994 Tennessee turned against the Clinton administration and produced a kind of political revolution. Republican Fred Thompson, famous as a Watergate investigator and movie actor, won the remainder of Gore's Senate term by a landslide, and heart transplant surgeon Bill Frist beat Sasser; Republican Don Sundquist was elected governor. Republicans won a majority of the vote for the U.S. House, gaining two seats and coming close in a third. The Republican trend was strong enough in 1996 that only after extraordinary efforts— Gore made 16 appearances here and the campaign pumped in money for late ads—was the Clinton-Gore ticket able to win by a narrow 48%-46% margin.

In 2000 the tide was even stronger. George W. Bush targeted the state early and worked it energetically; the Gore campaign, though headquartered in Nashville, seemed to assume it would come around in the end, and only campaigned hard here in the last few days. Bush carried the state 51%-47% and Gore became only the fourth major party nominee to lose his home state in 85 years (the others were South Dakota's George McGovern in 1972, Kansas's Alf Landon in 1936 and New Jersey's Woodrow Wilson in 1916). In his gracious concession speech, Gore noted that he had some fence-mending to do in Tennessee, but the problem was not that he was personally unpopular; the problem was that the issue positions and cultural tone of the Clinton-Gore administration was alien and grating in rural Tennessee and in the suburban subdivisions expanding from Nashville and other cities out into the countryside. The 2002 election saw some movement back to Tennessee Democrats: Former Nashville Mayor Phil Bredesen won the governorship by 51%-48%: Tennessee has now alternated the parties in the governor's office at eight-year intervals for a quarter-century. Democrats, aided by partisan redistricting, also picked up one congressional district and maintained control of the legislature. But Republican Lamar Alexander, 20 years after he won his second election as governor, was elected to the U.S. Senate by a 54%-44% margin. In 2004 Bush carried Tennessee by a solid 57%-43% margin and Republicans won the popular vote for the House and, for the first time since Reconstruction, elected a majority of state senators. In 2006 Bredesen, after spending political capital trimming the TennCare health insurance program, was reelected 69%-30%, carrying all 95 counties. But Republican Bob Corker, after winning a bitter primary, was able to beat Democratic Congressman Harold Ford 51%-48%—the one Republican victory in closely fought 2006 Senate contests. This, despite an effective and attractive campaign by Ford, who carried his fellow blacks 95%-4%; Corker carried white evangelicals (a majority of voters) 58%-41%. Ford ran especially strong in the state's urban cores, Memphis's Shelby County and Nashville's Davidson County. But Corker managed to carry some historically Democratic counties in Middle and West Tennessee, and got between 53% and 67% in the ring of six counties around Davidson County and 58% in the two suburban counties adjoining Shelby County.

This is a Tennessee that is expanding economically but is not abandoning its cultural roots. If its economy lagged behind the nation's through much of the 20th century, its respect for hard work and its open climate for entrepreneurism have enabled it to grow mightily in its last decades and in the first years of the 21st. The expansion started in the early 1980s, when Alexander helped bring big auto plants to middle Tennessee. The lack of strong unions and of bitter racial divisions— Tennessee was mostly untouched by the racial strife of the 1930s and the civil rights strife of the 1960s—attracted Japanese companies here, which in turn attracted General Motors's Saturn division. In the past few years, as the Big Three auto companies' problems sank Michigan's economy, Tennessee's mostly Japanese auto companies have maintained a vital and growing auto parts industry; there are an estimated 125,000 auto-related jobs in the state. In 2006 Nissan moved its American headquarters from the Los Angeles suburbs to Nashville. Some of Tennessee's old industries have fallen behind: apparel and textile factories have closed, and the tobacco harvest in 2006, after the federal tobacco buyout, was down 72% from its peak in 1982. But country music has boomed, and Nashville has become a major health care center. Unemployment has been low, and Tennessee's population increased 19% between 1990 and 2006. Growth has been particularly robust in the ring of counties around Nashville, which have been attracting significant Hispanic immigration.

Despite or because of all that growth, Tennessee state politics has become, well, a battleground. Tennessee has been growing more than neighboring in part because of its low taxes. It has no income tax (the state Supreme Court ruled in 1931 that the state Constitution didn't list the income tax as one the legislature could impose, and so it couldn't) and it ranks low on the list of state and local taxes as a percentage of per capita income. But in 1994 Governor Ned Ray McWherter created TennCare, an extension of Medicaid, and TennCare spending accelerated far above projections from $2.5 billion in 1995 to $8 billion in 2004. Republican Governor Don Sundquist, elected on a no-income-tax platform, nonetheless pressed unsuccessfully for an income tax. Democratic Governor Phil Bredesen, also elected on a no-income-tax platform, kept his promise and scaled TennCare back significantly in 2005. In 2006 he was resoundingly reelected; Democrats got a party-switcher's seat back in the state Senate, but one Democrat voted with Republicans to oust Senate leader (and under Tennessee rules, Lieutenant Governor) John Wilder, who at 85 had held that position, sometimes with Republican votes, since 1971—the longest-serving legislative leader in the nation.

The People		Race/Ethnic Origin			Military veterans: 560,141 (13.1%)	
Pop. 2006 (est):	6,038,803	4,505,930	79.2%	White	WWII: 17.3%	Korea: 12.8%
Pop. 2000:	5,689,283	928,204	16.3%	Black	Vietnam: 33.9%	Gulf War: 11.0%
Pop. 1990:	4,877,185	56,077	1.0%	Asian	**Most populous cities (2006):**	
Change 1990-2000:	Up 16.7%	13,820	0.2%	Native Am.	1. Memphis	670,902
% of U.S. total:	2.0%	1,810	0.0%	Hawaiian	2. Nashville	578,698
Pop. rank:	16th of 50	54,824	1.0%	Two+ races	3. Knoxville	182,337
Area size:	42,143 sq. mi.	4,780	0.1%	Other	4. Chattanooga	155,190
State Native:	64.7%	123,838	2.2%	Hisp. Origin	5. Clarksville	113,175
Non-citizen:	1.9%	**Ancestry**				
Language		USA: 14.7%		Irish: 7.8%	Urban population: 63.6%	
English: 93.5%	Spanish: 3.3%	English: 7.6%		German: 7.0%	Rural population: 36.4%	
Other Eur.: 2.0%		Scotch-Irish: 2.2%				

Education		Work Sector			General Assembly		
H.S. Grad:	75.9%	Private: 78.4%		Govt: 13.9%	Senate	16 D 16 R 1 I	
College Grad:	19.6%	Self: 7.3%		Family: 0.3%	House	53 D 46 R	
Industry		Unemployment: 5.4%			Legislative Term Limits: No		
Agri: 1.4%	Con: 7.3%	**Household Income**			**Registered Voters**		
Fin: 5.8%	Info: 2.4%	<15k: 19.2%		15-35k: 28.9%	No party registration		
Mfg: 25.2%	Prof: 26.0%	35-50k: 17.4%		50-100k: 26.2%			
Public: 4.0%	Trade: 15.6%	100-150k: 5.2%		>150k: 3.1%			
Other: 12.3%		Median: $36,360					
Occupation		Poverty status: 13.5%					
Blue collar: 30.2%	White collar: 55.6%	**Home Value**					
Gray collar: 14.2%		<50k: 19.0%	50-100k: 40.1%	100-200k: 29.9%	200-300k: 6.8%		
		300-500k: 2.9%	>500k: 1.3%	Median: $88,300			

Presidential politics   Tennessee has been about evenly divided in presidential politics at several different points in the last half-century, even as its basic political leanings have switched from Democratic to Republican. It was close in the Eisenhower-Stevenson races in the 1950s, in the Carter-Reagan race of 1980 and again in 1992, 1996 and 2000. But the fact that native son Al Gore was unable to win here as the representative of the incumbent party in a time of peace and prosperity suggests that Tennessee may be out of reach for presidential Democrats in the near future. Tennessee was not a battleground state in the 2004 presidential election, and George W. Bush carried it 57%-43%. John Kerry carried the counties including Memphis and Nashville, but lost heavily in the suburban ring around Nashville and otherwise carried only 15 ancestrally Democratic rural counties; Bush carried 81 of 99 counties altogether.

2004 Presidential Vote		
Bush (R)	1,384,375	(57%)
Kerry (D)	1,036,477	(43%)
Nader (I)	8,992	(0%)
Other	7,475	(0%)

2004 Democratic Presidential Primary		
Kerry (D)	151,527	(41%)
Edwards (D)	97,914	(27%)
Clark (D)	85,315	(23%)
Dean (D)	16,128	(4%)
Sharpton (D)	6,107	(2%)
Other	12,394	(3%)

2000 Presidential Vote		
Bush (R)	1,061,949	(51%)
Gore (D)	981,720	(47%)
Nader (Green)	19,781	(1%)
Other	12,731	(1%)

For several cycles Tennessee held its presidential primary on Super Tuesday (though Tennessee holds its state primaries on Thursdays, the only state to do so). But it was far from the biggest state to vote that day, and so received little attention. In 2004 it voted earlier, on February 10, just two weeks after New Hampshire; the only other primary that day was in Virginia. This was just a week after John Edwards had won in South Carolina and Wesley Clark had led Edwards and Kerry in a virtual three-way tie in Oklahoma. Edwards's and Clark's home states were both contiguous to Tennessee, and as southerners and, in Clark's case, as a general, they would seem to have special appeal in the state. But Kerry won the primary with 41% of the vote to 27% for Edwards and 23% for Clark. Kerry had big pluralities in the largest counties but carried most small counties as well. Turnout was 369,000—far lower than the record Democratic primary turnout in 1988 of 576,000, when Al Gore was running.

But even if it is not competitive in November, Tennessee remains a force in presidential politics. Al Gore's political base is still his large house in Nashville. Tennessee is also a hotbed of presidential candidates. Senator Howard Baker ran for president in 1980, without much success, but his proteges in Tennessee Republican politics have also entered the presidential field. Lamar Alexander ran a strong campaign in 1996 and claimed to be the candidate most feared by the Clintons; he came close to finishing second in New Hampshire, which would have left him the main rival to Patrick Buchanan, and thus the likely nominee. He set out to run again in 2000, but withdrew after the August 1999 Iowa Republican straw poll. Bill Frist, after becoming Senate Majority Leader in 2003, seemed well positioned to run in 2008 as a candidate in line with the Republican base that had nominated George W. Bush in 2000. But the frustrations he encountered in the Senate left him with little support, and shortly after the November 2006 election he announced he would not run and returned to Nashville. Then, in March 2007, Fred Thompson appeared on "Fox News Sunday" and announced that he was giving serious consideration to running. On September 5, Thompson launched his campaign with an appearance on NBC's "Tonight Show With Jay Leno" where he told the host, "I'm running for president of the United States." Thompson, like other Tennessee Republicans, can look to his home state for financial support. The Nashville establishment traditionally supported Democrats in Tennessee politics, but now Nashville money has become heavily Republican: metro Nashville gave $9.3 million, mostly to Republicans, in the 2004 cycle, with $4.6 million coming from just three zip codes—37205, 37215 and 37027.

Congressional districting

| 110th Congress Lineup |
| 5 D   4 R |
| 109th Congress Lineup |
| 5 D   4 R |

Tennessee's Democratic legislature controlled redistricting after the 2000 Census; Republican Governor Don Sundquist's veto could be overridden by majority votes in both houses. But in January 2002 the Democrats, with help from 6th District Democrat Bart Gordon, drew lines which were agreed to by most Republicans. The congressional district plan cut across party lines far more often than ever before in Tennessee. It took six Democratic-leaning counties out of Republican Zach Wamp's 3d District and placed them in the 4th District, whose incumbent Republican Van Hilleary was running for governor. That enabled Democratic state Senator Lincoln Davis to win the 4th: He led by only 2,000 votes in the counties formerly in the district, but by nearly 8,000 in the counties added, and would probably have trailed in the Republican East Tennessee counties that were subtracted. Heavily Republican Williamson County south of Nashville was taken out of Gordon's 6th and split between the 4th and the heavily Republican 7th District.

Tennessee will elect a new governor in 2010, and the legislature is closely enough divided now that it's risky to forecast which party will control either chamber when it comes time to redistrict in 2011-12.

Governor

Phil Bredesen (D)

Elected 2002, term expires Jan. 2011, 2d term; b. Nov. 21, 1943, Oceanport, NJ; home, Nashville; Harvard U., B.S. 1967; Catholic; married (Andrea Conte).

Elected Office: Lexington, MA, City Cncl., 1972-73; Nashville Mayor, 1991-99.

Professional Career: Founder, HealthAmerica Corp., 1975-86.

Office: State Capitol, Nashville, 37243, 615-741-2001; Fax: 615-532-9711; Web site: www.state.tn.us/governor.

Election Results

2006 general	Phil Bredesen (D)	1,247,491	(69%)
	Jim Bryson (R)	540,853	(30%)
	Other	30,205	(2%)
2006 primary	Phil Bredesen (D)	393,004	(89%)
	John Jay Hooker (D)	31,933	(7%)
	Other	19,117	(4%)
2002 general	Phil Bredesen (D)	837,284	(51%)
	Van Hilleary (R)	786,803	(48%)

Phil Bredesen is a Democrat who was elected governor of Tennessee in 2002, on his second try. Bredesen grew up far from Nashville, in Shortsville, New York, 30 miles southeast of Rochester; his parents were divorced and his mother worked as a bank teller; his grandmother lived with him and took in sewing for a living. He got a scholarship at Harvard and graduated with a degree in physics, and in 1967 he moved to Lexington, Massachusetts, and went to work for Itek; it was classified work and he got a draft deferment for it. He caught the political bug early. In 1968 he volunteered for Eugene McCarthy in New Hampshire and then for Robert Kennedy and for John Lindsay for mayor in New York in 1969. In 1970 he ran for the Massachusetts state Senate and lost to a longtime incumbent. In 1972 he won a seat on the Lexington Town Meeting. He went to work for Searle, a pharmaceutical firm, and moved to London, where he met his wife. She was recruited by Hospital Corporation of America; he quit his job to follow her to Nashville in 1975. There he got a job with Hospital Affiliates International, negotiating management contracts with hospitals. He wanted to start his own business and in 1980, with $50,000 cash and $250,000 in backing from local venture capitalists, operating from a computer in his den, he started HealthAmerica, which began acquiring and operating HMOs across the country. When it went public in 1983, it ran 20 HMOs with 400,000 members. His backers decided to sell the firm in 1986, and got $400 million from MaxiCare; Bredesen pocketed $47 million, while MaxiCare, under other management, later went bankrupt.

The political bug bit again. This time his goal was not the Lexington Town Meeting, but the mayoralty of Nashville, a particularly powerful position since the city includes all of Davidson County and the mayor has broad powers. Bredesen spent $2 million on his 1987 mayoral campaign but lost in the runoff to Congressman Bill Boner. Bredesen ran again in the January 1988 special election to succeed Boner, but lost the primary 40%-36% to former gubernatorial candidate Bob Clement. In 1991 Bredesen ran for mayor again and won with 71%. As mayor, Bredesen had some spectacular successes. He lined up financing for a hockey arena and, later, a football stadium and brought the NHL Predators and NFL Tennessee Titans to Nashville. He enticed Dell to locate a facility in Nashville. Nashville boomed in the 1990s and he took credit for 106,000 new jobs. Once a regional center, Nashville now seemed to be a major national metro area.

Nashville is Tennessee's largest media market, covering almost all of Middle Tennessee, and a successful Nashville mayor is a natural candidate for statewide office. In 1994 Bredesen spent $6 million on running for governor and won the Democratic nomination with 53% of the vote in a 10-candidate field. He did not campaign heavily in East and West Tennessee and lost to Republican Don Sundquist by a 54%-45% margin. But in the years that followed, Bredesen had a more successful record than Sundquist. The state government's problem is that it had an increasingly expensive health care program, TennCare, and one of the nation's lowest revenue bases, with no state income tax. TennCare, established in 1994 with federal waivers, covered not only those eligible for Medicaid but others with relatively low incomes or who were uninsured; enrollment zoomed and costs increased higher than average. In his second term, Sundquist went back on a campaign promise and sought an income tax. Most Republicans opposed him, arguing that Tennessee's low taxes helped account for the fact that the state had had much more economic growth than most neighboring states. The legislature, barraged at critical points by honking motorists and slogan-chanting anti-tax crusaders mobilized by radio talk show hosts, refused to pass one.

Against this background Bredesen, who had not run for reelection as mayor in 1999, decided to run for governor again. He said that he opposed an income tax and argued that his experience managing health care systems would enable him to straighten out TennCare. He won the Democratic primary easily, but the favorite was Republican Congressman Van Hilleary, who based his campaign on opposition to an income tax. Hilleary charged that Bredesen was a rich northerner who didn't really understand Tennessee. Bredesen undercut that by sitting down with folks over coffee and telling how he had grown up poor in a small town. Unusual for a Democrat, he appeared on conservative talk radio shows and made a favorable impression.

Much of Hilleary's campaign was based on the premise that Bredesen didn't really oppose an income tax. In September Hilleary ran an ad saying that "Phil BredeSundquist" had raised property taxes three times in Nashville (as indeed Bredesen had). Bredesen responded the next day with an on-camera ad: "Well, Mr. Hilleary, I'll say it again as clearly as I know how. I do not support an income tax." Bredesen focused more on fixing TennCare. "Everybody in the state of Tennessee knows somebody on TennCare they don't think should be on TennCare. It needs to be the bronze package, not the platinum package," he said. Hilleary, who said TennCare was "not my passion," said he would cut $300 to $400 million from TennCare. On other issues, there was agreement: Both candidates opposed gun control, supported scheduled teacher pay raises, called for children to learn to read by the third grade, wanted more spending on higher education, more spending to promote tourism and expansion of the Tennessee Industrial Infrastructure Program.

Bredesen spent $3 million of his own money on his campaign, to counter, he said, money raised for Hilleary by George W. Bush. This turned out to be the closest Tennessee governor's race since 1896; Bredesen won 51%-48%. This time he had campaigned across the state, raising money in small fundraisers, holding chili suppers in rural counties. He broke into the Republican base in East Tennessee, carrying Knoxville's Knox County—and holding Hilleary to a narrow lead in his own region. Bredesen carried Nashville solidly, had a big lead in Memphis and carried rural West Tennessee, often a swing area in Tennessee elections.

Facing a predicted $800 million budget shortfall, Bredesen got the legislature to cut state spending 9% across the board in 2003 and to vote in a lottery to pay for college scholarships. He supported changes in workmen's comp supported by businesses and opposed by trial lawyers. He got the legislature to limit driver's licenses to citizens and aliens with permanent resident status; others could get certificates of driving which would not be valid identification.

In 2004 he proposed selective increases in spending; he pushed through a $174 million education increase, raising teacher pay above the Southeastern average and starting voluntary pre-kindergarten. The big elephant remained in the room: TennCare. By early 2004 it consumed nearly one-third of the state budget and its 2005 cost was estimated to be $650 million over what was budgeted. In May 2004 the legislature approved Bredesen's proposed changes. One reason TennCare had so many benefits and cost so much was that self-styled public interest groups, notably the Tennessee Justice Center, kept going to court to enforce old consent decrees. In June 2004 the Tennessee Justice Center went to court again. In September Bredesen asked the Centers for Medicare and Medicaid Services for approval of all his changes. But the lawsuits went on, and on November 10 Bredesen announced that he was ready to abolish TennCare and move back to standard Medicaid, which would eliminate coverage for 430,000 people, one-third of beneficiaries.

Twice in the next weeks Bredesen met with the head of the Tennessee Justice Center to get concessions. But they would make none. On January 10, 2005, he announced that all non-Medicaid-eligible adults would be removed from TennCare and that strict limits would be imposed on prescription drugs and doctor visits, with no appeals. Bredesen proposed taking 323,000 adults off TennCare rolls, but he later scaled back that number by 97,000. Federal courts twice halted the proposed cuts, but the governor had won approval for his plan and by the end of the year the state trimmed 191,000 people from the program. By 2006 the overhaul of TennCare had reduced the cost increase from $650 million to $115 million and resulted in state budget surpluses. Bredesen sought to ease the pain of the cuts by using money saved from TennCare to establish a "safety net" to fund health clinics, indigent hospital care and prescription drug assistance for the mentally ill. Bredesen also used the savings to boost state education spending in his 2006 budget by $366.5 million, targeting pre-kindergarten initiatives with $55 million to fund 528 new pre-kindergarten class-rooms.

The governor in 2006 also launched Cover Tennessee to fund health care for those with pre-existing medical conditions, uninsured children and working adults. Unlike TennCare, the new state program would not receive federal money, except to cover children, and would tap some of the TennCare savings to get the program started. Bredesen said he would consider a tobacco tax increase in the future, but not an income tax. (In June 2005, Bredesen had vetoed a 50 cent per-pack increase on certain small brands because it might have interfered with payments from a settlement with the tobacco industry.) Fixing the state's health care system, a preoccupation for much of his first term, became a personal cause for Bredesen in December 2006. The governor had returned home to New York to watch his younger brother, an alcoholic, die of liver disease. Dean Bredesen, a vacuum cleaner salesman, had never asked his older brother, the multimillionaire former health care executive, for the $10,000 deposit that would have gotten him access to health care. Bredesen grieved publicly. He said he did not know if better care would have saved his brother but said the death gave him insight into what it is like to be an uninsured American. "If you're inside, it is warm and comforting. If you're outside with your face pressed to the window looking in, it's cold and scary," he said.

Bredesen's administration has faced criticism on ethics matters, although the governor sought to address the issues before they became major distractions. He ordered a shake-up of hiring practices at the Tennessee Highway Patrol after the Nashville *Tennessean* ran a story in 2005 about political insiders who were given official-looking identification that recognized them as "honorary captains" in the police force. Some tried to use them to get out of traffic violations, and two highway patrol officers were promoted after testifying on behalf of an "honorary captain" charged with a DUI, but Bredesen halted their rise. An outside review found evidence of corruption and cronyism at the THP, and Bredesen backed reform recommendations. His administration also faced scrutiny for getting involved in sexual harassment cases that involved two political appointees and Bredesen ordered Personnel Department employees to stop shredding documents related to their cases. In early 2006, Bredesen called the state legislature back in to session so lawmakers could finish an ethics bill that included limits on cash contributions from lobbyists. The new rules were prompted by the FBI's Tennessee Waltz bribery investigation that led to the May 2005 arrests of five current and former state legislators.

Some national Democrats, given pause by their defeats in November 2004, began to give Bredesen a lookover. *The New Republic* ran a laudatory cover story on him in January 2005. Bredesen seemed not totally uninterested, but said, "The people who have the opportunities are the ones who put their heads down and do the best job they can at the job at hand, and that produces the kind of opportunities that people who put their heads up don't have." But first he had to win reelection in 2006. Bredesen, a strong fundraiser who also could spend his own millions, ended up with weak Republican opposition. He faced freshman state Senator Jim Bryson, who ran negative television ads accusing Bredesen of not doing enough to crack down on illegal immigrants. But Bredesen had distinguished himself by making difficult decisions about TennCare and restoring the state's fiscal health. He carried all 95 counties and won 69%-30%.After the election, Bredesen made no move to join the early Democratic jockeying for the 2008 presidential nomination. But his status as one of the South's few Democratic governors, his insistence on fiscal restraint and thoughtful problem-solving could earn him a spot on the Democratic nominee's vice presidential short list.

Senior Senator

Lamar Alexander (R)

Elected 2002, seat up 2008, 1st term; b. July 3, 1940, Maryville; home, Nashville; Vanderbilt U., B.A. 1962, N.Y.U., J.D. 1965; Presbyterian; married (Honey).

Elected Office: TN Governor, 1978-86.

Professional Career: Pres., Univ. of TN, 1988-91; U.S. Edu. Sect., 1991-93; Co-director, Empower America, 1994-95; Prof., Harvard U. JFK Schl. of Govt., 2001-02.

DC Office: 455 DSOB, 20510, 202-224-4944; Fax: 202-228-3398; Web site: alexander.senate.gov.

State Offices: Blountville, 423-325-6240; Chattanooga, 423-752-5337; Jackson, 731-423-9344; Knoxville, 865-545-4253; Memphis, 901-544-4224; Nashville, 615-736-5129.

Committees: *Appropriations* (14th of 14 R): Legislative Branch; State, Foreign Operations & Related Programs; Commerce, Justice, Science & Related Agencies; Homeland Security; Interior, Environment & Related Agencies; Transportation, Housing and Urban Development & Related Agencies. *Environment & Public Works* (8th of 9 R): Public Sector Solutions to Global Warming, Oversight & Children's Health Protection (RMM); Clean Air & Nuclear Safety. *Health, Education, Labor & Pensions* (3d of 10 R): Children & Families (RMM); Retirement & Aging. *Rules & Administration* (8th of 9 R).

Group Ratings

	ADA	ACLU	AFS	LCV	ITIC	NTU	COC	ACU	CFG	FRC
2006	5	18	13	29	100	80	92	72	78	87
2005	5	—	0	15	—	71	100	88	79	—

National Journal Ratings

	2005 LIB	—	2005 CONS		2006 LIB	—	2006 CONS
Economic	36%	—	61%		20%	—	77%
Social	23%	—	64%		33%	—	64%
Foreign	0%	—	74%		26%	—	67%

Key Votes of the 109th Congress

1. Bar ANWR Drilling	N	5. Confirm Samuel Alito	Y	9. Limit Interstate Abortion	Y
2. FY06 Spending Curb	Y	6. Path to Citizenship	N	10. CAFTA	Y
3. Estate Tax Repeal	Y	7. Bar Same Sex Marriage	Y	11. Urge Iraq Withdrawal	N
4. Raise Minimum Wage	N	8. Stem Cell Research $	Y	12. Provide Detainee Rights	N

Election Results

2002 general	Lamar Alexander (R)	891,420	(54%)	($3,761,804)
	Bob Clement (D)	728,295	(44%)	($2,832,990)
2002 primary	Lamar Alexander (R)	295,052	(54%)	
	Ed Bryant (R)	233,678	(43%)	
	Other	19,752	(3%)	
1996 general	Fred D. Thompson (R)	1,091,554	(61%)	($3,469,369)
	Houston Gordon (D)	654,937	(37%)	($795,969)
	Other	32,173	(2%)	

Lamar Alexander, former governor of Tennessee and secretary of education, was elected Tennessee's junior senator in 2002. Alexander grew up Maryville, in East Tennessee between Knoxville and the Smoky Mountains, the son of a principal and a teacher; he started piano lessons at 4 and still plays.

Like Bill Clinton, he was elected governor of Boys State. He graduated from Vanderbilt, where he wrote editorials in the *Hustler* urging integration, and New York University Law School; he clerked for Judge John Minor Wisdom of the Fifth Circuit federal appeals court. Alexander was always a Republican, and in 1966 he wrote Howard Baker, then the Republican candidate for Senate, and volunteered for his Senate campaign against Frank Clement; Baker gave him a job—the critical connection in Alexander's career. In 1967 he served on Baker's staff in Washington; briefly he lived in a group house with a Democratic congressional staffer named Trent Lott. In 1969, on Baker's recommendation, Alexander got a job working for Richard Nixon's congressional liaison Bryce Harlow. On a trip back to Tennessee to scout the possibilities of running against Senator Albert Gore Sr. in 1970, he met Memphis dentist Winfield Dunn, who was running for governor; Alexander agreed to manage his campaign and Dunn became the first Republican elected governor in 50 years. He decided that next time he would be the candidate, so in 1974, at 34, he ran for governor. He ran a conventional campaign and in that Watergate year lost 55%-44% to Democratic Congressman Ray Blanton.

He ran again in 1978, but differently this time: Wearing a red plaid shirt, he walked 1,000 miles across Tennessee. This time he won 56%-44%. After the election Blanton started issuing many pardons of criminals: It turned out that he was taking bribes. To stop him, the U.S. attorney, a Democrat, urged that Alexander be sworn in three days early; Democratic legislative leaders and the state's chief justice agreed. In a hurried ceremony, Alexander took the oath and announced that he was naming Fred Thompson, famous from his work as Baker's chief counsel in the Senate Watergate hearings, as a special prosecutor. As governor, Alexander got Nissan to build its first American plant in Rutherford County and General Motors to build its Saturn plant in Williamson County; they became the sparkplugs of rapid growth in the counties around Nashville. He was reelected 60%-40% in 1982. After leaving office, he spent six months living in Australia, about which he wrote a graceful book called *Six Months Off*. In 1988 he became president of the University of Tennessee and in 1991 he became George H.W. Bush's education secretary. In these years he also reaped big profits from small investments: An option to buy the *Knoxville Journal* was sold to Gannett and yielded $620,000; an option given for his consultant work at Whittle Communications became $330,000. Alexander started a company called Corporate Child Care and is still part-owner.

In 1993 he went to work at the Nashville office of Baker's law firm. The next year turned out to be a good Republican year in Tennessee: Fred Thompson and Bill Frist were elected to the Senate and Don Sundquist was elected governor. Alexander probably could have won either office. But he was after bigger things: He was running for president. His 1996 campaign was keyed to the mood of 1994: He campaigned as an outsider, wore his red plaid shirt and called, as Baker often had, for citizen-politicians. Of members of Congress, he said, "Cut their pay and bring them home!" His bumper stickers said, "Lamar!" But he also had a sophisticated message, based on the idea that the nation needed more decentralized government; he had a superb fundraising organization that made Nashville one of the leading Republican money sources in the nation. He hired top notch political consultants and brilliant organizers in Iowa and New Hampshire. Alexander finished third in the Iowa caucuses, behind Bob Dole and Pat Buchanan and ahead of Steve Forbes. New Hampshire was his best chance for a breakthrough. Dole, the favorite, had been concentrating his fire on Buchanan. But five days before the primary Dole began running ads attacking Alexander. This was shrewd strategy: Buchanan was likely to do well in New Hampshire but obviously could never be nominated; the candidate who finished second in New Hampshire would likely be his chief rival and would easily win the nomination. So it turned out. But the second-place finisher in New Hampshire nearly wasn't Dole. Buchanan did win, with 27% of the vote, to 26% for Dole and 23% for Alexander.

In 1999 Alexander started running for president again. But the plaid shirt and the 1994-style themes failed to resonate. George W. Bush, with his celebrity and his fundraising, dominated the race and Forbes's extensive, expensive campaigning in Iowa left little room for Alexander. His fundraising faltered and after his disappointing sixth-place finish in the August 1999 Ames, Iowa, straw poll, he dropped out within days and endorsed Bush. He didn't go to the 2000 Republican National Convention, though, he revealed later, he was interviewed by Dick Cheney as a possible vice presidential nominee; he said he had run his last race for public office.

Then, on Friday, March 8, 2002, just 27 days before the filing deadline, Senator Fred Thompson announced that he would not run for reelection. He gave Alexander a heads-up on his decision, and on Monday, March 11, Alexander announced. Alexander's candidacy was welcome to the Bush White House and to Bill Frist, chairman of the Republicans' Senate campaign committee; a 2001 poll by Alexander's pollster Whit Ayres showed that 93% of voters could identify him, though he had not campaigned in Tennessee in 20 years, and that 66% of voters had favorable feelings toward him and only 16% unfavorable. Nashville's Democratic Congressman Bob Clement, son of three-term Governor Frank Clement, also made it clear he was interested. When suburban Memphis Congressman Ed Bryant said he might run, some Republicans tried to talk him out of it; it was clear he would start out behind in a four-month race. But on April 1 he announced.

Bryant's campaign theme was that he was the real conservative in the race. But Alexander campaigned as a conservative, backing individual investment accounts in Social Security, permanent tax cuts, school vouchers (a "G.I. Bill for kids") and a two-year federal budget cycle. On talk radio shows, whose listeners are very likely to be Republican primary voters, he ran a series of "plain talk" ads taking conservative stands on taxes, campaign finance, the Pledge of Allegiance, Judge Charles Pickering, charter schools and oil drilling in the Arctic National Wildlife Refuge. Bryant's ads called him "the one without the plaid shirt" and urged, "Don't be plaid. Be solid for Bryant." Alexander was endorsed on March 12 by Governor Don Sundquist, unpopular with many of his fellow Republicans for his advocacy of a state income tax. Bryant charged that Alexander had favored an income tax when he was governor. Alexander replied that he had considered an income tax as one of several alternatives and "rejected it." Bryant noted that he did increase the sales and gasoline taxes. Alexander won 54%-43%.

Alexander began running ads immediately after the primary and did not stop until November; Clement didn't put ads up until mid-September. But Clement started with good name identification: He had been elected congressman from Nashville, the center of the state's largest media market, starting in January 1988. He like Alexander was a university president (Cumberland University). Clement had a relatively moderate voting record: He voted for the Bush tax cuts and in October 2002 for the Iraq war resolution. They differed on Social Security, prescription drugs, and campaign finance regulation. But much of the campaign dialogue concerned their business investments. Clement said Alexander was a political insider who became wealthy through political connections. Alexander charged that Clement, while public service commissioner in the 1970s, served on the board of one of the banks of Jake Butcher—Alexander's 1978 opponent, whose banks imploded in scandal in the 1980s. Clement at first denied that he'd served on the board, then said it was just an advisory board, and that he had served a decade before the scandal. Alexander said that Clement had voted 143 times to raise taxes and attacked him for backing Senate Democrats' stand on homeland security; he said Clement would be part of "that crowd" voting against George W. Bush.

Alexander led in polls all along, though the lead narrowed as partisan lines strengthened: He won 54%-44%. He won 63% in his native (and ancestrally Republican) East Tennessee, which cast nearly 40% of the votes. Clement carried Nashville's Davidson County and rural counties in Middle Tennessee, but Alexander carried the fast-growing ring of suburban counties around Nashville and held Clement to 53% in his home area. In West Tennessee, Alexander made some inroads among Memphis blacks and carried the rural counties, for 50% in this (ancestrally Democratic) region. Memphis Mayor Willie Herenton introduced him at his victory party.

And so a politician who ran for governor at 34 became a senator at 62. On his office wall he mounted not the usual array of framed photographs but a 27-foot authentic barn wall, with 40 antique items (a guitar made of matches, a banjo made from a fruitcake tin) on loan of the Museum of Appalachia in Norris, Tennessee. As a former governor and cabinet secretary, he got a little seniority over other freshmen, and he joined his Tennessee colleague, Majority Leader Bill Frist, on the Health, Education, Labor, and Pensions Committee. There he worked on small bills, sponsoring three that became law in 2003 and 2004—to help states ensure special education teachers meet federal standards, to permit parents more choice in special education services for small children, to create summer academies for teachers and students to study American history and civics. He mostly supported the Bush administration. But he differed on air pollution. He joined Democrat Tom Carper's bill that would limit emissions not only of sulphur dioxide, nitrous oxide and mercury (as in the Bush bill), but also carbon dioxide, with a Kyoto-style cap and emissions trading. Air pollution has been high in the Knoxville and Smoky Mountains area, threatening the tourism industry; Alexander said Bush's bill "does not go far enough, fast enough in my back yard."

In the deliberations on the energy bill in 2005, Alexander sought to put $450 million of revenues from drilling in the Arctic National Wildlife Refuge into the Land and Water Conservation Fund. That became moot when ANWR drilling was dropped. Alexander moved successfully with Tim Johnson to give to states that allowed coastal oil and gas drilling 12.5% of production revenues, with another 12.5% going to the Land and Water Conservation Fund. He proposed an amendment to give local governments a veto over wind power projects and to require environmental impact statements of such projects in offshore areas and within 20 miles of scenic areas and military bases. "At a time when America needs large amounts of low-cost reliable power, wind produces puny amounts of high-cost unreliable power." Alexander opposed Bingaman's amendment to require that 10% of energy be produced from renewable sources, including wind power, by 2020, but it passed 52-48 in June 2005. He had better success on amendments streamlining the siting process for liquefied natural gas terminals and providing a 30% solar investment tax credit for homeowners. He cosponsored successful measures to fund schooling for the children displaced by Hurricane Katrina and fund presidential summer academies for K-12 history and civics teachers. He and Edward Kennedy hosted historian David McCullough in a hearing on students' low test scores on NAEP history exams. After the well-publicized singing of the national anthem in Spanish ("Nuestro Himno"), Alexander sponsored a successful resolution stating that the anthem and similar songs should be sung in English, and he supported the successful amendment to the immigration bill designating English as the national language. Other successful Alexander amendments to the immigration bill included $500 payments for English courses for legal immigrants, a reduction from five years to four for the citizenship qualification for those who are fluent in English and codification of the Oath of Allegiance.

Early in the controversy over filibusters of judicial nominees, Alexander said, "I've already said I'll never filibuster. So if six of my friends on the other side will say the same thing, I'll go get five Republicans. There can't be a filibuster, and there'd be no need to change the rules." This got several Democrats thinking about bipartisan action, but they and likeminded Republicans insisted on only qualified pledges not to filibuster. Alexander wanted absolute pledges, and did not join the Gang of 14.   On Tennessee issues, Alexander worked with Bill Frist for $10 million for a replacement lock on Chickamauga Dam and for $5 million in homeland security study grants for the University of Tennessee.

With his Tennessee colleague Frist retiring, and Whip Mitch McConnell likely to replace him as Senate leader, Alexander started in summer 2005 to gather votes for the position of Republican Whip. His likely opponent seemed to be Rick Santorum, and in mid-October 2006, when Santorum was trailing badly in polls for reelection in Pennsylvania, Alexander said he had enough support to win. He said he wouldn't run later for party leader: "I'm glad at this stage in my career to play second fiddle." Santorum, as predicted, lost, but six days after the election Trent Lott, former Senate Majority and House Minority Whip, as well as Senate Majority and Minority Leader, announced he was running. Alexander said he still had enough votes and, "We know each other well, and will be good friends after." On November 15, Lott won by a 25-24 secret ballot vote. "Senators, like most Americans, like a comeback. Trent proved he is a better vote counter," Alexander said. "I wish the vote had been taken at 11 o'clock last night."

In the 110th Congress Alexander got seats on the Appropriations and Environment and Public Works Committees. He formed a Bipartisan Members Group with Joe Lieberman, to meet at breakfast every Tuesday. He continued to press for reductions of sulfur dioxide, nitrous oxide and mercury emissions and for carbon dioxide caps—a general cap at current levels by 2010 and at 2001 levels by 2015. Other Alexander proposals: $4,000 scholarships for private schools of choice for students in failing schools, or $3,000 for intensive tutoring for such students if they wished to stay in those schools; a measure making it easier for state and local governments to terminate or modify consent decrees; allowing seniors to opt to continue Health Savings Accounts rather than going into Medicare.

Alexander announced in April 2007 that he would run for reelection in 2008. One viable candidate would be former Congressman Harold Ford, who won 48% against Bob Corker in 2006; but in early 2007 Ford became head of the Democratic Leadership Council, a position which seemed likely to preclude a Senate candidacy. Former state Democratic Chairman Bob Tuke, Nashville attorney Kevin Doherty and Mike McWherter, son of former Governor Ned McWherter, were considering running; all seemed to indicate they were trying to avoid a contested primary.

Junior Senator

Bob Corker (R)

Elected 2006, seat up 2012, 1st term; b. Aug. 24, 1952, Orangeburg, SC; home, Chattanooga; U. of TN, B.S. 1974; Protestant; married (Elizabeth).

Elected Office: Chattanooga Mayor, 2001-05.

Professional Career: Owner, Bencor Corp., 1978-90; Commissioner, TN Dept. of Fin. and Admin., 1995-96; Owner, Corker Group, 1982-2006.

DC Office: 185 DSOB, 20510, 202-224-3344; Fax: 202-228-0566; Web site: corker.senate.gov.

State Offices: Blountville, 423-323-1252; Chattanooga, 423-756-2757; Jackson, 731-424-9655; Knoxville, 865-637-4180; Memphis, 901-683-1910; Nashville, 615-279-8125.

Committees: *Aging (Special)* (9th of 10 R). *Armed Services* (12th of 12 R): Readiness & Management Support; Airland. *Energy & Natural Resources* (6th of 11 R): Water & Power (RMM); National Parks; Energy. *Foreign Relations* (4th of 10 R): Western Hemisphere, Peace Corps & Narcotics Affairs (RMM); International Development & Foreign Assistance, Economic Affairs & International Environmental Protection; European Affairs. *Small Business & Entrepreneurship* (7th of 9 R).

Group Ratings and Key Votes: Newly Elected

Election Results

2006 general	Bob Corker (R)	929,911	(51%)	($18,565,935)
	Harold Ford (D)	879,976	(48%)	($15,302,455)
	Other	23,806	(1%)	
2006 primary	Bob Corker (R)	231,541	(48%)	
	Ed Bryant (R)	161,189	(34%)	
	Van Hilleary (R)	83,078	(17%)	
	Other	5,309	(1%)	
2000 general	Bill Frist (R)	1,255,444	(65%)	($4,664,737)
	Jeff Clark (D)	621,152	(32%)	($173,406)
	Other	52,017	(3%)	

Bob Corker, the only Republican elected to the Senate in 2006, is the junior senator from Tennessee. He was born in South Carolina, grew up in Chattanooga and graduated from the University of Tennessee in 1974 with a degree in industrial management. Just a few years out of college, he started his own successful construction company, which he sold before he turned 40. Before that, Corker took a church mission trip to Haiti which inspired him to help create Chattanooga Neighborhood Enterprise, a non-profit organization designed to get low-income families into affordable housing. In 1994, he ran for the Senate, finishing second in the Republican primary to Bill Frist, who went on to defeat Democratic incumbent Jim Sasser. Fresh off that race, Republican Governor Don Sundquist named him state finance commissioner, which gave Corker responsibility for state government spending. After 18 months in state government, he returned to private business by purchasing two real estate and development companies in Chattanooga. In 2001 he won election as Chattanooga mayor, where he got credit for a decline in crime and for the success of the city's revitalized waterfront.

Corker was not yet through his first term as mayor when in October 2004 he announced he was running for Senate in 2006 to succeed Frist, by then the Senate Majority Leader, who stuck to his initial campaign promise to serve just two terms. By the end of the year, Corker had raised $2 million. Other Republicans joined the field, including two conservative former congressmen: Ed Bryant, who lost to Lamar Alexander in the 2002 Senate primary, and Van Hilleary, who lost to Democrat Phil Bredesen in the 2002 governor's race. The more moderate Corker drew on his personal wealth and spent $5 million through mid-July alone, in an effort to introduce himself to voters and defend against charges that he was insufficiently conservative. Bryant and Hilleary claimed he raised property taxes in Chattanooga and criticized his position on abortion, noting that he supported abortion rights during his 1994 Senate campaign. Corker responded by calling his opponents "ineffective career politicians" and talked about his background as a successful businessman and mayor. He said he was "wrong" on abortion in 1994 and now held a "pro-life" position, though, unlike Bryant and Hilleary, he would make exceptions in cases of rape and incest. Corker ended up winning by a comfortable margin as Bryant and Hilleary split the conservative vote. Corker, who carried nearly every county east of Nashville and a half-dozen to the west, won 48% to Bryant's 34%; Hilleary finished third with 17%.

The Democratic nominee was Congressman Harold Ford of Memphis, who in the absence of serious primary opposition was able to conserve his resources for the general election. Youthful, ambitious and telegenic, Ford was an immensely attractive candidate. The son of Congressman Harold Ford Sr., he was first elected to the House in 1996, just months after graduating from law school, and his record was sufficiently moderate to make him a competitive statewide candidate. The national media took great interest in the race: Ford was seeking to become the first African-American senator popularly elected in the South and from a state that had never before elected a black candidate to statewide office. For much of the general election campaign, it appeared as if Corker might defy Tennessee's recent Republican trend in national elections and lose a seat that was critical to the party's hopes of retaining its Senate majority. Corker struggled to unify the party after the contentious primary and failed to gain traction in the two months following the August primary. While Ford ran a nearly flawless campaign, Corker's efforts to frame Ford as too liberal for Tennessee fell flat in the face of Ford's centrist positions on illegal immigration, the Iraq war, border security and gay marriage. Ford also put Corker on the defensive about his business dealings and his tenure as Chattanooga mayor.

The national media tended to view the race through a racial prism, but Ford faced two more daunting obstacles. The first was the state's political landscape. The last Democrat Tennessee elected to the Senate was Al Gore in 1990; George W. Bush embarrassed Gore by defeating him 51%-47% on his home turf in 2000, then Bush widened his Tennessee margin in 2004 with a 57%-43 reelection victory. Then there was the Ford family. The scion of a Memphis political dynasty, Ford had to weather distractions caused by several family members, including his uncle, former state Sen. John Ford, who was indicted on federal corruption charges the day after Harold Ford filed his paperwork to run for the U.S. Senate; John Ford later resigned from office. John Ford's sister— Harold's aunt—won the special election to replace him but she was ousted by the state Senate in April amid allegations of voter fraud. Meanwhile, in the racially-charged House race to succeed Harold Ford, his brother Jake unexpectedly ran as independent candidate against white Jewish Democratic nominee Steve Cohen.

Heading into the final weeks of the campaign, the election appeared to be a dead heat. But Corker gained momentum after Republicans began zeroing in on Ford's personal story —he went to prep school in Washington, graduated from an Ivy League university and attended law school in Michigan before taking over his father's seat in Congress—and characterizing it as a life of privilege. Corker offered his own background as a contrast, with ads that described his rise from a laborer who poured concrete. In late October, the Republican National Committee weighed in with a controversial ad featuring purported on-the-street interviews with regular people, all of whom had unpleasant things to say about Ford. But one individual, an attractive young blonde woman, drew all the attention, saying that she "met Harold at the Playboy party," a reference to news stories that Ford had attended a Super Bowl party hosted by Playboy magazine. The commercial ended with the woman saying, "Harold, call me." Critics insisted this was an attempt at racial politicking; Republicans responded that it was about values. Corker's campaign asked television stations not to air the spot. Earlier, after Ford had run an ad filmed in a Memphis church, the National Republican Senatorial Committee responded with a commercial asking, "What kind of man parties with Playboy playmates in lingerie, then films political ads from a church pew?"

More votes were cast in this election, 1.83 million, than in two other high-profile state contests—the governor's race and an amendment to ban same-sex marriage, which passed by an overwhelming 81%-19%. Corker won 51%-48%; whites voted 59%-40% for Corker and blacks voted 95%-4% for Ford. Ford won 61%-38% in the Memphis area while Corker carried the Nashville area 50%-49%. Corker far outpaced Ford in East Tennessee, winning 58%-40%. Ford carried Middle and West Tennessee 52%-46%.

FIRST DISTRICT

Rep. David Davis (R)

Elected 2006, 1st term; b. Nov. 6, 1959, Johnson City; home, Johnson City; Milligan Col., B.A. 1991; Baptist; married (Joyce).

Elected Office: TN House, 1998-2006.

Professional Career: Owner, Advanced Homecare, 1986-95; Owner, Shared Health Service, 1996-2006.

DC Office: 514 CHOB, 20515, 202-225-6356; Fax: 202-225-5714; Web site: daviddavis.house.gov.

District Offices: Kingsport, 423-247-8161.

Committees: *Education & Labor* (20th of 22 R): Health, Employment, Labor & Pensions; Healthy Families & Communities. *Homeland Security* (14th of 15 R): Emergency Communications, Preparedness & Response. *Small Business* (12th of 15 R): Contracting & Technology (RMM); Rural & Urban Entrepreneurship.

Group Ratings and Key Votes: Newly Elected

Election Results

2006 general	David Davis (R)	108,336	(61%)	($518,037)
	Rick Trent (D)	65,538	(37%)	($77,838)
	Other	3,404	(2%)	
2006 primary	David Davis (R)	16,583	(22%)	
	Richard Venable (R)	16,010	(21%)	
	Richard Roberts (R)	13,580	(18%)	
	Phil Roe (R)	12,864	(17%)	
	Larry Waters (R)	7,885	(11%)	
	Vance Cheek (R)	3,334	(4%)	
	Other	4,457	(6%)	
2004 general	Bill Jenkins (R)	172,543	(74%)	($160,643)
	Graham Leonard (D)	56,361	(24%)	($27,775)
	Other	4,656	(2%)	

The People		Race/Ethnic Origin	Ancestry	
Area size:	4,174 sq. mi.	95.0% White	USA: 18.9%	English: 8.2%
Urban population:	55.4%	2.1% Black	Irish: 7.8%	
Rural population:	44.6%	0.4% Asian	**2004 Presidential Vote**	
Pop. 2000:	632,143	0.2% Native Am.	Bush (R)	172,079 (68%)
Pop. 2005 (est):	653,327	0.0% Hawaiian	Kerry (D)	79,507 (31%)
Median income:	$31,228	0.7% Two+ races	Other	1,800 (1%)
Poverty status:	14.8%	0.1% Other	**2000 Presidential Vote**	
Military veterans:	14.2%	1.5% Hispanic Origin	Bush (R)	132,304 (61%)
			Gore (D)	81,335 (37%)
			Other	3,441 (2%)
			Cook Partisan Voting Index: R +14	

Occupation	Blue collar: 34.4%	White collar: 50.0%	Gray collar: 15.6%

Between the corduroy-like ridges of the Appalachian chains, as they bend west and then south, the valley of Virginia extends far into northeastern Tennessee. The communities of this region—a hilly patchwork of industrial centers, small farms and federal land—were largely shaped by the building of railroads in the 1850s. The land rush immediately after the Revolutionary War populated the area; here in tiny Jonesborough the early settlers established the free state of Franklin in 1784, and many pioneer cabins, federal mansions and Greek Revival churches are lovingly preserved. It was the railroads, however, that determined the winners and losers. Other Appalachian areas were cut off from the rest of America, with tracks running only to the coal mines, but the small industrial cities that had grown up here—Johnson City, Kingsport, Bristol—were on the main lines of national commerce even before the Civil War. As President, Abraham Lincoln talked about building a

150-mile railroad through these hills, partly as a political gesture to Union supporters; the route, now known as "the Rathole" because of its topography, was not completed until after the Civil War. The War had a different political effect here than in most of the South: Northeast Tennessee, the home of wartime Governor and then Vice President Andrew Johnson, had few slaves and with its connection to northern industry was Union territory. It remains heavily Republican to this day.

The political continuity may be surprising because this area has had continuous economic growth and has developed the sort of industrial economy that produced unions and Democrats in the North. Its growth has been helped by modest wage levels, a skilled and hard-working labor force, low electric power rates because of the Tennessee Valley Authority and good transportation routes (rail lines and now Interstate 81). Its small cities boast major paper and printing plants, and have the look of comfortable, clean, 1920s factory towns. They continue to grow, and growth has been rapid in Sevier County near Knoxville, where Gatlinburg and Pigeon Forge (home of Dolly Parton's Dollywood theme park) have more than 14,000 hotel rooms at the entry point to the Great Smoky Mountains National Park, the nation's most-visited national park. The area surrounding the park suffers from heavy acid rain and ozone pollution from nearby power plants and factories.

The 1st Congressional District takes in the far northeastern end of Tennessee, a district so heavily Republican that it has not elected a Democrat to the House for more than 100 years. Nonetheless, it has had turbulent politics on occasion. For almost 40 years (1921-61, with one four-year and one two-year hiatus), the seat was held by B. Carroll Reece, a fierce mountain politician who was Republican national chairman from 1946-48. After Reece died in 1961, and his widow was elected to fill out his term, there was a hotly contested primary in 1962. The winner, Jimmy Quillen, a bread-and-butter politician, homebuilder and former owner of the *Johnson City Times*, represented the 1st for the next 34 years, a record tenure for the Tennessee delegation.

The new congressman from the 1st District is David Davis, a Republican elected in 2006, a decade after his first run for Congress. Davis grew up in the mountains around Limestone Cove in humble circumstances. His mother was a factory worker; his father worked for the state transportation department and did some farming on the side. Davis studied respiratory therapy at East Tennessee State University and California College. He earned a management degree from Milligan College in 1991. Davis started two health care businesses, including Shared Health Services, a company that provides oxygen therapy.

Davis first ran for the 1st District seat in 1996 as one of 11 Republicans—the Quillen 11—who filed to run in the primary. Tennessee has no runoff, and this was what political scientist V.O. Key called a "friends and neighbors" primary: There were few perceptible differences on issues, and candidates struggled to get enough votes out in their home areas to win. Bill Jenkins won the primary, just 331 votes ahead of his closest rival, and went on to hold the seat for a decade. Davis finished fourth, but the campaign served as a springboard for his successful run for the state House in 1998. During his next eight years in the legislature, he sponsored government ethics measures, opposed a state income tax and sought to limit eminent-domain powers.

Jenkins's retirement attracted a crowded field just as Quillen's had a decade earlier. Davis announced his campaign just a day after Jenkins announced his intention to step down. He was joined on the primary ballot by a dozen others, including Sullivan County Mayor Richard Venable, who finished fifth in the 1996 GOP primary, just 183 votes behind Davis. Venable had a geographic advantage because he hailed from the district's most populous county, which includes Kingsport. Davis represented the second most populous, Washington County, and won the Tennessee Right to Life endorsement. Wealthy businessman Richard Roberts spent over $1.2 million of his own money and borrowed nearly $1 million more. But in the August 3 primary, Davis once again finished just ahead of Venable, winning 22%-21% by just 573 votes. Roberts finished third with 18%. Davis won Washington and Unicoi Counties handily and did well enough in the rest of the district to counters Venable's dominance in Sullivan County. Like Jenkins, Davis will likely be a reliable conservative vote in Congress. He opposes abortion and gay marriage; he supports gun owners' rights and voluntary prayer in schools. In this solidly Republican district, last represented by a Democrat when Grover Cleveland was president, Democrat Rick Trent, a Morristown City Council member, had little chance of winning. Davis won 61%-37%.

SECOND DISTRICT

Rep. John Duncan (R)

Elected 1988, 10th full term; b. July 21, 1947, Lebanon; home, Knoxville; U. of TN, B.S. 1969, George Washington U., J.D. 1973; Presbyterian; married (Lynn).

Military Career: Army Natl. Guard & Army Reserves, 1970-87.

Professional Career: Practicing atty., 1973-81; Knox Cnty. judge, 1981-88.

DC Office: 2207 RHOB, 20515, 202-225-5435; Fax: 202-225-6440; Web site: www.house.gov/duncan.

District Offices: Athens, 423-745-4671; Knoxville, 865-523-3772; Maryville, 865-984-5464.

Committees: *Natural Resources* (4th of 22 R): National Parks, Forests & Public Lands. *Oversight & Government Reform* (9th of 18 R): Government Management, Organization & Procurement; National Security & Foreign Affairs. *Transportation & Infrastructure* (5th of 34 R): Highways & Transit (RMM); Water Resources & Environment; Aviation.

Group Ratings

	ADA	ACLU	AFS	LCV	ITIC	NTU	COC	ACU	CFG	FRC
2006	10	18	0	8	71	77	87	88	82	100
2005	5	—	13	0	—	80	81	92	95	92

National Journal Ratings

	2005 LIB	—	2005 CONS		2006 LIB	—	2006 CONS
Economic	35%	—	64%		26%	—	73%
Social	41%	—	59%		41%	—	59%
Foreign	52%	—	48%		58%	—	42%

Key Votes of the 109th Congress

1. Estate Tax Repeal	Y	5. Limit Interstate Abortion	Y	9. Build Border Fence	Y
2. Limit CAFE Standards	Y	6. Extend Patriot Act	N	10. CAFTA	Y
3. FY06 Spending Curb	Y	7. Bar Same Sex Marriage	Y	11. Oppose Iraq Withdrawal	N
4. Drilling in ANWR	Y	8. Stem Cell Research $	N	12. Detainee Tribunals	Y

Election Results

2006 general	John Duncan (R)	157,095	(78%)	($569,762)
	John Greene (D)	45,025	(22%)	
2006 primary	John Duncan (R)	55,295	(87%)	
	Ralph McGill (R)	7,994	(13%)	
2004 general	John Duncan (R)	215,795	(79%)	($418,308)
	John Greene (D)	52,155	(19%)	
	Other	4,978	(2%)	

Prior Winning Percentages: 2002 (79%); 2000 (89%); 1998 (89%); 1996 (71%); 1994 (90%); 1992 (72%); 1990 (81%); 1988 (57%); 1988 (56%)

The People		Race/Ethnic Origin	Ancestry	
Area size:	2,492 sq. mi.	90.1% White	USA: 14.0%	English: 8.9%
Urban population:	71.4%	6.2% Black	German: 8.9%	
Rural population:	28.6%	1.0% Asian	**2004 Presidential Vote**	
Pop. 2000:	632,144	0.3% Native Am.	Bush (R) 185,450	(64%)
Pop. 2005 (est):	679,926	0.0% Hawaiian	Kerry (D) 100,032	(35%)
Median income:	$36,796	1.0% Two+ races	Other 2,377	(1%)
Poverty status:	12.2%	0.1% Other	**2000 Presidential Vote**	
Military veterans:	13.5%	1.3% Hispanic Origin	Bush (R) 144,412	(59%)
			Gore (D) 95,100	(39%)
			Other 4,246	(2%)
			Cook Partisan Voting Index: R +11	

Occupation   Blue collar: 25.9%   White collar: 59.6%   Gray collar: 14.5%

Knoxville, the largest city in East Tennessee, is nestled between mountain ridges where the Holston and French Broad Rivers join to form the Tennessee River. It was established not long after the first wave of pioneers came through the gaps and down between the mountains of the Appalachian chain. During the Civil War it was Union territory, and it has remained Republican in allegiance and progressive on civil rights ever since: The ancestral tug of Tennessee politics. But its Republican heritage is tempered by another tradition, that of the Tennessee Valley Authority. A venturesome program when created in the 1930s, it is now part of the fabric of life in East Tennessee, sometimes criticized as its cheap hydroelectric power capacity was filled and more of its production came from expensive and sometimes poorly functioning nuclear plants. The area's largest cash crop remains tobacco.

Both TVA and the region have undergone turbulent changes in recent years. In competitive electricity market, and laboring under billions of dollars in debt mostly incurred in building its nuclear plants, TVA has cut its payroll sharply and held down rates. Heavy ozone pollution in Knoxville led the Environmental Protection Agency to impose growth limits. TVA spent several billion dollars to reduce pollution at its coal-fired power plants and the result has been marked improvement in recent years in local air quality—due, in part, to TVA emission controls. Delay in construction of a national nuclear-waste repository at Yucca Mountain in Nevada has forced TVA to spend tens of millions of dollars for new storage pools. Tellico Lake, formed by a once-controversial dam, attracts Midwestern retirees looking for lakefront property. Knoxville has overcome setbacks and grown robustly without much notice in the national press. In 2006, it ranked ninth on *Expansion Management* magazine's list of the best cities for business expansion and relocation, with growth in construction and services. The 1982 World's Fair site is the home of the Women's Basketball Hall of Fame. And the University of Tennessee's football stadium on fall Saturdays contains one of the nation's largest crowds—it qualifies as the state's 5th largest city during games—cheering the Vols. The city is also the home base of Instapundit.com, the popular blog of University of Tennessee law professor Glenn Reynolds.

The 2d Congressional District of Tennessee includes Knoxville and Knox County, plus four mountainous counties and part of another to the south; most of its people live within the Knoxville metro area. Its less populated areas span the foothills of the Great Smoky Mountains. The seat is heavily Republican and has not elected a Democratic congressman since the Civil War. Knox County surprised many by giving a narrow plurality to Democratic Governor Phil Bredesen in 2002, but Republican Van Hilleary carried the rest of the district by a wider margin; in 2006, Bredesen swept the county 71%-27%, as well as the district.

The congressman from the 2d District is John "Jimmy" Duncan, a Republican first elected in 1988; his father, who was senior Republican on the House Ways and Means Committee, represented the 2d from 1964 until his death in May 1988. Jimmy Duncan got a bachelor's degree in journalism at the University of Tennessee and a law degree from George Washington, practiced law and was a trial judge in the 1980s. When his father died, he won the seat despite a spirited challenge from Democrat Dudley Taylor, a scion of another prominent East Tennessee political family. Taylor attacked Duncan for signing up with the National Guard in 1970 and for his ties to scandal-tarred banker and Democratic politician Jake Butcher. But Duncan won with 57% in November. He has not been seriously challenged since then.

Duncan has been a frequent maverick on economic and foreign policy issues. He opposed normal trade relations with China, trade promotion authority, the No Child Left Behind Act, and he was one of 10 Republicans to vote against the new Homeland Security Department. In October 2002, he was one of six Republicans—and the only Tennessean—who voted against the use of force in Iraq. He said that this was his most difficult vote in the House and argued that there was not sufficient proof that Saddam Hussein had weapons of mass destruction. A year later, he opposed the $87 billion spending package for Iraq. "There is just no enthusiasm for this war," he said in August 2005. "It certainly is not going to help Republican candidates." In June 2006, he was one of three House Republicans who voted against a non-binding resolution in support of the war; in February 2007, he was one of 17 who voted to express disapproval of President Bush's troop surge.

Citing privacy concerns, he was the only Tennessee Republican to oppose continued authority for federal investigation of library records. After chairing for six years the Aviation Subcommittee on Transportation and Infrastructure, he became chairman for another six years of the Water Resources Subcommittee, a pork-dispensing panel of great interest to many members. After the devastation of Hurricane Katrina, he backed a large trust fund to finance wastewater projects. But his independence had its price. He was a candidate for the chairmanship of the Resources Committee in 2003, but Speaker Dennis Hastert's Steering Committee passed over Duncan and five other senior members and gave the post to Richard Pombo. Perhaps mindful of that setback, he voted for the Medicare/prescription drug bill in November 2003. In 2006, he made a big push for the top Republican position on the Transportation Committee. But he lost to John Mica, who is more junior but more of a party regular.

Duncan brings a thrifty approach when it comes to government expenditures but he hasn't been shy about seeking funding for local projects, from resurfacing the Foothills Parkway in the Great Smoky Mountains National Park to a rail and trolley system for downtown Knoxville.

In Knoxville, Duncan's annual barbecue dinner draws as many as 10,000 people, and reinforces his local popularity. Another local touch: At the Tennessee Valley Fair, where there are no water fountains, the Duncans have handed out more than 2 million drinks of water over 40 years.

THIRD DISTRICT

Rep. Zach Wamp (R)

Elected 1994, 7th term; b. Oct. 28, 1957, Fort Benning, GA; home, Chattanooga; U. of NC, 1976-77, 1979-80, U. of TN, 1978-79; Baptist; married (Kim).

Professional Career: Regional Sales Super., 1981-82, Partner, Wamp Alliance Architectural Devel. Co., 1983-89; Real Estate broker, 1989-94.

DC Office: 1436 LHOB, 20515, 202-225-3271; Fax: 202-225-3494; Web site: www.house.gov/wamp.

District Offices: Chattanooga, 423-756-2342; Oak Ridge, 865-576-1976.

Committees: *Appropriations* (13th of 29 R): Legislative Branch (RMM); Energy & Water Development.

Group Ratings

	ADA	ACLU	AFS	LCV	ITIC	NTU	COC	ACU	CFG	FRC
2006	5	14	0	0	71	56	87	88	53	100
2005	0	—	13	11	—	62	88	88	74	92

National Journal Ratings

	2005 LIB	—	2005 CONS		2006 LIB	—	2006 CONS
Economic	35%	—	64%		32%	—	68%
Social	26%	—	74%		23%	—	74%
Foreign	34%	—	61%		0%	—	94%

Key Votes of the 109th Congress

1. Estate Tax Repeal	Y	5. Limit Interstate Abortion	Y	9. Build Border Fence	Y
2. Limit CAFE Standards	N	6. Extend Patriot Act	Y	10. CAFTA	Y
3. FY06 Spending Curb	Y	7. Bar Same Sex Marriage	Y	11. Oppose Iraq Withdrawal	Y
4. Drilling in ANWR	Y	8. Stem Cell Research $	N	12. Detainee Tribunals	Y

Election Results

2006 general	Zach Wamp (R)	130,791	(66%)	($1,439,487)
	Brent Benedict (D)	68,324	(34%)	($19,588)
2006 primary	Zach Wamp (R)	57,569	(87%)	
	June Griffin (R)	3,579	(5%)	
	Doug Vandagriff (R)	3,112	(5%)	
	Other	1,702	(3%)	
2004 general	Zach Wamp (R)	166,154	(65%)	($1,003,532)
	John Wolfe (D)	84,295	(33%)	($92,074)
	Other	6,187	(2%)	

Prior Winning Percentages: 2002 (65%); 2000 (64%); 1998 (66%); 1996 (56%); 1994 (52%)

The People		Race/Ethnic Origin	Ancestry	
Area size:	3,597 sq. mi.	85.2% White	USA: 16.4%	Irish: 8.0%
Urban population:	64.2%	11.1% Black	English: 7.9%	
Rural population:	35.8%	0.9% Asian	**2004 Presidential Vote**	
Pop. 2000:	632,143	0.3% Native Am.	Bush (R) 163,612	(61%)
Pop. 2005 (est):	648,224	0.0% Hawaiian	Kerry (D) 102,390	(38%)
Median income:	$35,434	1.0% Two+ races	Other 2,063	(1%)
Poverty status:	13.4%	0.1% Other	**2000 Presidential Vote**	
Military veterans:	13.6%	1.6% Hispanic Origin	Bush (R) 132,792	(57%)
			Gore (D) 96,441	(41%)
			Other 3,843	(2%)
			Cook Partisan Voting Index: R + 8	

Occupation Blue collar: 31.7% White collar: 54.3% Gray collar: 14.0%

Through some of the most vivid scenery of the Appalachian chain, etching its way through the serrated ridges of East Tennessee, is the river that gave Tennessee its name. From Knoxville, the river cuts through a ridge and then plunges down a long valley to the city of Chattanooga at the Georgia line. There it switches course again, winding around the tabletop Lookout Mountain and then moving into northern Alabama. At the base of the mountain, Chattanooga was just a village when it was a Civil War battlefield; it then became the industrial "Dynamo of Dixie." Four decades ago it was labeled America's most polluted city. But regional political leaders, prodded by influential and civic-minded remnants of its Industrial Age aristocracy, used creative measures, such as a locally built electric shuttle bus, to reduce pollution and spruce up the city's scenic river banks; reduction in ozone levels moved ahead of schedule. With big job cuts at the Tennessee Valley Authority, the region has pinned its hopes for growth more on the private sector, including a large food-service industry (the district is home to both the MoonPie and Little Debbie confectioners). Downtown Chattanooga is the home of the 12-story-high Tennessee Aquarium, the world's largest fresh water aquarium, with an exhibit in which you can follow the course of a drop of rain from the headwaters of the Tennessee until it flows out the Mississippi River into the Gulf. At Lookout Mountain, the popular century-old Incline Railway climbs at a 72.7% grade; nearby are the 145-foot waterfall of Ruby Falls, as well as the rock formations and native gardens at Rock City. Grainger County, north of the Interstate 75 and Interstate 40 split, was the home of President Andrew Johnson and the south's first paper mill.

The 3d Congressional District of Tennessee includes Chattanooga and runs northeasterly from the Tennessee-Georgia border to the Virginia border, making this one of three Tennessee districts that span the state from north to south. Most of the population is in Chattanooga and the counties around it. Its thin strip of land to the north includes Dayton, the "buckle of the Bible Belt" where John Scopes was tried for teaching evolution in 1925 and was defended by Clarence Darrow and prosecuted by William Jennings Bryan. Farther north is Oak Ridge, which was secretly constructed in virgin Appalachian forest during World War II to house the nuclear facility that made uranium isotopes for the Hiroshima bomb and is now the Oak Ridge National Laboratory. For years, it did not appear on maps; the city had a tongue-in-cheek reputation for people who "glow in the dark." Politically, this area was split historically, with Chattanooga voting Democratic and the mountain counties Republican; today, it is solidly Republican, with none of its counties voting less than 57% for George W. Bush in 2004.

The congressman from the 3d District is Zach Wamp, a Republican first elected in 1994. Wamp left college before graduating to become a salesman for a local film company and a real estate developer in Chattanooga, selling $22 million in real estate in five years. Years later, he spoke about his heavy cocaine use during this period, including weeks in drug rehabilitation. In 1992 he ran for Congress against 20-year Democratic incumbent Marilyn Lloyd. She won by just 49%-47%, the closest margin of her career, and retired in 1994. Wamp ran again as a strong conservative; one of his proposals was to pay members of Congress the same as a lieutenant colonel and billet them in officer housing. Democrat Randy Button attacked Wamp's character. Wamp accused Button of flip-flopping on issues and, like many Republicans that year, ran an ad showing his opponent's face morphing into Bill Clinton's. Wamp won 52%-46%.

In the House, Wamp got a seat on the Appropriations Committee. He has a moderate-to-conservative record that is a bit more conservative on social issues. He called himself "a heat-seeking missile on behalf of Tennessee and my district." He has won additional benefits for employees with work-related illnesses at Oak Ridge National Laboratory. Wamp has taken some maverick stances. His support for TVA, including opposition to attempts to sell off its non-hydro power plants, annoyed many conservatives. He is co-chairman of the House Renewable Energy and Efficiency Caucus, which he uses to cite Chattanooga's successes in this area, and says that Congress has not done enough to address the nation's energy security. He vocally supported the McCain-Feingold campaign finance bill, a stance that irritated the Republican leadership and prompted the National Right to Life Committee to run radio ads against him, even though he is opposed to abortion; the committee feared that the new law would prevent it from running issue-advocacy ads at campaign time. Later, he reversed his policy against taking PAC contributions, which he said was no longer practical following the elimination of "soft money." He tacked toward social conservatives in sponsoring a bill to permit local governments to post the Ten Command-ments in public buildings, and he sought to restrict Internet access to pornography for children.

Wamp believes that he is one-sixteenth Cherokee, and he has taken an interest in the tribe; he helped deliver $1.3 million from the highway reauthorization bill for an interpretive visitors' center and memorial wall at Cherokee Removal Memorial Park in Meigs County. Wamp's Trail of Tears Study Act, designed to include additional routes on the Trail of Tears National Historic Trail, was signed into law in December 2006.

Wamp tried unsuccessfully after the 2000 election to repeal the House Republicans' three-term limit on chairmanships. With John Tanner, he called for independent commissions to supervise redistricting. He rented a home on Capitol Hill with three other House Republicans and three Democrats. "My attitude toward the Congress has changed," Wamp told *The New York Times Magazine*. "We must realize public service is a great way of life. I came in with the attitude there were a bunch of thieves here. That's not true." An avid user of the House gym, he founded the Congressional Fitness Caucus.

In 1996 he faced a spirited challenge from the second-place finisher in the 1994 Democratic primary. With Marilyn Lloyd's endorsement, Wamp won 56%-43%. Since then, he has won easily. In 1994 Wamp said he would serve only 12 years in the House and Bill Frist, running for the Senate, said he would only serve two terms. Frist seemed bent on keeping his promise, and in 2004 Wamp spent months traveling across the state. But Chattanooga Mayor Bob Corker said he was running for the Senate and within two months of filing for the seat raised $2 million; Wamp said he would remain in the House, where he is positioned to wield influence on the Appropriations Committee for many years. In 2007, he became ranking Republican on the Legislative Branch Subcommittee. After Tom DeLay was indicted in Texas and stepped down as Majority Leader in 2005, Wamp said that the status quo was unacceptable for the GOP, and he talked about running for party Whip. But the position did not become open.

FOURTH DISTRICT

Rep. Lincoln Davis (D)

Elected 2002, 3d term; b. Sept. 13, 1943, Pall Mall; home, Pall Mall; TN Tech. U., B.S. 1966; Baptist; married (Lynda).

Elected Office: Byrdstown Mayor, 1978-82; TN House of Reps, 1980-84; TN Senate, 1996-2002.

Professional Career: Owner, Diversified Construction Co.

DC Office: 410 CHOB, 20515, 202-225-6831; Fax: 202-226-5172; Web site: www.house.gov/lincolndavis.

District Offices: Columbia, 931-490-8699; Jamestown, 931-879-2361; McMinnville, 931-473-7251; Rockwood, 865-354-3323.

Committees: *Agriculture* (21st of 25 D): Department Operations, Oversight, Nutrition & Forestry; Horti-culture & Organic Agriculture. *Financial Services* (25th of 37 D): Capital Markets, Insurance & Government Sponsored Enterprises; Financial Institutions & Consumer Credit.

Group Ratings

	ADA	ACLU	AFS	LCV	ITIC	NTU	COC	ACU	CFG	FRC
2006	35	32	57	42	57	32	93	80	40	100
2005	70	—	75	33	—	29	78	64	34	85

National Journal Ratings

	2005 LIB — 2005 CONS		2006 LIB — 2006 CONS	
Economic	52% —	47%	54% —	46%
Social	48% —	52%	46% —	54%
Foreign	57% —	42%	58% —	41%

Key Votes of the 109th Congress

1. Estate Tax Repeal	Y	5. Limit Interstate Abortion	Y
2. Limit CAFE Standards	Y	6. Extend Patriot Act	Y
3. FY06 Spending Curb	N	7. Bar Same Sex Marriage	Y
4. Drilling in ANWR	Y	8. Stem Cell Research $	N

9. Build Border Fence	Y
10. CAFTA	N
11. Oppose Iraq Withdrawal	Y
12. Detainee Tribunals	Y

Election Results

2006 general	Lincoln Davis (D)	123,666	(66%)	($810,397)
	Kenneth Martin (R)	62,449	(34%)	
2006 primary	Lincoln Davis (D)	56,618	(86%)	
	Norma Cartwright (D)	6,564	(10%)	
	Harvey Howard (D)	2,511	(4%)	
2004 general	Lincoln Davis (D)	138,459	(55%)	($1,145,419)
	Janice Bowling (R)	109,993	(44%)	($322,815)
	Other	4,194	(2%)	

Prior Winning Percentages: 2002 (52%)

The People		Race/Ethnic Origin	Ancestry		
Area size:	10,155 sq. mi.	92.6% White	USA: 20.0%	Irish: 8.1%	
Urban population:	32.1%	4.4% Black	English: 7.2%		
Rural population:	67.9%	0.3% Asian	**2004 Presidential Vote**		
Pop. 2000:	632,143	0.3% Native Am.	Bush (R)	154,457	(58%)
Pop. 2005 (est):	660,378	0.0% Hawaiian	Kerry (D)	109,802	(41%)
Median income:	$31,645	0.8% Two+ races	Other	1,935	(1%)
Poverty status:	15.2%	0.0% Other	**2000 Presidential Vote**		
Military veterans:	13.2%	1.6% Hispanic Origin	Bush (R)	111,639	(50%)
			Gore (D)	109,559	(49%)
			Other	3,507	(2%)
			Cook Partisan Voting Index: R + 3		

Occupation	Blue collar: 40.4%	White collar: 45.1%	Gray collar: 14.4%

The invisible line between Civil War Republican and Civil War Democratic territory runs along the Cumberland Plateau, the westernmost upswelling of the Appalachians, west of the valley where the Tennessee River runs south from Knoxville to Chattanooga. This is cave country: under its green hills Tennessee has 8,500 caves, more than any other state, with 15 species of bats and more than 100 species of rare insects. This invisible line separates the Tennessee Valley, which had few slaves and whose economic ties were with the North, from the rolling farmlands of middle Tennessee, first settled by Andrew Jackson in the 1790s and resolutely Democratic from the time he became the first president to call himself a Democrat in 1829. Here are places like Sewanee, the pleasant home of the University of the South, which angered traditionalists when it changed its name to Sewanee: The University of the South; Bledsoe County, the pumpkin capital of the world; Columbia, home of President James K. Polk and the site of Maury County's Mule Day celebration every April, where a nearby Saturn plant has accelerated growth; Decherd in Franklin County, with a large Nissan engine assembly plant; and Lynchburg in dry Moore County, where Jack Daniel's sour-mash whiskey—the nation's number-two spirit in overseas sales, behind Johnny Walker Red Label Scotch—has been distilled for generations and which is every bit the idealized small town that the distillery's folksy, black-and-white advertisements make it out to be. In Campbell County, the construction of the Tennessee Valley Authority's Norris Dam in 1933 forced the evacuation of 153,000 acres of land and the resettlement of 3,000 families, and left some of the lowest standards of living in the state, but the area has since become a retirement and tourist haven. Cattle are the district's number-one commodity.

The 4th Congressional District of Tennessee runs across this line and crosses the state for some 200 miles. It reaches almost to Virginia in the northeast and almost to Mississippi in the southwest and ranks as the fourth most rural district in the nation.

The congressman from the 4th District is Lincoln Davis, a Democrat first elected in 2002. Davis grew up in Fentress County on his family farm, which was purchased from World War I hero Sergeant Alvin York, a great celebrity in the 1920s and 1930s who was played by Gary Cooper in an Oscar-winning performance in the 1941 movie *Sergeant York*. Davis started his own construction company, which builds homes and businesses, and develops land. He also has been a soil scientist, and farms cattle and tobacco. He began his political career in 1978 as mayor of Byrdstown near the Kentucky border and was elected to the state House in 1980. In 1984, when Al Gore left the House to run for the Senate, Davis ran for the House but lost the Democratic primary to Bart Gordon 28%-22%. He lost the 4th District House primary 31%-27% in 1994, for the seat won by Republican Van Hilleary. After he returned to office as a state senator, the third time proved a charm.

In 2002 Hilleary ran for governor, and Davis was the early favorite to replace him. He won support in the Democratic primary from national and local party leaders, organized labor, anti-abortion groups, and the National Rifle Association. But he had a difficult time against Democratic newcomer Fran Marcum. A wealthy businesswoman with EMILY's List backing, she spent $1.6 million of her own money. Her ads depicted Davis as a political retread, and tied him to the legislature's unpopular handling of budget problems. Davis won, 57%-43%. In the general, Janice Bowling, a Tullahoma alderwoman and self-described "pistol-packing Mama," attempted to seize on Gore's endorsement of Davis in the primary by asking voters to vote against Gore one more time. As part of her folksy message, she campaigned in a white chenille dress, red boots and an American flag scarf. She was significantly outspent by Davis, and complained that Republican financial backing came too late. Davis promised not to let any opponent "out-gun me, out-pray me, or out-family me." In the words of *The Tennessean*, Davis combined a "folksy, slap-on-the-back attitude with the oratorical punch of a revival preacher." He won 52%-46%. Redistricting made the difference. Davis carried the counties added to the district in 2002 by nearly 8,000 votes—almost all of his 10,000-vote margin. Bowling would probably have carried the Republican counties removed by redistricting.

In the House, Davis fit near the center and toward the conservative end of the Democratic Caucus. He appeared to keep his pledge to stay in close touch with the grass roots and keep his distance from most national Democrats, especially on cultural issues. To discourage abortions, he filed the Pregnant Women Support Act. He worked with other Democrats to promote their interest in "faith-based" issues. When Republicans forced a vote on a gay-marriage ban, he sarcastically suggested that they also include bans on divorce and adultery to highlight the partisan debate. Davis joined the Blue Dogs and supported pay-as-you-go rules to encourage budget discipline. He was one of 16 House Democrats to vote for the 2003 Medicare/prescription drug bill, citing the need to reduce the high local cost of prescription drugs. He opposed the Central American Free Trade Agreement because he feared the local impact. On Iraq, he initially supported George W. Bush; in 2006, he questioned whether the war was necessary. In 2007, he joined the Financial Services Committee, with a plan to focus on identity theft and terrorism financing.

In 2004, Bowling ran again but again received little party support. Davis emphasized his independence and willingness to listen to constituents. With endorsements from the Chamber of Commerce, National Right to Life and the NRA, he increased his victory margin to 55%-44%. In 2006, he rejected a run for the Senate, which would have forced a primary with Harold Ford Jr.; in November, Davis had his first relatively easy win.

FIFTH DISTRICT

Rep. Jim Cooper (D)

Elected 2002, 9th term; b. June 19, 1954, Nashville; home, Nashville; U. of NC, B.A. 1975, Oxford U., B.A./M.A. 1977, Harvard U., J.D. 1980; Episcopalian; married (Martha).

Elected Office: U.S. House of Reps., 1982-94.

Professional Career: Practicing atty., 1980-82; Investment banker, 1995-99; Founder and partner, investment bank, 1999-2002.

DC Office: 1536 LHOB, 20515, 202-225-4311; Fax: 202-226-1035; Web site: www.cooper.house.gov.

District Offices: Nashville, 615-736-5295.

Committees: *Armed Services* (16th of 34 D): Terrorism, Unconventional Threats & Capabilities; Strategic Forces; Oversight & Investigations. *Budget* (4th of 22 D). *Oversight & Government Reform* (18th of 23 D): National Security & Foreign Affairs.

Group Ratings

	ADA	ACLU	AFS	LCV	ITIC	NTU	COC	ACU	CFG	FRC
2006	70	77	86	100	100	36	53	40	19	28
2005	80	—	100	67	—	33	59	24	22	8

National Journal Ratings

	2005 LIB	—	2005 CONS		2006 LIB	—	2006 CONS
Economic	61%	—	38%		68%	—	31%
Social	61%	—	39%		60%	—	39%
Foreign	58%	—	42%		62%	—	38%

Key Votes of the 109th Congress

1. Estate Tax Repeal	N	5. Limit Interstate Abortion	Y	9. Build Border Fence	Y
2. Limit CAFE Standards	N	6. Extend Patriot Act	Y	10. CAFTA	Y
3. FY06 Spending Curb	N	7. Bar Same Sex Marriage	Y	11. Oppose Iraq Withdrawal	Y
4. Drilling in ANWR	N	8. Stem Cell Research $	Y	12. Detainee Tribunals	N

Election Results

2006 general	Jim Cooper (D)	122,919	(69%)	($732,657)
	Thomas Kovach (R)	49,702	(28%)	
	Other	5,521	(3%)	
2006 primary	Jim Cooper (D)	38,148	(92%)	
	Jason Pullias (D)	3,518	(8%)	
2004 general	Jim Cooper (D)	168,970	(69%)	($1,169,268)
	Scott Knapp (R)	74,978	(31%)	

Prior Winning Percentages: 2002 (64%); 1992 (66%); 1990 (69%); 1988 (100%); 1986 (100%); 1984 (75%); 1982 (66%)

The People		Race/Ethnic Origin	Ancestry	
Area size:	932 sq. mi.	68.2% White	USA: 10.8%	Irish: 7.6%
Urban population:	88.7%	23.4% Black	English: 7.6%	
Rural population:	11.3%	2.0% Asian	**2004 Presidential Vote**	
Pop. 2000:	632,143	0.3% Native Am.	Kerry (D) 140,874	(52%)
Pop. 2005 (est):	640,668	0.1% Hawaiian	Bush (R) 129,455	(48%)
Median income.	$40,419	1.6% Two+ races	Other 1,994	(1%)
Poverty status:	12.2%	0.2% Other	**2000 Presidential Vote**	
Military veterans:	11.7%	4.2% Hispanic Origin	Gore (D) 130,111	(57%)
			Bush (R) 95,309	(42%)
			Other 4,015	(2%)
			Cook Partisan Voting Index: D + 6	

Occupation   Blue collar: 21.9%   White collar: 64.2%   Gray collar: 13.8%

Nashville is the home of country music and is in almost every way the heart of Tennessee. This was one of the first American cities established west of the Appalachians; Andrew Jackson built his Hermitage nearby above the banks of the Cumberland River, and his political home base has remained Democratic ever since. It was the capital of Tennessee early on, just as it was, and still is, the center of the state's political life and discourse, the so-called "Athens of the South": home to *The Tennessean,* a classically partisan Democratic paper, and the state's biggest television market. Nashville is proud of its universities and its columned Capitol and its Parthenon; this is perhaps the greatest center of Greek Revival architecture in America. Nashville is firmly established as the religious publishing center of the country, producing more bibles than any other city in the world. Country music, an art form that emerged from the hardscrabble, mountainous counties of East Tennessee, is a more than $2 billion-a-year business and one of the nation's dominant radio formats; it creates local jobs with music publishers and recording studios that extend far into Middle Tennessee. The industry, run from a series of deceptively modest homes-turned-offices on what's called Music Row, congregated in Nashville because local radio station WSM had a clear channel in the 1920s from which to beam its weekly "barn dances" throughout the South; these later became known as the Grand Ole Opry, the longest continuously running radio show (since 1925). Opryland includes a modern home northeast of town, though its original Ryman auditorium continues. An expanded Country Music Hall of Fame and Museum opened as part of the downtown revitalization project, and the city now offers good music of all sorts, sushi bars and a lively and cool cafe scene.

For years, both the city's Parthenon-building elite and its religious leaders resented the growing local influence of country music; the former looked down on the music's uneducated practitioners, while the latter cringed at the musicians' unwholesome travails and occasional indecorous deaths. But all three groups made their peace in the 1970s, and since then Nashville has become one of the South's boom cities—the fastest growing metropolitan area between the still-larger Atlanta and Dallas-Fort Worth. New-generation industry moved in; a large local employer is the Corrections Corporation of America, the world's largest operator of private prisons and a prime government contractor. This also is a center of the for-profit health industry, led by the family of former Senate Majority Leader Bill Frist. An agreeable quality of life, plenty of medium-wage, high-skill labor, a central location, and absence of urban strife and militant unions have all helped make Nashville the largest metropolitan area in the state, with suburban growth in all directions. The dominant cultural tone remains conservative, and fast-growing surrounding counties have become increasingly Republican, but Nashville and Davidson County remain Democratic bulwarks of Republican-trending Tennessee.

The 5th Congressional District of Tennessee includes most of Nashville-Davidson County, plus the bulk of suburban Wilson County to the east and Cheatham County to the west. The 5th is reliably Democratic in statewide elections; to Congress it has elected rather liberal Democrats—this is, after all, the home of the first Democratic president. It was the home of Al Gore when he was a divinity student at Vanderbilt and reporter for *The Tennessean*, and was the site of his 2000 presidential campaign headquarters; in June 2002, he and Tipper bought a house in the elegant Belle Meade neighborhood.

The congressman from the 5th District is Jim Cooper, a Democrat elected in 2002; he served in the very different 4th District from 1982 to 1994, when he ran unsuccessfully for the Senate. His father, Prentice Cooper, was governor for six years. Jim Cooper, educated at the University of North Carolina, Oxford and Harvard Law School, won the 4th District seat in 1982 by beating the bearer of another famous name, Cissy Baker, the daughter of then-Senate Majority Leader Howard Baker. When he first took office at age 28, he was the youngest member of the House. Notable for his frankness, he spoke out against tobacco use and opposed the National Rifle Association. He partici-pated actively in the "group of nine" Democrats on the Energy and Commerce that helped to produce a compromise between John Dingell and Henry Waxman on the Clean Air Act of 1990. In 1994, after writing the chief—and less universal—alternative to Hillary Clinton's health care proposal, he ran against Fred Thompson for the Senate seat Gore vacated when he was elected vice president. Ads captured a personal contrast between the two candidates: Thompson appeared in workshirts, speaking confidently to the camera while walking up porch stairs; the much shorter and youthful-looking Cooper appeared before a church in starched white shirt and tie. Thompson won 60%-39%.

Cooper then went to work as an investment banker in Nashville and as a teacher in Vanderbilt's business school. In 2002, when Congressman Bob Clement jumped into the open Senate race, Cooper joined a flurry of Democratic candidates. His toughest opponent was Davidson County Sheriff Gayle Ray, the first woman sheriff in Tennessee, who had support from EMILY's List. Ray attacked Cooper's voting record on health care, particularly on women's health issues. Cooper, an abortion-rights supporter, recalled his actions as a key player on health care initiatives and said that Ray's charges were inaccurate. He ran an ad showing his children describing what he does well (banjo playing, helping with homework, getting health care for senior citizens) and what he doesn't do well (cooking, playing basketball). The AFL-CIO and *The Tennessean* endorsed Ray; Cooper had support from the Sierra Club and several smaller newspapers. Cooper raised twice as much money as Ray and spent $700,000 of his own money. He won the primary with 47%, with 23% for Ray in the seven-candidate field. Cooper won the general easily and has not been seriously challenged.

Back in the House, Cooper was unable to get back his old seat on the Commerce committee, where 6th District colleague Bart Gordon is now a member. Instead, he joined the Armed Services, Budget, and Government Reform committees. He helped to found the bipartisan Congressional China Caucus to increase dialogue on bilateral relations, and was 1 of 15 Democrats to vote for the Central American Free Trade Agreement, which he said was good for local business. With the Blue Dogs, he sought limits on budget earmarks and enforcement of PAYGO rules; he continued to seek earmarks for his district, but he published their details on his congressional website. He has highlighted the Treasury Department's grim annual Financial Report—information that the "White House does not want you to read." A budget hawk, he urged expanded presidential use of budget rescissions. He criticized "cronyism" with presidential appointments to the Tennessee Valley Authority. With John Tanner, he pushed for non-partisan redistricting reform. In the current system, he said, "There are two things you don't mess with: my wife and my district, not necessarily in that order."

Still relatively young, he seems to have abandoned his interest in statewide office and is more focused on being a leader within the Blue Dogs and a consensus-builder within the national Democratic party.

SIXTH DISTRICT

Rep. Bart Gordon (D)

Elected 1984, 12th term; b. Jan. 24, 1949, Murfreesboro; home, Murfreesboro; Middle TN St. U., B.S. 1971, U. of TN, J.D. 1973; United Methodist; married (Leslie).

Military Career: Army Reserves, 1971-72.

Professional Career: Practicing atty., 1974-84; Chmn., TN Dem. Party, 1981-83.

DC Office: 2310 RHOB, 20515, 202-225-4231; Fax: 202-225-6887; Web site: www.house.gov/gordon.

District Offices: Cookeville, 931-528-5907; Gallatin, 615-451-5174; Murfreesboro, 615-896-1986.

Committees: *Energy & Commerce* (7th of 31 D): Health; Telecommunications & the Internet. *Science & Technology* (Chmn. of 24 D).

Group Ratings

	ADA	ACLU	AFS	LCV	ITIC	NTU	COC	ACU	CFG	FRC
2006	50	50	57	75	71	27	80	60	29	57
2005	90	—	75	61	—	29	74	40	29	50

National Journal Ratings

	2005 LIB	—	2005 CONS		2006 LIB	—	2006 CONS
Economic	55%	—	45%		60%	—	40%
Social	53%	—	47%		53%	—	46%
Foreign	63%	—	36%		64%	—	35%

Key Votes of the 109th Congress

1. Estate Tax Repeal	Y	5. Limit Interstate Abortion	Y	9. Build Border Fence	Y
2. Limit CAFE Standards	Y	6. Extend Patriot Act	Y	10. CAFTA	N
3. FY06 Spending Curb	N	7. Bar Same Sex Marriage	Y	11. Oppose Iraq Withdrawal	Y
4. Drilling in ANWR	N	8. Stem Cell Research $	Y	12. Detainee Tribunals	Y

Election Results

2006 general	Bart Gordon (D)	129,069	(67%)	($939,722)
	David R. Davis (R)	60,392	(31%)	
	Other	2,919	(2%)	
2006 primary	Bart Gordon (D)	53,916	(92%)	
	Patrick Lyons (D)	4,490	(8%)	
2004 general	Bart Gordon (D)	167,448	(64%)	($852,690)
	Nick Demas (R)	87,523	(34%)	($37,399)
	Other	5,671	(2%)	

Prior Winning Percentages: 2002 (66%); 2000 (62%); 1998 (55%); 1996 (54%); 1994 (51%); 1992 (57%); 1990 (67%); 1988 (76%); 1986 (77%); 1984 (63%)

The People		Race/Ethnic Origin	Ancestry	
Area size:	5,576 sq. mi.	89.0% White	USA: 19.0%	English: 8.1%
Urban population:	53.2%	6.3% Black	Irish: 8.1%	
Rural population:	46.8%	0.9% Asian	**2004 Presidential Vote**	
Pop. 2000:	632,143	0.3% Native Am.	Bush (R) 167,372	(60%)
Pop. 2005 (est):	706,282	0.0% Hawaiian	Kerry (D) 111,203	(40%)
Median income:	$39,721	0.8% Two+ races	Other 1,721	(1%)
Poverty status:	11.1%	0.1% Other	**2000 Presidential Vote**	
Military veterans:	12.3%	2.6% Hispanic Origin	Bush (R) 112,096	(49%)
			Gore (D) 111,872	(49%)
			Other 3,729	(2%)
			Cook Partisan Voting Index: R + 4	

Occupation   Blue collar: 33.9%   White collar: 52.9%   Gray collar: 13.1%

The rolling countryside of Middle Tennessee, west of the Cumberland Plateau and the last chain of Appalachians, has been called "the dimple of the universe." This is hilly and fertile land, cut by deep rivers ambling along in S-curves. The terrain here was never much suited for plantation crops; this has long been a land of small farmers and small county seat towns, nestled amid what people here regard as some of the loveliest scenery on earth. Middle Tennessee has also been one of the heartlands of the Democratic Party. It was the political home base of Andrew Jackson and supported him nearly unanimously; during the Civil War, though it had very few slaves, it resisted the invading Union armies. For 140 years after Jackson, it voted solidly Democratic and elected as its congressmen some of the luminaries of the national Democratic Party: James K. Polk (1825-39), speaker of the House and later president; Cordell Hull (1907-21, 1923-31), later senator and secretary of state; Albert Gore Sr., (1939-53), later senator; and Albert Gore Jr., (1977-85), later senator and vice president.

The 6th Congressional District includes 14 Middle Tennessee counties north, east and south of Nashville, plus the eastern half of Wilson County just east of Nashville. The heritage here is old and rural, but economic growth has fanned out into the farmland from Nashville, evident in thousands of jobs created by Japanese companies and American startups, firms fleeing the North and entre- preneurs fleeing taxes. Nearby is Smyrna and its Nissan plant, which has the largest automobile production capacity in the nation and is the home of the Altima, the fourth best-selling car in the nation. In Rutherford County, Murfreesboro, which is the largest city, has grown from a crumbling town in the 1980s to a thriving community and the home of Middle Tennessee State University, the second-largest in the state. This is one of 2 fast-growing Tennessee congressional districts; the other is the neighboring 7th District. The new voters here are Republican, but Democrats in control of redistricting in 2002 removed rapidly growing Republican suburbs in Wilson and Williamson Counties from this district. They added Robertson County north of Nashville, which is significantly less Republican. But it was not enough to halt Republican advances. Without its former representa- tive, Al Gore, on the Democratic ticket, Bush carried the 6th by 60%-40% in 2004, representing a 20-point swing in Bush's margin of victory in four years.

The congressman from the 6th District is Bart Gordon, a Democrat first elected in 1984 when Gore gave up his House seat to run for the Senate. Gordon grew up in Murfreesboro, and graduated from Middle Tennessee State University and the University of Tennessee law school. He practiced law and became Tennessee Democratic chairman in 1981: Politics has been most of his life. In 1984, he ran a computerized fund-raising operation and voter contact system—then a novelty in this district where a personal handshake from a candidate was the norm. He won a multi-candidate primary with 28% of the vote (Lincoln Davis, now the 4th District's congressman, was second with 22%) and won the general 63%-37%.

In the House, Gordon has built a moderate record and used his insider skills to pass legislation and build a close relationship with Democratic leaders. Gordon has worked to protect the Tennessee Valley Authority from proponents of electricity deregulation. He has voted with Republicans to make permanent the repeal of the marriage penalty and the estate tax, and was 1 of 9 Democrats to support the tax-cut package in December 2005; but he opposed trade promotion authority and the Central American Trade Agreement, and seeks to repeal tax breaks for companies that send jobs overseas. He voted to authorize the use of force in Iraq, but voted to make reconstruction funds a loan rather than a grant. He won enactment of his proposal for Federal Trade Commission oversight of the practices of sports agents representing student athletes. The House defeated Gordon's proposal to increase funds for the Manufacturing Extension Partnership program, a nationwide network of non-profit centers that assists small and medium-sized manufacturers; the Bush administration phased out the program's grants. He assisted Nissan in securing an exemption from a change in fuel economy regulations that would have cost hundreds of local jobs. He would ban the use of tax credits for windmills in national parks.

On the Science and Technology Committee, where he is now chairman, Gordon raised questions about whether George W. Bush's support for human space flight to Mars and the moon would "cannibalize" other space programs that he supports. Following the Columbia shuttle disaster, he helped to reshape NASA by extending the life of the shuttle fleet. He also helped to convene an advisory panel for the committee that urged broad efforts to strengthen the nation's scientific competitiveness. As chairman, he said that his priorities include more funds for science education. On other issues, Gordon is a Civil War buff who has talked about creating a Congressional Battlefield Caucus to preserve the nation's military history.

When Gordon first won the seat it seemed safely Democratic. But, with the population surge in metro Nashville and the unpopularity of the Clinton administration in the mid-1990s, it suddenly became marginal. Gordon's close ties to the Democratic leadership were no longer an asset. In 1994 he was challenged by Steve Gill, a lawyer from heavily Republican Williamson County. Gordon spent $1.4 million, more than twice what Gill spent altogether; he carried the smaller rural counties 58%-42%, for a slim overall margin of 51%-49%. In a 1996 rematch, Gordon won 54%-42%. As the Democrats' point man in the 2002 redistricting, he drew new district lines that have seemed to make him invulnerable; in the three elections since then, he won with at least 64% of the vote. A notable accomplishment in the increasingly fit House: Gordon has won Congress's 5K race an impressive 18 times; at age 58, his time was 18 minutes and 24 seconds.

SEVENTH DISTRICT

Rep. Marsha Blackburn (R)

Elected 2002, 3d term; b. June 6, 1952, Laurel, MS; home, Brentwood; MS St. U., B.S. 1973; Presbyterian; married (Chuck).

Elected Office: TN Senate, 1998-2002.

Professional Career: Retail marketing consultant, 1973-98.

DC Office: 509 CHOB, 20515, 202-225-2811; Fax: 202-225-3004; Web site: blackburn.house.gov.

District Offices: Clarksville, 931-503-0391; Franklin, 615-591-5161; Memphis, 901-382-5811.

Committees: *Energy & Commerce* (26th of 26 R): Oversight & Investigations; Commerce, Trade & Consumer Protection; Health. *Select Committee on Energy Independence and Global Warming* (5th of 6 R).

Group Ratings

	ADA	ACLU	AFS	LCV	ITIC	NTU	COC	ACU	CFG	FRC
2006	0	9	0	0	100	81	100	96	88	100
2005	0	—	0	6	—	74	89	100	95	100

National Journal Ratings

	2005 LIB	—	2005 CONS		2006 LIB	—	2006 CONS
Economic	3%	—	94%		12%	—	86%
Social	0%	—	89%		6%	—	92%
Foreign	11%	—	86%		0%	—	94%

Key Votes of the 109th Congress

1. Estate Tax Repeal	Y	5. Limit Interstate Abortion	Y	9. Build Border Fence	Y
2. Limit CAFE Standards	Y	6. Extend Patriot Act	Y	10. CAFTA	Y
3. FY06 Spending Curb	Y	7. Bar Same Sex Marriage	Y	11. Oppose Iraq Withdrawal	Y
4. Drilling in ANWR	Y	8. Stem Cell Research $	N	12. Detainee Tribunals	Y

Election Results

2006 general	Marsha Blackburn (R)	....	152,288	(66%)	($855,416)
	Bill Morrison (D)	....	73,369	(32%)	($67,214)
	Other	....	4,925	(2%)	
2006 primary	Marsha Blackburn (R)	.... unopposed			
2004 general	Marsha Blackburn (R)	.... unopposed			($575,587)

Prior Winning Percentages: 2002 (71%)

The People		**Race/Ethnic Origin**	**Ancestry**	
Area size:	6,349 sq. mi.	83.5% White	USA: 12.3%	English: 9.1%
Urban population:	61.0%	11.4% Black	Irish: 9.1%	
Rural population:	39.0%	1.5% Asian	**2004 Presidential Vote**	
Pop. 2000:	632,139	0.2% Native Am.	Bush (R) 206,410	(66%)
Pop. 2005 (est):	707,771	0.1% Hawaiian	Kerry (D) 104,792	(33%)
Median income:	$50,090	1.1% Two+ races	Other 2,216	(1%)
Poverty status:	8.0%	0.1% Other	**2000 Presidential Vote**	
Military veterans:	14.2%	2.2% Hispanic Origin	Bush (R) 146,213	(59%)
			Gore (D) 99,423	(40%)
			Other 3,098	(1%)
			Cook Partisan Voting Index: R +12	

Occupation	Blue collar: 24.0%	White collar: 64.0%	Gray collar: 12.0%

Rural Tennessee north of Mississippi is one of the most sparsely settled areas in the state. Along each side of the Tennessee River, as it flows north and widens out into Kentucky Lake amid heavy forests, are small rural communities; many go back to pre-Civil War days and some have not grown much since. One of those towns is Waynesboro, where Davy Crockett delivered campaign speeches from the base of a huge natural stone double bridge overlooking the Buffalo River. Farther west is McNairy County, where Sheriff Buford Pusser of *Walking Tall* fame carried his big stick until his untimely death in 1974; in Fayette County, outside of Memphis, black sharecroppers in 1959 were removed from white-owned land and they created a "tent city" that extended for a decade and was the longest civil rights protest in the nation. Here, the land is flatter and more open, a northward extension economically and demographically of the northern Mississippi farmlands. This mostly empty land is bounded on two sides by large metropolitan areas, Nashville to the east and Memphis to the west. South of Nashville is booming Williamson County, which had more slaves than whites prior to the Civil War, was occupied by the Union Army for three years and was a scene of devastation; now, though some pockets of poverty linger, its bedroom communities of Franklin and Brentwood make it the most affluent, highly educated and fastest-growing county in Tennessee. To the north, along the Cumberland River, is fast-growing Clarksville, with many well-restored 19th century homes, a large industrial park and the sprawling Fort Campbell army base, which is home to the 101st Airborne Division and has more than 20,000 military personnel just across the Kentucky border.

The 7th Congressional District of Tennessee spans this territory, packing Republican voters from Montgomery County's seat of Clarksville, south through the western half of Cheatham County and most of Williamson County plus a bite of Nashville-Davidson, then rambling west across the Tennessee River and south to the Mississippi border and finally to the white neighborhoods on the east side of Memphis and Shelby County. On the map, this looks like a rural district. Demographically, it's mostly suburban. The 7th grew by 12% between 2000 and 2005, making this the fastest-growing district in the state. Almost 40% of its votes are cast in metro Memphis and 30% in metro Nashville, mostly in the Republican stronghold of Williamson County; another 11% are in Montgomery County and only 21% in the smaller rural counties. The 7th is nearly as solidly Republican as the 1st District in faraway East Tennessee. In 2004, when John Kerry won Nashville by about 25,000 votes (55%-45%), George W. Bush carried the four rapidly growing counties in the southern and eastern suburbs of Nashville by 91,000 votes (66%-33%), with 72% in Williamson.

The congresswoman from the 7th District is Marsha Blackburn, a Republican first elected in 2002. She grew up in a Farm Bureau family in Laurel, Mississippi, where her father sold oil-field production equipment. Her interest in gardening and canning won her a 4-H college scholarship at Mississippi State University, where she majored in merchandising and clothing. She helped pay her way through college by selling books door-to-door and then became a sales manager with South-western Company, which sells educational materials, and moved to Williamson County. (Her hilltop home is known as "Up Yonder," named by its former owner, Grand Ole Opry star Minnie Pearl).

Blackburn became director of retail fashion for a Nashville department store and was appointed by Governor Don Sundquist as executive director of the Tennessee Film, Entertainment and Music Commission. In 1992, she was the Republican nominee against Bart Gordon in the 6th District and attacked his spending record and the congressional pay raise; she lost 57%-41%. She was elected in 1998 to the Tennessee Senate, where she became an outspoken opponent of Sundquist's proposed income tax. She was well known there for her appearances on conservative radio talk shows and for organizing rallies opposed to the income tax.

When Congressman Ed Bryant decided to run for the Senate, Blackburn sought to replace him. Seven candidates ran in the Republican primary; three were familiar figures in the Memphis area. Blackburn was the only well-known candidate from the Nashville area. She benefited from $100,000 in advertising and another $90,000 in contributions by the anti-tax Club for Growth, and from attacks by the Shelby County candidates on one another. She ran as pro-life, pro-gun and pro-military. The Memphis area cast 50% of the votes and the Nashville area only 25%. But Blackburn won 40% to 20% for the runner-up. She took 78% in the Nashville area, and was competitive in the Memphis area, with 24%. Blackburn easily won the general election and has not been seriously challenged since.

In the House, Blackburn continued her low-tax message and her voting record was among the most conservative. She urged across-the-board cuts for non-defense discretionary spending. She cosponsored the bill to make sales taxes deductible in states that have no income tax; it was passed as part of the corporate tax bill. On telecom issues, she urged renewal of the federal ban on Internet access taxes and filed the Video Choice Act, to create more diversity in cable programming by reducing regulations. She became an outspoken advocate of securing the nation's borders, including the 700-mile fence along the Mexican border.

Blackburn was mentioned as a possible candidate for the Senate or governor in 2006. But once she won a seat on the Energy and Commerce Committee, she had sufficient incentive to remain in the House. After the 2006 election, she was one of four candidates to chair the Republican Conference, but she was eliminated on the second ballot. Instead, she became a deputy whip and communications chairwoman for both the National Republican Congressional Committee and the Republican Study Committee.

EIGHTH DISTRICT

Rep. John Tanner (D)

Elected 1988, 10th term; b. Sept. 22, 1944, Halls; home, Union City; U. of TN, B.S. 1966, J.D. 1968; Disciples of Christ, married (Betty Ann).

Military Career: Navy, 1968-72; TN Natl. Guard, 1974-2000.

Elected Office: TN House of Reps., 1976-88.

Professional Career: Practicing atty., 1973-88.

DC Office: 1226 LHOB, 20515, 202-225-4714; Fax: 202-225-1765; Web site: www.house.gov/tanner.

District Offices: Jackson, 731-423-4848; Millington, 901-873-5690; Union City, 731-885-7070.

Committees: *Chief Deputy Majority Whip. Foreign Affairs* (14th of 27 D): Europe. *Ways & Means* (8th of 24 D): Trade; Oversight.

Group Ratings

	ADA	ACLU	AFS	LCV	ITIC	NTU	COC	ACU	CFG	FRC
2006	55	67	71	42	67	34	86	58	33	42
2005	75	—	100	50	—	33	70	50	37	46

National Journal Ratings

	2005 LIB	—	2005 CONS		2006 LIB	—	2006 CONS
Economic	56%	—	44%		55%	—	45%
Social	56%	—	44%		59%	—	40%
Foreign	55%	—	44%		55%	—	44%

Key Votes of the 109th Congress

1. Estate Tax Repeal	N	5. Limit Interstate Abortion	Y	9. Build Border Fence	Y
2. Limit CAFE Standards	Y	6. Extend Patriot Act	N	10. CAFTA	Y
3. FY06 Spending Curb	N	7. Bar Same Sex Marriage	Y	11. Oppose Iraq Withdrawal	N
4. Drilling in ANWR	Y	8. Stem Cell Research $	Y	12. Detainee Tribunals	Y

Election Results

2006 general	John Tanner (D)	129,610	(73%)	($804,767)
	John Farmer (R)	47,492	(27%)	
2006 primary	John Tanner (D)	unopposed		
2004 general	John Tanner (D)	173,623	(74%)	($614,785)
	James Hart (R)	59,853	(26%)	($47,892)

Prior Winning Percentages: 2002 (70%); 2000 (72%); 1998 (100%); 1996 (67%); 1994 (64%); 1992 (84%); 1990 (100%); 1988 (62%)

The People		Race/Ethnic Origin	Ancestry		
Area size:	8,528 sq. mi.	74.4% White	USA: 15.8%		Irish: 7.6%
Urban population:	47.0%	22.3% Black	English: 6.3%		
Rural population:	53.0%	0.4% Asian	**2004 Presidential Vote**		
Pop. 2000:	632,142	0.3% Native Am.	Bush (R)	131,524	(53%)
Pop. 2005 (est):	649,980	0.0% Hawaiian	Kerry (D)	116,327	(47%)
Median income:	$33,001	0.8% Two+ races	Other	1,423	(1%)
Poverty status:	15.0%	0.1% Other	**2000 Presidential Vote**		
Military veterans:	13.5%	1.6% Hispanic Origin	Gore (D)	109,221	(51%)
			Bush (R)	102,998	(48%)
			Other	2,633	(1%)
			Cook Partisan Voting Index: D + 0		

Occupation   Blue collar: 37.0%   White collar: 47.7%   Gray collar: 15.3%

West of Nashville and the lakes along the Tennessee River and north of Memphis, the rivers roll lazily through flat or gently rolling land that almost could be the northern end of Mississippi. Cotton and soybeans are the main crops, and they often are abundant; more blacks remain in rural areas here than in any other part of Tennessee, a reminder of its old plantation economy. The towns here are small, edged in by farm fields; the river bottoms, often flooded, are heavily forested. Here is Henning, the hometown of Alex Haley, where he used to sit on his porch and listen to his aunts tell him stories about slave ships and the Civil War that became *Roots*.

The 8th Congressional District of Tennessee includes much of this West Tennessee farmland, from the lakes west to the Mississippi. Its largest city is Jackson, which manufactures Delta faucets and Toyota parts; it also includes the northern fringes of Memphis. Historically, this is Democratic country; Republicans haven't represented most of the counties that make up the 8th since the end of Reconstruction. The region trended Republican in national races in the 1960s and 1970s, then turned back toward the Democrats with the help of some smart local politicians. One of them was Ned Ray McWherter, Tennessee House speaker from 1973-86, then governor for eight years. Recent movement has been back toward Republicans. Rural Carroll County is filled with small factories and is something of a bellwether in Tennessee politics, voting 50%-49% for George W. Bush in 2000 and 56%-43% in 2004. Lamar Alexander won the county by 22 votes in 2002, and Bob Corker in 2006 defeated Harold Ford 52%-47%. Overall, the district voted 51%-48% for Al Gore in 2000 but switched to Bush 53%-47% in 2004.

The congressman from the 8th District is John Tanner, a Democrat first elected in 1988. Tanner, who is a cousin of McWherter, grew up in Obion County, went to college and law school at the University of Tennessee, served four years in the Navy, then practiced law in Union City; he served in the Army National Guard, and retired as a colonel. In 1976, at 32, he successfully ran for the Tennessee House, where he served 12 years. In 1988, when the incumbent retired, Tanner ran for Congress and won with a whopping 66% in a four-candidate primary and 62% in the general.

Tanner's voting record put him solidly in the middle of the Democratic House and slightly to the left of midpoint when Republicans were in control. He has a seat on Ways and Means; his 8th District predecessor Jere Cooper served there from 1932 to 1957, the last three years as chairman. He has worked on tax issues, including elimination of estate taxes on family-owned farms and small businesses. When Bill Clinton was president, Tanner was a leading Democrat advocating elimination of the estate tax. George W. Bush signed a bill eliminating it in 2010, though the changes are "sunset" and will revert to the old rates the next year unless Congress acts. Because of its overall size, Tanner voted against it as a centerpiece of Bush's broader tax cuts. He consistently supported trade promotion authority, plus normal trade relations with China and the Central American Free Trade Agreement. His advocacy of those measures at Ways and Means angered many Democrats and their interest-group allies.

In 1992 Tanner could have been a senator for the asking. McWherter was ready to appoint him to succeed Al Gore. But Tanner chose to stay in the House, where he has become a major force. He was a founder of the moderate-to-conservative Democrats called the Blue Dogs. Tanner helped to create their welfare proposal, which he claims was the genesis for the broad welfare reform plan that Clinton signed in 1996. His modifications won the support of half the House's Democrats; that bipartisanship, as well as Tanner's support, later disappeared when House Republicans sought to extend the law with tougher requirements for eligibility. He became a harsh critic of Republican deficit policies, and offered alternatives to make their tax cuts revenue-neutral. He has sponsored a resolution to require a three-fifths vote in the House to pass any bill that would increase the federal deficit. To encourage more oversight, he filed a bill to make federal agencies more accountable for reports by Inspectors General. As part of his non-partisan approach, he took up the cause of redistricting reform, which would switch control from state legislators to independent commissions and prevent mid-decade redistricting; in 2005, he got 48 cosponsors. He supported the war in Iraq, but got the House to pass his amendment requiring the Army to consider a shift to six-month deployments, to improve soldier morale and ease the strain on their families. Tanner has been a chief deputy whip for Steny Hoyer and James Clyburn, and has urged inclusion of centrists' views.

In the 8th District, Tanner has been re-elected by wide margins. In 2000, the United Steelworkers backed his Democratic primary opponent because of Tanner's free trade votes; Tanner won the primary 87%-13%. In 2004, the Republican was James Hart, a eugenicist who called for reducing birth rates among racial minorities; Republican leaders publicly denounced him and his views. Tanner won 74%-26%. In 2006, local GOP leaders helped to keep him off the ballot.

NINTH DISTRICT

Rep. Steve Cohen (D)

Elected 2006, 1st term; b. May 24, 1949, Memphis; home, Memphis; Vanderbilt U., B.A. 1971, U. of Memphis, J.D. 1973; Jewish; single.

Elected Office: Shelby Cnty. Comm., 1977-78, TN Senate, 1982-2006.

Professional Career: Practicing atty., 1974-2006.

DC Office: 1004 LHOB, 20515, 202-225-3265; Fax: 202-225-5663; Web site: cohen.house.gov.

District Offices: Memphis, 901-544-4131.

Committees: *Judiciary* (13th of 23 D): Commercial & Administrative Law; Courts, the Internet & Intellectual Property; The Constitution, Civil Rights & Civil Liberties. *Transportation & Infrastructure* (39th of 41 D): Economic Development, Public Buildings & Emergency Management; Aviation; Highways & Transit.

Group Ratings and Key Votes: Newly Elected

Election Results

2006 general	Steve Cohen (D)	103,341	(60%)	($619,935)
	Jake Ford (I)	38,243	(22%)	($169,084)
	Mark White (R)	31,002	(18%)	($227,222)
2006 primary	Steve Cohen (D)	23,629	(31%)	
	Nikki Tinker (D)	19,164	(25%)	
	Joseph Ford (D)	9,334	(12%)	
	Julian Bolton (D)	8,055	(11%)	
	Ed Stanton (D)	6,927	(9%)	
	Other	9,250	(12%)	
2004 general	Harold Ford (D)	190,648	(82%)	($1,225,931)
	Ruben Fort (R)	41,578	(18%)	

The People		Race/Ethnic Origin	Ancestry	
Area size:	340 sq. mi.	34.9% White	English: 4.9%	Irish: 4.7%
Urban population:	99.6%	59.5% Black	USA: 4.5%	
Rural population:	0.4%	1.5% Asian	**2004 Presidential Vote**	
Pop. 2000:	632,143	0.2% Native Am.	Kerry (D) 171,547	(70%)
Pop. 2005 (est):	611,980	0.0% Hawaiian	Bush (R) 74,020	(30%)
Median income:	$33,806	0.9% Two+ races	Other 899	(0%)
Poverty status:	19.4%	0.1% Other	**2000 Presidential Vote**	
Military veterans:	11.2%	3.0% Hispanic Origin	Gore (D) 147,898	(63%)
			Bush (R) 83,531	(36%)
			Other 2,758	(1%)
			Cook Partisan Voting Index: D +18	
Occupation	Blue collar: 24.0%	White collar: 60.4%	Gray collar: 15.6%	

Memphis, the largest city in Tennessee though its metropolitan area is second to Nashville, is in the state's far southwestern corner, 500 miles from the Appalachian border with Virginia but only 20 miles from Mississippi's cotton fields and riverboat casinos. Metropolitan Memphis has one of the highest percentages of blacks in the country—evidence of the city's economic heritage as a capital of the Cotton Kingdom. Big Mississippi planters used to come north to sell their crop in the courtyard of the Peabody Hotel where the ducks march each day, then make financial arrangements for the next growing season.

Such facts have shaped the city's most celebrated tradition, the blues—a musical form worlds apart from Nashville's country music, which emerged from mountainous, mainly white Middle and East Tennessee. The Memphis sound originated from the self-taught musical stylings of poor, rural blacks in the Mississippi Delta. Throughout the first half of the 20th century, the most talented black musicians migrated north to Memphis and congregated downtown on Beale Street. The blues sound was later adapted by Elvis Presley, a poor white from rural Mississippi, in pivotal sessions in July 1954 at Sam Phillips' Sun Studio in Memphis—the birth of rock 'n' roll. In the early 1960s Memphis once again became the crucible of a new sound, soul music, which emerged as a counterpoint to rock, its increasingly white-dominated cousin. For some years Memphis tried to live down this musical heritage; much of Beale Street was razed and set on a misguided path toward urban renewal. But the city has come to recognize its history as an asset. Graceland, Presley's garishly decorated mansion, attracts hordes of musical pilgrims from all over the world, and a Museum of American Soul Music opened in 2003 on the site of the Stax studio, demolished in 1989, where Otis Redding, Isaac Hayes, the Staple Singers and Sam & Dave once made their records.

Music is not the city's only asset. Geographically central, Memphis is the home of the first supermarket chain (the Piggly Wiggly, founded in 1916; its symbol, Mr. Pig, has slimmed down) and the first Holiday Inn. Home of the world's busiest cargo airport, Memphis calls itself "America's distribution center": by far its biggest employer, and still growing, is FedEx, which ships its domestic packages in and out of Memphis Airport every night. The airport pumps nearly $21 billion into the economy every year, but its success also depends on Northwest Airlines, which makes Memphis one of its three domestic hubs and emerged from bankruptcy at the end of May 2007. For some years racial discord has scarred the political life of Memphis. It is the city where Martin Luther King Jr. was assassinated in 1968; the site of the murder, the Lorraine Motel, was converted into a civil rights museum. Even today, resurgent Beale Street is one of the few racially integrated spaces in the city, a division that holds equally true in voting. Blacks vote almost unanimously Democratic; whites vote Republican by margins almost as great. Blacks now outnumber whites in Shelby County; many have moved into the middle class, although Memphis continues to have the highest poverty rate in Tennessee.

The 9th Congressional District of Tennessee consists of most of the city of Memphis, some of its suburban fringe and about 30 precincts in east Shelby County. This black-majority 9th remains the strongest Democratic district in the state and is essential to the success of Democrats running statewide. In 2004, Bush bettered his 2000 performance in every Tennessee district except this one, where he ran much worse.

The new congressman from the 9th District is Steve Cohen, a Democrat elected in 2006. Cohen is a fourth-generation Memphian, the son of a psychiatrist. At age five Cohen was diagnosed with polio, an illness that would shift his focus from sports to politics. Cohen studied at Vanderbilt University and went onto law school at the University of Memphis. After graduation in 1973, he worked as a legal advisor for the Memphis Police Department and then started a law practice in

1978. He was elected to the Shelby County Commission and in 1982 to a Memphis-based state Senate seat, where he served for the next 24 years. He became known as the father of the Tennessee State Lottery for his successful efforts in 2002 to pass a referendum repealing a lottery ban and for passing legislation that used the lottery revenue to fund college scholarships.

Cohen had sought a promotion to Congress in 1996 when 22-year Congressman Harold Ford Sr. announced his retirement, but he found his path to Washington blocked by the incumbent's 26-year-old son. Cohen, who is white and Jewish, sought to highlight the obstacles facing him in the majority-black, Memphis-based district by running an ad with famous footage of a single Chinese protester standing in front of a tank in Tiananmen Square. This may not have been the most prudent approach: Harold Jr. defeated Cohen decisively, 60%-34%, and Cohen publicly expressed frustration over the inexperienced Ford's strong performance in black precincts. But the seat opened up a decade later in 2006, when Ford ran for Senate. While other candidates leaped into the race, Cohen weighed his options carefully before joining the contest three days before the filing deadline. As the only serious white contender among the 15 candidates who filed to run, Cohen faced considerable criticism from several prominent candidates and local black leaders, who publicly asserted that an African-American should represent the district. "For the first time in 30 years Memphis could be without African-American representation," Democratic candidate Ron Redwing's campaign told voters in an e-mail. Cohen's supporters charged that another primary foe paid for a push poll that asked, "Are you more likely to vote for a born-again Christian or a Jew?" Cohen quipped that his staunchly liberal record would make people mistake him for a black woman.

The district's black leaders were unable to narrow the crowded field and the primary results splintered along racial lines. In the August primary, Cohen won with 31%. Nikki Tinker, the former campaign manager for Ford Jr., finished second with 25%. The incumbent's cousin, Joe Ford Jr., finished third with 12%.

The Democratic primary is typically the only election that matters in this solidly Democratic district, but Cohen faced a challenge in November from yet another Ford—Jake Ford, the younger brother of the incumbent, who ran as an independent candidate. Jake Ford was a high school dropout who had had a few scrapes with the law, but he carried the support of his father and other African-American leaders who opposed Cohen. He argued that he was in better sync with the community, noting that more than two-thirds of the primary vote went against Cohen. Cohen's critics also suggested that Cohen, who is single and supports same-sex marriage, is gay but he has said that he is not. "Girls know I'm straight and gay guys know I'm straight," he said in October.

Cohen won the general election with 60%, ending the Ford family's 32-year hold on the district and becoming the only white member of Congress who represents a majority-black district. Among Cohen's priorities is a proposal for a national lottery that could be used to reduce the national deficit. He also introduced a resolution apologizing for slavery. Cohen attracted attention during the campaign when, in response to a reporter's question, he said he would try join the Congressional Black Caucus, but backed off when CBC leaders made it clear he would not be allowed to join. Cohen will have to navigate the minefield of racial politics once again in 2008 if a black consensus candidate emerges to challenge him in the 2008 Democratic primary. Second-place primary finisher Nikki Tinker was the only candidate running aggressively through September 2007.

★ TEXAS ★

Texas is a nation-sized state, one of four to have been an independent republic (the others are California, Vermont and Hawaii) and the one that stuck to it the longest. It is a state with an international image and international impact. The nation has voted for president 11 times since 1960: four times it has elected Californians and four times Texans. These two largest states have put their stamp on national politics in our times, just as New York did up from 1900 to 1960, when it was the residence of five of the winners and eight of the losers in 15 elections. Texas has been the second-largest state in area since Alaska was admitted to the Union in 1959; it became the second-largest in population in 1994, when it passed New York. The key to Texas's history is that this is a society with no aristocratic past, a state not formed by plantation owners or plutocrats but by dirt farmers. Texas was founded by Southerners, particularly Tennesseans, who wanted to establish their own republic in what were empty spaces within the borders of Mexico, a republic with Anglo-Saxon freedoms and black slavery. They defended their dream to the death at the Alamo and to a bloody victory at San Jacinto; they entered the Union willingly in 1845 and left it

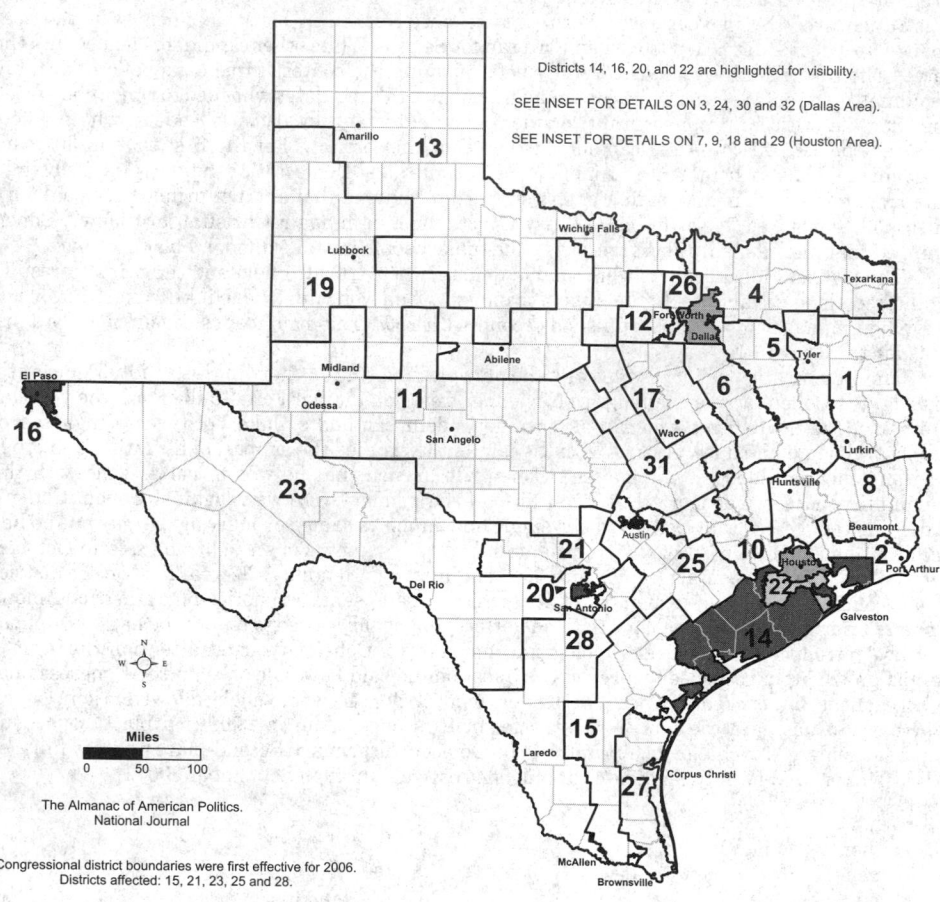

Districts 14, 16, 20, and 22 are highlighted for visibility.

SEE INSET FOR DETAILS ON 3, 24, 30 and 32 (Dallas Area).

SEE INSET FOR DETAILS ON 7, 9, 18 and 29 (Houston Area).

The Almanac of American Politics.
National Journal

Congressional district boundaries were first effective for 2006.
Districts affected: 15, 21, 23, 25 and 28.

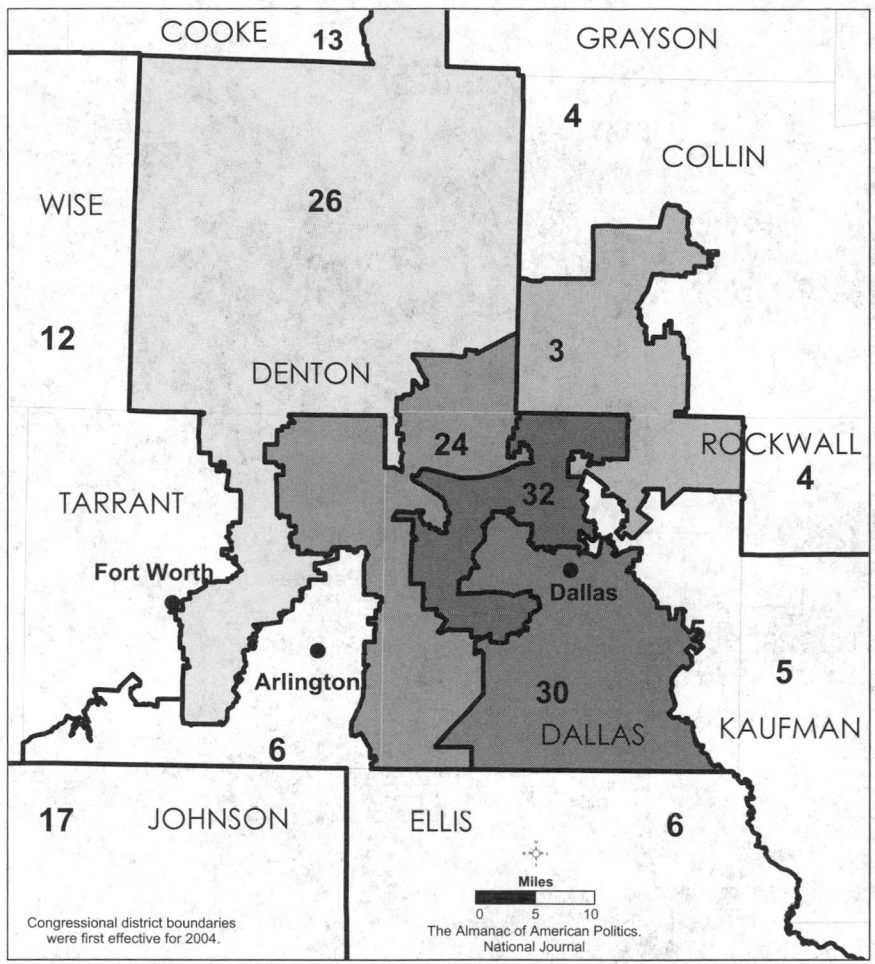

enthusiastically in 1861. The Texas that emerged from the Civil War was still young and poor; it was only in 1901 that oil was discovered at Spindletop, and the Texas wildcatters made their first fortunes.

Without the underpinnings and burdens of tradition, 20th century Texas produced fabulous wealth, generously rewarding success while being unforgiving of failure. It has respect for learning and style—think of its great universities, or Neiman Marcus—and it revels in rough manners and western wear. Texans are prone to wild swings in fortune—think of Sam Houston, or the great wildcatters, or Lyndon B. Johnson. And as the 20th century ended, Texans, for all their history of slavery and segregation, have proved open to immigrants and friendly with their neighbors in Mexico. NAFTA, the opening up of the border and the coming together of these two countries which are at such different economic levels and have such different cultures, is a project mainly of Texans of both political parties, of President George H. W. Bush and Treasury Secretary Lloyd Bentsen, Governors Ann Richards and George W. Bush. At the same time, Texas has become a high-tech powerhouse, a country with some of the nation's most creative businesses. But its success is not just economic. There are large elements of heroism—some mythical, some genuine—in the Texas history that every grade and high school student here learns.

Texas started off as a marchland on the border of the Third World, with an economy based on commodities, mainly cotton, whose prices were in long-term decline. Its farmers felt like part of a colonial economy controlled by bankers and Wall Street financiers. After Spindletop, Texas became the nation's—and for a time the world's—leading producer of oil. But oil prices, too, fell in free

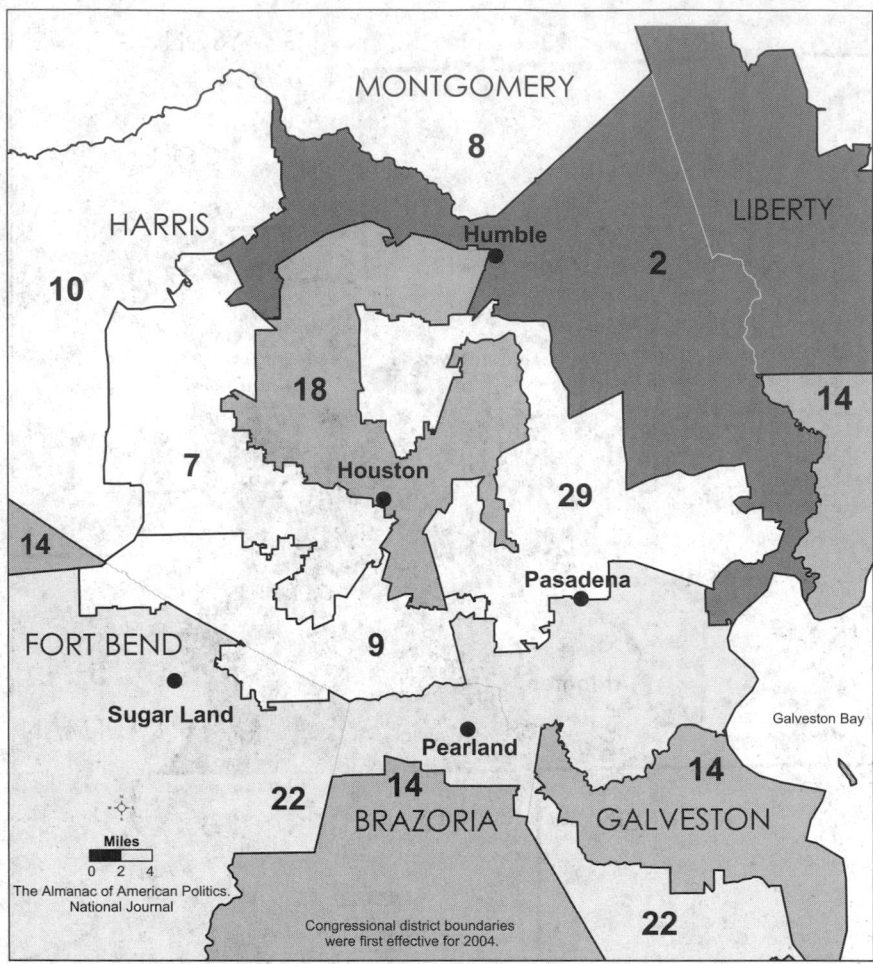

markets, and were propped up by politicians—the 1936 "hot oil" act that Sam Rayburn, as chairman of the House Commerce Committee, pushed through and the oil depletion allowance maintained for years by Rayburn when he was speaker, Senate Majority Leader Johnson, Senate Finance Committee Chairman Bentsen and others. These politicians also got subsidies for cotton growers and contracts for defense plants and space facilities in World War II and through the long years of the Cold War. Most Texas voters stayed Democratic up to 1970 because of Confederate memories, New Deal affections and the clout and competence of Texas's Democratic politicians.

But as Texas's economy became complex and creative, Texas's politics changed from a mostly Democratic effort to prop up the price of commodities to an increasingly Republican push to open up markets. By the 1970s Texas's economy was no longer dependent on raw commodities. The "awl bidness" here is less a matter of extracting oil from Texas; instead, Texas has the greatest concentration of high-skill specialists in extracting oil and natural gas in any part of the world. Also, beginning in the 1960s Texas has become a center for high tech, with the critical mass of knowledge and finances needed to produce firms like Texas Instruments and Dell Computer, and a university infrastructure in the University of Texas and Texas A&M to match the highway system that ties the state together. The Dallas-Fort Worth Metroplex is rich with defense contractors and with small firms that have become large with exports to Mexico. Houston is home to firms like Schlumberger, to many of the high-tech spinoffs from the space program, and to the enormous Texas Medical Center. San Antonio, with the Air Force's prime hospital, has significant medical technology and biotech industries. Austin, as UT doubled its number of engineering professors, became a high-tech center vying for second place after Silicon Valley in California; in 2006 Samsung announced it would build a $4 billion computer memory chip plant there. Texas state courts, once a happy hunting ground for trial lawyers, have been transformed by changes in tort law passed by the legislature in 1995 and 2003, while the federal court in Marshall, Texas, thanks to a fast discovery process and the willingness of juries to bring in big verdicts against patent violators, has become one of the nation's prime venues for patent cases. Texas's low taxes (and lack of a state income tax) helped attract corporate headquarters like American Airlines, GTE, J.C. Penney and Exxon. Oil is just a small part of the Texas economy now. As a result Dallas-Fort Worth and Houston have moved on the list of the top ten metro areas ahead of old industrial centers like Detroit, Cleveland, Pittsburgh and St. Louis, and in the process of overtaking Philadelphia and San Francisco and will stand behind only New York, Los Angeles and Chicago.

Texas has surged ahead despite the crash of oil prices in the early 1980s and the savings and loan crisis in the late 1980s, the defense cuts of the early 1990s and the WTO ruling against cotton subsidies in 2005. Job growth has been double the national average and Texas exports more goods to other countries than any other state. Growth has been most rapid in the exurban counties at the edges of its big big metro areas; between 2000 and 2006, populations have risen 30% in Collin County north of Dallas, 28% in Fort Bend County west of Houston, 29% in Williamson County north of Austin and 23% in Comal County northeast of San Antonio. Rural counties in West Texas, like so many in the Great Plains to the north, have been emptying out, but there has been steady growth in much of East Texas and rapid growth on the Lower Rio Grande from Laredo to Brownsville. Texas has surged in part because, in vivid contrast to that other onetime republic, California, it has nurtured and profited from its relationship with its southern neighbor, Mexico. California has shown its scorn, disgust and, worst of all, indifference to Mexico; it has portrayed its southern neighbor as generating illegal aliens and criminals California taxpayers must pay for; both its right and its left have done little to assimilate Mexican-Americans and other Latinos into a united America. Texas has taken a different course. Its border with Mexico is longer, some 1,200 miles long, and more often crossed; southern Texas along the Rio Grande is a transition zone between two very different economies. Despite a history of racial segregation, Texas has shown a friendly face to Mexicans, while Mexican immigrants have shown they wanted to become Texans and Americans. Fewer Latinos have crossed the border here to take advantage of welfare programs, which are much less generous in Texas than in California. Political leadership has made a difference. Governor George W. Bush, like Governor Ann Richards before him, journeyed often to Mexico and invited Mexican leaders to Texas, emphasizing the positive in public and leaving any negative details to private negotiations. Governor Rick Perry, who prepared for his office by taking Spanish lessons, has followed Richards's and Bush's lead. So, increasingly, has the Texas economy. Nearly half of U.S. merchandise exports to Mexico are from Texas, significantly more than California; 70% of U.S. exports to Mexico go through Texas. The NAFTA secretariat of labor is in Dallas, the North American Development Bank is headquartered in San Antonio, the Border Environmental Cooperation Commission is in Juarez, across the Rio Grande from El Paso, and the busiest truck crossing between the countries is the new World Trade Bridge near Laredo and Nuevo Laredo. The only thing marring the relationship was a recently-settled dispute over the distribution of Rio Grande water.

Texas is proud of its history and requires a year of Texas history in its high schools. But it also stands as a model for the American future, a model admired by many and disparaged by others. In 1845, when the Republic of Texas was annexed by the United States, New Englander Edward Everett Hale wrote a pamphlet entitled "How to Conquer Texas Before It Conquers Us," calling for emigration from the North to dilute "an unprincipled population of adventurers." But the newcomers joining ancestral Texans—think of the Bushes—have put the stamp of Texas on the whole United States. Texas is an open society, unpretentious, liberated from its heritage of racial and ethnic discrimination. It has a vast and rapidly growing economy. It presents a contrast with and a challenge to the traditions of other megastates—New York which pioneered the American welfare state, California with its high taxes and liberal social policies, the Great Lakes industrial states with their big labor unions. For Texas has some of the lowest taxes in the country and some of the lowest welfare levels; it has few union members and a relatively small public sector; it has resisted court-ordered moves to equalize spending among school districts; it continues to be a violent state, with a high crime rate and the highest number of executions. For years, liberals outside and inside Texas have called on the state to become more like New York or California or Michigan. But most Texans prefer their own model and over the past dozen years those states have in some respects been trying to become more like Texas.

Politically, Texas is now an indisputably Republican state: George W. Bush carried it 59%-38% in 2000 and 61%-38% in 2004. It was not always so: both George Bushes, Senator Kay Bailey Hutchison and former Senator Phil Gramm each lost an election before they started winning. One-party Democratic dominance ended in the 1960s, and for two decades Democratic victories were largely the product of Lloyd Bentsen, when he was on the ballot in 1970, 1976, 1982 and 1988 and when he exerted his influence for Ann Richards for governor in 1990. Metro Dallas-Fort Worth and Houston were the first parts of Texas to go Republican, and Bentsen relied on Democratic strength in the Texas countryside to win. But that is a thing of the past. George W. Bush carried 230 of 254 counties in 2000 and 236 in 2004; he carried rural Texas, outside the four big metro areas and the Rio Grande border country 65%-33% in 2000 and 66%-33% in 2004. At the same time, Republicans have retained a strong hold on the big metro areas: in 2004 the Dallas-Fort Worth Metroplex voted 62%-38% for Bush and metro Houston 58%-41%. Bush also carried metro San Antonio 59%-40% and, despite increased anti-Bush voting in the university precincts of Austin, he carried metro Austin 49.3%-48.9%. The border counties, heavily Hispanic, voted 58%-40% against Bush in 2000; he reduced that margin to 52%-48% in 2004.

Republicans now hold all 29 statewide elective offices, including all seats on the state Supreme Court. They have majorities in both houses of the legislature. The Republican Speaker of the House, Tom Craddick, is from Midland, the Permian Basin town in the west Texas desert which is also the hometown of George W. Bush, Laura Bush, former Commerce Secretary Donald Evans and General Tommy Franks. Who in the late 1950s and early 1960s, when they were all in Midland public schools, imagined that this one small town (there were 25,000 people in Midland County in 1950 and 67,000 in 1960) would produce so many leaders?

There are two threats to this Republican dominance. The first is the inevitable increase in the number of Latino voters. In 2000, 32% of Texas residents were Hispanic; more than half of Texas's population increase in the 1990s was accounted for by the increase in the number of Hispanics. To be sure, very many of these people are not U.S. citizens, and many who are citizens do not vote. White House political strategist Karl Rove has long been aware that Republicans must win a large share of the Latino vote if they are to remain dominant in the state. George W. Bush has cultivated Latino voters, starting in 1994 when he had little chance of reducing Ann Richards's margins among them; in 1998 the two exit polls showed him winning 49% and 39% of Hispanic votes. In 2000 the VNS exit poll showed Al Gore carrying Texas Hispanics 54%-42%. But in 2004 the NEP exit poll showed Bush winning 49% of Hispanic votes, just behind John Kerry's 50%, and he carried three heavily Hispanic congressional districts. West Texas rural counties where Hispanics are 30% to 50% of the population voted 2–1 and 3–1 for Bush, but it's not clear how many Hispanics there voted. Not all Republicans will do as well with Hispanics as Bush. But it seems unlikely that they will be an overwhelmingly Democratic bloc as Texas blacks have been—and in 2004 Bush increased his share of votes among Texas blacks according to NEP from 5% to 17%. In 2006 Governor Rick Perry won only 31% of the Hispanic vote, but Republican Carole Keeton Strayhorn, running as an Independent, got 18%, and together they got more than Democrat Chris Bell's 41%. Senator Kay Bailey Hutchison got 44% of the Hispanic vote and ran nearly even in the Border area.

The other threat to Republican dominance is the very fact that Republicans are plainly in control, in a position to be held responsible for any failures in public policy or ethics. In October 2003, U.S. House Majority Leader Tom DeLay, Texas Speaker Tom Craddick and Lieutenant Governor David Dewhurst slammed through a bill redrawing Texas's 32 congressional districts that was as partisan a gerrymander as the Democrats' 1991 plan. As a result, Texas's House delegation, which was 17-15 Democratic after the 2002 election, was 21-11 Republican after the 2004 election. That produced negative feedback in the form of indictments by Austin District Attorney Ronnie Earle of three of DeLay's allies on campaign finance charges. DeLay resigned as Majority Leader and then resigned from Congress in June 2006, but a judge blocked Republicans from picking another candidate, and Democrats won that seat on November 7 and a South Texas seat, redistricted by another court ruling, in a November runoff. Democrats also gained seats in the state House, but were still far from a majority.

On substantive issues, Governor Rick Perry and the now solidly Republican legislature faced difficult choices in early 2005 on the budget, school finance and state water policy. And Republicans faced intraparty fights. In the 1960s and 1970s divisive fights between conservative and liberal Democrats gave Republicans openings to capture statewide office, as Senator John Tower did in 1961 and Governor Bill Clements in 1978. Now divisive fights between more or less conservative Republicans may give Democrats similar openings. Texas politics is played for keeps, but it doesn't stand still.

The People		Race/Ethnic Origin			Military veterans: 1,754,809 (11.7%)	
Pop. 2006 (est):	23,507,783	10,933,313	52.4%	White	WWII: 17.1%	Korea: 11.7%
Pop. 2000:	20,851,820	2,364,255	11.3%	Black	Vietnam: 34.6%	Gulf War: 13.3%
Pop. 1990:	16,986,510	554,445	2.7%	Asian	**Most populous cities (2006):**	
Change 1990-2000:	Up 22.8%	68,859	0.3%	Native Am.	1. Houston	2,144,491
% of U.S. total:	7.4%	10,757	0.1%	Hawaiian	2. San Antonio	1,296,682
Pop. rank:	2nd of 50	230,567	1.1%	Two+ races	3. Dallas	1,232,940
Area size:	268,581 sq. mi.	19,958	0.1%	Other	4. Austin	709,893
State Native:	62.2%	6,669,666	32.0%	Hisp. Origin	5. Fort Worth	653,320
Non-citizen:	9.5%	**Ancestry**				
Language		German: 8.4%		USA: 6.3%	Urban population: 82.5%	
English: 68.6%	Spanish: 25.9%	Irish: 6.1%		English: 6.0%	Rural population: 17.5%	
Other Eur.: 2.8%		French: 1.9%				

Education		Work Sector		Legislature	
H.S. Grad:	75.7%	Private: 78.0%	Govt: 14.6%	Senate	20 R 11 D
College Grad:	23.2%	Self: 7.1%	Family: 0.3%	House	81 R 69 D
Industry		Unemployment: 6.0%		Legislative Term Limits: No	
Agri: 2.7%	Con: 8.1%	**Household Income**		**Registered Voters**	
Fin: 6.8%	Info: 3.1%	<15k: 17.0%	15-35k: 27.0%	No party registration	
Mfg: 17.6%	Prof: 28.8%	35-50k: 16.5%	50-100k: 27.9%		
Public: 4.5%	Trade: 15.9%	100-150k: 7.2%	>150k: 4.3%		
Other: 12.5%		Median: $39,927			
Occupation		Poverty status: 15.4%			
Blue collar: 24.1%	White collar: 60.6%	**Home Value**			
Gray collar: 15.3%		<50k: 27.6%	50-100k: 38.4%	100-200k: 24.6%	200-300k: 5.5%
		300-500k: 2.6%	>500k: 1.3%	Median: $77,800	

Presidential politics   Texas is now solidly Republican in presidential politics and a massive counterweight to the state it replaced in 1994 as the second largest, New York. The contrast can be seen in the results of the 2000 and 2004 elections. In 2000 New York cast 33 electoral votes for Al Gore and Texas cast 32 for George W. Bush; Gore's 1.5 million popular vote margin in New York overshadowed Bush's 1.36 million vote margin in Texas. In 2004 it was the other way around. Texas cast 34 electoral votes for Bush and New York 31 for John Kerry; Bush's 1.7 million popular vote margin in Bush overshadowed Kerry's 1.35 million margin in New York. Texas seems at least as far out of reach for Democrats as New York does for Republicans. The best the Democratic ticket has done here in recent years was 43% in 1988, when Lloyd Bentsen was on the ticket, and 44% in 1996, as Ross Perot split the opposition to Bill Clinton and Bob Dole carried the state anyway with 49%.

2004 Presidential Vote

Bush (R) 4,526,917   (61%)
Kerry (D) 2,832,704   (38%)
Badnarik (Lib) 38,787   (1%)
Other 12,341   (0%)

2004 Democratic Presidential Primary

Kerry (D) 563,237   (67%)
Edwards (D) 120,413   (14%)
Dean (D) 40,035   (5%)
Sharpton (D) 31,020   (4%)
Lieberman (D) 25,245   (3%)
Other 59,281   (7%)

2000 Presidential Vote

Bush (R) 3,799,639   (59%)
Gore (D) 2,433,746   (38%)
Nader (Green) 137,994   (2%)
Other 36,258   (1%)

Texas's presidential primary, originally in May, was moved to March for Super Tuesday in 1988. The Republican primary electorate is heavily conservative; the Democratic primary electorate is increasingly liberal—and shrinking. Texas does not have party registration, and so turnout in each party's primaries is a fair index of party preference. In 1988, 1.7 million Texans voted in the Democratic primary; Michael Dukakis led with 33% of the vote and Jesse Jackson got 25%, ahead of Al Gore, running as a southern moderate, with 20%. In 1992, nearly 1.5 million voted in the Democratic primary, 66% of them for Bill Clinton. In 1996, 2000 and 2004, when the Democratic nomination was uncontested by the time Texas voted, although there were still live contests for state office, turnout continued to fall—921,000 in 1996, 786,000 in 2000 and 839,000 in 2004.

The Texas legislature considered moving the state's presidential primary from March 4 to February 5, 2008, but did not do so.

Congressional districting

110th Congress Lineup
19 R   13 D

109th Congress Lineup
21 R   11 D

Before 2001, redistricting in Texas had always been the prerogative of Democrats. For many years it was not particularly partisan; there weren't enough Republicans to matter. By the 1990s there were, and in 1991 the Democrats produced their masterpiece. Modified slightly by a 1996 court ruling, it clumped heavily Republican areas into hugely Republican districts, then carved out with incredibly convoluted lines three new districts for Democrats. Starting in 1994, Republicans outpolled Democrats in House races and Anglo Democrats found themselves increasingly imperiled. Still, Democrats held a 17-13 majority in the delegation after the 2000 election.

Texas gained two new seats after the 2000 Census, and Republicans like House Majority Whip Tom DeLay predicted that their party would pick up six to eight seats. It didn't happen. The legislature was unable to agree on a map in 2001; a three-judge federal court in Tyler, with two Democratic- and one Republican-appointed judges, later took control and on November 14 came up with its own plan.

The plan protected all incumbents and created two new Republican districts. But in effect, the partisan Democratic plan of 1991 was given new life, with the Republicans given two new seats as a consolation prize. The result was, predictably, a 17-15 Democratic delegation.

In 2002 Republicans won big majorities in the legislature. In early 2003 Tom DeLay, now House Majority Leader, urged the legislature to pass a new plan; Senate Republicans were reluctant. DeLay continued to press new House Speaker Tom Craddick, a longtime ally. As the legislative session neared adjournment, the House Redistricting Committee approved a new map on May 6. The disciplined Republican majority ignored Democrat protests. On the eve of the House's scheduled May 12 debate, 51 Democrats fled the state and secretly settled in a Holiday Inn in Ardmore, Oklahoma, to prevent the Republicans from getting the two-thirds required for a quorum. This spectacle attracted national attention; the state police—possibly with the assistance of the new federal Homeland Security Department personnel—were dispatched to track down the self-styled "Killer D's." Once their location was revealed, the Democrats insisted they would not return to Austin until after May 15, the final day the House could take up the bill in its regular session. The maneuver worked, temporarily. Governor Rick Perry convened a special session on June 30 and in late July the House approved the redistricting plan and sent it to the Senate. Then 11 Senate Democrats skedaddled.

When enough Democrats showed up to make a quorum, Republicans started arguing about the plan. Craddick insisted on a district in which his hometown of Midland would be the largest city; Midland candidates (including George W. Bush) have lost in the past to candidates from Lubbock or from districts that sprawled to San Antonio. DeLay insisted on splitting Austin's Democratic Travis County among three districts, two of them Republican. Republicans in Williamson County, just north of Austin, insisted that their county dominate a district. Finally all the arguments were resolved and details of the final plan were unveiled on October 9. Passage was perfunctory.

The plan was obviously intended to benefit Republicans: 22 of the 32 districts had voted Republican in statewide races, and two others came close to doing so. The 2003 plan also shuffled around counties, so that Democrats who had been representing districts carried by Bush suddenly found themselves running in unfamiliar territory.

The plan attempted to comply with the Voting Rights Act by drawing safe districts for Texas's two black and five Hispanic incumbent Democrats. The previous plan had two districts that were more than 40% black; so did the new plan, but it added a 38% black district in Houston (which elected a black Democrat in 2004), while the next highest black percentage in the old plan was 23%. The old plan had seven districts with Hispanic majorities; the new plan had eight. What the plan did was make what Texans called WD-40s—white Democrats over 40—an endangered species. There were 15 of them in the Texas delegation elected in 1992, 11 in 2000, 10 in 2002 and only three in 2004.

Democrats quickly went into federal court and drew a panel with two Republican-appointed and one Democratic-appointed judges. On December 19 the Justice Department ruled the plan was in compliance with the Voting Rights Act; the court ruled that it was permissible to redistrict more than once in the 10 years between censuses. On January 2, 2004, Congressman Ralph Hall, a

Democrat elected from a heavily Republican district, announced that he was switching parties. On January 6 the court approved the plan 2–1. That same day 2d District Democrat Jim Turner announced his retirement. In September three DeLay associates who pushed the redistricting plan were indicted by Austin District Attorney Ronnie Earle on campaign finance charges related to the 2002 state House elections; Earle had been criticized by Republicans when an indictment he brought in 1993 against Senator Kay Bailey Hutchison was summarily dismissed. In October 2004 the U.S. Supreme Court ordered the three-judge court to reconsider the case in light of its decision in a redistricting case arising in Pennsylvania, in which the Supreme Court upheld a Republican plan as egregiously partisan as this one. In June 2005, the federal court again rejected the legal challenge, and elections went ahead under the plan.

But by then the election had already been held and the new House had taken office. George W. Bush carried Texas 61%-38%; in the 32 House races Republicans won 58% of the votes to Democrats' 39%. Five WD-40s were defeated; only three survived, Chet Edwards of Waco and two others, Lloyd Doggett and Gene Green, in majority-Hispanic districts. The Texas delegation, 17-15 Democratic before Hall's party switch, was 21-11 Republican in January 2005. Overall, Republicans gained three seats in the House, with the help of Texas, to bring their total to 232, the most won by Republicans in any biennial election since 1946; if Texas had not redistricted and Hall had not switched parties, there would have been only 226.

In December 2005 the Supreme Court agreed to hear the appeal, and in June the Court upheld the basic plan, rejecting by a 7–2 vote the charge that it was "an unconstitutional political gerrymander." But it ruled 5–4 that the fact that the 23d District, held by Republican Henry Bonilla, had a population that was only 55% Hispanic violated the Voting Rights Act, and it suggested that the 25th District, stretching from Austin to the Rio Grande, which was 69% Hispanic and reelected Austin Democrat Lloyd Doggett, might also have to be redrawn. It left the lines to be redrawn by the three-judge district court, which adopted a new plan, giving a larger portion of San Antonio to the 23d District and keeping the 25th District within easy driving distance of Austin. Filing was reopened for the five new districts, with primaries to be held on Election Day and runoffs between the party nominees later in December.

The overall result was a victory for Republicans, but with two offsetting losses. Democrat Nick Lampson, ousted in the 2d District in 2004, came back and won in Tom DeLay's old 22d District despite its heavy Republican leanings. And Henry Bonilla, running after the Republicans had lost the House, lost his 23d District seat to Democrat Ciro Rodriguez, who in 2004 had lost by a narrow and disputed margin the Democratic nomination in the 28th to Henry Cuellar. That left Republicans with a 19-13 majority in the delegation.

Governor

Rick Perry (R)

Assumed office Dec. 2000, term expires Jan. 2011, 2d full term; b. Mar. 4, 1950, Paint Creek; home, Austin; Texas A&M U., B.S. 1972; United Methodist; married (Anita).

Military Career: Air Force, 1972-77.

Elected Office: TX House of Reps., 1984-90; Comm., TX Dept. of Agriculture, 1990-98; Lt. Gov., 1998-2000.

Professional Career: Farmer & rancher.

Office: State Capitol, P.O. Box 12428, Austin, 78711, 512-463-2000; Fax: 512-463-1849; Web site: www.governor.state.tx.us.

Election Results

2006 general	Rick Perry (R)	1,716,803	(39%)
	Chris Bell (D)	1,310,353	(30%)
	Carole Keeton Strayhorn (I)	797,577	(18%)
	Kinky Friedman (I)	546,869	(12%)
	Other	27,466	(1%)
2006 primary	Rick Perry (R)	552,545	(84%)
	Larry Kilgore (R)	50,119	(8%)
	Rhett Smith (R)	30,225	(5%)
	Star Locke (R)	23,030	(4%)
2002 general	Rick Perry (R)	2,632,541	(58%)
	Tony Sanchez (D)	1,819,843	(40%)
	Other	101,598	(2%)

Rick Perry succeeded George W. Bush as governor of Texas on December 21, 2000, and was elected to full terms in 2002 and 2006; in December 2008 he will become the longest-serving governor in Texas history. Perry grew up on his family's farm in Paint Creek, in Haskell County, near where his great-great grandfather settled after fighting in the Civil War, and was elected to the Texas House in the 1890s. His family owns a 10,000-acre ranch, and his father served 28 years as a county commissioner, as a Democrat, like pretty much everyone in these parts. Rick Perry was an Eagle Scout and went to Texas A&M to study to be a veterinarian; that didn't pan out, though he did receive a degree in animal science. There, he became a yell leader—cheerleader on lesser campuses, and a coveted position at A&M. These were the years of great student rebellions, but apparently not at College Station; Perry says he never saw a war protest. After college he served five years in the Air Force, piloting C-130 transports. In 1977 he returned to work on the family ranch; after a season of drought he was ready to sign up as a pilot for Southwest Airlines, but the rains came and he stayed on the ranch. In 1984 he was elected to the state House, as a Democrat naturally. He was part of a group called the Pit Bulls who loved to cut state agency budgets. In 1989 he was passed over for a leadership position and switched to the Republican Party. In 1990 he ran for agriculture commissioner against the picaresque incumbent Jim Hightower. Perry, with the help of Karl Rove, got the support of the Farm Bureau and won an upset victory. In an increasingly Republican Texas, Perry was easily reelected in 1994.

Then in 1998, when storied Democratic incumbent Bob Bullock retired, Perry ran for lieutenant governor. This is an important position in Texas, more powerful than the governorship, some say; the lieutenant governor not only presides over the state Senate but controls its proceedings and appoints its committee members and chairmen. Governors and lieutenant governors are elected separately in Texas, and Bush and Perry ran separate campaigns; Karl Rove worked for Perry in 1990 and 1994 but not in 1998. Perry, interestingly, had no Republican primary opposition for a post that obviously could lead directly to the governorship. Perry and his Democratic opponent, state Comptroller John Sharp, managed to raise $15 million for the campaign. Sharp was a new Democrat who had done some interesting work on government reform, and served as student body president at A&M when Perry was yell leader. Perry's 50%-48% victory opened the way to the governor's office.

For five weeks after the 2000 presidential election it was not clear whether he would become governor, but he was obviously preparing. On December 21 he was sworn in—the first Aggie governor of Texas. In 2002, Democrats believed that Perry was vulnerable and gamely tried to put together a winning ticket. The chief organizer was John Sharp, who decided to run for lieutenant governor again, not governor, and worked to get a gubernatorial candidate who could swell Democratic turnout among Latinos. His dream candidate was Tony Sanchez, chief shareholder of International Bank of Commerce and Sanchez Oil & Gas in Laredo, who was said to have a net worth of $600 million. Sanchez was no political naif: in the early 1970s, he had worked for Lieutenant Governor Ben Barnes, one of Texas's canniest politicians and still a major lobbyist today. Sanchez returned to Laredo and with his father developed a huge pool of natural gas on the Mexican border near Laredo and started International Bank of Commerce and Tesoro Savings & Loan. Sharp and former San Antonio Mayor Henry Cisneros persuaded Sanchez to run for governor; they helped to push aside former UT quarterback Marty Akins, who in September 2001 announced he would run for comptroller instead. Sanchez spent $18 million on ads and beat former Attorney General Dan Morales in the Democratic primary 61%-33%. Meanwhile, in the April 2002 runoff, Democrats nominated for senator the black and business-friendly former mayor of Dallas, Ron Kirk. Sharp had got his "dream team," which he hoped would drive Latino and black turnout up even while he maintained appeal to Anglo voters at the top of the ticket.

Perry and Sanchez agreed on many issues but much of the campaign consisted of vitriolic negative ads. Sanchez's general theme was that Perry was beholden to campaign contributors and did their bidding. Perry hit Sanchez for not voting in some elections and for his business practices. In the fall he ran a number of hard-hitting ads linking Sanchez to drug kingpins' money laundering. It was undisputed that some $25 million was laundered through Tesoro Savings & Loan in the early 1980s; Sanchez claimed that the S&L followed regulations and that he did not know of the transactions and that no one in the S&L was charged with a crime. Nevertheless Perry ads linked the money laundering to the murder in 1985 of a Drug Enforcement Administration agent in Mexico. In one Perry ad another DEA agent said, "We investigated the murder. The same drug dealers who killed Kiki laundered millions in drug money through Tony Sanchez's bank." Sanchez was outraged. He said that Perry was "by far the most disgusting human being I have ever known."

Election night was a nightmare for the "dream team." Perry beat Sanchez 58%-40%, although Sanchez spent $67 million to Perry's $28 million, and Republicans won up and down the line. Ron Kirk and John Sharp, who led the Democratic ticket, both lost. The high Latino turnout that Democrats had hoped for did materialize, but only in the Rio Grande Valley. Elsewhere in the state, turnout in Latino neighborhoods in Houston, Dallas and San Antonio was not up much; the big increases were in the fast-growing heavily Republican counties at the edge of metro areas. Republicans won big margins in the legislature—19-12 in the state Senate and 88-62 in the state House. The new leaders of the legislature were Lieutenant Governor David Dewhurst in the Senate and Speaker Tom Craddick in the House—the first Republican speaker since 1871. Perry called his victory a mandate for restricting tort lawsuits, providing rate relief on homeowner insurance and changes in medical malpractice law; he also sought a school vouchers program. Facing forecasts that state revenues would fall $10 billion short of the cost of maintaining current levels of spending, he ordered 7% cuts for the rest of the fiscal year in all programs except education, Medicaid and children's health in January 2003. The state Senate voted for disclosure of homeowners insurance rates to regulators in February 2003.

Redistricting dominated the Texas political landscape in 2003. In early 2003 House Majority Leader Tom DeLay urged the legislature to pass a new plan; Senate Republicans and Dewhurst, the presiding officer, were reluctant. DeLay continued to press Craddick, a longtime ally. As the legislative session neared adjournment, the House Redistricting Committee approved a new map on May 6. It would have added five to seven new Republican seats and jeopardized each of the delegation's 10 Anglo Democrats, though it protected the five incumbent Latino Democrats and two African-Americans; it appeared to create two additional open seats designed for Latinos and one for a black candidate. On the eve of the House's scheduled May 12 debate, 51 Democrats fled the state and secretly settled in a Holiday Inn in Ardmore, Oklahoma, to prevent the Republicans from getting the two-thirds required for a quorum. This spectacle attracted national attention; the state police were dispatched to track down the self-styled "Killer D's." Once their location was revealed, the Democrats insisted they would not return to Austin until after May 15, the final day the House could take up the bill in its regular session. The maneuver worked, temporarily. Perry then convened a special session on June 30; after House Republicans passed their plan, that 30-day session deadlocked when Senators abided by their traditional rule for two-thirds approval to debate legislation. But Perry called a second 30-day session. When Republicans threatened to take action this time with a simple majority, 11 Senate Democrats fled to Albuquerque to prevent a quorum for legislative action or apprehension by state law-enforcement officers. With cheers from Democrats nationwide and growing anger from Republicans, they remained there for the month of August. When Perry indicated in early September that he would call a third special session, Democratic state senator John Whitmire effectively broke the deadlock by returning to Houston and to his legislative duties. When enough Democrats showed up to make a quorum, Republicans started arguing about the plan; on October 9, all the arguments were resolved and details of the final plan were formally posted. Passage was perfunctory. Perry's view: "For too long millions of Texans have lived in gerrymandered districts that were drawn to protect incumbents rather than the public interest. Starting today, the voters of Texas can know that their power to choose their congressman or congresswoman will not be hampered by an incumbent protection scheme."

School finance has long been a major issue in Texas government and politics. In 1993 Governor Ann Richards and the Democratic legislature passed a "Robin Hood" plan to distribute money from high-property-value school districts to poorer ones. By 2004 many school districts had reached their maximum taxing levels; voters were complaining about high property taxes while others were saying the schools were starved for money. In 2004 Perry advanced a package with property tax reductions, more spending on schools and a $1 cigarette tax increase, but it was criticized fiercely by Comptroller Carole Keeton Strayhorn. It failed to pass, and in September 2004, a state trial judge ruled that the school finance system was unconstitutional and gave the legislature a year to come up with a solution; the state appealed directly to the Texas Supreme Court, which had previously issued several orders on education funding. In 2005, Perry declared school financing a "legislative emergency." But the House and Senate were unable to come to agreement, this time coming close to a deal but failing in the final hours of the session. He vetoed a $35 billion education bill in June 2005 and called a special session to consider the issue. A couple more special sessions failed to come to a solution. In November 2005, the state Supreme Court ruled the current financing system unconstitutional on the grounds that it amounted to a statewide property tax. In September Perry appointed a commission headed by his old political foe John Sharp. It recommended a plan which Perry brought before a special session in April 2006. The Senate passed a bill in May with a one-third property tax cut, a $2,000 pay raise for teachers, a 4% spending increase, new math and science initiatives and a cigarette tax increase. It also incorporated changes in business taxes, expanding the franchise tax and reaching every significant business operation, with revenues to be used to finance property tax reductions.

Perry took other initiatives as well. Texas's growth has choked its roads with traffic, and I-35 from the Dallas-Fort Worth Metroplex on south has been pounded by trucks headed for the border at Laredo, the busiest crossing point for truck traffic between the United States and Mexico. Perry argued that the state's 20-cent gas tax is no longer adequate to build needed infrastructure, and the legislature in 2005 authorized his Trans-Texas Corridor plan to have the Spanish company Cintra build a network of toll highways, with rail corridors, at a cost of something on the order of $184 billion. The first segment of the Central Texas Turnpike bypassing Austin opened in September 2006; the plan is to build a highway corridor just east of and parallel to I-35. This has sparked protests from local governments, landowners and others; Strayhorn called it the "Trans-Texas Catastrophe." But Perry plunged ahead. Another problem was border enforcement. Perry ordered video surveillance cameras emplaced on the border in June 2006 and sent large numbers of state troopers to protect Texans from the Mexican drug cartels operating just south of the border. "Enforcing the border is the federal government's responsibility, but Texas will not wait for them to act." He denounced proposals for a border fence and for taking away birthright citizenship. The legislature also passed major changes in tort law, building on earlier laws. Perry sought increased spending for the CHIP children's health insurance program and increased financial aid to college students, together with required exit exams and other measures to hold students and colleges financially accountable for performance. He issued an order requiring girls to receive the HPV vaccine. He worked to accommodate tens, if not hundreds of thousands, of Katrina evacuees.

All this still left Perry's job approval under 50% going into the 2006 campaign cycle. Senator Kay Bailey Hutchison gave long thought to challenging Perry in the March 2006 primary, as she had in 2002, but in June 2005 she announced she would not run. The next day, Strayhorn made it clear she would. "I am not a weak leadin', ethics ignorin', pointin' the finger at everyone blamin', special session callin', public school slashin', slush fund spendin', toll road buildin', special interest panderin', rainy day fund raidin', fee increasin', no property tax cuttin', promise breakin', do-nothin' Rick Perry phony conservative." She called for repealing Perry's business tax and called the property tax reductions a "$23 billion hot check." Also entering the race was musician Kinky Friedman. "How hard could it be?" was his theme. "The far religious right and the politically correct left are holding the greatest state in the Union hostage. . . . Musicians can run this state better than politicians. We didn't put the train in the ditch. We'll work late at night. We won't work in the morning, though." Democrats had more difficulty coming up with a candidate. Finally one-term Houston Congressman Chris Bell, who had been defeated as a result of the 2003 redistricting plan, stepped forward. Just before the filing deadline, Strayhorn said she would run as an Independent rather than against Perry in the Republican primary. Early 2006 polls showed Perry running around 40% and these three opponents each receiving about half as many votes.

Despite a long and raucous campaign, that was pretty much how it turned out. In the March primary 656,000 votes were cast on the Republican side and 509,000 on the Democratic—a bit of a decline in Republican strength. In November Perry received 39% of the vote, to 30% for Bell, 18% for Strayhorn and 12% for Friedman. Perry carried metro Dallas (41%-31%), Houston (38%-31%) and San Antonio (36%-28%), which together cast nearly 60% of the state's votes, by solid margins over Bell. Bell carried metro Austin (39%-31%) and the Border counties (38%-33%). Whites voted

44%-24% for Perry; blacks 63%-16% for Bell; Hispanics, who cast 15% of the votes, 41%-31% for Bell. Republicans gained one seat in the state Senate, for a 20-11 margin, and lost five seats in the state House, leaving their majority at 81-69.

Senior Senator

Kay Bailey Hutchison (R)

Elected June 1993, seat up 2012, 3d full term; b. July 22, 1943, Galveston; home, Dallas; U. of TX, B.A. 1962, J.D. 1967; Episcopalian; married (Ray).

Elected Office: TX House of Reps., 1972-76; TX Treasurer, 1990-93.

Professional Career: Political & legal corresp., KPRC–TV, 1967-70; Vice Chmn., Natl. Transp. Safety Bd., 1976-78; V.P. & Gen. Cnsl., RepublicBank Corp., 1978-82; Owner, McCraw Candies, 1984-88.

DC Office: 284 RSOB, 20510, 202-224-5922; Fax: 202-224-0776; Web site: hutchison.senate.gov.

State Offices: Abilene, 325-676-2839; Austin, 512-916-5834; Dallas, 214-361-3500; Harlingen, 956-425-2253; Houston, 713-653-3456; San Antonio, 210-340-2885.

Committees: *Appropriations* (11th of 14 R): Military Construction, Veterans Affairs & Related Agencies (RMM); Labor, Health and Human Services, Education & Related Agencies; Transportation, Housing and Urban Development & Related Agencies; Commerce, Justice, Science & Related Agencies; Energy & Water Development; Defense. *Commerce, Science & Transportation* (4th of 11 R): Space, Aeronautics & Related Sciences (RMM); Aviation Operations, Safety & Security; Science, Technology & Innovation; Surface Transportation & Merchant Marine Infrastructure, Safety & Security. *Rules & Administration* (5th of 9 R). *Veterans' Affairs* (3d of 7 R).

Group Ratings

	ADA	ACLU	AFS	LCV	ITIC	NTU	COC	ACU	CFG	FRC
2006	5	17	13	0	100	69	92	84	58	87
2005	15	—	0	5	—	69	94	92	73	—

National Journal Ratings

	2005 LIB	—	2005 CONS		2006 LIB	—	2006 CONS
Economic	35%	—	64%		42%	—	56%
Social	23%	—	64%		28%	—	71%
Foreign	26%	—	65%		26%	—	67%

Key Votes of the 109th Congress

1. Bar ANWR Drilling	N	5. Confirm Samuel Alito	Y	9. Limit Interstate Abortion	Y
2. FY06 Spending Curb	Y	6. Path to Citizenship	N	10. CAFTA	Y
3. Estate Tax Repeal	Y	7. Bar Same Sex Marriage	Y	11. Urge Iraq Withdrawal	N
4. Raise Minimum Wage	N	8. Stem Cell Research $	Y	12. Provide Detainee Rights	N

Election Results

2006 general	Kay Bailey Hutchison (R)	2,661,789	(62%)	($5,734,146)
	Barbara Radnofsky (D)	1,555,202	(36%)	($1,432,107)
	Other	97,672	(2%)	
2006 primary	Kay Bailey Hutchison (R)	unopposed		
2000 general	Kay Bailey Hutchison (R)	4,082,091	(65%)	($3,518,862)
	Eugene Kelly (D)	2,030,315	(32%)	($4,602)
	Other	164,246	(3%)	

Prior Winning Percentages: 1994 (61%); 1993 (67%)

Kay Bailey Hutchison, senior senator from Texas, is a Republican who first won her seat in a June 1993 special election. She is of old Texas stock, the great-great-granddaughter of Charles S. Taylor, a signer of the Texas Declaration of Independence, who was a friend and business partner of Senator Thomas Jefferson Rusk, the first man to hold this seat; Hutchison is the first woman. She grew up in LaMarque, near the refinery town of Texas City, a prom queen who went to college and then law school at the University of Texas. Unable to get a law job in 1967, she worked for a Houston TV station as a reporter. In 1972, she won a seat in the legislature, its first Republican woman. In 1976 she went to Washington to fill the number two position at the National Transportation Safety Board. She married her former colleague Ray Hutchison, moved to Dallas and went into banking and became a small business owner in 1978. In 1982, she lost a House race to Steve Bartlett, later mayor of Dallas. But she stayed active in Republican politics and in 1990 was elected state treasurer, a breakthrough race for state Republicans who had not been able to win downballot statewide races before. Hutchison began her political career when it was no advantage to be a woman and has been mocked by liberals for her tight-lipped good manners and by Washington conservatives as a "Texas pompom girl." Her response: "This is what I have faced all my life—the trivialization of me—which I have not ever let bother me. I have always been able to rise above the expectations." Indeed: She is a senator from the nation's second-largest state, one of five senators in history (Barbara Boxer, Dianne Feinstein, Daniel Patrick Moynihan and Charles Schumer are the others) to have been elected with 4 million votes or more.

Her big break came in January 1993 when Lloyd Bentsen resigned his Senate seat after 22 years to become Secretary of the Treasury. To replace him, Governor Ann Richards appointed Bob Krueger, a two-term congressman in the 1970s who was elected railroad commissioner (actually, oil regulator) in 1990. Running against him in the May 1993 all-party primary were three Republicans, Hutchison and Congressmen Joe Barton and Jack Fields. Krueger opposed the Clinton budget and tax plan, but Democrats were so unpopular in Texas then—Bill Clinton had a 73% negative job rating—that Krueger won only 29% of the total vote, just behind Hutchison, also with 29%; Barton and Fields won 14% each. Hutchison kept the focus on Clinton and won the June runoff by an astonishing 67%-33%. Three serious Democrats were running as she entered the race for the full term in 1994. The potentially strongest candidate, moderate Houston Congressman Mike Andrews, was eliminated in the March primary. In the April runoff, former Attorney General Jim Mattox lost 54%-46% to Richard Fisher, a free-spending moderate who campaigned extensively in the Border counties in Spanish. Hutchison cruised to a solid 61%-38% victory.

Hutchison has a mostly conservative voting record. She is opposed to outlawing abortion and favors embryonic stem cell research, but voted for the partial-birth abortion ban. She has supported the Bush energy bills, including oil drilling in the Arctic National Wildlife Refuge. Hutchison has long sought to repeal the marriage penalty; in 1997 she sponsored a bill to do so that was vetoed by Bill Clinton. She supported it as part of the 2001 Bush tax cut and advanced her own version with relief for homemakers. In January 2003 she cosponsored with Evan Bayh a bill to repeal it immediately and permanently. She also cosponsored with two Democrats a bill to allow IRA holders over 59 1/2 to withdraw money for charitable donations without paying tax.

On the Aviation Subcommittee, she sponsored a 2000 law strengthening airport security that was being put into effect on September 11. After that she worked with Chairman Jay Rockefeller and strongly supported federalization of airport security. Hutchison had hoped to be chairman of the Aviation Subcommittee, but in January 2003 Trent Lott returned to the committee and with greater seniority, claimed the post; she became chairman of the Surface Transportation Subcommittee instead. In 2006, she supported the pension bill that gave Delta and Northwest, which went through bankruptcy, more time to fund their pensions than Texas-based American and Continental, which had not gone through bankruptcy. The idea was to amend the bill later and, in May 2007, Congress agreed to provide further pension assistance to airlines whose pension plans are not frozen. She worked to forge a compromise on changing the Wright amendment, which barred many interstate flights from Dallas's Love Field; Southwest, based in Love, wanted more such flights, while American, based in DFW, wanted fewer. She has been a longtime supporter of the Amtrak system and of Amtrak lines in Texas, but has argued that Amtrak should get tougher on its unions. In 2005, when Bush's budget cut Amtrak funding, she disagreed. "We need to either commit to a national railroad or abandon the pretense of one. National or nothing. The budget represents an inadequate middle ground." Hutchison is also a strong supporter of the manned space program; she grew up near what is now the Johnson Space Center. Before the February 2003 Columbia disaster she warned of underfunding, and afterwards she expressed confidence in the program and called for more funding. She hailed the appointment of Michael Griffin as NASA administrator in April 2005, and the June 2005 Commerce committee decision to keep the space shuttle flying past 2010 and until the expected date of the first crew exploration vehicle in 2014. Griffin in December 2005 said there would be only a two-year gap between the retirement of the space shuttle and the CEV, but in March 2007 said the CEV would be delayed until 2015. Hutchison has suggested including China in the space station and in May 2006, when there was doubt about the delivery date of the CEV, said, "Maybe that is where the private sector can come forward and be a major player in the space program."

During the Clinton years, Hutchison was critical of administration foreign policy; she was wary of U.S. involvement in the former Yugoslavia, called for an eventual pullout from Bosnia, and decried Clinton administration policy in Kosovo. She has supported the foreign policy of the Bush administration. In October 2006 she said there was "chaos" in Iraq and suggested that more consideration should be given to dividing Iraq into semi-autonomous regions. When George W. Bush announced the surge in January 2007 she said, "He is working with the Iraqi leadership to implement this new approach, and it is critical that the initiative be given a chance to succeed. I respect the president for admitting mistakes, correcting the course." But she noted that, "People in my state see me as having a few degrees of separation" from Bush. She serves on the Appropriations Committee and over the years has shepherded the Military Housing Privatization Initiative, in which the government hires private firms to build military housing; in February 2004 she helped get $1.37 billion for housing at San Antonio's Fort Sam Houston. She has sponsored a bill to expand federal funding of stem-cell research but to ban the creation of new embryos. In December 2006 she worked furiously to get the provision allowing taxpayers in states with no state income taxes (like Texas) to continue to be able to deduct state sales taxes; it passed both houses at nearly the last possible moment by wide margins.

Hutchison was reelected in 2000 by a 65%-32% margin; she carried 237 of 254 counties. After the election she showed some interest in running for governor in 2002, but that would have meant a primary against Governor Rick Perry and in March 2001 she announced she would not do so. From 2003 to 2005 Perry and the legislature grappled with difficult issues of school finance and transportation without resolution. Hutchison, busy in Washington and traveling around the state, remained above the legislative fray but let Republicans know she might run for governor and asked for their support. Into the November 2004 omnibus appropriation she, or someone, inserted a provision allowing money raised for federal campaigns to be spent in state campaigns; at the end of 2004 she had $6.7 million, not much less than Perry's $7.9 million but more than Comptroller Carole Keeton Strayhorn's $5.7 million. Her favorable ratings in polls in late 2004 and early 2005 were higher than Perry's. But in June 2005 she announced she would not run for governor and would instead run for reelection in 2006. Her opponent, Houston lawyer Barbara Ann Radnofsky, made a game effort at campaigning but was not financially competitive. Hutchison won 62%-36%, carrying 238 of 254 counties, losing only some Border and south Texas counties (while running about even in the area as a whole) and Austin's Travis County (but she carried Williamson County, just to the north, by more votes than she lost by in Travis). In November 2006 she was elected chairman of the Senate Republican Conference, the number three position in the leadership. She has been mentioned occasionally as a possible candidate for vice president. Her response in January 2007: "If our party's nominee called me and said we are putting everything in the grid, and we think you are the best person, would I say no? I can't imagine that I would say no. Would I seek it or do something to promote it? Absolutely not."

Junior Senator

John Cornyn (R)

Elected 2002, seat up 2008, 1st term; b. Feb. 2, 1952, Houston; home, San Antonio; Trinity U., B.A. 1973, St. Mary's Law Schl., J.D. 1977, U. of VA, L.L.M. 1995; Church of Christ; married (Sandy).

Elected Office: San Antonio Dist. Ct. judge, 1984-90; TX Sup. Ct., 1990-97; TX Atty. Gen., 1998-2002.

Professional Career: Practicing atty., 1977-84.

DC Office: 517 HSOB, 20510, 202-224-2934; Fax: 202-228-2856; Web site: cornyn.senate.gov.

State Offices: Austin, 512-469-6034; Dallas, 972-239-1310; Harlingen, 956-423-0162; Houston, 713-572-3337; Lubbock, 806-472-7533; San Antonio, 210-224-7485; Tyler, 903-593-0902.

Committees: *Armed Services* (9th of 12 R): Airland (RMM); Emerging Threats & Capabilities; Seapower. *Budget* (10th of 11 R). *Ethics (Select)* (Vice Chmn. of 3 R). *Judiciary* (7th of 9 R): Immigration, Refugees & Border Security (RMM); Constitution; Terrorism, Technology & Homeland Security; Human Rights & the Law.

Group Ratings

	ADA	ACLU	AFS	LCV	ITIC	NTU	COC	ACU	CFG	FRC
2006	0	8	0	0	100	83	83	96	87	100
2005	10	—	0	0	—	79	89	96	85	—

National Journal Ratings

	2005 LIB	—	2005 CONS		2006 LIB	—	2006 CONS
Economic	32%	—	67%		0%	—	97%
Social	0%	—	77%		18%	—	74%
Foreign	0%	—	74%		0%	—	92%

Key Votes of the 109th Congress

1. Bar ANWR Drilling	N	5. Confirm Samuel Alito	Y	9. Limit Interstate Abortion	Y
2. FY06 Spending Curb	Y	6. Path to Citizenship	N	10. CAFTA	Y
3. Estate Tax Repeal	Y	7. Bar Same Sex Marriage	Y	11. Urge Iraq Withdrawal	N
4. Raise Minimum Wage	N	8. Stem Cell Research $	N	12. Provide Detainee Rights	N

Election Results

2002 general	John Cornyn (R)	2,496,243	(55%)	($9,769,780)
	Ron Kirk (D)	1,955,758	(43%)	($9,426,763)
	Other	62,011	(1%)	
2002 primary	John Cornyn (R)	478,825	(77%)	
	Bruce Lang (R)	46,907	(8%)	
	Douglas Deffenbaugh (R)	43,611	(7%)	
	Dudley Mooney (R)	32,262	(5%)	
	Other	17,757	(3%)	
1996 general	Phil Gramm (R)	3,027,680	(55%)	($14,078,131)
	Victor M. Morales (D)	2,428,776	(44%)	($978,862)

John Cornyn, a Republican, was elected to the Senate in 2002. He was born in Houston and grew up in San Antonio. He graduated from high school in Japan; his father was an oral pathologist in the Air Force stationed there and after retiring from the service settled in San Antonio and taught at the University of Texas Health Science Center. John Cornyn graduated from Trinity University and St. Mary's University law school, both in San Antonio, in the 1970s. He practiced law for five years with a firm that defended doctors and insurance companies in medical malpractice cases. In 1984 he ran for district court judge on the Republican ticket in Bexar County and upset a strong favorite in the race.

In 1990 he was elected to the state supreme court as a Republican. Cornyn generally ruled for defendants in tort cases, but not always; he dissented in 1995 from a decision that stripped juries of the right to determine the credibility of expert witnesses. The same year he wrote a 5–4 decision upholding the "Robin Hood" school finance system in which property-wealthy school districts had to send money to property-poor districts. In 1997 he resigned from the court to run for attorney general. In the March 1998 Republican primary and runoff he defeated two better-known opponents. In the general election he faced a grizzled veteran of Texas politics, Jim Mattox, a populist-sounding Democrat, congressman from Dallas from 1976 to 1982, attorney general from 1982 to 1990, second-place finisher to Ann Richards in the 1990 primary and runoff for governor. Cornyn won 54%-44%. Cornyn was the first Republican attorney general since Reconstruction. He argued two cases before the U. S. Supreme Court, including the Santa Fe Independent School District's defense of reading the Lord's Prayer at football games (the Court nixed it).

Cornyn had been planning to run for reelection in 2002. But on September 4, 2001, Senator Phil Gramm announced that he would not run for reelection. Cornyn immediately set out to run for the Senate and seemed to have the support of George W. Bush. Cornyn announced September 21 and said he hoped to raise $6 million for the March primary; he had no serious opposition there and didn't raise that much until later. National Democrats found a Texas candidate they liked: Dallas Mayor Ron Kirk. Kirk had an interesting life story: he is black, the son of the first black mailman in Austin and a teacher; he graduated from the University of Texas and its law school and was an aide to Senator Lloyd Bentsen. In 1995 he was elected mayor of Dallas and in 1999 he was reelected by a wide margin. In 2001 he announced he was resigning as mayor and in January 2002 he announced he was running for the Senate.

Kirk was not the only Democrat who ran. Another was Congressman Ken Bentsen of metro Houston, nephew of Senator and Treasury Secretary Lloyd Bentsen. But neither Kirk nor Bentsen ran first in the March primary. That place went to Victor Morales, a geography teacher and track coach from the Dallas suburb of Crandall, who raised $7,000 for his campaign. Morales had won the nomination to run against Gramm in 1996 with 36% of the vote against two former congressmen; his main assets were his Hispanic identity and the fact that he had the same last name as Attorney General Dan Morales. (This scenario may recur as more Hispanics enter politics. There are many fewer surnames among American Hispanics than among American Anglos.) In 2002 Morales won 33.2% of the vote in the primary, to 33.1% for Kirk and 27% for Bentsen. In the four weeks before the runoff, Kirk was endorsed by Bentsen and Houston Mayor Lee Brown. In the lower-turnout runoff, Kirk won 60%-40%.

In the general election Cornyn ran as a supporter of George W. Bush, and of making the 2001 tax cuts permanent, extending the research and development tax credit and raising Texas's share of gas tax funds from 90.5 cents to 95 cents per dollar of gas tax revenues. He supported school vouchers, individual investment accounts as part of Social Security and colorblind standards nationally in college and university admissions. Kirk took an opposite stand on all these issues, but portrayed himself as a moderate Democrat who would often support Bush. On Iraq, Kirk equivocated, taking different stands at different times. Kirk was a favorite of Democratic contributors and spent much time—50 days, Cornyn's spokesman charged—outside Texas schmoozing with Democratic contributors in Washington, on the Upper East Side of Manhattan, in Beverly Hills and similar venues. Republicans ran ads linking him to Hillary Rodham Clinton and liberal out-of-state contributors. Eventually he spent $8.9 million—almost as much as Cornyn's $9.5 million, most of it raised in Texas.

Kirk was helped here by his sense of humor and a considerable charm, making fun of his bald pate and answering—mindful of Texas mores—when asked whether he owned a gun, "I have a wife and two little girls. You figure it out." But in the course of the campaign Kirk made some mistakes. He opposed the nomination to a federal judgeship of Texas Supreme Court Justice Priscilla Owen— something Republicans seized on in ads. He refused to disclose his income tax returns, except for allowing reporters one peek at his 2001 return. When Cornyn came out for a bill in the legislature requiring district attorneys to seek the death penalty for killers of law enforcement officials (the Austin district attorney had not sought the death penalty for the killer of a Travis County sheriff's deputy), Kirk said Cornyn was acting like he was running for district attorney—and then had to apologize abjectly to a convention of law enforcement officials a few days later, while Cornyn met with the deputy's widow. In San Antonio on September 12 he said that Cornyn might not support military action in Iraq if our military forces were not "disproportionately ethnic [and] disproportionately minority." He said he supported military action only if it met with international approval. Four days later he apologized and then said he backed Bush's position; he endorsed the Iraq war resolution in October.

Texas Democrats called their ticket of Kirk for senator and Tony Sanchez for governor the "dream team." They hoped it would draw a large turnout of blacks and Hispanics. Meanwhile Republicans quietly registered thousands of new voters in the heavily Republican fast-growing suburban counties around Dallas-Fort Worth, Houston, San Antonio and Austin. Polls showed the race close in the spring, with Cornyn well under 50%; one nonpartisan firm and Kirk's pollster showed Kirk ahead or leading in the summer and fall. Democrats operated on the assumption that Kirk had to win 85% of blacks, 65% of Hispanics and 35% of whites to win. He clearly achieved the first and probably achieved the second of those goals, but failed by a solid margin to achieve the third. Cornyn won 55%-43%—almost the same numbers as in his race for attorney general in 1998, and a fair reflection of basic party identification in Texas in recent years. Kirk carried historically Republican Dallas County 50%-49%. But Cornyn carried the entire Dallas-Fort Worth Metroplex 58%-41%. Cornyn carried metro Houston 55%-43% and the combined San Antonio and Austin metro areas 51%-47%. The Border went 69%-29% for Kirk, a 148,000-vote margin. But rural Texas, much larger, went 62%-37% for Cornyn, a 346,000-vote margin. Kirk may have increased black turnout in Dallas, and Sanchez clearly increased Hispanic turnout in Laredo, but otherwise black and Hispanic turnout does not seem to have risen much above that in 1994, the last big-turnout off-year election. In contrast, turnout was up from 25% to 52% in fast-growing counties around Dallas-Fort Worth, Houston, San Antonio and Austin. Cornyn holds the seat once held by Sam Houston, Lyndon B. Johnson and John Tower and is the first Texas senator to come from San Antonio, which in the state's first decades was its largest city and which he argues is its most representative.

In the Senate Cornyn has been an active member of the Judiciary Committee. In 2003 and 2004 he chaired the Constitution Subcommittee and held hearings on continuity of government, hostility to religious expression in the public square and same-sex marriage. He proposed a constitutional amendment to give each house of Congress the authority to decide how vacancies would be filled if one-quarter or more of its members were killed or incapacitated. He was a lead sponsor of the amendment, which got less than 50 votes, to ban same-sex marriage. He also supported amendments to expand the rights of crime victims and to overturn the Ninth Circuit decision banning the phrase "one nation under God" in the Pledge of Allegiance. He cosponsored the class action and bankruptcy bills opposed by trial lawyers but passed by the Senate and signed by Bush in 2005. He sought to amend the bankruptcy bill to require companies to file for bankruptcy in the state where their primary business or assets are located; this was a response to Enron's filing in New York, and Edward Kennedy, miffed that Massachusetts's Polaroid filed out of state, joined him. But Joseph Biden and Tom Carper of Delaware, legal home of 500,000 corporations, threatened to kill the bankruptcy bill, and Cornyn withdrew the amendment. Cornyn took a lead role in seeking to confirm Bush appellate judgeship appointees and urged colleagues to change the Senate rules to stop the Democrats' filibusters. With Democrat Patrick Leahy he moved to strengthen the Freedom of Information Act with a bill that would penalize federal agencies and employees that fail to respond to requests in a timely manner. A bill establishing a commission to consider changes in FOIA was approved unanimously by the Senate in June 2005. But a more specific bill, to penalize federal agencies for delayed response, create an ombudsman to review cases and create a hotline to track requests didn't go anywhere after passing in committee in September 2006. In March 2007, the House passed a similar bill despite a veto threat by the Bush administration.

Cornyn's hometown of San Antonio is only 150 miles from Mexico, and he has taken an interest in immigration and citizenship issues; in January 2005 he became chairman of the Immigration Subcommittee. (Its ranking Democrat, Edward Kennedy, floor managed his first bill, on immigration, in 1965.) One of Cornyn's first successful bills reduced from three years to one the waiting period for citizenship for legal aliens serving in the armed forces. He sponsored a bill to increase the time Mexicans with border crossing cards can remain in the United States from 72 hours to six months, the same time allowed for Canadians. And he proposed guest worker legislation, to allow workers with willing employers to get either seasonal visas (primarily farm workers) or non-seasonal visas for 12 months which could be extended to 36 months; some of their wages would be taken by the government and placed in bank accounts in their home countries, for their use when they return. This proposal was criticized by some who want to put guest workers on the path to citizenship and by others who argue that we should deport illegal aliens and not let guest workers in. Cornyn argues that it is unrealistic to expect that we will deport the estimated 8 to 10 million illegal aliens in the country and that people who want to work should be encouraged. He has opposed military patrol of the border or building a fence along most of its length—these would disrupt life in South Texas, he argues—but backed the measure passed by the House in February 2005 that would allow completion of the 14-mile fence in San Diego despite the objections of the California Coastal Commission and that would bar driver's licenses for illegal aliens being recognized by airport screeners or federal building security agents. Cornyn argued that these security measures should be treated as part of a larger immigration bill, despite the contrary arguments of House Judiciary Chairman James Sensenbrenner. During 2005 Cornyn pressed Majority Leader Bill Frist to bring immigration legislation to the floor without success. Frustrated, he told the San Antonio Rotary Club in August 2005, "I used to think Social Security was the third rail of American politics. I no longer think that. I think it's immigration." In March 2006 the Judiciary Committee began working on a bill, but did not imediately support the draft advanced by Kennedy and John McCain because it did not require illegal immigrants to return to their countries of origin before legalization. He voted for the 700-mile border fence in September 2006, though he questioned whether it would be a "practical use" of federal money. In spring 2007, as Jon Kyl negotiated another version with Kennedy, Cornyn stayed out of the negotiations because of the lack of a "touchback" provision requiring return to the country of origin, and he opposed Kennedy-Kyl when it came to the floor in May 2007; he also opposed the compromise bill that was defeated in June.

Cornyn has supported Bush judicial nominees opposed by Democrats. "I want judges on the Supreme Court who will not use their position to impose a political agenda on the American people." In April 2005 he stirred some controversy when he asked "whether there may be some connection between the perception in some quarters on some occasions where judges are making political decisions yet are unaccountable to the public, that it builds up and builds up and builds up to the point where some people engage in violence." He supported Bush's three Supreme Court nominees, including Harriet Miers, whom he had known in Texas. "Harriet Miers is a brilliant legal mind. She is a woman of outstanding character who clearly understands what it means to follow the law." In March 2006, Justice Sandra Day O'Connor spoke out "against those who would strong arm the judiciary. It takes a lot of degeneration before a country falls into dictatorship, but we should avoid these ends by avoiding these beginnings"—a remark many took as a criticism of Cornyn's statement 11 months before. It was "hyperbole, to say the least," said Cornyn. "There's no danger of dictatorship while people feel free to express their views." After the Supreme Court's *Kelo* decision, Cornyn sponsored a bill to bar the federal government and federally financed state and local governments to take property by eminent domain for economic development. He supported the Bush administration on Iraq, and after the surge was announced he said, "We know that if things spiral out of control in Iraq, that if we decide to precipitously leave Iraq and it becomes a failed state, or if it becomes a killing field for ethnic cleansing, that we will more likely have to return at even greater loss of blood and treasure." But in March 2007 he criticized Attorney General Alberto Gonzales for his handling of the firings of U.S. attorneys, and he sponsored an amendment to allow states to opt out of testing requirements from the reauthorization of the No Child Left Behind law. In November 2006 he was elected vice chairman of the Senate Republican Conference.

Cornyn comes up for reelection in 2008. Some Democratic strategists, noting that his job approval had not risen much above 50%, argued that he could be vulnerable. But attempts to attract a well-known challenger did not meet with success through summer 2007. It was widely thought that Houston Mayor Bill White or former Comptroller John Sharp might be formidable opponents, but neither made a move to run; former Texas Speaker Ben Barnes, a prolific Democratic fundraiser, said it was "highly unlikely" that he would do so. In June, wealthy San Antonio trial lawyer Mikal Watts formed an exploratory committee and won notice by launching his effort with $3.8 million of his own money. State Representative Rick Noriega, with grass roots support from party activists, was also pursuing a bid.

FIRST DISTRICT

Rep. Louie Gohmert (R)

Elected 2004, 2d term; b. Aug. 18, 1953, Pittsburg; home, Tyler; TX A&M U., B.A. 1975, Baylor U. Law Schl., J.D. 1977; Baptist; married (Kathy).

Military Career: Army, 1978-82.

Elected Office: Smith Cnty. Dist. Ct. judge, 1992-2002.

Professional Career: Practicing atty., 1982-92; Chief Justice, TX 12th Ct. of Appeals, 2002-03.

DC Office: 510 CHOB, 20515, 202-225-3035; Fax: 202-226-1230; Web site: www.gohmert.house.gov.

District Offices: Longview, 903-236-8597; Lufkin, 866-535-6302; Marshall, 866-535-6302; Tyler, 903-561-6349.

Committees: *Judiciary* (16th of 17 R): Crime, Terrorism & Homeland Security; Immigration, Citizenship, Refugees, Border Security & International Law. *Natural Resources* (14th of 22 R): Energy & Mineral Resources; National Parks, Forests & Public Lands. *Small Business* (10th of 15 R): Investigations & Oversight (RMM).

Group Ratings

	ADA	ACLU	AFS	LCV	ITIC	NTU	COC	ACU	CFG	FRC
2006	5	10	0	0	100	72	100	96	86	100
2005	0	—	0	6	—	67	85	96	82	100

National Journal Ratings

	2005 LIB	—	2005 CONS	2006 LIB	—	2006 CONS
Economic	28%	—	72%	24%	—	75%
Social	26%	—	74%	0%	—	94%
Foreign	0%	—	89%	38%	—	59%

Key Votes of the 109th Congress

1. Estate Tax Repeal	Y	5. Limit Interstate Abortion	Y	9. Build Border Fence		Y
2. Limit CAFE Standards	Y	6. Extend Patriot Act	Y	10. CAFTA		Y
3. FY06 Spending Curb	Y	7. Bar Same Sex Marriage	Y	11. Oppose Iraq Withdrawal		Y
4. Drilling in ANWR	Y	8. Stem Cell Research $	N	12. Detainee Tribunals		Y

Election Results

2006 general	Louie Gohmert (R)	104,099	(68%)	($955,344)
	Roger Owen (D)	46,303	(30%)	
	Other	2,668	(2%)	
2006 primary	Louie Gohmert (R)	unopposed		
2004 general	Louie Gohmert (R)	157,068	(61%)	($1,829,275)
	Max Sandlin (D)	96,281	(38%)	($1,690,816)
	Other	2,158	(1%)	

The People		Race/Ethnic Origin	Ancestry	
Area size:	8,916 sq. mi.	70.6% White	USA: 12.1%	Irish: 7.4%
Urban population:	50.9%	18.3% Black	English: 6.8%	
Rural population:	49.1%	0.5% Asian	**2004 Presidential Vote**	
Pop. 2000:	651,619	0.3% Native Am.	Bush (R)	178,409 (69%)
Pop. 2005 (est):	685,914	0.0% Hawaiian	Kerry (D)	78,609 (31%)
Median income:	$33,461	0.9% Two+ races	**2000 Presidential Vote**	
Poverty status:	16.0%	0.0% Other	Bush (R)	152,963 (68%)
Military veterans:	13.3%	9.3% Hispanic Origin	Gore (D)	73,596 (32%)
			Cook Partisan Voting Index: R +17	

Occupation   Blue collar: 30.3%   White collar: 53.3%   Gray collar: 16.4%

The gently rolling land of East Texas, cut by rivers headed south to the Gulf of Mexico, has been part of the United States for 160 years. Settled early on by farmers from Tennessee, it has been part of Scots-Irish America, a land of people of fighting faith, given to graceful courtesy but unwilling to endure a slight without recompense. One hundred years ago this was one of the poorest parts of America, a place where farmers scratched a living off the land and hoped for good prices in the marketplace and good weather for its crops. When a peach blight in the early 20th century wiped out much of the local fruit industry, many farmers turned to growing roses, which proved ideally suited to the climate and soil of the area around Tyler, one of the larger East Texas towns. By the 1940s, more than half the nation's supply of rose bushes was grown within 10 miles of Tyler, which has become known for its annual Texas Rose Festival and the East Texas State Fair. Longview, which in the 1870s was the western terminus of the Southern Pacific Railroad, became a trading center for wagon trains and local cotton growers and timber cutters; then, in 1943, the Big Inch pipeline began sending millions of barrels of crude oil from the "Black Giant" oil field near Longview—the largest ever in the state—to the East for refining. Since then, the Longview area has become an industrial center for earth-moving equipment and chemicals, and home to the Stroh Brewery, the largest in Texas. Marshall, the hometown of the late Lady Bird Johnson, participates in the Holiday Trail of Lights, a Christmas festival that stretches from towns in Louisiana to Texas. It was in the fields and woodlands of Nacogdoches and other nearby counties that the debris fell when Space Shuttle *Columbia* was lost in February 2003; an organized search by 25,000 people recovered more than 84,000 pieces—38% of *Columbia*. More than a year later, when NASA already had reached its conclusion over the cause of the failure and the pieces had little investigative value, local farmers and hunters were still retrieving small particles of tile, metal or plastic debris.

The 1st Congressional District of Texas includes the heart of East Texas; it's a rectangular collection of 12 counties, of which the most populous are Tyler's Smith County, Longview's Gregg County and Lufkin's Angelina County in the south. Also included is the southeast corner of Cass County east of Route 59, which is primarily the McLeod school district. East Texas is ancestrally Democratic, a region that nodded to the rhetoric of William Jennings Bryan and Franklin D. Roosevelt. But Tyler and Longview moved toward the Republican party as long ago as the 1950s, and the rest of East Texas followed, seemingly convinced that the party of Andrew Jackson and Sam Houston had abandoned bellicose alertness for emollient conciliation and celebration of ordinary people's values for elitist disdain. When George H. W. Bush ran for the Senate against Lloyd Bentsen in 1970 East Texas was solidly Democratic; by the time George W. Bush ran for reelection as governor in 1998, it was solidly Republican. Until 2004 East Texas was represented by Democrats in the House. The 2003 Republican redistricting changed that by reshaping the old 1st District, removing counties that had become used to voting for the Democratic incumbent and adding heavily Republican Smith and Gregg Counties. In 2004, George W. Bush carried 69% of the district vote.

The congressman from the 1st District is Louie Gohmert, a Republican elected in 2004 when he defeated four-term Democrat Max Sandlin. Gohmert grew up in Mount Pleasant, got an Army scholarship at Texas A&M, where he was class president, and then attended Baylor law school. After law school he served as a captain in the Army, then practiced law in Tyler and spent a decade as a district court judge before Governor Rick Perry in July 2002 named him chief justice of the local appeals court. While on the bench, he earned a reputation as a tough law-and-order judge with a knack for attracting attention. In 1996 he ordered an HIV-positive convicted car thief, as a condition of probation, to notify future sexual partners of his HIV status and to obtain written consent from each before engaging in sexual activity. After the 2003 redistricting, Gohmert was one of six Republicans who filed in the primary to challenge Sandlin, who had a moderate voting record and was politically close to Minority Leader Nancy Pelosi. Gohmert led in the primary with 42% of the vote to 30% for lawyer John Graves. In the month-long runoff campaign, few differences separated the two conservatives. Gohmert voiced reservations about the privacy threats posed by new law enforcement tools in the Patriot Act. Graves carried 9 of the 13 counties, but Gohmert prevailed by winning 77% in his Smith County, which cast 47% of the total vote; overall he won 57%-43%.

In the general, Gohmert linked Sandlin to the national Democratic party and presidential nominee John Kerry. In one debate, Gohmert repeatedly asked Sandlin about his choice for president; Sandlin sidestepped the question. Sandlin kept his distance from House Democrats, but he cited his work on the Ways and Means Committee to expand health care services in rural areas. Gohmert frequently mentioned his strong support for Bush and, unlike Sandlin, attended his party's national convention. He ran a TV spot that claimed that Sandlin's campaign ads "had more holes in them than a CBS story by Dan Rather"—a reference to the discredited CBS report about Bush's National Guard service. Sandlin criticized Gohmert for support from Tom DeLay. The result wasn't close: Gohmert won 61%-38%, with 79% in Smith County and 64% in Gregg County. Sandlin led in only two small rural counties plus the sliver of Cass in the new district.

In the House, Gohmert had a mostly conservative voting record. He was the only freshman Republican to get a seat on the Judiciary Committee. The House passed his bill to increase protection for judges, prosecutors and witnesses, and add penalties for carrying weapons in a courthouse; some Democrats objected to the mandatory minimum sentences in the measure. The Judiciary Committee rejected his amendments to authorize funding for faith-based organizations to programs aimed at reducing repeat criminal offenders. When the House voted to extend the Voting Rights Act, Gohmert unsuccessfully backed amendments to apply it nationwide and extend it for only 10 years; he voted for the final version. On Resources, his legislation to establish a memorial in the National Park System to the space shuttle *Columbia* passed the House in March 2007. To reduce federal spending after Hurricane Katrina, he called for stopping all other government building. Gohmert was reelected 68%-30% against a Democratic challenger who had served seven months in a Florida prison for a burglary conviction.

SECOND DISTRICT

Rep. Ted Poe (R)

Elected 2004, 2d term; b. Sept. 10, 1948, Temple; home, Humble; Abilene Christian U., B.A. 1970, U. of Houston, J.D. 1973; Church of Christ; married (Carol).

Military Career: Air Force Reserve, 1970-76.

Elected Office: Harris Cnty. Judge, 1981-2003.

Professional Career: Asst. dist. atty., 1973-81.

DC Office: 1605 LHOB, 20515, 202-225-6565; Fax: 202-225-5547; Web site: poe.house.gov.

District Offices: Beaumont, 409-212-1997; Humble, 281-446-0242.

Committees: *Foreign Affairs* (20th of 23 R): Terrorism, Nonproliferation & Trade; Europe. *Transportation & Infrastructure* (24th of 34 R): Coast Guard & Maritime Transportation; Aviation; Highways & Transit.

Group Ratings

	ADA	ACLU	AFS	LCV	ITIC	NTU	COC	ACU	CFG	FRC
2006	10	11	14	17	86	67	87	84	66	85
2005	0	—	0	6	—	65	89	92	79	100

National Journal Ratings

	2005 LIB	—	2005 CONS		2006 LIB	—	2006 CONS
Economic	26%	—	73%		39%	—	61%
Social	26%	—	73%		26%	—	74%
Foreign	0%	—	89%		33%	—	63%

Key Votes of the 109th Congress

1. Estate Tax Repeal	Y	5. Limit Interstate Abortion	Y	9. Build Border Fence	Y
2. Limit CAFE Standards	Y	6. Extend Patriot Act	Y	10. CAFTA	Y
3. FY06 Spending Curb	Y	7. Bar Same Sex Marriage	Y	11. Oppose Iraq Withdrawal	Y
4. Drilling in ANWR	Y	8. Stem Cell Research $	N	12. Detainee Tribunals	Y

Election Results

2006 general	Ted Poe (R)..	90,490	(66%)	($787,878)
	Gary Binderim (D)	45,080	(33%)	($14,945)
	Other...	2,295	(2%)	
2006 primary	Ted Poe (R)..................................... unopposed			
2004 general	Ted Poe (R)..	139,951	(56%)	($1,522,863)
	Nick Lampson (D)	108,156	(43%)	($2,405,430)
	Other...	3,931	(2%)	

The People		Race/Ethnic Origin	Ancestry	
Area size:	2,180 sq. mi.	64.2% White	German: 8.8%	Irish: 7.4%
Urban population:	89.5%	19.0% Black	USA: 6.8%	
Rural population:	10.5%	2.6% Asian	**2004 Presidential Vote**	
Pop. 2000:	651,620	0.3% Native Am.	Bush (R) 160,365	(63%)
Pop. 2005 (est):	709,126	0.0% Hawaiian	Kerry (D) 92,842	(37%)
Median income:	$47,029	1.1% Two+ races	**2000 Presidential Vote**	
Poverty status:	11.4%	0.1% Other	Bush (R) 140,442	(63%)
Military veterans:	12.9%	12.6% Hispanic Origin	Gore (D) 83,347	(37%)
			Cook Partisan Voting Index: R +12	
Occupation	Blue collar: 23.4%	White collar: 62.9%	Gray collar: 13.7%	

The spongy land of the Texas Gulf Coast, where the French explorer LaSalle and the Spanish colonizer Galvez dreamed of thriving settlements, remained mostly unsettled until well into the 19th century. When oil was found at the Spindletop field near Beaumont in 1901, the area all around boomed. First oil exploration, then petroleum refining, then petrochemicals: The straight-edged metal of oil rigs and the intricate curving metalwork of refineries shine through the swampy landscape of southeast Texas. The rig workers and mechanical engineers they brought here have given a kind of permanent roughneck air to the region. In the early days of Spindletop, the town was so overrun by boomers who drained the local water supply that some doctors advised people to drink whiskey instead of water. The Woman's Christian Temperance Union jumped in to create a counterforce. But oil drilling has declined in this area. From 1994 to 2004, annual production in East Texas from the Red River to the Gulf of Mexico dropped from 90.5 million barrels to 43.5 million barrels. Production was limited further by the damage inflicted in 2005 by Hurricanes Katrina and Rita.

The 2d Congressional District of Texas occupies much of this territory. Nearly 40% of its people live in and around Beaumont, Port Arthur and Orange, still very much oil country, the "Golden Triangle" industrial area with some of the country's largest oil refineries and chemical plants and dense pollution. It is among the few places in Texas where labor unions have had any strength. Beaumont is the home of several trial lawyers who have become billionaires through asbestos and tobacco cases; local juries are known for their willingness to bring in large verdicts against big corporations. The American Tort Reform Association calls the area a "judicial hellhole." Port Arthur was the home of 1960s blues and rock singer Janis Joplin, who is memorialized with a bust in the city library. These cities increasingly are in the shadow of Houston, and the majority of the people in the district live in Harris County, in suburbs north and east of Houston, where oil is an important part of the economy but hardly all of it. The Humble oil field was once the largest in Texas and the local Humble Oil and Refining Company is now known as Exxon; the community of Humble now serves as a retail and shipping center for the nearby George Bush Intercontinental Airport. In the 2003 redistricting, this district was created by adding parts of the old 8th District in Harris County and the old 9th District in Jefferson County. Only a sliver was taken from the old 2d District, which was carved into six separate pieces; 2d District Democrat Jim Turner announced his retirement the day the redistricting plan was upheld by a federal court. In 2004, George W. Bush got 63% of the vote here, relatively low for a Republican-held seat in Texas.

The congressman from the 2d District is Ted Poe, a Republican elected in 2004. A former prosecutor who served 22 years as a Houston-area district court judge, Poe became a publicity magnet and a judicial celebrity for meting out humiliating "Poe-tic justice" punishments to criminals: he required murderers to hang pictures of their victims in their prison cells and car thieves to give their vehicles to victims. He ordered drunken drivers and shoplifters to stand at the entrances to stores and taverns carrying signs publicizing their offenses; this became known as "shame sentencing." He also gained national recognition as a legal commentator on cable television channels such as Fox, MSNBC and CNN. He appeared on *Dateline NBC* and *60 Minutes*. In 2003, Poe stepped down as judge to run for Congress. In the six-way Republican primary, Poe's opponents couldn't buy that kind of attention, although some tried. Poe didn't put up a penny of his own in the primary. Thanks to name recognition and bench experience, he won 61% of the vote.

In the general, Poe faced incumbent Democrat Nick Lampson, first elected in 1996 in the old 9th District (in 2006, Lampson was returned to the House in the 22d District). Lampson had a moderate voting record, a low-key style and was a big booster of NASA. At first it was not clear whether Poe would be able to capitalize on the favorable redistricting. National Republicans fretted about his fundraising and his seemingly complacent campaign. Some of his positions were in tension with those of George W. Bush: he was skeptical about the federal role in education, he opposed Bush's proposal to grant temporary work permits to immigrants and he supported a national sales tax to replace the income tax. Lampson outspent Poe nearly 2-to-1 and worked feverishly to make inroads in the Republican Harris County suburbs. But on Election Day, the district's solid Republican bent and its geography were too much to overcome. Lampson led 68%-31% in Jefferson County, where 36% of votes were cast. But Poe won 70%-28% in Harris County, where 58% of the votes were cast. Overall Poe won 56%-43%.

In the House, Poe had a relatively moderate voting record for a Republican from Texas. He became the Houston-area Republican on the Transportation and Infrastructure Committee, where he sought to reduce local noise from Houston's international airport, and worked to restore funding to maintain and dredge the Sabine-Neches Waterway. He joined a bipartisan group that passed a House amendment to block the Bush administration from easing requirements for foreign ownership of U.S. airlines. He founded the Congressional Victims' Rights Caucus and became a leader of the Immigration Reform Caucus. After Hurricanes Katrina and Rita led to a large migration to Texas, he filed legislation to create a national registry of convicted child molesters who have been released from prison; the idea was to make it easier to identify newcomers who were criminals. He joined Democrats and libertarian Republicans to restrict access to library records under the Patriot Act. Seeking a market for local rice farmers, he sought to expand trade with Cuba. He often ends speeches on the House floor with his trademark, "And that's just the way it is." Poe had an easy reelection in 2006.

THIRD DISTRICT

Rep. Sam Johnson (R)

Elected May 1991, 8th full term; b. Oct. 11, 1930, San Antonio; home, Dallas; S. Methodist U., B.B.A. 1951, George Washington U., M.S. 1974; Methodist; married (Shirley).

Military Career: Air Force, 1950-79 (Korea & Vietnam).

Elected Office: TX House of Reps., 1984-91.

Professional Career: Home builder.

DC Office: 1211 LHOB, 20515, 202-225-4201; Fax: 202-225-1485; Web site: www.samjohnson.house.gov.

District Offices: Richardson, 972-470-0892.

Committees: *Ways & Means* (5th of 17 R): Social Security (RMM); Health.

Group Ratings

	ADA	ACLU	AFS	LCV	ITIC	NTU	COC	ACU	CFG	FRC
2006	5	0	0	0	86	73	91	90	78	85
2005	0	—	0	0	—	69	88	96	94	100

National Journal Ratings

	2005 LIB	—	2005 CONS		2006 LIB	—	2006 CONS
Economic	8%	—	92%		20%	—	80%
Social	0%	—	89%		0%	—	94%
Foreign	0%	—	89%		0%	—	94%

Key Votes of the 109th Congress

1. Estate Tax Repeal	Y	5. Limit Interstate Abortion	Y	9. Build Border Fence	*
2. Limit CAFE Standards	Y	6. Extend Patriot Act	Y	10. CAFTA	Y
3. FY06 Spending Curb	*	7. Bar Same Sex Marriage	*	11. Oppose Iraq Withdrawal	*
4. Drilling in ANWR	Y	8. Stem Cell Research $	N	12. Detainee Tribunals	Y

Election Results

2006 general	Sam Johnson (R)	88,690	(63%)	($974,859)
	Dan Dodd (D)	49,529	(35%)	($40,491)
	Other	3,662	(3%)	
2006 primary	Sam Johnson (R)	13,348	(85%)	
	Bob Johnson (R)	2,292	(15%)	
2004 general	Sam Johnson (R)	180,099	(86%)	($771,636)
	Paul Jenkins (I)	16,966	(8%)	($9,017)
	James Vessels (Lib)	13,287	(6%)	

Prior Winning Percentages: 2002 (74%); 2000 (72%); 1998 (91%); 1996 (73%); 1994 (91%); 1992 (86%); 1991 (53%)

The People		Race/Ethnic Origin	Ancestry	
Area size:	266 sq. mi.	63.3% White	German: 10.7%	English: 7.9%
Urban population:	99.0%	9.2% Black	Irish: 7.6%	
Rural population:	1.0%	8.3% Asian	**2004 Presidential Vote**	
Pop. 2000:	651,619	0.4% Native Am.	Bush (R) 174,711	(67%)
Pop. 2005 (est):	797,302	0.0% Hawaiian	Kerry (D) 86,718	(33%)
Median income:	$60,878	1.6% Two+ races	**2000 Presidential Vote**	
Poverty status:	7.0%	0.1% Other	Bush (R) 139,717	(70%)
Military veterans:	9.5%	16.9% Hispanic Origin	Gore (D) 60,386	(30%)
			Cook Partisan Voting Index: R +17	

Occupation	Blue collar: 15.2%	White collar: 74.7%	Gray collar: 10.1%

North Dallas, the subject of a trashy novel in the 1970s, the putative location of the 1980s TV program "Dallas," conjures up a certain image: of sudden affluence and insolent disdain for those who do not partake in it, of shady dealings and immoral trysts in an environment in which all visible expressions endorse traditional values, of a ruthless drive for money and power overriding all human sympathy. But all this is caricature. Dallas was named, improbably, for the stuffy and otherwise forgotten Philadelphia lawyer who was James K. Polk's vice president. It got its start as a railroad junction and cotton-shipping center. Dallas was at the cutting edge of high-tech, the home of Texas Instruments—where an integrated circuit on a silicon chip was invented in 1958—and of Ross Perot's EDS and many defense contractors. The high-tech, telecom, and defense businesses are less robust than in the 1980s, but the Dallas-Fort Worth Metroplex has thrived. Growth has come from corporate headquarters relocated from less business-friendly precincts, from small businesses growing quickly in an entrepreneur-friendly climate with no state income tax, and from companies making money trading with Mexico; Dallas is the nation's chief beneficiary of NAFTA. Health care and universities have become large job creators. The Metroplex, one way or the other, continues to thrive.

Dallas's growth has extended far into the countryside. The home of the city's elite may still be in the mansion-lined streets of Highland Park, only a few miles north of downtown, though they have lost municipal influence to south Dallas communities. But the center of Dallas's entrepreneurial economy has moved north to the LBJ Freeway and edge cities beyond, and the residential center of Dallas's business and professional classes has moved ever farther north in Dallas County, and to the rolling, scrub-covered hills, as they recently were, of Collin County to the north. Back in 1960 it was mostly rural, still part of the district that sent Speaker Sam Rayburn to the House. It had 41,000 people then and actually lost population in the 1950s. Then the Dallas-Fort Worth Metroplex moved in, with a force that can be discerned in the numbers: 66,000 in 1970, 144,000 in 1980, 264,000 in 1990, 491,000 in 2000, 699,000 in 2006. Collin County is the wealthiest county in Texas; its 42% increase since 2000 is the largest for a county of its size in the nation. The biggest city here is Plano, with 252,000 people, a former farming community that became a corporate headquarters and edge city with DART light-rail service, site of mega-mansion subdivisions, the state's ninth-largest city and the new face of successful Texas. Plano is 16% Asian, many of Chinese ancestry, and they outnumber Latinos. Today Plano is mostly built up, and the fastest growth is in the old county seat of McKinney. Politically, Collin County is very Republican, indeed more Republican than Dallas County ever was: it cast more votes in 2004 than all but five other Texas counties, and gave 71% of them to George W. Bush.

The 3d Congressional District of Texas includes most of Collin County and centers on Plano. It also covers the northeastern corner of Dallas County, beyond the LBJ Freeway, including much of Garland and Rowlett. This was the fastest-growing district in Texas in the 1990s, and one of the state's fastest-growing between 2000-05, and is solidly Republican, casting 67% for George W. Bush in 2004.

The congressman from the 3d District is Sam Johnson, a Republican first elected in 1991. Johnson grew up in Dallas, graduated from SMU and George Washington University. He was a director of the Air Force (Top Gun) Fighter Weapons School, and a fighter pilot who flew 87 combat missions in the Korean and Vietnamese wars. After his F-4 was shot down over North Vietnam during his 25th mission there, he was imprisoned from 1966 to 1973 in the "Hanoi Hilton", where he spent 42 months in solitary confinement; he weighed 120 pounds on his release, and was left with a slight stoop in his walk and a disfigured hand. On his return, Johnson started a homebuilding company and was elected to the state House in 1984. He was elected to Congress in a special election after Steve Bartlett was elected mayor of Dallas. Johnson ran second in the primary, behind former Peace Corps director Tom Pauken. In the runoff he emphasized his war record and, although he was less familiar with legislative issues, won 53%-47% over Pauken, who as Texas Republican chairman later was a sharp critic of Governor George W. Bush.

In the House, Johnson typically has been among members with the most conservative voting record. He was a founder and chair of the Conservative Action Team, which pressed Republican leaders to stick with goals ranging from budget targets to shutting down the National Endowment for the Arts; now known as the Republican Study Committee, the group suffered internal divisions after the 2006 election. Every Congress he offers a constitutional amendment to repeal the 16th Amendment, which authorized the federal income tax. On the Ways and Means Committee, he sponsored the successful repeal in 2000 of the earnings limit for Social Security recipients. He was a leading advocate of expanding tax-free savings accounts, and of personal retirement accounts for Social Security. He helped to enact the Military Family Tax Relief Act, which doubled the death benefit and reduced taxes on families that suffer death by an active member of the military. On the now-renamed Education and Labor Committee, the House passed his bill to encourage small businesses to join forces to purchase health insurance at lower costs and he was a leading proponent of pension reform that was enacted in 2006. With Mac Thornberry, he filed a bill to ease the voting process for military personnel. Johnson has been a defender of the F-22 fighter jet, partly produced at the Lockheed Martin plant in Fort Worth.

Even though he was a POW with John McCain for a year and a half, Johnson strongly backed George W. Bush in the 2000 primaries; McCain "cannot hold a candle to George Bush," he said. He was an outspoken critic in the 2004 campaign of John Kerry and his military record in Vietnam, which Johnson said was "nothing short of aiding and abetting the enemy." On the House floor he called Kerry "Hanoi John." After revisiting Vietnam for the first time in January 2006, he said, "I'm glad to leave and come back to the United States." In February 2007, when Democrats barred his amendment to guarantee military funds, he gained national attention when he spoke emotionally on the House floor against the plan of Speaker Nancy Pelosi to set a timetable to withdraw from Iraq. He invoked memories of Vietnam: "I know what it's like to be far from home and hear that your country and your Congress don't care about you. Our troops stand up for us every minute of every day. We must stand up for them in Congress." Republicans welcomed his depiction as the alternative to the Democrats' Vietnam vet John Murtha.

Johnson originally pledged to serve only 12 years, but changed his mind. This is one of the safest Republican seats in the country and it didn't seem to bother his constituents. In October 2006, beleaguered Speaker Dennis Hastert made one of his few campaign appearances that month at a fundraiser for Johnson.

FOURTH DISTRICT

Rep. Ralph Hall (R)

Elected 1980, 14th term; b. May 3, 1923, Fate; home, Rockwall; U. of TX, TX Christian U., S. Methodist U., LL.B. 1951; United Methodist; married (Mary Ellen).

Military Career: Navy, 1942-45 (WWII).

Elected Office: Rockwall Cnty. Judge, 1950-62; TX Senate, 1962-72.

Professional Career: Practicing atty., 1951-80; Pres. & CEO, TX Aluminum Corp., 1967-68; Spec. Cnsl., Howmet Corp., 1970-74.

DC Office: 2405 RHOB, 20515, 202-225-6673; Fax: 202-225-3332; Web site: www.house.gov/ralphhall.

District Offices: McKinney, 214-726-9949; New Boston, 903-628-8309; Rockwall, 972-771-9118; Sherman, 903-892-1112; Sulphur Springs, 903-885-8138; Texarkana, 903-794-4445.

Committees: *Energy & Commerce* (2d of 26 R): Energy & Air Quality; Health. *Science & Technology* (RMM of 20 R).

Group Ratings

	ADA	ACLU	AFS	LCV	ITIC	NTU	COC	ACU	CFG	FRC
2006	5	5	0	0	86	52	93	84	49	100
2005	5	—	0	0	—	56	92	92	55	100

National Journal Ratings

	2005 LIB	—	2005 CONS	2006 LIB	—	2006 CONS
Economic	17%	—	82%	30%	—	68%
Social	11%	—	88%	0%	—	94%
Foreign	27%	—	73%	47%	—	51%

Key Votes of the 109th Congress

1. Estate Tax Repeal	Y	5. Limit Interstate Abortion	Y	9. Build Border Fence	Y
2. Limit CAFE Standards	Y	6. Extend Patriot Act	Y	10. CAFTA	Y
3. FY06 Spending Curb	Y	7. Bar Same Sex Marriage	Y	11. Oppose Iraq Withdrawal	Y
4. Drilling in ANWR	Y	8. Stem Cell Research $	N	12. Detainee Tribunals	Y

Election Results

2006 general	Ralph Hall (R)	106,495	(64%)	($942,635)
	Glenn Melancon (D)	55,278	(33%)	($63,897)
	Other	3,496	(2%)	
2006 primary	Ralph Hall (R)	unopposed		
2004 general	Ralph Hall (R)	182,866	(68%)	($1,152,827)
	Jim Nickerson (D)	81,585	(30%)	($199,803)
	Other	3,491	(1%)	

Prior Winning Percentages: 2002 (58%); 2000 (60%); 1998 (58%); 1996 (64%); 1994 (59%); 1992 (58%); 1990 (100%); 1988 (66%); 1986 (72%); 1984 (58%); 1982 (74%); 1980 (52%)

The People		Race/Ethnic Origin	Ancestry	
Area size:	9,839 sq. mi.	79.2% White	USA: 12.7% Irish: 8.3%	
Urban population:	49.6%	10.4% Black	German: 7.5%	
Rural population:	50.4%	0.6% Asian	**2004 Presidential Vote**	
Pop. 2000:	651,619	0.7% Native Am.	Bush (R) 192,926	(70%)
Pop. 2005 (est):	730,027	0.0% Hawaiian	Kerry (D) 81,269	(30%)
Median income:	$38,276	1.1% Two+ races	**2000 Presidential Vote**	
Poverty status:	12.8%	0.0% Other	Bush (R) 146,416	(66%)
Military veterans:	14.4%	7.9% Hispanic Origin	Gore (D) 74,476	(34%)
			Cook Partisan Voting Index: R +17	

Occupation	Blue collar: 28.3%	White collar: 56.4%	Gray collar: 15.3%

The Red River Valley is just one of the hearts of Texas. This is hardscrabble farm country along an unnavigable river. First settled in the 1830s, in the days of the Texas Republic, many counties here reached their population peak around 1900, when a large extended farm family worked every 160 acres. It included towns like Denison, which was the birthplace of Dwight Eisenhower and has become a manufacturing center, plus Sherman, which was the site of a major race riot in 1930 when a black farm worker accused of rape was trapped in the courthouse after an angry white mob set it on fire. To the east is Texarkana, noteworthy because its neat grid streets cross the Texas-Arkansas state line, which is straddled by the downtown post office. This small city and its hinterland produced two presidential candidates in the 1990s: Ross Perot grew up in Texarkana, Texas, while Bill Clinton's boyhood home of Hope, Arkansas, is 30 miles east. This was the part of Texas that sent Sam Rayburn to Congress in 1912; he served as speaker from 1940 until his death in 1961, except for two terms when Republicans had the majority. The Red River Valley was one of the strongest Democratic parts of the country, with a sentimental regard for Confederate veterans and a seething hatred of Wall Street bankers. This was Rayburn's politics, and he arguably was the most skillful lawmaker of the 20th century: He helped write the securities laws that for 70 years have provided the basis for confidence in American securities markets, and other regulatory measures that have fared less well. Today Rayburn's politics has almost completely vanished from the area. The cause of the Confederacy has been left behind, populist suspicion of Wall Street has been replaced by active brokerage accounts and allegiance to the Democratic Party is a thing of the distant past.

The 4th Congressional District of Texas is the lineal descendant of the seat that Rayburn held, and still includes his hometown of Bonham in Fannin County, which houses a Rayburn museum. But it is quite a different district. In Rayburn's time it was a farm district, separate and distinct from citified Dallas. Today it still has its farm counties, but they are only a short Interstate ride away from the Dallas-Fort Worth Metroplex, and nearly half the district's people live in the Metroplex itself. The counties at the edge of the Metroplex, Collin (only part of which is in the district) and Rockwall, are among the fastest-growing in the country; with 61% growth from 2000 to 2006, Rockwall ranked third among the fastest-growing counties in the nation. The two counties are home now to upwardly-mobile families, far more trusting of free markets than of government regulation, and more than 2–1 Republican. In 1940, when Rayburn became Speaker, his district voted 90% for Franklin D. Roosevelt. In 2004, the 4th District voted 70% for George W. Bush.

The congressman from the 4th District is Ralph Hall, who was born in 1923 and first elected in 1980. He is currently the oldest member of the House. Hall grew up in Rockwall County, served in the Navy during World War II as a lieutenant and aircraft carrier pilot, and had a 30-year career in local politics and business; he got his law degree from Southern Methodist, was a county judge as long ago as 1950, and from 1962 to 1972 served in the Texas Senate. In 1980 he was elected to the House as a Democrat. His evolution to the Republican Party was a long time in gestation. He supported just about everything in the Contract with America and was one of five House Democrats who voted to impeach Bill Clinton. He voted with Bush on key tax, trade and foreign policy votes. During the 2002 campaign he promised to vote for Republican Speaker Dennis Hastert if his vote decided which party would control the House. In January 2003 he voted "present" rather than for Nancy Pelosi, because "she just don't think like we do." But Hall is not a pure free marketeer: He voted against NAFTA. In 2005, he successfully urged the base closing commission to reverse the Pentagon's recommendation to close the Red River Army Depot, with 5,000 jobs in Texarkana.

Republicans restlessly waited for years for Hall to join them. When he failed to switch after the 2001 redistricting, local and national Republicans expressed interest in a serious challenge to Hall. But they backed off after Hall met with Bush at the White House and said that the president strongly opposed a challenge. In March 2003, Hall was the only Democrat to vote for the Republican budget, which barely passed. Bush called to thank him. "I didn't want him to have a setback in Washington, D.C., when he's working his heart out two oceans away to win a war," Hall said. The 2003 redistricting finally convinced Hall to change. With Republican candidates lined up to run against him, he switched parties on January 2, 2004, the final day for filing because, he said, his Democratic affiliation was limiting his ability to get appropriations for his district. And so he moved from being the most conservative Democrat in the House to a relatively centrist Republican who seemed more comfortable with his new team and being part of the majority. When he joined their side, Republicans rewarded him with the chairmanship of the Energy and Air Quality Subcommittee, an attractive perk for a Texan, where he helped to enact the energy bill in 2005. In January 2007, when Democrats raised taxes on oil companies, he voiced fear "it's just the initial attack on an industry that's going to have other attacks this year." In the minority, he became ranking Republican on the Science and Technology Committee.

Party-switching has played well at home. With support from Bush and Speaker Dennis Hastert, he won 77% against two opponents in the Republican primary in 2004; in the general, he won 68%-30%, his largest margin in more than a decade. The *Dallas Morning News* was less impressed, urging Hall to retire. He didn't take the hint in 2006, and was easily reelected. Hall announced in April 2007 that he would run for reelection in 2008; former Frisco Mayor Kathy Seei, racing team owner Gene Christensen and businessman Kevin George all said they would challenge him in the primary. If Hall does retire, it would be no surprise if his son, Rockwall County District Judge Brett Hall, a Republican, runs for this seat.

FIFTH DISTRICT

Rep. Jeb Hensarling (R)

Elected 2002, 3d term; b. May 29, 1957, Stephenville; home, Dallas; TX A&M U., B.A. 1979, U. of TX, J.D. 1982; Christian; married (Melissa).

Professional Career: Practicing atty., 1982-84; TX Dir., U.S. Sen. Phil Gramm, 1985-89; Exec. Dir., NRSC, 1991-93; Communications Exec., 1993-02.

DC Office: 132 CHOB, 20515, 202-225-3484; Fax: 202-226-4888; Web site: www.house.gov/hensarling/.

District Offices: Athens, 903-675-8288; Dallas, 214-349-9996.

Committees: *Budget* (6th of 17 R). *Financial Services* (17th of 33 R): Domestic and International Monetary Policy, Trade & Technology; Financial Institutions & Consumer Credit; Capital Markets, Insurance & Government Sponsored Enterprises.

Group Ratings

	ADA	ACLU	AFS	LCV	ITIC	NTU	COC	ACU	CFG	FRC
2006	10	9	0	8	100	86	93	100	100	100
2005	0	—	13	6	—	79	81	100	100	100

National Journal Ratings

	2005 LIB	—	2005 CONS	2006 LIB	—	2006 CONS
Economic	14%	—	83%	37%	—	62%
Social	31%	—	69%	0%	—	94%
Foreign	0%	—	89%	6%	—	86%

Key Votes of the 109th Congress

1. Estate Tax Repeal	Y	5. Limit Interstate Abortion	Y	9. Build Border Fence	Y
2. Limit CAFE Standards	Y	6. Extend Patriot Act	Y	10. CAFTA	Y
3. FY06 Spending Curb	Y	7. Bar Same Sex Marriage	Y	11. Oppose Iraq Withdrawal	Y
4. Drilling in ANWR	Y	8. Stem Cell Research $	N	12. Detainee Tribunals	Y

Election Results

2006 general	Jeb Hensarling (R)	88,478	(62%)	($1,129,059)
	Charlie Thompson (D)	50,983	(36%)	($19,753)
	Other	3,791	(3%)	
2006 primary	Jeb Hensarling (R)	unopposed		
2004 general	Jeb Hensarling (R)	148,816	(64%)	($1,043,478)
	Bill Bernstein (D)	75,911	(33%)	($18,538)
	Other	6,118	(3%)	

Prior Winning Percentages: 2002 (58%)

The People		Race/Ethnic Origin	Ancestry	
Area size:	5,609 sq. mi.	71.5% White	USA: 11.3%	Irish: 7.7%
Urban population:	67.7%	12.4% Black	German: 7.6%	
Rural population:	32.3%	1.5% Asian	**2004 Presidential Vote**	
Pop. 2000:	651,619	0.4% Native Am.	Bush (R) 160,240	(67%)
Pop. 2005 (est):	694,989	0.0% Hawaiian	Kerry (D) 77,952	(33%)
Median income:	$41,007	1.2% Two+ races	**2000 Presidential Vote**	
Poverty status:	11.0%	0.1% Other	Bush (R) 137,553	(66%)
Military veterans:	13.2%	12.9% Hispanic Origin	Gore (D) 69,894	(34%)
			Cook Partisan Voting Index: R +16	

Occupation   Blue collar: 26.0%   White collar: 59.6%   Gray collar: 14.4%

Not all of Dallas is glitz and postmodern marble. East of downtown on one of the three street grids that skew to each other is an older Dallas, with neighborhoods of high-ceilinged old mansions, modest bungalows and shotgun houses running out past the old airport at Love Field or the State Fair Grounds and the Cotton Bowl in east Dallas. Some of this older Dallas is being renovated and rebuilt, with chic cafes and trendy stores serving those who make their livings catering to the rich farther north. Other once middle-class neighborhoods are filling up with immigrants from Mexico and other parts of Latin America, once again noisy with children as they were in the 1950s when people moved here not from Mexico or Central America but from the almost all-Anglo counties of north and central Texas.

The 5th Congressional District includes much of east and southeast Dallas County, including many such neighborhoods in Dallas and suburban Mesquite, which has become a destination for Asians moving up the economic ladder. It also covers a more upscale slice of Dallas inside the Freeway, including parts of Lakewood and White Rock Lake, which was rescued by FDR's Civilian Conservation Corps during the New Deal. Nearly half of the population is in Dallas County. The 5th District also contains six counties in East Texas, the largest of which are Henderson and Kaufman, which looms as one of the next high-growth areas in the Metroplex. As rural areas have swung away from the Democrats, the district switched from being a battleground in the early 1990s to safely Republican. In 2004, George W. Bush won 67% of the vote here.

The congressman from the 5th District is Jeb Hensarling, a Republican first elected in 2002. Hensarling grew up in Morris County in East Texas and Lubbock County in West Texas. He worked on his father's poultry farm near College Station as a teenager and decided that he did not want to be a farmer. In high school, he started a Republican club and began organizing political events. He graduated from Texas A&M and the University of Texas law school and practiced law for two years in San Antonio. Then he got a job on the staff of Senator Phil Gramm. He managed Gramm's 1990 campaign and was executive director of the National Republican Senatorial Committee when Gramm was chairman. He returned to Texas to become vice president of communications for Green Mountain Energy, a local utility, and he was co-founder of Family Support Assurance, a firm that sought to modernize child support collections.

After the 2001 redistricting, Pete Sessions, who had represented the 5th District for the previous six years, decided to run in the new and more compact 32d District on the north side of Dallas, even though the new 5th included 74% of his old district while the 32d included only 16%. Hensarling became the frontrunner for the Republican nomination. Like his mentor, he listed cutting taxes as his top priority. Against four opponents, he won the nomination with 54% of the vote. Democrats nominated Ron Chapman, a former Dallas County appellate judge who had been on the Dallas County ballot since 1978 and shared the name of a popular Dallas radio disc jockey. Chapman described himself as a loyal Democrat who could work with Republicans. By fall, Hensarling referred to his opponent as "Judge Softie" for twice allowing a man charged with attempted murder to go free from his courtroom. The folksy Chapman emphasized his public service, fiscal conservatism and deep local roots. He tried to paint Hensarling as too extreme for the district, but his message failed to take hold as Republican luminaries paraded into the district on his behalf, including George W. Bush, Dick Cheney, Bush adviser Karen Hughes and, of course, Phil Gramm. Perhaps the most significant endorsement came when Ron Chapman the disc jockey backed Hensarling at a press conference and emphasized that he was not the Democrat running for Congress. Hensarling won 58%-40%. He has been reelected easily.

In the House, Hensarling has a solidly conservative voting record. He styled himself as a fiscal conservative in the mold of Gramm and was not afraid to push Republican leaders to take more conservative positions, though he usually voted with them in the end when they didn't. With fellow freshmen Republicans Mario Diaz-Balart and Tom Feeney of Florida, he created "Washington Waste Watchers" to root out waste, fraud and abuse in the federal bureaucracy. On the Republican Study Committee, he took the lead in working with other conservatives on budget legislation designed to promote spending discipline; his efforts did not endear him to Republican appropriators and others in the party establishment. In the majority, his challenge was to influence Republican strategy without abandoning his own beliefs or stirring the pot too much. That dilemma was apparent when he struggled over the Medicare/prescription drug bill, which many conservatives criticized for creating a costly new government entitlement but which was strongly supported by Bush and Tom DeLay. Even though he claimed credit for a cost-containment provision of limited impact, Hensarling waited until the final hours before deciding to vote for the bill. With the huge costs resulting from Hurricane Katrina, he led an effort to find spending offsets, which was well-publicized but had little impact, especially after DeLay said that he was open to such cuts, but, "No one's been able to come up with any yet." On the Financial Services Committee, Hensarling warned against undue subsidies for insurance policyholders during Katrina relief. An avid foe of campaign regulations, he sought unsuccessfully to exempt bloggers from campaign finance rules, in response to a court ruling that said they were subject to them. In 2006, he spearheaded an effort of Texas-based members that repealed the Wright Amendment that limited long-distance flights from Love Field in Dallas, and had been designed to promote the expanded DFW Airport; the action was a major boost for Southwest Airlines.

In December 2006, he defeated Todd Tiahrt, an appropriator, in the contest for RSC chairman, a post that Hensarling called "keeper of the conservative flame." He managed the losing campaign of Mike Pence against John Boehner for Republican Leader. In the minority, he faced fewer constraints in spotlighting earmarks and big budget deficits, and said that Republicans needed to regain their commitment to limited government. "There is nothing quite like a two-by-four smacked across your head to get your attention," he told *Congress Daily* in January 2007.

SIXTH DISTRICT

Rep. Joe Barton (R)

Elected 1984, 12th term; b. Sept. 15, 1949, Waco; home, Ennis; Texas A&M U., B.S. 1972, Purdue U., M.S. 1973; United Methodist; married (Terri).

Professional Career: Asst. to V.P., Ennis Business Forms, 1973-81; White House Fellow, U.S. Dept. of Energy, 1981-82; Consultant, Atlantic Richfield Co., 1982-84.

DC Office: 2109 RHOB, 20515, 202-225-2002; Fax: 202-225-3052; Web site: joebarton.house.gov.

District Offices: Arlington, 817-543-1000; Crockett, 936-544-8488; Ennis, 817-543-1000.

Committees: *Energy & Commerce* (RMM of 26 R).

Group Ratings

	ADA	ACLU	AFS	LCV	ITIC	NTU	COC	ACU	CFG	FRC
2006	15	0	0	8	86	63	93	88	71	85
2005	0	—	0	0	—	69	92	92	83	75

National Journal Ratings

	2005 LIB	—	2005 CONS	2006 LIB	—	2006 CONS
Economic	3%	—	94%	26%	—	74%
Social	31%	—	68%	28%	—	70%
Foreign	0%	—	89%	6%	—	86%

Key Votes of the 109th Congress

1. Estate Tax Repeal	Y	5. Limit Interstate Abortion	Y	9. Build Border Fence	Y
2. Limit CAFE Standards	Y	6. Extend Patriot Act	Y	10. CAFTA	Y
3. FY06 Spending Curb	Y	7. Bar Same Sex Marriage	Y	11. Oppose Iraq Withdrawal	Y
4. Drilling in ANWR	Y	8. Stem Cell Research $	Y	12. Detainee Tribunals	Y

Election Results

2006 general	Joe Barton (R)	91,927	(60%)	($2,351,932)
	David Harris (D)	56,369	(37%)	($26,993)
	Other	3,740	(2%)	
2006 primary	Joe Barton (R)	unopposed		
2004 general	Joe Barton (R)	168,767	(66%)	($1,883,891)
	Morris Meyer (D)	83,609	(33%)	($101,080)
	Other	3,251	(1%)	

Prior Winning Percentages: 2002 (70%); 2000 (88%); 1998 (73%); 1996 (77%); 1994 (76%); 1992 (72%); 1990 (66%); 1988 (68%); 1986 (56%); 1984 (57%)

The People		Race/Ethnic Origin	Ancestry	
Area size:	6,336 sq. mi.	65.8% White	German: 8.7%	USA: 8.6%
Urban population:	80.0%	12.8% Black	Irish: 7.3%	
Rural population:	20.0%	3.4% Asian	**2004 Presidential Vote**	
Pop. 2000:	651,619	0.4% Native Am.	Bush (R) 173,476	(66%)
Pop. 2005 (est):	738,288	0.1% Hawaiian	Kerry (D) 87,454	(34%)
Median income:	$45,857	1.5% Two+ races	**2000 Presidential Vote**	
Poverty status:	10.4%	0.1% Other	Bush (R) 140,140	(66%)
Military veterans:	12.4%	15.9% Hispanic Origin	Gore (D) 71,283	(34%)
			Cook Partisan Voting Index: R +15	

Occupation   Blue collar: 24.1%   White collar: 62.4%   Gray collar: 13.5%

The Dallas-Fort Worth Metroplex—yes, the name is part of everyday speech there—has spread outward from its historic nodes in downtown Dallas and Fort Worth. Although Dallas is the larger population center, much of the development has moved west, across the dusty plains where one crosses the barely perceptible Balcones Escarpment, the geologist's boundary between green and grassy East Texas and the brown, barren and hilly West. This was empty territory a few decades ago; now it has mostly been filled in, with subdivisions and shopping centers that leave some feeling of the shape of this land under the enormous Texas sky. The biggest city here is Arlington, once seemingly all suburban, home to a General Motors assembly plant since 1954 and newer all-American attractions like Six Flags over Texas, Hurricane Harbor, and the Ballpark in Arlington, commissioned by the former part-owner of the Texas Rangers, George W. Bush. But this is not just white bread suburbia anymore. Arlington's population of 360,000 in 2005 was 24% Hispanic, 17% black and 5% Asian; just a couple miles south of Six Flags is a mixed Latino-Vietnamese area with Mexican restaurants and Asian delis. Arlington provides extra pay to police officers who can speak Spanish or Vietnamese. Arlington today is mostly developed; the big growth now comes to the south in Crowley and Mansfield, where the population has increased dramatically since 2000. Growth in the area has been so robust that Tarrant County, the third-largest county in Texas, was in 2004 the 18th largest in the country, just ahead of New York County (Manhattan), and just behind Clark County (Las Vegas).

The 6th Congressional District of Texas includes all of Arlington and the southern fringe of Fort Worth to the west. Two-thirds of its people live in Arlington and Tarrant County. Much of the rest are in Ellis County, directly south of Dallas County, which also has been growing rapidly. The district includes all or part of six counties running to the southeast, most of the way to Houston. Politically, this territory was ancestrally Democratic for many years; all of it voted for John F. Kennedy over Richard Nixon in 1960. But those days are gone. In 2004, the 6th District voted 66% for George W. Bush.

The congressman from the 6th District is Joe Barton, a Republican first elected in 1984. Barton grew up in Ennis, in then rural Ellis County just south of Dallas. He graduated from Texas A&M and Purdue, worked as an oil company engineer and was a White House Fellow. When Phil Gramm ran for the Senate in 1984, Barton ran for his 6th District House seat, and won the Republican runoff by only 10 votes and the general with 57% of the vote. At first, Barton had two great causes, one defunct, the other successful—in a way. The first was the superconductor Supercollider, an enormous scientific laboratory that was to have been built in Waxahachie, in Ellis County. In retrospect this was a purely Texas project, alive only so long as George H.W. Bush was president; despite Barton's efforts, the House voted 282-143 to zero it out in 1993. His other cause has been sponsorship of a constitutional amendment requiring a two-thirds vote to raise taxes. When the House took up the issue in early 1995, leadership whispered there was no way the tax limitation measure could win the needed 290 votes. In fact it got 253. Barton claimed progress across the country, where many states approved tax-limitation plans. But the budget surpluses starting in 1998 followed by Republican governance changed the conversation, and the amendment has been mostly forgotten. Although he remains a solid conservative, he sometimes strays toward the center on cultural issues.

In 1995 Barton became chairman of the Energy and Commerce Oversight and Investigation Subcommittee and conducted extensive hearings on food and drug laws. These resulted in enactment, with bipartisan support, of significant FDA modernization, encouraging the agency to more quickly review innovative drugs and medical devices. In 1999 he became chairman of the Energy and Power Subcommittee. His subcommittee had jurisdiction over various Bush energy plans, which Barton generally supported. He surprised some by reaching agreement in 2001 with Michigan Democrat John Dingell on higher fuel economy standards. All the while, Barton pressed for action on electricity regulation. He retreated from requiring utilities to join regional transmission organizations and sought to encourage them to do so, to produce an easy basis for exchanges of traded electricity. His version repealed the 1930s Public Utility Holding Company Act. This was an issue on which a Republican like Barton tried to increase federal regulatory power while Democrats like John Dingell and Henry Waxman were maintaining state primacy. In September 2002, Republicans pushed it through the House. But it went no farther.

In February 2004, Energy and Commerce chairman Billy Tauzin announced he would retire from Congress; Barton was selected to succeed him as chairman—the only Texan other than Sam Rayburn to hold the post. He said he wanted to focus on investigations, as Dingell had when he was chairman from 1981 to 1995. He aroused partisan feelings sometimes, as when in September 2004 he blocked committee Democrats' demand for information on Dick Cheney's 2001 energy task force. But he also worked successfully to win Democratic votes on some issues and to defend and expand the committee's jurisdiction. Not all his efforts were successful. In November 2004 he said he would no longer grant committee members waivers to serve on other committees; several, including some who had seats on Financial Services to follow their issues when the committee jurisdictions were altered in 2001, protested, and Barton issued waivers on a case-by-case basis. Conflicts with other committees are inevitable on Energy and Commerce. Barton clashed with Judiciary Chairman James Sensenbrenner on database privacy; a founder of the Congressional Privacy Caucus, Barton pushed a bill seeking consumers' access to information; Sensenbrenner backed one allowing less access, which was backed by content providers.

Telecommunications issues are a major responsibility of Energy and Commerce. Barton and Chip Pickering asked the FCC to assert jurisdiction over VoIP Internet phoning. After Janet Jackson's "wardrobe malfunction" during the 2004 Super Bowl broadcast, the committee voted to increase the fines on broadcast indecency. Barton tried to put the bill raising the maximum fine for one incident from $32,500 to $500,000 in the defense authorization. That failed, but the House passed the bill in February 2005. In June 2006, the House passed his bill to make it easier for telephone companies to enter the broadband market; but influential Democrats opposed the measure, and it died in the Senate. Barton called for a stand-alone bill to require broadcasters to return the analog spectrum to the government by the end of 2006; existing law allowed them to delay until 85% of households have digital TV. In January 2007, he said that remaining analog TVs for sale should have a warning label for consumers.

On the energy bill, Barton insisted on retaining provisions barring liability of the manufacturers of MTBE, the fuel additive that federal regulations encouraged oil companies to put in gasoline; that provision prevented passage in the Senate in 2003. While he seemed to despair of a comprehensive energy bill, the Bush administration and Senate Energy Chairman Pete Domenici kept pressing. Barton still seemed wary of provisions that might kill the bill in the Senate. He called for keeping oil drilling in the Arctic National Wildlife Refuge out of the bill and he removed immunity for MTBE manufacturers; each was a bitter pill for Barton and his allies, and a measure of the limitations that they faced. But Barton was pleased and took some credit when the bill was enacted in August 2005, with $12 billion in incentives, an inventory of oil and natural gas reserves, plus a one-month extension of daylight savings time. In October 2005, the House narrowly passed Barton's bill to encourage the construction of new refineries, but it died in the Senate. He has been an ardent skeptic of global-warming claims of environmentalists and climate scientists. At a September 2006 hearing, he led the criticism of British Petroleum for its pipeline leaks in Alaska.

Energy and Commerce is a great platform for generating contributions, and Barton raised much more money than he is ever likely to need to spend in his district. In June 2004 he hosted a fundraiser for Billy Tauzin III, who was running for his father's seat, as Tauzin had hosted a fundraiser for Barton's son when he ran for Congress (both sons lost). At home he was criticized by Democrats for seeking in 2003 and 2004 to keep Ellis County outside EPA's Dallas region for purposes of the Clean Air Act; Ellis County is home to three cement producers and other companies whose PACs or executives contributed to Barton's campaigns, and the county produces 40% of the industrial emissions in North Texas. Barton said there was no connection between the contributions and his action and argued that there was no scientific basis for Ellis County's inclusion. But in April 2004, the EPA decided otherwise and that Ellis County must work to reduce air pollution.

Barton has had some political disappointments. He ran for the Senate in 1993 after Lloyd Bentsen resigned to be Treasury secretary but finished third with just 14% of the vote in the May all-party primary. In September 2001, when Phil Gramm announced his retirement from the Senate, Barton considered running for his seat. But in early October, busy with electricity and energy legislation and amid talk that the Bush White House favored Attorney General John Cornyn, he announced he would not run. After the 2006 election, he made a belated bid for Minority Leader. But he quickly discovered that John Boehner had wrapped up the votes, and Barton withdrew after six days; although he has become their dean, his failure to alert them in advance caused resentment among Texas Republicans.

Barton has been reelected easily in the 6th District. He suffered a heart attack in December 2005, but quickly recovered.

SEVENTH DISTRICT

Rep. John Culberson (R)

Elected 2000, 4th term; b. Aug. 24, 1956, Houston; home, Houston; Southern Methodist U., B.A. 1981, S. TX Col. of Law, J.D. 1988; Methodist; married (Belinda).

Elected Office: TX House of Reps., 1986-2000, Maj. Whip, 1999-2000.

Professional Career: Jim Culberson Advertising, 1981-85; Practicing atty., 1988-2000.

DC Office: 428 CHOB, 20515, 202-225-2571; Fax: 202-225-4381; Web site: www.culberson.house.gov.

District Offices: Houston, 713-682-8828.

Committees: *Appropriations* (23d of 29 R): Commerce, Justice, Science & Related Agencies; Homeland Security.

Group Ratings

	ADA	ACLU	AFS	LCV	ITIC	NTU	COC	ACU	CFG	FRC
2006	10	5	0	8	86	57	93	88	61	100
2005	0	—	0	0	—	61	88	92	68	100

National Journal Ratings

	2005 LIB	—	2005 CONS	2006 LIB	—	2006 CONS
Economic	26%	—	73%	32%	—	67%
Social	0%	—	89%	0%	—	94%
Foreign	11%	—	86%	0%	—	94%

Key Votes of the 109th Congress

1. Estate Tax Repeal	Y	5. Limit Interstate Abortion	Y	9. Build Border Fence	*
2. Limit CAFE Standards	Y	6. Extend Patriot Act	Y	10. CAFTA	Y
3. FY06 Spending Curb	Y	7. Bar Same Sex Marriage	Y	11. Oppose Iraq Withdrawal	Y
4. Drilling in ANWR	Y	8. Stem Cell Research $	N	12. Detainee Tribunals	Y

Election Results

2006 general	John Culberson (R)	99,318	(59%)	($734,383)
	Jim Henley (D)	64,514	(38%)	($122,145)
	Other	3,953	(2%)	
2006 primary	John Culberson (R)	unopposed		
2004 general	John Culberson (R)	175,440	(64%)	($617,860)
	John Martinez (D)	91,126	(33%)	($26,993)
	Other	7,085	(3%)	

Prior Winning Percentages: 2002 (89%); 2000 (74%)

The People		Race/Ethnic Origin	Ancestry	
Area size:	198 sq. mi.	67.5% White	German: 11.3%	English: 9.3%
Urban population:	99.7%	5.6% Black	Irish: 7.4%	
Rural population:	0.3%	6.9% Asian	**2004 Presidential Vote**	
Pop. 2000:	651,620	0.2% Native Am.	Bush (R) 179,456	(64%)
Pop. 2005 (est):	719,784	0.0% Hawaiian	Kerry (D) 99,422	(36%)
Median income:	$57,846	1.6% Two+ races	**2000 Presidential Vote**	
Poverty status:	7.4%	0.2% Other	Bush (R) 172,336	(69%)
Military veterans:	9.9%	18.0% Hispanic Origin	Gore (D) 76,046	(31%)
			Cook Partisan Voting Index: R +16	
Occupation	Blue collar: 11.2%	White collar: 79.4%	Gray collar: 9.3%	

When George H. W. Bush moved from Midland in West Texas to Houston in 1960, he bought a house in Briarwood, in what was then the western edge of the fast-growing city, beyond Memorial Park and Loop 610, before the Galleria and high-rises went up around the intersection of Post Oak and Westheimer. Bush returned to Houston in 1993 and built a new house a mile from his old one, just west of lush Memorial Park. Bush's favorite shopping mall was nearby on Sage and San Felipe, and his favorite barbecue joint a mile east on Memorial; his office is atop the Park Laureate building at 10000 Memorial. Today these landmarks are no longer at the edge of the vastly bigger and economically vibrant Houston metropolitan area, but near its epicenter, certainly its retail center and not far from its commercial center, though the industrial center of gravity remains far to the east, near the Ship Channel. Downtown has survived the Enron collapse and is sprouting residential apartments, with many cultural amenities and a new campaign to preserve urban landmarks. Near the lavish Galleria, business leaders have made this area more than a shopping center. With extensive landscaping and art, they have sought to give it a unique and inviting image, and they have made improvements on the 610 to increase mobility for commuters and shoppers. The economy of Houston is once again strong; oil company revenues are up and many businesses moved here from the New Orleans-area following the devastation of Hurricane Katrina.

The 7th Congressional District of Texas is the lineal descendant of the district that elected Republican county chairman George H.W. Bush as its first member of the House in 1966 and the first Republican to represent Houston. It occupied far more territory then, half of Harris County. In successive redistrictings, its boundaries have been pared back, as the population of the west side of Houston has skyrocketed. Today more than 1.5 million people live in the area where 350,000 lived when Bush was first elected. The 7th District today touches the western edge of downtown Houston and includes most of the land between the Katy Freeway (Interstate 10) and Westheimer running straight west to Highway 6. To the south it includes the affluent neighborhoods southwest of downtown Houston, Rice University and the Texas Medical Center, Belleaire and a swatch of Houston southwest of 610. It extends north to include Jersey Village and the villages along Buffalo Bayou west of the 610 Loop. Within its boundaries live most of Houston's business and professional elite, the partners of the big law firms and the people you read about on the society page. Back in the 1980s, the 7th District was one of the most Republican districts in the country, and it still is heavily Republican. But as with many precincts of the very elite, from Greenwich, Connecticut, to Bloomfield Hills, Michigan, and Hillsborough, California, it—or at least a significant minority of longtime Republicans living here—has not taken a liking to George W. Bush's brand of Republicanism. Within these boundaries he won 69% of the vote in 2000 but dropped to 64% in 2004, a lower percentage than he won in 14 other Texas districts. The younger Bush now runs much stronger in the modest-income counties of West Texas than he does in the high-income precincts of Houston, where his parents live and where he spent some of what he admits now were his misspent years.

The congressman from the 7th District is John Culberson, a Republican first elected in 2000 and only the second man to hold the seat after the senior Bush. Culberson grew up in Houston and graduated from Southern Methodist University, then worked for his father's advertising agency. He graduated from South Texas College of Law and worked as a civil defense attorney. In 1986, at 29, Culberson won a seat in the Texas House, where he served for 14 years. In 2000 Bill Archer, Bush's successor in the House, retired when he was term-limited after six years as chairman of the Ways and Means Committee. In this safe Republican seat, the frontrunners in the primary were Culberson and Peter Wareing, a Houston merchant banker and son-in-law of Texas oilman Jack Blanton. Culberson led Wareing in the first round 38%-27%. Wareing spent nearly $4 million to Culberson's $650,000. But Culberson had an extensive grassroots campaign and won the runoff four weeks later 60%-40%. The general election was no contest.

Culberson calls himself a "Jeffersonian Republican" and is passionate about transferring power from the federal to local governments; he has had a mostly conservative voting record. He opposes racial quotas and preferences, gun control, and abortion (except in cases of rape, incest, or to save the life of the mother). In the Archer tradition, his goal is to junk the current tax system and replace it with a national sales tax. An amateur astronomer and self-proclaimed science buff since he got a telescope when he was 12, Culberson is an enthusiast for NASA and has an interest in nanotechnology research. "My eyes are too bad and my feet too flat for me to be an astronaut," he told the *Houston Chronicle*, with evident regret.

On Appropriations since 2003, he battled with Houston officials who wanted to increase spending for light rail. He insisted on expanded highway capacity, including the Katy Freeway, as part of the plan to relieve gridlock. In November 2003, he opposed the referendum in Houston to authorize $640 million in revenue bonds for 22 additional miles of light rail transit; the proposal passed narrowly. In 2005, Culberson, once an opponent of federal funding for local rail projects, reached agreement with area officials to seek $1 billion toward a $2 billion transit plan with a mix of highway and public-transit projects.

In the House, Culberson has often gone his own way. He ruffled feathers as one of only two Texas Republicans to oppose the 2003 Medicare/prescription drug bill. Also in the face of White House opposition, he proposed an appropriations rider to prohibit funding of a regulation to permit banks to accept Mexican *matricula consular* documents as identification; in September 2004, the House defeated his proposal, 222-177. He was outraged when immigration officials in Houston said that their agents would not perform random workplace raids and would respect "sanctuaries" for illegal aliens. "If they expected to get funded, they must enforce the immigration laws." He favors allowing border states to create militias to apprehend illegal aliens. Despite the pioneering research at medical centers in his district, he voted against embryonic stem cell research, which he said would encourage "production and harvesting of human embryos like a crop of corn, which is creepy and unacceptable." Though the district lines have changed twice since he was first elected, he has not faced serious competition. In 2006, Culberson was held to a 59%-38% win by Jim Henley, a debate instructor at a local middle school—Culberson's poorest election performance to date.

EIGHTH DISTRICT

Rep. Kevin Brady (R)

Elected 1996, 6th term; b. Apr. 11, 1955, Vermillion, SD; home, The Woodlands, TX; U. of SD, B.S. 1990; Catholic; married (Cathy).

Elected Office: TX House of Reps., 1990-96.

Professional Career: Exec., Woodlands Chamber of Commerce, 1978-96.

DC Office: 301 CHOB, 20515, 202-225-4901; Fax: 202-225-5524; Web site: www.house.gov/brady.

District Offices: Conroe, 936-441-5700; Huntsville, 936-439-9542; Orange, 409-883-4197.

Committees: *Joint Economic Committee* (6th of 10 R). *Ways & Means* (10th of 17 R): Social Security; Trade.

Group Ratings

	ADA	ACLU	AFS	LCV	ITIC	NTU	COC	ACU	CFG	FRC
2006	5	5	0	8	100	64	100	88	72	100
2005	0	—	0	0	—	68	89	96	89	92

National Journal Ratings

	2005 LIB	—	2005 CONS	2006 LIB	—	2006 CONS
Economic	7%	—	92%	25%	—	74%
Social	0%	—	89%	11%	—	85%
Foreign	16%	—	83%	27%	—	72%

Key Votes of the 109th Congress

1. Estate Tax Repeal	Y	5. Limit Interstate Abortion	Y	9. Build Border Fence	Y
2. Limit CAFE Standards	Y	6. Extend Patriot Act	Y	10. CAFTA	Y
3. FY06 Spending Curb	Y	7. Bar Same Sex Marriage	Y	11. Oppose Iraq Withdrawal	Y
4. Drilling in ANWR	Y	8. Stem Cell Research $	N	12. Detainee Tribunals	Y

Election Results

2006 general	Kevin Brady (R)	105,665	(67%)	($527,711)
	Jim Wright (D)	51,393	(33%)	
2006 primary	Kevin Brady (R)	unopposed		
2004 general	Kevin Brady (R)	179,599	(69%)	($670,875)
	Jim Wright (D)	77,324	(30%)	
	Other	3,705	(1%)	

Prior Winning Percentages: 2002 (93%); 2000 (92%); 1998 (93%); 1996 (59%)

The People		Race/Ethnic Origin	Ancestry	
Area size:	8,415 sq. mi.	80.1% White	USA: 10.8%	German: 9.1%
Urban population:	49.6%	8.7% Black	Irish: 8.4%	
Rural population:	50.4%	0.7% Asian	**2004 Presidential Vote**	
Pop. 2000:	651,620	0.5% Native Am.	Bush (R) 194,696	(72%)
Pop. 2005 (est):	741,712	0.0% Hawaiian	Kerry (D) 73,946	(28%)
Median income:	$40,459	0.9% Two+ races	**2000 Presidential Vote**	
Poverty status:	12.6%	0.1% Other	Bush (R) 155,003	(69%)
Military veterans:	13.8%	9.0% Hispanic Origin	Gore (D) 68,522	(31%)
			Cook Partisan Voting Index: R +20	
Occupation	Blue collar: 28.7%	White collar: 55.7%	Gray collar: 15.6%	

When Houston Intercontinental Airport opened in 1969, it was located 25 miles away from downtown Houston or from just about any other concentration of population, at the northern edge of Harris County and just south of the Montgomery County line. What is known now as George Bush Intercontinental is still a jaunt from downtown Houston. But rapid expansion and growth of commercial office space and upscale residential subdivisions have continued even farther to the north in once rural Montgomery County, rising on land that once held roadside stands and barbecues and unpainted farmhouses with water pooling on low swampy fields. The arrival of railroads in the late 19th century made timber production the first major local industry, but much of the land was stripped by the 1920s and it was turned over to livestock. Fortunes rose again in 1931 when wildcattter George Strake struck oil near Conroe. Thousands of other wildcatters and roughnecks quickly joined in the boom; this became one of the richest oil producing areas in the nation, and active production continues. In 1972, construction began on a planned community called The Woodlands; development of this new city has barely slowed since then. Greater Houston has spread far out into this countryside, past the now mislabeled Farm-Market Route 1960, out past The Woodlands and Conroe. Montgomery County had 49,000 people in 1970, just after the airport opened. Since then its population has risen to 128,000 in 1980, 182,000 in 1990, 293,000 in 2000 and 398,000 in 2006, and it is the fifth fastest-growing county in Texas.

The 8th Congressional District includes all of Montgomery County, which contains about half its people. Before the 2003 redistricting 60% of its population was in Harris County; now none is, and it extends east to the Sabine River on the Louisiana border, including all of eight counties and parts of two others. It covers the Big Thicket National Preserve, a primeval swamp described as

"America's Ark" because of its vast array of animals and plants. It includes the town of Huntsville, with one of Texas's oldest prisons, and the oil refinery town of Orange on the Sabine River, which is popular for bass fishing. This area was hard-hit in late September 2005 by Hurricane Rita, though it received limited attention because of the Katrina devastation. The redistricting changes have made the district less affluent and metropolitan, and a little less Republican. The old 8th District voted 78% for George W. Bush in 2000, his highest figure in the nation. Within the new 8th District, he won 69% in 2000 and 72% in 2004.

The congressman from the 8th District is Kevin Brady, a Republican first elected in 1996. Brady grew up and went to college in South Dakota, moved to Montgomery County in 1978 and headed The Woodlands Chamber of Commerce for 18 years. In 1990 he was elected to the Texas House. When Congressman Jack Fields announced in 1995 he was retiring, Brady decided to run. His main opponent in the decisive Republican primary was Eugene Fontenot, a physician who wanted "to restore America to its Christian heritage." Brady was the choice of party regulars; Fontenot was endorsed by religious conservatives. Fontenot attacked Brady for being one of two Republicans to vote against the state's concealed weapons law. Brady had opposed most gun control bills, but not this one; when he was 12, his father was shot and killed while trying a case in a South Dakota courtroom. Brady and Fontenot ran against each other four separate times in that one year. After Fontenot led Brady in the March primary, Brady won the April runoff 53%-47%. After the U.S. Supreme Court in June ordered a redrawing of 13 districts, Brady led Fontenot 41%-39% in an all-party primary in November. Finally, in the December runoff, turnout was sharply down and party regular Brady won 59%-41%.

In the House, Brady has compiled a conservative voting record, though a bit less so on foreign issues. He gained a reputation as more of a pragmatist than other Texas Republicans. With the murder of his father always a fresh memory, he has been an advocate of victims' rights and the death penalty. In January 2001 he took Bill Archer's seat on Ways and Means; he is an advocate of abolishing the IRS and moving toward a consumption tax. But while waiting until that distant day arrives, Brady has tinkered successfully with the status quo. He strongly backed the Bush tax cuts and helped to pass a scaled-back version of Bush's plan to give tax breaks for contributions to faith-based groups. Brady was a central figure in the successful effort in 2004 to make state and local sales taxes deductible in the seven states, including Texas, that have no personal income tax. He was the chief House sponsor of the Central America Free Trade Agreement; Texas would benefit, he argued, because it has become the nation's largest export state, with especially rapid growth in trade with Central America. "America chose engagement and building bridges instead of isolation and turning our back on Central America," he said after the House approved the deal in July 2005. He won committee approval of his bill to sunset all federal programs every 12 years unless Congress renews them, but opposition from Republican moderates led leadership to pull the bill from the schedule in July 2006. In addition to his energetic work on Ways and Means, Brady has been a deputy whip to Roy Blunt.

Since his four contests in 1996, Brady has had no problem winning reelection, even after district was radically redrawn. With his relatively young age and growing seniority at Ways and Means, he is positioned to wield House influence for many years to come.

NINTH DISTRICT

Rep. Al Green (D)

Elected 2004, 2d term; b. Sept. 1, 1947, New Orleans, LA; home, Houston; TX Southern U., J.D. 1973; Baptist; single.

Elected Office: Harris Cnty. justice of the peace, 1977-2004.

Professional Career: Practicing atty., 1973-77; Pres., Houston NAACP, 1986-95.

DC Office: 425 CHOB, 20515, 202-225-7508; Fax: 202-225-2947; Web site: www.house.gov/algreen.

District Offices: Houston, 713-383-9234.

Committees: *Financial Services* (21st of 37 D): Housing & Community Opportunity; Financial Institutions & Consumer Credit. *Homeland Security* (17th of 19 D): Emerging Threats, Cybersecurity & Science and Technology; Border, Maritime & Global Counterterrorism.

Group Ratings

	ADA	ACLU	AFS	LCV	ITIC	NTU	COC	ACU	CFG	FRC
2006	95	100	100	67	29	14	60	20	18	0
2005	100	—	100	56	—	13	48	16	6	8

National Journal Ratings

	2005 LIB	—	2005 CONS		2006 LIB	—	2006 CONS
Economic	65%	—	34%		63%	—	36%
Social	87%	—	12%		78%	—	22%
Foreign	88%	—	11%		77%	—	20%

Key Votes of the 109th Congress

1. Estate Tax Repeal	N	5. Limit Interstate Abortion	N	9. Build Border Fence	N
2. Limit CAFE Standards	Y	6. Extend Patriot Act	N	10. CAFTA	N
3. FY06 Spending Curb	N	7. Bar Same Sex Marriage	N	11. Oppose Iraq Withdrawal	N
4. Drilling in ANWR	Y	8. Stem Cell Research $	Y	12. Detainee Tribunals	N

Election Results

2006 general	Al Green (D) .... unopposed			($392,972)
2006 primary	Al Green (D) .... unopposed			
2004 general	Al Green (D) 114,462	(72%)		($838,834)
	Arlette Molina (R) 42,132	(27%)		($133,372)
	Other... 1,972	(1%)		

The People		Race/Ethnic Origin	Ancestry
Area size:	154 sq. mi.	17.4% White	SubSaharan: 3.1% German: 3.1%
Urban population:	99.8%	37.0% Black	USA: 2.5%
Rural population:	0.2%	10.7% Asian	**2004 Presidential Vote**
Pop. 2000:	651,619	0.1% Native Am.	Kerry (D) 112,065 (70%)
Pop. 2005 (est):	674,267	0.0% Hawaiian	Bush (R) 48,052 (30%)
Median income:	$34,870	1.7% Two+ races	**2000 Presidential Vote**
Poverty status:	18.4%	0.2% Other	Gore (D) 99,394 (69%)
Military veterans:	7.1%	32.8% Hispanic Origin	Bush (R) 45,579 (31%)
			Cook Partisan Voting Index: D +21

Occupation	Blue collar: 22.7%	White collar: 58.0%	Gray collar: 19.2%

Spreading out in all directions from its historic center at Allen's Landing on Buffalo Bayou, Houston has become one of the great metropolises of North America. A half-century ago, the steaming flatlands south of Houston running down to the Gulf of Mexico did not seem a likely site for one of the world's most advanced civilizations. But they are today. It was Houston where most of the scientific work was done that put the first man on the moon—the first word spoken on the moon was "Houston." Houston is the undisputed center of expertise in the oil business, where the greatest concentration of experts in the world is within a few miles of each other. Houston has also become one of the great medical centers of the world, with the giant Texas Medical Center and its 13 hospitals looming as impressively massive as any great office skyscraper complex.And Houston lately has become one of the great surprise growth cities, creating thousands of small businesses, many owned by immigrants. All this success and sophistication are testimony to human—and Texan—creativity, and to the triumph of air conditioning, which facilitated the growth of what is now the fourth-largest city in the nation. For who supposed that all these people would move here if they had to sweat through Houston's steamy five-month summer?

The 9th Congressional District of Texas slices across the southern part of metro Houston on the streets and freeways and waterways spreading out from the center of the city. It occupies much of the territory that was in the 25th District before the 2003 redistricting; it was redrawn to include more blacks and Asians. The 9th begins just southwest of where I-45 crosses the I-610 Loop; it continues west with a slight intrusion inside 610 near the Reliant Astrodome and Reliant Stadium, and then heads past Meadows Place and Mission Bend outside Beltway 8 toward the western end of Harris County. It includes two wedges of Fort Bend County, which form a crescent around the 22d District. The district includes many heavily black neighborhoods, low-income and middle-income, in Harris and Fort Bend Counties; its population is 37% black, the third highest in any Texas district. It also includes many Asians, who form 11% of the total, the highest percentage in Texas, and one of the highest in any district east of California or west of New York. Along Belleaire Boulevard is a Chinese-American community, with signs in Chinese characters over the stores and banks. In the Alief neighborhood of southwest Houston on Bray's Bayou, entrepreneurial Vietnamese boat people settled, created quality schools, an Asian-oriented shopping mall and businesses that serve the largest Vietnamese community in the nation outside of California; in 2004, the Vietnamese Democratic challenger from Alief narrowly ousted a long-time Anglo Republican stalwart in the state House. Nearby, a Pakistani Muslim was elected to the Houston city council. And of course there are many Hispanics in the district, 33% of the total population, though many are not citizens or not voters. The devastation of Katrina that emptied out New Orleans moved perhaps 200,000 of its residents to Houston, where tens of thousands have remained; many of them spent their first few days at the Astrodome, in far more orderly and secure arrangements than they escaped at the Superdome. Overall this is a heavily Democratic district, which voted 70% for John Kerry in 2004.

The congressman from the 9th District is Al Green, a Democrat first elected in 2004 when he was the surprise winner of a bitter Democratic primary. Green grew up in New Orleans, attended college at Florida A&M and graduated from Texas Southern law school, where he later taught. From 1986 to 1995 he was president of the Houston chapter of the NAACP. In 1977 he was elected justice of the peace and served 26 years. After the new district boundaries were approved, Green saw an obvious opening and resigned to run for Congress. The congressman from the old district that covered much of this area was Chris Bell, an Anglo Democrat first elected in 2002. That year, he ran with liberal support and beat a more conservative black candidate. The primary against Green was a different matter. Green said that he wanted to fight racial profiling and discrimination in law enforcement, frequently used subtle racial references on the campaign trail (including his promise to bring "a mountain of soul" to the new district) and amassed an impressive roster of endorsements from prominent local and national black leaders. Bell responded by asking voters "not to focus on the color of my skin, but on the size of my heart." He spent more than $1 million on the primary, while Green spent less than half as much, and Bell was endorsed by the AFL-CIO, Texas teachers, abortion rights groups and Minority Leader Nancy Pelosi. But he struggled as a white candidate running in a district where minorities constituted two-thirds of the electorate and in a two-month campaign where slightly more than half of the district was new to him.

As the primary neared, the racially charged atmosphere intensified. When state Democratic chairman Charles Soechting endorsed Bell, Green said that it reminded him of "the double standards when African-Americans had to ride on the back of the bus and drink from colored-only water fountains." Bell said Green accepted money from a former Republican official who worked against black interests; Green claimed that Bell wrongly informed voters that the NAACP endorsed him. The Congressional Black Caucus was drawn into the campaign after California's Maxine Waters hand-delivered a $5,000 check to Green from the caucus's political action committee; she announced that nearly a dozen CBC members backed Green over Bell. Bell said that Black Caucus Chairman Elijah Cummings had earlier promised to support him. Although the caucus itself never made a formal endorsement, its role in the primary angered other Democratic members, who argued that all incumbents should be supported. In the end, it may not have mattered. Green won the primary in a landslide, 66%-31%. "It's been a divisive race and in some ways a rather ugly race," Bell said in conceding. The general election was a foregone conclusion. After his primary defeat, Bell filed ethics charges against Tom DeLay that ultimately played a role in DeLay's downfall; some Republicans made the absurd argument that Bell was not entitled to file charges because he was a lame duck.

In the House, Green had a relatively moderate voting record, especially on economic issues. On the Financial Services Committee, he worked to eliminate housing practices that discriminated against minorities. He passed an amendment in the House to add $7.7 million to fight housing discrimination. He broke with most House Democrats by voting to permit oil drilling in the Arctic National Wildlife Refuge—probably the smart vote for a Houston-based district. More than a year after Katrina, he worked with FEMA to assist thousands of families in Houston displaced by the disaster. In March 2005, Houston airport security officials pulled him out of a line, and questioned and searched him; Green said that he may have been the target of ethnic profiling. In May 2006, he considered it a badge of honor when he was arrested for protesting with other Black Caucus members at the Embassy of Sudan.

In 2006, he was reelected without opposition.

TENTH DISTRICT

Rep. Michael McCaul (R)

Elected 2004, 2d term; b. Jan. 14, 1962, Dallas; home, Austin; Trinity U., B.A. 1984, St. Mary's U., J.D. 1987; Catholic; married (Linda).

Professional Career: Fed. prosecutor, 1990-99; Dep. Atty. Gen., 1999-2003; Chief, Western Div. of TX., U.S. Attys. Office, 2003-04.

DC Office: 131 CHOB, 20515, 202-225-2401; Fax: 202-225-5955; Web site: www.house.gov/mccaul.

District Offices: Austin, 512-473-2357; Brenham, 979-830-8497; Katy, 281-398-1247; Tomball, 281-255-8372.

Committees: *Foreign Affairs* (19th of 23 R): Western Hemisphere; Africa & Global Health. *Homeland Security* (10th of 15 R): Emerging Threats, Cybersecurity & Science and Technology (RMM); Management, Investigations & Oversight; Border, Maritime & Global Counterterrorism. *Science & Technology* (15th of 20 R): Investigations & Oversight; Space & Aeronautics; Energy & Environment. *Standards of Official Conduct* (5th of 5 R).

Group Ratings

	ADA	ACLU	AFS	LCV	ITIC	NTU	COC	ACU	CFG	FRC
2006	0	10	0	17	100	56	100	83	55	100
2005	5	—	0	0	—	60	93	96	73	85

National Journal Ratings

	2005 LIB	—	2005 CONS		2006 LIB	—	2006 CONS
Economic	3%	—	94%		37%	—	63%
Social	14%	—	85%		17%	—	79%
Foreign	17%	—	79%		30%	—	67%

Key Votes of the 109th Congress

1. Estate Tax Repeal	Y	5. Limit Interstate Abortion	Y	9. Build Border Fence	Y
2. Limit CAFE Standards	Y	6. Extend Patriot Act	Y	10. CAFTA	Y
3. FY06 Spending Curb	Y	7. Bar Same Sex Marriage	Y	11. Oppose Iraq Withdrawal	Y
4. Drilling in ANWR	Y	8. Stem Cell Research $	N	12. Detainee Tribunals	Y

Election Results

2006 general	Michael McCaul (R)	97,726	(55%)	($1,111,980)
	Ted Ankrum (D)	71,415	(40%)	($64,633)
	Michael Badnarik (Lib)	7,614	(4%)	($440,537)
2006 primary	Michael McCaul (R)	unopposed		
2004 general	Michael McCaul (R)	182,113	(79%)	($2,988,391)
	Robert Fritsche (Lib)	35,569	(15%)	
	Lorenzo Sadun (WI)	13,961	(6%)	($40,613)

The People		Race/Ethnic Origin	Ancestry	
Area size:	3,846 sq. mi.	66.5% White	German: 13.9%	English: 7.6%
Urban population:	80.8%	9.1% Black	Irish: 7.6%	
Rural population:	19.2%	3.9% Asian	**2004 Presidential Vote**	
Pop. 2000:	651,620	0.3% Native Am.	Bush (R) 177,555	(62%)
Pop. 2005 (est):	804,053	0.0% Hawaiian	Kerry (D) 109,287	(38%)
Median income:	$52,465	1.3% Two+ races	**2000 Presidential Vote**	
Poverty status:	8.2%	0.1% Other	Bush (R) 152,201	(67%)
Military veterans:	10.9%	18.7% Hispanic Origin	Gore (D) 76,643	(33%)
			Cook Partisan Voting Index: R +13	

Occupation   Blue collar: 18.6%   White collar: 69.9%   Gray collar: 11.5%

Two of Texas's major cities are named for pioneer leaders of the Texas Republic, Sam Houston and Stephen Austin. They are not entirely attractive characters today: Houston had episodes of alcoholic depression, Austin was a slaveholder who argued that Mexico infringed Texas's liberty when it freed its slaves. But they were also men of courage and determination, with a passion for liberty and a willingness to fight for it, who built a distinctively American culture in what was then the northeast of Mexico. Today the two metropolises named for them have quite different characters. Houston is about commerce, the world capital of the "awl bidness," an entrepreneurial paradise spread out over the swampy, humid plains just north of the Gulf of Mexico. Austin is the creature of the state government headquartered in the grand Capitol and of the University of Texas, with a huge endowment of land in West Texas that turned out to be underlaid with oil. But Austin in recent years has taken on some of Houston's character. North of the Capitol and the University, in land that was vacant when Lyndon Johnson celebrated his 87-vote victory in the 1948 primary in the Driskill Hotel, there has grown up an entrepreneurial Austin, high-tech and free-market oriented, spreading out over the hills and into adjacent Williamson County. The historic Austin is a liberal enclave in the heart of a conservative state; this new Austin is more in line with the mores and manners of most of Texas, with plenty of jobs for young professionals. Curiously, there is no superhighway between Austin and Houston. To get from one to the other you travel over roads through rural counties with monuments and plaques recalling the days of the Texas Republic. Only in recent years has metropolitan growth spread to these historic places.

The 10th Congressional District of Texas connects the western edge of Houston with the new northern precincts of Austin through a corridor of still mostly rural counties. It is split into three roughly equal parts. The largest of these is in Austin and Travis County, where the district includes the northern third of Austin, with one tentacle reaching southwest beyond the city limits and another dropping south to Austin State Hospital, where one city block near Guadalupe and 38th Streets is shared by three congressional districts: the 10th, the 21st and the 25th. The second largest is the western edge of Houston's Harris County, "21st century suburban America in its most common and oft-replicated form," sniffed the *Austin American-Statesman*. This is a fast-growing area, with lots of young families, new subdivisions and sparkling megachurches. In between are the six lightly populated rural counties, some of which (Austin and Washington) surprisingly enough have historic Republican voting traditions. Overall this is a heavily Republican district—and one of the fastest-growing in the state between 2000 and 2005.

The congressman from the 10th District is Michael McCaul, a Republican first elected in 2004. He grew up in Dallas, studied business and history at Trinity University and went to law school at St. Mary's University, both in San Antonio. He worked as a federal prosecutor, then became in 1999 a deputy attorney general to John Cornyn in Austin. In 2002, he joined the U.S. Attorney's office and was chief of the Terrorism and National Security Section for Western Texas. McCaul was one of eight candidates in the Republican primary; no Democrat even bothered to file in this district. The top contenders were McCaul, mortgage company owner Ben Streusand and former Judge John Devine. McCaul, who is from Austin and whose father-in-law is Clear Channel Communications chairman Lowry Mays, focused on his anti-terrorism work in the U.S. Attorney's office. "I'm the only candidate that's had a top-secret security clearance," he said. "I won't have a learning curve." Streusand, based in Harris County, called for less government regulation and opposed the Bush administration's immigration proposals. Devine, who had refused to remove a Ten Commandments display from his Harris County courtroom, had the support of Christian conservatives and called for a crackdown on illegal immigration. In the primary, Streusand carried 7 of the 8 counties to finish with 28% of the vote, to 24% for McCaul and 21% for Devine, who led in Harris County and ran behind everywhere else. McCaul won the runoff spot over Devine by just 857 votes.

In the runoff, McCaul and Streusand agreed on most issues. Both supported the Bush tax cuts and favored replacing the federal income tax with either a flat tax or a sales tax. In the absence of clear distinctions, they traded accusations about each other's background. McCaul criticized Streusand's past donations to Democratic candidates; Streusand, who was supported by Gary Bauer but few in the Republican establishment, questioned why McCaul served in the Clinton administration's Justice Department. Streusand spent $3.6 million, nearly all of it his own money. McCaul spent $2.9 million, of which $1.9 million was his own; he ended up with the second-largest campaign debt of all freshman members. But he sounded more thoughtful and had endorsements from former President George H.W. Bush, Governor Rick Perry and Senators Kay Bailey Hutchison and John Cornyn. McCaul won 63%-37% in a contest in which only 24,000 votes were cast. He carried every county except one, which he lost by 7 votes; he won 73% of the vote in Travis County and 52% in Harris County, which between them cast 72% of the votes. With no Democratic opponent, McCaul spent the fall helping Republicans against Democratic incumbents in other Texas districts.

In the House, McCaul had a moderate-to-conservative voting record. Freshman Republicans chose him as their liaison to the House leadership. He was assigned to Homeland Security, where he chaired the Investigations Subcommittee, and to the International Relations and Science committees. He gained headlines with hearings that revealed more than $1 billion in fraud in Katrina disaster relief. At the request of Republican leaders, he took the lead in enacting a bill to overhaul FEMA, especially its payments to victims. He filed a bill to require the imprisonment of all captured illegal immigrants until they are deported to their home countries. On the Science Committee, he called for a return to "the same enthusiasm" that accompanied the first landing on the moon. In 2007, he was assigned to the Ethics committee.

In 2006, McCaul won an unimpressive reelection victory that suggests he needs to work harder back home to secure this seat. Against retired Navy Captain Ted Ankrum, an underfunded challenger who served four tours in Vietnam and later worked on John Kerry's presidential campaign, McCaul won 55%-40%. Two Democrats have stepped forward to challenge McCaul in 2008: Dan Grant, an international affairs consultant from Austin, and Larry Joe Doherty, a Houston lawyer who stars as a judge in a courtroom reality television show called "Texas Justice."

ELEVENTH DISTRICT

Rep. Mike Conaway (R)

Elected 2004, 2d term; b. June 11, 1948, Borger; home, Midland; E. TX St. U., B.B.A. 1970; Baptist; married (Suzanne).

Military Career: Army, 1970-72.

Elected Office: Midland Schl. Bd., 1985-88.

Professional Career: Tax mgr., Price Waterhouse & Co., 1972-80; CFO, Keith G. Graham, 1980-81; CFO, Lantern Petroleum Comp., 1981; CFO, Arbusto Energy Inc./Bush Exploration Comp., 1982-84; CFO, Spectrum 7 Energy Corp., 1984-86; CFO, United Bank, 1987-90; Sr. VP, TX Comm. Bank, 1990-92; Board member, TX Bd. of Pub. Accountancy, 1995-2002, Chmn., 1997-2002; Owner, K. Michael Conaway, CPA, 1993-2004.

DC Office: 511 CHOB, 20515, 202-225-3605; Fax: 202-225-1783; Web site: www.conaway.house.gov.

District Offices: Brownwood, 866-882-3811; Llano, 325-247-2826; Midland, 432-687-2390; Odessa, 866-882-3811; San Angelo, 325-659-4010.

Committees: *Agriculture* (16th of 21 R): General Farm Commodities & Risk Management; Horticulture & Organic Agriculture; Livestock, Dairy & Poultry. *Armed Services* (27th of 29 R): Terrorism, Unconventional Threats & Capabilities; Oversight & Investigations. *Budget* (11th of 17 R).

Group Ratings

	ADA	ACLU	AFS	LCV	ITIC	NTU	COC	ACU	CFG	FRC
2006	0	0	0	0	100	65	100	88	69	100
2005	0	—	0	0	—	62	93	96	66	85

National Journal Ratings

	2005 LIB	—	2005 CONS		2006 LIB	—	2006 CONS
Economic	21%	—	79%		7%	—	91%
Social	30%	—	70%		17%	—	79%
Foreign	27%	—	71%		0%	—	94%

Key Votes of the 109th Congress

1. Estate Tax Repeal	Y	5. Limit Interstate Abortion	Y	9. Build Border Fence	N
2. Limit CAFE Standards	Y	6. Extend Patriot Act	Y	10. CAFTA	Y
3. FY06 Spending Curb	Y	7. Bar Same Sex Marriage	Y	11. Oppose Iraq Withdrawal	Y
4. Drilling in ANWR	Y	8. Stem Cell Research $	N	12. Detainee Tribunals	Y

Election Results

2006 general	Mike Conaway (R) .... unopposed		($737,564)
2006 primary	Mike Conaway (R) .... unopposed		
2004 general	Mike Conaway (R) 177,291	(77%)	($1,573,274)
	Wayne Raasch (D) 50,339	(22%)	
	Other 3,347	(1%)	

The People		Race/Ethnic Origin	Ancestry	
Area size:	35,185 sq. mi.	64.6% White	German: 9.5%	USA: 8.6%
Urban population:	70.8%	4.0% Black	English: 6.9%	
Rural population:	29.2%	0.5% Asian	**2004 Presidential Vote**	
Pop. 2000:	651,620	0.4% Native Am.	Bush (R) 188,929	(78%)
Pop. 2005 (est):	669,529	0.0% Hawaiian	Kerry (D) 52,174	(22%)
Median income:	$32,711	0.8% Two+ races	**2000 Presidential Vote**	
Poverty status:	15.8%	0.0% Other	Bush (R) 163,488	(75%)
Military veterans:	13.5%	29.6% Hispanic Origin	Gore (D) 55,244	(25%)
			Cook Partisan Voting Index: R +25	

Occupation	Blue collar: 26.8%	White collar: 54.8%	Gray collar: 18.4%

More than 400 years ago, in the 1540s, the conquistador Francisco Coronado and his men rode their horses over the plains of the land they called the Llano Estacado, land that is now the plains of west Texas. What they saw was a vast empty land, gradually and imperceptibly rising in elevation to the west, with only scrub vegetation and small bands of Comanche Indians. What they did not see, lying far beneath the surface, was oil, discovered in the 1940s in large amounts in the Permian Basin. When oil was found, two tiny county seats 25 miles apart suddenly became small cities—Odessa, home of the roughneck oil well workers, and Midland, the more upscale town where oil entrepreneurs lived and started their own Petroleum Club. The Permian Basin boomed in the years just after World War II: in 1940, Ector and Midland Counties had a population of 26,000, in 1950 it was 67,000 and in 1960, 159,000. Since then growth has slowed, as new discoveries have grown fewer; in 2000, Ector and Midland Counties had 237,000 people. It was to the Permian Basin in 1948 that George and Barbara Bush moved, in search of oil wealth and to raise a growing family. They moved around a lot, to three rented houses in Odessa (two since torn down and the third pretty grim) and then, after a year in Bakersfield, California, to three larger but by no means grand houses in Midland (typical 1950s ranches, one of 1,400 square feet now restored as a museum). Those houses, the Bushes' previous houses in New Haven and Houston and the Adams farmhouse in Braintree, Massachusetts, are the only houses in the United States where one president of the United States has raised another.

Midland in the 1950s was an affluent town by west Texas standards, but hardly a luxurious town to today's tastes; air conditioning had not yet become standard in homes or schools, and there were no mansions at the edge of town, just barren desert and oil derricks. There was a lively civic culture, with lots of volunteer organizations and new churches; today Midland has the Museum of the Southwest and the Petroleum Museum (the largest such museum in the world). This small city in the 1950s produced more than its share of the leaders of America today. Passing through the Midland public schools were George W. Bush, Laura Bush, former Commerce Secretary Donald Evans and General Tommy Franks. Odessa, too, has gained its place in the modern culture. In the 1956 movie *Giant*, James Dean played the hard-scrabble farmer who struck oil; Elizabeth Taylor and Rock Hudson co-starred. More recently, the popular movie *Friday Night Lights*, based on a non-fiction best seller, depicted the passion of its high school football, though perhaps not to local liking.

The 11th Congressional District of Texas covers much of West Texas. The district sweeps 400 miles across much of the state, from the hills of fast-growing Burnet County just north of Austin and the Texas German area of Gillespie County, on the eastern edge of which you can find the sprawling LBJ Ranch; to the west across wide open space at the New Mexico line is oil-producing Loving County, which with 60 people in 2006 was the smallest county in Texas and, for that matter, the United States. There are 36 counties here. Geographically the district is larger than 12 states; 54% of the population is in Midland, Ector and Tom Green (San Angelo) Counties; none of the other counties has more than 39,000 people. Politically, west Texas in the 1940s was, like every place in Texas except a few Texas German counties, almost totally Democratic. That began to change in the 1950s as Midland moved toward Republicans; newcomers like the Bushes were an important part of this trend. In 1962 a Republican was elected to the U.S. House in a district then made up of the

Permian Basin and El Paso, but that was mostly because the incumbent was ensnared in the Billie Sol Estes scandal, and he was defeated in 1964. That same year Midland elected a Republican to the state House, where Democrats outnumbered him by 149–1. He was replaced in 1968 by another Republican, Tom Craddick, who has remained in the legislature ever since and in January 2003 was elected Speaker; by this time Republicans outnumbered Democrats 88-62. The current 11th District is the first district in which Midland and Odessa were dominant: Craddick insisted on that. It is overwhelmingly Republican. When George W. Bush ran for the House in 1978, from a district that included Midland and Lubbock, he lost to Democrat Kent Hance: rural West Texas was still voting Democratic. In 2004 though, the 11th District cast 78.3% of its votes for Bush—his highest percentage in the nation.

The congressman from the 11th District is Mike Conaway, a Republican elected in 2004. Conaway grew up in Odessa and graduated from East Texas State University, before it became known as Texas A&M-Commerce. He worked as a certified public accountant for, among others, George W. Bush, and was chief financial officer in Arbusto/Bush Exploration during the 1980s; Governor Bush named him to the state Board of Public Accountancy, and he later chaired the National Association of State Boards of Accountancy. In May 2003, he finished second in the all-party special primary election in the old 19th District, which included nearly half of the new 11th. In June, he lost by less than 600 votes in a hard-fought runoff with Randy Neugebauer of Lubbock. After the new redistricting plan was passed in October, he was the obvious frontrunner for this seat. Democrat Charles Stenholm, who represented much of this area in the old 17th District, decided to run against Neugebauer in the new 19th District. Conaway's Republican primary opponent Bill Lester was a political science professor who campaigned against Bush's proposed guest worker program. Lester called for militarization of the border, with helicopter patrols. Conaway, a supporter of the Bush proposal, said that increased documentation would strengthen national security by separating "those who are seeking economic opportunity" from "those who would do us harm." Conaway won 75%- 25%. He carried 33 of the 36 counties, losing only in the eastern part of the district. In the general election he won 77%-22% over Wayne Raasch and carried every county.

Conaway has a conservative-leaning voting record. He is well-positioned with seats on Agriculture, Armed Services and Budget. On Social Security reform, he sought to convene a bipartisan group of House members to discuss the issue in April 2005, but Minority Leader Nancy Pelosi discouraged participation by Democrats. He authored the "No New Programs" bill, which requires that creation of any new federal program be joined with the elimination of another program of at least that cost. He sought to give oilfield drivers an exemption from rules that limit the hours that they could drive in a day. He hasn't been shy about his personal connections. "I believe I will be more effective if the president knows my first name than if he didn't," he told his hometown newspaper. He was reelected without opposition. In 2007, he joined the executive committee of the NRCC to take charge of auditing.

TWELFTH DISTRICT

Rep. Kay Granger (R)

Elected 1996, 6th term; b. Jan. 18, 1943, Greenville; home, Ft. Worth; TX Wesleyan Col., B.S. 1965; Methodist; divorced.

Elected Office: Ft. Worth City Cncl., 1989-91; Ft. Worth Mayor, 1991-96.

Professional Career: Teacher, 1965-78; Life Insurance Agent, 1978-85; Chmn., Ft. Worth Zoning Comm., 1981-88; Founder & Pres., Kay Granger Insurance Co., Inc., 1985-present.

DC Office: 440 CHOB, 20515, 202-225-5071; Fax: 202-225-5683; Web site: kaygranger.house.gov.

District Offices: Ft. Worth, 817-338-0909.

Committees: *Republican Conference Vice Chairman. Appropriations* (17th of 29 R): Homeland Security; Military Construction, Veterans Affairs & Related Agencies; Energy & Water Development.

Group Ratings

	ADA	ACLU	AFS	LCV	ITIC	NTU	COC	ACU	CFG	FRC
2006	5	5	0	0	100	57	100	76	50	71
2005	0	—	0	0	—	56	89	80	52	67

National Journal Ratings

	2005 LIB	—	2005 CONS		2006 LIB	—	2006 CONS
Economic	24%	—	74%		6%	—	93%
Social	36%	—	63%		32%	—	66%
Foreign	16%	—	83%		17%	—	73%

Key Votes of the 109th Congress

1. Estate Tax Repeal	Y	5. Limit Interstate Abortion	Y
2. Limit CAFE Standards	Y	6. Extend Patriot Act	Y
3. FY06 Spending Curb	Y	7. Bar Same Sex Marriage	Y
4. Drilling in ANWR	Y	8. Stem Cell Research $	Y

9. Build Border Fence	Y
10. CAFTA	Y
11. Oppose Iraq Withdrawal	Y
12. Detainee Tribunals	Y

Election Results

2006 general	Kay Granger (R)	98,371	(67%)	($1,350,752)
	John Morris (D)	45,676	(31%)	($13,708)
	Other	2,888	(2%)	
2006 primary	Kay Granger (R)	unopposed		
2004 general	Kay Granger (R)	173,222	(72%)	($895,146)
	Felix Alvarado (D)	66,316	(28%)	($15,948)

Prior Winning Percentages: 2002 (92%); 2000 (63%); 1998 (62%); 1996 (58%)

The People		Race/Ethnic Origin	Ancestry	
Area size:	2,217 sq. mi.	66.5% White	USA: 9.0%	German: 8.3%
Urban population:	82.8%	5.6% Black	Irish: 7.4%	
Rural population:	17.2%	2.3% Asian	**2004 Presidential Vote**	
Pop. 2000:	651,619	0.5% Native Am.	Bush (R) 162,192	(67%)
Pop. 2005 (est):	747,109	0.0% Hawaiian	Kerry (D) 79,862	(33%)
Median income:	$41,735	1.2% Two+ races	**2000 Presidential Vote**	
Poverty status:	11.3%	0.1% Other	Bush (R) 128,635	(64%)
Military veterans:	13.0%	23.7% Hispanic Origin	Gore (D) 72,219	(36%)
			Cook Partisan Voting Index: R +14	

Occupation   Blue collar: 28.0%   White collar: 58.0%   Gray collar: 14.0%

Fort Worth, Texas, has a fair claim to being the quintessential mid-American city: halfway across the continent, just west of the Balcones Escarpment that divides the dry treeless grazing lands of West Texas from the humid green croplands of East Texas, "where the blue sky begins," as its 19th century boosters proclaimed. This was the last stop for cattle drives before they returned to Kansas. It is Southern in heritage and Northern in its advanced post-industrial economy. It has the nation's longest row of Western wear shops and one of the nation's richest families, the Basses, whose steel-sheen skyscrapers, outlined at night by lights, dominate the skyline. This is where the West begins, Fort Worth boosters say; they add, as Will Rogers said, that Dallas is "where the East peters out."

Cowtown, as the city is sometimes called, is not the primitive West. In 2006, it was the 19th largest city in the nation: bigger than Boston, Charlotte and Seattle. Fort Worth has a high-tech economy and has been an aviation center since the 1940s, though one hard hit by defense cuts. The big Lockheed Martin (formerly General Dynamics) plant has produced the B-24, B-36, B-52, F-111, F-16 and F-22 bombers and fighters. Lockheed Martin is building the Joint Strike Fighter; despite cutbacks, it might stay in production for two decades. Next door is Carswell Air Force Base, the home of B-52s for years, slated for closure in 1993 but turned into a Joint Reserve Base, and expanded in the base review of 2005. The assembly lines at Bell Helicopter Textron's nearby plant were rescued when the Texas delegation and others overruled the cancellation of the accident-prone V-22 Osprey; since then, it won the contract for a new reconnaissance helicopter. There is much more to Fort Worth: *The New York Times* has called the city "an irresistible combination of cowboys and culture", in part because it has some of the nation's premier small museums, the Amon Carter Museum of Western Art designed by Philip Johnson, the Kimbell Museum designed by Louis Kahn, the Museum of Modern Art and the Sid Richardson Museum with more western art. And it has Texas-sized watering holes and eateries, like Billy Bob's Texas, the world's largest honky-tonk in the

Stockyards. Other cities have their claims, but the visitor from abroad who wants to see what is quintessentially American would be well advised to fly to Dallas/Fort Worth International Airport and head west.

The 12th Congressional District of Texas includes two-thirds of Fort Worth and western suburban Tarrant County, plus all of Parker and Wise Counties to the west and northwest. It includes the northern and western neighborhoods of the city and the affluent southwest quarter beyond Texas Christian University, downtown and the Stockyards; the heavily black areas on the east side are in the 26th District. Parker County was once windswept open land around the courthouse town of Weatherford, where former Speaker Jim Wright grew up and was first elected to the House in 1954; now it is sprouting subdivisions and growing rapidly. Fort Worth and Tarrant County stayed Democratic in the 1950s when Dallas went Republican; with Dallas recently swinging back to Democrats, Fort Worth and Tarrant have remained Republican. The 12th, represented by the Democratic Speaker of the House as recently as 1989, is now solidly Republican—67% for George W. Bush in 2004, when he got the second largest number of votes (behind Harris) of any county in Texas.

The congresswoman from the 12th District is Kay Granger, a Republican first elected in 1996. Granger grew up in Fort Worth, graduated from Texas Wesleyan College, worked as a teacher in North Richland Hills, raised three children and started her own insurance agency. In 1989 she was elected to the Fort Worth Council, and two years later was elected as the nonpartisan mayor. In 1995 Pete Geren, a conservative Democrat elected to replace Wright in 1989, announced he would not seek reelection; both Republican and Democratic leaders tried to recruit Granger. She said she was a Republican and ran in the Republican primary. Attacked as a liberal, partly for her pro-choice stand on abortion, she won 69% in a three-candidate race. Granger's Democratic opponent was Hugh Parmer, a former Fort Worth mayor and the Democratic nominee against Senator Phil Gramm in 1990. Parmer attacked Republican Medicare plans and Newt Gingrich. Granger called for a balanced budget and tax cuts for business, and ran on her record as mayor. Granger won 58%-41%, a stunning victory in Jim Wright's old district.

In the House, Granger's voting record has tended to be moderate on cultural issues and more conservative on economics. She became a favorite of Republican leaders, winning enactment of tax-free savings accounts for higher education expenses and serving as the only freshman on the health care task force. She split with most Republicans in applauding the FDA's approval of the RU-486 abortion pill and supporting embryonic stem-cell research. In response to criticism of the Wright Amendment's protection of Dallas/Fort Worth International Airport from competition by Dallas's Love Field, Granger worked to create a local regional airport authority to encourage cooperation between the DFW and Love; in 2006, she joined others from the Metroplex in repealing the Wright Amendment. Granger served on the Appropriations Committee, where her seat on the Military Construction Subcommittee allowed her to keep a close eye on local Pentagon spending. She has worked to maintain production of the F-16, the F-22, the F-35, the V-22 and the Joint Strike Fighter; Lockheed Martin has a big plant in the district. In February 2005 the Pentagon announced that production of the F-22 would cease in 2008, with only 179 of the 381 planes the Air Force wanted; Granger and others worked to reverse that decision. In June 2006, the House approved her proposal to lift the ban on sales of the F-22 to allies. Granger has come forward with original initiatives. In 2003 she and Sander Levin proposed a national gynecological cancer detection program; in January 2005 she journeyed to Iraq, where she and Ellen Tauscher conducted a training session for women candidates in their election. She has helped to create the bipartisan Anti-Terror Caucus and in 2007 Granger was elected vice-chair of the Republican Conference, the most senior woman in the House Republican leadership.

Granger has been reelected by wide margins in former Speaker Jim Wright's old district. Redistricting treated her kindly; she got some new territory, but it was solidly Republican. She is the author of the book, *What's Right About America: Celebrating Our Nation's Values*, published in 2006.

THIRTEENTH DISTRICT

Rep. Mac Thornberry (R)

Elected 1994, 7th term; b. July 15, 1958, Clarendon; home, Clarendon; TX Tech. U., B.A. 1980, U. of TX Law Schl., J.D. 1983; Presbyterian; married (Sally).

Professional Career: Legis. Cnsl., U.S. Rep. Tom Loeffler, 1983-85; Chief of Staff, U.S. Rep. Larry Combest, 1985-88; Dpty. Asst. Secy. of State for Legis. Affairs, 1988-89; Practicing atty., 1989-94; Rancher 1989-94.

DC Office: 2457 RHOB, 20515, 202-225-3706; Fax: 202-225-3486; Web site: www.house.gov/thornberry.

District Offices: Amarillo, 806-371-8844; Wichita Falls, 940-692-1700.

Committees: *Armed Services* (7th of 29 R): Terrorism, Unconventional Threats & Capabilities (RMM); Strategic Forces. *Permanent Select Committee on Intelligence* (4th of 8 R): Intelligence Community Management; Technical & Tactical Intelligence.

Group Ratings

	ADA	ACLU	AFS	LCV	ITIC	NTU	COC	ACU	CFG	FRC
2006	5	0	0	0	100	69	100	88	78	85
2005	0	—	0	0	—	67	85	100	88	100

National Journal Ratings

	2005 LIB	—	2005 CONS		2006 LIB	—	2006 CONS
Economic	0%	—	97%		16%	—	81%
Social	12%	—	86%		31%	—	68%
Foreign	27%	—	71%		17%	—	73%

Key Votes of the 109th Congress

1. Estate Tax Repeal	Y	5. Limit Interstate Abortion	Y	9. Build Border Fence	Y
2. Limit CAFE Standards	Y	6. Extend Patriot Act	Y	10. CAFTA	Y
3. FY06 Spending Curb	Y	7. Bar Same Sex Marriage	Y	11. Oppose Iraq Withdrawal	Y
4. Drilling in ANWR	Y	8. Stem Cell Research $	N	12. Detainee Tribunals	Y

Election Results

2006 general	Mac Thornberry (R)	108,107	(74%)	($551,841)
	Roger Waun (D)	33,160	(23%)	($27,384)
	Other	3,829	(3%)	
2006 primary	Mac Thornberry (R)	unopposed		
2004 general	Mac Thornberry (R)	189,448	(92%)	($383,724)
	M. J. Smith (Lib)	15,793	(8%)	

Prior Winning Percentages: 2002 (79%); 2000 (68%); 1998 (68%); 1996 (67%); 1994 (55%)

The People		Race/Ethnic Origin	Ancestry	
Area size:	40,403 sq. mi.	73.7% White	USA: 10.8%	German: 9.3%
Urban population:	69.9%	5.7% Black	Irish: 7.6%	
Rural population:	30.1%	1.1% Asian	**2004 Presidential Vote**	
Pop. 2000:	651,620	0.6% Native Am.	Bush (R) 183,375	(78%)
Pop. 2005 (est):	659,813	0.0% Hawaiian	Kerry (D) 52,431	(22%)
Median income:	$33,501	1.2% Two+ races	**2000 Presidential Vote**	
Poverty status:	14.0%	0.1% Other	Bush (R) 158,529	(74%)
Military veterans:	13.6%	17.6% Hispanic Origin	Gore (D) 56,229	(26%)
			Cook Partisan Voting Index: R +25	
Occupation	Blue collar: 27.1%	White collar: 53.3%	Gray collar: 19.7%	

Heading west in Texas, the population thins out, the land becomes browner until you can travel through whole counties containing only a few hundred people each—plus quite a few more head of cattle. And then the land rises nearly 1,000 feet in elevation, up steep hillsides from the gullies that surround the rivers that for most of the year are just tiny trickles, to the tilted tableland that is the High Plains of West Texas. The winds here sweep down from the Rockies, the land is barren except where irrigated, often with the now dangerously depleted waters of the Ogallala Aquifer, and so one passes through grazing land to cotton fields and then grazing land again. But here and there in this demanding environment—sticky-hot in the summer, swept by north winds from Canada in winter, always threatened in "Tornado Alley"—comfortable cities have been built to house the people and businesses that bring forth some of the nation's most abundant oil, natural gas, helium and other elements from the earth.

The 13th Congressional District of Texas covers more than 40,000 square miles; it extends from the New Mexico border to just north of Dallas and includes all of 42 counties and parts of two others. Population declined here in the 1980s, in some rural counties by as much as 30%, with only small gains in and around two of the three biggest cities, Wichita Falls and Amarillo. In the 1990s, the district's population increased 5%, but that was the smallest gain in any Texas district, with population still declining in most rural counties; between 2000-2005, this was one of the slowest-growing districts in the state. Around Wichita Falls is the agricultural land of the Red River Valley, dusty land with empty skylines, and one of Bell Helicopter's V-22 Osprey plants; Sheppard Air Force Base, a medical facility and pilot training center, was hit hard by cutbacks in the 2005 base review. The area claims to produce more cotton than any other congressional district, produces much of the world's milo (a variety of sorghum) and is home to one of the nation's oldest and largest cattle auctions. This was long white Anglo Texas: few blacks got this far west and there were not many Latinos either. But Latinos lately have been moving here in large numbers, to work in the fields or in crop processing. Today, the district is 6% black and 18% Hispanic. Much of the High Plains economy is based on natural resources. The largest city here is Amarillo, once the helium capital of North America (before Congress shut down production), now the center of the largest natural gas development in the world, and still—not Chicago—the windiest city in the United States. Just outside town is the Pantex plant that secretly assembled the nation's thousands of nuclear warheads and was the epicenter of American defense in the Cold War; its 16,000 acres have been used to dismantle some disarmed weapons and now maintain the remainder of the arsenal.

The Red River Valley, settled by Confederate veterans, was heavily Democratic up through the 1970s. The High Plains, settled overland from Kansas wheatlands, was for years more Republican. Both parts are now solidly Republican. The 78% that George W. Bush won here in 2004 was his third-best performance in the nation; thinly populated Ochiltree County, on the Oklahoma border, gave Bush 92%, his highest percentage of any county in the nation.

The congressman from the 13th District is Mac Thornberry, a Republican first elected in 1994. His great-great-grandfather Amos Thornberry, a Union Army veteran and staunch Republican, moved to Clay County, just east of Wichita Falls, in the 1880s; a year after Amos died in 1925, his son bought the cattle ranch that Mac Thornberry, his brothers and father now run. From the window of his ranch house, writes *The Texas Techsan*, "as far as the eye can see is the Golden Spread of Texas for which this part of the state is named. There are no buildings, no roadways, no signs of life. Gaze out long enough and you begin to think you can actually see the curvature of the earth." After college and law school in Texas, Thornberry worked for Congressmen Tom Loeffler and Larry Combest and at the State Department in Washington. He returned to practice law in West Texas. In 1994, he took on Democratic Congressman Bill Sarpalius, whom he attacked for voting for the Clinton budget and tax package. He profited from news stories about how Sarpalius did not pay a moving company that shipped his furniture to Washington, then accepted a fee for speaking at the company's convention in Las Vegas. Thornberry won 55%-45%.

In the House, Thornberry has compiled a conservative voting record, though hardly the most ideological in the Texas delegation. His hard work on defense and homeland security issues has earned him a reputation as one of the brainiest and most accessible lawmakers on those issues. In March 2001 he took the recommendations of a commission chaired by former Senators Gary Hart and Warren Rudman and sponsored the first bill to create a homeland security agency; in 2002, with Joseph Lieberman, he played a key role in creating the new department. As chairman of the Cybersecurity Subcommittee on Homeland Security, he later said that the new department had been "a huge disappointment," criticized delays in integrating its computer networks and intelligence analysis, and said that Congress must establish ways to measure how spending is deterring terrorists. On the Armed Services Committee he has championed missile defense and called for better coordination of military space programs, and became ranking Republican on the Terrorism, Unconventional Threats and Capabilities Subcommittee. On the Intelligence Committee, he chaired its oversight subcommittee and in September 2006 helped to enact new rules for the handling of terror suspects and detainees.

On domestic issues, Thornberry has pressed hard for estate tax repeal and tax credits to encourage production in marginal wells. In 2005, he introduced a bill to establish separate courts to handle medical malpractice cases. On a panel of House Republicans that investigated the aftermath of Hurricane Katrina, he called it "a chain reaction of failure." Thornberry makes the point that he is among the few members of Congress who remains personally involved in agriculture; in February 2006, he filed a bill to extend the 2002 farm bill until the Doha round of WTO negotiations is complete.

He has been reelected easily every two years.

FOURTEENTH DISTRICT

Rep. Ron Paul (R)

Elected 1996, 9th full term; b. Aug. 20, 1935, Pittsburgh, PA; home, Surfside; Gettysburg Col., B.A. 1957, Duke U., M.D. 1961; Protestant; married (Carol).

Military Career: Flight Surgeon, Air Force, 1963-68.

Elected Office: U.S. House of Reps., 1976, 1978-84.

Professional Career: Practicing physician, 1968-96.

DC Office: 203 CHOB, 20515, 202-225-2831; Web site: www.house.gov/paul.

District Offices: Galveston, 409-766-7013; Lake Jackson, 979-285-0231; Victoria, 361-576-1231.

Committees: *Financial Services* (8th of 33 R): Domestic and International Monetary Policy, Trade & Technology (RMM); Oversight & Investigations. *Foreign Affairs* (10th of 23 R): International Organizations, Human Rights & Oversight; Western Hemisphere. *Joint Economic Committee* (8th of 10 R).

Group Ratings

	ADA	ACLU	AFS	LCV	ITIC	NTU	COC	ACU	CFG	FRC
2006	45	55	17	25	33	84	60	76	83	57
2005	40	—	57	44	—	84	33	76	82	75

National Journal Ratings

	2005 LIB	—	2005 CONS		2006 LIB	—	2006 CONS
Economic	54%	—	46%		48%	—	51%
Social	55%	—	45%		56%	—	44%
Foreign	72%	—	28%		77%	—	20%

Key Votes of the 109th Congress

1. Estate Tax Repeal	Y	5. Limit Interstate Abortion	N	9. Build Border Fence	Y
2. Limit CAFE Standards	Y	6. Extend Patriot Act	N	10. CAFTA	N
3. FY06 Spending Curb	N	7. Bar Same Sex Marriage	N	11. Oppose Iraq Withdrawal	N
4. Drilling in ANWR	Y	8. Stem Cell Research $	N	12. Detainee Tribunals	N

Election Results

2006 general	Ron Paul (R)	94,380	(60%)	($1,469,488)
	Shane Sklar (D)	62,429	(40%)	($552,798)
2006 primary	Ron Paul (R)	24,086	(78%)	
	Cynthia Sinatra (R)	6,935	(22%)	
2004 general	Ron Paul (R)	unopposed		($744,969)

Prior Winning Percentages: 2002 (68%); 2000 (60%); 1998 (55%); 1996 (51%); 1982 (99%); 1980 (51%); 1978 (51%); 1976 (56%)

The People		Race/Ethnic Origin	Ancestry	
Area size:	9,369 sq. mi.	62.1% White	German: 10.7% Irish: 7.0%	
Urban population:	71.1%	9.8% Black	USA: 6.4%	
Rural population:	28.9%	1.7% Asian	**2004 Presidential Vote**	
Pop. 2000:	651,619	0.3% Native Am.	Bush (R) 169,480	(67%)
Pop. 2005 (est):	718,862	0.0% Hawaiian	Kerry (D) 82,792	(33%)
Median income:	$41,335	1.0% Two+ races	**2000 Presidential Vote**	
Poverty status:	13.3%	0.1% Other	Bush (R) 140,826	(64%)
Military veterans:	13.5%	24.9% Hispanic Origin	Gore (D) 78,634	(36%)
			Cook Partisan Voting Index: R +14	

Occupation	Blue collar: 27.8%	White collar: 56.2%	Gray collar: 16.1%

Retreating east from the Alamo, the ragtag army led by Sam Houston passed over what would become, after their bloody and conclusive victory at San Jacinto, some of the prime cropland in the Republic and later the state of Texas. The hilly and river-crossed land between Houston and Austin, named after Texas' first two leaders, was settled early. The first capital of the Republic of Texas was in Brazoria County. The flat coastal plains, steamy and humid so much of the year, were settled later when the railroads came in. Rice is grown along the coast, with cotton and cattle production inland. The Gulf of Mexico coastline, though it has plenty of inlets, never had any important ports in the stretch between Houston and Corpus Christi until the discovery of oil here made it worthwhile to build channels to ship the oil out.

This is the land of the 14th Congressional District of Texas. With rural countrysides and the cities of Victoria and El Campo, it runs along the Gulf Coast between Corpus Christi and Port Arthur. Victoria is a rail hub that serves Gulf ports; it also includes large industrial plants, such as DuPont, Union Carbide, Alcoa and BP Chemicals. Redistricting added most of hurricane-prone Galveston, on a barrier island on the Gulf. It was an immigrant port known as the Ellis Island of the West until a 1900 hurricane devastated the area and killed thousands; the city is now guarded by a 17-foot seawall and connected to the mainland by a hurricane-resistant bridge. This is a district that is mostly small-city Texas, but much of it now surrounds the suburban fringes of metropolitan Houston. This country is ancestrally Democratic but it has trended Republican since the 1980s, and voted 67% for George W. Bush in 2004.

The congressman from the 14th District is Ron Paul, a Republican first elected to Congress more than three decades ago. He failed in his only attempt to win statewide office yet twice he has run for President, once as a Libertarian candidate and once as a Republican. Paul grew up in Pennsylvania, graduated from Duke Medical School, served as an Air Force flight surgeon, then moved to Texas to practice obstetrics and gynecology in Brazoria County. Paul was dismayed when Richard Nixon cut the connection between the dollar and gold in 1971 and became interested in politics. He was elected to the House in an April 1976 special election, lost the seat by less than 300 votes in the general election seven months later, and then won the seat back in 1978. He ran for the Senate in 1984 and lost the Republican primary to Phil Gramm 73%-16%. His House seat was won by a young legislator and exterminating firm owner, Tom DeLay. In 1988, as the Libertarian candidate for president, Paul ran third with 432,000 votes, 0.47% of the total. In his first stint in the House, Paul advanced some ideas that by the mid-1990s had almost become mainstream—term limits and abolition of the income tax. Other Paul ideas remain outside the political pale: endorsing a group that wants to end all government funding of education, cutting $150 billion from the defense budget and returning to the gold standard. Paul practices what he preaches. He will not accept payment by Medicare or Medicaid, he wouldn't let his children accept federal student loans and he refuses his congressional pension. He has written several books.

Paul reentered electoral politics after Congressman Greg Laughlin switched to the GOP in June 1995. Laughlin had a moderate voting record, by no means the most conservative of Texas Democrats. Republicans offered him a seat on Ways and Means if he switched, and he did. Paul ran in 1996, raising money from his nationwide network of Libertarians, gold bugs and subscribers to the *Ron Paul Political Report*. Laughlin led in the primary with 43% of the vote, but Paul won the runoff 54%-46%. Democrats ran Charles "Lefty" Morris, a former president of the state trial lawyers' association. Morris ("Lefty is right") hit Paul for favoring abolition of the minimum wage, repealing federal anti-drug laws and anti-prostitution laws. Paul ran 1% ahead of Bob Dole and won 51%-48%.

With his libertarian views, Paul's voting record is anything but rock-solid Republican; *National Journal* ratings place him near the middle of the House. He never votes for legislation that is not expressly authorized by the Constitution, he says. Frequently, his insistence on limited government made Paul the House's lonely dissenter—against bills to require states to report on their progress in improving student achievement, to award Congressional Gold Medals to Rosa Parks and Pope John Paul II, to pass the Patriot Act after September 11, to spend money on homeland security. He favors relaxation of restrictions on illegal drugs, and he filed a lawsuit challenging the McCain-Feingold campaign finance act as a violation of the First Amendment. After his district in September 2005 was rocked by Hurricane Rita, he voted against hurricane relief.

Paul voted against the constitutional ban on same-sex marriages; and says that the states should set such policy. He deliberately delivers little pork to his district. Paul's isolationist views on foreign policy made his voting record on those issues indistinct from many liberal Democrats. He was the only Republican to vote "present" on the resolution expressing support for the military forces at the start of the war with Iraq. In June 2005, he cosponsored with Dennis Kucinich and others a resolution to withdraw from Iraq. In February 2007, he was one of 17 House Republicans who voted for the resolution opposing the military surge in Iraq. He supports virtually no role for the U.S. government overseas—from military defense to international trade; he calls himself a "non-interventionist," not an isolationist. In a July 2003 speech in the House, which he called "Neo-Conned!", he harshly attacked the Bush administration and its supporters. "The so-called conservative revolution of the past two decades has given us massive growth in government size, spending and regulation." His iconoclasm makes him probably the least dependable and persuadable Republican in the House, and it explains why many liberals have begun to praise him. And he does offer alternatives: He has been among the most prolific legislators, sponsoring dozens of bills and amendments each year. Typically, none have passed.

For a while, Paul appeared on House Democrats' target lists, but he easily survived. Democrats have virtually no chance in this district but Paul is not impervious to a serious challenge in the Republican primary. In January 2007, he announced his candidacy for the Republican presidential nomination, with his slogan, "The Taxpayers' Best Friend." Paul drew widespread attention—and the ire of former New York City Mayor Rudy Giuliani—when he suggested during a May 2007 Republican debate that interventionist American foreign policy led to the 9/11 attacks. "They attack us because we've been over there," he said. "We've been bombing Iraq for 10 years."

Despite the long odds against him, it may be unwise to underestimate someone who has managed to be elected to the House 10 times in four decades. If he did not win the presidential nomination, he said that he would seek reelection to the House in 2008. It seemed likely that he would face primary opposition because of his anti-war stance; former Paul aide Eric Dondero and Chris Peden, a Friendswood city councilman, both said they were running for the Republican nomination.

FIFTEENTH DISTRICT

Rep. Ruben Hinojosa (D)

Elected 1996, 6th term; b. Aug. 20, 1940, Mercedes; home, Mercedes; U. of TX, B.B.A. 1962, M.B.A. 1980; Catholic; married (Marty).

Elected Office: TX Bd. of Educ., 1974-84.

Professional Career: Pres. & CEO, H&H Foods Inc., 1962-present.

DC Office: 2463 RHOB, 20515, 202-225-2531; Fax: 202-225-5688; Web site: www.house.gov/hinojosa.

District Offices: Beeville, 361-358-8400; Edinburg, 956-682-5545.

Committees: *Education & Labor* (7th of 27 D): Higher Education, Lifelong Learning & Competitiveness (Chmn.); Early Childhood, Elementary & Secondary Education. *Financial Services* (14th of 37 D): Capital Markets, Insurance & Government Sponsored Enterprises; Financial Institutions & Consumer Credit. *Foreign Affairs* (19th of 27 D): Europe; Asia, the Pacific & the Global Environment.

Group Ratings

	ADA	ACLU	AFS	LCV	ITIC	NTU	COC	ACU	CFG	FRC
2006	60	79	86	42	86	21	87	36	29	42
2005	80	—	100	33	—	21	74	44	27	25

National Journal Ratings

	2005 LIB	—	2005 CONS		2006 LIB	—	2006 CONS
Economic	58%	—	42%		59%	—	41%
Social	65%	—	35%		64%	—	36%
Foreign	74%	—	26%		63%	—	36%

Key Votes of the 109th Congress

1. Estate Tax Repeal	Y	5. Limit Interstate Abortion	Y	9. Build Border Fence	N
2. Limit CAFE Standards	N	6. Extend Patriot Act	*	10. CAFTA	Y
3. FY06 Spending Curb	N	7. Bar Same Sex Marriage	*	11. Oppose Iraq Withdrawal	N
4. Drilling in ANWR	Y	8. Stem Cell Research $	Y	12. Detainee Tribunals	N

Election Results

2006 special	Ruben Hinojosa (D)	43,236	(62%)	($497,420)
	Paul Haring (R)	16,601	(24%)	
	Eddie Zamora (R)	10,150	(15%)	($13,841)
2006 primary	Ruben Hinojosa (D)	unopposed		
2004 general	Ruben Hinojosa (D)	96,089	(58%)	($818,826)
	Michael Thamm (R)	67,917	(41%)	($49,898)
	Other	2,352	(1%)	

Prior Winning Percentages: 2002 (100%); 2000 (88%); 1998 (58%); 1996 (62%)

The People		Race/Ethnic Origin	Ancestry	
Area size:	10,849 sq. mi.	19.7% White	German: 4.6%	USA: 2.7%
Urban population:	82.1%	1.7% Black	English: 2.4%	
Rural population:	17.9%	0.5% Asian	**2004 Presidential Vote**	
Pop. 2000:	651,625	0.1% Native Am.	Bush (R) 81,280	(51%)
Median income:	$26,840	0.0% Hawaiian	Kerry (D) 77,011	(49%)
Poverty status:	30.5%	0.3% Two+ races	**2000 Presidential Vote**	
Military veterans:	9.3%	0.0% Other	Gore (D) 78,001	(54%)
		77.6% Hispanic Origin	Bush (R) 65,409	(46%)
			Cook Partisan Voting Index: D + 3	

Occupation   Blue collar: 25.9%   White collar: 52.1%   Gray collar: 22.0%

The Lower Rio Grande Valley of south Texas is one of America's 20th century frontiers. A century ago, there was little here but desert wilderness. Only a handful of people lived anywhere near the shallow, sluggish Rio Grande; there was no Border Patrol because in this desert land very few people bothered to cross it. Then came pioneers like Lloyd Bentsen Sr., father of the former senator and Treasury secretary, who arrived after World War I with $5 in his pocket and became one of the biggest Valley landowners. Bentsen and others cleared the land and dug canals, hired Mexican and Mexican-American workers, and with irrigated water from the Rio Grande planted citrus groves, cornfields and palm windbreaks, ran cattle and drilled for oil and gas. Along U.S. 83 north of the Rio Grande these pioneers built a string of towns with Anglo names and storefronts. But most of the people here were Latino in culture and language. Wage levels higher than in Mexico (though low by U.S. standards) brought more Mexicans over the border. Though incomes are low, so is the cost of living—which makes this a haven for shoppers and for "winter Texan" retirees coming from the North in their RVs. The days are past when ranchers and oilmen wielded absolute political power here. There is instead a robust, mostly Hispanic, politics.

The 15th Congressional District of Texas is one of three districts dividing up the Lower Rio Grande Valley. It has gone through four iterations in this decade alone; the court-drawn redistricting plan in August 2006 imposed modest changes. Some 72% of its residents live just north of the river in Hidalgo and Cameron Counties, in or near the string of towns from McAllen to Harlingen. Reasonably priced real estate has helped make this the third-fastest growing metro area in the nation: Hidalgo and Cameron Counties' population rose 60% from 1990 to 2004, from 644,000 to 1,030,000. The local infrastructure has barely kept up as subdivisions have replaced citrus groves and traffic congestion has become routine. In the McAllen area, some who live in these new suburbs work just across the border as corporate managers in the low-wage *maquiladora* factories. Yet there is great poverty here also: Hidalgo County, which is the most heavily populated county along the border, and Cameron County, are among the poorest counties in the nation. Hidalgo has the lowest median family income of any large county in the nation.

The 15th also stretches north through a narrow corridor of rural land between Corpus Christi and San Antonio, including Duval County, which occasionally has been the most Democratic county in the United States, and where boss George Parr provided the key votes Lyndon Johnson needed for his 87-vote victory in the 1948 Democratic Senate runoff. The latest redistricting eliminated Bastrop County, which had been added in 2003. The changes reduced the number of counties in the 15th from 13 to 12 and increased its Hispanic percentage to 78%. The changes made the 15th more favorably Democratic.

The congressman from the 15th District is Ruben Hinojosa, a Democrat first elected in 1996. His background is not in politics but in business and civic affairs. He grew up in Mercedes, where his family owns H&H Foods, which produces Mexican foods and beef patties and is one of the largest employers in the Valley. Hinojosa graduated from the University of Texas, then went into the family business and was active in civic affairs, primarily in education and regional development. He served on the state Board of Education and led an effort to create three regional magnet schools. After former House Agriculture Committee Chairman Kika de la Garza announced he would not seek reelection, Hinojosa ran. In the Democratic primary he led Anglo lawyer Jim Selman 34%-33%. Selman questioned Hinojosa's Democratic credentials and said he profited from government contracts. Hinojosa emphasized his interest in improving educational opportunities and extending highways to the Lower Rio Grande Valley. Not the kind of liberal who leads most national and Texas Hispanic organizations, he called for reducing the capital gains tax and giving investment tax credits to those making capital improvements. Hinojosa won the runoff 52%-48% and easily won the general.

Hinojosa has had a moderate-to-conservative voting record among House Democrats. He has sought to protect benefits for legal immigrants, to promote NAFTA and to demand that Mexico deliver on its agreement for water to south Texas farmers. He has a proclivity for holding out on votes to make last-minute legislative deals. He was one of only two undecided congressmen, the other was Democrat Gregory Meeks, who took up Bill Clinton's offer of a visit to China to assess whether to approve normal trade relations; Hinojosa got assurances of funding for the Cross-Border Institute for Regional Development before voting for it. He again was one of the final members to decide on George W. Bush's proposal for trade promotion authority. He went along after a handshake with Tom DeLay on the House floor in a deal for earmarked funding for a job training project that Hinojosa wanted. Likewise, he was a late decider for the Central American Free Trade Agreement.

He had support in 2003 from the Texas delegation for a Democratic opening on Ways and Means, but it went to Max Sandlin, and Hinojosa became ranking Democrat on the Select Education Subcommittee, with jurisdiction over historically black and Hispanic colleges; in the majority, Hinojosa chaired the Higher Education, Life Long Learning and Competitiveness Subcommittee, and focused on families traditionally left behind in American education. He has called efforts to make English the official language of the nation "a code for official discrimination." With Judy Biggert, he co-founded the Financial and Economic Literary Caucus. In 2006, he helped to enact a revision of the Older Americans Act, with national guidelines for nutrition and transportation services.

In early 2005, Hinojosa made an unsuccessful leadership bid. He announced that he was running for vice-chairman of the Democratic Caucus, whenever James Clyburn moved up to replace Bob Menendez as caucus chairman. But he abandoned his candidacy within two weeks, a sign that Hinojosa's politics are not a perfect fit in the Democratic Caucus.

After breezing to reelection in 2000 and 2002, Hinojosa faced serious opposition in 2004, largely because of redistricting. Republican Michael Thamm, a plumbing contractor and former mayor of Cuero in DeWitt County, one of the counties added to the district, received little national attention or party support. He sounded standard Republican themes and spent only $50,000; Hinojosa spent $819,000 and devoted more time than in the past to reminding voters that he favored school prayer and opposed abortion. Thamm won the six most northern counties 60%-38%. But in Hidalgo County, which cast 37% of the vote (though it had 50% of the population), Hinojosa won 70%-29%. He won 58%-41% overall. He reached out to constituents in the northern end of the district, who before 2003 had no reason to know anything about him; he impressed local officials, even Republicans, with his hard work and moderate voting record. In 2005 he switched and voted for the Republicans' class action bill. "Some of my colleagues said, 'Ruben, you are not being consistent,' but it is a different congressional district." The 2006 redistricting returned Hinojosa to firmer footing—it removed 4 of the 6 troublesome northern counties Hinojosa lost in 2004, including Bastrop County. Hinojosa then resumed his tradition of an easy reelection, winning 62% in a special November 2006 election against two Republican candidates who opposed abortion and backed a ban on gay marriage.

SIXTEENTH DISTRICT

Rep. Silvestre Reyes (D)

Elected 1996, 6th term; b. Nov. 10, 1944, Canutillo; home, El Paso; El Paso Commun. Col., A.A. 1977; Catholic; married (Carolina).

Military Career: Army, 1966-68 (Vietnam).

Elected Office: Canutillo Schl. Board, 1968-70.

Professional Career: Border Patrol Agent, 1969-95.

DC Office: 2433 RHOB, 20515, 202-225-4831; Fax: 202-225-2016; Web site: www.house.gov/reyes.

District Offices: El Paso, 915-534-4400.

Committees: *Armed Services* (6th of 34 D): Readiness; Strategic Forces; Air & Land Forces. *Permanent Select Committee on Intelligence* (Chmn. of 12 D).

Group Ratings

	ADA	ACLU	AFS	LCV	ITIC	NTU	COC	ACU	CFG	FRC
2006	80	71	100	33	43	17	57	36	18	14
2005	80	—	100	39	—	19	60	41	15	25

National Journal Ratings

	2005 LIB	—	2005 CONS		2006 LIB	—	2006 CONS
Economic	59%	—	41%		60%	—	40%
Social	63%	—	36%		65%	—	35%
Foreign	62%	—	38%		70%	—	30%

Key Votes of the 109th Congress

1. Estate Tax Repeal	N	5. Limit Interstate Abortion	Y	9. Build Border Fence	N
2. Limit CAFE Standards	Y	6. Extend Patriot Act	Y	10. CAFTA	N
3. FY06 Spending Curb	*	7. Bar Same Sex Marriage	N	11. Oppose Iraq Withdrawal	N
4. Drilling in ANWR	Y	8. Stem Cell Research $	Y	12. Detainee Tribunals	N

Election Results

2006 general	Silvestre Reyes (D)	61,116	(79%)	($681,551)
	Gordon Strickland (Lib)	16,572	(21%)	
2006 primary	Silvestre Reyes (D)	unopposed		
2004 general	Silvestre Reyes (D)	108,577	(68%)	($618,785)
	David Brigham (R)	49,972	(31%)	($27,985)
	Other	2,224	(1%)	

Prior Winning Percentages: 2002 (100%); 2000 (68%); 1998 (88%); 1996 (71%)

The People		Race/Ethnic Origin	Ancestry	
Area size:	582 sq. mi.	17.4% White	German: 3.9%	Irish: 2.6%
Urban population:	98.3%	2.9% Black	USA: 2.4%	
Rural population:	1.7%	0.9% Asian	**2004 Presidential Vote**	
Pop. 2000:	651,619	0.3% Native Am.	Kerry (D) 92,792	(56%)
Pop. 2005 (est):	695,655	0.1% Hawaiian	Bush (R) 71,454	(44%)
Median income:	$31,245	0.7% Two+ races	**2000 Presidential Vote**	
Poverty status:	23.6%	0.1% Other	Gore (D) 81,874	(59%)
Military veterans:	11.6%	77.7% Hispanic Origin	Bush (R) 56,283	(41%)
			Cook Partisan Voting Index: D + 9	

Occupation   Blue collar: 24.7%   White collar: 58.1%   Gray collar: 17.2%

El Paso, Texas, and Juarez, Mexico, face each other across the narrow Rio Grande, their tree-shaded streets spread out below the rough brown face of Comanche Peak. The two border cities are surrounded by hundreds of miles of some of North America's most rugged and desolate landscape, 600 miles from Dallas-Fort Worth. There is much history here: Texas claims the first Thanksgiving took place in San Elizario near El Paso in 1598, and there were Spanish conquistadors coming through the pass of the north, El Paso del Norte, on their way to Santa Fe years before that. In the 1950s, El Paso and Juarez each had a population of 140,000; the 2006, there were 736,000 in El Paso County (about 80% Hispanic) and the Mexican census counted 1.2 million in metro Juarez. This is a bilingual, bicultural pair of cities, where most people have a Mexican heritage; the thrust of growth comes from the fertile union of a Spanish-speaking people and an English-speaking economy. El Paso is one of the lowest-wage and lowest-education locales in the U.S., and the fourth-poorest county in the nation; Juarez is one of the highest-wage in Mexico. Cotton is the predominant local crop, and the city is known as a boot-making center. Maquiladora plants pioneered a cross-border economy and NAFTA strengthened it, and it is not all low-skill either; south of the border, there are a big General Motors technical center and manufacturers from around the world. Big companies have moved back-office jobs to El Paso. The local Tigua Indians, who built a large casino here, were among the victims of convicted lobbyist Jack Abramoff.

The 16th Congressional District of Texas is made up of 96% of El Paso County—the city itself, the suburban fringe and giant Fort Bliss to the north and the colonias, most without electricity and running water, spread out to the east and south. Fort Bliss was a big winner in the 2005 base closing review, with a net gain of about 16,000 soldiers, including the First Armored Division that was based in Germany. A key factor: The military and the city cooperated to build the largest inland desalination facility in the world. El Paso feels distant from the rest of Texas—it's closer to Los Angeles than to Beaumont, and El Paso is in a different time zone from the rest of the state. As governor, George W. Bush paid close attention to El Paso, and in his 1998 reelection he won the county 50%-49%—notable, given the overwhelmingly Latino electorate. Bush got 41% against Al Gore and 44% against John Kerry in this district. With its geographic isolation and heavily Hispanic population, this was the only district unchanged by redistricting since 2003.

The congressman from the 16th District is Silvestre Reyes, a Democrat first elected in 1996. He grew up on a farm in Canutillo, five miles north of El Paso, the oldest of 10 children; he went to college in El Paso and Austin. He served in the Army in Vietnam, where he lost hearing in one ear during an enemy rocket attack; then he "took as many civil service tests as I could, and the Border Patrol called" in 1969. He worked for the Immigration and Naturalization Service in four cities in Texas and Glynco, Georgia, and returned to El Paso in 1993 as chief patrol agent. When he got there he found that "people could basically cross the border at any time, wherever they wanted to." More than 40 boatmen ran "what were essentially international ferries" with 8,000 illegals crossing the border every day. Reyes started Operation Hold the Line, positioning 400 officers on the border instead of trying to intercept illegals after they had already crossed into El Paso (amazingly enough, that had been firmly-rooted INS policy). Mexico complained about threats to its sovereignty, merchants worried about loss of sales, homeowners fretted about finding domestic help, border agents feared losing credit for apprehending aliens. But the innovative Reyes reduced the flow of illegals here by more than half; the move was almost universally popular north of the border and was accepted to the south.

With local name recognition at 65%, Reyes retired from the INS in November 1995 and ran for Congress. He talked of the need for integrity and common sense. His target was Ron Coleman, a Democrat around whom scandals swirled: he had 673 overdrafts at the House bank and Texas Attorney General Dan Morales accused him of trying to block prosecution of a local developer. In December, Coleman announced he was retiring, and he and labor unions backed Jose Luis Sanchez, his legislative assistant. Sanchez attacked Reyes as a crypto-Republican and for backing a capital gains tax cut. Reyes hewed to his moderate platform, including more high-tech jobs, more highways and border crossings. Reyes led the primary 42%-28%; Sanchez and the unions pressed hard in the runoff, but Reyes won 51%-49% and easily took the general.

In the House, Reyes' voting record has been moderate-to-conservative among Democrats. He said that the permanent solution for the border is economic stabilization for Mexico and spoke out against decertification of Mexico for its drug enforcement record, saying it would upset the Mexican economy. He backed retraining for workers displaced by NAFTA, which he said has been a great success overall, and he praised President Bush for calling for a guest-worker program. On the Armed Services Committee, Reyes has been a supporter of the missile-defense program; he worked to protect Fort Bliss from possible base closing, and he claimed credit when additional soldiers were stationed there. He opposed the use of force in Iraq, and criticized the intelligence failures in Iraq in the months before the war, but he later called for a troop increase in Iraq to dismantle the militias. He criticized the embedding of reporters with military units as a bad idea because "it provides the enemy with propaganda." With California's David Dreier, Reyes proposed a digitized Social Security identification card for all immigrants seeking a job in the United States. He opposed placing a fence along the border as impractical and "a waste of federal dollars," and preferred an increase in federal personnel and resources. In December 2006, Nancy Pelosi bypassed Jane Harman and Alcee Hastings for their separate transgressions, and selected "Silver" to chair the Select Intelligence Committee. She cited his "impeccable national security credentials . . . .When tough questions are required, whether they relate to intelligence shortcomings before the 9/11 attacks or the war in Iraq, or to the quality of intelligence on Iran or North Korea, he does not hesitate to ask them." As chairman, he got the Justice Department to turn over previously withheld documents from the surveillance program of the National Security Agency, and he voiced doubt about the "hyped" claims of the Bush administration that Iran was interfering in Iraq. But Reyes drew unflattering news coverage after a reporter asked him whether the al Qaeda network is Sunni or Shia and he answered, "Al Qaeda, they have both...Predominantly—probably Shiite"—an egregious mistake for the Intelligence Committee chairman to make.

As then-chairman of the all-Democratic Hispanic Caucus, Reyes set a goal of electing an additional six to 10 Hispanics to Congress in the 2002 election. But Anglo and black Democrats concentrated on protecting incumbents in California, Texas and Florida, and only two new Hispanic Democrats were elected, in California and Arizona. Reyes urged the four Hispanic Republicans to return to the Hispanic Caucus, but they demanded that the caucus support free elections in Cuba; the deep divisions on Fidel Castro among Hispanic Democrats made that a non-starter. At home, Reyes has not been seriously challenged. In 2006, one potential challenger in the primary failed to pay the filing fee, and another lacked enough signatures on his petition.

SEVENTEENTH DISTRICT

Rep. Chet Edwards (D)

Elected 1990, 9th term; b. Nov. 24, 1951, Corpus Christi; home, Waco; TX A&M U., B.A. 1974, Harvard U., M.B.A. 1981; Methodist; married (Lea Ann).

Elected Office: TX Senate, 1982-90.

Professional Career: Legis. & Dist. Dir., U.S. Rep. Olin Teague, 1975-77; Marketing Rep., Trammell Crow Co., 1981-85; Pres., Edwards Communications, 1985-90.

DC Office: 2369 RHOB, 20515, 202-225-6105; Fax: 202-225-0350; Web site: edwards.house.gov.

District Offices: Cleburne, 817-645-4743; College Station, 979-691-8797; Waco, 254-752-9600.

Committees: *Appropriations* (14th of 37 D): Military Construction, Veterans Affairs & Related Agencies (Chmn.); Energy & Water Development; Homeland Security. *Budget* (3d of 22 D).

Group Ratings

	ADA	ACLU	AFS	LCV	ITIC	NTU	COC	ACU	CFG	FRC
2006	55	55	57	17	71	28	87	68	38	42
2005	85	—	100	39	—	22	74	36	22	31

National Journal Ratings

	2005 LIB	—	2005 CONS	2006 LIB	—	2006 CONS
Economic	55%	—	45%	55%	—	45%
Social	56%	—	43%	56%	—	43%
Foreign	63%	—	36%	51%	—	48%

Key Votes of the 109th Congress

1. Estate Tax Repeal	Y	5. Limit Interstate Abortion	Y	9. Build Border Fence	Y
2. Limit CAFE Standards	Y	6. Extend Patriot Act	Y	10. CAFTA	N
3. FY06 Spending Curb	N	7. Bar Same Sex Marriage	Y	11. Oppose Iraq Withdrawal	Y
4. Drilling in ANWR	Y	8. Stem Cell Research $	Y	12. Detainee Tribunals	Y

Election Results

2006 general	Chet Edwards (D)	92,478	(58%)	($3,138,215)
	Van Taylor (R)	64,142	(40%)	($2,515,527)
	Other	2,504	(2%)	
2006 primary	Chet Edwards (D)	unopposed		
2004 general	Chet Edwards (D)	125,309	(51%)	($2,664,661)
	Arlene Wohlgemuth (R)	116,049	(47%)	($2,562,877)
	Other	3,390	(1%)	

Prior Winning Percentages: 2002 (52%); 2000 (55%); 1998 (82%); 1996 (57%); 1994 (59%); 1992 (67%); 1990 (53%)

The People		Race/Ethnic Origin	Ancestry	
Area size:	7,808 sq. mi.	71.4% White	German: 10.6%	USA: 8.2%
Urban population:	64.2%	10.3% Black	Irish: 7.4%	
Rural population:	35.8%	1.4% Asian	**2004 Presidential Vote**	
Pop. 2000:	651,620	0.4% Native Am.	Bush (R) 172,355	(70%)
Pop. 2005 (est):	705,902	0.1% Hawaiian	Kerry (D) 74,358	(30%)
Median income:	$35,253	1.0% Two+ races	**2000 Presidential Vote**	
Poverty status:	17.0%	0.1% Other	Bush (R) 140,611	(68%)
Military veterans:	12.6%	15.4% Hispanic Origin	Gore (D) 66,307	(32%)
			Cook Partisan Voting Index: R +18	

Occupation	Blue collar: 26.5%	White collar: 57.2%	Gray collar: 16.3%

Waco, at the intersection of lines from Dallas to Austin and Houston to Amarillo, is arguably the geographic and cultural heart of Texas. The city was named after Indians the Mexicans called Huacos; by the late 19th century it was one of the largest cotton markets in the world, a rip-roaring town with legalized prostitution and with a graceful ox-cart-wide suspension bridge across the Brazos which, when it opened in 1870, was the longest single-span suspension bridge in the United States and the second longest in the world. The bridge brought the Chisholm Trail to Waco. In 1885 a Waco pharmacist concocted the first Dr. Pepper; you can still visit the Dr. Pepper Museum downtown. Not far away is Baylor University, the oldest college in Texas and the largest Baptist university in the world, which moved here in 1886. Waco was the home in these years of atheist William Cowper Brann, author and publisher of The Iconoclast magazine, who was shot down in the streets but managed to kill his attacker. Waco is remembered now as the site of the tragedy of February 1993, when agents of the Bureau of Alcohol, Tobacco and Firearms moved in on David Koresh's Branch Davidian compound, Ranch Apocalypse, near Waco, and Koresh and many of his followers were burned to death in the ensuing fire. In Waco's McLennan County also is the tiny town of Crawford, with its Rainey Creek, which traverses George W. Bush's 1,583-acre Prairie Chapel Ranch. Waco is only a little more than an hour away from the gallerias of the Dallas-Fort Worth Metroplex, but it is still in touch with Texas's rural roots, with the days when cotton was the basis of Texas's economy.

The 17th Congressional District of Texas includes all of nine counties and parts of three more but is centered on Waco and two other population centers. To the north is fast-growing Johnson County, directly south of Fort Worth, and Hood and Somervell Counties just to the west. Once almost entirely rural, with odd settlements like the Mennonites in Grandview, this is now exurban territory. The other population center is Brazos County, whose largest city, College Station, is home to Texas A&M University. Its agricultural and military tradition sets it apart from the University of Texas; it has a more conservative atmosphere and is the site of the George H.W. Bush Presidential Library. It is a world-class university, with 49,000 students; its president until December 2006 was Robert Gates, former CIA director and now Defense Secretary, and it has opened a campus in Qatar. The political tradition in central Texas for over a century was Democratic, heavily so. This area voted for Democrat Hubert Humphrey in 1968, when most of the rural South went for George Wallace and Richard Nixon; it voted Democratic when Texas first elected a Republican governor in 1978 and voted for Democrat Ann Richards, a Waco native, in 1990. But it seems to have followed most of Texas and become Republican. George W. Bush carried the area when running for governor in 1994 and 1998; the district voted 68% for him for president in 2000 and 70% in 2004. This was in effect a new district created by the Republican redistricters in October 2003. Only 7% of its residents lived in the old 17th District, which stretched far to the west; it includes parts of six old districts.

The congressman from the 17th District is Chet Edwards, a Democrat first elected in 1990, and only the third congressman from the Waco-centered district since 1937. Edwards is one of those highly skilled and motivated Democrats who has made politics his life—and who kept the Texas legislature and the U.S. House Democratic for so many years. He grew up in Corpus Christi, was a junior golf champion; he played against Ben Crenshaw and decided not to become a golf pro. "After playing in the same junior events he did, I realized the Lord had a different plan for me, and I'd better spend more time in the library." He graduated from Texas A&M, where he studied economics under Phil Gramm, then a conservative Democrat. He got the attention of 6th District Congressman Olin Teague when he invited Ralph Nader to a campus event: Teague berated Edwards at first, but was impressed enough to hire him as his district director when he graduated from A&M. In 1978, Teague retired after 42 years in the House and Edwards, at 26, ran for the seat. In the Democratic primary, Edwards wound up in third place, just 115 votes behind Phil Gramm, who went on to win the seat; if Edwards had won just 116 more votes, a lot of Texas and national political history would be different. Edwards went off to Harvard to get an M.B.A., returned and moved to Duncanville in southwest Dallas County, and at age 31 ran for the state Senate in 1982 and won.

In 1990 when 11th District Democrat Marvin Leath retired, Edwards moved his residence to Waco, and ran for the 11th District seat unopposed in the Democratic primary. With a promise of an Armed Services Committee slot from Speaker Thomas Foley and strong support from Leath, Edwards won a 53%-47% victory. In the House, Edwards worked for Fort Hood and eventually won a seat on Appropriations, where he claims credit for more than $700 million in construction there. When Democrats were in the majority Edwards took conservative stands on some but by no means all issues. He voted against the Brady bill but for the assault weapons ban and the 1994 crime bill.

After Democrats lost their majority in 1994, Minority Leader Dick Gephardt asked Edwards to serve as one of four chief deputy whips. Edwards accepted, but promptly voted for the Contract with America's balanced budget amendment and line-item veto. In 1998 and 1999 he led opposition to the school-prayer constitutional amendment and opposed a resolution for a national day of prayer and fasting after the Columbine shootings in 1999. Later that year, he sponsored an amendment to ban government funds for "pervasively sectarian" groups. He has been critical of George W. Bush's proposals to fund services provided by faith-based organizations; he also opposed the partial-birth abortion ban. On several measures, he has worked with the Democratic leadership, supporting a waiting period for sales at gun shows and opposing repeal of the estate tax. He has voted for oil drilling in the Arctic National Wildlife Refuge and for the constitutional amendment to ban same-sex marriage. He has not been shy about using his seat on Appropriations to fund local projects.

In the years running up to the 2003 redistricting, Edwards won reelection in an increasingly Republican district by narrowing margins. In 2000, against retired Texaco executive Ramsey Farley, who raised over $500,000 and attacked him on education, taxes and abortion, he won 55%-44%. In 2002 Farley ran again and national Republicans ran ads against Edwards arguing that he had the voting record of a Northeastern liberal. Edwards argued that he supported Bush on terrorism, education, welfare, energy and the Iraq war resolution. Edwards gleefully pointed out that Farley had said he "very vehemently" opposed Bush's education bill. Edwards spent $1.6 million to Farley's $614,000. Yet he won by only a 52%-47% margin.

In January 2003 Edwards resigned his position as chief deputy whip to spend more time on district affairs. When the new district lines were announced in October 2003 it was obvious he would face a serious challenge. The Republicans nominated state Representative Arlene Wohlgemuth from Johnson County. She made a name in the legislature for the "Memorial Day massacre" in 1997, when in retaliation for the defeat of a parental consent bill she made a point of order that killed 52 bills, many sponsored by Republicans; the parental consent law was passed in 1999. In 2003, when Republicans finally won a majority in the state House, she shepherded through a reorganization of the state's health and human services department which, among other things, reduced enrollment in the CHIP children's health program.

Now Edwards was facing an experienced and aggressive challenger in a district sure to vote for its local president by more than a 2–1 margin. "I am proud that I will be receiving the vote of President George W. Bush," Wohlgemuth frequently proclaimed. In the race for speaker, she said, she would not vote for "Nancy Pelosi of San Francisco." Her ads showed her with George W. Bush at the top of the stairs to Air Force One. She attacked Edwards for voting against the partial-birth abortion ban. "This is a Republican district. It deserves to have a conservative Republican representing it." Edwards responded aggressively. He attacked her as overly partisan. "While Mrs. Wohlgemuth is focusing on partisanship on every breath in this campaign, I find voters feel strongly, including Republicans, that we need less partisanship in Washington, not more." And he repeatedly charged that her health and human services bill had removed 147,000 children from the CHIP program; she said the real number was 26,000. He argued that his seniority and his seat on the Appropriations Committee made him much better positioned to help the district, and he cited the projects he had funded; he pledged to fight to keep the threatened Waco VA hospital open. "I respect President Bush, and I have strongly supported him in his war on terror and his energy and education bills. But my philosophy has never changed. When I think an administration is doing right for district and country, I will support them. When it is not, I respectfully disagree."

It seemed obvious that both candidates would carry their home bases and so they campaigned heavily elsewhere, with frequent debates—two in one day in October. Brazos County was a key battleground. Edwards signed off in his ads for the Bryan-College Station TV market by saying, "I'm Chet Edwards, Class of '74, and I approved this message." Wohlgemuth reminded locals that her two daughters had graduated from A&M and that therefore she was an "Aggie mom." Both candidates stayed off expensive Dallas-Fort Worth TV for most of the campaign, but advertised elsewhere. Edwards spent $2.7 million to her $2.6 million. Wohlgemuth raised money from local and national conservatives and was the beneficiary of $325,000 in national Republican ads. Edwards raised large sums from the unions and trial lawyers who had been his allies since his days in the Texas Senate. Edwards was one of six white male Democratic incumbents in Texas seriously threatened by the 2003 redistricting (another one retired), and he was the only one to win, by a 51%-47% margin. In McLennan and Bosque Counties, the only two counties in his old 11th District, he led 63%-36%, a big improvement over his 2002 showing there, and an impressive 30% ahead of John Kerry. In Johnson County and the two adjacent counties in the DFW media market, Wohlgemuth led 61%-37%, running 13% behind Bush. Edwards ran ahead of Wohlgemuth by 268 votes in Brazos County and carried all but one of the smaller counties, running ahead 55%-44%.

After the election Edwards continued to talk about the need for bipartisanship and approached DeLay on the House floor and urged that they cooperate on Texas issues. He said he would continue to look after Fort Hood on the Military Construction Subcommittee though it is no longer in his district. As ranking Democrat on the appropriations subcommittee handling veterans' programs and military construction, he supported an additional $1.2 billion for veterans health care beyond discretionary spending limits after Veterans Affairs admitted in June 2005 that it had underestimated those costs by $1 billion. After the House passed an $82.6 billion appropriation in November 2005 he warned that VA was still underestimating demand for health care services. He and Republican Walter Jones sponsored a bill in March 2006 to block the Defense Department from raising Tricare fees for military retirees under 65. Although a VA commission recommended closing the Waco veterans hospital in 2003, it was ordered kept open in December 2006 after a lobbying effort by Edwards and Senators Kay Bailey Hutchison and John Cornyn. Edwards was not always successful. He failed to get the Republican leadership to pass his subcommittee's appropriation in December 2006 and was unable to prevent the transfer of a net 5,000 troops from Fort Hood in June 2005. But he did get $16 million for Waco-based L 3 Communications to refurbish border security planes and $1.6 million for nuclear terrorism research at Texas A&M.

In April 2005 Edwards accepted an invitation from his most famous constituent to take his first ride on Air Force One. But this did not mean an end to Republican efforts to defeat him. Two candidates ran in the March 2006 primary, Iraq war veteran Van Taylor and former Dallas Congressman Pete Sessions aide Tucker Anderson. Anderson had roots in the College Station area; Taylor grew up in Midland, graduated from Harvard and served in the Marine Corps, and in 2005 moved from Dallas to a town near Waco. Taylor far outspent Anderson in the primary and ran negative ads. But despite the support of NRCC Chairman Tom Reynolds, who perhaps belatedly realized that Taylor was the only Iraq war veteran running as a Republican in the country while at least nine were running as Democrats, Taylor won the primary by only a 54%-46% margin. Some 32,000 voted in the Republican primary and only 12,000 in the uncontested Democratic primary— not a good sign for Edwards. But he promptly unleashed attacks on Taylor, pointing out that he had only recently moved into the district (although Edwards himself moved from Dallas County to Waco to run in 1990) and asking exactly how much Exxon Mobil stock Taylor owned (his disclosure forms said it was between $5 million and $25 million). Once again Dick Cheney and Dennis Hastert came into the district to campaign for the Republican, while Edwards raised some $3 million. In the more Democratic climate of 2006, Edwards won by his widest margin in the decade, 58%-40%. Taylor carried Johnson County by 7 votes and Hood County by 981 votes; Edwards carried McLennan County by 16,006 votes and Brazos County by 4,792 votes.

Now Edwards is chairman of the Military Construction, Veterans Affairs and Related Agencies Subcommittee; he complained still about the 2003 redistricting, which cost Texas several chairmanships. "New York, Minnesota and Mississippi should send us a giant thank-you card." In January 2007 he reacted cautiously to George W. Bush's troop surge. "I have serious concerns about the ability of a U.S. troop surge to solve the sectarian violence. But I think the Congress should be extremely careful before it stops the commander-in-chief from implementing the plan." In March 2007 he resisted fellow Appropriations subcommittee chairman John Murtha's attempt to put readiness requirements into the supplemental that would prevent scheduled troops from reaching Iraq, and Murtha's plan was stopped.

EIGHTEENTH DISTRICT

Rep. Sheila Jackson Lee (D)

Elected 1994, 7th term; b. Jan. 12, 1950, Queens, NY; home, Houston; Yale U., B.A. 1972, U. of VA Law Schl., J.D. 1975; Seventh Day Adventist; married (Elwyn).

Elected Office: Houston City Cncl., 1990-94.

Professional Career: Practicing atty., 1975-77, 1978-87; Staff Cnsl., U.S. House Select Assassinations Cmte., 1977-78; Houston Assoc. Municipal Judge, 1987-90.

DC Office: 2435 RHOB, 20515, 202-225-3816; Fax: 202-225-3317; Web site: jacksonlee.house.gov.

District Offices: Houston, 713-691-4882; Houston, 713-861-4070; Houston, 713-655-0050.

Committees: *Foreign Affairs* (17th of 27 D): Africa & Global Health; Middle East & South Asia. *Homeland Security* (10th of 19 D): Transportation Security & Infrastructure Protection (Chmn.); Border, Maritime & Global Counterterrorism. *Judiciary* (8th of 23 D): Immigration, Citizenship, Refugees, Border Security & International Law; Courts, the Internet & Intellectual Property; Crime, Terrorism & Homeland Security.

Group Ratings

	ADA	ACLU	AFS	LCV	ITIC	NTU	COC	ACU	CFG	FRC
2006	100	100	100	75	29	18	53	16	18	0
2005	100	—	100	61	—	20	56	14	13	17

National Journal Ratings

	2005 LIB	—	2005 CONS		2006 LIB	—	2006 CONS
Economic	64%	—	36%		67%	—	33%
Social	88%	—	11%		85%	—	14%
Foreign	88%	—	11%		72%	—	27%

Key Votes of the 109th Congress

1. Estate Tax Repeal	Y	5. Limit Interstate Abortion	N	9. Build Border Fence	N
2. Limit CAFE Standards	Y	6. Extend Patriot Act	N	10. CAFTA	N
3. FY06 Spending Curb	N	7. Bar Same Sex Marriage	N	11. Oppose Iraq Withdrawal	N
4. Drilling in ANWR	N	8. Stem Cell Research $	Y	12. Detainee Tribunals	*

Election Results

2006 general	Sheila Jackson Lee (D)	65,936	(77%)	($502,818)
	Ahmad Hassan (R)	16,448	(19%)	
	Patrick Warren (Lib)	3,667	(4%)	
2006 primary	Sheila Jackson Lee (D)	unopposed		
2004 general	Sheila Jackson Lee (D)	136,018	(89%)	($370,856)
	Tom Bazan (I)	9,787	(6%)	($10,666)
	Brent Sullivan (Lib)	7,183	(5%)	

Prior Winning Percentages: 2002 (77%); 2000 (76%); 1998 (90%); 1996 (77%); 1994 (73%)

The People		Race/Ethnic Origin	Ancestry	
Area size:	228 sq. mi.	19.7% White	German: 3.7%	USA: 2.6%
Urban population:	99.9%	40.1% Black	Irish: 2.6%	
Rural population:	0.1%	3.3% Asian	**2004 Presidential Vote**	
Pop. 2000:	651,619	0.2% Native Am.	Kerry (D) 125,155	(72%)
Pop. 2005 (est):	645,342	0.0% Hawaiian	Bush (R) 48,753	(28%)
Median income:	$31,291	1.0% Two+ races	**2000 Presidential Vote**	
Poverty status:	23.3%	0.1% Other	Gore (D) 118,488	(72%)
Military veterans:	8.3%	35.6% Hispanic Origin	Bush (R) 45,151	(28%)
			Cook Partisan Voting Index: D +23	

Occupation	Blue collar: 30.0%	White collar: 52.1%	Gray collar: 17.8%

Houston contains, within its vast bounds, disparities of income and wealth as striking as any city in the United States. This is what one must expect in an expanding city with dynamic economic growth, vast immigration, absence of centralized planning and openness to cultural diversity. The contrast is most glaringly apparent at the edge of Houston's gleaming downtown with its keynote Pennzoil, Heritage Plaza and Bank of America buildings, plus Minute Maid Park (formerly Enron Field) for baseball's Astros to play outdoors and the Toyota Center for indoor sports, and newly renovated housing in what was once the city's warehouse district. Only a few blocks away are slums where many blacks and Mexican-Americans live in unpainted frame houses full of cracks wide enough to let in Houston's humid, smoggy air. But the contrasts are less obvious as one moves out from Houston's historic center. Half a century ago, when Houston pioneers like Jesse Jones, millionaire cotton broker and newspaper publisher, built downtown skyscrapers, they were operating in a town with a Third World economy, a low-skill producer of basic commodities, where a few got rich and many lived near subsistence level. Since then, Houston has gained a high-tech economy offering a myriad of opportunities and wide range of economic outcomes. As Houston's blacks and Hispanics have moved beyond the city, increasingly they live in comfortable middle-class neighborhoods. Highway congestion has increased the demand for additional mass transit. The area has suffered from a series of man-made and natural disasters. The biggest headlines came with the collapse and bankruptcy of Enron, the local energy and energy trading company whose executives famously cooked the books to conceal huge debt. Its collapse cost thousands of Houstonians their jobs, as did the merger of Compaq into Hewlett-Packard. But several factors have led the city to rebound: the increase of energy research and profits, expansion of the port, and real estate investment in the downtown. Even the announcement by Halliburton that it was moving its headquarters to Dubai did not mean a net loss of local jobs.

The 18th Congressional District of Texas contains central Houston and many of these outlying neighborhoods. The district includes Houston's downtown and the black and Latino neighborhoods immediately south toward Loop 610. On the north it has two spokes running out from Loop 610 and beyond: northeast between the Eastex Freeway and Beaumont Highway and then south to near Jacinto City and Galena Park, and northwest between the Northwest Freeway and Hempstead and then heading east to include George Bush International Airport. The 2003 redistricting reduced the African-American percentage to 40%, with about 60,000 black residents south of Loop 610 added to the new 9th District; nearly as many blacks were added from the old 29th District north of downtown. The Hispanic population increased to 36%. This and the 30th District in Dallas are the two most heavily Democratic districts in Texas.

The congresswoman from the 18th District is Sheila Jackson Lee, a Democrat first elected in 1994. A native of Queens, New York, she was educated at Yale and Virginia law school, worked on Capitol Hill and practiced law in Houston, served as a local judge and won two terms in an at-large seat on the Houston city council. After a local term limits law took effect in 1994, she ran for Congress. The incumbent was Craig Washington, a talented but storm-tossed legislator, an iconoclast who voted against the space station and NAFTA, both of which are big pluses for the Houston area economy. Jackson Lee supported NAFTA and raised lots of money from business interests who favored it—including Kenneth Lay, then a rising star at Enron. She won the Democratic primary unambiguously, 63%-37%, and has been re-elected easily since.

In the House, Jackson Lee has a liberal voting record, though she has been leaning toward the center on economic issues. She is prolific in proposing bills and offering amendments on the floor. Several of those that passed required studies, added small amounts to spending bills, or were non-controversial, such as prohibiting the use of children as soldiers in Afghanistan. In the Republican House, her more substantive proposals—for example, in favor of NASA funding and abortion rights—were usually defeated. She remained just as eager to file legislation after Democrats gained control. Jackson Lee emerged into national prominence as an outspoken and contentious defender of President Clinton during impeachment; she has modeled herself on Barbara Jordan, the first black representative elected by the 18th District and an eloquent advocate of the impeachment of Richard Nixon in the Judiciary Committee. But Jackson Lee has been embarrassed by revelations of regal pretensions, such as that she had an aide drive her one block to and from her Capitol Hill apartment every day. After she joined five other House Democrats who filed a pre-war lawsuit to prevent George W. Bush from invading Iraq without action by Congress, she was raucously jeered at a "Rally for America" held in her district by a local radio station. She joined anti-war protestors near President Bush's ranch in August 2005, and was an outspoken member of the Out of Iraq Caucus. In April 2006, she was arrested at a rally protesting genocide at the Sudanese Embassy. When White House press secretary Tony Snow confused her with Cynthia McKinney, Jackson Lee alerted him to the mix-up; an apologetic Snow said that she was "absolutely charming."

Under Republican control, Jackson Lee was ranking Democrat on the Immigration, Border Security and Claims Subcommittee. Facing conflicting desires from Latino constituents who favor more generous treatment of immigrants and some African-Americans who see immigrants as dangerous competition for jobs, she frequently took the pro-immigrant side; she favored increased visas and access to permanent resident status, but additional resources for the Border Patrol to identify immigrants with "bad intentions." In the majority, Zoe Lofgren claimed seniority and took the subcommittee chairmanship. Jackson Lee remained active on immigration issues, and stepped in as chairman of the Homeland Security Subcommittee on Transportation Security and Infrastructure Protection, an assignment that fits Houston.

NINETEENTH DISTRICT

Rep. Randy Neugebauer (R)

Elected June 2003, 2d full term; b. Dec. 24, 1949, Lubbock; home, Lubbock; TX Tech. U., B.B.A. 1972; Baptist; married (Dana).

Elected Office: Lubbock City Cncl., 1992-98; Mayor Pro Tempore, Lubbock, 1994-96.

Professional Career: Mgr., Sentry Property Mngt., 1972-75; Instructor, South Plains College, 1975-78; V.P., First National Bank, 1975-82; Pres., Prestige Homes, 1983-87; Pres., Lubbock Land Co., 1987-present.

DC Office: 429 CHOB, 20515, 202-225-4005; Fax: 202-225-9615; Web site: randy.house.gov.

District Offices: Abilene, 325-675-9779; Big Spring, 432-264-0722; Lubbock, 806-763-1611.

Committees: *Agriculture* (12th of 21 R): Horticulture & Organic Agriculture (RMM); Department Operations, Oversight, Nutrition & Forestry; General Farm Commodities & Risk Management. *Financial Services* (23d of 33 R): Housing & Community Opportunity; Financial Institutions & Consumer Credit. *Science & Technology* (12th of 20 R): Research & Science Education; Energy & Environment.

Group Ratings

	ADA	ACLU	AFS	LCV	ITIC	NTU	COC	ACU	CFG	FRC
2006	5	9	0	0	100	78	100	100	92	100
2005	0	—	0	0	—	67	93	100	86	100

National Journal Ratings

	2005 LIB	—	2005 CONS		2006 LIB	—	2006 CONS
Economic	0%	—	97%		21%	—	77%
Social	0%	—	89%		0%	—	94%
Foreign	0%	—	89%		0%	—	94%

Key Votes of the 109th Congress

1. Estate Tax Repeal	Y	5. Limit Interstate Abortion	Y	9. Build Border Fence	Y
2. Limit CAFE Standards	Y	6. Extend Patriot Act	Y	10. CAFTA	Y
3. FY06 Spending Curb	Y	7. Bar Same Sex Marriage	Y	11. Oppose Iraq Withdrawal	Y
4. Drilling in ANWR	Y	8. Stem Cell Research $	N	12. Detainee Tribunals	Y

Election Results

2006 general	Randy Neugebauer (R)	94,785	(68%)	($1,203,930)
	Robert Ricketts (D)	41,676	(30%)	($88,830)
	Other	3,546	(3%)	
2006 primary	Randy Neugebauer (R)	unopposed		
2004 general	Randy Neugebauer (R)	136,459	(58%)	($3,245,173)
	Charlie Stenholm (D)	93,531	(40%)	($2,479,274)
	Other	3,524	(2%)	

Prior Winning Percentages: 2003 (51%)

The People		Race/Ethnic Origin	Ancestry	
Area size:	25,356 sq. mi.	63.6% White	USA: 9.9%	German: 7.7%
Urban population:	74.0%	5.3% Black	English: 6.7%	
Rural population:	26.0%	0.8% Asian	**2004 Presidential Vote**	
Pop. 2000:	651,619	0.4% Native Am.	Bush (R) 181,516 (77%)	
Pop. 2005 (est):	649,385	0.0% Hawaiian	Kerry (D) 52,800 (23%)	
Median income:	$31,575	0.9% Two+ races	**2000 Presidential Vote**	
Poverty status:	17.5%	0.1% Other	Bush (R) 152,237 (75%)	
Military veterans:	11.6%	29.0% Hispanic Origin	Gore (D) 51,302 (25%)	
			Cook Partisan Voting Index: R +25	

Occupation	Blue collar: 23.8%	White collar: 56.8%	Gray collar: 19.4%

Until water was discovered in the giant Ogallala Aquifer that lies under the area around Lubbock, this was Indian country, then a land of Army forts and cattle ranches. When the water was tapped, well into the 20th century, what had been grazing land suddenly became cotton fields, with green crops grown in circles where sprinklers reached, separated by parched land. Lubbock became a regional center, the home of Texas Tech, and grew rapidly at mid-century: Lubbock County's population increased from 51,000 in 1940 to 101,000 in 1950 and 156,000 in 1960—lots of people in sparsely settled west Texas. Since then the regional economy has grown more slowly, as the Aquifer seemed to be going dry; in 2000, Lubbock County's population reached 242,000, and populations of neighboring, much smaller, counties declined. Cotton growers struggled with international competitors and trade rulings, plus pressure to reduce agricultural subsidies, which growers contend are a small fraction of the overall economic return. Wind power has become a source of energy, with dozens of towers between Abilene and Sweetwater. Lubbock has made an outsized contribution to American popular culture. This small city and nearby counties have produced a slew of fine musicians: Buddy Holly, Tanya Tucker, Jimmy Dean, Waylon Jennings, Mac Davis, Joe Ely, Roy Orbison, Don Williams. A discordant note came from Lubbock's Natalie Maines of the Dixie Chicks, who told a London audience in March 2003 that she was ashamed that George W. Bush came from Texas; the Dixie Chicks quickly disappeared from the playlists of some country stations. Later, they criticized their hometown in the recording, "Lubbock or Leave It." As a local congressman once noted in his website, people around here are "fiercely independent as Texans, steeped in patriotism when it comes to Flag and Country."

Lubbock is separated from the great metropolises of Texas by hundreds of miles of mostly, but not entirely, empty land. Nearly 200 miles southeast of Lubbock, over gully-ridden territory, are Abilene and the surrounding cattle country, with ranches specializing in Angora goats and sheep and exotic animals like ostriches, emus and aoudad sheep; there also are cotton fields and pecan trees and mesquite, and many oil wells. Archer City, the boyhood and current home of novelist Larry McMurtry, was chronicled in The Last Picture Show and Texasville. At Dyess Air Force Base near Abilene some of the nation's B-1 bombers are stationed. The communities here maintain their traditions and keep close to the land: Sweetwater has an annual Rattlesnake Roundup, while Olney in Young County stages a One-Armed Dove Hunt for amputees.

The 19th Congressional District of Texas connects these two wide-open regions. The population in Lubbock and its surrounding area is about twice as large as the Abilene area. The district, a product of the 2003 redistricting, was designed to safeguard the just-elected Republican incumbent from Lubbock against the likely challenge from a savvy and veteran Democrat from Abilene, and to allow the creation to the south of a new solidly Republican district dominated by Midland and Odessa, which had been in the old 19th District. Both goals were achieved. As recently as 1978, these parts of West Texas were Democratic enough that in an open seat election they rejected the candidacy of an attractive young Midland oilman named George W. Bush in favor of Lubbock Democrat Kent Hance. Today they are heavily Republican: Bush received 77% of the votes for president in this district in 2004.

The congressman from the 19th District is Randy Neugebauer (pronounced NAW-ga-bauer), a Republican who won the seat in a June 2003 special election. Neugebauer graduated from Texas Tech, became a banker and then ran his own land-development company. From 1992 to 1998, he was a Lubbock city councilman. The contest was prompted by the unexpected resignation, announced a week after the November 2002 election, of Larry Combest, who had chaired the House Agriculture Committee. In the primary, the four leading contenders in the all-party 17-candidate contest to succeed Combest were all Republican. They were Mike Conaway, a Midland accountant, plus three from Lubbock: Neugebauer, state representative Carl Isett, and former Mayor David Langston. Neugebauer was the biggest spender and in his advertising emphasized homeland defense. He focused on his business connections to oil and farming, and was helped because Isett—the only active office-holder—was tied down by legislative business in Austin. Langston, who previously won election as a Democrat, pitched himself as a Bush-like "compassionate conservative." Neugebauer finished first, with 821 more votes than Conaway. In third place, Isett trailed Conaway by 1,255 votes; Langston finished farther back. In Lubbock County, which cast nearly half of the total vote, Neugebauer won 30% to 28% for Isett and 21% for Langston. Conaway swept the Midland and Odessa areas. The runoff featured few differences on the issues. Not surprisingly, both supported Combest's farm bill and Bush's national security policy. Regional patterns held firm, as the Lubbock native again prevailed in the showdown with a Midland contender. In the combined vote from Midland and Odessa areas, Conaway won 85% of the vote; in Lubbock County, which cast 47% of the vote, Neugebauer led 71%-29%. Overall, Neugebauer won 51%-49%.

In the House, Neugebauer got a seat on the Agriculture Committee and later was appointed to Financial Services. He has been a reliable conservative. The House passed his amendment to add $3 billion for drought assistance to farmers, which was offset by a reduction in payments from a farm conservation program; it was part of the disaster aid bill, chiefly for hurricane victims, that Bush signed in October 2004. But he barely had a chance to get settled before the Texas legislature redistricted in October 2003. The new lines placed the home of Democrat Charlie Stenholm, congressman from the old 17th District since 1978, in the new 13th District; but that district was almost entirely unfamiliar territory for him, and heavily Republican to boot, and he decided to run in the 19th. Stenholm was arguably the last conservative Democrat from Texas in the House. He and Phil Gramm were leaders of the "Boll Weevils," backing the 1981 Reagan budget and tax cuts; he was one of five Democrats who voted to impeach Bill Clinton. But he stood with Democrats on tax issues. As the years went by, Republican leaders decided that Stenholm talked a good game but rarely delivered, though as ranking Democrat on the Agriculture Committee he did work closely with Combest in fashioning the 2002 farm bill. At home, his reelection margins had grown closer as the Republican tilt in his district grew even more pronounced. Most of the advantages—the district's partisan tilt, the fact that Neugebauer had represented 58% of its residents and Stenholm only 31%—favored the Republican. Both candidates promised to protect farm subsidies. Neugebauer called for cuts in other spending programs, such as food stamps; Stenholm was open to tax increases. Stenholm emphasized his social conservatism, his dedication to West Texas constituent services, and his independence as a Democrat; he criticized Neugebauer ads suggesting that Stenholm was not pro-life on abortion, and sought to link Neugebauer with Tom DeLay. Although Neugebauer ran as a loyal White House ally, his support for drug reimportation from Canada showed his willingness to go his own way; he sought to link Stenholm with John Kerry. The Texas Farm Bureau, which earlier honored Stenholm as "one of the giants of Texas agriculture," endorsed Neugebauer. He won 58%-40%, with 22 of the 27 counties. In Lubbock, Stenholm trailed 65%-33%. In his base of Abilene, which cast half as many votes as Lubbock, Stenholm led 50%-48%.

On Financial Services, Neugebauer said that post-Katrina reconstruction of public housing in New Orleans would be "the second worst disaster" in the city's history. In 2006, he won 68%-30% against an accounting professor at Texas Tech. About the only thing that could jeopardize his tenure is a radically different redistricting plan. In 2007, he was positioned to play a role on the farm bill as ranking member of the Agriculture Subcommittee on Horticulture and Organic Agriculture. During farm bill debate, he introduced amendments, knocked down by Democrats, to prevent indexing food stamps to inflation and to bar congressmen from directing Environmental Quality Incentives Program funds to specific industries. He defended farm subsidies to his district after the Environmental Working Group listed it as the nation's fourth-highest in crop subsidy program spending.

TWENTIETH DISTRICT

Rep. Charles Gonzalez (D)

Elected 1998, 5th term; b. May 5, 1945, San Antonio; home, San Antonio; U. of TX, B. A. 1969; St. Mary's Law Schl., J.D. 1972.; Catholic; married (Belinda Trevino).

Military Career: TX Air Natl. Guard, 1969-75.

Elected Office: Judge, San Antonio Municipal Court; Judge, Bexar Cnty. Court at Law, 1983-87; Judge, 57th State Judicial Dist. Court, 1988-97.

Professional Career: Elem. schl. teacher, 1969-71; Practicing atty., 1972-82.

DC Office: 303 CHOB, 20515, 202-225-3236; Fax: 202-225-1915; Web site: gonzalez.house.gov.

District Offices: San Antonio, 210-472-6195.

Committees: *Energy & Commerce* (21st of 31 D): Telecommunications & the Internet; Commerce, Trade & Consumer Protection; Energy & Air Quality. *House Administration* (4th of 6 D). *Small Business* (3d of 18 D): Regulations, Healthcare & Trade (Chmn.); Investigations & Oversight.

Group Ratings

	ADA	ACLU	AFS	LCV	ITIC	NTU	COC	ACU	CFG	FRC
2006	95	91	100	67	71	16	57	16	20	0
2005	90	—	100	61	—	13	63	16	5	0

National Journal Ratings

	2005 LIB	—	2005 CONS		2006 LIB	—	2006 CONS
Economic	60%	—	39%		63%	—	37%
Social	78%	—	22%		72%	—	27%
Foreign	69%	—	31%		70%	—	28%

Key Votes of the 109th Congress

1. Estate Tax Repeal	N	5. Limit Interstate Abortion	N	9. Build Border Fence	N
2. Limit CAFE Standards	Y	6. Extend Patriot Act	N	10. CAFTA	N
3. FY06 Spending Curb	N	7. Bar Same Sex Marriage	N	11. Oppose Iraq Withdrawal	N
4. Drilling in ANWR	N	8. Stem Cell Research $	Y	12. Detainee Tribunals	N

Election Results

2006 general	Charles Gonzalez (D)	68,348	(87%)	($694,162)
	Michael Idrogo (Lib)	9,897	(13%)	
2006 primary	Charles Gonzalez (D)	unopposed		
2004 general	Charles Gonzalez (D)	112,480	(65%)	($757,300)
	Roger Scott (R)	54,976	(32%)	($13,447)
	Other	4,348	(3%)	

Prior Winning Percentages: 2002 (100%); 2000 (88%); 1998 (63%)

The People		Race/Ethnic Origin	Ancestry	
Area size:	184 sq. mi.	23.4% White	German: 6.0% Irish: 3.5%	
Urban population:	99.8%	6.6% Black	English: 2.9%	
Rural population:	0.2%	1.4% Asian	**2004 Presidential Vote**	
Pop. 2000:	651,619	0.2% Native Am.	Kerry (D) 96,539	(55%)
Pop. 2005 (est):	645,740	0.1% Hawaiian	Bush (R) 78,757	(45%)
Median income:	$31,937	1.1% Two+ races	**2000 Presidential Vote**	
Poverty status:	19.9%	0.1% Other	Gore (D) 90,541	(58%)
Military veterans:	14.2%	67.1% Hispanic Origin	Bush (R) 64,927	(42%)
			Cook Partisan Voting Index: D + 8	

Occupation	Blue collar: 24.0%	White collar: 56.6%	Gray collar: 19.4%

San Antonio, with its antique past and theme-park future, its Hispanic heritage, its military superstructure and its high-tech hopes, is unlike any other city in the United States. Here on a plaza is the Alamo, preserved by the Daughters of the Republic of Texas, where Davy Crockett, Jim Bowie and 184 others were wiped out in 1836 (Crockett was a Tennessee congressman for three terms; if he had not lost his reelection in 1834, he presumably would not have left Tennessee for Texas). The Spanish architecture recalls San Antonio's days as the most important town in Texas, when the state was part of Mexico, and contrasts with the 31-story Tower Life Building, which contrasts with the armadillo-like Alamodome; the stark terrain contrasts with the lushness of the Paseo del Rio, the 1970s-redeveloped Riverwalk along the tiny San Antonio River. The city includes old neighborhoods redolent of the Texas Germans who were its chief Anglo citizens for many years.

For most of the 20th century, San Antonio's economy was built on the military. What the locals call "Military City, U.S.A." remains the home of Lackland Air Force Base, Fort Sam Houston and a giant military hospital. In 1995 Bill Clinton bent the rules of the base closing process to keep in San Antonio the thousands of depot jobs at Kelly Air Force Base, a move so resented that Congress blocked new rounds of base closings until 2005. Kelly was finally closed in 2001. In the 2005 base review, the Pentagon closed a local facility—Brooks City Base—but Fort Sam Houston was a big winner. Fort Sam's renowned Brooke Army Medical Center was transformed into a regional military medical center, for a net gain of more than 4,000 jobs in the area. The local health industry, which includes the Texas Health Science Center, has been thriving and is the largest local employer. The shift to privatization in the military has been a boon to local contractors. San Antonio also has many military retirees and it is the largest tourist center in Texas. The city also is the home of telecom-giant AT&T, which took over SBC Communications and announced in March 2006 that its merger with Bell South would remain based locally. In 2004, San Antonio surpassed Dallas as Texas's second-largest city and the eighth-largest in the country, though its metro area of 1.7 million is only about one-third the size of metro Houston or the Dallas-Fort Worth Metroplex. Its low education and income levels are affected by the proximity of the Mexican border, which has become a source of major commercial growth. Yet it has mostly avoided polarized politics and ethnic anger as it has made progress as a low-wage, high-tech center, with some linkage to nearby Austin.

The 20th Congressional District of Texas includes most of central San Antonio and its west side. The district is wholly contained within Bexar County; affluent Anglo neighborhoods are set off and placed in the 21st or 23d Districts. On the west it extends beyond Lackland Air Force Base toward the county line. Despite its impact on adjacent districts, redistricting had little impact on the partisan or ethnic compositions of the 20th, now 67% Hispanic. This is one of the state's seven Hispanic-majority districts, and it was the first to elect a Hispanic congressman in 1961. It is Democratic, but not overwhelmingly so: George W. Bush won 45% of the vote here in 2004.

The congressman from the 20th District is Charles Gonzalez, a Democrat first elected in 1998. He is one of eight children of Henry B. Gonzalez, who held the seat for 37 years. Charles Gonzalez grew up in San Antonio, graduated from the University of Texas and St. Mary's University School of Law, and served in the Texas Air National Guard. He was an elementary school teacher, practiced law and served as a judge from 1982 to 1997. When his father announced his retirement, Charles Gonzalez was the frontrunner for the seat, but the contest was more competitive than many had expected. Gonzalez campaigned as a consensus-builder, emphasizing his background in negotiation and compromise. Symbolizing the economic transformation of San Antonio, he said he would work for the entire district, not simply the low-income groups. Taking a more feisty tone was Maria Berriozabal, a former city council member, who called for more outspoken leadership. She displayed a picture of Henry Gonzalez in her campaign literature and claimed that she was more his model than was Charles. Just before the March primary, his father issued a brief statement endorsing his son. Gonzalez led Berriozabal in the primary 44%-22%. In the April runoff, he benefited from a fundraising advantage of more than 2–1 and mostly ignored his opponent. He won 62%-38% and easily won the general election.

In the House, Gonzalez has a relatively moderate voting record, especially on economic issues. After taking his father's seat on the Financial Services Committee, he moved to Energy and Commerce after Ralph Hall switched parties in January 2004 and created a Democratic vacancy. He backed a proposal to force satellite television operators to end a practice that forced users to have two satellite dishes to receive Spanish language channels. He called for stiffer penalties on businesses that hire undocumented workers. For both the Democratic Caucus and the Hispanic Caucus—which his father had refused to join—Gonzalez has been a leading proponent of census sampling. But he opposed Latino activists who wanted to create an additional Hispanic-majority district for Texas in the 2001 redistricting; because of low voter turnout among Hispanics, he said, such a step would reduce the Democratic majorities in other districts, an argument corroborated by subsequent redistricting in the state. In the majority, he led the House Administration Committee review of the contested 2006 result in the 13th District of Florida in which Democrat Christine Jennings lost by 369 votes, with more than 18,000 ballots not recorded.

In 2004, Gonzalez faced his first reelection challenge since he took office. Initially his ex-wife Becky Whetstone, a marriage and family therapist, said that she would run so that voters would have a choice and he would be "held accountable." But she failed to get the 500 signatures required to get on the ballot as an Independent. Gonzalez beat Republican Roger Scott 65%-32%. In 2006, he had no major-party opposition.

TWENTY-FIRST DISTRICT

Rep. Lamar Smith (R)

Elected 1986, 11th term; b. Nov. 19, 1947, San Antonio; home, San Antonio; Yale U., B.A. 1969, S. Methodist U., J.D. 1975; Christian Scientist; married (Beth).

Elected Office: TX House of Reps., 1981-82; Bexar Cnty. Comm., 1982-85.

Professional Career: U.S. Small Business Admin., 1969-70; Business writer, *Christian Science Monitor*, 1970-72; Practicing atty., 1975-76.

DC Office: 2409 RHOB, 20515, 202-225-4236; Fax: 202-225-8628; Web site: lamarsmith.house.gov.

District Offices: Austin, 512-306-0439; Kerrville, 830-896-0154; San Antonio, 210-821-5024.

Committees: *Homeland Security* (2d of 15 R). *Judiciary* (RMM of 17 R): Courts, the Internet & Intellectual Property. *Science & Technology* (3d of 20 R).

Group Ratings

	ADA	ACLU	AFS	LCV	ITIC	NTU	COC	ACU	CFG	FRC
2006	0	5	0	17	100	56	100	84	51	100
2005	0	—	0	0	—	57	93	96	57	85

National Journal Ratings

	2005 LIB	—	2005 CONS		2006 LIB	—	2006 CONS
Economic	9%	—	88%		21%	—	77%
Social	14%	—	85%		9%	—	90%
Foreign	0%	—	89%		27%	—	72%

Key Votes of the 109th Congress

1. Estate Tax Repeal	Y	5. Limit Interstate Abortion	Y	9. Build Border Fence	Y
2. Limit CAFE Standards	Y	6. Extend Patriot Act	Y	10. CAFTA	Y
3. FY06 Spending Curb	Y	7. Bar Same Sex Marriage	Y	11. Oppose Iraq Withdrawal	Y
4. Drilling in ANWR	Y	8. Stem Cell Research $	N	12. Detainee Tribunals	Y

Election Results

2006 special	Lamar Smith (R)	122,486	(60%)	($1,632,039)
	John Courage (D)	49,957	(25%)	($352,243)
	Gene Kelly (D)	18,355	(9%)	
	Other	12,984	(6%)	
2006 primary	Lamar Smith (R)	unopposed		
2004 general	Lamar Smith (R)	209,774	(61%)	($606,121)
	Rhett Smith (D)	121,129	(36%)	
	Other	10,216	(3%)	

Prior Winning Percentages: 2002 (73%); 2000 (76%); 1998 (91%); 1996 (76%); 1994 (90%); 1992 (72%); 1990 (75%); 1988 (93%); 1986 (61%)

The People		Race/Ethnic Origin	Ancestry	
Area size:	5,181 sq. mi.	68.1% White	German: 14.7%	English: 9.0%
Urban population:	81.0%	6.2% Black	Irish: 8.1%	
Rural population:	19.0%	2.6% Asian	**2004 Presidential Vote**	
Pop. 2000:	651,615	0.3% Native Am.	Bush (R) 212,196	(66%)
Median income:	$49,036	0.1% Hawaiian	Kerry (D) 110,288	(34%)
Poverty status:	9.2%	1.4% Two+ races	**2000 Presidential Vote**	
Military veterans:	16.8%	0.1% Other	Bush (R) 182,551	(69%)
		21.3% Hispanic Origin	Gore (D) 80,610	(31%)
			Cook Partisan Voting Index: R +16	

Occupation	Blue collar: 15.0%	White collar: 72.5%	Gray collar: 12.5%

The Balcones Escarpment is a bulwark of cracked and weathered rock that crosses Texas diagonally from the Dallas-Fort Worth Metroplex southwest to Austin and San Antonio and then to the Rio Grande in Del Rio. It separates the flatlands of central Texas from the stony hills to the north and west. It is a boundary between cropland and grazing land, between acres rich with greenery and acres whose rolling brown hills blaze out in color when the wildflowers bloom in Texas's early spring, between places where the sky is hemmed in by trees and buildings and places where the sky seems all around you, to the horizon far in the distance. The Balcones Escarpment separates Dallas and Fort Worth; it runs through Austin and the western edge of San Antonio. But it is less familiar to Texans today than the highway that runs pretty much along the same line: Interstate 35. This is one of the most heavily traveled and congested Interstates in America, thick with truck traffic in the populated stretches between the Metroplex and the Mexican border even as it passes through the lightly populated near-desert between San Antonio and Laredo. For this is one of the great routes of commerce in America, or rather between the United States and Mexico, and Laredo is the greatest freight crossing on America's southern border.

I-35 connects Austin and San Antonio, two Texan cities with very different beginnings and different characters now. Austin is the creation of state government, with the pink marble Capitol and the sprawling University of Texas. But it has gone beyond its roots, becoming one of America's leading high-tech centers with an office building boom downtown and in the suburbs to the north; after falling in the tech bust of 2000, its commercial real estate is now some of the most expensive in Texas. San Antonio was the creation of Texas's Mexican settlers, a town with a Spanish accent and a heavily Latino population. It is proud of the Alamo (which strikes most visitors as tinier than expected) and the Riverwalk, but it also has its corporate headquarters and an array of military bases: three Air Force bases, Fort Sam Houston, where the Army settled in back in 1876, and two military medical centers. In the counties between these two cities and in the Hill Country to the west, beyond the Balcones Escarpment, is the Texas German country, originally settled by Germans fleeing the reaction against the failed revolutions of 1848. The Texas German country has always been a set of orderly communities in rip-roaring Texas, economically prosperous in a state that considered itself poor until it struck oil. It was anti-slavery and politically Republican in a state whose enthusiasm for the Democratic Party had roots in Confederate loyalties and populist rebellions. The Texas German heritage is still visible, and an antique German sometimes heard on the streets (there are about 10,000 speakers now, compared to 159,000 in the 1940s), in towns like New Braunfels, Boerne and Fredericksburg, even as these communities with their neat houses, low cost of living and Hill Country ambiance attract new residents in shining new subdivisions and lake communities.

The 21st Congressional District of Texas, as redrawn for the 2006 election, includes much of this territory. A little more than half its people are in San Antonio and Bexar County. It includes the northeast corner of the city and county, Fort Sam Houston plus some predominantly Anglo neighborhoods on the north side (with many houses being bought up by rich Mexicans from Monterrey). This is mostly Anglo San Antonio, though 27% of the Bexar County residents in the district are Hispanic. About one-fifth of the residents are in Austin and Travis County, mostly in affluent neighborhoods on the west side of Austin and to the hilly country beyond. This is a primarily Anglo area, the most Republican part of a Democratic county. The district includes all of New Braunfels and Comal County just northeast of San Antonio, and several Hill Country counties to the west: Blanco County, where Lyndon Johnson was born in Johnson City and which was his legal residence when he was first elected to the House in 1937 (but only a sliver of the LBJ Ranch near Fredericksburg, just to the west); Kendall County, a fast-growing area north of San Antonio; Kerr County, the most populous part of the Hill Country, and two smaller counties to the south. The political heritage of the district is mixed. While Travis County was always Democratic and the Texas German country Republican, San Antonio, with a significant German heritage, was mixed. In 1931 the death of Bexar County's Republican Congressman Harry Wurzbach gave Democrats a majority in the House and enabled them to elect John Nance Garner of Uvalde as Speaker, while Wurzbach's replacement in the House, Democrat Richard Kleberg (of the King Ranch family) gave the then 23-year-old Johnson his first Washington job. Overall, the district is heavily Republican.

The congressman from the 21st District is Lamar Smith, a Republican first elected in 1986. Smith is from an old San Antonio and south Texas ranching family; their Jim Wells County ranch has been in the family for four generations. He graduated from Texas Military Institute (now TMI—The Episcopal School of Texas), Yale and SMU law school, worked as a reporter for the *Christian Science Monitor* and a lawyer in San Antonio. He was elected to the Texas House in 1980 and the Bexar County Commission in 1982. In 1986, when Congressman Tom Loeffler ran for governor, Smith ran for the House. At that time the 21st District ranged far west and had more acreage than Ohio; Smith decided to run after a Midland oilman named George W. Bush decided not to. Smith won by beating two other San Antonio-based candidates in the primary and then winning the runoff 54%-46% against a religious conservative; his campaign was run by then little-known Texas political consultant Karl Rove.

Smith compiled a conservative voting record and pursued original initiatives when Democrats held the majority. One bill added 100,000 acres to Big Bend National Park along the Rio Grande; another sponsored the first Bush administration's government-wide ethics act. In the majority, Smith chaired the Immigration Subcommittee of Judiciary from 1995 to 2001. He's long been a believer in stronger action to stop illegal immigration and to reduce legal immigration; he opposed Bill Clinton's proposal for, and George W. Bush's suggestion of legalization of, illegal immigrants living in the United States for many years. But he has supported some liberalizing immigration provisions. His bill to split the INS into two agencies, one concentrating on law enforcement, the other on aid to immigrants, was passed as part of the homeland security bill in November 2002. He opposed the Bush guest worker program in 2004 and charged that it "opens up every job in America" to low-wage competition; he called for enforcement of the law prohibiting employers from hiring illegal aliens. In June 2005 he hailed the administration for improving border enforcement and beginning to track down those who overstay visas, but criticized it for hiring only a small fraction of the new Border Patrol officers authorized by Congress and for the Treasury's decision to honor Mexican *matricula consular* identity cards. In July 2005, he co-sponsored John Culberson's bill to provide $6.8 million to train militias to serve under border state governors. Like other House Republican leaders, he insisted that better border enforcement must be in place before any guest worker or legalization policies were authorized. His reaction to the bill passed by the Senate in May 2006: "It's hard to justify legislation that would reward millions of lawbreakers, attract more illegal immigrants and depress American workers' wages." In June 2006 he and Henry Bonilla sponsored a bill to overturn a 1998 court decision giving illegal immigrants from El Salvador the right to an asylum hearing, on the ground that the political situation in that country had improved. He hailed the 700-mile border fence bill that passed in September 2006: "This is part of the overall solution. It is an important first step and shows that Republicans are serious about border security."

In 2001, having served the six years permitted by House Republican rules as chairman of the Immigration Subcommittee, Smith became chairman of what was then the Crime Subcommittee. There he focused on cybercrime and high-tech issues. He strongly supported the Patriot Act, which passed in October 2001, and produced the provisions allowing extended wiretaps. He has worked with Senator John Cornyn and Patrick Leahy on amending the Freedom of Information Act to obtain more and speedier disclosure of information. His bill to provide up to 20-year sentences for those who fraudulently obtain consumer and business phone records and distribute them over the Internet passed the House 409–0 in April 2006 and was given unanimous consent by the Senate in December 2006. In February 2007 he introduced a bill to require Internet service providers to keep records on their subscribers.

In 2003, Smith became chairman of the Courts, the Internet and Intellectual Property Subcommittee. He cosponsored with John Conyers and Howard Berman a bill to create new judgeships to determine copyright royalty rates and distribution of royalties and to remedy defects in Copyright Arbitration Royalty Panels; it was signed into law in December 2004. In July 2004 Smith passed a bill allowing firms to sell software that could delete offensive passages from movie DVDs; it became law in April 2005 as part the Family Entertainment and Copyright Act. Also passed by the House in April 2005 was his bill to lower the burden of proof for companies seeking to block dilution of trademarks. In 2004, Smith passed a Patent and Trademark Office Fee Act that devoted fees paid by those registering copyrights and trademarks to the operation of the office.

In 2006, when James Sensenbrenner faced the Republicans' term limits on committee chairmen, Smith made it plain that he wanted the post. He pointed out that he had chaired three of the five subcommittees. He had only minimal competition from the more senior Howard Coble who said, "I'm senior, but that alone will not prevail. Lamar and I will both give it a go. Either way is fine." Smith, who contributed more than $450,000 to Republican candidates in the 2005-06 cycle, won the post. He also became ranking minority member on the Courts, the Internet and Intellectual Property Subcommittee.

Smith is third in seniority among Republicans on the Science Committee. Most Texans have been strongly supportive of the manned space program. But after the loss of space shuttle Columbia in February 2003, he expressed some skepticism. Those who see Smith as an inveterate conservative may have been surprised when in June 2006 he sponsored a bill to provide matching grants up to 40% of cost for new solar panels for utility companies.

From January 1999 to January 2001, Smith chaired the ethics committee but the practice of bringing ethics complaints for partisan reasons had been discontinued, and Smith had few cases to contend with. In January 2005 he accepted an assignment to serve on the ethics committee again, but not as chairman. In May 2005 he stepped aside from the investigation of Tom DeLay, to whose defense fund he had contributed. In May 2006 he chaired the ethics subcommittee investigating Bob Ney. In February 2007 he was one of eight members chosen for a panel to determine whether the House required an outside body to police its ethics.

Smith has been easily reelected by wide margins. After the 2003 redistricting added much of Travis County to the district, his margin went down, to 61%-36% in 2004. For 2006, much of Travis County was removed, some of Bexar County was added and the district was stretched west into the Hill Country. Redistricting changed the normal election timetable and mooted the results of the March primary. Smith, as the only Republican candidate, got 60% of the vote in the special election November 7, well above the threshold needed to avoid a runoff. He won 59% of the vote in Bexar County, 47% in Travis County and 72% in the rest of the district.

TWENTY-SECOND DISTRICT

Rep. Nick Lampson (D)

Elected 2006, 5th term; b. Feb. 14, 1945, Beaumont; home, Beaumont; Lamar U., B.S. 1968, M.Ed. 1971; Catholic; married (Susan).

Elected Office: Jefferson Cnty. Assessor, 1977-95; U.S. House of Reps., 1996-2004.

Professional Career: Public schl. teacher, 1968-71; Instructor, Lamar U., 1971-76; Pres., Jefferson Cnty. Home Health Care, 1993-95.

DC Office: 436 CHOB, 20515, 202-225-5951; Fax: 202-225-5241; Web site: lampson.house.gov.

District Offices: Clear Lake, 281-461-6300; Stafford, 281-240-3700.

Committees: *Agriculture* (23d of 25 D): Department Operations, Oversight, Nutrition & Forestry; Livestock, Dairy & Poultry. *Science & Technology* (10th of 24 D): Energy & Environment (Chmn.); Space & Aeronautics. *Transportation & Infrastructure* (27th of 41 D): Railroads, Pipelines & Hazardous Materials; Aviation.

Group Ratings and Key Votes: Newly Elected

Election Results

2006 general	Nick Lampson (D)	76,775	(52%)	($3,578,097)
	Shelley Sekula-Gibbs (R)	61,938	(42%)	($912,977)
	Other	9,526	(6%)	
2006 special	Shelley Sekula-Gibbs (R)	76,924	(62%)	
	Bob Smither (Lib)	23,425	(19%)	
	Steve Stockman (R)	13,600	(11%)	
	Don Richardson (R)	7,405	(6%)	
	Other	2,568	(2%)	
2006 primary	Nick Lampson (D)	unopposed		
2004 general	Tom DeLay (R)	150,386	(55%)	($3,143,559)
	Richard Morrison (D)	112,034	(41%)	($685,935)
	Other	10,200	(4%)	

Prior Winning Percentages: 2002 (59%); 2000 (59%); 1998 (64%); 1996 (53%)

The People		Race/Ethnic Origin	Ancestry	
Area size:	1,002 sq. mi.	60.6% White	German: 10.6%	Irish: 7.1%
Urban population:	94.6%	9.3% Black	English: 7.0%	
Rural population:	5.4%	8.0% Asian	**2004 Presidential Vote**	
Pop. 2000:	651,619	0.3% Native Am.	Bush (R)	177,378 (64%)
Pop. 2005 (est):	799,101	0.0% Hawaiian	Kerry (D)	98,180 (36%)
Median income:	$57,932	1.4% Two+ races	**2000 Presidential Vote**	
Poverty status:	7.3%	0.1% Other	Bush (R)	151,311 (67%)
Military veterans:	11.1%	20.3% Hispanic Origin	Gore (D)	73,845 (33%)
			Cook Partisan Voting Index: R +15	

Occupation Blue collar: 19.8%   White collar: 69.1%   Gray collar: 11.0%

Those seeking the story of Houston's booming growth over the last dozen years would be well advised to go out the Southwest Freeway 45 minutes or so (if the traffic is not too bad) to Sugar Land. There has been a big change from the locale of *The Sugarland Express,* a B-movie in the 1970s about a fugitive convict—or, the sugar plantations that flourished here before the Civil War. Here in once rural Fort Bend County, on the site of the old Imperial Sugar Mill, is a privately planned city of 70,000, with privatized water and other services, immaculately clean and fast-growing (there were 33,000 people here in 1990). The entrepreneurial spirit is alive and well, with thousands of new and growing businesses, and so is a communitarian spirit, with dozens of churches and civic associations buzzing with activity. People welcome the new freeways and toll roads being built, to link them with Houston's airports and other business nodes. The image of suburbia has long been one of an all-white haven, but Sugar Land and Fort Bend County are welcoming to immigrants and minorities. Some 20% of the county population is black, and 77% of its blacks own their own homes; another 21% are Hispanic and 11% are Asian, the highest of any county in Texas. A reporter from the *San Francisco Chronicle* came to Sugar Land (then represented by Tom DeLay) to see "the anti-San Francisco" and seemed charmed by a community that "welcomes immigrants, shopping centers and jogging paths."Sugar Land has elected Daniel Wong, from Macao, to the city council; Dinesh Shah, from India, recently served on the board of the Chamber of Commerce. People came from around the world to construct and consecrate the huge new Hindu temple. This is 21st century America.

The 22d Congressional District of Texas covers more than two-thirds of Fort Bend County, including Sugar Land; in the 2003 redistricting, small pieces along the border with Harris County were moved to the new 9th District, to facilitate the election of a black Democrat. It also includes one-quarter of Brazoria County, centering on fast-growing Pearland, just south of Houston, plus parts of Galveston County including Santa Fe, La Marque and Hitchcock. Nearly one-half of its residents are in Harris County: working class Deer Park, Pasadena and LaPorte south of the Houston Ship Channel; and the more upscale Webster, Clear Lake and Taylor Lake Village surrounding the Johnson Space Center. Overall the district's population is 61% Anglo, 9% black, 20% Hispanic and 8% Asian. Politically, the 22d District continued to lean Republican, but not quite so heavily as before the 2003 redistricting. George W. Bush won here 67%-33% in 2000, but his majority fell to 64%-36% in 2004—still comfortable, but Bush won a higher share of the vote in 16 of the 32 Texas districts.

The new congressman from the 22d District is Nick Lampson, who previously served four terms in the old 9th District, part of which is now in the 22d. Lampson grew up in Beaumont; he got his first job sweeping floors at age 12 when his father died. After graduating from Lamar University, he taught science in Beaumont schools, leading the first local Earth Day celebration in 1979, and then taught a real estate management course at Lamar; he also headed a home health care company. In 1977, he was elected Jefferson County tax assessor; he claimed to cut the cost of tax collections during his 18 years on the job. In Lampson's previous House stint, he had a moderate voting record and was a member of the New Democrat Coalition. He promoted the Johnson Space Center from his Science Committee assignment and also looked after local needs from his perch on the Transportation and Infrastructure Committee. In 2003, Lampson fell victim to the 2003 redistricting plan that was designed to oust Anglo Democrats like him. Republican Ted Poe defeated him 56%-43% the next year in the newly formed 2d District.

Lampson sought and won election in a third and very different district following a tumultuous series of events involving the prior incumbent in the 22d District, Tom DeLay, the House majority leader and a Republican powerhouse. Lampson announced his challenge to DeLay in May 2005, at a time when DeLay was already under a cloud of scandal after three admonishments by the House Standards of Official Conduct (Ethics) Committee in the fall of 2004. Then, in September 2005, a Texas grand jury indicted DeLay on campaign finance charges, and he was required to step down from his leadership post. He nevertheless ran for renomination in the Republican primary in March and won with 62 percent of the vote. He faced a tough fight for reelection, but it was still a surprise when DeLay announced a month later that he would resign from the House in June. He had faced growing pressure following the guilty pleas of two of his former top aides in the Jack Abramoff lobbying scandal. In his farewell House speech, DeLay departed with his usual bravado: "There's only one thing I would change. I would fight even harder." But his exit was less than graceful. He changed his legal residence to Virginia in an orchestrated effort with the Texas Republican Party to replace him on the general election ballot; Texas Democrats sued and eventually won an appellate court ruling that Republicans could not replace DeLay on the ballot. Instead, he was permitted to withdraw from the race in August, and voters got a ballot with a blank space next to 22d District "Republican." Local Republican leaders endorsed Shelley Sekula-Gibbs (not the easiest name for write-in purposes), a Houston City Council member, as their write-in candidate; her name did, however, appear on the November 7 ballot for Republican nominee in the special election to complete the remaining two months of DeLay's term. (Thus her slogan, "Vote Twice for Shelley.") Lampson chose not to run in the special election to fill DeLay's unexpired term. Although President Bush and Vice President Cheney campaigned for Sekula-Gibbs, no write-in candidate had ever won a congressional election in Texas. And Lampson had raised some $3.7 million for his campaign, while Sekula-Gibbs was at a disadvantage with $994,000.

Lampson mostly kept his distance from the Republican chaos while he went about introducing himself to a new set of voters, a few of whom were from his old 9th District. He took advantage of the opening that DeLay inadvertently created for him and focused on the issues on which he had spent eight years in the House: homeland security, fiscal responsibility, and NASA. President Bush joined Sekula-Gibbs at a Sugar Land rally a week before the vote in an attempt to rally the base. But the write-in campaign turned out to be hopeless. Lampson got 52% of the votes, while the Sekula-Gibbs write-in effort drew 42%. Lampson won each of the four counties—including, amazingly, 51%-44% in DeLay's stronghold of Fort Bend, which had the largest turnout. In what became a fruitless consolation prize, she won 62% against four other candidates (not including Lampson) to fill the remaining two months of DeLay's term.

In the House, Lampson sought a seat on the Appropriations Committee. But Democratic leaders instead rewarded Ciro Rodriguez, another returning former member from Texas. Instead, he returned to Transportation and Infrastructure, plus the Agriculture and Science committees. In March 2007, Lampson had quadruple coronary bypass surgery.

He faced what appeared likely to be a tough reelection. In 2007, there was talk that Lampson might run for the Senate against John Cornyn—the thinking was that, since Lampson would need to raise at least several million dollars to win reelection to the House, he might as well run for a statewide seat. But he decided against it. Several Republicans voiced interest in challenging Lampson, including Pete Olson, former chief of staff to Cornyn, former Sugar Land Mayor Dean Hrbacek, District Judge Jim Squier, state Representative Robert Talton and Sekula Gibbs (she dropped the hyphen after the election), though she may have damaged herself with headline-grabbing escapades during her brief tenure in the House.

TWENTY-THIRD DISTRICT

Rep. Ciro Rodriguez (D)

Elected 2006, 4th full term; b. Dec. 9, 1946, Piedras Negras, Coah., Mexico; home, San Antonio; St. Mary's U., B.A. 1973, Our Lady of the Lake U., M.S.W., 1978; Catholic; married (Carolina).

Elected Office: Harlandale Schl. Bd., 1975-87; TX House of Reps., 1986-97; U.S. House of Reps. 1997-2004.

Professional Career: Substance Abuse Counselor, 1971-74, 1978-80; Educ. Consultant, 1980-87; Faculty, Our Lady of the Lake U., 1987-97; Founder, Rio Strategy Group, 2005.

DC Office: 2458 RHOB, 20515, 202-225-4511; Fax: 202-225-2237; Web site: rodriguez.house.gov.

District Offices: Del Rio, 830-774-5500; Eagle Pass, 830-757-8398; Fort Stockton, 432-336-3975; San Antonio, 210-922-1874.

Committees: *Appropriations* (37th of 37 D): Transportation, HUD & Related Agencies; Homeland Security. *Veterans' Affairs* (12th of 16 D): Disability Assistance & Memorial Affairs; Oversight & Investigations.

Group Ratings and Key Votes: Newly Elected

Election Results

2006 spec. runoff	Ciro Rodriguez (D)	38,256	(54%)	($963,647)
	Henry Bonilla (R)	32,217	(46%)	($3,821,285)
2006 special	Henry Bonilla (R)	60,175	(49%)	
	Ciro Rodriguez (D)	24,584	(20%)	
	Albert Uresti (D)	14,552	(12%)	($56,313)
	Lukin Gilliland (D)	13,728	(11%)	($1,055,818)
	Other	10,750	(9%)	
2004 general	Henry Bonilla (R)	170,716	(69%)	($1,211,717)
	Joe Sullivan (D)	72,480	(29%)	($9,335)
	Other	3,307	(1%)	

Prior Winning Percentages: 2002 (71%); 2000 (89%); 1998 (91%); 1997 (46%)

The People		Race/Ethnic Origin	Ancestry	
Area size:	48,562 sq. mi.	30.0% White	German: 7.1%	English: 4.0%
Urban population:	76.4%	2.8% Black	Irish: 3.9%	
Rural population:	23.6%	0.9% Asian	**2004 Presidential Vote**	
Pop. 2000:	651,612	0.3% Native Am.	Bush (R) 120,672	(57%)
Median income:	$33,574	0.0% Hawaiian	Kerry (D) 90,057	(43%)
Poverty status:	20.9%	0.7% Two+ races	**2000 Presidential Vote**	
Military veterans:	12.3%	0.1% Other	Bush (R) 94,736	(54%)
		65.1% Hispanic Origin	Gore (D) 82,173	(46%)
			Cook Partisan Voting Index: R +4	

Occupation   Blue collar: 26.0%   White collar: 55.6%   Gray collar: 18.4%

The Mexican-American tradition in the part of South Texas radiating from San Antonio is anchored in two culturally conservative but adaptive institutions, the Catholic Church and the United States military. Both are a major presence in San Antonio, just 150 miles north of the border, which for many years had the largest Mexican-American population of any American city, where Spanish has long been widely spoken and political refugees from Mexico's revolution could be sure of freedom. The church in San Antonio was led for years by liberal bishops who also ran St. Mary's University, which educated many Hispanic politicians and leaders, including two longtime House Democratic committee chairmen, Henry B. Gonzalez and Kika de la Garza—and also Republican Senator John Cornyn, who graduated from St. Mary's law school. Just as visible a presence in San Antonio are the Army and Air Force, with huge Fort Sam Houston, Lackland Air Force Base, and the Randolph Air Force Base, all in or near the city limits. At the site of the former Brooks Air Force Base, Toyota opened in November 2006 a $1.2 billion plant to manufacture Tundra pickup trucks; about 55% of the nearly 2,000 workers were Hispanic. Mexican-Americans have long volunteered for military service in numbers higher than most ethnic groups, and for many years Mexican-Americans in San Antonio worked in civilian jobs for the military service: Uncle Sam has long been an equal opportunity employer. San Antonio's Mexican-American community has produced many politicians who are liberal on economic issues, civil rights and civil liberties. But it has not produced many who are hostile to the military or to traditional religious and cultural values.

Fifty or so miles west of San Antonio, the hills flatten out and become the parched uplands of West Texas. This is a borderland, just north of Mexico, where people are concentrated in tiny hamlets amid the empty ranchlands and most residents are Latino. Once Indians were the threat on this frontier; now the challenge is assimilation and the threat is lack of water. The aquifers of West Texas are being drained; state law allows landowners to pump out as much water as they want. The Rio Grande, dried out by a dam in New Mexico, gets most of its water from the Rio Conchos in the Mexican state of Chihuahua; Mexico owes the United States hundreds of thousands of acre-feet under a 1944 treaty. Big cities have sprung up on the border. But in the hundreds of miles between El Paso and Juarez, Chihuahua (which between them have about 2 million people), and Laredo and Nuevo Laredo, Tamaulipas (which between them have about 800,000), there are only a few border crossings and much wilderness. The mountains of Big Bend National Park rise above the Rio Grande, where in the clean air you can find dozens of species of birds and can see for 180 miles; eccentrics have built an art colony in Marfa and stage a chili cookoff in Terlingua. Texas's frontier in many ways is thriving. But all this activity makes people thirsty. Private companies are buying ranchland so they can pump water out to Texas's growing cities, and some Texans have even talked about building a pipeline from Hoover Dam in Nevada.

The 23d Congressional District of Texas is geographically the largest in the state, larger than almost any state east of the Mississippi. It stretches from San Antonio to the outskirts of El Paso, from Eagle Pass and Maverick County to the New Mexico border. The August 2006 court redistricting shifted strongly Democratic Laredo to the 28th and the strongly Republican Hill Country to the 21st, and added a large portion of the south side of Bexar County, which includes many Latinos. That increased the Latino population here from 55% to 65%, and reduced the Anglo percentage from 41% to 30%. Many of the border counties are Democratic and heavily Hispanic. With the changes, this district voted 57% for George W. Bush in 2004 compared to 65% within the old boundaries.

The new congressman from the 23d District is Ciro Rodriguez, who served four terms in the old 28th District. Rodriguez grew up in San Antonio, was a social worker, teacher and educational consultant, and spent 12 years on the Harlandale school board. In 1986, he was elected to the Texas House, where he had a liberal voting record. He started running for the U.S. House soon after incumbent Frank Tejeda died of a brain tumor in January 1997. Critical in the campaign was his endorsement by the San Antonio Central Labor Council. His only serious competition for the seat came from San Antonio Councilman Juan Solis. Like Tejeda, Solis was pro-life on abortion and against gun control; he called Rodriguez "more of a wild-eyed liberal, and that's not what we need in Congress." Rodriguez was backed by several prominent politicians, and House Democratic leaders promised Tejeda's seat on the Armed Services Committee. In the March primary, he led Solis 46%-27%, and he won the low-turnout runoff 67%-33%. In the House, Rodriguez had the most liberal voting record of Texas's six Hispanic congressmen.

Rodriguez lost the 28th District in 2004 in a bitter contest with Henry Cuellar, after the district was revamped to include half of Laredo's Webb County. When the ambitious Cuellar announced, Rodriguez had a hard time believing that a friend and former legislative colleague for whom he had raised money in 2002 would run against him. In their five-month campaign, Cuellar campaigned more aggressively; he mobilized voters more effectively from his base in Laredo than Rodriguez did in San Antonio. After recounts and court reviews that took four months to resolve, Rodriguez lost by 203 votes. Their bitter conflict resumed in the 2006 primary for the 28th District. Without incumbency, Rodriguez raised less money than Cuellar and his campaign skills seemed stale. He lost again, this time by 53% to 40%. With the March 2006 result, the political obituary appeared to be written for Rodriguez.

But a court-ordered redistricting gave Rodriguez the unusual opportunity to run for the second time in 2006, against a new opponent and in a very different district. The contest was hardly a straight line to victory. Republican incumbent Henry Bonilla, first elected in 1992, was chairman of the Agriculture Appropriations Subcommittee, and also served on the Defense Appropriations Subcommittee. He had earmarked money for many district projects. He also had had good relationships with President Bush and Majority Leader Tom DeLay, though those alliances had become less useful by 2006. When the August redistricting added large sections of south San Antonio to the 23d, Rodriguez became a logical challenger to Bonilla. But five other Democrats also entered the contest, including Democratic fundraiser Lukin Gilliland, retired San Antonio district fire chief Albert Uresti, and Rick Bolanos of El Paso, who was unopposed in the March 2006 primary under the old boundaries. On August 30, upon hearing that the AFL-CIO, usually one of his strongest backers, might withhold its endorsement in the race, he announced he would abandon his campaign and the endorsement went to Uresti. Within 48 hours, Rodriguez changed his mind again after supporters urged him back into the contest. "We can turn this around," he said. In the Election Day all-party primary, the main question was whether Bonilla could get the 50% required to avoid a runoff. He fell just short, with 48.6%, winning 46.7% in Bexar County, which cast 65% of the primary vote. Rodriguez was runner-up with 20% to 12% for Uresti.

For the December runoff, Bonilla began with nearly $2 million in campaign funds, while Rodriguez typically had all but depleted his account. But Rodriguez had some factors in his favor: the enthusiasm generated by Democrats taking control of the House, and the sense by unified Texas Democrats that Bonilla was ripe for the taking. Rodriguez agreed to have the national party send in professionals to run the campaign, in place of his wife Carolina, who typically had run an old-fashioned volunteer effort. Rodriguez criticized Bonilla for voting in 2003 against a $1,500 bonus to soldiers serving in Iraq and Afghanistan. Bonilla said that Rodriguez showed "dangerous judgment" for opposing a law to allow the use of secret evidence in immigration hearings. With late polls showing a tight contest, Bonilla ran an ad in the closing days that depicted Rodriguez as a terrorist sympathizer. The DCCC dumped nearly a million dollars in the contest, and Bill Clinton made a last-minute campaign appearance in San Antonio. Rodriguez won 54%-46% over Bonilla and the dispirited Republicans. He took 56% in Bexar County; his 5,700 vote lead there was nearly the margin of his victory district-wide. Bonilla won 13 of the other 19 counties, but Rodriguez ran especially well around Eagle Pass and Big Bend, where Bonilla was hurt by his support for a border fence. Rodriguez was the final winner in the historic 2006 election.

Back in the House, Rodriguez sealed his remarkable comeback when House Democrats gave him a seat on the Appropriations Committee, which other Texas Democrats had been seeking. He appeared likely to face a competitive reelection challenge in 2008. Republican Bexar County Commissioner Lyle Larson said that he was interested in running; in 2007, retired marketing executive Jim McGrody and attorney Francisco (Quico) Canseco both declared their intentions to run.

TWENTY-FOURTH DISTRICT

Rep. Kenny Marchant (R)

Elected 2004, 2d term; b. Feb. 23, 1951, Bonham; home, Coppell; Southern Nazarene U., B.A. 1973, attended Nazarene Theol. Sem. 1975-76; Nazarene; married (Donna).

Elected Office: Carrollton City Cncl., 1980-84; mayor, 1984-86; TX House of Reps., 1986-2004.

Professional Career: Homebuilder, developer, 1975-2004.

DC Office: 1037 LHOB, 20515, 202-225-6605; Fax: 202-225-0074; Web site: marchant.house.gov.

District Offices: Irving, 972-556-0162.

Committees: *Education & Labor* (13th of 22 R): Health, Employment, Labor & Pensions; Healthy Families & Communities. *Financial Services* (31st of 33 R): Domestic and International Monetary Policy, Trade & Technology; Capital Markets, Insurance & Government Sponsored Enterprises. *Oversight & Government Reform* (12th of 18 R): Federal Workforce, Postal Service & the District of Columbia (RMM); National Security & Foreign Affairs.

Group Ratings

	ADA	ACLU	AFS	LCV	ITIC	NTU	COC	ACU	CFG	FRC
2006	0	5	0	8	100	65	100	92	69	100
2005	0	—	0	0	—	63	93	92	69	100

National Journal Ratings

	2005 LIB	—	2005 CONS	2006 LIB	—	2006 CONS
Economic	19%	—	79%	7%	—	91%
Social	0%	—	89%	10%	—	90%
Foreign	0%	—	89%	14%	—	85%

Key Votes of the 109th Congress

1. Estate Tax Repeal	Y	5. Limit Interstate Abortion	Y	9. Build Border Fence	Y
2. Limit CAFE Standards	Y	6. Extend Patriot Act	Y	10. CAFTA	Y
3. FY06 Spending Curb	Y	7. Bar Same Sex Marriage	Y	11. Oppose Iraq Withdrawal	Y
4. Drilling in ANWR	Y	8. Stem Cell Research $	N	12. Detainee Tribunals	Y

Election Results

2006 general	Kenny Marchant (R)	83,835	(60%)	($554,709)
	Gary Page (D)	52,075	(37%)	($10,135)
	Other	4,228	(3%)	
2006 primary	Kenny Marchant (R)	unopposed		
2004 general	Kenny Marchant (R)	154,435	(64%)	($781,923)
	Gary Page (D)	82,599	(34%)	($15,255)
	Other	4,340	(2%)	

The People		Race/Ethnic Origin	Ancestry	
Area size:	354 sq. mi.	63.9% White	German: 10.5%	English: 8.0%
Urban population:	99.2%	9.6% Black	Irish: 8.0%	
Rural population:	0.8%	6.2% Asian	**2004 Presidential Vote**	
Pop. 2000:	651,620	0.4% Native Am.	Bush (R) 161,864	(65%)
Pop. 2005 (est):	744,756	0.2% Hawaiian	Kerry (D) 86,786	(35%)
Median income:	$56,098	1.5% Two+ races	**2000 Presidential Vote**	
Poverty status:	6.3%	0.1% Other	Bush (R) 142,930	(68%)
Military veterans:	10.9%	17.9% Hispanic Origin	Gore (D) 66,587	(32%)
			Cook Partisan Voting Index: R +15	

Occupation	Blue collar: 17.0%	White collar: 72.9%	Gray collar: 10.0%

The gigantic (larger than Manhattan Island) Dallas-Fort Worth International Airport, the third-busiest in the world, bisects the Metroplex and its two adjacent counties with its large terminals and the Texas-sized highway network that feeds them. DFW, as nearly everyone calls it, also has been a focal point for the huge local development in both Dallas and Tarrant Counties. "DFW is no longer solely an airport. DFW is our home," the *Fort Worth Star-Telegram* wrote. Whole new Dallases and Fort Worths, with as many people as the central cities had in the 1950s—Grand Prairie and Irving—grew up around the airport during the next two decades in these once impoverished lands and became central to one of America's richest and most productive metropolitan areas. For years, DFW and its supporters fiercely opposed efforts to repeal the Wright Amendment, which limited the number of cities that can be reached from flights at the old Love Field in Dallas. In 2006, a political consensus in Texas and in Washington agreed to repeal it, partly at the behest of locally-based airlines seeking to throw off its anti-competitive shackles in a rapidly changing transportation world.

North of DFW are newer and more upscale suburbs: Grapevine and Southlake, with its huge shopping malls, in northeast Tarrant County; Coppell, Farmers Branch and Carrollton across the International Parkway in northwest Dallas County. To the north are the fast-growing suburbs and exurbs of Denton County. The Dallas-Fort Worth-Arlington Metropolitan Statistical Area has passed Philadelphia as the nation's fourth-largest MSA and is more diverse than one might expect—44% of its residents are African-American, Asian or Hispanic, compared to only 30% in the Philadelphia MSA.

The 24th Congressional District of Texas contains much of this area. The district includes three large spokes that reach out from DFW. The largest extends northeast through Dallas County and into Denton County, up to Route 121, including one-third of Irving and almost all of Farmers Branch, Coppell and Carrollton. To the west, another spoke reaches into Tarrant County out to Precinct Line Road, including Grapevine, Bedford, Colleyville and Southlake. South of the airport it includes almost all of Grand Prairie, part of Irving, Cedar Hill and part of Duncanville. About half of the population is in Dallas County, a third is in Tarrant County and the rest are in Denton County. The district was transformed by the October 2003 redistricting. Before that it included heavily

Democratic areas like the Oak Cliff neighborhood in Dallas and the black neighborhoods in eastern Fort Worth. That plan was designed by 24th District Democrat Martin Frost in 1991 and was largely carried over by the court which set the district lines in 2001. Frost, one of his party's most effective and durable partisans, was one of the chief targets of Majority Leader Tom DeLay, who pressed hard for the 2003 redistricting. The plan left Frost with no good choices. The new 24th District had voted 68% for George W. Bush in 2000. If he had followed his black constituents in Fort Worth, he would have to run in the 26th District, which had voted 62% for Bush. In something of a surprise, he decided to run in the new 32d District in Dallas County, which had voted 64% for Bush. That left the new 24th without an incumbent.

The congressman from the 24th District is Kenny Marchant, a Republican elected in 2004. He graduated from Southern Nazarene University. A local homebuilder and successful developer, Marchant served a quarter-century in elected offices: on the Carrollton City Council and then as mayor, then in the state House. He also has been active in private humanitarian projects around the world; the Ken Marchant Foundation funds church loans, mission projects and scholarships. In contrast to other upwardly mobile Republicans in Austin, he enjoyed a reputation on both sides of the aisle as a levelheaded peacemaker. Despite serving in some of the Legislature's most partisan posts, the mild-mannered and deeply religious Marchant managed to maintain a cool demeanor, even as his colleagues descended into acrimonious conflict. As *Texas Monthly* wrote: "His role was that of the genial, kindly sheriff in a western who allows the cowboys to gamble, drink and fight—but when they show up at the jail, rope in hand, he stands on the steps and says, 'Boys, just go on home and cool off.'"

Marchant had been chairman and floor leader of the Texas House Republican caucus and served on the House Redistricting Committee during the bitter 2003 redistricting battle. Unsurprisingly, the redistricting plan couldn't have been more favorable to him. In their effort to draw a Dallas-area seat that Martin Frost could not win, Republicans designed a district where Marchant could not lose. He denied that the new 24th was created specifically for him, but it incorporated nearly all of his state legislative district and was heavily Republican. He campaigned as "a proven leader for George W. Bush," a reference to his close legislative relationship with the former governor. Marchant drew no serious major-party opposition. In the primary, he defeated three other candidates with 73% of the vote. In November Marchant won 64%-34%. This was a welcome change from 2002, when he set out to run in the new 32d District only to withdraw when 5th District incumbent Republican Pete Sessions unexpectedly decided to run there.

In the House, Marchant cast a solidly conservative voting record, though without the hard edge or rhetoric employed by many Texas Republicans. As the only one of the five House Republicans elected as the result of DeLay's redistricting plan who had prior legislative experience, he settled comfortably into what could be a productive career. Like the others, Marchant defended DeLay from ethics charges, but he was not a DeLay stalwart. He quickly developed a fruitful relationship with John Boehner, joining the Education and the Workforce Committee that Boehner chaired in 2005 and serving as one of the few Texans to back Boehner when he was elected Majority Leader. His legislative priorities have been localized. As the only north Texas Republican on the Transportation Committee, he helped to coordinate the eight-year phased repeal of the Wright Amendment. He was one of two Republicans from Texas who voted to restore $100 million to the Corporation for Public Broadcasting.

TWENTY-FIFTH DISTRICT

Rep. Lloyd Doggett (D)

Elected 1994, 7th term; b. Oct. 6, 1946, Austin; home, Austin; U. of TX, B.B.A. 1967, J.D. 1970; Methodist; married (Libby).

Elected Office: TX Senate, 1972-84; TX Supreme Ct. Justice, 1989-94.

Professional Career: Practicing atty., 1970-89; Adjunct Prof., U. of TX Law Schl., 1989-94.

DC Office: 201 CHOB, 20515, 202-225-4865; Fax: 202-225-3073; Web site: www.house.gov/doggett.

District Offices: Austin, 512-916-5921.

Committees: *Budget* (9th of 22 D). *Joint Economic Committee* (5th of 10 D). *Ways & Means* (10th of 24 D): Health; Select Revenue Measures; Social Security.

Group Ratings

	ADA	ACLU	AFS	LCV	ITIC	NTU	COC	ACU	CFG	FRC
2006	90	95	100	100	50	15	23	8	13	0
2005	90	—	100	94	—	18	38	4	7	0

National Journal Ratings

	2005 LIB	—	2005 CONS		2006 LIB	—	2006 CONS
Economic	81%	—	18%		94%	—	0%
Social	78%	—	21%		78%	—	22%
Foreign	85%	—	14%		95%	—	0%

Key Votes of the 109th Congress

1. Estate Tax Repeal	N	5. Limit Interstate Abortion	N	9. Build Border Fence	N
2. Limit CAFE Standards	N	6. Extend Patriot Act	N	10. CAFTA	N
3. FY06 Spending Curb	N	7. Bar Same Sex Marriage	N	11. Oppose Iraq Withdrawal	N
4. Drilling in ANWR	N	8. Stem Cell Research $	Y	12. Detainee Tribunals	N

Election Results

2006 special	Lloyd Doggett (D)	109,911	(67%)	($570,699)
	Grant Rostig (R)	42,975	(26%)	($7,074)
	Barbara Cunningham (Lib)	6,942	(4%)	
	Other	3,596	(2%)	
2006 primary	Lloyd Doggett (D)	unopposed		
2004 general	Lloyd Doggett (D)	108,309	(68%)	($1,969,528)
	Rebecca Armendariz Klein (R)	49,252	(31%)	($804,160)
	Other	2,656	(2%)	

Prior Winning Percentages: 2002 (84%); 2000 (85%); 1998 (85%); 1996 (56%); 1994 (56%)

The People		Race/Ethnic Origin	Ancestry	
Area size:	6,182 sq. mi.	52.9% White	German: 11.8%	Irish: 6.4%
Urban population:	75.2%	9.6% Black	English: 6.2%	
Rural population:	24.8%	1.8% Asian	**2004 Presidential Vote**	
Pop. 2000:	651,618	0.3% Native Am.	Kerry (D) 140,063	(54%)
Median income:	$39,794	0.0% Hawaiian	Bush (R) 120,715	(46%)
Poverty status:	15.1%	1.2% Two+ races	**2000 Presidential Vote**	
Military veterans:	10.8%	0.2% Other	Bush (R) 105,867	(53%)
		33.9% Hispanic Origin	Gore (D) 92,698	(47%)
			Cook Partisan Voting Index: D +1	

Occupation	Blue collar: 22.7%	White collar: 61.5%	Gray collar: 15.8%

Austin, the capital of the second-largest state in the U.S. and site of its largest Capitol building, is also the southernmost capital in the continental 48 states. It is one of many capitals with a first-rate university, but one of the few (Nashville is the other) with its own musical tradition. Not long ago, Austin seemed as laid-back and countrified. There had never been much commerce here, and for much of the year the Capitol basked in a sun that seemed to ban gainful employment. Its skies were untainted with the smoke of industry, its ground unpocked with pumping oil rigs, its downtown streets lined not with business offices but with buildings holding a few lobbyists and the antique Driskill Hotel. Its biggest industry was the University of Texas—with 50,000 students and endowed with thousands of west Texas acres that turned out to sit on top of oil. The university has long had a distinguished faculty and some of the world's great scholarly collections; it houses the LBJ Presidential Library with its 35 million documents, has spawned a community of liberal intellectuals since the 1940s and helped spark Austin's high-tech boom in the 1980s and 1990s. Half a century ago, in Lyndon B. Johnson's time, Austin had a metropolitan population of 132,000. The compact Austin that was Johnson's headquarters in 1948 when the Duval County returns came in and gave him the 87-vote victory that made his national career is a very different Austin from the metropolitan center of 1.2 million that waited up in the rain, alternatively enthused and downcast, hoping to celebrate the election of George W. Bush in 2000.

Growth has also brought political change. For many years Austin was the central focus of Texas's hardy but almost always outnumbered liberals, based in the university, state government and the *Texas Observer*. Confident that the future was theirs, that Texas would follow America into the New Deal and the welfare state, they mocked the conservative business lobbyists who called the shots when the "lege" was in session and celebrated Texas zaniness with the verve of a Sixth Street band. But history—or at least Austin—has not moved in the direction Texas liberals expected. As the Austin area grew, it became more conservative; as its private sector has led the local economy, the techies who settled in the Silicon Hills going from Austin's Travis County to once-rural Williamson County have tended to vote Republican. The city core and the University area are still Democratic and Texas liberals still are potent in the media. But this is a state capital, in which George W. Bush could feel more at home than he would have 30 years before (when his application for admission was rejected by the UT law school). Bush lost Austin and Travis County 59%-41% when he first ran for governor in 1994, but he carried Travis 60%-38% in 1998 for re-election and 47%-42% in 2000 for president (with 10% for Ralph Nader). In 2004 Austin's liberal community registered large numbers of new voters, and Bush lost Travis County 56%-42%, even as he increased his margin statewide; Kerry got 57% more votes in the county than Al Gore had.

The 25th Congressional District of Texas, a new seat created by the 2003 redistricting and revised significantly by a federal court in August 2006, includes 50% of Travis County, with most of the east side of Austin and the city's heavily Latino and declining black neighborhoods. The Capitol and the UT campus are just outside, in the 21st District, while the 10th District includes most of the Republican northern part of the city and county. It was part of Tom DeLay's redistricting strategy to split Travis County among three districts, two of them safely Republican and the other a new heavily Hispanic district. This was accomplished by extending the 25th District south to the Mexican border on the Rio Grande, with the district's two main population centers some 300 miles apart: the Travis County portion and the heavily Hispanic Hidalgo County portion. The new version cuts off what had been called the thin *fajita* strip between Travis and Hidalgo. Seven rural counties that extend to the south and east now account for the remaining 38% of the district. The largest of them are Hays and Bastrop, both of which are among the fastest-growing in the state and increased more than 20% from 2000 to 2005. The district is 34% Hispanic, compared to 69% Hispanic with the 2003 map. But it remains Democratic. Under the previous boundaries, John Kerry defeated Bush here 63%-37%, his best showing in Texas outside of the three urban districts with black pluralities. Now, the district lines gave Kerry a 54%-46% win over Bush.

The congressman from the 25th District is Lloyd Doggett, first elected in 1994 in the old 10th District. He is a liberal Democrat with a dream resume and a political career with some notable twists. Doggett grew up in Austin, finished first in his class and was president of UT's student body in 1967. In 1972, he was elected to the state Senate at 26, and as part of a surprisingly large liberal bloc in the 1970s, he pushed for laws against job discrimination and cop-killer bullets and for generic drugs; he has always been a close ally of trial lawyers, the one strong institutional force supporting liberal Democrats in Texas. In the "lege," he was one of the "killer bees" who hid out to prevent a quorum on changing the rules in the Democratic primary and filibustered—wearing sneakers—against what he called anti-consumer bills. In 1984 he ran for the U.S. Senate, narrowly edging two congressmen to win the Democratic nomination. Then, despite the campaign help of James Carville and Paul Begala, Doggett lost the general 59%-41% to party-switching Congressman Phil Gramm. Doggett came back and, with strong support from trial lawyers, was elected to the Texas Supreme Court in 1988. When Jake Pickle retired after 31 years, Doggett ran for Congress after his judgeship had expired. He won the Democratic primary with token opposition, and in the general won by the solid, but not quite overwhelming, margin of 56%-40%.

In the House, Doggett's voting record has placed him among the most liberal Texans. He was a vocal critic of Newt Gingrich, and a close ally of Minority Whip David Bonior and Nancy Pelosi, and backed her against Texan Martin Frost in her race for minority leader. In 1999, he gained a seat on the Ways and Means Committee. Along with other Democrats, he sought to restrict the use of offshore tax havens. He has voted against most of George W. Bush's major proposals. Three days after September 11, his parliamentary objections stymied late night action on a $15 billion airline aid bill and forced a more thorough debate. He was a leader in opposing the resolution authorizing the use of force in Iraq; even Doggett was surprised that 126 House Democrats voted to oppose it.

Doggett is not everyone's cup of tea, so Republicans were giddy in 2003 over the prospect that redistricting might end his congressional career. But Doggett took up the challenge. As some other dislocated Texas Democrats took their fight to the courts, Doggett took his case to the voters of his new district. He started by working hard to get the support of elected officials and party activists along the border. "I chose to spend not a few hours here in the Valley in the month of December [2003], but a few weeks, to resume old friendship," he said in McAllen. Meanwhile, the best-known

Hispanic challengers for a Democratic primary were outmaneuvered. State Representative Kino Flores of Mission cited a lack of money when he withdrew six weeks after declaring his candidacy. Veteran state Senator Gonzalo Barrientos, a long-time Doggett rival, made bold claims but never declared his candidacy. Instead, he endorsed Leticia Hinojosa, a former district court judge from McAllen who worked for Legal Aid before becoming the first female judge in the Valley. She called herself a "pragmatist," in contrast to the outspoken Doggett, and she claimed a closer identification with voters. "I'm Leticia Hinojosa, and I grew up poor in the Valley," she said in her radio ad. But Doggett's strong local base and relentless pursuit of new voters prevailed. He campaigned less against Hinojosa than against the redistricters. If he lost, Doggett told voters, "Tom DeLay will have won." He won the primary, 64%-36%. He led 88%-12% in Travis County, and held Hinojosa to a standoff in Hidalgo County.

Although the primary effectively sealed his reelection, Doggett faced a spirited challenge in the general from Becky Armendariz Klein. She called herself a conservative "new voice with new ideas," and cited her experience working at the Pentagon, as policy director for then-Governor George W. Bush and, most recently, as chairwoman of the Texas Public Utility Commission. Klein raised more than $800,000 and jabbed repeatedly at Doggett. She contended that she could deliver more as a member of the majority in Washington, and she criticized his inability to work across party lines. "I am a candidate that has access to the president and the leadership in Congress," she said. But her challenge never got seriously off the ground. Doggett tweaked her bid for ethnicity by pulling out her "long forgotten maiden name" and cited his many local endorsements. He won 68%-31%. Doggett won Travis 79%-19%, and Hidalgo 60%-40%.

Under the new district lines in 2006, Doggett had a more customary win: no opposition in the primary, and a Republican with no support from his party in the general. Doggett won 67%-26%. But the election cycle was not entirely painless: in February 2006, a former staffer admitted to embezzling over a five-year period more than $166,000 from his campaign (it happens more often than you might think). Then the Federal Election Commission piled on by fining Doggett's campaign $6,500 for failing to accurately report disbursements.

In the majority for the first time since winning election to Congress, he gained a seat on the Budget Committee as a liaison from Ways and Means, and set his priorities as cutting back tax shelters and loopholes and negotiating prescription drug prices for Medicare. He also sought tax incentives for purchasers of plug-in "hybrid" electric cars.

TWENTY-SIXTH DISTRICT
Rep. Michael Burgess (R)

Elected 2002, 3d term; b. Dec. 23, 1950, Rochester, MN; home, Highland Village; N. TX St. U., B.S. 1972, M.S. 1976, U. of TX Med. Schl., M.D. 1977, U. of TX Dallas, M.S. 2000; Episcopalian; married (Laura).

Professional Career: Practicing obstetrician, 1981-2003.

DC Office: 1224 LHOB, 20515, 202-225-7772; Fax: 202-225-2919; Web site: burgess.house.gov.

District Offices: Ft. Worth, 817-531-8454; Lewisville, 972-434-9700.

Committees: *Energy & Commerce* (25th of 26 R): Oversight & Investigations; Commerce, Trade & Consumer Protection; Health; Energy & Air Quality.

Group Ratings

	ADA	ACLU	AFS	LCV	ITIC	NTU	COC	ACU	CFG	FRC
2006	5	14	0	8	86	57	92	83	50	100
2005	0	—	0	0	—	66	88	96	83	100

National Journal Ratings

	2005 LIB	—	2005 CONS	2006 LIB	—	2006 CONS
Economic	6%	—	93%	35%	—	64%
Social	19%	—	80%	11%	—	85%
Foreign	0%	—	89%	17%	—	73%

Key Votes of the 109th Congress

1. Estate Tax Repeal	Y	5. Limit Interstate Abortion	Y	9. Build Border Fence	Y
2. Limit CAFE Standards	Y	6. Extend Patriot Act	Y	10. CAFTA	Y
3. FY06 Spending Curb	Y	7. Bar Same Sex Marriage	Y	11. Oppose Iraq Withdrawal	Y
4. Drilling in ANWR	Y	8. Stem Cell Research $	N	12. Detainee Tribunals	Y

Election Results

2006 general	Michael Burgess (R)	94,219	(60%)	($942,669)
	Tim Barnwell (D)	58,271	(37%)	($16,612)
	Other	3,993	(3%)	
2006 primary	Michael Burgess (R)	unopposed		
2004 general	Michael Burgess (R)	180,519	(66%)	($817,015)
	Lico Reyes (D)	89,809	(33%)	($9,564)
	Other	4,211	(2%)	

Prior Winning Percentages: 2002 (75%)

The People		Race/Ethnic Origin	Ancestry	
Area size:	1,377 sq. mi.	66.1% White	German: 10.3% Irish: 7.9%	
Urban population:	90.5%	15.5% Black	English: 7.5%	
Rural population:	9.5%	2.2% Asian	**2004 Presidential Vote**	
Pop. 2000:	651,619	0.5% Native Am.	Bush (R) 181,989	(65%)
Pop. 2005 (est):	765,119	0.1% Hawaiian	Kerry (D) 99,633	(35%)
Median income:	$48,714	1.3% Two+ races	**2000 Presidential Vote**	
Poverty status:	11.0%	0.1% Other	Bush (R) 134,189	(62%)
Military veterans:	12.0%	14.3% Hispanic Origin	Gore (D) 80,992	(38%)
			Cook Partisan Voting Index: R +12	

Occupation	Blue collar: 22.1%	White collar: 64.5%	Gray collar: 13.4%

Until the Texas Land and Immigration Company settled this portion of northeast Texas with a land grant from the Texas Congress in 1841, settlers were scarce and Indian raids were common. The area now known as Denton County takes its name from John Bunyan Denton, a Methodist pioneer preacher and lawyer killed in a skirmish with Indians. Today, this area on the northern edge of the Dallas-Fort Worth Metroplex is teeming with new arrivals: Denton County is part of one of America's fastest-growing metropolitan areas. It is booming and filled with young, well-educated, middle-class families. Its chief cities are Denton and Lewisville, Carrollton and Flower Mound, all north of the DFW Airport; truck-manufacturer Peterbilt Motors Company in Denton is among its largest private employers. And a quick look at the county map reveals that there is plenty more room for growth along the Interstate 35E and 35W corridors as they converge on the city of Denton in the heart of the county. Growth takes many shapes here; the arrival of gas drilling rigs, protected by age-old Texas law on drilling rights, has caused local controversy. Near Justin, in the southwest corner of Denton County, nearly 1 billion cubic feet of natural gas are produced daily. With sophisticated imaging and drilling technology, other natural-gas wells operate within 10 miles of downtown Fort Worth. In 1940, there were 33,000 people in Denton County and they voted 88% Democratic for president. In 2000 there were 432,000 people in Denton County and they voted 70% Republican for president. In 2004 there were 530,000 and they voted 70% Republican again.

The 26th Congressional District of Texas is at the heart of the northern expansion of the Dallas-Fort Worth Metroplex. It includes three-quarters of suburban and exurban Denton County (but not Carrollton), most of rural Cooke County on the Oklahoma border, and a large slice of urban Tarrant County dipping south of the DFW airport. The Tarrant County portion also includes booming new subdivisions north of Fort Worth and the Alliance Airport business parks, founded and operated by Ross Perot Jr., that employ about 20,000 people. The Veterans Administration plans to build in this area its largest out-patient clinic in the country. The district was changed significantly by the 2003 redistricting, with the replacement of some suburban precincts by predominantly black precincts on the east side of Fort Worth, increasing the African-American population from 5% to

16%. Under the previous boundaries, George W. Bush won 73%-27% in 2000; under the new map, his 2000 performance here declined considerably to 62%-38%. In 2004, Bush carried the district 65%-35%.

The congressman from the 26th District is Michael Burgess, a Republican first elected in 2002. When House Majority Leader Dick Armey announced in December 2001 that he would not run again, there was no doubt that he would be succeeded by a Republican. But almost no one expected that the winner would be Burgess. He grew up in Denton County as the son of a physician, and graduated from the University of North Texas and the University of Texas Medical School in Houston. He trained at Parkland Hospital in Dallas and set up an obstetrical-gynecological practice in Lewisville.

After 21 years of practice, in which he delivered more than 3,000 babies, Burgess decided to run for Congress—his first bid for elective office. He was so intimidated at his first campaign forum that he nearly walked out. The widespread expectation, in Texas and in Washington, was that the winner would be the majority leader's son Scott Armey, a former Denton County judge. He quickly made the rounds on Capitol Hill and among lobbyists: he was only 32 and it seemed likely he would be a congressman for many years to come. In the primary, Armey outspent Burgess by more than 6–1. But turnout was light, only 25,000 in a heavily Republican district with 456,000 voting age residents; there were no Republican primary contests at the top of the ticket and there didn't seem to be much suspense about the outcome. Armey won 45% of the vote, not enough to avoid a runoff. Burgess won 23%, just 91 votes ahead of the third place finisher, a margin that presumably can be credited to parents of babies he had delivered or to the babies themselves. In the four-week runoff campaign, Burgess benefited from a series of hard-hitting articles in the *Dallas Morning News* about Scott Armey's record as county judge. The paper reported that he used his position to steer county jobs and contracts to close friends, including a $1.5 million transportation consulting contract. Burgess focused primarily on two issues—health care and taxes. A patients' rights advocate, he helped draft and pass the Texas Patients' Bill of Rights, and he vowed to do the same on a national level. His campaign was helped by the support of medical societies and local physicians who urged their patients to vote for him. Only 19,000 people turned out to vote in the April runoff and Burgess won 55%-45%. Armey carried Collin and Tarrant Counties, but lost 60%-40% in Denton County, where he was known best. After the runoff, Dick Armey spoke bitterly of the *Morning News's* "vicious unprofessionalism" and said they had conducted a vendetta against the Armey family. In the general election Burgess won 75%-23% over a Democrat whose son he had delivered.

In the House, Burgess has a reliably conservative voting record. As the only Texas Republican on the Transportation and Infrastructure Committee during his first term, he worked to change the funding formula so that Texas "receives its fair share." But he is better known for his work on health care issues. He chaired the health subcommittee of the Republican Policy Committee, where he voiced caution about the safety risks of drug reimportation, and then became vice-chairman of the committee. He supported George W. Bush's call for limited federal funding of embryonic stem cell research. At home, he sought answers to the high infant mortality rate in Tarrant County, and looked into the costs to public hospitals of children born to illegal immigrants. He played a role in enacting a measure to prepare the nation for a possible bird-flu epidemic. In 2005, his health policy expertise helped him win a seat on the Energy and Commerce which other Texans had coveted. That assignment belied earlier speculation that Burgess would be a short-timer in the House, and a "place-holder" for his political ally, conservative state Senator Jane Nelson, who had encouraged him to run. He has been reelected comfortably, though with smaller margins since the 2003 redistricting.

TWENTY-SEVENTH DISTRICT

Rep. Solomon Ortiz (D)

Elected 1982, 13th term; b. June 3, 1937, Robstown; home, Corpus Christi; Del Mar Col., Natl. Sheriffs Training Inst., 1977; Methodist; divorced.

Military Career: Army, 1960-62.

Elected Office: Nueces Cnty. Constable, 1965-68, Commissioner, 1969-76, Sheriff, 1976-82.

DC Office: 2110 RHOB, 20515, 202-225-7742; Fax: 202-226-1134; Web site: ortiz.house.gov.

District Offices: Brownsville, 956-541-1242; Corpus Christi, 361-883-5868.

Committees: *Armed Services* (3d of 34 D): Readiness (Chmn.); Air & Land Forces. *Natural Resources* (5th of 27 D): Energy & Mineral Resources; Fisheries, Wildlife & Oceans.

Group Ratings

	ADA	ACLU	AFS	LCV	ITIC	NTU	COC	ACU	CFG	FRC
2006	65	60	100	33	71	20	80	40	24	57
2005	65	—	100	33	—	17	70	40	14	42

National Journal Ratings

	2005 LIB	—	2005 CONS	2006 LIB	—	2006 CONS
Economic	59%	—	41%	58%	—	41%
Social	59%	—	40%	61%	—	39%
Foreign	57%	—	43%	58%	—	41%

Key Votes of the 109th Congress

1. Estate Tax Repeal	N	5. Limit Interstate Abortion	Y	9. Build Border Fence	N
2. Limit CAFE Standards	Y	6. Extend Patriot Act	Y	10. CAFTA	Y
3. FY06 Spending Curb	N	7. Bar Same Sex Marriage	Y	11. Oppose Iraq Withdrawal	N
4. Drilling in ANWR	Y	8. Stem Cell Research $	Y	12. Detainee Tribunals	N

Election Results

2006 general	Solomon Ortiz (D)	62,058	(57%)	($712,499)
	Willie Vaden (R)	42,538	(39%)	($102,878)
	Robert Powell (Lib)	1,718	(4%)	
2006 primary	Solomon Ortiz (D)	unopposed		
2004 general	Solomon Ortiz (D)	112,081	(63%)	($654,660)
	Willie Vaden (R)	61,955	(35%)	($51,228)
	Other	3,500	(2%)	

Prior Winning Percentages: 2002 (61%); 2000 (63%); 1998 (63%); 1996 (65%); 1994 (59%); 1992 (56%); 1990 (100%); 1988 (100%); 1986 (100%); 1984 (64%); 1982 (64%)

The People		Race/Ethnic Origin	Ancestry	
Area size:	6,319 sq. mi.	27.6% White	German: 5.7% Irish: 3.9%	
Urban population:	88.6%	2.5% Black	English: 3.6%	
Rural population:	11.4%	0.8% Asian	**2004 Presidential Vote**	
Pop. 2000:	651,619	0.2% Native Am.	Bush (R)	99,087 (55%)
Pop. 2005 (est):	688,348	0.0% Hawaiian	Kerry (D)	81,201 (45%)
Median income:	$31,327	0.7% Two+ races	**2000 Presidential Vote**	
Poverty status:	25.3%	0.1% Other	Gore (D)	81,454 (50%)
Military veterans:	11.6%	68.1% Hispanic Origin	Bush (R)	80,755 (50%)
			Cook Partisan Voting Index: R + 1	

Occupation   Blue collar: 25.4%   White collar: 55.1%   Gray collar: 19.5%

South from Corpus Christi to the Rio Grande and the Mexican border are two Texas versions of dreamland. One, fronting the Gulf of Mexico, is the sand spit of Padre Island, for most of its 80-mile length a barrier reef island and national seashore, at the southern tip of which is a high-rise resort to which college students throng for spring break and where developers have built 5,500 rental units. Remains of a 1554 Spanish shipwreck have been found offshore, and Portuguese settlers began cattle ranching here not long after. The other, inland from the Laguna Madre in Kleberg County, is the vast grazing and oil lands of the 825,000-acre (that's 1,289 square miles) King Ranch. This still seemingly vacant land between the Nueces River and the Rio Grande was the territory in contention in the Mexican-American War. The United States won that war and declared its sovereignty. But today most people here are of Mexican ancestry, some from families who have lived for generations on this side of the border, some recent immigrants. Adjacent to the King Ranch is the Armstrong Ranch, where Vice President Cheney in February 2006 accidentally shot a hunting partner. The culture here is *Tejano*, proudly American but with Mexican flair and vitality.

The 27th Congressional District of Texas includes this land from Corpus Christi south to the Rio Grande. Its population is concentrated at the northern and southern ends of the district. In the north Corpus Christi and surrounding Nueces County, with a 59% Hispanic population, is the southernmost natural port on Texas's Gulf Coast and the nation's fifth largest in trading volume with big petrochemical plants; the bayfront, lined with palm trees, is a popular recreational spot. At the southern end is Cameron County, which includes South Padre Island; the population here is 86% Hispanic. The island has moved beyond tourism, with plans for the nation's largest offshore wind farm, in which more than 100 turbines would generate power for 100,000 homes. The biggest city is Brownsville, on the Lower Rio Grande opposite Matamoros, Mexico, one of the major border crossings in Texas; NAFTA has lifted the economy in parts of this area, and there has been a boom in commercial construction. But there are pockets of grinding poverty here: not far from the border is the colonia of Cameron Park, where people live in trailers or makeshift structures without water or sewage service, rated by the Census Bureau as one of the poorest places in the nation. Politically, the 27th District is Democratic, but not so Democratic as one might expect. In 2000, George W. Bush just barely lost the district to Al Gore, and in 2004 he carried it with 55% of the vote. This was one of four Democratic-held districts in Texas that Bush won in 2004, three with Hispanic majorities.

The congressman from the 27th District is Solomon Ortiz, a Democrat and the only representative for this district since its creation in the 1982 redistricting. He grew up inland from Corpus in the Canta Ranas (singing frogs) neighborhood of Robstown, which is known for its political activism. His father died when he was 14, leaving him the eldest of four children who scratched out a living as migrant farm workers, sometimes working as far away as Colorado and Michigan. Ortiz worked as an Army investigator and translator, using his Spanish to learn French, took a correspondence course in police work and returned home to run for constable. In 1976 he was the first Hispanic elected Nueces County sheriff. In his first run for Congress, he got only 26% in the primary, but he made a propitious alliance with Democratic leaders in the Brownsville area and won the runoff with 52%. He has not been seriously challenged since then.

Ortiz's voting record has leaned toward the conservative end of House Democrats. As the third-ranking Democrat on the Armed Services Committee, he has watched out for the large military installations in the Coastal Bend region around Corpus Christi. As chairman on the Readiness Subcommittee, he remains an advocate of depot maintenance and adamantly opposed additional rounds of base closings; the House-Senate conference committee on the defense spending bill in 2004 stripped his House-passed amendment to delay the new round from 2005 to 2007. As it turned out, he had good reason to fear the 2005 round: the Coastal Bend region was hit hard by those decisions. Naval Station Ingleside, which has supported the Navy's fleet of minehunters and minesweepers, was closed with a net loss of 7,000 civilian and military employees; Naval Air Station Corpus Christi was realigned, with a net loss of 1,000 jobs. Ortiz blamed the "mixed signals" from the Corpus Christi community, including some who saw opportunities for development of the prime real estate.

Ortiz is a sturdy internationalist: an enthusiastic supporter of NAFTA and normal trade relations with China, and one of 21 Democrats to vote for trade promotion authority in 2001, though he voted against the final version in 2002. He expressed reservations about George W. Bush's guest worker program as serving corporate interests, and preferred to focus on family reunification. He opposed the Bush administration's "catch and release" program for illegal immigrants caught along the border for whom there were insufficient detention centers.

Ortiz has faced his share of negative publicity back home. In 2001, five months after the Port of Corpus Christi dedicated its new conference center in his name, the *San Antonio Express-News* reported that Ortiz got favored treatment when the Port awarded a contract for security to a firm that he owned even though it was not the low bidder. Ortiz defended the contract as awarded in open competition and his supporters said that the original low bidder was unqualified. But more questions were raised after his enthusiastic support for the U.S. free trade agreement with Singapore in

2003; it turned out his business provided security guards to a subsidiary of a Singapore-owned firm doing business in Brownsville. In 2003, he agreed to sell his business. In November 2005, the *Los Angeles Times* reported that Ortiz and his top aide took a free trip to Asia after getting a court house named for the father of the lawyer who paid for the trip; Ortiz called it a coincidence. In 2000 and 2002 Ortiz's Republican opponent was former Brownsville Mayor Pat Ahumada, who tried to take advantage of the controversy over the Port's contract with Ortiz; Ortiz won with 63% and 61% of the vote. In 2004, he won 63%-35% against Ingleside Mayor Willie Vaden, who refused to take large campaign contributions in order to draw a contrast with Ortiz. In a 2006 rematch, Vaden criticized Ortiz for his lack of support for the local bases, and narrowed the margin to 57%-39%. Ortiz reportedly is grooming his son Solomon Ortiz Jr., who represents Nueces County in the Texas House and earlier chaired the county Democratic party, as his successor.

TWENTY-EIGHTH DISTRICT

Rep. Henry Cuellar (D)

Elected 2004, 2d term; b. Sept. 19, 1955, Laredo; home, Laredo; Georgetown U., B.S. 1976, U. of TX, J.D. 1981, Ph.D. 1998, TX A&M U., M.A. 1982; Catholic; married (Imelda).

Elected Office: TX House of Reps., 1986-2000; TX Secy. of State, 2001.

Professional Career: Practicing atty., 1981-2004.

DC Office: 336 CHOB, 20515, 202-225-1640; Fax: 202-225-1641; Web site: www.house.gov/cuellar.

District Offices: Laredo, 956-725-0639; McAllen, 956-631-4826; San Antonio, 210-271-2851; Seguin, 830-401-0457.

Committees: *Agriculture* (11th of 25 D): Conservation, Credit, Energy & Research; Specialty Crops, Rural Development & Foreign Agriculture. *Homeland Security* (14th of 19 D): Emergency Communications, Preparedness & Response (Chmn.); Border, Maritime & Global Counterterrorism. *Small Business* (8th of 18 D): Contracting & Technology.

Group Ratings

	ADA	ACLU	AFS	LCV	ITIC	NTU	COC	ACU	CFG	FRC
2006	35	48	57	8	100	35	100	68	48	71
2005	70	—	88	33	—	29	89	52	37	46

National Journal Ratings

	2005 LIB	—	2005 CONS		2006 LIB	—	2006 CONS
Economic	53%	—	47%		52%	—	48%
Social	60%	—	40%		57%	—	43%
Foreign	55%	—	45%		43%	—	55%

Key Votes of the 109th Congress

1. Estate Tax Repeal	Y	5. Limit Interstate Abortion	Y	9. Build Border Fence	N
2. Limit CAFE Standards	Y	6. Extend Patriot Act	N	10. CAFTA	Y
3. FY06 Spending Curb	N	7. Bar Same Sex Marriage	Y	11. Oppose Iraq Withdrawal	Y
4. Drilling in ANWR	Y	8. Stem Cell Research $	Y	12. Detainee Tribunals	Y

Election Results

2006 special	Henry Cuellar (D)	52,574	(68%)	($1,674,231)
	Frank Enriquez (D)	15,798	(20%)	($408,762)
	Ron Avery (CNP)	9,383	(12%)	
2006 primary	Henry Cuellar (D)	24,256	(53%)	
	Ciro Rodriguez (D)	18,484	(40%)	
	Victor Morales (D)	2,943	(6%)	
2004 general	Henry Cuellar (D)	106,323	(59%)	($1,372,833)
	Jim Hopson (R)	69,538	(39%)	($43,581)
	Other	4,305	(2%)	

The People		Race/Ethnic Origin	Ancestry		
Area size:	13,738 sq. mi.	20.3% White	German: 5.7%		USA: 2.7%
Urban population:	79.4%	1.1% Black	Irish: 2.5%		
Rural population:	20.6%	0.4% Asian	**2004 Presidential Vote**		
Pop. 2000:	651,627	0.1% Native Am.	Bush (R) 90,730		(54%)
Median income:	$28,866	0.0% Hawaiian	Kerry (D) 77,349		(46%)
Poverty status:	29.9%	0.4% Two+ races	**2000 Presidential Vote**		
Military veterans:	8.7%	0.0% Other	Bush (R) 69,190		(50%)
		77.5% Hispanic Origin	Gore (D) 69,143		(50%)
			Cook Partisan Voting Index: R + 1		

Occupation	Blue collar: 29.2%	White collar: 51.3%	Gray collar: 19.5%

Hard by the Mexican border is a different kind of place, one where singer Johnny Cash, in "Streets of Laredo", summoned up images of lonely cowboys on dusty streets outside a row of saloons in a tiny town. But this is not the Laredo of today. Laredo, on the Rio Grande 150 miles south of San Antonio, is the busiest border crossing for U.S.-Mexico trade. Some 9,000 trucks and 1,200 rail cars cross its three bridges (one 17 miles upriver) every day, with merchandise worth upward of $100 billion a year, more than through all the other border crossings combined. Laredo was America's second fastest-growing city in the 1990s, with more warehouse space than San Antonio and Austin combined; its old downtown streets with their bargain stores are still filled with Mexicans who cross the border on foot, but those with cars head up the freeway to malls, and the Wal-Mart here is said to be the chain's top producer per square foot. Incomes and housing prices in Laredo (population 209,000) are low by U.S. standards, but far above those of Nuevo Laredo (population 500,000 in 2000) across the Rio Grande, and there is money to be made here. Laredo's Tony Sanchez, proprietor of a family oil and gas business and owner of International Bank of Commerce, became rich enough to spend $60 million on his unsuccessful 2002 campaign for governor.

The border country along the Rio Grande is in some ways a zone all its own, a mixture of the U.S. and Mexico, where many people have roots on both sides of the border. As former Laredo Mayor Betty Flores has said, "The river for us is more like some street that we cross; it's really not a border." Laredo's Webb County, had a 95% Hispanic population in 2005; local fast food restaurants feature enchiladas more than hamburgers. Years ago, movements like La Raza Unida—which had its beginnings here in 1969 when Hispanic youngsters wanted to elect high school cheerleaders in Crystal City—wanted the border country to become more like Mexico, with its union and party apparatchiks. More recently, Mexico, with its economic reforms and NAFTA, has been trying to become more like the United States, and particularly like Texas, with open markets and privatized companies, less controlled by political or labor bosses. The region shares some problems, including a high crime rate from the trade in illegal immigration and drugs.

The 28th Congressional District of Texas is centered in Laredo and then extends in two directions. South along the Rio Grande, it crosses Starr County, one of the poorest in Texas and home of many blatant and wealthy drug smugglers, and it reaches Mission in a slice of the southwest corner of Hidalgo County; these border counties include more than two-thirds of the district. It moves north, through thinly-settled ranch and oil well country and a small piece of Bexar County to the east of San Antonio.

The redistricting plan imposed by a three-judge federal court in August 2006 made major changes in the district. Historically, the 28th District was based in Bexar County, anchored by the Hispanic community on the south side of San Antonio. But those neighborhoods were required to assure a sufficient number of Hispanic voters in the 23d District; the 28th was left with a 78% Hispanic population of its own. Laredo has had a tumultuous politics in recent years. When local businessman Tony Sanchez was the Democratic candidate for governor in 2002, turnout in Webb County surged from 16,000 in 1998 to 39,000 in 2002, and that outpouring of Democratic votes almost enabled an upset of 23d District Republican Henry Bonilla. In 2003, Republicans were obviously trying to shore Bonilla up by removing half the county from his district; they also changed the political balance in the 28th. But making Laredo the centerpiece of the new district was welcomed by some Democrats.

The congressman from the 28th District is Henry Cuellar, a Democrat elected in 2004 after a bitter primary contest. Cuellar was the oldest of eight children of migrant workers who had only elementary education. He graduated from Georgetown University and the University of Texas law school, and he later got a Ph.D. in government from UT. From his base in Laredo, he served 14 years in the Texas House from 1986 to 2000, where he helped to author the Texas Grant college-aid program. In December 2000 Governor Rick Perry appointed him secretary of state even though he was a Democrat. Cuellar resigned in January 2002 to run against Henry Bonilla in the 23d District. He was helped when Bonilla said he didn't need Laredo to win; the Webb County Republican chairman endorsed Cuellar. Cuellar attacked Bonilla for his votes against funding the CHIP program, passage of the Family and Medical Leave Act, funding Pell grants, student loans, work study and classroom construction. And he accused him of being insufficiently Hispanic. Bonilla had the money advantage. Cuellar carried Webb County 84%-15%, with a 26,000 popular vote margin; only when the Bexar County votes were finally counted a few days later was it clear that Bonilla won by 52%-47%.

The 2003 redistricting strengthened Bonilla but gave Cuellar an opportunity to run in the 28th District against incumbent Ciro Rodriguez of San Antonio, who had the most liberal voting record of Texas's Hispanic Democratic congressmen and was the chairman of the Hispanic Caucus. When Cuellar announced, Rodriguez had a hard time believing that a friend and former legislative colleague for whom he had raised money in 2002 would run against him. The ambitious Cuellar, on the other hand, explained his primary bid as a common political occurrence in South Texas. Besides, he told a local reporter, "nobody died and made [Rodriguez] king. . . . Democrats run against Democrats all the time, and that's what it's all about." Rodriguez had little time to get acquainted with the new district, since the March primary took place just five months after passage of the new map. He had the support of the Hispanic Caucus in Washington, but that delivered few votes in Texas. Cuellar criticized Rodriguez for voting against the Medicare/prescription drug bill. Rodriguez said that Cuellar sided with Republicans after he was appointed secretary of state. The initial vote count showed Rodriguez ahead by 145 votes, but Cuellar demanded a recount. When officials in Zapata County, the border county just south of Webb County, found 177 additional votes for Cuellar and none for Rodriguez, Cuellar went ahead by 203 votes. After a lawsuit, a second recount, and a state appellate court ruling in July, Cuellar was declared the Democratic nominee by 58 votes out of 49,000 cast. But if Zapata County put Cuellar over the top, the election was really decided in Webb County. It cast 31% of the primary votes; Cuellar won there 84%-16%, and got more than half of his total votes in a county with only 15% of the total population. Rodriguez carried his base of Bexar County 80%-20%, but the turnout was smaller than in Webb even though the local population was nearly three times as large. Rodriguez carried six counties in the northern part of the district, and Cuellar carried the three that bordered Webb County. The recounts along the border were especially controversial. When the state appeals court dismissed Rodriguez's case, the five Republicans sided with Cuellar and the two Democrats with Rodriguez. After the July decision the state's Democratic congressional delegation reluctantly rallied behind the election of Cuellar. Cuellar won in November 59%-39%, with 68% of the vote in Bexar County and 90% in Webb County.

In the House, Cuellar had a voting record that made him the most conservative of the Hispanic Democratic congressmen from Texas. Some House Democrats said that they did not trust Cuellar and there was speculation that he might switch parties. Cuellar said that he will always be a Democrat but, "I don't want anybody to take my vote for granted." He kept his distance from Democratic leaders, and voted for tax cuts. He worked his district aggressively, and emphasized a bipartisan approach. With Republican help, he passed 11 amendments on the House floor, including legislation to create a national gang intelligence center at the FBI, and worked to toughen penalties on sex offenders who break the terms of their release. His legislative work was mostly on the Agriculture Committee, and he backed the Central American Free Trade Agreement, which he called an opportunity for "real transformation and progress" in the region. He disagreed with Republicans in their call for a fence along the border.

In 2006, his conflicts with other Democrats continued. Even before he left office, Rodriguez said that he would challenge Cuellar, and state Representative Richard Raymond of Laredo also expressed interest in running. Each received encouragement from House Democrats. Never the strongest fundraiser when he was in office, Rodriguez suffered from a smaller campaign fund; he raised $750,000, compared to $1.1 million for Cuellar. Raymond also struggled with fundraising and trailed badly in polls, and he withdrew from the contest in December 2005. Cuellar won the endorsement of the Wall Street-friendly Club for Growth, but it was of little political value in this district. With his votes in Washington, Rodriguez said that Cuellar had "sold out" the district. Cuellar said that voters were tired of the usual partisanship. The *San Antonio Express-News* endorsed Cuellar for his "independent non-partisan mindset" and said that his willingness to place the district ahead of his party was "refreshing." Evidently, many voters agreed. He won the March primary more comfortably than two years earlier, with 53% to 40% for Rodriguez and 6% for perennial candidate Victor Morales. Cuellar won 85% in Webb County, where the turnout exceeded the vote in the Rodriguez's base of Bexar County. With the court-ordered redistricting changes, Rodriguez had another opportunity later in the year, when he decided to run against Bonilla in the court-ordered special election in the 23d. Defeating Bonilla was one goal on which he and Cuellar agreed. So, the two bitter enemies were drawn together by the Democrats' ultimate success in defeating the only Mexican-American Republican in Congress.

TWENTY-NINTH DISTRICT

Rep. Gene Green (D)

Elected 1992, 8th term; b. Oct. 17, 1947, Houston; home, Houston; U. of Houston, B.A., 1971, Bates Col. of Law at U. of Houston, 1973-77; Methodist; married (Helen).

Elected Office: TX House of Reps., 1972-84; TX Senate, 1985-92.

Professional Career: Practicing atty., 1977-92.

DC Office: 2335 RHOB, 20515, 202-225-1688; Fax: 202-225-9903; Web site: www.house.gov/green.

District Offices: Baytown, 281-420-0502; Houston, 713-330-0761; Houston, 281-999-5879.

Committees: *Energy & Commerce* (13th of 31 D): Oversight & Investigations; Health (Vice Chmn.); Environment & Hazardous Materials; Telecommunications & the Internet. *Foreign Affairs* (15th of 27 D): Terrorism, Nonproliferation & Trade; Western Hemisphere. *Standards of Official Conduct* (2d of 5 D).

Group Ratings

	ADA	ACLU	AFS	LCV	ITIC	NTU	COC	ACU	CFG	FRC
2006	85	86	100	58	29	18	50	33	13	14
2005	95	—	100	39	—	17	48	28	10	25

National Journal Ratings

	2005 LIB — 2005 CONS		2006 LIB — 2006 CONS	
Economic	63%	— 37%	64%	— 36%
Social	64%	— 36%	65%	— 35%
Foreign	64%	— 35%	60%	— 39%

Key Votes of the 109th Congress

1. Estate Tax Repeal	N	5. Limit Interstate Abortion	N	9. Build Border Fence	N
2. Limit CAFE Standards	Y	6. Extend Patriot Act	Y	10. CAFTA	N
3. FY06 Spending Curb	N	7. Bar Same Sex Marriage	N	11. Oppose Iraq Withdrawal	Y
4. Drilling in ANWR	Y	8. Stem Cell Research $	Y	12. Detainee Tribunals	N

Election Results

2006 general	Gene Green (D)	37,174	(74%)	($703,804)
	Eric Story (R)	12,347	(24%)	($27,434)
	Other	1,029	(2%)	
2006 primary	Gene Green (D)	unopposed		
2004 general	Gene Green (D)	78,256	(94%)	($684,970)
	Clifford Messina (Lib)	4,868	(6%)	

Prior Winning Percentages: 2002 (95%); 2000 (73%); 1998 (93%); 1996 (68%); 1994 (73%); 1992 (65%)

The People		Race/Ethnic Origin	Ancestry	
Area size:	249 sq. mi.	21.9% White	USA: 4.1%	German: 3.1%
Urban population:	99.4%	9.7% Black	Irish: 2.8%	
Rural population:	0.6%	1.3% Asian	**2004 Presidential Vote**	
Pop. 2000:	651,619	0.2% Native Am.	Kerry (D) 59,897	(56%)
Pop. 2005 (est):	657,242	0.0% Hawaiian	Bush (R) 47,734	(44%)
Median income:	$31,751	0.7% Two+ races	**2000 Presidential Vote**	
Poverty status:	21.9%	0.1% Other	Gore (D) 61,303	(57%)
Military veterans:	7.2%	66.1% Hispanic Origin	Bush (R) 45,626	(43%)
			Cook Partisan Voting Index: D + 8	

Occupation   Blue collar: 43.1%   White collar: 40.3%   Gray collar: 16.6%

"What built Houston," wrote John Gunther in *Inside U.S.A.*, "was a combination of cotton, oil, and the ship canal." The cotton and oil were gifts of nature, though they required much human effort and ingenuity to produce in commercial quantities; the 54-mile Houston Ship Channel, by contrast, was almost totally man's creation. After the sand spit port of Galveston was destroyed by a hurricane and tidal wave in 1900, Houston's elders decided to dredge out Buffalo Bayou and make their inland city a seaport. When the channel officially opened in November 1914, a sluggish, 6-foot-deep creek became a 40-foot-deep channel—recently deepened to 45 feet, and widened from 400 feet to 530 feet—and Houston turned into one of the nation's biggest ports, today with more than 740 vessels daily generating 287,000 jobs and $11 billion a year for the local economy; about 60% of the big ships are tankers, with a capacity of 800,000 barrels of crude oil. The port also is the site of the largest petrochemical complex in the world. On its west side, Houston seems entirely a white-collar, office-bound city. But on the east and north, around the turning basin in the port and through the maze of refinery towers and tubing, Houston remains vibrant and blue collar, with blacks, Mexican-Americans and large numbers of whites from the rural South and even Michigan and California, who have come here to move up in the world.

The 29th Congressional District of Texas covers much of the Ship Channel area and working-class Houston—like a rough-edged wrench on the east side of the city. Included is much of the area on Houston's Northside, between the Eastex and North Freeways almost out to George Bush Intercontinental Airport and FM 1960, and blue-collar neighborhoods in northeast Houston. Neighborhoods in this area have ballooned in size as more than 200,000 Hurricane Katrina refugees temporarily or permanently relocated to Houston. The 2003 redistricting didn't have much of an impact here, increasing the Hispanic percentage from 62% to 66% and reducing the black percentage from 15% to 10%. This part of Houston has always been considered heavily Democratic, but in 2004 Bush lost it by only a 56%-44% margin. "The civil rights movement isn't part of their culture," a local Democratic consultant said of these voters. "It's as simple as, 'This president appointed Alberto Gonzalez to be Attorney General. That sounds good to me.'"

The congressman from the 29th District is Gene Green, a Democrat first elected in 1992. Green grew up in the largely Hispanic Lindale section of north Houston, worked as a printer's apprentice, got his business and law degrees from the University of Houston, and was admitted to the bar; he was elected to the state House in 1972, at 25, and to the state Senate in a special election in 1985. He has been a faithful friend to unions and trial lawyers in Austin and Washington, and also an opponent of gun control, a politician whose natural political base is Texas' small, unionized blue-collar class. He is committed to constituent service (his office hosts an annual "Immunization Day" to provide free vaccines) and a compulsive campaigner—the kind who goes door-to-door and carries lawn signs and a hammer in his trunk. It's a good thing, for as an Anglo he probably never would have won otherwise in the minority-majority 29th. In the 1992 primary he faced Ben Reyes, a tempestuous Houston councilman who once protested official inaction by demolishing a crack house. In the primary, Reyes led 34%-28% over Green. In the runoff, Green came out ahead by 180 votes out of 31,508 cast. Reyes went to court and charged that Republican voters had illegally crossed over and voted in the runoff. That got him a July re-runoff, but to no avail. This time Green won with 52%; he won the general election with 65%.

In the House, Green has had a relatively moderate voting record for a member in a heavily minority urban district. He enacted a bill to declare the Buffalo Bayou a national heritage area. After a spirited fight with other Texas Democrats in 1996, he won a seat on the Energy and Commerce Committee. Despite the importance of international trade to the Port of Houston, Green has sided with labor and opposed trade promotion authority, CAFTA and NAFTA. He criticized Republican proposals to encourage new oil refineries because their environmental exemptions could jeopardize the clean-air program in Houston. In January 2007, he cast a "difficult" vote for the Democratic bill to roll back subsidies for the oil industry. In the majority, he had an easier time enacting the bill to name the Department of Education building for Lyndon Johnson.

At a time when national and state Hispanic leaders are pressing for more Hispanic members, the anomalous 29th remains an inviting opportunity for an ambitious Hispanic politician. Perhaps in anticipation, Green organized a Spanish language class for members of Congress. But since 1996, no other Democrat has challenged him and he has been reelected easily. He has survived the state's redistricting chaos, with no major party opposition in 2002 and 2004. In 2006, he did not break a sweat against Republican challenger Eric Story, an oil-services manager.

THIRTIETH DISTRICT

Rep. Eddie Bernice Johnson (D)

Elected 1992, 8th term; b. Dec. 3, 1935, Waco; home, Dallas; St. Mary's at Notre Dame, B.A. 1955, TX Christian U., B.S. 1967, S. Methodist U., M.P.A. 1976; Baptist; divorced.

Elected Office: TX House of Reps., 1972-1977; TX Senate, 1986-92.

Professional Career: Registered nurse; Regional Dir., U.S. Dept. of HEW, 1977-80; Mgmt. consultant, Sammons Corp., 1979-81; Owner, Eddie Bernice Johnson & Assoc., 1981-present.

DC Office: 1511 LHOB, 20515, 202-225-8885; Fax: 202-226-1477; Web site: www.house.gov/ebjohnson.

District Offices: Dallas, 214-922-8885.

Committees: *Science & Technology* (3d of 24 D): Research & Science Education; Investigations & Oversight. *Transportation & Infrastructure* (9th of 41 D): Water Resources & Environment (Chmn.); Railroads, Pipelines & Hazardous Materials; Aviation.

Group Ratings

	ADA	ACLU	AFS	LCV	ITIC	NTU	COC	ACU	CFG	FRC
2006	95	100	100	75	43	16	60	16	18	0
2005	100	—	100	89	—	12	37	0	3	0

National Journal Ratings

	2005 LIB	—	2005 CONS	2006 LIB	—	2006 CONS
Economic	82%	—	16%	68%	—	31%
Social	87%	—	12%	80%	—	19%
Foreign	82%	—	18%	83%	—	14%

Key Votes of the 109th Congress

1. Estate Tax Repeal	N	5. Limit Interstate Abortion	N	9. Build Border Fence	N
2. Limit CAFE Standards	Y	6. Extend Patriot Act	N	10. CAFTA	N
3. FY06 Spending Curb	N	7. Bar Same Sex Marriage	N	11. Oppose Iraq Withdrawal	N
4. Drilling in ANWR	N	8. Stem Cell Research	$	12. Detainee Tribunals	N

Election Results

2006 general	Eddie Bernice Johnson (D)	81,348	(80%)	($410,117)
	Wilson Aurbach (R)	17,850	(18%)	($73,614)
	Other	2,250	(2%)	
2006 primary	Eddie Bernice Johnson (D)	unopposed		
2004 general	Eddie Bernice Johnson (D)	144,513	(93%)	($405,453)
	John Davis (Lib)	10,821	(7%)	

Prior Winning Percentages: 2002 (74%); 2000 (92%); 1998 (72%); 1996 (55%); 1994 (73%); 1992 (72%)

The People		Race/Ethnic Origin	Ancestry	
Area size:	319 sq. mi.	21.9% White	German: 3.2%	USA: 3.1%
Urban population:	98.8%	41.4% Black	Irish: 2.9%	
Rural population:	1.2%	1.3% Asian	**2004 Presidential Vote**	
Pop. 2000:	651,620	0.3% Native Am.	Kerry (D) 136,116	(75%)
Pop. 2005 (est):	645,039	0.0% Hawaiian	Bush (R) 45,148	(25%)
Median income:	$33,505	0.9% Two+ races	**2000 Presidential Vote**	
Poverty status:	21.4%	0.1% Other	Gore (D) 113,747	(74%)
Military veterans:	8.4%	34.2% Hispanic Origin	Bush (R) 39,468	(26%)
			Cook Partisan Voting Index: D +26	

Occupation   Blue collar: 30.7%   White collar: 52.1%   Gray collar: 17.2%

Dallas is, among other things, the westernmost city of the Deep South. Cotton was originally the major crop in this part of Texas, and many of Dallas's first enterprising businessmen, when the railroad reached the Trinity River here in the 1870s, were cotton brokers. Railroads made Dallas rich and helped it to grow. Geographically, Dallas is directly west of the Black Belt of Alabama and the Mississippi Delta, both heavy cotton-producing areas in the days before the boll weevil. Many blacks and whites came west on U.S. 80—and now Interstate 20—to the Dallas-Fort Worth Metroplex, now the largest metro area in the South. The south side of Dallas, not much visited by tourists, is predominately black. The Trinity River Corridor project, which has been discussed for decades, is moving toward reality and will change many features of Dallas with its ambitious plans for flood control, recreational features and transportation improvements, including three new suspension bridges.

The 30th Congressional District of Texas, designed as the Dallas-Fort Worth Metroplex's black-majority district, includes most of Dallas's black neighborhoods. Its creation in 1991 was insisted on by the then-chairman of the Texas Senate's redistricting committee (details to follow), and the result was one of the most grotesquely shaped districts in the country: Attached to the central body in south and east Dallas were tentacles that appeared as complex and attenuated as a series of DNA molecules. Since then, lawsuits and two more rounds of redistricting have smoothed out the lines and left this as the only Democratic district in the Metroplex. Today the 30th District includes two compact geographic units centered in downtown Dallas. One consists of most of the south side of Dallas; the other runs northwest out Stemmons Freeway. In between is the "mixmaster," where three busy interstates—I-30, 35E and 45—come together within a square mile, surrounding many of the prominent sites in Dallas. The district's population is 41% black and 34% Hispanic; local Hispanic population growth suggests redistricting in 2011 may produce a Hispanic-majority district in the Dallas area. The growing influence of racial minorities in the big city has been a major factor in the Democrats' recent capture of control of many Dallas County offices. In 2004, George W. Bush lost here 75%-25%, his worst performance in Texas.

The congresswoman from the 30th District is Eddie Bernice Johnson, who as a member of the state legislature created the district in 1991. She grew up in Texas, graduated from Texas Christian University as a registered nurse, and later got a master's in public administration at Southern Methodist. She worked at St. Paul Hospital and was chief psychiatric nurse at the VA Hospital in Dallas. In 1972 she was elected to the Texas House—the first black woman elected to anything in Dallas. She became a regional HEW director in the Carter administration and was elected to the state Senate in 1986; as Redistricting Committee chairman in 1991, she was instrumental in creating the new 30th District. She won the Democratic primary with 92% of the vote and has never had effective opposition.

In the House, Johnson has a mostly liberal voting record, but she has been attentive to business interests in Dallas. She claims to have sponsored or cosponsored more than 120 bills that have become law. She shows sharp political instincts: Johnson has chaired the Congressional Black Caucus and she supported Nancy Pelosi for minority leader over her former Metroplex colleague Martin Frost, with whom Johnson had a testy relationship, particularly on redistricting issues. Though Johnson once pledged to unions to oppose NAFTA, she changed her mind and voted for it; Dallas probably exports more to Mexico than any other American city, and many jobs depend on those exports. Johnson also sided with business on normal trade relations with China, but she later opposed trade promotion authority. On the Science Committee, where she was ranking Democrat on the Research Subcommittee, she shared credit for passing the Networking and Information Research and Development Act to double federal information research spending. She also sought to double spending for the National Science Foundation. As a health care professional, Johnson has taken an interest in minorities' health care problems. In 2001-2002, she chaired the Congressional Black Caucus. In 2004 she called for the United Nations to monitor the presidential election in Florida. "Too often, this country is rightly seen internationally as one who writes the rules and enforces them, but refuses to abide by them," she wrote on her website. She has gained attention with her "Women for World Peace" initiative.

On the Transportation and Infrastructure Committee, she got a seat on the Aviation Subcommittee, of great importance here: The 30th District is not far from Dallas-Fort Worth International Airport and includes three others, Love Field, Lancaster, and Dallas Executive Airport. Although she initially had objections, which included concerns about additional air traffic, she eventually cooperated with the Republican members of the Metroplex in repealing the Wright Amendment, named for former House Speaker Jim Wright, a Democrat; Johnson helped to broker the deal by encouraging more local coordination between the airports. As one of her top priorities, she worked to secure funds in the highway bill for construction of the I-30 suspension bridge over the Trinity River. In the majority, she chairs the Water Resources and Environment Subcommittee, where she has delivered for local projects, including the elevation and extension of levees. Asked what would be her agenda, she replied: "It's called the Trinity River."

THIRTY-FIRST DISTRICT

Rep. John Carter (R)

Elected 2002, 3d term; b. Nov. 6, 1941, Houston; home, Round Rock; TX Tech. U., B.A. 1964, U. of TX, J.D. 1969; Christian; married (Erika).

Elected Office: Dist. Ct. judge, 1982-2001.

Professional Career: Practicing atty., 1969-81.

DC Office: 408 CHOB, 20515, 202-225-3864; Fax: 202-225-5886; Web site: www.house.gov/carter/.

District Offices: Round Rock, 512-246-1600; Temple, 254-933-1392.

Committees: *Republican Conference Secretary. Appropriations* (27th of 29 R): Homeland Security; Military Construction, Veterans Affairs & Related Agencies.

Group Ratings

	ADA	ACLU	AFS	LCV	ITIC	NTU	COC	ACU	CFG	FRC
2006	0	10	0	0	100	59	100	88	57	100
2005	0	—	0	0	—	60	89	92	68	85

National Journal Ratings

	2005 LIB	—	2005 CONS		2006 LIB	—	2006 CONS
Economic	9%	—	88%		9%	—	91%
Social	0%	—	89%		21%	—	79%
Foreign	0%	—	89%		28%	—	71%

Key Votes of the 109th Congress

1. Estate Tax Repeal	Y	5. Limit Interstate Abortion	Y	9. Build Border Fence	Y
2. Limit CAFE Standards	Y	6. Extend Patriot Act	Y	10. CAFTA	Y
3. FY06 Spending Curb	Y	7. Bar Same Sex Marriage	Y	11. Oppose Iraq Withdrawal	*
4. Drilling in ANWR	Y	8. Stem Cell Research $	N	12. Detainee Tribunals	Y

Election Results

2006 general	John Carter (R)	90,869	(58%)	($908,827)
	Mary Beth Harrell (D)	60,293	(39%)	($207,294)
	Other	4,221	(3%)	
2006 primary	John Carter (R)	unopposed		
2004 general	John Carter (R)	160,247	(65%)	($899,885)
	Jon Porter (D)	80,292	(32%)	($15,618)
	Other	6,888	(3%)	

Prior Winning Percentages: 2002 (69%)

The People		Race/Ethnic Origin	Ancestry	
Area size:	7,194 sq. mi.	66.1% White	German: 12.6% Irish: 7.6%	
Urban population:	77.9%	13.0% Black	English: 6.8%	
Rural population:	22.1%	2.1% Asian	**2004 Presidential Vote**	
Pop. 2000:	651,619	0.4% Native Am.	Bush (R) 170,234	(67%)
Pop. 2005 (est):	760,702	0.2% Hawaiian	Kerry (D) 85,574	(33%)
Median income:	$43,381	1.8% Two+ races	**2000 Presidential Vote**	
Poverty status:	9.6%	0.1% Other	Bush (R) 136,116	(69%)
Military veterans:	16.4%	16.3% Hispanic Origin	Gore (D) 62,493	(31%)
			Cook Partisan Voting Index: R +16	

Occupation	Blue collar: 22.7%	White collar: 62.6%	Gray collar: 14.7%

Williamson County, Texas, long a rural backwater almost no one elsewhere had ever heard of, has become a major population and business center deep in the heart of Texas. Its population has virtually doubled in every recent decade: 37,000 in 1970, 77,000 in 1980, 140,000 in 1990, 250,000 in 2000, 354,000 in 2006. From 2000 to 2006 it was the nation's 16th fastest-growing county. Williamson County is just north of Austin, and much of this growth has been generated by the Austin area's high-tech boom; hugely successful Dell Computer is headquartered in Round Rock, with 18,000 local employees and still growing. And more growth will be generated by Texas 130, a 49-mile 10-lane toll road near completion in empty farmland a few miles east of congested I-35, the state's key north-south corridor. Bell and Coryell Counties, just north of Williamson County, are the site of Fort Hood, the largest U.S. military base in the world and the largest employer in Texas. The base is the only post in the United States capable of supporting two full armored divisions, and is home to 65,000 Army soldiers and family members, though the base closing review in 2005 reduced that by several thousand. Established in 1942 as a tank destroyer tactical and firing center, it uprooted on short notice 300 farming and ranching families who had been living a quiet life; now, this land serves a Texas-sized facility that covers 218,000 acres (that's 340 square miles). Toward the end of World War II, about 4,000 German prisoners of war were interned at Hood. The primary mission of Fort Hood has become maintaining readiness for combat missions, including training Army Reservists in urban combat. East of Fort Hood is Temple, a rail center and the only city in the area with a downtown business district. Decades ago, the freight carried from its rail yards was mostly cotton; now, it serves a variety of industries, including plastics manufacturers.

The 31st Congressional District of Texas, newly created in the 2001 court redistricting and sharply altered in the 2003 Republican redistricting, is dominated by Williamson, Bell and Coryell Counties, which include 86% of its population. The district also includes two smaller counties north of Coryell County and two counties and part of another east of Williamson and Bell Counties. Historically this was solidly Democratic country, devoted to the party of first the Confederacy and then the New Deal, full of cotton farmers who distrusted Wall Street and railroads and trusted in politicians like Sam Rayburn and Lyndon Johnson, and later, Ann Richards and Lloyd Bentsen. But people here have taken a shine to George W. Bush's brand of Republicanism. In 2004, he carried the district 67%-33%.

The congressman from the 31st District is John Carter, a Republican first elected in 2002. He grew up in Houston and graduated from Texas Tech and the University of Texas law school. He practiced law in Williamson County and served as a municipal judge in Round Rock. He was appointed a district judge in 1981 by Governor Bill Clements and in 1982 stood for election; judicial elections are partisan in Texas, and he was the first Republican judge elected in Williamson County. For that, Carter became known as the father of the county Republican party.

In 2001, after a three-judge district court created a new Republican 31st District stretching from Williamson County to Houston, Carter retired from the bench and started running for Congress. The real contest in this district was among the eight candidates for the Republican nomination. Carter's main rivals were Peter Wareing, the son-in-law of Texas oilman Jack Blanton, and Brad Barton, son of 6th District Congressman Joe Barton. In the primary, Wareing led with 37% to 26% for Carter and 16% for Barton. Wareing got 67% in his home base in Harris County; Carter got 58% in Williamson County. In the four-week runoff campaign Carter attacked Wareing as a liberal in disguise for his campaign contributions to Democrats like Congresswoman Sheila Jackson Lee. When Wareing proposed that each candidate sign a "clean campaign pledge," Carter offered what he called a "homestead pledge"—a ploy to highlight his charge that Wareing was a Houston carpetbagger who rented an apartment in the district for the sole purpose of running for office. Barton endorsed Carter as "the only true conservative in this race." Wareing outspent Carter more than

2-to-1, but Carter won 57%-43%. He got 78% of the vote in Williamson County, which cast 33% of the vote; Wareing got 65% of the vote in Harris County, which cast 16% of the vote. Carter won the general election easily.

In the House, Carter has been a reliable conservative who opposes abortion rights and supports voluntary prayer in schools. He became the freshman class representative on the Republican Steering Committee, which makes committee assignments. On the Judiciary Committee, he passed a bill to establish penalties for aggravated identity theft. He won House passage, 344-72, of his Terrorist Penalties Enhancement Act as an amendment to the intelligence reorganization bill. He objected to continuing the Voting Rights Act requirement that Texas get federal approval of voting-law changes, but he voted to extend the law. In 2005, with help from Majority Leader Tom DeLay, Carter joined the Appropriations Committee. As a member of the Military Construction and Veterans Affairs Subcommittee, he was well-positioned—with Chairman Chet Edwards of the neighboring 17th District—to defend the interests of Fort Hood. He criticized Republican conservatives who objected to earmarks by the appropriators. In December 2006, Carter was elected without opposition to the party leadership as secretary of the Republican Conference.

In the 2003 redistricting, Williamson County was the only territory carried over from the old 31st District, which eliminated the possibility of a challenge from the Houston area. In 2006, he faced Mary Beth Harrell, a lawyer in Killeen whose son served in Iraq and who advocated withdrawal from the conflict; Carter won, 58%-39%.

THIRTY-SECOND DISTRICT

Rep. Pete Sessions (R)

Elected 1996, 6th term; b. Mar. 22, 1955, Waco; home, Dallas; SW U., B.A. 1978; Methodist; married (Juanita).

Professional Career: District Mgr., SW Bell Telephone Co., 1978-93; V.P., Public Policy, Natl. Center for Policy Analysis, 1994-95.

DC Office: 1514 LHOB, 20515, 202-225-2231; Fax: 202-225-5878; Web site: sessions.house.gov.

District Offices: Dallas, 972-392-0505.

Committees: *Rules* (4th of 4 R): Rules & Organization of the House.

Group Ratings

	ADA	ACLU	AFS	LCV	ITIC	NTU	COC	ACU	CFG	FRC
2006	0	0	0	0	100	77	100	96	86	100
2005	0	—	0	0	—	69	93	100	88	75

National Journal Ratings

	2005 LIB	—	2005 CONS		2006 LIB	—	2006 CONS
Economic	0%	—	97%		4%	—	96%
Social	0%	—	89%		17%	—	83%
Foreign	0%	—	89%		0%	—	94%

Key Votes of the 109th Congress

1. Estate Tax Repeal	Y	5. Limit Interstate Abortion	Y	9. Build Border Fence	Y
2. Limit CAFE Standards	Y	6. Extend Patriot Act	Y	10. CAFTA	Y
3. FY06 Spending Curb	Y	7. Bar Same Sex Marriage	Y	11. Oppose Iraq Withdrawal	*
4. Drilling in ANWR	Y	8. Stem Cell Research $	N	12. Detainee Tribunals	Y

Election Results

2006 general	Pete Sessions (R)	71,461	(56%)	($1,762,182)
	Will Pryor (D)	52,269	(41%)	($460,074)
	Other	2,922	(2%)	
2006 primary	Pete Sessions (R)	unopposed		
2004 general	Pete Sessions (R)	109,859	(54%)	($4,512,464)
	Martin Frost (D)	89,030	(44%)	($4,761,288)
	Other	3,347	(2%)	

Prior Winning Percentages: 2002 (68%); 2000 (54%); 1998 (56%); 1996 (53%)

The People		Race/Ethnic Origin	Ancestry	
Area size:	161 sq. mi.	50.1% White	German: 7.7%	English: 7.5%
Urban population:	99.9%	7.7% Black	Irish: 6.1%	
Rural population:	0.1%	4.2% Asian	**2004 Presidential Vote**	
Pop. 2000:	651,620	0.4% Native Am.	Bush (R) 120,970	(60%)
Pop. 2005 (est):	655,222	0.0% Hawaiian	Kerry (D) 81,846	(40%)
Median income:	$45,725	1.3% Two+ races	**2000 Presidential Vote**	
Poverty status:	12.5%	0.1% Other	Bush (R) 118,257	(64%)
Military veterans:	8.9%	36.2% Hispanic Origin	Gore (D) 66,003	(36%)
			Cook Partisan Voting Index: R +11	

Occupation   Blue collar: 21.3%   White collar: 65.9%   Gray collar: 12.8%

North Dallas has long been the home of the city's elite—indeed, of a good portion of the nation's elite. Early in the 20th century, Dallas's richest citizens started moving away from old neighborhoods next to downtown and out past Turtle Creek to the area around the suburbs of Highland Park and University Park—the Park Cities. Dallas grew lustily from mid-century on, and beyond the Park Cities miles of affluent neighborhoods were built, especially between the Central Expressway and the Dallas North Tollway. Galaxies and office complexes followed. Not all of North Dallas is like that; there is an entertainment and singles apartment corridor along Greenville Avenue, working class black neighborhoods here and there, pockets of Latino neighborhoods near the freeways. But overall the tone has been set by the Dallas elite. In the 1960s and 1970s this was one of the politically most conservative parts of the country: people believed firmly in free markets, personal responsibility and the Republican party. Since 1992, North Dallas has moved, like elite parts of other big metropolitan areas, toward Democrats, as has the overall county. The number of affluent women voting Democratic on the abortion issue is much smaller than in affluent quadrants of New York or Los Angeles; but there are some. A decade ago, both George W. Bush and Dick Cheney lived in North Dallas, in or near the Park Cities; Bush moved to Austin in January 1995 to become governor and Cheney changed his residence to Wyoming in July 2000 so that he could be nominated vice president.

The 32d Congressional District of Texas includes most of the area commonly thought of as North Dallas: the Park Cities and affluent North Dallas neighborhoods north to the Dallas County line. Most of the business and professional elite of Dallas live in this area. The district also includes affluent suburbs in Dallas County: parts of Richardson northeast of the city, and Addison to the northwest. The 2003 redistricting removed some suburban territory and added blue-collar Irving and the heavily Latino Oak Cliff neighborhoods south of the Trinity River, where Lee Harvey Oswald was captured inside the old Texas Theater on November 22, 1963, shortly after he killed President John F. Kennedy. As in the elite-class 7th District in Houston, Bush's vote declined here in 2004, to 60%; an increase in Democratic-voting Latino voters (redistricting raised the Hispanic percentage from 27% to 36%) may have contributed to this result.

The congressman from the 32d District is Pete Sessions, a Republican first elected in 1996. Sessions grew up in Waco, graduated from Southwestern University, then worked at Southwestern Bell in Dallas for 16 years; his father William Sessions, a federal judge, served as FBI director from 1987 to 1993. His ambition and the vagaries of redistricting have led Sessions to run for Congress in several different House districts. In 1991 he ran and finished sixth in the special election in the 3d District, which then included much of North Dallas. In 1993 he resigned from the phone company to run against Democratic incumbent John Bryant in the 5th District, which included much of the east side of Dallas and several rural counties to the south. The district had been drawn to reelect Bryant, a liberal legislator. Sessions ran a vigorous campaign, making a two-day, 12-city tour of the district's rural portions with a livestock trailer full of horse manure and a sign saying "the Clinton health care plan stinks worse than this trailer." Although he outspent Sessions 2–1, Bryant won by just

50%-47%. In 1996 Bryant ran unsuccessfully for the Senate; Sessions ran again and won the primary. He faced John Pouland, a former regional GSA administrator. Sessions charged that Pouland was a big government liberal and would abandon U.S. military bases overseas; Pouland criticized subsidizing the foreign bases while pursuing Medicare "cuts." This was a seriously contested race; Sessions won 53%-47%.

Sessions has a voting record that has been among the most conservative in the House. In 1999 he got a seat on the Rules Committee, a sign that he was a leadership loyalist. He sponsored the constitutional amendment to require a two-thirds vote to raise taxes and was a leading advocate of the Republican proposal to put Social Security and Medicare surpluses in a lockbox. He joined with Charles Grassley and Democrats Ted Kennedy and Henry Waxman on a bill to permit families with disabled children to keep their Medicaid coverage even if their income rises; Sessions and his wife have a son with Down's syndrome. He wants to abolish the IRS and scrap the income tax code. In 2006, he was instrumental in finding common ground with others in the Metroplex for the phased repeal of the Wright amendment.

Since winning office, Sessions has faced competitive challenges in various districts. In 2000, Democrats talked up his challenger Regina Montoya Coggins, a Clinton White House liaison to local elected officials whose husband was Clinton's U.S. attorney in the Dallas area; she was well known for her on-air work at KERA-TV in Dallas. In a strong Republican year in Texas, Sessions won 54%-44%. The next year, the federal court's redistricting plan made the 5th District more Republican; Sessions surprised almost everyone in the political world by leaving the 5th and running in the newly-created 32d, which had no incumbent but included only 16% of his old district. He said he wanted to spend less time traveling around his district (the new 32d was considerably more compact) and that the new district was compatible with his pro-business philosophy; the 32d certainly has a stronger fundraising base. Sessions's decision led state Representative Kenny Marchant to abandon his plan to run in the 32d; in 2004, Marchant was elected in the 24th District. Sessions had only token primary opposition in 2002 and won the general, 68%-30%.

In 2003, Sessions urged the legislature to order a new round of congressional redistricting to replace the "current partisan interim map," and he worked closely with Majority Leader Tom DeLay to make that happen. But in getting what he wished for, he found himself with a less Republican district and a reelection challenge from 13-term Democratic stalwart Martin Frost, whose 24th District had been shorn of its most Democratic precincts. Frost kept people guessing for several weeks which district he would run in and announced, shortly before the filing date, that he would run in the 32d. He chose the 32d because of the large Jewish population in the Park Cities and his view that Sessions was too conservative for the local establishment. From the start, Sessions voiced confidence that he would win by about 10 points, though he braced himself for negative attacks. Frost focused on his legislative accomplishments and his work on local issues to help the Dallas business community; he rarely mentioned John Kerry. This was the most expensive House campaign of 2004; Sessions spent $4.5 million and Frost $4.8 million; more was spent by party committees and independent groups. The candidates hurled charges at each other and tangential issues came into play. Frost criticized Sessions for a streaking incident in college. Sessions criticized Frost for scheduling a fundraiser with Peter Yarrow, the Peter, Paul and Mary singer who had been convicted of "taking indecent liberties" with a 14-year-old girl in 1969. Frost cited Sessions's vote, along with only eight other members, against a bill opposing establishment of new air passenger security rules after September 11, and ran an ad with images of the World Trade Center in flames and the message, "Protect America. Say No to Pete Sessions." Frost was endorsed by the *Dallas Morning News,* local police and firefighters groups, teachers' organizations, and the Sierra Club. Sessions had support from the Club for Growth and the National Federation of Independent Business. Sessions won by 10 points, 54%-44%, just as he predicted, capturing more than 80% of the vote in some precincts in the Park Cities. Frost failed to get the higher turnout he needed in Oak Cliff. In 2006, Sessions won 56%-41% against Will Pryor, a Dallas lawyer and cousin of Arkansas Senator Mark Pryor.

The investigation of lobbyist Jack Abramoff brought some unwanted scrutiny to Sessions, for it brought attention to his support for casino-operating tribes and a trip to Malaysia that was arranged by Abramoff. Sessions denied any wrongdoing, and there was no indication that the Justice Department was investigating him. Citing his victory over Frost, he ran in 2006 to become chairman of the National Republican Congressional Committee, but he lost to Tom Cole on the second ballot. Sessions said that he suffered because Texans Kay Granger and John Carter won other leadership posts before the NRCC vote.

★ UTAH ★

U tah is a triumph of man over nature, the creation of a productive and orderly civilization in a remote expanse of desert and mountain, arrayed around a desolate salt sea. Today's Utah and Mormonism have their roots in a very different landscape of more than 150 years ago, when a wave of religious enthusiasm, prophecy and utopianism swept across the "burnt-over district" of Upstate New York in the 1820s and 1830s. There Joseph Smith, a 14-year-old farmer, experienced a vision in which the angel Moroni appeared and told him where to unearth several golden tablets inscribed with hieroglyphic writings. With the aid of special spectacles, Smith translated the tablets and published them as the Book of Mormon in 1831. He later declared himself a prophet and founded the Church of Jesus Christ of Latter-day Saints. The Mormons, as they were called, attracted thousands of converts and created their own communities; persecuted for their beliefs, they moved west to Ohio, Missouri and then Illinois. In 1844, the Mormon colony at Nauvoo, Illinois, had some 15,000 members living under the theocratic rule of Smith. It was here that Smith received a revelation sanctioning the practice of polygamy, which led to his death at the hands of a mob in 1844. After the murder, the new church president, Brigham Young, decided to move the faithful, "the saints," farther west into territory that was still part of Mexico and far beyond white settlement. Young led a well-organized march across the Great Plains and into the Rocky Mountains on a path where Mormons reenacted the march 150 years later in 1997. In 1847, they stopped on the western slope of the Wasatch Range and, as Young gazed over the valley of the Great Salt Lake spread out below, he said, "This is the place."

The place was Utah. Young was governor of the territory for many years, and it is the only state that largely continues to live by the teachings of a church. The early pioneers laid out towns foursquare to the points of the compass with huge city blocks, built sturdy houses and planted dozens of trees. Young's home still stands a block away from Temple Square, where the Temple, closed to non-Mormons, stands in gleaming marble, topped by the golden angel Moroni, across from the oval Mormon Tabernacle where its great choir sings. For 150 years this "Zion" has attracted thousands of converts from the Midwest, the north of England and Scandinavia. The object of religious fear and prejudice, Utah was not granted statehood until 1896, after the church renounced polygamy. Utah has grown steadily since then, and remains heavily Mormon, its basic character stamped on the mountain-shadowed, desert landscape that without the Mormons would probably have remained as unpopulated as Nevada would have been without gambling.

The LDS church remains distinctive in many ways. It cares deeply about its past: In caves in the mountains of Utah, the church preserves America's most complete genealogical records in its Family History Library, which is also on the Internet. It tries to spread the faith: Young Mormons, 65,000 every year, spend missionary years in the United States and abroad, and their experiences in turn give Utah the biggest inventory of people with knowledge of obscure foreign languages of any state in the union, a nice commercial advantage. That prompted the NSA to set up language analyst offices in Utah in 2006. The church prohibits the consumption of tobacco, alcohol and caffeine; it encourages hard work and large families. Mormons are healthier than the average American; better educated, they work longer hours and earn more money. In an individualist country, the church fosters communitarian attitudes: The LDS Church has no clergy, but members serve in positions for which they are chosen, conducting religious services but also keeping in touch with members and counseling them when they need help. The church also maintains its own social service organizations. It evidently works: While American mainline denominations are losing members, the Mormon Church is growing. There were 2.9 million Mormons in 1970 and nearly 11 million in 2000, with more than half outside the United States and just 15% in Utah; this has been the fastest-growing church in the United States in recent decades and the nation's fifth largest denomination in 2003.

Mormons and Utahns are heavily Republican today, but this was not always so. In the 19th century Republicans led the fight to keep Utah out of the union and a Democrat, Grover Cleveland, signed the statehood act. Before World War II, Utah saw itself as a colonial victim of East Coast bankers and financiers and Mormons saw themselves as suffering religious discrimination and bigotry—all with some cause. Utah's income levels were well below the national average, its cost of living higher, the prices paid for the things it produced seemed to be controlled elsewhere. In political terms, this perspective translated into a Democratic allegiance: In 1940 Utah was represented by staunch New Dealers in Congress and cast 62% of its votes for Franklin D. Roosevelt. Today, Utah sees itself as a busy generator of wealth, with a raft of successful businesses and a knack for high-tech innovation—and longer work weeks than the rest of the nation.

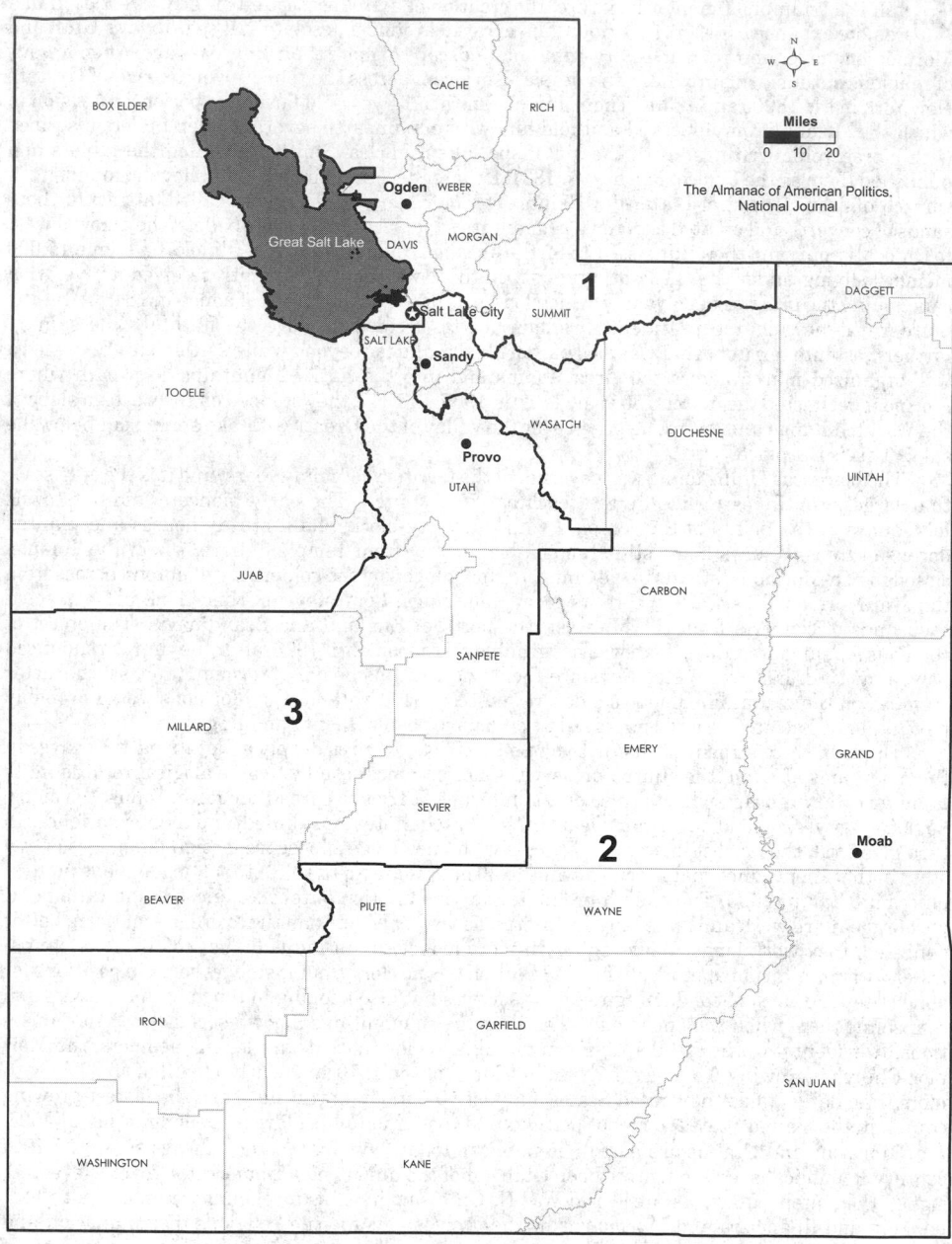

Congressional district boundaries were first effective for 2002.

Utah achieves all this with cultural attitudes and demographic patterns that resemble the America of the 1950s. Utah has the highest percentage of households headed by married couples, the highest fertility rate for non-Hispanic whites, the youngest median age of first marriage, and the lowest rate of birth to unmarried mothers. It has many more children per capita than any other state, and this can make its economic statistics misleading: Utah has a relatively low per capita income (because all those kids aren't earning salaries) but ranks much higher on median household incomes. It is the youngest state, with the largest families and one of the longest life expectancies, and the highest rate of volunteering. Some 62% of Utahns are Mormons, a percentage that has been declining but is still a solid majority, and pervading the cultural atmosphere of the state is the LDS Church. Its opposition to abortion is widely shared and it has always discouraged gambling: Utah has a law penalizing abortion if *Roe v. Wade* is overturned and is one of two states (Hawaii is the other) with no form of gambling. (Of course many Mormons are employed in the gaming industry across the line in Las Vegas.) Utah has some of the more restrictive laws on alcohol and has been way ahead of the rest of the nation in discouraging the use of tobacco. A large majority in 2004 voted for a constitutional amendment to ban same-sex marriage. Polls show about 80% of Mormons vote Republican, but church leaders made a point of stating that "principles compatible with the gospel may be found in the platforms of all political parties."

Between 2000 and 2006 Utah's population growth was the third-fastest among states, behind only Nevada and Arizona. Most of the growth comes from natural increase—all those kids—but there has also been substantial domestic inflow, especially from California, including Hispanics and high-income professionals. This has helped to reduce the Mormon percentage in Utah, even as the church continues making new converts in other states and around the world. Interestingly, the Salt Lake City neighborhoods close to the church headquarters, with gracious old houses and a smaller street grid that attract academic and professional newcomers, have become the most heavily "gentile" and politically liberal part of the state. Just as the Yankee hub of Boston filled up with Irish Catholic Democrats in the 1890s, so Salt Lake City has been getting secular liberal Democrats. Salt Lake City now is out of step with the rest of the state: It voted 58% for John Kerry in 2004 and its mayor since 2000, Rocky Anderson, has called George W. Bush a war criminal who should be impeached. But Salt Lake County grew just 8% in 2000-06, while Utah County, home of Provo and Brigham Young University, grew 20%. And Washington County, in the far southwest corner of the state just northeast of Las Vegas, is the fastest-growing region, with its own exploding private sector economy around the town of St. George, *Inc.* magazine's number one boomtown in 2007.

Politically, Utah has been indisputably the most Republican state since the 1980s. It does elect one Democratic congressman these days, Jim Matheson, who started off with the advantage of having a father who was a well-remembered Democratic governor. But it has not elected a Democratic governor since Matheson's father Scott in 1980, a Democratic senator since 1970 or a Democrat for president since 1964.

The People		Race/Ethnic Origin			Military veterans: 161,351 (10.6%)	
Pop. 2006 (est):	2,550,063	1,904,265	85.3%	White	WWII: 21.0%	Korea: 13.9%
Pop. 2000:	2,233,169	16,137	0.7%	Black	Vietnam: 31.7%	Gulf War: 11.5%
Pop. 1990:	1,722,850	36,483	1.6%	Asian	**Most populous cities (2006):**	
Change 1990-2000:	Up 29.6%	26,663	1.2%	Native Am.	1. Salt Lake City	178,858
% of U.S. total:	0.8%	14,806	0.7%	Hawaiian	2. West Valley City	119,841
Pop. rank:	34th of 50	31,308	1.4%	Two+ races	3. Provo	113,984
Area size:	84,899 sq. mi.	1,948	0.1%	Other	4. West Jordan	94,309
State Native:	62.9%	201,559	9.0%	Hisp. Origin	5. Sandy	94,203
Non-citizen:	4.9%	**Ancestry**				
Language		English: 21.4%		German: 8.5%	Urban population: 88.3%	
English: 83.1%	Spanish: 9.1%	USA: 5.0%		Danish: 4.8%	Rural population: 11.7%	
Other Eur.: 4.5%		Irish: 4.3%				

Education		Work Sector		Utah	
H.S. Grad:	87.7%	Private: 78.2%	Govt: 15.7%	Senate	21 R 8 D
College Grad:	26.1%	Self: 5.8%	Family: 0.3%	House	55 R 20 D
Industry		Unemployment: 4.9%		Legislative Term Limits: No	
Agri: 1.9%	Con: 8.2%	**Household Income**		**Registered Voters**	
Fin: 6.8%	Info: 3.3%	<15k: 10.8%	15-35k: 25.1%	No party registration	
Mfg: 17.0%	Prof: 28.6%	35-50k: 19.0%	50-100k: 33.9%		
Public: 5.5%	Trade: 16.3%	100-150k: 7.5%	>150k: 3.7%		
Other: 12.4%		Median: $45,726			
Occupation		Poverty status: 9.4%			
Blue collar: 24.1%	White collar: 61.4%	**Home Value**			
Gray collar: 14.5%		<50k: 4.8% 50-100k: 15.9% 100-200k: 57.0% 200-300k: 14.3%			
		300-500k: 5.9% >500k: 2.0% Median: $142,600			

Presidential politics   Utah has been the most Republican state in six of the last eight presidential elections. As recently as 1960, Richard Nixon carried Utah with just 55% of the vote, but by 1972 he won with 68%. Ronald Reagan won 73% here in 1980 and 75% in 1984; George Bush won 66% here in 1988 and George W. Bush 67% in 2000 and 72% in 2004. In 1992, this was also the least Democratic state: Ross Perot finished ahead of Bill Clinton, 27% to 25%.

Governor Mike Leavitt spent much time and effort promoting a Western regional primary for the Friday following Southern Super Tuesday, March 10, 2000. But only Colorado and Wyoming (with a caucus, not a primary) adopted the date, and candidates paid less attention to western issues than Leavitt had hoped. Bill Bradley and John McCain pulled out of their races before March 10, and only 10% of Utah's registered voters bothered to vote. In 2004 Utah held a Democratic primary February 24; 35,000 people voted in a state of 2.3 million, and John Kerry led John Edwards 55%-30%. For 2008, Utah was happy to schedule its primary for February 5, with hopes of attracting national candidates; but those hopes were surely dampened when California, New York and New Jersey picked the February 5 date and Florida January 29.

2004 Presidential Vote

Bush (R)	663,742	(72%)
Kerry (D)	241,199	(26%)
Nader (NPA)	11,305	(1%)
Other	11,598	(1%)

2004 Democratic Presidential Primary

Kerry (D)	19,232	(55%)
Edwards (D)	10,384	(30%)
Kucinich (D)	2,590	(7%)
Dean (D)	1,335	(4%)
Clark (D)	489	(1%)
Other	824	(2%)

2000 Presidential Vote

Bush (R)	515,096	(67%)
Gore (D)	203,053	(26%)
Nader (Green)	35,850	(5%)
Other	16,755	(2%)

Congressional districting   Utahns expected that the 2000 Census would give Utah a fourth seat in the House of Representatives. But, under the formula used for reapportionment, Utah fell 857 residents short of getting a new district; instead, North Carolina got an unexpected 13th seat. Utah did what comes naturally to Americans today: it sued, twice. The first lawsuit contended that if military personnel stationed abroad should be counted in their states of residence, so should Mormon missionaries, who also can be accurately tracked and matched with their home states. As it happens, North Carolina had thousands of military personnel stationed abroad and only 107 attributable Mormon missionaries. Utah had fewer military personnel stationed abroad but 11,176 Mormon missionaries. In April 2001 a three-judge federal court threw out Utah's case, and one judge called its theory "wildly unfair." In late November 2001 the Supreme Court affirmed that ruling without opinion. Utah's other theory was that the Census Bureau violated the Constitution's injunction that it conduct an "actual enumeration" of the population when it employed what statisticians call "hot-deck imputation": when Census takers after repeated efforts cannot contact residents of one housing unit, they assume that it contains

110th Congress Lineup
2 R   1 D

109th Congress Lineup
2 R   1 D

the same number of people in similar housing units nearby. Utah argued that this is "sampling", which, the Supreme Court ruled in another case, was prohibited by a 1957 statute. This argument did better in court: Utah lost by a 2–1 margin in a three-judge district court in early November 2001 and by 5–4 in the Supreme Court in June 2002. But the upshot was that North Carolina, not Utah, got the 435th district in the 2000 reapportionment.

Utah's legislature drew new congressional district lines in September 2001. Aware that the state was suing for another district, it adopted both three- and four-district plans. The large Republican majorities in the legislature argued that all districts should contain both urban and rural areas; this policy was followed when Utah had two congressional districts, but when it gained a third district in the 1980 Census, and then again after the 1990 Census, the legislature drew plans which had one district entirely inside Salt Lake County. This 2d District had had the temerity in 2000 to elect a Democratic congressman. The Republicans' principle, honored in the breach for the preceding 20 years, led them to draw three districts which combined urban and rural areas and which increased the Bush 2000 percentage in the 2d District from 57% to 67%. At the same time, the Republican legislators drew a four-district plan, which would go into effect should Utah win one of its then two pending court cases. This plan included a new 4th District entirely within Salt Lake County but within the southern portion of the county, which is heavily Republican. Utah conducted its 2002 election with the three-district plan in place, and the Supreme Court decision narrowly rejecting the state's attack on "hot-deck imputation" came just five days before the June 2002 primary.

In 2006 Utah's quest for a fourth House seat got raised again in Virginia Republican Tom Davis's bill to award the District of Columbia a full voting member of the House; it balanced that obvious gain for the Democrats by awarding another seat, until the next reapportionment after the 2010 Census, to the state entitled to the 436th district under the statutory formula—which of course happened to be Utah. But how would the new member from Utah be elected? House Judiciary Chairman James Sensenbrenner, when Republicans were in control, was wary of the legislation and insisted that the Utah legislature draw up a plan with four congressional districts before the bill would be considered. The Utah legislature did so in December 2006, with a plan that allayed Democrats' fears and gave Jim Matheson a much more Democratic district. But time was running out on the Republican Congress, and the D.C. bill never reached the floor.

The new Democratic leadership was much more favorable. A bill, with a proviso that the fourth Utah representative would be elected at-large, passed the Judiciary Committee 21-13 in March 2007; an amendment by Utah's Chris Cannon that would have required a 4-member districting plan for the 2008 and 2010 elections was rejected. Matheson and Cannon voted aye; 1st District Republican Rob Bishop voted present. After having been delayed when Republicans raised the issue of D.C.'s recently-declared-unconstitutional handgun ban, it passed the House 241-177 in April. Senator Orrin Hatch expressed reservations at first but later co-sponsored the bill along with Senator Bob Bennett; the White House suggested it would be vetoed if passed. Politically, some Republicans said that Utah would get a fourth seat anyway by 2012 and that it was a bad tradeoff to give D.C. a seat forever in return for just two terms. The constitutional issue, raised by many Republican opponents, is that the Constitution says that only "states" shall be represented in the House; supporters assembled conservative constitutional scholars who argue this is not a blank prohibition. Bishop raised the interesting question of whether Utah (or D.C.) would get an additional electoral vote. Alaska and Hawaii, on being admitted to the Union were granted one seat each in the House and two in the Senate, as required by the Constitution, and therefore, under another constitutional provision, three electoral votes each. It could be argued that if Utah were given an additional House member it should be allotted another electoral vote under the same provision, while D.C., which is not a state, would not be covered by that provision but would be limited by the Twenty-Third Amendment which provides that it get three and no more than three electoral votes. So a plan which would give Democrats an extra House seat in perpetuity starting in 2012 might give Republicans an extra electoral vote in 2008.

Governor

Jon Huntsman (R)

Elected 2004, term expires Jan. 2009, 1st term; b. Mar. 26, 1960, Palo Alto, CA; home, Salt Lake City; Attended U. of UT; U. of PA, B.A. 1987; Mormon; married (Mary Kaye).

Professional Career: Staff Asst., White House, 1982-83; Exec., Huntsman Corp., 1983-89; Dep. Asst. Sec. of Commerce, Trade Dev. Bureau, 1989-90; Dep. Asst. Sec. of Commerce for E. Asia & the Pacific, 1990-91; Amb. to Singapore, 1992-93; Pres., Huntsman Cancer Foundation, 1995-2001; U.S. trade amb., 2001-03; Chairman and CEO, Huntsman Family Holdings Co., 2003-04.

Office: East Office Building, Suite E220, PO Box 142220, Salt Lake City, 84114, 801-538-1000; Fax: 801-538-1528; Web site: www.utah.gov/governor.

Election Results

2004 general	Jon Huntsman (R)	531,190	(58%)
	Scott Matheson (D)	380,359	(41%)
	Other	8,411	(1%)
2004 primary	Jon Huntsman (R)	102,955	(66%)
	Nolan Karras (R)	52,048	(34%)
2000 general	Michael Leavitt (R)	424,837	(56%)
	Bill Orton (D)	321,979	(42%)
	Other	14,990	(2%)

Jon Huntsman Jr., a Republican, was elected governor of Utah in 2004. He was born in Palo Alto, California, the oldest of nine children, spent time in California and in Washington, D.C., where his father worked in the Nixon administration, then moved to Utah. He dropped out of high school to play keyboards in rock-and-roll bands; he attended the University of Utah briefly before leaving on a two-year Mormon mission to Taiwan. There he learned to speak fluent Mandarin Chinese. When he returned, he transferred to and graduated from the University of Pennsylvania. He is the son of billionaire philanthropist and industrialist Jon Huntsman, the wealthiest man in Utah (his company invented McDonald's Big Mac clamshell packaging), and the family owns a controlling interest in the Huntsman Corporation, a multinational petrochemical corporation headquartered in Salt Lake City. Jon Huntsman Jr. was an intern for Senator Orrin Hatch, a staff assistant to Ronald Reagan, served in the administration of George H.W. Bush as a deputy assistant secretary of Commerce and as ambassador to Singapore and was a deputy trade ambassador for George W. Bush. He also served as president of the Huntsman Cancer Foundation and as CEO of the Huntsman Family Holdings Co., the umbrella organization that holds the assets of the multibillion-dollar Huntsman chemical business.

Huntsman succeeded Republican Governor Olene Walker, who was the first woman to hold the position. Walker was governor for 13 months; as lieutenant governor, she assumed office in November 2003 when Governor Mike Leavitt stepped down with one year remaining in his term to become administrator of the federal Environmental Protection Agency. Walker would not say at first whether she planned to run for election in 2004, but she was no caretaker governor. After the 2004 legislative session, she vetoed a series of bills and then made the surprising announcement that she would run for a full term at age 74. Polls showed Walker was quite popular but she failed to get the 60% required to win the nomination outright at the state Republican convention in May and failed even to place among the top two candidates, thus preventing her from appearing on the June 22 primary ballot.

Huntsman led in the polls from the start against former Speaker and Board of Regents Chairman Nolan Karras. The primary lacked much drama: the two candidates agreed on most issues, were unusually civil to each other and Huntsman kept the focus on his top issue, economic development. He outspent Karras $1.3 million to $1 million and won easily with 66%, carrying every county but one and winning populous Salt Lake County by a more than 2–1 margin.

The Democratic nominee was Scott Matheson, the son of the state's last Democratic governor, brother of 2d District Congressman Jim Matheson, and a Rhodes Scholar who had managed his father's gubernatorial campaigns in 1976 and 1980. He served four years as U.S. Attorney for Utah and later became dean of the University of Utah law school. The tone of the general election campaign also was unusually civil. The two nominees shared similar views on many issues and even applauded each other during one debate. But they diverged on gay rights and school vouchers. Huntsman supported Amendment 3, a proposed state constitutional amendment that would ban same-sex marriage (a position held by the LDS Church, though it took no stand on the ballot measure itself; it passed in November with 66%), while Matheson opposed it. Huntsman advocated school choice, vouchers and a system of tuition tax credits; he claimed a vote for Matheson was a vote for the agenda of the state teachers' union, which had endorsed Matheson. Matheson emphasized the need to increase education spending.

Huntsman stayed focused on job creation and economic issues. He insisted that only an improved business climate would permit increased spending for highways and for the burgeoning public school system; revamping Utah's "dilapidated and anachronistic" tax system and phasing out the state sales tax on food was a necessary predicate. Huntsman closely aligned himself with the George W. Bush but parted company on two issues. Referring to the No Child Left Behind Act as an unfunded mandate, he argued that it "should be jettisoned out of the classroom"; the state has been a leader in the resistance to NCLB, with state officials arguing that the law is too rigid and a serious intrusion into Utah's right to control public schools. He also broke with the administration by suggesting he supported the importation of prescription drugs from Canada.

Huntsman outspent Matheson, $3.2 million to $2 million, loaning his campaign $275,000 but otherwise spent far less of his own money than other similarly situated candidates might have. He won all but four counties to win 58%-41%. Matheson carried Salt Lake County 51%-46%; Huntsman ran 14% behind George W. Bush there.

He began his term by breaking with tradition and delivering his first State of the State address in the historic statehouse in Fillmore, the territorial capital of Utah named in appreciation of President Millard Fillmore's decision to name Brigham Young as the first territorial governor. Huntsman proposed a phaseout of corporate income taxes and called for streamlining sales taxes. In his first legislative session as governor, he had a low-key style and got along well with legislators. He signed a bill banning Class B and C radioactive waste from Utah and vowed to prevent the shipment of mustard gas from Colorado to Utah for destruction. Broad tax reform was deferred but he raised salaries for state employees, got money for economic development and $18 million for tourism promotion. He also signed a measure to void undocumented immigrants' driver's licenses and replace them with a "driving privilege" card, which cannot be used as legal ID. He said he was open to relaxing the state's strict liquor laws. He called an April special session and then signed legislation limiting Utah's implementation of NCLB education requirements, despite warnings from the U.S. Education Department that the state eventually could lose millions in federal dollars.

Huntsman began his second year in office with high approval ratings and a healthy budget surplus. With a slightly more aggressive stance toward the legislature, he sought to fulfill his campaign promise to eliminate the sales tax on food and managed to reduce the state's portion of it by two percentage points. He failed in his effort to institute a "flatter" income tax but signed off on $20 million in business tax cuts. Huntsman also traveled to Iraq to visit soldiers and to China in October on a weeklong trade mission. There, the former diplomat impressed Chinese officials. "You're not the first governor who has come to promote tourism," said one Chinese official. "But you're definitely the first governor who came to China to promote your state in Mandarin Chinese." In December, Huntsman and his family traveled to India where they adopted a one-year-old girl who had been abandoned by the side of the road not long after her birth.

In 2007, with the state looking at a $1.7 billion surplus, Huntsman called for an 18% increase in education spending. This was a rare legislative session where there seemed to be money for almost everything: funding for all-day kindergarten, raises for teachers, $220 million in tax cuts (including another reduction in the food sales tax), hundreds of millions for transportation projects. Huntsman also achieved significant change in the state's tax structure. In 2008, the state will move to a 5% single-rate personal income tax system that relies on tax credits rather than deductions or exemptions. Another 2007 accomplishment was passage of an expansive school voucher bill which created a program open to all public school students and to private school students from low-income families; Huntsman signed the bill without fanfare and it quickly became embroiled in legal controversy.

Huntsman's successes have led to speculation about his political future. In April 2007, he insisted he was not interested in replacing Republican Senator Orrin Hatch in the event Hatch was selected by President George W. Bush to replace Alberto Gonzales as attorney general. But Huntsman did show an interest in national politics. He worked with other Western governors, including New Mexico Governor Bill Richardson, to establish a 2008 regional presidential primary though the effort met with limited success. Huntsman surprised some with his early endorsement of John McCain for Republican party 2008 presidential nomination, a notable choice given fellow Mormon Mitt Romney's widespread popularity in Utah—and Huntsman's father's strong support for Romney.

Senior Senator

Orrin Hatch (R)

Elected 1976, seat up 2012, 6th term; b. Mar. 22, 1934, Pittsburgh, PA; home, Salt Lake City; Brigham Young U., B.S. 1959; U. of Pittsburgh, J.D. 1962; Mormon; married (Elaine).

Professional Career: Practicing atty., 1962-76.

DC Office: 104 HSOB, 20510, 202-224-5251; Fax: 202-224-6331; Web site: www.senate.gov/~hatch.

State Offices: Cedar City, 435-586-8435; Ogden, 801-625-5672; Provo, 801-375-7881; Salt Lake City, 801-524-4380; St. George, 435-634-1795.

Committees: *Finance* (2d of 10 R): Health Care (RMM); Energy, Natural Resources & Infrastructure; Taxation & IRS Oversight & Long-Term Growth. *Health, Education, Labor & Pensions* (7th of 10 R): Children & Families; Retirement & Aging. *Intelligence (Select)* (5th of 7 R). *Joint Committee on Taxation* (5th of 5 R). *Judiciary* (2d of 9 R): Antitrust, Competition Policy & Consumer Rights (RMM); Terrorism, Technology & Homeland Security; Crime & Drugs.

Group Ratings

	ADA	ACLU	AFS	LCV	ITIC	NTU	COC	ACU	CFG	FRC
2006	5	17	13	14	100	74	92	84	66	87
2005	5	—	0	10	—	68	100	92	74	—

National Journal Ratings

	2005 LIB	—	2005 CONS		2006 LIB	—	2006 CONS
Economic	20%	—	78%		28%	—	69%
Social	0%	—	77%		18%	—	74%
Foreign	0%	—	74%		26%	—	67%

Key Votes of the 109th Congress

1. Bar ANWR Drilling	N	5. Confirm Samuel Alito	Y	9. Limit Interstate Abortion	Y
2. FY06 Spending Curb	Y	6. Path to Citizenship	N	10. CAFTA	Y
3. Estate Tax Repeal	Y	7. Bar Same Sex Marriage	Y	11. Urge Iraq Withdrawal	N
4. Raise Minimum Wage	N	8. Stem Cell Research $	Y	12. Provide Detainee Rights	N

Election Results

2006 general	Orrin Hatch (R)	356,238	(63%)	($3,340,902)
	Pete Ashdown (D)	177,459	(31%)	($255,729)
	Scott Bradley (CNP)	21,526	(4%)	($24,526)
	Other	16,029	(3%)	
2006 primary	Orrin Hatch (R)	unopposed		
2000 general	Orrin Hatch (R)	504,803	(66%)	($3,130,550)
	Scott N. Howell (D)	242,569	(31%)	($296,839)
	Other	22,332	(3%)	

Prior Winning Percentages: 1994 (69%); 1988 (67%); 1982 (58%); 1976 (54%)

Orrin Hatch, Utah's senior senator, was first elected to the Senate in 1976. Hatch grew up in Pittsburgh, where his father was a metal lather; he worked his way through Brigham Young University, then University of Pittsburgh law school, practiced law there and then moved to Salt Lake City. For a time he was an amateur boxer and at one point he and his wife lived in a refurbished chicken coop. He got into the 1976 Senate race late; an endorsement from Ronald Reagan helped him win the Republican nomination, and in the general he upset three-term

Democrat Frank Moss 54%-45%. His toughest re-election fight came in 1982, when he was opposed by Salt Lake City Mayor Ted Wilson; Hatch won 58%-41%.

Hatch's Senate career has been shaped by two impulses that are sometimes in tension with each other: a strong conservative philosophy and a sense of responsibility for the superintendency of legislation. He first attracted attention in a Senate dominated by Democrats when he successfully filibustered the AFL-CIO's labor law bill, which had been expected to pass. Then, after just four years, he became chairman of the Labor Committee after Republicans won a Senate majority in 1980. He remained a strong opponent of the striker replacement law sought by unions. On the Judiciary Committee, he fought abortion and a civil rights bill that produced racial quotas and preferences, and staunchly defended Supreme Court nominees Robert Bork and Clarence Thomas. In 1993 Hatch switched from ranking Republican on Labor to the same post on Judiciary, when it was vacated by Strom Thurmond; in 1995 he became chairman of Judiciary and left Labor altogether. On Judiciary he worked on limiting tort liability and regulatory law and managed the balanced budget amendment to one-vote defeats in 1995 and 1997. He worked also on the flag amendment, which fell four votes short of passage in March 2000, the anti-terrorism law and the Religious Freedom Restoration Act. On judicial appointments, Hatch promised in 1995 to cooperate with the Clinton administration; by early 1997 some Democrats were charging that he was stalling approval of nominees, while some Republicans were complaining that he was allowing too many liberal, activist judges on the bench. In 1997 Hatch again surprised some on both sides of the aisle when he joined Edward Kennedy in sponsoring a $24 billion program to get states to provide health insurance for children of low-income working parents who don't qualify for Medicaid.

Hatch has taken some surprising and bipartisan positions. He and Jeff Sessions sponsored a bill to increase the amount of crack cocaine required for an automatic five-year sentence from 5 grams to 20 grams. Despite his longstanding opposition to abortion, he has supported embryonic stem-cell research and argued that life is created in the womb, "not in a petri dish." In July 2006, as George W. Bush threatened to veto the embryonic stem-cell funding bill, Hatch sought to prevent a veto by allowing federally funded research on stem-cells created by private industry. After the November 2006 election he predicted there would be enough votes in the Senate to override another Bush veto, but not in the House; in spring 2007 he said he would nonetheless keep trying.

Hatch has sponsored bills to restrict class action lawsuits and to set limits on medical malpractice cases. In 2004 he gained wide acquiescence on setting up a trust fund to handle asbestos cases, but in 2005, when incoming Chairman Arlen Specter proposed a $140 billion trust fund, some businesses withdrew their support. In December 2006 the Senate passed a measure Hatch sponsored with Dick Durbin that required reporting to the FDA of bad side effects of dietary supplements and over-the-counter drugs. Hatch has expressed doubts about the use of mandatory minimum sentences in some drug cases and has interceded on behalf of those—a music producer arrested in the United Arab Emirates, a young Utahn who fled the country who he believes have been treated unjustly. He has worked successfully to extend tax credits for geothermal research and to extend the $250 deduction for school supplies bought by teachers. With Barack Obama, he got in a provision in a tax bill to bar bankruptcy courts from preventing the carrying out of charitable and tithing pledges.

As chairman and, from June 2001 to January 2003, ranking minority member of Judiciary, Hatch defended the Bush Justice Department and judicial nominees against Democrats' attacks; he decried their refusal to hold hearings on many appointees when they were in the majority and their filibusters of judicial appointees after January 2003. In 2005, though the Judiciary chairmanship had passed to Arlen Specter, Hatch continued aggressively to seek confirmation of filibustered appellate court nominees. After September 11, he was one of the framers of the USA Patriot Act, and in 2004 defended it against attempts to eliminate some provisions. "It seems to me that we should not make it any harder to go after suspected terrorists than after suspected drug dealers." He reintroduced the flag amendment but did not get another floor vote on it. He introduced another constitutional amendment to allow naturalized citizens to be eligible to serve as president and vice president 20 years after their naturalization. After the Supreme Judicial Court of Massachusetts ruled that its state constitution required legalization of same-sex marriages, Hatch proposed a constitutional amendment that would authorize states to refuse to recognize such marriages contracted in another state. But after same-sex couples in Massachusetts started obtaining marriage licenses, Hatch acquiesced in the amendment sponsored by Wayne Allard that would ban same-sex marriage altogether and supported it when it was brought to the floor, despite lack of action in the Judiciary Committee, in July 2004. Hatch has opposed federal gun control measures and in 2003 sponsored a bill to make it easier to carry handguns in the District of Columbia. In 2003, with Utah Congressman Chris Cannon, he sponsored a bill to allow children of illegal aliens to apply for conditional residency if they were in college, served in the military or performed 910 hours of community service; this would make them eligible for permanent residency and for in-state college tuition. In June 2006 he took the flag amendment once again to the floor of the Senate and once again fell short of the two-thirds needed for passage.

As Judiciary chairman and later on its Intellectual Property Subcommittee, Hatch has worked on the issue of protecting intellectual property in the face of technological advance. He supported the Digital Millennium Copyright Act of 1998 banning unlawful downloading of copyrighted music and movies and backed the record industry against the threat raised by Napster. In June 2004 the Senate passed his bill, co-sponsored with Patrick Leahy, to authorize the Justice Department to bring civil as well as criminal actions for illegal downloading. In June 2004 he drafted a bill barring technologies that were "intentionally inducing" copyright violations. Technology companies objected that this could make iPods illegal and on September 30 Hatch abandoned his markup and asked entertainment and technology representatives to come up with a mutually acceptable draft. He introduced his own version, with Leahy, Dianne Feinstein and John Cornyn in January 2005; it would also legalize movie filter technologies. In April 2007 he co-sponsored legislation revising patent law, with Patrick Leahy, Howard Berman, Lamar Smith and Chris Cannon.

Hatch's interest in these issues is not just theoretical. He has long written poetry and in 1995 began writing songs and has since written about 300. They have been recorded by a Utah firm, first in a 13-song album of Christmas music; some have been recorded by Gladys Knight, a convert to the LDS Church, and after Christian music publishers seemed uninterested in what Hatch has called his Latter-Day Sound, he began distributing his songs and has earned a platinum record for selling 1 million albums. He wrote a song for Edward Kennedy on his fifth wedding anniversary—very moving, Kennedy said. He appeared in the movie *Traffic*, but criticized it for its frequent obscenities; one of his songs was used in the recent movie *Ocean's 12*.

Hatch and Utah colleague Bob Bennett for some time supported a permanent nuclear waste repository in Yucca Mountain, Nevada: better to have the waste transported over Utah than deposited there. They worked together to prevent the Skull Valley Branch of the Goshute Indians' proposal to store radioactive waste on their reservation and in December 2005 helped to get a wilderness area provision in the defense bill which appeared to block railroad transport to the site; Bennett in the meantime had switched and was opposing Yucca Mountain. In April 2006 Hatch expressed concern about the proposed Divine Strake explosion at the Nevada Test Site; though the explosive was non-nuclear, it would have created a mushroom cloud and might have stirred up radioactive particles in the area. It was cancelled in February 2007.

Every senator, it sometimes seems, must run for president, and the time came for Hatch in June 1999. He admitted that it would take a "miracle" to win, but argued that he had more experience in federal office than the other candidates and could work with Democrats, and that he was not "beholden to the Republican establishment." At the August 1999 Iowa straw poll he came in last, with 2% of the votes. In the Iowa caucuses in January 2000 he won only 1% of the votes, fewer than John McCain, who did not campaign in the state. Two days later he withdrew from the race and endorsed George W. Bush.

In 2000, Hatch won 66%-31% and became the first Utahn popularly elected five times to the Senate; the only other five-term senator in Utah history, Reed Smoot, who served from 1903 to 1933, was elected to his first term by the legislature. In 2006, he won 63%-31% and after he was sworn into his sixth term became the longest-serving senator in Utah history. In March 2007, he endorsed Mitt Romney for president; at the American Society of Newspaper Editors convention he spoke out against what he considered religious bigotry and negative discourse on the LDS church. In April 2007, as Attorney General Alberto Gonzales was pressed to resign, there was speculation that Hatch would be appointed to the post. Under Utah law, should he resign, the state Republican party would have to provide Governor Jon Huntsman with a list of three possible nominees; Huntsman's choice would serve until a November 2008 election picked someone to serve out the rest of Hatch's term.

Junior Senator

Robert Bennett (R)

Elected 1992, seat up 2010, 3d term; b. Sept. 18, 1933, Salt Lake City; home, Salt Lake City; U. of UT, B.S. 1957; Mormon; married (Joyce).

Military Career: Chaplain, Army Natl. Guard, 1957-60.

Professional Career: Staff Aide, U.S. Rep. Sherm Lloyd, 1962; Staff Aide, U.S. Sen. Wallace F. Bennett, 1963; Cong. Liaison, U.S. Dept. of Transp., 1969-70; Pres., Robert Mullen P.R., 1970-74; P.R. Dir., Summa Corp., 1974-78; Pres., Osmond Communications, 1978-79; Chmn., American Computers Corp., 1979-81; Pres., Microsonics Corp., 1981-84; CEO, Franklin Quest Co., 1984-91; Chmn., UT Educ. Strategic Plng. Comm., 1988.

DC Office: 431 DSOB, 20510, 202-224-5444; Fax: 202-228-1168; Web site: bennett.senate.gov.

State Offices: Cedar City, 435-865-1335; Ogden, 801-625-5676; Provo, 801-851-2525; Salt Lake City, 801-524-5933; St. George, 435-628-5514.

Committees: *Appropriations* (9th of 14 R): Agriculture, Rural Development, Food and Drug Administration & Related Agencies (RMM); Energy & Water Development; State, Foreign Operations & Related Programs; Transportation, Housing and Urban Development & Related Agencies; Interior, Environment & Related Agencies; Military Construction, Veterans Affairs & Related Agencies. *Banking, Housing & Urban Affairs* (2d of 10 R): Financial Institutions; Securities, Insurance & Investment; Security & International Trade & Finance. *Joint Economic Committee* (7th of 10 R). *Rules & Administration* (RMM of 9 R).

Group Ratings

	ADA	ACLU	AFS	LCV	ITIC	NTU	COC	ACU	CFG	FRC
2006	15	25	13	14	100	71	100	72	71	75
2005	5	—	0	5	—	69	100	92	78	—

National Journal Ratings

	2005 LIB	—	2005 CONS		2006 LIB	—	2006 CONS
Economic	20%	—	78%		28%	—	69%
Social	0%	—	77%		33%	—	64%
Foreign	0%	—	74%		42%	—	54%

Key Votes of the 109th Congress

1. Bar ANWR Drilling	N	5. Confirm Samuel Alito	Y	9. Limit Interstate Abortion	Y
2. FY06 Spending Curb	Y	6. Path to Citizenship	Y	10. CAFTA	Y
3. Estate Tax Repeal	Y	7. Bar Same Sex Marriage	Y	11. Urge Iraq Withdrawal	N
4. Raise Minimum Wage	N	8. Stem Cell Research $	Y	12. Provide Detainee Rights	N

Election Results

2004 general	Robert Bennett (R)	626,640	(69%)	($2,649,234)
	Paul Van Dam (D)	258,955	(28%)	($116,959)
	Other	26,131	(3%)	
2004 primary	Robert Bennett (R)	unopposed		
1998 general	Robert Bennett (R)	316,652	(64%)	($1,546,219)
	Scott Leckman (D)	163,172	(33%)	($265,494)
	Other	15,085	(3%)	

Prior Winning Percentages: 1992 (55%)

Bob Bennett, Utah's junior senator, is a Republican who was first elected in 1992. He grew up in Salt Lake City, the grandchild of a president of the LDS Church (as is his wife). He was 17 when his father Wallace Bennett was elected in 1950 to the first of four terms in the Senate. He graduated from the University of Utah and worked as a congressional staffer and was the Transportation Department's chief lobbyist during the Nixon administration. He also headed the public relations firm (and CIA front) that employed Watergate burglar Howard Hunt, but was involved in no wrongdoing himself; some Watergate buffs wrongly believed that Bennett was Bob Woodward's "Deep Throat." After that, Bennett for three years headed Microsonics Corporation, which makes audio discs for talking toys, then became head of Franklin Quest, which produces the Franklin day planners and organizers; he increased it from four to 700 employees and brought in sales of $80 million, before selling his interest in 1991 for a reported $25 million. He headed a commission that produced Utah's Strategic Plan for Education and wrote *Gaining Control*, a book on how to control your daily life.

In 1992, when Jake Garn retired from the Senate, Bennett ran for the seat his father once held. He was not the only millionaire in the race. The initial favorite was Republican Joseph Cannon, who had taken over the old Geneva Steel plant and made it profitable, and who spent $5 million of his own money. But Bennett spent $1.4 million of his own, effectively attacked Geneva's environmental record and won the primary 51%-49%. The Democratic nominee, Congressman Wayne Owens, was a familiar face, with a voting record that was moderate—but evidently too liberal for Utah. Bennett won 55%-40%.

Bennett has had a moderate to conservative voting record and became chief deputy whip in 2003. He continued as a close adviser to Mitch McConnell, and officially became his counsel when McConnell became Minority Leader in 2007, which gave him a seat at the leadership table. Their friendship began when Bennett joined McConnell to oppose Orrin Hatch's constitutional amendment to bar desecration of the flag because of First Amendment concerns. Later they united in opposition to campaign finance reform for the same reason. Bennett has gained another Senate insider post as ranking Republican on the Rules and Administration Committee. Bennett has shown an interest in high-tech issues, and chaired the special Senate committee that responsible for steps to avoid problems in the Year 2000 computer switch. He has embraced some new technology himself: in 2001 he became the first member of Congress to own a hybrid vehicle and in 2006 he pushed for tax breaks for purchasers of fuel-efficient vehicles. He has favored sales taxes on Internet transactions; in his mail order business, he said, he charged customers sales tax in every state and no one protested.

In the debate on homeland security, Bennett strongly supported the personnel provisions backed by the Bush administration. Despite generally supporting the administration, in 2001 he voted against the education bill, which later became unpopular in Utah. As chairman of the Joint Economic Committee, he called for rewriting the nation's tax laws, starting from scratch. In 2005, on Social Security, he advocated progressively cutting future benefits and establishing personal retirement accounts. "You cannot solve the financial problems with personal accounts. But you cannot solve the long-term demographic problem without personal accounts." He drafted a plan that did not include personal accounts, but Democrats refused to join him. "The crisis is looming, and eventually the realities will reach a breaking point and Congress must act." In March 2006, he caused an uproar when he suggested that parts of Katrina-ravaged New Orleans should not be rebuilt. "I'm happy to appropriate money to help people who are in trouble . . . .Building a city 10 feet below sea level does not strike me as, inherently, basically a good idea." The New Orleans *Times-Picayune* editorialized against his "poor grasp of physics" and called him a "lunkhead." Four months later, he visited the city and concluded, "my instinct is to bulldoze [abandoned housing] and start over again."

Bennett has pressed for land exchanges between Utah and the federal government, to eliminate the checkerboard pattern of land ownership that prevents Utah from producing revenue for education from mining on state lands. He opposed the proposed nuclear waste depository on the lands of the Skull Valley Band of the Goshute Indians but he and Hatch supported the nuclear waste repository in Yucca Mountain, Nevada. In September 2005, however, Bennett changed his mind, saying he supported the Nevada senators' efforts to store nuclear waste where it is produced instead of transporting it to Yucca Mountain or Skull Valley. In 1999 he urged federal regulators to allow Envirocare to store nuclear waste in its hazardous material dump in Tooele County. But after House appropriators included a provision reclassifying waste from the Fernald, Ohio, and Niagara Falls nuclear sites so that it could be sent to Envirocare, he joined Governor Olene Walker in opposing such a transfer, and the provision was dropped in conference in 2003. In August 2004 he introduced a bill requiring input from Utah residents, radiation monitoring in Utah counties and advance notice before any testing of nuclear devices at the Nevada Test Site; Bennett has opposed new nuclear testing while backing development of new nuclear weapons.

On the Appropriations Committee Bennett is ranking Republican on the Agriculture Subcommittee. In 2005, he cited his successful sponsorship of $9 million for a 44-mile commuter rail project between Salt Lake City and Ogden, $4.25 million for statewide bus facilities, and $1 million to revitalize the historic district in Sandy. Citizens Against Government Waste has criticized Bennett for several projects, including $300,000 for a think tank started by former Governor Mike Leavitt, $1 million for an education initiative for Western Governors University, and $750,000 for the Range Creek ranch. Bennett has said that he is proud of the money that he directs to Utah.

In 1992 Bennett said he would run for only two terms. But in 1998 he said he would not rule out running again and he was reelected 64%-33% that year. In 2004 his Democratic opponent was former Attorney General Paul Van Dam, who rode around the state with his wife on a tandem bicycle. Bennett's campaign put up a series of billboards without the candidate's name: "Able. Articulate. Aerodynamic." "Big Heart. Big Ideas. Big Ears." "Better Looking than Abraham Lincoln. (Just Barely.)" He outspent Van Dam $2.6 million to $117,000 and won 69%-28%. He might be good for many more terms: his father lived to be 95.

FIRST DISTRICT

Rep. Rob Bishop (R)

Elected 2002, 3d term; b. July 13, 1951, Salt Lake City; home, Kaysville; U. of UT, B.A. 1974; Mormon; married (Jeralyn Hansen).

Elected Office: UT House of Reps., 1978-94; Speaker, 1993-94.

Professional Career: H.S.teacher, 1974-2002; Chair, UT Rep. Party, 1997-2001.

DC Office: 124 CHOB, 20515, 202-225-0453; Fax: 202-225-5857; Web site: robbishop.house.gov.

District Offices: Ogden, 801-625-0107.

Committees: *Armed Services* (17th of 29 R): Air & Land Forces; Readiness. *Education & Labor* (19th of 22 R): Early Childhood, Elementary & Secondary Education. *Natural Resources* (16th of 22 R): National Parks, Forests & Public Lands (RMM).

Group Ratings

	ADA	ACLU	AFS	LCV	ITIC	NTU	COC	ACU	CFG	FRC
2006	10	14	0	0	71	64	93	87	59	85
2005	10	—	0	0	—	63	81	100	80	100

National Journal Ratings

	2005 LIB	—	2005 CONS		2006 LIB	—	2006 CONS
Economic	0%	—	97%		14%	—	85%
Social	36%	—	64%		21%	—	78%
Foreign	11%	—	86%		16%	—	84%

Key Votes of the 109th Congress

1. Estate Tax Repeal	Y	5. Limit Interstate Abortion	Y	9. Build Border Fence			Y
2. Limit CAFE Standards	Y	6. Extend Patriot Act	N	10. CAFTA			Y
3. FY06 Spending Curb	Y	7. Bar Same Sex Marriage	Y	11. Oppose Iraq Withdrawal			*
4. Drilling in ANWR	Y	8. Stem Cell Research $	N	12. Detainee Tribunals			Y

Election Results

2006 general	Rob Bishop (R)	112,546	(63%)	($262,727)
	Steven Olsen (D)	57,922	(32%)	($60,103)
	Other	8,006	(4%)	
2006 primary	Rob Bishop (R)	unopposed		
2004 general	Rob Bishop (R)	199,615	(68%)	($435,494)
	Steven Thompson (D)	85,630	(29%)	($72,540)
	Other	8,716	(3%)	

Prior Winning Percentages: 2002 (61%)

The People		Race/Ethnic Origin	Ancestry	
Area size:	22,700 sq. mi.	83.3% White	English: 20.9%	German: 8.3%
Urban population:	88.7%	1.1% Black	USA: 5.0%	
Rural population:	11.3%	1.6% Asian	**2004 Presidential Vote**	
Pop. 2000:	744,389	0.7% Native Am.	Bush (R) 220,869	(73%)
Pop. 2005 (est):	815,207	0.6% Hawaiian	Kerry (D) 75,728	(25%)
Median income:	$45,058	1.4% Two+ races	Other 6,824	(2%)
Poverty status:	9.5%	0.1% Other	**2000 Presidential Vote**	
Military veterans:	11.7%	11.1% Hispanic Origin	Bush (R) 167,716	(68%)
			Gore (D) 66,792	(27%)
			Other 13,415	(5%)
			Cook Partisan Voting Index: R +22	

Occupation	Blue collar: 26.2%	White collar: 58.7%	Gray collar: 15.1%

In May 1869, a motley crowd of Irish and Chinese laborers, teamsters, engineers, train crews, officials and guests from California and Salt Lake City gathered at Promontory Summit, Utah, to watch the opening of the transcontinental railroad. The Union Pacific train was late and Leland Stanford's raised hammer totally missed the golden spike, but an alert telegrapher mimicked the sound over the wire and a photographer recorded the scene for posterity: United at last were the civilized East and the mostly untamed West. Here, beyond sight of the snow-capped mountains crossed by Mormon pioneers, where the rail line was bypassed a century ago, the salt flats still stretch out endlessly.

In Salt Lake City, the center of the Mormon Church—and of Utah—is Temple Square, illuminated by 300,000 lights during Christmas week and nestled beneath the towering mountains that flank Salt Lake City. Here you can find the Mormon Tabernacle, home of the famous choir, and the Temple itself, crowned with the golden angel Moroni. This area has been the focal point of Utah since Brigham Young, looking down at this valley, said, "This is the place." Ironically, this part of Salt Lake City is the least Mormon and most cosmopolitan part of Utah, with the state university and businesses bringing in outsiders who, flouting Mormon strictures, keep purveyors of alcohol and caffeine in business. Salt Lake County voted 60% for George W. Bush in 2004, up from 55% in 2000, but still modest compared to the rest of the state.

The 1st Congressional District of Utah consists of the northern end of the state. It includes most of Salt Lake City's historic downtown, its distinctive Avenues District and the airport, but little of the fast-growing suburbia that stretches south of the city. More than half the people in the district live in the stretch of the Wasatch Front, between the mountains and Great Salt Lake, just north of Salt Lake City, in Davis and Weber Counties. Davis County is suburban and fairly affluent; Ogden in Weber County is an old working class railroad town, an industrial center that depends on nearby Hill Air Force Base, home of the advanced F-22A fighter jets. Farther north in the Cache Valley is Logan, home of Utah State University. This is farming country and very heavily Mormon. Over the mountains to the east of Salt Lake City is Park City, the old mining town that is now a fashionable ski resort and home of Robert Redford's annual Sundance Film Festival. West of Salt Lake City are the lake, with a new 4,000 acre wetlands sanctuary, and the desolate Bonneville Salt Flats, where land speed records have been set. This land of stark beauty, much of it federally owned, has been used roughly by man: as a repository for hazardous wastes at civilian and military dumps in Tooele County and as a place for military experimentation on the Dugway Proving Ground, where scientists test defenses against chemical and biological agents, and the Wendover Range, where the designs of "Fat Man" and "Little Boy" were assessed before being dropped on Japan; new suburbs out Interstate 80 have made Tooele the state's second-fastest growing county, where real estate remains cheap. With continued delay in making Yucca Mountain in Nevada the nation's nuclear-waste repository, the Skull Valley temporary storage site—near Dugway—is looking less and less temporary. Politically this is a heavily Republican area, with patches of Democratic strength. The district's portions of Salt Lake County are trendy and working class Democratic; they were kept out of the 2d District by Republican redistricters who wanted to beat a Democratic incumbent. Park City is on its way to becoming another Aspen, Democratic with leftist voters; the mayor was a Vietnam war protestor who proudly kept a copy of Mao's Little Red Book. The Cache Valley is very heavily Republican, though, and overall the district voted 68% for George W. Bush in 2000 and 73% in 2004.

The congressman from the 1st District is Rob Bishop, a Republican first elected in 2002. He grew up in Davis County and graduated from the University of Utah. He became a high school history and government teacher in Box Elder County. In 1978, at 27, he was elected to the state House; in 1993 and 1994 he was Speaker. He continued working as a teacher after leaving the legislature and also worked as a lobbyist for state Republicans and for the National Rifle Association (though he did not own a gun). When the seat became open, Bishop ran and so did former House Majority Leader Kevin Garn. As a former state party chair for four years, Bishop won 58% of the vote at the Republican nominating convention. With mostly similar conservative views, their chief difference was a contentious issue in Utah, the ongoing battle between banks and credit unions. The credit union lobby endorsed Bishop who, as a lobbyist in 1999, helped defeat legislation to curtail the credit unions' tax-exempt status. Garn, as the wealthy chairman of a Layton bank, had the support of Utah bankers. The credit unions were the more valuable ally: They poured at least $100,000 in independent expenditures into an anti-Garn campaign, which helped even the financial balance since Garn outspent Bishop by 4–1. Bishop won the primary 60%-40%. Democrats believed they had a chance in the general with their nominee Dave Thomas, a wealthy advertising executive and an anti-abortion Mormon bishop who presented himself as a fiscal conservative and "a regular guy" not tied to special interests. Bishop won more easily than expected, 61%-37%.

In the House, Bishop usually has been a reliable conservative vote. With a few other House Republicans, he switched his vote under pressure from party leaders to help defeat an amendment that sought to deny funding to the Patriot Act provision authorizing access to library records; but in a March 2006 vote, he held firm with the civil libertarians. Although he voted for the constitutional amendment to bar same-sex marriages, he preferred a statute that would deny federal courts jurisdiction over state definitions of marriage. He also has worked on a variety of local issues: In 2005, he enacted his proposal to block private disposal of nuclear waste on the Skull Valley Goshute Indian reservation and convert the land to a wilderness area; he complained that the proposal was fought by members of the Nevada delegation, who were unhappy about support by the Utah delegation for the Yucca Mountain disposal site. He helped protect Hill Air Force Base from the base-closing review. He was criticized at home for supporting a change in federal law to permit Envirocare of Utah (now known as EnergySolutions) to dispose additional radioactive waste material from a bomb plant in Ohio. Envirocare, which was a client of his former lobbying firm, dropped the proposal after three months of controversy; Bishop later advocated recycling the waste.

In 2005, Speaker Dennis Hastert signaled that Bishop had favorably impressed party insiders by giving him for a seat on the Rules Committee. But the Democratic takeover of the House forced him from Rules; he moved to Armed Services, Education and Labor, and Natural Resources, where he became ranking Republican at the National Parks, Forests and Public Lands Subcommittee—a useful assignment in a state where the federal government controls nearly two-thirds of the land.

In 2006, Bishop defeated a Republican-turned-Democrat whose claim to fame was authorship of a pamphlet titled, "Why Most Utahns Are Democrats But Just Don't Know It Yet." Apparently local voters still don't know it: Bishop won 63%-32%.

SECOND DISTRICT

Rep. Jim Matheson (D)

Elected 2000, 4th term; b. Mar. 21, 1960, Salt Lake City; home, Salt Lake City; Harvard U., B.A. 1982, U.C.L.A., M.B.A. 1987; Mormon; married (Amy).

Professional Career: Staff, Environmental Policy Inst., 1982-85; Project Dev. Mgr., Bonneville Pacific, 1987-91; Sr. Assoc., Energy Strategies Inc., 1992-98; Founder & Pres., The Matheson Group, 1998-99.

DC Office: 1323 LHOB, 20515, 202-225-3011; Fax: 202-225-5638; Web site: www.house.gov/matheson.

District Offices: Price, 435-636-3722; Salt Lake City, 801-486-1236; St. George, 435-627-0880.

Committees: *Energy & Commerce* (27th of 31 D): Commerce, Trade & Consumer Protection; Energy & Air Quality; Health. *Science & Technology* (17th of 24 D): Technology & Innovation.

Group Ratings

	ADA	ACLU	AFS	LCV	ITIC	NTU	COC	ACU	CFG	FRC
2006	45	59	43	58	86	47	87	64	47	57
2005	75	—	100	56	—	37	78	40	34	38

National Journal Ratings

	2005 LIB	—	2005 CONS		2006 LIB	—	2006 CONS
Economic	54%	—	46%		56%	—	44%
Social	55%	—	44%		50%	—	49%
Foreign	53%	—	47%		53%	—	46%

Key Votes of the 109th Congress

1. Estate Tax Repeal	Y	5. Limit Interstate Abortion	Y	9. Build Border Fence	Y
2. Limit CAFE Standards	N	6. Extend Patriot Act	N	10. CAFTA	Y
3. FY06 Spending Curb	N	7. Bar Same Sex Marriage	Y	11. Oppose Iraq Withdrawal	Y
4. Drilling in ANWR	N	8. Stem Cell Research $	Y	12. Detainee Tribunals	Y

Election Results

2006 general	Jim Matheson (D)	133,231	(59%)	($1,624,165)
	LaVar Christensen (R)	84,234	(37%)	($834,661)
	Other	8,353	(4%)	
2006 primary	Jim Matheson (D)	unopposed		
2004 general	Jim Matheson (D)	187,250	(55%)	($2,021,524)
	John Swallow (R)	147,778	(43%)	($1,471,198)
	Other	6,940	(2%)	

Prior Winning Percentages: 2002 (49%); 2000 (56%)

The People		Race/Ethnic Origin	Ancestry	
Area size:	46,034 sq. mi.	88.0% White	English: 21.8%	German: 9.0%
Urban population:	84.9%	0.6% Black	Irish: 5.0%	
Rural population:	15.1%	1.5% Asian	**2004 Presidential Vote**	
Pop. 2000:	744,390	2.2% Native Am.	Bush (R) 227,668	(66%)
Pop. 2005 (est):	802,503	0.3% Hawaiian	Kerry (D) 108,286	(31%)
Median income:	$45,583	1.4% Two+ races	Other 8,434	(2%)
Poverty status:	9.0%	0.1% Other	**2000 Presidential Vote**	
Military veterans:	11.3%	5.9% Hispanic Origin	Bush (R) 183,387	(67%)
			Gore (D) 84,266	(31%)
			Other 6,573	(2%)
			Cook Partisan Voting Index: R +17	

Occupation   Blue collar: 20.1%   White collar: 65.6%   Gray collar: 14.3%

Demographically, Utah is an urban state; geographically, it is not just rural but, over most of its acreage, scarcely inhabited. Three-quarters of its people live in the Wasatch Front, from Ogden south through Salt Lake City to Provo, between the Great Salt Lake and Utah Lake and the Wasatch Mountains. The scenery here has grandeur, but is surpassed by the landscape of much of southern Utah, most of it preserved in five national parks, five national monuments and a national recreation area. The terrain of southern Utah ranges from the soaring cliffs of Zion National Park to the popsicle-like outcroppings of Bryce Canyon National Park to the red-walled river cuts of Canyonlands National Park to the surreal moonscape of Arches National Park. Monument Valley, on Navajo land in far southeastern Utah, has become familiar to Americans as the site of countless car commercials, and the land around Moab and Springdale has become a major tourist destination. Land here is mostly owned by one agency or another of the federal government, and there have been bitter fights between locals dependent on mining and environmentalists who want to preserve scenery: you can see evidence of old uranium mines in some of the national parks. Bill Clinton's campaign-year creation of the Grand Staircase-Escalante National Monument in 1996, in a ceremony across the border in Arizona, enraged many Utahns, since it effectively removed 1.7 million acres from mineral development, much of it land owned by the state that used the proceeds for schools; years later, local groups battled over access to the lands. Areas adjoining Dead Horse Point State Park and Arches National Park have been eyed for oil and gas projects by the Bush administration.

The 2d Congressional District of Utah includes these parts of the state, but the majority of its people live in Salt Lake County, east of a wobbling line between I-15 and the often dry Jordan River.

This area includes most of the affluent neighborhoods in Salt Lake City and the suburbs of South Salt Lake, Murray (an old smelter city settled by southern and central Europeans), Midvale, Sandy and Draper. The 2d stretches to include the eastern part of the state and the southwest corner, including the abundant scenic territories. In distant Washington County, the retirement haven of St. George grew by 40% from 2000 to 2006, the fastest-growing metro area in the nation, with expensive homes and traffic jams, and some spillover from Las Vegas; half of the new residents came from elsewhere in Utah. George W. Bush won the district with 67% in 2000 (though Moab's Grand County voted 15% for Ralph Nader) and 66% in 2004.

The congressman from the 2d District is Jim Matheson, a Democrat first elected in 2000. Matheson grew up in Salt Lake City, graduated from Harvard and interned on Capitol Hill for Speaker Tip O'Neill. His father Scott Matheson, a Salt Lake City lawyer, was elected governor of Utah in 1976 and 1980. Jim Matheson worked for the Environmental Policy Institute, and then earned an M.B.A. from UCLA. He returned to Salt Lake City to join Bonneville Pacific, an energy development company, where he was a project development manager. He moved in 1992 to Energy Strategies, a consulting firm, where he was a senior associate. He served four years on the Salt Lake Public Utilities Board. In 1998, he started the Matheson Group to help businesses adapt to electricity deregulation, but he closed it a year later to run for the House. Matheson ran in a district with a turbulent politics: From 1992 to 2000 it elected two Democrats and two Republicans to Congress. Much of the turbulence was caused by the volatile behavior of Congressman Merrill Cook. He was challenged in the 2000 Republican primary by businessman Derek Smith; Cook charged him with financial misconduct and aides had to pull them apart after a 45-minute confrontation near the end of the campaign. Smith won the primary 59%-41%. In the general, Matheson played down his party affiliation and criticized Al Gore's prescription drug plan. Smith denounced Bill Clinton's creation of the Grand Staircase-Escalante National Monument, and charged that Matheson was trying to look like a Republican. Smith spent more than four times what Democrats spent on Matheson. But Matheson won 56%-41%.

In the House, Matheson has a voting record that is among the most conservative of Democrats and he has crossed party lines on many issues. He supported the 2001 tax cuts, trade promotion authority, the use of force in Iraq, was one of 16 Democrats who voted for the Medicare/prescription drug bill, and one of 15 for the Central American free trade deal. But he voted against a constitutional amendment on flag burning, oil drilling in the Arctic National Wildlife Refuge and making the Bush tax cuts permanent. He has opposed cost of living pay increases for members of Congress and has given the money to charity, but he has failed to get a direct vote to stop them. He called for mandatory environmental reviews before resumption of nuclear weapons testing in Nevada and opposed allowing additional nuclear waste to be disposed by Envirocare in Tooele County. Matheson, whose father died of cancer as the result of radioactive fallout from nuclear tests, strongly opposed tests of a new nuclear warhead design. He has been a leader of the fiscally conservative Blue Dog Democrats and in 2006 continued his annual practice of donating his pay raise to district charities.

Matheson has been a prime Republican target. In 2002 John Swallow, a three-term state legislator, emphasized his strong support for tax cuts and gun ownership rights, and reminded voters of Matheson's Democratic Party affiliation at every opportunity; he harshly criticized Matheson's vote against a partial-birth abortion ban. Matheson reminded rural voters of his family's local connections and said that Swallow would harm public schools by giving tax money to parents who send their kids to private schools (the 2d has the lowest private school enrollment in the nation). Both national parties spent lavishly. Matheson won by 1,641 votes—49.4%-48.7%; this was the narrowest margin for any House incumbent that year. Swallow won most of the rural counties by huge margins, but lost 59%-39% in Salt Lake County, which cast 60% of the vote. In 2004 Swallow ran again and had support from the Club for Growth; the House Republican campaign committee spent nearly $1 million on the contest. But Swallow's more strident negative campaign apparently backfired, and Matheson won 55%-43%, with a 2–1 margin in Salt Lake County. In 2006, against state Representative LaVar Christensen, Matheson was reelected 59%-37%. But he cannot rest in this district.

With the prospect of frequent challenges, Matheson seems likely to run for statewide office. He deferred to his brother, Scott Matheson, who ran for governor in 2004 and lost to Republican Jon Huntsman; in 2005, he turned down calls that he run against Senator Orrin Hatch in 2006. Eager for him to stay in the House, Democratic leaders in 2007 gave him a seat on the Energy and

Commerce Committee. In the majority, he continued to show his independence, this time with more influence. He backed the bill to give a House member to the District of Columbia, combined with a new at-large seat for Utah until 2012.

THIRD DISTRICT

Rep. Chris Cannon (R)

Elected 1996, 6th term; b. Oct. 20, 1950, Salt Lake City; home, Mapleton; Brigham Young U., B.S. 1974, J.D. 1980; Mormon; married (Claudia).

Professional Career: Practicing atty., 1980-83; Asst. Assoc. Solicitor, Dept. of Interior, 1983-84, Assoc. Solicitor, 1984-86; Co–owner, Geneva Steel, 1987-90; Founder, Cannon Industries Inc., 1990-96.

DC Office: 2436 RHOB, 20515, 202-225-7751; Fax: 202-225-5629; Web site: chriscannon.house.gov.

District Offices: Provo, 801-851-2500; West Jordan, 801-569-5129.

Committees: *Judiciary* (8th of 17 R): Commercial & Administrative Law (RMM); Courts, the Internet & Intellectual Property. *Natural Resources* (6th of 22 R): National Parks, Forests & Public Lands. *Oversight & Government Reform* (8th of 18 R): Information Policy, Census & National Archives; Domestic Policy.

Group Ratings

	ADA	ACLU	AFS	LCV	ITIC	NTU	COC	ACU	CFG	FRC
2006	5	15	0	0	100	75	100	90	79	100
2005	0	—	0	0	—	66	93	100	89	100

National Journal Ratings

	2005 LIB	—	2005 CONS		2006 LIB	—	2006 CONS
Economic	0%	—	97%		3%	—	96%
Social	47%	—	52%		42%	—	57%
Foreign	0%	—	89%		0%	—	94%

Key Votes of the 109th Congress

1. Estate Tax Repeal	Y	5. Limit Interstate Abortion	Y	9. Build Border Fence	Y
2. Limit CAFE Standards	Y	6. Extend Patriot Act	Y	10. CAFTA	Y
3. FY06 Spending Curb	Y	7. Bar Same Sex Marriage	Y	11. Oppose Iraq Withdrawal	*
4. Drilling in ANWR	Y	8. Stem Cell Research $	N	12. Detainee Tribunals	Y

Election Results

2006 general	Chris Cannon (R)	95,455	(58%)	($1,159,603)
	Christian Burridge (D)	53,330	(32%)	($69,753)
	Jim Noorlander (CNP)	14,533	(9%)	($26,454)
	Other	2,080	(1%)	
2006 primary	Chris Cannon (R)	32,881	(56%)	
	John Jacob (R)	26,143	(44%)	
2004 general	Chris Cannon (R)	173,010	(63%)	($634,195)
	Beau Babka (D)	88,748	(33%)	($35,111)
	Other	11,170	(4%)	

Prior Winning Percentages: 2002 (67%); 2000 (59%); 1998 (77%); 1996 (51%)

The People		Race/Ethnic Origin	Ancestry	
Area size:	16,165 sq. mi.	84.5% White	English: 21.5%	German: 8.2%
Urban population:	91.2%	0.5% Black	USA: 5.2%	
Rural population:	8.8%	1.7% Asian	**2004 Presidential Vote**	
Pop. 2000:	744,390	0.7% Native Am.	Bush (R) 215,205	(77%)
Pop. 2005 (est):	850,120	1.1% Hawaiian	Kerry (D) 57,185	(20%)
Median income:	$46,568	1.4% Two+ races	Other 6,689	(2%)
Poverty status:	9.7%	0.1% Other	**2000 Presidential Vote**	
Military veterans:	8.8%	10.0% Hispanic Origin	Bush (R) 163,983	(75%)
			Gore (D) 51,878	(24%)
			Other 4,002	(2%)
			Cook Partisan Voting Index: R +26	

Occupation   Blue collar: 26.2%   White collar: 59.7%   Gray collar: 14.1%

Part of the heartland of the Mormon Church in America is in a geographically isolated valley between 11,000-foot peaks of the Wasatch Range and the shores of Utah Lake. Here is Provo, the home of Brigham Young University, an institution long known for the conservative views of its faculty, the old-fashioned moral standards it encourages and its welcoming of technological innovation. The Mormon commonwealth, after all, started off with a huge shortage of both labor and water, and was eager to use technology to compensate and prosper in this fearsome terrain. Provo produced Philo Farnsworth, the inventor of television, and Harvey Fletcher, inventor of the hearing aid. This has become one of America's high-tech centers, the home of Novell and hundreds of other computer-related firms, some fleeing California's high taxes and cultural liberalism. Overseas missionary work has bequeathed the area with unusual resources in foreign languages.

The 3d Congressional District of Utah includes all or part of seven counties in central and western Utah. Many of them are remote; during World War II, Japanese Americans were interned near Topaz in Millard County. About 90% of its people live in Utah or Salt Lake Counties. The 3d includes the west side of Salt Lake City and the suburbs south of the city, including West Valley City (the state's second-largest city, home to many recent Mormon converts from Polynesia), West Jordan, South Jordan and Riverton. Kennecott, the old mining conglomerate that owns 90,000 acres in Salt Lake and Tooele Counties, has been unloading its landholdings to real estate developers, who have built many subdivisions and the unique Sunrise, a "walkable" community of 30,000 in South Jordan. The district includes almost all of Utah County, with Provo and the string of counties between high-jutting mountains and Utah Lake; Eagle Mountain and Saratoga Springs were created here in the early 1990s and have grown rapidly. From 2000 to 2006, the youthful Provo area grew 26%, the sixth fastest among the nation's metro areas. Politically, Utah County is one of the most heavily Republican in the United States: Bill Clinton finished a poor third here in 1992 with 22% of the vote and lost 58%-29% to Bob Dole in 1996; George W. Bush carried the county 86%-12% in 2004. Overall the 3d District voted 77% for Bush in 2004, one of his half dozen best districts in the country.

The congressman from the 3d District is Chris Cannon, a Republican first elected in 1996. Cannon is a great-grandson of Utah's first territorial delegate and counselor to Church President Brigham Young, George Q. Cannon, who had five wives and a lot of progeny. Chris Cannon grew up in Salt Lake City, graduated from Brigham Young and its law school and practiced law. From 1983 to 1986 he worked, sometimes controversially, in the Reagan Interior and Commerce departments, on surface coal mining and other issues; he helped to shift oversight of coal mine reclamation from Washington to the states. In 1987, with his older brother Joe, he purchased and reopened the Geneva Steel plant near Provo, restoring 2,500 jobs. During a family dispute over the business in 1990, Chris Cannon was bought out and set up a venture capital investment firm. He was active in Republican politics, as was Joe, who ran for the Senate in 1992 and lost the primary 51%-49% to Bob Bennett. Joe Cannon served as Republican state chairman from 2001 to 2006 when he left to become editor of the *Deseret Morning News*. In 1996, Chris Cannon ran for the 3d District seat held by Democrat Bill Orton, a conservative Democrat. Cannon spent $1.8 million, $1.5 million of it his own money, against Orton's $709,000. He was helped when Bill Clinton in September, speaking in Arizona without consultation with Utah officials (including Orton), announced that he was establishing the 1.7 million-acre Grand Staircase-Escalante National Monument in southern Utah. This was heartily opposed in the area: much of the land was owned by a state school fund, which wanted to lease it for coal mining, and now would not get the revenue. Cannon ran an ad showing himself denim-clad, leading a horse, attacking Clinton, "I feel like I'm back in the 1850s again with the federal government encamped all around us." Orton said the designation was "a monumental blunder—pun intended." Cannon won 51%-47%.

In the House, Cannon has had a mostly conservative voting record and continued to attack the national monument, but he has moved toward the center on cultural issues. During the Clinton impeachment he served as one of the House managers in the Senate trial. He has chaired the Western Caucus, a group of more than 50 House members who advocate "rational, balanced and sound resource management." On Judiciary, Cannon worked to set up a regulatory framework for the Internet. As chairman of the Subcommittee on Commercial and Administrative Law, which handles bankruptcy and tort law, he helped to reach the final agreement on the oft-stalled bankruptcy bill that George W. Bush signed in April 2005.

Cannon served as a Mormon missionary in Guatemala, and that has lead to an interest in bills that promote "responsible increases" in immigration. He sponsored guest worker legislation, to allow more foreign nationals to come to work in the United States for willing employers who cannot find Americans to do their jobs and eventually achieve resident status. To charges that this amounts to amnesty for illegal immigrants, Cannon has said, "When you talk about amnesty, you can either put people in jail, fine them and throw them out of the country for 10 years, or you can give them a long term of duty and obligation. That seems to me to be a pretty substantial penalty for what they've done." In 2003 he sponsored a bill to allow states to charge in-state tuition to college students whose parents entered the country illegally. "We love immigrants in Utah. We don't make distinctions between legal and illegal," he said. The Farm Bureau and Chamber of Commerce backed his "Agjobs" bill to streamline the seasonal foreign agricultural workers programs. In 2007, he voiced hope that the Democratic takeover improved prospects for immigration legislation.

Cannon's immigration stance has generated considerable political opposition back home. In 2004 he faced a spirited primary challenge from former state Representative Matt Throckmorton, who attacked him on immigration and was strongly backed by national anti-immigration and "pro-borders" groups. At the state party convention in May Cannon won 57% but fell short of the 60% required to avoid a primary. Throckmorton said that Cannon was ignoring the views of his constituents but Cannon won the primary 58%-42%—a weak performance for an incumbent. He won the general election 63%-33%. In 2006, he had another competitive primary that revolved around immigration. Millionaire developer John Jacob charged that Cannon was "pro-amnesty;" but his campaign suffered after accusations that he once hired illegal immigrants and gambled to excess led him to comment that the devil was trying to undermine his campaign. Cannon won 56%-44%, and called the outcome a mandate for immigration reform. He won the general 58%-32%, with a conservative third-party candidate getting 9%.

Cannon seemed likely to face yet another tough primary in 2008. Jason Chaffetz, former chief of staff to Governor Jon Huntsman, and David Leavitt, a former Juab County prosecutor and the brother of former Governor Michael Leavitt, both indicated they would challenge Cannon for the Republican nomination. Jacob said it was "highly likely" that he would run again and former Congressman Merrill Cook was also mentioned as a prospective candidate.

★ VERMONT ★

Vermont is a mixture of the 19th and the 21st centuries—maple syrup and Ben & Jerry's Ice Cream, tiny clapboard villages and carefully zoned towns complete with unobtrusively signed outlet malls, covered bridges and civil unions—with much of the 20th, its factories and suburbs, skyscrapers and shopping malls, mostly left out. Not so long ago, Vermont seemed an entirely antique state, almost as carefully preserved as its Shelburne Museum, with a barn and jail, railroad station and blacksmith shop, covered bridge, and 37 buildings full of folk art. Yet it has been transformed by newcomers, who came here attracted to its antique look but have transformed its culture in their own image.

Vermont was first settled by flinty Yankees from Connecticut, and showed an independent streak from the beginning. After Ethan Allen's Green Mountain Boys repulsed the British in 1777, this was an independent republic for 14 years, claimed by New York and New Hampshire without avail. Allen conducted "international" negotiations with the British and tried to get George Washington to agree to make it a new state; several books argue that Vermont never voluntarily joined the United States. All this rugged independence paid off when when Vermont was admitted as the

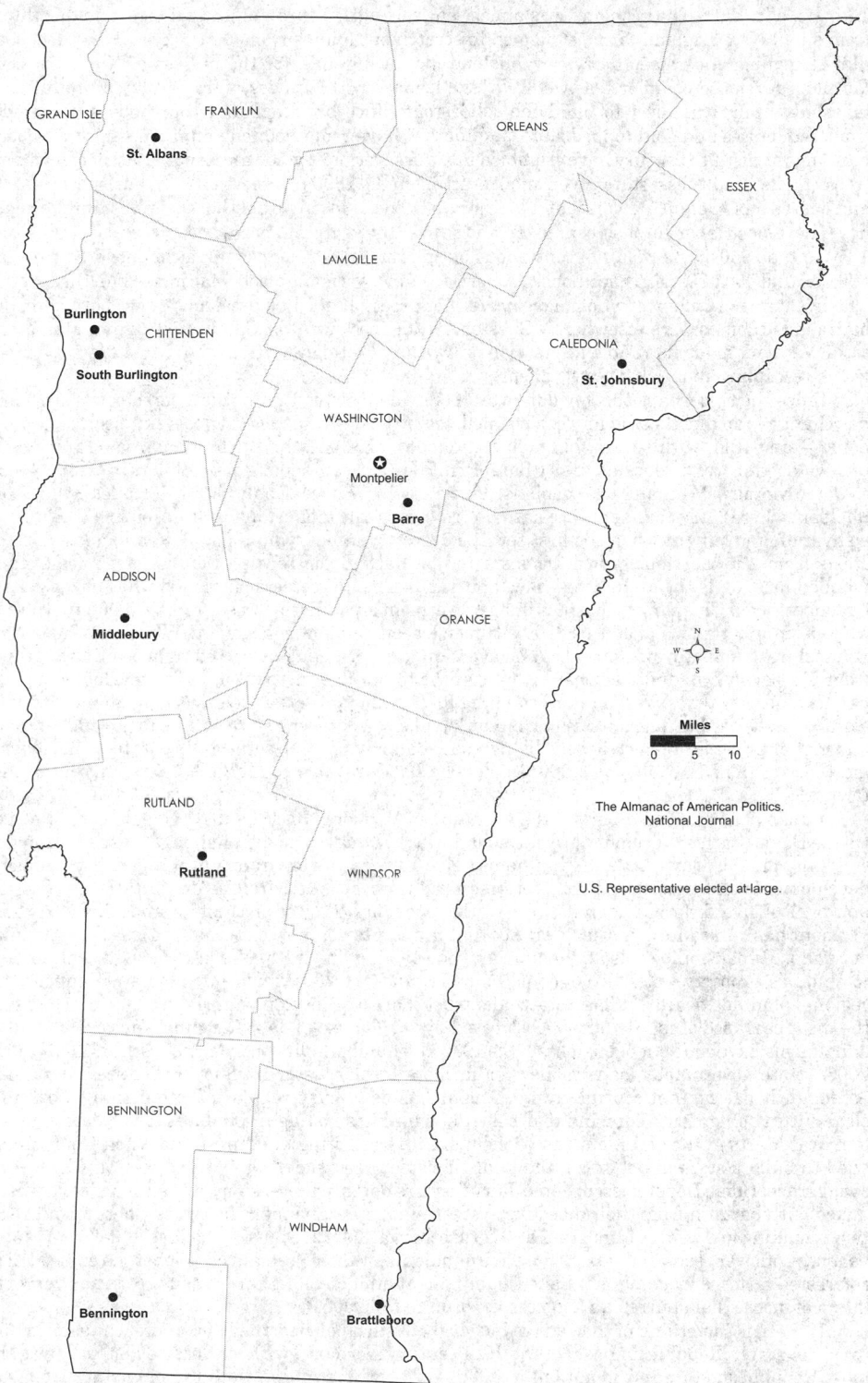

GRAND ISLE

FRANKLIN

ORLEANS

St. Albans

ESSEX

LAMOILLE

Burlington

CHITTENDEN

CALEDONIA

South Burlington

St. Johnsbury

WASHINGTON

Montpelier

Barre

ADDISON

ORANGE

Middlebury

Miles

0   5   10

The Almanac of American Politics.
National Journal

RUTLAND

WINDSOR

U.S. Representative elected at-large.

Rutland

BENNINGTON

WINDHAM

Bennington

Brattleboro

14th state in 1791. The economy was almost entirely agricultural, as second sons and daughters from small New England farms struggled to scratch out livings from the rocky soil. In time, they quit struggling and raised dairy cows instead, producing milk for the masses of New York City. Vermont developed commerce as well. With its legendary thriftiness, it accumulated capital that, invested wisely, was used to build the solid stone office buildings and courthouses, the thick-timbered houses and gold-topped state Capitol that have remained long after ramshackle wooden buildings of the 19th century have crumbled into dust. Vermont made an economic asset of its maple trees and its quaintness; state government starting in the 1890s promoted it as a tourist destination and passed a law requiring Vermont maple syrup to be made only from the local trees. But Vermont never developed labor-intensive industry, and so over the years it exported people, and it aged. From 1850 to the 1960s, as a result of continuous outmigration, Vermont's population hovered between 300,000 and 400,000. Today, millions of Americans have Vermont blood—far more than the 623,000 who live here now, many of whom have no Vermont roots at all. Two presidents were born here, but both made their careers elsewhere—Chester Arthur in New York, Calvin Coolidge in Massachusetts. Vermont made no visible impression on two great foreign writers who lived here for years—Rudyard Kipling and Aleksandr Solzhenitsyn.

Since then—perhaps the key date was 1963, when people first outnumbered cows—Vermont has changed rapidly. Its economy has boomed, led by leisure-time industries—ski resorts, summer homes—and IBM, with several big high-tech facilities around the Burlington area on the mostly undeveloped shores of glorious Lake Champlain. Here you can find big box retailers in Williston and ethnic diversity—Vietnamese, Bosnians, Koreans—in Winooski only 30 or 40 miles away from Sheldon, where 83% of residents are native Vermonters, the highest in the state, or tiny Buels Gore, a sliver of land left out when the first settlers drew town lines, whose population increased in the 1990s from 2 to 12. Homegrown firms started by Baby Boom rebels—Ben & Jerry's Ice Cream, founded in 1978, is the archetype—have flourished. The newcomers cherished what novelist Paul Greenberg calls "maple's homespun image." Vermont's population rose from 390,000 in 1960 to 511,000 in 1980 and 609,000 in 2000. It hasn't been random settlement: While next-door New Hampshire, trumpeting its low taxes and aversion to government, attracted right-leaning migrants from Massachusetts and elsewhere who were happy to live in spanking-new developments and ravenous for low taxes, Vermont, proclaiming its desire to preserve the environment and the past, attracted left-leaning migrants from New York and elsewhere who were willing to pay higher taxes and higher prices for the privilege of living in a seemingly pristine setting. Its greatest fans may be members of the 251 Club, the 4,000 people who have traveled to all 251 of Vermont's cities and towns.

Public policy played a part in the evolution of Vermont. Back in 1970, Republican Governor Deane Davis (the last Vermont native to hold the job), facing a primary challenge, pushed through a sweeping land use law (Act 250) that helped give Vermont its environmental reputation. Housing developments and new ski resorts were required to meet 10 environmental criteria and get the approval of five different commissions, with opponents granted a right to appeal. Since then, Vermont has passed its own Clean Air Act that levies a tax on new cars that get less than 20 miles per gallon. It bans billboards and rooftop air conditioning units. It passed Act 60, which attempted to equalize property taxes throughout the state, and Act 200, which provided state support for regional planning boards. It has a state land trust that buys development rights of farmland to stop the disappearance of family farms. Distressed by the demise of dairy farming—more than half of dairy farms have gone out of business since 1982 and numbers slipped from 1,800 in 2001 to 1,150 in 2006—state government loans money for farmers to buy water buffalo to produce mozzarella. Although it has no gun control laws, Vermont has been busy regulating other things: banning clear-cutting of forests, requiring seat belt use, banning smoking in public places. There are now four Wal-Marts in the state, but two of them are in preexisting buildings. And when Home Depot tried to build a store in one town, the locals insisted on a vegetation-covered roof on which cows could graze: Home Depot passed. Some dairy farmers now are processing their animals' solid waste, mixed with bacteria from their digestive systems, into methane fuel; the Grass Energy Collaborative is making fuel pellets from grass and corn; other farmers are making biodiesel fuel from canola beans, sunflower seeds and flax. Some environmental problems remain. Phosphorous embedded in reforested farms is leaching into Lake Champlain at an increasing rate. And there is an overpopulation of moose that spurred an "aggressive" hunt in fall 2006.

If there is something of the Yankee busybody in such policies, they also represent a departure from the state's Republican past. In the 19th century, Vermont, with its Yankee heritage, was the most Republican state in the nation; in 1936, Vermont and Maine were the only states to resist

Franklin D. Roosevelt's landslide. For three decades thereafter Vermont's Yankee Protestant Republicans outnumbered its French Canadian and Irish Catholic Democrats. But now, political issues slice Vermont on different lines—between liberal, highly educated newcomers and conservative, less educated old Vermonters. In the 2004 presidential election, Vermont was the third most Democratic state; its last Republican member of Congress switched to become an Independent in May 2001 and voted to make the Democrats the Senate majority party. In January 2003 former Governor Howard Dean set off to run for president; by July his opposition to the Iraq war (and not his relatively moderate fiscal record in Vermont) made him the leading fundraiser and frontrunner in the polls for the Democratic nomination. Vermont, valuing tradition, had become the leader of America's left.

One issue that made Dean attractive to left Democrats was civil unions. Ironically, it was one on which he had not taken the lead. In a lawsuit brought by three same-sex couples, the Vermont Supreme Court ruled that the legislature had to pass a gay marriage law or one which gave same-sex couples the same rights under state law as married couples. In April 2000 the legislature passed a law authorizing civil unions for same-sex couples and Dean signed it out of sight of cameras. Opposition to civil unions was fierce and vocal, though seldom articulated in the state's liberal press; groups were formed called Take Back Vermont and Who Would Have Thought. Backers of civil unions and other liberal policies formed a group called Move Vermont Forward. Civil unions and other liberal laws were opposed vociferously by Republican governor candidate Ruth Dwyer. Several pro-civil union Republican legislators lost their seats in the September primary, and Republicans won control of the state House in November. But Dwyer was beaten 50%-38% and Democrats held the state Senate.

Democrats have mostly prevailed since. Al Gore and John Kerry carried the state comfortably; Vermont was one of only two states in which George W. Bush's percentage of the vote declined between 2000 and 2004. In those years the controversy over civil unions has abated. Both major party candidates for governor in 2002 opposed repeal and the 2000 Census showed that only 1% of households were same-sex unions. The 2004 exit poll showed that 40% favored same-sex marriage, 36% civil unions and only 21% neither. Senator Patrick Leahy has won reelection by very wide margins, and Bernie Sanders, reelected easily to the House every two years, was elected to Jim Jeffords's Senate seat in 2006 by a 65%-32% margin, while Democrat Peter Welch won the House seat.

Yet at the same time Vermont may have become somewhat less liberal on economic issues. Job losses at IBM and slow economic growth in what had been the booming Burlington area were accompanied by a questioning of the costs of Act 250 and Act 60. In the 2002 election for governor, longtime Republican officeholder Jim Douglas beat Lieutenant Governor Doug Racine by 45%-42%. Douglas's prime goal was revision of Act 250, and in May 2004 the Democratic Senate and Republican House voted for major changes. But Vermont's cultural liberalism persisted. Douglas was proud of a law cleaning up Lake Champlain, and he let a medical marijuana bill become law without his signature. Republicans lost their majority in the state House in 2004; after the 2006 election, Democrats held a 93-49 margin there plus a 23–7 margin in the state Senate—margins that look almost like Massachusetts. But as Massachusetts, Rhode Island and Connecticut have done for many years, Vermont has voted to keep its Republican governor; Douglas was reelected by 59%-38% in 2004 and 56%-41% in 2006.

The People		Race/Ethnic Origin			Military veterans: 62,809 (13.6%)	
Pop. 2006 (est):	623,908	585,431	96.2%	White	WWII: 19.4%	Korea: 14.3%
Pop. 2000:	608,827	2,921	0.5%	Black	Vietnam: 32.2%	Gulf War: 7.4%
Pop. 1990:	562,758	5,160	0.8%	Asian	**Most populous cities (2006):**	
Change 1990-2000:	Up 8.2%	2,325	0.4%	Native Am.	1. Burlington	38,358
% of U.S. total:	0.2%	120	0.0%	Hawaiian	2. South Burlington	17,014
Pop. rank:	49th of 50	6,809	1.1%	Two+ races	3. Rutland	16,964
Area size:	9,614 sq. mi.	557	0.1%	Other	4. Barre	9,078
State Native:	54.3%	5,504	0.9%	Hisp. Origin	5. Essex Junction	8,902
Non-citizen:	1.8%	**Ancestry**				
Language		English: 13.1%		Irish: 11.7%	Urban population: 38.2%	
English: 90.8%	Other Eur.: 6.8%	French: 10.3%		German: 6.5%	Rural population: 61.8%	
Spanish: 1.6%		Fr. Canadian: 6.3%				

Education		Work Sector		General Assembly	
H.S. Grad:	86.4%	Private: 75.3%	Govt: 14.2%	Senate	23 D 7 R
College Grad:	29.4%	Self: 10.3%	Family: 0.3%	House	93 D 49 R 8 I
Industry		Unemployment: 4.2%		Legislative Term Limits: No	
Agri: 3.0%	Con: 6.7%	**Household Income**		**Registered Voters**	
Fin: 4.7%	Info: 2.7%	<15k: 14.5%	15-35k: 27.9%	No party registration	
Mfg: 18.8%	Prof: 31.2%	35-50k: 18.6%	50-100k: 30.3%		
Public: 4.6%	Trade: 15.1%	100-150k: 5.7%	>150k: 3.0%		
Other: 13.3%		Median: $40,856			
Occupation		Poverty status: 9.4%			
Blue collar: 23.3%	White collar: 60.8%	**Home Value**			
Gray collar: 15.9%		<50k: 8.6%	50-100k: 33.8%	100-200k: 43.9%	200-300k: 8.8%
		300-500k: 3.6%	>500k: 1.5%	Median: $111,200	

Presidential politics   Vermont was the most Republican state in the 1936 presidential election, when Franklin Roosevelt's campaign manager had a good laugh updating an old adage to say, "As goes Maine, so goes Vermont." Times have changed. In the 2004 presidential election Vermont was the third most Democratic state. As a new granola Vermont has grown in the Green Mountain and maple syrup atmosphere of the old, Vermont has become solidly liberal on cultural and foreign issues and not very conservative on economics. The change was apparent as long ago as 1980, when Ronald Reagan got his seventh lowest percentage here and John Anderson, more Vermont's kind of Republican, his best, 15%.

In 2004 the big presidential story here was the candidacy of Howard Dean, headquartered in Burlington. In 2000, only 49,000 Vermonters voted in the Democratic presidential primary and 81,000 in the Republican contest, which was not yet decided; John McCain beat George W. Bush 60%-35%. Four years later things were reversed. Although John Kerry clinched the Democratic nomination on March 2, 83,000 Vermonters voted in the Democratic primary a week later (it was the only primary Dean won in 2004), while only 27,000 voted in the (uncontested) Republican primary. In the fall this was one of only two states in which George W. Bush's percentage was lower than it had been in 2000.

2004 Presidential Vote		
Kerry (D)	184,067	(59%)
Bush (R)	121,180	(39%)
Nader (I)	4,494	(1%)
Other	2,568	(1%)

2004 Democratic Presidential Primary		
Dean (D)	44,393	(54%)
Kerry (D)	26,171	(32%)
Edwards (D)	5,113	(6%)
Kucinich (D)	3,396	(4%)
Clark (D)	2,749	(3%)
Other	1,059	(1%)

2000 Presidential Vote		
Gore (D)	149,022	(51%)
Bush (R)	119,775	(41%)
Nader (Green)	20,374	(7%)
Other	5,137	(2%)

The conflict between the old and new Vermonts is apparent in the NEP exit poll. In 2000, those without college degrees voted 48%-46% for Bush, but Gore carried college graduates 51%-36% and those with postgraduate degrees 62%-29%. The old divide between Protestants and Catholics has nearly vanished: in 2004, Bush carried Protestants 50%-47% and narrowly lost among Catholics 48%-52%. Kerry won 82%-15% among those with no religion.

The Vermont presidential primary, abolished for 1992, reappeared in 1996, but has achieved little notice; all the action is next door in New Hampshire.

Governor

Jim Douglas (R)

Elected 2002, term expires Jan. 2009, 3d term; b. June 21, 1951, Springfield, MA; home, Middlebury; Middlebury Col., B.A. 1972; Congregationalist; married (Dorothy).

Elected Office: VT House of Reps., 1972-79; Maj. Ldr., 1977-79; VT Secy. of St., 1980-92; VT Treasurer, 1994-2002.

Office: 109 State St., Montpelier, 5609s, 802-828-3333; Fax: 802-828-3339; Web site: www.vermont.gov/governor.

Election Results

2006 general	Jim Douglas (R)	148,014	(56%)
	Scudder Parker (D)	108,090	(41%)
	Other	6,420	(2%)
2006 primary	Jim Douglas (R)	unopposed	
2004 general	Jim Douglas (R)	181,540	(59%)
	Peter Clavelle (D)	117,327	(38%)
	Other	10,418	(3%)

Prior Winning Percentages: 2002 (45%);

The key decision that led to Jim Douglas being elected governor of Vermont in 2002 may have been his decision 34 years earlier to attend Middlebury College. Douglas grew up in Longmeadow, Massachusetts, a political junkie and a strong Republican, passing out AuH2O stickers for Barry Goldwater in 1964, at 13. In 1968, he enrolled at Middlebury and almost immediately decided to live in the town; his wife is from Middlebury and they have lived there ever since. Douglas's college years were a time of campus protests against the Vietnam War, but he became an active Republican and organized a rally for President Richard Nixon in Middlebury in 1970. In 1972, the year he graduated, he ran for state representative from Middlebury and was elected; he was elected majority leader in 1977. In 1979, he lost a race for Speaker and became an aide to Republican Governor Richard Snelling. In between sessions of the legislature he worked as a radio announcer and became executive director of the local United Way. In 1980, he was elected secretary of state and served for 12 years. In 1992, he ran against Senator Patrick Leahy and lost 54%-43%—the closest race Leahy has had since 1980. In 1994, after working for the Porter Medical Center in Middlebury, he spotted an opening for state treasurer and was elected to the first of four terms. The Democratic party produces many gifted political entrepreneurs who win office even in unlikely years and districts; the Republican party has one in Douglas. He has been on the Vermont ballot every two years since 1972, and for most of that time has gotten up before 6 a.m. to commute over the Green Mountains to the tiny state capital of Montpelier.

His opening to run for governor came when Democratic Governor Howard Dean announced on September 5, 2001 that he would not run again. Returned to office every two years—Vermont and New Hampshire are the last two states with two-year gubernatorial terms—he advanced a number of innovative policies which, in the minds of many observers, entitled him to serious consideration as a candidate for president in 2004.

But as Dean was preparing to leave Vermont politics, there was discontent with some of his policies. Not so much civil unions, which he embraced reluctantly (but which have become more popular as time goes on), but over the high property taxes engendered by Act 60, which levied a statewide property tax to provide each school district, the long delays in development caused by the environmental reviews under 30-year-old Act 250 and, most of all, by frequent news of job loss and a rising sense that Vermont has a reputation for being unfriendly to business. Douglas and his Democratic opponent, Lieutenant Governor Douglas Racine, agreed that Act 60 and Act 250 needed some changes; so did Con Hogan, former director of state human services, who started running for the Republican nomination but decided in February to run as an Independent. But there was a clear difference in emphasis. Douglas called for tax cuts, if spending cuts could be achieved, and promised to "create a more business-friendly environment." He advocated major modification in Act 60. It was "time for a change," he said, in a state which had had Democratic governors 17 of the last 18 years.

The result was something of an upset. Douglas led Racine 45%-42%, with 10% for Hogan. Under Vermont law, if no candidate receives 50% of the vote, the governor is chosen by a combined vote of the two houses of the legislature. Republicans entered the campaign with a large majority of legislative seats; Racine announced that he would not take his candidacy to the legislature if he won under 50%, while Douglas said he would. Then, contrary to most expectations, Democrats made gains in the legislature and their majority in the Senate was larger than the Republicans' narrow margin in the House. But Racine kept his word and Douglas became governor.

Douglas's great success as governor was in getting the legislature to pass in April 2004 a bill revising Act 250—the first major change in 34 years. The five citizen approval boards were abolished and their powers given to a single Environmental Court; opponents of development were no longer given an automatic right to intervene; developers could pay for stormwater runoff by offsetting reductions elsewhere. Douglas did not get the legislature to act on Act 60. He did institute increased tax collection from out-of-state corporations, combined with a 14% cut in the corporate tax rate. Douglas sought state reimportation of prescription drugs from Canada; when the FDA denied that, Vermont in August 2004 became the first state to sue.

Douglas's opponent in the 2004 election was Peter Clavelle, longtime mayor of Burlington, who got his political start in 1982 as an appointee of Socialist Mayor Bernie Sanders, now Vermont's junior senator. Clavelle was a longtime member of the left-wing Progressive party; deciding to run as a Democrat after Howard Dean announced his retirement, he arranged that the Progressive nomination would be won by an ally who would decline to run. Clavelle's major plank was health care. He proposed to use the $90 million the state spends on Medicaid on a universal health care insurance and said it could be paid for by greater efficiencies. To which Douglas said, "It's a $90 million plan that no one really understands, that its author can't explain and that they said is free. I think most Vermonters are pretty skeptical of that." He favored increasing competition by encouraging private insurers to reenter the state, health savings accounts and initiatives for chronic illness and encouraging healthy lifestyles in children. This issue, like renewable energy and smoking in bars (Clavelle favored a statewide ban, Douglas a local option), was a clear-cut conflict between a Republican backing market incentives and a Democrat favoring government decisionmaking. As the campaign went on Clavelle said that voters should back him because of his opposition to the war in Iraq. Douglas won 59%-38%, carrying all but one county. But Democrats increased their margin in the state Senate and replaced a small Republican majority with a large Democratic majority in the House. Douglas's solid reelection performance made him the Republicans' best chance for capturing the seat of retiring Senator James Jeffords in 2006 but Douglas announced in May 2005 that he would not run for Senate.

Health care remained a major issue after the election. In 2005, the legislature passed a sweeping plan providing near-universal coverage, paid for in part by a tax on payrolls of businesses that did not offer insurance; Douglas vetoed the measure. But in 2006 the legislature agreed to a more market-oriented version, the Catamount Health plan, that sought to curb health care costs while extending coverage to more uninsured residents and offering new approaches for those with chronic diseases; Douglas signed it. Also in 2006, the legislature and Douglas came to agreement on a plan to fund a college scholarship program. The year before, Douglas had sought to create a $175 million, 15-year college scholarship program funded by tobacco settlement money. The legislature had wanted the money to go toward health care. In the end, the two sides agreed to $5 million in scholarships for current high school seniors and established a commission to determine how to spend another $5 million on that class.

This pragmatic approach served Douglas well going into the 2006 election. His approval rating was above 60% in the summer. He ran on what he called his "Agenda of Affordability", which took aim at the increasingly high cost of living in Vermont, and highlighted what he called a Democratic willingness to raise taxes to afford more spending. His Democratic opponent, former state Senator Scudder Parker, struggled to make headway until the fall. Parker got a boost in September after Douglas played a role in scuttling a bill in Congress that would have designated more wilderness in the Green Mountain Forest. Parker criticized Douglas for not doing enough on renewable energy and consistently sought to tie him to President George W. Bush, who, with disapproval ratings over 70% in Vermont, was more unpopular here than just about anywhere else in the nation. "I'm not trying to say Jim equals George," Parker told the *Associated Press*. "What I am saying is that Jim has consistently supported Bush administration policies and those policies are coming home to have a direct impact on Vermont's budget, Vermont's quality of life."

Vermont is small enough that a governor facing a competitive reelection can raise and spend less than $1 million and still win. Douglas did just that, winning 56%-41%, again carrying all but one county. He has said he will run for a fourth term in 2008.

Senior Senator

Patrick Leahy (D)

Elected 1974, seat up 2010, 6th term; b. Mar. 31, 1940, Montpelier; home, Burlington; St. Michael's Col., B.A. 1961, Georgetown U., J.D. 1964; Catholic; married (Marcelle).

Elected Office: VT St. Atty., Chittenden Cnty., 1966-74.

Professional Career: Practicing atty., 1964-74.

DC Office: 433 RSOB, 20510, 202-224-4242; Fax: 202-224-3479; Web site: leahy.senate.gov.

State Offices: Burlington, 802-863-2525; Montpelier, 802-229-0569.

Committees: *Agriculture, Nutrition & Forestry* (2d of 11 D): Nutrition and Food Assistance, Sustainable and Organic Agriculture & General Legislation (Chmn.); Production, Income Protection & Price Support; Rural Revitalization, Conservation, Forestry & Credit. *Appropriations* (3d of 15 D): State, Foreign Operations & Related Programs (Chmn.); Commerce, Justice, Science & Related Agencies; Defense; Homeland Security; Interior, Environment & Related Agencies; Transportation, Housing and Urban Development & Related Agencies. *Judiciary* (Chmn. of 10 D): Antitrust, Competition Policy & Consumer Rights.

Group Ratings

	ADA	ACLU	AFS	LCV	ITIC	NTU	COC	ACU	CFG	FRC
2006	95	100	100	100	50	9	33	0	0	0
2005	100	—	100	95	—	7	28	0	0	—

National Journal Ratings

	2005 LIB	—	2005 CONS	2006 LIB	—	2006 CONS
Economic	88%	—	10%	83%	—	13%
Social	74%	—	25%	96%	—	0%
Foreign	90%	—	5%	94%	—	5%

Key Votes of the 109th Congress

1. Bar ANWR Drilling	Y	5. Confirm Samuel Alito	N	9. Limit Interstate Abortion	N
2. FY06 Spending Curb	N	6. Path to Citizenship	Y	10. CAFTA	N
3. Estate Tax Repeal	N	7. Bar Same Sex Marriage	N	11. Urge Iraq Withdrawal	Y
4. Raise Minimum Wage	Y	8. Stem Cell Research $	Y	12. Provide Detainee Rights	Y

Election Results

2004 general	Patrick Leahy (D)	216,972	(71%)	($1,531,833)
	Jack McMullen (R)	75,398	(25%)	($736,086)
	Other	14,838	(5%)	
2004 primary	Patrick Leahy (D)	27,459	(95%)	
	Craig Hill (D)	1,573	(5%)	
1998 general	Patrick Leahy (D)	154,567	(72%)	($1,014,751)
	Fred H. Tuttle (R)	48,051	(22%)	
	Other	11,418	(5%)	

Prior Winning Percentages: 1992 (54%); 1986 (63%); 1980 (50%); 1974 (50%)

Patrick Leahy, Vermont's senior and longest-serving senator, was first elected to the Senate in 1974. He has held public office for most of his adult life. He grew up in Burlington, went to Georgetown law school, then returned home to Burlington to practice law. He was elected Chittenden County state's attorney in 1966, at 26, and, after eight years in that post—and few public officials are scrutinized as closely as a local prosecutor—he was elected to the U.S. Senate at 34.

Leahy is the chairman of the Judiciary Committee once again, having been so during the Democrats' 18 months in the majority in 2001-03. He was also formerly chairman of the Agriculture

Committee. Judiciary handles many of the cultural issues which have polarized the two parties and their constituencies—issues like abortion and gun control—and the committee has been sharply polarized at least since the hearings on the Supreme Court nomination of Judge Robert Bork in 1987. In the 1990s, when Republicans were in the majority, Leahy criticized Republicans for holding up Bill Clinton's judicial appointments and stoutly defended Clinton on impeachment. When Leahy became chairman, he began to hold up judicial nominations himself. He led the rejection by party line votes of two nominees for the Fifth Circuit and demanded from another nominee the memos he had written while working in the office of the solicitor general during the Clinton administration—something never before sought. As ranking minority member in 2003-07, Leahy led filibusters against 10 appeals court nominees—the first in history—which were bitterly attacked by Republicans. Leahy points out that the large majority of appellate nominees and virtually every trial court nominee have been approved and cites statistics to argue that Democrats have been fairer to Bush appointees than Republicans were to Clinton's. In September 2005 Leahy asked tough questions of Supreme Court nominee John Roberts. But he surprised many when he voted to approve Roberts's nomination. It was "a close decision," he said. "I know this will not be popular with many of my constituency, and I understand that. . . I came here to do what I thought was right, and as a Vermonter I can do nothing different." He also asked tough questions of the next Supreme Court nominee, Samuel Alito. But this time he voted no. "This president is in the midst of a radical realignment of the powers of government and its intrusiveness into the private lives of Americans. This nomination is part of that plan."

This was in line with the approach Leahy has taken to legislation and administrative action after September 11; he has approached the task with some concern lest federal powers override individual rights. He and his staff worked with the Bush administration to hammer out the planks in the USA Patriot Act; it was essentially the Senate version, not the House version, which was passed in October 2001. But Leahy also criticized other Bush administration actions and proposals. He opposed the administration's first proposal for broader powers to detain and deport immigrants suspected of terrorism without presenting evidence in court. In September 2002, he said Justice should be required to disclose the number of U.S. citizens being spied on, the number of secret foreign intelligence wiretaps that had become part of criminal proceedings and the total number of persons targeted by foreign intelligence surveillance warrants. After the story broke on the Abu Ghraib prison scandal in April 2004 he sharply criticized the administration. He disagreed with Bush's declaration that the Geneva convention did not apply to unlawful combatants in Afghanistan and argued that methods authorized by Defense Secretary Donald Rumsfeld for Afghanistan prisoners in December 2002, though rescinded a month later, nonetheless migrated and were applied to prisoners in Iraq as well as in Afghanistan and at Guantanamo. In December 2005 he criticized the NSA surveillance of communications between suspected al Qaeda terrorists abroad and persons in the United States. In 2006 he opposed Arlen Specter's bill to open up the program to judicial review.

Leahy is a gadgeteer and fine amateur photographer, a "big fan" of Batman (he has a speaking role in the upcoming Batman film, due out in 2008) and the Grateful Dead. In 1995, he became the second senator (after Edward Kennedy) to set up a personal website; in 2003 he was the first member of Congress with a blog on its official website. Titled "More from the Floor", the blog is updated several times a day when the Senate is in session, informing readers about floor debates and roll call votes. He co-sponsored with Republican Orrin Hatch the Digital Millennium Copyright law, passed to comply with the WIPO treaty, and with Arizona Sen. Jon Kyl, the law making the theft of personal identification information a crime. Also with Hatch, he introduced a bill in 2006 to revise patent law, awarding patents to the first to file, limiting the defenses of willful infringement, expanding prior use rights and apportioning the rule for calculating damages.

Another Leahy cause has been the elimination of land mines. Since 1989, he has been crusading against the export and use of land mines, which are easy and cheap to implant yet difficult and expensive to remove, and which injure thousands of civilians long after hostilities have ended. In 1994, he got the United Nations to approve unanimously their eventual elimination. Leahy continues to work to aid land mine victims and to deactivate the thousands of land mines still active in many parts of the world and to find alternatives for them. On a similar issue, he and Dianne Feinstein in 2006 sponsored an amendment to ban the use of cluster bombs near civilian sites in Iraq and Afghanistan; it was defeated 70-30 in September. On foreign and defense issues, he tends to stand to the left of the Senate: He was one of three senators to vote against authorization of missile defense in March 1999 and has called for an end to the ban on travel to Cuba. He has been a staunch and outspoken critic of the Iraq war. He and Christopher Bond, as co-chairmen of the

National Guard Caucus, sponsored an amendment in June 2006 to promote the chief of the National Guard status to four-star status and to let the Guard identify differences with active forces; it was accepted by Armed Services Chairman John Warner but rejected in conference committee in September. He and Bond worked successfully to set aside $3 billion in the defense appropriation to replenish National Guard equipment stock.

Leahy has long been one of the few members of the Senate Agriculture Committee not from a state with heavily subsidized crops like wheat, corn, soybeans or cotton. As ranking Democrat, he worked with Richard Lugar in the 1990s to phase out the old subsidy system. Their great success was the Freedom to Farm Act of 1996, but soon crop prices fell and Congress took to voting huge annual subsidies in the form of emergency relief; the 2002 farm bill largely rolled back the 1996 act. In that act, Leahy shaped the bill's conservation provisions and tried to save the Northeast Dairy Compact, to set milk prices in the six New England states; the Compact, however, expired in September 2001. Working with his adversary on the Northeast Dairy Compact, Wisconsin's Herb Kohl, he did obtain MILC provisions (Milk Income Loss Compensation Program), which have brought $45 million to Vermont dairy farmers. His and Kohl's efforts to reauthorize MILC in October 2004, 11 months before its expiration, fell short. But in 2005 Leahy got it into the budget resolution, and in December 2005 the Senate passed an extension of MILC into September 2007. Leahy also pushed an amendment to the immigration bill providing year-round visas for foreign dairy workers; there were said to be 2,000 such workers on Vermont's 1,150 dairy farms.

Leahy serves on Appropriations and has procured funding for Vermont projects—$4 million to finish repairs on the dam on the Waterbury Reservoir, $750,000 for preserving historic buildings, a $7.1 million contract with a St. Johnsbury firm for advanced deployable shelters for combat zones. With the other members of the Vermont and New Hampshire delegations, he pushed successfully in 2006 for a wilderness designation for 42,000 acres in the Green Mountain National Forest. Vermont is a border state; it is less than a two-hour ride from Burlington to Montreal. In March 2006 he defeated a proposal for a study of a wall on the Canadian border—one of the wackiest ideas he had ever heard, he said. He has criticized the Bush administration's proposal for a passport-like PASS card to cross the border between the United States and Canada. In 2006 a Leahy amendment to postpone the PASS card to June 2009 passed; it provided that the PASS card would have to meet security standards (the Homeland Security Department wanted a radio-frequency identification chip readable from 20 feet away; Leahy wanted one with higher security readable from only four inches away). "Without even testing the technology for use as a passport or personal ID, they have chosen a weaker security standard that would make our borders less secure and that would risk the personal information of millions of Americans." Also in that bill, Leahy managed to steer millions of dollars in homeland security funds to small states like Vermont.

The one close call Leahy has had with Vermont voters came in 1980, when he narrowly survived the Republican sweep. He beat popular Governor Richard Snelling 63%-35% in 1986, and in 1992, against Jim Douglas, then state treasurer and now governor, Leahy won 54%-43%. In 1998, he had an easier time against 77-year-old dairy farmer Fred Tuttle, winning 72%-22%. In 2004, against the man Tuttle upset in the Republican primary six years before, Leahy won by a nearly identical 71%-25%.

Junior Senator

Bernie Sanders (I)

Elected 2006, seat up 2012, 1st term; b. Sept. 8, 1941, New York, NY; home, Burlington; Attended Brooklyn Col., U. of Chicago, B.A. 1964; Jewish; married (Jane O'Meara Sanders).

Elected Office: Burlington Mayor, 1981-89; U.S. House of Reps., 1990-2006.

Professional Career: Writer; Dir., Amer. People's Historical Soc., 1977-81; Lecturer, Harvard U., 1989; Prof., Hamilton Col., 1989-90.

DC Office: 332 DSOB, 20510, 202-224-5141; Fax: 202-228-0776; Web site: sanders.senate.gov.

State Offices: Brattleboro, 802-254-8732; Burlington, 802-862-0697; Montpelier, 802-223-2241.

Committees: *Budget* (11th of 12 D). *Energy & Natural Resources* (11th of 12 D). *Health, Education, Labor & Pensions* (10th of 11 D). *Veterans' Affairs* (5th of 8 D).

Group Ratings (as Member of U.S. House of Representatives)

	ADA	ACLU	AFS	LCV	ITIC	NTU	COC	ACU	CFG	FRC
2006	100	100	100	100	0	9	27	8	8	0
2005	100	—	100	94	—	18	33	8	3	0

National Journal Ratings (as Member of U.S. House of Representatives)

	2005 LIB	—	2005 CONS		2006 LIB	—	2006 CONS
Economic	94%	—	0%		91%	—	6%
Social	77%	—	23%		79%	—	20%
Foreign	94%	—	4%		87%	—	12%

Key Votes of the 109th Congress (as Member of U.S. House of Representatives)

1. Estate Tax Repeal	N	5. Limit Interstate Abortion	N	9. Build Border Fence	N
2. Limit CAFE Standards	N	6. Extend Patriot Act	N	10. CAFTA	N
3. FY06 Spending Curb	N	7. Bar Same Sex Marriage	N	11. Oppose Iraq Withdrawal	N
4. Drilling in ANWR	N	8. Stem Cell Research	$	Y	12. Detainee Tribunals	N

Election Results

2006 general	Bernie Sanders (I)	171,638	(65%)	($6,004,222)
	Richard Tarrant (R)	84,924	(32%)	($7,300,392)
	Other	5,857	(2%)	
2006 primary	Bernie Sanders (D)	35,954	(94%)	
	Other	2,232	(6%)	
2000 general	James Jeffords (R)	189,133	(66%)	($1,889,243)
	Ed Flanagan (D)	73,352	(25%)	($1,054,977)
	Other	26,015	(9%)	

Prior Winning Percentages: 2004 House (67%); 2002 House (64%); 2000 House (69%); 1998 House (63%); 1996 House (55%); 1994 House (50%); 1992 House (58%); 1990 House (56%)

Vermont's junior senator is Bernie Sanders, a Socialist elected as an Independent in 2006, but treated as a Democrat in the Senate. Sanders grew up in Flatbush, Brooklyn, the son of a paint salesman who had emigrated from Poland; his mother died while he was a teenager. He became involved in radical politics at the University of Chicago, then came to Vermont as part of the hippie invasion of 1968 and worked as a carpenter. Four years later, he ran in a special 1972 Senate election to replace Republican Winston Prouty, who died in office in 1971; Sanders won just 2% as the candidate of the socialist Liberty Union Party. His rumpled, tieless, sincere persona helped him win election as mayor of Burlington in 1981 by 10 votes, after losing four statewide races. In 1988, when Congressman Jim Jeffords ran for the Senate, Sanders ran for the House and lost to Republican Peter Smith. Two years later he ran again and reversed the result by capitalizing on Smith's support of the 1990 budget summit agreement and his vote for the ban on semiautomatic weapons. The National Rifle Association came out against Smith, and Sanders' opposition to gun control helped him carry 227 of Vermont's 251 cities and towns, plus three gores and one grant. Sanders became only the third Socialist elected to the House, after Victor Berger of Milwaukee (1911-13, 1923-29) and Meyer London of Manhattan's Lower East Side (1915-23). His views haven't changed much since his first election.

In the House, where Sanders served as Vermont's single House member, Democrats at first balked at accepting him in their caucus, but they granted him seniority as a Democrat when he arrived in 1991; he became ranking minority member on a subcommittee in 1997 over the objections of Elijah Cummings and, when a Banking subcommittee ranking position opened up in November 1997, he got that over the claims of Carolyn Maloney. He amassed a heavily liberal voting record and formed a Progressive Caucus, with what was at the time a quixotic agenda: progressive tax reform, a Canadian-style single-payer health care system, a 50% cut in military spending over five years, a national energy policy and—a Vermont touch—support for family farms.

He was at times a practical and sometimes successful legislator, gaining Republican allies in targeting what they consider corporate welfare. With Chris Smith of New Jersey, he passed an amendment barring spending for defense contractor mergers. In February 2001 he proposed a $300 per person income tax rebate; this quickly became Democratic party policy, and Republicans in assembling majorities for the Bush tax cuts included it in diluted form—a $300 rebate for income-tax-paying adults. Sanders and Democrats noted ruefully, and accurately, that Bush claimed credit for a tax cutting proposal which was initially theirs and which Republicans for a time resisted.

As much as any member of Congress, he made the cost of prescription drugs a national issue. Since the 1980s, he has called for government programs to pay for prescription drugs, and was the first member of Congress to lead bus trips to Canada to buy drugs there. He has denounced "the insatiable greed that consumes this runaway [pharmaceutical] industry." He objected consistently when Clinton HHS Secretary Donna Shalala and her Bush successor Tommy Thompson ruled that they could not certify that reimported Canadian drugs are safe. He argued that the safety threat is nonexistent and adds that "those who swear on the altar of free trade" are happy to let U.S. consumers eat imported fruits, vegetables and meat.

On trade issues, Sanders has called for repeal of NAFTA as well as PNTR and for a moratorium on free trade agreements. He argues that workers in both the United States and in foreign nations would be better off without free trade agreements. On national security, Sanders has been a critic of the Patriot Act and has focused on Section 215 which permits government investigators to obtain business records including those of library and bookstore patrons after obtaining an order from an intelligence court. As Vermont's sole representative, Sanders was naturally the House's leading backer of the Northeast Dairy Compact, which propped up Northeast dairy prices. After the Compact expired in September 2001, his bill to establish a national dairy compact passed the House but was killed in conference committee when Vermonters were unable to come up with a version acceptable to Midwestern dairy states.

All of this played well with Vermont voters, and by the late 1990s Sanders began winning by large margins as Democratic candidates failed to get support from the state party—if they filed to run against Sanders at all.

Sanders twice gave serious consideration to running against Senator Jim Jeffords, but that came before Jeffords left the Republican Party in May 2001, an event which gave Democrats a majority in the Senate for 18 months. Like Sanders in the House, Jeffords called himself an Independent but caucused with the Democrats; in April 2005, Jeffords announced he would not run for another term in 2006. Sanders became the early frontrunner and in no time had amassed endorsements from many Vermont Democrats, including former Governor Phil Hoff, Burlington Mayor Peter Clavelle, Senate President Pro Tempore Peter Welch and House Speaker Gaye Symington. Ever the loner, Sanders said he would neither seek nor accept the Democratic nomination—but, with his consent, Democrats ran his name on the primary ballot anyway. In the September 12 Democratic primary, he won 94 percent though he formally declined the nomination and petitioned the state to list him on the ballot as an Independent candidate. Still, national Democrats, including the Democratic Senatorial Campaign Committee, supported his election. Howard Dean, chairman of the Democratic National Committee and a former Vermont governor, declared that "a victory for Bernie Sanders is a win for Democrats."

On the Republican side, Governor Jim Douglas, considered the strongest possible Republican candidate, declined to run and Richard Tarrant, a multi-millionaire businessman and former high school basketball star, became the nominee. He waged an almost entirely self-funded campaign, spending $7.3 million of his own money, much of it on television commercials. His ads sought to portray Sanders as an ineffective radical who was soft on sexual predators and drug dealers and featured the tagline, "What's happened to Bernie?" This strategy might have worked elsewhere but not in Vermont where voters were already familiar with Sanders, who was making his 13th statewide run, and his iconoclastic ways. Despite the harsh attacks—or perhaps because of them—Tarrant was never able to close the gap in the polls. Tarrant outspent Sanders, but Sanders proved to be a well-funded socialist. He raised and spent over $6 million, many times more than he had ever raised or spent before, and enough to make this the highest-spending race in state history. Sanders won easily, 65%-32%.

Representative-At-Large

Peter Welch (D)

Elected 2006, 1st term; b. May 2, 1947, Springfield, MA; home, Hartland; Col. of the Holy Cross, A.B. 1969, U. of CA at Berkeley, J.D. 1973; Catholic; widowed.

Elected Office: VT Senate, 1980-88, 2001-2006; VT Senate Min. Ldr., 1982-84; VT Senate Pres. Pro Tempore, 1985-88, 2002-06.

Professional Career: Robert F. Kennedy Fellow, 1969-70; Practicing atty., 1974-2006.

DC Office: 1404 LHOB, 20515, 202-225-4115; Fax: 202-225-6790; Web site: www.welch.house.gov.

District Offices: Burlington, 802-652-2450.

Committees: *Oversight & Government Reform* (23d of 23 D): Government Management, Organization & Procurement; National Security & Foreign Affairs. *Rules* (6th of 9 D): Legislative & Budget Process.

Group Ratings and Key Votes: Newly Elected

Election Results

2006 general	Peter Welch (D)	139,815	(53%)	($1,737,958)
	Martha Rainville (R)	117,023	(45%)	($1,132,968)
	Other	5,888	(2%)	
2006 primary	Peter Welch (D)	unopposed		
2004 general	Bernie Sanders (I)	205,774	(67%)	($810,050)
	Greg Parke (R)	74,271	(24%)	($670,350)
	Larry Drown (D)	21,684	(7%)	
	Other	3,279	(1%)	

Vermont's single House member is Peter Welch, a Democrat first elected in 2006. He grew up in Springfield, Massachusetts and graduated from Holy Cross College. The summer before his junior year he worked for a Jesuit community organization in Chicago, where he heard Martin Luther King, Jr., speak in his campaign against racial discrimination there. After graduating he spent a year as a Robert F. Kennedy Fellow in Chicago. Then he attended law school in Berkeley and, after graduating, backpacked down the Pan-American Highway to Santiago, Chile, went overland to Salvador, Brazil, then worked on a freighter that sailed to Portugal. After these travels he practiced law in White River Junction, Vermont. He married a professor at Dartmouth, just across the river; she later taught at the University of Vermont. In 1980 he became just the second Democrat ever to represent Windsor County in the state Senate—and the first since the Civil War. In 1982 he became Senate minority leader. In 1984, after Democrats won a majority in the Senate for the first time ever, he was elected Senate President Pro Tem. He worked on environment, education and tax issues and helped establish the Housing and Land Conservation Trust, which worked for affordable housing and conservation of farm and forest land. In 1988, when Republican Congressman Jim Jeffords ran for the Senate, he ran for the U.S. House and lost the Democratic primary by just 266 votes, 34%-33%. If he had won, he would have faced not only the winning Republican, Peter Smith, but also Bernie Sanders, the longtime mayor of Burlington who was running as a Socialist. Sanders came close to winning, and in 1990 he capitalized on Smith's votes for gun control and tax increases and won the seat. In 1990 Welch ran for governor but lost 52%-46% to Republican Richard Snelling.

For some years after that Welch retired from political life. His wife, who had been his campaign manager, fought cancer for nine years and died in 2004. In 2001 Governor Howard Dean appointed him to the state Senate to fill a vacancy in Windsor County. In 2003 he became president pro tem once again and focused on health care; he helped negotiate an agreement on fuel rods in the Vermont Yankee nuclear power plant near Brattleboro.

In spring 2005, Senator Jim Jeffords announced he would not run for reelection in 2006; Bernie Sanders, after 15 years in the House, announced he would run for the seat and attracted little opposition. In June 2005 Welch announced he would run once again for the U.S. House. He was supported by many Democratic leaders and, while other potential candidates canvassed for support, none ended up running and he won the September 2006 primary unopposed. The winner of the Republican primary, by a 71%-28% margin, was Martha Rainville. She had an unusual background for a candidate. A Navy brat born on a base in Connecticut, she graduated from the University of Mississippi, enlisted in the Air Force in 1979 and after four years of active duty served in the Air National Guard. In 1997 she was elected by the legislature to serve as state Adjutant General, the first woman ever to command a state's National Guard. She announced her candidacy for the House in February 2006 and resigned from the Guard in April; state and national Republican leaders supported her. Welch campaigned as an opponent from the start of military action in Iraq and condemned the "corrupt" Republicans in Washington. He supported a universal health care program and called for the resignation of Defense Secretary Donald Rumsfeld. Rainville said she would have voted for military action in 2002 given what was known then, but criticized some of the Bush administration's decisions in Iraq. While Welch called for simplifying the Medicare prescription drug benefit, she supported it. Both candidates favored access to abortion.

Both candidates also pledged not to run negative campaigns, and this was probably the only seriously contested 2006 House race in the country in which no negative ads were run. But there was dispute. "Martha Rainville was hand-picked by the national Republicans," Welch said. "A Vermont Republican can be something very different," Rainville said. "The party has a lot of room for diversity." Welch's campaign spent $1.7 million to Rainville's $1.1 million. But the House Republican campaign committee outspent its Democratic counterpart by $750,000 to $300,000; this was one of the few Democratic seats (Sanders had always voted for the Democrats to organize the House) that the Republicans thought they had any chance of picking up. Though close in the polls throughout the summer, by late September Welch began opening up his lead; Rainville was embarrassed when she was forced to fire a speechwriter in early October for plagiarizing from, of all people, Hillary Rodham Clinton.

Welch won by a 53%-45% margin—decisive, but less than John Kerry's 59%-39% in Vermont in 2004. He said that his priorities were to work toward universal health care and a simplification of the Medicare prescription drug benefit. He called for withdrawing "a majority" of troops from Iraq in 2007 and for an "explicit acknowledgement that the U.S. will not maintain permanent military bases" there.

★ VIRGINIA ★

Traditions endure in Virginia. Through 400 years of history, Virginians have honored, and sometimes been fixated by, traditions going back to the Revolution and before. For the last half-century, Virginia has been growing lustily, in the first years after World War II thanks mainly to government, in recent years thanks more to a vibrant private sector, but the first state in the nation to elect a black governor still hews to a course close to its roots. The first Virginia was a commonwealth ruled by a landed gentry that was, in the words of historian David Hackett Fischer, "elitist and libertarian." From the tobacco-growing counties emerged in the 1770s a group of leaders—George Washington, George Mason, Patrick Henry, Thomas Jefferson, Richard Henry Lee, James Madison—who in learning, wisdom and strength of character, equal any such group from any similarly sized polity since Periclean Athens or republican Rome. They were slaveholders who insisted on liberty, armed men living on the marches of civilization who insisted on the rule of law, believers in racial inequality who set forth principles of equality that would in time form the basis of a non-racist society. The Virginia they led into the American Revolution was not only the most populous and the richest of the 13 colonies, it also was the indispensable creator of the Republic and the Constitution that has held together the world's greatest democracy.

After the Revolutionary War, gentry control continued even as Virginia was eclipsed in population and wealth by Pennsylvania and New York and, its tobacco fields all but exhausted, became a breeding ground for slaves. But Virginia had two more great heroes, Robert E. Lee and Stonewall Jackson, both of whom reluctantly and brilliantly fought for their state rather than the larger nation. Virginia's leadership class was impoverished and embittered by the Civil War, so much of which was fought on Virginia soil. Industrialization was haphazard: Railroads were constructed to ship cotton up from the South and coal east to the seaports; textile mills were built in Southside towns and tobacco factories in Richmond; the giant Newport News Shipbuilding & Drydock Company was built by railroad magnate Collis Huntington. Politically, Virginia was ruled by a local gentry who worshipped their Revolutionary past and mourned their Lost Cause. They were pessimists, looking not for economic growth but for stability, bent on maintaining Virginia's segregation and content with its second-class economy. County courthouse organizations became the political

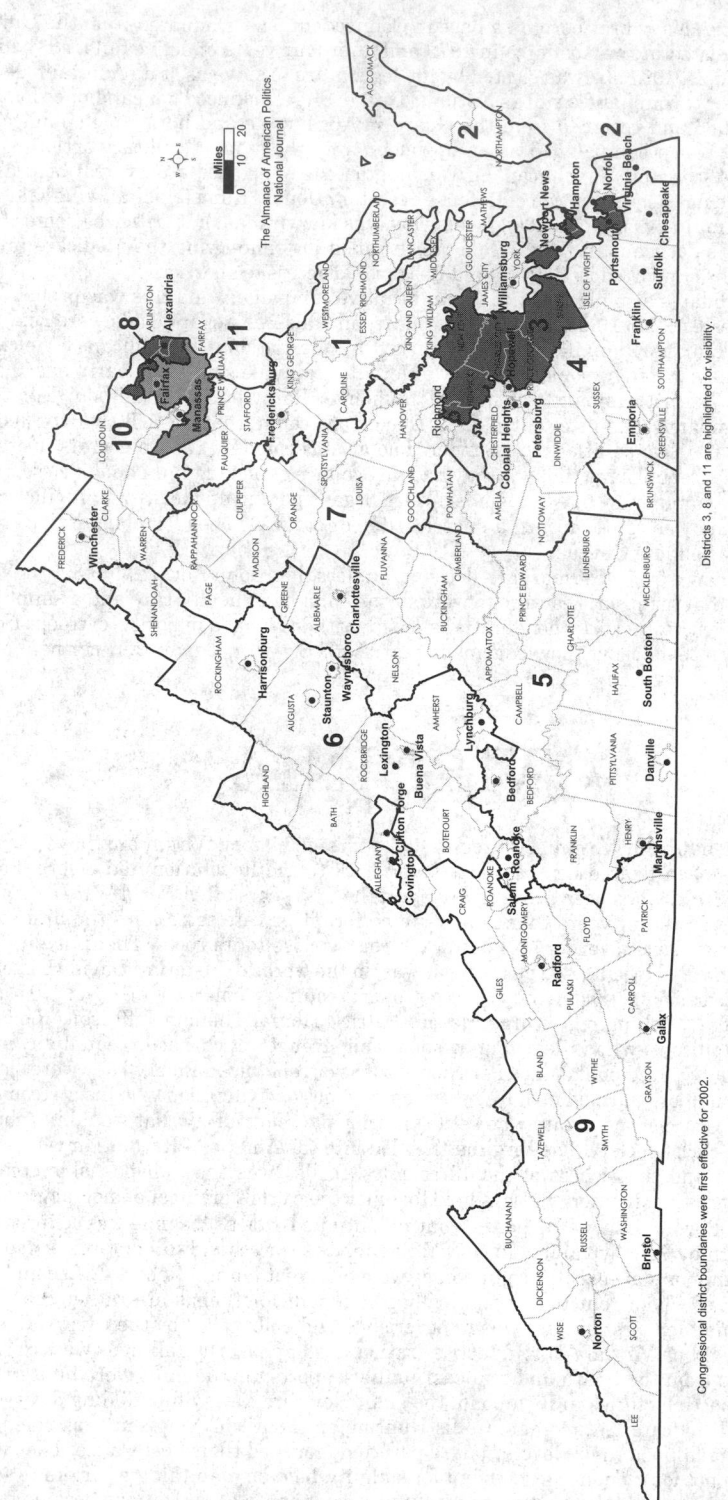

The Almanac of American Politics,
National Journal

Districts 3, 8 and 11 are highlighted for visibility.

Congressional district boundaries were first effective for 2002.

machine of Harry Byrd, who ran Virginia politics from 1925, when he was elected governor, until 1965, when he retired from the Senate. In national politics, this machine lost battles more often than Lee lost on the battlefield, and less gallantly. For years the machine succeeded in keeping most vestiges of the welfare state and racial equality out of Virginia, to the point of closing public schools in the 1950s rather than obeying federal court desegregation orders.

This "massive resistance" collapsed in the late 1950s; Virginia's demographics were changing and its politics went through a quarter-century of flux. The government-employee filled Northern Virginia suburbs of Washington D.C. and the industrial Tidewater region around Norfolk and Newport News, plus the enfranchisement of blacks, provided a political base for liberal Democrats. But they were never quite a majority. In the 1970s, conservatives who left the Democratic Party and ran as independents or Republicans held them at bay. In the 1980s, three moderate Democrats were elected governor—Charles Robb in 1981, Gerald Baliles in 1985, Douglas Wilder in 1989—because they did not represent an attempt to impose a labor-liberal agenda on an unwilling Virginia, and because they argued they could use government effectively to improve education and build Virginia's economy. Wilder's election was a national breakthrough, a successful attempt by a black politician to campaign and govern on equal terms. His fiscal conservatism, which resulted in sharp spending cuts in the early 1990s, like his elegant manners and thick Richmond accent, echoes Virginia's elitist and libertarian tradition; his insistence on the rule of law helped him win election as Richmond's mayor in 2004.

In the 1990s, Virginia developed ideological politics along party lines, and Republicans made historic strides by winning majorities with traditional party platforms. George Allen was elected governor by a wide margin in 1993 as a Republican who believed in lower taxes, traditional cultural values, longer prison terms, and teaching basic skills—he combined confrontational issue positions with a sunny temperament. In the 1997 contest for governor (Virginia is the last state which bars its governors from running for reelection, another tradition that endures), Republican James Gilmore made his centerpiece issue the phasing out of the property tax on automobiles, and won a 56%-43% victory over Democrat Don Beyer. Republicans for the first time swept the top three statewide offices. In 1999 Gilmore led Republicans to legislative majorities in both chambers for the first time ever. George W. Bush carried the state, to no one's surprise, by a solid 52%-44% margin in 2000.

In the years since Democrats have become more competitive and successful; Republicans haven't won a contested race for senator or governor since 2000 (Republican Senator John Warner had no Democratic opponent in 2002). The first Democratic winner was cell phone millionaire Mark Warner, who won in 2001 primarily due to an intensive 18-month campaign in rural Virginia—paying attention to the parts of the state not blessed by 1990s growth. Warner carried Northern Virginia and the Hampton Roads area only narrowly. But he also carried the rest of the state, which casts about half the vote, where Bush had won 56%-41% the year before. Warner's big success was persuading the legislature to raise taxes by a record amount in 2004; the Republican state Senate wanted to raise them even more, but a lot of arms had to be twisted to get the needed votes in the Republican House of Delegates. The key impetus for raising taxes was the demand for more roads and mass transit in Northern Virginia and Hampton Roads; as it turned out, revenues poured in and produced a big surplus. Warner left office with high ratings and a plan to run for president in 2008, as a moderate in touch with country music and NASCAR races; it helped him that Democratic Lieutenant Governor Tim Kaine was elected to succeed him in 2005.

Kaine's victory, and that of Democrat Jim Webb against Republican Senator George Allen in 2006, resulted from big Democratic margins in Northern Virginia. This was presaged in 2004, when John Kerry's campaign for a time was seriously contesting Virginia. Bush ended up winning again, 54%-45%, but contrary to the national pattern he ran worse in Northern Virginia than he had in 2000. Then Bush carried the area 49%-47%; in 2004 it went for John Kerry, 51%-48%. With a growing immigrant population in Fairfax County and a burgeoning number of singles in Arlington and Alexandria, Bush's cultural conservatism and country style were repelling Northern Virginia voters. In 2005, Kaine's opponent, Attorney General Jerry Kilgore, with a deep Southwest Virginia accent and very conservative stands, was an even harder sell; Kaine ran only 1% ahead of Warner's showing in Hampton Roads and failed to carry the half of the state outside the two big metro areas as Warner had. But he carried Northern Virginia 58%-40%, even carrying fast-growing exurban Loudoun and Prince William Counties. Webb duplicated that feat in 2006. Allen won 48% of the vote in Hampton Roads, the same as when he beat incumbent Senator Charles Robb in 2000, and in the area outside the two big metro areas he won 55%, just 1% less than six years before. But he was clobbered in Northern Virginia; he lost the area to Robb 51%-49% in 2000, but lost it 57%-42% to Webb in 2006.

Virginia, once the "mother of presidents" (eight of them were born in the state, more than any other) expected to have two 2008 presidential candidates, but both candidacies collapsed within a month. In October 2006, Mark Warner announced he was not running, and Allen's defeat in November, which gave Democrats a majority in the Senate, took him out of the race. A third Virginia candidate, former Governor Jim Gilmore, entered the race for the Republican nomination in January 2007 but exited in July.

The People		**Race/Ethnic Origin**			**Military veterans:** 786,359 (14.7%)	
Pop. 2006 (est):	7,642,884	4,965,637	70.2%	White	WWII: 14.1%	Korea: 10.5%
Pop. 2000:	7,078,515	1,376,378	19.4%	Black	Vietnam: 35.4%	Gulf War: 16.8%
Pop. 1990:	6,187,358	259,277	3.7%	Asian	**Most populous cities (2006):**	
Change 1990-2000:	Up 14.4%	18,596	0.3%	Native Am.	1. Virginia Beach	435,619
% of U.S. total:	2.5%	3,380	0.0%	Hawaiian	2. Norfolk	229,112
Pop. rank:	12th of 50	114,022	1.6%	Two+ races	3. Chesapeake	220,560
Area size:	42,774 sq. mi.	11,685	0.2%	Other	4. Arlington	199,776
State Native:	51.9%	329,540	4.7%	Hisp. Origin	5. Richmond	192,913
Non-citizen:	4.8%	**Ancestry**				
Language		German: 9.5%		USA: 9.2%	Urban population: 73.0%	
English: 87.3%	Spanish: 5.2%	English: 9.0%		Irish: 7.9%	Rural population: 27.0%	
Other Eur.: 4.0%		Italian: 2.9%				

Education		**Work Sector**		**General Assembly**	
H.S. Grad:	81.5%	Private: 74.7%	Govt: 19.6%	Senate	23 R 17 D
College Grad:	29.5%	Self: 5.5%	Family: 0.2%	House of Del.	57 R 40 D 3 I
Industry		Unemployment: 4.1%		Legislative Term Limits: No	
Agri: 1.3%	Con: 7.3%	**Household Income**		**Registered Voters**	
Fin: 6.6%	Info: 3.8%	<15k: 13.2%	15-35k: 23.5%	No party registration	
Mfg: 16.0%	Prof: 29.9%	35-50k: 16.5%	50-100k: 31.7%		
Public: 8.3%	Trade: 14.2%	100-150k: 9.4%	>150k: 5.7%		
Other: 12.6%		Median: $46,677			
Occupation		Poverty status: 9.6%			
Blue collar: 22.1%	White collar: 63.7%	**Home Value**			
Gray collar: 14.2%		<50k: 10.6%	50-100k: 30.2%	100-200k: 37.4%	200-300k: 12.9%
		300-500k: 6.7%	>500k: 2.3%	Median: $118,800	

Presidential politics   Virginia remains one of the more Republican states in presidential races, but not as solidly Republican as it once was. In 1996, Bill Clinton lost here by only 48%-46%. In 2000, George W. Bush won by 52%-44%. In 2004 Democrats, heartened by Mark Warner's victory in the 2001 governor election, targeted the state early; John Kerry spent $1 million in advertising here in the spring and early summer. But in August the polls showed Bush well ahead, and Virginia dropped off the target list. Bush carried the state by a seemingly comfortable margin, 54%-45%. But compared to 2000, he lost ground in Northern Virginia, which he lost 51%-48%, while gaining ground in Hampton Roads (53%-46%) and the rest of the state (58%-41%). But Virginia Democrats' victories in the 2005 governor and 2006 senate race may put Virginia on the Democrats' target list in 2008.

Until 2000, Virginia's national convention delegates were chosen at state conventions, but Republicans held an open primary in 2000, in which Bush won 53% of the vote to John McCain's 44%. In 2003, Virginia moved the presidential primary to February 2004, in order to gain the attention of presidential candidates and the national media; it was held February 10, two weeks

2004 Presidential Vote
Bush (R) 1,716,959   (54%)
Kerry (D).................... 1,454,742   (45%)
Badnarik (Lib)................ 11,032   (0%)
Other........................... 15,634   (0%)

2004 Democratic Presidential Primary
Kerry (D)..................... 204,129   (52%)
Edwards (D) 105,489   (27%)
Clark (D)..................... 36,566   (9%)
Dean (D) 27,634   (7%)
Sharpton (D)................... 12,863   (3%)
Other........................... 9,500   (2%)

2000 Presidential Vote
Bush (R) 1,437,490   (52%)
Gore (D)..................... 1,217,290   (44%)
Nader (Green) 59,398   (2%)
Other........................... 25,269   (1%)

after New Hampshire and on the same day as Tennessee. Wesley Clark concentrated on Tennessee and John Edwards spent time in Tennessee and southwest Virginia. They may have thought that Kerry had an insuperable lead in Northern Virginia; as it turned out Kerry carried every part of the state and won 52% of the votes, to 27% for Edwards and 9% for Clark.

Congressional districting

110th Congress Lineup		
7 R	3 D	1 V

109th Congress Lineup	
8 R	3 D

Republicans won control of both houses of the Virginia legislature in 1999 and, with Republican Jim Gilmore as governor, controlled the redistricting process in 2001 for the first time ever. Republican legislators promptly drew new lines, which made relatively minimal changes. They moved some black precincts from the 4th District to the 3d and increased its black majority while making the 4th more secure. They followed the wishes of the three Northern Virginia incumbents, two Republicans and one Democrat, who all strengthened themselves. They made the 9th District, held for many years by Democrat Rick Boucher, a little more Republican, but it would have been difficult to do otherwise without drawing a geographical monstrosity. Bobby Scott of the black-majority 3d District raised questions about the 3d and 4th District lines, but the Justice Department approved the plan, and a lawsuit challenging the plan was dismissed in September 2004.

In January 2007, the Republican House of Delegates rejected a proposal for a nonpartisan redistricting procedure. Democrats pointed out that Republicans had favored a similar plan 15 years before, when they were in the minority; Republicans pointed out that Democrats had failed to pass one while they held majorities for more than 100 years: both fair points. So redistricting in 2011 will fall to the governor and the House of Delegates elected in 2009 and the state Senate elected in 2007. Virginia is not expected to gain a seat from the 2010 Census.

Governor

Tim Kaine (D)

Elected 2005, term expires Jan. 2010, 1st term; b. Feb. 26, 1958, St. Paul, MN; home, Richmond; Univ. of MO, B.A. 1979, Harvard U., J.D. 1983; Catholic; married (Anne Holton).

Elected Office: Richmond City Cncl., 1994-98; Mayor, 1998-2001; Lt. Gov., 2001-05.

Professional Career: Practicing atty., 1983-2000

Office: Patrick Henry Bldg., 3rd Floor, 1111 E. Broad St., Richmond, 23219, 804-786-2211; Fax: 804-371-6351; Web site: www.governor.virginia.gov.

Election Results

2005 general	Tim Kaine (D)	1,025,942	(52%)
	Jerry Kilgore (R)	912,327	(46%)
	Other	45,509	(2%)
2005 primary	Tim Kaine (D)	unopposed	
2001 general	Mark Warner (D)	984,177	(52%)
	Mark Earley (R)	887,234	(47%)

Tim Kaine was elected governor of Virginia in 2005. He grew up in Overland Park, Kansas, a suburb of Kansas City, where his father was an electrical engineer who opened a small manufacturing business and his mother taught home economics. He attended the University of Missouri, where he graduated in three years, then went to Harvard Law School. Midway through, Kaine left to spend nine months teaching at a Jesuit mission in Honduras, then returned to Harvard and got his law degree in 1983. It was there that he met his wife, Anne Holton, the daughter of Linwood Holton, Virginia's first Republican governor in the 20th century. They settled in Richmond where Kaine went into private practice as a civil rights attorney. In 1994, he defeated an incumbent to win a seat on the Richmond city council and four years later he was elected mayor. His record as mayor was closely scrutinized in 2001 when he ran for lieutenant governor. His opposition to the death penalty and support for gun restrictions and abortion rights led his conservative opponent to paint him as an extreme liberal; Kaine talked about setting aside political divisions, focused on quality of life issues and won a narrow 50%-48% victory.

Virginia's lieutenant governorship does not confer much responsibility on the officeholder but it is an excellent platform for running for governor. So Kaine immediately was assumed to be the Democratic party's leading candidate for governor in 2005, when Democrat Mark Warner would be ineligible to run for a second term. Republicans also had a presumptive nominee: Jerry Kilgore, a conservative former prosecutor from Southwest Virginia who was elected attorney general at the same time Kaine was elected lieutenant governor.

Warner, who was making plans to run for president, took an interest in electing his successor. In a mutually beneficial arrangement, he campaigned across the state with Kaine and raised money for him in the hopes of polishing his own legacy and proving himself as a serious national candidate with an ability to connect with red-state voters. Kaine, in turn, sought to tap into Warner's popularity. He frequently touted the accomplishments of the "Warner-Kaine administration" and framed his candidacy as an opportunity to continue Warner's policies.

Yet Kaine ran with a dramatically different strategy than the one Warner successfully employed in 2001. Warner had called himself a "fiscal conservative" and pledged not to raise the income or sales taxes. He opposed any new gun control laws and wooed the National Rifle Association, which remained neutral—a victory for a Democrat. He ran ads featuring old pickup trucks and bluegrass music. He sponsored a NASCAR race truck. He traveled to all parts of rural Virginia as part of an attempt to win with an urban-rural coalition. That approach was hardly practical for Kaine, a former big-city mayor who held positions well to the left of Kilgore. Instead, Kaine pitched a quality-of-life agenda designed to appeal to urban and suburban voters, one that emphasized tax relief for homeowners, a statewide pre-K initiative, a balanced approach to growth, and new transportation solutions.

Kilgore took an opposite tack. He relied on hot-button issues like the death penalty and illegal immigration, dismissing Kaine as "too liberal for Virginia." In one tough ad, a man whose son and daughter-in-law were murdered by a killer whose death penalty appeal was assisted by Kaine, says, "Tim Kaine says that Adolf Hitler doesn't qualify for the death penalty. This was the worst mass murderer in modern times." Unlike the last two Republicans to win the governorship, Kilgore had no signature proposal such as ending parole (George Allen in 1993) or eliminating the car tax (Jim Gilmore in 1997). He criticized Kaine's support for a controversial, Warner-backed $1.3 billion tax increase that passed in 2004. Kaine talked frequently and openly about how his Catholic faith colored his positions; Kilgore noted a certain political convenience in Kaine's opposition to the death penalty and abortion on moral grounds but his insistence that he would not seek to change the laws or to infringe on a woman's right to choose. "We can't trust Tim Kaine," concluded Kilgore ads.

Kaine won 52%-46%, with state Senator H. Russell Potts, a moderate Republican who ran as an independent, finishing third with 2%. Kaine's victory was powered by large margins in suburban Northern Virginia where Kilgore's Appalachian twang may have seemed out of place. Kaine crushed Kilgore 60%-38% in suburban Fairfax County, the state's most populous; he took 74% in nearby Arlington County and 72% in the city of Alexandria. Kaine's focus on managing growth enabled him to carry six of the state's 10 fastest-growing counties, including two, Loudoun and Prince William, that are among the fastest-growing in the nation. Kaine's victory in one of only two governor's races that year was viewed by the national party as a harbinger for the 2006 midterm elections. Shortly after being sworn into office, he was asked to deliver the nationally-televised Democratic response to President George W. Bush's State of the Union address. In office, he faced Republican majorities in the state House and Senate and had some successes in his first year, which included legislation requiring rigorous teacher evaluations. But he was unable to deliver on his primary objective of finding a reliable source of transportation financing and relieving traffic congestion; resistance from House Republicans led to rejection of his package of tax and fee increases. Kaine did not stand in the way of four executions of death row inmates though he delayed the execution of a fifth after questions were raised about the inmate's mental capacity. He refused to sign a proposed constitutional amendment banning same-sex marriage that was approved by the General Assembly for placement on the November 2006 ballot—a symbolic move since vetoing it was not an option.

Kaine's second year was dominated by two events that occurred within a few weeks of each other in April 2007: the mass shootings at Virginia Tech and passage of a compromise $1.1 billion transportation package. Kaine, who was in Japan for an overseas trade mission at the time of the killings, immediately flew back home and won bipartisan praise for his handling of the tragedy. On the transportation package, Kaine managed to reach agreement with the Republican House and Senate on the biggest transportation funding increase in two decades. Since Republicans would not agree to a significant statewide tax increase, the plan called for borrowing up to $3 billion over 10 years and gave taxing powers to regional authorities in the two traffic-choked areas most in need of transportation dollars—Northern Virginia and Hampton Roads.

Virginia is the last state to limit its governors to non-consecutive terms. Like his predecessor Mark Warner, Kaine has been in discussion with legislators to end the ban on serving successive four-year terms but the change would not make him eligible to run again in 2009. Numerous potential candidates have drawn mention, including Virginia's last three governors: Warner, Allen and Gilmore.

Senior Senator

John Warner (R)

Elected 1978, seat up 2008, 5th term; b. Feb. 18, 1927, Washington, D.C.; home, Alexandria; Washington & Lee U., B.S., 1949, U. of VA, LL.B. 1953; Episcopalian; married (Jeanne Vander Myde).

Military Career: Navy, 1944-46 (WWII), Marine Corps, 1950-52 (Korea).

Professional Career: Law Clerk, U.S. Court of Appeals, Chief Judge Barrett Prettyman, 1953-54; Practicing atty., 1954-56, 1960-69; Asst. U.S. Atty., 1956-60; U.S. Navy, Undersecy., 1969-72, U.S. Navy, Secy., 1972-74; Dir., Amer. Rev. Bicentennial Comm., 1974-76.

DC Office: 225 RSOB, 20510, 202-224-2023; Fax: 202-224-6295; Web site: warner.senate.gov.

State Offices: Abingdon, 276-628-8158; Midlothian, 804-739-0247; Norfolk, 757-441-3079; Roanoke, 540-857-2676.

Committees: *Armed Services* (2d of 12 R): Emerging Threats & Capabilities; Airland; Seapower. *Environment & Public Works* (2d of 9 R): Private Sector & Consumer Solutions to Global Warming & Wildlife Protection (RMM); Transportation & Infrastructure. *Homeland Security & Governmental Affairs* (7th of 8 R): Oversight of Government Management, the Federal Workforce & the District of Columbia; Investigations (Permanent); State, Local & Private Sector Preparedness & Integration. *Intelligence (Select)* (2d of 7 R).

Group Ratings

	ADA	ACLU	AFS	LCV	ITIC	NTU	COC	ACU	CFG	FRC
2006	10	25	25	14	100	67	100	64	56	75
2005	10	—	0	20	—	67	100	88	72	—

National Journal Ratings

	2005 LIB	—	2005 CONS		2006 LIB	—	2006 CONS
Economic	43%	—	56%		45%	—	53%
Social	46%	—	53%		43%	—	55%
Foreign	26%	—	65%		42%	—	54%

Key Votes of the 109th Congress

1. Bar ANWR Drilling	N	5. Confirm Samuel Alito	Y	9. Limit Interstate Abortion	Y
2. FY06 Spending Curb	Y	6. Path to Citizenship	Y	10. CAFTA	Y
3. Estate Tax Repeal	Y	7. Bar Same Sex Marriage	Y	11. Urge Iraq Withdrawal	N
4. Raise Minimum Wage	Y	8. Stem Cell Research $	Y	12. Provide Detainee Rights	N

Election Results

2002 general	John Warner (R)	1,229,893	(83%)	($1,709,202)
	Nancy Spannaus (I)	145,102	(10%)	($61,984)
	Jacob Hornberger (I)	106,055	(7%)	($66,480)
2002 primary	John Warner (R)	unopposed		
1996 general	John Warner (R)	1,235,744	(52%)	($5,819,157)
	Mark Warner (D)	1,115,982	(47%)	($11,600,424)

Prior Winning Percentages: 1990 (81%); 1984 (70%); 1978 (50%)

John Warner, first elected in 1978, is the former chairman of the Senate Armed Services Committee. He grew up in Washington, D.C., with Virginia roots; his grandparents lived in Amherst County, Virginia. His father was a field surgeon in World War I; a great-uncle served in the Confederate Army and lost his arm in the Battle of the Wilderness. Warner volunteered for both the Army and Navy in 1944, at 17; the Navy snapped him up first. (There are only five World War II veterans left in the Senate: Ted Stevens, Daniel Inouye, Daniel Akaka, Frank Lautenberg and John Warner; 47 of the 100 senators were born after World War II ended). Warner went to college at Washington & Lee and then interrupted his years at the University of Virginia law school when he volunteered to serve in the Marine Corps in Korea. He worked as an assistant U.S. attorney and then practiced law in Washington and had a house in the horse country in Middleburg, Virginia. During the Nixon administration, he was Secretary of the Navy and negotiated with the Soviets the Incidents at Sea Executive Agreement, still in effect and a model often imitated. From 1974 to 1976 he headed the American Revolution Bicentennial Commission. He ran for the Senate in 1978 with few political assets other than his then-wife, Elizabeth Taylor. Finishing second at the huge Republican state convention, he graciously supported winner Richard Obenshain; then, when Obenshain died in a plane crash, Republican leaders reluctantly named Warner to fill his place. Warner won the general over Democrat Andrew Miller by a 4,721-vote margin.

Warner can be grandiloquent and showy, yet he works hard on important issues and has shown steadfastness in his beliefs. Warner became chairman of the Armed Services Committee in January 1999, when the more senior Strom Thurmond stepped down; he served in that post until June 2001, when Democrats regained a Senate majority, and from 2003 to 2007. For years on the committee he had worked closely with Democratic Chairman Sam Nunn; but he opposed Nunn and led the fight in 1991 for the Gulf War resolution, which passed by only 52-47. Warner made harsh criticisms of Clinton administration defense policy. He had supported previous rounds of base closings, but after Bill Clinton's politically-motivated tampering with the 1995 round of closings, he voted against another round in May 1999, saying, "Politics have destroyed the credibility of the process for closing bases." But in 2003 he foiled House Armed Services Chairman Duncan Hunter's attempt to postpone the 2005 base-closing round, and when asked to protect Virginia's Fort Monroe said, "There's nothing the law allows me to do. And I happen to be one who abides by the law. The concept of the BRAC process is to get Congress out—O-U-T—out of the business." In May 2005, Fort Monroe made the Pentagon's proposed closure list.

Warner has shown some prescience about problems others did not discern. In 1999, he created a new Emerging Threats Subcommittee to focus on terrorism, chemical and biological warfare and cyberwarfare. He strongly backs missile defense and in June 2004 sponsored an amendment to require the Pentagon to develop criteria for real-life operational missile tests by February 2005 and to begin testing no later than October 2005. In a secret markup session in May 2000, he got approval of five new nuclear submarines of the Virginia class—a major increase in the submarine fleet. In June 2004, over the opposition of Appropriations Chairman Ted Stevens, he got reinstatement of $140 million for a future carrier and $110 million for a carrier refueling project. The evening of September 11 he appeared at a press conference with Defense Secretary Donald Rumsfeld and the Joint Chiefs at the Pentagon. Defense authorization bills usually pass with bipartisan support, but in May 2002 he voted against the bill because Democrats led by Chairman Carl Levin shifted $812 million away from missile defense; his opposition, plus a Bush veto threat, got the Democrats to back down. Shipbuilding is a major Warner interest, and much of it is done at Virginia's Newport News Shipbuilding & Drydock. Warner put into the 2002 defense bill $229 million to keep on schedule the $10 billion CVNX aircraft carrier to be built at Newport News; this is a transformational ship, with a new nuclear plant and electromagnetic catapults to hurl planes into flight. Warner sponsored the Iraq war resolution in October 2002. "We cannot let the United Nations think in any way that they can veto the authority of this president or the ability of this nation to defend itself." He continued to support the Iraq effort as others questioned it. After Richard Lugar and Chuck Hagel criticized Bush policy in September 2004, Warner said, "I looked at those remarks and I looked at what our president has done and what he is trying to do today, and I'm solidly in the Bush corner."

But Warner has not been uncritical of the military. In May 2004 he held widely publicized hearings on the Abu Ghraib prison scandal and put Rumsfeld under oath, despite criticism from Hunter ("the Senate has been mesmerized by cameras") and committee member Jim Inhofe. Warner backed the administration plan to buy KC-767 refueling tankers from Boeing and, with Levin, in October 2003 proposed to lease 20 and buy 80, to solve a budgetary problem. But after Boeing was caught in scandal he and Levin withdrew their support in March 2004. In July 2004 Warner declared his flat-out opposition to a military draft and in December 2004, when many conservatives were attacking Rumsfeld, he said, "We should not at this point in time entertain any idea of changing those responsibilities in the Pentagon." Warner differed with the 9/11 Commission's conclusion that intelligence oversight was "dysfunctional" and fought to limit the authority of the new national intelligence director over the military. He joined John McCain and Lindsey Graham in 2005 when they pushed for tougher regulations on the treatment of prisoners, and in 2005 he supported a resolution that passed calling on Iraqis to take the lead in providing security, requiring progress reports to Congress and declaring that 2006 would be a year of transition to full Iraqi sovereignty. In September 2006 he voted with most Democrats on the military tribunals bill. In October 2006, after a trip to Iraq, he said that parts of the country had taken "steps backwards" and that the U.S. was in danger of losing. "I assure you, in two or three months, if this thing hasn't come to fruition and if this level of violence is not under control and this government able to function, I think it's a responsibility of our government internally to determine: Is there a change of course we should take? And I wouldn't take off the table any option at this time." After the November elections, when some Republican senators came out against a phased withdrawal, Warner did not. In January 2007 he introduced a resolution, with Susan Collins, Norm Coleman and Ben Nelson that stated that the Senate "disagrees with the 'plan' to augment our forces." He argued that "Several thousand could be put in, as a start" rather than "this massive plan, pushing forward all at once." This was advanced as an alternative to the Democratic nonbinding resolution calling for withdrawals, but did not come to a vote; Warner voted against the Democrats' resolution. In August 2007, he made headlines when he called for President Bush to begin withdrawing soldiers from Iraq by December 2007.

Warner's voting record has been moderately conservative and sometimes liberal on cultural issues. He has voted for government funding of abortions in some cases, but favors parental consent laws and the partial-birth abortion ban. He voted for the Brady gun control bill; in February 2004 he cosponsored renewal of the assault weapons ban and opposed the measure protecting gun manufacturers from lawsuits hold them responsible for crimes committed with their products. He put a late crimes provision in the 2004 defense authorization. Representing a state that still has a large number of public employees, he favors higher federal pay and supported repeal of the Hatch Act. Warner has voted against bills sponsored by John McCain and Joseph Lieberman to reduce carbon dioxide emissions, but he was one of 12 Republicans who supported a resolution added to the energy bill telling Congress to develop a mandatory plan for reducing those emissions. Under the Republican term limits rule, he had to step down as Armed Service Chairman in 2007, and in 2006 he moved to take the top Republican position on the Environment and Public Works Committee from the less senior Jim Inhofe. But in December 2006 he withdrew from that effort, saying, "I have decided to devote my full time to security responsibilities in the Senate and the demands of a vigorous and challenging reelection campaign." In January 2007 he was made ranking Republican on a new Subcommittee on the Private Sector and Consumer Solutions to Global Warming and Wildlife Protection, of which Lieberman was chairman. Lieberman and leaders of some environmental restriction groups hoped that they could get him to endorse a bill in some way limiting carbon dioxide emissions, although he said he was not inclined to support nationwide emission caps.

Warner has mostly won reelection easily. But for a time in the 1990s, Warner seemed to be in a war with many Virginia Republicans, which caused him some problems in the polls. In 1993, he refused to endorse lieutenant governor candidate Michael Farris, the leader of the national home schooling movement, and in 1994 he announced he could not support Senate nominee Oliver North, whose conviction on Iran-Contra charges was overturned on the grounds of inadmissibility of some critical evidence. In the 1994 Senate race Warner backed independent (and twice Republican gubernatorial candidate) Marshall Coleman, and many blamed Warner for North's narrow loss to Charles Robb. Farris and North backers hoped to deny Warner renomination in 1996 at the gigantic Virginia Republican state convention. But Warner invoked a Virginia law that entitled him to insist on a primary. There he defeated James Miller, budget director under President Ronald Reagan and North's opponent at the 1994 convention, by 66%-34%. In the general election, against former Democratic state chairman and now-Governor Mark Warner, John Warner called himself a "common sense conservative" and, citing seniority, said, "Virginia's got an investment in me." Warner was reelected, but only narrowly, 52%-47%. In 2002, in contrast, he had no serious opposition. Republicans had mostly forgotten Farris and North and Democrats were content not to run a candidate. Mark Warner, by then governor, called John Warner "a great guy and a great senator." For his part, Senator Warner joined Governor Warner in campaigning for passage of the November 2002 transportation tax referenda in Northern Virginia and Hampton Roads. The referenda were defeated, but John Warner was reelected with 83% of the vote. In February 2004 he supported Governor Warner's proposed tax increase. "Politics be damned! Let's consider what's best for the men and women of this great state and their families and children."

Warner campaigned for the reelection of his Republican colleague George Allen in 2006 and was disappointed when he lost to Jim Webb. With his own seat up for reelection in 2008 when he will be 81, in late August 2007 Warner announced he would not seek another term. Former Governor Mark Warner, the Democrats' top pick to run for the seat, declared his candidacy in September. It seemed likely that Congressman Tom Davis of Northern Virginia and former Governor Jim Gilmore would face off for the Republican nomination in a contest that would pit the party moderates against conservatives.

Junior Senator

Jim Webb (D)

Elected 2006, seat up 2012, 1st term; b. Feb. 9, 1946, St. Joseph, MO; home, Arlington; U.S. Naval Academy, B.S. 1968, Georgetown U., J.D. 1975; Christian; married (Hong Le).

Military Career: Marine Corps, 1968-72 (Vietnam).

Professional Career: Writer/Journalist; Counsel, U.S. House Cmte. on Veterans Affairs, 1977-81; Asst. Sec. of Defense for Reserve Affairs, 1984-87; Navy Sec., 1987-88.

DC Office: 144 RSOB, 20510, 202-224-4024; Fax: 202-228-6363; Web site: webb.senate.gov.

State Offices: Norton, 276-679-4925; Richmond, 804-771-2221; Roanoke, 540-772-4236; Virginia Beach, 757-518-1674.

Committees: *Armed Services* (12th of 13 D): Personnel; Airland; Seapower. *Foreign Relations* (11th of 11 D): Western Hemisphere, Peace Corps & Narcotics Affairs; African Affairs; East Asian & Pacific Affairs; International Operations & Organizations, Democracy & Human Rights. *Joint Economic Committee* (6th of 10 D). *Veterans' Affairs* (7th of 8 D).

Group Ratings and Key Votes: Newly Elected

Election Results

2006 general	Jim Webb (D)	1,175,606	(50%)	($8,559,590)
	George Allen (R)	1,166,277	(49%)	($16,071,564)
	Other	28,562	(1%)	
2006 primary	Jim Webb (D)	83,298	(53%)	
	Harris Miller (D)	72,486	(47%)	
2000 general	George Allen (R)	1,420,460	(52%)	($9,995,980)
	Charles S. Robb (D)	1,296,093	(48%)	($6,610,252)

James Webb, elected in 2006 as Virginia's junior senator, has an unusual background for a Democratic senator. He is of Scots-Irish descent, the son of an Air Force colonel who enlisted after Pearl Harbor; the family moved at least a dozen times when he was a child. He enrolled in the University of Southern California, then a year later in the U.S. Naval Academy. He was a reader who wanted to become a writer, but he was also a combative young man, and a boxing match in 1967 with Oliver North at Annapolis became a subject of legend (North won in a unanimous decision). He graduated in 1968 and in 1969 went into combat in Vietnam as a Marine lieutenant. He commanded 170 men and earned the Navy Cross, a Silver Star and two Purple Hearts; he suffered wounds which have left him with shrapnel in his body and a limp—and forced him to retire from active duty. He was one of the subjects of Robert Timberg's moving 1995 book, *The Nightingale's Song*. Webb entered Georgetown Law School in 1972 and was appalled by his antiwar schoolmates who he believed had shirked duty and then considered themselves morally superior because of their opposition to the war. He started writing and his novel about Vietnam, *Fields of Fire*, was published in 1978; many have called it the best Vietnam War novel. He has since written six other novels and his 2004 history-cum-memoir, *Born Fighting: How the Scots-Irish Shaped America*.

In the years after *Fields of Fire*, Webb wrote movie scripts and many articles and made many public statements, some of them controversial. He praised Confederate heroes, attacked feminists and Hollywood, academic elites and the news media. In 1979 he wrote an article for *Washingtonian* criticizing the new policy on women in the military. "I have never met a woman, including the dozens of female midshipmen I encountered during my recent semester as a professor at the Naval Academy, whom I would trust to provide those men with combat leadership." Bancroft Hall, he wrote, "which houses 4,000 males and 300 females" was "a horny woman's dream." The Navy banned him from speaking at the Academy. He helped lead the fight against Maya Lin's Vietnam War memorial and for an additional sculpture depicting soldiers. Disgusted with Jimmy Carter's amnesty for draft law violators, he left the Democratic party and became a Republican, and in 1980 supported Ronald Reagan for president. In interviews he said he wouldn't walk across the street to see Jane Fonda and for 20 years he refused to shake John Kerry's hand. In 1984 he won an Emmy for his coverage for the NewsHour of the barracks bombing that killed 241 Marines in Lebanon in 1983. He was appointed Assistant Secretary of the Navy for Reserve Affairs in 1984. In February 1987 Ronald Reagan appointed him Secretary of the Navy. He issued a directive that performance in combat be given greater weight in promotions, which was criticized by advocates of equality for women in the military. Webb publicly complained about budget cuts imposed by Congress, which angered Defense Secretary Frank Carlucci; Webb resigned in February 1988. "It's no secret that I'm not a person who wears a bridle well," he said.

Nor did he wear a political label well. Republicans recruited him to run for office in Virginia in 1988 and 1994; Democratic Senator Bob Kerrey asked him to run against Senator John Warner in 1996. He said no each time. In 1990 he opposed the pending Gulf war and said that it would open a Pandora's box in the Middle East; he has often said occupying a country was a misuse of U.S. troops and that the U.S. shouldn't try to export its system by gunpoint. In 1994 he backed Democratic Senator Charles Robb against his one-time sparring partner Oliver North. In 2000 he backed Republican George Allen against Robb; he argued that Robb had not done enough oversight of his party's administration. He wrote an article in the *Wall Street Journal* in 2000 attacking racial quotas and preferences as "a permeating state-sponsored racism that is as odious as the Jim Crow laws it sought to countermand." Of Bill Clinton he said, "Every time I see him salute a Marine, it infuriates me." After Clinton's 2001 pardons he added: "It is a pleasurable experience to watch Bill Clinton finally being judged, even by his own party, for the ethical fraudulence that has characterized his entire political career." Once the Republicans were in, he began thinking more like a Democrat. His research for *Born Fighting* convinced him that Scots-Irish people of modest means who willingly served in the military might better be served by the Democrats, and foresaw a coalition of Scots-Irish and blacks. "You measure the health of a society not at its apex, but at its base." In 2002 he opposed military action in Iraq in much the same language that he had opposed military action in the Gulf in 1990: it would destabilize the Middle East and mire the U.S. in a long occupation. His opposition continued even as his son dropped out of Penn State to join the Marine Corps. He supported John Kerry, a man he had refused to shake hands with for 20 years, against George W. Bush in 2004. The "last straw for me" in this political odyssey was the response to Hurricane Katrina, which reminded him how people of little means were treated.

All of which led him toward running against Senator George Allen, whom he had supported six years before. Allen began campaign year 2006 on the list of possible Republican presidential candidates in 2008—and on the top of some people's lists. His issue positions and his stance on cultural issues were both similar to Bush's and he had more experience in public office than Bush had at the beginning of 2000. He had served in the House, then ran for governor in 1993 and won 58%-41%. In 2000 he challenged Senator (and former Governor) Charles Robb and won 52%-48%. It was widely assumed that he would win by a bigger margin in 2006; as the year went on, he made ostentatious trips to Iowa and New Hampshire and on occasion told reporters that the job of senator was boring and that he preferred being an executive. In January 2006 the only visible Democratic candidate was Harris Miller, a former local government official in Northern Virginia who had spent 10 years as head of the Information Technology Association of America. He had serious credentials, some financial backing and some moderate issue positions. But he was universally regarded as the underdog.

In February 2006 Webb decided to run. He was encouraged by John Kerry and, more important, by DSCC Chairman Charles Schumer, who had already recruited a candidate at odds with the liberal Democratic base, Bob Casey, Jr., in Pennsylvania, and saw in Webb a similar opportunity to cut into the conservative vote. Webb announced on March 7, late in the season for such things. Noting that his son was being deployed to Iraq, but resisting invitations to say how he felt about this, he reiterated his opposition to military action there. "The invasion of Iraq was a double strategic blunder. First, it was a diversion from, not a response to, the war against international terrorism. Second, it has tied down our military in a costly occupation, fighting an insurgency that has strengthened not only the Shia population of Iraq, but also Iran itself." At the same time, he opposed a precipitous withdrawal. On cultural issues, he said, "My belief is that the power of government stops at the front door unless there is a compelling reason for it to come inside." He supported abortion rights; he said he wanted "to do better on rights for gays" and supported civil unions; he said racial preferences should be limited to blacks, because of their unique heritage, and not accorded to women or other ethnic groups. He strongly opposed new gun control laws, noting that his father had given him his first gun when he was 8 and that he had done the same with his son. He hired strategists Steve Jarding and Mudcat Saunders, who had vast experience in Democratic campaigns appealing to culturally conservative voters.

They had their work cut for them. Miller outspent Webb 3–1 and had far more ads on the air. Prominent African-Americans, nettled by Webb's statements on racial preferences, supported Miller. So did women military veterans, including General Claudia Kennedy. Webb was not a natural candidate, reluctant to handshake his way across a room, stiff in his public speeches. "I don't wake up in the morning wanting to be a U.S. senator. I wake up every morning very concerned about the country." His prime asset turned out to be support from antiwar activists, especially bloggers, who supported him strongly and who argued that he was the only candidate who could beat Allen. The word got around Northern Virginia, with its politically knowledgeable antiwar Democratic voters. Turnout was light in the June 13 primary, and Webb won 53%-47%. For a candidate who stressed his Scots-Irish roots and who had expressed scorn for Washington elites, he ran best in Northern Virginia, which he carried by 2–1 margins. He also ran well in the western part of the state, carrying most counties just east of the Blue Ridge and in the Shenandoah Valley and the valleys to the south. Miller carried the Richmond area and just about everything south of Fredericksburg and east of Lynchburg; he ran especially strong in cities and counties with high black percentages. In the days of the Byrd machine, this would have been enough to win a Democratic primary. In a time when one-third of voters live in Northern Virginia, it was not.

Webb had no money left after the primary; Allen had $7.5 million—and ultimately outspent him 2–1. But money was not decisive. On August 11 Allen was speaking in Breaks, Virginia, in Dickenson County, near the Kentucky border nearly 400 miles from Washington, D.C. He pointed at S. R. Siddarth, a 20-year-old student of Indian descent, who had been following him around for the Webb campaign, taping everything he said. "This fellow over here," Allen said, "with the yellow shirt, Macaca or whatever his name is, he's with my opponent....Let's give a welcome to Macaca here. Welcome to America, and welcome to the real world of Virginia." In another era, such an incident would have remained unknown. But it became the center of the campaign, thanks to YouTube and the *Washington Post*, which ran more than three dozen stories on the incident, with more than a dozen on the front page. The subtext was that "Macaca" was a racial epithet, evidence that Allen was a bigot. The ground for this charge had been prepared in an unflattering article in the *New Republic* in 2006, which recounted how Allen had put a Confederate flag on his wall as a young lawyer and relayed stories that he had used the n-word while as a student. (Webb's response, when asked if he used the word: "I don't think that there's anyone who grew up around the South that hasn't had the word pass through their lips at one time in their life.") Those stories were retold, as well as one in which he put a deer's head in a black family's mailbox; also relayed were accounts by other schoolmates that Allen never used such language or showed bigotry in any form. At a September debate, Washington area TV reporter Peggy Fox, a panelist, noted that "macaca" is a racial slur in Tunisia, where Allen's mother had grown up. She then asked Allen whether it was true, as had been reported by *The Forward*, that his mother's side of the family was Jewish. Allen replied that his religious background, or Webb's didn't matter, but the issue got much coverage. Eventually Allen revealed that his mother had concealed this for many years and only revealed it, tearfully, a month before.

Allen and his experienced campaign managers, Dick Wadhams and Chris LaCivita, had expected to run a campaign based on taxes and support of the military; now they were on the defensive. Webb was running closely behind or even with Allen in the polls by September. At the end of the month, Allen ran an ad with quotes from Webb's 1979 *Washingtonian* article on women in the military and showing three female academy graduates criticizing Webb. The strategy was to hold down the Webb vote in Northern Virginia, where the *Post's* Macaca coverage had clearly hurt Allen. Webb responded with an ad showing testimonials from military women. An Allen ad claimed that Webb wanted to raise taxes on married couples and families, costing the average Virginia family $2,000. Webb rebutted with an ad saying that Allen wanted to raise taxes on retirement savings, make college more expensive and give billions in tax cuts to oil companies. To charges that he was bigoted, Allen pointed to his pilgrimages to civil rights sites and to the work he had done to aid historically black colleges and universities. And Allen's campaign attacked Webb for the sexually racy passages in some of his novels.

This was one of the two closest Senate races in the nation, and the one which, when the result became clear two days after the election, gave the Senate majority to the Democrats. Webb won by 9,000 votes, 49.6%-49.2%. His victory was almost entirely due to Northern Virginia. Webb carried Hampton Roads 52%-46%, almost the same as Robb's 52%-48% margin there six years before. In the half of the state outside the two big metro areas, Allen won 55%-44%, down just slightly from his 56%-44% margin in 2000. Northern Virginia was a different story. Chuck Robb barely carried it, 51%-49%. Webb carried it 57%-42%. Robb's popular vote margin in the area was 21,000. Webb's was 110,000, five times larger. The exit poll showed Webb with 42% of whites and 85% of blacks, the latter a bit low for a Democrat. Webb's best income groups were the lowest and highest, his best education groups non-high school graduates and those with postgraduate degrees. White evangelical Protestants were 80% for Allen, whites with no religion 70% for Webb.

Webb's victory produced exultation among Democrats—and some curiosity as to what kind of Democratic senator he would be. Addressing Democrats' concerns, Webb said, "There are going to be times when I've got some strong ideas, but I'm not looking to simply be a renegade. I think people in the Democratic party leadership have already begun to understand that I know how to work inside a structure." His attitude toward George W. Bush was not friendly. When he attended a reception at the White House a few days after the election, Bush approached Webb and asked about his son in Iraq. "How's your boy?" Webb responded, "I'd like to get them out of Iraq, Mr. President." "That's not what I asked you," said the President. "How's your boy?" "That's between me and my boy, Mr. President," Webb replied.

Webb was chosen by Democratic leaders to give the rebuttal to Bush's State of the Union speech in January 2007, and gave a speech opposing Bush on Iraq and pointing to what he said was a widening difference between the rich and the poor. He said he would work with senior senators on a new G.I. bill of rights and with populists like Byron Dorgan on narrowing the rich-poor gap. "It's not healthy in a democracy such as ours to have such a wide gap between rich and poor."

FIRST DISTRICT
Vacant

Election Results

2006 general	Jo Ann Davis (R)	143,889	(63%)	($636,419)
	Shawn O'Donnell (D)	81,083	(35%)	($89,531)
	Other	3,562	(2%)	
2006 primary	Jo Ann Davis (R)	unopposed		
2004 general	Jo Ann Davis (R)	225,071	(79%)	($375,339)
	William Lee (I)	57,434	(20%)	
	Other	4,029	(1%)	

The People		Race/Ethnic Origin	Ancestry	
Area size:	4,612 sq. mi.	74.7% White	English: 10.7%	German: 10.4%
Urban population:	64.0%	18.4% Black	Irish: 8.8%	
Rural population:	36.0%	1.7% Asian	**2004 Presidential Vote**	
Pop. 2000:	643,514	0.4% Native Am.	Bush (R) 188,417	(60%)
Pop. 2005 (est):	736,121	0.1% Hawaiian	Kerry (D) 122,771	(39%)
Median income:	$50,257	1.6% Two+ races	Other 2,255	(1%)
Poverty status:	6.7%	0.2% Other	**2000 Presidential Vote**	
Military veterans:	17.7%	3.0% Hispanic Origin	Bush (R) 146,914	(58%)
			Gore (D) 98,731	(39%)
			Other 6,060	(2%)
			Cook Partisan Voting Index: R + 9	

Occupation	Blue collar: 22.1%	White collar: 62.8%	Gray collar: 15.0%

When English settlers first sailed up the estuaries that flow into the Chesapeake Bay, they were searching for gold, hoping to sail back soon with fortunes. But they couldn't help noticing that the spot where the James River feeds into the bay, now Hampton Roads, was a fine natural harbor, with calm, deep water and good anchorages. There they established a civilization whose elegance is recalled in the craftsmanship of restored Williamsburg and whose coarseness and brutality is brought to life by the four-century story of Jamestown and the other beleaguered settlements. Tidewater Virginia brought slavery to America and tobacco to the world, and slave-raised tobacco was the center of its economy in the colonial era and in the years afterward, when its most talented sons left its depleted soil for better opportunities elsewhere.

Now the economy and tone of life in Tidewater Virginia are set by the American military. More than six decades ago, as America faced world war, the Navy base at Norfolk and the shipbuilding centers in Newport News across Hampton Roads became the center of American naval might in the Atlantic. There were fewer than 370,000 people living then on both sides of Hampton Roads. Today there are nearly 1.6 million—a population collected from all over the country, making this a metropolitan area that is not so much Southern in atmosphere as it is, in the manner of military bases abroad, national.

The 1st Congressional District of Virginia contains much of this territory. The district ranges as far north from the Peninsula as rural Fauquier County, outside Washington, D.C., but the bulk of the population lives between the Potomac and James Rivers. Most of the major Hampton Roads military installations are in surrounding congressional districts, but the 1st remains steeped in military culture, both past and present, and the Department of Defense and NASA continue to be significant employers. Within the district lines, in 1781, George Washington's tattered and exhausted army at Yorktown finally pushed General Cornwallis to the sea where the French Navy waited: The final victory of the Revolutionary War. Today, historic Yorktown is adjacent to a Naval Weapons Station on the banks of the York River. To the north, in Caroline County, Fort A.P. Hill serves as a valuable training site for active and reserve-component units. Not far from there is Naval Surface Warfare Center in Dahlgren, located on the Potomac River, originally established as the Navy's main proving ground for large-caliber guns. The 1st includes within its boundaries all of 13 counties and parts of five others; all of the cities of Fredericksburg and colonial Williamsburg, with its booming vacation spots; the Marine Corps Base at Quantico; the more populous and developed part of Spotsylvania County; and the Northern Neck between the Rappahannock and Potomac Rivers, where Robert "King" Carter, one of the great landowners of colonial Virginia, reigned, and where George Washington and Robert E. Lee were born. In the Newport News area, the 1st runs primarily north of Mercury Boulevard, once known as Military Highway but renamed to honor the Mercury 7 astronauts. About 45% of the district's votes are cast in the Hampton Roads area and about 40% in the metro Washington orbit. Ancestrally, much of this area was Democratic. But with a large military population drawn from across the country (and with heavily black precincts placed in the adjoining 3d District), the 1st District is now reliably Republican in most elections.

The 1st District was temporarily vacant after the death of Republican Jo Ann Davis. Davis, who was in her 4th term, died on October 6, 2007, after a battle with breast cancer. Davis had grown up in the Hampton Roads area; her father worked at a gas station and drove city buses in Hampton. She graduated from Hampton Roads Business College and went to work as an executive secretary for a real estate firm for several years before becoming a stay-at-home mom, then started a real estate career in 1988. Davis was elected to the House of Delegates in 1997, defeating a 15-year incumbent who outspent her 3-to-1. When the 1st District Congressman Herb Bateman announced his retirement in January 2000, she jumped into the race 3 days later. She faced four other candidates for the Republican nomination, including real estate entrepreneur Paul Jost, who spent almost $1 million of his own money and won the endorsement of Governor James Gilmore. Davis, who spent less than one-tenth that sum, appealed to conservative activists, especially in the district's rural counties. She favored a Social Security lockbox, more flexibility to the states on education funding, elimination of the marriage penalty and estate taxes, and protection of Second Amendment rights. Davis won just 14,274 votes, but that was enough to defeat Jost 35%-30%. In the general, she faced Democrat Lawrence Davies, a Baptist minister and mayor of Fredericksburg for 20 years. The two biggest issues of the campaign were abortion rights—Davis against, Davies for—and the proposed King William reservoir, which Davis considered too expensive and Davies defended as necessary for growth. Davis won 58%-37%.

In the House, Davis was a firm conservative on cultural issues but toward the middle of Republicans on economic and foreign policy. On the Armed Services Committee, a useful post to represent what she called "America's First District," Davis reintroduced a bill to require the Navy to have no fewer than 375 vessels in active service, including 15 aircraft carrier battle groups and 15 amphibious ready groups; as of 2006, the Navy fleet had dropped to 276 ships. She defied Republican leaders by winning approval of her amendment to limit the Navy's ability to lease foreign-built ships. "When the Defense Department has a long-term need for ships," she said, "it ought to buy them from U.S. shipyards, or our industrial and skill capabilities will continue to erode." She led bipartisan efforts to oppose Pentagon plans to delay ship construction, including the new aircraft carrier to be built at Newport News. She also secured $47 million to scrap several dozen rusty naval ships from the "ghost fleet" that have been anchored on the James River, but the stockpile remains. Davis won passage of a bill to assure that survivors of military personnel killed on duty receive the full additional life insurance benefit up to $250,000. Davis initially defended the decision to invade Iraq as "a tough vote but the right one;" by 2006, she voiced second thoughts about faulty intelligence that was used to justify the conflict. Months before Defense Secretary Donald Rumsfeld stepped down, she urged him to resign because of his mishandling of the war. But her objections were within the limits of what leadership was prepared to tolerate: in 2007, Republican war opponent Walter Jones was passed over on the Readiness Subcommittee at Armed Services and Davis became ranking Republican instead. The House in 2006 passed her two amendments to improve accountability of the flood-insurance program. She also enacted a bill creating a national historic trail in the Chesapeake: the first all-water trail in the national parks.

In 2006, Davis faced her first major-party opposition since winning the seat: Democrat Shawn O'Donnell, a businessman who criticized the war in Iraq and called Davis a Republican "rubber stamp." She took all of the counties and cities except for Prince William, and won 63%-35%. Davis was diagnosed with breast cancer in October 2005. She had declared herself cancer-free in 2006 after undergoing chemotherapy treatment and a mastectomy, but in March 2007, she announced she was fighting breast cancer again. From January 2007 through July, she missed close to 80% of roll call votes; drawing on her personal experience, she filed legislation to require group health plans to include coverage for post-mastectomy reconstructive surgery.

In this conservative-minded district, the Republican nominee in the special election will be favored to succeed Davis.

SECOND DISTRICT

Rep. Thelma Drake (R)

Elected 2004, 2d term; b. Nov. 20, 1949, Elyria, OH; home, Norfolk; Elyria H.S.; United Church of Christ; married (Ted).

Elected Office: VA House of Del., 1995-2004.

Professional Career: Real estate agent, 1975-2004.

DC Office: 1208 LHOB, 20515, 202-225-4215; Fax: 202-225-4218; Web site: drake.house.gov.

District Offices: Accomac, 757-787-7836; Virginia Beach, 757-497-6859.

Committees: *Armed Services* (25th of 29 R): Military Personnel; Terrorism, Unconventional Threats & Capabilities. *Transportation & Infrastructure* (32d of 34 R): Water Resources & Environment; Highways & Transit.

Group Ratings

	ADA	ACLU	AFS	LCV	ITIC	NTU	COC	ACU	CFG	FRC
2006	0	9	0	17	100	54	100	88	56	100
2005	5	—	0	6	—	59	93	92	64	92

National Journal Ratings

	2005 LIB	—	2005 CONS	2006 LIB	—	2006 CONS
Economic	9%	—	88%	27%	—	71%
Social	0%	—	89%	23%	—	74%
Foreign	0%	—	89%	6%	—	86%

Key Votes of the 109th Congress

1. Estate Tax Repeal	Y	5. Limit Interstate Abortion	Y	9. Build Border Fence	Y
2. Limit CAFE Standards	Y	6. Extend Patriot Act	Y	10. CAFTA	Y
3. FY06 Spending Curb	Y	7. Bar Same Sex Marriage	Y	11. Oppose Iraq Withdrawal	Y
4. Drilling in ANWR	Y	8. Stem Cell Research $	N	12. Detainee Tribunals	Y

Election Results

2006 general	Thelma Drake (R)	88,777	(51%)	($2,348,983)
	Phil Kellam (D)	83,901	(48%)	($1,703,424)
2006 primary	Thelma Drake (R)	unopposed		
2004 general	Thelma Drake (R)	132,946	(55%)	($828,185)
	David Ashe (D)	108,180	(45%)	($436,620)

The People		Race/Ethnic Origin	Ancestry	
Area size:	2,776 sq. mi.	67.4% White	German: 10.1%	Irish: 9.1%
Urban population:	91.7%	21.4% Black	English: 9.0%	
Rural population:	8.3%	4.0% Asian	**2004 Presidential Vote**	
Pop. 2000:	643,510	0.4% Native Am.	Bush (R) 141,097	(58%)
Pop. 2005 (est):	653,242	0.1% Hawaiian	Kerry (D) 101,576	(42%)
Median income:	$44,193	2.2% Two+ races	Other 1,896	(1%)
Poverty status:	8.7%	0.2% Other	**2000 Presidential Vote**	
Military veterans:	20.3%	4.4% Hispanic Origin	Bush (R) 115,512	(55%)
			Gore (D) 90,256	(43%)
			Other 4,940	(2%)
			Cook Partisan Voting Index: R + 6	

Occupation   Blue collar: 21.1%   White collar: 63.0%   Gray collar: 15.9%

The United States Navy Atlantic fleet berthed in its homeport of Norfolk is one of the great awe-inspiring sights in America, or anywhere. The aggregation of destructive power in the line of towering gray ships is probably greater than in any other single port in history. Several dozen ships are based here—aircraft carriers, cruisers, destroyers, large amphibious ships, submarines, supply and logistics ships—and many more aircraft. Norfolk has been a Navy port since 1801, and has long been recognized as one of the best natural harbors on the East Coast, one that never freezes, has a channel 50 feet deep and is within 750 miles of three-quarters of U.S. manufacturing capacity. The Norfolk Naval Station is now the world's largest naval station, situated on 4,300 acres on Sewells Point, and the Hampton Roads region is the world's largest naval base, where residents are always within minutes of one naval installation or another. Norfolk, once a small city, is now the center of a metro area with 1.6 million people. The local Navy community—retirees, dependents, active duty and civilian personnel, workers at the Newport News Shipbuilding & Drydock—is estimated at more than 300,000 and military spending pours over $11 billion annually into the local economy. The port also has become a major commercial hub for East Coast shippers and distributors, with imports of containerized retail cargo increasing more than 50% since 2000.

Next-door Virginia Beach, once a beach resort and acres of swamp, is the state's largest city, with 436,000 people. It began attracting tourists when rail service to Norfolk began in 1883; with its rebuilt town center, it hosts the Williamsburg-style headquarters of Pat Robertson's Christian Broadcasting Network (the *700 Club* is produced here) and other Robertson operations. The city has a growing industrial base, including a large tool plant of the German-based Stihl company, but like Norfolk, Virginia Beach is infused with military culture. It is home to four military installations with 35,000 service and civilian employees and an annual payroll of over $1 billion. In 2005, the base-closing commission decided to remove more than 200 fighter jets from the Oceana Naval Air Station due to concerns over the vast development surrounding the base. After two years of local efforts to retain the jets at the 12,000-employee base, the Pentagon announced in January 2007 that the jets would remain at Oceana, though debate continued within the House Armed Services Committee over relocation efforts. East Coast Navy SEAL teams are based in Virginia Beach; these elite commandos endure punishing military training and have taken on some of the military's most secretive, daring and hazardous missions in Afghanistan and Iraq. They keep largely to themselves, deploying and returning quietly, and grieve amongst themselves when one of their own pays the ultimate price.

The 2d Congressional District of Virginia includes all of Virginia Beach, plus parts of Norfolk and Hampton with mostly white residents, including the Norfolk Navy base and Langley Air Force Base and, on a spit of land in the bay, Fort Monroe, where Jefferson Davis was confined after the Civil War. It covers more than 100 miles of Atlantic Ocean coastline and stretches from Maryland's Eastern Shore to North Carolina. About 86,000 active-duty military personnel are based here, which may be the largest of any congressional district in the nation. It also includes a more placid area, the two Virginia counties of the Delmarva Peninsula, Virginia's Eastern Shore, site of the annual roundup of wild Chincoteague ponies; these rural counties with their fishing villages are two of the state's poorest. Surrounded by water on three sides, they are connected to Virginia Beach by the Chesapeake Bay Bridge-Tunnel with its $12 toll. Back in the 1960s and 1970s, most people in the 2d District were in Norfolk, and the district often voted Democratic. Now the overwhelming majority live in Virginia Beach, and the district leans Republican. George W. Bush carried it with 55% of the vote in 2000 and 58% in 2004.

The congresswoman from the 2d District is Thelma Drake, a Republican first elected in 2004. She has a unique biography and won the seat in unusual circumstances. She grew up in Elyria, Ohio, got pregnant in high school and then married her Navy-bound high school boyfriend. They moved to Norfolk, where her husband soon divorced her and she was left to raise her child alone. Her experience as a single mother colors her outlook: "I always felt I was the only person responsible for myself. You don't turn to other people to help you." Drake declined to go on welfare, had a second divorce, remarried and worked for 20 years as a real estate agent and eventually became wealthy from real-estate investments. In 1995, she defeated an incumbent to win a seat in the House of Delegates. In April 2004 she voted against Governor Mark Warner's tax increase package, which nonetheless was enacted. Republican delegates split bitterly over the issue, and local conservative activists were eager to defeat those who supported the tax increase and to reward those who opposed it.

Drake had no plans to run for the House in 2004. Republican Ed Schrock, first elected in 2000, seemed likely to win reelection easily. Then on August 30, he abruptly announced his retirement amid allegations that he had engaged in homosexual activity. The married lawmaker and retired Navy captain never confirmed or denied the allegations; his statement noted simply that the charges "called into question my ability to represent the citizens of Virginia's 2nd Congressional District." The next day, the 12-member Second Congressional District Republican Committee met to choose a new nominee. Drake ran, as did state Senator Nick Rerras, who voted for the Warner tax increase, and Virginia Beach Sheriff Paul Lanteigne. Drake won a majority of the votes on the secret ballot, in large part because of her stand against the tax increase.

The Republican turmoil gave unexpected life to the candidacy of Democrat David Ashe, a lawyer and Marine reservist who had recently returned from a two-year tour in the Middle East, including six months in Iraq, where he worked on restoring the judicial system. Ashe was a political newcomer but proved to be an active candidate, and national Democrats elevated him on their priority list. Drake attacked Ashe for "weakening the war on terror" because he supported John Kerry. Democrats responded by highlighting Ashe's military credentials; the Democratic Congressional Campaign Committee ran ads urging voters to "send a Marine to Congress." Drake, in turn, promised to focus on military and national security issues and to vote to make the Bush tax cuts permanent. With help from national Republicans, she outraised Ashe by nearly 2–1 and won 55%-45%, carrying the four largest cities and counties by similar margins.

In the House, Drake had a conservative record. As promised by Speaker Dennis Hastert, she got a seat on the Armed Services Committee, where she sought expansion of the two local SEAL bases. Later, she also joined the Transportation and Infrastructure Committee. To reduce dependence on foreign sources, she advocated House-passed legislation to lift restrictions on offshore oil and gas drilling. "One of the ways that can be done is exploring the natural gas resources that exist off the coast of Virginia," she said.

In 2006, she faced another competitive contest—this time, against Phil Kellam, the Virginia Beach revenue commissioner and a member of a well-known local political family. The city's only elected Democrat, Kellam had the advantage of a much larger political base compared to Drake's Norfolk home; he emphasized the need for bipartisanship and criticized the corruption and gridlock in Washington. MoveOn.org ran TV ads that criticized Drake as beholden to big oil and pharmaceutical companies; Drake criticized the attacks as counter to Kellam's call for civility. She supported the war in Iraq, and got fundraising help from President Bush and Vice President Cheney. Kellam called on voters to register their disapproval of the war, though he did not back a change in course. He criticized Drake's support for offshore drilling. He withdrew from several late campaign debates, citing "shenanigans" by the Drake campaign. Both candidates were well-financed but Drake won 51.3%-48.5%. Oddly, Kellam won Norfolk 50%-49% while Drake won Kellam's Virginia Beach turf, 52%-48%. They split the outlying counties. Kellam announced in July 2007 that he will not seek a rematch.

THIRD DISTRICT

Rep. Bobby Scott (D)

Elected 1992, 8th term; b. Apr. 30, 1947, Washington, D.C.; home, Newport News; Harvard U., B.A. 1969, Boston Col., J.D. 1973; Episcopalian; single.

Military Career: Army Natl. Guard, 1970-73; Army Reserves, 1973-76.

Elected Office: VA House of Delegates, 1977-82; VA Senate, 1983-92.

Professional Career: Practicing atty., 1973-91.

DC Office: 1201 LHOB, 20515, 202-225-8351; Fax: 202-225-8354; Web site: www.house.gov/scott.

District Offices: Newport News, 757-380-1000; Richmond, 804-644-4845.

Committees: *Budget* (15th of 22 D). *Education & Labor* (5th of 27 D): Early Childhood, Elementary & Secondary Education; Higher Education, Lifelong Learning & Competitiveness. *Judiciary* (5th of 23 D): Crime, Terrorism & Homeland Security (Chmn.); The Constitution, Civil Rights & Civil Liberties.

Group Ratings

	ADA	ACLU	AFS	LCV	ITIC	NTU	COC	ACU	CFG	FRC
2006	100	100	100	100	29	9	27	4	7	0
2005	100	—	100	83	—	11	41	4	4	0

National Journal Ratings

	2005 LIB — 2005 CONS		2006 LIB — 2006 CONS
Economic	78% — 21%	79% — 18%
Social	98% — 2%	88% — 12%
Foreign	91% — 7%	80% — 18%

Key Votes of the 109th Congress

1. Estate Tax Repeal	N	5. Limit Interstate Abortion	N	9. Build Border Fence	N
2. Limit CAFE Standards	Y	6. Extend Patriot Act	N	10. CAFTA	N
3. FY06 Spending Curb	N	7. Bar Same Sex Marriage	N	11. Oppose Iraq Withdrawal	N
4. Drilling in ANWR	N	8. Stem Cell Research $	Y	12. Detainee Tribunals	N

Election Results

2006 general	Bobby Scott (D)	133,546	(96%)	($307,440)
	Other	5,448	(4%)	
2006 primary	Bobby Scott (D)	unopposed		
2004 general	Bobby Scott (D)	159,373	(69%)	($482,504)
	Winsome Sears (R)	70,194	(31%)	($205,812)

Prior Winning Percentages: 2002 (96%); 2000 (100%); 1998 (76%); 1996 (82%); 1994 (79%); 1992 (79%)

The People		Race/Ethnic Origin	Ancestry	
Area size:	1,306 sq. mi.	37.7% White	English: 5.6%	USA: 5.3%
Urban population:	92.2%	56.0% Black	German: 5.3%	
Rural population:	7.8%	1.4% Asian	**2004 Presidential Vote**	
Pop. 2000:	643,476	0.5% Native Am.	Kerry (D) 158,561	(66%)
Pop. 2005 (est):	635,459	0.1% Hawaiian	Bush (R) 79,302	(33%)
Median income:	$32,238	1.6% Two+ races	Other 1,517	(1%)
Poverty status:	18.9%	0.2% Other	**2000 Presidential Vote**	
Military veterans:	15.5%	2.6% Hispanic Origin	Gore (D) 134,020	(66%)
			Bush (R) 65,724	(32%)
			Other 3,603	(2%)
			Cook Partisan Voting Index: D +18	

Occupation	Blue collar: 25.8%	White collar: 55.4%	Gray collar: 18.7%

The history of African-American slavery literally began along the tidal expanse of the James River. In 1607, the first English colonists chose one of the marshiest, least healthy spots along the broad river as the site of their settlement at Jamestown. Only a dozen years later, the first slave ship sailed up the James and offloaded its human cargo, giving birth to the biracial society of the American South. In the 21st century, the great plantation houses of the Tidewater, entire communities once adorned by the most impressive architecture of the day and attended by hundreds of slaves, still dot the banks of the James. Charles City County—the site of William Byrd II's Westover, Benjamin Harrison III's Berkeley, and John Carter's Shirley—also was the birthplace of two successive presidents, William Henry Harrison and John Tyler. The county's population continues to be heavily black: The demography of the plantation remains.

The 3d Congressional District of Virginia is the descendant of a black-majority district formed in 1992, and redrawn twice in the 1990s after a federal court ruled it unconstitutional and then again after the 2000 Census. The district jumps back and forth across the James River to string together black precincts and communities in Norfolk, Hampton and Newport News; then, upriver on the Peninsula past Jamestown and Charles City County all the way to Richmond and eastern suburban Henrico County. It includes the Army's Fort Eustis and all of the majority-black city of Portsmouth—a Navy port and industrial town with a charming old section and a new cargo terminal in its shipyard. Politically, the 3d is the most Democratic district in Virginia and the only black-majority district. Its economy depends heavily on the Newport News Shipbuilding & Drydock Company, the largest industrial employer in Virginia, now owned by Northrop Grumman. The shipyard lies over the flat neighborhoods lining the baysides, with ships looming larger than life, their turrets and superstructures bristling with armored might. During the Cold War era, Newport News built two of the largest tankers ever made in the western hemisphere, in addition to its *Nimitz*-class nuclear aircraft carriers and *Los Angeles* class nuclear attack submarines; the USS George H.W. Bush, the tenth and final *Nimitz*-class aircraft carrier, was christened in October 2006.

The congressman from the 3d District is Bobby Scott, a Democrat first elected when the district was created in 1992. He grew up in Newport News, the son of a doctor, went to Harvard, where he was a classmate of Al Gore, and then to Boston College law school, where he preceded John Kerry. He served in the National Guard and Army Reserves, and returned home to practice law. In 1977, he was elected to the House of Delegates and in 1983 to the state Senate, representing a multi-racial district in a community where, because of the military tradition of integration, biracial politics came more naturally than in other places. In 1986 he ran a credible race for Congress and lost to Republican Herb Bateman, 56%-44%. In 1992, with his base in the Peninsula, and against two Richmond-based candidates, Scott won the crucial Democratic primary with 67% of the vote. He is the only black member of Congress elected from Virginia since Reconstruction.

Scott has a solidly liberal voting record, except on occasional economic and defense issues; he is one of the House's most outspoken civil libertarians. When bipartisan coalitions passed legislation to permit states to display the Ten Commandments in schools or government buildings, he raised First Amendment objections. After September 11 he opposed the USA Patriot Act, arguing that it might promote racial profiling. He opposes the death penalty and was one of 3 members to oppose condemnation of a federal court decision declaring unconstitutional the words "one nation under God" in the Pledge of Allegiance. "We ought to be standing up for unpopular decisions" and not voting for a resolution that "everyone knows is stupid, but it sounds popular." He unsuccessfully offered amendments to prohibit religious discrimination by faith-based organizations receiving government funds for Head Start centers, and to permit cab drivers and medical professionals to transport women across state lines for an abortion.   Scott has had some success on civil liberties, as with enactment of the bipartisan Death in Custody Act requiring states to report deaths of arrestees and prisoners. In 2003, he attended a White House signing ceremony for a bill designed to eliminate rape inside the nation's prisons. Scott and other members of the Congressional Black Caucus met with George W. Bush in January 2005, and Bush backed proposals to help children of offenders and to finance use of DNA evidence in death penalty appeals; later, on leaving the chamber after State of the Union address, he turned to Scott and said, "I heard what you said, Bobby."

At the start of the Iraq war, Scott was one of 11 members to oppose a resolution supporting the effort. He said that Bush had not stated a rationale, objected to clauses suggesting a link to the September 2001 terror attacks and said that the resolution was designed "to extract political advantage." In August 2006, he said that the public "has about had it" with Iraq, and said that troops should leave if Bush could not explain their rationale to be there. He has been formidable in raising questions about the budget deficit and big tax cuts. One of his goals is affordable health care for all. Remembering how his father had been denied staff privileges in a Newport News hospital, he vowed that any health care bill would prohibit racial discrimination against patients and health care providers. At home, he clashed with former Governor Douglas Wilder and other officials over their plan to strengthen the office of mayor of Richmond; the Justice Department overrode Scott's civil rights objections and Wilder was elected in 2004.

That year Scott faced his first Republican challenger since 1996, Winsome Sears, a former Marine and the first black Republican woman in the House of Delegates. Sears criticized Scott as "radical" on national security, education, gay rights and abortion; she called the war in Iraq a "battle for freedom." Scott focused on his record and criticized Republican policies, including an "overextended" military. In this strongly Democratic district, he won 69%-31%. In 2006, he ran unopposed. In the majority, he became chairman of the Judiciary Subcommittee on Crime, Terrorism and Homeland Security, where he planned tough oversight of criminal justice laws.

FOURTH DISTRICT

Rep. Randy Forbes (R)

Elected June 2001, 3d full term; b. Feb. 17, 1952, Chesapeake; home, Chesapeake; Randolph-Macon Col., B.A. 1974, U. of VA, J.D. 1977; Baptist; married (Shirley).

Elected Office: VA House of Del., 1989-97; VA Senate, 1997-2001.

Professional Career: Practicing atty., 1977-2001.

DC Office: 307 CHOB, 20515, 202-225-6365; Fax: 202-226-1170; Web site: forbes.house.gov.

District Offices: Chesapeake, 757-382-0080; Colonial Heights, 804-526-4969; Emporia, 434-634-5575.

Committees: *Armed Services* (12th of 29 R): Readiness; Seapower & Expeditionary Forces. *Judiciary* (12th of 17 R): Crime, Terrorism & Homeland Security (RMM); Immigration, Citizenship, Refugees, Border Security & International Law.

Group Ratings

	ADA	ACLU	AFS	LCV	ITIC	NTU	COC	ACU	CFG	FRC
2006	10	14	14	8	100	60	100	92	66	100
2005	5	—	0	6	—	58	89	92	69	100

National Journal Ratings

	2005 LIB	—	2005 CONS		2006 LIB	—	2006 CONS
Economic	29%	—	70%		27%	—	71%
Social	19%	—	80%		27%	—	73%
Foreign	17%	—	79%		30%	—	67%

Key Votes of the 109th Congress

1. Estate Tax Repeal	Y	5. Limit Interstate Abortion	Y	9. Build Border Fence	*
2. Limit CAFE Standards	Y	6. Extend Patriot Act	Y	10. CAFTA	Y
3. FY06 Spending Curb	Y	7. Bar Same Sex Marriage	Y	11. Oppose Iraq Withdrawal	Y
4. Drilling in ANWR	Y	8. Stem Cell Research $	N	12. Detainee Tribunals	Y

Election Results

2006 general	Randy Forbes (R)	150,967	(76%)	($566,651)
	Albert Durckard (IG)	46,487	(23%)	
2006 primary	Randy Forbes (R)	unopposed		
2004 general	Randy Forbes (R)	182,444	(64%)	($858,666)
	Jonathan Menefee (D)	100,413	(35%)	($30,215)

Prior Winning Percentages: 2002 (98%); 2001 (52%)

The People		Race/Ethnic Origin	Ancestry	
Area size:	4,575 sq. mi.	62.0% White	USA: 10.0%	English: 8.6%
Urban population:	70.9%	33.1% Black	German: 7.2%	
Rural population:	29.1%	1.3% Asian	**2004 Presidential Vote**	
Pop. 2000:	643,477	0.3% Native Am.	Bush (R) 166,689	(57%)
Pop. 2005 (est):	704,140	0.0% Hawaiian	Kerry (D) 125,164	(43%)
Median income:	$45,249	1.1% Two+ races	Other 1,713	(1%)
Poverty status:	9.5%	0.1% Other	**2000 Presidential Vote**	
Military veterans:	16.2%	2.0% Hispanic Origin	Bush (R) 131,834	(54%)
			Gore (D) 107,553	(44%)
			Other 3,690	(2%)
			Cook Partisan Voting Index: R + 5	

Occupation   Blue collar: 27.6%   White collar: 57.8%   Gray collar: 14.6%

The clash of arms resounds through much of the history of Tidewater Virginia. The Tidewater was the scene of the final victory of the Revolutionary War and saw bitter fighting more than 80 years later in the Civil War, as Union troops invested the battlements of the small industrial city of Petersburg, 25 miles south of Richmond; the Blackwater River was a prominent dividing line between Union and Confederate troops. Today, the Tidewater region boasts one of the densest concentrations of military power in the world: The Hampton Roads area has the nation's largest accumulation of Navy bases, while Fort Lee, the big Army base near Petersburg, has provided 6,800 local jobs and an estimated $862 million impact on the local economy. Local officials expect those jobs to double as a result of the 2005 base closing commission's decision to expand its military training facilities.

The 4th Congressional District of Virginia includes much of the Tidewater south of the James River. The district covers some heavily white Richmond suburbs but about half its people are in the Hampton Roads area, mostly in the fast-growing suburbs of Chesapeake and Suffolk. *Money* magazine named Chesapeake as among the best places to live in the country, with its quality schools, open local government and ample green space. Suffolk was the original home of the Planters Nut and Chocolate Company; its sandy loam soil is the eastern edge of Virginia's Peanut Belt, nearly all of which is in the 4th, though production has dropped markedly. The district also takes in the flat lands of Southside Virginia fanning south from the James River. These were tobacco lands after the English first settled them in the 17th century; today they also produce Smithfield hams in an area that calls itself the "Ham Capital of the World." The Great Dismal Swamp, which crosses into North Carolina, is a breathtaking national wildlife preserve that features long hikes into marshy woodland and the shallow Lake Drummond at its center; it was a sanctuary for runaway slaves. The district includes all of Petersburg and Hopewell, with its Honeywell plant facing 18th century plantations.

The congressman from the 4th District is Randy Forbes, a Republican who won a June 2001 special election. Forbes grew up in Chesapeake, majored in government at Randolph-Macon, graduated from the University of Virginia law school, and returned home to start a law firm which later merged with a larger Norfolk firm. His first job in politics was as an aide to the Democratic member of the House of Delegates from Chesapeake. When his boss retired in 1989, Forbes ran and won the seat as a Republican. Four years later, when Republicans were still in the minority, he became the party's floor leader. In 1997 he was elected to the state Senate. Forbes was a classmate and friend of Governors George Allen and Jim Gilmore in law school, and in 1996 Allen made him Republican state chairman; he helped engineer the historic Republican 1997 sweep of all three statewide offices.

In early 2001, Forbes was a leading candidate for lieutenant governor. When 10-term Democratic Congressman Norman Sisisky died in March after cancer surgery, national and state Republican leaders asked Forbes to run in what was then a competitive seat. The nominee was chosen at a convention, and Forbes won by forging unity in the delegations from Chesapeake and Portsmouth, then the district's two largest cities. He got a break when the strongest Democrat, Sisisky's son Mark, declined to run. Democrats chose state Senator Louise Lucas of Portsmouth, an African-American who held a majority-black seat. Lucas worked for 18 years at the Norfolk Naval Shipyard, where she became its first woman shipfitter. Both national parties and their interest-group allies spent heavily. Republicans attacked Lucas for opposing repeal of the sales tax on non-prescription drugs and for supporting a gasoline tax increase. Democrats criticized Forbes for backing "privatization" of Social Security. Forbes said that he favored George W. Bush's proposal to let younger workers invest some of their payroll taxes in individual investment accounts, but his ads emphasized that he would preserve current benefits—"every penny of it." Lucas carried Portsmouth 63%-37%. But Forbes took more populous Chesapeake 61%-39% and won majorities in seven of the 10 rural counties, for an overall win of 52%-48%.

In the House, Forbes has voted with conservatives and he sits on the Armed Services and Judiciary committees. His work on defense issues has ranged from pursuit of weapons of mass destruction to military mail. In a rare break with party leaders, he opposed the intelligence bill because it failed to address immigration problems. Forbes cosponsored the constitutional amendment to ban same-sex marriages, and spoke up for Representative Chris Smith's proposed Unborn Child Pain Awareness Act, which would require doctors to inform the mother of the pain that a fetus can feel from an abortion. The House in 2006 passed his bill to make any illegal alien found to be a member of a criminal gang detainable, deportable and ineligible to receive political asylum or other benefits. In 2007, he became ranking Republican on the Crime Subcommittee, where he unveiled a "law and order" agenda to address drug trafficking, child pornography and gang violence. With Susan Davis of California, he co-chaired the Navy and Marine Corps Caucus. With Armed Services Committee chairman Ike Skelton and others, he formed the China Caucus for members to learn more about its impact on U.S. defense and commerce.

After the Republicans' redistricting, Lucas decided against a rematch in 2002 and Forbes has faced only one Democratic challenger since then. And so a district held for 19 years by a Democrat has become safely Republican. Forbes wields influence as a political power broker in his hometown and has an interest in running for the Senate some day.

FIFTH DISTRICT

Rep. Virgil Goode (R)

Elected 1996, 6th term; b. Oct. 17, 1946, Richmond; home, Rocky Mount; U. of Richmond, B.A. 1969, U. of VA, J.D. 1973; Baptist; married (Lucy).

Military Career: VA Natl. Guard, 1969-75.

Elected Office: VA Senate, 1973-96.

Professional Career: Practicing atty., 1973-96.

DC Office: 1520 LHOB, 20515, 202-225-4711; Fax: 202-225-5681; Web site: www.house.gov/goode.

District Offices: Charlottesville, 804-295-6372; Danville, 804-792-1280; Farmville, 804-392-8331; Rocky Mount, 540-484-1254.

Committees: *Appropriations* (19th of 29 R): Legislative Branch; Interior, Environment & Related Agencies; Transportation, HUD & Related Agencies.

Group Ratings

	ADA	ACLU	AFS	LCV	ITIC	NTU	COC	ACU	CFG	FRC
2006	0	5	14	0	83	53	93	88	43	100
2005	15	—	13	28	—	56	81	88	51	92

National Journal Ratings

	2005 LIB	—	2005 CONS	2006 LIB	—	2006 CONS
Economic	44%	—	55%	38%	—	61%
Social	12%	—	86%	0%	—	94%
Foreign	40%	—	58%	42%	—	57%

Key Votes of the 109th Congress

1. Estate Tax Repeal	Y	5. Limit Interstate Abortion	Y
2. Limit CAFE Standards	Y	6. Extend Patriot Act	Y
3. FY06 Spending Curb	Y	7. Bar Same Sex Marriage	Y
4. Drilling in ANWR	Y	8. Stem Cell Research $	N

9. Build Border Fence	Y
10. CAFTA	N
11. Oppose Iraq Withdrawal	Y
12. Detainee Tribunals	Y

Election Results

2006 general	Virgil Goode (R)	125,370	(59%)	($1,064,515)
	Al Weed (D)	84,682	(40%)	($577,982)
	Other	2,027	(1%)	
2006 primary	Virgil Goode (R)	unopposed		
2004 general	Virgil Goode (R)	172,431	(64%)	($753,167)
	Al Weed (D)	98,237	(36%)	($481,071)

Prior Winning Percentages: 2002 (63%); 2000 (67%); 1998 (100%); 1996 (61%)

The People		Race/Ethnic Origin	Ancestry	
Area size:	9,054 sq. mi.	72.4% White	USA: 14.7%	English: 9.0%
Urban population:	36.0%	23.9% Black	German: 6.6%	
Rural population:	64.0%	1.0% Asian	**2004 Presidential Vote**	
Pop. 2000:	643,497	0.2% Native Am.	Bush (R) 158,568	(56%)
Pop. 2005 (est):	665,278	0.0% Hawaiian	Kerry (D) 121,960	(43%)
Median income:	$35,739	0.8% Two+ races	Other 3,097	(1%)
Poverty status:	13.2%	0.1% Other	**2000 Presidential Vote**	
Military veterans:	13.1%	1.6% Hispanic Origin	Bush (R) 137,223	(55%)
			Gore (D) 102,814	(41%)
			Other 8,907	(4%)
			Cook Partisan Voting Index: R + 6	

Occupation	Blue collar: 31.7%	White collar: 53.3%	Gray collar: 15.0%

Southside Virginia is a geographic name that for years was shorthand for a state of mind. Here is Appomattox Court House, in the serene little hamlet where Robert E. Lee surrendered to his one-time subordinate Ulysses S. Grant; here is Danville, where the tobacco auction originated in 1858; here also is Prince Edward County, where Harry Byrd's massive resistance shut down public schools in 1957 rather than obey a federal court desegregation order but where members of Congress recently have celebrated civil rights progress. This land north of the dividing line Colonel William Byrd surveyed in 1728 has some variety. Its eastern counties are flat and humid—frontier in the late colonial period, plantation country by 1800, now peanut fields and pine forests. Along U.S. 58, just north of Byrd's dividing line, are the vestiges of Virginia's Tobacco Road. In South Hill, the Tobacco Farm Life Museum pays tribute to that heritage, though only one tobacco warehouse is still in business. To the west, into the Piedmont, the land gradually gets more hilly. Here are the abandoned textile mills and furniture manufacturing centers of Danville and Martinsville, places that reminisce fondly about the last period of textile industry growth that peaked in 1973. Nearby is the D-Day Memorial in Bedford, which lost more men per capita, 23 of its 35 soldiers, in the Normandy invasion than any other town in the nation. Nearer to the mountains are more livestock and less tobacco, and the thick syrupy tones of the Southside Virginia accent turn to mountain twangs. Local officials have sought to add some of these areas to the federal map of Appalachia to make them eligible for anti-poverty funds.

The 5th District consists of much of Southside Virginia, west of metropolitan Richmond, and spreads as far north as the Blue Ridge Mountains. It includes all of liberal Charlottesville and surrounding Albemarle County and fast-growing Fluvanna County, but skirts around Lynchburg. Historically, politics here were Democratic, segregationist and conservative, run by chain-smoking local bankers and courthouse lawyers. Such Democrats are a rare breed these days, on the way to becoming extinct, and Southside is becoming part of the Republican heartland of Virginia.

The congressman from the 5th District is Virgil Goode (rhymes with mood), elected as a Democrat in 1996, an Independent for two years and officially a Republican since February 2002. Goode grew up in Franklin County, where his father was a prominent enough figure that part of U.S. 220 was named after him. He graduated from the University of Richmond and from the University of Virginia law school in 1973. That same year, he was elected to the Virginia Senate, at 27. In 1994, he ran against scandal-beleaguered Senator Charles Robb in the Democratic primary; Goode lost 58%-34%, but showed local strength. In 1995, his reelection in a Republican-leaning district enabled Democrats to hold control of the state Senate. In 1996, when conservative Democrat L.F. Payne retired, Goode seemed the only Democrat with a strong chance to win the district. He emphasized bipartisan cooperation with the slogan on the pencils and emery boards he handed out to voters: "Work together in Congress." Republicans ran George Landrith, a former Albemarle County school board member, who lost 53%-47% to Payne in 1994. Goode won by an impressive 61%-36%.

In his first years in the House, Goode had the most conservative voting record of any House Democrat. He passionately opposed one of the Clinton White House's favorite projects, the bill to curb tobacco consumption. He voted to impeach Bill Clinton, evidently not a close issue for him. "The party line says that lying under oath in a court proceeding is not an impeachable offense. I disagree with that." In January 2000, Goode announced that he would no longer be a member of the Democratic Caucus and would run for reelection as an Independent. He said that he would attend meetings of the House Republican Conference and contribute to their campaign committee. Republicans promptly gave him a seat on the Appropriations Committee. In his 2000 campaign, he attacked the Clinton administration for neglecting the woes of the Southside textile and apparel industries and campaigned with George Allen. Opposed by a Democrat who headed a black farmers' advocacy group, he won 67%-31%. When Goode formalized his affiliation as a Republican, he offered a practical explanation: On certain voting machines, independents are listed "off-center," and "we had to do significant advertising" to alert voters. He said that the switch would not change his stand on issues. Some observers thought that redistricting was the reason Goode left the Democratic party; Republicans, who controlled the process, could have placed his Franklin County home into the 9th District. Instead, they made only minor adjustments to existing lines.

As a Republican, Goode's voting record has become more conservative, especially on social issues. He organized the Second Amendment Caucus to advocate for gun owners. Claiming that "we are under an invasion," he won House passage of amendments for the military to assist border security agents to prevent entry of terrorists, drug traffickers and illegal aliens. Pentagon officials opposed his proposal as unnecessary and potentially disruptive, and critics called the proposal "anti-immigrant." In March 2006, he said that illegal aliens who waved the Mexican flag during immigration protests should return to Mexico. He was a leading advocate of the federal tobacco buyout, which was enacted in October 2004; Goode won a commitment for the measure from Republican leaders in exchange for his vote for the 2003 Medicare/prescription drug bill. Goode has voted against free trade agreements, including normal trade relations with for China and trade promotion authority, and he has called for the U.S. to withdraw from the North American Free Trade Agreement.

In 2006, Democratic nominee Al Weed, a farmer and vintner, ran for a second time and was well-funded. He clashed with Goode on issues ranging from Iraq to same-sex marriage; he said that Goode was stirring fear on immigration. Goode ran ads that he was an "independent," and won 59%-40%, though he lost Charlottesville by 75%-24%. In November 2006, lobbyists for defense companies pled guilty to making illegal campaign contributions to Goode; he said that he did not know that they were illegal and he gave the $90,000 to charity. In early 2007, he sparked national controversy when he objected to plans by freshman Democratic Rep. Keith Ellison to take his oath of office with the Koran. Americans needed to "wake up" and restrict immigration, or there would "likely be many more Muslims elected to office," Goode wrote to constituents.

SIXTH DISTRICT

Rep. Bob Goodlatte (R)

Elected 1992, 8th term; b. Sept. 22, 1952, Holyoke, MA; home, Roanoke; Bates Col., B.A. 1974, Washington & Lee Law Schl., J.D. 1977; Christian Scientist; married (Maryellen).

Professional Career: Dist. Dir., U.S. Rep. Caldwell Butler, 1977-79; Practicing atty., 1979-92.

DC Office: 2240 RHOB, 20515, 202-225-5431; Fax: 202-225-9681; Web site: www.house.gov/goodlatte.

District Offices: Harrisonburg, 540-432-2391; Lynchburg, 804-845-8306; Roanoke, 540-857-2672; Staunton, 540-885-3861.

Committees: *Agriculture* (RMM of 21 R). *Judiciary* (5th of 17 R): Immigration, Citizenship, Refugees, Border Security & International Law; Courts, the Internet & Intellectual Property.

Group Ratings

	ADA	ACLU	AFS	LCV	ITIC	NTU	COC	ACU	CFG	FRC
2006	0	9	0	0	100	62	100	92	67	100
2005	5	—	0	0	—	62	93	96	74	100

National Journal Ratings

	2005 LIB	—	2005 CONS		2006 LIB	—	2006 CONS
Economic	24%	—	74%		0%	—	98%
Social	12%	—	86%		6%	—	92%
Foreign	17%	—	79%		6%	—	86%

Key Votes of the 109th Congress

1. Estate Tax Repeal	Y	5. Limit Interstate Abortion	Y	9. Build Border Fence	Y
2. Limit CAFE Standards	Y	6. Extend Patriot Act	Y	10. CAFTA	Y
3. FY06 Spending Curb	Y	7. Bar Same Sex Marriage	Y	11. Oppose Iraq Withdrawal	Y
4. Drilling in ANWR	Y	8. Stem Cell Research $	N	12. Detainee Tribunals	Y

Election Results

2006 general	Bob Goodlatte (R)	153,187	(75%)	($1,029,538)
	Barbara Pryor (I)	25,129	(12%)	($2,585)
	Andre Peery (I)	24,731	(12%)	($8,140)
2006 primary	Bob Goodlatte (R)	unopposed		
2004 general	Bob Goodlatte (R)	206,560	(97%)	($797,676)
	Other	7,088	(3%)	

Prior Winning Percentages: 2002 (97%); 2000 (100%); 1998 (69%); 1996 (67%); 1994 (100%); 1992 (60%)

The People		Race/Ethnic Origin	Ancestry	
Area size:	5,664 sq. mi.	84.8% White	USA: 13.4%	German: 11.9%
Urban population:	64.7%	10.9% Black	English: 8.9%	
Rural population:	35.3%	0.9% Asian	**2004 Presidential Vote**	
Pop. 2000:	643,504	0.2% Native Am.	Bush (R) 177,133	(63%)
Pop. 2005 (est):	662,954	0.0% Hawaiian	Kerry (D) 100,561	(36%)
Median income:	$37,773	1.0% Two+ races	Other 2,883	(1%)
Poverty status:	11.0%	0.1% Other	**2000 Presidential Vote**	
Military veterans:	13.7%	2.0% Hispanic Origin	Bush (R) 147,961	(60%)
			Gore (D) 92,407	(37%)
			Other 6,984	(3%)
			Cook Partisan Voting Index: R +11	

Occupation   Blue collar: 28.5%   White collar: 55.9%   Gray collar: 15.6%

The sturdy men and women who settled the Valley of Virginia west of the Blue Ridge were quite different from the "second sons" of the European aristocracy who cleared the marshy forests of the Tidewater and built grand plantations there. Even before the Revolutionary War, Scots and Scots-Irish, German Protestants and Mennonites and Moravians—members of religious communities and fiercely independent farmers—poured down the great Wagon Road from Pennsylvania to the Valley. They were looking not for the flat, mahogany-brown land that eastern tobacco growers sought, but for fields, which could support wheat, corn and hay, crops that could be rotated, and that an individual farmer and his family could handle. That same independent spirit nurtured the growth of higher education here. In Lexington alone are Washington and Lee University, which Robert E. Lee headed, and the Virginia Military Institute, where Stonewall Jackson taught philosophy and artillery tactics, and which began admitting women in 1996 under order from the U.S. Supreme Court. A quartet of distinguished women's colleges is nearby: Mary Baldwin College at Staunton, Randolph-Macon Woman's College at Lynchburg, Sweet Briar College at Sweet Briar, and Hollins University at Roanoke, farther south in the Valley. A presidential library for Woodrow Wilson is planned for his birthplace of Staunton. Here, industry flourished more than in most of Virginia east of the Blue Ridge. In the 19th century the Norfolk and Western Railway established its chief junction at Roanoke; as the years passed the city became the headquarters of the railroad, now Norfolk Southern, and many major companies have plants here. Now there is a proposal to build a parallel to Interstate 81, which runs through the Valley, solely for trucks.

The 6th Congressional District of Virginia covers the heart of the Valley of Virginia, from Strasburg south to Roanoke, and crosses over the Blue Ridge to take in Lynchburg, the home of the late Jerry Falwell's Thomas Road Baptist Church and Liberty University. Politically, this area has a Republican tradition hospitable to economic assistance for the little guy, and it fiercely opposed Harry Byrd Democrats. In recent decades the ancestral conservatism of Byrd Democrats and the feisty politics of the mountain rebels have melded into a single conservative Republicanism, more populist than elite in tone, as concerned with moral values as economic freedom, prickly about interference from Washington or even Richmond. In 2004 the 6th District voted 63% for George W. Bush, his highest percentage in a Virginia district; in 2006, it voted 58%-40% for Senator George Allen, also his highest percentage, in his loss to Democrat Jim Webb.

The congressman from the 6th District is Bob Goodlatte, a Republican first elected in 1992, and past chairman of the House Agriculture Committee. Goodlatte grew up in Massachusetts, attended college in Maine and then law school at Washington & Lee, and went to work in Congressman

Caldwell Butler's office in Roanoke. Goodlatte practiced law in Roanoke and stayed active in politics; in 1992, when Democrat Jim Olin retired, Goodlatte was nominated by convention and won the general 60%-40%.

Goodlatte has compiled a mostly conservative voting record. On the Judiciary Committee, he sponsored the House-passed bill to limit class-action lawsuits against tobacco companies, gun makers and other companies, and a separate bill to give federal courts jurisdiction over large class-action suits. In response to conservatives' complaints over federal court decisions that cite legal rulings of other nations, he sponsored a bill stating that judicial decisions should not be based on foreign precedents. The House approved his plan to eliminate the visa lottery program from the immigration law.

With 9th District Democrat Rick Boucher, Goodlatte has been a leader among House members working on technology issues. He has chaired the GOP's High-Tech Working Group and co-chairs the Congressional Internet Caucus with Boucher, where they have encouraged open and non-taxed access to broadband technology. Goodlatte sponsored the Communications Decency Act, allowing censorship of obscene material on the Internet, which was overturned by the Supreme Court. To combat spyware software that tracks users' activities and identifying information, he won House passage of his "I-SPY Prevention Act" to criminalize the installation of such software without the owner's approval. In 2006, he helped to enact restrictions on Internet gambling by cutting off money to overseas operators.

In 2003, Goodlatte became chairman of the Agriculture Committee. The agriculture in his district, as he notes, is "free-market oriented: poultry, livestock, orchards. It gives me a pretty free hand to work with all the different regions of the country." He was the first Agriculture chairman since 1967 from east of the Mississippi River. He backed the Bush administration's appeal of a 2004 World Trade Organization ruling that U.S. cotton subsidies violated international trade rules. He worked to pass the Healthy Forests Initiative and got a two-year postponement of the country of origin labeling provisions in the 2002 farm act. In 2004, he worked with other tobacco state lawmakers to steer a perilous course in successfully attaching the tobacco buyout program—specifically, the end of Depression-era quotas and price supports—to the reform of corporate taxes, while rejecting Senate provisions to include FDA regulation of tobacco. He met major protests, including some at home, when he objected to a bill designed to stop the slaughter of horses; although he argued that it would produce increased horse abuse and neglect, the House passed the bill in September 2006. He has praised the impact of the 2002 farm bill, and hoped for bipartisan cooperation in its renewal. In the 109th Congress, he was one of only four members who did not miss a House vote.

Goodlatte has been consistently reelected without difficulty and has regularly donated his salary increases to local charities. He encountered no problem when he abandoned in 2002 his self-imposed 12-year term limit. He has not faced a Democratic challenger since 1998.

SEVENTH DISTRICT

Rep. Eric Cantor (R)

Elected 2000, 4th term; b. June 6, 1963, Richmond; home, Richmond; George Washington U., B.A. 1985, Col. of William & Mary, J.D. 1988, Columbia U., M.S., 1989; Jewish; married (Diana).

Elected Office: VA House of Del., 1991-2000.

Professional Career: Practicing atty., 1990-2000.

DC Office: 329 CHOB, 20515, 202-225-2815; Fax: 202-225-0011; Web site: cantor.house.gov.

District Offices: Culpeper, 540-825-8960; Richmond, 804-747-4073.

Committees: *Chief Deputy Minority Whip. Ways & Means* (13th of 17 R): Oversight; Select Revenue Measures.

Group Ratings

	ADA	ACLU	AFS	LCV	ITIC	NTU	COC	ACU	CFG	FRC
2006	5	5	0	8	100	61	100	92	72	100
2005	0	—	0	6	—	58	93	96	63	92

National Journal Ratings

	2005 LIB	—	2005 CONS		2006 LIB	—	2006 CONS
Economic	9%	—	88%		16%	—	81%
Social	12%	—	86%		11%	—	85%
Foreign	11%	—	86%		17%	—	73%

Key Votes of the 109th Congress

1. Estate Tax Repeal	Y	5. Limit Interstate Abortion	Y	9. Build Border Fence	Y
2. Limit CAFE Standards	Y	6. Extend Patriot Act	Y	10. CAFTA	Y
3. FY06 Spending Curb	Y	7. Bar Same Sex Marriage	Y	11. Oppose Iraq Withdrawal	Y
4. Drilling in ANWR	Y	8. Stem Cell Research $	N	12. Detainee Tribunals	Y

Election Results

2006 general	Eric Cantor (R)	163,706	(64%)	($3,499,247)
	James Nachman (D)	88,206	(34%)	($108,061)
	Other..	4,485	(2%)	
2006 primary	Eric Cantor (R)	unopposed		
2004 general	Eric Cantor (R)	230,765	(75%)	($2,193,388)
	W. Brad Blanton (I)............................	74,325	(24%)	

Prior Winning Percentages: 2002 (69%); 2000 (67%)

The People		Race/Ethnic Origin	Ancestry	
Area size:	3,556 sq. mi.	78.2% White	English: 12.1%	USA: 10.6%
Urban population:	70.0%	16.1% Black	German: 10.2%	
Rural population:	30.0%	2.3% Asian	**2004 Presidential Vote**	
Pop. 2000:	643,499	0.3% Native Am.	Bush (R) 204,273	(61%)
Pop. 2005 (est):	715,388	0.0% Hawaiian	Kerry (D) 128,166	(38%)
Median income:	$50,990	1.1% Two+ races	Other 2,148	(1%)
Poverty status:	6.1%	0.1% Other	**2000 Presidential Vote**	
Military veterans:	13.5%	2.0% Hispanic Origin	Bush (R) 172,425	(61%)
			Gore (D) 105,504	(37%)
			Other 6,261	(2%)
			Cook Partisan Voting Index: R +11	

Occupation   Blue collar: 19.4%   White collar: 68.4%   Gray collar: 12.2%

In the center of Virginia, on a hill in downtown Richmond above the James River, is Thomas Jefferson's Capitol, one of the first classical-style buildings in North America, chaste and simple in the Jefferson style. A mile or so west is Monument Avenue, Richmond's grand 140-foot-wide boulevard, punctuated by circles, each with a statue of a Confederate hero—Robert E. Lee (62 feet tall, dedicated Memorial Day 1890), Jeb Stuart, Jefferson Davis, Stonewall Jackson, Matthew Fountain Maury, "the Pathfinder of the Sea." Richmond is a monument to Jefferson and to the Confederacy; its metro area is only the third largest in the state, but it still sets the tone for Virginia, and is the home of many of the state's great institutions—Dominion Resources, Main Street banks, big law firms, and the *Richmond Times-Dispatch*. Richmond's metro area has grown far past its city borders, covering almost all of suburban Henrico and Chesterfield Counties and spreading into what was until recently countryside. For many years Richmond was riven by sharp racial differences. It was from here that Virginia's leaders called for massive resistance to desegregation in the 1950s; when Richmond elected its first black-majority council in the 1970s, the outgoing council deeded the statue of Lee to the state for fear it would be torn down. Now Richmond has come to a better place. Blacks have been a majority in the city for two decades now, and in 1989 Virginia elected a black governor, Douglas Wilder, who grew up on Church Hill, in a segregated neighborhood overlooking the Capitol. In 2005, Wilder made a triumphant return as mayor, elected by a biracial majority. A statue of Richmond-born African-American tennis champion Arthur Ashe has been added to Monument Avenue. Richmond has been thriving economically with banking, securities, and health care corporate offices and the Philip Morris headquarters. Politically, the city is solidly Democratic; Henrico, Chesterfield and the counties beyond are heavily Republican.

The 7th Congressional District of Virginia includes some city precincts and most of the area surrounding Richmond. The black precincts in the city and Henrico County are mostly in the black-majority 3d District. The 7th District extends past James Madison's home at Montpelier to fast-growing Spotsylvania and Culpeper Counties and as far north as Rappahannock County and the Blue Ridge Mountains. Like many other affluent areas, some of these locales have been struggling with illegal immigration. Although the 7th is only 16% black, 80% of its votes are cast in metro Richmond. This is one of the two most Republican districts in Virginia.

The congressman from the 7th District is Eric Cantor, a Republican first elected in 2000 and rapidly gaining influence in the House. He grew up in Henrico County, graduated from George Washington University and William and Mary law school, and got a master's degree in real estate from Columbia University. He then began practicing law in his family's real-estate firm in Richmond. In 1991, he was elected to the first of five terms in Virginia's House of Delegates. In the legislature, he was a leading ally of business, sponsoring a bill to limit the liability of Philip Morris in a Florida court decree and opposing restrictions on telemarketers. When Congressman Tom Bliley announced his retirement in 2000, after six years as chairman of the Energy and Commerce Committee, Cantor entered the race. He had interned for Bliley while in college, served as Bliley's campaign chairman and had the backing of his political organization. Cantor faced a serious contest in the Republican primary from state Senator Stephen Martin, who emphasized his low-income background and had a solid base of social and religious conservatives. Their contest turned negative: Cantor attacked Martin for supporting a back-door pay raise for legislators; Martin questioned Cantor's business dealings. Cantor put on a substantial advertising campaign. Martin raised less than $200,000—a quarter of what Cantor spent in the primary. Cantor won the primary by only 263 votes. He got 74% of the vote in Henrico, while Martin got 77% in his Chesterfield County base. In the general election, Cantor won 67%-33%.

In the House, Cantor has been reliably conservative in the Richmond tradition. His first bill provided a tax credit of $1,000 per child for all parents with school-age children in public or private schools until they graduate from high school. With his knowledge of the Middle East and his strong support for Israel, Cantor, the only Jewish Republican in the House, chaired the Republican task force on terrorism and unconventional warfare; he praises George W. Bush as more committed to Israel than any other president. But his more significant activity occurred outside the public spotlight as a member of the Republican Whip team. His efforts to assure support for Republican initiatives impressed House leaders and led to a meteoric rise to leadership. In December 2002, incoming Majority Whip Roy Blunt named Cantor as his chief deputy whip, giving him a seat at the party's leadership table and handing him the often thankless task of tracking his colleagues' sentiments on pending legislation. Cantor also won a seat on the Ways and Means Committee, where he was a booster of the Medicare/prescription drug bill and is an active proponent of health savings accounts.

Cantor has shown a sharp partisan edge. His tough attacks on Democratic leaders in the 2004 campaign led the state Democratic chairman to call Cantor "a Bush attack dog." He is a leader among junior Republicans seeking to confront Democrats; in February 2007, he offered an amendment to draw attention to Speaker Nancy Pelosi's request for a "luxury jetliner" and distributed stickers festooned with a drawing of a smiling tuna during the minimum wage debate to highlight what Republicans said was an exemption for a tuna plant owned by a company based in Pelosi's district.

When Blunt ran against John Boehner to replace DeLay as Majority Leader in early 2006, Cantor built an aggressive campaign to replace Blunt as Whip. It's widely conceded that Cantor would have won, though the contest never happened because Blunt lost to Boehner and remained as Whip, including in the minority. Cantor declined to break his pledge not to challenge Blunt and remained a respected and ambitious member of the leadership team. In 2007, he became finance chairman of the NRCC, a testament to his prodigious fundraising skills. He has faced only nominal opposition since his 2000 election but has raised more than $9 million. In 2006 alone, he raised $3.3 million—for a reelection campaign marked by Democrats' refusal to nominate a psychotherapist who used nudity as part of his "honesty workshops"; the candidate was replaced by the chairman of the Richmond Democratic Committee, who won 34% against Cantor.

EIGHTH DISTRICT

Rep. Jim Moran (D)

Elected 1990, 9th term; b. May 16, 1945, Buffalo, NY; home, Alexandria; Col. of Holy Cross, B.A. 1967, attended City U. of NY, 1967-68, U. of Pittsburgh, M.P.A. 1970; Catholic; married (LuAnn).

Elected Office: Alexandria City Cncl., 1979-82; Alexandria Vice Mayor, 1982-84, Alexandria Mayor, 1985-90.

Professional Career: Budget analyst & auditor, U.S. Dept. of H.E.W., 1968-74; Fiscal policy spec., Library of Congress, 1974-76; Staff, U.S. Senate Approp. Cmte., 1976-80; Investment broker, 1980-88.

DC Office: 2239 RHOB, 20515, 202-225-4376; Fax: 202-225-0017; Web site: moran.house.gov.

District Offices: Alexandria, 703-971-4700; Reston, 703-971-4700.

Committees: *Appropriations* (10th of 37 D): Interior, Environment & Related Agencies; Defense.

Group Ratings

	ADA	ACLU	AFS	LCV	ITIC	NTU	COC	ACU	CFG	FRC
2006	95	100	100	92	86	15	53	16	18	0
2005	90	—	100	89	—	15	65	4	19	0

National Journal Ratings

	2005 LIB	—	2005 CONS		2006 LIB	—	2006 CONS
Economic	71%	—	29%		74%	—	23%
Social	77%	—	22%		75%	—	25%
Foreign	73%	—	27%		77%	—	20%

Key Votes of the 109th Congress

1. Estate Tax Repeal	N	5. Limit Interstate Abortion	N	9. Build Border Fence	Y
2. Limit CAFE Standards	N	6. Extend Patriot Act	N	10. CAFTA	Y
3. FY06 Spending Curb	N	7. Bar Same Sex Marriage	N	11. Oppose Iraq Withdrawal	N
4. Drilling in ANWR	N	8. Stem Cell Research $	Y	12. Detainee Tribunals	N

Election Results

2006 general	Jim Moran (D)	144,700	(66%)	($1,054,506)
	Tom O'Donoghue (R)	66,639	(31%)	($113,782)
	Other	6,570	(3%)	
2006 primary	Jim Moran (D)	unopposed		
2004 general	Jim Moran (D)	171,986	(60%)	($1,677,506)
	Lisa Marie Cheney (R)	106,231	(37%)	($337,580)
	Other	9,702	(3%)	

Prior Winning Percentages: 2002 (60%); 2000 (63%); 1998 (67%); 1996 (66%); 1994 (59%); 1992 (56%); 1990 (52%)

The People		Race/Ethnic Origin	Ancestry	
Area size:	125 sq. mi.	57.1% White	German: 9.6%	Irish: 9.0%
Urban population:	100.0%	13.4% Black	English: 8.4%	
Rural population:	0.0%	9.5% Asian	**2004 Presidential Vote**	
Pop. 2000:	643,503	0.2% Native Am.	Kerry (D) 189,525	(64%)
Pop. 2005 (est):	646,683	0.1% Hawaiian	Bush (R) 104,298	(35%)
Median income:	$63,430	3.0% Two+ races	Other 2,782	(1%)
Poverty status:	7.5%	0.3% Other	**2000 Presidential Vote**	
Military veterans:	11.3%	16.4% Hispanic Origin	Gore (D) 152,940	(57%)
			Bush (R) 101,788	(38%)
			Other 11,692	(4%)
			Cook Partisan Voting Index: D +14	

Occupation	Blue collar: 10.7%	White collar: 77.0%	Gray collar: 12.3%

More than two hundred years ago, when George Washington trod the brick sidewalks of Alexandria on his way to market or court or church, this was the largest city in Northern Virginia, far larger than Georgetown, Maryland, just up the Potomac River; what are now Capitol Hill and downtown

Washington were hills above the river's mud flats. But Washington became the national capital, and as it grew, Northern Virginia seemed left behind. In 1846, the District of Columbia retroceded its land south of the Potomac—now Alexandria and Arlington—to Virginia because it seemed obvious that the federal government would never need it, and it was 97 years before the first federal building was built on the Virginia side—the Pentagon; Franklin Roosevelt wondered out loud what they would do with all that space after the war. When the Pentagon was built, Alexandria and the rural countryside of Northern Virginia were represented in Congress by Judge Howard W. Smith, a Harry Byrd Democrat, who saw as his mission the maintenance of the standards of George Washington, Thomas Jefferson and Robert E. Lee. Yet by the 1960s, the area was changing around him. New subdivision dwellers with white-collar jobs and lots of children wanted schools with good academic programs—not the segregated schoolhouses Judge Smith's friends were willing to finance. The new generation wanted freeways, parks and recreation facilities. As Smith's district was moved farther out into the countryside, two-party politics came to the suburbs.

Now the onetime suburbs of Alexandria and Arlington have themselves become central cities of a sort—"edge cities," as Joel Garreau put it. Giant office developments sprang up from rail yards in Crystal City and from used car lots up-river in Rosslyn. Vietnamese and Salvadorans moved into these neighborhoods, and Clarendon became one of America's biggest Vietnamese commercial districts. Then, many Vietnamese moved out a few miles to Seven Corners and Bailey's Crossroads, and Clarendon was gentrified with small shops, some national retailers, and skyrocketing real estate prices. Politically, Alexandria and Arlington, once hotly contested, are now solidly Democratic, with older subdivisions and huge rental apartment complexes that are filled with government employees and contractors. Arlington has a greater share of people with advanced degrees than any other county in the nation. Commuters find roads jammed, and there is a move to widen I-66 inside the Beltway, which was built with just four lanes as a compromise with opponents who didn't want the road at all. In 2005, the base closing commission decided to relocate many military offices from these high-rent neighborhoods; it's a good bet that the space will be filled.

The 8th Congressional District of Virginia consists of all of Arlington County and the cities of Alexandria and Falls Church. It takes in two separate parts of Fairfax County: A stretch of land from Tysons Corner west to Reston, and several areas south of Alexandria's Old Town—the gentle landscapes of Mount Vernon, lower-income Groveton along the old U.S. 1, suburban Springfield and the more rural areas around Fort Belvoir. The district now is solidly Democratic; in 2006, Democrat Jim Webb won 69% here in the Senate race against George Allen, Webb's highest percentage in any congressional district. Two local landmarks here were severely affected by the September 2001 attacks: The Pentagon was struck by American Airlines Flight 77 which caused a loss of 189 lives and nearly $1 billion in damage, and Ronald Reagan Washington National Airport was shut down because of security concerns for three weeks and did not return to nearly full operations for six months.

The congressman from the 8th District is Jim Moran, an oft-embattled Alexandria politician with traces in his accent of his Massachusetts roots. He graduated from Holy Cross and got a master's degree from the University of Pittsburgh, worked in Washington for HEW, the Library of Congress and the Senate Appropriations Committee. He was elected to the Alexandria City Council in 1979 and became vice mayor in 1982; in 1984 he pleaded no contest to a conflict of interest charge and resigned from the Council. The charges were later dropped, and in 1985 Moran was elected mayor. In 1990, he ran for Congress against Republican incumbent Stanford Parris. It was a nasty race: Parris said Moran was a supporter of Saddam Hussein; Moran said he wanted to "break [Parris's] nose," and called him "a deceitful, fatuous jerk." The major substantive issue was abortion, on which Moran ran a pro-choice ad portraying Lady Liberty behind bars. With a big margin in Alexandria, he won 52%-45%.

In the House, Moran has styled himself as a moderate among Democrats, though a bit more liberal on social issues. With Cal Dooley and Tim Roemer, he founded the New Democrat Coalition in 1997, made up of moderate Democrats to support alternatives to "traditional Democratic policies." Working with Virginians, he became a strong ally of the local high-tech industry. Among Democrats, he led the pro-CAFTA charge. Moran has criticized senior Democrat John Dingell for "doing the NRA's bidding" and harming Democrats on gun control legislation; Moran has called for a ban on the commercial sale of .50-caliber sniper rifles.

Moran has been known for his short temper and quick tongue. He jousted—literally—with other Republicans, shoving Californian Duke Cunningham off the floor and out the House chamber doors in 1995 after Cunningham said that Moran had "turned his back on Desert Storm." He was strongly critical of Bill Clinton's conduct in the Lewinsky scandal and in September 1998 suggested the president should resign, but he voted against impeachment in December. At an anti-war forum in March 2003, Moran said, "If it were not for the strong support of the Jewish community for this war with Iraq we would not be doing this. . . . The leaders of the Jewish community are influential enough that they could change the direction of where this is going and I think they should." The furious reaction to his remarks led Moran to apologize.

His personal finances have raised frequent problems. He received negative headlines in 2000 when the *Washington Post* reported that Maryland 8th District Democratic challenger—and pharmaceutical company lobbyist—Terry Lierman gave his friend Moran a $25,000 loan on generous terms; Moran quickly agreed to repay the loan and suffered no apparent political damage. More trouble followed in 2002 with reports that he borrowed $50,000 from the founder of America Online, and that MBNA, the big credit card company, had given him a favorable rate on a mortgage. In 2004, several local officials threatened to challenge him in the Democratic primary but they never actually filed. His one primary opponent was Alexandria attorney Andrew Rosenberg, a political newcomer who criticized Moran's character and rhetoric, and ran as the more progressive candidate. Moran cited his legislative experience and his advocacy of district interests. He prevailed 59%-41%, with his largest margin in Alexandria. The general election against defense consultant Lisa Marie Cheney was never in serious doubt. She accused Moran of giving the district "a black eye and a bloody nose," and promised to "not embarrass us." Moran won 60%-37%.

In June 2006, he was ridiculed by Republicans after he told local Democrats that if the party regained House control, "I'm going to earmark the shit out of" his Appropriations post. Otherwise, he appeared to have depleted his stock of personal crises, had remarried and moved into an expensive home along the Potomac. He worked actively on behalf of Jim Webb's Senate campaign, and was a close ally in John Murtha's unsuccessful contest against Steny Hoyer for Majority Leader. Following the vote, Moran contended that the Murtha team was lied to by some members who had indicated support in the secret-ballot race; he said freshmen who failed to vote for Murtha would "screw themselves for the rest of their lives" and threatened unwanted committee assignments as punishment.

NINTH DISTRICT

Rep. Rick Boucher (D)

Elected 1982, 13th term; b. Aug. 1, 1946, Abingdon; home, Abingdon; Roanoke Col., B.A. 1968, U. of VA, J.D. 1971; United Methodist; married (Amy Hauslohner).

Elected Office: VA Senate, 1975-1983.

Professional Career: Practicing atty., 1971-83.

DC Office: 2187 RHOB, 20515, 202-225-3861; Fax: 202-225-0442; Web site: www.boucher.house.gov.

District Offices: Abingdon, 540-628-1145; Big Stone Gap, 540-523-5450; Pulaski, 540-980-4310.

Committees: *Energy & Commerce* (4th of 31 D): Energy & Air Quality (Chmn.); Telecommunications & the Internet; Commerce, Trade & Consumer Protection. *Judiciary* (3d of 23 D): Courts, the Internet & Intellectual Property.

Group Ratings

	ADA	ACLU	AFS	LCV	ITIC	NTU	COC	ACU	CFG	FRC
2006	75	82	86	67	71	20	60	36	18	28
2005	90	—	100	56	—	18	59	25	19	8

National Journal Ratings

	2005 LIB	—	2005 CONS		2006 LIB	—	2006 CONS
Economic	63%	—	37%		60%	—	39%
Social	61%	—	38%		62%	—	38%
Foreign	67%	—	32%		66%	—	33%

Key Votes of the 109th Congress

1. Estate Tax Repeal	Y	5. Limit Interstate Abortion	N	9. Build Border Fence	Y
2. Limit CAFE Standards	Y	6. Extend Patriot Act	N	10. CAFTA	N
3. FY06 Spending Curb	N	7. Bar Same Sex Marriage	Y	11. Oppose Iraq Withdrawal	Y
4. Drilling in ANWR	N	8. Stem Cell Research $	Y	12. Detainee Tribunals	N

Election Results

2006 general	Rick Boucher (D) 129,705	(68%)	($1,249,993)
	Charles Carrico (R) 61,574	(32%)	($69,980)
2006 primary	Rick Boucher (D) .... unopposed		
2004 general	Rick Boucher (D) 150,039	(59%)	($1,628,026)
	Kevin Triplett (R) 98,499	(39%)	($646,669)
	Other 4,409	(2%)	

Prior Winning Percentages: 2002 (66%); 2000 (70%); 1998 (61%); 1996 (65%); 1994 (59%); 1992 (63%); 1990 (97%); 1988 (63%); 1986 (99%); 1984 (52%); 1982 (50%)

The People		Race/Ethnic Origin	Ancestry	
Area size:	8,838 sq. mi.	93.3% White	USA: 20.0%	English: 7.7%
Urban population:	34.1%	3.8% Black	German: 7.7%	
Rural population:	65.9%	0.8% Asian	**2004 Presidential Vote**	
Pop. 2000:	643,514	0.1% Native Am.	Bush (R) 153,868	(59%)
Pop. 2005 (est):	641,409	0.0% Hawaiian	Kerry (D) 101,662	(39%)
Median income:	$29,783	0.7% Two+ races	Other 3,078	(1%)
Poverty status:	16.2%	0.1% Other	**2000 Presidential Vote**	
Military veterans:	11.9%	1.1% Hispanic Origin	Bush (R) 129,110	(55%)
			Gore (D) 100,298	(42%)
			Other 7,011	(3%)
			Cook Partisan Voting Index: R + 7	

Occupation   Blue collar: 35.3%   White collar: 49.1%   Gray collar: 15.5%

One of the first areas to be settled from the seacoast to the great American interior was what is now Southwest Virginia. As early as 1765, settlements were carved out of the great Valley of Virginia, which bends westward and south toward Tennessee and the Cumberland Gap. Most founders were of Scots-Irish lineage, and they moved to a mountainous area that developed almost apart from the rest of Virginia. The fiercely independent settlers were first farmers, later often coal miners, as in West Virginia, which wasn't a separate state until 1863. Politically, this virtually all-white area opposed slavery and was skeptical if not hostile to the Confederacy. Out of the crucible of struggle between secessionists and unionists, Southwest Virginia developed a robust two-party politics after the Civil War, with both parties resembling their national counterparts more closely than in the rest of Virginia. It is a long way from here to plantation country: the state's extreme southwest corner is closer to the Mississippi River than to the Potomac.

The 9th Congressional District covers all of Southwest Virginia west of Roanoke. Over the years, the district became known as the "Fighting Ninth," because of its taste for raucous politics, culturally conservative and economically populist. Lately, it has become somewhat more like the rest of Virginia, as development has moved down Interstate 81 to, and even past, Blacksburg, home of Virginia Tech. It includes Patrick County, the site of the R.J. Reynolds Homestead as well as annual peach and cabbage festivals. Mountain counties farther west continue to depend on coal and to lose population. With encouragement from state officials, businesses have created jobs at high-tech companies and telephone call centers. The district voted narrowly for Bill Clinton twice, but by much wider margins for George W. Bush in 2000 and 2004. No other Virginia district voted for that combination.

The congressman from the 9th District is Rick Boucher, a Democrat first elected in 1982. Boucher grew up in the antique town of Abingdon, went to Roanoke College and then the University of Virginia law school; he practiced law in Abingdon and was elected to the Virginia Senate in 1975, at 29. Politics runs in the family: His father was the Republican commonwealth's attorney in Washington County, while his mother was county Democratic chairwoman; his grandfather and great-grandfather were Democratic members of the House of Delegates. In 1982 Boucher defeated veteran Republican Representative William Wampler with big margins in coal counties on the Kentucky border. Boucher tends to vote with House Democrats but he sometimes strays, especially on economic issues.

Boucher has devoted much of his legislative time to technology issues. Back in 1988, he cosponsored with then-Senator Al Gore a bill to allow phone companies to offer cable TV, and he sponsored the Satellite Home Viewers Act, so viewers without over-the-air network reception could subscribe to satellite services carrying network channels: The beginning of the now booming satellite TV business. Boucher sees new technologies, from satellite TV to the Internet, as a means for out-of-the-way places like the 9th to compete with urban areas on an equal commercial basis. On the 1996 Telecommunications Act, he helped write provisions to open competition in local telephone and cable TV markets. Boucher was a co-founder of the Congressional Internet Caucus and has been co-chairman with Bob Goodlatte of the next-door 6th District. He worked with Goodlatte on the Judiciary Committee to update copyright laws for the digital age and for a consensus on a National Information Infrastructure. He expressed concern that the recording industry's anti-piracy technology on CDs might override the consumer's ability to copy albums for personal use, as permitted by law, and he filed a bill to permit circumventing such technology in digital content for "fair use." He has sponsored legislation to provide journalists a legal shield from having to disclose confidential sources. (In 2006, he married his long-time girlfriend, the news editor of the local *Galax Gazette*.)

His votes against the party line have caused Boucher some discomfort. In November 2003, he was one of 16 House Democrats who voted for the Medicare bill because of its prescription drug coverage. He worked actively for passage of the tobacco buyout bill. But he has voted with Democrats against tax cuts and the partial-birth abortion ban. He opposed normal trade relations with China and trade promotion authority, expressing concern about the impact on jobs in his district. Boucher has worked for binding arbitration to settle Superfund suits, for allowing state and local governments to engage in interstate shipment of municipal waste, for promotion of coal liquefaction, and for electricity deregulation, which he hopes will benefit the coal industry and stimulate investment in mine facilities. In 2005, he helped to write parts of the big energy bill to promote smart meters and other efficient pricing technology. In the majority, he became chairman of the Energy and Commerce Subcommittee on Energy and Air Quality, which quickly became a focal point because of Speaker Pelosi's call for climate control legislation. The post gave Boucher added leverage to defend and promote development of clean-coal technology.

Boucher conducts an active constituency service operation and is highly popular despite his low-key style. He has helped his district to gain many telecom support jobs, though they have been imperiled by outsourcing overseas. His Commerce committee seat also helps him to raise large sums of money. He usually wins comfortably, but he faced spirited opposition in 2004 from challenger Kevin Triplett, a former NASCAR executive with significant support from national Republicans. Triplett promised to bring more energy to local economic development and criticized Boucher for voting in 2003 against $87 billion for the war in Iraq; Boucher said that he opposed the reconstruction projects. He was supported by organized labor and the National Rifle Association and won 59%-39%. In 2006, Boucher trounced state Delegate Bill Carrico, a former state trooper who was forced to retire after a car wreck, 68%-32%.

TENTH DISTRICT

Rep. Frank Wolf (R)

Elected 1980, 14th term; b. Jan. 30, 1939, Philadelphia, PA; home, Vienna; PA St. U., B.A. 1961, Georgetown U., LL.B. 1965; Presbyterian; married (Carolyn).

Military Career: Army, 1962-63, Army Reserves 1963-67.

Professional Career: Legis. Asst., U.S. Rep. Edward Biester, 1968-71; Asst., U.S. Interior Secy. Rogers Morton, 1971-74; Dep. Asst. Secy., U.S. Dept. of Interior, 1974-75; Practicing atty., 1975-80.

DC Office: 241 CHOB, 20515, 202-225-5136; Fax: 202-225-0437; Web site: wolf.house.gov.

District Offices: Herndon, 703-709-5800; Winchester, 540-667-0990.

Committees: *Appropriations* (5th of 29 R): State, Foreign Operations & Related Programs (RMM); Transportation, HUD & Related Agencies.

Group Ratings

	ADA	ACLU	AFS	LCV	ITIC	NTU	COC	ACU	CFG	FRC
2006	10	14	14	25	86	45	67	64	36	100
2005	5	—	0	28	—	48	89	60	48	75

National Journal Ratings

	2005 LIB	—	2005 CONS		2006 LIB	—	2006 CONS
Economic	47%	—	53%		45%	—	55%
Social	39%	—	60%		38%	—	61%
Foreign	34%	—	61%		33%	—	63%

Key Votes of the 109th Congress

1. Estate Tax Repeal	Y	5. Limit Interstate Abortion	Y
2. Limit CAFE Standards	N	6. Extend Patriot Act	Y
3. FY06 Spending Curb	Y	7. Bar Same Sex Marriage	Y
4. Drilling in ANWR	Y	8. Stem Cell Research $	N

9. Build Border Fence	Y
10. CAFTA	Y
11. Oppose Iraq Withdrawal	Y
12. Detainee Tribunals	Y

Election Results

2006 general	Frank Wolf (R)	138,213	(57%)	($1,793,567)
	Judy Feder (D)	98,769	(41%)	($1,573,523)
	Other	4,152	(2%)	
2006 primary	Frank Wolf (R)	unopposed		
2004 general	Frank Wolf (R)	205,982	(64%)	($1,611,149)
	James Socas (D)	116,654	(36%)	($921,094)

Prior Winning Percentages: 2002 (72%); 2000 (84%); 1998 (72%); 1996 (72%); 1994 (87%); 1992 (64%); 1990 (62%); 1988 (68%); 1986 (60%); 1984 (63%); 1982 (53%); 1980 (51%)

The People		Race/Ethnic Origin	Ancestry	
Area size:	1,864 sq. mi.	77.2% White	German: 12.9%	Irish: 10.5%
Urban population:	83.3%	6.7% Black	English: 9.5%	
Rural population:	16.7%	6.6% Asian	**2004 Presidential Vote**	
Pop. 2000:	643,512	0.2% Native Am.	Bush (R) 182,210	(55%)
Pop. 2005 (est):	779,047	0.0% Hawaiian	Kerry (D) 145,741	(44%)
Median income:	$71,560	1.9% Two+ races	Other 2,736	(1%)
Poverty status:	4.4%	0.2% Other	**2000 Presidential Vote**	
Military veterans:	13.5%	7.1% Hispanic Origin	Bush (R) 148,211	(56%)
			Gore (D) 109,063	(41%)
			Other 8,106	(3%)
			Cook Partisan Voting Index: R + 5	

Occupation   Blue collar: 15.9%   White collar: 72.5%   Gray collar: 11.6%

When George Washington decided to place the new nation's capital on the Potomac just upriver from Mount Vernon, where the falls blocked navigation above the port of Georgetown, the land above the fall line on the Virginia side of the river—the rolling green Piedmont of northern Virginia and the fertile mountain-bound lands of the Shenandoah Valley—was buzzing with new settlers. They came up the Potomac and the runs (a Virginia word for small rivers) that flow into it and into the Valley from the great Wagon Road south from Pennsylvania, moving onto lands speculated on by Washington and his peers. During the Civil War, this was some of the most heavily contested land on the continent. The Piedmont, historian C. Vann Woodward wrote, "soaked up more of the blood, sweat and tears of American history than any other part of the country. It has bred more founding fathers, inspired more soaring hopes and ideals and witnessed more triumphs, failures, victories and lost causes than any other place in the country." But after the Civil War, the land was quiet. The frontier was very far to the west, and on these lands farmers quietly raised hay and grazed cattle and kept horses and hounds for fox hunting. During World War II and immediately after this was still open country: General George Marshall, driving from his office in the Pentagon to the old house he bought in the courthouse town of Leesburg 30 miles away, would pass a few gas stations and crossroads villages and hundreds of acres of farm fields. If he could make the trip today, he would see something very different. For metropolitan Washington has spread out into this bucolic land. There are still some horse farms in the Piedmont, long the first or second homes of some of the richest people in America, but they are increasingly flanked by subdivisions that sprout up in the fields overnight. Fairfax County, by some measures the highest-income county in the nation, had 98,000 people in 1950 and passed the 1 million mark in November 2003. But Fairfax's explosive growth stopped earlier; from 2000 to 2006, the Census Bureau estimates that a net 91,000 Americans moved out and a net 68,000 immigrants moved in. The explosive growth for the last decade or so has been in Loudoun County, just past Dulles Airport, the fourth fastest-growing county in the United States from 2000 to 2006, up 59% from 169,000 to 268,000. The Washington metropolitan area now extends past Fairfax and Loudoun and over the Blue Ridge into the Shenandoah Valley.

In the 1950s and 1960s, the Northern Virginia suburbs of Washington were just that: Bedroom communities where most workers headed into the District of Columbia and where one-third of them were employed by the federal government. Today Northern Virginia is an employment center and focus of innovation on its own. The Dulles Access Road, which ran through rural-looking territory 20 years ago, is now lined with office buildings holding high-tech firms and entrepreneurial startups. Along intersecting Route 28, crossing the Fairfax-Loudoun County line, are the headquarters of tech giants such as AOL and Telos Corp. The federal government is no longer the dominant employer here. Some of Northern Virginia's private sector is the spawn of government—"Beltway Bandits" and defense contractors—but this area has also become one of the nation's major centers of high-tech and telecommunications firms.

The 10th Congressional District covers much of Northern Virginia. It starts inside the Capital Beltway and includes most of McLean, home of much of Washington's political and lawyer-lobbyist elite, and goes beyond the Beltway to include woodsy Great Falls, Herndon and the Route 28 corridor around Dulles Airport. It includes Manassas, site of the Civil War's first battle and now of a spruced up Old Town, in Prince William County; all of Loudoun County, heavily built-up in the east with some still rural areas west of Leesburg; and the northern half of Fauquier County, which has limited development and is still mostly horse farms. It includes three counties in the northern end of the Shenandoah Valley, the country around Front Royal and Winchester. In 2004, 34% of the votes were cast in Fairfax County, 33% in Loudoun County, 11% in Prince William and Manassas, 5% in Fauquier and 18% in the Shenandoah Valley. Northern Virginia, home of more defense than domestic government agencies, was long more Republican than the Maryland suburbs, and Fairfax County in 2000 voted 49%-47% for George W. Bush. But since then Fairfax has changed and the Washington suburbs, apparently repelled by religious conservatives and rural-oriented candidates, have become more Democratic. Fairfax, running contrary to the national trend, voted 53%-46% for John Kerry in 2004; Bush carried the 10th District by 15% in 2000 but by only 11% in 2004. The 10th District voted for Republican Mark Earley over Democratic Governor Mark Warner in 2001, but in 2005 it preferred Democrat Tim Kaine to a Republican from far-off southwest Virginia. In 2006, the district narrowly voted for Democrat Jim Webb over Senator George Allen, 50%-49%.

The congressman from the 10th District is Frank Wolf, first elected in 1980. Wolf grew up in Philadelphia, went to law school at Georgetown, worked as a staffer on Capitol Hill and as an Interior Department appointee in the Nixon and Ford administrations and practiced law. In 1976 he ran for Congress and lost the Republican primary. In 1978 he won the nomination to run against Joseph Fisher, a liberal who had won the district (then not extending beyond Fairfax County) in 1974, and lost 53%-47%; in 1980 Wolf ran again and won 51%-49%. He started off, in the suburban Washington manner, maintaining an active constituency service operation and concentrating on issues affecting federal employees.

Over the years Wolf has come to specialize in three other areas—transportation, human rights and gambling. He used his seat on the Transportation Appropriations Subcommittee to work on projects in traffic-choked Northern Virginia. He has sought funding for a Metro rail link to Dulles Airport which, astonishingly, was not foreseen by the system's planners. Wolf has helped obtain funding for the project, $5 million in 2004 and $215 million in all; approval went ahead for preliminary engineering in July 2004. In 2006 Wolf persuaded Governor Tim Kaine to build the Tysons Corner portion above-ground rather than in a tunnel, for fear the increased cost would jeopardize the whole project. In June 2003 Wolf and Tom Davis asked for an additional outbound lane on I-66 in Arlington; in 2006 he got $2 million for the widening for a total of $32 million for the project. From 1995 to 2001, Wolf was chairman of the Transportation Appropriations subcommittee. He opposed earmarking proposals for specific congressmen, even as the chairman of the authorizing committee, Bud Shuster, made the practice an art form; Wolf thus lost much of the appropriators' leverage. He used the subcommittee chairmanship to put through a national .08% blood alcohol limit for drunk driving and to promote truck safety. In January 2001, House Republicans' six-year limits on chairmanships caught up with both Wolf and Shuster: Shuster resigned from Congress, while Wolf took the chairmanship of the Commerce, Justice and State Subcommittee.

In that capacity he has worked since the September 11 attacks to change the culture of the FBI. He assisted Director Robert Mueller's reorganization and called for sharing information across international lines. He opposed the bill to require destruction within 24 hours of gun buyer background checks because he thought the information should be available to terrorism investigators. He is now ranking minority member on the renamed State, Foreign Operations and Related Programs Subcommittee.

Wolf has been one of the House's leading crusaders for human rights and is co-chairman of the Congressional Human Rights Caucus. With Nancy Pelosi, he led the annual moves in the 1990s to withdraw normal trade relations with China because of human right violations; he strongly opposed normal trade relations in 2000, citing China's acts of jailing dissidents, killing Catholic priests, jailing evangelical pastors, persecuting Tibetan Buddhists and aiming missiles at the United States. In 1998 he sponsored the law setting up a religious freedom office in the State Department and requiring annual reports on religious freedom throughout the world. He traveled to El Salvador in 1982, Sudan in 1989, Romania in 1990, East Timor and Tibet in 1997 (only the second time a congressman has been there since the Chinese takeover in 1959), Sierra Leone in 1999 and Ethiopia in 2003, where he saw starvation as ghastly as he had in 1984. He has made five visits to Sudan and reported on how the Sudanese government blocked food shipments, bombed civilians and supported slave raids first in the South and then in Darfur. In September 2006 the House passed sanctions against Sudan because of its actions in Darfur; Wolf said, "Bold action is warranted. The United Nations is working to try to get desperately needed UN troops on the ground but the government of Sudan continues to reject this deployment. Targeted divestment from companies doing business in Sudan is an action that should be taken. The genocide in Sudan can be stopped and it is up to every American to do his or her part. The United States Congress and the president have called it genocide. Therefore anything that can be done should be done." In October 2005 he began criticizing lobbyists who worked for the governments of Sudan and Saudi Arabia and the Chinese oil company CNOC; he urged members to show caution in meeting with them. Pelosi in 2005 said he was "an unmatched leader in his commitment to human rights."

Wolf is probably Congress's leading opponent of gambling. He first proposed the National Gambling Impact Study Commission, passed in 1997; he hailed its call in June 1999 for a pause in granting licenses for new casinos and for federal oversight of Indian and Internet gambling. He has opposed federal recognition of Indian tribes in Virginia.

Wolf and Chris Shays have been the only two members of the House to travel widely in Iraq without Defense Department escorts. On his third visit, in September 2005, he was unable to get around without escorts; he was especially alarmed when he saw armed security guards in a maternity ward in Tikrit. On his return he wrote an article in the *Washington Post* calling for "fresh eyes" to look at policy, a bipartisan study group. He pressed this idea successfully first with Condoleezza Rice and then with Donald Rumsfeld and National Security Adviser Stephen Hadley; the result was the Iraq Study Group, headed by former Secretary of State James Baker and former Congressman Lee Hamilton. But many of the committee's recommendations, released in September, were rejected, some by the Bush administration, some by the new Democratic leaders in Congress.

With his seat on Appropriations, Wolf has funded many projects in the 10th District. In 2007, with Senator John Warner, he proposed a 175-mile Journey Through Hallowed Ground National Heritage Trail running from Gettysburg south to Charlottesville, passing by eight presidential houses, 15 national historic landmarks and many Revolutionary War and Civil War battlefields.

Wolf has generally been reelected by wide margins. In 2004 and 2006 he had more vocal challengers than usual. In 2004 James Socas, who made a fortune as an investment banker in San Francisco in the tech boom, moved to the Washington area to work as a Senate staffer and then ran against Wolf. Socas spent $921,000 in all, $499,000 of it his own money, on radio ads harshly attacking Wolf on transportation issues and charging that he was part of an "extremist" Christian group whose members "admire the strength and personal leadership" shown by Adolf Hitler, Vladimir Lenin, Ho Chi Minh and Osama bin Laden. Wolf spent $1.6 million on the race and pointed out that Socas had only recently moved to Northern Virginia and did not own a home in the district. Wolf won 64%-36%, a lesser margin than his 72%-28% win in 2002. In 2006 his opponent was Judith Feder, dean of Georgetown's Public Policy Institute, who worked at HHS during the Clinton administration. She spent $1.5 million, with help from Hillary Clinton and Edward Kennedy, and attacked Wolf for supporting George W. Bush on Iraq and for voting with the administration 90% of the time. Wolf spent $1.7 million and criticized her for backing the Clinton health care plan and said she had no transportation policy. Feder did not get the DCCC to put this district on its "Red to Blue" target list, but she trimmed Wolf's majority. He won 57%-41%; he carried every county and independent city, but won by only 53%-46% in Fairfax County. Feder has said she will run again in 2008.

ELEVENTH DISTRICT

Rep. Tom Davis (R)

Elected 1994, 7th term; b. Jan. 5, 1949, Minot, ND; home, Annandale; Amherst Col. B.A. 1971, U. of VA, J.D. 1975; Christian Scientist; married (Jeannemarie Devolites).

Military Career: Army, 1971-72; Army Reserves, 1972-79.

Elected Office: Fairfax Cnty. Bd. of Supervisors, 1979-94, Chmn., 1991-94.

Professional Career: Vice Pres. & Gen. Cnsl., PRC Inc., 1977-94.

DC Office: 2348 RHOB, 20515, 202-225-1492; Fax: 202-225-3071; Web site: tomdavis.house.gov.

District Offices: Annandale, 703-916-9610; Prince William, 703-590-4599.

Committees: *Homeland Security* (5th of 15 R): Management, Investigations & Oversight. *Oversight & Government Reform* (RMM of 18 R).

Group Ratings

	ADA	ACLU	AFS	LCV	ITIC	NTU	COC	ACU	CFG	FRC
2006	15	19	0	50	100	49	80	56	47	71
2005	5	—	0	33	—	49	85	57	44	62

National Journal Ratings

	2005 LIB — 2005 CONS		2006 LIB — 2006 CONS	
Economic	47%	— 53%	45%	— 55%
Social	45%	— 55%	47%	— 52%
Foreign	39%	— 60%	29%	— 71%

Key Votes of the 109th Congress

1. Estate Tax Repeal	Y	5. Limit Interstate Abortion	Y	9. Build Border Fence	Y
2. Limit CAFE Standards	N	6. Extend Patriot Act	Y	10. CAFTA	Y
3. FY06 Spending Curb	Y	7. Bar Same Sex Marriage	Y	11. Oppose Iraq Withdrawal	Y
4. Drilling in ANWR	N	8. Stem Cell Research $	Y	12. Detainee Tribunals	*

Election Results

2006 general	Tom Davis (R)	130,468	(55%)	($3,301,041)
	Andrew Hurst (D)	102,511	(44%)	($360,563)
	Other	2,301	(1%)	
2006 primary	Tom Davis (R)	unopposed		
2004 general	Tom Davis (R)	186,299	(60%)	($1,835,379)
	Ken Longmyer (D)	118,305	(38%)	($71,661)
	Other	4,629	(1%)	

Prior Winning Percentages: 2002 (83%); 2000 (62%); 1998 (82%); 1996 (64%); 1994 (53%)

The People		Race/Ethnic Origin	Ancestry	
Area size:	404 sq. mi.	66.8% White	German: 11.5%	Irish: 10.0%
Urban population:	95.9%	10.1% Black	English: 9.4%	
Rural population:	4.1%	10.9% Asian	**2004 Presidential Vote**	
Pop. 2000:	643,509	0.2% Native Am.	Bush (R) 161,104 (50%)	
Pop. 2005 (est):	724,285	0.1% Hawaiian	Kerry (D) 159,055 (49%)	
Median income:	$80,397	2.6% Two+ races	Other 2,561 (1%)	
Poverty status:	3.8%	0.2% Other	**2000 Presidential Vote**	
Military veterans:	15.9%	9.1% Hispanic Origin	Bush (R) 140,961 (52%)	
			Gore (D) 123,702 (45%)	
			Other 8,087 (3%)	
			Cook Partisan Voting Index: R + 1	

Occupation   Blue collar: 11.7%   White collar: 76.5%   Gray collar: 11.8%

When author and *Washington Post* reporter Joel Garreau coined the term "edge city" to describe the autonomous urban centers developing on the rims of some of the nation's oldest municipalities, his prime example was Tysons Corner, Virginia. Rising on a hill west of Washington, Tysons Corner was a back-country intersection 50 years ago and a junction of several suburban roads 30 years ago; today it is home to the largest concentration of office space to be found anywhere between Washington and Atlanta, with a modern skyline and busy multi-lane avenues that serve as arteries to the Capital Beltway. Fairfax County, which includes all of Tysons Corner, has changed just as dramatically since the end of World War II. At first only a few District of Columbia residents seeking breathing room in the suburbs trickled into Northern Virginia; initially they went to Arlington and Alexandria. But that trickle became a rush as young marrieds with large families and whites avoiding the increasingly high-crime District pushed farther out into Fairfax. Now Fairfax County is no longer Washington's country cousin. By 2000 it had 969,000 residents, nearly twice D.C.'s. 572,000; it reached 1 million by 2003. It had in 1999 the nation's highest median household income ($81,050), over half its residents have a bachelor's degree or more and 71% of its households have two or more vehicles. Fairfax County is taking on most of the aspects of a city, with new high-density cluster developments around Metro stops and plenty of immigrants, from Koreans and Vietnamese to Afghanis and Africans, and with growth slowing because most of its land has been developed. There is even faster growth to the west in Loudoun County and to the south in Prince William County, growth not only in housing but in jobs; in 2003-04, the number of jobs in Prince William grew 8%, the most of any county in the nation, and not far behind were Loudoun (5.5%) and Fairfax (4.2%). Prince William is growing more affluent too, as megahouse subdivisions spring up in the western part of the county its median household income rose to Fairfax's high level.

The 11th Congressional District of Virginia consists of much of Fairfax County and most of Prince William County. The district straddles the Capital Beltway and includes Tysons Corner. Inside the Beltway is Annandale; beyond are Vienna, Fairfax, much of Springfield, Burke, Clifton, Centreville, part of Mount Vernon. In Prince William County it includes Woodbridge and Dale City and stretches west to Haymarket. This is a cosmopolitan district: 10% black, 9% Hispanic, 11% Asian in 2000; some 25% of residents speak a language other than English at home. The district is made up largely of two-income families, many with at least one spouse employed in one of the many divisions of high-tech companies that dot Fairfax County. The district was first created in 1991, after Virginia got a new seat in the 1990 Census. It was originally designed to be equally divided between the parties, and within its 1991 boundaries it voted 43%-42% for George H.W. Bush in 1992, 49%-47% for Bill Clinton in 1996 and 49%-47% for Al Gore in 2000. In its post-redistricting 2002 form, the district voted 52%-45% for George W. Bush in 2000 but only 50%-49% for him in 2004. In 2006, Democrat Jim Webb won 55%-44% here over Senator George Allen.

The congressman from the 11th District is Tom Davis, a Republican first elected in 1994. Davis was born in Minot, North Dakota, grew up in Northern Virginia, and was always interested in politics; by seventh grade he could name every member of the House. He got a job as a Senate page and was president of his class at the Capitol Page School; he was a roommate of David Eisenhower at Amherst College, where almost everyone else was a Democrat or something further left; he served on active duty in the Army before earning a law degree. He practiced law in Northern Virginia and was general counsel to computer services firm PRC. In 1979 he was elected to the Fairfax County Board of Supervisors, a high visibility position. In 1991 he was elected board chairman, something in the nature of a mayor. In 1994 Davis ran for the 11th District seat against Democrat Leslie Byrne, who had won 50%-45% in 1992. Byrne had voted solidly for Clinton administration positions and called for discipline against members of the Democratic Caucus who did not; she had strong support from labor and feminist groups and spent $1.1 million. But Davis raised and spent even more, $1.4 million. He won 53%-45%.

As soon as he arrived on Capitol Hill, Davis was handed by Speaker Newt Gingrich one of the hottest potatoes of the new Republican Congress: Dealing with the affairs of the troubled District of Columbia government and its reelected mayor, Marion Barry. As chairman of the Government Reform and Oversight Committee's D.C. Subcommittee, Davis first rejected Barry's request for massive federal aid, and worked closely with Gingrich and D.C. Delegate Eleanor Holmes Norton to cut District spending. Together they passed a law establishing a five-member control board to oversee the local government. He opposed the appropriators' detailed policy prescription as micromanagement, but went along with giving power over nine agencies to the control board. In 1999 Davis and Norton speedily passed a bill restoring full management powers to the District and its new mayor, Anthony Williams.

In 2003 Davis became chairman of the Government Reform Committee and abolished the D.C. subcommittee, allowing him to take the lead on District issues himself. He pushed through, against opposition from Norton and teachers' unions, but with the support of Mayor Williams and D.C. school board head Peggy Cooper Cafritz, a voucher program for the District of Columbia. Davis managed to get the House to agree to eliminate riders to D.C. appropriations bills and let Government Reform oversee its activities; he opposed the House's symbolic repeal of the District's gun laws (the Senate didn't go along) as a "dangerous assault on home rule." He was less successful in his attempt to give the District voting representation in the House. His idea was to add two members, one for the District and the other for the state entitled under the statutory formula to the 436th seat in the House, which after the 2000 Census happened to be Utah; that pretty much guaranteed that the District's Democrat would be balanced by a Utah Republican. But Speaker Dennis Hastert said, "Davis floats things from time to time," and Majority Leader Tom DeLay said, "It would require a constitutional amendment." Norton, in favor of full House and Senate representation, initially declined to endorse it, and other Democrats feared the Utah legislature would produce a redistricting that would threaten the state's single Democrat, Jim Matheson. Davis continued to push: He got a legal opinion from conservative scholars that the proposal was constitutional, and Matheson won reelection by a wide enough margin in a Republican-leaning district to suggest he was impervious to challenge. The Government Reform committee unanimously approved his bill in May 2006, but Republican leaders refused to schedule floor action.

Despite Republican resistance, Davis launched some oversight of the Bush administration, including limited review of the Iraq war. Following Hurricane Katrina, he issued a thorough and scathing account of the administration's botched response. "Katrina was a failure of initiative. It was a failure of leadership," said the report. One notable aspect of that review was the involvement of some Democrats, despite objections to their participation from then-Minority Leader Nancy Pelosi. The committee also held well-publicized hearings in March 2005 that spotlighted steroid abuse in major league baseball. Davis scored a major legislative accomplishment in the 2006 lame-duck session, when Congress finally enacted a wide-ranging overhaul of the postal system.

Davis is a political buff with a detailed knowledge of political statistics across the country. When the chairmanship of the NRCC became an elective post in 1998, he ran against incumbent John Linder and won 130-77. He raised and spent $1 million on 1999 state legislative races in Virginia, in which Republicans captured both houses and won control of redistricting; within a few months conservative incumbent Congressman Virgil Goode left the Democratic Party and announced he would caucus with Republicans and conservative Democrat Owen Pickett retired—a quick two-seat gain. In the 1999-2000 cycle Davis spotted open seats that had long voted Democratic but where conservative non-economic issues helped Republicans—Pennsylvania's 4th, West Virginia's 2d, Missouri's 6th, Michigan's 8th, Virginia's 2d—and won them all. Against party-switcher Michael Forbes in New York's 1st, he spent money on billboards thanking him for his solid support of Newt Gingrich and the Contract With America; Forbes was upset in the September Democratic primary, and the seat went Republican in November. He spotted the weakness of 20-year incumbent Democrat Sam Gejdenson in Connecticut's 2d, which led to another gain. The Republican nomination in Florida's open 8th District was not determined until the October runoff; but for two months before the NRCC spent heavily on ads attacking the Democratic nominee, who lost 51%-49%. Only four Republican incumbents lost, three in California and one in Arkansas. In a year when Senate Republicans lost five seats and the chamber tied at 50-50, the House GOP lost only two and emerged with 221 seats.

Davis was reelected campaign committee chairman in November 2000. Republicans far outraised Democrats in the 2001-02 cycle, and once again Davis did a fine job of targeting vulnerable seats, but his most valuable work was on redistricting. Not since the death of California Democrat Phillip Burton in 1983 has a member of Congress with such a detailed knowledge of the political demography of the entire country taken such a lead role in redistricting. Davis and White House political strategist Karl Rove persuaded the chief Democratic redistricter in California, Michael Berman, brother of Congressman Howard Berman, to settle for a plan that gave the state's one new seat to Democrats but otherwise maintained the status quo. After Democrats put through an aggressively partisan plan in Georgia, Davis worked to see that Republicans in Pennsylvania put through a similarly aggressive plan. As a result, Republicans gained seats in a state that lost two seats while Democrats failed to achieve the gains they expected in a state that gained two seats. In an impressive performance, House Republicans increased their majority to 229-205.

In selecting Davis for the Government Reform Committee chairmanship, though he was only ninth in seniority, Republican leaders rewarded his work as campaign chairman and recognized his expertise on civil service and procurement law. He has long been attentive to federal employee issues, a prerequisite for representing a district with so many federal workers. He opposed the Contract with America tax cut in 1995 because it would have required higher pension payments by federal employees. He has pushed successfully for civilian employees to get the same percentage pay increase as the military and to have better dental and vision benefits offered on federal employees' health insurance policies; when the Medicare/prescription drug bill was pending, he sponsored a guarantee that federal retirees would get the same prescription drug benefits as federal employees. Against the opposition of federal employees unions, Davis has backed the Bush administration policies for competitive sourcing in the Defense and Homeland Security Departments, with access to the GAO's protest forums, but he accepted not having these procedures in the new national intelligence director's office.

Fairfax County has been trending Democratic, but Davis so far has escaped political trouble in the 11th District. In 2004, against an underfunded Democrat, he won 60%-38%, even as George W. Bush became the first Republican presidential candidate to lose Fairfax since 1964. As Davis said, "The city is moving out to the suburbs. We all recognized that Fairfax was going to turn. How big it would turn was unclear." In 2006, his victory margin was cut to 55%-44% against little-known Democratic challenger Andrew Hurst, a Washington lawyer who sought to link Davis to the unpopular president. In Prince William County, which cast 28% of the vote, Davis led 57%-42%.

Davis has made no secret that he has statewide ambitions and the opportunity presented itself when Senator John Warner announced in late August 2007 that he would not seek reelection. Davis was widely expected to run for the seat in 2008, though his prospects may have been clouded by his strong support in 2004 for Governor Mark Warner's tax increases. A minority of House of Delegates Republicans as well as almost all Senate Republicans provided critical support for the increases; one of them was Davis's wife, state Senator Jeannemarie Devolites Davis, who is a possible lieutenant governor candidate in 2009. Winning Warner's Senate seat will be a heavy lift even for a highly-skilled pol like Davis. In September 2007, it seemed likely that he would have to defeat two former governors: Republican Jim Gilmore and Democrat Mark Warner. Davis has conceded that Republicans will face a struggle to hold his House seat if it becomes open.

★ WASHINGTON ★

W ashington state, for a moment in the late 1990s, seemed to be the national trend-setter. From Starbucks coffee to grunge music, from America's leading exporter, Boeing, to the world's leading software maker, Microsoft, to America's most visible dot-com, amazon.com, Washington seemed to be on the cutting edge of innovation. What was for many years an odd far corner of America had become a model for the rest of the nation. An unusual environment and human creativity combined to produce these achievements: Seattle's cold misty air and 225 overcast days a year stimulate the appetite for strong aromatic coffee, and the shapeless blue jeans and sweatshirts worn year-round in this moist climate by professionals and teenagers alike created a trend made famous by Nirvana and Soundgarden and other grunge artists. Boeing's airframe business took off during World War II because the Pacific Northwest's abundant hydroelectric power made cheap aluminum possible, and the boom in air travel in the 1980s and 1990s kept Boeing's huge assembly lines humming. Microsoft, founded by the usually tie-less and tousle-haired Bill Gates and based in

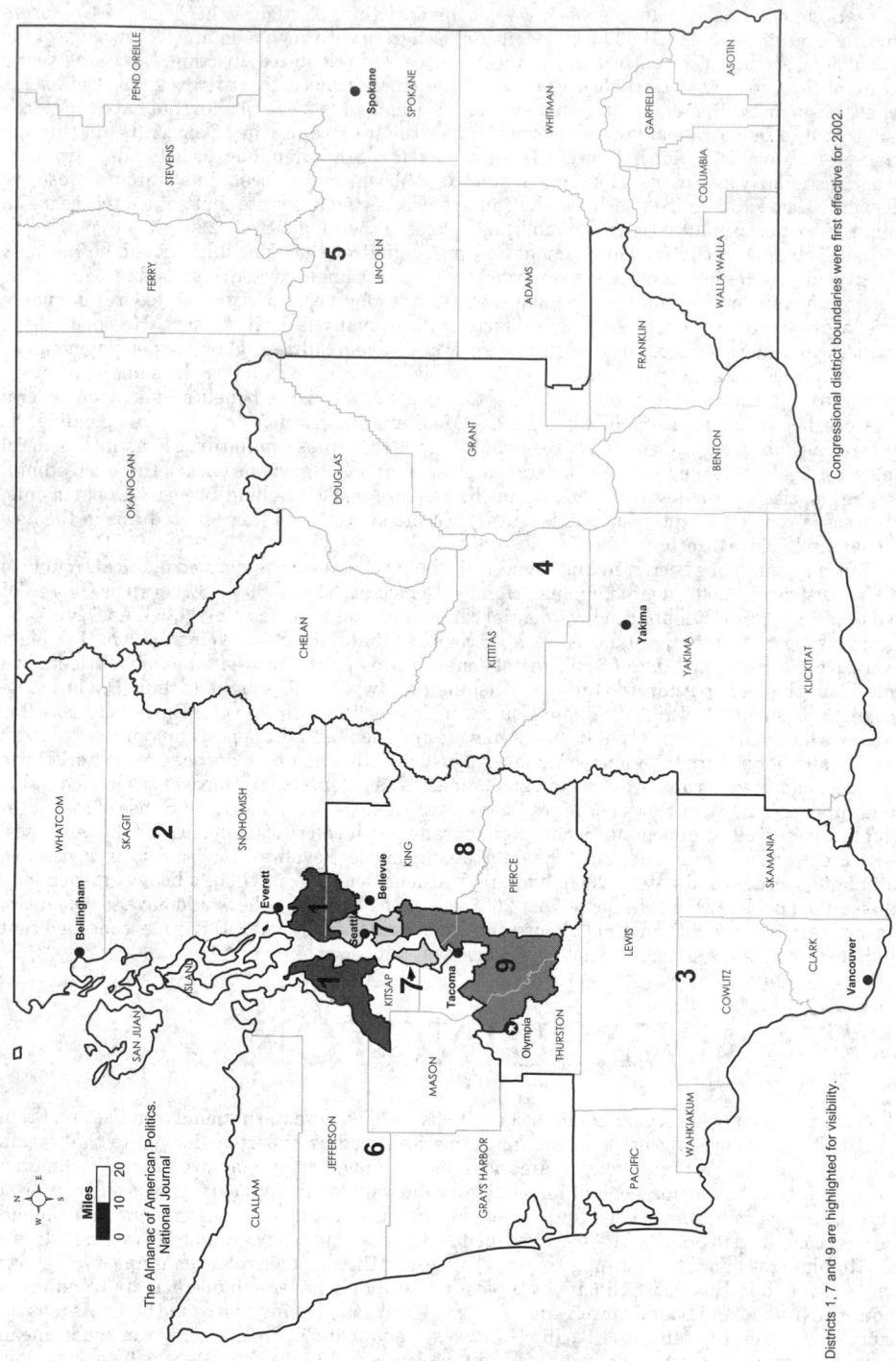

The Almanac of American Politics.
National Journal

Congressional district boundaries were first effective for 2002.

Districts 1, 7 and 9 are highlighted for visibility.

Redmond, across Lake Washington from Seattle, became one of America's great success stories as its software became embedded in the vast majority of the world's computers. With flannel shirts and umbrellas, blue-collar types working off hangovers as if in a Raymond Carver story, and professionals relaxing on woodsy acreage, Washington set a tone for the late 1990s, a style plainly Middle American but with attitude, an ordinariness so hip it is no longer ordinary. As the end of the century approached, Washington was a commonwealth of nearly 6 million people, economically booming, pleased to the point of smugness with its physical environment and lifestyle. Since that high point Washington has had its woes, and has bounced back again, perhaps not so fashionable as it was for a moment, but with strengths that have proved to be more durable than fashion.

Washington is a state which is not much more than a century old, one which in the two decades after statehood in 1889 built a new civilization, as transcontinental railroads reached the great ports of Puget Sound, the wheat-processing city of Spokane inland, orchard towns and fishing ports and lumber settlements. Shielded from the storms of the Pacific by the Olympic Mountains and the Sound, Seattle quickly became a serious American city, a lusty town full of lumbermen and railroad workers. When gold was struck in the Klondike and Alaska, Seattle became a metropolis of miners, prospectors and get-rich-quick operators, the site of the original "Skid Road" (skid row is a corruption propagated by a 1937 magazine article), where logs were rolled downhill to the port; today it's the focus of the restored Pioneer Square area. Thriving young Seattle had a turbulent class-warfare politics in the years before World War I, pitting the Industrial Workers of the World (the IWW, or Wobblies) against city business and civic leaders; the businessmen, after some violence, prevailed. Adding to the area's distinctiveness was its large number of Scandinavian immigrants, with their favorable views of cooperative enterprises and government ownership.

Over time, Washington was transformed by a series of national decisions that set its course for decades. One was government development of hydroelectric power. The Columbia River and its tributary, the Snake, falling thousands of feet in a relatively short distance, had far greater hydroelectric potential than any other American river system, and Franklin D. Roosevelt, who grew up in a great river valley, was always interested in these river valley projects. In 1937 Bonneville Dam was completed on the lower Columbia; in 1940 Grand Coulee Dam, the largest man-made structure in the world at the time and still the nation's single greatest producer of electricity, was opened where the Columbia cuts through the arid, surrealistically contoured plains of eastern Washington. Washington proved hospitable to the industrial union movement of the 1930s and became one of the nation's most heavily unionized states. When war came, Washington's hydroelectric power—the cheapest electricity in the country—made it the natural site for huge aluminum production plants, which required vast amounts of electricity, and the Seattle area became the home not only of shipbuilders, but of what became the biggest aircraft manufacturer in the country, Boeing, founded in 1916 by William Boeing after he bought a shipyard on the Duwamish River and turned it into an airplane factory. After the war, the Hanford plant on the Columbia was one of the government's main nuclear weapons manufacturing sites. Cheap power, aluminum, aircraft, nuclear weapons and high unionized wages: these became Washington's economic foundations in the post-World War II years.

Today's Washington lives less off the brawn of hydroelectric power and rail and ship tonnage and more off the brains that made Boeing the world leader in aircraft and Microsoft the world leader in software. Yet there has been some trouble in this misty paradise. A turning point came in December 1999, when Seattle hosted a meeting of the World Trade Organization. This was supposed to be an occasion for the city to shine in the international spotlight. But 50,000 demonstrators took control of the streets, smashing Starbucks' windows and preventing leaders from Bill Clinton on down from attending meetings; Seattle's police chief and mayor did little to stop the violence. Seattle became a symbol of mindless protest and lawless violence. The image was reinforced in the Mardi Gras riots in February 2001; voters responded, and Mayor Paul Schell carried only 22% of the vote in the September 2001 primary to become the first Seattle mayor in 45 years to lose a reelection bid. Washington was hurt also by the dot-com bust; the high-tech industry boomed as businesses retooled to avoid Y2K problems, then it suddenly became apparent that customers had all the technology they needed, the stock market started tanking in March 2000, and thousands of dot-coms were taken down. Microsoft was sued by the Justice Department's Antitrust Division in 1998; in March 2001, Boeing's chairman announced that the firm's headquarters would be moved out of Seattle, to Chicago. Then, after September 11, the airline industry was hard hit and cut back its orders; Boeing cut back its Seattle area employment from 102,000 in 1997 to 62,000 in 2002. Boeing continued to suffer from the airline recession, competition from Airbus and congressional opposition to the proposal to lease KC-767 aerial refueling tankers, a proposal that failed amid revelations of corruption. Recovery from the recession was slow: Washington's unemployment for a couple of years was the second highest in the nation, after Oregon's, and the state lost 84,000 jobs between 2001 and 2003. Amid this turbulence, the fundamentals undergirding Washington's affluent life seemed threatened. Proposals by Clinton administration officials to breach the dams on the Snake River threatened to reduce hydroelectric supply and to choke the agriculture of eastern Washington just as the court decision to protect the endangered spotted owl largely shut down Washington's logging industry in the early 1990s. Light snowpacks and melting glaciers threatened to reduce the supply of hydroelectric power even as demand from energy-starved California seemed likely to draw down supply. The Hanford Nuclear Reservation, which produced plutonium for the military, for years leaked radioactive waste and has been in the midst of a multiyear cleanup costing billions a year.

All these problems may turn out to be no more than footnotes to what is mainly a story of success. Look at a map that shows elevation of mountains and density of population. On both sides of the Pacific, vast numbers of people are squeezed into small margins of level land between steeply rising volcanic mountains and the sea, or tucked into valleys. These islands of settlement are surrounded by vast wildernesses—desert and mountains, open sea and Arctic lands. Yet the inhabitants of these pockets of the Pacific Rim in the last three decades have produced more economic growth than anywhere else in the world and, if there are occasional slumps, the Pacific Rim has always come surging back. And, as it has turned out, Washington's laid-back tolerance was not so excessive as to undermine its impressive achievements. Boeing overcame the 767 scandal and its 787 Dreamliner has clobbered Airbus's troubled A350 in advanced orders; the new aircraft was unveiled to the public in July 2007 at the final assembly factory in Everett. Microsoft has survived the federal antitrust case and continues to expand its 35,000-employee Redmond campus. Starbucks, with 10,000 stores in the U.S. in May 2007, has proved to be the fastest growing retail business of all time; there is presumably some limit to the number of people willing to spend $4 on a cup of coffee, but it hasn't been reached yet. Hydroelectric power may have reached its capacity, but in 2006 Washington ranked second in the amount of generated wind power added in the past year.

Politically, Washington, with its Scandinavian and labor union heritage, was in the 1930s one of the most Democratic northern states: Franklin D. Roosevelt's campaign manager James Farley used to refer to "the 47 states and the Soviet of Washington." Its mainstream Democrats—notably Warren Magnuson and Henry Jackson, who represented the state in Congress for a total of 87 years—believed in an active and compassionate federal government that built dams, aluminum plants and the Hanford Works at home, and an internationalist, anti-Communist foreign policy abroad. Their political strength was built on a blue-collar base, augmented by the respect big businesses had for their political clout. Today, the fulcrum of the electorate has moved from blue collar to white collar, from economic class warfare to cultural wars, with the balance favoring the Democrats. In presidential races, Washington leans Democratic. Washington's governor and both of its senators are all Democrats and all women. Democrats hold six of Washington's nine U.S. House seats. Four different Democrats have held the governorship since 1984, but the party almost lost it in 2004. The official count, after many shenanigans and legal challenges, declared that Christine Gregoire had been elected governor by 129 votes, and while Republicans lost control of the state Senate, they gained the attorney general's office. But in 2006 the pendulum swung hard in favor of the Democrats. They nearly captured the 8th District U.S. House seat, which would have eliminated Republican representation west of the Cascades, and Senator Maria Cantwell was reelected by a solid 57%-40% margin, sweeping western Washington and carrying Spokane County in the east as well. Democrats increased their majorities from 3 to 15 in the state Senate and from 14 to 28 in the state House. Gregoire attributed these gains to the Democrats' moderation, their resolution of a water dispute in eastern Washington, passage of tax relief for farmers and timber sellers, a compromise settlement on unemployment insurance and tough penalties for sex offenders. But with bigger margins, some Democrats and their union allies are pressing for big public sector pay increases and state health care funding.

The political lines are fairly clear. The central city of Seattle is increasingly the liberal bastion, the upscale suburbs have been trending Democratic, while old blue-collar lumber country strongholds have soured on many Democrats. Seattle's King County, by a wide margin the most affluent county in the state, is also its liberal stronghold: 65% for John Kerry in 2004, with a popular vote margin of 279,000, the sixth highest of any county in the nation. Republicans run best in the arid country east of the Cascades with far lower income levels. This is a marchland between the culturally liberal Pacific Rim and the culturally conservative Rocky Mountains: it voted 60% for George W. Bush in 2004. Long-range demographic trends may favor Republicans: King County grew only 5% from 2000 to 2006, and the fastest-growing counties were in the Republican Tri-Cities area and in increasingly conservative Clark County north of Portland. (Washington has no income tax and Oregon no sales tax, so you can avoid both taxes by living in Clark County and shopping across the line in Oregon.) But Democrats' advantage is so large at this point that it seems impervious to incremental demographic change.

A footnote on Washington's primaries. Washington does not have party registration, and from 1935 to 2000 Washington allowed voters to choose candidates of various parties in its primaries; the top Democrat and top Republican in each constituency was deemed nominated, and the percentage of total votes won by incumbents in September primaries was often a harbinger of their performance in the November general election. But in 2000 the U.S. Supreme Court by a 7–2 vote threw out a similar California primary system, and in 2003 a federal appeals court ruled Washington's invalid. The Supreme Court's theory was that this arrangement somehow violates the political parties' right to self-expression, which seems to mean the exclusion of voters that party leaders don't want voting in their primaries; why the parties' right to self-expression takes precedence over the voters' right to self-expression seems unclear. In 2004, Washington voters passed Initiative 872, which allows voters to select a candidate from either party, with the two candidates with the most votes moving to the general election, regardless of party. In anticipation of the 2005 off-year primaries, both parties held nominating conventions to avoid application of 872; in July 2005, a federal appeals court ruled it invalid. That seemed to be the end of that, but in February 2007 the Supreme Court agreed to hear a case on the validity of 872. Had the court perhaps changed its mind?

The People		Race/Ethnic Origin			Military veterans: 670,628 (15.3%)	
Pop. 2006 (est):	6,395,798	4,652,490	78.9%	White	WWII: 16.3%	Korea: 11.4%
Pop. 2000:	5,894,121	184,631	3.1%	Black	Vietnam: 35.9%	Gulf War: 12.2%
Pop. 1990:	4,866,692	319,401	5.4%	Asian	**Most populous cities (2006):**	
Change 1990-2000:	Up 21.1%	85,396	1.4%	Native Am.	1. Seattle	582,454
% of U.S. total:	2.1%	22,779	0.4%	Hawaiian	2. Spokane	198,081
Pop. rank:	15th of 50	175,926	3.0%	Two+ races	3. Tacoma	196,532
Area size:	71,300 sq. mi.	11,989	0.2%	Other	4. Vancouver	158,855
State Native:	47.2%	441,509	7.5%	Hisp. Origin	5. Bellevue	118,186
Non-citizen:	6.1%	**Ancestry**				
Language		German: 13.7%		English: 8.8%	Urban population: 82.0%	
English: 84.2%	Spanish: 6.1%	Irish: 8.3%		Norwegian: 4.6%	Rural population: 18.0%	
Asian: 4.6%		USA: 3.9%				

Education		Work Sector		Legislature	
H.S. Grad:	87.1%	Private: 76.1%	Govt: 16.5%	Senate	32 D 17 R
College Grad:	27.7%	Self: 7.2%	Family: 0.3%	House	63 D 35 R
Industry		Unemployment: 6.1%		Legislative Term Limits: No	
Agri: 2.5%	Con: 7.0%	**Household Income**		**Registered Voters**	
Fin: 6.1%	Info: 3.4%	<15k: 13.1%	15-35k: 24.2%	No party registration	
Mfg: 17.9%	Prof: 29.1%	35-50k: 17.1%	50-100k: 33.0%		
Public: 5.0%	Trade: 16.2%	100-150k: 8.3%	>150k: 4.3%		
Other: 12.8%		Median: $45,776			
Occupation		Poverty status: 10.6%			
Blue collar: 22.1%	White collar: 61.4%	**Home Value**			
Gray collar: 16.4%		<50k: 5.8% 50-100k: 15.2% 100-200k: 45.7% 200-300k: 19.3%			
		300-500k: 10.1% >500k: 3.9% Median: $158,800			

Presidential politics   For three decades Washington was one of the most contrarian states in presidential politics, voting for losers Richard Nixon in 1960, Hubert Humphrey in 1968, Gerald Ford in 1976 and Michael Dukakis in 1988. In the 1990s it was in sync with the nation, voting for Bill Clinton twice, but now Washington seems contrarian once again. It gave Al Gore a 50%-45% victory in 2000 and John Kerry a victory by the wider margin of 53%-46% in 2004. Both times the winning margin and more came from just one of the state's nine congressional districts, the 7th District which includes all of Seattle and close-in suburbs to the north and south in King County. Gore carried the 7th District 72%-21%; Kerry

2004 Presidential Vote		
Kerry (D)	1,510,201	(53%)
Bush (R)	1,304,894	(46%)
Nader (I)	23,283	(1%)
Other	20,706	(1%)
2000 Presidential Vote		
Gore (D)	1,247,652	(50%)
Bush (R)	1,108,864	(45%)
Nader (Green)	103,002	(4%)
Other	27,915	(1%)

carried it 79%-19%. Politics in Washington was once almost class warfare, with union members favoring Democrats and more comfortable folk Republicans. No more. John Kerry ran better—a whopping 63%—among voters with incomes over $100,000 than those below, while voters in union households (27% of the total; in the 1960s it was more like 50%) gave Kerry only 55% of their votes. Kerry carried voters with college degrees; George W. Bush carried those without. Those who identified their religion as "other" or none were 25% of the electorate, an unusually high percentage, and they voted 72% for Kerry. A 53% majority of voters attend religious services never or only a few times a year, and they voted 65% for Kerry. Only 35% attend religious services weekly or more often, and they voted 64% for Bush.

Washington switched from a caucus system to primaries in 1992, after Pat Robertson won among Republicans and Jesse Jackson finished a solid second among Democrats in 1988. But Democrats have never chosen to allocate delegates according to the results, preferring to use the results from party caucuses for that. In 2000 Bill Bradley, having lost in Iowa and New Hampshire and having no other states to contest for five weeks, came into Washington for the February 29 contest. To no avail; Al Gore won by about 2–1. George W. Bush beat John McCain by a razor-thin margin in a contest that counted a little toward delegate selection. In 2004 Washington's Democrats held caucuses February 7, which counted for nothing and got little notice.

In early 2007 the parties were divided on what to do in 2008. Republicans and Secretary of State Sam Reed wanted to hold a primary on February 5 that would count toward electing delegates; Democrats were divided, with many for eliminating the primary. In June, a bipartisan panel of state lawmakers and party leaders came to agreement and voted unanimously to hold the primary on February 19, 2008, in the hopes of being early enough to be relevant but not so early as to get lost amid the many states holding February 5 contests. Both parties also will hold caucuses on February 9. Republicans will allocate roughly half of their delegates based on primary results; Democrats will only use caucus results to allocate delegates.

Congressional districting   In 1983 Washington voters approved a constitutional amendment which provided that congressional and legislative districts be drawn by a bipartisan commission; the lines can be changed by a two-thirds vote of the legislature. If the commission is deadlocked, the issue goes to the state Supreme Court. In 1991 the commission created four districts that were pretty evenly divided between the parties: only three of the nine districts were won by the same party in the five elections during which the lines were in effect. The problem was that even minor alterations in the closely divided districts—the 1st, 2d, 3d and 9th—can make changes that will turn out to be of partisan significance at some point in the next decade. But 6th District Democrat Norm Dicks and then-8th District Republican Jennifer Dunn pressed the commissioners to compromise. Just before the constitutional deadline expired on January 1, 2002, they reached agreement. Attorney General Christine Gregoire pushed the legislature to change the statutory December 15 deadline to eliminate any question of the plan's legality; the legislators were happy to do so and made no changes in the plan. This 2002 plan followed pretty

110th Congress Lineup
6 D   3 R

109th Congress Lineup
6 D   3 R

closely the lines drawn in 1991. The Washington plan has been lauded by many for taking partisanship out of redistricting and for creating more districts that both parties can win. But in Washington, where the commission is not bound by the mathematical requirements that in Iowa have resulted in districts not tailored to incumbents, incumbent protection has been the result.

Governor

Christine Gregoire (D)

Elected 2004, term expires Jan. 2009, 1st term; b. Mar. 24, 1947, Adrian, MI; home, Olympia; U. of WA, B.A. 1969; Gonzaga U., J.D. 1977; Catholic; married (Mike).

Elected Office: WA Atty. Gen., 1992-2004.

Professional Career: Dep. Atty. Gen., 1982-88; Dir., WA Dept. of Ecology, 1988-92.

Office: P.O. Box 40002, Olympia, 98504, 360-902-4111; Fax: 360-753-4110; Web site: www.governor.wa.gov.

Election Results

2004 general	Christine Gregoire (D)	1,373,361	(49%)
	Dino Rossi (R)	1,373,232	(49%)
	Other	63,465	(2%)
2004 primary	Christine Gregoire (D)	504,018	(66%)
	Ron Sims (D)	228,306	(30%)
	Other	35,742	(5%)
2000 general	Gary Locke (D)	1,441,973	(58%)
	John Eric Carlson (R)	980,060	(40%)
	Other	47,819	(2%)

Christine Gregoire is a Democrat elected governor in 2004 in the closest race in Washington history. She was born in Adrian, Michigan, but grew up on a small farm in Auburn, Washington, just south of Seattle. Her mother was a short-order cook who moved west to escape an abusive husband. Christine Gregoire graduated from the University of Washington and, unable to find a teaching position, took a job as a clerk-typist for the state parole board. She worked as a welfare caseworker, attended law school at Gonzaga University in eastern Washington, then worked for Republican Senator Slade Gorton in his Spokane office. There she drew the attention of another Republican, Attorney General Ken Eikenberry, who hired her as a deputy attorney general in Olympia. In 1988, she was Democratic Governor Booth Gardner's unexpected choice to head the Department of Ecology. In 1992, nationally a good year for women candidates but especially good in Washington where Patty Murray was elected to the Senate and Maria Cantwell to the House, Gregoire ran as a Democrat and won election as attorney general.

She served three terms in that office and won national headlines as the lead negotiator in 1998 for the 46-state, $206 billion settlement with the tobacco industry. With high name recognition from her role in the tobacco settlement and three successful statewide races behind her, Gregoire came to be viewed as a governor-in-waiting. When Democrat Gary Locke, elected governor in 1996 and 2000, announced in 2003 that he would not run for a third term, Gregoire became the frontrunner to succeed him. But Gregoire almost didn't run. One week after announcing her candidacy in July 2003, her doctors told her she needed a mastectomy to remove an early form of breast cancer. She considered dropping out of the race, sought counsel from Janet Napolitano and Heidi Heitkamp, both former attorneys general and breast cancer survivors who had run for governor (Napolitano won in Arizona in 2002; Heitkamp lost in North Dakota in 2000), decided to have the surgery and then returned to the campaign trail a month later.

Gregoire figured to have tough primary opposition from former state senator and state Supreme Court Justice Phil Talmadge and from King County Executive Ron Sims in the September 14 primary. But Talmadge dropped out of the race in April for health reasons. That left Sims, who ran to Gregoire's left and whose political base was in the state's most populous county and biggest media market.

Washington's economy was hard-hit in the economic downturn; the industries that are central to the state economy—high-tech, aviation and natural resources—were slow to recover, leaving the state with the nation's second-highest unemployment rate in 2003. That made jobs, education, taxes and the environment the staples of the primary debate until August, when it was reported that Gregoire's sorority at the University of Washington excluded African-Americans. The Gregoire campaign charged that the Sims campaign was behind the story; Sims, who would have been the state's first African-American governor, denied being the source. Local black leaders harshly criticized Gregoire. She responded angrily to the charges of racism and claimed that she fought within the system to eliminate the sorority's exclusionary policy. Voters didn't seem to hold it against her: She defeated Sims 66%-30%, carrying every county in the state including Seattle's King County, which she won 59%-38%.

Republicans nominated state Senator Dino Rossi, a former Senate Ways and Means Committee chairman from the Seattle suburbs, who billed himself as a "fiscal conservative with a social conscience." He credited his outlook to a humble background: The grandson of an Italian immigrant coal miner, he grew up in a family that endured financial hardship while living through the alcoholism of his mother. Rossi, the only serious candidate in the Republican primary, had been personally lobbied to run by George W. Bush in 2003 when the state party was scrambling to come up with a viable candidate.

Rossi campaigned as a moderate and as an agent of change in a state where Republicans had not won the governorship since John Spellman's victory in 1980. He portrayed Gregoire as the representative of "a failed status quo." Business interests lined up with Rossi, a successful commercial real estate investor who said he wanted to change the culture in Olympia to a "free enterprise model" and promised to create a cabinet-level office of regulatory reform. Gregoire, who ran as a fiscal moderate, received strong support from the state's largest labor unions. Rossi's support for a constitutional amendment banning same-sex marriage and his opposition to abortion spurred abortion rights groups to donate heavily to Gregoire's campaign and led Democrats to characterize him as a right-wing extremist – the same tactic that worked against the last two Republican nominees. But as a youthful suburban legislator with four children who focused on economic, rather than social, issues, Rossi was not so easily caricatured.

The 2003 budget that he helped draft as Ways and Means chairman was a matter of contention. With the state facing a $2.6 billion deficit, Rossi won praise for brokering a deal with Locke that did not raise taxes or inflict severe cuts to social programs. Gregoire claimed the budget favored business interests over funding for social programs. Rossi framed it as a move designed to make the state more business-friendly. Each continued to take aim at the other's record in office, with Gregoire accusing Rossi of voting to cut health care benefits for children and Rossi lobbing charges about Gregoire's stewardship as attorney general.

By October, the race seemed to be moving in Gregoire's direction. She had built a double-digit lead in most public polls and national Republicans, who early in the campaign had high hopes for the ticket of Bush, Senate nominee George Nethercutt and Rossi, began to write off the state as a lost cause. But Rossi's change theme gained traction in the final weeks against Gregoire, a cautious candidate who had spent nearly her entire career in one government job or another.

Washington is one of just two states that allow absentee ballots to be postmarked as late as Election Day. So it took nearly three weeks for all the votes to be counted. Rossi was up by about 1,000 votes the morning after the election, but by evening Gregoire was ahead by 14,000. The lead see-sawed for days and in the ensuing weeks the election began to take on an eerie, Florida-like hue, replete with protesters, legal challenges, allegations of ballot fraud and the intervention of national parties. On November 12, the state Democratic Party sued the King County Elections Department over its handling of provisional ballots, seeking the names of those whose ballots were invalidated. Three days later, Seattle's King County, the state's Democratic stronghold, discovered 10,000 uncounted ballots and Gregoire took a 158-vote lead. Republicans sought a restraining order to stop the counting of provisional ballots; a King County judge denied the request. On November 17, after all counties had reported their results with the state, Dino Rossi was the winner by just 261 votes out of 2.8 million cast.

Washington state law requires a machine recount if the margin of victory is under 2,000 votes and half of one percent. Here the race was decided by 0.0093%. So a machine recount began and on November 24 Rossi was again the winner, this time by 42 votes. Rossi called on Gregoire to concede, but she refused; on November 29, he was certified as governor-elect. Gregoire still had another option for contesting the results. State election law allowed for a hand recount under the circumstances, provided that the party requesting it pays the costs. The state party wanted to do just that, but only in the counties where Gregoire stood to gain the most votes. This made it look as if Democrats were planning to cherry-pick only Democrat-friendly counties and Republicans were quick to criticize them for it. Gregoire would not go along with the party's plan; she said she would concede the race unless the party could raise enough to do a full statewide recount. State Democratic Chairman Paul Berendt responded, "That would be irrelevant. Concessions have no legal standing."

With leftover money contributed from Senator John Kerry's presidential campaign and with the financial assistance of MoveOn.org and the Democratic National Committee, enough money was raised to pay for a full, $730,000 statewide hand recount. But before it was finished, the state Democrats filed another lawsuit, this one requesting that county canvassing boards be ordered to reconsider thousands of ballots rejected in the first two vote counts; Gregoire denied any involvement with that suit. Rossi said she was trying to distance herself from a legal action that "left a bad taste in the public's mouth." The vote-counting slogged on through December as the action shifted back and forth between county election offices and the courts. King County suddenly discovered 561 wrongly-disqualified ballots on December 13. The next day, the state supreme court rejected the state Democratic party's request to order counties to reconsider rejected ballots. Then King County found even more uncounted ballots. Republicans filed suit in neighboring Pierce County, which they said was a fairer venue than King County, to prevent the counting of all the newfound ballots; a Pierce County judge found in their favor and kept the votes out. Democrats appealed to the state supreme court, which unanimously ruled that the disputed King County ballots could be counted. The votes were enough to put Gregoire over the top; on December 30, 58 days after Election Day, she was declared governor-elect by 129 votes. She won 48.8730% to Rossi's 48.8685%.

In January, just days before Gregoire's inauguration, Rossi and the Republican party filed suit in Chelan County Superior Court in central Washington asking that Gregoire's victory be nullified and a new election held. They presented evidence of allegedly improper votes including hundreds of votes cast by felons ineligible to vote, votes cast in the names of dead persons, votes cast by non-citizens and double votes. But on June 6 Chelan County Superior Court Judge John Bridges upheld Gregoire's election, finding that while there was evidence of 1,678 illegal votes, there was no evidence that Gregoire benefited from them and thus the standard for court intervention in the election was not met. Later that day, Rossi announced he would not file an appeal. "With today's decision, and because of the political makeup of the Washington state Supreme Court, which makes it almost impossible to overturn this contest, I am ending this contest," he said.

Working with solid Democratic majorities in both the House and Senate, Gregoire had an accomplished first year. In one of her first acts as governor, Gregoire created an election reform task force; in March 2005, the task force findings called for a statewide voter database, mandatory audits of local election systems by the Secretary of State and an earlier primary date. She signed a controversial labor-backed unemployment insurance bill for seasonal workers, a mental health parity bill, and legislation requiring the state to adopt the same car emissions standards used by California, which are stricter than the federal government's. She followed through on a campaign promise to create a $350 million Life Sciences Discovery Fund that would use tobacco settlement money for biotechnology research. But the big news was passage of a contentious $8.5 billion transportation package that paid for scores of highway and bridge projects with a 9.5-cent increase in the gas tax over four years. The measure generated considerable hostility and it didn't take long for opponents to get enough signatures to place a repeal initiative on the November 2005 ballot. But the initiative—opposed by Gregoire, big business, labor and environmental groups—lost 55%-45%, thanks in large part to Seattle's King County, where nearly half the money was to be spent on crumbling transportation infrastructure.

Gregoire had played a key role in getting the transportation package enacted. On that and a variety of other issues, legislators from both parties found themselves impressed by her level of engagement and her behind-the-scenes dealmaking skills. Yet by the end of her first year Gregoire's job approval ratings remained low, a vestige of her tainted victory but also a reflection of a style that was not inclined toward glad-handing and a record marked by several tax increases. There was talk that Gregoire, who often came across as intense and stiff, needed a "makeover." Her press releases late in the year suddenly referred to her as "Chris", rather than the customary and more formal Christine; the state Democratic party commissioned focus groups to better understand and remedy negative impressions about the governor.

In 2006, Gregoire helped pass a compromise medical malpractice bill and signed off on a landmark agreement for water storage in eastern Washington, a gay rights bill and various environmental measures, including one that made Washington the first state with an electronics-waste recycling mandate. In 2007, Gregoire proposed a $30 billion budget, up $3 billion from her first two-year budget. But amidst criticism of the increase in state spending under her watch, Gregoire muted opposition by proposing a "rainy day fund" to put aside one percent of revenues each year to soften the blow during times of fiscal crisis. The legislation sets aside $134 million in 2008 if voters approve it as a constitutional amendment in November 2007.

By mid-2007, Gregoire's approval ratings had finally broken the 50% mark, according to a SurveyUSA poll. It was widely assumed that Republican Dino Rossi, who wrote a book after the 2004 election and traveled the state giving speeches, would seek a rematch in 2008. He said he wouldn't announce his plans until December 2007; if he does not run, Gregoire's chances of winning reelection will improve dramatically.

Senior Senator

Patty Murray (D)

Elected 1992, seat up 2010, 3d term; b. Oct. 11, 1950, Seattle; home, Seattle; WA St. U., B.A. 1972; Catholic; married (Rob).

Elected Office: Shoreline Schl. Bd., 1985-89, Pres., 1985-86; WA Senate, 1988-92.

DC Office: 173 RSOB, 20510, 202-224-2621; Fax: 202-224-0238; Web site: murray.senate.gov.

State Offices: Bellevue, 425-462-4460; Everett, 425-259-6515; Seattle, 206-553-5545; Spokane, 509-624-9515; Tacoma, 253-572-3636; Vancouver, 360-696-7797; Yakima, 509-453-7462.

Committees: *Appropriations* (7th of 15 D): Transportation, Housing and Urban Development & Related Agencies (Chmn.); Financial Services & General Government; Energy & Water Development; Labor, Health and Human Services, Education & Related Agencies; Military Construction, Veterans Affairs & Related Agencies; Homeland Security; Defense. *Budget* (2d of 12 D). *Health, Education, Labor & Pensions* (6th of 11 D): Employment & Workplace Safety (Chmn.); Children & Families. *Rules & Administration* (9th of 10 D). *Veterans' Affairs* (3d of 8 D).

Group Ratings

	ADA	ACLU	AFS	LCV	ITIC	NTU	COC	ACU	CFG	FRC
2006	95	92	100	86	75	13	50	4	4	0
2005	95	—	100	95	—	7	44	0	7	—

National Journal Ratings

	2005 LIB	—	2005 CONS		2006 LIB	—	2006 CONS
Economic	88%	—	10%		87%	—	0%
Social	83%	—	10%		96%	—	0%
Foreign	66%	—	29%		76%	—	23%

Key Votes of the 109th Congress

1. Bar ANWR Drilling	Y	5. Confirm Samuel Alito	N	9. Limit Interstate Abortion	N
2. FY06 Spending Curb	N	6. Path to Citizenship	Y	10. CAFTA	Y
3. Estate Tax Repeal	N	7. Bar Same Sex Marriage	N	11. Urge Iraq Withdrawal	Y
4. Raise Minimum Wage	Y	8. Stem Cell Research $	Y	12. Provide Detainee Rights	Y

Election Results

2004 general	Patty Murray (D)	1,549,708	(55%)	($11,556,148)
	George Nethercutt (R)	1,204,584	(43%)	($7,726,296)
	Other	64,359	(2%)	
2004 primary	Patty Murray (D)	709,497	(92%)	
	Warren Hanson (D)	46,490	(6%)	
	Other	13,527	(2%)	
1998 general	Patty Murray (D)	1,103,184	(58%)	($5,600,592)
	Linda Smith (R)	785,377	(42%)	($5,159,527)

Prior Winning Percentages: 1992 (54%)

Patty Murray is the senior senator from Washington, first elected in 1992. Murray grew up in the Seattle suburb of Bothell, one of seven children of a disabled World War II veteran. She graduated from Washington State University in 1972, married and stayed home to raise her children. In 1980, when she was in Olympia trying to save from budget cuts a parent education class she was teaching at Shoreline Community College, a state legislator told her gruffly, "You're just a mom in tennis shoes; you can't make a difference." As she had said later, "Almost every woman I've ever met in politics got into it because she was mad about something." But like many committed public employees, she won her fight; then she ran for the Shoreline School District board, lost, was appointed and then elected, and served as president. In 1988 she challenged a Republican state senator, knocked on 17,000 doors and won the seat. Then in late 1991 she decided to run against U.S. Senator Brock Adams, who was under a cloud from charges of sexual harassment and later decided not to seek reelection.

Amid a crowd of better-known conventional male politicians, Murray, with her flat accent and "mom in tennis shoes" line, attracted most of the attention and most of the votes. In the all-party primary, her main Democratic opponent was former Congressman Don Bonker, who had narrowly lost a Senate nomination in 1988. But Murray won 28% of the total vote to Bonker's 19%. Murray then sprinted to a big lead in polls against Republican Congressman Rod Chandler, and in November won 54%-46%.

In the Senate Murray has had a largely liberal voting record. In her first years she was criticized as too staff-reliant and she refused to see Washington industry lobbyists. She got a seat on Appropriations and became involved in Washington issues. Murray was one of the Senate's strongest proponents of normal trade relations with China—a position strongly backed by Boeing; she also favors relaxing export restrictions on encryption technology.

When Democrats gained their Senate majority in June 2001, Murray became chairman of the Transportation Appropriations Subcommittee. She delivered for the state, and then some: By December 2001 her appropriation had $190 million of projects for Washington, more than twice as much as in 2000. In fiscal 2006, Washington state ranked 17th in per capita earmarks, according to Citizens Against Government Waste—this despite not having a single Republican member in a congressional leadership role. For her efforts, Murray has been called the "Queen of Pork" by Taxpayers for Common Sense, but Murray is unapologetic about using her Appropriations seat to steer funding to her state, arguing that lawmakers, not bureaucrats, should make funding decisions. "Earmarks are how those of us who lives 2,500 miles from the nation's Capitol ensure projects critical to our state are funded," she said. In 2005 she defended the spending priorities of Ted Stevens by threatening to take away Democratic projects if Democrats supported an amendment to strip "pork" from spending bills.

Murray strongly backed the Air Force's controversial proposals to either lease or buy KC-767 aerial refueling tankers from Boeing. To proposals that Airbus be allowed to bid on the contract, she decried "the outsourcing of our national defense" and said, "As long as they are employing Europeans and taking over America's market share, they don't care. That's not competition. That's subsidized slaughter, and we have to wake up before it's too late for America's aerospace companies and workers." She and Richard Shelby took the lead in trying to keep Mexican trucks from venturing into the U.S. beyond a 20-mile border zone, as provided by NAFTA. This was strongly supported by the Teamsters Union and opposed by the Bush administration.

Murray also has worked to remove restrictions on abortion, and has prevailed in the Senate on allowing abortions in military hospitals. With Hillary Clinton, Murray waged a fight with the Bush administration over the approval of over-the-counter sales of the Plan B contraceptive by threatening to put a hold on nomination of Lester Crawford to head the FDA. They dropped the hold when HHS Secretary Michael Leavitt assured them the FDA would make a decision, but became incensed when the FDA again postponed its decision, citing regulatory complications for sales to teenagers. "This is not only a broken promise to us, but another frightening example of politics trumping science at the FDA," Murray said. When Crawford resigned, Murray and Clinton again threatened to hold up the nomination of Andrew von Eschenbach until the FDA made a firm decision on its sale. The FDA in August 2006 gave its approval to Plan B sales for women 18 years and older; von Eschenbach was confirmed in December.

Murray in 2002 voted against using force in Iraq and has been a vociferous critic of the administration's war policy, accusing the administration of failing to plan for the full costs of the Iraq war. She has emerged as one of the Senate's most persistent advocates for veterans funding. She has sponsored bills for more benefits for National Guard and Reserve troops called up to active duty—permanent TRICARE, tax credits for employers who make up their lost pay, child care for their families. She worked to stop the closing of VA hospitals in Washington and to block a Veterans Affairs nominee in 2004 when the department missed a deadline on a report on health care in north central Washington. In April 2005 Murray attempted to add $2 billion for veterans health care to a bill funding the Iraq and Afghanistan wars. Republicans rejected the amendment but confronted the issue again when the VA acknowledged it had used 2002 estimates that underestimated the costs of soldiers returning from war and reported a $1 billion shortfall for the 2005 fiscal year. The Senate voted in June 96–0 to approve $1.5 billion in veterans funding, leading Rick Santorum to concede, "We were in error. Senator Murray was right."After a laptop containing personal information on veterans was stolen, Murray pressed the administration to protect veterans from identity theft, but later protested its plan to pay for credit monitoring for veterans by reducing funds for food stamps and student loan aid. After Democrats won the majority, Murray pressed the Defense Department to fully implement a medical tracking system to ensure returning veterans get complete treatment when they transfer from one facility to another. She also advocated specialized care for soldiers returning from Iraq with traumatic brain injuries, a common hazard for troops exposed to roadside bombings.

Murray and Maria Cantwell voted against estate tax repeal legislation in August 2006 after Republicans enticed them to support the measure by including tax breaks for timber companies and making Washington's sales tax deductible on federal income taxes. She sponsored with Susan Collins the Greenlane Maritime Cargo Security Act to provide port security grants and to improve port security at U.S. and foreign ports.

In the 2002 cycle Murray chaired the Democratic Senatorial Campaign Committee. Murray nearly doubled the committee's fundraising and brought in $158 million during the cycle. She also did a fine job of recruiting candidates. But she did less well at the polls. Democrats took only one seat from Republicans and lost three to them—and the Senate majority.

Murray has won reelection twice by impressive margins. In 1998 she was opposed by Congresswoman Linda Smith, another mom in tennis shoes—a strong opponent of abortion, backer of campaign finance regulation and opponent of free trade, a favorite of Ross Perot who was mistrusted by the House Republican leadership. Murray raised far more money than Smith, who spent much of her money on direct mail rather than TV ads, and won 58%-42%.

In 2003 eastern Washington Congressman George Nethercutt announced he was running against Murray. But the "mom in tennis shoes" had become an excellent fundraiser. A Murray aide put out word to lobbyists that she would regard contributions to Nethercutt as hostile even if the contributor gave to her too. In the end she raised and spent $11.5 million—far more than Nethercutt who spent $7.7 million. Nethercutt campaigned vigorously, and big name Republicans came in for him. He tried to put his own stamp on one of Murray's issues. For years she had been trying to create a Wild Sky wilderness area in Snohomish County, west of the Cascades. Nethercutt had never supported this (it's outside his district), but in 2004 he sponsored the bill and persuaded then-Resources Chairman Richard Pombo, who had bottled it up, to allow a vote on it. But Pombo insisted on eliminating 13,000 acres of low-level forest, and leaders of environmental groups strenuously objected. At the end of September, Nethercutt started running a spot featuring Murray's controversial December 2002 comments on Osama bin Laden's good works; speculating about bin Laden's popularity in some corners of the world, Murray had been perhaps a bit too kind in crediting him with the building of local infrastructure, health care and day care facilities. At the end of the ad, Nethercutt said, "Winning a war on terror means fighting terrorists, not excusing them." The *Seattle Times* and other newspapers denounced the ad. Nethercutt responded, "I defy her to find a day care center that Osama bin Laden has built." But the ad did not seem to move votes, and he remained well behind in the polls.

Murray ran a series of attack ads, charging that Nethercutt had missed House votes, characterizing him as an extreme conservative, referring to his opposition to abortion by showing a woman being booked into jail on an abortion charge. Murray agreed to only two debates, one of which was broadcast only in eastern Washington, another in Seattle on the same night as a big baseball game. Eastern Washington casts only 20% of the state's votes, and no one from eastern Washington has been elected to the Senate since 1928. The 2004 election did not break the string. Nethercutt reduced Murray's 1998 margin, but not by much: she won 55%-43%. It was almost as if the election were held in two states: Nethercutt carried every county east of the Cascades; Murray carried all but two counties to the west. Nethercutt's verdict: "There was an absolute protective network across the Puget Sound area that I don't think wanted to look at any other leadership options."

Following that election, Murray's influence grew considerably. In December 2004, Harry Reid appointed Murray assistant floor leader, and after Democrats took the majority in 2006, her colleagues elected her Democratic Conference Secretary, the fourth-ranking position in Democratic leadership. Once again she took the gavel of the Transportation Appropriations Subcommittee, and was also appointed to Defense Appropriations Subcommittee. She became a party spokeswoman on veterans' issues, particularly in the wake of the high-profile scandal involving the Walter Reed Army Medical Center; she managed the Senate floor debate on the Iraq war supplemental funding bill in the spring of 2007. Only in her mid-50s, Murray is young enough to advance far up the chain on Appropriations. And she is well-positioned to one day become the first woman to chair the Veterans' Affairs Committee.

Junior Senator

Maria Cantwell (D)

Elected 2000, seat up 2012, 2d term; b. Oct. 13, 1958, Indianapolis, IN; home, Edmonds; Miami U. (OH), B.A. 1981; Catholic; single.

Elected Office: WA House of Reps., 1986-92; U.S. House of Reps., 1992-94.

Professional Career: Owner, Cantwell & Assoc. PR firm, 1985-91; RealNetworks, 1995-2000.

DC Office: 511 DSOB, 20510, 202-224-3441; Fax: 202-228-0514; Web site: cantwell.senate.gov.

State Offices: Everett, 425-303-0114; Richland, 509-946-8106; Seattle, 206-220-6400; Spokane, 509-353-2507; Tacoma, 253-572-2281; Vancouver, 360-696-7838.

Committees: *Commerce, Science & Transportation* (7th of 12 D): Oceans, Atmosphere, Fisheries & Coast Guard (Chmn.); Consumer Affairs, Insurance & Automotive Safety; Surface Transportation & Merchant Marine Infrastructure, Safety & Security; Interstate Commerce, Trade & Tourism; Science, Technology & Innovation; Aviation Operations, Safety & Security. *Energy & Natural Resources* (7th of 12 D): Water & Power; Public Lands & Forests; Energy. *Finance* (10th of 11 D): Taxation & IRS Oversight & Long-Term Growth; Energy, Natural Resources & Infrastructure; Health Care. *Indian Affairs* (6th of 8 D). *Small Business & Entrepreneurship* (6th of 10 D).

Group Ratings

	ADA	ACLU	AFS	LCV	ITIC	NTU	COC	ACU	CFG	FRC
2006	95	83	100	100	100	19	58	12	6	12
2005	95	—	88	90	—	17	56	8	17	—

National Journal Ratings

	2005 LIB — 2005 CONS	2006 LIB — 2006 CONS
Economic	68% — 31%	79% — 18%
Social	90% — 0%	80% — 14%
Foreign	66% — 29%	75% — 24%

Key Votes of the 109th Congress

1. Bar ANWR Drilling	Y	5. Confirm Samuel Alito	N	9. Limit Interstate Abortion	N
2. FY06 Spending Curb	N	6. Path to Citizenship	Y	10. CAFTA	Y
3. Estate Tax Repeal	N	7. Bar Same Sex Marriage	N	11. Urge Iraq Withdrawal	Y
4. Raise Minimum Wage	Y	8. Stem Cell Research $	Y	12. Provide Detainee Rights	Y

Election Results

2006 general	Maria Cantwell (D)	1,184,659	(57%)	($14,013,932)
	Mike McGavick (R)	832,106	(40%)	($10,842,132)
	Other	66,969	(3%)	
2006 primary	Maria Cantwell (D)	570,677	(91%)	
	Hong Tran (D)	33,124	(5%)	
	Other	24,950	(4%)	
2000 general	Maria Cantwell (D)	1,199,437	(49%)	($11,533,295)
	Slade Gorton (R)	1,197,208	(49%)	($6,402,488)
	Other	64,734	(3%)	

Prior Winning Percentages: 1992 House (55%)

Maria Cantwell is a Democrat elected in the closest Senate race of 2000. Cantwell grew up in Indianapolis, where her father Paul Cantwell, a construction worker, served as county commissioner, city councilman and state legislator. As a child, Cantwell observed politics first hand as her father dispensed advice to the union members, laborers and politicians who stopped by to talk politics. During her father's stint as an aide to Congressman Andrew Jacobs, she woke one morning to the laughter of Ted Kennedy downstairs. Cantwell graduated from Miami University (Ohio) in 1980—the first in her family to graduate from college—and worked in Ohio for Jerry Springer's 1982 campaign for governor. (In 2003, when Springer was considering running for senator in Ohio, she said, "I think people will be surprised by his intellect. There's much more to him than his TV show.") Then she worked for Senator Alan Cranston's presidential campaign and went to Seattle to set up a regional campaign office. The Cranston campaign went nowhere, and so did Cantwell: she loved the Pacific Northwest and decided to stay. She moved to Mountlake Terrace, a suburb in Snohomish County just north of Seattle, where she organized a coalition to build a new library. In 1986, at 28, she was elected to the Washington House.

In 1992 Cantwell ran for an open U.S. House seat and won a solid 55%-42% victory. In the House she did not support the Clinton health care plan and supported NAFTA only at the last minute. She was a strong supporter of abortion rights and of stands backed by environmental advocacy groups. But by fall 1994 some of those positions had become unpopular. In November she lost 52%-48% to Republican nominee Rick White.

Back in the Seattle area, she joined a startup firm called Progressive Networks in 1995; five years later it had become RealNetworks, a leader in Internet-based audio and visual software. In late 1999 her stock was worth about $40 million, and she decided to run against Republican Senator Slade Gorton. Gorton, Microsoft's leading advocate on Capitol Hill, had an increasingly conservative record on environmental and economic issues. Cantwell was an answer to Democrats' prayers; their well-known House members had declined to run, and Insurance Commissioner Deborah Senn, who was running, was widely considered too liberal to win. The real difference was money. Cantwell, who liquidated more than $5 million of her RealNetworks stock, spent freely, while Senn was on TV only during the last two weeks before the September all-party primary. Cantwell won 37% of the total vote, to only 13% for Senn; Gorton, with 44% of the vote, was ahead but short of a majority.

For the general Cantwell said she would spend "whatever it takes" to win. At the same time, she made her support of McCain-Feingold-type campaign finance regulation a major issue, and refused to take contributions from PACs or soft money from the Democratic Party (though it put $640,000 into the state before Cantwell won the primary). She charged that Gorton was beholden to special interest contributors, singling out his late-night amendment to open a cyanide-leach gold mine in Okanogan County. Gorton called Cantwell an old-style liberal Democrat who would have government meddling in health care, education and local environmental issues. Cantwell highlighted her experience in the high-tech private sector. Overall, Cantwell spent $11.5 million, $10.3 million of it her own money; Gorton spent $6.4 million.

Gorton led on election night, but not by much. Washington allows absentee voting, and 54% of the votes were cast absentee; two days after the election, one-quarter of the votes had yet to be counted. During the three weeks of counting, Gorton seemed to have the advantage. But the last two days' absentee ballots from heavily Democratic King County put Cantwell over the top by 1,953. A mandated recount left the margin at 2,229 for Cantwell, out of 2.4 million cast. Cantwell carried only five counties—King, Snohomish, Thurston (which includes the state capital of Olympia) and two small counties in the west. She won King County 59%-39%; she also carried the rest of western Washington 50%-47%. Gorton carried eastern Washington 61%-36%—a lot but not quite enough to win. Cantwell's victory created a tie in the Senate, until James Jeffords became an independent in May 2001 and gave Democrats a razor-thin majority. This race was a very big loss for the Republican Party.

In the Senate Cantwell worked hard on campaign finance in the March 2001 two-week session on the issue. In October 2002 she voted for the Iraq war resolution, unlike her colleague Patty Murray. In May 2004 she tried to add to the corporate tax bill an extension of unemployment benefits. Republicans agreed to allow the vote on the amendment only if Democrats agreed to limit debate on the bill. Because of budget resolution rules, the amendment required 60 votes, but got only 59; John Kerry, who surely would have voted for it, was out campaigning for president.

In February 2003 Cantwell and Kay Bailey Hutchison of Texas introduced a bill to allow taxpayers to deduct state sales taxes as well as state income taxes on their federal income tax forms; Texas like Washington has a sales tax but no income tax. That became law for two years as part of the corporate tax bill in November 2004; in 2005 she called for making it permanent. In January 2003 she moved off the strife-torn Judiciary Committee to Commerce, where she promised to look after Washington interests. In June 2004, after Lindsey Graham added to the defense authorization an amendment allowing reclassification of nuclear waste so that it could be kept in storage tanks in the Savannah River Site in his state, Cantwell offered a competing amendment. She said that Graham's measure might be a precedent for similar action in Washington, which has nuclear waste stored at the Hanford Site. Cantwell's amendment failed 48-48. In September 2004 she held up an Energy Department appointment to try to get the department to continue the Former Hanford Workers Medical Screening Program, scheduled to be discontinued and replaced with a centralized support program accessible through an 800 number.

A strong supporter of campaign finance regulation, Cantwell had campaign finance problems of her own. To finance her 2000 campaign she had sold $5.6 million of her RealNetworks stock and had borrowed $3.8 million from a bank with RealNetworks stock as collateral. That enabled her to run the last minute ads that surely were essential to her victory. The FEC ruled in January 2004 that she violated the law by failing to disclose the terms of these decisive loans, but it evidently saw the offense as minor because it took no action against her. Paying off the loans should have been easy; Cantwell's net worth at one point was around $40 million. But RealNetworks, like so many high-tech firms, saw its stock price plummet, from $80 in spring 2000 to $6 in spring 2001. Suddenly she owed far more than the collateral was worth. She negotiated another loan due December 2001, guaranteed by the DSCC. And she began raising money, from committed Democrats and from Washington lobbyists. Between 2001 and 2004 she raised some $16.8 million; Cantwell maintained that she did not accept PAC donations, but she did accept from lawmaker committees and from individual lobbyists. By the end of 2004 she had reduced the debt to $2.5 million. With $435,000 in cash she was in position to pay off the remaining $130,000 in bank loans; the rest of the money is owed to her, and she seemed uninterested in being repaid before the 2006 election.

Democrats tapped Cantwell to spearhead the party's position on energy in the wake of Hurricane Katrina and she sponsored a measure to prevent gas companies from gouging consumers at the pump. In May 2005 she attached an amendment to the transportation bill that would require the EPA to modernize its fuel economy testing to reflect gas mileage performance for new cars. She also sought to protect Snohomish County electricity customers from paying $122 million in termination fees that Enron Corp. sought in a lawsuit after a public utility canceled its contract with the defunct company. Business and anti-tax groups in 2005 targeted Cantwell with ads urging her to support a permanent estate tax repeal, but she and Patty Murray in 2006 rejected a repeal measure, even though it included enticements including tax breaks for the timber industry and making Washington's sales tax deductible on federal income taxes.

Cantwell waged a series of floor fights with then-Senate Commerce Chairman Ted Stevens over drilling in the Arctic National Wildlife Refuge that antagonized the powerful Alaska senator. Republicans narrowly rebuffed attempts by Cantwell in March and November 2005 to remove ANWR from the budget reconciliation bill. Stevens retaliated by introducing a bill that would expand oil tanker traffic in the environmentally sensitive Puget Sound. Washington politicians of both parties protested the move and a furor erupted when e-mails from BP were later leaked that showed the oil giant, a Stevens contributor, had worked with Stevens for a year to open Puget Sound to more tankers to BP's Cherry Point refinery. Cantwell did little to defuse the conflict: she sponsored a bill that would require more tugboats to escort tankers into Puget Sound and send the bill to oil companies. The final battle over ANWR occurred in December 2005 when Republicans attached an ANWR measure to a defense spending bill. Cantwell worked the phones to round up votes among moderate Republicans to thwart the move. Republicans needed 60 votes to cut off debate; they got 56 votes. Stevens was incensed and suggested there would be political retribution: "I hope the senator from Washington likes my visits to Washington state, because I'm gonna visit there often."

Stevens was no doubt aware that Cantwell's narrow victory in 2000 placed her high on the Republicans target list for 2006. National Republicans hoped businessman and former state Senator Dino Rossi, who lost an extremely tight race for governor in 2004, would run against Cantwell. He declined and Republicans found their candidate in Safeco insurance chairman and CEO Mike McGavick. McGavick was a smart, successful businessman, with moderate positions, personal wealth and speaking ability. He also had political smarts, having managed Gorton's 1988 campaign and served as his chief of staff. McGavick ran on a pledge of civility and emphasized how his personal qualities would make him an effective lawmaker. McGavick in August 2006 acknowledged he had been charged with drunken driving in 1993. Cantwell faced lingering discontent from liberals in the party for her 2002 vote on Iraq. Cantwell had also voted for Democratic measures reducing the U.S. military commitment in Iraq; she crushed an anti-war candidate in the September primary, winning 91% of the vote.

The Cantwell-Stevens dispute served as a backdrop for her reelection campaign, and it worked to her advantage for it allowed the reserved and cautious Cantwell to show she could stand up to Stevens and the oil lobby in defense of Washington's environment. "Cantwell never had it so good until she had it so bad with Stevens," *Seattle Times* columnist Joni Balter wrote in January 2006. Stevens withdrew his tanker bill in March 2006 saying McGavick persuaded him to pull the bill. When McGavick attended a fundraiser in April in Anchorage hosted by the Alaska delegation, the news made the front page of the *Seattle Times*.

Even though Cantwell spent freely on her 2000 campaign, Cantwell asked the FEC to allow her an early start on raising general election funds in excess of normal contribution limits, in anticipation that McGavick would trigger the "millionaires amendment." The FEC declined the request. McGavick did pour $2.5 million of own money in race, but in the end was still outspent $14 million to $10.8 million. In a Democratic year in a Democratic-leaning state, Cantwell won 57%-40%. In the new Democratic majority, she became chairwoman of the Senate Commerce subcommittee that oversees the Coast Guard, and introduced a bill to revamp the Coast Guard's $24 billion Deepwater program to replace its aging fleet.

FIRST DISTRICT

Rep. Jay Inslee (D)

Elected 1998, 6th term; b. Feb. 9, 1951, Seattle; home, Bainbridge Island; Stanford U., 1969-70, U. of WA, B.A. 1973, Willamette U., J.D. 1976.; Christian; married (Trudi).

Elected Office: WA House of Reps., 1988-92; U.S. House of Reps., 1992-94.

Professional Career: Practicing atty., 1976-92, 1995-96; Regional Dir., U.S. Dept. of H.H.S., 1997-98.

DC Office: 403 CHOB, 20515, 202-225-6311; Fax: 202-226-1606; Web site: www.house.gov/inslee.

District Offices: Poulsbo, 360-598-2342; Shoreline, 206-361-0233.

Committees: *Energy & Commerce* (22d of 31 D): Telecommunications & the Internet; Oversight & Investigations; Energy & Air Quality. *Natural Resources* (22d of 27 D): National Parks, Forests & Public Lands. *Select Committee on Energy Independence and Global Warming* (3d of 9 D).

Group Ratings

	ADA	ACLU	AFS	LCV	ITIC	NTU	COC	ACU	CFG	FRC
2006	90	95	86	100	71	18	47	12	9	0
2005	95	—	100	100	—	20	37	0	8	0

National Journal Ratings

	2005 LIB — 2005 CONS		2006 LIB — 2006 CONS	
Economic	82%	16%	79%	18%
Social	79%	21%	77%	22%
Foreign	79%	20%	83%	14%

Key Votes of the 109th Congress

1. Estate Tax Repeal	N	5. Limit Interstate Abortion	N	9. Build Border Fence	N
2. Limit CAFE Standards	N	6. Extend Patriot Act	N	10. CAFTA	N
3. FY06 Spending Curb	N	7. Bar Same Sex Marriage	N	11. Oppose Iraq Withdrawal	N
4. Drilling in ANWR	N	8. Stem Cell Research $	Y	12. Detainee Tribunals	N

Election Results

2006 general	Jay Inslee (D)	163,832	(68%)	($929,507)
	Larry Ishmael (R)	78,105	(32%)	($43,036)
2006 primary	Jay Inslee (D)	unopposed		
2004 general	Jay Inslee (D)	204,121	(62%)	($882,639)
	Randy Eastwood (R)	117,850	(36%)	($64,780)
	Other	5,798	(2%)	

Prior Winning Percentages: 2002 (56%); 2000 (55%); 1998 (50%); 1992 (51%)

The People		Race/Ethnic Origin	Ancestry	
Area size:	616 sq. mi.	81.6% White	German: 13.6%	English: 10.0%
Urban population:	95.4%	1.8% Black	Irish: 8.7%	
Rural population:	4.6%	7.9% Asian	**2004 Presidential Vote**	
Pop. 2000:	654,904	0.8% Native Am.	Kerry (D) 189,566	(56%)
Pop. 2005 (est):	708,286	0.3% Hawaiian	Bush (R) 143,146	(42%)
Median income:	$58,565	3.1% Two+ races	Other 4,414	(1%)
Poverty status:	5.6%	0.2% Other	**2000 Presidential Vote**	
Military veterans:	14.5%	4.3% Hispanic Origin	Gore (D) 154,583	(53%)
			Bush (R) 123,879	(42%)
			Other 13,803	(5%)
			Cook Partisan Voting Index: D + 7	

Occupation	Blue collar: 18.0%	White collar: 69.4%	Gray collar: 12.6%

In the past 30 years, metropolitan Seattle spread out to the north and the east, as a growing wave of newcomers arrived seeking this area's distinctive blend of natural environmental beauty, free-wheeling culture and briskly expanding economy. In the process some of the distinctiveness of the old Seattle is left behind. The fishy odor of its docks does not permeate the new subdivisions built on what were once vegetable fields or vineyards; the Scandinavian heritage of old neighborhoods like Ballard has been mixed into a Pacific Northwest blend.

The heart of this new Seattle is east of Lake Washington, in the edge city of Redmond. Here are the turquoise, pine-shaded, low-rise buildings of the Microsoft campus—a tranquil environment for a booming and boisterously aggressive company. With more than 35,000 employees in Redmond, the company expanded its 300-acre campus and plans 14 new buildings with 3.1 million square feet of new office space in Redmond by 2010. A town of 1,426 people in 1960 has stretched its limits to 47,500. Not far away is the eastern shore of Lake Washington, home to many of the newly-rich "Microsoft millionaires", who got wealthy by exercising company stock options.

The 1st Congressional District of Washington includes most of Redmond, Kirkland (where Google has an R&D center that produced Google Maps), many of the other suburbs east of Seattle, plus Shoreline in the northwest corner of King County; it also includes suburban territory—Edmonds, Lynnwood, Mukilteo and biotech-heavy Bothell—in Snohomish County to the north. Booming growth during the 1990s has been followed by some resistance to increased urbanization. Across Puget Sound, the 1st includes the northern tip of Kitsap County and Bainbridge Island, where you can commute by ferry to downtown Seattle each day and return home to what looks like the perfect American small town in the evening, and the Trident Submarine Base in Bangor. Politically, this area has been torn by forces of roughly equal strength, cultural liberalism and economic conservatism, though the former seems predominant. Most Seattle area residents appreciate, and want to preserve, the region's unique natural aura: the evergreen smell of a well-watered land; the subtle regional style that is plainly American yet distinct from most of the nation. But it is impossible not to recognize the spectacular success of market economics in the 1st District.

The congressman from the 1st District is Jay Inslee, a Democrat first elected here in 1998. Inslee grew up in north Seattle, the son of a high school biology teacher and football coach, and graduated from the University of Washington and Willamette School of Law. He moved to Selah, in Yakima County east of the Cascades, to practice law and served on the State Trial Lawyers board of directors. In 1988, at 37, he was elected to the state House over a former Yakima mayor. In 1992, when 4th District Congressman Sid Morrison ran for governor, Inslee won the general 51%-49% over Doc Hastings, a conservative supported by the Christian Coalition. In the House, Inslee voted for the Clinton budget and tax increase and for the crime bill with the assault weapons ban, despite promising to vote against other gun control bills. In 1994 Hastings ran again and beat Inslee,

53%-47%. After his defeat, Inslee moved to Bainbridge Island and practiced law in Seattle. In 1996 he ran for governor and finished fifth, with 10% of the total vote, in the all-party primary. Briefly he was a regional director of HHS.

In 1998, Inslee ran in the 1st District against Republican Congressman Rick White. White was an economic conservative with liberal votes on some cultural issues, but he had problems. In April 1998 he was divorced, though he had portrayed himself as a family man in his first campaign in 1994. And Bruce Craswell, whose wife Ellen Craswell lost to Governor Gary Locke in 1996, ran on the line of the conservative American Heritage Party. Inslee attacked White for voting to reduce spending on education and the environment and for supporting electricity deregulation, claiming that White was "willing to sell our reasonably priced electricity to California." White tried to paint Inslee as a carpetbagging opportunist. Inslee replied that he had grown up in the 1st District and had lived there more years than White. In the September all-party primary, White led 50%-44%. By November, two issues changed the balance. One was White's divorce: Inslee's ad claimed that White intended to spend 10 years in the House and then be a lobbyist—a reference to a statement by his wife in the divorce papers. The second was impeachment: After White voted for the Clinton inquiry, Inslee ran an ad saying, "Rick White and Newt Gingrich shouldn't be dragging us through this. Enough is enough." In the acrimony, the primary numbers were reversed in November: Inslee won 50%-44%.

In the House, Inslee has voted as a moderate-to-liberal Democrat and worked on high-tech issues. He joined in protecting the privacy of consumer financial records—a cause that is important to Microsoft. When Congress passed the electronic signature bill, Inslee included an amendment to require that terms of consumer consent to receive electronic records be obvious and separate from other terms. He called for increased congressional oversight of the use of spyware by federal agencies. On other issues, he voted for normal trade relations with China but against trade promotion authority. He voted to override Bill Clinton's veto of the estate tax and marriage penalty repeal, but opposed estate tax repeal after George W. Bush became president. After the devastating Indian Ocean tsunami in December 2004, he called for an expanded warning system; the bill was enacted in December 2006. He has called for a national monument at an old ferry dock where 227 Japanese Americans in 1942 were marched at gunpoint to internment camps.

On the Energy and Commerce Committee, he has focused on conservation and increasing renewable energy sources. In June 2005, he filed the New Apollo Energy Act, aimed at addressing global warming and ending the nation's addiction to foreign oil. Speaker Pelosi appointed him to the Select Committee on Energy Independence and Global Warming, and he reacted that he hoped to make 2007 "an action year." At the House Democrats' retreat in February, he was tapped to raise the issue during an appearance there by George W. Bush. Inslee is co-authoring a book on turning the U.S. economy away from fossil fuels. In March 2007, he won House passage of the Charles Norwood Living Organ Donation Act, to make paired kidney donations legal.

In 2000 against former state Senate Republican leader Dan McDonald, Inslee won 55%-43%. His margins have grown wider as local antipathy to President Bush has increased. He gave serious thought to running again for governor in 2004, but decided against it. With the governor and two senators all Democrats, his statewide ambitions are on hold for now.

SECOND DISTRICT

Rep. Rick Larsen (D)

Elected 2000, 4th term; b. June 15, 1965, Arlington; home, Lake Stevens; Pacific Lutheran U., B.A. 1987, U. of MN, M.P.A. 1990; Methodist; married (Tiia).

Elected Office: Snohomish City Cncl., 1998-2000, Pres., 1999-2000.

Professional Career: Econ. Dev. Ofcl., Port of Everett, 1990-91; Dir., Pub. Affairs, WA St. Dental Assn., 1991-98.

DC Office: 107 CHOB, 20515, 202-225-2605; Fax: 202-225-4420; Web site: www.house.gov/larsen.

District Offices: Bellingham, 360-733-4500; Everett, 425-252-3188.

Committees: *Armed Services* (15th of 34 D): Seapower & Expeditionary Forces; Strategic Forces. *Small Business* (4th of 18 D): Rural & Urban Entrepreneurship; Regulations, Healthcare & Trade. *Transportation & Infrastructure* (16th of 41 D): Coast Guard & Maritime Transportation; Aviation.

Group Ratings

	ADA	ACLU	AFS	LCV	ITIC	NTU	COC	ACU	CFG	FRC
2006	85	91	86	83	86	16	67	20	22	0
2005	90	—	100	89	—	18	59	16	15	8

National Journal Ratings

	2005 LIB	—	2005 CONS		2006 LIB	—	2006 CONS
Economic	66%	—	34%		65%	—	34%
Social	70%	—	29%		70%	—	30%
Foreign	76%	—	23%		64%	—	35%

Key Votes of the 109th Congress

1. Estate Tax Repeal	Y	5. Limit Interstate Abortion	N	9. Build Border Fence	N
2. Limit CAFE Standards	N	6. Extend Patriot Act	N	10. CAFTA	N
3. FY06 Spending Curb	N	7. Bar Same Sex Marriage	N	11. Oppose Iraq Withdrawal	Y
4. Drilling in ANWR	N	8. Stem Cell Research $	Y	12. Detainee Tribunals	N

Election Results

2006 general	Rick Larsen (D)	157,064	(64%)	($1,550,524)
	Doug Roulstone (R)	87,730	(36%)	($698,209)
2006 primary	Rick Larsen (D)	unopposed		
2004 general	Rick Larsen (D)	202,383	(64%)	($1,412,604)
	Suzanne Sinclair (R)	106,333	(34%)	($38,740)
	Other	7,966	(3%)	

Prior Winning Percentages: 2002 (50%); 2000 (50%)

The People		Race/Ethnic Origin	Ancestry	
Area size:	7,976 sq. mi.	85.6% White	German: 13.7%	English: 9.2%
Urban population:	69.4%	1.1% Black	Irish: 8.4%	
Rural population:	30.6%	2.8% Asian	**2004 Presidential Vote**	
Pop. 2000:	654,903	1.9% Native Am.	Kerry (D) 169,420	(51%)
Pop. 2005 (est):	706,427	0.2% Hawaiian	Bush (R) 156,632	(47%)
Median income:	$45,441	2.4% Two+ races	Other 5,904	(2%)
Poverty status:	10.0%	0.2% Other	**2000 Presidential Vote**	
Military veterans:	16.3%	5.8% Hispanic Origin	Gore (D) 133,216	(48%)
			Bush (R) 129,027	(46%)
			Other 16,765	(6%)
			Cook Partisan Voting Index: D + 3	

Occupation   Blue collar: 27.6%   White collar: 55.1%   Gray collar: 17.3%

The 172 San Juan Islands, in the waters of Puget Sound at the far northwest corner of Washington, were the last part of the continental United States to be turned over to this country; these waters were great whaling grounds and not until 1860 did the British relinquish them. Today, ferryboats ply the waters of the Sound, connecting the islands to mainland Washington, and to British Columbia directly to the west; the publicly operated Washington State Ferries system has more than 25 million passengers annually. Whale watching is popular not only with tourists, but also among scientists on both sides of the border. This is some of the most beautiful land and water of North America, the steely blue Sound with green forested hills rising behind; shielded from the full force of Pacific rains by the Olympic Mountains, but still seldom dry. The little towns, on bits of level land between the water and mountains, have the look of pristine New England villages or Midwestern historic towns, but are better preserved than the originals; the stores are full of fresh produce and local seafood. Here the Seattle metropolitan area has marched north along the shore of Puget Sound, beyond the old lumber port and railroad terminus of Everett, with the huge Boeing plant— the largest building in the world—where 747s, 777s and the new long-range twin-engine 787s are built; amid intense competition with French-based Airbus, sales of 787 Dreamliners have been especially strong. To the north are the small city of Bellingham and the town of Blaine (named for the House Speaker and 1884 presidential nominee) on the 49th parallel, with America's most attractively landscaped border crossing and International Peace Arch, just south of British Columbia. Local studies have raised fears that global warming will raise the water level of the Sound higher than in most areas because of ocean wind patterns. But for now, the area's deepwater ports are booming with container cargo, as they benefit from a sail that is two days closer to Asia than are southern California ports.

The 2d Congressional District of Washington includes the San Juan Islands, 45-mile long Whidbey Island and Puget Sound from Everett north, plus most of the margin of mainland along the Sound and the huge Cascade mountains, topped by snow-capped Mount Baker in northeast King County. The district has several military installations, including a relatively new and high-tech navy base at Everett and naval air station on Whidbey Island. The political tradition in most of the lumbering and fishing areas here is Democratic, while the rich agricultural areas, like the flower-bulb-growing Skagit Valley, are more Republican. Everett tends to be Democratic, some of the nearby new suburban towns Republican. Overall, this is a nearly evenly balanced district that tends to vote close to the state average. George W. Bush lost here 51%-47% in 2004, and 48%-46% in 2000.

The congressman from the 2d District is Rick Larsen, a Democrat first elected in 2000. He grew up in Arlington, in Snohomish County, graduated from Pacific Lutheran University and got a masters degree at the University of Minnesota. He spent a year doing research on economic development for the Port of Everett. For six years he was director of public affairs for the Washington State Dental Association. In 1998 he won a seat on the Snohomish County Council and he later became its president. In 2000, Republican Jack Metcalf kept his promise to retire after three terms. The Democratic field was cleared for Larsen when a state legislator unpopular with labor leaders withdrew. The Republican field was cleared for conservative state Representative John Koster when a moderate legislator failed to raise much money and dropped out. In the September all-party primary, Koster unexpectedly led 49%-46%. The election became a battleground for political action committees and one of the premier contests in the nation: anti-abortion groups and the National Rifle Association backed Koster, and unions and abortion rights groups fought for Larsen. Larsen said that the contest offered "a clear choice" on abortion, and he criticized Koster for referring to "our American holocaust." He won 50%-46%, improving his performance in each major county from the primary.

In the House, Larsen joined the New Democrat Coalition and leans toward the center in his voting record. He voted for the Bush tax cuts in 2001. He voted against trade promotion authority in December 2001 but he was one of five Democrats who switched to vote for the conference agreement in July 2002. He has pushed to secure funds for upgraded border security at Bellingham and, on the highway bill, for increased support for the Puget Sound ferries; he worked with the state congressional delegation in its successful effort to preserve the Everett and Whidbey Island naval stations during the 2005 base closing reviews. He is a cofounder of the Methamphetamines Caucus; trafficking in meth has been a big problem in his district. With Mark Kirk, he organized the U.S.-China Working Group in the House to focus on a long-term diplomatic strategy. After voting against the Iraq war resolution in 2002, Larsen became a staunch supporter of the military effort but the 2006 election results led him to oppose George W. Bush's military surge. "The president does not understand the meaning of the election in 2006," he said in January 2007.

In 2002 Larsen was opposed by Norma Smith, a former top aide to Metcalf. Smith criticized Larsen's vote on Iraq and his vote against creation of the Homeland Security Department. She ran an ad that morphed the face of liberal Seattle Congressman Jim McDermott, who traveled to Baghdad that September and said that he believed Saddam Hussein more than George W. Bush, into Larsen's. Larsen spent three times as much money as Smith, who received no money from the national party. He won 50%-46%, almost exactly the same as his margin in 2000. In April 2006, Vice President Cheney attended a fundraiser in Everett for retired Navy Captain Doug Roulstone, but Roulstone turned out to be a weaker than expected candidate, and Larsen won 64%-36%.

THIRD DISTRICT

Rep. Brian Baird (D)

Elected 1998, 5th term; b. Mar. 7, 1956, Chama, NM; home, Olympia; U. of UT, B.A. 1977, U. of WY, M.S. 1980, Ph.D. 1984; Protestant; married (Rachel).

Professional Career: Prof., Pacific Lutheran U., 1986-98.

DC Office: 2443 RHOB, 20515, 202-225-3536; Fax: 202-225-3478; Web site: www.house.gov/baird.

District Offices: Olympia, 360-352-9768; Vancouver, 360-695-6292.

Committees: *Budget* (18th of 22 D). *Science & Technology* (7th of 24 D): Research & Science Education (Chmn.); Investigations & Oversight; Energy & Environment. *Transportation & Infrastructure* (15th of 41 D): Water Resources & Environment; Coast Guard & Maritime Transportation; Highways & Transit.

Group Ratings

	ADA	ACLU	AFS	LCV	ITIC	NTU	COC	ACU	CFG	FRC
2006	80	95	86	83	86	16	53	20	18	0
2005	95	—	100	94	—	18	56	9	5	15

National Journal Ratings

	2005 LIB	—	2005 CONS		2006 LIB	—	2006 CONS
Economic	69%	—	31%		70%	—	30%
Social	69%	—	31%		70%	—	30%
Foreign	75%	—	25%		67%	—	31%

Key Votes of the 109th Congress

1. Estate Tax Repeal	N	5. Limit Interstate Abortion	N	9. Build Border Fence	Y
2. Limit CAFE Standards	N	6. Extend Patriot Act	N	10. CAFTA	N
3. FY06 Spending Curb	N	7. Bar Same Sex Marriage	N	11. Oppose Iraq Withdrawal	N
4. Drilling in ANWR	N	8. Stem Cell Research $	Y	12. Detainee Tribunals	N

Election Results

2006 general	Brian Baird (D)	147,065	(63%)	($735,464)
	Michael Messmore (R)	85,915	(37%)	($147,274)
2006 primary	Brian Baird (D)	unopposed		
2004 general	Brian Baird (D)	193,626	(62%)	($850,014)
	Thomas Crowson (R)	119,027	(38%)	($55,727)

Prior Winning Percentages: 2002 (62%); 2000 (56%); 1998 (55%)

The People		Race/Ethnic Origin	Ancestry	
Area size:	7,961 sq. mi.	87.7% White	German: 14.3%	English: 8.9%
Urban population:	70.9%	1.2% Black	Irish: 8.3%	
Rural population:	29.1%	2.6% Asian	**2004 Presidential Vote**	
Pop. 2000:	654,898	1.0% Native Am.	Bush (R) 164,643	(50%)
Pop. 2005 (est):	736,411	0.3% Hawaiian	Kerry (D) 158,503	(48%)
Median income:	$44,426	2.5% Two+ races	Other 5,301	(2%)
Poverty status:	10.5%	0.1% Other	**2000 Presidential Vote**	
Military veterans:	16.2%	4.6% Hispanic Origin	Bush (R) 131,958	(48%)
			Gore (D) 127,292	(46%)
			Other 15,732	(6%)
			Cook Partisan Voting Index: D + 0	
Occupation	Blue collar: 26.8%	White collar: 57.0%	Gray collar: 16.2%	

From the Pacific Ocean to the majestic row of active and inactive volcanoes from Mount Rainier to Mount St. Helens to Oregon's Mount Hood, southwest Washington was long one of America's most productive lumber areas. The moist air and almost constant rains blown in from the Pacific keep the trees on the coast growing rapidly; precipitation remains heavy in the valleys just past the Coast

Range, and the forests there are also fast-growing. Then come the high mountains: The Cascades are a genuine divide, wrenching almost all precipitation out of the air so the climate eastward for a thousand miles is arid. Americans were reminded of the force of the volcanoes when Mount St. Helens, dormant for 123 years, erupted in 1980, killing 65 people, destroying its own peak and paving the land around with lava. Americans had long been taught that the lower 48 states had no active volcanoes; Mount St. Helens proved that wrong. Today, life is surging back with the abundant return of plants, animals and fish.

Lewis and Clark came here in 1805, down the Columbia River to a rainy and foggy winter by the ocean; for many years this part of Washington was sparsely settled, with lumber-mill and fishing-boat towns interspersed between mountains and water. It was flannel shirt country, Democratic since the New Deal days. In the early 1990s its resource-based economy was threatened by the environmental movement, which restricted fishing practices and got a court decision shutting down old growth forest logging to save spotted owl habitat. This roiled local politics and gave Republicans an opening. An important demographic shift has been the spread of two great metropolitan areas into these valleys. Clark County across the Columbia from Portland, Oregon, has filled up with new residents, eager to avoid Oregon's income tax and still able to make big purchases in Oregon free of sales tax; its population grew by 45% in the 1990s and another 20% since 2000, the largest increase in the state; although it is the fifth biggest county, people in Clark complain that they are disconnected from the rest of the state. From the north, the Seattle-Tacoma conurbation has been moving past the increasingly trendy and fast-growing state capital of Olympia. This is one of America's great international trading areas, with big exports of logs and timber and vast imports on the docks of Portland and the Puget Sound. The Columbia River Gorge features spectacular outdoor activities, including some of the finest windsurfing in the nation.

The 3d Congressional District of Washington covers the land between the ocean and the Cascades, from Olympia on an inlet of Puget Sound, south to Vancouver, site of the Hudson Bay Company headquarters in the 19th century. Economic growth and diversification and the coming of many new residents with no roots in the old industries have made the 3d a politically marginal district; George W. Bush won here with 48% of the vote in 2000 and 50% in 2004.

The congressman from the 3d District is Brian Baird, a Democrat first elected in 1998. Baird was born in northern New Mexico and grew up in western Colorado. He earned a Ph.D. in clinical psychology from the University of Wyoming, and worked with veterans, brain-injured patients and families dealing with cancer, with juvenile delinquents in prison and in psychiatric hospitals. He has written *The Internship and Practicum Handbook* to help interns in the social services professions, and *Are We Having Fun Yet?* for couples and families on vacation. He moved to Washington in 1980 and was a professor at Pacific Lutheran University in Tacoma and living in Olympia when he ran for the House in 1996 against Republican incumbent Linda Smith, who had strong support from Christian conservatives. Baird got little national party help, but he led on election night and was pronounced the winner by an overeager media. When the more than 40,000 absentee votes outstanding were counted, Smith won by 887 votes, 50.2%-49.8%. Taking a leave from his job, Baird never stopped running, while Smith ran unsuccessfully against Senator Patty Murray in 1998. Republicans nominated state Senator Don Benton, who called for a flat tax and respect for gun rights and property rights. Baird spent twice as much money and won 55%-45%.

In the House, Baird has a mostly moderate voting record and goes his own way on occasion. He kept a campaign promise by sponsoring a bill to restore income tax deductibility for state sales taxes; with a big boost from the Texas delegation, a modified version was passed in the 2004 corporate tax bill. He proposed incentives for owners of gas-electric hybrid cars and owns one himself. He sought middle ground with a medical malpractice proposal with incentives for mediation and high caps on damages. Baird voted against the use of force in Iraq in 2002 but in 2007 he returned from a visit there and said progress was being made and that the troop surge needed more time to work. "I think the consequences of pulling back precipitously would be potentially catastrophic for the Iraqi people themselves, to whom we have a tremendous responsibility," he told *The Olympian* newspaper. His change of heart drew tough criticism at home and from his Democratic House colleagues.

After September 11, Baird gained national attention when he focused on the issue of continuity of government—what would happen if many members of Congress were killed or incapacitated by an attack? He proposed a constitutional amendment providing that, if one-fourth of House seats became vacant, governors must appoint a successor within seven days from a list of replacements proposed by existing members. This would be quite a change; as House members like to note, under the Constitution no one has ever served in the House without winning an election. Baird said that his amendment is designed to preserve the constitutional checks and balances and maintain prior party balance, while ensuring the right of the people to be represented. He argued that if many members were killed or incapacitated, the House might not be able to achieve the quorum of half the living members required to act. Congress usually moves cautiously on constitutional amendments, only 17 of which have been ratified since 1792. In July 2004, the House defeated a modified version, 63-353. But some members of both parties proposed modest rules changes to help the House adjust to such a catastrophe. When Baird objected to additional procedural changes to redefine a House "quorum," he lost several attempts to defeat the "continuity" proposal. Baird opposed House-passed legislation that would require special elections to fill House seats within 49 days following a catastrophe. On another institutional issue, he sought to tighten "insider trading" restrictions against members of Congress and their aides. Citing his own professional experience in treating substance abuse, he has been outspoken about the need to fight methamphetamine abuse; in 2005, the House passed his amendment to add $20 million for that goal. Also that year, he enacted a bill to protect a 20-mile stretch of the upper White Salmon River system.

Baird has been reelected easily, even as George W. Bush has twice carried the district. He suffered no harm at home, when an environmental group in early 2006 ran radio ads attacking the proposal that he filed with Greg Walden to expedite logging in national forests. The House passed that measure in May 2006. Baird won the "Funniest Celebrity in Washington" contest in 2005 for his spot-on impersonation of Bush.

FOURTH DISTRICT

Rep. Doc Hastings (R)

Elected 1994, 7th term; b. Feb. 7, 1941, Spokane; home, Pasco; Columbia Basin Col., 1959-61, Central Washington U., 1963-64; Protestant; married (Claire).

Military Career: Army Reserves, 1964-69.

Elected Office: WA House of Reps., 1979-87.

Professional Career: Pres., Columbia Basin Paper & Supply, 1967-94.

DC Office: 1214 LHOB, 20515, 202-225-5816; Fax: 202-225-3251; Web site: www.house.gov/hastings.

District Offices: Pasco, 509-543-9396; Yakima, 509-452-3243.

Committees: *Rules* (3d of 4 R): Rules & Organization of the House (RMM). *Standards of Official Conduct* (RMM of 5 R).

Group Ratings

	ADA	ACLU	AFS	LCV	ITIC	NTU	COC	ACU	CFG	FRC
2006	0	10	0	0	100	56	100	88	50	85
2005	5	—	0	0	—	54	96	92	46	77

National Journal Ratings

	2005 LIB	—	2005 CONS		2006 LIB	—	2006 CONS
Economic	23%	—	76%		4%	—	94%
Social	44%	—	56%		35%	—	63%
Foreign	0%	—	89%		6%	—	86%

Key Votes of the 109th Congress

1. Estate Tax Repeal	Y	5. Limit Interstate Abortion	Y	9. Build Border Fence	Y
2. Limit CAFE Standards	Y	6. Extend Patriot Act	Y	10. CAFTA	Y
3. FY06 Spending Curb	Y	7. Bar Same Sex Marriage	Y	11. Oppose Iraq Withdrawal	Y
4. Drilling in ANWR	Y	8. Stem Cell Research $	N	12. Detainee Tribunals	Y

Election Results

2006 general	Doc Hastings (R)	115,246	(60%)	($621,673)
	Richard Wright (D)	77,054	(40%)	($293,969)
2006 primary	Doc Hastings (R)	54,968	(77%)	
	Claude Oliver (R)	16,661	(23%)	
2004 general	Doc Hastings (R)	154,627	(63%)	($557,536)
	Sandy Matheson (D)	92,486	(37%)	($404,802)

Prior Winning Percentages: 2002 (67%); 2000 (61%); 1998 (69%); 1996 (53%); 1994 (53%)

The People		Race/Ethnic Origin	Ancestry	
Area size:	19,430 sq. mi.	67.8% White	German: 13.1%	English: 7.8%
Urban population:	70.5%	0.8% Black	Irish: 6.9%	
Rural population:	29.5%	1.2% Asian	**2004 Presidential Vote**	
Pop. 2000:	654,901	1.9% Native Am.	Bush (R) 160,310	(63%)
Pop. 2005 (est):	710,061	0.1% Hawaiian	Kerry (D) 90,083	(35%)
Median income:	$37,764	1.7% Two+ races	Other 3,716	(1%)
Poverty status:	16.2%	0.1% Other	**2000 Presidential Vote**	
Military veterans:	13.3%	26.4% Hispanic Origin	Bush (R) 141,891	(62%)
			Gore (D) 78,768	(34%)
			Other 8,629	(4%)
			Cook Partisan Voting Index: R +13	

Occupation   Blue collar: 23.7%   White collar: 52.8%   Gray collar: 23.5%

The rugged peaks of the Cascade Mountains divide Washington State into two starkly different climate zones and two almost as starkly different political cultures. West of the Cascades, Washington is moist, green, full of watery inlets; to the east it is barren and brown, except where irrigation ditches feed the waters of the Columbia River into thirsty valleys, or where mountaintop waters fall east, as they do to water the apple orchards in the Yakima Valley. The federal government has been a presence east of the Cascades since the 1930s, when it began to build dams that provided cheap power and boosted economic development in this forbidding, often surreal, landscape. A giant bust of Franklin D. Roosevelt gazes from a bluff on the Columbia out over 550-foot-high Grand Coulee Dam, which Roosevelt initiated and which was one of his favorite projects. Other dams are strung along downriver, like beads on the necklace of the Columbia, most of the way to Bonneville Dam near Portland, where the river breaks through the Cascades.

The one exception is the Hanford Reach, the last undammed, undeveloped stretch of the upper Columbia River, near the 640-square mile Hanford Nuclear Reservation, north of the Tri-Cities of Richland, Kennewick and Pasco, which were originally a rail center. Hanford was built by the Army to manufacture plutonium for the Manhattan Project and was where the Nagasaki bomb was constructed. After the war, the Hanford Works became the primary producer of materials for America's nuclear weapons and eastern Washington's largest employer. Then in 1989 Hanford's plutonium plant, which produced two-thirds of the nation's plutonium, was shut down because of hazardous leaks and contaminated waste; the spent fuel is scheduled to be shipped to Yucca Mountain in Nevada, when the nuclear waste repository there is completed. Workers have completed the removal of millions of gallons of liquid radioactive waste from old tanks. In 2004, voters approved a referendum to prohibit the Energy Department from sending more radioactive waste into Washington until the existing sites have been cleaned up. A new plant is scheduled to convert million of gallons of nuclear waste to glass, with the cost increased to perhaps $10 billion and the original completion date of 2011 delayed by several years. Total clean-up costs could be much more than that may take another three decades to complete. President Clinton created the Hanford Reach National Monument, which is the first to be managed by the Fish and Wildlife Service.

The 4th Congressional District of Washington covers much of the center of the state east of the Cascades, running from Grand Coulee and the Columbia River through the Hanford Works down to the Dalles Dam and the Columbia River Gorge. One tends to think of this area as ethnically unvaried, but 26% of the district's residents, and 36% in Yakima County, are Hispanic: farm workers, in many cases, who have picked fruits for generations, or their children who have gone on to other things. Sentiment toward the federal government has soured across the district. Farmers in the Yakima Valley, which produces most of the nation's apples and many other crops, were enraged when environmentalists proposed to breach the Snake River dams upriver to save salmon. Lumber towns in the Cascades responded angrily when those who wanted to preserve the spotted owl tried to shut down logging businesses. In an area once narrowly split between the parties and that as recently as 1992 elected a Democrat to Congress, this has become the most Republican district in the state and one where Democrats have little hope; the cultural liberalism of Seattle, an hour or two distant on I-90, seems very far away here. Said one Democrat when he looked at a party poll, "I don't know what Democrats did to these people, but it sure must have been bad."

The congressman from the 4th District is Doc Hastings, a Republican first elected in 1994. He got the nickname because an older brother could not pronounce his real name of Richard when they were kids. Hastings grew up in the Tri-Cities, went to college in Ellensburg and is one of the few members of Congress without a college degree. He served in the Army Reserves and for 27 years ran the Columbia Basin Paper and Supply Company in Pasco, where he was president of the chamber of commerce. In 1979 he was elected to the state House, served as a Republican leader, then retired in 1987. In 1992 he won the Republican nomination for Congress, but was beaten 51%-49% by Democrat Jay Inslee. But Inslee voted for the Clinton budget and tax package and the crime bill with its gun-control provisions—big liabilities when Hastings ran again in 1994. In their second contest, Hastings won 53%-47%. Since then, Democrats have not seriously competed here and this has become a safe Republican seat.

In the House, Hastings has had a mostly conservative voting record, though more centrist on cultural issues. With a seat on the Rules Committee, he has usually been a leadership loyalist. Much of his time has been spent on issues surrounding the Hanford Nuclear Reservation. When George W. Bush proposed cuts in the Energy Department budget, Hastings warned that cuts in the Hanford cleanup program were not acceptable; within a few months, he secured sufficient funding for local projects to avoid an overall reduction. He formed and chairs the congressional nuclear cleanup caucus to fight for Hanford funding. Congress enacted his proposal for the Interior Department to study preservation of the Manhattan Project's historic sites at Hanford as part of the national park system. He said that his proudest legislative achievement was the enactment in 2003 of the Citizens' Soldier Act, which makes legal immigrants serving in the military eligible for citizenship after one year in uniform.

Hastings has been a prominent behind-the-scenes presence in Republican leadership circles. As chairman of the Investigating Subcommittee of the Ethics Committee, he had the thankless task of reviewing the case against James Traficant, who was convicted of bribery in federal court in April 2002. The panel voted unanimously to expel him from the House, only the second such action since the Civil War; just before the House voted 420–1 for expulsion, Traficant called Hastings "a very fair man." He was part of the unanimous 10-member panel in 2004 that voted three admonishments of Majority Leader Tom DeLay, the mildest possible sanction. But many Republicans were incensed because the panel also ruled that DeLay had violated no House rules. Speaker Dennis Hastert removed Joel Hefley as chairman—after the usual four-year period, members said—and replaced two other Republicans on the committee. Hastings was named chairman: a member who said that he had never previously called a press conference suddenly found himself in the public spotlight.

Democrats complained when Republicans in January 2005 changed the House's ethics rules to require a majority vote before an investigation could proceed; on this one committee that is made up of equal numbers of members of both parties, Democrats charged that this would give Republicans veto power over investigations. Hastings supported the rules changes and ousted the committee's top staffers, often a routine move for a new chairman. When the Democrats on the committee refused to attend committee meetings and prevented the establishment of a quorum there, Republicans in April agreed to restore the earlier rules. Hastings got a big increase in committee funding to assist members with compliance. But conflicts remained, including over the selection by Hastings of committee staff. When Democrats accused him of running the panel for partisan gain, Republicans were incensed. Additional months passed until the two sides could resolve procedural arrangements. After Tom DeLay was indicted in Texas, Hastings said that the panel would not investigate him while the criminal case was pending. Then, in April 2006, news stories described questionable financial investments by Alan Mollohan, the panel's ranking Democrat; under pressure, Nancy Pelosi replaced him with Howard Berman, who was experienced on ethics issues and had a reputation for bipartisanship. That proved to be a positive move for the committee, which quickly became busy with investigations of several members, including Bob Ney and William Jefferson. After Mark Foley resigned in September 2006, Hastings and Berman led a high-profile subcommittee investigation of what Republican leaders and their staff knew about Foley's dealings with House pages, with Hastert and others testifying in the committee's pre-election probe. All of the testimony was behind closed doors, but the investigation became a major partisan distraction for House Republicans. Following the election, the committee in December 2006 issued a unanimous report that no members or employees violated House rules but concluded that it was "disturbed" by the conduct of some of those who dealt with allegations regarding Foley's conduct. "In all, a pattern of conduct was exhibited among many individuals to remain willfully ignorant of the potential consequences of former Representative Foley's conduct with respect to House pages."

His friendship with John Boehner could position Hastings for leadership opportunities, such as Rules Committee chairman, if Republicans regain the majority. At home, Democratic challenger Richard Wright in 2006 criticized him for his handling of ethics issues; Hastings won 60%-40%, not a bad performance in a rough year for Republicans.

FIFTH DISTRICT

Rep. Cathy McMorris Rodgers (R)

Elected 2004, 2d term; b. May 22, 1969, Salem, OR; home, Deer Lake; Pensacola Christian Col., B.A. 1990, U. of WA, M.B.A. 2002; Christian; married (Brian Rodgers).

Elected Office: WA House of Reps., 1994-2004; Min. Ldr. 2002-04.

Professional Career: Owner-operator, Peachcrest Fruit Basket orchard, 1984-98; state legislative aide, 1990-94.

DC Office: 1708 LHOB, 20515, 202-225-2006; Fax: 202-225-3392; Web site: www.mcmorris.house.gov.

District Offices: Colville, 509-684-3481; Spokane, 509-353-2374; Walla Walla, 509-529-9358.

Committees: *Armed Services* (26th of 29 R): Air & Land Forces; Readiness. *Education & Labor* (12th of 22 R): Higher Education, Lifelong Learning & Competitiveness; Health, Employment, Labor & Pensions. *Natural Resources* (12th of 22 R): Water & Power (RMM); Fisheries, Wildlife & Oceans.

Group Ratings

	ADA	ACLU	AFS	LCV	ITIC	NTU	COC	ACU	CFG	FRC
2006	5	17	0	0	100	65	100	96	77	100
2005	5	—	0	0	—	61	93	100	72	100

National Journal Ratings

	2005 LIB	—	2005 CONS		2006 LIB	—	2006 CONS
Economic	19%	—	79%		23%	—	77%
Social	24%	—	74%		0%	—	94%
Foreign	17%	—	79%		6%	—	86%

Key Votes of the 109th Congress

1. Estate Tax Repeal	Y	5. Limit Interstate Abortion	Y	9. Build Border Fence	Y
2. Limit CAFE Standards	Y	6. Extend Patriot Act	Y	10. CAFTA	Y
3. FY06 Spending Curb	Y	7. Bar Same Sex Marriage	Y	11. Oppose Iraq Withdrawal	Y
4. Drilling in ANWR	Y	8. Stem Cell Research $	N	12. Detainee Tribunals	Y

Election Results

2006 general	Cathy McMorris Rodgers (R)	134,967	(56%)	($1,931,501)
	Peter Goldmark (D)	104,357	(44%)	($1,198,156)
2006 primary	Cathy McMorris Rodgers (R)	unopposed		
2004 general	Cathy McMorris (R)	179,600	(60%)	($1,537,540)
	Don Barbieri (D)	121,333	(40%)	($1,628,666)

The People		Race/Ethnic Origin	Ancestry	
Area size:	23,166 sq. mi.	87.7% White	German: 16.5%	Irish: 9.0%
Urban population:	71.9%	1.3% Black	English: 8.8%	
Rural population:	28.1%	1.7% Asian	**2004 Presidential Vote**	
Pop. 2000:	654,904	2.3% Native Am.	Bush (R) 177,311	(57%)
Pop. 2005 (est):	682,916	0.1% Hawaiian	Kerry (D) 127,162	(41%)
Median income:	$35,720	2.3% Two+ races	Other 5,705	(2%)
Poverty status:	14.4%	0.2% Other	**2000 Presidential Vote**	
Military veterans:	16.2%	4.5% Hispanic Origin	Bush (R) 150,013	(56%)
			Gore (D) 106,610	(40%)
			Other 13,262	(5%)
			Cook Partisan Voting Index: R + 7	

Occupation   Blue collar: 21.1%   White collar: 60.0%   Gray collar: 18.9%

Eastern Washington is a land of great rivers and bare parched land, where the Columbia, Spokane and Snake Rivers wind among vast plateaus, bringing water from the Rockies to the desert. Spokane grew up at the falls of the Spokane River when the railroads first came through, and became a major wheat, mining, electrical and railroad center early in the 20th century, the center of the so-called "Inland Empire"; it celebrated with the 1974 World's Fair and Exposition on the downtown riverfront. Nearby are some of the most fascinating landscapes in the United States: undulating yellow wheat fields, the rolling ridges of the Palouse where the wheat-growing topsoil is 200 feet deep, the bare-rock coulees rising above dammed-up lakes and barren desert, the vast wilderness of Okanogan County that has long been gold country and where plans for a new mine gained fresh momentum after operators proposed an underground mine that would minimize the environmental impact. This is remote and inhospitable land: the summers can be blazing hot and winters bitter cold; many rivers run wildly. But much of it has been tamed by man, and the water from the Grand Coulee and other dams irrigates some of the richest farmland in the country.

The 5th Congressional District of Washington covers the easternmost part of the state. Two-thirds of the people here live in greater Spokane, a city whose voting habits have grown apart from the Washington west of the Cascades, especially on resource issues and the role of government. Several Spokane area politicians have called for creating a 51st state of Eastern Washington, with 60% of the current state's land and 22% of its population. Near the Oregon border is Walla Walla, long dependent on wheat and sweet onions but now attracting tourists with its growing wine industry. The political inclinations are Republican, but not as Republican as most of the nearby Rocky Mountain states. Spokane County voted for Bill Clinton in 1992 and 1996, but George W. Bush won the county 56%-44% in 2004 and won 57% in the entire 5th District.

The congresswoman from the 5th District is Cathy McMorris Rodgers, a Republican elected in 2004. She spent much of her childhood in northern British Columbia, graduated from Pensacola Christian College in Florida and got an MBA from the University of Washington: a lot of moving around. The last time that eastern Washington elected a 35-year-old to Congress—Thomas Foley in 1964—he rose through the ranks and eventually became Speaker of the House. No one is yet predicting a similar ascent for Cathy McMorris Rodgers, elected at 35, but her background suggests that she is primed for the leadership track. While working in the family-owned orchard and fruit stand in Kettle Falls, she was appointed then later elected to the state House, where she served for 10 years and chaired the Commerce and Labor Committee; she served her final two years as House Minority Leader, the first female House leader in state history. In 2004 George Nethercutt, who beat Foley in 1994, the first congressional candidate to defeat a Speaker since Charles Denison defeated Galusha Grow in 1862, ran for the Senate; McMorris Rodgers and two other Republicans filed to compete for his seat in the Republican primary. McMorris Rodgers was backed by the economic conservatives of the Club for Growth; that prompted the moderate Republican Main Street Partnership to launch a highly unusual direct-mail and radio attack on her, though it did not support either of her opponents. The three primary candidates agreed on most major issues. Each opposed abortion and favored a constitutional amendment banning same-sex marriage. All three supported tort law changes and making the Bush administration tax cuts permanent; all criticized the Endangered Species Act. McMorris Rodgers won 50% of the vote in the primary to 27% for state senator Larry Sheahan and 23% for Spokane lawyer Shaun Cross.

The Democratic nominee, Don Barbieri, a wealthy businessman, had a geographical edge over McMorris Rodgers; he is from Spokane while she is from rural northeastern Washington. Barbieri also had a heavy financial advantage. He had no primary opposition and was well funded going in the general. The National Republican Congressional Committee spent heavily on McMorris Rodgers's behalf. One NRCC-sponsored ad charged that Barbieri put "profits before jobs" when his hotel development company laid off workers following a merger with another company. McMorris Rodgers highlighted her pro-business credentials and agricultural background as a farmer's daughter. That was enough to put her in by a comfortable margin, 60%-40%, another sign of how much has changed in Tom Foley's old district, where Democrats these days rarely win anything. She carried every county, with margins over 2–1 in many counties. She carried Spokane County 57%-43%.

Showing her political skill, she was elected the freshman representative to the Republican Steering Committee, which makes House committee assignments. Under Democratic rule, she kept seats on the Armed Services Committee, Education and Labor and Resources committees, becoming the ranking Republican of the Water and Power Subcommittee.

During her first term, Republicans appointed McMorris Rodgers as head of a taskforce to review the National Environmental Policy Act, which recommended mandatory deadlines for completing assessments that environmentalists have used to challenge projects. She continued the work of Foley and Nethercutt to compensate the Spokane Tribe for land flooded after the completion of the Grand Coulee Dam. She also sponsored a bill requiring utilities to let customers know how much of their electricity bills go to fund Endangered Species Act programs. She co-sponsored an amendment to the electronic medical records bill requiring a report on the impact of information technology for Medicaid chronic disease patients and moved through the House a measure to increase the number of qualified teachers for advanced placement courses. McMorris Rodgers has backed Bush's Iraq war policies, but she also criticized the administration on veterans health care, delayed rules for country of origin labeling for meat, and a budget proposal forcing the Bonneville Power Administration to use revenues to pay off debt rather than lower rates.

In 2006 McMorris Rodgers faced opposition from Democrat Peter Goldmark, a rancher who got a late start to his campaign. The two candidates argued in TV commercials about whether the incumbent had saved the Fairchild Air Force Base in the 2005 base closing round. In another ad she claimed she had "bucked party leadership" when she authored an amendment with Nita Lowey to restore budget cuts to the Perkins loan program. The candidates sparred over the Medicare prescription drug program, Bush tax cuts and veterans funding. The DCCC put the race on its "emerging races" list and spent $320,000 in independent ads, but Democratic candidates elsewhere seemed more promising to the party. Goldmark raised a respectable $1.2 million, but was still outspent by $750,000. McMorris Rodgers won 56%-44%, carrying every county.

McMorris Rodgers got married in August 2006. After the election she decided to add Rodgers to her name and announced that she was expecting a baby. She endured morning sickness on the campaign trail; in April she gave birth to a boy, Cole McMorris Rodgers, who was born four weeks premature and was diagnosed with Down syndrome. Only five women, all of them in the House, have given birth while serving in Congress. In 1996, Susan Molinari of New York gave birth to a daughter, followed six weeks later by then-Congresswoman, now Senator, Blanche Lincoln of Arkansas, who delivered twin sons. California's Yvonne Brathwaite Burke in 1973, and Enid Greene of Utah in 1995, also delivered daughters while members of Congress. McMorris Rodgers began raising money for reelection in the first quarter of 2007, dispelling Democratic hopes that she might retire from the seat.

SIXTH DISTRICT

Rep. Norm Dicks (D)

Elected 1976, 16th term; b. Dec. 16, 1940, Bremerton; home, Bremerton; U. of WA, B.A. 1963, J.D. 1968; Lutheran; married (Suzanne).

Professional Career: Legis. Asst., U.S. Sen. Warren Magnuson, 1968-73, A.A., 1973-76.

DC Office: 2467 RHOB, 20515, 202-225-5916; Fax: 202-226-1176; Web site: www.house.gov/dicks.

District Offices: Bremerton, 360-479-4011; Port Angeles, 360-452-3370; Tacoma, 253-593-6536.

Committees: *Appropriations* (3d of 37 D): Interior, Environment & Related Agencies (Chmn.); Defense; Military Construction, Veterans Affairs & Related Agencies. *Homeland Security* (4th of 19 D): Intelligence, Information Sharing & Terrorism Risk Assessment; Emergency Communications, Preparedness & Response.

Group Ratings

	ADA	ACLU	AFS	LCV	ITIC	NTU	COC	ACU	CFG	FRC
2006	85	95	100	83	86	14	50	8	13	0
2005	85	—	100	83	—	16	52	0	10	0

National Journal Ratings

	2005 LIB	—	2005 CONS		2006 LIB	—	2006 CONS
Economic	75%	—	24%		68%	—	32%
Social	73%	—	27%		77%	—	22%
Foreign	60%	—	40%		62%	—	37%

Key Votes of the 109th Congress

1. Estate Tax Repeal	N	5. Limit Interstate Abortion	N	9. Build Border Fence	N
2. Limit CAFE Standards	N	6. Extend Patriot Act	N	10. CAFTA	Y
3. FY06 Spending Curb	N	7. Bar Same Sex Marriage	N	11. Oppose Iraq Withdrawal	N
4. Drilling in ANWR	N	8. Stem Cell Research $	Y	12. Detainee Tribunals	N

Election Results

2006 general	Norm Dicks (D)	158,202	(71%)	($995,770)
	Doug Cloud (R)	65,883	(29%)	
2006 primary	Norm Dicks (D) .... unopposed			
2004 general	Norm Dicks (D)	202,919	(69%)	($871,608)
	Doug Cloud (R)	91,228	(31%)	

Prior Winning Percentages: 2002 (64%); 2000 (65%); 1998 (68%); 1996 (66%); 1994 (58%); 1992 (64%); 1990 (61%); 1988 (68%); 1986 (71%); 1984 (66%); 1982 (63%); 1980 (54%); 1978 (61%); 1976 (74%)

The People		Race/Ethnic Origin	Ancestry
Area size:	8,592 sq. mi.	77.7% White	German: 13.2% English: 8.5%
Urban population:	78.8%	5.5% Black	Irish: 8.5%
Rural population:	21.2%	4.4% Asian	**2004 Presidential Vote**
Pop. 2000:	654,902	2.2% Native Am.	Kerry (D) 163,145 (53%)
Pop. 2005 (est):	683,511	0.7% Hawaiian	Bush (R) 137,891 (45%)
Median income:	$39,205	4.1% Two+ races	Other 5,365 (2%)
Poverty status:	13.2%	0.2% Other	**2000 Presidential Vote**
Military veterans:	10.8%	5.1% Hispanic Origin	Gore (D) 139,643 (52%)
			Bush (R) 115,736 (43%)
			Other 15,098 (6%)
			Cook Partisan Voting Index: D + 6

Occupation   Blue collar: 25.3%   White collar: 54.8%   Gray collar: 19.8%

The rainiest part of the continental United States is at its far northwest corner, where the Olympic Mountains of Washington thrust into the Pacific Ocean. The waters of the Pacific evaporate, condense and then mist or rain down on the hills and mountains that jut up from the ocean and Puget Sound. The mountains here are always green, the trees that line the inlets towering, and during heavy rainfalls the rivers can rise six feet a day. This has long been lumbering and fishing country, where men go out to work at 6 a.m. in air cold enough to see your breath year-round, and where dependence on the vagaries of nature plus harsh environmental laws—like the ban on old-growth logging to protect the habitat of the spotted owl—have strengthened a traditional surly independence and suspicion of authority. Still, respect for the beauty of Nature endures at the 3,310-square-mile Olympic Coast National Marine Sanctuary, which probes a vast underwater reserve. Some here fear that melting glaciers are a sign of a disastrously warming climate, others that farmland is being bought up to build subdivisions and second homes.

The inlets of Puget Sound, winding sinuously through the mountains, are among America's most picturesque waterways and strategically among its most important. Here during World War II, shipyards built and sheltered much of the U.S. Navy's Pacific fleet, and here during the Cold War much of the nuclear submarine fleet anchored at the giant Bremerton Navy base, where the naval shipyard was opened in 1891. To the south is the Tacoma Straits Bridge, the replacement of the narrow span that, in a scene preserved on newsreel (and still viewed by civil engineering students), started vibrating on the wrong harmonic in high winds and collapsed in 1940. On the other side is Tacoma, long the second-ranking city on Puget Sound, with its massive docks, former pulp mills, pleasant hilly residential neighborhoods and the recently revived waterfront.

The 6th Congressional District of Washington includes the Olympic Peninsula, Bremerton and much of surrounding Kitsap County amid various inlets of Puget Sound, and most of Tacoma. Politically, the Olympic Peninsula and Bremerton are working-class Democratic. Kitsap County is the site of a proposed NASCAR track, the first in the area. Tacoma also is traditionally Democratic. But as cultural issues have become more important, and as Seattle latte liberals come to symbolize the Democratic party, these areas trended a little away from the party; Seattle and King County were somewhat more Republican than Tacoma and Pierce County as late as the early 1980s, and now they are much more heavily Democratic. In 2004 the 6th District cast 45% of its votes for George W. Bush, far more than the 19% cast for him in Seattle's 7th District.

The congressman from the 6th District is Norm Dicks, a Democrat first elected in 1976. Dicks grew up in Bremerton, the son of a shipyard worker, graduated from the University of Washington where he was a 185-pound linebacker on the football team and played in two Rose Bowls. After graduation from the university's law school, he joined Senator Warren Magnuson's staff, then regarded as one of the very best on Capitol Hill, the model of activist staffs that have served talented legislators of both parties. This was a fast track and Dicks seems to have been a fast learner who kept an eye on local politics. The 6th District's congressman was Floyd Hicks, a Democrat who was a surprise winner in 1964 and who held the seat into the 1970s even though it was widely known he would rather be a judge. In 1976 he got his judgeship, and Dicks got his chance to jump from staffer to member. He entered the race and ran a hard-charging campaign. The Pierce County Democratic chairman announced he had a policy of not endorsing in the primary; Dicks charged into a meeting with him and got the endorsement. He won a four-candidate primary, then cruised to a 73%-25% general election victory. With the examples of Magnuson and Jackson before him, Dicks could promise his constituents that he would accumulate seniority and be in a position to work for their interests over many years. Unlike Magnuson and Jackson, who took advantage of opportunities to run for the Senate while in their 30s, Dicks has stayed in the House. He signaled his intentions early on, by the unusual feat of winning a seat on the Appropriations Committee in his first term, over a fellow freshman named Al Gore. In his second term he got a seat on the Defense Subcommittee, of vital interest to the 6th District and to the nation.

Dicks has had a moderate voting record, and has been considered more supportive of military spending and an interventionist foreign policy than most House Democrats: the Scoop Jackson tradition. Like Jackson, he has supported free trade agreements and was one of the few House Democrats to vote for the Central American Free Trade Agreement in July 2005. He has often quoted Jackson: "I'm not a hawk or a dove. I just don't want my country to be a pigeon." In these posts Dicks has exerted pivotal influence on vital policies, usually operating behind the scenes. In the early 1980s Dicks took the lead in restoring Export-Import Bank loan authority—Boeing is America's biggest exporter and user of the loans—when the Reagan administration wanted to cut it, and led a campaign that switched 80 House votes overnight. During the post-Cold War downsizing of the Pentagon, he worked with Gore and Les Aspin in support of the MX missile and successfully looked out for the F-117 Stealth aircraft and especially for expanded production of the B-2 Stealth bomber. He was vindicated when the B-2 was used in the bombing of Serbia and Kosovo in 1999, Afghanistan in 2001 and Iraq in 2003, delivering weapons with pinpoint accuracy and sometimes flying halfway around the world to do so. Dicks was a strong supporter of normal trade relations with China; Washington accounts for one-quarter of U.S. exports to China and in January 2005 China agreed to buy 60 Boeing 7E7s for $7.2 billion. He worked hard to promote a a $23 billion, 10-year lease of up to 100 Boeing 767s to replace aging KC-135 tankers. Opponents, notably Senator John McCain, argued it would be cheaper in the long run to design a new tanker. The deal came undone after convictions of a top Boeing official and the Air Force's top procurement officer on bribery charges. Dicks's response: "Misconduct blew the deal. It is painful. It would have been the greatest thing I had done." He has been harshly critical of the Army's record on procurement of the Future Combat System and opposed Donald Rumsfeld's National Security Personnel System's changes in collective bargaining and union agreements. He has consistently supported the acquisition of more C-17 transports than the Pentagon has requested; in September 2006 Congress appropriated $4 billion for an additional 22 of the planes.

Dicks certainly does not neglect the 6th District's military facilities. The Bremerton Naval Shipyard, by far the largest employer in Kitsap County, is also the largest naval shore facility in the Pacific Northwest, and the 2005 base closing procedure moved two nuclear subs from Groton,

Connecticut, to Bremerton, in line with the nation's increasingly Pacific Rim-oriented military stationing. The base closing round also increased personnel at Fort Lewis near Tacoma, Bremerton Naval Station and Whidbey Island Naval Air Station. Dicks has promoted jointness between Fort Lewis and the adjacent McChord Air Force Base and the result has been increased joint operations, joint housing programs and even, Dicks has suggested, a merger. Dicks voted for and rounded up support for the Iraq war resolution in October 2002. In November 2005 he said he was misled about the claims of Iraqi weapons and regretted his past support though, unlike his Defense Subcommittee colleague John Murtha, he did not favor withdrawing all U.S. troops within six months. But he was angry at Republicans' attacks on Murtha, with whom he had served on the subcommittee since 1979. "Of course I am skeptical. I am worried about this, particularly when it comes to troop rotations," he said after meeting with George W. Bush on the surge in January 2007. "We will know quickly whether this will work, and there may be no practical way for Congress to act." He voted for the nonbinding resolution calling for withdrawal and for the supplemental appropriation with a timetable, but voted against a version of the supplemental promising immediate withdrawal. He said he expected conditions would be imposed on military operations in the defense appropriation that would come up in fall 2007. He has called for something like the World War II Truman committee to investigate wartime spending.

Dicks is the chairman of the Interior Subcommittee on Appropriations. As its ranking Democrat he worked amicably with Republican subcommittee Chairman Charles Taylor, who was defeated for reelection in 2006. Dicks clearly relishes the collegiality and relative bipartisanship of Appropriations; as he said in March 2006, "Heck, I wouldn't even be in Congress if I were on the House Ways and Means Committee." Over the years he has worked to help many Washington communities, funneling $1.2 billion to lumber mill towns when logging in old-growth forests was banned because of alleged damage to the spotted owl, passing timber salvage riders to keep mills going, dealing with the cost of maintaining salmon runs in dammed rivers. He also added the Clearwater area to the Washington wilderness bill. He has worked to fund the multi-billion dollar Hanford Reservation cleanup and to get funding for light rail in Tacoma and for the proposed NASCAR track in Kitsap County. He hammered out a deal with the Skokomish tribe and a Bellingham seafood company to end the dumping of salmon carcasses into Hood Canal, which suffered from algae growth; he wants to designate it as critical habitat for orcas and whales. He made sure that the energy bill continued the 1977 Magnuson Act limit of just 600 oil tankers a year in Puget Sound. He worked for five years on settling the land claims of the Puyallup Tribe near Tacoma. He has worked to revitalize Tacoma's once-grimy waterfront, building I-705 (the last of the original interstate highways), cleaning up the Thea Foss Waterway (once one of the Superfund's most polluted waterways), rehabilitating the Pantages Theater, and converting the old Union Station into a federal courthouse. In July 2005 he got $2 million for an EPA study of a possible comprehensive program to clean up Puget Sound, like those for the Great Lakes and Chesapeake Bay; in May 2006 he got $6 million in funding; this is how an appropriator plants the seeds for a long-term government initiative. In December 2005 he and neighbors Adam Smith and Dave Reichert got $200 million in grants for law enforcement agencies to prevent domestic violence committed by their officers; this was a response to the Tacoma police chief's murder of his wife and suicide in front of his young children in 2003. He fought for $36 million to reopen Mount Rainier National Park in May 2007, which was closed after suffering severe storm damage in November 2006.

Dicks had something of a close election in 1980, when his mentor Senator Warren Magnuson was defeated for reelection after 46 years in Congress. Dicks has been reelected by wide margins ever since and in 2006 won 71%-29%.

SEVENTH DISTRICT

Rep. Jim McDermott (D)

Elected 1988, 10th term; b. Dec. 28, 1936, Chicago, IL; home, Seattle; Wheaton Col., B.S. 1958, U. of IL, M.D. 1963; Episcopalian; married (Therese Hansen).

Military Career: U.S. Navy Medical Corps., 1968-70.

Elected Office: WA House of Reps., 1970-72; WA Senate, 1974-87.

Professional Career: Asst. Prof., U. of WA, Practicing psychiatrist, 1970-83; Medical Officer, U.S. Foreign Svc., Zaire, 1987-88.

DC Office: 1035 LHOB, 20515, 202-225-3106; Fax: 202-225-6197; Web site: www.house.gov/mcdermott.

District Offices: Seattle, 206-553-7170.

Committees: *Ways & Means* (4th of 24 D): Income Security & Family Support (Chmn.); Select Revenue Measures.

Group Ratings

	ADA	ACLU	AFS	LCV	ITIC	NTU	COC	ACU	CFG	FRC
2006	95	100	100	100	43	18	20	4	11	0
2005	100	—	100	94	—	21	37	0	7	0

National Journal Ratings

	2005 LIB	—	2005 CONS		2006 LIB	—	2006 CONS
Economic	94%	—	0%		94%	—	0%
Social	97%	—	2%		96%	—	3%
Foreign	93%	—	7%		88%	—	10%

Key Votes of the 109th Congress

1. Estate Tax Repeal	N	5. Limit Interstate Abortion	N	9. Build Border Fence	N
2. Limit CAFE Standards	N	6. Extend Patriot Act	N	10. CAFTA	N
3. FY06 Spending Curb	N	7. Bar Same Sex Marriage	N	11. Oppose Iraq Withdrawal	N
4. Drilling in ANWR	N	8. Stem Cell Research $	Y	12. Detainee Tribunals	N

Election Results

2006 general	Jim McDermott (D)	195,462	(79%)	($496,250)
	Steve Beren (R)	38,715	(16%)	($22,032)
	Linnea Noreen (I)	11,956	(5%)	($79,946)
2006 primary	Jim McDermott (D)	95,065	(91%)	
	Donovan Rivers (D)	4,837	(5%)	
	Joshua Smith (D)	4,526	(4%)	
2004 general	Jim McDermott (D)	272,302	(81%)	($437,147)
	Carol Cassady (R)	65,226	(19%)	($23,632)

Prior Winning Percentages: 2002 (74%); 2000 (73%); 1998 (88%); 1996 (81%); 1994 (75%); 1992 (78%); 1990 (72%); 1988 (76%)

The People		Race/Ethnic Origin	Ancestry	
Area size:	246 sq. mi.	66.9% White	German: 11.1%	Irish: 8.5%
Urban population:	98.5%	8.3% Black	English: 8.2%	
Rural population:	1.5%	13.2% Asian	**2004 Presidential Vote**	
Pop. 2000:	654,902	0.9% Native Am.	Kerry (D) 288,161	(79%)
Pop. 2005 (est):	648,613	0.6% Hawaiian	Bush (R) 70,167	(19%)
Median income:	$45,864	3.9% Two+ races	Other 5,436	(1%)
Poverty status:	11.5%	0.3% Other	**2000 Presidential Vote**	
Military veterans:	10.6%	5.8% Hispanic Origin	Gore (D) 228,988	(72%)
			Bush (R) 66,066	(21%)
			Other 23,952	(8%)
			Cook Partisan Voting Index: D +30	

Occupation	Blue collar: 14.7%	White collar: 70.9%	Gray collar: 14.4%

Seattle rises from the Puget Sound harbor of Elliott Bay on steep hills, once covered with 300-foot-high Douglas firs. Behind the hills and buildings you can see on a clear day, from almost anywhere, the nimbus of Mount Rainier. On the picturesque waterfront, below gleaming high-rises, is the Pike Place market, where you can get fresh salmon and Dungeness crabs; nearby is Pioneer Square, where stores and warehouses from the turn of the 20th century have been restored; and Yesler Way, America's original "Skid Road," now has upscale shops but still some homeless people. Seattle's upper class, like San Francisco's, continues to be anchored downtown, with its upscale stores and busy sidewalks. Seattle first zoomed into the national consciousness with the 1897 Klondike gold strike, has been a major American city since around 1910 and hosted its own World's Fair in 1962. In the 1990s its combination of economic growth and creativity plus its physical beauty and distinctive style made it a national leader. Seattle has had old ethnic neighborhoods, like once heavily Scandinavian Ballard that has been moving toward boutiques and nightspots, and the countercultural Capitol Hill neighborhood, with shoppers jamming busy stores, galleries and clubs. But it has a new ethnic mix, with thousands of Asian immigrants. The dominant tone is set by highly educated, affluent, single professionals, many of them gay—the kind of people who have made the Victorian houses of Queen Anne overlooking the harbor or the 1940s houses lining the streets of Capitol Hill among the nation's highest-priced residential real estate. There are still blue-collar workers on the south side of the city and in valleys; factories, warehouses and railroad yards are concentrated in a flat plain near Puget Sound and south of downtown. Boeing, long based in Seattle, is America's biggest exporter, but Seattle has exported other institutions such as Nordstrom department stores with their famously polite service and fashionable goods. Seattle also is the headquarters, in an old industrial district, of Starbucks coffee and its more than 13,000 stores.

As the 21st century dawned, all was not well in Seattle. In December 1999 rioters protesting globalism made a shambles of an international trade meeting at which Bill Clinton had hoped to chart new reductions in trade barriers. The city cancelled its New Year's Eve gala at the Space Needle because of terrorist threats. Then a federal judge back in the other Washington ruled that Microsoft was a monopoly. In perhaps the most stunning blow, Boeing announced in May 2001 that it would relocate its corporate headquarters to Chicago. That decision followed a series of bitter labor disputes and less than hospitable treatment by Seattle area officials. Seattle's affinity for protest politics and unionism seemed, in post-September 11 America, an indulgence that could no longer be afforded. In November 2006, voters approved a referendum ending subsidies for professional sports teams, which led the pro basketball Supersonics to look elsewhere for a home.

The 7th Congressional District of Washington includes nearly all of the city of Seattle, some industrial suburban fringe to the south and white collar suburban fringe to the north and artsy, rural-looking Vashon Island in Puget Sound. Seattle is one of the whitest major cities in the nation, so this district—13% Asian, 8% black and 6% Hispanic—is the closest thing to a minority district in the Seattle area. It shares more with San Francisco than hills and scenery: it is heavily populated by singles, gays, young professionals and elderly pensioners; it has one of the nation's lowest percentages of married couples and children. A generation ago, Seattle was roughly split between the parties; today, it is heavily Democratic and liberal. Al Gore carried this district 72%-21% and John Kerry won overwhelmingly 79%-19%.

The congressman from the 7th District is Jim McDermott, one of the most liberal members of the House and its only (credentialed) psychiatrist, first elected in 1988. McDermott grew up in a Chicago suburb and was the first in his family to attend college; his father ministered a fundamentalist church out of the garage. He graduated from conservative religious Wheaton College, also the alma mater of former Speaker Dennis Hastert. After service in the Navy and stints in New York and Illinois hospitals, he came to the University of Washington Hospital in Seattle. Almost immediately, he was elected to the state House in 1970, ran for governor in 1972 and finished third in the primary, and was elected to the state Senate in 1974. He ran for governor again in 1980, beat incumbent Dixy Lee Ray in the primary, then lost to Republican John Spellman; in 1984 he ran for governor a third time and lost the primary to Booth Gardner. In 1987 he retired from the legislature and went to Zaire (now Congo) as a medical officer in the Foreign Service. When the House seat opened in 1988, McDermott returned to Seattle and easily won, beating Norm Rice 38%-29% in the primary and taking 76% in the general.

In his early years in the House, McDermott rose quickly in influence as Tom Foley tapped him for influential assignments. His great cause has been health care but he has shared the frustration that many have met on the issue. He has long backed a single-payer, Canadian-style national health insurance program. In August 1994, as the Clinton health care plan was failing and Democratic leaders scrambled to come up with an alternative, McDermott urged Congress to abandon all health care bills for the year. He evidently expected a more favorable political environment after the election, and, like many, was surprised by the results. After Republicans took control, he said: "A lot of people around here have never been in the minority. I have. I know what to do: attack." While keeping to that promise, he has been called the father of another measure that first seemed quixotic but was enacted in 2000. This was the African Growth and Opportunity Act, which reduced import quotas and tariffs on African goods and included investment funds. He was among the handful of Democrats who actively supported normal trade relations with China. But he opposed trade promotion authority for George W. Bush and the Central American free trade deal.

After the September 11 attacks, McDermott had trouble sleeping and believed that he was having symptoms of post-traumatic stress disorder. When Bush ordered military strikes against Afghanistan, he was the first member to criticize him for acting too quickly. In September 2002, he went to Baghdad with former Minority Whip David Bonior and Mike Thompson of California. There, much to the astonishment of George Stephanopoulos, he told the audience of *This Week* that Bush was willing to "mislead the American people" and that he found Saddam Hussein more credible. This sparked harsh criticism from Republicans and dismay from those Democrats who sensed, probably accurately, that his comments hurt their party's chances in the November elections. "He combined the judgment of Neville Chamberlain before World War II and Jane Fonda in Hanoi," Texas Democrat Chet Edwards told *The New York Times*. McDermott retreated a bit and argued that Bush had failed to make the case for military action. He opposed the Iraq war resolution and joined five other Democrats in bringing a lawsuit to stop military action. In March 2003, he was one of 11 Democrats who voted against the resolution supporting the troops and the president at the start of the war. In March 2007, House Democrats added to the Iraq war funding bill his prohibition of an attack on Iran, though it was later removed.

McDermott again stirred controversy in April 2004, when he omitted the words "under God" as he led the House in its daily pledge of allegiance to the flag. After leaders of both parties criticized him, he replied that his omission was not deliberate, but that the reaction "ain't fun" and was "a diversion from looking at real issues facing this country."

McDermott is upfront about his legislative interests, which tend not to include the parochial matters and pork-barreling that consume some of his congressional colleagues. He has promoted health issues overseas and founded and chaired the Congressional Task Force on International HIV/AIDS. He also joined the crusade against the use of depleted uranium in war munitions. For a decade, McDermott has dealt with a controversy that arose when he was ranking minority member on the ethics committee during its consideration of charges brought against Speaker Newt Gingrich. McDermott was angry that Republicans would not make public the report of special counsel James Cole before the House voted for speaker in January 1997. A few days later, the committee voted for a House reprimand and a $300,000 penalty. In the midst of the controversy, a Florida couple, both Democratic activists, happened to tape from a police scanner a conversation between Ohio's John Boehner, talking on a cell phone, and other House Republican leaders. They presented the tape to their congresswoman, Karen Thurman, who suggested they turn it over to McDermott. A few days later excerpts from the tape appeared in *The New York Times* and the *Atlanta Journal-Constitution*. Evidence suggested that McDermott was the source, and in 1998 Boehner sued him in federal court for invasion of privacy. The trial judge ruled that the suit would infringe McDermott's First Amendment rights, but the D.C. Circuit Court of Appeals reversed. The trial judge ruled in December 2002 that McDermott's conversations with a committee lawyer were not privileged. McDermott approached Boehner in 2002 (they had not spoken in the 12 years they served together) and sought to settle the case. He agreed to one of Boehner's demands, that he apologize to the House, but would not agree to the other two, that he admit he was wrong and that he make a contribution to charity. On the eve of the 2004 election, the judge found McDermott guilty of violating the federal wiretapping law and ordered that he pay $60,000 in damages and $500,000 in attorneys' fees; he appealed the ruling, which friends in Seattle said they would help to pay. In November 2004, Boehner ally David Hobson filed an ethics complaint against McDermott. After the 2006 election, the ethics committee found that he did not violate House rules but it rebuked him for actions that "risked undermining the ethics process." But the court case took yet another turn against McDermott when the divided D.C. Circuit Court concluded in May 2007 that House rules on confidentiality barred him from disclosing the contents of the tape; the judges ordered payment of the damages to Boehner. McDermott claimed the ruling infringed on his free speech rights and in September 2007 he took his case to the Supreme Court.

With the Democrats' return to the majority, legislative life for McDermott again became more enjoyable. As a senior member on Ways and Means, he chaired the Income Security and Family

Support Subcommittee, with plans to address issues such as foster care, the social safety net, and training and benefits to workers who lose their jobs because of trade. He ranked fourth in seniority among committee Democrats, with each of the other three at least five years older than him. A long-time ally of Nancy Pelosi, he again had a friendly ear in high places. In the opening days of the 110th Congress, he helped to shape the House-passed bill to rescind some tax breaks for oil companies.

At home, McDermott considered running against Senator Slade Gorton in 2000, but backed away soon after he underwent open-heart surgery; he said that he didn't want to raise the $8 million that would be required. His outspokenness has not hurt McDermott in Seattle, where he regularly wins reelection with more than 70% of the vote.

EIGHTH DISTRICT

Rep. Dave Reichert (R)

Elected 2004, 2d term; b. Aug. 29, 1950, Detroit Lakes, MN; home, Auburn; Concordia Lutheran Col., A.A. 1970; Lutheran; married (Julie).

Military Career: Air Force Reserve, 1971-76.

Elected Office: King Cnty. Sheriff, 1997-2004.

Professional Career: King Cnty. police officer, 1972-1997.

DC Office: 1223 LHOB, 20515, 202-225-7761; Fax: 202-225-4282; Web site: www.house.gov/reichert.

District Offices: Mercer Island, 206-275-3438.

Committees: *Homeland Security* (9th of 15 R): Intelligence, Information Sharing & Terrorism Risk Assessment (RMM); Border, Maritime & Global Counterterrorism. *Science & Technology* (14th of 20 R). *Transportation & Infrastructure* (25th of 34 R): Aviation; Highways & Transit.

Group Ratings

	ADA	ACLU	AFS	LCV	ITIC	NTU	COC	ACU	CFG	FRC
2006	25	23	0	67	100	46	73	56	39	71
2005	10	—	0	28	—	48	88	64	36	62

National Journal Ratings

	2005 LIB — 2005 CONS		2006 LIB — 2006 CONS	
Economic	45%	54%	46%	53%
Social	44%	56%	50%	50%
Foreign	45%	54%	45%	54%

Key Votes of the 109th Congress

1. Estate Tax Repeal	Y	5. Limit Interstate Abortion	Y	9. Build Border Fence		Y
2. Limit CAFE Standards	Y	6. Extend Patriot Act	Y	10. CAFTA		Y
3. FY06 Spending Curb	Y	7. Bar Same Sex Marriage	Y	11. Oppose Iraq Withdrawal		*
4. Drilling in ANWR	N	8. Stem Cell Research $	Y	12. Detainee Tribunals		Y

Election Results

2006 general	Dave Reichert (R)	129,362	(51%)	($3,051,918)
	Darcy Burner (D)	122,021	(49%)	($3,048,902)
2006 primary	Dave Reichert (R)	unopposed		
2004 general	Dave Reichert (R)	173,298	(52%)	($1,569,196)
	Dave Ross (D)	157,148	(47%)	($1,446,406)
	Other	6,053	(2%)	

The People		Race/Ethnic Origin	Ancestry		
Area size:	2,621 sq. mi.	82.1% White	German: 14.0%	English: 9.4%	
Urban population:	87.6%	2.0% Black	Irish: 8.3%		
Rural population:	12.4%	7.8% Asian	**2004 Presidential Vote**		
Pop. 2000:	654,905	0.8% Native Am.	Kerry (D) 177,601	(51%)	
Pop. 2005 (est):	719,454	0.3% Hawaiian	Bush (R) 168,291	(48%)	
Median income:	$63,854	2.8% Two+ races	Other 4,273	(1%)	
Poverty status:	5.1%	0.2% Other	**2000 Presidential Vote**		
Military veterans:	14.0%	4.0% Hispanic Origin	Gore (D) 140,387	(49%)	
			Bush (R) 136,575	(47%)	
			Other 11,838	(4%)	
			Cook Partisan Voting Index: D + 2		
Occupation	Blue collar: 19.7%	White collar: 68.6%	Gray collar: 11.8%		

The land east of Seattle's Lake Washington half a century ago was quiet countryside. Orchards and vineyards flourished in the rich, moist soil just below the rise of the Cascades Mountains, while farms and broad pasturelands spread toward 14,410-foot Mount Rainier like a living green quilt. But as Seattle has grown over the years, people have crossed the pontoon bridge across Mercer Island to Bellevue and have made this Eastside area one of the most vibrant parts of metropolitan Seattle. Bellevue, with 115,000 people, a quarter of them of Asian descent, and enough office space to make it an edge city, has grown out of the shadow of Seattle; its tallest skyscraper has hit the city's 450-foot height limit, a departure from the strip malls and parking lots that that defined downtown a quarter century ago. While downtown Seattle specialized in banks and law firms and trading companies, Bellevue and other communities in Overlake specialized in high-tech startups. Redmond, just to the north in the 1st Congressional District, is the headquarters of Microsoft, and there are dozens of other firms here that make this one of America's leading high-tech centers.

The 8th Congressional District of Washington includes most of the eastern edge of metro Seattle. It includes most of Bellevue, Mercer Island and the affluent suburbs on Lake Washington—Medina, Clyde Hill, Yarrow Point, Hunts Point, Beaux Arts—where Bill Gates has built his $60 million, 66,000-square foot high-tech home with a trampoline room with vaulted ceilings, video walls that can be electronically programmed with art from the world's great museums, and a garage large enough to hold 30 cars: Seattle's Xanadu. The 8th also includes the suburbs to the south in King and Pierce Counties. It goes east to the crest of the Cascades Mountains and includes all of Mount Rainier, one of the nation's last inland old-growth rain forests. This is the most affluent district in Washington, rivaled only by the 1st; politically it is market-oriented on economics, more liberal on the environment and other cultural issues. Historically it is Republican, but George W. Bush lost this district twice, with 47% of the vote in 2000 and 48% in 2004.

The congressman from the 8th District is Dave Reichert, a Republican elected in 2004. Reichert was born in Detroit Lakes, Minnesota, but his family moved to the Seattle area a year later. He graduated from Concordia Lutheran College in Portland and then joined the Air Force Reserves. He worked for 32 years in the King County sheriff's office and was elected sheriff in 1997; he was a national leader on gun-crime reduction and methamphetamine prevention. During the riots that accompanied the 1999 international trade meeting in Seattle, he criticized city leaders and the police force for inadequate preparation. He gained national attention for his prominent role in capturing Gary Ridgway, the "Green River Killer" who had terrorized the Seattle area with a two-decade spree in which he murdered 48 women. After Ridgway's capture in 2001, Reichert was featured on national television shows and documentaries, and he published a book about the experience during the campaign titled, *Chasing the Devil: My Twenty-Year Quest to Capture the Green River Killer*.

In January 2004 Congresswoman Jennifer Dunn announced that she was retiring after 12 years in the House. Republicans actively recruited Reichert to run. He had three opponents in the September Republican primary. Two of them ran TV ads criticizing his call for harsher gun ownership requirements and for being too close to Democrats; he refused to appear with them in any public forum. He won the Republican nomination with 43% of the vote; state senator Luke Esser and former U.S. Attorney Diane Tebelius each got 23%. The leading Democrat in the race was Dave Ross, a New York native and longtime Seattle radio talk-show host who stayed on the air until July, when he filed papers with the FEC. He won the September primary with 48% of the vote.

The general election thus featured two candidates who were widely known. Reichert argued that local law enforcement agencies should receive more money and equipment for homeland security. Sounding like a talk-show host, Ross said that he wanted to be the eyes and ears of the public "into what's going on, who's making the trades, where the money is going and whether it's being wisely spent." The national parties each swarmed in with well over $5 million in spending, visits by prominent leaders and ads to boost their respective nominees. Each candidate tried to portray the other as lacking in public policy experience and holding views too extreme for the swing district. A TV ad by the National Republican Congressional Committee suggested that Ross's opposition to the proposed missile defense system would "empower terrorists." On the other side, the DCCC ran an ad criticizing Reichert's opposition to abortion. Both Seattle newspapers, with strong liberal traditions, endorsed Ross for his greater familiarity with issues, and suggested that Reichert was too conservative for this district. But Reichert won 52%-47%.

He got seats on the Homeland Security, Science, and Transportation and Infrastructure committees. After Reichert backed his bid to chair the Homeland Security Committee, Peter King rewarded Reichert with the Emergency Preparedness Subcommittee, making him the only fresh-man in his class to chair a subcommittee. He moved legislation that established standards for interoperable communications. After President Bush signed the bill, Reichert sent a letter to the White House to protest Bush's "signing statement" that he planned to ignore a part of the bill that established employment standards for the FEMA administrator. Reichert voted to override Bush's veto of the stem cell research bill after seeking input from female staffers in his office, and voted against a bill that would have kept the brain-damaged Terri Schiavo on life support. He also opposed a plan to allow more oil tankers in Puget Sound, but it was his vote against drilling in the Arctic National Wildlife Refuge that helped him demonstrate his independence from the national party, an asset in the 2006 elections.

Reichert's polite demeanor stood out in the often partisan House, but he experienced some growing pains. He angered Appropriations cardinal Frank Wolf, when he proposed shifting law enforcement funding to restore $78 million in cuts to the COPS program; afterward he vowed to work with Wolf next time. He had more success with Don Young, when he approached the prickly Alaskan on the House floor to urge him to reconsider his plan to move the home port of the icebreaker Healy from Seattle to Alaska. The Coast Guard also opposed the expense and Young conceded.

The Democratic Congressional Campaign Committee left little doubt the race would be a target in 2006 when it ran radio ads 18 months before Election Day hitting Reichert for a vote on military health care. Former Microsoft executive Darcy Burner, a political novice who was not recruited by national Democrats, banked over $330,000 in the first quarter of 2006 and got the attention of party leaders. In a competitive district where dissatisfaction with Bush would likely be a major liability, Reichert was unapologetic about appearing with Bush. "I know it's controversial to have the president come to the northwest part of the United States. I don't care. He's the president." Burner's campaign called him a "Bush Republican" and ran an ad that featured "Rubber Stamp Reichert" stepping off Air Force One with Bush. The candidates each spent $3 million on television ads and mail pieces; the national parties together poured in more than $4 million. Early results gave Reichert a slim lead, but uncounted absentee ballots delayed Burner's concession for another week. Reichert won 51%-49%. Reichert has now successfully fought two competitive races in a swing district, but he can expect further opposition. Burner said she was running again in 2008, when Democrats hope to benefit from presidential coattails; state Senator Rodney Tom was also running for the Democratic nomination, but Burner's aggressive fundraising led him to drop out of the race in September 2007.

NINTH DISTRICT

Rep. Adam Smith (D)

Elected 1996, 6th term; b. June 15, 1965, Washington, DC; home, Tacoma; Fordham U., B.A. 1987, U. of WA, J.D. 1990; Christian; married (Sara).

Elected Office: WA Senate, 1990-96.

Professional Career: Practicing atty., 1991-92; city prosecutor, 1992-95.

DC Office: 2402 RHOB, 20515, 202-225-8901; Fax: 202-225-5893; Web site: www.house.gov/adamsmith.

District Offices: Tacoma, 253-896-3775.

Committees: *Armed Services* (8th of 34 D): Terrorism, Unconventional Threats & Capabilities (Chmn.); Air & Land Forces. *Foreign Affairs* (12th of 27 D): Asia, the Pacific & the Global Environment; Africa & Global Health.

Group Ratings

	ADA	ACLU	AFS	LCV	ITIC	NTU	COC	ACU	CFG	FRC
2006	75	95	83	100	86	20	57	21	25	0
2005	85	—	88	100	—	18	50	12	13	8

National Journal Ratings

	2005 LIB	—	2005 CONS		2006 LIB	—	2006 CONS
Economic	68%	—	31%		79%	—	21%
Social	75%	—	25%		66%	—	34%
Foreign	73%	—	27%		65%	—	34%

Key Votes of the 109th Congress

1. Estate Tax Repeal	N	5. Limit Interstate Abortion	N	9. Build Border Fence	Y
2. Limit CAFE Standards	N	6. Extend Patriot Act	N	10. CAFTA	N
3. FY06 Spending Curb	N	7. Bar Same Sex Marriage	N	11. Oppose Iraq Withdrawal	Y
4. Drilling in ANWR	N	8. Stem Cell Research $	Y	12. Detainee Tribunals	N

Election Results

2006 general	Adam Smith (D)	119,038	(66%)	($642,549)
	Steven Cofchin (R)	62,082	(34%)	($42,875)
2006 primary	Adam Smith (D)	unopposed		
2004 general	Adam Smith (D)	162,433	(63%)	($527,669)
	Paul Lord (R)	88,304	(34%)	($7,660)
	Other	5,934	(2%)	

Prior Winning Percentages: 2002 (59%); 2000 (62%); 1998 (65%); 1996 (50%)

The People		Race/Ethnic Origin	Ancestry	
Area size:	691 sq. mi.	73.3% White	German: 13.2%	Irish: 7.9%
Urban population:	95.0%	6.3% Black	English: 7.7%	
Rural population:	5.0%	7.1% Asian	**2004 Presidential Vote**	
Pop. 2000:	654,902	1.1% Native Am.	Kerry (D) 146,494	(53%)
Pop. 2005 (est):	687,041	0.9% Hawaiian	Bush (R) 126,428	(46%)
Median income:	$46,495	4.2% Two+ races	Other 3,867	(1%)
Poverty status:	9.2%	0.3% Other	**2000 Presidential Vote**	
Military veterans:	17.2%	6.7% Hispanic Origin	Gore (D) 128,076	(53%)
			Bush (R) 104,549	(43%)
			Other 10,874	(4%)
			Cook Partisan Voting Index: D + 6	

Occupation	Blue collar: 24.7%	White collar: 59.4%	Gray collar: 15.9%

The misty shores of Puget Sound have seen some of America's most vibrant economic growth over the last two decades. It has spread south and west from Seattle, over the mixed suburban territory, to the outskirts of the once industrial city of Tacoma. The subdivisions along the Sound, which have some of the loveliest views in America, tend to be high-income. But much of greater Seattle's prime industrial territory lies between the ridges that run north and south inland. Weyerhaeuser, the world's largest private owner of softwood timber, has its headquarters here in Federal Way. Boeing is a major presence in Renton, on the south end of Lake Washington. Its aircraft and electronic components plants have made it America's number one exporter for many years. Renton, which has gained renown as the home of 1960s' guitarist Jimi Hendrix, manufactures the 737s, which has been the best-selling commercial jet in history and whose sales continue to soar. A host of smaller factories cluster near the rail lines that run from Minneapolis-St. Paul across the Great Plains to Puget Sound.

The 9th Congressional District of Washington covers much of this area. It includes Sea-Tac Airport, Burien and Renton, not far south of Seattle, and Kent, Des Moines, most of Auburn and Federal Way farther south in King County. It includes the expanded and more automated container port of Tacoma, though most of the rest of the city is in the 6th District; in surrounding Pierce County (the nation's largest producer of rhubarb) it includes Edgewood and Puyallup, plus Fort Lewis, the largest Army base in the West, and McChord Air Force Base, home of the C-17. It also includes a part of Thurston County outside the state capital Olympia, including the Nisqually National Wildlife Refuge, an important transit point for migratory birds. This district was created after the 1990 Census and politically was almost perfectly balanced in the mid-1990s: it elected a Democratic congressman in 1992, a Republican in 1994 and a Democrat in 1996. But as the Seattle region trended toward Democrats, the district has done likewise.

The congressman from the 9th District is Adam Smith, a Democrat first elected in 1996. He grew up in the Sea-Tac area; his father, a baggage handler for United Airlines and active in the Machinists' Union, died when Smith was 17. The family went on welfare; Smith worked his way through Fordham driving trucks for UPS, then went to the University of Washington Law School. He worked as a lawyer, then as a Seattle prosecutor, handling drunk driving and domestic abuse cases. In 1990, at 25, he was elected to the state Senate, beating an incumbent Republican by doorbelling the district twice. In 1995, he decided to run against first-term Congressman Randy Tate. The two were born the same year, to families of modest backgrounds, were first elected to office at young ages and were firm believers in doorbelling. Tate, a religious conservative and strong supporter of Speaker Newt Gingrich, was a prime target of the AFL-CIO. Smith campaigned as a moderate Democrat, a supporter of the death penalty and three-strikes legislation. He attacked Tate for supporting Gingrich on 96% of House votes and for backing Medicare "cuts." Tate attacked Smith for opposition to channeling youthful offenders to adult courts and prisons and for voting for Governor Mike Lowry's $1.2 billion tax increase in 1993. This was one of the closest races in the country. In the September all-party primary, Smith led 49%-48%. In November, he won 50%-47%.

In the House, Smith won a seat on the Armed Services Committee, a locally useful assignment, and joined the New Democrat Coalition. He has a decidedly moderate voting record and has shown a willingness to take on established interests within his party. He voted for charter schools, but against school vouchers. He voted to authorize military action in Iraq, and sought to improve compensation and other quality of life benefits for military personnel. In 2004, he stirred controversy when he was one of only four House Democrats who opposed changes in the Patriot Act. A few days later, he told liberal activists that he should have voted the other way. In the majority, he became chairman of the Subcommittee on Terrorism and Unconventional Threats and Capabilities, which he called the "tip of the spear" in the war on terrorism. Although he has a pro-free-trade record by Democratic standards, he voted against the Central American Free Trade Agreement because it did not adequately protect the rights of workers.

Smith's independence has worked well for him back home. He has won reelection easily, and Republicans have quit targeting this district. In the 2004 campaign, he was one of the first congressional supporters of John Kerry and chaired his campaign in Washington; his centrist rhetoric occasionally offended supporters of Howard Dean and Dennis Kucinich. In 2008, he was an early supporter of Barack Obama for president.

★ WEST VIRGINIA ★

Almost heaven—that's what the song says about West Virginia. And indeed some things are looking up for this state, whose people have never lost their sense of hope or their affection for the hills and mountains that make this the most unhorizontal state in the nation. But West Virginia has had more than its share of tragedy and heartbreak. It was born out of the tragedy of the Civil War, when 55 mountain counties with few slaves seceded from Virginia, and it has made its living most of the years since on that cruelest of minerals, coal. West Virginia is laced with coal: there are coal seams in 53 of its 55 counties, and production even today, after many mines have closed, in 26. Coal kept the sons of large mountaineer families here for much of the 20th century, men who would otherwise have left for big cities; coal brought immigrants in, a few from odd corners of Europe, but more from adjacent areas of the South where the local farming economies were stagnant when West Virginia's coal economy was booming. Coal and local rock salt and brines brought the large concentration of chemical plants 50 years ago to the Kanawha Valley around Charleston; it built steel mills and glass factories in the panhandle and the Monongahela River valley, not far south of Pittsburgh.

But coal did not build a self-sustaining economy. When America was beleaguered abroad, demand for coal increased and energy prices rose, and West Virginia boomed, during World War II (the state reached its all-time population peak of 2 million in 1950) and the oil shocks of the 1970s. Coal changed the state's politics too. West Virginia's heritage from the Civil War days was Republican, though some counties tilted toward the Confederacy and the Democrats. But after John L. Lewis's United Mine Workers organized most of the West Virginia mines, the coal country shifted toward the New Deal Democrats, and West Virginia for more than half a century was one of the most Democratic states, deserting the national ticket only in Republican landslide years (1956, 1972, 1984) until George W. Bush carried it in 2000; its legislature has been controlled by Democrats since 1930. But neither Democratic administrations nor the pensions and medical benefits the UMW negotiated for retired miners were able to provide the economic growth to keep thousands of West Virginians from leaving their mountains to find work elsewhere—now more often south on I-77 to the booming Carolinas or over U.S. 33 to Columbus than farther north to the Great Lakes industrial cities. As underground miners were replaced by strip-mining machines, coal tonnage went way up but coal mine employment dropped from 22% of the state's work force in 1950 to 10% in 1980 and only 4% in the late 1990s; coal mines employed 126,000 West Virginians in 1948, 63,000 in 1978, 13,500 in 2002. The state's population, 2.0 million in 1950 and 1.95 million in 1980, fell to 1.8 million in 2000—the largest decrease over that period, absolutely and in percentage terms, of any state. Of the state's 55 counties, 38 had fewer people in 2006 than they did in 1950, 76% and 53% fewer in coal-mining McDowell and Logan Counties; the only big population increases over that half-century have been in the eastern panhandle, the university town of Morgantown and several Ohio River counties. In the 2000 Census, West Virginia ranked 50th among states in household income, 50th in median value of housing (but first in percentage of home ownership), 48th in percentage of adults with a high school diploma and second in percentage living in poverty. Still, West Virginians have a strong attachment to this unique state, where the accent sounds Southern and the early 20th century factories and houses look Northern, where the landscape is rural and the economy industrial.

In the 1990s West Virginia was on the rebound, only to be threatened at the end of the decade with economic disaster. Population increased during the decade and the number of jobs rose by 8%. Unemployment since 2000 has been only slightly above and often below the national average, down to 4.5% in April 2007. Government has played a role. Senator Robert Byrd, as both chairman and ranking Democrat on the Appropriations Committee, achieved his career goal of channeling $1 billion of federal projects into West Virginia, and more. Forest products are replacing coal in rural counties, health care is growing as everywhere and telemarketing is growing as well. West Virginia has finally completed its interstate highway network and in a computer age it is no longer isolated. Still, West Virginia is losing young people. Even during the growing 1990s the number of people aged 25 to 34 fell by 33,000, while the number of those under 18 plunged by 41,000; from 2000 to 2006, more people died than were born in West Virginia. The state's median age rose to 38.9, the highest in the nation, even above Florida's. Young people in close-packed Huntington and Wheeling are moving across the Ohio River to more spread-out subdivisions in Ohio.

One threat to West Virginia's economy came in October 1999 when, in a case brought by environmental groups, federal judge Charles Haden ruled that mountaintop mining violates federal environmental laws. Far fewer miners are needed for this work than in underground mining,

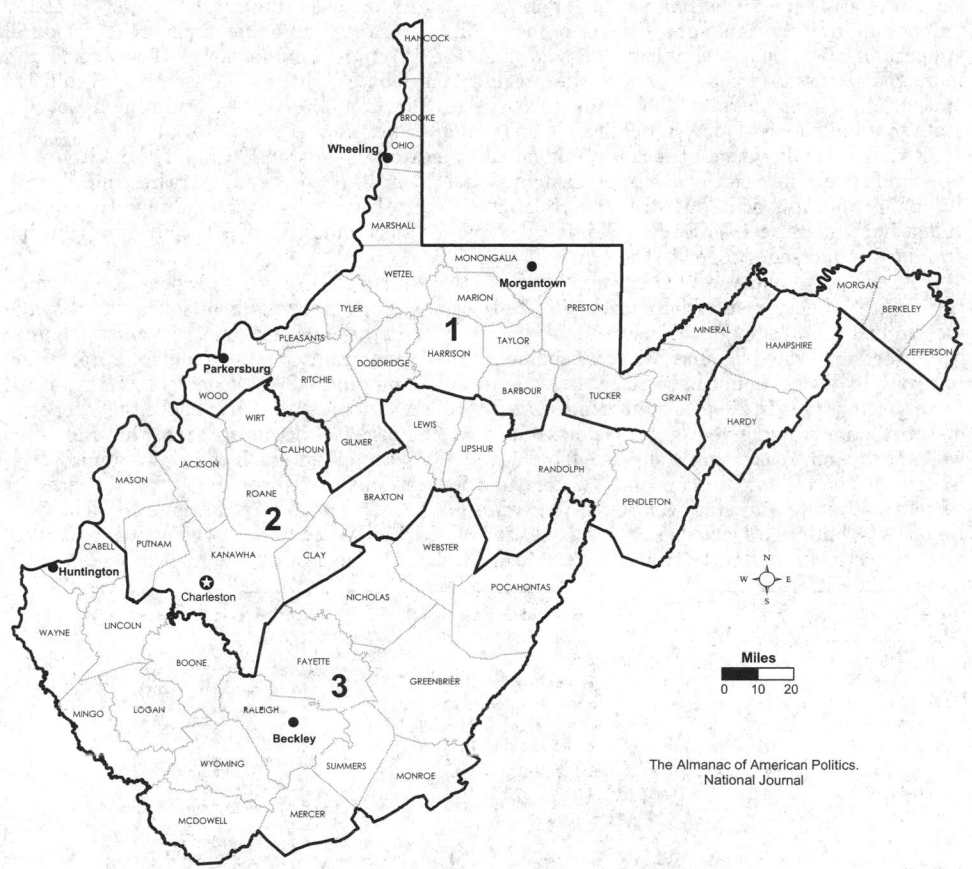

Congressional district boundaries were first effective for 2002.

but the pay is good and the jobs highly valued in counties which, in some cases, have half as many people as they did 50 years ago. Mining companies said that Judge Haden's decision would end coal mining in West Virginia. Senator Byrd threatened to overturn the decision in an appropriations bill; Bill Clinton said he would veto any such bill, and the provision was dropped. But the issue became important—arguably crucial—in the 2000 presidential race. In April 2000 the Clinton administration came out against a ban on mountaintop mining, but for stricter regulation; Al Gore was caught in the middle between environmentalists who supported it and West Virginia's all-Democratic congressional delegation which opposed it. George W. Bush, spotting an opening quickly, came out in favor of mountaintop mining and called for increased federal support of clean coal technology; he said that the Clinton administration "fears coal" and managed to mention coal in one of the presidential debates. Bush's support of coal and his opposition to gun control enabled him to carry West Virginia 52%-46%—a stunning upset in a state that hadn't voted for a Republican in an open presidential race since 1928. Its five electoral votes were crucial: Without them, it would not have mattered who won Florida. The environmental stands which helped Gore in large East and West Coast states proved fatal to his candidacy in West Virginia. In April 2001, the Fourth Circuit Court of Appeals reversed Judge Haden and ruled that under the 1977 Surface Mining Control and Reclamation Act, West Virginia's mining standards superseded federal standards.

As president, George W. Bush was attentive to coal. He got Congress to spend $2 billion on clean coal technology and from March 2002 to December 2003 slapped import quotas to help the steel industry, still a major coal user. All this helped Bush in the 2004 election. Democratic nominee John Kerry had voted against Byrd's amendment to save mountaintop mining and for air pollution control bills which would have cut coal usage by something like 40%. Democrats who regarded Bush's victory here in 2000 as a fluke made West Virginia a target state. They hoped that economic dissatisfaction would give Kerry a victory. But by September 2004 it was apparent that Bush was well ahead, and West Virginia slipped off both candidates' target list. Bush ended up winning 46 of 55 counties on his way to a 56%-43% victory, and Republicans won surprise victories in races for secretary of state and state Supreme Court. Most West Virginia voters continue to identify as Democrats, but Bush's victory raises the question of whether West Virginia is going to follow other mountain states like Kentucky and Tennessee and become predominantly Republican.

The People		Race/Ethnic Origin			Military veterans: 201,701 (14.3%)	
Pop. 2006 (est):	1,818,470	1,709,966	94.6%	White	WWII: 21.4%	Korea: 14.9%
Pop. 2000:	1,808,344	56,825	3.1%	Black	Vietnam: 32.5%	Gulf War: 8.4%
Pop. 1990:	1,793,477	9,356	0.5%	Asian	**Most populous cities (2006):**	
Change 1990-2000:	Up 0.8%	3,456	0.2%	Native Am.	1. Charleston	50,846
% of U.S. total:	0.6%	335	0.0%	Hawaiian	2. Huntington	49,007
Pop. rank:	37th of 50	14,983	0.8%	Two+ races	3. Parkersburg	31,755
Area size:	24,230 sq. mi.	1,144	0.1%	Other	4. Wheeling	29,330
State Native:	74.2%	12,279	0.7%	Hisp. Origin	5. Morgantown	28,654
Non-citizen:	0.5%	**Ancestry**				
Language		USA: 14.8%		German: 11.0%	Urban population: 46.1%	
English: 95.5%	Other Eur.: 2.0%	Irish: 8.6%		English: 7.7%	Rural population: 53.9%	
Spanish: 1.8%		Italian: 3.0%				

Education		Work Sector		Legislature	
H.S. Grad:	75.2%	Private: 75.8%	Govt: 17.9%	Senate	23 D 11 R
College Grad:	14.8%	Self: 5.9%	Family: 0.4%	House of Del.	72 D 28 R
Industry		Unemployment: 7.3%		Legislative Term Limits: No	
Agri: 4.1%	Con: 7.0%	**Household Income**		**Registered Voters**	
Fin: 4.6%	Info: 2.2%	<15k: 25.4%	15-35k: 32.0%	D: 648,889	(57.1%)
Mfg: 17.9%	Prof: 29.7%	35-50k: 16.4%	50-100k: 21.2%	R: 342,970	(30.2%)
Public: 5.8%	Trade: 15.9%	100-150k: 3.3%	>150k: 1.8%	O: 145,512	(12.8%)
Other: 12.9%		Median: $29,696			
Occupation		Poverty status: 17.9%			
Blue collar: 28.7%	White collar: 54.0%	**Home Value**			
Gray collar: 17.3%		<50k: 35.4%	50-100k: 41.0%	100-200k: 19.0%	200-300k: 3.0%
		300-500k: 1.0%	>500k: 0.5%	Median: $66,000	

Presidential politics   George W. Bush carried West Virginia twice, the first time since the 1920s that the state has voted Republican in two consecutive presidential elections. Between 1928 and 2000 the only Republican nominees it voted for were incumbents headed for landslide victories—Dwight Eisenhower in 1956, Richard Nixon in 1972, Ronald Reagan in 1984. In 2000 Bush cultivated the state assiduously, while Al Gore's campaign ignored it until the last weeks. In 2004 Democrats targeted the state early, and John Kerry made many appearances in the state; it was in Huntington, two weeks after he clinched the Democratic nomination, that he said, "I did actually vote for the $87 billion before I voted against it." But Kerry's record on coal issues and Bush's strong support from evangelical Christians and the National Rifle Association in a state in which 48% of voters are evangelical or born-again Christians and 71% are in gun-owning households put it far out of his reach. Bush won here 52%-46% here in 2000 and by a wider 56%-43% in 2004; turnout was

2004 Presidential Vote		
Bush (R)	423,778	(56%)
Kerry (D)	326,541	(43%)
Nader (I)	4,063	(1%)
Other	1,504	(0%)

2004 Democratic Presidential Primary		
Kerry (D)	175,065	(69%)
Edwards (D)	33,950	(13%)
Lieberman (D)	13,881	(5%)
Dean (D)	10,576	(4%)
Clark (D)	9,170	(4%)
Other	10,197	(4%)

2000 Presidential Vote		
Bush (R)	336,475	(52%)
Gore (D)	295,497	(46%)
Nader (Green)	10,680	(2%)
Other	5,472	(1%)

up 17% in a state with virtually no population growth. Bush carried every income group over $15,000, lost union households by only 53%-47% and carried 30% of self-identified Democrats. One possible glitch was South Charleston Mayor Richie Robb, a Republican elector who said he might not vote for Bush; but by Election Day he had changed his mind.

West Virginia's presidential primary, held in May, has not attracted much attention in years. But in 1960 it was the focus of the nation's attention when John F. Kennedy, reportedly fortified with large injections of cash from his father, took on Hubert Humphrey and beat him, proving that a Catholic could carry a virtually all-Protestant state. For 2008, West Virginia Republicans will hold a party convention on February 5, when so many other states will be voting; it is expected to be over early in the afternoon, so West Virginia will have the first of the day's results.

Congressional districting   West Virginia's three congressional districts, created after the state lost one House seat in the 1990 Census, were not significantly altered in redistricting—even though the process was dominated by Democrats and the sole Republican, Shelley Moore Capito, who won an open seat narrowly in 2000, could have been harmed by a partisan redrawing of the lines. But one or both of the state's two Democratic incumbents might have been weakened, if not for the general election, then in a possible primary, by such a plan. One Democratic legislator suggested removing the eastern panhandle counties from Capito's 2d District, and her 2000 opponent, trial lawyer Jim Humphreys, called for a plan that removed three Republican counties west of Charleston and substituted three heavily Democratic coal-mining counties to the south. But most legislators, preoccupied with redrawing their own districts, were content to please all three incumbents. In a September 2001 special session, the legislature with one dissenting vote removed Gilmer County from the 2d and placed it in the 1st and removed Nicholas County from the 2d and placed it in the 3d: Both are Democratic counties that had no significant impact on the 2002 results.

110th Congress Lineup
2 D   1 R

109th Congress Lineup
2 D   1 R

Projections based on 2000-06 population growth suggest that West Virginia will not lose a district in the reapportionment following the 2010 Census. If it does, the almost inevitable result is that the central 2d District represented now by Republican Shelley Moore Capito will be split between the 1st and 3d Districts now represented by Democrats Alan Mollohan and Nick Rahall.

Governor

Joe Manchin (D)

Elected 2004, term expires Jan. 2009, 1st term; b. Aug. 24, 1947, Farmington; home, Charleston; WV U., B.S. 1970; Catholic; married (Gayle).

Elected Office: WV House, 1982-84; WV Senate 1986-96; WV Sec. of State, 2000-04.

Professional Career: Co-owner, Manchin's Carpet and Tile, 1968-82; Owner, Enersystems, 1989-2000.

Office: 1900 Kanawha Blvd. E., Charleston, 25305, 888-438-2731; Fax: 304-558-2722; Web site: www.wvgov.org.

Election Results

2004 general	Joe Manchin (D)	472,758	(64%)
	Monty Warner (R)	253,131	(34%)
	Other	18,505	(2%)
2004 primary	Joe Manchin (D)	149,362	(53%)
	Lloyd Jackson (D)	77,052	(27%)
	Jim Lees (D)	40,161	(14%)
	Other	16,687	(6%)
2000 general	Robert Wise (D)	324,822	(50%)
	Cecil H. Underwood (R)	305,926	(47%)
	Other	17,299	(3%)

Joe Manchin, elected governor of West Virginia in 2004, comes from a family involved in politics for many years. Manchin grew up in Farmington, a few miles up Buffalo Creek from the industrial city of Fairmont on the Monongahela River. He remembers working in his grandfather's grocery store; he also worked in his father's carpet and furniture store, and took a semester off from college to rebuild it after a fire. His grandfather and father were elected mayor of Farmington; his uncle, A. James Manchin, was elected to the House of Delegates and, statewide, as secretary of state and state treasurer. After graduating from West Virginia University, Joe Manchin went to work in the carpet and furniture business, helping to send his four siblings to college. Then he started a coal brokerage company and eventually moved to Fairmont.

In 1982, at age 35, Joe Manchin was elected to the House of Delegates. In 1986 he was elected to the state Senate; a friend there was "Buffy" Warner, a Republican from next-door Monongalia County, the older brother of Manchin's 2004 Republican opponent Monty Warner. In 1996, after 10 years in the state Senate, Joe Manchin ran for governor. The Democratic primary was a riproaring contest between Manchin and legislator Charlotte Pritt, who had the support of organized labor. She attacked Manchin as the business candidate; unions opposed him because of his votes on workmen's comp. Pritt beat Manchin in the 11-candidate primary by 40%-32%. He declined to support her in the general election and attacked her in October; she lost to 74-year-old Republican Cecil Underwood, who had also been elected governor as a 34-year-old in 1956.

Manchin returned to Fairmont and seemed out of politics. But in 2000, when 86-year-old Secretary of State Ken Hechler ran for the U.S. House (where he had served from 1958 to 1976), Manchin ran for his office. So did Charlotte Pritt. This time Manchin beat her in the primary by 51%-29%. He worked with Republican U.S. attorneys to prevent vote fraud and was one of the few secretaries of state to comply with the federal requirement of a statewide voter registry. In May 2003, he announced he was challenging Democratic Governor Bob Wise in the 2004 primary. That seemed a daunting task, for Wise had already raised $1.2 million. But timing is everything: later in the month Wise announced that he had had an extramarital affair and would not seek reelection. In quick time eight Democrats and 10 Republicans joined the race.

In the 1996 governor's race, Manchin had been tagged as the business candidate. This time he worked successfully to get support from both labor and business. His stands on cultural issues were impeccably conservative: against abortion, gun control, same-sex marriage. But he emphasized economic issues, with a platform for concentrated state effort to spur economic development.

The cast of characters in the May 2004 Democratic primary was not unfamiliar. Manchin's best financed opponent was former state Senator Lloyd Jackson, who had started running against him in 1996 and then bowed out; another was Charleston lawyer Jim Lees, who had also run in 1996. Jackson ran tough negative ads against Manchin, but they apparently didn't have much impact. Manchin won with 53% of the vote to 27% for Jackson and 14% for Lees. In the more fragmented Republican primary, Monty Warner, a retired Army colonel and Monongalia County developer, won with 23% of the vote.

Manchin and Warner were old friends; Manchin substituted for the absent Buffy Warner at a family ceremony honoring Monty Warner on his retirement from the Army. They pledged to run a positive campaign, and mostly did. But the advantage was all with Manchin. He had far more money, and his implicitly low-tax platform undercut Warner's tax-cut, stop-lawsuit-abuse theme. Warner wasn't invited to appear on stage with George W. Bush during many of his frequent appearances in West Virginia, and Manchin's business support, plus the formation of a Republicans for Manchin group that included top Bush backers, helped convince the usually Republican *Daily Mail* to endorse him. The business community concentrated on an ultimately successful attempt to defeat Democratic state Supreme Court Justice Warren McGraw. Republicans also made gains in state legislative races—a dividend, perhaps, of George W. Bush's 56%-43% victory in the state. But Manchin won by a wider margin, 64%-34%, carrying 52 of 55 counties.

Manchin had been in office for just a year when he gained national renown as the public face of desperate attempts to rescue 13 trapped coal miners after the January 2, 2006 explosion at the Sago Mine in central West Virginia. Manchin, whose uncle was killed in a 1968 accident that claimed 78 men, arrived at the Sago mine within hours of the accident to offer comfort to the families of the miners and act as their main conduit of information. During the two-day ordeal, the governor appeared frequently at news conferences and gave numerous television interviews to national and international media outlets. But he also made an astounding mistake, announcing "the miracle of all miracles," that 12 of the miners had survived when in fact they had died, an almost unforgivable error considering the temporary euphoria it generated among the grief-stricken families. This was the kind of blunder that would seem a career-ending mistake. But in fact his standing skyrocketed in the polls, largely due to his sincerity and tirelessness but also in small part because West Virginia Republicans decided that the mining accident was a line that they would not cross. Asked by *USA Today* to comment on Manchin's performance, the state Republican party chairman said, "There's nothing political about this crisis. The governor represents the state, and we're all united in the heartache that we're all experiencing."

On January 26, Manchin signed into law a package of mine safety improvements, including wireless emergency communication devices, tracking devices and extra air supplies, and a $100,000 penalty for mine operators that fail to report mine fires and explosions to a central hotline within 15 minutes. After two other deadly mining accidents in the state, Manchin in early February ordered safety inspections at all West Virginia mines. In April 2007, Manchin signed new coal safety laws mandating certain ventilation practices and giving the state the authority to temporarily shut down mines with safety violations.

Taking advantage of his floor privileges and his experience as a former delegate, Manchin has achieved legislative success on other issues. In April 2006, he signed into law eight bills designed to improve state health care, including a new mental health commission, a low-income health care plan providing basic care at clinics around the state, and a catastrophic health care insurance program. He approved a bill that increased the minimum wage from $5.15 an hour to $7.25 over two years, though a loophole restricted benefit of the increase to just 2,000 workers. He also signed legislation restricting city governments in taking property in eminent domain cases.

Increased coal mining and video lottery revenue helped boost state tax revenues, which Manchin persuaded the legislature to use to pay down the state's portion of debt it owes to teacher and other state employee pension funds. Manchin also proposed a law increasing penalties for sex offenders. The bill died in the regular session after Senate Republicans added strict mandatory sentencing language and renamed the bill "Logan's Law" after an abused child who had been killed. After legislators met in a special June session and approved a compromise bill, Manchin signed it. During a second special session in November 2006, legislators delivered to Manchin a series of tax cuts, including a cut in the food tax and a reduction of business franchise and corporate income taxes.

Manchin enjoyed high approval ratings as Democrats headed into the 2006 elections and he proved to be a popular draw for Democratic candidates. In a bid to shift control of the House of Delegates to Republicans, coal executive Don Blankenship pumped more than $2 million into state delegate races; Democrats ended up improving their majority in the state House by four seats, giving them a 72-28 advantage. After the elections, Manchin added to his legislative success: He raised teacher pay by 3.5%, approved changes to campaign finance law and placed new limits on lawsuits from out-of-state plaintiffs.

Manchin's popularity has sparked discussions about his political future beyond the governor's office. He has been mentioned as a future Senate candidate if Jay Rockefeller opts for retirement. Other scenarios envision Manchin appointing himself to succeed Robert Byrd if that Senate seat becomes vacant, as a cabinet member in a future Democratic White House or even as a vice presidential candidate. But Manchin seems far more likely to run for reelection in 2008, and began raising money again in early 2007. The governor will be formidable: he had over $1 million left over from his 2004 race and Republicans have no ready candidate to challenge him.

Senior Senator

Robert Byrd (D)

Elected 1958, seat up 2012, 9th term; b. Nov. 20, 1917, North Wilkesboro, NC; home, Sophia; American U., J.D. 1963, Marshall U., B.A. 1994; Baptist; widowed.

Elected Office: WV House of Delegates, 1946-50; WV Senate, 1950-52; U.S. House of Reps., 1952-58; U.S. Senate Majority Whip, 1971-76, Majority Ldr., 1977-80, 1987-88, Minority Ldr., 1981-86.

DC Office: 311 HSOB, 20510, 202-224-3954; Fax: 202-228-0002; Web site: byrd.senate.gov.

State Offices: Charleston, 304-342-5855; Martinsburg, 304-264-4626.

Committees: *Appropriations* (Chmn. of 15 D): Homeland Security (Chmn.); Defense; Energy & Water Development; Interior, Environment & Related Agencies; Transportation, Housing and Urban Development & Related Agencies; Military Construction, Veterans Affairs & Related Agencies. *Armed Services* (3d of 13 D): Strategic Forces; Readiness & Management Support; Emerging Threats & Capabilities. *Budget* (5th of 12 D). *Rules & Administration* (2d of 10 D).

Group Ratings

	ADA	ACLU	AFS	LCV	ITIC	NTU	COC	ACU	CFG	FRC
2006	80	75	75	57	25	10	25	21	0	62
2005	95	—	100	65	—	10	44	20	0	—

National Journal Ratings

	2005 LIB	—	2005 CONS	2006 LIB	—	2006 CONS
Economic	60%	—	39%	66%	—	33%
Social	55%	—	44%	51%	—	47%
Foreign	76%	—	15%	92%	—	6%

Key Votes of the 109th Congress

1. Bar ANWR Drilling	Y	5. Confirm Samuel Alito	Y	9. Limit Interstate Abortion	Y
2. FY06 Spending Curb	N	6. Path to Citizenship	N	10. CAFTA	N
3. Estate Tax Repeal	N	7. Bar Same Sex Marriage	Y	11. Urge Iraq Withdrawal	Y
4. Raise Minimum Wage	Y	8. Stem Cell Research $	Y	12. Provide Detainee Rights	Y

Election Results

2006 general	Robert Byrd (D)	296,276	(64%)	($4,944,546)
	John Raese (R)	155,043	(34%)	($3,147,967)
	Other	8,565	(2%)	
2006 primary	Robert Byrd (D)	159,154	(86%)	
	Billy Hendricks (D)	26,609	(14%)	
2000 general	Robert Byrd (D)	469,215	(78%)	($1,045,993)
	David T. Gallaher (R)	121,635	(20%)	
	Other	12,627	(2%)	

Prior Winning Percentages: 1994 (69%); 1988 (65%); 1982 (69%); 1976 (100%); 1970 (78%); 1964 (68%); 1958 (59%); 1956 House (57%); 1954 House (63%); 1952 House (56%)

Robert Byrd, the longest-serving member of the United States Senate in history, may come closer to the kind of senator the Founding Fathers had in mind than any other. He comes from the humblest of beginnings, and when first elected to the Senate, as part of the large and talented Democratic class of 1958, he was scarcely noticed. Now he is the last member of that class still in the Senate, the President Pro Tempore of the Senate (and thus third in line for the presidency) and the chairman of the Senate Appropriations Committee. On June 12, 2006, he became the longest-serving senator in history, a landmark made bittersweet by the fact that it was the birthday of his wife of nearly 69 years who had died in March. When he cast his 17,000th vote in March 2004 (he has now cast more than 18,000 votes), his erstwhile rival Edward Kennedy noted, "Every time Bob casts a vote, he sets a new record. It is not fair, though, that he counts the votes he cast in the Roman Senate too, but we love him anyway and we never stop learning from him." But Byrd is also capable of having a little fun. He played a Confederate general in the film *Gods and Generals*, shot in 2001.

Robert Byrd comes from a background as grindingly poor as that of any American politician, as he recalls in his autobiography *Robert C. Byrd: Child of the Appalachian Coalfields*. "I lived in a house without electricity," he once explained. "No running water, no telephone, little wooden outhouse." Son of a coal miner in southern West Virginia, he was a welder in wartime shipyards and a meat cutter in a coal company town when he won his seat in the House of Delegates in 1946; he campaigned in every hollow in the county, playing his fiddle and even going to the length of joining the Ku Klux Klan (which he quickly quit and has for many years regretted joining). He worked hard in the legislature, and won a U.S. House seat when the incumbent retired in 1952; he made such a name for himself in West Virginia that by 1958, when he was 40, he was elected to the Senate—even though the United Mine Workers initially opposed him and the coal companies never supported him.

In the Senate, he became a supporter of Majority Leader Lyndon B. Johnson and in return got a seat on Appropriations his first year. He backed Hubert Humphrey against John Kennedy in the 1960 West Virginia presidential primary not because he shared Humphrey's liberal politics—his voting record then was as conservative as any Southerner's and he opposed the Civil Rights Act of 1964—but because Johnson wanted to stop Kennedy. In his early years he took care to master the Senate's arcane rules; as he said in 2002, "Nobody has ever used the rules of the Senate more than I have." In the 1960s, Byrd's career took what in retrospect was a helpful detour. He became assistant majority whip, an unimportant position in 1965; in 1971, when Edward Kennedy neglected his duties as whip after Chappaquiddick, Byrd quietly lined up support and, with Richard Russell's deathbed vote, ousted Kennedy. There Byrd performed ably, managing Senate business and accommodating colleagues' needs, and when Majority Leader Mike Mansfield retired in 1976, Byrd easily won the job. All the while Byrd was working hard to keep in touch with West Virginians, to the point that he won 78% of the vote in 1970, becoming the first West Virginian in history to carry all 55 counties. Byrd did not like being majority leader. Contrary to most people's assumptions, the post carries little power, because Senate rules requiring unanimous consent or supermajorities allow minorities and even individual senators to block action. Byrd was aware that his power came from meeting other senators' needs and did not have a national issues agenda of his own, though his voting record became notably less conservative. In 1987, with Democrats back in the majority after six years out of power, Byrd established some legislative priorities and then announced he would leave the post after the 1988 election.

In 1989, Byrd got the position he had been aiming for all along—chairman of the Appropriations Committee. He has been chairman or ranking minority member ever since. "I want to be West Virginia's billion dollar industry," he announced in 1990, and he has succeeded handsomely. Citizens Against Government Waste, a critic of Byrd's, reported in June 2006 that West Virginia had gotten $2.95 billion in spending since 1991, and that 33 projects were named after Byrd, including the Robert C. Byrd Highway, the Robert C. Byrd Green Bank Telescope and the Robert C. Byrd Hardwood Technologies Center. An FBI office went to Clarksburg, Treasury and IRS offices to Parkersburg, a Fish and Wildlife Training Center to Harper's Ferry, a Bureau of Alcohol, Tobacco and Firearms office to Martinsburg, a NASA Research center to Wheeling. The December 2000 final appropriations included more than $1 billion of spending in West Virginia. Some of it represents the ordinary operations of government, but much of it is Byrd's work. Since 1990, he has attached more than $270 million to appropriations bills for the construction of one interstate highway alone. He boasts that when he was in the state House of Delegates in 1947, West Virginia had just four miles of divided, four-lane highway. Today, there are 1,087 miles. Byrd has worked hard to find funds for the depleted United Mine Workers health care program for retired miners and their widows. He has supported the state's coal mining industry, seeking funds for miners displaced by the Clean Air Act in 1990, co-sponsoring the 1997 resolution opposing the Kyoto Protocol so long as it excluded developing countries like China, and opposing EPA's 1999 proposed air quality standards. When a federal judge ruled in October 1999 that mountaintop mining violated federal environmental laws, Byrd tried to pass an appropriations rider reversing the decision; he was angry when the Clinton administration, at first agreeable, decided to oppose such a rider with a veto. In April 2001, a federal appeals court reversed the decision and ruled that state laws governed mountaintop mining.

It should be noted that Byrd's positions are not just parochial but are the product of serious study of the Constitution and of history. He always carries a copy of the Constitution in his left breast pocket. With the assistance of Senate historian Richard Baker, he wrote *The Senate 1789-1989*, a two-volume history, plus two volumes of classic speeches and statistics; based on impressive research, gracefully written, full of arresting anecdotes and sound insights, it surpasses any previous work on the subject. Byrd earned his law degree while in the Senate and had his diploma presented to him by President Kennedy at the 1963 American University commencement where Kennedy delivered his most important foreign policy speech. In 1994, he was awarded his B.A. summa cum laude by Marshall University, which he had attended for one semester 43 years before and could not afford to continue, and where he earned A's in all eight courses he took. Byrd has been educating himself as well, systematically reading the classics, and takes to quoting Shakespeare, Thucydides or Cato the Younger in debates on the balanced budget amendment and the line-item veto.

If Byrd is determined to uphold the prerogatives of the Senate, he is determined also to uphold the prerogatives of the Appropriations Committee. He sees the Senate as part of a separate and equal branch of government, and he believes strongly in the prerogatives of appropriators. The Appropriations Committee operates mostly on a bipartisan basis and appropriators have worked together for years and cooperate across party lines against institutional adversaries like OMB and the authorizing and Budget committees. Byrd has served on Appropriations with his predecessor and successor as chairman, Ted Stevens, since 1973. When the Republican takeover of the Senate in 2003 cost Byrd his position as President Pro Tempore and his first-floor office suite, his colleagues elected him President Pro Tempore Emeritus and appropriated money for a new office. In December 2006, as he prepared to become Appropriations chairman again, he and his House counterpart David Obey announced that they would pass a continuing resolution maintaining previous spending levels for all appropriations except defense and homeland security, and would drop earmarks inserted into other appropriations earlier in the year. "While the results will be far from ideal, this path provides the best way to dispose of the unfinished business quickly, and allow governors, state and local officials, and families to finally plan for the coming year with some knowledge of what the federal government is fundng." He warned of significant cuts in earmarks in the 2008 appropriations but remained steadfast in his opposition to the line-item veto. In the 1990s he was lead plaintiff in a lawsuit challenging the line-item veto signed by Bill Clinton; the Supreme Court declared it unconstitutional. In January 2007 he stood like Cato in the Roman Senate against the latest line-item veto proposal. "I will stand back here and let my bones crumble under me, until I no longer have any breath in me," he said, rather than let it become law. "Such a process is a lethal, lethal, lethal aggrandizement of the chief executive's role in the legislative process. Lethal. Deadly....It is a gross, gross, colossal distortion of the congressional power of the purse. It is a dangerous, dangerous proposition, a wolf in the sheep's clothing of fiscal responsibility." Similarly, when Majority Leader Bill Frist threatened to change the filibuster rule in the confirmation fight over Samuel Alito, Byrd reacted furiously, even though he ended up voting to confirm. He has opposed just as strongly what he sees as a breach of Senate rules. When Ted Stevens attempted to attach a provision authorizing oil drilling in the Arctic National Wildlife Refuge into a military appropriation in December 2005, Byrd, although an Appropriations colleague of Stevens for more than 30 years, opposed it. "I abhor this idea. Shame!" he said. "If permitted today, the process could be utilized again and again, with terrible consequences for the Senate rules." Byrd said that the rules "must come first, before political party and before legislative maneuvering. Those battles are fleeting, but the Senate must stand forever."

His relations with the previous five or six administrations have been strained. George W. Bush went out of his way to shake Byrd's hand at his first speech to a joint session of Congress; Byrd had not attended State of the Union addresses since 1994 out of distaste for Bill Clinton. But Byrd opposed Bush's tax cut as "sheer madness," arguing that it was based on inevitably untrustworthy economic forecasts and complaining that it would cut off funds for appropriators. Byrd's insistence on maintaining what he regards as the Senate's constitutional prerogatives and his distaste for Bush administration policies led him to embark on two crusades in 2002 which may have helped lead to the Democrats' loss of their Senate majority in November. One was his opposition to the bill setting up the Department of Homeland Security. He insisted that the biggest reorganization of the federal government since the creation of the Department of Defense required more scrutiny, and he opposed giving the president authority to shift money between agencies without regard for congressional appropriators. His persistent speeches meant that the Senate, unlike the House, couldn't vote on it before the August recess or the September 11 anniversary that many senators had as a goal. In September, Byrd spoke frequently and at great length on the issue. He never used the word filibuster, but this was one in effect. It also gave government unions time to unite Democrats against the provisions for flexibility insisted on by Bush—a stand that hurt Democratic senators gravely in Georgia and Missouri on Election Day. In September, Byrd sought to require the president to get approval of the new department in three stages over the next year; that lost 70-28. After the election, Democrats realized it was in their political interest to pass the bill, and a motion to limit debate passed 65-29.

The other crusade was against military action in Iraq. In September 2002, he accused Bush of political motivation, saying out loud what some other Democrats believed but were too politick to say. "All of a sudden the president was dropping in the polls, and the domestic situation was such that the administration was appearing to be much like the emperor who had no clothes," he said. "All of a sudden, bam! All of this war talk—the war fervor, the drums of war, the bugles of war, the clouds of war, this war hysteria—has blown in like a hurricane. And what has that done to the president's polls? Seventy percent." In October, he threatened to delay action on the Iraq war resolution by insisting on votes on individual clauses; he was foiled when Connecticut Sen. Joe Lieberman and Daschle made a change in wording that made his motion out of order. His attempt to filibuster lost 75-25, and the Senate passed the resolution 77-23. Byrd did not give up. In January 2003 he and Edward Kennedy sought to require Bush to get congressional approval again. In June 2003 he called Bush's landing on the carrier "flamboyant showmanship." In July 2004 he said Bush was "dangerous, reckless and arrogant." In September 2004 he drew on his knowledge of history and said, "The Roman Senate lost its nerve, lost its way and succumbed. That's what we are seeing here in our own country. Our own Senate lost its way when it voted for the Iraq resolution." In February 2006, amid debate over NSA surveillance of communications between suspected terrorists abroad and persons in the United States, he said the Intelligence Committee had "jettisoned its constitutional responsibility to make certain that our laws are not being breached, and that the spirit and text of our revered Constitution remain in force." In January 2007 he sponsored a resolution to bar extension of the war to Syria or Iran without congressional approval. In February 2007 he complained of inaction on the nonbinding resolution opposing President Bush's proposed "surge" of troops in Iraq. "While our brave fighting men and women put their lives on the line in Iraq, the Senate stands paralyzed."

Byrd's umbrage at the Bush administration is clear. "I've never seen an administration so discourteous, so arrogant toward the legislative branch, as this one is. I've been here 51 years, so why shouldn't I speak out?" He opposed the Bush energy bill, even though it included money for clean coal research and utilization. He attended the Democratic National Convention in 2004, his first since 1988, and plugged his just-published book *Losing America: Confronting a Reckless and Arrogant Presidency*. He fumed when a trade amendment he placed in a 2000 agricultural appropriation was found by the WTO to be in violation of international trade rules, and in 2005 he tried to block the Senate from joining the House in repealing it. Of the promoters of the Family Marriage Amendment, he said, "The people who put this out [are] taking West Virginians to be gullible, ignorant fools." But he has, with West Virginia colleagues Jay Rockefeller and Nick Rahall, sponsored a constitutional amendment to allow voluntary prayer in schools.

West Virginia has had only three U.S. senators in nearly 50 years—since 1958, which saw the election of both Byrd and Jennings Randolph, who retired in 1984, 52 years after he first entered Congress (he spent some years in the private sector). In November 2000, Byrd was re-elected by a 78%-20% margin, his largest percentage margin ever, carrying all 55 counties for the third time. At a spirited rally at the end of the campaign he said, "West Virginia has always had four friends. God Almighty, Sears Roebuck, Carter's Liver Pills and Robert C. Byrd." He thus became only the second senator to be elected to eight six-year terms; the other was Strom Thurmond. In September 2005 he announced he was running for a ninth. Republicans, noting that George W. Bush had carried the state twice and that Byrd would turn 89 two weeks after the 2006 election, hoped for a strong opponent. But Congresswoman Shelley Moore Capito, Secretary of State Betty Ireland and former West Virginia University basketball coach Gale Catlett declined to run. In January 2006 a candidate stepped forward, John Raese, a businessman from Morgantown who had financed a campaign against Jay Rockefeller in 1984 which he lost by only a 52%-48% margin. Raese noted that he had his own connections with Byrd, who used to visit with his father, Dyke Raese, who coached the WVU basketball team to its only national championship and who lived in a house built by 1880s West Virginia (and Virginia) Senator Waitman Willey. "My dad would come down and say, 'Guess who called me on my birthday?' I'd say, 'I'll take three guesses. Two of them don't count. It was Robert Byrd.'" Raese took a seemingly laid-back attitude toward the campaign. "I'm running for U.S. Senate, not against Senator Byrd. I have a lot of different ideas, not that his are right or wrong. Mine might be better." Not, it appears, in the eyes of West Virginia voters. Byrd won 64%-34%, carrying 54 counties this time.

Junior Senator

Jay Rockefeller (D)

Elected 1984, seat up 2008, 4th term; b. June 18, 1937, New York, NY; home, Charleston; Harvard U., B.A. 1961, Intl. Christian U., Tokyo, Japan, 1957-60; Presbyterian; married (Sharon).

Elected Office: WV House of Delegates, 1966-68; WV Secy. of State, 1968-72; WV Gov., 1976-84.

Professional Career: Natl. Advisory Cncl., Peace Corps, 1961; Asst., Peace Corps Dir. Sargent Shriver, 1962-63; VISTA worker, 1964-66; Pres., WV Wesleyan Col., 1973-75.

DC Office: 531 HSOB, 20510, 202-224-6472; Fax: 202-224-7665; Web site: rockefeller.senate.gov.

State Offices: Beckley, 304-253-9704; Charleston, 304-347-5372; Fairmont, 304-367-0122; Martinsburg, 304-262-9285.

Committees: *Commerce, Science & Transportation* (2d of 12 D): Aviation Operations, Safety & Security (Chmn.); Surface Transportation & Merchant Marine Infrastructure, Safety & Security; Interstate Commerce, Trade & Tourism; Science, Technology & Innovation; Consumer Affairs, Insurance & Automotive Safety. *Finance* (2d of 11 D): Health Care (Chmn.); Social Security, Pensions & Family Policy; International Trade & Global Competitiveness. *Intelligence (Select)* (Chmn. of 8 D). *Joint Committee on Taxation* (2d of 5 D). *Veterans' Affairs* (2d of 8 D).

Group Ratings

	ADA	ACLU	AFS	LCV	ITIC	NTU	COC	ACU	CFG	FRC
2006	60	70	100	71	50	15	83	10	6	12
2005	100	—	100	80	—	7	50	4	2	—

National Journal Ratings

	2005 LIB	—	2005 CONS	2006 LIB	—	2006 CONS
Economic	77%	—	22%	62%	—	37%
Social	73%	—	26%	*	—	*
Foreign	87%	—	10%	60%	—	39%

Key Votes of the 109th Congress

1. Bar ANWR Drilling	Y	5. Confirm Samuel Alito	N	9. Limit Interstate Abortion	N
2. FY06 Spending Curb	N	6. Path to Citizenship	*	10. CAFTA	N
3. Estate Tax Repeal	*	7. Bar Same Sex Marriage	*	11. Urge Iraq Withdrawal	*
4. Raise Minimum Wage	*	8. Stem Cell Research $	Y	12. Provide Detainee Rights	Y

Election Results

2002 general	Jay Rockefeller (D)	275,281	(63%)	($2,299,519)
	Jay Wolfe (R)	160,902	(37%)	($136,935)
2002 primary	Jay Rockefeller (D)	198,327	(90%)	
	Bruce Barilla (D)	11,178	(5%)	
	William Galloway (D)	11,173	(5%)	
1996 general	Jay Rockefeller (D)	456,526	(77%)	($5,819,157)
	Betty A. Burks (R)	139,088	(23%)	

Prior Winning Percentages: 1990 (68%); 1984 (52%)

Jay Rockefeller's full name, John D. Rockefeller IV, has a familiar ring to those who remember his great-grandfather as the oil billionaire who was America's richest man, and his grandfather as the heir who had more than enough money to build New York's Rockefeller Center, restore Colonial

Williamsburg, and found the Museum of Modern Art during the Depression of the 1930s. Jay Rockefeller's father and uncles were men of impressive achievement in different fields, his father John D. Rockefeller III as head of the family's philanthropic efforts and founder of the Asia Society, his uncle David as head of Chase Manhattan Bank, and two uncles who became governors of states—Nelson as governor of New York for 15 years, a man of great building projects and fitful presidential ambitions, and Winthrop, who moved to impoverished and out-of-the-way Arkansas and served four years as a reform governor when the state needed it most. At various points in his life, Jay Rockefeller has followed the example of each, up to a point, with emphases and achievements all his own.

John D. Rockefeller IV grew up in New York, graduated from Harvard, and lived and studied in Japan for three years: his father's Asiaphilia is evident here. He worked for a year in Washington running the early Peace Corps program in the Philippines. Then, like so many of the elite of those years, he turned his attention from abroad to at home, and in 1964 went to the impoverished hill country not of Arkansas but of West Virginia, to work as a VISTA volunteer in Emmons, on the Big Coal River in Kanawha and Boone Counties. "Although I went to Emmons to help that community," he reminisced in 2002, "they helped me much more. My experience in Emmons set the course for the rest of my life." He moved on, more quickly than his uncles Nelson and Winthrop, to electoral politics. He was elected to the House of Delegates in Kanawha County in 1966 and as secretary of state in 1968, and then had the chastening experience of losing a 1972 race for governor to Republican Arch Moore. He served three years as president of West Virginia Wesleyan College in Buckhannon, and became more practical, dropping his opposition to strip mining. He was not shy about spending his own millions—his net worth was estimated at $200 million in 2006—and was elected governor in 1976 and, against Moore, reelected in 1980, after which the state was plunged into deep recession. In 1984, he ran for the U.S. Senate and beat Republican businessman John Raese by just 52%-48% after spending $12 million.

In his first years in the Senate, Rockefeller deferred to Robert Byrd and compiled a conventional liberal voting record, somewhat inclined to free trade because of his experience in East Asia. Then he began to concentrate on health care. With a seat on the Finance Committee, he got a place on the Pepper Commission on long-term health care. As chairman, he got majorities on the commission to back long-term care for all Americans regardless of age and universal medical insurance coverage. But getting others to agree was harder. He was motivated in part by anger at his mother's treatment during a long terminal illness—an experience that would be much worse for people of ordinary incomes, he thought—and he worked to increase the number of general practitioners, especially in states like West Virginia and Arkansas. As he was working on health issues, Rockefeller in 1991 gave serious consideration to running for president. He was 54, an age at which his uncle Nelson was about to make his second stab at running, and when he had developed expertise on an issue that seemed likely to be a major domestic priority.

Rockefeller talked mostly about health care financing when he was mulling a presidential race, and after he decided not to run he warmly endorsed Bill Clinton and applauded his emphasis on health care. Efforts at compromise on the Clinton plan came far too late, after voters had turned against a government takeover of health care, and the health care bill crashed and burned in September 1994. Rockefeller still would like a system-wide health care reform but recognizes that it cannot pass, and so he works on incremental changes. He opposed the Medicare/prescription drug act in 2003 and in February 2006 called it a "national disaster." In early 2007, chairing the Finance subcommittee on health, he was preparing a reauthorization of the CHIP children's health insurance program. Perhaps his biggest legislative achievement was his 1992 law, passed over furious opposition from Western coal states, which forced union and non-union coal companies and "reachback" companies that had gone out of the coal business to pay for the exploding cost of the United Mine Workers' health care trust funds; he has worked ever since to continue funding of this program for retired miners and their widows. Steel has been a preoccupation of Rockefeller for a long time. He was one of those who helped Weirton Steel, now West Virginia's fourth largest employer, become employee-owned in 1984. In the late 1990s, he called for aid to steel makers in the face of what he regarded as a flood of subsidized steel imports, arguing that workers and companies that have "played by the book" should get government help to allow them to continue in their jobs and their homes. In 2002, he called for 40% tariffs for four years on steel imports. The Bush administration in March 2002 imposed a 24% tariff in the second year and 18% in the third; Rockefeller complained when the administration made exceptions and when it dropped the quotas. In December 2005, unhappy with Mittal Steel's layoff of 800 workers at Weirton, he and Robert Byrd requested a meeting with company officials.

In January 2003 Rockefeller became vice chairman of the Intelligence Committee. The previous October he wrote to Pat Roberts, who became chairman, suggesting that if Democrats retained the majority he might fire all staff members and hire partisan staff. In July 2003 he argued that National Security Adviser Condoleezza Rice, and not just CIA Director George Tenet, should be blamed for the "sixteen words" about British intelligence in Africa in George W. Bush's 2003 State of the Union address. But at the same time he was criticized by some Democrats for not being a partisan "team player" and for not opposing Roberts's opposition to a far-ranging investigation of intelligence before September 11 and on Iraq. In June 2003, when John Kerry said Bush had "lied" about intelligence, Rockefeller said, "The Senator is running for president. And I think that Pat Roberts and I make a distinction between people who are running for president and therefore need to capture attention and what we on the Intelligence Committee have to do."

Later Roberts decided to hold hearings and in October 2003 he agreed with Rockefeller to include witnesses from the State and Defense Departments as well as the CIA. On November 4, radio talk show host Sean Hannity obtained a copy of a memo by Democratic committee staffers recommending that Democrats "pull the majority along" in extracting damaging disclosures from Democratic officials and then "pull the trigger" in 2004 to use the material to discredit Bush. Rockefeller said he never passed the memo along but declined to apologize for it, and approached Roberts with a letter promising not to let partisan motives affect the hearings. Roberts was not mollified. On November 12 he cancelled the committee's weekly assessment meeting and the next day he wrote in *The Washington Post*, "The Democrats planned to undermine the integrity of the committee by conducting a partisan attack, which threatens to destroy the credibility of an institution that has served the U.S. Senate and the nation well for nearly 30 years. I oppose them, and I make no apologies." Rockefeller responded, "One has to confront the very real possibility that this whole war was predetermined, so that the intelligence had to fit with the policymaking plans. So the Republicans just pounce on this little, pathetic stolen memo as the perfect opportunity to cover up whether there was White House manipulation of intelligence or whether there was [a] predetermined plan for war." In October 2002 Rockefeller had voted for the Iraq war resolution, so bitterly opposed by his West Virginia colleague Robert Byrd. In March 2004 he said, "If I had known then what I know now, I would have voted against it. I have admitted that my vote was wrong ...The decision got made before there was a whole bunch of intelligence. I think the intelligence was shaped. And I think the interpretation of the intelligence was shaped."

In December 2005, after *The New York Times* revealed NSA surveillance of communications between terrorist suspects abroad and persons in the United States, and that Rockefeller had been informed of the program several years before, Rockefeller charged that administration officials were misstating the facts and that they never offered him the opportunity to approve or disapprove of the program. In February 2006 he suggested that the *Times's* story resulted from leaks by administration officials, though it was undisputed that they tried to persuade the *Times* not to publish the story. Rockefeller protested vigorously that month when Chairman Pat Roberts adjourned a committee meeting after Democrats demanded an inquiry into the NSA surveillance program. The two later summarized their views. In *The Hill* newspaper, Roberts wrote, "I don't think it's a stretch to say that many in the minority would prefer to serve on 'the Committee Against Everything the Bush Administration Does.'" Rockefeller responded: "My Republican colleagues would prefer to operate in the dark."

In any case, Phase II of the investigation of the use of prewar intelligence was not completed before the end of the session; Roberts called for committee members to analyze prewar statements made by President Bush, members of his administration, members of Congress and Clinton administration officials without knowing who made them, and then to release a report detailing the comments and their sources. This might have embarrassed Democrats like Rockefeller, who in his October 2002 statement backing the Iraq war resolution left no doubt that he believed that Saddam Hussein possessed weapons of mass destruction.

The November 2006 election gave Democrats the Senate majority; Rockefeller ascended to the chairmanship, Roberts rotated off the committee and the vice chairman was Republican Christopher Bond. Rockefeller announced that his agenda included the NSA surveillance, CIA secret prisons, the administration's use of prewar intelligence and a "global counterterrorism plan for the next decade." He said that he and Bond would pursue a more bipartisan course, and that staffers would be shared without a partisan divide—of the kind that produced the 2003 electioneering memo. He proposed an agency-by-agency review of the law centralizing control in the Director of National Intelligence. Closed hearings in January 2007 focused on recommendations made by the Iraq Study Group. Rockefeller agreed to accept Bond's suggestions that it investigate shortcomings in human intelligence and radical Islamist ideology. He called for a separate warrant on every wiretap of a person in the United States and questioned whether the CIA should be running a secret prison network. He compared George W. Bush's statements on Iran with his pre-March 2003 statements on Iraq and said in January 2007 that the "whole concept of moving against Iran is bizarre."

On other issues, Rockefeller has co-sponsored with Robert Byrd and Nick Rahall a constitutional amendment to allow voluntary prayer in schools. He and Mike DeWine passed a bill in 2006 requiring labels on new cars showing their crashworthiness. He has introduced legislation to authorize the FCC to regulate violence on TV.

Rockefeller has been in strong shape politically—strong enough that in recent elections he has no longer spent any of his own money and still won handsomely. He won by 63%-37% in 2002. In November 2006, he said he intended to run for a fifth term in 2008. In early 2007 some Republicans were urging 2d District Congresswoman Shelley Moore Capito to run, but she announced in May 2007 that she would seek another term in the House. John Raese, who lost 52%-48% to Rockefeller in 1984 and 64%-34% to Robert Byrd in 2006, seemed interested in another bid. Other Republicans mentioned as possible candidates were Secretary of State Betty Ireland, former state Senator Steve Harrison and state Senator Mike Hall. If Rockefeller does not run, an obvious Democratic candidate would be highly popular Governor Joe Manchin.

FIRST DISTRICT

Rep. Alan Mollohan (D)

Elected 1982, 13th term; b. May 14, 1943, Fairmont; home, Fairmont; Col. of William & Mary, A.B. 1966, WV U., J.D. 1970; Baptist; married (Barbara).

Military Career: Army, 1970, Army Reserves, 1970-83.

Professional Career: Practicing atty., 1970-82.

DC Office: 2302 RHOB, 20515, 202-225-4172; Fax: 202-225-7564; Web site: www.house.gov/mollohan.

District Offices: Clarksburg, 304-623-4422; Morgantown, 304-292-3019; Parkersburg, 304-428-0493; Wheeling, 304-232-5390.

Committees: *Appropriations* (4th of 37 D): Commerce, Justice, Science & Related Agencies (Chmn.); Military Construction, Veterans Affairs & Related Agencies; Interior, Environment & Related Agencies.

Group Ratings

	ADA	ACLU	AFS	LCV	ITIC	NTU	COC	ACU	CFG	FRC
2006	60	73	86	58	29	21	50	46	21	57
2005	75	—	88	56	—	18	56	52	12	69

National Journal Ratings

	2005 LIB	—	2005 CONS	2006 LIB	—	2006 CONS
Economic	58%	—	42%	61%	—	39%
Social	63%	—	37%	59%	—	41%
Foreign	64%	—	35%	60%	—	39%

Key Votes of the 109th Congress

1. Estate Tax Repeal	N	5. Limit Interstate Abortion	Y
2. Limit CAFE Standards	Y	6. Extend Patriot Act	N
3. FY06 Spending Curb	N	7. Bar Same Sex Marriage	N
4. Drilling in ANWR	*	8. Stem Cell Research $	N

9. Build Border Fence Y
10. CAFTA N
11. Oppose Iraq Withdrawal N
12. Detainee Tribunals N

Election Results

2006 general	Alan Mollohan (D)	100,939	(64%)	($1,726,707)
	Chris Wakim (R)	55,963	(36%)	($729,046)
2006 primary	Alan Mollohan (D)	unopposed		
2004 general	Alan Mollohan (D)	166,583	(68%)	($524,011)
	Alan Parks (R)	79,196	(32%)	

Prior Winning Percentages: 2002 (100%); 2000 (88%); 1998 (85%); 1996 (100%); 1994 (70%); 1992 (100%); 1990 (67%); 1988 (75%); 1986 (100%); 1984 (54%); 1982 (53%)

The People		Race/Ethnic Origin	Ancestry	
Area size:	6,344 sq. mi.	95.8% White	German: 14.1% USA: 10.7%	
Urban population:	53.7%	1.7% Black	Irish: 10.0%	
Rural population:	46.3%	0.7% Asian	**2004 Presidential Vote**	
Pop. 2000:	602,545	0.2% Native Am.	Bush (R) 150,052	(58%)
Pop. 2005 (est):	597,570	0.0% Hawaiian	Kerry (D) 107,904	(42%)
Median income:	$30,303	0.8% Two+ races	Other 2,062	(1%)
Poverty status:	17.0%	0.1% Other	**2000 Presidential Vote**	
Military veterans:	14.8%	0.7% Hispanic Origin	Bush (R) 122,827	(54%)
			Gore (D) 97,432	(43%)
			Other 7,399	(3%)
			Cook Partisan Voting Index: R + 6	

Occupation   Blue collar: 28.5%   White collar: 54.0%   Gray collar: 17.5%

The northern part of West Virginia is in many ways an extension of the Pittsburgh metropolitan area. People here are Steelers and Pirates fans, they drink Iron City and Rolling Rock beer, they watch Pittsburgh TV, they live in the crevasses between hills cut by the Monongahela and Ohio rivers, on terrain that seems to forbid industrial and urban development. Yet this has been one of America's prime industrial areas; northern West Virginia is part of the same coal-and-steel economy that made Pittsburgh one of the nation's largest cities and filled the narrow bottomlands along the rivers with steel and glass factories, foundries and coal yards. These have been declining industries, or rather industries that have become far less labor-intensive; since 1980, the 12,000 mining jobs in this part of the state have dropped by more than two-thirds, with comparable fall-offs in manufacturing. The Weirton tin mill, which employed 14,000 in the mid-1970s and was the subject of an employee buyout at one point, was reduced to 1,300 in November 2005; it had three owners in three years. Replacing these jobs are service jobs—West Virginia's largest employer now is Wal-Mart—and the government jobs brought in by Senator Robert Byrd (the largest employer in Harrison County is the U.S. Dept. of Justice), plus a congressionally-aided high-tech spurt that some say will bring nearly 10,000 jobs to the Fairmont area.

The 1st Congressional District of West Virginia includes the northern third of the state and borders Maryland, Ohio and Pennsylvania. On the panhandle along the Ohio River are Victorian Wheeling, once one of the richest cities in the country with its steel and glass company investors and executives, and where the country music radio show "Jamboree U.S.A." has been broadcast every Saturday night for more than 50 years, and Weirton, named for Ernest T. Weir, the anti-union Pittsburgh industrialist who transformed it from a farming community to a steel town in the early 1900s. South of Pittsburgh on the Monongahela are Morgantown, site of West Virginia University and white-water rafting, plus Fairmont and Clarksburg. To the west, the district includes three lonely mountain counties—Doddridge, Ritchie and Tyler—that never heavily industrialized and have remained firmly Republican since the Civil War; Doddridge County was the only one of West Virginia's 55 counties to vote against Senator Robert Byrd in 2006. West of these, on the Ohio River, is the former oil-refining and shipping center of Parkersburg, which has become a plastics and manufacturing hub. For most of the 20th century, much of this territory was solidly Democratic. But dissatisfaction with the Clinton-Gore policies on coal and the environment helped George W. Bush carry this district twice. Bush's March 2002 decision to limit steel imports, as unpopular as it was among free trade advocates, foreign steel producers and domestic steel users, was popular in northern West Virginia.

The congressman from the 1st District is Alan Mollohan, a Democrat first elected in 1982. His father Robert Mollohan was elected congressman in 1952 and 1954, ran for governor and lost in 1956, and then won back the House seat a dozen years later when his Republican successor, Arch Moore, was elected governor. Alan Mollohan was born in Fairmont while his father served as superintendent of the State Industrial School for Boys, grew up in West Virginia and Washington, and graduated from William and Mary and West Virginia University's law school. He was working in Washington as a lawyer for Consolidated Coal, among other clients, when his father retired in 1982; he returned home and promptly won the seat. His one major challenge came in the 1992 primary, when he was redistricted into a seat with another congressman, Harley Staggers Jr., also the son of a congressman, and an ally of the National Rifle Association. Mollohan, who had represented more of the new district than Staggers, won 62%-38%.

Mollohan's voting record has become increasingly centrist and he has concentrated on bringing projects to the district. He got a seat on the Appropriations Committee in 1986 and today is chairman of the Commerce, Justice, Science, and Related Agencies Subcommittee. Over the next 20 years he was in the majority for eight years and the minority for 12, but the culture of Appropriations is bipartisan, and individual appropriations are usually hammered out by the chairmen and ranking minority members of each subcommittee. Many members earmark projects for their districts, a practice that became increasingly common when Republicans had the majority. Mollohan seems to have embarked on a long-range strategy of encouraging the creation of nonprofit organizations, many led by former staffers and close friends, through which he has funneled money into northern West Virginia. Critics of earmarks in 2006 set the five-year earmarks at $76 million for the Institute for Scientific Research, $31 million for the West Virginia High Technology Consortium Foundation, $28 million for the Vandalia Heritage Foundation, $6 million for the MountainMade Foundation and several million more for the Canaan Valley Institute. Altogether, Citizens Against Government Waste announced, Mollohan brought $480 million to the district between 1995 and 2006, more than half of it going to those five nonprofits. Mollohan argues that these nonprofits have created thousands of jobs in West Virginia, including high-tech jobs for 200 firms along the I-79 corridor from Morgantown to Weston, and in outfits like the Alan B. Mollohan Innovation Center, a computer software testing center in Fairmont. Mollohan defends his work: "The founding fathers gave Congress the power of the purse recognizing that the people's representatives were in a far better position than the executive branch to be responsive to the needs of people and communities," he said. "I am pleased to receive recognition for my efforts to support West Virginia, which is as deserving as any other state to receive federal assistance for community and economic development."

Others were critical of his practices. In April 2006 the conservative National Legal and Policy Center charged that Mollohan had failed to disclose all his assets, and issued a 500-page report that listed some 250 alleged misrepresentations and omissions. As amplified in a *Wall Street Journal* article, Mollohan had made real estate investments with nonprofit officials who were former staffers or contributors which had raised his assets from $565,000 in 2000 to at least $6 million (and perhaps as much as $24 million) in 2004. Federal prosecutors were investigating his finances, the *Journal* reported. Mollohan said that he had not been questioned and that he had profited from rapidly rising real estate properties in Washington and in North Carolina. In April he resigned as ranking minority member on the House ethics committee, explaining, "[O]ver the past two weeks I have been subjected to a concerted, politically motivated attack on my ethics that has been fomented by an ultra-conservative organization in Washington." Later in April the *Journal* reported that he had bought a farm on the Cheat River in Tucker County with the head of a defense contractor who had obtained a contract funded by a Mollohan earmark; Mollohan said they were old friends, and the contractor noted that Mollohan's other farm had been sold for development. In June 2006 Mollohan filed a revised personal disclosure statement, correcting 19 "unintentional" errors. In May, Republicans John Carter and Louis Gohmert said he should step down as ranking member of the Appropriations subcommittee with jurisdiction over the Department of Justice, and in December, the liberal-leaning Citizens for Responsibility and Ethics in Washington called on him to recuse himself from dealing with Justice appropriations; he said he would do the latter in January 2007.

Mollohan's service on the ethics committee was not uncontroversial. In September 2004 the committee unanimously voted to admonish—the weakest rebuke possible—House Majority Leader Tom DeLay for actions casting discredit on the House, though it found that he violated no House rules. Although Mollohan kept his customary low profile, he faced a no-win situation. Republicans complained about reports that he was sharing sensitive information with Democratic leaders, but when the committee later rebuked Texas Democrat Chris Bell for sloppy language in the complaint he filed against DeLay, Democrats privately charged Mollohan with seeking to protect West Virginia interests by cozying up to powerful Republicans. Locking arms with Chairman Joel Hefley, Mollohan defended the committee and criticized "erroneous" press reports. When Speaker Dennis Hastert and the new committee Chairman Doc Hastings tried to change ethics rules in January 2005, Mollohan resisted and the committee ceased to function. For months he resisted Hastings's desire to appoint his chief of staff as chief staffer on the committee; finally in June 2005 they agreed that the man would have a staff position, but that he would serve only as a liaison to Hastings. In November 2005, they hired as the committee's chief of staff a Washington lawyer with little involvement in politics who had made small contributions to Democratic candidates. The committee had only one live case, brought by David Hobson in November 2004 on behalf of John Boehner against Jim McDermott, but Mollohan indicated as late as March 2006 that the committee hadn't moved on possible investigations of DeLay, Bob Ney and William Jefferson, apparently because of lack of bipartisan agreement on setting up investigative subcommittees. Through all this, Boehner portrayed Mollohan and Minority Leader Nancy Pelosi as obstructionists, while Pelosi charged that Republicans "don't even honor a minimal standard."

On national issues, Mollohan voted against the war in Iraq and strongly opposed the initial Bush tax cut. He supported Bush's steel import restrictions as a vital step against unfair competition from foreign steelmakers, but protested when the administration subsequently granted a series of waivers in response to pressure from domestic steel users complaining about price increases. He has fought successfully to continue loan guarantees for steel companies, which has helped to keep Weirton Steel alive despite its financial troubles.

In the 2002 redistricting, Mollohan rebuffed Democrats who wanted a radical redrawing of West Virginia's district lines to disadvantage 2d District Republican Shelley Moore Capito, whose father had beaten Mollohan's father way back in 1958. In 2004, against his first Republican opponent since 1994, Mollohan won 68% of the vote, and carried all 20 counties except for Grant in the eastern Panhandle. In 2006, after the *Wall Street Journal* story broke and Mollohan resigned from the ethics committee, national Republicans made a major effort on behalf of the Republican candidate, Wheeling Delegate Chris Wakim. But Wakim was hurt by charges that he had overstated his military record, claiming to be a disabled Gulf War veteran when he served stateside during that conflict. Mollohan won 64%-36%, carrying all but Grant County and Doddridge County, the latter being the one West Virginia county where Senator Robert Byrd trailed that year.

SECOND DISTRICT

Rep. Shelley Moore Capito (R)

Elected 2000, 4th term; b. Nov. 26, 1953, Glen Dale; home, Charleston; Duke U., B.S. 1975, U. of VA, M.Ed. 1976; Presbyterian; married (Charles).

Elected Office: WV House of Del., 1996-2000.

Professional Career: Career counselor, WV State Col., 1976-78; Dir., Educ. Info. Center, WV Board of Regents, 1978-81.

DC Office: 1431 LHOB, 20515, 202-225-2711; Fax: 202-225-7856; Web site: capito.house.gov.

District Offices: Charleston, 304-925-5964; Martinsburg, 304-264-8810.

Committees: *Financial Services* (15th of 33 R): Housing & Community Opportunity (RMM); Capital Markets, Insurance & Government Sponsored Enterprises; Financial Institutions & Consumer Credit. *Transportation & Infrastructure* (21st of 34 R): Economic Development, Public Buildings & Emergency Management; Aviation; Highways & Transit.

Group Ratings

	ADA	ACLU	AFS	LCV	ITIC	NTU	COC	ACU	CFG	FRC
2006	15	18	14	33	86	51	100	80	47	57
2005	25	—	0	11	—	49	85	76	39	69

National Journal Ratings

	2005 LIB	—	2005 CONS		2006 LIB	—	2006 CONS
Economic	33%	—	66%		45%	—	55%
Social	45%	—	55%		41%	—	58%
Foreign	42%	—	55%		6%	—	86%

Key Votes of the 109th Congress

1. Estate Tax Repeal	Y	5. Limit Interstate Abortion	Y	9. Build Border Fence	Y
2. Limit CAFE Standards	Y	6. Extend Patriot Act	Y	10. CAFTA	N
3. FY06 Spending Curb	Y	7. Bar Same Sex Marriage	Y	11. Oppose Iraq Withdrawal	Y
4. Drilling in ANWR	Y	8. Stem Cell Research $	Y	12. Detainee Tribunals	Y

Election Results

2006 general	Shelley Moore Capito (R)	94,110	(57%)	($2,349,741)
	Mike Callaghan (D)	70,470	(43%)	($626,876)
2006 primary	Shelley Moore Capito (R)	unopposed		
2004 general	Shelley Moore Capito (R)	147,676	(57%)	($1,654,898)
	Erik Wells (D)	106,131	(41%)	($77,410)
	Other	3,218	(1%)	

Prior Winning Percentages: 2002 (60%); 2000 (48%)

The People		Race/Ethnic Origin	Ancestry	
Area size:	8,512 sq. mi.	93.9% White	USA: 14.7%	German: 11.7%
Urban population:	46.2%	3.6% Black	Irish: 8.1%	
Rural population:	53.8%	0.5% Asian	**2004 Presidential Vote**	
Pop. 2000:	602,243	0.2% Native Am.	Bush (R) 151,019	(57%)
Pop. 2005 (est):	624,919	0.0% Hawaiian	Kerry (D) 112,418	(42%)
Median income:	$33,198	0.9% Two+ races	Other 1,738	(1%)
Poverty status:	14.8%	0.1% Other	**2000 Presidential Vote**	
Military veterans:	14.8%	0.8% Hispanic Origin	Bush (R) 118,839	(54%)
			Gore (D) 96,524	(44%)
			Other 4,787	(2%)
			Cook Partisan Voting Index: R + 5	

Occupation   Blue collar: 28.9%   White collar: 55.1%   Gray collar: 16.1%

Not all of West Virginia has been coal country, not all of its valleys are industrial hollows choked with workingmen's homes and small factories, and not all of its hills are scarred with strip mining wounds or piled with tailings. It's true that for miles you can see gentle hills and rugged mountains, stands of green trees and vistas stretching to far horizons. Yet over another hill you may find, amid scenery primeval and rural, sudden evidence of industrialization: a pulp mill or charcoal factory in a clearing scraped out of the forest; a small factory town, built close to a river in a cleft bordered with hills, its houses built in the same 1910s style as in the factory suburbs of Pittsburgh; the entrance to an underground coal mine or a mountaintop blasted open to allow surface mining. Large parts of this naturally beautiful state look as verdant and unchanged as they must have when George Washington was speculating in land here or taking the waters in Berkeley Springs, or when John Brown launched his assault on the federal arsenal at Harper's Ferry in 1859.

The 2d Congressional District of West Virginia is a central slice of the state, a belt of land from Berkeley Springs and Harper's Ferry in the Washington exurbs all the way west to the Ohio River town of Point Pleasant, where the Kanawha River (pronounced *kuNAW*) flows into the Ohio. It could easily take a full day to drive through this mountainous district that, if ironed out, would probably spread across the continent. The 2d District includes the few fast-growing parts of West Virginia—the eastern panhandle counties, which are part of the Washington, D.C., metro area and have become home to some city folks seeking a quieter life, plus chemical-producing Putnam County just west of Charleston, where Toyota built an engine plant. The major urban center here is Charleston, where on the banks of the Kanawha rises West Virginia's Capitol, built in 1932 and designed by Cass Gilbert with a dome higher than the U.S. Capitol and a chandelier with 10,000 pieces of cut glass. Charleston, with its two partisan newspapers, the Democratic *Gazette* and the Republican *Daily Mail*, is the center of the state's political culture. It also is a major industrial center, with coal in the hills all around and, downriver from the Capitol, huge petrochemical plants that convert coal tar into everyday products. This was a center of American high tech in the 1940s, when it produced all the nation's lucite, polyethylenes and nylon, as well as much of its artificial rubber and anti-freeze. Today, the state boasts it is home to more polymer producers than any other place on the planet; the chemical industry makes products used in the manufacturing of cosmetics, detergents, shampoo, rubber, paints and coatings, fire retardants and agricultural products. Charleston is also West Virginia's professional center, with a few downtown skyscrapers and some affluent residential districts. But like much of the state, Kanawha County has continued to lose population since the 2000 Census. To the northeast is Upshur County, where a January 2006 explosion at Sago Mine attracted national attention as rescuers spent two days attempting to save 13 trapped miners; only one survived. Politically, this is an ancestrally Democratic district now trending Republican in many, though not all, races; Berkeley County, the fastest growing in the state, in the eastern panhandle votes like a Republican exurb. George W. Bush has carried the 2d District twice by comfortable margins, and it is the only district in the state to have elected a Republican House member in more than 20 years.

The congresswoman from the 2d District is Shelley Moore Capito, a Republican first elected in 2000. She grew up in northern West Virginia and in the Washington area, when her father, Arch Moore, served in the House from 1957-69. He was elected governor in 1968 and (over Jay Rockefeller) in 1972, and then again in 1984; later he was convicted and served three years in jail for fraud and extortion. Shelley Moore Capito graduated from Duke University and the University of Virginia, and is the first Cherry Blossom Princess elected to Congress. She worked for two years as a career counselor at West Virginia State College, and then was director of the state's Educational Information Center from 1978-81, when Rockefeller was governor. She served two terms in the West Virginia House of Delegates. Her opportunity to follow in her father's footsteps came when Bob Wise, a Democratic congressman first elected in 1982, ran for governor in 2000. She benefited from a divisive Democratic primary that was won by Jim Humphreys, a trial lawyer, former state senator and ally of labor unions, who made a fortune in asbestos litigation and spent $3 million of his own money to win the Democratic nomination. Capito, who supported abortion rights, started as the underdog but Humphreys, who spent another $6 million in the general, proved to be a poor candidate. One of the few beneficiaries of George W. Bush's coattails that year, she won 48%-46%, with big margins in the eastern panhandle counties.

In the House, Capito has received special attention from Republican leaders because of her precarious district. She was one of the few House Republicans to get a free pass to vote against trade promotion authority. Capito helped to make the case for her party's prescription drug plan for seniors and against the Democratic alternative. A firm Bush ally in the war on terror, she secured House commendation for Army Private Jessica Lynch, a district native who was rescued from captivity at the start of the war in Iraq. But the Bush administration rejected her proposal to distribute Iraqi assets to the former POWs. After the January 2006 Sago mining accident, Capito joined the West Virginia delegation in supporting legislation to improve mine safety by requiring that coal miners be given communications and tracking equipment and two-hour reserves of oxygen. After the Senate passed the measure, she persuaded House Republican leaders to schedule it for the floor, and President Bush signed the bill into law in June 2006.

At home, Capito has settled comfortably into her seat. In 2002, Democrats gave her a big break by again nominating Humphreys, who won another bruising and expensive primary; his 2002 campaign was even more ineffective than in 2000. Capito won 60%-40%. In 2004, her Democratic opponent was former television anchorman Erik Wells, but national Democrats abandoned interest in the district. The United Mine Workers endorsed Capito after praising her for blocking a Labor Department bid to weaken regulations on coal dust, and for legislation to protect medical benefits for retired miners, including 15,000 in West Virginia. Her victory margin fell to a still comfortable 57%-41%. National Republicans attempted to recruit Capito into the race against Senator Robert Byrd in 2006, but she declined.

In 2006, Capito faced attorney Mike Callaghan, a former state Democratic party chairman. In a year when Bush was a drag for many Republicans, Capito seemed unafraid to align herself with Bush on issues like energy policy and raised $560,000 at a July fundraiser with the president. As one of two Republicans on the House page board, Capito was forced to answer questions before the ethics committee in the final weeks of the campaign after revelations surfaced about Republican Congressman Mark Foley's sexually explicit communications with male pages. Capito ignored Callaghan's calls for her to resign from the board and said John Shimkus, the board's other Republican, did not tell her about Foley's contact with pages. Capito outspent her opponent by nearly 4-to-1 and won 57%-43%. She garnered almost 2,000 more votes than Callaghan in Charleston's heavily Democratic Kanawha County.

After Democrats took control of Congress in 2007, Capito voted for five of the Democratic "Six for '06" agenda items, voting only against requiring the government to negotiate with drug companies under the Medicare prescription drug program. Despite her labor-friendly voting record, Capito also voted against labor's signature bill, the Employee Free Choice Act, saying she believed in workers' rights to a secret ballot. Senate Republican strategists would love to see Capito challenge Jay Rockefeller in 2008, when she might benefit from the Republican-friendly current that recent presidential elections have created in the state, but she announced in May 2007 that she plans to seek a fifth House term. Capito remains a top Democratic target; Democrat John Unger, a state senator from Berkeley County, has announced he will challenge her in 2008.

THIRD DISTRICT

Rep. Nick Rahall (D)

Elected 1976, 16th term; b. May 20, 1949, Beckley; home, Beckley; Duke U., B.A. 1971; Presbyterian; married (Melinda).

Professional Career: Civil Air Patrol, 1977-88; Staff Asst., U.S. Sen. Robert Byrd, 1971-74; Bd. of Dir., Rahall Communications Corp. 1974-76; Pres., Mountaineer Tour & Travel Agency, 1974-76; Pres., WV Broadcasting Corp. 1980-present.

DC Office: 2307 RHOB, 20515, 202-225-3452; Fax: 202-225-9061; Web site: www.rahall.house.gov.

District Offices: Beckley, 304-252-5000; Bluefield, 304-325-6222; Huntington, 304-522-6425; Logan, 304-752-4934.

Committees: *Natural Resources* (Chmn. of 27 D). *Transportation & Infrastructure* (2d of 41 D): Highways & Transit; Railroads, Pipelines & Hazardous Materials; Aviation.

Group Ratings

	ADA	ACLU	AFS	LCV	ITIC	NTU	COC	ACU	CFG	FRC
2006	65	68	86	92	43	16	47	48	20	85
2005	90	—	88	83	—	19	56	44	14	67

National Journal Ratings

	2005 LIB	—	2005 CONS		2006 LIB	—	2006 CONS
Economic	64%	—	35%		63%	—	36%
Social	64%	—	36%		57%	—	43%
Foreign	81%	—	18%		67%	—	31%

Key Votes of the 109th Congress

1. Estate Tax Repeal	Y	5. Limit Interstate Abortion	Y	9. Build Border Fence	Y
2. Limit CAFE Standards	Y	6. Extend Patriot Act	N	10. CAFTA	N
3. FY06 Spending Curb	N	7. Bar Same Sex Marriage	Y	11. Oppose Iraq Withdrawal	N
4. Drilling in ANWR	N	8. Stem Cell Research $	N	12. Detainee Tribunals	N

Election Results

2006 general	Nick Rahall (D)	92,413	(69%)	($648,642)
	Kim Wolfe (R)	40,820	(31%)	($44,188)
2006 primary	Nick Rahall (D) .... unopposed			
2004 general	Nick Rahall (D)	142,682	(65%)	($930,079)
	Rick Snuffer (R)	76,170	(35%)	($89,312)

Prior Winning Percentages: 2002 (70%); 2000 (91%); 1998 (87%); 1996 (100%); 1994 (64%); 1992 (66%); 1990 (52%); 1988 (61%); 1986 (71%); 1984 (67%); 1982 (81%); 1980 (77%); 1978 (100%); 1976 (46%)

The People		Race/Ethnic Origin	Ancestry	
Area size:	9,375 sq. mi.	93.9% White	USA: 19.7%	Irish: 7.7%
Urban population:	38.4%	4.1% Black	English: 7.1%	
Rural population:	61.6%	0.4% Asian	**2004 Presidential Vote**	
Pop. 2000:	603,556	0.2% Native Am.	Bush (R) 122,707	(53%)
Pop. 2005 (est):	592,408	0.0% Hawaiian	Kerry (D) 106,219	(46%)
Median income:	$25,630	0.8% Two+ races	Other 1,668	(1%)
Poverty status:	21.9%	0.0% Other	**2000 Presidential Vote**	
Military veterans:	13.5%	0.6% Hispanic Origin	Gore (D) 101,541	(51%)
			Bush (R) 94,809	(47%)
			Other 3,942	(2%)
			Cook Partisan Voting Index: D + 0	

Occupation	Blue collar: 28.8%	White collar: 52.6%	Gray collar: 18.5%

Early in the 20th century, the coalfields of southern West Virginia were one of America's boom areas. Into rural farmland and hollows, inhabited by the same families since they first arrived at these mountains 100 years before, came coal company lawyers with mineral rights' leases to sign, coal company engineers to design and sink the mineshafts, and men from other mountain counties, as well as Europe, to work the mines. Company houses were built, company stores were stocked with goods as the company dictated and company paymasters kept close tabs on the finances of every employee. These conditions bred dull discontent, ignited into the fire of industrial unionism by the tongue of John L. Lewis, president of the United Mine Workers, who organized most of the mines in the 1930s. Lewis was not only a militant unionist, but also an isolationist, and during and after World War II he called out his coal miners on strikes, to the fury of Franklin Roosevelt and Harry Truman. The entire national war effort and postwar economic recovery seemed gravely threatened by these labor stoppages involving some 300,000 workers, centered in back corners of the country like southern West Virginia.

All that is history now. Coal is no longer central to the U.S. economy and there are only a few thousand coal miners left in southern West Virginia—and many are not UMW members anymore. Most of the old underground mines have been abandoned, leaving behind mineshafts and piles of tailings—and lives that were snuffed out by cave-ins or simple carelessness in America's deadliest industry. Manufacturing jobs in the area, which had been predominantly in the chemical industry, also have been reduced by more than half since 1980. There are few parts of the United States, apart from some central city neighborhoods and Great Plains farm counties, which have suffered such depopulation over the last half-century. But this region has still not hit bottom: Of seven counties in the nation with more than 20,000 residents that suffered more than 10% population loss in the 1990s, four—Logan, McDowell, Mingo and Wyoming—were in southern West Virginia, which has the oldest median age in the nation. To stem that tide, advocates of "clean coal" technology welcomed the Bush administration's 2004 unveiling of a $215 million project in Greenbrier County, which is designed to use waste coal to generate electric power with low pollution. But there are also vestiges of the past, as in the Bituminous Coal Heritage Foundation Museum in Boone County.

The 3d Congressional District of West Virginia includes most of the mountainous coal country in the southern part of the state that for years were among America's most heavily Democratic jurisdictions. Democratic voter registration is around 90% in Logan and McDowell Counties; nearby Mingo County—"Bloody Mingo," where coal company enforcers battled Matewan miners seeking to escape economic serfdom—is equally monolithic. But the coal mining counties now make up less than half of the 3d District. About a quarter of the population is in and around the industrial city of Huntington on the Ohio River, which includes Marshall University. Another quarter is to the east, at the interstate junction at Beckley and in the farming uplands around the resorts of White Sulphur Springs where, at the Greenbrier Hotel resort, the government built a massive secret fallout shelter (code-named "Project Greek Island," the bunker was intended to house the entire U.S. Congress in the event of nuclear war) that was finally opened to the public in 1992. The population of the 3d District in 1950 was 847,000—enough for two and a half districts at that time. In 2005 the population was 592,000, down 30% in a half-century, and possibly the biggest population loss over that period of any current congressional district in the United States.

The congressman from the 3d District is Nick Rahall, a Democrat first elected in 1976, at 27; he was the youngest member of the 95th Congress whose incoming members included Al Gore and Dick Gephardt. He comes from the thin economic upper crust of the coal country; his family owned radio and TV stations in Beckley and in St. Petersburg, Florida. He graduated from Duke, worked on Senator Robert Byrd's staff and then in the family's businesses. In 1976, when Congressman Ken Hechler, ran for governor, Rahall ran for the House and won a five-candidate Democratic primary with 37% of the vote. Hechler, having predictably lost the primary to Jay Rockefeller, returned to the district and ran as a write-in. Rahall spent $236,000 of his own money on his campaign—an enormous sum in those days and, at 27, beat Hechler 46%-37%; the hapless Republican got 18%. Rahall got seats on the Interior and Public Works Committees in his first term, fine assignments for a young member from a district with low incomes and poor roads. He is now (the committees have been renamed) chairman of Natural Resources and the number two Democrat on Transportation and Infrastructure.

Rahall has worked over the years to help the coal industry and coal miners. He was the chief House sponsor of the law requiring union and non-union coal operators to bail out the United Mine Workers health care funds and has continued efforts to secure federal funds for retired mineworkers. He chaired the Mining Subcommittee from 1985 to 1993 and developed the Abandoned Mine Reclamation program, the Coalbed Methane Development Program and the National Geologic Mapping Act. He and Robert Byrd passed an amendment to the Export-Import Bank reauthorization forbidding financing of foreign mining ventures. In May 2006, after the horrendous Sago mine disaster in Upshur County, he and Shelley Moore Capito co-sponsored legislation requiring companies to have updated mine emergency response plans, wireless two-way communication and electronic tracking systems, two rescue teams within one hour of each mine and to notify emergency officials within 15 minutes of an accident. It quickly passed both houses and became law in June. From 1993 to 2001, he was chairman and ranking minority member on the Surface Transportation subcommittee and was involved in reauthorizing the transportation act. For West Virginia he established the Rahall Transportation Institute, a consortium of five colleges at Marshall University and obtained $90 million for the Heartland Corridor, the old Norfolk Southern route through southern West Virginia connected to the Port of Virginia, where the double-stacking of trains is now possible.

Environmental groups were disappointed when Rahall in 2001 became ranking Democrat on the Resources Committee, because he had shown little support for their views. But he had worked to establish the New River Gorge National River as part of the National Park Service in 1978 and a decade later created the Gauley River National Recreation Area and the Bluestone National Scenic River. While he promotes the use of coal, he has by no means been a reliable supporter of measures sought by oil companies. He has opposed oil drilling in the Arctic National Wildlife Refuge and in December 2006 called the offshore oil and gas bill "a bumper sticker" bill. He has favored expanding wilderness areas in the West and opposed the Bush administration's energy package in 2003. In 2004, he received the Wilderness Society's Ansel Adams award for being "forceful, energetic and wise in preventing special interests from exploiting places that Americans hold dear." The Democratic victory in November 2006 meant that he became chairman of Natural Resources; Edward Markey, who has slightly more seniority (he was first elected in 1976 not only to a full term but to fill an unexpired term), did not make a push for the post. Rahall's agenda included increasing the royalties that oil and gas companies pay to the federal government for rights to deepwater exploration and overhauling the Mining Law of 1872. He said that he had no plans to rewrite the Endangered Species Act or to change the law on mountaintop mining. He reassured Western land users that he was not hostile to them. "My chairmanship will be about giving hope to that rancher . . . to those thirsting for adequate water and to that fisherman."

Rahall's family roots are in Lebanon, and he is often in the small minority of members voicing support for Arab causes and voting against Israel. In October 2002 he opposed military action in Iraq, saying, "I feel the Iraqis want to give peace a chance." In July 2006 he called for a cease fire between Israel and Hezbollah. He has consistently opposed trade agreements and in 2007 became a member of the Congressional Oversight Group that reviews trade negotiations. With Robert Byrd and Jay Rockefeller, he sponsored a constitutional amendment to allow voluntary school prayer.

Since his first election in 1976, Rahall has dropped below 61% of the vote only once. In October 2004, his Republican challenger said his polls showed him "neck and neck" with Rahall, and that voters wanted someone who "represents their interests ahead of his own." Rahall was reelected 65%-35% but failed to carry his home Raleigh County; he got 68% of the vote elsewhere. In 2006 he won 69% 31% with 70%-30% beyond Raleigh County.

★ WISCONSIN ★

Wisconsin, tucked off north of the main east-west routes across the country and squeezed between Lake Michigan and the Mississippi River, was at the beginning of the 20th century—and at the century's end—one of America's premier "laboratories of reform," in Justice Louis Brandeis's phrase: a state originating new public policies, seeing how they work, serving as an example for others. Wisconsin's first fame as a laboratory came during the Progressive era that began around 1900, and its primacy was due to an extraordinary governor, Robert LaFollette Sr., and to the state's unique history and German heritage. Wisconsin is the first state of that vast stretch of the United States reaching all the way to the Pacific, settled first by New England Yankees but even more by immigrants from Germany and Scandinavia. The German language is seldom heard now, the once plainly German beer brands now seem quintessentially American and few ties remain with the old country after two world wars, though in 2000 30% of Wisconsin residents said they were of German descent. But in the late 19th and early 20th centuries, Germans were among America's most numerous immigrants and until the 1890s probably the most distinct. They implanted, on the rolling dairyland of Wisconsin and the orderly streets of Milwaukee, their separate religions, often retaining their language and maintaining old customs, from country weddings to drinking beer—a source of friction in temperance-minded America—to eating bratwurst.

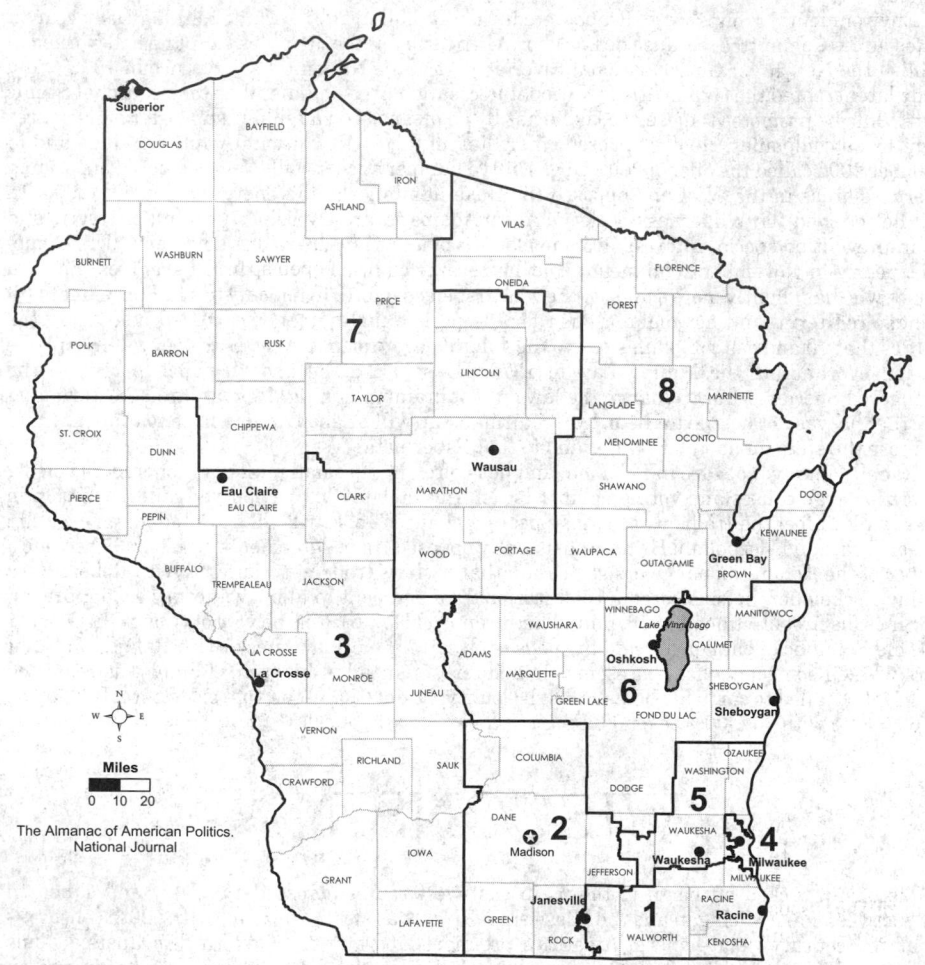

Congressional district boundaries were first effective for 2002.

Politically, the Germans were not monolithic. Their origins were diverse and they were spread too widely across the nation. But where they were concentrated, there was a distinctive politics, basically American, but with echoes of progressive ideas current in German-speaking countries in Europe. Nowhere was the politics of German-Americans more apparent than in Wisconsin. This is one of the two states that gave birth to the Republican Party in 1854 (the other is Michigan), and Germans, then arriving in America in vast numbers, heavily favored it. They abhorred slavery and welcomed the free lands Republicans advocated in the Homestead Act, the free education promised by setting up land grant colleges, and the transportation routes constructed by subsidizing railroad builders. Then came the Progressive movement of LaFollette, elected governor of Wisconsin in 1900. Up to that time a conventional Republican politician, LaFollette completely revamped the state government before going to the Senate in 1906. At a time when Germany was the world's leader in graduate education and the application of science to government, LaFollette had professors from the University of Wisconsin, just across town in Madison, help develop the state workmen's compensation system and income tax. The Progressive movement favored rational use of government to improve the lot of the ordinary citizen—an idea borrowed partly from German liberals and adopted by the New Dealers a generation later. All these programs were an attempt to bring bureaucratic rationality—Germanic systematization—to the seemingly disordered America of free markets and multiple cultures, gigantic fortunes and vast open spaces.

LaFollette became a national figure. He tried to run for president in 1912 as a Progressive, but was shoved aside by Theodore Roosevelt. He did run in 1924 on his Progressive ticket and won 18% of the vote, the best third-candidate showing between 1912 and 1992. He was strongest in the northern tier of states from Wisconsin west and along the West Coast—the same area of strength of later liberals George McGovern, Walter Mondale, Michael Dukakis and John Kerry. After LaFollette died in 1925, his sons carried on his tradition, progressive at home and isolationist abroad: Robert LaFollette Jr., for 22 years in the Senate; Philip, elected governor in 1930, 1934 and 1936. Philip created his own Progressive Party in 1934, with ominous overtones: a "Cross in Circle" symbol his critics called a circumcised swastika, huge rally-like parades reminiscent of some in Europe at the time and a call for the governor to propose all legislation. But Philip lost in 1938 and did not run again, and Robert Jr. decided to run for re-election in 1946 as a Republican but lost the primary to Joseph McCarthy. McCarthy's charges that Communists were influencing American foreign policy fed on the inarticulate convictions of many in Wisconsin and elsewhere that the U.S. should have been fighting Russia as well as Germany in World War II. McCarthy's national prominence made Wisconsin seem like a Republican state. But he won by narrow margins and the LaFollette Progressive tradition was taken up by liberal Democrats like Senators William Proxmire and Gaylord Nelson, and Governor Patrick Lucey. Like most liberals of their era, these progressives saw Washington rather than Madison as the main site of their laboratory of reform. Wisconsin, a mostly Republican state in the mostly Democratic years from 1944 to 1964, became a mostly Democratic state in the mostly Republican years from 1968 to 1988.

In the 1990s Wisconsin moved in another direction, and was a laboratory for different reforms, for which the state's economy provided a favorable environment. Wisconsin's high-skill, precision manufacturing economy jumped into gear in the late 1980s, and helped lead the nation's export boom of the 1990s. Yet much of the political focus remains on the dwindling number of dairy farmers. Wisconsin ranks number two in milk production, number one in cheese, but thanks to improved productivity the number of dairy farms has declined from 105,000 in 1960 to 45,000 in 1980 and 21,000 in 2000. For years the federal milk price fixing system was biased against Wisconsin, with prices higher the farther the farming operation is from Eau Claire; the Milk Income Loss Contract program adopted in 2002 is biased toward Wisconsin, with a limit on individual payments that works against big dairy farms in California. But California is threatening to overtake Wisconsin as the nation's number one cheese producer. One can't see Californians putting on the cheesehead hats you see at games in Milwaukee, Madison and Green Bay. But will Wisconsin continue to put the words "America's dairyland" on its license plates?

The motivating force for reform in the 1990s was, as in the early 1900s, a Republican governor, in this case Tommy Thompson, who beat a liberal Democrat in 1986. He cut taxes, sponsored a school choice program, and passed a series of welfare reforms—the nation's most thoroughgoing—which dramatically cut caseloads. Across the nation other governors and leaders of the Republican Congress looked to learn from Wisconsin's experiments: it's a fair question whether the 1996 federal welfare Act would have passed without Wisconsin's example to give its backers confidence.

Thompson did not carry all before him and left some fiscal problems behind him, while Wisconsin, proud of its clean politics since the LaFollette era, was suddenly beset by political scandal. Neither party is dominant. Al Gore carried the state by 47.8%-47.6% in 2000, John Kerry by 49.7%-49.3% in 2004. Wisconsin has two Democratic U.S. senators, one elected twice by narrow margins, and in 2006 Democrats picked up a 5–3 edge in U.S. House delegation. In 2002 it replaced Thompson's successor as governor, Scott McCallum, with Democrat Jim Doyle. But he won with less than a majority of the vote and Republicans gained control of the state Senate and made gains in the Assembly in 2002 and increased their margins in both in 2004. In 2006 Doyle was reelected 53%-45%, and Democrats picked up the state Senate and reduced Republicans' edge in the state House to 52-47. Wisconsin now has a political pattern the opposite of other Great Lakes states, where the biggest metro areas are Democratic and the countryside Republican. Doyle in 2006 won a large majority of Wisconsin's small counties and swept the relatively lightly populated western and northern counties. But the Milwaukee metro area was a dead heat, with three suburban counties casting the highest Republican percentages in the state, almost enough to overcome the Democratic majorities in Milwaukee County, where there was evidence of serious vote fraud in 2004. Governor Doyle resisted the efforts of Republican legislators to require photo identification of previously registered voters at the polls; the U.S. attorney in December 2005 found no evidence of major organized vote fraud.

The People		Race/Ethnic Origin			Military veterans: 514,213 (12.9%)	
Pop. 2006 (est):	5,556,506	4,681,630	87.3%	White	WWII: 21.1%	Korea: 14.5%
Pop. 2000:	5,363,675	300,245	5.6%	Black	Vietnam: 30.6%	Gulf War: 8.3%
Pop. 1990:	4,891,769	87,995	1.6%	Asian	**Most populous cities (2006):**	
Change 1990-2000:	Up 9.6%	43,980	0.8%	Native Am.	1. Milwaukee	573,358
% of U.S. total:	1.9%	1,346	0.0%	Hawaiian	2. Madison	223,389
Pop. rank:	18th of 50	51,921	1.0%	Two+ races	3. Green Bay	100,353
Area size:	65,498 sq. mi.	3,637	0.1%	Other	4. Kenosha	96,240
State Native:	73.4%	192,921	3.6%	Hisp. Origin	5. Racine	79,592
Non-citizen:	2.2%	**Ancestry**				
Language		German: 29.9%		Irish: 7.6%	Urban population: 68.3%	
English: 90.5%	Spanish: 4.1%	Polish: 6.5%		Norwegian: 5.9%	Rural population: 31.7%	
Other Eur.: 3.9%		English: 4.5%				

Education		Work Sector		Legislature	
H.S. Grad:	85.1%	Private: 81.1%	Govt: 12.5%	Senate	18 D 15 R
College Grad:	22.4%	Self: 6.1%	Family: 0.3%	Assembly	52 R 47 D
Industry		Unemployment: 4.7%		Legislative Term Limits: No	
Agri: 2.8%	Con: 5.9%	**Household Income**		**Registered Voters**	
Fin: 6.1%	Info: 2.2%	<15k: 13.0%	15-35k: 25.9%	No state voter registration	
Mfg: 26.7%	Prof: 26.6%	35-50k: 18.1%	50-100k: 33.6%		
Public: 3.5%	Trade: 14.8%	100-150k: 6.4%	>150k: 3.0%		
Other: 11.3%		Median: $43,791			
Occupation		Poverty status: 8.7%			
Blue collar: 28.4%	White collar: 56.6%	**Home Value**			
Gray collar: 15.0%		<50k: 10.0%	50-100k: 33.8%	100-200k: 43.6%	200-300k: 8.7%
		300-500k: 3.0%	>500k: 1.0%	Median: $109,900	

Presidential politics Wisconsin has been seriously contested in seven of the last eight presidential elections, and has voted narrowly for the Democratic nominee in six of them. The margins have been exceedingly narrow in the last two: 5,708 votes for Al Gore in 2000, 11,384 for John Kerry in 2004. The state was inundated by ads and lawn signs in both campaigns, and was especially heavily contested in 2004; Kerry stumbled when he came to Green Bay September 1 and referred to "Lambert Field" (it's Lambeau Field, as any Cheesehead can tell you). But Kerry perhaps atoned by abjuring the Northeast Dairy Compact and by spending three days later that month doing debate preparation in Spring Green.

2004 Presidential Vote		
Kerry (D)	1,489,504	(50%)
Bush (R)	1,478,120	(49%)
Nader (I)	16,390	(1%)
Other	12,993	(0%)
2004 Democratic Presidential Primary		
Kerry (D)	327,438	(40%)
Edwards (D)	283,376	(34%)
Dean (D)	150,548	(18%)
Kucinich (D)	27,306	(3%)
Sharpton (D)	14,691	(2%)
Other	22,891	(3%)
2000 Presidential Vote		
Gore (D)	1,242,987	(48%)
Bush (R)	1,237,279	(48%)
Nader (Green)	94,070	(4%)
Other	22,375	(1%)

In both these races some historic patterns were reversed. Bush carried metro Milwaukee, which casts about one-third of the state's votes, by narrow margins both times, thanks to big margins in the suburbs; while he ran far behind his father's 1988 showings in the nation's biggest metropolitan areas, he ran ahead in metro Milwaukee. But Gore and Kerry carried many historically Republican or marginal counties in western Wisconsin, just as they carried many rural counties across the Mississippi River in eastern Iowa. Indeed, this was the only rural part of the country where Gore and Kerry carried large numbers of counties and ran ahead of Democratic norms. Their biggest percentage margins were in Madison's Dane County and in Menominee County, which is an Indian reservation. Bush carried the Fox River Valley, and the eastern half of the state has become fairly solidly Republican. Western Wisconsin, with ailing dairy farms and an economy not so dynamic, has become the Democratic bastion of the state, with metro Madison providing the big Democratic majorities that metro Milwaukee no longer provides in the east. In 2000 Bush ran well ahead of Republican norms in the far north, as he did in the Upper Peninsula of Michigan and northern Minnesota. But in 2004 ancestral Democrats in this north country went back to Kerry, providing votes essential to keeping the state in the Democratic column. The Bush campaign in 2004 succeeded in increasing his popular vote margins in eastern Wisconsin, around Wausau and also in suburban Minneapolis-St. Paul. But Democrats held steady or better in western Wisconsin and increased their margins by 28,000 in Milwaukee County and 25,000 in Madison's Dane County. Those margins kept Wisconsin in the Democratic column.

Wisconsin once had one of the nation's most influential presidential primaries. It knocked Wendell Willkie out of the race in 1944, helped John F. Kennedy establish his lead over Hubert Humphrey in 1960, prompted Lyndon B. Johnson to withdraw as Eugene McCarthy was about to beat him here in 1968 and gave George McGovern his first victory in 1972. After that Wisconsin's primary, even after it was moved from April to March, tended to be ignored. So in 2003 the legislature moved the date up another month to February 17, 2004—the only primary held that day. Wisconsin saw heavier campaigning than it had in years, at least for a few days. It may have proved crucial. John Kerry led John Edwards 40%-34%, with Howard Dean in third place with only 18%. Kerry ran stronger among self-identified Democrats, Edwards better with Independents and Republicans, who made up 40% of primary voters; Wisconsin does not have party registration and few people bothered to vote in the uncontested Republican primary. Edwards carried only 12 of 72 counties (and tied in one other) and did not do as well as he might have hoped in rural areas but, evidently with help from Independents and Republicans, he did carry the Milwaukee suburbs. After Wisconsin, Dean went back to Vermont and ended his campaign, while Edwards failed to get the momentum an early victory here might have given him.

In 2008 Wisconsin will hold its primary on February 19, two weeks after the February 5 date when about half the nation will vote. Most observers expect the two parties' nominations to be clinched February 5, but if one or both of them are not, you'll be able to find the national press in the German restaurants in Milwaukee and campus hangouts in Madison, out in the parking lot in Lambeau Field or trailing campaign buses through rolling dairyland.

Congressional districting   Wisconsin lost a congressional district in the 2000 Census. Ordinarily that would trigger a fierce battle between a Republican governor and Assembly and Democratic state Senate. But in May 2001 5th District Democrat Tom Barrett announced he was running for governor. His north Milwaukee district had lost population and was easy to eliminate. The result was a consensus plan, approved by the House delegation, passed by both houses of the legislature and signed by the governor in March 2002. A lawsuit brought a year earlier was dismissed a day later. This is one state that produced a plan with regularly shaped districts with obvious communities of interest; it was also a plan that enabled all eight incumbents running to win reelection easily, though when 8th District Republican Mark Green ran for governor in 2006 his seat was picked up by Democrat Steve Kagen.

110th Congress Lineup	
5 D	3 R
109th Congress Lineup	
4 D	4 R

Governor

James Doyle (D)

Elected 2002, term expires Jan. 2011, 2d term; b. Nov. 23, 1945, Washington, DC; home, Maple Bluff; Attended Stanford U. 1963-66, U. of WI, B.A. 1967, Harvard U., J.D. 1972; Catholic; married (Jessica).

Elected Office: Dane Cnty. D.A., 1976-82; WI Atty. Gen. 1990-02.

Professional Career: Peace Corps, Tunisia, 1967-69; Atty., Navajo Indian Reservation (Chinle, AZ), 1972-75; Practicing atty., 1982-90.

Office: 115 E. State Capitol, Madison, 53707, 608-266-1212; Fax: 608-267-8983; Web site: www.wisgov.state.wi.us.

Election Results

2006 general	James Doyle (D)	1,139,115	(53%)
	Mark Green (R)	979,427	(45%)
	Other	43,158	(2%)
2006 primary	James Doyle (D)	unopposed	
2002 general	James Doyle (D)	800,515	(45%)
	Scott McCallum (R)	734,779	(41%)
	Ed Thompson (Lib)	185,455	(10%)

James Doyle, a Democrat, was elected governor of Wisconsin in 2002. He grew up in Madison, in a political family. His parents were part of a group of Madison liberals in the rising Democratic party of the 1950s and the dominant Democratic party of the 1960s—Governor and Senator Gaylord Nelson, Senator William Proxmire, Governor Pat Lucey, Governor John Reynolds, *Capital Times* editor Miles McMillan. Doyle's mother was elected to the Wisconsin Assembly in 1948, only the second woman there, but the fourth generation of her family (the Bachhubers) to serve there. His father ran for governor in 1954 and lost the primary to Proxmire; in 1967 he became a federal judge, for years the only judge in the Western District of Wisconsin, and issued dozens of liberal rulings disallowing state and federal government actions. Jim Doyle was a star basketball player and top student in high school in Madison, went to Stanford for three years and then graduated from the University of Wisconsin. With his wife, a niece of Congressman and Defense Secretary Melvin Laird, he spent two years in the Peace Corps in Tunisia; back in the U.S. they marched in Washington in protest of the Vietnam War and then met Laird in his office in the Pentagon. Doyle graduated from Harvard Law School, then worked for three years as a lawyer on the Navajo Reservation in Arizona.

He returned to Madison in 1975 and in 1976 ran against Dane County District Attorney Humphrey Lynch, a Democrat, and beat him. He served for six years, then went into private practice in Madison. In 1990 he ran for attorney general and defeated the incumbent Republican. His best publicized accomplishment was the state's $6 billion tobacco settlement, but he was criticized for paying the state's lawyers $847 million; Ed Garvey, a Democrat who had run for governor, sued and got the fee blocked.

Governor Tommy Thompson, long the dominant figure in state politics and the author of the changes in welfare laws that became a model for the nation, left Madison in January 2001 after 14 years as governor to become Secretary of Health and Human Services, and Lieutenant Governor Scott McCallum became governor. He was faced with more serious budget problems than Thompson had faced in many years, and in January 2002 he proposed that the state cut $1 billion in aid to local governments over the next three years. The cut in local aid was unpopular and McCallum's job rating, hovering around 50% in fall 2001, fell to about 35% in spring 2002.

Four Democrats lined up to run against McCallum. Doyle was endorsed by former Governors Gaylord Nelson, Pat Lucey (who had managed his father's campaign for governor in 1954) and Martin Schreiber. But he was backed by few legislators, many of whom were angry at his prosecutorial attitude toward state Senate Majority Leader Chuck Chvala, who was in trouble because his staffers had been politicking in his state office. Doyle started off much better known than his Democratic rivals, none of whom had a statewide base. Milwaukee Congressman Tom Barrett was well known in his district and, from previous service in the state Senate and Assembly, popular among Democratic legislators, most of whom endorsed him. Dane County Executive Kathleen Falk ran as a candidate with executive experience and was relying on her Madison area base and EMILY's List. State Senator Gary George ran as the candidate with the most experience in state government and hoped to build on his base among teachers' unions and Milwaukee blacks. But Wisconsin's population is only 6% black (three-quarters of whom live in Milwaukee) and George was thrown off the ballot in July for invalid signatures.

The Democratic candidates avoided negative campaigning; the ads were mostly positive. Doyle's showed his two grown sons, who are adopted and of African-American descent, praising him. In the September primary Doyle ran pretty evenly statewide, in no county above 54% or below 30%; the others' support was mostly in their bases.

Doyle came out of primary night swinging at McCallum. "He's living proof that not all on-the-job training programs are successful," said Doyle. He continued to run on cutting $1 billion by reducing the number of state employees and attacked McCallum for spending the state's entire tobacco settlement on balancing one year's budget. McCallum, who emerged from the primary with three times as much money, ran an ad showing a messy desk and spilled coffee and attacked Doyle for missing deadlines while doing the state's legal business. McCallum said he would balance the budget through revenue growth and said Doyle had promised teachers' unions and other groups programs that would cost $2.7 billion on top of an anticipated $2.8 billion shortfall. Into the fray also stepped a third candidate, Libertarian nominee Ed Thompson, who ran the Tee-Pee Supper Club in Tomah and was elected mayor of the town. But the real reason Thompson attracted attention was because he is Tommy Thompson's brother. In public polls Doyle had the lead, but never took off, while McCallum never seemed to rise above his lackluster job rating and Thompson ran in the high single digits.

In November Doyle beat McCallum 45%-41%, with 10% for Ed Thompson; Thompson carried the county where he lived and the next-door county where he grew up. It was a narrow win for Doyle, and one accompanied by Republican gains in legislative races: Republicans won control of the state Senate 18-15 and enlarged their Assembly majority to 58-41. In many ways this was a different race in different media markets. In the Milwaukee market McCallum led 47%-44%, with Thompson at 7%; in the Fox River Valley McCallum led 47%-41%, with Thompson at 8%. This eastern part of Wisconsin, with 57% of votes, went Republican. Where Doyle won was in the Madison market, where he led 49%-30%, and Thompson got 17%, and in the Wausau and Eau Claire markets, where he led 44%-37%, and Thompson got 15%. These two areas cast 35% of the state's votes. In the farthest west counties, served by Twin Cities and Duluth TV, Thompson was not much of a factor, with just 5% of the votes; here Doyle led 50%-24%.

In office Doyle faced a $3.2 billion deficit but, working with Republican legislators, was able to balance the budget without increasing sales, income or corporate taxes. A tax on job creation was eliminated and a single-tax formula based on corporate sales established. So was a sales tax exemption for the cost of energy used in manufacturing. Doyle declared that taxes as a percentage of income were the lowest in Wisconsin in 34 years and said Republican legislators deserved some of the credit. In December 2004, he cut state employment by 1,500—a little below his goal. He sought to increase Wisconsin's trade with China (which is encouraging milk-drinking, despite its people's reputation for being lactose intolerant), Japan and Mexico. And in fact Wisconsin was gaining jobs, even manufacturing jobs, in 2003 and 2004 when job growth in nearby states like Michigan and Ohio was flagging.

Wisconsin's governor has broad and quirky veto powers, and he has exercised them all against a Republican legislature eager to advance its agenda. He vetoed 54 bills in his first session and then 47 bills in 2005-2006 session. He twice vetoed bills allowing residents to carry concealed weapons (and was just one vote away from being overridden) and three times vetoed a bill requiring voters to show a photo ID (he said seniors often have a hard time producing identification). In January 2005, facing a two-year projected deficit of $1.6 billion, Doyle again came out against a tax increase; he proposed increasing school aid while holding down property tax increases (Republicans wanted a freeze). Doyle threatened to veto the entire two-year $54 billion budget that Republicans had approved because it gave Doyle less than half of the additional $938 million he sought for school spending. Instead Doyle made creative use of his line-item veto authority to bring the bill more closely into line with his own priorities. He made 139 separate changes that redirected $360 million in other funding to boost school spending by $861 million, in addition to placing limits on property tax increases. Doyle also vetoed a measure to ban human cloning that he said would restrict stem cell research.

In March 2006 Doyle did sign the Real ID bill that requires those applying for driver's licenses to show proof of local residency. In the same month, he supported a bill to raise the cap on enrollment in Milwaukee's school choice program and another to cap non-economic damages in medical malpractice cases to $750,000. The state Supreme Court had struck down limits in July 2005, and Doyle had vetoed new caps established by the legislature in December 2005, saying they were too close to the caps the court had already struck down. Later that spring, he vetoed bills to allow lawmakers a say in approving new off-reservation Indian casinos and to give residents a tax deduction for health savings accounts.

Elected with 45% in 2002, Doyle had been unable to move his approval ratings above 50% since. That left him seemingly vulnerable in 2006 to Green Bay-area Congressman Mark Green, who had traveled the state stumping for Assembly candidates in 2004 and began the governor's race by transferring $1.3 million from his federal account. Doyle offered himself up as a problem-solver who cleaned up the problems from Republican administrations; Green ran on an anti-tax platform and said he would limit state spending. But it wasn't entirely clear until the summer that Green would be the Republican nominee. Milwaukee County Executive Scott Walker considered a bid before withdrawing in March 2006; former Governor Tommy Thompson flirted with returning to office as late as May 2006, confidently predicting: "If I run, I win." Thompson ultimately decided not to run, but just speculating about it had the effect of undermining Green's candidacy.

Doyle, an energetic supporter of the University of Wisconsin's pioneering stem cell research, made Green's votes against embryonic stem cell research a central line of attack; stem cell research was an untested political issue, but one that Doyle calculated would resonate with undecided voters who saw it as having the potential to cure a range of diseases. Doyle's second ad featured a mother who said Green's votes stood in the way of research that could help her daughter's juvenile diabetes; actor Michael J. Fox, afflicted with Parkinson's disease, cut an ad for Doyle just before Election Day. Republicans tried reminding voters of the state procurement official who was found guilty of steering travel contracts to Doyle contributors and of Doyle appointees who approved the sale of a nuclear power plant the same month the plants owners donated to Doyle's campaign. But Green ran into his own fundraising conflicts when the state elections board ordered him to return nearly $470,000 from out-of-state PACs that he had transferred from his federal campaign account. In the week before the election, Green and the Republican Governors Association ran spots charging Doyle had changed his position on Indian gaming when he negotiated 2003 agreements with tribal governments. "Jim Doyle opposed new casinos, but after tribal casinos spent millions to elect him, Doyle changed his tune," one ad alleged.

The Republican legislature had also placed same-sex marriage and death penalty initiatives on the November ballot, raising the prospect of increased conservative voter turnout. But Doyle won 53%-45%, becoming the first Democratic governor in over 30 years to win re-election. He won 70% in Madison's Dane County and 62% in Milwaukee County. Democrats also won four seats in the state Senate to claim an 18-15 majority, and picked up eight seats in the Assembly to narrow the Republican majority to a 52-47 margin.

Doyle began 2007 with ambitious plans for expanding access to affordable health care to 98% of residents by creating BadgerCare Plus, which would combine three programs to form one comprehensive program focusing on uninsured children and self-employed adults. Doyle proposed raising the per-pack cigarette tax by $1.25 to $2.02 and increasing funding for the University of Wisconsin system by $225 million over two years. Doyle proposed allowing local governments to increase their tax levies by 4% after the 2% cap expired January 1, 2007. He pledged the state would help control property taxes by paying two-thirds of public school costs, although a nonpartisan study concluded his proposed budget fell $100 million short of that goal.

Senior Senator

Herb Kohl (D)

Elected 1988, seat up 2012, 4th term; b. Feb. 7, 1935, Milwaukee; home, Milwaukee; U. of WI, B.A. 1956, Harvard U., M.B.A. 1958; Jewish; single.

Military Career: Army Reserves, 1958-64.

Professional Career: Businessman; Pres., Kohl Corp., 1970-79; Chmn., WI Dem. Party, 1975-77; Pres., Herbert Kohl Investments, 1979-88; Owner, Milwaukee Bucks pro basketball team, 1985-present.

DC Office: 330 HSOB, 20510, 202-224-5653; Fax: 202-224-9787; Web site: kohl.senate.gov.

State Offices: Appleton, 920-738-1640; Eau Claire, 715-832-8424; LaCrosse, 608-796-0045; Madison, 608-264-5338; Milwaukee, 414-297-4451.

Committees: *Aging (Special)* (Chmn. of 11 D). *Appropriations* (6th of 15 D): Agriculture, Rural Development, Food and Drug Administration & Related Agencies (Chmn.); Labor, Health and Human Services, Education & Related Agencies; Commerce, Justice, Science & Related Agencies; Transportation, Housing and Urban Development & Related Agencies; Homeland Security; Interior, Environment & Related Agencies; Defense. *Judiciary* (4th of 10 D): Antitrust, Competition Policy & Consumer Rights (Chmn.); Crime & Drugs; Terrorism, Technology & Homeland Security.

Group Ratings

	ADA	ACLU	AFS	LCV	ITIC	NTU	COC	ACU	CFG	FRC
2006	90	75	100	71	75	14	50	16	6	12
2005	100	—	88	75	—	14	67	13	0	—

National Journal Ratings

	2005 LIB	—	2005 CONS		2006 LIB	—	2006 CONS
Economic	72%	—	27%		75%	—	22%
Social	71%	—	28%		67%	—	32%
Foreign	90%	—	5%		67%	—	29%

Key Votes of the 109th Congress

1. Bar ANWR Drilling	Y	5. Confirm Samuel Alito	N	9. Limit Interstate Abortion	Y
2. FY06 Spending Curb	N	6. Path to Citizenship	Y	10. CAFTA	N
3. Estate Tax Repeal	N	7. Bar Same Sex Marriage	N	11. Urge Iraq Withdrawal	Y
4. Raise Minimum Wage	Y	8. Stem Cell Research $	Y	12. Provide Detainee Rights	Y

Election Results

2006 general	Herb Kohl (D)	1,439,214	(67%)	($6,347,126)
	Robert Lorge (R)	630,299	(29%)	($176,987)
	Other	68,784	(3%)	
2006 primary	Herb Kohl (D)	308,178	(86%)	
	Ben Masel (D)	51,245	(14%)	
2000 general	Herb Kohl (D)	1,563,238	(62%)	($4,991,364)
	John Gillespie (R)	940,744	(37%)	($582,221)
	Other	35,199	(1%)	

Prior Winning Percentages: 1994 (58%); 1988 (52%)

Herb Kohl, Wisconsin's senior senator, is a Democrat first elected in 1988. He grew up in Milwaukee, where his parents immigrated from Russia and Poland in the 1920s and opened a food store, which became a Wisconsin supermarket and retail chain. He graduated from the University of Wisconsin and Harvard Business School, worked at Kohl's and was president in the 1970s; the firm was sold in 1979, and today is one of the fastest-expanding national retail chains. Kohl was a Democratic contributor and chairman of the Wisconsin Democratic party in the mid-1970s. In 1985 he became a local celebrity, in a city smarting from sports franchises with lousy records and eager to move elsewhere, when he spent $18 million to buy the Milwaukee Bucks basketball team to keep it from moving out of town. In 2003 he considered selling the team to Michael Jordan, but talks broke down; rumors continue that he may sell the team, but he has made it clear he wants it to stay in Milwaukee (*Forbes* magazine in 2007 estimated the team was worth $260 million). In 1976 he bought a ranch near Jackson, Wyoming, from Senator Clifford Hansen, a Republican who says Kohl has been a "good steward of the land"; like the Bucks, the property is worth far more today than when he bought it. He is one of the richest members of Congress.

When Senator William Proxmire retired in 1988, Kohl decided to run for the Senate. He spent his own money liberally, running an extensive ad campaign with the theme, "Nobody's senator but yours." He won 47% in the primary to 38% for former Governor Tony Earl. In the general, against moderate Republican Susan Engeleiter, Kohl stressed his support of defense cuts—popular in dovish Wisconsin—and for requiring businesses to provide medical insurance; Engeleiter stressed her environmental stands, her legislative experience and her status as a wife and mother. This turned out to be one of the closest Senate races in the country, with Kohl winning 52%-48% after spending $7 million of his own money.

Kohl is a pleasant, shy, almost painfully earnest man, of transparent good will and seemingly little guile. Of the Senate, he told the Milwaukee *Journal Sentinel*, "There's too much of the I-I-I-I, me-me-me-me, and these are my needs and you have to do them and you have to take care of me. When I see that in other people I think it's a weakness." He personally funds the Herb Kohl Educational Foundation, which has given more than $3.6 million in scholarships and grants to Wisconsin students, teachers and schools. He donated $25 million to the University of Wisconsin for the Kohl Center arena which opened in 1998. His voting record has been moderate to liberal; he dislikes the clash of partisan fighting. He was one of 12 Democratic senators who voted for the Bush tax cut in 2001 but he opposed the Bush tax cut in 2003. Four days after September 11 he was wary of military action. "We would take a tragic situation and make it infinitely worse if we just lash out." But in October 2002 he voted for the Iraq war resolution. He later called the administration's handling of the war "mistake after mistake after mistake" but resisted proposals for a specific timetable for withdrawing troops.

Kohl has supported gun control and wrote the 1990 law banning guns in schools that was overturned by the Supreme Court in 1995. Kohl and Ohio's Mike DeWine, who lost reelection in 2006, ran the Antitrust Subcommittee on a bipartisan basis in both the Clinton and Bush years. In 1997, a joint letter to FCC Chairman Reed Hundt prompted him to kill the proposed AT&T-SBC merger; subcommittee hearings in 1998 helped prevent the proposed American Airlines-British Airways merger. In 2001 they helped prevent the USAirways-United Airlines merger. As the only sports team owner in the Senate, he has recused himself on the issue of Major League Baseball's antitrust exemption. In June 2003 he and DeWine held hearings on the FCC ruling allowing media companies to own larger shares of local stations. That month they urged the FCC and Justice Department to scrutinize News Corporation's proposed purchase of DirectTV and in September they said regulators should press for concessions. In March 2005 they co-sponsored a bill to allow the Justice Department to seek wiretaps on antitrust violators. In 2005, Kohl and DeWine again sent a letter to federal regulators raising concerns over proposed mergers of AT&T with SBC and MCI with Verizon. As chairman in 2007, Kohl introduced legislation that would repeal antitrust exemptions for the railroad industry and opposed the proposed Sirius-XM satellite radio merger. Kohl also criticized AirTran Airways' hostile takeover attempt of Midwest Airlines, which he flies to Washington, on the grounds that the low-cost carrier would reduce service.

On the Judiciary Committee Kohl has joined other Democrats in opposing several appellate court nominees and threatening to filibuster them on the floor. As Republicans threatened to change the rules to prevent such filibusters, Kohl in March 2005 said, "The Democrats are saying there will be a price to pay for that. We're not trying to quantify in every detail, because different senators have different ideas of what this all means. But we're saying it's a serious, serious move. We've never said we're going to shut the place down, nor would I, Herb Kohl, be a part of that." Kohl supported the nomination of John Roberts in 2005 to be chief justice and voted him out of committee, but in 2006 he opposed promoting Samuel Alito to the high court.

Kohl has fought with uncharacteristic fierceness to change what he considers the unfair treatment of Wisconsin dairy farmers. Since 1937, the Agriculture Department has fixed milk prices by a formula that allows higher prices the farther a farmer is from Eau Claire, Wisconsin. This increases prices to consumers, creates an oversupply of milk and reduces dairy prices in the Upper Midwest. Further aggravating the problem is the Northeast Dairy Compact set up in the 1980s, which allows the New England states to set even higher prices; other Northeastern states have sought to join. In debate on the 1996 Freedom to Farm Act, Kohl got the Senate to vote 50-46 to end the Northeast Dairy Compact, but in conference it was extended to 1999 and the Agriculture Secretary was ordered to set new milk marketing rules by then. In October 1999 New England senators inserted into an appropriations bill a two-year extension of the Northeast Dairy Compact and a rejection of Agriculture Secretary Dan Glickman's new rules; this was in part an effort to help then-Republican Jim Jeffords of Vermont, who was up for reelection in 2000. Kohl was outraged, and threatened to filibuster the bill and obstruct all business of the Senate. On November 18 and 19 he held the floor and filibustered. He was forced to desist, but got verbal support on the issue from party leaders Trent Lott and Tom Daschle and Agriculture Chairman Richard Lugar who promised the issue would be revisited. In 2001 he got 41 senators to sign a letter opposing the Northeast Dairy Compact, enough to threaten a filibuster if the issue was brought up, and on September 30 the compact expired. In its place Kohl helped to get in 2002 the Milk Loss Income Contract program, which pays dairy farmers if market prices fall. In its first three years it provided $2 billion to dairy farmers nationally, $413 million of that in Wisconsin. In October 2004 he attacked George W. Bush for inaction when House Republicans dropped renewal of MILC from the omnibus appropriation. In 2005 he and Republican Norm Coleman pushed for renewal of MILC with a doubled payment cap, and he was encouraged when the administration budget continued the program, though with a 5% decrease. In 2006, he criticized a Bush budget proposal for a "milk tax" that assessed producers with a 3-cent tax for every 100 pounds of milk sold; the proposal found little support in the Senate. With Patrick Leahy, Kohl succeeded in attaching a one-month extension of MILC to the 2007 war spending bill—to September 30, 2007—to coincide with the expiration of the farm bill and improve the chances of a long-term extension.

Kohl has been reelected easily. His sincere, unprepossessing demeanor has helped—and so has his money. He spent $6.5 million of his own money in 1994 (far more per voter, incidentally, than the much-ridiculed Michael Huffington was spending in California) and $5 million of his own money in 2000. His ability to self-finance has deterred many well-known Republicans from running against him and all but guaranteed Kohl's re-election in 2006. Former Governor and HHS Secretary Tommy Thompson, who polls showed would make a formidable opponent, flirted with the possibility of running against Kohl, but he ruled out a race in June 2006, leaving Republicans without an viable challenger. Construction executive Tim Michels, who challenged Russ Feingold in 2004, also said no. Republicans nominated attorney Robert Gerald Lorge, a perennial candidate who was facing a sexual misconduct lawsuit. Kohl spent more than $6 million on his re-election, nearly all of it his own money, and sailed to a fourth term with 67% of the vote. After Democrats won the majority, Kohl became chairman of the Special Committee on Aging, which he said he would use to improve the Medicare/prescription drug bill, including a change that would allow the government to negotiate for lower drug prices. Kohl also introduced a bill that encourages businesses to retain employers as workers beyond retirement age. If Kohl completes his fourth term, he would end up in a tie for Wisconsin's second-longest serving senator, still far short of Proxmire's 31-year tenure.

Junior Senator

Russell Feingold (D)

Elected 1992, seat up 2010, 3d term; b. Mar. 2, 1953, Janesville; home, Middleton; U. of WI, B.A. 1975, Rhodes Scholar, Oxford U., 1977, Harvard Law Schl., J.D. 1979; Jewish; divorced.

Elected Office: WI Senate, 1982-92.

Professional Career: Practicing atty., 1979-83; Prof., Beloit Col., 1985-93.

DC Office: 506 HSOB, 20510, 202-224-5323; Fax: 202-224-2725; Web site: feingold.senate.gov.

State Offices: Green Bay, 920-465-7508; LaCrosse, 608-782-5585; Middleton, 608-828-1200; Milwaukee, 414-276-7282; Wausau, 715-848-5660.

Committees: *Budget* (4th of 12 D). *Foreign Relations* (4th of 11 D): African Affairs (Chmn.); International Operations & Organizations, Democracy & Human Rights; Near Eastern & South & Central Asian Affairs; East Asian & Pacific Affairs. *Intelligence (Select)* (6th of 8 D). *Judiciary* (6th of 10 D): Constitution (Chmn.); Administrative Oversight & the Courts; Antitrust, Competition Policy & Consumer Rights; Human Rights & the Law; Crime & Drugs.

Group Ratings

	ADA	ACLU	AFS	LCV	ITIC	NTU	COC	ACU	CFG	FRC
2006	100	100	100	100	0	22	25	8	1	0
2005	100	—	100	90	—	20	17	13	5	—

National Journal Ratings

	2005 LIB	—	2005 CONS		2006 LIB	—	2006 CONS
Economic	76%	—	23%		75%	—	22%
Social	83%	—	10%		86%	—	12%
Foreign	90%	—	5%		88%	—	8%

Key Votes of the 109th Congress

1. Bar ANWR Drilling	Y	5. Confirm Samuel Alito	N	9. Limit Interstate Abortion	N
2. FY06 Spending Curb	N	6. Path to Citizenship	Y	10. CAFTA	N
3. Estate Tax Repeal	N	7. Bar Same Sex Marriage	N	11. Urge Iraq Withdrawal	Y
4. Raise Minimum Wage	Y	8. Stem Cell Research $	Y	12. Provide Detainee Rights	Y

Election Results

2004 general	Russell Feingold (D)	1,632,697	(55%)	($9,239,908)
	Tim Michels (R)	1,301,183	(44%)	($5,542,087)
	Other	15,863	(1%)	
2004 primary	Russell Feingold (D)	unopposed		
1998 general	Russell Feingold (D)	890,059	(51%)	($3,846,089)
	Mark W. Neumann (R)	852,272	(48%)	($4,373,953)

Prior Winning Percentages: 1992 (53%)

Russ Feingold is a Democrat first elected to the Senate in 1992. He grew up in Janesville, where his father and Republican Congressman Paul Ryan's father practiced law in the same building. There was politics in his blood: his father ran for district attorney as a Progressive and once lost an election to the county board by one vote. In the second grade he cast the only vote in his class for John F. Kennedy and decided he wanted to be president and often said he wanted to be senator some day. He nurtured his ambition at the University of Wisconsin, as a Rhodes Scholar, and at Harvard Law School; he moved to Middleton, a not-so-academic suburb of Madison, and in 1982, at 29, beat an 83-year-old veteran state senator by 31 votes. Feingold has a flair for publicity, and for political reform issues and novel arguments. His great goal in the legislature was to ban the use of bovine growth hormones, an attempt to hold down the productivity of dairy cows, who have grown more productive even as Americans drink less milk than they did in the 1950s. Feingold decided to run in 1992 for the Senate seat held by Bob Kasten, a free-market conservative who had won by narrow margins in 1980 and 1986. In the Democratic primary, while Milwaukee businessman Joseph Checota and Congressman Jim Moody battered each other with negative ads, Feingold ran clever, humorous spots: one showing Elvis, alive and endorsing Feingold; another showing Feingold at home, opening up a closet and saying, "No skeletons." He also had detailed position papers, including an 82-point plan for reducing the deficit. Near primary day, Checota apologized for his ads and asked voters to vote for Feingold if they didn't vote for him. Feingold, already ahead in polls, zoomed to an astonishing 70% win in this three-way race. Feingold also bounced way ahead of Kasten, who ran his own Elvis ads attacking Feingold on issues; Feingold attacked Kasten's negativity and avoided engaging on specifics. The race narrowed, but Feingold won 53%-46%.

In the Senate, Feingold has had a liberal record on cultural and foreign issues, somewhat more moderate on economics. He attacked many spending programs and did not respond in lockstep with other Democrats on the Clinton scandals. In February 1997 he called for an independent counsel on the Clinton-Gore fundraising operations. In January 1999 he was the only Democrat to vote against Robert Byrd's motion to dismiss the charges against Clinton.

Feingold has long said that the campaign finance system is "legalized bribery and influence-peddling"; democracy, he once said, "has been almost entirely corrupted in the last few years by soft money." In December 1995 he was surprised when John McCain called and asked if he would work with him against pork barrel spending. Out of this collaboration came the various versions of McCain-Feingold campaign finance bills, which were filibustered to death in July 1996 and in February 1998. The House passed one version in August 1998, but it was filibustered in the Senate in September. In October 1999 McCain-Feingold was again beaten, but McCain and Feingold did push through the bill requiring disclosure by Section 527 committees in June 2000. McCain's presidential campaign and his threats to bring up the issue at every turn forced Trent Lott to schedule two weeks of debate on campaign finance in March 2001. This time McCain and Feingold prevailed. They beat an amendment for lesser changes by Chuck Hagel by 60-40 and beat non-severability by 57-43, important because most senators considered at least some provisions consti-tutionally dubious. The bill passed 59-41 in April. In July it seemed about to come to the floor of the House, but the Republican leadership's rule was defeated and Speaker Dennis Hastert pulled it off the calendar. Then, after the Enron bankruptcy, pressure mounted. The bill's advocates got 218 signatures on a discharge petition and it was brought to the floor and passed. The Senate passed a final version in March. George W. Bush expressed doubts about the constitutionality of some provisions but signed it anyway, without ceremony and without inviting McCain and Feingold. Behind the scenes not all Democrats were happy; some thought it would hurt their party. The argument switched to the courts. In May 2003 a three-judge federal court, deeply divided, issued 1,700 pages of opinions and upheld some of the provisions but not others. The Supreme Court upheld most sections of the law in December 2003.

The campaign finance act had an impact, though not the expected impact, on the 2004 elections. Democrats, contrary to the expectations of many, were able to raise large sums, much of it over the Internet. And 527 organizations, not covered by the act, raised hundreds of millions, with most of the money going to anti-Bush efforts; three individuals, George Soros, Peter Lewis and Steve Bing contributed more than $60 million. Feingold and McCain asked the FEC to rule that the act covered 527s; it declined to do so. In September 2004 they called for amendments to cover the 527s; in January 2005 they and their co-sponsors Chris Shays and Marty Meehan in the House sponsored a bill to require 527s to register as political committees and use only hard money for any advertisements that mention federal candidates. It produced some interesting responses: left-leaning organizations like the Sierra Club and the League for Conservation Voters opposed it, other liberal organizations raised the question of whether 501(c) charitable organizations would be covered and Senate Rules Committee Chairman Trent Lott announced he was all for it and would shepherd it through his committee. The bill cleared the Senate Rules Committee in April 2005, but DSCC Chairman Charles Schumer abruptly withdrew his support, citing the effect of Republican amendments. In September 2005 McCain and Feingold opposed Christopher Bond's amendment to allow leadership PACs to give unlimited amounts to national party committees. Feingold crusaded against the Senate's unique practice of requiring the filing of campaign finance reports on paper, rather than electronically as the House does, and in April 2006 voluntarily submitted his own filing electronically to the secretary of the Senate. In March 2007 the Rules Committee approved an electronic filing bill sponsored by Feingold and Thad Cochran.

Feingold has pursued other ethics issues. He was one of the crusaders against lobbyists' gifts to lawmakers. He sought to prohibit members of Congress from using for personal travel frequent flier miles earned on business trips. He has tried to ban cost-of-living adjustments to congressional pay. He tried to attach repeal of the COLA to various measures and failed until he got a vote on it as an amendment to the homeland security bill in November 2002; it lost 58-36. In July 2006, when a lobbying bill stalled, Feingold and Barack Obama tried to get its provisions adopted as Senate rules, and in January 2007 they were pushing the limits on gifts, meals and travels from lobbyists again. Feingold and John McCain came out for an independent ethics authority in December 2006.

To the Patriot Act, Feingold tried to offer amendments to limit secret searches, computer surveillance and roving wiretaps. Majority Leader Tom Daschle got them all tabled, and Feingold cast the sole vote against the bill. In December 2005 he filibustered the renewal of the Patriot Act, and Republican leaders were unable to get the 60 votes required for cloture. Instead, the law was extended for five weeks and Feingold launched his filibuster again in February. This time many Democrats seemed miffed; Feingold lost a procedural motion 96–3 in February and the filibuster was ended 84-15 in March.

Casting sole votes is not an unusual posture for Feingold: he voted against the 1996 anti-terrorism bill and he was the only Democrat to vote against Robert Byrd's $15 billion homeland security package in 2001. He was the only Democrat on the Budget Committee to join Republicans and vote for five-year caps on spending in 2002. He fought to apply "paygo" rules to the budget, requiring that all spending increases or tax cuts be compensated for by corresponding spending cuts or tax increases, and succeeded in the Senate in 2003 and 2004; this blocked the passage of a budget resolution, since the Republican House wouldn't accept paygo on taxes.

Feingold has staked out some original positions on the Judiciary Committee. He has called for repeal of all federal death penalty statutes. He was one of eight Democrats who voted to confirm John Ashcroft; he argues that a president should be given great deference in Executive Branch appointments. But he voted against the confirmation of Alberto Gonzales in January 2005. He joined other Judiciary Democrats in opposing several Bush appellate judge appointees and threatening to filibuster them and opposed changing the rules on judicial filibusters. He voted for John Roberts in committee and on the floor in September 2005. He questioned the qualifications and independence of Harriet Miers in October. In January 2006 he supported the unsuccessful filibuster against Samuel Alito.

On foreign policy, he was one of three Democratic senators in March 1999 to vote against air strikes in Serbia and Kosovo and in October 2002 he voted against the Iraq war resolution. In June 2005 he sponsored a resolution demanding the development of a schedule for withdrawal from Iraq. In August he proposed withdrawal by the end of 2006, the first senator to do so. He sponsored a resolution in March 2006 censuring George W. Bush for the NSA surveillance of communications between al Qaeda suspects abroad and persons in the United States; only Barbara Boxer, John Kerry and Tom Harkin signed on. He decried the tendency of other Democrats to go "back into the foxhole" on Iraq. His amendment to require most troops to leave by July 2007 was defeated 86-13 in June 2006. When Democrats got their majority back, he held a hearing in January 2007 on exercising Congress's constitutional power to end a war. He urged Democrats not to support John Warner's nonbinding resolution in February. In April 2007 Majority Leader Harry Reid endorsed Feingold's measure to end funding by the end of March 2008, with troop withdrawals to begin in 120 days after passage.

As chairman of the Africa Subcommittee he traveled to Kenya, Tanzania and Mozambique in February 2002; his visa for Zimbabwe was revoked by the Mugabe government. He opposed the Australian Free Trade Agreement because it allowed some dairy exports into the United States and has opposed the Caribbean Area Free Trade Agreement as well. He and Herb Kohl held up a routine trade bill in October 2004 which provided non-discriminatory treatment of Laos, in protest of Laos's treatment of the Hmong. In April 2006, he said he supported same-sex marriage. In July 2006 the Senate adopted his amendment for external review of any Army Corps of Engineers project over $40 million, or of any project on which review was requested by a governor, a federal agency or the secretary of the Army. In August 2006, he sponsored a bill to allow states to establish pilot projects on health care.

Feingold has made it a practice to hold listening sessions in all 72 Wisconsin counties every year, speaking for five minutes and then taking all questions. And he has submitted voluntarily to some of the campaign restrictions he sought to place on all candidates. In 1998 he faced a strong opponent in Congressman Mark Neumann, a conservative elected in 1994. They agreed to limit their campaign spending, Feingold to $3.8 million, Neumann to $4.7 million (he actually spent $4.4 million), and to limit PAC money to 10% of donations and out-of-state contributions to 25% and to impose a $2,000 limit on candidate contributions (more of a handicap for Neumann, a self-made home-builder millionaire, who spent $700,000 of his own money on a losing race in 1992). Feingold's leads of 10% or so melted away by the fall and the race became about even. Neumann ran humorous ads attacking Feingold for sending dollars to Russia to study monkeys in space and for voting for a study of cow flatulence (the ad showed smock-clad scientists out in a field trying to isolate samples of cow gas). In one of the nation's closest Senate races, Feingold won 51%-48%.

In 2001 Feingold talked occasionally about running for president; in the fall he made a campus speaking tour. But he said it was unlikely and that he would decide by his 50th birthday in March 2003. He spent that evening at the Harmony Bar in Madison and, as he put it, "I turned to a couple of friends and family members and said, 'By the way, I'm not running for president in 2004.' They said, 'OK. Fine. Now listen to the band.'" All along he had said it was "extremely likely" that he would run for reelection in 2004. No well-known Republican was interested in running. The three serious candidates in their primary were state Senator Robert Welch, who lost 58%-41% to Herb Kohl in 1994, Milwaukee area car dealer Russ Darrow and businessman Tim Michels, a Waukesha County businessman who served 12 years as an Army Airborne Ranger. Michels campaigned as the most moderate of the candidates and spent $1.4 million. He won the primary with 42% of the votes, to 30% for Darrow and 23% for Welch.

This time Feingold decided not to be outspent as he was in 1998. By August 2004 he had raised $9 million, and he started running his characteristically humorous ads nonstop in June, knowing that Wisconsin would be inundated with presidential advertising in the summer and fall. Michels argued that Feingold had spent too much time on campaign finance and not enough on health care and jobs, and he attacked Feingold for his vote against the Patriot Act. He said he had real life experience while Feingold had been a career politician for 22 years. But Michels did not make much headway, and before mid-October the NRSC cancelled plans to spend $1.2 million on ads against

Feingold. Feingold's message that he was an independent vote and a candid voice seemed to have resonance. He won by a solid but not overwhelming 55%-44% margin and his 1,632,000 votes set an all-time Wisconsin record.

After the election Feingold once again showed interest in running for president. He spent time in Alabama and Florida; September 2005 found him in New Hampshire. Feingold had a clear profile, as an opponent of the Iraq war from the beginning and the only vote against the Patriot Act. But the response he received was not tumultuous. He raised $2 million in the first half of 2006 and said he would not decide whether to run until after the November elections. Four days afterwards, he announced he would not run. "I never got to the point where I'd rather be running around the country, running for president, than being a senator from Wisconsin," he said. "I began with the feeling that I didn't really want to do this but was open to the possibility that getting around the country would make me want to do it. That never happened."

FIRST DISTRICT

Rep. Paul Ryan (R)

Elected 1998, 5th term; b. Jan. 29, 1970, Janesville; home, Janesville; Miami U. of OH, B.A., 1992; Catholic; married (Janna).

Professional Career: Aide, U.S. Sen. Bob Kasten, 1992; Advisor & speechwriter, Empower America, 1993-95; Legis. Dir., U.S. Sen. Sam Brownback, 1995-97; Mktg. consultant., Ryan Inc. Central, 1997-98.

DC Office: 1113 LHOB, 20515, 202-225-3031; Fax: 202-225-3393; Web site: www.house.gov/ryan.

District Offices: Janesville, 608-752-4050; Kenosha, 262-654-1901; Racine, 262-637-0510.

Committees: *Budget* (RMM of 17 R). *Ways & Means* (12th of 17 R): Social Security; Select Revenue Measures.

Group Ratings

	ADA	ACLU	AFS	LCV	ITIC	NTU	COC	ACU	CFG	FRC
2006	0	14	0	17	100	78	100	92	84	85
2005	0	—	0	11	—	69	89	96	95	100

National Journal Ratings

	2005 LIB	—	2005 CONS		2006 LIB	—	2006 CONS
Economic	26%	—	73%		21%	—	77%
Social	38%	—	61%		34%	—	66%
Foreign	49%	—	50%		42%	—	57%

Key Votes of the 109th Congress

1. Estate Tax Repeal	Y	5. Limit Interstate Abortion	Y	9. Build Border Fence	Y
2. Limit CAFE Standards	Y	6. Extend Patriot Act	Y	10. CAFTA	Y
3. FY06 Spending Curb	Y	7. Bar Same Sex Marriage	Y	11. Oppose Iraq Withdrawal	Y
4. Drilling in ANWR	Y	8. Stem Cell Research $	N	12. Detainee Tribunals	Y

Election Results

2006 general	Paul Ryan (R)	161,320	(63%)	($1,316,881)
	Jeffrey Thomas (D)	95,761	(37%)	($20,581)
2006 primary	Paul Ryan (R)	unopposed		
2004 general	Paul Ryan (R)	233,372	(65%)	($849,365)
	Jeffrey Thomas (D)	116,250	(33%)	($41,246)
	Other	7,354	(2%)	

Prior Winning Percentages: 2002 (67%); 2000 (67%); 1998 (57%)

The People		Race/Ethnic Origin	Ancestry	
Area size:	1,724 sq. mi.	87.4% White	German: 27.0%	Polish: 8.5%
Urban population:	84.4%	4.6% Black	Irish: 8.3%	
Rural population:	15.6%	1.0% Asian	**2004 Presidential Vote**	
Pop. 2000:	670,458	0.3% Native Am.	Bush (R) 197,970	(54%)
Pop. 2005 (est):	705,360	0.0% Hawaiian	Kerry (D) 170,371	(46%)
Median income:	$50,372	1.0% Two+ races	Other 1,618	(0%)
Poverty status:	6.3%	0.1% Other	**2000 Presidential Vote**	
Military veterans:	13.2%	5.7% Hispanic Origin	Bush (R) 163,040	(51%)
			Gore (D) 144,138	(45%)
			Other 11,656	(4%)
			Cook Partisan Voting Index: R + 2	

Occupation	Blue collar: 29.4%	White collar: 57.4%	Gray collar: 13.2%

Rolling dairy country, blanketed by snow during most of the winter, gloriously green under sunny blue skies in summer, the southern tier of Wisconsin from Lake Michigan inland to the Rock River Valley, is some of America's prime industrial country. Settled by Yankee and German farmers 170 years ago, it was once primarily dairyland. By the early 20th century, the steady habits and high skills of the local dairy farmers provided a good labor pool for factories. Today there are still major plants here: the operations center for S. C. Johnson Wax (and its Frank Lloyd Wright-designed tower and Wingspread Center) in Racine, a DaimlerChrysler engine plant in Kenosha and a Chevrolet plant in Janesville. But many other factories have closed, especially in Racine, where thousands of workers lost auto jobs.

The lake resorts, most notably Lake Geneva, are a favorite of wealthy Chicagoans; this is the site of the University of Chicago's historic Yerkes Observatory, long one of the nation's largest centers for research in astronomy and referred to as the birthplace of modern astrophysics. Most of this area is becoming metropolitan, part of the almost continuously suburban zone where metro Milwaukee melds into metro Chicago. To the untrained eye, this part of southern Wisconsin looks much the same as nearby northern Illinois; politically, there is a vast difference. The dotted line on the map is the historic boundary between the once corruption-prone machine politics of Illinois and the once squeaky-clean progressive politics of Wisconsin. This is the land of the 1st Congressional District of Wisconsin, from Lake Michigan west into Rock County. It includes all of Racine and Kenosha Counties on the lake; inland is Walworth County, with Lake Geneva and new ethanol plants for booming corn production. It includes the southern Milwaukee County suburbs of Oak Creek and Greenfield and the southern tier of townships in suburban Waukesha County, including New Berlin. It extends west to Janesville in the middle of Rock County. Politically, it tilts a bit to the Republican side; Waukesha and Walworth Counties are heavily Republican. In this presidential battleground state, the district voted 51% for George W. Bush in 2000 and 54% in 2004.

The congressman from the 1st District is Paul Ryan, a Republican first elected in 1998 at age 28. He grew up in Janesville, where in 1884 his great-grandfather started a family construction firm now run by his cousins. His father and Democratic Senator Russ Feingold's father had their law offices in the same building. Ryan got started in politics early, as a staffer for Senator Bob Kasten while attending college at Miami of Ohio; then he worked as a speechwriter for Jack Kemp and William Bennett at Empower America and was legislative director to Kansas Senator Sam Brownback. Ryan returned to the 1st District in anticipation of the Senate candidacy of Congressman Mark Neumann, who lost to Feingold in 1998. Ryan won the Republican primary with 81% of the vote. Democrats renominated Kenosha County official Lydia Spottswood, who had lost to Neumann in 1996. Ryan was for local control, against tax increases, in favor of gun ownership rights. This was a strenuously contested election, one of the Democrats' top 10 priorities in the nation. Spottswood spent $1.33 million, Ryan $1.24 million. But the final result was not that close. Ryan won 57%-43%.

In the House, Ryan became a mainstream Republican who was unafraid to occasionally challenge his party and who votes toward the center on foreign policy. He lost on the House floor when he pressed for language to require that any funds cut from appropriations bills be set aside to reduce total spending; appropriators in both parties objected that the provision would tie their hands. One of the most effective communicators among Republican fiscal conservatives, he pressed for a line-item veto plus changes in the handling of the congressional budget to require more spending discipline. On the Ways and Means Committee, he advocated business tax cuts to spur economic growth and has been an ally of the Club for Growth in criticizing George W. Bush's tax cuts as too small. He pushed for increased competition in Medicare plans and health savings accounts, and was an eager proponent of personal retirement accounts in Social Security. With Senator John Sununu, he sponsored in 2005 a comprehensive plan to create payroll-tax funded private retirement accounts that would be financed largely through spending cuts and new revenues predicted to result from the accounts. He complained that threatened retribution from Democratic leaders made it difficult for him to secure Democratic supporters. Ryan supports tax changes, including a deferral of capital gains taxes on reinvested distributions for mutual fund investors. He enjoys fishing (walleye and muskie) and hunting, particularly bow hunting, and in 2004 he helped enact increased tariffs on imports of archery gear to assure prices equivalent to those of domestic manufacturers.

In 2007, Ryan became ranking Republican on the House Budget Committee, after a contest with Ander Crenshaw of Florida. "We lost our brand as the party of fiscal responsibility, and we've got to get it back," Ryan said after his selection. "It's important that we give voters a very clear choice on fiscal policy as to where the two parties stand." Under his leadership, House Republicans in March 2007 offered an alternative budget blueprint that would trim discretionary and entitlement spending and extend all expiring tax cuts, with a balanced budget in 2012; it lost 160-268, with 40 Republicans voting against.

Ryan has become entrenched with easy reelections in what was a Democratic district until 1994. National conservatives have held up his success as an example for Republicans across the nation. Ryan has been mentioned as a potential candidate for the Senate but he has been unwilling to challenge either of his state's two Democratic incumbents. He has not ruled out the possibility of a statewide race.

SECOND DISTRICT

Rep. Tammy Baldwin (D)

Elected 1998, 5th term; b. Feb. 11, 1962, Madison; home, Madison; Smith Col., A.B. 1984; U. of WI Law Schl., J.D. 1989; No religious affiliation; partner (Lauren Azar).

Elected Office: Dane Cnty. Bd. of Supervisors, 1986-94; WI Assembly, 1992-98.

Professional Career: Practicing atty, 1989-92.

DC Office: 2446 RHOB, 20515, 202-225-2906; Fax: 202-225-6942; Web site: www.tammybaldwin.house.gov.

District Offices: Beloit, 608-362-2800; Madison, 608-258-9800.

Committees: *Energy & Commerce* (23d of 31 D): Environment & Hazardous Materials; Health; Energy & Air Quality. *Judiciary* (23d of 23 D): Crime, Terrorism & Homeland Security.

Group Ratings

	ADA	ACLU	AFS	LCV	ITIC	NTU	COC	ACU	CFG	FRC
2006	95	95	100	100	14	15	20	0	0	0
2005	100	—	100	100	—	19	30	0	7	0

National Journal Ratings

	2005 LIB	—	2005 CONS	2006 LIB	—	2006 CONS
Economic	92%	—	6%	79%	—	18%
Social	88%	—	12%	91%	—	8%
Foreign	96%	—	0%	95%	—	0%

Key Votes of the 109th Congress

1. Estate Tax Repeal	N	5. Limit Interstate Abortion	N	9. Build Border Fence	N
2. Limit CAFE Standards	N	6. Extend Patriot Act	N	10. CAFTA	N
3. FY06 Spending Curb	N	7. Bar Same Sex Marriage	N	11. Oppose Iraq Withdrawal	N
4. Drilling in ANWR	N	8. Stem Cell Research $	Y	12. Detainee Tribunals	N

Election Results

2006 general	Tammy Baldwin (D)	191,414	(63%)	($1,617,301)
	Dave Magnum (R)	113,015	(37%)	($985,933)
2006 primary	Tammy Baldwin (D)	unopposed		
2004 general	Tammy Baldwin (D)	251,637	(63%)	($1,448,889)
	Dave Magnum (R)	145,810	(37%)	($658,153)

Prior Winning Percentages: 2002 (66%); 2000 (51%); 1998 (53%)

The People		Race/Ethnic Origin	Ancestry	
Area size:	3,602 sq. mi.	89.0% White	German: 28.4% Irish: 9.4%	
Urban population:	75.6%	3.6% Black	Norwegian: 9.1%	
Rural population:	24.4%	2.4% Asian	**2004 Presidential Vote**	
Pop. 2000:	670,457	0.3% Native Am.	Kerry (D) 250,151	(62%)
Pop. 2005 (est):	713,356	0.0% Hawaiian	Bush (R) 151,024	(37%)
Median income:	$46,979	1.3% Two+ races	Other 3,303	(1%)
Poverty status:	8.7%	0.1% Other	**2000 Presidential Vote**	
Military veterans:	11.1%	3.4% Hispanic Origin	Gore (D) 201,738	(58%)
			Bush (R) 125,442	(36%)
			Other 19,398	(6%)
			Cook Partisan Voting Index: D +13	

Occupation   Blue collar: 22.3%   White collar: 63.6%   Gray collar: 14.1%

On a narrow isthmus between Lakes Mendota and Monona is the center of Madison and, in many ways, the center of Wisconsin. Here the state Capitol rises at one end of State Street; at the other end of several commercial blocks is the main campus of the University of Wisconsin, on a beautiful, parklike, sometimes windswept setting above Lake Mendota. For most of the 20th century, Wisconsin politics was dominated by the Madison-based LaFollettes and their liberal Democratic successors. And the traffic on State Street was two-way, with university faculty devoted to Bob LaFollette's "Wisconsin idea" of an apolitical bureaucracy, his Wisconsin Tax Commission and workmen's compensation law—both firsts in the nation. In recent years there was division, with the liberal campus at odds with the welfare and school choice law enacted while Republican Tommy Thompson was governor and not entirely happy with the no-tax-increase policy of his Democratic successor Jim Doyle. A steady debate is carried on here between the very liberal Madison *Capital Times* and its more conservative rival, the *Wisconsin State Journal*; the two newspapers practice the kind of competitive journalism still seen in only a few major cities and state capitals. This is an urban capital set in the midst of farmland; the Dane County farmers' market is the largest in the nation.

Madison is the center of Wisconsin's 2d Congressional District, is roughly equal parts urban, suburban and rural. It includes surrounding Dane County and dairy and alfalfa country to the north and south, as well as several rural dairy counties that have traditionally been Republican; they include such picturesque scenes as the birthplace of the Ringling Brothers Circus in Baraboo, and the Swiss-settled town of New Glarus. With the largest indoor hydropark in the world, the Wisconsin Dells have become a popular year-round tourist destination. Madison spawned an activist and sometimes violent student movement (during the Vietnam War, a grad student was killed in a laboratory by a bomb set off by a protester) and a permanent postgraduate proletariat. In the 1990s, with double-digit job growth in both the public and private sectors, *Money* magazine rated Madison among the best places to live in America (though it has since dropped to 53rd). Median family income in Madison is nearly twice the level in Milwaukee, with its shrinking job base. But the industrial base in Madison also has declined, as evidenced by the Schwinn Bicycle Company, which once employed thousands here but now makes only a few custom bikes domestically; most are manufactured in China. In the early 1990s, Dane County was open to Republicans like Thompson and Congressman Scott Klug, first elected in 1990. But the contrast between Madison's Dane County and the rural counties has faded, as Madison area liberals have moved into the countryside: a map of the 2004 presidential election results shows the rural areas south and west of Madison as a solid Democratic blue. This makes the 2d now a very Democratic district, 62%-37% for John Kerry in 2004.

The congresswoman from the 2d District is Tammy Baldwin, a Democrat elected in 1998. She grew up in Madison, where she was raised by her mother (a University of Wisconsin student when Tammy was born) and her maternal grandparents, a UW biochemist and the theater department's head costume designer. She graduated first in her class at Madison West High School and went on to Smith College and UW law school. In 1986, at 24, while still in law school, she was elected to the

Dane County Board of Supervisors. In 1992 she was elected to the Wisconsin Assembly from a heavily Democratic Madison seat. In 1998, when moderate Republican Scott Klug honored his promise to serve only four terms, this seemed a good chance for Democrats to pick up an open seat. Four Democrats and six Republicans ran. Baldwin had special advantages. As a woman with great political skills, she was supported by EMILY's List, which helped raised about one-quarter of her $1.5 million. And as a lesbian, she had support from national gay and lesbian organizations, which raised money from a large and affluent national constituency. With 86% of Democratic primary votes cast in Dane County, Baldwin won with 37% of the vote. Republicans nominated former state Insurance Commissioner Jo Musser. Baldwin roused the enthusiasm of Madison liberals in a way not seen in years. She called for a single-payer health insurance system and suggested that Musser was dominated by cash from insurance companies; Musser, a nurse who founded the Madison Employers Health Care Alliance, argued that single-payer would reduce choices and create long waiting periods for elective surgery. Both sides were well-financed. Dane County went 57%-42% for Baldwin, and she won the district 53%-47%.

Baldwin came out as a lesbian during college, and thus became the first openly homosexual non-incumbent to win a seat in the House; Barney Frank, the other openly gay member of the House, revealed his sexual orientation after he had served several terms. The vast majority of voters care more about her positions on issues that affect their lives than about her sexual orientation, she has said. Befitting Madison, she has a strongly liberal voting record, though she prefers to be called a progressive; her driving motivation is guaranteed health care for all Americans. She sponsored the Health Security for All Americans Act to guarantee universal coverage. With a seat on the Energy and Commerce Committee and its Health Subcommittee, she has been a leader in urging additional federal support for embryonic stem-cell research, some of which has been done at UW. With Republican cosponsors, she filed a bill to encourage flexibility in how the states cover the uninsured. In March 2007, the House passed her bill to expand breast and cervical cancer screening for poor and uninsured women. Baldwin said that she did not want to be seen primarily as a lesbian congresswoman, but she was vocal—and visible—in her opposition to the constitutional amendment to bar same-sex marriages, and praised local jurisdictions that encouraged "people who have made lifelong, permanent commitments to one another." She joined a bipartisan initiative to bar workplace discrimination against gays, and sought to broaden hate crimes to include people targeted because of gender, sexual orientation or disability. Baldwin was an outspoken opponent of the Iraq war resolution, and cosponsored a proposal to investigate the possible impeachment of President George W. Bush.

In her first reelection campaign in 2000, Baldwin faced Republican John Sharpless, whose ads in UW newspapers called him "our professor, our Congressman, our voice"; he had students in senior campaign positions. He said that Baldwin had sparse accomplishments, had ignored farmers and raised most of her campaign money out of state. Baldwin ran far behind Al Gore and won by only 51%-49%, a smaller margin than when she was first elected, a reversal of the usual pattern. Since then, she appears to have secured the seat. In 2004 and 2006, Baldwin defeated radio broadcaster Dave Magnum—by 63%-37% each time.

THIRD DISTRICT

Rep. Ron Kind (D)

Elected 1996, 6th term; b. Mar. 16, 1963, La Crosse; home, La Crosse; Harvard U., B.A. 1985, London Schl. of Econ., 1986, U. of MN, J.D. 1990; Lutheran; married (Tawni).

Professional Career: Practicing atty., 1990-92; Asst. St. Prosecutor, La Crosse Cnty., 1992-96.

DC Office: 1406 LHOB, 20515, 202-225-5506; Fax: 202-225-5739; Web site: www.house.gov/kind.

District Offices: Eau Claire, 715-831-9214; La Crosse, 608-782-2558.

Committees: *Natural Resources* (20th of 27 D): Fisheries, Wildlife & Oceans; National Parks, Forests & Public Lands. *Ways & Means* (17th of 24 D): Oversight; Health.

Group Ratings

	ADA	ACLU	AFS	LCV	ITIC	NTU	COC	ACU	CFG	FRC
2006	85	95	100	92	86	17	53	25	17	0
2005	75	—	100	100	—	21	59	20	13	0

National Journal Ratings

	2005 LIB	—	2005 CONS		2006 LIB	—	2006 CONS
Economic	68%	—	32%		71%	—	28%
Social	67%	—	33%		65%	—	34%
Foreign	62%	—	38%		75%	—	23%

Key Votes of the 109th Congress

1. Estate Tax Repeal	N	5. Limit Interstate Abortion	N	9. Build Border Fence	Y
2. Limit CAFE Standards	N	6. Extend Patriot Act	N	10. CAFTA	N
3. FY06 Spending Curb	N	7. Bar Same Sex Marriage	*	11. Oppose Iraq Withdrawal	Y
4. Drilling in ANWR	N	8. Stem Cell Research $	Y	12. Detainee Tribunals	N

Election Results

2006 general	Ron Kind (D)	163,322	(65%)	($780,394)
	Paul Nelson (R)	88,523	(35%)	($247,922)
2006 primary	Ron Kind (D)	39,765	(84%)	
	Chip DeNure (D)	7,744	(16%)	
2004 general	Ron Kind (D)	204,856	(56%)	($1,186,471)
	Dale Schultz (R)	157,866	(43%)	($531,538)

Prior Winning Percentages: 2002 (63%); 2000 (64%); 1998 (71%); 1996 (52%)

The People		Race/Ethnic Origin	Ancestry	
Area size:	13,849 sq. mi.	96.1% White	German: 29.7%	Norwegian: 14.1%
Urban population:	43.1%	0.5% Black	Irish: 8.5%	
Rural population:	56.9%	1.2% Asian	**2004 Presidential Vote**	
Pop. 2000:	670,462	0.5% Native Am.	Kerry (D) 192,297	(51%)
Pop. 2005 (est):	699,451	0.0% Hawaiian	Bush (R) 178,367	(48%)
Median income:	$40,006	0.7% Two+ races	Other 3,656	(1%)
Poverty status:	9.8%	0.0% Other	**2000 Presidential Vote**	
Military veterans:	12.9%	0.9% Hispanic Origin	Gore (D) 155,832	(49%)
			Bush (R) 144,948	(46%)
			Other 16,626	(5%)
			Cook Partisan Voting Index: D + 3	

Occupation	Blue collar: 29.2%	White collar: 53.3%	Gray collar: 17.5%

On the rolling land of western Wisconsin, in the knobby hills just east of the Mississippi River, is some of the most beautiful river landscape in the country. This is where Laura Ingalls Wilder's family built the "little house in the big woods" in the 1870s, before the first railroad came steaming up the narrow floodplain alongside the Mississippi River. Today, it is hard to imagine the big woods: The trees have long since been cut and the hillsides are covered with grass grazed by placid dairy cattle. Where pioneers tried to scratch out diversified crops, farmers soon created America's premier dairy region, producing milk, butter and especially cheese. Some Amish communities from Pennsylvania have relocated here in recent years because land is less than half the price and there has been less modernity. But more than half of family dairy farmers have gone out of business since 1980. Cows are more productive, while demand for milk has decreased. And Wisconsin has trouble competing against the European Common Market's hugely subsidized cheese and butter. But other businesses have risen. Dodgeville in Iowa County (which is not on the Iowa border) is the headquarters of Lands' End, the catalog retailer that was sold to Sears Roebuck. In the 1980s, many communities here lost population, but there has been growth since 1990; the most rapid growth in the state has been in commuter-oriented St. Croix County, part of the Minneapolis-St. Paul metro area.

The 3d Congressional District of Wisconsin follows the Mississippi and St. Croix River counties from the southern border of the state to St. Croix County, just east of St. Paul, and extends east two or three counties. Eau Claire and La Crosse are its 2 largest cities. This is the nation's number two dairy district, with 6,000 dairy farms, but it is very different in character than the number one district (California's 21st District), which has more milk cows concentrated on just 400 farms. It was settled largely by German and Scandinavian immigrants (Laura's Yankee family moved away as

Swedes were moving into the area), and it once voted for LaFollette Progressives. More recently, it has been closely divided between Democrats and Republicans. Western Wisconsin was the one segment of rural America where Al Gore and John Kerry ran even with historic Democratic percentages, which was vital to the narrow victory that each won in this state; Gore carried the district 49%-46% and Kerry 51%-48%. It produced solid margins for other Democrats, Governor Jim Doyle in 2002 and 2006, and Senator Russ Feingold in 2004.

The congressman from the 3d District is Ron Kind, a Democrat first elected in 1996. He grew up in a large family in La Crosse, the son of a telephone repairman and a secretary in the local schools. He went to Harvard on scholarship and played quarterback, and worked as a summer intern for Senator William Proxmire, doing research for his Golden Fleece awards. He attended the London School of Economics and University of Minnesota law school, practiced law in a big firm in Milwaukee, then returned home to La Crosse to work as an assistant prosecutor on rape and sexual abuse cases. Kind started running for Congress soon after moderate Republican Steve Gunderson announced during the 1994 campaign that he would not run again. Former state Senator Jim Harsdorf won the Republican primary and took hard-edged stands for the balanced budget and Governor Tommy Thompson's "Wisconsin Works" welfare program. Kind talked of campaign finance regulation and presented his own balanced budget proposal. Gunderson was neutral in the contest; he didn't agree with Harsdorf's views on civil and human rights and thought him too close to the Christian Coalition. Kind won 52%-48%.

In the House, Kind has compiled a moderate voting record. Like other Wisconsin members, he worked to reform the Federal Milk Marketing Order System, instituted in 1937; it pays higher prices the farther the farmer is from Eau Claire, which is in the northern part of the district, which means that 3d District dairy farmers get the lowest prices in the nation. In September 2004, he charged that the Bush administration was planning to impose a tax on dairy producers or cut price supports after the election. He filed a proposal to give affordable health care coverage to small businesses and family farmers. In early maneuvering for a 2007 farm bill, he called for reduced support for commodities and more funds for land conservation, and school nutrition. Kind is a co-founder of the Upper Mississippi River Congressional Task Force. His own home is on the river and was flooded in 2001. With members from Illinois and Iowa, he got the House to pass a bill to establish a water quality monitoring network in the Upper Mississippi River Basin. As co-chairman of the New Democrat Coalition, he said that he wanted to expand access to broadband in rural areas and to make his area "the Silicon Valley of agricultural research." After he voted for the use of force in Iraq, he was criticized by liberals back home. In October 2003, he unsuccessfully offered an amendment to cut in half U.S. funding for reconstruction in Iraq and call for more contributions from other nations; in February 2007, he said that it was "time to stop asking [U.S. troops] to baby-sit a civil war."

Local union organizers have complained that Kind has not been sufficiently supportive on trade issues, but they have not put up a primary opponent; in 2005, he opposed the Central America Free Trade Agreement. In 2004, he had his first credible challenger: Republican state Senator Dale Schultz, a moderate in the legislature for more than two decades. Schultz ran with an unlikely Republican theme, criticizing Kind as a free trader who had been sending jobs overseas. Kind affirmed his support for trade agreements, but criticized the Bush administration for its failure to enforce their terms. Schultz backed Bush's handling of the war on terror and he promised to do more for agriculture, while Kind called for more support for education. Kind won, 56%-43%. In 2006, he had an easy time against real estate agent Paul Nelson, who ran an ad saying Kind's votes on sex research and military funding shows that he "pays for sex, but not for soldiers." The state Republican party disavowed the ad, and Kind won 65%-35%. After losing out in 2005 for a seat on Ways and Means to Rahm Emanuel of Illinois, Kind joined the committee two years later. Subsequently, he resigned his role as a chief deputy whip.

FOURTH DISTRICT

Rep. Gwen Moore (D)

Elected 2004, 2d term; b. Apr. 18, 1951, Racine; home, Milwaukee; Marquette U., B.A. 1978; Baptist; single.

Elected Office: WI Assembly, 1989-92; WI Senate, 1992-2004; Senate pres. pro tempore, 1997-98.

Professional Career: Housing and urban dev. specialist, 1985-89.

DC Office: 1239 LHOB, 20515, 202-225-4572; Fax: 202-225-8135; Web site: www.house.gov/gwenmoore.

District Offices: Milwaukee, 414-297-1140.

Committees: *Budget* (21st of 22 D). *Financial Services* (24th of 37 D): Domestic and International Monetary Policy, Trade & Technology; Housing & Community Opportunity; Capital Markets, Insurance & Government Sponsored Enterprises. *Small Business* (10th of 18 D): Contracting & Technology; Rural & Urban Entrepreneurship; Regulations, Healthcare & Trade.

Group Ratings

	ADA	ACLU	AFS	LCV	ITIC	NTU	COC	ACU	CFG	FRC
2006	100	100	100	100	29	15	20	4	7	0
2005	100	—	100	100	—	14	38	0	4	0

National Journal Ratings

	2005 LIB	—	2005 CONS		2006 LIB	—	2006 CONS
Economic	92%	—	6%		91%	—	6%
Social	91%	—	8%		93%	—	7%
Foreign	82%	—	17%		87%	—	13%

Key Votes of the 109th Congress

1. Estate Tax Repeal	N	5. Limit Interstate Abortion	N	9. Build Border Fence	N
2. Limit CAFE Standards	N	6. Extend Patriot Act	N	10. CAFTA	N
3. FY06 Spending Curb	N	7. Bar Same Sex Marriage	N	11. Oppose Iraq Withdrawal	N
4. Drilling in ANWR	N	8. Stem Cell Research $	Y	12. Detainee Tribunals	N

Election Results

2006 general	Gwen Moore (D)	136,735	(71%)	($668,855)
	Perfecto Rivera (R)	54,486	(28%)	($19,723)
2006 primary	Gwen Moore (D)	unopposed		
2004 general	Gwen Moore (D)	212,382	(70%)	($933,653)
	Gerald Boyle (R)	85,928	(28%)	($81,298)
	Other	6,832	(2%)	

The People		Race/Ethnic Origin	Ancestry	
Area size:	113 sq. mi.	50.4% White	German: 18.3%	Polish: 8.9%
Urban population:	100.0%	33.0% Black	Irish: 5.4%	
Rural population:	0.0%	2.7% Asian	**2004 Presidential Vote**	
Pop. 2000:	670,458	0.7% Native Am.	Kerry (D) 219,636	(70%)
Pop. 2005 (est):	647,079	0.0% Hawaiian	Bush (R) 94,090	(30%)
Median income:	$33,121	1.8% Two+ races	**2000 Presidential Vote**	
Poverty status:	19.8%	0.2% Other	Gore (D) 183,810	(66%)
Military veterans:	11.1%	11.2% Hispanic Origin	Bush (R) 84,823	(30%)
			Other 11,814	(4%)
			Cook Partisan Voting Index: D +20	

Occupation	Blue collar: 27.8%	White collar: 54.0%	Gray collar: 18.2%

Milwaukee is America's most German city, with an ethnic heritage noticeable not just in the names of its beers and its old German restaurants but in the solidness of its houses and the orderliness of its streets. Until World War I made this German character seem un-American, German was spoken on the streets and read in newspapers, German beer was produced in dozens of breweries and

German cultural traditions breathed in churches, union halls and parlors. There was a German-type politics, with a Socialist mayor and an efficient, honest city government. The world's largest four-sided clock faces outward from all sides of the tower on the Allen-Bradley factory, looking out over the industrial city. It is an apt symbol, a piece of precision engineering, in this high-skill manufacturing town, with its skyline of smokestacks and church steeples, the closest thing in America to the factory cities of the Germany whence so many Milwaukeeans' ancestors came. Milwaukee has led the nation in industrial control equipment, mining gear, cranes and independent foundries. The work force, with German, Polish and Mitteleuropean work habits, is highly skilled and hard-working. Harley-Davidson began manufacturing on the West Side a century ago. Though some neighborhoods here are beset by crime and drug use, most of Milwaukee is solid and upstanding, and some of it—Brewers Hill near the old Schlitz brewery—is gentrifying. There is an Oktoberfest (as well as an Irish Fest, a huge musical Summerfest, etc.), and there are large and efficiently run factories that pay high wages to highly-skilled and well-disciplined workers. Residential development along the Milwaukee River recently has brought more people downtown. Much of Milwaukee County's Latino population, which reached nearly 100,000 in 2005, has settled in the old immigrant neighborhoods of the city's south side; the north side is home to the city's African-American neighborhoods such as Bronzeville, home to America's Black Holocaust Museum, and Sherman Park.

The 4th Congressional District of Wisconsin covers the entire city of Milwaukee and a few of its working class suburbs—St. Francis, Cudahy and South Milwaukee on Lake Michigan and West Milwaukee and part of West Allis west of the Allen-Bradley tower. Of Wisconsin's eight congressional districts, the 4th is the only one to have lost population between 2000 and 2005.

The congresswoman from the 4th District is Gwen Moore, a Democrat elected in 2004. Moore was born in Racine, the eighth of nine children, and raised on the north side of Milwaukee. As an 18-year-old college freshman, she became a single mother who was forced to rely on welfare to help support her daughter. She graduated from Marquette University and worked as a housing and urban development specialist. Moore said she got active in politics when a rent-to-own center repossessed her washer and dryer even though she had paid three times their value in exorbitant interest rates; she responded by leading an effort to establish a community credit union. She was elected to the state House in 1988 and to the state Senate in 1992, where she was the first black woman to serve.

In 2003, when old-style neighborhood 4th District Democrat Gerald Kleczka announced that he was retiring after 20 years in the House, Moore became the early frontrunner. But she had serious competition in the September 2004 Democratic primary. Moore faced two political veterans, state Senator Tim Carpenter and former state party chairman Matt Flynn, both white. The candidates agreed on most issues: all three supported abortion rights, focused on jobs and economic concerns, and called for eliminating the Bush administration's tax cuts for those making more than $200,000 a year. In the absence of significant ideological clashes, the fallout from Milwaukee's mayoral primary earlier in 2004 played a key role. The nonpartisan election in April featured former Congressman Tom Barrett, who is white, and acting Mayor Marvin Pratt, who sought to become the city's first black elected mayor. Barrett narrowly emerged as the winner in a vote that divided along racial lines and caused hard feelings in the black community. In the House race Moore took advantage of the energized black voter base, and she leveraged her financial support from national women's, teachers and other liberal groups. Flynn had chaired John Kerry's campaign in Wisconsin, was endorsed by Kleczka and boasted that he had backed Pratt for mayor; but he was damaged by his work as general counsel for the local Roman Catholic archdiocese in the sex abuse scandal. Carpenter was the only openly gay member of the Senate and had the support of national gay-rights groups. Moore won 64% of the vote to 25% for Flynn and 10% for Carpenter. Flynn won the five aldermanic districts and 49% of the vote on the south side, but Moore won about 80% of the vote north of I-94. She was helped by the efforts of America Coming Together, a 527 anti-Bush organization that used the September primary as a rehearsal of its November get-out-the-vote operation in black precincts. Although ACT did not endorse a candidate, Moore was the obvious beneficiary of its efforts.

In the general election Republican Gerald Boyle tried to win over Democrats disaffected with Moore. But he got no national money and Moore won, 70%-28%. In the House, she got seats on the Financial Services and Small Business committees. The luster from Moore's victory was diminished when her 25-year-old son was one of five John Kerry campaign employees charged in January 2005 with slashing the tires of more than 20 vans rented by Republicans to drive voters and monitors to the polls on Election Day; the vehicles were in a parking lot next to the Bush campaign office and the incident took place a few hours before voting started. A jury deadlocked on the verdict, leading to a plea agreement, but a judge threw out the deal and sentenced her son to four months in jail on a charge of misdemeanor property damage.

Moore has a solidly liberal voting record. She sponsored a bill to provide funding to help low-income workers buy cars to increase their access to better jobs. As a member of the "Out of Iraq" caucus, Moore considered voting against the 2007 war funding bill, but with the urging of Appropriations Chairman David Obey, she voted for it and a timetable for withdrawing U.S. troops from Iraq. She was arrested along with other members of the Congressional Black Caucus at the Sudanese Embassy in 2006 in a protest of genocide in Darfur. Moore said she has developed an interest in foreign relations and defense but said she wanted to focus on a few issues or "you have little or no credibility, because you're just all over the place." Lawmakers in 2005 incorporated provisions of Moore's SHIELD Act into the reauthorization of the Violence Against Women Act that would protect the identity of domestic violence victims who receive homeless assistance. Moore, who is learning Spanish to reach out to the Hispanic population on Milwaukee's south side, appears well established in her district. She drew no primary opposition and won re-election to a second term with 71%. Moore has been mentioned as a potential mayoral challenger to Barrett in 2008, speculation that her aides have dismissed.

FIFTH DISTRICT

Rep. Jim Sensenbrenner (R)

Elected 1978, 15th term; b. June 14, 1943, Chicago, IL; home, Menomonee Falls; Stanford U., A.B. 1965, U. of WI, J.D. 1968; Episcopalian; married (Cheryl).

Elected Office: WI Assembly, 1968-74; WI Senate, 1974-78.

Professional Career: Practicing atty., 1968-69; Staff asst., U.S. Rep. Arthur Younger, 1965.

DC Office: 2449 RHOB, 20515, 202-225-5101; Fax: 202-225-3190; Web site: www.house.gov/sensenbrenner.

District Offices: Brookfield, 262-784-1111.

Committees: *Judiciary* (2d of 17 R): Courts, the Internet & Intellectual Property; Crime, Terrorism & Homeland Security. *Science & Technology* (2d of 20 R): Investigations & Oversight (RMM). *Select Committee on Energy Independence and Global Warming* (RMM of 6 R).

Group Ratings

	ADA	ACLU	AFS	LCV	ITIC	NTU	COC	ACU	CFG	FRC
2006	10	18	0	25	100	80	87	83	75	85
2005	0	—	13	17	—	76	77	96	93	100

National Journal Ratings

	2005 LIB	—	2005 CONS		2006 LIB	—	2006 CONS
Economic	42%	—	58%		42%	—	57%
Social	32%	—	66%		38%	—	61%
Foreign	39%	—	61%		50%	—	50%

Key Votes of the 109th Congress

1. Estate Tax Repeal	Y	5. Limit Interstate Abortion	Y	9. Build Border Fence	Y
2. Limit CAFE Standards	Y	6. Extend Patriot Act	Y	10. CAFTA	Y
3. FY06 Spending Curb	Y	7. Bar Same Sex Marriage	Y	11. Oppose Iraq Withdrawal	*
4. Drilling in ANWR	N	8. Stem Cell Research $	N	12. Detainee Tribunals	Y

Election Results

2006 general	Jim Sensenbrenner (R)	194,669	(62%)	($831,766)
	Bryan Kennedy (D)	112,451	(36%)	($353,166)
	Other	8,060	(3%)	
2006 primary	Jim Sensenbrenner (R)	unopposed		
2004 general	Jim Sensenbrenner (R)	271,153	(67%)	($655,901)
	Bryan Kennedy (D)	129,384	(32%)	($267,814)
	Other	6,754	(2%)	

Prior Winning Percentages: 2002 (87%); 2000 (74%); 1998 (91%); 1996 (74%); 1994 (100%); 1992 (70%); 1990 (100%); 1988 (75%); 1986 (78%); 1984 (73%); 1982 (100%); 1980 (78%); 1978 (61%)

The People		Race/Ethnic Origin	Ancestry		
Area size:	1,301 sq. mi.	94.0% White	German: 34.6%	Irish: 8.8%	
Urban population:	84.9%	1.3% Black	Polish: 7.7%		
Rural population:	15.1%	1.5% Asian	**2004 Presidential Vote**		
Pop. 2000:	670,458	0.2% Native Am.	Bush (R)	265,537	(63%)
Pop. 2005 (est):	699,877	0.0% Hawaiian	Kerry (D)	151,968	(36%)
Median income:	$58,594	0.7% Two+ races	Other	1,006	(0%)
Poverty status:	3.4%	0.1% Other	**2000 Presidential Vote**		
Military veterans:	12.4%	2.2% Hispanic Origin	Bush (R)	233,005	(62%)
			Gore (D)	132,310	(35%)
			Other	13,080	(3%)
			Cook Partisan Voting Index: R +12		

Occupation	Blue collar: 21.3%	White collar: 68.2%	Gray collar: 10.5%

For decades, the orderly, heavily German-American factory city of Milwaukee has been spreading slowly, mostly west and north, into Wisconsin dairy country. There are high-income enclaves here, like close-in Elm Grove and Oconomowoc spread out to the west around its lakes. There is office development in Brookfield; subdivisions spread out in Mequon and Menomonee Falls and farther, reaching to small towns with roots deep in the 19th century. This is comfortable but not fancy territory, and the economy here is still based heavily on skilled manufacturing. Not far from Milwaukee are Port Washington, with Allen-Edmonds shoes; West Bend, with West Bend kitchen appliances; Pewaukee, with Harken sailboat hardware. In Ozaukee County is the tiny town of Waubeka where a schoolteacher in 1885 proclaimed America's first Flag Day. Closer to Milwaukee are its tonier and increasingly liberal suburbs along Lake Michigan—Shorewood, Whitefish Bay, and Fox Point—where wealthy neighborhoods are just a few miles from the poorest neighborhoods in the state on the other side of I-43. In April 2006, Shorewood and Whitefish Bay voters approved referenda calling for withdrawal of U.S. troops from Iraq.

The 5th Congressional District of Wisconsin includes most of the western, northwestern and northern suburbs of Milwaukee. Among them are the close-in lakefront suburbs in Milwaukee County, Ozaukee County north of Milwaukee and Washington County to the west; most of the Milwaukee County suburbs of Wauwatosa and West Allis; most of the northern three tiers of townships in Waukesha County just to the west; and a part of Jefferson County further west. Farmland in Ozaukee and Washington counties has dropped by one-third since the 1970s. This is by far the most Republican district in the state; it voted 62% for George W. Bush in 2000 and 63% in 2004.

The congressman from the 5th District is Jim Sensenbrenner, a Republican first elected in 1978. Sensenbrenner grew up in the Milwaukee area, with strong Wisconsin roots; his great-grandfather was a founder of Kimberly-Clark. He graduated from Stanford and the University of Wisconsin law school, and has spent most of his adult life in politics. He served briefly as a staffer in the House, then was elected to the Wisconsin Assembly in 1968 and the Wisconsin Senate in 1974. When Bob Kasten ran for governor, he ran in this district and won the Republican primary by 589 votes. Of such narrow victories are long congressional careers made. Sensenbrenner reports a net worth of $10.8 million, and *Roll Call* ranks him the 24th richest member of Congress; but that may be misleading, since Sensenbrenner lists his investments in detail and calculates his net worth with precision, while most wealthy members value their assets within broad categories. Sensenbrenner isn't just loaded—he's lucky, too. In December 1997 he won $250,000 in the District of Columbia lottery after buying two tickets while picking up some beer for an office party at a Capitol Hill liquor store; he also won $1,000 in the Wisconsin Lottery in 2006 and again in 2007.

Sensenbrenner has a rough and often partisan edge, but his voting record has leaned toward the center and he prides himself on his legislative skills. He has long been a stickler for ethics, and was one of the first to urge that Congress apply to itself the laws it imposes on the rest of the country. In the Clinton impeachment, he was one of the 13 House managers and was chosen by chairman Henry Hyde to start the presentation to the Senate. As chairman of the Science Committee from 1997 to 2001 Sensenbrenner supported the space station and most manned space flight, but was persistently critical of the U.S.-Russia space agreement. In 2001, he became chairman of the Judiciary Committee. He sought to protect the committee's jurisdiction from raids by other House committees, notably Energy and Commerce. He was proud of enacting the first congressional authorization of the Department of Justice in many years, citing the vital role that it gave his committee in improving oversight of the department. "I am a hawk on oversight," he said. "I don't back down because the president is in my party." After September 11, he pressed for a thorough congressional review of Attorney General John Ashcroft's call for additional law enforcement investigative powers. Concerned about possible violations of civil liberties, he insisted on a sunset provision under which the Patriot Act would expire in four years.

On some legislation he worked for many years to gain enactment. He supported the bankruptcy bill, but was frustrated when abortion opponents voted it down in November 2002 because of a provision inserted by Senator Charles Schumer, making non-dischargeable in bankruptcy fines and damages for violence or protest against abortion providers. In 2005, after Schumer's provision was rejected in the Senate, the bill passed. He has backed limitations in tort law on class actions, medical malpractice, and asbestos liability, and has sought to increase penalties for frivolous lawsuits. But he has not always followed the party line. In 2003, he said he saw no need to amend the Constitution to ban same-sex marriages. After the Massachusetts Supreme Judicial Court ruled that such marriages were mandated by the state's constitution, the Republican leadership bypassed the committee and brought it to the floor in September 2004; the vote was 227-186 in favor, well short of the required two-thirds.

Sensenbrenner resisted calls for a constitutional amendment to permit in case of a catastrophic attack the appointment of members to fill House vacancies caused by death or incapacity. Instead he passed a bill requiring elections to fill vacancies within 49 days. On the intelligence reorganization bill in 2004 he inserted immigration provisions setting national standards for driver licenses, including denying them to illegal immigrants, prohibiting the use of Mexican *matricula consular* cards for identification, tightening standards for asylum and overriding state laws and regulations blocking border barriers. When he objected to the conference report with the Senate, Speaker Dennis Hastert promised that Sensenbrenner's immigration provisions would come to the floor in 2005 as the first must-pass legislation.

His final two years as chairman were busy. The House approved his immigration provision 261-161 in February 2005 and it became law in May. After the House later passed additional measures to penalize illegal aliens, he criticized the Senate-passed "comprehensive" immigration reform bill as "amnesty" and said that President Bush had failed to address conservative demands to toughen border enforcement; he kept the door open to a House-Senate conference agreement, but said that the two chambers were "oceans apart" and they made little progress before the election.

In March 2005, he was the chief sponsor of the bill to force federal court review of removal of the feeding tube that had sustained the life of Terri Schiavo. In June 2005, some questionable parliamentary maneuvering during a hearing on the Patriot Act led Democrats to file an unusual resolution condemning his abuse of power; the House rejected it on a party-line vote and Sensenbrenner refused demands for an apology. After a difficult conference committee with the Senate, he won extension of the Patriot Act. At his insistence, most of its provisions were made permanent and law-enforcement authority was enhanced. But Sensenbrenner had differences with Attorney General Alberto Gonzalez over the scope of the domestic surveillance program and demanded steps to protect "the freedoms we cherish." After the FBI's May 2006 raid of the congressional office of Representative Bill Jefferson, Sensenbrenner said that he was bothered that the decision to seize the records was made without consultation with House lawyers. "The [speech or debate] privilege does not belong to the executive branch." In July 2006, he spearheaded the 25-year extension of the Voting Rights Act.

In September 2006, he won House passage of the bill for presidential authority to conduct warrantless surveillance, but it died in the Senate. That same month, he had an angry clash with Milwaukee Mayor Tom Barrett, his former House colleague, after Barrett criticized a Judiciary Committee bill to limit review of gun data and Sensenbrenner responded that the city was becoming "the murder capital of the U.S."

Sensenbrenner has not been seriously challenged since the 1978 primary; his lowest reelection score came in 2006 when he won 62%-36% over Bryan Kennedy, a professor of Portuguese at the University of Wisconsin-Milwaukee, who also ran in 2004. The House Republicans' six-year term limit for senior committee members forced Sensenbrenner to step aside at Judiciary in January 2007, and he lost to Ralph Hall in the selection of the ranking Republican at the Science and Technology Committee. In March, Minority Leader John Boehner named Sensenbrenner ranking Republican on the Select Committee on Energy Independence and Global Warming. Some Republicans would not be surprised if he retires in 2008. If he does, they should have little trouble holding the seat.

SIXTH DISTRICT

Rep. Tom Petri (R)

Elected April 1979, 14th full term; b. May 28, 1940, Marinette; home, Fond du Lac; Harvard U., B.A. 1962, J.D. 1965; Lutheran; married (Anne).

Elected Office: WI Senate, 1972-79.

Professional Career: Peace Corps, Somalia, 1966-67; Law Clerk, Fed. Judge James Doyle, 1965-66; White House aide, 1969; Practicing atty., 1970-79.

DC Office: 2462 RHOB, 20515, 202-225-2476; Fax: 202-225-2356; Web site: www.house.gov/petri.

District Offices: Fond du Lac, 920-922-1180; Oshkosh, 920-231-6333.

Committees: *Education & Labor* (2d of 22 R): Higher Education, Lifelong Learning & Competitiveness. *Transportation & Infrastructure* (3d of 34 R): Aviation (RMM); Railroads, Pipelines & Hazardous Materials; Highways & Transit.

Group Ratings

	ADA	ACLU	AFS	LCV	ITIC	NTU	COC	ACU	CFG	FRC
2006	5	27	0	67	100	72	87	76	73	85
2005	5	—	0	17	—	67	85	72	83	92

National Journal Ratings

	2005 LIB	—	2005 CONS	2006 LIB	—	2006 CONS
Economic	46%	—	53%	42%	—	57%
Social	39%	—	60%	38%	—	61%
Foreign	45%	—	54%	47%	—	51%

Key Votes of the 109th Congress

1. Estate Tax Repeal	Y	5. Limit Interstate Abortion	Y	9. Build Border Fence	Y
2. Limit CAFE Standards	N	6. Extend Patriot Act	Y	10. CAFTA	Y
3. FY06 Spending Curb	Y	7. Bar Same Sex Marriage	Y	11. Oppose Iraq Withdrawal	Y
4. Drilling in ANWR	N	8. Stem Cell Research $	N	12. Detainee Tribunals	Y

Election Results

2006 general	Tom Petri (R)	.... unopposed		($913,108)
2006 primary	Tom Petri (R)	.... unopposed		
2004 general	Tom Petri (R)	 238,620	(67%)	($478,540)
	Jef Hall (D)	 107,209	(30%)	($4,333)
	Other	 10,166	(3%)	

Prior Winning Percentages: 2002 (100%); 2000 (65%); 1998 (93%); 1996 (73%); 1994 (100%); 1992 (53%); 1990 (100%); 1988 (74%); 1986 (97%); 1984 (76%); 1982 (65%); 1980 (59%); 1979 (50%)

The People		Race/Ethnic Origin	Ancestry		
Area size:	5,816 sq. mi.	94.1% White	German: 38.8%	Irish: 6.8%	
Urban population:	60.7%	1.0% Black	Polish: 5.4%		
Rural population:	39.3%	1.5% Asian	**2004 Presidential Vote**		
Pop. 2000:	670,440	0.4% Native Am.	Bush (R) 208,931	(56%)	
Pop. 2005 (est):	684,973	0.0% Hawaiian	Kerry (D) 157,212	(43%)	
Median income:	$44,242	0.7% Two+ races	Other 3,747	(1%)	
Poverty status:	6.1%	0.0% Other	**2000 Presidential Vote**		
Military veterans:	13.7%	2.3% Hispanic Origin	Bush (R) 170,134	(53%)	
			Gore (D) 134,926	(42%)	
			Other 13,499	(4%)	
			Cook Partisan Voting Index: R + 5		

Occupation	Blue collar: 35.4%	White collar: 49.1%	Gray collar: 15.5%

Central Wisconsin is solid country, a producer of basic commodities—milk, butter and cheese, paper products, Mercury outboard motors, Kleenex and military trucks in Oshkosh. Settled first by Yankee Protestants, it was one of the birthplaces of the Republican Party in February 1854, when a group of Whigs, Free Soilers and Democrats met in a small white schoolhouse in Ripon, Wisconsin, and proclaimed themselves Republicans; Jackson, Michigan, also claims to be the birthplace of the party. Whichever, the party grew rapidly, winning a near-majority in the House in the 1854 elections. But Republican roots here are not just Yankee. The 1850s brought the first surge of German migration into the United States, and central Wisconsin was a favorite destination. Here they built the dairy farms and factory towns that seemed steadfastly prosperous, and developed a manufacturing economy that has been booming recently. The German influence is still felt: Sheboygan is the Bratwurst Capital of the World, though it's also the home these days of more than 4,300 Asians (mostly Hmong) and 5,000 Hispanics (including the mayor). Here also was the testing ground, in Fond du Lac County, of Governor Tommy Thompson's W-2 welfare program; the welfare rolls there, never high, fell to zero after the program began in 1997.

The 6th Congressional District is a slice of central Wisconsin from Lake Michigan to the Wisconsin River. It has the highest percentage of residents of German ancestry (39%) in the nation and includes Sheboygan and Manitowoc on Lake Michigan, Oshkosh and Fond du Lac on Lake Winnebago in the Fox River Valley, and the towns of Menasha and Kimberly, just outside Appleton. It also includes five rural counties to the west and south. Oshkosh, the largest city in the district, is no longer the place where kids clothing maker Oshkosh B'Gosh manufactures its clothes. But it is home to the aviation enthusiasts of the Experimental Aircraft Association, which hosts the annual EAA fly-in. Politically, this has been Republican territory since that first meeting in Ripon and remains so today, and it has elected Republicans who have come up with thoughtful and original solutions to problems. One was William Steiger, first elected in 1966, who put on his staff a University of Wisconsin graduate student named Dick Cheney; Steiger's chief monuments were the all-volunteer military and the 1978 Steiger amendment cutting capital gains tax rates—considerable accomplishments for a member of the minority party, and especially for one who died at age 40 in 1978.

The congressman from the 6th District is Tom Petri, a Republican first elected in the 1979 contest to succeed Steiger. Petri grew up in Fond du Lac, graduated from Harvard, was a Peace Corps volunteer in Somalia and was elected to the state Senate in 1972, at 32. In 1974 he was the Republican nominee against Senator Gaylord Nelson; he walked across the state campaigning but in that Democratic year lost 62%-36%. When he ran for the House in 1979, Petri beat Tommy Thompson, then a state legislator, in the primary 35%-19% and then won the special election with 50.4%.

With a voting record that has been firmly centrist, some of Petri's ideas have been adopted. He long boosted the Earned Income Tax Credit, which results in payments to low-income people who work, targeting aid to families much better than the minimum wage; the Clinton administration agreed and increased the EITC when Democrats were in control. Petri called for expanding the EITC concept with a $1,000 tax credit per child, in place of the current deduction; Congress agreed with Clinton on a $500 per child credit, leaving the deduction in place. Later, he called for a review of what he called the poverty trap—as low income people increase their earnings, they lose eligibility for the EITC and other federal benefits and are in effect taxed at rates up to 100%. In 2004 he joined the bipartisan call for a $500 grant to all newborn children, to be held in an investment account and usable after age 18 for education or a first home.

Petri hoped to become chairman of the Education and the Workforce Committee after the 2000 elections. He was the most senior Republican on the committee, but the Republican Steering Committee passed over him and installed the fourth most senior Republican, John Boehner. Petri's office put out a statement saying this was part of a "purge of moderate Republicans," and Petri's voting record became more liberal than it was before 2000. He backed the Shays-Meehan campaign finance bill for some time and in July 2001 he was one of 19 Republicans who successfully voted against the rule for debate on the bill. Then in January 2002, after the Enron bankruptcy, he was one of two Republicans who signed to provide the 218 signatures that brought the issue to the floor. With George Miller, he sponsored in March 2005 a $1,000 increase in Pell grants, to $5,050. When Boehner stepped down as chairman to become Majority Leader in February 2006, Petri did not seek his post. In June 2005, he was one of 12 House Republicans to vote against the constitutional amendment to ban flag-desecration.

As chairman from 1995 to 2006 of the often-renamed Highways, Transit and Pipelines Subcommittee, the key subcommittee of Transportation and Infrastructure, Petri played a major role in highway and other transportation bills. With the reauthorization of TEA-21 in 2005, he argued from the start for increases in transportation spending. In subcommittee and full committee, he pushed for a $375 billion bill, funded by a 5-cent gas tax increase; he also pressed for ending the 5.2 cent lower tax on ethanol. One reason for the high spending was the need to propitiate both donor states—those who get back less than 100% of their gas tax revenues and whose members insisted on getting 95 cent—and donee states, whose members wanted to avoid any cuts. Another reason was the need to fund hugely expensive special projects. But the Bush administration threatened to veto any tax increase, and Congress finally passed a $286 billion bill. Included was $25 million for Sheboygan to link local centers with bicycle and pedestrian paths and $10 million to replace the Wisconsin Street Bridge in Oshkosh.

When the senior Republican position opened on the Transportation Committee following the 2006 election, Petri was the most senior member who was eligible. Once again, he lost in the leadership-controlled Steering Committee. The winner was the more partisan John Mica of Florida. "Maybe I'm missing something," Petri told the *Journal Sentinel.* "Sometimes I think you can be more effective by working with people." He became ranking Republican on the Aviation Subcommittee. Despite his setbacks in Washington, Petri has been reelected easily, and was among the few Republicans who ran without opposition in 2006. In February 2007, he was one of 17 Republicans who voted for the House-passed resolution opposing the military surge in Iraq.

SEVENTH DISTRICT

Rep. David Obey (D)

Elected April 1969, 19th full term; b. Oct. 3, 1938, Okmulgee, OK; home, Wausau; U. of WI, B.S. 1960, M.A., 1962; Catholic; married (Joan).

Elected Office: WI Assembly, 1962-69.

Professional Career: Asst., family-run supper club & motel, 1962-68.

DC Office: 2314 RHOB, 20515, 202-225-3365; Web site: www.obey.house.gov.

District Offices: Superior, 715-398-4426; Wausau, 715-842-5606.

Committees: *Appropriations* (Chmn. of 37 D): Labor, HHS, Education & Related Agencies (Chmn.).

Group Ratings

	ADA	ACLU	AFS	LCV	ITIC	NTU	COC	ACU	CFG	FRC
2006	90	91	100	100	43	13	20	20	6	14
2005	100	—	100	100	—	16	35	16	3	17

National Journal Ratings

	2005 LIB	—	2005 CONS		2006 LIB	—	2006 CONS
Economic	85%	—	15%		86%	—	11%
Social	71%	—	28%		66%	—	33%
Foreign	88%	—	12%		88%	—	10%

Key Votes of the 109th Congress

1. Estate Tax Repeal	N	5. Limit Interstate Abortion	Y	9. Build Border Fence	N
2. Limit CAFE Standards	N	6. Extend Patriot Act	N	10. CAFTA	N
3. FY06 Spending Curb	N	7. Bar Same Sex Marriage	N	11. Oppose Iraq Withdrawal	N
4. Drilling in ANWR	N	8. Stem Cell Research $	Y	12. Detainee Tribunals	N

Election Results

2006 general	David Obey (D) 161,903	(62%)	($1,400,489)
	Nick Reid (R) 91,069	(35%)	($211,609)
	Other.. 7,456	(3%)	
2006 primary	David Obey (D) .... unopposed		
2004 general	David Obey (D) 241,306	(86%)	($775,009)
	Mike Miles (Green) 26,518	(9%)	
	Larry Oftedahl (CNP) 12,841	(5%)	

Prior Winning Percentages: 2002 (64%); 2000 (63%); 1998 (61%); 1996 (57%); 1994 (54%); 1992 (64%); 1990 (62%); 1988 (62%); 1986 (62%); 1984 (61%); 1982 (68%); 1980 (65%); 1978 (62%); 1976 (73%); 1974 (71%); 1972 (63%); 1970 (68%); 1969 (52%)

The People		Race/Ethnic Origin	Ancestry	
Area size:	19,391 sq. mi.	95.1% White	German: 30.4%	Polish: 8.6%
Urban population:	42.0%	0.3% Black	Norwegian: 7.6%	
Rural population:	58.0%	1.5% Asian	**2004 Presidential Vote**	
Pop. 2000:	670,462	1.5% Native Am.	Kerry (D) 185,076	(50%)
Pop. 2005 (est):	683,930	0.0% Hawaiian	Bush (R) 179,963	(49%)
Median income:	$39,026	0.8% Two+ races	Other 3,987	(1%)
Poverty status:	8.6%	0.0% Other	**2000 Presidential Vote**	
Military veterans:	14.5%	0.9% Hispanic Origin	Gore (D) 152,177	(47%)
			Bush (R) 150,068	(47%)
			Other 18,294	(6%)
			Cook Partisan Voting Index: D + 2	

Occupation	Blue collar: 31.8%	White collar: 51.5%	Gray collar: 16.7%

In the late 19th century, on the rail lines radiating northwest from Chicago and Milwaukee, came thousands of migrants whose descendants have made the northern reaches of Wisconsin the most thickly settled land this far north in the United States east of the Mississippi. What brought people up so far was not cropland—there are no industrial-sized wheat farms as in the Red River Valley of North Dakota—but trees, iron and cows. This was one of America's largest virgin timberlands, and the river towns are still dotted with paper mills. Farther north, iron brought Finns and Italians to the port of Superior, Wisconsin, right next to Duluth, Minnesota, and to smaller towns on the chilly lake, like Bayfield near the Apostle Islands. Then on the cleared forestlands came dairy farms. Dairy cattle, properly cared for, thrive in these northern uplands, and the sons of Wisconsin dairymen, many of them immigrants from Germany and Norway, moved their dairy herds even farther north. On this base small cities grew, some with big enterprises. Wausau has paper mills and Wausau Insurance, Wisconsin Rapids has Stora Enso, and Stevens Point has Sentry Insurance. While many rural areas have declined, the area around Wausau, Wisconsin Rapids and Stevens Point has generated new businesses and jobs and retained a high-skill work force. The number of dairy farmers is in sharp decline, but farmers are turning to potatoes, vegetables, cranberries and ginseng.

All these places are in Wisconsin's 7th Congressional District, which stretches from Stevens Point in the south to Lake Superior in the north. The politics of northern Wisconsin and the 7th District has a rough-hewn quality, a certain lumberjack populist flavor. Ancestrally Republican, this area favored the progressivism of the LaFollettes. Today, the Superior and Stevens Point areas are heavily Democratic; Wausau's Marathon County and many of the smaller counties have been more Republican. This was a closely divided district in the last two presidential elections: Al Gore carried it by 47.5%-46.8% and John Kerry by 50.1%-48.7%.

The congressman from the 7th District is David Obey, a Democrat first elected in April 1969 and now chairman of the House Appropriations Committee, and one of the most capable and strongly motivated legislators on either side of the aisle. He grew up in Wausau, where his father worked in a roofing factory; he started off as a Republican, but was influenced by history teacher Arthur Henderson—who assigned papers on the politics of the 1920s and was attacked by McCarthyites—and between 1952 and 1956 Obey switched from supporting Dwight Eisenhower and Joe McCarthy to Adlai Stevenson and William Proxmire. Obey graduated from the University of Wisconsin, studied Soviet politics for three years in graduate school, and in 1962, when he was 24, he was elected to the Wisconsin Assembly even before he got his master's degree. When Melvin Laird resigned his House seat to become Richard Nixon's Defense secretary, Obey won an upset victory in the April 1969 special election.

In the state legislature, Obey was inspired by older New Deal Democrats who fought hard for the little guy; when he entered the House, the driving energy came from liberal Democrats opposed to the Vietnam War. Obey preserves something of the force of each group. He is not a sentimental liberal: He has a prickly personality and a vigorous temper and does not suffer gladly those he considers fools or knaves. But he can leaven that with humor: he likes to quote Archy the Cockroach, the supposed writer of Don Marquis's *Archy and Mehitabel*, and he is part of a band called The Capitol Offenses, which plays bluegrass music and gospel hymns. Even as he moved to the top of the seniority ladder, Obey has retained his sense of outrage and his eagerness to fight for what he believes in—a quality that even some Democrats complain has been too intense. But he continues to display abundant energy and leadership on a host of fronts. He has had his disappointments. He lost the Budget Committee chairmanship to Oklahoma's Jim Jones in 1980 by 121-116. In 1984 he wanted to become Democratic Caucus chairman, but demurred when it became clear that Dick Gephardt had the votes. Even so, informally Obey became a key leader of liberal Democrats, in 1989 pushing Gephardt for majority leader when Jim Wright and Tony Coelho were resigning. He has been a supporter of Nancy Pelosi's rise in the leadership, despite some friction with other Pelosi supporters like George Miller and John Murtha.

Obey remains a true believer in traditional liberalism, in Keynesian economics and economic redistribution. He thinks that government should provide economic security, create jobs and build infrastructure through public investment, that it should control health care costs and guarantee coverage and a choice of providers. He bucked the Clinton administration, vocally opposing NAFTA and, when Bill Clinton seemed to be backing away from universal health care coverage in July 1994, said "then I will walk away from the Clinton health care plan" and supported his real preference, a single-payer system. In June 1995, when Clinton accepted the Republicans' goal of a budget balanced in seven years, Obey immediately issued a written statement reading, "I think most of us learned some time ago that if you don't like the president's position on a particular issue you simply need to wait a few weeks." Obey also opposed some administration positions from the right. He has long opposed abortion, and has voted for the partial-birth abortion ban and other limits on abortion, but he is not for abolishing abortion rights. When former La Crosse Archbishop Raymond Burke admonished Catholic officeholders who do not seek to outlaw abortion, Obey wrote in the Jesuit publication *America*, "While I detest abortion and agree with Catholic teaching that in most instances it is morally wrong, I decline to force my views into laws that, if adopted, would be unenforceable and would tear this society apart. That judgment may be wrong, but it is a judgment honestly arrived at, and one that I am obligated to make." Representing the north woods, Obey opposes gun control, and once pointed out that one of the guns singled out in the assault weapons ban was owned by 23,000 residents of the 7th District, including two sheriffs.

Obey is above all an appropriator, and takes some justifiable pride in his skill at this work. He first got his seat on Appropriations in August 1969, when he was just 30. He first became chairman in March 1994, after the death of William Natcher; he was the youngest person to hold the post since James Good of Iowa in 1919. He got the job over the more senior Neal Smith, who had the support of other cardinals (Appropriatese for subcommittee chairmen), but Obey had more from non-committee liberals and less senior members, and won in the Democratic Caucus 152-106. Obey showed a determination to get things done on time—which is not always how appropriating works. For years much of his work was on the Foreign Operations Subcommittee, which he chaired from 1985 to 1995. This panel handles rather small sums of money but deals with some very sensitive issues, and it was often rocked in disputes about aid to the Nicaraguan Contras, the pace of negotiations in the Middle East, the treatment of the liberated nations of Eastern Europe. Obey has not always gotten his way, but in each case he worked to move appropriations bills forward in an orderly manner. He passed separate foreign operations appropriation bills nine out of 10 years, something that had only been accomplished twice in 10 years by his predecessors. Similarly, when Obey became chairman of the full committee in 1994, all 13 appropriations bills were signed into law prior to the beginning of the new fiscal year for the first time in 47 years; it hasn't happened since.

The Appropriations Committee has a bipartisan culture: there may be partisan votes between two sets of alternatives, but the subcommittees and the full committee tend to come to consensus on just how to spend the amounts they are allocated by budget resolutions and their own internal determinations. Obey worked relatively amicably with Chairman Bob Livingston from 1995 to 1999 and with Chairman Bill Young from 1999 to 2005; his relationship with Jerry Lewis, chairman in 2005-07 and now ranking minority member, has seemed more strained. After September 11, Obey and other Appropriations leaders backed George W. Bush's emergency appropriation of $40 billion, but put restrictions on spending—the first $10 billion could be spent after consultation with congressional leaders, the next $10 billion only after giving Congress 15 days of notice in which members could make objections, the last $20 billion only with congressional approval. In October Bush asked for $20 billion more for homeland security; Obey, like Robert Byrd in the Senate, thought that more was needed. He delayed the measure for two days in November because the Republican leadership would not allow a vote on his amendment for $7 billion more; Obey argued that more was needed for, among other things, protecting nuclear sites, but the Republicans passed a rule 216-211 blocking the amendment.

Obey was ranking Democrat on the Labor-HHS Subcommittee, the focus of the appropriations process in fall 2002; the conservative Republican Study Committee was pressuring the leadership to bring up Labor-HHS and hold it to the Bush budget limits, while Obey and subcommittee Chairman Ralph Regula, who worked together harmoniously, argued that they would be forced to cut worthy programs. Obey asked Speaker Dennis Hastert to allow four alternatives on the floor, in vain, and all but the defense and military construction appropriations were delayed until after the election and not passed until February 2003. In June 2003, Obey proposed to restore $1 billion to military housing and to increase homeland security spending by $1 billion, to be financed by reducing the tax cut on those earning more than $1 million a year; this was brushed aside as an invasion of Ways and Means's prerogatives. In June 2004 the House leadership gave him a floor vote on a proposal to increase discretionary spending, largely education, homeland security and veterans' health care, by $14 billion and scaling back tax cuts. It was defeated 184-230. But Obey did help facilitate the passage of other appropriations. When incoming Appropriations Chairman Jerry Lewis reduced the number of subcommittees from 13 to 10, Obey said Democrats "had no input whatsoever." "The result of this is you have not seen power this centralized since the days of Czar Cannon," he said.

Obey is not one of those appropriators who load up their districts with earmarked projects, though he has supported some. But he has paid close attention to district interests. Most important is the plight of Wisconsin dairy farmers; since 1937 the Agriculture Department has fixed milk prices by a formula that allows higher prices the farther a farm is from Eau Claire, Wisconsin. This increases prices to consumers, creates an oversupply of milk and reduces dairy prices in the Upper Midwest. Obey opposed the Northeast Dairy Compact, which allowed New England states to set higher prices, and it finally expired in September 2001. He voted against the farm bill in 2002; he supports its Milk Income Loss Contract provision but complained that it left in place unfair Federal Milk Marketing orders. In October 2004 he was miffed when House Republican leaders took the MILC program out of a drought and hurricane emergency appropriation and in January 2005 said that, despite George W. Bush's endorsement of the program, it would be hard to get an extension because of administration cuts in other farm programs. In 2005, he got it renewed as part of a disaster bill, but was angered when the Agriculture Committee in September decided to let it expire just before the end of the current farm bill, meaning it wouldn't be included in the budget baseline for the next farm bill, due to be reauthorized in 2007. "With all respect to the sainted authorizers, I have no intention of paying attention to their will. This ain't the way a rational legislative body would work." In May 2006 he got an extension of MILC passed so that it would be included in the budget baseline.

Obey has stirred controversy on a number of issues. In 2005 he got an amendment in appropriation condemning proselytizing at the Air Force Academy; when Republican John Hostettler said this was part of "the long war on Christianity in America," Obey demanded that he withdraw the remark. He supported the $51.8 billion emergency Katrina appropriation, but his amendment that FEMA report directly to the president was defeated along party lines. "The problem is that the agency that we are appropriating most of the money to has demonstrated with great clarity that it is spectacularly dysfunctional." He complained that Lewis did not clear with him a committee Surveys and Investigation staff review of the measure; he was said to be angry that Lewis had blocked the year before an S&I review of Donald Rumsfeld's Pentagon intelligence analysis operation. In February 2006, he called the Bush budget "wrongheaded and embarrassing" and said the administration had "the most fiscally irresponsible people to ever occupy the White House." He was especially critical of the freeze on Pell grants. In May 2006 he sought to cut military aid to Egypt after the arrest of democratic politician Ayman Nour; despite administration opposition, the committee cut $200 million. He has been a furious critic of the work of the Architect of the Capitol in constructing the Capitol Visitors Center. In May 2005 he blocked approval of office space plans for three weeks, under a provision requiring approval by both the committee's chairman and ranking member, and pushed an amendment to transfer all authority from the Architect to the GAO and appoint an inspector general in his office. The amendment passed the House with the legislative branch appropriation in June, but the Architect made the provision moot when he announced in August that he would not seek renomination at the end of his 10-year term in January 2007.

The practice of earmarking funds became vastly more common during the years Republicans held a majority in the House, and as an appropriator who did relatively little earmarking on district projects Obey seemed not necessarily averse to changes although, as he pointed out in May 2006, identifying earmarks would help rather than hurt many members in their districts. "You list earmarks and all that's going to do is to encourage more of them." When he and Robert Byrd took over as Appropriations chairmen, they faced the problem that only two appropriations had been passed by both houses; the House had passed all but one by July 4, but the Senate had not acted in the fall, and the House Republican leadership decided not to bring them up after the election. Obey criticized that decision. "Either the Congress will be consumed for months trying to pass those remaining bills . . . or it will be forced to pass some long-term continuing funding resolution. Either of those scenarios would represent lousy outcomes, but they would have been made unavoidable by Republican inaction today." Obey and Byrd decided to take the continuing resolution route, with "limited adjustments." And they announced they would not allow any earmarks to go into effect in the budget year ending September 30. "The best way to get people's attention that there needs to be serious reform is to say there won't be any earmarks. We have to build in some protection for when some idiot goes too far and fouls the nest. The problem is not earmarking. The problem is the abuse of earmarking." This of course was hailed by earmark opponent and conservative Republican Jeff Flake: "If Chairmen Obey and Byrd are serious about this, then they deserve some praise. If they're serious, they've managed to do something that Republican spenders have had a hard time doing lately: say no." But Obey did not rule out earmarks in the fiscal year 2008 appropriations. With more than 32,000 earmarking requests that he needed to approve, Obey extended the time for requests from March 16 to April 27 and announced that no earmarks would be added to appropriations bills until conference; he threatened to do away with them completely if the minority party "demagogues" the issue. The resulting uproar led Republicans to stall progress on the House floor for three days. Obey and party leaders brokered a compromise that let the first two appropriations bills go without earmarks until before the August recess (at which point they could be challenged on points of order on the floor) but allowed projects to be added up front to later bills. Republicans also agreed to let the bills proceed in a timely fashion.

Looking ahead as a member of the newly-minted majority, Obey was nettled when incoming Speaker Nancy Pelosi got the Democratic Caucus to limit members to six years as chairmen, a change Republicans made after they won their majorities in 1994. He told Pelosi he opposed the move; she said that if he had the votes to overturn it, she would let the caucus vote. Incoming Majority Leader Steny Hoyer said, somewhat vaguely, "It will be revisited at some point in time. When it will be revisited I don't know."

Obey voted against the Iraq war resolution in October 2002 and has been harshly critical of administration actions in Iraq. In September 2003 he said that Donald Rumsfeld and Paul Wolfowitz should resign. In March 2007 the task fell to him of constructing supplemental appropriations for Iraq with timetables for withdrawal but which also provided for the troops. In the halls of the Rayburn Building, Obey was approached by antiwar activist Tina Richards who asked him to defund the war now. "We can't get the votes. Do you see a magic wand in my pocket? We don't have the votes for it," he said in a six-minute interchange captured by a cellphone camera for public view on YouTube. He spoke of "idiot liberals" who didn't understand the bill and said, "We're trying to use the supplemental to end the war." Similarly, in a Democratic Caucus, when asked by aspiring presidential candidate Dennis Kucinich whether the supplemental allowed privatization of Iraqi oil, "I told him to read the goddamn language. If someone's ears are too tender for that language, that's too bad. I did it on purpose.... I'm sorry he's only at 1% in the polls. He simply does not like me and I don't like him. I make no apology [for] what I said to Kucinich. He had it coming."

Obey is the third most senior member of the House and one of three who served in the 1960s. He has been reelected by wide margins, except in 1994, when he won 54%-46%. He has said he plans to run at least through 2010, before the next round of redistricting. In 2006, against a 26-year-old Republican and a Green candidate, he won 62%-35%-3%.

EIGHTH DISTRICT

Rep. Steve Kagen (D)

Elected 2006, 1st term; b. Dec. 12, 1950, Appleton; home, Appleton; U. of WI, B.S. 1972, M.D. 1976; Jewish; married (Gayle).

Professional Career: Practicing allergist, 1979-2007; Founder, Kagen Allergy Clinics, 1981; Asst. clinical prof., Medical Col. of WI, 1983-2007; Allergy consultant, CNN, 1985-92.

DC Office: 1232 LHOB, 20515, 202-225-5665; Fax: 202-225-5729; Web site: kagen.house.gov.

District Offices: Appleton, 920-380-0061; Green Bay, 920-437-1954.

Committees: *Agriculture* (19th of 25 D): Livestock, Dairy & Poultry; Department Operations, Oversight, Nutrition & Forestry; Conservation, Credit, Energy & Research. *Transportation & Infrastructure* (38th of 41 D): Aviation; Water Resources & Environment.

Group Ratings and Key Votes: Newly Elected

Election Results

2006 general	Steve Kagen (D) 141,570	(51%)	($3,187,330)
	John Gard (R) 135,622	(49%)	($2,831,522)
2006 primary	Steve Kagen (D) 25,623	(48%)	
	Jamie Wall (D) 15,427	(29%)	
	Nancy Nusbaum (D) 12,731	(24%)	
2004 general	Mark Green (R) 248,070	(70%)	($433,513)
	Dottie Le Clair (D) 105,513	(30%)	($11,160)

The People		Race/Ethnic Origin	Ancestry		
Area size:	10,118 sq. mi.	92.2% White	German: 30.8%	Irish: 6.9%	
Urban population:	56.0%	0.6% Black	Polish: 6.5%		
Rural population:	44.0%	1.4% Asian	**2004 Presidential Vote**		
Pop. 2000:	670,480	2.6% Native Am.	Bush (R) 202,238	(55%)	
Pop. 2005 (est):	697,683	0.0% Hawaiian	Kerry (D) 162,793	(44%)	
Median income:	$43,274	0.9% Two+ races	Other 2,738	(1%)	
Poverty status:	6.8%	0.0% Other	**2000 Presidential Vote**		
Military veterans:	13.9%	2.2% Hispanic Origin	Bush (R) 165,819	(52%)	
			Gore (D) 138,056	(43%)	
			Other 13,974	(4%)	
			Cook Partisan Voting Index: R + 4		
Occupation	Blue collar: 31.3%	White collar: 53.9%	Gray collar: 14.8%		

In 1673, the French explorer and priest Father Marquette sailed from the open waters of Lake Michigan into what is now Green Bay. He had hoped to find the Northwest Passage to the Pacific. He actually found the Fox River, which leads to Lake Winnebago and, after a not-too-difficult portage, the Wisconsin River, which flows into the Mississippi. Green Bay and the Fox River Valley remained mostly wilderness and Indian country for more than 150 years. But once settled by Europeans, they became, as Father Marquette would have liked, one of the most heavily Catholic parts of the United States, though Indians still remain a presence; there was a long dispute over Chippewa Indian spearfishing rights and Green Bay's best hotel is now next to the Oneida Indian casino. This has been a thriving area economically, with traditional paper mills joined by high-skill manufacturing in Green Bay and Appleton in the Fox River Valley; a creative local business found a way to make the small packets that are filled with sugar and sugar substitutes, and took the business away from a South Korean firm. While paper products have long been an economic mainstay, the industry has experienced instability: in 2005, Procter & Gamble announced plans for a new toilet paper facility in Green Bay but at the same time Georgia-Pacific announced a round of job losses there.

No reference to Green Bay is complete without mention of pro football's Packers, owned by 110,000 shareholding Wisconsinites and never likely to move (under the team's charter, if the Packers are ever sold, the proceeds would go to the local Sullivan-Wallen American Legion Post 11 "for the purposes of erecting a proper soldier's memorial"). In September 2004, John Kerry became the butt of jokes when he came to Green Bay and referred to Lambeau Field, home of the Packers, as "Lambert Field", perhaps confusing it with the airport in St. Louis. Thirty miles south is Appleton, which has produced a number of famous Americans—Senator Joseph McCarthy, novelist Edna Ferber and escape artist Harry Houdini—and has a growing Hispanic population.

The 8th Congressional District of Wisconsin includes Green Bay and the Fox River Valley south to Appleton. It also includes sprawling north woods and dairy counties inland, plus the Door County peninsula that juts out into Lake Michigan, a favorite summer vacation spot for Chicago and Milwaukee families. Politically, this has often been malleable country. Democrats can win here: John F. Kennedy, with enthusiasm from local Catholics, carried the Fox River Valley in the primary and general election in 1960, and Bill Clinton carried it in 1996. But the 8th District these days more often votes Republican; George W. Bush won 52% of the vote in 2000 and 55% in 2004.

The new congressman from the 8th District is Steve Kagen, a Democrat elected in 2006, 40 years after his father ran unsuccessfully for the same seat. Kagen grew up in Appleton, was a competitive speed skater, earned his medical degree from the University of Wisconsin, and founded Kagen Allergy Clinics in the Fox River Valley. His clinics made him wealthy and two of them, in Appleton and Green Bay, are located in the district's population centers. Kagen taught at the Medical College of Wisconsin and, according to his congressional biography, served as "the exclusive allergy consultant to CNN." His first experience in politics came in 1966, when his father, dermatologist Marvin Kagen, a contemporary and friend of Gaylord Nelson and William Proxmire, ran unsuccessfully for Congress here. Steve Kagen's chance to run for the seat occurred when four-term Republican Mark Green announced he would vacate the seat to run for governor. Kagen entered the campaign in August 2005 running on a universal health care platform he called No Patient Left Behind, which proposed transparency and uniformity in health care pricing, a national insurance risk pool, a deductible set at 3% of a household's federal taxable income and government-sponsored coverage for the poor.

Kagen was hardly the Democrats' obvious nominee: in the primary he faced former Brown County Executive Nancy Nusbaum, who had wide name recognition and the backing of EMILY's List. Also running was business consultant Jamie Wall, who had the endorsement of Congressman David Obey from the neighboring 7th District. Kagen spent himself into contention by contributing nearly $1.5 million from his own pocket for the primary, allowing him to start running ads in March. While national Democrats remained neutral in the primary, the National Republican Congressional Committee recognized Kagen's outsider image and health care message might appeal to Republicans and independents; they sought to short-circuit his candidacy by running ads that referred to him as "Dr. Millionaire" and criticizing him for suing 80 patients for nonpayment of bills. Kagen explained that out of 60,000 patients, he took action only against those who refused to pay their bills. The NRCC's ploy didn't work. In the September 12 primary, Kagen carried 12 of the district's 15 counties, and won 48% to Wall's 29% and Nusbaum's 24%. Republicans nominated John Gard, Wisconsin's Assembly Speaker, who won early support from state and national party leaders and easily turned back primary opposition from state Representative Terri McCormick. Democrats used a March fundraising visit by Vice President Dick Cheney to attack Gard as a "rubber stamp" for the administration, and Gard's nearly two decades in the Assembly made it difficult to sidestep criticism that he was a "career politician." Kagen told the Appleton *Post-Crescent* he was happy to run as a political newcomer. "I'm an outsider in an outsider year. I'm not a professional politician. I'm the only candidate in this race, on both sides of the aisle, who hasn't been involved in government. I've never been part of the problem. I've been solving problems as a doctor." In the final weeks of the campaign, one Kagen ad called Gard "the most corrupt politician in Madison," though it offered no evidence to back up that claim.

Kagen's political inexperience wasn't always an asset. He had to apologize in late October for using the term "Injun time" in a campaign appearance. Republicans used the comment as evidence Kagen was ill-prepared to serve in Congress although the racially insensitive comment drew few condemnations from tribal leaders. They claimed Kagen would support higher taxes, amnesty for illegal immigrants and eliminate the Medicare/prescription drug benefit. In late October, Kagen spent another $720,000—thus triggering the "millionaires' amendment" allowing Gard to raise more than the regular legal limit. In a tough political environment for Republican candidates, even the 8th District's Republican leanings weren't enough to keep the seat under GOP control. Kagen won by nearly 6,000 votes, 51%-49%; he carried Brown County and Outagamie County, winning the latter by over 6,200 votes. He spent $3.2 million, $2.6 million out of his own pocket, compared to Gard's $2.8 million, making it the most expensive House race in Wisconsin history.

After the election, Kagen said he was mindful Republicans would work to make him a "one-timer" but he nevertheless found himself embroiled in controversy. Apparently unaware that an editor for an alternative monthly newspaper, *The Scene*, was present, Kagen bragged to local peace activists that he had confronted Karl Rove during a chance encounter in a bathroom during a White House reception. He told the group he had prevented Rove from leaving the bathroom and taunted him for the Republican ad campaign against him. "You're in the White House and you think you're safe, huh? You recognize me? My name's Dr. Multimillionaire and I kicked your ass." Kagen also claimed to have confronted Dick Cheney and then insulted President Bush by intentionally greeting First Lady Laura Bush as Barbara Bush. The White House denied Kagen's story, and Kagen's later statements to the press proved evasive. He then apologized in a letter to constituents, but not before newspaper editorialists questioned his judgment. Kagen faced other bad news: the FDA sent a letter to Kagen in December 2006 that said his clinics did not have a valid license to ship allergy shots across state lines.

If Kagen can steer clear of further controversy, he has opportunities to establish himself as a legislator. As the only Democratic physician in the House, he has a unique platform to speak on one of the party's leading issues. As the only Wisconsin member of the House Agriculture Committee, he had the chance to represent the state during the 2007 farm bill reauthorization. Republicans have already made the district a target in 2008. Kagen faces a possible repeat challenge from Gard; former Green Bay Mayor Paul Jadin and state Representatives Frank Lasee and Steve Wieckert were also mentioned as possible Republican candidates.

★ WYOMING ★

Wyoming is "the land of the cowboy," as the *WPA Guide* called it more than 60 years ago. "Its mountains, plains, and valleys are essentially livestock country. A cowboy astride a bucking bronco greets the visitor from enameled license plates, from newspapers, magazines and painted signs." The cowboy is still on the license plates, and Wyoming remains the most western of states in spirit—largely unsettled, the least populous state, a thin veneer of civilization stretched over a forbidding and beautiful land. But it is more than the land of the cowboy now; it is the land of the oil and gas worker, of the coal mine operator, of the tourism operator.

For Wyoming's economy now depends not on cowboys and cattle but on mining and minerals. Wyoming boomed with oil prospectors during the energy price surge of the 1970s, but was hit hard by drops in oil prices in the early 1980s and again in the late 1990s. As the exploration for oil slumped, the production of other minerals has surged. The Clean Air Act put a premium on Wyoming's low-sulfur coal, and this is now the number one coal state, producing one-third of the nation's coal, more than West Virginia and Kentucky combined. In the Powder River Basin 30-story high machines blast away the topsoil and scoop out the coal; it is hauled away by 65 unit trains a day by the Burlington Northern and Union Pacific, which can't handle all the traffic; but the Dakota, Minnesota & Eastern rail line proposed to run east to the Mississippi River, the biggest U.S. rail construction project in a century, was dealt a blow by its failure to get a federal loan. Wyoming is also the number seven oil and number four natural gas producer, and the nation's top producer of the mineral bentonite (used in oil drilling and cosmetics) and has the world's largest reserve of trona (used in glass and baking soda), on which Congress cut the royalty rate from 6% to 2% in September 2006. Much of the natural gas is coal-bed methane, mixed with water next to coal seams; only in 1989 did engineers figure out how to separate the natural gas from the water. Now 200-foot drilling rigs are sinking wells as deep as 25,000 feet, and production has jumped enormously since 2000. These are capital-intensive industries which produce relatively few jobs for highly educated young people. About one-quarter of people 25 to 34 left the state in the 1990s, and about two-thirds of the graduates of the University of Wyoming leave, which causes some unease. "For those unable to stay,

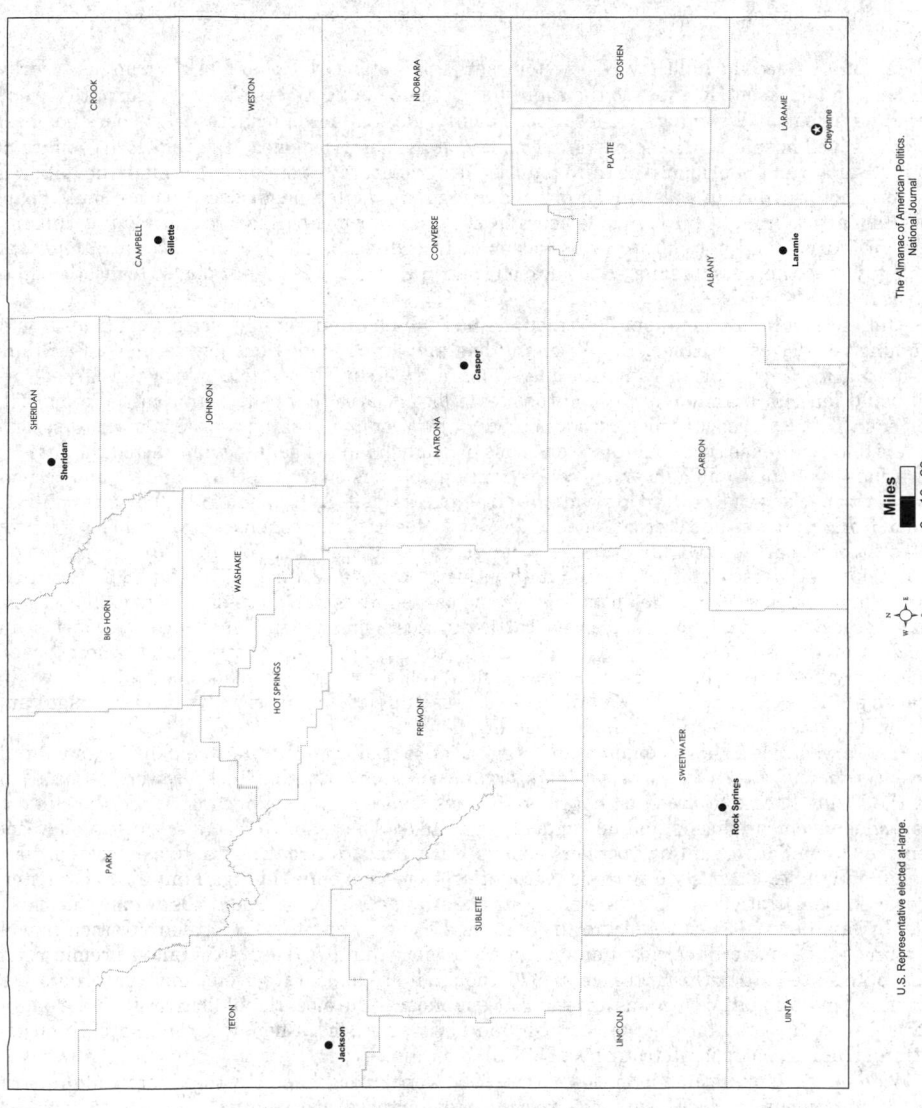

CROOK

WESTON

NIOBRARA

GOSHEN

PLATTE

LARAMIE

✪ Cheyenne

CAMPBELL

● Gillette

CONVERSE

ALBANY

● Laramie

SHERIDAN

JOHNSON

NATRONA

● Casper

CARBON

● Sheridan

WASHAKIE

BIG HORN

HOT SPRINGS

FREMONT

SWEETWATER

● Rock Springs

PARK

SUBLETTE

TETON

LINCOLN

UINTA

● Jackson

Miles

0 10 20

The Almanac of American Politics.
National Journal

U.S. Representative elected at-large.

hopefully some day you will return," Governor Dave Freudenthal told graduates at the university's commencement. But there's a unfulfilled demand for workers in the Powder River Basin and other boom areas, and Wyoming is busy sending recruiters out to places like Flint and Lansing, Michigan, to attract skillful blue collar workers not afraid to take their chances on the nation's energy frontier. Everything seems to be coming together for Wyoming: high oil and gas prices, continued demand for coal, rising beef prices, rapidly rising severance taxes and revenues from tourists. The American City Business Journal in 2005 rated Wyoming number one in economic vitality, tied with Nevada, in 2005.

Wyoming's second industry is now tourism. Yellowstone National Park continues to draw millions, and Jackson Hole just to the south has become one of America's elite resort areas year-round; its airport is Wyoming's busiest and the only one that accommodates jets. There has been growth as well in the scenic and pastoral country on the eastern slope of the Big Horn Mountains around Buffalo and Sheridan. The third industry is agriculture: Wyoming is second in the nation in wool production, third in sheep inventory and also produces hay, sugar beets, barley, pinto beans and beef cattle. Drought hurt some farmers in 2002, but farm exports were sharply up. This mix between tourism and agriculture leads to some cultural clash. The movie *Brokeback Mountain*, about gay sheep herders, premiered in Jackson Hole in December 2005, but played to mostly empty houses in the state.

Reliance on high-tech mineral extraction and high-end tourism may seem a contradiction of Wyoming's Old West heritage. But Wyoming has always depended on new technology to tame age-old nature. Cattle ranches after the open-range era were made possible only by the barbed wire that could fence in roaming herds, and the steam locomotives that could carry cattle to markets back east. This 19th century high tech was brought to Wyoming by large capitalist operators, some of them onetime Texas cowhands or second sons of English landed gentry, who started the first big operations after the Civil War. And of course mining depends on high-tech machinery and responsiveness to markets that reward innovation and penalize stasis. At the same time, Wyoming still is a kind of frontier: It was until recently one of the few states with more men than women—one reason it was the first part of the United States, when it was a territory in 1869, to give women the vote (exception: New Jersey allowed women with property to vote between 1776 and 1807, but there weren't many). There is a settled part of Wyoming as well, in the medium-sized towns that are the state's largest cities, and among sheep and cattle ranches, sugar beet and malting barley farms and denizens of tiny settlements. This is a small state, a single community really, where people remember who played what position, when and how well, for what high-school football team; where because all the locals know who your father's cousins married, you mostly live on the straight and narrow. The locals set the tone of life in Wyoming.

There was once a sharp economic and regional split traditionally reflected in partisan politics. The big economic interests—cattle ranchers, organized in the Wyoming Stock Growers' Association, and the Union Pacific Railroad management always favored the Republicans, as did the wildcatters, independent producers and oil company geologists. The main Democratic constituency had been the Union Pacific Railroad workers who built the first transcontinental line across southern Wyoming in the 1860s; the southern tier of counties, from Cheyenne through Laramie to Evanston, once voted Democratic. But now the Democrats are strongest in Teton County, the home of Jackson Hole, by far the wealthiest county in the state and the only one to vote for John Kerry in 2004. Wyoming has been one of the most Republican states since the 1970s; it hasn't elected a Democrat to the Senate since 1970 or the House since 1976, though it has had mostly Democratic governors over that time. In presidential elections it is solidly Republican—the most Republican state in the nation in 2000, when it voted for George W. Bush and native son Dick Cheney, a running back on the Natrona High School football team, by a 69%-28% margin.

Wyoming's Republican tendencies in the 1990s were strengthened by the Clinton administration's environmental policies—proposing grazing fee increases, the reintroduction of gray wolves into Yellowstone, proposing threatened species status on the black-tailed prairie dog, banning snowmobiles in national parks, the moratorium on road building in the national parks. But the policies of the Bush administration—removing endangered status from the gray wolves, opening the way to proving title to land currently controlled by the Bureau of Land Management—have removed some of these grievances. In a small state with not much more than half a million people—the nation's smallest population congressional district—Wyoming voters expect to talk person-to-person with their governors, senators and congressmen every so often. Personal campaigning is important, and Democrats have won six of the last eight races for governor. But party tends to trump personality when it comes to federal office.

The People

Pop. 2006 (est):	515,004			
Pop. 2000:	493,782			
Pop. 1990:	453,588			
Change 1990-2000:	Up 8.9%			
% of U.S. total:	0.2%			
Pop. rank:	50th of 50			
Area size:	97,814 sq. mi.			
State Native:	42.5%			
Non-citizen:	1.2%			

Language

English: 90.7%   Spanish: 5.7%
Other Eur.: 2.3%

Race/Ethnic Origin

438,799	88.9%	White
3,504	0.7%	Black
2,670	0.5%	Asian
10,238	2.1%	Native Am.
264	0.1%	Hawaiian
6,164	1.2%	Two+ races
474	0.1%	Other
31,669	6.4%	Hisp. Origin

Ancestry

German: 18.4%		English: 11.3%	
Irish: 9.4%		USA: 4.6%	
Norwegian: 3.0%			

Military veterans: 57,860 (15.8%)

WWII: 16.8%	Korea: 12.3%
Vietnam: 36.2%	Gulf War: 12.8%

Most populous cities (2006):

1. Cheyenne	55,314
2. Casper	52,089
3. Laramie	25,688
4. Gillette	23,899
5. Rock Springs	19,324

Urban population: 65.2%
Rural population: 34.8%

Education

H.S. Grad:	87.9%
College Grad:	21.9%

Industry

Agri: 10.7%		Con: 8.7%
Fin: 4.7%		Info: 2.2%
Mfg: 11.4%		Prof: 27.4%
Public: 6.3%		Trade: 14.1%
Other: 14.5%		

Occupation

Blue collar: 27.5%   White collar: 54.2%
Gray collar: 18.2%

Work Sector

Private: 70.2%		Govt: 20.4%
Self: 8.9%		Family: 0.5%
Unemployment: 5.2%		

Household Income

<15k: 16.7%	15-35k: 29.2%
35-50k: 18.3%	50-100k: 29.1%
100-150k: 4.5%	>150k: 2.2%
Median: $37,892	
Poverty status: 11.4%	

Home Value

<50k: 18.4%	50-100k: 39.0%	100-200k: 31.7%	200-300k: 6.0%
300-500k: 2.5%	>500k: 2.4%	Median: $91,500	

Legislature

Senate	23 R 7 D
House	43 R 17 D

Legislative Term Limits: No

Registered Voters

D: 67,246	(25.6%)
R: 162,952	(61.9%)
O: 32,885	(12.5%)

Presidential politics   Wyoming is one of the least likely states in the nation to be seriously contested in presidential general elections: it is too Republican, too remote and has only three electoral votes. Candidates have seldom visited, except when Dick Cheney has gone to his home in Jackson. This was George W. Bush's number one state in 2000, when he carried it 69%-28%, and his number two state in 2004, when he carried it 69%-29%.

Wyoming typically holds presidential caucuses in early March. In 2004 the Democratic caucuses were held March 20, apparently with no members of the national press in attendance. In 2008, Wyoming Republicans pledged to caucus "the same date as the New Hampshire Republican primary, whenever that may be." With New Hampshire's date still uncertain, the state party decided in August 2007 to caucus (actually it's a county-level delegate selection convention) on January 5. Democrats planned to caucus on March 8.

2004 Presidential Vote

Bush (R)	167,629	(69%)
Kerry (D)	70,776	(29%)
Nader (I)	2,741	(1%)
Other	2,282	(1%)

2000 Presidential Vote

Bush (R)	147,947	(69%)
Gore (D)	60,481	(28%)
Other	5,298	(2%)

Governor

Dave Freudenthal (D)

Elected 2002, term expires Jan. 2011, 2d term; b. Oct. 12, 1950, Thermopolis; home, Cheyenne; Amherst Col., B.A. 1973, U. of WY, J.D. 1980; Episcopalian; married (Nancy).

Professional Career: Practicing atty. 1980-94; U.S. Atty. for WY, 1994-2001

Office: State Capitol Bldg., Rm. 124, Cheyenne, 82002, 307-777-7434; Fax: 307-632-3909; Web site: governor.wy.gov.

Election Results

2006 general	Dave Freudenthal (D)	135,516	(70%)
	Ray Hunkins (R)	58,100	(30%)
2006 primary	Dave Freudenthal (D)	26,550	(90%)
	Al Hamburg (D)	3,062	(10%)
2002 general	Dave Freudenthal (D)	92,662	(50%)
	Eli Bebout (R)	88,873	(48%)
	Other	3,924	(2%)

Dave Freudenthal, a Democrat, was elected governor of Wyoming in 2002. He grew up on a farm north of Thermopolis, the seventh of eight children. Freudenthal (pronounced *FREE-den-thal*) graduated from Amherst College and then returned to Wyoming to work for the state Department of Economic Planning and Development. Ed Herschler, a Democrat elected to the first of his three terms as governor in 1974, appointed him state planning coordinator in 1975 and administrative aide in 1978. In 1980 he graduated from the University of Wyoming Law School. From 1981 to 1993 he practiced law in Cheyenne; from 1981 to 1985 he was Wyoming Democratic chairman. In 1994 he was appointed U.S. Attorney for Wyoming and served until 2001. Then he started running for governor.

The incumbent, Republican Jim Geringer, was ineligible to run for a third term. Five Republicans and four Democrats got into the race. All agreed that economic development was a key concern. Freudenthal's chief competitor in the Democratic primary was Paul Hickey, son of Joseph Hickey, who was elected governor in 1958 and who was appointed to the Senate in January 1961. In the August primary Freudenthal beat Hickey 54%-37%. The winner in the Republican primary was state House Speaker Eli Bebout.

The two nominees had similar positions on many issues—for the death penalty, against gun control, for economic diversification, against a state income tax. Bebout claimed there were "huge differences" between him and Freudenthal and pointed out that, as U.S. Attorney, Freudenthal was a Clinton nominee. But his business interests caused him some problems. One of his primary opponents attacked him because a company on whose board he served had applied to build a temporary storage facility for spent nuclear rods. After the August primary the *Casper Star-Tribune* reported that SEC documents showed that he had not repaid a $468,000 loan made in 1983 by a company on whose board he served; Bebout presented the paper with a copy of the loan with "PAID" stamped on it. Polls showed many voters undecided, and on Election Day Freudenthal won 50%-48%. He won 59%-39% in the five counties in the southern end of the state—the traditionally Democratic Union Pacific counties.

Freudenthal entered office with state government in a good fiscal position. Increases in land values due to mining activity had produced surging increases in state revenue and the state budget was in surplus. But Republicans had majorities in the legislature big enough to override vetoes. He angered environmentalists with several early appointments, including one that put a mining executive in charge of the Department of Environmental Quality.

Higher natural gas and oil prices gave the state a projected $1.2 billion surplus as the 2004 legislative session convened. While most other states struggled with budget deficits, Wyoming was in the best fiscal shape of all; the only issue was how much to put into savings and how much to spend. In the final $2 billion budget bill—large by Wyoming standards—20% was directed into various reserve funds, with $100 million for the Permanent Mineral Trust Fund, the interest earnings of which helps pay the cost of state government and keep taxes low.

At an August 2004 press conference announcing that state revenues could be as much as $474 million more than expected due in large part to mineral severance tax revenues, Freudenthal said the state could be looking at years of strong economic performance—the increase suggested a plateau, rather than a spike in revenues. Some school districts in mineral-rich regions were collecting so much from high mineral prices and production that it skewed the state's attempts to equalize school funding. Under an earlier constitutional amendment, these districts were allowed to keep some of the excess money (rather than send it to the state for redistribution to less wealthy districts) when it gets above a certain amount per pupil; a proposed constitutional amendment in 2004 would have corrected this and repealed the limit on property tax revenues that could be taken from the "recapture districts." Freudenthal supported a constitutional amendment abolishing the limit on redistribution of property tax revenues, but the measure failed.

In 2005, again handed a surplus of close to $1 billion—an "astonishingly healthy state fiscal picture," he said—Freudenthal proposed $293 million of additional general fund spending for the second year of Wyoming's two-year budget. His wildlife trust fund proposal passed, though he got only $30 million in funding for it not the $75 million he sought. Money went to raises for teachers, a college scholarship endowment, a University of Wyoming library complex, and new four-lane highways. Freudenthal also signed a suicide prevention bill in 2005; Wyoming has the highest rate in the country, about double the 11 per 100,000 national rate. All the while his approval ratings remained high—67% in 2005.

Fueled by booming natural gas prices, the state entered the 2006 fiscal year with yet another massive surplus—this one was estimated at $1.8 billion. Freudenthal proposed $772 million in new spending for school construction, highway projects, water projects, scholarship funding, tax cuts, heating assistance funding and a state employee pay hike. He also proposed growing the state's "rainy day" fund to $500 million by saving $415 million in surplus revenues. The Republican legislature approved a 2-year $7.5 billion budget that funded many of the governor's priorities, but opted to put only $183 million in the reserve fund and an extra $200 million into the Permanent Mineral Trust Fund. The budget also spent more than $2.2 billion on education funding and school construction and included a two-year repeal of grocery taxes.

Freudenthal showed sensitivity on some environmental issues, but was mindful of the importance of natural resources to the Wyoming economy and defended his state's economic prerogatives. He opposed a congressional proposal in 2005 that would lift restrictions on winter drilling on federal lands designed to protect wildlife and resisted a Forest Service plan to auction off 20,000 acres of Bridger-Teton National Forest for oil and gas development until conservation objections were resolved. In 2006 he expressed frustration with BLM priorities that emphasized an expansion of drilling over monitoring wildlife. Freudenthal has defended his state's interest in water disputes with neighboring Montana. When Montana attempted to establish rules that set limits on the amount of sodium, which is used in extracting natural gas, that Wyoming could puts into rivers that flow into Montana, Freudenthal asked the EPA to mediate the dispute and then filed a lawsuit. He has also argued with Montana Governor Brian Schweitzer over whether to increase the outflow of water from the Bighorn Lake reservoir, which straddles the two states, in order to provide more water into the Bighorn River. Freudenthal reluctantly signed in 2006 an agreement with Nebraska and Colorado over use of water from the Platte River that balanced the needs of water use and endangered species protection. Freudenthal and California Governor Arnold Schwarzenegger signed a memorandum of understanding in April 2006 that would tap federal funding to develop "clean coal" power plants in Wyoming that would generate electricity for power-hungry California and be transmitted via a new multi-billion dollar Frontier Line transmission project.

Having led the state through economic good times, Freudenthal in 2006 faced opposition from rancher and attorney Ray Hunkins, who had run unsuccessfully for the Republican nomination in 2002. Hunkins hit Freudenthal for running an ineffective fight against methamphetamine use and for failing to plan for the lean times by diversifying the economy. "I won't just pay lip service to our shared conservative ideals. I'll put them into action," Hunkins declared in his April 2006 campaign announcement. Freudenthal called Hunkins' anti-meth proposals too vague and his campaign mailed out an 11-page "Report to the Citizens of Wyoming" detailing his success and praising the Republican legislature for working with him. State Republican Chairman Drake Hill angered members of both parties when he conducted opposition research on Freudenthal and funded a negative radio ad that portrayed the governor as living a lavish lifestyle and using a state-financed "party plane." The plane, which Freudenthal never traveled on, was actually used by the state to conduct aerial surveying work, and the issue reinforced Freudenthal's attempt to portray himself as above partisan politics. Freudenthal campaigned as "Gov Dave" and a *Star-Tribune* poll showed him with a 33-point lead in the final weeks of the campaign. The poll proved only slightly inaccurate: Freudenthal won a second term by 70%-30%.

Freudenthal ended 2006 by proposing an additional $800 million in spending, along with a permanent repeal of the grocery tax. Declining natural gas prices reduced projected budget surpluses and forced lawmakers to consider spending some of the $200 million it had planned for the permanent fund. Freudenthal framed the spending debate by arguing that transportation costs were increasing faster than the rate of savings. By the end of the session in March 2007, the legislature approved a $470 million supplemental spending bill, which including $100 million for highway construction, and a permanent repeal of the grocery tax. Freudenthal also signed bills that increased fees for hunting and fishing licenses by 20%, an open container law prohibiting alcohol consumption in moving vehicles, state matching funds for rural hospitals and property tax relief for combat veterans.

Senior Senator

Michael Enzi (R)

Elected 1996, seat up 2008, 2d term; b. Feb. 1, 1944, Bremerton, WA; home, Gillette; George Washington U., B.S. 1966, Denver U., M.B.A. 1968; Presbyterian; married (Diana).

Military Career: WY Natl. Guard, 1967-73.

Elected Office: Gillette Mayor, 1975-82; WY House of Reps., 1986-90; WY Senate, 1990-96.

Professional Career: Owner, NZ Shoes, 1969-95; Dir. & Chmn., First WY Bank of Gillette, 1978-88; Accounting Mgr. & Computer Programmer, Dunbar Well Service, 1985-97; Educ. Comm. of States, 1989-93; Dir., Black Hills Corp., 1992-96; Western Interstate Comm. for Higher Educ., 1995-96.

DC Office: 379-A RSOB, 20510, 202-224-3424; Fax: 202-228-0359; Web site: enzi.senate.gov.

State Offices: Casper, 307-261-6572; Cheyenne, 307-772-2477; Cody, 307-527-9444; Gillette, 307-682-6268; Jackson, 307-739-9507.

Committees: *Banking, Housing & Urban Affairs* (4th of 10 R): Securities, Insurance & Investment; Security & International Trade & Finance; Housing, Transportation & Community Development. *Budget* (5th of 11 R). *Health, Education, Labor & Pensions* (RMM of 10 R). *Small Business & Entrepreneurship* (8th of 9 R).

Group Ratings

	ADA	ACLU	AFS	LCV	ITIC	NTU	COC	ACU	CFG	FRC
2006	5	10	0	0	75	87	91	96	99	100
2005	10	—	0	10	—	72	78	96	70	—

National Journal Ratings

	2005 LIB	—	2005 CONS		2006 LIB	—	2006 CONS
Economic	0%	—	94%		0%	—	97%
Social	0%	—	77%		0%	—	82%
Foreign	49%	—	50%		18%	—	76%

Key Votes of the 109th Congress

1. Bar ANWR Drilling	N	5. Confirm Samuel Alito	Y	9. Limit Interstate Abortion	Y
2. FY06 Spending Curb	Y	6. Path to Citizenship	N	10. CAFTA	N
3. Estate Tax Repeal	Y	7. Bar Same Sex Marriage	Y	11. Urge Iraq Withdrawal	N
4. Raise Minimum Wage	N	8. Stem Cell Research $	N	12. Provide Detainee Rights	N

Election Results

2002 general	Michael Enzi (R)	133,710	(73%)	($884,114)
	Joyce Corcoran (D)	49,570	(27%)	($8,467)
2002 primary	Michael Enzi (R)	78,612	(86%)	
	Crosby Allen (R)	12,931	(14%)	
1996 general	Michael Enzi (R)	114,116	(54%)	($953,572)
	Kathy Karpan (D)	89,103	(42%)	($814,258)
	Other	7,858	(4%)	

Michael Enzi, the senior senator from Wyoming, was first elected in 1996 and chaired for two years the Health, Education, Labor and Pensions Committee (HELP). Enzi grew up in Thermopolis and Sheridan, the son of a shoe salesman, got degrees in accounting and retail marketing, moved to Gillette and became an oil well servicing company accountant and founded NZ Shoes. In the 1970s, at a Jaycees meeting, he met Senator Alan Simpson, who was impressed by his volunteerism and asked him to consider running for public office. In 1975 Enzi was elected mayor of Gillette, the center of Wyoming's coal belt and its fastest-growing town, and served eight years. In 1986 he was elected to the state House and in 1990 to the state Senate. After Simpson announced his retirement in December 1995, Enzi was one of nine Republicans and two Democrats to run for the seat. With support from a grass roots network of conservatives, Enzi finished first in a straw poll at the May 1996 Republican state convention; in second place was John Barrasso, today his Senate colleague but then an orthopedic surgeon from Casper who had appeared on statewide TV discussing health issues for 12 years. Their chief difference was on abortion; Barrasso supported and Enzi opposed abortion rights. Barrasso had more money, but Enzi won 32%-30%. The Democratic nominee was former Secretary of State Kathy Karpan, who opposed gun control and abortion. But she had the liabilities of having supported the presidential candidacies of Bill Clinton in 1992 and Bruce Babbitt (unpopular in Wyoming as Clinton's Interior Secretary) in 1988. Enzi led in polls all the way and won 54%-42%.

Enzi started off in the Senate by presiding for 100 hours in the chair by July and seeking permission to bring his laptop on the floor: a workhorse. The Rules Committee said no by a 6–1 vote; Enzi renewed his request in June 2002, noting that even the Senate is in a new century but the rule still stands. He has opposed meatpacker ownership of livestock and has pushed for country of origin labeling of meat.

In 2002, his sixth year in the Senate, Enzi was still little known in most of Washington, but he played a key role on a major piece of legislation. The issue was corporate accountability, and as the only accountant in the Senate Enzi could claim special expertise. In July 2000 he was one of 13 senators who signed a letter urging then-SEC Chairman Arthur Levitt to delay a decision on his proposal to bar accounting firms from doing auditing and consulting work for the same corporation. After the Enron bankruptcy in December 2001 raised questions about accounting, Enzi still urged caution and said he feared overregulation. Banking Chairman Paul Sarbanes held extensive hearings on the issue and Enzi, the fifth ranking Republican, paid close attention. The bill Sarbanes introduced to the committee did not go so far as the Levitt proposal, but did go farther than the bill passed by the House in April 2002. It included an accounting board independent of the SEC with power to set rules, investigate, punish violations and conduct regular inspections of accounting firms' work. Enzi worked closely with lobbyists for the big accounting firms but kept the perspective of a Wyoming small business accountant. He decided that some bill needed to be passed and Sarbanes, not wanting to report a bill supported only by Democrats, consulted him. On the evening of June 17, Enzi flew in from Wyoming and went to Sarbanes's office where they negotiated a compromise. Enzi got Sarbanes to agree that two of the four members of the board must be accountants, that the board could adopt rules favored by the accounting industry and that the board would not be financed by accountants. Disciplinary proceedings would be confidential. On June 18, Enzi told committee Republicans that he would vote for Sarbanes's bill. Others agreed: six of the 10 Republicans supported it. On June 26 the WorldCom accounting scam was made public. The Senate wanted to act, and Sarbanes could go to the floor with bipartisan support. On July 15 the Senate approved the bill 97–0. The bill was passed and signed before the August recess.

In January 2005 Enzi became chairman of the HELP Committee. He earned a reputation as a hard worker, knowledgeable about the details of legislation and the views of those affected, not always following the lead of the Bush administration. His unassuming manner helped him manage the egos on a panel featuring 4 former chairmen of the committee (Judd Gregg; Orrin Hatch; James Jeffords; and Edward Kennedy) and 7 members who had run for president or had plans to in 2008. As chairman, he worked to put together a reauthorization of the Carl Perkins vocational and technical education bill that passed the Senate 99–0 in March 2005 and was enacted in August. Enzi has argued that in an economy where workers will typically hold 14 jobs over a lifetime, 10 of them in careers that are not yet invented, lifelong education is crucial. The Carl Perkins act is one leg, he argued, of a three-legged stool; the others are his Workforce Investment Act, a version of which passed the Senate unanimously in 2004, and reauthorization of the Higher Education Act, a more controversial matter. He sided with ranking minority member Edward Kennedy in opposing the White House proposal to encourage more use of school vouchers in the recovery following Hurricane Katrina. On the renewal of the No Child Left Behind Act, Enzi was open to modifications. Working with leaders of the Senate Finance Committee, he participated in the protracted negotiations with the House on pension reform. "Promises made will be promises kept by limiting when benefits may be increased," he said when Congress completed action in August 2006. On a committee issue of special interest back home, Enzi helped to enact a bill to expedite the clean-up of abandoned coal mines.

On health care issues, Enzi has favored market-oriented solutions with consumer choice and more information; an example is a bill funding state high risk pools. Opposition to the House-passed bill from many Democrats and some Republicans blocked Enzi's attempts to apply the bipartisan model from the 2002 accounting-reform law. He has supported federal medical malpractice bills and funding states to test alternatives to current tort law. On stem cell legislation, he offered an alternative to encourage research on embryos without destroying them. He has sponsored worker safety legislation to provide for third party consultants to OSHA, certificates of compliance for employers, posting of sample material safety data sheets and hazard information, but was unable to move those proposals during his chairmanship. In the closing days of the Republican majority, he helped to resolve conflicts over the funding formula to renew domestic AIDS programs.

Enzi did not have serious opposition in 2002. He won the Republican primary 86%-14% and the general election 73%-27%. The death of Craig Thomas in June 2007 set up an unusual situation in which each Wyoming senator faced election in November 2008. Enzi appeared secure for another term even before the appointment of John Barrasso, who would share the ballot with him.

Junior Senator

John Barrasso (R)

Appointed June 2007, seat up 2008, 1st term; b. July 21, 1952, Reading, PA; home, Casper; Georgetown U., B.A. 1974, M.D. 1978; Presbyterian; divorced.

Elected Office: WY Senate, 2002-07.

Professional Career: Orthopedic surgeon 1983-2007; RNC Committeeman, 1992-96; Chief of staff, WY Medical Center, 2003-05.

DC Office: 307 DSOB, 20510, 202-224-6441; Fax: 202-224-1724; Web site: barrasso.senate.gov.

State Offices: Casper, 307-261-6413; Cheyenne, 307-772-2451; Riverton, 307-856-6642; Rock Springs, 307-362-5012; Sheridan, 307-672-6456.

Committees: *Energy & Natural Resources* (11th of 11 R): National Parks; Water & Power; Public Lands & Forests. *Environment & Public Works* (6th of 9 R): Superfund & Environmental Health (RMM); Private Sector & Consumer Solutions to Global Warming & Wildlife Protection; Public Sector Solutions to Global Warming, Oversight & Children's Health Protection. *Indian Affairs* (4th of 7 R).

Group Ratings and Key Votes: Newly Appointed

Election Results

2006 general	Craig Thomas (R)	135,174	(70%)	($1,392,057)
	Dale Groutage (D)	57,671	(30%)	($141,164)
2006 primary	Craig Thomas (R)	unopposed		
2000 general	Craig Thomas (R)	157,622	(74%)	($762,833)
	Mel Logan (D)	47,087	(22%)	($4,187)
	Margaret Dawson (Lib)	8,950	(4%)	

John Barrasso was sworn in as the 100th member of the Senate on June 25, 2007, replacing Republican Craig Thomas, who died June 4 of complications from leukemia. Thomas was the fourth of Wyoming's 21 senators to die in office. Barrasso was born and grew up in Reading, Pennsylvania, the son of a World War II veteran who made a living as a cement finisher and who took his family to Washington every four years for the president's inauguration. He got his undergraduate and medical degrees from Georgetown University, then moved to Wyoming in the 1980s where he was an orthopedic surgeon in Casper. Barrasso quickly made his name in Wyoming, by getting involved in Republican politics, serving as a Republican National Committeeman and state party treasurer, and establishing himself as a broadcast personality dispensing practical medical advice. He also was the local host for the annual Jerry Lewis telethon for muscular dystrophy.

In 1996, he ran for the Senate when Republican Alan Simpson retired. He faced then-state Senator Mike Enzi in a crowded primary where the abortion issue played a key role. Running as a moderate, Barrasso favored abortion rights and had opposed a 1994 constitutional amendment to ban most abortions; Enzi, who had support from social conservatives, opposed abortion and narrowly edged Barrasso by 32% to 30%. Barrasso then became Enzi's finance chairman in the general election.

In 2002, Barrasso won election to the state senate, where he worked on health care issues and chaired the Transportation, Highways and Military Affairs Committee. His record there was conservative, and he sponsored a bill to increase the penalty for killing a pregnant woman; Governor Dave Freudenthal vetoed the measure. He occasionally crossed the political aisle, backed the exemption of food from the state sales tax and supported a ban on smoking in public buildings. He also sponsored the "I'm sorry" law, which enables physicians to talk freely with patients about medical complications, without the risk that the conversations would be used against them in a lawsuit.

After Thomas died, under Wyoming law the state Republican Central Committee had 15 days to select three candidates to fill the vacancy, from which the governor was required to pick the successor. That triggered a scramble by 31 candidates who applied for consideration; they conducted a week-long campaign among the 71 members of the party committee. The roster of applicants included state Representative Colin Simpson, the son of Alan Simpson, and numerous other state legislators, attorneys, ranchers, and other professionals. Barrasso emphasized his strong conservative credentials in his statement of interest to the committee: "I believe in limited government, lower taxes, less spending, traditional family values, local control, and a strong national defense." He noted he had an "A" rating from the National Rifle Association and had voted for prayer in schools, against gay marriage and "sponsored legislation to protect the sanctity of life."

At its June 19 meeting, the Republican committee heard brief speeches and then reduced the list to 10 candidates. More speeches followed and two more rounds of voting, before the committee agreed on Barrasso; Cynthia Lummis, who served 14 years in the legislature and two terms as state treasurer; and Tom Sansonetti, who had been chief of staff to Thomas and an assistant attorney general in the Bush administration. Freudenthal, a Democrat, then met the three candidates in private interviews, for which he had sent them a list of more than 40 topics for discussion. Sansonetti was an attorney who lobbied on behalf of mining, energy and ranching interests, and Lummis reportedly was not on good terms with the governor, while Barrasso had worked with him on health care issues. In announcing his selection of Barrasso on June 22, Freudenthal said his decision was based on many factors. "While I don't intend to indulge the speculation on why I made this decision, I will say that I hope I made the right choice."

After taking office, Barrasso said that he will run in the November 2008 special election to fill the remaining four years of Thomas's term. Sansonetti said that he would not challenge him, but Lummis left the door open to a Republican primary. Democrats promised a competitive contest. Freudenthal would be their strongest challenger; he is term-limited in 2010. The election will mark a busy year in Wyoming politics, as Enzi is also up for reelection in 2008.

Representative-At-Large

Barbara Cubin (R)

Elected 1994, 7th term; b. Nov. 30, 1946, Salinas, CA; home, Casper; Creighton U., B.S. 1969; Episcopalian; married (Frederick).

Elected Office: WY House of Reps., 1986-92; WY Senate, 1992-94.

Professional Career: Office Mgr., Dr. Frederick Cubin, 1975-94.

DC Office: 1114 LHOB, 20515, 202-225-2311; Fax: 202-225-3057; Web site: www.house.gov/cubin.

District Offices: Casper, 307-261-6595; Cheyenne, 307-772-2595; Rock Springs, 307-362-4095.

Committees: *Energy & Commerce* (8th of 26 R): Health; Telecommunications & the Internet.

Group Ratings

	ADA	ACLU	AFS	LCV	ITIC	NTU	COC	ACU	CFG	FRC
2006	0	18	0	0	80	63	100	91	64	100
2005	5	—	0	6	—	62	88	96	76	100

National Journal Ratings

	2005 LIB	—	2005 CONS	2006 LIB	—	2006 CONS
Economic	23%	—	77%	6%	—	93%
Social	30%	—	70%	10%	—	89%
Foreign	42%	—	55%	27%	—	72%

Key Votes of the 109th Congress

1. Estate Tax Repeal	Y	5. Limit Interstate Abortion	Y	9. Build Border Fence	Y
2. Limit CAFE Standards	Y	6. Extend Patriot Act	Y	10. CAFTA	N
3. FY06 Spending Curb	Y	7. Bar Same Sex Marriage	Y	11. Oppose Iraq Withdrawal	Y
4. Drilling in ANWR	Y	8. Stem Cell Research $	N	12. Detainee Tribunals	Y

Election Results

2006 general	Barbara Cubin (R)	93,336	(48%)	($1,268,578)
	Gary Trauner (D)	92,324	(48%)	($940,182)
	Thomas Rankin (Lib)	7,481	(4%)	
2006 primary	Barbara Cubin (R)	50,004	(60%)	
	Bill Winney (R)	33,287	(40%)	
2004 general	Barbara Cubin (R)	132,107	(55%)	($944,908)
	Ted Ladd (D)	99,989	(42%)	($373,436)
	Other	6,938	(3%)	

Prior Winning Percentages: 2002 (61%); 2000 (67%); 1998 (58%); 1996 (55%); 1994 (53%)

Wyoming, the nation's least populous state, has elected one congressman-at-large since it was admitted to the Union in 1890. The current incumbent is Barbara Cubin, a Republican first elected in 1994. The great-great-granddaughter of one of Wyoming's original homesteaders, she grew up in Casper, where she worked as a teacher, social worker, chemist and realtor; for 19 years she managed her husband's medical practice. She was divorced after an early first marriage, worked as a single mother, was subjected to sexual harassment, but insists: "I am not a feminist. I am not gender sensitive." She notes that Susan B. Anthony and all the early advocates of women's rights were opposed to abortion. In 1986 she was elected to the state House and in 1992 to the state Senate. In 1994, when Congressman Craig Thomas ran for the Senate, Cubin was one of five Republicans and two Democrats to run for the House. She sharply attacked "the Clinton-Babbitt war on the West." In the Republican primary, she won with 39%. The Democratic nominee was Bob Schuster, a law partner of high-profile Wyoming trial lawyer Gerry Spence. He spent $2.4 million, most of it his own money, on what was the third highest spending campaign in the country. Schuster's big issue was abortion; she called him a "a slick trial lawyer Clinton Democrat." Cubin won 53%-41%.

In the House Cubin has a solidly conservative voting record and became chairman of the Energy and Mineral Resources Subcommittee. She sponsored the successful bill to allow coal companies larger leases of federal lands. In November 2000 she was elected Republican Conference Secretary, the number six position in the House leadership. In April 2002 Cubin expressed interest in succeeding the retiring James Hansen as chairman of the Resources Committee. She was only the 12th Republican on the committee in seniority, but the most senior was James Saxton of New Jersey, who had voted against conservatives on many committee issues. She suggested reviving the old Merchant Marine and Fisheries Committee, abolished by Republicans in 1995, and making Saxton its chairman. She may have damaged her case in September 2002, when she sponsored a bill for $6 billion in drought relief; this was the position taken by Senate Democrats and opposed by the Bush administration and the House Republican leadership. The Republican Steering Committee interviewed Cubin and other candidates for the chairmanship in January 2003, and awarded it to Richard Pombo of California, who had been 11th in seniority; he held the post for four years until he was defeated for reelection in California in 2006.

In 2003 Cubin got a waiver to serve one more term as chairman of the Energy and Mineral Resources Subcommittee; she did not get another in 2005, and questioned Pombo's realignment of subcommittee jurisdictions. She has worked on some issues that have turned out to be more controversial than might have been expected. In 2004 Cubin joined with committee ranking Democrat Nick Rahall on a bill to reauthorize the Abandoned Mine Reclamation Fund and continue payments to Wyoming and Rahall's West Virginia even though mine cleanups in Wyoming were complete. Cubin has argued that the fund owes Wyoming $450 million in back payments and the bill removed the $70 million yearly cap on transfer of payments to retirees' health funds. "Many Western coal producers are frustrated that the interest on their [abandoned mine fund] fees is going to support retired miners they never employed in the first place, rather than moving dirt on actual reclamation projects. But unfortunately the health care and reclamation issues had a bit of a shotgun wedding in the early 1990s, and you can't just divorce the two and still get a bill with a broad bipartisan support." She worked in 2005 with John Peterson of Pennsylvania to get a compromise, and in July 2006 the House passed the bill, with $550 million for Wyoming, as an amendment to a tax measure. But it was opposed by Senate Budget Committee Chairman Judd Gregg, who said it would shift costs from coal companies to taxpayers and increase the budget deficit by $4 billion, and never passed in the Senate. Wyoming did win a victory there in September 2006 when the Senate lowered trona royalties from 6% to 2%.

In April 1999 Cubin announced that she would only serve six terms, for a total of 12 years. In 2001 and 2002 she missed many roll call votes, as she tended her husband, who had multiple surgeries. She made news when she missed the vote on Resources Chairman James Hansen's proposal to allow the Mormon Church to buy Martin's Cove in Wyoming, the site of the death of Mormon pioneers in a blizzard in 1856, a proposal opposed by the Wyoming delegation, because she had been caught in traffic returning from a doctor's appointment. She was reelected 61%-36% in 2002, but carried her home base in Natrona County by exactly 1 vote. She did not seek reelection to the Conference Secretary position. In 2004 she won just 55% of the vote in the primary against four little-known challengers, and she was reelected in November with just 55% of the vote, running better in Natrona County but running 14% behind George W. Bush. In July 2005 she had a heart attack while waiting for a plane at Dulles Airport, and remained in the Washington area over the Fourth of July recess. In 2005 and 2006 she missed more than 10% of all roll call votes. In October 2005 she announced she was running again, despite this heavy absenteeism and her pledge to serve only six terms. In January 2006 a Democratic opponent appeared, Gary Trauner, an Internet service entrepreneur and school board member from Jackson Hole who seemed to have good contacts with the liberal millionaires who had bought second homes or retired there—his donors listed occupations such as "self-employed philanthropist" or "asset manager." Trauner hired the campaign team that had worked for Democratic Governor Dave Freudenthal in 2002 and specialized in intensive, person-to-person campaigning, staying on in a community for as much as a week. He came out against a proposal to sell off federal lands for mining, which Cubin had supported and Senator Craig Thomas opposed. Trauner's fundraising was competitive with Cubin's, and he raised about as large a percentage of his funds from Wyoming, unlike many Democrats who raise most of their money on the East or West Coasts; however the great bulk of his Wyoming money came from Jackson Hole's Teton County, the only county in the state to vote for John Kerry. Cubin also had primary opposition from a retired Navy captain, who raised only $21,000; nonetheless, he held her to a 60%-40% margin in the August primary, an unimpressive showing for a 12-year incumbent. She lost Teton and Laramie (Cheyenne) Counties and nearly lost Natrona. The *Wyoming Tribune-Eagle*, which gave her as grudging an endorsement as can be imagined in the primary, endorsed Trauner heartily in October. Cubin charged that Trauner backed registration of guns, amnesty for immigrants and cuts in military spending; he said he backed the Second Amendment and favored reducing the deficit and the national debt. In late October, after a debate that included the Libertarian candidate, wheelchair-bound Thomas Rankin, Cubin came over to him afterwards and, in his version, "Barbara walked over to me and said, 'If you weren't sitting in that chair, I'd slap you across the face." She said that she had told him that anyone would have wanted to hit him after a remark he made. This made news in what was already a close race; a mid-October poll showed Cubin ahead of Trauner 44%-37%, a late October poll showed it 44%-40%.

The House race in Wyoming, which was George W. Bush's number one state in 2000 and number two state in 2004, proved to be one of the closest in the country. Cubin won by only 1,012 votes, 48.3%-47.7%. A Saturday-before-the-election appearance by Dick Cheney may have saved her seat. In 2007 Cubin continued to miss more votes than all but a few members, but a Cubin aide said she was running again for 2008. Trauner said in 2007 he might try again; it seemed likely in mid-2007 that if Cubin sought reelection she also would face stiff primary competition. Two Republicans drew mention as possible candidates: state Representative Colin Simpson, the son of former Senator Alan Simpson, and Matt Mead, former U.S. Attorney for Wyoming and the grandson of former Governor and Senator Clifford Hansen.

PUERTO RICO, VIRGIN ISLANDS, ★ GUAM, AMERICAN SAMOA ★

Four American insular territories—Puerto Rico, Virgin Islands, Guam, American Samoa—are represented in Congress by elected delegates who, like the District of Columbia's delegate, have floor privileges and votes on committees but not votes on the floor (though House Democrats let them vote in committee of the whole proceedings in the 110th Congress). Each territory's status—its relationship to the United States—is different, governed by a separate law, and status is often the pivot around which territorial politics turn.

PUERTO RICO

Puerto Rico has a unique history. For four centuries, from Columbus's landing here in 1493 until the Spanish-American War of 1898, Puerto Rico was a Spanish colony, and the port of San Juan was the gathering place for its annual convoy of gold and silver from the Americas to Spain. Today, with 3.9 million people, it is the largest American territory—about the same population as Oregon; and about 4 million people of Puerto Rican descent live on the mainland. Sixty years ago, it was "the poorhouse of the Caribbean," heavily populated, devoted almost entirely to sugar and coffee cultivation. Now it has a recognizably First World economy, with per capita incomes about half of those of the least affluent American states and among the highest in Latin America.

Puerto Rico has elected a resident commissioner to Congress since 1900 (the only member of Congress with a four-year term) and its residents have been American citizens since 1917, but it didn't elect its own governor until 1948. In the 1940s, 1950s and early 1960s, Puerto Rico was transformed by Governor Luis Munoz Marin and his Popular Democratic Party. Munoz initiated "Operation Bootstrap" (called "Operation Hands to Work" by Puerto Ricans) to lure businesses to Puerto Rico with promises of low-wage labor and government-built factories and tax exemptions. Munoz also developed Puerto Rico's commonwealth form of government—better understood in Spanish, Estado Libre Asociado (ELA): Free Associated State—approved by plebiscite in 1952. Under ELA, Puerto Rico is part of the United States for purposes of international trade, foreign policy and war, but has its own separate laws, taxes and representative government; it is not subject to federal income taxes and is not eligible for all federal benefits (though some have been approved by Congress). Some 200,000 Puerto Ricans have served in the U.S. military; 2,000 died in service and four were awarded the Congressional Medal of Honor. Puerto Rico has also developed its own political parties: Munoz's Popular Democrats (the Spanish acronym is PPD), the New Progressives (PNP) who favor statehood, and two Independence parties.

The commonwealth solution, by its own terms, was open to amendment; ever since Munoz retired in 1964, the central issue in Puerto Rico's politics has been status: Should this island continue or modify ELA, should it seek statehood, or should it seek independence? For many years there was gradual movement toward statehood. In the July 1967 referendum, conducted when the Popular Democrats were in power, Puerto Ricans voted for ELA over statehood by 60%-39%; in the November 1993 referendum, conducted with PNP Governor Pedro Rossello in office, the vote was 48% for ELA, 46% for statehood. In March 1998 the U.S. House voted 209-208 for a referendum setting terms for statehood; this was a project of Speaker Newt Gingrich, who hoped to attract Hispanic votes, and of Resources Committee Chairman Don Young, who saw in statehood backers' demands echoes of Alaska's fight for statehood. But the bill went nowhere in the Senate. Rossello ordered a referendum on his terms (which are unlikely ever to be accepted in Congress) in December 1998; 47% voted for statehood and 50% for "none of the above," the option favored by the Popular Democrats. Independence has negligible support—4% in 1993, 3% in 1998—primarily from university students; nor are there many pro-independence abstentions, voter turnout in the enthusiastic politics of Puerto Rico is the highest under the American flag, higher than in even the most affluent, long-settled suburbs of the mainland. The election of two PPD governors, Sila Calderon in 2000 and Anibal Acevedo Vila in 2004, seemed to halt the move toward statehood. For years younger and more affluent voters have tilted toward statehood, but as they have aged and the island has grown more prosperous, support for statehood seemed to have stopped growing.

More recently the action on status has moved from the island to the mainland. In December 2005 a White House task force, originally set up during the Clinton administration, finally reported. It recommended a two-step referendum, with Puerto Ricans both on the island and on the mainland, first voting on whether to consider a change in the current ELA status, and then, if they favored a change, choosing between statehood and independence. A bill incorporating this recommendation was sponsored by Jose Serrano of the Bronx and Luis Fortuno, elected the PNP Resident Commissioner from Puerto Rico in 2004. Among its mainland supporters were Steny Hoyer, Roy Blunt, Nick Rahall and Don Young. This approach was criticized by Governor Anibal Acevedo Vila, the only PPD candidate elected in 2004. He argued that the two-step approach would frustrate the wishes of the majorities or pluralities which had voted for ELA in previous referenda and would produce a verdict for an option, statehood, which clearly lacked majority support. Acevedo called for "enhanced commonwealth," under which Puerto Rico could set its own foreign and trade policies and opt out of federal law as negotiated with Congress. To advance this, Nydia Velazquez sponsored a bill authorizing a constitutional convention on the island in which delegates could decide on status and define Puerto Rico's relationship with the mainland. This was supported by Luis Gutierrez, Jimmy Duncan, Richard Burr, Roger Wicker, Charles Rangel, John Conyers, Bob Menendez, Trent Lott and Edward Kennedy. Critics said that it was unconstitutional for Puerto Rico to be able to abrogate or modify federal laws and for the federal government to cede such powers to a territory.

Both positions on status seem unrealistic. Congress is not likely to accept Puerto Rico as a state under the terms and conditions advocated by the PNP (Spanish as an official language, for example, and continuation of Puerto Rico's eligibility under certain welfare laws). And it's not apparent that it's feasible or desirable to let Puerto Ricans on the mainland—how many generations removed?— vote on the state of the island. Nor is Congress going to allow Puerto Rico to remain American and yet have a separate foreign policy. As Fortuno says, "Three administrations have told you what you are proposing is unconstitutional. What part of no don't you understand?" Status positions on the mainland have become a rallying point for partisan issues on the island. As for mainland politicians, Democrats and many Republicans assume that as a state Puerto Rico would be solidly Democratic (with five or six House members), though Fortuno, a Republican, and Puerto Rico Senate President Kenneth McClintock, a statehood backer and Democrat, argue that it would actually lean Republican. McClintock points out that in the 1950s almost everyone assumed that Hawaii would be Republican and Alaska Democratic, when it has turned to be the other way around; but Puerto Rico has no companion seeking statehood whose contrary leanings might balance it out.

As the debate over status has gone on, Puerto Rico's economy has been evolving, and not entirely in a positive direction. Operation Bootstrap took advantage of the fact that Puerto Rico is part of the U.S. market and encouraged the growth of apparel and other low-wage manufacturing industries. It also capitalized on Section 936 of the Internal Revenue Code, which sheltered earnings of some Puerto Rico manufacturers from federal taxes; this was seized on especially by pharmaceutical companies which produce a large percentage of their pills in Puerto Rico. In the 1970s, as Puerto Rican income topped half the levels in the lowest mainland state, Congress extended welfare benefits at mainland rates to the island. More than half the residents went on food stamps (*cupones*) and work force participation fell, even as apparel jobs were threatened by competition from the Dominican Republic and Honduras. Section 936, though it generated local taxes and deposits for local banks, did not produce all that many jobs. In 1995 Congress voted to phase it out over 10 years; this made less difference than people expected, since the pharmaceuticals set up foreign-based subsidiaries to run their Puerto Rico operations and shield them from mainland taxes. In the 1990s Governor Pedro Rossello moved Puerto Rico away from socialism, by selling off the government-owned Navieras shipping line, telephone company and hospitals. Governor Sila Calderon moved a bit in the other direction in 2002, with a program investing $1 billion in the 700 poorest communities in the island, in infrastructure—water, electricity, roads—and education and health care programs. But none of this has spurred enough private sector growth: with welfare benefits available, Puerto Rico has some of the lowest male work force participation in the world. Crime rates are much higher than on the mainland, and there is a new movement of bilingual professionals—nurses, policemen, doctors, teachers—from the island to mainland locations where fluency in Spanish is an asset.

One issue that has been removed from Puerto Rico politics is the Navy's bombing range and training ground on the island of Vieques. Established in 1941, it was an irritant to many in Puerto Rico. In June 2001 George W. Bush promised to halt all military exercises in May 2003; despite increased pressures after September 11, he kept his word. The base was closed and efforts were made to encourage local development; the Navy also closed the Roosevelt Roads base in San Juan Harbor, whose only mission was support of the Vieques bombing range.

Much of the political news out of Puerto Rico has come out of corruption charges against various high officials in the administrations of PPD Governor Pedro Rossello, elected in 1992 and

1996. Rossello was succeeded by PPD Governor Sila Calderon, who concentrated on getting the Navy out of Vieques and spurring development in Puerto Rico's poorest communities; she also ran a voter registration drive among Puerto Ricans on the mainland, which probably helped Democrats in the Northeast but Republicans in Florida. She chose not to seek reelection in 2004. The 2004 election resulted in the election of new leaders and was the first time Puerto Rico elected a split ticket: the PPD's Acevedo was elected governor over Rossello by a 48.4%-48.2% margin, after court battles over whether ballots should be counted on which voters marked the square for Acevedo and the square for the pro-independence PIP party. The PNP's Luis Fortuno was elected resident commissioner, Puerto Rico's non-voting member of the House, by a 48.5%-48.0% margin. The PNP won a majority in the Senate, and one PNP member resigned to allow Rossello to become a member. But Kenneth McClintock then resisted Rossello's move to replace him as Senate President. The government was shut down briefly in May 2006 in a dispute between Acevedo and the legislature; a commission set up to solve the problem recommended furloughing 95,000 employees and closing 1,500 schools. A 5.9% sales tax was enacted, with a new levy on large corporations to repay a $531 million loan from the Puerto Rico Government Development Bank to cover employee salaries. In December 2006 Resident Commissioner Luis Fortuno announced he would run for governor in 2008; Rossello also appeared interested but had to answer questions about whether he had claimed too much on his pension.

Puerto Rico stands in uneasy equipoise. Its ELA status is a compromise, and a considerable achievement; Luis Munoz Marin was able to create enthusiasm for what was a middle-of-the-road position, neither full independence nor assimilative statehood. The Puerto Rican people did develop a polity that is tolerant of divergence of opinion, determined to uphold personal liberty, increasingly intolerant of corruption and capable of fostering sustained economic growth: an achievement worthy of respectful attention in Latin America and on the mainland. But there continue to be tugs in both directions on status. Independentistas, though few in number, still are full of enthusiasm for the nonagenarian Lolita Lebron, the nationalist who led the gunfire attack on the U.S. House of Representatives in March 1954, and protested when police shot the aging fugitive Filiberto Ojeda Rios in September 2005, who was guilty of a car bombing and armed bank robbery. Governor Acevedo seeks an enhanced commonwealth and Fortuno and the PNP statehood, both on terms Congress seems highly unlikely to approve. Over the last century Congress has only admitted new states when there has been a widespread consensus there for statehood; that is and has been lacking in Puerto Rico, where people are split nearly down the middle over status. The Puerto Rican economy, which jumped so far ahead of the rest of Latin America in the 1950s and 1960s, is now growing more slowly, burdened with an overlarge public sector and overgenerous welfare benefits which sap work incentives. Passage of CAFTA and other free trade agreements in Latin America could lead to greater trade and to a role for Puerto Rico as a helpful elder sister, with money to invest and expertise gained from its own economic development—and wisdom gained from its own political development. But first Puerto Rico needs to get its own house in better order.

Presidential politics   One of the complaints of Puerto Rico's New Progressives is that it cannot vote for president, and in 2000 Governor Pedro Rossello tried to remedy that. On August 29, 2000, a federal judge in Puerto Rico ruled that Puerto Rican voters have a right to vote for president emanating from their U.S. citizenship and ordered that a vote be held and that Congress count eight electoral votes for Puerto Ricans' choice (eight was the number of electoral votes Puerto Rico would have had under the 1990 Census if it were a state). This ruling went against precedent and the language of the Constitution, which gives votes only to states that have been admitted to the Union and, in an amendment, to the District of Columbia. But Rossello and the New Progressive legislature were happy to pass a law putting the presidential election on the November 7 ballot. On October 13, the First Circuit Court of Appeals predictably reversed the rules and ordered the presidential contest off the ballot. So no one knows for sure which candidate Puerto Rico would have preferred, George W. Bush (who nominally favored statehood, as Republican platforms long have) or Al Gore (who favored "self-determination" for Puerto Rico), although almost everyone assumes Gore would have won.

Puerto Rico does send delegates to the two mainland parties' national conventions. The Republicans, long identified with the New Progressives, though some of its leaders identify with the Democrats, held a primary in February in which the Spanish-speaking George W. Bush beat John McCain 93%-6%. That gave him 14 convention delegates, more than were elected by Vermont or Delaware and the same number as Maine, Rhode Island and Hawaii. Al Gore won the March

Democratic caucus, giving him 59 delegates, more than 24 states. In 2004, local Democrats canceled the June caucus. By then, John Kerry had no remaining opposition; all 58 delegates were designated as Kerry delegates. Since Puerto Rico's Democratic delegates in the past have voted as a bloc, while Democratic rules require most other states' delegates to be split proportionately, in a divided Democratic convention (if there ever is one again) Puerto Rico actually has more leverage than all but a half dozen or so states, as it did in the bitterly split convention in 1980.

Governor   Anibal Acevedo Vila was elected governor of Puerto Rico in 2004. He is a former president of the Popular Democrats (PPD), was elected to a four-year term as Puerto Rico's Resident Commissioner—actually, non-voting delegate in the U.S. House—in 2000. He was born in San Juan and graduated from the University of Puerto Rico and Harvard Law School and was a law clerk in the Puerto Rico Supreme Court and the First Circuit Court of Appeals in Boston, which has jurisdiction over Puerto Rico. He returned to Puerto Rico to work on the staff of Governor Rafael Hernandez Colon from 1989 to 1992. In 1992 he was elected to the Puerto Rico House. In 2000 he was the PPD candidate for resident commissioner; his opponent was incumbent Carlos Romero Barcelo, who was elected mayor of San Juan in 1968 and 1972, governor in 1976 and 1980 and resident commissioner in 1992 and 1996. Romero was known for his pugnacious temperament and strong advocacy of statehood, and unlike many other New Progressives always identified with the mainland Democratic Party. Puerto Ricans tend to vote on straight party lines, and as the Popular Democrats' Sila Maria Calderon was winning the governorship 49%-46%, Acevedo Vila was elected by a 50%-45% margin, with 5% for the Independence Party candidate. In May 2003, Calderon unexpectedly announced she would not seek reelection in 2004; she immediately backed lawyer Jose Alfredo Hernandez Mayoral, son of the former three-term Governor Rafael Hernandez Colon, for the PPD nomination. But Hernandez Mayoral later withdrew from the race and the nomination went to Acevedo Vila. Acevedo-Vila showed his independence of Calderon when in September 2003 he criticized her selection of Ferdinand Mercado as chief justice of the Puerto Rico Supreme Court. The PNP had a primary in November 2003 in which former Governor Pedro Rossello, elected in 1992 and 1996, defeated former Transportation Secretary Carlos Pesquera, the party's candidate in 2000. Rossello campaigned as a strong supporter of statehood and said he would bring a lawsuit against the federal government citing civil rights cases and seeking a decision declaring Puerto Rico a state—an unlikely prospect. Acevedo Vila said he would let voters decide whether to call a constitutional convention on state to define options for a referendum or would ask Congress to authorize a plebiscite. He also frequently attacked Rossello for corruption in his administration; PNP supporters said the corruption prosecutions were a form of persecution of statehood advocates. Rossello led in the polls through much of the campaign. Acevedo Vila urged supporters of the PIP independence party to make their ballots for the PIP and then for him. A PPD ballot was traditionally known as a *pavaso*, after the party symbol of the peasant's hat, or *pava*; a vote for the PIP and Acevedo became known as a *pivaso*.

The *pivasos* made all the difference. The initial count showed Acevedo Vila leading by 3,880 votes, or 48.4%-48.2%, with 28,000 *pivasos*. Rossello said that *pivaso* ballots should not be counted for Acevedo Vila; Acevedo Vila said they should and that such ballots had been routinely counted in the past. Rossello sued and the Puerto Rico Supreme Court, most of whose members were PPD appointees, ruled that *pivasos* should be counted. Rossello went to federal court and Judge Daniel Dominguez, a PNP supporter, said that his court, not the Puerto Rico Supreme Court, had jurisdiction. Amid cries from both sides that the other was stealing the election, the PNP appealed to the First Circuit Court of Appeals in Boston, which ruled in late December that the Puerto Rico Supreme Court had jurisdiction. Acevedo Vila was declared the winner and Rossello stopped contesting the election, but said, "We reaffirm that his certification is an illegitimate one." The PNP won a majority of seats in the Senate and elected its candidate Luis Fortuno as Resident Commissioner; this is the first time a governor of Puerto Rico has had to deal with a legislature and a representative in Congress of the opposite party. In April 2005 Acevedo Vila vetoed a bill that would have called a referendum on whether to request the federal government honor any future decision by Puerto Rico to seek statehood. Acevedo Vila and the PNP legislature had a major struggle over the budget in 2006, which resulted in a government shutdown in May. A commission set up to solve the budget problem recommended substantial layoffs of employees and school closures. These struggles will likely continue through 2008. Acevedo Vila has said he is running for reelection, though he has some opposition in the PPD. Resident Commissioner Luis Fortuno is running for the PNP nomination, and may have serious competition from Pedro Rosello. In the meantime, many in Puerto Rico will be watching to see whether the Democratic Congress takes action on Puerto Rico's status. Fortuno has backed a bill which would follow the recommendations of a White House task force and have a two-step referendum, the first vote on whether Puerto Rico wants to continue its current status, the second if it wants to change to choose between independence and statehood. Acevedo Vila is backing an "enhanced commonwealth" and backs Nydia Velazquez's bill authorizing a constitutional convention in Puerto Rico. Both are supported by many mainland Democrats and Republicans.

Resident Commissioner

Luis Fortuno (R)

Elected 2004, 1st term; b. Oct. 31, 1960, San Juan; home, Guaynabo; Georgetown U., B.S.F.S. 1982; U. of VA, J.D. 1985; Catholic; married (Luce).

Professional Career: Practicing atty., 1985-2004; Sec., PR Dept. of Econ. Dev. and Comm., 1994-97.

DC Office: 126 CHOB, 20515, 202-225-2615; Fax: 202-225-2154; Web site: www.house.gov/fortuno.

District Offices: Old San Juan, 787-723-6333.

Committees: *Education & Labor* (15th of 22 R): Healthy Families & Communities; Early Childhood, Elementary & Secondary Education. *Foreign Affairs* (22d of 23 R): Western Hemisphere; Europe. *Natural Resources* (11th of 22 R): Insular Affairs (RMM).

Luis Fortuno was elected Puerto Rico's resident commissioner in 2004, the first Puerto Rican to hold that office who identified with the Republican party in 100 years. Fortuno grew up in San Juan and graduated from Georgetown University and the University of Virginia law school. He practiced corporate law at a San Juan law firm until a gubernatorial appointment in 1993 as executive director of the Puerto Rico Tourism Company; in 1994 he became Puerto Rico's first Economic Development and Commerce Secretary. In 1996 he quit, as scandal charges began striking the administration of Pedro Rossello, and returned to private practice. In 2001 he became Puerto Rico's Republican National Committeeman and in 2003 he became the PNP nominee for resident commissioner; the incumbent PPD incumbent Anibal Acevedo Vila was running for governor and the PPD nominee was Senator Roberto Prats Palerm. This was the first Puerto Rico campaign in which the National Republican Congressional Committee and the Democratic Congressional Campaign Committee became involved. The previous PNP resident commissioner, Carlos Romero Barcelo, elected in 1992 and 1996, and former Governor Pedro Rossello, the PNP gubernatorial candidate again in 2004, identified with the Democratic party and were strong backers of Bill Clinton, while PPD officeholders have almost always identified with the Democratic party; an exception was former Governor Sila Calderon, who identified with neither mainland party and, after resolution of the Vieques issue, had good things to say about George W. Bush. Fortuno identified with the Republican party. "Hispanic values are Republican values, to a great degree," he said. "Family values are extremely important in our community. . . . I campaigned on a conservative platform of fiscal conservatism, family values, school vouchers, a five-minute moment of silence in the schools." He also campaigned for George W. Bush in central Florida, which has a large Puerto Rican population, and Bush carried or ran about even among non-Cuban Hispanics in that state. NRCC Chairman Tom Reynolds recruited Fortuno, and Illinois's Jerry Weller and Florida's Tom Feeney came to Puerto Rico to campaign for him. Fortuno spent $1.6 million and Prats $1.1 million.

Puerto Ricans tend to vote straight party tickets, and the result in this race was very close. Fortuno won 48.5% of the vote, 0.5% ahead of his party's losing candidate for governor; Prats won 48.0% of the vote, 0.4% behind his party's winning candidate for governor. That made Fortuno the first Republican to represent Puerto Rico in the House since Frederick Degetau, who served from 1901 to 1904. Fortuno was named vice president of the Republican freshman class. This was the first time Puerto Rico has elected a split ticket: Governor Anibal Acevedo Vila of the PPD backs some form of commonwealth status; Fortuno of the PNP favors statehood. Both pledged to work together, but have backed sharply different approaches on status. Fortuno backed a bill sponsored by Jose Serrano based on the December 2005 White House task force recommendation for a two-step referendum, the first vote on whether to retain the current status, the second, if it is rejected, to choose between independence and statehood. He opposed Nydia Velazquez's bill for a constitutional convention in Puerto Rico, which would presumably lead to Governor Acevedo's choice of "enhanced commonwealth." He argued that Acevedo Vila's proposal that Puerto Rico set its own foreign and trade policies was unrealistic. "Three administrations have told you what you are proposing is unconstitutional. What part of no don't you understand?"

On other legislation, Fortuno got committee approval of an amendment prohibiting for-profit colleges from receiving funding for programs designed for historically black colleges and universities. He sponsored with Rick Santorum and Mary Landrieu a bill giving Puerto Rico equal treatment in the Medicare Prospective Payment System. He got both houses to agree to a bill designating 10,000 acres of the Caribbean National Forest as wilderness, protecting the Karst region and the buffer zone around El Yunque. In February 2007, he announced he would run for governor in 2008.

VIRGIN ISLANDS

The United States's other insular territory in the Caribbean is the Virgin Islands, a very different sort of place from Puerto Rico, and the only place under the U.S. flag where people drive on the left. It is much smaller, with a resident population of only 110,000, mainly on the three islands of St. Thomas, St. John and St. Croix. They were settled not by Spaniards but by Dutch and Danes, and had a polyglot colonial society with one of the oldest Jewish communities in the Western Hemisphere; their most famous son is Alexander Hamilton, who grew up in St. Croix. Puerto Rico is multiracial and not self-conscious about it, but most Virgin Islanders are black and resent the clear divide between the races. While Puerto Rico has attracted all kinds of light industry, the Virgin Islands has lived primarily off tourism and refineries (the Hovensa refinery on St. Croix is the largest refinery in the Western Hemisphere; it was built by Amerada Hess in the 1960s and is now half-owned by the Venezuela government oil company and thus by Hugo Chavez). These are industries that have produced high incomes for a few employees but have not provided the basis for a steady economy. Tourism, hurt by hurricanes in the 1990s, has recovered from September 11 and was up sharply in 2004, when the Virgin Islands were largely unscathed by the hurricanes that battered so much of the Caribbean and Florida. There has been a construction boom and new hotels and resorts have been opening. St. Thomas remains the number one cruise ship port in the world, with nearly 400 ships coming in each year, and in 2004 cruise ships returned to St. Croix after a two-year hiatus because of high crime. In terms of homeland security the Virgin Islands is, according to the *Economist*, "perhaps America's most vulnerable point," with weak infrastructure, unconnected electric grids and almost total dependence on shipping for fuel, food and medicine.

Nor does economic salvation seem likely to come from the investment businesses attracted to the Virgin Islands by tax breaks established by Congress and the Virgin Islands government. Individuals and businesses that qualify under the Economic Development Authority pay a maximum of 3.5% in income tax, which has yielded revenues of about $100 million a year to the island government. To qualify, you must live and do business in the Virgin Islands, under rules which Virgin Islands officials asked the Treasury to clarify but which the Treasury said were clear. In 2002 and 2003 nearly 100 businesses were set up to qualify, but in 2004 the IRS started investigating whether investors really lived in the Virgin Islands; agents queried office and household staff on the location of their owners and how frequently they were in the islands. The first indictment came in February 2004 and the IRS in June said that lawyers and estate planners were making false claims. In October 2004 Congress passed a law that changed the rules which required investors to live here for 183 days in one year rather than 122 days over three years to qualify for the tax break. Virgin Islands Governor Charles Turnbull said the change could cost the Islands government $80 million in revenue; Delegate Donna Christensen said, "This is the number one issue for us in terms of our economic prosperity going forward."

That could be a serious problem, because the Virgin Islands government has been running structural deficits estimated at between $50 and $100 million on budget of around $600 million. One problem is the crushing burden of a $1 billion bond debt, which requires $45 million in debt service. Another is that the local government has largely ignored the recommendations of federal auditors; one agency had a 70% rate of delinquency on its loans. One-third of workers are employed by government. Virgin Island Delegate Donna Christensen, saying the government was on the brink of financial collapse, persuaded the U.S. House to pass in September 2004 and again in March 2005 a bill to establish a financial overseer with veto power over Virgin Islands government spending for five years; Charles Turnbull, then governor, strongly opposed this, and the U.S. Senate did not act.

Governor John deJongh, a Democrat, is governor of the Virgin Islands. He grew up in St. Thomas and in Detroit. He graduated from Antioch College and participated in work study programs in various places including the Virgin Islands. He returned to St. Thomas and worked on the Tri-Island Development Council's historic redevelopments projects, then ran all consumer banking for Chase Bank in the U.S. and British Virgin Islands and St. Maarten. In 1984 he was appointed to the Industrial Development Commission. From 1987 to 1990 he was Commissioner of Finance (a position once held by his grandfather Percy deJongh) and headed the U.S. Virgin Islands Public Finance Authority. From 1990 to 1992 he was executive assistant to Governor Alexander Farrelly. For the next dozen years he worked in the private sector in the Virgin Islands, including a stint as president of the chamber of commerce.

In 2002 he ran for governor as an independent and finished second to incumbent Charles Turnbull, nearly forcing Turnbull into a runoff. But in 2006, after eight years dealing with the Virgin Islands' massive financial problems, Turnbull was ineligible to run. At one point in 2005 things were so bad that the local Water and Power Authority threatened to cut off services to public buildings unless the government started paying $16 million in overdue bills.

This was a close race: on November 7 deJongh was just 2 votes short of winning the required absolute majority. Two weeks later he defeated Kenneth Mapp 57%-43%. Just before he took office, the Senate approved 7–6, with two members not voting, a bill to raise its members' salaries to $85,000 and the governor's to $150,000, and to issue $600 million in bonds to finance the predicted deficit in the Government Employees Retirement System. In his inaugural deJongh said that the structural deficit was over $50 million and unpaid retroactive pay obligations amounted to $400 million. Obviously the bill just signed by Turnbull did not help matters; local businessmen launched a recall petition against the seven senators who voted for it. All of this probably strengthened the case for the bill, which Delegate Donna Christensen persuaded the U.S. House to pass in October 2004 and March 2005 but which was strongly opposed by Turnbull, setting up a federal overseer to control the Virgin Islands finances for five years.

Delegate

Donna Christensen (D)

Elected 1996, 6th term; b. Sept. 19, 1945, Teaneck, NJ; home, St. Croix; St. Mary's Col., B.S. 1966, George Washington U., M.D. 1970; Moravian; married (Christian).

Professional Career: Practicing physician, 1975-97; Territorial Asst., Commissioner of Health, 1988-94; Acting Commissioner of Health, 1994-95.

DC Office: 1510 LHOB, 20515, 202-225-1790; Fax: 202-225-5517; Web site: www.house.gov/christian-christensen.

District Offices: St. Croix, 340-778-5900; St. Thomas, 340-774-4408.

Committees: *Homeland Security* (11th of 19 D): Emerging Threats, Cybersecurity & Science and Technology; Emergency Communications, Preparedness & Response. *Natural Resources* (7th of 27 D): Insular Affairs (Chmn.); National Parks, Forests & Public Lands.

The delegate from the Virgin Islands is Donna Christensen, first elected in 1996, when she beat Victor Frazer, a Republican who ran as an independent and was the upset winner in 1994. Christensen is from an old St. Croix family; her father was Virgin Islands Chief District Court Judge Almeric Christian. She graduated from St. Mary's College and George Washington Medical School; she practiced medicine for more than 20 years in the Virgin Islands, in a family practice and in several public positions, and is the first female physician to serve in Congress. She was elected a Democratic national committeewoman in 1984 and ran one losing race for delegate in 1994. In 1996 she attacked Frazer, who after some hesitation caucused with the Democrats, for foreign travel (11 trips to four continents) and for inaction in opposing the welfare bill. Christensen led Frazer 38%-34% on November 5; in the runoff two weeks later she won 52%-48%. It was a regional race: Christensen won 69% on St. Croix, Frazer 64% on St. Thomas and St. John.

In the House, Christensen has forged alliances with the Congressional Black Caucus to achieve her goals; she works on health issues for the Black Caucus. She opposed Bill Clinton's designation in January 2001 of 12,708 undersea acres as the U.S. Virgin Islands Coral Reef National Monument, arguing that it would hurt local fishermen. As ranking minority member of the Parks Subcommittee, she got a hearing on the issue in the Virgin Islands in July 2002.

Christensen has argued that the Virgin Islands government, with $1 billion in debt, is on the verge of bankruptcy. In October 2004 and once again in March 2005 she persuaded the House to vote for her bill to establish a financial overseer with veto power over government spending for five years. On this she was strongly opposed by then-Governor Charles Turnbull. She has pressed for passage of a bill to recognize as Virgin Island residents investors who spend 122 days there over three years, rather than the Treasury's requirement of 183 days in one year. In August 2004 she advanced a constitutional amendment, co-sponsored by the delegates from Guam and American Samoa, allowing residents of U.S. territories overseas to vote for president. "Every conflict this country has been in, we have sent our young men and women to serve or to die in, per capita, some of the highest numbers you will find." In 2005 she hailed an FDA advisory panel for recommending approval of a combination of two generic drugs for blacks only. In April 2006 she passed amendments to the port act creating a border patrol unit for the Virgin Islands and a homeland security report on the impact of the advanced passenger information system on charter boat operators. In September 2006 she sought to make permanent the Virgin Islands's $13.25 rum tax payment.

Christensen was reelected by wide margins in 2002, 2004 and 2006.

GUAM

Some 3,700 miles west of Hawaii, 19 hours of flying time from Washington, D.C., is Guam, where America's day begins. Guam lies west of the International Date Line, and it is in the early hours of Tuesday there when the rest of us are just trying to get through Monday afternoon; the Interior Department came to Guam to see whether there were Y2K problems, as the clock struck midnight, January 1, 2000, while it was 9 a.m., December 31, in Washington. Geographically in the center of the Mariana Islands, Guam is legally separate: The Northern Marianas were administered by the U.S. as a United Nations trust territory until they became the Commonwealth of the Northern Marianas (CNMI) in 1978. Guam was ruled by Navy captains from 1898 to 1949, except for 32 months of Japanese occupation during World War II; in 1950 the Guam Organic Act made Guamanians U.S. citizens. Guam's first civilian governor, Carlton Skinner, who as a captain integrated the crew of his Navy ship in 1943, established the University of Guam and wrote its constitution; he died in June 2004. Guam elects its local government, but Congress still retains final power over the territory. It authorized Guam to start electing a non-voting delegate to the House in 1972.

Guam is 36 miles long by four to nine miles wide, with 171,000 people; 37% are Chamorro (descendants of the original islanders), 26% Filipino, 13% other Asian and 10% Caucasian; 85% of Guamanians are Catholic. The Catholic Church helped defeat a proposal for casino gambling 61%-39% in 2004, despite the competition for tourists from Japan and now China from the Tinian Dynasty casino in the CNMI, and a proposal for slot machines in race tracks in 2006. Guam is tropical, but not an easy environment: in August 1993 it lived through an earthquake rated at 8.2 on the Richter scale, comparable to San Francisco in 1906; in December 2002, Supertyphoon Pongsona, with winds up to 184 miles per hour, cut off all electric power and caused hundreds of millions in damage. In July 2004 Typhoon Tingting pelted the island with 20 inches of rain in 48 hours. And it suffers from an invasive species, the brown tree snake, which apparently arrived on a military plane some time in the 1940s or 50s, and has caused the extinction of nine of 12 native forest birds and two native lizards.

Economically, Guam depends heavily on U.S. military bases; military bases occupy one-third of the land, 60% of income comes from the federal government and it makes for a pretty good living. Guam's gross domestic product per capita is the second highest in the Pacific, after Hawaii's. The slump in the Japanese economy hit Guam too: tourism was down from 1.3 million in 2000 to 1 million in 2002 and rose to just 1.15 million in 2004. Tourism seemed like the wave of the future when the military was being drawn down, from 30,000 personnel at the time of the Vietnam War to 5,000 after the end of the Cold War. Housing values plummeted and unemployment rose to as much as 15%. But September 11 changed that. Popular protests in South Korea and Japan against the

U.S. military presence there, the threats of the North Korean government and the need to supply operations in South Asia have made Guam much more important militarily. Guam, 3,700 miles closer to Asia than Hawaii, reduces "the tyranny of distance" and is now a "power projection hub," in militaryspeak. And it has one additional advantage: as Air Force General William Begert put it, "Guam, first of all, is U.S. territory. I don't need overflight rights. I don't need landing rights. I always have permission to go to Guam. It might as well be California or New Jersey."

By 2004 military spending here was nearly double the levels of the mid-1990s. In fall 2002 two Los Angeles class submarines were stationed in Guam, and another followed in 2003; the USS Buffalo is scheduled to follow in 2007. In February 2003 12 B-52s and 12 B-1s were stationed on Guam. The Navy spent $30 million dredging Apra Harbor and repairing World War II-era wharves; $500 million was spent on construction at Andersen Air Force Base, including a $32 million air-conditioned hangar for the humidity-sensitive B-2. Guam is a good site for training: the Marines rent typhoon-damaged structures for urban warfare exercises and the southern jungles, so thick that the last Japanese holdout was not flushed out until 1972, are good for rural warfare training. There are proposals to station a carrier group in Guam, which would bring in $423 million to the local economy and create 4,000 local jobs, and to station a flight wing there as well. In October 2005 the United States and Japan agreed that 8,000 Marines would be relocated from Okinawa to Guam by 2012. They would more than double the military presence, and bring 9,000 family workers and 15,000 construction workers to make Guam the strategic "tip of the spear," as Rear Admiral John Bird put it. Andersen Air Force Base has plenty of ramp space and extensive open space that can be developed; Guam has the Air Force's largest fuel supply, the largest supply of weapons in the Pacific.

For much of the 1990s Guam sought a change in status, to give the Guam government control over immigration. Chamorros said they want to block others from coming in, establishing citizenship and making them a minority; another motive was to bring in guest workers as the surrounding Commonwealth of the Northern Marianas Islands has done, with local enforcement of labor laws. The first Bush administration rejected the bill as inconsistent with the constitutional provision giving Congress full powers over territories. For a time the Clinton administration seemed sympathetic and inclined to agree to "mutual consent." But the election of the Republican Congress abruptly changed the provision's prospects. In October 1997 a Clinton official said he saw no constitutional way to do what Guam wanted. There has been no revival of this issue since George W. Bush became president.

Instead then-Delegate Robert Underwood sought increased Compact-Impact Aid and a War Reparations Commission. The latter, a goal of Guam delegates since 1972, was finally signed in December 2002, as Underwood was leaving office (he ran for governor and lost). It set up a five-member commission to decide whether Guamanians who were victims of torture, forced labor, internment and deprivation during the Japanese occupation should get more than the $5,000 that was paid them under the 1940s Guam Meritorious Claims Act. In April 2005 Delegate Madeleine Bordallo sponsored a bill with 82 cosponsors for reparations for those who suffered during the Japanese occupation (the 1951 treaty between the U.S. and Japan absolved Japan of any claims). It would provide for payments of $12,000 to each of 9,000 survivors and lump sums of $25,000 to children of the 1,000 Guamanians killed by the Japanese. The bill passed the House in May 2007.

The Democratic Congress in 2007, aware that disgraced Republican lobbyist Jack Abramoff was the great promoter of the CNMI's economic status, made sure to impose the federal minimum wage on the CNMI as well as Guam (but not on American Samoa, where local Democrats were opposed).

Guam votes for Democrats more often than Republicans, but politics here is a family matter. Governor Camacho's father was also governor; his lieutenant governor, Kaleo Moylan, is the son of the elder Camacho's lieutenant governor. Robert Underwood ascribed his first victory as delegate to his large number of cousins; he was weakened in the 2002 governor race by primary competition from Geri Gutierrez, wife of term-limited Governor Carl Gutierrez. The 2002 Republican candidate for delegate, Joseph Ada, was elected governor in 1986 and 1990. His opponent in the latter race was Madeleine Bordallo, who beat him for delegate and whose husband Ricardo Bordallo was elected governor in 1974 and 1982. Bordallo won the 2002 Democratic nomination by beating Judith Won Pat, daughter of Antonio Borja Won Pat, Guam's first elected delegate who served from 1972 to 1984 and after whom Guam's civilian airport is named; Won Pat in 2006 led the ticket in the race for the Guam legislature. In 2006 there were two primary contests for governor, on the Republican side between Camacho and Moylan, whom he had dumped from the ticket; on the Democratic side between Underwood and Gutierrez. Camacho beat Moylan by nearly 2–1, but the Democratic contest was close, and in November Camacho beat Underwood by only 50%-48%.

Guam of course does not cast any electoral votes for president, but has a part in presidential politics. It elects delegates to party national conventions—6 for Bush and 6 for Kerry in 2004. In November Guam has conducted a straw poll for president, and has voted for the winner every time since 1984. In 2000 George W. Bush beat Al Gore 52%-47%; in 2004, after the big military buildup, Bush beat John Kerry 65%-35%. That was a bigger increase in the Bush percentage he achieved in any state and, among congressional districts, was only equaled in the 9th District of New York.

Governor   Felix Camacho, a Republican, was elected governor of Guam in 2002. Camacho grew up in Guam and attended Catholic schools; his father Carlos Camacho was appointed governor in 1969 and elected to a single term in 1970. Felix Camacho graduated from Marquette University in Milwaukee and returned to Guam and worked for Pacific Financial Corporation and IBM. When he was 31, IBM proposed to transfer him off island, and he paused to set out his short-term and long-term goals; one of the long-term goals was "governor of Guam." Republican Joseph Ada was governor, and in March 1988 he appointed Camacho deputy chief of the Public Utility Agency, and in November 1988 he was appointed executive director of the Civil Service Commission. In 1992 he was elected to the Guam Legislature, where he was assistant majority leader.

In 2002 Governor Carl Gutierrez was ineligible to run for a third term, and Camacho ran. In the Republican primary he defeated Tony Unpingco, the Speaker of the Guam Legislature, 54%-46%. In the Democratic primary, between Delegate Robert Underwood and Geri Gutierrez, Carl Gutierrez's wife, both Democrats spent more than $400,000 on this race; Underwood won 64%-36%. The candidates debated in both English and Chamorro; Underwood spoke in Chamorro the whole time, while Camacho had to break into English. They disagreed on issues like casinos, waste treatment and return of military land. Camacho won 55%-45%, carrying some normally Democratic areas, but Democrats won a 9–6 majority in the Legislature.

Camacho urged Congress to include Guam in the Radiation Exposure Compensation Program because of the 67 nuclear tests conducted from 1946 to 1958 at the Marshall Islands atoll of Eniwetok. In September 2004 Camacho vetoed the Legislature's $447 million budget, saying it would overspend revenue by $50 million; the Legislature partially overrode his veto. Perhaps his biggest achievement was the privatization of the Guam Telephone Authority, sold for $150 million in December 2004 to TeleGuam Holdings, part of a private investment fund of the Roy Disney family. Budget fights continued in 2005, as Camacho issued an executive order allowing Guam's hospital authority to set its own pay scales and personnel rules and reinstated pay increases to 2,700 government employees. It included $1.46 million to retire Guam Memorial Hospital's debt to the GovGuam Retirement Fund. In 2006 Camacho declined to challenge a court ruling requiring millions in delinquent cost of living payments to GovGuam retirees. Not surprisingly, in September 2006 the Pacific Command said the government of Guam was a "financial mess" because of its reluctance to lay off public employees and because of "borrowing in financial markets to pay employees."

In December 2005 Camacho announced he wouldn't run again with Lieutenant Governor Kaleo Moylan; he had already fired some members of Moylan's staff. He chose state Senator Michael Cruz, a physician and an Iraq war veteran, to be his 2006 running mate. They were opposed in the primary by Moylan and Francis Santos. Camacho and Cruz won by a 63%-36% margin. The Democrats had a closer race, between former Governor Carl Gutierrez and former Delegate Robert Underwood; the latter won by a 53%-47% margin. There were some negative undertones to this race. Camacho was attacked for having worked with disgraced Republican lobbyist Jack Abramoff, whose emails showed a contempt for Chamorros; he admitted having received political advice from Abramoff when he was Governor Joseph Ada's running mate in 1998. Meanwhile, charges that Underwood was anti-Filipino were widely circulated; Underwood said Camacho was spreading them. Five major business groups endorsed Camacho a week before the November election.

Camacho won by less than 1,000 votes, 50%-48%. Underwood requested a runoff, on the grounds that if overvotes were counted, Camacho had received only 49.6% of the vote, less than the absolute majority required. On December 19 the Guam Supreme Court ruled against him.

Delegate

Madeleine Bordallo (D)

Elected 2002, 3d term; b. May 31, 1933, Graceville, MN; home, Tamuning; St. Mary's Col. 1952, St. Katherine's Col., A.A. 1953; Catholic; widowed.

Elected Office: GU Senate, 1981-82, 1986-94; GU Lt. Gov., 1994-2002.

DC Office: 427 CHOB, 20515, 202-225-1188; Fax: 202-226-0341; Web site: www.house.gov/bordallo.

District Offices: Hagatna, 671-477-4272.

Committees: *Armed Services* (18th of 34 D): Seapower & Expeditionary Forces; Readiness. *Natural Resources* (11th of 27 D): Fisheries, Wildlife & Oceans (Chmn.); Insular Affairs.

Madeleine Bordallo, a Democrat, was elected delegate from Guam in 2002. She grew up in Minnesota and, from age 14, on Guam. She graduated from St. Katherine's College in St. Paul with a degree in vocal music and worked as a program director and program host on Guam radio stations. In 1953 she married Ricardo Bordallo, from a prominent Guam family, who owned an auto dealership and had many business interests and was well connected in island politics. Madeleine Bordallo became Guam's Democratic National Committeewoman in 1964 and has held that position ever since (she is the most senior member of the Democratic National Committee). Ricardo Bordallo was elected governor in 1974, defeated for reelection in 1978, then elected governor again in 1982. With her husband's encouragement, Madeleine Bordallo ran for the Guam Legislature and was elected in 1980, 1986, 1988, 1990 and 1992. In 1990 Ricardo Bordallo wrapped himself in the Guam flag, chained himself to the statue of Chief Quipuha and shot himself to avoid a prison term for bribery. Madeleine Bordallo was a candidate for governor that year, but lost 57%-43% to incumbent Joseph Ada. In 1994 she was elected lieutenant governor and was reelected in 1998.

In 2002, when Delegate Robert Underwood decided to run for governor, Bordallo ran for delegate. In the primary she faced Judith Won Pat, daughter of Guam's first delegate, Antonio Borja Won Pat, who served from 1974 to 1986. In this contest between longtime friends, Bordallo won 59%-41%. In the general she faced Joseph Ada, who beat her in 1990. This time Bordallo won by an impressive 65%-35% margin.

Bordallo got a seat on the Armed Services Committee and proceeded to lobby her colleagues there for more military deployments in Guam. "All I have to say is location, location, location." She urged Defense Secretary Donald Rumsfeld to visit the island on an "instructional tour" in 2003, which she saw as a turning point. She got a bill signed in 2003 giving Guam and other insular areas the same access to guaranteed loans as the 50 states; this seemed likely to bring in $13.5 million, a significant chunk of money for GovGuam (the name for Guam's government). She sought $157 million of debt relief for Guam but her request was denied by the Bush administration. Working closely with Senator Daniel Inouye, who she said was her mentor in Congress, she successfully got $30 million annual compact aid for 20 years, to be divided among Guam, Hawaii, the CNMI and American Samoa; this is to compensate Guam for the costs imposed by immigrants from Micronesia and the Marshall Islands, allowed in the United States by a 1986 compact which gave the U.S. military access to their territories.

The 2004 defense reauthorization included $90 million in military construction for Guam. It also included $250,000 for Bordallo's invasive species pilot project; Guam has been plagued by the voracious and repulsive brown tree snake, which has no natural enemies there and which has wiped out most of the island's native birds. In April 2005 she sponsored a bill, with 82 co-sponsors, for reparations for Guamanians who suffered during the Japanese occupation—$12,000 to some 9,000 survivors and lump sums of $25,000 to children of the 1,000 Guamanians killed by the Japanese; this was approved by the House in May 2007. In January 2006 she called for an independent counsel to investigate the demotion of U.S. Attorney Frederick Black, who had been investigating disgraced lobbyist Jack Abramoff and his relations with clients in the CNMI. In March 2006 she called for Japan to pay three-quarters of the cost of relocating 8,000 Marines from Okinawa to Guam.

Bordallo was unopposed for reelection in 2004 and 2006. In 2007, she became chair of the Natural Resources Subcommittee on Fisheries, Wildlife and Oceans.

AMERICAN SAMOA

American Samoa, the only American territory south of the Equator, has been relatively little influenced by Western settlers and remains almost as Polynesian today as it was when the United States took possession in 1900 at the request of tribal chiefs. These seven islands with a hot and rainy climate are 2,300 miles southwest of Hawaii, 1,600 miles northeast of New Zealand. American Samoa has 57,000 people, 90% of them on the island of Tutuila, 89% of them Polynesian, mostly Christian (50% Congregationalist, 20% Catholic); they are U.S. nationals but not U.S. citizens; they can serve in the U.S. military, but not as officers. An estimated 50,000 Samoans live on the U.S. mainland and 20,000 in Hawaii, including Honolulu Mayor Mufi Hannemann. American Samoa's population has doubled in the last 20 years, and fear that outsiders will change the culture has prompted some demands for stricter immigration standards. American Samoa is an unincorporated territory administered by the Interior Department since 1951; minimum wages have been set for industries by the U.S. Department of Labor. American Samoa elects a governor and a two-house legislature known as the Fono. It is a bilingual society and government: Government is mostly conducted in English, Fono proceedings are in Samoan, and court sessions are conducted in English with each sentence then translated into Samoan.

The market economy has not made much progress here: American Samoa lives off the federal government, which contributed 60% of its government revenues in fiscal year 2004, plus varying amounts for construction (the Army in 2002 pitched in $1 million for a 55-year lease of six acres at Pago Pago Airport for a Reserve County), and two big StarKist and Chicken of the Sea tuna canneries, which employ 5,150 workers and provide one-third of all U.S. canned tuna. Another 4,000 work for the American Samoan government, most at $7.99 an hour. Residents are eligible for U.S. food stamps and welfare; local agriculture is minimal and sheltered (the territorial government in 2000 wanted to quadruple tariffs on bananas and taro). The bedrock of the local economy is the territorial government. Congressional Democrats excluded American Samoa from their 2007 minimum wage increase, although Guam and the Commonwealth of the Northern Marianas Islands were included; this was done at the request of American Samoa's Delegate Eni Faleomavaega, who cited much lower-wage competition from Thailand. House Republicans attacked the Democrats as hypocritical and noted that StarKist is headquartered in Speaker Nancy Pelosi's district, though there was nothing to suggest that Pelosi was doing the company any favors.

Tourism has been minimal: Governor Togiola Tulafono says he hopes to develop "controlled tourism in a way that won't affect our fragile environment." The first McDonalds opened in 2000, followed by a Kentucky Fried Chicken and a Quality Inn. A second McDonalds was proposed in 2005 on Utelei Beach, with a playground and a traditional Samoan fala (house), but was opposed by the Senate which sued to force Tulafono to seek legislative approval.

One cause celebre is the renaming of nearby Samoa, formerly British Samoa and Western Samoa. The single name suggests to many in American Samoa that they are regarded as not full Samoans, and the legislature threatened not to recognize Samoan passports—a problem, since 85% of the cannery work force is from Samoa. Similarly, residents of American Samoa must have visas to visit Samoa. Tulafono would like to have controls over immigration. As he said in 2005, "The problem we have is everyone wants to come to American Samoa and we don't have much land and can be overcrowded very easily. But our people that go from here to Samoa, even people with Samoan ties, they're very slow in camping out over there and not coming back, so we inherit the problem and they don't."

But if American Samoans are proud Samoans, they are also proud Americans: On April 17, 2000, they celebrated the 100th anniversary of the American takeover, with a 60-foot American flag raised on Sogelau Hill, where the American flag was first raised; there was traditional singing and dancing at Veterans Stadium and a long boat race in Pago Pago Harbor, and a commemorative stamp was unveiled showing a Samoan alia (two-hull canoe) sailing in easterly winds near Suniatu Mountain in the Manu'a island group. And Samoans have become devoted to one staple of American life: football. The island has six high school football teams and a 5,000-seat stadium where just about everyone comes to cheer. The style of play is aggressive, with lots of body contact. Of 900 boys who graduated from high school in 2002 and 2003, 97 left the island to play at four- or two-year colleges in the mainland; 41 players of Samoan descent were listed on NFL rosters in 2007. In contrast, American Samoa is not much given to soccer; FIFA ranked it the very last team in the runup to the 2006 World Cup.

American Samoa does not cast electoral votes for president, but does send delegates to the parties' national conventions. In February 2000, George W. Bush won four delegates in a caucus. In March 2000, Al Gore beat Bill Bradley by 21–4—those are not percentages, but the actual number of votes; Bradley got one convention vote split between four delegates. On March 8, 2004, John Kerry got 2.5 convention votes divided between 5 delegates and Dennis Kucinich got the remaining half-vote from the sixth delegate. The week before, Bush won all 6 Republican delegates.

Governor   Togiola T.A. Tulafono was sworn in as American Samoa's governor on April, 7, 2003, after the sudden death of Governor Tauese Sunia March 26. Togiola grew up in American Samoa and after high school graduated from Honolulu Police Academy and worked as a policeman for a year. He graduated from Chadron State College in Nebraska, worked in the American Samoan attorney general's office and graduated from the Washburn University law school in Topeka, Kansas, and National Judicial College in Reno, Nevada.   He returned to American Samoa, where he practiced law for 20 years and served as a judge and a senator and in a variety of executive posts: administrative assistant to the Secretary of Samoan Affairs, Samoan Assistant to the Attorney General, the first chairman of the American Samoa Power Authority, and the first chairman of the Board of High Education. Togiola was elected lieutenant governor in 1996 and served under Tauese until his 2003 death. In April 2003, one of his first acts as governor was to appoint Treasurer Aitofele Toese Sunia, Tauese's brother, as lieutenant governor.

As governor, Togiola took action on a number of issues. In December 2003 he issued an order prohibiting shark finning, importing shark fins, prized by many Asians, without the entire shark carcass. In March 2004 he sponsored a statute criminalizing human trafficking, to complement the federal statute under which a Korean garment factory operator was prosecuted in 2001. In April 2004 he said he would appoint a commission to review American Samoa's relationship to the United States. In July 2004 he expressed concern that all the 200 Army reservists in American Samoa would be called to active duty at the same time. He wrote the Army "asking that they modify that policy to allow for partial deployments." In December 2004 56 were deployed, including his daughter Olita Tulafono. In the November 2 election, Togiola won 48% of the vote to 39% for Afoa Moega Lutu and 12% for Senator Teo Fuavai. Togiola won the November 16 runoff with 56% of the vote.

In October 2005 Togiola called for controls on immigration from Samoa. "The problem we have is everyone wants to come to American Samoa and we don't have much land and can be overcrowded very easily. But our people that go from here to Samoa, even people with Samoan ties, they're very slow in camping out over there and not coming back, so we inherit the problem and they don't." He has also drawn notice for his attempt to get a new airline to serve American Samoa. Only Hawaiian Airlines serves American Samoa, with four flights weekly between Pago Pago and Honolulu. Togiola has charged that the airline charges too much and frequently reschedules flights at great inconvenience; he has called for a cut off in air service from Hawaiian Airlines, which receives a federal subsidy under the Essential Air Services program for serving American Samoa. The airline said that the cost of providing service to the territory was high and after Togiola issued an executive order ending service it petitioned the Department of Transportation for declaratory relief.

Delegate

Eni F.H. Faleomavaega (D)

Elected 1988, 10th term; b. Aug. 15, 1943, Vailoatai; home, Pago Pago; Brigham Young U., B.A. 1966, U. of Houston, J.D. 1972, U. of CA, LL.M. 1973; Mormon; married (Hinanui).

Military Career: Army, 1966-69 (Vietnam).

Elected Office: AS Lt. Gov., 1984-89.

Professional Career: A.A., U.S. Del. from AS, 1973-75; Cnsl., U.S. House Interior Cmte., 1975-81; AS Dpty. Atty. Gen., 1981-84.

DC Office: 2422 RHOB, 20515, 202-225-8577; Fax: 202-225-8757; Web site: www.house.gov/faleomavaega.

District Offices: Pago Pago, 684-633-1372.

Committees: *Foreign Affairs* (4th of 27 D): Asia, the Pacific & the Global Environment (Chmn.); Western Hemisphere. *Natural Resources* (3d of 27 D): Energy & Mineral Resources; Insular Affairs; Fisheries, Wildlife & Oceans.

American Samoa has elected a delegate to Congress since 1980. Delegate Eni F. H. Faleomavaega is a Democrat first elected in 1988. He went to high school in Hawaii, to Brigham Young University, then to law school in Houston and Berkeley; he served in Vietnam in the Army. In the 1970s he worked on the Natural Resources Insular subcommittee staff and for Utah Democrat Gunn McKay. In 1981 he became deputy attorney general of American Samoa, and in 1985 lieutenant governor. He is one of four Mormon Democrats in Congress (the others are Harry Reid, Tom Udall and Jim Matheson) and he has campaigned in Utah among Samoans who have been living or studying there.

Faleomavaega (he uses his last name in his press releases, rather than the first name used to refer to Samoan chiefs) serves on the Natural Resources Committee, where was ranking minority member on three subcommittees—Native Americans and Insular Affairs in 1995; National Parks and Public Lands in 1997; Fisheries, Conservation, Wildlife and Oceans in 1999. He is also a member of Foreign Affairs and chairman of its Subcommittee on Asia, the Pacific and the Global Environment. He led the congressional protest against the French nuclear tests in the Pacific, and was stopped by the French for approaching the French nuclear testing site at Mururoa Atoll and imprisoned in Tahiti in 1996. In February 2005 he called for the IAEA to review the health and environmental effects of France's 30-year nuclear testing program. In December 2006 he and three other members visited North Korea's Kaesong industrial complex. He has called for hearings on West Papua and whether it should be independent from Indonesia; his relatives were Christian missionaries there.

For several years, Faleomavaega pressed for a bill to exempt interest on American Samoa bonds from state and local taxes—the same treatment enjoyed by bonds issued by Puerto Rico, Guam and the Virgin Islands—and it was signed into law in October 2004. When the Interior Department tightened conditions for funding capital improvement projects in the territories, Faleomavaega objected in March 2004. "What is the sense of having an elected governor if the deputy assistant secretary is going to be the one controlling the use of funds?" In October 2004, he called for an extension of Section 936 for tuna canneries; the provision, which provides favorable tax treatment, was scheduled to expire in October 2006. He was concerned that tariffs on Ecuador's tuna exports might be rescinded in order to ease disputes between Ecuador and large U.S. companies operating there; he warned that Ecuador's tuna production capacity could "wipe out" American Samoa's economy. In September 2005 he met with the StarKist and Chicken of the Sea CEOs in Washington about extending 936; in November, Ways and Means Chairman Bill Thomas agreed to keep 936 for American Samoa for a year. In 2006, Faleomavaega convinced House members and StarKist and Chicken of the Sea officials to agree on replacing 936 with Section 30A tax credits, which offer similar benefits. The two-year extension was signed into law in December.

Faleomavaega favored a minimum wage increase in June 2005 and contrasted high executive salaries with the wages paid to workers in American Samoa. But in January 2007 he urged his fellow Democrats not to include American Samoa in their minimum wage increase. "The truth is that the global tuna industry is so competitive that it is no longer possible for the federal government to demand mainland minimum wage rates for American Samoa without causing the collapse of our economy and making us welfare wards of the federal government." He has introduced bills to prohibit human trafficking in American Samoa and succeeded, with the help of Republicans Dan Burton and Joe Barton, in 2005 in almost doubling Medicaid payments to American Samoa. He opposed the building of American Samoa's second McDonalds on Utelei Beach. He argued in October 2006 that discussions of the territorial status of American Samoa should not begin until the issue of the treaties or deeds of cession signed in Tutuila in 1900 and Manu'a in 1904 are addressed; he noted that there is no officially declared union between the two.

American Samoa's election law provides for no primary contests and requires a runoff 14 days later if no candidate wins 50% of the vote in the November election. In 1996, 2000 and 2002, Faleomavaega was forced into runoffs. He protested that 14 days was not enough time to get ballots to and back from military personnel serving abroad. In 2002 this posed an additional problem: because of the infrequency of flights to and from American Samoa, Faleomavaega was unable to campaign and to return to Washington to vote in the November 14 Democratic Caucus where Bob Menendez defeated Rosa DeLauro for Caucus chairman by one vote (he would have voted for Menendez). In 2004 he sponsored a bill to abolish the runoff unless the Fono (the two-house legislature) created a primary election for delegate. This passed the House and Senate unanimously and was signed into law October 30. It was moot for the November 2 election, since Faleomavaega had just one opponent, longtime Republican House staffer Aumua Amata Coleman, who also ran against him in 2000 and 2002. This time Faleomavaega won 53%-47%. It applied in 2006, however, when Faleomavaega won 47% of the vote to 41% for Coleman and 12% for Ae Ae Jr., Muavaefa'atasi. Fewer votes are cast in American Samoa than in any other House race—11,502 in November 2004, 11,033 in November 2006.

BY THE NUMBERS
THE 110TH CONGRESS
(As of January 4, 2007)

House: 233D, 202R
Senate: 50D, 49R, 1I

Oldest member of the Senate:	Robert Byrd (born Nov. 20, 1917)
Youngest member of the Senate:	John Sununu (born Sept. 10, 1964)
Longest service in the Senate:	Robert Byrd (since Jan. 3, 1959)
Oldest member of the House:	Ralph Hall (born May 3, 1923)
Youngest member of the House:	Patrick McHenry (born Oct. 22, 1975)
Longest service in the House:	John Dingell (since Dec. 13, 1955)
Largest House delegation:	California (53 seats; 34D, 19R)
Female members of Congress:	70 (House) 16 (Senate)
Black members of Congress:	40 (House) 1 (Senate)
Hispanic members of Congress:	23 (House) 2 (Senate)

Democratic-held districts carried by George W. Bush in 2004: 62
Republican-held districts carried by John Kerry in 2004: 8

Top Ranked Congressional Districts

Largest (*excluding at-large districts*):	105,635 sq. miles	Nevada 2
Smallest:	12 sq. miles	New York 11
Rural:	78.7%	Kentucky 5
One-person households:	49.6%	New York 14
Graduate/professional degrees:	28.1%	Maryland 8
Government workers:	29.0%	Maryland 4
Military veterans:	21.7%	Florida 1
Black, non-Hispanic:	65.2%	Illinois 1
Asian, non-Hispanic:	53.6%	Hawaii 1
American Indian, non-Hispanic:	18.0%	Arizona 1
Hispanic:	77.7%	Texas 16
Social Security beneficiaries:	250,771	Florida 5

2004 PRESIDENTIAL ELECTION

George W. Bush (R)   50.7%
John Kerry (D)   48.3%

States carried by Bush   31
States carried by Kerry   19
Counties carried by Bush: 2,530
Counties carried by Kerry: 583
Top Bush county:
Ochiltree County, TX   92.0%
Top Kerry county:
Shannon County, SD   84.6%

Congressional districts carried by Bush in 2004:   255
Congressional districts carried by Kerry in 2004:   180

Districts carried by Bush in 2000 and Kerry in 2004: 2
Districts carried by Gore in 2000 and Bush in 2004: 17

Top 10 Best-Performing Bush Districts in 2004

District	Member	Bush %
TX 11	Conaway (R)	78.4
AL 6	Bachus (R)	78.0
TX 13	Thornberry (R)	77.8
TX 19	Neugebauer (R)	77.5
UT 3	Cannon (R)	77.1
GA 9	Deal (R)	76.6
NE 3	Smith (R)	74.9
UT 1	Bishop (R)	72.8
TX 8	Brady (R)	72.5
KS 1	Moran (R)	72.1

Top 10 Worst-Performing Bush Districts in 2004

District	Member	Bush %
NY 15	Rangel (D)	9.3
NY 16	Serrano (D)	10.1
PA 2	Fattah (D)	12.4
CA 9	Lee (D)	12.8
NY 10	Towns (D)	13.1
NY 11	Clarke (D)	13.1
CA 8	Pelosi (D)	14.1
NY 6	Meeks (D)	15.0
PA 1	Brady (D)	15.4
CA 33	Watson (D)	15.9
IL 2	Jackson, Jr. (D)	15.9

Note: Presidential performance by congressional district data reflects recently redrawn maps in Georgia and Texas.

CONGRESSIONAL LEADERSHIP

U.S. SENATE

Democrats

Majority Leader	Harry Reid (NV)
President Pro Tempore	Robert Byrd (WV)
Assistant Majority Leader	Richard Durbin (IL)
Conference Vice Chair/DSCC Chairman	Charles Schumer (NY)
Conference Secretary	Patty Murray (WA)
Policy Committee Chairman	Byron Dorgan (ND)
Steering and Outreach Committee Chair	Debbie Stabenow (MI)

Republicans

Minority Leader	Mitch McConnell (KY)
Assistant Minority Leader	Trent Lott (MS)
Conference Chairman	Jon Kyl (AZ)
Conference Vice Chairman	John Cornyn (TX)
Policy Committee Chairman	Kay Bailey Hutchison (TX)
NRSC Chairman	John Ensign (NV)

U.S. HOUSE OF REPRESENTATIVES

Democrats

Speaker of the House	Nancy Pelosi (CA-8)
Majority Leader	Steny Hoyer (MD-5)
Majority Whip	James Clyburn (SC-6)
Senior Chief Deputy Whip	John Lewis (GA-5)
Chief Deputy Whip	G.K. Butterfield (NC-1)
Chief Deputy Whip	Joseph Crowley (NY-7)
Chief Deputy Whip	Diana DeGette (CO-1)
Chief Deputy Whip	Ed Pastor (AZ-4)
Chief Deputy Whip	Jan Schakowsky (IL-9)
Chief Deputy Whip	John Tanner (TN-8)
Chief Deputy Whip	Maxine Waters (CA-35)
Chief Deputy Whip	Debbie Wasserman Schultz (FL-20)
Caucus Chairman	Rahm Emanuel (IL-5)
Caucus Vice Chairman	John Larson (CT-1)
Steering Committee Co-Chair	Rosa DeLauro (CT-3)
Steering Committee Co-Chair	George Miller (CA-7)
Chairman, Committee on Rules	Louise Slaughter (NY-28)
DCCC Chairman	Chris Van Hollen (MD-8)

Republicans

Minority Leader	John Boehner (OH-8)
Minority Whip	Roy Blunt (MO-7)
Chief Deputy Minority Whip	Eric Cantor (VA-7)
Conference Chairman	Adam Putnam (FL-12)
Conference Vice Chairman	Kay Granger (TX-12)
Conference Secretary	John Carter (TX-31)
Policy Committee Chairman	Thaddeus McCotter (MI-11)
NRCC Chairman	Tom Cole (OK-4)

Closest 2006 House Elections

		2006 %	2004 Bush % in District			2006 %	2004 Bush % in District
KY-2	Lewis (R)	55	65	MI-9	Knollenberg (R)	52	51
TX-10	McCaul (R)	55	62	NY-29	Kuhl (R)	51	56
MI-8	Rogers (R)	55	54	WA-8	Reichert (R)	51	48
IL-11	Weller (R)	55	53	IA-2	Loebsack (D)	51	44
IA-1	Braley (D)	55	46	IL-6	Roskam (R)	51	53
LA-3	Melancon (D)	55	58	NH-1	Shea-Porter (D)	51	51
NE-3	Smith (R)	55	75	VA-2	Drake (R)	51	58
CO-7	Perlmutter (D)	55	48	NY-19	Hall (D)	51	54
NJ-5	Garrett (R)	55	57	CT-4	Shays (R)	51	46
NE-2	Terry (R)	55	60	IL-8	Bean (D)	51	56
IN-3	Souder (R)	54	68	WI-8	Kagen (D)	51	55
TX-23	Rodriguez (D)	54	57	FL-22	Klein (D)	51	48
AZ-8	Giffords (D)	54	53	NY-25	Walsh (R)	51	48
MI-11	McCotter (R)	54	53	PA-6	Gerlach (R)	51	48
OR-5	Hooley (D)	54	50	KY-3	Yarmuth (D)	51	49
IN-2	Donnelly (D)	54	56	KS-2	Boyda (D)	51	59
NY-24	Arcuri (D)	54	53	GA-8	Marshall (D)	51	61
NC-11	Shuler (D)	54	57	OH-2	Schmidt (R)	50	64
IN-7	Carson (D)	54	42	AZ-5	Mitchell (D)	50	54
PA-3	English (R)	54	53	NV-2	Heller (R)	50	57
PA-15	Dent (R)	54	50	PA-8	Murphy (D)	50	48
IL-10	Kirk (R)	53	47	GA-12	Barrow (D)	50	50
CA-11	McNerney (D)	53	54	NM-1	Wilson (R)	50	48
VT-AL	Welch (D)	53	39	OH-15	Pryce (R)	50	50
CA-50	Bilbray (R)	53	55	NC-8	Hayes (R)	50	54
NY-20	Gillibrand (D)	53	54	FL-13	Buchanan (R)	50	56
PA-10	Carney (D)	53	60	MN-6	Bachmann (R)	50	57
FL-8	Keller (R)	53	55	CT-2	Courtney (D)	50	44
MN-1	Walz (D)	53	51	IN-9	Hill (D)	50	59
NH-2	Hodes (D)	53	47	ID-1	Sali (R)	50	69
OH-1	Chabot (R)	52	51	MI-7	Walberg (R)	50	54
NY-26	Reynolds (R)	52	55	FL-16	Mahoney (D)	50	54
PA-4	Altmire (D)	52	54	NJ-7	Ferguson (R)	49	53
IA-3	Boswell (D)	52	50	CA-4	Doolittle (R)	49	61
TX-22	Lampson (D)	52	64	NV-3	Porter (R)	48	50
AZ-1	Renzi (R)	52	54	WY-AL	Cubin (R)	48	69
KY-4	Davis (R)	52	63	CO-4	Musgrave (R)	46	58

Closest 2006 Senate Elections

Winner	2006 %	2004 Bush % in State
John Ensign (R-NV)	55	50
Ben Cardin (D-MD)	54	43
Sheldon Whitehouse (D-RI)	54	39
Robert Menendez (D-NJ)	53	46
Jon Kyl (R-AZ)	53	55
Bob Corker (R-TN)	51	57
Joe Lieberman (ID-CT)	50	44
Jim Webb (D-VA)	50	54
Claire McCaskill (D-MO)	50	53
Jon Tester (D-MT)	49	59

CONGRESSIONAL CLASS OF 2006

Senate		House
8 D 1 R 1I	Party breakdown	42 D 13 R
2	Number of women	10
0	Number of African-Americans	3
0	Number of Hispanics	2
1	Number with military service	6
6	Number who defeated an incumbent	24
3	Number with prior House service	3

New Senate Members

Sherrod Brown, D-Ohio
Ben Cardin, D-Md.
Bob Casey, D-Pa.
Bob Corker, R-Tenn.
Amy Klobuchar, D-Minn.

Claire McCaskill, D-Mo.
Bernie Sanders, I-Vt.
Jon Tester, D-Mont.
Jim Webb, D-Va.
Sheldon Whitehouse, D-R.I.

New House Members

Jason Altmire, D-Pa.
Michael Arcuri, D-N.Y.
Michele Bachmann, R-Minn.
Gus Bilirakis, R-Fla.
Nancy Boyda, D-Kan.
Bruce Braley, D-Iowa
Vern Buchanan, R-Fla.
Christopher Carney, D-Pa.
Kathy Castor, D-Fla.
Yvette Clarke, D-N.Y.
Steve Cohen, D-Tenn.
Joe Courtney, D-Conn.
David Davis, R-Tenn.
Joe Donnelly, D-Ind.
Keith Ellison, D-Minn.
Brad Ellsworth, D-Ind.
Mary Fallin, R-Okla.
Gabrielle Giffords, D-Ariz.
Kirsten Gillibrand, D-N.Y.
John Hall, D-N.Y.
Phil Hare, D-Ill.
Dean Heller, R-Nev.
Baron Hill, D-Ind.
Mazie Hirono, D-Hawaii
Paul Hodes, D-N.H.
Hank Johnson, D-Ga.
Jim Jordan, R-Ohio
Steve Kagen, D-Wis.

Ron Klein, D-Fla.
Doug Lamborn, R-Colo.
Nick Lampson, D-Texas
Dave Loebsack, D-Iowa
Tim Mahoney, D-Fla.
Kevin McCarthy, R-Calif.
Jerry McNerney, D-Calif.
Harry Mitchell, D-Ariz.
Chris Murphy, D-Conn.
Patrick Murphy, D-Pa.
Ed Perlmutter, D-Colo.
Ciro Rodriguez, D-Texas
Peter Roskam, R-Ill.
Bill Sali, R Idaho
John Sarbanes, D-Md.
Joe Sestak, D-Pa.
Carol Shea-Porter, D-N.H.
Heath Shuler, D-N.C.
Albio Sires, D-N.J.
Adrian Smith, R-Neb.
Zack Space, D-Ohio
Betty Sutton, D-Ohio
Tim Walberg, R-Mich.
Tim Walz, D-Minn.
Peter Welch, D-Vt.
Charlie Wilson, D-Ohio
John Yarmuth, D-Ky.

FILING DEADLINES

STATE	CONGRESSIONAL FILING DEADLINE	CONGRESSIONAL PRIMARY DATE	RUNOFF DATE	ELECTIONS DIVISION PHONE NUMBER
Alabama	April 4, 2008	June 3, 2008	July 15, 2008	334-242-7210
Alaska	June 2, 2008	August 26, 2008		907-465-4611
Arizona	June 4, 2008	September 2, 2008		602-542-8683
Arkansas	March 10, 2008	May 20, 2008	June 10, 2008	501-682-1010
California	March 7, 2008	June 3, 2008		916-657-2166
Colorado	TBD	August 12, 2008		303-894-2200
Connecticut	TBD	August 12, 2008		860-509-6100
Delaware	July 25, 2008	September 9, 2008		302-739-4277
Florida	June 20, 2008	August 26, 2008		850-245-6200
Georgia	May 2, 2008	July 15, 2008	August 5, 2008	404-656-2871
Hawaii	July 22, 2008	September 20, 2008		808-453-8683
Idaho	March 21, 2008	May 27, 2008		208-334-2852
Illinois	November 5, 2007	February 5, 2008		217-782-4141
Indiana	February 22, 2008	May 6, 2008		317-232-3939
Iowa	March 14, 2008	June 3, 2008		515-281-0145
Kansas	June 10, 2008	August 5, 2008		785-296-4561
Kentucky	January 29, 2008	May 20, 2008		502-564-3490
Louisiana	July 11, 2008	September 6, 2008	October 4, 2008	225-922-0900
Maine	March 15, 2008	June 10, 2008		207-624-7736
Maryland	December 3, 2007	February 12, 2008		410-269-2840
Massachusetts	May 6, 2008	September 16, 2008		617-727-2828
Michigan	May 13, 2008	August 5, 2008		517-373-2540
Minnesota	July 15, 2008	September 9, 2008		651-215-1440
Mississippi	January 11, 2008	March 11, 2008	April 1, 2008	601-576-2550
Missouri	March 25, 2008	August 5, 2008		573-751-2301
Montana	March 20, 2008	June 3, 2008		406-444-4732
Nebraska	March 1, 2008	May 13, 2008		402-471-2555
Nevada	May 16, 2008	August 12, 2008		775-684-5705
New Hampshire	June 13, 2008	September 9, 2008		603-271-3242
New Jersey	April 7, 2008	June 3, 2008		609-292-3760
New Mexico	February 12, 2008	June 3, 2008		505-827-3600
New York	July 10, 2008	September 9, 2008		518-473-5086
North Carolina	February 29, 2008	May 6, 2008	June 24, 2008	919-733-7173
North Dakota	April 11, 2008	June 10, 2008		701-328-4146
Ohio	January 4, 2008	March 4, 2008		614-466-2585
Oklahoma	June 4, 2008	July 29, 2008	August 26, 2008	405-521-2391
Oregon	March 11, 2008	May 20, 2008		503-986-1518
Pennsylvania	February 12, 2008	April 22, 2008		717-787-5280
Rhode Island	June 25, 2008	September 9, 2008		401-222-2345
South Carolina	March 31, 2008	June 10, 2008	June 24, 2008	803-734-9060
South Dakota	March 25, 2008	June 3, 2008	June 17, 2008	605-773-3537
Tennessee	April 3, 2008	August 7, 2008		615-741-7956
Texas	January 2, 2008	March 4, 2008	April 8, 2008	800-252-8683
Utah	March 17, 2008	June 24, 2008		801-538-1041
Vermont	July 21, 2008	September 9, 2008		800-439-8683
Virginia	April 16, 2008	June 10, 2008		804-864-8901
Washington	June 6, 2008	August 19, 2008		360-902-4180
West Virginia	January 26, 2008	May 13, 2008		304-558-6000
Wisconsin	July 8, 2008	September 9, 2008		608-266-8005
Wyoming	May 30, 2008	August 19, 2008		307-777-7186

TBD: To be determined

Compiled from information provided by state election offices; all dates and deadlines as of September 14, 2007.

PRESIDENTIAL NOMINATING EVENTS

2008 DATE	STATE AND EVENT	
January		
TBD	Iowa caucuses	
TBD	New Hampshire primary	
5	Wyoming caucuses (R)	
15	Michigan primary	
19	Nevada caucuses	South Carolina primary (R)
29	Florida primary	South Carolina primary (D)
February		
1	Maine caucuses (R)	
5	Alabama primary	Minnesota caucuses
	Alaska caucuses	Missouri primary
	Arizona primary	New Jersey primary
	Arkansas primary	New Mexico caucuses (D)
	California primary	New York primary
	Colorado caucuses	North Dakota caucuses
	Connecticut primary	Oklahoma primary
	Delaware primary	Tennessee primary
	Georgia primary	Utah primary
	Idaho caucuses (D)	West Virginia convention (R)
	Illinois primary	
9	Lousiana primary	Washington caucuses
	Nebraska caucuses (D)	
10	Maine caucuses (D)	
12	Maryland primary	Virginia primary
19	Hawaii caucuses (D)	Wisconsin primary
	Washington primary	
March		
4	Massachusetts primary	Texas primary
	Ohio primary	Vermont primary
	Rhode Island primary	
8	Wyoming caucuses (D)	
11	Mississippi primary	
April		
22	Pennsylvania primary	
May		
6	Indiana primary	North Carolina primary
13	Nebraska primary	West Virginia primary
20	Kentucky primary	Oregon primary
27	Idaho primary	
June		
3	Montana primary	South Dakota primary
	New Mexico primary	

All dates as of October 5, 2007.
TBD = To be determined
NOTES: Kansas will not hold a primary or caucuses in 2008; Hawaii Republican caucuses run from January 25 through February 5.

SENATE SEATS

2008 ELECTION CYCLE

Republicans (22)	Previous %	Democrats (12)	Previous %
Lamar Alexander (TN)	54%	Max Baucus (MT)	63%
Wayne Allard (CO)*	51%	Joseph Biden (DE)	58%
John Barrasso (WY)	#	Richard Durbin (IL)	60%
Saxby Chambliss (GA)	53%	Tom Harkin (IA)	54%
Thad Cochran (MS)	85%	Tim Johnson (SD)	50%
Norm Coleman (MN)	50%	John Kerry (MA)	80%
Susan Collins (ME)	58%	Mary Landrieu (LA)	52%
John Cornyn (TX)	55%	Frank Lautenberg (NJ)	54%
Larry Craig (ID)*	65%	Carl Levin (MI)	61%
Elizabeth Dole (NC)	54%	Mark Pryor (AR)	54%
Pete Domenici (NM)*	65%	Jack Reed (RI)	78%
Michael Enzi (WY)	73%	Jay Rockefeller (WV)	63%
Lindsey Graham (SC)	54%		
Chuck Hagel (NE)*	83%		
James Inhofe (OK)	57%		
Mitch McConnell (KY)	65%		
Pat Roberts (KS)	83%		
Jeff Sessions (AL)	59%		
Gordon Smith (OR)	56%		
Ted Stevens (AK)	78%		
John Sununu (NH)	51%		
John Warner (VA)*	83%		

*Will not seek reelection in 2008.
#Barrasso was appointed in June 2007 to fill the seat left vacant by the death of Sen. Craig Thomas.

2010 ELECTION CYCLE

Republicans (19)	Previous %	Democrats (15)	Previous %
Robert Bennett (UT)	69%	Evan Bayh (IN)	62%
Christopher (Kit) Bond (MO)	56%	Barbara Boxer (CA)	58%
Sam Brownback (KS)	69%	Christopher Dodd (CT)	66%
Jim Bunning (KY)	51%	Byron Dorgan (ND)	68%
Richard Burr (NC)	52%	Russell Feingold (WI)	55%
Tom Coburn (OK)	53%	Daniel Inouye (HI)	76%
Mike Crapo (ID)	99%	Patrick Leahy (VT)	71%
Jim DeMint (SC)	54%	Blanche Lincoln (AR)	56%
Charles Grassley (IA)	70%	Barbara Mikulski (MD)	65%
Judd Gregg (NH)	66%	Patty Murray (WA)	55%
Johnny Isakson (GA)	58%	Barack Obama (IL)	70%
Mel Martinez (FL)	49%	Harry Reid (NV)	61%
John McCain (AZ)	77%	Ken Salazar (CO)	51%
Lisa Murkowski (AK)	49%	Charles Schumer (NY)	71%
Richard Shelby (AL)	68%	Ron Wyden (OR)	63%
Arlen Specter (PA)	53%		
John Thune (SD)	51%		
David Vitter (LA)	51%		
George Voinovich (OH)	64%		

GOVERNORSHIPS

2007, 3 States

Kentucky (R)　　　　　　　Mississippi (R)
Louisiana (D)

2008, 11 States

Delaware (D)　　　　　　North Dakota (R)
Indiana (R)　　　　　　　　Utah (R)
Missouri (R)　　　　　　　Vermont (R)*
Montana (D)　　　　　　　Washington (D)
New Hampshire (D)*　　　West Virginia (D)
North Carolina (D)

2009, 2 States

New Jersey (D)　　　　　　**Virginia (D)**

2010, 36 States

Alabama **(R)**　　　　　　Minnesota (R)
Alaska (R)　　　　　　　　**Nebraska (R)**
Arizona (D)　　　　　　Nevada (R)
Arkansas (D)　　　　　　　New Hampshire (D)*
California (R)　　　　　**New Mexico (D)**
Colorado (D)　　　　　　　New York (D)
Connecticut (R)　　　　　Ohio (D)
Florida (R)　　　　　　　　**Oklahoma (D)**
Georgia (R)　　　　　　**Oregon (D)**
Hawaii (R)　　　　　　**Pennsylvania (D)**
Idaho (R)　　　　　　　　**Rhode Island (R)**
Illinois (D)　　　　　　　**South Carolina (R)**
Iowa (D)　　　　　　　　**South Dakota (R)**
Kansas (D)　　　　　　**Tennessee (D)**
Maine (D)　　　　　　　Texas (R)
Maryland (D)　　　　　　Vermont (R)*
Massachusetts (D)　　　　Wisconsin (D)
Michigan (D)　　　　　**Wyoming (D)**

Partisan control of governorships (as of September 14, 2007): 22 Republicans, 28 Democrats
*New Hampshire and Vermont have two-year terms. All others are four years.
Boldface indicates governors who cannot succeed themselves in the next election.

CAMPAIGN FINANCE

All data is derived from candidate and party reports as well as other official studies available from the Federal Election Commission. Individuals listed in italics were unsuccessful candidates in that election. Zip code analysis is based on research by The Center for Responsive Politics, as of June 4, 2007.

Top Donor Zip Codes for 2005-2006 Election Cycle

Rank	Zip Code	Location	Total Amount	Democrat	Republican
1.	10021	New York, NY	$16,165,587	74%	26%
2.	10022	New York, NY	$ 8,132,153	73%	27%
3.	10028	New York, NY	$ 5,334,990	78%	22%
4.	10024	New York, NY	$ 5,037,223	87%	13%
5.	20007	Washington, DC	$ 4,930,720	73%	27%
6.	22101	McLean, VA	$ 4,824,791	34%	66%
7.	10128	New York, NY	$ 4,764,844	80%	20%
8.	10023	New York, NY	$ 4,548,179	87%	13%
9.	20854	Potomac, MD	$ 4,541,553	55%	45%
10.	10019	New York, NY	$ 4,507,850	75%	25%
11.	90210	Beverly Hills, CA	$ 4,008,714	68%	32%
12.	20815	Chevy Chase, MD	$ 3,978,964	73%	27%
13.	85253	Paradise Valley, AZ	$ 3,933,766	26%	74%
14.	20016	Washington, DC	$ 3,813,568	58%	42%
15.	33480	Palm Beach, FL	$ 3,717,907	37%	63%
16.	20008	Washington, DC	$ 3,499,353	72%	28%
17.	06831	Greenwich, CT	$ 3,463,513	53%	47%
18.	20036	Washington, DC	$ 3,405,611	62%	38%
19.	10017	New York, NY	$ 3,362,139	69%	31%
20.	60093	Winnetka, IL	$ 3,340,457	55%	45%
21.	75205	Dallas, TX	$ 3,140,541	28%	72%
22.	22102	McLean, VA	$ 3,064,155	49%	51%
23.	06830	Greenwich, CT	$ 3,014,479	47%	53%
24.	22207	Arlington, VA	$ 2,988,236	48%	52%
25.	22314	Alexandria, VA	$ 2,965,257	46%	54%

U.S. SENATE

The following charts show the 15 top 2006 Senate candidates in terms of the highest total net receipts, net expenditures, political action committee (PAC) contributions, individual contributions, cash-on-hand and debts owed during the 2005-2006 election cycle as of August 7, 2007.

2006 Senate: Top Raisers

1. Hillary Rodham Clinton (D-NY) $39,833,526
2. *Rick Santorum (R-PA)* $24,796,718
3. *Ned Lamont (D-CT)* $20,580,703
4. Joe Lieberman (ID-CT) $18,996,689
5. Bob Casey (D-PA) $17,941,395
6. Bob Corker (R-TN) $16,831,072
7. Bill Nelson (D-FL) $15,355,490
8. *George Allen (R-VA)* $14,994,264
9. *Jim Pederson (D-AZ)* $14,709,628
10. *Harold Ford (D-TN)* $14,306,467
11. Jon Kyl (R-AZ) $14,123,880
12. *Jim Talent (R-MO)* $14,098,563
13. Maria Cantwell (D-WA) $13,725,773
14. *Pete Ricketts (R-NE)* $13,424,896
15. *Mike DeWine (R-OH)* $12,094,898

2006 Senate: Top Spenders

1. Hillary Rodham Clinton (D-NY) $34,358,255
2. *Rick Santorum (R-PA)* $25,832,567
3. *Ned Lamont (D-CT)* $20,557,217
4. Bob Corker (R-TN) $18,565,935
5. Bob Casey (D-PA) $17,592,210
6. Joe Lieberman (ID-CT) $17,210,710
7. Bill Nelson (D-FL) $16,116,224
8. *George Allen (R-VA)* $16,071,564
9. Jon Kyl (R-AZ) $15,571,727
10. *Harold Ford (D-TN)* $15,302,455
11. *Jim Pederson (D-AZ)* $14,709,241
12. *Jim Talent (R-MO)* $14,340,762
13. *Mike DeWine (R-OH)* $14,161,402
14. Maria Cantwell (D-WA) $14,013,932
15. *Pete Ricketts (R-NE)* $13,417,690

2006 Senate: Top PAC Recipients

1. *Rick Santorum (R-PA)* — $4,007,539
2. *Jim Talent (R-MO)* — $3,472,930
3. *Mike DeWine (R-OH)* — $2,906,920
4. *George Allen (R-VA)* — $2,843,031
5. Jon Kyl (R-AZ) — $2,802,011
6. *Conrad Burns (R-MT)* — $2,586,600
7. Ben Nelson (D-NE) — $2,527,378
8. Joe Lieberman (ID-CT) — $2,324,109
9. Robert Menendez (D-NJ) — $2,151,084
10. *Mark Kennedy (R-MN)* — $2,135,457
11. Kent Conrad (D-ND) — $2,033,240
12. John Ensign (R-NV) — $1,851,877
13. Bill Nelson (D-FL) — $1,804,712
14. Orrin Hatch (R-UT) — $1,765,142
15. Jeff Bingaman (D-NM) — $1,609,084

2006 Senate: Top Cash-On-Hand

1. Hillary Rodham Clinton (D-NY) — $11,021,087
2. Kay Bailey Hutchison (R-TX) — $7,317,742
3. Edward Kennedy (D-MA) — $6,588,065
4. Dianne Feinstein (D-CA) — $3,220,232
5. Orrin Hatch (R-UT) — $2,345,102
6. Joe Lieberman (ID-CT) — $2,215,537
7. Richard Lugar (R-IN) — $2,110,478
8. Kent Conrad (D-ND) — $2,015,853
9. Trent Lott (R-MS) — $1,495,343
10. Bill Nelson (D-FL) — $1,316,224
11. John Ensign (R-NV) — $1,302,036
12. Thomas Carper (D-DE) — $1,296,077
13. Olympia Snowe (R-ME) — $1,077,665
14. Jeff Bingaman (D-NM) — $1,066,204
15. Craig Thomas (R-WY) — $617,077

2006 Senate: Top Individual Contributions

1. Hillary Rodham Clinton (D-NY) — $37,136,715
2. *Rick Santorum (R-PA)* — $19,246,928
3. Joe Lieberman (ID-CT) — $16,554,248
4. Bob Casey (D-PA) — $16,122,113
5. Maria Cantwell (D-WA) — $12,915,252
6. Bill Nelson (D-FL) — $12,690,628
7. *Harold Ford (D-TN)* — $12,321,864
8. Jon Kyl (R-AZ) — $10,967,596
9. *George Allen (R-VA)* — $10,660,532
10. Bob Corker (R-TN) — $10,452,658
11. Claire McCaskill (D-MO) — $9,806,337
12. Robert Menendez (D-NJ) — $9,394,154
13. *Jim Talent (R-MO)* — $8,947,400
14. *Mike DeWine (R-OH)* — $8,169,121
15. Jim Webb (D-VA) — $7,675,639

2006 Senate: Top Debts Owed

1. *Pete Ricketts (R-NE)* — $7,575,000
2. Bob Corker (R-TN) — $5,911,767
3. *John Raese (R-WV)* — $2,715,069
4. *Katherine Harris (R-FL)* — $2,575,000
5. *Jim Pederson (D-AZ)* — $2,533,729
6. Maria Cantwell (D-WA) — $2,350,098
7. *Edward Cox (R-NY)* — *$1,272,000*
8. *Lincoln Chafee (R-RI)* — $1,128,734
9. *Jeanine Pirro (R-NY)* — $854,194
10. *John Spencer (R-NY)* — $419,058
11. *Matt Brown (D-RI)* — $417,245
12. *Keith Butler (R-MI)* — $400,000
13. Sherrod Brown (D-OH) — $366,136
14. *Michael Steele (R-MD)* — $349,528
15. Claire McCaskill (D-MO) — $339,610

U.S. HOUSE OF REPRESENTATIVES

The following charts show the 25 top 2006 House candidates in terms of the highest total net receipts, net expenditures, political action committee (PAC) contributions, individual contributions, cash-on-hand and debts owed during the 2005-2006 election cycle as of August 7, 2007.

2006 House: Top Raisers

1. Vern Buchanan (R-FL) — $8,123,186
2. *David McSweeney (R-IL)* — $5,140,197
3. Dennis Hastert (R-IL) — $5,064,847
4. Heather Wilson (R-NM) — $4,904,809
5. Clay Shaw (R-FL) — $4,707,676
6. *Tammy Duckworth (D-IL)* — $4,563,409
7. *Richard Pombo (R-CA)* — $4,547,779
8. *Charles Taylor (R-NC)* — $4,397,723
9. Tom Reynolds (R-NY) — $4,337,295
10. Melissa Bean (D-IL) — $4,337,073
11. Deborah Pryce (R-OH) — $4,278,439
12. Geoff Davis (R-KY) — $4,198,788
13. Ron Klein (D-FL) — $4,186,909
14. *Lois Murphy (D-PA)* — $4,120,102
15. *Nancy Johnson (R-CT)* — $4,055,866
16. Christopher Shays (R-CT) — $3,827,216
17. Nick Lampson (D-TX) — $3,730,044
18. *Francine Busby (D-CA)* — $3,636,717
19. *Henry Bonilla (R-TX)* — $3,600,091
20. Peter Roskam (R-IL) — $3,443,597
21. *Anne Northup (R-KY)* — $3,397,906
22. *Patricia Madrid (D-NM)* — $3,396,045
23. Jim Gerlach (R-PA) — $3,353,282
24. Eric Cantor (R-VA) — $3,310,828
25. Joe Sestak (D-PA) — $3,285,954

2006 House: Top Spenders

1. Vern Buchanan (R-FL) — $8,112,752
2. Tom Reynolds (R-NY) — $5,275,474
3. *Clay Shaw (R-FL)* — $5,226,161
4. Dennis Hastert (R-IL) — $5,206,105
5. *David McSweeney (R-IL)* — $5,140,109
6. *Nancy Johnson (R-CT)* — $5,095,844
7. Heather Wilson (R-NM) — $4,906,596
8. Deborah Pryce (R-OH) — $4,696,772
9. *Richard Pombo (R-CA)* — $4,629,983
10. *Tammy Duckworth (D-IL)* — $4,556,495
11. *Charles Taylor (R-NC)* — $4,425,482
12. Melissa Bean (D-IL) — $4,299,589
13. Geoff Davis (R-KY) — $4,255,379
14. Ron Klein (D-FL) — $4,185,922
15. *Lois Murphy (D-PA)* — $4,097,663
16. *Henry Bonilla (R-TX)* — $3,821,285
17. Christopher Shays (R-CT) — $3,804,187
18. *Francine Busby (D-CA)* — $3,596,185
19. Nick Lampson (D-TX) — $3,578,097
20. Bobby Jindal (R-LA) — $3,573,550
21. Mark Kirk (R-IL) — $3,512,971
22. Eric Cantor (R-VA) — $3,499,247
23. Jim Gerlach (R-PA) — $3,492,402
24. *John Sweeney (R-NY)* — $3,425,841
25. *Anne Northup (R-KY)* — $3,421,281

2006 House: Top PAC Recipients

1.	Deborah Pryce (R-OH)	$2,437,580
2.	Dennis Hastert (R-IL)	$2,400,128
3.	*Nancy Johnson (R-CT)*	$2,211,881
4.	John Boehner (R-OH)	$1,936,911
5.	Roy Blunt (R-MO)	$1,880,294
6.	Heather Wilson (R-NM)	$1,871,677
7.	Joe Barton (R-TX)	$1,826,166
8.	*Richard Pombo (R-CA)*	$1,801,011
9.	Tom Reynolds (R-NY)	$1,777,245
10.	Jim McCrery (R-LA)	$1,734,600
11.	*Henry Bonilla (R-TX)*	$1,733,012
12.	Jim Gerlach (R-PA)	$1,717,641
13.	Steny Hoyer (D-MD)	$1,705,074
14.	Eric Cantor (R-VA)	$1,702,925
15.	*Clay Shaw (R-FL)*	$1,676,114
16.	Geoff Davis (R-KY)	$1,518,827
17.	Melissa Bean (D-IL)	$1,498,972
18.	Chet Edwards (D-TX)	$1,493,323
19.	*Chris Chocola (R-IN)*	*$1,483,299*
20.	*Mike Fitzpatrick (R-PA)*	*$1,471,649*
21.	*Rob Simmons (R-CT)*	$1,468,491
22.	*John Sweeney (R-NY)*	$1,405,648
23.	*J.D. Hayworth (R-AZ)*	$1,402,368
24.	Steve Chabot (R-OH)	$1,380,081
25.	John Spratt (D-SC)	$1,326,864

2006 House: Top Cash-On-Hand

1.	Martin Meehan (D-MA)	$5,119,677
2.	Frank Pallone (D-NJ)	$2,409,251
3.	Edward Markey (D-MA)	$2,393,515
4.	Cliff Stearns (R-FL)	$2,258,097
5.	David Dreier (R-CA)	$2,227,487
6.	Robert Andrews (D-NJ)	$2,153,336
7.	Bill Delahunt (D-MA)	$2,033,691
8.	Lloyd Doggett (D-TX)	$2,015,867
9.	Don Young (R-AK)	$1,858,542
10.	Joe Barton (R-TX)	$1,818,345
11.	Ed Royce (R-CA)	$1,726,822
12.	Steven Rothman (D-NJ)	$1,710,579
13.	*Mark Foley (R-FL)*	$1,677,548
14.	Bud Cramer (D-AL)	$1,628,862
15.	Chris Van Hollen (D-MD)	$1,480,939
16.	Jerry Costello (D-IL)	$1,431,138
17.	John Duncan (R-TN)	$1,389,600
18.	Brad Sherman (D-CA)	$1,388,845
19.	Adam Schiff (D-CA)	$1,376,605
20.	Tom Lantos (D-CA)	$1,367,651
21.	Richard Neal (D-MA)	$1,351,434
22.	Frank LoBiondo (R-NJ)	$1,332,006
23.	Ileana Ros-Lehtinen (R-FL)	$1,274,416
24.	Mark Udall (D-CO)	$1,262,370
25.	Paul Ryan (R-WI)	$1,258,377

2006 House: Top Individual Contributions

1.	*Tammy Duckworth (D-IL)*	$3,716,121
2.	Ron Klein (D-FL)	$3,468,070
3.	*Lois Murphy (D-PA)*	$3,397,372
4.	*Francine Busby (D-CA)*	$2,980,780
5.	*Patricia Madrid (D-NM)*	$2,725,745
6.	*Clay Shaw (R-FL)*	$2,701,783
7.	Melissa Bean (D-IL)	$2,692,227
8.	Joe Sestak (D-PA)	$2,663,352
9.	Heather Wilson (R-NM)	$2,654,938
10.	Christopher Shays (R-CT)	$2,640,745
11.	Dennis Hastert (R-IL)	$2,610,059
12.	Nick Lampson (D-TX)	$2,609,396
13.	*Patty Wetterling (D-MN)*	$2,569,246
14.	*Richard Pombo (R-CA)*	$2,496,312
15.	*Diane Farrell (D-CT)*	$2,492,593
16.	Mark Kirk (R-IL)	$2,473,576
17.	Tom Reynolds (R-NY)	$2,452,778
18.	*Darcy Burner (D-WA)*	$2,423,984
19.	Vern Buchanan (R-FL)	$2,227,217
20.	*Mary Jo Kilroy (D-OH)*	$2,226,989
21.	Allyson Schwartz (D-PA)	$2,188,918
22.	Ed Perlmutter (D-CO)	$2,112,652
23.	Geoff Davis (R-KY)	$2,110,470
24.	*Christine Jennings (D-FL)*	$2,109,582
25.	Marilyn Musgrave (R-CO)	$2,098,670

2006 House: Top Debts Owed

1.	*Jack Davis (D-NY)*	$2,505,376
2.	Vern Buchanan (R-FL)	$1,612,274
3.	*Mike Erickson (R-OR)*	$1,567,605
4.	*Frank Guglielmi (R-OH)*	$1,562,850
5.	*Charles Taylor (R-NC)*	$1,506,785
6.	Darrell Issa (R-CA)	$1,500,000
7.	*Bob Shamansky (D-OH)*	$1,400,000
8.	*David McSweeney (R-IL)*	$1,284,967
9.	*Mike Sodrel (R-IN)*	$1,243,712
10.	*Dave Magnum (R-WI)*	$890,391
11.	John Yarmuth (D-KY)	$708,127
12.	*Lukin Gilliland (D-TX)*	$700,000
13.	*Chris Chocola (R-IN)*	$661,096
14.	*John Jacob (R-UT)*	$616,549
15.	*LaVar Christensen (R-UT)*	$590,599
16.	Tim Mahoney (D-FL)	$503,162
17.	*Capri Cafaro (D-OH)*	$500,538
18.	Rick Renzi (R-AZ)	$490,322
19.	Steve Kagen (D-WI)	$482,500
20.	*Tan Nguyen (R-CA)*	$472,000
21.	Rahm Emanuel (D-IL)	$463,562
22.	*Mike Whalen (R-IA)*	$448,950
23.	Rodney Frelinghuysen (R-NJ)	$441,079
24.	*Bob McEwen (R-OH)*	$425,400
25.	*Francisco (Quico) Canseco (R-TX)*	$402,100

SENATE COMMITTEE LEADERSHIP

Aging (Special)
Herb Kohl (WI)
RMM: Gordon Smith (OR)

Agriculture, Nutrition, & Forestry
Tom Harkin (IA)
RMM: Saxby Chambliss (GA)

Appropriations
Robert Byrd (WV)
RMM: Thad Cochran (MS)

Armed Services
Carl Levin (MI)
RMM: John McCain (AZ)

Banking, Housing, & Urban Affairs
Christopher Dodd (CT)
RMM: Richard Shelby (AL)

Budget
Kent Conrad (ND)
RMM: Judd Gregg (NH)

Commerce, Science & Transportation
Daniel Inouye (HI)
RMM: Ted Stevens (AK)

Energy & Natural Resources
Jeff Bingaman (NM)
RMM: Pete Domenici (NM)

Environment & Public Works
Barbara Boxer (CA)
RMM: James Inhofe (OK)

Ethics (Select)
Barbara Boxer (CA)*
RMM: John Cornyn (TX)

Finance
Max Baucus (MT)
RMM: Charles Grassley (IA)

Foreign Relations
Joseph Biden (DE)
RMM: Richard Lugar (IN)

Health, Education, Labor, & Pensions
Edward Kennedy (MA)
RMM: Mike Enzi (WY)

Homeland Security & Governmental Affairs
Joe Lieberman (CT)
RMM: Susan Collins (ME)

Indian Affairs
Byron Dorgan (ND)
RMM: Lisa Murkowski (AK)

Intelligence (Permanent Select)
Jay Rockefeller (WV)
RMM: Christopher (Kit) Bond (MO)

Judiciary
Patrick Leahy (VT)
RMM: Arlen Specter (PA)

Rules & Administration
Dianne Feinstein (CA)
RMM: Robert Bennett (UT)

Small Business & Entrepreneurship
John Kerry (MA)
RMM: Olympia Snowe (ME)

Veterans' Affairs
Daniel Akaka (HI)
RMM: Richard Burr (NC)+

Committee leadership information as of September 11, 2007.
Committee chairmen are noted in boldface
RMM: Ranking Minority Member
acting chair   *+ temporary RMM*

SENATE COMMITTEES

Aging (Special)
aging.senate.gov
Majority (D 11): Kohl (WI), Chmn.; Wyden (OR), Lincoln (AR), Bayh (IN), Carper (DE), Nelson (FL), Clinton (NY), Salazar (CO), Casey (PA), McCaskill (MO), Whitehouse (RI)
Minority (R 10): Smith (OR), RMM; Shelby (AL), Collins (ME), Martinez (FL), Craig (ID), Dole (NC), Coleman (MN), Vitter (LA), Corker (TN), Specter (PA)

NO SUBCOMMITTEES

Agriculture, Nutrition & Forestry
328A Russell
agriculture.senate.gov
202–224–2035
Majority (D 11): Harkin (IA), Chmn.; Leahy (VT), Conrad (ND), Baucus (MT), Lincoln (AR), Stabenow (MI), Nelson (NE), Salazar (CO), Brown (OH), Casey (PA), Klobuchar (MN)
Minority (R 10): Chambliss (GA), RMM; Lugar (IN), Cochran (MS), McConnell (KY), Roberts (KS), Graham (SC), Coleman (MN), Crapo (ID), Thune (SD), Grassley (IA)

SUBCOMMITTEES

Domestic & Foreign Marketing, Inspection, & Plant & Animal Health
Majority (D 6): Baucus, Chmn.; Conrad, Stabenow, Nelson, Salazar, Casey
Minority (R 5): Graham, RMM; McConnell, Roberts, Crapo, Thune

Energy, Science & Technology
Majority (D 6): Conrad, Chmn.; Nelson, Salazar, Brown, Casey, Klobuchar
Minority (R 5): Thune, RMM; Lugar, Graham, Coleman, Grassley

Nutrition and Food Assistance, Sustainable and Organic Agriculture & General Legislation
Majority (D 6): Leahy, Chmn.; Lincoln, Stabenow, Brown, Casey, Klobuchar
Minority (R 5): Coleman, RMM; Lugar, Cochran, McConnell, Crapo

Production, Income Protection & Price Support
Majority (D 6): Lincoln, Chmn.; Leahy, Conrad, Baucus, Brown, Klobuchar
Minority (R 5): Roberts, RMM; Cochran, Coleman, Thune, Grassley

Rural Revitalization, Conservation, Forestry & Credit
Majority (D 6): Stabenow, Chmn.; Leahy, Baucus, Lincoln, Nelson, Salazar
Minority (R 5): Crapo, RMM; Lugar, Cochran, McConnell, Graham

Appropriations
S-131 The Capitol
appropriations.senate.gov
202–224–7363
Majority (D 15): Byrd (WV), Chmn.; Inouye (HI), Leahy (VT), Harkin (IA), Mikulski (MD), Kohl (WI), Murray (WA), Dorgan (ND), Feinstein (CA), Durbin (IL), Johnson (SD), Landrieu (LA), Reed (RI), Lautenberg (NJ), Nelson (NE)
Minority (R 14): Cochran (MS), RMM; Stevens (AK), Specter (PA), Domenici (NM), Bond (MO), McConnell (KY), Shelby (AL), Gregg (NH), Bennett (UT), Craig (ID), Hutchison (TX), Brownback (KS), Allard (CO), Alexander (TN)

SUBCOMMITTEES

Agriculture, Rural Development, Food and Drug Administration & Related Agencies
Majority (D 8): Kohl, Chmn.; Harkin, Dorgan, Feinstein, Durbin, Johnson, Nelson, Reed
Minority (R 7): Bennett, RMM; Cochran, Specter, Bond, McConnell, Craig, Brownback

Commerce, Justice, Science & Related Agencies
Majority (D 9): Mikulski, Chmn.; Inouye, Leahy, Kohl, Harkin, Dorgan, Feinstein, Reed, Lautenberg
Minority (R 8): Shelby, RMM; Gregg, Stevens, Domenici, McConnell, Hutchison, Brownback, Alexander

Defense
Majority (D 10): Inouye, Chmn.; Byrd, Leahy, Harkin, Dorgan, Durbin, Feinstein, Mikulski, Kohl, Murray
Minority (R 9): Stevens, RMM; Cochran, Specter, Domenici, Bond, McConnell, Shelby, Gregg, Hutchison

Energy & Water Development
Majority (D 9): Dorgan, Chmn.; Byrd, Murray, Feinstein, Johnson, Landrieu, Inouye, Reed, Lautenberg
Minority (R 8): Domenici, RMM; Cochran, McConnell, Bennett, Craig, Bond, Hutchison, Allard

Financial Services & General Government
Majority (D 5): Durbin, Chmn.; Murray, Landrieu, Lautenberg, Nelson
Minority (R 4): Brownback, RMM; Bond, Shelby, Allard

Homeland Security
Majority (D 9): Byrd, Chmn.; Inouye, Leahy, Mikulski, Kohl, Murray, Landrieu, Lautenberg, Nelson
Minority (R 8): Cochran, RMM; Gregg, Stevens, Specter, Domenici, Shelby, Craig, Alexander

Interior, Environment & Related Agencies
Majority (D 9): Feinstein, Chmn.; Byrd, Leahy, Dorgan, Mikulski, Kohl, Johnson, Reed, Nelson
Minority (R 8): Craig, Stevens, Cochran, Domenici, Bennett, Gregg, Allard, Alexander

Labor, Health and Human Services, Education & Related Agencies
Majority (D 8): Harkin, Chmn.; Inouye, Kohl, Murray, Landrieu, Durbin, Reed, Lautenberg
Minority (R 7): Specter, RMM; Cochran, Gregg, Craig, Hutchison, Stevens, Shelby

Legislative Branch
Majority (D 3): Landrieu, Chmn.; Durbin, Nelson
Minority (R 2): Allard, RMM; Alexander

Military Construction, Veterans Affairs & Related Agencies
Majority (D 7): Johnson, Chmn.; Inouye, Landrieu, Byrd, Murray, Reed, Nelson
Minority (R 6): Hutchison, RMM; Craig, Brownback, Allard, McConnell, Bennett

State, Foreign Operations & Related Programs
Majority (D 8): Leahy, Chmn.; Inouye, Harkin, Mikulski, Durbin, Johnson, Landrieu, Reed
Minority (R 7): Gregg, RMM; McConnell, Specter, Bennett, Bond, Brownback, Alexander

Transportation, Housing and Urban Development & Related Agencies
Majority (D 11): Murray, Chmn.; Byrd, Mikulski, Kohl, Durbin, Dorgan, Leahy, Harkin, Feinstein, Johnson, Lautenberg
Minority (R 10): Bond, RMM; Shelby, Specter, Bennett, Hutchison, Brownback, Stevens, Domenici, Alexander, Allard

Armed Services
armed-services.senate.gov

228 Russell
202–224–3871

Majority (D 13): Levin (MI), Chmn.; Kennedy (MA), Byrd (WV), Lieberman (CT), Reed (RI), Akaka (HI), Nelson (FL), Nelson (NE), Bayh (IN), Clinton (NY), Pryor (AR), Webb (VA), McCaskill (MO)
Minority (R 12): McCain (AZ), RMM; Warner (VA), Inhofe (OK), Sessions (AL), Collins (ME), Chambliss (GA), Graham (SC), Dole (NC), Cornyn (TX), Thune (SD), Martinez (FL), Corker (TN)

SUBCOMMITTEES

Airland
Majority (D 7): Lieberman, Chmn.; Akaka, Bayh, Clinton, Pryor, Webb, McCaskill
Minority (R 6): Cornyn, RMM; Warner, Inhofe, Sessions, Chambliss, Corker

Emerging Threats & Capabilities
Majority (D 7): Reed, Chmn.; Kennedy, Byrd, Nelson (FL), Nelson (NE), Bayh, Clinton
Minority (R 6): Dole, RMM; Warner, Collins, Graham, Cornyn, Martinez

Personnel
Majority (D 5): Nelson (NE), Chmn.; Kennedy, Lieberman, Webb, McCaskill
Minority (R 4): Graham, RMM; Collins, Chambliss, Dole

Readiness & Management Support
Majority (D 6): Akaka, Chmn.; Byrd, Bayh, Clinton, Pryor, McCaskill
Minority (R 5): Thune, RMM; Inhofe, Chambliss, Dole, Corker

Seapower
Majority (D 6): Kennedy, Chmn.; Lieberman, Reed, Akaka, Nelson (FL), Webb
Minority (R 5): Martinez, RMM; Warner, Sessions, Collins, Cornyn

Strategic Forces
Majority (D 5): Nelson (FL), Chmn.; Byrd, Reed, Nelson (NE), Pryor
Minority (R 4): Sessions, RMM; Inhofe, Graham, Thune

Banking, Housing & Urban Affairs
banking.senate.gov

534 Dirksen
202–224–7391

Majority (D 11): Dodd (CT), Chmn.; Johnson (SD), Reed (RI), Schumer (NY), Bayh (IN), Carper (DE), Menendez (NJ), Akaka (HI), Brown (OH), Casey (PA), Tester (MT)
Minority (R 10): Shelby (AL), RMM; Bennett (UT), Allard (CO), Enzi (WY), Hagel (NE), Bunning (KY), Crapo (ID), Sununu (NH), Dole (NC), Martinez (FL)

SUBCOMMITTEES

Economic Policy
Majority (D 2): Carper, Chmn.; Brown
Minority (R 1): Bunning, RMM

Financial Institutions
Majority (D 8): Johnson, Chmn.; Tester, Menendez, Akaka, Reed, Schumer, Bayh, Carper
Minority (R 7): Hagel, RMM; Bennett, Allard, Sununu, Bunning, Crapo, Dole

Housing, Transportation & Community Development
Majority (D 8): Schumer, Chmn.; Akaka, Casey, Reed, Carper, Brown, Tester, Menendez
Minority (R 7): Crapo, RMM; Dole, Martinez, Allard, Enzi, Hagel, Sununu

Securities, Insurance & Investment
Majority (D 8): Reed, Chmn.; Menendez, Johnson, Schumer, Bayh, Casey, Akaka, Tester
Minority (R 7): Allard, RMM; Enzi, Sununu, Bennett, Hagel, Bunning, Crapo

Security & International Trade & Finance
Majority (D 5): Bayh, Chmn.; Brown, Johnson, Casey, Dodd
Minority (R 4): Martinez, RMM; Enzi, Dole, Bennett

Budget
budget.senate.gov

624 Dirksen
202-224-0642

Majority (D 12): Conrad (ND), Murray (WA), Wyden (OR), Feingold (WI), Byrd (WV), Nelson (FL), Stabenow (MI), Menendez (NJ), Lautenberg (NJ), Cardin (MD), Sanders (VT), Whitehouse (RI)

Minority (R 11): Gregg (NH), Domenici (NM), Grassley (IA), Allard (CO), Enzi (WY), Sessions (AL), Bunning (KY), Crapo (ID), Ensign (NV), Cornyn (TX), Graham (SC)

NO SUBCOMMITTEES

Commerce, Science & Transportation
commerce.senate.gov

508 Dirksen
202-224-5115

Majority (D 12): Inouye (HI), Chmn.; Rockefeller (WV), Kerry (MA), Dorgan (ND), Boxer (CA), Nelson (FL), Cantwell (WA), Lautenberg (NJ), Pryor (AR), Carper (DE), McCaskill (MO), Klobuchar (MN)

Minority (R 11): Stevens (AK), V. Chmn.; McCain (AZ), Lott (MS), Hutchison (TX), Snowe (ME), Smith (OR), Ensign (NV), Sununu (NH), DeMint (SC), Vitter (LA), Thune (SD)

SUBCOMMITTEES

Aviation Operations, Safety & Security

Majority (D 11): Rockefeller, Chmn.; Kerry, Dorgan, Boxer, Nelson, Cantwell, Lautenberg, Pryor, Carper, McCaskill, Klobuchar

Minority (R 10): Lott, RMM; McCain, Hutchison, Snowe, Smith, Ensign, Sununu, DeMint, Vitter, Thune

Consumer Affairs, Insurance & Automotive Safety

Majority (D 8): Pryor, Chmn.; Rockefeller, Nelson, Cantwell, Lautenberg, Carper, McCaskill, Klobuchar

Minority (R 7): Sununu, RMM; McCain, Lott, Snowe, Smith, Vitter, Thune

Interstate Commerce, Trade & Tourism

Majority (D 7): Dorgan, Chmn.; Rockefeller, Kerry, Boxer, Cantwell, Pryor, McCaskill

Minority (R 6): DeMint, RMM; McCain, Snowe, Smith, Ensign, Sununu

Oceans, Atmosphere, Fisheries & Coast Guard

Majority (D 7): Cantwell, Chmn.; Kerry, Boxer, Nelson, Lautenberg, Carper, Klobuchar

Minority (R 6): Snowe, RMM; Lott, Smith, Sununu, DeMint, Vitter

Science, Technology & Innovation

Majority (D 8): Kerry, Chmn.; Rockefeller, Dorgan, Boxer, Cantwell, Pryor, McCaskill, Klobuchar

Minority (R 7): Ensign, RMM; McCain, Hutchison, Smith, Sununu, DeMint, Thune

Space, Aeronautics & Related Sciences

Majority (D 4): Nelson, Chmn.; Kerry, Dorgan, Pryor

Minority (R 3): Hutchison, RMM; Lott, Sununu

Surface Transportation & Merchant Marine Infrastructure, Safety & Security

Majority (D 9): Lautenberg, Chmn.; Rockefeller, Kerry, Dorgan, Cantwell, Pryor, Carper, McCaskill, Klobuchar

Minority (R 8): Smith, RMM; McCain, Lott, Hutchison, Snowe, DeMint, Vitter, Thune

Energy & Natural Resources
energy.senate.gov

304 Dirksen
202-224-4971

Majority (D 12): Bingaman (NM), Chmn.; Akaka (HI), Dorgan (ND), Wyden (OR), Johnson (SD), Landrieu (LA), Cantwell (WA), Salazar (CO), Menendez (NJ), Lincoln (AR), Sanders (VT), Tester (MT)

Minority (R 11): Domenici (NM), RMM; Craig (ID), Murkowski (AK), Burr (NC), DeMint (SC), Corker (TN), Sessions (AL), Bunning (KY), Smith (OR), Martinez (FL), Barrasso (WY)

SUBCOMMITTEES

Energy

Majority (D 9): Dorgan, Chmn.; Akaka, Wyden, Johnson, Landrieu, Cantwell, Menendez, Sanders, Tester

Minority (R 8): Murkowski, RMM; Craig, Burr, DeMint, Corker, Sessions, Bunning, Martinez

National Parks

Majority (D 8): Akaka, Chmn.; Dorgan, Landrieu, Salazar, Menendez, Lincoln, Sanders, Tester

Minority (R 7): Burr, RMM; Murkowski, Corker, Barrasso, Sessions, Smith, Martinez

Public Lands & Forests

Majority (D 9): Wyden, Chmn.; Akaka, Johnson, Landrieu, Cantwell, Salazar, Menendez, Lincoln, Sanders

Minority (R 8): Craig, Murkowski, Burr, DeMint, Barrasso, Sessions, Smith, Bunning

Water & Power

Majority (D 7): Johnson, Chmn.; Dorgan, Wyden, Cantwell, Salazar, Lincoln, Tester

Minority (R 6): Corker, RMM; Craig, DeMint, Barrasso, Smith, Bunning

Environment & Public Works
epw.senate.gov

410 Dirksen
202-224-8832

Majority (D 10): Boxer (CA), Chmn.; Baucus (MT), Lieberman (CT), Carper (DE), Clinton (NY), Lautenberg (NJ), Cardin (MD), Sanders (VT), Klobuchar (MN), Whitehouse (RI)

Minority (R 9): Inhofe (OK), RMM; Warner (VA), Voinovich (OH), Isakson (GA), Vitter (LA), Barrasso (WY), Craig (ID), Alexander (TN), Bond (MO)

SUBCOMMITTEES

Clean Air & Nuclear Safety
Majority (D 4): Carper, Chmn.; Lieberman, Clinton, Sanders
Minority (D 3): Voinovich, RMM; Isakson, Alexander

Private Sector & Consumer Solutions to Global Warming & Wildlife Protection
Majority (D 4): Lieberman, Chmn.; Baucus, Lautenberg, Sanders
Minority (R 3): Warner, RMM; Barrasso, Isakson

Public Sector Solutions to Global Warming, Oversight & Children's Health Protection
Majority (D 5): Boxer, Chmn.; Lieberman, Carper, Klobuchar, Whitehouse
Minority (R 4): Alexander, RMM; Craig, Bond, Barrasso

Superfund & Environmental Health
Majority (D 4): Clinton, Chmn.; Baucus, Lautenberg, Cardin
Minority (R 3): Barrasso, RMM; Craig, Vitter

Transportation & Infrastructure
Majority (D 5): Baucus, Chmn.; Carper, Clinton, Cardin, Sanders
Minority (D 4): Isakson, RRM; Warner, Voinovich, Vitter

Transportation Safety, Infrastructure Security & Water Quality
Majority (D 4): Lautenberg, Chmn.; Cardin, Klobuchar, Whitehouse
Minority (R 3): Vitter, RMM; Bond, Voinovich

Ethics (Select)   220 Hart
ethics.senate.gov   202–224–2981
Majority (D 3): Boxer (CA), acting chair; Pryor (AR), Salazar (CO)
Minority (R 3): Cornyn (TX), Vice Chmn.; Roberts (KS), Isakson (GA)

NO SUBCOMMITTEES

Finance   219 Dirksen
finance.senate.gov   202–224–4515
Majority (D 11): Baucus (MT), Chmn.; Rockefeller (WV), Conrad (ND), Bingaman (NM), Kerry (MA), Lincoln
    (AR), Wyden (OR), Schumer (NY), Stabenow (MI), Cantwell (WA), Salazar (CO)
Minority (R 10): Grassley (IA), RMM; Hatch (UT), Lott (MS), Snowe (ME), Kyl (AZ), Smith (OR), Bunning
    (KY), Crapo (ID), Roberts (KS), Ensign (NV)

SUBCOMMITTEES

Energy, Natural Resources & Infrastructure
Majority (D 7): Bingaman, Chmn.; Conrad, Kerry, Lincoln, Wyden, Cantwell, Salazar
Minority (R 6): Bunning, RMM; Smith, Hatch, Lott, Crapo, Ensign

Health Care
Majority (D 8): Rockefeller, Chmn.; Kerry, Bingaman, Lincoln, Wyden, Stabenow, Cantwell, Salazar
Minority (R 7): Hatch, RMM; Grassley, Snowe, Kyl, Roberts, Bunning, Ensign

International Trade & Global Competitiveness
Majority (D 6): Lincoln, Chmn.; Baucus, Rockefeller, Bingaman, Stabenow, Schumer
Minority (R 5): Smith, RMM; Crapo, Snowe, Roberts, Bunning

Social Security, Pensions & Family Policy
Majority (D 4): Kerry, Chmn.; Rockefeller, Conrad, Schumer
Minority (R 3): Ensign, RMM; Lott, Kyl

Taxation & IRS Oversight & Long-Term Growth
Majority (D 7): Conrad, Chmn.; Baucus, Wyden, Cantwell, Schumer, Stabenow, Salazar
Minority (R 6): Kyl, RMM; Lott, Roberts, Snowe, Crapo, Hatch

Foreign Relations   450 Dirksen
foreign.senate.gov   202–224–4651
Majority (D 11): Biden (DE), Chmn.; Dodd (CT), Kerry (MA), Feingold (WI), Boxer (CA), Nelson (FL), Obama
    (IL), Menendez (NJ), Cardin (MD), Casey (PA), Webb (VA)
Minority (R 10): Lugar (IN), RMM; Hagel (NE), Coleman (MN), Corker (TN), Sununu (NH), Voinovich (OH),
    Murkowski (AK), DeMint (SC), Isakson (GA), Vitter (LA)

SUBCOMMITTEES

African Affairs
Majority (D 5): Feingold, Chmn.; Nelson, Obama, Cardin, Webb
Minority (R 4): Sununu, RMM; Coleman, Vitter, Hagel

East Asian & Pacific Affairs
Majority (D 5): Boxer, Chmn.; Kerry, Feingold, Obama, Webb
Minority (R 4): Murkowski, RMM; Isakson, Vitter, Hagel

European Affairs
Majority (D 5): Obama, Chmn.; Dodd, Menendez, Cardin, Casey
Minority (R 4): DeMint, RMM; Voinovich, Corker, Murkowski

International Development & Foreign Assistance, Economic Affairs & International Environmental Protection
Majority (D 5): Menendez, Chmn.; Kerry, Boxer, Obama, Casey
Minority (R 4): Hagel, RMM; Corker, Murkowski, DeMint

International Operations & Organizations, Democracy & Human Rights
Majority (D 5): Nelson, Chmn.; Feingold, Menendez, Casey, Webb
Minority (R 4): Vitter, RMM; Voinovich, DeMint, Isakson

Near Eastern & South & Central Asian Affairs
Majority (D 5): Kerry, Chmn.; Dodd, Feingold, Boxer, Cardin
Minority (R 4): Coleman, RMM; Hagel, Sununu, Voinovich

Western Hemisphere, Peace Corps & Narcotics Affairs
Majority (D 5): Dodd, Chmn.; Kerry, Nelson, Menendez, Webb
Minority (R 4): Corker, RMM; Isakson, Coleman, Sununu

Health, Education, Labor & Pensions
help.senate.gov

428 Dirksen
202–224–5375

Majority (D 11): Kennedy (MA), Chmn.; Dodd (CT), Harkin (IA), Mikulski (MD), Bingaman (NM), Murray (WA), Reed (RI), Clinton (NY), Obama (IL), Sanders (VT), Brown (OH)
Minority (R 10): Enzi (WY), RMM; Gregg (NH) Alexander (TN), Burr (NC), Isakson (GA), Murkowski (AK), Hatch (UT), Roberts (KS), Allard (CO), Coburn (OK)

SUBCOMMITTEES

Children & Families
Majority (D 7): Dodd, Chmn.; Bingaman, Murray, Reed, Clinton, Obama, Sanders
Minority (D 6): Alexander, RMM; Gregg, Murkowski, Hatch, Roberts, Allard

Employment & Workplace Safety
Majority (D 7): Murray, Chmn.; Dodd, Harkin, Mikulski, Clinton, Obama, Brown
Minority (R 6): Isakson, RMM; Burr, Murkowski, Roberts, Allard, Coburn

Retirement & Aging
Majority (D 6): Mikulski, Chmn.; Harkin, Bingaman, Reed, Sanders, Brown
Minority (D 5): Burr, RMM; Gregg, Alexander, Isakson, Hatch

Homeland Security & Governmental Affairs
hsgac.senate.gov

340 Dirksen
202–224–2627

Majority (D 9): Lieberman (CT), Chmn.; Levin (MI), Akaka (HI), Carper (DE), Pryor (AR), Landrieu (LA), Obama (IL), McCaskill (MO), Tester (MT)
Minority (R 8): Collins (ME), RMM; Stevens (AK), Voinovich (OH), Coleman (MN), Coburn (OK), Domenici (NM), Warner (VA), Sununu (NH)

SUBCOMMITTEES

Disaster Recovery
Majority (D 3): Landrieu, Chmn.; Carper, Pryor
Minority (R 2): Stevens, RMM; Domenici

Federal Financial Management, Government Information, Federal Services & International Security
Majority (D 6): Carper, Chmn.; Levin, Akaka, Obama, McCaskill, Tester
Minority (R 5): Coburn, RMM; Stevens, Voinovich, Domenici, Sununu

Investigations (Permanent)
Majority (D 6): Levin, Chmn.; Carper, Pryor, Obama, McCaskill, Tester
Minority (R 5): Coleman, RMM; Coburn, Domenici, Warner, Sununu

Oversight of Government Management, the Federal Workforce & the District of Columbia
Majority (D 5): Akaka, Chmn.; Levin, Carper, Pryor, Landrieu
Minority (R 4): Voinovich, RMM; Stevens, Coburn, Warner

State, Local & Private Sector Preparedness & Integration
Majority (D 6): Pryor, Chmn.; Akaka, Landrieu, Obama, McCaskill, Tester
Minority (R 5): Sununu, RMM; Voinovich, Coleman, Domenici, Warner

Indian Affairs
indian.senate.gov

836 Hart
202–224–2251

Majority (D 8): Dorgan (ND), Chmn.; Inouye (HI), Conrad (ND), Akaka (HI), Johnson (SD), Cantwell (WA), McCaskill (MO), Tester (MT)
Minority (R 7): Murkowski (AK), V. Chmn.; McCain (AZ), Coburn (OK), Barrasso (WY), Domenici (NM), Smith (OR), Burr (NC)

NO SUBCOMMITTEES

Intelligence (Select)
intelligence.senate.gov

211 Hart
202–224–1700

Majority (D 8): Rockefeller (WV), Chmn.; Feinstein (CA), Wyden (OR), Bayh (IN), Mikulski (MD), Feingold (WI), Nelson (FL), Whitehouse (RI)
Minority (R 7): Bond (MO), RMM; Warner (VA), Hagel (NE), Chambliss (GA), Hatch (UT), Snowe (ME), Burr (NC)

NO SUBCOMMITTEES

Judiciary
judiciary.senate.gov

224 Dirksen
202–224–7703

Majority (D 10): Leahy (VT), Chmn.; Kennedy (MA), Biden (DE), Kohl (WI), Feinstein (CA), Feingold (WI), Schumer (NY), Durbin (IL), Cardin (MD), Whitehouse (RI)
Minority (R 9): Specter (PA), RMM; Hatch (UT), Grassley (IA), Kyl (AZ), Sessions (AL), Graham (SC), Cornyn (TX), Brownback (KS), Coburn (OK)

SUBCOMMITTEES

Administrative Oversight & the Courts
Majority (D 4): Schumer, Chmn.; Feinstein, Feingold, Whitehouse
Minority (R 3): Sessions, RMM; Grassley, Graham

Antitrust, Competition Policy & Consumer Rights
Majority (D 6): Kohl, Chmn.; Leahy, Biden, Feingold, Schumer, Cardin
Minority (R 5): Hatch, RMM; Specter, Grassley, Brownback, Coburn

Constitution
Majority (D 5): Feingold, Chmn.; Kennedy, Feinstein, Durbin, Cardin
Minority (R 4): Brownback, RMM; Specter, Graham, Cornyn

Crime & Drugs
Majority (D 7): Biden, Chmn.; Kennedy, Kohl, Feinstein, Feingold, Schumer, Durbin
Minority (R 6): Graham, RMM; Specter, Hatch, Grassley, Sessions, Coburn

Human Rights & the Law
Majority (D 6): Durbin, Chmn.; Kennedy, Biden, Feingold, Cardin, Whitehouse
Minority (R 5): Coburn, RMM; Kyl, Graham, Cornyn, Brownback

Immigration, Refugees & Border Security
Majority (D 5): Kennedy, Chmn.; Biden, Feinstein, Schumer, Durbin
Minority (R 4): Cornyn, RMM; Grassley, Kyl, Sessions

Terrorism, Technology & Homeland Security
Majority (D 7): Feinstein, Chmn.; Kennedy, Biden, Kohl, Schumer, Durbin, Cardin
Minority (R 6): Kyl, RMM; Hatch, Sessions, Cornyn, Brownback, Coburn

Rules & Administration
rules.senate.gov

305 Russell
202–224–6352

Majority (D 10): Feinstein (CA), Chmn.; Byrd (WV), Inouye (HI), Dodd (CT), Schumer (NY), Durbin (IL), Nelson (NE), Reid (NV), Murray (WA), Pryor (AR)
Minority (R 9): Bennett (UT), RMM; Stevens (AK), McConnell (KY), Cochran (MS), Lott (MS), Hutchison (TX), Chambliss (GA), Hagel (NE), Alexander (TN)

NO SUBCOMMITTEES

Small Business & Entrepreneurship
sbc.senate.gov

428A Russell
202–224–5175

Majority (D 10): Kerry (MA), Chmn.; Levin (MI), Harkin (IA), Lieberman (CT), Landrieu (LA), Cantwell (WA), Bayh (IN), Pryor (AR), Cardin (MD), Tester (MT)
Minority (R 9): Snowe (ME), RMM; Bond (MO), Coleman (MN), Vitter (LA), Dole (NC), Thune (SD), Corker (TN), Enzi (WY), Isakson (GA)

NO SUBCOMMITTEES

Veterans' Affairs
veterans.senate.gov

412 Russell
202–224–9126

Majority (D 8): Akaka (HI), Chmn.; Rockefeller (WV), Murray (WA), Obama (IL), Sanders (VT), Brown (OH), Tester (MT), Webb (VA)
Minority (D 7): Burr (NC), RMM; Specter (PA), Craig (ID), Hutchison (TX), Graham (SC), Ensign (NV), Isakson (GA)

NO SUBCOMMITTEES

HOUSE COMMITTEE LEADERSHIP

Agriculture
Collin Peterson (MN-7)
RMM: Bob Goodlatte (VA-6)

Appropriations
David Obey (WI-7)
RMM: Jerry Lewis (CA-41)

Armed Services
Ike Skelton (MO-4)
RMM: Duncan Hunter (CA-52)

Budget
John Spratt (SC-5)
RMM: Paul Ryan (WI-1)

Education & Labor
George Miller (CA-7)
RMM: Buck McKeon (CA-25)

Energy & Commerce

John Dingell (MI-15)
RMM: Joe Barton (TX-6)

Financial Services
Barney Frank (MA-4)
RMM: Spencer Bachus (AL-6)

Foreign Affairs
Tom Lantos (CA-12)
RMM: Ileana Ros-Lehtinen (FL-18)

Homeland Security
Bennie Thompson (MS-2)
RMM: Peter King (NY-3)

House Administration
Robert Brady (PA-1)
RMM: Vernon Ehlers (MI-3)

Judiciary

John Conyers (MI-14)
RMM: Lamar Smith (TX-21)

Natural Resources
Nick Rahall (WV-3)
RMM: Don Young (AK-AL)

Oversight & Government Reform
Henry Waxman (CA-30)
RMM: Tom Davis (VA-11)

Rules
Louise Slaughter (NY-28)
RMM: David Dreier (CA-26)

Science & Technology
Bart Gordon (TN-6)
RMM: Ralph Hall (TX-4)

Small Business
Nydia Velazquez (NY-12)
RMM: Steve Chabot (OH-1)

Standards of Official Conduct
(Ethics)
Stephanie Tubbs Jones (OH-11)
RMM: Doc Hastings (WA-4)

Transportation & Infrastructure
James Oberstar (MN-8)
RMM: John Mica (FL-7)

Veterans' Affairs
Bob Filner (CA-51)
RMM: Steve Buyer (IN-4)

Ways & Means
Charles Rangel (NY-15)
RMM: Jim McCrery (LA-4)

Intelligence (Permanent Select)
Silvestre Reyes (TX-16)
RMM: Pete Hoekstra (MI-2)

Energy Independence and Global Warming
(Select)
Edward Markey (MA-7)
RMM: Jim Sensenbrenner (WI-5)

Committee chairmen are noted in boldface
RMM: Ranking Minority Member

HOUSE COMMITTEES

Agriculture
agriculture.house.gov

1301 Longworth
202–225–2171

Majority (D 25): Peterson (MN), Chmn.; Holden (PA), Vice Chmn.; McIntyre (NC), Etheridge (NC), Boswell (IA), Baca (CA), Cardoza (CA), Scott (GA), Marshall (GA), Herseth Sandlin (SD), Cuellar (TX), Costa (CA), Salazar (CO), Ellsworth (IN), Boyda (KS), Space (OH), Walz (MN), Gillibrand (NY), Kagen (WI), Pomeroy (ND), Davis (TN), Barrow (GA), Lampson (TX), Donnelly (IN), Mahoney (FL)

Minority (R 21): Goodlatte (VA), RMM; Everett (AL), Lucas (OK), Moran (KS), Hayes (NC), Johnson (IL), Graves (MO), Bonner (AL), Rogers (AL), King (IA), Musgrave (CO), Neugebauer (TX), Boustany (LA), Kuhl (NY), Foxx (NC), Conaway (TX), Fortenberry (NE), Schmidt (OH), Smith (NE), McCarthy (CA), Walberg (MI)

SUBCOMMITTEES

Conservation, Credit, Energy & Research
Majority (D 14): Holden, Chmn.; Herseth Sandlin, Cuellar, Costa, Ellsworth, Space, Walz, Scott, Salazar, Boyda, Gillibrand, Cardoza, Kagen, Donnelly
Minority (R 12): Lucas, RMM; Rogers, King, Fortenberry, Schmidt, Walberg, Everett, Moran, Hayes, Graves, Bonner, Musgrave

Department Operations, Oversight, Nutrition & Forestry
Majority (D 6): Baca, Chmn.; Pomeroy, Davis, Lampson, Kagen, Boyda
Minority (R 5): Bonner, RMM; Moran, King, Neugebauer, Boustany

General Farm Commodities & Risk Management
Majority (D 10): Etheridge, Chmn.; Scott, Marshall, Salazar, Boyda, Herseth Sandlin, Ellsworth, Space, Walz, Pomeroy
Minority (R 8): Moran, RMM; Johnson, Graves, Boustany, Conaway, Lucas, Neugebauer, McCarthy

Horticulture & Organic Agriculture
Majority (D 6): Cardoza, Chmn.; Etheridge, Davis, Mahoney, Barrow, Gillibrand
Minority (R 5): Neugebauer, RMM; Kuhl, Foxx, McCarthy, Conaway

Livestock, Dairy & Poultry
Majority (D 10): Boswell, Chmn.; Gillibrand, Kagen, Holden, Baca, Cardoza, Lampson, Donnelly, Costa, Mahoney
Minority (R 8): Hayes, RMM; Rogers, King, Foxx, Conaway, Schmidt, Smith, Walberg

Specialty Crops, Rural Development & Foreign Agriculture
Majority (D 6): McIntyre, Chmn.; Marshall, Cuellar, Salazar, Barrow, Pomeroy
Minority (R 5): Musgrave, RMM; Everett, Smith, Fortenberry, Hayes

Appropriations
www.house.gov/appropriations

H-218 The Capitol
202–225–2771

Majority (D 37): Obey (WI), Chmn.; Murtha (PA), Dicks (WA), Mollohan (WV), Kaptur (OH), Visclosky (IN), Lowey (NY), Serrano (NY), DeLauro (CT), Moran (VA), Olver (MA), Pastor (AZ), Price (NC), Edwards (TX), Cramer (AL), Kennedy (RI), Hinchey (NY), Roybal-Allard (CA), Farr (CA), Jackson (IL), Kilpatrick (MI), Boyd (FL), Fattah (PA), Rothman (NJ), Bishop (GA), Berry (AR), Lee (CA), Udall (NM), Schiff (CA), Honda (CA), McCollum (MN), Israel (NY), Ryan (OH), Ruppersberger (MD), Chandler (KY), Wasserman Schultz (FL), Rodriguez (TX)

Minority (R 29): Lewis (CA), RMM; Young (FL), Regula (OH), Rogers (KY), Wolf (VA), Walsh (NY), Hobson (OH), Knollenberg (MI), Kingston (GA), Frelinghuysen (NJ), Wicker (MS), Tiahrt (KS), Wamp (TN), Latham (IA), Aderholt (AL), Emerson (MO), Granger (TX), Peterson (PA), Goode (VA), LaHood (IL), Weldon (FL), Simpson (ID), Culberson (TX), Kirk (IL), Crenshaw (FL), Rehberg (MT), Carter (TX), Alexander (LA), Calvert (CA)

SUBCOMMITTEES

Agriculture, Rural Development, FDA & Related Agencies
Majority (D 8): DeLauro, Chmn.; Hinchey, Farr, Boyd, Bishop, Kaptur, Jackson, Rothman
Minority (R 5): Kingston, RMM; Latham, Emerson, LaHood, Alexander

Commerce, Justice, Science & Related Agencies
Majority (D 8): Mollohan, Chmn.; Kennedy, Fattah, Ruppersberger, Schiff, Honda, DeLauro, Price
Minority (R 5): Frelinghuysen, RMM; Culberson, Rogers, Latham, Aderholt

Defense
Majority (D 9): Murtha, Chmn.; Dicks, Visclosky, Moran, Kaptur, Cramer, Boyd, Rothman, Bishop
Minority (R 6): Young, RMM; Hobson, Frelinghuysen, Tiahrt, Wicker, Kingston

Energy & Water Development
Majority (D 9): Visclosky, Chmn.; Edwards, Pastor, Berry, Fattah, Israel, Ryan, Serrano, Olver
Minority (R 5): Hobson, RMM; Wamp, Emerson, Simpson, Granger

Financial Services & General Government
Majority (D 8): Serrano, Chmn.; Kilpatrick, Ruppersberger, Wasserman Schultz, Visclosky, Cramer, Hinchey, Schiff
Minority (R 5): Regula, RMM; Kirk, Rehberg, Alexander, Calvert

Homeland Security
Majority (D 9): Price, Chmn.; Serrano, Kilpatrick, Rodriguez, Lowey, Edwards, Roybal-Allard, Farr, Fattah
Minority (R 6): Rogers, RMM; Carter, Aderholt, Granger, Peterson, Culberson

Interior, Environment & Related Agencies
Majority (D 8): Dicks, Chmn.; Moran, Hinchey, Olver, Mollohan, Udall, Chandler, Pastor
Minority (R 5): Tiahrt, RMM; Peterson, Emerson, Goode, Calvert

Labor, HHS, Education & Related Agencies
Majority (D 11): Obey, Chmn.; Lowey, DeLauro, Jackson, Kennedy, Roybal-Allard, Lee, Udall, Honda, McCollum, Ryan
Minority (R 6): Walsh, RMM; Regula, Peterson, Weldon, Simpson, Rehberg

Legislative Branch
Majority (D 6): Wasserman Schultz, Chmn.; Lee, Udall, Honda, McCollum, Ruppersberger
Minority (R 3): Wamp, RMM; LaHood, Goode

Military Construction, Veterans Affairs & Related Agencies
Majority (D 8): Edwards, Chmn.; Farr, Dicks, Mollohan, Kennedy, Boyd, Bishop, Berry
Minority (R 5): Wicker, RMM; Crenshaw, Young, Carter, Granger

Select Intelligence Oversight
Majority (D 8): Holt, Chmn.; Obey, Murtha, Reyes, Dicks, Lowey, Cramer, Schiff
Minority (R 5): LaHood, RMM; Lewis, Young, Hoekstra, Frelinghuysen

State, Foreign Operations & Related Programs
Majority (D 8): Lowey, Chmn.; Jackson, Schiff, Israel, Chandler, Rothman, Lee, McCollum
Minority (R 5): Wolf, RMM; Knollenberg, Kirk, Crenshaw, Weldon

Transportation, HUD & Related Agencies
Majority (D 8): Olver, Chmn.; Pastor, Rodriguez, Kaptur, Price, Cramer, Roybal-Allard, Berry
Minority (R 5): Knollenberg, RMM; Wolf, Aderholt, Walsh, Goode

Armed Services   2120 Rayburn
armedservices.house.gov   202–225–4151
Majority (D 33): Skelton (MO), Chmn.; Spratt (SC), Ortiz (TX), Taylor (MS), Abercrombie (HI), Reyes (TX), Snyder (AR), Smith (WA), Lo. Sanchez (CA), McIntyre (NC), Tauscher (CA), Brady (PA), Andrews (NJ), Davis (CA), Larsen (WA), Cooper (TN), Marshall (GA), Bordallo (GU), Udall (CO), Boren (OK), Ellsworth (IN), Boyda (KS), Murphy (PA), Johnson (GA), Shea-Porter (NH), Courtney (CT), Loebsack (IA), Gillibrand (NY), Sestak (PA), Giffords (AZ), Cummings (MD), Meek (FL), Castor (FL)
Minority (R 28): Hunter (CA), RMM; Saxton (NJ), McHugh (NY), Everett (AL), Bartlett (MD), McKeon (CA), Thornberry (TX), Jones (NC), Hayes (NC), J. Davis (VA), Akin (MO), Forbes (VA), Miller (FL), Wilson (SC), LoBiondo (NJ), Cole (OK), Bishop (UT), Turner (OH), Kline (MN), Miller (MI), Gingrey (GA), Rogers (AL), Franks (AZ), Shuster (PA), Drake (VA), McMorris Rodgers (WA), Conaway (TX), Davis (KY)

SUBCOMMITTEES

Air & Land Forces
Majority (D 15): Abercrombie, Chmn.; Spratt, Ortiz, Reyes, Smith, McIntyre, Tauscher, Brady, Marshall, Boren, Johnson, Sestak, Giffords, Meek, Castor
Minority (R 13): Saxton, RMM; McKeon, Miller (FL), Wilson, LoBiondo, Cole, Bishop, Turner, Miller (MI), Gingrey, McMorris Rodgers, Davis (KY), Akin

Military Personnel
Majority (D 6): Davis, Chmn.; Snyder, Sanchez, Boyda, Murphy, Shea-Porter
Minority (R 5): McHugh, RMM; Kline, Drake, Jones, Wilson

Oversight & Investigations
Majority (D 9): Snyder, Chmn.; Spratt, Sanchez, Tauscher, Andrews, Davis, Cooper, Johnson, Sestak
Minority (R 7): Akin, RMM; Bartlett, Jones, Miller (FL), Gingrey, Conaway, Davis (KY)

Readiness
Majority (D 15): Ortiz, Chmn.; Taylor, Reyes, Sanchez, Brady, Marshall, Bordallo, Udall, Boren, Boyda, Shea-Porter, Courtney, Loebsack, Giffords, Cummings
Minority (R 13): Davis (VA), RMM; Jones, Forbes, Rogers, McHugh, McKeon, Hayes, LoBiondo, Cole, Bishop, Miller (MI), Franks, McMorris Rodgers

Seapower & Expeditionary Forces
Majority (D 8): Taylor, Chmn.; Abercrombie, Larsen, Bordallo, Ellsworth, Courtney, Gillibrand, Sestak
Minority (R 6): Bartlett, RMM; Everett, Davis (VA), Forbes, Wilson, Shuster

Strategic Forces
Majority (D 6): Tauscher, Chmn.; Spratt, Reyes, Larsen, Cooper, Loebsack
Minority (R 5): Everett, RMM; Franks, Thornberry, Turner, Rogers

Terrorism, Unconventional Threats & Capabilities
Majority (D 9): Smith, Chmn.; McIntyre, Andrews, Cooper, Marshall, Udall, Ellsworth, Gillibrand, Castor
Minority (R 7): Thornberry, RMM; Hayes, Kline, Drake, Conaway, Saxton, Shuster

Budget
207 Cannon
budget.house.gov
202–226–7200
Majority (D 21): Spratt (SC), Chmn.; DeLauro (CT), Edwards (TX), Cooper (TN), Allen (ME), Schwartz (PA), Kaptur (OH), Becerra (CA), Doggett (TX), Blumenauer (OR), Berry (AR), Boyd (FL), McGovern (MA), Andrews (NJ), Scott (VA), Etheridge (NC), Hooley (OR), Baird (WA), Moore (KS), Bishop (NY), Moore (WI)
Minority (R 16): Ryan (WI), RMM; Barrett (SC), Bonner (AL), Garrett (NJ), M. Diaz-Balart (FL), Hensarling (TX), Lungren (CA), Simpson (ID), McHenry (NC), Mack (FL), Conaway (TX), Campbell (CA), Tiberi (OH), Porter (NV), Alexander (LA), Smith (NE)

NO SUBCOMMITTEES

Education & Labor
2181 Rayburn
edlabor.house.gov
202–225–3725
Majority (D 27): Miller (CA), Chmn.; Kildee (MI), Payne (NJ), Andrews (NJ), Scott (VA), Woolsey (CA), Hinojosa (TX), McCarthy (NY), Tierney (MA), Kucinich (OH), Wu (OR), Holt (NJ), Davis (CA), Davis (IL), Grijalva (AZ), Bishop (NY), Li. Sanchez (CA), Sarbanes (MD), Sestak (PA), Loebsack (IA), Hirono (HI), Altmire (PA), Yarmuth (KY), Hare (IL), Clarke (NY), Courtney (CT), Shea-Porter (NH)
Minority (R 22): McKeon (CA), RMM; Petri (WI), Hoekstra (MI), Castle (DE), Souder (IN), Ehlers (MI), Biggert (IL), Platts (PA), Keller (FL), Wilson (SC), Kline (MN), McMorris Rodgers (WA), Marchant (TX), Price (GA), Fortuno (PR), Boustany (LA), Foxx (NC), Kuhl (NY), Bishop (UT), Davis (TN), Walberg (MI), Heller (NV)

SUBCOMMITTEES

Early Childhood, Elementary & Secondary Education
Majority (D 16): Kildee, Chmn.; Scott, Kucinich, Davis (CA), Davis (IL), Grijalva, Payne, Holt, Sanchez, Sarbanes, Sestak, Loebsack, Hirono, Hare, Woolsey, Hinojosa
Minority (R 13): Castle, RMM; Hoekstra, Souder, Ehlers, Biggert, Fortuno, Bishop, Platts, Keller, Wilson, Boustany, Kuhl, Heller

Health, Employment, Labor & Pensions
Majority (D 13): Andrews, Chmn.; Miller, Kildee, McCarthy, Tierney, Wu, Holt, Sanchez, Sestak, Loebsack, Hare, Clarke, Courtney
Minority (R 10): Kline, RMM; McKeon, Marchant, Boustany, Davis, Hoekstra, McMorris Rodgers, Price, Foxx, Walberg

Healthy Families & Communities
Majority (D 8): McCarthy, Chmn.; Clarke, Shea-Porter, Kucinich, Grijalva, Sarbanes, Altmire, Yarmuth
Minority (R 6): Platts, RMM; McKeon, Marchant, Fortuno, Davis, Heller

Higher Education, Lifelong Learning & Competitiveness
Majority (D 13): Hinojosa, Chmn.; Miller, Tierney, Wu, Bishop, Altmire, Yarmuth, Courtney, Andrews, Scott, Davis (CA), Davis (IL), Hirono
Minority (R 10): Keller, RMM; Petri, McMorris Rodgers, Foxx, Kuhl, Walberg, Castle, Souder, Ehlers, Biggert

Workforce Protections
Majority (D 5): Woolsey, Chmn.; Payne, Bishop, Shea-Porter, Hare
Minority (R 3): Wilson, RMM; Price, Kline

Energy & Commerce
2125 Rayburn
energycommerce.house.gov
202–225–2927
Majority (D 31): Dingell (MI), Chmn.; Waxman (CA), Markey (MA), Boucher (VA), Towns (NY), Pallone (NJ), Gordon (TN), Rush (IL), Eshoo (CA), Stupak (MI), Engel (NY), Wynn (MD), Green (TX), DeGette (CO), Vice Chmn.; Capps (CA), Doyle (PA), Harman (CA), Allen (ME), Schakowsky (IL), Solis (CA), Gonzalez (TX), Inslee (WA), Baldwin (WI), Ross (AR), Hooley (OR), Weiner (NY), Matheson (UT), Butterfield (NC), Melancon (LA), Barrow (GA), Hill (IN)
Minority (R 26): Barton (TX), RMM; Hall (TX), Hastert (IL), Upton (MI), Stearns (FL), Deal (GA), Whitfield (KY), Cubin (WY), Shimkus (IL), Wilson (NM), Shadegg (AZ), Pickering (MS), Fossella (NY), Buyer (IN), Radanovich (CA), Pitts (PA), Bono (CA), Walden (OR), Terry (NE), Ferguson (NJ), Rogers (MI), Myrick (NC), Sullivan (OK), Murphy (PA), Burgess (TX), Blackburn (TN)

SUBCOMMITTEES

Commerce, Trade & Consumer Protection
Majority (D 15): Rush, Chmn.; Schakowsky, Butterfield, Barrow, Hill, Markey, Boucher, Towns, DeGette, Gonzalez, Ross, Hooley, Weiner, Matheson, Melancon
Minority (R 12): Stearns, RMM; Hastert, Whitfield, Pickering, Fossella, Radanovich, Pitts, Bono, Terry, Myrick, Burgess, Blackburn

Energy & Air Quality
Majority (D 17): Boucher, Chmn.; Butterfield, Melancon, Barrow, Waxman, Markey, Wynn, Doyle, Harman, Allen, Gonzalez, Inslee, Baldwin, Ross, Hooley, Weiner, Matheson
Minority (R 14): Hastert, RMM; Hall, Upton, Whitfield, Shimkus, Shadegg, Pickering, Buyer, Bono, Walden, Rogers, Myrick, Sullivan, Burgess

Environment & Hazardous Materials
Majority (D 15): Wynn, Chmn.; Pallone, Stupak, Capps, Allen, Solis, Baldwin, Butterfield, Barrow, Hill, DeGette, Weiner, Waxman, Green, Schakowsky
Minority (R 12): Shimkus, RMM; Stearns, Deal, Wilson, Shadegg, Fossella, Radanovich, Pitts, Terry, Rogers, Sullivan, Murphy

Health
Majority (D 17): Pallone, Chmn.; Waxman, Towns, Gordon, Eshoo, Green, DeGette, Capps, Allen, Baldwin, Engel, Schakowsky, Solis, Ross, Hooley, Weiner, Matheson
Minority (R 14): Deal, RMM; Hall, Cubin, Wilson, Shadegg, Buyer, Pitts, Ferguson, Rogers, Myrick, Sullivan, Murphy, Burgess, Blackburn

Oversight & Investigations
Majority (D 8): Stupak, Chmn.; DeGette, Melancon, Waxman, Green, Doyle, Schakowsky, Inslee
Minority (R 6): Whitfield, RMM; Walden, Ferguson, Murphy, Burgess, Blackburn

Telecommunications & the Internet
Majority (D 17): Markey, Chmn.; Doyle, Harman, Gonzalez, Inslee, Hill, Boucher, Towns, Pallone, Gordon, Rush, Eshoo, Stupak, Engel, Green, Capps, Solis
Minority (R 14): Upton, RMM; Hastert, Stearns, Deal, Cubin, Shimkus, Wilson, Pickering, Fossella, Radanovich, Bono, Walden, Terry, Ferguson

Financial Services
financialservices.house.gov
2129 Rayburn
202–225–4247

Majority (D 37): Frank (MA), Chmn.; Kanjorski (PA), Waters (CA), Maloney (NY), Gutierrez (IL), Velazquez (NY), Watt (NC), Ackerman (NY), Carson (IN), Sherman (CA), Meeks (NY), Moore (KS), Capuano (MA), Hinojosa (TX), Clay (MO), McCarthy (NY), Baca (CA), Lynch (MA), Miller (NC), Scott (GA), A. Green (TX), Cleaver (MO), Bean (IL), Moore (WI), Davis (TN), Sires (NJ), Hodes (NH), Ellison (MN), Klein (FL), Mahoney (FL), Wilson (OH), Perlmutter (CO), Murphy (CT), Donnelly (IN), Wexler (FL), Marshall (GA), Boren (OK)
Minority (R 32): Bachus (AL), RMM; Baker (LA), Pryce (OH), Castle (DE), King (NY), Royce (CA), Lucas (OK), Paul (TX), LaTourette (OH), Manzullo (IL), Jones (NC), Biggert (IL), Shays (CT), Miller (CA), Capito (WV), Feeney (FL), Hensarling (TX), Garrett (NJ), Brown-Waite (FL), Barrett (SC), Gerlach (PA), Pearce (NM), Neugebauer (TX), Price (GA), Davis (KY), McHenry (NC), Campbell (CA), Putnam (FL), Bachmann (MN), Roskam (IL), Marchant (TX), McCotter (MI)

SUBCOMMITTEES

Capital Markets, Insurance & Government Sponsored Enterprises
Majority (D 26): Kanjorski, Chmn.; Ackerman, Sherman, Meeks, Moore, Capuano, Hinojosa, McCarthy, Baca, Lynch, Miller, Scott, Velazquez, Bean, Moore, Davis, Sires, Hodes, Klein, Mahoney, Perlmutter, Murphy, Donnelly, Wexler, Marshall, Boren
Minority (R 22): Pryce, RMM; Baker, Shays, Castle, King, Lucas, Manzullo, Royce, Capito, Putnam, Barrett, Brown-Waite, Feeney, Garrett, Gerlach, Hensarling, Davis, Campbell, Bachmann, Roskam, Marchant, McCotter

Domestic and International Monetary Policy, Trade & Technology
Majority (D 14): Gutierrez, Chmn.; Maloney, Waters, Kanjorski, Sherman, Moore, Meeks, Moore, Clay, Ellison, Wilson, Wexler, Marshall, Boren
Minority (R 12): Paul, RMM; Castle, Lucas, LaTourette, Manzullo, Jones, Hensarling, Price, McHenry, Bachmann, Roskam, Marchant

Financial Institutions & Consumer Credit
Majority (D 25): Maloney, Chmn.; Watt, Ackerman, Sherman, Gutierrez, Moore, Kanjorski, Waters, Carson, Hinojosa, McCarthy, Baca, Green, Clay, Miller, Scott, Cleaver, Bean, Davis, Hodes, Ellison, Klein, Mahoney, Wilson, Perlmutter
Minority (R 21): Price, Baker, Pryce, Castle, King, Royce, LaTourette, Jones, Biggert, RMM; Capito, Feeney, Hensarling, Garrett, Brown-Waite, Barrett, Gerlach, Pearce, Neugebauer, Davis, McHenry, Campbell

Housing & Community Opportunity
Majority (D 14): Waters, Chmn.; Velazquez, Carson, Lynch, Cleaver, Green, Clay, Maloney, Moore, Sires, Ellison, Wilson, Murphy, Donnelly
Minority (R 11): Biggert, Pearce, King, Shays, Miller, Capito, RMM; Garrett, Neugebauer, Davis, Campbell, McCotter

Oversight & Investigations
Majority (D 10): Watt, Chmn.; Gutierrez, Waters, Lynch, Velazquez, Capuano, McCarthy, Klein, Mahoney, Wexler
Minority (R 9): Miller, RMM; McHenry, Royce, Paul, LaTourette, Barrett, Price, Bachmann, Roskam

Foreign Affairs
foreignaffairs.house.gov
2170 Rayburn
202–225–5021

Majority (D 27): Lantos (CA), Chmn.; Berman (CA), Ackerman (NY), Faleomavaega (AS), Payne (NJ), Sherman (CA), Wexler (FL), Engel (NY), Delahunt (MA), Meeks (NY), Watson (CA), Smith (WA), Carnahan (MO), Tanner (TN), Green (TX), Woolsey (CA), Jackson Lee (TX), Crowley (NY), Hinojosa (TX), Wu (OR), Miller (NC), Sanchez (CA), Scott (GA), Costa (CA), Sires (NJ), Giffords (AZ), Klein (FL)
Minority (R 23): Ros-Lehtinen (FL), RMM; Smith (NJ), Burton (IN), Gallegly (CA), Rohrabacher (CA), Manzullo (IL), Royce (CA), Chabot (OH), Tancredo (CO), Paul (TX), Flake (AZ), Davis (VA), Pence (IN), Wilson (SC), Boozman (AR), Barrett (SC), Mack (FL), Fortenberry (NE), McCaul (TX), Poe (TX), Inglis (SC), Fortuno (PR), Bilirakis (FL)

SUBCOMMITTEES

Africa & Global Health
Majority (D 6): Payne, Chmn.; Watson, Woolsey, Jackson Lee, Smith, Miller
Minority (R 5): Smith, RMM; Tancredo, Boozman, Fortenberry, McCaul

Asia, the Pacific & the Global Environment
Majority (D 7): Faleomavaega, Chmn.; Smith, Ackerman, Meeks, Watson, Hinojosa, Sires
Minority (R 6): Manzullo, RMM; Burton, Rohrabacher, Royce, Chabot, Flake

Europe
Majority (D 8): Wexler, Chmn.; Tanner, Hinojosa, Miller, Sanchez, Costa, Engel, Sires
Minority (R 6): Gallegly, RMM; Wilson, Poe, Inglis, Fortuno, Bilirakis

International Organizations, Human Rights & Oversight
Majority (D 5): Delahunt, Chmn.; Carnahan, Payne, Meeks, Crowley
Minority (R 3): Rohrabacher, RMM; Paul, Flake

Middle East & South Asia
Majority (D 10): Ackerman, Chmn.; Berman, Scott, Costa, Klein, Sherman, Wexler, Engel, Carnahan, Jackson Lee
Minority (R 9): Pence, RMM; Chabot, Davis, Wilson, Barrett, Fortenberry, Inglis, Mack, Bilirakis

Terrorism, Nonproliferation & Trade
Majority (D 6): Sherman, Chmn.; Wu, Scott, Klein, Green, Crowley
Minority (R 5): Royce, RMM; Boozman, Poe, Manzullo, Tancredo

Western Hemisphere
Majority (D 10): Engel, Chmn.; Meeks, Sanchez, Sires, Giffords, Faleomavaega, Payne, Delahunt, Klein, Green
Minority (R 8): Burton, RMM; Mack, McCaul, Fortuno, Smith, Gallegly, Paul, Davis

Homeland Security   176 Ford HOB
hsc.house.gov   202–226–2616
Majority (D 18): Thompson (MS), Chmn.; Lo. Sanchez (CA), Markey (MA), Dicks (WA), Harman (CA), DeFazio (OR), Lowey (NY), Norton (DC), Lofgren (CA), Jackson Lee (TX), Christensen (VI), Etheridge (NC), Langevin (RI), Cuellar (TX), Carney (PA), Clarke (NY), A. Green (TX), Perlmutter (CO)
Minority (R 15): King (NY), RMM; Smith (TX), Shays (CT), Souder (IN), Davis (VA), Lungren (CA), Rogers (AL), Jindal (LA), Reichert (WA), McCaul (TX), Dent (PA), Brown-Waite (FL), Bilirakis (FL), Davis (TN), Broun (GA)

SUBCOMMITTEES

Border, Maritime & Global Counterterrorism
Majority (D 7): Sanchez, Chmn.; Harman, Lofgren, Jackson Lee, Langevin, Cuellar, Green
Minority (R 5): Souder, RMM; Jindal, Reichert, McCaul, Bilirakis

Emergency Communications, Preparedness & Response
Majority (D 7): Cuellar, Chmn.; Sanchez, Dicks, Lowey, Norton, Christensen, Etheridge
Minority (R 5): Dent, RMM; Souder, Rogers, Jindal, Davis

Emerging Threats, Cybersecurity & Science and Technology
Majority (D 5): Langevin, Chmn.; Lofgren, Christensen, Etheridge, Green
Minority (R 4): McCaul, RMM; Lungren, Brown-Waite, Broun

Intelligence, Information Sharing & Terrorism Risk Assessment
Majority (D 5): Harman, Chmn.; Dicks, Langevin, Carney, Perlmutter
Minority (R 3): Reichert, RMM; Shays, Dent

Management, Investigations & Oversight
Majority (D 4): Carney, Chmn.; DeFazio, Clarke, Perlmutter
Minority (R 3): Rogers, RMM; Davis, McCaul

Transportation Security & Infrastructure Protection
Majority (D 6): Jackson Lee, Chmn.; Markey, DeFazio, Norton, Clarke, Perlmutter
Minority (R 4): Lungren, RMM; Brown-Waite, Bilirakis, Broun

House Administration   1309 Longworth
cha.house.gov   202–225–2061
Majority (D 6): Brady (PA), Chmn.; Lofgren (CA), Capuano (MA), Gonzalez (TX), Davis (CA), Davis (AL)
Minority (R 3): Ehlers (MI), RMM; Lungren (CA), McCarthy (CA)

NO SUBCOMMITTEES

Judiciary   2138 Rayburn
judiciary.house.gov   202–225–3951
Majority (D 23): Conyers (MI), Chmn.; Berman (CA), Boucher (VA), Nadler (NY), Scott (VA), Watt (NC), Lofgren (CA), Jackson Lee (TX), Waters (CA), Delahunt (MA), Wexler (FL), Li. Sanchez (CA), Cohen (TN), Johnson (GA), Sutton (OH), Gutierrez (IL), Sherman (CA), Weiner (NY), Schiff (CA), Davis (AL), Wasserman Schultz (FL), Ellison (MN), Baldwin (WI)
Minority (R 17): Smith (TX), RMM; Sensenbrenner (WI), Coble (NC), Gallegly (CA), Goodlatte (VA), Chabot (OH), Lungren (CA), Cannon (UT), Keller (FL), Issa (CA), Pence (IN), Forbes (VA), King (IA), Feeney (FL), Franks (AZ), Gohmert (TX), Jordan (OH)

SUBCOMMITTEES

Commercial & Administrative Law
Majority (D 7): Sanchez, Chmn.; Conyers, Johnson, Lofgren, Delahunt, Watt, Cohen
Minority (R 5): Cannon, RMM; Jordan, Keller, Feeney, Franks

Courts, the Internet & Intellectual Property
Majority (D 12): Berman, Chmn.; Conyers, Boucher, Wexler, Watt, Jackson Lee, Cohen, Johnson, Sherman, Weiner, Schiff, Lofgren
Minority (R 11): Coble, RMM; Feeney, Sensenbrenner, Smith, Gallegly, Goodlatte, Cannon, Chabot, Keller, Issa, Pence

Crime, Terrorism & Homeland Security
Majority (D 9): Scott, Chmn.; Waters, Delahunt, Nadler, Johnson, Weiner, Jackson Lee, Davis, Baldwin
Minority (R 6): Forbes, RMM; Gohmert, Sensenbrenner, Coble, Chabot, Lungren

Immigration, Citizenship, Refugees, Border Security & International Law
Majority (D 9): Lofgren, Chmn.; Gutierrez, Berman, Jackson Lee, Waters, Delahunt, Sanchez, Davis, Ellison
Minority (R 6): King, RMM; Gallegly, Goodlatte, Lungren, Forbes, Gohmert

The Constitution, Civil Rights & Civil Liberties
Majority (D 8): Nadler, Chmn.; Davis, Wasserman Schultz, Ellison, Conyers, Scott, Watt, Cohen
Minority (R 5): Franks, RMM; Pence, Issa, King, Jordan

Natural Resources
resourcescommittee.house.gov

1324 Longworth
202–225–6065

Majority (D 27): Rahall (WV), Chmn.; Kildee (MI), Faleomavaega (AS), Abercrombie (HI), Ortiz (TX), Pallone (NJ), Christensen (VI), Napolitano (CA), Holt (NJ), Grijalva (AZ), Bordallo (GU), Costa (CA), Boren (OK), Sarbanes (MD), Miller (CA), Markey (MA), DeFazio (OR), Hinchey (NY), Kennedy (RI), Kind (WI), Capps (CA), Inslee (WA), Udall (CO), Baca (CA), Solis (CA), Herseth Sandlin (SD), Shuler (NC)
Minority (R 22): Young (AK), RMM; Saxton (NJ), Gallegly (CA), Duncan (TN), Gilchrest (MD), Cannon (UT), Tancredo (CO), Flake (AZ), Pearce (NM), Brown (SC), Fortuno (PR), McMorris Rodgers (WA), Jindal (LA), Gohmert (TX), Cole (OK), Bishop (UT), Shuster (PA), Heller (NV), Sali (ID), Lamborn (CO), McCarthy (CA), Fallin (OK)

SUBCOMMITTEES

Energy & Mineral Resources
Majority (D 8): Costa, Chmn.; Faleomavaega, Ortiz, Holt, Boren, Hinchey, Kennedy, Solis
Minority (R 6): Pearce, RMM; Jindal, Gohmert, Shuster, Heller, Sali

Fisheries, Wildlife & Oceans
Majority (D 9): Bordallo, Chmn.; Kildee, Faleomavaega, Abercrombie, Ortiz, Pallone, Kennedy, Kind, Capps
Minority (R 7): Brown, RMM; Saxton, Gilchrest, McMorris Rodgers, Jindal, Cole, Sali

Insular Affairs
Majority (D 4): Christensen, Chmn.; Faleomavaega, Grijalva, Bordallo
Minority (R 3): Fortuno, RMM; Gallegly, Flake

National Parks, Forests & Public Lands
Majority (D 15): Grijalva, Chmn.; Kildee, Abercrombie, Christensen, Holt, Boren, Sarbanes, DeFazio, Hinchey, Kind, Capps, Inslee, Udall, Herseth Sandlin, Shuler
Minority (R 13): Bishop, RMM; Duncan, Cannon, Tancredo, Flake, Pearce, Brown, Gohmert, Cole, Heller, Sali, Lamborn, McCarthy

Water & Power
Majority (D 5): Napolitano, Chmn.; Costa, Miller, Udall, Baca
Minority (R 4): McMorris Rodgers, RMM; Heller, Lamborn, Fallin

Oversight & Government Reform
oversight.house.gov

2157 Rayburn
202–225–5051

Majority (D 23): Waxman (CA), Chmn.; Lantos (CA), Towns (NY), Kanjorski (PA), Maloney (NY), Cummings (MD), Kucinich (OH), Davis (IL), Clay (MO), Watson (CA), Lynch (MA), Higgins (NY), Yarmuth (KY), Braley (IA), Norton (DC), McCollum (MN), Cooper (TN), Van Hollen (MD), Hodes (NH), Murphy (CT), Sarbanes (MD), Welch (VT)
Minority (R 18): T. Davis (VA), RMM; Burton (IN), Shays (CT), McHugh (NY), Mica (FL), Souder (IN), Platts (PA), Cannon (UT), Duncan (TN), Turner (OH), Issa (CA), Marchant (TX), Westmoreland (GA), McHenry (NC), Foxx (NC), Bilbray (CA), Sali (ID), Jordan (OH)

SUBCOMMITTEES

Domestic Policy
Majority (D 9): Kucinich, Chmn.; Lantos, Cummings, Watson, Murphy, Davis, Tierney, Higgins, Braley
Minority (R 7): Issa, RMM; Burton, Shays, Mica, Souder, Cannon, Bilbray

Federal Workforce, Postal Service & the District of Columbia
Majority (D 7): Davis, Chmn.; Norton, Sarbanes, Cummings, Kucinich, Clay, Lynch
Minority (R 5): Marchant, RMM; McHugh, Mica, Issa, Jordan

Government Management, Organization & Procurement
Majority (D 5): Towns, Chmn.; Kanjorski, Murphy, Welch, Maloney
Minority (R 3): Bilbray, RMM; Platts, Duncan

Information Policy, Census & National Archives
Majority (D 5): Clay, Chmn.; Kanjorski, Maloney, Yarmuth, Hodes
Minority (R 3): Turner, RMM; Cannon, Sali

National Security & Foreign Affairs
Majority (D 12): Tierney, Chmn.; Maloney, Lynch, Higgins, Yarmuth, Braley, McCollum, Cooper, Van Hollen, Hodes, Welch, Lantos
Minority (R 10): Shays, RMM; Burton, McHugh, Platts, Duncan, Turner, Marchant, Westmoreland, McHenry, Foxx

Permanent Select Committee on Intelligence
intelligence.house.gov

H-405 The Capitol
202–225–7690

Majority (D 12): Reyes (TX), Chmn.; Hastings (FL), Vice Chmn.; Boswell (IA), Cramer (AL), Eshoo (CA), Holt (NJ), Ruppersberger (MD), Tierney (MA), Thompson (CA), Schakowsky (IL), Langevin (RI), Murphy (PA)
Minority (R 8): Hoekstra (MI), RMM; Everett (AL), Wilson (NM), Thornberry (TX), McHugh (NY), Tiahrt (KS), Rogers (MI), Issa (CA)

SUBCOMMITTEES

Intelligence Community Management
Majority (D 5): Eshoo, Chmn.; Holt, Ruppersberger, Thompson, Murphy
Minority (R 3): Issa, RMM; Thornberry, Tiahrt

Oversight & Investigations
Majority (D 5): Cramer, Chmn.; Hastings, Tierney, Schakowsky, Ruppersberger
Minority (R 3): Everett, RMM; Wilson, McHugh

Technical & Tactical Intelligence
Majority (D 5): Ruppersberger, Chmn.; Cramer, Langevin, Holt, Murphy
Minority (R 3): Wilson, RMM; Everett, Thornberry

Terrorism, Human Intelligence, Analysis & Counterintelligence
Majority (D 5): Thompson, Chmn.; Boswell, Langevin, Murphy, Hastings
Minority (R 3): Rogers, RMM; Everett, McHugh

Rules
www.rules.house.gov

H-312 The Capitol
202–225–9091

Majority (D 9): Slaughter (NY), Chmn.; McGovern (MA), Hastings (FL), Matsui (CA), Cardoza (CA), Welch (VT), Castor (FL), Arcuri (NY), Sutton (OH)
Minority (R 4): Dreier (CA), RMM; L. Diaz-Balart (FL), Hastings (WA), Sessions (TX)

SUBCOMMITTEES

Legislative & Budget Process
Majority (D 5): Hastings, Chmn.; Cardoza, Welch, Sutton, Slaughter
Minority (R 2): Diaz-Balart, RMM; Dreier

Rules & Organization of the House
Majority (D 5): McGovern, Chmn.; Matsui, Castor, Arcuri, Slaughter
Minority (R 2): Hastings, RMM; Sessions

Science & Technology
science.house.gov

2320 Rayburn
202–225–6375

Majority (D 24): Gordon (TN), Chmn.; Costello (IL), Johnson (TX), Woolsey (CA), Udall (CO), Wu (OR), Baird (WA), Miller (NC), Lipinski (IL), Vice Chmn.; Lampson (TX), Giffords (AZ), McNerney (CA), Kanjorski (PA), Hooley (OR), Rothman (NJ), Honda (CA), Matheson (UT), Ross (AR), Chandler (KY), Carnahan (MO), Melancon (LA), Hill (IN), Mitchell (AZ), Wilson (OH)
Minority (R 20): Hall (TX), RMM; Sensenbrenner (WI), Smith (TX), Rohrabacher (CA), Bartlett (MD), Ehlers (MI), Lucas (OK), Biggert (IL), Akin (MO), Bonner (AL), Feeney (FL), Neugebauer (TX), Inglis (SC), Reichert (WA), McCaul (TX), M. Diaz-Balart (FL), Gingrey (GA), Bilbray (CA), Smith (NE), Broun (GA)

SUBCOMMITTEES

Energy & Environment
Majority (D 9): Lampson, Chmn.; Costello, Woolsey, Lipinski, Giffords, McNerney, Udall, Baird, Kanjorski
Minority (R 7): Inglis, RMM; Bartlett, Biggert, Akin, Neugebauer, McCaul, Diaz-Balart

Investigations & Oversight
Majority (D 6): Miller, Chmn.; Costello, Johnson, Hooley, Rothman, Baird
Minority (R 4): Sensenbrenner, RMM; Rohrabacher, Feeney, McCaul

Research & Science Education
Majority (D 7): Baird, Chmn.; Johnson, Lipinski, McNerney, Hooley, Carnahan, Hill
Minority (R 5): Ehlers, RMM; Bartlett, Lucas, Neugebauer, Bilbray

Space & Aeronautics
Majority (D 7): Udall, Chmn.; Wu, Lampson, Rothman, Ross, Chandler, Melancon
Minority (R 5): Feeney, RMM; Rohrabacher, Lucas, Bonner, McCaul

Technology & Innovation
Majority (D 7): Wu, Chmn.; Matheson, Mitchell, Wilson, Chandler, Ross, Honda
Minority (R 5): Gingrey, RMM; Ehlers, Biggert, Bonner, Smith (NE)

Select Committee on Energy Independence and Global Warming
globalwarming.house.gov

H2-250 Ford
202–225–4012

Majority (D 9): Markey (MA), Chmn.; Blumenauer (OR), Inslee (WA), Larson (CT), Solis (CA), Herseth Sandlin (SD), Cleaver (MO), Hall (NY), McNerney (CA)
Minority (R 6): Sensenbrenner (WI), RMM; Shadegg (AZ), Walden (OR), Sullivan (OK), Blackburn (TN), Miller (MI)

NO SUBCOMMITTEES

Small Business
www.house.gov/smbiz

2361 Rayburn
202–225–4038

Majority (D 16): Velazquez (NY), Chmn.; Shuler (NC), Gonzalez (TX), Larsen (WA), Grijalva (AZ), Michaud (ME), Bean (IL), Cuellar (TX), Lipinski (IL), Moore (WI), Altmire (PA), Braley (IA), Clarke (NY), Ellsworth (IN), Johnson (GA), Sestak (PA)
Minority (R 15): Chabot (OH), RMM; Bartlett (MD), Graves (MO), Akin (MO), Shuster (PA), Musgrave (CO), King (IA), Fortenberry (NE), Westmoreland (GA), Gohmert (TX), Heller (NV), Davis (TN), Fallin (OK), Buchanan (FL), Jordan (OH)

SUBCOMMITTEES

Contracting & Technology
Majority (D 6): Braley, Chmn.; Cuellar, Moore, Clarke, Sestak
Minority (D 5): Davis, RMM; Bartlett, Graves, Akin, Fallin

Finance & Tax
Majority (D 6): Bean, Chmn.; Grijalva, Michaud, Johnson, Sestak, Ellsworth
Minority (R 5): Heller, RMM; Buchanan, Jordan, Shuster, King

Investigations & Oversight
Majority (D 3): Altmire, Chmn.; Gonzalez, Grijalva
Minority (R 2): Gohmert, RMM; Westmoreland

Regulations, Healthcare & Trade
Majority (D 7): Gonzalez, Chmn.; Lipinski, Larsen, Altmire, Bean, Moore, Sestak
Minority (R 6): Westmoreland, RMM; King, Fallin, Musgrave, Buchanan, Jordan

Rural & Urban Entrepreneurship
Majority (D 7): Shuler, Chmn.; Larsen, Ellsworth, Michaud, Moore, Clarke, Johnson
Minority (R 5): Fortenberry, RMM; Musgrave, Bartlett, Heller, Davis

Standards of Official Conduct
www.house.gov/ethics

HT-2 The Capitol
202–225–7103

Majority (D 5): Tubbs Jones (OH), Chmn.; G. Green (TX), Roybal-Allard (CA), Doyle (PA), Delahunt (MA)
Minority (R 5): Hastings (WA), RMM; Bonner (AL), Barrett (SC), Kline (MN), McCaul (TX)

NO SUBCOMMITTEES

Transportation & Infrastructure
transportation.house.gov

2165 Rayburn
202–225–4472

Majority (D 40): Oberstar (MN), Chmn.; Rahall (WV), DeFazio (OR), Costello (IL), Norton (DC), Nadler (NY), Brown (FL), Filner (CA), Johnson (TX), Taylor (MS), Cummings (MD), Tauscher (CA), Boswell (IA), Holden (PA), Baird (WA), Larsen (WA), Capuano (MA), Carson (IN), Bishop (NY), Michaud (ME), Higgins (NY), Carnahan (MO), Salazar (CO), Napolitano (CA), Lipinski (IL), Matsui (CA), Lampson (TX), Space (OH), Hirono (HI), Braley (IA), Altmire (PA), Walz (MN), Shuler (NC), Arcuri (NY), Mitchell (AZ), Carney (PA), Hall (NY), Kagen (WI), Cohen (TN), McNerney (CA)
Minority (R 34): Mica (FL), RMM; Young (AK), Petri (WI), Coble (NC), Duncan (TN), Gilchrest (MD), Ehlers (MI), LaTourette (OH), Baker (LA), LoBiondo (NJ), Moran (KS), Miller (CA), Hayes (NC), Brown (SC), Johnson (IL), Platts (PA), Graves (MO), Shuster (PA), Boozman (AR), Gerlach (PA), Capito (WV), M. Diaz-Balart (FL), Dent (PA), Poe (TX), Reichert (WA), Mack (FL), Kuhl (NY), Westmoreland (GA), Boustany (LA), Schmidt (OH), Miller (MI), Drake (VA), Fallin (OK), Buchanan (FL)

SUBCOMMITTEES

Aviation
Majority (D 24): Costello, Chmn.; Filner, Boswell, Larsen, Carnahan, Salazar, Lipinski, Lampson, Space, Braley, Mitchell, Hall, Kagen, Cohen, Rahall, DeFazio, Norton, Brown, Johnson, Tauscher, Holden, Capuano, Matsui, Hirono
Minority (R 21): Petri, RMM; Coble, Duncan, Ehlers, LaTourette, LoBiondo, Moran, Hayes, Graves, Boozman, Capito, Gerlach, Diaz-Balart, Dent, Poe, Reichert, Mack, Kuhl, Westmoreland, Fallin, Buchanan

Coast Guard & Maritime Transportation
Majority (D 7): Cummings, Chmn.; Taylor, Larsen, Brown, Higgins, Baird, Bishop
Minority (R 6): LaTourette, RMM; Young, Coble, Gilchrest, Poe

Economic Development, Public Buildings & Emergency Management
Majority (D 7): Norton, Chmn.; Michaud, Altmire, Arcuri, Carney, Walz, Cohen
Minority (R 5): Graves, RMM; Shuster, Capito, Dent, Kuhl

Highways & Transit
Majority (D 27): DeFazio, Chmn.; Rahall, Nadler, Tauscher, Holden, Capuano, Carson, Bishop, Michaud, Higgins, Napolitano, Hirono, Altmire, Walz, Shuler, Arcuri, Carney, McNerney, Filner, Cummings, Baird, Lipinski, Matsui, Cohen, Space, Braley, Mitchell
Minority (R 23): Duncan, RMM; Young, Petri, Coble, Baker, Miller (CA), Hayes, Brown, Johnson, Platts, Boozman, Capito, Gerlach, Diaz-Balart, Dent, Poe, Reichert, Boustany, Schmidt, Miller (MI), Drake, Fallin, Buchanan

Railroads, Pipelines & Hazardous Materials
Majority (D 16): Brown, Chmn.; Nadler, Boswell, Carson, Napolitano, Lampson, Space, Braley, Walz, Rahall, DeFazio, Costello, Johnson, Cummings, Michaud, Lipinski
Minority (R 13): Shuster, RMM; Petri, Gilchrest, LaTourette, Moran, Miller (CA), Brown, Johnson, Platts, Graves, Gerlach, Diaz-Balart, Westmoreland

Water Resources & Environment
Majority (D 21): Johnson, Chmn.; Taylor, Baird, Matsui, Costello, Bishop, Higgins, Carnahan, Salazar, Hirono, Shuler, Mitchell, Hall, Kagen, McNerney, Norton, Filner, Tauscher, Capuano, Napolitano, Arcuri
Minority (R 17): Baker, RMM; Duncan, Gilchrest, Ehlers, LoBiondo, Miller (CA), Hayes, Brown, Platts, Shuster, Boozman, Mack, Kuhl, Boustany, Schmidt, Miller (MI), Drake

Veterans' Affairs
335 Cannon
veterans.house.gov
202–225–9756
Majority (D 16): Filner (CA), Chmn.; Brown (FL), Snyder (AR), Michaud (ME), Herseth Sandlin (SD), Mitchell (AZ), Hall (NY), Hare (IL), Doyle (PA), Berkley (NV), Salazar (CO), Rodriguez (TX), Donnelly (IN), McNerney (CA), Space (OH), Walz (MN)
Minority (R 13): Buyer (IN), RMM; Stearns (FL), Moran (KS), Baker (LA), Brown (SC), Miller (FL), Boozman (AR), Brown-Waite (FL), Turner (OH), Bilbray (CA), Lamborn (CO), Bilirakis (FL), Buchanan (FL)

SUBCOMMITTEES

Disability Assistance & Memorial Affairs
Majority (D 4): Hall, Chmn.; Rodriguez, Hare, Berkley
Minority (R 3): Lamborn, RMM; Turner, Bilirakis

Economic Opportunity
Majority (D 4): Herseth Sandlin, Chmn.; Donnelly, McNerney, Hall
Minority (R 3): Boozman, RMM; Baker, Moran

Health
Majority (D 7): Michaud, Chmn.; Brown, Snyder, Hare, Doyle, Berkley, Salazar
Minority (R 5): Miller, RMM; Stearns, Moran, Baker, Brown

Oversight & Investigations
Majority (D 4): Mitchell, Chmn.; Space, Walz, Rodriguez
Minority (R 3): Brown-Waite, RMM; Stearns, Bilbray

Ways & Means
1102 Longworth
waysandmeans.house.gov
202–225–3625
Majority (D 24): Rangel (NY), Chmn.; Stark (CA), Levin (MI), McDermott (WA), Lewis (GA), Neal (MA), McNulty (NY), Tanner (TN), Becerra (CA), Doggett (TX), Pomeroy (ND), Tubbs Jones (OH), Thompson (CA), Larson (CT), Emanuel (IL), Blumenauer (OR), Kind (WI), Pascrell (NJ), Berkley (NV), Crowley (NY), Van Hollen (MD), Meek (FL), Schwartz (PA), Davis (AL)
Minority (R 17): McCrery (LA), RMM; Herger (CA), Camp (MI), Ramstad (MN), Johnson (TX), English (PA), Weller (IL), Hulshof (MO), Lewis (KY), Brady (TX), Reynolds (NY), Ryan (WI), Cantor (VA), Linder (GA), Nunes (CA), Tiberi (OH), Porter (NV)

SUBCOMMITTEES

Health
Majority (D 8): Stark, Chmn.; Doggett, Thompson, Emanuel, Becerra, Pomeroy, Tubbs Jones, Kind
Minority (R 5): Camp, RMM; Johnson, Ramstad, English, Hulshof

Income Security & Family Support
Majority (D 8): McDermott, Chmn.; Stark, Davis, Lewis, McNulty, Berkley, Van Hollen, Meek
Minority (R 5): Weller, RMM; Herger, Camp, Porter, English

Oversight
Majority (D 8): Lewis, Chmn.; Tanner, Neal, Becerra, Tubbs Jones, Kind, Pascrell, Crowley
Minority (R 5): Ramstad, RMM; Cantor, Linder, Nunes, Tiberi

Select Revenue Measures
Majority (D 8): Neal, Chmn.; Doggett, Thompson, Larson, Schwartz, McDermott, Emanuel, Blumenauer
Minority (R 5): English, RMM; Reynolds, Cantor, Linder, Ryan

Social Security
Majority (D 8): McNulty, Chmn.; Levin, Pomeroy, Schwartz, Davis, Becerra, Doggett, Tubbs Jones
Minority (R 5): Johnson, RMM; Lewis, Brady, Ryan, Nunes

Trade
Majority (D 9): Levin, Chmn.; Tanner, Larson, Blumenauer, Pascrell, Berkley, Crowley, Van Hollen, Meek
Minority (R 6): Herger, RMM; Weller, Lewis, Brady, Reynolds, Hulshof

JOINT COMMITTEES

Joint Committee on Taxation
1015 Longworth
www.house.gov/jct
202–225–3621
House (5): Rangel (NY), Chmn.; Stark (CA), Levin (MI), McCrery (LA), Herger (CA)
Senate (5): Baucus (MT), Vice Chmn.; Rockefeller (WV), Conrad (ND), Grassley (IA), Hatch (UT)

Joint Economic Committee
433 Cannon
www.house.gov/jec
202–226–3234
House (10): Maloney (NY), Vice Chmn.; Hinchey (NY), Hill (IN), Sanchez (CA), Cummings (MD), Doggett (TX),
    Brady (TX), Saxton (NJ), RMM; English (PA), Paul (TX)
Senate (10): Schumer (NY), Chmn.; Kennedy (MA), Bingaman (NM), Klobuchar (MN), Casey (PA), Webb (VA),
    Bennett (UT), Brownback (KS), Sununu (NH), DeMint (SC)

INDEX

A

Aaron, Hank, 493
Abercrombie, Rep. Neil, 507–10
Aberdeen Proving Grounds, 767
Abramoff, Jack, 86, 98, 114, 173, 281, 1581
Acevedo Vila, Gov. Anibal, 1806–07
Ackerman, Rep. Gary, 1142–44
Acoma, NM, 1088
Aderholt, Rep. Robert, 60–61
Afro–American, 779
Air Force Academy, 323
Akaka, Sen. Daniel, **505**–07
Akin, Rep. Todd, 952–54
Akron, OH, 1308–09
Alabama Inst. For the Deaf and Blind, 59
Alamo (TX), 1591, 1594
Albany, NY, 1183, 1185–86
Albuquerque, NM, 1102–03
Alcoa, 1420, 1576
Alexander, Sen. Lamar, 1502–05
Alexander, Rep. Rodney, 728–30
Alfred P. Murrah Federal Bldg., 1344
Allard, Sen. Wayne, **307**–09
Allen, Rep. Tom, 748–50
Allentown, PA, 1422
Altmire, Rep. Jason, 1394–96
Amana colonies, 644
Amarillo, TX, 1574
American Gothic, 642
American Graffiti, 212
Ames, IA, 647
Amherst, MA, 799
Amon Carter Museum of Western Art (TX), 1571
Amoskeag Mills (NH), 1025, 1038
Anaconda Mining Co., 971
Anaheim, CA, 284
Anchorage, AL, 70–73
Anchorage Daily News, 78, 86
Anderson, IN, 617

Andrews, Rep. Robert, 1058–60
Andy Griffith Show, The, 1223
Ann Arbor, MI, 874
Annan, Kofi, 929, 1016, 1081
Anniston Army Depot (AL), 58
Apple Computer, Inc., 205
Apple, R.W., Jr., 248
Appleseed, Johnny, 1316
Arafat, Yassir, 1128
Arctic Natl. Wildlife Refuge (AK), 71, 77–78, 82–83, 85
Arcuri, Rep. Michael, 1192–93
Area 51, 1021
Argus Leader, 1491
Arkansas Democrat–Gazette, 125–26, 135–36
Arlington, TX, 1557
Arlington, VA, 1685
Armey, Dick, 1608
Armstrong, Louis, 1143
Army Corps of Engineers, 702, 726, 1366
Army Military Intelligence Center, 120
Asbury Park, NJ, 1072
Ashcroft, John, 947, 965
Asheville, NC, 1245
Aspen, CO, 318
AT&T, 1592
Athens, GA, 486
Atlanta, GA, 451, 471–79, 493
Atlanta Journal–Constitution, 482
Atlantic City, NJ, 1061–62
Atwater, Lee, 1451–52
Auburn Univ., 59
Augusta, GA, 486, 491
Austin, TX, 1567, 1594, 1604–05, 1619
Austin, Stephen, 1567
Austin American–Statesman, 1567

B

B.F. Goodrich, 1308
Baca, Rep. Joe, **273**–75
Bachus, Rep. Spencer, 64–66
Bachmann, Rep. Michele, 902–03
Bada Bing (NJ), 1078

Baird, Rep. Brian, 1715–17
Baker, Rep. Richard, 730–34
Bakersfield, CA, 217, 220–21
Baldacci, Gov. John, 740–43
Baldwin, Rep. Tammy, 1771–73
Ballance, Frank, 1222
Baltimore, MD, 755, 767, 769, 779
Bangor, ME, 752
Barbour, Gov. Haley, 916–19
Barkley, Charles, 47
Barksdale Air Force Base (LA), 726
Barnum, P.T., 354
Barrasso, Sen. John, 1798–99
Barrett, Rep. Gresham, 1468–69
Barrow, Rep. John, **490**–92
Barry, Marion, 372–73
Bartlett, Rep. Roscoe, 776–78
Barton, Rep. Joe, **1556**–59
Basketball Hall of Fame, 801
Batelle Memorial Institute, 1313
Bath Iron Works, 738
Batman, 1650
Baton Rouge, LA, 731
Baucus, Sen. Max, **977**–80
Bauer, Gary, 693
Bayh, Birch, 599, 601–03
Bayh, Sen. Evan, **601**–03
Baylor Univ., 1583
Beach Boys, 255, 258, 281
Bean, Rep. Melissa, **560**–62
Beaumont, TX, 1548
Beaverton, OR, 1360
Becerra, Rep. Xavier, 244–46
Beebe, Gov. Mike, **125**–26
Bell, Art, 1021
Bennett, Sen. Robert, 1633–35
Bentonville, AR, 138
Bentsen, Lloyd, 1540
Berger, Sandy, 244
Berkeley, CA, 189–90

Berkley, Rep. Shelley,
1017–19
Berlin, NH, 1041
Berman, Rep. Howard,
233–37
Berman, Michael, 235, 237
Berry, Rep. Marion, 132–34
Bethlehem, PA, 1422
Beverly Hills, CA, 242
Biden, Sen. Joseph, 363–67
Big Chill, The, 1467
Big Dig (MA), 820
Biggert, Rep. Judy, 571–73
Bilbray, Rep. Brian, 289–92
Bilirakis, Rep. Gus, 410–12
Billings, MT, 971
Biloxi, MS, 936–37
Bingaman, Sen. Jeff,
1099–1101
Bird, Larry, 624
Bird–in–Hand, PA, 1425
Birmingham, AL, 41, 64–65,
67
Bishop, Rep. Rob, 1635–37
Bishop, Rep. Sanford,
466–68
Bishop, Rep. Tim, 1133–35
Black, Hugo, 41
Black Hawk, CO, 316
Black Metropolis, 559
Black Panthers, 190
Blackburn, Rep. Marsha,
1521–23
Blagojevich, Gov. Rod,
532–35
Blair, Diane, 123
**Blanco, Gov. Kathleen
Babineaux, 706**–09
Bloomberg, Michael, 1124,
1150, 1167
Blue Ball, PA, 1425
Blue Diamond, NV, 1023
Blumenauer, Rep. Earl,
1364–66
Blunt, Gov. Matt, 943–45
Blunt, Rep. Roy, 963–66
Bob Jones Univ. (SC), 1471
Boehner, Rep. John,
1294–97
Boeing, 235, 1713
Boise, ID, 523, 525
**Bond, Sen. Christopher
(Kit), 945**–47
Bonner, Rep. Jo, 53–55
Bono, Rep. Mary, 277–79
Bono, Sonny, 255, 279
Book of Virtues, 342

Boozman, Rep. John,
137–39
Bordallo, Del. Madeleine,
1813
Boren, David, 1323, 1338
Boren, Rep. Dan, 1337–39
Bork, Robert, 1381
Boston, MA, 813, 817–20
Boston Globe, 818, 820
Boston Herald, 796, 820
Boswell, Rep. Leonard,
643–45
Boucher, Rep. Rick,
1686–88
Boulder, CO, 315–16
Boulder City, NV, 1023
Boulder School of Massage
Therapy, 316
Boustany, Rep. Charles,
734–36
Bowles, Erskine, 1216, 1219
Boxer, Sen. Barbara,
161–64
Boyd, Rep. Allen, 395–97
Boyda, Rep. Nancy, 665–67
Boys Town (NE), 999
BP Chemicals, 1576
Bradlee, Ben, 1083
Bradley, Bill, 941
Brady, Rep. Kevin, 1561–63
Brady, Rep. Robert,
1387–90
Braley, Rep. Bruce, 639–40
Brandeis Univ., 813
Brann, William Cowper, 1583
Branson, MO, 964–65
Bredesen, Gov. Phil,
1499–1502
Brentwood, NY, 1136
Brigham Young Univ. (UT),
1641
Broadhurst, Billy, 127
Broadview Heights, OH, 1309
Broder, David, 547
Broiler litter, 358
Bronx, NY, 1148, 1174–77
Brookline, MA, 805
Brooklyn, NY, 1150, 1153,
1156–61
Brooklyn Bridge (NY), 1150,
1158
Brooks, David, 326
Broun, Rep. Paul, 485–87
Brown, Rep. Corrine,
397–99
Brown, Rep. Henry,
1463–65
Brown, Jerry, 145

Brown, Pat, 144
Brown, Sen. Sherrod,
1276–78
Brown, Willie, 145, 184
Brown Univ., 1444
Brown v. Board of Education,
666, 1467
Brownback, Sen. Sam,
656–59
Brown–Waite, Rep. Ginny,
401–03
Brunswick Naval Air Station,
749
Bryan, William Jennings,
1513
Buchanan, James, 1407, 1425
Buchanan, Pat, 1503
Buchanan, Rep. Vern,
420–22
Buckley v. Valeo, 746
Bucks County, PA, 1404
Buffalo, NY, 1198, 1201
Buffett, Warren, 986, 989, 999
Bull Durham, 1229
Bunning, Sen. Jim, 682–85
Burgess, Rep. Michael,
1606–08
Burr, Aaron, 1087, 1123, 1219
Burr, Sen. Richard,
1218–21
Burton, Rep. Dan, 613–15
Burton, Phillip, 185
Bush, Laura, 1569
Bustamante, Cruz, 147
Butte, MT, 971
Butterfield, Rep. G.K.,
1221–23
Butternuts, 594, 623
Buyer, Rep. Steve, 610–12
Byrd, Harry, 1657, 1678
Byrd, Sen. Robert, 1740–44

C

Cabrini–Green, 559
Cairo, IL, 570
California Coastal
Commission, 242
Calle Ocho, 433, 440
Calvert, Rep. Ken, 275–77
Camacho, Gov. Felix, 1812
Cambridge, MA, 817–18
Camden, NJ, 1059–60
Camp, Rep. Dave, 847–48
Camp Pendleton (CA), 289
Campbell, Ben Nighthorse,
303
Campbell, Carroll, 1451, 1453

Campbell, Rep. John, 284–86
Campbell Soup Co., 1059
Cannon, Rep. Chris, 1640–42
Cannon, Clarence, 970
Cannon, Lou, 145
Cannon Air Force Base (NM), 1109
Canton, OH, 1315–16
Cantor, Rep. Eric, **1681**–83
Cantwell, Sen. Maria, 1707–10
Cape Canaveral (FL), 426
Cape Cod (MA), 822
Cape Girardeau, MO, 968
Cape May, NJ, 1062
Capito. Rep. Shelley Moore, 1750–52
Capone, Al, 551
Capote, Truman, 54
Capps, Rep. Lois, **222**–24
Capuano, Rep. Michael, 816–18
Carcieri, Gov. Donald, 1437–39
Card, Andrew, 1036
Cardin, Sen. Ben, 761–63
Cardoza, Rep. Dennis, 211–13
Carnahan, Rep. Russ, 954–56
Carney, Rep. Christopher, 1408–10
Carper, Sen. Thomas, 367–69
Carson, Rep. Julia, **618**–21
Carson City, NV, 1020–21
Carswell Air Force Base (TX), 1571
Carter, Jimmy, 41, 451
Carter, Rep. John, 1618–20
Cascade Mountains, 1363
Case, Ed, 501, 507, 511
Case Western Reserve Univ., 1301, 1304
Casey, Sen. Bob, **1385**–87
Cash, Johnny, 1612
Castle, Rep. Michael, 369–72
Castor, Rep. Kathy, **416**–18
Castro, Fidel, 433
Cather, Willa, 986, 994, 1001
Catskills (NY), 1188
Cedar Rapids, IA, 641
Central Command, 415, 417
Center Township, IN, 620
Centralia, PA, 1411

Central Park (NY), 1166–67
Chabot, Rep. Steve, **1278**–81
Chadds Ford, PA, 1402
Chafee, John, 1433, 1442
Challenger Space Shuttle, 387
Chambliss, Sen. Saxby, **459**–61
Champaign–Urbana, IL, 581
Chandler, Rep. Ben, **698**–700
Chao, Elaine, 679
Charles City, IA, 647
Charleston, SC, 1464–65, 1477
Charleston, WV, 1751
Charleston Naval Base (SC), 1465
Charlotte, NC, 1239–41, 1248
Charlottesville, VA, 1678
Chattanooga, TN, 1513
Chavez, Hugo, 1175
Cheney, Dick, **39**, 1610, 1782, 1792
Cherokee Nation, 1338
Cherry Hill, NJ, 1064
Cherry Point Marine Corps Air Station (NC), 1226
Chertoff, Michael, 932, 1130
Chesapeake Bay, 764, 1671
Chicago, IL, 527–30, 544–59, 565
Chicago Heights, IL, 547
Chicago Sun–Times, 547
Chicago Tribune, 540, 547, 555
Chiles, Lawton, 387, 419
Chillicothe, OH, 1322
Chincoteague, VA, 1671
Chisholm, Shirley, 1159
Christensen, Del. Donna, **1809**–10
Church of Scientology, 411
Churchill, Winston, 970
Cianci, Buddy, 1433
Cincinnati, OH, 1279–82
Clarendon (VA), 1685
Clark, Wesley, 1029, 1039
Clark County, NV, 1023
Clark County, OH, 1292
Clarke, Rep. Yvette, **1157**–60
Clay, Rep. William Lacy, **950**–52
Cleaver, Rep. Emanuel, **959**–61
Cleland, Max, 460
Clemson Univ., 1469

Cleveland, OH, 1301–04
Cleveland Clinic, 1304
Clinton, Bill, 121–24, 138, 1127
Clinton, Sen. Hillary Rodham, 138, **1126**–32
Clooney, George, 694
Clotilde, 67
Club for Growth, 854
Clyburn, Rep. James, **1476**–78
Coast Guard Academy (CT), 349
Coble, Rep. Howard, **1233**–35
Coburn, Sen. Tom, **1332**–35
Cochran, Sen. Thad, **919**–22
Coeur d'Alene, ID, 523
Cohen, Rep. Steve, **1525**–27
Colbert Report, The, 436
Cole, Rep. Tom, **1341**–43
Coleman, Michael, 1306
Coleman, Sen. Norm, **885**–87
College Station, TX, 1583
Collins, Sen. Susan, **745**–48
Colorado Springs, CO, 323
Columbia, SC, 1466–67, 1477
Columbia River Gorge (OR), 1363, 1365
Columbia Space Shuttle, 387,1546
Columbine High School, 326
Columbus, OH, 1306–07, 1313
Comstock Lode (NV), 1003, 1020
Conan the Barbarian, 153
Conaway, Rep. Mike, **1568**–70
Concord, NH, 1041
Concord Monitor, 1030
Condit, Gary, 212
Congress from the Inside, 1277
Connor, Bull, 41, 65
Conrad, Sen. Kent, **1258**–61
Conroe, TX, 1562
Constitutional Convention, 1371
Continental Congress, 1371, 4132
Conyers, Rep. John, **869**–73
Cooper, Rep. Jim, **1516**–19
Corker, Sen. Bob, **1506**–07
Cornyn, Sen. John, **1541**–45
Corpus Christi, TX, 1609–10
Corzine, Gov. Jon, **1047**–51

Costa, Rep. Jim, **215**–17
Costello, Rep. Jerry, 569–71
Cotton Bowl (TX), 1555
Cotton Kingdom, 1526
Coughlin, Charles, 866
Council Bluffs, IA, 649
Country Music Hall of Fame & Museum (TN), 1518
Courier–Journal (KY), 684
Courtney, Rep. Joe, **348**–50
Craddick, Tom, 1532, 1537
Craig, Sen. Larry, **517**–20
Cramer, Rep. Bud, **62**–64
Crapo, Sen. Mike, **520**–22
Crawford, TX, 1583
Crenshaw, Rep. Ander, 399–401
Crist, Gov. Charlie, **384**–86
Crockett, Davy, 1522, 1591
Cross, Al, 674
Crowley, Rep. Joseph, 1147–49
Crucible, The, 811
Crump, Edward, 1496
Cubin, Rep. Barbara, 1800–02
Cuellar, Rep. Henry, 1611–14
Culberson, Rep. John, 1559–61
Culver, Gov. Chet, 631–32
Cumberland Plateau (TN), 1515
Cummings, Rep. Elijah, 778–80
Cuomo, Andrew, 1117, 1172
Custer, George, 1322, 1478

D

Dakota County, MN, 893
Daley, Richard J., 527, 529–30, 549, 556, 558
Daley, Richard M., 530, 534, 545, 556, 558
Dallas, 1550
Dallas, TX, 1550–51, 1555, 1617
Dallas Morning News, 1554, 1608
Dallas/Fort Worth Intl. Airport (TX), 1602
Dallas–Fort Worth Metroplex (TX), 1550, 1553, 1557, 1602, 1607
D'Amato, Alfonse, 1123, 1138
Danforth, John, 1381
Daniels, Gov. Mitch, **596**–98

Dartmouth College (NH), 1041
Daschle, Tom, 1481, 1489–90
Dating Game, The, 830
Davenport, IA, 639–40
Davis, Rep. Artur, **66**–68
Davis, Rep. Danny, **557**–59
Davis, Rep. David, **1508**–09
Davis, Rep. Geoff, **692**–94
Davis, Jefferson, 41, 1671, 1682
Davis, Jo Ann, 1667–69
Davis, Rep. Lincoln, 1514–16
Davis, Mac, 1589
Davis, Rep. Susan, **298**–300
Davis, Rep. Tom, **1692**–95
Dayton, OH, 1284–85, 1294–95
Dayton, TN, 1513
Daytona Beach, FL, 406, 447
Deal, Rep. Nathan, **483**–85
Dean, Howard, 1647
Dean, Jimmy, 1589
Dearborn, MI, 871
Death of a Salesman, 279
Deer Hunter, The, 1420
DeFazio, Rep. Peter, 1366–69
DeGette, Rep. Diana, 312–14
DeJongh, Gov. John, 1809
Delahunt, Rep. Bill, **821**–23
DeLauro, Rep. Rosa, 350–52
Delaware County, PA, 1389, 1402
Delaware Turnpike, 358
DeLay, Tom, 1537, 1598
Dell Computer, 1619
Delray Beach, FL, 442, 445
DeMint, Sen. Jim, **1461**–63
Denison, TX, 1553
Dent, Rep. Charlie, 1421–23
Denver, CO, 313–14, 325–26, 328
Denver Post, 305
Dept. of Peace, 1302
Des Moines, IA, 644
Des Moines Register, 627, 645
Detroit, MI, 868–71
Detroit Free Press, 872
Dewey Defeats Truman, 848
Dewhurst, David, 1532, 1537
Diaz–Balart, Rep. Lincoln, **439**–41

Diaz–Balart, Rep. Mario, 448–51
Dickinson, Bill, 57
Dicks, Rep. Norm, **1722**–25
Digital Millennium Copyright Act, 1632, 1650
Dingell, Rep. John, **873**–77
Dinkytown (MN), 900
DiPrete, Edward, 1438
Disney, Walt, 283, 408–09, 447
Disney World (FL), 409, 426
Disneyland (CA), 267, 283–84
Ditka, Mike, 1395
Divided Highways, 1407
Dixie Chicks, 1589
Dixon, IL, 575
Dixville Notch, NH, 1041
Do the Right Thing, 1156
Dobson, James, 1382
Dodd, Sen. Christopher, 336–39
Dodge City, KS, 664
Dodger Stadium (CA), 245
Doggett, Rep. Lloyd, 1603–06
Dole, Bob, 1216
Dole, Sen. Elizabeth, 1215–18
Dollywood (TN), 1509
Domenici, Sen. Pete, 1096–99
Donnelly, Rep. Joe, **606**–08
Doolittle, Rep. John, 171–74
Doonesbury, 795
Dorgan, Sen. Byron, 1261–63
Dornan, Robert, 281, 283
Douglas, Gov. Jim, **1647**–49
Dover, NH, 1039
Doyle, Gov. James, **1760**–63
Doyle, Rep. Mike, **1419**–21
Dr. Pepper, 1583
Drake, Rep. Thelma, 1670–72
Dreier, Rep. David, **228**–31
Drums Along the Mohawk, 1192
Duke, David, 703, 713
Duke Univ. (NC), 1229
Dulles Intl. Airport, 1690
Duluth, MN, 908
Duncan, Rep. John, 1510–12
DuPont, 358
Durbin, Sen. Richard, 535–37

Durham, NC, 1229
Dust Bowl, 1323, 1340
Dyess Air Force Base (TX), 1589
Dylan, Bob, 900

E

Earle, Ronnie, 1532, 1535
Earlham College, 617
Easley, Gov. Michael, 1212–14
East Cleveland, OH, 1304
East St. Louis, IL, 570
Eau Claire, WI, 1774
Edgar Springs, MO, 968
Edina, MN, 895
Edison, Thomas, 1042, 1071
Edwards, Rep. Chet, 1582–86
Edwards, Edwin, 703, 735
Edwards, John, 1210, 1219
Ehlers, Rep. Vernon, 844–46
Eisenhower, Dwight, 664
El Dorado, AR, 140
El Paso, TX, 1581
Election Systems & Software, 991
Eli Lilly & Co., 593, 602, 615
Ellington, Duke, 1143, 1156
Ellis Island (NJ), 1086
Ellison, Rep. Keith, 899–901
Ellsworth, Rep. Brad, 621–23
Ellsworth Air Force Base (SD)
Elmendorf Air Force Base (AK), 68
Ely, Joe, 1589
Emanuel, Rep. Rahm, 553–55
Embarrassment of Riches, The, 1109
Emerson, Bill, 968
Emerson, Rep. Jo Ann, 967–69
Engel, Rep. Eliot, 1176–77
Engler, John, 826, 830
English, Rep. Phil, 1392–94
Enron, 1560, 1587
Ensign, Mike, 1013–14
Ensign, Sen. John, 1014–17
Enterprise Rent–A–Car, 963
Environmental Protection Agency, 1511, 1559
Enzi, Sen. Michael, 1796–98
Erie County, NY, 1198
Erie, PA, 1393

Eshoo, Rep. Anna, 201–03
ESPN, 347
Etheridge, Rep. Bob, 1223–25
Eugene, OR, 1367–68
Evans, Donald, 1569
Evanston, IL, 563
Evansville, IN, 621–22
Everett, WA, 1713
Everett, Rep. Terry, 55–57
Everglades, 449–50
Everglades: River of Grass, The, 382
Exeter, NH, 1039

F

Face the Nation, 366
Fahrenheit 9/11, 1054
Fairfax County, VA, 1693
Fairfield, CA, 192
Faith of My Fathers, 95
Faleomavaega, Del. Eni F.H., 1815–16
Fall River, MA, 803
Fallin, Rep. Mary, 1344–45
Fallon Naval Air Station (NV), 1021
Falwell, Jerry, 1680
Farr, Rep. Sam, 208–10
Fattah, Rep. Chaka, 1390–92
Fayetteville, AR, 138
FedEx, 1526
Feeney, Rep. Tom, 446–48
Feingold, Sen. Russell, 1765–69
Feinstein, Sen. Dianne, 157–61
Fenty, Adrian, 374
Ferguson, Rep. Michael, 1073–75
Ferris Bueller's Day Off, 565
Field of Dreams, 625
Fillmore, UT, 1629
Filner, Rep. Bob, 292–94
Fingerhut, Eric, 1276, 1311
Fitzgerald, Peter, 530, 541, 589
Flagstaff, AZ, 104
Flake, Rep. Jeff, 115–17
Fletcher, Gov. Ernie, 676–78
Flint, MI, 850
Flint Hills (KS), 664
Focus on the Family, 323
Foley, Mark, 428, 578, 903, 1182, 1199, 1314
Folsom, Jim, 41

Forbes, 1336, 1764
Forbes, Rep. Randy, 1675–77
Forbes, Steve, 1384, 1503
Foreign Affairs, 992
Forest County, PA, 1397
Forest Hills, NY, 1153
Forrest Gump, 54, 465
Fort A.P. Hill (VA), 1668
Fort Bend County, TX, 1564, 1597
Fort Benning (GA), 467
Fort Campbell (TN), 1522
Fort Carson (CO), 323
Fort Collins, CO, 321
Fort Dix (NJ), 1064
Fort Greely (AK), 68
Fort Knox (KY), 688
Fort Lauderdale, FL, 436–38, 442
Fort Leavenworth (KS), 665
Fort Monroe (VA), 1671
Fort Myers, FL, 423–24
Fort Payne, AL, 61
Fort Rucker (AL), 56
Fort Sam Houston (TX), 1594
Fort Sill (OK), 1342
Fort Wayne, IN, 609
Fort Worth, TX, 1571–72
Fortenberry, Rep. Jeff, 996–98
Fortuno, Del. Luis, 1807–08
Fossella, Rep. Vito, 1163–65
Fox River Valley (WI), 1782, 1788–89
Foxx, Rep. Virginia, 1231–33
Frank, Rep. Barney, 804–08
Frank, Thomas, 650
Franks, Tommy, 1569
Franks, Rep. Trent, 106–108
Frederick, MD, 777
Freedom fries, 1227
Frelinghuysen, Rep. Rodney, 1081–83
Fresno Bee, 215, 219
Fresno, CA, 212, 214, 218
Freudenthal, Gov. Dave, 1794–96
Friday Night Lights, 1569
Fried Green Tomatoes, 481
Frist, Bill, 1498, 1503, 1506

Fulbright, William, 123
Furniture Mart, 1234
Future Farmers of America, 1327

G

Gadsden, AL, 61
Gainesville, FL, 398
Gallegly, Rep. Elton, 224–26
Galveston, TX, 1576, 1615
Gannett, 1503
Garfield, James, 1301, 1311
Garreau, Joel, 1693
Garrett, Rep. Scott, 1068–70
Gary, IN, 605
Gates, Bill, 1730
Gateway Arch (MO), 951
Gatlinburg, TN, 1509
Genentech, 197
General Electric, 799, 811
General Motors, 826, 850, 866, 868, 1557
George Bush Intercontinental Airport (TX), 1562
George H.W. Bush Presidential Library (TX), 1583
George Washington Bridge (NJ), 1078
Gerlach, Rep. Jim, 1399–1401
Geronimo, 120
Gerry, Elbridge, 757, 788, 811
Gibbons, Gov. Jim, 1008–10
Giffords, Rep. Gabrielle, 119–21
Gilchrest, Rep. Wayne, 763–66
Gillibrand, Rep. Kirsten, 1182–84
Gilligan, John, 654
Gillmor, Paul, 1288–89
Gingrey, Rep. Phil, 487–89
Gingrich, Newt, 576
Giuliani, Rudolph, 1109, 1113, 1128–29
Glendale, AZ, 107
Glenn, John, 1274, 1276, 1295
Glickman, Dan, 671
Glory, 465
Goddard Space Flight Center (MD), 760, 774
Gods and Generals, 1741
Gohmert, Rep. Louie, 1545–47
Goldman Sachs, 1048

Goldwater, Barry, 87, 109, 115
Gone with the Wind, 451, 470
Gonzales, Alberto, 311, 344, 793, 1545, 1632
Gonzales, Elian, 431
Gonzalez, Rep. Charles, 1591–93
Goode, Rep. Virgil, 1677–79
Goode, Wilson, 1377, 1388
Goodlatte, Rep. Bob, 1679–81
Goodyear, 1308
Google, 203, 874, 1363, 1711
Gordon, Rep. Bart, 1519–21
Gore, Al, 1496, 1518
Gore, Albert Sr., 1496
Gorton, Slade, 1708
Goss, Porter, 424
Graceland (TN), 1494, 1526
Graham, Sen. Lindsey, 1457–60
Gramm, Phil, 1542, 1590
Grand Canyon, 104
Grand Ole Opry, 1517
Grand Rapids, MI, 845
Granger, Rep. Kay, 1570–72
Granholm, Gov. Jennifer, 830–32
Grant, Ulysses S., 1678
Grapes of Wrath, The, 209, 221
Grassley, Sen. Charles, 632–35
Graves, Rep. Sam, 961–63
Gray Panthers, 1354
Great Falls, MT, 971
Great Gatsby, The, 1143
Green Bay, WI, 1788–89
green chile diplomacy, 1094
Green, Rep. Al, 1563–64
Green, Rep. Gene, 1614–16
Greenberg, Paul, 135
Greensboro, NC, 1234, 1248
Greenwich, CT, 354
Gregg, Sen. Judd, 1032–34
Gregoire, Gov. Christine, 1701–04
Grey, Zane, 1322
Grijalva, Rep. Raul, 117–19
Guardian, 1227, 1270, 1292
Guinn, Kenny, 1006
Guinness Book of World Records, 1093
Gunite/EMI, 1393
Gutierrez, Carlos, 854
Gutierrez, Rep. Luis, 550–52
Gwinnett County, GA, 478–79

H

Hagel, Sen. Chuck, 990–93
Haggard, Merle, 1338
Hahn, James, 246, 255–56
Haley, Alex, 1524
Hall, Rep. John, 1180–82
Hall, Rep. Ralph, 1552–54
Halliburton, 1587
Hamburger Univ., 572
Hamilton, Alexander, 1076, 1087, 1808
Hampton Roads (VA) 1668, 1676
Hamptons (NY), 1134
Hamtramck, MI, 866, 871
Hanover, NH, 1041
Hare, Rep. Phil, 585–86
Harkin, Sen. Tom, 635–38
Harlem, NY, 1169–70
Harlingen, TX, 1578
Harman, Rep. Jane, 257–60
Harris County, TX, 1548
Harrisburg, PA, 1427
Hart, Gary, 127
Hartford, CT, 347
Hartford Courant, The, 355
Hastert, Rep. Dennis, 574–79
Hastings, Rep. Alcee, 444–46
Hastings, Rep. Doc, 1717–20
Hatch, Sen. Orrin, 1630–32
Hayes, Rep. Robin, 1237–39
HealthAmerica, 1499
Heineman, Gov. Dave, 988–90
Helena, MT, 971, 973
Heller, Rep. Dean, 1020–22
Hemingway, Ernest, 559, 840
Henderson, NV, 1023
Hendrix, Jimi, 1733
Henry, Gov. Brad, 1327–29
Hensarling, Rep. Jeb, 1554–56
Herenton, Willie, 1504
Herger, Rep. Wally, 167–69
Herseth Sandlin, Rep. Stephanie, 1492–94
Hershey, PA, 1427
Heston, Charlton, 46
Hewlett–Packard, 1359, 1587
Higgins, Rep. Brian, 1200–02
High Point, NC, 1234
Hill Air Force Base (UT), 1636
Hill, Lister, 41
Hill, Rep. Baron, 623–24

Hillsdale College (MI), 854
Hinchey, Rep. Maurice,
    1187–89
Hindenburg, 1066
Hinojosa, Rep. Ruben,
    1577–80
Hirono, Rep. Mazie, 500,
    510–12
Hoboken, NJ, 1087
Hobson, Rep. David,
    1291–93
Hodes, Rep. Paul, 1040–42
Hodges, Jim, 1453–54
Hoekstra, Rep. Peter,
    841–44
Hoeven, Gov. John,
    1256–58
Holden, Rep. Tim, 1426–28
Hollings, Ernest, 1451, 1462
Hollins Univ. (VA), 1680
Holloman Air Force Base
    (NM), 1101, 1106
Holly, Buddy, 1589
Hollywood, CA, 239, 242
Holt, Rep. Rush, 1083–85
Home on the Range, 664
Honda, Rep. Mike, 204–06
Honeymooners, The, 1164
Honolulu, HI, 508
Hooley, Rep. Darlene,
    1369–71
Hoosiers, 624
Hooters Air, 583
Hoover Dam (NV), 1023
Hopi Tribe, 87
Houston, TX, 1560–67, 1587,
    1615
Houston, Sam, 1567
Houston Chronicle, 1561
Houston Ship Channel, 1615
*How to Conquer Texas Before
    It Conquers Us*, 1531
Hoyer, Rep. Steny, 772–75
Huckabee, Mike, 123, 125–26
Huffington, Michael, 160
Hughes, Howard, 254, 258
Hulshof, Rep. Kenny,
    969–71
Hunt, J.B., 123
Hunter, Rep. Duncan,
    295–98
Huntsman, Gov. Jon,
    1628–30
Huntsville, AL, 43, 63
Hurston, Zora Neale
Hustler, 1282, 1503
**Hutchison, Sen. Kay
    Bailey, 1539**–41

I
IBM, 1112, 1179
Iconoclast, The, 1583
Idaho Statesman, 514,
    519–20, 526
Imus, Don, 1051
Incline Village, NV, 1021
Independence Hall (PA), 1388
Indian Territory (OK), 1338,
    1340
Indiana Univ., 624
Indianapolis, IN, 614, 619–20
Indianapolis Star, 620
Inglis, Rep. Bob, 1470–72
Inhofe, Sen. James,
    1329–32
Inouye, Sen. Daniel, 502–04
Inslee, Rep. Jay, 1710–12
Instapundit.com, 1511
Intel, 1360
Intercourse, PA, 1425
Intl. Criminal Court, 1383
Intl. Paper, 1393
Intl. Surfing Museum (CA),
    280
Intl. UFO Museum (NM),
    1105
Iowa Caucuses, 628–30
Iowa City, IA, 641–42
Iowa State Fair, 627
Iowa State Univ., 629
Iron Range (MN), 908
Isakson, Sen. Johnny,
    462–64
Israel, Rep. Steve, 1135–37
Issa, Rep. Darrell, 287–89
It Takes a Village, 1128

J
Jackson, MS, 931, 934
Jackson, TN, 1524
Jackson, Andrew, 41, 1473,
    1515
Jackson, Rep. Jesse, Jr.,
    545–47
Jackson Hole, WY, 1792
Jackson Lee, Rep. Sheila,
    1586–88
Jacksonville, FL, 398, 400,
    404
Jamestown, VA, 1668
Janklow, Bill, 1480–81,
    1483–84
Jefferson, Thomas, 672, 1655,
    1682
Jefferson, Rep. William,
    718–21, 1248
Jennings, Christine, 422

Jennings, Waylon, 1589
Jeopardy!, 1085
Jersey City, NJ, 1080, 1087
Jersey Shore, 1062
Jindal, Rep. Bobby, 707–09,
    715–17
Johanns, Mike, 988
John Deere, 640
John F. Kennedy Intl. Airport
    (NY), 1145
Johnson, Hiram, 183–84
Johnson, Magic, 251
**Johnson, Rep. Eddie
    Bernice, 1616**–18
Johnson, Rep. Hank,
    471–73
Johnson, Rep. Sam,
    1549–52
Johnson, Rep. Tim, 580–82
Johnson, Sen. Tim, 1485–88
Johnson City, TN, 1496, 1508
Johnson Space Center (TX),
    1597
Johnstown, PA, 1413–14
Joliet, IL, 568
**Jones, Rep. Stephanie
    Tubbs, 1303**–05
Jones, Rep. Walter,
    1225–28
Jonesboro, AR, 133
Joplin, Janis, 1548
Jordan, Rep. Jim, 1286–88
Jordan, Michael, 540, 558,
    1764
Joshua Tree Natl. Park, 279
Journal Sentinel (WI), 1764,
    1783
Juarez, Mexico, 1581
Juneau, AK, 70

K
Kagen, Rep. Steve, 1788–90
Kaine, Gov. Tim, 1659–61
Kaiser, Henry J., 180
Kalispell, MT, 971–73
Kanjorski, Rep. Paul,
    1410–12
Kansas City, KS, 668
Kansas City, MO, 960, 962
Kansas State Univ., 666
Kaptur, Rep. Marcy,
    1298–1300
Keating, Frank, 1326–27
Kefauver, Estes, 1496
Keller, Rep. Ric, 408–10
Kellogg, 854
Kelly, Jim, 1395
Kelly Air Force Base, 1592

Kempthorne, Dirk, 512, 514, 516

Kennedy, Sen. Edward, 790–93

Kennedy, John F., 785

Kennedy, Rep. Patrick, 1443–46

Kennedy Space Center (FL), 447

Kent State Univ., 1319

Kerry, Sen. John, 794–97

Key, V.O., 43, 1509

Kildee, Rep. Dale, 849–51

Kilpatrick, Rep. Carolyn Cheeks, 867–69

Kilpatrick, Kwame, 869

Kind, Rep. Ron, 1773–75

King, Martin Luther, Jr., 41, 474–75

King, Rep. Peter, 1137–39

King, Rodney, 145

King, Rep. Steve, 648–50

King of the Hill, 1214

Kingsport, TN, 1508

Kingston, Rep. Jack, 464–66

Kipling, Rudyard, 1644

Kirk, Rep. Mark, 564–67

Kirk, Ron, 1536–37, 1542

Kiryas Joel, NY, 1181

Klein, Rep. Ron, 441–43

Kline, Rep. John, 892–94

Klobuchar, Sen. Amy, 888–89

Knollenberg, Rep. Joe, 857–60

Knowles, Tony, 72, 75

Knoxville, TN, 1511

Kohl, Sen. Herb, 1763–65

Kotkin, Joel, 225, 269

Ku Klux Klan, 58, 65, 471

Kucinich, Rep. Dennis, 1300–03

Kuhl, Rep. Randy, 1205–07

Kulongoski, Gov. Ted, 1350–53

Kyl, Sen. Jon, 100–03

L

La Crosse, WI, 1774

La Grande, OR, 1363

Lackland Air Force Base (TX), 1592, 1599

Lafayette, IN, 611

LaGuardia, Fiorello, 1112, 1166, 1170

LaHood, Rep. Ray, 587–89

Lake Havasu City, AZ, 107

Lake Minnetonka (MN), 895–96

Lake Shore Drive, 558

Lake Tahoe, NV, 1003, 1021

Lambeau Field (WI), 1789

Lamborn, Rep. Doug, 322–24

Lamont, Ned, 344–45

Lampson, Rep. Nick, 1596–98

Landon, Alf, 1496

Landrieu, Sen. Mary, 709–12

Langevin, Rep. Jim, 1446–49

Langley Air Force Base (VA), 1671

Lansing, MI, 856

Lantos, Rep. Tom, 196–99

Laredo, TX, 1612

Larsen, Rep. Rick, 1712–14

Larson, Rep. John, 346–48

Las Cruces, NM, 1105–06

Las Vegas, NV, 1003, 1018, 1023

Las Vegas Sun, 1010

Last Picture Show, 1589

Latham, Rep. Tom, 646–47

LaTourette, Rep. Steven, 1310–12

Lautenberg, Sen. Frank, 1051–55

Lawrence, KS, 668

LAX, 162, 255

Lay, Kenneth, 1587

Lazio, Rick, 1129

LBJ Presidential Library (TX), 1604

LBJ Ranch (TX), 1569

Leahy, Sen. Patrick, 1649–51

Leatherstocking Tales, 1192

Leave it to Beaver, 234

Leaves of Grass, 1059

Lee, Rep. Barbara, 189–91

Lee, Robert E., 1669, 1680, 1682

Levin, Sen. Carl, 833–36

Levin, Rep. Sander, 865–67

Levittown, NY, 1138

Levy, Chandra, 213

Lewis, Rep. Jerry, 268–70

Lewis, Rep. John, 473–75

Lewis, John L., 590

Lewis, Rep. Ron, 687–89

Lexington, KY, 699

Liberty Univ. (VA), 1680

Lieberman, Sen. Joe, 340–46

Life on the Mississippi, 716

Limbaugh, Rush, 968

Lincoln, Abraham, 527, 568, 583, 1508

Lincoln, Sen. Blanche, 127–29

Lincoln, NE, 997

Lincoln Park, IL, 554

Lindbergh, Charles, 1074, 1141

Linder, Rep. John, 478–80

Lindsay, John, 1113, 1153

Lineville, AL, 58

Lingle, Gov. Linda, 499–501

Lipinski, Bill, 549

Lipinski, Rep. Daniel, 548–50

Little Dixie (MO), 940, 970

Little Dixie (OK), 1338

Little League World Series, 1409

Little Rock, AR, 135

Little Texas (NM), 1088, 1105

Livonia, MI, 863–64

L.L. Bean, 749

LoBiondo, Rep. Frank, 1061–63

Locher, Ralph, 1304

Lockheed Martin, 488, 1571

Loeb, William, 1025

Loebsack, Rep. Dave, 641–43

Lofgren, Rep. Zoe, 206–208

London, Jack, 190

Long, Huey P., 729

Long Beach, CA, 260–61, 281

Long Branch, NJ, 1071

Long Island, NY, 1133–34

Lookout Mountain (TN), 1494, 1513

Lopez, Jennifer, 1148

Lorain, OH, 1308–09

Lordstown, OH, 1319

Los Angeles, CA, 239, 241–42, 245–64, 271

Lost City, The, 549

Lott, Sen. Trent, 923–27

Loudon County, VA, 1690

Louisville, KY, 690–91

Love Field (TX), 1540, 1555

Lowell, MA, 809

Lowey, Rep. Nita, 1178–80

Lubbock, TX, 1589

Lucas, Rep. Frank, 1339–41

Lugar, Sen. Richard, 598–601

Luke Air Force Base (AZ), 107
Lungren, Rep. Dan, 169–71
Lynch, Gov. John, **1030**–32
Lynch, Rep. Stephen,
    819–21
Lyon, Matthew "Spitting", 686

M

Macaca, 1666
MacDill Air Force Base (FL),
    415, 417
Mack, Rep. Connie, **423**–25
Macomb County, MI, 861, 866
Macon, GA, 481
Madison, WI, 1772
Madison County, IA, 647
Mahoney, Rep. Tim, **427**–29
Mahoning Valley (OH), 1268,
    1290, 1319
Major League Baseball, 364,
    373, 683
Malcolm X, 1143
Mall of America (MN), 877,
    895
Maloney, Rep. Carolyn,
    1165–68
Man in Full, A, 467
Manalapan, NJ, 1084
Manchester, NH, 1038–39,
    1041
Manchin, Gov. Joe, **1738**–40
Manhattan, KS, 666
Manzullo, Rep. Don, **582**–84
Marchant, Rep. Kenny,
    1601–03
March Madness, 1229
Marin County, CA, 162, 178
Marino, Dan, 1395
Marion, AR, 133
Markey, Rep. Edward,
    812–16
Marshall, George, 1689
Marshall, Rep. Jim, **480**–82
Marshall, TX, 1531, 1546
Marshall Space Flight Center
    (AL), 41, 63
Marshfield, MO, 957
Martinez, Sen. Mel, **389**–92
Mary Baldwin College (VA),
    1680
Matheson, Rep. Jim,
    1637–40
Matsui, Rep. Doris, **174**–76
Matsui, Robert, 176
Mayo Clinic (MN), 890
Mayport Naval Station (FL),
    400
MBNA, 358

McAllen, TX, 1578
McCain, Sen. John, 94–100
McCarthy, Rep. Carolyn
McCarthy, Rep. Kevin,
    220–221
McCaskill, Sen. Claire, 944,
    948–49
McCaul, Rep. Michael,
    1566–68
McClellan, John, 123
McClintock, Tom, 146, 154
McCollum, Rep. Betty,
    897–99
McConnell, Sen. Mitch,
    679–82
McCook, NE, 994
McCotter, Rep. Thaddeus,
    863–65
McCrery, Rep. Jim, **725**–28
McDermott, Rep. Jim,
    1295, **1726**–29
McEwen, Bob, 1283
McGovern, George, 1480,
    1482
McGovern, Rep. Jim,
    802–04
McGreevey, Jim, 1045, 1049
McHenry, Rep. Patrick,
    1242–44
McHugh, Rep. John,
    1189–91
McIntyre, Rep. Mike,
    1235–37
McKeon, Rep. Buck, **226**–28
McKinley, William, 1265,
    1313
**McMorris Rodgers, Rep.
    Cathy**, **1720**–22
McNairy County, TN, 1522
McNerney, Rep. Jerry,
    193–96
McNulty, Rep. Michael,
    1185–87
McWherter, Ned Ray, 1496–97
Meehan, Martin, 809–10
Meek, Rep. Kendrick,
    430–31
Meeks, Rep. Gregory,
    1144–46
Meet Me in St. Louis, 951
Meet the Press, 131, 542, 1130,
    1415
Melancon, Rep. Charlie,
    722–24
Memphis, TN, 1526
Mencken, H.L., 753
Menendez, Sen. Robert,
    1055–58

Merrimack River Valley, 809
Mesa, AZ, 116
Miami, FL, 430–34, 440
Miami Vice, 433
Mica, Rep. John, **405**–07
Michaud, Rep. Michael,
    294, **751**–53
Microsoft, 1695, 1711
Midland, TX, 1569
*Midnight in the Garden of
    Good and Evil,* 491
Midway Airport (IL), 549
Mikulski, Sen. Barbara,
    759–61
Millender–McDonald,
    Juanita, 259–60
Miller, Rep. Brad, **1249**–51
Miller, Rep. Candice,
    860–62
Miller, Rep. Gary, **271**–73
Miller, Rep. George, **179**–82
Miller, Rep. Jeff, **392**–94
Miller, Zell, 451, 454, 460–63
Mills, Wilbur, 123, 135
Milwaukee, WI, 1776–77,
    1779
Minneapolis, MN, 879, 900,
    902
Minner, Gov. Ruth Ann,
    361–63
Minuteman Project, 121, 286,
    327
Miramar Marine Corps Air
    Station (CA), 290
Missoula, MT, 971
Mitchell, Rep. Harry,
    113–14
Mizner, Addison, 428, 435,
    442
Mobile, AL, 43, 54
Modesto, CA, 212
Mollohan, Rep. Alan,
    1747–50
Mondale, Walter, 877, 886
Money, 572, 1365, 1676
Monkey Business, 127
Monmouth, NJ, 1084
Montana, Joe, 1395
Montana Power, 971, 973
Montgomery, AL, 41, 56
Montgomery County, MD,
    771, 781
Montgomery County, PA,
    1417–18
Moongate, 427
More From The Floor, 1650
Moore, Rep. Dennis, **667**–69
Moore, Rep. Gwen, **1776**–78

Moore, Michael, 850
Moore, Roy, 43, 47
Moran, Rep. Jerry, **663**–65
Moran, Rep. Jim, **1684**–86
Morgantown, WV, 1748
Moses, Robert, 1138
Most Superior Land, A, 839
Mount Rainier (WA), 1715
Mount Rushmore (SD), 1478
Mount St. Helens (WA), 1715
Mount Washington, NH, 1041
Mount Vernon, VA, 1685
Moynihan, Daniel Patrick,
    1125, 1128
Mt. Hood (OR), 1360, 1365
Muncie, IN, 616–17
Murfreesboro, TN, 1520
Murkowski, Sen. Lisa,
    80–83
Murphy, Rep. Chris, **356**–57
Murphy, Rep. Patrick,
    1403–05
Murphy, Rep. Tim, **1428**–30
Murray, Sen. Patty,
    1704–07
Murtha, Rep. John,
    1412–16
Muscle Shoals, AL, 63
Museum of Appalachia (TN),
    1504
Musgrave, Rep. Marilyn,
    320–22
Music Man, The, 605, 647
Music Row (TN), 1517
Myrick, Rep. Sue, **1240**–42
Myrtle Beach, SC, 1465
Mystic Seaport (CT), 349
Myths of Free Trade, 1277

N

Nadler, Rep. Jerrold,
    1149–52
Namath, Joe, 1395
Nampa, ID, 523
Napa County, CA, 166
Naperville, IL, 572
Napoleonville, LA, 723
Napolitano, Rep. Grace,
    261–63
Napolitano, Gov. Janet,
    92–94
NASCAR Hall of Fame, 1241
Nashua, NH, 1033, 1041
Nashville, TN, 1517–18
Nassau County, NY, 1136,
    1138, 1140–43
National Journal, 723, 1491

National Party No More, A,
    454
National Review, 1456
Natl. Advanced Driving
    Simulator, 638
Natl. Automobile Museum
    (NV), 1021
Natl. Bowling Stadium (NV),
    1021
Natl. Football League, 400,
    1501
Natl. Inventors Hall of Fame,
    1308
Natl. Negro Leagues Baseball
    Museum, 960
Natl. Prisoner of War
    Museum (GA), 467
Natl. Underground Railroad
    Freedom Center (OH),
    1280
Navajo Nation, 104–05
Naval Submarine Base New
    London (CT), 350
Naval Undersea Warfare
    Center (RI), 1444
Naval Surface Warfare Center
    (CA), 277
Naval War College (RI), 1440
NCAA, 581, 593
Neal, Rep. Richard, **800**–02
Neiman Marcus Co., 235
Nellis Air Force Gunnery
    Range, 1021
Nelson, Sen. Ben, **994**–96
Nelson, Sen. Bill, **386**–89
Nethercutt, George, 1706
Neugebauer, Rep. Randy,
    1588–90
Nevada Test Site, 1021
New Bedford, MA, 805
New Brunswick, NJ, 1072
New Deal, 660
New Haven, CT, 351
New Madrid, MO, 968
New Orleans, LA, 716, 719–20
New Republic, The, 97, 358,
    875, 1666
New York City, NY, 1112–14
New York Times Magazine,
    1514
Newark, NJ, 1080, 1087
Newark Airport, 1071, 1080
Newport, KY, 693
Newport, RI, 1444
Newport News, VA, 1673
Newsom, Gavin, 184
Newton, MA, 805
Ney, Bob, 1267, 1322

Niagara Falls, NY, 1203–04
Nickles, Don, 1333
Nightingale's Song, The, 95
Nike, 1346, 1360, 1367
Nirvana, 1695
Nixon Library (CA), 272
Nordstrom, 1727
Norfolk, VA, 1670–73
Norfolk Naval Station (VA),
    1671
Norman, OK, 1342
Norquist, Grover, 973
Norris Dam (TN), 1515
North Carolina State Univ.,
    1229
North Royalton, OH, 1309
Northwestern Univ. (IL), 563
Norton, Del. Eleanor
    Holmes, **375**–76
Norton, Gale, 310
Norwood, Charlie, 968
Notes on Virginia, 672
Notre Dame Univ. (IN), 607
Nunes, Rep. Devin, **217**–219

O

Oahu, HI, 508–11
Oak Park, IL, 559
Oak Ridge, TN, 1513
Oak Ridge Natl. Laboratory,
    1513
Oakland, CA, 189–90
Oakland County, MI, 858,
    864, 866
Obama, Sen. Barack,
    538–43
Oberlin College, 1299
Oberstar, Rep. James,
    907–10
Obey, Rep. David, **1783**–88
OC, The, 267
Odessa, TX, 1569
Official Negligence, 145
Offutt Air Force Base (NE),
    1000
O'Hare Intl. Airport, 556, 563
O'Keeffe, Georgia, 1108
Oklahoma City, OK, 1342
Oklahoma City Natl.
    Memorial, 1344
Olver, Rep. John, **798**–800
Olympic Coast Natl. Marine
    Sanctuary (WA), 1723
Omaha, NE, 999–1000
Omaha World–Herald, 649,
    988
O'Malley, Gov. Martin,
    757–59

On the Waterfront, 1087
Operation Hold the Line, 1581
Orange County, CA, 267, 272, 283–84, 286
Orbison, Roy, 1589
Oregon State Univ., 1370
Oregon Trail, 1370
Orlando, FL, 398, 409, 447, 449
Orlando Sentinel, 409
Ortiz, Rep. Solomon, 1609–11
Osawatomie, KS, 657
Oshkosh, WI, 1782
Oskaloosa Independent, 660
Otter, Gov. Butch, 516–17
Outer Banks (NC), 1226
Owensboro, KY, 688
Oxford, MS, 928
Ozarks (MO), 965

P

Packwood, Bob, 1354, 1357
Paducah, KY, 686
Palin, Gov. Sarah, 74–76
Palisades Park, 1078
Pallone, Rep. Frank, 1070–72
Palm Beach, FL, 428, 435, 442
Palm Springs, CA, 279
Palo Alto, CA, 203
Paris Air Show, 1064
Parks, Rosa, 41
Pascrell, Rep. Bill, 1075–77
Pastor, Rep. Ed, 111–12
Pataki, George, 1119–21
Paterno, Scott, 1428
Paterson, NJ, 1076
Patrick, Gov. Deval, 789–90
Patrick Air Force Base (FL), 426
Patuxent River Complex (MD), 773
Paul, Rep. Ron, 1575–77
Pawlenty, Gov. Tim, 882–85
Payne, Rep. Donald, 1079–81
Pearce, Rep. Steve, 1104–07
Pearl, Minnie, 1522
Pearl Harbor, HI, 508
Pease Intl. Tradeport (NH), 1039
Pelosi, Rep. Nancy, 182–88
Pence, Rep. Mike, 616–18
Pendleton, OR, 1363
Penn, William, 1371, 1388, 1391, 1404

Pennsylvania Dutch Country, 1424–25
Pennsylvania State Univ., 1398
Pensacola, FL, 393–94
Pensacola News Journal, 394
Pentagon (VA), 1685
Peoria, IL, 587–88
Perdue, Gov. Sonny, 457–59
Perlmutter, Rep. Ed, 327–29
Perry, Gov. Rick, 1535–39
Peterson, Rep. Collin, 904–07
Peterson, Rep. John, 1396–98
Petri, Rep. Tom, 1781–83
Phenix City, AL, 58
Philadelphia, PA, 1371, 1388, 1391, 1404, 1417–18
Philadelphia Daily News, 1389
Philadelphia Inquirer, The, 1390, 1418
Philadelphia Museum of Art, 1391
Phillip Morris, 1682
Phillips, Sam, 1526
Phoenix, AZ, 109, 111–13, 115–16
Pickering, Rep. Chip, 933–35
Piggly Wiggly, 1494
Pikes Peak, 323
Pine Barrens (NJ), 1064
Pittman, Key, 1005
Pitts, Rep. Joe, 1424–26
Pittsburgh, PA, 1420, 1429
Pittsburgh International Airport (PA), 1429
Plano, TX, 1551
Platts, Rep. Todd, 1431–33
Playboy Mansion (CA), 283
Pluto, 760
Plymouth, MA, 822
Poe, Rep. Ted, 1547–49
Politico, 327, 1457
Polk County, FL, 419
Pombo, Richard, 195–96
Pomeroy, Rep. Earl, 1263–64
Pony Express, 938, 962
Porgy and Bess, 1464
Port Arthur, TX, 1548
Porter, Rep. Jon, 1022–24
Portland, ME, 749
Portland, OR, 1360–61, 1365
Portland *Oregonian*, 1352

Portman, Rob, 1282
Portsmouth, NH, 1038–39
Portsmouth Naval Shipyard (ME), 738, 749
Powell, Colin, 365, 833
Presley, Elvis, 1494, 1526
Price, Rep. David, 1228–30
Price, Rep. Tom, 475–77
Primary Colors, 723
Prince George's County (MD), 472, 771
Princeton Univ. (NJ), 1084
Promise Keepers, 1014
Proposition 187, 146, 150
Providence, RI, 1444
Provincetown, MA, 822
Provo, UT, 1641
Prudhoe Bay, 70–71
Pryce, Rep. Deborah, 1312–14
Pryor, Sen. Mark, 129–32
Puget Sound (WA), 1727
Punxsutawney, PA, 1397
Purdue Univ. (IN), 611
Pusser, Buford, 1522
Putnam, Rep. Adam, 418–20

Q

Quad Cities (IL), 585–86
Quakers, 1371, 1388, 1399
Quantico Marine Corps Base (VA), 1668
Quayle, Dan, 609, 614
Queen Nicotina, 773
Queens, NY, 1143, 1145, 1148, 1153, 1161
Quillen, Jimmy, 1509
Qwest, 308

R

Racine, WI, 1770
Radanovich, Rep. George, 213–15
Rahall, Rep. Nick, 1753–55
Raimondo, Tony, 993
Raleigh, NC, 1224, 1229, 1250
Ramstad, Rep. Jim, 894–96
Randolph Air Force Base (TX), 1599
Rangel, Rep. Charles, 1168–73
Ransom, John Crowe, 1494
Rather, Dan, 1547
Rauch, Jonathan, 723
Rayburn, Sam, 1551, 1553
RCA Victor, 1059
Reading, PA, 1400

Reagan, Ronald, 145, 225, 242, 639
Real Majority, The, 1285
Redmond, WA, 1711
Redneck Riviera (FL), 393
Redstone Arsenal (AL), 63
Reed, Sen. Jack, 1439–41
Reed, Ralph, 454
Reforma, 711
Regula, Rep. Ralph, 1315–18
Rehberg, Rep. Denny, 982–84
Reichert, Rep. Dave, 1729–31
Reid, Sen. Harry, 1010–13
Rell, Gov. M. Jodi, 334–36
Rendell, Gov. Ed, 1377–80
Reno, Janet, 398, 615
Reno, NV, 1020–21
Renzi, Rep. Rick, 103–06
Republican National Convention, 98, 157, 454
Research Triangle Park (NC), 1229
Reyes, Rep. Silvestre, 1580–82
Reynolds, Glenn, 1511
Reynolds, Rep. Tom, 1197–1200
Rhode Island School of Design, 1433
Rice, Condoleezza, 159, 365, 1180
Rich, Denise, 1129
Richardson, Gov. Bill, 1092–95
Richardson, Rep. Laura, 259–61
Richmond, CA, 180
Richmond, VA, 1673, 1682
Richmond Times–Dispatch, 1682
Riddick's Senate Procedure, 1334
Ridge, Tom, 1393
Riley, Gov. Bob, 45–47
Ringling Bros. Circus, 421
Ripken, Cal, 767
Ritter, Gov. Bill, 305–06
River Runs Through It, A, 977
Riverside, CA, 277
Rizzo, Frank, 1377, 1418
Roanoke, VA, 1680
Roberts, Sen. Pat, 659–62, 1746
Robertson, Pat, 1671
Robinson, Jackie, 1158

Rochester, NY, 1203
Rockefeller, Sen. Jay, 661–62, **1744**–47
Rockefeller, John D., 1179, 1745
Rocky, 1388, 1391
Rodriguez, Rep. Ciro, 1599–1601
Rogers, Rep. Harold, 694–98
Rogers, Rep. Mike (AL), 57–59
Rogers, Rep. Mike (MI), 855–57
Rogers, Roy, 269
Rogers, Will, 1338, 1571
Rohrabacher, Rep. Dana, 279–81
Roll Call, 123, 158, 520, 796, 1100
Romney, Mitt, 788–89
Ron Paul Political Report, 1576
Ronald Reagan Library (CA), 225
Roots, 1524
Rose Bowl (CA), 239
Roseville, CA, 173
Roskam, Rep. Peter, 555–57
Ros–Lehtinen, Rep. Ileana, 432–34
Ross, Rep. Mike, 139–41
Rossi, Dino, 1702
Rostenkowski, Dan, 533, 554
Rothman, Rep. Steven, 1077–79
Rounds, Gov. Mike, 1483–85
Rove, Karl, 1536
Roybal–Allard, Rep. Lucille, 251–53
Royce, Rep. Ed, 265–68
Ruppersberger, Rep. Dutch, 766–68
Rush, Rep. Bobby, 543–45
Russell, KS, 650
Russert, Tim, 542
Rutgers (NJ), 1084
Ryan, George, 530, 533
Ryan, Rep. Paul, 1769–71
Ryan, Rep. Tim, 1318–20

S

Sabo, Martin Olav, 901
Sacramento, CA, 170, 172, 175–76
Salazar, Rep. John, 317–19

Salazar, Sen. Ken, 309–12
Salem, MA, 811
Salem, OR, 1370
Sali, Rep. Bill, 523–24
Salinas, CA, 210
Salt Lake City, UT, 1636–39
Salt of the Earth, 1105
San Antonio, TX, 1591–94, 1599–1600
San Bernardino, CA, 274
San Diego, CA, 290–91, 293, 295–96, 299–300
San Francisco, CA, 177–78, 180, 183–84, 197
San Francisco Chronicle, 201
San Jacinto, TX, 1527, 1576
San Jose, CA, 204–05, 207
San Juan Islands, WA, 1713
Sanchez, Rep. Linda, 263–65
Sanchez, Rep. Loretta, 282–84
Sanders, Sen. Bernie, 1651–53
Sandia National Laboratories (NM), 1102
Sanford, Gov. Mark, 1454–57
Santa Anita race track, 229
Santa Barbara, CA, 222–23
Santa Cruz, CA, 209
Santa Fe, NM, 1090, 1108
Sarasota, FL, 421
Sarbanes, Rep. John, 768–70
Saturday Night Fever, 1164
Saugus Iron Works, 811
Savannah, GA, 490–91
Saxton, Rep. Jim, 1063–65
S.C. Johnson Wax, 1770
Scalia, Antonin, 915
Scarborough, Joe, 394
Schakowsky, Rep. Jan, 562–64
Schaumburg, IL, 560–61
Schiavo, Terri, 392
Schiff, Rep. Adam, 238–40
Schmidt, Rep. Jean, 1281–83, 1415
Schumer, Sen. Charles, 1122–26
Schumpeter, Joseph, 699
Schwartz, Rep. Allyson, 1417–19
Schwarzenegger, Gov. Arnold, 153–57
Schweitzer, Gov. Brian, 975–77

Scotia, CA, 166
Scott, Rep. Bobby, 1672–75
Scott, Rep. David, 492–94
Scott Air Force Base, 571
Scottsdale, AZ, 113–14
Scranton, PA, 1411
Searchlight, NV, 1023
Sears Tower (IL), 558
Seattle, WA, 1711, 1727
Seattle Times, 1710
Sebelius, Gov. Kathleen, 654–56
Sedona, AZ, 104
Seinfeld, 1151
Selma, AL, 41
Seminoles, 423
Sensenbrenner, Rep. Jim, 1778–81
Sergeant York, 1516
Serrano, Rep. Jose, 1173–75
Sessions, Sen. Jeff, 51–53
Sessions, Rep. Pete, 1620–22
Sestak, Rep. Joe, 1401–03
700 Club, 1671
Seward, William, 68
Shadegg, Rep. John, 108–110
Shaker Heights, OH, 1304
Shanksville, PA, 1406
Shannon County, SD, 1478
Sharon, Ariel, 1037
Shays, Rep. Christopher, 353–56
Shea–Porter, Rep. Carol, 1038–40
Shelby, Sen. Richard, 48–51
Shepard, Alan, 63
Shepard, Matthew, 1359
Shepherd of the Hills, The, 964
Sheppard Air Force Base (TX), 1574
Sherman, TX, 1553
Sherman, Rep. Brad, 231–33
Sherman, William, 1287
Shimkus, Rep. John, 589–90
Shriver, Maria, 153, 157
Shuler, Rep. Heath, 1244–46
Shuster, Rep. Bill, 1405–08
Shuster, Bud, 1407
Sideways, 225
Siegel, Bugsy, 1003, 1018

Silicon Forest (OR), 1361, 1365
Silicon Valley (CA), 202–03
Silos and Smokestacks National Heritage Area (IA), 639
Simon, Paul, 531, 540
Simplot, J.R., 512
Simpson, Rep. Mike, 524, 525–27
Sinatra, Frank, 1087
Sinn Fein, 802, 1139, 1196
Sioux City, IA, 649
Sires, Rep. Albio, 1086–87
60 Minutes, 552
Skelton, Rep. Ike, 956–59
Skokie, IL, 563
Slaughter, Rep. Louise, 1202–05
Smith, Rep. Adam, 1732–33
Smith, Rep. Adrian, 1001–02
Smith, Rep. Chris, 1065–68
Smith, Sen. Gordon, 1357–59
Smith, Joseph, 1623
Smith, Rep. Lamar, 1593–96
Smith, Nick, 854, 862
Snowe, Sen. Olympia, 743–45
Snyder, Rep. Vic, 134–36
Solis, Rep. Hilda, 247–249
Solzhenitsyn, Aleksandr, 1644
Song of the Chattahoochee, 484
Sopranos, The, 1078
Souder, Rep. Mark, 608–10
Soundgarden, 1695
South Bend, IN, 607
South Carolina State Univ., 1477
Southern Manifesto, 1496
Southern Poverty Law Center (AL), 67
Space, Rep. Zack, 1321–22
Sparkman, John, 63
Sparks, NV, 1020–21
Spartanburg, SC, 1471
Specter, Sen. Arlen, 1380–85
Spindletop (TX), 1548
Spitzer, Gov. Eliot, 1118–21
Spokane, WA, 1721
Spratt, Rep. John, 1472–75
Springer, Jerry, 1276, 1708
Springfield, MA, 801
Springfield, MO, 964–65

Springfield, OR, 1367–68
Springsteen, Bruce, 1072
St. Augustine, FL, 406
St. Joseph, MO, 962
St. Louis, MO, 950–55
St. Paul, MN, 879, 897–98, 902
St. Petersburg, FL, 402, 411, 413
St. Petersburg Times, 413, 415–16
Stabenow, Sen. Debbie, 836–38
Standard Oil, 1265, 1301
Starbucks, 1695, 1724
Stark, Rep. Pete, 199–201
Stassen, Harold, 1349
State, The, 1463
Stateline, NV, 1003, 1021
Staten Island, NY, 1164
Statue of Liberty, 1086
Stearns, Rep. Cliff, 403–05
Stevens, Sen. Ted, 76–80
Stockton, CA, 194–95, 212
Straub, W.L., 413
Strayhorn, Carole Keeton, 1538
Strickland, Gov. Ted, 1272–73
Strip, The (NV), 1018
Strongsville, OH, 1309
Stupak, Rep. Bart, 838–40
Suffolk County, NY, 1134, 1136, 1138
Sugar Land, TX, 1597
Sugarland Express, The, 1597
Sullivan, Rep. John, 1335–37
Sun Studio (TN), 1526
Sun Valley, ID, 512, 526
Sun, The (MD), 758, 762
Sundquist, Don, 1500
Sununu, Sen. John, 1035–37
Sutton, Rep. Betty, 1308–09
Sweet Briar College (VA), 1680
Sweetwater, TX, 1589
Syracuse, NY, 1194–95

T
Tacoma, WA, 1724, 1732
Tahlequah, OK, 1338
Tallahassee, FL, 395–96
Tallgrass Prairie National Preserve, 664
Tampa, FL, 402, 411, 417

Tancredo, Rep. Tom,
325–27
Tanner, Rep. John, 1523–25
Taos, NM, 1108
Tate, Allen, 1494
Tauscher, Rep. Ellen,
191–93
Taxpayers for Common Sense,
414–15
Taylor, Rep. Gene, 936–38
Telluride, CO, 318
Telos Corp., 1690
Tempe, AZ, 113–14
Ten Commandments, 43, 47
Tenet, George, 1339
TennCare, 1497
Tennesee Aquarium, 1513
Tennessee Barn Dance, 1494
Tennessee Justice Center,
1501
Tennessee Valley Authority,
62
Tennessean, The, 1517
Terre Haute, IN, 622
Terry, Rep. Lee, 998–1000
Tester, Sen. Jon, 980–82
Texarkana, AR, 140
Texarkana, TX, 1553
Texas A&M Univ., 1583
Texas Instruments, 1550
Texas Monthly, 1603
Texas Rose Festival, 1546
Texas Techsan, 1574
Texasville, 1589
Thimerosal, 615
Thomas, Bill, 219, 221
Thomas, Clarence
Thomas, Craig, 1798–99
Thompson, Fred, 1496, 1498
Thompson, Rep. Bennie,
930–33
Thompson, Rep. Mike,
165–67
Thompson, Tommy, 1757
Thoreau, Henry David, 783,
798
Thornberry, Rep. Mac,
1573–75
Three Mile Island (PA)
Thune, Sen. John, 1488–92
Thurmond, Strom
Tiahrt, Rep. Todd, 670–72
Tiberi, Rep. Patrick,
1305–07
Tierney, Rep. John, 810–12
Tillman, Pat, 206
Times Square (NY), 1150
Timken, 1316

Timonium, MD, 767
Tinker Air Force Base (OK),
1342
To Kill a Mockingbird, 54
Tobacco Road, 491
Tocqueville, Alexis de, 823
Toledo, OH, 1298–99
Tombstone, AZ, 120
Tonight Show, The, 147
Toomey, Pat, 1382, 1384
Topeka, KS, 666
Torricelli, Bob, 1052–53
Towns, Rep. Edolphus,
1155–57
Traffic, 1632
Traficant, Jim, 1320
Trail of Tears, 1323, 1338
Traverse City, MI, 848
Travis County, TX, 1567,
1595, 1605
Trenton, NJ, 1066
Tribune–Review (PA), 1430
Truman, Harry, 957, 960, 970
Trump, Donald, 1152
Tucker, Tanya, 1589
Tucson, AZ, 118–21
Tufts Univ., MA, 813
Tulafono, Gov. Togiola T.A.,
1815
Tulsa, OK, 1336
Turner, Rep. Mike, 1284–86
Tuskegee Institute (AL), 58
Twain, Mark, 170
Twentynine Palms Marine
Corps Base, 269
251 Club, 1644
Tyler, TX, 1546
Tysons Corner, VA, 1685, 1693

U

U.S.S. *Alabama,* 54
U.S.S. *Arizona,* 508
U.S.S. *Cole,* 49
U.S.S. *Constitution,* 817
U.S.S. *John F. Kennedy,* 401
Udall, Rep. Mark, 315–17
Udall, Morris, 112, 316
Udall, Stewart, 316
Udall, Rep. Tom, 1107–09
Uncle Tom's Cabin, 1282
Undaunted Courage, 971
Underground Railroad, 823,
852
Union Carbide, 1576
Union Leader, The (NH),
1025, 1030
United Auto Workers, 826–27,
850

United Mine Workers,
695–96, 1414
United Steelworkers, 1414
Univ. of Alabama, 67
Univ. of Chicago, 544
Univ. of Colorado, 315
Univ. of Florida, 398
Univ. of Georgia, 486
Univ. of Illinois, 581
Univ. of Iowa, 629, 641
Univ. of Kansas, 668
Univ. of Michigan, 874
Univ. of Minnesota, 900
Univ. of Mississippi, 928
Univ. of Nebraska, 997
Univ. of North Carolina, 1229
Univ. of Tennessee, 1511
Univ. of Texas, 1604
Unto the Sons, 1062
Upper East Side (NY),
1166–67
Upper Peninsula (MI), 839
Upton, Rep. Fred, 851–53
US Steel, 605
USA Today, 172, 1739
USAirways, 1429
Utz Quality Foods, 1432

V

Vallejo, CA, 180
Valley Forge, PA, 1400
Valley of the Sun (AZ), 112–13
Van Hollen, Rep. Chris,
780–82
Vandenberg, Arthur, 845
Vanderbilt Univ., 1518
Vedic City, IA, 642
Velazquez, Rep. Nydia,
1160–63
Ventura, Jesse, 879, 882
Vieux Carre (LA), 720
Villaraigosa, Antonio, 246,
256
Vilsack, Tom, 629–31
Virginia Beach, VA, 1671
Virginia City, NV, 1020
Virginia Tech Univ., 1687
Visclosky, Rep. Peter,
604–06
Vitter, Sen. David, 712–15
Voinovich, Sen. George,
1273–76

W

Wabash Cannonball, 611
Waco, TX, 1583
Waikiki, HI, 508
Wakefield, NE, 997

Walberg, Rep. Tim, 853–55
Walden, Rep. Greg, **1362**–64
Walking Tall, 1522
Wall Street Journal, 86, 683,
    1009–10, 1109, 1119, 1196
    1246, 1749
Wallace, George, 41
Wal–Mart, 123, 138
Walsh, Rep. James, **1194**–97
Walsh, Thomas, 971
Walton, Sam, 123
Walz, Rep. Tim, **890**–92
Wamp, Rep. Zach, **1512**–14
War on Poverty, 777
Warner, Sen. John, **1661**–64
Warner, Mark, 1660, 1664
Warren, Earl, 144
Warren Commission, 1381
Washington, George, 1400,
    1655, 1668–69, 1684, 1689
Washington Monthly, 97
Washingtonian, 224, 1666
**Wasserman Schultz, Rep.
    Debbie**, **437**–39
Waters, Rep. Maxine,
    253–56
Watson, Rep. Diane, **249**–51
Watt, Rep. Melvin, **1247**–49
Waxman, Rep. Henry,
    240–44
Waynesboro, TN, 1522
Weather Channel, 476
Webb, Sen. Jim, **1664**–67
Weekly Standard, The, 657
Weiner, Rep. Anthony,
    1152–54
Welch, Rep. Peter, **1654**–55
Weldon, Rep. Dave, **425**–27
Weller, Rep. Jerry, **567**–69
Wellstone, Paul, 879, 886, 893
West Orange, NJ, 1045, 1076
West Point (NY), 1181
Westchester County, NY, 1179

Westminster College (MO),
    970
Westmoreland, Rep. Lynn,
    469–71
Wetterling, Patty, 903
Wexler, Rep. Robert,
    435–37
*What's the Matter with
    Kansas?*, 650
Wheeler, Burton, 971
Wheeling, WV, 1748
Where the Boys Are, 437
White Sands Natl. Monument
    (NM), 1105
Whitehouse, Sen. Sheldon,
    1441–43
Whitfield, Rep. Ed, **685**–87
Whitman, Christine Todd,
    1044, 1048
Whitman, Walt, 1158
Whitney, Eli, 351
Whitney Glacier, 168
Whitten, Jamie, 929
Wichita, KS, 670–71
Wichita Falls, TX, 1574
Wicker, Rep. Roger, **928**–29
Wilder, Douglas, 789, 1682
Wilkes–Barre, PA, 1411
Williamsburg, VA, 1668
Williamson County, TN
Williamson County, TX
Wilmington, NC, 1236
Wilson, Rep. Charlie,
    1289–91
Wilson, Rep. Heather,
    1101–04
Wilson, Rep. Joe, **1466**–68
Wilson, Pete, 145, 151, 239
Winston–Salem, NC, 1248
Wizard of Oz, The, 650
Wolf, Rep. Frank, **1688**–92
Wolfe, Tom, 1174

Woman's Christian
    Temperance Union, The,
    1548
Women's Basketball Hall of
    Fame (TN), 1511
Woodlands, TX, 1562
Woolsey, Rep. Lynn, **177**–79
Worcester, MA, 803
World Trade Center (NY),
    1150
Worth the Fighting For, 98
Wright, Frank Lloyd, 559
Wright, Harold Bell, 964
Wrigley Field (IL), 554
Wu, Rep. David, **1359**–62
Wyden, Sen. Ron, **1353**–56
Wynn, Rep. Albert, **770**–72

X

Xerox, 1112–14

Y

Yakima Valley, WA, 1718
Yarmuth, Rep. John,
    690–92
Yearling, The, 398
Yellowstone Natl. Park, 1792
York, Myrth, 1437, 1442
Yorktown, VA, 1668
Young, Rep. Bill, **412**–16
Young, Brigham, 1623
Young, Rep. Don, **84**–87
Youngstown, OH, 1319
Youngtown, AZ, 89
Yucca Mountain (NV),
    1005–06
Yuengling, 1427
Yuma, AZ, 118

Z

Zanesville, OH, 1322
Zephyr Cove, NV, 1021
Zion, IL, 561

THE AUTHORS

Michael Barone is a senior writer at *U.S. News & World Report* and a Fox News Channel contributor. The *Chicago Tribune* says, "Michael Barone is to politics what statistician-writer Bill James is to baseball, a mix of historian, social observer, and numbers cruncher who illuminates his subject with perspective and a touch of irreverence." His most recent book is *Our First Revolution: The Remarkable British Upheaval That Inspired America's Founding Fathers*, published by Random House in 2007.

Richard E. Cohen brings to the *Almanac* 30 years of experience covering Capitol Hill. He is the 1990 winner of the Everett McKinley Dirksen Award for distinguished reporting on Congress and *National Journal's* congressional correspondent since 1977. Cohen is the author of several books about Congress, including a biography of former Rep. Dan Rostenkowski.

THE PUBLISHER

Since 1969, National Journal Group has provided "insight for insiders" through nonpartisan publications that cover all the power players in Congress, the executive branch, the lobbying world, and beyond.

This 2008 edition of *The Almanac of American Politics* marks the thirteenth volume to be published by National Journal Group.

In addition to the *Almanac*, National Journal Group properties include *National Journal*, *CongressDaily*, *The Hotline*, *NationalJournal.com* and *Technology Daily*.

600 New Hampshire Ave. NW, Washington, DC 20037 Telephone (202) 739-8400